A Genealogical and Heraldic Dictionary of the Landed Gentry of Great Britain and Ireland, Volume 1

A

GENEALOGICAL AND HERALDIC DICTIONARY

OF THE

LANDED GENTRY

OF

GREAT BRITAIN AND IRELAND.

BY

SIR BERNARD BURKE,

ULSTER KING OF ARMS,

AUTHOR OF THE DICTIONARIES OF "THE PEERAGE AND BARONETAGE," "THE EXTINCT AND DORMANT PEERAGE," ETC. ETC.

LONDON:
HARRISON, PALL MALL.

1858.

PREFATORY NOTICE.

My "Dictionary of the Landed Gentry" is now, for the first time, presented to the public complete in a single volume, exactly similar to that of my "Peerage and Baronetage." The book may appear large, yet, its contents, in the same manner, as with the Dictionary of the Peerage and Baronetage, have been compressed into the smallest compass consistent with the full information such productions should necessarily possess, to be historically, genealogically, and generally useful.

This work, the subject of which is of deep, and I may say, national interest, has been a favourite occupation of my past life, and has been cheered in its course by great and flattering success: I have laboured in this new edition, with a spirit fully alive to the importance of perpetuating such prosperity. I have spared in the task neither toil nor devotion; every page has been re-written, every memoir carefully revised, and every pedigree minutely examined. Communications in emendation have been received from all parts of the kingdom, and new information of great value obtained: these means of perfection, when acquired, have been carefully attended to.

I may, therefore be pardoned in the agreeable and sanguine hope that "The Dictionary of the Landed Gentry," thus submitted to further public approval, will be deemed a more comprehensive, faithful, and worthy record, than can be obtained from any other source, of that class of gentlemen, who, though undistinguished by hereditary titles, possess an undeniable right, from antiquity of race, extent of property, and brilliancy of achievement, to take foremost rank among the lesser nobility of Europe.

J. BERNARD BURKE,
ULSTER.

A

GENEALOGICAL AND HERALDIC

DICTIONARY

OF THE

LANDED GENTRY.

ABADAM OF MIDDLETON HALL.

ABADAM, EDWARD, Esq. of Middleton Hall, co. Carmarthen, *b.* 28 April, 1809; *m.* Louisa, dau. of — Taylor, Esq., and has issue,

I. EDWARD-HAMLIN. II. Conrad.
III. Francis-Walrond. And other issue.

Lineage.—WILLIAM ADAMS, Esq., son of Capt. Conrad Adams, of Barbadoes, derived from the old baronial family of Abadam, *d.* in 1703. He *m.* 23 Dec. 1697, Frances, dau. and co-heir of Col. Thomas Walrond, by Frances, dau. of Sir Jonathan Atkins, Knt., governor of Barbadoes from 1674 to 1680, and by her (who *m.* subsequently George Græme, Esq.) left at his decease a son,

THOMAS ADAMS, Esq. of Christchurch, Barbadoes, who *m.* 9 June, 1727, Margaret, dau. of Lt.-Gen. Thomas Maxwell, a descendant of the Nithsdale family, and by her had issue,

WILLIAM, of whom presently.
Thomas-Maxwell, of Adam's Castle, Barbadoes, *m.* in 1770, Mrs. Anne Fonblanque.
Elizabeth, *m.* in 1728, to James Monk, chief justice of Canada.
Frances, *m.* in 1757, to Samuel Sedgwick, Esq. M.D.

The eldest son,

WILLIAM ADAMS, Esq., *m.* 1st, in 1759, Eleanor Rosiman, by whom he had no issue to survive; and 2ndly, Elizabeth-Anne, dau. of the Rev. Thomas Coxeter, by whom (who *m.* 2ndly, Robert Gordon, M.D.) he had issue,

William Maxwell, *b.* 19 Oct. 1775; who *d.* *unm.* in 1795.
Edward-Hamlin, of Middleton Hall.
Thomas-Maxwell, who *m.* 4 July, 1792, Anne-St.-John Trefusis (sister of Lord Clinton).
Anne-Margaretta, who *d.* *unm.* in 1789.

The 2nd son,

EDWARD-HAMLIN ADAMS, Esq. of Middleton Hall, *b.* 30 April, 1777; served as high-sheriff of Carmarthenshire in 1832, and was M.P. for that county in 1833-4. He *m.* 5 Jan. 1796, Amelia-Sophia, eldest dau. of Capt. John MacPherson, by Mary-Anne Macneil, his 2nd wife, and granddau. of William MacPherson, descended from Gallichattan More, chief of the clan Æhattan, and had issue,

EDWARD, now of Middleton Hall, who has resumed the surname of ABADAM.
William, *b.* 15 Sept. 1814; *d.* 15 Oct. 1851.
Mary-Anne. Sophia. Caroline. Matilda.

Mr. Adams *d.* 2 Jan. 1842.

Arms—Arg., on a cross gu., five mullets (or, estoilles), or.
Crest—Out of a ducal coronet, or, a demi-lion, affronté, gu.
Motto—Aspire—Persevere—and Indulge not.
Seat—Middleton Hall, co. Carmarthen.

ABNEY OF MEASHAM HALL.

ABNEY, WILLIAM-WOTTON, of Measham Hall, co. Derby, Esq., *b.* 5 Jan. 1807; *m.* 6 May, 1828, Helen-John-Sinclair, eld. dau. of James Buchanan, Esq. of Craigend Castle, co. Stirling, by the Lady Janet Sinclair, his wife, and had one son, who *d.* in early infancy, Dec. 1829. Mr. Abney *s.* his grandfather in 1827.

Lineage.—The Abneys were seated at Abney in the Peak about the time of the Conquest.

JOHN DE ABENEY (son of William de Abeney, and grandson of John de Abeney, living at Wivelislie in 1318), *m.* about 1400, the elder dau. and co-heir of William de Ingewardeby, of Willesleye, co. Derby, and was ancestor of the ABNEYS *of Willesley*, of which were SIR EDWARD ABNEY, a well known judge, and his younger brother, SIR THOMAS ABNEY, lord-mayor and M.P. for London, one of the founders of the Bank of England.

WILLIAM ABNEY, of the Inner Temple, Esq. (fourth in descent from Robert Abney, of Newton Burguland, 2nd son of George de Abeney, of Willesley), purchased the estate of Measham, co. Derby, and erected the family mansion there. He was *b.* 25 Nov. 1713, and *d.* in 1800. He *m.* Catherine, dau. and heir of Thomas Wotton, of Little Cannons, Herts, Esq., and had (with two daus., Mary, wife of John Swinfen, of Swinfen, Esq., and Catherine, wife of the Rev. Thomas Burnaby) four sons: the two youngest *d.* *unm.*; the eldest, Robert, of Measham, *b.* in 1748, high-sheriff of Derbyshire in 1777, *m.* Anne, dau. of the Rev. Philip Bracebridge, and left an only dau. and heir, Anne, wife of Samuel-B. Heming, Esq. The second son,

EDWARD ABNEY, of Measham, Esq., *b.* in 1751, *d.* in 1827; having had by Hephzibah, his 2nd wife, dau. of Samuel Need, Esq. of Nottingham, two sons and a dau.,

I. WILLIAM-WOTTON, capt. royal horse-guards blue; *m.* Elizabeth, dau. of W. Richardson, Esq. of Fulford House, co. York; and dying *v. p.*, in 1821, left issue,

1 WILLIAM-WOTTON, present proprietor.
2 Edward-Henry, in holy orders; *m.* in 1833, Catherine, dau. of Jedediah Strutt, Esq. of Belper, co. Derby, and has issue.
1 Catherine, *m.* in 1835, to the Rev. William Sandys.

II. Edward, *m.* in 1822, Ellen, dau. of Hyla Holden, of Wednesbury, Esq., and left two daus., Hephzibah-Constance, and Ellen-Clarke.
I. Elizabeth, *m.* to Henry Walker, of Blythe Hall, Notts, Esq.

Arms—Or, on a chief, gu., a lion, passant, arg.
Crest—A demi-lion, rampant, or, a pellet between the paws.
Motto—Fortiter et honeste.
Seat—Measham Hall, Derbyshire.

ACKERS OF MORETON HALL.

ACKERS, GEORGE-HOLLAND, Esq. of Moreton Hall, co. Chester, *b.* 10 Aug. 1812; *m.* 23 Jan. 1838, Harriott-Susan, 2nd dau. of Henry-William Hutton, Esq. of Beverley, co. York, and has

I. GEORGIANA-HARRIOTT. II. Constance-Marianne.

Mr. Ackers *s.* his father, 22 Nov. 1836.

Lineage.—HOLLAND ACKERS, Esq. of Bank House, Manchester, *b.* 6 Feb. 1744, son of George Ackers, by Ellen Bonney, his 1st wife, purchased the Moreton property. He *m.* 23 Oct. 1787, Elizabeth Filkin, and by her (who *d.* 15 Feb. 1800), had a son and successor,

GEORGE ACKERS, Esq. of Moreton Hall, *b.* 19 Aug. 1788; *m.* 8 Nov. 1811, Harriott Dell, 2nd dau. of Henry Hutton, Esq. of Lincoln, and by her (who *m.* 2ndly, in 1841, the late William-Edward Powell, of Nanteos, Esq., M.P. for Cardiganshire), left at his decease, 22 Nov. 1836, an only child, GEORGE-HOLLAND ACKERS, Esq., now of Moreton Hall.

Arms—Arg., on a bend, sa., three acorns, or, husked, vert.
Crest—A dove rising, in the beak an olive branch, all ppr.
Motto—La liberté.
Seat—Moreton Hall, Congleton.

ACTON OF GATACRE PARK.

ACTON, EDWARD-FARRER, Esq. of Gatacre Park, co. Salop, J.P. and D.L., major in the Shropshire militia; *m.* in 1832, Mary-Anne, youngest dau. of the Rev. Horace Suckling, rector of Barsham, Suffolk, and has issue,

I. EDWARD-WILLIAM-FREDERICK, an officer in the army, *b.* in 1834.
I. Mary-Henrietta.

Lineage.—THOMAS ACTON, Esq., of Gatacre Park, 2nd son of Sir Edward Acton, 1st Bart. of Aldenham, by Sarah his wife, dau. of Richard Mytton, Esq., of Halston, *m.* Mabell, dau. of Clement Stoner, Esq. of London, and *d.* in 1677, leaving a son, CLEMENT, who *d.* in 1726, and was father of EDWARD, of Gatacre Park, who *d.* in 1767, and was grandfather of EDWARD-ACTON ACTON, Esq. of Gatacre Park, who *d.* in 1822, and was *s.* by his son, the present E.-F. ACTON, Esq. of Gatacre Park.

Arms—Gu., two lions passant, arg., between nine-cross-crosslets, fitchée, or.
Crest—Within a torse, a human leg and thigh in armour, couped, and dropping blood, all ppr.
Seat—Gatacre Park, Bridgnorth.

ACTON OF WEST ASTON.

ACTON, THOMAS, Esq. of West Aston, co. Wicklow, *b.* in 1826; *s.* his father, 10 April, 1854.

Lineage.—THOMAS ACTON, Esq. of West Aston (son of William Acton, Esq., by Jane Parsons, his wife, granddau. of Sir Wm. Parsons, Bart. of Birr, and grandson of Thos Acton, Esq., by Eleanor his wife, dau. of Col. Kempston), *m.* in 1780, Sidney, dau. of Joshua Davis, Esq., barrister-at-law, of Dublin, and had issue,

WILLIAM, his heir.
Thomas, *m.* Sidney, dau. of Hampden Evans, Esq. of Portrane, co. Dublin.
Anna-Maria, *m.* to Major Warburton, of Aughrim, co. Galway.
Jane, *m.* to George Drought, Esq. of Glencorry, co. Wicklow.

The eldest son,

WILLIAM ACTON, Esq. of West Aston, M.P. for co. Wicklow, lt.-col. of the co. militia, and its high sheriff in 1820; *b.* in 1789; *m.* in 1817, Caroline, dau. of Thomas Walker, Esq., master in Chancery, and has issue,

I. THOMAS, now of West Aston.
II. Charles, *b.* 1830. III. William, *b.* 1828.
I. Jane.

Motto—Adjuvante Deo.
Seat—West Aston, co. Wicklow.

ACTON OF WOLVERTON.

ACTON, WILLIAM-JOSEPH, Esq. of Wolverton, co. Worcester, *b.* 27 June, 1803; *m.* 22 Oct. 1833, Mary, widow of William Trafford, Esq., brother of the late Sir Thomas-Joseph de Trafford, Bart. of Trafford Park, Lancashire, and has surviving issue,

I. WILLIAM-ROBERT, *b.* 16 Nov. 1835.
II. Thomas-Vincent, *b.* 15 Oct. 1836.
III. Edward-Charles, *b.* 13 Oct. 1839.

Mr. Acton is a magistrate for the co. of Worcester.

Lineage.—The Actons, whose antiquity of descent is equalled by few existing families, are of Saxon origin, and were in Worcestershire, according to Mr. Abingdon, previously to the Conquest. Soon after that great event, we find them seated at Ombersley; and in the 3rd HENRY III. the name of Elias de Acton, of Acton Hall, in Ombersley, appears with those of other knights and gentlemen summoned to serve upon a jury.

From a common ancestor with the ACTONS *of Acton* sprung the ACTONS *of Sutton*, of which family that of Wolverton is a scion, being founded by a younger son of Sir Roger Acton, of Sutton (the heir of Sir John Mortimer), who *m.* Alice, sister of William Cokesey, Esq., and was father of JOHN ACTON, who acquired the estate of Wolfrinton, or Wolverton, in Worcestershire, as heir to his uncle, the last of the Cokeseys.

WILLIAM ACTON, Esq. of Wolverton (son and heir of William Acton, of Wolverton, by Margaret his wife, dau. and co-heir of Richard Perkins, Esq. of Beenham, Berks,) and grandson (by Barbara his wife, dau. and co-heir of John Vincent, Esq.) of William Acton, Esq. of Wolverton, who *d.* 12 April, 1679); *m.* Anne, dau. of William Tyler, descended from the Ardens of Warwickshire; and, dying 6 Sept. 1763, left a son and successor,

WILLIAM ACTON, Esq. of Wolverton, who *m.* in 1801, Ann-Constantia Davies, descended from the family of Fowler, of St. Thomas, co. Stafford; and, dying 22 Feb. 1814, left, with a dau. Mary, who *d. unm.*, a son, the present WILLIAM ACTON, Esq. of Wolverton.

Arms—Gu., a fesse, erm., within a bordure, engrailed, of the second.
Crest—An arm in armour, embowed, ppr., holding in the hand a sword, arg., hilt, or, thereon a boar's head, couped at the neck, sa., distilling blood.
Motto—Vaillance avance l'homme.
Seat—Wolverton, Worcestershire.

ADAIR OF BELLEGROVE.

ADAIR, GEORGE, Esq. of Bellegrove, and Rath, Queen's County, *b.* 13 Sept. 1784; *m.* 16 May, 1822, Elizabeth, 2nd dau. of the Very Rev. Thos. Trench, Dean of Kildare, 2nd brother of the late Lord Ashtown, and by her, who *d.* 21 March, 1823, has an only son,

JOHN-GEORGE, *b.* 3 March, 1823.

Mr. Adair, who *s.* his father 14 July, 1809, is J.P. and D.L. for the Queen's County, and was high-sheriff in 1822.

Lineage.—The traditional origin of the ADAIRS *of Bellegrove* is this:

THOMAS, the 6th Earl of Desmond, having gone on a hunting expedition, lost his way, and was benighted between Tralee and Newcastle, co. Limerick, where he was received and hospitably entertained by William M'Cormic, whose dau. he subsequently married. At this alliance his family and clan, it is said, were much offended, and compelled him to fly to France, and resign his title and estates to his younger brother, in 1418. He *d.* of grief at Rouen, A.D. 1420, the king of England attending his funeral. The family account proceeds to state that his grandson,

ROBERT, returning to Ireland, with the hope of regaining his family title and estates, killed Gerald, the White Knight (2nd son of Gerald, the then Earl of Desmond) in single combat, at Athdare (Ford of the Oaks), co. Limerick, but was subsequently defeated, and fled to Scotland, where he assumed the name of ADAIRE. From him descended

THOMAS ADAIRE, Esq. (son of Archibald Adaire), who *m.* Mary Hamilton, of the Scotch noble family, and settled in the Queen's County, his patrimonial estates being much diminished, in consequence of his father having been attainted by King JAMES. He had issue, Archibald, William, John,

Robert, and a large family, all of whom *d.* without issue, except

ARCHIBALD ADAIRE, Esq., who *m.* in 1731, Jane, dau. of Mark Antony Chateneuf, and had issue, 1 John; 2 Mark Antony, *d.* young; 1 Mary, *d. unm.* The eldest son,

JOHN ADAIR, Esq. of Rath, Queen's County, *m.* 26 Feb. 1776, Rebecca, eldest child of George Maquay, of the city of Dublin, Esq., and his wife Elizabeth, dau. of Eccles Disney, Esq. of Churchtown, co. Waterford, and dying 14 July, 1809, left issue,

I. GEORGE, heir to his father.
II. John, *b.* 3 Jan. 1792; *d. unm.* 3 Jan. 1839.
I. Elizabeth.
II. Jane, *m.* to F.-W. Fortescue, of Miltown Grange, co. Louth, Esq.
III. Mary. IV. Sarah. V. Charlotte.

Arms—Per bend, or and arg., three dexter hands, couped at the wrist, two and one, gu.
Crest—A man's head, couped and bloody, ppr.
Motto—Loyal au mort.
Seat—Bellegrove, Ballybrittas, Queen's County, Ireland.

ADAIR OF HEATHERTON PARK.

ADAIR, ALEXANDER, Esq. of Heatherton Park, co. Somerset, and Colehouse, Devon, *b.* 15 Sept. 1791; *m.* 17 June, 1828, Harriet-Eliza, dau. of George Atkinson, Esq. of Temple Sowerby, Westmorland, and has issue,

I. ALEXANDER-WILLIAM, *b.* 28 Oct. 1829.
II. Robert-Desmond, *b.* 19 Jan. 1831.
III. Hugh-Jenison, *b.* 21 March, 1835.
IV. Allan-Shafto, *b.* 20 Dec. 1836.
V. Henry-Atkinson, *b.* 17 March, 1839.
I. Harriet-Camilla. II. Henrietta-Mary.

Mr. Adair is younger brother of Sir Robert-Shafto Adair, Bart., being 2nd surviving son of the late Hugh (commonly called William) Adair, Esq. of Ballymena, co. Antrim, by Camilla his wife, dau. and heir of Robert Shafto, Esq. of Benwell, Northumberland.

Arms—Per bend, or and arg., three dexter hands, couped at the wrist, two and one, gu.
Crest—A man's head, couped and bloody, ppr.
Motto—Loyal à mort.
Seats—Heatherton Park, near Taunton; and Cole House, near Bovey Tracey.

ADAIR OF LOUGHANMORE.

ADAIR, THOMAS-BENJAMIN, Esq. of Loughanmore, co. Antrim, *b.* 1776; *m.* in 1806, Amelia, 2nd dau. of Lieut.-Col. Benjamin Adair, R.M., and has,

I. CHARLES, late capt. 33rd foot.
II. Henry. III. Benjamin-Clements.
IV. Thomas-Benjamin, in holy orders.
V. William-Robert, lieut. in the 67th foot.
I. Millicent. II. Amelia.
III. Susanna. IV. Eleanor-Margaret.

Mr. Adair, J.P. for the county of Antrim, served as high-sheriff in 1801.

Lineage.—BENJAMIN ADAIR, Esq. of Loughanmore, who *m.* Anne, dau. of Waterhouse Crymble, Esq. of Ballygillock, co. Antrim, was father of

THOMAS-BENJAMIN ADAIR, Esq. of Loughanmore, who *m.* Margaret, eldest dau. of Charles Crymble, Esq. of Ballygillock, co. Antrim, and had (with two other sons, Benjamin and William-Robert, and two daus., Anne and Elizabeth) an eldest son and successor,

CHARLES ADAIR, Esq. of Loughanmore, who *m.* in 1776, Millicent, eldest dau. of Henry Ellis, Esq. of Prospect, in the county of the town of Carrickfergus, and had issue, THOMAS-BENJAMIN, now of Loughanmore, and Henry.

Arms—Per bend, or and arg., three dexter hands, couped at the wrist, gu.
Crest—A man's head, couped at the neck, ppr.
Motto—Loyal au mort.
Seat—Loughanmore, near Antrim.

ADAM OF BLAIR ADAM.

ADAM, WILLIAM-PATRICK, Esq. of Blair Adam, co. Kinross, *b.* 14 Sept. 1823; *s.* his father, Sir Charles Adam, K.C.B., 16 Sept. 1853.

Lineage.—The surname of Adam is of great antiquity in Scotland, as proved by many documents in the public records.

DUNCAN ADAM, son of Alexander Adam, lived in the reign of King ROBERT BRUCE, and had four sons, Robert, John, Reginald, and Duncan, from whom all the Adams, Adamsons, and Adies, in Scotland, are descended.

WILLIAM ADAM, an eminent architect (son of John Adam, by Helen Cranston his wife, and grandson of Archibald Adam, of Fanno, who purchased, *temp.* CHARLES I., the lands of Queensmanour, co. Forfar), became possessed of many lands, particularly those of Blair, co. Kinross, where he built a house and village, to which he gave the name of Maryburgh. He *m.* Mary, dau. of William Robertson, Esq., of Gladney, and had issue, JOHN, his heir; Robert, architect to GEORGE III., returned to parliament for Kinrosshire in 1768; James, William, Janet, Helen; Mary, wife of Dr. John Drysdale, Dean of the Chapel Royal; Susannah, *m.* to John Clerk, Esq., 3rd son of Sir John Clerk, Bart. of Penneyculck; and Margaret. Mr. Adam *d.* in 1748, and was *s.* by his son,

JOHN ADAM, Esq. of Maryburgh, who *m.* in 1750, Jean, dau. of John Ramsay, Esq., by Jean his wife, dau. of Robert Whyte, Esq. of Bennochy, and left at his decease, 25 June, 1792, with other issue, a son and successor,

THE RIGHT HON. WILLIAM ADAM, of Blair-Adam, lord-lieut. of Kinrosshire, lord chief commissioner of the Jury Court of Scotland, a bencher of Lincoln's Inn, &c.; who *m.* 7 May, 1777, the Hon. Eleanora Elphinston, 2nd dau. of Charles, 10th Lord Elphinston, and sister of Adm. Lord Keith, by which lady (who *d.* 4 Feb. 1800) he had a numerous family, of whom were VICE-ADM. SIR CHARLES ADAM, K.C.B., and LIEUT.-GEN. SIR FREDERICK ADAM, G.C.B. and G.C.M.G., colonel 57th regiment, a gallant military officer, who served with high distinction in the Peninsula and at Waterloo; and *d.* 17 Aug. 1853. The elder,

VICE-ADMIRAL SIR CHARLES ADAM, K.C.B., governor of Greenwich Hospital; *b.* in 1780, *m.* 4 Oct. 1822, Elizabeth, dau. of Patrick Brydone, Esq., F.R.S.; and *d.* 16 Sept. 1853, having had,

WILLIAM-PATRICK, now of Blair Adam.
Charles-Brydone, Mid. R.N.; *b.* 1825; lost at sea in H.M.S. "Fairy," 1840.
Mary.

Arms—Arg., a mullet, az., pierced, of the field, between three crosses-crosslet, fitchée, gu.
Crest—A cross-crosslet, as in the arms, surmounted of a sword in saltier, ppr., hilted and pommelled, or.
Motto—Crux mihi grata quies.
Seat—Blair Adam, co. Kinross.

ADAMS OF ANSTY.

ADAMS, HENRY-WILLIAM, Esq. of Ansty Hall, co. Warwick, and Morton Pinkney, co. Northampton, brigadier-gen. and col. in the army, lieut.-col. 49th regt., C.B., *b.* 31 Jan. 1805; *m.* 28 Nov. 1843, his cousin, Catharine, dau. of the late Rev. Thomas Coker Adams, vicar of Ansty. He *s.* his father in 1842.

Lineage.—SIMON ADAMS, merchant and vintner, *d.* in 1448, leaving several houses and other property in the City of London, to the Vintner's Company, to found two chaplaincies, and distribute the surplus to the poor. His descendant

SIMON ADAMS, Lord of the Manor of Great Packham, Essex, *d.* 1598, leaving a grandson,

SIMON ADAMS, who became possessed of Morton Pinkney, co. Northampton, he *d.* in 1644, leaving a son,

THE REV. SIMON ADAMS, co. Northampton, rector of Aston-le-Walls, who *d.* in 1678, leaving by Cecily Abbys, his wife (with four daus.), two sons, SIMON, his heir, and Thomas, ancestor of the family of ADAMS *of Lavendon*, Bucks. The eldest son,

SIMON ADAMS, Esq. of Morton Pinkney, co. Northampton, *b.* in 1631, *m.* twice, and by his 2nd wife, Anne, dau. of Robert Cooper, of Lubbenham, Esq., had (with four daus.) two sons, of whom the elder,

SIMON ADAMS, M.D. of Daventry and East Haddon, *b.* in 1667, *m.* 1692, Anne, dau. of the Rev. William Gilbert, of Culworth, and had by her one son, SIMON, and two daus. Dr. Adams *d.* in 1748, aged 80. His son,

THE REV. SIMON ADAMS, vicar of Welton, in Northamptonshire, *b.* in 1693, *m.* 1717-18, Anne, dau. of John Clarke, Esq. of Welton, and left, at his decease in 1731, two sons, of whom the elder,

Clarke Adams, Esq. of East Haddon and Morton Pinkney, lieut.-col. of the Northamtonshire militia, *b.* in 1718-19, *m.* 1st, 15 Aug. 1744, Elizabeth Dobbins, dau. and heir of the Rev. William Tayler, of Ansty Hall, co. Warwick, rector of Malpas, in Cheshire, and had a son, Simon, his heir, and a dau. Elizabeth Dobbins, *m.* to Charles Watkins, Esq. of Daventry. Col. Adams *m.* 2ndly, 29 Aug. 1751, Frances, only dau. and heir of Richard Clarke, Esq. of Welton, but by her, who *d.* 20 Aug. 1781, had no issue. He *d.* 26 June, 1776, and was *s.* by his son,

Simon Adams, Esq. of Ansty Hall, co. Warwick, barrister-at-law, deputy recorder of Northampton, and recorder of Daventry. This gentleman, in 1780, sold the estate of East Haddon to Henry Sawbridge, Esq. He *m.* 3 Jan. 1778, Sarah, dau. of Cadwallader Coker, Esq. of Bicester, and by her, who *d.* 17 July, 1833, aged eighty, had issue,

Henry-Cadwallader, his heir.
Thomas-Coker, vicar of Anstey, Shelton, and Foleshill, A.M., *b.* in 1782; *d.* in 1851; *m.* 16 Sept. 1806, Mary, dau. of Johnson Pistor, Esq. of Bath, and has issue, Simon-Thomas, *b.* in 1807; Cadwallader-Coker, *b.* in 1817; and Daniel-Charles-Octavius, *b.* in 1822; all in holy orders; Mary Philadelphia, Catherine and Sarah-Coker.
John, serjeant-at-law and assistant-judge of the Middlesex quarter sessions, *b.* in 1786, *m.* 1st, in 1811, Eliza, only dau. of William Nation, Esq. of Exeter, and by her, who *d.* 12 Aug. 1814, had issue, John, barrister-at-law, and author of *The Doctrine of Equity*, *b.* in 1813, *m.* 21 Dec. 1843, Emily, dau. of Sir John Riddell, Bart. of Riddell, Roxburghshire, and *d.* 18 Sept. 1848, leaving issue, John-Walter and Emily-Eliza-Charlotte; and William, in holy orders, and author of *The Shadow of the Cross*, &c., *b.* in 1814, *d.* 17 Jan. 1848. He *m.* 2ndly, in 1817, Jane, dau. of Thomas Martin, Esq. of Nottingham, and by her, who *d.* 19 June, 1825, had another son, Henry-Cadwallader, in holy orders, *b.* in 1817, *m.* 1852, Esther, dau of the Rev. R. Edmonds. Mr. Serjeant Adams *m.* 3rdly, in 1826, Charlotte-Priscilla, dau. and heir of John Coker, Esq. (*See* Coker *of Bicester*), and has by her, Coker, *b.* in 1827, in holy orders, fellow of New College, Oxford; Charles-Warren, *b.* in 1833; Walter-Marsham, *b.* in 1837.
Sarah-Coker, *m.* 17 May, 1800, to James Beck. Esq. of Allesley Park, Warwickshire.

Mr. Adams *d.* 10 March, 1801, and was *s.* by his son,

Henry-Cadwallader Adams, Esq. of Ansty Hall, co. Warwick, *b.* 11 Dec. 1779; *m.* 18 June, 1803, Emma, eldest dau. of Sir William Curtis, Bart. and had issue,

I. Henry-William, his heir.
II. George-Curtis, commander R.N., *b.* 1807, *m.* 1847, Mary-Susan, dau. of Edward Woolmer, Esq. of Exeter, and has,
  1. Henry-Cadwallader, *b.* 28 July, 1850.
  1. Emma-Louisa. 2. Catharine-Anne.
III. Frank, lieut.-col. 28th foot, *b* in 1809, *m.* in 1845, Ellen, relict of J. Straith, Esq., and has issue,
  1. William-Ormond, *b.* 16 Jan. 1847.
  2. Frank-Reginald, *b.* 14 Sept. 1852.
  Ellen-Georgina, Emma-Catharine, } twins.
IV. Arthur-Robarts, A.M., Fellow of St. John's College, Oxford, *b.* in 1812.
V. Cadwallader, capt. 49th foot, *b.* in 1825.
I. Emma-Curtis. II. Laura-Coker.
III. Anna-Delicia.

Mr. Adams, a magistrate and deputy-lieutenant for Warwickshire, served as sheriff of the county in 1837. He *d.* in March, 1842.

Arms—Vert, a cross, or, charged with an estoile, sa.
Crest—A talbot, passant, az., semé of bezants, and collared, arg.
Motto—Sub cruce veritas.
Seat—Ansty Hall, near Coventry.

ADAMS OF BOWDON.

Adams, William-Dacres, Esq., of Bowdon, co. Devon, *b.* 16 Dec. 1775; *m.* 10 March, 1804, Elizabeth, 2nd dau. of Mayow-Wynell Mayow, Esq. of Sydenham, in Kent, and by her, who *d.* 4 Feb. 1814, has issue,

I. William-Pitt, Chargé d'Affaires and Consul-General to the Peruvian Republic; *b.* 11 Dec. 1804; *m.* 16 Sept. 1847, Georgiana-Emily, dau. of Robert Lukin, Esq.; and *d.* at Lima, 1 Sept. 1852, leaving one daughter.
II. Dacres, in holy orders, vicar of Bampton, co. Oxford; *b.* 26 July, 1806; *m.* 15 Aug. 1832, Anna-Maria, eldest dau. of Baldwin Fulford, Esq. of Fulford, co. Devon, and has issue, William-Fulford and Philip-Dacres.
III. Mayow-Wynell, *b.* 11 Oct. 1808; *m.* 19 May, 1841, Anna-Maria, dau. of Major Edward Hodge, 7th light-drag. (killed at Waterloo), and Maria his wife, dau. of Sir Edmund Bacon, Bart., and has one dau., Edith-Maria.
IV. Herbert-George, in holy orders, vicar of Cornwood, Devon; *b.* 23 Jan. 1814; *m.* 3 Aug. 1843, Eleanor, dau. of Baldwin Fulford, Esq. of Fulford; and *d.* at Bowdon, 25 Nov. 1851, leaving issue, Charles-Herbert, Baldwin-Dacres, George-Francis, and Anna-Maria.
I. Elizabeth-Mary.

Mr. Adams was confidential secretary to the Right Hon. William Pitt during his last administration, and was subsequently a commissioner of the Woods, Forests, and Land revenues.

Lineage.—William Adams, Esq., son of the Rev. Samuel Adams, by Susan his wife, dau. of Bartholomew Parr, of Silverton, Devon, *m.* Mary Chadder, and had,

I. William, his heir.
II. Samuel, of Totness, in Devon, *b.* 1 Jan. 1770; *m.* 27 Jan. 1800, Elizabeth Bentall, and has, 1 William, *b.* in 1802; 2 Edward, in the army, *b.* in 1804; 3 Henry-Bentall, *b.* in 1806, who *m.* in 1835, Harriot, dau. of the late Joseph Bickham, Esq., and has issue; 4 George, E. I. Co.'s civil service, *b.* in 1808, who *m.* in 1833, Amelia, dau. of the late Captain Reid, and has issue; 5 Frederick, E. I. Co.'s military service, *b.* in 1814; 6 Francis, *b.* in 1821; 1 Mary; 2 Louisa; and 3 Elizabeth.
I. Mary, *m.* to Giles Welsford, Esq.
II. Sarah-Chadder, *m.* to James Hodge, Esq.
III. Susan, *m.* to John-Parr Welsford, Esq.

The elder son,

William Adams, Esq. of Bowdon, in Devon, M.P. for Totness; *m.* 24 June, 1774, Anna-Maria, dau. of Richard Dacres, Esq., descended from Dacres, of Leatherhead, in Surrey, supposed to be a branch of the noble line of Dacre of the North, and by her (who *d.* at Bowden, 19 April, 1830), had issue,

William Dacres, his heir.
George Pownoll (Sir), K.C.H., gen. in the army; *m.* Elizabeth, dau. and co-heir of Sir William Elford, Bart., and has issue, William-Elford, capt. Royal Irish regt., *b.* 10 June, 1822, *m.* 1849, Anna-Maria, dau. of Patrick Bannerman, Esq.; George-Dacres, *b.* 1 Nov. 1823, in holy orders; Arthur-Fulford, *b.* 6 April, 1825, *m.* 1847, Henrietta, 2nd dau. of William F. Bowman, Esq.; and Henry Cranstoun, *b.* 25 Nov. 1826, *m.* Matilda-Winsloe, 3rd dau. of Thomas Palton, Esq., and has issue.
Anna-Maria, *m.* to Baldwin Fulford, Esq. of Great Fulford.
Louisa-Sawyer.

Mr. Adams *d.* 21 Sept. 1811, and was *s.* by his elder son, the present William-Dacres Adams, Esq. of Bowdon.

Arms—Or, a lion, rampant, gu., between semée of cross-crosslets fitchée, within a bordure, engrailed, sa.
Crest—A dexter arm in armour, embowed, grasping a cross-crosslet of the arms, charged on the elbow with a torteau.
Motto—Libertas et natale solum.
Seat—Bowdon, near Totness.

ADAMS OF HOLYLAND.

Adams, John, Esq. of Holyland, co. Pembroke, *b.* in 1796; *m.* 24 July, 1828, Anne, eldest dau. of the late Henry Gibbons, 2nd son of John Gibbons, Esq. of Oswestry, and has issue,

I. John-Alexander-Philipps, *b.* 10 Jan. 1831.
II. Henry-Joseph, *b.* in Sept. 1835.
I. Augusta-Mary. II. Agnes-Anne.
III. Frances-Louisa. IV. Mary-Charlotte.

Lineage.—This is a very ancient Pembrokeshire family. The first recorded ancestor,

Nicholas Adams, or Adames, was of Buckspool, about the year 1370. His son and successor,

John Adams, marrying Ellen, one of the co-heiresses of David de Paterchurch, became seated at Paterchurch, where his descendants continue to reside.

William Adams, Esq. of Holyland (son and heir of William Adams, Esq. of Holyland, descended in a direct line from the Paterchurch family), *m.* Anne, 2nd dau. of Joseph Rixson, Esq., and had issue, 1 John-Philipps, his heir; 2 Joseph, major in the army, who *m.* Elizabeth, dau. of John Campbell, Esq. of Stackpool Court, and was father of Lieut.-Gen. Alexander Adams, who *m.* Frances-Louisa, dau. of the Rev. William Holcombe, canon of St. David's; 3 Roger; 4 Anne, *m.* 1st, to the Rev. William Thomas, and 2ndly, to Matthew Campbell, Esq., son of J. H. Campbell, Esq. of Bangeston, Lion king-at-arms. The eldest son,

John-Philipps Adams, Esq. of Holyland, a deputy-lieutenant for Pembrokeshire; *m.* Charlotte, dau. of William Corbet, Esq. of Darnhall, in Cheshire, and left two sons, JOHN and William. The elder,

JOHN ADAMS, Esq. of Holyland, m. in 1795, Sophia, dau. of the Ven. Archdeacon Holcombe, and left, with a dau., Augusta, m. to Vaughan Lloyd, Esq., R.N., a son and successor, the present JOHN ADAMS, Esq. of Holyland.

Arms—Quarterly: 1st and 4th, sa., a martlet, arg.; 2nd and 3rd, arg., a cross, gu., thereon five mullets, or.
Crest—A martlet, arg.
Motto—Certior in cœlo domus.
Seat—Holyland, near Pembroke.

ADAMS OF NORTHLANDS.

ADAMS, THE VERY REV. SAMUEL, A.M., of Northlands, co. Cavan, Dean of Cashel, and prebendary of Terebrine, diocese of Elphin, J.P. for the counties of Cavan and Monaghan, b. 15 Feb. 1783; m. 4 Jan. 1809, Frances, youngest dau. of Capt. John Hervey, of Killiane Castle, co. Wexford, and has issue,

I. Benjamin-William, b. 13 Feb. 1816; d. 4 March, 1822.
II. JOHN-HERVEY, a barrister, J.P. for the cos. of Cavan and Monaghan, and high-sheriff of the former county, 1854; b. 28 April, 1818; m. 31 March, 1846, Elizabeth, 3rd dau. of Ambrose Going, Esq., J.P. of Ballyphilip, co. Tipperary, and has issue, Samuel-Allen, Ambrose-Going, Margaret, and Elizabeth-Frances.
III. Charles-Steuart, b. 12 July, 1820; m. Elizabeth, only dau. of Charles McMahon, Esq., and has issue two sons.
IV. Benjamin-William, A.M.; b. 31 March, 1827; in holy orders, rector of Cloghran, Swords, diocese of Dublin; m. 14 Dec. 1854, Georgina-Roberta, dau. of John-Drew Atkin, Esq. of Merrion Square Dublin, and granddau. of the late Sir Thomas Roberts, Bart.
I. Dorothea-Anne, m. 31 March, 1833, Le Chevalier Charles-A. Zander, of Munich, and has issue.
II. Elizabeth-Frances, m. 21 March, 1833, John-J.-D. McDonnell, Esq., an officer in the army, and has issue.
III. Caroline-Matilda, m. 2 May, 1837, Thomas-R. Barry, Esq., and has issue.

Lineage.—This family claims to be a branch of the old Scottish house of ADAM, which was closely allied in ancient times to the illustrious race of Douglas. In the 17th century, tradition records that there were three brothers of the family of ADAM *of Fanno*. The eldest continued the line in his native country, while the two younger, annexing the letter *s* to their patronymic, left home, one settling in Wales, and the other in Ireland. The latter, who m. Catherine Magennis, dau. of Arthur Magennis, 1st Viscount Iveagh, by his wife Sarah, dau. of Hugh, Earl of Tyrone, was father of

CAPTAIN JAMES ADAMS, who was an officer in the army of King WILLIAM III., and distinguished himself at the battle of the Boyne. His son,

JAMES ADAMS, Esq. of Corneary House, co. Cavan, b. in 1673, m. Jane Allen, and d. 19 Nov. 1744, aged 71. His only son,

ALLEN ADAMS, Esq. of Corneary House, b. 1708, m. Martha, dau. of Captain Higginbotham, and granddau. of General Scurlogh Williams,* of Clongill Castle, co. Meath, and dying 15 Dec. 1755, left issue,

I. RICHARD, J.P. for the cos. of Cavan and Monaghan, of Shircock House, co. Cavan, of which county he was high-sheriff in 1788, and of Monaghan in 1784. He m. Matilda, dau. of Thomas Cosby, Esq., and had a numerous issue.
II. James, of Corneary House, d. unm. in 1809, aged 64.
III. William, of Castletown House, m. and dying 28 Feb. 1815, left issue.
IV. Samuel, settled in Dublin, and m. Miss Leslie, by whom he had issue. He d. 7 June, 1799.
V. Benjamin.

The fifth son,

THE REV. BENJAMIN ADAMS, b. 1756; rector of Kellinick, J.P. for the co. of Cavan; m. 14 April, 1777, Elizabeth, dau. of John Clark, Esq., son of the celebrated metaphysician, Dr. Samuel Clark, rector of St. James, London, and chaplain to Queen ANNE, and by her (who d. 28 Feb. 1833, aged 77) had issue four sons and six daus.,

I. William-Allen, b. 15 May, 1783; d. 3 March, 1784.
II. John, J.P. for co. Cavan; b. 16 May, 1785; was high-sheriff for Cavan in 1811; m. 1807, Joyce, eldest dau. of his uncle Richard; and d. in 1827, without issue.
III. SAMUEL, the present dean of Cashel.
IV. Charles-James, lieut. R.N., J.P. for co. Cavan, of Shinan House; b. 29 April, 1792; entered the navy in 1807, where he served with distinguished merit for some years: he was high-sheriff for Cavan in 1833; m. Anne-Jane (d. 4 March, 1834, aged 36), dau. of William Foster, Esq. of Dowdstown, co. Louth, and d. 23 Aug. 1854, having had issue,
1 Benjamin-Samuel, b. 22 June, 1828; lieut. 12th regt.
2 William-John, b. 14 Feb. 1831; d. 29 March, 1832.
3 Charles-James, b. 13 Feb. 1832.
1 Rebecca-Horatia, m. Thomas Coote, Esq., D.L., and J.P., of the co. Monaghan, of Brandrum, and has issue.
2 Elizabeth, m. Rev. Wm. Deering, and has issue.
3 Caroline-Martha, m. Edgar Brodin, Esq., J.P., and has issue.
4 Anne-Jane, m. Rev. Stephen Radcliff, and has issue.
I. Elizabeth, d. 25 April, 1780.
II. Elizabeth, d. 28 Oct. 1780, an infant.
III. Emelia, d. 5 Sept. 1782.
IV. Charlotte, d. 16 Aug. 1790.
V. Matilda, d. 15 July, 1794.
VI. Caroline, m. John Leonard, Esq., J.P., of Claremont House, co. Wicklow, and has issue.

Mr. Adams d. 10 June, 1840, aged 84.

Arms—(duly registered in the Office of Arms, Dublin Castle)—Gu. a heart, between three crosses-crosslet, fitchée, or.
Crest—On a mount, vert, a cross-crosslet, fitchée, or, charged with a bleeding heart, gu.
Motto—In cruce salus.
Seat—Northlands, co. Cavan.

* In consideration of the distinguished service rendered by this officer to the inhabitants of Drogheda in the war of 1688, they granted the freedom of their borough to him and his heirs for ever, which privilege the ADAMS family, in consequence of this marriage, still enjoy.

ADAMS OF JAMESBROOK.

ADAMS, RICHARD-WALLIS-GOOLD, Esq. of Jamesbrook, co. Cork, J.P., b. 27 March, 1802, m. 4 Nov. 1852, Mary-Sarah, dau. of the late Sir William Wrixon-Becher, Bart. of Ballygiblin, and has a son and heir,

WILLIAM-RICHARD, b. 30 Aug. 1853.

Lineage.—The late MICHAEL-GOOLD ADAMS, Esq. of Jamesbrook, son of Wallis Adams, Esq., and Frances Goold his wife, m. in 1800, Martha, sister of the 1st Earl of Bantry, and dau. of Simon White, Esq. of Bantry House, co. Cork, by Frances-Jane his wife, dau. of Richard-Hedges Eyre, Esq., of Mount Hedges, and had issue,

RICHARD-WALLIS, his heir.
Michael, late capt. Scots Greys.
Robert-Hedges.
Samuel-Hamilton, m. 1st, in 1846, Frances-Margaret, dau. of Colonel and Lady Katharine Bernard of Castle Bernard, King's County, and has by her, a dau., Katharine-Charlotte. He m. 2ndly, in Nov. 1852, Frances-Louisa, dau. of the late Dean of Cloyne and the Lady Anna De Burgh.
Frances-Jane.

Mr. Goold Adams d. in 1817 (his widow survived until 1841), and was s. by his son, the present RICHARD-WALLIS-GOOLD ADAMS, Esq. of Jamesbrook.

Seat—Jamesbrook, near Cloyne.

ADAMS OF AHAVAGURRAH.

ADAMS, THOMAS-TRAVERS, Esq. of Ahavagurrah, co. Limerick, J.P., b. in Oct. 1790; m. June, 1822, Hannah, dau. of Captain Evans, of Tipperary.

Lineage.—WILLIAM ADAMS, Esq., a younger son of Roger Adams, Esq. of the co. of Limerick, m. Frances Cox, of Ballinoe, in that county, and was father of

WILLIAM ADAMS, Esq. of Ahavagurrah, who m. in July, 1789, Jane Travers, and by her, who d. in Sept. 1846, had issue,

I. THOMAS-TRAVERS, now of Ahavagurrah.
II. William, d. young. III. George. IV. Hugh.
I. Maria, m. to Major Travers.
II. Frances, m. to Llewellyn Nash, Esq. of Ballyquane, co. Cork.
III. Harriette, m. to Jonathan-Wigmore Sherlock, Esq. of Fermoy.
IV. Jane, d. unm. V. Wilhelmina, d. young.

Mr. Adams d. in Dec. 1846.

Arms—Az., three mountain-cats, passant, or.
Crest—A griffin's head, erased, az.
Motto—Malo mori quam fœdari.
Seat—Ahavagurrah, Kilfinane, co. Limerick.

ADDERLEY OF HAMS HALL.

ADDERLEY, CHARLES-BOWYER, Esq. of Hams Hall, co. Warwick, b. 2 Aug. 1814; m. 28 July, 1842, Julia-Anne-Eliza, eldest dau. of Chandos, Lord Leigh, of Stoneleigh Abbey, and has issue,

I. Charles-Leigh, b. 10 March, 1846.
I Anna-Maria-Margarette. II. Caroline-Jane.
III. Frances-Georgina-Mary.
IV. Evelyn-Augusta. V. Isabel.

Mr. Adderley, who is M.P. for North Staffordshire, s. his great-uncle, Charles-Bowyer Adderley, Esq. of Hams Hall, 12 April, 1826.

Lineage.—The family of Adderley is of considerable antiquity in Staffordshire. The manor of Coton, in that county, was purchased in 1558, by Ralph Adderley, Esq., an eminent lawyer, who served as high sheriff, 17 Elizabeth. From his eldest son, Richard, derived the Adderley's of Coton, and from his 2nd, Ralph, the Adderley's of Hams Hall, co. Warwick, an estate purchased by Sir Charles Adderley, Knt. (Ralph's son and heir). Sir Charles's great grandson,

Bowyer Adderley, Esq. of Hams Hall (son of Charles Adderley, Esq. of Hams, by Mary, his wife, dau. and co-heir of Sir William Bowyer, Bart.), m. 1st, 1726, Elizabeth, dau. of Christopher Horton, Esq. of Catton, co. Derby, and had two daus., Mary and Frances. He m. 2ndly, 14 July, 1741, Lettice, dau. and co-heir of Ralph Adderley, Esq. of Coton Hall, co. Stafford, and had issue,

I. Charles-Bowyer, heir to his father.
II. Ralph, of Coton, who m. 4 Aug. 1778, Dorothy, dau. of Thomas Kynnersley, Esq. of Loxley Park, and widow of Thomas Byrche Savage, Esq. of Elmley Castle, co. Worcester, by whom he left at his decease in 1819,
1 Charles Clement, who m. 6 June, 1811, Anna-Maria, eldest dau. of Sir Edmund Cradock Hartopp, Bart. of Four Oaks Hall, Warwickshire, and dying 30 June, 1818, (his widow survived until April, 1827), left issue,
Charles-Bowyer, heir to his grand-uncle.
Edmund-James, b. in February, 1816, m. Marian, dau. of Sir Joseph Leeds, Bt.
Anna-Maria-Letitia, m. in 1834, to Forster-Alleyne M'Geachy, Esq., and d. in 1841.
Mary.
2 Ralph, of Barlaston and Coton. (*See that family.*)
3 Arden, admiral R.N., m. 21 Oct. 1823, Anne, only dau. of W.-R. Bishton, Esq. of Shakerley House, co. Salop.
4 George-William Bowyer, of Fillongley Hall, co. Warwick. (*See that name.*)
1 Letitia-Penelope, m. 1st, Andrew Hacket, Esq. of Moxhull Park, in Warwickshire, and 2ndly, in 1820, the Hon. Berkeley Noel, 6th son of Sir Gerard-Noel Noel, Bart., by the Baroness Barham.

Mr. Adderley d. 3rd Nov. 1747, and was s. by his son,

Charles-Bowyer Adderley, Esq. of Hams Hall, who m. in 1779, Mary, only dau. of Robert Hotchkin, Esq. of Uppingham, co. Rutland, but dying s. p. 12th April, 1826, was s. by his grandnephew Charles-Bowyer Adderley, Esq. of Hams Hall.

Arms—Arg., on a bend, az. three mascles, of the field.
Crest—On a chapeau, gu., turned up, erm., a stork, arg.
Seat—Hams Hall, Warwickshire.

ADDERLEY OF BARLASTON AND COTON.

Adderley, Ralph-Thomas, Esq. of Barlaston Hall and Coton Hall, both in the county of Stafford, b. 18 March, 1826.

Lineage.—Ralph Adderley, Esq. of Coton Hall, b. 15 June, 1781, uncle of Charles-Bowyer Adderley, Esq. of Hams Hall, m. 4 July, 1816, Rosamond, eldest dau. and co-heir (with her sister, Catherine-Penelope, wife of Sir J.-C.-Browne Cave, Bart.) of William Mills, Esq. of Barlaston Hall, grandson of Thomas Mills, Esq., by Hester his wife, dau. and co-heir of Samuel Bagnall, Esq. of Barlaston Hall, and had issue,

Ralph-Thomas, now of Barlaston and Coton.
Randolph-Ralph, lieut. 60th rifles, b. 15 Feb. 1832.
Mylles-Bagnall-Bowyer, b. 6 June, 1835.
Sophia-Catherine, d. 28 July, 1835.
Mary-Elizabeth, m. 19 April, 1853, to Andrew Corbet, Esq., 2nd son of Sir Andrew Corbet, Bart.
Anne-Selina.

Mr. Adderley d. 31 Jan. 1851.

Seats—Barlaston and Coton Halls, Staffordshire.

ADDERLEY OF FILLONGLEY HALL.

Adderley, The Rev. George-William-Bowyer, of Fillongley Hall, co. Warwick, b. 9 Jan. 1787; m. 11 Dec. 1823, Caroline, youngest dau. of the late John Taylor, Esq. of Moseley Hall, co. Worcester. Mr. Adderley is 4th son of the late Ralph Adderley, Esq. of Coton Hall, co. Stafford, by Dorothy, his wife, dau. of Thomas Kynnersley, Esq. of Loxley Park, and widow of Thomas Byrche Savage, of Elmley Castle, co. Worcester, and youngest uncle of Charles-Bowyer Adderley, Esq. of Hams Hall, co. Warwick. (*See that family.*)

Arms and Crest—Same as Adderley *of Hams Hall.*
Seat—Fillongley Hall, co. Warwick.

ADEANE OF BABRAHAM.

Adeane, Henry-John, Esq. of Babraham, co. Cambridge, b. 9 June, 1833.

Lineage.—General James-Whorwood Adeane, M.P. for the town and afterwards for the co. Cambridge, son of Simon Adeane, Esq. by Mary, his wife, dau. of the Hon. and Rev. Dr. Henry Brydges, brother to the 1st Duke of Chandos, m. Anne, only child and heiress of Robert Jones, Esq. of Babraham, co. Cambridge, and had with three daus., viz., Jane, m. to George-Henry Law, D.D., Bishop of Bath and Wells; Margaret, m. to John Osborne, Esq. of Malshot Park, Hants, and Mary-Anne, m. to General Tinling, an only son and heir,

Robert-Jones Adeane, Esq. of Babraham, m. in 1785, Annabella, dau. of Sir Patrick Blake, Bart. of Langham Hall, co. Suffolk, and had issue,

Charles-James, b. 14 June, 1786, d. young.
Henry-John, heir to his father.
Annabella, m. to Captain Francis Warde, Rl. H. Art.
Louisa, m. Rev. William Barlow, Prebendary of Chester.

The son and heir,

Henry-John Adeane, Esq. of Babraham, b. 18 June, 1789; m. 1st, 24 Oct. 1822, Catherine-Judith, dau. of John King, Esq. of Aldenham House, Herts, but had by this marriage no surviving issue. He m. 2ndly, 6 Oct. 1828, the Hon. Matilda-Abigail Stanley, dau. of Lord Stanley, of Alderley, co. Chester, and by her (who d. 28 July, 1850,) had,

I. Robert-Jones, of Babraham, b. 9 Sept. 1830; d. unm. 7 Dec. 1853.
II. Henry-John, now of Babraham.
III. Edward-Stanley, b. 7 Dec. 1836.
IV. Frederic-Carus, d. 5 Dec. 1852.
I. Matilda-Annabella-Maria, d. 11 Sept. 1853. } twins.
II. Alethea-Louisa. }
III. Lucy-Elizabeth. IV. Emmeline-Augusta.
V. Isabel. VI. Louisa-Amabel.
VII. Jane-Henrietta. VIII. Constance-Maria-Josepha.

Mr. Adeane, M.P. co. of Cambridge, d. 11 May, 1847.

Arms—Sa., on a chevron between three griffins' heads, erased, arg., as many estoiles; quartering Jones, Brydges, and Chandos.
Crest—A griffin's head, collared, between two wings.
Seat—Babraham, co. Cambridge.

VANS-AGNEW OF BARNBARROCH.

Vans-Agnew, Robert, Esq. of Barnbarroch, co. Wigton, s. his father in 1842.

Lineage.—The family of Vans or Vaus claims to be a branch of the great house of Vaux, so celebrated in every part of Europe. (*See* Burke's *Extinct and Dormant Peerage.*) A younger branch of the Dirleton line of the family was that of Barnbarroch, derived from Robert Vans, who acquired from the Earl of Douglas a charter of the lands of Barnbarroch, in 1451. This

Robert Vans, who was eldest son of John Vans, ambassador to England from King James II., in 1437, left issue, Blaize, his heir; Thomas, ambassador to England, in 1457, dean of Glasgow, secretary to the King, and keeper of the Privy Seal; George, Bishop of Galloway, and Patrick, Prior of Whitehorne. The eldest son,

Blaize Vans, of Barnbarroch, m. Elizabeth, dau. and heiress of Sir John Shaw, of Haillie, and widow of Sir John Stewart, of Garlies, by whom he had a son, Patrick Vans, of Barnbarroch, who m. Margaret, dau. of Gilbert, 2nd Lord Kennedy, and great-granddau. of King Robert III., and left at his decease, in 1528, a son and successor, Sir John Vans, of Barnbarroch, slain at Pinkie, whose son, Sir Patrick Vans, of Barnbarroch, ambassador to Denmark, was father of Sir John Vans, of Barnbarroch, who d. in 1642, and was s. by his son, Patrick Vans, of Barnbarroch, who d. in 1673, leaving a son, John Vans, Esq. of Barnbarroch, who dissipated the greater portion of the family estates. His brother and heir, ALEXANDER VANS, Esq. of Barnbarroch, was father of

PATRICK VANS, Esq. of Barnbarroch, M.P. for Wigtonshire, who died suddenly in 1733, owing to the breaking out of a wound received at the Battle of Almanza. He was s. by his son,

JOHN VANS, Esq. of Barnbarroch, who m. Margaret, only child and heiress of Robert Agnew, Esq. of Sheuchan, (of the Agnews of Lochnaw,) by Margaret, dau. of Patrick M'Dowall, of Freugh, and upon his marriage, under a mutual entail, assumed the additional surname and arms of AGNEW. He d. in 1780, and was s. by his son,

ROBERT VANS-AGNEW, Esq. of Barnbarroch and Seuchan, who m. Frances, dau. of John Dunlop, Esq of that ilk, and had issue, JOHN, his heir; PATRICK, successor to his brother; Henry-Stewart, an advocate at the Scottish bar; Margaret, Frances-Georgiana, and Anna-Maria. Mr. Vans-Agnew d. in 1809, and was s. by his eldest son,

JOHN VANS-AGNEW, Esq. of Barnbarroch and Seuchan, who d. unm. in 1825, and was s. by his next brother,

PATRICK VANS-AGNEW, Esq. of Barnbarroch and Seuchan, col. in the East India Company's service, Companion of the Bath, and one of the East India directors, b. 6 Jan. 1783, m. 7 Sept. 1813, Miss Catherine Fraser, of Inverness, and had issue, ROBERT, his heir; Patrick-Alexander, William, John, James, George, Frances, Mary, Elizabeth and Catherine. Col. Vans-Agnew d. in 1842.

Arms—Quarterly: 1st and 4th, arg., a bend, gu.; 2nd and 3rd, arg., a chevron, between, in chief, two cinquefoils, gu., with a cross-crosslet fitchée, sa., in centre and in base, a saltier couped.

Crests—1st, a lion, rampant, holding scales in the dexter paw; 2nd, an eagle, issuant and regardant, ppr.

Supporters—Two savages, with clubs in their hands, and wreathed about the middle with laurel.

Mottoes—Be faithful—for VANS. Consilio, non impetu—for AGNEW.

Seats—Barnbarroch, near Wigton; Park House, near Stanraer.

AINSWORTH OF SMITHILLS HALL.

AINSWORTH, PETER, Esq. of Smithills Hall, co. Lancaster, b. 24 Nov. 1790; m. 15 Aug. 1815, Elizabeth, 3rd dau. and co-heir of Ashton Byrom, Esq. of Fairview, Liverpool. He s. his father, 1 April, 1833. He is a magistrate and deputy-lieut. of the county, and was M.P. for Bolton from 1834 to 1847.

Lineage.—This family has been resident in the township of Halliwell for two hundred years.

PETER AINSWORTH, Esq. of Lightbounds, co. Lancaster, son of Peter Ainsworth, of The Moss, m. 17 July, 1761, Alice Aspinall, of Carrington, co. Chester, by whom he had a son,

RICHARD AINSWORTH, Esq. of Moss Bank, Halliwell, a deputy-lieutenant for the co. of Lancaster, who m. Sarah, dau. of James Noble, Esq. of Lancaster, and had issue,

PETER, his heir.
John-Horrocks, of Moss Bank, m. in 1833, Elizabeth, dau. of John Shaw, Esq. of London, and has issue, Richard-Henry, Gertrude-Sophia, Emily-Alice, Louisa-Sarah and Florence.
Sarah, m. to the Hon. Arthur Annesley, 2nd son of the late Earl of Mountnorris. Alice.
Hannah, m. 3 July, 1834, to Edward Webster, of Lincoln's Inn, Esq.

Mr. Ainsworth d. 1 April, 1833, and was s. by his son, the present PETER AINSWORTH, of Smithhills Hall, Esq.

Arms—Gu., three battle-axes, arg.
Crest—A man in armour, holding a battle-axe, ppr.
Motto—Mea gloria fides.
Seat—Smithills Hall, near Bolton, co. Lancaster.

AKERS OF MALLING ABBEY.

AKERS, ARETAS, Esq. of Malling Abbey, co. Kent, J.P. and D.L. of that county, and also J.P. for Sussex, b. 15 May, 1799; m. 9 May, 1821, Isabella, dau. (by Dorothy, his wife, only dau. of Sir Charles Style, Bart.) of the late John Larking, Esq. of Clare House, high sheriff in 1800, and has had six sons and four daus., of whom three sons and five daus. survive, viz.,

I. ARETAS, b. 18 Nov. 1824, m. 7 Aug. 1849, Frances-Maria, dau. of Frances Brandram, Esq. of Tonbridge Wells.
II. Charles-Style, Lt. R. Eng., b. 21 Sept. 1828, m. 16 Oct. 1851, Henrietta-Margaret, dau. of Col. Despard, C.B.
III. George, b. 18 Dec. 1837.
I. Isabella-Dorothea. II. Jane-Mary.
III. Caroline-Ramsay, m. to the Rev. W. Lewis Wigan, eldest son of J. A. Wigan, Esq., of Clare House, Kent.
IV. Mary-Elizabeth. V. Dorothy.

Mr. Akers is eldest son of Aretas Akers, Esq., formerly of St. Christopher and St. Vincent, in the West Indies, the descendant of a family which was among the earliest settlers in those colonies, by Jane, his wife, youngest dau. of the Rev. James Ramsay, vicar of Teston and rector of Nettlested, in Kent, the celebrated writer on the African slave trade, and the originator of the discussion which terminated in the abolition of that traffic on the part of this country. The late Mr. Akers derived, through his paternal grandmother, from the DOUGLASES *of Baads*, co. Lanark. He left, besides the present Aretas Akers, Esq., another son, James-Ramsay, who m. Maria, dau. of — Goodrich, Esq., late of The Rookery, Dedham, Essex, and one dau., Caroline, m. to John Borton, Esq., of Blofield, Norfolk.

Arms—Gu., three escallops, or.
Crest—An arm, vested, bendy, az. and or, holding a pennon, bendy, of the same and or, charged with a Saracen's head, ppr., between eight crosses-crosslet, counterchanged.
Motto—Je vive en esperance.
Seat—Malling Abbey, Kent.

ALCOCK OF WILTON.

ALCOCK, HARRY, of Wilton Castle, co. Wexford, Esq., b. 27 July, 1821; s. his father 3 Dec. 1840.

Lineage.—HARRY ALCOCK, of Wilton, Esq., b. 22 Feb. 1792 (youngest son of Henry Alcock, Esq. of Wilton, by Elizabeth-Catherine, his wife, dau. of Beverley Ussher, Esq. M.P., and grandson of Col. William Alcock, by Mary, his wife, dau. of Nicholas, 1st Viscount Loftus), s. to the family estates at the death, in 1812, of his elder brother, William-Congreve Alcock, Esq. of Wilton, M.P. for the co. of Wexford. He m. Margaret, dau. and heir of James Savage, Esq. of Kilgibbon, co. Wexford, and had issue, 1 HARRY, now of Wilton Castle; 2 Ussher-William; 3 Philip-Savage; 4 George-Augustus; 1 Elinor-Catherine; 2 Henrietta, m. to Wm. Russell Farmar, Esq. of Bloomfield, co. Wexford; 3 Elizabeth-Louisa; 4 Margaret-Charlotte, m. to David-Vandeleur Beatty, Esq. of Borodale, co. Wexford; and 5 Sarah, m. to Sir Thos.-John Fetherston, Bt. Mr. Alcock, who was sheriff of the co. of Wexford, d. 3 Dec. 1840.

Arms—Arg., a fesse, embattled, az., between three cocks' heads, erased, gu.
Crest—A cock, arg., standing on a globe, armed, combed, and gilled, or.
Motto—Vigilate.
Seat—Wilton, Enniscorthy.

ALCOCK, THE REV. ALEXANDER, A.M., rector of Kilculliheen, co. Kilkenny, m. Anne, eldest dau. of the Rev. John Kennedy, of Fethard Castle, co. Wexford, and has had issue,

I. LETITIA, who m. 1st, in 1833, Jacob-William Goff, Esq., J. P. and D. L., of Horetown House, co. Wexford, and 2ndly, 16 Nov. 1847, D. Beaty, Esq. of the same co., but d. s. p. in 1848.
II. ELIZA, m. Samuel-Thomas Grubb, Esq. of Killaspey, and has one son and two daus.

Lineage.—THE VERY REV. ALEXANDER ALCOCK, Dean of Lismore, brother of William Alcock, Esq. of the city of Dublin, ancestor of Alcock of Wilton, m. Miss Mason, dau. of Sir John Mason, and had issue,

I. Henry, m. the sister of the 1st Viscount Jocelyn.
II. John, dean of Ferns, m. Miss C. Burgh, aunt of Walter Hussey Burgh, lord chief baron, and had with two daus.,
1 Alexander, who m. Miss Cumberland, dau. of the bishop of Clonfert.
2 Robert, who m. Miss Kelly, dau. of John Kelly, Esq., by whom he had issue, John-Henry, of Richmond, co. Waterford, major in that county militia, m. 29 Aug. 1853, Deborah, eldest dau. of the Rev. C. Campbell, rector of Ardglass, co. Down; and Richard, R.N.; and
3 John Dormer, who m. Miss Ashe.
III. ALEXANDER.

The 3rd son,

The Venerable Alexander Alcock, Archdeacon of Waterford, m. a sister of Viscount Jocelyn, Lord Chancellor of Ireland, and had issue, Robert, Alexander, Thomas, Mason, and Jane, m. to Sir Simon Newport. The 2nd son,

Alexander Alcock, Esq. of Elysium, co. Waterford, m. Miss Wall, dau. of James-Wall, Esq., and had, with five younger sons and three daus, Alexander, present representative.

ALCOCK OF KINGSWOOD WARREN.

Alcock, Thomas, Esq. of Kingswood Warren, co. Surrey, b. in 1801; m. in 1831, a dau. of the late Rear-Admiral Stuart. This gentleman, formerly M.P. for Newton, and now one of the Knights of the Shire for East Surrey, is son of the late Joseph Alcock, Esq. of Roehampton.

Seat—Kingswood Warren, Epsom, Surrey.

ALDERSEY OF ALDERSEY.

Aldersey, Samuel, of Aldersey Hall and Spurstow, co. Chester, Esq., b. 17 Sept. 1776; s. his father in 1802; high-sheriff in 1816; m. 9 Aug. 1824, Lucy, dau. of George Baylis, of Shiffnal, Esq., and has issue,

I. Hugh-Robert, b. 19 Nov. 1828; d. 24 Dec. 1848.
II. Thomas, b. 30 March, 1830.
I. Susan-Mary, m. 4 July, 1850, to Augustus, 3rd son of Robert-Kelham Kelham, Esq. of Bleasby, Notts.
II. Lucy-Anne.

Lineage.—The Alderseys have been seated at Aldersey since the Conquest.

William Aldersey, of Aldersey, Esq., living *temp.* Henry VI., the lineal descendant of Hugh de Aldersey, who flourished under Henry III., m. Margaret, dau. and heir of John Stalker, of Lower Spurstow, Esq., and was father of

Henry Aldersey, of Aldersey and Spurstow, Esq., who m. Jane, dau. of John Hockenhull, of Hockenhull, Esq., and had four sons. The 2nd, Robert, was ancestor of the Alderseys of Kent and Staffordshire; and the fourth, Richard, father of William Aldersey, a celebrated antiquary, mayor of Chester in 1614. The eldest son and heir,

John Aldersey, of Aldersey and Spurstow, Esq., m. Anne, dau. and eventual heir of Thomas Bird, of Clutton, Esq., and d. in 1528, leaving *inter alios*, two sons; John, his heir, and Thomas, founder of the school of Bunbury. The former,

John Aldersey, of Aldersey and Spurstow, Esq., m. Anne, dau of Hugh Aston, of Aston Green, Esq., and was great-great-great-grandfather of

The Rev. Samuel Aldersey, of Aldersey and Spurstow, rector of Wigan, co. Lancaster, who m. Henrietta, dau. of Henry Bridgman, D.D., Bishop of Sodor and Man, and d. in 1742, leaving several children. The last surviving son and eventual heir,

The Rev. Samuel Aldersey, of Aldersey and Spurstow, m. Margaret, youngest dau. and co-heir of Cornelius Hignet, of Darland, Esq., and dying in 1802, was s. by his son,

Robert Aldersley, of Aldersey and Spurstow, Esq., b. in 1738, a bencher of the Inner Temple, who d. *unm.* in 1802, and was s. by his brother,

Samuel Aldersey, of Aldersley and Spurstow, Esq., who m. Elizabeth, only child of William Wotton, of Haddenham, co. Bucks, Esq., and dying in 1802, left issue, Samuel, Thomas, d. s. p., Catherine, Margaret, and Elizabeth (all deceased). The eldest son is the present

Samuel Aldersley, of Aldersley and Spurstow, Esq.

Arms—Gu., on a bend, engrailed, arg., between two cinquefoils, or, three leopards' faces, vert.
Crest—A demi-griffin, segreant, gu., beaked and armed, issuing from a plume of five ostrich feathers, or.
Seats—Aldersey Hall, and Spurstow Hall, Cheshire.

ALDWORTH OF NEWMARKET.

Aldworth, Richard-Oliver, Esq. of Newmarket, co. Cork, b. 2 Feb. 1794; m. 22 Jan. 1824, the Lady Letitia Hare, eldest dau. of the late Viscount Ennismore (eldest son of the late Earl of Listowel), and has issue,

I. Richard-William, b. 31 Jan. 1825.
II. Robert, b. 11 June, 1827.
III. William-St. Leger, b. 21 Feb. 1829; m. in June, 1853, Mary, 3rd dau. of the late William-Stark Dougall, Esq. of Scotscaig, Fifeshire.
IV. John, b. 8 Sept. 1832.
I. Katherine-Anne.

Mr. Aldworth is a magistrate and deputy-lieut. for co. Cork, and served as high-sheriff in 1832-3.

Lineage.—This family, of considerable antiquity, was early seated in the county of Berks, where the immediate representative, Richard Aldworth, resided at Stanlakes, and on succeeding to the barony of Braybrooke, assumed the names of Neville and Griffin.

The Irish branch settled in the co. of Cork, in the reign of Elizabeth, and in various female lines trace their descent from some of the noblest families in England, and through the houses of Neville of Abergavenny, Stafford of Buckingham, and Percy of Northumberland, from the Plantagenets and King Henry III.

Richard Aldworth, who obtained a grant of part of the Earl of Desmond's forfeited estate near Short Castle, Mallow, m. Ellen Poer, dau. of the ancestor of the Earl of Tyrone, and niece of Roche, Viscount Fermoy, and was father of Sir Richard Aldworth, Knt., provost-marshal and vice-president of Munster, to whom the manor and estate of Newmarket was granted, 1 March, 1621. That property devolved in succession to

Richard Aldworth, Esq. of Newmarket, b. in 1694, son of Boyle Aldworth, Esq., and grandson of Sir Richard Aldworth, of Newmarket, by Martha Stannard, his wife, dau. of Sir Robert Travers, and niece of Dr. Michael Boyle, Primate of Ireland. He m. Elizabeth, dau. of Arthur, 1st Lord Doneraile, and had issue, Boyle, his heir; and St. Leger, who was created Lord Doneraile, (*see* Burke's *Peerage and Baronetage.*) Mr. Aldworth d. 25 April, 1776, and was s. by his eldest son,

Boyle Aldworth, Esq. of Newmarket, who m. 1st, Jane, dau. of Robert Oliver, Esq. of Cloughnodfoy, co. Limerick, and by her had,

Richard, who m. Anne, dau. of Dr. John Ryder, Archbishop of Tuam, and relict of Admiral Cotes, and d. s. p. 4 April, 1824.
Robert, d. *unm.*
Jane, m. to Phineas Bury, Esq. of Little Island, Cork.
Elizabeth, m. to John Flood, Esq. of Flood Hall, co. Kilkenny.
Mary. Susan.

He m. 2ndly, Martha, dau. of Colonel Christopher Rogers, of Lota, co. Cork, and by her had,

St. Leger, d. s. p. in 1823.
Christopher, d. s. p. in 1796.
Robert-Rogers, of whom we treat.

Mr. Aldworth d. 7 Dec. 1788. His son,

Robert-Rogers Aldworth, Esq. of Newmarket, m. 11 March, 1793, Elizabeth, dau. of the Ven. John Oliver, Archdeacon of Ardagh, and granddau. of John Ryder, Archbishop of Tuam, and had issue,

I. Richard-Oliver, present proprietor.
II. John, in holy orders, rector of Youghal, m. 1st, Anne, dau. of Charles-Deane Oliver, Esq., and 2ndly, Miss Mary Jackson, by the former he has issue, 1. Charles-Oliver; 2. Robert-St. Leger; 3. Richard-Fitz-John; 4. St. Leger-Hewitt; 1. Elizabeth-Catherine; 2. Sarah-Maria; and 3. Letitia-Agnes.
III St. Leger, m. Alicia, dau. of Charles-Deane Oliver, Esq., and has issue, Robert-Oliver and Alicia-Emily-Hester.
IV. Robert, m. Olivia, widow of George Wood, Esq., and dau. of the Rev. James Morton.

Mr. Alworth d. 28 Jan. 1836.

Arms—Arg., a fesse, engrailed, between six billets, gu.
Crest—A dexter arm embowed, in armour, the hand grasping a straight sword, all ppr.
Motto—Nec temere, nec timide.
Seat—Newmarket, co. Cork.

ALEXANDER OF POWIS.

Alexander, Sir James-Edward, of Powis, K.C.L.S., K.C.S.J., lieut.-col. Portuguese service, and on the staff of the British army; m. in 1837, Eveline-Marie, dau. of Col. Charles Cornwallis Michell, K.H., K.C.T.S., surveyor-gen. of the Cape of Good Hope, and has issue.

Lineage.—This family, which claims to be a branch from the same root as the EARLS OF STIRLING, acquired the lands of Powis from the heiress of MAYNE, whose progenitors, descending from the MAYNES *of Lockwood*, were settled near Stirling, and have been landed proprietors in that neighbourhood since the commencement of the fifteenth century.

The late EDWARD ALEXANDER, Esq. of Powis, son of James Alexander, Esq., Provost of Stirling, by Euphemia, his wife, widow of James Henderson, Esq., and only dau. of James Mayne, Esq. of St. Ninians (*see family of* MAYNE), *b.* in 1768, *m.* 1st, in 1801, Miss Colquhoun, dau. of R. Colquhoun, Esq., and sister of Gideon Colquhoun, Esq., late resident at Bussorah, but had no issue. He *m.* 2ndly, in 1808, Catherine, dau. of John Glass, Esq., and niece of Major-General Sir Alexander Bryce, K.C.H., inspector-general of fortifications, and of Dr. Bryce, dean of the chapel royal. By this lady he had,

- JAMES-EDWARD, (Sir) his heir
- John, major in the rifle brigade, who assumed the surname of HENDERSON, on succeeding to the estate of Westerton, at the decease of his uncle, John Henderson, Esq., in whose family the lands of Westerton had been for several hundred years.
- Euphemia-Mayne, who *d. unm.* in 1823.
- Mary-Bryce, *m.* to J. Colquhoun, Esq., barrister-at-law.
- Catherine-Glas, *m.* to J. Mac Arthur Moir, Esq. of Milton.

Arms—Quarterly; 1st and 4th, per pale, arg. and sa., a chevron, and in base a crescent, all counterchanged; 2nd and 3rd, or, a galley, sa., three cross-crosslets, fitchée, gu.
Crest—A beaver.
Motto—Per mare, per terras.

ALINGTON OF SWINHOPE.

ALINGTON, GEORGE-MARMADUKE, Esq. of Swinhope, co. Lincoln, *b.* 17 Feb. 1798; *m.* 17 May, 1825, Mary, dau. of Mathew-Bancroft Lister, Esq. of Burwell Park, co. Lincoln, and has had,

- I. GEORGE-HUGH, *b.* in 1826, an officer, 68th Light Infantry, *d.* at Malta, 8 June, 1852.
- II. Charles-Argentine, in holy orders, rector of Burwell. *b.* 22 March, 1828.
- III. Arthur-Hildebrand, mids. R.N., *b.* 10 Oct. 1839.
- IV. Albert-Edward, *b.* 24 Nov. 1841.
- V. Frederick-William, *b.* 29 July, 1845.
- I. Sophy-Anne. II. Ellen-Fanny.

Mr. Alington, J.P. and D.L. for Lincolnshire, *s.* his father, the late Marmaduke Alington, Esq., 2 Aug. 1840.

Lineage.—Sir Hildebrand de Alington was under-marshal to WILLIAM THE CONQUEROR. His descendant,

GEORGE ALINGTON, Esq of Swinhope, co. Lincoln, son of George Alington, Esq., younger brother of Sir Giles Alington, of Horseheath, ancestor of the Lords Alington, *d.* in 1633, leaving the large property in that shire, of which he was possessed, to his grand-nephew,

HENRY ALINGTON, Esq. of Swinhope, son of Metcalfe Alington, Esq., and grandson of Henry Alington, younger son of George Alington, who *d.* in 1558. He *m.* Penelope, dau. of Sir Maximilian Dalyson, of Kent, and devised his estates to his two sons,

- Hugh, who *m.* in 1668, Jane, dau. of Sir Martin Lister, of Burwell, and had an only surviving dau., Barbara, *m.* at an early age to Richard Pye, Esq., a younger son of Sir Robert Pye, of Farringdon, from whom the SARAH ROWE who bequeathed her estate to the late Mr. Alington's second son, derived her descent.
- HENRY.

The 2nd son,

HENRY ALINGTON, Esq. of Swinhope, *m.* Elizabeth Boyer, and had (with another son, Marmaduke, who *d. unm.*) a son and successor,

WILLIAM ALINGTON, Esq. of Swinhope, who *m.* Elizabeth, sister of Sir Thomas Cookes Winford, of Glasshampton, in the co. of Worcester, and niece of Sir Thomas Cookes, founder of Worcester College, Oxford, and had (with another son, Hildebrand, who *d. unm.*, and a dau., *m.* to Mr. Threader) a son,

HENRY ALINGTON, Esq. of Swinhope, who *m.* Frances, dau. of Robert Baron, Esq. of Letchworth, in Herts, by whom (who *d.* in 1809) he had issue,

- MARMADUKE, his heir.
- William, in holy orders, who *m.* Sarah, dau. of John Williamson, Esq. of Baldock, in Hertfordshire, and had, with a dau. Frances, a son, John. (*See* ALINGTON *of Little Barford.*)
- Henry, of Hertford.
- Mary, *m.* to Colonel George Maddison, and had an only son, George-Wilson Maddison.
- Frances.
- Sarah, *m.* to the Rev. John Robinson, of Faldingworth.

Mr. Alington was *s.* by his eldest son,

MARMADUKE ALINGTON, of Swinhope, Esq., who *m.* Anne, dau. of the Rev. John Emeris, of Louth, co. Lincoln, and by her (who *d.* in 1851) had issue,

- GEORGE-MARMADUKE, present proprietor.
- Henry, *b.* 3 Aug. 1800, who assumed the surname and arms of PYE, in compliance with the testamentary injunction of Mrs. Sarah Rowe, who bequeathed to him an estate at Bosbury, derived from the Pye family. He *m.* 1st, Charlotte, dau. and co-heiress of John Yarburgh, Esq. of Frampton, and has by her, one dau., Charlotte, *m.* to the Rev. Charles-Cary Barnard. He *m.* 2ndly, in 1854, Lady Albinia-Frances Hobart, eldest dau. of the present Earl of Buckinghamshire.
- John, in holy orders, rector of Candlesby, co. Lincoln, *m.* Charlotte, 3rd dau. of the late and sister of the present Sir Allan Bellingham, Bart. of Castle Bellingham, co. Louth.
- Hildebrand-William, of Boston, who *m.* Katherine, dau. of Francis Overton, Esq. of Louth.
- Richard Pye, in holy orders, rector of Swinhope, *m.* Emily, dau. of William Medland, Esq. of Hertford.
- Anne, *m.* to the Rev. William Cooper, of West Rasen.
- Sarah-Penelope, *m.* to the Rev. George Robinson, rector of Irby.

Arms—Sa., a bend, engrailed, between six billets arg.
Crest—A talbot, passant, ermine.
Seat—Swinhope, near Binbrook.

ALINGTON OF LITTLE BARFORD.

ALINGTON, THE REV. JOHN, M.A. of Little Barford, Manor House, Beds, and Letchworth Hall, Herts, *b.* 4 May, 1795; *m.* 3 Oct. 1822, Eliza-Frances, 2nd dau. of the Rt. Hon. Sir Thomas Plumer, Master of the Rolls, and has issue,

- I. WILLIAM, *b.* 6 April, 1826.
- II. Henry, *b.* 23 July, 1831.
- III. Charles, *b.* 22 April, 1833.
- IV. Julius, *b.* 6 Dec. 1836.
- I. Frances, *m.* to the Rev. George Yalden, M.A., rector of Twywell.
- II. Mary. III. Emily.

Mr. Alington is only son of the Rev. William Alington, 2nd son of Henry Alington, Esq. of Swinhope, by Frances Baron, his wife.

Arms—As ALINGTON *of Swinhope*.
Seat—Little Barford Manor House, Beds.

ALLAN OF BLACKWELL GRANGE.

ALLAN, WILLIAM, Esq. of Blackwell Grange, co. Durham, J.P., *b.* 21 May, 1796; *s.* his relative, George Allan, Esq., 21 July, 1828.

Lineage.—This is a branch of the ancient family of ALLAN *of Buckenhall and Brockhouse*, in the co. of Stafford, whose descent is deduced in an unbroken line from Henry Allan, or Alleyne, Lord of Buckenhall, in 1290.

GEORGE ALLAN, Esq. of Yarm, in Yorkshire, living in 1630, (son of George Allan, "who went to settle in the county of Durham," and who was 2nd son of William Allen, Esq. of Brockhouse, who *d.* 2 July, 1589,) *m.* a dau. of — Clifton, and had (with other children, who *d. s. p.*)

- I. THOMAS, (eldest son,) *b.* in 1651, of Newcastle-upon-Tyne, who amassed a large fortune in the collieries, and purchased estates, a part of which still retains the name of Allan's Flatts, near Chester-le-Street. He left four sons, 1 John, *d. unm.*; 2 George, of Newcastle-on-Tyne, *d.* 1729, leaving four daus., his co-heirs; 3 Lionel, of Rotterdam; and 4 Thomas, of Allan Flatts, *d.* 1740, leaving a son, Thomas, who *d. unm.*, and four daus., co-heirs—viz., Susan, *m.* to Ralph Jennison, Esq., M.P. of Walworth Castle, co. Durham, Master of the Stag-hounds to GEORGE II.; Margaret, *m.* to Jennison Shafto, Esq., M.P of Wratting Park, co. Cambridge; Dorothy, *m.* to James Garland, Esq., of Michael Stow Hall, co. Essex; and Camilla, who *m.* in 1752, Robert Shafto, Esq. of Benwell, and was mother of a dau., Camilla, heiress to her brother, *m.* to William Adair, Esq., father of the present Sir Robert Shafto Adair, Bart.
- II. John, bapt. 18 June, 1653, whose only dau. and heir *m.* Mr. Swainston.
- III. Henry, bapt. 6 Nov. 1665, who *m.* twice: by his first wife he had an only dau. *m.* to Capt. Mewse, and by his second, another dau. *m.* to Wm. Francis, Esq. of London.

IV. George, (sixth son,) *b.* in 1663, who making a large fortune by government contracts, built Blackwell Grange, "a handsome, spacious mansion," in 1710, and purchased estates. He *d.* in 1744. His granddau., Anne Allan, who eventually became sole heiress, *d.* universally lamented, in Oct. 1785, and devised all her estates in Durham and Yorkshire to her cousin and nearest male relation of her name, James Allan, Esq. of Darlington.

V. Robert, (seventh son,) who *d.* at Antigua, leaving an only dau. and heiress, Elizabeth, who *m.* John Burke, Esq.

VI. NICHOLAS, (eighth son,) of whom presently.

The eighth son of George Allan, of Yarm,

NICHOLAS ALLAN, Esq. of Staindrop, co. Durham, *b.* in 1668, *m.* in 1691, Elizabeth, only dau. of William Sober, Esq. of Cockerton, co. Durham, and had fifteen children, who all *d. unm.* except the youngest son,

JAMES ALLAN, Esq. of Blackwell Grange, upon whom the family estates eventually devolved. He was *b.* 23 Oct. 1712, and *m.* 18 Nov. 1734, Elizabeth, dau. of William Pemberton, Esq. (*see* BURKE's *Royal Families*), by Elizabeth, dau. of John Killinghall, Esq. of Middleton St. George, in the co. Durham. Mr. Allan *d.* in 1790, and left issue,

I. GEORGE, his successor.

II. James, *d. unm.* 26 Sept. 1800.

III. Robert, of Sunniside, co. Durham; lord of the manor of Barton, co. York, *m.* Elizabeth, dau. and co-heir (with her sister Mary, wife of William Russell, Esq. of Brancepeth Castle) of Robert Harrison, Esq., a wealthy merchant at Sunderland, and dying 28 March, 1806, left issue,

1 ROBERT, of Newbottle, co. Durham, *b.* 10 April, 1769, who *m.* 20 Dec. 1792, Hannah, (who *d.* 9 Jan. 1837, aged 70,) dau. of William Havelock, Esq. of Sunderland, and sister of William Havelock, Esq., late of Ingress Park, Kent, and left at his demise, 27 Dec. 1813,

WILLIAM, who *s.* to Blackwell Grange at the demise of his relative, Geo. Allan, Esq., 21 July, 1828, and is the PRESENT REPRESENTATIVE OF THE FAMILY.

ROBERT-HENRY, F. S. A., of Blackwell Hall (*See* ALLAN *of Blackwell Hall*).

John, of Dalton-upon-Tees, co. York, *b.* 25 June, 1803, *m.* Elizabeth, dau. of Mr. Jeffries, and *d. s. p.* 25 March, 1844.

George-Thomas, of Eryholme, co. York, D.L. for co. Durham, *b.* 11 Oct. 1804, *m.* 11 Oct. 1843, Maria, dau. of the Rev. Thomas Ramshay, vicar of Brampton.

James, *b.* 2 Dec. 1807; *d unm.* 26 March, 1833.

Elizabeth-Anne, *m.* 21 May, 1832, to Benjamin Dunn, Esq. of Hurworth, co. Durham.

Ann.

Joanna-Mary, *m.* 22 Sept. 1836, Edward-Haygarth Maling, Esq., and has one son and one dau.

Mary-Emma, *m.* 10 July, 1837, to William Wheatley, Esq., who *d. s. p.* 30 Sept. 1850.

Caroline-Jane, *m.* 1st, 28 Sept. 1831, to William-Hunter Burne, Esq., and by him, who *d.* 8 July, 1844, has a son, Freville-Lambton. She *m.* 2ndly, 23 Oct. 1845, John Murray, Esq., and *d.* 30 Nov. 1849.

2 JOHN, of Blackwell, co. Durham, M.A., J.P. for that shire, and for the North Riding of York, *b.* 29 Aug. 1778, *d. unm.*

1 Elizabeth, *m.* to John Maling, Esq. of Hylton, co. Durham; and *d.* in 1810.

2 Anne, *d. unm.* in 1807.

3 Mary, *m.* 13 June, 1802, to John-Henry Johnson, Esq., a capt. in the North York militia.

The eldest son,

GEORGE ALLAN, Esq. of Blackwell Grange, F.S.A., who is designated in Sir John Prestwick's *Republica*, as "a learned, studious, and careful preserver of English antiquities, and a favourer of literature;" and by Mr. Surtees, as "an eminent antiquary and collector," was *b.* 7 June, 1736. He *m.* 18 Sept. 1766, Anne, only dau. and heir of James Colling Nicholson, Esq. of Scruton, co. York, and had,

GEORGE, his successor.

James, *b.* 27 Feb. 1772; capt. 29th regt. of foot; *d.* 28 May, 1795.

Anne, *m.* to John Wright, Esq. of Bolton-on-Swale, co. York, and *d.* in 1797.

Elizabeth, *m.* in Nov. 1791, to Seymour Hodgson, Esq. of Richmond, co. York.

Hannah, *d.* young.

Dorothy, *d. unm.* 18 Sept. 1821.

Mr. Allan *d.* 17 May, 1800, and was *s.* by his elder son,

GEORGE ALLAN, Esq. of Blackwell Grange, M.A., F.S.A., M.P. for Durham, a gentleman not more distinguished for his literary talents than for an elegant, accomplished, and generous mind. He *m.* Prudence, dau. of William Williams, Esq., but had no issue. Mr. Allan, who *d. s. p.* at St. Omer, in France, 21 July, 1828, was *s.* by his relative, WILLIAM ALLAN, Esq., now of Blackwell Grange.

Arms—Sa., a cross potent, quarter pierced, or, charged with four guttes de sang, in chief two lions' heads erased, of the second, all within a bordure engrailed, erminois; quartering PEMBERTON, HINDMARSH, KILLINGHALL, HERDEWYK, LAMBTON, and DODSWORTH.

Crest—A demi-lion, rampant, arg., ducally crowned, gu., holding in the dexter paw a cross potent, or, and supporting with the sinister paw a rudder of the second.

Motto—Fortiter gerit crucem.

Seat—Blackwell Grange, co. Durham.

ALLAN OF BLACKWELL HALL.

ALLAN, ROBERT HENRY, Esq. of Blackwell Hall, co. Durham, and of Barton, co. York, F.S.A., D.L., high-sheriff of the co. of Durham in 1851, and a justice of the peace for the co. of Durham and North Riding of the co. York; *b.* 22 Jan. 1802; *m.* 14 July, 1841, Elizabeth, dau. of John Gregson, Esq. of Marton and Burdon, co. Durham, by Elizabeth, dau. and heiress of Lancelot Allgood, Esq., and had one son,

Robert-Killinghall, *b.* 25 Dec. 1842; *d.* 25, and buried in Bishop Wearmouth church, 28 Sep. 1843.

Robert Henry Allan, Esq. of Blackwell Hall, is next brother of the present William Allan, Esq. of Blackwell Grange, the head of the family.

Arms, Crest, and *Motto*—Same as the preceding.

Seat—Blackwell Hall, Darlington.

ALLARDICE.—*See* BARCLAY.

ALLEN OF CRESSELLY.

ALLEN, SEYMOUR-PHILIPPS, Esq. of Cresselly, co. Pembroke, *b.* 24 May, 1815; *s.* his father 9 April, 1843; *m.* 29 July, 1843, Lady Catherine, dau. of the late and sister of the present Earl of Portsmouth, and has issue,

I. Henry-Hugh, *b.* 19 Nov. 1845; *d.* 8 May, 1847.

II. HENRY-SEYMOUR, *b.* 30 Aug. 1847.

III. Frederick-Seymour, *b.* 23 Aug. 1849.

IV. Francis-Seymour, *b.* 29 March, 1853.

I. Gertrude-Catherine.

II. Camilla-Frances-Henrietta, *d.* young, 1858.

Lineage.—JOHN ALLEN, Esq., 2nd son of David Allen, Esq. of Fobstone, by Anne his wife, sister and heir of John Laugharne, Esq. M.P., which David Allen was younger brother of William Allen, Esq. of Galliswick; *m.* Joan Bartlett, of Cresselly and left issue,

JOHN-BARTLETT, his heir.

Roger, who *m.* Miss Margaret Davis, and had a son, JAMES ALLEN, Esq. of Freestone Hall.

Joshua. (*See* ALLEN *of Bicton.*)

Margaret, wife of A. Leach, Esq.

The eldest son,

JOHN-BARTLETT ALLEN, Esq. of Cresselly, co. Pembroke, *m.* 1763, Elizabeth, only child of John Hensleigh, Esq. of Panteague, and had issue,

JOHN-HENSLEIGH, his heir.

Lancelot-Baugh, one of the six clerks in Chancery, *b.* 1 Jan. 1774; *m.* 1st, 13 May, 1813, Caroline, dau. of Mr. Romilly, of Dulwich, brother of Sir Samuel Romilly, and by her, who *d.* in 1830, has two sons, George and Edward-Edmund. Mr. L.-B. Allen *m.* 2ndly, in July, 1841, Georgiana-Sarah, dau. of Charles-Nathaniel Bayley, Esq., by the Lady Sarah, his wife, dau. of George, 4th Earl of Jersey, and has by her a son, Charles, *b.* in May, 1842.

Elizabeth, *m.* to Josiah Wedgwood, Esq.

Catherine, second wife of Sir James Mackintosh.

Mary, *d.* young.

Caroline, *m.* to the Rev. Edward Drewe, rector of Broadhembury.

Harriet, *m.* to the Rev. Matthew Surtees, M.A., prebendary of Canterbury and Gloucester, younger son of Aubone Surtees, Esq. of Newcastle and Headley, and brother-in-law of Lord Eldon.

Jessie, *m.* to Sismondi, the historian.

Emma. Frances.

Mr Allen was *s.* at his decease by his elder son,

JOHN-HENSLEIGH ALLEN, Esq. of Cresselly, *b.* 29 Aug. 1769, J.P. and D.L., who filled the office of high sheriff for co. Pembroke, in 1809, and represented that shire in parliament from 1819 to 1826. He *m.* 12 Nov. 1812, Gertrude, youngest dau. of Lord Robert Seymour, 3rd son of Francis, 1st Marquis of Hertford, and by that lady, who *d.* 13 Jan. 1825, had issue,

SEYMOUR-PHILIPPS, his heir.

Henry-George, *b.* 29 July, 1816.

John-Hensleigh, *b.* 3 Nov. 1818.

Gertrude-Elizabeth, *d.* in 1824.

Isabella-Georgina, m. in 1840, to George-Lort Phillips, Esq. of Lawrenny Hall, descended, in the female line, from the LORTS of *Stackpole Court.*

Mr. Allen d. 9 April, 1843.

Arms—Per bend, rompu, arg. and sa., six martlets, counterchanged.
Crest—A dove and olive branch.
Motto—Amicitia sine fraude.
Seat—Cresselly, co. Pembroke.

ALLEN OF BICTON.

ALLEN, JOSHUA-JULLIAN, Esq. of Bicton, co. Pembroke, J.P., b. 25 March, 1799; m. 8 July, 1821, Martha, only surviving dau. of John Brooke, Esq. of London, and has had issue,

I. JOSHUA-BIRD, of Trinity Coll. Camb., b. 15 May, 1823; m. 13 April, 1848, Margaretta-Anne, only dau. of Lt.-Col. William Morison, R.I.C.S., of Portclew House, co. Pembroke.
II. Charles-John, b. 2 March, 1832.
I. Mary-Anne, d. 19 July, 1833.

Lineage.—JOSHUA ALLEN, 3rd son of John-Allen, of Cresselly, by Joan Bartlett, his wife, m. his first cousin, Margaret, dau. and co-heiress of William Allen, of Fobstone, by Margaret Bird, his wife, and had, with other issue, DAVID BIRD, his heir; Frances, m. to George Bowling, Esq.; Julia, m. to Major William Slater, of the 82nd regt.; and Lucy, m. to Lt.-Col. William Morison, Bombay Army. The son and heir,

THE REV. DAVID-BIRD ALLEN, M.A., Rector of Burton, co. Pembroke, b. 16 Feb. 1769; m. 24 Oct. 1796, Mary-Anne-Harriot, dau. of Peter-Bartholomew Jullian, Esq. of London; and d. 31 Dec. 1831, leaving issue,

JOSHUA-JULLIAN, now of Bicton.
William, b. 27 Sept. 1800; M.A., rector of Bosherston, co. Pembroke; m. 5 July, 1831, his second cousin, Frances-Margaret, eldest dau. of James Allen, Esq. of Freestone Hall, and has issue, Robert-James, b. 20 May, 1832; Alfred-Bird, b. 11 Nov. 1834; Charles-Stanley, b. 22 Aug. 1838; William-Frederick, b. 15 April, 1840; Thomas-Cecil, b. 11 April, 1846; Elizabeth-Jane; Francis-Charlotte; and Jessie-Emily.
James, b. 15 July, 1802; M.A., vicar of Castlemartin, co. Pembroke; m. 28 April, 1852, Isabella-Dorothea Hoare.
Bird, comm. R.N.; d. unm. at Fernando Po, on his return with Captain Trotter from the Niger Expedition, 25 Oct. 1841.
Charles, b. 29 July, 1808; in the Bengal civil service; m. 11 Aug. 1840, Mary, youngest dau. of James Allen, Esq. of Freestone Hall, and has issue a son, Herbert-James.
John, b. 25 May, 1841; M.A., chaplain of King's College, London, and Her Majesty's inspector of schools; he m. 31 July, 1834, Harriet, dau. of J.-W. Higgins, Esq., and has issue, John-Higgins, and several daus.

Seat—Bicton, co. Pembroke.

ALLFREY OF WOKEFIELD PARK.

ALLFREY, ROBERT, Esq. of Wokefield Park, co. Berks, J.P., b. 10 Oct. 1809; m. 20 Oct. 1834, Caroline, dau. of William Hobson, Esq. and has,

I. GOODRICH-HOLM'SDALE, b. 27 Sept. 1835.
II. Irving-Stening, b. 5 April, 1837.
III. Ernest-Herbert, b. 30 April, 1839.
IV. Walter-Mortimer, b. 6 Dec. 1843.
V. Rodney-Charles, b. 13 March, 1847.
VI. Gerald-Moubray, b. 10 Sept. 1848.
VII. Beauclerk-Cyril, b. 10 Feb. 1851.
VIII. Sidney-Reginald, b. 26 Nov. 1852.
I. Ellen. II. Constance-Louisa.

Lineage.—The family of Allfrey has been long settled in the county of Sussex, as appears by family papers dated in the reign of HENRY VIII., and from the Heralds' Visitations. The immediate ancestor of the family before us,

EDWARD ALFREY, of Westdean, co. Sussex, m. Eleanor Tutt, and d. in 1696, aged 65, leaving issue, of which the youngest son,

RICHARD ALFREY, or ALLFREY, of Deptford, had, by Mary his wife, besides daus., three sons, of which the youngest,

GEORGE ALLFREY, of Westdean, b. in 1705, m. Catharine Woodhams, and d. in 1764, aged 59, having had, besides a dau., Mary, who m. 19 Feb. 1765, Stening Beard, of Seaford, co. Sussex, a son,

GEORGE ALLFREY, Esq. of Westdean, and afterwards of Friston Place, co. Sussex, who m. Mary, dau. of William Stone, Esq. of Stonebridge, Sussex, and d. in 1794, having had by her (who d. at Seaford in 1810) five daus., of whom the 3rd, Catherine, m. Thomas-R. Willard, Esq. and the 4th, Harriet, Capt. Thomas Mortimer; and two sons,

I. GEORGE, of Friston Place; m. Kitty, dau. of Stening Beard, Esq. of Seaford, and Mary Allfrey, his wife; and d. at Brighton, in 1802, having had issue, 1 George, of Stamford Hill, Middlesex, m. 1st, Marianne, dau. of Nicholas St. Croix, of Guernsey, and by her (who d. in 1828) has issue, George, b. in July, 1824, and Margaret. He m. 2ndly, Elizabeth, dau. of Henry Richmond, Esq. of Chester-street, London, and by her has, John-Octavius, b. 6 May, 1833; Edward-Richmond, b. 6 Oct. 1835; Charles-Henry, b. in 1838; Katherine-Elizabeth; and Frances; 2 Edward-Thomas; 3 John-Stening; 4 William.
II. EDWARD, of whom we treat.

The 2nd son,

EDWARD ALLFREY, Esq. of Bryanstone-square, London, Salehurst, co. Sussex, and Banstead, co. Surrey, m. 3 Dec. 1807, Margaret, dau. of Robert Shedden, Esq. of Gower-street, and d. in June, 1834, having had issue,

ROBERT, now of Wokefield Park.
Henry-Wells, b. 17 Sept. 1817; m. 6 Dec. 1845, Adeline-Frances, dau. of Sir Robert Moubray, K.H., of Cockairney, co. Fife.
Frederick-William, b. 15 May, 1819; m. 4 Sept. 1845, Emily, dau. of Sir Robert Moubray, K.H., of Cockairney.
Edward, b. 16 Dec. 1822.

Arms—Per fesse, sa. and erm., a pale, counterchanged, three ostrich's heads, erased, arg., gorged with crowns and lines, or.
Crest—An ostrich's head and neck, gorged with a crown, as in the arms, between two ostrich's feathers, arg.
Seat—Wokefield Park, Reading, Berkshire.

ALLGOOD OF NUNWICK.

ALLGOOD, LANCELOT-JOHN-HUNTER, Esq. of Nunwick, co. Northumberland, an officer, 13th light-dragoons, b. 22 Feb. 1823.

Lineage.—The ALLGOODS *of Nunwick* are descended from John Allgood, of Salerne, co. Devon, living in 1386, who accompanied John, Duke of Lancaster, in his expedition to Spain, against the pretended king of Castile.

SIR LANCELOT ALLGOOD, Knt. high-sheriff of Northumberland, *temp.* GEORGE II., and M.P. for that county in 1748, son of Isaac Allgood, of Brandon White House, and grandson of the Rev. Major Allgood, rector of Simonburn, was knighted by GEORGE III, in 1760. Sir Lancelot m. 22 Feb. 1738-9, his relative, Jane, dau. and heir of Robert Allgood, of Nunwick and Simonburn, co. Northumberland, Esq., and was father, *inter alios*, of two daus. (Hannah, wife of Sir William Loraine, Bart.; and Isabella, m. to Lambton Loraine, Esq.) and of a son and heir,

JAMES ALLGOOD, Esq. of Nunwick, LL.D., b. in 1749, m. 2 Oct. 1790, Martha, dau. of Christopher Reed, of Chipchase Castle, co. Northumberland, Esq. and by her had issue,

ROBERT-LANCELOT, his heir.
James, vicar of Felton, and rector of Ingram, co. Northumberland.
Sarah. Jane. Margaret.

Mr. Allgood d. 14 May, 1807, and was s. by his eldest son,

ROBERT-LANCELOT ALLGOOD, of Nunwick, Esq, b. 17 Sept. 1794, m. 1st, 2 May, 1816, Mary-Neville (who d. 2 Sept. following), eldest dau. of John Reed, of Chipchase Castle, co. Northumberland, Esq., and 2ndly, 26 Aug. 1820, Elizabeth, 2nd dau. and co-heiress of John Hunter, of The Hermitage, in the same county, Esq., by whom he had,

LANCELOT-JOHN-HUNTER, now of Nunwick.
James, in holy orders, b. 30 June, 1826, m. 4 May, 1854, Isabella, 3rd dau. of the late Charles-A. Williamson, Esq.
George, b. 1 Nov. 1827.
William-Isaac, b. 1 Nov. 1837.
Elizabeth-Martha, m. in 1840, to Henry Eyre, Esq. major 98th regt.
Anne-Jane. Isabella.

Mr. Allgood, a deputy-lieut. for Northumberland, for which county he was high-sheriff in 1818, d. 25 May, 1854.

Arms—Arg., a cross, engrailed, gu., between four mullets, az.; on a chief, or, three damask roses of the second, seeded gold, barbed, vert.
Crest—Two arms, embowed, in armour, ppr, holding in the hands a human heart, gu., inflamed, or, charged with a tower, triple towered, arg.
Motto—Age omne bonum.
Seat—Nunwick, co. Northumberland.

ALLIX OF WILLOUGHBY.

Allix, Charles, Esq. of Willoughby Hall, co. Lincoln, *b.* 20 Jan. 1783; *m.* 3 June, 1808, Mary-Elizabeth, 2nd dau. of William Hammond, Esq. of St. Albans Court, Kent, and has issue,

- I. Charles-Hammond, *b.* 27 July, 1810, lieut. Grenadier guards, *d.* in 1830.
- II. Frederick-William, *b.* 11 April, 1816, *m.* Sophia-Mary, only child of C. H. Noel, Esq. of Wellingore, co. Lincoln, and has issue, a son, *b.* 15 May, 1851.
- III. William-Kent, *b.* 9 April, 1823.
- IV. Wager-Townley, *b.* 1 March, 1825.
- I. Mary-Catherine-Elizabeth, *m.* to her cousin, Charles Allix, Esq. and *d.* in 1842.
- II. Charlotte-Francis.
- III. Caroline-Isabella, *d.* 25 Jan. 1836.
- IV. Louisa-Margaret, *m.* to the Rev. James Griffith.
- V. Juliana-Jemima, *m.* 15 Aug. 1839, to Francis Capper Brooke, Esq. of Ufford-place, Suffolk, and *d.* in 1840.
- VI. Emily-Persia, *m.* to A. D.. Veasey, Esq. eldest son of David Veasey, Esq. of Castle Hall, co. Huntingdon.

Mr. Allix, who is in the commission of the peace, and deputy-lieutenancy for Lincolnshire, *s.* his father in Nov. 1795.

Lineage.—The Very Rev. Peter Allix, rector of Shudy Camps, in Cambridgeshire, and dean of Ely, (son of the eminent divine, Dr. Peter Allix, of Alençon, head of the Protestant Church in France, banished that kingdom at the revocation of the Edict of Nantes) *m.* Miss Elizabeth Wager, niece and co-heir of Admiral Sir Charles Wager, first Lord of the Admiralty, *temp.* King George I., and was *s.* by his son,

Charles Allix, Esq. of Swaffham, co. Cambridge, who *m.* Catherine, dau. of Thomas Green, D.D., Bishop of Ely, and had issue, Charles Wager, his heir; John-Peter (*see* Allix *of Swaffham House*); and Jane, who *m.* the Rev. George Wilson, and *d.* in 1794. He was succeeded by his eldest son,

The Rev. Charles-Wager Allix, of Willoughby Hall, who *m.* Catherine, 2nd dau. of Richard Townley, Esq. of Belfield, co. Lancaster, and by her, who *d.* 6 Oct. 1839, had issue, Charles, his heir; Richard-Wager; Catherine-Anne; and Margaret-Elizabeth, *m.* to the Rev. George Yate.

Mr. Allix *d.* in Nov. 1795, and was *s.* by his elder son, the present Charles Allix, Esq. of Willoughby Hall.

Arms—Arg., a wolf's head, erased at the neck, ppr.; in the dexter chief point, a mullet, gu.
Crest—A wolf's head, erased, as in the arms.
Seat—Willoughby Hall, near Grantham.

ALLIX OF SWAFFHAM HOUSE.

Allix, John-Peter, Esq. of Swaffham House, co. Cambridge, late M.P. for that shire; *b.* 2 Dec. 1785; *m.* 7 March, 1816, Maria, dau. of John Pardoe, Esq. of Leyton, co. Essex. Mr. Allix, J.P. and D.L., served as high-sheriff in 1828.

Lineage.—John Peter Allix, Esq. of Swaffham House, co. Cambridge, younger brother of the Rev. Charles-Wager Allix, of Willoughby Hall, co. Lincoln, (*see that family,*) *m.* in 1782, Sarah, dau. of the Rev. William Collier, vicar of Swaffham, co. Cambridge, and had issue,

John-Peter, now of Swaffham House.
Charles, colonel in the guards: who *m.* Mary-Catherine-Elizabeth, dau. of Charles Allix, Esq. of Willoughby, co. Lincoln, by Mary his wife, dau. of William Hammond, Esq., St. Alban's Court, Kent, and had issue one son.
William. Thomas. Wager.
Catherine, *m.* to Robert Wilkinson, Esq.
Charlotte, *m.* to John Pardoe, Esq., Leyton, Essex.
Matilda, *m.* to Thomas Roberts, Esq.
Juliana. Mariana.

Seat—Swaffham House, co. Cambridge.

ALLOTT OF HAGUE HALL.

Allott, The Rev. John, of Hague Hall, co. York, rector of Maltby, co. Lincoln, *b.* 21 March, 1812; *m.* 27 Oct. 1836, Catherine, dau. of William Wilson, Esq. of Louth, co. Lincoln, and has issue,

- I. John-George, *b.* 15 July, 1839.
- II. Henry-Hepworth, *b.* 25 June, 1842.

- III. Robert-James, *b.* 22 Nov. 1847.
- I. Catherine-Mary.
- II. Marianne-Ludlam.
- III. Sarah-Frances.
- IV. Elizabeth-Ann.

Lineage.—When this family became first seated at Elmley, it is difficult to ascertain on good authority, but that they were settled there in the time of Henry VI., the strongest evidence exists, in deeds dated 11, 16, and 24 Henry VI.

Edmund Allot, lineally descended from Robert Allot, of Sedfull, *m.* Bridget, dau. of Thomas Arthington, and had two sons, John, and Thomas, who *m.* the dau. of Thomas Merfield, and was grandfather of Richard Allot, of Greenfield, co. Middlesex, as well as of Syles Allot, of Micklefield, Suffolk. The elder son,

John Allot, whose will is dated in 1509, *m.* Elizabeth, dau. and heir of Sir John Allington, Knt., and was father of

Robert Allott, of Beutley Grange, whose will was proved in 1541. He *m.* Elizabeth, sister of Armigael Waad, the navigator, and niece of Alvared Comyn, prior of Nostel, and had two sons,

Robert, of Bentley Grange, whose eldest son, John, of Bentley Grange, aged 43, 14 Oct. 1606, was ancestor of the Rev. Richard Allott, Fellow of Trinity College, Cambridge, son of Richard Allott, late dean of Raphoe.
John, of whom we treat.

The 2nd son,

John Allott, of Crigleston, which estate had been purchased by his mother, *m.* Elizabeth, dau. of Richard Spight, of Heaton, and had issue, Edward, of whom presently; Robert, M.D., of St. John's College, living in 1626; Elizabeth. The elder son,

Edward Allott, of Crigleston, *m.* Susanna, dau. of Johnson of Dercarne, and had, besides other issue, an eldest son,

George Allott, of Crigleston, whose will was dated in 1683. His son,

Edward Allott, of Crigleston, *m.* 13 Dec. 1677, Rebecca Swallow, and had, with younger issue,

George, his heir, of Crigleston and South Kirkby, who *m.* Jane, dau. and heir of Thomas Slack, of South Elmsall, and had two daus., Rebecca, and Anne (his heiress), who *m.* in Oct. 1739, William Bowes, Esq. of York, and *d. s. p.* in 1790, leaving the Crigleston and South Elmsall estates to her kinsman, James Allott, Esq. of Hague Hall. George Allott *d.* in 1716.
Robert, of whom presently.

The 2nd son,

The Rev. Robert Allott, M.A., fellow of St. John's College, Cambridge, and vicar of South Kirkby, *m.* Frances, dau. of Francis Hall, Esq. of Swaith Hall, and *d.* 29 July, 1783, having had three sons,

- I. James, in holy orders, vicar of South Kirkby; bapt. 5 May, 1723; *m.* Elizabeth, dau. and heir of the Rev. Henry Green, of the Hague; and *d.* in 1756, leaving a son and heir,
  - 1 James Allott, of Hague Hall, devisee of the Crigleston and Elmsall estates, from his kinswoman, Anne Bowes. He *d. unm.* 28 Sept. 1811, and devised his estates of Crigleston and Elmsall to his cousin, Robert Allott; and Hague Hall to his cousin, Captain John Allott.
- II. Robert, of Painthorpe, bapt. 15 April, 1730; *m.* 24 April, 1769, Elizabeth, dau. of the Rev. — Sidwell, and had issue,
  - 1 Robert, who *s.* to Crigleston and Elmsall, under the will of his cousin, James. He *m.* Sarah, dau. of William Hodgson, Esq. of Taxal Lodge, co. Derby; and *d.* 14 May, 1847, having had issue one son and one dau., viz., James, *d. unm*; Frances-Dorothy.
  - 2 George, *m.* Mary Neal, and had a dau., Mary, *d. unm.*
- III. John, of whom we treat.

The youngest son,

The Rev. John Allott, vicar of South Kirkby, bapt. 1734, *m.* in Nov. 1768 or 1769, Anne, dau. of Hugh Hammersley, Esq. of Doncaster, and *d.* in 1813, having had issue,

- I. John.
- II. George.
- III. James, in holy orders, chaplain to the forces; *d. unm.* in 1814.
- I. Sarah, *d. unm.*
- II. Anne.

The eldest son,

John Allott, Esq. captain in the army, *s.* to the Hague Hall estate, under the will of his cousin, James Allott, in 1811. He *m.* Elizabeth, dau. of James Emmerson, Esq. of South Kirkby, and dying *s. p.* in 1824, was *s.* by his brother,

The Rev. George Allott, of Hague Hall, vicar of South Kirkby, *b.* 8 Oct. 1776, *m.* 10 Oct. 1805, Mary, eldest dau. of James Emmerson, Esq. of South Kirkby, and had issue,

JAMES, b. 29 Sept. 1810; m. 14 Jan. 1847, Hannah, eldest dau. of the late John Webster, Esq. of Springfield House, Morley, near Leeds, and d. s. p.
JOHN, now of Hague Hall.
George, in holy orders, vicar of South Kirkby, co. Lincoln; b. 7 June, 1818; m. June, 1851, Miss Sarah Webster.
Catherine-Ann, m. to W.-Platt Bradshaw, Esq. of Comston Bank, co. Lancaster.
Sarah-Cope, m. to Joshua Hepworth, Esq. of Bogerthorpe Hall, near Pontefract.
Mary-Elizabeth, m. to Henry Orme, Esq. of Louth, co. Lincoln.
Frances-Jane, m. to Robert Shipman, Esq. of Grantham, co. Lincoln.

Mr. Allott d. 13 June, 1848.

Arms—Or, a plain fesse, double cotised, wavy, az.; on a canton of the second, two bars, arg., charged with three swallows, volant, sa.
Crest—A dexter arm, couped at the elbow, habited, or, charged with a fesse, double cotised, wavy, az., cuff, arg., the hand, ppr., holding a mullet, gold.
Motto—Fortiter et recte.
Seat—Hague Hall, near Wakefield, co. York.

ALLOWAY OF BALLYSHANDUFFE.

ALLOWAY, ROBERT-MORELLET, Esq. of Ballyshanduffe, otherwise The Derries, in the Queen's Co., J.P., s. his father, the late William-Johnson Alloway, Esq., 2 Oct. 1829; m. 19 June, 1832, Mary-Anne, only dau. of William Lewis, Esq. of Harlech, co. Dublin, and has issue,

ROBERT-MARMADUKE, b. 9 June, 1840.
Grace-Montgomerie.

Lineage. THEOPHILUS ALLOWAY, son of Marmaduke, laird of Alloway, in Ayrshire, left Scotland, and became possessed of property at Minehead, in Somersetshire, about the year 1640. He was father of

ROBERT ALLOWAY, who m. Katharine, dau. of Sir John Watson, of Staffordshire, and was father of

THEOPHILUS ALLOWAY, who m. Dorothy Warren, of Devonshire, and had a son,

BENJAMIN ALLOWAY, who m. Una, dau. of Peter Godwin, of Ben, in Somersetshire. He left Minehead, and settled in Dublin, about the year 1700. His son,

WILLIAM ALLOWAY, m. Grace, dau. of Archibald Montgomerie, Esq. of Ayrshire, of the Eglinton family, and had (with a dau. Hannah, who m. Jonas Duckett, Esq. and was grandmother to John-Dawson Duckett, Esq. of Duckett's Grove, co. Carlow) a son,

BENJAMIN ALLOWAY, Esq. who m. 1st, Lydia, granddau. of Robert Barclay, of Urie, Aberdeenshire, the celebrated "Apologist," by whom he left a son, the late John-Barclay Alloway, Esq., of Mount Pleasant, co. Dublin, who d. in 1831, without issue. He m. 2ndly, Anne, dau. of William Johnson, Esq. of Dublin, by whom he left a son,

WILLIAM-JOHNSON ALLOWAY, Esq. of The Derries, Queen's County, who m. Margaret, eldest dau. of the late Hon. Robert Johnson, a judge of the Court of Common Pleas in Ireland, and by her (who d. in April, 1834) left,

ROBERT-MORELLET, now of Ballyshanduffe.
Arthur-William, late of the 4th or King's Own regiment; m. his cousin, Miss Mary Johnson, and has issue.
George-Holmes, M.D.; m. in 1849, Florence-Gertrude, dau. of the late Henry McClintock, Esq. of Dundalk.
Anna.

Seat—Ballyshanduffe, Ballybrittas, Queen's County.

ALSTON OF ELMDON HALL.

ALSTON, WILLIAM-CHARLES, Esq. of Elmdon Hall, co. Warwick, b. 22 March, 1796; m. 8 Dec. 1841, Elizabeth-Ann, dau. of Col. Fetherston, of Packwood, and has issue,

I. WILLIAM-CHARLES, b. 2 Nov. 1842.
II. James-Fetherston, b. 19 Oct. 1844.
And three daughters.

This gentleman is son of the late James Alston, Esq. of Winson Hill, by his wife, Anne Holt, of The Woodhouses, Shropshire.

Arms—Az., ten estoiles, or, four, three, two, and one; on a chief, arg., a crescent reversed, gu., between two boars' heads, sa.
Crest—A demi-eagle, wings displayed, or; on each wing a crescent reversed, gu.
Motto—In altum.
Seat—Elmdon Hall, Warwickshire.

AMERY OF PARK HOUSE.

AMERY, JOHN, Esq., F.S.A., of Park House, Stourbridge, co. Worcester, J.P. and D.L., barrister-at-law, b. 10 Feb. 1799; m. 1 Nov. 1824, Anna-Dorothea, eldest dau. of the Rev. Frederick-William Foster, of Derbyshire, elder brother of John Foster, Esq. of Brickhill, co. Bedford, and has issue,

I. JOHN-FREDERICK FOSTER, B.A., b. 24 Dec. 1825.
II. Edmund-Verdon, M.A. in holy orders, b. 21 July, 1827.
III. Henry Dickinson, b. 28 Sept. 1831.
IV. William-D'Amery, b. 1 Dec. 1839.
I. Anna-Eleonora, d. 10 Aug. 1844.
II. Caroline-Amelia. III. Henrietta-Louisa-Gertrude.
IV. Mary-Emmeline.

Lineage.—The family of D'Amery came to England with the CONQUEROR, from Tours; and different branches were subsequently seated in the counties of Somerset, Oxford, Devon, and Gloucester.

ROGER D'AMERY, of Yate, co. Gloucester, and his descendants, held the manor of Weston Birt, in the same co., from the 22nd EDWARD III., until it was alienated by RICHARD D'AMERY, of Codrington, about the year 1610: from this Richard descended ROGER D'AMERY, whose son, JOHN, was father of RICHARD AMERY, of Stoney Stainton, co. York, father of an only son, RICHARD AMERY, Esq. of Fishlake, who m. Miss Conway, and had two sons, of whom the elder, RALPH AMERY, Esq. of Womersley, m. Ann Banks, and was father of an only son, JOHN AMERY, Esq. who m. Ann Eccles, and left, with other issue, a son and successor, the present JOHN AMERY, Esq. of Park House, Stourbridge.

Arms—Arg., three bars, nebulé, gu.; over all a bend, engrailed, az.
Crest—Out of a mural crown, a talbot's head.
Motto—Tu ne cede malis.
Seat—Park House, Stourbridge, co. Worcester.

AMES OF THE HYDE.

AMES, LIONEL, Esq. of The Hyde, co. Bedford, b. 13 July, 1810; m. 10 June, 1848, Augusta-Percy, dau. of Col. Sir John-Morillyon Wilson, C.B., K.H., and has issue,

I. LIONEL-NEVILLE-FREDERICK, b. 21 Feb. 1850.
II. Percy-George, b. 7 May, 1851.
III. Gerard-Vivian, b. 7 Aug. 1852.

Mr. Ames is lieut.-col. of the Herts militia, and a magistrate for the counties of Herts and Bedford. He s. his father in 1846.

Lineage.—LEVI AMES, Esq. mayor of Bristol in 1789, son of Jeremiah Ames, m. 1st, in 1770, Anna-Maria, dau. of Chauncy Poole, Esq. also of Bristol, by Anna-Maria his wife, sister of Sir Lionel Lyde, Bart. of Ayot St. Lawrence, and had issue,

LIONEL, who assumed the surname of LYDE on succeeding to the estates of Sir Lionel Lyde, Bart. He d. in Jan. 1851.
Jeremiah, who m. Mary, youngest dau. of J.-F. Pinney, Esq. of Somerton, co. Somerset; and d. without issue in 1820.
LEVI, late of The Hyde. John.
George-Henry, who m. Anna, dau. of G. Acland, Esq.
Maria, m. to Richard Llewellyn, Esq. of Westbury, co. Gloucester.
Sarah, m. to her cousin, John Olive, Esq. of Beach Hill, co. Monmouth.
Phœbe, m. to her cousin, the Rev. James Olive.
Harriet, d. unm.

The 3rd son,

LEVI AMES, Esq. of The Hyde, b. 30 Nov. 1778; m. 13 June, 1808, Anne-Bird, dau. of Henry Metcalfe, Esq. of Murton and Seatonville, co. Northumberland, and has issue,

LIONEL, now of The Hyde.
Henry-Metcalfe, m. in Nov. 1852, Elizabeth-Sarah, dau. of Major Hodgson Cadogan, of Brinkburn Priory, co. Northumberland.
Emily-Anne, m. to the Rev. Frederick Sullivan.
Mary, m. to Col. Codrington, of the Coldstream guards.
Margaret-Rose, m. to Capt. R. Blane, 2nd life-guards.
Harriet-Elizabeth, m. to Captain Sidley Burdett, Coldstream guards.

Mr. Ames, a magistrate for the cos. of Bedford and Herts,

and a dep.-lieut. of the latter, served as sheriff of Bedfordshire in 1840. He *d.* in 1846.

Arms—Arg., on a bend, cotised, sa., three roses of the field, seeded, or, barbed, vert.
Crest—A rose, arg., stalked and leaved, vert.
Seat—The Hyde, Beds.

AMHERST OF FIELD GATE HOUSE.

AMHERST, THE REV. FRANCIS-KERRIL, of Field Gate House, co. Warwick, *b.* 17 July, 1819.

Lineage.—This is an ancient Essex family. The late WILLIAM-KERRIL AMHERST, Esq. of Parndon, in that county, *m.* in May, 1817, Mary-Louisa, dau. of Francis Fortescue Turvile, Esq. of Bosworth Hall, co. Leicester, and left issue,

FRANCIS-KERRIL, now of Field Gate House.
William-Joseph, *b.* 7 July, 1820.
Caroline, } nuns.
Mary-Barbara, }
Mary-Louisa. Harriet-Ann.

Arms—Gu., three tilting spears or lances, erect, in fesse, or, headed, az.
Crest—On a mount, vert, three like spears, one erect, and two in saltier, girt with a wreath of laurel, ppr.
Seat—Field Gate House, Kenilworth.

AMCOTTS OF HACKTHORN.

See CRACROFT.

AMOS OF ST. IBBS.

AMOS, ANDREW, Esq. of St. Ibbs, co. Hertford, barrister-at-law; *m.* 1 Aug. 1826, Margaret, dau. of the Rev. Professor Lax, of the University of Cambridge, and has issue,

I. WILLIAM. II. James.
III. Gilbert-Andrew. IV. Sheldon.
I. Margaret-Isabella.

This distinguished lawyer, son of James Amos, Esq., by Frances-Cornelia Bonté, his wife, dau. of General Bonté, governor of Negapatam, *s.* to St. Ibbs, at the decease of his father-in-law, in 1836, and is a magistrate for Herts. He was lately member of the Supreme Council of India.

Crest—A stag's head.
Motto—Sapere aude.
Seat—St. Ibbs, Hitchen.

AMPHLETT OF CLENT HOUSE.

AMPHLETT, JOHN, Esq. of Clent House, co. Worcester, *b.* 20 March, 1820; *m.* 18 May, 1844, Jane, dau. of the late Robert Smithson, Esq. of Skipwith, co. York, and has issue,

I. JOHN, *b.* 22 March, 1845.
II. Charles-Hugh, *b.* 19 March, 1847, *d.* an infant.
I. Jane-Elizabeth.

Lineage.—This family anciently resided at Salwarpe, co. Worcester.

WILLIAM AMPHLETT, Esq. lord of the manor of Hadsor, in that shire, son of William Amphlett, of Salwarpe, *temp.* JAMES I. *m.* Frances, dau. of John Sparrow, of Clent, co. Stafford, and was father of

RICHARD AMPHLETT, Esq. of Hadsor, who *m.* Anne, dau. of Edward Cookes, of Bentley Paunceforte, Esq. and had, with three daus. (Elizabeth, wife of Robert Clive, of Styche, Esq.; Anne, wife of John Hunt, Esq., of Chester; and Frances, wife of John Doughtie), three sons, viz.

I. JOHN, who *m.* Lucy Perrot, and *d. s. p.*
II. WILLIAM, of Astley, co. Worcester, who *m.* Anne, dau. of the Rev. Thomas James, of Sedgeley, and had five sons, Richard, John, William, Joseph, and Thomas, and one dau., Anne, wife of the Rev. Thomas Bell, rector of Quat. The eldest son, RICHARD AMPHLETT, Esq. of Hadsor, *m.* Sarah, dau. of Nicholas Hyett, of Amely, and had a son and heir,
WILLIAM AMPHLETT, Esq. of Hadsor, who *m.* Christian, dau. of John Amphlett, of Clent, Esq., and had, with a dau. (Harriet, wife of Captain John Edwards), four sons, 1 RICHARD, his heir; 2 John, D.D., rector of Doderhill, co. Worcester (father of John, *d. s. p.*, Aubrey, *d. s. p.*, Richard, Joseph, Elizabeth, *m.* to Henry Burslem, Esq., and Penelope, of Monmouth); 3 Joseph, of Dudley (father of Edward, of Broma, co. Stafford, who *m.* Caroline, dau. of Jacob Turner, Esq. of Park Hall, in Kidderminster, and had issue); and 4 Martin, rector of Stamford, co. Lincoln. The eldest son, RICHARD AMPHLETT, Esq. of Hadsor, living in 1780 *m.* Lydia, dau. and co-heir of John Holmden, of Crowle, co. Worcester, and had a son and successor, THE REV. RICHARD HOLMDEN AMPHLETT, of Hadsor, who *m.* 1st, a dau. of Paul, of Finedon, co. Northampton; and 2ndly, Jane, dau. of Thomas Dudley, of Shutend, in Himley, by both of whom he has issue. The children by his first wife are, 1 Richard-Paul, of Lincoln's Inn, M.A., barrister-at-law; *m.* 2 Dec. 1840, Frances, only child of the late Edward Ferrand, Esq. of St. Ives, co. York: 2 Holmden, of Birmingham; 3 Martin; 4 Charles, of London; 5 William; 1 Sarah; 2 Louisa; and 3 Julia.
III. JOSEPH, of whose line we have to treat.

The 3rd son,

JOSEPH AMPHLETT, Esq. of Clent, *m.* Anne, dau. of Sir Charles Lyttelton, of Frankley, and had, with other issue, a son and successor,

JOHN AMPHLETT, Esq. of Clent, who *m.* Mary, dau. of John Cardale, Esq. of Dudley, and widow of Edward Martin, of Leigh Court, co. Worcester, and had, with a dau. (Christian, *m.* 1st, to Wm. Amphlett, Esq. of Hadsor, and 2ndly, to Thomas Holbeach, Esq.) a son and successor,

JOHN AMPHLETT, Esq. of Clent, who *m.* Mary, dau. and co-heir of Thomas Hopwood, Esq. of Droitwich, and had,

JOHN, his heir.
Mary, *m.* to Henry, son of Dr. Cameron, of Worcester.
Elizabeth, *m.* to Col. Andrews, barrack-master at Gibraltar.
Christian, *m.* to William Wilkinson, Esq.
Margaret, *m.* 1st, to John-Perrott Noel, of Bell Hall, Esq.; 2ndly, to Henry Andrews, Esq.; and 3rdly, to John Gwinnell, Esq.

Mr. Amphlett *d.* in 1777, and was *s.* by his son,

JOHN AMPHLETT, Esq. of Clent, *b.* in 1763, who *m.* in 1789, Eliza-Anne, eldest dau. of Thomas Hill, Esq. of Dennis, in the same county, by whom (who *d.* in 1837) he had issue,

I. JOHN, *b.* 1795; *m.* in 1816, Eliza, eldest dau. and co-heir of Benjamin Benyon, Esq. of Haughton, in Shiffnall, co. Salop, M.P. for Stafford; and *d.* 9 Dec. 1826, leaving issue,
1 JOHN, present representative. 1 Eliza-Maria.
II. Thomas.
I. Margaret, *d.* 1839. II. Eliza-Anne. III. Mary.
IV. Harriet, *m.* to John-Perrott Noel, Esq. of Bell Hall.
V. Caroline. VI. Sophia, *d.* young. VII. Louisa.

Mr. Amphlett was *s.* at his decease by his grandson, the present JOHN AMPHLETT, Esq. of Clent House.

Arms—Arg., a fesse between three lozenges, az.; in chief a cinquefoil, sa.
Crest—A dromedary, ppr.
Seat—Clent House, co. Stafford.

ANDERSON OF JESMOND HOUSE.

ANDERSON, THOMAS, Esq. of Jesmond House, co. Northumberland, and Wallington Lodge, co. Surrey, *b.* 21 Sept. 1789; *m.* 7 June, 1527, Isabella, dau. of Robert Simpson, M.D., of St. Petersburgh, formerly of Sebrigham Hall, Cumberland, and has issue,

I. JOHN-SOULSBY, *b.* 22 June, 1828.
II. Robert-Gerard, *b.* 9 June, 1830.
III. Thomas-Goldsborough, *b.* 5 April, 1833.
IV. Charles-King, *b.* 24 Aug. 1836.

Mr. Anderson *s.* his father 1829, and served as sheriff of Newcastle in 1812.

Lineage.—This family was settled in Newcastle from the time of ELIZABETH, until about the year 1690, when they removed to North Shields, where they held property, a portion of which still continues in possession of the family. About the middle of the last century they returned to Newcastle.

GERARD ANDERSON, *b.* in 1646, *m.* Elizabeth Nicholson and *d.* in 1711, leaving, with a dau. Barbara, *m.* to Capt. Valentine Wye, a son,

THOMAS ANDERSON, who was father of two sons, Edward, who emigrated to America, and

THOMAS ANDERSON, *b.* in 1710, who *m.* 27 Sept. 1736, Eleanor Soulsby, of Newcastle, and had, with two daus., three sons,

I. Thomas, who *d. unm.* in 1789.
II. Matthew, *b.* in 1754; who settled in St. Petersburg about the end of the last century; and *d.* in 1834, leaving issue three sons, 1 Thomas, *b.* at St. Petersburg, 1793;

2 John, *m.* Frances, dau. of Robert Simpson, M.D., and has issue, Robert-Alexis, *m.* Harriet, dau. of Robert Cattley, Esq., Thomas-Gerard, and other children; 3 Matthew, *m.* Annie-Elizabeth Maine, and has issue; 1 Eleanor, *m.* to Joseph Stother, Esq.
III. JOHN, of whom we treat.

JOHN ANDERSON, Esq. of Jesmond House, J.P., *b.* 1 Nov. 1757, *m.* 12 May, 1787, Hannah, dau. of James King, Esq. of Newcastle, and had issue,

THOMAS, now of Jesmond House.
Matthew, of Jesmond Cottage, J.P., *b.* 18 April, 1792.
James-Crosby, of Little Benton, *m.* in 1822, Alice, dau. of William Losh, Esq. of Point Pleasant, and *d.* in 1837, leaving issue, 1 John, *b.* 2 Feb 1825; 2 William-Losh, *b.* 16 July, 1826; 3 James-Crosby, *b.* 12 July, 1828; 1 Alice; and 2 Eleanor-Adelaide.
JOHN, of Coxlodge Hall, Northumberland, J.P., sheriff of Newcastle, 1820; *m.* in 1827, Dorothy-Diana, dau. of Charles-Dalston Purvis, and sister of Thomas Purvis, Esq., Q.C., and has issue, 1 Charles-Dalston, *b.* 16 March, 1836; 1 Dorothy-Elizabeth; 2 Hannah-Emily, *m.* 3 May, 1851, to W.-F. Carter, Esq., capt. 63rd regt.; 3 Marianne-Purvis; 4 Eleanor; and 5 Florence.
Eleanor. Ann. Mary.

Mr. Anderson *d.* 6 May, 1829.

Arms—Per nebulée, az. and vert, a bugle horn stringed, between three stags, couchant, or.
Crest—On a mount, vert, a stag couchant, wounded in the breast by an arrow, and holding in his mouth an ear of wheat, all ppr., charged on his side with a bugle horn, or.
Motto—Nil desperandum, auspice Deo.
Seats—Jesmond House, co. Northumberland; and Wallington Lodge, Surrey.

ANDERSON OF GRACE DIEU.

ANDERSON, THE REV. JOSHUA, A.M., rector of Myshall, co. Carlow, *b.* 8 Dec. 1770; *m.* Oct. 1807, Anne, eldest dau. of Capt. William Perceval, (*see* PERCEVAL *of Temple House*), and has issue,

I. JAMES, of Grace Dieu Lodge, co. Waterford, J.P., *m.* April, 1842, Margaret, youngest dau. of Thomas Carew, Esq. of Ballinamona, and has issue, James-Paul, *b.* 21 Jan. 1850; Thomas-William; and Jane-Margaret.
II. William.
III. Robert-Carew, M.D., 90th light infantry, *m.* 13 Oct. 1853, Jane-Wallis, only dau. of the Rev. Henry Bolton.
IV. Paul-Christmas, of Prospect, co. Kilkenny.
V. Alexander, lieut. R.N.
I. Anne, *m.* 4 Feb. 1845, Charles-Newport Bolton, Esq.
II. Jane-Ellen. III. Ellen. IV. Catherine.
V. Henrietta. VI. Susan.

Lineage.—ALEXANDER ANDERSON, Esq. of Grace Dieu, descended from Anderson of Wester-Airderbeck, was nephew of the Rev. Arthur Anderson, chaplain to WILLIAM III., and Major Anderson, of Grace Dieu. He *m.* 2 Feb. 1721, Miss Brewster, dau. and co-heir of Wm. Brewster, Esq. son of Sir Francis Brewster, twice lord-mayor of Dublin. By her (who *d.* in 1754), Mr. Anderson left (with two daus., of whom the elder, Jane, *m.* Robert Carew, Esq. of Woodenstown, co. Tipperary) a son and heir,

JAMES ANDERSON, Esq. of Grace Dieu, *m.* in 1764, Susanna, youngest dau. of Christmas Paul, Esq. by Ellen his wife, daughter of Robert Carew, Esq. M.P., of Castle Boro', co. Wexford, great-uncle of Lord Carew, and had issue,

JAMES, his heir.
Paul (Sir), C.B., K.C., general, colonel of the 78th Highlanders, and governor of Pendennis Castle; *d. s. p.* 1851.
Alexander, capt. in the army; *d.* in Bath, in 1833, *s. p.*
Henry, R.N.; *d. s. p.*
JOSHUA, in holy orders, present representative of the family.
Robert, an officer in the 42nd regt., who was killed at the battle of Alexandria, *s. p.*
Ellen.

The eldest son,

JAMES ANDERSON, Esq. of Grace Dieu, *d.* in London, in 1838, *s. p.*, and left his estates to his brother, the present REV. JOSHUA ANDERSON.

Arms—Quarterly: 1st and 4th, arg., a saltier, engrailed, az., between two mullets in chief, gu., and as many boars' heads, erased, in the flanks, of the last; 2nd and 3rd, gu., a chevron, erm., between three estoiles, arg.
Crest—An oak-tree, ppr.
Motto—Over the crest, "Stand sure." Under the arms, "Dum spiro spero."
Residence—Myshall Glebe, co. Carlow.

AND

ANDERTON OF EUXTON.

ANDERTON, WILLIAM-INCE, Esq. of Euxton and Ince, both in co. Lancaster; *m.* 14 Nov. 1823, Frances, only dau. of Christopher Crook, Esq. of London, and first cousin to Thomas Gillebrand, Esq. of Gillebrand Hall, by whom he has an only son,

WILLIAM-MICHAEL-INCE, *b.* 29 Sept. 1825, *m.* 12 Sept. 1850, Lady Emma-Frances Plunkett, dau. of the Earl of Fingall.

Mr. Anderton *s.* his father in 1811.

Lineage.—JAMES ANDERTON, Esq. of Euxton, descended from a 2nd son of Anderton of Anderton, wedded Ann, dau. of Henry Banister, Esq. of The Bank, in the co. of Lancaster, and relict of Thomas Farington, Esq. of Farington. He was *s.* by his son,

HUGH ANDERTON, Esq. of Euxton, who *m.* 1st, a dau. of — Butler, Esq. of Rawcliffe; and 2ndly, Alice, dau. of Alexander Standish, Esq. of Standish. He had (besides four daus., Dorothy, *m.* to Edward Rigby, Esq. of Bury; Jane, who *d. unm.*; Anne, *m.* to William Hesketh, Esq. of Maines; and Alice, *m.* to Cuthbert Clifton, Esq. of Westby), two sons, WILLIAM and Hugh, of Clayton. Hugh Anderton *d.* about the year 1652, and was *s.* by his grandson,

HUGH ANDERTON, Esq. of Euxton, son of William Anderton, Esq. by Isabel his wife, dau. and heir of William Hancock, Esq. of Pendle Hall. He *m.* Margaret, dau. of Roger Kirkby, Esq. and left at his decease in 1664, a dau., Dorothy, *m.* to John Bradshaw, Esq. of Daniog, in Anglesea, and a son,

HUGH ANDERTON, Esq. of Euxton, who *m.* Catherine, dau. of Francis Trapa, Esq. of Nidd, and left, at his demise (with other issue), Margaret, the wife of Robert Blundell, Esq. of Ince Blundell, in the co. of Lancaster, and a son and successor,

WILLIAM ANDERTON, Esq. of Euxton, who *m.* Mary, dau. of Richard, 5th Viscount Molyneux, and relict of Thomas Clifton, Esq. of Lytham, by whom (who *d.* in 1752) he had (with two daus., Catherine, wife of Sir Robert Gerard, Bart., and Ann, a nun at Calais) two sons, WILLIAM, his heir, and Francis, a monk, who *d.* at Linley, in Salop.

WILLIAM ANDERTON, Esq. of Euxton, the elder son, *m.* Frances, dau. and heir of Christopher Ince, Esq. of Ince Hall, in the co. of Lancaster, representative of one of the most ancient families in that shire, and had (with three other sons, Robert, Thomas, and Francis), a successor, at his decease in 1811, the present WILLIAM-INCE ANDERTON, Esq. of Euxton and Ince.

*** From a third son of the House of ANDERTON *of Anderton* descended LAWRENCE ANDERTON, who founded the family of Lostock. (*See* BURKE's *Extinct Baronetage*).

Arms—Sa., a chevron, between three shackbolts, arg.
Crest—A curlew, ppr.
Motto—We stoop not.
Seats—Euxton Hall, near Chorley; and Ince Hall, near Wigan.

ANDREWS OF LITTLE LEVER AND RIVINGTON.

ANDREWS, ROBERT, Esq. of Little Lever and Rivington, co. Lancaster, J.P., *b.* at Rivington Hall, 13 Jan. 1785.

Lineage.—This is a branch of the ancient family of ANDREW *of Charwelton*, co. Northampton, founded by RALPH ANDREW, of Gray's Inn, son of Thomas Andrew, of Carlisle, *anno* 1286, as appears from a certificate under the hand and seal of John Andrew, son of Sir John Andrew, of Charwelton, now among the archives of the College of Arms.

JOHN ANDREW, Esq. of Little Lever Hall, son and heir of Nicholas Andrew, citizen of London, by Hoth, dau. of Thos. Lever, Esq. of Little Lever, co. Lancaster, a captain in CROMWELL's army, entered his pedigree at the visitation of Lancashire, 16 May, 1664, by Sir William Dugdale, Norroy King-at-Arms. He *m.* for his 2nd wife, in 1653, Jane, dau. and heiress of Robert Lever, Esq. of Darcy Lever, co. Lancaster, and had issue. The son and heir,

JOHN ANDREW, otherwise ANDREWS, of Little Lever and Rivington, *m.* 6 July, 1682, Anna, dau. of Robert Mort, Esq. of Little Hulton, co. Lancaster, and had issue,

ROBERT ANDREWS, of Bolton-le-Moors, co. Lancaster, 2nd son, *m.* Dec 30, 1712, Hannah, dau. of Joseph Crompton, Esq. of Hackin, co. Lancaster, afterwards of Bolton-le-Moors, in the same county, and had, with other issue,

I. JOSEPH, of whom presently.
II. Robert, b. 29 June, 1723; minister of the presbyterian chapel, Bridgenorth, co. Salop; m. Hannah, dau. of — Haslewood, of Bridgenorth; d. s. p.
III. James, of Manchester, and afterwards of Bolton-le-Moors, co. Lancaster, b. 4 Feb. 1728; m. 31 Oct. 1750, Susanna, second dau., and eventually co-heiress, of Robert Dukinfield, Esq. of Manchester, son of Sir Robert Dukinfield, Bart., and had issue two daus. and co-heiresses (he d. in Nov. 1768; she d. in Jan. 1787), viz.,
  1 Susanna, b. 26 June, 1755; m. 8 July, 1776, the Rev. Jonathan Hodgkinson, of Hindley, co. Lancaster, and had issue, James-Andrews, b. 25 Jan. 1783; William, b. 1? March, 1786; and Susanna-Andrews, b. 8 April, 1791; m. her cousin, Thomas Hibbert, Esq. of Everton, co. Lancaster.
  2 Frances, b. 11 June, 1761; m. at Wigan, co. Lancaster, 23 Feb. 1789, the Rev. Nathaniel Hibbert, of Rivington, co. Lancaster, and had with junior issue, Thomas, of Everton, co. Lancaster, b. 21 Aug. 1791; m. his cousin, Susanna-Andrews Hodgkinson, as before mentioned, and has issue, Thomas-Dorning, b. 29 July, 1821, of the Middle Temple, barrister-at-law.

JOSEPH ANDREWS, of Bolton-le-Moors, son and heir, b. 25 Nov. 1715, m. Hannah, dau. of Edward Kenyon, of that place, and had issue,

I. ROBERT.
I. Hannah, b. 13 April, 1740; m. in 1766, John Fletcher, of Liverpool, and had, with three daus., four sons,
  1 Thomas, of Liverpool, b. 22 June, 1767; m. Anna, dau. of William Enfield, LL.D., and has issue.
  2 Joseph, of Liverpool, b. 19 Oct. 1768; m. Eliza, dau. of Robert Nicholson, of Liverpool, and has issue.
  3 John, of Liverpool, b. 20 April, 1773; d. 24 Aug. 1844. He m. 1st, Eliza, dau. of Thomas Hodgson, of Caton, co. Lancaster, and had issue. He m. 2ndly, Sarah, dau. of Eli Jagger, of Liverpool, and had issue.
  4 Robert, of Toxteth Park, near Liverpool; b. 5 Sept. 1776; m. his cousin, Hannah-Maria, dau. of Robert Andrews, Esq., of whom hereafter.

Mr. Joseph Andrews, d. 29 Oct. 1749, and was s. by his son and heir,

ROBERT ANDREWS, Esq. of Little Lever and Rivington; he having s. to the estates, on the death of Mr. Wilson, as great-nephew and heir-at-law of John Andrews aforesaid; b. 30 Dec. 1741, m. 1st, Mary, dau. of Samuel Darbishire, of Bolton-le-Moors, by whom he had no issue. He m. 2ndly, Sarah, dau. of Thomas Cockshott, Esq. of Marlow, co. York, and by her (who d. 29 April, 1791) had issue,

ROBERT, his heir.
John, b. 25 July, 1786.
Anna-Maria, b. 21 July, 1783; m. her cousin, Robert Fletcher, of Toxteth Park, as before mentioned, and has issue.

Mr. Andrews, J.P. for Lancashire, d. 13 Aug. 1793, and was s. by his son and heir, the present ROBERT ANDREWS, Esq. of Little Lever and Rivington.

Arms—Quarterly: 1st and 4th, gu., a saltier, or, surmounted of another, vert; in chief, a trefoil, arg., for difference, for ANDREWS; 2nd and 3rd, arg., two bends, sa., the one in chief, engrailed, for LEVER *of Darcy Lever.*
Crest—A Moor's head, in profile, couped at the shoulders, ppr.; in the ear a pendant, arg.
Motto—Fortiter defendit.
Seat—Rivington Hall, co. Lancaster.

ANKETELL OF ANKETELL GROVE.

ANKETELL, WILLIAM, Esq. of Anketell Grove, co. Monaghan, J.P. and D.L.; m. Sarah, dau. of John Waring Maxwell, Esq. of Finnebrogue, co. Down, and has issue,

I. MATTHEW-JOHN, b. 31 Oct. 1812, high-sheriff for the county of Monaghan, in 1834; m. 6 Feb. 1840, Frances-Anne, eldest dau. of David Ker, Esq. of Portavo, co. Down, by the Lady Selina his wife, sister of the late Marquess of Londonderry, and has issue.
II. William. III. Oliver. IV. Fitzameline.
V. Maxwell. VI. Moutray.
I. Anne-Dorothea, m. in 1833, to the Rev. Robert Loftus Tottenham, 2nd son of Lord Robert Tottenham, Bishop of Clogher.
II. Maria, m. in 1839, to the Rev. John Bunbury, eldest son of Sir James Richardson-Bunbury, Bart., of Augher Castle, co. Tyrone.
III. Matilda.

Lineage.—The family of which we are about to treat, was of high station in the co. of Dorset at a very remote period (its name appearing in Doomsday Book), and so early as the reign of EDWARD I., we find Fitzameline Anschetil representing the borough of Shaftesbury in parliament. The English line has long since passed away, but a branch of the ancient stem having been planted in the north of Ireland *temp.* CHARLES I., the Anketells maintain in the land of their adoption as distinguished a position as did their English progenitors in the land of their extraction.

MATTHEW ANKETELL, Esq. acquired in 1636, a grant of land in the co. of Monaghan, and emigrated to Ireland, where he m. Matilda, dau. of Robert Moore, Esq. of Garvy Castle, in Tyrone, and had a son,

MATTHEW ANKETELL, Esq. of Anketell Grove, who lost his life during the contest between King JAMES and King WILLIAM in 1689, fighting on the side of the latter monarch. His son,

OLIVER ANKETELL, Esq. of Anketell Grove, M.P. for the borough of Monaghan, m. 28 Feb. 1716, the Hon. Sarah Caulfeild, 2nd dau. of William, 2nd Viscount Charlemont (the gallant and well-known participator in the triumphs of the Earl of Peterborough in Spain), by Anne his wife, only dau. of James Margetson, Lord Archbishop of Armagh. By this lady, who d. in Dec. 1742, Mr. Anketell left, with other issue, a son and successor,

MATTHEW ANKETELL, Esq. of Anketell Grove, who m. 11 March, 1748, Anne, dau. of Charles Coote, Esq. of Coote Hill, M.P. for the co. of Cavan, and sister of Charles, Earl of Bellamont; by this lady he had a son and heir,

MATTHEW ANKETELL, Esq. of Anketell Grove, who m. 1st, in 1780, Prudentia, only dau. of Thomas Steward Corry, Esq. of Rockcorry Castle, in the co. of Monaghan, by whom he had a dau. Prudentia, who d. in youth. He wedded 2ndly, Mary, dau. of the Rev. Richard Norris, and had, with other issue, a son and heir, the present WILLIAM ANKETELL, Esq. of Anketell Grove.

Arms—Or, a cross, ragulée, vert.
Crest—An oak-tree, ppr.
Motto—Vade ad formicam.
Seat—Anketell Grove.

ANNESLEY OF ARLEY CASTLE.

ANNESLEY, ARTHUR-LYTTELTON, Esq. of Arley Castle, co. Stafford, capt. in the army, b. 30 Nov. 1802; m. 18 March, 1835, Mary, 3rd dau. of John Bradley, Esq. of Colborne Hall, co. Stafford, and has,

I. ARTHUR-LYTTLETON, b. 2 Sept. 1837.
II. John-George, b. 8 Aug. 1839.
I. Georgiana-Lyttleton. II. Annabella-Lucy.
III. Augusta-Mary.

This gentleman, son of Major-Gen. Norman Macleod (great-grandson of Sir Roderick Macleod, of Macleod), by Hester-Annabella his wife, dau. of the 1st Earl of Mountnorris, took the name and arms of ANNESLEY, by royal license, in 1844, having s. to the estates of his maternal uncle, George Annesley, last Earl of Mountnorris. Mr. Annesley is a magistrate for the cos. of Stafford, Worcester, Salop, and Wexford.

Arms—Paly of six, arg. and az., over all a bend, gu.
Crest—A Moor's head in profile, couped, ppr., wreathed about the temples, arg. and az.
Motto—Virtutis amore.
Seats—Arley Castle, co. Stafford; and Camolin Park, co. Wexford.

ANSTRUTHER-THOMPSON.

See THOMSON *of Charleton.*

ANSTRUTHER OF HINTLESHAM HALL.

ANSTRUTHER, JAMES-HAMILTON-LLOYD, Esq. of Hintlesham Hall, co. Suffolk, b. 21 Dec. 1807; m. 1st, 6 Dec. 1838, Georgiana-Charlotte, eldest dau. of the Hon. Lindsey Burrell, and by her (who d. 21 Sept. 1843), has issue,

ROBERT-HAMILTON, b. 27 April, 1841.
Priscilla-Barbara-Elizabeth.

He m. 2ndly, 1 Nov. 1847, the Hon. Georgiana-Christiana, dau. of George, 5th Viscount Barrington, and by her has,

Francis-William, *b.* 20 Feb. 1849.
James, *b.* 9 Jan. 1852.
Basil and Cecil (twins), *b.* 1 Dec. 1852.

Mr. Anstruther is next brother of the present Sir Ralph-Abercrombie Anstruther, Bart. of Balcaskie, co. Fife, being 2nd son of the late General Anstruther, by Charlotte-Lucy his wife, only dau. of Col. James Hamilton (grandson of James, 4th Duke of Hamilton), by Lucy his wife, dau. of Sir Richard Lloyd, of Hintlesham.

Arms—Arg., three piles issuing from the chief, sa.
Crest—Two arms in armour, holding in the gauntlets a battle-axe, all ppr.
Motto—Periissem ni periissem.
Seat—Hintlesham Hall, Suffolk.

ANTROBUS OF EATON HALL.

Antrobus, Gibbs-Crawfurd, Esq. of Eaton Hall, co. Chester, *b.* 27 May, 1793; *m.* 1st, 23rd June, 1827, Jane, 2nd dau. of Sir Coutts Trotter, Bart., and by her (who *d.* 24 Nov. 1829), had one son and heir,

I. John-Coutts, *b.* 23 Nov. 1829.

He *m.* 2ndly, 12 Jan. 1832, Charlotte, 2nd dau. of Sir Edward Crofton, Bart., and sister of the present Lord Crofton, and by her (who *d.* 29 Sept. 1839), had issue,

I. Edward-Crawfurd, *b.* 28 Feb. 1835.
II. Charles, *b.* 26 Aug. 1836.
I. Susan-Emily. II. Anna-Maria.

Mr. Antrobus, who is younger brother of Sir Edmund-William Antrobus, Bart., is a magistrate and deputy-lieut. of Cheshire, and was high-sheriff in 1834.

Lineage.—For descent, see Burke's *Peerage and Baronetage.*

Arms—Losengy, or and az., on a pale, gu., three estoiles of the first.
Crest—A unicorn's head, couped, arg., horned and maned, or, gorged with a wreath of laurel, vert, issuing out of rays, ppr.
Motto—Dei memor, gratus amicis.
Seat—Eaton Hall, Congleton, co. Chester.

ARABIN OF BEECH HILL PARK.

Arabin, Richard, Esq. of Beech Hill Park, co. Essex, and Drayton House, Middlesex, *b.* 1 March, 1811; *m.* 10 Oct. 1839, Elizabeth-Mary, eldest dau. of the late Sir Henry Meux, Bart. of Theobalds Park, Herts, and has issue,

I. William-St. Julian, *b.* 23 Nov. 1843.
I. Marianne-Elizabeth. II. Alice-Charlotte.

Mr. Arabin, J.P. for the cos. of Middlesex, Herts, and Essex, and D.L. for the last-named shire, *s.* his father in 1841.

Lineage.—William-St. Julien Arabin, Esq. of Beech Hill Park, serjeant-at-law, *m.* Mary, sister of the late Sir Henry Meux, Bart. and had a son, Richard, his heir. Serjeant Arabin, who was judge-advocate-general in 1838-9, *d.* in 1841, and was *s.* by his son, the present Richard Arabin, Esq. of Beech Hill Park.

Arms—Quarterly; 1st and 4th, az.; in base an arm, couped at the wrist, lying fesseways, holding a sword, all ppr.; on the point thereof a crescent, arg., between two mullets in chief, or; in the dexter base point a heart, gu.; 2nd and 3rd, an eagle, displayed, sa., ducally crowned, or.
Crest—An eagle's head, erased, between two wings, sa., ducally crowned, or.
Motto—Nec temere nec timide.
Seat—Beech Hill Park, co. Essex.

ARCEDECKNE OF GLEVERING HALL.

Arcedeckne, Andrew, Esq. of Glevering Hall, co. Suffolk.

Lineage.—Chaloner Arcedeckne, Esq. of Glevering Hall, high-sheriff of Suffolk, and M.P. for Westbury, son and heir of Andrew Arcedeckne, attorney-general of the island of Jamaica, where he died about the year 1765, *m.* Catherine, 2nd dau. and co-heiress of John Leigh, Esq. of North Court House, Isle of Wight, and *d.* 13 Dec. 1809, leaving issue, Andrew, his heir, Chaloner, *d. unm.*, Walter, Frances-Katherine, *m.* 2 April, 1810, to Lord Huntingfield; and Mary-Louisa, *d. unm.* in July, 1816.

The eldest son, Andrew Arcedeckne, Esq. of Glevering Hall, co. Suffolk, *b.* in Jan. 1780, *m.* 29 Aug. 1816, Harriet, only dau. of Francis-Love Beckford, Esq. of Basing Park, Hants, by whom he had issue,

Andrew, now of Glevering.
Louisa, *m.* 6 July, 1839, the Hon. Joshua Vanneck, eldest son of Lord Huntingfield.

Mr. Arcedeckne, who sat in parliament for Dunwich, *d.* 8 Feb. 1849.

Arms—Arg., three chevrons, gu.
Crest—A dexter arm, holding in the hand a sword.
Seat—Glevering Hall, Suffolk.

ARCHBOLD OF DAVIDSTOWN.

Archbold, Robert, Esq. of Davidstown, co. Kildare, late M.P. for that county; *m.* Miss Copeland, and became a widower without issue in 1842.

Lineage.—The Archbolds were, in early times, titular Barons of Timolin, in the co. of Kildare. The late

James Archbold, Esq. of Dublin, *s.* to the estate of Davidstown and the representation of his ancient family, on the demise of his cousin, John Archbold, Esq. of Blackrath, co. Kildare. He *m.* Eleanor, dau. of Thomas Kavanagh, Esq. of Borris, co. Carlow, by the Lady Susan his wife, sister of John Butler, Earl of Ormonde and Ossory, and dying about the year 1804, left, with a dau. *m.* to Robert Cassidy, Esq. of Monasterevan, three sons, Robert, now of Davidstown; James, who *m.* in 1842, Miss Power, of Faithlegue, co. Waterford; and John.

Seat—Davidstown House, co. Kildare.

ARCHDALL OF CASTLE ARCHDALL.

Archdall, William, Esq. of Castle Archdall, co. Fermanagh, late lieut.-col. 4th or King's Own infantry; *s.* his brother, Gen. Mervyn Archdall, in 1839; *m.* Martha-Hawley, dau. of James Clarke, Esq. of Castle Carey, co. Somerset, and is a widower without issue.

Lineage.—The first of the family of Archdall, who settled in Ireland *temp.* Elizabeth, was John Archdall, Esq. of Norsom or Norton Hall, in the co. of Norfolk. His two sons were,

Edward, his heir, and John, vicar of Luske in 1664, great-grandfather of the Rev. Mervin Archdall, author of the *Monasticon Hibernicum.*

Angel Archdall (the eventual heiress), only sister of Edward Archdall, Esq. of Castle Archdall, *m.* Nicholas Montgomery, Esq. of Derry Gonnelly, co. Fermanagh, M.P. for that shire, son of Hugh Montgomery, Esq. by Katherine his wife, dau. and heir of Richard Dunbar, Esq. of Derrygonelly. Mr. Montgomery assumed the surname and arms of Archdall, and left by the heiress of Archdall, who *d.* about 1742 or 1743, an only son,

Mervyn Archdall, Esq. of Castle Archdall and Trillic, M.P. for the co. of Fermanagh, who *m.* in 1762, Mary, dau. of William-Henry, Viscount Carlow, and sister of John, 1st Earl of Portarlington, by whom he had issue,

I. Mervyn, his heir.
II. William, present representative of the family.
III. Edward, of Riversdale, co. Fermanagh, high-sheriff in 1813; *m.* 2 Oct. 1809, Matilda, 2nd dau. of William Humphrys, Esq. of Ballyhaise, co. Cavan, and has had issue,
 1 Mervyn, late capt. 6th dragoons, M.P. for the co. of Fermanagh; *b.* in 1812.
 2 William-Humphrys, B.A.; *m.* Emily, dau. of the Hon. and Rev. Charles Maude.
 3 Edward, capt. in the army, late 14th infantry; *m.* 21 Nov. 1846, Caroline-Anne, dau. of Charles-Claude Clifton, Esq. of Tymawr, co. Brecon.
 4 Henry-Dawson, B.A., in holy orders; *m.* a dau. of James-Blackwood Price, Esq. of Saintfield, and has issue.
 5 Nicholas-Montgomery, *m.* the 4th dau. of the Rev. John-Gray Porter, son of the Bishop of Clogher, and has issue.

6 John, in the 52nd light infantry; *d.* of yellow fever, at Berbice, in 1841.
7 Hugh-Montgomery, capt. 52nd regt.
8 Audley-Mervyn, *m.* a dau. of Philip-John Miles, Esq. of Leigh Court, Bristol.
9 James-Mervyn, *d.* in 1840.
1 Mary.
2 Letitia-Jane, *m.* to the Rev. Butler Brooke, rector of Aghaven, next brother of Sir H.-B. Brooke, Bart.
3 Richmall-Magnall. 4 Matilda, *d. unm.* 1852.

IV. Henry, late capt. 6th dragoon-guards; *m.* Jane, dau. of Philip Doyne, Esq., which lady *d. s. p.*
I. Mary, *m.* Sir John Stewart, Bart., M.P., and is deceased.
II. Angel, *m.* John Richardson, Esq. of Rossfad House, co. Fermanagh; and *d.* leaving issue.
III. Caroline. IV. Anne. V. Catherine.
VI. Elizabeth, *m.* to Dacre Hamilton, Esq. of Cornacassa, co. Monaghan; and *d.* leaving issue.
VII. Sidney, *m.* Robert Hamilton, Esq. of the city of Dublin, and has issue, 1 Maxwell, who *m.* in 1854, the dau. and co-heir of the late John Graves, Esq. of Mickleton Manor House, co. Gloucester; 2 Robert, in holy orders, widower, with issue; 3 Chetwode; 4 Mervyn; 5 Dawson; and several daughters.
VIII. Wilhelmina-Henrietta, *m.* to Augustine Macnamara, Esq. of Dublin, and is deceased.

Mr. Archdall *d.* in 1818, and was *s.* by his eldest son,

MERVYN ARCHDALL, Esq. of Castle Archdall and Trillic, a general officer in the army, lieutenant-governor of the Isle of Wight, and M.P. in eleven parliaments for the co. Fermanagh, *b.* in 1763, *m.* 1805, Jane, dau. of Gustavus Rochfort, Esq. of Rochfort, co. of Westmeath, but *d.* without issue in 1839.

Arms—Quarterly: 1st and 4th, for ARCHDALL, az., a chevron, erm., between three talbots, or; 2nd, for MONTGOMERY, quarterly, az. and gu., in the 1st and 4th, three fleurs-de-lis, or; in the 2nd and 3rd, three annulets of the last; 3rd, for MERVYN, party per pale, or and arg., three lions, passant-guardant, sa.
Crests—ARCHDALL—Out of a ducal coronet, an heraldic tiger's head, ppr. MONTGOMERY—On a cap of maintenance, ppr., a hand, vested, az., grasping a sword, ppr., pommel and hilt, gold. MERVYN—A squirrel, segreant, ppr.
Mottoes—ARCHDALL—Data fata secutus. MONTGOMERY—Honneur sans repos. MERVYN—De Dieu tout.
Seats—Castle Archdall, co. Fermanagh; and Trillic, co. Tyrone.

ARCHER-BURTON OF WOODLANDS.

ARCHER-BURTON, BURTON, Esq., M.A. of Woodlands, Emsworth, Hants, J.P., barrister-at-law, *b.* 10 July, 1820; *m.* 30 Sept. 1845, Henrietta, 4th dau. of the late Henry Taylor, Esq., Madras Civil Service, and has,

I. JAMES-GREAM. II. James-Henry.
I. Katharine-Edith. II. Georgina-Emma.
III. Evelyn-Mary.

Lineage.—The late LANCELOT ARCHER-BURTON, Esq. of Emsworth, son of John South, Esq. of Latton, in Essex, by Ann his wife, sole heiress of John Archer, Esq. of Ongar Park Hall, in the same county, *b.* 9 Sep. 1789, assumed the surnames of ARCHER and BURTON, under the King's sign-manual, in lieu of SOUTH, at the decease, and on his succession to the property, of Lancelot Burton, Esq. of Maida Vale, Middlesex. He was J.P. and D.L. for Hants, and served as High Sheriff in 1847. He *m.* 2 Sept. 1817, Jane, youngest dau. of James Gubbins, Esq. of Epsom, and had issue,

BURTON, now of Woodlands.
James-Gubbins, late capt. 6th dragoon guards.
Richard.
Susan-Jane. Mary-Ann-Elizabeth. Emma.

Mr. Archer-Burton *d.* 7 Feb. 1852.

Arms—ARCHER and BURTON, quarterly.
Crests—1st, BURTON: 2nd, ARCHER.
Motto—Amicus vitæ solatium.
Seats—Woodlands, Emsworth, Hants; and Brook Lodge, Sunninghill, Berks.

ARCHER OF TRELASKE.

ARCHER, EDWARD, Esq. of Trelaske House, co. Cornwall, *b.* 8 Nov. 1816; *m.* 24 July, 1838, Sarah-Lydia, eldest dau. of the Rev. Walter Radcliffe, of Warlegh, co. Devon, and has issue,

I. CHARLES-GORDON, *b.* 1 Nov. 1846.
II. Addis-Edward, *b.* 18 Aug. 1851.
I. Alice. II. Emily-Augusta.
III. Sarah-Constance.

Mr. Archer *s.* his father 16 May, 1834, and is a magistrate and deputy-lieut. for Cornwall.

Lineage.—The Archers came over at the time of the CONQUEST, and the name is to be found in the Battle Abbey Roll. A branch of this family was ennobled, *anno* 1747, in the person of THOMAS ARCHER, Esq. M.P. for Warwick, who was created BARON ARCHER, *of Umberslade*, in Warwickshire. The line more immediately before us appears to have been settled in Cornwall for at least 400 years, a John Archer having represented Helston in parliament as far back as the time of HENRY VI.

RICHARD ARCHER, of St. Kew, who possessed considerable property in St. Kew, St. Ewe, Bodmin, and other parishes, devised Trelewack, in St. Ewe, and all his estates to his nephew, Nicholas Archer, eldest son of his brother John, rector of Carhayes, and to this Nicholas, his father, by will, bequeaths "his silver cup, to remayne for ever in the keeping of the eldest son of my family." The rector of Carhayes, the REV. JOHN ARCHER, had three sons, Nicholas, who *d. s. p.*; Edward, vicar of Manaccan, who *m.* Judith Swete; and John; and three daus., Amy, *m.* to George Slade, Anne, and Mary.

The late EDWARD ARCHER, Esq. of Trelaske, *b.* 25 April, 1792, high-sheriff of Cornwall in 1832 (son of Samuel Archer, Esq. of Trelaske, by Dorothy-Ayre his wife, dau. of the Rev. John Yonge, of Postlynch, Devon, and great-grandson of John Archer, Esq., by Sarah his wife, dau. and co-heir of John Addis, Esq. of Whiteford, which John Archer was eldest son of the Rev. Edward Archer, vicar of Manaccan, and Judith his wife, dau. of John Swete, Esq. of Modbury), *m.* 2 Aug. 1814, Charlotte-Catherine, only child and heiress of Capt. Charles Harward, of the 3rd foot guards, of Hayne House, Devon, by Charlotte-Augusta his wife, 3rd dau. of Sir Wm. Chambers, surveyor-general of the Board of Works, and by her (who *m.* 2ndly, Charles Gordon, Esq. of Wiscombe Park, Devon) had issue,

I. EDWARD, his heir.
II. Charles-Harward, *b.* in Aug. 1819.
III. Samuel-Harward, *b.* in Jan. 1821.
IV. Fulbert, *b.* in April, 1825.
V. Henry-Swete, *b.* in Jan. 1834.
I. Charlotte-Dorothea. II. Jane.
III. Anne-Augusta. IV. Elizabeth.
V. Catherine. VI. Marianne.

Mr. Archer *d.* 16 May, 1834.

Arms—Sa., a chevron, engrailed, arg., between three pheons, or.
Crest—A quiver, fessewise, ppr.
Seat—Trelaske, near Launceston.

ARCHIBALD OF RUSLAND HALL.

ARCHIBALD, CHARLES-DICKSON, Esq. of Rusland Hall, co. Lancaster, F.R.S., F.S.A., *b.* at Truro, in the province of Nova Scotia, 31 Oct. 1802; *m.* 16 Sept. 1832, Bridget, only child and heiress of Myles Walker, Esq. of Rusland Hall, and has issue,

I. CHARLES-WILLIAM, *b.* 20 July, 1838.
II. Edward-Stanley-Fitzgerald, *b.* 5 Dec. 1846.
III. Clarence-Holford, *b.* 12 Nov. 1847.
IV. Alfred-George, *b.* 6 Aug. 1849.
I. Elizabeth-Jane. II. Florence-Mary.
III. Juliet-Augusta. IV. Clara-Susanna.

Mr. Archibald is a magistrate and deputy-lieut. for the county of Lancaster.

Lineage.—The family of ARCHIBALD has been established for centuries in Ireland.

SAMUEL ARCHIBALD, Esq. of Coleraine, co. Londonderry, son of David Archibald, Esq. of Coleraine, *m.* Rachel, dau. of James Duncan, Esq. of Haverhill, Massachusetts, New England, and was father of

THE HON. SAMUEL-GEORGE-WILLIAM ARCHIBALD, LL.D., her Majesty's attorney and advocate-general, speaker of the Assembly, master of the rolls, &c. of the province of Nova Scotia, who *m.* 1st, in 1802, Elizabeth, dau. of Charles Dickson, Esq. of Onslow, and by her, who *d.* in May, 1830, had issue,

CHARLES-DICKSON, now of Rusland Hall.

He *m.* 2ndly, in 1832, Joanna, widow of W. Brinky, Esq. and *d.* 26 Jan. 1840.

Motto—Palma non sine pulvere.
Seat—Rusland Hall, co. Lancaster.

ARDEN OF LONGCROFT.

ARDEN, THE REV. FRANCIS-EDWARD, of Gresham, co. Norfolk, m. Rachael, dau. of John Pinkard, Esq., and has issue,

I. EDWARD. II. Henry. III. Hamer.
I. Rachel. II. Emma.

Lineage.—This family boasts of Saxon blood, and claims distinction for a full century at least before the CONQUEST, deriving, in direct descent, from SIWARD DE ARDEN, eldest son of Turchill de Warwick. The senior line, the ARDENS *of Park Hall*, in Warwickshire, became extinct at the decease, in 1643, of ROBERT ARDEN, of Park Hall, Esq. who left his four sisters his co-heirs—viz., ELIZABETH, m. to Sir Wm. Poley, of Boxted, in Suffolk; GODITHA, wife of Herbert Price, Esq.; DOROTHEA, m. to Henry Bagot, Esq.; and ANNE, m. to Sir Charles Adderley, of Lea.

The late REV. JOHN ARDEN, of Longcroft Hall, b. in March, 1752, was son of Henry Arden, Esq. of Longcroft, by Alathea his wife, dau. of Robert Cotton, Esq. of Worcester, and grandson (by Anna-Catherine his first wife, eldest dau. of John Newton, Esq. of King's Bromley) of John Arden, Esq. of Longcroft, sheriff of Staffordshire in 1730, 5th in descent from Simon Arden, Esq., 2nd son of Thos. Arden, Esq. of Park Hall. He m. Margaret-Elizabeth, only child of Rear-Admiral Hamer, and had,

JOHN, his heir.
FRANCIS-EDWARD, present representative of the family.
Henry, lieutenant 61st foot, slain at Toulouse.
Samuel, major in the East India Company's service, m. Jane, dau. of James Franklyn, Esq., of Bristol, and d. leaving issue.
William, of Barton-under-Needwood, m. Lettice, dau. of the Rev. John Weston, of Prestbury, co. Chester, and has issue.
George-Humphrey, deceased.
George, lieutenant R.N., died in the West Indies.
Thomas, in holy orders.
Eliza.
Emma-Catherine, m. to Walter-William Fell, Esq., barrister-at-law.
Anne-Diana, m. to the Rev. Francis Close, of Cheltenham.
Mary-Jane, m. to George-Woodroofe Franklyn, Esq.

Mr. Arden d. 10 Feb. 1803, aged 51, and was s. by his eldest son,

MAJOR-JOHN ARDEN, of the 3rd or King's Own dragoons, who m. Anne-Maria, dau. of John Hodgson, Esq. of Wellingborough, co. Northampton, and had issue,

JOHN-HUMPHREY-COTTON, died in India.
Margaret-Mary-Anne, m. to James Challen, Esq., and has issue.
Susanna-Maria, m. to John Bott, Esq., of Coton Hall, co. Stafford, and has issue.

Major Arden d. 2 Aug. 1809, aged 33.

Arms—Erm., a fesse, chequy or and az.
Crest—On a chapeau, purpure, turned up, ermine, a wild boar, passant, or.
Motto—Quo me cunque vocat patria.
Seat—Longcroft Hall, Staffordshire.

ARKWRIGHT OF SUTTON SCARSDALE.

ARKWRIGHT, ROBERT, Esq. of Sutton, co. Derby, J.P. and D.L., b. 7 March, 1783; m. Frances-Crawford, dau. of Stephen-George Kemble, Esq. of Durham, and has issue,

I. GEORGE, barrister-at-law, a magistrate for Derbyshire, and M.P. for Leominster, b. 20 Aug. 1807.
II. William, capt. in the army, b. 12 Sept. 1809.
III. Godfrey-Harry, b. 10 Oct. 1814.
IV. Eustace, b. 27 Dec. 1818.
I. Fanny-Elizabeth.

Lineage.—SIR RICHARD ARKWRIGHT, to whom we owe the compilation and completion into a connected whole, of the different parts of the invention called the spinning-frame, was born at Preston, in Lancashire, in 1732; he m. 1st, Patience, dau. of Robert Holt, of Bolton, by whom he had one son, RICHARD, his heir, and 2ndly, in 1760, Margaret Biggens, by whom he had one other child, Susannah, m. to Charles Hurt, Esq. of Wirksworth. Sir Richard Arkwright was knighted on presenting an address to GEORGE III., and served as sheriff of Derbyshire in 1787. He d. 3 Aug. 1792, and was s. by his son,

RICHARD ARKWRIGHT, Esq. of Willersley, b. 19 Dec. 1755, J.P. and D.L., high sheriff in 1801, m. in 1780, Mary, dau. of Adam Simpson, Esq. of Bonsall, and had issue,

I. RICHARD, b. 30 Sept. 1781; m. Maria, dau. of the Rev. Mr. Beresford, d. s. p., in 1832.
II. ROBERT, of Sutton Scarsdale.
III. PETER, of Willersley Castle.
IV. JOHN, of Hampton Court.
V. CHARLES, of Dunstall.
VI. JOSEPH, of Mark Hall.
I. Elizabeth, m. Francis Hurt, Esq., of Alderwasley, co. Derby, and d. in 1838, leaving issue.
II. Anne, m. Sir James Wigram.
III. Frances.

Mr. Arkwright d. in 1843.

Arms—Arg., on a mount, vert, a cotton tree, fructed, ppr., on a chief, az., between two bezants, an escutcheon of the field, charged with a bee, volant, ppr.
Crest—An eagle, rising, or, in its beak an escutcheon, pendent by a riband, gu., thereon a hank of cotton, arg.
Motto—Multa tuli fecique.
Seat—Willersley.

ARKWRIGHT OF WILLERSLEY.

ARKWRIGHT, PETER, Esq. of Willersley, co. Derby, J.P., b. 17 April, 1784; m. 1805, Mary-Anne, dau. of Charles Hurt, Esq. of Wirksworth, and has issue,

I. FREDERIC, b. 16 Aug. 1806; m. in 1845, Susan-Sabrina, dau. of the Ven. Archdeacon Burney, and has one son two daus.
II. Edward, b. 15 Dec. 1808; m. in 1845, Charlotte-Wilmot, dau. of Robert Sitwell, Esq., and d. in 1850, leaving three daus.
III. Henry, b. 16 March, 1811, in holy orders, m. 1st, Henrietta, dau. of the Rev. Charles Thornicroft, of Thornicroft, co. Chester, and by her (who d. in 1844) has one son and three daus., Henrietta-Beck, Sophia-Mary, and Mary-Anne-Louisa: he m. 2ndly, in 1847, Ellen, dau. of John-Home Purves, Esq., and has by her five children.
IV. Alfred, b. 19 June, 1812; m. in 1845, Elizabeth, dau. of Henry Crutchley, Esq. of Sunning Hill Park, and has two daus.
V. James-Charles, b. 1 Oct. 1813.
VI. Ferdinand-William, b. 10 Dec. 1814.
VII. Augustus-Peter, lieut. R.N., b. 6 March, 1821.
VIII. John-Thomas, b. 2 Nov. 1823.
I. Mary-Anne, m. in 1852, to Robert Strange, Esq. of Naples.
II. Susan-Maria, m. to Ven. Archdeacon Joseph Wigram, and has issue.
III. Fanny-Jane.
IV. Margaret-Helen, m. to Jas.-Richard Wigram, Esq.
V. Caroline-Elizabeth, m. in 1852, to John Clowes, Esq., 2nd son of W.-Legh Clowes, Esq. of Broughton Hall, co. Lancaster.

Mr. Arkwright of Willersley is 3rd son of the late Richard Arkwright, Esq. of Willersley (*see preceding article*).

Seat—Willersley, co. Derby.

ARKWRIGHT OF HAMPTON COURT.

ARKWRIGHT, JOHN, Esq. of Hampton Court, co. Hereford, b. 27 Aug. 1785, J.P. and high-sheriff 1831; m. 13 April, 1830, Sarah, eldest surviving dau. of Sir Hungerford Hoskyns, Bart. of Harewood, and has issue,

I. JOHN-HUNGERFORD, b. July, 1833.
II. Richard, b. 22 Jan. 1835.
III. George, b. 29 July, 1836.
IV. Henry-John, b. 16 Dec. 1837.
V. Edwyn, b. 2 May, 1839.
VI. Arthur-Chandos, b. 8 March, 1843.
VII. Charles-Leigh, b. 6 June, 1846.
I. Caroline-Sarah. II. Mary.
III. Frances-Catherine. IV. Emily-Sophia.
V. Alice-Eden.

Mr. Arkwright of Hampton Court is the 4th son of the late Richard Arkwright, Esq. of Willersley Castle.

Seat—Hampton Court, co. Hereford.

ARKWRIGHT OF DUNSTALL.

ARKWRIGHT, CHARLES, Esq. of Dunstall, co. Stafford, J.P., 5th son of the late Richard Arkwright, Esq. of Willersley Castle, *b.* 22 Nov. 1786; *m.* Mary, dau. of Edward-S. Sitwell, Esq. of Stainsby.

Seat—Dunstall, Staffordshire.

ARKWRIGHT OF MARK HALL.

ARKWRIGHT, THE REV. JOSEPH, of Mark Hall, Essex, and Normanton Turville, co. Leicester, 6th son of the late Richard Arkwright, Esq. of Willersley Castle, *b.* 9 Aug. 1791; *m.* 29 Oct. 1818, Anne, dau. of Sir Robert Wigram, Bart., and has issue,

I. ROBERT-WIGRAM, *b.* 15 April, 1822; *m.* 30 Dec. 1847.
II. Charles, *b.* 9 Sept. 1823.
III. Julius, *b.* 28 Sept. 1825; *m.* 5 Sept. 1851.
IV. Loftus-Wigram, *b.* 29 Sept. 1829.
V. Arthur-William, *b.* 20 Feb. 1831.
I. Eleanor-Harriett, *m.* 4 Feb. 1851, to Capt. George-G. Randolph.
II. Anne-Mary, *m.* 16 Sept. 1841, Rev. G. Bruxner, and has issue.
III. Anna-Frances. IV. Catherine-Elizabeth.
V. Susan-Ellen. VI. Gertrude.
VII. Agnes-Isabella.

Seats—Mark Hall, Essex, and Normanton Turville, co. Leicester.

ARMITAGE OF ATHERDEE, COOLE, AND DRUMIN.

ARMITAGE, WHALEY, Esq. of Coole and Drumin, co. Louth, barrister-at-law, *b.* 9 June, 1767; *m.* 7 April, 1796, Eleonora, eldest dau. and co-heir of the late Edward Haistwell, Esq. of Kensington, by Eleonora Brickenden his wife, maternally descended from the Hungerfords; and has had issue,

I. BRAITHWAITE. II. Robert. III. Edward.
IV. Whaley. V. Arthur.
I. Caroline. II. Eleonora. III. Rachel.
IV. Grace. V. Cecilia. VI. Emma.
VII. Frances, *d. unm.* VIII. Octavia. IX. Henrietta.

Mr. Armitage, who resides at Moraston, near Ross, co. Hereford, is in the commission of the peace for that shire.

Lineage.—This family, which claims descent from the senior branch of the ARMITAGES *of Yorkshire*, was established in Ireland, *temp.* Queen ELIZABETH, upon grants of land then received, situated at Atherdee, Coole, Cardiston, and Drumin, all in the co. Louth.

The late ROBERT ARMITAGE, Esq. of Coole and Drumin, who resided at Kensington, co. Middlesex, and was there buried, was son and heir of Robert Armitage, of Liverpool, a considerable merchant there, and nephew of Timothy Armitage, Esq. of Atherdee, whose granddau., Miss Armitage, *m.* R.-C. Whaley, Esq. M.P. He *m.* in 1766, Caroline, eldest dau. of Colonel Braithwaite, by Sylvia Cole, his wife, a descendant of the family of COLE *of Colchester*, and had issue, WHALEY, his heir, now representative of the family, William, deceased, Caroline, and Priscilla-Cecilia.

Motto—Fractum non abjicio ensem.
Residence—Moraston, near Ross.

ARMITAGE OF MILNSBRIDGE HOUSE.

ARMITAGE, JOSEPH, Esq. of Milnsbridge House, co. York, J.P. and D.L., *b.* 9 Feb. 1778; *m.* 25 Sept. 1804, Anne, eldest dau. of Joseph Taylor, Esq. of Blackley Hall, co. Lancaster, and by her (who *d.* 3 Feb. 1854) has issue,

I. GEORGE, *b.* 24 Sept. 1806; *m.* Caroline-Jane, eldest dau. of James Dowker, Esq. of North Dalton, East Riding, co. York.
II. Joseph-Taylor, of Birkby, near Huddersfield, *b.* 24 April, 1809, *m.* Ellen, 2nd dau. of Henry Ingram, Esq. of Halifax, co. York.
III. John, *b.* 20 Feb. 1817, *m.* Harriet, 2nd dau. of Thomas Calrow, Esq. of Bury, co. Lancaster.
IV. Henry, *b.* 21 May, 1818, *m.* Amelia, 3rd dau. of Thomas Ramsay, Esq. commissary-general, N.S.W.
V. Edward, *b.* 27 Aug. 1819, *m.* Eliza-Anne, 3rd dau. of Thomas Calrow, Esq. of Bury.
VI. James, *b.* 19 Aug. 1823.
I. Sarah-Anne, *m.* to John Starkey, Esq. of Huddersfield.
II. Emma, *m.* to the Rev. Dr. James, incumbent of Marsden, near Huddersfield.
III. Charlotte, *m.* to William-Leigh Brook, eldest son of James Brook, Esq. of Meltham Hall, West Riding, co. York.
IV. Ellen, *d.* in Feb. 1812. V. Eliza, *d.* 17 May, 1818.
VI. Mary, *m.* to the Rev. Edward Sandford, incumbent of Elland, near Halifax, 4th son of the Rev. Humphrey Sandford.
VII. Helen, *d.* 1 June, 1818.
VIII. Anne-Taylor, *m.* to Humphrey Sandford, Esq. eldest son of the Rev. Humphrey Sandford.
IX. Emily, *m.* to W. L. Brook, Esq.

Lineage.—GEORGE ARMITAGE, Esq. *b.* 1674, who resided at Highroyd House, parish of Almondbury, left at his decease in 1742 (by Alice his wife), an only son,

JOSEPH ARMITAGE, Esq. of Highroyd House, who *m.* Mary, dau. of the Rev. Mr. Wilson, incumbent of Holmfirth, and by her had, with two daus., viz.: Sarah, *m.* to William Fenton, Esq. of Spring Grove, Huddersfield; and Martha, *m.* to Richard Bassett, Esq. of Glentworth Hall, near Gainsborough, an only son,

GEORGE ARMITAGE, Esq. of Highroyd House, *b.* in 1736, who *m.* in 1776, Sarah, dau. of Joseph Walker, Esq. of Lascelles Hall, and had by her (who *d.* in 1815), with two daus., Marianne, and Sarah, *m.* in 1808, to Richard Wilson, Esq. of Leeds, and *d.* in 1809, an only son, the present JOSEPH ARMITAGE, Esq. of Milnsbridge House.

Arms—Gu. a lion's head, erased, between three cross-crosslets, arg.
Crest—A dexter arm, embowed, couped at the shoulder, habited, or, cuffed, arg., holding in the hand, ppr., a staff, gu., headed and pointed, or.
Motto—Semper paratus.
Seat—Milnsbridge House, Huddersfield, co. York.

ARMSTRONG OF BALLYCUMBER.

ARMSTRONG, JOHN-WARNEFORD, Esq. of Ballycumber, King's County, J.P., *b.* 28 Aug. 1770; *m.* 18 Oct. 1806, Anne, dau. of William Turner, Esq. of Gloucester, and has two daus.,

I. MARY-DROUGHT, *m.* 12 July, 1837, to Charles-Edmund Wilkinson, Esq. lieut.-col. royal engineers, son of Jacob Wilkinson, Esq. of Springfield House, co. Somerset, and has issue, William-Edmund, *b.* 22 April, 1839, Charles-St.Lo, *b.* 12 May, 1849, Anne-Frances-Louisa, and Lora-St.Lo-Elizabeth.
II. ANNE-FRANCES, *m.* 17 Dec. 1844, Wm. Bigoe Buchanan, Esq.

Lineage.—The family of Armstrong was, in ancient times, settled on the Scottish border; and springing from this parent stock, several branches, at a very early era, became located in the northern counties of England. One, established at Corby, in Lincolnshire, had continued there for seven descents; and another at Tynedale, in Northumberland, for nine generations, at the period of the Visitation, in 1623. A third scion, Thoroton, in his *History of Nottinghamshire*, mentions as fixed at Thorpe, in that co., so early as the eleventh year of RICHARD II., and gives the pedigree, in an interrupted succession, to the year 1672; and Leland, in the first volume of his *Itinerary*, speaks of a family of Armstrong settled in Yorkshire, whose representative he calls "a gentleman of many lands." Tradition states that the original surname was Fairbairn.

CHRISTOPHER ARMSTRONG, laird of Mangerton, younger brother of the famous John Armstrong, laird of Giltnock, who was executed at Carlingrig, about the year 1530, *m.* and had two sons, the younger of whom, William, left Scotland some years after the death of Queen ELIZABETH, and seated himself in the co. Fermanagh, where he became the founder of a numerous family, whose branches flourished in those parts. The eldest son of the laird of Mangerton was father of

ANDREW ARMSTRONG, born in the castle of Mangerton in 1576, who migrated to the north of Ireland, and established himself near his uncle in the co. Fermanagh. He *m.*, 1st, a lady named Alexander, of Scottish descent, and had by her, ANDREW, who *m.* and had (with two daus., Rebecca, *m.* to Mr. Johnston, and Mary, wife of Thomas Robinson, of Knockshegowna, Esq.), one son, Richard, who *m.* and had issue. Andrew Armstrong *m.* 2ndly, Elizabeth, dau. of M. Johnston, Esq. and had by that lady, with daus., five other sons, EDMUND, ancestor of the ARMSTRONGS *of Gallen Priory;* THOMAS, of whom presently; William, who had three sons and two daus.; Robert, father of (with two daus., Elizabeth, *m.* to Philip Henzell, Esq., and Lydia, wife of John Fleetwood, Esq.) three sons, 1. The celebrated founder of the Royal Arsenal at Woolwich, the gallant GENERAL JOHN ARMSTRONG, so distinguished as an engineer officer in Marlborough's wars; 2. Samuel, who *d.* under age; and 3. Michael, whose son was the late General Bigoe Armstrong; John, *d. unm.* Andrew Armstrong *m.* 3rdly, in the seventy-fourth year of his age, Mrs. Jane Stephenson, and had, by her, two other sons, MICHAEL, who *m.* and *d.* at Banagher; ARCHIBALD, for whose descendants see ARMSTRONG *of Garry Castle and Castle Iver.* Andrew Armstrong *d.* in 1671, aged ninety-five: his son,

THOMAS ARMSTRONG, Esq. *b.* in the co. Fermanagh, in 1639, was taken prisoner at the battle of Worcester, 3rd September, 1651, and conveyed to London. He subsequently returned to Ireland, and settled at Banagher, in the King's Co., of which he was one of the burgesses, and several times sovereign of the corporation. He *m.* Grissel, sister of Capt. Charles Beatty, of the co. Longford, and by her, who *d.* in 1680, had, with four daus. (Margaret, *m.* to Capt. William Charlston; Catherine, *m.* to Oliver Crofton, Esq.; Anne, *m.* to William Beatty, Esq.; and Elizabeth, *m.* to Mr. Courts), three sons, JOHN, killed at the siege of Gibraltar, in 1704; ANDREW, heir to his father; and James, who *d. unm.* The 2nd, but eldest surviving son,

ANDREW ARMSTRONG, Esq. of Ballycumber, in the King's Co., *b.* in 1669, *m.* 9 June, 1697, Lucy, widow of William Mason, an officer in King WILLIAM's army, and eldest dau. of George Charnock, Esq. 8th son of Sir George Charnock, Knt. of Gloucestershire, by Jane his wife, sister of William Clent, Esq. of the city of Worcester; and had by her, who *d.* 15th Sept. 1733, aged 62, and was buried in Rahan Church, four sons and four daus., viz.: 1. WARNEFORD, his heir; 2. Thomas, *b.* in 1702, who became first director of his Majesty's engineers, chief engineer of Minorca, and senior engineer in the service: he *d. unm.*; 3. George, who *d. s. p.* in 1752; 4. John, governor of Minorca, who *d. unm.*; 1. Mary, *m.* to Edward Wallen, Esq. of Snugborough; 2. Grissel, *m.* to Alexander Armstrong, Esq.; 3. Jane, *m.* to Capt. Supple; and 4. Letitia, *m.* 1st, to Mr. Slaughter, and 2ndly, to the Rev. Geo. Wallen. Andrew Armstrong *d.* 14 May, 1717, aged 48, and was *s.* by his eldest son,

WARNEFORD ARMSTRONG, Esq. of Ballycumber, J.P. *b.* 27 Sept. 1699, sheriff for King's Co. in 1738, *m.* first, 15 March, 1719, Elizabeth, eldest dau. of Milo Bagot, Esq. of Newtown, by Margaret his wife, younger dau. of Edmund Armstrong, Esq. of Stonestown, and had by her, who *d.* 23 Oct. 1739,

- I. ANDREW, *b.* 28 May, 1727, *m.* 9 Sept. 1756, Deborah, dau. and heiress of Samuel Simpson, Esq. of Oatfields, co. Galway, and by her, who *d.* in April, 1808, left at his decease, 16 July, 1802,
  - 1 ANDREW, of Clara, J.P., King's County, and captain of the Kilcourcy corps of yeomanry cavalry, *m.* Eleanor, dau. and heir of Edward Briscoe, Esq. of Scraggan, and dying 25 Aug. 1796, left issue,
    - EDWARD-GEORGE, *b.* in 1788, *d.* 28 July, 1834.
    - Eliza, *m.* to the Rev. Mr. Jones, rector of Macroom.
    - Deborah.
  - 2 Samuel, *b.* 16 Sept. 1762, for some time of Clara House, and subsequently of Spring Garden, J.P. for the King's County. He *m.* Euphemia-Frances Wright, of the co. of Longford, and *d.* at Birr, 16 March, 1832, leaving two sons and two daus.
  - 1 Margaret, *m.* to William Hodson, Esq. of Dublin, brother to Sir Robert Hodson, Bart. of Holly Park, in Wicklow, and had issue.
  - 2 Elizabeth, *m.* to John-Hardiman Burke, Esq. of St. Clerans, co. Galway, and *d.* 3 Jan. 1835, leaving issue.
- II. Milo, *b.* 19 March, 1729, of the E. I. Co.'s service, *d.* at Bengal, 27 Sept. 1751.
- III. Thomas, *b.* 23 Oct. 1731, who made two voyages to China. He *d.* at Clara, *unm.*, and was buried at Banagher.
- IV. GEORGE, of whom presently.
- V. John, *b.* 28 June, 1736, *d.* in infancy.
- I. Margaret, *b.* 8 Jan. 1720, *m.* to Frank Brown, Esq. of Riverstown, co. Kildare, barrister-at-law, and had issue.
- II. Caroline, *b.* 14 Nov. 1728, *m.* in 1752, to Thomas Drought, Esq., eldest son of John Drought, Esq. of The Heath, King's County.
- III. Elizabeth, *b.* 28 June, 1736; *m.* to Richard, son of Richard Vicars, Esq. of Levally, in the Queen's County; and *d.* at Clifton, 19 Jan. 1810, leaving issue.

Warneford Armstrong *m.* 2ndly, Jane, eldest dau. of Lewis Jones, Esq. of Dublin, by whom he had two sons, who both died in infancy; and 3rdly, in Jan. 1760, Fanny, dau. of William Grey, Esq. by whom, who *d.* in Dublin, Nov. 1807, he had, with two daus., Fanny, who *d. unm.* in 1834, and Lucinda, who *d.* an infant, two sons,

- I. John, *b.* 15 Sept. 1761, capt. in the 8th foot, and subsequently major in the 5th dragoon guards. He *m.* 6 March, 1806, Mary-Anne, dau. and co-heir of Jonathan Gurnell, Esq. of Ealing House, Middlesex, and dying in Cornwall, in May, 1835, left issue,
  - 1 John, of Baliol College, Oxford, *b.* 2 April, 1810, in holy orders.
  - 2 Mary-Anne-Gurnell.
  - 3 Fanny.
- II. William, *b.* in 1763, a military officer, who served in America and India, and obtained a majority in the 80th regiment. He was afterwards appointed inspecting field officer of yeomanry for the co. Longford. Col. William Armstrong *m.* in Aug. 1791, Charlotte, 5th dau. of the Very Rev. Dean Arthur Champagné, of Portarlington.

Warneford Armstrong's 4th son,

GEORGE ARMSTRONG, Esq., *b.* 19 June, 1734, *m.* Constantia-Maria, eldest dau. of Andrew Armstrong, Esq. of Gallen, and by her, who *d.* in April, 1826, had issue,

- I. JOHN-WARNEFORD, his heir.
- II. Andrew-George, *b.* 12 Sept. 1773, a capt. in the 104th regiment, purchased the house and demesne of Ballycumber. He *d. unm.* 26 Sept. 1821.
- I. Constantia.
- II. Elizabeth, *d. unm.* in 1799.
- III. Frances, *m.* 25 April, 1805, to Samuel John Bever, Esq., a lieut. 38th regt., and had issue.

Mr. Armstrong *d.* 23 Aug. 1780, and was *s.* by his son, the present JOHN-WARNEFORD ARMSTRONG, Esq. of Ballycumber.

Arms—Gu., three dexter arms, vambraced in armour, arg., hands, ppr.

Crest—A dexter arm, vambraced in armour, arg., hand, ppr.

Motto—Vi et armis.

Seat—Ballycumber, King's County.

ARMSTRONG OF GARRY CASTLE.

ARMSTRONG, THOMAS-ST.-GEORGE, Esq. of Garry Castle House, King's County, high-sheriff in 1809, *b.* 14 Nov. 1765; *m.* 14 Feb. 1792, Elizabeth, dau. of Thomas Priaulx, Esq. of the island of Guernsey, of an ancient Norman family, and has surviving issue,

- I. CARTERET-ANDREW, barrister-at-law, *b.* in 1796.
- II. Thomas-St. George, *b.* in 1797, *m.* Donna Justa de Villanueva, dau. of Don Pedro de Villanueva, a Castilian of noble descent, settled in Buenos Ayres.
- III. William-Bigoe, *b.* 13 April, 1800.
- IV. John-Priaulx, *m.* his cousin-german, Emma, dau. of Thomas Priaulx, Esq. of Montil House, in Guernsey, and has issue.

Lineage.—ARCHIBALD ARMSTRONG, Esq. of Ballylin, 2nd son of Andrew Armstrong, Esq. by Jane Stephenson, his 3rd wife, *b.* in 1655, *m.* in 1681, Letitia, youngest dau. of Col. Edward Playsted, and had issue,

- I. WILLIAM, *b.* in 1691; who *m.* in 1715, Rebecca, dau. of Bigoe Henzell, Esq., and left issue,
  - 1 Archibald, *b.* at Barnagratty in 1716; *m.* Rebecca, only dau. of Captain Michael Armstrong, and sister of General Bigoe Armstrong, and had, with two daus., Jane, *m.* to Hugh Coulaghan, Esq., and Catherine, *m.* to Daniel Coulaghan, Esq., three sons, of whom the third, Bigoe, an officer in the army, *m.* Susannah, dau. of Thomas Bernard, Esq. of Birr, and by her (who *d.* in July, 1819), left at his decease, 15 March, 1773, aged 28, two sons, Bigoe, an officer in the guards, who *m.* Sophia, widow of Sir David Williams, Bart., and *d.* at Boulogne, in 1824, leaving a dau., Caroline; and Thomas, lieut.-col. in the Coldstream guards.
  - 2 William, an officer in the army; *m.* 1st, 3 July, 1747, Mary, dau. of William Hunt, Esq. of Petworth, in Sussex; and 2ndly, Miss Hill, sister of Colonel Hill, of London, but had issue only by the first, viz., four daus.; Fanny, *m.* to Edmund Armstrong, Esq. of Percy Street, London; Charlotte, *m.* to Richard Hassell, Esq., barrister-at-law; Rebecca, *m.* and had issue; Mary, *m.* to Dr. Blair, and had issue. Mr. William Armstrong *d.* in London, 10 Oct. 1784, aged 62.
  - 3 Andrew, capt. E.I.C.S., of Castle Armstrong, King's County, high-sheriff in 1777; *m.* Mary, relict of Governor George Scot, of Bengal, and dau. of a Mr. Bidwell, by whom (who *d.* 2 July, 1781) he left at his decease, 31 July, 1789, aged 65, William, who went as a writer to Bengal, where he *m.* and *d.*; Thomas, *b.* in

1765, of Castle Armstrong, who *m.* Elizabeth, dau. of John Puget, Esq. of London, banker, and left a dau. and heiress, Elizabeth, *m.* to Thomas Raikes, Esq.; Andrew, who *d.* at St. Croix, in 1805, leaving, by Anne his wife, eldest dau. of James Brady, Esq. of the city of Dublin, two surviving sons and two daus. (William-Andrew, J.P. of Rathmacknee, co. Wexford, J.P., *b.* 30 March, 1793, who *m.* 8 Feb. 1848, Marianne-Stuart, dau. of John Flood, Esq. of View Mount, co. Kilkenny; Thomas-Bagot, in holy orders, vicar of Ballyvaldon, co. Wexford, *m.* 24 Jan. 1845, Isabella, youngest dau of Richard Fothergill, Esq. of Carleon, co. Monmouth; Harriet; and Catherine); Rebecca, *m.* to Nicholas Gamble, Esq. of Derrinboy, and had issue; and Harriet, *m.* in 1796, to George Armstrong, Esq.

4 Edward, *b.* 14 June, 1724, who lived at Clara, and was in the commission of the peace for the King's County. He *m.* Anne, dau. of Michael M'Evoy, Esq. of the co. Longford, and had issue.

1 Rebecca, *m.* to Frank Conrahy, Esq. of Birr.

II. Edmund, capt. E.I.C.S., who *d.* leaving issue.

III. Charles, in General Wynne's regiment of dragoons; killed in a duel.

IV. ANDREW, of whose line we have to treat.

V. Thomas, of Ballylin, in the King's County, inspector-general of barracks, and a justice of the peace, who served the office of sheriff. He *m.* twice, but left at his decease, in 1750, issue only by his second wife, Lucy, third dau. of George Holmes, Esq.—viz.,

1 Andrew, of Ballylin, an officer in the E.I.C.S.; *d. s. p.*

2 Thomas, lieut.-col. in the 17th regt. of foot; *d. unm.*

3 George, of the island of Jamaica; who *m.* 1st, Elizabeth, dau. of Mr. Philips, and widow of Andrew Waller, Esq., by whom he had issue,

Thomas, capt. in the Longford militia; *m.* Miss Armstrong, of Ennis, in the co. of Clare, and had issue, George-Knox; Edmund, M.D.; Robert-Wallace, M.D., who *d. unm.*; Thomas-Holmes, merchant in Manchester (who *m.* in 1831, Anna, eldest dau. of the Rev. Blayney Mitchell, of Monaghan, and has issue, Lydia, Anna-Sophia, Harriet, Lucy-Ellen, and Ellen-Stewart); John-Simpson, barrister-at-law; James-Henry; Anna, *m.* to Sir Benjamin Morris, Knt., late capt. 25th regiment; Jane; and Dorothea.

Lucy-Mary, *d. unm.* at Sidmouth, 7 Jan. 1810.

George Armstrong *m.* 2ndly, in 1796, Harriet, 2nd dau. of Andrew Armstrong, Esq., and left by her, at his decease (being killed by falling into a dock at Bristol), three daus., viz., Harriet, Mary-Elizabeth, Isabella.

1 Elizabeth, *m.* in 1780, to Thomas Woods, Esq.; and *d.* at Parsonstown, 28 Feb. 1808, leaving issue.

I. Margaret, *m.* to George Brereton, Esq., and had issue.

II. Elizabeth, *m.* to Matthew Hyde, Esq. of Newtown, in the King's County, and had issue.

Archibald Armstrong, who had been treasurer of the King's County, *d.* at a very advanced age, April 18, 1747, and was buried in the family burial place at Banagher. His 4th son,

ANDREW ARMSTRONG, Esq. was treasurer of the King's Co., and for some time comptroller of the household to the Lord-lieutenant of Ireland. He *m.* 1 Aug. 1724, Alphra, youngest dau. of Bigoe Henzell, Esq. of Barnagrotty, and by her, who *d.* 13 July, 1783, had issue,

I. Archibald, *b.* at Barnagrotty, in 1726; *m.* Margaret, dau. of John Bagot, Esq. of Ard, in the King's County; and dying 13 June, 1798, left, with other children, who *d. unm.*

1 Andrew-Edmund-Bigoe, *b.* 1 June, 1774, who assumed the surname of BAGOT, in consequence of his uncle, William Bagot, having left him a share of his estate at Ard. He *m.* Mrs. Sidney Stretch, and left three daus., viz.,

Sidney-Mary, *m.* in 1840, to Charles Bagot, Esq. of Kilcoursey, King's County.

Fanny-Anne, *m.* to Abraham Fuller, eldest son of Abraham Fuller, Esq. of Woodfield, in the King's County.

Sidney-Blanche.

2 Charlotte-Margaret, *m.* in 1780, to Richard Crosbie, Esq.

II. Thomas, a captain in the army; *b.* 27 Dec. 1729; who lived at Derrycooly, and afterwards at Ballycumber, where he *d.* 7 Nov. 1795, leaving by his wife, the dau. of Hugh Campbell, Esq., and widow of Hugh M'Laughlin, Esq., an only surviving child, Lucinda, *b.* at Dundee; *m.* to Benjamin Bird, Esq., and had issue.

III. ANDREW, of whom presently.

IV. Edmund, *b.* in 1735, of Fortie Hall, Enfield, Middlesex, and of Percy Street, London; army-agent, appointed 25 Jan. 1794, groom of the privy chamber to GEORGE III., and made subsequently husband of the 4½ per cent. duties of the customs. He *m.* 1st, Miss Mackie, by whom he had an only dau., who *d.* young; and 2ndly, Fanny, dau. of William Armstrong, Esq. of Petworth, by whom he had three children, viz.,

1 William-Archibald, of Pengelly Lodge, *b.* in 1770; A.B., F.S.A., in holy orders, rector of Hykham, in Lincolnshire, a magistrate for the cos. of Hertford and Middlesex; *m.* in 1796, Charlotte E.-M. Hassell, younger dau. of Richard Hassell, Esq., and had issue,

Edmund-John, lieut. R.N.; *b.* in Aug. 1798; *m.* in 1825, Miss Watson.

Henry-William, of St. John's College, Oxon.

George-Craven, *b.* 2 April, 1806; lieut. in the E.I.C.S.

Augustus, *b.* 19 April, 1810.

William-Matthew, *b.* 2 March, 1814.

Charles-Frederick, *b.* 6 Dec. 1814.

Harriet-Frances.

Avarilla-Alphra, *m.* in 1825, to Artemidorus-Cromwell Russell, Esq., eldest son of T.-A. Russell, Esq. of Cheshunt Park, Herts.

Helen-Marianne-Monk.

Fanny-Eliza-Raikes.

2 George-Andrew, *b.* in Oct. 1771; lieut.-general in the army; *m.* 1st, Elizabeth, dau. of George Hayward, Esq.; and 2ndly, Mary-Esther, dau. of T.-A. Russell, Esq. of Cheshunt Park; but *d. s. p.* 12 Nov. 1834.

1 Harriet-Ann.

V. Bigoe, *b.* 1737; *d. unm.* 1756.

I. Rebecca, *b.* in 1728; *m.* to Theriagh Magrath, Esq., and had three sons, and one dau., *m.* to Richard Warburton, Esq.

II. Lucy, *m.* to Humphrey Ellis, and had issue.

The 3rd son of Andrew Armstrong, by Alphra his wife,

ANDREW ARMSTRONG, Esq. *b.* in 1732, was an officer in the 14th regiment, but being severely wounded at the siege of Louisburg, he retired from the army. He resided at Garry Castle, in the King's Co., whereof he was treasurer, and J.P. He *m.* 5 May, 1756, Elizabeth, only dau. of Capt. James Buchanan, of Craigavern and Dromakill, in Scotland, of the family of that ilk, and by her, who *d.* 21 Sept. 1818, aged seventy-two, had issue,

I. Archibald, *b.* 1 Nov. 1763; capt. in the E.I.C.S.; *d. s. p.*

II. Andrew, *b.* 20 Oct. 1764; lieut. 54th regt.; *m.* 14 Jan. 1793, Anne, dau. of Andrew Armstrong, Esq. of Gallen, and had issue,

1 William-Bigoe, *b.* in 1801. 2 John.

1 Constantia-Maria. 2 Elizabeth.

III. THOMAS-ST. GEORGE, of Garry Castle.

IV. WILLIAM-BIGOE, of Castle Iver.

V. James, *b.* 20 Aug. 1769; formerly lieut. 46th regt., and subsequently paymaster 57th. He *m.* in the West Indies, and now resides in France.

VI. Edmund, *b.* 10 Jan. 1772; major in the E.I.C.S.; *m.* Miss Leonora Lucas; and *d.* in India, in 1809, having had one son and three daus., viz.,

1 Andrew-Bigoe, in the E.I.C.S.: *b.* 11 June, 1802; *d.* in the East Indies.

1 Leonora. 2 Mary-Elizabeth.

3 Catherine-Rebecca.

VII. Bigoe-Charles, *b.* 17 May, 1775; capt. in the 57th regt.; *d. unm.*

I. Catherine-Rebecca, *m.* 27 Jan. 1784, to Hugh Conrahy, Esq., and had issue.

II. Mary, *m.* in 1792, to Capt. William Grant, of the Clare militia, son of James Grant, Esq., and had issue.

III. Elizabeth, *m.* in 1794, to John Armstrong, Esq., lieut. royal Irish artillery, of the co. Fermanagh, and had issue.

The 3rd son is the present THOMAS-ST. GEORGE ARMSTRONG, Esq. of Garry Castle.

Arms, &c.—See ARMSTRONG *of Ballycumber.*
Seat—Garry Castle House.

ARMSTRONG OF CASTLE IVER.

ARMSTRONG, JAMES-FERRIER, Esq. of Castle Iver, King's County, treasurer of the King's County, *m.* 14 Jan. 1838, Honoria, eldest dau. of John Fleming, Esq. of Stoneham Park, Hants, M.P. for the southern division of that county.

Lineage.—WILLIAM-BIGOE ARMSTRONG, Esq. of Castle Iver, treasurer of the King's County, (next younger brother of Thos.-St. George Armstrong, Esq. of Garry Castle), *b.* 19 July, 1768, *m.* in 1796, Jane-Wilhelmina, only child of James Ferrier, Esq. Gen. Royal Engineers, and by her (who *d.* 16 April, 1829, aged 65), left at his decease, an only child, the present JAMES-FERRIER ARMSTRONG, Esq. of Castle Iver.

Arms—See ARMSTRONG *of Ballycumber.*
Estates—In the King's County.
Seat—Castle Iver.

ARMSTRONG OF KIPPURE PARK.

ARMSTRONG, WILLIAM-JONES, Esq. of Batleagh Lodge, Tynan, co. Armagh, *b.* 22 May, 1794; *m.*

3 Feb. 1842, Frances-Elizabeth, Lady M'Creagh, relict of the late Col. Sir Michael M'Creagh, C.B., K.C.H., &c., and only dau. of Major Christopher Wilson, late of the 22nd foot. Mr. Armstrong served the office of high-sheriff for the county of Armagh in 1840.

Lineage.—This is another branch of the ancient border family of Armstrong, deriving, traditionally, from a common ancestor with the King's County family.

The Rev. William - Jones Armstrong, M.A. rector of the Union of Termonfeckan, co. Louth, son of Edward Armstrong, Esq. by Grace Jones, his wife, and grandson of William Armstrong, Esq. by Jane Garvey, his wife; *m.* in 1784, Margaret, 3rd dau. of Alderman John Tew, of Dublin, at one time its lord-mayor, and granddau. of Alderman David Tew, of the same place, lord-mayor in 1752, by whom he had issue,

- William-Jones, late of Kippure Park, co. Wicklow, and now of Batleagh Lodge.
- John-Tew, who *m.* Anne, only dau. of Ralph Tew, Esq., late of Baddinstown, co. Meath, and has issue, Maxwell, John, and Thomas.
- Thomas-Knox, who *m.* Catherine-Frances, 2nd dau. of the late Wallop Brabazon, Esq. of Rath House, co. Louth, by Jane, his 1st wife, dau. of the late Josias Dupré, Esq. of Wilton Park, Bucks, and *d.* at Rome in Jan. 1840, leaving issue, Jane-Rebecca and Catherine-Diana-Lucinda.
- Helen, *m.* to the Rev. John Kerr, rector of the Union of Termonfeckan, and has issue.
- Anne, *m.* to Walter Newton, Esq., late of the 21st light dragoons, and has issue.
- Diana-Jane.

Arms } *Crest* } As Armstrong *of Ballycumber.*
Motto—Invictus maneo.
Seat—Batleagh Lodge, Tynan, co. Armagh.

ARMSTRONG OF NEW HALL AND KILKEE, (Formerly of Mount Heaton).

Armstrong, William Edward, Esq. of New Hall, Clare, *b.* 10 May, 1826; *s.* 29 June, 1850, to the extensive estates of his maternal uncle, the late John MacDonnell, Esq. of New Hall. Mr. Armstrong is a magistrate for the county of Clare, and filled the office of high-sheriff in 1853.

Lineage.—This family has long held a leading position in the counties of Tipperary and King's, where it acquired considerable property, as also in the counties of Limerick and Fermanagh. Its progenitors were formerly Scotch, and bore the name of Fairbairn, which was changed to that of Armstrong. The Armstrongs of the border were at the head of a numerous and warlike clan, the most famed of whose chieftains was John Armstrong, of Gilnockie, in the parish of Cannonby, Eskdale. His castle was built on a promontory washed on three sides by the Esk, which being steep and rocky, was scarcely accessible but on the land side, where it was fenced with a deep ditch. This powerful border chieftain lived in the reign of James V. (1513 to 1545) and was the terror of the Western Marches of England, having forced the inhabitants of Cumberland, Westmorland, and a great part of Northumberland, to become his tributaries. At length, his power having grown too great for a subject, he became an object of jealousy to the Scottish king, who levied an army for the avowed purpose of punishing Gilnockie and his followers, and marched at their head to the parish of Elves. There John was summoned to attend the king, upon the promise of security, and having accordingly obeyed his summons, in violation of the public faith pledged for his personal safety, as observed by Buchanan, he and his attendants were hanged at Castlewick rigg, two miles to the north of Mosspaul, on the road between Hawick and Langholm. After this execution, the family dispersed, and some of them settled in different parts of England, one branch in Lincolnshire: the present family trace their descent from Sir Thomas Armstrong, who was the representative of that line.

Sir Thomas Armstrong, Knt., *b.* at Nimeguen, in Holland, had been a great sufferer in the royal cause, and was very active for Charles II. before the restoration. His enterprising spirit excited the jealousy of Cromwell, who threw him into prison and even threatened his life. He engaged with all the zeal that was natural to him in the service of the Duke of Monmouth. Finding himself obnoxious to the court, he fled the kingdom and went to Holland, and his flight was soon followed by outlawry. He was seized abroad and sent to London, where he was condemned by Chief Justice Jeffries, and executed at Tyburn, without a trial, and with peculiar circumstances of rigour. He at his death denied having ever had any intention against his Majesty's life. The attainder was subsequently reversed. Sir Thomas was gentleman of the horse to the king, captain of the first troop of royal horse guards, and served as a burgess in parliament for Stafford and Leicester town. He had no issue male.

Captain William Armstrong, brother to Sir Thomas, and founder of the family in Tipperary, went over to Ireland shortly after the battle of Worcester, and settled in the old castle at Farney Bridge, near Thurles, where he was followed by his brother's widow, Lady Armstrong. William Armstrong we find was captain of the troop of horse attached to the Tipperary militia in 1688. He *m.* Alice, dau. of Sir Thomas Deane, of the county of Suffolk, and by her had issue, two sons,

- John, his successor.
- Thomas, *m.* a dau. of Robert Carew, Esq. of Ballinamona, and had issue. From Thomas are descended the Mealiffe branch, now represented by George Armstrong, Esq. of Chaffpoole and Mealiffe, high sheriff of the county of Sligo.

John Armstrong, Esq. of Farney Castle, *s.* his father, and *m.* in 1677, Julianna, dau. of Robert Carew, Esq. of Ballinamona, co. Waterford, by Mary his wife, dau. of John Shapland, Esq. He purchased, in 1677, the lands of Ballycahill and Holycross, and *d.* in 1717, leaving issue four sons,

- William, his successor.
- Robert, *d. unm.*
- John, ancestor of the present Farney Castle branch (now represented by Major W. Armstrong, of Farney Castle).
- James-William, in holy orders, *d. unm.*

Colonel William Armstrong, M.P., of Farney Castle and Mount Heaton (the eldest son), col. Tipperary militia, *m.* in 1730, Mary, dau. and co-heir of Francis Heaton, Esq. of Mount Heaton, King's County (and formerly of the co. of York), by Elizabeth his wife, dau. of — Cartwright, Esq. The family residence was then changed to Mount Heaton (otherwise called Ballyskennagh); and Farney Castle was given over to his brother John. William (having survived his wife) *d.* in 1772, leaving issue, a son and a daughter,

- John, (of whom presently).
- Mary, *m.* 12 Sept. 1755, the Rev. George Thomas, and had issue.

The son and heir,

The Right Hon. John Armstrong, of Farney Castle and Mount Heaton, *s.* his father in 1772. He *m.* 17 July, 1770, Letitia, dau. and co-heir of Henry Greene, Esq. of Ballymacreese, co. Limerick, (late of Desternane, co. Fermanagh). (Mrs. Armstrong *m.* 2ndly, the Rev. James Hobson, of Sidmouth, son of Mr. Hobson, M.P. city of Waterford, and *d.* 28 Jan. 1820). John rose to considerable distinction at the bar, to which he was called 1759: he served in several parliaments for the boroughs of Fore and Kilmallock, and was a member of the king's privy council in Ireland. He was twice urged by the Irish government to take a baronetcy (which he declined), in consideration of important services he had done the country. It was subsequently arranged that he was to be made a peer, under the title of *Baron of Dunamase*, in Ireland, and the patent is stated to have been lodged at the Hanaper office, when he *d.* at Mount Heaton, on 12 Sept. 1791, and is buried in the churchyard at Ballycahill. His son and successor was

William-Henry Armstrong, Esq. of Mount Heaton, M.P., *b.* at Toulouse, in France, 21 June, 1774. He *m.* 7 April, 1809, Bridget, only dau. of the late Colonel Charles MacDonnell, of New Hall, co. Clare, M.P., by Bridget his wife, dau. of John Bayly, Esq. of Debsborough, co. Tipperary. From the year 1816, he resided almost entirely on the continent, and not intending to return to Ireland, he sold, in 1817, Mount Heaton, in 1827, his Fermanagh and nearly all his Tipperary and Limerick property. He *d.* at Passy, near Paris, 21 Sept. 1835, and is buried in the cimetière Montmartre, at Paris, leaving issue,

- John, *b.* at Mount Heaton, 1 May, 1815, *m.* 29 May, 1849, Mlle. Josephine Von Mayr, a German lady, and has issue, John-Childe, *b.* 1 Jan. 1850; Louisa-Bids.
- Charles-William, *b.* 19 April, 1819, *d.* at Abbeville, 31 May, 1819.
- William-Edward, now of New Hall.
- Charles, J.P. for Clare, *b.* 7 May, 1830.

Letitia-Mary, d. 11 July, 1811, and is buried at Ballycahill.
Letitia-Charlotte, m. 1 June, 1841, Charles-William, eldest son of Charles Hamilton, Esq. of Hamwood, co. Meath, by Mary-Anne-Caroline his wife, dau. of William Tighe, Esq. of Woodstock, co. Kilkenny, M.P., and has issue.
Catherine-Gertrude, m. 7 Oct. 1839, John Bayly, Esq. of Debsborough, co. Tipperary, by Mary-Elizabeth-Helena his wife, dau. of Richard Uniacke, Esq. of Mount Uniacke, co. Cork, and has issue.
Bridget, m. 28 March, 1849, James Dobrée, Esq. of Rock Lodge, Devonshire, eldest son of the late Peter Dobrée, Esq. of Clapham Common, London, (and grandson of the late Peter Dobrée, Esq. of Beauregard, in the island of Guernsey), and has issue.
Mary, m. 12 July, 1842, Evans Johnson, archdeacon of Ferns, second son of the late judge Johnson, and has issue.
Emily-Dorothea, d. at Paris, 5 Feb. 1838, and is buried near her father.
Louisa.

Arms—Gu., three arms in armour vambraced, hands ppr., quartering Heaton, Greene, and MacDonnell.
Crest—An armed hand and arm; in the hand a leg and foot, in rich armour, couped at the thigh.
Motto—Vi et armis.
Seats—New Hall, and Kilkee, co. Clare.

ARMSTRONG OF MEALIFFE AND CHAFFPOOL.

Armstrong, George-De la Poer, Esq. of Mealiffe, co. Tipperary, and Chaffpoole, co Sligo; s. his father 2 Dec. 1846.

Lineage.—This is a branch of the Armstrongs *of Farney Castle*, springing from the marriage of Thomas Armstrong, high sheriff of the co. Tipperary, *temp.* Queen Anne, (next brother of John Armstrong, Esq. of Farney Castle), with a dau. of Robert Carew, Esq. of Bellinamona. *(see preceding genealogy)*. The grandfather of the present possessor of Mealiffe,

The Rev. William Armstrong, of Mealiffe, m. in 1791, the Hon. Catherine-Eleanor Beresford, eldest dau. of William, Lord Decies, archbishop of Tuam, and by her, who d. in 1837, left at his decease, May, 1839, a son and successor,

John Armstrong, Esq. of Mealiffe, who m. Catherine, dau. and heir of T. Somers, Esq. of Chaffpoole, co. Sligo, and had by her, besides two sons, deceased, viz., Captain William Armstrong, who m. Madamoiselle de Labrosse, and d. 7 March, 1849, and Thomas, lieut. 60th Rifles, who d. 7 June, 1847, four other sons, still surviving, viz.,

George-De la Poer, now of Mealiffe and Chaffpoole.
James-W., lieut. R.N.
Edward-Marcus, lieut. 55th regt.
Francis-Henry.

Mr. Armstrong d. 8 Dec. 1846.

Arms—Gu., three arms in armour vambraced, hands ppr.
Crest—An armed hand and arm; in the hand a leg and foot, in rich armour, couped at the thigh.
Motto—Vi et armis.
Seats—Mealiffe, Thurles; and Chaffpoole, Ballymote.

ARMSTRONG OF WILLOW BANK AND ADZAR HOUSE.

Armstrong, Edmund-John, Esq. of Willow Bank, co. Clare, and Adzar House, co. Dublin, b. in May, 1808; m. in April, 1840, Jane-Catherina, 3rd dau. of Thomas-Hayter Longden, Esq., D.L., of co. Kent, of Ennismore Place, Hyde Park, London, and has issue,

I. Edmund-James, b. 1844.
II. John-Henry-Maxwell, b. 1850.
III. Thomas-Conyngham, b. 1852.
I. Mario-Lavinia-Cecilia.
II. Jane-Longden,
III. Ellen-Louisa.
IV. Agnes-Georgina.

Mr. Armstrong, a magistrate and deputy-lieut. for co. Clare, served as high-sheriff for that county in 1852. He s. his uncle, the late E.-B. Armstrong, Esq., who d. unm. in 1833. He is only son of the late Rev. John Armstrong (who d. in 1820), by Maria-Cassandra Young his wife, niece to the Very Rev. Dr. Young, bishop of Clonfert, and grandson (by Hannah Westropp his wife, sister of the late M. R. Westropp, Esq. of Monkstown Castle, co. Cork) of Edmund Armstrong, Esq. of Buncraggy, whose father, James Armstrong, was the first of the family who settled in co. Clare, in the early part of the 17th century, and who was brother of Major-General John Armstrong, surveyor-general of the Ordnance and chief engineer of England, and colonel-in-chief of the royal regiment of foot in Ireland.

Arms—Gu., three arms vambraced in armour, hands ppr.
Crest—An arm vambraced in armour.
Motto—In Deo robur meus.
Seats—Willow Bank, Ennis, co. Clare; and Adzar House, co. Dublin.

ARMSTRONG OF HEMSWORTH.

Armstrong, The Rev. Charles-Edward, M.A. of Hemsworth, co. York, b. 1807; m. 18 April, 1838, Mary-Anne, dau. of John Clayton, Esq. of Enfield Old Park, co. Middlesex. The Rev. Mr. Armstrong, master of Hemsworth Hospital, and perpetual curate of St. Forckley-cum-Clayton, co. York, s. in 1852, on the decease of his aunt (wife of William Busfield, Esq., M.P.), to the estates of his grandmother, Mrs. Wood (heiress of Lacon Barker, Esq.), at Otley, in Yorkshire. He is son of Charles-Edward Armstrong, Esq., of the E.I.C.S., by Dorothy his wife, dau. of Capt. Wood, R.N., and sister of Sir F. Wood, Bart. of Hemsworth Hall, and grandson of Dr. Charles Armstrong, of London, and great-grandson of Dr. John Armstrong, of Godalming, co. Surrey, whose dau., Elizabeth, m. in 1778, Edward, Earl of Winterton. This Dr. John Armstrong was son of Dr. Richard Armstrong, of Dumfries, who left that place and settled in Guildford, co. Surrey. He was son of David Armstrong, advocate, of Edinburgh, and grandson of David Armstrong, of Kirtle Town, Dumfries, whose grandfather, Christopher Armstrong, settled in Dumfries, and was living 1530.

Arms—Gu., three dexter arms vambraced, in pale, ppr.
Crest—An arm vambraced.
Motto—Vi et armis.
Seat—Hemsworth, Pontefract.

ARNOLD OF LITTLE MISSENDEN ABBEY.

Arnold, The Rev. Edward-Gladwin, of Little Missenden Abbey, co. Bucks, rector of Stapleford, Herts, b. 25 April, 1823; m. 27 April, 1852, Charlotte-Georgiana, eldest dau. of Lord Henry Cholmondeley.

Lineage.—General Benedict Arnold m. 8 April, 1779, Margaret, dau. of Edward Shippen, Chief Judge of Pennsylvania, and d. in 1801, having had issue,

Edward-Shippen, lieut. 6th Bengal cavalry, and paymaster of Muttra; d. at Dinapoor, in India, 13 Dec. 1813.
James-Robertson, lieut.-general, K.H. and K. Crescent, m. Virginia, dau. of Bartlett Goodrich, Esq. of Saling Grove, Essex, which lady d. 14 July, 1852.
George, lieut.-col. 2nd Bengal cavalry, m. Anne Brown, and d. in India, 1 Nov. 1828.
William-Fitch, of Little Missenden Abbey.
Sophia-Matilda, m. to Col. Pownall Phipps, E. I. C. Service, (related to the Mulgrave family) and d. in 1828.

The youngest son,

William-Fitch Arnold, Esq. of Little Missenden Abbey, capt, 19th Lancers, b. 25 June, 1794; m. 19 May, 1819, Elizabeth-Cecilia, only dau. of Alexander Ruddach, Esq. of Tobago, and had issue,

Edward-Gladwin, his heir.
William-Trail, b. 23 Oct. 1826, capt. 4th regt.
Margaret-Steuart, m. to the Rev. Robert-H.-S. Rogers.
Elizabeth-Sophia, m. to the Rev. Bryant Burgess.
Georgiana-Phipps, m. to the Rev. John Stephenson.
Louisa-Russell.

Capt. Arnold, a magistrate for Bucks, d. 7 Nov. 1846.

Arms—Gu., three pheons, arg.; on a chief of the second, a bar nebulée, az.
Crest—A demi-tiger, sa., bezantée, maned and tufted, or., holding a broad arrow, stick, gu., feathers and pheon, arg.
Motto—Nil desperandum.
Seat—Little Missenden Abbey, Bucks (now belonging to the widow of Capt. Arnold).

ARTHUR OF GLANOMERA.

Arthur, Thomas, Esq. of Glanomera, co. Clare, b. 10 Sept. 1806; s. his father in 1845.

Lineage.—It is not clearly ascertained at what period the Arthurs settled in Ireland, but it is certain that they long held large possessions in that kingdom, especially in the co. of Limerick, until their estates in that county were confiscated by CROMWELL, for their loyalty to the royal cause, when they removed to the co. of Clare, and became seated at Glanomera.

The history of Limerick records that two members of the family sat in parliament for that city, *temp.* Queen ELIZABETH, viz., Edward Arthur, in 1559, and Thomas Arthur, in 1585.

THOMAS ARTHUR, Esq. of Glanomera, representative of this ancient house, *m.* Mary Butler, heiress of the BUTLERS *of Kilmoyler*, co. of Tipperary, lineally descended from the noble house of Ormonde, and was father of

THOMAS ARTHUR, Esq. of Glanomera, who *m.* Lucy, fourth dau. of Sir Edward O'Brien, Bart. of Dromoland, and left by her at his decease, in 1801 (with a dau. Mary, *m.* to Richard Henn, Esq. of Paradise, co. of Clare, who *d.* without surviving issue), an only son and successor,

THOMAS ARTHUR, Esq. of Glanomera, *b.* April, 1778, *m.* 10 April, 1803, Harriet, 2nd dau. and co-heir (with her only sister, Charlotte, wife of Sir Edward O'Brien, Bart. of Dromoland) of William Smith, Esq., of Cahirmoyle, co. of Limerick, by whom he had issue,

- THOMAS, his heir.
- William-Smith, *b.* 13 June, 1809, *m.* in 1839, Caroline-Sydney, eldest dau. of Frederick-Saintbury Parker, Esq. of Saintbury, co. Dublin, and *d.* without issue in March, 1840.
- Lucius, in holy orders, *b.* 31 July, 1810, *m.* 21 April, 1840, Caroline-Elizabeth, third dau. of John Jervis, Esq. of Moseley, Warwickshire, by whom he has had three sons, Thomas-Lucius-Jervis; Edward-Henry-Frederick (who *d.* an infant); and Charles-William-Augustus; with five daus.
- Edward, barrister-at-law, *b.* 7 Jan. 1817, *d.* 6 Aug. 1853.
- Augustus, a magistrate for the co. Clare, *b.* 27 Aug. 1819.
- Henry, in holy orders, *b.* 12 Nov. 1820, *m.* 13 April, 1847, Ellen, 2nd dau. of the late Henry-Joy Tombe, Esq.
- Frederick-B.-B., in holy orders, *b.* 13 Sept. 1822.
- Together with nine daus., four of whom are deceased.

Mr. Arthur *d.* 6 May, 1845, and was *s.* by his eldest son, the present THOMAS ARTHUR, Esq. of Glanomera.

Arms—Gu., a chevron between three rests (or clarions), or, quartering BUTLER and SMITH.
Crest—A falcon, rising, ppr., jessed and belled, or.
Motto—Impelle obstantia.
Seat—Glanomera, co. Clare.

ASH OF ASHBROOK.

ASH, WILLIAM-HAMILTON, Esq. of Ashbrook, co. Londonderry, J.P. and D.L., *b.* 3 May, 1801; *m.* 10 July, 1827, Lady Elizabeth-Emma Douglas, sister of the present Earl of Morton, and has issue,

Caroline-Hamilton, *m.* 7 July, 1853, to John-Barre Beresford, Esq. of Learmont, co. Londonderry.

Lineage.—WILLIAM HAMILTON, Esq., son of William-Hamilton, Esq., by Jane his wife, dau. of George Ash, Esq., took the additional name of ASH, on succeeding to the estates of his uncle, the late George Ash, Esq. of Ashbrook. He *m.* 29 May, 1795, Miss Elizabeth-Harriet Benderson, by whom (who *d.* in 1805) he had issue,

- WILLIAM-HAMILTON, now of Ashbrook.
- George, in holy orders, rector of Ballyscullion, co. Londonderry, *m.* in 1828, Mary, dau. of the late Rev. Thomas Spotswood, and *d.* 28 Oct. 1852, having had issue two sons and a dau.
- Anne, *m.* to (the late) Rev. William Dixon.
- Jane, *m.* to Robert Algar, Esq., collector of Customs at Berwick-upon-Tweed, and *d.* in 1848.

Mr. Hamilton Ash *d.* 29 May, 1821.

Arms—ASH and HAMILTON, quarterly.
Crest—A squirrel.
Motto—Non nobis sed omnibus.
Seat—Ashbrook, near Londonderry.

ASHBY OF NASEBY.

ASHBY-MADDOCK, GEORGE, Esq. of Naseby, co. Northampton, and of Greenfields, co. Salop, an officer 11th Hussars, *b.* 3 June, 1834.

Lineage.—This is the senior line of the very ancient family of Ashby, which can be authentically traced from RICHARD DE ASHBY, lord of the manors of South Croxton and Queniby, co. Leicester, A.D. 1297.

ROBERT ASHBY, Esq., grandson of William Ashby, Esq. of Quenby, living in 1489, *s.* in 1536 to the family estates, at the decease of his cousin, Anne Ashby, of Quenby, wife of George Skevington, of Skevington. He *m.* Barbara, dau. George Ashby, Esq. of Loseby, co. Leicester, and sister of Edward Ashby, Esq. of Loseby, whose son, William Ashby, Queen ELIZABETH'S ambassador to JAMES VI., *d. s. p.* in Scotland, in 1589.

By Barbara his wife, Robert Ashby left at his decease, 24 Aug. 1557, four daus. and one son, viz.:—

GEORGE ASHBY, Esq. of Quenby and Loseby, high sheriff of Leicestershire in 1601, who *m.* Mary, dau. of Andrew Gedney, Esq. of Enderby, and left, with other issue, a son and heir,

GEORGE ASHBY, Esq. of Quenby, who erected, in 1636, the present mansion-house, and sold the lordship of Loseby to Mr. Paramour. He *m.* Elizabeth, dau. of George Bennet, Esq. of London, and of Welby, co. Lincoln, and *d.* in 1653, leaving issue, three sons and three daus. The eldest son,

GEORGE ASHBY, Esq. of Quenby, *b.* 29 July, 1629, served as high sheriff of Leicestershire, 18 and 19 CHARLES II. He *m.* 24 June, 1652, Mary, dau. and heir of Euseby Shukbrugh, Esq. of Naseby, co. Northampton, and by her (who *m.* 2ndly, George Hewett, Esq. of Rotherby, and *d.* 15 April, 1721, aged 93) had issue,

- GEORGE, his heir.
- Shukbrugh, whose son (by Mary, his wife, dau. of Nele Hewett, Esq.) Shukburgh, *m.* Mary, dau. and heir of Nathaniel Cradock, of Cossington, and *d.* in 1752, leaving a son, Shukbrugh Ashby, Esq., F.R.S., M.P. for Leicester, who *m.* Elizabeth, dau and heir of Richard Hinde, Esq., and *d.* in 1792, leaving two daus., his co-heiresses, viz., Mary-Elizabeth, *m.* to William Latham, Esq., F.R.S., F.S.A., of Eltham; and Dorothea, *m.* to Sir Thomas Hussey Apreece, Bart. (*See* ASHBY *of Quenby*).
- Euseby, Fellow of Trinity College, *d. s. p.*
- Mary, *m.* to John Ekins, Esq. of Rushden.
- Elizabeth, *m.* to Sir Nathan Wrighte, the lord keeper.
- Lucy, *d.* young.
- Margaret, *m.* to William Boothby, Esq. of Marston.

George Ashby, sen., *d.* 29 May, 1672, and was *s.* by his eldest son,

GEORGE ASHBY, Esq. of Quenby, *b.* 16 July, 1656, M.P. for Leicestershire in 1695 and 1707, and high sheriff in 1688-9. This gentleman *m.* 7 Nov. 1682, Hannah, dau. and co-heir of Major Edward Waring, of Humphreston, high sheriff of Shropshire in 1657, and M.P. for Bridgenorth in 1658, by Elizabeth his wife, dau. of John Ashe, Esq. of Freshford, co. Somerset, and had, with other children, who *d. s. p.*

- JOHN, of whom presently.
- Edmund, father of the Rev. George Ashby, president of St. John's College, Cambridge.
- Waring, who *s.* to Quenby, and served as high sheriff of Leicestershire, in 1733. By Elizabeth Cumberland, his wife, sister of the Bishop of Dromore, he left at his decease in 1770, one son, GEORGE, of Hazlebeech Hall, near Naseby, who sold Quenby to Shukbrugh Ashby, Esq., and *d. s. p.* in 1802, having bequeathed the Naseby estate to his cousin, Hannah Maria, the wife of John Maddock, Esq.
- Elizabeth, who *m.* 17 Feb. 1706, John Freeman, Esq. of Wellingborough, and had two daus., viz., Elizabeth, wife of Pudsey Jesson, Esq. of Langley, co. Warwick; and Hannah, who *m.* William Ash, Esq. of Paston, near Peterborough, and was mother of three daus.; Hannah, *m.* to William Jesson, Esq. of Sutton Coldfield; Elizabeth, wife of Edmund Ashby, Esq. of The Lynches; and Mary, wife of the Rev. Richard-Bliss Riland, rector of Sutton Coldfield.
- Mary, *m.* to Henry Hall, of London.
- Hannah, *m.* to George Cheselden, M.D.
- Anne, *m.* to Robert Norton, of Leicester.

The eldest son,

JOHN ASHBY, Esq. of The Lynches, near Shrewsbury (his mother's jointure), *b.* 27 Nov. 1687, *d.* 20 July, 1756, leaving by Hannah his wife, two sons and one dau., viz.,

- JOHN, of The Lynches, *b.* 9 May, 1722, one of the esquires to Lord Clive, on his installation as a Knight of the Bath. He *m.* Jane Wingfield, relict of Anthony Kinnersley, Esq. of Leighton, but *d. s. p.*, 29 Jan. 1779.
- EDMUND, of whom we treat.
- Hannah, *b.* 14 Aug. 1728, *m.* to Charles Stamford, Esq. of Wellingborough.

The 2nd son (but the only one to leave issue),

EDMUND ASHBY, Esq. of The Lynches, *m.* Elizabeth Ash, his cousin, dau. of William Ash, Esq. of Paston, near Peterborough, and by her (who *m.* 2ndly, Æmilian Holbech,

Esq.) he left at his decease, 20 Nov. 1785, two daus. his co-heiresses (in whom vested the representation of the ancient house of ASHBY *of Quenby*), viz.:

ELIZABETH-FREEMAN ASHBY, who *m.* in 1784, Robert Hale, Esq., and had four daus., Elizabeth, Lucia, Jane, and Frances. Of these the third *m.* Capt. Whitfield, 18th regt., and had issue, Major Henry Whitfield, of the 2nd West India regt., and Robert-Philpote Whitfield, who *d. unm.*, 23 June, 1842, aged 31 years.

HANNAH-MARIA ASHBY, *m.* 9 Jan. 1787, John Maddock, Esq. of Shrewsbury, son of John Maddock, also of Shrewsbury, by Elizabeth his wife, and grandson of John Maddock, of Shrewsbury, who was son of Thomas Maddock, of Chester.

The 2nd dau. and co-heiress,

HANNAH-MARIA ASHBY, wife of JOHN MADDOCK, Esq. of Shrewsbury, *d.* 25 Nov. 1830, leaving a son and heir,

THE REV. GEORGE ASHBY MADDOCK, of Greenfields, Shrewsbury, and of Naseby, co. Northampton, who *m.* July 22, 1833, Anne, dau. of Mr. George Procter, of Carron Cottage, Argyllshire, and *d.* in 1836, leaving an only child, the present

GEORGE ASHBY MADDOCK, Esq. of Naseby, co. Northampton, and of Greenfields, co. Salop.

Arms—Quarterly: 1st, per pale, az. and gu., two lions, passant in pale, or, for MADDOCK. 2nd, or, three boars' heads sa., a chief indented of the last, for JENKS. 3rd, az. a chevron, erm., between three leopards' faces, or, for ASHBY. 4th, sa., a chevron, engrailed, between three mullets, arg., for SHUKBRUGH. 5th, sa., a chevron, between three pewits' heads, erased, arg., for WARING. 6th, ASH, arg., two chevronels, and in chief as many crescents, sa.

Crests—1st, a demi-lion rampant, holding a sword erect, for MADDOCK. 2nd, on a mural crown, arg., a leopard's head, or, for ASHBY.

Motto—Be just and fear not.

ASHBY OF QUENBY.

ASHBY, WILLIAM-ASHBY, Esq. of Quenby Hall, co. Leicester, *b.* 6 Feb. 1775; *m.* 15 July, 1797, Mary, dau. of Michael Miller, Esq. of Bristol, and has issue,

I. SHUKBRUGH-ASHBY, } twins.
II. William, }
III. Edward-Quenby, in holy orders, *m.* Eliza, 2nd dau. of the Rev. Henry Palmer, of Withcote, co. Leicester.
I. Agnes-Eliza, *m.* to George Pochin, Esq. of Barkby, co. Leicester.

This gentleman, whose patronymic was LATHAM, assumed the surname and arms of ASHBY on inheriting the estates of that family. He is a magistrate for the counties of Leicester and Derby.

Lineage.—MARY-ELIZABETH ASHBY, *b.* in 1747, elder dau. and co-heir of Shukbrugh Ashby, Esq., M.P. (*see page* 25) *m.* in 1770, William Latham, Esq. of Eltham, F.R.S., and F.S.A., and by him, who *d.* about 1805, and was buried at Hungerton, had issue,

WILLIAM-ASHBY LATHAM, his heir.
Maria-Elizabeth Latham, *m.* to the Rev. George Osborne, of Haselbeech, Northamptonshire.
Harriet Latham, *m.* to Thomas Byron, Esq., who is deceased.
Dorothea-Hinde Latham.

Mrs. Latham *d.* in 1815, and was buried with her husband. Her son, having assumed the surname of ASHBY, is the present WILLIAM-ASHBY ASHBY, of Quenby, Esq.

Arms—Az., a chevron, erm., between three leopards' faces, or.

Crest—Out of a mural crown, a leopard's face, affrontée.

Motto—Be just, and fear not.

Seat—Quenby Hall.

ASHE OF ASHFIELD.

ASHE, WILLIAM-WELLESLEY, Esq. of Ashfield, co. Meath; *m.* in 1828, Maria-Walker, only dau. of George Haigh, Esq. of Halifax, descended from an ancient Scottish family, and had one son and one dau., both of whom *d.* in infancy. This gentleman is a brevet lieut.-col. foreign service.

Lineage.—The ancient and eminent family of ESSE, ASHE, or D'ESSECOURT, which came over with WILLIAM THE CONQUEROR, appears by certified extracts under the seal of Ulster king-of-arms,—by the authority of the Herald's College,—and from the pages of our old historians, to have held large estates in the co. of Devon, so early as the

eleventh century; and the line is deducible through more than eighteen generations. From

SIR OLIVER D'ESSE or ASHE, living towards the close of the thirteenth century, lineally descended

SIR THOMAS ASHE, of St. John's, and of Dromshill, co. Cavan (eldest son of Thomas Ashe, Esq., by his wife, the dau. and heiress of Nicholas Bailey, Esq. of the Abbey of St. John's, co. Meath, and grandson of Nicholas Ashe, of Clyst Fornyson, from whose youngest son, James, derived the ASHES *of Freshford and Heytesbury*, and the ASHES *of Ashgrove*, co. Limerick), was knighted at Dublin Castle by Sir George Carew, lord deputy, on St. James's day, 25 July, 1603. He *d.* without issue, 14 Oct. 1626, and was *s.* by his grand-nephew,

NICHOLAS ASHE, Esq. of Moyrath, *b.* in 1603, at whose decease without issue, in 1656, the estates were inherited by the heir of entail, his cousin,

WILLIAM ASHE, Esq. of Summerstown (son of Richard Ashe, Esq., and Alice his wife, dau. of Lewis Jones, D.D. Bishop of Killaloe, and grandson of Nicholas Ash, Esq. of Newtown, who was brother of Sir Thomas Ash, of St. John's). He *m.* 1st, Martha Leigh, and by her had one son, RICHARD, and four daus., Mary, *m.* to Edward Crofton, Esq. of Clonard, in Meath; Martha, *m.* Joseph Fish, Esq. of Kilcullen; Alice, and Elizabeth. He *m.* 2ndly, Mary, dau. of Dudley Colley, Esq. of Castle Carbery, and sister of Henry Colley, Esq. great-grandfather of Arthur, 1st Duke of Wellington. By this lady he had one son, Dudley, and a dau. Mary, who *m.* one of Lord Darnley's family. Mr. Ashe *d.* in 1682, was buried at Trim, and *s.* by his son,

RICHARD ASH, Esq. of Ashfield, in the co. of Meath, M.P. for Trim. He *m.* Anne, dau. of — Deane, Esq., and dying in 1727, left (with three daus., Anne, *m.* in 1734, to Hans Bailey, Esq.; Mary, *m.* in 1740, *m.* to William Lynden, Esq.; and Elizabeth, *m.* to Benjamin Fish, Esq.), five sons, of whom the eldest was

JOSEPH ASHE, Esq. of Ashfield, high-sheriff of Meath, M.P. for Trim. He *m.* Susanna, dau. of Dudley Loftus, Esq. of Killian, had issue,

I. RICHARD, barrister-at-law, and M.P. for Trim; *m.* a dau. of Richard Warren, Esq. of Grangebeg, in Kildare, and relict of Thomas Cooper, Esq., registrar of the court of Chancery; but *d. s. p.* in the lifetime of his father.
II. Dudley, killed at the storming of Moro Castle.
III. Thomas (Sir), Knt., M.P., bapt. 10 Sept. 1732; high-sheriff for the co. Meath; *m.* Mary, dau. of Sir David Kinloch, Bart. of Gilmartin, in Scotland, and left,
   1 Joseph, of Drogheda, who *m.* in 1802, Catherine, dau. of — Sheppard, Esq., but has no issue,
   1 Harriet, *m.* to Robert Shepherd, Esq., formerly secretary to Lord Castlereagh.
   2 Catherine, *m.* to James Sterling, Esq., British consul at Genoa.
IV. Joseph, killed in storming the battery of Mora Castle.
V. WILLIAM, of whom presently.
I. Alice, *m.* to Damer Edgeworth, Esq. of Longwood, in the co. Westmeath.
II. Anne, *m.* Dudley Loftus, Esq of Clara Castle, in Meath.

The 5th son,

WILLIAM ASHE, Esq., major in the army, inherited, at his father's decease, a portion of the Ashfield estate. He *m.* in 1793, Mary, dau. of Archdeacon Mockler, and relict of John Rawlins, Esq. of Dublin, and had, with two other sons and three daus., all now deceased, the present LIEUT.-COL. WILLIAM-WELLESLEY ASHE, of Ashfield.

Arms—Quarterly of six: 1st and 6th, arg., two chevronels, sa., for ASHE; 2nd, vert, a lion rampant, arg., for FORNYSON; 3rd, gu., a cross, erm.; 4th, arg., a bend and three mullets in chief, sa.; 5th, gu., a fesse, vair, arg. and az. between, in chief, a bezant charged with an anchor, sa., between two stars, or, and in base three martlets, two and one, of the last, for BAILEY.

Crest—A cockatrice, or, crested, armed, &c., gu.

Mottoes—Above the shield, "Fight." Below, "Non nobis sed omnibus.

Seat—Ashfield, co. Meath.

ASHHURST OF WATERSTOCK.

ASHHURST, JOHN HENRY, Esq. of Waterstock, co. Oxford; *s.* his father 3 June, 1846; *m.* Elizabeth, dau. of Thomas Duffield, Esq. of Marcham, Bucks, and has a son and heir,

WILLIAM-HENRY.

Lineage.—Soon after the Conquest, ADAM DE ASSHEHURST obtained from Roger de Leyland a grant of all Roger's claim of lands in Dalton, and from that remote period to the present, the Ashhursts have preserved a male succession; several members of the family received the honour of knighthood in early times, and were distinguished in the wars of the Plantagenets. SIR ADAM DE ASSHEHURST, Knt. direct ancestor of the present family, was appointed clerk-marshal to EDWARD III., in 1339, for life, and formed part of the suite of that king at the battle of Cressy. For a detailed pedigree refer to BURKE's *Extinct and Dormant Baronetage.*

THOMAS ASHHURST, of Ashhurst, Esq. living in the reign of CHARLES II., 1671, son of William Ashhurst, Esq.* member of the Long Parliament, and representative of the county of Lancaster in 1654, and grandson of Henry Ashhurst, Esq. of Ashhurst; m. Susanna, dau. and co-heiress of Thomas Bosvile, Esq. of Edlington, co. York, and was father of

THOMAS-HENRY ASHHURST, Esq. of Ashhurst, in Lancashire, b. in 1672, Vice-Chancellor of the Duchy of Lancaster, and recorder of Liverpool and Wigan, b. in 1672, who m. Diana, dau. of Sir Richard Allin, of Somerleighton, co. Suffolk, Bart., by Frances his wife (only dau. of the 1st Sir Henry Ashhurst, Bart. of Waterstock, in right of whom Mr. Ashhurst became possessed of Waterstock, Oxon), and by her left at his decease, in 1744, with five daus., a son and heir,

SIR WILLIAM-HENRY ASHHURST, Knt., one of the judges of the King's Bench in the reign of GEO. III., from 1770 to 1800, and twice (in 1783 and 1792), one of the lords commissioners of the great seal. His lordship was b. at Ashhurst, Lancashire, in Jan. 1725, m. 21 April, 1772, Grace, dau. of Robert Whalley, of Oxford, M.D., and had issue,

WILLIAM-HENRY, heir to his father.
James-Henry, d. in the East Indies, unm.
Thomas-Henry, D.C.L., Fellow of All Souls' College, Oxford.
Grace, m. 6 Oct. 1796, to George Dorrien, Esq.; and d. leaving two sons and four daus.

Mr. Ashhurst d. at Waterstock, Nov. 1807, and was s. by his eldest son,

WILLIAM-HENRY ASHHURST, Esq. of Waterstock, b. 19 Oct. 1778, m. 1st, 19 Dec. 1806, Elizabeth, eldest dau. of Oswald Mosley, Esq. of Bolesworth Castle, Cheshire, by whom he had issue,

WILLIAM-HENRY, d. unm.
JOHN-HENRY, now of Waterstock.
James-Henry, in holy orders, vicar of Great Milton, Oxon.
Henry-George, in Australia.
Frederick-Thomas-Henry, in Canada.
Frances-Elizabeth, m. 13 Aug. 1836, to Thomas-George Harriot, Esq. of Twickenham; and d. 15 May, 1839, leaving a son, George-Thomas.
Caroline, m. to the Venerable Charles-Carr Clerke, Archdeacon of Oxford. Mary.

He m. 2ndly, 15 Aug. 1839, Selina, eldest dau. of Sir John Morshead, Bart. of Trenant Park, Cornwall, and widow of Sir Charles Mill, Bart. of Newton Bury, Hants. Mr. Ashhurst is J.P. and D.L. for the co. of Oxford, and sheriff in 1810; he represented this county in parliament from 1815 to 1830. He d. 8 June, 1846.

Arms—Gu., a cross, arg., between four fleurs-de-lis, arg.
Crest—A fox, statant, ppr.
Motto—Vincit qui patitur.
Seat—Waterstock, co. Oxford.

ASHWORTH OF ASHWORTH, ELLAND, AND HALL CARR.

ASHWORTH, THE REV. JOHN-HARVEY, of East Woodhay, Hants, and Craggan Tower, co. Clare, late of Elland, co. York, a magistrate for Hampshire; m. Mary, eldest dau. of Thomas-Hippon Vavasour, Esq. of Rochdale, co. Lancaster, descended from the very ancient house of VAVASOUR *of Haslewood*, co. York.

Lineage.—The Ashworths are one of the oldest families in England: the earliest notice of them which we have discovered, is in 1244. In the middle of the reign of HENRY III, Barnard de Hesseworth devised the manor of Ashworth to his sons Robert and Stephen de Assheworth. Stephen's moiety was alienated by his daughter Margery (22 EDWARD I.) to her cousin Robert, son of Robert de Assheworth; and Matilda, dau. and co-heir of Robert, having married before 1349, Hugh, son of John de l'Holt, conveyed the whole to him. The senior line thus became extinct in 1349, with the heiress marrying Holte, but younger branches have preserved a male succession even to the present time. One offshoot has long been seated at Hall Carr, co. Lancaster, and another at Elland Bank, co. York, from which springs by direct descent, the present Rev. JOHN-HARVEY ASHWORTH, M.A. of East Woodhay, Hants. His grandfather, John Ashworth, Esq. of Elland Bank, died seized of certain lands in Whitworth, which formed part of the ancient possessions of the family. During the civil wars, the Ashworths were engaged with Fairfax in support of the Parliament.

Arms—Gu. a cross humetté and engrailed, or, between four fleur-de-lys, arg.
Crest—On a mount, vert, a fox ppr.
Seat—Craggan Tower, co. Clare.

ASKEW OF REDHEUGH.

ASKEW, HENRY-WILLIAM, Esq. of Conishead Priory, co. Lancaster, and of Glenridding, co. Cumberland, b. in 1808; m. in 1832, Lucy, 3rd dau. of The Hon. and Rt. Rev. Hugh Percy, D.D., bishop of Carlisle, and has issue,

I. HENRY-HUGH, b. 23 July, 1847.
II. Edmund-Adam, b. 25 May, 1849.
I. Charlotte-Elizabeth. II. Emily-Mary.
III. Frances-Louisa.

Lineage.—ADAM ASKEW, M.D. (son of Anthony Askew, M.D. of Kendal, by Anne his wife, dau. of Adam Storrs, Esq. of Storrs Hall, co. Lancaster, and the lineal descendant of Hugh Askew, of Greymanes, Cumberland), settled at Newcastle-upon-Tyne, about the year 1725, and acquired extensive practice. He m. Anne, dau and co-heir of Richard Crakenthorp, Esq. of Newbiggin, in Westmorland, and had issue, ANTHONY, his heir; Adam, M.A., rector of Plumland; Henry, of Redheugh; John, of Pallinsburn; Deborah, who d. unm.; and Anne, who d. also single. Doctor Askew d. in 1773, and was s. by his eldest son,

ANTHONY ASKEW, M.D. of London, so celebrated for his extensive collection of books and manuscripts, b. in 1722. Doctor Askew m. 1st, Margaret, dau. of Cuthbert Swinburne, Esq. of Longwitton, and the West Gate, in Northumberland, but had no issue. He m. 2ndly, Elizabeth, dau. of Robert Holford, Esq., one of the masters in chancery, by whom he had,

ADAM, his heir.
Anthony-Linacre, M.A., Fellow of King's College, Cambridge; d. in 1818.
Henry, in holy orders, rector of Greystock, in Cumberland; m. 1799, Anne, dau. of Thomas Sunderland, Esq. of Little Croft, Ulverstone; d. 25 Dec. 1852, leaving issue, HENRY-WILLIAM, now of Conishead Priory; Anne-Elizabeth, m. in 1830, John-Dalrymple Murray, Esq. of Murraythwaite, and d. in 1845; and Eleanora, m. to Capt. Washington, R.N.
Richard, formerly major, 27th regiment.
Thomas, m. to Lucy, dau. of Robert Carey, Esq. of London, merchant.
Anne-Elizabeth, m. to George-Adam Askew, Esq. of Pallinsburn. Sarah, d. unm.
Deborah, m. to Sir Lucas Pepys, Bart., M.D.
Amy, to the Rev. John Washington, of Winchester.
Mary, d. unm. in 1786.
Elizabeth, m. to Henry-Percy Pulleine, Esq. of Carleton Hall, in Yorkshire.

Doctor Askew d. at Hampstead, in 1774, and was s. by his eldest son,

ADAM ASKEW, Esq. of Redheugh, high-sheriff of the co. of Durham in 1809; m. 1st, Amy, dau. of Robert Carey, Esq. of London, and 2ndly, Elizabeth, dau. of the late Rev. Sir Richard Rycroft, Bart., but d. s. p. His nephew is the present HENRY-WILLIAM ASKEW, Esq. of Conishead Priory.

Arms—Sa., a fesse, or, between three asses, passant, arg.
Crest—An arm holding a sword transfixing a Saracen's head.
Seats—Conishead Priory, Ulverston; and Glenridding, Penrith.

ASKEW OF PALLINSBURN.

ASKEW, RICHARD CRASTER, Esq. of Pallinsburn, co. Northumberland, barrister-at-law, recorder of Newcastle-on-Tyne, b. 5 Sept. 1778; s. his brother 25 June, 1847.

* William Ashhurst's brother, HENRY ASHHURST, of London, Esq., an eminent merchant, distinguished for benevolence, humanity, and piety, was father, *inter alios*, of two sons, SIR HENRY ASHHURST, Bart. of Waterstock, and Sir William Ashhurst, Knt., lord-mayor and M.P. for London.

Lineage.—John Askew, Esq. of Pallinsburn, 4th son of Doctor Adam Askew, of Storrs Hall, by Anne, dau. and co-heir of Richard Crakenthorp, Esq. of Newbiggen, m. 29 Sept. 1770, Bridget, dau. and heir of John Watson, Esq. of Goswick, co. Durham, by Elizabeth, dau. of John Craster, Esq. of Craster, in Northumberland, and had issue,

George-Adam, his heir.
John-Watson, A.M., Fellow of University College, Oxford, in holy orders; d. unm. 17 Nov. 1810.
Henry (Sir), K.C.B., late of Pallinsburn.
William, lieut. R.N.; d. in Dec. 1805.
Richard-Craster, now representative of the family.
Christopher-Crakenthorp, capt. R.N.; b. 23 May, 1792; m. in Feb. 1828, Sarah Dickson, and has issue.
Hugh-Bertram, in the E.I.C.S.
Elizabeth-Anne. Isabella.

Mr. Askew d. 28 Oct. 1794, and was s. by his eldest son,

George-Adam Askew, Esq. of Pallinsburn, b. 19 July, 1771, sheriff of Northumberland in 1800, m. in 1795, his cousin, Anne-Elizabeth, dau. of Anthony Askew, M.D. of London, but d. s. p. in 1806, when he was s. by his brother,

Sir Henry Askew, K.C.B. of Pallinsburn, lieut.-gen. in the army, b. 7 May, 1775, d. s. p. 25 June, 1847.

Arms—Sa., a fesse, or, between three asses, passant, arg.
Crest—An arm holding a sword transfixing a Saracen's head.
Motto—Patientia casus exuperat omnes.
Seat—Pallinsburn House, Northumberland.

ASPINALL OF STANDEN HALL.

Aspinall, John, Esq. of Standen Hall, co. Lancaster, b. 7 Aug. 1779; m. 1st, 23 April, 1804, Jane, dau. of — Robinson, of Sabden; and 2ndly, Harriet, widow of Ralph Bligborough, M.D., by the former of whom he has issue,

I. John-Thomas-Walshman, who m. 20 May, 1851, Ellinor, dau. of Nicholas Aspinall, Esq. of Liverpool.
I. Mary, m. to J.-L. Hammond, Esq.
II. Helen, m. to John Lomax, Esq. of Clayton Hall.
III. Elizabeth-Walshman. IV. Jane.

Mr. Aspinall, who s. his great-uncle, John Aspinall, Esq., serjeant-at-law, 1 March, 1784, is J.P. and D.L. for Lancashire and the west riding of Yorkshire.

Lineage.—This family has been for several centuries seated in the parish of Whalley; its ancestor, James Aspinall, was seised of lands in Clitheroe, prior to the reign of Elizabeth.

James Aspinall, Esq. (elder son of Alexander Aspinall, Esq. of Clitheroe, and brother of the late Mr. Serjeant John Aspinall), m. Anne, widow of Henry Lonsdale, Esq., and was father of

John Aspinall, Esq. who m. in 1744, Miss Hannah Cooper, and had two sons, John, now of Standen Hall; and Nicholas, of Liverpool, who m. Elizabeth Sowden, and has issue, Edward, Margaret, Alice, and Ellinor.

Arms—Or, a chevron, between three griffins' heads, erased, sa.
Crest—A demi-griffin, erased, sa., collared, winged, and beaked, or.
Motto—Ægis fortissima virtus.
Seat—Standen Hall, Lancashire.

ASSHETON OF DOWNHAM HALL.

Assheton, William, Esq. of Downham Hall, co. Lancaster, J.P. and D.L., b. 16 March, 1788; m. 9 Aug. 1816, Frances-Annabella, dau. of the Hon. William Cockayne, of Rushton Hall, co. Northampton, and by her (who d. 25 July, 1835) has surviving issue,

I. Ralph, b. 20 Dec. 1830.
II. Richard-Orme, b. 12 July, 1835.

Lineage.—Ashton-under-Lyne, a market town in Salford hundred, county palatine of Lancaster, gave name to the ancient family of Assheton, which was founded by Orme FitzEward, to whom Albert de Gresley gave one carucate of land in Assheton, besides a knight's fee in Dalton, Parbold, and Wrightington, *temp.* Henry III.

Radcliffe Assheton, Esq. b. in 1582, 2nd son of Ralph Ashheton, Esq. of Great Lever, co. Lancaster, by Johanna his 1st wife, dau. and co-heir of Thomas Radcliffe, Esq. of Wimbersley (see Burke's *Extinct Baronetage*); m. Elizabeth, dau. of John Hyde, of London, and had, with other issue,

John Assheton, Esq. col. in the service of Charles I., who m. Anne, dau. of Richard Shuttleworth, Esq. of Gawthorpe, and had a son,

Richard Assheton, Esq. of Downham, under a deed of settlement, dated in 1678, of his kinsman, Sir Ralph Ashheton, of Whalley, Bart. Richard Assheton m. Mary, dau. of George Pigot, Esq. of Preston, by whom he had numerous issue; of whom

Ralph Assheton, Esq. m. Sarah Bruen of Stapelford, and (with a son, Richard, who d. s. p.) was father of an elder son,

Ralph Assheton, Esq., who m. Mary, dau. of Thomas Lister, Esq. of Arnoldsbiggin, co. York, and had issue,

Ralph, his heir.
Richard, D.D., warden of Manchester, and rector of Middleton; b. 19 Aug. 1727; d. 1800, leaving by his wife Mary, younger dau. of William Hulls, Esq. of London, Richard, d. s. p.; Mary; Elizabeth, m. to James Whalley, Esq. of Clerkhill, who d. 1785; Caroline; and Catherine.
Elizabeth, m. to Richard Assheton, Esq., brother of Sir Ralph Assheton, of Middleton.
Mary, m. to the Rev. John Witton, of Lupset Hall; and 2ndly, to Peregrine Wentworth, Esq. of Tolston Lodge, Yorkshire.

The eldest son,

Ralph Assheton, Esq. of Downham, m. Rebecca, dau. of William Hulls, Esq. of London, and dying 3 Jan. 1759, aged 47, left issue, William, his heir, Anne, m. to Dr. W. Cleaver, Bishop of Bangor, Rebecca, m. to — Penniston, Esq. of Oxfordshire, Mary, and Elizabeth. The son and heir,

William Assheton, Esq. of Downham, b. in 1758, served as sheriff of Lancashire in 1792. He m. in 1786, Lettice, 2nd dau. of Sir Richard Brooke, Bart. of Norton Priory, co. Chester, and left (with a dau. Mary, wife of John Armytage, Esq., eldest son of Sir George Armytage, Bart.) a son and successor, the present William Assheton, of Downham Hall, Esq.

Arms—Arg., a mullet, sa., pierced, of the field.
Seat—Downham Hall, near Clitheroe.

ASTELL OF EVERTON.

Astell, Richard William, Esq. of Everton House, co. Huntingdon, lieut.-col. Grenadier guards, s. his father 7 March, 1847.

Lineage.—William Thornton, Esq. 2nd son of Godfrey Thornton, Esq. of Mogerhanger House, co. Beds. (see *family of* Thornton), b. 13 Oct. 1774, assumed by sign-manual the surname and arms of Astell in 1807. He m. 15 July, 1800, Sarah, only dau. of John Harvey, Esq. of Ickwellbury in Beds., and of Finningly Park, co. York, and by her (who d. 15 May, 1841) has had issue,

Richard-William, now of Everton House.
John-Harvey, H.E.I.C. factory at Canton, now M.P. for Cambridge, b. in 1806.
Henry-Godfrey, m. Louisa-Maria, dau. of Major-Gen. Wynyard, C.B.
Charles-Edward, a military officer.
Sarah.
Caroline, m. to the Rev. W.-H. Rooper, of Abbots Repton, Huntingdonshire, and is deceased.
Louisa, m. to Thomas St. Quintin, Esq., jun., of Hatley Park, in the co. of Cambridge.
Harriet.

Mr. Astell was colonel of the Royal East India Volunteers, a director of the East India Company, and frequently filled the chair of the court. He d. 7 March, 1847.

Arms—Quarterly: 1st and 4th, gu., a lion, passant, per pale, or and arg., between four cross-crosslets, of the last, for Astell; 2nd, arg., on a chevron, gu., between three trees, ppr., three-crosses patée-fitchée, arg., for Thornton; 3rd, for Godin.
Crests—1st, a cross-crosslet, or, entwined with a serpent, vert; 2nd, a lion's head, erased, purpure; round the neck, a coronet, or.
Motto—Sub cruce glorior.
Seat—Everton House.

ASTLEY OF FELFOOT.

Astley, Francis-Dukinfield-Palmer, Esq. of Felfoot, co. Lancaster, and Dukinfield Lodge, co. Chester, b. 24 April, 1825; m. 7 Oct. 1847, Gertrude-Emma, 2nd dau. of Col. H.-D. Jones, Royal Engineers, and has issue,

I. Francis-Dukinfield, b. 29 May, 1853.
I. Gertrude-Susan.
II. Constance-Charlotte.

Mr. Astley is son of the late Francis-Dukinfield Astley, Esq. (who *d.* 29 July, 1825), by Susan Palmer his wife, and grandson (by his 1st wife, Lady Dukinfield-Daniel) of John Astley, Esq., son of Richard Astley, a physician, who was cousin of Sir John Astley, Bart. of Patshull.

Arms—Az., a cinquefoil, erm.
Crest—Out of a ducal coronet, or, a plume of seven ostrich feathers, gu.
Seats—Fellfoot, Lancashire; and Dukinfield Lodge, Cheshire.

ASTON OF ASTON.

ASTON, SIR ARTHUR, G.C.B. of Aston, co. Chester, formerly envoy-extraordinary and minister-plenipotentiary at the court of Spain; *s.* his nephew in 1839.

Lineage.—CATHERINE ASTON, eldest sister and heir of Sir Thomas Aston, 4th Bart. of Aston, who *d.* in 1744 (see BURKE'S *Extinct Baronetage*), *m.* the Hon. and Rev. John Hervey, D.D., 5th son of John, 1st Earl of Bristol. Dr. Hervey assumed, in consequence, the surname of ASTON, by act of parliament, and left a son and heir,

HENRY-HERVEY ASTON, Esq. of Aston, sheriff of Cheshire in 1768, who *m.* Miss Dickonson, of Wrightington Hall, co. Lancashire, and had, with a dau., Anna-Sophia, *m.* in 1782, to Anthony Hodges, Esq., a son,

HENRY-HERVEY ASTON, Esq. of Aston, a col. in the army, who *m.* 16 Sept. 1789, the Hon. Harriet-Ingram Shepherd, 4th dau. and co-heir of Charles 9th Viscount Irvine, and left at his decease (having fallen in a duel, 23 Dec. 1798) two sons, HENRY-CHARLES, his heir, and ARTHUR (Sir) now of Aston. The elder,

HENRY-CHARLES-HERVEY ASTON, of Aston Hall, *m.* Margareta, dau. of the late William Barron, Esq. of Carrick Barron, and left at his decease (with a dau., Harriet, *m.* 17 July, 1833, to the Hon. and Rev. Arthur Talbot), a son,

ARTHUR-WELLINGTON-HERVEY ASTON, Esq. of Aston, Lieut. 1st life-guards, *b.* in 1815, who *d. unm.* 28 Aug. 1839, and was *s.* by his uncle, the present ARTHUR ASTON, Esq. now of Aston Hall.

Arms—Per chevron, sa. and arg.
Crest—An ass's head, ppr.
Motto—Prêt d'accomplir.
Seat—Aston Hall, Cheshire.

ATCHERLEY OF MARTON.

ATCHERLEY, DAVID-FRANCIS, Esq. of Marton, co. Salop, *b.* 1 July, 1818; *s.* his father in 1846.

Lineage.—The family of ATCHERLEY *of Marton* has been settled in that neighbourhood at least as far back as the reign of HENRY VII. Their ancestor, Sir Roger Atcherley, Knt., who was born at Stanwardine, in the parish of Baschurch, within about a mile from Marton, was elected sheriff of Middlesex and London, 21 Sept. 1504, 20th HENRY VII., and was chosen lord-mayor of London, 13 Oct. 1511, 3rd HENRY VIII. He is mentioned in Fuller's *Worthies*, vol. ii. p. 263, and also in Stow's *Survey of London*, edition 1598, p. 530, as having munificently stored Leadenhall for the relief of the poor. He filled several civic offices of high trust with distinction, and died in the month of July, 1521, 13th HENRY VIII.

His descendant, Richard Atcherley, who was also *b.* at Stanwardine, went to live at Marton, and afterwards lived at Wycherley Hall, in the same parish of Baschurch. Thomas Atcherley, the eldest son of Richard Atcherley, added certain parts of the Marton property in 1611, 9th JAMES I., and purchased more in 1620; and upon his death, was *s.* by his eldest son,

THOMAS ATCHERLEY, who was baptized 31 Dec. 1609, and *m.* in 1642, Eleanor, a dau. of Roger Griffiths, Esq., alderman of Shrewsbury. This Thomas rebuilt Marton Hall, which has ever since been in the possession of his lineal descendants, and which still remains as he built it, with some recent additions. The last male descendant of this gentleman,

RICHARD ATCHERLEY, Esq., who *m.* Elizabeth Edwards, dau. of Arthur Edwards, of Bosbury, co. Hereford, Esq., *d.* without issue, 27 Feb. 1834, and by his will devised his estates to his nephew, David-Francis Jones, now Atcherley, the only son of his sister Jane, by her husband, David-Francis Jones, Esq. of Cymman, co. Flint, directing him to take the name and arms of ATCHERLEY only. This he accordingly did, by royal license, 21 March, 1834, and became

DAVID-FRANCIS ATCHERLEY, Esq. of Marton, F.R.S., serjeant-at-law, and attorney-general of the counties palatine of Lancaster and Durham. He was *b.* 13 June, 1783, and *m.* 20 May, 1817, Anne-Margaret, 2nd dau. of the late James Topping, Esq. of Whatcroft Hall, co. Chester, K.C., and *d.* in 1846, leaving a son and heir, the present DAVID-FRANCIS ATCHERLEY, Esq. of Marton, and seven other surviving children.

Arms—Gu., on a fesse, engrailed, arg., between three griffins' heads, erased, or, as many crosses patée-fitchée, sa.
Crest—A demi-bustard, couped, gu., wings elevated, or; in the beak a lily, arg., slipped, vert.
Motto—Spe posteri temporis.
Residences—Marton and Cymman.

ATHORPE OF DINNINGTON.

ATHORPE, JOHN-CARVER, Esq. of Dinnington, co. York, *b.* 9 Aug. 1803; *m.* 8 Feb. 1831, Mary, dau. of Thomas-Gibbon FitzGibbon, Esq. of Ballyseeda, co. Limerick, and granddau. of Sir Henry Osborne, Bart., and has issue,

I. JOHN, *b.* 31 March, 1833.
II. George-Middleton, *b.* 1 Nov. 1835.
III. Henry, *b.* 6 March, 1837.
IV. Robert, *b.* 16 Oct. 1841.
V. Marmaduke, *b.* 27 May, 1843.
I. Mary-Anne-Eliza, *m.* 5 April, 1858, to Edward Walter, Esq., late capt. 8th Hussars.
II. Harriet. III. Emily-Jane. IV. Catherine-Agnes.
V. Clara-Isabella. VI. Nannette-Fanny.
VII. Ellen-Ethelred. VIII. Blanche.
IX. Alice-Nina.

This gentleman, who is elder son of the late Marmaduke-Middleton Middleton, Esq. of Leam, co. Derby, (who *d.* 6 Nov. 1848), by Mary-Anne his wife, dau. of Robert Athorpe-Athorpe, Esq. of Dinnington, assumed, upon attaining his majority, the surname and arms of ATHORPE, in pursuance of the will of his maternal uncle, Thomas Athorpe, Esq.

Arms—Quarterly: 1st and 4th, per pale, nebulée, arg. and az., two mullets in fess, counterchanged, for ATHORPE; 2nd, erm., on a saltier, engrailed, sa., an eagle's head, erased, or, for MIDDLETON; 3rd, or, on a chevron, between three crosses cluchée, sa., a fleur-de-lis between two stags' heads, caboshed, of the first, for CARVER.
Crests—1st, ATHORPE, a falcon, ppr., belled, or, the dexter claw resting on an escutcheon, per pale, nebulée, and two mullets, in fesse, as in the arms; 2nd, MIDDLETON (*see* MIDDLETON *of Leam*); 3rd, CARVER, a mount, vert, thereon a cross cluchée, or, charged in the centre with a fleur-de-lis, sa.
Seat—Dinnington, Yorkshire.

ATHY OF RENVILLE

ATHY, RANDLE-EDMOND-LYNCH, Esq. of Renville, co. Galway, representative of one of the Tribes of Galway, is son and heir of the late Philip-Lynch Athy, Esq., by Bridget his wife, elder dau. of Randle M'Donnell, Esq., an eminent merchant of the city of Dublin. He has one brother, Myles, and two sisters, Elizabeth and Catharine.

Seat—Renvill, co. Galway.

ATKIN OF LEADINGTON.

ATKIN, JOHN-THOMAS, Esq. of Leadington, co. Cork, *m.* Sophia, dau. of J. Wright, Esq. of Dublin, and has (with three daus.) a son and heir,

MAURICE.

Lineage.—This family have been settled in the co. of Cork for more than two centuries. They removed from the neighbourhood of Minehead, Somerset, at the time when the royalists were beginning to be roughly handled by the dominant parliamentary soldiery.

JOHN ATKIN, Esq., whose father was of Billbrook, Old Cleave, co. Somerset, was of Polemore, now called Redbarn, near Youghal, which estate he purchased. By Jeane his wife (who *d.* 7 Dec. 1675), he had with five daus., of whom the eldest, Jane, *m.* Jasper Lucas, Esq. of Youghal, and the second, Elizabeth, Samuel Hayman, Esq. of South Abbey. He *d.* 14 Feb. 1642, and was *s.* by his son,

JOHN ATKIN, Esq. an alderman of Youghal, *b.* in 1638. He *d.* 20 May, 1708, leaving a son,

THE REV. WALTER ATKIN, of Ballinleaden, or Leadington, incumbent of Middleton, and vicar-general of the diocese of Cloyne. He *m.* Elizabeth, dau. of — Coningsby, Esq. of Hampton Court, co. Hereford, and by her (who *d.* 4 Nov. 1713), had four sons and three daus.; the youngest of the latter, Elizabeth, *m.* in 1742, the Rev. Atkin Hayman (*see* HAYMAN *of South Abbey*), and *d.* in Jan. 1756. Mr. Atkin *d.* 1 Nov. 1741, and was *s.* by the next son,

THE REV. JOHN-THOMAS ATKIN, of Leadington, who *m.* Margaret, 2nd dau. of the Rev. Matthew Jones, archdeacon of Lismore (by Bridget his wife, dau. of Sir Richard Kennedy, Bart., 2nd baron of the Exchequer), and niece to Dr. Edward Jones, Bishop of Cloyne (1682—1692), by whom he left at his decease, in 1765, an only son,

WALTER ATKIN, Esq. of Leadington and Windsor, both in co. Cork, who *m.* 1st, in June, 1751, Barbara, only child of Maurice Uniacke, Esq. of Woodhouse, and had, I. JOHN-THOMAS, his heir; II. MAURICE-UNAICKE, heir to his brother; III. Walter, *m.* Gertrude, dau. of R.-U. Fitzgerald, Esq. of Corkbeg, M.P. for co. Cork, by whom he had, Robert, deceased; Louisa, *m.* to William-M. Hickson, Esq. of co. Kerry; Margaret, *m.* to Sir William Hamilton, governor of Heligoland. Mr. Atkin *m.* 2ndly, Mary, 2nd dau. of George Dunscombe, Esq. of Mount Desert, and had further issue,

I. George, of Kilwinny, *m.* Miss Burke, of Galway, and had issue, Mary, *d. unm.*
II. Edward, capt. in the 50th regt.; *m.* Miss O'Sullivan.
III. William.
IV. Matthew, drowned in North America.
V. Nicholas, *m.* Miss Kildahl.
VI. James, *m.* 1st, Mary, dau. of — Bleasley, Esq.; and 2ndly, the widow Roe.
I. Harriette, *m.* 1st, Val. Kildahl, Esq.; and 2ndly, the Rev. Thomas Nolan, A.M., of Youghal. To the former she bore,
   SOBIESKI KILDAHL, Esq. of Prospect Hill, Youghal, *m.* Mary-Harriette, elder dau. of Lieut. Atkin Hayman, R.N., and has issue.
II. Eliza, *m.* 1st, 6 Feb. 1813, Atkin Hayman, Esq., lieut. R.N., by whom (who *d.* 25 March, 1817) she had issue,
   1 Samuel, a posthumous son, *d.* in infancy.
   1 Mary-Harriette, *m.* to her cousin, Sobieski Kildahl, Esq.
   2 Elizabeth.
   She *m.* 2ndly, 17 May, 1821, William-Andrews Lamb, Esq. of Bandon, J.P., and has further issue.

He was *s.* by his eldest son,

JOHN-THOMAS ATKIN, Esq. of Leadington, *m.* in June, 1785, Martha, 2nd dau. of William Purefoy, Esq. of Cork, and *d.* in 1786, having had issue, a dau.,

Martha, *m.* to Graves-Chamney Swan, Esq. of Newtown Park.

MAURICE-UNIACKE ATKIN, lieut.-col. in the North Cork militia, *s.* to the family estates on his elder brother's death, without male issue. He *m.* Elizabeth-De Courcy, only dau. of Daniel M'Carty, Esq. of Carrignavar (*see that family*), by the Hon. Elizabeth-Geraldine De Courcy, his wife, dau. of Gerald, 24th Lord Kingsale, and had issue,

Walter, *d. unm.* in Jan. 1821.
JOHN-THOMAS, present representative.
Robert, *d.* in 1825.
Elizabeth-Geraldine-De Courcy, *m.* 23 June, 1808, William-Cooke Collis, Esq. of Castle Cooke (*see that title*)
Barbara, *m.* to the Rev. Charles Harte; and *d.* 3 Feb. 1845.
Ellen, *d. unm.* in 1844.

Arms—Arg., three conies, gu.; a chief, vairy, or and az.
Seat—Leadington, near Middleton, co. Cork.

ATKINS OF FIRVILLE.

ATKINS-GOING, THE REV. PHILIP-GOING, of Firville, co. Cork, and of Monaquil, co. Tipperary, *b.* 21 June, 1804; *m.* 16 Aug. 1830, Jane, 2nd dau. of the late Rowland Morrison, Esq. of Cork, by Maria his wife, 2nd dau. of Robert Davies, M.D., and has surviving issue,

I. ROBERT, *b.* in 1833.
II. Philip, *b.* in 1834.
III. John, *b.* in 1840.
I. Maria-Jane.
II. Charlotte-Elizabeth.
III. Henrietta-Louisa.

Mr. Atkins-Going *s.*, at his grandmother, Mrs. Going's decease, to the Monaquil estates, and to Firville, at the death of his father, 13 Sept. 1839.

Lineage.—RICHARD ATKINS, Esq., the first of the family who settled in Ireland, is believed to have been 2nd son of Sir Jonathan Atkins, Knt., governor of Guernsey, by Mary his wife, sister of Charles Howard, 1st Earl of Carlisle. He obtained a grant of lands in the co. of Kerry, between the years 1640 and 1660, which he soon afterwards alienated, and purchased several debentures, which were confirmed to him as a loyal subject, when Sir Peter Courthorpe was governor of Munster, about 1660. He *m.* a dau. of — Fuller, Esq. of The Sandbanks, co. Cork, and had,

I. CHARLES, his heir.
II. William, of Rossagh, co. Cork, *m.* a dau. of John Nowlan, of Doneraile, and had issue. His descendants intermarried with the Crofts, Purcell, Crone, and other families of respectability in the neighbourhood; George, John, and Roger, were family names.
III. John, of Ballyandrew, near Doneraile. He *m.* Elizabeth, dau. of John Nowlan; and dying before 1757, left a son, Richard, of Ballyandrew, near Doneraile, and of Marlow; who *m.* Anne, only dau. of the O'Sullivan Beare, of Glennarought, and by her (who was *b.* in 1712, and *d.* 8 Nov. 1756, aged 44) Mr. Atkins left at his decease, being killed by a fall from his horse returning from hunting, an only child, John, of Fountainville, *b.* about 1729; who *m.* 5 Nov. 1757, Mary, 2nd dau. of Robert Atkins, Esq. of Fountainville and Copstown, by Elizabeth his wife, dau. and co-heir of Jacob Ringrose, Esq., and Elizabeth his wife, dau. of George Crofts, Esq. of Velvetstown, co. Cork. Jacob Ringrose was 3rd son of Col. Richard Ringrose, of Moynoe House, co. Clare. Mr. Atkins *d.* 10 Jan. 1788, having had issue,
   1 Robert, capt. in the South Cork militia; *b.* 13 March, 1762; *m.* Jane-Purdon, 2nd dau. of Richard Ringrose Bowerman, Esq. of Moynoe House, co. Clare, by Avarina his wife, dau. of Simon Purdon, Esq. of Tinnerana, co. Clare; and *d.* 20 May, 1802, leaving a dau.,
      Avarina, *m.* to the Rev. Henry Gubbins, of Limerick, eldest son, by his 2nd wife, of Joseph Gubbins, Esq. of Kenmare Castle.
   Thomas, lieut. 89th regiment, who inherited from his father the property of Ballydaniel. He *d.* of a wound in one of his feet, in 1795, at St. Lucia. He was never married.
   1 Anne, *m.* 2 April, 1782, to John Cole, Esq. of Oldwood, co. Cork.
   2 Elizabeth, *d. unm.* at Mallow, 30 April, 1836.
   3 Margaret.
   4 Mary, *m.* 8 July, 1802, to James-Thomas Davis, Esq., surgeon Royal Artillery, and acting deputy-inspector of ordnance hospitals in the Peninsula, representative of an ancient Buckinghamshire family, originally from Wales; and had by him, who *d.* at Exeter, aged 40, 27 Sept. 1814, three sons and one dau.,
      JOHN-NICHOLAS-CROFTS-ATKINS DAVIS, senior surgeon royal artillery.
      James-Robert Davis, of Lower Baggot Street, Dublin. *m.* 17 Oct. 1844, Charlotte-Eliza, sister of the Rev. Philip-G. Atkins-Going, of Firville.
      Thomas-Osborne Davis, barrister-at-law, *d. unm.*
      Charlotte-Melina Davis.
   5 Charlotte, *m.* to John-Frederick Ridley, Esq., surgeon Royal Artillery, of Hawthorn, co. Durham.
IV. Samuel, who lived in London; he *m.* and had issue, two sons, Robert and Thomas, and a dau., Charlotte, (Mrs. Bradshaw.)
I. Margaret, *m.* Richard Chapman, Esq. of Gurtnagrum, co. Cork, (now called Firville) and had issue.

The eldest son of Richard Atkins,

CHARLES ATKINS, Esq. of Fountainville, sheriff of Limerick in 1694, *m.* 1st, a dau. of John Westropp, Esq. of Cahirdowgan, co. Cork, who was the eldest brother of Westropp of Attyflyn, in the co. of Limerick, but had no issue by her. He *m.* 2ndly, Hannah, eldest dau. of Robert Minnitt, Esq. of Knygh Castle, Blackfort, co. Tipperary. Mr. Atkins *d.* before 1733-4, but his widow, who was *b.* in 1682, lived till 26 Aug. 1762 (and *m.* again, but by her second husband had no issue); by her first husband, Mr. Atkins, she had, with a dau. Barbara, *m.* to Mr. Barnes, an Englishman, three sons, viz., ROBERT, his heir, John, who *d. s. p.*, and Thomas, of Virginia, in America. The eldest son,

ROBERT ATKINS, Esq. of Fountainville, Ballyngnearane, Clashgariffe, Ballyhowra, &c. was *b.* 1704. He *m.* Elizabeth, only child of Jacob Ringrose, Esq 3rd son of Col. Richard Ringrose, of Moynoe House, in the co of Clare. He *d.* 17 May, 1783, having had a numerous issue, viz.,

I. CHARLES, *b.* 18 Oct. 1729, who *m.* Elizabeth, sole child (by his 1st wife) of William Beere, Esq. of Ballyboy, co. Tipperary. He *d.* 1762, aged 32, in the lifetime of his father, leaving issue,
   WILLIAM ATKINS, Esq., *b.* in May, 1757, who *s.* to

Fountainville on the demise of his grandfather in 1788. He m. Mary, dau. of John Roberts, Esq. of Ardmore House, co. Cork, and had issue, a son, William, who d. unm., and six daus., of whom the eldest, Sarah, m. her cousin, Ringrose Atkins, M.D., and the youngest, Frances, m. William Lysaght, Esq. of Hazlewood, co. Cork.

II. Ringrose, of Prospect Hill, near Mallow, justice of the peace, co. Cork, m. 1st, in 1769, Catharine, only dau. and heir of John Brookes, Esq., by whom he had no issue, and 2ndly, Elizabeth, eldest dau. of William Baker, Esq. of Ballydavid, co. Tipperary. Mr. Atkins d. 24 Feb. 1789, and left issue several children, viz.,

1 Robert-Baker, his heir, of Prospect Hill, d. unm.

2 Ringrose, M.D., was surgeon of the Tipperary militia, b. in 1783, m. in 1804, Sarah, eldest dau. and co-heiress of William Atkins, Esq. of Fountainville and of Mallow, and d. 18 Feb. 1818, aged 85, leaving issue,

Thomas-Ringrose, now of Monkstown, co. Cork, b. Oct. 1809, a captain in the Imperial Lancers of Austria; he sold Prospect Hill, and other property in Mallow and its vicinity; he m. July, 1837, Susanna-Augusta, dau. of Colonel Nuttal Greene, of Kilmanahan Castle, near Clonmel, co. Tipperary, and has issue.

John-Roberts, of Coolmahon, co. Cork, barrister-at-law, b. in 1810.

Ringrose, late a major in the Queen of Spain's Rifles, and now lieut.-col. by brevet, and a knight of San Fernando.

William, on whom half of Fountainville is settled by his grandfather's will.

Walter-Baker, of Trinity College, Dublin.

Elizabeth-Ringrose, } twin sisters.
Maria-Ringrose, }

Henrietta. Anne.

3 Thomas, lieut. in the army, now a settler in Van Dieman's Land, m. Bertha-Sarah, dau. of — Luttrell, Esq., staff-surgeon in that colony, and has Robert; Ringrose; Eliza, wife of Thomas Nicholson, Esq.; and other issue.

1 Anne, m. to Thomas Gelston, Esq., assistant-commissary-general, now of Adelaide Place, Cork.

2 Elizabeth, m. to Henry Franks, Esq., her cousin.

3 Margaret, m. to G.-B. Pain, Esq., and has one child.

III. Jacob, who was port-surveyor, Baltimore, co. Cork. He m. in 1772, Phœbe, sole child and heiress of John Dobbs, Esq. of Mallow, (see Dobbs of Castle Dobbs,) and had issue one son, Robert, d. unm., and one dau. Phœbe, m. 1st, to John Lynch, Esq., and 2ndly, to the Rev. J.-B. Grey.

IV. Thomas, merchant at Jamaica, in the West Indies, d. unm.

V. Robert, of Firville, of whom hereafter, as founder of that branch.

I. Margaret, b. in 1739, m. to William Devereux, Esq. of Deerpark, co. Clare, a scion of the ancient family of Devereux of Carrigmenan, in Wexford.

II. Mary, m. as before stated, to her relative, John Atkins, Esq.

III. Elizabeth, of Meadestown, m. to Henry Franks, Esq. of Moorestown, co. Limerick.

The 5th surviving son,

Robert Atkins, Esq. b. 1 Aug. 1749, of Firville, near Mallow, in the co. of Cork, J.P. for that co., and major in the Mallow cavalry. He m. in 1773, Mary, dau. of George Hastings, Esq., and sister and co-heiress by blood, and sole heiress in property, to her brother, Stephen Hastings, Esq. of Forthenry, in the co. of Tipperary, J.P. for the counties of Tipperary, Clare, and Limerick, a descendant of Sir Edward Hastings, 4th son of Francis, 2nd Earl of Huntingdon, and had issue,

I. Robert, his heir.

II. Stephen-Hastings, of Forthenry, co. Tipperary, J.P. for several years for the cos. Tipperary, Clare, and Limerick; he was b. 29 March, 1798, and m. 1 Dec. 1815, Elizabeth, eldest dau. of Myles O'Reilly, Esq. and sister of Dowel-John O'Reilly, Esq. of Heath House, Queen's County. Mrs. Atkins dying in 1816, left an only child,

Stephen-Hastings, in holy orders, b. 12 Sept. 1816.

Mr. Atkins m. 2ndly, July, 1825, Mary-Anne, eldest dau. of Major William Greene, of the 61st regiment, of Cottage, near Swords, co. Dublin, and has by her,

William, b. 17 Jan. 1836.

Romulus-Robert, } twins, b. in 1840.
Remus-Henry, }

Elizabeth-Adela. Margaret-Grace. Mary-Anne.

III. George, d. a student in Trinity College, Dublin, unm.

I. Mary, m. to Thomas Lidwill, Esq. of Cormackstown, co. Tipperary.

II. Elizabeth, m. to Robert Twiss, Esq., justice of the peace, of Cordal House, co. Kerry, high-sheriff of the said co. in 1802.

III. Anne, m. to Richard-Harding Wigmore, Esq. of Ballynona and Brookdale, co. Cork.

IV. Margaret, m. Arthur Ormsby, Esq. of Bird Hill House, co. Tipperary, and now of Brookdale, co. Cork.

V. Hannah, m. to William Fitzgerald, Esq. of Adrival, co. Kerry, and of Blackfort, co. Tipperary.

VI. Henrietta, m. 1st, to the Rev. Warham Leader, rector of Upper Shandon, Cork, 2nd son of William Leader, Esq of Mount Leader, co. Cork, and 2ndly, to the Rev. Matthew Moore, now rector of Cahirconlish, co. Limerick, 2nd brother of M.-Crosbie Moore, Esq. of Mooresfoot, co. Tipperary, justice of the peace and deputy-lieutenant.

The eldest son,

Robert Atkins, Esq. of Firville, co. Cork, b. 21 Jan. 1775, m. 1st, 31 Dec. 1798, Charlotte, 2nd dau. and co-heir of Philip Going, Esq. of Monaquil, co. Tipperary, by Grace his wife, dau. of Thomas Bernard Esq. of Castle Bernard, King's Co., and by her, who d. in 1812, had issue,

Robert, b. in 1802, d. in 1812, unm.

Philip-Going, now of Firville.

Hastings, b. 5 March, 1807.

Thomas, b. 22 April, 1808, lieut. 19th foot, d. unm. at Demerara, 1827.

John-Bennett-Robert, b. 30 Oct. 1812, in holy orders, curate of Mallow, d. unm. in 1840.

Charlotte-Eliza, m. in 1844, to Jas.-Robert Davies, Esq.

Mr. Atkins m. 2ndly, 31 Oct. 1816, Catherine, dau. and eventually co-heir of John Ridley, Esq. of Hawthorn, co. Durham, but had no further issue. He d. 13 Sept. 1830.

Arms—Arg., on a chevron, sable, three unicorns' heads, erased, of the field; quartering Hastings, Minnitt, (through the same family, Woollaston, and many others) Going, Ringrose, &c.

Crest—A demi-heraldic tiger, ppr., erminée, ducally collared and chained, or.

Seats—Firville, near Mallow, co. Cork; Monaquil, co. Tipperary.

ATKINS OF WATERPARK.

Atkins, Robert, Esq. of Waterpark, co. Cork, late capt. 60th Rifles, b. March, 1802; m. 3 Dec. 1840, Sarah-Elizabeth, dau. of James Penrose, Esq. of Woodhill, co. Cork, and has issue,

I. Robert-St. Leger, b. 12 Nov. 1842.

I. Louisa-Petitot-St. Leger.

II. Mary-Elizabeth-St. Leger.

III. Henrietta-Geraldine-St. Leger.

Lineage.—Margaret Atkins, heiress of Waterpark (elder dau. of Robert Atkins, Esq. of Highfield, who purchased Carrigaline, now Waterpark, and granddau. of Robert Atkins (son of Augustine Atkins, a gentleman of English ancestry), who obtained various grants of land at the commencement of the 18th century), m. in 1742, Heyward St. Leger, Esq. of Heyward's Hill, and had several children (see *family of* St. Leger). The 2nd son,

Robert-Atkins St. Leger, Esq. succeeding to Waterpark, assumed the surname of Atkins, in compliance with his grandfather's will. He m. Jane, dau. and co-heir of Philip Lavallin, Esq. of Waterstown, co. Cork, and had (with two daus., Sarah m. to Robert Berkeley, Esq. great grandson of the celebrated Bishop Berkeley; and Jane, m. to Michael-Bustead Westropp, Esq.) six sons; of whom the eldest

Robert St. Leger-Atkins, Esq. of Waterpark, was killed by a fall from his horse. He d. unm., and was s. by his brother,

Warham Atkins, Esq. of Waterpark, who m. Mary, dau. of Dennis McCarthy, Esq. of Macksgrove, co. Cork, and had an only son, the present Robert Atkins, Esq. of Waterpark.

Arms—Arg., two bars, gu.; on a chief, of the first, three roundles, of the second.

Crest—A pelican wounding herself, ppr.

Motto—Be just, and fear not.

Seat—Waterpark, co. Cork.

ATKINSON OF LORBOTTLE.

Atkinson, Adam, Esq. of Lorbottle, co. Northumberland, J.P., and captain in the militia, b. 7 April, 1817; m. 4 June, 1850, Charlotte-Eustatia, only child of John Collett, Esq. of Upper Belgrave-street, London, by Emma his wife, eldest dau. of Sir Thomas Gage, Bart. of Hengrave, Suffolk, and by this lady (who is of founder's kin to William of Wykeham, *see* Burke's *Collegiate Foundations*) has issue,

I. John-Collett, b. 23 April, 1854.

I. Louisa-Edith. II. Gertrude.

Lineage.—This family is of considerable antiquity on the English border, as may be seen from various old records. In one of the earliest heraldic visitations of Northumberland, a document is recorded, in which William Adekyson, of Fenwick, is mentioned, 13 Nov. 1397; and in a manuscript possessed by the late Robert Surtees, Esq. of Mainsforth, F.A.S., is given a list of all the castles and towers in the county of Northumberland, with the names of their proprietors, made about the year 1460; and under the head, "Nomina Fortalicinum infra com. Northumb.:" we find "Turris de Bukton," the property of William Atkynson.

There are records of this family in various places; but a fire having occurred at Brankston, which destroyed a number of the family registers, it would be difficult to make a connected history with precision.

ADAM ATKINSON, Esq. *b.* in 1755, J.P. for Northumberland, purchased the estate of Lorbottle in 1796. He *m.* in 1776, Isabella, eldest dau. of Robert Curry, Esq., and *d.* 15 July, 1844. His eldest son,

ADAM ATKINSON, Esq. of Lorbottle, *b.* 1 May, 1794, J.P., and major-commandant of a corps of yeomanry cavalry, *m.* 25 June, 1816, Eleanor, 4th dau. of Nathaniel Davison, Esq., British consul at Nice, and afterwards at Algiers, and had issue,

ADAM, present representative.
Nathaniel, in holy orders; *b.* 30 April, 1822.
John, an officer in the army; *b.* 12 April, 1829.
Margaret, *m.* 11 June, 1845, to the Rev. David Bruce, M.A., 2nd son of Thomas Bruce, Esq. of Arnot, N.B., by Clementina his wife, dau. of Gen. Thomas and Lady Eleanor Dundas.
Isabella-Eliza-Cook, *m.* to Thomas Renny, eldest son of Alexander-Renny Tailyour, Esq. of Borrowfield, co. Forfar.
Eleanor. Louisa-Elizabeth.

Arms—Erm., a fesse, sa., between three pheons, or.
Crest—A pheon, or.
Seat—Lorbottle House, co. Northumberland.

ATKINSON OF REHINS.

ATKINSON, CHARLES, Esq. of Rehins, co. Mayo, *b.* in Feb. 1820.

Lineage.—WILLIAM ATKINSON, Esq. of Rehins (son of Charles, of Rehins, by Deborah his wife, dau. of Capt. John Vaughan, and fourth in descent from Capt. Charles Atkinson, who settled in Ireland, *temp.* Queen ELIZABETH), *m.* Jane, widow of Joseph Shardlowe, Esq. of the co. Kildare, and had, with two daus., Debora, wife of Charles Gardiner Esq. of Cloona, co. Mayo, and Martha, wife of William Rogers, Esq. of the co. Galway, two sons, William, who *d.* in minority, and his successor,

CHARLES ATKINSON, Esq. of Rehins, who *m.* in 1785, his cousin Mary, dau. and heir of his uncle, George Atkinson, Esq. of Ballina, co. Mayo, and had issue,

WILLIAM, his heir.
Charles, who *m.* Mary, dau. of Major Hill, of Bellaghy Castle, co. Antrim, and left one son, Charles.
Matthew, of Mountjoy Square, Dublin, barrister-at-law; *m.* Miss Cruice, dau. of D.-J. Cruice, Esq., R.M.
Thomas, in holy orders, rector of Doone, co. Limerick.
Elizabeth, *m.* to Fergus Langley, Esq. of Lickfine, co. Tipperary.
Mary, *m.* to William Leech, Esq. of the co. of Dublin.
Anne, *m.* to the Rev. Charles-P. Coote, brother of Chidley Coote, Esq. of Mount Coote, co. Limerick.

Mr. Atkinson was *s.* at his decease by his eldest son,

WILLIAM ATKINSON, Esq. of Rehins, *b.* 28 Dec. 1790, *m.* 16 Feb. 1816, Frances, dau. of Charles Langley, Esq. of Coalbrook, co. Tipperary, and has issue,

CHARLES, now of Rehins.
William, *b.* in Dec. 1827.
Frances-Wilhelmina. Mary-Georgina.
Elizabeth. Charlotte-Anne.

Mr. Atkinson was a magistrate for the counties of Mayo and Sligo, and a deputy-lieutenant of the former.

Arms—Erm., on a fesse, vert, three fleurs-de-lis, arg.
Crest—An eagle, with two heads, displayed, arg.
Motto—Est pii Deum et patriam diligere.
Seat—Rehins, co. Mayo.

ATKINSON OF CANGORT.

ATKINSON, GUY, Esq. of Cangort, King's County, *b.* 14 July, 1800; *m.* 24 Oct. 1839, Anne-Moore, 2nd dau. of William Trench, Esq. of Cangort Park, brother of the late Lord Ashtown, and has had issue,

I. Charles-Newcomen, *d.* young.
II. GUY-NEWCOMEN, *b.* 4 Jan. 1847.
III. William-Henry, *b.* 28 Aug. 1848.
IV. Richard-Frederick, *b.* 11 Dec. 1849.
I. Sarah-Harriet. II. Emily. III. Caroline-Sophia.

Mr. Atkinson *s.* his father 14 Aug. 1846, and is a magistrate for the King's County.

Lineage.—This family has been settled in the King's Co. since the reign of ELIZABETH, holding its lands under a patent from the crown.

ANTHONY ATKINSON, Esq. of Cangort (son of William Atkinson, Esq. of Cangort, by Anne Hamilton his wife, granddau. of Sir Francis Hamilton, Knt. of Killishandra, co. Cavan), and grandson (by Anne his wife, dau. of Sir Robert Newcomen, Bart.) of Anthony Atkinson, Esq. of Cangort, (whose father, Lieut. Anthony Atkinson, of the island of Kiltobret, King's Co., made his will 16 May, 1626) *m.* in 1709, Mary, dau. of Admiral John Guy, of Greenwich, in Kent (celebrated for having relieved Derry by breaking the boom), and had, with other issue, GUY, successor to his father, and Charles, ancestor of ATKINSON *of Ashley Park (which see)*. Mr. Atkinson *d.* in Dec. 1743, and was *s.* by his eldest surviving son,

THE REV. GUY ATKINSON, of Cangort, rector of Aghoghill, co. Antrim, and vicar of Trim, who *m.* 1st, in 1746, Jane, dau. of Charles Maule, Esq., and niece of Henry, Bishop of Meath, and had by her an only child, Anthony, who *d.* before his father. Mr. Atkinson *m.* 2ndly, Jane, dau. of Jackson Wray, Esq. of the co. Donegal, and had by her, 1 HUGH, who *d.* in India; 2 Guy, an officer in the navy, blown up by the explosion of a ship on fire; 3 JACKSON, of whom presently; 4 Charles, in holy orders, rector of Creggan, co. Armagh; *m.* Thomasina, dau. of the Rev. Mr. Downing, of the co. of Londonderry; 5 George, who *m.* Leonora, dau. of Jackson Wray, Esq. of Bentford, co. Antrim, and assumed, by royal license, the surname and arms of WRAY; and 1 Maria, *m.* to — Golding, Esq. The third son,

JACKSON-WRAY ATKINSON, Esq. of Cangort, lieut.-col. of the King's Co. militia, *m.* in 1794, Sarah, dau. of Richard Caddell, Esq. of Downpatrick, and had issue,

GUY, his heir.
Henry, *b.* in July, 1806, *m.* in April, 1839, Elizabeth-Jane, eldest dau. of the Rev. William-Brownlow Savage, rector of Shinrone, King's County, and has two daus., Elizabeth-Barbara and Sarah-Anne.
Charles, an officer 10th Native cavalry, E.I.C.S., *d.* in India from the bite of a snake, in 1840.
Richard, *b.* in 1819, *m.* Mary-Jane, dau. of George Golding, Esq., and has a dau., Georgiana.
Sarah. Maria. Mabella-Jane.
Caroline-Steuart, *m.* to William L'Estrange, Esq. of Kilcummin.
Emily-Rebecca. Harriet-Anne.

Col. Atkinson *d.* 14 Aug. 1846, and was *s.* by his eldest son, the present GUY ATKINSON, Esq. of Cangort.

Arms—Or, an eagle, displayed, with two heads, az., beaked and legged, gu.; in chief, a rose, of the last, seeded, gold, between two martlets, sa.
Crest—An eagle, displayed, with two heads, az., beaked and legged, gu.
Motto—Deo et regi fidelis.
Seat—Cangort, King's County.

ATKINSON OF ASHLEY PARK.

ATKINSON, GEORGE-GUY, Esq. of Ashley Park, co. Tipperary, a magistrate for that shire and for the King's County.

Lineage.—ANTHONY ATKINSON, Esq. of South Park, co. Tipperary, (son of Charles Atkinson, Esq. King's Co., by Mary his wife, dau. of Robert Saunderson, of Clover Hill, co. Cavan, and grandson of Anthony Atkinson, Esq. of Cangort), who *d.* in 1743, *m.* Catherine, dau. of Dominick Blake, Esq. of Castlegrove, by Frances his wife, dau. of Nicholas, 5th Viscount Netterville, and had, with a dau. Charlotte, who *d. unm.*, two sons, GEORGE-GUY ATKINSON, Esq. of Ashley Park, and CHARLES ATKINSON, Esq. of South Park.

Arms, &c.—*See* ATKINSON *of Cangort.*
Seat—Ashley Park, co. Tipperary.

ATKINSON OF ANGERTON.

ATKINSON, JAMES-HENRY-HOLLIS, Esq. of Angerton, co. Northumberland, *b.* 9 March, 1819; *m.* 12 March, 1840, Anne-Louisa, dau. of the late William Ellice, Esq. He took the name of ATKINSON on succeeding to the estates of his maternal granduncle, Ralph Atkinson, Esq. of Angerton, in 1827, and was lately a cornet in the royal horse-guards.

Lineage.—Sir Thomas Bradford, G.C.B., G.C.H., a lieut.-gen. in the army, (son of the late Thomas Bradford, Esq. of Woodlands near Doncaster, and of Ashdown Park, Sussex, and brother of Lieut.-Col. Sir Henry Bradford, who d. 1816, from the effects of wounds received at Waterloo), m. 1st, Mary-Anne, widow of Lieut.-Col. Philip Ainslie, and niece of Ralph Atkinson, Esq., by whom he had issue, James-Henry-Hollis, now of Angerton; Ralph, b. 1824; Elizabeth-Mary; Georgiana-Augusta-Frederica; and Barbara. Sir Thomas m. 2ndly, 13 July, 1840, Anne-Elizabeth, widow of B. Good, Esq. of Harley Street.

Arms—Erm., on a fesse, double cotised, gu., between three pheons, az., a lion, passant, between two roses, arg.
Crest—On a mount, between two roses, stalked and leaved, ppr., a pheon, az.
Motto—Crede Deo.
Seat—Angerton near Morpeth, co. Northumberland.

ATKINSON OF RAMPSBECK LODGE AND MORELAND.

Atkinson, Francis-Baring, Esq. of Rampsbeck Lodge, co. Cumberland, and Moreland, co. Westmoreland, b. 30 Dec. 1805; m. 1st, in Dec. 1831, Mary-Anne, dau. of Sir John Stoddart, Knt., chief justice of Malta, which lady d. in Nov. the following year. He m. 2ndly, 8 Aug. 1837, Ellen-Francis, dau. of John Home, Esq. of Edgbaston (son of John, who was son of the last Home of Whitfield, a branch of Home (or Hume) *of Ninewells*), and by her has issue,

i. George, b. 24 Nov. 1838.
ii. Francis-Home, b. 2 March, 1840.
iii. Thomas, b. 2 Aug. 1841.
iv. William } twins, b. 18 Oct. 1844.
v. Richard-Clayton }
vi. Alexander-Henry, b. 16 Aug. 1846.
vii. Robert-Septimus, b. 15 Feb. 1848.
viii. Edward, b. 19 July, 1850.
i. Ellen-Frances. ii. Mary-Jane. iii. Bridget-Harriet.

Mr. Atkinson is a deputy-lieutenant for Cumberland, for which shire he was high-sheriff in 1853.

Lineage.—This family inherits at Temple Sowerby, by direct descent, from William Atkinson, who with his mother is included in a lease for 999 years, granted in the 18th of Elizabeth, by the then lords of the manor, on the compromise of suits at York, which had originated out of questions on the tenures of the landholders at Temple Sowerby, which manor had formerly belonged to the Knights of St. John and to the Templars. Mr. Atkinson's great-grandfather,

Matthew Atkinson, of Temple Sowerby, was father (besides a younger son, Richard Atkinson, b. in 1738, a merchant of London, and admitted to the freedom of the goldsmiths' company, who sat in parliament for Romney, and was senior alderman present at the mansion-house during the attack on the Bank in Lord George Gordon's riots, after Kennet, the lord mayor, had absconded; and who d. unm. in May, 1785) of an elder son,

George Atkinson, Esq. b. 16 Aug. 1730, who was receiver-general for Cumberland and Westmoreland. He m. 7 Jan. 1758, Bridget, dau. and heiress of Michael Maughan, Esq. of Wolsingham, and Dorothy his wife, co-heiress of George Lowthian, Esq. of Staffold, and d. 12 Oct. 1781, having had, with other children who d. in infancy,

Michael, of Mount Mackal, Kent, and London, d. 1821.
George, of whom presently.
Richard, d. unm. 1793.
Matthew, of Carr Hill, near Newcastle-on-Tyne, d. 1829.
John, d. unm. 1798.
Dorothy, m. to N. Clayton, Esq. of Chesters, Northumberland, and d. in 1827.
Bridget, m. to H. Tulip, Esq. of Brunton, Northumberland, and d. 1850.
Jane, of Temple Sowerby.

The 2nd surviving son,

George Atkinson, Esq. of Morland, called also of Lee, in Kent, b. 17 Sept. 1764, was secretary at Jamaica, and A.D.C. to Lord Balcarres, when governor of that island, and afterwards agent-general for that colony in England. He m. 30 July, 1794, Susan-Mackenzie Dunkley, of Clarendon, Jamaica, and d. in Feb. 1830, having had,

George, b. 6 June, 1795, d. unm. 1849.
Thomas, b. 14 Sept. 1800, capt. 13th light dragoons, d. unm. 1828.

Francis-Baring, now of Rampsbeck Lodge and Moreland.
William, in holy orders, rector of Gateshead Fell, Durham, and hon. canon of Durham; b. 13 June, 1809, m. Jane-Elizabeth, dau. of William Clarke, Esq. of Belford Hall, co. Northumberland, and has issue.
Richard, b. 5 Aug. 1813, m. Caroline, dau. of the Rev. J. Landon, of Aberford.
Bridget, m. to Robert Robertson, Esq. of Auchleeks, co. Perth, and Memblands, Devon.
Mary, m. to Alex. Turnbull, Esq., H.B.M. Consul at Marseilles.
Jane, m. to Edward Johnson, Esq. of Newcastle-on-Tyne.
Harriet-Eliza, m. to Alex. Adair, Esq. of Heatherton Park, Somerset.

Arms—Gu., an eagle, displayed, with two heads, arg.; on chief, of the second, three mullets, of the first.
Crest—A falcon, wings expanded.
Seats—Rampsbeck Lodge, Cumberland; and Moreland, co. Westmoreland.

ATTHILL OF BRANDISTON HALL.

Atthill, The Rev. William, of Brandiston Hall, co. Norfolk, A.M., vicar of Horsford, and perpetual curate of Horsham St. Faith's, Norfolk, b. 11 July, 1807; m. 1st, 14 Dec. 1835, Sarah-Bircham, eldest dau. of the late Guy Lloyd, Esq. of Croghan House, co. Roscommon, and by her, who d. in 1837, has one son,

William, b. 2 Dec. 1836.

He m. 2ndly, in 1840, Catherine, only dau. of the late Christopher Topham, Esq. of Middleham Hall, Yorkshire, by whom (who d. 19 Oct. 1844) he has,

Robert-Christopher-Topham, b. 13 Sep. 1841.
Jane-Catherine.

He m. 3rdly, 28 June, 1849, Dorothea, dau. of the late Robert Radclyffe, Esq. of Foxdenton Hall, co. Lancaster.

Lineage.—This family deduces its descent from the time of the Conquest, and is stated by some authorities to have been of Saxon origin.

Richard Att'ehill, of Bareworth, in the co. of Berks, (whose name, &c. are recorded in the *Abbreviatio Rotulorum Originalium*, 31st Edward I.) m. Maude, dau. of Sir John Harley, of South Wales, and was grandfather of

John Att'ehill, the first of his family who settled in the co. of Norfolk, where his descendants have since continued to reside. His great-great-grandson,

Henry Att'ehill, appears among the list of the gentry of England returned by the commissioners in the reign of Henry VI. He m. in 1448, Mary-Therese, dau. of Sir Hugo de Montmorencie, a French officer, and by her left, with three daus., two sons. The elder,

Henry Att'ehill, fell in the wars of the Roses, leaving an only son, who d. in infancy. The family estates then devolved upon his only brother,

Thomas Att'hill, who m. in 1471, Lucy, dau. of Sir Ralph Mordaunt, and had, with four daus., an only son, his successor,

Sir Richard Att'hill, Knt. who d. in 1505, leaving two sons and two daus. and was interred in the church of Geystwick, where his effigy in brass still remains. Sir Richard was s. at his demise by his elder son,

Anthony Att'hill, Esq. The family residence having become dilapidated, this gentleman settled at Cawston, in the co. of Norfolk. He m. in 1540, and had issue, four sons and two daus. of whom the eldest,

Richard Att'hill, Esq. b. in 1545, succeeded his father, and marrying in 1569, had, *inter alios*, a dau. Cicely, wife of William Custance, Esq. and a son and successor,

Edward Att'hill, Esq. captain in the army of Charles I. who m. the dau. and heir of Peterson, of Aylsham and Brandiston, and d. in 1676, leaving an only surviving son,

Anthony Att'hill, Esq. of Cawston, who m. in 1684, Anne, dau. of Sir Thomas Lombe, Knt. and left, besides several daus., two sons, viz.

Anthony-Lombe.
John, ancestor of the Cawston branch, from which are descended Edward Atthill, Esq., seised of estates in Cawston and Bewley, and the Rev. Lombe Atthill, of Halesworth.

Mr. Att'hill was s. at his decease, by his eldest son,

Anthony-Lombe Atthill, Esq. of Brandiston, who m. Maria, dau. of — Capon, Esq. and had issue,

i. Anthony, who m. Mary, dau. of Charles Wethorall, Esq. and, dying before his father in 1758, left issue.

1 ANTHONY-JOHN, successor to his grandfather.
2 William, M.D., of Spottisham Hall, co. Norfolk, *d. unm.*
3 Jermyn, H.E.I.C.S., *d.* abroad, *unm.*
4 Maria, *m.* to — Bond, Esq., co. Middlesex.

II. Edward, A.M., in holy orders, rector of Sparham and Foxley, co. Norfolk, *d. unm.*
III. John, R.N., *d.* at sea, *unm.*
IV. Lombe, *m.* Elizabeth, dau. of — Johnson, Esq., and left issue four sons and three daus.
I. Mary, *m.* to — Smith, of Cottis Hall, co. Norfolk, and had, with other issue,

1 Mary, *m.* to the Right Rev. John Porter, D.D., Lord Bishop of Clogher.

Mr. Atthill was *s.* at his decease in 1760, by his grandson,

ANTHONY-JOHN ATTHILL, Esq. of Brandiston, who *m.* in 1773, Sarah, dau. of Mr. Howlett, of Marsham, in the co. of Norfolk, deceased, and dying, 1780, left with a dau. Martha, an only son,

THE REV. WILLIAM ATTHILL, of Brandiston Hall, A.M. prebendary of Clogher, rector and vicar of the parishes of Fintona, co. Tyrone, and of Magheraculmony, co. Fermanagh, *b.* in April, 1774; *m.* 1st, April, 1805, Henrietta-Margaret-Eyre, eldest dau. of the Very Rev. Geo. Maunsell, D.D. Dean of Leighlin, niece of Robert-Hedges Eyre, Esq. of Macroom Castle, co. Cork, and cousin to the Earl of Bantry, by whom he had issue,

WILLIAM, present representative.
Robert, A.B., *b.* 9 Feb. 1810; *d.* abroad in 1839.
Richard, *b.* 11 Aug. 1811, A.B., in holy orders, canon of the collegiate church of Middleham, Yorkshire; *m.* Dec. 1844, Martha, eldest dau. and co-heir of the late Robert Cookson, Esq. of Ellery, Westmoreland, and has issue.
John-Grey-Porter, *b.* 31 Dec. 1812, barrister-at-law, judge of the royal court at St. Lucia, and of the court of Vice-Admiralty there; *m.* 15 Sept. 1840, Veronica-Montgomerie, dau. and co-heir of John-Henry Blennerhassett, Esq. of Tralee, and has a dau., Veronica-Montgomerie.
Edward-Eyre, J.P. for Fermanagh, *m.* 1847, Jane, eldest dau. and co-heir of the late Lowther Brien, Esq. of Ardvarney, Fermanagh, and has issue.
Henry-Maunsell.
Lombe, M.D., *m.* in 1848, Elizabeth, dau. of Jas. Dudgeon, Esq. of Dublin, and has issue.
Henrietta-Elizabeth, *m.* in 1833, to the Rev. Richard Stainforth, A.M.
Emily, *m.* in Feb. 1843, to Joseph Jones, Esq. of Hathershaw House, Oldham, J.P. and D.L. for Lancashire and Yorkshire.
Jemima-Grace, *m.* in June, 1842, to the Rev. Howard-Boyle St. George.

This gentleman was elected in 1796, a fellow of Caius and Gonville College, Cambridge; whence, removing to Ireland, he obtained the preferment above mentioned. He *d.* 7 March, 1847.

Arms—Arg., on a chevron, gu., three crescents, or, quartering LOMBE.
Crests—1st, a demi-griffin, rampant; 2ndly, a falcon, or, ducally gorged, az., belled and leashed, of the first.
Mottoes—Honorantes me honorabo; and Monte de alto.
Seat—Brandiston Hall, co. Norfolk.
Residence—Hcrsford Vicarage, near Norwich.

ATTY OF PENLEY HALL.

ATTY, JAMES, Esq. of Rugby, co. Warwick, and Pinchbeck, co. Lincoln, J.P. for the former shire, and major 2nd regt. of Warwickshire militia, *b.* in 1810; *m.* in 1831, Catherine-Adeline, dau. of Adlard Welby, Esq. of North Rauceby, co. Lincoln, and has issue,

I. JAMES, an officer, 43rd light infantry.
II. George-Robert.
III. Charles.
I. Adeline.
II. Harriot.
III. Charlotte.

Mr. Atty was formerly capt. 52nd light infantry.

Lineage.—JAMES ATTYE, Esq., second son of JAMES ATTYE, Esq. of Whitby, by Isabella his wife, dau. of G. Weatherill, Esq., *m.* Harriot, dau. of Robert Middleton, Esq., and had issue,

JAMES, of whom presently.
George, *d. unm.* 1797, aged 25.
Robert Middleton, of Ingon Grange, co. Warwick.

The eldest son,

JAMES ATTYE, Esq., *m.* 1st, in 1807, Harriot, dau. of Sir Thomas Whichcote, Bart., of Oswarby, co. Lincoln, by Diana his wife, dau. of Edmond Turnor, Esq. of Stoke Rochfort, by whom, who *d.* in 1810, he had one son, JAMES, now of Rugby. He *m.* 2ndly, Catherine, dau. of the Rev. Thomas Hall, rector of Westborough, and vicar of Doddington, co. Lincoln, and had by her one son, George, M.A., of Brazenose College, Oxford, and now of the Middle Temple.

Arms—Az., a bend between two lions, rampant, or.
Crest—An ermine, passant, on a ducal coronet.
Motto—Eamus que ducit fortuna.
Seat—Penley Hall, co. Flint.

ATTYE OF INGON GRANGE.

ATTYE, ROBERT-JAMES, Esq. of Ingon Grange, co. Warwick, B.A. of St. John's College, Cambridge, J.P. and D.L. co. Warwick, *b.* in 1812.

Lineage.—The late ROBERT-MIDDLETON ATTYE, Esq., of Ingon Grange, J.P., and D.L., and high sheriff for the co. of Warwick in 1824, (youngest son of James Attye, Esq., of Whitby, by Harriot his wife, dau. of Robert Middleton, Esq.), *m.* in 1810, Margaretta-Lucy, youngest dau. of the Venerable William Willes, archdeacon of Wells, third son of Edward, 2nd bishop of Bath and Wells, younger brother of the Right Hon. Sir John Willes, lord chief justice of the Common Pleas. He had issue,

ROBERT-JAMES, now of Ingon Grange.
Henry-Gould, *d.* in 1832.
William-F.-Willes, lieut. in 31st regt., present at the occupation of Cabul in 1842, throughout the campaigns in the Punjaub and on the Sutlej, in the actions of Moodkee, Ferozeshah, Aliwal (where he was wounded), and Sobraon; and *d.* aged 23 years.
Francis-Lionel-Octavius, capt. in the 2nd or Queen's Royals.
Hannah-Lucy.
Harriett-Caroline.
Ellen-Margaret.
Augusta-Jeana.

Mr. Attye *d.* in 1838.

Arms, &c.—See preceding family.
Seat—Ingon Grange, co. Warwick.

AUFRERE OF FOULSHAM.

AUFRERE, GEORGE-ANTHONY, Esq. of Foulsham Old Hall, co. Norfolk, *b.* 18 June, 1794; *m.* 3 Sept. 1828, Caroline, dau. of John Wehrtmann, Esq. of Hamburgh. Mr. Aufrère is a magistrate for the county, and *s.* his father in Nov. 1833.

Lineage.—ANTHONY AUFRERE, an advocate in the Parliament of Paris, who left France on the revocation of the edict of Nantes, was grandfather of

THE REV. ANTHONY AUFRERE,* (presented in 1731, to the rectory of Heigham, in Norfolk) who *d.* in 1781. His only son,

ANTHONY AUFRERE, Esq. of Hoveton, *m.* 17 Feb. 1756, Anna, only dau. of John Norris, Esq. of Witton, by Anne his wife, one of the daus. of Thomas Carthew, Esq., of Benacre in Suffolk, and dying 11 Sept. 1814, had issue,

ANTHONY, *b.* in 1757, of whom hereafter.
George-John, *b.* in 1769, in holy orders, rector of Ridlington and Bacton, Norfolk.
Charles-Gatten, R.N., *b.* in 1760, drowned.
Thomas-Norris, deceased.
Philip-DuVal, in holy orders, rector of Scarning and Bawdeswell, Norfolk, *m.* 1st, Mary, dau. of the Rev. Mr. Beevor, who *d.* in 1818, *s. p.*; and 2ndly, Ann-Margaret, dau. of the Rev. Marmaduke Smith; by the latter of whom he left at his death, 4 June, 1849, one child, Philip-Norris.
Anne, *d. unm.*
Sophia, *m.* to William Dawson, Esq.
Harriett, *m.* to Sir Robert Baker, Knt., some time chief magistrate at Bow Street.
Caroline, *m.* to the Rev. Mr. Flavell, rector of Stody and Hunworth, Norfolk.
Louisa, *m.* to — Minshull, Esq., one of the magistrates in London.
Amelia-Jane.
Maria, *m.* to Paul Squires, of Mulbarton Lodge.

The eldest son and heir,

ANTHONY AUFRERE, Esq. *b.* 30 Nov. 1757, sold the Hoveton estate. He *m.* in 1791, Matilda, dau. of General Count Lockhart, of Dryden and Lee House, co. Lanark, N.B., and *d.* in Nov. 1833, leaving a son and dau., viz.,

GEORGE-ANTHONY, his heir, now of Foulsham.
Matilda, *m.* in 1818, to George Barclay, Esq.

Motto—Esto quod esse videris.
Seat—Foulsham Old Hall.
Residences—Burnside, near Bowness; Windermere, co. Westmoreland.

* His next brother, George Aufrère, Esq. of Chelsea, M.P., left an only dau. and heir, Sophia, Baroness Yarborough.

AUSTEN OF SHALFORD.

AUSTEN, SIR HENRY-EDMUND, Knt. of Shalford House, co. Surrey, J.P. and D.L., high-sheriff in 1810, *b.* 20 May, 1785; *m.* 1st, in 1805, Anne-Amelia, only dau. of the late Robert-Spearman Bate, Esq. of the H.E.I.C.S., and by her (who *d.* 5 Sept. 1839) has surviving issue,

I. ROBERT-ALFRED-CLOYNE, *b.* 17 March, 1808, a magistrate and deputy-lieut. for Surrey, *m.* in 1832, Maud-Elizabeth, dau. of Col. Godwin, C.B., gentleman-usher to Prince ALBERT, and has, besides daus., a son, Henry-Haversham.
II. Henry-Edmund, *b.* 4 March, 1809, capt. in the 71st light infantry.
III. Frederick-Lewes, *b.* 16 Oct. 1813.
IV. Algernon-Stuart, lieut. R.N., *b.* 3 Aug. 1815.
V. John-Wentworth, lieut. 49th regt., *b.* 5 July, 1820.
IV. Albert-George, lieut. E.I.C.'s service, *b.* 9 Sept. 1822.
I. Amelia, *m.* in 1832, to James Brabazon, Esq. of Mornington House, co. Meath.

Sir Henry Austen *m.* 2ndly, in 1843, Lady Pocklington, widow of Sir Robert Pocklington, K.M.T., of Chelsworth, Suffolk.

Lineage.—The late ROBERT AUSTEN, Esq. of Shalford, who was a munificent benefactor to the parish of Shalford, by rebuilding its church at his own expense, in 1788, *m.* in 1772, Frances-Annesley, dau. and heir of John-Wentworth-Nasimsen Gregory, Esq., and had surviving issue,

I. HENRY-EDMUND, his heir.
I. Frances-Ann, *m.* to the Hon. John Bedford, judge of the Vice-Admiralty Court in Barbadoes, and had (with a dau., who *d.* in 1805) two sons,
1 Edward-Henry Bedford.
2 Paul-Austen Bedford, in holy orders.
II. Elizabeth-Smith.

Mr Austen *d.* 3 Nov. 1797, and was *s.* by his son, the present SIR HENRY-EDMUND AUSTEN, of Shalford.

Arms—Azure, a chevron, arg., between three Cornish choughs, or.
Crest—On a leopard's head, az., a falcon rising, or.
Motto—Ne quid nimis.
Seat—Shalford House, near Guildford.

AWDRY OF SEEND.

AWDRY, AMBROSE, Esq. of Seend, co. Wilts, *b.* 14 Sept. 1816; *m.* 24 Oct. 1839, Eliza, dau. of G.-B. Clapcott, Esq. of Keynstone, co. Dorset, and has issue,

I. AMBROSE, *b.* 9 March, 1843.
II. Edward-Seymour, *b.* 2 Aug. 1850.
III. Henry-Shield, *b.* 3 Oct. 1851.
I. Fanny-Eliza. II. Ellen-Louisa.

Mr. Awdry *s.* his uncle 15 June, 1842.

Lineage.—The first recorded ancestor of this respectable Wiltshire family, THE REV. JOHN AWDRY, was instituted to the vicarage of Melksham, 21 Sept. 1601, and *d.* in 1629, leaving, by Hester his wife, a son, GODWIN AWDRY, Esq., father, by Alice his wife, dau. of Sandley Holmes, of AMBROSE AWDRY, Esq. of Melksham and Seend, bapt. in 1627, who *m.* Cicel, dau. of Jeremiah Gough, and had issue, 1. JOHN, of Melksham; 2. Ambrose, of whom presently; 3. Jeremiah; 1. Mary, *m.* to Thomas Goddard, Esq. of Rudloe, co. Wilts. The second son,

AMBROSE AWDRY, Esq. of Seend, *m.* Mary, dau. of Isaac Selfe, Esq., and *d.* in 1728, aged 75, leaving (with two daus., Mary, *m.* to George Penney, Esq., and Elizabeth, *m.* to Ambrose Goddard, Esq. of Swindon) a son and successor,

AMBROSE AWDRY, Esq. of Seend, co. Wilts, who *m.* 14 Jan. 1724, Jane, dau. of John Awdry, Esq. of Melksham, and had (with two daus. Mary, *b.* 8 Feb. 1725, and Jane, *b.* 9 Dec. 1730) three sons, AMBROSE, his heir; John, of Notton, co. Wilts, *(see that family)*; Jeremiah, fellow of Oriel College, Oxford. The eldest son,

AMBROSE AWDRY, Esq. of Seend, *m.* in 1761, Christiana, dau. of Peter Delmé, Esq. of Erle Stoke Park, Wilts, and by her (who *d.* in 1784) had issue,

I. AMBROSE, his heir.
II. PETER, *b.* 3 March, 1771, who *m.* 1st, 16 May, 1794, Hester-Maria, dau. of Lord William Seymour, 3rd son of Edward, Duke of Somerset, which lady *d.* in the following year; and 2ndly, 2 Nov. 1813, Elizabeth, dau. of Anthony Guy, Esq. of Chippenham; and *d.* 1 June, 1826, leaving by this lady (who *d.* 31 March, 1851) a son, the present AMBROSE AWDRY, of Seend, and two daus., Elizabeth, *m.* to the Rev. Alston-William Radcliffe; and Ellen-Seymour, *m.* to the Rev. Edward Everett.
III. William-Henry, *b.* 1 Dec. 1778; *m.* in 1801, Eliza, dau. of West Hill, M.D. of Devizes, and has surviving issue,
1 West, *b.* in 1807, who *m.* in 1834, Mary-Remington, 2nd dau. of John Smith, Esq. of Clapham, and has, William Henry, *b.* in 1835; West-Stewart, *b.* in 1840; Caroline, Bella-Delmé, and Georgiana.
2 Edward-Charles, in holy orders, *b.* in 1811.
3 Frederick, *b.* in 1817. 4 Justly-William, *b.* in 1818.
5 Peter, *b.* in 1820. 6 Charles-Hill, *b.* in 1825.
1 Georgiana. 2 Arabella.
IV. Charles, *b.* 23 Aug. 1784; *d.* 5 May, 1840.
I. Christian, *d. unm.* 8 May, 1841.
II. Georgiana, *m.* in 1800, to her kinsman, James-Henry Arnold, LL.D.

The eldest son,

AMBROSE AWDRY, Esq. of Seend, *b.* 12 Aug. 1762, was a magistrate and deputy-lieut. for Wilts, and served as high sheriff in 1821: he *m.* Hannah, dau. of Anthony Guy, Esq. of Chippenham, but dying *s. p.* 15 June, 1842, was *s.* by his nephew, the present AMBROSE AWDRY, of Seend, Esq.

Arms—Arg., three cinquefoils, or, on a bend, az., cotised, of the same.
Crest—Out of a ducal coronet, a lion's head, az.
Motto—Nil sine Deo.
Seat—Seend, near Melksham.

AWDRY OF NOTTON.

AWDRY, SIR JOHN-WITHER, Knt. of Notton House, co. Wilts, *b.* 21 Oct. 1795; *m.* 1st, 29 June, 1830, Sarah-Maria, dau. of the Rev. Jeremiah Awdry, vicar of Felsted, in Essex, and by her had issue,

I. JOHN, *b.* 13 Feb. 1834. I. Jane.

He *m.* 2ndly, 24 July, 1839, Frances-Ellen, 2nd dau. of the Rt. Rev. Thomas Carr, D.D., late bishop of Bombay, and by her has,

I. Thomas, *b.* 6 July, 1840.
II. William, *b.* 24 Jan. 1842.
III. Ambrose, *b.* 28 April, 1844.
IV. Charles, *b.* 12 Feb. 1847.
V. James, *b.* 8 Sept. 1849.
VI. Herbert, *b.* 20 Oct. 1851.
I. Sarah. II. Frances. III. Elizabeth.

Sir John Awdry, formerly fellow of Oriel College, Oxford, and subsequently chief justice of the Supreme Court of Judicature at Bombay, *s.* his father 23 Dec. 1844.

Lineage.—JOHN AWDRY, Esq. of Notton, co. Wilts, lieut.-col. of yeomanry, younger son of Ambrose Awdry, Esq. of Seend, by Jane his wife, dau. of John Awdry, Esq. of Melksham, was devisee of his maternal uncle, Jeremiah Awdry, Esq., who *d.* in 1754. He *m.* 1st, 25 June, 1765, Priscilla, dau. of Ambrose Goddard, Esq. of Swindon, and had by her, who *d.* 2 Dec. 1768, a son, JOHN, his heir. He *m.* 2ndly, Mary-Magdalene, dau. of James Massé, Esq., by whom he had no issue; and 3rdly, Sarah-Susannah, widow of the Rev. Mr. Derbyshire, prebendary of Chester, and dau. of Thomas Roston, Esq. of Barton, co. Stafford, by which lady he had another son,

Jeremiah, in holy orders, vicar of Felsted, in Essex, who *m.* 1st, Maria-Emelia, eldest dau. of J. May, Esq. of Hale House, Hants, and had by her,
John-Dea, major in the Madras service, who *m.* Margaret Currie, and has one son and one dau.
Charles-Roston, who *m.* Jane, dau. of the Rev. W. Thring, D.D., and has issue.
Sarah-Maria, late wife of Sir John-Wither Awdry.
Harriet-May, *m.* to Quintin Jamieson, Esq., Madras medical service.
Mary-Catherine, *m.* to Capt. M.-J. Rowlandson, Madras N.I.
Eliza-Coppindale, *m.* to the Rev. J. Peck.
Louisa-Frances, *m.* to George Stiles, Esq.
The Rev. Jeremiah Awdry *m.* 2ndly, Rosina-Osborne, only dau. of the late Capt. Weller, of the Bengal service, by whom he has a dau., Rosina-Osborne-Law; and 3rdly, Mary-Sibella, eldest dau. of John Wilkinson, Esq. of Springfield, Bath, by whom he has two daus, Sarah and Louisa-Caroline.

Col. Awdry, who was a magistrate and dep.-lieut. of the county of Wilts, served as high-sheriff in 1791. His elder son and successor,

JOHN AWDRY, Esq. of Notton House, J.P. and D.L. for Wilts, *b.* 7 April, 1766, *m.* 19 Dec. 1794, Jane, 2nd dau. of Lovelace Bigg, Esq. of Chilton Foliat, (who afterwards took the name of Wither, and became of Marydown Park, Hants), and had issue to survive,

JOHN-WITHER (Sir), his heir.
Charles, in holy orders, B.C.L., rector of Worthen, co. Salop, *b.* 19 Dec. 1802.
Henry-Goddard, *b.* 21 Aug. 1804; *m.* 10 April, 1834, Mary, dau. of the Rev. Kenrick Peck, of Notton Lodge, Wilts, and has issue, Henry-Short, *b.* 17 July, 1836; Kenrick-Wither, *b.* 21 Nov. 1837; William, *b.* 14 Jan. 1840; and Mary-Catherine.
Walter-Herbert, *b.* 1 Aug. 1812; *m.* 3 Jan. 1854, Mary-Llewellyn, dau. of the Rev. William Evans, vicar of Rhayader, co. Radnor.
Jane, *m.* in May, 1827, to the Rev. William Short, M.A., then vicar of Chippenham, Wilts, now rector of St. George-the-Martyr, Queen-square, London, and has issue, William-Awdry; Walter-Francis; Ambrose; Charlotte-Augusta; Mary-Jane; and Elizabeth-Laura.
Catherine, *m.* 4 March, 1837, to Frederic Stainforth, Esq., Bengal civil service, and has issue, Biscoe and Ellen-Catherine.
Alethea-Sophia. Margaret-Lucy.

Mr. Awdry *d.* 23 Dec. 1844, and was *s.* by his eldest son, the present SIR JOHN-WITHER AWDRY, Knt. of Notton. Mrs. Awdry *d.* 14 April, 1846.

Arms and *Crest*—Same as AWDRY *of Seend.*
Seat—Notton House, Chippenham.

AYLMER OF LYONS.

AYLMER, MICHAEL-VALENTINE, Esq. of Derry House, co. Tipperary, *b.* 8 March, 1812; *s.* his father, as head and lineal representative of this ancient family, 9 Jan. 1837; *m.* 26 April, 1841, Marianne, dau. and heir of the late William Conolly, Esq. of the city of Dublin, and has had issue,

I. GERALD-JOSEPH, *b.* 27 Oct. 1849.
II. Michael-Valentine, *b.* 25 June, 1851.
III. Reginald-Arnulph, *b.* 3 Feb. 1853.
I. Mary, *d.* young, in 1847.
II. Valentina. III. Teresa-Marguerita.
IV. Henrietta-Sabilla.
V. Alathea-Josephine-Victoria, *d.* 1851.

Lineage.—The family of Aylmer has been long seated in Ireland, and particularly at Lyons, in the county of Kildare, where it occupied for many generations a high station amongst the gentry of that shire.

In the year 1300, we find the two brothers, Radulph and William Aylmer, living at Lyons.

In 1421, RICHARD AYLMER, Esq. of the same place, was one of the keepers of the peace of the counties of Dublin and Kildare, and in 1432, sovereign of the town of Tassagard. From him lineally derived

RICHARD AYLMER, of Lyons, Esq. who was made chief serjeant of the county of Kildare, 1 June, 1535. His descendant,

GEORGE AYLMER, Esq., was (in conjunction with John Wogan, Esq. of Rathcoffey), one of the representatives returned by the co. of Kildare, to the memorable parliament convened to assemble in Dublin, 7 May, 1689, and at the Revolution was comprehended within the Articles of Limerick; he *m.* in 1685, Mary, eldest dau. of Sir Valentine Browne, 1st Viscount Kenmare, and dying 21 Jan. 1729, left (with three daus., of whom the eldest, Jane, *m.* Pierce Bryan, Esq. of Jenkinstown) three sons, of whom the eldest,

GERALD AYLMER, *d.* 10 March, 1729, two months after his father's decease, leaving, by Mary his wife, dau. and coheiress of Michael Moore, of Drogheda, Esq., two sons and two daus., George, who *d.* a minor, in Oct. 1732, Michael, Mary, and Alice. The surviving son and heir,

MICHAEL AYLMER, Esq. of Lyons, *m.* 1st, in 1756, Margaret, only child of George Mathew, of Thomastown, Esq., by whom he had issue, George and Gerald, who both *d.* young; Mary, *m.* in 1783, to Valentine, the late Earl of Kenmare; and Margaret, *m.* in 1788, to Robert Ffrench, of Rahasane, co. Galway, Esq. Mr. Aylmer *m.* 2ndly, 8 June, 1765, Honora, dau. of Matthew Hore, of Shandon, co. Waterford, Esq., and Agbrahane, co. Galway, by whom he had no issue; and 3rdly, in 1770, Mary, dau. of the Hon. Thomas de Burgh, younger brother to Michael, 10th Earl of Clanricarde, and had issue. Mr. Aylmer *d.* at Brussels, in the 80th year of his age, 6 Aug. 1808, and was *s.* by his son and heir,

GERALD AYLMER, Esq., who *m.* in April, 1811, Catherine, eldest dau. of Patrick Lambert, of Carnagh, co. Wexford, Esq. and had,

MICHAEL-VALENTINE, his heir.
Henry, *m.* 28 Feb. 1842, Esmay, only dau. of the late Bryan Brady, Esq. of Stonefield, co. Meath.
Mary-Anne.
Margaret, *m.* 2 July, 1850, to Ambrose Nugent, Esq. of Killasona, co. Longford.
Frances. Georgina, deceased.
Jane-Eliza, *d.* 18 Feb. 1849.
Letitia, *m.* 9 Oct. 1844, to Charles Barnewall, Esq. of Meadstown, co. Meath.

Mr. Aylmer *d.* 9 Jan. 1837, and was *s.* by his elder son and heir, the present MICHAEL-VALENTINE AYLMER, Esq.

Arms—Arg., a cross, sa., between four Cornish choughs, ppr.
Crest—A Cornish chough, rising out of a ducal coronet, all ppr.
Motto—Hallelujah.
Seat—Derry House, Rathcabbin.

AYLMER OF WALWORTH CASTLE.

AYLMER, JOHN-HARRISON, Esq. of Walworth Castle, co. Durham, *b.* 19 Jan. 1812; *s.* his father, General Aylmer, in 1831, *m.* 7 Feb. 1849, Rosanna-Louisa, dau. of Vice-Admiral Sir J. Coghill-Coghill, Bart., and has issue,

I. ARTHUR-FITZGERALD-HARRISON, *b.* 26 Jan. 1850.
II. Herbert-Willoughby-Coghill, *b.* 31 Jan. 1851.

Lineage.—LIEUTENANT-GENERAL ARTHUR AYLMER, (2nd son of Sir Fitzgerald Aylmer, Bart. of Donadea, who derived from a branch of the AYLMERS *of Lyons*), *m.* 9 June, 1807, Anne, only dau. and heiress of John Harrison, Esq. of Walworth Castle, co. Durham, by whom he had issue,

JOHN-HARRISON, present proprietor.
Elizabeth-Margaret, *m.* 5 Jan. 1833, to the Rev. John James Scott, and *d.* 24 July, 1853, leaving two sons and two daus.
Grace-Anna, *m.* 21 Oct. 1828, to the Rev. Charles-Pasley Vivian, of Hatton Hall, Wellingborough, Northamptonshire, and has issue.
Louisa-Lucy-Eleanor. Catherine-Dorothy.
Augusta-Anne, *m.* in 1845, to the Rev. John-Davie Eade, vicar of Aycliffe.

General Aylmer *d.* in 1831.

Arms—Arg., a cross, sa., between four Cornish choughs, ppr.
Crest—A Cornish chough, rising out of a ducal coronet, all ppr.
Motto—Hallelujah.
Seat—Walworth Castle, near Darlington.

AYLWARD OF SHANKILL CASTLE.

AYLWARD, JAMES-KEARNEY, Esq. of Shankill Castle, co. Kilkenny, J.P. and high-sheriff in 1837; *m.* in 1853, Mrs. Newton.

Lineage.—This family is of great antiquity in Ireland, and was settled in the co. of Waterford at a very early period, where, for more than three centuries, it was in the enjoyment of large possessions. The first on record is,

RICHARD AYLWARD, who, by Joan Fitzgerald, his wife, was father of RICHARD AYLWARD, of Faithlecke, or Fathlegg, co. Waterford, who *m.* Catherine, sister to Sir Almare Gras (Baroul de Gras), of Kilkenny, and who was appointed, 16 Jan. 1385, commissioner of the peace for the co. Waterford. From this Richard descended

PETER AYLWARD, who settled at Shankill, co. Kilkenny, son of John Aylward of Fathlegg. He *m.* Elizabeth, eldest dau. and eventual co-heir of Sir Richard Butler, Bart. of Poolestown, co. Kilkenny, and had a son and successor,

NICHOLAS AYLWARD, Esq. of Shankill, M.P. for Thomastown, sheriff of the co. Kilkenny in 1742. He *m.* 5 Aug. 1719, Catherine, 2nd dau. of Maurice Keating, Esq. of Narraghmore, co. Kildare, and *d.* in 1756, leaving two sons, NICHOLAS, his heir, and Peter, who *d. unm.* in 1801, and was interred at Gloucester. The elder son,

NICHOLAS AYLWARD, Esq. of Shankill, high-sheriff in 1757, *m.* Mary, dau. of B. Kearney, Esq., by whom he had issue, PETER, his heir; Nicholas, *d. unm.*; and Catherine. He was *s.* at his death, in 1768, by his eldest son,

PETER AYLWARD, Esq. of Shankill, who *m.* Anne, dau. of — Kearney, Esq. of New Ross, co. Wexford, and *d.* in 1792, having had a son and heir,

NICHOLAS AYLWARD, Esq. of Shankill, who *m.* in 1805, Elizabeth, eldest dau. of James Kearney, Esq. of Blanchville, co. Kilkenny, and had issue, JAMES-KEARNEY, present representative; Nicholas, *d.* young; Peter-Charles; Marianne, *m.* to the Rev. P. Toler, and has issue; Elizabeth, *m.* to the Rev. Clopton-Henry Keogh, and has issue, Susanna-Waller; and Merial.

Arms—Quarterly: 1st and 4th, arg., a fleur-de-lis, az.; in the dexter chief and sinister base a sun in its glory, or; in the sinister chief and dexter base an increscent, of the last, for AYLWARD; 2nd and 3rd, or, a chief, indented, az., for BUTLER *of Poolestown*.

Crest—Out of a ducal coronet, a dexter arm in armour, embowed, couped at the shoulder, ppr., grasping an anchor, az.

Motto—Verus et fidelis semper.

Seat—Shankill Castle, co. Kilkenny.

BABINGTON OF ROTHLEY TEMPLE.

BABINGTON, THOMAS-GISBORNE, Esq., A.M., of Rothley Temple, co. Leicester, *b.* 24 July, 1788; *m.* 27 April, 1814, Augusta-Julia, 4th dau. of Sir Gerard Noel-Noel, Bart. of Exton Park, Rutland, by his 1st wife, Diana, Baroness Barham, and by her (who *d.* 19 June, 1833) has issue,

I. THOMAS-ARTHUR, *b.* 25 Nov. 1820.
II. Charles-Edward, *b.* 23 Feb. 1828.
I. Augusta-Diana, *m.* 9 April, 1839, to Frederic Lewin, Esq., of The Hollies, Kent.
II. Louisa, *m.* at Rothley, 3 Feb. 1842, to the Rev. Francis-C.-P. Reynolds, chaplain to the E. I. C.

Mr. Babington *m.* 2ndly, 18 June, 1841, Augusta-Theresa, dau. of Francis-Gerard Vecqueray, one of the secretaries of state to the King of Prussia for the Grand Duchy of the Rhine, by whom he has a dau.,

I. Julia-Mary.

Mr. Babington, J.P. for Leicestershire, *s.* his father 21 Nov. 1837.

Lineage.—The family of Babington was settled at Babington in Northumberland, *temp.* WILLIAM the Conqueror. The first who is known to have seated in Northumberland, is JOHN DE BABINGTON, Lord of Babington, in the barony of Umfraville, where he resided in the reigns of Kings JOHN and HENRY III.

SIR JOHN BABINGTON, Knt. of East Bridgeford, Notts, (son of Sir John de Babington, chief captain of Morlaix in Brittany, *temp.* EDW. III.) *d.* in 1409, leaving, by Benedicta his wife, dau. and heir of Sir Simon Ward, of the co. Cambridge, five sons, THOMAS, his heir; William (Sir), Knt. of Chilwell, Notts, and Kiddington, Oxfordshire, K.B., chief justice of the Common Pleas; Arnold, a citizen of Norwich; Norman, of East Bridgeford; John, of Aldrington, county Devon. Sir John Babington's eldest son,

THOMAS BABINGTON, Esq., after serving with HENRY V. in the French wars, returned home, and purchased the manor of Kingston, Notts. The sword which he wore at Agincourt is still preserved. He was M.P. for Nottingham in 1459. He *m.* Isabel, dau. and heir of Robert Dethick, of Dethick, in Derbyshire, and by her, who *d.* in 1485, left at his decease in 1464, a son and successor,

SIR JOHN BABINGTON, Knt. of Dethick and Kingston, sheriff of the counties of Derby and Nottingham in 1480, who *m.* Isabel, dau. of Henry Bradburne, Esq. of Bradburne, and The Hough, in Ashbourn; and by her, who *d.* 18 March, 1486, had issue. Sir John Babington was slain at the battle of Bosworth, and *s.* by his son,

THOMAS BABINGTON, Esq. of Dethick, sheriff of Derbyshire and Notts in 1498, who *m.* Editha, dau. of Ralph Fitzherbert, Esq. of Norbury, and dying 13 March, 1518, had issue. From Sir Anthony, the eldest son, descended the BABINGTONS *of Dethick*, of whom was Anthony Babington, attainted in 1586; the 2nd son was Sir John Babington, commander of the preceptory of Dalby and Rothley, co. Leicester; and the 5th son was

HUMFREY BABINGTON, Esq. of Rothley Temple, co. Leicester: he *m.* Eleanor, 3rd dau. and co-heir of John Beaumont, Esq. of Wednesbury, in Staffordshire, grandson of Henry, Lord Beaumont, and dying 22 Nov. 1544, was *s.* by his son,

THOMAS BABINGTON, Esq. of Rothley Temple, and of Cossington, both in Leicestershire: he joined in the fruitless attempt to advance the Lady Jane Grey to the throne, but on payment of a large fine, obtained a pardon under the great seal, in the first year of Queen MARY's reign. He *m.* Eleanor, dau. of Richard Humfrey, Esq. of Barton, in Northamptonshire, and dying 27 Oct. 1567, was *s.* by his son,

HUMFREY BABINGTON, Esq. of Rothley Temple, *b.* in 1544, who *m.* Margaret, dau. of Francis Cave, LL.D. of Baggrave, in Leicestershire, brother to Sir Thomas Cave, of Stanford, and left at his decease (10 June, 1610), a son and successor,

THOMAS BABINGTON, Esq. of Rothley Temple, lord of the manor, and patron of the church, of Cossington, at the decease of his uncle Matthew. He was *b.* in 1575, and *m.* Catherine, only dau. of Henry Kendall, Esq. of Smithesby, in Derbyshire, and dying in 1645, left, with other issue, a son and successor,

MATTHEW BABINGTON, Esq. of Rothley Temple, *b.* 17 May, 1612, M.P. for the co. of Leicester in 1660, who *m.* Anne, youngest dau. of Samson Hopkyns, Esq. of Stoke-by-Coventry, and dying in 1669, was *s.* by his son,

THOMAS BABINGTON, Esq. of Rothley Temple, M.P. for Leicester in 1685 and 1688, and sheriff for the co. in 1677. He was *b.* in 1635, and *m.* 1st, Elizabeth, dau. of William Jesson, Esq. of Coventry, by whom, who *d.* in 1669, he had no surviving child, and 2ndly, Margaret, dau. and co-heir of Henry Hall, Esq. of Gretford, in Lincolnshire, by whom, who *d.* 12 Feb. 1723–4, he left at his decease, 16 April, 1708, a son and heir,

THOMAS BABINGTON, Esq. of Rothley Temple, *bapt.* 10 Oct. 1682, who *m.* in 1711, Elizabeth, dau. of Ralph Keeling, Esq. of London, and by her, who *d.* 30 Jan. 1729–30, left at his decease, 31 July, 1745, with other issue, who *d. unm.*, a son and successor,

THOMAS BABINGTON, Esq. of Rothley Temple, *b.* 26 May, 1715, high-sheriff of Leicestershire in 1750. He *m.* at Wanlip, 9 Jan. 1758, Lydia, dau. of the Rev. Joseph Cardale, A.M., vicar of Hinckley, and by her, who *d.* 4 May, 1791, aged 64, had issue,

I. THOMAS, his heir.
II. Matthew, A.M., fellow of St. John's College, Cambridge, vicar of Rothley, *b.* 24 June, 1761, *m.* in 1787, Elizabeth, only child of Richard-Roberts Drake, Esq. of Leicester, and by her, who *d.* 26 June, 1793, left at his decease, 6 May, 1796, a son and dau.,
   Matthew-Drake, A.M. rural dean of Ackley, in Leicestershire, *b.* 11 July, 1788, *m.* 7 June, 1820, Hannah, dau. of B.-Fleetwood Churchill, Esq. of Northampton, by whom he has a son,
      Churchill, *b.* 11 Mar. 1821, of St. John's College, Cambridge.
   Elizabeth, *m.* in 1829, to Robert Strange, Esq., M.D. of Naples.
III. William, A.B., rector of Cossington, *b.* 11 March, 1763, *m.* in 1787, Elizabeth Newbold, dau. of the Rev. Henry-Lovell Noble, A.M., patron and rector of Frowlesworth, in Leicestershire, and by her, who *d.* 13 Mar. 1832, left at his decease three sons and one dau.,
   1 William, of the E.I.C.C.S., *b.* 10 Dec. 1790, *m.* 12 Jan. 1824, Catharine, dau. of the Rev. Wm. Ravenscroft, prebendary of Rasharkin, and rector of Finvoy, in the co. of Armagh, by whom he has issue,
      William, a midshipman in H.M.S. "Indus," *b.* 1 Feb. 1825.
      George-Matthew, *b.* 13 Feb. 1829.
      Samuel-Henry, *b.* 29 Dec. 1830.
      Henry-Gisborne, *b.* 5 Nov. 1832.
      Gisborne, *b.* 20 March, 1835.
      Alfred, *b.* 30 Dec. 1839.
      Redmond, *b.* 29 Aug. 1842.
      Elizabeth-Ravenscroft. Catharine.
   2 Samuel, of the E.I.C.C.S., *b.* 28 Nov. 1792, *m.* 1st, Martha, dau. of John Dickinson, Esq., of London, who *d.* 31 Jan. 1826; he *m.* 2ndly, Florence, dau. of Thomas Waddy, Esq. of Norton Grange, Yorkshire. By his 1st wife he had issue,
      Samuel-Robert, *b.* 26 Jan. 1826, *d.* in infancy.
      Martha. Jane.
   3 Gisborne, *b.* 7 March, 1812.
   1 Eliza, *m.* 23 Sept. 1834, to Henry-William Ravenscroft, Esq., son of the Rev. W. Ravenscroft, by whom she has issue.
IV. Joseph, M.D. of Ludlow, *b.* 2 Jan. 1768, *m.* Catherine, dau. of John Whitter, Esq. of Bradninch, Devon, and by her, who *d.* 18 Nov. 1833, left at his decease, 16 Dec. 1826, an only son,
   Charles-Cardale, of St. John's College, Cambridge, *b.* 23 Nov. 1808, A.M., F.L.S., and F.G.S.
I. Mary, *m.* 1 March, 1788, to the Rev. Thomas Gisborne, A.M. of Yoxall Lodge, Staffordshire, Prebendary of Durham, by whom she has issue.

Mr. Babington *d.* 20 June, 1776, aged 61, and was *s.* by his son,

THOMAS BABINGTON, Esq. of Rothley Temple, high-sheriff of Leicestershire in 1780, M.P. for Leicester in five successive

Elizabeth-Ursula, *m.* 23 June, 1853, to Henry-St. John, eldest son of Sir Henry Halford, Bart.
Caroline-Anne. Helen-Gertrude. Cecilia-Margaret.

He *d.* 1 June, 1851.

Arms—Per pale, erminois and gu., a bugle stringed between three roses, all counterchanged, barbed, and seeded, ppr. quartering the ensigns of GILL, WESTBY, and DRAKE.
Crest—A dexter cubit arm issuing out of the clouds, the hand, ppr., holding a bugle horn, or, the handle, sa., within the strings a rose, gu.
Motto—Forma, flos; fama, flatus.
Seats—The Oaks, in Norton, near Sheffield; Wormhill Hall, near Buxton.

BAGWELL OF MARLFIELD.

BAGWELL, JOHN, Esq. of Marlfield, co. Tipperary, and of East Grove, co. Cork, J.P. and D.L., high-sheriff of the co. of Tipperary in 1834, *b.* 3 April, 1811; *s.* his uncle, the Right Hon. William Bagwell, M.P., in 1825; *m.* 21 June, 1838, Fanny, youngest dau. of the Hon. F.-A. Prittie, brother of Lord Dunalley, and has issue,

I. RICHARD, *b.* 9 Dec. 1840.
II. William, *b.* 5 March, 1849.
I. Elizabeth. II. Margaret.
III. Emily. IV. Fanny.

Lineage.—WILLIAM BAGWELL, Esq. M.P. for Clonmel (son of John Bagwell, Esq. of Clonmel and Burgagery, banker, and grandson of William Bagwell, Esq. of Ballyloughane, living in 1707, whose father, John Backwell, a captain in CROMWELL'S army, is stated to have been brother of Backwell, the original proprietor of the London bank, now known as Child's), *m.* in 1749, Jane, dau. and co-heir of John Harper, Esq. of Belgrove, co. Cork, and dying in 1756, left, with three daus., a son and heir,

JOHN BAGWELL, Esq., who purchased Marlfield, in the co. of Tipperary. He was M.P. for the co. of Tipperary, and col. of the militia. He *m.* in 1774, Mary, dau. of Richard Hare, Esq. of Ennismore, and sister of William, Earl of Listowel, by whom he had issue (with four daus., Margaret, *m.* to John Kelly, Esq. of Shangally Castle; Jane, *m.* to Lieut.-Gen. Sir Eyre Coote; Catherine, *m.* to John Croker, Esq. of Ballinaguard; and Mary, *m.* to Henry Langley, Esq. of Brettas Castle), two sons, WILLIAM, his heir; and Richard, who *m.* in 1808, Margaret, eldest dau. of Edward Croker, Esq. of Ballinaguard, and had issue, JOHN, successor to his uncle; Edward, an officer in the 3rd dragoon guards; Margaret, *m.* to Joseph Gore, Esq. of Derrymore, co. Clare; Mary, *m.* to George Gough, Esq. of Woodstown, co. Tipperary; and Jane, *m.* to Benjamin B. Frend, Esq. Colonel Bagwell was *s.* at his decease by his eldest son,

THE RIGHT HON. COLONEL WILLIAM BAGWELL, of Marlfield, M.P., a privy councillor and muster-master-general for Ireland, at whose decease, *unm.*, in 1825, the estates devolved on his nephew, the present JOHN BAGWELL, Esq. of Marlfield.

Arms—Paly of six, arg. and az.; on a chief, gu., a lion, passant, arg.
Crest—Out of a mural crown, a demi-bull, all ppr.
Motto—In fide et in bello fortis.
Seats—Marlfield, near Clonmel, and Eastgrove, Queenstown.

BAILEY OF ABERAMAN.

BAILEY, CRAWSHAY, Esq. of Aberaman, co. Glamorgan, J.P. and D.L., elected M.P. for Monmouth in 1852; *m.* Anne, dau. of the late Joseph Moore, Esq. of Mitcham, Surrey. This gentleman, brother of the present Sir Joseph Bailey, Bart. of Glanusk, is son of the late Joseph Bailey, Esq., and nephew of the late Richard Crawshay, Esq. of Cyfartha. He served as sheriff of Brecknockshire in 1837, and of Monmouthshire in 1850.

Arms—Arg., between two bars, three annulets, in fesse gu., all between as many martlets, of the last.
Crest—A griffin, sejant, arg., semée of annulets, gu.
Motto—Libertas.
Seat—Aberaman, near Pontypridd.

BAILLIE OF JERVISWOOD.

BAILLIE, GEORGE, Esq. of Jerviswood, co. Lanark, and Mellerstain, co. Berwick, *b.* 14 April, 1802; *m.* 16 Sept. 1824, Georgina, dau. of the late Archdeacon Robert Markham, and has issue,

I. GEORGE, *b.* 26 July, 1827.
II. Robert, lieut. Rifle brigade, *b.* 8 Oct. 1828.
III. Clifton, *b.* 5 March, 1831.
IV. Henry, R.N., *b.* 20 Aug. 1832.
V. Arthur-Charles, *b.* in 1838.
I. Mary. II. Frances.
III. Georgina-Sophia.

Mr. Baillie *s.* his father, 11 Dec. 1841. He is eldest son of the late George Baillie, Esq. of Jerviswood and Mellerstain, by Mary his wife, youngest dau. of Sir James Pringle, Bart., and grandson of the Hon. George Hamilton (2nd son of Charles, Lord Binning), who assumed the surname of his maternal ancestors, the BAILLIES *of Jerviswood and Mellerstain.* (See BURKE'S *Peerage,* "HADDINGTON.")

Arms—Az., nine stars, three, three, two, and one, or.
Crest—A crescent, or, surmounted of a sun.
Motto—Major virtus quam splendor.
Seat—Mellerstain, co. Berwick.

BAILLIE OF DOCHFOUR.

BAILLIE, EVAN, Esq. of Dochfour, co. Inverness, *m.* in 1823, Lady Georgiana-Frederica Montagu, 4th dau. of William, Duke of Manchester, and has issue.

Lineage.—SIR WILLIAM BAILLIE, of Lamington, by Marian his wife, dau. of Sir John Seton, of Seton, had a numerous issue. The three eldest sons had maimed a clergyman, who had been taken into the house as tutor, for a grievous offence which he had committed in their family, of which injury he died. The power of the church at this time being great in Scotland, the three brothers were obliged to fly.

The eldest settled in Inverness-shire; the second in Ireland: from him springs the family of Inshhaugy. The third went to the isle of Anglesey, and founded the family of which the Marquess of Anglesey is a descendant.

ALEXANDER BAILLIE, the eldest son, fought at the battle of Brechin, and was for his services rewarded with the baronies of Dunain and Torbreck, part of the castle lands of Inverness, in the year 1452. From him derived, fourth in descent,

WILLIAM BAILLIE, of Dunane, who *m.* Catherine, dau. of Robert More Munro, of Fowlis, chief of the clan Munro, and left two sons, ALEXANDER, of Dunain, and John, ancestor of the family of Leys. The elder,

ALEXANDER BAILLIE, Esq. of Dunain, sheriff of the county from 1585 to 1593, *m.* Catherine, dau. of Munro of Miltown, and left two sons, WILLIAM, his heir, of Dunain, ancestor of the BAILLIES *of Dunain*, now represented by WILLIAM BAILLIE, Esq. of that place; and DAVID, ancestor of the family of Dochfour. The second son,

DAVID BAILLIE, 1st of Dochfour, *m.* Margaret, fourth dau. of the Lord Lovat, and was *s.* by his eldest son,

ALEXANDER BAILLIE, of Dochfour, who *m.* in 1709, Hannah, dau. of Fraser of Relig, and left four sons, HUGH, of Dochfour; William, of Rosehall, in Sutherland, father of the late General Sir Ewan Baillie, Bart., and General Charles Baillie; Evan, of Aberiachan; and David. The eldest son,

HUGH BAILLIE, Esq. of Dochfour, *m.* 10 June, 1730, Emilia, dau. of Fraser of Relig, and left, ALEXANDER, his heir, of Dochfour, *d.* in 1798; James; EVAN, of whom presently; Duncan; Catherine, *m.* to Provost Chisholm, of Inverness, younger brother of Chisholm of Chisholm; Isabella, *m.* to Duncan Grant, of Bught; Hannah, *m.* to James Fraser, of Belladrum; Christin, *m.* to Duff of Muirtown. The third son,

EVAN BAILLIE, of Dochfour, *s.* his elder brother, Alexander, in 1798, and becoming an eminent West India merchant at Bristol, was M.P. for that city, and colonel of the Bristol regiment of volunteer infantry. He *m.* Mary, dau. of Peter Gurley, Esq. of the island of St. Vincent, and left three sons,

PETER, of Dochfour.
Hugh-Duncan, of Redcastle, M.P. for Honiton, and lord-lieutenant of the co. Ross.
James-Evan, formerly M.P. for Tralee and Bristol.

The eldest son,

PETER BAILLIE, of Dochfour, M.P., *m.* in 1797, Elizabeth, dau. of John Pinney, Esq. of Somerton, and left,

EVAN, now of Dochfour.
John-Frederick, of Leys, *m.* Annie Baillie, dau. and heiress of Col. John Baillie, of Leys.

Jane, m. to the Hon. and Rev. Baptist-Wriothesley Noel, brother of the Earl of Gainsborough.
Mary, m. 1st, to John Morritt, Esq. of Rokeby; and 2ndly, to Capt. George-St. John Mildmay, R.N.

Arms—Az., nine stars, three, three, two, and one.
Crest—A boar's head, couped.
Motto—Quid clarius astris.
Seat—Dochfour, Inverness.

BAILLIE OF REDCASTLE.

BAILLIE, COL. HUGH-DUNCAN, of Redcastle and Tarradale, co. Ross, *b.* 31 May, 1777; *m.* 1st, 13 Dec. 1796, Elizabeth, dau. of the Rev. Henry Reynett, D.D., and by her has issue,

I. HENRY-JAMES, M.P. for Inverness-shire, *b.* in March, 1803, *m.* 29 Dec. 1840, Philippa-Eliza-Sydney, elder dau. of Percy, present Viscount Strangford.
I. Maria-Ann, *m.* 8 March, 1831, to the Hon. William Ashley, second son of the Earl of Shaftesbury.
II. Augusta-Vesey.
III. Eliza, *m.* to William Brodie, Esq. of Brodie, N.B.

Colonel Baillie *m.* 2ndly, 2 July, 1821, Mary, dau. of Thomas Smith, Esq. of Castleton Hall, and by her has issue,

I. Hugh-Smith. II. Duncan-James.
III. Alfred-William.
I. Frederica-Penelope, *m.* to Philip Perceval, Esq., eldest son of Col. Perceval, of Temple House, co. Sligo.

For lineage, &c., see BAILLIE *of Dochfour*.

Seats—Redcastle, and Tarradale, Ross-shire.

BAILY OF HALL PLACE.

BAILY, THOMAS-FARMER, Esq., of Hall Place, Leigh, co. Kent, *b.* 24 Sept. 1823, is only son and heir (by Amelia Perkins his wife, who *m.* 2ndly, in Sept. 1832, William Smith, Esq. of Sydenham) of FARMER BAILY, Esq., who purchased, in 1821, the estate of Hall Place, in the parish of Leigh, co. Kent, and *d.* in Oct. 1828.

Arms—Or, on a fesse, engrailed, between three nags' heads, erased, az., as many fleurs-de-lis, of the first.
Crest—A goat's head, erased, az., bezantée, attired, or.
Motto—Vestigia nulla retrorsum.
Seat—Hall Place, Leigh, co. Kent.

BAINBRIGGE OF LOCKINGTON.

BAINBRIGGE, THOMAS-PARKER, Esq. of Hill House, Derby, *b.* 6 March, 1791; *m.* 1st, 3 May, 1820, Eliza, dau. of Lieut.-Gen. Sir Dyson Marshall, K.C.B., which lady *d. s. p.* 3 May, 1822. He *m.* 2ndly, 11 May, 1830, Lorina-Anne, dau. of Charles Dashwood, Esq. of Beccles, co. Suffolk. Mr. Bainbrigge *s.* his father 23 Jan. 1842.

Lineage.—This family, of great antiquity in the north of England, came to Lockington about the close of the reign of HENRY VII. "In the year 1583, William Flower Norroy, granted to William Baynbrigge, of Lockington, (descended from the ancient family of the Bainbrigges in the north), a crest to his ancient arms, which were then confirmed."

JOHN BAYNBRIGGE, of Wheatley, co. of York, otherwise called Bainbrigge del North, and afterwards of Leicestershire, had three children, ROBERT, Thomas, and John. From the eldest,

ROBERT BAINBRIGGE, Esq. of Lockington, co. of Leicester (buried 21 Aug. 1572), the sixth in descent was

THOMAS BAINBRIGGE, Esq. of Woodseat and Rocester, *b.* July, 1714, who purchased the manor of Rocester, 1778; built Woodseat, 1767; was sheriff for the co. of Derby in 1760, and proclaimed King GEORGE III. on his accession to the throne. He *m.* Anne, dau. of Isaac Borrow, Esq. of Castlefields, co. of Derby, by his 2nd wife, Honor Burton, who was directly descended from EDWARD III. of England. He *d.* in 1796, and was buried at Rocester, leaving issue, I. THOMAS, *b.* 8th Aug. 1751, sheriff for the co. of Stafford in 1801, *d. unm.* 1818. II. JOSEPH, of whom presently. III. John, of Hales Green, co. Derby, captain in the Derby militia, *d.* 1834, aged 71. IV. Philip, *b.* 1756, lieut.-col., killed commanding the 20th regiment of foot, at the battle of Egmont-op-Zee, in Holland, 6th Oct. 1799, aged 43. He *m.* Rachel, dau. of Peter Dobree, Esq. of Beauregard, in the isle of Guernsey, by whom he left issue, 1 Philip, col. in the army, *b.* in 1786, *m.* in 1816, Sarah-Mary, dau. of Joseph Fletcher, Esq. of Liverpool; 2 John-Hankey, captain in the army, who *m.* his cousin, Sophia, dau. of Bonamy Dobree, Esq. of Guernsey; 3 Peter, who took the name of LE HUNT in 1832; 4 Thomas, an officer in the army, who *m.* Sarah, dau. of — Bate, Esq.; 1 Anne, who *d.* young; 2 Harriet, *m.* to Lieut.-Col. Robert Dale; 3 Honor-Elizabeth; 4 Rachel-Dobree; 5 Anne, *m.* 31 Oct. 1815, to her cousin, Samuel Dobree, Esq. of Walthamstow, and *d.* in the Dec. following. The second son,

JOSEPH BAINBRIGGE, Esq. of Derby, capt. in the Staffordshire militia, *b.* 27 Sept. 1752, *m.* 1st, his cousin Honor, dau. of Philip Gell, M.D. of Wirksworth, co. Derby, who *d. s. p.*, and 2ndly, Miss Hannah Harrison, of Yielderaley, by whom (who *d.* in April, 1841) he had issue,

THOMAS-PARKER, present representative of the family.
William-Henry, now of Liverpool, *b.* in Dec. 1805, to whom his elder brother has given up Woodseat and Rocester: he *m.* 1st, 26 April, 1838, Miss Maria-M. Thompson, of Liverpool, and has issue, Thomas-Parker-Borough, and Anne-Honora. He *m.* 2ndly, 7 June, 1851, Emma, dau. of Joseph Yates, Esq. of Liverpool.
Anne-Elizabeth.
Hannah-Maria-Jane, *m.* 31 Dec. 1835, to the Rev. Wm. Fletcher, D.D.
Mary-Barbara, *m.* 20 Dec. 1838, to William Dixon, Esq., a magistrate for Liverpool.

Mr. Bainbrigge *d.* 23 Jan. 1842.

Arms—1st and 4th, arg., a fesse embattled, between three battle-axes, sa., BAINBRIDGE; 2nd and 3rd, gu., a chevron between three leopards' heads, or.
Crest—A goat, sa., horned and unguled, arg., around his neck a collar of the same, standing on a hill, vert.
Residence—Hill House, Derby.

BAIRD OF CAMBUSDOON.

BAIRD, JAMES, Esq. of Cambusdoon, co. Ayr, *b.* 1803; *m.* in 1852, Charlotte, dau. of Robert Lockhart, Esq. of Castle Hill, co. Lanark. Mr. Baird, who represents the Falkirk district of burghs in parliament since 1851, is son of the late Alexander Baird, of Lockwood (who *d.* in 1833), by Jane Moffat his wife; and brother of William Baird, Esq. of Elie, co. Fife, who sat in parliament for Falkirk from 1841 to 1847; of Douglas Baird, Esq. of Closeburn, co. Dumfries; of George Baird, Esq. of Auchmedden; and of David Baird, Esq. of Urie.

Crest—An eagle's head, erased.
Motto—Dominus fecit.
Seat—Cambusdoon, co. Ayr.

BAKER OF ELEMORE HALL AND CROOK HALL.

BAKER, HENRY-JOHN-BAKER, Esq. of Elemore Hall and Crook Hall, co. Durham, *b.* 29 June, 1822; *m.* Isabella, dau. of R. S. Allgood, Esq. of Nunwick, co. Northumberland. Mr. Baker, an officer in the 4th dragoon guards, eldest son of Henry Tower, Esq., by Isabella his wife and cousin, only child and heiress of George Baker, Esq. of Elemore Hall, Durham, assumed, in 1844, the surname of BAKER only, with the arms of Baker quarterly with Tower, in accordance with the will of his maternal grandfather.

Lineage.—SIR GEORGE BAKER, Knt., recorder of Newcastle-on-Tyne, one of the loyal defenders of that town for King CHARLES, was second son of Oswald Baker, of Durham, by Mary Heron his wife. He purchased, about the year 1635, Crook Hall, in which estate he was *s.* in 1667, by his son,

GEORGE BAKER, Esq. of Crook Hall, father, by Margaret his wife, dau. of Thomas Forster, Esq. of Edderstone, Northumberland, of a son and successor,

GEORGE BAKER, Esq. of Crook Hall, *b.* 1 Aug. 1654, who *m.* Elizabeth, only dau. and heir of Samuel Davison, Esq. of Wingate Grange, co. Durham, and dying in 1699, left an only son,

GEORGE BAKER, Esq. of Crook Hall, M.P. for the city of Durham, who *m.* Elizabeth, only dau. and heiress of Thomas Conyers, Esq. of Elemore, co. Durham, M.P., and *d.* 1 June, 1723, leaving, with a dau. Margaret, wife of

Edward Shipperdson, Esq. of Piddington Hall Garth, a son.

GEORGE BAKER, Esq. of Elemore Hall, who m. Judith, dau. and co-heir of of Cuthbert Routh, Esq. of Dinsdale, co. Durham, and d. in 1774, leaving a dau. Elizabeth, m. to Christopher Tower, Esq. of Weald Hall, Essex, and a son,

GEORGE BAKER, Esq. of Elemore Hall, who m. Isabella, dau. of John Dalton, Esq. of Sleningford, co. York, and had an only dau. and heiress,

ISABELLA BAKER, who m. 15 Feb. 1816, her cousin, Henry Tower, Esq, (*see family of* TOWER *of Weald Hall*), and d. in Nov. 1842, leaving, with other issue, (*see* TOWER), an eldest son, the present HENRY-JOHN BAKER BAKER, Esq. of Elemore.

Arms—Quarterly: 1st and 4th, erm., on a saltire, engrailed, az., a maunch between four escallops, or; on a chief, sa., a lion, passant, of the third, for BAKER; 2nd and 3rd, sa., a tower, or, charged with a peahen, of the field, within a bordure, of the second, charged with ten cross-crosslets, also of the field, for TOWER.

Crests—1st, BAKER, a lion, rampant, arg., charged on the shoulder with a saltier, az., and supporting between the paws a shield of the last, thereon a maunch, or; 2nd, TOWER, a griffin, passant, per pale or and erm., the dexter claw resting on a shield, sa., charged with a tower, as in the arms.

Motto—Love and dread.

Seats—Elemore Hall, and Crook Hall, both co. Durham.

BAKER OF BAYFORDBURY.

BAKER, WILLIAM-ROBERT, Esq. of Bayfordbury, co. Hertford, b. 8 Oct. 1810; m. 4 Oct. 1839, Anna-Emma-Katherine, eldest dau. (by Katherine, his 2nd wife, dau. of the Right Rev. Wm. Magendie, bishop of Bangor) of Henry-Fynes Clinton, Esq., eldest son of the Rev. Chas.-Fynes Clinton, D.D., representative of the Hon. Sir Henry-Fynes Clinton, 3rd son of the 2nd Earl of Lincoln, and by her has a son and heir,

WILLIAM-CLINTON.

Mr. Baker is a magistrate for the county of Hertford, of which shire he was high-sheriff in 1836.

Lineage.—SIR WILLIAM BAKER, Knt. purchased, in 1757, the manor and estate of Bayford; and between the years 1758 and 1762, built the present mansion-house of Bayfordbury, which he surrounded with a park. He m. 19 Jan. 1742, Mary, dau. of Jacob and Mary Tenson, and had six sons and a dau. The eldest son,

WILLIAM BAKER, Esq. of Bayfordbury, co. Herts, M.P. for that county in five successive parliaments, m. 1st, 23 May, 1771, Juliana, eldest dau. of Thomas Penn, of Stoke Pegeis, Esq., by Juliana his wife, dau. of Thomas, 1st Earl of Pomfret, and by her had one dau.,

Juliana.

He m. 2ndly, 7 Oct. 1775, Sophia, third dau. of John and Lady Henrietta Conyers, of Copt Hall, Essex, by whom he had nine sons and six daus., of whom three sons and four daus. still survive. The eldest son,

WILLIAM BAKER, Esq. of Bayfordbury, m. at Palermo, 2 Aug. 1809, Ester, dau. of Robert Fagan, Esq., consul-general of H. B. M. for Sicily and Malta, and had issue,

Edward, d. Oct. 1811.
WILLIAM-ROBERT, now of Bayfordbury.
Mary-Anne-Concordia, d. in 1836.

Arms—Per pale, ermine and gules, a greyhound, courant, between two bars invecked; in chief, two quatrefoils, and another in base, all counterchanged.

Crest—A cockatrice, per fesse, indented, erminois and pean, combed and wattled, gu., gorged with a collar, az., and in the beak a quatrefoil, slipped, vert.

Motto—So run that you may obtain.

Seat—Bayfordbury, co. Herts.

BAKER OF WEST HAY.

BAKER, ROBERT, Esq. of West Hay, co. Somerset, J.P. and D.L., b. 26 Nov. 1786; m. 5 April, 1826, Dorothea, dau. of the Rev. John Wylde, rector of Aldridge-with-Barr, co. Stafford, and has issue,

I. ROBERT-LOWBRIDGE, b. 22 Feb. 1831.
I. Fanny. II. Mary. III. Lucy.
IV. Emily-Dorothea.

Lineage.—JOHN-INNES BAKER, Esq., b. 5 July, 1746 (2nd son of Slade Baker, Esq., by Elizabeth his wife, dau. of Jeremy Innes, Esq. of Redland Court, Bristol, one of the grandsons of Sir Robert Innes, Bart.), m. 9 Dec. 1775, Mary, dau. of Robert Bright, of Brockbury, co. Hereford, Esq., and by her, who d. 13 Feb. 1825, had issue, five sons and five daus. Mr. Baker d. 31 Jan. 1805.

Arms—Az., on a fesse, engrailed, between three swans' necks, erased, or, gorged with ducal coronets, gu., as many cinquefoils, of the last.

Crest—A dexter arm in mail, the under vest seen at the elbow, vert, the hand, ppr., grasping a swan's neck, as in the arms, beaked, gu.

Seat—West Hay, in the parish of Wrington, co. Somerset.

BAKER OF ORSETT HALL.

BAKER, WILLIAM, Esq. of Orsett Hall, Essex, b. in June, 1772; m. 1st, in 1795, Lady Charlotte-Maria Digby, eldest dau. of Henry, 1st Earl of Digby, and by her (who d. in 1807) has issue,

I. GEORGE-DIGBY WINGFIELD, b. in 1796, m. Lucy-Mabella, sister of Lord Portman.
II. John-Digby Wingfield, in holy orders, b. 1798. m. 20 April, 1826, Anne-Eliza, elder dau. of Sir John-Wyldbore Smith, of Sydling, Dorset, Bart., and has,
  1 John-Digby. 2 William-George-Digby.
  3 Richard-Henry.
  1 Lydia-Lucy. 2 Anne-Eliza. 3 Harriet.
III. Richard-Baker Wingfield, b. 1801.
I. Mary, m. to William Gordon, Esq. of Haffield, co. Hereford.
II. Caroline, m. to the late Earl of Cottenham, Lord Chancellor.
III. Frances-Eliza, m. to her cousin, E.-W. Mills, Esq.

Mr. Baker m. 2ndly, 2 June, 1813, Elizabeth, dau. of William Mills, Esq. of Bisterne, co. Hants, and by her has issue,

I. William-Wriothesley-Digby.
II. Charles-John-Wingfield. III. Frederick-Wingfield.
IV. Henry-Wingfield. V. Kenelm-Digby.
I. Julia, m. to J. Fletcher, Esq. II. Lucy.

Mr. Baker is a Queen's counsel, and was formerly one of the masters in ordinary in the court of Chancery, and chief justice of the Brecon circuit in Wales. He assumed the surname of BAKER, in lieu of his patronymic, WINGFIELD, by royal license, 29 Dec. 1849.

Lineage.—WILLIAM WINGFIELD, Esq. of Washington, co. Durham, and Humbleton, co. Northumberland, claiming descent from the WINGFIELDS *of Suffolk*, m. in 1734, Anne, dau. of Sir William Williamson, Bart., of Whitburn Hall, co. Durham, by Elizabeth his wife, dau. of John Hedworth, Esq. of Harraton, and had (besides a dau. ELIZABETH, m. to Sir J. St. Aubyn, of Clowance, co. Cornwall) a son,

GEORGE WINGFIELD, Esq. who m. Mary, dau. of G. Sparrow, Esq., and d. in 1774, having had, besides the present Mr. Baker, of Orsett Hall, another son, George, capt. in the 7th Hussars, who assumed his maternal surname of SPARROW, under the will of his grandfather, on inheriting his estate, and three daus.

Anne, m. to the Rev. T.-H. Hume, canon of Salisbury.
Eliza, m. to J. James, Esq.
Mary, m. to the Rev. John Bassett.

Arms—Quarterly: 1st and 4th, arg., a greyhound, courant, between two bars, sa., for BAKER; 2nd and 3rd, arg., on a bend, gu., between two cotises, sa., three pairs of wings, of the first, for WINGFIELD.

Crests—1st, a cockatrice, erm., combed and wattled, gu., for BAKER; 2ndly, a griffin, passant, vert.

Seat—Orsett Hall, Essex.

BAKER OF HARDWICKE COURT.

BAKER, THOMAS-BARWICK-LLOYD, Esq. of Hardwicke Court, co. Gloucester, b. 14 Nov. 1807; m. 10 March, 1840, Mary, dau. of Nicholas-Lewis Fenwick, Esq. of Besford Court, co. Worcester, by Mary-Anne-Saunders, dau. of Sir John Sebright, Bart., and has issue,

I. GRANVILLE-EDWIN-LLOYD, b. 10 Feb. 1841.
II. Henry-Orde-Lloyd, b. 1 June, 1842.

Lineage.—THE REV. WILLIAM-LLOYD BAKER, late of Stouts Hill, co. Gloucester (son of the Rev. Thomas Baker, vicar of Bibury, co. Gloucester, by Mary his wife, sister of the Rev. John Lloyd, of Ryton), *m.* Mary, dau. of the Rev. John Lloyd, rector of Ryton, in Durham, a descendant of Dr. William Lloyd, Bishop of St. Asaph, Lichfield, Coventry, and Worcester, by whom he had issue, an only son,

THOMAS-JOHN-LLOYD BAKER, Esq. of Hardwicke Court, *b.* 17 May, 1777, *m.* 1st, in May, 1800, Mary, dau. of William Sharpe, Esq., of Fulham, co. Middlesex, and niece of Granville Sharpe, and had issue,

THOMAS-BARWICK-LLOYD, now of Hardwicke Court.
Catherine, *m.* in 1834, to the Rev. Thomas-Murray Browne, vicar of Standish, co. Gloucester.
Mary-Anne-Lloyd, *m.* in 1832, to Col. Benjamin Chapman Browne.

He *m.* 2ndly, in Sept. 1815, Annabella, dau. of the Rev. William Ralfe, rector of Maldon, co. Bedford. Mr. Baker, who was high-sheriff in 1824, *d.* in 1841.

Arms—Az., three swans' heads, erased, arg., gorged with ducal coronets, or.
Crest—A naked dexter arm, ppr., holding a swan's head, erased, arg.
Seat—Hardwicke Court, near Gloucester.

BAKER OF COTTESMORE.

BAKER, RICHARD-WESTBROOK, of Cottesmore and Langham, co. Rutland, Esq., *b.* 4 July, 1797; *m.* 6 Dec. 1820, Ann, dau. of Henry-Hind Brown, Esq., of Melton Mowbray, and has had issue,

I. Richard, *b.* 17 April, 1825; *d.* 22 Oct. 1833.
II. WILLIAM-HENRY, *b.* 16 Aug. 1832.
III. Edward-George, *b.* 13 Nov. 1835.
I. Ann-Catherine, *m.* 9 Nov. 1850, to John Startin, Esq., H.E.I.C.S.
II. Sarah-Jane.

Mr. Baker is a life-governor of the Royal Agricultural Society, and commissioner of land-tax, and was high-sheriff in 1842-3.

Lineage.—In the fifteenth century the Bakers were a family of property in the North, and subsequently, about the year 1650, were resident at and near Ailesbury, Bucks, at which period the greater number of them became the followers of the celebrated George Fox, the Quaker, and with him suffered imprisonment, by order of CROMWELL. Of this, the Ailesbury branch of the family, was

WILLIAM BAKER, M.D., *b.* in 1721, son of Francis Baker, by his wife Mary Burr, of an ancient Hertfordshire family. He *m.* Miss Anne Leete, of Cambridgeshire descent, and had issue,

WILLIAM, *b.* in 1751; *d. unm.* in 1789.
RICHARD, of whom presently.
Ann, *b.* in 1746; *m.* to Robert Jermyn; and dying in 1824, left an only dau., the wife of Samuel James, M.D.

The 2nd son,

RICHARD BAKER, *b.* in 1762, *m.* 1st, Miss Ann Reynolds, by whom he had one son and one dau., viz.,

WILLIAM, captain E.I.C.S., a magistrate, and commissioner of land-tax for the co. of Surrey; *b.* in March, 1789; *m.* and has issue.
Ann.

He *m.* 2ndly, 27 Feb. 1793, Catherine, only dau. of William Richards, M.D., and by her had issue,

Richard-Westbrook, now of Cottesmore and Langham.
Joseph-Francis, lieutenant R.N.; *b.* 31 July, 1798; *m.* and has issue.
Catherine. Sarah-Isabella, *m.* and has issue.

Arms—Erm., on a fesse, invecked, between two greyhounds, courant, sa., a garb, or, between two fleurs-de-lis, arg.
Crest—A greyhound's head, erased, ppr., charged with a fesse, as in the arms, between six ears of wheat, or.
Motto—Non sibi sed patriæ.
Seats—Cottesmore, and Langham, co. Rutland.

BALDWIN OF CLOHINA.

BALDWIN, HERBERT, Esq., M.D. of Clohina, co. Cork, formerly M.P. for the city of Cork, *b.* 24 June, 1782; *m.* 1st, in 1809, Barbara, dau. of Edward Dunne, Esq., M.D. of Tralee, and has by her one surviving dau., viz.,

Mary-Anne, *m.* to John O'Sullivan, Esq. of Bere, in the co. of Cork.

Dr. Baldwin *m.* 2ndly, in 1818, Julia, dau. of Edward Herrick, Esq. of Bellemount, and has a son,

HERBERT-JAMES-HENRY, *b.* 19 April, 1822, *m.* in Nov. 1845, Miss O'Driscoll.

Lineage.—The first of this family who came to Ireland, or, at least, to the south of that kingdom, were two brothers, who settled there in the reign of Queen ELIZABETH; the elder of whom was Ranger of one of the royal parks, and *m.* to the dau. of Herbert of Powis, a house ennobled under that title, and illustrious under those of Pembroke, Montgomery, and Cherbury (*see* BURKE's *Extinct Peerage*). From this alliance the Christian name of Herbert has been transmitted in the family, which has also continued to quarter the arms of Herbert with those of Baldwin. These two brothers purchased property, and fixed their residence in the vicinity of Bandon, in the co. of Cork; the elder at Mossgrove, the younger at Lisnagart. The former left three sons, of whom the 2nd,

HERBERT BALDWIN, Esq. of Currovoldy, *m.* Mary, dau. of Dr. Dives Downes, Bishop of Cork and Ross, and had three sons and two daus., viz., 1 Henry; 2 Herbert; 3 Walter; 1 Mary, *m.* to Col. Foot, of Mallow; and 2 Elizabeth, *m.* to John Ware, Esq. Of the sons, Henry and Walter are the progenitors of several considerable families in the co. of Cork. The 2nd,

HERBERT BALDWIN, Esq., who, inherited the estate of Clohina, under the bequest of his uncle, Col. James Baldwin, *m.* in 1689, Mary, dau. of Col. Hungerford, of The Island, and had issue, 1 JAMES, his heir; 2 Herbert, who *d. s. p.*; and 3 Richard, whose son Richard *m.* Miss Germain, of Affadown. Herbert Baldwin was *s.* at his decease by his eldest son,

JAMES BALDWIN, Esq., who *m.* in 1726, Elizabeth Langton, of Bury, in the co. of Limerick, and left at his decease, in 1776, 1 JAMES, his heir; 2 Herbert, M.D., who *m.* Miss Collis, and had, *inter alios*, a son, Michael, M. D., who *m.* Miss Shea; Anne, *m.* to Mr. Thomas Oliffe, of Cork; and Mary, *m.* to Charles M'Carthy, Esq. The elder son,

JAMES BALDWIN, Esq., *m.* in 1763, Mary, dau. of Daniel O'Connell, Esq. of Derrynane, in the co. of Kerry, and left, at his decease, three sons and five daus., 1 Walter, *d. unm.*; 2 Connell-James, late capt. 50th regiment, now of Toronto, Upper Canada; 3 HERBERT; and five daughters, 1 Eliza, *m.* to Daniel M'Carthy, Esq. of Glenarough; 2 Alice, *m.* to Matthew-Hale-Adderly Minhear, Esq.; 3 Mary-Anne, *m.* to Richard Newton, Esq.; 4 Anne, *m.* to Major Broderick; and 5 Bridget, *m.* to William Hickey, Esq. of Lisbon. Mr. Baldwin's 3rd son is the present DR. HERBERT BALDWIN, of Cork.

Arms—Arg., a chevron, erm., between three oak branches, ppr.
Crest—A dove with the olive branch, ppr.
Motto—Est voluntas Dei.
Seat—Clohina, co. Cork.

BALFOUR OF BALFOUR.

BALFOUR, DAVID, Esq. of Balfour and Trenabie, co. Orkney, D.L., convener of that county, *b.* 14 Oct. 1811; *m.* 12 Dec. 1844, Eleanor-Alder, dau. of Capt. Samuel-Barker Edmeston.

Lineage.—The very ancient family of Balfour, long heritable sheriffs of Fife, derive their name from Balfour Castle in that county, built upon their earliest possessions in Scotland, the vale, or strath, of the Or, a tributary of the Leven. Their first recorded ancestor was SIWARD, probably a Northumbrian, living in the reign of DUNCAN I. His son, OSULF, living *temp.* MALCOLM CEAN-MOHR, was father of SIWARD, "cui dat EDGAR Rex vallem de Or (Strathor) et Macy, pro capite Ottar Dani." He had a son, OCTRED, who founded an altarage to St. Michael for the souls of his father and grandfather, and of his son, MICHAEL DE BALFOR, "qui obiit obses in Angliâ," leaving two sons, between whom Octred de Strathor, their grandfather, divided his lands, viz.,

WILLIAM (Sir) of that ilk, sheriff of Fife, ancestor of the BALFOURS *of Balfour*, extinct in the male line, but represented through the female by the BETHUNES *of Balfour*.
MICHAEL, of whose line we are about to treat.

The 2nd son,

SIR MICHAEL DE BALFOR, Knt., 1st Baron of Strathor, was father of

SIR DAVID DE BALFOR, Knt., of Strathor, "qui ob cruce signatus apud Tunigiam," in 1269. His son and successor,

SIR MICHAEL DE BALFOR, Knt., of Strathor, seneschal of the Earl of Fife, fell in Wallace's defeat at Falkirk, in 1298, leaving a son,

SIR DAVID DE BALFOR, Knt., o Strathor, seneschal of Fife, who sat as a baron in the parliaments of Cambuskonnoth, 1314, and of Ayr, 1315. He *m.* Isabella, dau. of

Macduff of Reres, second son of Malcolm, 8th Earl of Fife, and was *s.* at his decease, in 1318, being then with BRUCE'S army in Ireland, by his son,

SIR MALCOLM DE BALFOR, Knt., of Strathor, seneschal of Fife, who was slain by the English, leaving a son,

SIR MICHAEL DE BALFOR, who was brought up by his kinsman, Duncan, 12th Earl of Fife, who gave, in 1353, "consanguineo suo Michaeli de Balfour," in exchange for Pittencrieff, the much more valuable lands of Munqhanny. The Countess Isabella, dau. of Earl Duncan, also bestowed many grants upon her "cousin" Sir Michael, who *s.* as chief of the family, in 1379, at the decease of Sir John Balfour of Balfour. He was *s.* by his eldest son,

SIR LAURENCE DE BALFOUR, of Strathor and Munqhanny, who, by Marjory his wife, had three sons: the 3rd, John, was of Balgarvey; the 2nd, David, was of Carroldstone; and the eldest,

GEORGE DE BALFOUR, *s.* at his father's decease, to Munqhanny. He had two sons: James, the younger, was of Ballo; the elder, SIR JOHN BALFOUR, fell at the siege of Roxburgh, in 1460, during his father's lifetime, leaving a son and heir,

SIR MICHAEL BALFOUR, 9th baron of Strathor, who *m.* Janet, dau. of Sir Andrew Ogilvy, of Inchmartin, and was father of

MICHAEL BALFOUR, of Munqhanny, an especial favourite of JAMES IV., who, in 1493, erected his lands into a barony, to be called the Barony of Munqhanny. Sir Michael *m.* Marjory, dau. of George Dury of that ilk, and falling at Flodden, was *s.* by his only son,

ANDREW BALFOUR, of Munqhanny, who *m.* Janet, third dau. of Sir Alexander Bruce, of Earlshall, and had seven sons, viz., 1 MICHAEL; 2 Sir Gilbert, of Westra, master of Queen MARY'S household; 3 Sir James, of Pittendriech, who *m.* Margaret, dau. and heiress of Michael Balfour, of Burleigh, and from him descended the Lords Balfour of Burleigh, James, Lord Balfour of Clonawley, &c.; 4 David, ancestor of the BALFOURS *of Grange*; 5 George, Prior Commendator of Charterhouse; 6 Robert, Provost of St. Mary's; and 7 John. The eldest son,

MICHAEL BALFOUR, younger of Munqhanny, *m.* Janet, dau. of Sir David Boswell, of Balmuto, and dying in 1570, was *s.* by his son,

SIR MICHAEL BALFOUR, of Munqhanny, who removed, in 1588, to Noltland Castle, in the island of Westra, in Orkney, which he inherited from his cousin-german, Archibald Balfour, of Westra. He *m.* Mariota Adamson, dau. of Patrick, Archbishop of St. Andrew's, and had two sons; the elder, Sir Andrew, of Strathor and Munqhanny, *m.* in 1589, Mary, dau. of Sir James Melville, of Halhill, but *d. s. p.* The younger.

MICHAEL BALFOUR, of Garth, *m.* in 1598, Margaret, dau. of Malcolm Sinclair, of Quendal, Arch-dean of Zetland, and was *s.* by his eldest son,

PATRICK BALFOUR, of Pharay, *m.* a stanch royalist, and severe sufferer in the cause, who *m.* Barbara, dau. of Francis Mudy, of Breckness, and was *s.* at his decease, in 1664, by his elder son,

GEORGE BALFOUR, of Pharay, *m.* 1st, in 1657, Marjory, dau. of James Baikie, Esq. of Tankerness, and his only surviving son by that lady, WILLIAM, of Pharay, left an only child, Isabel, wife of Archibald Stewart, of Brough. He *m.* 2ndly, in 1678, Mary Mackenzie, only dau. of Murdoch, Bishop of Orkney, and dying in 1706, left, by her several sons, of whom the eldest,

JOHN BALFOUR, of Trenaby, *s.* to a portion of his father's estates, and on the death of his half-brother William, became chief of the family. He *m.* Elizabeth, dau. of Thomas Traill, of Skaill, and had five sons and one dau.; WILLIAM, his heir; Thomas, of Huip; Archibald; John, M.D.; Robert; and Mary, *m.* to John Traill, of Westness. He *d.* in 1741, and was *s.* by his eldest son,

WILLIAM BALFOUR, of Trenaby, *b.* in 1719, who *m.* 9 Feb. 1744, Elizabeth Coventry, heiress of Newark, dau. of the Rev. Thomas Coventry, and had (with three daus., Elizabeth, *m.* in 1787, to William Manson, Esq.; Margaret, who *d. unm.*; Catherine, who *d. unm.*; and Mary, *m.* to Capt. George Craigie,) three sons, viz.,

I. JOHN, his heir.
II. Thomas, of Elwick, a col. in the army; *b.* 3 Feb. 1752; and *d.* at Bath in 1799. He *m.* in 1776, Frances Ligonier, niece of Field-Marshal John, Earl Ligonier, commander-in-chief of the British forces, and only sister of Edward, 2nd Earl Ligonier, by whom he had, John-Edward-Ligonier, capt. in the 9th foot, *b.* 11 Jan. 1780, killed at Alkmaar, 19 Sept. 1799; WILLIAM, of Elwick, present representative of the family; and Mary, *m.* to the Rev. Alexander Brunton, D.D.
III. David, *b.* 8 Nov. 1754; *m.* Marion, dau. of George M'Intosh, Esq. of Dunchattan; and *d.* 25 May, 1813, leaving issue, William, late lieut.-col. of the 82nd regt., *m.* and has issue; and Mary, *m.* to Godfrey Meynell, Esq. of Langley Meynell.

Mr. Balfour *d.* in Oct. 1786, and was *s.* by his eldest son,

JOHN BALFOUR, Esq. of Trenaby, *b.* in 1750, M.P. for the co. of Orkney, who *m.* 1783, Henrietta, sister of Sir Richard Sullivan, Bart., but dying *s. p.* in 1842, was *s.* by his nephew,

WILLIAM BALFOUR, Esq. of Trenaby, capt. R.N., and vice-lieutenant of Orkney, *b.* 8 Dec. 1781, *m.* 1st, in 1806, his cousin, Mary-Balfour, only child of William Manson, Esq. of Kirkwall, and by her, who *d.* in 1820, had issue,

THOMAS, late M.P. for Orkney; *b.* 2 April, 1810; *d.* in 1838, *unm.*
DAVID, now of Trenabie and Balfour.
William, late lieut. 79th Highlanders; *b.* 19 Aug. 1818; *m.* Jessy-Alexina, dau. of the Rev. Thomas Steele.
George-Craigie, *b.* 18 Feb. 1818; *m.* and has issue.
James-Traill, *d.* in 1826.
Mary-Henrietta, *m.* to James Kinnear, Esq. of Edinburgh, and has issue.
Elizabeth, *d. unm.* in 1823.

Capt. Balfour *m.* 2ndly, in 1823, Mary-Margaret, dau. of Andrew Baikie, Esq., and has, by her, two sons, James-William, 7th dragoon-guards, *b.* in 1827, *m.* Isabella, dau. of Col. Craster, and Edward, *b.* in 1831, and five daus., Margaret-Craigie, Frances-Ligonier, Isabella-Traill, Janet-Edmestone, and Harriett. Capt. Balfour *d.* 10 Feb. 1846.

Arms—Arg., on a chevron, *sa.*, an otter's head, erased, of the first.
Crest—A dexter arm, ppr., couped at the elbow, holding a baton, arg.
Motto—Forward. (Supposed to refer to the tenure of the wardenship of the Forth, held by the Balfours as proprietors of the Isle of May at the mouth of the Firth of Forth.)
Seats—Balfour Castle, and Noltland Castle, co. Orkney.

BALFOUR OF BALBIRNIE.

BALFOUR, JOHN, Esq. of Balbirnie, co. Fife, *b.* 23 April, 1811; *m.* 25 June, 1840, Lady Georgiana-Isabella Campbell, 2nd dau. of the Earl of Cawdor, and has issue,

I. ROBERT-FREDERICK, *b.* 30 April, 1846.
II. Edward, *b.* 23 Jan. 1849.
III. John-William, *b.* 20 Aug. 1850.
I. Emily-Eglantine.
II. Georgiana-Elizabeth.
III. Mary-Louisa.

Lineage.—The late Lieut.-Gen. ROBERT BALFOUR, of Balbirnie, co. Fife, son of John Balfour, Esq., by Mary-Ellen his wife, was descended from the ancient family of Balfour. He *m.* 8 Aug. 1808, Eglantine-Katherine Fordyce, and by her (who *d.* 9 Jan. 1852) had issue,

JOHN, now of Balbirnie.
Charles-James, commander R.N.; *m.* 16 May, 1850, Frances-Harriet, dau. of Rear-Admiral Wemyss, of Wemyss Castle, co. Fife.
Robert-William, major 88th regt.
George-Gordon, H.E.I.C.S.; *m.* Julia Lamb.
Mary-Georgiana.
Katherine-Jane, *m.* to Edward Ellice, Esq., M.P., son of the Right Hon. Edward Ellice.
Eglantine-Charlotte-Louisa, *m.* to Robert Ellice, Esq., son of Gen Ellice.
Elizabeth-Anne, *m.* 1 Nov. 1842, to the Hon. Edward-Pleydell Bouverie, 2nd son of the Earl of Radnor.

General Balfour *d.* 31 Oct. 1837.

Arms—Arg., on a chevron, engrailed, between three mullets, *sa.*, a sealch's head, erased, of the first.
Crest—A palm-tree, ppr.
Motto—Virtus ad æthera tendit.
Seat—Balbirnie, Markinch, Fife.

BALFOUR OF WHITTINGHAME.

BALFOUR, JAMES MAITLAND, Esq. of Whittinghame, East Lothian, and Strathconan, co. Ross, *b.* 5 Jan. 1820; *m.* 15 Aug. 1843, Lady Blanche-Gascoyne-Cecil, 2nd dau. of James, 2nd Marquess of Salisbury, and has issue,

I. ARTHUR-JAMES, *b.* 24 July, 1848.
II. Cecil-Charles, *b.* 22 Oct. 1849.
III. Francis-Maitland, *b.* 11 Nov. 1851.
IV. Gerald-William, *b.* 9 April, 1853.
I. Eleanor-Mildred.

II. Evelyn-Georgiana-Mary.
III. Alice-Blanche.

Mr. Balfour is son of the late James Balfour, Esq. (who d. in April, 1845), by the Lady Eleanor Maitland his wife, dau. of James, 8th Earl of Lauderdale, which James Balfour was a younger son of John Balfour, Esq. of Balbirnie, co. Fife. The present Mr. Balfour of Whittinghame has one brother and two sisters, viz., Charles, of Balgonie and Newton Don, co. Berwick; Mary, m. to Henry-Arthur Herbert, Esq. of Muckross, co. Kerry; and Anna, m. to Lord Augustus-Charles-Lennox Fitzroy, 2nd son of Henry, 5th Duke of Grafton.

Arms—Arg., on a chevron, engrailed, between three mullets, sa., a seaich's head, erased, of the first.
Crest—A palm-tree, ppr.
Motto—Virtus ad æthera tendit.
Seats—Whittinghame, co. East Lothian; and Strathconan, co. Ross.

BALFOUR OF TOWNLEY HALL.

BALFOUR, BLAYNEY-TOWNLEY, Esq. of Townley Hall, co. Louth, J.P. and D.L., b. 28 May, 1769; m. 17 Oct. 1797, Lady Florence Cole, dau. of William Willoughby, 1st Earl of Enniskillen, and has issue,

I. BLAYNEY-TOWNLEY, b. 1799, formerly lieut.-gov. of the Bahama Islands, m. Elizabeth-Catherine, dau. and heir of Richard-Molesworth Reynell, Esq. of Reynella, co. Westmeath, and has two sons.
II. Willoughby-William-Townley, b. 1801, in holy orders.
III. Francis-Leigh, b. in 1805, d. at Honduras, in 1833.
IV. Arthur-Lowry-Townley, b. in 1809, major in the army, d. in India.
V. Lowry-Vesey-Townley, secretary of the Order of St. Patrick, b. in 1819.
I. Anne-Mary-Townley.
II. Letitia-Frances-Townley.
III. Florence-Henrietta-Townley.
IV. Elizabeth-Sarah-Townley, d. 1838, unm.

Mr. Balfour, who s. his grandfather, Blayney-Townley Balfour, Esq., in 1788, was formerly member in the Irish parliament in 1797-8, for the borough of Belturbet; he served the office of high-sheriff for Louth in 1792.

Lineage.—The Balfours of whom we are treating are a younger branch of the BALFOURS *of Burleigh*, in Scotland, and and were established by Sir William Balfour, who purchased property in the co. of Fermanagh, from Lord Balfour of Clonawley. The Townleys spring from a scion of the ancient stock of TOWNLEY *of Townley Hall*, in Lancashire. Their representative,

BLAYNEY TOWNLEY, Esq. assumed the surname of BALFOUR on the death of his nephew, William Balfour, Esq., whom he succeeded. He m. his cousin, Mary Townley, heiress of Hamilton Townley, of Townley Hall, Esq., and relict of — Tennison, Esq., by whom he left an only son,

BLAYNEY TOWNLEY, b. in 1743; who m. 20 Feb. 1768, Letitia, dau. of Francis Leigh, Esq., M.P. for Drogheda, by Anne his wife, dau. of Henry Bingham, Esq. of Newbrook, co. Mayo, and predeceasing his father, left issue,

BLAYNEY-TOWNLEY, successor to his grandfather.

ANNA-MARIA, m. in 1796, to the late Rev. Thomas-Vesey Dawson, dean of Clanmorris, and nephew to Thomas, 1st Lord Cremorne. He d. s. p. in 1820.

Mr. Balfour d. at the age of 84, in 1788, and was s. by his grandson, (having survived his only son), BLAYNEY-TOWNLEY BALFOUR, Esq. of Townley Hall.

Arms—Quarterly: 1st and 4th, arg., on a chevron, sa., an otter's head, erased, of the first; 2nd and 3rd, arg., a fesse, sa.; in chief, three mullets of the 2nd, for TOWNLEY.
Crests—1st, a lady standing on a rock, holding in her right hand an otter's head, and in her left a swan's head; 2nd, on a perch, or, a hawk close, ppr., beaked and belled, of the first, round the perch a ribbon, gu.
Supporters—Dexter, an otter; sinister, a swan, both ppr.
Motto—Omne solum forti patria.
Seat—Townley Hall, near Drogheda, co. Louth.

BALGUY OF DUFFIELD.

BALGUY, JOHN, Esq. of Duffield, co. Derby, Q.C., Recorder of Derby, J.P. and D.L., b. 14 Sept. 1782; m. 1 May, 1819, Barbara, eldest dau. of the Rev. John-Francis-Seymour-Fleming St. John, one of the prebendaries of Worcester Cathedral, and relict of John Baker, Esq. of Waresley House, co. Worcester, and has issue,

I. JOHN, barrister-at-law, b. 16 Dec. 1821.
II. Henry, capt. 4th or King's Own regt., b. 23 Aug. 1823.
III. Charles-Yelverton, capt. 42nd Highlanders, b. 20 Aug. 1827.
IV. Francis-St. John, b. 7 Jan. 1832.
I. Barbara-Elizabeth, m. in 1852, to F. G. O'Reilly, Esq.
II. Caroline-Amy.

Lineage.—The Balguys have been seated in Derbyshire for twenty generations, and are described as a branch of the BAGULEYS *of Baguley*, in Cheshire. The estate of Darwent Hall, sold by the late John Balguy, Esq., had been held by the family for several hundred years, and was the remnant of large possessions in the High Peak, formerly belonging to them. JOHN BALGUY, who served the office of high-sheriff for Derbyshire three or four years after the Restoration. is described as of Darwent Hall. In 1594, Thomas Balguy was member for Stamford, in Lincolnshire, and recorder of that borough. To the latter office John Balguy was elected in 1623, and his son, of the same name, in 1649. The late representative of the family,

JOHN BALGUY, Esq. of Darwent Hall and Duffield, co. Derby, recorder of Derby, chairman of the quarter sessions for that county, and one of his majesty's judges upon the Carmarthen circuit, m. in Sept. 1781, Elizabeth, youngest dau. of Edward Gould, Esq. of Mansfield Woodhouse, co. Notts, by whom, who d. 8 Dec. 1821, he had (with three daus., Mary; Elizabeth, wife of Cockshutt Heathcote, Esq.; and Charlotte) three surviving sons, viz., JOHN, now of Duffield; Bryan-Thomas, town-clerk of Derby; and Charles-George, registrar of the archdeaconry of Nottingham. Mr. Balguy d. 14 Sept. 1833.

Arms—Or, three lozenges, az.
Crest—A bear, passant, ppr., collared and chained, or.
Seat—Duffield, co. Derby.

BALLANTYNE OF HOLYLEE.

BALLANTYNE, JAMES, Esq. of Holylee, Scotland, b. 22 May, 1789; m. 17 Aug. 1821, Anne, dau. of Andrew Henderson, Esq. of Midgehope, and has issue,

I. JAMES-GEORGE, b. 28 May, 1837.
I. Helen-Turnbull. II. Elizabeth-Burnet.
III. Ann-Williams.

Mr. Ballantyne is son of Thomas Ballantyne, Esq., by Elizabeth Burnet his wife; and grandson of George Ballantyne and Katharine his wife.

Arms—Arg., on a cross, az., between four mullets, gu., a crescent, or.
Crest—A demi-griffin, holding in the dexter claw a sword, erect, ppr.
Motto—Nec cito, nec tarde.
Seat—Holylee, N.B.

BAND OF WOOKEY HOUSE.

BAND, EDWARD-WRIGHT, Esq. of Wookey House, co. Somerset, J.P., b. 23 April, 1779; m. 9 June, 1800, Sarah-Elizabeth, eldest dau. and co-heir (with his sister, Mary, m. to the Rev. Lewis Way) of the Rev. Herman Drewe, rector of Combe-Raleigh, in Devon, 7th son of Francis Drewe, Esq. of Broadhembury Grange, by his first wife, Mary, dau. and heiress of Thomas Rose, Esq. of Wotton-Fitspain, Dorsetshire, and has issue,

I. CHARLES-EDWARD, of St. John's College, Cambridge, in holy orders, rector of Combe Raleigh, in Devonshire, m. 1st, 4th June, 1827, Henrietta-Mary-Bourke, eldest dau. of the Rev. Henry Fellowes, vicar of Sidbury, and by her, who d. 5 Jan. 1841, has issue. He m. 2ndly, Harriott-Louisa, dau. of the Rev. John Bond, rector of Freston, co. Suffolk.
I. Elizabeth-Drewe, m. 8 May, 1833, to Pierce-Rogers Nesbit, M.D., and d. in 1835.
II. Hermana-Drewe. III. Mary-Rose.
IV. Dorothea-Penruddocke, d. unm.
V. Wright-Drewe.

Lineage.—John Band, Esq. of Wookey House, (whose mother was a Miss Wright, of the family of that name, near Andover, Hants), for many years an acting magistrate, and deputy-lieut. for Somersetshire, served the office of high-sheriff for that co. in 1801. He *m.* and had issue,

Edward-Wright, now of Wookey House.
Martha, *m.* to Charles Penruddocke, Esq.

Arms—Gu., three eagles, displayed, or; on a chief, three leopards' heads.
Crest—An eagle, or.
Motto—Dieu est mon aide.
Seat—Wookey House, Somersetshire.

BANKES OF KINGSTON HALL.

Bankes, William-John, Esq., M.A., of Kingston Hall, co. Dorset, and of Soughton Hall, in Flintshire, *s.* his father in 1834; formerly M.P. for the University of Cambridge, and afterwards for Dorsetshire.

Lineage.—Sir John Bankes, constituted lord chief justice of the Common Pleas in 1640, (the son of John Bankes, a merchant, by his wife Elizabeth Hassel), had been in the celebrated cause instituted in the Exchequer against the patriot Hampden, for his refusal to pay the arbitrary imposition of ship-money. By his wife Mary, (the gallant defender of Corfe Castle for King Charles), only dau. of Robert Hawtrey, Esq. of Riselip, Sir John Bankes left at his decease in 1644, a son and successor,

Sir Ralph Bankes, of Corfe Castle, Knt., who *m.* Mary, only dau. and heir of John Bruen, Esq., of Athelhampton, and had, with a dau. Mary, who *d. unm.*, an only son, John, his heir. Sir Ralph dying about the year 1679, was *s.* by his son,

John Bankes, Esq. of Kingston Ball, M.P. for Corfe Castle, who *m.* Margaret, dau. of Sir Henry Parker, by whom (who *m.* 2ndly, Thomas Lewis, Esq. of London), he had, with other children, who died issueless, two sons, John and Henry, and a dau. Mary, *m.* to Sir Thomas l'Anson, Bart. He *d.* in 1714,, and was *s.* by his elder son,

John Bankes, Esq. of Kingston Hall, M.P. who dying issueless, in 1772, was *s.* by his brother,

Henry Bankes, Esq. of Kingston Hall, barrister-at-law, king's counsel, M.P. for Corfe Castle, and one of the commissioners of the customs. He *m*, 1st, Eleanor, dau. of Richard Symonds, Esq. of London, and 2ndly, Margaret, dau. of the Right Rev. John Wynne, D.D., Bishop of Bath and Wells, and co-heir of her brother, the Right Hon. Sir W. Wynne, Knt., chief judge of the Prerogative Court and dean of the Arches. By the first lady, he had no issue. By the second he had a son, Henry, his heir, and a dau. Anne. Mr. Bankes *d.* in 1776, and was *s.* by his only surviving son,

Henry Bankes, Esq. of Kingston Hall, M.P. for Corfe Castle from 1780 to 1826, and for the co. of Dorset from that time until 1831. Mr. Bankes *m.* in 1784, Frances, dau. of William Woodley, Esq., governor of the Leeward Islands, and had (with two daus., Anne-Frances, *m.* to Edward, Earl of Falmouth; and Maria-Wynne, *m.* to the Hon. Thomas Stapleton) four sons, viz,

i. Henry, lost at sea in 1806.
ii. William-John, now of Kingston Hall.
iii. George, of Studland, in the Isle of Purbeck, Cursitor Baron, M.P. for co. Dorset. He *m.* Georgina-Charlotte, dau. and heir of Sir Charles-Edmund Nugent, Knt., G.C.H., and Admiral of the Fleet, and has had issue,
  1 Edmund-George, *b.* 24 April, 1826.
  2 Henry-Hyde-Nugent, *b.* 10 April, 1828.
  3 Edward-Dee, *b.* 12 Jan. 1830; *d.* 24 June, 1844.
  4 Frederick-Wynne, *b.* 15 April, 1834; *d.* 22 June, 1836.
  5 William-George-Howbrey, *b.* 11 Sept. 1835.
  6 Wynne-Albert, *b.* 31 May, 1840.
  1 Georgina-Charlotte-Frances, *m.* 20 Feb. 1844, to John Floyer, Esq. of West Stafford, co. Dorset.
  2 Mary-Margaret, *d.* 23 May, 1836.
  3 Adelaide.
  4 Augusta-Anne, } twins.
  5 Octavia-Elizabeth, }
iv. Edward, rector of Corfe Castle, prebendary of Gloucester; who *m.* 1st, in 1820, Lady Frances-Jane Scott, dau. of John, Earl of Eldon, by whom he has issue, John-Scott, Eldon-Surtees, and Frances; and 2ndly, in 1839, Maria, 3rd dau. of the Hon. and Very Rev. Edward Rice, D.D.

Mr. Bankes *d.* 17 Dec. 1834.

Arms—Sa., a cross, engrailed, erm., between four fleurs-de-lis, or; quartering Bruen, Martin, Pydel, Wynne, and Jones.

Crest—A Moor's head, full faced, couped at the shoulders, ppr., on the head a cap of maintenance, gu., turned up, erm., adorned with a crescent, whence issues a fleur-de-lis.
Seat—Kingston Lucy, Dorsetshire.

BANKES OF WINSTANLEY HALL.

Bankes, Meyrick, Esq. of Winstanley Hall and Up-Holland House, Lancashire, *b.* 22 Nov. 1811.

Lineage.—Simon Bankes, the first of this family on record, *m.* in 1335, the dau. and heiress of Katherton of Bank Newton, in Craven, Yorkshire, and acquired, *jure uxoris*, the manor of Bank Newton, which remained in the Bankes' family till sold by the elder branch, about the middle of the seventeenth century. to Nicholas Townley, Esq. of Royle. The last male heir of the Bankes's *of Winstanley Hall*, who were the second branch of the stock,

William Bankes, Esq. of Winstanley Hall, high-sheriff of Lancashire in 1784; *m.* Mary-Anne, dau. of Joseph Bunney, Esq. of Leicester, and *d. s. p.* in 1800, when the male line of the Bankes family became extinct; but Mr. Bankes bequeathed his property to his first-cousin and nearest heir,

The Rev. Thomas Holme,* of Up-Holland House, and then of Winstanley Hall, the son of Anne-Bankes, the first-cousin of the testator. He was *b.* in 1732, and *m.* Mary, dau. of Richard Meyrick, Esq., fourth son of Owen Meyrick, Esq of Bodorgan, co. Angleses, and by her left issue,

i. Meyrick, his heir.
ii. Frederick-William, in holy orders, B.D.; *b.* 12 Jan. 1772, fellow of Corpus Christi College, Oxford, and afterwards rector of Meysey Hampton, co. Gloucester; *m.* 1st, May, 1811, Mary-Elizabeth, eldest dau. of Thomas Pigot, Esq. of Almington Hall, Staffordshire, and left issue,
  1 Frederick, *b.* 10 June, 1812; M.A. and F.Z.S., fellow of Corpus Christi College, Oxford; *d. unm.*
  2 Meyrick, in holy orders; *b.* 18 April, 1815; B.A. of Brazennose College, Oxford.
  1 Mary-Elizabeth, *m.* to the Rev. Mr. Lee.
  2 Jane, *m.* in 1842, to Henry-Leigh Trafford, Esq.
iii. Cholmondeley, *b.* 23 Jan. 1779; *d.* 12 Aug. 1793.
i. Jane, *m.* Lieut.-Col. Burgh Leighton; who *d.* in 1836, *s. p.*
ii. Anne, *m.* the Rev. G. Borlase, who *d.* in 1809, *s. p.*
iii. Mary-Meyrick, *d. unm.* in 1834, buried at Up-Holland.
iv. Harriet.

He *m.* 2ndly, in 1800, Miss Anne Leighton, sister of Sir Baldwin Leighton, Bart., but by her (who survived him and *d.* his widow in 1820) he had no issue. Mr. Holme *d.* at Winstanley, 17 Aug. 1808, and was *s.* by his third, but eldest surviving son,

Meyrick Holme, Esq. of Winstanley Hall, who took the name and arms of Bankes only, in 1804; *b.* 12 Aug. 1768, served the office of high-sheriff of Lancashire in 1895. He *m.* 1st, his first-cousin, Catherine, dau. of the Rev. Edward Lally, vicar of Whitegate, Cheshire, by whom he had issue an only son, who *d.* an infant. He *m.* 2ndly, in 1810, Maria-Elizabeth, eldest dau. of Thomas Langford-Brooke, Esq. of Mere Hall, Cheshire. Mr. Bankes *d.* 1 March, 1827, and was *s.* by his only surviving son, the present Meyrick Bankes, Esq. now of Winstanley Hall.

Arms—Sa., a plain cross, or, between four fleurs-de-lis, arg., and a canton of the second.
Crest—On a stump of a tree, a stork, statant, ppr., ducally gorged, gu.
Seat—Winstanley Hall, near Wigan.

BARCLAY-ALLARDICE OF ALLARDICE.

Barclay-Allardice, Robert, Esq. of Urie and Allardice, co. Kincardine, *b.* 19 May, 1841; *s.* his grandfather in 1854.

Lineage.—This family claims descent from the Berkeleys *of Berkeley Castle.*

David Barclay, *b.* in 1610, colonel under Gustavus Adolphus, purchased, in 1648, the estate of Urie, from William,

---

* The family of Holme has been seated in Lancashire, in different branches, from a period shortly subsequent to the Norman conquest. The surname, which was originally and properly spelt Hulme, is local, and derived from the manor of that name between Trafford and Manchester, formerly possessed by the family.

In the third volume of Holinshed's *Chronicle*, among the Norman gentlemen attending William the Conqueror, is mentioned the "Seigneur de Hulme," but whether he was the father of Ranulph or Randulphus, who was possessed of Hulme about the end of the 11th century, is not clearly ascertained.

Earl-Mariechal. He was eldest son of David Barclay, of Mathers, the representative of the old house of BARCLAY *of Mathers*. He *m.* Katharine, dau. of of Sir Robert Gordon, of Gordonstoun, and had, with two daus., Lucy and Jean, *m.* to Sir Ewen Cameron, of Lochiel, three sons, ROBERT, his heir; John, who settled in America, and left issue; and David; the eldest,

ROBERT BARCLAY, of Urie, the celebrated apologist of the Quakers, *b.* in 1648, *m.* Christian, dau. of Gilbert Molleson, of the MOLLESONS *of Aberdeenshire*, and had, with four daus. (Patience, *m.* to Timothy Forbes, of Dublin, merchant; Katharine, *m.* to Alexander Forbes, brother of Timothy; Christian, *m.* to Alexander Jaffray, of King's Wells; and Jean, *m.* to Alexander Forbes) three sons, ROBERT, his heir; David, of London, from whom descend the BARCLAYS *of Bury Hill*, &c. (*see that family*); John, who settled in Dublin, and married there, Anne, dau. of Amos Strettell, by whom he had issue. The eldest son,

ROBERT BARCLAY, Esq. of Urie, *b.* in 1672, *m.* Elizabeth, dau of John O'Brien, Esq, and had, with three daus., two sons, ROBERT, his heir; and David, who *m.* Mary, dau. of John Pardoe, Esq. of Worcester, but *d. s. p. m.* The elder son,

ROBERT BARCLAY, Esq. of Urie, *b.* in 1699, *m.* Une, dau. of Sir Ewen Cameron, of Lochiel, and had three sons, ROBERT, his heir; Evan, who *d. s. p.*; and Alexander, who *d. s. p.* The eldest son,

ROBERT BARCLAY, Esq. of Urie, *b.* in 1731–2, M.P. for Kincardineshire, *m.* 1st, Lucy, dau. of David Barclay, Esq., by whom he had a dau, Lucy, *m.* to Samuel Galton, Esq. of Duddeston House, co. Warwick; and 2ndly, SARAH-ANNE ALLARDICE, only dau. of James Allardice, of Allardice, heiress of line of the Earls of Airth and Menteith, by whom he had,

- ROBERT, his heir.
- James, *d.* at Madras, in 1804, *unm.*
- David-Stuart, *d. unm.*
- Une-Cameron, *m.* to John Innes, Esq. of Cowie.
- Margaret, *m.* in 1809, to Hudson Gurney, Esq. of Keswick.
- Rodney.

Mr. Barclay *d.* in 1797, and was *s.* by his son,

ROBERT BARCLAY-ALLARDICE, Esq. of Urie and Allardice, *b.* 25 Aug. 1779, who *m.* in 1819, Mary Dalgarno, and had an only child,

- MARGARET, who *m.* 2 April, 1840, Samuel Ritchie, and has a son and heir, ROBERT BARCLAY-ALLARDICE, now of Allardice.

Mr. Barclay-Allardice being general and of line of William, 1st Earl of Airth, as such claimed the Earldoms of Strathern, Menteith, and Airth. He was sole heir of the body of Prince David, son of ROBERT II. King of Scotland.

Arms of BARCLAY—Az., a chevron, and in chief, three crosses-patée, arg.
Crest of BARCLAY—A mitre.
Supporters of BARCLAY—Two old men, with clubs, ppr.
Motto—In cruce spero.

Arms of ALLARDICE—Arg., a fesse wavy, gu., between three boars' heads, erased, sa.; quartering GRAHAM, Earls of Monteith and Airth, and the Royal Arms of Scotland differenced by a label, arg.
Crest of ALLARDICE—A naked arm from the middle, holding in the dexter hand a scimitar, all ppr.
Motto of ALLARDICE—In the defence of the distressed.
Supporters of ALLARDICE—Dexter, an eagle; sinister, a bear, both ppr.

BARCLAY OF BURY HILL.

BARCLAY, CHARLES, Esq. of Bury Hill, co. Surrey, late M.P. for that shire, *b.* in 1780; *m.* Anna-Maria, dau. of Thomas Kett, Esq. of Seething, co. Norfolk, and has issue,

- I. ARTHUR-KETT, *b.* in 1806, who *m.* 20 Dec. 1836, Maria-Octavia, dau. of Ichabod Wright, Esq. of Mapperley, Notts, and has issue.
- II. Robert, *b.* in 1808, who *m.* Rachel, dau. of Osgood Hanbury, Esq. of Holfield Grange, Essex, and has issue.
- III. George, *b.* in 1810.
- I. Caroline, *m.* to John-Gurney Hoare, Esq.
- II. Rachel-Juliana.

Lineage.—DAVID BARCLAY, 2nd son of Robert Barclay, of Urie, the apologist of the Quakers, settled in London, and entertained successively Queen ANNE, GEORGE I., GEORGE II., and GEORGE III. when they visited the city on lord-mayor's day. He *m.* 1st, Anne, dau. of James Taylor, of London, by whom he had two sons,

- James, who *m.* Sarah Freame, and had two sons, Joseph and Alexander, both *d. s. p.*, and one dau., Anne, wife of James Allardice, of Allardice.
- ALEXANDER, of whom presently.
- Elizabeth, *m.* to Timothy Bevan, Esq.
- Christiana, *d. unm.*
- Anne, *m.* to James Collison, Esq.
- Patience, *m.* 1st, to John Stedman, Esq., and 2ndly, to Thomas Weston, Esq.

He *m.* 2ndly, in 1723, Priscilla, dau. of John Freame, of London, by whom he had two sons,

- David, of Youngbury, Herts, who *m.* 1st, Martha Hudson, and 2ndly, Rachael, dau. of Samson Lloyd, banker at Birmingham, the last-named lady *d. s. p.*; but by his 1st wife, David Barclay left at his decease, in 1809, an only dau. and heiress, Agatha, who *m.* Richard Gurney, Esq. of Keswick, co. Norfolk, and had a son, the present HUDSON GURNEY, Esq. of Keswick, and a dau., Agatha, widow of Sampson Hanbury, Esq. of Poles, Herts.
- John, who *m.* Susannah Willett, and had a son, Robert, *b.* in 1758, who *m.* Anne Satterthwaite, and had a son, Robert, who *m.* Elizabeth Gurney, and had issue.
- Priscilla.
- Catharine, *m.* to Daniel Bell, Esq. of Tottenham.
- Lucy, *m.* to Robert Barclay, Esq., M.P., of Urie.
- Caroline, *m.* to John Lindoe, Esq. of Norwich.
- Richenda, *m.* to Nathaniel Springall, Esq.
- Christiana, *m.* 1st, to Joseph Gurney, Esq.; 2ndly, to John Freame, Esq.; and 3rdly, to Sir William Watson, of London.

The 2nd son,

ALEXANDER BARCLAY, Esq. who *d.* at Philadelphia, in 1768, aged 57, left, by Ann Hickman his wife, a son,

ROBERT BARCLAY, Esq. of Bury Hill, co. of Surrey, *b.* in 1751, who *m.* 1st, Rachel, dau. of John Gurney, Esq. of Keswick, and 2ndly, Margaret Hodgson, by the former of whom he had (with daus., of whom Anne, *m.* to Jacob-Foster Reynolds, Esq.; Lucy, *m.* to George Croker Fox, Esq. of Grove Hill; and Maria, *m.* to Robert-Were Fox, Esq.) four sons,

- CHARLES, his heir.
- David, *b.* in 1784, of Eastwick Park, co. Surrey, formerly M.P. for Sunderland, who *m.* 20 Oct. 1818, Maria-Dorothea, dau. of the late Sir Hedworth Williamson, Bart., and has issue.
- Gurney, *b.* in 1786, who *m.* Mary Freshfield, and *d.* leaving an only child, Gurney, *b.* in 1819.
- Alexander, *b.* 1791; *d. unm.* in 1812.

Mr. Barclay was *s.* at his decease by his eldest son, the present CHARLES BARCLAY, Esq. of Bury Hill.

Arms, Crest, and Motto—Same as BARCLAY *of Allardice*.
Seat—Bury Hill, Dorking, Surrey.

BARCLAY OF WAVERTREE LODGE.

BARCLAY, THOMAS-BROCKHURST, Esq. of Wavertree Lodge, co. Lancaster, J.P., *b.* 5 Sept. 1783; *s.* his father 18 June, 1819; *m.* 12 Dec. 1820, Sarah, dau. of Henry Peters, of Betchworth Castle, co. Surrey, Esq.

Lineage.—GEORGE BARCLAY, Esq. of Burford Lodge, co. Surrey, M.P. for Bridport (son of Thomas Barclay, Esq. of London, by Dorothy, dau. of Robert Thomson, Esq. of Kilham, co. York, and grandson of George Barclay, Esq. of Collairnie, co. Fife, by his 2nd wife, Alice Rigbye, of Goosnargh, co. Lancaster), *m.* 13 July, 1782, Rebecca, only child of Benjamin Brockhurst, of London, Esq., by Sarah his wife, dau. of Latham Arnold, of London, Esq., and had issue,

- THOMAS-BROCKHURST, of Wavertree.
- George-Pearkes, *b.* 1784, *m.* in 1810, Maria, dau. of Henry Boulton, of Givon's Grove, co. Surrey, Esq., and has issue, George-Barnard; Frederick; Maria; Rebecca-Andalusia; Juliana-Elizabeth; Emily.
- Frederick-Maude, *b.* 1787, *d. unm.* 1835.

Mr. Barclay d. 18 June, 1819.

Arms—Arg. a chevron between three crosses-patée, gu.
Crest—A cross-patée, gu., surmounted by a Moorish crown, or.
Motto—Mieux être que paroître.
Seat—Wavertree Lodge, near Liverpool.

BARKER OF KILCOOLY ABBEY.

PONSONBY-BARKER, WILLIAM, Esq. of Kilcooly Abbey, co. Tipperary, J.P. and D.L., *b.* 9 Nov. 1795; *m.* 8 Aug. 1816, Elizabeth-Selina, 4th dau. of the late Hon. and Rt. Rev. William Knox, Bishop of Derry.

Lineage.—The Hon. Major-General Henry Ponsonby, of Ashgrove, 2nd son of William, 1st Viscount Duncannon, m. Lady Frances Brabazon, dau. of Chambre, Earl of Meath, and dying in 1745 (being slain at Fontenoy), left, with a dau., Juliana, m. to William Southwell, Esq. a son and successor,

Chambre-Brabazon Ponsonby, Esq., who m. 1st, Elizabeth, dau. and heir of Edward Clarke, Esq., by whom he had a dau., Frances, m. in 1767, to George Lowther, Esq. of Kilrue, in Meath; 2ndly, Louisa, dau. of John Lyons, Esq. of Morant, in Westmeath, by whom he had another dau., Sarah, of Llangollen Vale, who d. in 1831; and 3rdly, Mary, dau. of Sir William Barker, Bart. of Kilcooly, by whom he left, with a dau., Mary, wife of Folliot Barton, Esq., a son,

Chambre-Brabazon Ponsonby, Esq., b. 12 June, 1762, who inherited Kilcooly from his maternal family, and assumed the additional surname of Barker; he m. 4 June, 1791, Lady Henrietta Taylor, eldest dau. of Thomas, 1st Earl of Bective, and by her, who d. 12 Jan. 1838, had issue,

William, his heir, now of Kilcooly.
Chambre-Brabazon, late capt. 8th hussars, m. 30 April, 1834, Mary, dau. of the late Col. David Latouche, and became a widower in Aug. 1840.
Thomas-Henry, capt. 6th dragoon guards, m. 21 Feb. 1838, Fanny-Mary, 2nd dau. of Major R.-L. Dickson, late of the life-guards, and has issue.
Catherine-Jane, m. 25 May, 1819, to Edward-Michael Conolly, Esq.

Mr. Ponsonby-Barker d. 13 Dec. 1834.

Arms—Quarterly: 1st and 4th, per fesse, nebulée, az. and sa., three martlets, or, a canton, erm., for Barker; 2nd and 3rd, gu., a chevron between three combs, arg., for Ponsonby.
Crests—1st, a bear, sejant, or, collared, sa., for Barker; 2nd, in a ducal coronet, az., three arrows, one in pale, and two in saltier, points downwards, enveloped with a snake, ppr., for Ponsonby.
Seat—Kilcooly Abbey, co. Tipperary.

BARKER OF FAIRFORD PARK.

Raymond-Barker, John-Raymond, Esq. of Fairford Park, co. Gloucester, b. 30 March, 1801; m. 1st, 6 May, 1825, Harriot-Ives, dau. of William Bosanquet, Esq. of London, banker, by whom he had issue,

i. Augusta. ii. Leonora.

He m. 2ndly, 14 Dec. 1841, the Lady Catherine Moreton, youngest dau. of Thomas, 1st Earl of Ducie, and has by her a son,

i. Percy-Fitzhardinge, b. in Feb. 1842.

Lineage.—Esther Barker, lady of the manor of Fairford, dau. and co-heir of Samuel Barker, Esq., high-sheriff of Gloucestershire in 1691, and granddau. of Andrew Barker, who purchased Fairford from the Traceys, m. James Lamb, Esq. of Hackney, but d. s. p. in 1789, having devised her estates to

John Raymond, Esq., who took the surname of Barker in addition to his patronymic, by sign-manual. He m. 1st, Martha, co-heir of Daniel Booth, Esq. of Hutton Hall, co. Essex, by whom he had twelve children; he m. 2ndly, Margaret Boddington, and had by her two daus. His son,

Daniel Raymond-Barker, Esq. m. in 1797, Sophia-Anne, youngest dau. of John Ives, Esq. of Norfolk, and had issue,

John-Raymond, now of Fairford Park.
George Ives.
Henry-Charles, rector of Daylingworth, co. Gloucester.
Sophia-Anne, m. to Bernard Brocas, Esq. of Beaurepaire, Hants.
Harriet-Ives, m. to the Rev. F. Rice, vicar of Fairford.

Arms—Az., five escallops in cross, or, quartering Raymond.
Crests—1st, on a rock, arg., a hawk close, or, for Barker; 2nd, out of a mural crown, a demi-eagle displayed.
Motto—Virtus tutissima cassis.
Seat—Fairford Park, co. Gloucester.

BARNARD OF CAVE CASTLE.

Barnard, Henry-Gee, Esq. of Cave Castle, co. York, b. 22 Feb. 1789; m. 8 April, 1834, Elizabeth-Mary, dau. of Henry Elliot, Esq.

Lineage.—Edward-Gale Boldero, Esq., supposed to have been a descendant of the Suffolk Bolderos, had, by his wife Mary Lewyns, who d. in 1758, aged 63 (with two daus., Mrs. Hutchinson and Mrs. Fallowfield), four sons, viz:

i. Lewyns, his heir.
ii. John, first of Stapleton Hall, in Yorkshire, and subsequently of Aspeden Hall, in the co. of Herts. He m. Esther, dau. of D. Stone, Esq., and had (with two other sons, who d. unm., and three daus., the eldest, Esther, m. to Sir Stephen Lushington, Bart.; the 2nd, to Thomas Hibbert, Esq. of Chalfont; and the 3rd, to General Denzil Onslow) Charles; and William, in holy orders, who d. in 1833.
iii. Edward-Gale, m. and had one dau.
iv. Henry, of Aviary Hill, near Eltham, in Kent, who m. Miss Randall, and had an only surviving child, the present Edward-Gale Boldero, Esq., who m. Sophia, dau. of John Cornwall, Esq. of Hendon, and had issue,
1 Henry, who m. Margaret, dau. of the late William Christian, Esq. of Hoddesdon, Herts, and has a dau.
2 John-Stephen, in the E.I.C.C.S., who m. in India, Louisa, dau. of — Templeton, Esq., and has issue,
Edward-James. John-Cornwall.
Tempe-Stanley. Louisa-Margaret.
3 Lonsdale, captain and lieut.-colonel in the grenadier guards.
1 Sophia.

The eldest son,

Lewyns Boldero, Esq. assumed the surname and arms of Barnard.* He espoused Miss Anne Papplewell, and by her, who d. in 1797, aged 68, had issue,

i. Henry, his heir.
ii. Lewyns, who d. in 1820, leaving an only child,
Mary-Anne, who m. in June, 1821, Captain John Ditmas, and by him, who d. 29 Aug. 1827, aged 27, has issue,
1 Mary-Henrietta Ditmas. 2 Georgiana Ditmas.
3 Frances Ditmas. 4 Laura Ditmas.
i. Anne, who m. Robert, Lord Carrington, and d. in Feb. 1827.
ii. Mary, m. in 1808, to James Bankes, Esq., cousin to Sir Joseph Bankes, K.B.

Mr. Boldero-Barnard d. in 1783, aged 75, and was s. by his son,

Henry Boldero-Barnard, Esq. of Cave Castle, who m. 23 April, 1788, Sarah-Elizabeth, elder dau. and co-heir of Roger Gee, Esq. of Bishop Burton, representative of the ancient Yorkshire family of Gee, of which was Sir William Gee, Knt. of Bishop Burton, secretary to the Council of the North, who d. in 1611. By this lady, Mr. Boldero-Barnard had issue,

i. Henry-Gee, his heir.
ii. Charles-Lewyns, b. 19 Jan. 1790, capt. Scotch Greys; killed at Waterloo, 1815.
iii. Edward-William, in holy orders, b. 16 March, 1791, held the family living of South Cave. He m. 27 April, 1821, Philadelphia-Frances-Esther, dau. of the late Venerable Archdeacon Wrangham, and dying at Chester, in Jan. 1827, left issue,
1 Edward-Charles-Gee, b. 23 March, 1822.
1 Rosamond. 2 Caroline.
i. Sarah-Elinor, b. 11 Aug. 1810, m. 10 Oct. 1832, to Joseph Delpratt, Esq., only surviving son of the late Samuel Delpratt, Esq., of the island of Jamaica.

Mr. Boldero-Barnard d. 6 Feb. 1815 (his widow surviving until 28 Nov. 1832), and was succeeded by his eldest son, the present Henry-Gee Barnard, Esq. of Cave Castle.

Arms—Quarterly: 1st and 4th, quarterly, 1st and 4th, arg. a bear, rampant, sa., muzzled, or; 2nd, and 3rd, per pale, or and az., a saltier counterchanged, surmounted by a saltieret; 2nd and 3rd, gu., a sword in bend, arg., for Gee.
Crests—A bear, as in the arms, for Barnard; a greyhound, courant, for Boldero.
Seat—Cave Castle, Yorkshire.

BARNARD OF BARTLOW.

Barnard, Thomas, Esq. of Bartlow, co. Cambridge, J.P., formerly capt. in the army, b. 30 July, 1792; m. 12 Aug. 1822, Christian, dau. of Thomas Porter, Esq. of Rockbeare House, co. Devon, and has issue,

i. Thomas, b. 29 July, 1823, 65th regt.
ii. William, b. 21 May, 1825.
iii. Robert-Cary, b. 13 Dec. 1827.
i. Charlotte-Christina.

Lineage.—The Rev. Thomas Barnard, of Leeds, who m. Miss Drake, had, with a dau. Frances, wife of the Rev. Mr. Jackson, two sons, Thomas, his heir, and Charles, who m. and had issue. The elder son,

* The great-grandfather of Lewyns Boldero had, besides his son and successor, a dau., Mrs. Barnard, mother of Henry Barnard, M.D., who d. unm. in 1769, and was buried in St. Mary's Church, Beverley. From this gentleman the family derive the surname of Barnard.

THE REV. THOMAS BARNARD, rector of Withersfield, Suffolk, m. Meloaine Rosenhagen, and had issue.

I. ROBERT-CARY, of whom presently.
II. Robert, in holy orders, prebendary of Winchester, who m. in 1793, Louisa, only dau. of John-Peyto, 6th Lord Willoughby de Broke, and d. 3 Feb. 1835, leaving issue,
1 ROBERT, Lord Willoughby de Broke.
1 Louisa, m. to Joseph Townsend, Esq.
III. Thomas, in holy orders, who m. Everilda, 2nd dau. of the late Sir Mordaunt Martin, Bart.
IV. Charles-Drake, in holy orders, who m. Anna-Maria, relict of Sir Griffith Boynton, Bart.
I. Charlotte-Anne.

The eldest son,

THE REV. ROBERT-CARY BARNARD, rector of Withersfield, Suffolk, and justice of the peace, m. 10 June, 1790, Elizabeth, dau. of Robert-Cary Elwes, Esq. of Throcking, co. Herts, and by her (who d. in 1813), had issue,

THOMAS, of Bartlow, as above.
Charles-James, in holy orders, who m. in 1827, Caroline-Arabella-Elizabeth, dau. of Robert-Cary Elwes, Esq. of Billing, co. Northampton.
Henry-Anthony. Philip-Adolphus.
Charlotte-Elizabeth, m. to Henry-Lindow Lindow, Esq.

Arms—Arg., a bear, rampant, sa., muzzled, or.
Crest—A demi-bear, rampant, sa., muzzled, or.
Seat—Bartlow, co. Cambridge.

BARNARDISTON OF THE RYES.

BARNARDISTON, NATHANIEL-CLARKE, Esq. of The Ryes, co. Suffolk, b. 5 Nov. 1799; m. 1 March, 1826, Sophia, dau. of George-Robert Eyres, Esq. of Cavenham House, co. Norfolk, by Louisa his wife, dau. of the late Sir Harry Parker, Bart. of Melford, and has issue,

I. NATHANIEL, an officer 27th regt., b. 24 April, 1832.
II. Thomas, R.N., b. 4 Dec. 1833.
III. Arthur, b. 7 June, 1835.
IV. Charles-Francis, b. 8 June, 1841.
I. Louisa-Elizabeth, m. 19 Feb. 1852, to John Greenwood, Esq. of Swarcliffe, near Ripley, co. York.
II. Anne-Sophia, d. 1 Feb. 1832.
III. Sophia-Mary. IV. Frances-Maria.
V. Laura-Caroline. VI. Edith-Charlotte.

Mr. Barnardiston s. his father in 1837.

Lineage.—The family of Barnardiston, one of the most ancient of the equestrian order in the kingdom, having flourished in a direct line for nearly thirty generations, assumed its name from the town of Barnarston, or Barnston, contiguous to Ketton, of which the Barnardistons were proprietors from the CONQUEST. By marrying, *temp.* EDW. II., the heiress of Willoughby, the family obtained the noble manor of Great Cotes, co. Lincoln, which they held for several centuries. Ketton Hall they acquired with the heiress of the family of Newmarch, which surname it appears they adopted, and anciently bore, in conjunction with that of Barnardiston, as exhibited on the monument of Anne, dau. of Sir Thomas Barnardiston, the wife of Sir Hugh Everard, in the church of Great Waltham, Essex. She d. in 1609.

SIR THOMAS BARNARDISTON, Knt. of Witham, co. Essex, who s. to the representation of this distinguished race at the decease of his father, Sir Thomas, in 1619, m. twice, but had issue only by his first wife, Mary, dau. of Sir Richard Knightley, Knt. of Fawsley, several sons and daus. Of the former, the eldest, SIR NATHANIEL BARNARDISTON, of Ketton, five times knight of the shire for Suffolk, was ancestor of the extinct baronets of Ketton and Brightwell, while the 2nd,

THOMAS BARNARDISTON, Esq., founded the family before us. He m. 1st, Anne, dau. of Henry Austen, Esq. of London, by whom he had daus. only, and 2ndly, Anne, dau. of Henry Polstead, Esq. of London, by whom he had four sons and seven daus. The eldest son,

THOMAS BARNARDISTON, a merchant of London, d. 31 Oct. 1704, aged 67, leaving by his wife Eliza, dau. of John Clarke, Esq., M.P. for Bury, with numerous other children, a 2nd son,

NATHANIEL BARNARDISTON, b. in 1681, who m. Bethia Fowler, and was father of four sons, all of whom d. s. p., except the youngest, viz.:

JOHN BARNARDISTON, of Lincoln's Inn, who m. 31 May, 1734, Anne, dau. of Edward Leeds, Esq. of Croxton Park, co. Cambridge, serjeant-at-law, and by her left an only surviving son,

NATHANIEL BARNARDISTON, Esq. of The Ryes, near Sudbury, b. 28 Sept. 1755, who m. 25 Feb. 1783, Elizabeth-Joanna, only child of John Styles, Esq. of Kingston, Surrey, and d. 23 Dec. 1837, having had issue,

NATHANIEL-CLARKE, present representative.
Elizabeth, m. in 1811, to Charles-Raymond Barker, Esq., and d. 8 Jan. 1825.
Ann, m. in 1815, to the Rev. Thomas Mills, rector of Stutton, co. Suffolk.

Arms—Az., a fesse dancettée, erm., between six cross-crosslets, arg.
Crest—An ass's head, arg.
Seat—The Ryes, near Sudbury.

BARNE OF SOTTERLEY AND DUNWICH.

BARNE, FREDERICK, Esq. of Sotterley and Dunwich, co. Suffolk, late M.P. for Dunwich, and capt. in the 12th lancers, b. 8 Nov. 1805; m. 4 Feb. 1834, Mary-Anne-Elizabeth, eldest dau. of the late Sir John-Courtenay Honywood, Bart., and has issue,

I. FREDERICK-ST.JOHN-NEWDIGATE, b. 5 Sept. 1841.
II. Philip-Julius-Honywood-Ayscogh, b. 19 Jan. 1843.
I. Alice-Mary-Honywood. II. Edith.

Lineage.—MILES BARNE, Esq. of Sotterley, in the co. Suffolk, M.P. for Dunwich, b. in 1718 (6th in descent from Sir George Barne, lord-mayor of London in 1552), m. 1st, Elizabeth, dau. and co-heir of Nathaniel Elwick, Esq. of May Place, near Crayford, Kent, formerly governor of Fort Saint George, in the East Indies, and had a son, MILES, his heir. Mr. Barne m. 2ndly, Mary, eldest dau. of George Thornhill, Esq. of Diddington, in Huntingdonshire, and had, with other children, Barne, M.P. d. unm. in 1829; Snowdon, M.P., a lord of the Treasury, d. unm. in 1825; MICHAEL, successor to his brother; Thomas, M.A., rector of Sotterley, Suffolk; Mary, m. to W. Sawbridge, Esq. of East Haddon; Sarah, m. to John Harding, Esq.; Elizabeth; and Anne, wife of Drake Garrard, of Lamer, Esq. Mr. Barne d. 20 Dec. 1780, and was s. by his eldest son,

MILES BARNE, Esq. of Sotterley, Suffolk, and May Place, Kent, M.P. for Dunwich from 1791 to 1796, at whose decease, unm., 8 Sept. 1825, the estates devolved upon his half-brother,

MICHAEL BARNE, of Sotterley and Dunwich, Esq., lieut.-col. 7th hussars, and M.P. for Dunwich, b. in 1759, m. in 1798, Mary, dau. of Ayscogh Boucherett, of Willingham and Stalingborough, co. Lincoln, and d. in 1837, leaving, with a dau., Emilia-Mary, m. to Lieut.-Gen. Sir Edward Bowater, a son, the present FREDERICK BARNE, of Sotterley and Dunwich, Esq.

Arms—Quarterly: 1st and 4th, az., three leopards' heads, arg.; 2nd and 3rd, arg., a chevron, az., between three Cornish choughs, sa.
Crest—An eagle displayed, sa.
Motto—Nec timide, nec temere.
Seats—Dunwich and Sotterley Park, Suffolk; and May Place, Kent.

BARNEBY OF BROCKHAMPTON.

BARNEBY, JOHN-HABINGTON, Esq. of Brockhampton, co. Hereford, b. 2 May, 1840.

Lineage.—Dr. Nash, in his *History of Worcestershire* (vol i. p. 116, art. "*Bockelton*,") has the following note respecting the Barnebys:—" Mr. Habingdon says this family came originally from Yorkshire, and if so, were probably a younger branch of the ancient family BARNBY *of Barnby Hall*, in the parish of Calthorne, in the East Riding of that co., where they continued to flourish till the last century, when they expired in co-heirs."

JOHN BARNEBY, Esq. (3rd son of Richard Barneby, Esq. of Brockhampton, by Isabella his wife, dau. of Nicholas Lechmere, Esq. of Hanley Castle, co. Worcester, and grandson of John Barneby, Esq. of Brockhampton, returned among the persons qualified for the Order of the Royal Oak), baptised 6 May, 1684, d. in 1726, s. p., having devised his estates to his nephew,

BARTHOLOMEW-RICHARD-LUTLEY, Esq., who assumed in consequence the surname and arms of BARNEBY by act of parliament in 1735. He m. at Whitbourne, 21 Oct. 1756, Betty, dau. of John Freeman, Esq. of Gaines, and by her (who d. 14 May, 1785, aged 50), had (with two daus., Penelope, m. to Thomas Newnham, Esq. of Broadwas; and Abigail, who d. unm. in 1805) JOHN, his heir; Philip, b. in 1763, late receiver-general for the co. of Hereford, who m.

Eleanor, dau. of William Lilly, Esq., and had a dau. Anne; Lutley, b. in 1764; Richard, b. in 1769, who m. Betty Dansie, niece and devisee of Richard-Sweeting Dansie, Esq., and had issue, Richard, Thomas, Elizabeth, wife of the Rev. John Lingard, and Mary; and Thomas, rector of Stepney, b. in 1773. Mr. Barneby, who was high-sheriff of Herefordshire in 1739, d. 21 Dec. 1783, and was s. by his son,

JOHN BARNEBY, Esq. of Brockhampton, baptised there 16 Dec. 1757, high-sheriff of Herefordshire in 1797. He m. at St. George's, Hanover Square, 17 July, 1792, Elizabeth, dau. and sole heir of Robert Bulkeley, Esq. of Bulkeley, in Cheshire, and by her (who d. at Buckenhill, 18 Jan. 1833), had issue,

JOHN, his heir. William, b. 27 Nov. 1801.
Edmund, b. 15 Dec. 1802, devisee of his great-uncle, William Higginson, Esq. of Saltmarsh, under whose will he has taken the name of HIGGINSON.
Elizabeth, devisee of Buckenhill under her mother's will, m. 5 Aug. 1834, to Robert-Biddulph Phillipps, Esq. of Longworth.

Mr. Barneby d. in London, 11 Feb. 1817, was buried at Brockhampton, and s. by his eldest son,

JOHN BARNEBY, Esq. of Brockhampton, M.P. for Droitwich, and afterwards for Worcestershire, b. 20 Nov. 1799, m. 24 July, 1838, Susan, eldest dau. of Henry Elwes, Esq. of Colesborne, co. Gloucester, and had a son and heir, JOHN-HABINGTON, now of Brockhampton.

Arms—Quarterly: 1st and 4th, sa., a lion, passant-guardant, between three escallops, arg., for BARNEBY; 2nd and 3rd, quarterly, or and az., four lions, rampant, counterchanged, together with upwards of forty quarterings, chiefly brought in by Habingdon and Shirley.
Crest—A lion, couchant-guardant, sa.
Motto—Virtute non vi.
Seat—Brockhampton, in Herefordshire.

BARNETT OF STRATTON PARK.

BARNETT, CHARLES, Esq. of Stratton Park, co. Bedford, b. 31 Oct. 1796; m. 1 Feb. 1826, Elizabeth, 3rd dau. of Sir Peter Payne, Bart., and has issue,

I. CHARLES-FITZROY, b. 12 Oct. 1830.
II. George-James, b. 8 Dec. 1831.
III. Clayton, b. 15 Sept. 1839.
IV. Rosewell, b. 3 May, 1841.
I. Harriet-Anne-Maria-Stanhope. II. Elizabeth.
III. Laura-Janet-Emma. IV. Louisa.

Mr. Barnett was high-sheriff of the county of Bedford in 1821.

Lineage.—CURTIS BARNETT, Esq., son of Lieut. Barnett, who was lost in the "Stirling Castle" man-of-war, in 1703, m. 18 May, 1725, Elizabeth, dau. of Benjamin Rosewell, Esq., and d. 29 April, 1746, at Fort St. David's, in the East Indies, being commander-in-chief of his majesty's ships designed on a particular service, leaving a son,

CHARLES BARNETT, Esq. of Stratton Park, co. Bedford, who m. 17 Feb. 1756, Bridget, 3rd dau. of Alexander Clayton, Esq., and had (with other children deceased), CHARLES, his heir; James, banker, of Lombard Street; and Bridget. The eldest son and heir,

MAJOR-GEN. CHARLES BARNETT, of Stratton Park, b. in March, 1758, m. 22 Feb. 1796, Harriet, eldest dau. of Admiral Sir Richard King, Bart., by whom, who d. 17 Sept. 1799, he had a dau., Caroline, wife of J. McGrath, M.D., and an only son and successor, the present CHARLES BARNETT, Esq. of Stratton Park. Gen. Barnett d. 10 Oct. 1804, at Gibraltar, of which garrison he was then second in command.

Arms—Arg., a saltier, sa.; in chief, a leopard's head, of the second.
Crest—A trefoil.
Seat—Stratton Park, Biggleswade.

BARNSTON OF CHURTON.

BARNSTON, ROGER, Esq. of Crewe Hill, co. Chester, b. 4 Dec. 1826, capt. 90th light infantry.

Lineage.—The ancestors of this family were seated at Churton at least as early as the reign of HENRY VI., when URIAN DE BARNSTON appears as a trustee in the deeds of the LECHES *of Carden*. This Urian de Barnston had issue, by Catherine his wife, dau. of Edward de Crewe, of Crewe.

ROBERT BARNSTON, Esq. of Churton, b. 1714, son and heir of Roger Barnston, Esq. of Churton, by Jane his 1st wife, dau. and heir of Edward Gregge, Esq. of Hapsford, was 9th in descent from Thomas Barnston, of Churton, *temp.* HENRY VII. He m. Elizabeth dau. of Sir Whitmore Acton, 4th bart. of Aldenham and Round Acton, in the co. Salop, and was father of

ROGER BARNSTON, Esq. of Churton, high-sheriff of Cheshire in 1800, b. 1749, m. Anne, dau. of the Rev. John Parker, of Astle, co. Chester, and d. 4 Feb. 1837, having had two daus., Anne-Elizabeth-Mary and Alice-Emma, m. to the Hon. Charles Napier, and a son and heir,

ROGER-HARRY BARNSTON, Esq. of Churton, J.P. and D.L., b. 29 Sept. 1803, who m. in 1825, Selina-Martha, dau. of William-M. Thackeray, M.D. of Chester, and by her, who d. 13 Jan. 1835, left at his decease, 22 May, 1849, ROGER, now of Crewe Hill; William, lieut. 55th regt.; Harry; Selina; Eliza; Mary; and Emma.

Arms—Az., a fesse dancettée, erm., between six cross-crosslets, fitchée, or.
Seat—Crewe Hill, Farndon, Cheshire.

BARRETT OF MILTON HOUSE.

BARRETT, JOHN-BASIL, Esq. of Milton House, Berks, is son of the late James Barrett, Esq. of the same place, and grandson of John-Briant Barrett, Esq., who purchased the estate of Milton, about the year 1768, from the family of Calton.

Arms—Quarterly: 1st and 4th, gu., on a chief, indented, arg., three escallops of the 1st, for BARRETT; 2nd and 3rd, arg., a chevron, engrailed, ermines, between three greyhounds' heads, erased, erm., for BELSOM.
Crest—A wyvern, wings erect, or, chained and collared, az.
Motto—Honor, virtus, probitas.
Seat—Milton House, Berks.

BARNWELL OF MILEHAM.

BARNWELL, THE REV. CHARLES-BARNWELL, of Mileham Hall, lord of the manors of Mileham and Beeston, and patron of those churches, rector of Mileham, J.P. for the co. of Norfolk; b. 7 July, 1801; m. 28 Oct. 1829, Sophia, one of the daus. of George-Thomas Wyndham, of Cromer, Esq., and has issue,

I. CHARLES-WYNDHAM, b. 31 Aug. 1836.
I. Sophia-Catherine. II. Adelaide-Horatia.

Mr. Barnwell, whose original name was HERRING, assumed the name of BARNWELL on succeeding to the estates of Charles Barnewell, Esq., and the Rev. William Barnwell, his great-uncles, in 1825.

Lineage.—WOLFRAM DE BARNWALL, lord of Dromnagh, co. Dublin, 14 EDWARD I., was descended from MICHAEL DE BARNWALL, who settled in Ireland *temp.* HENRY II.

REGINALD, his son (28 EDWARD I.) had, with a 2nd son Reginald, an elder son and heir,

WOLFRAM, who m. Nicola, dau. of Robert Clahull, lord of Balrothery, Dublin, and had issue, Reginald; Walter; and NICHOLAS. The last,

NICHOLAS BARNWALL, of Crickstown, co. Meath, m. a dau. of Clifford, and left two sons, CHRISTOPHER, of Crickstown; and JOHN, of Frankstown, created *Viscount Kingsland*. The elder,

CHRISTOPHER BARNWALL, Esq. of Crickstown, was a judge of the King's Bench in Ireland; he m. the widow of Drake of Drakestown, and had two sons: the younger, Robert, was created *Baron Trimlestown, (See Peerage)*. The elder,

SIR NICHOLAS BARNEWALL, m. Ismay, dau. and heir of Sir John Sarjeant, of Castle Knock. Christopher, his elder son, was ancestor of the present SIR REGINALD BARNEWELL, Bart. of Crickstown. His second son,

THOMAS BARNWELL, was of Offalye, in Ireland, and by Blanche Nugent his wife had three sons, Morris, Gerrard, and THOMAS. The last named,

THOMAS BARNWELL, is said to have m. Alice, dau. of James Eustace, Master of the Rolls, and to have had issue by her, with two other sons, Thomas and Richard, a third son,

ROBERT BARNWELL, who migrated to Lenton, co. Nottingham, and m. Abigail, dau. of Thomas Manly, and left two sons, SIMON and Thomas. The elder,

SIMON BARNWELL, was of Cransley, co. Northampton. He was father, besides two younger sons, John and Richard, of

THOMAS BARNWELL, of Cransley, his heir, who by his wife Elizabeth, dau. of Thomas Cradock, of Dyngley, co. Northampton, had issue, five sons, EDWARD; Gyles; Thomas; Gerrard; and William; and one dau. Mary. The eldest son,

Edward Barnwell, of Cransley, Gent., m. 1st, Ellen, dau. of Thomas Brook, of Ogeley, whose only child, Jane, d. unm.; he m. 2ndly, Ann, dau. of John Spencer, of Blunham, co. Beds., and by her had issue, six sons, Stephen; Thomas; Edward; John; William; and Angus; and three daus., Mary; Elizabeth; and Ann. He d. in 1602, at Walgrave, having, in conjunction with his eldest son Stephen, exchanged the Northamptonshire estate with Sir Thomas Cecil, Knt., (afterwards Marquess of Exeter), for that of Mileham and Beeston, in Norfolk. The eldest son,

Stephen Barnwell, came into Norfolk, and made his residence at Mileham, in 1585. He m. Mary, dau. of Nicholas Calton, of Little Catworth, Hants, and was buried at Mileham, 19 Sept. 1628, leaving three sons, of whom the eldest,

Edward Barnwell, Esq. of Mileham, m. Anne, dau. of Sir Thomas Playters, of Sotterley, Suffolk, Bart., and d. at Mileham, where he was buried, 30 Nov. 1666. His issue were eight sons and four daus. His eldest surviving son and heir,

Charles Barnwell, of Mileham, b. 1626, m. Susan, dau. of William Sydnor, of Blundeston, Suffolk, and was s. (Edward his eldest son dying an infant) by his only other son,

Charles Barnwell, of Mileham, Gent., who m. in 1678, Ann, one of the daus. of Clement Heigham, of Barrow, Suffolk, and dying in 1702, (buried Dec. 19), left issue (two other sons having d. in infancy), with a dau. Ann, wife of Henry Mingay, of Woodton, his 2nd son and heir,

Charles Barnwell, of Mileham, Esq., who was thrice married; by his 1st wife, Elizabeth, dau. of Rev. John Neale, rector of Mileham, who d. 19 Dec. 1705, he had an only son,

Charles, of whom hereafter.

He m. 2ndly, Mary, dau. of Sir Thomas Burney, of Reedham, Bart., who d. 17 Dec. 1720, having had several children all of whom d. in infancy, except the second,

Edward, b. 1712; in holy orders, rector of Mileham; d. 1738, unm.

He m. 3rdly, in 1728, Mary, dau. of Rev. John Nowell, rector of Hillington, Norfolk, and by this lady (who survived him and d. his widow in 1787), with a son John who d. an infant, had,

I. Frederick, of Bury St. Edmunds, bapt. at Mileham 22 June, 1730; in holy orders, rector of Brackley, Lawshall, and Stanningfield, in Suffolk; succeeded, under his mother's marriage settlement, to a portion of the Mileham estate, including the Old Park and the site of the ancient castle of the FitzAlans; m. 1769, Susanna-Maria, dau. and co-heir of Rev. Thomas Ewin, rector of Swanton Morley, Norfolk, who d. 23 Aug. 1806. He d. 4 March, 1800, and left issue,

1 Frederick-Henry, of Bury St. Edmunds, who in 1826, on succeeding to the property of Henry Turnor, late of Bury, took the name of Turnor before Barnwell; and d. unm. 24 Oct. 1843, when he was s. in his inheritance of Mileham Park by his only brother,

2 Charles-Frederick, keeper of antiquities in the British Museum; who m. Jane, dau. of Rev. John Lowry, and by her left, Frederick-Lowry, solicitor, of Lincoln's Inn Fields; John-Lowry, d. an infant; Charles-Lowry; Edward-Lowry, in holy orders; Henry-Lowry; Susanna-Lowry, wife of Rev. Edward Parker, of Oxendon, co. Northampton; Jane-Lowry, wife of Charles-Lewis Parker, of Oxford.

I. Anna-Maria, m. William Donne, an eminent surgeon at Norwich.

Mr. Barnwell d. 24 July, 1750, and was s., as to the manors of Mileham and Beeston, the mansion of Mileham Hall, and the advowsons of the rectories of Mileham and Beeston, by his eldest son,

The Rev. Charles Barnwell, b. 1705, rector of Beeston-next-Mileham. He m. in 1735, Catherine, dau. of Samuel Sparrow, of Lavenham, Suffolk, who d. 28 April, 1774, and he following within three days after, they were both buried in Beeston church, on the 29th of same month. Their issue were,

I. Charles.
II. Edward, d. an infant.
III. William, who took holy orders, and on his father's death became rector of Beeston. He d. 6 Jan. 1810, leaving by his wife Mary, dau. of George Patteson, of Lynn Regis (who d. 31 July, 1825), an only son, George-Barnwell, rector of Mileham; who d. 25 Dec. 1822, unm.
IV. John, of Bale, in Norfolk; m. Anne Wilson, dau. and co-heir of Thomas Wright, of Stiffkey, Norfolk, Esq., and relict of Thomas-Lee Warner, of Walsingham, Esq.; and his only dau. and heir, Catherine Barnwell, m. John Herring, Esq., alderman of Norwich; and d. in 1840, leaving issue,

1 Charles-Barnwell Herring, who has assumed the surname of Barnwell on succeeding to the family estates, and is the present possessor of Mileham Hall.
2 Henry-Lee-Warner-Herring, m. Joanna, dau. of William Harlock, Esq. of Ely.
3 John-Barnwell-Herring, d. unm. 1838.
1 Catherine-Barnwell Herrring, m. to the Rev. John-Thomas Batcheler, 2nd son of Horner Batcheler, Esq. of Horstead, Norfolk; and is now deceased.

V. Neale, } both d. infants.
VI. Samuel, }
I. Theodosia, d. unm.　　II. Elizabeth, d. unm.
III. Catherine, m. John Webster, of Norwich, surgeon.
IV. Sarah, m. Samuel Pye, of Norwich, Gent.

Charles Barnwell, Esq., eldest son, was of Mileham Hall, and d. 1 Dec. 1802: his widow Mary, dau. and co-heir of William Barwick, of Norwich, surgeon, d. 17 Dec. 1808, and leaving no issue, the estates came to his brother,

The Rev. William Barnwell, above mentioned, who was s. by his son,

The Rev. George Barnwell, on whose death, unm., 25 Dec. 1822, the property devolved, under the will of Charles Barnwell, Esq., on the present Rev. Charles Barnwell Herring, who 3 Oct. 1825, obtained the royal license to bear the name and arms of Barnwell.

Arms—Gu., a saltier, embattled, between four crescents, arg.
Crest—A wolf's head, erased, arg., gorged with a collar, embattled, gu., studded, or, and chained, of the same.
Motto—Loyal au mort.
Seat—Mileham Hall, co. Norfolk.

BARRON OF GLENVIEW.

Barron, Pierse-Marcus, Esq. of Glenview and Killoen, co. Waterford, J.P., b. 3 July, 1806; m. 9 Oct. 1824, Catherine-Lucinda, dau. of Laurence Crowe, Esq. of Stephen's Green, Dublin, and has issue,

I. Pierse-Laurence.
II. Joseph-Manuel.　　III. William-Justin-Archbold.
IV. Arthur-Hervey-Aston.
I. Catalina-Lucinda-Mary-Anne.
II. Maria-Matilda.　　III. Margarita-Louisa.
IV. Emily-Eliza-Mary.

Lineage.—James Barron, Esq. of Carrick Barron, co. Waterford, brother of John Barron, Esq., grandfather of the present Sir Henry-Winston Barron, Bart., m. and had two sons, John and William. The elder m. Miss Power, heiress of the Georgetown estate, and had a son, James Barron, Esq. of Georgetown. The younger,

William Barron, Esq. of Carrick Barron, and afterwards of Cadiz, in Spain, m. Margarita Power, whose mother, Margarita Archbold, was aunt to Robert Archbold, Esq. of Davidstown, M.P. By this lady, who m. 2ndly, Col. Le Chevalier Fitzgerald, of the Spanish service, Mr. Barron had issue,

Pierse-Marcus, his heir, now of Glenview.
William-Eustace, b. in 1808; d. at Malaga in 1835.
Margarita, m. 1st, to Arthur-Hervey Aston, Esq. of Aston Hall, Cheshire; 2ndly, to the Chevalier de Poggenhofel, Chargé d'Affaires from Russia to the court of Spain; and 3rdly, to Le Chevalier de Montenegro, lieut.-gen. and chamberlain to H.R.H. Don Francisco de Paula.

Arms—Erm., on a saltier, gu., five annulets, or.
Crest—A boar, passant, az., on a cap of maintenance, ppr.
Motto—Audaces fortuna juvat.
Seats—Glenview, and Killoen, co. Waterford.

BARROW OF SOUTHWELL.

Barrow, William-Hodgson, Esq. of Southwell, co. Lincoln, J.P. and D.L., M.P. for South Notts, b. 1 Sept. 1784.

Lineage.—John Barrow, who m. Isabel, dau. of William Hodgson, had, with other issue, two sons, the younger, William, in holy orders, late archdeacon of Nottingham, and

The Rev. Richard Barrow, who m. 1 Jan. 1778, Mary dau. of George Hodgkinson, Esq., and had issue,

George-Hodgkinson, b. Jan. 1779; m. Mrs. Elizabeth Lowe; and d. in May, 1853, leaving two sons and two daus.
William-Hodgson, of Southwell, as above.

Richard, of Ringwood Hall, co. Derby, b. July, 1787.
John, of Normanton Hall, Southwell, b. Aug. 1790.
James, in holy orders, rector of Lopham, Norfolk; b. Oct. 1793; m. Louisa, dau. of the late Sir C. Malet, and has a son and a dau.
Mary-Anne, widow of the Rev. William Lawson.
Arabella, d. Sept. 1850. Sutten-Bullen.

Arms—Per pale, indented, sa. and az., two swords in saltier, ppr., pommels and hilts, or, between four fleurs-de-lis, two in pale, of the last, and two in fesse, arg.
Crest—On a perch, ppr., a squirrel, sejant, or, collared and chained, cracking a nut, all ppr.
Motto—Non frustra.
Residence—Southwell, Lincolnshire.

BARRY OF ROCLAVESTON.

BARRY, PENDOCK-BARRY, Esq. of Roclaveston Manor, co. Nottingham, D.L., b. 6 May, 1783; s. his father, Pendock Barry, Esq., LL.D., 13 March, 1833.

Lineage.—This family derives, in direct descent, from Godfridus, "qui floruit apud Teversal, *temp.* Conquest." In the 14th EDWARD III., SIR JOHN BARRY, of Tollerton, served as one of the knights of the shire in parliament, and is probably the Sir John Barry mentioned in the siege of Caerlaverock. The eventual heiress of this long descended house,

MATILDA BARRY, only child of WILLIAM BARRY, of Tollerton, Esq., m. RICHARD PENDOCK, Esq., of Gotherington, co. Gloucester, decended from Pendock of Pendock, and their descendant and representative,

ANN PENDOCK, of Tollerton, m. John Neale, Esq. of Mansfield Woodhouse, b. 18 Sept. 1657, (son of Richard Neale of the same place, who came from Ireland with the Duke of Newcastle), and dying in 1692, left a son,

JOHN NEALE, of Tollerton, Esq., b. at Mansfield Woodhouse, in 1686, who m. Elizabeth Major, of Belper, co. Derby, and had issue,

I. PENDOCK, of whom presently.
II. John, in holy orders, rector of Tollerton and Sibson; who m. Elizabeth Lowe, dau. of Lowe of Park Hall, co. Derby, and had a son,
PENDOCK, of whom hereafter, as successor to his uncle.
III. Thomas, in holy orders, rector of Sibson, co. Leicester, and of Tollerton; bapt. 11 Dec. 1733; who m. Susanna, dau. of Philip Falkner, Esq. of Lincoln, by whom he had issue,
1 Thomas, who m. Bridget Glen, and had two sons, Thomas-Pendock, and Pendock-William, and two daus.
2 Pendock, who m. Sarah Wright; and d. s. p.
3 John, in holy orders, rector of Tollerton; b. 29 March, 1771; who m. Sarah, dau. of the Rev. Jonathan Dennis, rector of Bramshot, Hants, and has a son, Philip-Pendock, b. in 1798.
1 Susanna, m. to her cousin, Pendock Barry, LL.D., of Roclaveston.

The eldest son,

PENDOCK NEALE, of Tollerton, Esq., m. Harriet, sister of Richard, 1st Lord Eliot, of Port Eliot, d. s. p. in 1773, and was s. by his nephew,

PENDOCK NEALE, Esq., LL.D., b. 27 Aug. 1757, who m. his cousin, Susanna, dau. of his uncle, the Rev. Thomas Neale, and by her (who d. 22 April, 1811), had issue,

PENDOCK-BARRY, now of Roclaveston.
Susanna-Falkner-Neale, d. unm. in 1821.

Mr. Neale, who assumed, in 1812, by sign-manual, the surname of BARRY, in lieu of his patronymic, d. 13 March, 1833.

Arms—Gu., three bars, embattled, arg.
Crest—The embattlement of a tower, gu., charged with three roses in fesse, arg.
Motto—A Rege et victoriâ.
Seat—Roclaveston Manor, Notts.

BARRY OF BALLYCLOUGH.

BARRY, JAMES, Esq. of Ballyclough, co. Cork, b. 28 July, 1805; m. 2 March, 1841, Olivia-Maria, dau. and sole heiress of Francis Drew, Esq. of M'Collop Castle, co. Waterford. Captain Barry was high-sheriff of co. Cork in 1841.

Lineage.—This family, formerly seated at Lisnegar, near Rathcormack, claims to be senior to the Barrymore family.

REDMOND BARRY, Esq. of Lisnegar and Rathcormack, co. Cork, ("M'Adam Barry,") m. 1st, Mary, dau. of John Boyle, Esq. of Castle Lyons, co. Cork, and had issue a son and two daus.,

JAMES, his heir.
Anne, m. to Samuel Hartwell, Esq., capt. in the army, slain at Landen, in 1693.
Catherine, m. to Alan Brodrick, 1st Viscount Midleton, and had issue.

Mr. Barry m. 2ndly, in 1666, Jane, eldest dau. of Sir Nicholas Purdon, Knt., of Ballyclough, co. Cork, M.P. for Baltimore, and had, with two daus., another son,

REDMOND, of Ballyclough, co. Cork, who m. 1700, Catherine, dau. of William Taylor, Esq. of Brucheny and Ballintemple (near Buttevant), co. Cork, and by her had an elder son and heir,

REDMOND, of Ballyclough, high-sheriff of co. Cork in 1734; who m. Henrietta, 2nd dau. of William Dunscombe, Esq. of Mount Desart, co. Cork, and had issue,
JAMES, his heir, of whom hereafter, as successor to his cousin, Redmond Barry, Esq. of Rathcormack, as M'ADAM BARRY.
Mary, m. to Richard-Aldworth St. Leger, Viscount Doneraile.

Mr. Barry was s. by his eldest son by his 1st wife,

JAMES BARRY, Esq. of Rathcormack, ("M'Adam Barry"), col. in the army, who m. 1st, Mary, dau. of Abraham Anselm, Esq. of London, and had issue, two sons and a dau., viz., JAMES, his heir; REDMOND, successor to his brother, as hereafter; Mary, d. unm. Col. Barry m. 2ndly, Susanna, dau. of John Townsend, Esq. of Timoleage, co. Cork, by Lady Catherine Barry, his wife, dau. of Richard, Earl of Barrymore, and by her had issue two sons, David, M.D., d. s. p.; Patrick, M.D., d. s. p.; and two daus., Elizabeth, m. to Noblett Dunscombe, Esq. of Mount Desart, co. Cork, and had issue; and Catherine, m. to John Townsend, Esq., her cousin. On the death of Col. Barry, he was s. by his elder son,

JAMES BARRY, Esq., who d. unm., when his next brother,

REDMOND BARRY, Esq. became of Rathcormack, (M'Adam Barry). He d. s. p. in 1750, and was s. by his cousin,

JAMES BARRY, Esq. of Ballyclough, who then became the M'Adam Barry. He m. Elizabeth, dau. and co-heiress of Abraham Green, Esq. of Ballymachree, co. Limerick, and d. in 1793, leaving issue. The eldest son and heir,

REDMOND BARRY, Esq. of Ballyclough, (M'Adam Barry,) d. unm. 10 Feb. 1812, when the representation devolved upon his brother,

HENRY-GREEN BARRY, Esq. of Ballyclough, a major-general, H.M.S., who m. 21 Sept. 1804, Phœbe, dau. of John-Armstrong Drought, Esq. of Lettybrook, King's Co., and had issue,

JAMES, his heir.
Henry, capt. E.I.C.'s service, killed in Burmah, 1854.
Redmond, barrister-at-law, judge at Melbourne, Victoria.
St. Leger, late capt. 65th foot, now commissioner Gold Fields, Australia.
John-Richard, lieut. 86th foot; d. in India unm.
William-Wigram, capt. royal artillery.
Letitia, m. to the Rev. Robert Bury, of Carrigrenane, co. Cork.
Eliza, m. Murray Simpson, Esq. Caroline.
Catherine, m. to Major Osborne Broadley.
Phœbe, d. unm. Charlotte. Louisa, d. unm.

Gen. Barry d. 18 May, 1838, and was s. by his eldest son and heir, the present JAMES BARRY, Esq. of Ballyclough.

Arms—Barry of six, arg. and gu.
Crest—Out of a castle, arg., a wolf's head, sa.
Motto—Boutez en avant.
Seat—Ballyclough, co. Cork.

BARRY OF FOATY ISLAND AND MARBURY HALL.

SMITH-BARRY, JAMES-HUGH, Esq. of Foaty Island, co. Cork, and of Marbury Hall, co. Chester, b. in 1816; m. in Sept. 1841, Eliza, eldest dau. of Shallcross Jacson, Esq. of Newton Bank, Cheshire. Mr. Smith-Barry served as high-sheriff of Cheshire in 1846.

Lineage.—THE HON. JOHN BARRY, b. in 1725, youngest son of James, 4th Earl of Barrymore, m. in 1746, Dorothy, dau. and co-heir (with her sister Lucy, wife of James, Lord Strange) of Hugh Smith, Esq. of Weald Hall, in Essex, and had two sons, JAMES-HUGH, his heir, and Richard, who d. s. p. The elder,

JAMES-HUGH SMITH-BARRY, Esq. of Marbury Hall and Foaty Island, b. in 1748, was high-sheriff of Cheshire in 1725. He d. leaving two sons and three daus., viz.,

JOHN, of whom presently.
James, of Lota Lodge, co. Cork, m. but has no issue.

Caroline-Augusta, m. to George, eldest son of Robert Courtenay, Esq. of Ballyedmond.
Narcissa, m. to the Hon. William Massy, brother of the late Lord Massy.
Louisa, m. to the Right Hon. Thomas-B. Cusack-Smith, Master of the Rolls in Ireland.

The elder son,

John Smith-Barry, Esq. of Marbury Hall and Foaty Island, b. 1793, succeeded to the estates by bequest. He m. 1st, Eliza, second dau. of Robert Courtenay, Esq. of Ballyedmond, and had,

James-Hugh, his heir, now of Marbury Hall.
John-Hugh, deceased.
Robert-Hugh, } officers in the army.
Richard-Hugh, }
Anna, deceased. Elizabeth, also deceased.

Mr. Smith-Barry m. 2ndly, Eliza-Felicia, second dau. of General Heron, of Moor, in Cheshire, but by her had no issue. He d. in 1837.

Arms—Quarterly: 1st and 4th, barry of six, arg. and gu.; 2nd and 3rdly, quarterly, 1st and 4th, gu., on a chevron; or, between three bezants, as many crosses formée-fitchée, sa.; 2nd and 3rd, a fesse, between three urchins, or.
Crest—Out of a castle, arg., a wolf's head, sa.
Motto—Boutez en avant.
Seats—Marbury Hall, Cheshire; and Foaty Island, co. Cork.

BARTON OF THREXTON HOUSE.

Barton, Thomas-Edward-Walter, Esq. of Threxton House, co. Norfolk, b. 14 Sept. 1811; m. 27 June, 1844, Eliza, only child of John Allday, Esq. of Griston, and has issue,

I. Thomas-Allday, b. 21 June, 1845.
II. Walter-May, b. 18 Nov. 1846.

Mr. Barton s. his father 22 Aug. 1837.

Lineage.—Thomas Barton, Esq. of Hadlow, younger brother of John Barton, Esq., grandfather of the present Walter-Barton May, Esq. of Hadlow Castle, Kent, (*see that family*); b. 13 Oct. 1726, m. Susanna Ellis, and had issue a son, Walter, and a dau. who m. John Burcham, of Holt, Norfolk. The son,

Walter Barton, Esq., m. Anne-Hannah Pigge, and had issue, three sons and four daus.; of the former,

Thomas Barton, Esq. of Threxton House, m. 16 Jan. 1810, Hannah Clark, and had issue,

Thomas-Edward-Walter, now of Threxton.
Sarah-Anne-Hannah. Elizabeth.

Arms—Erm., on a fesse, gu., three annulets, or.
Crest—A griffin's head, erased, ppr.
Motto—Fortis est veritas.
Seat—Threxton House, near Watton, co. Norfolk.

BARTON OF STAPLETON PARK.

Barton, John Hope, Esq. of Stapleton Park, co. York, and Saxby Hall, co. Lincoln, b. 3 Oct. 1833.

Lineage.—This family claims to be a branch of the ancient house of Barton *of Smithills*, in Lancashire, recorded in the Heralds' Visitation of 1567.

Henry Barton, Esq., descended from William Andrew Barton, Esq. of Deanwater, Cheshire, acquired considerable property as a merchant at Manchester, and purchased, about the end of the century, the estates of Swinton and Ward Hall, in Lancashire. He m. in 1768, Mary, dau. of Joseph Bushell, Esq. of Neston, in Cheshire, and had issue. The eldest son,

John Barton, Esq. of Swinton in Lancashire, and Saxby in Lincolnshire, b. in 1770, m. in 1796, Margaret, dau. of John Watson, Esq. of Preston, in Lancashire, and dying in 1831, left, (with two daus., Mary, wife of Thomas Heywood, Esq. of Hope End, and Sophia, of Jeremiah Taylor, Esq. of The Grange, co. Worcester,) a son,

John-Watson Barton, Esq., J. P. and D. L., of Stapleton Park, co. York, and of Swinton, in Lancashire, b. 29 Aug. 1798, m. 29 Jan. 1830, Juliana, 2nd dau. of James Hope, Esq. of Moray Place, Edinburgh, and had issue,

I. John Hope. I. Mary-Jane.
II. Julia-Sophia, m. 21 Sept. 1854, to the Rev. Charles-Augustus Hope, youngest son of the late Sir John Hope, Bart. of Craig Hall.
III. Margaret. IV. Louisa. V. Caroline.
VI. Frances.

Mr. Barton d. 22 Jan. 1840.

Arms—Az., on a fesse, between three bucks' heads, caboshed, or, a martlet, gu., between two acorns, leaved, ppr.
Crest—An acorn, or, leaved, vert.
Motto—Crescitur cultu.
Seat—Stapleton Park, near Pontefract.

BARTON OF GROVE.

Barton, William, Esq. of Grove, co. Tipperary, J.P. and D.L., b. 21 June, 1790; m. in April, 1815, Catherine, dau. of Samuel Perry, Esq. of Woodrooffe, by Deborah his wife, dau. of Lord Dunalley, and has issue,

I. Thomas-Barker, b. in 1816.
II. Samuel-Harry, b. in 1817.
III. William-Hugh, b. in 1820.
I. Deborah, m. to John Wade, Esq., 2nd son of William Blaney Wade, Esq. of Clonabrany, co. Meath.
II. Mary-Frances. III. Catherine-Grace.
IV. Anne-Margaret. V. Emily-Martha.

Mr. Barton was high-sheriff in 1825.

Lineage.—This family, which claims to be a branch of the ancient Lancashire house of Barton *of Barton Hall*, was established in Ireland by Thomas Barton, who accompanied the Earl of Essex's army to that kingdom, and obtained a grant of land, comprising the district called Drumminshin and Necairn, in the co. of Fermanagh. He m. Margaret Loyd, and had a son, Anthony Barton, father of

William Barton, b. about 1630, who m. Jane-Hannah Forster, and had two sons,

Edward, m. and had issue, William and Edward. The latter m. his cousin, Elizabeth Barton, and was father of John, who was brought up by his uncle Thomas, at Bordeaux. The elder son, William, had three sons, John, Edward, and Gustavus. The latter was father of the Rev. Edward Barton, archdeacon of Ferns.
William.

The second son,

William Barton, had (with a daughter, Elizabeth, wife of her cousin, Edward Barton) a son,

Thomas Barton, Esq. of Curraghmore, co. Fermanagh, b. 21 Dec. 1694, who settled as a merchant at Bordeaux A.D. 1725. He m. 1 Nov. 1722, Margaret, youngest dau. of Robert Delap, Esq. of Ballyshannon, and had one son,

William Barton, Esq. of Grove, co. Tipperary, who m. 1 Aug. 1754, Grace, eldest dau. of the Rev. Charles Massey, of Doonas, co. Clare, Dean of Limerick, and sister of Sir Hugh-Dillon Massey, the first baronet of Doonas, and had issue,

I. Thomas, his heir,
II. William, of Clonelly. (*See that branch.*)
III. Charles. (*See* Barton *of Waterfoot.*)
IV. Hugh, of Straffan, co. Kildare, (*See that family.*)
V. Robert (Sir), K.C.H., a lieutenant-general in the army, b. in 1770, m. 1st, Maria, dau. and co-heir of John Painter, Esq., and had issue,
1 Hugh, a major in the army.
1 Grace, m. to Captain Addison. 2 Maria.
He m. 2ndly, Colette, relict of Col. McPherson, and had by her a dau., Alexandrine.
VI. Dunbar, of Rochestown, co. Tipperary. (*See that branch.*)
I. Grace, m. to John Palliser, Esq. of Derryluskan, co. Tipperary, and has issue.
II. Elizabeth, m. to the late Lieut.-Gen. Sir Augustine Fitzgerald, Bart., many years M.P. for Clare county.
III. Margaret, m. to Lord Massy, and d. in 1818, leaving issue.

The eldest son,

Thomas Barton, Esq. of Grove, M.P. for Fethard before the Union, m. Mary, dau. of the Hon. General Ponsonby, and sister of Chambre-Brabazon Ponsonby Barker, Esq. of Kilcooly Abbey, and d. in 1820, leaving issue,

William, now of Grove.
Chambre-Brabazon, lieutenant-colonel in the 2nd life guards, d. in 1834.
Charles-Robert, a field-officer in the army.
Mary, m. to George, youngest son of the late Lord Robert Fitzgerald.
Grace, m. 1st, to Lieut.-Col. Pennefather, of Newpark, co. Tipperary, and had issue. She was m. 2ndly, to Major Michael-Angelo Galliazzi, of the Austrian service.
Catherine, m. to Edmond Staples, Esq. of Dunmore, Queen's County.

Arms—Arg., a rose, three boars' heads, erased, gu.
Crest—A boar's head, gu.
Motto—Quod ero spero. *Ancient Motto*—Vis fortibus arma.
Seat—Grove, near Fethard, co. Tipperary.

BARTON OF CLONELLY.

Barton, Folliot-Warren, Esq. of Clonelly, co. Fermanagh, J.P. and D.L., b. 15 Sept. 1798; s. his

5 HUMPHREY, of Aberedow and Lambedr, co. Radnor, which estates he acquired in marriage with Eleanor, dau. and heir of John ap Gwillim. His son and heir,

JOHN BASKERVILLE, Esq. of Aberedow, m. in 1578, Sarah, dau. of Thomas Lewis, of Harpton Court, in Radnorshire, and was father of

THOMAS BASKERVILLE, Esq. of Lambedr in 1610, m. Eleanor, dau. of John Lewis, of Lanwenny, and was s. by his son,

JAMES BASKERVILLE, Esq. of Aberedow, who m. Dorothy, dau. of David Blayney, and by her, who d. in 1697, left a son,

JAMES BASKERVILLE, Esq. of Aberedow, who m. in 1664, Elizabeth, dau. of Edward Griffin, Esq. of Bickmarsh, and was s. by his son,

THOMAS BASKERVILLE, Esq., who m. in 1700, Sybill, dau. of — Collins, Esq. of Bryngwyn, in the co. of Radnor, and was s. by his son,

THOMAS BASKERVILLE, Esq. of Aberedow Court, who m. in 1726, Meliora, eldest dau. of Richard Baskerville, Esq. of Richardston, in Wiltshire, by Jane, dau. of Sir William Gore, Knt. of Barrow Court, and left at his decease in 1740, an only dau. and heiress,

PHILIPPA, who m. in 1767, the Rev. John Powell, of Penland, co. Radnor, by whom (who d. in 1819) she had an only dau. and heiress,

MELIORA, m. in 1787, to Peter Rickards-Mynors, Esq. of Treago.

II. John, who left a son, Henry.
III. Thomas, of Pontrilas.
IV. Elizabeth, wife of Kynard Delabere, or according to some, of Sanacre Delabere, of Kynardsley.

Sir Walter m. 2ndly, Elizabeth, dau. of Henry ap Milo ap Harry, of Poston, by whom he had, with other issue, PHILIP (see BASKERVILLE *of Crosley Park*), and SIMON. This

SIMON BASKERVILLE, Esq. m. Elizabeth, dau. of — Brand, Esq. of Wanborough, in the co. of Wilts, and left three sons, of whom the youngest,

GEORGE BASKERVILLE, Esq. of Tewkesbury, co. Gloucester, m. Eleanor, dau. of — Quarrel, Esq. of Blockland, of Evesham, co. Worcester, and had a son,

THOMAS BASKERVILLE, Esq. of Richardston, in the co. of Wilts, m. in 1604, Johan Lor, by whom he had (with five daus., Jenevora, m. to John Grubbe, Esq. of Potherne; Catharine, m. to Henry Grubbe, Esq.; Elizabeth, m. to John Lambe, Esq.; Anne, wife of John Polwhele, of Polwhele, Esq.; and Mary, m. to William Riven, Esq.) an only surviving son and heir,

FRANCIS BASKERVILLE, Esq. b. in 1615, m. in April, 1635, Margaret, 2nd dau. of John Glanville, Esq. of Broadhinton, in the co. of Wilts (afterwards Sir John Glanville, Knt.) by whom, who d. 28 March, 1696, he left, with four daus., three sons, Walter, who d. s. p. in 1696; THOMAS, successor to his father; and Francis, M.P. for Marlborough. The 2nd son,

THOMAS BASKERVILLE, Esq. m. Mary, dau. of Richard Jones, Esq. of Hanham, in the co. of Gloucester, and had,

I. RICHARD, his heir.
II. George, of Winterbourne Basset, who d. 20 May, 1755, at the age of 73, leaving, with other issue, a dau.,
1 Jane, m. to her cousin, Thomas Baskerville, Esq.

Thomas Baskerville was s. by his son,

RICHARD BASKERVILLE, Esq of Richardston, who m. Jane, dau. of Sir William Gore, Knt. of Barrow Court, in the co. of Somerset, and widow of — Raymond, Esq., by whom he had issue,

I. THOMAS, his successor.
II. MELIORA, b. in 1701, who m. in 1726, Thomas Baskerville, Esq. of Aberedow Court, and left an only child and heiress, PHILIPPA, who m. in 1767, the Rev. John Powell, of Penland, and had an only dau. and heiress,

MELIORA POWELL, who m. 1st, in 1787, Peter Rickards-Mynors, Esq. of Treago, by whom (who d. in 1794) she had issue; 1 PETER RICKARDS-MYNORS, Esq. of Treago, (*See that family*); 2 THOMAS BASKERVILLE, of whom presently, as successor to his relative, Col. Baskerville; 3 Meliora, m. in 1815, to Hugh-Hovell Farmar, Esq. of Dunsinane, in the co. Wexford, and has issue. Mrs. Rickards-Mynors m. 2ndly, Jaspar Farmar, Esq., but dying in 1829, left no further issue.

III. Jane, m. to Thomas Roding, Esq. of Salisbury, and d. s. p.

Mr. Baskerville, of Richardston, d. 14 Sept. 1739, aged 72, and was s. by his only surviving son,

THOMAS BASKERVILLE, Esq. who m. his cousin Jane, dau. of George Baskerville, Esq. of Winterbourne Basset, and left issue at his decease, in 1758 (with a dau., Meliora, who d. unm., in 1773), a son and successor,

THOMAS BASKERVILLE, Esq., lieut.-col. of the 60th regt. of foot, who m. 1st, Anne, only dau. of the Rev. James O'Neale, of Ballyshannon, in the co. of Donegal, and 2ndly, Jane, youngest dau. of Thomas Bishop, Esq. of Kinsale, but d. s. p. in 1817, when his estates devolved upon his cousin, the present THOMAS-BASKERVILLE-MYNORS-BASKERVILLE, Esq. of Clyrow Court.

Arms—Arg., a chevron, gu., between three hurts.
Crest—A wolf's head, erased, arg., holding in its mouth a broken spear, staff, or, head, arg., imbrued, gu.
Motto—Spero ut fidelis.
Seat—Clyrow Court, in the co. Radnor.

BASKERVILLE OF CROWSLEY PARK.

BASKERVILLE, HENRY, Esq. of Woolley House, co. Wilts, and Crowsley Park, co. Oxford, J.P. and D.L., b. 6 Jan. 1793; m. 14 Feb. 1839, Mary-Anna, 2nd dau. of John Burton, Esq. of Cheltenham, and grand-niece of Tolmin North, Esq. of Thurland Castle, co. Lancaster, and has,

I. JOHN, b. 9 Nov. 1839.
I. Mary-Anna. II. Jessie.
III. Helen-Jane. IV. Florence-Emma.

Mr. Baskerville, formerly a civilian at Madras, s. to the estates of his cousin, the late John Baskerville, Esq. of Woolley House, and assumed, by royal license, 5 March, 1838, the surname and arms of BASKERVILLE, in lieu of his paternal one, VIVEASH. He served as high-sheriff of Oxfordshire in 1847.

Lineage.—This is a branch of the great and ancient family of Baskerville.

PHILIP BASKERVILLE, who settled in Wiltshire (son of Sir Walter Baskerville, of Erdisley, K.B., by Elizabeth his 2nd wife, dau. of Henry ap Milo ap Henry, had, by Agnes his wife, dau. of John Hamlyn, of that co.,

JOHN BASKERVILLE, who settled at Malmesbury. He m. and had two sons, Francis and John; the latter,

JOHN BASKERVILLE, of Malmesbury, co. Wilts, buried there, 3 Nov. 1681, was father, by Rebecca his wife, of

JOHN BASKERVILLE, Esq. of Burton Hill, Malmesbury, Wilts, whose eldest surviving son, by his first wife, Elizabeth Wallis, of Slaughterford, was

JOHN BASKERVILLE, Esq. of Woolley, Bradford, Wilts, b. 7 July, 1678, who m. 1st, 19 June, 1701, Anne Webb, of Bradford, which lady d. 26 Dec. following. He m. 2ndly, 6 July, 1710, Rachel, dau. of Joseph Sargent, Esq. of Calne, Wilts, and by her (who d. 18 March, 1744, aged 59), had issue. The 3rd son,

THOMAS BASKERVILLE, Esq. of Woolley, b. 7 March, 1718, m. Anne, dau. of Thomas Dyke, Esq. of Bradford, co. Wilts, and d. in 1779, having had issue,

I. Thomas, an officer in the army.
II. JOHN, of whom presently.
I. Elizabeth, m. 13 March, 1782, to Thomas Todd, Esq. of the General Post Office, London, and of Tunniside, near Lanchester, co. Durham. He d. 11 March, 1827.
II. Susannah, m. to Henry Headley, Esq., M.D., of Devizes, Wilts, who d. s. p. 12 March, 1838.
III. Rachel, d. unm. IV. Anne, d. unm.
V. Sarah, m. 21 April, 1788, to Oriel Viveash, Esq. of Calne, co. Wilts, 2nd son of Simeon Viveash, Esq. of Calne, and Mary Bailey, his wife; and by him (who d. 30 April, 1836, aged 72) had issue,
1 Samuel, b. 19 Jan. 1791, d. in London, 25 Nov. 1830, unm.
2 Henry, who s. his cousin in the Woolley House estate, and assumed the surname and arms of BASKERVILLE. He is the present HENRY BASKERVILLE, Esq. of Woolley House and Crowsley Park.
3 Oriel, of Calne, and the Middle Temple, barrister-at-law, b. 6 Jan. 1795.
4 Charles-Baskerville, of Calne, b. 27 Jan. 1799, m. 19 April, 1824, Eleanor, eldest surviving dau. of Henry Tanner, Esq. of Overton, Wilts: she d. 14 June, 1842.
1 Catherine-Anna, d. young, in 1792.
2 Anne, d. unm. in 1819, aged 25.
3 Eliza-Susannah.
4 Hester, m. 15 Oct. 1829, to William Tanner, Esq. of Overton, Wilts.

The 2nd son,

JOHN BASKERVILLE, Esq. of Woolley, J.P. and D.L. for Wilts, m. in Oct. 1771, Hester, dau. of Nicholas Webb, of Gloucester, and d. 15 March, 1800, aged 54, leaving two sons, JOHN, his heir; and Joseph, of Woolley House, d. unm. 7 Oct. 1812. The elder son,

JOHN BASKERVILLE, Esq. of Woolley House, and of Bath, d. unm., 20 Dec. 1837, and was s. by his cousin, HENRY VIVEASH, Esq., who thereupon assumed the surname and sons of BASKERVILLE, and is the present HENRY BASKERVILLE, Esq. of Woolley House and Crowsley Park.

Arms, Crest, and *Motto*—See preceding family.

Seats—Woolley House, parish of Bradford, Wilts; and Crowsley Park, Henley-on-Thames, Oxfordshire.

BASSET OF UMBERLEIGH AND WATERMOUTH.

BASSETT, ARTHUR-DAVIE, Esq. of Umberleigh and Watermouth, co. Devon, *b.* 14 May, 1801; *m.* 4 Dec. 1828, Harriet-Sarah Crawfurth, descended from the CRAWFURTHS *of Crawfurth Hope*, co. Berwick, and has issue,

I. ARTHUR CRAWFURTH, in holy orders, *b.* 11 Aug. 1830.
I. Harriet-Mary. II. Eleanora-Susan.

Lineage.—On the roll of Battel Abbey appears the name of BASSET, and in the Conqueror's survey, THURSTAN (or, as he is commonly written, THURSTINE) a Norman, held six hides of land in Drayton, co. Stafford. This Thurstine, according to Dugdale, was paternal ancestor of the several families bearing the name of BASSET, which rose into power and distinction very shortly after the Conquest, Ordericus Vitalis stating them to have been previously of baronial rank in Normandy.

JOHN BASSET, Esq. eldest son and heir of Sir John Basset, brother of George Basset, of Tehidy, Cornwall, and grandson of Sir John Basset, who acquired Umberleigh and Heanton Court, Devon, by his marriage with Joan, sister and heir of Philip Beaumont, of Shirwel, Devon, *m.* Frances, dau. and co-heir of Arthur Plantagenet, Viscount Lisle, who surviving him, remarried Thomas Monk, of Potheridge, co. Devon, Esq., and was great-grandmother of the celebrated George Monk, Duke of Albemarle. By Frances Plantagenet Mr. Basset had issue,

SIR ARTHUR BASSET, of Umberleigh, Knt., who *m.* Eleanor, dau. of Sir John Chichester, of Raleigh, Knt., and was father of

SIR ROBERT BASSET, Knt. of Umberleigh, living in 1620, "who," says Prince, "being by his grandmother descended from the Plantagenets, and of the blood royal, in the beginning of King JAMES I.'s reign, made some pretensions to the crown of England, but not being able to make them good, he was forced to fly into France, to save his head" To compound for this as well as to maintain his expensive style of living, Sir Robert greatly injured his estate, and was necessitated to sell White Chapple, the ancient inheritance of his ancestors, and no less than thirty manors. He *m.* Elizabeth, 2nd dau. and co-heir of Sir William Peryam, Knt. chief baron of the Exchequer, and by her, who *d.* in 1633, aged 64, he had issue,

COL. ARTHUR BASSET, his son and heir, *b.* at Heanton Court, in 1597, and *d.* 7 Jan. 1672, having *m.* a dau. and co-heir of Leigh of Burrough, co. Devon, by whom he had a son, who *d. v. p.* Col. Basset was a zealous royalist, and Prince, in his *Worthies*, gives a lengthened memoir of him. He was governor of St. Michael's Mount, when it was surrendered to the parliamentary forces, under Col. Hammond, in 1646, and is buried in the parish church of Heanton Punchardon, co. Devon, where a handsome monument is erected to his memory.

JOHN BASSET, Esq. his son, *d.* in 1660, aged 30, and is buried in Heanton church. He *m.* Susannah, dau. of Bluett, of Holcombe Rogis, co. Devon, and left one son and heir,

JOHN BASSET, who succeeded to the estates on the decease of his grandfather. He was *b.* 1652, and *d.* 1686, having *m.* Elizabeth, dau. of Arthur Acland, of Bittadon, co. Devon, Esq., by whom he left issue,

JOHN BASSET, Esq., who *m.* a dau. of Sir Nicholas Hooper, of Fullabrook, co. Devon, Knt., and *d.* in 1721, leaving

FRANCIS BASSET, Esq. his son and heir, of Heanton Court, who *m.* Eleanora, dau. of Sir William Courtenay, of Powderham, co. Devon, and had three children,

I. FRANCIS BASSET, of Heanton Court, Esq., only son and heir, who dying *unm.*, devised his estates as before mentioned.

I. Eustachia, who *m.* John-Hooke Campbell, Esq., Lord Lyon king of arms, by whom she had issue, Eustachia, *m.* to Admiral Sir George Campbell, G.C.B.; Charlotte, *m.* Sir Thomas Gage, of Suffolk, Bart.; and Louisa-Caroline, *m.* to Henry Hulton, Esq.

II. Eleanora, *m.* John Davie, of Orleigh, in the parish of Buckland Brewer, co. Devon, Esq., and *d.* leaving fourteen children,

1 JOSEPH DAVIE, who took the name of BASSET in pursuance of his uncle's will, and was the late JOSEPH-DAVIE BASSET, of Umberleigh and Watermouth, Esq.

2 Rev. Charles Davie, rector of Heanton Punchardon, co. Devon, *m.* Bridget, dau. of — Boyfield, of Lee, co. Kent, Esq., and *d.* leaving issue, Charles-Christopher Davie, captain 67th regiment; and Mary-Jane, *m.* John May, Esq. of Broadgate, near Barnstaple, deputy-lieutenant and magistrate for the co. of Devon.

3 John Davie, Esq., post-captain in the R.N., who *m.* and *d.*, leaving one dau.

4 Francis Davie, a lieut. in the R. M., who *d. unm.*

5 Peregrine Davie, Esq., in the H.E.I.C.S., *m.* and *d.* in India, leaving one child, a dau.

6 Henry Davie, Esq., also in the H.E.I.C.S., was lost at sea on his return from India. He *d. unm.*

7 Thomas Davie, *d.* young.

1 Eleanora, the eldest dau., *m.* Rev. Lewis Lewis, of Gwinfe, co. Carmarthen, and *d.* leaving issue.

2 Julia, *m.* Rev. Mr. Beadon.

3 Eustatia, *m.* Captain Sharp, of H.M. 29th regt. of foot, and has issue.

4 Frances, *d. unm.* 5 Harriet, *d. unm.*

6 Charlotte, *m.* General Debrisay, and has issue.

7 Mary, *m.* twice, 1st, to — Lumsden, Esq. of the E.I.C.S., and 2ndly, — Jones, Esq., and has issue by both husbands.

JOSEPH DAVIE, Esq., nephew and heir of Colonel Francis Basset, *s.* to the estates of the Basset family upon the demise of his uncle, in 1802, and thereupon assumed the additional surname of BASSET. He *m.* Miss Mary Irwin, of Barnstaple, co. Devon, and had issue,

ARTHUR, now of Watermouth.
Francis, in holy orders, rector of Heanton Punchardon, co. Devon, *m.* Mary, dau. of William Cartwright, Esq. of Teignmouth, co. Devon.
John, *m.* Elizabeth, dau. of Robert Smith, Esq. of Gloucester.
Augusta-Mary, *m.* in 1827, to the Rev. William-Bickford Coham, of Coham and Dunsland, co. Devon.
Mary, *m.* to General Sir Hopton Scott, K.C.B., of the Hon. E.I.Co.'s service.

Arms—Quarterly: 1st and 4th, Barry-wavy of six, or and gu., for BASSET; 2nd and 3rd, az., a ship with two masts, or, the sails trussed up and hoisted to the yards, arg., adorned with flags charged with the cross of England; on a chief of the second, three cinquefoils, pierced, gu., for DAVIE.

Crests—1st, a unicorn's head, couped, arg., mane, beard, and horn, or, on the neck two bars indented, gu., for BASSET; 2ndly, a mount, vert, thereon a lamb, passant, arg., in the mouth a sprig of cinquefoil, gu., slipped vert, for DAVIE.

Seats—Watermouth, in the parish of Ilfracombe, and Umberleigh, near Exeter.

BASSET OF BEAUPRÉ.

BASSET, RICHARD, Esq. of Beaupré, co. Glamorgan, *b.* 6 Dec. 1797, capt. in the royal artillery; *d.* 8 Nov. 1849, leaving his widow, the present proprietrix of the estate of Beaupré.

Lineage.—The BASSETS *of Beaupré* descend from THURSTINE DE BASSET, the Norman who accompanied WILLIAM the Conqueror, as his grand-falconer, to England, and whose name appears on the Roll of Battel Abbey. His son, SIR JOHN BASSET, Knt., was Chancellor and Vice-comes in Glamorganshire, to Robert Fitzhamon, from whom he received the lordship of St. Hilary, in which Beaupré is situated. The representative of this gallant knight,

WILLIAM BASSET, Esq. of Beaupré, son of Edward Basset, Esq. of Brovishin, co. Glamorgan, and Katherine his wife, second dau. of Edward Carne, Esq. of Nash, in the same co., *m.* Cecil, dau. of Thomas Van, Esq. of Penbrey, and with other children, left at his decease, before 1646, a son and heir,

SIR RICHARD BASSET, of Beaupré, Knt., high-sheriff of Glamorganshire, and governor of the town and castle of Cardiff, who *m.* 1st, Mary, dau. of Edward Thomas, of Wenvoe, and had issue, WILLIAM (Sir), his heir; Katherine, *m.* to Edward Matthew, Esq. of Aberman, co. Glamorgan; and Mary, *m.* 1st, to William Games, and 2ndly, to James Lory, Esq. Sir Richard *m.* 2ndly, Elizabeth, dau. of Edward Vanne, Esq. of Marcrosse, and relict of James Matthew, Esq. of Aberman and Roos, and by her had issue, RICHARD (Sir), successor to his half-brother, John, and Edward; Jane, wife of the Rev. Anthony Jones, archdeacon of St. David's; and Eliza, wife of William Andrews, of Cadoxton. Sir Richard Basset was *s.* by his eldest son,

SIR WILLIAM BASSET, of Beaupré, Knt., who *m.* in 1662-3, Martha, third dau. and co-heir of Sir Hugh Wyndham, of Pilsden, co. Dorset, Bart., and relict of Edward Carne, Esq. of Ewenny, co. Glamorgan, but dying *s. p.*, 8 Sept. 1667, was *s.* by his half-brother,

SIR RICHARD BASSET, of Beaupré, knighted at Whitehall, 8 Feb. 1681, who *m.* 1st, Philippa, dau. of James Campbell, of Woodford, co. Essex, and 2ndly, Priscilla, dau. of Col. Phillip Jones, of Fonmon, co. Glamorgan; by the latter only he had issue, viz., PHILIP, of Beaupré, living 1709; RICHARD, of whom presently; Jane, wife of Charles Gibbs; Elizabeth, wife of Thomas Powell, Esq. of Landow, co. Glamorgan; Anne; and Priscilla, *m.* to Thomas Cross. The younger son,

RICHARD BASSET, Esq., a major in Sir John Brull's regiment, baptized 12 Nov. 1690; *m.* 1st, Elizabeth Apprice, and 2ndly, Barbara, dau. of William Bainbrigge, Esq. of Lockington, co. Derby, and by the latter only had issue, an only son,

LIEUT-COL. HENRY BASSET, *b.* in 1730, who *m.* Katherine, dau. of Thomas Bainbrigge, Esq. of Woodseat, co. Derby, and had issue, 1 James, capt. in the army; 2 RICHARD (Sir), brigadier-general and lieut.-colonel 6th West India regiment, *d. unm.* in 1806; 3 THOMAS; and 4 Catherine, who *m.* William King, Esq., and had three sons, William, major in the army; Richard, lieut.-colonel royal artillery; and Henry. The 3rd son,

THOMAS BASSET, Esq., lieut.-col. in the army, sometime Governor of the Military Knights of Windsor, *m.* 1 March, 1790, Elizabeth, dau. of the late Alexander Cruikshanks, Esq. of the co. of Aberdeen, and had issue,

- RICHARD, late of Beaupré.
- William-Alexander, *b.* 1 June, 1810.
- Catherine, *m.* to Capt. Brookes, of Appledore, Devon.
- Hannah-Augusta.
- Isabella, *m.* Major William Bruce, K.H., and has a son, William-West-James Bruce, Esq., on whom Beaupré is entailed.
- Georgiana-Anne-Mansel.

Col. Basset *d.* 7 Jan. 1842.

Arms—Arg., a chevron, between three bugle horns, stringed, sa.

Crest—A stag's head, cabossed; between the attires a cross fitched at the foot, arg.

Motto—Gwell angau na chywilydd.

Seat—Beaupré, co. Glamorgan.

BASSET OF TEHIDY.

BASSET, JOHN, Esq. of Tehidy, co. Cornwall, J.P. and D.L., *b.* in 1791, high-sheriff of Cornwall in 1837; *m.* in 1830, Mary-Elizabeth, dau. of the late Sir Rose Price, Bart. of Trengwainton.

Lineage.—THE REV. JOHN BASSET, rector of Illogan and Camborne, Cornwall, next brother of Francis, 1st Lord de Dunstanville, *b.* in 1760, *m.* 4 Oct. 1790, Mary, dau. of George Wingfield, Esq., and dying 20 May, 1816, left a son, the present JOHN BASSET, Esq.

Arms—Or, three bars, wavy, gu.

Crest—A unicorn's head, couped, arg.; as BASSETT *of Umberleigh*. *Motto*—Pro rege et populo.

BASSETT OF BONVILSTONE.

BASSETT, RICHARD, Esq. of Bonvilstone, co. Glamorgan, J.P. and D.L., *b.* 21 June, 1820; *m.* 24 Oct. 1843, Ann-Maria, 2nd dau. of John Homfray, Esq. of Penlline Castle, co. Glamorgan, by Ann-Maria, dau. and heir of John Richards, Esq. of Corner House, Cardiff, and has issue,

- i. JOHN-RICHARD, *b.* 31 May, 1847.
- ii. Ralph-Thurstine, *b.* 15 Jan. 1851.
- i. Mary-Elizabeth-Constance.

Lineage.—This is a branch of the ancient family of BASSETT *of Beaupré*, which was founded by Thurstine the Norman, grand-falconer to WILLIAM the Conqueror), whose son, Sir John Bassett, Knt., was vice-chancellor to Robert Fitzhamon. Eleventh in descent from this Sir John, was WILLIAM BASSETT, Esq. of Beaupré and St. Hilary, who was father of five sons, of whom the youngest, THOMAS BASSETT, Esq., *m.* Jennet, dau. and heir of Thomas ap Evan ap Vychan, and thus became possessed of the estate of Llantrythyd. His son and heir,

JOHN-THOMAS BASSETT, Esq. of Llantrythyd, *m.* 1st, Alice, dau. of Thomas Love, Esq. of Dynaspowis, and 2ndly, Elizabeth Norton, by the former of whom he was father of a son,

THOMAS BASSETT, Esq. of Llantrythyd, whose son, by Joan Gwillim his wife, was JOHN BASSETT, Esq., father, by Margaret Williams his wife, of the REV. WILLIAM BASSETT, rector of Newton Nottage, living 1624, who *m.* Jennet, dau. of the Rev. Roger Williams, and had a son, the REV. THOMAS BASSETT, prebendary of Llandaff, who *d.* 1666, leaving by his wife, Rachel Mathews, a son, THOMAS BASSETT, father of the REV. JOHN BASSETT, prebendary of Llandaff, whose son,

JOHN BASSETT, Esq. of Bonvilstone, *b.* in 1745, high sheriff of Glamorganshire in 1824, *m.* Anne Morgan, and dying 11 Dec. 1827, was *s.* by his son,

JOHN JAMES, who *d. s. p.* 1838, and was *s.* by his brother,

THOMAS-MORGAN BASSETT, Esq. of Bonvilstone, *b.* in Feb. 1780, who *m.* in 1817, Anne, eldest dau. of the Rev. Dr. Morgan, and had issue,

- RICHARD, now of Bonvilstone.
- John-Morgan, *d. unm.* 23 Jan. 1841.
- William-Watkin, an officer 56th regt.
- Mary, *m.* the Rev. Charles Rumsey Knight, of Tithegstone Court; and *d.* in 1848, leaving a dau. Florence.
- Susannah, *m.* Louis Thowroude, and has issue.
- Louisa-Catherine, *m.* the Rev. Louis Thomas, and has issue.

Mr. Bassett *d.* 5 Nov. 1840.

Arms, Crest, and *Motto*—Same as BASSETT *of Beaupré*.

Seat—Bonvilstone House, Cardiff.

BASTARD OF KITLEY.

BASTARD, EDMUND-RODNEY-POLLEXFEN, Esq. of Kitley and Buckland Court, both in co. Devon, *b.* 7 Sept. 1825; *s.* his father 8 June, 1838; *m.* 22 Nov. 1853, Florence-Mary, eldest dau. of Simon Scrope, Esq. of Danby Hall, co. York.

Lineage.—The family of BASTARD has been seated in Devonshire ever since the Conquest. Robert Bastard appears in Domesday Book to have had large grants in that county. His descendants have intermarried with the heiresses of Crispin and of Killiowe, in the co. of Cornwall, and into the families of FitzStephen, Besilles, Damarell, Gilbert, Reynell, Hele, and Bampfylde, and have at different periods served as sheriffs of the county. Their seat, for many generations, was at Garston, near Kingsbridge, until, about the end of 17th century,

WILLIAM BASTARD, Esq., by marriage with the heiress of Pollexfen of Kitley, acquired that estate, which has since been the family residence. His son,

POLLEXFEN BASTARD, Esq. of Kitley, *m.* Lady Bridget Poulett, dau. of John, 1st Earl Poulett, and was *s.* at his decease, in 1733, by his eldest son,

WILLIAM BASTARD, Esq. of Kitley. He *m.* Ann, dau. of Thomas Worsley, Esq. of Ovingham, in the co. of York, and was *s.* at his decease, in 1782, by his elder son,

JOHN-POLLEXFEN BASTARD, Esq., M.P. for Devon, who *m.* Sarah, widow of — Wymondesold, Esq. of Lockinge, in the co. of Berks, but dying without issue, 4 April, 1816, he was *s.* by his brother,

EDMUND BASTARD, Esq., sometime M.P. for Dartmouth, who *m.* Jane, dau. and heiress of Captain Pownoll, R.N., of Sharpham, Devon, and had issue,

- EDMUND-POLLEXFEN, his heir.
- John, of Sharpham, capt. R.N., and M.P. for Dartmouth, who inherited the Pownoll estates. He *m.* Frances, dau. and co-heiress of Benjamin Wade, of The Grange, co. York, Esq.; and *d.* 11 Jan. 1835, leaving an only child and heiress, Frances, *m.* 2 July, 1850, to Wm.-Frederick, Viscount Chewton, who *d.* 1854, of wounds received at the Battle of the Alma.
- Philemon-Pownoll, in holy orders; *m.* Mary, eldest dau. of Mr. Justice Park.

Mr. Bastard *d.* in 1816, and was *s.* by his son,

EDMUND-POLLEXFEN BASTARD, Esq. of Kitley, M.P. for Devon, *b.* 12 July, 1784, who *m.* 22 Jan. 1824, the Hon. Anne-Jane Rodney, only surviving dau. of George, 2nd Baron Rodney, of Rodney Stoke, and had by her (who *d.* 25 April, 1833), three sons,

- EDMUND-RODNEY-POLLEXFEN, now of Kitley.
- Baldwin-John-Pollexfen, *b.* 11 March, 1830.
- William-Pollexfen, *b.* 12 Jan. 1832.

Mr. Bastard *d.* 8 June, 1838.

Arms—Or, a chevron, az.

Crest—A dexter arm, embowed, in plate armour, ppr., garnished, or, the elbow towards the sinister, the hand in a gauntlet, grasping a sword, also ppr., pommel and hilt, gold, in bend sinister, the point downwards.

Motto—Pax potior bello.

Seats—Kitley, near Yealmpton, and Buckland Court, near Ashburton, both in Devon.

BASTARD OF CHARLTON MARSHALL.

BASTARD, THOMAS-HORLOCK, Esq. of Charlton Marshall, co. Dorset, J.P. and D.L., *b.* in 1772; *m.* 1st, in 1793, Elizabeth Biggs, of Blandford, and by her (who *d.* in 1810) had issue,

I. Thomas-Horlock, b. in in 1796.
II. Elizabeth-Horlock, m. in 1819, to John Brine, commander, R.N.

Mr. Bastard m. 2ndly, in 1811, Eliza Muston, of Blandford, and had issue,

I. Henry-Horlock, b. in 1812, M.A., in holy orders, of Wakehill House, Ilminster, m. 20 July, 1854, Anna-Catharine, dau. of the late Edward Sanders, Esq. of Maidstone.

This gentleman, who was high-sheriff in 1812, is only son of the late Thomas Bastard, Esq. of Blandford Forum, and subsequently of Charlton Marshall, who was 2nd son of Thomas Bastard, Esq. of Blandford, by Mary his wife, dau. of Henry Horlock, Esq. of Charlton Marshall, and grandson of Thomas Bastard, originally of Belchalwell, by Bridget Creech his wife, sister of the poet Creech.

Arms—Or, a chevron, az.
Crest—A griffin's head, collared and armed, or.
Residence—Charlton Marshall, near Blandford.

BATEMAN OF KNYPERSLEY HALL.

Bateman, John, Esq. of Knypersley Hall, co. Stafford, and of Tolson Hall, Westmoreland, high-sheriff for Staffordshire in 1830, b. 31 Oct. 1782; m. 30 May, 1810, Elizabeth, 2nd dau. of the late George Holt, Esq. of Redivals, in Lancashire, and has issue,

James, b. 18 July, 1812.

Lineage.—John Bateman, Esq. of Tolson Hall, son of Thomas Bateman, of the same place, who d. in 1736, m. Elizabeth, dau. of Edward Branthwaite, Esq. of Carlinghill, in the co. of Westmoreland (direct lineal descendant from, and inheritor of the estates of, Robert Branthwayt, of Carlinghill, keeper of the Tower of London, *temp.* James I., and dying in 1783, was s. by his elder son,

James Bateman, Esq. of Tolson Hall, who m. Margaret, dau. of Edward Nicholson, of Kendal, merchant, and granddau. to the Rev. William Nicholson, of Old Hutton, by Margaret, first-cousin to Secretary Craggs, and had issue, John, his heir; James, who d. in 1800; Elizabeth, m. to William Thorpe, Esq.; Margaret, m. to O.-P. Wathen, Esq., 4th son of Sir Samuel Wathen; and Susanna, m. to Richard Gould, Esq. Mr. Bateman d. in 1824, and was s. by his elder son, John Bateman, Esq., of Knypersley Hall.

Arms—Az., on a fesse, embattled, between three crescents, issuant from each an estoile, arg., the chemical character of Mars, sa.
Crest—A tower, arg., issuant therefrom a demi-eagle, wings elevated, sa., charged on the breast with the chemical character of Mars, or; in the beak, a wreath of oak, ppr.
Seats—Knypersley Hall, co. Stafford; and Tolson Hall, Westmoreland.

BATEMAN OF MIDDLETON HALL.

Bateman, Thomas, Esq. of Middleton Hall, co. Derby, b. 8 Nov. 1821; m. 2 Aug. 1847, Sarah, dau. of Mr. William Parker, and has issue,

I. Thomas-William, b. 9 March, 1852. I. Sarah.

Lineage.—Richard Bateman, Esq. of Hartington, b. in 1727, lineal descendant of William Bateman, of South Winfield, living 4th Richard II., m. in 1758, Elizabeth, dau. of Ralph Leek, Esq. of The Heath House, Chaddleton, in Staffordshire, and by her, who d. in 1784, had issue,

I. Thomas, his heir.
II. Richard, b. in 1763; m. twice, but d. s. p. in 1808: his widow m. 2 Nov. 1810, John Stringer.
III. William, of Manchester, merchant; b. in 1774; m. in 1799, Mary, dau. of Samuel Swire, merchant, by Isabella his wife, dau. and co-heir of Richard Bent, of Manchester, and of Isabel his wife, dau. and co-heir of Thorpe, of Hopton, in Yorkshire. Mr. William Bateman d. at Ardwick, 14 July, 1817, leaving issue,
   1 Henry, of Trinity College, Cambridge, M.A.; b. 5 Oct. 1801.
   2 Thomas, b. 6 April, 1806.
   3 William, b. 18 July, 1806; d. 10 Jan. 1818.
   4 Samuel, b. 4 Oct. 1810.
   5 Frederick, b. in 1815; d. in 1818.
   1 Mary, m. in 1832, to William Kay, M.D., of Cheltenham.
   2 Elizabeth. 3 Isabella-Anne.
I. Elizabeth, d. young.
II. Nancey, m. 1st, in 1796, to Nathan Sutton, of Leek; and 2ndly, to John Gibson, of Tattershall, in Lincolnshire, merchant.

Mr. Bateman d. in 1774, and was s. by his son, Thomas Bateman, Esq. of Middleton Hall, high sheriff of Derbyshire in 1823, b. 27 Sept. 1760; m. 13 April, 1786, Rebekah, dau. and co-heir of Arthur Clegg, of Manchester, merchant, and by her (who d. in 1797) had issue,

William, F.A.S.; b. 25 July, 1787; m. 19 June, 1820, Mary, dau. of James Crompton, of Brightmet, in Lancashire; and dying 11 June, 1835, left an only child,
   Thomas, now of Middleton Hall.
Thomas, b. in 1792; d. in 1810.
Rebekah, m. 1816; to Samuel Hope, Esq. of Liverpool, and has issue.

Arms—Or, three crescents, each surmounted by an estoile, gu.
Crest—A crescent and estoile, as in the arms, between two eagles' wings, or.
Seat—Middleton Hall, Derbyshire.

BATEMAN OF HARTINGTON HALL.

Bateman, Richard-Thomas, Esq. of Hartington Hall, co. Derby, b. 9 Sept. 1794; m. 26 May, 1820, Madelene, dau. of Robert Willoughby, Esq. of Cliffe, in Warwickshire, and has issue,

I. Hugh. II. Richard. III. Thomas.
IV. Francis-Willoughby.
I. Elizabeth. II. Madeleine.

Lineage.—That the family of Bateman was settled at Hartington before the year 1600, appears by the entries in the Heralds' College, as well as by a letter of Sir Anthony Bateman, lord-mayor of London in 1664, dated in Jan. 1644, in which, after stating that his father is "just dead at an advanced age," he says, that the deceased had remembered in his will "the poor of Hartington, where he was born."

Hugh Bateman, Esq. of Hartington (4th in descent from Hugh Bateman, elder brother of Richard Bateman, chamberlain of London, and sometime M.P., father of Sir Thomas Bateman, created a Baronet, 1664), m. Elizabeth, dau. and co-heir of John Osborne, Esq. of Derby, by Elizabeth his wife, dau. and eventual co-heir of William Sacheverell, Esq. of Barton, Notts, and of Morley in Derbyshire, and had a son,

Richard, of Derby, b. in 1719; who m. 11 June, 1755, Catherine, dau. of William Fitzherbert, Esq. of Tissington, in Derbyshire, and had two sons,
   1 Hugh, successor to his grandfather.
   2 Richard, a deputy-lieut., and magistrate for the counties of Derby and Stafford, and high-sheriff for the former shire in 1812; who m. 12 Oct. 1792, Elizabeth, only child and sole heiress of the Rev. Thomas Keelinge, of Uttoxeter, in Staffordshire; and dying 29 March, 1821, leaving issue,
      Richard-Thomas, of whom presently.
      John, b. in Feb. 1800; in holy orders; m. Emily, dau. of E. Shewell, Esq.
      James-Alleyne-Sacheverel, b. 10 Dec. 1805; a deputy-lieutenant for Derbyshire.
      Thomas-Osborne, b. 1 March, 1809.
      Joyce-Osborne, d. in 1808.
      Mary-Elizabeth, m. 20 March, 1829, to the Rev. James-Hamilton Chichester, of Arlington, in Devonshire; and d. in 1830.
      Eliza-Catherine, d. in 1819 unm.

Hugh Bateman d. 24 Nov. 1777, and was s. by his grandson,

Hugh Bateman, Esq. of Hartington Hall, b. 21 March, 1756, who was created a Baronet 15 Dec. 1806, with remainder, on failure of the issue male of his body, to the heirs male of his daughters. He m. 4 Feb. 1786, Temperance, dau. of John Gisborne, Esq. of Derby, and had two daus.,

I. Catherine Juliana, who m. in 1815, Edward-Dolman Scott, Esq., eldest son of Sir Joseph Scott, Bart., and had a son,
   Francis-Edward Scott, Esq., b. in 1824; who s. his maternal grandfather, and is the present baronet.
II. Amelia-Anne, m. to Sir Alexander Hood, Bart.

Sir Hugh Bateman d. in March, 1824, and was s. at Hartington by his nephew, the present Richard-Thomas Bateman, Esq. of Hartington Hall.

Arms—Or, three crescents, with an estoile of six points above each crescent, gu.; a canton, az.
Crest—A crescent and estoile, as in the arms, between two eagles' wings, or.

BATEMAN OF GUILSBOROUGH.

Bateman, The Rev. Edmund-Hazelrigg, M.A., of Guilsborough, co. Northampton, b. 25 Dec. 1803; m. 23 Nov. 1842, Magdalene Leckner.

Lineage.—This family of Bateman is of antiquity in Warwickshire.

JOHN BATEMAN, de Clifton, co. Garwick, (whose will, dated 24 Feb. 1579, was proved 15 June, 1580), *m.* Alice Page, and had four sons, William, of Pulkington, co. Warwick; John, devisee of estates at Clifton; Thomas; and Richard.

Subsequently, by the Visitation of 1678, there was a Bateman of Tottenham Court, co. Middlesex, one of the six clerks in Chancery, and his brother,

EDMUND BAREMAN, of Clifton, co. Warwick, and of Windsor, co. Berks, who was father of

EDMUND BATEMAN, of Windsor and Shawell, lord of the manor of Guilsborough, and auditor of the king's exchequer. From him descended

MARY BATEMAN, of Guilsborough, only dau. and heir of John Bateman, Esq. of Guilsborough, who *d.* in 1784. She *m.* the Rev. Joshua Wigley, D.D., rector of Clifton, near Guilsborough, who was directly descended from the ancient family of WIGLEY *of Wigwell*, co. Derby, and *d.* in Nov. 1822, leaving by her husband (who *d.* in 1790) two daus. and co-heirs; Elizabeth, *d. unm.* 15 Feb. 1838, and

MARY WIGLEY, of Guilsborough, *m.* to the Rev. John Buckley, of Kilworth, who assumed, by royal license, in 1824, the surname of BATEMAN, in pursuance of the will of his wife's grandfather, John Bateman. Their issue were,

EDMUND, present representative.
John, in holy orders, M.A. of Oxford; *b.* 3 Sept. 1805.
Richard, *b.* 12 Feb. 1807.
Joshua-Wigley, M.A. of Cambridge; *b.* 27 Nov. 1808, receiver-general of the Duchy of Cornwall; *m.* 1 Jan. 1841, Emma-Louisa-Rosa, dau. of General Blacker, and has issue a dau., Grace.
Thomas, M.A. of Cambridge; *b.* 16 March, 1810; *m.* 29 June, 1840, Marianne, dau. of John Daubeny, Esq., LL.D., of Doctors' Commons, London, and has issue, Arthur-Wigley and Mary-Daubeny.
Charles, *b.* 28 Dec. 1812; *m.* Catherine Needham, of Manton, and has a dau., Elizabeth.
Mary-Anne.

Arms—Or, three stars, issuing from crescents, gu.
Crest—A star, issuing from a crescent, gu., as in the arms, between two wings, gold.
Motto—Sidus adsit amicum.
Seat—Guilsborough, co. Northampton.

BATEMAN OF OAK PARK.

BATEMAN, JOHN, Esq. of Oak Park, Killeen, and Ardravale, co. Kerry, high-sheriff in 1820, and at one time M.P. for Tralee, *b.* 26 Nov. 1792; *m.* 25 Sept. 1824, Frances, youngest dau. of Nathaniel Bland, Esq. of Randalls Park, Leatherhead, co. Surrey, and has,

ROWLAND DE CONINGSBY, J.P., *b.* 16 May, 1826.

Lineage.—This family, claiming descent from the De Baudements, Seigneurs de Braine-sur-Visle, is directly descended from

ROWLAND BATEMAN, an officer in Hierome Sankey's regiment of horse, who settled in Kerry about 1654, and was subsequently high-sheriff of the county. His son,

JOHN BATEMAN, Esq. of Killeen, co. Kerry, *m.* 1st, a dau. of William Trenchard, Esq. of Mount Trenchard, co. Limerick, but had no issue. He *m.* 2ndly, Anne, 2nd dau. of the Right Hon. George Evans, and sister of the 1st Lord Carbery, by whom he had issue,

ROWLAND, of whom presently.
George, *m.* a dau. of Anthony Stoughton, of Rattoo, and settled at Dromaltin, co. Kerry.
John, who settled in co. Limerick, and was ancestor of the BATEMANS *of Alta Villa*, in that county.

The eldest son,

ROWLAND BATEMAN, Esq. of Oak Park, *b.* in Jan. 1705, *m.* in 1727, Elizabeth, eldest dau. of Nicholas Colthurst, Esq. of Ballyhaly, co. Cork, eldest son of John Colthurst, Esq. of Cooleneshanavalley, and uncle of Sir John-Conway Colthurst, created a Baronet in 1744; and by her had issue,

ROWLAND, *s.* to his father.
COLTHURST. (*See* BATEMAN *of Bartholey*.)
John, *m.* Olivia, dau. and co-heiress of Hugh Edwards, Esq., and relict of Richard Parsons, 2nd Earl of Rosse, but had no issue.
Elizabeth, *m.* to Anthony Stoughton, of Rattoo, and had issue two sons, Thomas and Anthony, and four daus.
Anne, *m.* to Francis Crosbie, Esq. of Rusheen, *s. p.*
Penelope, *m.* to Richard Smyth, Esq. of Ballynatray, co. Waterford, and had issue.
Mary, *m.* to Thomas Fitzgerald, Knight of Glyn, and had issue.
Sarah, *m.* to the Rev. Dr. Barry, of Cork, and had issue.
Francis, *m.* to Pierce Crosbie, Esq. of Ballyheigue, and had, with daus., two sons, of whom the elder, Colonel Crosbie, *m.* his cousin Elizabeth, 2nd dau. of Rowland Bateman.
Jane, *m.* to Richard Dunscombe, Esq., co. Cork, and had issue.

The eldest son,

ROWLAND BATEMAN, Esq. of Oak Park, M.P. for the co. of Kerry, and also for the borough of Tralee, *m.* in 1758, Letitia, eldest dau. of Sir Thomas Denny, Knt. of Tralee Castle, by Agnes his wife, dau. of John Blennerhassett, Esq. of Ballyseedy. The issue of this marriage was,

ROWLAND, *b.* 1760; *d.* young.
ROWLAND, successor to his father.
Thomas, *b.* 1767; *d.* young.
Agnes, *m.* to Richard Chute, Esq. of Tallygarron, and had issue, two sons, Francis and Rowland, and three daus.

The only surviving son,

ROWLAND BATEMAN, Esq. of Oak Park, *m.* in 1790, his first-cousin, Arabella, 2nd dau. of Sir Barry Denny, of Tralee Castle, Bart., descended in a direct line from the celebrated Sir Anthony Denny, Knt., groom of the stole and privy councillor to HENRY VIII. By this lady Mr. Bateman had issue,

JOHN, present representative.
William, *b.* 1 May, 1797.
Thomas, *b.* 26 Aug. 1802; *d.* 1820.
Jane, *d.* 26 Jan. 1792.
Letitia, *m.* 8 Sept. 1831, to Emanuel-Hutchinson Orpen, Esq.

Arms—Or, on a chevron, between three escallops, gu., an ostrich feather, arg.
Crest—A pheasant, ppr.
Motto—Nec pretio nec prece.

BATEMAN OF BARTHOLEY.

BATEMAN, COLTHURST, Esq. of Bartholey House, co. Monmouth, high-sheriff in 1832-40, *b.* 2 Oct. 1780; *m.* 2 Nov. 1809, Jane-Sarah-Gardner, only surviving child and heiress of John-Kemeys Gardner-Kemeys, Esq. of Bartholey House, and has issue,

I. JOHN, *b.* Feb. 1814.
II. George-Colthurst, *b.* Aug. 1815.
III. Rowland, *b.* Nov. 1816, an officer in the navy, *d.* on board H. M. S. "Wellesley," in the Persian Gulf, in 1839.
IV. Robert, *b.* Aug. 1819.
V. Reginald, of the R.N. *b.* Dec. 1820.
VI. Thomas, *b.* March, 1823.
VII. Frederick, *b.* April, 1825.
I. Jane, *m.* in Aug. 1836, to John Gwalter Palairet, B.A., Christ Coll., Camb.
II. Sarah.

Lineage.—COLTHURST BATEMAN, Esq. of Bedford House, near Listowel, co. Kerry, 2nd son of Rowland Bateman, of Oak Park, Esq., by Elizabeth his wife, dau. of Nicholas Colthurst, Esq., *m.* in Sept. 1779, Jane, dau of Robert Dobson, Esq. of Angrove, co. Cork, and had issue,

COLTHURST, now of Bartholey.
Rowland, in holy orders; *m.* Eliza, dau. of Maurice Fitzmaurice, Esq. of Duagh, and relict of James Erdington, Esq. of Scotland.
John, a lieut. in the 13th Bengal N.I.; *d. unm.*
Jane, *m.* to Robert-R. Dobson, Esq., late captain in the 5th foot.
Anne, *m.* to Patrick Maitland, Esq., since deceased.
Elizabeth, *m.* to Daniel Staunton, Esq., deceased.
Dorothea, *m.* to Admiral John Maitland.

Arms, Crest, and *Motto,* as BATEMAN *of Oak Park.*
Seat—Bartholey House, near Uske, co. Monmouth.

BATES OF MILBOURNE.

BATES, NATHANIEL, Esq. of Milbourne Hall, co. Northumberland, *b.* 16 June, 1805.

Lineage.—The family of BATES has been established many centuries in the co. of Northumberland.

THOMAS BATES, Esq. of Ovington Hall, in Northumberland, M.P. for Morpeth, which he continued to represent in the reigns of MARY and ELIZABETH, appears to have been high in favour with the former queen, for we find her majesty addressing a complimentary letter to him in 1556-7. Thomas Bates was subsequently, during the reign of ELIZABETH, appointed supervisor of all her majesty's houses, lordships, manors, lands, and tenements in Northumberland. His great great-grandson,

RALPH BATES, Esq. of Halliwell, East Hartford, &c., co.

Northumberland, bapt. at Earsdon, 29 Aug. 1613, transmitted in 1666, to the Herald's Office, a pedigree of his family. He *m.* Margaret, dau. of Thomas Chatour, of Butterby, and dying 11 March, 1690, aged 78, was *s.* by his eldest son,

RALPH BATES, Esq. of Halliwell, bapt. 16 Feb. 1646, whose son (by his 2nd wife, Anne, dau. of William James, Esq. of Washington),

RALPH BATES, Esq. of Halliwell, *b.* 8 Jan. 1688, succeeded to the family estates at the death, *s. p.*, in 1734, of his half-brother, Thomas. He *m.* 1st, 6 May, 1714, Mary, dau. of John Bacon, Esq. of Staward, in Northumberland, by whom (who *d.* in March, 1723), he had issue, Anne, wife of the Rev. Charles Stoddart; Isabella, *m.* to William Watson, Esq.; and Margaret, wife of Cuthbert Watson, Esq. Mr. Bates *m.* 2ndly, in 1725, his cousin, Isabel, eldest dau. of Richard Bates, Esq. of Newcastle-on-Tyne, and had further issue, RALPH, his heir; Thomas, whose eldest son, Col. Thomas Bates, *m.* a dau. of Sir Robert Waller, Bart., and has issue, Mary, *m.* in 1754, to Henry Wilson, Esq. of Newbottle; Esther, *m.* to Richard Wharton, Esq.; Elizabeth, *d. unm.*; and Dorothy, *m.* 1st, to William Clayton, Esq., of Newcastle, and 2ndly, to — Brick, Esq. Ralph Bates, of Halliwell, a very active magistrate, *d.* 23 Nov. 1754, and was buried at St. Dunstan's in the West, London. His elder son and successor,

RALPH BATES, Esq., *b.* 14 May, 1730, sheriff for Northumberland in 1762, *m.* 1st, 16 July, 1759, Jane Mitford, by whom (who *d.* in childbed, 6 May, 1760) he had an only dau., Isabella-Jane, *m.* in 1786, to the Rev. Henry Ingilby, brother to the late Sir John Ingilby, Bart. of Ripley Castle. Mr. Bates *m.* 2ndly in 1762, Anne, sister of the late Henry Ellison, Esq. of Hebburn Hall, and had (with other children who *d. unm.*), RALPH, his heir; Richard, killed on board the "Argo" man-of-war, in 1783; Cuthbert; Hannah, *m.* in 1786, to John Hunter, Esq. of Lisburn; and Mary-Anne, *m.* in 1795, to the Rev. John Fawcett. Mr. Bates *d.* 2 Aug. 1783, and was *s.* by his el lest son,

RALPH BATES, Esq. of Milbourne Hall, Halliwell, &c., *b.* 22 Oct. 1764, for many years lieut.-col. of the 6th (Enniskillen) dragoons. This gentleman, col.-commandant of the southern regiment of Northumberland local militia, J.P. and D.L., served as high-sheriff in 1812. He *m.* 4 Dec. 1798, his second-cousin, Sarah, 3rd dau. of the late Rev. Nathaniel Ellison, vicar of Bolam and Doddington, by Jane his wife, dau. and heiress of Col. Furye, of Faringdon, Berks, and had two sons and three daus, viz.: RALPH, NATHANIEL, Jane-Anne, Sarah, and Georgiana, *m.* 8 March, 1848, the Rev. John Elphinstone Elliot, 3rd son of James Elliot, Esq. of Wolflee, co. Roxburgh. Col. Bates *d.* 6 June, 1813, and was *s.* by his eldest son,

RALPH BATES, Esq. of Milbourne Hall, *b.* 13 Dec. 1799, who *d.* 6 June, 1853, and was *s.* by his brother, the present Nathaniel Bates, Esq. of Milbourne.

Arms—Sa., a fesse engrailed, or, between three dexter hands, couped at the wrist, bendways, arg.
Crest—A naked man, holding in his dexter hand a willow wand.
Motto—Et manu et corde.
Seat—Milbourne Hall, co. Northumberland.

BATES OF DENTON.

BATES, HENRY-WILLIAM, Esq. of Denton, co. Sussex, J.P., a capt. in the royal Sussex militia, *b.* in 1807; *s.* his father, John-Henry Bates, Esq., in 1828.

Lineage.—JOHN BATES, Esq. of Beaconsfield, co. Bucks, *b.* in 1722, an alderman of the city of London, *d.* in 1785, during his year of serving the office of sheriff for that city, and was buried in Beaconsfield church. He *m.* Miss Ellison, and left a son, HENRY, and two daus., viz.: Martha, *m.* to Samuel Ferns, M.D. of Beaconsfield, whose only son, Col. Sir Bates Ferns, *d.* in 1836; Anne, *m.* to M. Staples, banker, of London.

HENRY BATES, Esq. of Denton, co. Sussex, the son and heir, *b.* in 1754, *m.* Sarah, only dau. of Jonathan Ellison, Esq. of Cheshire, and *d.* in 1826, leaving by his wife, who *d.* in 1835, an only son,

JOHN-HENRY BATES, Esq. of Denton, co. Sussex, J.P. and D.L., *b.* in 1775, capt. in the 2nd life-guards, who *m.* in 1806, Harriet-Eliza, 3rd dau. of Wm. Smith, Esq. of Chiswick, co. Middlesex, and had by her (who *d.* in 1826),

HENRY-WILLIAM, his successor.
John-Ellison, in holy orders, incumbent of Crosby, co. Lancaster, *b.* in 1809, *m.* in 1836, Ellen, dau. of F. Carlton, Esq. of Dublin, and has issue, Henry; Charles-Ellison; and Mary.
Francis-Edward, *b.* 1811, a midshipman R.N., *d.* in 1824.
Charles-Chester, B.A., Trinity Coll., Cambridge, *b.* in 1816.

Mr. Bates *d.* in 1828.

Arms—Sa., a fesse, between three hands, arg.
Crest—An arm in armour, embowed, in the hand a truncheon.
Motto—Manu et corde.
Seat—Denton, co. Sussex.

BATHURST OF LYDNEY PARK.

BATHURST, CHARLES, Esq. of Lydney Park, co. Gloucester, J.P., *b.* 15 Jan. 1790; *m.* 27 Aug. 1819, Mary, dau. of William Trendall, Esq. of Gloucester, and of Hall Court, Marcle, co. Hereford, by Jane his wife, dau. of the Rev. James Benson, D.D., and the Lady Anne his wife, dau. of Allen, 1st Earl Bathurst.

Lineage.—BENJAMIN BATHURST, Esq. of Lydney, co. Gloucester, 3rd son of Sir Benjamin Bathurst, Knt. cofferer of the household to Queen ANNE, by Frances his wife, dau. of Sir Allen Apsley, Knt. of Apsley, in Sussex, *m.* 1st, Finetta, dau. and co-heir of Henry Poole, Esq. of Kemble, in Wiltshire, and by her (who *d.* in 1738) had two sons, THOMAS and POOLE, and four daus., all of whom *d. s. p.*, except a dau. ANNE, who *m.* 25 Jan. 1752, Charles Bragge, Esq. of Cleve Hill, Mangotsfield, co. Gloucester, and was mother of a son, CHARLES BRAGGE, heir to his uncle. Mr. Bathurst *m.* 2ndly, Catherine, dau. of Laurence Brodrick, D.D., brother of Alan, Viscount Midleton, and had, with other issue, a son, HENRY, late bishop of Norwich. (*See* BURKE'S *Peerage*). The eldest son,

THOMAS BATHURST, Esq. of Lydney Park, *d. unm.*, and was *s.* by his brother,

POOLE BATHURST, Esq. of Lydney Park, who also *d.* without issue, having bequeathed his estates to his nephew,

THE RIGHT HON. CHARLES BRAGGE, M.P., who assumed, by sign-manual, in 1804, the surname and arms of BATHURST. He was chancellor of the duchy of Lancaster in 1812. He *m.* 1 Aug. 1788, Charlotte, youngest dau. of Anthony Addington, M.D., father of Viscount Sidmouth, and dying 18 Aug. 1831, left surviving issue,

CHARLES, now of Lydney Park.
William-Hiley, in holy orders, of Barwick-in-Elmet, Yorkshire, who *m.* Mary-Anne Rhodes, and has two sons, the elder named Charles; and four daus.
Charlotte. Anne.

Arms—Sa., two bars, erm.; in chief, three crosses-patée, or.
Crest—A dexter arm in mail, embowed, holding a club with spikes, all ppr.
Motto—Tien ta foy.
Seat—Lydney Park, co. Gloucester.

BATT OF PURDYSBURN AND OZIER HILL.

BATT, ROBERT, Esq. of Purdysburn, co. Down, and Ozier Hill, co. Wexford, *b.* in 1795; *m.* in 1841, Charlotte, dau. of Samuel Wood, Esq., and has issue,

ROBERT, *b.* in 1844; and four daus.

Mr. Batt is a magistrate and deputy-lieut. for co. Down.

Lineage.—This family, originally from Cornwall, was founded in Ireland, by an officer in CROMWELL'S army, who acquired considerable property in the co. of Wexford. His grandson,

THOMAS BATT, of Ozier Hill, *m.* in 1718, Jane, dau. of Thomas Devereux, and was *s.* by his eldest son,

SAMUEL BATT, Esq., father of Major Thomas Batt, who was killed in the American war, when the property devolved on his youngest brother,

ROBERT BATT, Esq. of Ozier Hill, co. Wexford, captain in the 18th regt., who *m.* in 1765, Hannah, dau. of Samuel Hyde, Esq., and *d.* in 1783, having had issue five sons, NARCISSUS, his heir, William, Samuel, Robert, and Thomas. The eldest son,

NARCISSUS BATT, Esq. of Purdysburn, co. Down, and Ozier Hill, co. Wexford, *m.* in 1793, Margaret, dau. of Thomas Greg, Esq., and by her, who *d.* in 1848, had issue, ROBERT, now of Purdysburn; Thomas; Elizabeth; and Mary, *m.* to Thomas Greg, Esq. Mr. Batt *d.* in 1840.

Arms—Arg., on a cross, between four bats, displayed, sa., three escallops, in pale, or.
Crest—A crescent, arg., charged with an escallop, gu.
Motto—Virtute et valore.
Seats—Purdysburn, co. Down; and Ozier Hill, co. Wexford.

BATTEN OF THORN FAULCON.

BATTEN, JOHN, Esq. of Thorn Faulcon and Yeovil, co. Somerset, J.P. and D.L., *b.* in 1775; *m.* in March, 1818, Sarah, youngest dau. of John Copeland, Esq. of Iver, co. Bucks, and Lingfield Lodge, co. Surrey, and by her (who *d.* in 1821) had issue,

I. JOHN, *b.* in Feb. 1815, *m.* in May, 1841, Grace-Elinor, only surviving dau. of John White, Esq. of Upcerne, co. Dorset, and Fairlee, Isle of Wight, and had issue, JOHN-MOUNT, *b.* in April, 1843, and a dau.
II. Edmund, *b.* in Nov. 1817, M.A., barrister-at-law, *m.* in Aug. 1843, Jemima, only dau. of The Chisholm, of Erchless Castle, co. Inverness, by Elizabeth his wife, dau. of Macdonell of Glengarry, and has issue, James-Forbes-Chisholm, *b.* 13 Jan. 1847, and Jemima-Emily.
III. Herbert-Butler, *b.* in July, 1819.
I. Emily.

Lineage.—This family has been seated for nearly six centuries in the county of Somerset.

Its origin appears to have been Flemish. In the reign of EDWARD I., the leading merchants of the wool staple, trading with Flanders and of Flemish origin, were Ingeram de Beteyn, William de Beteyn, and John Beteyn.

Ingeram de Beteyn also held lands in Wendover, co. Bucks, where Andrew Batyn, probably his son, was M.P. for Wycombe in 1307.

William Beteyn was sheriff of London, 1289, and a member of the Goldsmiths' Company. Richard Beteyn, goldsmith, probably his son, served as mayor of London in 1327, and twice represented the city in parliament. He bore a conconspicuous part in the dethronement of EDWARD II., and in sequence the city received extensive charters from EDWARD III. on his accession. His arms were for many hundred years in the Grey Friars' Church, Newgate, where he was interred.

Henry Batyn settled in Somersetshire, and was M.P. for Bath, 1297; from that time to the present his descendants have remained in that county.

For a period of 250 years, this family occupied an important station at Bath, and in the adjoining counties. Thomas Batten was steward of the priory of Bath in 1534. After the dissolution of monasteries, the family seem to have quitted Bath, one branch to have settled in Wiltshire, of which was SIR HENRY BATTEN, Knt., gentleman-pensioner to JAMES I., and another to have gone to the more western parts of the county, of which were ANDREW BATTEN, of Easton St. George, and JOHN BATTEN, of Michael Church, co. Somerset.

ANDREW BATTEN, of Easton, had a son, SIR WILLIAM BATTEN, Knt., one of the most eminent naval commanders in the civil wars; he was surveyor of the navy, 1638, vice-admiral of England from 1642 to 1647, and particularly distinguished himself at the sieges of Dartmouth, Lyme, and Portland Castle. He was appointed governor of Mount Batten, a fort which he built at Plymouth, and which is still existing. Though he served the parliament, he was sincerely attached to a constitutional monarchy, and averse to the designs of the army, to stop whose attempts upon the king's life, he revolted with the fleet to Prince CHARLES. On the Restoration, however, he was merely reinstated in his post of surveyor, and became M.P. for Rochester, till his death, in 1667. His issue in the male line is extinct.

JOHN BATTEN, of Michael Church, is the immediate ancestor of the line before us. In 1597, he is returned as having lands in Michael Church. From him sprang, in a direct line (with a dau., Grace, *m.* to John Fletcher), a son,

NATHANIEL-BUTLER BATTEN, Esq., *b.* 1713 (son of Robert Batten, the friend of Sir Richard Steele, and the author of the letters in the *Spectator*, vol. i., signed R B.), sold his estate at Pitminster, and purchased the manor and advowson of Thorn Faulcon. He *m.* in 1738, Joanna, dau. and co-heiress of John Prigge, Esq., and had issue, JOHN-PRIGGE, who *m.* Miss Wallis, and had issue, with daus., an only son, the present JOHN BATTEN, Esq. Mr. Butler Batten *m.* 2ndly, Miss Adams, and had issue,

NATHANIEL.
Robert, *m.* Hannah, dau. of John Copeland, Esq. of Peckham, and Lingfield Lodge, co. Surrey, high-sheriff for that co. in 1735, but *d. s. p.*
EDMUND.

Mr. Butler Batten *d.* in 1790: his eldest son, by his first marriage, having succeeded to his mother's property, the estate of Thorn Faulcon came to his son,

NATHANIEL BATTEN, Esq. of the Inner Temple and Thorn Faulcon; he *d. unm.* in 1819, and was *s.* by his brother,

EDMUND BATTEN, Esq. of Thorn Faulcon and Yeovil, a deputy-lieutenant for Somersetshire, who *m.* Miss Chaffey, of Stoke, and dying in 1836, *s. p.* (his widow survived until 1845), was *s.* by his nephew, JOHN BATTEN, Esq.

Arms—Quarterly: 1st and 4th, az., a chevron, erm., between three anchors, ppr.; 2nd and 3rd, gu., a saltier, or, between four fleurs-de-lis of the 2nd, quartering DRAKE and ASHE.

Crest—The trunk of an oak tree, couped at the top, issuing from towards the top two branches, all ppr. The family also use a sea-lion, erect, holding in his paws an anchor, all ppr.

Seats—Thorn Faulcon, near Taunton; and Hollands, near Yeovil, both co. Somerset.

BATTERSBY OF LISLIN AND ASHGROVE.

BATTERSBY, ROBERT, Esq., M.D., of Ashgrove and Lislin, co. Cavan, *b.* 9 Oct. 1805; *m.* 20 April, 1835, Susanna-Maria, dau. of the late Henry Woodward, Esq. of Drumbarrow, co. Meath, by his wife, Sarah-Catherine Wade, and has issue,

I. CHARLES-HENRY, *b.* 16 Jan. 1836.
II. Robert-William, *b.* 26 Dec. 1840.
III. Henry-Wade, *b.* 26 Jan, 1843.
IV. William-Edward, *b.* 24 May. 1847.
I. Sarah-Catherine. II. Frances-Esther.
III. Elizabeth-Mary.

Lineage.—This family, which came over to Ireland with WILLIAM III., claims to derive from an ancient house of the same name, formerly seated in the co. of York, of which was Nicholas Battersby, of Harrabeare, in Cornwall, who entered his pedigree in the Herald's visitation of that county, in 1620, grandson of Nicholas Battersby, of Battersby Hall, co. York.

WILLIAM BATTERSBY, Esq. of Clonabrany, son of the first settler in Ireland, was *b.* in 1676, *m.* Mary, dau. of Ambrose Sharman, Esq., and *d.* in 1762, having had issue,

William, of Smithstown, *m.* Miss Garnett; and *d. s. p.*
ROBERT, heir to his father.
JOHN, of Lakefield, *b.* in 1722; *m.* 1st, Elizabeth Shiel, of Monaghan, by whom he had one son; and 2ndly, Sarah Leslie, by whom he left at his decease, in 1803, seven sons and five daus.
Thomas, *d. unm.*
Charles, *m.* Miss Hastings, and left at his decease, in 1756, a son, James, capt. 29th regt., who *d. s. p.*, and a dau., *m.* 1st, — Hanna, Esq., and 2ndly, W. Campbell, Esq.
Elizabeth. Caroline.

The 2nd but eldest surviving son,

ROBERT BATTERSBY, Esq. of Bobsville, *b.* in 1721, *m.* in 1763, Marianne, dau. and co-heiress of Haynes Wade, Esq. of Lislin, co. Cavan, and had issue,

I. HAYNES-WADE, his heir.
II. William, of Bobsville, *b.* 1767; lieut.-col., J.P., and dep.-gov. for Meath, for which co. he served as high-sheriff in 1804. He *m.* in 1794, Anna-Maria, dau. of Long, of Longfield, co. Tipperary; and *d.* in 1837, having had issue, 1 Robert, in holy orders, rector of Killeagh, *b.* in 1796; 2 Richard, in the army, *b.* in 1798; 3 William, in holy orders, *b.* in 1800, *m.* in 1840, Mary, dau. of Col. William Caulfeild, of Benown; 4 Thomas, *b.* in in 1804, *d.* in 1837; 5 Henry, *b.* 1806, *d.* in 1826; 6 Francis, *b.* 1810, J.P.; 7 Charles, *b.* 1811; 8 John, *b.* 1814, *m.* in 1841, Catherine, dau. of the Rev. Thomas Blakeney, of Holywell, co. Roscommon: she *d.* in 1842; 9 Hercules-Soame-Jenyns, *b.* in 1820; 1 Marianne, *d.* in 1841; and 2 Harriett.
III. Thomas, in the army, deceased.
IV. Robert, *b.* 1793; *m.* Penelope, dau. of John Battersby, Esq. of Lakefield, and left at his decease, in 1824, surviving issue, ROBERT, M.D. in the army, *b.* 1802; Sarah; Marianne; Penelope, *m.* to Robert Roberts, Esq.; Elizabeth; and Catherine, *m.* to Thomas Gerrard, Esq.
V. Edward, *m.* Elizabeth, dau. of Rev. Wm. Ryan, and has issue, Robert; William, *m.* Harriette Ormonde, dau. of Rev. J. Phelan; and Jenyns, *m.* and has two daus., Mary-Elizabeth and Virginia.
I. Francis, *d.* young.
II. Mary. III. Abigail, *m.* to A. Morland, Esq.
IV. Catherine, *m.* to Edward-J. Smith, Esq. of Chiswick.

Mr. Battersby *d.* in 1785, and was *s.* by his son,

HAYNES-WADE BATTERSBY, Esq., J.P., late of Ballard, co. Westmeath, *b.* in 1765, who *m.* in Oct. 1804, Judith, dau. of the Rev. Charles Woodward, D.D. of Drumbarrow, by whom (who *d.* in 1847) he left at his decease, in 1841,

ROBERT, now of Lislin and Ashgrove.
Charles, *d. unm.* 1833.
Esther, *m.* in 1832, to Hugh Gaullagher, Esq.; and *d.* in 1840, leaving one dau.

Arms—Or, a saltier, paly of twelve, erm. and gu.; a crescent for difference.

Crest—A ram, passant, armed and unguled, gold.

Motto—Ante honorem humilitas.

Seat—Lislin, co. Cavan.

BATTERSBY OF LOUGH BANE, NEWCASTLE, &c.

BATTERSBY, GEORGE, Esq. of Lough Bane, co. Westmeath, Q.C., LL.D., *b.* 8 Sept. 1802; *m.* 10 Dec. 1830, Charlotte-Sarah, dau. of the Right Hon. John Radcliff, LL.D., late judge of the Prerogative Court in Ireland, and has issue,

I. THOMAS-GEORGE, *b.* 9 Oct. 1832.
II. John-Radcliff, *b.* 30 Sept. 1839.
I. Betanna-Catherine, *m.* 10 Jan. 1852, John-Colley Pounden, Esq. of Ballywalter, co. Wexford, and has issue, Charlotte, Elizabeth, and Alice-Betanna.

Lineage.—JOHN BATTERSBY, Esq. of Lakefield, co. Meath, J.P., 2nd son of William Battersby, Esq. of Smithstown House, by Mary his wife, dau. of Ambrose Sharman, Esq., *b.* in 1722, *m.* 1st, Elizabeth Shiel, of Monaghan, and by her had an only child, WILLIAM, of Freffans, co. Meath, *b.* 16 Nov. 1764, who *m.* Frances, dau. of Nathaniel Preston, Esq. of Swainstown, and by her had two sons and two daus., viz.: Francis, *d. unm*; Arthur, *m.* Eliza, dau. of Major Dillon, and *d.* leaving a son, William, and a dau.; Anna, *m.* to Lambert Disney, Esq.; and Frances, *m.* to Chas.-John Battersby, Esq. John Battersby *m.* 2ndly, 7 Sept. 1765, Sarah, dau. of the Rev. Henry Leslie, of Nutfield, co. Fermanagh, and by her had issue,

LESLIE, in holy orders, of Skreene, co. Sligo, *b.* 20 July, 1766, *m.* 5 July, 1796, Anna-Maria, dau. of Patrick Palmer, Esq., barrister-at-law, and *d.* leaving issue, John, lieut. R.N., settled at Hamilton, Upper Canada; Leslie; Joseph, *d. s. p.*; Edwin, of Dublin; George, of Dublin, and William, settled at Hamilton, Upper Canada.
THOMAS, of whom hereafter.
Francis, lieut.-col., C.B., of Listoke House, Drogheda, *b.* 19 Sept. 1795; served under the Duke of York in Holland, subsequently at Alexandria, Copenhagen, and the capture of the West India Islands, as major in the 8th foot. He commanded the Glengarry light infantry at the battle of Niagara, and throughout the last American war, and at its termination was presented with an address of thanks and a sword of great value, by the houses of legislature of Canada, for his services. He *m.* Eliza, 2nd dau. of George Rotherham, Esq. of Crossdrum, co. Meath, and had issue a son, John Prevost, lieut. 60th Royal rifles, *b.* in 1826, and a dau., Frances, *m.* in June, 1848, to Mathew Coates, Esq. of Newtown Prospect, co. Meath.
John, *b.* 28 June, 1781, a J. P. for Meath, raised and commanded the Athboy and Clonmullon Yeomanry during the rebellion of 1798. He *m.* Frances, dau. of Robert Wade, Esq. of Clonabrany, co. Meath, and *d.* in 1839, leaving issue, John, in holy orders, of Drumelton, co. Westmeath; Robert, of Lakefield; and Thomas.
Alexander, *b.* 10 Aug. 1783, *m.* 10 July, 1807, Eliza, dau. of James Cusac, Esq. of Lara, co. and Kildare, *d.* leaving an child, John, of Miltown, co. Westmeath.
Henry-Robert, post-capt. R.N., *m.* 10 May, 1810, Miss Chapman, dau. of William Chapman, Esq., and niece of Sir Thomas Chapman, of Killua Castle, co. Westmeath, Bart., *d. s. p.*
George, *b.* 20 April, 1788, capt. 23rd light dragoons, and aide-de-camp to General Howard during the war in Spain. He was severely wounded at Toulouse, and fell returning from the last charge of the cavalry at Waterloo. There has been a splendid monument erected to his memory in the church of Waterloo, by "a mourning friend," whose name is unknown to his family. Capt. Battersby *d. unm.*

The 2nd son,

THOMAS BATTERSBY, Esq. *b.* 23 Oct, 1767, *m.* 16 Oct. 1799, Margaret-Catharine, eldest dau. of George Rotherham, Esq. of Crossdrum, co. Meath, and *d.* 26 Feb. 1839, leaving fourteen children,

GEORGE, now of Lough Bane.
Thomas, now of Newcastle, co. Meath, J. P., *b.* 16 Oct. 1803, *m.* 17 May, 1837, Henrietta-Mary-Anne, dau. of John Rotton, Esq. of Bath.
Edward, lieut. R.N., *b.* 3 May, 1805, *d.* on board H.M.S. "Satellite," at Barbadoes, 4 Oct. 1839, *unm.*
Henry, *b.* 4 April, 1806, *m.* Frances, dau. of T. Rutherfoord, Esq. of St. Doolagh's, co. Dublin.
Francis, M.D.
Frederick-William.
Charles-John.
William-Alexander, scholar of Trinity Coll., Dublin.
Catherine, *m.* 16 Nov. 1836, to William-Smith Harman, Esq. of Crossdrum.
Sarah, *m.* 29 Jan. 1841, to the Rev. Hugh-Henry O'Neill, of Monter Conaught, co. Cavan.
Elizabeth-Jane.
Isabella.
Barbara.

Arms, Crest, and *Motto,* as BATTERSBY *of Lislin.*

Seat—Lough Bane, Collinstown, Westmeath.

BATTY OF BALLYHEALY.

BATTY, ESPINE, Esq., late of Ballyhealy, co. Westmeath, *s.* his brother in 1847; *m.* 1st, in 1832, Jane, dau. of Michael Harris, Esq. of Dublin, by whom he has a dau., JANE; and 2ndly, in 1835, Belissa, dau. of John Smyly, Esq., Q.C.

Lineage.—This family, which came originally from England, has been seated at Ballyhealy, since about 1690, when Charles Batty, Esq., was the head of the family. His son, CHARLES BATTY, Esq. of Ballyhealy, *m.* Margaret Espine, of the co. of Wicklow, and *d.* in 1737, leaving two sons, the Rev. John Batty, rector of Timolin, co. Kildare, who *d. s. p.*, and

ESPINE BATTY, Esq., who *m.* in 1753, Alicia Whittingham, by whom he had two sons, PHILIP, his heir, and John-Espine, who *m.* Letitia, dau. of — Bolton, Esq. of Brazil, co. Dublin, and had two sons, John, *d. s. p.*, and Arthur-Henry; and six daus., Eliza; Letitia, deceased; Louisa; Annette; Caroline; and Florence. The eldest son,

PHILIP BATTY, Esq. of Ballyhealy, *m.* twice, 1st in 1780, Catherine, dau. of Gaynor Barry, Esq. of the co. of Dublin, and 2ndly, in 1811, Louisa, dau. of John Nugent, Esq. of Clonlost, co. Westmeath, but had issue by his first wife only, several children, viz.,

ROBERT-FITZHERBERT, his heir, who *d. unm.* in 1836.
Gaynor-Barry, *d. unm.*
FITZHERBERT, successor to his father, *d. unm.* in 1847.
ESPINE, now representative of the family.
Michael-William, who *d. unm.* in 1822.
Edward, in holy orders, vicar of Duleek, co. Meath, to whom the estate of Ballyhealy was transferred in 1853: he *m.* 1st, Mary-Anne, widow of Capt. Caulfeild, and by her had two daus., Louisa, *m.* to Nicholas Evans, Esq., and Emily, who *d. unm*; he *m.* 2ndly, Catherine Kincaid, by whom he has a son, PHILIP, and two daus., viz., Anna-Maria and Frances.
William-Barry.
Catherine-Hannah.

Family Seat—Ballyhealy, Castletown Delvin, Ireland.

BAYLY OF BALLYARTHUR.

BAYLY, EDWARD-SYMES, Esq. of Ballyarthur, co. Wicklow, J.P. and D.L., formerly capt. 34th regt., high-sheriff in 1837, *b.* 9 April, 1807; *m.* 20 June, 1835, Catherine, youngest dau. of the Right Hon. Maurice Fitzgerald, Knight of Kerry, by Maria his wife, youngest dau. of the Rt. Hon. David Latouche, of Marlay, co. Dublin, and has issue,

I. HENRY-NICHOLAS, *b.* 2 Oct. 1843.
II. Edward-Richard, *b.* in June, 1846.
III. Maurice-Spring-Rice, *b.* in 1850.
I. Maria-Elizabeth-Frances-Gertrude, *d.* 20 April, 1853.
II. Gertrude-Caroline.
III. Selina-Emily.
IV. Julia-Catherine, *d.* 20 March, 1854.

Lineage.—The Baillies or Baylys derived their name and origin from their ancestors having anciently been bailiffs of the districts of Carrick, Kyle, and Cunningham, in Scotland. The BAILIES *of Lamington*, co. Lanark, became seated there by marriage with the only dau. and heiress of the Scottish patriot, Sir William Wallace, of Lamington. From this alliance descended

LAMBART BAYLY, Esq., barrister-at-law, third son of Sir Edward Bayly, Bart. of Plasnewyd, co. Anglesey, by Dorothy his wife, dau. of the Hon. Oliver Lambart; and younger brother of Sir Nicholas Bayly, Bart., father of Henry, 1st Earl of Uxbridge; *m.* Elizabeth, dau. of John Rotton, Esq., and had two sons: the younger, John, dean of Killaloe, *m.* Mary, dau. of William Wall, Esq. of Coolnamuck, co. Waterford, and *d.* in July, 1831, having had issue, Paget, capt. in the 7th hussars; and a dau., Letitia. The elder son,

THE REV. EDWARD BAYLY, rector of Killurin, co. Wexford, *b.* in 1743, *m.* 1st, in 1773, Elizabeth, dau. of Richard Symes, Esq. of Ballyarthur, co. Wicklow, by Eleanor his wife, dau. of Loftus Cliffe, Esq. of Ross, and had issue an only son, HENRY-LAMBART, of whom hereafter. He *m.* 2ndly, in 1783, Mildred, dau. of Joshua Davis, Esq., barrister-at-law, by whom he had issue,

Edward, in holy orders, rector of Hoartown, co. Wexford; m. in Jan. 1827, Ellen, dau. of Rev. Joseph Miller, and has several children.
Henry-Albert.
Anna-Lucinda, m. to Bartholomew Warburton, Esq. of Birrview, King's Co.
Elizabeth-Jane, m. to Col. Skerritt, of the 55th regiment.

The Rev. Mr. Bayly d. in Dec. 1825. His only son by his first marriage,

The Rev. Henry-Lambart Bayly, of Ballyarthur, co. Wicklow, heir to his maternal uncle, the Rev. James Symes, of Ballyarthur, co. Wicklow, m. 29 Aug. 1802, Selina, eldest dau. of Sir Charles Levinge, Bart., and dying 25 July, 1827, left issue,

Edward-Symes, present representative.
Henry-Lambert, b. 9 Dec. 1808; for many years in the E.I.Co.'s service; m. Margaret, dau. ot the Rev. Thomas Acton.
Charles-James, in holy orders; b. 9 Sept. 1811; rector of Collinstown, co. Westmeath.
Richard-William, b. 11 Nov. 1817.
George-Augustus, b. 26 May, 1819; m. 1851, Elizabeth, dau. of Sir Nicholas Colthurst, Bart.
Elizabeth-Frances, m. 24 Nov. 1830, to the Rev. William Aylmer, 3rd son of the late Sir Felton Aylmer, Bart.
Anna-Selina, m. 1830, to Capt. William Congreve, of the 3rd light dragoons, eldest son of Richard Congreve, Esq. of Burton, co. Chester.
Caroline-Sarah. Elizabeth-Mary.

Arms—Az., nine estoiles, arg.
Crest—A boar's head, erased, ppr.
Motto—Quid clarius astris.
Seat—Ballyarthur, Blessington, co. Wicklow.

BAYLY OF DEBSBOROUGH.

Bayly, John, Esq. of Debsborough, co. Tipperary, J.P. and D.L., b. 3 Sept. 1805; m. 1st, 13 May, 1829, Catherine, youngest dau. of Thomas Yates, Esq. of Barry, co. Lancaster, first-cousin of the late Sir Robert Peel, Bart., and by her (who d. 22 Sept. 1833) he has one son,

John, b. 30 Nov. 1831.

He m. 2ndly, 17 Oct. 1839, Gertrude-Catherine, 3rd dau. of the late William-Henry Armstrong, Esq. of Mount Heaton, King's County, by his wife, the only dau. of the late Col. Charles M'Donell, of New Hall, M.P. for the co. of Clare, and has by her a son,

Lancelot-Peter, b. 9 Feb. 1842.

Lineage.—This influential family has long maintained a leading position in the co. of Tipperary.

John Bayly, Esq. of Debsborough, b. 17 June, 1691, m. 7 July, 1720, Deborah, dau. and co-heir of Benjamin O'Neale, archdeacon of Leighlin, by Hannah his wife, dau. of Sir Joshua Paul, Bart., and by her, who m. 2ndly, in 1736, Henry Prittie, Esq. of Dunalley Castle, M.P., had issue, John; Benjamin (whose only son, Benjamin-O'Neale, m. Letitia Archer, and had issue); O'Neale; Henry; Paul; Hannah; Constantia; and Elizabeth. The eldest son, John Bayly, Esq. of Debsborough, b. 4 Dec. 1724, m. Bridget, dau. of Robert Holmes, Esq. of Johnstown, co. Tipperary, and had issue, John; Henry; Benjamin; Peter; William; Deborah; Lucinda; and Bridget, wife of Charles M'Donell, of New Hall, M.P. for the co. of Clare. The eldest son,

John Bayly, Esq. of Debsborough, b. in 1755, m. in 1776, Catherine, eldest dau. and co-heir of Lancelot Crosbie, Esq. of Tubbrid, co. Kerry, and by her, who inherited the estates of her uncle, John Gustavus Crosbie, Esq., M.P., was father of

John Bayly, Esq. of Debsborough, b. 15 Dec. 1777, who m. 1 May, 1800, Mary-Elizabeth-Helena, only child and heir of Richard Uniacke, Esq. of Mount Uniacke, co. Cork, and had issue,

John, now of Debsborough.
Richard-Uniacke, of Ballynaclogh, co. Tipperary, J.P.; b. 1 Nov. 1806; m. 7 Feb. 1837, Harriet, only dau. of the Very Rev. John Head, dean of Killaloe, by Susanna his wife, dau. of Edward Darby, Esq., of Leap Castle, King's Co., and has issue, Richard-Uniacke, b. 15 Dec. 1838; and John-Prittie, b. 4 July, 1842.
Lancelot-Peter, b. 27 Sept. 1807; m. 12 Oct. 1841, Lydia-Catherine, only dau. of the Very Rev. Gilbert Holmes, dean of Ardfert, by Lydia-Waller his wife, youngest dau. of the late Francis Saunderson, Esq. of Castle Saunderson, co. Cavan, and has issue, Lancelot-Gilbert-Alexander, b. 27 Aug. 1842.

Seat—Debsborough, co. Tipperary.

BEACH OF OAKLEY HALL.

Beach, William, Esq. of Oakley Hall, co. Hants, and Keevil House, co. Wilts, J.P. and D.L., b. 24 July, 1783; m. 1 Feb. 1826, Jane-Henrietta, dau. of John Browne, Esq. of Salperton, co. Gloucester, and by her (who d. 11 Aug. 1831) has issue,

I. William-Wither-Bramston, b. 25 Dec. 1826.
I. Mary-Jane. II. Henrietta-Maria.

Mr. Beach (who is nephew of the late Sir William Hicks, Bart., uncle to Sir Michael-Hicks Hicks-Beach, the present baronet, and 2nd son of the late Michael Hicks, Esq. of Beverstone Castle, who assumed the additional surname of Beach, upon his marriage with Henrietta-Maria, only dau. of William Beach, Esq. of Netheravon) dropped, by sign-manual, in 1838, the name Hicks, retaining that of Beach only.

Arms—Vairé, arg. and gu., on a canton, az., a pile, or.
Crest—A demi-lion, rampant, couped, or, holding in the paws an escocheon, az., charged with a pile, or.
Seats—Oakley Hall, Hants; and Keevil House, Wilts.

BEADLE OF SOUTH ELLA.

Beadle, John, Esq. of South Ella, East Riding co. York, b. 17 Dec. 1786; a magistrate for Kingston-upon-Hull, and chairman of the Hull Dock Company from 1840 to 1847.

Arms—Sa., a chevron, between three escallops, arg., all within a bordure, engrailed, of the last.
Crest—A stag's head, erased, ppr., ducally gorged, or.
Seat—South Ella, East Riding of Yorkshire.

BEADON OF GOTTEN HOUSE.

Beadon, William, Esq. of Gotton House, co. Somerset, J.P., m. in 1802, Martha-Anna, only child of John Hammet, Esq., lieut. R.N., by Elizabeth his wife, dau. and co-heir of Thomas Musgrave, Esq., of Gotten House, and has issue,

I. William, of Otterhead, co. Devon, b. 10th Nov. 1803, m. 1 June, 1827, Anne, eldest dau. of William Oliver, Esq. of Hope Corner, co. Somerset, by Anne Ruddock his wife, and has issue,
  1 William-Hammet, barrister-at-law, b. 18 May, 1829; m. 14 Sept. 1852, Fanny-Adele-Lambart, dau. of the late John-Clayton Cowell, Esq., 1st Royals, by Frances-Anne-Hester his wife, granddau. of Richard, Earl of Cavan.
  2 Edward-Musgrave, b. 9 Dec. 1833, 85th regt.
  3 Robert-John, b. 11 April, 1844.
  1 Anne-Oliver, m. 28 Dec. 1852, to Woodforde Ffooks, Esq.
  2 Martha-Anna. 3 Mary-Musgrave.
  4 Emily-Ruddock.
II. John Hammet, capt. 1st Somerset militia, m. in Sept. 1845, Emma-Harriet, only dau. of James Whiting, Esq. of The Grove, Carshalton, Surrey, and has issue, Emma-Alice.
III. George, comm. R.N., m. 17 Oct. 1833, Sarah, youngest dau. of William Oliver. Esq. of Hope Corner (sister of his brother William's wife), and has issue two sons two daus.,
  1 George-Robert. 2 Oliver-Armitage.
  1 Georgiana. 2 Annabella.

Lineage.—The family of Beadon, variously written Beaudin, Beaudyn, or Beadyn, was of considerable importance at a very early period, and enjoyed extensive property in Devonshire; in particular the manor of Egge Buckland, and Compton, in the hundred of Roborough. This estate was held by them until conveyed in marriage to Roger Whitleigh, of Efford, by Margaret, dau. and heir of Sir Robert de Beadyn, once high-sheriff of Devon, *temp.* Edward I., and twice during the reign of Edward II.

Robert Beadon, living at Pinkworthy, about 1645, m. Agnes Spurway, of the ancient family of Spurway *of Spurway*, (a pedigree of which may be found in the *Visitations of Devon*), and by her had (besides a dau., who m. Pincombe of Oakford, co. Devon) five sons, of whom the 2nd,

Richard Beadon, Esq., m. Joan, dau. and co-heir of John Radford, Esq. of Oakford, (derived, through the marriage of John Radford, Esq. of Oakford, living in 1620, with Dorothy, dau. of John Beare, Esq. of Beare, from Richard Radford, Esq. of Oakford, with whom the entry in the *Visitation of Devon* commences). By this lady Mr. Beadon had issue, The eldest son,

ROBERT BEADON, Esq., *m.* in May, 1728, Mary, dau. of the Rev. Dr. F. Squire, and niece of Dr. Samuel Squire, bishop of St. David's,* and had issue,

I. Edwards, in holy orders, rector of North Stoneham, Hants, and domestic chaplain to Lord Bute; *m.* Mary, dau. of Sir William Watson, M.D., and had issue,

1 John-Watson, in holy orders, rector of Christian Malford, Wilts: *m.* Juliana, sister of Joseph-Davie Bassett, Esq. of Umberleigh and Watermouth, co. Devon.
2 William, drowned accidentally at Cambridge.
3 Frederick, in holy orders, rector of North Stoneham, Hants; *m.* Mary-Anne, eldest dau. of the Rev. Henry Wilder, LL.D. of Purley Hall, Berks, and had issue a son, Richard, *d.* an infant, and two daus., of whom, Anne *m.* the Rev. Mr. Heathcote, son of Sir John Heathcote, Bart.
1 Mary-Anne, *m.* to the Rev. Edward Bernard, only son of Dr. Bernard, provost of Eton.
2 Charlotte, *m.* to George Norman, Esq. of Bromley, Kent, high-sheriff for that county.
3 Harriet, *m.* to J. Wilder, Esq. of Purley Hall, Berks.

II. GEORGE, of whom presently.
III. Richard, D.D., Bishop of Gloucester, and subsequently of Bath and Wells; *m.* Rachel, dau. and co-heir of the Rev. John Gooch, prebendary of Ely, son of Sir Thomas Gooch, Bart., Bishop of Ely; and *d.* in April, 1824, leaving an only son,

Richard, *m.* 15 May, 1805, Annabella, dau. of the late Sir William-P.-Ashe A'Court, Bart., M.P., and sister of Lord Heytesbury, and has issue,

William-Frederick, barrister-at-law, of the Inner Temple; *m.* Jessie, dau. of General Cockburn.
Richard-A'Court, in holy orders, vicar of Cheddar, vicar and prebendary of Wiveliscombe, co. Somerset; *m.* Isabella, dau. of Dr. White, D.D., and has issue two daus.
Hyde-Wyndham, in holy orders, vicar of Latton, Wilts, and of Haselling, co. Somerset; *m.* Frances, dau. of Lieut.-Gen. Sir William Ponsonby, K.B., and has a dau., Mary.
Cecil, E. I. Co.'s civil service; *m.* Harriet, dau. of Major Ralph Sneyd, and has issue four sons.
Annabella, *m.* Henry Bruce, Esq., and has issue.

IV. Robert, *d. unm.*, having perished on board the "Prince George" packet, which was burnt in Plymouth Sound.
I. Sarah, *m.* Richard Buller, Esq., and had issue.
II. Mary, *m.* George Turner, Esq., and has issue, George, and other children.
III. Susanna, *m.* to John Otway, Esq.
IV. Agnes, *m.* John Blake, Esq., and has issue.

The second son,

GEORGE BEADON, Esq. of Oakford, *b.* in 1733, *m.* Rebecca, eldest dau. of William Leigh, Esq. of Bardon, co. Somerset, grandson of Robert Leigh, Esq. of Bardon, by Margaret his wife, dau. of John Collard, Esq. of Spaxton, and fifth in descent from Robert Leigh, Esq. of Ridge. who, removing from Devonshire, settled at Bardon in 1595. By this lady Mr. Beadon had issue,

I. Robert, of Taunton and Corfe, co. Somerset, *m.* Hannah, dau. of Hugh Petten, Esq.; and *d.* in Aug. 1845, aged 83, having had issue,

1 Robert.
2 Edwards, *m.* Anne, relict of the late Rev. Richard-F. Follett, cousin of the late Sir William Follett, attorney-general.
3 Richard-John, in holy orders, rector of Sherwell, co. Devon, *m.* in 1848, Charlotte-Elizabeth, eldest dau. of the late Sir Arthur Chichester, Bart.
1 Mary. 2 Charlotte, *d. unm.*
3 Susanna, *d. unm.*

II. George, *m.* Charlotte, dau. of the Rev. Jeremiah Griffiths, and had issue,

1 George, in holy orders, rector of Axbridge, co. Somerset.
2 Charlotte. 3 Frances.

III. WILLIAM, of Gotten House.
I. Rebecca, *d. unm.*
II. Mary-Anne, *m.* to Robert Franklin, Esq.; and *d.* 5 March, 1846, *s. p.*

* Through this marriage the Beadons have become related to the families of Whalley, Rogers, and Twyford, the last of which is now represented by the Rev. T.-R. Joliffe, of Ammerdown Park, co. Somerset, only surviving son of the late Thomas-Samuel Joliffe, Esq., M.P., by Mary-Anne his wife, dau. and heiress of the Rev. Robert Twyford, of Kilmersdon, by Eleanor Squire his wife.

BEALE OF THE HEATH HOUSE.

BEALE, THOMAS, Esq. of The Heath House, co. Salop, *m.* 18 May, 1815, Constance-Isabella, dau. of the late Richard Salwey, Esq. of The Moor Park, co. Salop, and has issue.

Lineage.—BARTHOLOMEW BEALE, Esq. of Gray's Inn, clerk of the signet, and lord of the manor of Walton, Bucks, purchased that estate from the family of Longueville, and *d.* in 1660, aged 77, leaving four sons; Henry; Theodore, rector of Walton; BARTHOLOMEW; and Charles, (father, by Mary Cradock, his wife, who *d.* in 1697, aged 65, of two sons, Charles, *b.* in 1660, and Bartholomew, D.D.). The third son,

BARTHOLOMEW BEALE, Esq. auditor of imprests in the Exchequer, purchased the manor of Hopton Castle, co. Salop, and *d.* at his house in Hatton Garden, London, 8 May, 1674, leaving, by his wife, a dau. of Col. Hunt, a son,

BARTHOLOMEW BEALE, Esq. of The Heath House, co. Salop, who *m.* Elizabeth, dau. Sir Walter Yonge, Bart. of Culleton, co. Devon, and had a son and successor,

THOMAS BEALE, Esq. of The Heath House, father of

THOMAS BEALE, Esq. of The Heath House, who *m.* and had issue. His eldest dau., Mary, *m.* in 1806, the Rev. John-Bright Bright, and his eldest son is the present THOMAS BEALE, Esq. of The Heath House.

Arms—Sa., on a chevron, or, between three griffins' heads, erased, arg., as many estoiles, gu.
Crest—A unicorn's head, erased, arg., charged on the neck with three estoiles, gu.
Seat—The Heath House, Shropshire.

BEAMISH OF RAHEROON.

BEAMISH-BERNARD, ARTHUR, Esq. of Palace Anne, co. Cork, the present head of the Beamish family. (For his birth, maternal descent, &c., see BERNARD *of Palace Anne.*)

Lineage.—The family of Beamish has been settled in the co. Cork for nearly three centuries. Catherine, widow of the first of the name of whom we find mention, *d.* in 1642 (will proved in Cork same year), having had issue,

Thomas Beamish, patentee under act of settlement of the lands of Allaghmore jointly with his stepson-in-law John Franks: will dated 1681; proved in Cork: he had issue (with two daus.), a son, Daniel, *m.* in 1688, Elizabeth Williams, of Kilbrogan, but is supposed to have died *s. p.*
Richard Beamish, joint patentee with his brother Francis, of the lands of Kilmalooda and Maulbrack; he had issue (with one dau.) a son, Richard, *d. s. p.*
JOHN BEAMISH, of whom hereafter.
Francis Beamish, joint patentee with his brother Richard, of the lands of Kilmalooda and Maulbrack, ancestor of the present Thomas Beamish, of Kilmalooda House, Esq. (*See* BEAMISH *of Kilmalooda*).
Catherine, *m.* William Wright, Esq.

The 3rd son,

JOHN BEAMISH of West Gully, *m.* Elizabeth, sister of Isaac Philpot, Esq. and *d.* 1669, when he was *s.* by his eldest son (he had besides three younger sons and five daus.),

THOMAS BEAMISH, of West Gully, who was father of THOMAS BEAMISH, of Raheroon, who, by Elizabeth his wife, had a son and successor,

THOMAS BEAMISH, of Raheroon, who *m.* in 1728, Jane, dau. of Richard Beamish, of Garranlowghane, Esq., by whom he had issue (with three daus.), an only son,

RICHARD BEAMISH, of Raheroon, who *m.* Elizabeth, eldest dau. of Arthur Bernard, Esq. of Palace Anne, co. Cork, and was father of the present ARTHUR-BEAMISH BERNARD, of Palace Anne and Raheroon, (for his other issue, see BEAMISH-BERNARD *of Palace Anne.*)

Arms—BEAMISH: 1st and 4th, arg., a lion, rampant, gu.; 2nd, or, a chevron, between three fleurs-de-lis, gu.; 3rd, or, a fesse, gu., between six laurel leaves, vert.
Crest—A demi-lion, rampant, gu.
Motto—Virtus insignit audentes.

BEAMISH OF KILMALOODA.

BEAMISH, THOMAS, of Kilmalooda House, co. Co Esq., justice of the peace for co. Cork.

Lineage.—FRANCIS BEAMISH (*see preceding article*), joint patentee of the lands of Kilmalooda and Maulbrack, and next brother to John, of West Gully, ancestor of

Arthur-Beamish Bernard, of Palace Anne, *m.* Catherine, dau. of Francis Bernard, of Castle Bernard, Esq. (ancestor of the Earls of Bandon), and had issue (with three daus.),

I. FRANCIS, *s.* his father.
II. John, of Keelworrough, *m.* in 1698, Jane Wood, of Kenneigh, and had issue,

1 FRANCIS, *s.* his cousin at Kilmalooda.
2 John, of Lisgibba, *m.* in 1736, Mary Good, of Kilmeen, and was father of Richard Beamish, of Cork, merchant.
3 Richard, *m.* in 1730, Margaret Coveney, and had issue,

John, of Cashelmore, who had a son, John Beamish, of Cashelmore and Hare Hill, co. Cork, who *m.* 1st, a dau. of — Howe, of Glounavorrane, Esq., and 2ndly, a dau. of — Hewitt, of Cork, Esq., and has issue.
George, of Clogheen, *m.* in 1789, Catherine, dau. of Henry Baldwin, of Old Court, Esq., by Catherine his wife, dau. of Jonas Morris, of Dunkettle, Esq., and had issue (with five daus.), Rev. Thomas, of Reengarrigeen, *m.* Eliza, dau. of Boyle Travers, of Ballymacowen, Esq.; Richard, J. P., co. Cork, *m.* Susan, dau. of Richard Hungerford, of Cappen, Esq., and has issue; George, M.D., *m.* Sophia, dau. of Samuel Orpen, Esq.; Henry-Baldwin, of Dunmore, J. P., co Cork, *m.* Anne, dau. of Thomas Marmion, Esq.: and John, of Maulbrack.

4 Thomas, *m.* 1726–7, Jane Kingston, of Rathclarin, but *d. s. p.*
5 William.

III. Richard, of Garranloughane, ancestor of the present BENJAMIN-SWAYNE BEAMISH, of Mount Beamish, Esq. (*See* BEAMISH *of Mount Beamish*).
IV. Thomas.

Mr. Beamish of Kilmalooda *d.* 1679 (will, in which he leaves Maulbrack to his son John, dated and proved in Cork same year), and was *s.* by his eldest son,

FRANCIS BEAMISH, of Kilmalooda, who *m.* in 1677-8, Anne, dau. of John Freke, Esq. (ancestor of the Lords Carbery), by whom he had a son, FRANCIS, *s.* his father, and a dau. Anne, *m.* Freke Smyth, Esq. Mr. Beamish of Kilmalooda was *s.* on his decease (will dated 25 Jan. 1681, and proved in Cork), by his only son,

FRANCIS BEAMISH, of Kilmalooda, who *m.* in 1726, Elizabeth, dau. of Jervois, of Brade, Esq., and widow of Percy Smyth, of Headborough, Esq. but *d. s. p.* Will dated 1750, and proved in Cork. He was *s.* by his cousin,

FRANCIS BEAMISH, of Kilmalooda (eldest son of John Beamish, of Keelworrough), who *m.* in 1727, Mary Warren, of Kilmichael, and had issue (with three daus.), an only son,

FRANCIS BEAMISH, of Kilmalooda, who *m.* in 1758, Elizabeth, dau. of John Sealy, of Richmount, Esq., and had issue; I. FRANCIS, *s.* his father; II. SAMPSON, *s.* his nephew, Townsend Beamish; and III. John of Killinea and Bandon, M.D., who *m.* a dau. of — Teulon, Esq., and had, with other issue, two sons, Francis, of Killinear and Bandon, barrister-at-law, Charles, major 35th regiment; I. Eleanor, *m.* in 1784, William Austin, Esq; II. Elizabeth, *m.* Richard Gillman, of Gurteen and Bandon, Esq.; III. A dau., *m.* Boyle Travers, of Ballymacowen, Esq. The eldest son,

FRANCIS BEAMISH, of Kilmalooda, *m.* Mary, dau. of Francis Townsend, of Clogheen, Esq., and had (with three daus.) an only son,

TOWNSEND BEAMISH, Esq. who *m.* Mary, dau. of Walter Atkins, Esq., and had two sons, Francis and John, who both predeceased him, *s. p.* Mr. Townsend Beamish dying without issue, was *s.* in the Kilmalooda estates by his uncle,

SAMPSON BEAMISH, of Kilmalooda, who *m.* in 1800, Catherine, dau. of the Rev. Thomas-Waller Evans (nephew of George, 1st Lord Carbery) and had issue,

THOMAS, now of Kilmalooda.
Sampson, *m.* Elizabeth, dau. of Andrew Poole, of Kilrush, Esq., and has issue, Thomas; Andrew-Poole; Lydia-Maria, and another dau.
Elizabeth, *m.* Francis Bennett, of Clognakilty, Esq.

Mr. Beamish of Kilmalooda was *s.* on his decease by his eldest son, THOMAS BEAMISH, Esq., now of Kilmalooda House, co. Cork.

Arms, Crest, and *Motto*—Same as BEAMISH *of Raheroon.*

BEAMISH OF MOUNT BEAMISH.

BEAMISH, BENJAMIN-SWAYNE, of Mount Beamish, co. Cork, Esq., *m.* Charity-Margaret, dau. of Thomas Little, Esq., M.D.

Lineage. — RICHARD BEAMISH, of Garranloughane (purchased by him in 1696), 3rd son of Francis Beamish, of

Kilmalooda, Esq., *m.* in 1695, Mary Townsend, of Clognakilty, by whom he had issue,

John (Rev.), of Maulbrack, *m.* in 1740, Elizabeth, dau. of William Morris, of Benduffe, Esq., and had issue, Francis; John (Rev.), of Bantry, *m.* Mary, dau. of William Purcell, of Park, Esq.
GEORGE, of whom hereafter.
WILLIAM, progenitor of the Willsgrove branch of the Beamish family.
Thomas, *m.* in 1738, Dorothy Swete, but *d. s. p.*
Jane, *m.* in 1728, Thomas Beamish, of Raheroon, Esq.

The 2nd son,

GEORGE BEAMISH, of Mount Beamish, *m.* 1st, in 1746, Rebecca Scheolfield, of Fanlobus, and 2ndly, in 1748, Miss Frances Jones, by whom he had two sons, SAMUEL (Rev.), his heir, and George, who had (with two daus.) a son, George Beamish. Mr. Beamish, of Mount Beamish, was *s.* on his decease by his eldest son,

THE REV. SAMUEL BEAMISH, of Mount Beamish, who *m.* 1st, 14 July, 1774, Mary, dau. of John Stamers, of Bandon, Esq., by whom he had issue,

George, *d. s. p.*
JOHN-SAMUEL, *s.* his father.
William, *m.* 1 Sept. 1809, Harriett, dau. of John Newman, of Dromore, Esq., and had issue, Samuel-George, *m.* 19 Feb. 1834, Miss Hannah Slingsby, and has issue; John-Newman, of Cork; Adam-Newman, in holy orders; and William, *m.* a dau. of Rev. James Kingston, LL.D.
Sarah, *m.* Edward Rogers, Esq.
Frances-Anne, *m.* Major-General Hamilton, of Newry.

The Rev. Samuel Beamish *m.* 2ndly, a dau. of Joshua Hamilton, Esq. (by Mary, dau. of Sir Richard Cox, Bart.), and had by her,

Henry-Hamilton, (Rev.), *m.* 1st, Miss Spread, and 2ndly, Mrs. D[illegible]k, and has issue.
Mary, *m.* to the Rev. Richard-F. Webb.

The Rev. Samuel Beamish was *s.* on his decease by his eldest surviving son,

JOHN-SAMUEL BEAMISH, of Mount Beamish, M.D., who *m.* in Sept. 1802, Arabella, dau. of Benjamin Swayne, Esq., and had issue,

Samuel (Rev.), *d. unm.*
Benjamin-Swayne, *s.* his father.
John, *d. s. p.*
George, of Dublin, *m.* in Nov. 1844, Lucy, dau. of Samuel Crosthwait, of Bagnalstown, co. Carlow, Esq.
William, of Cork, M.D., *m.* in May, 1840, Ellen, dau. of Lieut.-Colonel David Gregory, 45th regt., and has issue, David-Gregory; William; Arabella-Swayne; Ellen-Catherine, and another dau.
Elizabeth, *m.* in July, 1837, to Henry Herrick, of Farranlough, Esq.
Isabella, *m.* in Feb. 1846, to Henry C. Jones, Esq.
Harriett, *m.* in Feb. 1854, to William Hamilton, Esq., late captain 37th regt.
Frances-Anne, *m.* in 1845, to Frederick Mc Carthy, of Carrignavar, Esq., M.D.

Dr. Beamish, of Mount Beamish, *d.* in 1853, and was *s.* by his eldest surviving son, BENJAMIN-SWAYNE BEAMISH, Esq., now of Mount Beamish.

Arms, Crest, and *Motto*—Same as BEAMISH *of Raheroon.*

BEAMISH OF WILLSGROVE.

BEAMISH, ROBERT-DELACOUR, of Ditchley, co. Cork, Esq., *b.* 1791; high-sheriff of co. Cork in 1841; *m.* Maria-Anne, dau. of Lieut.-Col. Archibald Macdonald, adjutant-gen. H. M. forces in India, by whom he has issue,

I. WILLIAM-DELACOUR.
II. Norman-Macdonald.
III. Caulfield.
IV. Grenville.

Lineage.—WILLIAM BEAMISH, of Willsgrove, co. Cork, Capt. R.N., next brother of George Beamish, of Mount Beamish, Esq., *m.* in 1750, Alice, dau. of Major North-Ludlow Bernard, of Castle Bernard, co. Cork (ancestor of the Earls of Bandon), by whom (who *d.* 1792) he had issue,

FRANCIS-BERNARD, *s.* his father.
Richard, *b.* 11 Feb. 1755.
WILLIAM, of whom hereafter.
Charles (Rev.), *b.* 14 Aug. 1761, rector of St. Anne, Shandon, Cork, *d.* at Florence *circa* 1841, leaving issue.
James, *b.* 25 June, 1764.
Isaac, *b.* 10 July, 1767.
Rose, *m.* to Wm. Cuthbert, of Bloomfield, Esq.
Mary, *m.* to Thos. Ware, of Woodfort, Esq.

Captain Beamish *d.* in 1773, and was *s.* by his eldest son,

FRANCIS-BERNARD BEAMISH, of Willsgrove, M.P. for Rathcormack, who sold the paternal property of Willsgrove to his cousin, Lord Bandon, and dying *unm.* in 1805, was *s.* by his brother,

WILLIAM BEAMISH, of Beaumont House, co. Cork, Esq., *b.* 13 May, 1760, who *m.* in 1788, Anne-Jane-Margaret, dau. of Robert De la Cour, of Short Castle, co. Cork, Esq., by whom (who *d.* 8th Aug. 1852), he had issue,

WILLIAM, *s.* his father.
ROBERT-DELACOUR, of whom hereafter.
North-Ludlow, of Lota Park, co. Cork, *b.* 31 Dec. 1797, Lieut.-Colonel à-la-suite in the Hanoverian service, and Knight of the Royal Hanoverian Guelphic Order, late captain in the 4th (Royal Irish) dragoon guards, and major unattached, J. P. for co. Cork, and F.R.S., *m.* at Stockholm, 27 May, 1841, Aline-Marie, dau. of Rev. John-Eric Forsström, M.A. and M.D., by Petronella-Elizabeth his wife, only child and heir of Casparus-Adrianus Robertson, Governor of Voorschooten and Veur, in Holland. Colonel Beamish has issue, North-Ludlow-Axel, *b.* 1842; William-Adolphus, *b.* 1844; George-Horatio-Townsend, *b.* 1847; Aline-Mathilde-Hulda; and Alice.
Richard, of Suffolk Square, Cheltenham, co. Gloucester, late of Sans Souci, co. Cork, *b.* 1798, formerly of the Coldstream guards, F.R.S., F.S.S., M.I.C.E., M.R.I., &c., *m.* at Quainton, Bucks, 27 Sept. 1831, Theodosia-Mary, only surviving child and heir of Lieut.-Colonel Augustus Heise, C.B. and K.H., of the King's German Legion, by Theodosia-Arabella his wife, dau. and co-heir of the Rev. William King, rector of Mallow, co. Cork. Mr. Richard Beamish has issue, Richard-Pigott, *b.* 1832; Alten-Augustus-William, *b.* 1841; Anne-Theodosia; and Emily-Isabella.
Charles, of Delacour Villa, Crookstown, co. Cork, and Buckingham Square, Cork.
Francis-Bernard, of Grenville House, Cork, high-sheriff of Cork in 1852, M.P. for Cork, J.P. for co. Cork, *m.* 3 May, 1827, Hon. Katherine-Savery-De Lisle De Courcy, dau. of the Hon. Captain Michael De Courcy, R.N., and sister of John Stapleton, 28th Lord Kingsale (who had the precedence of a baron's dau. granted to her by royal license, dated 14 July, 1836), by whom he has issue, Francis-Bernard-Servington, *b.* 1839.
James-Caulfield, of South Devon Place, Plymouth, *m.* Louisa-Erskine, 2nd dau. of Lieut.-Colonel Archibald Macdonald, by whom he has issue, Caulfield-Francis, *b.* 1834, ensign 45th regt.; and Louisa-Kate.
Dorcas, *m.* to Frederick Meade, of Belmont, co. Cork, Esq., lieut.-colonel unattached, late of the 88th Connaught rangers, and aide-de-camp to Major-Gen. Sir Thomas Reynell, K.C.B.

Mr. Beamish, of Beaumont, *d.* 17th April, 1828, and was *s.* by his eldest son,

WILLIAM BEAMISH, of Beaumont, *b.* 14 Oct. 1790, who *m.* at Lochnaw Castle, Scotland, 15 Sept. 1814, the Hon. Mary De Courcy, dau. of John, 26th Lord Kingsale (who *d.* 17 April, 1835), and by her had issue,

WILLIAM, *s.* his father.
JOHN-DE COURCY, *s.* his brother.
Susan, *d. unm.* 1831.
Anne-Jane-Margaret, *m.* in May, 1846, to the Rev. Wm.-Hamilton Thompson, and has issue. Mrs. Thompson *s.* to the Beaumont estates on the death of her brother, John-De Courcy Beamish, Esq.

Mr. Beamish, of Beaumont, *d.* 1 Oct. 1838, and was *s.* by his eldest son,

WILLIAM BEAMISH, of Beaumont, M.A. Trin. Coll., Cambridge, *b.* 1821, who *d. unm.* 1847, and was *s.* by his only brother,

JOHN-DE COURCY BEAMISH, of Beaumont House, *b.* 1822, who *d. unm.* in 1848, when the representation of this branch of the family devolved upon his uncle, ROBERT-DELACOUR BEAMISH, Esq. of Ditchley, as above mentioned.

Arms, Crest, and *Motto*—Same as BEAMISH *of Raheroon.*

BEARCROFT OF MEER HALL.

BEARCROFT, EDWARD, Esq. of Meer Hall, co. Worcester.

Lineage.—The estate of Meer Hall was possessed by the Bearcrofts, in lineal male descent, from 1337—and probably from a period long anterior—up to the year 1822, when it passed into the female line, whose heirs assumed the name and arms of BEARCROFT.

Meer Hall was built by Thomas Bearcroft in 1337, the tenth year of EDWARD III.'s reign. It is a half-timber mansion, approached by a fine avenue of elms, with a wooded hill behind, forming a picturesque background.

In the great civil war, the Bearcroft of the day had the ill-luck to make himself somewhat too conspicuous on behalf of royalty. The consequence was, that Cromwell's troopers took possession of his house, converting the hall into stables, and applying the rest to purposes for which they were most certainly never intended by the original builder. Being set down, in the phrase of the triumphant party, for an inveterate and confirmed malignant, he was heavily fined, and his name still appears in the catalogue of those who were obliged to compound for their estates.

Seat—Meer Hall, Worcestershire.

BEARDMORE OF UPLANDS.

BEARDMORE, JOHN, Esq. of Uplands, co. Hants, M.A., J.P., high-sheriff in 1846, *b.* 8 Sept. 1816, barrister-at-law.

Lineage.—The late JOHN BEARDMORE, Esq., *b.* in 1751, only son of JOHN BEARDMORE, Esq., and grandson of JOHN BEARDMORE, Esq., of Somersetshire, *m.* Maria-Margaret, eldest dau. of John Parke, Esq., by Hannah his wife, dau. of Col. Burnett, (a descendant of Bishop Burnett), and by her (who *d.* the August previous) he left at his decease an only son, the present JOHN BEARDMORE, Esq. of Uplands.

Arms—Or, a chevron, sa., between three Moors' heads, ppr.
Crest—A griffin's head, erased.
Motto—Providentiæ nec committo.
Seat—Uplands, near Fareham, Hants.

BEATSON OF KILLRIE.

BEATSON, ALEXANDER-JOHN, Esq. of Rossend, co. Fife, *b.* 17 Jan. 1833.

Lineage.—JAMES BEATSON, Esq., the first laird of Killrie, co. Fife, was *b.* 1598, and *d.* 1674, leaving issue,

ROBERT, his heir.
David, first of the family of Vicarsgrange.
William, first of the family of Glasmount, now represented by WILLIAM-STUART BEATSON, Esq., an officer Bengal light infantry; who *m.* 1851, Cornelia, only dau. of Major Brownlow, and has issue.

ROBERT BEATSON, son and heir, *m.* Isabell, dau. of — Cunynghame, Esq., and left issue,

JAMES, of Pitkennie, his heir.
John, first of the family of Pitcadie.
And other children.

JAMES BEATSON, Esq., son and heir, *m.* 1672, Janet, dau. of Alex Orrock, Esq. of that ilk, Fifeshire, and was *s.* by his eldest son,

ROBERT BEATSON, Esq. of Pitkennie, who *m.* Margaret, only child of the 2nd marriage of William Beatson, Esq. of Glasmount, and had issue, *inter alios,*

ROBERT, his heir.
Jean, *m.* Beatson of Vicarsgrange.

ROBERT BEATSON, Esq., son and heir, *m.* 7 Aug. 1728, Helen, eldest dau. of Alex Orrock, Esq. of that ilk, Fifeshire, and had issue, *inter alios,* a dau. Isabell, *m.* Beatson of Glasmount; and a son and successor,

ROBERT BEATSON, Esq., *b.* 10 Aug. 1730, *m.* 175–, Jean, dau. of Read of Turfbeg, co. Forfar, by Elizabeth his wife, dau. of Sir Alexander Wedderburn, Bart., and had issue,

I. ROBERT, his heir, *b.* at Dundee, 2 Oct. 1758.
II. Alex, major-gen. H. E. I. C. S., of Knowle Farm, and Henly, co. Sussex, governor of St. Helena, 1808–13, author of *Tracts on St. Helena*, and a *History of the Origin and Conduct of the War with Tippoo Saib*; *m.* 1806, Davidson, 2nd dau. of David Reid, Esq., commissioner of His Majesty's Customs for Scotland, and had issue,
  1 Alex, H.E.I.C.S., engineers; *d. unm.*
  2 Theodore, capt. in the Bengal cavalry; *m.* in 1843, Louisa, only dau. of Col. Stephen Reid.
  3 Davidson, *m.* 1841, Anne-Henrietta, 2nd dau. of John Campbell, Esq. of Liston Hall, Norfolk; and has issue, a son and dau.
  4 Stephen, *d.* young.
  5 Douglas, Bengal infantry: *d. s. p.*
  6 Albert, Bengal infantry.
  1 Jane-Helena, *m.* 1830, James-Whitwell Torre, Esq. of Snydale Hall, Yorkshire.
  2 Catherina, *d. unm.*
  3 Dora, *m.* 1838, John Pryce, Esq. of Tunbridge Wells, and has issue.
  4 Caroline, *m.* 1842, John Lysaght, Esq. of Mallow, co. Cork.
  5 Adelaide, *m.* 1846, James Lysaght, Esq. of Carrigmore, co. Cork.
  6 Georgiana, *m.* Samuel Newington, Esq., M.D.
  7 Letitia.

F 2

III. John, b. Nov. 1760, d. s. p.
I. Helena, m. Sir Charles Oakeley, Bart.; and d. 1837.

The eldest son,

ROBERT BEATSON, Esq. of the Royal Engineers, m. Jane, only child of Murdoch Campbell, Esq. of Rossend Castle, Fifeshire, by Margaret his wife, dau. of John Taylor, Esq. of Pitcairlie and the heiress of Carbiston, and had issue,

Robert, who d. young.
ALEX-CAMPBELL, his heir.
Robert-Wedderburn, capt. in the Indian army; d. s. p. 11 Dec. 1848.
William-Fergusson, lieut.-col. in the service of the Queen of Spain, and knight of San Fernando, lieut.-col. in the Indian army, recently employed as brigadier commanding the cavalry of His Highness the Nizam, and subsequently in the Turkish army; m. 1840, Marian, youngest dau. of Lieut.-Col. Humfrays, of the Bengal engineers; has two daus., Jane; and Harriet, m. to Wm.-A. Laurin, Esq.
Margaret, d. young.
Barbara, m. Major-Gen. Edward-Swift Broughton, H.E.I.C.S.; issue, daus.
Harriette, m. Wm.-Alex. Lawrie, Esq.
Jane.

The eldest surviving son,

ALEX-CAMPBELL BEATSON, of Rossend, captain in the Indian army, m. 22 Dec. 1831, Eliza, 3rd dau. of John Baird, Esq. of Camelon, and d. 14 August, 1832, leaving issue a posthumous son, the present representative of the family.

Arms—Gu., a chevron between three spear-heads (points upwards), arg.
Crest—A bee, volant en arrière, ppr.
Motto—Cum prudentia sedulus.

BEAUCLERK OF ARDGLASS CASTLE.

BEAUCLERK, AUBREY-DE VERE, Esq. of Ardglass Castle, co. Down, b. 28 Sept. 1837; s. his father 1 Feb. 1854.

Lineage.—TOPHAM BEAUCLERK, Esq., b. in 1739, (son of Lord Sydney Beauclerk, vice-chamberlain to the king, by Mary his wife, dau. of Thomas Norris, Esq. of Speke, and grandson of Charles, 1st Duke of St. Albans, by Diana his wife, dau. and heir of Aubrey de Vere, 20th Earl of Oxford), m. in 1768, Lady Diana Spencer, dau. of Charles, Duke of Marlborough, and had (with two daus., Mary, m. to Francis, Count Jenison Walworth; and Elizabeth, m. to George, Earl of Pembroke) a son,

CHARLES-GEORGE BEAUCLERK, Esq. of St. Leonard's Forest, Horsham, Sussex, who m. in 1799, Emily-Charlotte, second dau. of William Ogilvie, Esq., by Emily-Mary his wife, Duchess Dowager of Leinster, and had issue, AUBREY-WILLIAM, his heir; Charles-Robert, fellow of Caius College, Cambridge, b. in 1802; George-Robert, b. in 1803; Caroline, Anna, m. in 1829, to Robert Aldridge, Esq.; Georgiana, m. in 1826, to John-Dean Paul, Esq.; Diana-Olivia, widow of Sir Francis-Fletcher Vane, Bart.; Jane-Elizabeth, m. in 1830, to Henry Fitzroy, Esq.; Isabella-Elizabeth, m. in 1840, to Capt. John-William Montagu, R.N.; and Katherine-Katinka. The eldest son,

AUBREY-WILLIAM BEAUCLERK, Esq. of Ardglass Castle, co. Down, and St. Leonard's Forest, Horsham, Sussex, b. 20 Feb. 1801; m. 1st, 13 Feb. 1834, Ida, 3rd dau. of Sir Charles-Forster-Goring, Bart., and 2ndly, 7 Dec. 1840, Rosa-Matilda, dau. of Joshua Robinson, Esq. of Kew Green; by the former of whom (who d. 23 April, 1839), he had issue, AUBREY-DE VERE, now of Ardglass; Diana-Arabella; and Augusta; and by the latter (who survives) he had two daus., Louisa-Catherine and Isabella-Julia. Major Beauclerk, formerly M.P. for East Surrey, d. 1 Feb. 1854.

Arms—Quarterly: 1st and 4th, France and England, quarterly; 2nd, Scotland; 3rd, Ireland; over all a sinister baton, gu., charged with three roses, arg., seeded and barbed, ppr.
Crest—On a chapeau, gu., turned up, erm., a lion, statant-guardant, or, crowned with a ducal coronet, per pale, arg. and of the first, gorged with a collar of the last, thereon three roses, also arg., barbed and seeded, ppr.
Motto—Auspicium melioris ævi.
Seat—Ardglass Castle, co. Down.

BEAUMAN OF HYDE PARK.

BEAUMAN, MATHEW-FORDE, Esq. of Hyde Park, in the co. of Wexford, s. his brother 24 Sept. 1840; m. 7 July, 1841, Harriet, youngest dau. of the late Rev. Thomas Quin, of Wingfield, co. Wicklow, and has,

I. JOHN-CHRISTOPHER, b. 3 March, 1846.
I. Ellen.
II. Jane-Emily.
III. Harriet.
IV. Anne-Margaret.
V. Isabella.
VI. Elizabeth.
VII. Mary-Emily.

Lineage.—The BAUMANS, originally of Bohemia, where they possessed considerable property, expatriated themselves in consequence of the persecutions to which, as Lutherans, they were exposed on the expulsion of the ELECTOR-PALATINE, and took refuge in various parts of Germany and Holland.

MELCHIOR-CHRISTOPHER BAUMAN, accompanying General de Ginkell, to whom he was nearly allied by marriage, into Ireland, settled in the co. of Wexford, *anno* 1691.* He married and had two sons, viz., JOHN, his heir; and Francis, who m. a sister of the Comte de Serans, and settled at Nantes, in Bretagne. The eldest son,

JOHN BAUMAN, Esq., of the co. of Wexford, m. Margaret, dau. of Edward Barty, Esq. of Rathrush, co. Carlow, and dying in 1761, was s. by his son,

JOHN BAUMAN, Esq. of the co. of Wexford, who altered the spelling of the family name from Bauman to BEAUMAN. He m. in 1758, Anne, dau. of Edmond Rice, Esq. of Ahere, in the same shire, and by her, who d. 10 May, 1812, had,

I. JOHN-CHRISTOPHER, his heir.
II. Edward-Barry, who d. in 1800, in India.
III. Michael, a capt. in the Madras artillery; m. Mary, dau. of General Wahab, and had several children, of whom the only surviving is,
  Edward-John-Barry Beauman, Esq. of Furness, co. Kildare, a justice of the peace; who m. 29 March, 1833, Elizabeth, dau. of George Moore, Esq. of the co. Wicklow, and has issue.
  Capt. Michael Beauman, who held the situation of superintendant of the arsenals at Madras, was lost on his passage home from India, on board the "Lady Dundas" Indiaman, in 1809.
IV. William, of Rutland Square, Dublin, m. in 1796, Charity, widow of Tennison Edwards, Esq. of Old Court, in Wicklow, and dau. of John Barrington, Esq., and had issue,
  1 John, in holy orders, vicar-choral of St. Patrick's Cathedral, and vicar of Julianstown, co. Meath; d. unm. 15 April, 1828.
  1 Anne, m. 9 Oct. 1827, to the Rev. Brabazon-William Disney, rector of Stackallen, in Meath.
  2 Maria, m. 19 March, 1819, to Sir John Kennedy, Bart. of Johnstown-Kennedy; and d. 7 Nov. 1828, leaving five sons and one dau.
V. Francis, capt. R.N.
I. Margaret, m. to Barry Lawless, Esq. of Cherrywood, co. Dublin; and d. in March, 1818, s. p.
II. Anne, m. to William Talbot, Esq. of Castle Talbot, co. Wexford.
III. Mary.

Mr. Beauman d. 13 Dec. 1802, and was s. by his eldest son,

JOHN-CHRISTOPHER BEAUMAN, Esq. of Hyde Park, b. 29 Oct. 1764, high-sheriff of the co. of Wexford in 1821, who m. 2 Oct. 1795, Jane, dau. of Matthew Forde, Esq. of Seaforde, co. Down, and had issue,

JOHN, who d. s. p. 24 Sept. 1840.
MATHEW-FORDE, present possessor.
Elizabeth-Anne, m. in 1841, to Sir John Kennedy, Bart.
Anne-Margaret.
Charity-Isabella, m. in 1835, to Henry-Cavendish Hore, Esq., R.N., 4th son of the late William Hore, Esq. of Harperstown.
Jane-Emily.

Motto—Fortiter.
Seat—Hyde Park, co. Wexford.

BEAUMONT OF BARROW-UPON-TRENT.

BEAUMONT, JOHN, Esq. of Barrow-upon-Trent, co. Derby, b. 22 July, 1826; s. his father 11 Mar. 1834.

Lineage.—EDWARD BEAUMONT, Esq., who settled at Barrow-upon-Trent, co. Derby, about the year 1550, was 2nd son of Thomas Beaumont, Esq. of Thringston, co. Leicester, and younger brother of John Beaumont, of Grace Dieu, Master of the Rolls, and grandfather of Francis Beaumont, the dramatic poet. He m. Anne, dau. and heir

* Another member of the family, the REV. JOHN BAUMAN, a native of Prague, came to England about the year 1646, with ample testimonials from many of the principal German divines. He d. about 1668, leaving one dau., then of tender years, who afterwards m. Daniel Doddridge, of London, and was mother of the celebrated PHILIP DODDRIDGE, D.D., the very eminent dissenting divine.

of Millgate of Lockington, in Leicestershire, and had a son and successor,

William Beaumont, Esq. of Barrow-upon-Trent, who *m.* Elizabeth Sutton, of Derby, and dying 30 July, 1592, was *s.* by his son,

Francis Beaumont, Esq. of Barrow-upon-Trent, a major in the service of Charles I., who *m.* Elizabeth, dau. and heir of Simon Bracebridge, Esq. of Twyford, co. Derby, and had issue, two sons—viz., Edward, who was disinherited, and *d.* in 1660, and his heir, at his decease, in 1661, aged ninety-two,

John Beaumont, Esq. of Barrow-upon-Trent, who *m.* 1st, Dorothy, dau. of John Powtrell, Esq. of West Hallom, in Derbyshire, by whom he had no issue, and 2ndly, Barbara, dau. of Edward Willoughby, Esq. of Cotham, in Nottinghamshire, by whom he left at his decease, with other issue, a son and successor,

Robert Beaumont, Esq., of Barrow-upon-Trent, *b.* in 1655, who *m.* 1st, Cecily, dau. and co-heir of Sir Thomas Beaumont, Bart. of Gracedieu, and had by her, who *d.* in 1697, John, his heir, and Barbara, lady abbess of a convent in Flanders. Mr. Beaumont *m.* 2ndly, Jane, widow of Francis Lowe, Esq. of Old Greaves, and dau. and heir of John Middleton, Esq. of Wandesley, Notts, by whom he had a son, Francis, who *d. unm.*; and 3rdly, Winifred, dau. of Francis Lowe, Esq., without issue. He *d.* 2 Jan. 1726–7, and was *s.* by his son,

John Beaumont, Esq., of Barrow-upon-Trent, *b.* in 1694, who *m.* Miss Joyce Johnson, niece of Thomas Allestree, Esq. of Elvaston, and dying 11 Oct. 1763, was *s.* by his eldest son,

John Beaumont, Esq. of Barrow-upon-Trent, who *d. unm.*, 21 July, 1806, and was *s.* by (the son of his brother Robert) his nephew,

John Beaumont, Esq. of Barrow-upon-Trent, *b.* 23 Jan. 1779, who *m.* 29 Aug. 1825, the Hon. Mary-Elizabeth Curzon, 3rd dau. of Nathaniel, 2nd Lord Scarsdale, and had

John, now of Barrow.
Robert-Curzon, *b.* 10 Dec. 1827.
Edward, *b.* 22 July, 1829.
Henry.

Mr. Beaumont *d.* 11 March, 1834.

Arms—Az., semée of fleurs de lis, a lion, rampant, or.
Crest—On a chapeau, gu., turned up, erm., a lion, passant, or.
Motto—Erectus non elatus.
Seat—Barrow-upon-Trent.

BEAUMONT OF WHITLEY BEAUMONT.

Beaumont, Richard-Henry, Esq. of Whitley, co. York, *b.* 5 Aug. 1805; *m.* 3 Dec. 1831, Catherine, dau. of Timothy Wiggin, Esq. of the United States of America.

Lineage.—The last direct male representative of the ancient and eminent house of Beaumont *of Whitley Beaumont*,

John Beaumont, Esq. of Whitley Beaumont, *b.* 29 Aug. 1752, had issue by Sarah Butler (whom he married in 1778), dau. of Humphrey Butler, of Hereford, and granddau. of the Rev. Humphrey Butler, rector of Keir, one son and two daus., viz.:

I. Charles-Richard, LL.D.; *b.* 22 May, 1777, constituted tenant for life of the Whitley Beaumont estates, after the death of his father and his aunt Bernard, with remainder to the heirs of his body, by the will of his uncle, Richard-Henry Beaumont, Esq. He *m.* in 1802, Martha, dau. of Stephen Hemsted, M.D.; and dying 18 March, 1813, left a son and dau.,
   1 Richard-Henry, heir to his grandfather.
   1 Martha, *m.* to Patrick M'Mahon, Esq. of Addlestone, Surrey.

I. Charlotte, *b.* in 1779; *m.* 14 April, 1801, to John M'Cumming, Esq., seigneur of Grande Vallée des Montes, in Lower Canada, capt. 81st regt.; and *d.* 16 Aug. 1815, leaving one son, the present Richard-Henry-John-Beaumont M'Cumming, Esq., seigneur of Grande Vallée des Montes, a major in the army; and three daus.
II. Elizabeth-Sarah, *b.* in 1781; *m.* in 1813, to Joseph-Thomas Tuite, Esq. of Pocklington, afterwards of Deighton Grove, near York.

Mr. Beaumont *d.* 3 Dec. 1831, and was *s.* by his grandson, the present Richard-Henry Beaumont, Esq. of Whitley.

Arms—Gu., a lion, rampant, arg., langued and armed, az., between eight crescents, of the second.
Crest—A bull's head, erased, quarterly.
Motto—Fide sed cui vide.
Seat—Whitley Hall, near Huddersfield, co. York.

BEAUMONT OF BRETTON.

Beaumont, Wentworth-Blackett, Esq. of Bretton Hall, co. York, and Bywell Hall, Northumberland, *b.* in 1829, M.P. for South Northumberland. Mr. Beaumont *s.* his father in 1849.

Lineage.—George Beaumont, Esq. of The Oaks, *b.* in 1696 (eldest son of George Beaumont, Esq. of Chapel Thorpe, by Gertrude his wife, dau. of John Bagshaw, Esq. of Hucklow, and grandson of William Beaumont, Esq. of The Oaks, in Darton, co. York, whose father, George Beaumont, of The Oaks, *d.* in 1664), *m.* in 1723, Frances, dau. of Richard Beaumont, Esq. of Whitley Beaumont, and had two sons and a dau., viz.:

Thomas, his successor.
George, in holy orders; *m.* Elizabeth, dau. of John Green, of Leeds, merchant; and *d.* 17 May, 1773, leaving issue.
Susanna, *m.* to the Rev. John Walter, and *d. s. p.*

He *d.* 27 Jan. 1735, and was *s.* by his elder son,

Thomas Beaumont, Esq. of The Oaks, *b.* at Whitley, 18 Feb. 1723, *m.* Anne, dau. and co-heir of Edward Ascough, Esq. of Louth, in Lincolnshire, and dying 6 Feb. 1785, was *s.* by his son,

Thomas-Richard Beaumont, Esq. of The Oaks, *b.* 29 April, 1758, col. in the army, M.P. for Northumberland from 1795 to 1818. He *m.* Diana, dau. and heir, by will, of Sir Thomas Wentworth Blackett, Bart., and had issue, Thomas-Wentworth, his heir; William; Richard; Edward-Blackett, *m.* Jane, dau. of William Lee, Esq. of Grove; Henry; Diana; Marianne; and Sophia. Col. Beaumont *d.* at Bretton Hall, 31 July, 1829, and Mrs. Beaumont subsequently, when the estates devolved upon her eldest son,

Thomas-Wentworth Beaumont, Esq. of Bretton Hall, M.P. for Northumberland, *b.* 5 Nov. 1792, who *m.* Henrietta-Jane-Emma, dau. of J. Atkinson, Esq. of Maple Hayes, and *d.* 18 Dec. 1849, leaving issue, Wentworth-Blackett, now of Bretton and Bywell; Walter; Somerset-Archibald; Dudley; Emma-Diana; and Florence.

Arms, &c., as Beaumont *of Whitley*.
Seats—Bywell Hall, Newcastle-on-Tyne; and Bretton Hall, Wakefield.

BECKETT OF THE KNOLL.

Beckett, John-Staniforth, Esq. of The Knoll, Torquay, Devon, formerly of Barnsley, co. York, deputy-lieut., *b.* 5 April, 1794; *m.* 24 May, 1842, Gertrude-Elizabeth, elder dau. of Capt. Sir William-Howe Mulcaster, R.N., K.C.H., K.T.S., C.B.

Lineage.—Joseph Beckett, Esq. younger brother of Sir John Beckett, the 1st Bart. of Leeds and Somerby Park, co. Lincoln, *m.* 23 June, 1785, Mary, dau. and co-heir of John Staniforth, Esq. of Hull, and by her had (with five daus., Eleanor; Caroline, *m.* in 1825, to Sir Thomas Beckett, Bart.; Mary-Anne; Eliza, *m.* to William-Creed Fairman, Esq. of Lynsted, Kent; and Augusta) one son, the present John-Staniforth Beckett, Esq. of The Knoll.

Arms—Quarterly: 1st and 4th, gu., a fesse between three boars' heads, couped, erminois, a crescent, arg., for difference; 2nd and 3rd, erminois, on a fesse, wavy, gu., three lions, rampant, arg.
Crest—A boar's head, couped, or, pierced by a cross patée-fitchée, erect, sa.
Motto—Prodesse civibus.
Seat—The Knoll, Torquay.

BECKWITH OF THURCROFT AND TRIMDON.

Beckwith, William, Esq. of Thurcroft, co. York, and of Trimdon, co. Durham, *b.* in 1772; *m.* in 1794, Caroline, dau. of John Neasham, Esq. of Houghton-le-Spring, and by her, who *d.* at St. Omer, in France, 10 April, 1832, had surviving issue,

I. William, K.H., lieut.-col. unattached, late major of the 14th light-dragoons, who *m.* 1831, Priscilla-Maria, dau. and heiress of Thomas Hopper, Esq. of Silksworth, in Durham.
II. John.
III. Henry, in holy orders, rector of Eaton Constantine, near Shrewsbury, *m.* Miss Rose-Anne Eyton.

I. Caroline.
II. Mary.

Lineage.—This very ancient family bore, originally, the name of Malbie or Malbysse, being lineally descended from the marriage, *temp.* Henry III., of Hercules de Malbie, grandson of Sir Simon de Malbie, Lord of Cawton in Craven, with Beckwith, one of the daus. of Sir William Bruce, Lord of Uglebarby, derived from Sir Robert Brus, Lord of Skelton Castle, in Cleveland, a noble Norman knight, ancestor of the BRUCES *of Scotland*.

MATTHEW BECKWITH, Esq. of Tanfield and Sleningford, a captain in the parliamentary army, living 9 April, 1666, 3rd son of Roger Beckwith, of Clint, co. York, Esq. and younger brother of Arthur Beckwith, of Aldborough, Esq., father of SIR ROGER BECKWITH, Bart. (*see* BURKE'S *Extinct Baronetage*) *m.* Elizabeth, dau. of Sir John Buck, Knt. of Filey, and dying in 1679, left, with other issue, a son,

WILLIAM BECKWITH, Esq. *b* 22 Nov. 1664, who inherited the property of his uncle, William Beckwith, Esq. of Thurcroft, and became of that place. He *m.* Mary, dau. of Sir Edward Chaloner, of Guisborough, by whom, who *d.* 4 Dec. 1702, he left at his decease in 1713, with other issue, a son and successor,

WILLIAM BECKWITH, Esq. of Thurcroft and Sleningford. He *m.* 28 April, 1715, Elizabeth, only dau. and heiress of John Woodifield, Esq. of Fishburn and Trimdon, in the co. palatine of Durham, and had issue,

WOODIFIELD, his heir.
William, of Carey-street, London, barrister-at-law; who *m.* and had one son, William, an ensign in the 27th regt. of foot, *d. unm.* in 1776; and two daus., Maria and Elizabeth.
John, a lieut.-col. in Abercrombie's regt.
Jane, *m.* to Thomas Westley, Esq. of Howarth.
Elizabeth, *m.* to W. Horsfall, Esq. of Storth's Hall; and *d.* 21 April, 1798, aged 72.

Mr. Beckwith *d.* at Thurcroft, 10 April, 1760, aged 74, and was *s.* by his eldest son,

WOODIFIELD BECKWITH, Esq. of Thurcroft and Trimdon, baptized at Laughton, 12 Sept. 1719, who *m.* 1 June, 1771, Dorothy, dau. of Christopher Robinson, Esq. of Easington, co. Durham, and by her (who *m.* 2ndly, Major Patrick Campbell, and was buried at Easington), left at his decease, in 1779, aged 60, an only surviving child, WILLIAM BECKWITH, Esq. of Thurcroft and Trimdon.

Arms—Arg., a chevron between three hinds' heads, erased, gu.
Crest—An antelope, ppr., in the mouth a branch, vert.
Motto—Joir en bien.
Seat—Trimdon House, near Sedgefield, Durham.

BECKFORD OF FONTHILL AND BASING PARK.

BECKFORD, WILLIAM, Esq. of Ruxley Lodge, Surrey, *b.* 23 March, 1790; *m.* 12 Jan. 1822, Maria-Elizabeth, only dau. of the Rev. John Bramston Stane, of Forest Hall, Essex, and has issue,

I. FRANCIS-JOHN-BRAMSTON, *b.* at Rome, 2 Feb. 1842.
I. Maria-Harriet. II. Joanna-Elizabeth.
III. Harriette-Marian.

Lineage.—The family of Beckford was established at an early period in Gloucestershire, and the name occurs so far back as the 12th century, when Robert de Beckeford granted certain tithes to the abbey of Gloucester. Among the principal adherents of RICHARD III. at Bosworth, was Sir William Beckford. The family appears to have been settled afterwards near Oxford, and to have removed thence to Berkshire.

After the conquest of Jamaica, in 1656, COL. PETER BECKFORD, son of Peter Beckford, Esq., who was brother to Sir Thomas Beckford, of Ashtead, rose to the highest station in that colony. Having, during the reign of CHARLES II., filled the important office of president of the council, he was, by WILLIAM III., appointed lieut.-governor and commander-in-chief of the island. He *d.* in 1710, possessed of immense wealth, leaving two sons, viz.: PETER, of whom presently; and Thomas, *b.* in 1682, *m.* Mary, dau. and heir of Thomas Ballard, Esq., and dying in 1731, left issue. The elder son,

PETER BECKFORD, Esq. Speaker of the House of Assembly of Jamaica, *d.* in 1735. Having *m.* Bathshua, dau. and co-heir of Col. Julines Hering, he had issue,

PETER, his heir; *d. s. p.* 1737.
WILLIAM, successor to his brother, of Fonthill, twice lord-mayor of the city of London, and representative in parliament for the metropolis; *d.* during his mayoralty, in 1770, having *m.* Maria, dau. and co-heir of the Hon. George Hamilton, M.P. for Wells, second surviving son of James, 6th Earl of Abercorn, and left an only child,
WILLIAM BECKFORD, Esq. of Fonthill Abbey, M.P. author of *The Caliph Vathek*; who *d.* in 1844, having had, by Margaret his wife, dau. of Charles, 4th Earl of Aboyne, two daus., his co-heirs, viz., Margaret-Maria-Elizabeth, *m.* in 1811, to Lieut.-Gen. James Orde; and Susannah-Euphemia, *m.* in 1810, to Alexander, Duke of Hamilton and Brandon, K.G.
Richard, M.P. for Bristol; *d. unm.*
Nathaniel, *d. unm.*
Julines, of Stapleton, M.P., grandfather of HORACE-WILLIAM, 3rd Lord Rivers.
FRANCIS.
Anne, *m.* to George Ellis, Esq., chief-justice of the island of Jamaica.
Elizabeth, *m.* 1st, to Thomas Howard, 2nd Earl of Effingham; and 2ndly, to Field-Marshal Sir George Howard, K.B.

The 6th son, FRANCIS BECKFORD, Esq. of Basing Park, Hants, *m.* 1st, Lady Albinia Bertie, dau. of Peregrine, Duke of Ancaster and Kesteven, but by her, who *d.* in 1754, he had no issue. He *m.* 2ndly, in 1755, Susannah, dau. and heir of Richard Love, Esq. of Basing, and by her, had (with two daus., Charlotte, wife of John Middleton, Esq. of Hildersham House, co. Cambridge, and Maria), a son,

FRANCIS-LOVE BECKFORD, Esq., late of Basing Park, *b.* 1764, *m.* in 1788, Joanna, 3rd dau. and co-heir of John Leigh, Esq. of Northcourt House, Isle of Wight, and relict of Richard-Bennett Lloyd, Esq., by which lady (who *d* in 1814), he had issue,

FRANCIS-LOVE, late of the Coldstream guards, *b.* 1789
WILLIAM, of Ruxley Lodge, Surrey.
John-Leigh, capt. R.N.; *m.* in Nov. 1829, Harriette, 4th dau. of George Ward, Esq. of Northwood House, Isle of Wight.
Carleton, *d. unm.* in 1829.
Charles-Douglas, in holy orders; *m.* in 1831, his cousin, Charlotte-Maria, 2nd dau. of John Middleton, Esq. of Hildersham House, Cambridge, and has a dau., Lucy.
Harriet, *m.* in 1816, to her cousin, Andrew Arcedeckne, Esq. of Glevering Hall, Suffolk.

Mr. F.-Love Beckford *d.* 24 Feb. 1838.

Arms—Per pale, gu. and az., on a chevron, arg., between three martlets, or, an eagle, displayed, sa., within a bordure, of the fourth, charged with a double tressure, flory-counter-flory, of the first.
Crest—A heron's head, erased, or, gorged with a collar, flory-counterflory, gu.; in the beak a fish, arg.
Motto—De Dieu tout.
Seat—Ruxley Lodge, Surrey.

BEDINGFELD OF DITCHINGHAM.

BEDINGFELD, JOHN-LONGUEVILLE, Esq. of Ditchingham Hall, co. Norfolk, *b.* 19 Oct. 1800; *m.* 24 July, 1829, Mary, 2nd dau. of John, Lord Henniker, and has,

I. PHILIP, *b.* 25 April, 1830. II. John, *b.* 16 Aug. 1831.
III. Francis-William, *b.* 26 Oct. 1837.
IV. George-Longueville, *b.* 1841.
I. Mary-Henniker. II. Sarah-Sophia.
III. Anne-Eliza. IV. Louisa-Jemima.

Lineage.—The family of Bedingfeld is one (as Camden says) of undoubted antiquity, deriving its name from a town in Suffolk; and deducing its lineage from the era of the Conquest, through an uninterrupted line of distinguished ancestors. From OGERUS DE PUGEIS, *alias* LONGUEVILLE, a Norman knight, and fellow soldier of Duke WILLIAM, lineally descended

JAMES BEDINGFELD (2nd son of Sir Peter, and brother of Sir Thomas Bedingfeld, ancestor of the Oxburgh family), who was living in 1350. He *m.* Alice, dau. and heir of Peter de Fleming, by whom he acquired Fleming's Hall and Manor, and had, with a dau., Margaret, wife of Thomas Appleyard, of Dunstan, in Norfolk, a son and successor,

WILLIAM BEDINGFELD, living *temp.* HENRY VI., who *m.* Mary, dau. of Thomas Playters, of Sotterly, in Suffolk, and was ancestor of the BEDINGFELDS *of Ditchingham*, whose representative at the beginning of the 18th century,

THE REV. JOHN BEDINGFELD, LL.D. of Ditchingham, built the present mansion there. He *m.* Catherine, dau. of Clere Garneys, Esq. of Hedenham, but dying *s. p.* in 1729, was *s.* by his brother,

JAMES BEDINGFELD, Esq. of Ditchingham, who *m.* Mary, dau. of Francis Maskull, Gent. of London, and left (with a younger son, James, and three daus., Elizabeth, Anne, and Mary) a successor,

PHILIP BEDINGFELD, Esq. of Ditchingham, *b.* 31 May, 1716, who *m.* 1st, Mary, dau. of Sir Edmund Bacon, Bart. of Gillingham, and had, by her, three sons and two daus.,

PHILIP, his heir.
BACON, successor to his brother.
James, who *m.* Miss Pierson; but *d. s. p.*

John.
Mary, m. to Brampton Gurdon, Esq. of Dillingham and Letton.
Ann, m. to William Leigh, Esq. of Rushall, Staffordshire.

Mr. Bedingfeld m. 2ndly, Mrs. Forster, dau. of — Spendlove, Esq. of Norwich, and had further issue,

Francis-Philip, b. in 1763; who m. Catherine, dau. of Thomas Havers, Esq. of Thelton, in Norfolk, and had three sons, Francis, Thomas, and Richard, and two daus., Catherine and Mary.
Elizabeth, m. 1st, to Capt. Addison; and 2ndly, to the Rev. E. Forster.

Mr. Bedingfeld d. in 1791, and was s. by his son,

PHILIP BEDINGFELD, Esq. of Ditchingham, who m. Henrietta-Priscilla, dau. of Robert Hamby, Esq. of Ipswich, but d. without issue, shortly after his father, in Sept. 1791, when the estate devolved on his brother,

THE REV. BACON BEDINGFELD, of Ditchingham, b. 16 May, 1746, who m. 19 June, 1770, Susannah, dau. of Donatus O'Brien, Esq. of Blatherwycke Park, in Northamptonshire, and had by her, who d. 9 May, 1812,

Philip-Bacon, who d. s. p.
JOHN-JAMES, his heir.
Susanna-Harriot, m. 1st, to John Talbot, brother to the Earl of Shrewsbury; and 2ndly, to Henry Roper, 15th Lord Teynham.
Lucy-Eleanor.
Caroline-Elizabeth, widow of Joseph Mortimer, Esq. of Wiltshire.
Matilda-Stafford-Sophia, widow of Donatus O'Brien, Esq. of Tixover.

Mr. Bedingfeld d. 13 July, 1797, and was s. by his son,

JOHN-JAMES BEDINGFELD, Esq. of Ditchingham, J.P. and D.L., b. 14 Feb. 1773, m. 1 Jan. 1800, Sarah, dau. and co-heir of Paul Piersy, Esq. of Fairhill, co. Cork, and had issue,

JOHN-LONGUEVILLE, now of Ditchingham.
Philip, b. in 1803; major E.I.C.S.
William, b. in 1805, lost his life while serving as a midshipman, R.N.
James, b. 19 Sept. 1809; rector of Bedingfeld, in Suffolk; m. in 1839, Frances, dau. of the late Lord Henniker.
Lucinda-Caroline, m. 19 Oct. 1824, to Rev. John-Robert Hopper, rector of Wells, in Norfolk, and has issue.

Arms—Erm., an eagle displayed, gu., armed, or.
Crest—A demi-eagle, gu.
Motto—Aquila non capit muscas; or, Despicio terrena.
Seat—Ditchingham Hall, Norfolk.

BEECH OF BRANDON LODGE.

BEECH, JAMES, Esq. of Brandon Lodge, co. Warwick, and The Shawe, co. Stafford; m. Miss Madocks, of the ancient family of Glanywern, co. Denbigh.

The estate of The Shaw came into the Beech family through the eldest of three co-heiresses (sisters of the name of Stubbs), who married the uncle of the present proprietor's grandfather. The mansion was built by the late James Beech, Esq., about sixty years since.

Arms—Arg., on a bend, gu., three bucks' heads, caboshed, or.
Crest—A stag's head, caboshed.
Motto—Sub tegmine fagi.
Seats—Brandon Lodge, Coventry; and The Shawe, near Cheadle.

BELGRAVE OF PRESTON HALL.

BELGRAVE, THE REV. WILLIAM, M.A. of Preston Hall, co. Rutland, J.P., rector of Preston, b. 24 Aug. 1791; m. 3 Nov. 1814, Sophia-Elizabeth, dau. of the late William Belgrave, Esq. of Preston Hall, co. Rutland, and has issue,

I. WILLIAM, b. 8 Dec. 1822, m. 9 April, 1847, Ellen-Mary, dau. of Perceval-Hare Earle, Esq. of Torquay.
I. Sophia-Elizabeth. II. Jane-Susanna.
III. Frances, m. 21 Nov. 1848, to the Rev. Charles Lucas, of Filby House, co. Norfolk.
IV. Marianne, d. 11 Feb. 1852.
V. Henrietta.

Lineage.—THE REV. CORNELIUS BELGRAVE, M.A., rector of Ridlington, co. Rutland, and of North Kilworth, co. Leicester, b. 18 Aug. 1676, the 5th son of William Belgrave, of North Kilworth, great-great-great-great-grandson of William Belgrave, of North and South Kilworth, who was 2nd son of Belgrave of Belgrave, m. 2 Dec. 1703, Mary, dau. and co-heir of William Sheild, of Preston, co. Rutland, Gent., and d. 17 Feb. 1757, leaving, besides four other sons and four daus.,

THE REV. JEREMIAH BELGRAVE, rector of Preston, co. Rutland, and of North Kilworth, co. Leicester, b. in 1706, who m. in Aug. 1742, Frances, dau. of Richard Taylor, of the parish of St. George, Middlesex, capt. of an Indiaman, and had issue,

Charles, in holy orders, rector of Ridlington, co. Rutland, and of North Kilworth, co. Leicester; d. unm. 20 Feb. 1804.
William, of Preston Hall, co. Rutland, high-sheriff in 1788. He d. 1824, leaving daus. only.
George, D.D. of Preston Hall, rector of Cockfield; d. s. p. March, 1831.
JEREMIAH, of whom presently.
Thomas, of Louth, co. Lincoln, d. 1789, leaving issue.
Samuel, of Preston, d. 1758.
Cornelius, of Lutterworth, d. 1794, leaving a dau.
Frances, of Stamford. Mary, of Stamford.

Mr. Belgrave d. in 1802. His 4th son,

JEREMIAH BELGRAVE, Esq. of Stamford, co. Lincoln, b. 2 June, 1753, m. 26 Feb. 1786, Jane, eldest dau of William Barker, Esq. of Stamford, co. Lincoln, and by her (who d. 4 May, 1796), had issue,

WILLIAM.
Frances-Elizabeth, m. in 1814, to Edward Tryon, Esq. of Southampton.
Mary-Anne, m. in 1814, to Egerton Cutler, Esq. of London, who d. in March, 1833.

Mr. Belgrave d. 19 Aug. 1819, and his son William s. to the estates of his uncle, George Belgrave, D.D., at his decease in 1831.

Arms—Gu., a chevron, erm., between three mascles, arg.
Crest—A ram's head.
Seat—Preston Hall, near Uppingham, co. Rutland.

BELL OF WOOLSINGTON.

BELL, MATTHEW, Esq. of Woolsington, co. Northumberland, D.L. and high-sheriff in 1816, formerly M.P. for Northumberland, b. 18 April, 1793; m. 10 Oct. 1816, Elizabeth-Anne, only child and heiress of Henry-Utrick Reay, Esq. of Killingworth, Northumberland.

Lineage.—MATTHEW BELL, of Newcastle-on-Tyne, m. the dau. of Salkeld, and had, with a dau., Elizabeth, who m. John Stephenson, Esq. also of Newcastle, and Knaresdale Hall, co. Northumberland, an only son,

MATTHEW BELL, Esq. alderman of Newcastle, sheriff in 1736, and mayor in 1757. He m. Jane, dau. of Richard Ridley, Esq. of Heaton, co. Northumberland, ancestor of Sir M.-White Ridley, Bart., and was father of

MATTHEW BELL, Esq. of Woolsington, colonel of the Northumberland Militia, who m. in 1767, Dulcibella, dau. of Sir John Eden, Bart. of Windlestone, co. Durham, and had, with three daus., four sons, MATTHEW; Stephen; Robert, mayor of Newcastle in 1822; and Henry. The eldest,

MATTHEW BELL, Esq. of Woolsington, high-sheriff of Northumberland in 1797, m. 9 June, 1792, Sarah-Frances, sister of Charles-J. Brandling, Esq. of Gosforth House, co. Northumberland, and had issue,

MATTHEW, now of Woolsington.
Charles, m. 1st, Mary, youngest dau. of the Rev. Ralph-Henry Brandling, of Gosforth House, which lady d. in 1828; and 2ndly, Rachel, fourth dau. of William Brandling, Esq. of Low Gosforth. Mr. Charles Bell d. in 1844.
Robert-John, d. in 1826.
Henry, m. Helen, only child of Sir William-Bagnel Burdett, Bart.
John, m. Isabella, only dau. of Sir Charles Loraine, Bart., of Kirkharle, Northumberland, and has issue.
William, m. Jane, 3rd dau. of John Ridley, Esq. of Park End, co. Northumberland.
Elizabeth-Jane. Dulcibella.
Frances, m. to Sir John-James Walsham, Bart. of Knill Court, co. Hereford.

Mr. Bell d. in 1811, and was s. by his eldest son, MATTHEW BELL, Esq. now of Woolsington.

Arms—Sa., a fesse, erm., between three bells, arg.
Crest—A hawk, erect, and belled.
Seat—Woolsington, Newcastle-upon-Tyne.

BELL OF MELLING HALL.

BELL, WILLIAM-GILLISON, Esq. of Melling Hall, co. Lancaster, J.P. and D.L., b. 23 Aug. 1803; m. 5 March, 1828, Harriot, 2nd dau. of the Rev. Ralph Worsley, rector of Finchley, and has issue surviving

I. WILLIAM-GILLISON, b. 12 Dec. 1828.
II. Henry-James, b. 27 Oct. 1831.
III. George-Constable-Gildart, b. Sept. 1843.
I. Harriot.

Mr. Bell is only son of the late William-Gillison Bell, Esq., by Rebecca his wife, dau. of William Saunders, grandson of William Bell and Marion Dalgliesh his wife, and great-grandson of James Bell, Esq., and Elizabeth his wife.

Motto—Prænuntia pacis
Seat—Melling Hall, near Lancaster.

BELLAIRS OF KIRKBY BELLARS.

BELLAIRS, REV. HENRY, A.M., rector of Bedworth, co. Warwick, rural dean and honorary canon of Worcester cathedral, vicar of Hunsingore, co. of York, domestic chaplain to the Earl of Strafford, and J.P., b. 29 Aug. 1790; entered the royal navy, and was wounded at Trafalgar; was afterwards in the 15th hussars; and subsequently entered holy orders; m. 30 May, 1811, Dorothy-Parker, dau. and co-heir (with Mary, 1st wife of John, Earl of Strafford, and Sarah, wife of Captain Carmichael) of Peter Mackenzie, Esq. of Grove House, Middlesex, descended from the Mackenzies, barons of Kintail, and by her has issue,

I. HENRY-WALFORD, in holy orders, one of H.M. Inspectors of Schools, b. 14 March, 1812, m. 15 July, 1839, Mary-Hannah-Albina, dau. of George-Watkin Kenrick, Esq. of Woore Hall, Salop, by Isabella, dau. of William ffarington, Esq. of Werden, Lancaster, and has issue.
II. William-Oswald-Mackenzie, b. 22 July, 1814.
III. Charles, in holy orders, b. 3 March, 1818, m. 5 Dec. 1839, Anna-Maria, eldest dau. of John Isherwood, Esq. of Marple Hall, Cheshire, and of Bradshaw Hall, Lancashire, and has issue.
IV. Arthur-Heathcote, b. 27 Sept. 1826.
V. George-Byng, b. 7 March, 1828.
I. Dora-Ennis, m. Reginald-Simpson Graham, Esq. eldest son of Reginald Graham, Esq. of Etterby, in Cumberland. She was drowned with her husband and only child in the river Amazon, on Easter Monday, 1845, by the accidental upsetting of a canoe.
II. Mary-Ellen, m. Thomas-Bradshaw Isherwood, Esq. of Marple and Bradshaw, and has issue.
III. Rosamira, m. Benjamin Lancaster, Esq. of Chester Terrace, Regent's Park. IV. Laura-Parker.
V. Frances-Lake, m. the Rev. John-Morgan Brown.
VI. Nona-Maria-Stevenson.
VII. Agnes, m. the Rev. Bertram-Brooke Hulbert, of Exhall, co. Warwick.

Lineage.—This family (spoken of by Dugdale as "royally connected") deduce their origin from Judith, niece to King WILLIAM the Conqueror, and sister to Hugh Lupus, Count of Avranches, and Earl of Chester. She m. Richard de Aquila, and had issue, Maud de Aquila, m. 1st, to Robert de Mowbray, Earl of Northumberland, and 2ndly, to Nigel de Albini, younger brother of William de Pincerna. By him she had two sons,

Roger Mowbray, ancestor of the ducal house of Norfolk, a great benefactor to the Knights Templars, and a famous warrior; he marched in the second crusade with King LOUIS to Palestine, fought under the banner of the Temple, and on his return home gave many possessions to the order.
Hamon de Beler, ancestor of the Bellairs family. He was Lord of Eye Kettleby, A.D. 1160, and left a son,

RALPH DE BELER, of Eye Kettleby, m. Emma, dau. of Sir Walter de Folvile, of Ashby Folvile, Knt., and had issue, two sons. The younger,

Roger, sheriff of Lincolnshire 1256; d. 1277; grandfather of Roger, Lord de Beler, an itinerant judge, who was killed in a valley near Reresby, *anno* 1326, by Eustace de Folvile, of Ashby Folvile, his two brothers, and Eudo de la Zouch, who waylaid and barbarously murdered him. His vast estates descended in the female line to the family of Lord Cromwell. His chief seat was Wingfield Manor House, co. Derby, where was a magnificent mansion, dismantled during the civil wars.

The elder son of Ralph,

WILLIAM DE BELER, of Eye Kettleby, living in 1235 and 1273, m. Isabel, dau. of Sir Robert Dangervile, Knt., and had issue two sons, Hamon, and WILLIAM, of whom presently. The descendants of Hamon were,

Hamon, d. 1304.
Sir Ralph, m. Emma, dau. of Sir Walter de Folvile, Knt., d. 1345.
Sir Richard, m. Agatha, dau. of Sir Richard Bingham, Knt., d. 1388.
Sir James Bellars, m. Margaret, dau. of Richard Barnard, of Hoffingham, whose son, John, m. Elizabeth, dau. of Antony Howby: d. 1461, leaving issue, 1 John, d. s. p.; 1 Marina, m. to Sir Thomas Greene; 2 Joanna, m. to Jasper Villiers, ancestor of the ducal house of Buckingham; 3 Margaret, prioress of Langley; 4 Eleanor, m. William Ruskin, of Melton Mowbray.

WILLIAM, above-mentioned, founded a religious house of Black Canons at Kirkby Bellars, and left descendants: Roger, 1351; Roger, 1380; Ralph Bellars, 1438; Sir John, 1476; John, 1515; Reginald, 1546; John, m. 1575, Dorothy Petre, and d. 1597; John, b. 1581, m. Elizabeth Madleye, d. 1647; John, b. 1603.

JOHN BELLARS, b. 1640, m. Esther Greene, and had issue, John, b. 1677, d. 1677; JAMES, his heir; Tobias, d. 1632; Elizabeth; Ann, m. John Goodyear, Esq. The eldest son,

JAMES BELLARS, Esq. of Uffington, co. Lincoln, and of Billesdon, co. Leicester, b. May, 1680, d. in 1744. He m. 1714, Catharine, dau. and heiress of John Lea, of Bracebrough (by Catharine, dau. and heiress of Thomas Foot, of Ryhall, Esq.) and by her, who d. 21 Jan. 1757, had issue,

JAMES, his heir.
Elizabeth, m. William Pank, Esq. of Wansford, whose dau. Mary m. John Mansfield, Esq., M.P. for Leicester.
Esther, b. 1716; m. Richard Boar, Esq. of Maxey.
Alice, b. 1718; m. William Clark, Esq. of Lobthorpe; and was grandmother of William Stevenson, who d. 1845, leaving his large possessions to the Bellairs family.
Ann, b. 1723; m. J.-W. Davie, Esq. of Stamford.

The son and heir,

JAMES BELLARS, Esq. of Uffington and Billesdon, b. 5 Sept. 1720, d. 5 Dec. 1799, married twice (his 2nd wife was Martha, dau. of William Barker, Esq. of the family of Sir Abel Barker, Bart.): his 1st wife was Mary, dau. and heiress of Abel Walford, Esq., by Susanna, dau. of J. Venour, Esq.: by her he had issue,

ABEL-WALFORD, his heir.
John, capt. 46th regt.; m. Jane Judd, and left, John-Harry, lieut. R.N.; and other issue.
James, major 12th regt.; d. s. p. 1799.

The eldest son,

ABEL-WALFORD BELLAIRS, Esq. (inserted the letter "I," into the spelling of the name), of Uffington and Billesdon, b. 8 Feb. 1755. He was high-sheriff for Rutlandshire, D.L. and J.P. for Lincolnshire and Northamptonshire; he d. 23 April, 1839, having m. in 1781, Susanna, only dau. of Miles Lowley, Esq. of Oakham, and had issue,

I. James, of Uffington, who assumed, by royal sign-manual, in 1844, the name and arms of STEVENSON. He was b. 9 Aug. 1782; and d. 18 Aug. 1853; he m 29 Jan. 1807, Elizabeth-Ann, eldest dau. of Laurence Peel, Esq., and niece of Sir Robert Peel, Bart., and left issue,
James-Peel Stevenson, Esq. of Uffington. He was b. 20 June, 1808; and m. Maria, dau. of Col. Mackenzie, and has issue.
II. George, of Stockerston, co. Leicester, b. 25 Feb. 1787; m. Miss Linwood, and has issue,
1 Stevenson-Gilbert, in holy orders, b. 1825.
2 George-Clarke.
1 Dora-Mary, m. to the Rev. William Alford.
III. Henry, in holy orders (*vide supra*).
IV. William (Sir), Knt., of Mulbarton Lodge, co. Norfolk, capt. 15th hussars, served in the Peninsular war, and at Waterloo; m. Cassandra, dau. and heir of Edmund Hooke, Esq. of Mulbarton Lodge, and has issue, 1 Edmund, capt. 7th fusiliers, m. Emilia Bellairs, dau. of James Stevenson, Esq. of Uffington; 2 Leopold, capt. 49th regt.; 3 William, capt. in the 49th regt.
I. Emilia, m. Rev. John Wood, of Swanwick Hall, Derby.
II. Frances, m. James Higgon, Esq. of Scolton House, co. Pembroke.
III. Catherine, m. 1st, Rev. J.-Lindsay Young; and 2ndly, Rev. George MacLear.
IV. Anna-Maria, m. W.-M. Harries, Esq. of Haverfordwest.

Arms—Per pale, gu. and sa., a lion rampant, arg.
Crest—A lion's gamb, erased, gu.
Motto—In cruce mea fides.

BELLEW OF STOCKLEIGH COURT.

BELLEW, JOHN-PRESTWOOD, Esq. of Stockleigh Court, co. Devon, b. 19 July, 1803; m. 8 May, 1827, Mary-Ann, dau. of William Hancock, Esq. of Wiveliscombe, in Somersetshire, and has issue,

I. JOHN-FROUDE. II. William-Legassicke.
I. Louisa-Philippa. II. Fanny.
III. Mary-Anne-Prestwood. IV. Camilla-Carrington.

Lineage.—The Bellews, of whom there were eighteen knights in a direct line of succession, and who were renowned in the middle ages, settled in Ireland, at Bellewstown, in the co. of Meath, and in the adjoining co. of Louth, in 1470. From SIR RICHARD BELLEW descended Sir John Bellew, of Willystown, ancestor of Lord Bellew of Barmeath, of Sir Michael-Dillon Bellew, Bart. of Mount Bellew, in the co. of Galway, and of Sir Christopher Bellew, Knt., whose eldest son, Sir John, was created Baron Bellew, of Dulech. The BELLEWS *of Devonshire* derive from a common ancestor with the ennobled branches, and have for centuries held a very high position amongst the landed aristocracy of the West of England. Their pedigree can be traced in an unbroken line up to the period of the Norman Conquest.

JOHN BELLEWE, lineally descended from Roger Bellewe, of Bellewstown, *m. temp.* King EDWARD IV., Amy, eldest dau. and co-heir of John Fleminge, Esq. (of the very ancient house of FLEMINGE *of Bratton Fleminge*), by his wife, the dau. and co-heir of Martin Ferrers, descended from Henry Ferrers, who held the manor of Beer Ferrers, in the co. of Devon, in the reign of EDWARD II., and had his castle there. By the co-heiress of Fleminge, John Bellewe had a son and successor,

PATRICK BELLEWE, of Alverdiscott, in Devon, who *m.* Anne, dau. of John Dennys, Esq. of Orleigh, in that shire, and had a son and heir,

HENRY BELLEWE, Esq. of Alverdiscott, who *m.* Alice, dau. and heir of William Colebrooke, by Jane his wife, dau. and heir of Robert Calley, Esq. of Chymney, and had a son and successor,

WILLIAM BELLEWE, Esq. of Ash Rogus, in Brampton, in Devonshire, who *m.* Anne, dau. of Sir Hugh Stukely, of Aston, in that co., and had a son,

HENRY BELLEW, Esq. of Stockleigh English, in the co. of Devon, living in 1564, who *m.* Elizabeth, dau. of Amyas Chichester, Esq. of Arlington, and dying in 1597, left a son,

PHILIP BELLEW, Esq. of Stockleigh Court, father of

WILLIAM BELLEW, Esq. of Yarnscombe, who *m.* Rose Hill, and dying in 1700, was *s.* by his son,

HENRY BELLEW, Esq. of Stockleigh Court, who *m.* and had one son, Henry, who *d. s. p.* in 1711. Mr. Bellew, surviving his only child, was *s.* at his decease, in 1719, by (the son of his brother William) his nephew,

HENRY BELLEW, Esq. of Stockleigh Court, who *m.* Frances, dau. of William Barbor, Esq. of Lary and Raleigh, in the co. of Devon, by Frances his wife, the heiress of Poyntz of Northcote and Bettadown, and dying in 1752, left, with a dau., Frances, wife of Horatio Hele, Esq., three sons, of whom

HENRY BELLEW, Esq., captain R.N., *s.* his nephew at Stockleigh Court, and was a distinguished naval officer. He *m.* Anne, widow of Thomas Wentworth, Esq., but dying issueless, 18 April, 1791, aged 63, was *s.* by his brother,

JOHN BELLEW, Esq. of Stockleigh Court, who *m.* Philippa Le Comte, an heiress, and *d.* in 1821, having had issue, John-Pillet, who *d. unm.* in 1815; Henry, who *d.* in 1806; WILLIAM, successor to his father; Frances, who *d.* 22 Dec. 1840; and Philippa, who *d.* 6 Feb. 1841. The son and heir,

WILLIAM BELLEW, Esq. of Stockleigh Court, *m.* in 1798, Prestwood-Love, dau. of the Rev. John Froude, rector of Knowstone and Molland (of the family of FROUDE *of Edmeston*, in Devon), by his wife Miss Legassicke, and had issue, JOHN-PRESTWOOD, his heir; Henry, of Oakhampton Park, Somersetshire, *m.* Mary, 2nd dau. of H. Bawden, Esq., J.P., and has a dau., Ada-Mary; Frances; and CAROLINE, whom her aunt, Miss Bellew, made her heiress. Mr. Bellew *d.* 17 June, 1826, and was *s.* by his son, the present JOHN-PRESTWOOD BELLEW, Esq. of Stockleigh Court.

Arms—Sa., fretty, or, quartering FLEMINGE, FERRERS, COLEBROOKE, CALLEY, &c.
Crest—An arm, embowed, habited, the hand, ppr., grasping a chalice pouring water (*belle eau*, in allusion to the name) into a basin, also ppr. *Motto*—Tout d'eu haut.
Seat—Stockleigh Court, co. Devon.

BENCE OF THORINGTON HALL.

BENCE, HENRY-BENCE, Esq. of Thorington Hall, Suffolk, J.P. and D.L., col. in the East Suffolk militia, *b.* 12 March, 1788; *m.* 5 May, 1815, Elizabeth-Susanna, 2nd dau. and co-heir of the late Nicholas Starkie, Esq. of Frenchwood, Lancaster, and has had,

I. HENRY-ALEXANDER-STARKIE, *b.* 15 May, 1816, *m.* in 1850, the dau. of John Barclay, Esq.
II. Edward-Robert-Starkie, late of the King's dragoon guards, *b.* 27 Aug. 1823, *m.* in 1850, a dau. of George Sulivan, Esq.
III. Thomas-Starkie, in holy orders, *b.* 1 Oct. 1824, rector of Thorington.
Marianne-Susanna-Starkie, *d.* in 1838.

Lineage.—The family of Bence is one of considerable antiquity in Suffolk, deriving immediately from

JOHN BENCE, of Aldeburgh, co. Suffolk, youngest son of Edmund Bence, of the same place, who *d.* before 1587. The eventual heiress,

ANN BENCE, dau. of Robert Bence, Esq. of Henstead, *b.* in 1707, *m.* 16 Dec. 1740, Robert Sparrow, Esq. of Worlingham and Kettleborough, in Suffolk, and by him, who *d.* in 1764, had issue,

I. ROBERT SPARROW, Esq. of Worlingham Hall, who *m.* twice, and had by his first wife, Mary, dau. and heir of John Barnard, Bart. of Brampton Park, one son and one dau., viz.,
1 ROBERT-BERNARD SPARROW, Esq. of Worlingham Hall, bapt. in 1773; who *m.* 14 May, 1797, Lady Olivia Acheson, dau. of Arthur, 1st Earl of Gosford; and *d.* a brigadier-general in the West Indies in 1805, leaving a dau. and heiress,
MILICENT, *m.* in 1822, to George, present Duke of Manchester; and *d.* 21 Nov. 1848.
1 Mary Sparrow, *m.* to Archibald, Earl of Gosford.
II. BENCE SPARROW, of whom we are about to treat.

The 2nd son,

THE REV. BENCE SPARROW, rector of Beccles, in Suffolk, inheriting the Thorington estate, assumed by sign-manual 2 May, 1804, the surname and arms of BENCE. He *m.* in 1786, Harriet, dau. and heir of William Elmy, Esq. of Beccles, and had issue,

HENRY BENCE, now of Thorington.
Anna-Maria, *m.* in 1809, to the Rev. Lancelot Brown, rector of Kelsale and Carlton, co. Suffolk, and has three daus.
Matilda, *m.* in 1811, to Lieut.-Col. Wm. Jones, of the 5th dragoon guards, and has three sons.

Mr. Bence *d.* in Sept. 1824.

Arms—Arg., on a cross, between four frets, gu., a castle, of the first.
Crest—A castle, triple-towered.
Motto—Virtus castellum meum.
Seat—Thorington Hall, Suffolk.

BENDYSHE OF BARRINGTON.

BENDYSHE, JOHN, Esq. of Barrington, co. Cambridge, lieut. R.N., J.P. and D.L., at one time high-sheriff of Cambridgeshire, *b.* 10 April, 1791; *m.* 1st, 10 May, 1820, Catherine, eldest dau. of George Matcham, Esq. of Ashfold Lodge, Sussex, by Catherine his wife, sister of the great Earl Nelson, and by her (who *d.* in 1831) he has issue,

I. JOHN, *b.* 10 May, 1821. II. Richard, *b.* 8 Sept. 1822.
III. Nelson, *b.* 17 Oct. 1823. IV. Thomas, *b.* 7 July, 1827.
I. Caroline. II. Laura. III. Susanna.
IV. Circe. V. Catherine.

He *m.* 2ndly, 21 Oct. 1833, Anna-Maria, 3rd dau. of Sir Charles Watson, Bart. of Wratting Park, Cambridgeshire.

Lineage.—The surname, originally DE WESTLEY, was changed to that of BENDISH, from a considerable lordship in Radwinter, whereof the family became possessed sometime in the twelfth century. The first whose name occurs in ancient writings that may be certainly depended upon, is,

PETER DE WESTLEY, alias BENDISH. He flourished about the reigns of King JOHN and of HENRY III. His descendant,

EDMUND BENDYSHE, Esq., eldest son of Thomas Bendyshe, Esq., by Margaret his wife, dau. and co-heir of Thomas Bradfield, Esq. of Barrington, inherited his mother's estate, and founded the family of BENDYSHE *of Barrington*, co. Cambridge, whose representative in the early part of the last century,

RALPH BENDYSHE, Esq. of Barrington, *m.* Mary, dau. of John Aylaff, of the parish of St. James's, Westminster, and was father of

RICHARD BENDYSHE, Esq. of Barrington, who *m.* 17 Feb. 1783, Jane, dau. of John Jervis, Esq. of Darlaston, co. Stafford, and had (with two other sons, Richard, an officer in the 1st foot-guards, who *d.* at Chatham; and Robert, lieut. R.N., drowned in the "Blenheim" with Sir Thomas Trowbridge) a successor, the present JOHN BENDYSHE, Esq. of Barrington.

Arms—Arg., a chevron, sa., between three rams' heads, erased, az.
Crest—Out of a ducal coronet, or, a talbot's head.
Motto—Utrâque Pallade.
Seat—Kneesworth House, near Royston.

BENNET OF LALESTON.

BENNET, JOHN-WICK, Esq. of Laleston, co. Glamorgan, J.P. and D.L., m. Anna-Maria-Charlotte, relict of Thomas Wyndham, Esq. of Dunraven Castle, and dau. of Thomas Ashby, Esq., by Charlotte his wife, dau. of Robert Jones, Esq. of Fonmon Castle, co. Glamorgan.

Lineage.—SIR BENET DE PENCLAWDD accompanied the CONQUEROR to England, and received for his services the lordship of Penclawdd, in Gower, (the western extremity of Glamorgan.)

That the family of which we are treating was settled there at that period, divers records fully substantiate.

Fuller, in his *Church History*, pp. 165, 166, quotes a MS. of Thomas Scriven, Esq.; also Fox, and the *Chronicle* of John Brompton; in proof that, amongst others, Bonet, or Benet was one of "such persons as after the battle were advanced to seigneuries in this land" [Glamorgan].

SIR HUMPHREY BENET (son of Sir Benet de Penclawdd), m. Elinor, dau. of Morgan Llewellyn ap Ivor, and thus acquired the estate of Kilfigin, in the parish of Llanbader, in Monmouthshire. He was ancestor of

JOHN BENNET, Esq., b. 1630 (2nd son of David Bennet, and uncle of John Bennet, of Kettle Hill, sheriff of Glamorganshire in 1695). He m. Mary Jones, of Laleston, dau. of Captain Thomas Jones, of Frampton, in Glamorganshire, by his wife, Mary Turbervill, of Ogmore. By the heiress of Laleston (who d. 10 Dec. 1726), Mr. Bennet left, at his decease, in 1707, with other issue, a son,

WILLIAM BENNET, Esq. of Laleston, who m. Mary, dau. of Richard Llewellyn, Esq. of Ynis-y-gerwn, in Glamorganshire, and had (with two daus., Jane, m. to Edward Gwynne, Esq. of Llantrissant; and Anne, m. to the Rev. Robert Davies) several sons, of whom the eldest,

THOMAS BENNET, Esq. of Laleston, served the office of sheriff for Glamorganshire in 1768. He m. Mary, dau. of Edward Walters, Esq. of Pitcot, sheriff in 1754, but dying issueless, 29 Jan. 1772, was s. by his brother,

WILLIAM BENNET, Esq. of Laleston, who m. 1st, the dau. of Robert Morris, Esq. of Gnisarwad, high-sheriff for Glamorganshire in 1742; and 2ndly, Catherine, dau. of Edward Wilkins, Esq. of Lantwit; by the latter of whom he left, at his decease in 1801, aged 80, a dau., Mary, wife of Morgan-Price Smith, Esq. of Newhouse, and a son,

JOHN BENNET, Esq. of Laleston, m. 17 July, 1791, Selenah-Maria-Anne, dau. of Jacob Grose, Esq. of Appleshaw, Hants (brother to Captain Francis Grose, the celebrated antiquary and Richmond herald), by Frances Andrews his wife, of the family of ANDREWS *of Porton*, in Hampshire, and had issue,

JOHN-WICK, now of Laleston.
Selenah-Catherine-Frances.
Louisa-Mary-Anne.
Caroline-Susan, m. to the Rev. Henry Windsor-Richards, rector of St. Andrew's and St. Lythan's, in Glamorganshire, and has issue.
Elinor. Matilda.
Eliza, m. to William Head-Deacon, Esq. of Longcross House, Glamorganshire.

Mr. Bennet served the office of high-sheriff for the co. of Glamorgan in 1825.

Arms—Arg., three goats' heads, erased, sa., barbed and double armed, or; langued, gu.
Crest—A goat's head, as in the arms.
Motto—Aut nunquam tentes, aut perfice.
Seat—Laleston House, Glamorganshire.

BENNET OF ROUGHAM HALL.

BENNET, PHILIP, Esq. of Tollesbury, co. Essex, and Rougham Hall, co. Suffolk, J.P. and D.L., M.P. for West Suffolk; m. in 1822, Anne, 2nd dau. and co-heir of Sir Thomas Pilkington, Bart. of Chevet, and has a son and heir,

PHILIP, b. in 1837.

Lineage.—PHILIP BENNET, Esq. of Widcombe, co. Somerset, son of Philip Bennet, Esq., by Mary his 2nd wife, dau. of Thomas Hallam, Esq. of Tollesbury, and grandson of Philip Bennet, by Jane his wife, dau. of Scarborough Chapman, Esq. of Widcombe, co. Somerset, m. 14 Dec. 1769, Mary, dau. of the Rev. Christopher Hand, B.D., and by her, who d. 16 April, 1822 aged 75, had a son,

PHILIP BENNET, Esq. of Tollesbury, J.P., high-sheriff of Suffolk in 1821; b. in 1771; who m. in 1794, Jane-Judith, only child of the Rev. R. Kedington, of Rougham Hall, and had issue,

PHILIP, now of Rougham.
James-Thomas, rector of Chevelly, co. Cambridge, m. 6 April, 1826, Henrietta-Eliza, dau. of James Jackson, Esq. of Doncaster, and has issue.
Jane-Fanny, m. 4 Dec. 1821, to the Rev. Samuel Alderson, rector of Risby, brother of Mr. Baron Alderson.

Arms—Gu., a bezant between three demi-lions, rampant, couped, arg.
Crest—In a mural crown, or, a lion's head, couped, charged on the neck with a bezant.
Motto—Bene tenax.
Seats—Rougham Hall, Bury St. Edmunds, co. Suffolk; and Tollesbury, co. Essex.

BENNETT OF THOMASTOWN.

BENNETT, FRANCIS-VALENTINE, Esq. of Thomastown, King's County, b. 28 Jan. 1826; s. as representative of the family, upon the death of his father, Valentine Bennett, Esq., in May, 1839.

Lineage.—NICHOLAS BENNETT, Esq., m. Mabel O'Kelly, co. Roscommon, and had issue, Thomas, d. unm.; FRANCIS, his heir; Mabel, m. to John Ball, Esq., father of the present Rt. Hon. Nicholas Ball, one of the judges of the Common Pleas in Ireland; Anne, d. unm. The eldest surviving son,

FRANCIS BENNETT, Esq., m. Elizabeth Laffan, of the co. of Kilkenny, and had issue, Thomas, unm.; VALENTINE; Mary-Catherine, m. to Lieut.-Col. L'Estrange, of Moystown, King's County; Elizabeth-Emily, m. to John Farrell, Esq., of Moynalty, co. Meath. The youngest son,

VALENTINE BENNETT, Esq., J.P. and D.L., of the King's County, and high-sheriff in 1830, m. 7 Jan. 1824, Elizabeth-Helen, dau. of the late George Ryan, Esq. of Inch House, co. Tipperary, and had issue,

FRANCIS-VALENTINE, now of Thomastown.
George Henry. Valentine.
Thomas-Joseph. Frederick-Philip.
Henry-Grey. Albert, (a posthumous child.)
Elizabeth-Marian, d. 1833.

Mr. Valentine Bennett d. in May, 1839.

Seat—Thomastown House, King's County.

BENNETT OF THORPE PLACE.

BENNETT, THE REV. HENRY-LEIGH, of Thorpe Place, co. Surrey, b. 17 May, 1795; m. 11 Sept. 1845, Caroline, 2nd dau. of George-Henry Crutchley, Esq. of Sunning Hill Park, Berks, and has had issue,

I. HENRY-CURRIE-LEIGH, b. 25 July, 1852.
I. Grace-Leigh, d. young. II. Julia-Leigh, d. young.
III. Mary-Leigh.

Lineage.—On the dissolution of the monasteries by HENRY VIII., the manor of Thorpe, Surrey, became vested in the crown, and so remained until granted in 1590, by Queen ELIZABETH, to Sir John Wolley, her Latin secretary. His only son and heir, Sir Francis Wolley, M.P. for Haslemere, d. in 1609, having devised this estate to his cousin William Minterne, with remainder to another cousin, Elizabeth Minterne. This lady, Elizabeth Minterne, m. SIR FRANCIS LEIGH, whose ancestors had long been settled at Addington, co. Surrey. With the descendants of Sir Francis Leigh, and Elizabeth his wife, Thorpe remained, until, by the marriage of the two co-heiresses, Mary and Anne, in the years 1731 and 1737 respectively, it devolved to the families of BENNETT and SPENCER. Eventually a division of the Leigh estates took place, and in 1768, under the provisions of an act of parliament, Thorpe was allotted to

THE REV. WOLLEY-LEIGH BENNETT. His son,

THE REV. JOHN-LEIGH BENNETT, of Thorpe, pulled down the old mansion at Hall Place, and built a new and handsome house in its stead, to which he gave the name of Thorpe Place. By Harriott-Eliza his wife, who d. 11 Dec. 1846, he had issue,

JOHN-LEIGH, now of Thorpe.
Edward-Leigh, m. 1st, Ellenor Coddrington; and 2ndly, Anne Huntingford.
Frederick-Leigh, deceased.
Mary-Anne, m. in 1824, to Sir Richard-Torin Kindersley.

Arms—Gu., a bezant between three demi-lions, rampant, couped, arg.
Crest—A lion's head, issuing out of a mural crown.
Motto—Dux vitæ ratio.
Seat—Thorpe Place, Chertsey.

BENNETT OF FARINGDON HOUSE.

BENNETT, DANIEL, Esq. of Faringdon House, co. Berks, b. 29 June, 1823; m. 28 Oct. 1847, Mary-Elizabeth, eldest dau. of Uvedale Corbett, Esq. of Aston Hall, co. Salop.

Lineage.—WILLIAM BENNETT, Esq. of Faringdon House, Berks, b. in 1790, son of Daniel Bennett, Esq. of Faringdon House, who d. in 1826, served as high-sheriff of Berks in 1837. He m. 25 Sept. 1817, Marianna, dau. of the late John Dunkin, Esq. of Fryerning, Essex, and by her (who d. in 1840) has issue,

DANIEL, now of Faringdon House.
William, lieut. 15th hussars, d. in India, 29 Sept. 1848.
John-Dunkin, d. 6 Nov. 1851.
Elizabeth-Emma, m. 29 July, 1845, Richard-Meredyth Richards, Esq., only son of R. Richards, Esq., M.P. of Caerynwch; and d. s. p. 10 Dec. 1852.
Marianne, d. unm. 22 March, 1837.

Mr. Bennett d. 18 Jan. 1844.

Arms—Gu., a bezant, between three demi-lions, rampant, arg.
Crest—A lion's head, charged with a bezant.
Motto—De bon vouloir servir le roi.
Seat—Faringdon House, co. Berks.

BENNETT OF BENNETT'S COURT.

BENNETT, JOSEPH-HENRY, Esq. of Bennett's Court, co. Cork, m. Theodosia-Ann, dau. and co-heiress of John Smith, Esq. of Summer Castle, co. Lancaster, and had one son,

I. JOSEPH-HENRY, who d. 4 July, 1843, aged 30, and was interred with his mother at the Abbey Church at Bath.

This gentleman, eldest son of George Jackson, Esq. of Glanbeg, co. Waterford, by Susannah his wife, dau. and sole heiress of Joseph Bennett, Esq., recorder of Cork, assumed the name and arms of his maternal grandfather, to whose estates he succeded.

Arms—Gu., a bezant, between three demi-lions, or.
Crest—Out of a mural coronet, or, a demi-lion, rampant, arg., holding a bezant.
Motto—Serve the King.
Seat—Bennett's Court, near Queenstown.

BENNITT OF STOURTON HALL.

BENNITT, WILLIAM, Esq. of Stourton Hall, near Stourbridge, b. 15 Nov. 1799; m. in Aug. 1834, Sarah-Louisa, dau. of John Dawes, Esq., and has issue,

I. PYESON-WILMOT, b. 17 June, 1836.
II. William-Ward, b. 24 Nov. 1839.
III. Thomas-George-Dawes, b. 19 Oct. 1847.
IV. Joseph-Bourne, b. 17 July, 1849.
I. Louisa-Jane. II. Sarah-Maria.
III. Emma-Naomi. IV. Eleanor-Harding.

Mr. Bennitt is an active magistrate for the counties of Worcester, Stafford, and Salop, and deputy-lieut. of the first-named shire. He is captain of the Dudley troop of Worcestershire yeomanry cavalry, and had presented to him, in 1846, two pieces of plate on behalf of the county troop, for his efficient discharge of the duties in command of it since its formation in 1831.

Arms—Az., on a chevron, or, between three martlets in chief, and one in base, arg., three annulets, of the field.
Crest—Upon a mount, vert, a horse's head, couped, arg., pierced through the neck by an arrow, in bend sinister, point downwards, ppr.
Motto—Irrevocabile.
Seat—Stourton Hall, near Stourbridge.

BENSON OF UTTERBY HOUSE.

BENSON, THE REV. HENRY, A.M. of Utterby House, co. Lincoln, J.P., late vicar of Heckinton, b. 9 Aug. 1793; m. 15 Oct. 1829, Mary-Catherine, only child of the late Sapsford Harrold, Esq. of Utterby House.

Lineage.—This family, originally resident in Yorkshire, was a near branch of that from which Robert Benson, Lord Bingley, descended.

GEORGE BENSON (cousin of his lordship) was b. in 1662, m. in 1692, Anne Coulton, and d. in 1738, being then lord mayor of York. He left, with other issue, a son,

ROBERT BENSON, b. at York, 14 Jan. 1708, who m. 1st, 6 Jan. 1742, Elizabeth, dau. of Isaac Handcock, of Leeds, and by her (who d. 24 Nov. 1743), had one son, John, who died the same day. He m. 2ndly, 27 June, 1754, Mary, dau. of Mr. Thomas Bridges, of Leeds, and by her (who d. 22 Dec. 1816), had issue,

ROBERT, of whom presently.
John, b. 22 June, 1756, m. 8 Aug. 1780, Martha, dau. of Paul Tate, Esq. of Gauber Hall, Yorkshire, and had issue, Robert-Michael; James; William; John; Thomas; Richard; Mary-Ann; and Martha.
Thomas, b. 11 Nov. 1757, one of the hon. band of gentlemen pensioners, d. unm. 9 April, 1794, accidentally drowned.

The eldest son,

THE REV. ROBERT BENSON, A.M., patron and vicar of Hockington, co. Lincoln, b. 11 May, 1755, m. 8 Dec. 1778, Lucinda, only dau. of Matthew Fretwell, Esq. of Snaith, and had issue,

Robert-Haggard, formerly of University College, Oxford, d. s. p. 2 Feb. 1829.
HENRY, now of Utterby House.
Lucinda-Maria, d. unm. 21 Jan. 1816.
Harriet-Frances, m. 27 July, 1820, John Skipworth, Esq. of York, and has issue, George, an officer in the army, b. in 1825; Harriett-Mary; and Lavinia, m. to the Rev. Wm.-George Jorvis, only son of Lieut.-Colonel Jervis, of Barley Hall, Herts.

Arms—Arg., three trefoils, sa., between two bendlets, gu.
Crest—A bear's head erased, arg., muzzled, gu.
Motto—Inconcussa virtus.
Seat—Utterby House, co. Lincoln.

BENSON OF LUTWYCHE HALL.

BENSON, MOSES-GEORGE, Esq. of Lutwyche Hall, co. Salop, J.P. and D.L., b. 20 Jan. 1798; m. 11 April, 1826, Charlotte-Riou, only child (by Dorothy* his wife, dau. of Stephen Riou, Esq., captain 1st regt. horse grenadier-guards) of the late Colonel Lyde Browne, 21st Fusiliers (2nd son of Lyde Browne, Esq., by Margaret his wife, dau. and heiress of Richard Barwell, Esq. of Esher, Surrey). By this lady Mr. Benson has issue,

I. RALPH-AUGUSTUS, b. 11 Aug. 1828.
II. Edward-Riou-George, b. 1 Dec. 1834.
III. Philip-Riou-Henry, b. 4 June, 1842.
IV. Lyde-Ernest-George, b. 27 May, 1845.
I. Dora-Georgina-Harington, m. 22 Nov. 1853, to the Rev. Frederic-J. Richards, vicar of Boxley, grandson of Chief Baron Richards.
II. Charlotte-Julia-Mary.
III. Mary-Elizabeth. IV. Fanny-Mary.
V. Madeline-Barbara.

Lineage.—RALPH BENSON, Esq. of Lutwyche Hall (elder son and heir of Moses Benson, of Liverpool, and grandson of John Benson, Esq. of Ulverston, Furness), m. Barbara, 3rd dau. and co-heiress of Thomas Lewin, Esq. of Cloghans, co. Mayo, by Eliza his wife, dau. of Harry-Ross Lewin, of Fort Fergus, co. Clare, and Hannah his wife, dau. of John Westropp, Esq. of Attyflin, co. Limerick, and had by her (who d. in 1852) issue,

I. MOSES-GEORGE, his heir.
II. Ralph-Lewin, formerly rector of Easthope; b. 6 May, 1799, m. in 1827, Amelia-St. George-Browne, only child of John Dyer, Esq., by Amelia-St. George, his wife, 2nd dau. of the late Gen. Sir Sackville Browne, K.C.B.; and d. 28 Aug. 1849, leaving two sons,
1 George-Sackville, b. in Oct. 1828.
2 William-Ralph, b. in 1830.
I. Elizabeth-Mary, } d. young.
II. Barbara, }

Mr. Benson, for some time M.P. for Stafford, d. 23 Oct. 1845.

Arms—Arg., on waves of the sea, an old English galley, all ppr.; on a chief, wavy, az., a hand, couped at the wrist, supporting on a dagger the scales of justice, or.
Crest—A horse, caparisoned, passant, ppr.
Motto—Leges arma tenent sanctas.
Seat—Lutwyche Hall, co. Salop.

* Dorothy Riou was descended from the ancient and honourable family of DE RIEUX, in Languedoc. Her mother was Dorothy, dau. of George Dawson, Esq. of Ferriby. Her brothers were Col. Philip Riou, royal engineers, and Capt. Riou, R.N., killed at the battle of Copenhagen.

BENT OF WEXHAM LODGE.

Bent, John, Esq. of Wexham Lodge, co. Bucks, J.P., major in the army, *b.* 26 April, 1782; *m.* 24 April, 1823, Elizabeth, youngest dau. of Robert Paul, Esq., president of the Council, St. Vincent's, West Indies, and has issue,

I. George, *b.* 31 May, 1824, an officer in the 25th regt.
II. Robert-Paul, *b.* 1 Feb. 1826, in holy orders; *m.* 8 Aug. 1854, Lucy-Helen, only surviving dau. of B. Dowson, Esq. of Great Yarmouth.
III. William-Roberts, *b.* 31 July, 1829, in the R.N.
IV. John-Oxenham, *b.* 12 Oct. 1831.
V. Stephen-Weston, *b.* 25 April, 1835.
I. Elizabeth-Adeline. II. Mary-Granger.
III. Frances-Rebecca. IV. Georgina-Sarah.

Lineage.—The Rev. George Bent, rector of Jacobstowe and Highbray, co. Devon, and chaplain of Sandford, in the same shire (son of George Bent, M.D. of Exeter, by Mary his wife, dau. of Wm. Oxenham, Esq. of Oxenham, the descendant of a very ancient Devonshire family), *m.* 1st, in 1773, Mary, dau. of John Milton, Esq. of Bristol, and by her (who *d.* in 1784) had issue, George, *d. unm.* in 1803, capt. 60th rifles; John, now of Wexham Lodge; Mary, *d. unm.* in 1841; Frances; Elizabeth, *d.* in 1784. He *m.* 2ndly, in 1785, Hannah, widow of Thomas Marsh, Esq., and by her (who *d.* in 1794) had issue,

I. Hugh, in holy orders, *s.* to his father's livings of Jacobstowe and Highbray, *m.* 1st, Sarah Lane, by whom he had two daus.,
  1 Elizabeth, *m.* to the Rev. R. Hutton, rector of Ringmore.
  2 Mary-Frances, *m.* to William Deans, Esq.
  He *m.* 2ndly, Emily Hutton, and by her had a dau., Hannah-Matilda, and *d.* in 1836.
II. William-Henry, lieut.-colonel royal artillery, *m.* Charlotte, dau. of the late Lieut.-General Samuel Rimmington, royal invalid artillery, and has issue,
  1 John, assistant-surgeon royal artillery.
  2 William-Henry, assistant-surgeon, R.N.
  3 George, an officer in the royal engineers.
  4 Hugh, an officer in the royal artillery.
  5 Frederick. 6 Thomas.
  1 Anna. 2 Charlotte.
  3 Mary-Anne, *m.* to Capt. Travers, royal artillery.
  4 Frances.
I. Rebecca, *m.* to William-Teer Hawke, Esq.
II. Charlotte, deceased.
III. Georgina, *m.* to Stephen Shute, Esq.

The Rev. George Bent *d.* in 1814.

Arms—Per pale, az. and gu., on a fesse, engrailed, or, between six bezants, a lion's head, erased, of the second, between two annulets, of the first.
Crest—A demi-lion rampant, per fesse, az. and gu., gorged with a collar, indented, and holding between the paws a bull's head, cabossed, or.
Motto—Tutamen Deus.
Seat—Wexham Lodge, near Slough, Bucks.

BENTINCK OF TERRINGTON St. CLEMENT.

Bentinck, George-William-Pierrepont, Esq. of Terrington St. Clement, Norfolk, M.P. for the western division of that county, *b.* 17 July, 1803. This gentleman is eldest son of Vice-Admiral William Bentinck, by the Lady Frances-Augusta-Eliza Pierrepont, only dau. of Charles, 1st Earl Manvers, and grandson of Captain John Albert Bentinck, R.N., Count of the Empire, whose father, the Hon. William Bentinck, a noble of Holland, was son of William Bentinck, 1st Earl of Portland, by his 2nd wife, Jane, Dowager Lady Berkeley. (*See* Burke's *Peerage.*)

Arms—Az., a cross-moline, arg.
Crest—Out of a marquess's coronet, ppr., two arms counter-embowed, vested, gu., on the hands, gloves, or, each holding an ostrich feather, arg.
Seat—Terrington St. Clement.

BENTLEY OF BIRCH HOUSE.

Bentley, John, Esq. of Birch House, co. Lancaster, J.P. and D.L., *b.* 11 April, 1797; *m.* 11 Oct. 1836, Emma, eldest dau. of Clement Royds, Esq. of Mount Falinge, high-sheriff of Lancashire in 1850, and has issue,

I. Francis-John-Royds, *b.* 12 May, 1850.
II. Clement-Edward-Royds, *b.* 24 Nov. 1852.
III. Algernon-Royds, *b.* 7 Aug. 1854.
I. Emma-Rhoda. II. Adela-Constance.

Lineage.—The Bentlyes are an old Lancashire family, and their residence was for some centuries at Bentley Hall, near Bury.

John Bentley, living about the middle of the 18th century (son of John Bentley), *m.* Mary, dau. of — Craven, Esq., and had six children, John, Richard, Thomas, Sarah, Mary, and Lydia. The eldest son,

John Bentley, Esq. of Birch House, *b.* 22 Sept. 1758, *m.* in 1793, Ellen, dau. of Richard Lomax, Esq. of Harwood, near Bolton, and dying in June, 1821, left an only surviving child, the present John Bentley, Esq. of Birch House.

Arms—Arg., on a bend, sa., three wolves, passant, or.
Crest—A wolf, rampant, erm., ducally collared, or.
Motto—Benigno numine.
Seat—Birch House, near Bolton.

BENYON OF ENGLEFIELD.

Benyon, Richard, Esq. of Englefield House, co. Berks. This gentleman, 2nd surviving son of the late William-Henry Fellowes, Esq. of Ramsey Abbey, by Emma his wife, dau. of Richard Benyon, Esq., *s.* to the Benyon estates under the will of his uncle, Richard Benyon De Beauvoir, Esq., and has assumed the name and arms of Benyon.

Lineage.—Richard Benyon, Esq., Governor of Fort St. George, in the East Indies, son of Daniel Benyon, Esq. by Mary his wife, *b.* 26 Nov. 1698, *m.* for his 3rd wife, Mary, dau. of Francis Tyssen, Esq. of Balmes House, Hackney, and relict of Powlett Wrighte, Esq. (by which gentleman, who was grandson of Sir Nathaniel Wrighte, lord keeper of the Great Seal, he had one son, Powlett Wrighte, who *d. s. p.* in 1779, and bequeathed his estates to his uncle, Nathaniel, for life, with remainder to his half-brother, Richard Benyon), and by her had an only son,

Richard Benyon, Esq., devisee of the estates of his half-brother, Powlett Wrighte, *b.* 28 June, 1746, *m.* 8 Sept. 1767, Hannah, eldest dau. of Sir Edward Hulse, Bart. of Breamore House, and by her (who *d.* 27 April, 1828) left at his death, 22 Aug. 1796, with daus. (of whom, Hannah-Elizabeth *m.* Vice-Admiral Fellowes; and Emma *m.* William-Henry-Fellowes, Esq. of Ramsey Abbey, Huntingdon) an only son,

Richard Benyon-De Beauvoir, Esq. of Englefield House, *m.* 27 Sept. 1797, Elizabeth, only dau. of Sir Francis Sykes, of Basildon Park, co. Berks, and by this lady (who *d.* 29 Oct. 1822), had no issue. Mr. Benyon-De Beauvoir, who assumed the surname of Powlett-Wrighte in 1814, and that of De Beauvoir in 1822, was a magistrate and deputy-lieut. for Berkshire, and was high-sheriff in 1816. He *d.* in 1854, having devised a portion of his estates to (the son of his sister) his nephew Richard Fellowes, who, having assumed the name of Benyon, is now of Englefield.

Arms—Vairé, sa. and or; on a chief, wavy, of the last, an eastern crown between two mullets, gu., for Benyon, quartering Fellowes.
Crest—A griffin, sejant, or, collared with an eastern crown, gu., holding in the beak a Guernsey lily, ppr.
Motto—Vincam vel moriar.
Seat—Englefield House, Berks.

BEYNON OF CARSHALTON.

Beynon, The Rev. Edmund-Turner, A.M. of Carshalton, and Slines Oaks, Chelsham, co. Surrey, *b.* 29 April, 1777; *m.* 31 July, 1805, Martha, only child of Edward Beynon, Esq. of Carshalton,* and has,

I. Edmund-Batley Beynon, *b.* 24 June, 1806, M.A.
II. Edward-Francis Beynon, *b.* 9 Dec. 1808, M.A. Trin. Coll., Cambridge, rector of Creaton, co. Northampton.

Mr. Beynon (son of the late Henry Batley, Gent., of Carshalton, by Jane his wife, dau. and heir of Edmund Turner, Esq. of Stockwell, and grandson of Benjamin Batley, Gent. of Newington Butts, originally from the neighbourhood of Halifax) having acquired the estate at Carshalton upon his marriage, assumed his present surname.

* Mr. Beynon was 2nd son of Francis Beynon, Esq. of Shrewsbury, and younger brother of Francis Beynon, of Spratton Place, co. Northampton, Esq., whose only dau. and heir, Elizabeth-Anne, *m.* Andrew Hacket, Esq. of Moxhull Park, co. Warwick.

Arms—Per pale, wavy, az. and gu., on a bend, cotised, or, three cross-crosslets, vert, for BEYNON; quartering BATLEY.

Crest—A lion, rampant, arg., semée of cross-crosslets, vert, holding between his fore paws an escocheon, of the first, charged with a griffin's head, erased, pean, for BEYNON; a griffin's head, erased, pean, in the beak a millrind, as in the arms, for BATLEY.

Seat—Carshalton, co. Surrey.

BERE OF MOREBATH.

BAKER-BERE, MONTAGUE, Esq. of Morebath, co. Devon, D.L., barrister-at-law, and one of the commissioners of Bankruptcy, *b.* 15 July, 1798; *m.* 12 Aug. 1822, Wilhelmina-Jemima, 3rd dau. of Daniel Sandford, D.D., bishop of Edinburgh, and has issue,

I. MONTAGUE, barrister-at-law, *b.* 9 July, 1824; *m.* 12 Aug. 1852, Cecil-Henrietta, 2nd dau. of Capt. Thomas-Wentworth Buller, R.N., of Whimple, Devon, and has a dau., Alice-Julia.
II. Charles-Sandford, *b.* 25 Jan. 1829.
I. Frances-Anne-Julia.
II. Wilhelmina-Adelaide-Georgiana.

Lineage.—The family of Bere was seated at Huntsham as early as the reign of EDWARD II., and its pedigree appears recorded in the Heralds' Visitations.

MONTAGUE-BERE BAKER, Esq. of Morebath (son and heir of William Baker, Esq. of Timberscomb, co. Somerset, by Anne his wife, dau. and eventual heir of Davy Bere, Esq. of Morebath, grandson of Richard Bere, Esq., who purchased the manor of Morebath), assumed the surname and arms of BERE, by royal license, 9 Dec. 1775. He *m.* 1st, in 1795, Anne, eldest dau. of the Rev. Thomas-Edward Clarke, of Trimlet House, co. Somerset, and by her, who *d.* 1802, had issue,

MONTAGUE, now of Morebath.
William, M.A., vicar of Morebath, and perpetual curate of Upton, *m.* Mary-Emily, 2nd dau. of the Rev. John Sprye, vicar of Ugborough, co. Devon, but by her (who *d.* 16 April, 1854) left no issue at his decease, 5 Oct. 1844.
Edward, major in the army, *m.* Arabella-Elizabeth, eldest dau. of William Pigou, Esq. of Hounslow, and has issue.
Anne-Clarke, *m.* 1st, in 1821, to the Rev. R.-F. Follett, M.A., and 2ndly, in 1836, to Edwards Beadon, Esq. of Taunton.

Mr. Baker *m.* 2ndly, 25 Jan. 1804, Anne, dau. of Robert Lee, Esq. of Bardon, co. Somerset, by which lady (who *m.* 2ndly, John-Burgess Kerslake, Esq.; and 3rdly, Richard Campion, Esq.) he had no issue. He *d.* 29 Jan. 1804.

Arms—Arg., three bears' heads, sa., muzzled, or.
Motto—Bear and forbear.
Seat—Morebath House, Devon.

BERE OF TIMEWELL HOUSE.

BERE, JOHN, Esq. of Timewell House, co. Devon, J.P., *m.* Mary, dau. of the Rev. James Randolph, of Tiverton, and has issue.

Lineage.—THE REV. JOHN BERE, vicar of Morebath (younger brother of Davy Bere, Esq. of Morebath, whose dau. Anne, *m.* William Baker, Esq., grandfather of the present Montague Baker-Bere, Esq.), *m.* Mary Hayman, and was father of JOHN, his heir, and Richard, B.D., vicar of Carhampton, *d. unm.* in 1831. The elder,

THE REV. JOHN BERE, M.A. vicar of Morebath, and rector of Skilgate, co. Somerset, *m.* Anne, dau. and co-heir of Robert Pearce, Esq. of Morebath, and had (with two daus., Anne, *m.* in 1814, to Stukeley-Tristram Lucas, Esq., and Elizabeth, who *d. unm.*) two sons, JOHN, his heir, now of Timewell House, and Richard, LL.B., rector of Skilgate, co. Somerset.

Arms and Motto—As BERE *of Morebath.*
Seat—Timewell House, Morebath.

BERESFORD OF LEARMOUNT.

BERESFORD, JOHN-BARRÉ, Esq. of Learmount, co. Londonderry, J.P. and D.L., *b.* 19 April, 1815; *m.* 1st, 23 April, 1840, Sophia, sister of Hugh Lyons-Montgomery, Esq., M.P. co. Leitrim, and had by her (who *d.* 21 March, 1850),

I. HENRY-BARRÉ-BLACKER, *b.* 4 May, 1848.
II. John-Claudius-Montgomery, *b.* 3 Feb. 1850.

He *m.* 2ndly, 17 July, 1853, Caroline, only dau. of William-Hamilton Ash, Esq. of Ashbrook, co. Londonderry.

Lineage.—THE RIGHT HON. JOHN BERESFORD, 2nd son of Marcus, 1st Earl of Tyrone, by Catherine his wife, Baroness Le Poer, left, by Barbara his 2nd wife, dau. of Sir William Montgomery, Bart. of Magbie Hill, two sons and five daus. Of the former, the elder,

HENRY-BARRÉ BERESFORD, Esq., *b.* 25 Sept. 1874, *m.* 29 Feb. 1812, Eliza, youngest dau. of John Bayly, Esq. of the city of Bristol, and by her (who *d.* 22 Dec. 1831), had issue,

JOHN-BARRÉ, now of Learmount.
Henry-Barrè, lieut. R.N., *b.* 23 July, 1816.
William-Montgomery, in holy orders, *b.* 31 Oct. 1817, *m.* 18 Feb. 1851, Rosa, dau. of John Turner, Esq. of Brighton, and has a dau.
James-David, late 76th regt., *b.* 2 April, 1819.
George-De la Poer, capt. 16th regt., *b.* 13 Feb. 1826, *m.* 15 Dec. 1849, Anne, dau. of Major-Gen. Conyers, and has issue, three sons.
Mary-Barbara, *m.* 9 Feb. 1836, to Thomas-William Fountaine, Esq. of Narford Hall, co. Norfolk.
Eliza-Frances.

Arms—Quarterly: 1st and 4th, arg., crusilly-fitchée, three fleurs-de-lis, within a bordure, engrailed, sa., for BERESFORD; 2nd and 3rd, arg., a chief, indented, sa., for DE LA POER.

Crests—A dragon's head, erased, arg., pierced through the neck with a broken spear, or, point, arg., thrust through the upper jaw, for BERESFORD; and a stag's head, cabossed, ppr., attired, or, between the horns a crucifix, of the last, thereon the resemblance of Jesus, ppr., for LA POER.

Motto—Nil nisi cruce.

Seat—Learmount, co. Londonderry.

BERINGTON OF WINSLEY.

BERINGTON, JOHN, Esq., *m.* 1 March, 1850, Georgina-Deborah, dau. of the late J.-S. Coxon, Esq. of Flesk Priory, Killarney.

Lineage.—The Shropshire family of Berington, seated at Motehall, near Shrewsbury, has always been considered to have a common origin with branches seated in Herefordshire, and is the senior branch.

Blount, in his *MS. Collections from Herefordshire*, speaking of Winsley, anciently Windesley, says: "In EDWARD III.'s time, Beryton of Stoke Lacy married the daughter and heir of Rowland de Windesley, and had by her this ancient seat, with other lands, which has continued in the family ever since. But in later tymes the name has been changed to Berington. This house lyes in the parish of Hope-under-Dinmore, and as a badge of its antiquity there is carved in wood, in old characters, over the porch, a cross with these words: 'Per signum Taw libera nos Domine.' Upon the crossbeams of the hall is carved an ancient coat of arms, consisting of bendy of five pieces, which haply was the arms of Windesley before the Beringtons were owners of it."

SIMON BERINGTON, Esq. (eldest son of William Berington, of Stoke Lacy, by Elizabeth Kittleby his 2nd wife, and grandson of John Berington, Esq. of Stoke Lacy, by Eleanor his wife, dau. and heir of Rowland Wyndesley, of Wyndesley) *m.* 1st, Winifred Coningsby, of Hampton, co. Hereford; and 2ndly, Elizabeth, dau. of John Blount, of Eye, co. Hereford, and by the latter had issue, WILLIAM, of whom we treat; Humphrey, of London, merchant, *m.* and left a son, John; and Philippa, *m.* to William Carpenter, of Coleford, co. Gloucester. The elder son,

WILLIAM BERINGTON, of Winsley, *m.* Eleanor, dau. and heir of Richard Goodman, chief yeoman of the buttery to Queen ELIZABETH, and *d.* about 1636, aged about 55, leaving (besides two daus., Elizabeth; and Anne, *m.* to John Harpur, of Chilston, co. Hereford) a son and heir,

JOHN BERINGTON, Esq. of Winsley, aged 72 in 1683, who *m.* Jane, dau. of Henry Casey, of Whitfield, co. Gloucester, and had issue a son, JOHN, and three daus., viz., Winifred, *m.* to Bellingham Slaughter, of Cheneys Court, co. Hereford; Anne, *m.* to Thomas Berington, of Motehall, co. Salop; and Mary, *m.* to John Street, of Gatertop, co. Hereford. The son,

JOHN BERINGTON, Esq. of Winsley, living in 1683, aged 35, *m.* Elizabeth, dau. of Sir Thomas Woolrych, Knt.

and Bart., of Dudmaston, co. Salop, and had, with other issue,

- JOHN, his heir.
- Thomas, living in 1683, who m. Elizabeth, dau. of John Russell, of Little Malvern, and had (besides a son, who d. s. p.) an only dau. and heir, Elizabeth, m. to Thomas Williams, Esq. of Trellynnie, co. Flint, who acquired, with her, Little Malvern, and left an only dau. and heir, Mary, who m. — Wakeman, and d. s. p., devising Little Malvern to her kinsman, William Berington, Esq. of Hereford, (the son of her second-cousin, Charles.)
- Elizabeth.

The eldest son and heir,

JOHN BERINGTON, Esq. of Winsley, m. the dau. and heir of Andrews of Hereford, and had, with a younger son, Simon, in holy orders, an elder son and heir,

JOHN BERINGTON, Esq. of Winsley and Devereux Wotton, who m. Winifred, dau. of John Hornyold, Esq. of Blackmoor Park, co. Worcester, and by her (who d. 12 Jan. 1791) had issue,

- John, d. s. p. at Bristol.
- THOMAS, of whom presently.
- Joseph, in holy orders.
- Charles, of Wintercott, co. Hereford, (See BERINGTON of *Little Malvern Court.*)
- Winifred, d. unm. 24 Sept. 1826.
- Elizabeth, m. to Lacon Lambe, Esq., and d. 30 Sept. 1823.
- Mary, m. 1 Dec. 1770, to John Eldridge, of London.
- Catharine, Bridget, and another dau., all nuns.
- Henrietta, d. unm. 5 July, 1825.
- Jane, d. unm. 1 Jan. 1820.

Mr. Berington d. 2 Feb. 1794, aged 87, and was s. by his 2nd but eldest surviving son,

THOMAS BERINGTON, Esq. of Winsley, who m. Jane, only dau. of Francis Ridon, Esq. of Howfield, co. Essex, and by her (who d. in Feb. 1812) had issue,

- JOHN, his heir.
- Thomas-Risdon, of Hereford.
- William, m. Mary Hughes, and has issue, John and Harriet.
- Rowland, d. s. p.
- Caroline. Maria. Louisa. Harriet.

Mr. Berington d. 14 March, 1824, aged 82, and was s. by his eldest son,

JOHN BERINGTON, Esq., D.L., and lieut.-col. Hereford militia, m. Mrs. Frances Dickenson, and d. 25 Jan. 1852, leaving, JOHN, present representative of the family; Rowland; Thomas; William; and Charles.

Arms—Sa., three greyhounds, courant, arg., collared, gu., within a bordure, of the last.

BERINGTON OF LITTLE MALVERN COURT.

BERINGTON, CHARLES-MICHAEL, Esq. of Little Malvern Court, co. Worcester, b. 15 Feb. 1830.

Lineage.—CHARLES BERINGTON, of Wintercott, co. Hereford, 4th surviving son of John Berington, Esq. of Winsley, by Winifred Hornyold, his wife (see BERINGTON *of Winsley*), m. 1 Dec. 1770, Mary Jay, of Wintercott, a co-heiress, and d. 7 Feb. 1809, having had by her (who d. 5 Jan. 1810) issue, besides four sons, who d. s. p.

- James.
- WILLIAM, of whom presently.
- Mary, m. to Hooper, of co. Hereford.
- Winifred, lady abbess at Taunton.
- Anne. Frances.
- Elizabeth, m. in 1814, to John Davis, of Demdale, co. Hereford.
- Theresa.
- Catherine, lady abbess at Spetsbury, co. Dorset.
- Jane, m. to Clement Lorymer, of Perthea, co. Monmouth.

The 2nd surviving son,

WILLIAM BERINGTON, Esq., acquired the Little Malvern estate, under the will of his cousin, Mrs. Mary Wakeman, dau. and heir of Thomas Williams, Esq. of Trellynnie, co. Flint, and Little Malvern, which latter estate he acquired by his wife Elizabeth, only dau. and heir of Thomas Berington (2nd son of John Berington, of Winsley, by Elizabeth his wife, dau. of John Russell, of Little Malvern. Mr. William Berington m. 18 May, 1829, Mary-Frances Brun, a Spanish lady, and d. 16 April, 1847, having had issue, CHARLES-MICHAEL, now of Little Malvern Court; William; and Josephine.

Arms—Sa., three greyhounds courant, arg., collared, or, within a bordure, gu.

BERKELEY OF SPETCHLEY.

BERKELEY, ROBERT, Esq. of Spetchley, co. Worcester, m. in 1822, Henrietta-Sophia, eldest dau. and co-heir of the late Paul Benfield, Esq. of Grosvenor Square, M.P., by Mary-Frances his wife, granddau. of Sir John Swinburne, of Capheaton, Bart., and has,

- I. ROBERT, b. 8 Oct. 1823, m. 4 March, 1851, Lady Catherine Browne, dau. of Thomas, Earl of Kenmare.
- II. John-Edward.
- III. Henry-William.
- I. Mary-Frances.
- II. Harriet-Eliza.
- III. Agnes-Caroline.
- IV. Emily-Jane.

Lineage.—THE HON. THOMAS BERKELEY, *fourth son* of James, 4th Lord Berkeley, by Isabel his wife, dau. and co-heir of Thomas Mowbray, 1st Duke of Norfolk, was seated at Dursley, co. Gloucester. He m. Mary, dau. of Richard Guy, Esq. of Minsterworth, in the same shire, and dying in 1484, was s. by his son,

RICHARD BERKELEY, Esq. of Dursley, (named in the will of his uncle the Marquess of Berkeley), who m. Margaret Dyer, and was father of

WILLIAM BERKELEY, Esq., mayor of Hereford, and M.P. for that city in 1547. He m. Elizabeth, dau. of William Bunghill, of Cowarne, and was s. by his son,

ROWLAND BERKELEY, Esq., M.P. for the city of Worcester, who became possessor of the estates of Cotheridge and Spetchley, in Worcestershire. He m. Catherine, dau. of Thomas Hayward, Esq., and dying in 1611, had, with five younger sons and nine daus.,

- WILLIAM, of Cotheridge (*See that family*).
- ROBERT (Sir).

The second son,

SIR ROBERT BERKELEY, Knt. of Spetchley, b. in 1584, became one of the judges of the court of King's Bench. He m. Elizabeth, dau. and co-heir of Thomas Conyers, Esq. of East Barnet, and left, in 1656, an only son and successor,

THOMAS BERKELEY, Esq. of Spetchley, who m. Anne, dau. of William Darell, Esq. of Scotney, in Sussex, (descended from a niece of Archbishop Chicheley, founder of All Souls' College, Oxford). Their son,

THOMAS BERKELEY, Esq., m. Elizabeth, dau. and sole heir of William Holyoke, Esq. of Morton Basset, co. Warwick. He d. in 1719, and was s. by his son,

THOMAS BERKELEY, Esq., who m. Mary, dau. and heiress of Robert Davis, Esq. of Clytha, co. Monmouth, and dying in France, left two sons, viz.,

- ROBERT, his heir.
- John, who m. 1st, Catherine, dau. of Charles Bodenham, Esq. of Rotherwas, co. Hereford, and had an only son, ROBERT, successor to his uncle. He m. 2ndly, Jane, dau. and co-heir of Sir William Compton, Bart., and had two daus., Catherine, wife of Robert Canning, Esq. of Foxcote; and Jane, m. to Thomas-Anthony, Viscount Southwell.

The elder son,

ROBERT BERKELEY, Esq. of Spetchley, m. 1st, Anne, sister and co-heir of John Wyborne, Esq. of Flixton, co. Norfolk; 2ndly, Catherine, dau. of Thomas Fitzherbert, Esq. of Swinnerton, in Staffordshire; and 3rdly, Elizabeth, dau. of Peter Parry, Esq. of Twysog, in Denbighshire. Mr. Berkeley d. without issue, in 1804, and was s. by his nephew,

ROBERT BERKELEY, Esq. of Spetchley, who m. in 1702, Apolonia, 3rd dau. of Richard Lee, Esq. of Llanfoist, co. Monmouth, and left at his decease, an only surviving son, the present ROBERT BERKELEY, Esq. of Spetchley.

Arms—Gu., a chevron, arg., between ten crosses patée, of the second.
Crest—A bear's head, couped, arg., muzzled, gu.
Motto—Dieu avec nous.
Seat—Spetchley, Worcestershire.

BERKELEY OF COTHERIDGE.

BERKELEY, WILLIAM, Esq. of Cotheridge Court, co. Worcester, m. in 1809, Lucy-Frederica, 2nd dau. and co-heir of John-Richard Comyns, Esq. of Hylands, co. Essex, and has issue,

- I. WILLIAM-COMYNS, in holy orders, m. Harriet-Elizabeth, 3rd dau. of John-Bowyer Nicholls, Esq., F.S.A., and has four sons,
  - 1 Rowland-Comyns.
  - 2 William-Nicholls.
  - 3 Edmund-Robert.
  - 4 Herbert-Bowyer.

II. Comyns-Rowland, of Gray's-inn, m. Mary, 2nd dau. of the Rev. Frederic Lateward, rector of Perivale, Middlesex, and has issue.
III. Charles-Clement, of Lincoln's-inn, barrister-at-law.
IV. George-Brackenbury. V. Augustus.
I. Emily-Conyers.

Lineage.—WILLIAM BERKELEY, Esq., b. in 1582, eldest son of Rowland Berkeley, Esq. of Worcester and Spetchley, M.P., (*see* BERKELEY *of Spetchley*), m. Margaret, dau. of Thomas Chettle, Esq. of Worcester. In the 13th of JAMES I., he purchased from Sir John Acton, the manor and estate of Cotheridge, in Worcester, and served the office of high-sheriff in 1618. At his decease in 1658, he left, with two daus., Jane, m. to William Jeffreys, Esq. of Holme Castle; and Katherine, m. to John Verney, Esq. of Kingston, co. Warwick; a son and heir,

SIR ROWLAND BERKELEY, Knt. of Cotheridge, b. in 1613, a cavalier officer, and M.P. for the city of Worcester. In 1646 he paid a fine of £2080, for having been a commissioner of array, and for having raised money to maintain the enemies of the parliament. In Dugdale's *Usage of Arms*, he is mentioned as one of the intended knights of the Royal Oak. He m. Dorothy, dau. of Sir Thomas Cave, Knt. of Stanford, co. Northampton, and had a son, Thomas, who d. unm. in 1669, and five daus., Elizabeth, m. to Henry Green, Esq. of Wykin, co. Warwick; Penelope, m. Sir Thomas Street, Knt., lord chief justice of the King's Bench; Rebecca, m. to Henry Townsend, Esq. of Elmley-Lovet; Mary, m. to Richard Nash, Esq. of Droitwich; and Margaret, m. to William Bromley, Esq. of Holt Castle. Sir Rowland was s. at his decease, by his grandson,

ROWLAND GREEN, Esq., who assumed the surname of BERKELEY. He was high-sheriff for the co. of Worcester in 1711. He m. Mary, dau. and co-heir of George Bohun, Esq. of Newhouse and Coundon, co. Warwick, (founder's kin at Winchester), and had two sons, Rowland, and Lucy, M.A., rector of Great Whitley and Acton-Beauchamp, co. Worcester; and eight daus., Margery, d. unm.; Dorothy, wife of William Calcott, of Berwick, Shropshire; Penelope, wife of William Green, Esq.; Eliza, d. unm.; Susanna, d. unm.; Margaret, wife of Scarlett Lloyd, Esq. of Harlscott; Jane, m. to William, 5th Lord Craven, of Combe Abbey, co. Warwick; and Katherine, wife of Thomas, 4th Lord Leigh, of Stoneleigh Abbey, co. Warwick. Mr. Green-Berkeley was s. at his decease by his elder son,

ROWLAND BERKELEY, Esq. of Cotheridge, who m. Lucy, dau. of Anthony Lechmere, Esq. of Severn End, and had issue, ROWLAND; Henry-Rowland; Anne, wife of the Rev. Richard Tomkyns; Mary, m. to Joseph Severne, Esq. of Bromyard, co. Hereford; and Margaret, m. to William Yeomans, Esq. Mr. Berkeley was s. by his eldest son,

ROWLAND BERKELEY, Esq. of Cotheridge, who served as high-sheriff in 1764. He m. Sarah, dau. of William Carbonnel, Esq., and dying s. p. in 1805, was s. by his brother,

THE REV. HENRY-ROWLAND BERKELEY, of Cotheridge, D.C.L., rector of Onibury, Shropshire, and of Shelsley-Beauchamp, co. Worcester, and a fellow of Winchester. He m. Miss Mary Jones, of New Woodstock. co. Oxford, and at his decease s. p., 17 Sept. 1832, aged 92, the estates passed under his brother Rowland's will, to (his eldest sister's son) his nephew,

THE REV. RICHARD TOMKYNS, who assumed the surname of BERKELEY, in the October following. He m. Louisa, dau. of the Rev. James Peesdy, and had (with a son who d. in infancy) a dau., Louisa-Anne, who m. Edward-Russell Ingram, Esq. of Wareley. Mr. Tomkyns-Berkeley d. 2 Jan. 1840, and was s. by his cousin,

THE REV. JOHN-ROWLAND BERKELEY, of Cotheridge, fellow of New College, Oxford, rector of Much-Cowarne, co. Hereford, grandson of the Rev. Lucy Berkeley before mentioned, and eldest son of the Rev. Rowland Berkeley, LL.D., fellow of New College, Oxford, vicar of Writtle and Roxwell, and rector of Rochford, co. Essex, by Elizabeth his wife, dau. of — Wathen, Esq. He d. unm. 31 March, 1856, and was s. by his brother, the present WILLIAM BERKELEY, Esq. of Cotheridge.

Arms—Gu., a chevron, arg., between ten crosses-patée, of the second.
Crest—A bear's head, couped, arg., muzzled, gu.
Motto—Dieu avec nous.
Seat—Cotheridge Court, Worcestershire.

BERNARD OF CASTLE BERNARD.

BERNARD, THOMAS, Esq. of Castle Bernard, King's County, late capt. 12th lancers, b. in Sept. 1816; s. his father, the late Col. Bernard, in May, 1834

Lineage.—CHARLES BERNARD, b. in 1615, stated to have been grandson of Francis Bernard, Esq. of Abingdon, in Northamptonshire, accompanied CROMWELL to Ireland, and settled in the co. of Carlow. He m. Elizabeth, dau. and heir of Philip Sheppard, Esq., and by her was father of

THOMAS BERNARD, Esq. of Oldtown and Clonmulsh, co. Carlow, who m. Deborah, dau. of Charles Franks, Esq. of Clapham, and dying in 1720, left issue, 1 CHARLES, of Bernard's Grove, Queen's Co., high-sheriff of Carlow in 1718, who d. 1728, leaving issue; 2 Franks, of Castletown, King's Co. m. and had issue; 3 JOSEPH, of whom we treat. The third son,

JOSEPH BERNARD, Esq. of Straw Hill, co. Carlow, and Castletown, King's County, high-sheriff of the former in 1730, b. in 1694, m. Mary, dau. of John Edwards, Esq of Old Court, co. Wicklow, and had, with five daus., (Jane (Mrs. Galbraith); Mary, wife of John Bennett, Esq.; Deborah; Jemima (Mrs. Moffatt); and Anne) three sons,

THOMAS, his heir.
John, capt. R.N., who m. his cousin, Miss Pickering, and left one son, Joseph, of Frankford, King's Co.
William, of Straw Hall, co. Carlow, m. his cousin, Mary Bernard, by whom he had, Thomas, of Straw Hill, who d. in 1807, leaving, besides daus., two sons.

Mr. Bernard d. in 1764, and was s. by his eldest son,

THOMAS BERNARD, Esq. of Castletown, who m. 1st, Miss Stephens; 2ndly, Mrs. Bernard, widow of Franks Bernard, Esq.; and 3rdly, Miss Palmer; and d. in 1788, leaving (with six daus., Mrs. Palmer; Mrs. Going; Mrs. Armstrong; Mrs. Lauder; Mrs. Smith; and Mrs. Clarke) one son,

THOMAS BERNARD, Esq. of Castle Bernard, who m. 1st, Mary, dau. of — Willington, Esq. of Castle Willington, King's County, and 2ndly, Miss Biddulph, by the former of whom he left, at his decease in 1815, (with four daus., Mary, m. to Sir Robert Waller, Bart.; Anne; Eliza; and Barbara, wife of John Poe, Esq. of Salsborough), one son,

THOMAS BERNARD, Esq. of Castle Bernard, colonel of the King's County militia, and for more than thirty-two years knight of the shire in parliament. Colonel Bernard, b. in 1769, m. 1st, in 1800, Elizabeth, dau. of Henry, 1st Lord Dunalley, which lady d. s. p. in 1802; and 2ndly, 29 July, 1814, Lady Catherine-Henrietta Hely-Hutchinson, sister of the present Earl of Donoughmore, by whom he had four sons and two daus., viz.

THOMAS, now of Castle Bernard.
Francis, b. in Dec. 1818.
John-Henry-Scrope, b. May, 1820, an officer in the army.
Richard-Wellesley, b. in March, 1822, who was present at the battles of Alma, Balaklava, and Inkerman.
Frances. Marguerite, d. in 1842.

Colonel Bernard d. in May, 1834.

Seats—Castle Bernard, King's Co.; and Youghall Lodge, Nenagh.

BERNARD OF PALACE ANNE.

BERNARD-BEAMISH, ARTHUR, Esq. of Palace Anne, co. Cork, J.P., s. his maternal uncle, Thomas Bernard, Esq., in 1795, and assumed, in consequence, the surname and arms of BERNARD.

Lineage.—ARTHUR BERNARD, Esq. of Palace Anne, near Bandon, co. Cork, b. in 1666, next brother of Francis Bernard, of Castle Bernard, co. Cork, Esq., judge of the Common Pleas, ancestor of the Earls of Bandon, m. Anne, dau. and heir of Roger Le Poer, or Power, of Mount Eglantine, co. Waterford, and had issue, ROGER, his heir; Francis; George, father of the late General George Bernard, of Heton Lodge, Leeds, who d. in 1820; ARTHUR, successor to his nephew; Anne, m. to William Conner, Esq.; Elizabeth, m. to Major Gibbon; Alicia, m. to Benjamin Green, Esq.; ——, m. to Charles Gooken, Esq.; Catherine, m. to Edward Martin, Esq. of Cork; Thomasine, m. to William Coghlan, Esq.; Margaret, m. to Edward Barret, Esq.; Henrietta, m. to Arthur Bernard, Esq.; and Arabella, who d. unm. Mr. Bernard erected, in 1714, the family mansion of Palace Anne, near the river Bandon, where his successors have been since seated.

ROGER BERNARD, Esq. of Palace Anne, m. a dau. of — Harpur, and left at his decease an only child,

ROGER BERNARD, Esq. of Palace Anne, high-sheriff for

the co. of Cork in 1767, at whose decease, unm., the estates passed to his uncle,

ARTHUR BERNARD, Esq. of Palace Anne, b. in 1716, who m. his cousin, Mary Adderley, great-granddau. of Sir Matthew Hale, and had issue,

I. THOMAS, his heir.
II. Arthur, who m. Margaret, — Warren, Esq., of Castle Warren, co. Cork, and has, with other issue, a son,
1 Arthur, major, h.-p., 84th regt.
I. Elizabeth, m. to Richard Beamish, Esq., of Baharoon, co. Cork, and had issue,
1 Thomas Beamish, late major 83rd regt. (deceased).
2 ARTHUR BEAMISH, successor to his uncle, Thomas Bernard, Esq.
3 Vincent Beamish, lieut. 8th (King's) regt., d. in the West Indies.
4 George Beamish, late capt. 31st regt.
5 Bernard Beamish, late lieut. 84th regt.
6 Samuel Beamish, late capt. 84th regt., m. Ellen, dau. of George Byrne, Esq., and has issue.
7 Adderley Beamish, late capt. 31st regt.
8 Richard Beamish, deceased.
1 Elizabeth Beamish, m. to Thomas Austen, Esq. of Sheaf, co. Cork.
2 Mary Beamish, m. to William Sullivan, Esq., late major 79th regt. (deceased).
3 Jane Beamish, deceased. 4 Anne Beamish.
II Alicia, m. to the Rev. John Hingston, of Aglis, co. Cork.
III. Anne, d. unm.

Mr. Bernard, who was provost of Bandon for many years, d. at an advanced age in 1793, and was s. by his son,

THOMAS BERNARD, Esq. of Palace Anne, who m. Harriet, dau. of — Lucas, Esq., but dying without issue, was s. by his nephew, Arthur Beamish, Esq., now ARTHUR-BEAMISH-BERNARD, Esq. of Palace Anne.

Arms—Arg., a bend, az., charged with three escallop shells, of the first.
Crest—A demi-lion, arg., holding between his paws a snake, ppr.
Motto—Virtus probata florescit.
Seat—Palace Anne, near Bandon.

BERNERS OF WOOLVERSTONE PARK.

BERNERS, JOHN, Esq. of Woolverstone Park, co. Suffolk, b. in July, 1800; m. in 1832, Mary-Henrietta, dau. of the Rev. Joshua Rowley, rector of Bergholt, Suffolk, and niece of the late Sir William Rowley, Bart.

Lineage.—This family claims descent from Hugo de Berners, who accompanied the CONQUEROR to England, and received grants of land in Essex.

JAMES BERNERS, son of JOSIAS BERNERS, m. Mary, dau. and heiress of William Robinson, Esq. and, with other issue, was father of

WILLIAM BERNERS, Esq., b. in 1679, who m. a dau. of R. Roworth, Esq., and d. in 1712, leaving an only surviving son,

WILLIAM BERNERS, Esq. who m. Mary, dau. of Henry Bendysh, Esq. of South Town, Great Yarmouth, great-great-granddau. of the Protector CROMWELL, and had issue,

CHARLES, of whom presently.
Henry, rector of Hambleton, co. Bucks, who m. Elizabeth Weston, and d. in 1810, having had issue a dau., Emma.
William, d. an infant.
Martha.

The elder son,

CHARLES BERNERS, Esq. of Woolverstone Park, b. in 1740, m. 11 June, 1765, Katherine, dau. of John Laroche, Esq. of Egham, M.P. for Bodmin, and had issue.

CHARLES, his heir.
HENRY-DENNY, late of Woolverstone Park.
William, of London, banker, b. in 1771, m. Rachel, dau. of John Jarrett, Esq., of Freemantle, Hants, and d. in 1841, having had issue, with two daus., three sons, William, capt. R.H.A.; Henry, m. Miss Saunders, of London; and Arthur.
Maria, m. in 1793, to Herbert-Newton Jarrett, Esq., of the island of Jamaica, and d. in 1831.

Mr. Berners d. in 1815, and was s. by his son,

CHARLES BERNERS, Esq. of Woolverstone Park, who d. unm. 19 Aug. 1831, aged 61, and was s. by his brother,

THE VEN. HENRY-DENNY BERNERS, of Woolverstone Park, J.P., archdeacon of Suffolk, b. 18 Sept. 1769, m. in July, 1799, Sarah, dau. of John Jarrett, Esq. of Freemantle, and had issue,

JOHN, now of Woolverstone.
Hugh, capt. R.N., b. in July, 1801, m. in 1832, Julia, dau. of John Ashton, Esq. of The Grange, Cheshire, and has issue a son and three daus.
Ralph, b. in March, 1803, in holy orders, rector of Harkstead, co. Suffolk, m. 27 June, 1831, Eliza, dau. of Sir Cornelius Cuyler, Bart. of Welwyn, Herts, and has issue three sons and two daus.
Alice, d. unm. in 1820.

Arms—Quarterly, or and vert.
Crest—A monkey, ppr., environed about the loins, and lined, or, holding a scroll with the motto.
Motto—Del fugo I avola—I escape from the fire.
Seat—Woolverstone Park, co. Suffolk.

BERNEY OF MORTON HALL.

BERNEY, THOMAS-TRENCH, Esq. of Morton Hall, co. Norfolk, b. 27 July, 1784; m. 15 June, 1812, Mary, dau. of Thomas Penrice, Esq. of Great Yarmouth, and of Wilton House, co. Norfolk, and has issue,

I. GEORGE-DUCKET. II. Thomas, in holy orders.
III. John. IV. Augustus.
I. Mary. II. Elizabeth-Emily. III. Susannah.
IV. Caroline. V. Julia.

Mr. Berney is a magistrate for Norfolk, and was high-sheriff in 1813.

Lineage.—This very ancient family is of Norman origin, and derived its name from the town of Berney, near Walsingham, Norfolk.

THOMAS BERNEY, Esq. high-sheriff of Norfolk in 1647 (younger brother of Sir Richard Berney, 1st Bart. of Park Hall, in Reedham), m. Dorothy, dau. of John Smith, Esq. of Arminghall, and was grandfather of

THOMAS BERNEY, Esq. of Swardestone Hall, bapt. 28 April, 1674, who m. 29 May, 1700, Anne, dau. of Robert Suckling, Esq. of Wotton Hall, co. Norfolk, by Sarah his wife, dau. of Maurice Shelton, Esq. of Barningham, Suffolk, and was father of

JOHN BERNEY, Esq. of Bracon Hall, bapt. 14 July, 1717, high-sheriff of Norfolk in 1760, who m. 1st, 28 May, 1745, Susan, dau. and sole heir of Samuel Trench, Esq., and had by her a son, THOMAS, his heir; and two daus., Anne, m. to Robert Fellowes, of Shottesham Hall, M.P.; and Susanna, m. to Peter-John-Tremeaux, Esq. He m. 2ndly, in 1756, Margaret, dau. and heir of Sir Daniel Dolens, Knt., but had no further issue. His son and successor,

THOMAS BERNEY, Esq. of Bracon Hall, b. 18 March, 1753, m. 8 May, 1774, Elizabeth, 3rd dau. and co-heir of Sir George Jackson, Bart., some time under-secretary of state, and M.P. for Colchester, by Mary his wife, dau. and sole heir of William Ward, Esq. of Guisborough, in Yorkshire, and left at his decease (with a dau., Elizabeth) a son and successor, the present THOMAS-TRENCH BERNEY, Esq. of Morton Hall.

Arms—Quarterly, gu. and az., over all, a cross, engrailed, erm.
Crest—A plume of ostrich feathers, per pale, arg. and gu.
Motto—Nil temere, neque timore.
Seat—Morton Hall, co. Norfolk.

BERRY OF BALLYNEGALL.

BERRY, JAMES-WILLIAM-MIDDLETON, Esq. of Ballynegall, co. Westmeath, b. 17 March, 1812; m. 16 Sept. 1851, Caroline-Augusta, 4th dau. of the Right Hon. T.-B. Cusack Smith, Master of the Rolls in Ireland. Mr. Berry is a magistrate and deputy-lieut., and served as high-sheriff of Westmeath in 1848. He s. by will to the estate of Ballynegall in 1846, on the death of James Gibbons, Esq.

Lineage.—The family of Berry, originally from Wales, where they possessed a large estate called Middleton, settled in Ireland in the time of CROMWELL, and received from CHARLES II. a grant of Eglish Castle, where they resided for several years. John Berry, of Middleton, in Wales, disinherited his son (John) for marrying a Miss Sweetman, a Roman Catholic lady: by her he had a son, THOMAS, who settled at Mnockerville, and purchased, with several other townlands, Millelan, which he called Middleton. He m. Miss Dames, of Green Hills, in the King's Co., and by her had issue, a son,

JOHN BERRY, who settled at Roundwoods, co. Westmeath. He m. Hester, dau. of Capt. Fleetwood, son to Gen. Fleetwood, by Bridget, dau. of Oliver CROMWELL, widow of Gen. Ireton (thus this family not only went to Ireland with

Oliver CROMWELL, Ireton, &c., as stated by Hume in his *History of England*, but are, by its present members, *lineally* descended from Oliver CROMWELL himself, through his dau. Bridget): by Hester, his wife, Mr. Berry left at his decease, in 1768, three sons,

Thomas, of Rathgibbon and Eglish Castle, in the King's Co., *b.* in 1731.
JAMES-MIDDLETON, of whom we treat.
Michael, *d. unm.*

The 2nd son,

JAMES-MIDDLETON BERRY, Esq., *b.* in 1745, *m.* Mary, dau. of Thomas Longworth (who assumed the surname of DAMES, on succeeding to the estates of his maternal grandfather, Thomas Dames) and dying in 1823, was *s.* by his only son,

JOHN-MIDDLETON BERRY, Esq., *b.* in 1787, who *m.* in 1810, Letitia-Catherine, dau. of William Smyth, Esq. of Drumcree (who represented Westmeath in several successive parliaments, both before and after the Union). Mr. Berry served as sheriff in 1814, and dying in 1830, left an only child, JAMES-WILLIAM-MIDDLETON BERRY, Esq. now of Ballynegall.

Arms—Quarterly: 1st and 4th, gu., three bars, or, a trefoil, vert; 2nd and 3rd, arg., a lion, rampant, gu., debruised by a bend, az., charged with three escallops, or.
Crests—1st, a griffin's head and neck, per palo indented, gu. and arg., charged with a trefoil, counterchanged; 2nd, a demi-lion, rampant, az., holding in his paws an escallop, or.
Motto—Nihil sine labore.
Seat—Ballynegall, co. Westmeath.

BEST OF DONNINGTON.

BEST, HEAD-POTTINGER, Esq. of Donnington, co. Berks, J.P., *b.* 18 July, 1808; *m.* 1st, 11 June, 1839, Maria, 2nd dau. of Thomas Duffield, Esq. of Marcham Park, in the same shire, M.P. for Abingdon, by Emily his wife, only child and heir of George Elwes, Esq., and by this lady (who *d.* 5 Jan. 1845) has issue,

Rosamond-Head.

Mr. Best *m.* 2ndly, 22 Sept. 1846, Jane, eldest dau. of George Stratton, Esq., E. I. Co.'s civil service, and a member of the council of Fort St. George, and has a son and heir,

MARMADUKE-HEAD, *b.* 27 June, 1847.

Lineage.—The family of Best was for several generations settled at Middleton Quernhow, in the parish of Wath, co. York. Sir Christopher Best, chantry-priest of Wath, made his will in 1557.

JAMES BEST, of Hutton Cranswick, eldest son of Richard Best, of Middleton Quernhow, bought, in 1598, the manor of Elmswell from his brother Henry, who was ancestor of the respectable family which continued at Middleton Quernhow till about 1745 (*see* BEST *of Eastbury*). James Best *d.* in 1617. His son, HENRY, of Elmswell, who *d.* in 1645, was father of JOHN, who *d.* in 1669, leaving, by Sarah Lambert his wife, a son,

CHARLES BEST, Esq. of Elmswell, J. P.; *b.* 7 May, 1650; *m.* Charlotte, sister of Sir Charles Hotham, Bart., and by her (who *d.* in 1710), was father of

FRANCIS BEST, Esq. of Elmswell, J.P and D.L., *b.* in 1699. He *m.* in 1727, Rosamond, dau. of Yarburgh Constable, Esq. of Wassand, and by her (who *d.* 6 March, 1787) had, with a dau., Rosamond, *m.* to William Tulloh, Esq., three sons, 1 Francis, of Elmswell, rector of SouthDalton, J.P., whose last surviving son, Charles, M.D., of York, *m.* in 1807, Mary-Norcliffe-Dalton, dau. of Thomas Norcliffe, Esq. of Langton, and left at his decease, in 1817, two daus., Rosamond, *m.* in 1830, to Henry, 3rd son of Rear-Admiral Robinson; and Mary-Ellen, *m.* 1840, to John-Anthony Sarg, Esq.; 2 Marmaduke, *d. s. p.*; and 3 CHARLES. The youngest son,

CHARLES BEST, Esq. of Baglake Manor, co. Dorset, *b.* in 1732, *m.* 7 April, 1764, Henrietta-Harriett, dau. of William Light, Esq. of Baglake, by Susan his wife, dau. of Thomas Broadrepp, Esq. of Meipash, Dorset, and by this lady (who *d.* 5 May, 1816) had, with a dau., Catherine, three sons, 1 Francis, *b.* in 1765, *d. unm.* in 1782; 2 Charles, *b.* in 1773, *m.* Mary, dau. of R. Godfrey, D.D., of Bath, and *d.* 7 Jan. 1819, leaving a son, Charles-John, *m.*, and has issue; and a dau., Harriott-Mary-Rosamond, *m.* John-Richard Beste, Esq. of Botleigh Grange, Hants, and *d.* in 1848, leaving issue; 3 JAMES, of whom we treat. Mr. Best *d.* 13 May, 1813, aged 80. His youngest son,

THE REV. JAMES-WILKES BEST, M.A., of Bath, and Chieveley, Berks, *b.* 7 March, 1777, *m.* 30 July, 1807, Eliza-Head, dau. and sole heir of the Rev. Head Pottinger, vicar and impropriator of Compton, co. Berks, and by her had a son and heir, HEAD-POTTINGER BEST, Esq. of Donnington, co. Berks.

Arms—Gu., a Saracen's head, couped at the neck, ppr., navally crowned, or, between eight lions' gambs, chevronways, in pairs, paws inwards, of the second.
Crest—A cubit arm, vested, gu., cuff, arg., a faulchion, ppr.
Motto—Optimus est qui optimè facit.
Seat—Donnington, Berks.

BEST OF EASTBURY HOUSE.

BEST, GEORGE, Esq. of Eastbury House, Compton, co. Surrey, J.P. and D.L., *b.* 9 March, 1799; *m.* 1st, Nov. 1827, Mabel-Anne, only surviving dau. and heir of John-Britland Hollings, Esq. of Eaton Mascott, Shropshire, which lady *d. s. p.* in 1832; and 2ndly, in 1834, Elizabeth-Georgina, 2nd dau. of the late General William Loftus, lieutenant of the Tower of London, by Lady Elizabeth Townshend, his 2nd wife; by this lady he has issue,

I. GEORGE-HOLLINGS, *b.* 5 May, 1835.
II. Henry-Compton, *b.* July, 1837.
III. William-Grosvenor, *b.* 25 Jan. 1841.
IV. Francis-Wittingham, *b.* 17 Aug. 1842.
I. Emilie-Jane.

Lineage.—This family (the present head of which is JOHN-RICHARD BEST, Esq. of Botleigh Grange, Hants, second-cousin of George Best, Esq. of Eastbury,) was settled at Middleton Quernhow, in Richmondshire, in the latter part of the sixteenth century.

THE REV. HENRY BEST, D.D., prebendary of Lincoln, *m.* 1st, Judith, dau. of the Rev. E. Segar, of Sowerby Park, Thirsk, by whom he had no issue, and 2ndly, Mercy, dau. and co-heir of Richard Whittingham, of Sutterton, co. Lincoln, Esq., by whom he had two sons, HENRY and WHITTINGHAM. Dr. Best *d.* in 1755, and was buried in Lincoln Cathedral. His 2nd son,

THE REV. WHITTINGHAM BEST, vicar of Sunbury, co. Middlesex, *m.* Anne, 2nd dau. of Christopher Jones, Esq. of Weston, in Shropshire, by Sarah his wife, dau. and heir of Thomas Fenton, Esq. of Hollin House, co. Stafford, and had two sons, THOMAS, and GEORGE-NATHANIEL. Mr. Best *d.* in 1769, and was buried at Sunbury. His 2nd son,

GEORGE-NATHANIEL BEST, Esq. of Bayfield Hall, Norfolk, a barrister of eminence, one of the benchers of the Middle Temple, *m.* 1st, in 1796, Elizabeth, 2nd dau. of Col. John Wood, commandant of Trichinopoly, in the East Indies, and by her, who *d.* in 1804, had (with another son, the Rev. Nathaniel Best, M.A., who *d. s. p.* in 1841) the present GEORGE BEST, Esq. of Eastbury House. Mr. G.-N. Best *m.* 2ndly, Joanna-Elizabeth, widow of Henry Jodrell, Esq., and eldest dau. of John Weyland, Esq. of Wood Eaton, co. Oxford.

Arms—Arg., a chevron, gu., between three sheaves of arrows, two in saltier and one in pale.
Crest—A griffin's head, erased, sa.
Motto—Haud nomine tantum.
Seat—Eastbury House, Compton, Surrey.

BEST, LATE OF CHILSTON AND WIERTON.

BEST, (the late) THOMAS-FAIRFAX, Esq. of Chilston, and of Wierton, co. Kent, *b.* 15 Oct. 1786; *m.* Margaret-Anna, dau. of Joseph-George Brett, Esq. of Old Brompton, Middlesex. He *d.* in London, 30 June, 1849, and was buried at Boughton-Malherbe, co. Kent, leaving issue four daus., his co-heirs, viz.,

I. CAROLINE-GEORGIANA.　　II. ISABELLA-DOROTHY.
III. MARGARET-ANNA.　　IV. FRANCES.

Mr. Best had been an officer in the Grenadier guards, had served in Spain under Sir John Moore, and was at the battle of Corunna; he was also a magistrate and deputy-lieut. for the co. of Kent.

Lineage.—The earliest recorded ancestor of this family is

JOHN BEST, who *d.* 20 July, 1408, and was buried at Boughton-under-Bleane, co. Kent, as appears by the inscription to his memory, and that of his wife Joane, in Weever's *Funeral Monuments*. From him we pass to

RICHARD BEST, Esq. of Bibrooke, in the co. of Kent, who

m. Dorothy, the dau. and co-heir of John Barrow, Esq. of Hinxhill, co. Kent, and had issue,

JOHN, his heir.
Magdalen, wife of John Fowle, Esq.

JOHN BEST, Esq., the son and heir, was of Allington Castle, co. Kent, of St. Lawrence, near Canterbury, and of Wellcourt, in the parish of Cosmusbleane, Kent, which last he purchased in 1610. He is also described as of London, in 1633, and of Kennington, near Charing, in Kent, where he was buried. He m. 1st, Anne, the dau. of Reginald Knatchbull, Esq. of Saltwood Castle, and had issue,

RICHARD, his heir, of whom hereafter.
Dorothy, who m. at St. Paul's Church, Canterbury, 24 March, 1614, Thomas Gibbon, Esq. of Westcliffe, co. Kent, and was buried at Westcliffe, 27 Jan. 1634, where her husband was also interred, 19 Nov. 1671, aged 81.
Anne, wife of John Odiarne, Esq. of Maidstone, Kent.
Frances, wife of Henry Stourton, Esq.

The 2nd wife of Mr. John Best was Anne, dau. of Laurence Rooke, Esq. of Horton-Monachorum, and afterwards of Christchurch, co. Kent; to this lady (who was granddau. of Sir Reginald Scott, Knt., of Scott's Hall, co. Kent) he was m. in 1598, and by her he had issue,

I. John, who was aged 17 at the Visitation of 1619, and is described as "the younger," of Allington Castle, in 1626. He m. twice; his 1st wife was Anne, dau. of George (otherwise Gore) Tucker, Esq. of Milton-next-Gravesend, Kent, who d. 19 Dec. 1626, and was buried in the chancel of Allington Church, having had one dau., Anne, who was "half a-year old" at the Visitation of 1625. His 2nd wife was Elizabeth, dau. of Humfrey Clarke, Esq. of Bredgar and of Great Chart, co. Kent. widow of William Tonge, Esq.; and by this lady he had,
1 John, d. an infant in 1633, buried at Allington.
2 Humphrey, also buried at Allington.
1 Mary.
2 Elizabeth, m. 20 Sept. 1650, to Herbert Randolph, Esq. of Canterbury; he d. 15 Aug. 1685, aged 56, and was buried at Biddenden, Kent; she survived till 12 April, 1697.

II. George, also described as of Allington Castle, aged 16 at the Visitation of 1619. He subsequently settled in London, and is there recorded in 1633, but on the 26th June, 1641, he is described as of St. Lawrence, near Canterbury, when he had a lease of the vicarage of St. Paul's. He m. Anne, dau. of Thomas Barming, of Wodnesborough, co. Kent, and had issue, George; William; and Anne.
Ursula, wife of Thomas Finch, of Coptree, in Allington.

RICHARD BEST, Esq., the eldest son of the 1st marriage, was "aged 21 and upwards" at the Visitation of 1619. He is described as of Wringleton, co. Kent, in 1625, and of St. Lawrence, near Canterbury, in 1633. He m. Elizabeth, dau. of Andrew Hughes, Esq. of Wringleton, in Winsborough, co. Kent, and had issue,

JOHN, his heir.
Mary, joint-executrix of her mother, 1662.
Anne, wife of — Day, Esq. named in her sister Dorothy's will (1689).
Elizabeth, m. at St. Paul's, Canterbury, 17 Sept. 1657, Henry Pettit, Esq. of Dent-de-Lyon, Isle of Thanet (who d. in 1661, æt. 33); she was executrix of her sister Dorothy, in 1689.
Ursula, bapt. 1627.
Millicent, bapt. at St. Paul's, Canterbury, 18 May, 1630.
Dorothy, bapt. 1631, joint-executrix of her mother in 1662; described as "of the parish of St. John the Baptist, in the Isle of Thanet, spinster," in her will, dated 8 Feb. 1689, which was proved 3 May, 1690.
Frances, bapt. 1632, joint-executrix of her mother, in 1662, and named in her sister Dorothy's will, 1689.

Mr. Richard Best was buried in the chancel of St. Paul's, Canterbury, 18 Oct. 1633; his wife survived him, and resided in the parish of St. Cosmas and Damian-upon-the-Bleane, Kent; her will was dated 5 Oct. 1662, and proved 29 Oct. same year; she d. at Wellcourt, and was buried in the chancel of St. Paul's church, Canterbury, near her husband, 13 Oct. 1662.

JOHN BEST, Esq. of St. Lawrence, near Canterbury, the son and heir of Richard, s. his father in 1633, but sold the St. Lawrence estate before 1654, to William Rooke, Esq. He m. Katherine, dau. of John Allanson, Esq. of Norwood, in Middlesex, and had issue,

Richard, aged 12 at the Visitation of 1663.
John, living in 1663.
William, bapt. at St. Paul's, Canterbury, 21 Aug. 1655, living in 1663.
THOMAS, of whom presently.
Charles, bapt. 12 June, 1659, buried same year, both at St. Paul's, Canterbury.
Charles, bapt. at St. Paul's, Canterbury, 17 Feb. 1662, living at the Visitation in that year.
Henry, bapt. at St. Paul's, 25 April, 1665.
Elizabeth, bapt. at St. Paul's, 22 Nov. 1660, living at the Visitation of 1662.

Mr. John Best d. in 1666, and was buried at St. Paul's, Canterbury, 14 Dec. in that year. Mrs. Best survived him, and is named in the will of Dorothy, in 1689. Their 4th son,

THOMAS BEST, Esq., was bapt. 2 June, 1657, at St. Paul's, Canterbury, subsequent to the alienation of the St. Lawrence estate. In consequence of his marriage, he settled at Chatham, and was eventually described as of Cowling Castle, co. Kent. He m. 1st, Elizabeth, dau. of John Mawdistly, Esq. of Chatham, and by her had issue, one son and five daus., viz.,

MAWDISTLY, his heir.
Sarah, wife of Admiral Edward Vernon.
Dorothy, wife of Capt. John Myhell.
Mary, wife of John Tyhurst, Esq. of Chatham.
Anne, wife of Charles Taylor, Esq.
Elizabeth, wife of Thomas Pearce, Esq.

Mrs. Best d. 30 Oct. 1702, aged 45, and was buried at Chatham, 3 Nov. in that year. Her husband m. 2ndly, Elizabeth, widow of William Nurse, Esq., but by that lady had no issue; she d. 20 Dec. 1706, aged 38, and was buried at Chatham, on the 27th of the same month. Mr. Thomas Best d. 22 Aug. 1740, and was buried at Chatham, on the 31st of the same month, where his monument bears the old arms of the BESTS *of Allington*, viz., sa., a cinquefoil, between eight cross-crosslets, fitchée, or. His will is dated 29 Oct. 1737, and was proved 25 Aug. 1740.

MAWDISTLY BEST, Esq. of Park House, Boxley, Kent, high-sheriff in 1730, s. his father in 1740; and, 18 Dec. 1742, obtained a new grant of arms, viz., sa., in chief two cross-crosslets, fitchée, and in base a cinquefoil, pierced, or. He m. Elizabeth, dau. of — Fearne, and had issue,

Thomas, of Chilston Park, co. Kent, eldest son, lieut.-governor of Dover Castle, M.P. for Canterbury from 1741 to 1754, and from 1761 to 1768; b. 1713, m. 8 Jan. 1743, Caroline, dau. of Geo. Scott, Esq. of Scott's Hall, co. Kent, who d. 29 April, 1782, æt. 64. Mr. Best d. s. p. 26 March, 1795, and was buried at Boughton Malherbe, co. Kent.
JAMES, of whom presently, continuing the male line.
Dorothy-Sarah, m. 18 July, 1740, Robert, 7th Baron Fairfax, of Leeds Castle, co. Kent.

The 2nd son,

JAMES BEST, Esq. of Park House, Boxley, co. Kent, high-sheriff in 1751, m. Frances, dau. and co-heir of Richard Shelley, Esq. of Michelgrove, co. Sussex, and by her (who d. 30 Oct. 1808, aged 77, buried at Boxley) had issue,

I. THOMAS, who continued the senior male line, (vide BEST *of Park House*.)
II. James, who m. twice, but d. s. p., 1828.
III. Richard, who m. twice, and d. 1801, leaving issue.
IV. GEORGE, of whom hereafter, as continuing this line.
I. Elizabeth, wife of the Rev. Maurice Lloyd, vicar of Lenham.
II. Frances, m. 4 June, 1779, the Rev. Henry Hardinge, and d. 27 Oct. 1837, leaving issue,
1 REV. SIR CHARLES HARDINGE, Bart. of Bounds Park, co. Kent.
2 GEN. VISCOUNT HARDINGE, the commander-in-chief, with other issue, (vide BURKE's *Peerage*.)
III. Dorothy, wife of William Twopenny, Esq. of Woodstock Park, co. Kent.
IV. Charlotte, d. 4 Aug. 1791, aged 27.

Mr. James Best d. in 1782, aged 62, and was buried at Boxley, Kent. His 4th son,

GEORGE BEST, Esq. of Chilston Park, in the parish of Boughton Malherbe, co. Kent, a magistrate and deputy-lieutenant for that co., was M.P. for Rochester from 1790 to 1796, and m. Caroline, dau. of Edward Scott, Esq. of Scott's Hall, co. Kent (which Caroline was b. 3 March, 1751, bapt. at Smeeth, co. Kent, 28 March, 1751, and m. at Boughton-Malherbe, 7 Dec. 1784; she d. at Chilston, 24 Oct. 1809, aged 58, and was buried at Boughton-Malherbe). By this alliance, Mr. George Best had issue,

Thomas-George, twin with Caroline-Frances, d. in infancy, 1786.
THOMAS-FAIRFAX, his heir.
George, an officer in the 10th foot, d. at Lancaster, s. p., 1814.
William-Baliol, d. s. p., 1832.
Caroline-Frances, twin with Thomas-George, d. in infancy, 1786.
Caroline, living 1854.
Dorothy, wife of the Rev. Joseph-George Brett.
Louisa, wife of George-Matcham Tarlton, Esq., late of the 6th foot.

Mr. George Best d. at Chilston, 8 Sept. 1818, and was

buried at Boughton-Malherbe, co. Kent, being *s.* by his son, THOMAS-FAIRFAX BEST, whose name is at the head of this article.

Arms—Sa., in chief two cross-crosslets, fitchée, and in base a cinquefoil, pierced, or, for BEST; quartering Barrow, Shelley, Petitt, Hawkwood, Michelgrove, Belknap, Boteler, Pantulf, De Sudley, De Montfort, De la Plaunch, Haversham, Gage, Sudgrove, St. Clere, Louvayne, Darcy, Fitz Langley, Harleston, Berdwell, Hethe, Durward, Kytson, Donnington, Pye, Tankerville, Chamberlain, Gatesden, Morteyn, Ekney, St. John, Louvayne, Abell, and Bourchier.

Crest—A demi-ostrich, arg., issuing out of a mural crown; in the beak a cross-crosslet, fitchée, or.

Residence—37, Westbourne Terrace, Hyde Park.

BEST OF PARK HOUSE.

BEST, JAMES, Esq. of Park House, co. Kent, *s.* his father in 1815; *m.* 23 Sept. 1817, Harriet, dau. of S.-R. Gaussen, Esq. of Hertfordshire, and has issue,

I. JAMES, *b.* 27 Oct. 1822.
II. Mawdistly-Gaussen, *b.* 23 Aug. 1826.
III. Thomas-Charles-Hardinge, *b.* 22 May, 1828.

Mr. Best is major of the West Kent militia.

Lineage.—THOMAS BEST, Esq. of Park House, eldest son of James Best, Esq. of Park House, high-sheriff of Kent in 1751, *(see preceding genealogy)*, *m.* Miss Elizabeth Irwin, of Winchester, and dying 27 May, 1815, aged 61, left (with three daus., Frances-Julia; Elizabeth-Charlotte; and Dorothy) two sons, JAMES, now of Park House, and Thomas, capt. 26th foot, who *d.* at Gibraltar, 8 Oct. 1813, aged 29, leaving by Anne his wife, two sons, William-Mawdistly, *b.* in 1809, and James-John, *b.* in 1811.

Arms—Sa., a cinquefoil, pierced, and in chief, two crosses-crosslet, fitchée, or.

Crest—A demi-ostrich, arg., issuing out of a mural crown, and holding in the beak a cross-crosslet, fitchée, or.

Seat—Park House, Kent.

BESWICK OF GRISTHORPE.

BESWICK, WILLIAM, Esq. of Gristhorpe, co. York, *b.* 7 June, 1817, a magistrate for the East Riding of Yorkshire.

Lineage.—WILLIAM BESWICK, Esq. of Gristhorpe, where the family have been seated for upwards of four centuries, *m.* 21 Oct. 1755, Mary, dau. of William Darley, of Muston, co. York, and had issue an only son,

LIEUT.-COL. GEORGE BESWICK, of Gristhorpe, a deputy-lieut. for the North Riding of Yorkshire, who *m.* 2 Oct. 1789, Jane, dau. of John Wilson, of Filey, co. York, and had issue,

I. WILLIAM, his heir.
II. George, *b.* 15 Dec. 1791, *m.* Anne, dau. of John Bell, Esq. of Scarborough, and had issue,
 1 George, *m.* 21 March, 1846, Emma, youngest dau. and co-heiress of William Darley, of Muston, Esq., and has issue,
  Godfrey-Darley, *b.* 26 Nov. 1847.
  George-William-Darley, *b.* 12 June, 1851.
  Arthur-Bell-Darley, *b.* 10 Oct. 1852.
 2 John-Wilson, *d.* 16 Dec. 1850, *s. p.*
 1 Jane, *m.* to James-Arthur, son of the Hon. Jonathan Sewell, late chief-justice of Lower Canada.
 2 Anne-Bell, *d.* 17 Aug. 1833.

The elder son,

WILLIAM BESWICK, Esq. of Gristhorpe, a magistrate for the North Riding of Yorkshire, *m.* 28 Sept. 1809, Mary, dau. of Thomas Keld, Esq. of Scarborough, by Mary Beswick, of Gristhorpe, his wife, and had issue,

George, his heir, *b.* 16 Dec. 1815, *d. unm.*, 8 April, 1851.
WILLIAM, present representative.
Thomas-Keld.
Mary-Elizabeth, *m.* to W.-H.-N. Myers, Esq. of Leeds.
Jane, *d.* 22 Aug. 1821. Ann, *d.* 30 April, 1833.

Arms (Ancient)—Arg., on a fesse, sa., cotised, gu., three bezants, between three battering-rams in chief, az.; in base, a crow upon the stump of a tree, ppr.

Crest—A dexter hand couped at the wrist, ppr; surmounted by an estoile, radiated, or.

Motto—Denique coelum.

Arms (Ordinary)—Gu., ten bezants, four, three, two, and one; on a chief, or, a lion, passant-guardant, az.

Crest—A demi-lion, rampant, holding between the paws a bezant.

Motto—Denique coelum.

Seat—Gristhorpe, near Scarborough, North Riding, co. York.

BETHELL OF RISE.

BETHELL, RICHARD, Esq. of Rise and Walton Abbey, co. York, late M.P. for the East Riding of that shire, *b.* 10 May, 1772; *m.* 26 April, 1800, Mary, 2nd dau. of William Welbank, Esq. of the city of London. Mr. Bethell *s.* to the estates under the will of the late William Bethell, Esq., who *d.* in July, 1799.

Lineage.—THOMAS BETHELL, or AP ITHILL, of Maunsel, in the co. of Hereford, was father of

THOMAS BETHELL, Esq. of Maunsell, who *m.* Elizabeth, dau. of George Rogers, Esq., and had, with other issue,

Hugh (Sir,) Knt., of Ellerton, co. York.
ROGER, of whom presently.
Andrew, whose grandson was
 RICHARD, devisee of his uncle, John Bethell. This gentleman was grandfather of
 JOHN BETHELL, Esq., *b.* in 1659, who *m.* Catherine Jay, of Dearndale, co. Hereford, and was *s.* by his son,
 RICHARD BETHELL, Esq., *b.* in 1687, who *m.* Frances Bond, of Hereford, by whom he left, at his decease, in 1762, a son,
 THE REV. RICHARD BETHELL, who *m.* in 1771, Ann, dau. of James Clitherow, Esq. of Boston House, Middlesex, and dying in 1806, left (with three daus., Anne, Frances, and Philippa, who all *d. unm.*) four sons,
  1 RICHARD, the present RICHARD BETHELL, Esq., M.P., of Rise.
  2 Christopher, D.D., consecrated, in 1824, Bishop of Gloucester, and translated to the see of Bangor, in 1830.
  3 James, *d.* 1854.
  4 George, in holy orders, M.A., Fellow of Eton College, *m.* Miss Ann Lightfoot.

The son,

ROGER BETHELL, Esq., acquired the estate of Rise, in Holderness. He *d.* and was buried there, 22 March, 1625. His great-grandson *m.* for his second wife, Sarah, dau. and co-heiress of William Dickenson, Esq. of Walton Abbey, in the co. of York, by whom he left, at his decease in 1716, a son and heir,

HUGH BETHELL, Esq. of Rise and Walton Abbey, high-sheriff of Yorkshire in 1734, who *m.* Ann, dau. of Sir John Coke, Bart. of Bramshill, and dying in 1752, was *s.* by his son,

HUGH BETHELL, Esq. of Rise, high-sheriff of Yorkshire in 1761, who *d. unm.* 8 May, 1772, and was *s.* by his brother,

WILLIAM BETHELL, Esq. of Rise, sheriff in 1780, who *m.* Charlotte, dau. of Ralph Pennyman, Esq., but dying *s. p.* 25 July, 1799, devised his estates to his kinsman, the present RICHARD BETHELL, Esq. of Rise.

Arms—Arg., on a chevron, between three boars' heads, couped, sa., an estoile, or.

Crest—Out of a ducal coronet, or, a boar's head, couped, sa.

Seats—Rise, and Walton Abbey, both near Beverley.

BETTON OF GREAT BERWICK.

BETTON, RICHARD, Esq. of Overton House, co. Salop, *b.* 3 Oct. 1808; *m.* 13 Oct. 1831, Charlotte-Margaretta, youngest dau. of the late Richard Salwey, Esq. of Moor Park, near Ludlow.

Lineage.—By deed, dated the 2nd of RICHARD II. (1378), we learn that John de Betton was then dead, having left Margaret, his widow, and Richard de Betton, his son and heir. This Richard was father of

WILLIAM BETTON, of Great Berwick, near Shrewsbury, whose residence there in the year 1403 is proved by the records in the Exchequer of the town of Shrewsbury. From him derived, 7th in descent,

RICHARD BETTON, Esq., bapt. at St. Mary's, Shrewsbury, 6 Feb. 1614-15, who, by his wife Elizabeth, had issue, RICHARD, his heir; John, whose son, James Betton, was father of John Betton, the father of Sir John Betton, Knt. late of Shrewsbury; and Nathaniel, whose son John was father of Nathaniel Betton, Esq. late of Shrewsbury, who by Mary his wife, had issue, John capt. 3rd dragoon-guards, *d.* in Spain, in 1809; Richard, *d. unm.*; Nathaniel, of Shrewsbury; and Mary, wife of Thomas G. Gwyn, Esq. Mr. Betton was *s.* by his son,

RICHARD BETTON, Esq. of Great Berwick, who *d.* in 1726, and was *s.* by his only surviving son,

RICHARD BETTON, Esq. of Great Berwick, *b.* in 1684, *m.* 20 Feb. 1706-7, Dorothy, dau. of Edward Lloyd, Esq. of Leaton, in the co. of Salop, and left at his decease, in 1764, a dau. Elizabeth, m. to John Watkins, Esq., and a son,

Richard Betton, Esq. of Great Berwick, b. in 1710, who m. Mary, dau. of Charles Maddox, Esq. of Whitcott, in the co. of Salop, and had, with a dau. Anne, m. to Thomas Bayley, Esq., two sons, Richard, his heir, and Charles, of Whitchurch, near Ross. Mr. Betton d. in 1767, and was s. by his eldest son,

Richard Betton, Esq. of Great Berwick, b. in 1744, who m. Priscilla, dau. and eventually sole heir of John Bright, Esq. of Totterton House, in the co. of Salop, by whom he had issue,

Richard, his heir.
John-Bright Betton, M.A., vicar of Lydbury North, b. in 1773, who, in succeeding to the Totterton &c. estates, took by royal sign-manual, 12 Oct. 1807, the name of Bright, and used the arms of Bright only. He m. 22 Jan. 1806, Mary, eldest dau. of Thomas Beale, Esq. of Heath House, and dying 22 Dec. 1833, left issue, John, b. in 1811, Eliza, Mary, Frances, Amelia, Louisa.

Mr. Betton d. 7 Feb. 1796, and was s. by his eldest son,

Richard Betton, Esq. of Great Berwick, b. 16 Nov. 1768, major in the Shropshire regiment of militia, who m. 17 Feb. 1795, Mary-Anne, dau. of the Rev. Aaron Foster, of Taunton, co. Somerset, and d. 15 June, 1819, leaving, (with two daus., Mary-Anne, wife of Thomas Foster, Esq., royal engineers; and Harriet, m. to Thomas-H. Rimington, Esq., royal engineers) a son and successor, the present Richard Betton, Esq.

Arms—Arg., two pales, sa., each charged with three crosslets, fitchée, or.
Crest—A demi-lion, rampant.
Motto—Nunquam non paratus.
Seat—Overton, near Ludlow, co. Salop.

BETTS OF PRESTON HALL.

Betts, Edward-Ladd, Esq. of Preston Hall, co. Kent, b. 5 June, 1815; m. 6 July, 1843, Ann, dau. of William Peto, Esq., and has issue,

I. Edward-Peto, b. 2 Aug. 1844.
II. Morton-Peto, b. 30 Aug. 1847.
III. Ernest-William, b. 29 Oct. 1850.
I. Elizabeth-Peto. II. Alice-Peto.

Mr. Betts is son of William Betts, Esq., by Elizabeth-Hayward Ladd his wife, whom he m. in Aug. 1814, and who d. 25 Jan. 1844.

Arms—Sa., on a bend between two bendlets indented, arg., an annulet, between two cinquefoils, of the first.
Crest—Out of battlements of a tower, ppr., a stag's head, arg., charged with a cinquefoil, ppr.
Motto—Ostendo non ostento.
Seat—Preston Hall, near Maidstone.

BETTS OF WORTHAM.

Betts, The Rev. Thomas-D'Eye, of Wortham Hall, co. Suffolk, b. 1789; m. Harriet, dau. of George-Clarke Doughty, Esq. of Theberton Hall, co. Suffolk, and has issue,

I. George. I. Mary.
II. Catherine-Harriet.

Lineage.—John Betts, son of John Betts, Esq. of Withenden, co. Suffolk, settled at Wortham, 1490. He m. Elizabeth, dau. of John Wright, Esq. of Wortham, and was father of

Richard Betts, who d. in 1558, having had, by Alice his wife, with other issue, George, who by Susan his wife, had a son, John; and Richard, whose son, John, was father of

George Betts, living 1656, m. Susan Gascoigne, and was father of

Edmund Betts, who m. Abigail Vincent, and d. in 1733, leaving issue, George, his heir, and Edmund. The elder son,

George Betts, m. Anne Shuckford, and d. in 1766, leaving, with other issue, a son and heir,

George Betts, b. in 1752, who m. his cousin Mary, dau. of Edmund Betts and Martha D'Eye, his wife, and by her (who d. in 1814) had issue, of whom he only left surviving at his decease, in 1822,

Thomas-D'Eye, now of Wortham Hall.
James, m. to Sophia Borradaile.
Harriet. Sophia, d. 1842.

Arms—Sa., on a bend, arg., three cinquefoils, gu., all within a bordure, engrailed, of the second.
Crest—Out of a ducal coronet, or, a buck's head, gu., attired, gold.
Seat—Wortham Hall, co. Suffolk.

BEVAN OF FOSBURY AND TRENT PARK.

Bevan, Robert-Cooper-Lee, Esq. of Fosbury House, co. Wilts, and Trent Park, East Barnet, Herts, b. 8 Feb. 1809; m. 24 Feb. 1836, Lady Agneta-Elizabeth Yorke, sister of the Earl of Hardwicke, and by her (who d. 8 July, 1851) has issue,

I. Sydney, b. 6 Oct. 1838.
II. Francis-Augustus, b. 17 Jan. 1840.
III. Wilfred-Arthur, b. 21 Oct. 1845.
IV. Roland-York, b. Sept. 1848.
I. Lucy-Agneta, d. 7 Sept. 1845.
II. Alice-Lee. III. Edith-Agneta.

Lineage.—Silvanus Bevan, Esq. (son of Timothy Bevan, Esq., by Elizabeth his wife, dau. of David Barclay, Esq.) d. in 1830, leaving, by Louisa Kendall his wife, (with six other sons, viz., Henry; Frederick; Charles; George; Robert; and Richard) the late

David Bevan, Esq. of Belmont, Middlesex, b. 6 Nov. 1774, who m. in 1797, Miss Favell Bourke, dau. of Robert-Cooper Lee, Esq. of Bedford-square, and had issue,

Robert-Cooper-Lee, now of Fosbury.
Richard-Lee, m. Isabella, dau. of the Rev. Loraine Smith.
David-Barclay, in holy orders, m. Agnes, dau. of the Rev. W.-Carus Wilson, of Casterton Hall.
Louisa-Priscilla, m. to Augustus-Henry Bosanquet, Esq.
Favell-Lee, m. to the Rev. Thos. Mortimer.
Frederica-Emma, m. to Ernest-Augustus Stephenson, Esq.
Frances-Lee, m. to Capt. William Morier, R.N.

Arms—Az., a dove, ppr.; on a chief, erm., three annulets, or, each enriched by a ruby.
Crest—On a mural crown, arg., a griffin, passant, or, gorged with an eastern coronet, gu.
Seats—Fosbury, near Hungerford; and Trent Park, East Barnet, Herts.

BEVERLEY OF BEVERLEY.

Beverley, Robert-Mackenzie, Esq. of Beverley, co. York, J.P. and D.L.

Lineage.—This ancient family can be traced amongst the corporation records of the town of Beverley to the time of King John. In the reign of Henry VIII. the Beverleys had increased in consideration, and one of them was a commissioner appointed by the king to inquire into the northern monasteries. They received some grants of church property, and became soon after divided into two branches, one settled in Selby, the other at Beverley. In the reign of Charles I., John Beverley, of Beverley, adhered to the cause of royalty; and at the Restoration, his name appears on the list of those on whom it was intended to confer the order of the Royal Oak.

Robert Beverley, Esq. of Beverley, the representative of the family, sold his property in Beverley to the Pennyman family, and retired, with a large fortune, to Pennsylvania, in America, of which he was appointed Governor, and where he purchased very extensive estates. He erected a large mansion, now occupied by his grandson, Robert Beverley, Esq., and called the place Blandford. His only son,

Robert Beverley, Esq.,* was sent to England to be educated at the Beverley grammar-school. He m. Miss Bland, of Yorkshire descent, and had a large family, of which the eldest,

William Beverley, Esq. of Beverley, East Riding of Yorkshire, J.P. and D.L., was appointed in 1832, vice-lieut. by the Earl of Carlisle. He m. about the year 1795, Mary, dau. and co-heir (with her sister, Anna-Margaretta, wife of Lord Grantley) of Jonathan Midgley, Esq. of Beverley, a gentleman of large landed estate, and had issue,

Robert Mackenzie, present representative of the family.
Maria (great-niece and sole heiress of Anne, Dowager Lady Denison, widow of Sir Thomas Denison, Knt., one of the judges of the court of King's Bench), m. in 1814, to Edmund, 4th son of Sir John Beckett, Bart. of Leeds, and assumed with her husband the name and arms of Denison.

* Mr. Beverley was first-cousin of General Washington. The family of Washington had estates near South Cave, in the East Riding of Yorkshire, about the end of the last century.

Mr. Beckett-Denison represents the West Riding of Yorkshire in parliament.
Anna-Margaretta.

Arms—Erm., a chevron, sa.; on a chief of the second, three bulls' heads, caboshed, arg.
Crest—A bull's head, erased, arg.
Motto—Ubi libertas ibi patria.

BEWICKE OF CLOSE HOUSE.

BEWICKE, MRS. MARGARET, of Close House, co. Northumberland, and of Urpeth Lodge, co. Durham, widow of Calverley Bewicke, Esq. At the death, in 1815, of that gentleman, without issue, he bequeathed his estates to his widow for her life, and afterwards to his nephew, Calverley-Bewicke Anderson, Esq. of Coleby Manor, co. Durham, who, in compliance with the will of his uncle, relinquished the patronymic of ANDERSON, and assumed the surname of BEWICKE, by sign-manual, 16 Dec. 1815. This Calverley-Bewicke Bewicke, Esq., *m.* Elizabeth-Philadelphia, dau. of Thomas Wilkinson, Esq. of Coxhoe, co. Durham, by Anne his wife, dau. and co-heiress of Robert Spearman, Esq. of Old Acres, and has issue,

I. CALVERLEY. II. Robert-Caverley.
III. Thomas, *d. s. p.* IV. William.
I. Margaret. II. Elizabeth.

Lineage.—This family anciently possessed lands at Bewicke, co. Northumberland, whence it derived its surname; but in the reign of EDWARD II., the then Bewicke of Bewicke confederating with the Scots, forfeited his patrimonial estate.

PETER BEWICKE, sheriff of Newcastle-upon-Tyne in 1476, and mayor in 1490, married, and was father of

ANDREW BEWICKE, sheriff of Newcastle-upon-Tyne in 1528, mayor in 1538, *m.* Margaret, dau. of Cuthbert Hunter, merchant, in the same borough, and by her (who *m.* 2ndly, Ralph Jennison, mayor of Newcastle) had issue, 1 ROBERT, his heir; 2 Cuthbert, *m.* 1599, Barbara, dau. of Edmund Cra'ster, of Cra'ster Tower, Northumberland (*see* CRA'STER), and had a dau. and heiress, Jane, *b.* in 1600, who *m.* Edward Stole, Esq., captain of foot in the service of CHARLES I., and was grandmother of Frances Stole, wife of William Shippen, the celebrated orator and patriot. The elder son,

ROBERT BEWICKE, Esq., *b.* 18 Oct. 1561, sheriff of Newcastle in 1615, mayor in 1628 and 1629, purchased the manor of Chantre and chapel of Abbey le Close, otherwise Close House, and the whole hamlet of Houghton. He *m.* in 1596, Eleanor, dau. of William Huntley, alderman of Newcastle, and had a son and heir,

THOMAS BEWICKE, Esq. of Close House and Urpeth Lodge, sheriff for co. Durham in 1655. At the Restoration, he was one of the gentlemen selected for the proposed order of the Royal Oak. He *m.* Jane, dau. of Sheffield Calverley, Esq., a younger son of the house of Calverley, co. York, and had with other issue, Robert, his heir, and Benjamin, rector of Barrow and Hallaton (*see* BEWICKE *of Hallaton*). The eldest son,

ROBERT BEWICKE, Esq. of Close House and Urpeth Lodge, *b.* in 1643, high-sheriff of Northumberland in 1695, *d. unm.* in 1706, and was *s.* by his brother,

CALVERLEY BEWICKE, Esq. of Close House and Urpeth Lodge, *b.* in 1661, *m.* Dorothy Izard, and *d.* in 1729, leaving issue, 1 ROBERT, his heir; 2 Caverley (*see* BEWICKE *of Hallaton*); 1 Dorothy, *m.* to Thomas Lambton, Esq. of Hardwick (*see* BURKE'S *Peerage*); 2 Elizabeth. The son and heir,

ROBERT BEWICKE, Esq. of Close House and Urpeth Lodge, *b.* in 1689, high-sheriff of Northumberland in 1726, *m.* in 1724, Jane, dau. of Robert Lynn, Esq. of Mainsforth, and heiress, through her mother, of Joseph Wilson, Esq. of Cassop, and left issue, two sons. The elder,

SIR ROBERT BEWICKE, *b.* in 1728, high-sheriff of Northumberland in 1760, when he was knighted, *m.* Mary, dau. of Robert Hurst, Esq. of Nottingham, *d.* in 1771, leaving (with seven daus., viz., I. Jane, *m.* Sir Paul Joddrell, Bart.; II. Mary, *m.* to Alexander Anderson, Esq. of Highgate, and had issue; 1 John-Robert, *b.* in 1775, *m.* in 1809, Elizabeth, dau. of Robert Boswell, Esq. of Edinburgh; 2 Calverley-Bewicke, who, by his uncle's will, will succeed to the property on the death of Mrs. Bewicke, now of Close House; 3 Paul; 1 Charlotte; 2 Mary-Anne; III. Anne, *m.* to James Woodmason, Esq. of Belcamp, near Dublin, *d. s. p.* IV. Margaret, *m.* to Thomas Bond, Esq. of Norton House, Devon, *d. s. p.*; V. Alicia, *d. unm.*; VI. Dorothy, *m.* to William Lynn, Esq. of Clapham; and VII. Eleanor) a son and heir,

CALVERLEY BEWICKE, Esq. of Close House and Urpeth Lodge, lieut.-col. of the Durham militia, M.P. for Winchester, high-sheriff of Northumberland in 1782, *m.* 1st, Deborah, dau. of Thomas Wilkinson, Esq. of Brancepeth, in Durham, and 2ndly, Margaret, youngest dau. and co-heiress of Robert Spearman, Esq. of Old Acres, Northumberland, and dying without issue in 1815, bequeathed his estates to his widow, the present Mrs. Bewicke, of Close House and Urpeth Lodge, for her life, and afterwards to his nephew, Calverley Bewicke Anderson, of Coleby Manor.

Arms—Arg., five lozenges, in fesse, gu., each charged with a mullet, of the first, between three bears' heads, erased, sa.
Crest—A bugle's head, erased at the neck, arg., armed, maned, and gorged with a mural crown, gu.
Seats—Close House, Northumberland, and Urpeth Lodge Durham.

BEWICKE OF HALLATON.

BEWICKE, CALVERLEY, Esq. of Hallaton Hall, Leicestershire, *b.* in 1816; *m.* Mary-Amelia, youngest dau. of the Rev. Nathaniel-John Hollingsworth, rector of Boldon, co. Durham, and has issue,

I. CALVERLEY-THEODORE, *b.* in 1848.
I. Caroline-Emily. II. Menina-Honoria.
III. Alicia-Ellen-Neve.

Lineage... THE REV. BENJAMIN BEWICKE, 5th son of Thomas Bewicke, Esq. of Close House (*see* BEWICKE *of Close House*), purchased the manor and advowson of Hallaton in 1713, and dying *unm.*, bequeathed them to his nephew,

CALVERLEY BEWICKE, Esq. of Hallaton Hall, 2nd son of Calverley Bewicke, Esq. of Close House, *b.* in 1694, high-sheriff for the county of Leicester in 1762, *m.* Alice, dau. of Robert Smith, Esq. He *d.* in 1774, leaving issue,

I. BENJAMIN, his heir.
II. Calverley, of Clapham, *m.* Jane, dau. of Robert Thornton, Esq; *d.* in 1814, leaving issue,
 1 Henry, *d. unm.*
 1 Jane, *m.* Henry Blackburn, Esq. of Ramsgate, and had issue,
I. Anne, *m.* the Rt. Rev. Philip Young, Bishop of Norwich.
II. Alice, *m.* Daniel Eyre, Esq. of Wiltshire, and left issue.

BENJAMIN BEWICKE, Esq. of Hallaton Hall, and of Ormond-street, London, *b.* in 1728, *m.* 1st, Elizabeth Smith, without issue, and 2ndly, Anne, dau. of John Gleson, Esq. of London. He *d.* in 1815, leaving issue,

I. CALVERLEY-JOHN, his heir.
II. Thomas, in holy orders; *m.* in 1797, Sarah, dau. of the Rev. R. Etheridge, rector of Stanton, Norfolk; *d.* in 1842, leaving issue, with five daus., a son,
 1 Calverley-Richard, *b.* in 1798.
I. Rebecca, *m.* William-Augustus Standert, Esq.
II. Anna-Letitia, *d. unm.* in 1841.

CALVERLEY-JOHN BEWICKE, of Hallaton Hall, *b.* in 1765, in holy orders, rector of Hallaton-cum-Blaston, and Loddington, in the co. of Leicester, *m.* 1st, Mary-Elizabeth, widow of James Vaughan, Esq. of Leicester, dau. of Sir Everard Buckworth, Bart., without issue; and 2ndly, Caroline, dau. of Col. Nathaniel Newnham, of Barn Rocks House, Sussex, by whom he left issue,

I. CALVERLEY, his heir.
II. Thomas, *b.* in 1822.
I. Emma, *m.* her cousin, Calverley-Richard Bewicke, Esq. of Barsham, Suffolk, and has issue,
 1 Arthur-Newnham.
 2 Lionel-Calverley.
 1 Ada-Philippine-Anna.
 2 Minna-Harvey.
 3 Madeline-Emma-Collingwood.
II. Sophia.

The Rev. Calverley-John Bewicke *d.* in 1843, and was *s.* by his eldest son, the present CALVERLEY BEWICKE, Esq. of Hallaton Hall, who is the direct male representative of the family of BEWICKE *of Close House*.

Arms and *Crest*—The same as BEWICKE *of Close House*.
Seat—Hallaton Hall, Leicestershire.

BIDDULPH OF BURTON.

WRIGHT-BIDDULPH, ANTHONY-JOHN, Esq. of Burton Park, co. Sussex, *b.* 29 Jan. 1830.

Lineage.—"The BIDDULPHS do derive themselves," says Erdeswick, "from one ORMUS LE GUIDON, the son of

RICARDUS FORESTARIUS," of Norman race, who held, as appears by Domesday, ten lordships in Staffordshire, which were conferred on him in reward of his services. The 2nd son of

EDWARD, of Middle Biddulph, first took the surname of BIDDULPH, and was ancestor of the eminent family of BIDDULPH, which, in the reign of HENRY VIII., became divided into two branches, the elder line represented by SIR RICHARD BIDDULPH, Knt., who adhered steadily to the principles and faith of their ancestors, during all the religious revolutions of that and the succeeding reigns, with many of the ancient families in the northern parts of England.

RICHARD BIDDULPH, of Biddulph, son of William, of Biddulph, and the direct descendant of Ormus le Guidon, had two sons, SYMON, the younger, ancestor of the BIDDULPHS *of Ledbury*, and the elder,

SIR RICHARD BIDDULPH, of Biddulph, Knt., living *temp.* HENRY VIII., whose son and successor,

RICHARD BIDDULPH, of Biddulph, *m.* Margaret, dau. and co-heir of Sir John Salwey, by Margaret his wife, dau. of Hugh Erdeswick, and was father of FRANCIS, of Biddulph, who erected the noble mansion of Biddulph, *temp.* ELIZABETH. This FRANCIS was grandfather of JOHN BIDDULPH, Esq. of Biddulph, a devoted royalist, whose grandson,

RICHARD BIDDULPH, Esq. of Biddulph, *m.* Anne, dau. and eventual heiress of Sir Henry Goring, Bart. of Burton, the lineal descendant and representative of John Goring, of Burton, Esq., by Margaret, his 1st wife, dau. of Ralph Radmylde, Esq., and Margaret his wife, sister and co-heir of Hugh Lord Camoys. Mr. Biddulph *d.* before 1679, leaving (with a dau., Elizabeth, *m.* to Charles, Lord Dormer) a son and successor,

JOHN BIDDULPH, Esq. of Biddulph and Burton, who *m.* Mary, dau. of Charles Arundel, Esq. of Horningsham, and had issue, I. RICHARD, his heir; II. CHARLES, successor to his brother; I. MARY, *b.* 1710, who *m.* Thomas Stonor, Esq. of Stonor, co. Oxford, and was great-grandmother of THOMAS STONOR, now Lord Camoys; II. ANNE, *b.* in 1717, who *m.* Anthony Wright, Esq. of Wieldside, in Essex, and had, with other issue, ANTHONY WRIGHT, Esq., who *m.* Lucy, 2nd dau. of Edmund Plowden, Esq. of Plowden, and by her, who *d.* in 1786, left at his decease in the same year; 1 ANTHONY-GEORGE, of Burton Park; 2 John, *b.* 20 June, 1786, *m.* Henrietta, eldest dau. of the late Michael Blount, Esq. of Maple Durham, and has issue; 1 Lucy; 2 Mary, *m.* to Vincent Eyre, Esq.; 3 Anne, *m.* to Sir Charles Wolseley, Bart. of Wolseley, co. Stafford, and *d.* in 1838. He *d.* in May, 1720. The elder son,

RICHARD BIDDULPH, Esq. of Biddulph, *d. unm.* in 1767, aged 60, and was *s.* by his brother,

CHARLES BIDDULPH, Esq. of Biddulph and Burton, who *m.* 1st, Elizabeth, dau. of Sir Henry Bedingfeld, Bart. of Oxburgh, and 2ndly, Frances-Apollonia, dau. of George-Brownlow Doughty, Esq. of Snarford Hall, co. Lincoln, and widow of Henry Wells, Esq. By the former, who *d.* in 1769, he left at his decease, in 1763, a son and heir,

JOHN BIDDULPH, Esq. of Biddulph and Burton, who *d. unm.* 2 Aug. 1835, leaving his estates to his kinsman,

ANTHONY-GEORGE WRIGHT, Esq. *b.* 20 April, 1785, who took the additional surname of BIDDULPH. He *m.* 15 Jan. 1827, Catherine-Dorothy, dau. of the late Simon-Thomas Scrope, Esq. of Danby Hall, co. York, and *d.* leaving, with three daus., Catherine-Charlotte-Mary, Clementina-Maria, and Geraldine-Mary, a son and successor, the present ANTHONY-JOHN WRIGHT-BIDDULPH, Esq.

Arms—Quarterly: 1st and 4th, vert, an eagle displayed, arg., for BIDDULPH; 2nd and 3rd, az., two bars, arg., and in chief, a leopard's face, or, for WRIGHT; quartering GORING, COMPTON, and CAMOYS.

Crests—1st, a wolf, salient, arg.; 2nd, out of a ducal coronet, or, a dragon's head, ppr.

Seat—Burton Park, Sussex.

BIDDULPH OF CHIRK CASTLE.

BIDDULPH, ROBERT-MYDDELTON, Esq. of Chirk Castle, co. Denbigh, and Burghill, co. Hereford, *b.* 20 June, 1805; *m.* 31 May, 1832, Fanny, 2nd dau. of William Owen, Esq. of Woodhouse, co. Salop, and has issue,

I. RICHARD, *b.* 13 Feb. 1837.

I. Fanny. II. Alice. III. Mary-Caroline.

Mr. Biddulph is lieutenant and custos-rotulorum of Denbighshire, and colonel of the county militia.

Lineage.—*See* BIDDULPH *of Ledbury.*

The Myddeltons are said to have descended from Ririd Vlaydd, Lord of Penlyn, in Merionethshire, whose descendant, Ririd, *m.* Cicely, sister and heir of Sir Alexander Middleton, of Middleton, co. Salop, and was father was Ririd, whose great-grandson,

DAVID MYDDELTON, of Gwaynenog, in Denbighshire, Receiver of North Wales, *temp.* EDWARD IV., *m.* Ellen, dau. of Sir John Done, Knt. of Utkington, co. Chester, and had, with other issue,

ROGER MYDDELTON, of Gwaynenog, ancestor of the MYDDELTONS *of Gwaynenog.* (*See that family*).

And

FULKE MYDDELTON, Esq., who *m.* Margaret, dau. of Thomas Smith, alderman of Chester, and had, with other issue,

RICHARD MYDDELTON, Esq. of Denbigh, who *m.* Jane, dau. of Hugh Dryhurst, of the same place, by Lucy his wife, dau. of Robert Groensdyke, and had several children, of whom

THOMAS (the eldest surviving son) was ancestor of the MYDDELTONS *of Chirk Castle*; and

HUGH (the 6th son), of Ruthyn, co. Denbigh, was the celebrated SIR HUGH MIDDELTON, the projector of the New River. *See* BURKE'S *Extinct Baronetage.*

The eldest son,

SIR THOMAS MYDDELTON, was sheriff and alderman of London, and filled the civic chair in 1613. He was a munificent benefactor of the Goldsmiths' Company. His son and heir,

SIR THOMAS MYDDELTON, Knt. of Chirk Castle, suffered severely during the Commonwealth. From him descended the extinct Baronets, the MYDDELTONS *of Chirk Castle* (*see* BURKE'S *Extinct Peerage*), whose last male heir,

RICHARD MYDDELTON, Esq. of Chirk Castle, lieut. of the county, and M.P. for the town of Denbigh, *m.* thrice, but had issue only by his 2nd wife, the Hon. Anne Rushout, sister of Lord Northwick, one son and three daus., viz., RICHARD, his heir; CHARLOTTE, of whom hereafter; MARIA, *m.* to the Hon. Frederick West, brother of Lord Delawarr; and HARRIET. Mr. Myddelton *d.* in 1795, and was *s.* by his eldest son,

RICHARD MYDDELTON, Esq. of Chirk Castle, who *d. unm.* in 1796, leaving his three sisters his co-heirs; of whom the eldest,

CHARLOTTE MYDDELTON, *m.* in 1801, Robert Biddulph, Esq. of Ledbury, co. Hereford, and Cofton Hall, co. Worcester, who thereupon assumed the additional name and arms of MYDDELTON, and had issue,

ROBERT MYDDELTON, now of Chirk Castle.

Thomas Myddelton, lieut.-col. in the army, Master of the Household to the Queen.

Charlotte-Elizabeth.

Arms—Quarterly: 1st and 4th, vert, an eagle displayed, arg., armed and langued, gu., for BIDDULPH; 2nd and 3rd, arg., on a bend, vert, three wolves' heads, erased, of the field, for MYDDELTON.

Crests—A wolf, salient, arg., charged on the shoulder with a trefoil, slipped, vert, for BIDDULPH; out of a ducal coronet, or, a bloody hand, ppr., for MYDDELTON.

Motto—In veritate triumpho.

Seats—Chirk Castle and Nantyr Hall, co. Devon.

BIDDULPH OF LEDBURY.

BIDDULPH, ROBERT, Esq. of Ledbury, co. Hereford, J.P. and D.L., formerly M.P. for Hereford; *m.* 25 Feb. 1830, Elizabeth, dau. of George Palmer, Esq. of Nazing Park, Essex.

Lineage.—SYMON BIDDULPH, Esq. of Elmhurst, 2nd son of Richard Biddulph, Esq. of Biddulph, *m.* Joyce, dau. of Sir Robert Weston, Knt., and was father of

SYMON BIDDULPH, Esq. of Elmhurst, whose son,

SYMON BIDDULPH, Esq. of Elmhurst, *d.* in 1632, leaving, by Joyce his wife, dau. of Richard Floyer, Esq., several sons, of whom the eldest, Michael, was father of SIR THEOPHILUS BIDDULPH, created a Baronet in 1664, and the 3rd,

ANTHONY BIDDULPH, Esq., bapt. at Stowe in 1584, *m.* Elizabeth, dau. of Robert Palmer, Esq., alderman of London, and was father of

MICHAEL BIDDULPH, Esq., who *m.* Frances, dau. of Sir William Kingston, Bart., and had a son and successor,

ROBERT BIDDULPH, Esq., who *m.* Mary, dau. of Sir William Cullen, Bart., of East Sheen, and dying in 1670, was *s.* by his son,

ANTHONY BIDDULPH, Esq., who first settled at Ledbury, in the co. of Hereford, and served as high-sheriff in 16?4.

He m. Constance, dau. and co-heir of Francis Hall, Esq., and dying in 1718, left three sons,

I. ROBERT, his heir.

II. Francis, m. thrice. By his 1st and 2nd wives he had two daus., Constance, m. to the Rev. Thomas Salwey, LL.D., and Anne, m. to Benjamin Baugh, Esq. of Ludlow. By the 3rd, Margaret, widow of Reginald Pindar, Esq. of Kempley, co. Gloucester, and dau. and heir of William Lygon, Esq. of Madresfield, representative of Richard, last Lord Beauchamp of Powick, he had a son, THE REV. THOMAS BIDDULPH, who m. 1st, Martha, dau. and co-heir of the Rev. John Tregenna, and had by her a son, THOMAS-TREGENNA, his heir. He m. 2ndly, Sarah, dau. of Chauncey Townsend, Esq., and had by her two daus., Frances-Phipps, m. to James Townsend, Esq., commander, R.N.; and Charlotte-Louisa, m. to George Vizard, Esq. Mr. Biddulph was s. by his son, THE REV. THOMAS-TREGENNA BIDDULPH, M.A., b. at Worcester, minister of St. James's, Bristol, who m. Rachel, dau. of Zachary Shrapnel, Esq. of Bradford, Wilts, and sister of Major-Gen. Henry Shrapnel, R.A., and had issue, THOMAS SHRAPNEL, of Amroth Castle, prebendary of Brecon, m. Charlotta, dau. of the Rev. James Stillingfleet, prebendary of Worcester, and had issue, FRANCIS-JOHN; Michael-Anthony; Thomas-Edward-Stillingfleet; Margaret-Anne; Frances-Augusta-Charlotte; Zachariah-Henry, B.D., vicar of Shoreham, Sussex, and Blackwell, Somersetshire, late fellow of Magdalen College, Oxford; Theophilus, who m. Catherine, dau. of John Linden, Esq.; Rachel-Lydia, m. to the Rev. Charles Henning; and Henrietta, m. to William Pinchard, Esq.

III. Michael, a bencher of Lincoln's Inn, who d. s. p. in 1758.

The eldest son,

ROBERT BIDDULPH, Esq. of Ledbury, bapt. Oct. 1682, m. Anne, dau. of Benjamin Joliffe, Esq. of Cofton Hall, co. Worcester, and dying in 1772, left three sons, MICHAEL, his heir; Benjamin, in holy orders (father of Benjamin, of Burghill, co. Hereford); and Francis, banker, of Charing Cross, who d. s. p. in 1800. The eldest son,

MICHAEL BIDDULPH, Esq. of Ledbury and Cofton Hall, m. Penelope, eldest dau. of John Dandridge, Esq. of Balden's Green, Malvern, Worcestershire, and had (with four daus., Penelope, widow of Adam Gordon, Esq.; Mary-Anne, widow of Robert Phillips, Esq. of Longworth, co. Hereford; Anne, widow of David Gordon, Esq. of Abergeldie; and Harriet, m. to Thomas Woodyatt, Esq., R.N.) two sons, ROBERT, father of the present ROBERT-MYDDELTON BIDDULPH, Esq. of Chirk Castle (see that family), and JOHN, of Ledbury. Mr. Biddulph d. 6 Dec. 1800. His 2nd son,

JOHN BIDDULPH, Esq. of Ledbury, b. in 1768, m. 9 Sept. 1797, Miss Augusta Roberts, and had, with six daus., four sons, viz., ROBERT, now of Ledbury; John; Francis-Thomas; and Ormus.

Arms—Vert., an eagle displayed, arg., armed and langued, gu.

Crests—1st, a wolf, salient, arg., charged on the shoulder with a trefoil slipped, vert; 2nd, a wolf, sejant-regardant, arg., vulned on the shoulder, gu.

Motto—Sublimiora petamus.

Seat—Ledbury, co. Hereford.

BIGGE OF LINDEN.

BIGGE, CHARLES-SELBY, Esq. of Linden, co. Northumberland, b. 21 July, 1834.

Lineage.—WILLIAM BIGGE, of Newcastle-upon-Tyne, presumed to have descended from an ancient house seated for many generations in Essex, m. in 1666, Isabell, dau. and co-heir of Thomas Dent, Esq., and d. in 1690, leaving two daus. (Mary, wife of Edward Collingwood, Esq. of Byker and Dissington; and Anne, m. to Edward Ward, Esq.) and two sons, John, who d. s. p. in 1721, and

THOMAS BIGGE, Esq., who m. *circa* 1706, Elizabeth, dau. of Edward Hindmarsh, Esq. of the Six Clerks' Office, and had (with three daus., of whom the eldest, Grace, m. Sir Robert Carr, Bart.) three sons, viz., WILLIAM, his heir; Edward, of Brinkley, who d. unm.; and Thomas, of Ludgate Hill, London, who m. Elizabeth, sister of the late Phillip Rundell, and dying in 1791, left a son, Thomas, b. in 1766, who m. Maria, dau. of Thomas Rundell, Esq. of Bath, and had issue, Thomas-Edmund, Philip-Edmund, James-Rundell, Charles-Richard; John; Elizabeth, m. to Col. Anderson; Jane, who d. unm. in 1812; Augusta, Emily, Maria, Georgiana, Emily-Jane, and Fanny. The eldest son and heir,

WILLIAM BIGGE, Esq. of Benton, b. in 1707, one of the six clerks in Chancery, was high-sheriff for Northumberland in 1750. He m. 29 Jan. 1736, Mary, dau. and eventually sole heiress of Charles Clarke, Esq. of Ovingham, and had issue, THOMAS-CHARLES, his heir; William-Edward, who d. unm.; John, of Brinkley, who d. s. p. in 1797. Mr. Bigge d. 30 June, 1758, and was s. by his eldest son,

THOMAS-CHARLES BIGGE, Esq. b. in 1739, sheriff of Northumberland in 1771, who m. in the following year Jemima, dau. of William Ord, Esq. of Fenham, by his wife Anne, dau. of William Dillingham, Esq. of London, and had, with six daus., of whom one only married, viz., Grace-Julia, widow of Thomas-Christopher Glyn, Esq., three sons, CHARLES-WILLIAM, his heir; John-Thomas, b. in 1780, formerly chief-justice of Trinidad; Thomas-Hanway, of Newcastle-on-Tyne, banker, who m. Charlotte, dau. of the Rev. James Scott, and d. in 1824, leaving four sons and two daus. Mr. Bigge d. at Bath, 10 Oct. 1794, and was s. by his eldest son,

CHARLES-WILLIAM BIGGE, Esq. of Linden, a deputy-lieut. and late chairman of the quarter sessions there, lieut.-col. in the Northumberland Militia, and high-sheriff in 1802, b. 28 Oct. 1773, m. 27 Jan. 1802, Alicia, only dau. of Christopher Wilkinson, Esq. of Newcastle-upon-Tyne, of the family of WILKINSON *of Thorpe*, co. York, and d. in 1849, having had issue,

I. CHARLES-JOHN, b. 11 April, 1803, m. Lewis-Marianne, eldest dau. of Prideaux-John Selby, of Twizell House, and d. 16 March, 1846, having issue,

1 CHARLES-SELBY, present representative of the family.

1 Mary-Lewis, b. 7 May, 1836.

2 Fanny-Alice, b. 11 March, 1842.

3 Sybil-Constance (posthumous), b. 6 April, 1846.

II. Henry-Lancelot, b. 10 May, 1806, d. in India, 9 Dec. 1844, in the E. I. Co.'s military service.

III. Edward-Thomas, b. 19 Oct. 1807, d. 3 April, 1844, in holy orders, first archdeacon of Lindisfarne, and vicar of Edlingham, co. Northumberland.

IV. William-Matthew, b. 9 Oct. 1812, in the army, lieut.-col. of the 7th regt. of foot.

V. John-Frederick, in holy orders, vicar of Stamfordham, co. Northumberland, b. 12 July, 1814, m. 14 Dec. 1843, Caroline-Mary, only dau. of Nathaniel Ellison, Esq., and has issue.

VI. Arthur, b. 18 May, 1818, barrister-at-law.

VII. Matthew-Robert, b. 30 March, 1822.

VIII. George-Richard, b. 2 Oct. 1825.

I. Mary, d. 3 Feb. 1821.

II. Charlotte-Eliza.

III. Julia-Katherina, m. the Rev. H.-J. Maltby, son of Edward Maltby, D.D., Lord Bishop of Durham, d. 27 April, 1843, leaving issue,

1 Edward-Charles. 1 Julia.

IV. Jemima, d. in 1835.

Arms—Arg., on a fesse, engrailed, between three martlets, sa., three annulets, or.

Crest—A cockatrice's head, turretted, or, wings erect, sa.

Seat—Linden.

BIGGS OF STOCKTON.

BIGGS, HARRY, Esq. of Stockton, co. Wilts, high-sheriff in 1819, b. 4 Dec. 1767; m. 16 Sept. 1802, Margaretta-Ann, sole dau. and heir of Godolphin-William Burslem, Esq. of Alton Grange, co. Leicester, and has had issue,

I. HENRY-GODOLPHIN, b. 4 July, 1803, m. 20 June, 1837, Marianne, 2nd dau. of William Wyndham, Esq. of Dinton.

II. Arthur-William, major 7th hussars, b. 9 Aug. 1804, d. 2 Nov. 1840.

I. Margaretta, b. 11 Oct, 1805, d. 11 Oct. 1819.

II. Emma, m. in 1837, to Harry-Farr Yeatman, Esq. of Stock House, co. Dorset, who d. 22 May, 1852.

Lineage.—The village of Stapleford, in the immediate vicinity of Stockton, was long the residence of the family of Biggs, of which,

THOMAS BYGGS, of Stapleford, in the co. of Wilts, d. in 1551, 5th EDWARD VI. In this parish the family continued to reside, and had there their place of sepulture, until

TRISTRAM BIGGS removed to the adjoining parish of Little Langford, in the same co. He was b. in 1634, and m. Lucy, dau. of Beach, of Wiltshire, who d. in 1704: he d. 1 Sept. 1720, and was buried at Stapleford, having had issue, three sons and three daus. The eldest son,

TRISTRAM BIGGS, Esq., s. his father at Little Langford. He was twice married: by his 1st wife he had, with two daus. (Hannah, m. to Henry Hunt, Esq. of Littleton; and Mary, m. to Flower Sainsbury, Esq. of Lavington) two sons, Tristram, who d. in infancy in 1706; and Thomas, of Heytesbury, whose only son, Thomas-Morris Biggs, d. s. p. The 2nd wife of Mr. Tristram Biggs was Jane, dau. of Henry Miles, of Maddington, in the co. of Wilts, and co-heir of her brother, Henry Miles, Esq. of the same place, by whom he had two daus. and an only son,

Henry Biggs, Esq. of Little Langford, b. in 1723. Having purchased the neighbouring manor and estate of Stockton, he removed thither. By Diana his wife, dau. of John Davis, Esq. of Bapton, and relict of John Potticary, Esq. (whom he m. 8 June, 1766), he had issue,

Harry, present possessor.
Jane, m. the Rev. William Bond, of Tyneham, co. Dorset, 4th son of John Bond, Esq. of Grange; and d. 6 March, 1854.

Mr. Biggs d. 31 March, 1800, and his widow, 30 June, 1818, aged 89 years.

Arms—Per pale, erm. and az., a lion, passant, within a bordure, engrailed, gu., the latter charged with fleurs-de-lis, or.
Crest—A leopard's face, ppr.
Seat—Stockton, near Salisbury, co. Wilts.

BIGLAND OF BIGLAND.

Bigland, Wilson-Braddyll, Esq. of Bigland Hall, co. Lancaster, capt. R.N., and K.H.; m. 8 Jan. 1822, Emily, sister of Capt. Sir Henry Leeke, R.N., and has had issue,

I. George Kelsey, ensign 46th regt., accidently killed, 23 Jan. 1842.
II. Wilson Henry-John, b. 7 Jan. 1824.
I. Sophia-Georgiana.

Lineage.—The Biglands, one of the most ancient families in Lancashire, traditions affirm to have been seated at Bigland as early as the Norman conquest.

Edward Bigland, of Bigland, grandson of Edward Byglande, of Byglande, living *temp.* Henry VII., m. a dau. of the ancient family of Sandys *of Furness Fell*, and had, with two daus., three sons, from the second of whom, George, of Cartmel, derived through the female line, the late Sir Ralph Bigland, Garter king-at-arms. Edward Bigland d. in 1563, and was s. by his eldest son,

Henry Bigland, Esq. of Bigland, from whom the seventh in descent was

George Bigland, Esq. of Bigland, b. 5 May, 1750, m. 1st, in 1781, Anne, 2nd dau. and co-heir of Robert Watters, Esq. of Whitehaven, high-sheriff for Cumberland, and had by her, who d. in 1783, one son, George, his heir. He m. 2ndly, at Ulverstone, 23 Nov. 1784, Sarah, dau. of John Gale, Esq. of Whitehaven, high-sheriff for Cumberland, and sister of the late Wilson Bradyll, Esq. of Conishead Priory, and by her, who d. in 1830, had, (with four daus., who all d. unm., except the eldest, Sarah, wife of Pudsey Dawson, Esq. of Langcliff Hall) two sons, John, capt. 3rd regt. of Lancashire militia, who is married, and has issue; and Wilson-Braddyll, now of Bigland. Mr. Bigland d. in Jan. 1831, s. by his eldest son,

George Bigland, Esq. of Bigland, b. in 1782, who d. unm., and was s. by his brother, the present Wilson-Braddyll Bigland, Esq. of Bigland.

Arms—Az., two ears of big wheat, or, quartering, arg., three wolves' heads, sa., for Wilson.
Crest—A lion passant regardant, gu., holding in his fore-paw an ear of big wheat, as in the arms.
Mottoes—Above the crest, Gratitude; below the shield, Spes [illegible] vita.
Seat—Bigland Hall, near Cartmel.

BILLAM OF YORKSHIRE.

Billam, Francis, Esq. of Newall Hall, co. York, J.P., b. 3 May, 1800; m. 10 Jan. 1828, Anne, relict of Thomas Wilkinson, Esq. of Winterburne, co. York, and only dau. and heiress of Thomas Clifton, Esq. of Newall and Clifton, and has issue,

Thomas-Clifton, J.P. of Yorkshire, m. 30 Sept. 1852, Julia-Jemima, 2nd dau. of the Hon. Henry Butler, and has, Thomas Clifton, b. in 1853, and other issue.
Mary-Anne-Wilkinson.

Lineage.—John Billam, Esq. of Billam and Wales, both in co. York, D.L. (claiming descent from John de Billam, who is stated to have been granted estates at Billam and Wales, for his services at Agincourt), m. Mary, dau. of Thomas Robinson, Esq. of Wales, and was father of John Billam (eldest son), who d. unm., and

Francis Billam, Esq. of Wales and Leeds, senior surgeon to the General Infirmary at Leeds, from its institution till his resignation in 1783. He m. Anne, dau. and co-heir of

the Rev. John Jackson, rector of Rossington, co. York, prebendary of Wherwell, master of Wigton Hospital, Leicester, and domestic chaplain to Queen Caroline, wife of George II.; and by her had two sons and a dau., viz.,

John, his heir; Francis-Thomas, lieut. in the 62nd regt., d. unm., 10 Feb. 1840; and Anne, who m. Edward Kenion, Esq. of Knayton, co. York, and by her (who d. in 1805) left an only dau., Anne-Billam, m. to Charles-Bissett Walker, Esq. The eldest son,

John Billam, Esq. of Wales, co. York, M.D., of Trinity College, Cambridge, m. Mary, eldest dau. of George Baron, of Leeds, merchant, and by her (who d. 31 Jan. 1827) left at his decease, 29 Dec. 1825,

Francis, of Newall Hall.
John-Baron, m. 20 Sept. 1814, Maria, youngest dau. of Harper Soulby, Esq. of Cliffe House, co. York, and has issue, John; Harper-Soulby; Frank-Baron; Maria; Dorothy; and Sarah-Jane.

Arms—Gu., three bows, ppr.
Crest—A dexter arm, grasping an arrow, ppr.
Motto—Azincour.
Seat—Newall Hall, Yorkshire.

BINGHAM OF MELCOMBE BINGHAM.

Bingham, Richard-Hippisley, Esq. of Bingham's Melcombe, co. Dorset, J.P., D.L., and colonel of the Dorset militia, b. 1 Oct. 1804; m. 6 April, 1836, Harriet-Georgiana, 3rd dau. of his maternal uncle, the Rev. Montagu-John Wynyard, B.D., chaplain to the Queen.

Lineage.—The family of Bingham, of Saxon origin, was originally seated at Sutton Bingham, in the co. of Somerset, and thence removed to Melcombe, in Dorsetshire.

Robert Bingham, Esq. of Melcombe (son and heir of Robert Bingham, Esq. of Melcombe, by Joan his wife, dau. of John Delalynde, Esq., and ninth in descent from Sir Ralph de Bingham, elder brother of Robert, Bishop of Salisbury, who d. in 1246) m. Alice, dau. of Thomas Coker, Esq. of Mapouder, and had, with two daus., eight sons, viz., Robert, his heir; Christopher; Richard (Sir), one of the most eminent soldiers of the time in which he lived, who d. in 1598; George (Sir), who served under his brother in the Irish wars, and was ancestor of the Earls of Lucan; Roger, who d. s. p.; John (Sir); Thomas; and Charles. Robert Bingham d. in 1561, and was s. by his eldest son,

Robert Bingham, Esq. of Melcombe, who m. Jane, dau. of Robert Williams, Esq. of Herringston, in Dorsetshire, and dying in 1593, was s. by his grandson,

Richard Bingham, Esq. of Melcombe, (son of Robert Bingham and Anne his wife, dau. of William Chaldecot, Esq. of Quarrelston), who m. Jane, dau. of Sir Arthur Hopton, Knt. of Witham Abbey, in Somersetshire, and dying in 1636, was s. by his eldest son,

John Bingham, Esq. of Melcombe, the parliamentarian, who was, during the civil war, colonel of a regt., Governor of Poole, and commander at the last siege and demolition of Corfe Castle; he was also a member of the Long Parliament at its dissolution, April, 1653. He m. 1st, Frances, dau. and co-heir of John Trenchard, Esq. of Warmwell, and 2ndly, Jane Norwood, of Gloucestershire, but had issue only by the former, viz., five daus., Elizabeth; Jane; Penelope, m. to John Michel, Esq. of Kingston Russell; Frances, who d. in 1681, and Grace, m. to Thomas Skinner, Esq. Col. Bingham d. in 1673, and was s. by (the son of his brother, Strode Bingham) his nephew,

Richard Bingham, Esq. of Melcombe Bingham, who m. Philadelphia, dau. and heir of John Potenger, Esq. by Philadelphia his wife, dau. of Sir John Ernle, Knt., chancellor of the Exchequer, and by her, who d. in 1737, aged 78, had, with other issue,

I. Richard, his heir.
II. George, B.D., fellow of All Souls' College, Oxford, rector of Pimperne and More Critchel, a distinguished and learned divine, m. in 1748, Sarah Bode, and by her left at his decease, in 1800, aged 85, a dau., Sarah, and one son,
1 Peregrine, LL.B., fellow of New College, rector of Edmondsham and of Radclive, who m. Amy, dau. of William Bowles, Esq., and d. in 1826, having had two sons,
Peregrine, b. in 1788, of the Middle Temple, barrister-at-law and one of the police magistrates, m. in [illegible], dau. of James Bolton, and sister of the late Lady Thurlow, and has issue, Peregrine, b. in 1824, and Eliza.

Edward, *b.* in 1789, a lieut. R.N., *d.* at Lima, in Peru, in 1823, *s. p.*

Mr. Bingham, for more than forty years in the commission of the peace, represented Bridport, and subsequently the co. of Dorset, in parliament. He *d.* in 1735, aged 69, and was *s.* by his eldest son,

RICHARD BINGHAM, Esq. of Melcomb Bingham, barrister-at-law, who *m.* Martha, dau. of William Batt, Esq. of Salisbury, and by her (who wedded 2ndly, Perry Buckley, Esq. of Winkfield Place, Berks, and *d.* in 1765) had three sons, namely,

I. RICHARD, his heir.
II. William, D.D., archdeacon of London, who *m.* Agnes, dau. of — Dorrien, Esq., and had issue,
1 Robert-Turberville, *b.* in 1777, lieut.-col. grenadier-guards, *m.* Mary, only dau. and heir of Thomas Elliott, Esq. of The Vines, Rochester, and had a dau., who *d.* in 1817.
2 Arthur-Batt, *b.* in 1784, capt. R.N., who was drowned in 1830, leaving, by Emily his wife, dau. of W.-L. Kingsman, Esq., of Petworth, four sons and one dau., viz., Arthur-Maunsel, R.N., *b.* in 1814, *d.* in 1838; Thomas-Henry, R.N., *b.* in 1816, lost at sea; George-William, *b.* in 1817, in the 95th regt.; Francis-Robert-Bertie, *b.* in 1819, *d.* in 1839; and Emily-Agnata-Harriet.
3 John-Batt, *b.* in 1787, in holy orders, *m.* Frances, 2nd dau. of the Rev. Croxton Johnston, rector of Wilmslow, Cheshire, and has a son, Henry, *b.* in 1837, and a dau., Maria-Maunsel.
1 Martha-Caroline-Buckley. 2 Agnata-Maria.
III. John, *d.* at Calcutta, in 1760.

Mr. Bingham *d.* in 1755, aged 58, and was *s.* by his son,

RICHARD BINGHAM, Esq. of Melcombe Bingham, colonel of the Dorsetshire militia, *b.* in 1750, who *m.* 1st, in 1766, Sophia, dau. of Charles Halsey, Esq. of Great Gaddesden, in Herts, and had by her, who *d.* in 1773, two sons and one dau., viz.,

I. RICHARD, his heir.
II. William, fellow of New College, Oxford, *b.* in 1771, rector of Cameley, in Somersetshire, and of Melbury Babb, in Dorsetshire, *m.* 20 April, 1797, Sarah-Emily, dau. of General William Wynyard, and *d.* 27 May, 1810 (his widow survived until 14 June, 1852), leaving issue,
1 William-Wynyard, *b.* 18 Jan. 1798, fellow of New College, Oxford, *d. unm.* 1821.
2 GEORGE, *b.* in 1803, in holy orders, *m.* Frances, dau. of Anthony Blagrave, Esq., and *d.* in 1838.
3 RICHARD-HIPPISLEY, present head of the family.
4 Charles-William, rector of Melcombe Horsey, co. Dorset, *b.* 23 Sept. 1810, *m.* 28 May, 1839, his cousin, Caroline-Damer, 2nd dau. of the Rev. Montagu-John Wynyard, which lady *d.* without surviving issue, 1 Jan. 1852.
1 Emily-Georgiana, deceased.
2 Sophia-Matilda, *m.* in 1826, to Robert-Francis Wright, Esq. of Hinton Blewett, co. Somerset, and has Augustus-Robert-Bingham, Arthur-Francis-Bingham, and Sophia-Leonora.
III. Charles-Cox, *b.* in 1772, *d.* at the Royal Arsenal, Woolwich, in 1835, colonel R.A., *m.* Sarah, dau. of Samuel Hayter, Esq., and had issue,
1 George-William, royal artillery, *b.* 15 Sept. 1801.
2 Richard-Clavell, an officer in the army, *b.* 10 May, 1810.
3 Charles, royal artillery, *b.* in 1815.
4 Edmund-Hayter, *b.* in 1820.
1 Mary-Frances, *m.* in 1833, to the Rev. Henry Stevens, eldest son of the Dean of Rochester.
2 Emma. 3 Sophia.
I. Sophia, *m.* to William-Richards Clavell, Esq. of Smedmore.

Mr. Bingham *m.* 2ndly, 26 Oct. 1775, Elizabeth, dau. of John Ridout, Esq. of Dean's Lease, and had by her,

George-Ridout (Sir), K.C.B. and T.S. of Dean's Lease, *b.* 21 July, 1777, major-general in the army, and col. of the Rifle corps, *m.* in Sept. 1814, Emma-Septima, youngest dau. of Edmund-Morton Pleydell, Esq. of Whatcombe House, in Dorsetshire, but *d. s. p.* 3 Jan. 1833.
John, *b.* 18 March, 1785, lieut. R.N., *m.* Fanny, dau. of C. Woolcombe, Esq., and has issue.
Mary, *m.* to Nathaniel-Tryon Still, Esq., capt. in the army, and had issue.
Leonora, *m.* twice, without issue.

Mr. Bingham *d.* in 1823, and was *s.* by his eldest son,

RICHARD BINGHAM, Esq. of Melcombe Bingham, *b.* in 1768, who attained the rank of lieut.-gen. in the army. He *m.* Miss Priscilla Carden, a relation of Sir John Carden, Bart., but dying without issue in 1829, (his widow survided until 1 Feb. 1848) was *s.* by his nephew,

THE REV. GEORGE BINGHAM, *b.* 4 June, 1803, who *m.* Frances-Anna-Byam, only dau. of Anthony Blagrave, Esq., and had a son, George-Henry, who *d.* in infancy. He *d.* himself in May, 1833, and was *s.* by his brother, the present representative of the family.

Arms—Az., a bend, cotised, between six crosses-patée, or.
Crest—On a rock, ppr., an eagle rising, or.
Motto—Spes mea Christus.
Seat—Melcombe Bingham, Dorset.

BIRCH OF WRETHAM.

BIRCH, WYRLEY, Esq. of Wretham Hall, co. Norfolk, *b.* 11 Sept. 1781; *m.* 19 July, 1804, Katharine-Sarah, 3rd dau. and co-heir of Jacob Reynardson, Esq. of Holywell, co. Lincoln, by Anne his wife, dau. of Sir John Cust, Bart., Speaker of the House of Commons, and has issue,

I. GEORGE-WYRLEY, *b.* in April, 1805, *m.* 17 Jan. 1833, Jane, 3rd dau. of Richard Congreve, Esq. of Burton, co. Chester, and has, with other issue, a son, WYRLEY, *b.* in 1837.
II. Thomas-Jacob, *b.* in 1806, called to the bar, 18 Nov. 1831, judge of the county court circuit No. 32, recorder of Thetford.
III. Henry-William, *b.* in 1809.
IV. Frederick-Lane, rector of East and West Wretham, *b.* in 1812, *d.* May, 1850.
V. Peregrine, *b.* in 1817, *m.* in 1843, Anna, dau. of Gen. James Grant, of Hayes Park, Middlesex.
VI. Lawrence, *b.* in 1823.
I. Katherine-Mary-Anne.
II. Jemima-Lucy, *m.* 31 Aug. 1841, to Richard Longfield, Esq. of Longueville, co. Cork.
III. Charlotte-Ethelred.
IV. Frances-Augusta, *m.* 23 July, 1833, to William-Peere Williams-Freeman, Esq. late of Fawley Court, co. Bucks, now of Pylewell, Hants.
V. Juliana-Maria, *m.* 3 Nov. 1840, to Henry-Fowler Broadwood, Esq.
VI. Elizabeth-Caroline, *m.* in Aug. 1844, to Robert Pryor, Esq.
VII. Agnes-Ellen, *m.* in Sept. 1850, to the Rev. James Parke Whalley, rector of East and West Wretham.

Lineage.—THOMAS BIRCH, Esq. of Birchfield, in the parish of Handsworth, co. Stafford, and of Birch Green and Aston, co. Warwick, was living at Birchfield, 7th ELIZABETH, and was buried at Aston in 1618. His son and heir, THOMAS BIRCH, Esq. of Harborne, bapt. at Handsworth in 1565, was father of GEORGE BIRCH, of Harborne Hall, bapt. at Handsworth in 1616, and buried there in 1660. His son,

GEORGE BIRCH, Esq., *m.* Mary, dau. of Thomas Foster Esq., and dying in 1721, left issue.

THOMAS (Sir), his heir.
John, rector of Handsworth, *d. s. p.*
James, of Wolston, co. Warwick, *m.* Jane, dau. and co-heir of Abraham Owen, Esq., and *d.* in 1772, leaving a son, GEORGE BIRCH, Esq. of St. Leonard's Hill, co. Berks, who *m.* Mary, dau. of Thomas Newell, Esq., and *d.* in 1803, leaving issue.
Another son, in holy orders, who *d.* leaving issue.
Mary, *m.* to William Green, Esq. of Eccles, co. Norfolk.
Sarah, *m.* 1st, in 1769, to Godfrey-Woodward Vane, Esq., and 2ndly, to Sir Wadsworth Bush.

The eldest son,

SIR THOMAS BIRCH, Knt., judge of the Common Pleas, *b.* at Harborne, in 1690, *m.* in 1733, Sarah, dau. and co-heir of J. Teshmaker, Esq., and dying in 1757, left, with two daus., Mary, who *d. unm.*, and Esther-Barbara, *m.* to the Rev. Thomas Lane, rector of Handsworth, three sons, GEORGE, his heir; Thomas, who *d. s. p.*; and John, capt. in the horse-guards (Blue), who *d. unm.* The eldest son,

GEORGE BIRCH, Esq. of Hamstead Hall and Handsworth, *b.* in July, 1739, *m.* in 1776, Anne, 3rd dau. of Thomas Lane, Esq. of Bentley, (and granddau. of John Lane, Esq., by Mary his wife, eldest dau. of Humphrey Wyrley, Esq.; and co-heir with her sister Sybill, *m.* to the Rev. Peter Birch, D.D., prebendary of Westminster). By her (who *d.* in Feb. 1806) Mr. Birch left, at his decease, in Feb. 1807, one son, the present WYRLEY BIRCH, Esq. of Wretham Hall, and three daus., viz., Mary-Ann, *m.* to Richard Congreve, Esq. of Burton, Cheshire; Sarah, who *d.* in 1846; and Ann, *m.* Major Joseph-Jeanes Durbin (son of Sir John Durbin), and *d.* in 1848.

Arms—Az., three fleurs-de-lis, and a canton, arg.
Crest—A fleur-de-lis, with shamrock and serpent entwining, ppr.
Motto—Prudentia simplicitate.
Seat—Wretham, near Thetford.

BIRCH OF HENLEY PARK.

NEWELL-BIRCH, JOHN-WILLIAM, Esq. of Henley Park, co. Oxford, *b.* 30 April, 1775; *m.* 13 Dec. 1821, Diana-Eliza, dau. of the late James Bourchier, Esq. of Little Berkhampstead, Herts. Mr. Newell-Birch assumed the name of NEWELL before his patronymic, BIRCH, in compliance with the will of Mrs. Frances Webb, from whom he derives the family estate of Adwell, co. Oxford.

Lineage.—This is a branch of the house of BIRCH *of Wretham, (see that name).*

GEORGE BIRCH, Esq. of St. Leonard's Hill, Berks, son of James Birch, of Wolston, co. Warwick, 2nd brother of Sir Thomas Birch, Knt., justice of the Common Pleas, *(see* BIRCH *of Wretham)*, *m.* Mary, dau .of Thomas Newell, Esq., and *d.* in 1803, leaving,

- Thomas, general in the army, who *m.* Etheldred-Anne, eldest dau. and co-heir of Jacob Reynardson, Esq. of Holywell Hall, co. Lincoln, and assumed, on the death of his father-in-law in 1811, the additional surname of REYNARDSON. He *d.* in 1847, leaving issue (*See* BIRCH-REYNARDSON).
- JOHN-WILLIAM, the present JOHN-WILLIAM NEWELL-BIRCH, Esq. of Henley Park.
- Mary-Jane, *m.* to the Rev. William Canning, canon of Windsor, and brother of Lord Stratford de Redcliffe.

Arms, Crest, and *Motto*—As BIRCH *of Wretham*: quartering NEWELL.
Seat—Henley Park, co. Oxford.

BIRD OF DRYBRIDGE HOUSE.

BIRD, THE REV. CHARLES-JOHN, A.M. and F.A.S., of Drybridge House, co. Hereford, rector of Mordiford and Dynedor, J.P., and late rural dean of Ross, *b.* 11 July, 1777; *m.* 1st, 19 May, 1803, Harriet Jones, of Upton Castle, co. Pembroke, great-niece of John Tasker, Esq. of Upton Castle, high-sheriff of Pembrokeshire, and has had issue,

- I. Charles - William - Tasker, *b.* 10 Feb. 1804, *m.* his cousin, Mary-Anne, dau. of G.-G. Bird, Esq., and *d. s. p.*
- II. THOMAS-HUGH, *b.* 12 May, 1806, A.M., in holy orders, *m.* 8 Sept. 1846, Jane, 2nd dau. of Samuel Bell, Esq. of Hopton Hall, Suffolk, and by her, who *d.* 27 Dec. 1850, has two sons, Charles-Pavin and Reginald-Hereford.
- I. Harriett-Jane-Eliza, *d. unm.* in 1818.
- II. Sophia-Maria-Jane, *m.* to the Rev. John Evans, A.M., of Aylestones Hill, co. Hereford.
- III. Frances-Anne, *m.* 26 June, 1845, Thomas Cooper, Esq. of Hampstead.
- IV. Julia-Hannah, *m.* to the Rev. John Purton, A.M., rector of Oldbury, near Bridgnorth.

Mr. Bird *m.* 2ndly, 4 Feb. 1823, Rachel, dau. of the Rev. Edward Glover, A.M. of Barmer, co. Norfolk, and by her has a dau.

- I. Christiana-Rachael.

Lineage.—RICHARD BIRD, Esq. *b.* in 1640, claimed descent from the BYRDES *of Broxton*, co. Chester. By Elizabeth his wife, he had, with numerous other issue, a son,

BENJAMIN BIRD, Esq. of Drybridge House, *b.* 18 April, 1682, who *m.* 1st, Miss Smith, of Crockey Hill, co. Hereford, by whom he had issue. He *m.* 2ndly, Jane, dau. of Thomas Gwynne, Esq. of Cunghordy, co. Carmarthen, brother of Glynne of Glanbrane, and by her had three sons and four daus. The last surviving son of the 2nd marriage,

WILLIAM BIRD, Esq. of Drybridge House, *m.* 15 Dec. 1757, Hannah, eldest dau. and co-heiress of William Boulton, Esq. of Sillens, co. Worcester, and *d.* 15 Aug. 1795, having had issue,

- William, *b.* 12 May, 1759, *d. unm.* 14 Feb. 1784.
- James, *b.* 22 Jan. 1771, of Magdalen Hall, Oxon, *d. unm.* 31 Aug. 1798.
- Thomas, D.L., F.A.S., late of Drybridge House, *b.* 2 March, 1772, *m.* in 1798, Hannah-Maria, dau. of the Rev. Edward Phillips, A.M., rector of Patching, and vicar of West Tarring, co. Sussex, and *d. s. p.* 5 March, 1836.
- CHARLES-JOHN, of Drybridge House, as above.
- George-Gwynne, *b.* 19 Aug. 1779, *m.* Elizabeth Preece, and has issue, George, William, Charles, Thomas, Benjamin, Richard, Mary-Anne, Julia, and Elizabeth.
- Anne, *m.* to the Hon. Benning Wentworth, Secretary of the province of Nova Scotia, member of council, &c., both deceased.
- Catherine, *m.* to Henry Allen, Esq., son of the Rev. William Allen, D.D., prebendary of Hereford, and *d.* 18 June, 1842.
- Harriet, *m.* to James Nicholls, Esq. and *d.* 6 Feb. 1800.
- Mary-Anne, *m.* to Charles Betton, Esq., and *d.* Oct. 1803.

Arms—Arg., a cross-flory, between four martlets, gu.; on a canton, az., a mullet of five points, or, a crescent for difference.
Crest—A martlet, gu.
Motto—Cruce spes mea.
Seat—Drybridge House, co. Hereford.

BIRLEY OF CUMBERLAND AND LANCASHIRE.

BIRLEY, JOHN, Esq. of Woodend, near Egremont, co. Cumberland, *b.* at Kirkham, 1 March, 1769; *m.* 1 Dec. 1808, Mary-Ann, dau. of Simon Grayson, Esq. of Maryport, and widow of John Linden; by this lady (who *d.* 30 April, 1818) he had issue,

- I. Thomas, *b.* 9 Sept, 1809, *m.* Agnes Evans, and *d. s. p.* 18 Aug. 1847.
- II. Hutton, *b.* 14 Sept. 1816, *d.* 18 March, 1818.
- III. Hutton, *b.* 28 March, and *d.* 19 Aug. 1818.
- I. Anne, *m.* to her cousin, Thomas-Langton Birley, Esq. of Carr Hill.
- II. Margaret, *m.* to Joseph Dickson, Esq. of Preston, and *d.* 24 May, 1835.
- III. Ellen, *m.* to Henry Smith, Esq. of Fleetwood.

Lineage.—The locality from which this name is derived is mentioned in the charters of the Osbaldiston family, *temp.* EDWARD II. and III., as Beroclegh and Birclogh, in the township of Balderston, in the parish of Blackburn; the grantor being called Rob. de Birclogh and Rob. de Byrlogh. Adam de Birleye and others were witnesses, in 1335, to a judgment respecting the repair of the chancel at Chirche, in the parish of Whalley. In Kuerden's MSS., W. fil. R. de Birley is named, 4th HENRY IV., and James Birley, as a tenant of Sir John Southworth, of Samlesbury, 22nd HENRY VII. In 1621, Isabel, wife of Thomas Birley, of Kirkham, gave "seventy gold pieces," as an incitement to a general contribution throughout the parish for the erection and endowment of a Free School. The Free Grammar School of Kirkham was thus founded, now a rich and flourishing institution, whose funds have been augmented by the gifts and bequests of more recent benefactors.

JOHN BIRLEY, of Skippool, in the parish of Poulton-le Fylde, co. Lancaster, (whose will bears date 6 Nov. 1732), was father of

JOHN BIRLEY, of Kirkham, a West India merchant, who *d.* 12 May, 1767. By his 1st wife, Ellen Harrison, he had four children, who all *d.* without issue. His 2nd wife was Elizabeth, dau. of Thomas Shepherd, *m.* 6 May, 1741, *d.* 27 Jan. 1780, and by her he had, with four daus., four sons, THOMAS, his heir; Richard, of Blackburn *(see* BIRLEY *of Manchester)*; John, of Kirkham *(see* BIRLEY *of Kirkham)*; and William, *b.* 24 April, 1750, *d. unm.* 10 March, 1792.

THOMAS BIRLEY, of Kirkham, son and heir, *b.* 22 Feb. 1741–2, *m.* 23 Sept. 1765, Margaret, dau. of Henry Lawson, by Isabel Crookall his wife; she *d.* 30 March, 1797. Thomas Birley *d.* 1 March, 1817. His issue were,

- JOHN, now of Woodend, Egremont.
- Henry, of Whitehaven, bapt. 9 July, 1771, *d.* 31 Jan. 1830, *unm.*
- Richard, bapt. 5 Jan. 1774, *d.* 17 Nov. 1794.
- James, of Restalrig, near Edinburgh, bapt. 8 June, 1784, *m.* to Jane, dau. of Rev. Abraham Brown, and widow of John Richardson;—issue, Isabel, *m.* to Francis O'Brien, of Liverpool.
- Martha, *m.* Rev. George Lewthwaite, rector of Adel, in co. York.
- Cicely, *m.* Charles Buck, Esq. of Preston, and *d.* 6 Dec. 1840.

Arms—Sa., on a fess, engrailed, between three boars' heads, couped, arg., a mascle, between two cross-crosslets, of the field.
Crest—A demi-boar, sa., collared, az., chain reflexed over the back, or, supporting a branch of wild teazle, ppr., and charged on the shoulder with a millrind, arg.
Motto—Omni liber metu.

BIRLEY OF MANCHESTER.

Lineage.—RICHARD BIRLEY, of Blackburn, second surviving son of of John Birley, of Kirkham, *(vide preceding article)*, *b.* 4 Dec. 1748, *m.* 15 Dec. 1772, Alice, dau, of Hugh Hornby, Esq. of Kirkham, by his wife Margaret, dau. of Joseph Hankinson. Mr. Birley *d.* 11 Jan. 1812, and his wife in the following month of April. Their issue were,

I. John Birley, a deputy-lieut. of the co. Lancaster, *b.* 30 Aug. 1775, *m.* 4 Feb. 1800, Margaret, dau. of Daniel Backhouse, Esq. of Liverpool. He *d.* 25 Dec. 1833, leaving issue,

1 Richard, *b.* 15 March, 1801, *m.* 10 March, 1825, Mary-Anne, dau. of John Hardman, Esq. of Manchester, and of Mary his wife, dau. of Jos. Tipping. He *d.* in Canada, 3 Nov. 1845, leaving issue,

John-James, *b.* 7 July, 1828.
Charles, *b.* 2 Oct. 1830.
Richard-William, *b.* 7 Oct. 1835, *d.* 3 Jan. 1836.
Margaret, *m.* Andrew-Tosach Smith, of Dumfries, Canada West.
Mary-Anne, *d.* 27 Feb. 1835.
Sarah-Maria.
Eliza-Jane, *d.* 3 Oct. 1841.

2 Daniel, *b.* 26 Jan. 1807, *d.* 19 Oct. 1839.
3 Hornby, *b.* 18 Jan. 1811, *m.* Margaret, 2nd dau. of Dr. Roberts, M.D., of Beaumaris.
4 William, in holy orders, incumbent of Chorlton-cum-Hardy, *b.* 16 Feb. 1813, *m.* 8 Sept. 1836, Maria, 3rd dau. of Thomas Barrow, Esq. of Pendleton, and of Harriet his wife, dau. of James Hardman. They have issue,

William Carew, *b.* 22 June, 1843, *d.* 15 Nov. 1843.
William-Carew, *b.* 8 Dec. 1844.
Harriet-Elizabeth.
Caroline-Margaret. Mary-Jane.

5 John, *b.* 30 Oct. 1814, *d.* 16 Feb. 1851.
6 George, *b.* 4 June, 1816.
1 Elizabeth, *m.* Rev. John Williams, of Beaumaris, *d.* 24 May, 1845.
2 Alice, *m.* Charles Buck, Esq. of Preston, being his 2nd wife.
3 Margaret, *m.* Charles Pochin, *d.* 30 Dec. 1840.
4 Frances, *m.* Daniel Hornby, Esq. of Raikes Hall.

II. Hugh-Hornby Birley, of Broomhouse, a deputy-lieut. and magistrate for the co. Lancaster, *b.* 10 March, 1778, *m.* 5 March, 1822, Cicely, dau. of Thomas Hornby, Esq. of Kirkham, and of Cicely his wife, dau. of Thomas Langton. Mrs. Birley *d.* 15 Jan. 1843, and Mr. Birley, 31 July, 1845, leaving issue,

1 Thomas-Hornby, of Broomhouse, *b.* 16 June, 1824.
2 Hugh-Hornby, in holy orders, *b.* 31 Aug. 1825.
3 Joseph-Hornby, *b.* 12 March, 1827.
4 William-Hornby, } twins, *b.* 22 Dec. 1834, *d.* 26 Jan.
5 Edward-Hornby, } 1838.
6 Frederick-Hornby, *b.* 23 March, 1837.
7 Edward-Hornby, *b.* 17 Jan. 1842.
1 Cicely-Margaret, *d.* 28 Sept. 1823.
2 Cicely-Margaret. 3 Alicia-Marian.
4 Mary-Isabella. 5 Emily-Jane.

III. Joseph Birley, of Ford Bank, a deputy-lieut. for the co. Lancaster, *b.* 31 May, 1782, *m.* 22 Aug. 1809, and *d.* 24 Jan. 1847. His wife was Jane, eldest dau. of Thomas Hornby, of Kirkham, by Cicely Langton, his wife. Their issue are,

1 Richard, of Manchester, J.P. and deputy-lieut. co. Lancaster, *b.* 11 March, 1812, *m.* 2 Aug. 1836, Amelia-Garforth, dau. of James Kennedy, Esq. of Manchester, and of his wife, Jane, dau. of Matthew Brown, of Paisley. Their issue are,

Richard-Kennedy, *b.* 16 March, 1845.
Amelia-Josephine, *d.* 3 March, 1841.
Helen. Margaret.
Amelia-Jane, *d.* 7 Dec. 1842.
Mary-Louisa. Josephine. Janet.
Henrietta. Amelia-Gertrude.

2 Thomas-Hornby, *b.* 13 Nov. 1813, *d.* 8 Nov. 1814.
3 Thomas-Hornby, of Manchester, *b.* 11 May, 1815, *m.* 2 Aug. 1843, Anne, dau. of Capt. James Leatham, 1st dragoon guards, and of his wife, Catherine-Frances, dau. of Henry White, Esq. of Carrick-on Suir, and widow of George Hobbs, of Waterford. Their issue are,

James-Leathom, *b.* 22 Dec. 1847.
Francis-Hornby, *b.* 4 March, 1850.
Anne-Katharine.

4 Hugh, *b.* 4 Sept. 1816, *d.* 4 Nov. following.
5 Hugh, of Manchester, *b.* 21 Oct. 1817, *m.* 7 July, 1842, Mabella, dau. of Joseph Baxendale, Esq., and of Mary his wife, dau. of Richard Birley. Their issue are,

Hugh-Arthur, *b.* 29 Aug. 1846.
Joseph-Reginald, *b.* 8 April, 1850.
Mary-Alice. Edith-Mabella.

6 Herbert, } twins, *b.* 10 April, 1821.
7 Henry, }
8 Robert, in holy orders; *b.* 1 Nov. 1825.
9 Alfred, *b.* 19 July, 1827; *d.* young.
10 Alfred, of Baliol College, Oxford; *b.* 18 May, 1832.
11 Arthur, of Pembroke College, Oxford; *b.* 25 April, 1834.
1 Jane. 2 Cecilia. 3 Elizabeth.

4 Louisa, *d.* 7 Aug. 1824.
5 Louisa-Margaret. 6 Adelaide.

I. Margaret, *d.* in infancy.
II. Elizabeth, *m.* John Cardwell, Esq. of Liverpool.
III. Margaret, *d.* 23 Jan. 1844.
IV. Jane, *d.* 2 April, 1823.
V. Mary, *m.* Joseph Baxendale, Esq. of Woodside, co. Middlesex.

Arms, Crest, and Motto—As Birley *of Woodend.*

BIRLEY OF KIRKHAM.

Birley, The Rev. John-Shepherd, M.A. of Halliwell Hall and Kirkham, co. Lancaster, J.P., *b.* 11 Oct. 1805; *m.* 22 Aug. 1836, Anne, dau. of John Hargreaves, Esq. of Hart Common, and has issue,

Lucy-Mary-Shepherd.

Lineage.—John Birley, of Kirkham, 3rd surviving son of John Birley, of Kirkham (*see before*), *b.* 20 Nov 1747; *m.* 16 Dec. 1776, Margaret, dau. of John Yate, Esq. of Liverpool, by Hannah his wife, dau. of Hugh Parr, and widow of John Potter. She *d.* 13 Nov. 1830, and Mr. Birley *d.* 31st of the following month of May. Their issue were,

I. William, of Kirkham.
II. Thomas, of Millbank, *b.* 4 Aug. 1782, *m.* 9 July, 1810, Anne, dau. and co-heir of John Langton, Esq. of Kirkham, by his wife Betty, dau. and heir of Cuthbert Bradkirk: she *d.* in Feb. 1833, and Mr. Birley, 1 April, 1847, leaving issue,

1 Thomas-Langton Birley, of Carr Hill, *b.* 18 June, 1811, *m.* 31 Aug. 1836, Anne, dau. of John Birley, of Woodend, and has issue,

Henry-Langton, *b.* 11 Aug. 1837.
Hutton, *b.* 6 Aug. 1840.
Edwin-Grayson, *b.* 12 Jan. 1847, and *d.* 16 Dec. 1849.
Margaret-Louisa, *d.* 19 Sept. 1842.
Cicely-Anne.

2 Charles, of Kirkham, *b.* 20 Nov. 1812, *m.* 23 Feb. 1843, Elizabeth, dau. of Richard Addison, Esq. of Liverpool, by Betty his wife, dau. of John-Bridge Aspinall. They have issue,

Charles-Addison, *b.* 11 Sept. 1844.
Richard-Bradkirk, *b.* 10 April, 1846.
Aspinall, *b.* 9 June, 1847.
Thomas-Shepherd, *b.* 18 Feb. 1850.

3 James-Webber, in holy orders, *b.* 5 May, 1814.
4 Francis-Bradkirk, of Canton, *b.* 19 Oct. 1817, *m.* at Hong Kong, 30 March, 1847, Melicina-Eleanor, dau. of Lieut.-Col. Thornton.
5 Edward, *b.* 12 Oct. 1818, *d.* 22 Nov. 1842.
6 Arthur-Leyland, of Millbank, *b.* 5 Aug. 1820.
7 Frederick, of Wrea Green, *b.* 11 Dec 1822, *m.* 14 Dec. 1848, to Mary, dau. of Richard Addison, of Liverpool, and has issue,

Mary-Louisa.

8 Gilmour-Robert, *b.* 13 Oct. 1823, *d.* the following day.
1 Louisa, *d.* 10 Sept. 1830.
2 Maria-Joanna, *m.* the Rev. G.-L. Parsons, vicar of Kirkham.

III. Edward, of Kirkham, *b.* 19 April, 1784, *m.* 8 Aug. 1808, Elizabeth, dau. of John Swainson, of Preston. Mr. Birley *d.* 13 Nov. 1811, and Mrs. Birley in 1836. They had issue,

1 Edward, bapt. 2 March, 1812, buried 26 Dec. 1817.
1 Margaret-Susannah, wife of William-Henry Hornby, Esq. of Blackburn.

IV. Charles, *b.* 27 Aug., *d.* 29 Sept. 1787.
V. Charles, *b.* 3 Aug., *d.* 5 Oct. 1789.
VI. Yate, of Ramsay, Isle of Man, *b.* 9 July, 1791, *m.* 28 Dec. 1815, Nancy, dau. of William Fisher, of Westby, and has issue,

1 John, *b.* 18 Sept. 1818, *d.* 26 Aug. 1843.
2 William-Henry, *b.* 25 Nov. 1826.
3 Robert, *b.* 10 Jan. 1829.
4 Walter, *b.* 14 Nov. 1832.
5 Edward, } twins, *b.* 8 Nov. 1836.
6 Charles, }
7 Septimus, *b.* 20 Feb. 1841.
1 Frances. 2 Margaret-Elizabeth.
3 Mary-Anne. 4 Hannah, *d.* 26 Jan. 1832.
5 Hannah-Catherine. 6 Emma-Jane.

I. Hannah, *d.* 18 June, 1778.
II. Hannah, *m.* Richard Harrison, Esq. of Bankfield.
III. Elizabeth.

William Birley, of Kirkham, J.P., *b.* 2 June, 1779, *m.* 30 Oct. 1804, Mary, dau. of John Swainson, Esq. of Preston, by his wife Susannah, dau. of Charles Inman, Esq. of the island of Jamaica: by her (who *d.* 6 Feb. 1819), he had issue,

I. John-Shepherd, of Halliwell Hall.
II. William, of Preston, *b.* 5 Dec. 1811, *m.* 18 Jan. 1854 Eliza, dau. of John Hastings, Esq. of Downpatrick.

III. Edmund, of Clifton Hall, J.P., *b.* 19 Aug. 1817, *m.* 17 June, 1846, Caroline-Dorothea, dau. of Rev. Richard Moore, by Mary-Anne his wife, dau. of Richard Hodgson, and has issue,
  1 Edmund-William.
  1 Emily-Marian. 2 Caroline-Margaret.
  3 Another daughter.
I. Mary, *m.* to Richard Pedder, Esq. of Preston.

Mr. Birley *m.* 2ndly, 4 Feb. 1823, Margaret, dau. of Robert Greene, of Liverpool. He *d.* 29 May, 1850.

Arms—Quarterly: 1st and 4th, sa., on a fesse, engrailed, between three boars' heads, couped, arg., a mascle, between two cross-crosslets, of the field, for BIRLEY. 2nd, az., on a chevron, between three fleurs-de-lis, arg., as many estoiles, gu., for SHEPHERD. 3rd, per chevron, or and sa., three gates, counterchanged, for YATE.
Crest—A demi-boar, sa., collared, arg., chain reflexed over the back, or, supporting a branch of wild teasle, ppr., and charged on the shoulder with a millrind, arg.
Motto—Omni liber metu.
Seats—Kirkham and Halliwell Hall, co. Lancaster.

BLAAUW OF BEECHLAND.

BLAAUW, WILLIAM-HENRY, Esq. of Beechland, co. Sussex, M.A., F.S.A., *b.* 25 May, 1793; *m.* 1st, 14 June, 1825, Harriet, dau. of John King, Esq., formerly M.P. and under-secretary of state, and by her (who *d.* 26 May, 1828) had issue,

I. Louisa-Henrietta, *d.* 14 July, 1841.
II. Caroline-Jane, *d.* 6 May, 1828.

He *m.* 2ndly, 16 June, 1832, Margaret-Emily, dau. and co-heiress of Sir John-St. Leger Gillman, Bart. of Curraheen, co. Cork, by Hannah, dau. of Sir Thomas Miller, Bart., and by her has issue,

I. HENRY-WILLIAM-GILLMAN, *b.* March 9, 1834 (in the light infantry battalion of the Royal Sussex Militia).
II. Thomas-St. Leger, *b.* July 1, 1839.
I. Emily-Hannah.

Mr. Blaauw, who *s.* his father in 1808, is a magistrate and deputy-lieut. for co. Sussex.

Lineage.—This family is of ancient Dutch extraction, many of whom have been burgomasters of Amsterdam.

GERARD BLAAUW, *b.* in 1708, *m.* 13 June, 1730, Maria-Agneta, dau. of David Van Heyst, and *d.* 13 Dec. 1775, leaving issue,

I. WILLIAM, *b.* 9 Nov. 1748, who settled in England, and *m.* 1st, in 1772, Anne-Charlotte, dau of M. Charles Le Maitre, by whom he had issue,
  1 Maria-Anne, *m.* 6 Feb. 1796, to Thomas-Gardiner Bramston, Esq., M.P. of Skreens, co. Essex, who *d.* in 1831. She *d.* 6 Feb. 1821.
  2 Charlotte-Julia, *d.* in 1787.
  Mr. Blaauw *m.* 2ndly, in 1789, Louisa, dau. of Christopher Puller, Esq. of Woodford, co. Essex, and by her (who *d.* 26 Oct. 1842), had issue,
  1 WILLIAM-HENRY, his successor, now of Beechland.
  2 Louisa-Agnes, *m.* 24 April, 1813, Capt. Charles-R.-Manners Molloy, grenadier-guards, son of Capt. Molloy, R.N., by Juliana, dau. of Sir John Laforey, Bart. He *d.* in 1820.
  3 Frances-Elizabeth, *m.* 14 June, 1817, Frederick-Burmester, Esq. of Gwynne House, co. Essex.
  Mr. Blaauw *d.* 27 Dec. 1808.
II. Gerard, for many years burgomaster of Amsterdam, *m.* and had issue.

Arms—Az., a human foot, couped, arg.; on a canton, or, an anchor, gu.
Crest—A demi-lion, rampant, arg.
Motto—Festina lente.
Seat—Beechland, Newick, co. Sussex.

BLACKBURNE OF HALE.

BLACKBURNE, JOHN-IRELAND, Esq. of Orford and Hale, co. Lancaster, J.P. and D.L., lately M.P. for Warrington, *b.* 26 May, 1783; *m.* in April, 1811, Anne, dau. of William Bamford, Esq. of Bamford, in the same county, and has issue,

I. JOHN-IRELAND, capt. 5th dragoon-guards, *b.* in 1815, *m.* in 1846, Mary, dau. of Sir Henry Hoghton, Bart. of Hoghton Tower, co. Lancaster, and has one son and four daus.
I. Emily. II. Harriott-Elizabeth. III. Ellinor-Avena.

Lineage.—This branch of the Blackburn family came from Yorkshire, temp. ELIZABETH, and settled at Garstang, in Lancashire.

WILLIAM BLACKBURN, an extensive Russia merchant, originally from Yorkshire, was of Thistleton, in Lancashire: he was father, with two other sons, William* and Thomas, of

RICHARD BLACKBURNE, Esq. first of Scorton Hall, near Garstang, then of Thistleton, and lastly, of Newton, all in Lancashire. He *m.* Jane, dau. of John Aynesworth, of Newton, and their 3rd son,

THOMAS BLACKBURNE, Esq. of Orford and Newton, *b.* in 1605, *m.* Margaret, dau. of Robert Norris, Esq. of Boston, and had nine daus. and seven sons: of the latter, the 2nd,

JONATHAN BLACKBURNE, Esq. of Orford, *b.* in 1646, *m.* twice, 1st, Anne, dau. of Thomas Lever, Esq., and relict of C. Lockwood, Esq. of Leeds, by whom he had three sons, Thomas; JOHN, of whom presently; and Jonathan. He *m.* 2ndly, Bridget, dau. of Thomas Bloomfield, of Little Leigh, co. Chester, and had by her four daus., Margaret, *m.* 20 July, 1686, to Thomas Patten, Esq. of Warrington; Bridget, *m.* to Henry Richmond, Esq., grandfather of Bishop Richmond; Martha, *m.* to J. Blinstone, Esq.; and Catharine, *d. s. p.* The 2nd son of the first marriage,

JOHN BLACKBURNE, Esq. of Orford Hall, became by purchase lord of the manor of Warrington. He *m.* Catharine, dau. and co-heiress of the Rev. William Ashton, B.D., rector of Prestwich, Lancashire, and by her (who *d.* in 1740) had issue,

I. THOMAS, his heir.
II. John, of Liverpool, merchant, mayor in 1760, who *m.* Dorothy, dau. of L. Barrett, Esq. of Appleby, co. Westmoreland, and had issue,
  1 JOHN, of Hawford House, co. Worcester, and of Wavertree Hall, Lancashire, lord of the manor of Garston, Lancashire, and mayor of Liverpool in 1788. He *m.* 1st, Mary, dau. of Jonathan Blundell, Esq. of Liverpool, and had an only dau. and heiress, Alice-Hannah, *m.* in 1814, to Thomas Hawkes, of Himley House, co. Worcester, M.P. for Dudley. Mr. Blackburne *m.* 2ndly, Ellinor, dau. of Matthew Stronge, Esq., mayor of Liverpool, 1768, and sister of the late Sir James Stronge, Bart. of Tynan Abbey, co. Armagh.
  2 Miles, *d. s. p.*
  3 Thomas, settled at Lynn Regis, co. Norfolk, *m.* 1st, Sarah, dau. and heiress of Thomas Steward, Esq. of Lynn, by whom he had one son, who *d.* young. He *m.* 2ndly, Lucy, dau. of the Rev. Brooke Hurlock, of Lemarsh, co. Essex, and by her had two sons, Jonathan and Thomas.
  4 Ashton, of Liverpool.
  1 Catherine, *d.* 22 Oct. 1816.
III. Jonathan, an eminent antiquary, who had a very famous collection of prints; they were sold in March, 1786.
IV. William, of Leeds, *m.* Miss Preston, of The Park, and had two sons in the East Indies.
V. Ashton. VI. James.
I. Anne, of Fairfield, near Warrington, the great naturalist and correspondent of Linnæus, *d. unm.*

The eldest son,

THOMAS BLACKBURNE, Esq. of Orford Hall, high-sheriff of Lancashire in 1763, *m.* Ireland, dau. and co-heiress of Isaac Green, Esq. of Childwall and Hale, by Mary his wife, dau. and eventual heir of Edward Aspinwall, Esq., grandson of Edward Aspinwall, Esq. of Aspinwall, and Eleanor his wife, elder sister and co-heir of Sir Gilbert Ireland, of The Hutt and Hale, lineally descended from Sir John de Ireland, *temp. Conquestoris*. Mr. Blackburne *d.* in 1768, leaving issue,

JOHN, of whom presently.
Thomas, LL.D., a magistrate for the co. of Chester, and warden of the collegiate church of Manchester. He resided at Thelwall Hall, Cheshire, and *m.* Margaret, eldest dau. of Sir Richard Brooke, Bart., and *d.* in 1823, leaving two daus., Mary, *m.* to the Rev. Peter Leigh, rector of Lymm; and Anne, *m.* to Ralph Peters, Esq., and is now living, his widow, at Southport.
Isaac, of Warrington, high-sheriff in 1803, *m.* Alicia, sole dau. and heiress of Walter Kerfoot, and *d.* in 1830.
Anne, *m.* to William Bamford, Esq. of Bamford.

Mrs. Blackburne survived her husband until 1795, when the Hale estate devolved upon her eldest son,

JOHN BLACKBURNE, Esq. of Orford Hall and Hale, F.R.S. &c., *b.* 5 Aug. 1754, high-sheriff of Lancashire in 1781, which county he represented in parliament for forty-six years. He *m.* 19 April, 1781, Anne, dau. of Samuel Rodbard, Esq. of Shepton Mallet, and had issue,

JOHN-IRELAND, present representative.
Thomas, M.A., in holy orders, rector of Prestwich, late

* William was ancestor of the BLACKBURNS *of Bridge End and Blackley Hurst*, the last of which family *m.* John Gildart, Esq., and their only child, Sophia, *m.* the Hon. Richard Jones, brother to the 5th and 6th Viscounts Ranelagh.

vicar of Eccles, co. Lancaster, *b.* 1790, Emma, dau. of Henry Hesketh, Esq. of Newton, co. Chester, and died, leaving issue.

Gilbert-Rodbard, M.A., rector of Crofton, co. York, *b.* in 1800, *m.* 31 Aug. 1832, Charlotte, eldest dau. of the late Gen. Sir Montagu Burgoyne, Bart. of Sutton Park, Bedfordshire.

Mary, *m.* to George-John Legh, Esq. of High Legh, Cheshire.

Anna, *m.* to Edwin Corbett, Esq. of Darnhall, Cheshire.

Elizabeth. Harriet.

Mr. Blackburne *d.* 11 April, 1833.

Arms—Arg., a fesse, nebulée, between three mullets, sa.
Crest—A cock, ppr., standing on a trumpet, or.
Seats—Hale Hall, and Orford Hall, near Warrington.

BLACKER OF CARRICK BLACKER.

BLACKER, WILLIAM, Esq. of Carrick Blacker, co. Armagh, M.A., lieut.-col. of the Armagh militia, J.P. and D.L., high-sheriff in 1811; *b.* 1st Sept. 1777; *m.* Nov. 1810, Anne, eldest dau. of Sir Andrew Ferguson, Bart., M.P. for Londonderry. Colonel Blacker was appointed vice-treasurer of Ireland in Jan. 1817, and held office until 1829, when he resigned. He *s.* his father in 1826.

Lineage.—CAPTAIN VALENTINE BLACKER, of Carrick, co. Armagh, *b.* in 1597, *m.* Judith, dau. of George Harrison, Esq. of Ballydorgan, co. Down, and had one son, GEORGE, and a dau. Violetta. Capt. Blacker purchased, in 1660, from Anthony Cope, Esq. of Loughall, the manor of Carrowbrack, subsequently known as Carrick-Blacker. He *d.* 17 Aug. 1677, and was interred in Seagoe church. His only son and successor,

MAJOR GEORGE BLACKER, of Carrick, a firm adherent of King WILLIAM III., *m.* Rose, dau. of Rowland Young, Esq. of Drakestown, co. Louth, and by her, who *d.* in 1689, left two sons; the younger, Robert, was ancestor of the BLACKERS *of Drogheda* and *of the co. Meath*; the elder,

WILLIAM BLACKER, Esq. of Carrick and Ballytroan, *m.* 1st, about the year 1666, Elizabeth, daughter of Col. the Hon. Robert Stewart, of Irry and Stewart Hall, in the co. of Tyrone, 3rd son of the 1st Baron Castlestewart, and by her, who *d.* 11 Jan. 1678, he had an only son, STEWART, his heir. Mr. Blacker *m.* 2ndly, late in life, Miss Mathers, and had another son,

Samuel, of Tandragee, barrister-at-law; who *m.* 29 April, 1734, Mary, dau. of Corry, of Rock Corry, co. Monaghan, and by her (who *d.* 30 Oct. 1771), he left issue,

ST. JOHN BLACKER, M.R.I.A., rector of Moira, co. Down, and afterwards prebendary of Inver, in Donegal; *b.* 28 Sept. 1743; *m.* 1st, in 1767, Grace, dau. of Maxwell Close, Esq. of Elm Park, in Armaghshire; and 2ndly, Susan, dau. of Dr. Messiter, of London. By his 1st wife he had five sons and four daus., viz.,

SAMUEL, in holy orders, LL.D., prebendary of Mullabrack, co. Armagh, *b.* 1771, *m.* 1st, Mary-Anne, dau. of David Ross, Esq. of Rosstrevor, by whom he had, with a son, Henry, who *d. s. p.*, one dau., Elizabeth, *m.* to the Rev. N. Calvert, of Hunsdon House, Herts Dr. Samuel Blacker *m.* 2ndly, Elizabeth, eldest dau. of Thomas Douglas, Esq. of Grace Hall, co. Down, and *d.* 3 Jan. 1849, leaving issue, St. John-Thomas, of Ballylongford, J.P. and D.L. for Kerry; Thomas-Samuel, of Castle Martin, co. Kildare, *m.* 1852, Frances-Mary-Anne, dau. of Thomas-A. Forde, Esq., and has issue; Theodosia, *d. unm.*; and Frances-Elizabeth, *m.* 1851, to M.-M. Blacker, Esq.; and Isabella.

Maxwell, of Dublin, Q.C., late chairman of Kilmainham, *b.* 14 March, 1773, *d. s. p.* in 1843.

William, of Armagh, *b.* 1776; M.R.I.A.; *d. s. p.* 20 Oct. 1850.

Valentine, C.B., lieut.-col. of the 1st regiment of light infantry in the E. I. Co.'s service, quartermaster-general of the Madras army, surveyor-general of India, &c., *b.* in 1778, *m.* 22 Dec. 1813, Emma, dau. of Robert Johnson, Esq. of Liverpool, and had three sons, Valentine-Samuel-Barry, in holy orders; Maxwell-Julius, in holy orders, married; and Murray-Macgregor, *m.* in 1851, Frances-Elizabeth, dau. of the Rev. Dr. Blacker, and has issue; and one dau., Emma-Louisa-Rosa. He *d.* in 1823.

St. John, lieut.-col. in the 1st regt. of Madras native infantry, *b.* 14 March, 1786, *m.* in 1828, Anne-Hammond, only child of Sir Charles Morgan, and *d.* in 1842, leaving two sons, St. John-Maxwell, lieut. 71st fusiliers, *d.* 1852; and William; and two daus., Charlotte and Isabella.

Mary.

Catherine, *m.* 1st, 10 Jan. 1804, to the Rev. Charles Barker, canon of Wells, and 2ndly, to the Rev. Robert Ball.

Grace, *m.* 6 May, 1809, to Robert Alexander, Esq., representative of the elder branch of the Caledon family; and *d.* in 1835, leaving issue.

Charlotte, *m.* 8 Dec. 1808, to Major-Gen. Munro, of Teaninich, and has issue.

William Blacker, of Carrick, was *s.* at his decease, in 1732, by his elder son,

STEWART BLACKER, Esq. of Carrick, *b.* in 1671, who *m.* in 1704, Elizabeth, dau. of the Rev. Henry Young, A.M., and niece and heiress of William Latham, Esq. of Brookend, co. Tyrone, and had issue,

I. WILLIAM, his heir.

II. Latham, *b.* 1711, *m.* Martha, dau. of Peter Beaver, Esq. of Drogheda, by whom (who *d.* in Sept. 1802) he left issue,

1 William-Latham, *m.* 1773, Mary, eldest dau. of Thomas Hamlin, Esq.; and *d.* in 1810, leaving, Latham (who took the name of HAMLIN), and other issue.

2 Henry, capt. 65th regt., *d. s. p.* in America.

3 Beaver, who *m.* in Dec. 1789, his cousin, Miss Susan Blacker, and *d.* in 1808, leaving issue,

Latham, of London, *b.* 25 Oct. 1793; who *m.* 13 April, 1820, Catherine, dau. of the Rev. George Miller, D.D., late fellow of Trinity College, Dublin, vicar-general of Armagh, and by her (who *d.* 14 Dec. 1853), has surviving issue, 1 Beaver-Henry, M.A. in holy orders, *b.* 31 May, 1821, *m.* 20 Feb. 1850, Isabella, eldest dau. of Martin-Brownly Rutherfoord, Esq. of Dublin, and by her (who *d.* 19 Dec. 1850) has an only child, Latham-Brownly Rutherfoord, *b.* 5 Dec. 1850; 2 George-Miller, *b.* 10 Aug. 1827; 3 Latham-William, *b.* 18 June, 1829, *m.* 10 Dec. 1851, Harriet-De Maine, youngest dau. of Charles Smith, Esq.; 1 Anna, *m.* 29 Dec. 1849, to Richard-Tipping Hamilton, Esq.; 2 Catherine-Georgina-Elizabeth; 3 Florinda-Martha; 4 Elizabeth-Mildred.

Susan.

Martha-Beaver, *m.* the Rev. Thos.-Blacker-Owens; and *d.* in 1830.

Frances-Anne, *m.* to John-Shaw McCulloch, Esq.

4 Latham, major 65th regt., Newent, co. Gloucester, *m.* Catherine, dau. of Col. Maddisson, of Lincolnshire; and *d.* 11 June, 1846, having had issue,

George, *d. unm.*, ensign 65th regt. 1827.

Martha, *m.* to the Rev. John Fendall, M.A.

Catherine, *m.* to Richard Onslow, Esq., son of Archdeacon Onslow.

Mary.

Theodosia, *m.* in 1832, to Frederick-John, 6th Lord Monson, who *d.* in 1841.

5 Elizabeth, *m.* to Henry Coddington, Esq., M.P., of Oldbridge, and had issue.

III. Henry, in holy orders, M.A.; *b.* 10 July, 1713; *m.* Miss Martin, and had a dau. Frances, who *d. unm.* in 1829.

IV. George, of Hallsmill, in Downshire, *b.* 26 Sept. 1718, *m.* 1st, in 1744, Mary, only surviving dau. of Joseph Nicolson, LL.D., and 2ndly, in 1746, Alicia, only child of Edward Dowdall, Esq. of Mountown, in Meath (by Alicia Haughton, relict of — Parsons, Esq., brother of Sir William Parsons, Bart., father to the Earl of Rosse), and had, with other issue, James Blacker, magistrate of Dublin, *b.* 14 Aug. 1759, who *m.* Miss Mansergh, and had, *inter alios*, the Rev. George Blacker, chaplain to the city of Dublin, and rector of Taghadoe, co. Kildare.

I. Barbara, *b.* 23 Oct. 1706, *m.* to James Twigg, Esq. of Rohan Castle, co. Tyrone.

Mr. Blacker *d.* in 1751, aged 80, and was buried at Sego. He was *s.* by his eldest son,

WILLIAM BLACKER, Esq. of Carrick and Brookend, *b.* 12 Sept. 1709. He *m.* 8 Aug. 1738, Letitia, elder dau. of Henry Cary, Esq. of Dungiven Castle, M.P. for the co. of Londonderry, and *d.* in 1783, leaving issue,

I. STEWART, his heir.

II. William, capt. 105th regt., served in the American war. He *m.* the dau. and heiress of Arthur Jacob, Esq. of Killane, co. Wexford, and had, 1 WILLIAM BLACKER, Esq. of Woodbrook, co. Wexford, whose son is the present Major Blacker, of Woodbrook (*see that family*); 2 Edward; 1 Letitia; 2 Jane; 3 Hannah; and 4 Susan.

III. Henry, a capt. in the 62nd regt., who served in the American war, and was wounded and taken prisoner with General Burgoyne, at Saratoga. He inherited from his maternal uncle, the Right Hon. Edward Cary, the house and property of Milburn, co. Derry. He *d.* 1 Sept. 1827, and was buried at Coleraine, leaving his estates to his nephew, the Rev. Richard Olpherts.

IV. George, in holy orders, who *d.* vicar of Sego, 1 May, 1810, aged 46.

I. Eliza, *b.* in 1739, *m.* Sir William Dunkin, judge of the Supreme Court of Judicature in Bengal.

II. Barbara, *m.* to Richard Olpherts, Esq. of Armagh, and had issue.

III. Martha.

IV. Alicia, *m.* in 1772, to General Sir James Stewart Denham, Bart., G.C.H.

V. Jane, *m.* to James Fleming, Esq. of Belleville, co. Cavan, and has issue.

VI. Letitia, *m.* Gen. the Hon. Edward Stopford, brother to the Earl of Courtown, and has issue.
VII. Lucinda.

The eldest son and successor,

THE VERY REV. STEWART BLACKER, of Carrick, dean of Leighlin, and latterly rector of Dumcree and vicar of Seagoe, *b.* 1740, *m.* Eliza, dau. of Sir Hugh Hill, Bart., M.P. for Londonderry, by whom, who *d.* 27 Feb. 1797, he had four sons and five daus., viz.,

I. WILLIAM, now of Carrick-Blacker.
II. George, *b.* 27 Dec. 1784, captain in the Hon. E. I. Co.'s 17th infantry, *m.* Anne, dau. of Capt. William Sloane, Royal Bengal artillery, and had issue,
  1 Stewart, A.M., barrister-at-law, *b.* 1 Jan. 1808.
  1 Eliza-Hill. 2 Hester-Anne.
  3 Sophia-Maria, *d.* 30 April, 1838.
  Capt. George Blacker *d.* 31 Aug. 1815.
III. Stewart, capt. R.N., posted in 1821, *d. unm.* 25 April, 1826.
IV. James-Stewart, A.M., in holy orders, rector of Keady, co. Armagh, *b.* 16 Feb, 1797, *m.* 30 Nov. 1824, Eliza, eldest dau. of Conyngham Gregg, Esq. of Ballymenoch, in Downshire, and dying in 1835, left issue,
  1 Stewart-Beresford, *b* in Dec. 1826.
  2 James-Conyngham, *b.* in April, 1832.
  1 Eliza. 2 Sophia.
I. Letitia, *m.* to George Studdert, Esq. of Bunrotty Castle, co. Clare, and *d.* 8 April, 1831, leaving issue.
II. Sophia, *m.* 1st, to Matthew Forde, Esq. of Seaforde, in co. Down, and 2ndly, in 1818, to William-Stewart Hamilton, Esq. of Brownhall, co. Donegal. She *d.* in June, 1829, leaving issue.
III. Eliza, who *m.* 1st, Hugh Lyons-Montgomery, Esq. of Belhavel, co. Leitrim, and of Lawrencetown, in Downshire, by whom (who was killed by a fall from his horse, 26 April, 1826) she had issue. She *m.* 2ndly, at Tours, in France, 29 Sept. 1830, Monsieur de Chomprè, Royal Cuirassiers.
IV. Louisa, *m.* to John Rea, Esq., of St. Columbs, co. Derry, by whom (who *d.* in 1832) she left, at her decease in 1815, two daus.
V. Caroline, *d. unm.* 30 April, 1828.

Dean Blacker *d.* 1 Dec. 1826, aged 86.

Arms—Arg., gutté-de-sang, a Danish warrior, armed with a battle-axe in the dexter, and a sword in the sinister hand, all ppr.
Crest—Anciently a Danish battle-axe. Latterly, the same, supported by an arm in armour, ppr.
Motto—Pro Deo et Rege.
Seat—Carrick, Portadown.

BLACKER OF WOODBROOK.

BLACKER, WILLIAM-JACOB, Esq. of Woodbrook, co. Wexford, J.P., major of the Wexford militia, and high-sheriff in 1852; *b.* in 1823; *m.* 26 May, 1849, Elizabeth, dau. of Hervey-Pratt De Montmorency, Esq. of Castle Morres, co. Kilkenny. Major Blacker is eldest son (by Anne his wife, dau. of the late Robert-Shapland Carew, Esq., M.P. for co. Wexford, and sister of Robert, Lord Carew) of the late William Blacker, Esq. of Woodbrook, who was son of Captain William Blacker, of the 105th regiment, 2nd son of William Blacker, Esq. of Carrick and Brookend, by Letitia his wife, dau. of Henry Cary, Esq. of Dungiven Castle, M.P. for co. Londonderry. (*See* BLACKER *of Carrick-Blacker*). Major Blacker has one brother, Robert-Shapland-Carew, B.A., in holy orders, and five sisters, viz., Anne, *m.* in 1848, to Sir Robert Joshua Paul, Bart.; Susan, *m.* in 1840, to the Rev. A.-L. Kirwan, dean of Limerick (son of the celebrated Dean Kirwan); Ellen-Letitia; Hannah-Dorothea; and Jane-Mary.

Arms, &c.—Same as BLACKER *of Carrick-Blacker.*
Seat—Woodbrook, co. Wexford.

BLACKETT OF WYLAM.

BLACKETT, JOHN-FENWICK-BURGOYNE, Esq. of Wylam, co. of Northumberland, *b.* in 1821; M.P. for Newcastle-on-Tyne.

Lineage.—NICHOLAS BLACKETT, Esq. of Woodcroft (4th in descent from Sir John Blackett, Knt., of Woodcroft, who fought at Agincourt), *m.* Alyson, dau. and co-heir of Sir Rowland Tempest, Knt., and one of the representatives of the noble family of Umfreville, Earls of Angus. His great-grandson,

WILLIAM BLACKETT, Esq. of Hoppyland, in the co. of

Durham, first possessed the lead mines in Durham, which have produced great wealth to the junior branches of his descendants. He had issue three sons, viz., CHRISTOPHER, his heir; Edward, whose issue is extinct; and William, M.P. for Newcastle-upon-Tyne, created a Bart. in 1673, ancestor of the present SIR EDWARD BLACKETT, Bart. of Matfen. The eldest son,

CHRISTOPHER BLACKETT, Esq. of Hoppyland, an officer in the army of King CHARLES I., *m.* Alice, dau. and sole heir of Thomas Fenwick, Esq. of Matfen, in the co. of Northumberland, and dying in 1675, left issue, WILLIAM, of Hoppyland, for many years envoy at the court of Sweden, where he *m.* the dau. of the Duc de Boys, but *d. s. p.* 25 Dec. 1695; and JOHN BLACKETT, Esq. of Hoppyland and Wylam, Northumberland, high-sheriff in 1692. He *m.* Mary, dau. and heir of Richard, son of John Errington, Esq. of Errington Hall and Beaufront, by Dorothy his wife, sister of Sir Henry Widdrington, Knt. of Widdrington Castle, and was *s.* at his decease, in 1707, aged seventy-two, by his eldest son,

JOHN BLACKETT, Esq. of Hoppyland and Wylam, high-sheriff in 1714. He *d.* in the same year, leaving, by Elizabeth his wife, dau. of John Bacon, Esq. of Staward Peel (with two daus., Isabella, *m.* to William Clavering, Esq. of Bevington; and Alice, *m.* to her cousin, Blackett Burton, Esq. of Kiverston), an only son and successor,

JOHN BLACKETT, Esq. of Wylam, high-sheriff in 1738. He *m.* 1st, Dorothy, dau. of Edward Grey, Esq., by Anne his wife, dau. of Robert Lambton, Esq., 5th son of Sir William Lambton, Knt., slain at Naseby Moor, and had four sons, JOHN, heir; Edward, an officer in the army, *d. unm.*; William, an officer in the army, *d. unm.*; and THOMAS, successor to his brother. He *m.* 2ndly, Elizabeth Crosbie, and had another son, CHRISTOPHER, who *s.* his half-brother Thomas. Mr. Blackett was *s.* at his decease, in 1769, by his eldest son,

JOHN BLACKETT, Esq. of Wylam, who *d. unm.* in 1791, and was *s.* by his next surviving brother,

THOMAS BLACKETT, Esq. of Wylam, who dying also without issue, in 1801, was *s.* by his half-brother,

CHRISTOPHER BLACKETT, Esq. of Wylam, who *m.* Alice, dau. of William Ingham, Esq., and had issue,

CHRISTOPHER, late of Wylam.
William-Fenwick, who *m.* Catherine-Porterfield, dau. of Robert Stewart, Esq. of St. Fort, co. Fife, and has issue.
John-Alexander, in holy orders, vicar of Heddon-on-the-Wall, Northumberland, *m.* Annie, only child of Lieut.-Col. Hamilton, by Anne his wife, eldest sister of William Ord, Esq. of Whitfield Hall.
Alice, *m.* to Anthony Surtees, Esq. of Hamsterley Hall, co. Durham, and *d.* in 1827.
Elizabeth. Dorothy-Christian.

Mr. Blackett *d.* 25 Jan. 1829, and was *s.* by his son,

CHRISTOPHER BLACKETT, Esq. of Wylam, formerly capt. 18th hussars, and M.P. for South Northumberland; *b.* 22 June, 1788; who *m.* 15 Aug. 1818, Elizabeth-Younge, dau. and co-heir of Montagu Burgoyne, Esq., younger son of Sir Roger Burgoyne, Bart.; by this lady (who *d.* 29 March, 1833) Mr. Blackett had issue,

JOHN-FENWICK-BURGOYNE, now of Wylam.
Edward-Algernon, R.N.; *m.* 25 May, 1852, Lucy, dau. of the Rev. T. Minchin.
Montagu. Frances-Mary.

Arms—Arg., on a chevron between three mullets, pierced, sa., three escallops of the field.
Crest—A hawk's head, erased, ppr.
Motto—Nous travaillerons dans l'espérance.
Seat—Wylam, Newcastle-on-Tyne.

BLAGRAVE OF CALCOT PARK.

BLAGRAVE, JOHN, Esq. of Calcot Park, Berks, J.P. and D.L., col. of the Berkshire militia, *b.* 14 March, 1781; *m.* 1st, Sept. 1827, Mary-Anne, dau. of Henry Parsons, Esq., and relict of the Rev. Matthew Robinson, brother of Lord Rokeby; and 2ndly, 30 Nov. 1841, Georgiana, dau. of the late Sir William Rowley, of Tendring Hall, co. Suffolk, Bart.

Lineage.—JOHN BLAGRAVE, Esq. of Highworth, who *m.* Agnes, dau. of John Kibblewhite, Esq. of South Fawley, co. Berks (living 12th HENRY VII., and aunt of Sir Thomas Whyte, lord-mayor in 1554, founder of St. John's College, Oxford) was father of THOMAS BLAGRAVE, Esq. of Watchfield, whose son, Thomas Blagrave, of Shrivenham, had a son, GEORGE BLAGRAVE, living 1594, who was great-great-grandfather of

JOHN BLAGRAVE, Esq. of Watchfield, who m. in 1723, Anne Hussey, and had an only son and heir,

THOMAS BLAGRAVE, Esq. of Watchfield, who m. Catherine, only dau. and eventual heiress (through the death s. p. of her three brothers) of Charles Garrard, Esq. of Kingwood, by Mary his wife, only child and heir of Edward Batten, Esq. of Lambourn Woodlands, co. Berks. By this lady he had (with two daus., Catherine, m. to Samuel Pococke, Esq. of Beanham, co. Berks, and Agnes-Anne) an only son and heir,

JOHN BLAGRAVE, Esq. of Watchfield, parish of Shrivenham, who m. in 1778 or 1779, Frances, eldest dau. and co-heir of Anthony Blagrave, son and heir of Anthony Blagrave, Esq. of Southcot, and grandson of John Blagrave, Esq. of Reading, M.P. by Hester his wife, dau. of Wm. Gore, Esq. of Barrow. By her had surviving issue,

JOHN, now of Calcot Park.
Anthony, m. Mrs. Dayley, dau. of — Yates, Esq., and has issue a son, John-Henry, and a dau., Frances-Anna-Byam, m. to the Rev. George Bingham, of Dorsetshire.
James.
Charles-George, in the civil service of the E. I. Co., m. a dau. of — Colvin, Esq., and has issue, Charles-Alexander, b. 17 June, 1816; Thomas-Colvin, b. 25 March, 1818; two other sons and five daus., Elizabeth-Helen-Russel, Jean-Maria-Ann, Frances-Elizabeth-Colvin, Catherine-Calverly, and another.
Catherine, m. to Sir Robert Pocklington, Knt. of Chilsworth, co. Suffolk.
Eliza-Agnes, m. in 1820, to the Rev. Martin-Joseph Routh, D.D., President of Magdalen College, Oxon.
Anne, m. to the Rev. Henry Pole, son of Sir Charles Pole, Bart.
Agnes. Harriet.
Charlotte, m. to Job Hanmer, Esq. of Holbroke Hall, co. Suffolk.

Mr. Blagrave d. 28 Feb. 1827.

Arms—Or, on a bend, sa., three legs in armour, couped at the thigh, and erased at the ancle, ppr.
Crest—A falcon, ppr., belled, or. (*Another crest*—An oak tree, eradicated, ppr. *Another*—Three palm branches, ppr).
Motto—Pro marte et arte.
Seat—Calcot Park, co. Berks.

BLAIR OF BLAIR.

BLAIR, WILLIAM-FORDYCE, Esq. of Blair, co. Ayr, J.P. and D.L., captain R.N., b. 10 Sept. 1807; m. 23 July, 1840, Caroline-Isabella, youngest dau. of the late John Sprot, Esq. of London, and sister of Mark Sprot, of Riddell, and has issue,

I. WILLIAM-AUGUSTUS, b. 24 June, 1843.
II. Frederick-Gordon, b. 11 Nov. 1852.
I. Mary. II. Caroline-Madelina.

Lineage.—The BLAIRS *of Blair*, connected by intermarriages with the first families in the west of Scotland, have maintained, for upwards of six centuries, a high position in the co. of Ayr. They claim the chiefship of all the Blairs in the south and west of Scotland; but the BLAIRS *of Balthyock*, settled in the counties of Fife, Perth, and Angus, dispute the honour with them. JAMES VI., to whom the point was referred, determined that "the oldest man, for the time being, of either family, should have the precedency." Both families appear to be equally ancient, but the belief that they spring from the same ancestry is extremely doubtful, their arms bearing no affinity.

So far back as 1205, William de Blair occurs in a contract between Ralph de Eglinton and the town of Irvine. His grandson, SIR BRYCE BLAIR, of Blair, was one of the patriots associated with Wallace, in defence of the liberties of Scotland; and in more recent times, the troublous period of the great civil war, another Sir Bryce Blair, of Blair, adhered with unshaken loyalty to King CHARLES I., by whom he was knighted.

MADALENE BLAIR, (the eventual heiress of this eminent house, only dau. of William Blair, of Blair, son and heir of William Blair, of Blair, by the Lady Margaret Hamilton, his wife, dau. of William, 2nd Duke of Hamilton), m. William Scott, Esq., advocate, second son of John Scott, Esq. of Malleny, in Midlothian, (an ancient branch of Buccleuch), and had a son, WILLIAM, her heir. The heiress of Blair d. probably before the year 1715, and Mr. Scott, her widower, who had assumed the surname of BLAIR, m. 2ndly, Catherine, only dau. of Alexander Tait, of Edinburgh, merchant, and had by her five sons and six daus.; viz., 1 HAMILTON, heir to his half-brother; 2 Alexander, surveyor of the customs at Port Glasgow, m. Elizabeth, only dau. of John Hamilton, Esq. of Grange, and had issue; 3 John, captain of infantry, killed at Minden, in 1759; 4 Thomas, cornet in the Scots Greys, killed at the battle of Vald, in 1747; 5 William, an officer, slain at Oswego, in India, in 1756; 1 Ann, m. to David Blair, Esq. of Adamton; 2 Madaline, m. to Sir William Maxwell, Bart. of Monreith; 3 Janet, m. to Alexander Tait, Esq., one of the principal clerks of session; Barbara, m. to William Fullarton, Esq. of that ilk; 5 Catherine, d. unm.; 6 Mary, m. to Sir John Sinclair, Bart, of Stevenston. Madalene Blair was s. at her decease by her son,

WILLIAM BLAIR, Esq. of Blair, who d. unm. in 1732, and was s. by his half-brother,

HAMILTON BLAIR, Esq. major, Scots Greys. He m. Jane, dau. of Sydenham Williams, Esq. of Herringston, co. Dorset, and dying in 1782, left (with two daus., Agatha, m. to Lieut.-General Avarne; and Jane, m. to Robert Williams, Esq. of Cerne Abbas, co. Dorset) a son and successor,

WILLIAM BLAIR, Esq. of Blair, M.P. for Ayrshire. He m. Madalene, dau. of the late John Fordyce, Esq. of Ayton, co. Berwick, and by her, who d. in 1817, had

Hamilton, capt. R.N., d. 21 May, 1816.
John-Charles, capt. R.N., d. 6 July, 1836.
WILLIAM-FORDYCE, present representative.
Henry-Melville, lieut. R.N., d. 18 July, 1837.
Augustus, capt. Scotch fusiliers.
Catharine, m. to Matthew Fortescue, Esq. of Stephenstown, co. Louth, and d. 17 Dec. 1847.
Madaline, m. to Alexander Scot, Esq. of Trinity, Midlothian.
Louisa, m. to Colonel Jackson, of Enniscoe, co. Mayo.
Elizabeth. Charlotte.
Jane-Gordon, d. in 1829.
Georgiana, m. to James Hamilton, Esq. of Cornacassa, co. Monaghan.

Col. Blair d. 21 Oct. 1841.

Arms—Quarterly: 1st and 4th, arg., on a saltier, sa., nine mascles, of the field, for BLAIR; 2nd and 3rd, or, on a bend, az., a star between two crescents, of the field, and in base an arrow, bend-wise, ppr., feathered, headed, and barbed, arg., for SCOTT.
Crest—A stag, lodged, ppr.
Motto—Amo probos.
Seat—Blair, near Dalry.

BLAIR OF BALTHAYOCK.

BLAIR, NEIL-JAMES-FERGUSSON, Esq. of Balthayock, co. Perth, J.P., b. 9 June, 1814.

Lineage.—ALEXANDER DE BLAIR, who lived in the reigns of WILLIAM the Lion, and his son, ALEXANDER II. m. Ela, dau. of Hugh de Nyden, of that ilk, and d. in 1230, leaving a son, SIR WILLIAM DE BLAIR, who was Steward of Fife, and was knighted by King ALEXANDER II. He was s. by his son, SIR ALEXANDER BLAIR, whose son and heir, (by Helen his wife, sister of Sir William Ramsay), JOHN BLAIR, was father of DAVID DE BLAIR, who d. in the reign of King DAVID, leaving two sons, Thomas, the younger, ancestor of the BLAIRS *of Ardblair*; and the elder, his heir,

PATRICK DE BLAIR, the first designed of Balthayock. From this Patrick, who was living in 1370, derived the distinguished family of BLAIR *of Balthayock*, and its offshoots, the BLAIRS settled in France, the BLAIRS of *Pittendreich, Glascuney, Balmyle, &c.*

MARGARET BLAIR, of Balthayock, (only dau. and heir of John Blair, of Balthayock, son of Sir Alexander Blair, of Balthayock, by Elizabeth his wife, only child of Thomas Fotheringham, of Powrie), m. in 1723, David Drummond, (son of David Drummond, advocate), who, upon his marriage, assumed the name and arms of BLAIR. He d. in 1728, leaving by the said Margaret, a son and successor,

JOHN BLAIR, of Balthyock, who m. Patricia, dau. of John Stevens, Esq. of Edinburgh, and had issue a son, David, and five daus., of whom the oldest dau.

MARGARET BLAIR, m. Major Johnston, and had an only dau. and heir,

JEMIMA JOHNSTON, who became representative of the family of BLAIR *of Balthayock*, and m. 26 Nov. 1811, Adam Fergusson, Esq.,* and had issue, NEIL-JAMES, now of Balthayock; Adam; David; John; James; George; and Robert.

Arms—Arg., a chevron, sa., between three tortoises, gu.
Crest—A dove with wings expanded, ppr.
Motto—Virtute tutus.
Seat—Balthayock, co. Perth.

* Mr. Fergusson m. 2ndly, Jessy, eldest dau. of the late M. Tower, of Aberdeen, merchant.

BLAKE OF HORSTEAD.

BLAKE, THOMAS, Esq. of Horstead, co. Norfolk, LL.D., J.P. and D.L., *b.* 13 March, 1790.

Lineage.—This family, supposed to have come from Wilts, shortly previous to the civil war, *temp.* CHARLES I., have been resident for several generations at Bunwell and at Scottow, in Norfolk.

ROBERT BLAKE, *b.* in 1655, (4th son of John Blake, Gent. of Bunwell, by Anne his wife, dau. of Thomas Welbee; and grandson of John Blake, who was admitted to copy-hold lands in Bunwell, A.D. 1638) settled at Scottow, where he erected a good house. He *m.* in 1681, Margaret, eldest dau. of William Durrant, Esq. of Scottow, (ancestor of the Durrants, Barts.) and *d.* in Dec. 1729, leaving two sons, Robert and THOMAS, of whom the younger,

THOMAS BLAKE, *b.* in 1689, *s.* his father at Scottow. He *m.* Elizabeth, dau. of John Jex, Esq. of Lowestoft, and Mary his wife, dau. and co-heir of William Coulson, of Swanton Abbots, and had two sons, THOMAS, and William, of Swanton Abbots, who *d. s. p.* Mr. Blake *d.* in Aug. 1755, and was *s.* by his elder son,

THOMAS BLAKE, Esq. of Scottow, *b.* 18 June, 1726, who *m.* Judith, dau. of William Clarke, Esq. of Loddon, and *d.* 26 June, 1806, leaving two sons,

THOMAS, his heir.
William, to whom his uncle William bequeathed the estate of Swanton Abbots, and who assumed (by sign-manual, dated 17 Aug. 1837) the additional surname and arms of JEX. (*See* JEX-BLAKE *of Swanton Abbots.*)

The elder son and heir,

THOMAS BLAKE, Esq., barrister-at-law, of Scottow, J.P. and D.L. for co. Norfolk, *b.* 22 June, 1755, *m.* 1st, Margaret, only child of the Rev. Thomas Weston, rector of Cookeley and Halesworth, co. Suffolk; and 2ndly, Theodora-Martha, dau. of David Colombine, Esq. of Norwich, (descended from an ancient family of Dauphiny, from whence his grandfather, a physician, withdrew after the revocation of the edict of Nantes, in 1685, and settled at Norwich). By the latter lady only (who *d.* 28 July, 1801) Mr. Blake had issue,

I. THOMAS, now of Horstead.
II. Robert, *b.* 23 Nov. 1795, of Swafield, and Wroxham House, co. Norfolk, J.P., an officer in the army, severely wounded, and lost his leg in action near Bayonne, 13 Dec. 1813. He assumed, by royal sign-manual, 10 Aug. 1847, the additional surname and arms of HUMFREY. He *m.* Charlotte, youngest dau. of Lieut.-Colonel Harvey, of Thorpe Lodge, near Norwich, and has issue,
   1 Robert-Harvey, *b.* 28 Jan. 1843.
   2 Thomas, *b.* 3 March, 1844.
   3 John, *b.* 23 Jan. 1847.
   1 Margaret. 2 Eleanor.
III. Henry-William, *b.* 22 Dec. 1798, in holy orders, rector of Thurning, co. Norfolk, late fellow of Corpus Christi College, *m.* 1st, Louisa, only dau. of the Rev. Charles Day, of Horsford, and granddau. of Lieut.-Col. Harvey, of Thorpe Lodge, and by her (who *d.* 11 March, 1845) had surviving issue, Henry, *b.* 4 Jan. 1843. He *m.* 2ndly, Mary, dau. of Major Heitland, of the Bengal artillery.
IV. Francis-John, of Norwich, *b.* 31 March, 1801, *m.* Sarah, eldest dau. of the Rev. George Norris, of Woodnorton, co. Norfolk, and by her (who *d.* 30 July, 1827) has two daus., Frances and Susanna-Margaret.
I. Theodora Martha, *m.* to the Rev. Robert-Fountaine Elwin, rector of Wilby and Hargham, Norfolk.
II. Maria-Margaret, *m.* the Rev. George Howes, rector of Spixworth, co. Norfolk, and vicar of Gaseley, co. Suffolk, and *d.* 11 Feb. 1829, leaving issue, a son, Frederick Howes.
III. Judith-Elizabeth.

Mr. Blake *d.* 27 Sept. 1813.

Seat—Horstead, Norfolk.

BLAKE OF SWANTON ABBOTS.

See JEX-BLAKE OF SWANTON ABBOTS.

BLAKE OF RENVYLE.

BLAKE, HENRY, Esq. of Renvyle, co. Galway, J.P., *b.* 18 Nov. 1789; *m.* 22 Dec. 1810, Martha-Louisa, dau. of Joseph Attersoll, Esq. of Portland Place, London, and has issue,

I. EDGAR-HENRY, lieut. R.N., *b.* 19 Dec. 1834.

II. Harold-Henry, *b.* 1 July, 1817.
III. Ethelbert-Henry, M.D., in the 98th regiment, *b.* Dec. 1818, *m.* Oct. 1849, Jane-Caroline, dau. of Dr. Hay, E.I.C.S.
IV. Egbert-Henry, royal engineers, *b.* 15 Sept. 1821, lost in the wreck of the "Solway," April, 1843.
V. Ethelred-Henry, *d.* 1838, aged 14.
VI. Ethelstane-Henry, *b.* 3 April, 1826.
VII. Herbert-Henry, *b.* 4 May, 1828.
I. Emelie-Anna. II. Eleanor-Elizabeth.

Mr. Blake is a magistrate for the counties of Galway and Mayo.

Lineage.—RICHARD CADDLE *alias* BLAKE, sheriff of Connaught in 1306, was the ancestor of the many noble families of the name in Ireland, and of the BLAKES *of Langham, co. Suffolk, and Twisel Castle, co. Durham,* both English baronets.

The remarkable petition presented by John Blake *alias* Caddle, eldest and lineal descendant of Richard Caddle *alias* Blake, sheriff of Connaught, 1306, to the Commissioners of Plantation in Connaught, 1640, and the commissioners' report thereon, with other family documents, satisfactorily prove the origin and descent of this old family from their first coming to Connaught down to the present HENRY BLAKE, of Renvyle, who is the head of this ancient family.

RICHARD CADDLE, *alias* BLAKE, purchased several manors from Thomas Stobridge, in 1315, in addition to which he got grants in the reigns of EDWARD I. and II. He had four sons, Walter; John; Thomas-Niger; and Valentine.

WALTER, eldest son of Richard, got a grant of the customs of Galway; he had five sons, John; Henry, attainted for joining the rebellion of the De Burghs; Nicholas; Walter; and William Fitz Walter Fitz Richard, from whom Lord Wallscourt and the BLAKES *of Ballinafad* are descended.

JOHN-OGE BLAKE, eldest son of Walter, *m.* Margaret, dau. of Philip Le Brun, of Athenry, by whom he had three sons, Henry; Walter; and Geoffrey. In the 13th of RICHARD II., divers lands about Athenry were granted to John and Henry, his heirs. John *d.* 1420, and was *s.* by his eldest son,

HENRY-FITZ JOHN, who *m.* Mary, dau. of Bermingham of Athenry, and had five sons, John; Nicholas; Thomas; Walter; and Richard. He got a grant of land in the co. Galway, 2nd HENRY VI. This Henry and several members of the Blake family, in 1435, joined in giving grants to the church of Saint Nicholas, Galway, and subsequently, in 1445, they had an amicable division of their landed possessions.

JOHN BLAKE, eldest son of Henry, *m.*, and had two sons, Valentine and William, and a dau. Julian, *m.* to Peter Lynch. He *d.* in 1468, and was *s.* by his son and heir,

VALENTINE BLAKE, who *m.* Julian, dau. of Geoffrey Lynch, by whom he had, John, his heir; Valentine; Thomas, ancestor of the BLAKES *of Menlough* (Barts.) *Towerhill, and Drum;* William; and Annestasia, *m.* to William Browne, of Galway. He *d.* 1499, and was *s.* by

JOHN BLAKE, his eldest son, who *m.* Evelina Skerret, and had, Nicholas, his heir; Richard, ancestor of the BLAKES *of Kiltullagh* (now Frenchfort), and of the BLAKES *of Cregg Castle;* and John-Fitz-John; with a dau. Julian, *m.* to Bodkin. The eldest son,

NICHOLAS BLAKE, mayor of Galway, 1555, *m.* 1st, Gennet, dau. of James Ffrench, and 2ndly, 1556, Celia, dau. of Walter Lynch, by whom he had, John, his heir, and a dau., Evelina. He *d.* in 1564, and was *s.* by

JOHN BLAKE, who *m.* Celia Skerret, and had, Nicholas, and Walter-FitzJohn: he *d.* 1578, and was *s.* by his son,

NICHOLAS BLAKE, mayor of Galway, 1564, who *m.* Julian, dau. of Valentine Ffrench, and had, JOHN, his heir; Martin; James; Nicholas; and Mary. He *d.* 1622, and was *s.* by his eldest son,

JOHN BLAKE, who *m.* Mary Ffrench, and was mayor of Galway, 1646: in 1640 he presented a petition to the Commissioners of the Plantation of Connaught, accompanied by his pedigree and other ancient documents, upon which they certified that he was the lineal and eldest descendant of Richard Caddle, *alias* Blake, sheriff of Connaught, 1306, and awarded him the claimed properties. He had, Thomas, his heir; John; Nicholas; and Henry (John went to Montserrat, Nicholas and Henry to Barbadoes) and a dau. Catherine.

THOMAS BLAKE, (eldest son of John,) of Mullaghmore and Windfield, *m.* Mary, eldest dau. of Nicholas Blake, of Kiltullagh, in 1658, and had, JOHN, his heir; Nicholas;

Catherine; Julian, *m.* to Philip Butler; and Mary, *m.* to Bartly-Lynch Fitz Ambrose. The eldest son,

JOHN BLAKE, *m.* Julian Lynch, and had, with other issue, Thomas, his heir; and Marcus (whose eldest son, Valentine, became the head of the Blake family on the death of the three sons of Thomas Blake without issue, while John, his 2nd son, came into the possession of the Mullaghmore and Windfield estates under the will of his first-cousin John Blake, of Windfield).

THOMAS BLAKE, eldest son of John, *m.* Anne, dau. of John Bodkin, of Annagh, by his 1st wife, Miss Browne, of Coolarn, by whom he had, John, his heir; Martin; and Marcus, neither of whom had a family; Mary, *m.* Michael Browne, of Cloonkeely and Moyne; Ellen, *m.* James Kelly; Bridget, *m.* Andrew Concannon; Catherine, *m.* — McDermot; and Margaret, *m.* — FitzMaurice. The eldest son,

JOHN BLAKE, *s.* to his father's extensive estates; he *m.* Miss Kirwan, of Cregg. He *d. s. p.* in 1789. His uncle, MARK BLAKE, Esq. of Renvyle, *m.* Miss French, of Carrorea, co. Galway, and had, with other issue, of which one dau. *m.* George Davies, Esq. of Martinstown, co. Roscommon, and another *m.* George Taaffe, Esq. of Strokestown, two sons,

I. VALENTINE, his heir.
II. John, of Winfield, J.P., who *m.* Mary, dau. of Christopher Bowen, Esq. of Hollymount, co. Mayo, a branch of BOWEN *of Bowen's Court*, and *d.* in 1812, leaving issue,
 1 Christopher-John, of Winfield, who *m.* Elizabeth, dau. of John Burke, Esq. of St. Cleran's, and *d.* 14 March, 1820, leaving a son, John Bowen, who *d.* in minority in 1823, and two daus., Elizabeth, and Maria.
 2 Henry-Martin, of The Heath, co. Mayo, *b.* in 1796, who *m.* twice: by his first wife he has a son, John, *b.* in 1816; and by his second, Nichola-Frances-Charlotta, 3rd dau. of Robert French, Esq. of Monivae Castle, co. Galway, he has several children.
 1 Anna-Maria, *m.* to William-M. Burke, Esq. of Ballydugan, co. Galway. (*See that family.*)

The elder son,

VALENTINE BLAKE, Esq. of Lehinch and Renvyle, high-sheriff of Mayo, *m.* in 1788, Anna-Maria, dau. of the Hon. and Rev. Richard Henry Roper, of Clones, son of Henry, 8th Lord Teynham, by Anne, Baroness Dacre, his wife; and by her, who *m.* 2ndly, James Shuttleworth, Esq. of Barton Lodge, co. Lancaster, he had two sons, HENRY, now of Renvyle, and Marcus, who *d.* young; and three daus., Jane-Maria, *d. unm.*, 1815; Caroline, *d. unm.*, 1812; and Julia-Frances, *m.* to the Rev. Henry Burke, a younger son of the late Michael Burke, Esq. of Ballydugan. Mr. Blake *d.* in 1800.

Arms—Arg., a fret, gu.
Crest—A mountain-cat, passant, ppr.
Motto—Virtus sola nobilitat.
Seat—Renvyle, co. Galway.

BLAKE OF BALLYGLUNIN.

BLAKE, MARTIN-JOSEPH, Esq. of Ballyglunin Park, co. Galway, M.P. for the town of that name since 1833, is representative of a branch of the family of BLAKE *of Langham*, co. Suffolk.

Arms—Arg., a fret, gu.
Crest—A mountain-cat, passant, ppr.
Motto—Virtus sola nobilitat.
Seat—Ballyglunin Park, Athenry.

BLAKE OF TOWERHILL.

BLAKE, VALENTINE-O'CONNOR, Esq. of Towerhill, co. Mayo, and Bunown Castle, co. Galway, J.P. and D.L., high-sheriff of Mayo in 1839; *m.* in 1836, the Hon. Margaret-Mary, only dau. of Charles, Lord Ffrench, and has issue,

I. Maurice. II. Charles. III. Valentine.
IV. Robert. V. Thomas. VI. Martin-Joseph.
I. Mary. II. Margaret.

Lineage.—RICHARD CADDLE *alias* BLAKE, sheriff of Connaught in 1305-6, was ancestor of the BLAKES *of Connaught*, and of the BLAKES *of Langham*, in Suffolk, and of the BLAKES *of Twisel Castle*, co. Durham, both English Baronets.

From William, 5th son of Walter, eldest son of the above Richard, was descended the distinguished patriot Sir Richard Blake of Ardfry, ancestor to the Lords Wallscourt; while Thomas, 3rd son of Valentine, sixth in descent from the first Richard, was the founder of the BLAKES *of Menlo Castle*, Irish baronets, from whom the BLAKES *of Towerhill* are more immediately descended.

SIR VALENTINE BLAKE, of Menlo Castle, 3rd baronet, *m.* Elinor, dau. of Sir Henry Lynch, of Castle Carra, co. Mayo, Bart., and had four sons and several daus.,

Thomas (Sir), his heir.
Henry, whose descendants *s.* to the Baronetcy on the failure of male issue of the elder branch.
Francis, who left no family.
JOHN.

The 4th son,

JOHN BLAKE, was the founder of the Towerhill branch of the Blake family: he was an active and brave supporter of the cause of CHARLES II., and was rewarded for his services by grants of land in the counties of Galway, Mayo, and Clare. His attachment to the STUARTS induced him a second time to take up arms in their behalf, and he lost his life while leading his regiment against the besiegers of Athlone (1691), leaving an only son (by his wife Miss Lynch, of Drimcong) then under age,

ISIDORE BLAKE, father of

MAURICE BLAKE, of Towerhill, who *m.* his cousin Anne, dau. of Sir Walter Blake, of Menlo Castle, and had a numerous family: his eldest son,

ISIDORE BLAKE, Esq. of Oldhead and Towerhill, co. Mayo, *m.* Fanny, one of the three co-heiresses of R. Rutledge, of Bloomfield, co. Mayo (the 2nd Miss Rutledge *m.* Anthony Ormsby, Esq. of Ballinamore, co. Mayo; and the 3rd, *m.* William Bermingham, of Rosshill, and was mother of the Ladies Charlemont and Leitrim, co-heiresses). Isidore left six sons and four daus., viz.,

I. MAURICE, his heir.
II. Thomas, of Lakeview, *m.* Margaret Dowell, and had, Isidore, his heir; Edward, of Castlemoyle, co. Galway, *m.* Margaret, only dau. of John Nolan, Esq. of Ballinderry; Patrick; Fanny; and Elizabeth.
III. John, of Weston, *m.* Charlotte Blake, of Corbally, and has, Isidore-John, his heir, and other children.
IV. Peter, of Ballylahan, co. Mayo, *m.* Mary Mc Loughlin, and had, Isidore, his heir, and several children.
V. Anthony, of Dublin, *m.* Rebecca Skerrett, and left, Joseph, his heir (who *m.* his cousin, Miss Lynch, of Peterburgh), and a dau.
VI. Isidore, *m.* Anne Coleman, and has, Isidore and Anthony, and three daus.
I. Mary, *m.* Arthur Lynch, Esq. of Cloughballymore, by whom she had one son and several daus., all of whom, with the exception of Anne, *m.* to Maurice Blake, Esq. of Ballinafad, died young.
II. Anne, *m.* to Joseph Burke, Esq. of Carrow Keel.
III. Catherine, *m.* to Daniel Jones, Esq. of Banada, and had one dau.
IV. Fanny, *m.* to Arthur Lynch, Esq. of Peterburgh, and was mother of the present Charles Lynch, of Peterburgh.

The eldest son,

MAURICE BLAKE, Esq. of Towerhill, major of the North Mayo militia, and a magistrate for that county, *m.* Maria, only dau. of Valentine-O'Connor, of Dublin, and of Oakley Park, Blackrock, and had, VALENTINE O'CONNOR, present proprietor; Mary, who *m.* the late O'Connor Don, many years M.P. for the co. Roscommon; and Honoria, *m.* to Edward, brother of the O'Connor Don.

Arms—Arg., a fret, gu.
Crest—A mountain-cat, passant, ppr.
Motto—Virtus sola nobilitat.
Seats—Towerhill, Ballyglass, co. Mayo; and Bunown Castle, Clifden, co. Galway.

BLAKE OF CREGG CASTLE.

BLAKE, FRANCIS, Esq. of Cregg Castle, co. Galway, J.P., *b.* 7 Feb. 1789; *m.* 19 Jan. 1819, Georgina-Elizabeth, dau. of Richard Burke, Esq. of Glinsk, and has issue,

I. JAMES, *b.* 27 Dec. 1822, *m.* 12 Aug. 1851, Helena, dau. of Arthur French, Esq. of French Park.
II. John, *b.* 4 Oct. 1826.
III. Henry, *b.* 28 March, 1828.
IV. Richard, *b.* 18 Aug. 1829.
V. Francis, *b.* 18 Sept. 1835.
I. Jane, *m.* to Pierce Joyce, Esq. of Merview.
II. Johanna. III. Georgina. IV. Fanny.
V. Mary.

Lineage.—FRANCIS BLAKE, Esq., son of NICHOLAS BLAKE, Esq., and a descendant of the ancient family of

BLAKE of *Kiltulla*, co. Galway, *m.* Julia Tierny, and had two sons, Henry and

JAMES BLAKE, Esq. of Cregg Castle, who *m.* 16 June, 1787, Jane, only sister of Walter Joyce, Esq. of Merview, and had, with three sons, Henry, Pierce-Joseph, and Walter, and a dau., Mary, wife of James MacDermott, Esq. of Ramore, another son, the present FRANCIS BLAKE, Esq. of Cregg Castle.

Arms—Arg., a fret, gu.
Crest—A cat-a-mountain, ppr.
Motto—Virtus sola nobilitat.
Seat—Cregg Castle, co. Galway.

BLAKE OF FURBOUGH.

BLAKE, ANDREW-WILLIAM, Esq. of Furbough, co. Galway, J.P. and D.L., high-sheriff in 1841, *b.* 22 Aug. 1798; *m.* 26 Sept. 1832, Maria, 2nd dau. of Malachy Daly, Esq. of Raford, co. Galway, by Julia his wife, dau. of the late Sir Thomas Burke, of Marble Hill, Bart., and sister of the late Countess of Clanricarde, and has issue,

I. JOHN-ARCHER DALY, of Raford, *b.* 11 Jan. 1835, for whom the royal license was obtained, 24 April, 1837, to bear the name and arms of DALY only, in accordance with the testamentary injunction of his grand-uncle Hyacinth Daly, Esq. of Raford.
II. Malachy-Joseph, *b.* 5 Feb. 1836.
III. Andrew-William, *b.* 2 June, 1842.
I. Julia-Maria, *d. unm.*, 28 March, 1854.
II. Elizabeth-Anne. III. Emily-Margaret.
IV. Charlotte-Frances. V. Annabelle.

Lineage.—This is another branch of the ancient and eminent family of Blake.

ANDREW BLAKE, Esq. of Furbough, only son of John Blake, Esq., by his wife Sarah French, of Aggard, co. Galway, *m.* Honora, dau. of Michael Burke, Esq. of Ballydugan; and had, with a son, Andrew, a captain in the 88th foot, killed at the battle of Talavera, an elder son and successor,

COLONEL JOHN BLAKE, of Furbough, who *m.* in 1797, Maria-Eliza Blake, and by her (who *d.* Feb. 1849) had issue, viz.,

ANDREW-WILLIAM, present representative.
Edmond. John-Henry.

Col. Blake *d.* 8 Oct. 1836.

Arms—Arg., a fret, gu.
Crest—A cat, passant-guardant, ppr.
Motto—Virtus sola nobilitat.
Seat—Furbough, co. Galway.

BLAKE OF MERLIN PARK.

BLAKE, CHARLES, Esq. late of Merlin Park, co. Galway, J.P. and D.L., *m.* 7 May, 1839, Dorothea, only dau. of Thomas Ormsby, Esq. of Cummin House, co. Sligo, and has issue a son and heir, *b.* 28 March, 1840.

Lineage.—This is a branch of the great house of BLAKE founded in Ireland by Richard Blake, a soldier of fortune, who accompanied Prince John to that kingdom in 1185, and having obtained considerable grants of land in the counties of Galway and Mayo, settled there.

CHARLES BLAKE, Esq. of Merlin Park, co. Mayo, *m.* Margaret Daly, of the family of DALY *of Raford*, and had, with a son Dennis, and a dau. Frances, an elder son,

CHARLES BLAKE, Esq. of Merlin Park, who *m.* Georgina, dau. and co-heir (with her sister Anne, wife of Samuel Poer, Esq. of Belleville Park, co. Waterford) of Sir George Browne, of The Neale, co. Mayo, Bart., by Anastatia his wife, eldest dau. of Denis Daly, Esq. of Raford, and had issue,

CHARLES, of Merlin Park, as above.
Denis-John, who *m.* in April, 1831, the eldest dau. of Samuel Poer, Esq. of Belleville Park, co. Waterford, and has issue a son and a dau.
Martin, who *m.* the only dau. of the late John Blake, Esq. of Tuam, uncle to the present Joseph Blake, Esq. of Brook Lodge, co. Galway, M.P., and has issue two sons and two dans.
Margaret, *m.* to George Kirwan, Esq. of Dalgin Park, co. Mayo.
Georgina, *m.* to Walter Lawrence, Esq. of Bellevue, co. Galway.
Frances.

Arms—Arg., a fret, gu.
Crest—A cat-a-mountain, ppr.
Motto—Virtus sola nobilitat.
Seat—Merlin Park, co. Galway.

BLAKE OF KILTULLAGH AND FRENCHFORT.

BLAKE, THEOBALD-MICHAEL, Esq. of Kiltullagh and Frenchfort, *b.* Jan. 1829; *m.* Nov. 1854, Elizabeth, dau. and heir of James Blake, Esq. of Vermont, co. Galway.

Lineage.—This is another branch of the Blake family, descended from Richard Caddle, *alias* Blake, sheriff of Connaught in 1306; but more immediately from Richard, second son of John Blake (sixth in descent from the founder), by his wife Eveline Skerrett. Richard-FitzJohn filled the office of mayor of Galway in 1533. On a division of the property (between the Blakes), the castle of Kiltullagh and some of the adjoining townlands fell to the lot of Richard. This was part of the estate purchased by Richard Caddle, *alias* Blake, from Thomas Hobridge, in 1315.

The castle of Kiltullagh was built by a person of the name of McWelycke, whose grandson, John McWelycke, in 1553, filed a bill in Chancery against Richard and Nicolas Blake, seeking compensation for the loss his grandfather sustained in building the castle of Kiltullagh. The Lord Chancellor, Sir Thomas Cusack, ordered Richard Blake to pay to complainant, John McWelycke, a small annuity for life, inasmuch as his grandfather built the castle, under the impression that he held the lands in perpetuity, whereas he only held them for a term of fourscore years. This, perhaps, is the earliest instance of tenant-right on record.

JOHN-FITZRICHARD succeeded to his father's property. He served as mayor of Galway in 1578; and *m.* in 1580, Julian-Browne, by whom he had,

NICOLAS-FITZJOHN, his heir, who was *s.* by his eldest son,

ANTHONY-FITZNICOLAS, who was *s.* by his son,

NICOLAS-FITZANTHONY, alderman of Galway in 1639. He had four sons, PATRICK, his heir; Nicolas; James; and Henry; and an only dau., Mary, *m.* in 1658, to her cousin, Thomas Blake, of Mullaghmore, in the co. of Galway.

PATRICK BLAKE, eldest son of Nicolas FitzAnthony, was *s.* by his eldest son,

NICOLAS BLAKE, who was *s.* by his eldest son,

PATRICK BLAKE, living in 1737, who *m.* Mary Browne, and was father of

EDWARD BLAKE, Esq., who *m.* Eliza Cheevers, and had a son and heir,

MICHAEL BLAKE, Esq., who *m.* 1st, Anne Ffrench, and had issue by her, Edward, and Eliza: he *m.* 2ndly, Eliza Butler, and by her had, James, Michael, Patrick, Nicolas, Theresa, Mary-Anne, and Henrietta.

EDWARD BLAKE, Esq., eldest son of Michael by his first wife, *m.* Mary McDermott, by whom he had issue, and was *s.* by his eldest surviving son,

OWEN-EDWARD BLAKE, Esq. of Kiltullagh, who *d.* without issue, and was *s.* by his brother, THEOBALD-MICHAEL BLAKE, Esq., the present proprietor.

Arms—Arg., a fret, gu.
Crest—A mountain-cat, passant, ppr.
Motto—Virtus sola nobilitat.
Seats—Frenchfort and Kiltullagh, Oranmore, co. Galway.

BLAKENEY OF ABBERT.

BLAKENEY, JOHN-HENRY, Esq. of Abbert, Castle Blakeney, co. Galway, J.P., high-sheriff in 1819, *m.* 1 July, 1818, Charlotte, 3rd dau. of the late Sir Ross Mahon, Bart. of Castlegar, co. Galway, by Elizabeth, his 1st wife, sister of the late Marquess of Sligo, and has issue,

I. JOHN, late of the 23rd R. W. Fusiliers, *m.* in 1854, Fanny, dau. of James-H. Burke, Esq. of St. Cleran's.
II. Robert, capt. 48th regt. III. William, E.I.C.S.
IV. Edward. V. Henry.
I. Elizabeth-Margaret, *m.* 24 April, 1834, to Albemarle Cator, Esq., eldest son of John Cator, Esq. of Beckenham Place, Kent, and Woodbastwick Hall, Norfolk.
II. Sarah. III. Mary. IV. Louisa.
V. Harriette. VI. Margaret. VII. Anne.

Lineage.—The Blakeneys formerly resided in Norfolk where they were in possession of considerable landed property, a large proportion of which having been inherited by a female, the male ancestors of the Castle Blakeney and Mount Blakeney[*] families, settled in Ireland, *temp.* ELIZABETH. The ancestor of the elder of these two branches *m.* Sarah Hatton, of the family of the Lord Chancellor Hatton, and purchased Castle Blakeney, in the co. of Galway.

JOHN BLAKENEY, Esq., son of Robert Blakeney, Esq. of Castle Blakeney, A.D. 1671, *m.* Sarah, dau. of Dudley Persse, of Roxborough, dean of Kilmacduah, and had issue, ROBERT, of whom presently; John, capt. in the army, of Dislington, in Cumberland; Susanna, *m.* to John Colpoyse, Esq. The eldest son,

COLONEL ROBERT BLAKENEY, of Castle Blakeney, M.P. for Athenry, *m.* Sarah, dau. of Colonel William Ormsby, M.P., and had several children, the eldest of whom,

JOHN BLAKENEY, Esq. of Castle Blakeney, a colonel in the army, and member of parliament, *m.* Grace, dau. of Colonel Persse, of Roxborough, and had issue,

ROBERT, of Abbert, a major in the army, and M.P., *m.* in 1752, Gertrude, dau. of Major Robert Blakeney, of Mount Blakeney, and had issue, John *d. unm.*; Grace, *m.* to — Lyon, Esq.
John, *d. unm.*
THEOPHILUS, of whom presently.
William, a colonel in the army, and M.P., father, with other children, of the Rt. Hon. SIR EDWARD BLAKENEY, G.C.B., G.C.H., K.T.S., &c., Lieut.-General, Commander of the Forces in Ireland, *b.* in 1778, *m.* in 1814, a dau. of the late Col. Gardiner, E.I.C.S. This highly distinguished officer, who entered the army in 1794, served at the taking of Demerara, Berbice, and Essequibo, in 1796; in Holland, in 1799; at Minorca, in 1800 and 1801, and at the capture of Martinique, in 1809. Subsequently he joined the Peninsular forces and participated in the victories of Busaco, Ciudad Rodrigo, Badajos, Albuhera, Vittoria, and the Pyrenees. At Badajos and Albuhera, he was wounded. In 1814, he commanded the 1st battalion Royal Fusiliers against New Orleans; in 1815, accompanied the Duke of Wellington's army to Paris; and in 1826, had under his orders the 1st brigade, sent to Portugal under Sir W. Clinton.
Sarah, *m.* to Col. Persse, of Roxborough.
Martha, *m.* to M. Browne, Esq. of Shewel.
Mary, *m.* to Major Taylor, of Castle Taylor.

The 3rd son,

THEOPHILUS BLAKENEY, Esq. of Abbert, captain in the army, and M.P., *m.* in 1782, Margaret, eldest dau. of John Stafford, Esq. of Gillstown, co. Roscommon, and had issue,

JOHN-HENRY, now of Abbert.
Bridget, *m.* to Sir Richard-Bligh St. George, of Woodsgift, co. Kilkenny, Bart.
Grace, } both *d.* young.
Sarah, }
Margaret, *m.* John O'Dwyer, Esq., barrister-at-law.
Elizabeth, *m.* to Capt. De Hugo, of the French National Guard.
Harriet, *m.* Arthur St. George, Esq. of Kilrush House, co. Kilkenny.

Captain Blakeney *d.* 22 Sept. 1818, and was *s.* by his eldest son, the present JOHN-HENRY BLAKENEY, Esq. of Abbert.

Arms—Sa., a chevron, erm., between three leopards' faces, or.
Crest—Out of a ducal coronet, an arm, erect, couped at the elbow, vested, gu., cuffed, arg., in the hand a sword, ppr., hilt and pommel, or.
Motto—Auxilium meum ab alto.
Seat—Abbert, Castle Blakeney, co. Galway.

BLAMIRE OF THACKWOOD AND THE OAKS.

BLAMIRE, WILLIAM, Esq. of Thackwood and The Oaks, Cumberland, J.P., high-sheriff in 1828, formerly M.P. for Cumberland, and now Chief Tithe Commissioner, *b.* 13 April, 1790; *m.* 8 April, 1834, his cousin Dora, youngest dau. of John Taubman, Esq. of The Nunnery, Isle of Man, and relict of Col. Mark Wilks, of Kirby, in that island, governor of St. Helena.

Lineage.—WILLIAM BLAMIRE, Esq. of The Oaks, son and heir of John Blamire, Esq. of The Oaks, by Jane his wife, only child of John Ritson, Esq., *m.* 1st, in 1736, Isabella, only child and heir of George Simpson, Esq. of Thackwood, co. Cumberland, by Sarah his wife, dau. of Christopher Richmond, Esq. of Catterlen and Highhead Castle, in the same co., and had issue,

WILLIAM, his heir.
Richmond, *b.* in 1742, *m.* Frances, dau. of Richard Baynes, Esq. of Cockermouth.
Sarah, *m.* to Thomas Græme, Esq. of Gartmore, co. Stirling, col. of the 42nd Highlanders.
Susannah, *d. unm.*

He *m.* 2ndly, Bridget, widow of John Simpson, Esq. of Sebergham Hall, Cumberland, and by her had one dau., Bridget, *m.* to George Browne, Esq. of Newcastle-upon-Tyne. The eldest son and heir,

WILLIAM BLAMIRE, Esq. of The Oaks, *m.* in Aug. 1785, Jane, 3rd dau. of John Christian, of Milntown, Isle of Man, and of Ewanrigg Hall, co. Cumberland, by Jane his wife, dau. of Eldred Curwen, Esq., M.P., of Workington Hall, in the same co., and had issue,

WILLIAM, present representative of the family.
Mary-Simpson, *m.* in Sept. 1814, to the Rev. Thomas Young, rector of Gilling, co. York.
Jane-Christian.
Sarah-Susannah, *m.* in April, 1830, to the Rev. William Young, rector of Aller, co. Somerset.

Arms—Arg., a lion, rampant, within an orle, gu.
Crest—A wolf, sejant, ppr., chained, or.
Motto—Faire sans dire.
Seats—Thackwood and The Oaks, co. Cumberland.

BLAND OF KIPPAX PARK.

DAVISON-BLAND, THOMAS, Esq. of Kippax Park, co. York, *b.* 15 July, 1783; *m.* 20 Jan. 1812, Apollonia, 2nd dau. of Charles-Philip, 16th Lord Stourton, and has issue,

I. THOMAS, *b.* 23 Nov. 1812. II. Edward, *b.* 23 Aug. 1813.
III. Henry, *b.* 6 Dec. 1814.

Lineage.—The family of BLAND was anciently seated at Bland's Gill, in the co. of York, but the male line of the elder stock failing, the representation devolved upon the descendant of

ROBERT BLAND of Leeming, in the North Riding, a younger son of Bland of Bland's Gill. This Robert was great grandfather of

SIR THOMAS BLAND, Knt., who settled at Kippax Park, in the time of ELIZABETH, and was in the commission of the peace for the co. of York, in the 32nd of that reign. His grandson, SIR THOMAS BLAND, of Kippax Park, was created a baronet on the 30 Aug. 1642, by King CHARLES I., for his active zeal and devotion in the royal cause, and became ancestor of the BLANDS *of Kippax*, extinct baronets, the last of whom

SIR HUNGERFORD BLAND, 8th baronet, *d. unm.* in 1756, when the title became extinct, while the estate passed to his cousin,

THOMAS DAVISON, Esq., *b.* 8 June, 1744-5, son of Thomas Davison, Esq. of Blakestone, who was son of Thomas Davison, Esq. of the same place, by Anne his wife, eldest dau. of SIR JOHN BLAND, 5th Bart. He assumed the additional surname of BLAND, and *m.* in 1776, Jane, dau. and co-heir of Godfrey Meynell, Esq. of Yeldersley, in the co. Derby, by whom he had one son, THOMAS, now of Kippax Park; and five daus., Harriett, *m.* to Lieut.-Col. John-Sullivan Wood; Martha; Anne; Frances-Augusta; Judith-Selina; and Charlotte, *m.* to the Rev. Theophilus Barnes. Mr. Davison-Bland *d.* 27 April, 1794.

Arms—Arg., on a bend, sa., three pheons, or.
Crest—Out of a ducal coronet, a lion's head, ppr.
Seat—Kippax Park, near Leeds.

BLAND OF BLANDSFORT.

BLAND, LOFTUS-HENRY, Esq. of Blandsfort, Queen's County, M.P., Queen's Counsel, *b.* Aug. 1805; *m.* 1st, 20 Aug. 1840, Charlotte-Elizabeth, 2nd dau. of Gen. the Hon. Arthur-Grove Annesley, of Ann's Grove, co. Cork, and by her (who *d.* 26 March, 1842) has a son,

[*] William Blakeney, of Mount Blakeney, near Kilmallock, a younger brother of the Blakeney of Castle Blakeney, was father of two sons, William and George, the latter a colonel in the army: the former was father of four sons, William, Charles, John, and Robert. The eldest was the celebrated GENERAL SIR WILLIAM BLAKENEY, K.B., raised to the peerage in 1756, as BARON BLAKENEY, for his gallant conduct as Governor of Minorca; the youngest was Major Robert Blakeney, of Castle Blakeney, who *m.* Deborah, dau. of Richard Smyth, Esq., of Ballynatray, co. Waterford, and had two sons, 1. William, of Mount Blakeney, who *m.* his cousin, Gertrude, dau. of Richard Smyth, Esq. of Ballynatray, and had one son, father of the Rev. Robert Blakeney, who *d. s. p.* in 1824; 2. Grice, a lieut.-general in the army, who *d. unm.*; and 3. Gertrude, wife of Robert Blakeney, of Abbert, Esq.

I. JOHN-LOFTUS, b. 20 June, 1841.

He m. 2ndly, 2nd Dec. 1843, Annie-Jane, eldest dau. of the late John-Prendergast Hackett, Esq. of Stratford Place, London, and by her has,

I. Thomas-Dalrymple, b. 9 June, 1845.
I. Elizabeth-Emily.
II. Annie-Sophia-Alicia.

Mr. Loftus Bland graduated at Cambridge in 1825, became M.A. in 1828, was called to the bar in 1829, and created Q.C. in 1854. He was returned for the King's County in 1852, and continues to represent it in parliament. He s. his brother, John-Thomas Bland, Esq., in 1849.

Lineage.—COLONEL JOHN BLAND, a cadet of the baronetical house of BLAND *of Kippax*, co. York, in 1699 purchased land in the Queen's County, where he commenced the present mansion, which was finished in 1715, a date inscribed on a cut stone slab, beneath the family arms, at Blandsfort. Colonel Bland *d.* in 1728, *s. p.*, and was *s.* by his brother,

GENERAL HUMPHREY BLAND, who was governor of Gibraltar, and commander-in-chief in Scotland. General Bland, a distinguished writer on military tactics, commanded a troop of horse at Culloden. He *m.* at Edinburgh, 12 Jan. 1755 (being then commander-in-chief in Scotland), Elizabeth Dalrymple, eldest sister of John, 5th Earl of Stair (she *d.* in 1816, aged 95). General Humphrey Bland *d.* in 1763, *s. p.* His youngest brother,

CAPTAIN WILLIAM BLAND, *m.* 1st, 1720, Elizabeth Horsman (*née* Jones), and by her had a son, JOHN, heir to his uncle, General Humphrey. Captain Bland *m.* 2ndly, 1732, Letitia Davys, and by her had issue, 1 Humphrey, captain in the army, whose male line is extinct; 2 Neville, father of the gallant Loftus-Otway Bland, Captain R.N., and Lieut.-Colonel Humphrey Bland, 47th regt.; 3 Thomas, General in the army, and Colonel of the 5th dragoon guards, who *d.* in 1816, without issue. The eldest son (the heir to General Humphrey Bland),

JOHN BLAND, Esq. of Blandsfort, *m.* in 1763 (then a cornet of dragoons), Sarah, dau. of Charles Birch, Esq. of Birch Grove, co. Wexford; and *d.* in 1790, leaving a son and successor,

JOHN BLAND, Esq. of Blandsfort, who *m.* in 1790, Elizabeth, dau. of Robert Birch, Esq. of Turvey, co. Dublin, and by her (who *d.* in 1836), left at his decease, in 1810, three sons and three daus., viz.,

I. JOHN-THOMAS, his heir.
II. ROBERT-WINTRINGHAM, in holy orders, of Abbeyville, co. Antrim; *m.* Alicia, dau. of the Rev. Edward Evans, of Dungannon, co. Tyrone, and has issue,
  1 JOHN-HUMPHREY.
  2 Edward-Loftus, R.E.
  3 Robert-Henry.
  1 Mary-Anne-Sinclair.
  2 Sarah-Maria.
  3 Louisa-Jane.
III. LOFTUS-HENRY, now of Blandsfort.
I. Catherine-Jane, *m.* 1st, to Capt. Richard Croker, R.N., and 2ndly, to the Rev. Thomas-Frere Bowerbank, vicar of Chiswick, co. Middlesex.
II. Sarah-Anne, *d. unm.* 1823.
III. Georgina-Elizabeth, *m.* to James-Franck Rolleston, Esq. of Franckfort Castle, King's County.

The eldest son,

JOHN-THOMAS BLAND, Esq. of Blandsfort, *m.* Margaret, dau. of John Bond, Esq. of Bath, and dying *s. p.* in 1849, devised Blandsfort to his brother, LOFTUS-HENRY BLAND, Esq. of Blandsfort, M.P.

Arms (registered and confirmed in Ulster's Office)—Arg., on a bend, sa., three pheons, or; in the sinister chief point a crescent, gu.

Crest—Out of a ducal coronet, a lion's head, ppr., charged with a crescent, gu.

Motto—Quo fata vocant.

Seat—Blandsfort, Queen's County.

Town Residence—33, Merrion Square North, Dublin.

BLAND OF DERRIQUIN CASTLE.

BLAND, JAMES-FRANKLIN, Esq. of Derriquin Castle, co. Kerry, J.P., high-sheriff in 1835, *b.* 24 Jan. 1799; *m.* 27 Dec. 1825, Emma, dau. of Joseph Taylor, Esq. of Dunkerron Castle, Kerry, major Bengal artillery, and has issue,

I. FRANCIS-CHRISTOPHER, *b.* 8 Oct. 1826, *m.* 23 June, 1849, Jane, dau. of the Rev. Archibald-Robert Hamilton, of Cork.

II. James-Franklin, capt. 57th foot, *b.* 10 Jan. 1828, killed in action at the battle of Inkerman.
I. Alice-Phillis, *m.* 20 Dec. 1853, to Usher Williamson, Esq., eldest son of the Rev. Benjamin Williamson, of Old Dromore, co. Cork.

Lineage.—NATHANIEL BLAND, LL.D., Judge of the Prerogative Court at Dublin, and vicar-general of the diocese of Ardfert and Aghadoe, *m.* 1st, Diana, only dau. of Nicholas Kemeys, Esq., and had by her a son,

JAMES, his heir.

He *m.* 2ndly, Lucy, dau. of Francis Heaton, Esq., by whom he had issue,

Francis, father, by Catherine Mahony his wife, of Colonel James-Francis Bland, of Killarney, and of Frances, *m.* to the Rev. Robert Hewson.
Nathaniel, *m.* Mary Mead, but had no issue.
George, *m.* Hannah Westrop, but had no issue.
Lucy, *m.* to George Orpen, Esq., a military officer, distinguished at Minden, 4th son of the Rev. Thomas Orpen, of Killowen, co. Kerry.
Hester, *m.* to Robert Sinclair.
Dorothea, *m.* to Francis Crumpe, Esq., and had, with other issue, Nathaniel Crumpe, of Randalls Park, in Surrey, who took the additional surname of BLAND.

Dr. Bland was *s.* by his eldest son,

THE REV. JAMES BLAND, of Derriquin Castle, who *m.* 1st, Elizabeth, dau. of Christopher Julian; and 2ndly, Barbara, dau. of — Nash, Esq., by the former of whom he had, with other issue, a dau., *m.* to Major Nathaniel Bland, and a son and successor,

FRANCIS-CHRISTOPHER BLAND, Esq. of Derriquin Castle, who *m.* 15 March, 1798, Lucinda, dau. of Arthur-Bastable Herbert, Esq. of Brewsterfield, near Killarney, and by her (who *d.* 16 Sept. 1838) had

JAMES-FRANKLIN, now of Derriquin.
Arthur. John. Edward.
Elizabeth, *m.* Frederick Hyde, Esq.
Lucy, *m.* to Capt. Thomas Stuart, R.N.
Frances-Diana, *m.* to Thomas-Hartnett Fuller, Esq.
Lætitia, *m.* to Henry Stokes, Esq., C.E.
Mary-Matilda.
Christina-Frances, *m.* to Robert-Acheson Thompson, Esq.
Clara-Dalinda, *m.* to William Allen, Esq.

Mr. Bland *d.* 16 Sept. 1838.

Seat—Derriquin Castle, co. Kerry.

BLATHWAYT OF DYRHAM PARK.

BLATHWAYT, GEORGE-WILLIAM, Esq. of Dyrham Park, co. Gloucester, and of Langridge and Porlock, co. Somerset, J.P., a captain (h. p.) in the 1st Dragoon-guards, major of the royal Gloucestershire hussar yeomanry cavalry, *b.* 25 Feb. 1797; *m.* 21 Jan. 1822, Mary-Anne, dau. of the Rev. Thomas-Agmondisham Vesey (a branch of the De Vesci family), and has issue,

I. GEORGE-WILLIAM, *b.* 11 May, 1824, an officer in the 1st dragoon-guards.
II. Wynter-Thomas, *b.* in Sept. 1825.
III. Richard-Vesey, *b.* in Jan. 1827.
IV. Charles-Pye, *b.* in March, 1828.
V. William, *b.* in April, 1839.

Lineage.—The family of Blathwayt is of very ancient origin: the first of the name, originally spelt Brauthwait, are said to have come over to England with WILLIAM the Conqueror, and to have settled in the counties of Cumberland and Westmoreland, where they had grants of land for services rendered.

The family estates of Dyrham, &c., originally belonged to Sir Walter Dennis, Knt., who sold the manor in the 13th ELIZABETH, 1571, to GEORGE WYNTER, Esq., (youngest brother of Sir William Wynter, of Lidney, in the Forest of Dean.) He *m.* Anne, one of the sisters and co-heiresses of Robert Brayn, Esq., a merchant of Bristol, and dying in 1581, was *s.* by his son, JOHN WYNTER, a captain in the royal navy, who accompanied Sir Francis Drake in his famous voyage round the world, as his vice-admiral. His eldest brother, Sir William Wynter, of Lidney, Gloucestershire, was also a vice-admiral under Sir Francis Drake, in the ever-memorable destruction of the Spanish armada.

Capt. John Wynter *m.* Mary, dau. of Sir William Bruen, of Dorsetshire, and dying in 1619, was *s.* by his eldest son,

SIR GEORGE WYNTER, high-sheriff for Gloucestershire, 7 CHARLES I. He *m.* Mary, dau. of Edward Rogers, Esq.

of Cannington, co. Somerset, and dying in 1638, was s. by his eldest son,

John Wynter, Esq., who m. Frances, dau. of Thomas Gerard, Esq. of Trent, co. Somerset, and d. in 1668, leaving an only surviving dau.,

Mary Wynter, who m. 23 Dec. 1686, William Blaythwayt, Esq., of St. Martin's, "within the citty of London," and had (with a dau., Anne, m. the Hon. Edward Southwell, of King's Weston,) two sons, William, his heir; John, a col. in the army, m. Miss Penfield, and had issue. This Mr. Blathwayt was secretary-at-war, and also secretary of state, to King William, during his abode in Holland and Flanders; he was also one of the commissioners for trade and plantations, and clerk of the privy council in the reigns of King Charles, King James, King William, and Queen Anne. He likewise represented the city of Bath in parliament, from 1690 to 1710. He d. in Aug. 1717, and was s. by his son and heir,

William Blathwayt, Esq. of Dyrham, who m. in 1719, Thomasina Ambrose, and by her (who d. in 1774), left, at his decease in 1742, a son,

William Blathwayt, Esq. of Dyrham, who m. 1st, in 1750, Miss Penelope Jenkinson, and by her (who d. in July, 1755) has issue, I. William, his heir, b. in 1751; II. James, b. in 1754, a captain in the army, d. unm. in 1788; I. Penelope, b. in 1755, m. Mr. Crane, and had one son only, William, who took the name of Blathwayt in 1818, but d. s. p. in 1839. He m. 2ndly, Mrs. Elizabeth Le Pepre (whose maiden name was Clarke) and by her (who d. in Aug. 1764) had issue,

I. George-William, fellow of Merton College, Oxon, and rector of Langridge, co. Somerset, and of Dyrham, co. Gloucester, m. in 1795, Isabella, dau. of Charles Pye, Esq. of Wadley, co. Berks, a deputy-lieutenant and high-sheriff of that county, and had issue,
  George-William, now of Dyrham Park.
  William, b. 10 April, 1798, capt. 3rd light dragoons, m. Miss Filmer, and has issue.
  Charles, b. 6 Jan. 1800, rector of Langridge, m. Miss Rose, and has issue two sons.
  Wynter, d. young, in 1818.
  Anne-Sophia, m. Thomas Curtis, Esq. of London.
  Frances.

Mr. William Blathwayt m. 3rdly, Miss Mary Creighton, of London, but by her had no issue. He d. in May, 1787, and was s. by his eldest son of the first marriage,

William Blathwayt, Esq. of Dyrham, b. in 1751, who m. in July 1790 Frances, dau. of William Scott, Esq. of Great Barr, Staffordshire, but d. in May, 1806, without issue, leaving his widow surviving: she subsequently m. Admiral Douglas, who d. in 1839.

Arms—Or, two bends, engrailed, sa.
Crest—On a rock, ppr., an eagle rising, arg., wings, az.
Motto—Virtute et veritate.
Seat—Dyrham Park, Gloucestershire.

BLAYDES OF RANBY HALL.

Blaydes, Charles-Benjamin, Esq. of Ranby Hall, Notts, b. 9 April, 1812; m. Caroline-Martha, dau. of Captain Jackson.

Lineage.—Joseph Blaides, of Sutton, in the co. of York, J.P., b. 15 July, 1588, son and heir of William Blaides, and Margaret Appleyard his wife, heiress of Sutton, co. York, was mayor of Kingston-upon-Hull, in 1636. He m. Anne Booth, by whom he had a dau., Lydia, the wife of George Anson, Esq., ancestor of the circumnavigator, afterwards Lord Anson; and a son, his successor,

James Blaides or Blaydes, of Sutton, J.P., b. about the year 1625, m. Anne, dau. of the Rev. Andrew Marvel, and sister of the celebrated patriot, Andrew Marvel. He was s. at his decease by his son,

Joseph Blaydes, Esq., bapt. 28 Sept. 1671, m. Jane Mould, whose family likewise possessed estates in Sutton. Their 2nd son,

Hugh Blaydes, Esq., lord of the manors of Sutton-cum-Stoneferry, and part of Sculcoates, in the co. of York, b. in 1685, m. 23 April, 1728, Elizabeth, dau. of Peter de la Pryme, Esq. of Crowtrees Hall, by Frances, dau. of Francis Wood, Esq. of Hatfield-Levels. By this lady (who d. 21 Aug. 1772) he had issue, of whom, his successor, Benjamin, alone married. He d. 9 April, 1759, aged 74, and was s. by his son,

Benjamin Blaydes, Esq. of Melton and High Paull, in the co. of York, b. 5 March, 1735. He m. 13 May, 1775, Kitty, 2nd dau. and co-heiress of Christopher Scott, Esq. of Aldborough, in Holderness, and dying 29 Oct. 1805, was s. by his son,

Hughes Blaydes, Esq. of High Paull, in Yorkshire, and of Ranby Hall, Notts, high-sheriff in 1812. He was b. at Melton, 9 Aug. 1777, and m. 19 March, 1800, at Ripon Minster, Delia-Maria, 2nd dau. of Col. Richard Wood, of Hollin Hall, in the co. of York, by whom he had issue,

  Hugh-Marvel, who d. unm. in 1836.
  Charles-Benjamin, present representative.
  Frederick-Henry Marvel, in holy orders, b. 29 Sept. 1818, m. in 1843, Fanny-Maria, eldest dau. of the late Sir Edward-Page Turner, Bt., and has issue, Edward-Henry Frederick - Augustus, Arthur - Charles - Julius, George-Frederick-Handel, and Katharine-Louisa-Frances.
  Delia-Katherine.
  Louisa-Anne, m. to Henry-Thomas-Coggan Kerr, Esq., capt. in the army, son of the late Gen. Kerr, of Hartham House, co. Somerset; and by him (who d. in Sept. 1845) has issue, Harry-Kynaston; Mary; Kate, m. to Captain Cowell, 3rd dragoons; Emily; and Annie.
  Harriet-Elizabeth, d. unm. in 1824.
  Henrietta-Christian, m. in 1837, to Edward Parratt, Esq. clerk of the journals, House of Lords, and has one dau., Caroline-Lennox.
  Emmeline-Sophia, m. in 1838, to Frederick-Alexander Blachford, Esq., capt. 93rd Highlanders.

This gentleman was for some years major of the 3rd battalion of West Riding militia. He d. 15 Feb. 1829.

Arms—Az., a saltier, arg., between three pheons, ppr.; on a chief, or, a lion, passant.
Crest—A talbot's head, erased, and erect, sa.
Motto—Pro Deo, rege, et patria.
Seat—Ranby Hall, Notts.

BLAYNEY OF EVESHAM.

Blayney, Robert, Esq., M.A., of The Lodge, Evesham, co. Worcester, b. 23 March, 1818, a captain in the Worcestershire militia, and J.P. for the counties of Worcester and Gloucester.

Lineage.—This family claims to descend, through the Blayneys *of Kinsham*, co. Hereford, from the famed Elystan Glodrydd, Prince of Fferlys.

Robert Blayney (2nd son of Thomas Blayney, Esq., by Betty his wife, dau. of Benjamin Parkes, Esq. of Worcester, and younger brother of the Rev. Benjamin Blayney, D.D., Regius professor of Hebrew, and canon of Christchurch, Oxford), m. 13 July, 1756, Katherine, youngest dau. of Joseph Withers, Esq. of Worcester (of the Hampshire family of Withers), and had issue. The elder son,

The Rev. Robert Blayney, rector of Pitsford, co. Northampton, lord of the manor of Garlford, heir of his maternal uncle, Sir Charles-Trubshaw Withers, Knt., who had m. Frances, widow of Richard Nash, D.D., and dau. and heir of John Ravenhill, Esq., by Katherine Dansey his wife, lady of the manor of Strensham, granddau. and heir of Sir Francis Russell, Bart. of Strensham. The Rev. Robert Blayney m. in Sept. 1783, Catherine, eldest dau. of Henry Howard, Esq. of Arundel, and sister of Lord Effingham, but dying s. p. 24 Sept. 1824, was s. by his brother,

Thomas Blayney, Esq. of The Lodge, Evesham, Worcestershire, D.L., b. 9 Sept. 1762, m. 1st, 12 April, 1787, Margaret, 2nd dau. of Charles Welch, Esq. of Evesham, which lady d. s. p.; and 2ndly, 17 June, 1815, Anna-Harland, 2nd dau. of Thomas Harrison, Esq. of Fulford, in Yorkshire, by whom he had issue,

  John-Charles-Withers, b. 18 March, 1816, and d. in April, 1817.
  Robert, of Exeter College, Oxford, M.A., now of The Lodge, Evesham.
  Katherine-Emma, m. in 1848, to James F. Marett, Esq. of St. Helier's, Jersey, and H.M. Ordnance, Barbadoes.
  Mary-Eleanor, m. in 1841, to George Jackson, Esq. of Bushey, Herts.
  Anna, m. in 1844, to Thomas Colmore, Esq. of Sheldon House, Warwickshire.
  Jane-Margaret.

Mr. Blayney d. 1 Dec. 1838.

Arms—Quarterly: first and fourth, arg., three boars' heads, couped, sa., armed, gu.; second and third, gu., a lion, rampant-regardant, or; quartering Withers and Trubshaw.
Crest—A fox, arg.
Motto—I rest to rise.
Seat—The Lodge, near Evesham.

BLENCOWE OF BLENCOWE AND THOBY PRIORY.

BLENCOWE, HENRY-PRESCOTT, Esq., late of Blencowe Hall, co. Cumberland, and now of Thoby Priory, co. Essex, *b.* 1799; *s.* his father in 1847.

Lineage.—ADAM DE BLENCOWE distinguished himself in the French wars in the reign of EDWARD III., under the banner of William, Baron of Greystoke, who granted arms to him and his heirs by the following warrant:

"To all to whom these presents shall come to be seen or heard; William, Baron of Greystoke, Lord of Morpeth, wisheth health in the Lord: Know ye, that I have given and granted to Adam de Blencowe an escutcheon sable, with a bend closetted (or barred) argent and azure, with three chaplets gules; and with a crest closetted, argent and azure, of my arms; to have and to hold to the said Adam, and his heirs, for ever. And I, the said William, and my heirs, will warrant to the said Adam, and his heirs, the arms aforesaid; In witness whereof, I have to these letters patent set my seal. Written at the Castle of Morpeth, the 26th day of February, in the 30th year of the reign of King EDWARD III., after the Conquest." [A.D. 1357.]

ADAM DE BLENCOWE, 1327, *m.* twice. By his 1st wife, Emma, he had three sons, William, *d. v. p.*, *unm.*; THOMAS, his successor; John, whose wife's name was Johanna.

THOMAS DE BLENCOWE, *s.* his father, and *m.* Elizabeth, dau. and heiress of Nicholas Veteripont or Vipont, (1333,) Baron of Westmoreland, and to whom his Alston estates descended, in conjunction with her sister Joan, wife of William Whytlaw. They now belong to Greenwich Hospital. Their son and heir,

WILLIAM DE BLENCOWE, *m.*, *temp.* HENRY VI., Johanna, dau. of Robert Brisco, of Crofton, Cumberland.

RICHARD DE BLENCOWE, son and heir of William, living in the reign of EDWARD IV., was father of

CHRISTOPHER DE BLENCOWE, who *m.* and had issue, RICHARD, his heir, and Isabella, *m.* James Halton, of an ancient family resident at Greystoke, whose manor house still remains.

RICHARD BLENCOWE, Esq., son and heir of Christopher, *m.* Eleanor Crackenthorpe, of Newbiggin, dau. of John Crackenthorpe, Esq., and had issue, ANTHONY, his heir; Christopher, *d. unm.*; Cuthbert, *d. unm.*; Elizabeth, *m.* Richard Hoton, of Hoton Roof, Esq., a hamlet of Greystoke; and Marzen, *m.* Matthew Bec, Esq.

ANTHONY BLENCOWE, Esq., the eldest son and heir of Richard, *m.* Winifred Dudley, granddau. of the old Lord Dudley, of Yanwarth, co. Westmorland, by whom he had issue,

I. RICHARD, his heir, mentioned amongst the gentry of the county subject to Border service, 1543; *m.* Appoline ——, afterwards the wife of W. Allonby, of Allonby, Esq., by whom he left issue,
   1 HENRY, heir to his grandfather.
   2 Richard, *d. unm.*

II. Anthony, D.C.L., provost of Oriel College, Oxford, 45 years. He was chancellor or vicar-general of the cathedral church of Chichester. He *d.* 1618, and was buried in St. Mary's Church, Oxford. He was *unm.*, and left £1,300 to the rebuilding of his college, with which the west side of Oriel College, as it now stands, was accordingly built.

III. George, M.P. for Chichester in 1603.

HENRY (afterwards SIR HENRY) BLENCOWE, *s.* his grandfather. He was high-sheriff of Cumberland in 1608, and was knighted by King JAMES I., on his return from Scotland in 1617. He was again high-sheriff of Cumberland, 1st CHARLES I., and *d.* 21 Nov. 1635. His 1st wife was Jane, dau. of Sir William Musgrave, of Hayton, Bart. (sister to Eleanor, wife of Sir Christopher Lowther, of Lowther, Knt., and great-grandmother to the 1st Lord Lonsdale,) by whom he had no issue that lived to succeed him. His 2nd wife was Grace, dau. of Sir Richard Sandford, of Howgill, by whom he had issue,

CHRISTOPHER, his successor.
Henry, *d. unm.* in his father's lifetime.
Anthony, to whom the estate at Harbybrow was first limited by Mr. Highmore. Harbybrow was for many generations the property and seat of the HIGHMORES. The BLENCOWES purchased it of them and possessed it for several descents. This estate was purchased of the latter about the year 1745, by — Steel, Esq. It is now the property of W. Charlton, Esq. A square tower, which is part of the old mansion at Harbybrow, still remains. Anthony *d.* soon after his father, *unm.*
John, *m.* and *d.* in his father's lifetime, leaving issue, by Anne —, his wife, Elizabeth, *m.* H. Thompson, Esq. of Hollin Hall, Ripon, York, grandfather of Sir W. Thompson, a baron of the Exchequer; Ann, *m.* George Barwick, Esq. of Carlisle.

SIR CHRISTOPHER BLENCOWE, Knt., son and heir of Sir Henry, *m.* Mary, dau. of Thomas Robinson, of Rokeby, Esq., Yorkshire, great-grandfather of Sir Thos. Robinson, of Rokeby, Bart., and his brother, Lord Bishop of Armagh, created Baron Rokeby; and had issue, Henry, *d. unm.* before his father; CHRISTOPHER, his successor; Thomas, *d. unm.*; Mary; Frances; Margaret; and Katherine.

CHRISTOPHER BLENCOWE, Esq., son and heir of Sir Christopher, Knt., *m.* Ann, eldest dau. and co-heiress of William Laton, of Dalemain, Esq., which this family had possessed before the time of HENRY III., and had issue a son and heir,

HENRY BLENCOWE, Esq., high-sheriff of Cumberland, *temp.* GEORGE I.: he *m.* 1st, Dorothy, dau. and heiress of George Sisson, Esq. of Penrith, she *d.* 29 Oct. 1707, aged 32, and was buried in the church of Penrith; by this lady he had issue,

CHRISTOPHER, who succeeded him.
Henry, *d. v. p.* George, *d. v. p.*
Dorothy, *m.* the Rev. Tobias Croft, vicar of Kirby Lonsdale.
Bridget, *m.* Utrick Reay, Esq. of Newcastle.
Mary, *d. unm.*

He *m.* 2ndly, Elizabeth, dau. of W. Todd, Esq. of Wath, Yorkshire, and had issue,

I. HENRY, who *s.* his half-brother, Christopher.

II. William, *m.* 1736, Elizabeth, dau. and co-heiress of Ferdinando Latus, Esq. of The Beck, in Millum, co. Cumberland, by Henrietta his wife, dau. of Sir John Tempest, Bart. of Tong, co. York, by whom he had issue,
   1 George, *d.* in the West Indies, *s. p.*
   2 Henry, *d. s. p.* 3 John, *d. s. p.*
   4 WILLIAM-FERDINANDO, son and heir.
   1 Elizabeth, *m.* J. Blain, Esq., M.D. of Carlisle, interred at St. Mary's, Carlisle.

III. Peter, *m.* Frances Benn, of Whitehaven, Cumberland, and had issue,
   1 Henry.
   1 Elizabeth.

Henry Blencowe, Esq., *d.* in 1721, and was *s.* by his eldest son,

CHRISTOPHER BLENCOWE, Esq. of Blencowe, who *d. unm.*, 1723, aged 25, and was *s.* by his half-brother. Such was the reputation of this gentleman as a lawyer that he was called to the bar at the age of 21, and three years after he was made one of the deputy-lieutenants of the Tower Hamlets, and chief steward or judge of the Court of Records, within the liberties of the same: he died while upon the circuit.

HENRY BLENCOWE, Esq., *s.* his half-brother, Christopher, and *m.* Mary, only surviving dau. and heiress of Alexander Prescott, Esq. of Thoby Priory, Essex, [at this point the BLENCOWES *of Blencowe* become again closely connected with the BLENCOWES *of Marston*]: he had issue,

HENRY-PRESCOTT, *b.* 1752, his heir.
Mary, *d. unm.*, at Billericay, Essex.

HENRY-PRESCOTT BLENCOWE, Esq., *s.* his father, and *m.* Elizabeth,* eldest dau. of Richard Barbor, Esq. of Brentwood, co. Essex. By this lady, who *d.* in 1843 (the last of the Barbor family), he had issue,

I. HENRY-PRESCOTT, his successor.

II. John-Prescott, *b.* 1778, *m.* Pleasance, youngest dau. of Edward Everard, Esq. of Lynn, Norfolk: he *d.* 9 Nov. 1840, leaving issue,
   1 John-Prescott, *b.* 1800.
   2 Edward-Everard, *b.* 17 April, 1806, rector of West Walton, Norfolk, and R.D.
   3 Edmond, *dec.* 4 Walter, *b.* 25 Aug. 1812.
   1 Pleasance, *dec.* 2 Elizabeth. 3 Mary.
   4 Agnes, *dec.* 5 Henrietta.

* There was in the possession of this lady a curious jewel, of which the account is as follows, copied from the will of Gabriel Barbor:

"Mr. Barbor (the father of my great-grandfather,) for his firm adherence to the Protestant religion, was in Queen Mary's reign brought into Smithfield to suffer at the stake, but whilst he was taking leave of certain friends, news came the queen was dead, so that the Popish party did not dare to put him to death. In remembrance of so eminent a preservation, the said Mr. Barbor had the effigies of Queen Elizabeth cut out upon a stone, bequeathing the jewel to his eldest son, if he had a daughter and named her Elizabeth, otherwise the jewel should descend to the 2nd son if the condition was fulfilled by him, but if not, then to the 3rd son, and so on. This is ye account as it has been handed down from father to son, and hitherto there has been an Elizabeth in the family." Aug. 24, 1724.

6 Jane, m. Rev. S. Allen, D.D.
7 Agnes. 8 Margaret. 9 Ellen.
I. Elizabeth, m. James Everard, Esq. of Lowestoft, and d. leaving issue, James, R.N., drowned; Mary, m. Rev. Isaac Gaskarth; Eleanor, m. Proudfoot Montagu, Esq.; Fanny; Caroline; Louisa; and Anna.
II. Margaret.

Mr. Blencowe d. 9 Feb. 1787, and was s. by his son,

HENRY-PRESCOTT BLENCOWE, Esq of Blencowe, m. Rebecca, eldest dau. of Edward Everard, Esq. of Lynn, co. Norfolk, and by her (who d. 20 Oct. 1854, aged 83) had issue, HENRY-PRESCOTT, his successor; John, dec.; Edward, dec.; Everard; Rebecca; Mary, m. George Bannatyne, Esq. of Bathford House, Somersetshire. Mr. Blencowe, in the year 1802, sold Blencowe to the Duke of Norfolk. He d. in 1847, and was s. by his eldest son, the present HENRY-PRESCOTT BLENCOWE, Esq.

Arms—1st, BLENCOWE, gu., a quarter, arg. 2nd, GREYSTOKE, augmentation with a difference. 3rd, LATON of Dalemain. 4th, PRESCOTT.

Crest—A sword in pale, arg., hilt in chief, or, enfiladed with a human heart, gu., all between two wings expanded, arg. [A legend in the family refers this curious crest to the circumstance that in the Border wars, a Blencowe, whose crest was a sword, having slain a Douglas (no small honour in those days), was permitted to unite it in the present form, with the bleeding heart of the Douglas.]

Motto—Quorsum vivere mori, mori vitæ.

Seat—Thoby Priory, Essex.

BLENCOWE OF MARSTON ST. LAWRENCE.

BLENCOWE, JOHN-JACKSON, Esq. of Marston St. Lawrence, co. Northampton, b. 5 Feb. 1810; m. 1st, 27 May, 1834, Gratia-Maria, dau. of the Rev. John Prowett, rector of Catfield, Norfolk, and by her, who d. 23 Dec. 1840, has an only surviving child,

Anna-Maria.

He m. 2ndly, 2 May, 1843, Cecilia, dau. of the Rev. Charles Prowett, rector of Stapleford, Herts, and has by her,

I. JOHN-ALEXANDER, b. 3 Sept. 1846.
II. Charles-Edward, b. 13 Oct. 1847.
III. Alfred-James, b. 16 Nov. 1848.
I. Mary-Cecilia.

Lineage.—The Blencowes (a branch of a very old Cumberland family, which had property at Greystock, in that county), have been seated at Marston earlier than 1446.

THOMAS BLENCOWE, grandson of John Blencowe, living at Marston St. Lawrence, *temp.* HENRY VI., obtained in the year 1540, a grant from the crown of the demesne lands and rectorial tithes of the manor of "Lawrence Marston, alias Marston St. Lawrence." His great-great-great-grandson was,

SIR JOHN BLENCOWE, of Marston St. Lawrence, an eminent judge, one of the justices of the Common Pleas. He m. Anne, eldest dau. of the Rev. John Wallis, D.D., F.R.S., the famous Savilian professor of Oxford, by whom (who d. in 1718) he had issue, JOHN, his heir; Thomas, a bencher of the Inner Temple (*see* BLENCOWE *of The Hooke*); William, who d. unm.; Mary, m. to Alexander Prescott, Esq. of Thoby Priory, Essex; Anne, m. in 1720, to Sir Edmund Probyn, of Newlands; Elizabeth; and Susannah, m. to Richard Jennens, Esq. of Princethorp. Judge Blencowe d. in 1726, at the age of 84, and was s. by his eldest son,

JOHN BLENCOWE, Esq. of Marston St. Lawrence, who m. Jane, dau. of William Holbech, Esq. of Farnborough, in Warwickshire, by whom (who d. in 1756) he left issue, a son, JOHN, his heir, and four daus., Jane, who m. the Rev. Samuel Jackson, rector of Stisted, in Essex, and had two sons, Samuel and John; Anne, m. to the Rev. Thomas Bree, M.A.; Elizabeth, who d. unm.; and Mary, who also d. unm. Mr. Blencowe d. in 1740, and was s. by his only surviving son,

JOHN BLENCOWE, Esq. of Marston St. Lawrence, who d. unm. in 1717, and devised his estates to his nephew,

SAMUEL JACKSON, Esq., who thus became of Marston St. Lawrence, and assumed the surname and arms of BLENCOWE. He m. 1st, Anne, youngest dau. of the Rev. Thomas Bree, of Allesley, by Anne Blencowe, and had by her (who d. in 1789) five sons—viz., 1 JOHN-JACKSON, his heir; 2 Thomas, in holy orders, vicar of Marston, b. in 1782; 3 Samuel-William, of Lincoln, b. in 1784, m. Miss Anne Bell; 4 James, in holy orders, b. in 1785, m. in 1818, Anne, relict of Jas. Nagle, Esq. dau. and co-heir of John Beauchamp, Esq. of Pengreep, in Cornwall; and 5 Henry, who d. unm. in 1808. Mr. (Jackson) Blencowe m. 2ndly, Elizabeth-Gramer, dau. of the Rev. Thomas Biker, rector of Culworth, by whom (who d. in 1814) he had further issue, Charles, in holy orders, b. in 1798; Peter-Gramer, in holy orders, m. 2 Jan. 1829, Loveday, eldest dau. of Isaac Sparkes, Esq. of Crewkerne, in Somersetshire; Robert, of the Inner Temple, London, b. in 1801; George, b. in 1803; Edward, b. in 1805; Elizabeth; Rhoda-Maria; and Sophia. Mr. Blencowe was s. by his eldest son,

JOHN-JACKSON BLENCOWE, Esq. of Marston St. Lawrence, high-sheriff in 1827, b. in 1780, who m. 16 Aug. 1804, Louisa-Anne, dau. and co-heiress of the Rev. Thomas Biker, rector of Culworth, by his 2nd wife, and by her (who d. 21 Feb. 1845) had issue,

JOHN-JACKSON, now of Marston.
Samuel, twin with John, d. unm. 2 Aug. 1833.
Thomas, m. in Dec. 1837, Ellen, dau. of R. Bathurst, Esq., and has, Thomas-Henry, and other issue.
James.
Louisa-Ann, relict of the Rev. Francis Gottwaltz, late vicar of Coughton, in Warwickshire.
Mary-Ann.
Susannah-Judith, m. 1 July, 1841, to the Rev. James Stafford, rector of Dinton, Wilts.

Mr. Blencowe d. 28 Aug. 1830.

Arms—Gu., a canton, arg.

Crest—A sword in pale, arg., hilt in chief, or, enfiladed with a human heart, gu., all between two wings expanded, arg.

Seat—Marston House, Northamptonshire.

BLENCOWE OF THE HOOKE.

BLENCOWE, ROBERT-WILLIS, Esq., M.A., of The Hooke, co. Sussex, J.P., b. 1791; m. in 1815, Charlotte-Elizabeth, youngest dau. and co-heir of the Rev. Sir Henry Poole, Bart. of The Hooke, and has one son,

JOHN-GEORGE, M.A., J.P. for Sussex, b. 1817.

Lineage.—THOMAS BLENCOWE, Esq. of Hayes, co. Middlesex, bencher of the Inner Temple, 2nd son of Sir John Blencowe, Knt., by Anne his wife, dau. of the Rev. John Wallis, D.D., the celebrated Savilian professor of Oxford (*see* BLENCOWE *of Marston St. Lawrence*), m. Martha, dau. and co-heir of William Perris, Esq. of Hayes, by his wife, dau. and heir of — Briggenshaw, Esq. of Hayes, and was eventually s. by his youngest son,

ROBERT BLENCOWE, Esq. of Northampton, M.D., b. 1732, who m. Margaret, dau. of — Danvers, Esq., and d. in 1774. His only surviving son,

ROBERT WILLIS BLENCOWE, Esq., b. in 1776, m. in 1780, Penelope, youngest dau. of Sir George Robinson, Bart. of Cranford, co. Northampton, and d. in 1842, having had issue,

John-George, b. 1790, d. unm.
ROBERT-WILLIS, now of The Hooke.
Harry-Charles.
William-Multon, in holy orders, rector of Shawell, co. Leicester, m. Maynard, dau. of Col. Rochfort.
Edward-Willis, d. in 1833.
Frances-Dorothea, m. 1st. to William-Peere Williams, only surviving son of Admiral Williams, of Clapton, co. Northampton, and 2ndly, to General Sir George Napier, K.C.B.
Mary, m. to Major-General Grant.
Ann-Elizabeth, d. unm. 1831.
Elizabeth. Louisa-Eleanor, d. 1803.
Caroline-Diana.
Emma, m. to the Rev. Sir George Robinson, Bart.
Charlotte-Louisa, m. to Henry Frampton, Esq.
Louisa-Isabella, m. to the Rev. J. Chichester, and d. in 1834.

Arms and *Crest*—As BLENCOWE *of Marston*, quartering WALLESTON, PERRIS, and BRIGGENSHAW.

Motto—Quorsum vivere mori, mori vitæ.

Seat—The Hooke, Chailey, near Lewes.

BLENKINSOPP OF HOPPYLAND CASTLE.

BLENKINSOPP, GEORGE-THOMAS LEATON, Esq. of Hoppyland Castle, co. Durham, and Humbleton Hall, Northumberland, J.P. and D.L., b. 21 Dec. 1783; m. 6 Oct. 1807, Harriot, dau. of Henry Collingwood, Esq. of Lilburn Tower, and Cornhill House, co. Durham, and has had issue,

I. RICHARD-BLENKINSOPP-GEORGE, b. 15 Jan. 1809, rector of Shadforth, Durham, m. 27 Sept. 1836, Mary-Emma, dau. of Sanderson Ilderton, Esq. of Ilderton, Northumberland, and has issue,

1 George-Ilderton, b. 8 May, 1840.
2 Edwin-Henry, b. 15 Jan. 1842.
1 Emma-Victoria.

II. George-Anthony, b. 24 Dec. 1813, captain in the 45th foot.

III. Henry-Wellington, b. 2 July, 1815, d. 27 April, 1841.

IV. Edward-Clennell, in holy orders, b. 31 Jan. 1819.

I. Harriet-Collingwood.

Lineage.—This is a branch of the ancient Northumbrian house of BLENKINSOPP *of Blenkinsopp*, which Camden styles "a right ancient and generous family." The heiress of the senior line, JANE, only dau. and heir of Thomas Blenkinsopp, of Blenkinsopp Castle, Esq., m. in 1727, WILLIAM COULSON, Esq., of Jesmond House *(see* COULSON *of Blenkinsopp Castle)*, while the heiress of the descendant of another branch,

ELIZABETH BLENKINSOPP, only dau. of GEORGE BLENKINSOPP, Esq. of Whickham House, co. Durham, and Humbleton Hall, co. Northumberland, by Elizabeth his wife, dau. of John Coulter, of Prestwich and Newcastle, merchant, m. 5 Dec. 1776, ANTHONY LEATON, Esq., son of John Leaton, Esq., by Elizabeth Rawlings his wife, and grandson of Anthony Leaton, Esq., by his wife, a dau. of the family of Orde, and had a son and heir, the present GEORGE-THOMAS-LEATON BLENKINSOPP, of Hoppyland Castle, Esq.

Arms—Quarterly: 1st and 4th, gu., a fesse between three garbs, or, for BLENKINSOPP; 2nd and 3rd, quarterly, 1st and 4th, arg., a fesse between six crosses-crosslet, fitchée, sa., for LAYTON or LEATON; 2nd and 3rd, sa., three swords in fesse, arg., two with their points in base, and the middle one in chief, for RAWLINS.

Crests—1st, a lion, rampant, or, for BLENKINSOPP; 2nd, out of a mural coronet, two wings expanded, arg., each charged with a cross-crosslet, fitchée, sa., for LEATON.

Motto—Dieu defende le droit.

Seats—Hoppyland Castle, co. Durham, and Humbleton Hall, Northumberland.

BLENNERHASSETT OF BALLYSEEDY.

BLENNERHASSETT, CHARLES-JOHN, Esq. of Ballyseedy, b. in July, 1830.

Lineage.—This family is of English origin, and has either received its surname from, or conferred it upon, Blennerhasset, co. Cumberland. It sent a representative for Carlisle to the parliaments of almost all kings from RICHARD II. to JAMES I. The Blennerhassetts settled in Ireland, *temp.* Queen ELIZABETH; and have, since that period, maintained the highest rank amongst the gentry of the co. Kerry, where the first settlers, THOMAS BLENNERHASSETT, with his son, ROBERT, obtained a part of the Earl of Desmond's large possessions. From the latter descended

JOHN BLENNERHASSETT, Esq. of Ballyseedy, who became knight of the shire, co. Kerry. He m. Margaret Lyn, and had, with other issue, JOHN, his heir, and Robert, ancestor of the present Sir Arthur Blennerhassett, Bart. The eldest son,

JOHN BLENNERHASSETT, Esq. of Ballyseedy, was progenitor of the late

ARTHUR BLENNERHASSETT, Esq. of Ballyseedy, M.P. for Kerry, son of Arthur Blennerhassett, Esq. of Ballyseedy, by Dorcas his wife, dau. of George Twiss, Esq. of Anna; he m. Frances-Deane Grady, and by her (who d. in 1834), had surviving issue, CHARLES-JOHN, now of Ballyseedy; Dorcas, m. to Robert-Conway Hurly, Esq.; Amelia, m. to the Hon. Chichester Skeffington; Ada, m. to Standish, 3rd Viscount Guillamore; and Frances. Mr. Blennerhassett d. in 1843.

Arms—Gu., a chevron, erm., between three dolphins, embowed, naint, arg.

Crest—A wolf, sejant, ppr.

Motto—Fortes fortuna juvat.

Seat—Ballyseedy House, Tralee, co. Kerry.

BLISS OF BRANDON PARK.

BLISS, HENRY, Esq. of Brandon Park, co. Suffolk, b. 28 May, 1809, assumed, by royal license, the surname and arms of BLISS, in lieu of those of ALDRIDGE, on succeeding to the property of his uncle, Edward Bliss, Esq.

Lineage.—The late EDWARD BLISS, Esq., J.P., lord of the manor of Brandon, co. Suffolk, high-sheriff of that shire in 1836, (son of Edward Bliss, Esq., M.D., by Mary Clark his wife, and grandson of Edward Bliss, and Elizabeth Brown his wife) was b. 20 Dec. 1774. He m. 28 Oct. 1797, Sarah,* 2nd dau. of the Rev. Acquila Scatchard, and Sarah his wife, but d. without issue, 2 April, 1845. Brandon Park, and the whole of his other property, passed under his will (subject to some life annuities) to his nephew, HENRY ALDRIDGE, Esq. (son of James Aldridge, Esq., by Elizabeth his wife, and grandson of John Aldridge, Esq. of Hampshire, justice of the peace, and deputy-lieutenant of the county), who by royal sign-manual, changed his name to BLISS.

Seat—Brandon Park, Suffolk.

BLOFELD OF HOVETON HOUSE.

BLOFELD, THE REV. THOMAS-CALTHORPE, M.A., of Hoveton House, co. Norfolk, J.P. and D.L., rector of Hellesden-with-Drayton, co. Norfolk, b. 16 Aug. 1777; m. 7 May, 1802, Mary-Caroline, 3rd dau. and eventually only surviving child of Francis Grose, Esq., F.A.S. (the celebrated antiquary), and by her (who d. 5 Jan. 1852) has issue,

I. THOMAS-JOHN, M.A., in holy orders, J.P. and D.L., vicar of Hoveton, co. Norfolk, b. 22 Feb. 1807, m. 1834, Catherine-Charlotte, dau. of the Rev. Anthony Collett, rector of Heveningham, and has issue,

1 Thomas-Calthorpe, b. 15 Dec. 1836.
2 Robert-Singleton, b. 7 Jan. 1839.
3 Francis-Grose, b. 8 April, 1845, d. 28 April, 1851.
1 Catharine-Mary.

I. Mary-Catherine.

Lineage.—The family of Blofeld was settled in Norfolk at a very early period. Thomas Blofeld possessed lands in North Repps, in that county, which he sold before 1466 to Robert Wende, of Northrepps; and a Robert Blofeld was living at Hickling in 1479.

THOMAS BLOFELD, Esq. of Sustead Hall and Beeston Priory, co. Norfolk, barrister-at-law (son of Thomas Blofeld, Esq. of South Repps, by Margaret his wife, dau. of Robert Doughty, Esq. and grandson of Robert Blofeld, of Cromer, whose grandfather, John Blofeld, of Cromer, living in 1528, was grandson of William Blofeld, of Norwich), m. 1st, Mary, dau. — of Wright, Esq. of Sculthorp, co. Norfolk, and by her had, with four daus.,

Thomas, of Beeston Priory, who m. Anne, dau. of William Hunt, Esq. of Hildoverstone, co. Norfolk, and had issue, William, of Beeston Priory.
ROBERT, of whom presently.

The 2nd son,

THE REV. ROBERT BLOFELD, M.A., rector of Westwick and of Thorpe-next-Norwich, m. Mary, dau. of T. Layer, Esq. of Booton, co. Norfolk, and had issue,

I. THOMAS, of whom presently.

II. John, of London, m. Mary, dau. and co-heir of — Richardson, Esq., and had issue; John, of London, m. Mary, dau. of Henry Negus, of Norwich, merchant; and Thomas, of Briston, m. Catherine, dau. of John Calthorpe, Esq. of Hickling Hall, and had issue; 1 THOMAS, of Hoveton, who s. his great-uncle, and of whom hereafter; 2 John, of Norwich, m. Mary, dau. of Thomas Munnings, Esq., and had a son, JOHN, of whom hereafter; 1 Catharine, m. to John Richer, Esq., M.D.

The elder son,

THOMAS BLOFELD, Esq. of Norwich and Hoveton, J.P. and D.L., and M.P. for Norwich, m. Elizabeth, dau. of Henry Negus, Esq. of Hoveton-St. Peter, co. Norfolk, and dying s. p., 17 Oct. 1708, was s. by his grand-nephew,

THOMAS BLOFELD, Esq. of Hoveton, co. Norfolk, J.P. and D.L., who m. Sarah, dau. of Henry Negus, Esq. of Hoveton-St. Peter, and had an only child, SARAH, m. to her cousin JOHN. This

JOHN BLOFELD, Esq., b. 6 Feb. 1725, s. under the will of his great-great-uncle, to the estate of Hoveton. He m. his cousin, Sarah, only child of Thomas Blofeld, Esq. of Hoveton, and d. in Aug. 1805, leaving a son,

THOMAS BLOFELD, Esq. of Hoveton, barrister-at-law, and a magistrate and deputy-lieut., b. 24 Dec. 1753, m. Mary, dau. of Henry Spencer, Esq. of Dulwich, and by her (who d. 14 April, 1824) had issue,

John-Spencer, b. 5 July, 1776, capt. in the E. I. Co.'s service, d. unm. at Hyderabad, 22 Sept. 1803.

* This lady's elder sister, Mary, m. 1st, the Rev. James Bentham, prebendary of Ely, and 2ndly, the Rev. Dr. Hatt.

Thomas, now of Hoveton.
Maria, d. unm.

Mr. Blofeld d. 7 Aug. 1817.

Arms—Sa., a chevron, arg., between three fleurs-de-lis, or.
Crest—Three ostrich feathers, arg.
Motto—Domino quid reddam.
Seat—Hoveton House, co. Norfolk.

BLOUNT OF MAPLE-DURHAM.

BLOUNT, MICHAEL-HENRY-MARY, Esq. of Maple-Durham, co. Oxford, J.P. and D.L., high-sheriff in 1832, b. 8 Aug. 1789; m. 1st, 15 May, 1817, Elizabeth-Anne-Mary, 4th dau. of Robert-Edward, 10th Lord Petre, and has surviving issue,

I. MICHAEL-CHARLES, b. 19 April, 1819.
II. Charles-John, b. 21 Aug. 1821.
III. John, b. 22 Feb. 1833.
IV. Robert-Martin, b. 25 Oct. 1837.
I. Mary-Catherine.
II. Charlotte-Elizabeth.
III. Georgiana-Frances.
IV. Henrietta-Matilda.

Mr. Blount m. 2ndly, Lucy-Catherine, 4th dau. of James Wheble, Esq.

Lineage.—This ancient and distinguished family can be traced from the Counts of Guisnes, in Picardy, a race of nobles descended from the Scandinavian rulers of Denmark. RODOLPH, 3rd Count of Guisnes, had three sons by his wife Rosetta, dau. of the Count de St. Pol, all of whom accompanied the Norman in his expedition against England, in 1066. One of the brothers returned to his native country; the other two adopted that which they had so gallantly helped to win, and abided there; of these, SIR WILLIAM LE BLOUNT, the younger, was a general of foot, at Hastings, and was rewarded by grants of seven lordships in Lincolnshire; his son was seated at Saxlingham, in Norfolk, and the great-granddau. of that gentleman, sole heiress of her line, MARIA LE BLOUNT, marrying in the next century, Sir Stephen le Blount, the descendant and representative of her great-great-great-uncle, SIR ROBERT LE BLOUNT, united the families of the two brothers,

SIR WALTER BLOUNT (son of Sir John le Blount, of Sodington, by Eleanor his 2nd wife, dau. and co-heir of John, Lord Beauchamp of Hache), so celebrated for his martial prowess in the warlike times of EDW. III., RICH. II., and HENRY IV., and immortalized by the muse of Shakspeare for his devotion, even unto death, to King HENRY, fell at the battle of Shrewsbury, 22 June, 1403, leaving, by his wife, Donna Sancha de Ayala, dau. of Don Diego Gomez de Toledo, with two daus., four sons, viz., JOHN (Sir), his heir, K.G., who d. s. p.; THOMAS, successor to his brother; JAMES (Sir), ancestor of the BLOUNTS *of Grendon, Eldersfield, Orleton, &c.*; and Peter, who d. s. p. The 2nd son,

SIR THOMAS BLOUNT, treasurer of Normandy, dying in 1456, left, with three daus., two sons, SIR WALTER BLOUNT, LORD MOUNTJOY, and

SIR THOMAS BLOUNT, of Milton Ross, co. Leicester, who d. in 1468, and was s. by his son,

RICHARD BLOUNT, who m. Elizabeth, only dau. and heir of William de la Ford, of Iver, in the co. of Buckingham, by whom he acquired the estate in that place, and purchasing the manor of Maple-Durham Gurney, in the co. of Oxford, 1 Feb. 1489, fixed his permanent abode there. He served the office of sheriff for Bucks and Bedfordshire in 1502. He d. 31 Nov. 1508, and was s. by his son,

SIR RICHARD BLOUNT, of Maple-Durham Gurney, one of the gentlemen of the chamber to King HENRY VIII.; of the privy chamber to EDWARD VI., and lieutenant of the Tower, *temp.* ELIZABETH. He m. Elizabeth, dau. of Sir Richard Lister, chief-justice of England, and sister of Sir Michael Lister, K.B., and dying 11 Aug. 1564, was s. by his elder son,

SIR MICHAEL BLOUNT, of Maple-Durham, b. in 1529, lieutenant of the Tower. In 1581 (4 Feb.) he purchased the manor of Maple-Durham Chawsey, for 900*l.*, and soon after erected the fine mansion of Maple-Durham, still existing in the most perfect state. He was sheriff of Oxfordshire in 1586 and 1597. He m. Mary, sister and co-heir of Thomas Moore, Esq. of Bicester, in Oxfordshire, by whom (who d. 23 Dec. 1592) he had, with other issue, a son and successor,

SIR RICHARD BLOUNT, Knt. of Maple-Durham, b. 28 June, 1564, m. 1st, Cicily, dau. of Sir Richard Baker, of Sisinghurst, in Kent, and had, with other issue, CHARLES (Sir), his heir. He m. 2ndly, Elizabeth, dau. of Sir Francis Moore, Knt. of Fawley, in Berkshire, and had by her a dau., Jane, m. to Sir William Moore, of Fawley, and two sons, of whom the elder, WILLIAM, of Kidmore End, m. Elizabeth, dau. of Sir Ralph Delaval, and had a son, LISTER, of whom presently. Sir Richard d. 22 Nov. 1619, and was s. by his eldest son,

SIR CHARLES BLOUNT, Knt. of Maple-Durham, who was slain fighting under the king's banner, at Oxford, 1 June, 1644. He m. Dorothy, dau. and sole heir of Sir Francis Clerke, Knt. of Houghton Conquest, in Bedfordshire, and by her had (with two daus., of whom the elder Anne, m. 1st, John Swinburne, Esq. of Capheaton, and 2ndly, Francis Godfrey, Esq.) two sons, MICHAEL, who was killed in 1649, and WALTER. The 2nd son,

WALTER BLOUNT, Esq. of Maple-Durham, m. 1st, Philippa Benlowes, of Essex, who d. in 1667 (issueless), and 2ndly, Dorothy, dau. of Edmund Plowden, Esq. of Plowden, co. Salop, by whom he had a dau., Elizabeth, who d. an infant. He d. himself in May, 1671, having, by deed, of the 5th February, in the previous year, settled the estates of Maple-Durham on his cousin,

LISTER BLOUNT, Esq, b. in 1654, who thus became of Maple-Durham. This gentleman m. in 1683, Mary, dau. of Anthony Englefield, Esq. of White Knights, and had issue, one son, MICHAEL, his heir, and two daus., well known as the friends of the poet Pope, viz., Teresa, b. at Paris, 15 Oct. 1688, and d. in 1759; and Martha, b. 15 June, 1690, and d. in 1763. Mr. Blount d. 25 June, 1710, and was s. by his son,

MICHAEL BLOUNT, Esq. of Maple-Durham, b. 26 March, 1693, m. 1715, MARY-AGNES, dau. and co-heir of Sir JOSEPH TICHBORNE, of Tichborne, co. Hants, by which lady (who d. in May, 1777, aged 82) he had, with two daus., Mary, m. to Sir Henry Tichborne, Bart., and Francis, who d. a nun at Brussels, in 1740, three sons, MICHAEL, his heir; Henry Tichborne, a priest, president of Douay College in 1770, who d. in 1810; and Walter, a Benedictine monk, who d. in 1746. He d. 2 Nov. 1739, and was s. by his eldest son,

MICHAEL BLOUNT, Esq. of Maple-Durham, b. in 1719, who m. in 1742, Mary-Eugenia, eldest dau. of Mannock Strickland, Esq. of Lincoln's Inn, by whom (who was b. 10 July, 1723, and d. 12 Dec. 1762) he had issue,

I. MICHAEL, his heir.
II. Joseph, b. 15 July, 1752, m. Mary, dau. of Francis Canning, Esq. of Foxcote, co. Warwick, by whom he left at his decease,
   1 Joseph, b. in 1779, m. 1st, Jane, dau. of John Saterthwaite, Esq. of Mansergh Hall, Westmoreland, but there was no issue of that marriage. He m. 2ndly, 19 Feb. 1816, Anne, only dau. of Mr. Richard Martin, of Hurstborne Tarrant, in Hampshire, and by this lady had an only dau.
   2 Michael, m. Catharine, dau. and co-heir of Francis Wright, Esq. of Bedford Square, London, (by his wife, Catharine Petre, who m. after the death of Mr. Wright, Michael Blount, Esq. of Maple-Durham,) and has issue.
   1 Elizabeth, m. in July, 1802, to Ralph Riddell, Esq. of Felton Park, in Northumberland.
   2 Frances.
I. Mary-Eugenia, b. 14 Feb. 1745, m. 1st, 15 Nov. 1765, to Charles Stonor, Esq. of Stonor, and 2ndly, in 1783, to Thomas Canning, second son of Thomas Canning, Esq. of Foxcote, in Warwickshire.
II. Martha, b. in 1762, d. unm. 5 Feb. 1780.

Mr. Blount d. 5 Feb. 1792, and was s. by his eldest son,

MICHAEL BLOUNT, Esq. of Maple-Durham, b. 4 July, 1743, m. 1st, at Bristol, 15 April, 1781, Eleanora, 2nd dau. of Maurice Fitzgerald, Esq. of Puncher's Grange, co. Kildare. By this lady, who d. 12 May in the next year, he had a dau., Maria-Eugenia, b. in Jan. 1782, d. 2 Aug. 1791. He m. 2ndly, 27 Aug. 1787, Catharine, dau. and sole heir of John Petre, Esq. of Belhouse, Essex, and widow of Francis Wright, Esq. of Bedford Square, and had

MICHAEL-HENRY-MARY, his successor.
Walter-Thomas-Mary.
Henrietta, m. 16 Sept. 1811, to John Wright, Esq. of Belsize Park, Hampstead.
Juliana-Mary, m. to Thomas Nolan, Esq. of the ancient family of Ballykealy, co. Carlow.

Mr. Blount d. 29 Oct. 1821, and was s. by his son, the present MICHAEL-HENRY-MARY BLOUNT, Esq. of Maple-Durham.

Arms—Barry-nebulée, or and sa.; quartering AYALA, CASTILE, and BEAUCHAMP.
Crest—A wolf, passant, sa., between two cornets, out of a ducal coronet, or; also, a foot in the sun, with the motto, "Lux tua, via mea." The latter is the crest now generally adopted.
Seat—Maple-Durham.

BLOUNT OF ORLETON.

Blount, William, Esq. of Orleton, co. Hereford, *b.* in April, 1799; *m.* 1st, in 1821, Eliza, dau. of Thomas Wright, Esq. of Fitzwalters, co. Essex, by which lady he has a son,

I. William.

And 2ndly, 31 March, 1839, Lady Charlotte-Jane St. Maur, eldest dau. of Edward-Adolphus, Duke of Somerset, and has by her two sons,

I. Archibald. II. Henry.

Mr. Blount *s.* his elder brother in 1831, and was M.P. for Totness in 1839.

Lineage.—Myles Blount, Esq. of Orleton, 6th son of Roger Blount, Esq. of Grendon, by Maria his wife, dau. of W. Berington, Esq. of Winsley, *d.* in 1663, leaving, by his wife, Anne Bustard, of Addlebury, *inter alios*, two sons, Thomas Blount, the lawyer, an antiquary and writer of celebrity, who *d.* at Orleton, having been frightened to death by Titus Oates' plot, and Myles Blount, Esq. father of

Thomas Blount, Esq., who *m.* Mary Mostyn, and dying in 1781, left a son,

Edward Blount, Esq., who *m.* Miss Cotham, and had issue. The fourth son,

William Blount, Esq., M.D. of Orleton, *b.* in 1760, *m.* Mary, only dau. of Lacon Lambe, Esq. of Bidney, co. Hereford, and had (with other issue, of which a dau. Emma, *m.* Henry Matthews, Esq., the author of *The Diary of an Invalid*, who *d.* a judge in the island of Ceylon, in 1829) a son and successor, the present William Blount, of Orleton, Esq.

Arms—Barry-nebulée of six, or and sa.; in chief, eight pellets.
Crest—A cross in the sun.
Motto—Mors crucis mea salus.
Seat—Orleton, co. Hereford.

BLUETT OF HOLCOMBE COURT.

Bluett, Peter, Esq. of Holcombe Court, co. Devon, J.P. and D.L., high-sheriff in 1800, *b.* 25 July, 1768; *m.* 20 Sept. 1794, Elizabeth, dau. of Edward Phelips, Esq. of Montacute House, co. Somerset, and relict of John Clarke, Esq. of Halton, co. Cornwall.

Lineage.—John Bluett, descended from the Bluetts, lords of Ragland, acquired Holcombe Rogus in the 15th century, by marriage with a co-heiress of Chiselden. His ancestors had married heiresses or co-heiresses of Ragland, Greenham, and Beaupeny. Richard Bluett, great-grandson of this John, had two sons, Sir Roger, his heir, who *d.* in 1566, and Francis, ancestor of the Bluetts *of Cornwall*, Arthur, great-grandson of Sir Roger, *m.* the heiress of Lancaster. The elder branch of the direct line became extinct in 1636, by the death of his son, John Bluett, Esq., whose daus. and co-heirs *m.* Jones, Wallop, Lenthall, and Basset. John, the son of Francis (a younger son of Arthur), who was killed at the siege of Lyme, in 1644, dying *s. p.* in 1700, the elder line was supposed to be extinct, and he bequeathed his estates to Robert Bluett, Esq., then the representative of the Bluetts *of Colan*, in Cornwall, descended from the younger brother of Sir Roger. Buckland-Nutcombe Bluett, Esq. (son of Robert) who *d.* in 1786, bequeathed his estates to their present possessor, Peter Bluett, Esq. of Falmouth, supposed to be a descendant of Francis Bluett, half-brother of Colan Bluett, who lived in the early part of the 17th century. Mr. Bluett is son of the late James Bluett, Esq., by Anna his wife, dau. of Capt. Peter Hill; and grandson of William Bluett, Esq., by Mary his wife. He has had one brother and three sisters, viz.,

William, who *m.* Elizabeth-Maria, dau. of John Clarke, Esq. of Halton, Cornwall, and had issue, Peter-Frederick, James, Lauretta-Maude, Amelia, and Christiana.
Elizabeth, *m.* to John Walsby, Esq.
Anna, *m.* to Capt. Stephen-Banfield Bell.

Arms—Or, a chevron, between three eagles displayed, vert.
Crest—A squirrel, sejant, or, in his paw an acorn, vert, fructed, or.
Motto—In Deo omnia.
Seat—Holcombe Court, co. Devon.

BLUNDELL OF CROSBY.

Blundell, Nicholas, Esq. of Crosby Hall, co. Lancaster, *s.* his father 11 July, 1854; *m.* in Nov. 1847, Agnes, 3rd dau. of Sir Edward Smythe, Bart. of Acton Burnell, and has issue,

I. William, *b.* in April, 1851.
II. Francis-Nicholas, *b.* in May, 1853.
I. Mary-Agnes.

Lineage.—Osbertus de Aynosdale, living in the 12th century, the first ancestor of this family on record, was great-grandfather of

Sir Robert Blundell de Crosby, living 5th Edward I., who gave to Allan, the son of Allan Norras (Norreys) all his land in Watton Dale, Breck, and Bold, for six marks, which the said Allan had lent him. In the 5th Edward I. Sir Robert made over to his son Nicholas, all his lands in Annosdale, now called Ainsdale, saving to himself the right of shipwreck (a valuable appendage in those days) to an estate on the coast, and likewise all his lands in Ravensmeales and Liverpoole, still reserving the produce of shipwreck.

Nicholas Blundell, Esq. of Crosby, the last male representative of this long-descended family, *m.* Frances, dau. of Marmaduke, 2nd Lord Langdale, and had two daus., viz.,

Mary, who *m.* John Coppinger, Esq. of Ballyvolane, co. Cork, and had an only son, who *d.* in infancy, in 1745.
Frances.

Mr. Blundell *d.* in 1737, and was *s.* by his daus., of whom the younger,

Frances Blundell, *m.* Henry Peppard, Esq. (grandson of Thomas Peppard, Esq., who *d.* M.P. for Drogheda, in 1640), and had issue. The heiress of Crosby *d.* 17 April, 1773, having outlived her husband about eighteen months, and was *s.* by her eldest surviving son,

Nicholas Peppard, Esq. of Crosby, who assumed, in 1772, the surname and arms of Blundell only. He *m.* Clementina, 3rd dau. of Stephen-Walter Tempest, Esq. of Broughton, co. York, by Frances-Olive his wife, dau. and co-heir of George Meynell, Esq. of Aldborough, and by her, who *d.* 21 July, 1821, left at his decease in 1795, (with two daus., Frances, wife of Sir Edward Mostyn, Bart., and Clementina, who *d.* *unm.* in 1821) a son and successor,

William Blundell, Esq. of Crosby, J.P. and D.L., *m.* Catherine, dau. of the late Sir Thomas Stanley-Massey-Stanley, Bart. of Hooton, in Cheshire, by Catherine his wife, dau. of William Salvin, Esq., of Croxdale, and had issue,

I. Nicholas, now of Crosby.
II. William, capt. 51st infantry, killed in action at Rangoon, 18 April, 1852.
III. Charles, major Austrian service.
IV. John, *m.* Catherine, dau. of Peter Middleton, Esq. of Middleton Lodge, and Stockwell Park, co. York.
V. Thomas.
I. Clementina. II. Catharine-Frances.
III. Mary-Emily. IV. Anna-Maria.

Mr. Blundell *d.* 11 July, 1854.

Arms—Sa., ten billets, arg.
Crest—A demi-lion, rampant, sa., in the paws a tau, fitchée, erect, arg.
Seat—Crosby Hall, near Liverpool.

BLUNDELL OF INCE.

See Weld-Blundell.

BLUNT OF WALLOP HOUSE.

Blunt, The Rev. Walter, of Wallop House, co. Hants, J.P., *b.* 23 Jan. 1802; *m.* 16 Oct. 1827, Marian, eldest dau. of William Pearce, Esq. of Whitehall Place, London, and has had issue,

I. Ronald-Pearce, *b.* in 1828, *d.* the same year.
I. Emily-Anna-Maria. II. Agnes Rebecca.

Lineage.—Walter Blunt, Esq. of Croydon, (3rd son of Sir Henry Blunt, 2nd bart., by Dorothy his wife, eldest dau. of William Nutt, Esq. of Walthamstow), *m.* 1st, Anne, dau. of James Dandridge, Esq. and by her had two sons, Walter, who *d.* young, and James, of whom presently. He *m.* 2ndly, in 1774, Hanna-Maria, dau. of Sir Thomas Gatehouse, of Headly Park, Hants and granddau. of

William Huggins, Esq. of the same place, and by her had issue,

George, b. 4 Jan. 1778, d. at Agra, in the East Indies, 3 June, 1829, s. p.
EDWARD-WALTER, now of Kempshott Park (see that article).
Eliza-Maria, m. 17 Nov. 1804, to John Greathed Harris, Esq., Commissioner of the Insolvent Court.
Harriet.

The only son of the first marriage,

JAMES BLUNT, Esq. of Wallop House, co. Hants, m. 1st, 3 Oct. 1799, Henrietta, dau. of Robert Garden, Esq. of Clifton, and had issue,

WALTER, now of Wallop House.
Edward-Powlett, in holy orders, b. 24 April, 1806, m. July, 1831, Caroline-Anne, dau. of the Rev. Roger Clavell, of Manston, co. Dorset, and has issue, Francis, Grant, Henrietta, Charlotte, and Mary-Anne.
Emily-Dorothea, d. 7 July, 1831.

He m. 2ndly, 9 April, 1810, Sarah, dau. of Richard Little, Esq., and by her had issue,

Harriet-Louisa, m. to Hulbert Wathen, Esq. of Streatham, Surrey.
Charlotte-Maria, d. in April, 1833.
Caroline-Arabella, m. to the Rev. Alfred Wilkinson, of Downside, co. Somerset.
Sarah-Selina, m. to the Rev. Alexander Annand, of Roade, co. Northampton.

Mr. Blunt d. 28 Sept. 1832.

Arms—Barry-nebulée of six, or and sa.
Crest—The sun in glory, charged on the centre with an eye, issuing tears, all ppr.
Motto—Inter lachrymas micat.
Seat—Wallop House, near Andover.

BLUNT OF KEMPSHOTT PARK.

BLUNT, EDWARD-WALTER, Esq. of Kempshott Park, co. Hants, b. 28 Nov. 1779; m. 9 March, 1813, Janet-Shirley, dau. of James Allan, Esq. of The Hall, co. Stirling, and has issue,

I. Edward-Walter, b. 2 Sept. 1818, d. unm. 30 July, 1840.
II. George-Allan, b. 28 June, 1822, d. 11 Feb. 1840.
III. HENRY, b. 15 Sept. 1823.
IV. Charles-Harris, b. 7 Sept. 1825.
V. James-St.John, b. 5 June, 1827.
VI. Arthur, b. 1 Jan. 1829.
VII. Alexander-Colvin, b. 14 Nov. 1831.
VIII. David, b. 29 Dec. 1833.
I. Elizabeth-Maria, m. 8 May, 1839, to the Rev. H.-J. Bigg Wither, rector of Worting, Hants, 2nd son of the late Henry-Bigg Wither, Esq. of Marydown Park, Hants.
II. Harriet, m. 17 Aug. 1841, to the Rev. John Lawrell, M.A., rector of Hampreston, co. Dorset, youngest son of the late James Lawrell, Esq. of Frimley, co. Surrey.
III. Shirley-Anna.

Mr. Blunt is a magistrate and deputy-lieutenant.

Lineage.—This is a junior branch of the Blunts, Baronets, of London.

WALTER BLUNT, Esq., 3rd son of Sir Henry Blunt, 2nd baronet, by Dorothy his wife, eldest dau. of William Nutt, Esq. of Walthamstow, married twice; by his first wife he was grandfather of the REV. WALTER BLUNT, of Wallop House, (see that name), and by his second, Anna-Maria, dau. of Sir Thomas Gatehouse, of Headly Park, Hants, and granddau. of William Higgins, of that place, Esq., he had issue,

George, b. 4 Jan. 1778, d. at Agra, E.I., 3 June, 1829.
EDWARD-WALTER, of Kempshott Park, as above.
Eliza-Maria, m. in 1805, to John Greathed Harris, Esq., Commissioner of the Insolvent Court.
Harriet.

Arms—Barry-nebulée of six, or and sa.
Crest—The sun in glory, charged on the centre with an eye, issuing tears, all ppr.
Motto—Inter lachrymas micat.
Seat—Kempshott Park, near Basingstoke.

BODENHAM OF ROTHERWAS.

BODENHAM, CHARLES-THOMAS, Esq. of Rotherwas, co. Hereford, J.P., b. 15 Feb. 1783; m. 29 Nov. 1810, Elizabeth-Mary, 5th dau. of Thomas Weld, Esq. of Lulworth Castle, co. Dorset, and has a son,

CHARLES-DE LA BARRE, b. 4 May, 1813, m. 28 April, 1850, the Countess Irena-Maria Dzierzykraj-Morawska, dau. of the late Joseph, Count Dzierzykraj-Morawska, of Operon, Grand Duchy of Posen.

Lineage.—SIR JOHN BODENHAM, Lord of Monington, Walterston, Cheriston, and Dewchurch, 5th in descent from Hugh de Bodham, alias Bodenham, Lord of Bodenham Rogeri, temp. STEPHEN, m. 1st, Margaret, dau. of John Ragon, Lord of Walterston and Cheriston, and had by her two sons, viz., John, of Monington, whose dau. and heir, Margaret, m. Hugh Hargest, of Hargest, and Robert, ancestor of the BODENHAMS of Biddenden and Ryal. Sir John m. 2ndly, Isabella, dau. and sole heir of Walter de la Barre, and by her (who m. 2ndly, Walter Coykin, without issue), left at his decease, 49th EDWARD III., a son and successor,

ROGER BODENHAM, of Dewchurch, great-grandfather of

ROGER BODENHAM, Esq. of Rotherwas, b. 3rd HEN. VII., who m. Jane, 3rd dau. and co-heir of Thomas Whyttington, of Pauntly, and left at his decease in 1579, Thomas, his heir, who d. s. p. 1583; ROGER, successor to his brother; Elizabeth, m. to Thomas Morgan, of Machen, co. Monmouth; and Margaret, m. 1st, to William Games, and 2ndly, to John Pye. The 2nd son,

SIR ROGER BODENHAM, of Rotherwas, b. in 1545, K.B. at the coronation of JAMES I.; m. in 1582, Bridget, youngest dau. of Sir Humphrey Baskerville, Knt. of Erdisley Castle, co. Hereford, and had (with a dau. Blanch, m. 5 Oct. 1611, to Edward Lingen, of Stoke Edith and Sutton, co. Hereford) two sons, 1 THOMAS, his heir; and 2 William, of Bryngwyn, bapt. 21 Sept. 1592, who signed the Visitation of 1634. Sir Roger's elder son and heir,

THOMAS BODENHAM, Esq. of Rotherwas, living in 1634, m. Mary, dau. of Sir Francis Lacon, of Kinlet Hall, in Salop, and had, with two daus. (Bridget, m. before 1634, to Walter James, of Treyvor; and Blanch, m. after 1634, to Edmund Hawley), a son and successor,

ROGER BODENHAM, Esq. of Rotherwas, who m. Anne Draycot, of Paynesley, in Staffordshire, and had issue. The second son,

JOHN BODENHAM, Esq. m. Mary, dau. of Charles Trinder, of Bourton-on-the-Water, in Gloucestershire, and had (with a dau. Anne, m. to Henry Tasburgh, Esq. of London, and d. s. p.), two sons, of whom the younger, John, a Jesuit, named in the settlement of 1712, d. unm; while the elder,

CHARLES BODENHAM, Esq. of Rotherwas, m. 1st, Anne, dau. of John Stonor, Esq. of Stonor, co. Oxford, and by her (who d. in April, 1714) had a son, CHARLES STONOR, his heir, and Margaret-Catherine, a nun at Brussels. He m. 2ndly, in 1731, Catherine, dau. of Henry Huddlestone, Esq. of Sawston, in Cambridgeshire, and by her had issue, John, d. s. p.; Catherine, m. to John Berkeley, Esq. of Spetchley, co. Worcester; Mary, m. to John Tancred, Esq.; and Anne, d. an infant. Mr. Bodenham d. 15 May, 1762, and was s. by his son,

CHARLES-STONOR BODENHAM, Esq. of Rotherwas, who m. Frances Pendrill, descended from Richard Pendrill, who saved King CHARLES II., and dying 16 April, 1764, was s. by his son,

CHARLES BODENHAM, Esq. of Rotherwas, b. 2 June, 1757, who m. Bridget, dau. of Thomas Hornyold, Esq. of Blackmore Park, in Worcestershire, and by her, who d. 21 April, 1825, had one son and a dau., viz.,

CHARLES-THOMAS, now of Rotherwas.
Eliza-Mary, Canoness of the order of St. Anne of Bavaria.

Mr. Bodenham d. 5 April, 1826.

Arms—Az., a fesse between three chess-rooks, or, quartering twenty-five coats.
Crest—A dragon's head, erased, sa.
Motto—Veritas liberabit.
Seat—Rotherwas, co. Hereford.

BODKIN OF ANNAGH.

BODKIN, ROBERT, Esq. of Annagh, co. Galway, J.P., high-sheriff in 1833-4, b. 20 March, 1809; m. 30 June, 1842, Elizabeth, youngest dau. and co-heiress of the late Thomas Redington, Esq. of Ryehill, in the county Galway.

Lineage.—The family name was originally FITZGERALD. A younger son of the ancient and powerful family, the FITZGERALDS of Desmond and Kildare, came to Connaught in the 13th century, and settled in Athenry, as most of the Anglo-Normans did at that period. A descendant of his had BOWDEKINE added to his name, which was retained, and the original discontinued in a similar manner to that by which the descendants of the Caddles took the name of Blake. The motto of their ancestors the Fitzgeralds is that of the Bodkins of the present day.

The Bodkins took an active part in the affairs of Athenry in the time of EDWARD III.: many of the family removed to Galway in the succeeding reign, that of RICHARD II., where they gave their name to a street, and at that early period Thomas Bodkin and his son Henry were, in and about the town, extensive proprietors. In 1455, John Bodkin was compositor of the customs. Members of the family were frequently elected provosts of Athenry; Richard Bodkin, a burgess of Galway, was provost of Athenry in 1454. A great many of the family became mayors and sheriffs for the town of Galway up to the time when it surrendered to Sir Charles Coote in 1652. So attached were they to their religion and king, that not a single member of the Bodkin family signed the articles of assent on that occasion; it appears by the returns of the town-major of Galway to the commissioners of the Commonwealth, in 1652, that the representatives of six of the Bodkin family refused to sign, and that ten others were absent. During the short reign of JAMES II., many of the ancient Roman Catholic families returned to Galway; amongst them, JOHN BODKIN FITZ-AMBROSE, of Annagh, who is mentioned in the charter that JAMES II. granted to the citizens of Galway.

JOHN BODKIN, mayor of Galway, 1518, was *s.* by his eldest son,

AMBROSE BODKIN, sheriff of Galway in 1570, who *m.* Julian, dau. of John Blake, by his wife Evelina Skerrett, and was father of

JOHN BODKIN, who had two sons, JOHN FITZ-JOHN, his heir, and Richard Fitz-John.

JOHN BODKIN FITZ-JOHN, was father of Ambrose, his heir; Dominick Fitz-John; Andrew Fitz-John; and Marcus Fitz-John. The eldest son,

AMBROSE BODKIN FITZ-JOHN, *m.* the dau. of Alderman Andrew Browne Fitz-Dominick, of Galway. This Ambrose absented himself from Galway on the surrender to Sir Charles Coote in 1652; he got grants of the following lands, that is to say, Annagh, Kilmoyland, and several other denominations. He *d.* in 1679, and was *s.* by his son,

JOHN BODKIN FITZ-AMBROSE, who *d.* in 1689, leaving three sons, Richard Fitz-John, his heir; John Fitz-John; and Patrick Fitz-John. He was admitted a freeman of Galway by charter of JAMES II. John was *s.* by his son,

RICHARD BODKIN FITZ-JOHN, whose son,

JOHN BODKIN, *m.* 1st, Miss Browne, dau. of Martin Browne, of Coolarne, by his wife Miss Brown, of Castle Mount Garret, and had by her, RICHARD-BLAKE, his heir; Robert, successor to his brother; Austin; Anne, *m.* in 1719, to Thomas Blake, Esq. of Mulloughmore and Windfield; and another dau. *m.* to Nicholas Bermingham, of Bachersfort. He *m.* 2ndly, Margaret, dau. of R. Blake, of Ardfry, ancestor to the present Lord Wallscourt, and had three daus., Julia, *m.* 1st, to Peter Lynch, Esq., and 2ndly, to P. Martyn, Esq.; a dau. *m.* to John Browne, of Galway; and Mary-Anne, *m.* to Richard Geoghegan, Esq. of Bunown Castle, co. Galway.

RICHARD-BLAKE BODKIN, the elder son, *d. unm.*, and was *s.* by his brother,

ROBERT BODKIN, who *m.* 1st, a dau. of Sir Anthony Brabazon, of Brabazon Park, co. Mayo, by whom he had an only dau., Anne, *m.* to Henry Bingham, brother of John, Lord Clanmorris, of Newbrook, in the co. Mayo. He *m.* 2ndly, Elizabeth, dau. of John Kirwan, Esq. of Castlehacket, in the co. Galway, by whom he had JOHN, his heir; Denis, who *d. unm.*; and Margaret, who *m.* John Bodkin, of Bungarra, in the co. Galway.

JOHN BODKIN, of Annagh, son and heir, *m.* Harriet, dau. of Martin Kirwan, of Blindwell, in the co. Galway, and had issue,

ROBERT, the present proprietor.
Martin, a barrister, who *d. unm.*
Denis.
Mary, a nun.
Elizabeth, *m.* to John Blake, Esq. of Ballyglunin, now deceased.
Harriet, *m.* to Hyacinth Daly, Esq. of Raford, in the county of Galway.
Margaret, a nun. Catherine. Anne.

Arms—Arg., a saltire, gu.
Crest—A wild boar, ppr.
Motto—Crom-a-boo.
Seat—Annagh, co. Galway.

BOLDEN OF HYNING.

BOLDEN, JOHN, Esq. of Hyning, co. Lancaster, J.P. and D.L., *b.* 25 Aug. 1776; *m.* in 1801, Mary, dau. of John Satterthwaite, Esq. of Rigmaden Hall, Westmoreland, and has issue,

WILLIAM-BOLDEN, his heir, *b.* 29 Sept. 1808.
And six other sons and two daus.

Lineage.—This family was possessed of the estate of Bolden, in Ellel, co. Lancaster, for more than two centuries, until it was sold about the year 1750, by

WILLIAM BOLDEN, Esq., who afterwards settled in Liverpool. His son and heir,

WILLIAM BOLDEN, Esq. of Hyning, co. Lancaster, *b.* 25 Dec. 1730, *m.* Agnes Fleming, of Rayrigg, co. Westmorland, a descendant of the Rydal family, but *d. s. p.* in 1800, when his estate devolved on (the son of his sister, Alice, by her husband, John Leonard, of Liverpool) his nephew, JOHN LEONARD, who assumed the surname and arms of BOLDEN, and is the present JOHN BOLDEN, Esq. of Hyning.

Arms—Quarterly: 1st and 4th, or, on a fesse, gu., three fleurs-de-lis of the field; 2nd and 3rd, per fesse dancettée, gu. and vert, three swans, or.
Crests—1st, out of a ducal coronet, or, a tiger's head, arg.; 2nd, a swan, or.
Motto—Pour bien désirer.
Seat—Hyning, co. Lancaster.

BOLDERO OF WHITE HOUSE.

BOLDERO, JOHN, Esq. of White House, Rattlesden, co. Suffolk, *b.* 3 Oct. 1806; *m.* 16 Oct. 1829, Sarah-Maria, eldest dau. of Mr. John Raynham, sometime of Drinkstone Hall, co. Suffolk, son of James Raynham, of Ofton Wallow and Burnt House, in the same county, and has issue,

I. JOHN-SIMON, *b.* 12 Nov. 1830.
II. George-Thomas, *b.* 20 Feb. 1832.
III. Frederic, *b.* 2 May, 1841.
IV. Arthur-Herbert, *b.* 20 Oct. 1845.
V. Joseph-John, *b.* 18 July, 1847.
VI. Alexander-Samuel, *b.* 2 Nov. 1848.
VII. Henry-Francis, *b.* 23 Nov. 1852.
I. Mary-Anne. II. Sarah-Maria.
III. Anna-Caroline. IV. Helen.
V. Isabella-Jane. VI. Alice-Emma.

Lineage.—EDMUND BOLDERO, living at Fornham St. Martin, Suffolk, in 1501, son and heir of Richard Boldero, and grandson of William Boldero, of Fornham St. Martin, *m.* Isabel, dau. of Jenkyn Smith, Esq., and *d.* in or about 1523, leaving (with younger issue) two sons, JOHN, his heir, and Thomas, who *d.* in 1583, leaving, by Margery Bettes, his wife, a son and heir, John, of Bury St. Edmunds, father of Edmund Boldero, M.A., rector of Westerfield, Glemsford, and Snaylwell, who *d.* 5 July, 1679:—he is referred to by Roger North, Walker, and Evelyn.

JOHN BOLDERO, (son and heir of Edmund Boldero and Isabel Smith his wife) living at Fornham St. Martin in 1537, *m.* in 1546, Margaret Howard, of Norfolk, and *d.* in 1584, leaving, with other issue, EDMUND BOLDERO, who *m.* Elizabeth Page, of Framlingham, and *d.* in 1602, leaving several children, and

GEORGE BOLDERO, Gent. bapt. at Fornham St. Martin, in 1561, who *d.* in 1609, leaving, by Margaret his wife, several children, of whom was

GEORGE BOLDERO, Gent., bapt. at Bury in 1596, whose wife's name was Ann. He *d.* in 1665, and was father of

SIMON BOLDERO, M.A. of Jesus College, Cambridge, bapt. at Ixworth in 1636, who *m.* in 1658, Frances, dau. of John Godbould, Esq., M.P. for Bury, and *d.* in 1701, leaving issue,

SIMON, his heir.
George, *b.* in 1665, *m.* in 1701, Esther Fiske, of Rattlesden, and *d.* in 1737, leaving, with other issue, Roger, of Ixworth, *b.* in 1714, who *m.* in 1750, Elizabeth Cocksedge, and *d.* in 1794, leaving a son, George, *b.* in 1753, who *m.* in 1780, Hester, dau. of the Rev. Edward Griffin, and *d.* in 1818, having had, George, perpetual curate of Ixworth, *d. s. p.* at Brussels, 1836; Hester, *m.* to the Rev. Henry Adams, rector of Bardwell, Suffolk; Frances, *m.* to the Rev. Edward-René Payne, rector of Hepworth, Suffolk; and Mary, *m.* to the Rev. Mr. Dodson.

The eldest son,

THE REV. SIMON BOLDERO, A.M., vicar of Great Barton,

and subsequently rector of Wolpit, b. in 1660, m. in 1688, Joan Cooke, of Little Livermere, and was s. at his decease in 1722, by his son and heir,

THE REV. JOHN BOLDERO, rector of Woolpit, who m. 17 Oct. 1828, Martha Taylor, of Woolpit, sister of Maria-Rebecca Taylor, wife of Richard Dillon, Esq. of Dillon Grove, co. Roscommon, and had by her

JOHN, rector of Ampton, b. 16 Oct. 1729, whose sons were, JOHN; William; George (rector of Raynham, Norfolk); and Edmund. The eldest son, the Rev. John Boldero, rector of Ampton, was father of COLONEL HENRY-GEORGE BOLDERO, M.P. for Chippenham.
SIMON, of whose family we treat.
Roger, d. unm. 1756.
Martha, m. 6 Oct. 1757, to Simon Hunt, of Norton, Suffolk, and d. in 1807.
Ann. Mary, d. young. Elizabeth, d. young.

John Boldero d. 17 Oct. 1758. His 2nd son,

SIMON BOLDERO, Esq., b. 30 Dec. 1730, m. 6 Oct. 1757, Elizabeth-Susannah, dau. of — Gardner, Gent. of Woolpit, a descendant of Sir R. Gardner, Knt., sometime lord of the manors of Elmswell and Woolpit, and founder of almshouses in the former parish, in the church of which is a splendid monument to his memory. By her (who d. 5 July, 1784) Mr. Boldero left at his decease, 25 March, 1784, three sons, viz.,

ROGER, b. 28 May, 1766, who m. Deborah Poole, and d. 2 July, 1810, leaving issue.
SIMON, of whom presently.
John, of Bury St. Edmunds, b. 31 March, 1771, m. Susan Cocksedge, and d. in 1838.

The second son,

SIMON BOLDERO, Esq. of Drinkstone, b. 30 Jan. 1769, m. twice. By Elizabeth-Susan, his 1st wife, who d. in 1801, he had a dau. Elizabeth, m. to Thomas Markham; and by his 2nd, Mary Hazlewood, of Woolpit, three sons and two daus., viz.,

JOHN, now of White House, Rattlesden.
George, of Ashfield, b 21 July, 1811, m. 25 Nov. 1830, Sophia, dau. of James Ransom, of Bury St. Edmunds, by his wife, a dau. of James Stewart, Esq., and has, GEORGE-WILLIAM, eldest surviving son, b. in 1837, and other issue.
William, b. in 1818, m. Anna-Caroline, dau. of Mr. Raynham, of Drinkstone Hall, and d. s. p. in 1851.
Susan, m. to George Pledger, late of Bury.
Martha, d. unm.

Arms—Per pale, or and az., a saltire counterchanged.
Crest—A greyhound, sejant.
Motto—Audax ero.
Seat—White House, Rattlesden, Woolpit, Suffolk.

BOLGER OF BALLINABARNA.

BOLGER, JAMES, Esq. of Ballinabarna, co. Kilkenny, b. 7 April, 1828; s. his father 18 Aug. 1847.

Lineage.—RICHARD BOLGER, Esq., m. Margaret, dau. of Patrick Wall, Esq. of Pollardstown, co. Carlow, and had, with a dau. Bridget, an only son and heir,

EDWARD BOLGER, Esq., who m. Christian, dau. of Harry Lambert, Esq. of Carnagh, co. Wexford, and by her had two sons. RICHARD, the elder, d. s. p., and was s. by his only brother,

JAMES BOLGER, Esq., who m. about 1795, Catherine, dau. of James Winter, Esq. of London and Pilgrim Hatch, and had issue,

EDWARD, his heir.
Richard, m. Henrietta, dau. of James O'Reilly, Esq. of Baltrasna, and had issue, four sons and one dau.
James.
Christina-Maria. Catherine.
Mary, m. to William de Rinzy, Esq. of Wexford.

The eldest son,

EDWARD BOLGER, Esq. of Ballinabarna, co. Kilkenny, J.P., b. 10 July, 1802, s. his father 1 Sept. 1824. He m. 12 June, 1827, Maria, only dau. of Francis McCrohon, Esq. of co. Kerry, and had issue,

I. JAMES, now of Ballinabarna.
II. Edward. III. Francis.
IV. Richard. V. George.
VI. William-Henry.
I. Jane. II. Maria-Lucinda. III. Catherine.
IV. Christina. V. Ellen. VI. Victoria-Anna.
VII. Lucinda. VIII. Anne.

Motto—Deus providebit.
Seat—Ballinabarna, co. Kilkenny.

BOLTON OF BECTIVE ABBEY.

BOLTON, RICHARD, Esq. of Bective Abbey, co. Meath, J.P., m. Frances, dau. of George Bomford, Esq. of Rahinstown, co. Meath, and sister and co-heir of Robert-George Bomford, Esq. of Rahinstown, who d. s. p. in 1846.

Lineage.—SIR RICHARD BOLTON, Knt., recorder of Dublin in 1607, was son of John Bolton, Esq. of Great Fenton, co. Stafford, by Margaret his wife, dau. of Richard Ash, of Ash, and derived from a branch of the family of BOLTON *of Bolton*, in Lancashire. In 1625, he was appointed chief baron of the Exchequer, and in 1639, became lord-chancellor of Ireland. He m. 1st, Frances, dau. of Richard Walter, Esq. of Stafford, and 2ndly, Margaret, dau. of Sir Patrick Barnewall, Knt. of Turvey; by the former he left at his decease, 1648, two daus., Anne, m. to Arthur Hill, Esq. of Hillsborough, and Mary, m. 1st, to Patrick Nangle, baron of Navan, and 2ndly, to Edward Bermingham; and seven sons, of whom the eldest,

SIR EDWARD BOLTON, of Brazeel, co. Dublin, knighted 2 Feb. 1635, was constituted chief baron of the Exchequer in Ireland, but was removed by the usurping powers. By Isabella his wife, dau. of Mr. Sergeant Ayloffe, he had NICHOLAS, his heir; Edward, of Clouneek, Queen's Co.; and one dau. The eldest son,

NICHOLAS BOLTON, Esq. of Brazeel, m. 1 May, 1649, Anne, 2nd dau. of Nicholas Loftus, Esq. of Fethard, and had issue, EDWARD, of Brazeel, who d. s. p. in 1705; RICHARD, successor to his brother; Isabella, m. 16 May, 1695, to Sir Mark Rainsford, Knt.; Frances, m. to John Madden, M.D.; and Margaret, m. 1st, to Theophilus Jones, Esq. of Ballynamore, co. Leitrim, and 2ndly, to John Atkyns, Esq. of Roper's Rest. Mr. Bolton d. 1 Aug. 1692. His 2nd son,

RICHARD BOLTON, Esq. of Brazeel, heir to his brother, m. Anne-Catherine, dau. of Stein Bill, of Copenhagen, and dying in 1721, was s. by his eldest son,

EDWARD BOLTON, Esq. of Brazeel, M.P. for Swords, b. in 1695, m. Letitia, youngest dau. of Robert, Viscount Molesworth, and d. 5 Aug. 1758, leaving (with five daus., of whom Letitia m. the Rev. Gustavus Hamilton, and Anna-Maria m. Capt. Archibald Grant) four sons, viz., ROBERT, his heir; Theophilus, a commissioner for managing the state lottery in Dublin; Richard; and Edward, who died young. The eldest son,

ROBERT BOLTON, Esq. of Brazeel, m. 13 July, 1754, Elizabeth, dau. of John Blennerhassett, and had two sons, EDWARD, his heir; and Robert-Compton, who m. in 1778, Elizabeth, eldest dau. of Jas.-Massey Dawson, Esq. of Ballynacourt, co. Dublin, and had a son, John-Bolton Massey, Esq. of Balliwire, co. Tipperary, and a dau., Maria, wife of John Arthur, Esq. of Seafield, co. Dublin. Mr. Bolton d. in 1798, and was s. by his son,

EDWARD BOLTON, Esq. of Brazeel, who m. 1st, Miss Donaldson, and 2ndly, Frances, dau. of Joseph Neynoe, Esq., and had issue by both: by the 1st, he was father of a dau., Anna-Maria, m. to W.-B. Neynoe, Esq., and of two sons, Robert-Compton, his heir, and Edward-Compton, who m. and had issue. The eldest son,

ROBERT-COMPTON BOLTON, Esq. of Brazeel, had two wives, by the 2nd, Charlotte, dau. of Joseph Neynoe, Esq. (whom he m. in 1800), he had a dau., Anne, m. to Loftus Neynoe, Esq. of Castle Neynoe, co. Sligo, and two sons, RICHARD, now of Bective Abbey, and Robert, who m. Maria, dau. of John Arthur, Esq. of Seafield, co. Dublin, and has issue.

Arms—Or, on a chevron, gu., three lions couchant, of the field.
Crest—A hawk belled, arg.
Seat—Bective Abbey, co. Meath.

BOLTON OF MOUNT BOLTON.

(FORMERLY OF FATLOCK CASTLE.)

BOLTON, JANE, of Mount Bolton, co. Waterford, s. her brother, Major John Bolton, in 1841.

Lineage.—The founder of this family in Ireland* was, CAPTAIN WILLIAM BOLTON, an officer of dragoons in the Protector's army, who stormed and took Fatlock Castle,

* It is presumed that the BOLTONS *of Mount Bolton*, co. Waterford, are descended from the ancient family of De Bolton, represented in the year 1300 by John de Bolton, bow-bearer of the royal forest of Bowland, Lancashire, who was (according to Sir William Dugdale) the lineal representative of the Saxon Earls of Mercia.

Oct. 1649, and obtained a large grant of land in the co. of Waterford in 1667. He held the office of mayor of Waterford in 1662. By Abigail his wife, dau. of Col. Prittie, he had several children; from the eldest son, Cornelius, captain in Col. Collingwood's regt., descends the present CORNELIUS-HENRY BOLTON, captain in the Waterford Militia. Capt. William Bolton's brother,

THOMAS BOLTON, Esq., mayor of Waterford in 1671, and recorder of that city, *d.* about 1697, leaving issue. The eldest son,

WILLIAM BOLTON, of Fatlock Castle, Esq., capt. in Col. Edward May's troop of dragoons. He *d.* 12 March, 1750, leaving (with two daus., Mary, *m.* to — Lymbery, Esq., of Killcopp House, co. Waterford, and Eleanor, *d. unm.* in 1783) a son,

JOHN BOLTON, Esq., first of Fatlock Castle, and afterwards of Mount Bolton, who *m.* 5 Dec. 1745, Anne, dau. of — Snow, Esq. of Snowhaven, co. Kilkenny, and had issue,

CHARLES, his heir.
Robert (Sir), lieut.-gen., G.C.H., of Swerford Park, Oxfordshire, aide-de-camp to GEORGE III., and equerry to GEORGE IV. He *d.* 15 March, 1836.
Hannah, *m.* 21 May, 1772, to Maunsell Bowers, Esq., and had issue, three sons and six daus.

The son and heir,

CHARLES BOLTON, Esq., bapt. 18 April, 1759, *m.* 1st, Jane, sister of Lieut.-Gen. Doyle, of Waterford, by whom he had one son,

I. JOHN, his heir.

Mr. Bolton *m.* 2ndly, Ellen, eldest dau. of Henry Wallis, of Drishane Castle, co. Cork, Esq., by Elizabeth, dau. of Christmas Paul, Esq., and Ellen, dau. of Robert Carew, Esq., M.P. of Ballinamona, co. Waterford. By this second marriage he had two sons and one dau.,

I. HENRY, A.M., vicar of Dysart, Enos, and Kilteale, Queen's Co., *b.* 3 April, 1787, *m.* 19 Dec. 1814, Frances, 2nd dau. of Sir Simon Newport, Knt., by Jane his wife, younger dau. of the Ven. Archdeacon Alcock, and had issue,

1 Charles-Newport, of Brook Lodge, co. Waterford, B.A. of St. Edmund Hall, Oxford, *b.* 15 March, 1816, *m.* 4 Feb. 1845, Anne, eldest dau. of the Rev. Joshua Anderson, of Grace Dieu, co. Waterford (brother of Gen. Anderson, C.B., K.C.) by Anne his wife, eldest dau. of Capt. William Perceval, and has issue,
Henry-Anderson, *b.* 7 March, 1848.
Charles-Perceval, *b.* 18 Sept. 1849.
Anne-Frances-Ellen.
2 Robert-Wallis, *b.* 2 May, 1819, *d.* 25 Feb. 1820.
1 Jane-Wallis, *m.* 13 Oct. 1853, Robert-Carew Anderson, Esq., M.D., 90th light infantry, 3rd son of the Rev. Joshua Anderson, rector and vicar of Myshall, co. Carlow, son of James Anderson, Esq. of Grace Dieu, by his wife Susanna, youngest dau. of Christmas Paul, Esq.

II. Charles, *d.* young.
I. Elizabeth, *m.* in 1828, Sir Simon Newport, Knt. of Waterford, but *d. s. p.* 1 Dec. 1844.

The eldest son,

JOHN BOLTON, Esq. of Mount Bolton, *m.* Eliza, 2nd dau. of Maunsell Bowers, Esq., and dying in 1807, aged 24, was *s.* by his son,

JOHN BOLTON, Esq. of Mount Bolton, major 7th dragoon-guards, *b.* in 1807, who *d.* suddenly in London in 1841, and was *s.* by his sister, the present Mrs. Bolton, of Mount Bolton.

Arms—Arg., on a chevron, gu., three lions, passant-guardant, or.
Crest—A buck's head, erased, attired, or, gorged with a chaplet, vert, and pierced through the neck with an arrow, of the second.
Motto—Vi et virtute.
Seat—Brook Lodge, co. Waterford.

BOMFORD OF OAKLEY PARK.

BOMFORD, GEORGE, Esq. of Oakley Park, co. Meath, *b.* 11 April, 1811; *m.* 23 July, 1832, Arabella, dau. of John-Pratt Winter, Esq. of Agher, and has issue,

I. GEORGE-WINTER, *b.* 12 Nov. 1834.
II. John-Francis, *b.* 22 Dec. 1837.
III. Samuel-Stephen, *b.* 27 July, 1841.
IV. Arthur-Chichester, *b.* 27 July, 1851.
I. Anne. II. Arbella-Anna. III. Elizabeth.
IV. Victoria-Adela.

Lineage.—In 1692, LAURENCE BOMFORD, descended from a good English family, was living at Clonmahon, in the co. Meath: he *d.* in 1720, at the advanced age of 108, having had issue by his wife Eleanor, four sons and four daus. His eldest son,

THOMAS BOMFORD, Esq. of Rahinstown, co. Meath, secretary of the Court of Claims, *d. s. p.*, 4 Feb. 1740, and was *s.* by his brother,

STEPHEN BOMFORD, Esq. of Gallow, co. Meath, who *m.* Anne Smith, of Violetstown, co. Westmeath, by whom he had issue, Thomas; Stephen; John; David, ancestor of Isaac-North Bomford, of Gallow; and Isaac; and four daus. He *d.* in 1756, and was *s.* by his eldest surviving son,

STEPHEN BOMFORD, Esq., J.P. of Rahinstown, who *m.* Elizabeth, dau. of Stephen Sibthorpe, of Brownstown, co. Louth, by Margaret his wife, sister of the Right Hon. Anthony Foster, chief baron of the Exchequer in Ireland, and grand-dau. of William Fortescue, of Newragh, co. Louth: by her he had, with other issue,

I. ROBERT, his heir, of Rahinstown, who *m.* in 1792, Maria, dau. of the Hon. James-Massey Dawson, 2nd son of Hugh, 1st Lord Massy, and had issue,

1 ROBERT-GEORGE, of Rahinstown, *b.* in 1802, high-sheriff of Meath in 1832, who *m.* in 1826, Elizabeth, only child of James-Trail Kennedy, Esq. of Annadale, co. Down, and *d. s. p.* in 1846.
1 Annette, *m.* to Sir Thomas-H. Hesketh, Bart., of Rufford Hall, co. Lancaster.
2 Jane, *m.* to Richard Mansergh, Esq. of Greenane, co. Tipperary.
3 Frances, *m.* to Richard Bolton, Esq. of Bective Abbey, co. Meath.
4 Jemima, *m.* to Richard Bolton, Esq., co. Waterford.
5 Sarah, *m.* to the Hon. Frederick Tollemache.
6 Susan, *m.* to the Rev. Charles Martin.

II. GEORGE, of Drumlargan.

This

GEORGE BOMFORD, Esq. of Drumlargan, *m.* in 1809, Arbella, dau. of Samuel Winter, Esq. of Asher, and by her, who *d.* 11 Sept. 1815, had issue,

GEORGE, now of Oakley Park.
Samuel, of the 3rd dragoon-guards, *m.* 11 July, 1839, Frances-Jane, dau. of Samuel-Pratt Winter, Esq., 3rd son of Samuel Winter, Esq. of Agher, and has issue.
Rodon-Charles. Laurence-George.
Trevor. Gerald.
Caroline-Frances.

Mr. Bomford *d.* Jan. 1814.

Motto—Justus et fidelis.
Seat—Rahinstown House, co. Meath.

BONAR OF BONARE, KELTYE, KILGRASTON, AND KIMMERGHAME.

BONAR, JAMES, Esq. of Kimmerghame, co. Berwick, and Warriston, in Mid-Lothian, *b.* in 1795, chief of the name, and twentieth in descent from William de Bonare, founder of the family in Scotland; heir male and representative of Bonar of that ilk, of Keltye, and of Kilgraston, and heir of line and representative of Oliphant of Dron, and of Grahame of Callander; *m.* 11 Sept. 1839, Mary, dau. of Sir Patrick Murray, 7th baronet of Ochtertyre.

Lineage.—SIR GUILHEM DE BONARE, the first of this family, with whom we commence the Scottish branches, settled in North Britain under King WILLIAM the Lion (*ante* 1200), as feudal Baron of Bonare, in Perthshire, having given to the lands assigned to him in fief his own name, which is still borne to this day by the village of Bonar, situate at the foot of a hill, on the summit of which stand the ruins of Castle Bonar. This knight, whom we may call in this pedigree WILLIAM, 1st feudal Lord of Bonare, bore "Azure, two swords crossed saltier-ways, argent." He was *s.* by his son,

WILLIAM, 2nd feudal lord, who lived *temp.* King ALEXANDER II. (1230), and was *s.* by his son,

WILLIAM-ROGER DE BONAR, 3rd feudal lord, who took the cross (in 1248-9), and joined the sixth Crusade, with the other Scottish knights, whom King ALEXANDER III. sent to Palestine under the banner of St. Louis. Of the issue of William-Roger, the Crusader, two sons alone are known, viz.,

WILLIAM, Master of Bonare.
John, of Laindes, who migrated to Flanders, and was author of several lines which flourished both in that country and in Sweden, Poland, Moravia, Silesia, and Breslau.

The eldest son,

WILLIAM BONAR, 4th feudal lord, royal seneschal of

Kyngshorne, on the coast of Fife, *temp.* King ALEXANDER III., was *s.* by his son,

WILLIAM BONAR, 5th feudal lord, royal seneschal of Kyngshorne, *temp.* King ROBERT I., a zealous follower of Sir William Wallace. He fought at Bannockburn in 1314, under the banner of ROBERT THE BRUCE. His only son,

WILLIAM-ROBERT BONAR, 6th feudal lord, royal seneschal of Kyngshorne, *temp.* Kings ROBERT I. and DAVID II. He fought at the battle of Halidon Hill in 1333. By Margaret his wife, of the family of Wemyss of that ilk, he had issue, I. JOHN, his heir; II. JAMES, of Bonarton, founder of that line, and ancestor of other branches, which flourished in Poland and Silesia. The last seneschal of Kyngshorne was killed at the battle of Durham in 1346. His son and heir,

JOHN BONAR, 7th feudal lord of Bonare, was at the siege of Carlaverock in 1355, and was still living in 1380. He *m.* Anne, of the RAMSAYS *of Dalhousie*, and left the following issue,

WILLIAM, his heir.
James, of Rossye, founder of the Rossye family. From the line of Rossye also derived the Barons of Cairnbaddy, who held their barony immediately from the crown; also the Lairds of Bonarfield (of whom David, the first, was killed at Flodden), and the Lairds of Balgershaw, and the Lairds of Easter Rossye (of whom John, the first, was killed at Flodden), and the legitimated line of Coltye, and the lines of the Lairds of Forgundenny, and Lairds of Cowbyres.
John, of Friarton, anthor of that line (of which James, the first, was killed at Flodden).

Sir John de Bonare was *s.* by his son,

WILLIAM BONAR, of Bonare, who is the first of this family whom we find designated as feudal lord of Keltye (which afterwards became the chief barony of the family). He served in the French wars under the Bastard of Orleans, who led a body of Scottish knights to the king's aid, and thus gained the victories of Beaugé, in 1421, and of Verneuil, in 1424, over the English. By his marriage with Christian Balfour, of the BALFOURS *of Burleigh*, he left,

I. JOHN, his heir.
II. William, of Keltye, who fought with his father and brother at Arbroath and Bannockburn. He *d.* in 1478, leaving issue,
1 NINIAN, successor to his uncle.
2 David, of Wester Keyth, who was wounded and made prisoner at Flodden. He *m.* Janet Barclay, of Touch, and left a son, DAVID, of Wester Keyth, living in 1548. whose wife was Mary Kircaldy, heiress of Lumquhat, By her he had David, of Wester Keyth, who *d. s. p.*; Alexander, *d. s. p.*; John, of Lumquhat, living in 1578, father of JOHN, 2nd of Lumquhat, who appears in several charters of the years 1589, 1592, 1593, 1594, and 1597. He had issue,
JOHN, 3rd of Lumquhat, A.D. 1610, whose son, JOHN, 4th of Lumquhat, *d. s. p.*
HARRYE, of Gregstou, ancestor of the BONARS *of Gregston*, now represented by WILLIAM-GRAHAM BONAR, of Gregston.
3 John, abbot of Balmerinoch.
III. Robert, of Strathy Bonar, ancestor of the BONARS *of Strathy and Cvulls*, both extinct.
IV. James, of Bonahalffe, living in 1502, who *m.* Anne Inglis, dau. of Tarvat, and left (with another son, William, of Drumdowane), a successor,
JOHN, of Kilgraston, who was at Flodden. By Jean his wife, of the Arnots of that ilk, he left a son,
JOHN, of Kilgraston, living in 1581, who loft by Agnes, dau. of Grahame of Garvock, a dau., Isobel, *m.* to Blair of Pitskellie, and a son and heir,
JOHN, of Kilgraston, living in 1542, who left, by Janet, dau. of Logan of that ilk, an only dau. and heir,
EUPHEMIA, Lady of Kilgraston. He also left,
John, of Colbyne, author of that line, bastard of Kilgraston, who was legitimated under the great seal of Scotland, *post mortem patris*, 25 Feb. 1584.
Euphema, Lady of Kilgraston, *m.* her kinsman, James Bonar, of Trevor, who *s.* at Kilgraston, as
JAMES, of Kilgraston and Trevor. He left by her, I. JOHN, his heir; II. David, *d. s. p.*; III. Bessetta, *m.* to Murray of Blackbarony; IV. Eupheme, *m.* to her kinsman, John of Bonarton. The Lady of Kilgraston predeceasing him, James was remarried to his cousin, Margaret, of the COLVILLES *of Culross*, and left by her, Patrick, who continued the line of Trevor. The elder son succeeded as
JOHN, of Kilgraston. He *m.* previously to 1606, Rosina, of the MURRAYS *of Auchtertyre*, and left, I. JOHN, his heir; II. Robert; III. Matthew; IV. Walter, fiar of Garvock, whose only son, Andrew, of Glassmouth, was tutor of Keltye, and left a son, David, of Burntisland, also tutor of Keltye; V. Helen, *m.* to Craigie of Dumbarney; VI. Katherine, *m.* to Maitland. The elder son who *s.* his father, as
JOHN, of Kilgraston, *m.* in 1634, Agnes, dau. and heir of Laurence Grahame, of Callander, a scion of Montrose; and left by her, I. JOHN, Master of Kilgraston, in right of his mother, representative and heir of line of GRAHAME *of Callander*; II. Alexander, of Tullochmaire, author of that line; III. James, of Gregston, who carried on that line, having *m.* his kinswoman, Mary, heiress of Gregston. The elder son,
JOHN BONAR, of Kilgraston, became eventually, at the decease of William Bonar, of Keltye, chief of the house of Bonar: of him in the sequel.

William Bonar dying in 1469, was *s.* by his eldest son,

JOHN BONAR, 2nd feudal lord of Keltye, who had fought with his father and brother at Arbroath, in 1445, and at Bannockburn in 1448. By his marriage with Margaret, of the SETONS *of Parbroath*, he had an only son, Ninian, Master of Bonare, who *d.* in infancy, whereupon the representation of the family devolved on John's nephew,

NINIAN BONAR, Baron of Keltye, eldest son of William of Keltye, and grandson of William, of Bonare. He was created knight-banneret on the field of Cauglor (or Sauchyburn, as it is often called), in 1488, in which he saved the life of King JAMES, by whose side he was afterwards killed at Flodden, in 1513. He *m. ante* 1505, Margaret Oliphant, Lady of Dron, sole dau. and heritrix of John Oliphant, of Dron, Dumbarney, Pitcaithly, and Binsean, son and heir of Thomas, of Dron, who was 2nd son of Walter, 5th of Aberdalgye, who was son of John, of Aberdalgye, and grandson of Walter, 4th of Aberdalgye, eldest son and heir of Walter, 3rd of Aberdalgie, Gask, &c., by the Princess Elizabeth of Scotland, dau. of King ROBERT I. Sir Ninian fell at Flodden, 9 Sept. 1513. Sir Ninian was *s.* by

WALTER BONAR, 2nd Baron of Keltye, who had been at Flodden under his father's banner. He *m.* Beatrice, of the HAYS *of Errol*, by whom he had a dau., Isabel, *m.* to Charles, of the RUTHERFORDS *of Fairnylee*, and two sons,

WILLIAM, Master of Keltye.
John, of Trevor.

Sir Walter resigned his barony into the Queen's hands by deed dated at Keltye, 23 Feb. 1535, in favour of his son,

WILLIAM BONAR, who fought at the battle of Pinkie, in 1547. He *m.* his cousin Margaret, Lady Abercairney, dau. of Lord Oliphant, by whom he had, I. NINIAN, Master of Keltye; II. Robert, of Cardness, of whom hereafter, as 7th Baron of Keltye; I. Janet, *m.* in 1571, to her cousin Grahame, 5th Baron of Garvock. After the death of Lady Abercairney, he *m.* 2ndly, his cousin Nicoline, dau. of Murray of Philiphaugh, by whom he had Margaret, *m.* to Henderson, treasurer of the Orkneys. He resigned his barony into the king's hands, by deed of 13 Nov. 1586, dated at Keltye, in favour of his son,

NINIAN BONAR, who having no male issue, and the barony of Keltye being a male fief, resigned the barony by act dated at Keltye, 28 Nov. 1610, in favour of his brother,

ROBERT Bonar, who *m.* Margaret, of the SANDILANDS *of Torphichen*, by whom he had six children, of whom Isobel, *m.* her cousin, Oliphant of Over Cultuquhaine, (and their dau., Isobel, *m.* Ninian, 10th Baron of Keltye;) Margaret, *m.* Stewart of Cuthills, sheriff of Perth; Catherine, *m.* her cousin Rutherford, of Nether Balquhandie. Robert of Keltye resigned his barony, by instrument dated Keltye, 3 Feb. 1630, in favour of his eldest son,

WILLIAM BONAR, who *m.* his cousin Catherine, dau. of Blair of South Corbe, by whom he left Jean, *m.* to her cousin Arnot; NINIAN, of whom presently, as 10th Baron of Keltye; and his eldest son, who succeeded him,

ROBERT BONAR, who dying *unm.* was *s.* by his brother,

NINIAN BONAR, who *m.* his cousin Isobel, dau. of Oliphant of Over Cultuquhaine, by whom he had an only son, WILLIAM. He eventually resigned his barony by act, dated Keltye, 4 May, 1680, in favour of his son, who succeeded, as

WILLIAM BONAR. He *m.* his cousin Helen, dau. of Grahame of Balgowane, and had an only son, Ninian, Master of Keltye, who *d.* the year of his birth, 1689. This last Baron of Keltye *d.* in Dec. 1691, and in his person the second line of the family ended, and the representation devolved on his kinsman, JOHN, 6th of Kilgraston. This

JOHN BONAR, 6th of Kilgraston, by Jean his wife, dau. of Reyd of Carse, had issue, I. JOHN, Master of Kilgraston and titular Master of Keltye; II. Catherine, *m.* to her kinsman, David, 2nd of Kintillo; and III. Anne, *m.* to Sinclair of Kennyarde. He *d.* in 1694, and was *s.* by his son,

JOHN BONAR, *b.* 16 Jan. 1670, *m.* 16 Dec. 1693, Grizzell, dau. of Gilbert Bennett, of Beath, by whom he had seven children, of whom William, Ebenezer, Margaret, Griseldis, and Marjorie *d.* young; ANDREW was founder of the line of

Camden (*see* CAMDEN), and JOHN, the eldest, was his father's heir. He *d.* 7 Aug. 1747, and was *s.* by his eldest son,

JOHN BONAR, of Kilgraston, *b.* 4 Aug. 1696, *m.* 13 Oct. 1720, Jean, dau. to Smythe of Monypenny; by her he left six sons: I. JOHN, his heir; II. James, *d. s. p.*; III. Ebenezer, *d. s. p.*; IV. William, *d. s. p.*; V. Andrew, *b.* 17 March, 1734, who left, by Patience Redbourne, two sons, James, who left by Janet, of the LAURIES *of Maxwelton*, Thomson; and William, of Gogar, who left by Janet, of the MAITLANDS *of Pitrichie*, four sons, Thomson, John, Archibald, all *unm.*, and Andrew, who *m.* Anne, of the DIXONS *of Ingo*, and has issue. He was *s.* in 1750, by his eldest son,

JOHN BONAR, titular Baron of Keltye, and 10th laird of Kilgraston, *b.* 4 Nov. 1721, who *m.* 18 Nov. 1746, Christian Currier, co-heritrix of Peppermills, and left issue, I. JOHN, of Kimmerghame; II. Andrew, of Warriston, of whom presently, as Kimmerghame; III. ALEXANDER, of Ratho, whose son, John, of Ratho, left a dau., Helen, heiress of Ratho; IV. Archibald, who left James and Archibald; V. Thomson, of Grove, who left Thomson, John, and Andrew; VI. James, who left John, who has left Andrew, Thomson, John, William, Archibald, and James. This last titular of Kilgraston *d.* 21 Dec. 1761, and the representation of the family devolved on his eldest son,

JOHN BONAR, of Kimmerghame, *b.* 24 Aug. 1747. He *d. unm.* in 1807, and was *s.* by his brother,

ANDREW BONAR, *b.* 6 Oct. 1748, who had acquired the estate of Warriston, in Mid-Lothian. He *m.* Anne, dau. of Carr of Esholt, by whom he had, I. JOHN, his heir; II. JAMES, now of Kimmerghame; III. William, *b.* in 1797, *m.* 20 May, 1831, Lilias, dau. of the late Alexander Cuninghame, of Craigends (sister to the Duchess of Argyll), and has one dau., Margaret-Cuninghame; and IV. Andrew, *b.* in 1802, *m.* 22 Oct. 1833, Marcelline, dau. of M'Donnell of Glengarry, and has two sons, John-Andrew and Alexander M'Donnell, and two daus., Euphemia-Rebecca and Anne-Jane. Andrew Bonar, on his demise, 5 Aug. 1825, was *s.* by his elder son,

JOHN BONAR, of Kimmerghame, *b.* in 1798, who dying *unm.*, in July, 1834, was *s.* by his brother, JAMES BONAR, now of Kimmerghame and Warriston.

Arms—Quarterly: 1st grand quarter, BONAR, *ancient*, quartering BONAR, *modern*; 2nd grand quarter, OLIPHANT *of Dron*, quartering the Royal ensigns of Scotland; 3rd grand quarter, GRAHAME *of Callander*, quartering GRAHAME *of Montrose*; 4th grand quarter, BONAR *of Keltye*, quartering BONAR *of Kilgraston*; over all BONAR *of Kimmerghame*.
Crests—Two swords, BONAR, *ancient*; a Crusader's sword, BONAR, *modern*; two banners crossed, as honourable augmentation, granted to the family by the King of France.
Seat—Kimmerghame, co. Berwick.

Bonar of Camden, co. Kent.

This is a branch of BONAR *of Kilgraston*, derived from

ANDREW BONAR (3rd son of John Bonar, 7th of Kilgraston, *b.* 24 June, 1708, *m.* Anne, dau. of Thomson of Crichton, (which family anciently bore the name of M'Tavish, and was a scion of the house of M'Farlane of that ilk), by whom he left, I. JOHN, who *d. unm.*; II. THOMSON, of Camden; III. Harrye, *d. s. p.* Of these, the 2nd son,

THOMSON BONAR, Esq., *b.* in 1743, acquired the lands of Camden and Elmstead, co. Kent. He *m.* Anne Thomson, dau. of his mother's brother, Andrew Thomson, Esq., and left issue by her, I. THOMSON, of Camden; II. Henry, *b.* in 1793; I. Agnes, *b.* in 1796, *m.* to Count di Moretti, in Italy. The elder son,

THOMAS BONAR, Esq., *s.* his father in 1811. He was *b.* in 1780, and *m.* 3 Nov. 1807, Anastasia-Jessye, dau. and (with her sister, the Dowager Lady Hay) co-heritrix of Guthrie of Hawkerton, falconer to the crown in Fife, heir-male, and ninth in descent from James Guthrie, 1st of Hawkerton, next brother to David, 1st Baron of Guthrie, armour-bearer to King JAMES III., and lord high-treasurer of Scotland. By this lady Mr. Bonar had issue,

ERNEST, present possessor of Camden.
Alfred-Guthrie, secretary of legation at Munich.
Lionel-Ninian, *b.* in 1816.
George-Douglas, *b.* in 1817.
Anastasia-Mary, *m.* to her kinsman, Patrick-Fraser Tytler, Esq., son of the late Lord Woodhouselee.
Emily-Anne. Mary-Anne.

The elder son, who *s.* his father in 1828, is the present

ERNEST-AUGUSTUS BONAR, Esq. of Camden and Elmstead, *b.* in 1808, chief of the second branch of the Bonars, twentieth in descent from William, first founder of the family in Scotland, and heir of line and representative of Guthrie of Hawkerton, heritable falconer to the crown in Fife. He was several years an officer in the service of the Emperor of Austria, and received the Cross of the Sovereign Hospitaller Order, as Chevalier de Justice of the Britanno-Bavarian Langue, upon the verification of his proofs of knightly extraction and gentle blood on either side, showing the filiation and alliances of this paternal line of BONAR, up to James, 1st of Trevor, and his wife Eupheme, dau. of Kilgraston, and the filiation and alliances of his maternal line of GUTHRIE, up to Harrye, 1st of Hawkerton, and his wife Mary, dau. of Ogilvye of Newton. He *m.* 11 Jan. 1834, Rosalia-Juliana-Henrietta de Wullerstorff-Urbair, dau. of Charles-Leopold de Wullerstorff-et-Urbair, a nobleman of Moravia and of the Holy Roman Empire.

BOND OF BONDVILLE.

BOND, HENRY-COOTE, Esq. of Bondville, co. Armagh, *b.* in March, 1786; *m.* in Dec. 1812, Eliza, eldest dau. of the Rev. Edward Stanley, of Tyholland, co. Monaghan, and grand-dau. of Arthur Stanley, Esq. of Dublin, late governor of the Bank of Ireland, and has issue,

I. EDWARD-W., *b.* 12 Dec. 1813.
II. Handcock-Stanley, *b.* 18 March, 1815, *m.* 28 July, 1840.
III. Wadham-Wyndham, *b.* 1 Nov. 1817, *m.* in June, 1845.
IV. Arthur-Henry, *b.* 21 April, 1819.
V. Thomas, *b* 24 March, 1824, *d.* 1850.
I. Charlotte-Stanley, *m.* to Thomas Bond, Esq. of co. Longford.
II. Jane-Caroline, *m.* to Ralph-Smith Obré, Esq. of co. Armagh.

Mr. Bond is only surviving son of the late Thomas Bond, who *d.* in 1784, by Sarah Donelly his wife, and grandson of Dr. John Bond, by his wife, Margaret Coote, of Belamont Forest, co. Monaghan. He had one brother, Thomas, who *d. unm.* in 1828; and one sister, Margaret, *m.* to Edward Younge, of Knockburn, co. Armagh.

Crest—A lion, sejant, arg.
Seat—Bondville, co. Armagh.

BOND OF GRANGE.

BOND, THE REV. NATHANIEL, of Grange, co. Dorset, rector of Steeple-with-Tyneham, *b.* 24 Nov. 1804; *m.* 31 Oct. 1835, Mary, 2nd dau. of the late John Hawkesworth, Esq. of Forest, in the Queen's County, and has issue,

I. NATHANIEL, *b.* 18 Sept. 1840.
II. Denis-William, *b.* 22 Jan. 1842.
III. George-Hawkesworth, *b.* 13 May, 1845.
I. Leonora-Sophia.

Lineage.—The family of Bond were of great antiquity in the co. of Cornwall, and are said to have been originally seated at Penryn in that co., but removed thence, at a very early period, to Earth, in the parish of St. Stephen's, an estate they acquired in marriage with the dau. and heiress of a very ancient house, which took its name from that place.

From this match descended

ROBERT BOND, who removed to Beauchamp's Hache, in Somersetshire, and in the year 1431 (9th HENRY VI.) was seated at Lutton, in the Isle of Purbeck, in the co. of Dorset, an estate which he acquired in marriage with the dau. and heiress of a family of that name, and which has ever since continued in the possession of his descendants. He had issue two sons, viz., ROBERT, his heir; and William, of Buckland, co. Somerset, who had two sons, William, of Crosby Palace, alderman of London, who *d.* in 1576; and George (Sir), lord-mayor of London in 1587, ancestor of SIR THOMAS BOND, created a BARONET by CHARLES II. The elder son,

ROBERT BOND, of Lutton, *m.* in 1453, Mary, dau. of Sir John Hody, Knt. of Pilledon, in the co. of Dorset, lord chief-justice of England in the 18th HENRY VI., and was father of WILLIAM, his successor, and John Bond, of Buckland, in the co. of Dorset, whose son, Sir Nicholas Bond, Knt., *d. s. p. m.*

WILLIAM BOND, of Lutton, eldest son of Robert, was *b.* in 1455, and *m.* in 1496, Elizabeth, dau. and co-heiress of John Prows, of Bredy, in the co. of Dorset, of the ancient family of PROWS *of Gedleigh Castle*, in Devonshire, and had DENIS, his heir, and John, ancestor of the BONDS of *Essex*. William Bond dying in 1530, was *s.* by his son,

DENIS BOND, of Lutton, *b.* in 1500, who *m.* in 1532, Alice, dau. of Robert Samways, of Toller, Dorset, and had several children: the 3rd son, William, left three daus., his co-heirs, of whom the eldest, Edith, *m.* Sir White Beckonshaw, of Moyle's Court, and was mother of Alice, *m.* to John Lisle, Esq. This lady was unjustly beheaded at Winchester in 1685. Denis Bond's 4th son,

JOHN BOND, Esq. of Lutton, *b.* in 1556, continued the line of the family, and was appointed, in 1588, captain of the Isle of Portland, at the time of the expected invasion by the Spanish armada. He *m.* in 1583, Margaret, dau. of Richard Pitt, Esq. of North Crickett, in the co. of Somerset, and dying in 1632, was *s.* by his son,

DENIS BOND, Esq. of Lutton, *b.* in 1588, a staunch parliamentarian, high in favour with Cromwell. From the commencement of the civil war he was of the committee for his own county, and from 1654 to 1656 he was M.P. for Weymouth, and one of the council of state from 1648 to 1652. He was likewise comptroller of the receipts of the Exchequer. Mr. Bond *m.* 1st, in 1610, Joane, dau. of John Gould, Esq. of Dorchester, by whom he had issue, JOHN, LL.D., M.P. for Melcombe Regis, 16th CHARLES I., who *d. s. p.* in 1676; and William, of South Bestwall, co. Dorset, of whose daus. and co-heirs the elder, MARY, by her 2nd husband, James Gould, Esq., was mother of an only child, Anna-Maria, *m.* 1st, to Gen. Charles Churchill, brother of John, 1st Duke of Marlborough, and 2ndly, to Montagu, 2nd Earl of Abingdon; and the 2nd, MARGARET, *m.* William Speke, Esq. He *m.* 2ndly, in 1622, Lucy, dau. of William Lawrence, Esq. of Steepleton, co. Dorset, and had, with other issue, Samuel, sometime M.P. for Poole and Melcombe Regis; and NATHANIEL, his successor at Lutton. Mr. Denis Bond dying 30 Aug. 1658, was buried in Westminster Abbey, and succeeded at Lutton by his son by his 2nd marriage,

NATHANIEL BOND, Esq. of Lutton, *b.* 1634, who was bred to the bar, and became king's serjeant. He purchased, in 1686, the adjoining estate of Grange, which has since been the chief residence of the family. He had also bought Tyneham, where a branch of his descendants still continue to reside. He *m.* Mary, dau. of Lewis Williams, Esq. of Chitterton, Dorset, and relict of Thomas Browne, Esq. of Frampton, by whom (who *d.* in 1728) he had issue,

DENIS, his successor.
John, of Tyneham, in the Isle of Purbeck, M.P. for Corfe Castle, *m.* in 1715, his cousin Margaret, 3rd dau. of John Williams, Esq. of Herringston, co. Dorset, by whom (who *d.* in 1775) he had, with other issue, JOHN, heir to his uncle.

Mr. Nathaniel Bond, who was M.P. for Corfe Castle, 31st CHARLES II., and subsequently for Dorchester, *d.* in 1707, and was *s.* by his eldest son,

DENIS BOND, Esq. of Grange, M.P. for Dorchester, 7th ANNE; for Corfe Castle, 1st and 8th GEORGE I.; and for Poole, 1st GEORGE II. He *m.* in 1729, Leonora-Sophia, relict of Edmund Dummer, Esq., and youngest dau. of Sir William-Dutton Colt, Knt., envoy at the court of Hanover, by Mary, his 3rd wife (of whom she was co-heir), eldest surviving dau. of John, and co-heir of her brother, Wentworth Garneys, Esqrs. of Boyland Hall, in Norfolk, and Kenton Hall, in Suffolk. Mr. Denis Bond *d. s. p.* in 1746, and the estates devolved upon his nephew,

JOHN BOND, Esq. of Grange, *b.* 1717, M.P. for Corfe Castle, from 21st GEORGE II. to 14th GEORGE III., who *m.* in 1749, Mary, eldest dau. and co-heir (with her sister, Elizabeth, wife of Valentine Knightley, Esq. of Fawsley Park, in the co. of Northampton) of Edmund Dummer, Esq. of Swathling, Hants, by the above-mentioned Leonora-Sophia, dau. of Sir William-Dutton Colt, and had issue,

I. JOHN, his successor.
II. NATHANIEL (RIGHT HON.), of Holme, *b.* 1754, sometime M.P. for Corfe Castle, one of the most hon. privy council, judge-advocate-general, a king's counsel, one of the lords of the Treasury, and a bencher of the Inner Temple, *d. unm.* in 1823.
III. Thomas, of Egliston, *b.* in 1756, vicar of Coombe-with-Wool, co. Dorset, *d. unm.* in 1833.
IV. William, of Tyneham, *b.* in 1757, rector of Steeple-with-Tyneham, and a canon of Bristol Cathedral, who *m.* Jane, only dau. of Henry Biggs, Esq. of Stockton House, co. Wilts, and had issue,
1 William, of the Inner Temple, barrister-at-law, a police magistrate, recorder of Poole and Wareham, *d. unm.* 1846.
2 John, vicar of Bath Weston, in Somersetshire, now of Tyneham.
3 Henry, vicar of South Petherton, in Somersetshire, *m.* Editha-Augusta-Mary, only dau. of the late Hon. Henry Pomeroy, and has issue, William-Henry; and Edith-Mary.
4 Thomas, barrister-at-law, recorder of Wareham.
1 Jane. 2 Mary.
I. Margaret-Sophia, *m.* in 1801, to the Rev. John Rogers, of Berkeley House, co. Somerset, and *d. s. p.* in 1820.
II. Mary, *m.* in 1796, to Nicholas-Cæsar Corsellis, Esq. of Wivenhoe Hall, co. Essex, and *d. s. p.* 1842.

The eldest son,

JOHN BOND, Esq. of Grange, *b.* 1753, *s.* his father, in 1784. He *m.* in 1798, Elizabeth, dau. and heiress of John Lloyd, Esq. of Cefncoed, co. Cardigan, and by her (who *d.* in 1846) had issue,

JOHN, his heir.
NATHANIEL, now of Grange.
Elizabeth, *m.* in 1840, to the Rev. Charles Onslow.
Leonora-Sophia, *m.* in 1835, to the Rev. William Buller.

Mr. Bond, who was M.P. for Corfe Castle, *d.* 12 May, 1824, and was *s.* by his elder son,

JOHN BOND, Esq. of Grange, M.P. for Corfe Castle, who served as high-sheriff of Dorsetshire in 1830. He *d. unm.* 18 March, 1844, and was *s.* by his brother, the present REV. NATHANIEL BOND, of Grange.

Arms—1st and 4th, BOND (ancient), sa., a fesse, or; 2nd and 3rd, BOND *of Cornwall*, arg., on a chevron, sa., three bezants.
Crests—1st, an eagle's wing, sa., charged with a fesse, or; 2nd, a demi-pegasus, az., winged, and semée of estoiles, or.
Motto—Non sufficit orbis.
Seat—Grange, in the Isle of Purbeck.

BOOKER OF THE LEYS AND VELINDRA HOUSE.

BOOKER, THOMAS-WILLIAM, Esq. of The Leys and Cobrey Park, co. Hereford, and Velindra House, co. Glamorgan, *b.* 28 Sept. 1801; *m.* 4 Oct. 1824, Jane-Anne, only dau. of the late John Coghlan, Esq., an officer in the army, and has issue,

I. RICHARD-BLAKEMORE, *b.* 26 June, 1828.
II. Thomas-William, *b.* 7 Jan. 1831.
III. John, *b.* 17 Nov. 1833.
I. Anna. II. Mary.

Mr. Booker was returned M.P. for co. Hereford in 1850. He is son of the Rev. Luke Booker, LL.D., F.R.L.S., vicar of Dudley, co. Worcester, and rector of Tedstone de la Mere, co. Hereford, by Anna his wife, dau. of Thomas Blakemore, Esq. of Darlaston, co. Stafford, and sister of the late Richard Blakemore, Esq. of The Leys, M.P. for Wells. Mr. Booker has one half-brother, John-Key Booker, and three sisters, viz.,

Harriet-Esther, *m.* to James Willington, Esq. of Bristol.
Catherine, *m.* to Leopold Tildasley, Esq. of Westbromwich.
Mary.

Arms—Or, an eagle, displayed, vert, ducally crowned, of the first, beaked and membered, gu., within a bordure, az., charged with three fleurs-de-lis, gold.
Crest—A demi-eagle, displayed.
Seats—The Leys and Cobrey Park, co. Hereford; and Velindra House, near Cardiff, co. Glamorgan.

BOOTH OF GLENDON HALL.

BOOTH, RICHARD, Esq. of Glendon Hall, co. Northampton.

Lineage.—JOHN BOOTH, of London, *d.* at his seat, Cheshunt, Herts, 14 Aug. 1733, leaving, by Anne his wife, dau. and co-heir of William Lloyd, Esq. of Liverpool, four sons, John, William, Montagu, and Benjamin, and several daus. The eldest son,

JOHN BOOTH, Esq. of Theobalds, co. Herts, then of Glatton, co. Huntingdon, and lastly of Glendon, co. Northampton, *b.* in May, 1721, *m.* Phœbe Wilkinson, of London, an heiress, by whom (who *d.* about 1764,) he had issue. The 4th son, Robert, of Huntingdon, and of Alconbury Hill, *b.* about 1758, *m.* Mrs. Maule, of Huntingdon, and *d.* 7 Aug. 1798, leaving issue, a dau., Phœbe (who *m.* and had issue), and a son, Robert, *b.* in 1794; *m.* Miss Edwards, dau. of the Rev. Mr. Edwards, by whom he had two sons and six daus. Mr. Booth was *s.* at his decease, in 1782, by his son,

RICHARD BOOTH, Esq. of Glendon Hall, co. Northampton, b. in March, 1756, high-sheriff in 1794, m. Janet, dau. of Sir Gillies Payne, of Tempsford, co. Bedford, Bart., and had issue, I. JOHN, his heir; II. Richard, b. in 1799, d. 1821, unm.; III. George-Neville; I. Janet, m. 1 Jan. 1823, to the Rev. Henry-Rule Sarel, rector of Balcombe, co. Sussex; II. Anne, d. unm.; III. Lætitia-Mary, d. unm.; IV. Caroline-Matilda, m. in 1834, to Richard Palmer, Esq. (of the family of PALMER of Grantham); V. Eliza-Purefoy. Mr. Booth d. 24 Feb. 1807, and was s. by his eldest son,

JOHN BOOTH, Esq. of Glendon Hall, b. 25 March, 1794, m. 14 Oct. 1835, Augusta De Capell-Brooke, 4th dau. of the late Sir Richard-Brooke De Capell-Brooke, of Oakley House, co. Northampton, Bart., and left a son and heir, the present RICHARD BOOTH, Esq. of Glendon. Mr. Booth was a deputy-lieutenant for Northamptonshire, and sheriff in 1818.

Arms—Arg., three boars' heads, erect and erased, sa.
Crest—A lion, passant, arg.
Motto—Quod ero, spero.
Seat—Glendon Hall, co. Northampton.

BORRER OF HENFIELD.

BORRER, WILLIAM, Esq. of Henfield, Sussex, J.P., F.R.S., and F.L.S., b. in May, 1781; m. 28 March, 1810, Elizabeth, dau. of Nathaniel Hall, Esq., and has issue,

I. WILLIAM, of Brook Hill, Cowfold, M.A. J.P., m. Margaret, dau. of J. H. Borrer, Esq. of Brighton, and has issue.
II. Dawson.
III. Lindfield.
I. Ann, m. to Nicholas Hall, Esq. of Portslade.
II. Fanny, m. to the Rev. Charles Dunlop, M.A., vicar of Henfield, deceased.
III. Elizabeth.
IV. Isabel.
V. Adelaide.

Lineage.—WILLIAM BORRER, of Rusper, Sussex, who m. in 1698, Sarah Smith, of Hurstpierpoint, was father of two sons, William Borrer, of Rusper, and

JOHN BORRER, of Rusper, who had, by Susanna his wife, WILLIAM, his heir; John, of Ditchling; and other issue. The eldest son,

WILLIAM BORRER, Esq. of Parkyns Manor, b. 1724; m. 1750, Barbara, dau. and co-heir of Edward Hardess, Esq. of Albourne House (of the ancient family of Hardess), and d. 21 Jan. 1797, leaving by her (who d. 12 April, 1795), William; John, of Henfield; and other issue. The eldest son,

WILLIAM BORRER, Esq. of Parkyns Manor, J.P. D.L., and high-sheriff of Sussex in 1801, was b. 7 March, 1753. He m. 1 Aug. 1780, Mary, dau. and co-heir of Nathaniel Lindfield, of Dean House, by Mary Clifford his wife, and by her (who d. 4 Sept. 1807) had issue,

I. WILLIAM, now of Barrow Hill, Henfield.
II. John, of the Manor House, Portslade, Sussex, J.P., b. 25 Dec. 1784, m. 1st, Kitty, 2nd dau. of John Beckett, of Henfield: she d. 7 April, 1811. He m. 2ndly, Mary-Anne, only dau. of John Upperton, of Amberley, which lady d. 18 July, 1819, and 3rdly, Sarah-Anne, 3rd dau. of Nathaniel Hall of New Hall: he has issue.
III. NATHANIEL, of Parkyns Manor, co. Sussex, J.P., b. 24 March, 1790, m. 4 April, 1811, Mary-Anne, dau. of Richard Weekes, Esq. of Hurstpierpoint, by Charity his wife, dau. and heir of the Rev. William Hampton, rector of Plumpton, Sussex, and by this lady (who d. 5 Jan. 1854) has issue,
   1 CAREY-HAMPTON, in holy orders, rector of Hurstpierpoint, M.A., and rural dean, b. 13 Nov. 1814, m. 17 Aug. 1837, Elizabeth, 3rd dau. of James Orr, Esq. of Holyhead House, co. Down, by Jane his wife, dau. of Richard Stewart, of Ballintoy Castle, and has issue,
      Carey-Hampton, b. 18 July, 1838.
      Clifford-Fortescue, b. 5 March, 1841.
      Charles-Alexander, b. 4 Dec. 1843.
      Jane-Clifford.
      Isabella-Emily.
      Mary-Anne-Alice.
      Helen-Henrietta.
      Elizabeth-Catharine.
      Charlotte-Augusta.
      Ida-Frances.
   2 Henrietta, m. 31 March, 1817, to George Octavius Pollard, of Lower Seymour Street, London, youngest son of the late Rev. John Pollard, M.A., D.D., rector of Bennington, Herts, by Sophia his wife, dau. of the late General and Lady Frances Morgan.
   3 Emily, m. 26 March, 1844, to Charles-Hoskyns, only son of C.-H.-L. Master, of Barrow Green House, co. Surrey, and Codnor Castle, co. Derby, Esq.

Arms—Az., a lion rampant, erminois, holding an auger (borer), ppr., in his dexter paw, a chevron, arg., charged with three inescutcheons, of the field, the centre bearing a white rose, seeded and pointed, ppr.
Crest—A buck's head, ppr., erased, fretty, arg., holding an auger, ppr., in its mouth.
Motto—Fide laboro.
Seat—Barrow Hill, Henfield, Sussex.

BOROUGH OF HULLAND AND CHETWYND PARK.

BOROUGH, JOHN-CHARLES-BURTON, Esq. of Hulland Hall, co. Derby, and Chetwynd Park, co. Salop, b. 30 July, 1810; m. 11 July, 1848, Elizabeth-Charlotte, dau. of Rear-Admiral Robert Gawen, and has issue,

1 JOHN-SIDNEY, b. 25 April, 1852.
1. Jane-Charlotte.

Lineage.—THOMAS BORROW, Esq. of Castlefield, co. Derby, barrister-at-law, b. 3 June, 1709 (eldest son of Isaac Borrow, Esq. of Hulland, by Honora his 2nd wife, only dau. of Thomas Burton, Esq., and eventually sole heiress of her brother, Robert Burton, of the elder branch of the Burtons, descended from Jacobus de Burton, which Isaac Borrow was son of John Borowe, Esq. of Hulland, high-sheriff of Derbyshire in 1688, by Mary his wife, dau. of Curwen Rawlinson, Esq. of Cark Hall, co. Lancashire), was recorder of Derby for forty years. He m. Anne, dau. and heir of John Alt, Esq. of Loughborough, co. Leicester, and d. 6 August, 1786, leaving a son,

THOMAS BOROUGH, Esq. of Castlefield, who first recorded in the College of Arms the change in the spelling of the name from Borrow. He was of University College, Oxford, a barrister-at-law of the Middle Temple, and was sometime captain in the Leicester Militia. He m. 26 April, 1788, Jane, only dau. of William Smithson, Esq. of Ledstone Park, Ferrybridge, co. York, and by her had issue,

JOHN-CHARLES-BURTON, his heir.
Jane, m. 3 May, 1832, to George Hill, Esq., captain royal horse artillery, eldest son of Sir Robert-Chambre Hill, of Rees Hall, co. Salop.
Anna-Honora, d. unm. 19 Oct. 1852.

Mr. Borough, who removed from Castlefield to Chetwynd Park, in 1803, was s. at his decease by his only surviving son and heir, the present JOHN-CHARLES-BURTON BOROUGH, Esq. of Chetwynd Park.

Arms—Gu., the root of an oak-tree, eradicated and couped, in pale, sprouting out two branches, ppr., with the shield of Pallas hanging thereon, or.
Crest—An eagle, ppr., holding the shield of Pallas in its claws.
Motto—Virtute et robore.
Seat—Hulland Hall, Ashbourne, Derbyshire.

BORTHWICK OF CROOKSTON AND BORTHWICK CASTLE.

BORTHWICK, JOHN, Esq. of Crookston and Borthwick Castle, co. Edinburgh.

Lineage.—The surname of Borthwick is apparently local, assumed from lands of that name on Borthwick Water, co. Selkirk. Thomas de Borthwick obtained some lands near Lauder, in Berwickshire, from Robert Lauder, of Quarrelwood, in the reign of King DAVID II. Sir William Borthwick was possessor of the lands of Catkune, in the reign of King ROBERT II. which appears by a charter dated in 1378.

SIR WILLIAM BORTHWICK, junior, ambassador at Rome in 1425, was created BARON BORTHWICK, in 1433, and d. in 1458, leaving two sons, viz., WILLIAM, second Lord Borthwick, and JOHN DE BORTHWICK, who acquired the estate of Crookston in 1446, and from whom descended, through nine generations, (as set forth in the petition presented to the House of Lords, regarding the succession to the peerage,)

JOHN BORTHWICK, Esq. of Crookston, who m. in 1787, Grisel, eldest dau. of George Adinston, Esq. of Carcant, and left, at his decease, a son and successor,

JOHN BORTHWICK, Esq. of Crookston and Borthwick Castle, J.P. and D.L., who m. 1st, 16 March, 1819, Anne, eldest dau. of the Right Hon. Robert Dundas, of Arniston, and by her had issue, 1 JOHN, now of Borthwick and Crookston; 2 Robert; 3 William-Henry; 1 Elizabeth; 2 Grace-Henrietta, d. in 1828; and 3 Grace. He m. 2ndly, Mrs. Simpson, widow of Col. Simpson, of Plean, co. Stirling, and had issue by her.

Arms—Arg., three cinquefoils, sa.
Supporters—Two angels, ppr., winged, or.

Crest—A Moor's head, couped, ppr.
Mottoes—"Qui conducit," and "Fide et spe."
Seat—Crookston, co. Edinburgh.

BOSANQUET OF FOREST HOUSE.

BOSANQUET, SAMUEL-RICHARD, Esq. of the Forest House, Epping Forest, co. Essex, and of Dingestow Court, co. Monmouth, *b.* 1 April, 1800; *m.* 4 Feb. 1830, Emily, eldest dau. of George Courthope, Esq. of Whiligh, Sussex, and has issue,

I. SAMUEL-COURTHOPE, *b.* 2 March, 1832.
II. Claude, *b.* 8 Nov. 1833.
III. George-Stanley, *b.* 18 April, 1835.
IV. Frederick-Albert, *b.* 8 Feb. 1837.
V. Walter-Henry, *b.* 10 Jan. 1839.
VI. Edmund-Fletcher, *b.* 2 Sept. 1840.
VII. Reginald-David, *b.* 24 Jan. 1847, deceased.
VIII. William-David, *b.* 3 June, 1849.
IX. Richard-Arthur, *b.* 25 May, 1852.
I. Emily-Letitia. II. Fanny-Elizabeth.
III. Ellen-Edith.

Lineage.—PIERRE, grandson of Foulcrand Bosanquet, or de Bosanquet, *m.* about 1628, Antoinette Mainvielle, and was father of

PIERRE, of Lunel, in Languedoc, who had seven children. At the revocation of the Edict of Nantes, the family became divided; the two elder sons of Pierre, John and David, sought refuge in England, where John was subsequently naturalised, by private act of parliament, in 1708. The 2nd son,

DAVID BOSANQUET, *m.* 1697, Elizabeth, dau. of Claude Hayes, Esq., and *d.* 1732, leaving issue, I. DAVID, *b.* 1699, a merchant in London, and a learned antiquary. He *d.* in 1741, leaving an only child, Richard, who *d. unm.*; II. SAMUEL, *b.* 1700, of whom presently; III. Claude, *d. s. p.*; IV. Benjamin, M.D., F.R.S., one of the council of the Royal Society, in 1749, *d. s. p.*; V. JACOB. (*See* BOSANQUET *of Broxbournbury.*) I. Susannah, *b.* 1698, *m.* Charles Van Notten, Esq. of Amsterdam; and II. Elianor, *m.* Henry Lannoy Hunter, Esq., and had issue. The 2nd son of David Bosanquet,

SAMUEL BOSANQUET, Esq. of the Forest House, lord of the manor of Low Hall, co. Essex, *m.* in 1733, Mary, dau. and sole heiress of William Dunster, Esq. (son of Henry Dunster, Esq., and Mary, dau. and sole heiress of Henry Gardiner, Esq. M.P. for Ilchester, in the 12th of CHAS. II.) by Ann, dau. of Sir Peter Vandeput, and had issue, SAMUEL; William, who *d. unm.* in 1813; Anna-Maria, *m.* to her cousin Peter Gaussen, Esq.; and Mary, *m.* to the Rev. John-William de la Flechere. The eldest son,

SAMUEL BOSANQUET, of Forest House, and also of Dingestow Court, co. Monmouth, lieutenant of the Forest of Waltham, J.P. and D.L. for Essex, *b.* in 1744, was high-sheriff of that shire in 1770: he *m.* in 1767, his cousin Eleanor, dau. of Henry Lannoy Hunter, Esq. Mr. Bosanquet was Governor of the Bank of England in 1792. He *d.* in 1806, leaving issue,

SAMUEL, his heir.
Charles, of Rock, co. Northumberland, J.P. and D.L., high-sheriff of Northumberland, in 1828. He *m.* Charlotte, dau. of Peter Holford, Esq., Master in Chancery, and had surviving issue, Robert-William, in holy orders, who *m.* Frances, dau. of Col. Pulleine, of Crake Hall, Yorkshire, and has issue; George-Henry, also in holy orders; and Mary-Anne.
JOHN BERNARD (Sir), one of the judges of the Common Pleas, and a member of the privy council. He *m.* in 1804, Mary-Anne, eldest dau. of Richard Lewis, Esq. of Llantilio Grossenny, co. Monmouth, and had a son, Lewis-Bernard, who *d. s. p.*

The eldest son,

SAMUEL BOSANQUET, Esq. of the Forest House and Dingestow Court, *b.* in Aug. 1768, *m.* 19 Jan. 1798, Lætitia-Philippa, the younger of the two daus. (the elder, Camilla, *m.* to Sir Charles Style, Bart.) of James Whatman, Esq. of Vinters, Kent, by his 1st wife, Sarah, eldest dau. of Edward Stanley, Esq., LL.D., cousin of the 11th Earl of Derby, and had issue,

SAMUEL-RICHARD, now of Forest House.
James-Whatman, *b.* Jan. 1804; *m.* in 1840, Merelina, only dau. of the Right Hon. Sir Nicholas-Conyngham Tindal, Lord Chief Justice of the Common Pleas, and has a son, James-Tindal, *b.* in 1841.
William-Henry, *b.* Feb. 1805.
Edward-Stanley, *b.* March, 1806, in holy orders.
Charles-John, *b.* 5 May, 1807, of Wildwood, Middlesex, capt. R.N., *m.* 6 June, 1832, his cousin, Charlotte Eliza, youngest dau. of Jacob Bosanquet, Esq. of Broxbournbury, Herts, and has issue, Henrietta-Lætitia-Eliza; and Amelia-Elinor.
Frederick-Bernard, *b.* Nov. 1813.
Eleanor-Lætitia, *m.* in 1852, to William, third son of Samuel Gaussen, Esq. of Brookmans, Herts.
Camilla, *m.* to William Needham, Esq. of Lenton, Notts.
Georgiana, *m.* to Thomas, fourth son of Sir John Ogilvy, Bart.
Anna-Maria-Nelly.

Mr. Bosanquet, a magistrate and deputy-lieutenant for the counties of Essex and Monmouth, served the office of high-sheriff of the latter county in 1816. He *d.* in June, 1843.

Arms—Or, on a mount, vert, a tree, ppr.; on a chief, gu., a crescent between two mullets, arg.; quartering DUNSTER and GARDINER.
Crest—A demi-lion, rampant, couped, gu.
Seats—Dingestow Court, Monmouthshire; Forest House, Essex.

BOSANQUET OF BROXBOURNBURY.

BOSANQUET, GEORGE-JACOB, Esq. of Broxbournbury, co. Herts, high-sheriff of that shire in 1833, *b.* 1 July, 1791; *m.* 28 Oct. 1831, his cousin Cecilia, dau. of William Franks, Esq. of Beech Hill, and widow of Samuel-Robert Gaussen, Esq. of Brookmans, Herts, and has a dau.,

Cecilia-Jane-Wentworth.

Mr. Bosanquet was his Majesty's chargé d'affaires at Madrid from 1828 to 1830.

Lineage.—JACOB BOSANQUET, 5th son of David Bosanquet, the first settler in England, *m.* in 1748, Elizabeth, dau. of John Hanbury, Esq. of Kelmarsh, co. Northampton, and had issue,

I. JACOB, his heir.
II. William, banker of London, *m.* in 1787, Charlotte-Elizabeth, dau. of John Ives, Esq., and had issue,
1 William-George-Ives, *m.* Eliza, dau. of Patrick Cumming, Esq., and has issue.
2 Augustus-Henry, *m.* Louisa, dau of David Bevan, Esq. of Belmont, Herts, and has issue.
3 John, *m.* Elizabeth, dau. of Thomas Boileau, Esq., and has issue.
4 Samuel, *m.* Sophia, dau. of James Broadwood, Esq.
5 Edwin, in holy orders, *m.* Eliza, dau. of Thomas Terry, Esq. of Dummer House, Hants, and has issue.
1 Charlotte-Elizabeth-Ives.
2 Emma, *m.* to the Chevalier de Kantzow, His Swedish Majesty's minister at Lisbon.
3 Sophia, *m.* to her cousin, William-John, eldest son of John-William Commerell, Esq. of Strood, Sussex.
4 Harriet, *m.* to John-Raymond Barker, Esq. of Fairford Park, Gloucestershire, and is deceased.
III. Henry, of Clanville, Hants, served the office of high-sheriff of that co. in 1815, *m.* in 1790, Caroline, dau. of Christopher Anstey, Esq., the poet, and had issue, Henry, *m.* Mary, dau. of William Richards, Esq., and has issue.
IV. Susannah, *m.* to James Whatman, Esq. of Vinters, Kent.
V. Mary, *m.* to John-William Commerell, Esq. of Strood, Sussex.
VI. Elizabeth, *m.* to her cousin, Samuel-Robert Gaussen, Esq. of Brookmans, Herts.

The elder son,

JACOB BOSANQUET, Esq. of Broxbournbury, co. Herts, forty-five years an East India Director, served as sheriff of the county in 1803. He *m.* in 1790, Henrietta, dau. of Sir George Armytage, Bt., and had, with two daus. (Henrietta-Maria, *m.* to her cousin John Wentworth, Esq., and Charlotte-Eliza, *m.* to her cousin, Capt. Charles-John Bosanquet, R.N.) two sons, GEORGE-JACOB, now of Broxbournbury, and Richard-Godfrey, *b.* 29 Sept. 1793, *m.* Grace, dau. of William Browne, Esq. of Brownes Hill, co. Carlow.

Arms, &c.—As BOSANQUET *of Forest House.*
Seat—Broxbournbury, Herts.

BOSVILE OF RAVENFIELD.

BOSVILE, THOMAS-BOSVILE, Esq. of Ravenfield Park, co. York, *b.* 4 May, 1799; *m.* in Aug. 1829, Harriet, dau. of William Jackson, Esq., deputy-com.-gen., and widow of Samuel Petrie, Esq. Mr. Bosvile, who is 2nd son of the late Robert-Newton Lee, Esq. of Louth and Littlecoate, assumed, by royal license, in 1829, the surname of BOSVILE, in lieu of his patronymic, LEE, upon succeeding to the Ravenfield estate, on the death of his kinsman, the late Lieut.-Col. Thomas-James Bosvile, in accordance with the will of the Rev. Thomas Bosvile, of Raven-

12

field. He is a magistrate for the West Riding of Yorkshire.

Lineage.—There are few families in England which can be traced, by means of authentic evidences, through so many centuries, as that of Bosvile.

The surname is found in England from nearly the time of the Conquest, when, in all probability, it was introduced. In a charter of Humphrey de Bohun, dated in 1126, a William de Bosvile appears as a witness. In a chartulary of the abbey of Warden, in Bedfordshire, a William de Bosvile is spoken of as his knight by Geffrey de Maundevile, the Earl, that is, of Essex; and Michael, son of William de Bosvile, was an early benefactor to the same house. The senior branches, seated at New Hall, Darfield, at Gunthwaite, co. York, and at Bradbourn, co. Kent, are all now extinct in the male line.

THE REV. THOMAS BOSVILE, vicar of Braithwell, eldest son of Thomas Bosvile, Esq. of Braithwell, by Alice his wife, who recorded his pedigree at Sir William Dugdale's Visitation in 1666, *d.* in 1674, leaving (with two daus.) an only son,

THE REV. THOMAS BOSVILE, vicar of Braithwell, and rector of Sandal Parva, near Doncaster, who *m.* Elizabeth, only child of Alexander Hatfield, Esq., and dying in 1711, left, with four daus., six sons,

I. Thomas, B.D., retor of Ufford, co. Northampton; who *d.* in 1718, aged 49, leaving, by Elizabeth his wife, sister and co-heir of John Bolle, Esq. of Thorpe Hall, co. Lincoln, three daus., his co-heirs,
   1 Margaret, who *m.* James Birch, Esq. of Coventry; and *d.* in 1778, leaving two sons and one dau.; the 2nd son, the Rev. James Birch, *d.* in 1828, aged 84; the eldest son, THOMAS BIRCH, of Thorpe Hall, Esq., was father of LIEUT.-COL. THOMAS-JAMES BIRCH, of Thorpe, of whom presently, as successor to the Ravenfield estate; the only dau., Elizabeth Birch, *m.* Robert Lee, of Louth and Littlecoate, and *d.* in 1819, leaving an only son, Robert-Newton Lee, Esq. of Coldrey, Hants, who *m.* in 1793, Harriet-Elizabeth, dau. of the Rev. Joseph Warton, D.D., head-master of Winchester College, and *d.* in 1837, leaving, with junior issue, Robert-Newton Lee, Esq. of Taunton, and THOMAS-BOSVILE LEE, who *s.* to Ravenfield at the decease of his kinsman, Col. Bosvile, in 1829, and having assumed the surname and arms of BOSVILE, is the present THOMAS-BOSVILE BOSVILE, of Ravenfield, Esq.
   1 Elizabeth, *m.* 1st, to Alexander Emmerson, Esq. of Retford; and 2ndly, to the Rev. Stephen Ashton.
   2 Bridget, *m.* to her cousin, Thomas Bosvile, Esq.
II. Alexander, who had an only dau., Elizabeth.
III. Jasper, who *d.* *unm.* in Barbary.
IV. JOHN, of whom presently. V. Anthony.
VI. Hugh, of the city of York, whose only dau. and heir, Mary, *m.* Thomas Place, Esq.

The 4th son,

JOHN BOSVILE, of London, *m.* Mary, dau. of Henry Robins, and had, with a dau., Mary, an only son,

THOMAS BOSVILE, who became possessed of the estate of Ulverscroft Abbey, co. Leicester, by the will of his distant relation, Charles Bosvile, Esq. of Byanna, in Staffordshire. He *m.* his cousin Bridget, 3rd dau. and co-heir of the Rev. Thomas Bosvile, rector of Ufford, and dying in 1771, was *s.* by his elder son,

WILLIAM-PARKIN BOSVILE, Esq. of Ulverscroft Abbey and Ravenfield Hall, who *d.* without issue in 1811, and was *s.* by his brother,

THE REV. THOMAS BOSVILE, of Ravenfield, who *d.* *unm.* in 1824, having made by will a settlement of his estates on the descendants of his eldest aunt, Margaret Bosvile, wife of James Birch, Esq.: under that disposition, he was *s.* by his cousin,

THOMAS-JAMES BIRCH, of Thorpe Hall, lieut.-col. 1st life-guards, who assumed the surname of BOSVILE, by sign-manual. He *d.* *s. p.* in 1829, and was *s.* by his cousin THOMAS-BOSVILE LEE, the present possessor of Ravenfield.

Arms—Arg., five fusils in fesse, gu.; in chief, three bears' heads, sa.

Crest—An ox issuing from a knoll of trees, ppr.

Motto—Intento in Deum animo.

Seat—Ravenfield Hall, near Doncaster, co. York.

BOTELER OF EASTRY.

BOTELER, WILLIAM, Esq. of Brook Street, Eastry, co. Kent, *b.* 23 Oct. 1810, M.A., barrister-at-law.

Lineage.—This family is of very ancient standing in the co. of Kent. So far back as the commencement of the fifteenth century, we find John Boteler, of Sandwich, co. Kent, mayor of that corporation, *annis* 1440-3-4, and 1445; one of the burgess in parliament for Sandwich in 1445 and 1447, and one of the supporters of the canopy at the coronation of MARGARET, Queen of HENRY VI., 30 May, 1445. He was buried in St. Peter's Church, Sandwich. His descendant,

WILLIAM BOTELER, Esq., F.S.A. of Brook Street, in Eastry, *b.* 4 Oct. 1745 (son of Richard Boteler, Esq. of Brook Street, in Eastry), who *d.* in 1792), *m.* 1st, 26 April, 1774, Sarah, dau. of Thomas Fuller, Esq. of Statenborough, co. Kent, by whom (who *d.* 9 Jan. 1777,) he had a son, WILLIAM-FULLER, late of Eastry. Mr. Boteler *m.* 2ndly, 15 March, 1785, Mary, dau. of John Harvey, Esq. capt. R.N. (who died of wounds received in the action of the 1st of June, 1794), and by her had,

Richard, lieut.-col. royal engineers; *b.* 24 Oct. 1786; lost at sea on his return from Halifax, in 1833.
Henry, comm. R.N.; *b.* 15 Feb. 1793; *m.* 1 Dec. 1829, Henrietta, dau. of the late Allan Bellingham, Esq., and niece of the late Sir William Bellingham, of Castle Bellingham, Bart., and has issue one dau., Mary-Julia-Monique.
John Harvey, comm. R.N.; *b.* 11 Feb. 1796; *m.* 15 Aug. 1832, Helen-Agnes, 5th dau. of the late James West, Esq. of Bryanstone-square, London, and has issue, WILLIAM-JOHN, *b.* 12 Nov. 1842; Emma-Mary; Julia-Elizabeth; Helen-Agnes; Annie-Adelaide.
Thomas, comm. R.N; *b.* 1 Mary, 1797; *d.* 28 Nov. 1829, while in command of H.M.S. "Hecla," employed on a surveying and exploring expedition on the coast of Africa.
Edward, M.A., and fellow of Sidney Sussex College, Cambridge, vicar of St. Clement's, Sandwich; *b.* 29 April, 1798; *d.* 9 Aug. 1831.
Robert, capt. royal engineers; *b.* 11 Sept. 1801, *m.* 3 Dec. 1835, Maria-Anne, only dau. of the Rev. John-Thomas Casbard, D.C.L.
Eliza, *m.* 5 July, 1819, to the Rev. C.-J. Burton, M.A., vicar of Lydd, co. Kent, and has issue.
Julia, *m.* 18 Jan. 1820, to the Rev. Thomas-Stephen Hodges, M.A., late rector of Little Waltham, Essex; and *d.* 20 Nov. 1824, leaving issue.
Maria. Agnes. Bertha.

Mr. Boteler *d.* 4 Sept. 1818, and was *s.* by his son,

WILLIAM-FULLER BOTELER, Esq. of Brook Street, in Eastry, Q.C. and bencher of Lincoln's Inn, recorder of the city of Canterbury, and towns and ports of Sandwich, Hythe, and New Romney, and of the borough of Deal, and steward of the town of Fordwich; *b.* 5 Jan. 1777, *m.* 29 Nov. 1808, Charlotte, dau. of the late James-Leigh Joynes, Esq. of Mount Pleasant, near Gravesend, and had issue,

I. WILLIAM, present representative.
II. Richard, *b.* 2 May, 1821, now of St. John's College, Cambridge.
III. Thomas, *b.* 10 Sept 1823; *d.* the following day.
I. Charlotte-Grace. II. Mary.
III. Elizabeth-Catherine. IV. Sarah.
V. Catherine. VI. Anne, *d.* 1839.

Arms—Arg., three escocheons, sa., each charged with a covered cup, or.

Crest—A covered cup, or, between a pair of wings, endorsed, the dexter, arg., sinister, az.

Motto—Do not for to repent.

Seat—Brook-street, Eastry, Kent.

BOTFIELD OF NORTON HALL.

BOTFIELD, BERIAH, Esq. of Norton Hall, co. Northampton, and Decker Hill, co. Salop, J.P., M.A., F.R.S., and F.S.A., *b.* 5 March, 1807; *s.* his father, 27 April, 1813; high-sheriff of Northamptonshire in 1831, and M.P. for Ludlow from 1840 to 1847, Chevalier of the Order of Albert the Brave of Saxony, and Knight of the Order of Leopold of Belgium.

Lineage.—This is a branch of the ancient family of BOTEVYLE *of Botevyle*, in Shropshire, founded by Geoffry and Oliver Botevyle, who came over from Poitou to assist King JOHN in his wars with the barons in 1210.

THOMAS BOTEFELDE, living 5th HENRY V., 5th in descent from Sir Geoffrey Botevyle, living A.D. 1210, was father of two sons, WILLIAM BOTEFELDE, *alias* William "de la Inn," ancestor of the Thynnes, Marquesses of Bath; and JOHN BOTEFELDE, 18th HENRY VI., grandfather of

WILLIAM BOTEVYLE, of Botevyle, Church Stretton, Shropshire, who *m.* Joyce, dau. of Jenkyn Sankey, of Lebotwood, and had, with younger issue, a son and heir,

THOMAS BOTEVYLE, of Botevyle, who *m.* twice: by his 1st wife, Margaret, dau. of Thomas Palmer, of Hughley, he had a son, THOMAS, ancestor of the BOTEVYLES *of Botevyle*; and by Joan, his 2nd wife, he left, Peter, living 1623; John, of Leighton; Richard, of Shrewsbury; and Humphrey, of Frodaley. The 2nd son, JOHN BOTEVYLE, of Leighton, was father of WILLIAM BOTEVYLE, *alias* WILLIAM BOTFIELD, of Leighton, who *d.* before 3 May, 1639, leaving a son, THOMAS BOTFIELD, of Eaton Constantine, co. Salop, A.D. 1665, father, by Mary his 1st wife, of

THOMAS BOTFIELD, of Dawley, buried there 28 May, 1735. By Abigail his wife, he left a dau., Agnes Botevyle, *m.* at Madeley, 17 Nov. 1728, and a son,

BERIAH BOTFIELD, Esq. of Dawley, *b.* 28 Feb. 1702. He *m.* Margaret, dau. of John and Ann Adams; and *d.* 8 April, 1754, leaving a son,

THOMAS BOTFIELD, Esq. of Dawley and Ditton Stoke, co. Salop, and Norton Hall, co. Northampton, *b.* 14 Feb. 1736; who *m.* 29 Sept. 1761, Margaret, only dau. of William Baker, Esq. of Bromley, in the parish of Worfield, Salop, and by her (who *d.* 5 Nov. 1803) had issue,

THOMAS, his heir.
WILLIAM, of Decker Hill, co. Salop, *b.* 7 May, 1766; *m.* 14 Jan. 1794, Lucy, dau. of John Bishton, Esq. of Kilsall. Mr. Botfield served as high-sheriff in 1806. He *d. s. p.* 25 Dec. 1850; and his widow 9 Dec. 1851.
BERIAH, of Norton Hall, co. Northampton, *b.* 27 July, 1768; *m.* 26 July, 1806, Charlotte, dau. of William Withering, M.D., of The Larches, Edgbaston, near Birmingham, by Helena his wife, only dau. of George Cookes, Esq., and Ruth Amery his wife; and dying 27 April, 1813, left a son, the present BERIAH BOTFIELD, of Norton Hall and Decker Hill, Esq.

Mr. Botfield *d.* 5 April, 1841, and was *s.* by his son,

THOMAS BOTFIELD, Esq. of Hopton Court, co. Salop, *b.* 14 Feb. 1762; *m.* 14 Feb. 1800, Lucy, dau. of William Skelhorne, of Liverpool. Mr. Botfield, a magistrate and deputy-lieutenant of Shropshire, served as high-sheriff of the county in 1818. He *d. s. p.* 17 Jan. 1843.

Arms—Barry of twelve, or and sa.
Crest—A reindeer, statant, or.
Motto—J'ay bonne cause.
Seat—Norton Hall, co. Northampton; and Decker Hill, co. Salop.

BOUCHERETT OF WILLINGHAM.

BOUCHERETT, AYSCOGHE, Esq. of Willingham and Stallingborough, co. Lincoln, J.P., high-sheriff in 1820, *b.* 24 Sept. 1791; *m.* 11 May, 1816, Louisa, dau. of Frederick-John Pigou, Esq. of Dartford, in Kent, and Hill Street, Berkeley Square, London, and his wife, Louisa, dau. of Humphrey Minchin, Esq. of Stubbington, Hants, by whom he has had issue,

I. Ayscoghe, *b.* 22 June, 1817; *d.* 6 Aug. 1832.
II. HENRY-ROBERT, *b.* 23 Aug. 1818; in the 17th lancers.
III. Hugo, *b.* 31 Dec. 1819.
I. Louisa. II. Emilia. III. Jessie.

Lineage.—The Boucheretts are of ancient French descent. Armon de Boucherat, who *d.* in 1564, Avocat du Roi; and Louis Boucherat, of the same family, son of Jean Boucherat, Maitre des Comptes, was Chancelier de France and Garde des Sceaux in 1685. The first who settled at Willingham was MATHEW BOUCHERET, naturalised in 1644. His descendant,

MATHEW BOUCHERETT, Esq. of Willingham, co. Lincoln, *m.* Sarah, dau. of Sir — Hungerford, Knt., and was father of

MATHEW BOUCHERETT, Esq. of Willingham, who *m.* Isabella, 2nd dau. and co-heiress of Sir Edward Ayscoghe, Knt., of Stallingborough and South Kelsey, co. Lincoln, by Mary his wife, dau. and co-heiress of William Harboard, Esq., and had an only son,

AYSCOGHE BOUCHERETT, Esq. of Willingham and Stallingborough, who *m.* Mary, dau. of — White, Esq., and had issue (with a dau. Mary, *m.* to Michael Barne, Esq. of Sotterley and Dunwich, lieut.-col. of the 7th light dragoons, and M.P. for Dunwich) a son and successor,

AYSCOGHE BOUCHERETT, Esq. of Willingham and Stallingborough, who *m.* 17 March, 1789, Emilia, dau. of Charles Crockatt, Esq. of Luxborough Hall, Essex, and Anne his wife, dau. and heiress of Henry Muilman, Esq. of Dagenham Park, co. Essex, and Anne his wife, dau. and co-heir of Sir John Darnall, Knt., and his wife, the dau. and heiress of Sir Thomas Jenner, Knt., Justice of the Common Pleas. By this marriage he had a son and three daus., AYSCOGHE, now of Willingham; Emilia-Mary; Maria, widow of Charles-Newdigate Newdegate, Esq. of Harefield, co. Middlesex; and Juliana. Mr. Boucherett *d.* 15 Sept. 1815.

Arms—Quarterly: 1st and 4th, az., a cock, or, armed, &c., for BOUCHERETT; 2nd and 3rd, sa., a fesse, or, between three asses, passant, arg., for AYSCOGHE.
Crest—A cockatrice, or.
Motto—Primâ voce salutat.
Seat—Willingham, co. Lincoln.

BOULTBEE OF SPRINGFIELD.

BOULTBEE, JOSEPH-MOORE, Esq. of Springfield, co. Warwick, *m.* 5 Aug. 1815, the Lady Elizabeth-Margaret-Ferrers Townshend, 3rd dau. of the late Marquess Townshend, and has issue,

I. HENRY-TOWNSHEND, *b.* 8 March, 1827; an officer in the royal horse artillery.
I. Charlotte-Elizabeth. II. Henrietta.
III. Elizabeth, *m.* to James Roberts-West, Esq. of Alscot Park, co. Warwick.
IV. Emily, *m.* to Capt. E.-V. Mackinnon, 5th dragoon-guards.

Mr. Boultbee is lieut-col. of the Warwickshire militia. He is son of Joseph Boultbee, Esq. and Elizabeth Moore his wife, and has three brothers and two sisters, viz.,

I. Richard-Moore, *m.* Mary, dau. of Sir Christopher Pegge.
II. Edward-Moore, *m.* Beatrice, dau. of John Boultbee, Esq. of Baxterly, co. Warwick.
III. Frederick-Moore, capt. R.N.
I. Charlotte-Anna, *m.* to Lieut.-Col. Dundas.
II. Helena-Maria, *m.* to the Rev. J.-W. Bree, of Allesley.

Motto—Spes in Deo.
Seat—Springfield House, near Knowle, co. Warwick.

BOULTON OF MOULTON.

BOULTON, REV. ANTHONY, of Moulton, co. Lincoln, rector of Preston Capes, in Northamptonshire, *b.* 4 June, 1788; *m.* 29 June, 1819, Harriet, 3rd dau. of Thomas Lane, Esq. of Selsdon, in Surrey, by Anne his wife, only dau. and heiress of Henry Bowyer, Esq.,* and has two daus.,

I. ANTONIA-MARIA. II. MARY.

Mr. Boulton *s.* his father 11 March, 1828.

Lineage.—This family was formerly possessed of considerable property at Stixwold, in Lincolnshire; and in the 56th of HENRY III., we find Thomas de Bolton sheriff of that county.

HENRY BOULTON, Esq. of Moulton, J.P. for Rutland and Lincoln, member of the Board of Green Cloth, &c., son of Henry Boulton, Esq., by Alice Bolton, of Moulton, his wife; *m.* 1st, Mrs. Elizabeth Berridge, but had no issue. He *m.* 2ndly, Miss Sarah Buckworth, and had one dau., Elizabeth, *m.* to the Rev. Charles Knightley. Mr. Boulton *m.* 3rdly, Mary, dau. of D'Arcy Preston, Esq. of Askham, in Yorkshire, and had three sons, viz.,

HENRY, his heir.
D'Arcy, one of Her Majesty's judges in Upper Canada.
George, in holy orders, rector of Oxenden, Northamptonshire.

He was *s.* by his eldest son,

HENRY BOULTON, Esq. of Moulton, of the Middle Temple, barrister-at-law; who *m.* 1st, 17 April, 1781, Susannah, eldest dau. and co-heir of Mr. Serjeant James Forster, by Susannah his wife, dau. of Sir John Strange, Master of the Rolls, and had one son and one dau., viz., Anthony, his heir, and Mary. He *m.* 2ndly, Mary, dau. of John Francklin, Esq. of Great Barford, in Bedfordshire; and 3rdly, Harriet, youngest dau. of the Rev. Baptist Isaac, of Whitwell, in the co. of Rutland: by the latter he had two daus., viz.,

Harriet, *m.* to the Rev. Henry-De Foe Baker, of Greetham, in Rutlandshire.
Elizabeth, *m.* to her cousin, George-Strange Boulton, Esq. of Cobourg, Upper Canada.

---

* By Anne his wife, sole dau. and heiress of J. Bennet, Esq of East Grinstead, Sussex.

Mr. Boulton wedded, 4thly, Mary-Winifreda, dau. of Lieut.-Col. Durell, and had another dau.,

Anne-Maria, m. to Donald-Christopher Baynes, Esq., 3rd son of Sir Christopher Baynes, Bart.

He m. 5thly, Emma, 4th dau. of the late Thomas Lane, Esq. of Selsdon, and younger sister of his eldest son's wife, by whom he had one son,

James, b. in May, 1816.

Mr. Boulton d. 11 March, 1828, and was s. by his son, the present REV. ANTHONY BOULTON, of Moulton.

Arms—Az., three bird-bolts, or; quartering FORSTER, viz., arg., a chevron, vert, between three bugle-horns, sa.

Crest—The bolt in tun.

Motto—Dux vitæ ratio.

BOURKE OF THORNFIELD.

BOURKE, LIEUT.-GEN, SIR RICHARD, K.C.B. of Thornfield, co. Limerick, J.P., high-sheriff in 1839, b. 4 May, 1777; m. 1 March, 1800, Elizabeth-Jane, youngest dau. of John Bourke, Esq. of Carshalton, co. Surrey, receiver-general of the land tax for Middlesex; and by her, who d. at Paramatta, New South Wales (where she is interred), 7 May, 1832, has issue,

I. JOHN, b. 11 Feb. 1808.
II. Richard, b. 30 May, 1812, barrister-at-law, m. 8 Oct. 1844, Anne, dau. of De Courcy O'Grady, Esq. of Kilballyowen.
I. Mary-Jane, m. in 1827, to Dudley-Montagu Perceval, Esq., 4th son of the late Rt. Hon. Spencer Perceval, chancellor of the Exchequer, and has issue.
II. Anne, m. in 1833, to Edward-Deas Thomson, Esq., colonial secretary in New South Wales, and second son of the late Sir John Thomson, K.C.H., formerly a commissioner of the navy; and has issue.
III. Frances, m. in 1831, to the Rev. John Jebb, eldest son of the late Hon. Richard Jebb, a justice of the King's Bench in Ireland.
IV. Georgina, d. young.
V. Lucy, d. in 1832, unm.

Sir Richard Bourke, who s. his father in 1795, served with great distinction in Holland in 1799, when he was severely wounded in the face; was present at Buenos Ayres in 1807, at the storming of Monte Video, and subsequently served in the Peninsular war. He was lieutenant-governor of the Cape of Good Hope from 1825 to 1828, and governor-in-chief of New South Wales and Van Dieman's Land from 1831 to Dec. 1837.

Lineage.—JOHN BOURKE, Esq., grandson of Richard Bourke, Esq. of Drumsally, co. Limerick, half-uncle to Sir Richard de Burgho, Bart., m. in 1775, Anne, dau. of Edmund Ryan, of the city of Dublin, and of Boscobel, co. Tipperary, and by her (who d. in 1837) had issue,

RICHARD, his heir.
Edmund and John, both d. young.
Frances-Emma, m. to the Rev. Heneage Horsley, only son of the Right Rev. Samuel Horsley, D.D., formerly Lord Bishop of St. Asaph. She d. in 1831, leaving issue.

Mr. Bourke d. in 1795.

Arms—Or, a cross, gu.; in the first quarter a lion, rampant, sa.

Crest—A cat-a-mountain, sejant-guardant, ppr., collared and chained, or.

Motto—In cruce salus.

Seat—Thornfield, co. Limerick.

BOURNE OF WYERSDALE AND STALMINE.

BOURNE, CORNELIUS, Esq. of Stalmine Hall, co. Lancaster, J.P. and D.L., b. 2 Jan. 1807; m. 27 July, 1841, Alice, eldest dau. of William Sharp, Esq., J.P., of Linden Hall, co. Lancaster, by Jane his wife, dau. and heir of William Taylor, Esq. of Borwick, and Jane his wife, dau. and co-heir of Henry Parkinson, Esq., representative of PARKINSON *of Bleasdale*, and has issue,

I. JOHN-WILLIAM, b. 30 Jan. 1845.
I. Mary.

Lineage.—The family of Bourne is one of great antiquity: so far back as the reign of King JOHN its ancestors appear to have been settled and to have enjoyed estates in the township of Nether Wyersdale. The tything of a district there situate, called "Bourne's tenement," has descended to, and is still possessed by the present Mr. Bourne, of Stalmine. Crosshill school, in the same township, was founded by one of the Bournes. The representative of the family, about the middle of the seventeenth century, left, by Unis his wife, five sons,

JOHN, of whom presently.
Titus, of Lincolnshire, from whom the family seated at Dalby, in that county, is descended.
Timothy, of Buxton, whose descendants settled in London.

The eldest son,

JOHN BOURNE, Esq. of Wyersdale, d. in 1714, leaving a son,

JOHN BOURNE, Esq. of Stalmine, b. in 1706, who m. Jane, dau. and co-heiress of Cornelius Fox, Esq. of Fern Hill and Stalmine Hall, and d. 30 Jan. 1783, having had issue,

I. JOHN, his heir.
II. JAMES, heir to his brother.
III. CORNELIUS, b. 2 April, 1747; d. 1 March, 1806. He m. 21 July, 1774, Anne, dau. of Thomas Rymer, Esq., and widow of Edmund Glover, Esq., and by her (who d. 12 June, 1828) had issue,
  1 JOHN, heir to his uncle.
  2 THOMAS, of Hackinsall, d. unm. 1821.
  3 JAMES, of Liverpool.
  4 PETER (see BOURNE of *Hackinsall*).
  1 Mary-Ann, m. to James Molyneux, Esq.; and d. s. p. 22 July, 1851.
I. Agnes, m. to James Smith, Esq.
II. Margery, m. Robert Lawe, Esq. of Preston.

The eldest son,

JOHN BOURNE, Esq. of Stalmine, b. 1741, d. unm. in 1790, and was s. by his brother,

JAMES BOURNE, Esq. of Stalmine, b. in 1742, m. Dorothy, dau. of Thomas Parkinson, Esq., and had issue, two daus., Jane and Elizabeth, both d. unm. He d. in 1816, and was s. by his nephew,

JOHN BOURNE, Esq. of Stalmine, b. 29 Aug. 1777, who m. in July, 1804, Mary, dau. of John Bury, Esq. of Salford, and d. in 1841, having had by her (who d. in 1833)

CORNELIUS, now of Stalmine Hall.
John-Bury, in holy orders, rector of Colmere, Hants; m. Margaret, eldest dau. of Henry Wood, Esq. of Littleton, Middlesex, and has issue.
James-Thomas, of Newsham Hall, co. Lancaster, J.P.
Thomas-Rymer, m. Anna, dau. of Alex. Haliburton, Esq. of Wigan.
Margaret, m. to T.-K. Hassell, Esq.
Ann, m. to Arthur-Yates Williams, Esq.
Jane, m. to F. Whitelock, Esq.

Arms—Arg., a chevron, sa., gutté-d'eau, between, in chief, two lions, rampant; and in base an heraldic tiger, also rampant, gu.

Crest—An heraldic tiger, sejant, or, gutté-de-sang, resting the dexter paw on a cross-patée, gu.

Motto—Esse quam videri.

Seat—Stalmine Hall, Lancaster.

BOURNE OF HACKINSALL.

BOURNE, JAMES, Esq. of Hackinsall, co. Lancaster, J.P. and D.L., major royal Lancashire artillery, b. 8 Oct. 1812; m. 11 Oct. 1841, Sarah-Harriet, dau. of Thomas-Fournis Dyson, Esq. of Everton and Willow Hall, co. York, and has issue,

I. JAMES-DYSON, b. 29 July, 1842.
I. Harriet-Anne-Dyson.
II. Helen-Dyson, d. 1 Jan. 1853.
III. Emily-Dyson.

Mr. Bourne s. his father 3 Feb. 1846.

Lineage.—This is a junior branch of the family of BOURNE *of Stalmine*.

THOMAS BOURNE, Esq. (2nd son of Cornelius Bourne, Esq. of Liverpool, by Anne his wife, dau. of Thomas Rymer, Esq.) became joint lord of the manor of Preesall-with-Hackinsall, co. Lancashire. He was b. in 1779, and d. unm. in 1821. His brother,

PETER BOURNE, Esq. of Liverpool, became of Hackinsall,

He was *b.* 13 Oct. 1783, and *m.* 14 May, 1810, Margaret, only dau. of James Drinkwater, Esq. of Liverpool (descended from the DRINKWATERS *of Bent*), by whom he had issue,

Cornelius, M.A., of Oxford; *b.* in 1811, *d. unm.* in 1839.
JAMES, now of Hackinsall.
Thomas, *b.* 28 Feb. 1814. Peter, *b.* in 1819.
George-Drinkwater, in holy orders, rector of Weston-sub-Edge, co. Gloucester, J.P. and D.L., *b.* 31 Aug. 1821, *m.* Jane, only dau. of Francis Hole, Esq. of Tiverton, Devon, and has issue, Francis-Hole, *b.* 2 April, 1850; and Margaret-Hole.
Elinor, *d.* young.
Anne, *m.* to the Rev. W.-H. Brandreth, rector of Standish.
Elinor-Drinkwater, *m.* to her cousin, W.-L. Drinkwater, Esq., barrister-at-law.
Margaret, *m.* to Henry Royds, Esq.

Mr Bourne *d.* 3 Feb. 1846, and was *s.* by his eldest surviving son, the present JAMES BOURNE, Esq. of Hackinsall.

Arms, Crest, and *Motto*—Same as BOURNE *of Stalmine.*
Seats—Hackinsall; and Heathfield House, Wavertree.

BOURNE OF HILDERSTONE HALL.

BOURNE, JAMES, Esq. of Hilderstone Hall, co. Stafford, *b.* 17 July, 1796.

Lineage.—JAMES BOURNE, Esq. of Fenton, in the parish of Stoke-upon-Trent, co. Stafford, descended from a respectable family in that shire, *m.* in 1766, Jane, dau. of John Dayson, Esq. of Shelton, by Mary his wife, relict of James Stannaway, Esq., and had issue,

I. RALPH, his heir.
II. John, of Fenton, merchant, *b.* 4 April, 1774, deceased.
III. Charles, of Fenton, merchant, *b.* 21 Nov. 1776, who *m.* in 1798, Mary, dau. of William Edwards, Esq. of Lane Delph, co. Stafford, and had issue, Charles; Ralph; John; Mary; and Charlotte.
I. Mary, *m.* 4 Oct. 1794, to William Baker, Esq. of Fenton Culvert, co. Stafford, and has issue,
  1 William Baker, Esq.
  2 THE REV. RALPH-BOURNE BAKER, M.A., rural dean of Stone, and incumbent of Hilderstone. This gentleman now resides at Hilderstone Hall, and has also the landed property of Doveridge Woodhouse, co. Derby.
  1 Harriot Baker, deceased.
  2 Charity Baker, *m.* to Philip-Barnes Broode, Esq. of Fenton Manor House.
  3 Mary Baker, *d. unm.*
  4 Jane Sarah Baker, *m.* to John Hitchman, Esq. of Leamington.
  5 Charlotte Baker. 6 Elizabeth Baker, deceased.
II. Charlotte, *m.* in 1804, to John Pratt, Esq. of Lane Delph, and had issue.

Mr. Bourne *d.* 23 Aug. 1789, and was buried at Stoke-upon-Trent. His eldest son and successor,

RALPH BOURNE, Esq. of Hilderstone Hall, a magistrate and deputy-lieut. for Staffordshire, *b.* 2 March, 1772, *m.* 21 Dec. 1793, Sarah, relict of William Baker, Esq., and dau. of Thomas Bagnall, Esq., and had an only child, JAMES. Mr. Bourne, founder of two churches built and endowed at his own expense, one at Hilderstone, the other at Fenton, *d.* 30 Nov. 1835.

Arms—Arg., on a mount, vert, and in base, barry-wavy of four, of the field and az., a castle, triple-towered, gu., two flaunches, of the last; on a chief, nebuly, of the third, the sun in splendour, between two estoiles of the first.
Crest—On a mount, vert, a pegasus, saliant, per fesse, or and gu., charged on the body with two fountains, ppr.; in the mouth a trefoil slipped, vert.
Motto—Hæc omnia transeunt.
Seat—Hilderstone Hall, Staffordshire.

BOUVERIE OF DELAPRÉ ABBEY.

BOUVERIE, EDWARD, Esq. of Delapré Abbey, co. Northampton, J.P. and D.L., sheriff in 1800, *b.* 26 Oct. 1767; *m.* 10 March, 1788, Catherine, only dau. and heir of William Castle, Esq., and has issue,

I. EVERARD-WILLIAM, col. in the army, equerry to Prince ALBERT, *b.* 18 Oct. 1789, *m.* 3 April, 1816, Charlotte, dau. of the late Col. Hugh O'Donel, of Newport Pratt, co. Mayo.
II. Charles, *d. unm.* in 1827.
III. Francis-Kenelm, *m.* 21 Nov. 1836, Eliza, dau. of — Sheil, Esq. of Castle Dawson, co. Derry, and *d.* 19 Sept. 1837.
IV. James, lieut.-col. in the 17th foot, *m.* 11 July, 1826, Miss Elizabeth-Alston Stewart, dau. of Col. Alston, of Urrard House, Perthshire, and *d.* in 1845.
I. Catherine-Mary-Charlotte. II. Elizabeth-Anne.
III. Caroline-Margaret.
IV. Mary-Elizabeth, *d.* 1 Oct. 1834.

Lineage.—HON. EDWARD BOUVERIE (2nd son of Jacob, 1st Viscount Folkestone, by Mary his wife, dau. of Bartholomew Clarke, Esq. of Hardingstone, and of Delapré Abbey), who was returned at the general elections in 1761 and 1768, M.P. for New Sarum. He *m.* 30 June, 1764, Harriot, only dau. of Sir Everard Fawkener, Knt., many years ambassador at the Porte, and had issue,

EDWARD, his heir, of Delapré.
John, in holy orders, *b.* 18 Jan. 1779, prebendary of Lincoln, and rector of Woolbeding, Sussex.
Henry-Frederick (Sir), K.C.B., G.C.M.G., a general officer, Governor of Malta, &c., *b.* 11 July, 1783, *m.* 8 July, 1826, Julia, dau. of Lewis Montolieu, Esq., and widow of Captain William Wilbraham, R.N., and *d.* 14 Nov. 1852, leaving a son, Henry-Montolieu, capt. Coldstream-guards, killed in action at the battle of Inkerman; and a dau., Henrietta, *m.* in 1851, to Hugh-Montolieu Hammersley, Esq.
Harriet-Elizabeth, *m.* to the Earl of Rosslyn, and *d.* in 1810.
Frances-Anne.
Mary-Charlotte, *m.* in 1800, to William Maxwell, Esq., and *d.* in 1816.
Jane, *m.* in 1802, to Sir Francis Vincent, Bart., and *d.* in 1809.
Diana-Juliana, *m.* to the Hon. George Pensonby.

Mr. Bouverie *d.* 8 Sept. 1810.

Arms—Per fesse, or and arg., an eagle displayed, sa.; on the breast an escutcheon, gu., charged with a bend, vair.
Crest—A demi-eagle with two heads, displayed, sa., ducally gorged, or: on the breast a cross-crosslet, arg.
Motto—Patria cara, carior libertas.
Seat—Delapré Abbey, near Northampton.

BOWDON OF SOUTHGATE AND BEIGHTON-FIELDS.

BOWDON, HENRY, Esq. of Southgate House and Beightonfields, co. Derby, J.P. and D.L., *b.* 7 Aug. 1814; *m.* Henrietta-Matilda, 4th dau. of Michael Blount, Esq. of Maple Durham, co. Oxford. He *s.* his father in 1850.

Lineage.—The Bowdons of Bowdon Hall, near Chapel-en-le-Frith, co. Derby, were settled there, according to many writers, upwards of four hundred years. Lysons mentions them as a very wealthy and ancient family. It is generally supposed that the Bowdons came over at the Conquest, as the name Bodin or Bowdon appears on the roll of Battel Abbey. During the times of persecution carried on against the Catholics, most of the family papers were either lost or destroyed, and we are therefore compelled to begin only at the year 1500, when

GEORGE BOWDON, son of Thomas Bowdon, was of Bowdon. He *m.* Barbara, dau. of Nicholas Bagshawe, of Abney, and was father of

GEORGE BOWDON, Esq. of Bowdon Hall, *b.* in 1537, who *m.* Ellen, dau. of Augustine Pole, Esq. of Langley, and had, with a dau., Anne, wife of Rowland Smith, of Waterford, three sons,

I. THOMAS, who *d. v. p.*, leaving, by Anne his wife, dau. of Henry Bagshawe, Esq. of Ridge, *inter alios*,
  1 GEORGE, of Bowden, aged twelve, in 1611, *m.* in 1622, Dorothy, dau. of Nicholas Brown, of Marsh Hall, Esq., and dying in 1679, left a son and heir,
    NICHOLAS, of Bowdon, who *d.* about 1670, leaving issue only by his second wife, the dau. of Thomas Barnby, of Barnby, *viz.*, three sons, Barnby; Thomas; and Robert; who all *d. s. p.*
  2 Nicholas, } *d. s. p.*
  3 Edward, }
  4 THOMAS, of whose line we treat.
II. George, *m.* Alianor, dau. and heir of George Bowdon, Esq. of Downs, co. Chester, and was father of two sons, William, the elder, whose dau. *m.* Augustine Pole, of Langley; and Edward Bowdon, living in 1611, whose only son, George Bowdon, *m.* his cousin, Ellen, dau. of Augustine Pole, of Langley.
III. German, who *m.* Florence, dau. of Nicholas Bradburne.

The 4th son of Thos. Bowdon and Anne Bagshawe his wife,

THOMAS BOWDON, Esq. of Whetstone, co. Derby, capt. in the army, and commander of the garrison at Bolsover Castle, *m.* Helen, dau. of J. Shrigley, Esq., and had (with a younger son, John, capt. in the army, who *m.* Alice, dau. of Richard Beard, Esq. of Beard Hall, co. Derby, and *d. s. p.* of the plague in 1665), an elder son,

HENRY BOWDON, Esq. of Whetstone, co. Derby, who *m.* the sister and heiress of John Alleyne, Esq. of Whetston Hall, and had a son and successor,

HENRY BOWDON, Esq. of Whetstone, heir to his uncle, John Alleyne, m. in 1691, Mary, dau. and heir of John Hewet, Esq. of Beightonfields, of the family of HEWET *of Shireoaks*, Notts, and had a son and heir,

JOHN BOWDON, Esq. of Beightonfields, b. 31 Aug. 1695, who m. 1st, Mary, dau. of John Barker, of Barlborough, and had by her, with a dau., Elizabeth, m. to George Johnson, Esq. of Shelfield, brother to her father's third wife, an only son and heir,

JOHN, of whom presently.

He m. 2ndly, Margaret, dau. of — Nelson, Esq. of Fairhurst, co. Lancaster, and relict of John Sherburne, of Stonyhurst, by whom he had a son, Thomas, b. 20 Aug. 1731, d. unm. 1779. Mr. Bowdon m. 3rdly, Mary, dau. of George Johnson, Esq. of Shelfield, co. Warwick, and had, with other issue,

I. George, of Radford, co. Oxford, b. 9 Oct. 1748, m. Elizabeth Clements, of Oxfordshire, and had issue,
 1 George, of Barlborough, m. Eleanora Harrison, of Lancashire, and dying 18 Feb. 1822, left issue, Mary, d. in 1842; Eliza, m to Philip Hickin, Esq. of Wolverhampton; and Anne, m. to James Vinn, Esq. of Brussels, and d. s. p. in 1842.
 2 John, d. unm.
 3 Joseph, in holy orders, D.D., president of Sedgely Park, d. 1844.
 4 Mary.
II. James, of Staveley, co. Derby, b. 14 Nov 1744, m. Elizabeth, dau. of the Rev. Samuel Yates, rector of Clown, co. Derby, and d. s. p.
I. Charlotte, m. to Richard Butler, Esq. of Pleasington Hall, co. Lancaster.

Mr. Bowdon d. 1 March, 1764, and was s. by the only son of his first marriage,

JOHN BOWDON, Esq. of Beightonfields, b. 14 May, 1722, who m. Alice, dau. of George Johnson, Esq. of Shelfield, and sister to his father's 3rd wife, and was father of

HENRY BOWDON, Esq. of Southgate House and Beightonfields, b. in 1754, who m. Mary, only dau. and heir of Joseph Erdeswick, of Hartley Green, Esq., co. Stafford, representative of that very ancient family, and son of Sampson Erdeswick, of Hartley, Esq., by Elizabeth his wife, dau. of Thomas Whitegreave, Esq. of Moseley. Mr. Bowdon d. 26 Feb. 1833, and was s. by his only surviving son,

JOHN-PETER-BRUNO BOWDON, Esq. of Southgate and Beightonfields, J.P., high-sheriff 1841, b. 23 April, 1787, who m. 26 Feb. 1812, Mary-Martha, eldest dau. of Edward Ferrers, Esq. of Baddesley Clinton, co. Warwick, and had issue,

HENRY, now of Southgate House.
JOHN, of Pleasington Hall, co. Lancaster. (*See* BUTLER-BOWDON, *of that place*).
Helena-Mary, m. to Peter Constable Maxwell, Esq., third son of M. C. Maxwell, Esq. of Everingham Park, co. York, and has issue.
Barbara-Magdalen, m. 24 April, 1849, to Edward Wright, Esq., third son of John Wright, Esq. of Kelvedon, and has issue.
Fanny-Willoughby, a nun. Eliza-Jemima.
Caroline-Erdeswick, d. 1842.

Arms—Quarterly: 1st and 4th, sa. and or; in the first quarter, a lion, passant, arg., langued, gu., for BOWDON; 2nd, gu., a bordure, erm.; 3rd, arg., on a chevron, gu., five besants, for ERDESWICK.
Crests—1st, a heron's head, erased, ppr., beaked, and charged on the neck with three ermine spots, sa.; 2nd, out of a ducal coronet, or, a demi-eagle displayed, ppr.
Motto—Vanus est honor.
Seats—Southgate House and Beightonfields, co. Derby.

BUTLER-BOWDON OF PLEASINGTON HALL.

BUTLER-BOWDON, JOHN, Esq. of Pleasington Hall, co. Lancaster, b. 14 Sept. 1815, 2nd son of the late John-Peter-Bruno Bowdon, Esq. of Southgate House and Beightonfields, by Mary his wife, eldest dau. of Edward Ferrers, Esq. of Baddesley-Clinton, co. Warwick, s. to the Pleasington estate by the bequest of his cousin, Mary-Anne, only surviving child and heir of the late Richard Butler, Esq. of Pleasington Hall (who purchased that property in 1777), by Charlotte his wife, dau. of the late John Bowdon, Esq. of Beightonfields. Mr. Bowdon, upon his succession to the Butler estate, assumed, by sign-manual, dated 21 Jan. 1841, the name of BUTLER, in addition to and before his patronymic, as also the arms of Butler quarterly with Bowdon. He m. Amelia-Catherine-Frances, eldest dau. of G.-T. Whitgreave, Esq. of Moseley Court, co. Stafford, and has issue,

I. JOHN-ERDESWICK, b. 16 Feb. 1850.
II. Lancelot-George, b. 28 March, 1851.
III. Jermyne-Thomas, b. 18 Sept. 1853.
I. Mary-Frances-Amelia.

Arms—Quarterly: 1st and 4th, sa. and or, in the first quarter a lion, passant, arg., langued, gu., for BOWDON; 2nd and 3rd, az., a chevron between three covered cups, or, for BUTLER.
Crests—1st, for BOWDON; 2nd, a covered cup, or, for BUTLER.
Motto—Comme je trouve.
Seat—Pleasington Hall, co. Lancaster.

BOWEN OF CAMROSE.

BOWEN-WEBB, CHARLES-WHEELER-TOWNSEND, Esq. of Camrose House, co. Pembroke, J.P., high-sheriff in 1836-7, b. 9 March, 1798; s. his father in May, 1833.

Lineage.—The family of Bowen has been established in Pembrokeshire for a great number of years, and various branches have become dispersed over South Wales and elsewhere.

HUGH WEBB, Esq., son of George Webb, Esq. of Hackard, co. Pembroke, by ANNE his wife, eldest dau. of the Rev. James Bowen, 3rd son of the Rev. Charles Bowen, of Camrose, s. to Camrose in 1801, and assumed the additional surname and arms of BOWEN, in the Nov. following. He m. 1st, Miss Child, of Haverfordwest, by whom he had one dau., Elizabeth; and 2ndly, 2 Oct. 1795, Emma, youngest dau. (by Elizabeth his wife, dau. and co-heir of Robert Townsend, Esq.) of Thomas Ince, Esq. of Stoneydale, Christleton, co. Chester, by whom he had issue,

CHARLES-WHEELER-TOWNSEND, now of Camrose.
Bell.
William, in holy orders, widower, with three sons and two daus.
Townsend.
Thomas, lieut. 64th regiment, d. unm. at Kingston, Jamaica.
Emma, m. to J.-M. Child, Esq. of Bigelly House, co. Pembroke.
Augusta, widow of John Howell, M.D., of Tigfynydd, co. Carmarthen.
Caroline, m. to D.-P. Callan, Esq. of Molleston, co. Pembroke.

Mr. Webb-Bowen d. in May, 1833.

Arms—Quarterly: 1st and 4th. arg., a lion, rampant, sa., for BOWEN; 2nd and 3rd, gu., a fesse, between three owls, or, for WEBB.
Crest—A lion, rampant, as in the arms.
Seat—Camrose House, near Haverfordwest.

BOWEN OF TROEDYRAWR.

BOWEN, THE REV. THOMAS, of Troedyrawr, co. Cardigan, b. 25 Jan. 1757; m. 1st, in 1792, Sarah-Malvina Vaulker, of Hampton, co. Middlesex, but has no issue. He m. 2ndly, in 1801, Frances Norton, of Hampton. The rev. gentleman, who s. his mother in 1793, is rector of Troedyrawr, and a magistrate and deputy-lieutenant.

Lineage.—JOHN BOWEN, Esq., whose grandfather changed the name of Owen into that now in use by this family, was father of

WILLIAM BOWEN, Esq., high-sheriff of Cardiganshire in 1755, who m. Rebecca, eldest dau. and co-heiress of — Willy, Esq. of Whitehouse, co. Pembroke, and had, besides the REV. THOMAS BOWEN, of Troedyrawr, two other sons and four daus., viz.,

John, barrister-at-law, m. 1st, Mary, youngest dau. of David-Lloyd Morgan, Esq. of Cardigan, and 2ndly, Miss Hughes, heiress of Aber Molwyn, co. Cardigan. He d. s. p. in 1815.
William, M.D., at Bath, m. Miss Boycott, of Shropshire, sister of the late Countess of Guildford. He d. s. p. in 1815.
Mary-Anne, Rebecca, Hester, and Elizabeth, all d. unm.

Arms—Gu., a lion, rampant-regardant, or.
Crest—A nag's head, bridled.
Seat—Troedyrawr, co. Cardigan.

BOWER OF IWERNE HOUSE.

BOWER, THOMAS-BOWYER, Esq. of Iwerne House, co. Dorset, high-sheriff in 1847, b. 1 July, 1803; m.

9 Aug. 1828, Eliza, only dau. of William Creed, Esq. of Ballygrennan Castle, co. Limerick, by whom he has issue,

I. Thomas-Bowyer, formerly an officer, 73rd regt., b. 6 Sept. 1829.
II. William-Henry, b. 14 Dec. 1838.
I. Eliza-Harriott. II. Charlotte-Frances.

Lineage.—Edmund Bower, Esq., living 22nd Edw. IV., great-grandson of John Bower, m. Agnes, dau. of Hugh Weston, and had three sons, Edmund, Walter, and William, of Mere, in Wiltshire, who had issue. The eldest son,

Edmund Bower, Esq., living 3rd Henry VIII., was mayor of Shaftesbury, to which town he appears to have been a great benefactor, having built the Guild Hall and Market-place. He m. Joan, dau. of Richard Moggeridge, of Sarum, and had two sons, I. Walter, canon of Wells, who m. Elizabeth, dau. of Adrian Hawthorne, Esq., and had issue; and II. Thomas, of Lower Dunhead, Wilts, father of Edmund, of Dunhead St. Andrew, whose son, by Margaret his wife, dau. and co-heir of William Kirle, of Wilton, was Thomas, of Ewen Minster, great-great-great-grandfather of

Thomas Bower, Esq., b. 20 Feb. 1744, who m. 1st, 19 Oct. 1767, Anne-Catharina, dau. of the Rev. Edward Napier, rector of More Critchill, co. Dorset, and had two sons and three daus., all deceased. He m. 2ndly, Dorothy-Elizabeth, dau. of the Rev. Samuel Elliott, by whom he also had issue a son, George-Edmund, b. 11 March, 1781, who m. Emma-Letitia, dau. of John Boys, M.D., and had issue, two daus., Louisa-Dorothy and Lucy. The eldest son,

Thomas-Bowyer Bower, Esq. of Iwerne House, J.P., high-sheriff in 1796, and lieut.-col. Dorset yeomanry cavalry, b. 26 April, 1771, m. 29 May, 1792, Harriett, dau. of Walter Whitaker, Esq., recorder of Shaftesbury, and by her (who d. 27 May, 1841) had issue,

I. Thomas-Bowyer, now of Iwerne House.
II. Henry-Tregonwell, in holy orders, b. 22 Nov. 1808, m. 22 June, 1837, Elizabeth-Synderoombe, dau. of the Rev. Thomas Fox, rector of Abbas Combe, co. Somerset, and South Newton, Wilts, and has issue,
Henry-Synderoombe, b. 14 July, 1839.
I. Harriett-Catherina, m. 17 Feb. 1826, the Rev. Christopher Nevill, rector of East Grinstead, co. Sussex, and has issue.
II. Elizabeth-Anne, m. 2 Oct. 1828, to the Rev. Edward Bower, rector of Closworth, co. Somerset, and has issue.

Mr. Bower d. 21 Sept. 1840.

Arms—Sa., three talbots' heads, couped in chief, arg., langued, gu.; in the middle point a cinquefoil, erm.
Crest—A talbot's head, arg.
Motto—Hope well and have well.
Seat—Iwerne House, Dorsetshire.

BOWER OF WELHAM.

Bower, Robert, Esq. of Welham, co. York, D.L., m. 23 June, 1824, Helen, eldest dau. of John Hall, Esq. of Scarborough, and has issue,

I. Robert-Hartley, b. 9 July, 1832.
II. Henry-John, b. 14 Sept. 1834.
III. George-Cuthbertson, b. 1 Nov. 1835.
IV. Leonard-William.
I. Lucy-Margaret. II. Charlotte-Philadelphia.

Lineage.—The family of Bower was originally settled at Bridlington, East Riding of Yorkshire. In the earliest registers of its church we find the name of Bower, and it is continued in regular succession of entries from 1568 to the latter part of the last century, when the more immediate connexion of the family with that place appears to have ceased. The first advancer of the family was,

William Bower, of Bridlington, merchant (son of John Bower, of the same place, and Jean [Bonfeylde], his wife), whose baptism occurs on the 14th May, 1598. He was a considerable benefactor to his native town. His eldest son,

John Bower, Esq. of Bridlington, m. in 1652, Catherine, widow of — Rogers, and dau. of William Bower, of Cloughton, and had several sons and daus.: of the latter, Priscilla m. 10 Aug. 1700, to Ralph Creyke, Esq. of Marton, near Bridlington; and of the former, the eldest,

William Bower, Esq. of Bridlington, b. in 1654, m. 1st, in 1676, Sarah, dau. of Jasper Belt, Esq. of Pocklington, son of Sir Robert Belt, of Bossall, Knt., and had issue, William, who left three daus.; Leonard, of whom presently; and other issue. Mr. Bower m. 2ndly, Catherine, dau. of Edward Trotter, Esq. of Skelton Castle, by Mary his wife, dau. of Sir John Lowther, Bart., and by that lady had issue,

Henry, of York, who purchased the estate of Killerby Hall, near Scarborough. He d. unm. in 1770.
George, of Bridlington, b. in 1708, m. Henrietta, dau. of Samuel Freeman, Esq. of Dublin, and relict of William Heblethwaite, Esq. of Bridlington, and had issue.
Freeman, of Killerby Hall and Bawtry, co. York, J.P. and D.L., m. 1st, Margaret, dau. of Richard-Burdon, Esq. of Doncaster, and had one son, Edward-Trotter, d. an infant. He m. 2ndly, 18 Jan. 1777, Mary, eldest dau. and co-heiress of Nathaniel Pearson, Esq. of Tyers Hill, Darfield, by Priscilla his wife, sister and co-heir of Thomas Rayney, Esq. of Tyers Hill, and by this lady left, at his decease, 29 July, 1786, one son and three daus., viz.,
1 Henry, of Tickhill and Doncaster, F.S.A., deputy-lieut. of the West Riding, d. unm. 25 Feb. 1842; 2 Frances-Mary, m. to the Rev. Henry Watkins, vicar of Silkstone, co. York, and Beckingham, Notts, and has issue; 3 Henrietta-Priscilla, widow of James Jackson, Esq. of Doncaster, who d. 14 March, 1821, leaving issue; and 4 Wilhelmina-Elizabeth.
Robert, of Sleights, near Whitby, and Welham, b. in 1705, who m. Tabitha, dau. and co-heir of Richard Burdett, Esq. of Sleights, by Idonea his wife, dau. of Fiennes Twisleton, Esq. of Broughton Castle, co. Oxford, but d. s. p. in 1777, leaving his estate of Welham to his kinsman, Robert, grandson of his half-brother Leonard.
Mary, m. 1st, in 1727, to Peter Whitton, Esq., lord-mayor of York in 1728, and 2ndly, in 1742, to George Perrott, Esq., an eminent barrister, afterwards one of the barons of the Exchequer.

The 2nd son of the 1st marriage,

Leonard Bower, Esq., b. 26 April, 1682, settled at Scorton. He m. 2 Aug. 1720, Elizabeth, dau. of Richard Woolfe, Esq. of Bridlington Quay, and had (with three daus., of whom the eldest, Hannah, m. 17 Sept. 1751, George Cuthbertson, jun., Esq. of Newcastle-on-Tyne; and the youngest, Sarah, m. Gen. Montgomery Agnew) two sons: the elder, William, d. s. p.; the younger,

John Bower, Esq. of Scorton, b. in 1730, m. 10 July, 1759, Philadelphia, dau. of George Cuthbertson, Esq. of Newcastle-upon-Tyne, and had issue. The eldest surviving son,

Robert Bower, Esq., b. 2 Feb. 1767, s. to the Welham estate, under the will of his kinsman, Robert Bower, half-brother of his grandfather, Leonard Bower. He was major of the East Riding local militia, and deputy-lieut. He m. Elizabeth-Amy, only surviving child of John Clubbe, Esq., M.D., of Ipswich, and by her (who d. 17 Jan. 1802) had issue,

Robert, present representative.
John-William, M.A., in holy orders, rector of Barmston, co. York, and a magistrate for the East Riding, m. 3 Sept. 1828, Eugenia, youngest dau. of John Hall, Esq. of Scarborough, and has issue, John; Mary-Elizabeth; Elizabeth; Margaret; and Eugenia.
George-Henry, M.A., in holy orders, rector of Rossington, co. York.
Elizabeth-Amy. Sarah-Anne.

Mr. Bower d. 29 April, 1835.

Arms—Sa., a human leg, couped at the thigh, transpierced by a broken spear, in bend, ppr.; on a canton, arg., a tower, gu.
Crest—A human leg, transpierced, as in the arms.
Motto—Esse quam videri.
Seat—Welham, East Riding, co. York.

BOWES OF STREATLAM CASTLE.

Bowes, John, Esq. of Streatlam Castle, Gibside Park, and Hilton Castle, all in the county of Durham, b. 19 June, 1811; s. to the estates of John, 10th Earl of Strathmore, under the will of that nobleman. These great possessions in the north came into the Strathmore family by the intermarriage of John, the 9th earl, in 1767, with Mary-Eleanor, dau. and heiress of George Bowes, Esq. of Streatlam Castle. Mr. Bowes represented for some time the southern division of the county of Durham in parliament.

Seats—Streatlam Castle and Gibside Park, co. Durham.

BOWLES OF NORTH ASTON.

Bowles, Charles-Oldfield, Esq. of North Aston, co. Oxford, J.P. and D.L., lieut.-col. of the militia, *b.* 30 Aug. 1785; *m.* 9 April, 1815, Elizabeth, eldest dau. of Matthew, Lord Rokeby, and has issue,

I. CHARLES, lieut. 3rd light dragoons, *b.* 5 May, 1816, *m.* Martina, dau. of Dr. William-Lewis Grant, H.I.C.S., and widow of Capt. Alfred Jackson, H.I.C.S.

II. Henry-Oldfield, rifle brigade, *b.* 7 Jan. 1818, *m.* Barbara, dau. of Pelham Warren, M.D.

III. Edward, *b.* 27 Aug. 1825.

I. Jane-Lydia, *m.* to Leopold, Baron Gronys de Frimdonstein.

II. Laura-Gertrude-Anna.

Lineage.—This family claims descent from William Bolles or Bowles, 3rd son of John Bowles, of Swineshead and Hough, co. Lincoln, who was sheriff of that shire, 16th EDWARD IV. The great-grandfather of the present representative,

WILLIAM BOWLES, Esq. of Windsor and Clewer, co. Berks, *m.* Elizabeth, dau. of Sir Charles Modyford, Bart., by Mary his wife, dau. of Sir Thomas Norton, Bart. of Coventry, and had a son and successor,

CHARLES BOWLES, Esq., who *m.* Jane, dau. of — Clark, Esq. of Northamptonshire, and had, with a dau., Anne, *m.* to Robert Graham, Esq., a son and successor,

OLDFIELD BOWLES, Esq. of North Aston, who *m.* 1st, in 1768, Gertrude, dau. of Sir Richard Bamfylde, Bart. of Poltimore, which lady *d. s. p.* the following year. Mr. Bowles *m.* 2ndly, Mary, dau. of Sir Abraham Elton, Bart. of Clevedon Court, co. Somerset, and had issue,

CHARLES-OLDFIELD, now of North Aston.
Jane, *m.* to Richard Palmer, Esq. of Holme Park.
Mary, *m.* to Sir George Armytage, Bart. of Kirklees.
Anne, *m.* to the Right Hon. William-Sturges Bourne, of Testwood, Hants.
Emma, *m.* to the Rev. Ralph-H. Brandling, of Gosforth, co. Northumberland.
Elizabeth, *m.* to William Markham, Esq. of Becca Hall, co. York.
Lucy, *m.* to William Holbech, Esq. of Farnborough, co. Warwick.
Laura Gertrude, *m.* to Frederick Moysey, Esq. of West Wickham, Kent.
Frances, *m.* to Edward Golding, Esq. of Maiden Erlegh, Berks.

Arms—Az., out of three cups, or, as many boars' heads, couped, arg.
Crest—A demi-boar, wounded in the breast with a broken spear.
Seat—North Aston, co. Oxford.

BOYCOTT OF BOYCOTT, HINTON, AND RUDGE.

BOYCOTT, THOMAS, Esq. of Boycott, Hinton, and Rudge, co. Salop, *b.* in 1771; *m.* 10 Aug. 1801, Jane, eldest dau. of Thomas Tarleton, Esq. of Bolesworth Castle, co. Chester, by Mary his wife, dau. and co-heir of Lawrence Robinson, Esq. of Clitheroe, co. Lancaster, and by her (who *d.* 18 Feb. 1843) has had issue,

I. THOMAS, *b.* 22 May, 1806, *d. unm.* in 1827.

I. Emma. II. Charlotte, *d. unm.* in 1824.

III. Harriet, *m.* 24 June, 1826, Francis Harries, Esq., jun. of Benthall.

IV. Louisa-Mary-Catherine, *m.* 28 Jan. 1841, Andrew Wight, Esq. of Ormiston, N.B., and has had issue,

1 Andrew-Boycott, *b.* 4 June, 1842, *d.* 12 July, 1847.
2 Hamilton-Belfast-Boycott, *b.* 11 Aug. 1846.

Lineage.—The family of Bigot, or Boycott, is of great antiquity in Shropshire, in which county, and in those adjacent, they held extensive estates from the period of the Conquest, part of which, including Boycott, whence the name is taken, is still in the possession of the present representative.

FRANCIS BOYCOTT, Esq. of Boycott and Buildwas, in Shropshire, in 1543, was father of

WILLIAM BOYCOTT, Esq. of Boycott, Buildwas, and Hinton, who *m.* 1st, in 1624, Elizabeth, dau. and heir of John Tyrer, Esq. of Hinton, and had issue,

I. Elizabeth, *m.* to Thomas Holland, Esq., a magistrate for Shropshire in 1663.

II. Sarah, *m.* in 1654, William Warter, Esq. of Cruckmeole, and had issue,

1 John Warter, Esq. of Rudge Hall, whose only child, Catherine, *m.* in 1745, William Boycott, Esq., after mentioned.

William *m.* 2ndly, in 1651, Eleanor, dau. of Sylvanus Lacon, Esq. of West Coppice, by Grace his wife, dau. of Sir Edward Littleton, Bart. of Pillaton, co. Stafford, and had issue, Sylvanus, of Hinton and Buildwas, and FRANCIS, of Boycott, of whom presently. William Boycott was one of those Shropshire gentlemen who, with his sons, Sylvanus and Francis, materially assisted their majesties, CHARLES I. and II. in their distresses, and as a reward for which, CHARLES II., in 1663, granted to the said Sylvanus and Francis Boycott, a special patent of arms. William Boycott *d.* in 1658. His second son,

FRANCIS BOYCOTT, of Boycott, *m.* in 1659, Catherine, dau. and sole heir of Richard Ward, Gent. of The Lowe and of Uppington, and had issue, with other children, his eldest son,

WILLIAM BOYCOTT, Esq. of Boycott, *b.* in 1661, who *m.* in 1692, Sarah, sole dau. and heir of Robert Kirkby, Esq., co. Nottingham, and had issue, with other children, three sons, viz., Francis, of Boycott, whose issue became extinct; William, *d.* in 1762, *s. p.*; and RICHARD (the Rev.), of whose descendants we treat. The third son,

THE REV. RICHARD BOYCOTT, *b.* in 1698, rector of Whittington, near Oswestry, *m.* in 1732, Gertrude, 2nd dau. of Thomas Jenkins, Esq. by Gertrude, dau. of Richard Wingfield, Esq. of Bauxley, and dying in 1751, left, with two daus., Anne, who *d. unm.*, and Sarah, wife of Edward Jenkins, Esq. of Charlton Hill, co. Salop, three sons, of whom the eldest,

THOMAS BOYCOTT, Esq. of Boycott, Hinton, and Rudge, *m.* in 1768, Jane, youngest dau. of John Puleston, Esq. of Pickhill, co. Denbigh, and by her (who *d.* in Oct. 1803) had issue,

THOMAS, of Boycott, Hinton, and Rudge.
Richard, *b.* in 1773, capt. in the 34th regt., *d. unm.* in the island of St. Vincent.
Charles, *b.* in 1777, major in the 29th regt., *d.* in 1809, having *m.* Wilhelmina, dau. of Christopher Smyth, Esq., and granddau. of Christopher Smyth, Esq. of Northampton.
Frances, *m.* in 1797, John Hayman, Esq., major in the 9th regt.
Emma, *m.* in 1793, to Edward Ravenscroft, Esq.
Harriet, *m.* in 1801, Henry-Lannoy Hunter, Esq. of Beech Hill, co. Berks.
Sophia, *m.* in 1810, to William Bowen, Esq., M.D., *d.* in 1829, *s. p.*
Maria, *m.* in July, 1810, to Francis, 4th Earl of Guilford, *d.* in 1821, *s. p.*
Charlotta, *d. unm.* in 1842.
Louisa-Victoria, *m.* in 1807, Walter Smythe, Esq. of Brambridge, co. Hants.

Mr. Boycott *d.* 29 June, 1798.

Arms—Gu., on a chief, arg., three grenadoes, ppr.
Crest—An armed arm, ppr.; issuing out of a mural crown, and casting a grenado.
Motto—Pro rege et religione.
Seat—Rudge Hall, Wolverhampton.

BOYD OF ROSSLARE.

BOYD, JAMES, Esq. of Rosslare, co. Wexford, J.P., high-sheriff in 1831, major in the army, *m.* in 1813, Georgiana, dau. and co-heir of the Hon. George Jocelyn, next brother to Robert, 2nd Earl of Roden, by whom, who *d.* in 1819, he has issue,

I. JAMES-JOCELYN, an officer in the army, *m.* in 1842, Isabel, dau. of Major Cooper, and *d.* in 1849, leaving issue, JAMES, Charles, and Isabel-Lucy.

I. Georgiana, *m.* to Philip Bagenal, Esq. of Benekerry Park, co. Carlow, and has issue.

II. Elizabeth, *m.* to William-H. Glascott, Esq. of Alderton, co. Wexford, and has issue.

Lineage.—HIGATT BOYD, Esq., *b.* before 1677, to whom his cousin, John Highgate, of Rosslare, bequeathed all his estates, claimed descent from the BOYDS of *Kilmarnock*. He *m.* Margaret, 3rd dau. of Henry Loftus, Esq. of Loftus Hall, co. Wexford, the father of Nicholas, 1st Viscount Loftus, and had, with four sons, seven daus., of whom, Mary, *m.* in 1713, Robert Clifford, Esq. of Wexford; Margaret, Samuel French, Esq.; Anne, Samuel Batt, Esq.; and Jane, Joseph Atwood, Esq. Higatt Boyd was one of the commissioners for raising money in the co. of Wexford for King WILLIAM III., in 1695. His will is dated 20 June, 1728, and was proved in the diocese of Ferns, 16 May, 1733. His son and heir,

JAMES BOYD, Esq. of Rosslare, *b.* 1702, had, by Lucy his wife, two sons and four daus. James Boyd's will is dated 25 March, 1774, and was proved in the diocese of Ferns, 7 March, 1776. His eldest son,

HIGATT BOYD, Esq. of Roslare, bapt. 5 Feb. 1729, m. 1768, Miss Amy-Phillips, and had issue,

JAMES BOYD, Esq. of Roslare, J.P., m. Elizabeth, only dau. of Col. Walter Hore, of Harperstown, co. Wexford, by Lady Anne Stopford his wife, 4th dau. of James, 1st Earl of Courtown, and had issue, I. JAMES, now of Roslare; II. Higatt, lieut. 4th foot, 16 Aug. 1810; III. Charles, an officer of the E. I. Co.'s service, d. unm.; I. Anne, d. unm. 17 Feb. 1835; II. Amy; and III. Lucy. Mr. Boyd was M.P. for Wexford in the Irish parliament, and served the office of sheriff of the co. of Wexford.

Arms—Az., a fesse, chequy, or and gu.
Crest—A dexter hand, couped at the wrist, erect, third and fourth fingers turned down, ppr.
Motto—Confido.
Seat—Roslare, seven miles from Wexford.

BOYD OF MIDDLETON PARK.

BOYD, GEORGE-AUGUSTUS, Esq. of Middleton Park, co. Westmeath, J.P. and D.L., high-sheriff in 1843, b. 13 March, 1817; m. 4 July, 1843, Sarah-Jane, eldest dau. of George Woods, Esq. of Milverton, co. Dublin, by Sarah his wife, dau. of the late Hans Hamilton, Esq., for many years M.P. for the co. of Dublin, and has issue,

I. ROCHFORT-HAMILTON, b. 25 Sept. 1844.
II. Charles-Augustus-Rochfort, b. 4 Oct. 1850.
I. Alice-Jane. II. Edith-Sarah-Hamilton.
III. Florence.

Mr. Boyd inherits from his mother, the late Countess of Belvedere, a great portion of the Belvedere estates, situated in the co. of Westmeath.

Lineage.—THE REV. JAMES BOYD, rector of Erris, co. Mayo, b. in 1725, who claimed descent from the Boyds, Earls of Kilmarnock, m. in 1752, Mary, dau. of — Martin, Esq., and relict of Arthur Vernon, Esq., and d. in 1775, leaving an only son,

ABRAHAM BOYD, Esq., barrister-at-law and K.C., b. 1760, who m. in July, 1786, Catherine Shuttleworth, relict of John Davies, Esq., by whom he had one child, Helena, m. to Thomas Fenton, Esq. He m. 2ndly, in 1815, Jane, Countess of Belvedere, dau. and eventual sole heiress of the Rev. James Mackay, and by her, who d. in 1836, left at his decease, 4 Nov. 1822, an only son, the present GEORGE-AUGUSTUS BOYD, Esq., as above.

Arms—(confirmed 24 April, 1837) Quarterly: 1st and 4th, az., a fesse, chequy, arg. and gu., between three crescents, of the second, for BOYD; 2nd, gu., on a chevron, arg., between three bears' heads, couped, or, muzzled, of the first, a roebuck's head, erased, ppr.; between two hands, couped at the wrist, each grasping a dagger pointing to the centre, ppr., for MACKAY; 3rd, az., a lion, rampant, arg., and in chief, two redbreasts, ppr., for ROCHFORT.
Crests—1st, Out of a ducal coronet, or, a hand erect, with the third and fourth fingers folded, ppr., for BOYD; 2nd, A cubit arm, grasping a dagger in pale, ppr., for MACKAY; 3rd, A redbreast, ppr., for ROCHFORT.
Mottoes—Above the arms, "Manu forte." Underneath, "Confido."
Seat—Middleton Park, co. Westmeath.

BOYD OF BALLYMACOOL.

BOYD, JOHN-ROBERT, Esq. of Ballymacool, co. Donegal, J.P. and D.L., barrister-at-law, b. 24 June, 1808; m. 6 Aug. 1851, Mary-Louisa, eldest dau. of the Rev. William Knox, of Clonleigh.

Lineage.—JOHN BOYD, Esq. of Letterkenny, who claimed descent from a younger branch of the ancient Scottish family of Boyd, Earls of Kilmarnock, m. Ann, dau. of Alderman Gamble, of Derry, and had issue. The eldest son,

JOHN BOYD, Esq., major in the Donegal militia, m. Martha, eldest dau. of Col. Stewart, governor of the Bahama Islands, and was father of

JOHN BOYD, Esq., barrister-at-law, b. 20 Aug. 1769, who m. 26 Jan. 1799, Frances, 2nd dau. of Sir Samuel Hayes, Bart. of Drumboe Castle, and had issue,

JOHN-ROBERT, now of Ballymacool.
William, an officer in the 87th Royal Irish Fusiliers.
Mary, m. to William-H. Porter, Esq.
Patty Frances.
Anna-Maria, m. to William-Stewart Ross, Esq., of Sheep Hill, co. Derry.
Isabella.

Motto—Confido.
Seat—Ballymacool, Letterkenny, co. Donegal.

BOYD OF DUNDUAN HOUSE.

BOYD, JOHN, Esq. of Dunduan House, co. Londonderry, J.P. and D.L., and many years M.P. for Coleraine, b. 22 June, 1789; m. 3 Jan. 1821, Anna-Arabella, eldest dau. of the Rev. Robert Healet, rector of Killowen, J.P., and has issue.

BOYLE OF SHEWALTON.

BOYLE, PATRICK, of Shewalton, co. Ayr, M.A., Oriel College, Oxon, J.P. and D.L., member of the Faculty of Advocates, principal clerk of the High Court of Justiciary, b. 29 March, 1806; m. 17 Aug. 1830, Mary-Frances, 2nd dau. of Sir Robert Dalrymple-Horn-Elphinstone, Bart. of Horn and Logie Elphinstone, and has surviving issue,

I. DAVID, R.N., b. 31 May, 1833.
II. Robert-Elphinstone, b. 3 June, 1837.
III. Alexander-James, b. 26 Feb. 1842.
I. Elizabeth-Magdalene-Graeme.
II. Mary-Helen. III. Helen-Jane.

Lineage.—THE RIGHT HON. DAVID BOYLE, (2nd son of the Hon. Patrick Boyle, 3rd son of John, 2nd Earl of Glasgow, see BURKE'S *Peerage*), lord justice-general and president in the Court of Session, in Scotland, b. 26 July, 1772, m. 1st, 24 Dec. 1804, Elizabeth, eldest dau. of the late Alexander Montgomerie, Esq. of Annick Lodge, next brother of Hugh, 12th Earl of Eglinton, and had by her,

PATRICK, now of Shewalton.
Alexander, commander R.N., b. 9 March, 1810, m. 2 July, 1844, Agnes, 3rd dau of James Walker, Esq., C.E.
John, b. 9 Sept. 1819, barrister at-law, m. 6 Sept. 1853, Jane, 2nd dau. of Theodore Walrond, Esq. of Calder Park, co. Lanark.
William, capt. 89th regt., b. 25 Jan. 1821, m. 14 June, 1853, Louisa, eldest dau. of the Rev. Henry Parsons.
Archibald-Thomas, b. 14 April, 1822.
Elizabeth, m. in 1828, to James Hope, Esq., 3rd son of the Right Hon. Charles Hope.
Helen, m. in 1829, to Sir Charles-Dalrymple Fergusson, of Kilkerran, Bart., who d. in 1849.
Hamilla-Augusta. Eleanora-Charlotte.

Mr. Boyle m. 2ndly, 17 July, 1827, Camilla-Catherine, eldest dau. of the late Hon. David Smythe, of Methven Castle, Perthshire, a judge of the Court of Session, and had by her,

George-David, M.A., in holy orders, b. 17 May, 1828.
Robert, royal horse artillery, b. 2 Dec. 1830.
Henry-Dundas, b. 1 Feb. 1833, d. 19 April, 1853.
Amelia-Laura.

The Lord Justice-General, who s. to Shewalton, on the death of his elder brother, Col. John Boyle, in 1837, d. 4 Feb. 1853.

Arms—Quarterly: 1st and 4th, or, an eagle, displayed, with two heads, gu.; 2nd and 3rd, per bend embattled, arg. and gu.; over all, an escutcheon, or, charged with three stags' horns, erect, gu., two and one.
Crest—An eagle, displayed, with two heads, per pale embattled, arg. and gu.
Motto—Dominus providebit.
Seat—Shewalton, near Kilmarnock.

BOYSE OF BANNOW.

BOYSE, THE REV. RICHARD, of Bannow, co. Wexford, m. Winifred-Berners Plestow, of Watlington Hall, Norfolk, and has a son and heir,

AUGUSTUS-FREEMAN, b. 26 Sept. 1822.

Lineage.—THOMAS BOYSE, Esq., great-grandson of Nathaniel Boyse, who settled in the co. of Wexford about 1658, and purchased the estate of Bannow, m. Margaret, dau. and co-heir of Edmund Jackson, Esq. of Portnescolly, and left (with four daus., Nina, m. to John Green, Esq. of Greenville; Margaret, m. to William Watts, Esq.; Frances, m. to R.-T. Carew, Esq. of Ballinamona; and Jane) one son,

SAMUEL BOYSE, Esq. of Bannow, who *m.* in 1780, Dorothy, dau. of Robert-S. Carew, Esq. of Castleborough, and had issue, 1 THOMAS, his heir; 2 Shapland, lieut.-col. 13th light dragoons, C.B., commanded his regiment at Waterloo, *d. unm.* in 1832; 3 RICHARD, present representative; and five daus., of whom the 4th, Margaret, *m.* H.-H. Hunt, Esq. The eldest son,

THOMAS BOYSE, Esq. of Bannow, J.P., *b.* 25 Dec. 1781, *m.* Jane-Stratford, dau. of John Kirwan, Esq., barrister-at-law, and widow of Cæsar Colclough, Esq. of Tintern Abbey, co. Wexford; but *d. s. p.*; when he was *s.* by his brother.

Seat—Bannow, co. Wexford.

MOORE-BRABAZON OF TARA HOUSE.

MOORE-BRABAZON, THE REV. WILLIAM-JOHN, of Tara House, co. Meath, A.M., vicar of Sarrat, Herts, *b.* 29 April, 1789; assumed by sign-manual, in July, 1845, the additional surname and arms of BRABAZON.

Lineage.—In 1721, JOHN MOORE, Esq. of Dublin, acquired, under an act of parliament passed for the sale of the estates of William Graham, Esq. the town lands of Dalgatherine, Hill of Rath, Tullyhallen, and Drybridge, all in the barony of Mellifont, and co. of Louth. He *m.* Miss Campbell, second sister of the Right Hon. Charles Campbell, M.P. of New Grange, co. Meath, and had issue,

Charles, barrister-at-law, *d. s. p.*
JOHN, of whom we treat.
Alice, *m.* General Sir John Whiteford, Bart., and had several daus., of whom one, Alicia-Lucy, *m.* 29 Nov. 1795, Henry, 3rd Lord Vernon; and another, *m.* Col. Cunningham.

The younger son,

JOHN MOORE, Esq., M.D., of Tullyhallen, &c., *m.* 26 Aug. 1752, Frideswide, dau. of Dixie Coddington, Esq. of Athlumney Castle, co. Meath, and had,

JOHN, his heir.
Alice, *m.* Thomas Achmuty, Esq. of Madeira.
Jane, *m.* in July, 1799, the Hon. and Very Rev. John Hewitt, Dean of Cloyne.
Frideswide, *m.* in 1786, Col. the Hon. Robert-Henry Southwell, of Castle Hamilton.

Dr. Moore was shot at his own door by an unknown person, in 1788, and was *s.* by his son,

JOHN MOORE, Esq. of New Lodge, Herts, *b.* 20 Sept. 1763, who *m.* 1st, 24 May, 1788, Barbara, dau. of the Hon. William Brabazon, 2nd son of Edward, 7th Earl of Meath, and had issue,

WILLIAM-JOHN, now of Tara House, who has assumed the additional surname of BRABAZON.
John-Arthur, *b.* 24 Sept. 1791, R.N., for many years signal-officer to Admiral (then Captain) Blackwood, *m.* 31 July, 1827, Sophia, dau. of Col. Yates.
Charles-Henry, *b.* 21 March, 1798.

Mr. Moore *m.* 2ndly, 26 April, 1839, Charlotte, dau. of George-Samuel Collyer, Esq. and *d.* in April, 1842.

Arms—Gu., on a bend, or, three martlets, sa., quartering, az., a chief, indented, or, charged with three mullets, pierced, gu.

Crest—1st, on a mount, vert, a falcon rising, or, belled, of the last; 2nd, out of a ducal coronet, or, a Moor's head, ppr., filleted round the temples, az. and or; a jewel pendent in the ear, arg.

Motto—Durum patientiâ frango.

Seat—Tara House, co. Meath.

BRABAZON OF BRABAZON PARK.

BRABAZON, HUGH, Esq. of Brabazon Park, co. Mayo, late a capt. in the 15th hussars, *m.* 9 Feb. 1827, Ellen-Ambrosia, youngest dau. of the late Sir William-Henry Palmer, Bart., of Palmerstown, and Kenure Park, and has issue,

I. LUKE-BRABAZON, *b.* 23 March, 1832.
II. John-Palmer, *b.* 12 Feb. 1843.
I. Elizabeth-Louisa.
II. Augusta.
III. Emma.
IV. Kate.

This gentleman, eldest son of Luke Higgins, Esq., late of Castlebar, co. Mayo, by Catharine his wife, sister of Sir Anthony Brabazon, Bart. of Brabazon Park, assumed by royal license, in 1852, the surname and arms of BRABAZON.

Arms—Quarterly, 1st and 4th, gu., on a bend, or, three martlets, sa., with a fleur-de-lis, arg., for difference, for BRABAZON; 2nd and 3rd, arg., guttée-de-poix, on a fesse, sa., three towers, of the first, for HIGGINS.

Crest—On a mount, vert, a falcon, rising, belled, or, charged with a fleur-de-lis, az.

Motto—Vota vita mea.

Seat—Brabazon Park, co. Mayo.

BRACEBRIDGE OF ATHERSTONE HALL.

BRACEBRIDGE, CHARLES-HOLTE, Esq. of Atherstone Hall, co. Warwick, *b.* 19 March, 1799; *m.* 24 March, 1824, Selina, dau. of William Mills, Esq. of Bisterne, co. Hants.

Lineage.—This family establishes a Saxon descent, deriving from TURCHILL DE WARWICK, who enjoyed the dignity of Earl prior to the advent of the Normans, and afterwards, in conformity with the invaders, assumed the surname of ARDEN, from a woodland tract in Warwickshire.

OSBERT DE ARDEN, son of Turchill, by his 2nd wife, inherited the manor of Kingsbury, the principal seat of his father, which property passed eventually to his only dau.,

AMICIA DE ARDEN, wife of

PETER DE BRACEBRIDGG, so called from a place near Lincoln, of which he was lord. His elder son,

JOHN DE BRACEBRIDGG, Lord of Kingsbury, *d.* issueless, 2nd HENRY III., and was *s.* by his brother,

WILLIAM DE BRACEBRIDGG, Lord of Kingsbury, constituted, 19th HENRY III., a justice of assize at Warwick. He was *s.* by his son,

SIR RALPH DE BRACEBRIGG, Knt., Lord of Kingsbury, knighted in the 33rd of HENRY III. His dau., Matilda, *m.* Thomas de Clinton, and he was *s.* by his son,

SIR JOHN DE BRACEBRIGG, Knt. From SIR JOHN we pass to

SIR RALPH DE BRACEBRIGG, Knt., styled, in an inquisition taken in the 1st of HENRY IV., "frater Johannis de Bracebrigg militis." In the 7th Henry V., Sir Ralph was summoned the first, amongst other persons of note, to attend the king in person, for the defence of the realm. Sir Ralph de Bracebrigg, it appears, attended, in 1414, with eleven other knights of ancient family, HENRY V. to Paris, on the occasion of the coronation of CHARLES VI. of France. His descendant in the fifth degree was,

THOMAS BRACEBRIGG, Esq. (a son of Simon Bracebrigg, by Elizabeth, dau. of William Harewell, of Wotton-Waven). He *m.* twice, and disinherited the children* of his 1st wife, on marrying the 2nd, Jocosa Wilson. His son and heir, THOMAS, by that lady, becoming deeply involved in debt, the remainder of Kingsbury was alienated to Sir Francis Willoughby, Knt. of Middleton. He *d.* 1 March, in the 11th of ELIZABETH. The 3rd son of the 2nd marriage,

ANKETIL BRACEBRIGG, Esq., *m.* Anna, dau. of Thomas Corbin, Esq. of Hall End, and was grandfather of

SAMUEL BRACEBRIDGE, Esq. of Atherstone, who *m.* Elizabeth, dau. of John Moore, Esq. of Shakston, and had, with younger children, ABRAHAM, his heir, and Thomas, in holy orders, who *m.* Jane, dau. of John Ludford, Esq.; and his son, SAMUEL, who assumed the name of LUDFORD, was great-grandfather of Elizabeth-Juliana Ludford, the wife of John, eldest son of Sir John Chetwode, Bart.; Frances-Millicent Ludford; and Mary-Anne Ludford, wife of the Rev. Francis Astley, of Everley, co. Wilts. These ladies were the daus. and co-heirs of John Ludford, of Ansley Hall, Esq., who *d.* in 1822. The eldest son, and successor in 1692, of Samuel Bracebridge,

ABRAHAM BRACEBRIDGE, of Atherstone, Esq., *m.* Maria, dau. of Thomas Charnell, of Snareston, co. Leicester, Esq., and was father of Samuel,† of Lindley, and

ABRAHAM BRACEBRIDGE, Esq. of Atherstone, who was *s.* by his son (by his 2nd wife, Maria, dau. and co-heir of the Rev. Walter Jennings, of Onparva, in Staffordshire),

ABRAHAM BRACEBRIDGE, Esq. of Atherstone, who *m.* Mary, dau. of John Stiles, Esq. of Uxbridge, and had issue,

ABRAHAM, his successor.
Walter (see BRACEBRIDGE of Morville)

* The eldest son, William Bracebridge, *m.* Anne, dau. of Julian Nethermill; and *d.* 2 ELIZABETH, leaving a son, Michael, who *d. s. p.*, and two daus., Margery, *m.* 1st, to Waklyve Willington, of Hurley, Esq.; and 2ndly, to Barnaby Easte, Esq.; and Jane, *m.* to Lionel Skipwith, Esq.

† This gentleman had, with other issue,

SAMUEL, M.P. for Tamworth: who *d.* in the isle of Scio, in 1786.
PHILIP, in holy orders; who *d.* in 1762, leaving two daus.
ANNE, *m.* to Robert Abney, Esq.
AMICIA, *m.* to George Henning, Esq.

He was s. at his decease, in 1789, by his eldest son,

ABRAHAM BRACEBRIDGE, Esq. of Atherstone, who m. in 1775, Mary-Elizabeth, only dau. and heiress of Sir Charles Holte, Bart. of Aston, co. Warwick, and had a son and a dau., viz.,

CHARLES-HOLTE, present proprietor.
Mary-Holte, who m. in 1803, her cousin, Walter-Henry Bracebridge, Esq. of Morville House.

Mr. Bracebridge d. in 1832.

Arms—Vairé, arg. and sa., a fesse, gu.
Crest—A staff raguly, arg. (*Note*: "The Bear and ragged Staff" belonged to Turchil de Warwick, as descendant of the chivalrous Guy, Earl of Warwick.)
Motto—Be as God will.
Seat—Atherstone Hall, co. Warwick.

BRACEBRIDGE OF MORVILLE.

BRACEBRIDGE, WALTER HENRY, Esq. of Morville Hall, co. Warwick, and Chetwode Priory, Bucks, b. in 1781; m. in 1803, Mary-Holte, dau. of Abraham Bracebridge, Esq. of Atherstone Hall.

Lineage.—WALTER BRACEBRIDGE, Esq., 2nd son of Abraham Bracebridge, Esq. of Atherstone, m. Harriet, dau. of Henry Streatfeild, Esq. of Chiddingstone, Kent, and by her (who d. 4 March, 1824), he left at his decease, 27 Oct. 1820, a son, WALTER-HENRY, now of Morville and Chetwode Priory; and one surviving dau., Harriet-Anne, of Sea Beach House, Eastbourne, Sussex, widow of Henry Ogle, Esq., son of the Rev. John Ogle, of Kirkley, Northumberland.

Arms, &c., same as BRACEBRIDGE *of Atherstone*.
Seats—Morville Hall, Warwickshire; and Chetwode Priory, Bucks.

BRACKENBURY OF SKENDLEBY HOUSE.

BRACKENBURY, SIR EDWARD, Knt. of Skendleby House, co. Lincoln, J.P. and D.L., lieut.-col. in the army, m. 1st, 9 June, 1827, Maria, dau. of the Rev. Edward Bromhead, of Repham, co. Lincoln, and had issue,

EDWARD-BROMHEAD, b. 18 Oct. 1828; d. in 1845.

He m. 2ndly, Eleanor, widow of the late William-B. Clark, Esq. of Belford Hall, Northumberland, and dau. of the late Addison Fenwick, Esq. of Bishop-wearmouth. In 1824, he was invested with the order of the Tower and Sword, and also with that of St. Bento d'Avis.

Lineage.—This family, which descends immediately from Sir Robert Brackenbury, the famous lieutenant of the Tower, *temp.* RICHARD III., was founded in England by Sir Perse de Brakenbury, one of the companions in arms of WILLIAM the Conqueror.

The grandfather of Sir Edward Brackenbury, CARR BRACKENBURY, Esq. of Panton Hall, co. Lincoln, eldest son of CARR BRACKENBURY, Esq. of Spilsby, was father of the REV. EDWARD BRACKENBURY, of Skendleby, who d. s. p., and of

RICHARD BRACKENBURY, Esq. of Aswardby, co. Lincoln, who m. Janetta Gun, of Edinburgh, and has issue,

JOHN-MACPHERSON (Sir), K.H., late H. B. M.'s consul at Cadiz; m. in 1801, Miss Nichelson, dau. of William Nichelson, Esq.
EDWARD (Sir), of Skendleby House.
William, of Whitby House, co. Lincoln, formerly of the 101st regiment; deceased.
Janetta, m. to Charles Brackenbury, Esq., elder brother of the Rev. Henry Brackenbury, of Scremby.

Arms—Arg., three chevrons, interlaced in base, sa.
Crest—A lion, couchant, sa., at the foot of an oak-tree, ppr.
Motto—Sans recueiller jamais.
Seat—Skendleby House, near Spilsby, co. Lincoln.

BRACKENBURY OF SCREMBY HALL.

BRACKENBURY, HENRY, Esq. of Scremby Hall, co. Lincoln, b. 11 Dec. 1790; m. 28 May, 1821, Anne, only dau. of John Atkinson, Esq. of Ansthorpe Hall, co. York.

Lineage.—CARR BRACKENBURY, Esq. of Spilsby, co. Lincoln, m. 1st, Miss Anne Gace, by whom he had six sons and one dau., viz., CARR, of Panton Hall (*see preceding family*), Joseph, THOMAS, Langley, Charles, John, and Anne; and 2ndly, Anne, dau. of Sir John Tyrwhitt, Bart., by whom he had one son, James. The third son,

THOMAS-CARR BRACKENBURY, Esq., m. 1st, Elizabeth Ostler, who d. in 1760; and 2ndly, in 1761, Margaret, eldest dau. of John Mottram, Esq. He was s. by his son,

CHARLES BRACKENBURY, Esq. of Scremby Hall, who m. in 1780, Caroline Hairby, and had issue, 1 Charles, m. Miss Janetta Brackenbury, and had one dau., Janetta; 2 George; 3 HENRY, of Scremby Hall; 4 Augustus; 5 Evelyn; 1 Anne; 2 Caroline; 3 Sophia; and 4 Louisa. He d. 16 March, 1816.

Arms—Arg., three chevrons, braced in base, sa.
Crest—A lion, couchant-guardant, sa., under an oak-tree, vert.
Motto—Sans recueller jamais.
Seat—Scremby Hall, Spilsby, co. Lincoln.

BRACKENRIDGE OF ASHFIELD PARK.

BRACKENRIDGE, GEORGE-CHARLES, Esq. of Ashfield Park, co. Tyrone, J.P., barrister-at-law, b. 18 June, 1814; assumed by royal license, 9 March, 1846, the surname of BRACKENRIDGE, in lieu of that of Trimble, and the arms of Brackenridge quarterly with those of Trimble.

Lineage.—JOSEPH TRIMBLE, Esq. of Ashfield Park, whose mother, Margaret, was dau. of George Brackenridge, of Ballymacan, co. Tyrone, d. 8 Sept. 1841, leaving, by Catherine his wife, a son, the present GEORGE-CHARLES BRACKENRIDGE, Esq. of Ashfield Park, and two daus., Jane, m. 1st, 7 May, 1830, to James King, Esq. of Doughmore, and 2ndly, 20 Oct. 1847, to Charles Stanley, Esq. of Armagh; and Margaret, m. 22 July, 1841, to James-C. Bell, Esq.

Arms—Quarterly: 1st and 4th, az., three roses, arg., seeded, or, barbed, vert; from the chief, a pile, of the third, charged with a rose, gu; 2nd and 3rd, per fesse, arg and or, a bull's head, caboshed, sa.
Crest—Between two eagle's wings, displayed, az., a pile, gu., charged with a white rose, as in the arms.
Motto—Labore et industria.
Seat—Ashfield Park, co. Tyrone.

BRADDON OF TREGLITH.

BRADDON, JOHN, Esq. of Treglith, co. Cornwall, J.P. and D.L., b. in May, 1777; m. July, 1805, Judith, dau. of Richard Kingdon, Esq. of Holsworthy, co. Devon, and has issue three sons.

Lineage.—The Braddons were originally of Northamptonshire: the first of the family recorded in the Heralds' College, as living in Cornwall, is

STEPHEN BRADDON, barrister of the Inner Temple, of Treworgey, in St. Genny's. He m. Alice, dau. of William Beleawe, and was elected member of parliament for the neighbouring town of Bossiney, in the first year of Queen ELIZABETH (1558), as he also was in the fifth of the same reign.

WILLIAM BRADDON, grandson of Stephen, rebuilt the old house of Treworgey, and was M.P. for Cornwall in 1651. He d. at Treworgey in 1694. By Ann his wife (who d. 21 Oct. 1672), he left issue two sons and one dau., HENRY; Lawrence, barrister of the Middle Temple; Ann, m. Harrington, of Devon, grandson of Sir John Harrington, Knt., godson of Queen ELIZABETH. The elder son,

HENRY BRADDON, Esq., d. 26 Sept. 1711, leaving a son,

THE REV. JOHN BRADDON, who, in 1713, was inducted to the livings of Luffincott and St. Giles-on-the-heath, Devon. He m. Mary, dau. of Nicholas Mill, Esq. of Grimscott, co. Cornwall, and left two sons and three daus. The elder son,

JOHN BRADDON, Esq., m. Mary, only child of Richard Martyn, Esq. of Milford, Devon; and d. at Milford in 1788, leaving three sons and a dau., viz., WILLIAM, of whom we treat; John, in holy orders, rector of Werrington, co. Cornwall, d. s. p. in 1842; HENRY, father of WILLIAM BRADDON, Esq. of Skisdon Lodge (*see that branch*); Mary, m. to the Rev. Thomas-Tregenna Hamley, and d. in 1815, s. p. The eldest son,

WILLIAM BRADDON, Esq. of Treglith, co. Cornwall, m. in 1774, Mary, dau. of — Spettigue, Esq. of Treglith; and d. in 1823, leaving three sons surviving, viz.,

JOHN, now of Treglith.
Thomas-Anstis.
Richard-Martyn.

Arms—Sa., a bend, fusilly, arg.
Motto—Aut mors aut libertas.
Seat—Treglith, near Launceston.

BRADDON OF SKISDON LODGE.

BRADDON, WILLIAM, Esq. of Blacklands, Devon, and Skisdon Lodge, Cornwall, J.P., late H.E.I.C.S., *m.* Hannah-Maria, dau. of John Daniells, Esq., and has issue,

I. WILLIAM-CLODE, *m.* Margaret-Selina, dau. of John-Wogan Patton, Esq., and has issue, two sons.
II. Henry-Edward, *m.* Alicia-Elizabeth, dau. of John Chapman, Esq. of Bloomfield, co. Tipperary, and has two sons. III. John-Clode.
I. Mary-Maynard, *m.* to the Rev. James-Henry Chowne, (son of James Tilson, Esq. of Goring, co. Oxford), who, in compliance with the will of his uncle, General Christopher Chowne, assumed the surname of CHOWNE; they have issue, three sons and two daus.
II. Sarah, *d. unm.* in 1824. III. Maria.
IV. Annie-Frances, *m.* Richard-Strode Hewlett, capt. R.N.
V. Louisa-Charlotte. *d.* 8 July, 1847.

Lineage.—HENRY BRADDON, Esq. of Skisdon Lodge, 3rd son of John Braddon, Esq. of Milford, *m.* Sarah, dau. of William Clode, Esq. of Camelford, and *d.* in 1817, leaving five sons and two daus.

Richard, major E.I.C.'s service; *d. unm.* in 1837.
WILLIAM, present representative of this branch.
John-Clode, of Camelford and Skisdon Lodge; *d.* in 1850.
Henry, *m.* Fanny, dau. of J. White, Esq. of co. Cavan.
Edward-Nicholas, in holy orders, vicar of St. Mary's and St. Clement's, Kent; *m.* Charlotte, dau. of W. Wright, Esq. of Kent.
Sarah-Phillis-Clode, *m.* 1st, Edward Kelly, Esq., capt. 51st light infantry, 2nd son of the late Arthur Kelly, Esq. of Kelly, co. Devon, and by him (who *d.* 24 May, 1831) has a son, Edward-Henry-Kelly, of Camplehay, Devon. She *m.* 2ndly, the Rev. William Cowlard, who *d.* 17 June, 1844.
Mary, *m.* to Charles Basden, Esq., capt. R.N.

Arms, &c.—As BRADDON *of Treglith*.
Seats—Blacklands, Devon; and Skisdon Lodge, Cornwall.

BRADLEY OF SLYNE HOUSE.

BRADLEY, ROBERT-GREENE, Esq. of Slyne House, co. Lancaster, J.P., barrister-at-law, and a bencher of Gray's Inn, *b.* 14 April, 1788; *m.* 12 June, 1820, Lydia, only surviving child of the late Francis Boynton, Esq., by Charlotte his wife, eldest dau. and co-heiress of the late Sir Warton-Pennyman Warton, of Beverley Park, co. York, Bart. She *d.* at Slyne House, 12 April, 1836, *s. p.* Mr. Bradley and his sister Elizabeth are the children of Robert Bradley, Esq., by Margaret his wife, dau. of Thomas Greene, Esq. of Slyne.

Arms—Sa., a fesse, engrailed; and in chief, a mullet, between two crosses, formée-fitchée, arg.
Seat—Slyne House, co. Lancaster.

BRADSHAW OF BARTON.

BRADSHAW, FRANCIS, Esq. of Barton Blount, co. Derby, *b.* 8 July, 1800; *m.* 18 Dec. 1823, Mary-Anne, dau. of Robert Holden, Esq. of Nuttall Temple, Notts, and has issue,

I. FRANCIS, *b.* 1826. II. Henry-Holden, *b.* 1828.
III. Robert-Wilmot, *b.* 1836. IV. William, *b.* 1840.
I. Mary-Anne. II. Frances-Maria.
III. Caroline. IV. Helen. V. Alice.

Lineage.—The BRADSHAWS *of Barton Blount* are descended from the BRADSHAWS *of Bradshaw*, co. Lancaster, where the family have flourished from the time of the Saxons, the present owner thereof being Thomas Bradshaw-Isherwood, Esq. of Marple Hall, Cheshire.

GEORGE BRADSHAW, Esq., 2nd son of John Bradshaw, of Bradshaw, went, *circa* 1400, into Staffordshire, having *m.* the dau. and heiress of Sir William Skeffington. His son,

JOHN BRADSHAW, Esq., *m.* Cicely, dau. and heir of Thomas Foljambe, of Wyndley, co. Derby, and *d.* in 1523. His grandson,

HENRY BRADSHAW, Esq., *m.* Elizabeth, dau. of Robert Eyre, of Hassop, and had two sons, HENRY, of whose descendants we treat; and William, of Bradshaw Hall, co. Derby, ancestor of the Rev. C.-Bradshaw Bowles, and also of the Bradshaw-Isherwood, of Marple. The eldest son,

HENRY BRADSHAW, *m.* Eleanor, dau. of Richard Curzon, of Kedleston, and was father of

RICHARD BRADSHAW, of Alderwasley. His great-great-grandson,

HENRY BRADSHAW, Esq. of Holbrook, *d.* 1649, leaving, by Ellen Hill his wife, two sons, SAMUEL, his heir; and ANTHONY, of Belper, whose eldest dau., by Anne Lowe his wife, Anne, *m.* Joseph Baggiley, Esq. The son and heir,

SAMUEL BRADSHAW, Esq. of Holbrook, *m.* 1676, Mary, dau. of Robert Fearne, Esq.; and *d.* 1716, leaving a son,

THE REV. SAMUEL BRADSHAW, of Upminster, in Essex, *b.* in 1683; *m.* Mary, dau. of the Rev. Mr. Ellis, of Gunningstone, Notts, and dying *s. p.*, bequeathed his estate to his cousin,

JOSEPH BAGGALEY, Esq. of Holbrook, (son of Joseph Baggaley, Esq. of Holbrook, by Anne his wife, dau. of Anthony Bradshaw, of Belper) who assumed in 1767, the surname and arms of BRADSHAW, and served as sheriff for Derbyshire in 1777. He *m.* Frances, dau. of the Rev. Francis Bower, rector of Barlborough, and had issue, FRANCIS, heir; Joseph, *m.* Frances, dau. of Samuel Clowes, Esq. of Broughton, near Manchester; Anne, *m.* to Thomas-Porter Bonell, Esq. of Duffield, and *d.* 20 Oct. 1821; Elizabeth, *m.* 15 Jan. 1793, to John-Edwin Biscoe, Esq.; Mary; Harriet; and Frances. The eldest son,

FRANCIS BRADSHAW, Esq. of Barton Blount, high-sheriff, co. Derby, 1806, *m.* 1798, Eliza, dau. of Sir Robert Wilmot, Bart. of Chaddesden; and dying Aug. 1841, left issue, FRANCIS, now of Barton Blount; Charlotte-Anne, *m.* 19 Nov. 1821, to Robert-S.-Wilmot Sitwell, Esq. of Stainsby; Frances-Maria, *m.* 3 March, 1828, to the Rev. Charles-Evelyn Cotton, of Etwall Hall; and Elizabeth, *m.* 5 July, 1836, to the Rev. Pepioe-P. Mosley, of Rolleston.

Arms—Arg., two bendlets, between as many martlets, sa.
Crest—A hart, gu., standing under a vine-branch, vert.
Motto—Qui vit content tient assez.
Seat—Barton Hall, co. Derby.

BRADY OF MYSHALL LODGE.

BRADY, JOHN BEAUCHAMP, Esq. of Myshall Lodge, co. Carlow, J.P., *b.* 2 July, 1800; *m.* 25 Dec. 1825, Jane-Harriet, 3rd dau. of Sir Rupert George, Bart., and has issue,

I. J.-CORNWALL, late of the 23rd fusiliers, *b.* 26 March, 1827, *m.* 6 Oct. 1853, Elizabeth-Susan, dau. of the late Thomas H. Watson, Esq. of Serenclove, co. Carlow.
II. Henry-Beauchamp (69th regt.), *b.* 25 July, 1828.
III. Rupert-George (1st Royals), *b.* 25 July, 1831.
I. Frances-Margaret-Fetherstone, *m.* to John-Frederick Leeky, Esq., only son of John-James Leeky, Esq., J.P. and D.L., of Ballykealy, co. Carlow.

Mr. Brady has served as high-sheriff of co. Carlow. His father, HENRY BRADY, Esq. of Myshall Lodge, son of Hugh Brady, Esq., by Eliza Beauchamp his wife, *m.* in 1792, Sarah Pearson, and by her had a son, the present JOHN-BEAUCHAMP BRADY, of Myshall Lodge; and two daus., Jane, *m.* in 1810, to Major Cornwall; and Eliza, *m.* in 1817, to Sir Francis Ford, Bart.

Seat—Myshall Lodge, co. Carlow.

BRAILSFORD OF TOFT HILL.

BRAILSFORD, THOMAS, Esq. of Toft Hill and Toft Grange, co. Lincoln, D.L., *b.* 10 Oct. 1787; *m.* 1st, 14 Jan. 1815, Anne, dau. of James Shapley, Esq., by Elizabeth his wife, one of the co-heiresses of the late William Heathcote, Esq. of the colony of Demerara, and of Stancliffe Hall, co. Derby, and has issue,

I. Thomas, *b.* 2 Nov. 1815; *d.* 20 April, 1854.
II. SAMUEL, *b.* 1 May, 1819.
III. John-Arthur-Heathcote, *b.* in 1822; *d.* in 1844.
IV. William, *b.* 2 June, 1825.
I. Eliza.
II. Ellen, *m.* in 1841, to the Rev. Charles Holland, vicar of Burgh.
III. Alsina, *m.* 1843, to the Rev. Halford-Robert Burdett.
IV. Emma-Dorothea.

Mr. Brailsford *m.* 2ndly, 31 March, 1840, Mary-Anne, dau. of the Rev. John Hale, rector of Holton, and has by her a dau., Mary-Margaret.

Lineage.—THOMAS BRAILSFORD, of South Normanton, descended from the BRAILSFORDS *of Senior*, *m.* some time before the year 1689, Elizabeth Smyth, of Bolsover, an heiress, and had a son and successor,

THOMAS BRAILSFORD, of Bolsover and South Normanton,

father, by Frances Meacham, of Mansfield, his wife, whom he m. 30 Sept. 1718, of Samuel Brailsford, of Rowthorne, who d. in 1808, and of

THOMAS BRAILSFORD, of Bolsover and South Normanton, in the co. of Derby, who m. in 1740, Ellen Newbould, of Mansfield Woodhouse, Notts, and had two sons, THOMAS, his heir; and Samuel, who m. in 1786, Mary, dau. of Nicholas Christian, Esq. of Castleton, Isle of Man, and d. in 1793, leaving two sons, Thomas, and Samuel, who d. in 1809. Mr. Brailsford was s. by his elder son,

THOMAS BRAILSFORD, Esq. of South Normanton, b. in 1742, at whose decease, without issue, in 1820, the estates and representation of the family devolved on his nephew, the present THOMAS BRAILSFORD, Esq. of Barkwith House.

Arms—Or, a cinquefoil, sa., on a chief, indented, erm., two pommes, each charged with a cross, arg.

Crest—A unicorn's head, arg., erased, gu., armed and maned, or, entwined by a serpent, ppr., and charged on the neck with a pomme, and thereon a cross, as in the arms.

Motto—In Jehovah fides mea.

Seat—Toft Grange, Horncastle, Lincolnshire.

BRAMSTON OF SKREENS.

BRAMSTON, THOMAS-WILLIAM, Esq. of Skreens, co. Essex, M.P. for Essex, J.P. and D.L., b. 30 Oct. 1796; m. 12 Aug. 1830, Eliza, 5th dau. and co-heir of the late Admiral Sir Eliab Harvey, G.C.B., M.P., of Rolls Park, in the same county, and has issue,

I. THOMAS-HARVEY, b. 11 May, 1831.
II. John, b. 14 Nov. 1832.
III. William-Mondeford, b. 3 Feb. 1835.
IV. Henry, b. 4 July, 1836.
I. Georgina. II. Eliza-Harriet.
III. Emma-Alice.

Lineage.—SIR JOHN BRAMSTON, Knt., b. at Maldon, son of Roger Bramston, of that place, lineally descended from William Bramston, sheriff of London, 18th RICHARD II., was constituted lord chief justice of England in 1635. Sir John Bramston m. 1st, Bridget, dau. of Thomas Mondeford, an eminent physician (son of Sir Edmund Mondeford, Knt. of Feltwell, in Norfolk) by Mary his wife, dau. of Sir Richard Hill and Elizabeth his wife, the 20th dau. of Sir William Lock, lord-mayor of London. By her he had issue, 1 JOHN (Sir), his heir; 2 Mondeford (Sir), Master in Chancery, who m. Alice, dau. of Sir George le Hunt, and had issue: 3 Francis, one of the barons of the Exchequer, 1678; 1 Dorothy, m. to Sir William Palmer; 2 Mary, m. to John Parke, Esq.; and 3 Catherine, m. to Sir Thomas Dyke. The chief justice m. 2ndly, Elizabeth, widow of Sir John Bereton, Knt., serjeant-at-law, and dau. of Edward, Lord Brabazon, of Ardee, but by her (who d. 7 June, 1647) had no issue. He was s. at his decease by his eldest son,

SIR JOHN BRAMSTON, of Skreens, in Essex, Knight of the Bath at the coronation of King CHARLES II., having had a seat in the parliament (1660) which restored the monarchy, as member for the co. of Essex, for which shire he was again returned knight in 1661. Sir John m. Alice, eldest dau. of Anthony Adby, Esq., an alderman of London, and by her left at his decease, 4 Feb. 1699, (with two daus., Mary, wife of Sir Andrew Jenour, Bart. of Bigoods; and Elizabeth, wife of Mondeford Bramston, Esq.) an only surviving son,

ANTHONY BRAMSTON, Esq. of Skreens, who m. Catherine, dau. and co-heir of Sir Thomas Nutt, Knt. of Mayes, in Essex, and d. in 1722, having had, with other issue, JOHN, who d. v. p. in 1718, leaving three daus., of whom, Mary, m. 1730, Edward Byng, son of Lord Torrington, and

THOMAS BRAMSTON, Esq. of Skreens, who m. 1st, Diana, dau. of Edward Turnor, Esq. of Stoke, in the co. of Lincoln, and widow of Robert Ferne, Esq. of Locke, in Derbyshire, but had by her no issue. He m. 2ndly, Elizabeth, only dau. of Richard Berney, Esq. recorder of Norwich, and had (with a dau. Mary, the wife of William Deedes, Esq.) a son and heir,

THOMAS-BERNEY BRAMSTON, Esq. of Skreens, M.P. for the co. of Essex from 1779 to 1802, who m. Mary, dau. and heiress of — Gardiner, Esq. of Norfolk, and dying in 1812, aged 80, left (with a dau. Mary-Anne, wife of J.-A. Houblon, Esq. of Hallingbury Place, Essex) two sons, THOMAS-GARDINER, his heir; and JOHN, of Forest Hall, Essex, in holy orders, who has assumed the surname of STANE. The elder son,

THOMAS-GARDINER BRAMSTON, Esq. of Skreens, M.P. for the co. of Essex, m. Maria-Anne, dau. of William Blaauw, Esq. of Queen Anne Street, London, and had two sons and three daus., viz., 1 THOMAS-WILLIAM, now of Skreens; 2 John, in holy orders, vicar of Great Baddow, b. in 1804, who m. 1st, in 1832, Clarissa-Sandford, only dau. of Sir Nicholas Trant, and 2ndly, Anna Hanbury, and has issue; 3 Mary-Anne; 4 Charlotte, m. to the Rev. J. Davidson, and d. in 1841; and 5 Elizabeth, m. to W. Hooper, Esq., R.N., and d. in 1839. Mr. Bramston d. 3 Feb. 1831.

Arms—Or, on a fesse, sa., three plates, arg.

Crest—A lion, sejant, collared, sa., charged with three plates, arg.

Seat—Skreens, in Essex.

BRANFILL OF UPMINSTER HALL.

BRANFILL, BENJAMIN-AYLETT, Esq. of Upminster Hall, co. Essex, an officer in the 10th royal hussars, b. 26 Feb. 1828.

Lineage.—"The original name of this family," says Morant, "is supposed to have been Bamfield,"—a supposition borne out by the exact similarity of arms. The purchaser of Upminster Hall, in Essex, was

CAPT. ANDREW BRANFILL, Esq. of Dartmouth, in Devon, who bought the manor from the Earl of Gainsborough, in 1685. He m. in 1681, Damaris, eldest dau. of John Aylet, of Kelvedon Hatch, (son of the gallant Capt. Aylet, of Magdalen Laver, so distinguished in the cause of King CHARLES during the great civil war,) and by her had several children. He d. 27 July, 1709, aged 59. His eldest son and heir,

CHAMPION BRANFILL, Esq. of Upminster Hall, Essex, high-sheriff in 1734, m. Mary, dau. of Mr. Benjamin Braund, of the city of London, and had issue. The elder son,

CHAMPION BRANFILL, Esq. of Upminster Hall, m. Elizabeth James, and by her had two sons and a dau., viz., CHAMPION; Benjamin; and Frances, d. young. The elder son and heir,

CHAMPION BRANFILL, Esq. of Upminster Hall, m. 14 Oct. 1783, Charlotte, dau. of Edward Brydges, Esq. and Jemima his wife, youngest dau. and co-heir of William Egerton, LL.D., and by her (who m. 2ndly, 20 Jan. 1794, John Harrison, Esq.) had issue a son, CHAMPION-EDWARD, and a dau. Jemima-Elizabeth, m. to the Rev. Thomas Harrison. Mr. Branfill d. 7 Oct. 1792, and was s. by his son,

CHAMPION-EDWARD BRANFILL, Esq. of Upminster Hall, b. 13 July, 1789, who m. 26 Nov. 1818, Anne-Eliza, dau. of the Rev. Anthony-Egerton Hammond, lineally descended, maternally, from the Earls of Bridgewater. By this lady Mr. Branfill had issue,

CHAMPION, b. 19 Oct. 1820; succeeded to the estate of the late Joseph Russell, Esq., and assumed, in consequence, the surname and arms of RUSSELL.
Egerton-Anthony-Hammond, b. 28 March, 1825; d. 5 Oct. 1843.
BENJAMIN-AYLETT, of Upminster Hall.
Champion-Edward-Brydges, b. in 1829; d. in 1831.
Brydges-Robinson, b. 22 Nov. 1833.
John-Arthur-Capel, b. 22 March, 1838.
Eliza-Jemima-Mary, m. 28 May, 1851, to the Rev. Edward-Francis Gepp.
Charlotte-Jane. Agnes-Josepha.

Mr. Branfill d. 7 Oct. 1844.

Arms—Or, on a bend, gu., three mullets, arg., quartering AYLETT, viz., Gu., three annulets, arg., surmounted by a chief, arg.; on a canton, or, a rose of England, ppr.

Crest—A naked arm, holding a sword, rising out of a cloud, ppr.

Motto—Not in vain.

Seat—Upminster Hall, Upminster, Essex.

BRAY OF SHERE.

BRAY, EDWARD, Esq. of Shere, co. Surrey, b. 20 July, 1798.

Lineage.—The name of the SIEUR DE BRAY occurs in the roll of Battel Abbey, amongst the associates in arms of the CONQUEROR.

SIR RICHARD BRAY, the descendant and representative of the Norman knight, is said by some to have been of the privy council to HENRY VI.; by others he is called the King's physician; the former is the more probable, as he was buried in Worcester cathedral. He had two wives: by the 1st, Margaret, dau. of John Sandes, Esq. of Furness Fell, in Lancashire, he had an only son, JOHN (Sir), whose only dau. and heir, Margaret, m. Sir William Sandys, Baron Sandys of the Vine; by the 2nd, Joan, Sir Richard had two other sons, viz., SIR REGINALD BRAY, knight-banneret and K.G., lord-treasurer *temp.* HENRY VII., and

JOHN BRAY, Esq., who was buried in the chancel of the church at Chelsea, had (with a dau., the wife of Sir John

Norris), three sons, EDMUND (Sir), summoned to parliament as Baron Bray, 21st HENRY VIII., ancestor of the present BARONESS BRAYE; EDWARD (Sir), of whom presently; and Reginald, of Barrington, co. Gloucester, ancestor of the BRAYS *of Barrington*. The 2nd son,

SIR EDWARD BRAY, Knt. of Vachery Park, in Cranley, Surrey, was sheriff of Surrey and Sussex in the 30th of HENRY VIII., and represented the former county in the two parliaments of Queen MARY. He *d.* in 1558, and was *s.* by his son,

SIR EDWARD BRAY, Knt., M.P. for Helstone, in the 13th ELIZABETH, who *m.* 1st, Mary, dau. of Simon Elrington, Esq. of Northampton, and had by her an only son, Reginald, described as heir-apparent, and of the Inner Temple in 1557, being then of age, who appears to have *d.* issueless. Sir Edward *m.* 2ndly, Elizabeth, dau. of William Roper, Esq. of Eltham, in Kent, by Margaret his wife, dau. of the Chancellor Sir Thomas More, and had another son, also named REGINALD. He *m.* 3rdly, Magdalene, dau. of Sir Thomas Cotton, of Kent, by whom, who *d.* in 1563, he had no issue; and 4thly, a lady, named Mary, by whom (who wedded 2ndly, Sir Edmund Tylney, master of the revels to Queen ELIZABETH) he had three daus., Mary, *m.* to Sir George Chowne, Knt. of Wrotham, Kent; Magdalen, *m.* to George Bowes, Esq. of Durham; Frances, *m.* to George Gastrell, Esq. Sir Edward *d.* in 1581, and was *s.* by his son,

REGINALD BRAY, Esq. of Shere, bapt. 1 May, 1555, who *m.* Elizabeth, dau. of Richard Covert, Esq. of Hascombe, in Surrey, and left a son and successor,

EDWARD BRAY, Esq. of Shere, *b.* in 1577. He *m.* 1st, Jane, dau. of Edward Covert, Esq. of Tuynham, in Sussex, and was grandfather of

EDWARD BRAY, Esq. of Shere (son of Edward), bapt. 18 Oct. 1640, who *m.* Frances, dau. of Vincent Randyll, Esq. of Chilworth, and dying in 1714, was *s.* by his son,

EDWARD BRAY, Esq. of Shere, bapt. 4 Jan. 1687, who *m.* in 1727, Ann, dau. of the Rev. George Duncumb, rector of Shere, and dying in 1740, was *s.* by his eldest son,

THE REV. GEORGE BRAY, of Shere, who *d. unm.* 1 March, 1803, and was *s.* by his brother,

WILLIAM BRAY, Esq. of Shere, the learned antiquarian and historian of Surrey, bapt. 7 Nov. 1736. He *m.* Mary, dau. of Henry Stevens, Gent., and had (with three daus., Mary, Catherine, and Amelia-Caroline, who *d. unm.* in 1789) a son,

EDWARD, *b.* 31 Jan. 1768; who *m.* Mary-Anne-Catherine, dau. of Daniel Malthus, Esq. of Albury, in Surrey, and sister of the celebrated writer on population, and predeceasing his father in 1814, left issue,

1 EDWARD, now of Shere.
2 Reginald, *b.* in 1797; *m.* Frances, dau. of T.-N. Longman, Esq., and has a son, Reginald-More, and two daus., Mary and Henrietta-Louisa.
3 William, in holy orders.
1 Henrietta-Mary, *m.* to Augustus Warren, Esq.
2 Louisa. 3 Catherine.

Mr. Bray, who was treasurer to the Society of Antiquaries, and editor of *The Evelyn Memoirs*, *d.* in 1832.

Arms—Quarterly: 1st and 4th, arg., a chevron, between three eagles' legs, sa., erased à la cuisse, their talons, gu.; 2nd and 3rd, vairy, arg and az., three bends, gu.
Crest—A flax-breaker, or.
Seat—Shere, near Guildford.

BRAY OF LANGFORD HILL.

BRAY, CECIL-NICHOLAS, Esq. of Langford Hill, co. Cornwall, J.P., *b.* 14 July, 1804; *m.* 20 Dec. 1831, Miss Mary-Dennis Abraham, of Tavistock, co. Devon, and has issue,

I. CECIL, *b.* 14 Jan. 1835.
I. Margaret-Mary. II. Lucy. III. Mary.

Mr. Bray is son of the late Richard-Burdon Bray, Esq., and grandson of Nicholas Bray, by Elizabeth Burdon his wife.

Arms—Arg., three oak trees, ppr., acorned, or.
Crest—On a ducal coronet, az., a griffin's head, erm., beaked, or.
Seat—Langford Hill, Marhamchurch, co. Cornwall.

BRERETON OF BRINTON.

BRERETON, JOHN, Esq. of Brinton, co. Norfolk, *b.* 11 Sept. 1813; *m.* 29 June, 1841, Elizabeth-Ann, only dau. of Robert-John Brereton, Esq. of Blakeney, by Sarah his wife, younger dau. and co-heiress of Pearson Walton, Esq. of Walton House, co. York, and has issue,

I. JOHN-LLOYD, *b.* 22 April, 1842.
II. William-Robert-John, *b.* 16 Feb. 1845.
III. Robert-Pearson, *b.* 18 March, 1848.
IV. Cuthbert-Arthur, *b.* 17 Sept. 1850.
I. Elizabeth-Anna.

Lineage.—Ormerod, in his able *History of Cheshire*, mentions Grosvenor, Davenport, and Brereton as "three grantees who can be proved by ancient deeds to have existed at or near the Conquest, though unnoticed in Domesday." Of these, the family least favoured by fortune in later times (the peerage and the baronetcy in the Brereton family having both become extinct, and the heirship in lands and manors, in all the principal English lines, having descended to females) was, during the earlier centuries after the Conquest, among the most distinguished in the Palatinate; and by its fortunate and splendid marriages became entitled to prefer for its issue the highest claims, even to ducal and regal descent.

The Breretons appear to have arrived in England from Normandy with WILLIAM THE CONQUEROR, under Gilbert or Gislebert de Venables, surnamed *Venator* (the hunter), afterwards Baron of Kinderton, in the retinue of Hugh Lupus, or Hugh d'Avranches, nephew of the CONQUEROR, and afterwards Earl of Chester.

After the Conquest, the manor of Brereton (called Bretone in Domesday) was one of the six dependencies of the Barony of Kinderton. Very shortly after this period, says Ormerod, "the manor of Brereton was granted to a family which assumed the local name, and was probably descended from the same stock as the Norman grantee of the Barony of Kinderton, if an opinion may be formed from the arms which the Breretons subsequently used, arg., two bars, sa., differing only in tincture from the coat which the Barons of Kinderton had adopted." And what seems a decisive test of consanguinity is, that upon any intermarriage of the Venables with the Breretons, a dispensation was required.

On these grounds it is inferred, that the first grantee of the manor of Brereton, who assumed the local name, was a Venables, or a youthful kinsman engaged in the Norman adventure. What we find as a fact is, that, in reign of WILLIAM RUFUS, Ralf de Brereton witnessed a deed of Gilbert de Venables, and was probably his esquire.

The lineage of the direct line of the BRERETONS *of Brereton Hall*, and the Irish branch descended therefrom, is to be found in Ormerod's *History of Chester*, Lysons' *Magna Britannia*, Collins' *Peerage*, and Sir F. Dwarris' *Memoirs of the Brereton Family*.

From the branch seated at Shocklack and Malpas Hall, Cheshire, which separated from the elder branch of the family in the person of Sir Randle Brereton, of Ipstanes, descend the BRERETONS *of Norfolk*.

JOHN BRERETON, Esq., *m.* Cicely, eldest dau. and co-heir of Robert and Mary Cook, of Brinton, and was father of three sons. The eldest,

JOHN BRERETON, of Brinton, *m.* Anne Banbridge, but *d. s. p.*, and was *s.* by his brother,

WILLIAM BRERETON, Esq. of Brinton, who *m.* Anne, dau. of Thomas Shorting, collector of customs at the port of Cley, and niece of Admiral Sir Cloudesley Shovell, Knt., and was *s.* by his eldest son,

SHOVELL BRERETON, Esq., who left only two daus. His brother,

JOHN BRERETON, Esq. of Brinton, *m.* Bridget, younger dau. of John Brett, Esq. of Toft Trees, co. Norfolk, descended from the family of Sir Percy Brett, and had issue,

JOHN, his heir. Abel.
William, *m.* Anne, dau. of William Roberts, Esq.
Robert, of Blakeney, who *m.* Ann, dau. of — Hudson, Esq. of Tottenham, co. Middlesex, and had issue, ROBERT-JOHN, his heir, of Blakeney, who *m.* Sarah, younger dau. and co-heiress of Pearson Walton, Esq. of Walton House, co. York, and has issue a son, Robert-Pearson, *m.* in May, 1842, Anna-Margaretta, eldest sister of the present John Brereton, Esq., of Brinton, and a dau., Elizabeth-Anne, wife of the said John Brereton.
And several daus.

The eldest son,

JOHN BRERETON, Esq. of Brinton, *m.* his cousin, Anna-Margaretta, eldest dau. of David Lloyd, Esq. of Lanvaughan, co. Cardigan, by Mary his wife, younger dau. of William Brereton, Esq. of Brinton, and had,

WILLIAM-JOHN, his heir, of whom presently.
Charles-David, rural dean, rector of Little Massingham,

co. Norfolk; *b.* 4 July, 1790; *m.* 29 June, 1819, Frances, dau. of Joseph Wilson, Esq. of Highbury Hill, co. Middlesex, and Stowlangtoft Hall, co. Suffolk, and has, Charles-David, *b.* 19 April, 1820, *m.* Jan. 1844, Eliza, dau. of William Kent, Esq.; Henry, *b.* 23 May, 1821, *m.* 4 Sept. 1848, Emily, dau. of Henry Boulderson, Esq.; Joseph-Lloyd, *m.* 24 June, 1852, Frances, dau. of the Rev. William Martin; John-Alfred; William-Wilson; Robert-Maitland; Anna-Margaretta, *m.* 14 May, 1844, H.-G.-W. Sperling, Esq., and *d. s. p.*; Frances-Mary, *d.* 1848; Mary-Anne; Emma-Matilda; Henrietta-Lucy.

Randle, of Blakeney, merchant; *m.* Sarah, 2nd dau. of William Barwick, Esq. of Holt Lodge, Norfolk, and had issue a son, Randle-Barwick, and four daus.

Shovell, of Briningham, impropriator and rector of Great Poringland, Norfolk; *m.* Maria, dau. of Edward Colwell, Esq. of London, and has issue, two sons and a dau., viz., Shovell-Henry, Charles-John, and Anna-Margaretta-Jane.

Mary.

The eldest son,

WILLIAM JOHN BRERETON, Esq. of Brinton, a magistrate and deputy-lieut. for Norfolk, *m.* Elizabeth, dau. of John Hale, Esq. of Worcester, and had issue,

JOHN, now of Brinton.

Anna-Margaretta, *m.* in May, 1842, to Robert-Pearson Brereton, Esq.

Elizabeth, *m.* in May, 1842, to Richard Ward, Esq.

Mary-Brecknell. Emma-Frances.

Arms—Arg., two bars, sa.

Crest—A bear, ppr., muzzled, or.

Motto—Opitulante Deo.

Seat—Brinton, co. Norfolk.

BREWSTER OF WRENTHAM.

Lineage.—The Brewsters are one of the oldest of our East Anglian families: in the confirmation by Harvey, Clarenceux, A.D. 1561, of the original grant of arms (now in the possession of Cardinal Brewster, Esq. of Halstead, Essex), the house of Brewster is described as "most ancient;" the date of original grant is not known. In a list of the gentry of Norfolk, returned to King HENRY VII., A.D. 1483, we find the name of Galfridus Brewster, and in 1550, Sir John Brewster died at Kirton, in Lincolnshire. The family became connected with the county of Suffolk at a still earlier period, for in 1375, John Brewster was witness to a deed relating to land in the parish of Henstead. In the early part of the reign of EDWARD IV., the manor of Wrentham was purchased by this family; and in 1550, Humphrey Brewster, Esq., built Wrentham Hall, which was occupied by his descendants until 1797, when on the death of another Humphrey Brewster, the estate was sold and the mansion taken down.

In the county of Suffolk, this family possessed considerable influence; and in the great rebellion, became active partisans of the parliament. Colonel Humphrey Brewster raised and commanded a troop of horse against the king; and Robert Brewster, Esq. of Wrentham Hall, sat for Dunwich in the Long Parliament.

WILLIAM BREWSTER, Esq. of Rushmere, co. Suffolk, living *temp.* HENRY VI., *m.* Mary, dau. of William Hervey, Esq. of Olton, co. Suffolk, and was father of Robert Brewster, Esq. of Rushmere, who *m.* the dau. and co-heiress of Sir Christopher Edmonds, of Cressing Temple, co. Essex, and Lewknor, co. Oxon; and had two sons, Humphrey and James. The former, Humphrey Brewster, Esq. of Wrentham Hall, co. Suffolk, who built that edifice, *b.* in 1526, *m.* Alice, dau. of William Foster, Esq. of Copdock, co. Suffolk, and *d.* in 1593, having had by her (who *d.* in 1611), two sons and four daus., viz., FRANCIS, his heir; Humphrey, of Hadleigh, co. Suffolk, *m.* Grizel, dau. of Robert Rolf, Esq. of Hadleigh, and *d.* in 1613, aged 44; Elizabeth, *m.* 1st, to Thomas Brewse, Esq., son of Sir J. Brewse, of Wenham Hall, co. Suffolk, and 2ndly, to Francis Claxton, Esq. of Cheston, co. Suffolk; Susan, *m.* to John Hayward, Esq. of Gisleham, co. Suffolk; Mary; and Jane. The elder son and heir,

FRANCIS BREWSTER, Esq. of Wrentham Hall, *b.* in 1566, J.P. and D.L. for the co. of Suffolk, *m.* Elizabeth, dau. of Robert Snelling, Esq. of Ipswich, and *d.* in 1644, having had by this lady, who *d.* in 1638,

ROBERT, his heir.

Francis, of Wrentham, *b.* in 1600; *m.* Susanna Bunnen; and *d.* in 1657, having had issue, Francis, *b.* in 1627, *d.* in 1694; John, of Yarmouth, *b.* in 1632; Robert, *b.* in 1638; Nathaniel, *b.* in 1648; Benjamin, *b.* in 1644; Elizabeth; Mary; and Anne.

Humphrey, of Hedenham, co. Norfolk, and afterwards of Beccles, co. Suffolk, *b.* in 1602; lieut.-col. of infantry; *d.* in 1669; *m.* Ann, dau. of — Atkins, Esq. of Norwich, and had issue, Philip, of Wrentham Hall, who *d.* 1710; Samuel, of Norwich; and John, of Beccles, who *m.* Rebecca Cleeves, and *d.* in 1718.

John, of Wyfields, Barking, co. Essex, *b.* in 1604; *m.* Mary, dau. of Augustine Scottowe, Esq. of Norwich; and *d.* in 1677, having had issue, Augustine, of Wyfields, *b.* in 1642, and *d.* in 1708, æt. 66; Samuel, of St. Margaret's, Westminster, who *d.* in 1701, leaving, by Dorothy his wife, a son, John, of the Cursitor's Office, and two daus., Dorothy and Mary.

Elizabeth, *m.* to the Rev. Richard Taylor.

Mary, *m.* to — Mildmay, Esq.

The eldest son and heir,

ROBERT BREWSTER, Esq. of Wrentham Hall, *b.* in 1599, M.P. for Dunwich in 1640-45-49-54-58-59, and 1660, and for the co. of Suffolk in 1656; *m.* Amy, dau. of Sir Thomas Corbet, of Sprowston, co. Norfolk, and had two sons, FRANCIS, and Robert. He *d.* in 1663, and was *s.* by his eldest son,

FRANCIS BREWSTER, Esq. of Wrentham Hall, *b.* in 1623, M.P. for the co. of Suffolk, who *m.* Cicely, dau. and co-heiress of Sir Charles Crofts, of Bardwell, co. Suffolk, and had two daus.,

AMY, *m.* Sir Philip Skippon, M.P. for Dunwich, son of Major-Gen. Skippon, the republican general; and Cicely, *m.* 1st, to Sir Robert Hatton, of Ditton, Surrey; and, 2ndly, to Sir Harry Dutton Colt, Bart., M.P. for Westminster, *temp.* WILLIAM and ANNE. Mr. Francis Brewster *d.* in 1761, and was *s.* by his brother Robert, on whose decease in 1681, *s. p.*, PHILIP BREWSTER, Esq., eldest son of Col. Humphrey Brewster, of Beccles, became the proprietor of Wrentham Hall: he *d.* in 1710, leaving a son and heir,

HUMPHREY BREWSTER, Esq. of Wrentham Hall, who *m.* Elizabeth Molton, and *d.* in 1735, aged 53, having had by her, who *d.* in 1747, PHILIP; William, *b.* 1718, *d.* 1788, *s. p.*; Humphrey, *b.* 1721, *d.* 1751, *unm.*; Anne, *m.* John Wilkinson, Esq. of Halesworth, co. Suffolk; Francis, *m.* John Meadows, Esq. of Wortham, co. Suffolk; Mary; and Elizabeth. The eldest son,

PHILIP BREWSTER, Esq. of Wrentham Hall, *b.* in 1712, *m.* Isabella Crompton, of Doncaster, co. York, and *d.* in 1765, having had by her, who *d.* in 1778,

HUMPHREY BREWSTER, Esq. of Wrentham Hall, *b.* in 1752, *d.* 1797, *unm.* This family had many ramifications; one branch settled at Barking, in Essex, and possessed the manor of Withfield, in Great Ilford, and the manor of Condovers, in West Tilbury; another branch was established at Castle Hedingham, in Essex. There was also a branch of the family which, in the reign of ELIZABETH, owned land in Luddenham, Linstead, Lenham, Ospringe, and other parishes, in the county of Kent; another branch settled in Northamptonshire, in the reign of CHARLES I., where they possessed the manor of Welford, and other lands; and another branch, seated in Lincolnshire, gave birth to William Brewster, the ruling elder and chief pastor of the Pilgrim Fathers, who in 1620 went to America to avoid the religious persecutions to which they were exposed in this country, and became the founders of New England. In 1655, Nathaniel Brewster, of Aldby, in Norfolk, was appointed chaplain to Henry Cromwell, lord-lieutenant of Ireland, and was actively engaged in the service of the parliament; and in the same year, Hugh Brewster and Francis Brewster were acting as commissioners for securing the peace of the commonwealth at Bury St. Edmunds; their correspondence with CROMWELL and his secretary Thurloe may be seen in Thurloe's *State Papers*. In 1699, Sir Francis Brewster was appointed, in company with the Earl of Drogheda and others, a commissioner to take account of forfeited estates in Ireland.

The Hedingham branch of the Wrentham family settled at Castle Hedingham, Essex, early in the 16th century, and was allied to the ancient families of Clopton, Poley, Wentworth, Seckford, Hardwicke, Neville, Quarles, &c.

ROBERT BREWSTER, son of John, had four sons,

William, who *d.* 1583. Robert.

Richard, *d.* 1593; buried in St. Dunstan's in the West, with Alice his wife.

John.

WILLIAM BREWSTER, Esq., eldest son, *m.* 1st, Anne, dau. of Sir Wm. Clopton, of Liston Hall, Essex. By her he had,

William, *b.* 1562; *m.* a dau. of John Wells, Esq. of London, and had issue, John, Anthony, and William.

Cordel.

Catherine, *m.* 1st, to Thomas Hardwicke, Esq.; and 2ndly, to William Neville, Esq. of York.

The 2nd wife of William Brewster was Mirabel, dau. of Sir John Poley, of Badley, co. Suffolk, by Ann, dau. of Thomas, Lord Wentworth, of Nettlestead Hall, co. Suffolk; by her he had,

John, *b.* 1575; *d.* in Ireland.
Edmund, *d.* 1633, buried in Badley church.
William, of Great Bealings, Suffolk, *d.* 1624.
Edward, of Woodbridge, Suffolk, *d.* 1637.
Thomas, of Wickham Market, Suffolk, *d.* 1645.
Anne, *b.* 1579; *m.* 1st, to Thomas Kirby, Esq. of Kirby Hall, Castle Hedingham, and Henham, co. Essex; 2ndly, to Sir Thomas Seckford, of Seckford Hall, Great Bealings, co. Suffolk; and 3rdly, to Sir Robert Quarles, of Stewards, Romford, co. Essex, M.P. for Colchester, and brother of the poet Quarles.

JOHN BREWSTER, Esq., 4th son of Robert, was Secondary of the Office of Fines: he *m.* 1st, Thomasine, dau. of John Pierce, Esq. of London; she *d.* 1596; and 2ndly, Elizabeth, dau. of Richard Thornhill, Esq. of Bromley, co. Kent: she had been previously married, 1st, to Christopher Webb, eldest son of Sir William Webb, and first-cousin of Archbishop Laud; and 2ndly, to Sir James Deane. John Brewster had issue by his 1st wife,

I. Thomas. II. Richard.

THOMAS BREWSTER, Esq., his son and heir, of the Middle Temple, and of Burwell, co. Lincoln, and Trumpington, co. Cambridge; *m.* 1st, Dorothy, dau. of Sir Thomas Jocelyn, of High Roding Hall, co. Essex; he *m.* 2ndly, Dorothy, dau. of — Martin, Esq. of Barton, co. Cambridge, by whom he had, DOROTHY, his heir, who *m.* Henry Wingfield, Esq. of Crowfield, co. Suffolk. In 1653, John Brewster represented the co. of Essex in parliament, and in 1655, he was a member of the parliament committee formed for the preservation of the peace of the county of Essex.

Descendants of this branch of the family are still residing in the neighbourhood of Hedingham.

Arms—Sa., a chevron, erm., between three estoiles, arg.
Crest—A leopard's head, erased, az.
Seat—Halsted Lodge, Essex.

BRICKDALE OF BIRCHAMP HOUSE.

BRICKDALE, JOHN-FORTESCUE, Esq. of Birchamp House, co. Gloucester, J.P. and D.L., barrister-at-law, *b.* 17 Feb. 1788; *m.* 7 July, 1813, Catherine, dau. of Charles Gregorie, Esq., by Catherine-Sophia his wife, dau. and heir of George Macaulay, M.D., and has issue,

I. MATTHEW-INGLETT, barrister-at-law, *b.* 15 April, 1817.
II. Charles-John, lieut. in the navy.
III. John-Fortescue, lieut. in the 61st foot.
I. Anne.
II. Catherine-Sophia, *m.* in 1840, to Edward-Owen Jones, Esq. of Nass House, co. Gloucester.
III. Mary.

Lineage.—The Brickdales were originally of Brickdale, co. Lancaster, of which family were Ralph and Thomas Brickdale, first governors of Conway Castle, *temp.* EDWARD I.

JOHN BRICKDALE, lord of the manor of Filton, co. Gloucester, J.P. and D.L., *m.* Elizabeth, dau. and co-heir of Robert Bound, mayor of Bristol, and was father of two sons, JOHN, who *m.* and settled in Spain, where there are several of the family, and

MATTHEW BRICKDALE, lord of the manor of Filton, co. Gloucester, and of Stoodleigh, co. Devon, who had estates in the cos. of Somerset, Salop, and Montgomery, all of which he sold. He represented Bristol in several parliaments, and resided at West Monkton, Somersetshire. Mr. Brickdale *m.* Elizabeth, dau. of Thomas Smith, Esq. of Clifton, co. Gloucester, by Lucy his wife, dau. of Thos. Carew, Esq. of Carew Castle, co. Pembroke, and Crowcombe, co. Somerset, and by this lady was father of

JOHN BRICKDALE, Esq., J.P. and D.L. for Somerset and Devon, who *m.* in Feb. 1787, Anne-Inglett, youngest dau. of Richard-Inglett Fortescue, Esq. of Spridlestone, Buckland-Filleigh, and Dawlish, co. Devon, and had issue,

JOHN-FORTESCUE, now of Birchamp House.
Richard, in holy orders, rector of Felthorpe and vicar of Ringland, Norfolk, *m.* Elvire Baunsell.
Frances-Elizabeth. Anne. Lucy-Maria.

Mr. Brickdale *d.* 28 June, 1840.

Arms—(Granted by EDWARD II. to Jenkyn Brickdale, for his valiant services in the field)—Az., a chevron, between three sheaves of five arrows, or, flighted and pheoned, arg., pointed and banded, gu.
Crests—1st, a sheaf of arrows, as in the arms; 2nd, out of a ducal coronet, or, a demi-lion, rampant, supporting a spear, ppr., thereon a standard, az., fringed and tasselled, or, charged with a sheaf of five arrows, as in the arms.
Motto—Fide et fortitudine.
Seat—Birchamp House, Coleford, co. Gloucester.

BRI

BRIDGER OF BUCKINGHAM HOUSE.

BRIDGER, HARRY-COLVILL, Esq. of Buckingham House, Old Shoreham, co. Sussex, J.P., *b.* 11 June, 1799; *m.* 21 May, 1825, Sarah-Louisa, 3rd dau. of William Scrase, Esq., late of Withdean, co. Sussex, and has issue,

I. HARRY, *b.* 27 June, 1828, *m.* 9 March, 1850, Eliza-Ann, eldest dau. of George Orme, Esq. of Merton, co. Surrey, and has one son, Harry-Colvill, *b.* 21 Nov. 1850.
II. William, *b.* 14 Sept. 1834.
III. John, *b.* 14 March, 1836, *d.* 16 March, 1837.
IV. Frederick, *b.* 24 May, 1837.
V. Augustus-Goring, *b.* 24 July, 1841.
I. Louisa, *d.* 23 Sept. 1840. II. Mary.
III. Isabella, *d.* 19 Nov. 1841. IV. Emma.
V. Adela-Catharine.

Lineage.—HARRY BRIDGER, Esq., *m.* Katherine Bridger, and had issue, Harry, *b.* 10 Feb. 1720, *d.* young; Colvill, *b.* 6 May, 1726, *d.* young; COLVILL, his heir; Harry, *b.* 8 March, 1732; Richard, *b.* 16 June, 1734; Arthur, *b.* 13 Oct. 1737; Katherine; Anne; Elizabeth; and Mary. The eldest surviving son and heir,

COLVILL BRIDGER, Esq. of Buckingham House, co. Sussex, served as high-sheriff of Sussex in 1778. He *m.* Mary, 2nd dau. of Sir Charles-Mathews Goring, 4th Bart. of Highden, co. Sussex, by Mary his first wife, youngest dau. of William Blackburne, Esq. of High Ongar, and by this lady had, with several sons and daus., an eldest son and heir,

HARRY BRIDGER, Esq of Buckingham House, *b.* 16 Sept. 1768, who *m.* 8 June, 1797, Mary-Ann, 2nd dau. of the late Jeremiah Watson, Esq. of Great Portland-street, London, and had issue,

HENRY-COLVILLE, present representative.
Frank, *m.* Mary, dau. of Captain John Butler, of New Shoreham, and *d. s. p.*, 25 Feb. 1840.
Augustus, *d. unm.* 16 Nov. 1828.
John, *m.* Eliza-Pope, dau. of — Comper, Esq. of Chichester, and has issue one son.
Mary-Anne.
Isabella, *m.* to John-Sandys Penfold, Esq. and has issue.

Mr. Bridger *d.* 25 March, 1832.

Arms—Arg., a chevron, engrailed, sa., between three crabs, gu.
Crest—A crab, as in the arms.
Seat—Buckingham House, Old Shoreham, co. Sussex.

BRIDGER OF HALNAKER.

BRIDGER, WILLIAM-MILTON, Esq. of Halnaker, co. Sussex, a magistrate for that county, *m.* 10 Oct. 1837, Sophia, youngest dau. of Gorges Lowther, Esq., formerly of Kilrue, co. Meath, and Julia his wife, dau. of the Rev. Dr. Huntingford, and niece of George-Isaac Huntingford, late bishop of Hereford. By this lady Mr. Bridger has issue,

I. WILLIAM-MILTON, *b.* 1 Aug. 1838.
II. John-Huntingford, *b.* 13 Aug. 1839.
III. Robert-Lowther, *b.* 3 Dec. 1840.
I. Sophia.

Mr. Bridger, barrister-at-law, and recorder of Chichester, is son of the late WILLIAM BRIDGER, Esq., and Mary Pannel his wife, and great-nephew of Ann Streetin, wife of William Milton, Esq., for many years deputy-recorder of Chichester, which lady bequeathed to him the Milton property.

Arms—Arg., a chevron, between three crabs, gu.
Crest—A hand, grasping an eagle's neck and head.
Seat—Halnaker, Chichester.

BRIGHAM OF FOXLEY HOUSE,

FORMERLY OF BRIGHAM.

BRIGHAM, WILLIAM, Esq. of Foxley House, Lymm, co. Chester, *b.* 18 Feb. 1792; *m.* 5 Feb. 1834, Elizabeth, dau. of John Richardson, Esq. of Manchester, and has two daus.,

I. HENRIETTA-FELICIA. II. HELEN-ELIZABETH.

Mr. Brigham is male heir of the ancient Yorkshire family of BRIGHAM *of Brigham.*

Lineage.—RALPH BRIGHAM, of Brigham, co. York, son of Theobald, and grandson of William Brigham, of Brigham, living 9th HENRY VII., m. Elizabeth, dau. of Grimston of Cottingham, and was father of

FRANCIS BRIGHAM, of Brigham, living 1584, who m. Margaret, dau. of Gilbert Warter, of Cranswick, and left a son, RALPH BRIGHAM, b. in 1583, whose wife Mary was dau. of Ralph Creswell, of Nonkelling, co. York. By her he left at his decease in 1656, three sons and three daus.: of the latter, the eldest, Mary, m. Ralph Wilberfosse: of the former, the 2nd, but eldest to survive,

WILLIAM BRIGHAM, of Brigham and Wyton, both in Holdernesse, co. York, aged 53 years at the heralds' visitation of Yorkshire A.D. 1665; d. circ. 1670, having had, by Ursula his wife, dau. of Richard Langley, of Mellington, in the East Riding, two daus., Mary, m. to Leonard Metcalfe, and Dorothy; and three sons, JOHN, his heir; Richard, of Wyton, living in 1700, then m. with issue; and Peter. The eldest son, JOHN BRIGHAM, of Brigham and Wyton, aged 28 at the heralds' visitation, m. in 1669, Mary, dau. of Thomas Meynell, Esq. of North Kilvington, co. York; and d. in 1710. There were of this marriage two daus. and two sons; the younger, William, m. Catherine, dau. of Thomas Waterton, of Walton, Esq.: the elder,

ROGER BRIGHAM, Esq. of Brigham and Wyton, m. in 1711, Elizabeth, dau. of Edward Charlton, Esq. of Hesleyside, Northumberland; and dying in 1729, left issue, 1 William, of Brigham and Wyton, who m. Ursula, dau. of Ralph Brigham, Esq. of Wyton, and had issue an only child, Anne, who d. unm. 7 Jan. 1767, twenty-seven days before her father; 2 Nicholas, d. s. p.; 3 JOHN, of whom presently; and 4 Jerard, of Preston in Holdernesse. The third son,

JOHN BRIGHAM, Esq. of Brigham and Crathorne, m. Anne, dau. of Christopher Metcalfe, and had, with other children, who d. young or unmarried, a son, WILLIAM, his heir; and Anne, m. 4 July, 1791, to James Burchell, Esq., M.D., of Richmond, co. York. Mr. Brigham d. 9 Jan. 1792, aged 67, and was s. by his son,

WILLIAM BRIGHAM, Esq. of Brigham and Abberford, and afterwards of Manchester, b. 2 Aug. 1759; who m. 1 Sept. 1783, Sarah, dau. of John Cresswell, Esq., and by her (who d. 29 Oct. 1834) had issue,

- WILLIAM, present representative of this ancient family.
- Henry, in holy orders of the church of Rome; b. 23 Jan. 1796.
- Edward, of Manchester, b. 27 Sept. 1799; m. Mary, dau. of John Castree, of Manchester, and has issue.
- Charles, of Dodden Green, Westmoreland, a Catholic priest; b. 6 March, 1802.
- Octavius, d. 19 May, 1834.

Mr. Brigham, who sold the Brigham estate, d. 22 July, 1815.

Arms—Arg., a saltier, engrailed, vert.
Crest—Out of a ducal coronet, a plume of feathers.
Motto—In cruce salus.
Seat—Foxley House, Lymm, co. Chester.

BRINKLEY OF ARDAGH.

BRINKLEY, RICHARD GRAVES, Esq. of Ardagh, and Fortland, co. Sligo, b. 21 Sept. 1823; m. 2 Dec. 1845, Hester, dau. of James S.-D.-D. Lloyd, Esq., by Charlotte his wife, dau. of George Hepenstal, Esq., and has issue,

- I. JOHN-LLOYD, b. 8 June, 1852.
- II. James-William-Arthur, b. 15 March, 1854.
- I. Charlotte-Ida-Harriette.
- II. Louisa-Maria-Susan.
- III. Harriette-Adela.

Lineage.—MATTHEW BRINKLEY, Esq., b. 2 March, 1796, son of the Right Rev. JOHN BRINKLEY, Lord Bishop of Cloyne, the Astronomer Royal of Ireland, by Esther Weld his wife, m. 5 March, 1821, Harriette, dau. of the Very Rev. Richard Graves, dean of Ardagh, and had issue,

- RICHARD-GRAVES, now of Ardagh and Portland.
- Mathew, lieut. 97th foot.
- Esther, m. to John Alexander, Esq., M.P. of Milford, co. Carlow.
- Eliza, m. to William-H. Longfield, Esq. of Gravelmount, co. Meath.
- Harriette, m. to R.-H. Farrer, Esq. of Ashfield, Queen's County.

Arms—Az., a cross patonce, engrailed, and in chief three estoiles, or.
Crest—A cross patonce, engrailed, surmounted of an estoile, all or.
Motto—Mutabimur.
Seats—Ardagh and Fortland, co. Sligo.

BRISCOE OF TINVANE.

BRISCOE, HENRY-WHITBY, Esq. of Tinvane, co. Tipperary, J.P., b. 29 Sept. 1809; s. his father 7 Feb. 1834; m. 8 June, 1835, Miss Deborah Shaw, and has issue three sons and five daus.

Lineage.—This is a branch of the ancient Cumberland family of BRISCOE *of Crofton Hall*.

WILLIAM-MUSGRAVE BRISCOE, a younger son of the English house, accompanied his brother-in-law, Col. Ponsonby, to Ireland, an officer in the same regiment, and settled in the barony of Iverk, co. Kilkenny, A.D. 1650. His descendant,

HENRY BRISCOE, Esq., J.P. for the counties of Tipperary, Kilkenny, and Waterford, born in 1753, at Tybroughney Castle, co. Kilkenny, the residence and estate of his ancestors, entered the 1st regiment of horse, 31 Aug. 1770. He m. in 1775, Miss Margaret Sneyd, and had issue,

- HENRY-WHITBY, his heir.
- John, major royal artillery, deceased.
- Robert, an officer 27th foot, deceased.
- Edward-Whitby, J.P. co. Kilkenny, m. Miss N. Rivers.
- Abigail, (Mrs. Bowers,) deceased.
- Fanny, deceased.
- Margaret, m. to Major-Gen. Bredin, royal artillery.
- Dora, m. to J. Wilkie, Esq., Ordnance storekeeper, brother of Sir David Wilkie, R.A.
- Anne, m. to Capt. Gibson, R.N. Battalion.
- Catherine, m. to Capt. Christian, R.V.B.

The eldest son,

HENRY BRISCOE, Esq., J.P. for the counties of Tipperary, Kilkenny, and Waterford, b. in 1777, s. his father, Henry, in 1807. He m. in 1808, Miss Alicia White, and by her, who d. in 1816, had issue,

- HENRY, his heir.
- Francis, M.A., vicar of Kilmessan, and rector of Macetown, in the diocese of Meath, b. 14 Nov. 1810, m. in 1854, Dora, eldest dau. of John Cornwall, Esq. of Branstown House, co. Meath.
- Alicia-Louisa, m. 5 Jan. 1836, Richard-Bergoin Bennett, Esq., barrister-at-law, eldest son of Richard-Newton Bennett, Esq., barrister-at-law, formerly of Blackstoops, co. Wexford, and chief justice of Tobago, and has issue, three sons and two daus.
- Anne, m. in 1851, to Thomas-C. Waring, Esq., late of the co. Kilkenny, and has issue, one son.
- Fanny. Harriette.

Arms—Arg., three greyhounds, courant, in pale, sa.
Crest—A greyhound, courant, sa., seizing a hare, ppr.
Motto—Post virtutem curro.
Seat—Tinvane House, Carrick on-Suir, co. Tipperary.

BRISTOW OF BROXMORE PARK.

BRISTOW, ROBERT, Esq. of Broxmore Park, co. Wilts, M.A., J.P., s. his father 8 Dec. 1776; m. Sophia, dau. of Joseph Twine, Esq. of Ramsbury, and had a dau.,

- Ada-Sophia, b. 9 Jan. 1841.

Lineage.—In 1399, or about that period, JOHN DE BRISTOWE, a lineal descendant of Sir John de Burstow, of Burstow, in Surrey, assessor for that county in 1294, was cupbearer to HENRY IV. He was ancestor of JOHN BRISTOW, of Lee, mentioned in St. George's Visitation of Essex, A.D. 1634, as John Bristow, of Lee, Gent., the father of Nicholas Bristow, described as his 2nd son.

NICHOLAS BRISTOW, who was b. in 1494, held the appointment of clerk of the jewels to Kings HENRY VIII. and EDWARD VI., and to Queens MARY and ELIZABETH. In 1543 he purchased the manor and estate of Little Bibbesworth, Herts, and subsequently had grants of the manor of Ayot St. Lawrence, and the manor of Cannons, near Watford. Nicholas Bristow d. in 1584, aged 90, leaving, by his wife, dau. of Robert Barlye, of Great Bibbesworth, a son and successor,

NICHOLAS BRISTOW, Esq. of Ayot St. Lawrence and of Little Bibbesworth, clerk of the jewels to King JAMES I. He m. Margaret, dau. of Sir John Boteler, Knt. of Watton Woodhall, and was father of NICHOLAS, of Ayot St. Lawrence, whose son,

ROBERT BRISTOW, Esq. of Ayot St. Lawrence and Little Bibbesworth, b. in 1596, m. in 1641, Elizabeth, dau. of Richard Scriven, Esq. of London, and by her, who d. in 1690, had issue. The 2nd son,

ROBERT BRISTOW, Esq., b. in 1643, established himself in North America in 1660, on the restoration of CHARLES II., as is stated in Sir Edward Bysshe's Visitation of the County of Herts, in 1669. His only son,

Robert Bristow, Esq., became subsequently a Bank director, and sat as one of the members for Winchelsea, 1698 and 1700. He *m.* in 1684, Catherine, eldest dau. of Robert Woolley, Esq. of London, and by her, who *d.* 28 Oct. 1751, aged 84, had issue,

I. Robert, his heir.
II. William, a chief commissioner of revenue in Ireland, *d. unm.* in 1758.
III. John, of Quidenham Hall, co. Norfolk, Sub-Governor of the South Sea Company, M.P., &c., *m.* in 1733, Anne-Judith, dau. of Paul Folsin, an East India merchant in Paris, and dying at Lisbon in 1768, left issue,
  1 Henry Bristow, of Dover-street, Piccadilly, capt. and lieut-col. in the Coldstream-guards, *m.* his cousin, Anne Dashwood, one of the maids of honour to Queen Charlotte, and dying at Bath in 1786, left issue,
    George, page of honour to Queen Charlotte, lieut.-col. grenadier-guards, and afterwards aide-de-camp and private secretary to the Marquess of Wellesley, governor-general of India; *m.* in 1805, Elizabeth-Lacy, dau. of Lieut.-Col. Howe, of Bath, and *d.* at Fort William, in Calcutta, in 1833, leaving issue,
      Thomas-Henry, captain in the army, *b.* 25 Oct. 1807, *m.* 15 June, 1841, Susanna-Elizabeth, dau. of Lieut.-Col. Percy Groves, of Boughton, Kent.
      George-William Grant, *b.* in 1809, in the Hon. E. I. Co.'s military service, *m.* in 1832, Isabella, dau. of Major-Gen. Colin Campbell, commander of the forces at the Cape of Good Hope.
      Cerjat-Michael, *b.* in 1811, in the Hon. E. I. Co.'s military service, *d. unm.* in 1839.
      John-Samuel, *b.* in 1815, in the Hon. E. I. Co's military service.
      Pellegrine-Howe, *b.* in 1818, in the Hon. E. I. Co.'s military service, and *d.* in 1846.
      Elizabeth-Georgiana, *m.* in 1825, Col. Dundas, of Manor, and has issue.
      Anne-Catherine, *m.* in 1830, J.-Spencer Judge, Esq. of Calcutta, and has issue.
      Sabina-Maria, *m.* in 1834, to her cousin, Robert Neave, Esq. of the Hon. E. I. Co.'s service, nephew of Sir Thomas Neave, Bart., of Dagnam Park, co. Essex.
      Lacy-Ann, *m.* in 1836, Capt. Daniel, of the Hon. E. I. Co.'s military service.
    Madeline, *m.* in 1799, Lieut.-Col. Andrew Cerjat, of the life-guards, and left issue, Madeline, *m.* to Robert Baird, capt. R.N., brother of Sir David Baird, Bart. of Newbyth.
  2 John, President of the Board of Trade at Calcutta, who *m.* Emilia, dau. of William Wrangham, Esq., and dying in 1803, left issue, John-Charles, of Eusmere Hill, Ullswater, Cumberland; Emelia-Sophia, *m.* to Frederick Welstead, comm. R.N.; and Charlotte-Louisa, *m.* in 1809, to George Hannam, Esq.
  3 William, R.N., *b.* 17 Dec. 1750, *m.* in May, 1782, Mary, dau. of Anthony Sawyer, Esq. of Heywood Lodge, Berkshire, by Phœbe his wife, dau. and co-heir of Richard Harcourt, Esq. of Wigsell, M.P. and *d.* at Bath in 1803, having had issue,
    William, R.N., killed off Boulogne, under Lord Nelson, in 1801.
    Henry, lieut-col. in the army, *b.* 19 Feb. 1786, *m.* Elisabeth Alchorne, of the Kentish family of the name, and has a son, Henry-William, and a dau., Eliza.
  1 Anne-Margaret, *m.* in 1761, to her cousin, the Hon. H. Hobart, M.P.
  2 Catharine, *m.* to Lieut.-Gen. the Hon. Simon Fraser, M.P.
  3 Louisa, *m.* to Tillieux Girardot, Esq. of Putney.
  4 Frances, *m.* in 1761, to Sir Richard Neave, Bart.
  5 Caroline, *m.* in 1774, to William-Henry, Lord Lyttelton.
  6 Mary, *d. unm.*
  7 Harriet, *m.* to Gen. Slessor, Governor of Oporto.
  8 Sophia, *d. unm.* in 1778.
I. Katherine, *m.* to George Dashwood, Esq., M.P., of Heveningham Hall, Suffolk.
II. Averilla, *d. unm.* in 1762.
III. Elizabeth, *m.* to John, Earl of Buckinghamshire.
IV. Anne, *m.* in 1728, to Francis, Earl of Effingham.
V. Frances, *m.* to John Warde, Esq. of Squerries.
VI. Rebecca, *d. unm.* 5 Jan. 1775.

Robert Bristow *d.* 20 Sept. 1706, and was *s.* by his eldest son,

Robert Bristow, Esq. of Micheldever House, co. Hants, clerk-comptroller of the household, and M.P. for Winchilsea, who *m.* in 1709, Sarah, dau. of Sir John Warde of Squerries, co. Kent, M.P. for London, and had issue,

I. Robert, his heir. II. John, *d. unm.* 1798.
III. William, R.N., *d. unm.* in 1736.
IV. George, of Ashford, co. Middlesex, *b.* 13 June, 1727, who *m.* Elizabeth-Maria, dau. of George North, Esq., clerk to the Merchant Tailors' Company, and *d.* 5 Sept. 1815, leaving a dau., Elizabeth-Rebecca, *m.* in 1785, to the Rev. Bartholomew-Lutley Sclater.

Mr. Bristow *d.* 3 Nov. 1737, and was *s.* by his son,

Robert Bristow, Esq. of Micheldever House, clerk of the Board of Green Cloth, M.P. for Winchilsea, and afterwards for Shoreham, *b.* in 1712, who *m.* 1st, 7 June, 1746, Susannah, dau. and heir of John Philipson, Esq., surveyor-general of Woods and Parks, and M.P. for Harwich, and had by her a dau., Susanna, who *m.* Sir Brooke Boothby, Bart., but *d. s. p.* 13 Nov. 1822. He *m.* 2ndly, Mary, dau. of the Rev. Richard Harding, vicar of Micheldever, and had by her a son, Robert, and three daus., of whom only one *m.*, viz., Anna-Maria, wife of Frederick Booth, Esq., solicitor to the Tax Office. Mr. Bristow *d.* 8 Dec. 1776, and was *s.* by his son, Robert Bristow, Esq. of Broxmore Park.

Arms—Erm., on a fesse, cotised, sa., three crescents, or.
Crest—Out of a crescent, or, a demi-eagle, displayed, az.
Motto—Vigilantibus non dormientibus.
Seat—Boxmore Park, co. Wilts.

BRISTOWE OF BEESTHORPE HALL.

Bristowe, Samuel-Ellis, Esq. of Beesthorpe Hall, co. Nottingham, and of Twyford, co. Derby, J.P. and D.L., *b.* 10 March, 1800; *m.* 1st, in 1821, Mary-Anne, dau. of Samuel Fox, Esq. of Osmaston Hall, co. Derby; and 2ndly, 6 July, 1836, the Lady Alicia-Mary Needham, sister of the Earl of Kilmorey. By the former lady he has had issue,

I. Samuel-Boteler, *b.* 5 Oct. 1822.
II. Henry-Fox, *b.* 8 May, 1824.
I. Anna-Maria.

Lineage.—This very ancient family descends, through the Hertfordshire line, from the Bristowes or Burstows *of Burstow*, in Surrey, who derived, according to Sir Edward Bysshe, and other authorities, from Stephen Fitzhamon, *alias* Stephen de Burstow, *temp.* Richard I. The branch before us has long been seated in Nottinghamshire and Derbyshire; and so far back as 1569, Thomas Bristowe sat in parliament as knight of the former shire.

Samuel Bristowe, Esq. of Twyford, *b.* 23 June, 1694 (elder son of Samuel Bristowe, Esq. of Twyford, and 4th in descent from William Bristowe, a younger son of Bristowe *of Beesthorpe*), *m.* 19 Sept. 1730, Mary, dau. and heir of Thomas Savage, Esq. of Burton Nether Hall, co. Stafford, descended from the noble family of Savage, Earl Rivers, and had issue,

  Samuel, his heir.
  Thomas, of Twyford, *b.* 4 July, 1739, *m.* 29 Aug. 1765, Mary, 3rd dau. of Leonard Fosbrooke, Esq. of Shardlowe, co. Derby, and had, with a dau. Mary, a son,
    Samuel, *b.* 8 Aug. 1766, who *m.* Eliza-Anne Banks, and had (with two daus., Eliza, who *m.* and left issue; and Julia), four sons, Samuel-Ellis, heir to his great-uncle; Simon, barrister-at-law, *b.* in 1806, *m.* Mary, only dau. of the Rev. J. Stephenson, and has one son and one dau.; John, *b.* in 1813; Henry-Fosbrooke.

Mr. Bristowe *d.* 31 March, 1761, and was buried at Twyford. His elder son,

Samuel Bristowe, Esq. of Beesthorpe, co. Notts, and Twyford, co. Derby, *b.* 8 Sept. 1736, J.P. for both counties, served as high-sheriff of Nottinghamshire in 1799. He *d. unm.* 18 June, 1818, and was *s.* by his grand-nephew, the present Samuel-Ellis Bristowe, Esq. of Beesthorpe and Twyford.

Arms—Erm., a fesse, cotised, sa.; three crescents, or.
Crest—Out of a crescent, or, a demi-eagle, displayed, az.
Motto—Vigilantibus non dormientibus.
Seats—Beesthorpe Hall, Notts; and Twyford, co. Derby.

BROADLEY OF KIRK ELLA.

Broadley, John-Bourryan, Esq. of Kirk Ella, co. York, late captain 17th Lancers, *b.* 3 May, 1817, *m.* 22 June, 1854, Eleanor-Sarah, 2nd dau. of the Rev. Charles Lane, M.A., rector and vicar of Wrotham, and rural dean of Shoreham, Kent.

Lineage.—Henry Broadley, Esq., an officer, R.N. (3rd surviving son of Thomas Broadley, Esq. of Ferriby and Kingston-upon-Hull, and great-grandson of Thomas Broadley, Esq., by Frances his wife), *m.* 8 Dec. 1774, Betty-Anne, dau. and heiress of John Jarratt, Esq. of Beverley, and by her, who survived till 1807, had issue, Thomas, in holy orders, *d. unm.* 16 Feb. 1815; John, of whom presently; Henry, of Welton House and Ferriby, co. York, M.P. for the East Riding of the county, J.P. and D.L., *b.* in 1793, *d. s. p.* 9 Aug. 1851; Sarah, *d. unm.* in 1807; Mary, *m.* 4 Nov.

4 Isabella, *m.* in 1821, to Archibald-Erskine Patullo, Esq., captain in the Madras cavalry, who *d.* leaving issue.
5 Louisa, *m.* in 1825, to Hugh-Calveley Cotton, Esq., captain Madras engineers.

II. William-Douglass, consul in Spain, who *d.* at Madras, 14 Aug. 1826.
I. Jane-Ann-Catharine.
II. Margaret, *m.* to Lieut.-Col. Colquhoun Grant, of the 54th. They both *d.* in India, leaving one son.
III. Charlotte, *m.* to Colonel Keith Macalister, who left her a widow with one son.

James Brodie, of Brodie, *d.* 17 Jan. 1824, and was *s.* by his grandson, the present WILLIAM BRODIE, Esq of Brodie, the representative of a long line of ancestors, longer perhaps than any family in regular succession in the kingdom.

Arms—Arg., a chevron, gu., between three mullets, az.
Crest—A right hand holding a bunch of arrows, all ppr.
Supporters—Two savages, wreathed about the head and middle with laurel, each holding a club resting against his shoulder.
Seat—Brodie.

BRODIE OF LETHEN.

BRODIE, JAMES-CAMPBELL, Esq. of Lethen and Coulmony, co. Nairn, D.L., *b.* 22 Feb. 1801; *m.* 20 March, 1832, Mary-Catharine, youngest dau. of Stewart Souter, Esq. of Melrose, and by her (who *d.* 27 Feb. 1854,) has,

I. THOMAS-STEWART, *b.* 22 April, 1837.
II. James-Campbell-John, *b.* 26 March, 1848.

Lineage.—ALEXANDER BRODIE, 1st of Lethen, second son of David Brodie of that ilk, was *b.* about 1587, uncle of Lord Brodie; purchased, in 1630—1634, the estates of Pitgavenie, Eastgrange, and Lethen, in the cos. of Nairn and Moray, and in 1643, the estate of Kinloss, in the latter county. He *d.* 7 Nov. 1672, at a very advanced age, leaving issue by his 1st wife, Margaret Clerk (dau. of James Clerk, of Balbirnie, in Fife, and niece of Magdalen Clerk, wife of Edward, 1st Lord Bruce of Kinloss), five children.

ALEXANDER BRODIE, of Lethen, was M.P. for the county of Nairn in 1739, and great-grandson of Alexander, 1st of Lethen; *m.* in 1754, Henrietta, dau. of Colonel William Grant, of Ballindalloch; had issue five children, viz.,

ALEXANDER, his heir.
JOHN, afterwards of Lethen.
ANNE, also afterwards of Lethen.
Sophia, afterwards Mrs. Sophia Dunbar-Brodie, of Lethen and Burgie.
Henrietta-Brodie, *b.* 5 May, 1761; and *d.* a child.

He *d.* at Lethen, 28 April, 1770, and was survived by his wife, and *s.* by his eldest son,

ALEXANDER BRODIE, of Lethen, who was *b.* 16 July, 1756; and *d.* 28 Nov. 1770, in his fifteenth year, only a few months after his father. He was *s.* by his brother,

JOHN BRODIE, of Lethen, who was *b.* 15 Jan. 1758; and dying in his sixteenth year, 20 Sept. 1773, at Nice, was *s.* by his eldest sister,

MISS ANNE BRODIE, of Lethen. She was *b.* 17 June, 1755; and dying *unm.* in Oct. 1805, was *s.* by her youngest sister,

MRS. SOPHIA DUNBAR-BRODIE, of Lethen and Burgie, who was *b.* 12 Feb. 1759, and had *m.*, 14 June, 1796, her cousin-german, Lewis Dunbar, of Grange, afterwards Lewis Dunbar-Brodie, of Burgie and Lethen, who dying at Cheltenham, 9 Nov. 1827, left her his paternal estate of Burgie, which, however, on her own death, which happened at Burgie House, in Morayshire, 26 Sept. 1829, went, by the terms of his will, to his own heir-at-law. By her decease, the descendants of her father, Alexander Brodie, of Lethen, became extinct, and she was accordingly *s.* by the present JAMES-CAMPBELL BRODIE, Esq. of Lethen and Coulmony, son of Thomas Brodie, W.S., and grandson of Thomas Brodie, lyon-depute of Scotland, 3rd son of Alexander Brodie, of Lethen, whose grandfather, Alexander, was the 1st of Lethen.

Mr. James-Campbell Brodie has had three brothers, viz., 1 Major Thomas Brodie, Hon. East India Company's Bengal establishment, *b.* 23 May, 1805; 2 Ensign David-Hay Brodie, *b.* 29 Jan. 1809, *d.* in Bengal, *unm.*, 22 April, 1831; and 3 John-Clerk Brodie, writer to the signet, and crown-agent for Scotland, *b.* 20 May, 1811, *m.* 1st, 20 March, 1832, Bathia-Garden, eldest dau. of Stewart Souter, Esq. of Melrose, by whom (who *d.* 1844,) he has an only child, Thomas Brodie, *b.* at Edinburgh, 26 Dec. 1832. He *m.* 2ndly, 1848, Penelope-Marianne, 3rd dau. of the Rev. John Sneyd, M.A., and has issue. Mr. Brodie had also three sisters, viz., 1 Elizabeth Brodie, *b.* 7 Oct. 1793, *m.* Frederick Furnell, Esq., younger brother of Michael Furnell, Esq. of Cahir Elly Castle, co. Limerick; 2 Phœbe Brodie, *d.* in 1833, *unm.*; and 3 Anne Brodie, *m.* in 1827, David-Brown Wardlaw, Esq. of Gogarmount, in the county of Edinburgh.

Arms—Arg., on a chevron, gu., between three mullets, az., a galley or lymphad, sa.
Crest—A dexter hand holding a bunch of arrows, ppr.
Motto—Be mindful to unite.
Seats—Lethen House, and Coulmony House, co. Nairn.

BROME OF SALOP, HERTS, AND KENT.

BROME, CHARLES-JOHN-BYTHESEA, Esq. of West Malling, Kent, *b.* in Sept. 1811; *m.* in 1833, Miss Æmilia Hill, of the Staffordshire family of Hill, and has issue,

I. CHARLES-BYTHESEA, *b.* in 1833.
II. William-Edward-Saxton.
III. Francis-Heathcote.
I. Æmelia-Cecilia.
II. Agnes-Mary.
III. Julia-Bythesea.

Mr. Brome *s.* his father in 1830.

Lineage.—For some time previous to the year 1300, the family of which we are treating are stated to have resided at Broome, in Salop, and, in the sixteenth century, to have migrated thence into Kent, whence they subsequently removed into Hertfordshire, in consequence of the marriage of

JOHN BROME, Esq. (son of William Brome, Esq.), with Cordelia, dau. and co-heir of John Sandford, Esq. of Herts, by Anne his wife, dau. and co-heir of Edward Denny, Esq. of Bishop's Stortford. By Cordelia, Mr. Brome left at his decease, 30 Nov. 1734, aged 59, with other issue, a son,

JOHN BROME, Esq. of the Manor House, Bishop's Stortford, *b.* 12 Nov. 1717; who *m.* 1st, in 1739, Martha Osborne, by whom he had two children, a son and a dau., both *d. s. p.*; and 2nd'ly, in 1761, Mary, sister of Sir Charles Saxton, Bart., many years Commissioner of Portsmouth, by whom he left (with other children, who *d. unm.*) a son,

CHARLES BROME, Esq. of Malling House, West Malling, Kent, *b.* in 1770; who *m.* 1803, Cecilia, only dau. of William Bythesea, Esq. of Blackheath, Kent, and Week House, Wilts; and dying in 1830, left issue,

CHARLES-JOHN-BYTHESEA, present representative and only male descendant of this ancient family.
Cecilia-Bythesea, *m.* to the Rev. Edward Weigall, M.A.
Mary-Agnes-Bythesea, *m.* to Samuel-William Bythesea, Esq. of The Hill, Freshford.

Arms—Arg., a sinister hand erect, in pale, couped at the wrist; quartering, among many others, SANDFORD, DENNY, QUILTER, HODGES, &c.
Crest—An arm, vested, gu., turned up, arg., holding in the hand, ppr., a slip of broom, vert, flowered, or.
Motto—Domine dirige nos.
Residence—West Malling, Kent.

BROMLEY OF BAGINGTON.

(*See* DAVENPORT-BROMLEY.)

BROOKE OF MERE.

BROOKE, THOMAS-JOHN-LANGFORD, Esq. of Mere Hall, co. Chester, *b.* 16 March, 1820; *m.* 21 April, 1841, Catherine-Mary, dau. of Major Macleod, brother of Sir John Macleod, and has a son,

THOMAS-WILLIAM-LANGFORD, *b.* 8 May, 1843.

Lineage.—SIR PETER BROOKE, son of Thomas Brooke, Esq. of Norton, co. Chester, by Eleanor Gerard, his 3rd wife, purchased, in 1652, from John Mere, Esq., the manor of Mere, and established himself there. He received the honour of knighthood in 1660, was M.P. for Cheshire, 8th CHARLES II., and high-sheriff for that co. in 1669. He *m.* thrice, and by his 1st wife had two sons, THOMAS, his heir; and Richard, ancestor of the BROOKES *of Astley*. Sir Peter, who rebuilt and beautified the hall at Mere, was *s.* at his decease by his son,

THOMAS BROOKE, Esq. of Mere, father, by Margaret his first wife, dau. and heiress of Henry Brereton, Esq. of Eccleston, of a son and heir,

PETER BROOKE, Esq. of Mere, who *m.* Elizabeth, dau. and co-heir of Peter Venables, Esq. of Over Street, and left (with two daus., Margaret, and Elizabeth, the wife of

Thomas Ravenscroft, Esq. of Pickhill, in Flintshire) a son and successor,

PETER BROOKE, Esq. of Mere, high-sheriff of Cheshire in 1728; who m. Frances, dau. and heir of Francis Hollinshead, Esq. of Wheelock; and dying in 1764, aged 69, left (with three daus., Felicia, m. to George Heron, Esq.; Elizabeth, m. to the Rev. Thomas Patten, D.D., rector of Childrey; and Frances, who d. unm.) two sons; the younger, John, d. unm. in 1780. The elder,

PETER BROOKE, Esq. of Mere, high-sheriff of Cheshire in 1766; m. 1st, Anne-Meriel, dau. of Fleetwood Legh, Esq. of Lyme, which lady dying issueless in 1740, aged 21, he m. 2ndly, Elizabeth, dau. and heiress of Jonas Langford, Esq. of Antigua, and by her (who d. 15 Dec. 1809, aged 75) he left at his decease in 1783, with two sons, three daus., Elizabeth, m. to Randle Ford, Esq.; Frances, m. to Thomas Oliver, Esq.; and Jane, m. 1st, to William Hulton, Esq. of Hulton, and 2ndly, to William-Tyrell Boyce, Esq. The eldest son,

JONAS-LANGFORD BROOKE, Esq. of Mere, d. unm. at Milan, eighteen months after his father, and was s. by his brother,

THOMAS-LANGFORD BROOKE, Esq. of Mere, who m. Maria, dau. of the Rev. Sir Thomas Broughton, Bart. of Broughton and Doddington, and had issue, PETER-LANGFORD, his heir; THOMAS-LANGFORD, now of Mere; William-Henry-Langford, late capt. of the 31st regt., d. unm. in 1839; Jonas-Langford; Maria-Elizabeth, widow of Meyrick Bankes, Esq. of Winstanley Hall; and Jemima, m. to Sir Jeremiah Dickson, K.C.B. Mr. Brooke d. 21 Dec. 1815, and was s. by his eldest son,

PETER-LANGFORD BROOKE, Esq. of Mere, b. in 1793, high-sheriff in 1824; who m. 1st, in 1818, Elizabeth-Sophia, eldest dau. of Vice-Admiral Sir Charles Rowley, K.C.B.; and 2ndly, in 1836, Julia-Seymour Buccleuch, dau. of Col. John Campbell, of Shawfield; but d. s. p. 9 Jan. 1840, and was s. by his brother,

THOMAS-LANGFORD BROOKE, Esq. of Mere, b. 3 Sept. 1794; m. 3 June, 1817, Eliza, dau. of John-William Clough, Esq. of Oxton Hall, co. York; and d. 24 Jan. 1848, leaving issue, 1 THOMAS-JOHN-LANGFORD, now of Mere; 2 Frederick-Langford; 3 Charles-Langford; 1 Eliza-Maria; 2 H.-Langford, m. to William Smallcombe, Esq.; 3 Charlotte; and 4 Julia.

Arms—Or, a cross, engrailed, per pale, gu. and sa., quarterly with LANGFORD.
Crest—A badger, passant, ppr.
Motto—Vis unita fortior.
Seat—Mere Hall.

BROOKE OF HANDFORD.

BROOKE, RICHARD, Esq. of Handford, co. Chester, and of Liverpool, co. Lancaster, F.S.A., b. 19 July, 1791; m. 17 Dec. 1831, Eleanor-Elspit, dau. of Alexander Hadden, Esq. of Bramcote, co. Notts, and has,

I. RICHARD-ARNAUD, b. 12 Oct. 1832.
II. Alexander, b. 29 Aug. 1835.
I. Anne-Mary. II. Eleanor-Elizabeth.
III. Helen. IV. Clare-Trafford.

Lineage.—As early as the reign of King EDWARD I., the ancient family of Brooke, or Del Brooke, had a seat and estate at Leighton, in the parish of Nantwich, co. Chester, of which the direct male line terminated on the death of Thomas Brooke, Esq. of Leighton, very aged, in 1652, having sold his house and lands there to Lady Mary Cholmondeley in 1608, in the 6th of JAMES I. But although there was a failure of issue of the family in the direct male line, there are several branches remaining who claim descent from the collateral, or younger lines. One of these was located, in the last century but one, near Congleton, in the parish of Astbury; a member of which,

BENEDICT BROOKE, Esq., son of Richard Brooke, was b. in 1670, and acquired an estate at Handford, Cheadle, co. Chester, in the 12th Queen ANNE, to which he afterwards made considerable additions. He d. in Aug. 1728, and was s. by his son,

RICHARD BROOKE, Esq., b. in 1715; who d. 19 July, 1774,* aged 59 years, and was s. by his only son,

RICHARD BROOKE, Esq., b. 14 June, 1761; who m. 29 Dec. 1786, Mary, dau. of Peter Penny (formerly Pennee), Esq., by whom (who d. 15 Jan. 1847, in her 81st year), he had issue,

PETER, b. Dec. 1788; a lieut. R.N.; distinguished at Martinique, and in the attack on New Orleans, on the 7th January, 1815, where he was wounded. He m. in Nov. 1819, Frances, widow of Charles Bowns, Esq. of Darley Hall, co. York; and d. s. p. 25 March, 1841.
RICHARD, now of Handford and Liverpool.
Mary-Ann.

Arms—Or, a cross, engrailed, per pale, gu. and sa.
Crest—A badger, passant, ppr.
Motto—Pro avitâ fide.
Residences—Liverpool; and Handford Lodge, Cheshire.

BROOKE OF UFFORD PLACE.

BROOKE, FRANCIS-CAPPER, of Ufford Place, co. Suffolk, late capt. Grenadier guards, b. 18 Sept. 1810; m. 15 Aug. 1839, Juliana-Jemima, dau. of Charles Allix, of Willoughby Hall, co. Lincoln, Esq., and by her, who d. at Athens, 12 Dec. 1840, has an only child,

ALICE.

Lineage.—From REGINALD BROOKE, of Aspall, in the co. of Suffolk, 2nd son of Sir Thomas Brooke, Knt., and Joane his wife, Baroness Cobham, dau. and heir of Sir Reginald Braybrooke, m. Anne Everton, lineally derived, 9th in descent,

FRANCIS BROOKE, Esq. of Woodbridge, in Suffolk, who m. 1st, Anne, dau. and heiress of Samuel Thompson, Esq., of Ufford Place, by whom he had issue, with three other sons, who d. unm., CHARLES, his heir. He m. 2ndly, Mary, dau. of the Rev. John Sparrow, rector of Kettleburgh, by whom (who d. in 1817) he had issue, four daus., who all d. unm. At Mr. Brooke's decease, in 1799, the family estates devolved upon his eldest son,

THE REV. CHARLES BROOKE, M.A. of Ufford Place, b. in 1765, who m. in 1809, Charlotte, 3rd dau. of the Rev. Francis Capper, rector of Earlsoham and of Monksoham, co. Suffolk, and dying 30 March, 1836, left an only child, the present FRANCIS-CAPPER BROOKE, Esq. of Ufford Place.

Arms—Gu., on a chevron, arg., a lion, rampant, sa., crowned, or, armed and langued, of the first.
Crest—On a chapeau, gu., turned up, erm., a wing erect, of the first, charged with a chevron, arg., thereon a lion, rampant, sa., crowned, gold.
Seat—Ufford Place, near Woodbridge.

BROOKE OF HAUGHTON HALL.

BROOKE, THE REV. JOHN, of Haughton Hall, co. Salop, b. in March, 1803; m. Georgiana-Frances, dau. of the late John Cotes, Esq. of Woodcote, by the Lady Maria, his wife, and has issue,

I. JOHN-TOWNSHEND, b. in 1844.
II. Charles, b. in 1846.

Lineage.—GEORGE-SALESBURY TOWNSHEND, Esq. of Chester, b. 19 April, 1742, 6th son of John Townshend, Esq. of Hem, co. Denbigh, by Frances his wife, dau. and heir of Nathaniel Lee, Esq. of Darnhall, m. Frances, dau. of the Rev. John Brooke, vicar of Shiffnal, son of Leigh Brooke, Esq. of Blacklands, by Elizabeth his wife, sister and co-heir of Sir Hugh Brigges, Bart. of Haughton; and d. 21 Sept. 1801, leaving a son,

GEORGE-BROOKE-BRIGGES TOWNSHEND, Esq., who s. to Haughton, at the decease of his uncle, the Rev. John Brooke, in 1786, assumed by sign-manual, in 1797, the surname of BROOKE only, and served as high-sheriff of Shropshire in 1811. He m. in 1799, Henrietta, dau. of Richard Massey, Esq. of Walton-on-the-Hill, co. Lancaster, and had issue,

I. GEORGE, his heir. II. JOHN, now of Haughton Hall.

* Another part of the same branch of the family resided at Chelford, Cheshire.

The Rev. Thomas Brooke, LL.D., dean of Chester, was of this branch; he was the son of Benedict Brooke, of Buglawton, in Cheshire, Gent. He was rector of Winslow, co. Bucks, vicar of Nantwich, 30 June, 1720, and rector of Dodleston, 15 June, 1739, and dying at Nantwich, was there buried, 20 Dec. 1757. He was nearly related to the first-mentioned Benedict Brooke.

Another of this branch was Samuel Brooke, Esq. of Chelford, in Cheshire, who d. without issue in 1775, having devised his Chelford estate, in default of issue of his sister Catherine, to Thomas Brooke, the eldest son of his cousin, Dean Brooke, with remainder to the dean's second son, Robert-Salisbury Brooke, Esq., who came into possession of it. Another of his cousins, William Brooke, Esq., resided many years at Northwich; and d. without issue. Robert-Salisbury Brooke d. without issue, in May, 1814.

III. William, b. in 1804, d. in 1830. IV. Richard, b. in 1806.
V. Townshend, b. in 1807.
I. Harriet. II. Frances, d. in 1833.

Mr. Brooke d. in 1845, and was s. by his eldest son,

GEORGE BROOKE, Esq. of Haughton Hall, a magistrate for Shropshire, b. in 1802, who d. unm. 14 March, 1847.

Arms—Quarterly: BROOKE and TOWNSHEND.
Crest—A badger.
Motto—Virtus est Dei.
Seat—Haughton Hall, co. Salop.

BROOKS OF FLITWICK.

BROOKS, JOHN-THOMAS, Esq. of Flitwick Manor House, co. Bedford, J.P. and D.L., high-sheriff in 1821, b. 16 Dec. 1794; m. 20 April, 1816, Mary, eldest dau. (by Mary his wife, dau. of Sir Richard Perryn, Knt., one of the barons of the Exchequer) of Alexander Hatfield, Esq. of Twickenham, a lineal descendant of Adam de Hatfield, of Hatfield, and of Glossopdale, co. Derby, A.D. 1327, and has issue,

I. JOHN-HATFIELD, 1st Bengal light cavalry.
II. George-Henry, of Doctors' Commons.
III. Thomas-William-Dell, of Christ Church College, Oxford.
I. Mary-Anne.

Mr. Brooks served formerly in the 14th light-dragoons, and is now a magistrate and deputy-lieut. for co. Bedford, of which shire he was high-sheriff in 1821.

Lineage.—The late GEORGE BROOKS, Esq. of Flitwick Manor House, b. in 1741, J.P., high-sheriff in 1796; m. 1st, Mary, dau. of R. Kirton, Esq., and by her had issue, I. JOHN, who left at his decease, by Harriett his wife, surviving issue, 1 John; 2 George-William, in holy orders; 3 Francis; 4 Thomas; and, 1 Harriet-Anne-Sophia, m. to John-William-Egerton Green, Esq. of Colchester; II. Sophia, m. to the Rev. Francis Drake, D.D., of Langton, co. York. Mr. Brooks m. 2ndly, in 1789, Anne, dau. of Jeffrey Fisher, Esq. of Maulden, and by her had three sons, Francis, b. in 1790, d. in infancy; George, b. in 1792, also d. in infancy; and JOHN-THOMAS, now of Flitwick Manor House. Mr. Brookes d. in 1817, and was s. by his son, the present JOHN-THOMAS BROOKS, Esq.

Arms—Or, a cross, per pale, gu. and sa.
Crest—An otter, on a mural crown, ppr.
Motto—Ut amnis vita labitur.
Seat—Flitwick Manor House, near Ampthill.

BROUNCKER OF BOVERIDGE.

BROUNCKER, RICHARD, Esq. of Boveridge, co. Dorset, J.P., high-sheriff in 1833, b. 13 Sept. 1801; m. 1st, 24 July, 1827, Maryana, youngest dau. of the late Rev. Charles-William Shuckburgh, of The Moot, Downton, Wilts, and by her, who d. 29 Nov. 1833, has issue,

I. Mary-Frances-Ann.
II. Geraldine-Fanny-Winifred. III. Barbara-Harriet-Diana.

He m. 2ndly, in 1836, Catherine-Jane, dau. of the late Capt. George Burdett, R.N. of Longtown House, co. Kildare, by Catherine-Dorothea his wife, only child of Col. William Browne, and has by her, with four daus., two sons,

I. HENRY-FRANCIS, b. in 1841.
II. William-Edgar-Morley, b. in 1846.

Lineage.—LEWIS-WILLIAM BROUNCKER, Esq. (son of Henry Brouncker, Esq., and grandson of Francis Brouncker, who d. in 1739), m. and had issue, I. HENRY, of whom presently; II. Lewis-William, b. 25 Sept. 1763, who d. 29 Jan. 1812, leaving, by Harriott his wife, surviving issue, 1 RICHARD, heir to his uncle; 2 Francis; 1 Henrietta; 2 Catherine, m. to Thomas-Whitmore-Wylde Browne, Esq. of Woodlands, in Shropshire; 3 Mary; 4 Frances; 5 Annabella; and 6 Barbara, m. to Edgar Disney, Esq.; I. Catherine, m. to John Willett, Esq. of Merley House, Dorsetshire; and II. Mary, m. 1st, to the Hon. William Finch, of Aldbury, admiral, R.N., 2nd son of the Earl of Aylesford, and 2ndly, to William Strode, Esq. The elder son,

HENRY BROUNCKER, Esq. of Boveridge, in the co. of Dorset, b. 30 June, 1767, d. unm. in May, 1825, and was s. by his nephew, the present RICHARD BROUNCKER, Esq. of Boveridge.

Arms—Arg., six pellets, three, two, and one; a chief, embattled, sa., thereon a lozenge, fessways, of the field, charged with a cross-patee, of the second, between two crescents, of the first.
Crest—Out of battlements, sa., a dexter cubit arm, vested, arg., charged with two bendlets, wavy, of the first; in the hand, ppr., a lozenge, in pale, charged with a cross-patee, as in the arms.
Motto—Duty.
Seat—Boveridge, near Cranbourne.

BROUGHTON OF TUNSTALL.

BROUGHTON, PETER, Esq. of Tunstall Hall, Shropshire, J.P., high-sheriff in 1839, b. 1 Aug. 1788; m. 2 Nov. 1818, Anna Ogilvie, youngest dau. of the late John, 2nd son of the late William Smithwick, Esq. of Mount Katherine, co. Limerick, by whom he has issue,

I. PETER, b. 1 Aug. 1822.
II. John-Lambart, b. 19 Jan. 1831.
I. Anna-Jane. II. Maria-Catherine-Wilhelmina.
III. Harriet. IV. Anna-Maria-Frances.

Lineage.—PETER BROUGHTON, Esq. of Lowdham, co. Notts, son of Peter Broughton, Esq. of Lowdham, Notts, and grandson of Thomas Broughton,* Esq. of Broughton Hall, co. Stafford, and Lowdham, was father of

PETER BROUGHTON, Esq. of Lowdham, Notts, who m. Eleanor Church, youngest dau. and co-heiress of William Church, Esq. of Tunstall Hall, Shropshire, and by her had,

THE REV. PETER BROUGHTON, of Tunstall Hall, Shropshire, and Lowdham, co. Notts, who m. in 1785, Jane, dau. of John Alcock, Esq. of Market Drayton, and had issue,

PETER, the present representative of the family.
Emma, m. to William Charleton, Esq. of Chilwell Hall, co. Notts. She d. in May, 1818, leaving two sons and one dau.

Mr. Broughton, rector of East Bridgeford, co. Notts, d. 17 July, 1827, aged 82.

Arms—Arg., two bars, gu.; on a canton, of the second, a cross, of the field.
Crest—A sea-dog's head, gu., eared and finned, arg.
Seat—Tunstall Hall, Shropshire.

BROWN OF JARROW HALL.

BROWN, THOMAS-DREWETT, Esq. of Jarrow Hall, co. Durham, barrister-at-law, b. 2 June, 1807; m. 3 March, 1836, Isabella, eldest dau. of Sir William Chaytor, Bart., and has issue,

DREWETT-ORMONDE, b. 1 June, 1838.

Lineage.—THOMAS BROWN, Esq. eldest son of THOMAS BROWN, who was drowned at sea, m. Lydia Pearce, of Broadstairs, Kent, and left, with two younger sons, Robert and John, an elder son,

THOMAS BROWN, who m. twice; by his 2nd wife, Susanna, dau. and heir of Peter Drewett, Esq. of Colerne, Wilts, he left at his decease, 19 Feb. 1841,

THOMAS-DREWETT, of Jarrow Hall.
Frederick-William, of New Grove, co. Middlesex.
Lydia Frances, m. John-C. Chaytor, son of Sir William Chaytor, Bart.
Marguretta-Anne, m. to George Lee, Esq. of Garratt House, co. Surrey.
Simmonette-Susan, m. to C. Reynolds, Esq. of Carshalton House, co. Surrey.

Arms—Arg., a fesse, between three mullets, sa.
Crest—A stork's head, couped at the neck, nowed, ppr., between two wings, arg.
Seat—Jarrow Hall, co. Durham.

BROWN OF BEILBY GRANGE.

BROWN, WILLIAM, Esq. of Beilby Grange, co. York, and of Richmond Hill, co. Lancaster, b. 4 May, 1784, M.P.; m. 1 Jan. 1810, Sarah, dau. of Andrew Gihon, of Ballymena, co. Antrim, J.P., and has issue,

I. ALEXANDER, (HON.) M.A. Oxon, J.P., b. 13 July, 1815; m. at New York, 19 Dec. 1838, his cousin, Sarah, dau. of James Brown, Esq., and d. in 1850, leaving one dau., Sarah, and three sons, William-Richmond, b. 16 Jan. 1840; James; and Alexander.

* Thomas Broughton's eldest son was created a Baronet in 1660.

I. Grace, m. 16 Nov. 1831, to John Hargreaves, Esq. of Broad Oak, and Hall Barn, Bucks, and d. leaving issue.

Lineage.—WILLIAM BROWN, of the co. of Antrim, had three sons,

JOHN, of the city of London, insurance broker, d. leaving two children, a son and dau., who both have families.
ALEXANDER, of whom presently.
Stewart, of Baltimore, merchant, who m. twice, and had issue by both wives.

The 2nd son,

ALEXANDER BROWN, b. at Ballymena, leaving his native country towards the close of the year 1800, settled as a general merchant at Baltimore, in Maryland, and associated with him his four sons, whom he had sent to England to be educated. Mr. Brown m. 17 June, 1783, Grace, dau. of John Davison, Esq., and had issue,

I. WILLIAM, now of Beilby Grange.
II. George, b. 17 April, 1787, now residing in Baltimore, m. 17 Dec. 1818, Isabella Maclanigan, and has issue,
1 Alexander-Davison, b. 30 May, 1823.
2 George-Stewart, b. 7 May, 1834.
1 Grace-Ann. 2 Isabella. 3 Elizabeth-Johnston.
III. John-A., of Philadelphia, b. 21 May, 1788, m. 1st, Isabella Patrick, and has issue,
1 Alexander, b. 13 July, 1815.
Mr. John-A. Brown m. 2ndly, 9 Sept. 1823, Miss Grace Brown, and has by her a dau.,
1 Ellen.
IV. James, of New York, b. 4 Feb. 1791, m. Louisa Kirkland, and has issue,
1 James-Alexander, b. 28 July, 1823.
2 William-Benedict, b. 23 April, 1825.
1 Sarah, m. in 1838, to her cousin, Alexander Brown, Esq.
2 Grace-Davison. 3 Mary-Louisa. 4 Margaret.
Mr. James Brown m. 2ndly, 14 Sept. 1831, Maria Coe, and has by her,
1 George-Hunter, b. 9 Jan. 1835.
2 John-Crosby, b. 22 May, 1838.
3 Clarance, b. 7 May, 1840. 1 Maria.

Mr. Brown d. at Baltimore, 6 April, 1834.

Arms—Gu., a chevron, or, between two lion's gambs, in chief, arg., and four hands conjoined, in base, of the second; on a chief, engrailed, gold, an eagle, displayed, sa.
Crest—A lion's gamb, erect, and erased, arg., holding a hand, ppr.
Motto—Est concordia fratrum.
Seats—Richmond Hill, near Liverpool; and Beilby Grange, near Hetherby, Yorkshire.

BROWN OF HAREHILLS GROVE.

BROWN, JAMES, Esq. of Harehills Grove, co. York, b. 12 April, 1814.

Lineage.—JAMES BROWN, Esq., an eminent merchant at Leeds, m. 17 Oct. 1785, Anne, only dau. and heiress of Samuel Williams, Esq. of the same place, and had two sons, namely,

I. JAMES, his heir.
II. William - Williams, of Allerton Hall, near Leeds, a banker in Leeds and London, a magistrate and deputy-lieutenant for the West Riding of Yorkshire, b. 10 Feb. 1788, m. 23 Nov. 1812, Margaret-Brockden, only child of Isaac Duncan, of Philadelphia, in the United States, and by her, who d. 23 May, 1820, had one son and two daus., viz.,
1 Samuel - James, b. 25 Oct. 1814, m. 1 June, 1841, Jacobina - Maria - Sophia, eldest dau. of Sir Joseph Radcliffe, Bart.
1 Ann-Williams, m. to Thomas Benyon, Esq. of Gledhow Hall, near Leeds, and d. 18 Feb. 1852.
2 Margaret-Duncan, m. 10 Feb. 1842, to Lieut.-Col. Dunn, Royal Artillery.

Mr. Brown d. in 1813, and was s. by his elder son,

JAMES BROWN, Esq. of Harehills Grove, J.P. and D.L. West Riding of Yorkshire; b. 25 Sept. 1786; m. 10 June, 1811, Charlotte, 3rd dau. of Matthew Rhodes, Esq. of Campfield, near Leeds, and had issue,

JAMES, of Trinity College, Cambridge, now of Harehills Grove.
Charlotte-Anne, m. 11 June, 1833, to Richard Shuttleworth Streatfeild, Esq. of The Rocks, in Sussex.
Mary, m. 3 Aug. 1841, to Thomas Shiffner, Esq., youngest son of Sir George Shiffner, Bart.
Anne - Rhodes - Williams, m. 14 Sept. 1837, to James-Williams Scarlett, Esq., only surviving son of Sir William-A. Scarlett, Knt., late chief justice of Jamaica.

Arms—Arg., on a bend, sa., cotised, az., between two six-pointed mullets, pierced, sa., three lions, rampant, of the field; quartering WILLIAMS.
Crest—A demi-lion, rampant, or, between two elephants' trunks, ppr.
Motto—Persevera Deoque confide.
Seat—Harehills Grove, near Leeds.

BROWN OF CLONBOY.

BROWN, JOHN, Esq. of Clonboy, co. Clare, J.P., b. 23 Jan. 1802; m. 25 Aug. 1826, Mary-Charlotte, eldest dau. of Thomas Lidwill, Esq. of Clonmore, and has issue,

I. JOHN, b. 19 Sept. 1827, m. 1854, Miss Harriet-Vereker Westropp, of the Attyflin family.
II. Robert-Lidwill, b. 8 Aug. 1837.
III. William, b. 13 Oct. 1839.
IV. George, b. 25 March, 1841.
I. Mary-Atkins. II. Isma-Helen.
III. Constance-Margaret.

Lineage.—THE REV. JOHN BROWN, of ancient Scotch descent, was of Danesfort, and Mount Brown, co. Limerick. He m. in 1752, Meliora, dau. of the Hon. Col. Southwell, brother of Viscount Southwell, and had issue, two sons, HENRY, his heir, and John-Southwell, who inherited Mount Brown, and was ancestor of the family now residing there; and four daus., of whom Mary m. Robert Peppard, Esq. of Cappagh, co. Limerick; Phœbe, m. 1st, John Finch, Esq., a younger son of Finch of Kilcoleman, co. Tipperary, and 2ndly, George Hewson, Esq.; and the youngest, Frances, m. Michael Cantillon, Esq. of co. Limerick. The eldest son and heir,

HENRY BROWN, Esq. of Danesfort, and of Clonboy, co. Clare, and at one period of Richfield, m. in 1782, Sarah, dau. and heiress of Richard Pierce, Esq. of Liskmagry, co. Limerick (of a family originally from Wilts and Berkshire), and had issue,

JOHN, of Bridgetown (Clonboy,) captain in the Limerick militia, m. in 1801, Constance, 2nd dau. of Col. William Odell, of The Grove, co. Limerick, M.P. for the city of Limerick for thirty years, and a lord of the Treasury, and d. *vitâ patris*, leaving issue,
JOHN, present representative.
William, m. Mildred, dau. of Thomas Odell, Esq. of Fort William, co. Limerick, and d. leaving issue.
Henry, m. Sarah, dau. of Major Odell, of The Grove, co. Limerick, and has issue.
Thomas-Antony Southwell, who m. in 1836, Isma-Cowley, 4th dau. of Thomas Lidwill, Esq. of Clonmore, and has issue.
Richard Pierce, deceased.
Aphra, m. to William Scanlan, Esq. barrister-at-law.
Sarah, m. 1st March, 1834, to Hugh Scanlan, Esq.
Frances, m. to the Rev. Richard Maunsell, of Milford.
Phœbe, m. to William Odell, Esq.
Emily, m. to Matthew Scanlan, Esq.
Henry. Edward. Pierse.
William. Francis.
Meliora, m. to — Odell, Esq., co. Limerick.
Sarah. Anna. Catherine.

Mr. Brown d. in 1838.

Arms—Gu., on a chevron, between three fleurs-de lis, or, a thistle, ppr.
Crest—An eagle, displayed.
Motto—Virtus dabit, cura servabit.
Seat—Clonboy, co. Clare.

BROWNE OF MORLEY HOUSE.

GRAVER-BROWNE, JOHN-TURNER, Esq. of Morley House, co. Norfolk, m. Frances, dau. (by Frances his wife, youngest dau. of John Mackenzie, Esq. of Strathgarne, in Rosshire) of the late Ven. Henry Bathurst, archdeacon of Norwich, sister of Colonel Bathurst, 3rd Fusilier-guards, and granddau. of the late Bishop Bathurst, and by this lady has issue,

I. JOHN-BATHURST.
I. Frances-Henrietta. II. Anna. III. Cecilia.
IV. Grace-Emily. V. Laura-Adeline.

This gentleman, J.P. for Norfolk, is son of the late George Graver, Esq. of Wymondham, co. Norfolk, and Elizabeth his wife, dau. of Richard Dewing, Esq. of Carbrooke. He inherited his estates on the decease of his godfather, John Browne, Esq. of Tacolnestone, Norfolk, in 1813, and assumed the additional surname of BROWNE.

Arms—BROWNE and GRAVER.
Crests—BROWNE and GRAVER.
Motto—Sur espérance.
Seat—Morley House, near Wymondham, Norfolk.

BROWNE OF JANEVILLE.

BROWNE, PETER-RUTLEDGE-MONTAGUE, Esq. of Janeville, co. Down, J.P. and D.L., capt. half-pay 9th foot, *b.* 5 March, 1796; *m.* 7 July, 1830, Mary-Jane, only child and heiress of the late Thomas-Typping Smythe, Esq., J.P., major of the North Down militia, and has issue,

I. ANDREW-SMYTHE MONTAGUE, *b.* 12 June, 1836.
II. William-Henry-Seymour-Montague, *b.* 7 Nov. 1839.
I. Mary-Montague. II. Belinda-Anna.
III. Emma-Matilda.

Captain Montague Browne served in Spain, France, Canada, and on the staff in the West Indies.

Lineage.—This family claims to be a branch of the ancient and noble line of Browne, Lords Montague. The grandfather of the present Capt. Browne,

JOHN BROWNE, Esq., barrister-at-law, son of John BROWNE, Esq., a landed proprietor in both England and Ireland, by his wife, a dau. of the Blake family, held some important official situation in the colonies. He *m.* Miss Henderson, a lady of ancient descent in Fifeshire, and had a son,

PETER BROWNE, Esq., M.D., of Westport, co. Mayo, an eminent physician, who *m.* in 1777, Anna, dau. of Andrew Craufurd, Esq., capt. of dragoons in Marlborough's army, wounded at the battle of Blenheim, and by her, who *d.* in 1816, he left at his decease, in Dec. 1797, four sons and one dau., viz.,

ANDREW, inspector-gen. army medical department, *m.* but has no issue.
James, an officer in the army, *d.* in 1805.
William-Henry, also an officer in the army, *d.* in 1807.
PETER-RUTLEDGE-MONTAGUE, now of Janeville.
Belinda, who *m.* in 1806, James Burke, Esq. of Richmond, co. Galway, and *d.* in 1819, leaving two sons and three daus.

Arms—Sa., three lions, passant, in bend, between two double cotises, arg.; a crescent for difference.
Crest—An eagle displayed, vert.
Motto—Suivez la raison.
Seat—Janeville, near Killough, Downshire.

BROWNE OF BRONWYLFA.

BROWNE, LIEUT.-GEN. SIR THOMAS-HENRY, Knt., K.C.H. of Bronwylfa, co. Flint, J.P. and D.L., high-sheriff in 1830, *b.* 8 Sept. 1787; *m.* 13 March, 1828, Elizabeth, dau. of the Rev. Ralph-H. Brandling, of Gosforth House, near Newcastle-on-Tyne, and has issue,

I. HENRY-RALPH, capt. in the 9th regt., *b.* 29 Dec. 1828.
II. Ralph-Charles, lieut. 71st regt., *b.* 18 Feb. 1830.

Sir Thomas-Henry Browne is a lieut.-gen. in the army, colonel of the 80th foot, and Military Knight Commander of the Guelphic Order. This distinguished officer served at the siege of Copenhagen, in America, at the capture of Martinique, and in Portugal, Spain, and France; he was present at the battles of Salamanca, Vittoria, the Pyrenees, Nive, Nivelle, Orthes, Toulouse, &c.

Lineage.—GEORGE BROWNE, Esq., Imperial and Tuscan Consul at Liverpool, son of George Browne, Esq., late of Passage, co. Cork, and Mary his wife, dau. of John Cotter, Esq., *m.* in 1786, Felicity, dau. of the late Benedict-Paul Wagner, Esq. of North Hall, near Wigan, co. Lancaster, Imperial and Tuscan consul-general in Liverpool, by his wife Elizabeth Haydock, of Rivington, in the same shire, and had issue,

THOMAS-HENRY, the present possessor of Bronwylfa.
George-Baxter, lieut.-col. in the army, one of the Commissioners of Police in Ireland, *m.* Harriet-Anne, eldest dau. of the late Martin Whish, Esq., chairman of the Board of Commissioners of Excise.
FELICIA-DOROTHEA, *b.* 25 Sept. 1793, *m.* in 1812, to Capt. Hemans, of the 4th regiment of infantry, and *d.* in 1835. This lady was the celebrated poetess.
Harriet-Mary, *m.* to the Rev. W. H. Owen, vicar of the cathedral church of St. Asaph.

Arms—Sa., three lions, passant, in bend, between two double cotises, arg.
Crest—An eagle displayed, vert.
Motto—Spectemur agendo.
Seat—Bronwylfa, near St. Asaph, co. Flint.

BROWNE OF BROWNE'S HILL.

BROWNE, ROBERT-CLAYTON, Esq. of Browne's Hill, co. Carlow, J.P. and D.L., high-sheriff in 1831, *b.* 28 Jan. 1799; *m.* 28 Oct. 1834, Harriette-Augusta, 3rd dau. of the late Hans Hamilton, Esq., many years M.P. for the county of Dublin, and has issue,

I. WILLIAM-CLAYTON, *b.* 20 Nov. 1835.
II. Charles-Henry, *b.* 13 Nov. 1836.
III. Robert-Clayton, *b.* 8 May, 1838.
I. Annette-Caroline.

Lineage.—This family of Browne was originally established in England; and derives from the branch seated since the year 1422, at Rokewoode and Weald Hall, Essex.

ROBERT BROWNE, younger son of John, (who was 2nd son of John Browne, Esq. of Wickham, co. Bucks, and Weald, co. Essex) by Margaret his wife, dau. and co-heir of Thomas D'Arcy, of Tolleshunt D'Arcy, co. Essex, Esq., went to Ireland in the parliamentary army, attached to Col. Henry Prittie's regiment, during the civil war in 1650, and settled at Carlow soon after that period, about 1654. He *d.* in 1677, leaving, by Jane his wife, two sons, William, the younger, and

JOHN BROWNE, Esq., the elder, who *s.* his father. He *m.* about 1680, Mary, dau. of Robert Jennings, Esq. of Kilkea Castle, co. Kildare, of the family of JENNINGS *of Selden*, co. York. Their son and successor,

WILLIAM BROWNE, Esq. of Browne's Hill, *m.* Elizabeth, dau. of Dr. Clayton, dean of Derry, and sister to the learned Robert Clayton, bishop of Clogher. By this lady, who descended from the family of that name of Adlington Hall, co. Lancaster, he had, John, *d. unm.*; ROBERT, successor to his father; Anne, *m.* to the Right Rev. Thomas Bernard, D.D., Bishop of Limerick; Catherine, *m.* to the Rev. Abraham Symes; Mary, *m.* to Peter Gale, Esq. of Ashfield, Queen's County; and Juliana, *m.* to Thomas Cooper, Esq. of Newstown, co. Carlow. Mr. Browne *d.* in 1772, aged 88, and was *s.* by his son,

ROBERT BROWNE, Esq. of Browne's Hill, who *m.* 27 March, 1762, Eleanor, dau. of Redmond Morres, Esq., M.P. for Dublin, and had issue,

WILLIAM, his heir.
Redmond, col. in the army, *d. unm.*
Robert, a lieut.-gen. in the army, *m.* in 1804, Harriet, only dau. and heir of Sir Richard Clayton, of Adlington Hall, co. Lancaster, Bart., and on succeeding in right of his wife to the Adlington Hall estates, assumed the additional surname of CLAYTON. He *d.* in 1845, leaving issue a son, RICHARD-CLAYTON BROWNE-CLAYTON, Esq. of Adlington Hall and Carrigbyrne; and a dau. Eleanor, *m.* to the Rev. James Daubeny.
John, in holy orders.
Elizabeth and Anne, both *d. unm.*

Mr. Browne *d.* in Jan. 1816, aged 87, and was *s.* by his eldest son,

WILLIAM BROWNE, Esq. of Browne's Hill, J.P., and custos rotulorum of the co. of Carlow, M.P. for Portarlington. He was *b.* in Jan. 1763, *m.* 1st, in 1793, the Lady Charlotte Bourke, dau. of Joseph Deane, 3rd Earl of Mayo and Archbishop of Tuam, and by her (who *d.* in 1806) had issue,

ROBERT-CLAYTON, present representative.
Joseph-Deane, late capt. in the carabineers, *m.* Miss Thursby.
Elizabeth, *m.* to Sir Wheeler-Denny Cuffe, Bart., of Lyrath, co. Kilkenny, who *d.* in 1853.
Eleanor-Mary, *m.* to William-FitzWilliam Burton, Esq. of Burton Hall, co. Carlow, who *d.* in 1844.
Charlotte, *m.* to William Brownlow, Esq. of Knapton, Queen's County.
Annette, *m.* in 1826, to the Hon. and Ven. Henry Scott Stopford, archdeacon of Leighton, and *d.* in March, 1842.

He *m.* 2ndly, in 1815, the Lady Letitia Toler, dau. of John, 1st Earl of Norbury, lord chief justice of the Common Pleas in Ireland, by his wife, Grace Graham, Baroness of Norwood, and by this lady had issue,

John-Toler.
William-Raymond, capt. 7th fusiliers.
Hector-Graham.
Grace-Isabella, *m.* to Godfrey Bosanquet, Esq.

Mr Browne, high-sheriff of the co. of Carlow, in 1794, *d.* 1 April, 1840.

Arms—Gu., a chevron, between three lion's gambs, erect and erased, arg.; a bordure of the second; on a chief of the same, an eagle, displayed, sa., armed and crowned, or, quartering CLAYTON: arg, a cross, engrailed, sa.; between four torteaux.
Crest—The eagle of Sicily, displayed, with two heads, sa.
Motto—Fortiter et fideliter.
Seat—Browne's Hill, co. Carlow.

BROWNE OF KILSKEAGH.

Browne, Robert, Esq. of Kilskeagh, co. Galway, Ranger of the Curragh, *m.* Harriet, dau. of William-S. Dempster, Esq. of Skibo, co. Sutherland, and has issue,

I. Robert-John.
I. Charlotte. II. Harriet-Margaret.
III. Emily. IV. Rosa.

Lineage.—For the earlier pedigree, see Browne *of Moyne.*

Oliver Browne, eldest son of Dominick FitzWilliam-Browne, (who *d.* in 1596) served as sheriff of Galway in 1593, and as mayor in 1609. His eldest son,

Martin Browne, of Coolarn, a stanch adherent of royalty, had his property confiscated, including the splendid mansion he had erected in Galway. He left two sons, Oliver, and Dominick (Sir), Knt. The elder,

Captain Oliver Browne, of Coolarn, had, at the Restoration, a re-grant of a portion of his father's lands. He *d.* in 1686, leaving, with daus., one of whom, Elizabeth, *m.* Marcus Lynch, of Barna, three sons; of whom the eldest,

Martin Browne, Esq. of Coolarn, *m.* a dau. of Geoffrey Browne, Esq. of Castle McGarrett, co. Mayo, and had issue, Robert, his heir; Anthony; and several daus., one of whom *m.* 1717, John Bodkin, Esq. of Annagh. The elder son,

Robert Browne, Esq. of Coolarn, *m.* and had issue, Martin, of Coolarn, who *d. s. p. m.*; Dominick; and a dau., *m.* to Blake of Moorefield. The 2nd son,

Dominick Browne, Esq. of Kilskeagh, became eventually head of the family: he *m.* Emily, dau. of the Hon. John Browne, of Elm Hall, and had issue,

Robert, now of Kilskeagh.
John-William, of Mount Kelly.
Henry, resident in America. George, deceased.
Maria, *m.* to Edmund Peel, Esq. of Bonchurch, Isle of Wight, late of the 49th regt.

Arms—Quarterly: 1st and 4th, sa., three lions, passant, in bend, between two double cotises, arg.; 2nd and 3rd, arg., an eagle displayed, with two heads, sa.
Crest—An eagle displayed.
Motto—Suivez raison.
Seat—Kilskeagh, co. Galway.

BROWNE OF MOUNT KELLY.

Browne, John-William, Esq. of Mount Kelly, co. Galway, J.P., *m.* in Oct. 1832, Mary-Sophia, dau. of Nathaniel Cavenagh, Esq. of Bath, which lady *d. s. p.* 20 Aug. 1846. Mr. Browne is 2nd son of Dominick Browne, Esq. of Kilskeagh, co. Galway, J.P., by Emily his wife, eldest dau. of the Hon. John Browne, of Elm Hall, co. Mayo, youngest son of the 1st Earl of Altamont, ancestor of the Marquess of Sligo.

Arms—Sa., three lions, passant, in bend, arg., between two double cotises, of the last.
Crest—An eagle, displayed. *Motto*—Suivez la raison.
Seat—Mount Kelly, Barony of Ballymoe, co. Galway.

BROWNE OF MOYNE.

Browne, Michael-Joseph, Esq. of Moyne, Galway, J.P., high-sheriff in 1847.

Lineage.—This name Le Brun (afterwards Browne), stands 50th on the Battle Abbey Roll.

Sir Stephen Le Brun, eldest son of Sir Hugh Le Brun, one of the Lords of the Marches of Wales, *m.* Eva, sister to Griffith, Prince of Wales: he and his sons supported Stephen, against the Empress Matilda, after the death of that monarch.

Hugh Le Brun, eldest son of Sir Stephen, having rendered some important services to Henry II., on his invasion of Wales, was permitted by that monarch to inherit his father's manors: his younger brothers, Sir Philip and Sir William Le Brun, having been more distinguished in the civil wars in fighting against Henry, were not so easily forgiven; they joined their relatives in invading Ireland, and thus escaped Henry's resentment, and acquired extensive possessions in the invaded country.

Sir Philip's descendants became proprietors of many manors in the county of Wexford, in the affairs of which they took a distinguished part. Lawrence Browne, 2nd son of Nicholas, of Mulrankan Castle, was elected by the burgesses of Wexford, to represent them in the parliament assembled at Westminster, 1376. It appears by an inquisition, taken at Wexford, 30 Jan. 1665, that this ancient castle, and several manors, were confiscated under the pretence that William Browne, of Mulrankan, "an Irish papist," joined in the rebellion of 1641.

Sir William FitzStephen, youngest brother of Sir Philip Le Brun, held a command in the army that proceeded against Dublin, then in the possession of the Danes. Subsequent to its surrender, he settled in the county of Dublin: his descendants became seated at Clondalkin, one of whom, Fromond Le Brun, was chancellor of Ireland, 1259. The extensive estates of Fromond's descendants passed into the hands of the Barnwell family, on the marriage of Lady Anne Brun to Lord Kingsland, 1488.

Walter Le Brun, youngest son of Sir William FitzStephen, was father of

Stephen Le Brun, who had two sons,

Stephen FitzStephen, who became proprietor of Kilpatrick, in the county Meath, and

Sir David Le Brun or Browne, contemporary, and a companion in arms of the Red Earl of Ulster, with whom he was nearly connected by marriage; he was a distinguished warrior, and obtained extensive possessions, particularly near Athenry, then the capital of the Anglo-Norman settlers in Connaught. He *d.* 1303, on his acquired property, which up to the present day is known as "David's Castle." He was *s.* by his eldest son,

Stephen FitzDavid, who by his bravery at the battle of Athenry, 1316, added considerably to his possessions; he *m.* Catherine de Bermingham, dau. of Lord Athenry, by whom he had four sons, with daus.; Henry, his heir, of Bally David; John, of Stradbally; Robert; and William.

Henry FitzStephen, eldest son, joined his relatives, the Berminghams, in the civil wars between the Anglo-Irish nobles, and subsequently accompanied the Earl of Kildare to France, where he joined the forces of Edward III., and distinguished himself. On his return, he *m.* Christian, dau. of Sir Ambrose Browne, of Kent, by whom he had, with other issue,

Philip FitzHenry, his heir, who *m.* Sily, dau. of Walter Blake, eldest son of Richard Caddle, *alias* Blake, sheriff of Connaught, 1306. Philip was killed while still young, in an encounter with the natives, and was *s.* by his eldest son,

Thomas FitzPhilip: he *m.* Kate, dau. of John Bowdekine, provost of Athenry (ancestor of Robert Bodkin, of Annagh, and John Bodkin, of Quarrymount, late M.P. for the county Galway).

By a deed in the 49th Edward III., between Thomas FitzPhilip, and his son-in-law, John Browne, son of John, the younger, it appears that at that early period, several branches of the Browne family were proprietors in Connaught: he had a numerous family, and was *s.* by his son,

Henry Browne FitzThomas, of Aith-an-Ree, who acquired large tracts of land with his wife, Sheela, dau. of Donald Mullally: he was slain 1309, and was *s.* by his son,

Thomas Browne, who *m.* Mabel, dau. of William Browne, provost of Athenry, 7th Henry V. Another dau. of this William was *m.* to John Browne, son of Stephen Browne, mayor of London, who was distinguished for his patriotism and benevolence. This John settled in Ireland, and had a son named Eustace, from whom another branch of the Browne family claims descent.

John Browne, eldest son of Thomas, *m.* Mary, dau. of Walter Ffrench, mayor of Galway, 1445, and had a son and heir,

William Browne, who *m.* Mary Athy, whose ancestor was one of the earliest Anglo-Normans that settled in Galway: it is stated that the Athys erected the first stone house in that ancient city, of which many of them filled the offices of sheriff and mayor.

John Browne, eldest son of William, *m.* Honor de Burgo. He joined William de Burgo and others, who rose against the oppression of the English government, but fell with many other leaders of that party, at the battle of Knock-a-tuath, after which Athenry and Galway surrendered, when his son,

Stephen Browne, who had *m.* Eveline, dau. of Geoffrey Lynch, mayor of Galway, 1487, *s.* to the property. He had, with a dau., six sons, Andrew, who *d.* while mayor of Galway, 1574; William; John; James; Patrick; and Nicholas, four of whom were admitted to the freedom of Galway in 1539-40, and came to reside on their properties in and about Galway.

WILLIAM BROWNE, of Galway, 2nd son of Stephen, m. Annastasia, dau. of Valentine Blake, by his wife, Evelina ffrench, dau. of Geoffrey ffrench, by whom he had, Andrew, of Glones; Dominick, of Barna; Richard; and Thomas.

DOMINICK BROWNE, of Barna, served as mayor of Galway in 1575. He took a leading part in the affairs of Galway; and, with other chieftains, was a party to the composition which they entered into, in 1585, with Sir John Perrot, on the part of QUEEN ELIZABETH, for their properties in Connaught. He m. a dau. of Sir Morrogh O'Flaherty, by whom he had (with a dau., Jane, m. to Alderman Patrick Kirwan, ancestor of the KIRWANS *of Cregg*) a numerous family of seven sons, from whom most of the present Galway families of Browne are descended. He d. at an advanced age in 1596, and was buried in the family tomb at the Franciscan Abbey, Galway. His sons were,

OLIVER, ancestor of the Coolarn line (*which see*).
EDWARD, went to Germany: a son of his, Colonel Browne, in the service of the Duke of Lorraine, was to have commanded two thousand of the troops that prince proposed sending to aid CHARLES.
Geoffrey, father of Sir Dominick, ancestor to Lord Oranmore.
Marcus, ancestor of the BROWNES *of Annaghmore*, now extinct.
Thomas, from whom the families of Newtown, Ardskea, and Coeloo, are descended.
James, had four sons, Peter-FitzJames, sheriff of Galway, 1647; Thomas; Nicholas FitzJames, who was father of Michael, ancestor to the present John-Francis Browne, of Tuam. These three were proprietors in and about Galway, while Patrick, the 4th son, joined his relatives in foreign service.
ANDREW, of whose descendants we treat.

This

ALDERMAN ANDREW BROWNE FITZDOMINICK, was the founder of the family of Cloonkeely and Moyne. He m. a sister to Sir Henry Lynch, of Carrindulla and Castle-Carra, co. Mayo; and had (with a dau., Mary, m. to Ambrose Bodkin, of Annagh) three sons. Andrew was one of the independent jurors who found against the iniquitous claims of the crown, brought forward by Lord Wentworth. For this he suffered in common with his brother jurors, and was attainted. Andrew d. in 1647, leaving his three sons then alive, viz.,

I. FRANCIS, who had been educated on the continent, and was then in foreign service, returned to Ireland: he commanded troops at the sieges of Limerick and Galway. On the surrender of the latter town in 1652, Francis left the country, to which he returned on the Restoration; but he, in 1664, assigned to his brothers the comparatively small portions of his inheritance which had been recovered, and rejoined his companions in arms on the continent.
II. Dominick, m. his cousin Catherine, dau. of Sir Henry Lynch. He and his relative Geoffrey Browne, who m. Mary Lynch, sister to his wife, took an active part in the affairs of the confederate Catholics, particularly in defending their native town, Galway, which was the last of the towns in the United Kingdom that surrendered to the republican army. Dominick, as well as his brothers, got some grants on the Restoration, which he left to Edward, his only son, who entered the Spanish service, where he became a distinguished officer.
III. JOHN.

The 3rd son,

JOHN BROWNE, took an active part in opposing CROMWELL, for which he suffered during the Commonwealth; and on the restoration of CHARLES, he and his brothers recovered but a small portion of their inheritance. John m. in 1663, Angelina, dau. of Francis Athy, by whom he had two sons, Francis and Anthony. In 1664, John's eldest brother, Francis, whom we have mentioned before, determined on returning to foreign service; previous to which he settled most of his properties on his brothers, and appointed his younger brother, John, to manage the portion he reserved for himself in his absence. John d. while his sons were still young, leaving only his widow to protect their rights, in doing which she had many opponents to contend with. She succeeded in getting an additional grant. We find that Giles Athy, *alias* Browne, and Francis, her son, got a grant of Mullagh (the old name of Cloonkeely), 29 Feb. (22nd CHARLES II.), Francis being then a minor.

FRANCIS BROWNE joined the army of JAMES II., and is stated to have been killed in the wars, while defending Athlone, 1691. After his death, his mother went to reside with her only surviving son, Anthony, at Cloonkeely, hoping, by living in retirement, to escape further confiscation.

ANTHONY BROWNE, Esq., became the representative of this branch of the Brownes on the death of his elder brother, Francis; and heir to all that escaped confiscation of his father's, grandfather's, and uncle's estates; but these were small in comparison to what was confiscated. Anthony m. in 1695, his cousin, Annastasia, dau. of Nicholas Browne, of Newtown, and was s. by his eldest son,

JOHN BROWNE, Esq. of Cloonkeeloy and Moyne. He m. Julian, dau. of Michael Lynch, of Tubberoe, by whom he had an only son,

MICHAEL BROWNE, Esq. of Cloonkeely and Moyne, who m. in 1752, Mary, eldest dau. of Thomas Blake, Esq. of Mullaghmore and Windfield, and had, with John, his heir, Thomas, an officer in the East India service, killed while still young; and two daus., the elder, Julia, m. to Roderick McDermot, Esq. of Coolavin; and the younger, Anne, to John Browne, of Castlemoyle, in the county Galway, Esq.

JOHN BROWNE, Esq. of Moyne, J.P., eldest son of Michael, m. in 1790, Margaret, dau. of John Dolphin, of Turoe, by his wife, Eleanor Burke, of St. Clerans, dau. of John Burke, Esq. of St. Clerans, and had issue,

MICHAEL-JOSEPH BROWNE, Esq. now of Moyne.
Maria, m. in 1809, to the present Lord Ffrench, d. in 1827.
Anne.

Arms—Arg., an eagle, displayed, with two heads, sa.
Crest—A griffin's head, erased.
Motto—Fortiter et fideliter.
Seat—Moyne, Dangan, co. Galway.

BROWNE OF GREENVILLE AND TUAM

BROWNE, JOHN-FRANCIS, Esq. of Greenville and Tuam, co. Galway, J.P.

Lineage.—JAMES BROWNE, 6th son of Dominick Browne FitzWilliam, mayor of Galway, 1575, descended from Sir William Le Brun (for an account of whom and his ancestors, *see* BROWNE *of Moyne*), was the founder of this branch of the Browne family. His sons,

NICHOLAS FITZJAMES, and PETER FITZJAMES, sheriff of Galway, 1647, took an active part in the affairs of the confederate Catholics, particularly in defending their native town, Galway, which was the last town in the United Kingdom which surrendered to the parliamentary army.

It appears by returns then made, that Nicholas Browne FitzJames, and his son, Michael Browne, refused to sign the assent of capitulation; and we find in Cromwell's roll, 1657, the name of Nicholas-Browne FitzJames amongst those who had their property in the town of Galway confiscated. Michael Browne, to avoid further persecution on account of his religion, then went to live at Tuam.

After the restoration of CHARLES II., though named in the enrolment of the decrees of the Innocents, Michael Browne did not succeed in recovering his father's confiscated property. In the charter which JAMES II. granted to Tuam, and which he was active in procuring, Michael Browne appears second on the list of burgesses. His attachment to JAMES induced him, though advanced in life, to join the king's forces at Aughrim. After that battle, he retreated to Galway, and had the mortification of seeing his native town obliged to surrender a second time. Michael died soon after, and left by his wife, Julian Joyce, VALENTINE, his heir, and a dau., Mary, m. to James Browne, of Ardskea.

VALENTINE BROWNE succeeded to his father. He m. Mary, dau. to Valentine Blake, of Drum Castle, co. Galway, and was succeeded by his son,

JOHN FRANCIS BROWNE, Esq. of Tuam, who m. Anastasia Burke, of Newford, by whom he had,

I. JOHN-FRANCIS, present representative.
II. Valentine.
III. Thomas.

Arms—Arg., an eagle, displayed, with two heads, sa.
Crest—A griffin's head, erased.
Motto—Fortiter et fideliter.
Seat—Greenville, Mount Bellew Bridge, co. Galway.

BROWNE OF BROWNE HALL

BROWNE, JAMES-ARTHUR, Esq. of Browne Hall, co. Mayo, b. 30 April, 1810; m. 22 Jan. 1841, Emily-

Alice, 2nd dau. of Arthur Browne, Esq.* of Newtown, co. Roscommon, by Elizabeth his wife, dau. of the late Captain Clements, E.I.C.S., and has had issue,

I. Reginald-Llewellyn, b. 24 Aug. 1843; d. 17 Feb. 1848.
II. HANS-SLOANE-HUGHES, b. 12 Sept. 1853.
I. Augusta-Louisa. II. Alice-Laura.
III. Edith-Anne. IV. Florence.

Lineage.—The patents by which the lands of Browne Hall or Kilticulla are held were granted by King CHARLES I. to EDWARD BROWNE, one of the same family of Browne as that of Castle M'Garrett, represented by Lord Oranmore.

JACOB BROWNE, Esq. of Browne Hall, son of James Browne, by Margaret his wife, dau. of Richard Cox, Esq., m. Ellis, dau. of Dominick Browne, Esq. of Castlemacgarrett, grandfather of Dominick, Lord Oranmore, and was father of

JAMES BROWNE, Esq., of Browne Hall, who m. 8 May, 1774, Honoria, dau. of Josiah Shadwell, Esq. of Eyreville, co. Galway, and relict of John Donnellan, Esq. of Ballydonnellan, same county, and had issue,

DOMINICK, of Browne Hall.
Charles, b. 10 May, 1784, d. young.
Ellis, m. in July, 1797, to Christopher Ussher, Esq., since deceased. She d. in Sept. 1820, leaving issue.

The eldest son,

DOMINICK BROWNE, Esq. of Browne Hall, lieut.-colonel South Mayo militia, to which rank he was appointed in 1801, at the age of 28, and of which regiment Dominick Browne, Esq. of Castle M'Garrett, was at the time full colonel, m. in July, 1808, Augusta-Louisa, dau. of the Hon. Colonel Arthur Browne, M.P. for Mayo, 2nd son of the 1st Earl of Altamont, and by her (who d. in 1850) had issue,

JAMES-ARTHUR, his heir.
Dominick-Augustus, in holy orders, b. 24 April, 1811, m. in Nov. 1848, Lucy, only dau. of the late Mr. Lyle, of Armagh.
Arthur, b. 6 May, 1812.
Frederick-William, b. 1 April, 1814.
Henry-Augustus, b. 7 July, 1821.
Edward-Geoffrey, b. 14 Aug. 1824.
Louisa. Honorie, d. unm. 1845.
Laura, m. in March, 1853, to the O'Driscoll.

Arms—Arg., an eagle, displayed, with two heads, sa., langued, gu.
Crest—A griffin's head, erased, arg., langued, gu.
Motto—Fortiter et fideliter.
Seat—Browne Hall, co. Mayo.

BROWNE OF RAHEENS.

BROWNE, HUGH-JOHN-HENRY, Esq. of Raheens, co. Mayo, b. 6 Feb. 1800.

Lineage.—DODWELL BROWNE, Esq. of Raheens, brother of John, 1st Lord Kilmaine, and 3rd son of Sir John Browne, Bart., of The Neale, by Margaret, his 1st wife, dau. and co-heir of Henry Dodwell, Esq. of Athlone, m. Elizabeth, eldest sister and co-heir of James Cuff, Lord Tyrawley; and d. about the year 1796, leaving a son,

DODWELL BROWNE, Esq. of Raheens, lieut. R.N.; who m. Maria, dau. of Sir Neale O'Donnell, Bart. of Newport, and by her (who d. in 1809), had issue,

HUGH-JOHN-HENRY, now of Raheens.
Neal O'Donnell, who m. Sarah Labertouche.
Mary-Anne Moore, m. to Peter Digges La Touche, Esq.
Margaret-Elizabeth, m. to the Hon. Henry Caulfeild, of Hockley, co. Armagh, brother of the Earl of Charlemont.
Matilda-Dorcas, m. to Alexander Richey, Esq.
Louisa-Julia, m. to Dr. Benjamin Darley.
Maria, m. to Dr. Long.

Mr. Browne d. in Canada in 1819.

Arms—Sa., three lions, passant, in bend, between two double cotises, arg.
Crest—An eagle, displayed, vert.
Motto—Suivez raison.
Seat—Raheens, co. Mayo.

BROWNE OF BRAEFFEY.

BROWNE, DOMINICK-ANDREW, Esq. of Braeffey, co. Mayo, b. 30 June, 1824.

Lineage.—DOMINICK BROWNE, Esq. of Breafield, now Braeffey, co. Mayo (3rd son of Sir John Browne, 1st Bart. of The Neale, and brother of George, ancestor of the Barons Kilmaine, and John, ancestor of the Marquesses of Sligo), m. Barbara, dau. of Sir Henry Talbot, and niece of the Earl of Tyrconnell, and was father of ANDREW BROWNE, Esq. of Braeffey, whose son, by Eleanor his wife, dau. of Alexander Kerwan, Esq.,

DOMINICK BROWNE, Esq. of Braeffey, b. in 1701, m. Anne, dau. of Martin D'Arcy, Esq. of Houndswood, co. Mayo; and d. in 1776, leaving issue, ANDREW-NICHOLAS, his heir; and John-Edmond, created a Baronet of Ireland in 1797. The elder son,

ANDREW-NICHOLAS BROWNE, Esq. of Braeffey, who m. Mary Gilker, and had issue,

DOMINICK, major in the army, d. in 1808.
Edmund, lieut.-col., d. 18 April, 1838.
JOHN, of whom we treat.

The 3rd son,

LIEUT.-COL. JOHN BROWNE, of Braeffey, m. 2 Oct. 1823, Frances-Jane Hawthorn, and had issue,

I. DOMINICK-ANDREW, now of Braeffey.
II. Montague. III. Henry-John.
IV. Frederick-Augustus. V. Arthur-Wellesley-Wyndham.
VI. Edmund-Charles. VII. Augustus-Hawthorne.
I. Rose-Mary-Anne. II. Sarah-Jane.
III. Mary-Louisa.

Col. Browne d. 20 Nov. 1849.

Arms—Sa., three lions, passant, in bend, between two double cotises, arg.
Crest—An eagle, displayed.
Motto—Suivez raison.
Seat—Braeffey, Castlebar.

BROWNE OF CAUGHLEY.

BROWNE, THOMAS-WHITMORE WYLDE, Esq. of The Woodlands, co. Salop, J.P., b. Sept. 1800, m. Nov. 1821, Catherine, 2nd dau. of William Brouncker, Esq., and by her (who d. 1835,) has issue,

I. WILLIAM, b. March, 1823. II. Ralph, b. March, 1831.
III. Harry, b. Nov. 1833.
I. Catherine. II. Henrietta.
III. Agnes-Jane. IV. Mary-Anne.

Lineage.—This family has been one of influence in the county of Salop for several generations. RALPH BROWNE, Esq. of Caughley, was high-sheriff of Shropshire in 1687. EDWARD BROWNE, of Caughley, Esq., filled the same office in 1719; and RALPH-BROWNE WYLDE BROWNE, Esq. of Caughley, was high-sheriff in 1808. This gentleman, son of Thomas Wylde, Esq., by Elizabeth his wife, dau. and heir of Ralph Browne, Esq. of Caughley, took the additional surname and arms of BROWNE. He m. 1798, Mary-Anne, dau. of Thos. Whitmore, Esq. of Apley, and d. Dec. 1810, leaving issue, THOMAS-WHITMORE, now of The Woodlands; John-Edward; Mary-Anne; Jane, m. to Edward Finch, Esq.; and Elizabeth, m. to Sir Charles Williams, Knt.

Arms—Sa., three lions, passant, in bend, between two double cotises, arg.; a trefoil for difference.
Seat—The Woodlands, Salop.

BROWNE OF MONKTON FARLEIGH.

BROWNE, EDWARD-PENNEFATHER-WADE, Esq. of Monkton Farleigh, Wilts, b. 7 July, 1835.

Lineage.—WADE BROWNE, Esq. of Leeds, J.P. and D.L.; b. in 1760, son of John Browne, of Chapel Allerton, co. York, by the dau. and eventual heiress of John Wade, of Moortown, Esq., m. 1st, Rhoda, dau. of Jacob Smith, Esq. of Walsall (of the family of the SMYTHS *of Honington*, co. Worcester, who were settled there for the last two centuries), and had issue,

WADE, his heir, of Monkton Farleigh, who became also heir to his uncle, Joseph Smith, Esq. of Sion Hill, co. Worcester, and high-sheriff thereof.
Lydia, m. 1st, to Joseph Lea, Esq., and 2ndly, to John-Addenbrooke Addenbrooke, Esq.
Elizabeth.
Sarah, m. to the Rev. Charles-Collins Crump, rector of Halford, co. Worcester.

Mr. Brown m. 2ndly, Miss Elizabeth Jones, by whom he had a dau., Mary, wife of the Rev. William Farwell, rector of St. Austen's, Cornwall. He d. in Nov. 1821, and was s. by his only son,

WADE BROWNE, Esq., J.P. of Monckton Farleigh; b. 30 April, 1796; m. 23 June, 1831, Anne, eldest dau. of the

* Arthur Browne was son of John Browne, Esq., and Rosa-Mary, his wife, dau. of Admiral Sir Richard Hughes, under whom Lord Nelson served on the West India station. John Browne was eldest son of the Hon. Colonel Arthur Browne, M.P. for Mayo, 2nd son of the 1st Earl of Altamont.

Right Hon. Edward Pennefather, lord chief justice of the Queen's Bench in Ireland, and by her (who *d.* 29 Sept. 1837) had issue,

I. EDWARD-PENNEFATHER-WADE, now of Monkton Farleigh.
II. Cornwallis-Wade, *b.* 6 Sept. 1837.
I. Rhoda-Susan-Wade. II. Anne-Georgiana-Wade.

Mr. Wade Brown *d.* 2 Aug. 1851.

Arms—Quarterly: 1st and 4th, erm., a chevron, or, cotised, between three roses, gu., for BROWNE; 2nd, arg., a lion, passant-regardant, sa., for SMYTH; 3rd, az., on a bend, arg., three gillyflowers, ppr., for WADE.
Crest—A demi-eagle, displayed, or, surmounted by two palm branches in saltier, ppr.
Motto—Suivez raison.
Seat—Manor House, Monkton Farleigh, Bradford, Wilts.

BROWNE OF SALPERTON.

BROWNE, THOMAS-BEALE, Esq. of Salperton, co. Gloucester, and Cappagh White, co. Tipperary, J.P. for Gloucestershire, *b.* 6 Nov. 1810; *m.* 12 Aug. 1840, Mary-Eliza, 2nd dau. of George-James Sulivan, Esq. of Wilmington, near Ryde, and has issue,

I. JOHN, *b.* 8 May, 1841.
II. Thomas-Beale, *b.* 7 Oct. 1848.
III. George-Beale, *b.* 24 Aug. 1850.
I. Mary. II. Eliza. III. Ellen.

Lineage.—The family of BROWNE *of Gloucestershire* is of considerable antiquity, and long after its settlement at Norton, in that co., bore the Norman name of Le Brun. Its patriarch was one of the companions-in-arms of the CONQUEROR.

THOMAS BROWNE, Esq. of Salperton, son of the REV. JOHN BROWNE, rector of Coberley, co. Gloucester, by Mary his wife, was father (with a son, Thomas, who *d. unm.*, and a dau. Mary, *m.* to Edward Sampson, Esq. of Henbury) of an elder son,

JOHN BROWNE, Esq. of Salperton, who *m.* Mary, dau. and heiress of John Beale, Esq. of Temple Guiting, co. Gloucester, whose ancestors were there seated *temp.* STEPHEN, and had issue,

JOHN, of Salperton.
Thomas-Beale, *b.* 1 Dec. 1776, *d. unm.* 12 Jan. 1794.
Mary, *m.* to William-Gore Langton, Esq. of Newton Park, M.P. for co. Somerset, and has issue.

The eldest son,

JOHN BROWNE, Esq. of Salperton, J.P. and D.L., high-sheriff in 1801, *b.* 25 Aug. 1773, *m.* 2 Nov. 1793, Martha-Susanna, dau. of the Rev. John Pettat, rector of Stonehouse, by Martha his wife, eldest dau. of Sir Howe Hicks, Bart., and by her (who *d.* in 1843,) had issue,

John-Beale, *b.* 4 Nov. 1794, *d. unm.* 1823.
THOMAS-BEALE, now of Salperton.
Henrietta-Jane, *m.* Feb. 1826, to William Beach, Esq. of Oakley Hall, Hants, and *d.* 11 Aug. 1831, leaving issue.
Frances-Susanna.
Caroline-Anne, *m.* to her cousin, the Rev. Charles-Richard Pettat, rector of Ashe and Dean, co. Hants.

Mr. Browne *d.* in March, 1850.

Arms—Sa., three lions, passant, in bend, arg., between two double cotises, of the last.
Crest—An eagle, displayed, vert.
Seat—Salperton, co. Gloucester.

BROWNE OF TALLANTIRE HALL.

BROWNE, WILLIAM, Esq. of Tallantire Hall, co. Cumberland, J.P. and D.L., high-sheriff in 1817, *b.* 3 Dec. 1780; *m.* 11 Oct. 1803, Catherine, dau. of the late William Stewart, of Castle Stewart, co. Wigton, N. B., by his wife, the Hon. Euphemia Mackenzie, and has issue,

I. WILLIAM, *b.* 9 July, 1810, *m.* in 1847, Isabella Midford.
II. John-Stewart, *b.* 19 Oct. 1814.
I. Catherine. II. Jane-Euphemia.
III. Caroline, *m.* in 1833, to Lord Teignmouth.
IV. Harriette.

Lineage.—The family of Browne was settled at Woodhall, in the parish of Caldbeck, Cumberland, for many generations. WILLIAM BROWNE, Esq., *b.* 19 Sept. 1732, a younger son of William Browne, Esq. of Woodhall, and Orthwaite Hall, both in the co. Cumberland, purchased the lordships of Tallantire, Dovenby, and Papcastle, in the same co., and served as high-sheriff in the 30th GEORGE III. He *m.* 23 Sept. 1779, Mary, relict of Richard Lancaster, Esq., and *d.* in 1802, leaving a son, WILLIAM, the present possessor of the estate, and three daus., Mary-Dorothea, *m.* to John Pemberton, Esq. of Cherburn Hall, co. Durham; Elizabeth, *m.* to Capt. John Ponsonby, R.N.; and Isabella, *m.* to John Smith, Esq.

Arms—Arg., three martlets in pale, sa., between two flaunches, of the second, each charged with a lion, passant, or.
Crest—A griffin's head, vert, between two wings.
Motto—Traducere ævum leniter.
Seat—Tallantire Hall, Cockermouth, Cumberland.

BROWNE OF RATHBANE.

WILLIAM-BROWNE, THE REV. P., of Rathbane, co. Limerick, M.A. Trinity College, Dublin, incumbent of Blackrod, Bolton, Lancashire. This gentleman assumed, by royal license, dated 27 June, 1851, in obedience to the testamentary injunction of his father, the name of WILLIAM, in addition to the surname of BROWNE. Mr. William-Browne and his two sisters, Elizabeth and Jane-Catherine, are the only children of the late John Browne, Esq. of Rathbane, co. Limerick, and of Mountjoy Square, in the city of Dublin, by Catherine his wife, eldest dau. of Philip Walsh, Esq. of Fiddown, co. Kilkenny, descended from the ancient family of WALSH, and grand-children of James Browne, Esq. of Lurgan, co. Armagh, presumed to have sprung from a scion of the noble house of Browne.

Arms—Arg., three lions, passant, gu., between two bendlets, sa.
Crest—Rising from a marquess's coronet, ppr., an eagle, displayed, gu., winged and membered, or.
Motto—Suivez la raison.
Residence—Mountjoy Square, Dublin.

BRUCE OF KENNET.

BRUCE, ROBERT, Esq. of Kennet, co. Clackmannan, and Dunnogot, co. Perth, *b.* 8 Dec. 1795; *m.* 1st, 12 April, 1825, Anne, eldest dau. of the late William Murray, Esq. of Touchadam and Polmaise, in Stirlingshire, which lady *d. s. p.*; and 2ndly, 26 April, 1848, Jane-Hamilton, dau. of Sir James Fergusson, Bart. of Kilkerran, co. Ayr, and has by her,

I. ALEXANDER-HUGH, *b.* 13 Jan. 1849.
I. Henrietta-Anne.

This gentleman, formerly a captain in the Grenadier guards, and M.P. for the county, served in the Peninsula and at Waterloo.

Lineage.—ROBERT DE BRUS, a noble Norman knight, the first on record of this great and patriotic family, attending the CONQUEROR into England, was of such high estimation, that WILLIAM, after the victory at Hastings, commissioned him to subdue the northern parts of England. He first possessed the manor and castle of Skelton, in Yorkshire, and Hert and Hertness, in the bishopric of Durham; and soon increased his property in the former shire to such an extent, that before the end of the CONQUEROR'S reign, he had acquired no fewer than ninety-four lordships in that county.

The eldest branch of his descendants, the Lords of Skelton, expired, in the male line, with Peter de Brus, who *d.* without issue, *temp.* EDWARD I. From a younger son of Robert de Brus, son of the Norman knight, sprang the Scottish Bruces, the Bruces of Annandale, the progenitors of ROBERT BRUCE, King of Scotland. To his 2nd son,

THOMAS DE BRUYS, Sir Robert de Bruys, 2nd Baron of Clackmannan, granted the lands of Wester Kennet, Pitfolden, and Cruickitlands, in the shire of Clackmannan. The Laird of Kennet died *temp.* JAMES I. His great-great-great-grandson,

ROBERT BRUCE, of Kennet, served heir 13 June, 1556, *m.* a dau. of Andrew Kinninmont of that ilk, in Fifeshire, and had an only dau. and heiress,

MARGARET BRUCE, of Kennet, who *m.* Archibald Bruce, son of the deceased David Bruce, of Green, a younger son of Sir David Bruce, of Clackmannan, in 1506, and had a son,

Robert Bruce, of Kennet, served heir to his mother, 6 Feb. 1589. He *m.* in 1599, Elizabeth, dau. of Alexander Gall, of Maw, in Fifeshire, and left a son and successor,

Robert Bruce, of Kennet, who *m.* Agnes, dau. of Patrick Murray, of Perdowie, by Margaret Colville, his wife, dau. of Lord Colville, of Culross, and by her had issue,

I. David, his heir.

II. Alexander (the Rev.) had the estate of Gartlet, near Kennet, by charter from his father: *m.* Margaret, dau. of James Cleland, of Stonepath, co. Peebles, and by her, who died at Gartlet, in 1722, had a son (with two other sons, Alexander and David; as many daus., viz., Margaret, *d. unm.*, and Rachel, wife of John Cleland, whose dau. Margaret, was mother of the Rev. John Jamieson, D.D., F.R.S., author of the *Scottish Dictionary*, &c.) James, of Gartlet, chief judge of Barbadoes, who *m.* Keturah, dau. of Capt. Joseph French, and by her, who *d.* in London, 1775, left issue,

1 Joseph-Osborne Bruce, Esq. of Gartlet, a J.P., and for some time judge of the Court of Common Pleas, Barbadoes, *m.* Jane, dau. and heir of Lieut.-Gen. Samuel Barwick, Governor of Barbadoes, and by her had issue,

James-Conrade Bruce, *d. s. p. m.*

Samuel-La Roque (who left issue an only dau., Jane, wife of George Richards, Esq., who remarried, at her decease, a dau. of Samuel Hindes, Esq., president of the council at Barbadoes).

Barwick Bruce, who *m.* Amabel, dau. and co-heir of Nathaniel Walrond, Esq., and *d.* 1841, having had issue,

Alexander, major in the army, died in early life, and *unm.*

Samuel Barwick, M.D., a distinguished medical military officer, who served in America and the West Indies, the Peninsula, and at Waterloo; and *d.* in London in 1852, leaving, by Jane his wife, dau. of William Downing, Esq., two sons and two daus., viz., 1 William-Downing Bruce, of Lincoln's-inn, barrister-at-law, K.C.S., F.S.A., *m.* at Paris in 1847, Louisa-Emily, dau. of William Plomer, Esq. of Linbourne, N.B., J.P. and D.L., only son of Sir William Plomer, and brother of Lady Campbell, of Dunstaffnage Castle, Argyleshire; and by her has issue two sons and two daus., viz., Robert-Dalrymple-Barwick, William-Alexander-Beresford-Barwick, Laura-Elizabeth-Amabel-Walrond, Louisa-Emily-Keturah-French; 2 Robert-Cathcart Dalrymple, lieut. and adjt. 29th regt.; 1 Elizabeth-Jane; 2 Amabel-Emma.

Nathaniel French (the Rev.), D.D., *m.* at New York, Sarah-Eliza, dau. of Dr. Benton, and has, Alexander-Caleb, in holy orders; Edward-Livingston; Samuel-Barwick; Henry-Hobart; Stella-Eliza; Sarah-Barwick; Frances-La Roque; Mary-Jane-Walrond.

Frances-La Roque, *d. unm.* 1851.

Elizabeth-Keturah, *m.* James Beresford, Esq., an officer in the army, and *d.* in 1852.

Mary-Dalrymple, *m.* William-Watson Tudor, Esq., and has issue.

2 Robert, an officer in the 65th regt., *d. unm.*

3 Alexander, M.D., of Edinburgh, *m.* Dorothy, dau. of James Shephard, Esq., judge of the Court of Exchequer, Barbadoes, and by her, who *d.* in London, 1816, left issue,

Keturah Shephard, *m.* 1st, Capt. Devenish, R.N., (and had a son, James-Alexander, lieut. 53rd regt., killed at Salamanca, in Spain, 19 June, 1812, and a dau. Keturah, wife of Alexander-Grey Davison, Esq.) and 2ndly, William Murray, of the civil service, and had further issue, William; Alexander-Bruce; Dorothy-Bruce, wife of Samuel Harman, Esq., member of Her Majesty's Council in Antigua; and Elizabeth-Pilgrim, wife of Gen. S.-H. Berkeley, col. of the 75th regt., and commander-in-chief in the West Indies.

1 Elizabeth, *m.* James Straker, Esq., barrister-at-law, and left an only child, Marianne, *m.* to Col. Hew Dalrymple, major of the 49th regt., some time A.D.C. to the lord-lieutenant of Ireland, and grandson of Hew, Lord Drummore. (*See* Burke's *Peerage*: Stair.)

2 Keturah, wife of the Rev. John Pilgrim, M.A. of New Windsor, Berks, and *d. s. p.* at an advanced age in 1829.

David Bruce, of Kennet, who *m.* Margery, dau. of David Young, Esq. of Kirkton, in the co. of Fife, and had six sons and two daus., of whom the eldest son,

David Bruce, of Kennet, *d. unm.*, and was *s.* by his next surviving son,

James Bruce, of Kennet, who, in 1688, attended the Prince of Orange to England, in 1689 was appointed captain in the Earl of Leven's regiment of foot, and eventually, after serving many years with high reputation, attained the rank of brigadier-general. He wedded in 1690, Mary, dau. of Sir Alexander Swinton, of Mersington, one of the senators of the College of Justice, 2nd son of Sir Alexander Swinton, of that Ilk, and had (with three daus., Alice, *m.* to George Dundas, of Dundas; Mary; and Jean, *m.* to John Edgar, Esq.) four sons, Alexander, his heir; James, advocate before the Court of Session and master of the Mint, who *m.* and had children; William-Henry, captain R.N., who *m.* an English lady, but *d.* issueless; and John, a churchman, who *m.* Jean, dau. of James Bruce, of Powforls, and had issue. Brigadier-Gen. Bruce *d.* in Aug. 1728, and was *s.* by his son,

Alexander Bruce, of Kennet, who served several campaigns with reputation in Flanders, during Queen Anne's wars, and was appointed, in 1715, major of the regiment raised in support of the government by the town of Glasgow. He *m.* in 1714, Mary, 2nd dau. of Robert Balfour, 4th Lord Burleigh, and dying in 1747, left, with a dau., Margaret, *m.* to Sir Lawrence Dundas, Bart. of Kerse, a son and successor,

Robert Bruce, Esq of Kennet, an eminent lawyer, appointed, in 1764, one of the Senators of the College of Justice, under the title of Lord Kennet. He *m.* in 1754, Helen, dau. of George Abercromby, Esq. of Tullibody, and sister to Gen. Sir Ralph Abercromby, by whom he had six sons and two daus., Alexander, his heir; Lawrence-Dundas; James; Thomas; Ralph, lt.-col. in the army, *d.* 1854; Burnet; Mary; and Margaret, *m.* to Walter Watson, Esq. of Southfield, in the co. of Edinburgh. Lord Kennet was *s.* by his eldest son,

Alexander Bruce, Esq. of Kennet, who *m.* 15 Feb. 1793, Miss H. Blackburn, dau. of Hugh Blackburn, Esq. of Glasgow, and by her (who *d.* Dec. 1851), had issue,

Robert, now in Kennet.

George-Abercromby, *b.* 8 March, 1799, *d.* in the West Indies, March, 1817, *unm.*

Hugh, *b.* 10 Jan. 1800, advocate at the Scottish bar.

Lawrence-Dundas, *b.* 16 Nov. 1800, midshipman, *d.* at Deptford, in Nov. 1817, *unm.*

William, *b.* 8 April, 1807, *m.* Louisa, dau. of Thomas Hull, Esq.

Helen, *m.* to the Hon. Lord Handyside, one of the senators of the College of Justice.

Margaret.

Alexander Bruce *d.* in July, 1808.

Arms—Or, a saltier and chief, gu., the last charged with a mullet, arg.

Crest—A hand holding a sceptre, ppr.

Motto—Fuimus.

Seats—Kennet, in Clackmannanshire; and Dunnogot, Perthshire.

BRUCE OF KINNAIRD.

Cumming-Bruce, Charles-Lennox, Esq. of Kinnaird, co. Perth, and Roseisle, co. Moray, *m.* in 1820, Mary-Elizabeth, only dau. of James Bruce, Esq. of Kinnaird, and granddau. of James Bruce, the Abyssinian traveller, and has a dau.,

Elizabeth-Mary, *m.* 22 April, 1841, the Earl of Elgin, and *d.* in Jamaica, 1843, leaving a dau., Elma.

Major Cumming-Bruce, whose patronymic is Cumming, and who is brother of the late Sir William-Cumming Gordon, Bart. of Altyre and Gordonstown, assumed the additional surname of Bruce on his marriage. He formerly sat in parliament for Inverness.

Lineage.—The Bruces *of Kinnaird* were a scion of the great northern house of Bruce *of Airth*, deriving from Robert Bruce, of Kinnaird, a Presbyterian minister, who was 2nd son of Sir Alexander Bruce, of Airth, by Janet his wife, dau. of Alexander, 5th Lord Livingston, who *d.* about 1553. The male line continued until the decease of Alexander Bruce, of Kinnaird, whose dau. and heiress, Helen Bruce, of Kinnaird, *m.* David Hay, of Woodcockdale, and had a son and successor,

David Bruce, of Kinnaird, who *m.* a dau. of James Graham, Esq. of Airth, dean of the Faculty of Advocates, and judge of the High Court of Admiralty in Scotland, by whom, who *d.* in Nov. 1733, he left at his decease, a son and successor,

James Bruce, of Kinnaird, the celebrated traveller, and explorer of the Nile, *b.* 14 Dec. 1730, who *m.* 1st, in 1754, Miss Allan, who *d.* shortly after; and 2ndly, 20 May, 1776, Mary, dau. of Thomas Dundas, Esq. of Fingask, by whom he had two sons and a dau. He *d.* 27 April, 1794, and was *s.* by his son, James Bruce, of Kinnaird, whose dau. and heir, Mary-Elizabeth, *m.* Charles-Lennox Cumming, Esq.

Arms—Or, a saltier and chief, gu., the last charged with a mullet, of the field.

Seats—Kinnaird, Perthshire; Roseisle, Morayshire.

KNIGHT-BRUCE OF ROEHAMPTON PRIORY

KNIGHT-BRUCE, THE RIGHT HON. SIR JAMES-LEWIS, P.C., of Roehampton Priory, co. Surrey, D.C.L., F.R.S., F.S.A., one of the Lords Justices, *m.* Eliza, dau. of Thomas Newte, Esq. of Sutton, co. Surrey, and has issue,

I. HORACE-LEWIS-KNIGHT, M.A., in holy orders, vicar of Abbotsham, in Devon, deceased.
II. Lewis-Bruce-Knight, B.A., Balliol College, Oxford, of Lincoln's-inn.
III. George-Hamilton-Wyndham, cornet 3rd light-dragoons, killed at Moodkee.
I. Eliza-Julia, *m.* Francis-Samuel-Daniel Tyssen, Esq., late of the 4th dragoon-guards.
II. Rosalind-Margaret, *m.* John-George Phillimore, Esq., M.A., M P., barrister-at-law.

The right honourable gentleman, whose patronymic is KNIGHT, assumed, by royal license, dated 4 Sept. 1837, the additional surname and arms of BRUCE.

Lineage.—DAVID BRUCE, Esq., an officer in the army, a descendant of the BRUCES *of Kennet*, *m.* Margaret, dau. of William Holloway, Esq. of Stoke, co. Hants; and *d.* before 1725, having had two sons, Robert, *d. s. p.*, and

WILLIAM BRUCE, Esq., high-sheriff of co. Glamorgan, who *m.* 1st, Jane, eldest dau. of Gabriel Lewis, Esq. of Lanishen, co. Glamorgan; and 2ndly, Mary, dau. of Richard Turbervile, Esq., M.P., of Ewenny Abbey, in the same shire, and by the former only had issue,

Thomas, in holy orders, rector of St. Nicholas, co. Glamorgan, *d. unm.* in 1790.
Jane, *d. unm.* in 1826.
MARGARET, of whom we treat.

MARGARET BRUCE, co-heir of her brother, *m.* 29 Aug. 1779, JOHN KNIGHT, Esq., only son of James Knight, Esq., by Jane his wife, only dau. of Michael Wharton, Esq.; and *d.* 20 May, 1809, having had, with four sons who *d.* young,

JOHN-BRUCE-PRYCE, of Duffryn, co. Glamorgan.
WILLIAM-BRUCE-KNIGHT, M.A., in holy orders, chancellor and dean of the diocese of Llandaff; *m.* Maria-Eleanor, 2nd dau. of Llewelyn Traherne, Esq. of St. Hilary; and *d.* in 1846.
JAMES-LEWIS (Sir), one of the Lords Justices.
Frances, *m.* to William Davies, Esq.
Blanch-Bridget, *m.* to John-Digby Newbolt, the eldest son of Sir John-H. Newbolt, chief-justice of Madras, who is deceased.
Margaret, *d. unm.*

Arms—KNIGHT and BRUCE, quarterly.
Seat—Roehampton Priory, Surrey.

BRUCE OF SCOUTBUSH AND KILLROOT.

BRUCE, EDWARD, Esq. of Scoutbush and Killroot, co. Antrim, J.P., high-sheriff in 1836, *b.* 27 March, 1783; *m.* 29 Oct. 1807, Maria, eldest dau. of James Coghlan, Esq. of Castlegar, co. Mayo, and has issue,

I. EDWARD, *b.* 16 Nov. 1811; in holy orders; *m.* Maria, eldest dau. of the late Lieut.-Col. Head, of Derry Castle, co. Tipperary.
II. James-Alexander, *b.* 5 Jan. 1826.
I. Marianne. II. Rose.

Lineage.—EDWARD BRICE, *b.* about 1720-1, son of Lieut.-Col. Edward Brice, by Jane his wife, dau. of Richard Dobbs, Esq. of Castle Dobbs, co. Antrim, and great-grandson of the Rev. Edward Bryce, or Bruce, younger brother of a laird of Airth, was high-sheriff of Antrim in 1748; and *m.* 1st, in 1752, Rose, dau. of Alexander Stewart, Esq. of Acton, co. Armagh, and of Ballintoy, co. Antrim, by whom he had one son and successor, EDWARD. He *m.* 2ndly, Jane Adair, and by her had four sons, one of whom was a lieut.-col. in the guards, and killed in Egypt, under Sir Ralph Abercrombie; another *d.* a lieut. in the royal navy; a third *d.* shortly after his return from the West Indies; and the fourth, Archibald, was in holy orders, and beneficed in Norfolk (he left two sons; the elder *s.* him in one of his livings, and the younger, a barrister, resides in Bath; and two daus., the younger *d. unm.*, and the elder, Maria, *m.* the Right Hon. Sir John Anstruther, Bart., chief-justice of the Supreme Court, Bengal, and had issue). Mr. Brice's only son of his first marriage,

EDWARD BRICE, Esq. of Kilroot, *b.* in 1756; *m.* in 1772, Theodora, eldest dau. of Thomas Mullins, 1st Lord Ventry, and had issue,

EDWARD, present representative, who has resumed, by royal license, the original surname of BRUCE.
Thomas-Richard, *b.* in April, 1790; *m.* Jane, youngest dau. of the late Samuel-De la Cherois Crommelin, Esq. of Carrowdore Castle, co. Down.
Rose, *m.* to the late Sir John Blake, of Menlough Castle, co. Galway, Bart., and had issue.
Eliza, *m.* to Staff-Surgeon R. O'Connell.
Theodora, *m.* to Trevor Hill, Esq.
Charlotte, *m.* to Thomas-Johnson Smyth, Esq. of Lisburn.

Arms—Or, a saltier and chief, gu.; a mullet in the dexter canton, of the first.
Crest—A cubit arm, couped at the elbow, and erect, holding a scimetar, ppr.
Motto—Do well, doubt nought.
Seats—Scoutbush, Carrickfergus; and Kilroot, co. Antrim.

BRUCKSHAW OF HARRY TOWN HALL.

BRUCKSHAW, JOSHUA, Esq. of Harry Town Hall, co. Chester, J.P. and D.L., *b.* 12 July, 1789; *m.* 10 Oct. 1822, Susanna, dau. of the Rev. Charles Prescott, late rector of Stockport, co. Chester. Mr. Bruckshaw is only surviving son of the late Joshua Bruckshaw, Esq. of Harry Town Hall (who *d.* 27 November, 1816), by Frances Hollingworth his wife, of the Old Hall, within Hollingworth, co. Chester; and grandson of John Bruckshaw, and Susannah his wife.

The estate of Harry Town has been possessed by this family for a very long period, in the course of which we find the name variously written Brodockshaw, Brockshaw, and Brookshaw, until it finally settled down into Bruckshaw. The old mansion at Harry Town was erected in the 15th century, by Harry Bruckshaw, but was pulled down and rebuilt, in 1671, by John Bruckshaw.

Seat—Harry Town Hall, Stockport.

BRUEN OF OAK PARK.

BRUEN, HENRY, Esq. of Oak Park, co. Carlow, *b.* in 1828; *m.* 6 June, 1854, Mary-Margaret, 3rd dau. of the late Col. Conolly, of Castletown.

Lineage.—The late representative of this influential family,

COL. HENRY BRUEN, of Oak Park, son and heir of Lieut.-Col. Henry Bruen, M.P. of Oak Park, by Dorothea-Henrietta his wife, 2nd dau. of Francis Knox, Esq. of Rappa Castle, *m.* in 1820, Anne, dau. of Thomas Kavanagh, Esq. of Borris House, co. Carlow; and *d.* in 1852, leaving an only son and heir, the present HENRY BRUEN, Esq. of Oak Park; and two daus., Harriette, and Anne, *m.* in 1854, to Benjamin Burton, Esq.

Seat—Oak Park, Carlow.

BRUGES OF SEEND.

LUDLOW-BRUGES, WILLIAM-HEALD, Esq. of Seend, Melksham, Wilts, J.P. and D.L., recorder of Devizes, *b.* in April, 1796; *m.* 1st, in Nov. 1827, Augusta, youngest dau. of Samuel Heathcote, of Shaw Hill House, co. Wilts, Esq., and has two daus.,

I. Elizabeth-Heathcote, } who retain the name of Ludlow
II. Augusta, } only.

He *m.* 2ndly, in July, 1834, Agnes, 3rd dau. of Thomas Penruddock, Esq. of Winkton, near Christchurch, Hants, and has issue,

I. WILLIAM-PENRUDDOCK. II. Edmund.
I. Agnes. II. Juliana.

This gentleman took, by royal license, in 1835, the name of BRUGES, in addition to that of LUDLOW. He formerly represented Bath in parliament.

Lineage.—The family of Ludlow is of long standing in Wiltshire. The late

BENJAMIN-PENNELL LUDLOW, Esq., son of Benjamin Ludlow, Esq., by Anne, dau. of George Heald, Esq. of Horncastle, and grandson of Christopher Ludlow, Esq., by Catherine Lampard his wife, *m.* in 1795, Susanna, dau. of William Bruges, Esq. of Semington, co. Wilts (son of William Bruges, Esq., by his wife, Elizabeth, dau. of Lewis, of Semington, co. Wilts); and dying in Nov. 1802, left (with a dau., Anne, who m. W. Sainsbury, jun., M.D. of Corsham, co. Wilts, and is deceased) an only son, the present WILLIAM-HEALD-LUDLOW BRUGES, Esq. of Seend.

Arms—Arg., a cross, quarterly, pierced, of the field, erm.; in the centre point a leopard's face, sa., for BRUGES; quartering LUDLOW.
Crest—An anchor erect, sa., charged with a saltier, or, entwined by the cable, ppr.
Motto—Omne solum forti patria.
Seat—Seend, Melksham, co. Wilts.

BRYAN OF JENKINSTOWN.

BRYAN, GEORGE-LEOPOLD, Esq. of Jenkinstown, co. Kilkenny, *b.* 29 Nov. 1828; *m.* 6 Dec. 1849, Lady Elizabeth-Georgiana Conyngham, dau. of the Marquess Conyngham, and has one dau.,

MARY-MARGARET-FRANCES.

Lineage.—The immediate ancestor of this family, JOHN BRYAN, Esq. of Kilkenny, was younger brother of James Bryan, Esq. of Bawnmore, and son of John Bryan, of Bawnmore, (whose father, Lewis Bryan, had a grant from Thomas, Earl of Ormonde, of Whitewalls, *alias* Bawnmore, co. Kilkenny, and *d.* 15 Oct. 1568). He *m.* Anna, dau. and heir of Henry Stanes, Esq. of Jenkinstown, co. Kilkenny, and left a son, JAMES BRYAN, Esq. of Jenkinstown, 1673-4, father of

PIERCE BRYAN, Esq. of Jenkinstown, whose will, dated 11 Aug. 1753, was proved 20 Feb. 1777. He *m.* Jane, dau. of George Aylmer, Esq. of Lyons, co. Kildare, and had issue, 1 JAMES, his heir; 2 George, of Portland Place, London, *b.* in 1720, who *m.* Catherine, dau. and heir of Henry Byrne, Esq., son of Sir Gregory Byrne, Bart., by Alice his wife, only dau. of Randal, Lord Slane, and was father of GEORGE, successor to his uncle; 3 Aylmer, brig.-gen. in the French service; 4 Pierce; 1 Alice; 2 Rose; 3 Mary. The eldest son,

JAMES BRYAN, Esq. of Jenkinstown, *b.* in 1719, *d. unm.* Aug. 1805, and was *s.* by his nephew,

GEORGE BRYAN, Esq. of Jenkinstown, *b.* 3 Nov. 1770; who *m.* 1794, Maria-Louisa, Comtesse de Rutaut, dau. of the Count de Rutaut, of Lorraine, and left at his decease, 8 Oct. 1843, a dau., Mary, and a son and successor,

GEORGE BRYAN, Esq. of Jenkinstown, *b.* 25 Oct. 1796; who *m.* 21 March, 1820, Margaret, dau. of William Talbot, Esq. of Castle Talbot, co. Wexford, and had surviving issue,

GEORGE-LEOPOLD, now of Jenkinstown.
Augusta-Margaret-Gwendaline, *m.* 7 Feb. 1853, to the Hon. Edward-Joseph Bellew, eldest son of Lord Bellew.

Major Bryan claimed the Barony of Slane. He *d.* 5 Oct. 1848.

Arms—Gu., three lions, passant, two and one.
Crest—Two lions' gambs, gu., supporting between them a sword erect, arg., pommel and hilt, or.
Motto—Fortis et fidelis.
Seat—Jenkinstown, co. Kilkenny.

BUCHAN OF AUCHMACOY HOUSE.

BUCHAN, JAMES, Esq. of Auchmacoy House, co. Aberdeen, a magistrate for the shire, *b.* in June, 1800; *m.* 12 June, 1833, Helen, 2nd dau. of Gordon Duff, Esq. of Hatton, co. Aberdeen, and has issue,

I. THOMAS. I. Louisa.

Lineage.—The first of this family is stated to have been a son of the last and powerful Earl of Buchan, of the name of Comyn, upon whom King ROBERT BRUCE conferred the lands of Auchmacoy, on his changing his name to BUCHAN. From him was descended, in a direct male line, in the 17th century,

JAMES BUCHAN, of Auchmacoy, who *m.* Margaret, dau. of Alexander Seton, of Pitmedden, and had four sons,

ALEXANDER, of Auchmacoy.
JAMES, who *s.* his brother, and of whom presently.
Thomas, who served with distinction in France and Holland, and was appointed by CHARLES II., col. of a regiment of foot in Scotland. Subsequently he was promoted to Major-General by JAMES II., by whom he was appointed commander of the forces in Scotland, after the fall of Viscount Dundee at Killiecrankie. He *d.* in 1720.
John, who commanded a regiment of foot for the Prince of Orange.

The 2nd son,

JAMES BUCHAN *s.* his elder brother, Alexander. He was father of

JAMES BUCHAN, of Auchmacoy, major in the service of JAMES II., who *m.* a dau. of Sir John Forbes, Bart. of Craigievar, and had a son and heir,

THOMAS BUCHAN, of Auchmacoy, who *m.* his cousin, Nicola, dau. of Thomas Buchan, of Cairnbulg, by his wife the Hon. Grace Hamilton, dau. of the last Lord Bargany, and by her was father of

THOMAS BUCHAN, of Auchmacoy, who dying in 1819, was *s.* by his son, the present JAMES BUCHAN, Esq. of Auchmacoy.

Arms—Quarterly: 1st and 4th, arg., three lion's heads, erased, two and one, sa., langued, gu., for BUCHAN; 2nd and 3rd, quarterly: 1st and 4th, gu., three cinquefoils, erm.; 2nd and 3rd, arg., a galley with her sails furled, sa., all within a bordure, company, arg. and az.; the 1st charged with hearts, gu.; the 2nd with mullets, arg., being the arms of William, 3rd Lord Bargany, of whom Mr. Buchan is heir of line.
Crest—A sun shining on a sun-flower full blown, ppr.
Supporters—Dexter, a heron with an eel in its beak, all ppr.; sinister, an antelope, arg., collared, gu., the collar charged with three cinquefoils, erm.
Motto—Non inferiora secutus.
Seat—Auchmacoy House, co. Aberdeen.

BUCHANAN OF LENY.

See BUCHANAN-HAMILTON.

BUCHANAN OF ARDINCONNAL AND AUCHINTORLIE.

BUCHANAN, ANDREW, Esq. of Auchintorlie, co. Dumbarton, *s.* his father in 1832.

Lineage.—This is a branch of the ancient and distinguished families of BUCHANAN *of Buchanan*, or that ilk, and of BUCHANAN *of Leny*, now representative of that house, and chief of the clan Buchanan.

ALEXANDER BUCHANAN, 5th in descent from John of Leny, 3rd son of John Buchanan, Laird of Buchanan in the 15th century, had two sons, JOHN, his successor at Mochastel, and

WALTER BUCHANAN, of Glenny, whose grandson, Capt. James Buchanan, *s.* to the estate of Glenny, but dying in France without issue, his uncle, the 2nd son of Walter, of Glenny,

ALEXANDER BUCHANAN, became heir to his nephew, the Laird of Glenny. He had two sons, Andrew and George; the elder,

ANDREW BUCHANAN, purchased Gartacharan from Lord Napier. He had two sons, ALEXANDER, his successor, and

GEORGE BUCHANAN, a magistrate and merchant in Glasgow, who had four sons and one dau., viz.,

GEORGE, a merchant, who with his brothers Andrew, Niel, and Archibald, were the original promoters of the Buchanan Society in that city. He was twice *m.*; 2ndly, to a dau. of Sir John Forbes, Bart. of Foveran, Aberdeenshire, and had four sons and four daus., but his male line is now extinct.
Andrew, of Drumpellier, co. Lanark, who had two sons and five daus. The elder son, JAMES, *m.* Margaret Hamilton, granddau. of the Earl of Haddington, and sister of the Countesses of Morton and Selkirk, and of Lady Halket, of Pitferran. By this lady he had, with a son, who *d. unm.*, several daus., of whom, Helen *m.* Admiral Sir George Home, Bart. The Drumpellier branch of the Buchanan family is now represented by the descendant of Andrew's 2nd son, ROBERT-CARRICK BUCHANAN, Esq., of Drumpellier.
ARCHIBALD, of Auchintorlie, co. Dumbarton.
Neil, of Hillington, co. Renfrew, M.P. for the Glasgow district of Burghs, whose male line is now extinct. He left one son and three daus.: of the latter, Ann, the eldest, *m.* Oswald, Bishop of Raphoe; and Marion, the 3rd, became the wife of Oliphant of Rossie, in Perthshire, postmaster-general for Scotland.
Mary, *m.* to George Buchanan, of Auchintoshan, co. Dumbarton.

The 3rd son,

ARCHIBALD BUCHANAN, Esq., acquired Auchintorlie, in Dumbartonshire, from his brother Andrew, as also the lands of Hillington, in Renfrewshire, upon the death of his brother Neil. He *m.* Martha, dau. of Peter Murdoch, Esq., of Rosehill, Renfrewshire, lord provost of Glasgow, by whom he had issue,

Peter
GEORGE, successively of Auchintorlie.

Andrew, of Ardinconnal, and heir of destination of Auchintorlie, of whom presently.
Mary, m. Alexander Speirs, of Elderslie, co. Renfrew.

The eldest son and heir,

Peter Buchanan, Esq. of Auchintorlie, m. Miss Catherine Macpherson, who, after his death, m. Sir Ewen Cameron, Bart. of Fassifern, co. Inverness. Dying s. p. Mr. Buchanan was s. by his brother,

George Buchanan, Esq. of Auchintorlie, who was twice m. but had no issue. He left the family estates of Auchintorlie and others in the co. of Dumbarton, and Hillington, in the co. of Renfrew, as before-mentioned, to his nephew Archibald; his brother,

Andrew Buchanan, Esq. of Ardinconnal, co. Dumbarton, and Auchingray, co. Lanark, J.P. and D.L., b. 12 July, 1745, m. 3 July, 1769, Jane, eldest dau. of James Dennistoun, of Colgrain and Dennistoun, and had

I. Archibald, of Auchintorlie, co. Dumbarton, and Hillington, co. Renfrew, m. Mary, 2nd dau. of Richard Dennistoun, Esq. of Kelvin Grove, co. Lanark, and d. 16 Dec. 1832, leaving issue,
  1 Andrew, now of Auchintorlie.
  2 Richard-Dennistoun.
  1 Christiana. 2 Jane. 3 Mary. 4 Isabella.
  5 Georgina. 6 Archina.

II. James, of Blair Vadock, Ardinconnal, now seated at Craigend Castle, co. Stirling, m. Lady Janet Sinclair, eldest dau. of James, 12th Earl of Caithness, and has issue,
  1 Andrew, envoy extraordinary and minister plenipotentiary to the court of Denmark.
  1 Helen-John Sinclair, m. to William-Wootton Abney, Esq. of Measham Hall, co. Leicester.
  2 Jane-Dennistoun, m. to William Tritton, Esq.
  3 Jane-Campbell, m. to Richard Fox, Esq. of AwBawn, co. Cavan, grandson of Barry, 1st Earl of Farnham.
  4 Charlotte-Macgregor-Murray, m. to Charles-Henry Forbes, of Kingairlock, co. Argyle.
  5 Matilda-Frances-Harriet, m. to Patrick Maitland, of Freugh, great-grandson of Charles, 6th Earl of Lauderdale.

I. Jesse, m. to James Monteith, Esq. of Craighead, Lanarkshire.

II. Martha, m. to George Yuille, Esq. of Cardross Park, co. Dumbarton, 2nd son of George Yuille, of Darleith.

Arms—Quarterly: 1st and 4th, or, a lion, rampant, sa., armed and langued, gu., within a double tressure, flowered and counter-flowered with fleurs-de-lis, of the second, for Buchanan; 2nd and 3rd, sa., a chevron between two bears' heads, erased, in chief, and another in base, arg., muzzled, gu. On the chief-point of the chevron, a cinquefoil, of the first, for Lenny. This quartering, however, was omitted last matriculation at the Lord Lyon's office.

Crest—A hand, couped, holding a duke's coronet, with two laurel branches wreathed under it.

Motto—Clarior hinc honos. *Seat*—Auchintorlie.

BUCHANAN OF ARDOCH.

Buchanan, John, Esq. of Ardoch, co. Dumbarton, b. 24 March, 1799.

Lineage.—From John Buchanan, eldest son of the second marriage of Thomas Buchanan, of Carbeth, who was grandson of Thomas Buchanan, 3rd son of Sir Walter Buchanan, 13th Laird of Buchanan, sprang

William Buchanan, who acquired in 1693, the estate of Ardoch, co. of Dumbarton. He m. Jean, dau. of Kincaid of Auchenreoch, and dying in 1723, was s. by his grandson,

John Buchanan, of Ardoch, (son of Thomas Buchanan,) b. in 1706, who m. 1st, Mary, dau. of William Crawford, merchant, of Glasgow, and had one son and two daus., viz., Thomas, his heir; Mary, m. to the Rev. James Graham; and Agnes, m. to John Buchanan, of Ledrishmore. Mr. Buchanan m. 2ndly, in 1747, Elizabeth, dau. of Walter Buchanan, writer in Glasgow, and relict of Alexander Buchanan, of Cremannan, and by her had another dau., Frances, b. in 1751, m. to John Maxwell, of Dargaval, in the co. of Renfrew. This John, who was an eminent lawyer at Glasgow, d. 13 Jan. 1774, and was s. by his son,

Thomas Buchanan, of Ardoch, b. 6 Nov. 1733. This gentleman m. 1st, Margaret, dau. and heiress of Moses Buchanan, descended in a direct line from John, son of Alexander Buchanan, of Ibert, brother of George Buchanan, the historian and poet; and by her had a son, John, his successor. He m. 2ndly, Jean, dau. of John Gray, of Dalmarnoch, and had, James, who m. Anne, youngest dau. of John Parkes, Esq. of Warwick, and Elizabeth, m. to Alexander Gordon, Esq. Mr. Buchanan m. 3rdly, Helen, dau. of William Graham, of Birdstone, and had four other sons and two daus.,

William, m. the Honourable Elizabeth Murray, eldest dau. of Alexander, 7th Lord Elibank.
Robert, m. Margaret, dau. of Dunlop of Annanhill, co. Ayr.
Thomas.
Archibald, commander R.N., m. Matilda, dau. of — Dalbiach, Esq., and d. in 1822.
Helen, m. to John Balfour, Esq. Marion.

He d. 10 Dec. 1789, and was s. by his eldest son,

John Buchanan, Esq. of Ardoch, vice-lieutenant, lieutenant-commander of the local militia, and lately member of parliament for that shire, b. 8 Jan. 1761, m. 1 Nov. 1785, Elizabeth, dau. of John Parkes, Esq. of Netherton, in Worcestershire, by whom, who d. 4 Sept. 1807, he had issue,

John, now of Ardoch.
Mary, m. to Robert Findlay, Esq. of Easter Hill, co. Lanark.
Margaret, d. 25 Jan. 1825. Elizabeth.

Arms—Or, a lion, rampant, sa., in the dexter paw a dagger, ppr., within the royal tressure, flowered and counter-flowered with fleurs-de-lis, of the second, all within a bordure, invecked, gu.

Crest—Two hands grasping a two-handed sword, ppr.

Motto—Clariora sequor.

Seat—Ardoch, co. Dumbarton.

BUCK OF MORETON AND HARTLAND ABBEY.

Buck, Lewis-William, Esq. of Moreton and Hartland Abbey, co. Devon, J.P. and D.L., M.P. for North Devon, and at one time high-sheriff of the county, m. Anne, dau. of Thomas Robbins, Esq., and has surviving issue,

I. George-Stucley, lieut.-col. commanding Devon militia artillery, J.P. and D.L., b. 17 Aug. 1812, m. 22 Dec. 1835, Lady Elizabeth O'Bryen, youngest dau. of William, 2nd Marquess of Thomond, and has issue, William-Lewis Stucley, b. 27 Aug. 1836; Lewis-George-Orchard, b. 25 April, 1843; Edward-Arthur-George, b. 12 Feb. 1852; and Elizabeth-Anne-Georgiana.

I. Louisa, m. in 1839, to Samuel-Trehawke Kekewich, Esq., of Peamore, co. Devon.

Lineage.—This family, of Irish origin, settled in Devonshire towards the latter end of the 17th century.

George Buck, Esq., who m. Sarah, only dau. and heiress of Lewis Stucley, Esq. of Affeton, co. Devon, d. Nov. 1743, aged 71, and was s. by his son,

John Buck, Esq. of Daddon, co. Devon, who m. to his 1st wife, Judith, dau. and heiress of Hugh Pawley, of Bideford, descended from the ancient family of Pawley *of Gunwin*, in Cornwall. By her, who d. 5 Oct. 1739, he had issue three sons, George, Lewis, and William.

George Buck, Esq. of Daddon, the eldest son, m. Anne, dau. of Paul Orchard, Esq. of Hartland Abbey, by whom he was father of

George-Stucley Buck, of Moreton and Hartland Abbey, who m. Martha, dau. of the Rev. Richard Keates, and sister of Admiral Sir Richard Keates; and by her, who m. 2ndly, Col. Kirkman, had issue,

George-Pawley, deceased.
Lewis-William, now of Moreton and Hartland Abbey.
Richard, capt. R.N., m. Angelica, dau. of — Macdonald, Esq., and d. leaving issue, Richard; Lewis-Stucley; Thomas; and five daus.
Elizabeth, m. to Colonel Bailey, R.A.

Arms—Per fesse embattled, arg. and sa., quartering Pawley.

Crest—Between a buck's attire fixed to the scalp, a lion, rampant, holding over his shoulder a battle-axe, all ppr.

Motto—Bellement et hardiment.

Seats—Moreton and Hartland Abbey, co. Devon.

BUCK OF DENHOLME AND GLANARBETH.

Buck, William, Esq. of Denholme, co. York, and Glanarbeth, co. Cardigan, b. 18 March, 1817, D.L. for the West Riding of Yorkshire and for Cardigan, of which latter shire he is a magistrate, and served as high-sheriff.

Lineage.—This is the same family as Buck, extinct Baronets.

John-William Buck, Esq., b. 3 May, 1780, son of John Buck, Esq. of Townhill House, co. York, by Caroline his wife, dau. of John Travis, Esq. of Crofton, co. Lancaster, m. 28 May, 1812, Sophia, dau. of William-Owen Brigstocke,

Esq. of Blaenpont, co. Cardigan, and *d.* 23 Aug. 1821, leaving, besides the present WILLIAM BUCK, Esq. of Denholme and Glanarberth, two daus.,

Caroline, *m.* 6 June, 1834, to the Rev. William-Henry Rooper, of Abbotts Repton, co. Huntingdon.
Sophia, *m.* 3 July, 1847, to Charles-Augustus Parkinson, Esq. of Twyn-y-Caye, co. Brecon.

Arms—Paly bendy sinister of six, or and az., a canton, erm.
Crest—A portcullis.
Motto—Nosce teipsum.
Seats—Denholme, co. York, and Glanarbeth, co. Cardigan.

BUCKLE OF WHARTON HOUSE.

BUCKLE, JOHN, Esq. of Wharton House, co. Edinburgh, *b.* in 1792; *m.* 1st, in 1817, Isabella, dau. of Edward Hay-Mackenzie, Esq. of Tarbet House, Cromarty, brother of the 7th Marquess of Tweeddale, and has issue,

I. EDWARD, *b.* in 1818, *m.* Maria Shearsby.
II. Lewis-Barton, *b.* in 1824.
III. John-Manners, *b.* in 1826.
I. Isabella-Dorothea, *m.* to Matthew-Dysart Hunter, Esq. of Antons Hill, co. Berwick, and of Medomsley, co. Durham.
II. Eleanor-Frances. III. Maria-Emma.
IV. Georgina-Anne.

Mr. Buckle *m.* 2ndly, in 1834, Dorothea, eldest dau. of John Blackwell, Esq., advocate, and has by her,

I. Cuthbert, *b.* in 1835.
II. Alfred-John, *b.* in 1837.
III. Barton, *b.* in 1839.
III. Frederick-Lodwick, *b.* in 1841.
IV. Hubert, *b.* in 1849.

Lineage.—SIR CHRISTOPHER BUCKLE, *b.* in 1629, son of Sir Christopher Buckle, Knt. of Burgh in Banstead, Surrey, and grandson of Sir Cuthbert Buckle, lord mayor of London in 1593, who was son of Sir Christopher Buckle, of Burgh in Westmoreland, *b.* in 1533, purchased the estates at Mitcham, Burgh, and Banstead, in Surrey. He *m.* in 1653, Elizabeth, dau. of Sir William Lewis, Bart. of Borden Eastmeon, in Hants, and had four sons, Christopher, Lewis, William, and Martin. The eldest,

CHRISTOPHER BUCKLE, Esq. of Banstead, *m.* Sarah, dau. of Jacob Forster, merchant, and had (with four younger sons, and a dau., Sarah, the wife of Henry St. John, Esq.) a successor,

CHRISTOPHER BUCKLE, Esq., *b.* in 1684, who built Nork House, in the parish of Banstead, Surrey, in 1740. He *m.* Sarah, dau. of Lennard Wessel, merchant, by Anne Crawford his wife, and had issue,

I. CHRISTOPHER, *b.* in 1699, of Burgh in Banstead, who *m.* 1st, Sarah, sister of Sir Rowland Hill, Bart. of Hawkstone, in Salop, and had, with a dau., Sarah, who *d. unm.* in 1821, a son,

CHRISTOPHER, *b.* in 1742, who sold Nork House to Lord Arden, and *d. s. p.* in 1816, aged 74.

Mr. Buckle *m.* 2ndly, Ann, dau. of Henry St. John, Esq., and widow of Nathaniel Wessel, by whom he left at his decease, 10 Jan. 1783, aged 84, an only dau., Ann, *m.* to Col. Robert Crowe, of Kiplin, co. York, whose dau., Sarah Crowe, *m.* John-Delaval, last Earl of Tyrconnel.

II. LEWIS, of whom presently.
III. Matthew, *b.* in 1716, admiral R.N., *m.* in 1763, Hannah, dau. of Isaac Hughes, Esq. of Garret's House, Banstead, Surrey, and dying at Nork House, 7 July, 1784, left,

MATTHEW, capt. R.N., resident at Bath, who *m.* in 1798, Henrietta, dau. of Hugh Reveley, Esq., and has, (with five daus., Henrietta; Matilda; Georgina; Elizabeth-Margaret; and Jane) four sons,

1 MATTHEW-MASON-HUGHES, in holy orders, head master of the grammar-school, Durham.
2 Henry, R.N.
3 Edward, royal engineers. 4 Randolph.

Hannah, *m.* to her cousin, Matthew Buckle, Esq. of Norton House, near Chichester.

The 2nd son,

LEWIS BUCKLE, Esq., *b.* in 1713, of Borden in Eastmeon, Hampshire, *m.* in 1757, Eleanor, dau. of Dr. Dickins, physician, of Liverpool, and by her, who *d.* 9 Sept. 1811, had issue,

I. LEWIS, his heir.
II. William, *b.* in 1759, in holy orders, rector of Pyrton, Oxfordshire, and vicar of Banstead, Surrey, *m.* Grace, dau. of Sir John Stewart, Bart. of Grandtully, and had (with other issue, of which Jane-Frances *m.* George Ranking, Esq.) a son and heir,

William-Lewis, in holy orders, *s.* his father in the living of Banstead in 1832, *m.* Mary-Freeman, dau. of Mr. Serjeant Manley, of Henley, in Oxfordshire, and has issue, Stewart; Christopher; Charles; Edward; Mary; Matilda; and Louisa.

III. MATTHEW, of Norton House, Sussex, *b.* 14 Dec. 1760, *m.* 10 Feb. 1803, Hannah, dau. of Admiral Matthew Buckle, of Nork House, and has had issue, Christopher-Richard; Louisa, *d. unm.* in 1828; Emma; Frances-Martha, *m.* to the Rev. John Fearnley, of Yorkshire; Eleanor; and Mary-Elizabeth.
IV. Dickins, of Medina Cottage, Isle of Wight, *b.* in 1761, *m.* in 1814, Miss Martha Long, of the Isle of Wight, and has one dau., Frances-Martha, *m.* in 1827, to Capt. James Sargeantson, of the 30th regt.
I Eleanor, *m.* to Dr. Reeve, M.D. of Ireland, and had issue.

Mr. Buckle *d.* in 1785, and was *s.* by his eldest son,

LEWIS BUCKLE, Esq. of Rogate Lodge, Sussex, *b.* in 1758, who *m.* in 1782, Frances, dau. of — Bachelor, Esq. of Prior Court House, parish of Cheveley, Berks, and had issue,

LEWIS-BARTON, his heir, capt. in the 15th dragoons, *b.* 8 Dec. 1786, who *m.* in 1812, Gertrude, dau. of John Lockwood, Esq. of Cashel, co. Tipperary, but *d. s. p.* 1 Jan. 1819. His widow *m.* 2ndly, 8 Jan. 1821, James Scargill, Esq., lieut. in the 9th regt. of foot.
William, *d. unm.*
JOHN, now of Wharton House.
Frances-Martha, *m.* in 1818, to the Rev. James Tripp, of Fittleworth, Sussex, and *d.* in 1820.
Mary-Elizabeth, *m.* to Bevis Thelwall, Esq. of Brynyffynmon, North Wales.
Louisa, *m.* to George Whitley, Esq. of Ireland.
Sarah, *m.* in 1819, to the Rev. Edward Thelwall, rector of Llanbedr, co. Denbigh.

Arms—Sa., a chevron, between three chaplets, arg.
Crest—Out of a ducal coronet, or, a demi-ounce, arg.
Motto—Nil temere tenta nil timide.
Seat—Wharton House, Edinburgh.

BUCKLEY OF NEW HALL.

BUCKLEY, MAJOR-GEN. EDWARD-PERY, of New Hall, Salisbury, Wilts, J.P. and D.L., equerry to the Queen, *b.* 7 Nov. 1796; *m.* 13 May, 1828, Catharine, only child of William, Earl of Radnor, by Catherine, his 1st wife, only dau. of Henry, Earl of Lincoln, and has issue,

I. ALFRED, *b.* 13 Oct. 1829.
II. Duncombe-Frederick-Batt, *b.* 14 July, 1831.
III. Felix-John, *b.* 15 Oct. 1834.
IV. Victor, *b.* 28 April, 1838.
I. Frances-Gertrude.

Lineage.—EDWARD BUCKLEY, descended from a Welsh family, and supposed to have derived from a common ancestry with the Lord Bulkley, *d.* in 1730, leaving four sons. The youngest,

PERY BUCKLEY, Esq. of Winkfield Place, Berks, *m.* Martha, dau. of William Batt, Esq. of New Hall, co. Wilts, and relict of Richard Bingham, Esq. of Melcombe Bingham, co. Dorset; and by her, who *d.* in 1765, was father of

EDWARD-PERY BUCKLEY, Esq. of Woolcombe Hall, Dorset, and Minestead Lodge, Hants, *b.* April, 1760, lieut.-col. of the South-West Hants militia, who *m.* in 1782, Lady Georgiana West, dau. of John, 2nd Earl De la Warr, and by her, who was lady of the bed-chamber to the Princesses, daus. of GEORGE III., and *d.* in 1832, had issue,

EDWARD-PERY, now of New Hall.
George-Richard, *b.* in 1798, and *d.* in 1815.
Henry-William, in holy orders, *b.* 28 March, 1800, *m.* in Sept. 1831, Charlotte-Margaret, eldest dau. of the late Sir John Johnston, Bart., and has issue, Charles-Edward, *b.* in 1836; Georgiana-Elizabeth; Henrietta-Janet; and Lilias-Charlotte.
Georgiana-Henrietta, *m.* in 1814, to George-Lane Fox, of Bramham Park, co. York, who *d.* in 1848.

Col. Buckley filled for thirty years the office of first equerry, and afterwards groom of the bedchamber. He *d.* in 1840, aged 81.

Arms—Sa., a chevron between three bulls' heads, caboshed, arg.
Crest—Out of a ducal coronet, or, a bull's head, arg., armed, of the first.
Motto—Nec temere nec timide.
Seat—New Hall, Salisbury.

BUCKLEY OF ARDWICK AND GROTTON HALL.

BUCKLEY, EDMUND, Esq. of Ardwick, co. Lancaster, and Grotton Hall, Saddleworth, co. York, *b.* 24 Dec.

1780. Mr. Buckley is a magistrate for Lancashire, and for the city of Manchester; and sat in the parliament of 1841 for the borough of Newcastle-under-Lyme.

Lineage.—This family has long been resident at Grotton Head, and Lidgate, in Saddleworth, co. York. The late

JOHN BUCKLEY, Esq., son of Edmund Buckley, of Lidgate, *m.* Mary, dau. of James Lees, of Lane, in Saddleworth, and had issue,

EDMUND, now of Ardwick and Grotton Hall.
John, deceased. James, deceased.
Ralph, *m.* Miss Hadfield, and *d.* several years ago.
Sarah, *m.* to John Shaw, Esq.
Susannah, *m.* to James Wilkinson, Esq. of Staleybridge.
Elizabeth, *m.* to Walter Whitehead, Esq.

Seats—Ardwick, Manchester; and Grotton Hall, Saddleworth.

LINDSEY-BUCKNALL OF TURIN CASTLE.

BUCKNALL, JOHN-CHARLES LINDSEY, Esq. of Turin Castle, co. Mayo, J.P., *b.* 19 April, 1813; *m.* 24 May, 1838, Anne, only child of Charles Crawford, Esq. of Oatlands, co. Donegal, and has issue,

I. SAMUEL-CHARLES, *b.* 20 April, 1842.
II. Hamilton-Owen, *b.* 29 Jan. 1844.
III. John-Arbuthnot, *b.* 15 April, 1846.
I. Jane.

Lineage.—THOMAS LINDSEY, of Turin Castle, eldest son of SAMUEL LINDSEY, Esq. of Belleek, co. Mayo, *m.* a dau. of Crossdaille Miller, Esq. of Milford, in the same co., and had (with several daus.) four sons,

SAMUEL, his heir. Robert. Owen.
THOMAS, grandfather of THOMAS-SPENCER LINDSAY, Esq. of Hollymount. (*See that family.*)

The eldest son,

THE REV. SAMUEL LINDSEY, of Turin Castle, rector of Enniskillen, co. Fermanagh, *m.* Frances, eldest dau. of the Right Hon. Col. Charles Bucknall, and had (with three daus., Anne, Frances, and Letitia, all married, the eldest to Arthur-Chichester Macartney, Esq.) two sons, THOMAS BUCKNALL, his heir, and JOHN, successor to his brother. The elder son,

THOMAS-BUCKNALL LINDSEY, of Turin Castle, major of the South Mayo militia, *m.* Anne, elder dau. of Col. Arthur Browne, brother of the 2nd Earl of Altamont, and dying *s. p.* was *s.* by his brother,

JOHN LINDSEY, Esq. of Turin Castle, who took the surname of BUCKNALL, from his maternal grandfather, the Right Hon. Col. Bucknall. He *m.* in 1785, Mary, 2nd dau. of Capt. George Bingham, of Castlebar, Mayo, uncle to the 1st Lord Lucan, and left at his decease (with a dau. Georgina now living, a widow,) an only son and heir,

SAMUEL LINDSEY-BUCKNALL, Esq. of Turin Castle, J.P., *b.* 8 April, 1786, *m.* 11 June, 1811, Jane, 2nd dau. of Richard Holmes, Esq. of Prospect, King's Co., and had surviving issue,

JOHN-CHARLES, now of Turin Castle.
Thomas, *b.* 22 April, 1818, *m.* Jane, dau. of Sir James Dombrain.
Richard, *b.* 26 April, 1821, *m.* Isabella, dau. of Richard Garret, Esq.
Samuel, *b.* 20 May, 1830.
Anne, *m.* to Robert-John, eldest son of Capt. Thos. Montgomery, R.N.
Mary.

Mr. Lindsey-Bucknall *d.* 24 April, 1844.

Arms—Arg., two chevrons, gu., between three bucks' heads, cabossed, sa., attired, or.
Crest—A buck's head, cabossed, sa., attired, or.
Seat—Turin Castle, co. Mayo.

BUCKSTON OF BRADBORNE.

BUCKSTON, THE REV. GERMAN, of Bradborne, co. Derby, *b.* in Sept. 1797; *m.* in May, 1820, Ellen-Margaret, only child of the Rev. Richard-Rowland Ward, of Sutton-on-the-Hill, in the same shire, and has issue,

I. ROWLAND-GERMAN, *b.* in Nov. 1828.
I. Ellen-Martha. II. Emily-Frances-Anne.

Lineage.—The first of this family on record is HENRY DE BAWKESTONE, mentioned in a deed of the year 1256; and one Thomas Buxton was high-sheriff for Derbyshire in 1415. The regular pedigrees begin, however, about the year 1500, or somewhat earlier.

JOHN BUXTON, of Buxton, in Derbyshire, living 10th ELIZABETH, had two sons, WILLIAM, ancestor of the BUXTONS *of Buxton, Brassington, Bakewell,* and *Youlgrave;* and a 2nd son, HENRY BUXTON, of Bradborne, co. Derby, ancestor of

HENRY BUXTON, Esq. of Bradborne, *b.* in 1670, who *m.* Dorothy, sister of the Right Hon. Sir Richard Levinge, Bart., lord chief justice of the Court of Common Pleas in Ireland, and left at his decease, 6 May, 1721, an only child,

GEORGE BUXTON, Esq. of Bradborne, who *m.* Margaret, eldest dau. of Richard Stubbing, Esq. of West Broughton, and sister and co-heir of Thomas Stubbing, Esq., high-sheriff for Derbyshire in 1711, by whom he had three sons and three daus. Mr. Buxton *d.* in June, 1732, and was *s.* by his eldest son,

GEORGE BUCKSTON, Esq. of Bradborne, who adopted the present mode of spelling the name. He *m.* Sarah, dau. and co-heir of Richard Peacock, Esq. of Rodsley, in Derbyshire, and had two sons, GEORGE, his heir, and Richard, who *d.* young; and one dau. Martha, *m.* 1st, to Dr. Berridge, M.D., and 2ndly, to the Rev. Thomas-Francis Twigge, of Derby. Mr. Buckston *d.* 8 April, 1810, aged 89, and was *s.* by his son,

THE REV. GEORGE BUCKSTON, M.A. of Ashborne, rector of Shirland, and vicar of Bradborne, who *m.* Frances, dau. of Moreton Walhouse, Esq. of Hatherton, in Staffordshire, by Frances his wife, dau. of Sir Edward Littleton, Bart., of Pillaton, and had issue,

GERMAN, now of Bradborne.
John.
Henry-Thomas, in holy orders, *m.* Mary, dau. of John-Goodwin Johnson, Esq.
Martha-Frances, *m.* to the Rev. William Morgan, of Llandovery.
Georgiana, *m.* in 1816, to the Rev. George Milner, youngest son of the late Sir William Milner, Bart., of Nun Appleton, in Yorkshire.
Elizabeth.
Catharine, *m.* to Graves Archer, Esq. of the co. Wicklow.
Louisa-Ellen.

Mr. Buckston *d.* in Dec. 1826.

Arms—Sa., two bars, arg., between which three mullets, of the second; on a canton, also of the second, a buck, trippant, of the field.
Crest—A pelican vulning herself, or.
Motto—Fructum habet charitas.
Seat—Bradborne Hall, Derbyshire.

TATCHELL-BULLEN OF MARSHWOOD.

TATCHELL-BULLEN, JOHN, Esq. of Marshwood, co. Dorset, *b.* in 1808; *m.* 1st, in 1826, Sophia-Anne, dau. of William Cole Wood, Esq. of Martock, co. Somerset; and 2ndly, in 1843, Ann, dau. of W. Hoey, Esq., and relict of the late Capt. Forster, R.N. of Alnwick, co. Northumberland; he has issue,

I. JOHN, *b.* in 1847.
I. Sophia-Anne. II. Anne.

Mr. Tatchell-Bullen, J.P. and D.L. for Dorsetshire, assumed, by royal license, the surname of BULLEN after that of TATCHELL, and the arms of BULLEN quarterly with those of TATCHELL. He is eldest son and heir of the late William-Fitzherbert Bullen, Esq. of Stoke Abbott, co. Dorset (who *d.* in 1822), by Mary Tatchell his wife; and grandson of Simeon Bullen, Esq., and Elizabeth Fitzherbert his wife. He has one brother, Charles, lieut. R.N.

Arms—Quarterly, 1st and 4th: erm., on a chevron, az., between three bulls' heads, erased, sa., two swords, ppr., pommels and hilts, or, the points saltierways, encircled by a wreath of laurel, gold, for BULLEN; 2nd and 3rd, az., a cross-nebuly, or, in the first and fourth quarters, a lion, rampant, and in the second and third a cross-patée, arg., for TATCHELL.
Crest of BULLEN—Out of a naval crown, or, the sails arg., a bull's head, of the first, charged on the neck with an anchor, sa., between two wings, az.: of TATCHELL—on a mount, vert, in front of an oak-tree, fructed, ppr., a bow and arrow, in saltier, or, surmounted by a lion's face, gu.
Motto—A rege et Victoria.
Seat—Marshwood, co. Dorset.

BULLER OF DOWNES.

BULLER, JAMES-WENTWORTH, Esq. of Downes, co. Devon, J.P. and D.L., formerly M.P. for Exeter, *m.*

5 Oct. 1831, Charlotte-Juliana-Jane, 3rd dau. of the late Lord Henry Molyneux Howard (brother of Bernard-Edward, 15th Duke of Norfolk), and has issue.

Lineage.—The first of this ancient and honourable house, who settled in Cornwall, was

RICHARD BULLER, Esq. of Tregarrick, son of Alexander Buller, Esq. of Lillesdon, co. Devon, by Elizabeth his wife, dau. of Sir John Horsey, Knt. He *m.* Margaret, dau. and co-heir of Thomas Trethurffe, Esq. of Trethurffe, and cousin and co-heir of Edward Courtenay, Earl of Devon; and dying in Nov. 1555, left issue,

FRANCIS BULLER, Esq. of Shillingham, high-sheriff in 1600; who *m.* Thomasine, dau. of Thomas Williams, Esq. of Stowford, co. Devon, Speaker of the House of Commons, *temp.* ELIZABETH, by whom he left at his decease, in 1615, RICHARD, his heir; Thomasine, wife of Francis Rawle, lord of Tresparett, Cornwall; and Margaret, wife of Richard Kendall, Esq. of Treworgy. The son and heir,

SIR RICHARD BULLER, of Shillingham, high-sheriff of the county, and M.P. in 1637, *m.* Alice, dau. of Sir Rowland Hayward, and co-heir of her brother, Sir John Hayward, and by her had issue, FRANCIS, his heir; JOHN, of whom presently; Thomasine, *m.* to Josias Calmady, Esq. of Langdon Hall, co. Devon, eldest son and heir of Sir Shilston Calmady, and Honoria his wife, widow of Sir H. Prideaux. The eldest son and heir,

FRANCIS BULLER, Esq. of Shillingham and of Ospringe, co. Kent, *m.* Thomasine, dau. of Sir Thomas Honeywood, and had issue,

FRANCIS BULLER, Esq. of Shillingham, M.P. for Cornwall in 1640; who *m.* the sole dau. and heiress of Ezekiel Grosse, Esq. of Gowlden, by whom he acquired seventeen manors, and had issue,

James, who *d.* without surviving issue in 1710, when his estates went to the other branch, settled at Morval.
Anne, *m.* to W. Vivian, Esq. of Trewyn, and had a son, John, high-sheriff in 1678; who *m.* Anne, dau. of Sir Jonathan Trelawny, Bart.

JOHN BULLER, Esq. (2nd son of Sir Richard Buller), *m.* 1st, Anne, dau. and sole heir of John Coode, Esq. of Morval (through whom came this manor and the estates); and 2ndly, Jane, dau. and sole heir of Walter Langdon, Esq. of Keverell. By his first wife, Mr. Buller had issue, JOHN, his heir, and Mary, who *m.* Christopher Harris, Esq., M.P. of Hayne, co. Devon, whose brother, John, was master of the household to their Majesties GEORGE II. and GEORGE III. The son and heir,

JOHN BULLER, Esq. of Morval, M.P. for East Looe during the Protectorate; *m.* Mary, 3rd dau. and co-heir of the Hon. Sir Henry Pollexfen, chief justice of the Common Pleas, by whom he had issue, viz., JOHN-FRANCIS, his heir; Mary, *m.* to Thomas Dodson, Esq. of Tonkin, M.P. for Liskeard in 1702; and Elizabeth, *m.* to John Murth, Esq. of Talland. The son and heir,

JOHN-FRANCIS BULLER, Esq., of Morval, *m.* 22 July, 1716, Rebecca, dau. and co-heir of Sir Jonathan Trelawny, Bart., Bishop of Winchester; and *d.* in 1751, leaving issue,

I. JAMES, his heir.
II. Francis, M.P. for West Looe; *m.* Mary, dau. of Sir Copleston Bamfylde, Bart. (by Jane his wife, eldest dau. of Sir Courtenay Pole, Bart., M.P.), and relict of Sir Coventry Carew, Bart.; and *d. s. p.* in 1764.
III. John, *m.* 1st, 3 March, 1760, Mary, dau. of John St. Aubyn, Bart., M.P., by whom he had issue,
 1 John, M.P. for East Looe; who *m.* Augusta, dau. of R. Nixon, Esq.; but *d. s. p.* in 1807.
 2 Edward, of Trenant Park, vice-admiral of the Red, created a Baronet in 1808. (*See* BURKE'S *Extinct Baronetage*).
Mr. Buller *m.* 2ndly, 4 Nov. 1768, Caroline, dau. of John Hunter, Esq., and by her had GENERAL FREDERICK BULLER, of Lanreath.
III. William, Bishop of Exeter; *b.* in 1735; *m.* 19 April, 1762, Anne, dau. and co-heir of the Right Rev. John-Thomas, Bishop of Winchester, by whom he had issue,
 1 Anne, to her cousin, James Buller, Esq. of Downes.
 2 Susannah-Catherine, *m.* to Vice Admiral Sir John Duckworth, Bart., G.C.B.
I. Rebecca, *m.* in 1741, to Vice-Admiral Sir Charles Watson, and had issue, Charles, created a Baronet. (*See Peerage and Baronetage.*)
II. Anne, *m.* to Reginald Pole, Esq.
III. Mary, *m.* to Sir Joseph Copley, Bart.
IV. Elizabeth, *m.* to the Rev. John Sturges, D.D.

The eldest son and heir,

JAMES BULLER, Esq. of Morval, Downes, and Shillingham, M.P. for Cornwall; *m.* 1st, Elizabeth, dau. and co-heir of William Gould, Esq. of Downes, and by her (who *d.* in 1742, had a son, JAMES, his heir. He *m.* 2ndly, in 1744, Lady Jane Bathurst, 2nd dau. of Allen, 1st Earl Bathurst, and sister of the Lord Chancellor, by whom he had issue,

John. (*See* BULLER *of Morval.*)
Edward, who *m.* Mary, dau. and sole heir of John Hoskyn, Esq. of Port Looe; and *d.* 25 Oct. 1791, leaving issue.
John, in holy orders, of Perran, rector of St. Just.
Francis, the distinguished judge, created a Baronet, 29 Nov. 1789. (*See* BURKE'S *Peerage and Baronetage.*)
Catherine, *m.* to General Macarmick; and *d.* 17 Oct. 1807.
Jane, *m.* to Sir William Lemon, Bart.
Mary, *m.* to James Templer, Esq. of Stover Lodge, co. Devon.

The only son of the first marriage,

JAMES BULLER, Esq. of Downes, M.P. for Exeter; *b.* 1741; *m.* 1st, Husey, dau. of Thomas Gould, Esq. of Frome Wilet, co. Dorset, who *d.* in 1742; and 2ndly, Mary, 2nd dau. of John Hippisley-Coxe, Esq. of Stone Easton, co. Somerset, and sister of Lady de Dunstanville. Mr. Buller *d.* 11 Feb. 1772, leaving, by his 1st wife, a son and heir,

JAMES BULLER, Esq. of Downes and Shillingham, M.P. for Exeter for upwards of twenty years; who *m.* his cousin, Anne, dau. of the Right Rev. William Buller, Bishop of Exeter, and had issue,

JAMES-WENTWORTH, his heir, and present representative.
Thomas-Wentworth, commander R.N.
Hester-Eleanora, *m.* in 1827, to the Rev. Henry-Fox Strangways, nephew of the late Earl of Ilchester.

Arms—Sa., on a cross, arg., quarter-pierced, of the field, four eagles, displayed, of the first.
Crest—A Saracen's head couped, ppr.
Motto—Aquila non capit muscas.
Seat—Downes, co. Devon.

BULLER OF MORVAL.

BULLER, JOHN-FRANCIS, Esq. of Morval, co. Cornwall, *b.* 30 May, 1818.

Lineage.—JOHN BULLER, Esq. of Morval, eldest son of James Buller, Esq., by his 2nd wife, Lady Jane Bathurst, (*see* BULLER *of Downes*) was successively M.P. for Exeter, Launceston, and West Looe, and one of the lords of the Treasury. He *m.* Anne, sister of the late Sir William Lemon, Bart., M.P., and by her had issue,

JOHN, his heir.
William, *d. unm.* at Trinidad.
Richard, in holy orders, rector of Lanreath, *m.* Anne, dau. of James Templer, Esq. of Stover.
James, *m.* Mary, dau. of James Templer, Esq. of Stover.
Anthony (Sir), formerly a judge in Bengal, *m.* 4 Feb. 1805, Isabella-Jane, dau. of the late Sir William Lemon, Bart., M.P.
Charles, *m.* Barbara-Isabella, dau. of Col. Kirkpatrick, and has a son, Charles, late M.P. for West Looe and for Liskeard, chief secretary to Lord Durham, when in Canada.
Louisa, *m.* to Arthur Champernowne, Esq. of Dartington, co. Devon, M.P.
Maria, *m.* 5 July, 1808, to Sir Charles Hulse, Bart.
Charlotte, *m.* to Henry Clive, Esq.

The eldest son,

JOHN BULLER, Esq. of Morval, *m.* 1st, 1798, Elizabeth, younger dau. of the Hon. and Right Rev. James Yorke, Bishop of Ely, and niece of Philip, 2nd Earl of Hardwicke, who *d.* in 1802, and 2ndly, 29 June, 1814, Harriet, dau. of the late Sir Edward Hulse, Bart. of Breamore House, Hants, by whom he had issue a son, JOHN-FRANCIS, now of Morval, and four daus., viz., Harriet-Eliza, *m.* to the Rev. J.-B. Kitson; Frances-Anne, *m.* to W.-H. Pole-Carew, Esq; Charlotte-Jane; and Mary-Isabella, *m.* to Sir John-Thomas-Buller Duckworth, Bart. Mr. Buller, J.P. and D.L., formerly represented West Looe, and was high-sheriff of Cornwall in 1835. He *d.* 3 April, 1849.

Arms and *Motto*—As BULLER *of Downes.*
Seat—Morval, co. Cornwall.

BULLER OF LANREATH.

BULLER, FREDERICK, Esq. of Lanreath and Pelynt, co. Cornwall, a lieut.-gen. in the army, *m.* Charlotte, dau. of G. Tomlyns, Esq., and has issue,

I. FREDERICK-THOMAS, colonel in the army, *m.* 16 Aug. 1831, Lady Agnes Percy, elder dau. of the 2nd Duke of Northumberland.
II. William, in holy orders, *m.* 15 Sept. 1835, Leonora-Sophia, dau. of John Bond, Esq. of Grange, co. Dorset.

III. George, C.B., a major-general in the army.
IV. John, R.N., deceased.
I. Charlotte, *d. unm.*
II. Caroline, *m.* 16 March, 1836, to Lord Poltimore.
III. Agnes, deceased.
IV. Georgiana-Amelia, *m.* in 1836, to Charles, 2nd son of Sir Charles Hulse, Bart.

General Buller is son (by his 2nd wife, Caroline Hunter) of John Buller, Esq., 3rd son of John-Francis Buller, Esq. of Morval.

Arms and *Motto*—As BULLER *of Morval.*
Seat—Lanreath, co. Cornwall.

BULLOCK OF SHIPDHAM.

BULLOCK, DIANA, CATHERINE, MARY, and SUSANNA, of Shipdham, co. Norfolk, an estate which, with other lands in the same shire, they inherited as CO-HEIRS at the decease of their father, the Rev. Colby Bullock, 23 Sept. 1817. The youngest co-heir, SUSANNA, *m.* 20 June, 1820, the REV. WILLIAM GIRLING, of Scarning, in Norfolk, a magistrate of that county, and has issue,

I. WILLIAM GIRLING, *b.* 4 Nov. 1825.
I. Diana Girling. II. Mary-Girling.

Lineage.—In the 12th of HENRY VI., *anno* 1434, the name of John Bullock, Esq., occurs, among those returned as gentlemen of Norfolk; and in the year 1617, we find another John Bullock, who left a donation to the parish of Shipdham. *(See* BLOOMFIELD'S *Norfolk.)*

THOMAS BULLOCK, Esq. of Hingham Hall, son of William Bullock, and grandson of Thomas Bullock, of Shipdham, by Mary his wife, eldest dau. and co-heir of William Llewellyn, Esq., alderman of London, *m.* Catherine, dau. and sole heiress of John Berney, Esq. of Lynn, by his 1st wife, Catherine, 2nd dau. of George Townshend, Esq. of Wretham, by Mary, dau. of Sir Robert Baldock, Knt., and heiress of her brother, Robert Baldock, Esq. Mr. Bullock *d.* in Nov. 1766, leaving issue, COLBY; Thomas, who *m.* Catherine, dau. of — Morris, Esq.; Catherine, who *d. unm.*; Diana, *m.* to the Rev. Henry Lloyd, 3rd son of Guy Lloyd, Esq. of the co. Roscommon; and Elizabeth, *m.* to the Rev. John Beaver, rector of Scarning. The son and heir,

THE REV. COLBY BULLOCK, of Shipdham, heir to the TOWNSHENDS *of Wretham*, *m.* Elizabeth, dau. of Capel Brengies, Esq. of Hingham, whose mother was Elizabeth, sister and co-heir of George Bedell, Esq. of Woodrising, Norfolk, a descendant of the family of Sir Capel Bedell, Bart. of Huntingdonshire. The Rev. Colby Bullock *d.* 23 Sept. 1817, leaving four daus., Diana, Catherine, Mary, and Susanna, his co-heirs.

Arms—Gu., between a chevron, erm., three bulls' heads, caboshed, arg, armed, or.
Seat—Shipdham.

BULLOCK OF FALKBORNE.

BULLOCK, JONATHAN, Esq. of Falkborne Hall, co. Essex, J.P. and D.L., formerly capt. 1st dragoon-guards, *b.* 19 Oct. 1773; *m.* in April, 1811, Margaret, dau, of the Rev. Andrew Downes, eldest son of Robert, Lord Bishop of Raphoe, and grandson of Henry, Bishop of Derry, and of Elizabeth his wife, dau. of the Very Rev. Dr. Thomas Wilson, dean of Carlisle. By this lady Mr. Bullock has surviving issue,

I. HENRY, *b.* 26 July, 1815, *m.* 18 Aug. 1840, Cicely-Abigail, eldest dau. of Sir Edward Bowyer Smijth, Bart. of Hill Hall, Essex.
II. Walter-Trevelyan.
I. Elizabeth-Anne, *m.* 12 Oct. 1840, to her cousin, the Rev. John-Frederick Bullock, rector of Radwinter, Essex.
II. Henrietta-Maria, *m.* 9 Dec. 1851, to the Rev. Charles Eyres, rector of Melton, Norfolk.
III. Margaret-Emily, *m.* 1 July. 1845, to the Hon. and Rev. Llewellyn Irby, rector of Cottesbroke, Northamptonshire.
IV. Ellen-Rosetta, *m.* 8 Oct. 1846, to Henry-James, son and heir of the Rev. Henry Lee Warner, of Walsingham Abbey, Norfolk.

Lineage.—ROBERT BULLOCK, of Herburghfield, or Arborfield, co. Berks, who used the arms now borne by the Essex family, was sheriff of Berkshire and Oxfordshire, in the 8th of RICHARD II. He *d.* in 1405, leaving a son,

THOMAS BULLOCK, of Arborfield, whose great-grandson,

THOMAS BULLOCK, Esq., *m.* Alice, dau. of John Kingsmill, one of the justices of the King's Bench, and had, with six daus., as many sons, of whom the eldest, RICHARD, was of Arborfield; the 5th,

WILLIAM BULLOCK, Esq., *m.* Elizabeth, dau. and heir of Ralph Bellet, of Moreton, in Cheshire, and had a son and successor,

JOHN BULLOCK, Esq., the first of the family who settled at Great Wigborough, in Essex, where he *d.* 10 Feb. 1595, and was buried in the chancel of the church there. His grandson,

SIR EDWARD BULLOCK, Knt. of Loftes, in Great Totham, Essex, *b.* 1580, purchased from John Fortescue, Esq., about the year 1637, the manor and estate of Falkborne, in Essex.

LIEUT.-COL. JONATHAN BULLOCK, of Falkborne, the last direct male heir and descendant of Sir Edward, was M.P. for Essex. He *m.* in 1763, Miss Elizabeth Lante, but *d. s. p.* in 1809, when the estates devolved on (the eldest son of his sister Elizabeth, wife of Jonathan Watson, Esq.) his nephew,

JONATHAN-JOSIAH-CHRISTOPHER WATSON, Esq., who thus became of Falkborne Hall, and assumed in 1810, the surname and arms of BULLOCK. He *m.* Miss Juliana-Elizabeth Thomas, niece and heiress of Elizabeth Lante, wife of Lieut.-Col. Bullock, and had issue,

JONATHAN, now of Falkborne.
John, in holy orders, rector of Radwinter, in Essex, *m.* in 1806, Mary-Roberts, only dau. of Thomas Wilkinson, Esq., and *d.* 13 Aug. 1844, leaving issue.
Charles, who *m.* 11 May, 1807, Harriet, dau. of Thomas-Humphrey Lowe, Esq. of Bromsgrove, co. Worcester, and *d.* 22 Aug. 1842, leaving issue.
Henry-Robert, of Bury St. Edmunds, a major in the army, who *m.* in 1825, Charlotte, 2nd dau. of John Hall, Esq. of Weston Colville, Cambridgeshire, and *d.* in 1845, leaving issue.
Elizabeth-Lante, *m.* in 1819, to the Rev. Christopher-George Watson, rector of Melton, in Suffolk.

Mr. Bullock *d.* in Jan. 1832.

Arms—Gu., a chevron, erm., between three bulls' heads, caboesed, arg., armed, or; quartering WATSON.
Crest—Five Lochaber axes, ppr., bound with an escarf, gu., tassels, or.
Motto—Nil conscire sibi.
Seat—Falkborne Hall, Essex.

BULLOCK OF NORTH COKER.

BULLOCK, GEORGE, Esq. of North Coker House, co. Somerset, *b.* 15 Aug. 1797; *m.* 7 Dec. 1826, Maria-Caroline, youngest dau. of the late Charles Grove, Esq., M.D. (of the family of GROVE *of Zeals*, co. Wilts), and Elizabeth his wife, dau. of the late Arthur Acland, Esq. of Fairfield, co. Somerset, and sister of Sir John-Palmer Acland, Bart. (*see* BURKE'S *Baronetage*), and by her had issue,

I. GEORGE TROYTE-BULLOCK, of Christ Church, Oxford, *b.* 16 Oct. 1829; who, in conformity with the will of his maternal relative, the Rev. Edward-Berkeley Troyte, LL.D. of Huntsham Court, co. Devon, who *d.* 9 May, 1852, has assumed, by royal license, the surname of TROYTE, in addition to, and before that, of Bullock, and the arms of Troyte, quarterly, with his own family arms.
I. Mary-Elizabeth-Grove, who *d.* in infancy.

Mr. Bullock, J.P. and D.L., is son of the late John Bullock, Esq., by Sarah his wife, dau. of the late George Warry, Esq. of Shapwick, co. Somerset, and grandson of George Bullock, Esq., both of North Coker.

Arms—Gu., on a chevron, between three bulls' heads, caboesed, arg., armed, or, another chevron, erm., charged with as many annulets, az.
Crest—On a mount, vert, five black bills, erect, banded with a wreath of olive, ppr., therein pendent an escocheon, az., charged with a cross-crosslet, or.
Seat—North Coker, Yeovil.

BULTEEL OF FLETE.

BULTEEL, JOHN, Esq. of Flete, co. Devon, *b.* 26 June, 1827; *m.* 23 March, 1854, Euphemia-Emily, dau. of the late Lieut.-Col. Parsons, formerly Resident of Zante.

Lineage.—The late JOHN-CROCKER BULTEEL, Esq. of Flete and Lyneham, eldest son of John Bulteel, Esq. of the same places, was great-grandson of James Bulteel, Esq. of Flete, by Mary his wife, dau. and heir of Courtenay Crocker, Esq. of Lyneham, the last male representative of the senior branch of the ancient family of CROCKER *of Devon*:

"Crocker, Crewys, and Coplestone,
When the Conqueror came, were at home."

He sat in parliament for South Devon, and was high-sheriff of the county, 1841: he *m.* 13 May, 1826, Lady Elizabeth Grey, 2nd dau. of Charles, Earl Grey; and *d.* in Sept. 1843, leaving issue, JOHN, now of Flete; Mary-Elizabeth (the Hon.), maid of honour to the Queen; Georgiana-Frances; and Louisa-Emily-Charlotte.

Arms—Arg., a bend, between fourteen billets, gu., quartering CROCKER, viz., arg., a chevron, engrailed, gu., between three ravens, ppr.
Crest—Out of a ducal coronet, gu., a pair of wings, arg., billettée, of the first.
Seat—Flete, Devonshire.

BULWER OF HEYDON.

BULWER, WILLIAM-EARLE-LYTTON, Esq. of Heydon Hall, co. Norfolk, *b.* 28 April, 1799; *m.* 1st, 11 Dec. 1827, Emily, youngest dau. of General Gascoyne, late M.P. for Liverpool, and by her (who is deceased) has issue,

I. WILLIAM-GASCOYNE, Scots fusilier-guards; *b.* 1 Jan. 1829.
II. Edward-Gascoyne, 23rd Welsh fusiliers, *b.* in Dec. 1830.
III. Henry-Ernest.
I. Emily-Rose. II. Elizabeth-Maude.
III. Mary-Eleanor.

Mr. Bulwer *m.* 2ndly, in 1841, Elizabeth, dau. of William Green, Esq. of Forty Hill, Enfield.

Lineage.—The family of Bulwer, of Norman origin, was founded at the time of the Conquest, by TYRUS or TUROLD DE DALLING, who was enfeoffed of the lordships of Wood Dalling and Bynham, by Peter de Valoins, who held those lands from the CONQUEROR. When the Lord Valoins established the priory of Bynham, this Turold gave two parts of his tithes to that establishment; and his son, SIR RALPH DE DALLING, granted in some years after to the monks of the same monastery, the churches of Wood Dalling and of Little Ryburgh, with lands in each parish. The late

WILLIAM-EARLE BULWER, Esq. of Heydon Hall, a brigadier-general in the army, and colonel of the 106th foot; *m.* Elizabeth, dau. and sole heir of Richard-Warburton Lytton, Esq. of Knebworth Park, Herts, had three sons, viz.,

WILLIAM-EARLE-LYTTON, now of Heydon.
Henry-Lytton (The Right Hon. Sir), G.C.B., *b.* in 1804, *m.* 1848, the Hon. Georgina Wellesley, dau. of Lord Cowley.
Edward-Lytton (Sir), created a BARONET in 1838. (*See* BURKE'S *Peerage and Baronetage.*)

General Bulwer *d.* in 1807.

Arms—Gu., on a chevron, between three eaglets, regardant, or, as many cinquefoils, sa.
Crest—A horned wolf's head, erased, erm., crined and armed, or.
Motto—Adversis major, par secundis.
Seat—Heydon Hall, Norfolk.

BUNBURY OF MOYLE.

BUNBURY, KANE, Esq. of Moyle, co. Carlow, colonel in the army.

Lineage.—SIR HENRY BUNBURY, of Stanny, co. Chester, representative of the very ancient family of BUNBURY *of Bunbury*, received the honour of knighthood from Queen ELIZABETH. He *m.* 1st, Anne, dau. of Jefferey Shackerley, of Shackerley, co. Lancaster, and had a son, HENRY, his heir, of Stanny, ancestor of the Baronets of Stanny. By his 2nd wife, Martha, dau. of Sir William Norris, Knt. of Speke, Sir Henry had a son,

THOMAS BUNBURY, Esq., who *m.* Eleanor, dau. of Henry Birkenhead, Esq. of Backford, co. Chester, and was father of

BENJAMIN BUNBURY, Esq., who went to reside in Ireland, and settled at Killerigg, co. Carlow. By Elizabeth-Frances his wife, widow of Mr. Shepherd, he had a dau., Diana, *m.* to Mr. Barnes, and five sons,

JOSEPH, who *m.* Hannah, dau. of the Venerable Edward Hinton, archdeacon of Ossory, and had a dau., Henrietta, *m.* to Paul Minchin, Esq., and a son, HENRY BUNBURY, Esq. of Johnstown, co. Carlow.
Thomas, founder of the House of Cloghna, co. Carlow.
WILLIAM, of whom presently.
Matthew, of Kilfacle, co. Tipperary.
Benjamin, ancestor of the BUNBURYS *of Killerigg*, co. Carlow.

The 3rd son,

WILLIAM BUNBURY, Esq. of Lisnevagh, co. Carlow, whose will, dated 13 Oct., was proved 25 Oct. 1710, *m.* Elizabeth Penderell, and had a dau., Mary, *m.* to the Rev. Gibson Raymond, and two sons, WILLIAM, of Lisnevagh, who *d. unm.* in 1754, and THOMAS. The 2nd son,

THOMAS BUNBURY, Esq., settled at Kill, co. Carlow. He *m.* 1st, 1735, Catherine, dau. of Josias Campbell, Esq. of Drumsna, co. Leitrim, and by her, who *d.* in 1758, had issue, WILLIAM, his heir; George, who *d.* 7 May, 1820; Benjamin, who *m.* Margaret, dau. of the Rev. George Gowan, and had three children, who *d. unm.*; and Letitia, who *m.* George Gough, Esq., lieut.-col. of the Limerick Militia, and had a son, Hugh, present Lord Gough, G.C.B. Mr. Bunbury *m.* 2ndly, Susanna-Priscilla, sister of John Isaac, Esq., killed at Fontenoy, and by her had a son, Thomas, who *m.* Miss M. Green; and a dau., Jane, wife of the Rev. Benedict Arthur. The eldest son,

WILLIAM BUNBURY, Esq. of Lisnevagh, M.P. for the county of Carlow, *m.* in 1773, Katherine, dau. of R. Kane, Esq., and had issue,

THOMAS, his heir. KANE, now of Moyle.
Elizabeth, *d. unm.*
Jane, who *m.* in 1797, John McClintock, Esq. of Drumcar, co. Louth. (*See* MCCLINTOCK-BUNBURY *of Lisnevagh.*)

Mr. Bunbury *d.* in 1778, and was *s.* by his eldest son,

THOMAS BUNBURY, Esq., of Lisnevagh and Moyle, M.P. for the co. Carlow, who *d. unm.* 28 May, 1846, and was *s.* by his brother, the present Col. Kane Bunbury, of Moyle.

Arms—Erm., a chess-rook between two leopard's faces, in bend, between two bendlets, sa.
Crest—Two swords, saltierwise, through the mouth of a leopard's face, or.
Motto—Firmum in vitâ nihil.
Seat—Moyle, co. Carlow.

BUNBURY OF LISNEVAGH.

M'CLINTOCK-BUNBURY, WILLIAM-BUNBURY, Esq. of Lisnevagh, co. Carlow, M.P., capt. R.N., 2nd son of JOHN M'CLINTOCK, Esq. of Drumcar, co. Louth (*see that family*), *b.* in 1800; *m.* in 1842, Pauline-Caroline-Diana-Mary, 2nd dau. of Sir James-Mathew Stronge, Bart. of Tynan Abbey, co. Armagh, and has issue,

I. THOMAS, *b.* in Nov. 1849.
II. John-William, *b.* Sept. 1851.
I. Helen. II. Isabella.

Captain M'Clintock-Bunbury, in compliance with the will of his maternal uncle, Thomas Bunbury, Esq., M.P., of Moyle, who *d.* in 1846, assumed the name and arms of BUNBURY, in addition to those of M'CLINTOCK.

Arms—Quarterly: 1st and 4th, erm., a chess-rook between two leopard's faces in bend, between two bendlets, sa., for BUNBURY; 2nd and 3rd, per pale, gu. and az., a chevron, erm., between three escallop-shells, arg., for M'CLINTOCK.
Crest—In front of a tree, ppr., on a mount, vert, a leopard's head, paly of six, arg. and sa., transfixed by two arrows, in saltier, also ppr., for BUNBURY. A lion, passant, ppr., for M'CLINTOCK.
Motto—Virtus paret robor.
Seat—Lisnevagh, co. Carlow.

BUND OF WICK HOUSE.

BUND, THE REV. THOMAS-HENRY, of Wick House, co. Worcester, *s.* his father in 1854.

Lineage.—The first entry in the present registries of the family of Bund is dated 13 Jan. 1559, and records the marriage of Edwarde Frenche and Jone Bund. At that time the family possessed some of the property which they still hold.

THOMAS BUND, Esq., *m.* 1st, Eliza Pardoe, but had no

issue. He m. 2ndly, Susannah, dau. of the Rev. John Vernon, rector of Martley, co. Worcester, and had issue, WILLIAM, of whom presently; John, d. unm.; Thomas, rector of Woking, Surrey, m. and had a son, who d. s. p.; Henry, rector of Fladbury, who took the name of VERNON, d. unm.; Richard, d. young; Sarah, m. to W. Cooke, Esq. of Worcester; and Elizabeth, d. unm. The eldest son,

WILLIAM BUND, Esq., m. 1st, Mary, dau. and heiress of John Parsons, Esq. of Overbury, co. Worcester, and 2ndly, Alicia Cox, and by the former only had issue,

WILLIAM, m. Catharine, 3rd dau. of John Dandridge, Esq. of Great Malvern, and had issue a son, d. young, and two daus., Mary, m. to the Rev. William Probyn, vicar of Pershore, and Anna-Maria, m. George Palmer, Esq. of Nazing Park, co. Essex.

And another son,

THOMAS BUND, Esq., who m. 29 Nov. 1768, Susannah, youngest dau. of Benjamin Johnson, Esq. of Worcester, and d. 10 Aug. 1815, having had issue,

THOMAS-HENRY, of Wick House.
WILLIAM, m. Ann-Ryder Mainprise, and had issue a son, Wilmot-Johnson, d. young, and a dau., Susannah-Ursula.

The elder son,

THOMAS HENRY BUND, Esq. of Wick House, J.P. and D.L., col. of the Worcestershire Militia, b. 11 July, 1774, m. 16 Nov. 1802, Anne, dau. and only surviving child of the Rev. Pynson Wilmot, vicar of Halesowen, co. Salop, and has issue,

THOMAS-HENRY-BENJAMIN, in holy orders.
Ann-Susannah-Kent, m. to John-Walpole Willis, one of H. M. judges in New South Wales.
Ursula-Frances, m. to the Rev. Henry-Thomas Hill, incumbent of Lye, near Stourbridge, co. Worcester.
Eliza-Emily.

Arms—Quarterly: 1st and 4th, gu., three eagle's legs, erased à la cuisse, or, for BUND; 2nd, az., a chevron, erm., between three trefoils, arg., for PARSONS; 3rd, arg., a fesse, lozengy, between three lion's heads, erased, gu., for JOHNSON.
Crest—An eagle's head, erased, or.
Seat—Wick House, co. Worcester.

BUNNY OF SPEEN HILL.

BUNNY, EDWARD-BRICE, Esq. of Speen Hill, Newbury, co. Berks, J.P. and D.L.; m. 29 June, 1824, Emma, younger dau. and co-heir of James Piggott, Esq. of Fitz Hall, Iping, co. Sussex, and has,

I. EDWARD-JOHN, capt. royal Sussex light infantry militia, b. 27 Feb. 1828.

Lineage.—RICHARD BUNNY, Esq. of Ibdrope, co. Hants, of which estate his ancestors were in possession from the time of King JOHN, as appears by a deed of that date, was father (with four daus., Agnes, Thomason, Margaret, and Mary) of a son, ROBERT, who, by his wife Mary, was father of

EDMOND BUNNY, Esq. who m. Jane Buck, of Welford, and their only son,

BLANDY-BUCK BUNNY, Esq., dying 22 Feb. 1777, left, by his wife Sarah, dau. of Richard Brice, Esq., with two sons and a dau., all of whom d. s. p., two other sons, John Bunny, who m. Alice Pyke, of Wherwell, Hants, by whom he had an only dau., Alice, and

JOSEPH BUNNY, Esq., who m. Anne-Mariot, dau. of Capt. Bennett, E. I. Co.'s naval service; and by her, who d. in 1772, had

Joseph-Blandy, m. Elizabeth, dau. of Rev. Philip Worsley, of Cheshunt, Herts.
Mariot, m. to John Martineau, Esq. of Stamford Hill, near London.

He m. 2ndly, Elizabeth, dau. of John Rigby, Esq. of Chowbent, co. Lancaster, and by her, who also d. in 1836, had further issue,

EDWARD-BRICE, now of Speen Hill. John-Mort.
Jere, of Newbury, m. 2 April, 1813, Clara, only surviving dau. of the late Samuel Slocock, of Newbury, and by her, who d. 16 Nov. 1835, had issue surviving, Charles, Brice-Frederick, Edward-William, Henry-Arthur, Clara, Caroline-Eliza, Laura, Gertrude, and Alice.

Arms—Arg., a chevron, between three goat's heads, erased, sa.; on an escutcheon of pretence, per fesse, arg. and sa., a lion, rampant, between three pickaxes, all counterchanged, for PIGGOTT.
Crest—A goat's head, erased, sa., attired, or; on one of the horns two annulets conjoined, of the last.
Motto—Propositi tenax.
Seat—Speen Hill, Newbury, co. Berks.

BURCHALL OF BROADFIELD COURT.

BURCHALL, JOHN-HENRY, Esq. of Broadfield Court, co. Hereford, J.P., b. 27 June, 1777; m. 2 April, 1803, Katherine, dau. of William Cooke, Esq. of Church Hill, Walthamstow, a director of the Bank of England, and has one dau.,

I. SUSANNA-JANE, m. to William Helme, Esq. of Stroud, co. Gloucester.

Lineage.—THE REV. HENRY BURCHALL, D.D., rector of Norton-under-Hamdon, had, by Elizabeth his wife, two sons and two daus. The eldest son,

ROBERT BURCHALL, Esq., m. 1st, 8 April, 1775, Susanna, dau. of the Rev. Dr. Chapone, D.D., formerly minister at St. Mary's, Lee, Layton, Essex, and niece of Mrs. Chapone, authoress of *Chapone's Letters*, and by her had issue,

JOHN-HENRY, of Broadfield Court.
William-Mounteny. Robert.
Catharine, m. to Henry Cooke, Esq. of Walthamstow.
Susanna, m. to John Hawes, Esq. of Colchester.
Ann, m. to Joseph Ocllyer, Esq. of Castlebury, co. Herts.
Anna-Maria. Elizabeth-Towne. Harriet.

Mr. Burchall m. 2ndly, 13 Nov. 1800, Anne, widow of William Cooke, Esq. of Church Hill, Walthamstow, a Director of the Bank of England.

Arms—Arg., on a chevron, az., between three cross-crosslets, fitchée, sa., as many fleurs-de-lis, or.
Crest—A lion, rampant, az., supporting a tree, vert.
Seat—Broadfield Court, Herefordshire.

BURCHELL OF BUSHEY.

(*See* HERNE.)

BURDETT OF BALLYMANY AND BALLYWATER.

BURDETT, GEORGE, Esq. of Ballymany, co. Kildare, and Ballywater, co. Tipperary, b. 25 Sept. 1813.

Lineage.—This family derives from a common ancestor with that of BURDETT *of Foremark*, co. Derby. Its founders in Ireland were Thomas and Samuel Burdett, sons of Alderman Burdett, of London. The former, taking up his residence at Garrahill, was ancestor of the BURDETTS *of Dunmore*, Barts., and the younger was

SAMUEL BURDETT, who settled at Lismalin, co. Tipperary. His 2nd son,

THE VERY REV. JOHN BURDETT, dean of Clonfert, m. Margaret, 5th dau. of Sir John Cole, Bart. of Newland, co. Dublin, and dying in 1726, left, with other issue, a son,

ARTHUR BURDETT, Esq. of Lismalin, who m. Grace, dau. of John Head, Esq. of Derry Castle, and had (with three daus., the eldest of whom, Grace, m. Barry, 1st Earl of Farnham) a son,

GEORGE BURDETT, Esq. of The Heath House, Queen's Co., M.P. for Thomastown and Callan. He m. Jane, 2nd dau. of — Frend, Esq., and had issue,

I. ARTHUR, of whom presently.
II. George, of Longtown House, co. Kildare, capt. R.N., deceased, m. 1st, Mary-Jane, dau. of the late Lieut.-Gen. Whitelock; and 2ndly, Catherine-Dorothea, only dau. and heiress of the late Col. William Browne, of Glengarry, co. Dublin, by whom he had issue,
  1 George, m. to Harriett, dau. of William Willan, Esq.
  1 Frances-Elizabeth, m. to Thomas-Pery Knox, Esq.
  2 Catherine-Jane, m. in 1836, to Richard Brouncker, Esq. of Boveridge, co. Dorset.
III. JOHN (*see* BURDETT *of Hunstanton*).
I. Grace, m. to Henry-Peisley L'Estrange, Esq. of Moystown, King's County.
II. Jane, m. to Francis Brooke, Esq., lieut.-col. 4th or King's Own regt. of foot, and brother of the late Sir Henry Brooke, of Colebrook, Bart.

The eldest son,

ARTHUR BURDETT, Esq., m. in 1810, Anna, only dau. of William Ripley, Esq. of Liverpool, and had issue,

GEORGE, present representative. Arthur.
Mary-Jane.
Anna, m. in 1842, to Edward-John Collingwood, Esq., Lilburn Tower and Churton House, co. Northumberland.
Adelaide-Louisa, m. in 1842, to her cousin, John-Head Burdett, Esq. of Hunstanton, King's County.

Arms—Az., two bars, or; a crescent for difference.
Crest—A lion's head, erased, sa.

BURDETT OF HUNSTANTON.

BURDETT, JOHN-HEAD, Esq. of Hunstanton, King's Co., J.P., barrister-at-law, m. 20 July, 1842, his first-cousin, Adelaide-Louisa, youngest dau. of the late Arthur Burdett, Esq. of Great George's-street, Dublin, by Anna his wife, dau. of William Ripley, Esq. of Rodney-street, Liverpool.

Lineage.—THE REV. JOHN BURDETT, vicar of Rynach and Gallen, King's Co., and rector of Ballygarth, co. Meath, youngest son of Geo. Burdett, Esq. of The Heath House, Queen's Co., and of the city of Dublin, M.P., m. in Dec. 1802, Margaret-Anne, 6th dau. of Michael Head, Esq. late of Derry Castle, co. Tipperary, by Margaret his wife, 6th dau. of Henry Prittie, Esq. of Kilbury, in the same co., aunt to the 1st Lord Dunalley, and had issue,

JOHN-HEAD, now of Hunstanton.
Henry, in holy orders, m. in June, 1842, Sybilla, dau. of Thomas Fleetwood, Esq.
Arthur-Michael. George-Prittie. Francis-Robert.
Margaret-Anne. Jane.
Grace, m. 2 Jan. 1834, to John-Eyre Trench, Esq. of Clonfert House, co. Galway.
Maria. Louisa.

Arms, Crest, and *Motto*—As BURDETT *of Ballymany and Ballywater.*
Seat—Hunstanton, King's County.

BURDON OF CASTLE EDEN.

BURDON, ROWLAND, Esq. of Castle Eden, co. Durham, J.P., s. his father 17 Sept. 1838, and is married.

Lineage.—ROWLAND BURDON, Esq., descended from Thomas Burdon, of Stockton-upon-Tees, *temp.* EDWARD IV., was nine times mayor of Stockton-upon-Tees, between the years 1641 and 1655. He m. Elizabeth, dau. of John Swainston, and had, with several daus., two sons, viz., GEORGE, his heir, and Henry, whose granddau., Mary Burdon, m. in 1743, Wm. Webster, Esq. Mr. Burdon d. in 1657, and was s. by his elder son,

GEORGE BURDON, Esq. of Stockton-on-Tees, 1648, who m. Elizabeth, dau. of William Hutchinson, Esq. of Frindon, in the co. of Durham, and dying in 1681, was s. by his only surviving son,

THE REV. ROWLAND BURDON, some time of Sedgfield, in the co. of Durham, 1679, m. Sarah, dau. of John Reeve, Esq. of Great Milton, in the co. of Oxford, and dying in 1750, was s. by his son,

ROWLAND BURDON, bapt. 7 Jan. 1724, a merchant of Newcastle-upon-Tyne, who purchased Castle Eden in 1758. He m. 26 Aug. 1755, Elizabeth, dau. of George Smith, Esq. of Burnhall, in the co. of Durham, and dying 25 Oct. 1786, left an only child,

ROWLAND BURDON, Esq. of Castle Eden, M.P. for the co. Durham, who m. 1st, 27 June, 1780, Margaret, dau. of Charles Brandling, Esq. of Gosforth, in Northumberland, by whom (who d. 17 Feb. 1791) he had an only dau., Elizabeth, b. 18 Jan. 1788, d. 30 Jan. 1791. Mr. Burdon m. 2ndly, in 1794, Cotsford, dau. and sole heiress of General Richard Matthews, and had issue, ROWLAND, his heir; Richard; John; Cotsford; Elizabeth-Anne; Frances; and Mary-Cotsford. Mr. Burdon d. 17 Sept. 1838, in his 82nd year.

Arms—Az., three palmer's staves, inter-semée of cross-crosslets, gu.
Seat—Castle Eden.

BURGES OF PARKANAUR AND EAST HAM.

BURGES, JOHN-YNYR, Esq. of Parkanaur, co. Tyrone, and Thorpe Hall and East Ham, co. Essex, J.P. and D.L., high-sheriff of the co. of Tyrone in 1829, b. 31 Jan. 1798; m. 21 March, 1833, Lady Caroline Clements, youngest dau. of the late Earl of Leitrim, and has had issue,

I. YNYR-HENRY, b. 31 Jan. 1834.
II. Charles-Sheffington, b. 19 Aug. 1835, deceased.
III. Clements-Keppel, d. in March, 1840.
IV. Wamphay-John-Richard-Alexander, b. 25 Aug. 1843, deceased.
I. Mary-Anne-Margaret. II. Alice-Caroline.

Mr. Burges s. to the family estates upon the death, in 1838, s. p., of his relative, Margaret, Dowager Countess of Poulett, dau. and sole heir of his grand-uncle, Ynyr Burgess, Esq. of East Ham, by Margaret his wife, dau. of Governor Brown. Mr. Burges then assumed the additional arms of LLOYD.

Lineage.—The surname of this family, as appears from ancient documents, was formerly De Burges, afterwards Burches, and subsequently, in 1747, the present one was adopted.

JOSEPH BURGES, Esq., m. in 1716, Elizabeth, dau. of Ynyr Lloyd, Esq. of East Ham, co. Essex, and had (with two daus., Margaret; and Alice, wife of Francis Methold, Esq.) three sons, viz., Joseph, d. in 1746; JOHN, of whom hereafter; YNYR, of East Ham, m. in 1792, Margaret, dau. of Governor Brown, by whom he had issue, a dau. and heir, Margaret, m. 1st, to Sir John Smith, Bart., who took the additional surname of Burges, but d. s. p.; his widow m. 2ndly, in July, 1816, John, 4th and late Earl Poulett, of Hinton St. George, co. Somerset, but d. s. p. in May, 1838, when her kinsman, the present JOHN-YNYR BURGES, s. her in her estates. The 2nd son,

JOHN BURGES, Esq., m. 20 Nov. 1763, Martha, dau. of Robert Ford, Esq., and had issue, (with two daus., viz., Mary, m. in 1784, to George Perry, Esq. of Mullaghmore, co. Tyrone, and Martha, m. in 1787, to James Johnston, Esq. of Knappagh, co. Armagh,) a son,

JOHN-HENRY BURGES, Esq. of Wood Park, co. Armagh, b. 15 July, 1766, m. in 1794, Marianne, eldest dau. and eventually co-heir of the late Sir Richard Johnston, Bart. of Gilford, and had issue,

JOHN-YNYR, now of Parkanaur and East Ham.
Richard.
Margaret-Anne, m. in July, 1815, to Lieut.-Colonel (now General) Thomas Charretie, of the 2nd Life-guards.
Matilda, d. Nov. 1805.

Arms—Or, a fesse, chequy, arg. and az.; in chief, two cross-crosslets, gu., and in base a covered cup, of the last, for BURGES; quartering, paly of eight, or and gu., all within a bordure, pellettée, or, for LLOYD.
Crests—A dove, rising, arg., beaked and membered, gu., in its beak a palm-branch, ppr., for BURGES; a lion, rampant, gu., langued, az., in the dexter paw an annulet, enclosing a fleur-de-lis, arg., for LLOYD.
Motto—Tace aut face.
Seats—East Ham and Thorpe Hall, co. Essex; and Parkanaur, co. Tyrone, Ireland.

HUSSEY-BURGH OF DONORE AND DROMKEEN.

HUSSEY-BURGH, WALTER, Esq. of Donore House, co. Kildare, and of Dromkeen House, co. Limerick, J.P., high-sheriff of Kildare in 1839-40, b. 27 June, 1801; m. 1st, 18 May, 1820, Elizabeth-Jane, dau. of James Fitzgerald, of Stephenton, co. Clare, Esq., by whom he had,

I. JOHN-HAMILTON, b. 10 June, 1822.
I. Mary-Adelaide. II. Charlotte-Elizabeth.
III. Elizabeth-Jane. IV. Anna-Maria.
V. Louisa-Catharine. VI. Flora.
VII. Harriett.

He m. 2ndly, 11 Feb. 1840, Hessie, dau. of the Rev. Alexander M'Clintock, 2nd son of the late John M'Clintock, of Drumcar, co. Louth, Esq.

Lineage.—THE REV. ULYSSES BURGH, of Dromkeen, co. Limerick, son of Richard Burgh or Burke, of Dromkeen, Esq., and representative of the Dromkeen branch of the house of De Burgh, was consecrated bishop of Ardagh, in 1692. He m. Mary, dau. of William Kingsmill, Esq. of Ballibeg, co. Cork, and had issue,

I. RICHARD, of Dromkeen, in holy orders, prebendary of Kilbragh, who m. Elizabeth, dau. of — Griffin, Esq. of London, and by her, who d. in 1716, left at his decease, (with daus., of whom the eldest, Mary, m. Lloyd of Castle Lloyd,) two sons,
   1 THOMAS, of Dromkeen, whose will, dated 5 Dec. 1734, was proved in 1747. He m. his cousin, Mary Burgh, of Oldtown, and had, with a son, RICHARD, of Drumkeen, who d. s. p. in 1762, a dau., Mary, m. to Philpot Wolfe, eldest son and heir of John Wolfe, Esq. of Forenaghts, co. Kildare.
   2 Rickard, of Mount Bruis, co. Tipperary, in holy orders, who m. Martha, dau. of Peter Carew, Esq., and dying in 1778, left issue, Rickard-Ulysses, in holy orders; Thomas, rector of Ardcanny, co. Limerick; and Mary, m. to William Byam, Esq. of Byams, Antigua; and Woodborough, co. Somerset, an officer in the 68th regt. (*See that family.*)
II. WILLIAM, of Bert, ancestor of Lord Downes.
III. THOMAS, of Old Town, of whom presently.
IV. Charles.

v. John, of Troy House, co. Monmouth, father of two sons,

1 The Rev. Henry Burgh, whose only dau. and heir, Maria, m. Thomas Johnes, Esq. of Hafod.
2 Ashburnham Burgh, father of Henry Burgh, Esq. of Stanley Park, co. Gloucester.

I. Dorothy, m. to Thomas Smyth, bishop of Limerick, ancestor of the noble house of Gort.

The 3rd son,

THOMAS BURGH, Esq. of Old Town, co. Kildare, b. in 1670, engineer and surveyor-general, m. Mary, dau. of William Smith, bishop of Kilmore, and had (with a son, Thomas, of Old Town, grandfather of the VERY REV. JOHN-THOMAS BURGH, dean of Cloyne) two daus., of whom ELIZABETH BURGH m. Ignatius Hussey, Esq. of Donore, co. Kildare, and had a son and successor,

THE RIGHT HON. WALTER HUSSEY-BURGH, distinguished as one of the most eloquent advocates at the Irish bar. He became afterwards lord chief baron of the court of Exchequer in Ireland. Mr. Hussey-Burgh became possessed of one-half of the property of Dromkeen, on the death of Rickard Burgh, and assumed the name of BURGH, in accordance with that gentleman's will. He was b. 23 Aug. 1742, m. 4 July, 1767, Anne, dau. of Thomas Burgh, of Bert, co. Kildare, Esq., by Anne his wife, dau. of Dive Downes, bishop of Cork and Ross; and by her, who d. 1782, had issue,

JOHN, of whom presently.
Eliza, m. 4 Feb. 1797, to Archdeacon Hill.
Catherine, m. 4 Nov. 1794, to Sir John Macartney, Bart.; d. 10 Sept. 1840.
Mary, m. in Feb. 1793, to Richard Griffith, Esq.; d. 8 Sept. 1820.
Anne, m. 19 May, 1798, to B. M'Carthy, Esq.

Chief Baron Hussey-Burgh d. 29 Sept. 1783, and was s. by his son,

THE REV. JOHN-HUSSEY BURGH, of Dromkeen, m. 31 July, 1800, Mary, dau. of Robert Burgh, Esq., 3rd son of Thomas Burgh, of Bert, Esq., ancestor of Lord Downes, and had issue,

WALTER, now of Dromkeen.
Robert, b. 1 Sept. 1808, in holy orders; m. Louisa, dau. of James Fitzgerald, Esq. of Stephenton, co. Clare.
Edward, b. 30 Aug. 1811.
Thomas, b. 30 Nov. 1816, in the army.
Anne, m. to — Reardon, Esq. of Limerick.

Mr. Hussey-Burgh d. 7 May, 1830.

Arms—Or, a cross, gu., quartering HUSSEY.
Crests—A cat-a-mountain, sejant-guardant, ppr., collared and chained, or, for BURGH; a hind, passant, arg., on a mount, vert, and under a tree, ppr., for HUSSEY.
Motto—A cruce salus.
Seats—Donore House, co. Kildare; Dromkeen House, co. Limerick.

BURKE OF KNOCKNAGUR.

BURKE, WILLIAM, Esq. of Knocknagur, co. Galway, b. 20 March, 1794; m. 9 July, 1827, Fanny-Xaveria, only dau. of Thomas Tucker, Esq. of Brook Lodge, co. Sussex, by Marianne his wife, dau. of James Wiseman, Esq. of Seville, and sister of Cardinal Wiseman. By her he has issue,

I. RICKARD-CHRISTOPHER, b. 2 July, 1828.
II. Thomas-Henry, b. 29 May, 1829.
III. William, b. 15 Aug. 1831.
IV. Theobald-Edmund, b. 24 March, 1833.
V. Charles-Alfred, b. 15 July, 1834.
VI. Augustus-Joseph-Nicholas, b. 28 July, 1836.
VII. Adelm-Ulick, b. 1 April, 1840.
I. Marianne-Alice-Aline.

Lineage.—WILLIAM BURKE, Esq. of Keelogues, 3rd son, by his wife Mary Cheevers, of Killyan, of Rickard Burke, Esq., 4th son of Sir John Burke, 4th Bart. of Glinsk (see BURKE's *Peerage and Baronetage*), m. in 1762, Margaret, dau. of Thomas Coleman, Esq., and by her (who d. in 1826) left at his decease in 1796 (with two daus., Margaret, m. to William, Earl of Howth; and Mary, m. to Martin Kirwan, Esq of Blindwell) two sons, RICKARD, his heir, and William, who m. Lady Matilda St. Lawrence, and has issue. The eldest son,

RICKARD BURKE, of Keelogues, co. Galway, m. in 1792, Elizabeth, widow of William Bermingham, Esq., and eldest dau. of John Croghan, Esq. of Croghan, co. Roscommon, by Matilda his wife, dau. of Major Bermingham, a claimant to the Barony of Athenry; and by her, who d. in July, 1831, left at his decease in Aug. 1819, a son and successor, the present WILLIAM BURKE, Esq. of Knocknagur.

Arms—Or, a cross, gu.; in the 1st quarter, a lion, rampant, sa.
Crest—Out of a ducal coronet, or, a plume of five ostrich feathers, arg.
Motto—In hoc signo vinces.
Seat—Knocknagur, co. Galway.

BURKE OF OWER.

BURKE, JOSEPH, Esq. of Ower, co. Galway, b. 8 July, 1781; m. 9 April, 1823, Margaret, 3rd dau. of Oliver Martyn, Esq., M.D., of Galway, of the family of the MARTYNS *of Tolirea*, and has issue,

I. WILLIAM, barrister-at-law.
II. Oliver.
III. John.
IV. Richard.
I. Elisabeth.
II. Teresa.
III. Anna-Maria.

Mr. Burke s. his brother 3 Oct. 1849.

Lineage.—SIR REDMOND DE BURGH, son of Sir William or Ulick de Burgh, called *The Grey*, ancestor to the Marquess of Clanricarde, d. in 1324, leaving a son,

JOHN BUY, or *The Yellow*, from whom his descendants, a powerful clan in the barony of Clare, co. Galway, were termed the sept of John Buy M'Redmond. From him descended

MYLES DE BURGH or BURKE, living about the year 1480, whose son,

REDMOND DE BURGH, was father of

ULICK BURKE, who d. in 1571, as appears from an inquisition taken in Galway in 1586. He was s. by his son,

JOHN BURKE, who m. Margaret, dau. of Thady Kelly, of Mullaghmore, a descendant of the ancient princes of Hymaine, and by her left,

JOHN, of whom presently.
Catherine, m. to Andrew Browne, of Brownestown.
Isabella, m. to O'Connor Don.

The son and heir,

JOHN BURKE, forfeited, during the confiscations, the greater portion of his estates, retaining, however, Ower, part of the ancient property. He m. Mary Bermingham, dau. of the 17th Lord Athenry, premier Baron of Ireland, by whom he left at his death, in 1684 or 1685,

ULICK, of whom presently.
Francis, m. Margaret, dau. of Darby Daly, of Killimore.
Thomas, m. Mary, dau. of Edward Hearne, of Hearnesbrook.

The son and successor,

ULICK BURKE, Esq. of Ower, m. Catherine, dau. of Stephen Lynch, of Doughiskea, by Elliner, dau. of Sir John Browne, Bart. of The Neale, ancestor to Lord Kilmaine. By her he left at his death, in 1716,

I. John, d. s. p., a captain in General Dillon's regiment in France.
II. MYLES, of whom presently.
III. Dominick, whose son, Myles, m. Catherine, dau. of Sir Walter Blake, Bart. of Menlo, and left issue,
  1 Myles, m. Catherine, granddau. of Dominick Blake, Esq. of Castle Grove, by his wife, dau. of Sir Joseph Hoare, Bart., and left issue, Joseph, Walter, William, and Eliza, m. to Charles, son of Sir Charles Peshall.
  2 Stephen, m. Julia, sister of the foregoing Catherine, and has issue, Myles, Joseph, Walter, Stephen, Eliza, Catherine, and Elly.
  1 Maria, m. to Martin Kirwan, Esq. of Hillsbrook, co. Galway.

The 2nd son,

MYLES BURKE, Esq., who s. his father, m. Mary, dau. of Stephen-Lynch Fitz-Thomas, Esq. of Tubberoe, and niece of Sir Dominick Browne, and by her left issue,

John, a Franciscan friar.
Stephen, m. Marcella, dau. of James Martin, Esq. of Ross, and left issue, Barbara, m. to Mark Lynch, Esq., by whom she had the present Patrick Lynch, Esq. of Duras and Renmore Lodge, co. Galway.
Dominick.
Francis.
WILLIAM, of whom presently.
Jane, m. to Henry Jordan, Esq. of Rosslevin.
Barbara, m. to Sir Walter Blake, Bart. of Menlo Castle.

The 5th son,

WILLIAM BURKE, Esq., s. his father, and m. Teresa Kirwan, of Hillsbrook, co. Galway, by whom he left at his death, in 1801,

John, m. Maria, eldest dau. of Oliver Martyn, Esq., M.D., of Galway, and d. s. p. 3 Oct. 1849. He was an officer in the 79th and 38th regiments, and had a Peninsular medal with three clasps. He was many years a magistrate of the county.

JOSEPH, now of Ower.
Francis, m. Catherine, dau. of Ulick Jennings, Esq. of Ironpool, and having died, left issue by her, William, in holy orders in the Church of Rome; Ulick; John; Bessy; and Teresa.
Stephen and William, both d. without issue.
Mary, m. James Garvey, grandfather of James Garvey, Esq. of Tully, co. Mayo. She m. 2ndly, Major Allen, aide-de-camp at the viceregal court, and left issue, Mary, Caroline, and Teresa.
Julia, m. to Francis Leigh, surgeon in the 60th rifles, and left issue, William, Alexander (now of the island of Jersey), John, and Francis.
Barbara, m. to Bartholomew St. Leger, Esq. of Ballyheragh, co. Mayo, and has issue, Barbara, m. to Denis Clarke, Esq. of Larch Hill, and has issue.
Bridget, a nun.

Arms—Or, a cross, gu.; in the dexter canton, a lion, rampant, sa.
Crest—A chained cat, sejant-guardant, ppr.
Motto—Un roy, une foy, une loy.
Seat—Ower, near Headford, co. Galway.

BURKE OF TYAQUIN.

BURKE, JOHN-CHARLES-RAYMOND, Esq. of Tyaquin, co. Galway, *b.* 16 Dec. 1839.

Lineage.—JOHN BURKE, Esq., son of Thomas Burke, Esq., and his wife Miss Walsh, of Old Connaught, co. Wicklow, m. Elizabeth, dau. of Charles Lambert, Esq. of Creg Clare, by Margaret his wife, a dau. of Dominick Browne, of Castle Mc Garrett, and was father of

CHARLES BURKE, Esq. of Tyaquin, who m. in 1804, Arabella, dau. of Edmund Naghten, Esq. of Thomastown Park, co. Roscommon, and had issue,

JOHN-CHARLES, b. 10 Jan. 1805; d. 8 June, 1832.
EDMUND, late representative of the family.
Anne-Arabella, m. in 1829, to Edmund-Henry Naghten, Esq. of Thomastown Park, co. Roscommon.

The elder son,

JOHN-CHARLES BURKE, Esq. of Tyaquin, b. 10 Jan. 1805, d. unm. 8 June, 1832, and was s. by his brother,

EDMUND BURKE, Esq. of Tyaquin, J.P., b. 10 March, 1808; m. 19 June, 1833, Helen-Mary-Agnes, dau. of Thomas O'Mara, Esq., by Margaret his wife, relict of the late Mr. Fitzsimon, of Glancullen, and dau. and co-heir of B. O'Callan, of Osberstown, co. Kildare, Esq., and had issue,

JOHN-CHARLES-RAYMOND, now of Tyaquin.
Margaret-Cecil. Arabella-Mary.

Arms—Or, a cross, gu.; in the 1st quarter, a lion, rampant, sa.
Crest—A cat-a-mountain, sejant, ppr., collared and chained, or.
Motto—Ung Dieu, ung loi, ung foi.
Seat—Tyaquin, co. Galway.

BURKE OF BALLYDUGAN.

BURKE, THE REV. MICHAEL, A.M., of Ballydugan, co. Galway, m. 1848, Isabella, dau. of James Clarke, Esq., captain 12th lancers, and niece to the late Mrs. Archdall, of Castle Archdall, and has issue,

I. WILLIAM-MALACHY-JAMES, b. in March, 1851.
II. Michael-Henry, b. in July, 1853.
III. Henry-John, b. in June, 1854.
I. Eliza-Martha.

Mr. Burke s. his father in Jan. 1853.

Lineage.—This is another branch of the ancient and wide-spreading family of Burke, of which the noble house of Clanricarde is the chief.

MICHAEL BURKE, Esq., who purchased Ballydugan, in 1726, from the Lynch family, was son of William Burke,* Esq. of the Klorogue branch of the family, by his wife, a dau. of Daly of Cloncha. He m. 1st, Miss Flynn, 2ndly, Miss Dillon, of Clonbrock, and 3rdly, Mary, dau. of Burke of Meelick. By the first two he had no issue, but by the 3rd was father of WILLIAM, his heir; Honora, m. to Andrew Blake, Esq. of Furbough; and Marcella, who m. Malachy Daly, Esq. of Benmore. Mr. Burke's son and heir,

WILLIAM BURKE, Esq. of Ballydugan, m. Mabel, dau. of Malachy Donelan, Esq. of Ballydonelan, co. Galway, by Mary his wife, dau. of Thomas-Power Daly, Esq., eldest son of the Right Hon. Denis Daly, of Carrownekelly, 2nd justice of the Common Pleas, *temp.* JAMES II., and was father of

MICHAEL BURKE, Esq. of Ballydugan, M.P. for Athenry, a director of inland navigation and one of the surveyors-general for Ireland, who served as high-sheriff of the co. of Galway, in 1786, and for the town of Galway, in 1796. He m. Sarah, only child of John Morgan, Esq. of Monksfield, co. Galway, by Sarah his wife, 3rd dau. of Francis Ormsby, Esq. of Willowbrook, co. Sligo, and by her, who d. 11 Oct. 1813, had issue,

WILLIAM-MALACHY, barrister-at-law, late of Ballydugan.
John, in holy orders, vicar of Kilcolgan, co. Galway, provost of Kilmacduah, and prebendary of Kilconnell, m. Mary-Anne, sister of Arthur Guinness, Esq. of Beaumont, near Dublin, and dying in 1842, left MICHAEL-JOHN, barrister-at-law; Arthur; William, barrister-at-law; Edward-Frederick; John; Elizabeth; Mabel-Maria, wife of Thomas Trouton, Esq.; and Louisa.
Michael, collector of excise, and formerly a magistrate for the co. of Galway, d. unm. in 1846.
Thomas, of Belvidere-place, Dublin, m. Louisa, relict of Thomas Burke, Esq. of Spring Garden, co. Galway, and Blake, Esq. of Lehinch, co. Mayo, by Anna-Maria his wife, dau. of the Hon. and Rev. Richard-Henry Roper, son of Lord Teynham, and has, Michael-George, and other issue, dau. of Dominick Daly, Esq., by Johanna-Harriet his wife, sister of the 1st Lord Wallscourt.
Henry, in holy orders, m. Frances-Julia, only dau. of Val. Denis, of Fortlands, co. Galway, m. Maria, dau. of the late Major Graham, and has issue.
Sarah, d. unm. 1852.
Mabel, m. in 1832, to the Rev. James-Temple Mansel, and has issue.

Mr. Burke d. in 1833, and was s. by his eldest son,

WILLIAM-MALACHY BURKE, Esq. of Ballydugan, b. in 1784, high-sheriff of the co. of Galway in 1822. He m. Anna-Maria, only dau. of John Blake, Esq. of Windfield, and by her, who d. in 1847, had issue,

MICHAEL, now of Ballydugan.
John-William, A.B., in holy orders, A.B. University of Cambridge.
William-Malachy, M.D., of the city of Dublin, m. in 1852, Harriett-Isabella, only dau. of the Rev. Hugh Hamilton, of Churchhill, co. Fermanagh, by Elizabeth his wife, sister of the present Sir Thomas Staples, Bart., and has a dau., Grace-Elizabeth-Anna-Maria.
Thomas-James, in holy orders.
Edmund, scholar of Trinity College, Dublin.
Mary. Sarah. Caroline-Frances, d. in 1847.

Arms—Or, a cross, gu.; in the dexter canton, a lion, rampant, sa.
Crest—A cat-a-mountain, sejant-guardant, ppr., collared and chained, or.
Motto—Un roy, une foy, une loy.
Seat—Ballydugan, near Loughrea.

BURKE OF ELM HALL.

BURKE, JOSEPH, Esq. of Elm Hall, co. Tipperary, barrister-at-law, s. to the property at the decease of his father, the late Peter Burke, Esq., J.P., 13 Jan. 1836. Mr. Burke was appointed an Assistant Poor-law Commissioner in April, 1839, shortly after the introduction of the Poor-law into Ireland, and continued in office until March, 1855.

Lineage.—This family derive from the BURKES *of Meelick*, co. Galway, long one of the most important branches of the ancient house of DE BURGH.

DOMINICK BURKE, Esq. of Cloudagoff Castle, co. Galway, (which lands are mentioned in a Patent of the Earl of Clanricarde's possessions, registered in the Rolls Office), m. and had issue,

I. DOMINICK, of Clondagoff Castle, father of two sons, of whom the elder, PETER, of Clondagoff Castle, d. in 1770, leaving by his wife, a dau. of Madden of Fahy, four children, of whom the last surviving son, ANTHONY BURKE, Esq. of Clondagoff Castle, m. 1st, Mary, dau. of Patrick Skerrit, Esq. of Eyrecourt, and 2ndly, Frances, dau. of Carroll of Newlawn, co. Tipperary, cousin of the late Marchioness Wellesley. By the former he had an only dau., Maria; and by the latter an only son, James-Carroll, who m. in 1829, Bidelia, dau. of John Dowling, Esq. of Longford Castle, co. Galway.
II. PETER.

This 2nd son,

PETER BURKE, Esq., settled at Birr (Parsonstown), in the King's Co. He m. Elizabeth, dau. of Henry Comerford, Esq. of Faddenbegg, co. Tipperary, son and heir of George Comerford, Esq., by Jane his wife, only child of Richard Butler, Esq. of Tinlough, who possessed, besides, Tinnikelly and other lands in the barony of Lower Ormonde. Peter Burke d. about the year 1764, leaving issue,

I. DOMINICK, of Riverstown House, co. Tipperary, m. Catherine, dau. of Philip Langton, Esq. of Birr, and d. in June, 1786, leaving,

* A brother of this William Burke entered the Neapolitan service, and attained high military rank at Naples.

1 JOSEPH, of Rockville, who *m.* in 1772, Mary, sister of Edward Murphy, Esq. of Castle Annagha, co. Kilkenny, and left at his decease, 17 March, 1783, a dau., Margaret, and four sons, Dominick, who *d. unm.*; William, major, H.E.I.C.S., who served for twenty years in India, participating in the storming of Seringapatam: he *d.* 30 May, 1823; John, of Waterford, *d.* at Penzance, Cornwall, *unm.* in 1852; Edward, R.N., *d.s.p.*; and Margaret, who *m.* Jeremiah Ryan, Esq. of Bath, and had three daus., of whom the 2nd, Catherine, *m.* Michael-Theobald Langton, Esq., of Bath, only son of Michael Langton, Esq. of Cadiz.

2 John, of Clongowna, co. Tipperary, *m.* 3 June, 1779, Bridget, only child of Mathias Freeman, Esq. of Birr, and *d.* 16 June, 1815, leaving issue, Dominick, who served during the Peninsular war in the 16th light-dragoons, and *d.* at Fuentarabia, in Spain, 6 March, 1814; Joseph, civil engineer, *m.* 4 June, 1816, Anne, dau. of James Smith, Esq. of Sharow House, co. York, and had issue (with two daus., 1 John-Smith, *b.* at Clongowna, 27 Aug. 1817, *m.* a dau. of Major Marlow, R.E. 2 James-Baird, *b.* at Kilpoint, Scotland, 22 June, 1819, *m.* 7 May, 1850, Charlotte-Augusta, youngest dau. of Major Marlow, R.E.) Felix, *dec.*; and six daus., of whom the 2nd, Catherine, *m.* 1st, in 1808, John-Alexander Jones, Esq., and 2ndly, in 1815, the Hon. Augustus-Abraham Hely-Hutchinson, brother of the 1st Earl of Donoughmore.

II. JOHN, of whose descendants we treat.

I. Mary. II. Eleanor.

The 2nd son of Peter Burke of Birr,

JOHN BURKE, Esq., an officer in the Spanish army, served under his uncle, Brigadier-General John Comerford. He *m.* 1st, Eleanor, relict of John Burke, Esq. of Birr, and dau. of Keating of Shanballyduff, by whom he had a dau., Elizabeth, who *d. unm.* He *m.* 2ndly, Lucinda, eldest dau. of Oliver Plunket, Esq. of Bettyfield, co. Roscommon, and sister of Bartholomew Plunket, Esq., whose son, Major James Plunket, *m.* Miss Gunning, first-cousin of Elizabeth, Baroness Hamilton, wife, 1st, of James, Duke of Hamilton, and 2ndly, of John, Duke of Argyll. By Lucinda, his 2nd wife, John Burke had issue,

I. JOSEPH, of London, *b.* in 1749, *m.* in 1774, Jane, dau. of Simon-Arthur-Hyacinth French, Esq. of Frenchbrook, co. Roscommon, and niece of Jeffery French, Esq., M.P. of Clonequin. By this lady, who *d.* 20 Jan. 1829, he left an only son at his decease, 4 Jan. 1827.

II. PETER, of whom we treat.

I. Eleanor, *d. unm.*, 10 May, 1814.

II. Ellis, *m.* to John Antisell, Esq., and *d.* in 1836.

The 2nd son,

PETER BURKE, Esq. of Elm Hall, co. Tipperary, a justice of the peace for that county, and for the King's Co., *m.* 1st, Anne, 2nd dau. and co-heir of Matthew Dowdall, Esq., M.D. of Mullingar, by Bridget Barnewall his wife, sister of Bartholomew Barnewall, Esq., father of the late Sir Robert Barnewall, Bart. of Crickstown Castle, co. Meath. By this lady, who *d.* 18 Feb. 1818, he had issue,

I. JOHN, of London, *m.* Mary, 2nd dau. of Bernard O'Reilly, Esq. of Ballymorris, co. Longford, and *d.* in 1848, leaving surviving issue,

1 PETER, of the Inner Temple, barrister-at-law, author of *The Life of the Right Honourable Edmund Burke*, and of several legal and other works.

2 JOHN-BERNARD (Sir), Knt., Ulster King of Arms, and knight-attendant on the Order of St. Patrick, keeper of the Bermingham Tower Records, M.R.I.A., barrister-at-law, author of *The Landed Gentry*, *The Visitation of Seats*, *The General Armory*, *Family Romance*, &c.

3 Mary-Clarinda.

II. JOSEPH, now of Elm Hall.

I. Bridget, *m.* in 1817, to Michael Hoey, Esq., who *d.* 1838.

Mr. Burke *m.* 2ndly, 26 July, 1820, Clarinda, eldest dau. of the late Redmond Dolphin, Esq. of Corr, co. Galway, J.P., but by her, who *d.* 15 April, 1851, had no issue. He *d.* 13 Jan. 1836.

Arms, as registered in the Office of Arms, Dublin: Or, a plain cross, gu., in the 1st and 4th quarters a lion rampant, sa.

Crest—A cat-a-mountain, sejant, ppr., collared and chained, or, on the breast a cross, gold.

Motto—Ung roy, ung foy, ung loy.

Seat—Elm Hall, co. Tipperary.

BURKE OF PROSPECT VILLA.

BURKE, THOMAS-FITZMAURICE, Esq. of Prospect Villa, co. Cork, J.P., major-gen. in the army; *b.* in 1776; *m.* Elizabeth, dau. of Daniel Conner, Esq. of Ballybricken, co. Cork, and has issue,

I. JOHN-FITZMAURICE, *b.* in 1815, late an officer in the 56th regt.

II. Edmund. III. Thomas-Fitzmaurice.

I. Elizabeth-Mary, *m.* to Edward-Hoare Reeves, Esq. of Ballyglissane, co. Cork.

Lineage.—The patriarch of this family of Burke was WALTER DE BURGH, who it is stated landed in Ireland, *temp.* HENRY II., and obtained a grant of land near Limerick, at a place called Ballinaguard, which continued in the possession of his descendants for nearly 500 years, until forfeited to CROMWELL, by

THEOBALD BURKE, of Ballinaguard. This gentleman *m.* Ellen, dau. of Purcell of Creagh, co. Limerick, and had two sons and six daus. Of the former, the elder

THEOBALD BURKE, Esq., *m.* Mary, dau. of Timothy M'Mahon, of the co. of Clare, and had a son,

JOHN BURKE, Esq., who *m.* Margaret, dau. of Maurice Stack, Esq., by his wife Catherine Fitzmaurice, of Lixnaw, and was father of

REDMOND BURKE, Esq., who *m.* Johanna, dau. of John-MacRobert Fitzmaurice, Esq. of Lixnaw, (descended from the great house of Fitzmaurice, Lord Kerry,) by Alice his wife, dau. of Daniel O'Connell, Esq. of Derrynane, and *d.* at Durrine, about 1796, having had issue,

John-Fitzmaurice, formerly in the French service, resident at Lixnaw, co. Kerry, *d. unm.* in 1826.

THOMAS-FITZMAURICE, of Prospect Villa.

Alice, *m.* to Francis Segerson, Esq. of Dungagan, co. Kerry.

Margaret, *m.* to Richard Murphy, Esq. of Kerry.

Maria. Catherine, *d. unm.* Ellen.

Arms—Or, a cross, gu.; in the dexter quarter, a lion, rampant, sa.

Crest—A cat-a-mountain, sejant-guardant, ppr., collared and chained, or.

Motto—Ung roy, ung foy, ung loy.

Seat—Prospect Villa, co. Cork.

BURKE OF SLATEFIELD.

BURKE, DOMINICK-JOSEPH-BROWNE, Esq. of Slatefield, co. Galway, resident at Killimer Castle, Athenry, co. Galway, *b.* about 1808.

Lineage.—This is a branch of the ancient house of BURKE *of Meelick*.

HYACINTH BURKE, of Slatefield or Gorthmalaken, eldest son of DOMINICK-PATRICK BURKE, Esq., and his wife, dau. of MacHugo of Trienageera, co. Galway, by his wife, a dau. of Daly of the Red House, *m.* Margaret, dau. of Phelan of Shanballyduff, co. Tipperary, by his wife, a dau. of Ryan of Inch, and was father of

DOMINICK BURKE, Esq. of Slatefield, who *m.* about 1775, Margaret Dolphin, of Turoe, co. Galway, and *d.* in 1818, leaving a son,

HYACINTH-GEORGE BURKE, Esq., of Slatefield, who *m.* about 1807, Frances, dau. of George Browne, Esq. of Brownestown, co. Mayo, son of John Browne, Esq., and Catherine his wife, dau. of Denis Daly, Esq. of Raford, co. Galway, and by her (who *d.* Aug. 1841), left at his decease, 4 April, 1841, one son, the present DOMINICK-JOSEPH-BROWNE BURKE, of Slatefield; and two daus., Margaret-Gertrude and Frances-Josephine.

Arms, &c.—Same as the preceding.

Seat—Killimer Castle, Athenry.

BURKE OF ST. CLERANS.

BURKE, JOHN-HARDIMAN, Esq. of St. Clerans, co. Galway, *b.* in Oct. 1820; major in the army, and captain 88th, Connaught Rangers.

Lineage.—Derived from a common ancestor with the preceding families, was

JOHN BURKE, Esq. of Isserceleran, co. Galway, who *m.* Jane, dau. of Michael Burke, Esq. of Cloughanover, a descendant of the BURKES *of Castle Hacket*, had, with a dau. Ellen, wife of John Dolphin, Esq. of Turoe, a son and successor,

JAMES BURKE, Esq. of St. Clerans, who *m.* Penelope, dau. of Robert Hardiman, Esq. of Loughrea, co. Galway, and had, with a dau., who *m.* — Browne, Esq. of Gloves, co. Galway, a son,

JOHN BURKE, Esq. of St. Clerans, who *m.* in 1783 or 1784, Elizabeth, dau. of Andrew Armstrong, Esq. of Clara House, King's Co., by whom he had issue,

JAMES-HARDIMAN, his heir.

Robert. John.

Penelope, *m.* to John Kirwan, of Castle Hacket, co. Galway, Esq.

Elizabeth, *m.* to Christopher-John Blake, of Winfield, co. Galway, Esq.

Mr. Burke took the name of HARDIMAN, in addition to that of Burke, pursuant to the will of his maternal uncle, Robert Hardiman, Esq., whose estates and property he inherited upon that gentleman's death in 1800. He *d.* in Dec. 1808, and was *s.* by his son,

JAMES-HARDIMAN BURKE, Esq. of St. Clerans, *b.* in 1788, *m.* in Oct. 1817, Anne, dau. of Robert O'Hara, of Raheen, co. Galway, Esq., and has issue,

JOHN, now of St. Clerans.
Robert O'Hara, *b.* in 1821, an officer in the Austrian service.
James-Thomas, *b.* in 1828, an officer, R.E., killed in Turkey, 1854.
Fanny-Maria. Elizabeth.
Hester-Albinia. Anne-Celestine.

Mr. Burke, who served the office of sheriff, *d.* 9 Jan. 1854.

Arms—Or, a cross, gu.; in the 1st quarter, a lion, rampant, sa.
Crest—A cat-a-mountain, sejant, ppr., collared and chained, or.
Motto—Ung Dieu, ung loy, ung foy.
Seat—St. Clerans (formerly called Issercleran), co. Galway.

BURLEIGH OF CARRICKFERGUS.

BURLEIGH, WILLIAM, Esq. of Carrickfergus, co. Antrim, J.P., *b.* in 1797; *m.* in 1828, Lucretia, dau. of James Wills, Esq. of Plâs Bellin, co. Flint, by Lucretia-A. Kingsley his wife, and has issue six sons and six daughters.

Lineage.—WILLIAM BURLEIGH, capt. in Sir John Clotworthy's regiment of horse, who was wounded at the defence of Lisburn against O'Neil, in 1641, was subsequently lieut.-col. of the Earl of Kildare's regiment. His eldest son,

WILLIAM BURLEIGH, *m.* Anne, eldest dau. of Sir Roger Langford, and left by her two sons, the elder of whom,

HERCULES BURLEIGH, was captain in the army, and served at the siege of Londonderry. He *m.* 1st, Margaret, dau. of George Pearson, Esq. of Harwood Shields, co. Northumberland, and had by her three sons and several daus. A dau. of a second marriage *m.* Sir William Brown, Bart. He *d.* in 1744. His eldest son,

WILLIAM BURLEIGH, *b.* in 1700, *m.* Elizabeth, dau. and co-heiress of Thomas Clerk, Esq. of co. Armagh, and *d.* in 1750, leaving three sons and a dau. The 3rd son,

WILLIAM BURLEIGH, *b.* in 1730, *m.* Ellen, dau. of Hamlet Obins, Esq. of Castle Obins, and had one dau. He *m.* 2ndly, Anne, dau. and co-heiress of Andrew Boyd, Esq. of Prospect, co. Antrim, and by her left, at his decease in 1798, two sons and one dau.; the elder of the sons,

WILLIAM-DOBBS BURLEIGH, Esq., *b.* in 1765, was called to the bar in 1788. He *m.* in 1796, Anne, dau. of Thomas Wills, Esq. of Willsgrove, co. Roscommon, by Jane-Lucy Talbot his wife, and left at his decease, in 1829 (with a son, Henry, a capt. in the Hon. E.I.C.S., and three daus., one of whom, Jane, *m.* to the Rev. John-L. Chute) an elder son, the present WILLIAM BURLEIGH, Esq. of Carrickfergus.

Arms—Vert, three boar's heads, couped, arg., armed, or.
Crest—A demi-boar, ppr., armed, hoofed, and bristled, or, and gorged with a chain, of the last, supporting a thistle, ppr.

BURNABY OF BAGGRAVE HALL.

BURNABY, EDWYN, Esq. of Baggrave Hall, co. Leicester, *b.* 29 Sept. 1799; *m.* 28 Aug. 1829, Anne-Caroline, dau. of Thomas Salisbury, Esq., 2nd son of Thomas Salisbury, Esq. of Marshfield House, co. York, by Mary his wife, dau. of Thomas Lister, Esq., and has issue,

I. EDWYN-SHERARD, capt. 1st regt. grenadier-guards.
I. Caroline-Louisa. II. Cecilia-Florence.
III. Laura-Gertrude. IV. Ida-Charlotte.

Mr. Burnaby, who *s.* his father 1 Oct. 1825, is a gentleman of her Majesty's most honourable privy chamber, deputy-lieut. and magistrate for the co. of Leicester, and late capt. in the 3rd, or Prince of Wales's dragoon-guards.

Lineage.—HUGH BURNABY, 3rd son of Thomas de Burnaby, of Watford, co. Northampton, the representative of a very ancient family settled in Leicestershire shortly after the Conquest, *d.* at Manton, in Northamptonshire, 28 July, 1591, leaving, with other issue,

ROBERT BURNABY, bapt. at Manton, 15 Sept. 1577, who *d.* at Gulton, 18 May, 1643, and was father of

HUGH BURNABY, *b.* at Gulton, 30 Jan. 1620, fellow of St. John's College, Cambridge, and patron and rector of Asfordby, in the co. of Leicester. He *m.* Elizabeth, dau. of Sir Thomas Burton, of Stockerston, in the co. of Leicester, by Philippa his wife, dau. of Sir Edward Cobham, Knt., and by her, who *d.* 29 July, 1699, had issue, Hugh, of Asfordby, who *d.* in 1742, leaving a dau.; Benjamin, rector of Stainby, who *d. unm.*; Andrew; and Robert, of Brampton, who *d. s. p.* The 3rd son,

ANDREW BURNABY, *s.* to the estate and living of Asfordby, on the death of his father, 20 Jan. 1699, and *m.* Anne, widow of Maurice Camm, Esq., by whom he had a son,

THE REV. ANDREW BURNABY, *b.* 29 June, 1702, of Brampton Manor House, prebendary of Lincoln, vicar of St. Margaret's, Leicester, and rector of Asfordby, who *m.* Hannah, dau. of George Beaumont, Esq. of Darton, in the co. of York, and had issue, ANDREW, his heir; Robert, prebendary of Lincoln and vicar of St. Margaret's, who *m.* Catherine, dau. of T. Gee, Esq., and had issue; Thomas-Beaumont, rector of Asfordby, who *m.* Catherine, dau. of William Abney, Esq. of Measham; Anna-Maria, *m.* to Richard Walter, Esq.; and Hannah, *d. unm.* The eldest son,

ANDREW BURNABY, D.D. of Baggrave Hall, in the co. of Leicester, and of Brampton, in Huntingdonshire, archdeacon of Leicester and vicar of Greenwich, *m.* 26 Feb. 1770, Anna, dau. and heir of John Edwyn, Esq. of Baggrave Hall, high-sheriff of Leicestershire in 1750, and had issue, EDWYN-ANDREW, his heir; Sherard-Beaumont, D.C.L. of Brampton, co. Huntingdon, *d.* 25 March, 1848; John-Dick, of Evington, co. Leicester, col. 1st Grenadier-guards, who *m.* in 1798, Henry-Anne, dau. of Sir Thomas Fowke, Bart.; George-Freeman, who *d. unm.*; and Anna-Maria, *m.* to John Atkins, Esq. of Halstead House, Kent. The eldest son,

EDWYN-ANDREW BURNABY, Esq. of Baggrave Hall, *b.* 9 May, 1771, *m.* 30 Dec. 1794, Mary, dau. and heiress of the Rev. William Browne, rector and patron of Burrow, and granddau. of Suffield Browne, of Leesthorpe Hall, in the co. of Leicester, and had issue, I. EDWYN, now of Baggrave Hall; II. William-Edwyn, barrister-at-law, *d. unm.*, 23 Aug. 1830; III. Gustavus-Andrew, in holy orders, *m.* 19 Nov. 1833, Harriet, dau. of Henry Villebois, Esq. of Marham, and has Frederick-Gustavus, Evelyn, Mary, *m.* 22 April, 1853, to John-H.-Manners Sutton, Esq., M.P. of Kelham Hall, Notts, and Anna; I. Mary, *m.* 8 May, 1820, to John-Tylston Pares, Esq.; II. Selina, *d.* 12 Nov. 1836; III. Georgiana; and IV. Anna-Edwyn, *m.* 23 May, 1829, to Matthew Knapp, Esq. of Linford House, Bucks, and *d.* 28 Dec. 1835. Mr. Burnaby *d.* 1 Oct. 1825.

Arms—Arg., two bars; a lion, passant-guardant, in chief, gu.
Crest—A demi-man, sa., in the dexter hand a branch of columbine flowers, ppr., round the neck a rope, or, with the end hanging down on the sinister side.
Motto—Pro rege.
Seat—Baggrave Hall, Leicestershire.

BURNE OF LOYNTON HALL.

BURNE, THOMAS-HIGGINS, Esq. of Loynton Hall, co. Stafford, J.P. and D.L., *b.* 24 March, 1791; *m.* 10 Dec. 1814, Sophia, youngest dau. of the late George Briscoe, Esq. of Summer Hill, co. Stafford, and has issue,

I. THOMAS-SAMBROOKE-HIGGINS, *b.* 9 Sept. 1822.
II. Thomas, *b.* 7 May, 1824.
III. Richard-Higgins, *b.* 24 May, 1827.
I. Maria, *d.* in 1842.
II. Sophia. III. Eliza. IV. Caroline.
V. Diana-Patience. VI. Mary-Jane. VII. Georgiana.
VIII. Emily. IX. Rachel-Higgins.

Lineage.—The family of Higgins has been seated at Loynton for many generations.

CHRISTOPHER COMYN HIGGINS, Esq. of Loynton, son of John Higgins, Esq. of Loynton, by Mary his wife, dau. of the Rev. Christopher Comyn, vicar of Prees, and prebendary of Lichfield cathedral, assumed the surname of COMYN before that of HIGGINS, in pursuance of his grandfather's will. He *m.* 1st, Rachel, youngest dau. and co-heir of Francis Sambrooke, Gent. of Sambrooke, co. Salop, and 2ndly, Miss Mary Yonge, by both of whom he had issue. By the 1st he was father of two daus., Rachel and Margaret, who *d. unm.*, and of one son,

CHRISTOPHER HIGGINS, Esq., who *m.* Mary, dau. of Richard Blower, Esq. of Woodnorton, in Norfolk, and had,

Richard, b. in 1729; d. unm.
SAMBROOKE, in holy orders, rector of Norbury, co. Stafford, for 64 years, who d. 23 July, 1823, and was s. in the estate of Loynton by his grand-nephew, the present THOMAS-HIGGINS BURNE, Esq. of Loynton.
CATHERINE, of whom presently. Rachel. Dorothy.

The eldest dau.,

CATHERINE HIGGINS, bapt. in 1735, m. Thomas Burne, Esq of Penn, elder son (by Elizabeth his wife, dau. of John Shelton, Esq.) of Thomas Burne, Esq., whose ancestors had been resident on a patrimonial estate at Penn, co. Stafford, for several generations. By him she was mother of a son, THOMAS, of whom presently, and four daus., Catherine, Dorothy, Mary, and Anne. The son,

THOMAS BURNE, Esq., m. in 1787, Maria, eldest dau. of Richard Mee, Esq. of Himley, co. Stafford, and d. in Aug. 1791, having had by her (who d. in May, 1809,) a son, THOMAS-HIGGINS, now of Loynton Hall, and a dau., Maria, m. 19 Oct. 1809, to Edward Dixon, Esq. of Dudley, and Ashwood House, co. Stafford.

Seat—Loynton Hall, co. Stafford.

BURNELL OF WINKBURN HALL AND BEAUCHIEFF ABBEY.

PEGGE-BURNELL, EDWARD-VALENTINE, Esq. of Beauchieff Abbey, co. Derby, and Winkburn Hall, Notts, M.A., J.P. for Notts, b. 14 Feb. 1805; m. 12 Nov. 1833, Harriet, dau. of Hugh Parker, Esq. of Woodthorpe, co. York, and has issue,

I. EDWARD-STRELLEY, b. 7 April, 1835.
II. Hugh-D'Arcy, b. 16 July, 1836.
III. William-Acton, b. 24 May, 1842.
IV. Edward-Anneslеy, b. 9 Nov. 1844.
I. Harriet-Gertrude, d. young.
II. Elizabeth-Constance. III. Alice-Mary-Caroline.

Lineage.—The first mention we have of the family of Steade, living at, or being possessed of Onesacre, in the co. of York, where stands the old family mansion, appears, according to Dr. Hunter, in some old writings of the time of EDWARD III, between 1326 and 1377.

JOHN DE LA STEDE resided, as we find from several ancient deeds, at Onesacre, in 1417, as did his immediate successors, Thomas, John, John, and Nicholas de la Stede.

THOMAS STEADE, Esq., b. in 1728, (7th in descent from Nicholas Steade,) m. in 1768, Melliscent, dau. of Strelley Pegge, Esq. of Beauchieff Abbey, and sister of the late Peter Pegge, of Winkburn Hall, who devised his estates to his nephew, the late Mr. Pegge-Burnell. By her he had issue,

THOMAS, his successor, who d. unm. 1796.
BROUGHTON-BENJAMIN.

Mr. Steade d. in 1793. His 2nd son,

BROUGHTON-BENJAMIN STEADE, Esq. b. 3 July, 1774, J.P. and D.L., high-sheriff of Derbyshire in 1839, succeeded in Feb. 1836, to the estates in the counties of Nottingham and Derby, of his maternal uncle Peter Pegge-Burnell, Esq. of Winkburn, Notts, and then took by royal authority the names of PEGGE and BURNELL, instead of that of Steade, in compliance with an injunction contained in his uncle's will.

PETER PEGGE-BURNELL was 3rd and youngest son of Strelley Pegge, of Beauchieff Abbey, Derbyshire, to whose estates he succeeded, as also to those of his distant relative, D'Arcy Burnell, of Winkburn, Notts, in 1784. On his marriage with Mary, relict of J. Lee, Esq. of Chesterfield, he also became the possessor of considerable property in that neighbourhood. On the death of Mary, relict of D'Arcy Burnell, in 1784. the said Peter Pegge took the name of BURNELL in addition.

The Burnell family has been settled at Winkburn since the time of King EDWARD VI., when the monastery of Winkburn, together with the parish, formerly belonging to the Knights of St. John of Jerusalem, was granted to John Burnell, merchant, of London, in exchange for certain lands in Sussex. *(See THOROTON'S Nottinghamshire.)*

The Pegges were settled at Ashbourne, in Derbyshire, when Edward Pegge m. Gertrude, only dau. and heiress of Nicholas Strelley, of Beauchieff Abbey. By this marriage the Strelley estates, at Beauchieff, passed into the Pegge family.

Mr. Broughton-Benjamin Pegge-Burnell m. 21 Dec. 1802, Miss Elizabeth Dalton, and d. 20 May, 1850, leaving a dau., Mary-Milliscent, m. 22 March, 1831, to the Rev. Wm. Smith, of Dunston Hall, Derbyshire, and a son and successor, the present EDWARD-VALENTINE PEGGE-BURNELL, Esq. of Winkburn Hall and Beauchieff Abbey.

Arms—Quarterly: 1st and 4th, per fesse indented, or and arg., a lion, rampant, sa., a bordure, gu., charged with eight plates, for BURNELL; 2nd and 3rd, arg., a chevron, between three wedges, sa., for PEGGE.
Crest—A lion's gamb, erect and erased, sa., in the paw a bunch of violets, ppr., for BURNELL; the sun rising in splendour, the rays alternately, sa., or, and arg., for PEGGE.
Motto—Caritas fructum habet.
Seats—Beauchieff Abbey, co. Derby; and Winkburn Hall, Notts.

BURR OF ALDERMASTON.

BURR, DANIEL-HIGFORD-DAVALL, Esq. of Aldermaston Court, Berks, J.P. and D.L., high-sheriff in 1851, M.P. for Hereford from 1837 to 1851, b. 24 March, 1811; s. his mother 1 Feb. 1836; m. 18 Sept. 1839, Anne-Margaretta, only dau. of the late Captain E. Scobell, R.N., and has issue,

I. HIGFORD, b. 20 July, 1840.
II. Edward, b. 25 Sept. 1842.
III. James-Scudamore, b. 15 Jan. 1854.

Lineage.—DANIEL BURR, Esq., son of Daniel Burr, and his wife Elizabeth Dauchert, of Amsterdam, m. Elizabeth, dau. of John Davall, Esq. of Yarmouth, co. Norfolk, and was father of

DANIEL BURR, a lieut.-col., H.E.I.C.S., who captured the island of Ternate, the chief of the Moluccas, 21 June, 1801. He m. 1st, 26 April, 1804, Miss Lucy Parry, and by her, who d. 17 Nov. 1805, had one dau.,

Lucy-Mary-Anne, m. 2 May, 1826, to James Phillipps, Esq. of Bryngwyn.

He m. 2ndly, 29 Sept. 1808, Mary, dau. and heiress of James Davis, Esq. of Chepstow, (and co-heiress of Frances, late Dowager Duchess of Norfolk, being a descendant of John Higford, Esq. of Dixton, co. Gloucester, who m. Frances, sister of John, Lord Scudamore, of Holme Lacy, co. Hereford,) by whom he had issue,

DANIEL-HIGFORD-DAVALL, now of Aldermaston.
James-Henry-Scudamore, in holy orders, b. 10 Aug. 1816; m. in 1840, Jane, only child of Rear-Admiral Charles Gordon, and has issue.
Mary. Frances-Cornelia, m. to Charles Bushe, Esq.

Gen. Burr d. 19 Feb. 1828, and his wife d. 2 Feb. 1836.

Arms—Erm., on a mount, vert, issuing from park-palings, with gate, ppr., a lion, rampant, or, holding in the dexter paw a scimetar, all ppr.; on a chief, indented, sa., two lions, rampant, arg.
Crest—Out of a mural crown, inscribed with the word "Ternate," a Malay, holding in the dexter hand the colours of Ternate, all ppr., granted in commemoration of the capture, in 1801, of that island, the chief of the Moluccas, by the late Lieut.-General Daniel Burr, E.I.C.S.
Motto—Virtus verus honos.
Seat—Aldermaston, Reading.

BURRELL OF BROOMEPARK.

BURRELL, BRYAN, Esq. of Broomepark, Northumberland, A.M., F.S.A., b. 23 June, 1805, late a captain in the 4th dragoon-guards, J.P. and D.L.; m. 21 Sept. 1837, Frances-Mary, only dau. of John Quantock, Esq. of Norton House, co. Somerset, and has issue,

I. BRYAN, b. 15 July, 1839.
II. Henry-Matthew, b. 6 July, 1842.
III. William-John, b. 8 Feb. 1845.
IV. Walter-Charles, b. 18 April, 1849.
V. John, b. 25 Feb. 1852.
I. Frances-Eleanor. II. Georgina.

Lineage.—The Burrells are of very ancient date upon the borders of England and Scotland, particularly in that district formerly known by the name of the East Marches; their names occur in various records of the times and in family muniments, as Boraille, Borell, Burwell, but now generally Burrell.

THOMAS BURRELL, Esq. of Milfield and of Broomepark, b. 1654, son of Ralph Burrell, Esq. of Milfield, and great-grandson of Thomas Burrell, of Milfield, living *temp.* ELIZABETH, s. to his paternal property at Milfield in 1668, and in 1657, to his uncle Thomas's estates of Broomepark and Abberwick. He m. 1 July, 1680, Martha, dau. of George Revely, of Newton Underwood and Thropple, and dying in 1790, left fifteen children. The 4th son,

THE REV. WILLIAM BURRELL, A.M., vicar of Chatton, in the co. of Northumberland, from 1713 to 1752, s. to the family estates upon the death of his brother Robert, in July, 1751. He was b. 25 Jan. 1687, m. about 1726, Philadelphia, dau. of Bryan Grey, Esq. of Kyloe. He *d.* and was buried in his own church at Chatton, 14 Jan. 1752, leaving two sons and two daus., BRYAN, his heir; Robert, *d. s. p.* in 1751; Martha, *d. unm.* in 1806; and Frances, *m.* to Robert Smart, Esq. of Hobberlaw. The eldest son,

BRYAN BURRELL, Esq., *b.* about 1728, A.B., served as high-sheriff for the county in 1768. He *m.* in May, 1771, Mary, dau. of Henry Partridge, of King's Lynn, afterwards of Northwold, in Norfolk, and by her (who *d.* 12 July, 1778, aged 28) he left at his decease, 8 Nov. 1806, aged 78, two sons, WILLIAM, late of Broomepark; and Henry, A.M., barrister-at-law, one of the principal secretaries of Lord Eldon, *d.* in 1814. The elder son,

WILLIAM BURRELL, Esq. of Broomepark, *b.* in 1773, J.P. and D.L., served as high-sheriff in 1811. He *m.* in 1804, Eleanor, eldest dau. of Matthew Forster, Esq. of Bolton House, and by her, who *d.* 21 May, 1846, had two sons, BRYAN, now of Broomepark, and Matthew, A.M., in holy orders, vicar of Chatton, Northumberland. Mr. Burrell *d.* 2 Feb. 1847.

Arms—Or, a saltier, gu., between four leaves, vert; on a chief, az., a lion's head, erased, between two battle-axes, ppr.

Crest—An arm, armed, ppr., holding a bunch of burdock, vert.

Motto—Adhæreo.

Seat—Broomepark, Northumberland.

BURROUGHES OF BURLINGHAM.

BURROUGHES, HENRY-NEGUS, Esq. of Burlingham Hall, Norfolk, *b.* 8 Feb. 1791; *m.* 25 Aug. 1818, Jane-Sarah, dau. of the Rev. Dixon Hoste, rector of Titteshall-cum-Godwick, and sister of Sir William Hoste, Bart., and has,

I. JAMES-BURKIN, *b.* in 1819.
II. Henry-Negus, *b.* in 1821.
III. William, *b.* in 1827.
I. Jane. II. Mary.

Mr. Burroughes was high-sheriff for Norfolk in 1817, and is M.P. for East Norfolk.

Lineage.—JEREMIAH BURROUGHES, Esq. of Wymondham, *m.* 1st, Anne, dau. of Thomas Randall, Esq., and by her (who *d.* 10 Oct. 1734, aged 36) had issue,

JEREMIAH, his heir.
Randall, of Long Stratton, in holy orders, A.M., of Clare Hall, Cambridge, rector of Bressingham and Shelfanger, *m.* Elizabeth-Maria, dau. and sole heiress of William Ellis, Esq. of Kiddall Hall, co. York, and had issue.
Thomas, of Wymondham, surgeon, *d. v. p.*, leaving, by Elizabeth his wife (who *d.* 20 July, 1805), besides a dau., Elizabeth, *m.* to T. Norgate, a son,
Thomas-Cooke, M.A., in holy orders, sometime a senior fellow of Caius College, rector of Landbeach, co. Cambridge, and J.P. for that shire, *m.* Mary, dau. and co-heir of the Rev. Robert Masters, B.D., rector of Landbeach, and *d.* 23 April, 1821, aged 65, leaving two sons,
Thomas (the Rev.), of Rickinghall.
Thomas-Cooke, of Gazeley, co. Suffolk.

Mr. Burroughes *d.* 27 Nov. 1759, aged 67 (his will, dated 30 Jan. 1759, was proved 11 Dec. following), and was *s.* by his eldest son,

JEREMIAH BURROUGHES, Esq. of Wymondham, J.P. and deputy-lieut. for the co. Norfolk, who *m.* (settlement dated 19 and 20 Nov. 1754,) Diana, youngest dau. and co-heir of James Burkin, Esq. of North Burlingham, and had issue,

I. JAMES-BURKIN, his heir.
II. Randall, of Burfield Hall, in Wymondham, J.P. and deputy-lieut. for Norfolk, *m.* Anne, youngest dau. and co-heir of Samuel Denton, Esq., by Jane his wife, niece and heiress of Samuel Proctor, Esq. of Burfield Hall, and *d.* 9 Sept. 1817, aged 56, having had by this lady (who *d.* 30 Jan. 1827, aged 65) a son and three daus., viz.,
1 Randall-Proctor, M.A., and fellow of Emanuel College, Cambridge, J.P. for Norfolk, *d.* 16 Jan. 1820, aged 25.
1 Diana, *m.* to William Spinks.
2 ANN-DIANA, of Burfield Hall.
3 Jemima, *d. unm.* 9 Jan. 1820.

Mr. Burroughes *d.* at Bath, 7 Dec. 1767, aged 39, (will dated 2nd, was proved 19 Dec. 1767.) His eldest son and heir,

JAMES-BURKIN BURROUGHES, Esq. of Burlingham Hall, *m.* Christabel, dau. and heir of Henry Negus, Esq. of Hoveton Hall, and by her (who *d.* 25 Jan. 1848, aged 78) had issue,

HENRY-NEGUS, his heir.
Jeremiah, in holy orders, who *m.* in 1828, Pleasance, dau. of the late Sir Thomas Preston, Bart.
William.
Mary, *m.* to Lieut.-Col. Sir George-Charles Hoste, brother of the late Sir William Hoste, Bart.

Mr. Burroughes *d.* 30 Nov. 1803, and was *s.* by his eldest son, HENRY-NEGUS BURROUGHES, Esq. of Burlingham.

Arms—Arg., two chevrons, between three chaplets, vert.

Crest—A griffin's head, erased, arg., charged with two chevrons, vert.

Motto—Animo et fide.

Seat—Burlingham Hall.

BURROUGHES OF LONG STRATTON.

BURROUGHES, ELLIS, Esq. of The Manor House, Long Stratton, Norfolk.

Lineage.—RICHARD BURROUGHES, Esq. of Long Stratton, in Norfolk, 2nd son of Jeremiah Burroughes, Esq. (see BURROUGHES *of Burlingham*), *m.* Elizabeth-Maria, only dau. and heir of William Ellis, Esq. of Kidhall, co. York, the representative of the ancient Norman family of Ellys, and had (with two daus., Elizabeth-Maria, *m.* to the Rev. J. Ward, D.D., and Diana, *m.* to the Rev. W. Walford, A.M.) an only son,

THE REV. ELLIS BURROUGHES, of Long Stratton, who *m.* in 1795, Sarah-Nasmyth, only dau. of Robert Marsh, Esq., and had issue, ELLIS, his heir; Walter; and Randall-Ellis. He *d.* in 1831, and was *s.* by his eldest son,

THE REV. ELLIS BURROUGHES, of Long Stratton, J.P. and D.L., *b.* 17 Jan. 1797, *m.* 16 Sept. 1823, Elizabeth-Phillipa, eldest dau. of Lieut.-Gen. Sir Francis Wilder, late M.P. for Arundel, and had,

I. ELLIS. II. Randall-Robert.
I. Frances-Sarah.

Arms—Arg., two chevrons, between three chaplets, vert, quartering ELLIS.

Crest—A griffin's head, erased, arg., charged with two chevrons, vert.

Motto—Animo et fide. The ELLIS motto is, "Huic habeo non tibi."

Seat—Stratton House, Norfolk.

BURROWES OF STRADONE HOUSE.

BURROWES, ROBERT, Esq. of Stradone House, co. Cavan, J.P. and D.L., *b.* 19 March, 1810; *m.* 16 Oct. 1838, Anne-Frances, only dau. of the late John Carden, Esq. of Barnane, co. Tipperary, and has surviving issue,

I. ROBERT-JAMES, *b.* 9 Sept. 1846.
I. Frances-Susan. II. Honora.
III. Mary-Anne-Cecilia.

Mr. Burrowes filled the office of high-sheriff in 1838.

Lineage.—This family was first established in Ireland by Robert Borowes, who settled at Drumlane, co. Cavan, on the settlement of Ulster by King JAMES I. This Robert Borowes's eldest son and heir,

THOMAS BOROWES, became possessed of Stradone, of which estate he also received a patent of confirmation from King CHARLES I., A.D. 1633.

THOMAS BURROWES, Esq. of Stradone House, (great-grandfather of the present proprietor,) *m.* Jane, dau. of Thomas Nesbitt, Esq. of Lismore House, co. Cavan, and had issue, viz., ROBERT, Thomas, and Arnold, and two daus., Martha and Jane. The eldest son,

ROBERT BURROWES, Esq. of Stradone House, *m.* Sophia, dau. of the Rev. Joseph Story, archdeacon of Kilmore, and by her had (with four daus., viz., Jane, Anne, Frances, and Sophia,) a son and heir,

THOMAS BURROWES, Esq. of Stradone House, who *m.* in 1807, Susan, dau. of the Rev. Henry Seward, of Badsey, co. Worcester, and had issue,

ROBERT, now of Stradone.
James-Edward, *b.* in Nov. 1820.
Honora-Seward, *m.* in 1834, to the Hon. Thomas Leslie.

Arms—Or, on a cross, gu., five mullets, arg.; in the chief quarters, two lions, passant, sa., crowned and langued, of the second.

Crest—A lion, sejant-guardant, sa., crowned, or, langued, gu.

Motto—Non vi sed virtute.

Seat—Stradone House, co. Cavan.

BURTON OF LONGNER.

BURTON, ROBERT, Esq. of Longner Hall, co. Salop, *b.* in 1796; *m.* 1st, 1 Nov. 1821, Catherine, 2nd dau. of William Walcot, Esq. of The Moor Hall, co. Salop, by whom (who *d.* in 1830) he has a dau., Jemima-Anne; and 2ndly, 6 Aug. 1835, Catherine, eldest dau. of the Rev. Herbert Oakeley, D.D., of Oakeley, by whom he has issue,

I. ROBERT LINGEN, *b.* 28 Oct. 1836.
II. Robert-Henry-Lingen, *b.* in 1841.
III. Robert-Edward-Lingen, *b.* in 1842.
I. Constance-Lingen.

Lineage.—The BURTONS *of Longner* have been seated for many centuries in Shropshire. One antiquary, viz., William Burton, B.L., in his Commentary on Antoninus's *Itinerary*, says, "they were of Shropshire, a family for some time, for no ordinary relations, very gracious with the several princes of the royal house of York;" and another (Browne Willis, Esq., M.P., of Whaddon, Bucks,) tells us that "they were a family of great antiquity, being possessors of Longner in the time of EDWARD IV., and before that being seated at Burton, or Boerton, in the parish of Condover, Shropshire."

SIR EDWARD BURTON, of Longner, representative of the family, "was with King EDWARD IV. successful in fourteen set battles, between the houses of York and Lancaster; and for his great royalty (loyalty?) and service he was made knight-banneret, under the royal standard in the field," A.D. 1460. His direct male representative,

THOMAS BURTON, Esq. of Longner, son and heir of Robert Burton, Esq. of Longner, high-sheriff of the co. Salop, in 1709, was *b.* in 1705, and *d.* at Shrewsbury in 1780. His nephew (the son of his sister Anne, by her husband, Thomas Lingen, Esq., of Sutton Court, co. Hereford, and Radbrook, co. Gloucester), was

ROBERT LINGEN, *b.* in 1725, who assumed the name of BURTON, pursuant to the will of his great-uncle, Thomas Burton, by act of parliament, 1748. He *m.* 7 June, 1748, Anne, dau. of Thomas Hill, Esq. of Tern Hall, by whom (who *d.* in 1771) he had issue,

I. ROBERT, his heir.
II. Henry, *b.* in 1755, vicar of Atcham, of Madeley, and for some time of the Holy Cross and St. Giles, all in Shropshire, *d.* 16 Jan. 1831, leaving issue by his wife, Mary, dau. of William Gittins, Esq. of Chilton, co. Salop,
  1 ROBERT, heir to his uncle.
  2 Henry, M.A., rector of Upton Cressett, and vicar of Atcham and of Condover, Salop.
  1 Anne. 2 Elizabeth-Blanche.
III. Edward, *b.* in 1756; *d.* 18 April, 1827, leaving by his wife, Dorothy-Eliza, dau. of Joshua Blakeway, Esq. of Lythwood, co. Salop, surviving issue,
  1 Edward, *b.* in 1794; *m.* in 1825, Ellen, dau. of the Rev. Joseph Corbett, D.D., of Longnor, archdeacon of Salop, and *d.* without issue, 19 Jan. 1836.
  2 Robert-Lingen, M.A., vicar of the Holy Cross and St. Giles's, Shrewsbury, *m.* 1st, in 1829, Everilda, dau. of the Rev. Rigbye Rigbye, of Harrock Hall, co. Lancaster, which lady *d.* 22 April, 1833; and 2ndly, in 1835, Mary-Anne-Elizabeth, dau. of the Rev. C.-Pyne Coffin, of Eastdown House, co. Devon, and relict of the Rev. Orlando-Hamlyn Williams, of Clovelly, in the same shire, by whom he has a son, Edward-Lingen, *b.* 1836.
  1 Anna-Maria, *m.* in 1821, to the Rev. Charles-Gregory Wade, rector of Hanwood. 2 Anne.
IV. John.
I. Mary. *d.* in 1775.
II. Anna-Maria, *m.* in 1776, Edmund Plowden, of Plowden, co. Salop.

Mr. Burton served the office of sheriff of Salop in 1763, and dying in 1803, was *s.* by his eldest son,

ROBERT BURTON, Esq. of Longner, high-sheriff of Shropshire in 1804, who *m.* in 1798, Rose, 2nd dau. and co-heir of John Smitheman, Esq. of Little Wenlock, and dying *s. p.* in 1841, was *s.* by his nephew, the present ROBERT BURTON, Esq. of Longner Hall.

*** From a younger dau. of BURTON *of Longner* derives the noble house of CONYNGHAM.

Arms—Party per pale, azure and purpure, a cross, engrailed, or, between four roses, arg.
Crest—A dexter gauntlet, ppr., couped at the wrist.
Motto—Dominus providebit.
Seats—Longner Hall, near Shrewsbury; Radbrook, Gloucestershire.

BURTON OF BURTON HALL.

BURTON, WILLIAM-FITZWILLIAM, Esq. of Burton Hall, co. Carlow, *b.* 14 May, 1826; *m.* 17 June, 1848, Coralie-Augusta-Frederica, 3rd dau. of Henry Lloyd, Esq. of Farrinrory, co. Tipperary, by Harriette-Amelia his wife, dau. of Sir John-Craven Carden, Bart., and has issue,

I. WILLIAM-FITZWILLIAM, *b.* 30 April, 1849.
II. Alfred-Henry, *b.* 29 March, 1853.

Lineage.—SAMUEL BURTON, Esq., son of Thomas Burton, who settled in Ireland in 1610, *m.* Margery Harris, and had issue, 1 FRANCIS, grandfather of the 1st Lord Conyngham; and 2 BENJAMIN, of Burton Hall, M.P. for Dublin from 1703 to 1723, who *m.* Grace, dau of Robert Stratford, Esq., and had twelve children, of whom the 5th son, Charles, was created a BARONET in 1758, and the eldest,

SAMUEL BURTON, Esq., became of Burton Hall. He *m.* Miss Anne Campbell, and left with a dau., Catherine, wife of Nicholas, 5th Viscount Netterville, a son,

BENJAMIN BURTON, Esq. of Burton Hall, who *m.* 10 Jan. 1734, Lady Anne Ponsonby, dau. of the 1st Earl of Bessborough, and had issue, three sons and two daus., of whom Sarah *m.* John Hyde, Esq. of Castle Hyde, co. Cork. The eldest son, the Right Hon. Benjamin Burton, *d. unm.*: the second,

WILLIAM-HENRY BURTON, Esq. of Burton Hall, *m.* 12 Dec. 1765, Mary, only child of Henry Aston, of East Aston, co. Wicklow, Esq., and *d.* 7 Jan. 1818, leaving issue. The elder son and heir,

BENJAMIN BURTON, Esq. of Burton Hall, *b.* 12 Sept. 1766; *m.* 15 Dec. 1794, Anne, dau. of Thomas Mainwaring, of Goltho, co. Lincoln, Esq., and had issue,

WILLIAM-FITZWILLIAM, his heir.
Benjamin, *b.* 10 July, 1799; *d. unm.* 6 Nov. 1853.
Mary-Elizabeth, *m.* 19 Dec. 1819, to Sir Richard Sutton, of Norwood Park, Notts, Bart., *d.* 1 July, 1842.
Sophia-Catherine, *m.* 5 Aug. 1824, to Robert Thoroton, Esq., colonel in the Grenadier guards.

Mr. Burton *d.* 26 April, 1808, and was *s.* by his son,

WILLIAM-FITZWILLIAM BURTON, of Burton Hall, *b.* 22 Sept. 1796; J.P., who served as high-sheriff of Carlow in 1822. He *m.* 1st, 18 July, 1825, Mary, dau of the late Sir John Power, of Kilfane, Bart., and by her (who *d.* 25 Jan. 1839) had issue,

WILLIAM-FITZWILLIAM, now of Burton Hall.
Benjamin, *b.* 17 Sept. 1829; *m.* 27 April, 1854, Anne, dau. of the late Colonel Bruen, M.P., of Oak Park, co. Carlow.
John-Power, *b.* 3 Sept. 1833.
Charles, *b.* 24 Oct. 1836.
Harriet-Anne, *m.* 29 July, 1851, to Richard Sutton, Esq. of Skeffington Hall, co. Leicester, 2nd son of Sir Richard Sutton, Bart.
Mary-Frances. Sophia-Charlotta.
Helen-Mary.

Mr. Burton *m.* 2ndly, 5 Oct. 1840, Eleanor-Mary, dau. of the late William Browne, of Brownes Hill, co. Carlow, Esq. He *d.* 15 Nov. 1844.

Arms—Per pale, az. and purpure, a cross, engrailed, or, between four roses, arg.
Crest—On a ducal coronet, a dexter gauntlet, the palm inwards, all ppr.
Motto—Dominus providebit.
Seat—Burton Hall, co. Carlow.

BURTON OF CARRIGAHOLT CASTLE.

BURTON, HENRY-STUART, Esq. of Carrigaholt Castle, co. Clare, *b.* 16 Sept. 1808; *m.* 23 June, 1836, Alicia-Mary, dau. of the Rev. Dr. Simpson, and has issue,

I. FRANCIS-NATHANIEL-VALENTINE, *b.* 13 Sept. 1842.
II. William-Conyngham-Vandeleur, *b.* 18 Sept. 1846.
III. Henry-Stuart, *b.* 12 June, 1849.
I. Lucy-Anne. II. Valentina-Henrietta.
III. Elizabeth-Cecilia-Alice.

Mr. Burton, and his younger brother, William-Conyngham Burton, Esq., *b.* 31 Dec. 1809, are the sons of the late Hon. Sir Francis-Nathaniel Burton, G.C.H., brother of Henry, 1st Marquess Conyngham. (*See* BURKE's *Peerage.*)

Arms, &c.—Same as BURTON *of Burton Hall.*
Seat—Carrigaholt Castle, co. Clare.

BURTON OF SACKETT'S HILL HOUSE.

BURTON, SIR RICHARD, Knt. of Sackett's Hill House, co. Kent, *b.* 23 Nov. 1773; *m.* 27 April, 1802, Elizabeth, only dau. of the late Robert Crofts, Esq. of Dumpton House, Isle of Thanet, and has had issue,

I. JOHN, b. in 1804; m. in 1829, Mary-Helena, eldest dau. of Captain George Robinson, R.N.; and dying in 1833, left one son and one dau., viz., RICHARD, b. in 1830; and Elizabeth-Ann.

II. Richard, b. in 1805; captain 54th regiment of foot; d. in 1832.

III. Robert, b. in 1807; m. in 1828, Mary, youngest dau. of the late Rev. Robert Rastall, rector of Winthorpe, Notts, and has two sons, Robert-Heron, b. in 1829; and Richard-Crofts, b. in 1833; and two daus.

IV. Francis, b. in 1809.

V. Carr, b. in 1811; m. 16 Feb. 1843, Margaret, 2nd dau. of the late W.-H. Dearsley, Esq. of Shinfield, Berks.

I. Frances-Sarah, m. in 1831, to Latham Osborne, Esq.

II. Honor, m. in 1838, Lieut. Alexander Brown, R.N.

Sir Richard Burton received the honour of knighthood in 1831.

Lineage.—SIR JOHN BURTON, Knt. of Wakefield, co. York, b. in 1744, eldest son of Col. Richard Burton, of the York militia, and great-great-grandson of Arthur Burton, Esq. of Kelling Hall, near Ripley; who m. 1st, in 1770, Honor, dau. of John-Harvey Thursby, Esq. of Abington, in Northamptonshire, and had an only son, RICHARD, his heir. He m. 2ndly, Philippa-Irnham Forster, of Buxton Vale, in Northumberland, and by her had a son, John, b. and d. in 1801, and a dau., Philippa-Frances. Sir John d. in 1809.

Arms—Sa., on a chevron, between three owls, arg., ducally crowned, or, a mural crown, gu., between two wreaths of laurel, vert.
Crest—A beacon, or, fired, ppr., surmounted by two branches of laurel, in saltier, vert.
Motto—Vigilans.
Seat—Sackett's Hill House, near Margate.

BUSFEILD OF UPWOOD.

BUSFEILD, THE REV. WILLIAM, M.A., of Upwood, co. York, rector of Keighley, co. York, b. 21 Feb. 1802; m. 21 Sept. 1830, Sarah, youngest dau. of the Rev. Charles-Frederick Bond, of Margaretting, Essex, and has had issue,

I. WILLIAM, b. 20 Jan. 1837.
II. John, b. 18 Nov. 1839.
III. Frederick-Charles, b. 7 Sept. 1843.
IV. Edward-Harcourt, d. 1847.
I. Mary, d. unm. 1854. II. Ellen.
III. Harriet-Olivia.

Lineage.—ELIZABETH BUSFEILD, b. 1 Jan. 1747 (only dau. and heir of William Busfeild, Esq. of Ryshworth Hall, Bingley, co. York, son and heir of William Busfeild, Esq., of Gray's Inn, J.P., by Elizabeth his wife, dau. of Abraham Fothergill, Esq.), m. 7 Jan. 1765, Johnson Atkinson,* M.D. of Leeds, and afterwards of Ryshworth and Myrtle Grove, near Bingley, J.P. and D.L., who assumed, upon the demise of his wife's uncle, Thomas Busfeild, Esq., the surname and arms of BUSFEILD. The issue of the marriage were three sons and a dau., viz.,

I. WILLIAM, of Upwood.
II. Johnson-Atkinson, D.D., b. 8 July, 1775; m. in 1798, Mary-Susannah, 3rd dau. of Joseph Priestley, Esq. of White Windows; and 2ndly, Charlotte, dau. of — Irving, Esq. By the former, he left at his decease, 12 Jan. 1849,
1 WILLIAM, now of Upwood.
2 Charles, b. 6 Sept. 1804.
3 John-Lea, b. in 1806; d. in 1816.
4 Harcourt-Norris-Torriana, b. 5 Dec. 1811.
III. Currer-Fothergill, of Cottingley Bridge, b. 23 Jan. 1777, m. 12 Feb. 1805, Sarah, 2nd dau. of John Ferrand, Esq. of Stockton-upon-Tees, and sister of Edward Ferrand, Esq. of St. Ives, co. York, and d. 30 June, 1832, having had issue (see FERRAND).
I. Jane, m. 27 Oct. 1803, to Charles Jones, Esq., major in the 18th hussars, and d. 24 March, 1818, leaving issue.

The heiress of Busfeild d. 5 Nov. 1796, and was s. by her eldest son,

WILLIAM BUSFEILD, Esq., m. 13 May, 1800, Caroline, eldest dau. of Capt. Charles Wood, R.N. of Bowling Hall, and sister of Sir Francis Wood, Bart., but by her (who d. 8 April, 1839) had no issue. Mr. Busfeild, who is a magistrate and deputy-lieutenant of the West Riding of Yorkshire, was returned to parliament by the borough of Bradford in 1837.

Arms—Sa., a chevron, between three fleurs-de-lis, or.
Seat—Upwood, Yorkshire.

* He m. 2ndly, in 1800, Susannah, relict of John Dearden, Esq. of The Hollins.

BUSHE OF GLENCAIRN ABBEY.

BUSHE, GERVASE-PARKER, Esq. of Glencairn Abbey, co. Waterford, at one time high-sheriff of that county.

Lineage.—JOHN BUSHE, Esq., a colonel in the army, had grant of land in Kilfane, 10 Dec. 1670. By Mary his wife, dau. and co-heir of Col. John Grey, he left, with four daus., two sons, AMIAS, and Arthur, who m. twice, and had issue by both wives. The elder son,

AMIAS BUSHE, Esq. of Kilfane, co. Kilkenny, whose will, dated 29 Aug. 1724, was proved 2 March, 1730, m. twice and had issue, 1 Amias, d. unm.; 2 CHRISTOPHER, of whose line we treat; 3 Arthur, of Kilmurry, co. Kilkenny, father of the Rev. Thomas Bushe, of Kingston Cottage, co. Cork, who m. Catherine, dau. of Charles Doyle, Esq. of Bramblestown, co. Kilkenny, and left, with other issue, a son, the RIGHT HON. CHARLES-KENDALL BUSHE, lord-chief-justice of the Court of Queen's Bench in Ireland, who m. Anne, sister of Sir Philip Crampton, Bart., and left at his decease, John, and other issue; 1 Elinor, wife of Christopher Hewetson, Esq.; 2 Elizabeth, wife of Edward Doan, Esq. of Dangen and Tyrenure. The 2nd son,

CHRISTOPHER BUSHE, Esq., who d. *vitâ patris*, left, by Margaret his wife, a son,

AMIAS BUSHE, Esq. of Kilfane, who m. 2 May, 1737, Elizabeth, only dau. and heir of Gervais Parker, Esq., a general of horse, governor of Cork and Kinsale, commander-in-chief in Ireland; and dying in 1773, was s. by his son,

GERVAIS-PARKER BUSHE, Esq. of Kilfane, whose will, dated 30 June, 1792, was proved 30 Aug. 1793. He m. Mary, dau. of James Grattan, Esq. recorder of Dublin, and had issue, 1 HENRY-AMIAS; 2 William, in holy orders, rector of St. George's, Dublin; 3 Gervais-Parker, barrister-at-law, who m. Mrs. Eliza Hacket; 4 Richard; 5 Robert; 1 Charlotte, m. to the Rev. Dean Scott; and 2 Frances, m. to the Right Rev. George-De La Poer Beresford, Bishop of Kilmore. The eldest son,

HENRY-AMIAS BUSHE, Esq., m. Lavinia, eldest dau. of Richard Gumbleton, Esq. of Castle Richard (now called Glencairn Abbey), co. Waterford, and s., by the bequest of that lady's brother, Richard-Edward Gumbleton, Esq., who d. in 1819, to Glencairn Abbey. He served as high-sheriff of the co. of Waterford in 1826, and was s. at his decease by his son, the present MAJOR GERVAIS-PARKER BUSHE.

Arms—Quarterly: 1st and 4th, az., a wolf, rampant, arg., collared and chained, or; in chief, three crosses, patée-fitchée, of the second; 2nd and 3rd, barry of six, arg. and az., a bend, compony, or and gu.
Crest—A goat's head, arg.
Motto—Moderata durant.
Seat—Glencairn Abbey, co. Waterford.

BUSK OF FORD'S GROVE.

BUSK, EDWARD-THOMAS, Esq. of Ford's Grove, co. Middlesex, J.P., b. 21 May, 1805; m. 4 Nov. 1851, Susan, dau. of Thomas Benson, Esq., and has issue,

I. THOMAS-TESHMAKER, b. 18 Sept. 1852.
I. Lucy.

Lineage.—JACOB-HANS BUSCH, of an ancient family in Sweden, came to England early in the last century, and settled at Leeds. He m. in 1717, Rachel Wadsworth, and had ten children, none of whom had male descendants except the youngest,

SIR WADSWORTH BUSK, Knt., who m. in 1764, Alice, dau. and co-heir of Edward-Clark Parish, Esq. of Walthamstow, and had, with four younger sons, his heir, EDWARD. Sir Wadsworth m. 2ndly, Sarah, relict of Colonel Vane, and dau. of James Birch, Esq. He d. in 1811. The eldest son of the first marriage,

EDWARD BUSK, Esq., m. in 1800, Sarah Thomasin, dau. and co-heir of Thomas Teshmaker, Esq. of Ford's Grove, only son of Merry Teshmaker, Esq., and nephew and heir of James Gould, Esq. of Ford's Grove. By this lady he had issue,

EDWARD-THOMAS, now of Ford's Grove.
Henry-William, of the Middle Temple, barrister-at-law, m. Mary-Anne, dau. of the Rev. Philip Le Breton, and has issue.
Sarah-Alice.
Mary-Anne, m. to the Rev. Edward-Blackburn Warren, A.M. Caroline.

Arms—Arg., three trees, ppr.
Crest—A stag, regardant, ppr.
Motto—Suaviter sed fortiter.
Seat—Ford's Grove, Enfield, co. Middlesex.

BUTLER OF CREGG.

BUTLER, FRANCIS, Esq. of Cregg, co. Galway, J.P., *b.* 8 March, 1789; *m.* 14 Feb. 1814, Sarah, sister of Maurice-Crosbie Moore, Esq. of Mooresfort, co. Tipperary, and has issue,

I. WALTER-RICHARD, *b.* 3 Dec. 1816.
II. Edward-Walter, *b.* 12 Sept. 1820.
I. Elizabeth, *m.* to John Lopdell, Esq. of Derryowen.
II. Anna. III. Sarah-Ellen. IV. Frances-Pyne.

Lineage.—PIERCE BUTLER, Esq., son of Theobald Butler, and a descendant of a branch of the Ormonde family, obtained from King CHARLES II., 1 May, 1677, a confirmatory patent of his estate, which his ancestors had enjoyed time immemorial. He was father of

THEOBALD BUTLER, of Cregg, whose son,

FRANCIS BUTLER, of Cregg, *m.* a dau. of Walter Lambert, Esq. of Creg Clare, co. Galway, and had two sons and three daus. The elder son,

WALTER BUTLER, Esq. of Cregg, served as high-sheriff of the co. of Galway. He *m.* 1st, Miss Anne Mahon; and 2ndly, Anne, dau. of — Taylor, Esq. of Castle Taylor, co. Galway, by the former of whom he had issue,

FRANCIS, now of Cregg.
Walter, who *m.* Miss Sarah Jeffries, and has one surviving son, Theobald, who *m.* in 1839, his cousin, Anna-Maria, dau. of Andrew Blake, Esq. of Dunmacreena.
Theobald, who *m.* Nicola, sister of Arthur-St. George, Esq. of Tyrone, co. Galway, and has issue.
Belinda, *m.* to Andrew Blake, Esq. of Dunmacreena.

Arms—Quarterly: 1st and 4th, or, a chief, indented, az.; 2nd and 3rd, gu., three covered cups, or.
Crest—Out of a ducal coronet, or, a plume of five ostrich feathers, arg., therefrom issuant a falcon, rising, of the last.
Motto—Comme je trouve.
Seat—Cregg, co. Galway.

BUTLER OF PRIESTOWN.

BUTLER, THE REV. JAMES, of Priestown, co. Meath, *b.* in 1790; *m.* Isabella, eldest dau. of Thomas Rothwell, Esq. of Rockfield, co. Meath, Ireland, and has issue,

I. Richard. II. Thomas. III. James.
I. Helena. II. Matilda. III. Isabella.
IV. Augusta, *d.* young. V. Emma.

Lineage.—From the genealogy "furnished in the year 1712, for Theobald Butler, Knt., son of Peter, D.D., son of Theobald, son of James, Baron of Dunboyne and Mullingar," it appears that, before the year 1329, Theobald Butler *m.* Joanna, dau of John Walter, by whom he had two sons, Theobald, ancestor of the Ormonde family of Butlers; and Thomas, who *d.* in 1329, having *m.* Synolda, dau. and heiress of Peter Petit, of Dunboyne and Mullingar, whose son, Peter, or Pierce, besides other children, left a son, William, Baron of Dunboyne, *m.* in 1406, Elizabeth, by whom he left issue, James, who *m.* Morina, dau. of — Brian, and *d.* in 1445, leaving a son, Edmund (who was restored to the manor of Mullingar by act of parliament, HENRY VII.) He *m.* Katherine, dau. of Richard Boelieke, and left issue, "Peter, or Pierce, killed by James Tobyn in 1502;" and James, who *m.* Elinor, dau. of MacCarthy Reagh, and *d.* Baron of Dunboyne in 1508, leaving James, Baron of Dunboyne, who *m.* 31 HENRY VIII, Joanna, dau. of Peter, Earl of Ormonde, and left issue, Edmund, Lord Dunboyne, who *m.* Cecilia, dau. of Cormac MacCarthy, of Muskerry, whose son, James, Baron of Dunboyne, *d.* 18 Feb. 1625, having *m.* 1st, Margaret, dau. of Barnaby Fitzpatrick, Lord of Up Ossory, whose son, John, was "killed by Richard Grace in 1602," and whose dau., Joanna, *m.* Maurice Fitzgibbon, White Knight; and Catherine, *m.* N. Everard. James, Baron of Dunboyne, *m.* 2ndly, Margaret, dau. of Cornelius, Earl of Thomond, by whom he left issue, Pierce, who *m.* Margaret, dau. of Walter Blake, Esq. of the co. Galway, and left issue, James, who *d. s. p.*, and

THEOBALD BUTLER, of Priestown, co. Meath, who *m.* 1st, Maria O'Hara, who *d. s. p.*; and 2ndly, Maria, dau. of Nathaniel Whitwell, alderman of Dublin, by whom he left issue, 1 JAMES, of whom hereafter; 2 Whitwell, who settled in Kerry, and *m.* Belinda Yielding, by whom he left James, Whitwell, and Belinda; and 3 Ellen, who *m.* Robert Beatty, Esq. The elder son,

JAMES BUTLER, Esq. of Priestown, *m.* Dorothea, dau. of Sir Richard Steele, Bart., by whom he left issue,

RICHARD, of whom hereafter.
James, lieut.-gen. and governor of Sandhurst College, who *m.* 1st, Elizabeth, dau. of — Pitcairne, Esq., by whom he left issue, James, a major in the army; Alexander, a captain in the army; Jeannette; Elizabeth; Katherine; and Rosa. He *m.* 2ndly, Frances, dau. of — Glover, who *d. s. p.* in 1828; and 3rdly, a dau. of — Bateman, who survives him. He *d.* in August, 1836.
Theobald, *m.* Lucy, dau. of — Richards, Esq.
Whitwell, *d. s. p.* Pierce, *d. s. p.*
Nathaniel-Edward, *m.* Anne, dau. of the Rev. — Stone, *d. s. p.* in 1842.
Rose, *d. unm.*

The eldest son,

THE REV. RICHARD BUTLER, D.D., vicar of Burnchurch, co. Kilkenny, *m.* in 1792, Martha, 2nd dau. of Richard Rothwell, Esq. of Burford, co. Meath, and had,

JAMES, now of Priest-Town.
Richard (the Very Rev.), Dean of Clonmacnoise and vicar of Trim, *b.* 14 Oct. 1794; *m.* 14 Aug. 1826, Harriet, dau. of R.-L. Edgeworth, Esq. of Edgeworthstown, by Frances-Anne his wife, dau. of the Rev. D.-A. Beaufort, D.D.
Thomas-Lewis, capt. 79th Highlanders, *d.* in 1848.
Whitwell, *m.* in 1833, Elizabeth, 2nd dau. of John-Payne Garnett, Esq. of Arch Hall, co. Meath, and has issue, Whitwell, Richard, John, Mary, and Elizabeth.
Edward, in holy orders, *m.* 1st, in 1830, Henrietta, dau. of Henry Skryne, Esq. of Warleigh, Somersetshire, by whom (who *d.* in 1832) he had a son, Bagot, *d.* an infant; 2ndly, in 1835, Anne-Elizabeth, dau. of William Woodville, Esq., by whom (who *d.* in 1845) he had a son, Theobald-William; and 3rdly, in 1846, Blanche, dau. of Philip Perring, Esq. of Devon.
John. Mary.

Dr. Butler *d.* in 1841.

Arms—1st, or, on a chief, indented, az., eight escallop-shells, of the first, BUTLER; 2nd, arg., a fesse, sa., PETIT; 3rd, gu., three covered cups, or, BUTLER; 4th, gu., a fesse, company, or and az., cotised, of the second, for WHITWELL.
Motto—Timor Domini fons vitæ.

BUTTER OF FASKALLY.

BUTTER, ARCHIBALD, Esq. of Faskally, co. Perth, J.P. and D.L., *b.* 9th May, 1805; *m.* in Sept. 1834, Jemima, youngest dau. of the late James Richardson, Esq. of Pitfour, co. Perth, and has issue,

I. ARCHIBALD, *b.* 28 March, 1836.
II. Henry-Thomas, *b.* 17 Aug. 1840.
III. James, *b.* 28 May, 1843.
IV. Albert, *b.* 28 Sept. 1844.
I. Elizabeth-Vere. II. Jemima-Charlotte-Barbara.

Lineage.—The late ARCHIBALD BUTTER, Esq., a lieut.-col. in the army, *b.* in 1769 (eldest son of Henry Butter, Esq., by Katherine his wife, 2nd dau. of Peter Hay, Esq. of Leys and Randerston, co. Fife, and grandson of Archibald Butter, Esq., by Jean, dau. of Henry Balneaves); *m.* in 1803, Vere, only dau. of the late Sir Robert Menzies, of Menzies, Bart., and by her, who survived until Jan. 1847, left at his decease, in 1805, an only son and successor, the present ARCHIBALD BUTTER, Esq. of Faskally.

Arms—Arg., a cross, sa., between four hearts, gu.
Crest—Two arms issuing from clouds, drawing a bow with an arrow, paleways, all ppr.
Motto—Diriget Deus.
Seat—Faskally, co. Perth.

BUTTS OF CAMESWORTH.

BUTTS, THE REV. EDWARD-DRURY, of Camesworth, co. Dorset, *m.* Mary, dau. of James Hill, Esq. of Walthamstow, co. Essex, and has issue,

I. EDWARD-DRURY. II. William-Pitt.
III. Robert-Gosset. IV. Henry-Hill.
V. John-George.
I. Amy. II. Selina-Jane. III. Martha-Beatrice.

Mr. Butts is incumbent of Melplaish, co. Dorset.

Lineage.—The family of Butts held at a very early period, and for a considerable time, the manorial estates of Shouldham, Thorpe, and Thornage, the latter of which was carried out of the family by an heiress, who *m.* Sir N. Bacon, Bart.

THE RIGHT REV. ROBERT BUTTS, Lord Bishop of Ely (2nd son of the Rev. William Butts, rector of Hartest, Suffolk), *m.* 1st, Elizabeth, dau. of the Rev. Anthony Pitcher, rector of Hawsted; and 2ndly, Anne, dau. of the

Rev. James Reynolds, of Lackford, Suffolk. By the latter, his lordship had six daus., and by the former, two sons and three daus., viz.,

Eyton, in holy orders, dean of Cloyne.
ROBERT, of whom presently.
Martha, m. to Dr. Steadman, archdeacon of Norfolk.
Charlotte. Mary, m. to Dr. Owen.

The 2nd son,

THE REV. ROBERT BUTTS, rector of Long Melford, Suffolk, m. Jane, dau. of Dr. Reuben Clarke, dean of Westminster, and had (with a dau., Jane, wife of Roger Kedington, of Rougham, and another son, Robert),

THE REV. WILLIAM BUTTS, who m. Amy, 3rd dau. of the Rev. George Drury, A.M., rector of Overstone and Cladon, who d. in 1807, and had, besides the present REV. EDWARD-DRURY BUTTS, four sons and two daus., viz,

Robert. William, who m. Miss Robinson.
Charles-Salisbury. Henry-Owen.
Emily, m. to Thomas M'Dougall, Esq.
Jane-Elizabeth.

Seat—Camesworth House, Bridport.

BYAM OF ANTIGUA, AND OF SOMERSETSHIRE.

BYAM, WILLIAM, Esq. of Cedar Hill, Antigua, and of Westwood House, in the co. of Hants, president of the island of Antigua, and lieut.-col. of the local dragoons, m. 8 Feb. 1815, Martha, dau. of Thomas Rogers, Esq. of Antigua, and has issue,

I. EDWARD-GAMAGE, capt. 59th regt., b. 30 June, 1828.
II. William, b. 10 Feb. 1828.
I. Lydia, m. 18 March, 1837, to Francis Shand, Esq. of Everton, co. Lancaster.
I. Martha-Anne. II. Elizabeth-Christiana.

Mr. Byam served in the 15th hussars, in the south of France, and afterwards at Waterloo, where he was wounded.

Lineage.—The family of Byam ("antiquissima familia BYAMORUM") consists of two branches descended from two brothers, the sons of William Byam, a distinguished royalist, who was engaged on the king's side throughout the whole of the civil wars in the West of England, and afterwards became governor of Surinam, viz., Col. Willoughby Byam, who commanded the body-guard at the capture of St. Christopher, in 1690, and d. of his wounds there received; and Edward Byam, governor of the Leeward Islands, who, surviving to an advanced age, d. in 1741; the former being now represented by WILLIAM BYAM, Esq. of Cedar Hill, in Antigua, and of Westwood, in Hampshire, and the latter by the REV. RICHARD-BURGH BYAM, vicar of Kew and Petersham, in Surrey. The state of the family was duly registered by the Heralds in the Visitation of Somersetshire, A.D. 1623.

WILLIAM BYAM, b. 9 March, 1628 (2nd son of the Rev. Edward Byam, precentor of Cloyne, and grandson of the Rev. Lawrence Byam, of Luccombe, co. Somerset, who descended from Mainerch, Lord of Brecknock, who derived from CARADOC VRAICH VRAS, Earl of Hereford, Lord of Radnor); m. Dorothy, dau. of Francis Knollys, of Standford-in-the-Vale, co. Berks, Esq., by Alice his wife, sister and co-heir of Sir William Beecher, Knt., and granddau. of Richard, brother and heir of William Knollys, 1st Earl of Banbury. This gentleman was governor of Surinam, whence, on its being ceded to the Dutch, in 1667, he removed to Antigua, where he had grants of lands, and where he d., leaving, with other issue,

I. WILLOUGHBY, his heir.
II. Edward, governor of the Leeward Islands, and president of the council of Antigua in 1707; m. twice, and had issue by each marriage. By the first marriage, with Mary Winthorpe, he had a son, Edward, and a dau., Mary, wife of Col. Thomas Williams, son of Rowland Williams, Lieut.-Governor of Antigua. By his 2nd wife, Lydia, widow of Samuel Martin, Esq. of Green Castle, and aunt of Sir George Thomas, Bart., he left at his decease, 4 Dec. 1741, with two daus., Alice, m. to Robert Freeman, of Antigua, and Lydia, m. to her cousin, Edward Byam, of Cedar Hill, as hereafter, three sons,

1 George, of Antigua, b. 24 April, 1704, m. Henrietta-Maria, dau. of Col. John Frye, of Antigua, and d. in 1834, leaving, with other issue, a son, George, of Apps Court, co. Surrey, who m. Louisa, dau. of Peter Bathurst, Esq., M.P., of Clarendon Park, co. Wilts, and niece of Earl Bathurst, and by her had a son, George, d. 1774, and four daus., 1 Selina, m. to the Rev. William Hony, of Liskeard, co. Cornwall, and had issue; 2 Elizabeth, m. to Mark Batt, Esq. of Lawell House, Devon, and d. s. p; 3 Louisa; and 4 Henrietta, d. unm. The eldest sister of George, of Apps Court, Mary, m. Daniel Mathew, Esq. of Antigua, and of Felix Hall, Essex, and had issue, Daniel-Byam Mathew, of Felix Hall, who m. Elizabeth, dau. of Sir Edward Dering, Bart.; George, who m. Euphemia Hamilton; Elizabeth, m. Robert, 4th Viscount Galway; Louisa Mathew, who m. Admiral Lord Gambier; and Jane, m. Samuel Gambier, commissioner of the navy.

2 William, of Byams, in Antigua, and of Westbourne House, Paddington, co. Middlesex, col. in the army, and a member of the privy council of Antigua, b. 3 July, 1706, m. 19 June, 1735, Anne, dau. of Col. John Gunthorpe, member of the privy council of Antigua, and had issue,

Martin, of Antigua, member of council, b. 29 Sept. 1742, m. 2 Nov. 1711, Elizabeth, dau. of Stephen Blizard, judge of the Common Pleas in Antigua, and relict of William Warner, Esq., of that island, and d. in June, 1805, s. p.

Edward, b. 15 Sept. 1743, lieut. in the royal navy, was lost in the "Ville de Paris," after her capture in 1782, leaving, by Anne his wife, dau. of William Gunthorpe, Esq. of Antigua, a son, William-Henry, capt. R.N., m. his cousin, Alicia, dau. of Anthony Wyke, Esq., and d. s. p. 26 Nov. 1838; and a dau., Louisa, d. unm. in 1835.

William, b. 7 Nov. 1753, capt. in the 68th foot, m. in 1781, Mary, only dau. of the Rev. Richard Burgh, of Mount Bruis, co. Tipperary, and d. 27 April, 1830, having had issue, 1 Martin-William, b. 1783, m. Elizabeth, dau. of Thomas Bull, of Bostock Hall, co. Chester, and d. s. p., 22 April, 1836; 2 RICHARD-BURGH, in holy orders, vicar of Kew and Petersham, co. Surrey, member of council at Antigua, b. 26 Jan. 1785; 4 Edward-Samuel, a Celtic scholar, formerly commissary-general of the police in the island of Mauritius, b. 5 Aug. 1788, m. 26 March, 1818, Eleanor, eldest dau. of Andrew-Murray Prior, Esq. of Rathdowny, Queen's Co., and niece of Viscount Frankfort, and had issue, Edward-De Montmorency, b. 6 Aug. 1819, and d. Oct. following; 4 Martha; 5 Anna-Maria; and 6 Alicia-Juliana, m. to William Leeves, Esq. of Tortington House, Sussex.

Anne, m. in 1763, to Anthony Wyke, Esq. of the island of Montserrat, and has issue, George, captain in the Grenadier guards; Anne, wife of Daniel Hill, Esq.; Louisa, m. to Henry Mitford, Esq., capt. R.N., nephew of Lord Redesdale, and other issue.

Alice, m. 28 April, 1763, Samuel Elliot, Esq. of Antigua (derived from a branch of the family of Port Eliot, in Cornwall), and had four daus., 1 Anne, m. to Lieut.-Gen. Sir Henry Cosby, of Barnsville Park, co. Gloucester; 2 Elizabeth, m. to Sir Thomas Stapleton, Lord Le Despenser; 3 Mary, m. to Robert Camden Cope, Esq., col. of the Armagh militia; and 4 Alice, m. 3 Aug. 1796, to William Hay-Carr, Earl of Erroll, grandfather of the present peer.

3 Francis, in holy orders, fellow of Trinity College, Cambridge, rector of St. John's, Antigua, and member of council, b. 8 Aug. 1709, d. in 1757, having m. 2 Jan. 1738, Jane, dau. and co-heir of Edward Warner, Esq. of Eltham, co. Kent, col. in the army, and member of council in Antigua, and had, with other issue, 1 Edward, b. 21 Dec. 1740, m. 7 July, 1763, Rebecca, dau. of Stephen Blizard, judge of the Common Pleas in Antigua. This Edward was judge of the Vice-Admiralty Court, and president of the Council of Antigua. He d. 8 Feb. 1817, leaving an only child and heir, Jane, m. to Thomas-Norbury Kerby, president of the Council of Antigua, and had issue, Anne Byam, m. to the Hon. and Rev. Miles Stapleton, 3rd son of Lord Le Despenser, by whom she had four daus., co-heirs to the barony; 2 Ashton-Warner (Sir), Knt., attorney-general of Grenada, b. 1 June, 1744, d. unm.; 3 Richard-Scott, b. 24 Dec. 1753, d. unm. in 1832; 4 Grace-Johnson, m. 3 March, 1767, to Thomas Ottley, Esq. of the island of St. Vincent, and had issue.

The eldest son,

WILLOUGHBY BYAM, Esq., lieut.-col. in the army, commanded the body-guard of the commander-in-chief at the capture of St. Christopher's, in 1690, where he received a wound of which he died. He was father of two sons, WILLIAM, his heir, and Samuel, whose granddau. and heiress, Phillis Byam, m. 1st, Charlton Wollaston, physician to Queen CHARLOTTE, and 2ndly, James Frampton, Esq. of Moreton, co. Dorset. The elder son,

WILLIAM BYAM, Esq. of Cedar Hill, Antigua, col. in the army, and member of the privy council of the island, m. Mary, dau. of John Yeamans, lieut.-governor of Antigua, and had, with other issue, who d. young, three daus. (Mary, m. to Warner Tempest, Esq.; Anne, m. to Crooke Thomas, of London, merchant; and Rebecca, m. to Thomas Freeman, Esq.), and three sons, EDWARD, his heir; John-Sampson, d. unm. 1766; and Henry, D.D., d. 1760, leaving three daus, Anne; Hester, m. to Anthony Munton, Esq.;

and Mary-Gunthorpe, m. to Col. William Dundas, brother of the 1st Viscount Melville. The eldest son,

Edward Byam, Esq. of Cedar Hill, and of Clay Hill, Enfield, co. Middlesex, and sometime of Llanian, in the parish of St. Mary, Pembroke, where he was buried, b. 1712, m. in 1734, his cousin Lydia, dau. of Edward Byam, governor of the Leeward Islands, and dying in 1768, was s. by his son,

William Byam, Esq. of Cedar Hill, and sometime of Sunny Hill, co. Pembroke, who m. Martha, dau. of Edward Rogers, of Lanwnda, co. Pembroke, and d. in 1779, leaving, with a dau., who d. unm., two sons, Edward, his heir, and Samuel, D.D., vicar of Catterick, co. York, and chaplain in ordinary to the king, who d. in 1816, leaving, by Jane his wife, dau. of John Welsh, Esq. of St. Christopher's, three sons and two daus., viz., William-George-Munton, late of the 43rd light infantry; Adolphus-Elizabeth, capt. Madras artillery, d. s. p.; Henry-James, d. in Spain, unm.; Cornelia-Rachel, m. to Baron Augustus de Firkes; and Augusta-Louisa-Anne, m. Fredk.-Shallet Lomax, Esq. The elder son,

Edward Byam, Esq. of Cedar Hill, member of the House of Assembly of Antigua, b. 1767, m. Christiana-Matilda, dau. of Matthew Ryan, Esq. of Dublin, barrister-at-law, and d. in 1795, leaving two sons, William, now of Cedar Hill; and Edward, of Warblington Lodge, Hants, b. in 1794, late major 15th hussars, and now major-gen. in the army, served in the Peninsula and at Waterloo, who m. in 1829, Elizabeth-Augusta, sister of the late Sir Grenville Temple, Bart., and has, Willoughby-Temple, b. in 1832; Henry-Edward, b. in 1835; Arthur-Merick; Edward-Willoughby-Grenville; Temple-Knollys; Matilda-Augusta-Anne; Agnes-Welthian; Maria-Christiana-Elizabeth; Augusta-Temple; Ellen-Gladys; Christina-Laura; and Alice-Margaret.

Arms—Quarterly: 1st, arg., three dragons' heads, erased, vert, each holding in its mouth a dexter hand, erased, ppr., dropping blood; 2nd, sa, a chevron between three spears' heads, erect., arg., pointed, gu.; 3rd, gu., a lion, rampant-regardant, or; 4th, gu., three towers, triple-turretted, arg.; 5th, vert, a chevron between three wolves' heads, erased, or; 6th, as first.

Crests—1st, A squirrel, passant, or, collared and chained, vert; 2nd, a dragon's head, erased, vert, langued, gu., holding in its jaws a hand, ppr., dropping blood.

Motto—Claris dextera factis. "Y gwin yn-erbyn y byd," is the motto borne by Edward-Samuel Byam, Esq.

Seats—Cedar Hill, island of Antigua; Westwood House, and Warblington Lodge, Hants.

BYRNE OF CABINTEELY.

Byrne, Georgiana-Mary, of Cabinteely, co. Dublin. Miss Byrne inherited the estates at the decease of her sister.

Lineage.—From the earliest era of Irish history, to the invasion of Cromwell, the family of O'Broin, O'Byrne, or O'Birne, was amongst the most powerful and distinguished in the province of Leinster. It traces its descent from Hermon, the youngest son of Milesius, through Ugane More and Cathire More, two of the most renowned warriors that swayed the Irish sceptre.

Charles O'Byrne, representative of this great house, was deprived by Cromwell of his extensive domains. He m. Grizel, dau. of Byrne of Ballinacurbeg, and had three sons, Hugh, of Ballinacurbeg, whose line is extinct; John, of Ballenclough, co. Wicklow, who had three daus., his co-heirs; and Daniel. This

Daniel Byrne m. Anne, dau. of Richard Taylor, Esq. of Swords, and had, with two daus. (Mary, m. 1st, to John Walsh, of Old Connaught, Esq., and 2ndly, to Sir Luke Dowdall, Bart.; and Margaret, m. to Terence Dunn, of Brittas), four sons, 1 Gregory of Timogue, created a Bart. in 1671 (his male representative is George, Lord De Tabley); 2 John, of whom presently; 3 Walter, capt. in the army, d. at St. Germains; and 4 Joseph, of Dublin, killed at Aughrim. The 2nd son,

John Byrne, Esq. of Cabinteely, a barrister of eminence, served the office of high-sheriff of that shire. He m. in 1678, Mary, dau. of Walter Chevers, Esq. of Monkstown, by Alson his wife, dau. of Viscount Netterville, and d. suddenly in 1681, when he was s. by his elder son,

Walter Byrne, Esq. of Cabinteely, who m. Clare, dau. of Christopher Mapas, Esq. of Roachestown, but dying without issue, 21 Jan. 1731, was s. by his brother,

John Byrne, Esq. of Cabinteely, a merchant in Dublin. This gentleman m. Marianna, youngest dau. of Colonel Dudley Colclough, of Mohory, co. Wexford, and had, with four daus. (Mary, who m. Walter Blakeney, Esq., and was great-grandmother of the Rt. Hon. Thomas Wyse, H.M. minister-plenipotentiary at the court of Greece; Frances, m. to Edward Masterson, Esq.; Harriet, m. to Anthony Lynch, Esq.; and Marianne, m. to Adam Colclough, Esq.), eight sons, of whom the three eldest were,

George, his heir.
Dudley, who m. Elizabeth, dau. of James Dillon, Esq.
John, who, after the death of his father, resided with a merchant in Rotterdam, whence removing to Bordeaux, he commenced business there. This gentleman, who took out letters of nobility from the French government, in 1771, m. Mary, dau. of R. Gernon, Esq., an eminent merchant in Bordeaux, and was s. at his decease by his son,
Richard O'Byrne, Esq., who m. Elizabeth, dau. of Richard-William Stack, M.D. of Bath, and d., leaving a son and successor, the present
Robert O'Byrne, who m. Martha-Troughear, dau. of Joseph Clark, Esq. of Norwich, and has issue,
William-Richard, author of *The Naval Biography*, b. 27 Jan. 1823, m. 29 Oct. 1851, Emily, dau. of John Troughear Handy, Esq. of Malmesbury, Wilts, and has issue, Emily-Mary, and Kathleen-Elizabeth.
Robert, b. 23 Dec. 1825.

Mr. Byrne d. in 1741, and was s. by his eldest son,

George Byrne, Esq. of Cabinteely, who m. Clare, 2nd dau. of Captain Michael Nugent, of Carlanstown, co. Westmeath, and sister to Robert, Earl Nugent. By this lady, he left issue a dau., Mary, wife of William Skerrett, Esq. of Finvara, and three sons, Michael, his heir; Gregory, d. unm.; and Robert, successor to his brother. Mr. Byrne was s. by his son,

Michael Byrne, Esq. of Cabinteely, at whose demise, unm., the estates devolved upon his only surviving brother,

Robert Byrne, Esq. of Cabinteely, who m. Mary, dau. of Robert Devereux, Esq. of Carigmenan, co. Wexford, and left at his decease, in 1798, three daus., Mary-Clare, who d. unm. 1810; Clarinda-Mary, who d. unm.; and Georgiana-Mary, now of Cabinteely.

Arms—Gu., a chevron, between three dexter hands, arg.

Crest—A mermaid, in the dexter hand a mirror, in the sinister a comb, all ppr.

Motto—Certavi et vici. *Seat*—Cabinteely, co. Dublin.

BYTHESEA OF THE HILL, FRESHFORD.

Bythesea, Samuel-William, Esq. of The Hill, Freshford, Somersetshire, J.P., b. 14 July, 1801; m. his cousin, Mary-Agnes Bythesea, younger dau. of the late Charles Brome, Esq. of Malling House, West Malling, Kent, youngest and last surviving son of John Brome, Esq. of the Manor House, Bishop's Stortford, Herts, by Mary his wife, sister of Sir Charles Saxton, Bart. of Circourt, Berkshire, many years commissioner of Portsmouth. By this lady, Mr. Bythesea has one son,

Samuel-William-Charles-Brome, b. 9 April, 1831.

Lineage.—The first mayor of Axbridge, appointed under the charter of Elizabeth, dated 22 Feb. 1598, was a John Bythesea; and in the corporation records of that borough, the family is mentioned as the oldest and most respectable there.

Thomas Bythesea, of Compton Bishop, member of the corporation of Axbridge in 1645, afterwards mayor of that borough, and a magistrate for the co. of Wilts, m. Mary, dau. of the Rev. Oliver Chivers, prebendary of Sarum, grand-niece and co-heir of Richard Vyner, Esq., and great-granddau. of Sir Henry Vinour, who was grandson of Henry Vinour, Esq., by Anne his wife, dau. of Sir John Scrope, Knt. of Castlecombe, and Margaret Wrottesley his wife, which Margaret derived, through the Greys, Cecils, Nevils, &c., from King Edward III. By this lady, Mr. Bythesea had issue,

John, his heir.
Frances, m. to Mr. Milkin, and d. s. p.
Mary, m. to John Hopkins, of Bristol, merchant.

Mr. and Mrs. Bythesea both d. in 1672, and were s. by their only son, then an infant,

John Bythesea, Esq. of Week House, in the commission of the peace for Wilts, b. in 1672, who, on the death of his aunt, Susannah Lewis, inherited Chapmanslade, the other moiety of the Viner property. He m. Hester Halliday, of Bradford, in Wilts, and by her (who d. in 1737), left at his decease, in 1747, with five daus., of whom the 2nd, Grace, m. in 1727, Matthew Jervis, Esq. of Trowbridge, uncle of John, the gallant Earl St. Vincent, a son and successor,

John Bythesea, Esq. of Week House and Chapmanslade, a magistrate of the co. of Wilts, who m. Jane, dau. of the Rev. Thomas Leir (by his wife, a dau. of Ralph Freke, Esq.

of Hannington, and Cecilia his wife, dau. of Sir Thomas Colepeper, Knt.), by whom, who d. in 1782, aged 75, he had issue,

I. THOMAS, his heir.
II. William, b. 31 Jan. 1732, magistrate and deputy-lieut. for Kent, inherited from his father the estate of Chapman-slade. He m. Catherine, dau. of the Rev. Thomas Cobb, rector of Upper Hardres, of an ancient Kentish family, settled at Reculver, and dying 18 Dec. 1795, left one son and two daus., viz.,
1 George, b. in 1764, rector of Ightham, Kent, in the commission of the peace, who m. Anne, dau. of Thomas-Read Kemp, Esq. of Lewes Castle and Hurstmonceaux Park, Sussex, M.P. for Lewes, and d. in Dec. 1800, leaving an only son, George Kemp.
1 Catherine, d. aged 18.
2 Cecilia, m. in 1803, Charles Brome, Esq., R.N. (See family of BROME.)
III. Samuel, b. 31 Oct. 1744, who d. unm. 26 May, 1830, aged 85.
IV. Henry, b. 8 Oct. 1748, a magistrate for Wilts, m. 1st, Anne, dau. of Thomas Whittaker, Esq. of North Bradley, Wilts; 2ndly, her sister, Miss Fanny Whittaker; and 3rdly, Anne, dau. of John Budd, Esq. of Greenham, Berks. His first wife d. issueless; by the second he had,
1 Henry-Frederic, rector of Nettleton, in Wilts, b. 10 April, 1780, m. Eliza, dau. of General Meredith, and d. in July, 1850, having had one son, Henry-Edmund-Frederic, who m. Mary-Anne, youngest dau. of the late Miles Adams, of King's Capel, co. Hereford, Esq., and d. Sept. 1848, having had two children, Frederic-William, who d. young, and Emily.
By his 3rd wife, who d. in 1801, he left at his decease, in 1814, two other sons, namely,
1 George, in holy orders, of Grosvenor Place, Bath, rector and patron of Freshford, in Somersetshire, b. 29 May, 1792, who m. 9 March, 1815, Mary, dau. of Francis Glossop, Esq. of Glossopdale, co. Derby, and d. 13 Dec. 1853, having had issue,
George-Charles-Glossop, b. 29 May, 1819, lieut. 31st regt., killed in action at Ferozeshah.
Henry-Francis, b. 22 March, 1821, an officer in the army.
Samuel-Francis-Glossop, b. 30 July, 1822, late lieut. 31st regt.
Edwin, b. 29 Aug. 1824.
John, lieut. R.N., b. 15 June, 1827.
Georgina-Azelia, who d. Dec. 1841.
Frances-Anne, m. to Joseph Todd, Esq. of Moulsey Park, Surrey.
Charlotte, m. to Anthony Hammond, Esq., Bengal C.S.
2 SAMUEL-WILLIAM, now of The Hill, Freshford.
I. Jane, m. to Simon Halliday, Esq. of Iford House, Wilts, and of Westcombe Park, Kent.

Mr. Bythesea d. in 1769, and was s. by his eldest son,

THOMAS BYTHESEA, Esq. of Week House, b. 4 Feb. 1727, a magistrate for Wiltshire, who m. Elizabeth, dau. and co-heiress of — Lewis, Esq., proprietor of estates near Kidwelly and Carmarthen, and by her, who d. 9 Oct. 1809, had,

JOHN-LEWIS, his heir.
Thomas, who d. 11 Oct. 1811.
Charles, magistrate for Wilts, who m. Mary, dau. of William Eyles, Esq. of Shaw, near Melksham, Wilts, and d. in 1820, s. p.
Edmund, of Shirley Hall, near Southampton, d. 4 July, 1842.
Eliza, who m. 26 Jan. 1783, Edward-Horlock Mortimer, Esq. of Bellefield House, near Trowbridge, a magistrate for Wilts, and had issue.

Mr. Bythesea d. 10 April, 1783, and was s. by his eldest son,

REV. JOHN-LEWIS BYTHESEA, of Week House, rector of Lee Delamere, Wilts, and Bagington, co. Gloucester, J.P. and D.L., who d. s. p.

Arms—Arg., on a chevron, engrailed, sa., between three crabs, the claws towards the dexter, gu., the Roman fasces, erect, surmounting two swords in saltier, and encircled by a chaplet, or.

Crest—An eagle, displayed, arg., on the breast the Roman fasces, erect, surmounting two swords in saltier, and encircled by a chaplet, ppr., each wing charged with a cross-crosslet fitchée, gu.

Motto—Mutare vel timere sperno.

Seat—The Hill, Freshford.

CADOGAN OF BRENCKBURN PRIORY.

CADOGAN, WILLIAM HODGSON, Esq. of Brenckburn Priory, co. Northumberland, late major in the army, and captain in the 5th dragoon-guards. This gentleman, only son of the late RICHARD HODGSON, Esq. of Moorhouse Hall, co. Cumberland, assumed, by royal license, in 1835, the additional surname of CADOGAN, upon the demise of his father-in-law, the late Ward Cadogan, Esq. of Brenckburn Priory, whose only dau. and heir, Sarah, he had married. By this lady he has issue,

I. CADOGAN, b. 10 Nov. 1826; m. Isabel-Mary, dau. of Oswald Smith, Esq. of Blendon Hall, co. Kent, and has,
1 Arthur-Cadogan, b. 24 March, 1847.
2 Philip-Cadogan, b. 19 Feb. 1854.
1 Mary. 2 Eleanor-Margaret.
I. Sarah-Elizabeth, m. to Henry-Metcalf Ames, Esq.

Lineage.—This family claims descent from the senior line of the ancient house of Cadogan, founded by Cadwgan ap Elistan, chief of the 4th Royal Tribe of Wales.

THOMAS CADOGAN, Esq., who is understood to be a younger son of the family seated at Trostrey Vach, in the co. of Monmouth, left England at the period of the emigration of the Royalists, during the Commonwealth, and settled in the island of Barbadoes in 1679, where he acquired property in the parish of St. Lucy. In the destructive hurricane of 1776, the greater part of these parish registers were destroyed. He left an only son,

WILLIAM CADOGAN (d. in 1730), who m. Rebecca Rollock, by whom he had an only son,

THOMAS CADOGAN (b. in 1727, d. 1790), who m. Mary Sandiford, and by her had several children. The youngest,

WARD CADOGAN (b. 1772, d. 1835), m. Sarah Macintosh, by whom he had an only dau., SARAH CADOGAN, who m. Major William Hodgson, above mentioned.

Seat—Brenckburn Priory, Northumberland.

CALCOTT OF CAYNHAM COURT.

BERKELEY-CALCOTT, GEORGE, Esq. of Caynham Court, co. Salop, b. 14 Dec. 1787; m. 5 April, 1821, Jane, dau. of Dr. Beatty, of Dublin, and has issue,

I. JOHN-WILLIAM. II. George-Wallis.
III. Charles-Rowland. IV. Frederick-Mowbray.
I. Jane. II. Mary-Anne-Elizabeth.
III. Margaret-Emily.

Mr. Berkeley-Calcott (son of the Rev. Rowland Berkeley, LL.D., and brother of the Rev. John-Rowland Berkeley, of Cotheridge) assumed the latter surname of CALCOTT, in addition to his patronymic, Berkeley, in 1826, in accordance with the will of his late aunt, Jane Calcott.

Arms—Quarterly: 1st and 4th, per pale, or and gu., on a chief, arg., three shovellers, sa., for CALCOTT; 2nd and 3rd, gu., a chevron, arg., between ten crosses-patée, of the second, for BERKELEY.

Crests—1st, a demi-lion, or, holding between his paws a crescent; 2nd, a bear's head, couped, arg., muzzled, gu.

Motto—Dieu avec nous.

Seat—Caynham Court, Ludlow.

CALCRAFT OF ANCASTER HALL.

LUCAS-CALCRAFT, CHARLES-YORKE, Esq. of Ancaster Hall, co. Lincoln, D.L., b. 6 June, 1800; m. 29 Nov. 1838, Mary-Jane-Elizabeth, dau. of James-Lock Nixon, Esq., major in the army, and has issue,

I. ANTHONY-LUCAS, b. 17 Jan. 1842.
II. Edmund-James, b. 13 Jan. 1845.
III. Granby, b. 9 Jan. 1848.
I. Edith. II. Julia. III. Frances-Mary-Jane.
IV. Caroline. V. Coline-Mary-Christian-Sophia.

Lineage.—JOHN-CHARLES-LUCAS CALCRAFT, Esq. of Ancaster Hall, co. Lincoln, b. 9 Oct. 1770, son of Anthony Lucas, Esq. of Ancaster Hall (a younger son of Lucas of Fenton, co. Lincoln), by Christian, dau. of John Calcraft, Esq. of Grantham, took the name of CALCRAFT, in addition to that of LUCAS, on succeeding to the estate at Ancaster, in 1792. He m. 4 June, 1794, Sophia, 5th dau. and co-heir of the Rev. John-Neville Birch, rector of Leasingham, by Frances his wife, eldest dau. and co-heir of Thomas Yorke, Esq. of Leasingham Hall, who d. in 1782, he being the last male of the elder branch of the YORKES of Yorkshire, whose ancestor was Sir Richard Yorke, Knt., mayor of the Staple in Calais, lord mayor of York in 1469 and 1482, and M.P. for that city in 1472, which branch removed into Lincolnshire in the 16th century, and were first settled at Ashby-de-la-Laund, then at Burton Pedwardine, and finally at Leasingham. Thomas Yorke, Esq., through his grandmother, Penelope (wife of Sir William Yorke, Knt., M.P. for Boston from 1681 to 1702), a daughter of Richard Samwell,

Esq. of Gayton and Upton, co. Northampton (by Frances, eldest dau. and co-heir of Thomas Wenman, 2nd Viscount Wenman) descended from the ancient family of Neville, Earls of Westmoreland, and through them, from the illustrious house of Plantagenet. By Sophia his wife (who *d.* 30 May, 1837), Mr. Lucas Calcraft had issue,

I. CHARLES-YORKE, now of Ancaster Hall.
II. John-Neville, *b.* 7 July, 1801; rector of Haceby, co. Lincoln; *m.* 17 May, 1842, Marianne-Sophia, dau. of William Mansell, Esq., capt. in the army, and has issue,
1 Neville, *b.* 11 March, 1844.
2 Richard-Lucas, *b.* 1 April, 1846.
1 Penelope-Yorke. 2 Gertrude-Sophia.
3 Blanche-Eleanor. 4 Isabel-Marianne.
I. Sophia-Christiana, *m.* 25 May, 1825, the Rev. John Conington, and has issue.
II. Caroline, *m.* 25 May, 1825, the Rev. Charles-Thomas Plumptre, rector of Claypole, co. Lincoln (son of John Plumptre, Esq. of Fredville, co. Kent); *d.* 12 June, 1838, leaving issue,
III. Frances, *m.* 9 Oct. 1839, the Rev. Frederic Myers, incumbent of St. John's, Keswick; *d.* 12 Jan. 1840.

Arms—Per fesse, arg. and erm., three lions, passant-guardant, sa.
Crest—A greyhound, courant, sa., charged with a cross-crosslet, or.
Seat—Ancaster Hall, near Grantham.

CALCRAFT OF REMPSTONE.

CALCRAFT, JOHN-HALES, Esq. of Rempstone, co. Dorset, captain in the army, *b.* 13 Sept. 1796; *m.* 13 Feb. 1828, Lady Caroline-Katharine Montagu, 5th dau. of William, 5th Duke of Manchester, and has issue,

I. JOHN-HALES-MONTAGU, R.N., *b.* 4 May, 1831.
II. William-Montagu, *b.* 11 Oct. 1834.
III. Henry-George, *b.* 12 April, 1836.
I. Katharine. II. Georgiana-Emily.
III. Susan-Charlotte.

Lineage.—THE RIGHT HON. JOHN CALCRAFT, of Rempstone, co. Dorset, M.P. for Rochester, Wareham, and the county of Dorset, *b.* in 1766, who *s.* to the estates in Dorsetshire purchased by his father, JOHN CALCRAFT, Esq., the eminent army agent, was appointed clerk of the Ordnance in 1806, and became paymaster of the forces in 1828. He *m.* 5 March, 1790, Elizabeth, 3rd dau. and co-heir of Sir Thomas Pym Hales, Bart. of Beaksbourne, and by her (who *d.* in 1815), left, with three daus., Elizabeth-Mary, *m.* Sir John Burke, Bart. of Marble Hill; Caroline-Jane; and Arabella, *m.* to Capt. Rochfort, R.N., who *d.* in 1847; two sons, the present JOHN-HALES CALCRAFT, Esq. of Rempstone Hall; and Granby-Hales, late a captain in the army, and now on H. M. service as agent to Post-office packets, New York. Mr. Calcraft *d.* in 1831.

Arms—Per fesse, arg. and erm., three lions, passant-guardant, in pale, sa., all within a bordure, wavy, az.
Crest—A greyhound, courant, sa., collared and ringed, arg., on the body a palet, wavy, or.
Seat—Rempstone, co. Dorset.

CALDECOT OF HOLTON.

CALDECOT, HENRY, Esq. of Holton Hall, co. Lincoln, *m.* in 1825, Margaretta, dau. of the Rev. John Hale, of Holton, and has four sons and three daus.

Lineage.—This family, one of considerable antiquity, came originally from Melbourne, co. Derby. The late

GILBERT CALDECOT, Esq. of Holton Hall and Beckering, co. Lincoln, colonel of the Royal North Lincoln Militia, son of Charles Caldecot, Esq. of Fulnetby, in the same shire, by his wife, Miss Browne, of Lincoln, *m.* Miss Duncombe, dau. of T. Duncombe, Esq. of Duncombe Park, co. York, and by her, who *d.* in 1779, left at his decease, 6 July, 1796, aged 86, an only dau. and heir,

SARAH CALDECOT, who *m.* Thomas Reid, Esq., M.D., F.R.S. (son of John Reid, Esq. of Barra, co. Aberdeen), and by him, who assumed, in consequence, the surname and arms of CALDECOT, and *d.* at Bath, 15 Jan. 1802, she had issue,

HENRY, now of Holton Hall.
Charles, *m.* Mary, dau. of Dr. Williams, of Llanbedrog, co. Carnarvon, and has one son and two daus.
Elizabeth, *m.* to the late Gen. Sir Love Jones-Parry, of Madryn, co. Carnarvon.

The heiress of Holton *d.* in 1825.

Crest—A martlet.
Seat—Holton Hall, co. Lincoln.

CALDECOTT OF RUGBY.

CALDECOTT, THOMAS, Esq. of The Lodge, Rugby, co. Warwick, barrister-at-law, J.P. and D.L., *b.* 6 Oct. 1798; *m.* 8 Jan. 1828, Ann-Catherine, eldest dau. of the late Lieut.-Col. James West, R.A., and has issue,

I. THOMAS, *b.* 3 Oct. 1831. II. Henry, *d. s. p.*
I. Elizabeth. II. Emily. III. Ellen.
IV. Lucy. V. Laura. VI. Lelia, *d. unm.*

Lineage.—The ancient family of Caldecott takes its name from Calcot or Caldecote, co. Chester, of which place, *temp.* WILLIAM the Conqueror, its ancestors were mesne lords. From Sir Ralph de Caldecote, *temp.* HENRY III., was lineally descended

THOMAS CALDECOTT, Esq., who *m.* Isabel, dau. and sole heiress of John Caldecote, Esq. of Barrow and Whitwell, co. Rutland, high-sheriff of that county in 1515 and 1525, and had issue,

THOMAS CALCOTT or CALDECOTT, Esq., *b.* 1565, who, in 1617, purchased the manor of Calthorpe, co. Leicester, where he died, 1645, leaving, by his wife Abigail, dau. of John Huggeford, Esq. of Henwood Hall, co. Warwick, one son,

THOMAS CALCOTT or CALDECOTT, Esq., *b.* 1627, high-sheriff, co. Leicester, 1664, 1665. He *m.* Mary, dau. of Alexander Prescot, Esq. of Thoby Abbey, co. Essex, and *d.* 1703, leaving his successor,

THOMAS CALDECOTT, Esq., *b.* 1652, who *m.* Maud, dau. of John Evans, Esq. of Northampton, and dying 1720, left (with a dau., Mary, wife of John Ward, Esq. of Guilsbro) one son,

THOMAS CALDECOTT, *b.* in 1685, *m.* Elizabeth-Cheney, dau. and heiress of John Pettit, Esq. of Dartford, co. Kent, and left (with a dau., Merriel, wife of Abraham Turner, Esq., and a son, Thomas, barrister-at-law, and recorder of Northampton, who *d. s. p.*) his successor,

WILLIAM CALDECOTT, Esq. of Rugby, who *m.* 1st, Elizabeth, dau. of the Rev. Peter Senhouse, of Linton, co. Hereford, by whom he had one son, Thomas, of Dartford, co. Kent, barrister-at-law, who *d. s. p.*; and 2ndly, Anna, relict of William Boughton, Esq. of Rugby: he *d.* in 1777, leaving,

I. JOHN, of Holbrook Grange, co. Warwick, who *m.* twice, but dying in 1839, *s. p.*, left his estates to his nephew, CHARLES MARRIOTT.
II. William, *d. s. p.* III. Charles, *d. s. p.*
IV. Samuel, of Melton Mowbray, *d.* leaving one son, John-Thomas, *b.* 1790.
V. ABRAHAM, of whom presently.
I. Mary, deceased.
II. Catherine, *m.* the Rev. J. Parker, vicar of Newbold-upon-Avon, and had one son, the Rev. J. T. Parker, who *m.* Anna, eldest dau. of Sir Gray Skipwith, Bart., and left one son, John-Skipwith Parker, Esq.
III. Arabella, *m.* the Rev. Dr. James, and had issue,
1 John, late Bishop of Calcutta.
2 William, rector of Bilton, co. Warwick.
3 Edward, late canon of Winchester, and vicar of Alton, Hants.
4 George, lieut.-col. royal artillery.

The 4th son by the 2nd marriage,

ABRAHAM CALDECOTT, Esq., *b.* 21 Aug. 1768, purchased the manor of Rugby in 1801, and subsequently divers lands in the counties of Northampton and Oxford; he *m.* 4 Jan. 1797, Elizabeth, eldest dau. of the Rev. Dr. Marriott, of Cotrobach, co. Leicester, and had issue,

ABRAHAM, *d. s. p.* 1814.
THOMAS, now of The Lodge.
John-Marriott, retired from the army in 1825.
William-Marriott, in holy orders, *d. s. p.* 1840.
Robert-Marriott.
Charles-Marriott, of Holbrook Grange.
Elizabeth, *d.* 1828. Caroline, *unm.*

Mr. Caldecott served the office of high-sheriff for co. Warwick in 1821, and dying 8 Sept. 1829, was succeeded by his eldest surviving son, THOMAS CALDECOTT, Esq. of Rugby Lodge.

Arms—Arg., a fesse, az., fretty, or, between three cinquefoils, gu.
Crest—A demi-lion, rampant, gu., charged on the shoulder with a cinquefoil, arg.
Seat—The Lodge, Rugby.

CALDECOTT OF HOLBROOK GRANGE.

CALDECOTT, CHARLES-MARRIOTT, Esq. of Holbrook Grange, Little Lawford, Warwickshire, formerly H.E.I.C. Bengal civil service, J.P. and D.L., *b.* 9 June, 1807; *m.* 1 March, 1827, Margaret, only dau. of Thomas Smith, Esq., physician-general H.E.I.C. Bengal Establishment, and has issue,

I. Charles-Thomas, b. 24 Dec. 1831, H. M. 76th regt.
II. John-Alexander, b. 10 Dec. 1835.
III. Alexander-William-Bradfield, b. 9 Aug. 1837.
IV. Francis-James, b. 29 April, 1842.
V. Randolph, b. 29 July, 1847.
VI Sidney-Arthur, b. 4 April, 1852.
VII. Everard-Garfoot, b. 1 April, 1854.
I. Margaret-Elizabeth. II. Caroline-Selina.
III. Sophia-Catherine. IV. Merriel.

Arms, &c.—See preceding family.
Seat—Holbrook Grange, Warwickshire.

CALDWELL OF NEW GRANGE.

Caldwell, Charles-Andrew, Esq. of New Grange, co. Meath, b. 25 March, 1785; m. 1 Dec. 1808, Charlotte-Anne, sister of Sir William Abdy, Bart., and has issue,

I. Charles-Benjamin, b. 9 Oct. 1809.
II. James-Thomas, b. 28 Dec. 1810.
III. William-Charles, b. 1 May, 1812.
IV. Henry, b. 24 Feb. 1815.
I. Mary-Catherine. II. Charlotte-Louisa.

Lineage.—The family is of ancient Scottish descent.

Charles Caldwell, Esq. of Dublin, solicitor to the Customs, b. 14 June, 1707, son and heir of Andrew Caldwell, Esq., by Catherine his wife, sister of the Right Hon. Charles Campbell, M.P. of New Grange, co. Meath, m. in 1732, Elizabeth, dau. of Benjamin Heywood, Esq. of Liverpool, by Anne his wife, sister of General Arthur Graham, of Armagh, and by her (who d. 19 Nov. 1792) had issue,

I. Andrew, of Cavendish-row, Rutland-square, Dublin, barrister-at-law; b. 19 Dec. 1733; d. s. p. 2 July, 1808.
II. Charles, of Liverpool, b. in 1737; d. 10 Jan. 1814, leaving issue,
1 George, in holy orders, fellow of Jesus College, Cambridge; who m. 4 Dec. 1817, Harriot, dau. of the late Sir William Abdy, Bart., and has issue.
2 William, of Kingston, Jamaica, member of the House of Assembly for the parish of St. Dorothy; d. 29 Jan. 1819.
1 Anne, m. to George, 2nd son of Sir George Dunbar, Bart.
2 Harriot.
III. Benjamin (Sir), of whom presently.
IV. Ponsonby, b. 26 Nov. 1746; d. 7 Nov. 1819.
V. Arthur, b. 18 May, 1748; d. 18 June, 1749.
I. Amelia, m. 22 Jan. 1761, George Cookburn, Esq.
II. Catherine, m. 19 Nov. 1768, to Phineas Riall.
III. Mary-Elizabeth, m. 26 Jan. 1768, to Jacob Sankey, Esq. of Coolmore, co. Tipperary.
IV. Frances-Arabella, d. 9 March, 1807
V. Alice, d. in 1780. VI. Henrietta, d. in 1785.

The 3rd son,

Admiral Sir Benjamin Caldwell, G.C.B., b. 31 Jan. 1738-9; m. 7 June, 1784, Charlotte, dau. of Admiral Henry Osborn, vice-admiral of England (cousin of the late Sir George Osborn, of Chicksand, co. Bedford), and by her (who d. 22 Sept. 1819) had a son, Charles-Andrew, now of New Grange, co. Meath.

Arms—Or, in chief three piles, sa., each charged with a fountain, ppr.; in base four bars, wavy, alternately gu. and vert.
Crest—A demi-lion, grasping a broken scimitar, all ppr.
Motto—Ense libertatem petit inimico tyrannis.
Seat—New Grange, co. Meath.

CALDWELL OF BEACHLANDS.

Caldwell, Lieut.-Gen. Sir James-Lillyman, G.C.B., of Beachlands, Isle of Wight, b. 22 Nov. 1770; m. 18 Feb. 1794, Mademoiselle Maliard, of Dôle, in France, and relict of Richard Johnston, Esq., and by her had,

I. Arthur-James, who d. 11 June, 1848,
I. Eliza-Maria, m. to Edward Sulivan, Esq., 3rd son of Sir Richard Sulivan, Bart., by whom she has two sons and one dau., the latter m. to John, eldest son of Sir Harcourt Lees, Bart.

Sir James-Lillyman Caldwell, a general in the Indian army, and chief engineer of the Madras presidency, is son of Major Arthur Caldwell, of the Bengal Engineers, and nephew of General Sir Alexander Caldwell, G.C.B.

Arms—Or, three piles meeting in the centre fesse point, sa.; in base, barry-wavy, alternately gu., of the field, and vert, surmounted by a portcullis, of the second. On the centre pile, suspended by a riband, orange, a representation of the medal presented to Sir J. L. Caldwell, in commemoration of his services at the storming of Seringapatam, with the word "Seringapatam" underneath, gold; the whole within a bordure, embattled, of the third.
Crest—Out of an eastern crown, or, a demi-lion, gu., holding in the dexter paw a sword ppr., pommel and hilt, gold, supporting between the paws two flag-staves in bend sinister, the one being that of the union flag of Great Britain, surmounting the other with the staff broken, being a flag, swallow-tailed, vert, semée of mullets, arg.
Supporters—On the dexter, a grey horse supporting in bend a flag, swallow-tailed, vert, semée of mullets, arg., the staff broken, ppr.; on the sinister, a royal tiger of Tippoo Sultaun, vert, striped, ducally gorged and chained, or; supporting, in bend sinister, a flag, swallow-tailed, vert, semée of mullets, arg.
Motto—Virtus et spes.
Seat—Beachlands, Ryde, Isle of Wight.

CALDWELL OF LINLEY WOOD.

Caldwell, James-Stamford, of Linley Wood, co. Stafford, Esq., J.P., M.A. of the University of Cambridge, and a barrister-at-law; author of *A Treatise of the Law of Arbitration*, and other works; s. his father, James Caldwell, Esq., who d. 16 Jan. 1838.

Lineage.—James Caldwell, Esq. who was during many years a magistrate and deputy-lieut. for the co. of Stafford, and recorder of the borough of Newcastle-under-Lyme, m. Elizabeth, dau. and co-heiress (with a sister, Hannah, who d. unm.) of Thomas Stamford, of Derby, Esq., by Hannah his wife, eldest dau. of John Crompton, of Chorley Hall, co. Lancaster, Esq., which property was acquired by that branch of the Crompton family soon after the rebellion in 1715. Mrs. Stamford was a descendant of the Rev. John Crompton, M.A., b. in 1641, and cousin of Samuel Crompton, of Derby, Esq., and of Henry Coape, of Duffield, Esq.: a share of whose personal estate came to her dau., Mrs. Caldwell. By this lady, who d. 9 April, 1831, Mr. Caldwell had issue,

I. James-Stamford, his heir,
I. Hannah-Eliza, m. W.-Stanley Roscoe, Esq., eldest son of William Roscoe, Esq., at one time M.P. for Liverpool, and author of *The Life of Lorenzo de Medici*, &c., and left issue,
1 William-Caldwell. 2 Arthur.
3 Thomas-Stamford, 4 Francis-James.
1 Elizabeth-Jane, d. unm. 2 Anne-Mary, d. unm.
II. Mary, d. unm.
III. Anne, m. Arthur-Cuthbert Marsh, Esq. (deceased), and has issue,
1 Martin-William-James, deceased.
1 Eliza-Louisa.
2 Frances-Mary, m. to Richard-Henry Crofton, Esq., capt. royal artillery, and has issue.
3 Georgiana-Amelia. 4 Rosamond-Jane.
5 Mary-Emma, m. Leopold-G. Heath, Esq., comm. R.N., and has issue.
6 Hannah-Adelaide, m. to the Rev. Henry Loring, vicar of Cobham, Surrey, and has issue.
IV. Margaret-Emma, m. to Henry Holland, M.D. (now Sir Henry Holland, Bart.), of Lower Brook-street, London, and d. 2 Feb. 1830, leaving issue,
1 Henry-Thurston, m. a dau. of George Hibbert, Esq. of Munden Park, Surrey, and has issue.
2 Francis-James, in holy orders.
1 Emily-Mary, m. to Charles, 3rd son of the late Sir Thomas Fowell-Buxton, Bart., and has issue.
V. Catherine-Louiza, d. unm. VI. Frances, d. unm.

Arms—Quarterly: 1st and 4th, per pale, sa. and vert, a stag's head, couped, arg.; in chief, three cold wells, ppr., for Caldwell; 2nd and 3rd, arg., two bars, az.; on a canton, gu., a gauntlet, grasping a broken sword, ppr., hilt and pommel, gold, for Stamford.
Crest—A lion, couchant, arg., gorged with two bars, the upper, sa., the lower, vert, holding between the paws a cold well, ppr.
Motto—Niti, facere, experiri.
Seat—Linley Wood, co. Stafford.

CALLANDER OF CRAIGFORTH.

Callander, George-Frederick-William, Esq. of Craigforth, co. Stirling, and Ardkinglas, co. Argyll, b. 28 July, 1848.

Lineage.—The Ardkinlas family is a cadet branch of the ancient house of Argyll, as appears from a charter of Sir Duncan Campbell of Lochow, of the lands of Auchingown, dated 6 May, 1428, "dilecto et fideli nepoti suo Joanni Campbell, filio et hæredi fratris sui Colin Campbell de Ardkinlas." Of Ardkinlas, the Campbells *of Ardintennie, Dunoon, Carrick, Skipnish, Blythswood, Shawfield, Rachan, Achwillan*, and *Dergachy*, are branches.

The first Callander of Craigforth was master armourer to JAMES VI. of Scotland, and purchased Craigforth from the Earls of Livingstone and Callandar, about the time of JAMES VI.'s accession to the English crown (1603). His descendant,

JOHN CALLANDER of Craigforth, *m.* Margaret, dau. of Sir James Nasmyth, Bart. of New Posso, and had issue, JAMES, of whom presently; and Anne, *m.* 1st, to Col. Blackader (a name well-known to the religious world); and 2ndly, to Sir James Campbell, Bart. of Ardkinlas (who, by his 1st wife, Margaret Campbell, heiress of Gargunnock, was father of Helen Campbell, afterwards Lady Livingstone, of Glentirran,) Anne *d.* without issue. The only son,

JAMES CALLANDER, *m.* Catharine Mackenzie, of Cromarty, the lineal descendant of Sir George Mackenzie, the eminent lawyer and writer. James Callander predeceased his father, leaving an only son,

JOHN CALLANDER, of Craigforth, who *s.* his grandfather. He *m.* Mary Livingstone, eldest dau. of Sir James Livingstone, Bart. of Glentirran and Dalderse, by whom he had several children. He *d.* 1789, and was *s.* by his eldest son,

JAMES CALLANDER, of Craigforth, *b.* in 1744, who assumed the surname of CAMPBELL, on succeeding, in right of his mother, to his cousin-german, Sir Alexander Campbell, Bart., in the estate of Ardkinglas. He *m.* 1st, in 1768, Christian, youngest dau. of George Forbes, Esq. of Hitchener Hall, Surrey, and by her (who *d.* in 1771) had a son, GEORGE, of whom presently; and a dau. Mary, *m.* Capt. Lucius O'Brien, cousin of Sir Lucius O'Brien, of Dromoland Castle, co. Clare,) and had issue six sons and one dau. He *m.* 2ndly, Miss Harriet Dutens, and by her (who *d.* in 1772,) had an only child, Elisabeth, who *m.* Richard Magenis, Esq., M.P., and had issue an only son, He *m.* 3rdly, in 1776, Lady Elisabeth MacDonnell, dau. of the Earl of Antrim, and by her (who *d.* in 1796,) had two sons and three daus., viz.,

- Alexander-James, major in the 91st regt., *d. unm.*
- Randall-William, *m.* Miss Wilson, and had issue three sons and four daus.
- Georgina, *d. unm.* in 1839.
- Caroline, *m.* Thomas Sheridan, son of the Right Hon. Richard-Brinsley Sheridan (who *d.* in 1818), and had issue, four sons and three daus.
- Fanny, *m.* the Right Hon. Sir James-R.-G. Graham, Bart. of Netherby, and had issue three sons and three daus.

The eldest son,

GEORGE CALLANDER, Esq. of Craigforth, lieut.-col. of the Rifle brigade, *b.* in March, 1770, *m.* 21 Oct. 1801, Elisabeth-Crompton, eldest dau. of the Hon. Henry Erskine, of Ammondell (brother of the Earl of Buchan, and of Lord Chancellor Erskine), and had issue,

- JAMES-HENRY, his heir.
- John-Alexander, *b.* 19 Sept. 1809; *m.* in Aug. 1837, Emma, dau. of John Young, Esq. of Wesbridge, Isle of Wight, and has issue two sons and five daus.,
- Alicia-Christian, *d.* 24 March, 1824.
- Elizabeth-Anne, *m.* 11 Aug. 1831, Henry-William Vincent, Esq. of Lily Hill, Berkshire, and *d.* in 1839, leaving issue two daus.
- Mary-Henrietta, *d.* in 1838.
- Caroline-Frances, *m.* 17 Jan. 1832, Robert-Dunmore Napier, Esq. of Ballikinrain, Stirlingshire (who *d.* in 1846), and has issue one son and two daus.
- Agnes, *m.* in 1836, William Dunmore, Esq., E.I.C.S.; *d.* in 1837, leaving issue one dau.
- Margaret, *d.* in childhood.
- Georgiana, *d.* in 1838.

Col. Callander *d.* 18 Feb. 1824, in the lifetime of his father, and was *s.* in Craigforth by his elder son,

JAMES-HENRY CALLANDER, Esq. of Craigforth and Ardkinglas, *b.* 18 Aug. 1803, *m.* 1st, 29 Aug. 1837, the Hon. Jane-Plumer Erskine, youngest dau. of David Montague, Lord Erskine, and by her (who *d.* 30 March, 1846,) had,

I. Fanny-Jane. II. Mary-Hermione.
III. Jane-Sevilla.

He *m.* 2ndly, 1 July, 1847, Charlotte-Edith-Eleonora, only dau. of the late John-George Campbell, Esq., brother of Walter-Frederick Campbell, Esq. of Islay, and had by her two sons, GEORGE-FREDERICK-WILLIAM, present proprietor, and Henry-Barrington, *b.* 19 July, 1849. Mr. Callander represented the co. of Argyll in the first reformed parliament. He *d.* 31 Jan. 1851.

Arms—Quarterly: 1st and 4th, CALLANDER; 2nd and 3rd, CAMPBELL.

Seats—Craigforth House, co. Stirling; and Ardkinglas Lodge, co. Argyll.

CALLEY OF BURDEROP.

CALLEY, HENRY, Esq. of Blunsdon St. Andrew, co. Wilts, late major 19th regt., *b.* 22 May, 1818.

Lineage.—WILLIAM CALLEY, originally from Norfolk, but subsequently settled a merchant in London, *temp.* HENRY VII., was father of

JOHN CALLEY, of Leatherdean, Hants, who *m.* Isabel, dau. and co-heir of Edmund Brydges, and niece of Sir John Brydges, lord-mayor of London in 1521, and left a son and successor,

RALPH CALLEY, Esq. of Highway, in Wiltshire, whose son,

SIR WILLIAM CALLEY, Knt., became seated at Burderop Park, co. Wilts, an estate purchased in the reign of ELIZABETH from the family of Stephens. He *m.* Judith, dau. of Richard Bowdler, of London, and was *s.* by his son,

WILLIAM CAWLEY or CALLEY, Esq. of Burderop, *b.* in 1600, who was living at the Visitation in 1623. His eldest son,

SIR WILLIAM CALLEY, Knt. of Burderop, *d.* without issue, and was *s.* by his brother,

OLIVER CALLEY, Esq. of Burderop, who *m.* in 1667, Mary, dau. of J. Scott, Esq. of Bromham, Wilts, and was father of

OLIVER CALLEY, Esq. of Burderop, bapt. in April, 1672, who *m.* Isabella, dau. of Robert Codrington, Esq. of Codrington, co. Gloucester, and left at his decease, in 1715, a son and successor,

WILLIAM CALLEY, Esq. of Burderop, who *m.* Arabella, dau. and heir of Thomas Browne, Esq. of Minty, in Gloucestershire, and was father of

THOMAS-BROWNE CALLEY, Esq. of Burderop, *b.* in 1752, who *m.* in 1778, Elizabeth, only dau. of John Rowlls, Esq. of Kingston-upon-Thames, in Surrey, and had issue, 1 THOMAS, his heir; 2 William-Peter, who *d. unm.* in 1808; 3 John-James, of Blunsdon St. Andrew, co. Wilts, *b.* in 1788, *m.* in 1816, Elizabeth-Tunstall, eldest dau. and coheiress of the Rev. James Wyld, rector of Blunsdon St. Andrew, and by her has had issue, William-John, *b.* in 1817, *d. unm.* in 1838; HENRY, *b.* in 1818, major in her Majesty's 19th regt.; Charles-Benet, in holy orders, *b.* 19 April, 1820, *m.* in Oct. 1846, Julia-Susanna, dau. of the Rev. Jeremiah Scholefield, rector of Barton-on-the-Heath, and has issue, John-Henry, *b.* 1 Sept. 1849; Legh-Charles, *b.* 30 Dec. 1851; Gertrude-Margaret; Diana-Julia; 4 Arabella, *m.* in 1797, to Henry Bullock, Esq. of Shepperton, in Middlesex; and 5 Elizabeth-Poppea, *m.* in 1807, to Clement Tudway, Esq. of Wells. The eldest son,

THOMAS CALLEY, Esq. of Burderop, *b.* in 1780, high-sheriff of Wiltshire in 1807, and M.P. for Cricklade, *m.* in 1802, Elizabeth-Anne, only dau. of Anthony-James Keck, Esq. of Stoughton Grange, in Leicestershire, by Elizabeth his wife, 2nd dau. and co-heir of Peter Legh, Esq. of Lyme, in Cheshire, and had issue, JOHN-JAMES, his heir; Elizabeth-Anne-Benet, *m.* in 1827, to John-Neale Nott, Esq., R.N.; and Arabella, *m.* in 1825, to John-Mathews Richards, Esq. of Cardiff. Mr. Calley *d.* in 1836, and was *s.* by his son,

JOHN-JAMES CALLEY, of Burderop, Esq., *b.* 10 Nov. 1810, who *m.* in July, 1849, Agnes-Caroline, only dau. of Harry-Brereton Trelawny, Esq. of Saughall, Cheshire, but *d. s. p.* 16 Jan. 1854, and was *s.* in the representation of the family by his cousin, MAJOR HENRY CALLEY.

Arms—Quarterly: arg. and sa., on a bend, gu., three mullets, of the first.

Crest—A demi-lion, rampant, arg., charged with a bend, gu., thereon three mullets, of the first, holding a battle-axe, handle, of the second, head, arg.

Motto—Callide et honeste.

Seat—Burderop Park, near Marlborough.

CALMADY OF LANGDON.

CALMADY, CHARLES-BIGGS, Esq. of Langdon Hall, co. Devon, *b.* in March, 1791; *m.* in March, 1816, Emily, eldest dau. of the late William Greenwood, Esq. of Brookwood, Hants (of an ancient Yorkshire family), and has issue,

I. VINCENT-POLLEXFEN, *b.* in 1825,
I. Emily. II. Laura-Anne,
III. Honora-Mary, *m.* in 1850, to John-Augustus-Hugh, son and heir of Sir John Boyd, Bart.
IV. Cycill-Christiana, *m.* in 1854, to William-Frederick, 2nd son of the late John Collier, Esq. of Grimstone, Devon, M.P. for Plymouth.
V. Gertrude-Elizabeth.

Mr. Calmady *s.* his father, 5 March, 1807.

Lineage.—ELIZABETH CALMADY (eldest sister and coheir of Waldo Calmady, Esq. of Langdon, high-sheriff of Devon in 1728, and dau. of Josias Calmady, Esq. of Leawood, M.P. for Okehampton, who was lineally descended from John Calmady, of Calmady, living A.D. 1460) *m.* John Pollexfen, Esq. of Mothecombe, in Devonshire, high-sheriff for the co. in 1718, and left an only dau. and sole heiress,

Elizabeth Pollexfen, (the last survivor of that ancient house) who m.

Francis-Vincent Calmady, Esq. of Combshead, (son and heir of Francis Calmady, Esq. of Combshead, by Cecilia his wife, dau. of Warwick Pollexfen, Esq., and grandson of Francis Calmady, Esq., whose father, Francis, of Combshead, was 3rd son of Sir Shilston Calmady, son and heir of Josias Calmady, Esq. of Langdon, by Catherine his wife, dau. and heiress of Carew Courtenay, Esq.,) and had issue,

Francis, his heir.
Elizabeth, m. to Christopher Hamlyn, Esq. of Pascoe, co. Devon, and has a son, Calmady-Pollexfen Hamlyn, Esq.
Pollexfen, of whom hereafter.

Mr. Calmady was s. at his decease, in 1765, by his only son,

Francis Calmady, Esq. of Langdon, who d. unm., and bequeathed his estates to his youngest sister,

Pollexfen Calmady, b. 12 Aug. 1755, who thus became of Langdon. This lady m. Charles-Holmes Everitt, Esq. an admiral of the Red, who thereupon assumed the surname and arms of Calmady, in 1788. By the heiress of Calmady the admiral left at his decease, in 1807, (with a dau., Arabella-Philippa, who m. in 1822, Charles-Henry Hotchkys, Esq. of Prospect, near Plymouth, and d. in 1848, leaving one son and one dau.) a son and successor, the present Charles-Biggs Calmady, Esq. of Langdon Hall.

Arms—Az., a chevron between three pears, or.
Crest—A pegasus, arg.
Motto—Simili frondescit virga metallo.
Seat—Langdon Hall, near Plymouth.

CALROW OF WALTON LODGE.

Calrow, William, Esq. of Walton Lodge, co. Lancaster, J.P. and D.L., b. 24 Sept. 1786; m. 12 Sept. 1808, Margaret, 3rd dau. of the late Robert Town, Esq. of Ulverston, and has issue,

I. Richard, b. 17 April, 1815; m. Margaret, only dau. of John Grundy, Esq. of Bury, Lancashire; and d. in 1850.
II. William-Augustus, b. 2 Aug. 1820.
III. Robert-Francis, b. 28 Sept. 1823; m. 25 Aug. 1853, Eleanor, 3rd dau. of John Lewthwaite, Esq. of Broad Gate, Cumberland.
I. Eleanor, m. in 1830, to George-Johnson Wainwright, Esq. of Runshaw Hall, Lancashire.
II. Jane-Judith, m. to William Walker, Esq. of Woodlands, brother of Richard Walker, Esq., M.P.
III. Elizabeth, m. in 1846, to the Rev. Charles Bickmore, of Berkswell Hall, co. Warwick.
IV. Wilhelmina. V. Margaret.
VI. Frances-Rebecca-Holford.

William Calrow, Esq. of Walton Lodge, and Thomas Calrow, Esq. of Woodhill, near Bury (m. in 1815, to Harriet, dau. of Abraham Clegg, Esq. of Bent Grange), are the sons of the late Richard Calrow, Esq., and grandsons of Richard Calrow, of Adlington, co. Chester, where the family had resided for about three hundred years.

Arms—Az., on a fesse, arg., between a beehive, surrounded by bees, volant, in chief and a millwheel in base, or, a hank of cotton, of the field, between two roses, gu., barbed and seeded, ppr.
Crest—A beehive, thereon perched a dove, wings elevated, holding in the beak a sprig of olive, all ppr.
Motto—Industria.
Seat—Walton Lodge, co. Lancaster.

CALTHROP OF STANHOE.

Calthrop, John, Esq. of Stanhoe Hall, co. Norfolk, J.P. and D.L., m. Mary, dau. of John Palmer-Hollway, Esq. of Boston, and has an only dau.,

Mariette.

He is a justice of the peace for Norfolk, and deputy-lieut. of co. Lincoln.

Lineage.—From a branch of the ancient family of Calthrop *of Burnham and Gedney* descended the Rev. John Calthrop, vicar of Boston and of Kirton in 1746, and prebendary of Lincoln, who m. Mary, dau. of Benett Dobbs, Esq. of Bucknall, but d. s. p., whereupon a valuable property in that county came to Squier Calthrop, Esq., of Boston, and from him descended to his nephew, the present John Calthrop, Esq. of Stanhoe Hall. Mr. Calthrop became possessed of Stanhoe Hall, and of a considerable estate in Burnham (part of the family estates originally belonging to Sir Walter Calthrop) by purchase. His brother, the Rev. Henry Calthrop, is rector of Braxted, co. Essex, and prebendary of Lichfield.

Arms—Quarterly: 1st and 4th, chequy, or and az., a fesse, erm., for Calthrop; 2nd and 3rd, barry of eight, or and az., a bend, arg., for Stanhoe.
Crest—A salamander, or, in flames, ppr.
Motto—Victrix fortunæ sapientia.
Seat—Stanhoe Hall, co. Norfolk.

CALTHROP OF GOSBERTON.

Calthrop, The Rev. John, of Gosberton, co. Lincoln, J.P., b. 16 Feb. 1783; m. 6 July, 1807, Barbara-Calthrop, dau. of Charles Bonner, Esq. of Salisbury-square, and has issue,

I. John-George, b. 23 June, 1811.
II. Henry-James, b. 1 March, 1819.
III. Charles-Eamonson, b. 19 Jan. 1824.
IV. William-Henry, b. 29 May, 1830.
I. Anne-Barbara.

Lineage.—This family, which has been seated at Gosberton since the beginning of the sixteenth century, and of which many curious and ancient monuments exist in and near Norwich, and in several Lincolnshire churches, claim to descend from Walter de Calthrop, Bishop of Norwich, in the thirteenth century.

Richard Calthrop, Esq. of Gosberton, son of Robert Calthrop, Esq. of the same place, m. Mary Thompson, and had, with two daus. (Anne, m. to Luke Betham, Esq.; and Barbara, m. to C. Bonner, Esq.) a son,

John George Calthrop, Esq. of Gosberton, high-sheriff for Lincolnshire, early in the French revolutionary war. He m. 11 Aug. 1778, Anne Spurr, and by her, who predeceased him, had issue,

John, now of Gosberton.
Richard, of Swineshead Abbey, near Boston, m., and has numerous issue.
Henry, capt. in the 10th foot, deceased, leaving three sons, viz., Henry, William, and Calthrop-Johnson.
James, m., and has issue, Joe-George, James, and Edward.
George.
Mary. Anne, m. to Charles Bonner, Esq.

Arms—Chequy, or and az., a fesse, erm.
Crest—A salamander in flames, ppr.
Motto—Victrix fortunæ sapientia.
Seat—Gosberton, near Boston, co. Lincoln.

CALVERLEY OF OULTON HALL.

Calverley, John, Esq. of Oulton Hall, co. York, b. 11 Sept. 1789; m. 23 May, 1822, Ellen-Watson, dau. of Thomas Molyneux, Esq. of Newsham House, co. Lancaster, and has had issue,

I. John-Calverley, d. under age, 9 June, 1841.
II. Edmund, b. 14 Aug. 1826, m. 14 April, 1852, Isabella-Mary, elder dau. of John-Thomas Selwyn, Esq. of Down Hall, Essex.
I. Ellen. II. Charlotte.

This gentleman resumed, by royal license, 1852, the name and arms of Calverley.

Lineage.—John Calverley, Esq., next brother of Sir William Calverley, Knt. of Calverley, and 10th in direct descent from John Scot, *alias* Calverley, Lord of Calverley A.D. 1136, held lands in Chorwell in 1510. His son, Christopher Calverley, of Rothwell, who d. in 1546, was great-great-grandfather of Robert Calverley, Esq. of Oulton, who d. in 1674, leaving, by Anne his wife, four sons, of whom the 3rd, Matthew, b. in 1652, was father, by Elizabeth his wife, of William, b. in 1684, who m. in 1714, Frances, dau. and co-heir of John Grosvenor, and dying in 1739, left a son, John, mayor of Leeds, who m. Mary, dau. of Thomas Walker, Esq. of Dewsbury, and d. in 1783, leaving a son, John Calverley, Esq., who assumed by royal license, in 1807, the name and arms of Blayds. He m. Mary, dau. of the Rev. Charles Downes, and left at his decease, in 1827, three surviving sons, viz., John, the present John Calverley, Esq. of Oulton; Henry, in holy orders, prebendary of Wells, and rural dean, b. 1794, m. Elizabeth, dau. of John Meade, Esq.; and Thomas, b. 1795, m. Charlotte, eldest dau. of Martin Hind, Esq.

Arms—Sa., an inescutcheon, within an orle of owls, arg.
Crest—A horned owl, arg.
Seat—Oulton Hall, Wakefield.

CALVERT OF HUNSDON.

CALVERT, FELIX, Esq. of Hunsdon, co. Herts, major-general in the army, b. 16 Oct. 1790.

Lineage.—FELIX CALVERT, Esq. of Furneux-Pelham, co. Herts, b. in 1623, 2nd son of Felix Calverd, of Little Haddam, Herts, younger brother of Thomas Calvert, Esq., ancestor of the CALVERTS *of Albury;* m. Joan Day, and was father of

WILLIAM CALVERT, Esq. of Furneux-Pelham, b. 1667; high-sheriff of Cambridgeshire in 1690; who m. his cousin, Honor, dau. of Peter Calvert, Esq. of Nine Ashes, and had three sons, WILLIAM (Sir), LL.D., M.P. for London, and lord-mayor in 1749, d. 1761; FELIX, of whom presently; and Peter, of Great Hadham, who m. Susannah, dau. of Thomas Tooke, D.D., of Lamborne, Essex, and had issue. The second son,

FELIX CALVERT, Esq. of Furneux-Pelham, b in 1693; m. Christian, dau. of Josias Nicolson, Esq. of Clapham, and by her (who d. in 1759) had (with several daus., of whom Mary m. the Rev. William Hanmer, and Honor m. Thomas Tash, Esq.) two sons, NICOLSON and FELIX. He d. in 1756, and was s. by the elder,

NICOLSON CALVERT, Esq. of Hunsdon House, b. in 1725; high-sheriff of Herts in 1749, and M.P. for Tewkesbury in 1754 and 1761. He m. Rebecca, dau. of the Rev. John Goodwin, M.A., rector of Clapham; but d. s. p. in 1793, and was s. by his brother,

FELIX CALVERT, Esq. of Portland-place, London, who m. in 1763, Elizabeth, eldest dau. of Sir Robert Ladbroke; and dying in 1802, left issue, NICOLSON, his heir; Robert, who d. s. p. in 1821; Charles, of Ockley Court, co. Surrey, M P. for Southwark, who m. in 1823, Jane, dau. of Sir William Rowley, Bart., and is deceased; and Walter. The eldest son,

NICOLSON CALVERT, Esq. of Hunsdon, M.P. for Hertford; b. 15 May, 1764; m. 9 Jan. 1789, Frances, youngest dau. of Edmond-Sexton Pery, Viscount Pery, and had issue,

FELIX, now of Hunsdon.
Edmond-Pery-Sexton, b. 26 Oct. 1797.
Nicholas-Robert, b. 4 Aug. 1800.
William-Henry, b. 8 Feb. 1803.
Isabella, m. in 1810, to Sir James-Mathew Strong, Bart. of Tynan Abbey, co. Armagh.
Lavinia-Frances-Jane.
Mary-Caroline-Felicia. Harriet-Diana.

Arms—Paly of six, or and sa., a bend, counterchanged.
Crest—Out of a ducal coronet, or, two pennons, the dexter, or, the other, sa., staves, gu.
Seat—Hunsdon House, Herts.

CAMERON OF LOCHIEL.

CAMERON, DONALD, Esq. of Lochiel, co. Inverness, D.L., b. 25 Sept. 1796; m. in July, 1832, Lady Vere-Catherine-Louisa Hobart, sister of the Earl of Buckinghamshire, and has issue,

I. DONALD, b. in April, 1835.
II. George-Hampden, b. in Oct. 1840.
I. Anne-Louisa. II. Julia-Vere.
III. Sibilla-Matilda. IV. Albinia-Mary.

Lineage.—The surname of Cameron is of great antiquity in Scotland, and in ancient times was variously written, viz., Cameron, Cambron, Cambrun. "The Camerons have a tradition among them that they are originally descended of a younger son of the royal family of Denmark, who assisted at the restoration of King FERGUS II., anno 404; but it is more probable that they are of the aborigines of the ancient Scots or Caledonians that first planted the country."

"The earliest possession of the Camerons"—we quote Skene's *Highlanders of Scotland*—"was that part of Lochaber extending to the east of the loch and river of Lochy, and was held by them of the Lord of the Isles; their more modern possessions of Lochiel and Locharkaig, which lay on the west side of that water, had been granted by the Lord of the Isles to the founder of the clan Ranald, by whose descendants it was inhabited. Originally the clan Cameron consisted of three septs, the clan Ic Mhartin or MacMartins of Letterfinlay; the clan Ic Ilonobhy, or Camerons of Strone; and Sliochd Shoirle Ruaidh, or Camerons of Glenevis."

"The Camerons having, along with the clan Chattan, deserted Alexander, Lord of the Isles, when attacked by JAMES I. in Lochaber, and having subsequently refused to join Donald Balloch in his invasion of Scotland in 1431, that chief, after his victory at Innerlochy, resolved to revenge himself upon the Camerons, and attacked them with fury. The clan was unable to withstand his attack, and the chief was obliged to fly into Ireland, while the rest of the clan took refuge amongst the most inaccessible parts of the mountain country." When the return of Alexander from captivity had restored some degree of order to his wild dominions,

DONALD DHU, the then chief of the clan, appears to have raised the Camerons from the depressed state into which they had fallen by the vengeance of the Lords of the Isles, and to have re-acquired for the clan the estates which they had formerly possessed. From Donald Dhu we pass to his descendant,

SIR EWEN CAMERON, of Lochiel, b. in Feb. 1629, eclipsed in fame all his predecessors, and from a very early age became a stanch adherent of the royal cause. He m. thrice.

JOHN CAMERON, of Lochiel, called John MacEwen, joined the Earl of Mar in 1715, for which he suffered attainder and forfeiture. He m. Isabel, sister of Sir Duncan Campbell, of Lochnell, and had issue, DONALD, his heir; John of Fassifern, co. Argyll, father of Sir Ewen Cameron, of Fassifern, who was created a Bart. in 1817; and Archibald, a physician, who engaged in the rebellion of 1745, and was executed. By Jean his wife, dau. of Archibald Cameron of Dungallon, he left issue, four sons and a dau. John Cameron d. at Nieuport, in Flanders, in 1748, and was s. by his eldest son,

DONALD CAMERON, of Lochiel, captain of the clan Cameron, who had joined the young Pretender with a considerable body of his men in 1745, and fought at their head on several occasions. He m. Anne, dau. of Sir James Campbell, 5th Bart. of Auchinbreck, by whom he left at his death, in 1748, an eldest son and heir,

JOHN CAMERON, Esq. of Lochiel, who d. in 1762, and was s. by his only surviving brother,

CHARLES CAMERON, Esq. of Lochiel, father of

DONALD CAMERON, Esq. of Lochiel, who m. in 1795, Anne, dau. of Sir Ralph Abercromby, and sister of the late Lord Abercromby, by whom he had issue,

DONALD, his heir.
Alexander, in holy orders; who m. 1 Sept. 1835, Charlotte, dau. of the Hon. Edward Rice, D.D., Dean of Gloucester, and has issue, one son and two daus.
Mary-Anne. Matilda.

Lochiel d. in 1832.

Arms—Gu., three bars, or.
Crest—A dexter arm embowed in armour, the hand grasping a sword, all ppr.
Supporters—Two savages wreathed about the loins, each holding over his shoulder a pole-axe, all ppr.
Motto—Pro rege et patriâ.
Seats—Achnacarry, co. Inverness; and Hampden House, Bucks.

CAMPBELL OF ORMIDALE.

CAMPBELL, ROBERT-NUTTER, Esq. of Ormidale, co. Argyll, major 4th native infantry, H.E.I.C.S., for many years in command of the Nair Brigade, at Travancore.

Lineage.—Campbell of Ormidale, next in entail to Campbell of Otter, springs from John Campbell, of Kinochtree, a younger son of Campbell of Lundy, in Angus, whose ancestor was Thomas Campbell, 2nd son of Colin, 1st Earl of Argyll. The present MAJOR CAMPBELL, of Ormidale, is only surviving son of the late JOHN CAMPBELL, of Ormidale, by Catherine his wife, dau. of Gen. Campbell, of Strachur, and grandson of Alexander Campbell, of Ormidale, who was 2nd son of John Campbell, of Otter, by his 2nd wife, a dau. of John Steahouse, Esq. of Drummore.

Arms—Gyronny of eight, erm. and sa.
Crest—A boar's head, fessewise, couped, or.
Motto—Ne obliviscaris.
Seat—Ormidale, co. Argyll.

CAMPBELL OF MONZIE.

CAMPBELL, ALEXANDER, Esq. of Monzie Castle, co. Perth, and Inveraw, co. Argyll, b. 30 Dec. 1812; m. 27 May, 1844, Christina, only child of Sir Duncan Cameron, Bart. of Fassifern, and has had issue,

I. ALEXANDER, b. 30 March, 1847, d. young.
I. Christina. II. Louisa.
III. Mary, d. young.

Mr. Campbell is present representative of the Monzie branch of the house of Campbell, being son and heir (by Christina Menzies his wife) of the late LIEUT.-GEN. ALEXANDER CAMPBELL, of Monzie and Finnah, M.P., who derived from Archibald Campbell, of Monzie, 4th son of Sir Duncan Campbell, 1st bart. of Glenurchy. Mr. Campbell of Monzie has a brother, Robert; and a sister, Caroline, wife of Charles Swinfen, Esq. of Swinfen.

Arms—Quarterly: 1st and 4th, or, gyronny of eight, or and sa., for CAMPBELL; 2nd, arg., a lymphad or galley, sa., with oars in action, for LORN; 3rd, or, a fesse, chequy arg. and sa., for STEWART *of Lorn*.

Crest—A boar's head, erased, ppr.

Motto—Follow me.

Seat—Monzie, co. Argyll.

CAMPBELL OF LOCHNELL.

CAMPBELL, ARCHIBALD, Esq. of Lochnell, co. Argyll, b. Feb. 1777; m. 29 Nov. 1803, Louisa-Ann, dau. of Captain Duncan Macdougall, of Ardintrive, 2nd son of Macdougall of Lorn, and had issue,

I. DUNCAN.
II. Archibald-Argyll-Napier, H.E.I.C.S., d. in Bombay.
III. John-Cameron, late major in the 9th royal Lancers, distinguished himself when in command of a squadron of that regiment at the battle of Gujerat, 21 Feb. 1849, m. Isabella-Sophia, dau. of the late Charles Smith, Esq. banker, of Northampton.
IV. Hope, d. young.
V. Colin, in holy orders, m. Henrietta, dau. of Henry.-N. Hovy, Esq., consul at Bordeaux to His Majesty the King of The Netherlands.
VI. Alexander.
VII. Wellington, drowned in India. And eight daus.

Lineage.—Mr. Campbell is the 11th Laird of Lochnell, in a direct descent from the Hon. John Campbell, 2nd son of Colin, 3rd Earl of Argyll, by the Lady Jane Gordon his wife, dau. of Alexander, 3rd Earl of Huntly. The CAMPBELLS *of Lochnell* are the latest cadets of Argyll, and in default of male descendants of John, 4th Duke of Argyll, heirs to the titles and estates.

Arms—Quarterly: 1st and 4th, gyronny of eight, or and sa., for CAMPBELL; 2nd, az., a boar's head, couped, for GORDON; 3rd, arg., a lymphad, sa., her oars in action, for LORN.

Crest—A dexter hand grasping a horseman's lance, bendways, all ppr.

Motto—Arma parata fero.

Supporters—On the dexter side, a lion, guardant, ppr., and on the sinister, a swan, ppr.

CAMPBELL OF CESSNOCK AND TREESBANK.

CAMPBELL, GEORGE-JAMES, Esq. of Treesbank, co. Ayr, D.L. and J.P., b. in July, 1800; m. 1st, in Dec. 1822, Elizabeth M'Kerel, only child of Colonel John Reid, of the East India Company's service (by Elizabeth his wife, dau. of John M'Kerel, of Hillhouse), by whom (who d. in 1826) he has two surviving daughters. He m. 2ndly, in Aug. 1829, Miss C.-J. Jones, 2nd dau. of the late Major Jones, of the 25th light dragoons, and has issue,

I. GEORGE-JAMES. And a dau.

Lineage.—JAMES CAMPBELL, of Treesbank, co. Ayr, 2nd son of Sir Hugh Campbell, of Cessnock, by Elizabeth Campbell his wife, 2nd dau. and co-heir of John, Master of Loudoun, became male representative of the house of Cessnock, at the decease of his brother, Sir George. He d. after 1730 (he was then upwards of 90 years of age), leaving by Jean his wife, dau. of Sir William Mure, of Rowallan, a son and successor,

GEORGE CAMPBELL, Esq. of Treesbank, who m. in 1708, Anne, youngest dau. of David Boswell, of Auchinleck, and had (with two daus., Anne, d. unm., and Jean, m. in 1746, to the Rev. George Reid,) two sons. The elder,

JAMES CAMPBELL, Esq. of Treesbank, chief of the CAMPBELLS *of Cessnock*, m. 1st, in 1763, Helen, 2nd dau. of Andrew M'Credie, Esq. of Pierceton, by whom he had an only child, Jean, who m. in 1787, Robert Reid, Esq. of Adamton, and d. in Aug. 1789, leaving a dau. Helen, who d. in April, 1790. He m. 2ndly, in 1768, Mary, 2nd dau. of David Montgomery, of Lainshaw (by his wife Veronica, dau. of James Boswell, of Auchinleck), and had two sons, GEORGE-JAMES, his successor, and David, a col. in the army. He d. in 1776, and was s. by his elder son,

GEORGE-JAMES CAMPBELL, Esq. of Treesbank, who m. in 1797, his cousin, Elizabeth-Montgomery Beaumont, only dau. of Mrs. Elizabeth Montgomery, heiress of Lainshaw, and sister of Sir James-Montgomery Cunninghame, Bart. of Corse Hill, by whom he had issue, GEORGE-JAMES, his heir; John, David, Jane-Maxwell, Elizabeth-Montgomery, Mary, and Anne. The laird d. in Nov. 1815, and was s. by his eldest son, the present GEORGE-JAMES CAMPBELL, Esq. of Treesbank.

Arms—Gyronny of eight, or and sa., for ARGYLL: within a bordure, gu., charged with eight escallops, of the first; and a canton, also gyronny of eight, erm. and gu., for LOUDOUN.

Crest—A phœnix head, erased, or.

Motto—Constanter et prudenter.

Seat—Treesbank House, Kilmarnock.

CAMPBELL OF BARQUHARRIE AND SORNBEG.

CAMPBELL, JOHN, Esq. of Sornbeg, co. Ayr, J.P. and D.L., b. 11 March, 1785.

Lineage.—HUGH CAMPBELL, Esq., designed of Barquharrie, in Ayrshire, 3rd son of Sir Hugh Campbell, of Cessnock, by Elizabeth Campbell his wife, 2nd dau. and co-heir of John, Master of Loudoun, m. 5 June, 1702, Margaret, 2nd dau. of David Boswell, Esq. of Auchinleck, and had an only son,

HUGH CAMPBELL, Esq. of Barquharrie, who m. 10 Jan. 1727, Margaret, dau. of David Henderson, Esq. of Tinnochside, and was father of

BRUCE CAMPBELL, Esq. of Barquharrie, who m. in 1772, Annabella, dau. of James Wilson, Esq. of Kilmarnock, and had issue,

I. HUGH, of Barquharrie, a justice of the peace for the co. Ayr, and capt. in the 85th regt., who m. 18 Dec. 1797, Sophia, youngest dau. of Thomas Barber, Esq. of Greasley, in Nottinghamshire, and dying at Bath, 5 Jan. 1824, left issue,
 1 HUGH-BRUCE, of Barquharrie, now residing at The Park, Nottingham, b. 8 April, 1803, who m. 1st, 28 April, 1829, Ann, dau. of Philip Hurd, Esq. of Kentish Town, by whom (who d. 6 Sept. 1829) he had no issue; and 2ndly, 2 Oct. 1832, Elizabeth, dau. of Edwards Werge, Esq. of Hexgrave Park, co. Nottingham, by whom he has had issue, Hugh, d. 17 Oct. 1839; BRUCE, b. 14 June, 1839; Claud, b. 25 Nov. 1840; Elizabeth; Mary-Anne; and Janet.
 2 Thomas-Alexander, m. 3 June, 1835, Susannah, dau. of Mr. George Shelton, d. s. p., 10 Oct. 1844.
 3 William, m. 1 Aug. 1838, Sarah-Ann, dau. of Capt. Webb, R.N., and d. s. p. 29 March, 1843.
 4 John, d. unm. 15 Jan. 1841.
 1 Anne, m. to George Douglas, Esq. of Rodinghead, N.B.
 2 Annabella, m. to William-Nugent Comyn, Esq. of the co. Clare.
 3 Sophia-Elizabeth, m. to Denis Browne, Esq. of Brownestown, Ireland.
II. Bruce, b. 25 May, 1775, capt. E.I.Co.'s naval service, d. unm.
III. Alexander, b. 28 Sept. 1779, a capt. in the 74th regt., and of distinguished bravery; of his services, particularly at the memorable battle of Assaye, honourable mention is frequently made in Col. Welch's *Reminiscences of India*. He d. of his wounds, in Oct. 1805, unm.
IV. JOHN, now of Sornbeg.
V. William, b. 4 May, 1788, d. in Jan. 1830.
I. Euphemia, m. to her cousin, Hugh Wilson, Esq. of Kilmarnock, and d. in 1817, leaving a son, Hugh-Campbell Wilson.
II. Marianne, d. in April, 1825, unm.

Mr. Campbell d. in Feb. 1813, aged 79.

Arms—Gyronny of eight, or and sa., within a bordure, gu., charged with eight escallops, of the first, and a canton, also gyronny of eight, erm. and gu.

Crest—A phœnix head, erased.

Motto—Constanter et prudenter.

Seat—Sornbeg, co. Ayrshire.

CAMPBELL OF FAIRFIELD.

Campbell, William-Gunning, Esq. of Fairfield, co. Ayr, J.P. and D.L., *b.* 18 Jan. 1784; *m.* 18 April, 1811, Diana, 3rd dau. of Sir John Ingilby, Bart. of Ripley, in Yorkshire, and by her (who *d.* in 1840) had one son,

I. William-Ingilby, *b.* in Nov. 1812, late lieutenant, 6th dragoon-guards, lost at sea in 1835.

He *m.* 2ndly, 17 March, 1845, Maria-Anna, dau. of John-Henry McNaughton, 2nd son of John-Stewart Menzies, Esq. of Culdares, co. Perth.

Lineage.—William Campbell, Esq. of Fairfield, son of John Campbell, Esq. of Whitehaugh or Fairfield, and great-great-grandson of John Campbell, Esq. of Whitehaugh, who was 4th son of Sir Hugh Campbell, of Cesnock, by Elizabeth his wife, 2nd dau. and co-heir of John Campbell, Master of Loudoun, *m.* in 1747, Elizabeth Metcalf, of Northumberland, co. Virginia, and had a son,

William Campbell, Esq. of Fairfield, who *m.* 1st, in 1772, Sarah Cunninghame, of Cambridge, New England, by whom he had two daus., Martha, wife of Charles M'Vicar, Esq., and Elizabeth, *m.* to Lord John-Douglas-E.-H. Campbell (afterwards Duke of Argyll). He *m.* 2ndly, 15 Aug. 1782, Catherine Gunning, niece of Sir Robert Gunning, Bart. of Horton, and dau. of Captain Gunning, who fell at the storming of Guadaloupe, in 1757, aged 21. By this lady he had issue, 1 William Gunning, now of Fairfield; 2 George, E.I.Co.'s service, *d. unm.*; 3 Charles, major E.I.Co.'s service, who *m.* Jane-Wemyss, dau. of the Hon. Leveson-Granville-Keith Murray, and by her (who *m.* 2ndly, in 1836, Captain C.-S. Maling, E.I.Co.'s service), left at his decease, in 1832, three sons, viz., Leveson-Granville, *m.* and has issue; Gunning-Granville; and Fincastle-Argyle, who *d. unm.* 1850; 4 Alexander, E.I.Co.'s civil service, who *m.* Matilda, dau. of — Thursby, Esq., and has issue; 5 Napier, capt. horse artillery, E.I.Co.'s service, who *m.* Selina, dau. of — Gore, Esq., and *d.* in 1839, leaving issue; 6 James, lost at sea; 7 Andrew, capt. E.I.Co.'s service, who *d. unm.* in 1850; 8 Argyle, *d.* young; 1 Mary, *m.* to Sir Henry Jervis White-Jervis, Bart.; and 2 Catherine, *m.* to Duncan Hunter, Esq. Mr. Campbell *d.* in June, 1815.

Arms—Gyronny of eight, or and sa., and a canton, also gyronny of eight, erm. and gu.
Crest—An eagle's head, erased, ppr.
Motto—Constanter et prudenter.
Seat—Fairfield House, near Kilmarnock.

CAMPBELL OF ARDCHATTAN PRIORY.

Campbell, Jane-Elizabeth-Mary, of Ardchattan Priory, co. Argyll, *s.* her uncle, Colonel Thomas-Dundas Campbell, in 1845; *m.* in 1841, Strachan-Irving Popham, Esq., son of the late Admiral Sir Home Popham, and had issue,

Robert-Alexander and Elizabeth, who both died in infancy.

Lineage.—The chiefs of this branch of Argyll were for two or three centuries Priors of Ardchattan. The late representative,

Patrick Campbell, Esq. of Ardchattan Priory, *m.* Margaret, dau. of John Macfarlane, of Macfarlane, and had,

Charles, [illegible] capt. [illegible] highlanders, killed at the battle of Catawba, in the American war [illegible] Aug. [illegible]
Robert, heir to his father.
Alexander, successor to his brother.
Thomas-Dundas [illegible] Lt.-Col. Alexander Campbell, at Ardchattan, and *d.* [illegible] regt. [illegible]
Lawrence-Dundas [illegible] Emma Courtenay and *d.* leaving issue.
Anne, *m.* [illegible] to Andrew Taylor, Esq. of Comrie-Castle, co. Perth.
Mary *d. unm.*

Mr. Campbell *d.* [illegible] June [illegible] and was *s.* by his eldest son,

Robert Campbell, Esq. of Ardchattan Priory, captain E.I.Co.'s service [illegible] who *d.* [illegible] and was *s.* by his brother,

Col. Alexander Campbell, of Ardchattan Priory [illegible] May [illegible] *m.* [illegible] the [illegible] dau. and heiress of [illegible] Wemyss [illegible] Esq. of [illegible] wife, [illegible] and heiress of [illegible] and had issue,

Alexander-[illegible] Aug. [illegible] Sir Home [illegible] Popham [illegible]

Jane-Elizabeth-Mary, *m.* to Strachan Popham, Esq., E.I.Co.'s civil service, son of the late Sir Home Popham.
Sophia-Margaret, *d. unm.*, 11 Nov. 1827.

Arms—Quarterly: 1st and 4th, gyronny of eight, or and sa.; 2nd, a buck's head; 3rd, arg., a galley, sa., all within a bordure, or, charged with eight crescents.
Crest—A swan, ppr., crowned, or.
Seat—Ardchattan Priory, Argyllshire.

CAMPBELL OF DUNOON.

See Campbell-Wyndham.

CAMPBELL OF COLGRAIN.

Campbell, Colin, Esq. of Colgrain, co. Dumbarton, *b.* 8 Jan. 1782; *m.* 24 Oct. 1814, Janet Miller, eldest dau. of John Hamilton, Esq. of North Park, male representative of the old family of Hamilton *of Westport*, co. Linlithgow, and has issue,

I. John, capt. Royal Scots Greys; *b.* 9 Aug. 1815; *d.* in May, 1846.
II. Colin, *b.* 2 Sept. 1819; *m.* 3 June, 1845, Jessie, dau. of Wm. Middleton, Esq., son of John Middleton, Esq. of Shiels, Aberdeenshire, and has issue,
 1 Colin-John, *b.* 28 May, 1848.
 2 William-Middleton, *b.* in 1849.
 3 Henry-Alexander, *b.* in 1851.
 1 Jessie, *d.* in 1849.
III. Alexander-Henry, *b.* 31 July, 1822.
IV. Archibald-Hamilton, an officer in the Indian army; *b.* 17 Dec. 1823.
V. Thomas, *b.* 20 March, 1825; *m.* in Sept. 1851, his cousin, Mary, dau. of Col. Alexander Campbell, of Possil, co. Lanark, which lady *d.* in Aug. 1852.
VI. George-William, *b.* 3 June, 1826.
VII. James, *b.* 14 Oct. 1828.
VIII. Robert, an officer 34th regt.; *b.* 13 March, 1830.
IX. Mungo-Septimus, *b.* 31 March, 1831.
X. William, an officer 71st regt.; *b.* 18 June, 1832.
I. Helen-Bogle, *m.* 16 Jan. 1851, her cousin, John Campbell, Esq. of Possil; and *d.* 8 July, 1851.
II. Marion, *m.* 3 June, 1840, Alexander S. Finlay, Esq. of Castle Toward, and has issue,
 1 Kirkman, *b.* in 1841, *d.* in 1843.
 2 Colin-Campbell, *b.* in 1843.
 3 Alexander-Kirkman, *b.* in 1844.
III. Mary. IV. Elizabeth Anne.
V. Janet-Hamilton.

Mr. Campbell of Colgrain is 3rd son of John Campbell, Esq. of Morriston, Lanarkshire, West India merchant and proprietor, by Marion Murdoch his wife. John Campbell was 3rd son of Alexander Campbell, captain in the old "Black Watch," of the family of K[illegible], Perthshire, descended from Sir John Campbell, of Lawers, who was raised to the peerage, in 1633, by the title of Baron Farrinyeane and Mauchline, and *d.* in 1662; he was ancestor to the Earls of Loudoun. Sir John was 3rd son of Sir Colin Campbell, of Glenorchy, ancestor to the Earls of Breadalbane, by his 2nd wife, Margaret, [illegible] dau. of Lord Drummond, of Kerr. Mr. Campbell of Colgrain is a deputy-lieut. for Lanarkshire.

Arms—Gyronny of eight, or and sa. [illegible] a [illegible] [illegible] all within a bordure [illegible], charged with eight [illegible] of the first.
Crest—A swan's head, neck and wings [illegible], or, armed and [illegible] ppr.
Motto—[illegible]
Seat—[illegible] Colgrain, Dumbartonshire.

CAMPBELL OF [illegible]

Campbell, William-[illegible], Esq. of [illegible] [illegible] *m.* [illegible] [illegible] dau. of the late John [illegible] Esq. of [illegible] and has a son,

[illegible] *b.* [illegible] March [illegible] an officer in the army.

Lineage.—[illegible] son of [illegible] Campbell of [illegible] [illegible] Breadalbane [illegible] capt. of the clan Chattan, was killed at Stirling, leaving by his wife, a dau. of Campbell of Ardkinglas, a son and successor,

ROBERT CAMPBELL, of Glenfalloch, who m. Susannah, dau. of James Menzies, of Culdares, and was father of

COLIN CAMPBELL, Esq. of Glenfalloch, who m. Agnes, dau. of Campbell of Auchlyne, and had issue, Robert, d. young; James, lieut. 42nd regiment, d. s. p.; WILLIAM, heir to his father; Archibald, killed at Fontenoy; Robert (who m. Jean, dau. of Sir James Sinclair, Bart. of Dunbeath, and had issue, eight sons and three daus.) The eldest surviving son,

WILLIAM CAMPBELL, Esq. of Glenfalloch, m. Susan Campbell, dau. of — McPherson, Esq. of Argyllshire, and had issue. The second son,

JAMES CAMPBELL, Esq. of Glenfalloch, m. Elizabeth Blanchard, of Cirencester, relict of — Lulow, Esq. of Gloucester, and by her had issue,

WILLIAM-JOHN-LAMB, now of Glenfalloch.
Elizabeth-Marlborough, m. and had issue, d. in 1835.
Susan-Sophia, m. and had issue.

Arms—Quarterly: 1st and 4th, gyronny of eight, or and sa.; 2nd, arg., a galley with her sails furled, and oars in action, sa.; 3rd, or, a fesse, chequy, az. and arg., and for difference, in the centre point a hunting-horn, sa., garnished, gu.
Crest—A man's heart pierced through with a dart, ppr.
Motto—Thus far.
Seat—Glenfalloch House, co. Perth.

CAMPBELL OF SKIPNESS.

CAMPBELL, WALTER-WILLIAM-THOMAS-BEAUJOLOIS, Esq. of Skipness Castle, co. Argyll, J.P., b. 5 Nov. 1807; m. 13 Sept. 1838, Anna-Henrietta, eldest dau. of Lieut.-Col. Loring, and has issue one dau.,

CONSTANCE-GLENCAIRN.

Lineage.—Skipness Castle is situated in the district of Kintyre and co. Argyll.

WALTER CAMPBELL, Esq. of Skipness, chief of this ancient line, m. 1st, Eleanor Kerr, and had issue, John, Glencairn, ROBERT, Walter, Colin, Eleanor, Harriet, Margaret, Katherine, and Elizabeth. He m. 2ndly, Mrs. Hay, and also had issue, Hamilton, William, and Mary. The 3rd son,

ROBERT CAMPBELL, Esq. of Skipness, m. in July, 1806, Eugenia-Josephine, dau. of Richard Wynne, Esq. of Forkingham, co. Lincoln, and had issue,

WALTER-WILLIAM-THOMAS, now of Skipness.
George-Augustus, E.I.C.S., m. 2 Nov. 1834, Lady Sarah Lyon, dau. of Thomas, Earl of Strathmore, and had issue five children, all d. in infancy.
John-Francis-Glencairn, m. in Oct. 1836, Katherine-Alexander, and had issue, Robert, Cornwall-Henry, and Eleanor-Jane.
Mary-Agatha, m. in June, 1839, to Keith Macalister, Esq. of Glenbarr.

Arms—Gyronny of eight, or and sa., a bordure indented, of the first, charged with eight crescents, of the second.
Crest—Two oars, crossed in saltier.
Motto—Terra marque fide.
Seat—Skipness Castle, co. Argyll.

CAMPBELL OF ISLAY.

CAMPBELL, WALTER-FREDERICK, Esq. of Woodhall, co. Lanark, J.P. and D.L., M.P. for Argyllshire from 1821 to 1832, b. 10 April, 1798; m. 1st, 2 Feb. 1820, Lady Ellinor Charteris, eldest dau. of Francis, Earl of Wemyss and March (who d. 16 Sept. 1832), by whom he had issue,

JOHN-FRANCIS, b. 29 Dec. 1822. Margaret-Susan.

Mr. Campbell m. 2ndly, 11 March, 1837, Catherine, dau. of Stephen-Thomas Cole, Esq., by the Lady Elizabeth Stanley his wife.

Lineage.—This is a scion of CAMPBELL of *Skipness*. Its late representative,

WALTER CAMPBELL, Esq. of Shawfield, son of JOHN CAMPBELL, of Shawfield, and the Lady Harriet his wife, dau. of the Earl of Glencairn, s. his eldest brother, Daniel, who d. unm. in 1777. He m. 1st, in 1768, Eleanor, dau. of Lord Charles Kerr; and 2ndly, Mary, dau. of Nisbet of Dirlton; and d. in 1816, having had issue,

I. John, who m. in 1796, Lady Charlotte Campbell, youngest dau. of John, Duke of Argyll, and by her (who m. 2ndly, the Rev. Edward Bury,) left at his decease, v. p. in 1806, two sons and six daus.,

1 WALTER-FREDERICK, present representative of the family.
2 John-George, b. in 1800, m. Ellen, dau. of Sir Fitzwilliam Barrington, Bart., and dying 6 Aug. 1830, left one son and one dau.
1 Eliza-Maria, m. to Sir William-Gordon Cumming, Bart.
2 Eleanora, m. to Henry, Earl of Uxbridge, and d. in 1828.
3 Beaujolois-Harriet-Charlotte, m. to Charles, late Earl of Charleville.
4 Emma, m. to William Russell, Esq., youngest son of the late Lord William Russell.
5 Adelaide, m. to Lord Arthur Lennox.
6 Julia, m. to Peter-Langford Brooke, of Mere Hall, co. Chester.

I. Harriet, m. to Daniel Hamilton, of Gilkerkscleugh.
II. Glencairn, m. to Francis Carter, Esq. of Edgecott, Northamptonshire.
III. Katherine, m. to Sir Charles Jenkinson, Bart.
IV. Margaret, m. to the Earl of Wemyss.
V. Elizabeth, m. to Stewart-Moncreiff Threipland, Esq.
VI. Mary, m. to Lord Ruthven.
VII. Hamilton, m. to Lord Belhaven.
VIII. Ellinor, d. unm.

Arms—Gyronny of eight, or and sa., within a bordure, of the first, charged with as many crescents, of the second.
Crest—A griffin, erect, holding the sun between the fore paws.
Motto—Fidus amicus.
Seat—Island of Islay, Argyllshire; and Woodhall, in Lanarkshire.

CAMPBELL OF SKERRINGTON.

CAMPBELL, ROBERT, Esq. of Skerrington, co. Ayr, J.P., b. 19 Dec. 1814; m. 25 Jan. 1843, Anne, only surviving dau. of the late John Carr, Esq. of Dunston Hall, co. Durham.

Lineage.—This is one of the most ancient families in Ayrshire, and derived from the same stock as Loudoun.

SIR GILLESPICK CAMPBELL, of Lochow, who appears in a charter in 1266, and from whom the noble families of Argyll and Loudoun are descended, m. a dau. of William de Somerville, Baron of Carnwath, and was father of SIR COLIN CAMPBELL, of Lochow, who had several sons, of whom Sir Niel was progenitor of the Argyll family, and Donald was father of Sir Duncan, progenitor of the Loudoun family; from the above Sir Colin, the CAMPBELLS *of Skerrington* claim to be derived.

ELEANORA CAMPBELL (eldest sister of John Campbell, Esq. of Skerrington, who d. s. p., and dau. of John Campbell, Esq. of Skerrington, by Wilhelmina his wife, dau. of Lieut.-Gen. Sir Andrew Agnew, Bart. of Lochnaw), m. Charles Maxwell, of Cowhill, co. Dumfries, and had, with a dau., the late Miss Wilhelmina Maxwell, of Cowhill, a son,

DUGALD-JOHN CAMPBELL, Esq. of Skerrington, who m. 25 Aug. 1804, Janet, 4th dau. of the Hon. William Baillie, of Polkemmet, one of the senators of the College of Justice in Scotland, and had issue, Charles and William, both deceased; Robert, present representative; Dugald, b. 15 Aug. 1816; Margaret-Colquhoun, m. to Thomas-Durham Weir, Esq. of Boghead, co. Linlithgow; Susan-Dalrymple; Caroline; Jessy, m. to Patrick-George Skene, Esq. of Hallyards, co. Fife; Isabella, deceased; and Mary.

Arms—Quarterly: 1st, gyronny of eight, or and sa.; 2nd, az., three crosslets fitched, issuing out of as many crescents, arg.; 3rd, az., three boars' heads, erased, arg., between a lance, issuing out of the dexter base, and a Lochaber axe issuing out of the sinister, both erect, in pale, of the second; 4th, gyronny of eight, gu. and erm.
Crest—A dexter hand and arm in armour, holding a garland of laurels, all ppr.
Mottoes—Above the crest, "Campi fero præmia belli." Under the arms, "Wisdom's beginning is God's fear."

CAMPBELL OF AUCHMANNOCH.

CAMPBELL, ROBERT, Esq. of Auchmannoch, in Ayrshire, J.P., b. 26 Jan. 1782; s. his father 11 March, 1828.

Lineage.—"The Campbells of Auchmannoch," says Robertson, "have been respectable land owners, in the district of Kyle-Stewart, for several centuries. The lands of Auchmannoch and others, formerly and still belonging to them, are situate in the lordship of Kylesmuir, and in the north part of the parish of Sorn, about from three to four miles north-eastward of the town of Mauchline, and about six miles south-eastward of the castle of Loudoun, from which family they were originally derived."

GEORGE CAMPBELL, of Auchmannoch, son of Arthur Campbell, of Auchmannoch, and Janet his wife, dau. of John Campbell, of Eschawburn, was representative of the family in the 17th century, and, being an active supporter of the Presbyterian cause, became involved in the religious disputes and turmoils of the unhappy period in which he lived. He m. in June, 1682, Jean, dau. of John Mure, Esq. of Blacklaw, and granddau. of Sir William Mure, Knt. of Rowallan, by whom he had two sons, ARTHUR, his heir; and John, who acquired the lands of Netherton and Whitehaugh, in Ayrshire. The elder son,

ARTHUR CAMPBELL, of Auchmannoch, m. 28 Sept. 1671, Margaret, 2nd dau. of John Schaw, of Kiers, in Carrick, afterwards designed of Dalton, by whom he had three sons and two daus. Auchmannoch d. in 1703, and was s. by his eldest son,

JOHN CAMPBELL, of Auchmannoch, who m. Jean, eldest dau. of Hugh Mitchell, Esq. of Dalgain, by his wife Janet Campbell, only dau. of John Campbell, of Whitehaugh, by whom he had issue several children, who d. young, and two sons to survive him, JOHN and ARTHUR. He d. in 1740, and was s. by his eldest son,

JOHN CAMPBELL, of Auchmannoch, who resided many years in England, as a merchant at Bristol. He d. unm. in Feb. 1795, and was s. by his only brother,

ARTHUR CAMPBELL, of Auchmannoch, who m. in March, 1779, Burella, 2nd dau. of Robert Hunter, Esq. of Pisgah, Ayrshire (descended of Hunterston), late professor of Greek in the University of Edinburgh, and had four sons and one dau.,

JOHN, who d. at Calcutta, in the service of the Hon. E.I.Co. in Nov. 1808, unm.
ROBERT, now of Auchmannoch.
Andrew, of Avisyard, co. Ayr, late lieut.-col. in the service of the E.I.Co.; m. 1st, Margaret, 2nd dau. of Charles Hay, Esq. of the family of HAY *of Hopes*, co. Haddington. She d. in 1821, after having had a son, who is also dead: Colonel Campbell m. 2ndly, Nicola-Anne, dau. of the late Colonel Richard Maxwell, of Birdstown, co. Donegal, and has by her a son, ROBERT-MITCHELL.
Arthur, of Catrine House, Ayrshire, W.S.; m. Jane, dau. of the late Charles Barstow, Esq. of Kelso, and has, with several daus., one son, Arthur.
Elizabeth, m. to the late James Cuthbert, Esq. of Dalleagles, in Ayrshire, and has issue.

Mr. Campbell d. 11 March, 1828.

Arms—Gyronny of eight, gu. and erm.
Crest—A double-headed eagle rising from flames, looking towards the sun.
Motto—I bide my time.
Seat—Auchmannoch House, Mauchline.

CAMPBELL OF GLENLYON.

See GARDEN-CAMPBELL.

CAMPBELL OF JURA.

CAMPBELL, COLIN, Esq. of Jura and Craignish, co. Argyll, J.P. and D.L., heritable keeper of Craignish Castle, b. 8 Nov. 1772; m. 6 Aug. 1806, Isabella Hamilton, dau. of Richard Dennistoun, Esq. of Kelvin Grove, co. Lanark, son of James Dennistoun, Esq. of Dennistoun, co. Dumbarton, and had issue,

I. ARCHIBALD. II. Richard-Dennistoun.
III. Colin, an officer in the 91st foot.
IV. James. V. John.
I. Christiana-Alston, m. 27 April, 1831, to James Meiklem, Esq. of Carnbroe, co. Lanark, and has issue.
II. Sarah, m. 13 June, 1838, to W.-F. Gordon, Esq. of Milrig, co. Ayr.
III. Isabella-Hamilton-Dundas, m. 19 Jan. 1836, to Lachlan Macquarie, Esq. of Jarvisfield, co. Argyll, capt. in the Scots Greys, only son of the late Gen. Macquarie, governor of New South Wales.
IV. Anne-Caroline, d. 26 April, 1832.
V. Mary-Lyon. VI. Barbara.
VII. Duncan-Augusta-Lochnell.

Lineage.—This is a junior branch of the Lochnell line of the noble House of Argyll, derived immediately from DUNCAN CAMPBELL, 2nd son of Alexander Campbell, Esq. of Lochnell, grandson of John, 2nd son of Colin, 3rd Earl of Argyll.

DUNCAN CAMPBELL, first of the family of Jura, was b. in 1596; m. 1st, Mary, dau. of Sir Donald Campbell, of Ardnamurchan, by whom he had several daus., one of whom was m. to Malcolm of Poltalloch, co. Argyll. He m. 2ndly, Mary, dau. of Hector Maclean, of Torloisk, by whom he had, with several other daus., three sons, viz., JOHN, his successor; Archibald, ancestor of the CAMPBELLS *of Glendaruel*; and Alexander, d. unm. He d. 2 May, 1695, in his 99th year, and was s. by his eldest son,

JOHN CAMPBELL, Esq., who m. his cousin Catherine, dau. of Colin Campbell, Esq. of Lochnell, by whom he had an only son, ARCHIBALD, and several daus., one of whom, Anne, was m. in 1711, to Alexander Campbell, Esq. of Ardalignish, son of Lochnell, ancestor of the present family. He d. 18 July, 1736, aged 95, and was s. by his only son,

ARCHIBALD CAMPBELL, Esq., who m. 1st, Barbara, eldest dau. of Archibald Campbell, Esq. of Inveraw, co. Argyll, and had four sons, all of whom d. unm., except the second, ARCHIBALD, who s. his father; and several daus. He m. 2ndly, Flora, dau. of Donald Maclachlan, of Maclachlan, co. Argyll, but had no further issue. The only surviving son,

ARCHIBALD CAMPBELL, Esq. of Jura, d. in 1764, and was s. by his third son,

ARCHIBALD CAMPBELL, Esq. of Jura, J.P., heritable keeper of Craignish Castle; who m. Sarah, dau. of James Campbell, of St. Germains and Tofts, co. East Lothian, and cousin-german to John, 1st Marquess of Breadalbane, and had issue,

Archibald, lieut.-col. of the 84th foot; who d. unm. in India in 1817.
JAMES, of Jura, d. unm. 2 Dec. 1838.
John-Kirkpatrick, writer to the Signet, of Glenfeochan, co. Argyll; m. Mary-Kirkpatrick, only child of Alexander Campbell, Esq., by whom he left one dau. and heiress, Mary-Kirkpatrick-Aiskell.
COLIN, of Jura, b. 8 Nov. 1772.
Duncan, d. young.
Anne-Penelope, m. in 1797, to Robert Dennistoun, Esq., son of James Dennistoun, Esq. of Dennistoun.
Barbara, m. in 1800, to Alexander Campbell, Esq. of Hallyards, co. Peebles. He d. in May, 1817.

Mr. Campbell d. 15 July, 1835, aged 91.

Arms—Quarterly: 1st and 4th, gyronny of eight, sa. and or; 2nd, arg., a boar's head, couped, ppr.; 3rd, arg., a galley, sa., sails furled and oars in action, ppr.
Crest—A hand holding a spear, ppr.
Motto—Audacos juvo.
Seats—Jura House, and Craignish Castle, co. Argyll.

CAMPBELL OF STRACATHRO.

CAMPBELL, SIR JAMES, Knt. of Stracathro, co. Forfar, b. 3 June, 1790; m. 17 Jan. 1822, Janet, dau. of Henry Bannerman, Esq. of Manchester, and has surviving issue,

I. JAMES-ALEXANDER, b. 20 April, 1825.
II. Henry, b. 7 Sept. 1836.
I. Louisa.

Sir James Campbell was serving as Lord Provost of Glasgow at the birth of the Prince of Wales in 1842, and then received the honour of knighthood. He is son of JAMES CAMPBELL, Esq., and Helen his wife, dau. of John Forrester, Esq. of Ashentree, co. Perth, and grandson, by Mary Mackerecher his wife, of JAMES CAMPBELL, Esq. of Inchnock, co. Perth, who was son of JAMES CAMPBELL, Esq., of the family of CAMPBELL *of Melford*, a scion of the Argyll Campbells. Sir James has had, besides four sisters (Helen, m. to Alexander Fisher; Mary, m. to George Langlands; Janet, m. to Archibald Whitelaw; and Elizabeth, m. to James Blackburn), three brothers, viz.,

John, m. in America, Mary Kennedy, and has issue, John, William-Henry, Mary-Anne, and Helen.
Alexander, d. unm.
William, of Tullichawen, co. Dumbarton, m. Margaret, dau. of Archibald Roxburgh, Esq. of Glasgow, and has issue, James, Archibald, William, John, Elizabeth, and Helen.

Arms—Quarterly: 1st and 4th, gyronny of eight, or and sa.; 2nd and 3rd, arg., a lymphad, sails furled, and oars in action, all sa., flag and pennant flying, gu.
Crest—A boar's head, erased.
Motto—Ne obliviscaris.
Seat—Stracathro, Forfarshire.

CAMPION OF DANNY.

CAMPION, WILLIAM-J., Esq. of Danny, co. Sussex, *b.* 19 July, 1770, high-sheriff in 1820; *m.* 10 Jan. 1797, Jane, dau. of Fancis-Motley Austen, Esq. of Kippington, co. Kent, and has issue,

I. WILLIAM-JOHN, *b.* 16 Nov. 1804, *m.* 17 Jan. 1829, to Harriet, eldest dau. of Thomas-Read Kemp, Esq. of Brighton.
II. Charles-Heathcote, *b.* 14 Feb. 1814.
III. George-Edward, *b.* 1 Dec. 1816.
I. Jane-Bridget, *d. unm.* 24 Nov. 1840.
II. Margaretta. III. Frances-Henrietta.

Lineage.—WILLIAM CAMPION, Esq. of Combwell, son of HENRY CAMPION, of London, was father of SIR WILLIAM CAMPION, knighted in 1618, who settled at Colchester. He *m.* Elizabeth, dau. and co-heir of Sir William Stone, of London, Knt., and, with other children, was father of SIR WILLIAM CAMPION, of Combwell, knighted 7 Nov. 1644, whose eldest son (by Grace his wife, dau. of Sir Thomas Parker, of Ratton, co. Sussex), WILLIAM CAMPION, Esq., *m.* Frances, dau. of Sir John Glynde, Knt., serjeant-at-law to CHARLES II., and was father of HENRY CAMPION, Esq. of Campion Hall, Kent, who *m.* Barbara, dau. and heir of Peter Courthope, Esq of Danny, co. Sussex, and had, with other issue, a dau , Catherine, *m.* to George Courthope, Esq. of Whiligh, co. Sussex, and a son,

WILLIAM CAMPION, Esq., bapt. at Hurstpierpoint in 1700, and *d* in 1771, leaving, by Elizabeth his wife, dau. of Edward Partericbe, Esq. of the Isle of Ely, co. Cambridge, three sons and a dau.,

HENRY-COURTHOPE, of whom presently.
William, of Lewes, co. Sussex, *m.* 1st, Catherine, dau. of William Dawson, Esq. of Portugal, and by her (who *d.* in 1763), had a son, Henry, of The Deanery, South Malling, co. Sussex, *b.* 10 March, 1762, *m.* 1 Oct. 1807, Frances, dau. of the Rev. Henry Watkins, prebendary of York and Southwell, Notts, and is deceased. His widow *m.* 2ndly, in 1838, General Sir Fitzroy Maclean, Bart. He *m.* 2ndly, 5 Sept. 1774, Priscilla, dau. of John Page, Esq. of Oporto, and by her had two sons, William, *d.* an infant; William-Henry, *d. unm.* 1821; and three daus., of whom the youngest, Amelia, *m.* 20 Jan. 1808, George Courthope, Esq. of Whiligh.
Edward, *d.* in 1803, leaving an only child, Frances-Elizabeth, who *d.* in 1804.
Frances-Barbara, *m.* to George Courthope, Esq. of Whiligh.

The eldest son,

HENRY-COURTHOPE CAMPION, Esq. of Danny, *m.* Henrietta, dau. of Sir John Heathcote, Bart. of London, and by her (who *d.* in 1771), left at his decease, in July, 1811, an only son, the present WILLIAM CAMPION, Esq. of Danny.

Arms—Arg., on a chief, gu., an eagle displayed, or.
Crest—A turkey, in his pride, ppr.
Seat—Danny, co. Sussex.

CANDLER OF CALLAN.

CANDLER, WILLIAM, Esq., an officer in the royal navy, J.P. for the co. of Worcester, *s.* his brother in Feb. 1825; *m.* 1st, 4 June, 1829, Louisa, dau. of John Evered, Esq. of Hill House, co. Somerset, which lady *d.* 4 Oct. 1841; and 2ndly, 9 Aug. 1852, Emma-Catherine, youngest dau. of Sir Anthony Lechmere, Bart. of The Rhydd.

Lineage.—The family of Candler is of considerable antiquity in the counties of Norfolk and Suffolk.

WILLIAM CANDLER, Esq., the first of the family who settled in Ireland, was lieutenant-colonel in the army, under CROMWELL, and had considerable grants of land by patents, dated 18 and 20 June, and 28 Nov., 21 of CHAS. II., in the counties of Kilkenny and Wexford. He *m.* Anne, relict of Major John Villiers, and had issue. The elder son,

THOMAS CANDLER, Esq. of Callan Castle, co. Kilkenny, *m.* 1st, Elizabeth, dau. of Capt. William Burrell, by Elizabeth his wife, sister and co-heir of Benjamin Phipps, Dean of Ferns, but had no issue. He *m.* 2ndly, Jane, dau. of Sir Henry Tuite, Bart. of Sonagh, co. Westmeath (by Diana Mabbot, niece of Edward Hyde, the celebrated Earl of Clarendon, and first-cousin of her Royal Highness Anne, Duchess of York, mother of the Queens MARY and ANNE), by whom he had issue,

I. HENRY.
II. William, D.D., of Castlecomer, co. Kilkenny; who *m.* 1st, Miss Aston, and had by her a son, HENRY, LL.D.; and 2ndly, Mary, dau. and co-heir of Charles Ryves, Esq., by whom he had issue,

1 Edward-Candler-Brown, of Prior Park, and Combe Hill, co. Somerset, and of Aghamure, co. Kilkenny, who *d. s. p.*
1 Mary, *m.* — Dobbyn, Esq.
2 Jane, *m.* 1st, to Captain S. Barrett; 2ndly, to Oliver Grace, Esq.; and 3rdly, to James Hamilton, Esq. of Sheephill, co. Dublin.
3 Anne, *m.* to John Blunt, Esq. of Arches Grove, co. Kilkenny, and left an only dau., Mary, *m.* to John Helsham, Esq. of Legget's Rath, co. Kilkenny, by whom she had, with other issue, Edward, who inherited the English estates of his great-uncle, Edward-Candler Brown, and assumed the surname of BROWN; and William, who *s.* to the Irish property of the same gentleman, and took the name of CANDLER.

III. Thomas, of Dublin, *m.*, and left issue, John, of Castlewood, in the Queen's County, who *d. s. p.*

Thomas Candler, of Callan, was *s.* by his eldest son,

THE VENERABLE HENRY CANDLER, D.D., Archdeacon of Ossory, and rector of Callan, who *m.* Anne, dau. of Francis Flood, Esq. of Burnchurch, co. Kilkenny, sister of the Rt. Hon. Warden Flood, Lord Chief Justice of Ireland, and aunt to Sir Frederick Flood, Bart., by whom (who *d.* 11 Dec. 1761), he had issue,

I. THOMAS.
II. William, of Acomb, co. York, capt. 10th regt. of foot; *m.* Mary, only dau. of William Vavasour, Esq. of Weston Hall, co. York (by Anne, dau. of John Chaplin, of Tathwell, co. Lincoln, Esq.), by whom he had issue,

1 HENRY, of whom hereafter.
2 Thomas (Sir), knight of the several Russian Orders of St. Anne, St. George, and St. Vladimir, a rear-admiral in the service of His Imperial Majesty the Emperor of Russia; *m.* 1st, Marie de Lotaroff, a lady of a noble and ancient family of Russia, but had no issue; he *m.* 2ndly, Jane, eldest dau. of John Booker, Esq., His Britannic Majesty's Consul at Constadt, by Isabella, dau. of Captain James Hamilton, of the Isle of Arran, N.B., by whom (who *d.* in 1824) he had Agrapina-Isabella, Annabella-Cope, Jane-Greig, and Mary-Caroline-Catherine.
3 Annabella, *m.* to Sir Jonathan Cope, of Brewerne, co. Oxford, Bart.

III. Anne, *m.* to — Berry, Esq. of Dove Grove, in the King's County, and left issue.

Archdeacon Candler *d.* Dec. 1757, and was *s.* by his eldest son,

THE REV. THOMAS CANDLER, of Kilmoganny, *m.* Sarah, dau. of — Lechwood, Esq., but having no issue, was *s.* by his nephew,

HENRY CANDLER, Esq., eldest son of Capt. William Candler, of Acomb, co. York, by Mary Vavasour his wife. He *m.* Mary, only child of William Ascough, Esq. of Kirby Malzart, co. York, by whom (who *d.* 7 March, 1816), he had issue,

I. HENRY. II. William.
III. Jonathan-Thomas, a lieut.-col. in the Russian Imperial Guards; *d. unm.* 12 Feb. 1832.
IV. Edward, of Morton Pinkney, co. Northampton, deputy-lieut. of that shire; *m.* 14 June, 1836, the Right Hon. Baroness Sempill, and has assumed, by royal license, the surname of SEMPILL only.
V. Charles. VI. George.
I. Annabella. II. Mary.
III. Emma, *m.* the Rev. Charles-William-Henry Evered, rector of Exton, co. Somerset, and has issue, Charles-Edward-Ascough, *b.* in Nov. 1833, lieut. 87th regt.; and Walsingham, *b.* 6 July, 1838.
IV. Hester.

He *d.* 21 Oct. 1815, and was *s.* by his eldest son,

HENRY CANDLER, who *d. unm.* in Feb. 1825, and was *s.* by his brother, the present WILLIAM CANDLER, Esq., R.N., J.P.

Arms—Quarterly: 1st and 4th, parted in tierce, per fesse indented, the chief, per pale, arg. and az., the base, or, a canton, gu., for CANDLER; 2nd and 3rd, sa., a fesse, or, between three asses, passant, arg., for ASCOUGH.
Crest—The figure of an angel, ppr., vested, arg., holding in the dexter hand a sword, the blade wavy, of the first, pommel and hilt, gold.
Motto—Ad mortem fidelis.
Residence—Mavern Lodge, Worcestershire.

CAPRON OF STOKE DOYLE.

CAPRON, GEORGE, Esq. of Stoke Doyle, and Southwick Hall, co. Northampton, *b.* 16 June, 1783; *m.* 27 Oct. 1812, Martha, dau. of William Halliley, Esq. of St. Neots, co. Huntingdon, and has had issue,

I. John-Shukburgh, lieut. 23rd Royal Welsh Fusiliers, *b.* 26 July, 1815, *d. unm.* 18 Sept. 1847.
II. GEORGE-HALLILEY, in holy orders, rector of Stoke-

Doyle, and a magistrate for the co. Northampton, *b.* 23 Nov. 1816.

III. Thomas-William, of the Temple, *b.* 25 Aug. 1818, *m.* Caroline-Mary, eldest dau. of William-Fowler Jones, Esq. of Ashhurst Park, Kent, grandson of John Jones, Esq., by Lucy his wife, eldest sister and co-heir of Sir William Fowler, Bart. of Harnage Grange. By this lady Mr. Capron has one son and one dau., viz., CLAUDE-LYTTELTON, *b.* in 1846, and Ethel-Maud-Mary.

IV. Frederick-Lucas, *b.* 29 Oct. 1820.

V. Charles-Henry-Ward, of St. John's College, Cambridge, *b.* in March, 1826.

I. Martha, *m.* to G.-P. Smith, Esq. barrister-at-law.

II. Georgiana-Marian.

Lineage.—The late THOMAS CAPRON, Esq. of Stoke Doyle, who was buried there in 1829, in his 82nd year, *m.* Elizabeth, dau. of John Lucas, Esq. of Nortoft Manor, co. Northampton, by Anne his wife, dau. of John Ward, Esq. of Guilsborough, high-sheriff of Northamptonshire in 1780, and sister of Sir Thomas Ward, Knt. of Guilsborough. By this lady, who *d.* in 1832, aged 80, Mr. Capron had issue, Thomas-Ward, who *d.* young; William-Lucas, who *d. unm.* in 1802; GEORGE, now of Stoke Doyle and Southwick Hall; Frederick-Ward, who *d.* young; Charles-Thomas; and Ann-Maria, *m.* to Joseph-Charles Martin, Esq. of Oundle.

Arms—Quarterly: 1st and 4th, per chevron, gu. and az., on a chevron, engrailed, arg., between two lions, combatant, in chief, erminois, and a cross-flory, in base, or, three mullets, sa., for CAPRON; 2nd and 3rd, sa., on a chevron, between three losenges, arg., each losenge charged with an ermine spot, another chevron, gu., CAPRON (*ancient*).

Crest—A cross-flory, or, in front of a demi-man, affronté, in armour, ppr., garnished, gold, holding in the dexter hand an arrow, the barb downwards, also ppr., the sinister hand resting on the cross.

Mottoes—Above the crest, "Vigilate et orate;" under the arms, "Sub cruce salus."

Seat—Southwick Hall, Oundle, co. Northampton.

CAPEL OF THE GROVE.

CAPEL, WILLIAM, Esq. of The Grove, Painswick, co. Gloucester, J.P.

Lineage.—This family came originally from How Capel, co. Hereford, and were at a very early period settled at Gloucester, of which city John Capel was mayor in 1484. The same office was filled in 1619, by Christopher Capel, M.P. for Gloucester, from whom sprang the CAPELS *of Prestbury*, and

DR. RICHARD CAPEL, rector of Eastington, who was obliged to resign his parsonage in 1633, and retired to Pitchcombe, where he practised physic, and where he *d.* 1656, aged 75. It is stated on his tomb that he was a magistrate for the co. of Middlesex. He founded the family of CAPEL *of The Grove*.

Arms—Chequy, or and az., on a fesse, gu., three mascles, arg.

Crest—A plume of three ostrich feathers, two arg. and one gu.

Motto—Sic vita humana.

Seat—The Grove, Painswick, Gloucestershire.

CARDINALL OF TENDRING MANOR HOUSE.

CARDINALL, JOHN, Esq. of The Manor House, Tendring, co. Essex, *b.* 15 Sept. 1808.

Lineage.—So far back as 1598, we find William Cardinall, Esq., endowing in that year Queen Elizabeth's Grammar School at Dedham with a farm in Great Bromley, for the education of two poor scholars, who were to be sent to the University of Cambridge.

CLARKSON CARDINALL, Esq., who *m.* Elizabeth, dau. of the Rev. Talbot Lloyd, of the family of LLOYD *of Hintlesham, Suffolk*, was father of JOHN CARDINALL, Esq. of the Manor House, Tendring, who *m.* Sarah, dau. of Palmer Fisher, Esq., formerly of The Abbey, and *d.* in 1847, leaving issue, JOHN, now of the Manor House; Sarah; and Elizabeth.

Seat—Manor House, Tendring, Colchester.

POLE-CAREW OF ANTONY.

POLE-CAREW, WILLIAM-HENRY, Esq. of Antony, co. Cornwall, *b.* 30 July, 1811; *m.* 28 Aug. 1838, Frances-Anne, 2nd dau. of John Buller, Esq. of Morval, and has issue,

I. REGINALD, *b.* 1 May, 1849.

II. Charles-Edward, *b.* 26 Dec. 1853.

I. Geraldine-Maria. II. Fanny-Julia.

Lineage.—THE REV. CAROLUS POLE, rector of St. Breock, in Cornwall, 3rd son of Sir John Pole, 3rd bart. of Shute, *m.* Sarah, dau. of Jonathan Rashleigh, Esq. of Menabilly, by Sarah his wife, dau. of SIR JOHN CAREW, Bart. of East Antony, and left a son,

REGINALD POLE, Esq. of Stoke Damarel, co. Devon, who *m.* Anne, dau. of John-Francis Buller, Esq. of Morval, and had issue, REGINALD, his heir; Charles-Morice, K.C.B., admiral R.N., created a baronet in 1801; Edward; Anne, *m.* to Charles, 1st Earl Somers; and Sarah, *m.* to Henry-Hippisley Coxe, Esq. of Stone Easton, co. Somerset. The eldest son,

THE RIGHT HON. REGINALD POLE, *b.* in 1752, assumed the additional surname of CAREW, in compliance with the testamentary injunction of his kinsman, SIR COVENTRY CAREW, of Antony. He *m.* 1st, 18 Nov. 1784, Jemima, only dau. and heir of the Hon. John Yorke, 4th son of Lord Chancellor Hardwicke, and had by her (who *d.* in 1804), two sons and six daus., JOSEPH, his heir; John-Reginald, who *d.* in 1808; Charlotte-Jemima, *m.* 1st, to Charles-Garth Colleton, Esq. of Haines Hill, Berks, and 2ndly, to Comte Alphonse de Morel; Jemima; Elizabeth-Anne; Harriet, *m.* to John, 1st Earl of St. Germans; Agneta, *m.* to Thomas Somers Cocks, Esq.; and Amabel, *m.* to Francis Glanville, Esq. of Catchfrench, Cornwall. He *m.* 2ndly, 4 May, 1808, Caroline-Anne, dau. of William-Henry, 1st Lord Lyttelton, by whom (who *d.* 11 April, 1883) he had,

WILLIAM-HENRY, now of Antony.

Gerald, in holy orders; *m.* Harriet, 1st dau. of John Buller, of Morval, Esq.; and *d.* 14 March, 1845, *s. p.*

Caroline, *m.* to Major-Gen. Bucknall Estcourt, 2nd son of T.-G.-B. Estcourt, Esq., late M.P. for Oxford University.

Frances-Antonia, *m.* to Joseph Yorke, of Forthampton Court, Tewkesbury, Esq.

Juliana, *m.* to Thomas-James-Agar Robartes, of Lanhydrock, Cornwall, M.P. for East Cornwall.

Catherine, *unm.*

Anna-Maria, *d.* an infant.

Mr. Pole-Carew *d.* 3 Jan. 1835, and was *s.* by his eldest son,

JOSEPH POLE-CAREW, Esq. of Antony, who *m.* 1st, in 1810, Caroline, dau. of John Ellis, Esq., elder brother of Lord Seaford; and 2ndly, the widow of E. Cadogan, but *d. s. p.* 9 March, 1852.

Arms—Or, three lions, passant, sa., quartering the ensigns of POLE.

Crest—A main-mast, the roundtop set off with palisadoes, or, a lion issuing thereout, sa.

Seat—Antony, Cornwall.

CAREW OF CAREW CASTLE.

CAREW, THOMAS-GEORGE WARRINGTON, Esq. of Carew Castle, co. Pembroke, of Crowcombe, co. Somerset, and of Pentrepant, co. Salop, *m.* Mary, only child of the late Thomas Clarke, Esq. of Furnham House, co. Somerset, and has issue.

Lineage.—THOMAS CAREW, Esq. of Carew Castle, Camerton, Crowcombe, Clatworthy, and Stoadley, M.P. for Minehead in 1762, the lineal male descendant of SIR JOHN CAREW, knight banneret, grandson of NICHOLAS CAREU, *temp.* EDWARD I., *m.* Mary, dau. of Francis Drewe, Esq. of Grange, in the co. of Devon, and had an only surviving dau. and heiress,

ELIZABETH CAREW, who *m.* James Bernard, Esq. of the Middle Temple, but had no issue, whereupon the estates passed at her decease, under an entail, to her first-cousin, Mary Carew, eldest dau. of John Carew, of East Antony, in Cornwall. This Mary *m.* in 1794, George-Henry Warrington,* Esq. of Pentrepant, in Shropshire, who, having

* FAMILY OF WARRINGTON.

This family, formerly seated at Aigberth, co. Lancaster, is traceable, through an authenticated pedigree, to remote antiquity. The REV. GEORGE WARRINGTON, rector of Pleasley, co. Derby, and vicar of Hope, co. Flint, grandson of John Warrington, of Aigberth, Esq., *m.* Mary, only dau. and heir of Henry Strudwick, Esq., descended from the baronetical families of Hanmer and Broughton, and left, with other issue,

I. GEORGE-HENRY WARRINGTON, who, marrying the heiress of Carew, of Carew Castle and Crowcombe, assumed, by sign-manual, in 1811, the surname of CAREW only.

II. William Warrington, rector of Thirsk, in Yorkshire; who *m.* Miss Mainwaring.

III. Hanmer Warrington, major in the 4th dragoon-guards, consul-general at Tripoli; who *m.* Jane-Elisabeth, only

assumed the surname and arms of his wife's family, became

GEORGE-HENRY CAREW, Esq. of Carew Castle, co. Pembroke, and Crowcombe, co. Somerset, and had issue,

THOMAS-GEORGE WARRINGTON, his heir.
Henry, who m. Jane-Maria, only child of John Rogers, Esq. of Ayshford, and has a son and a dau.
John-Francis.
Gerald, in holy orders; who m. Miss Black, of Bath.
Nesta, m. to Gabriel Powell, Esq., eldest son of the Rev. Thomas Powell, of Peterstone Court, co. Brecknock.
Mary-Anne, m. to — Luxton, Esq.
Elizabeth-Louisa. Elizabeth. Ellinora.
Caroline-Harriet, m. 2 Jan. 1838, to Col. J.-C. Dansey, royal artillery.

Mr. Carew d. in 1842, and was s. by his son, the present THOMAS-GEORGE-WARRINGTON CAREW, Esq.

Arms—Or, three lioncels, passant, in pale, sa.
Crest—A main-mast, the roundtop set off with palisadoes, or, a lion issuing thereout, sa.
Supporters—Dexter, a lion, sa.; sinister, an antelope, gu.
Motto—J'espère bien.
Seats—Crowcombe Court, and Pentrepant.

CAREW OF BALLINAMONA.

CAREW, ROBERT, Esq. of Ballinamona, co. Waterford, b. 12 Nov. 1810.

Lineage.—A scion of the CAREWS *of Devon*, settling in Ireland, was the ancestor of the Carews of that kingdom, of whom

ROBERT CAREW, Esq., the immediate ancestor of the family before us, m. Elizabeth, dau. and co-heir (with her sister, Catherine, wife of William Hore, Esq. of Harperstown) of John Shapland, a wealthy merchant of Wexford, and had issue, SHAPLAND, of Castleborough (grandfather of Robert-Shapland, LORD CAREW); THOMAS, of Ballinamona; and Ellen, wife of Christmas Paul, Esq. of Paullsville, co. Carlow. The 2nd son,

THOMAS CAREW, Esq. of Ballinamona, co. Waterford, b. 11 Aug., 1718; m. 12 Nov. 1745, Eliza-Rickards, dau. of James May, Esq. of Mayfield, by Letitia his wife, dau. of William, 1st Viscount Duncannon, and had issue, ROBERT-THOMAS, his heir; John-Mutlow, m. Miss Jones, of Mullinabro; Ponsonby, who m. Miss Giles; Elizabeth (Mrs. Chartres); and Letitia, wife of the Rev. John Kennedy, of Fethard Castle, co. Wexford. The eldest son,

ROBERT-THOMAS CAREW, Esq. of Ballinamona, b. 22 May, 1747; m. 4 July, 1771, Frances, dau. of Thomas Boyse, Esq. of Bishop's Hall, co. Kilkenny, and had issue,

THOMAS, his heir.
Robert-Shapland, b. 25 Aug. 1777; capt. in the 18th Hussars, who fell at the battle of Vittoria, in June, 1813.
Margaret, m. to Robert Hunt, Esq., of Sidbury House, Devon.

Mr. Carew d. 11 April, 1834, and was s. by his son,

THOMAS CAREW, Esq. of Ballinamona, J.P., b. 23 Aug. 1775; m. 8 April, 1805, Jane, eldest dau. and co-heir of the late Sir John Alcock, of Waterford, and had issue, ROBERT-THOMAS, now of Ballinamona; John-Henry-Alcock, b. 2 Feb. 1820; Jane; Frances; Marianne; Henrietta, m. 22 Aug. 1842, to Thomas-Edward Ivers, Esq.; and Margaret, m. 25 April, 1842, to James Anderson, Esq. of Grace Dieu Lodge, Waterford. Mr. Carew d. 4 Oct. 1853.

Arms—Or, three lioncels, passant, in pale, sa.
Crest—An antelope, passant, gu.
Seat—Ballinamona Park, co. Waterford.

CAREW OF BEDDINGTON.

CAREW, CHARLES-HALLOWELL, Esq. of Beddington, co. Surrey, m. Mary, dau. of the late Captain Sir Murray Maxwell, R.N., and has issue.

Lineage.—SIR NICHOLAS CAREW, of Beddington, co. Surrey, great-great-grandson of Sir Nicholas Carew, Knt. of Beddington, son of Sir Nicholas Throckmorton, of Paulerspury, by ANNE his wife, dau. and eventual heiress. SIR NICHOLAS CAREW, K.G., of Beddington, represented the county of Surrey in parliament, and was created a Baronet in 1715. He m. Anne, dau. of Nicholas Hacket, Esq. of Bucks, and had one son and one dau., viz.,

NICHOLAS-HACKET, his heir.
Anne, m. 1st, to Thomas Fountayne, Esq. of Melton, in Yorkshire; and 2ndly, to Joshua Ward, Esq. of the Inner Temple.

Sir Nicholas d. in March, 1726-7 (his widow, who m. 2ndly, in 1728, William Chetwynd, Esq., M.P., d. in 1740), and was s. by his only son,

SIR NICHOLAS-HACKET CAREW, of Beddington, who m. April, 1741, the dau. of John Martin, Esq. of Overbury, in Gloucestershire, M.P. for Tewkesbury; but dying without male issue, 19 Aug. 1762, he devised his estates, first, to his dau. Catherine, who d. unm. in 1760, and subsequently to different relations. They ultimately devolved on Richard Gee, Esq., grandson of Richard Gee, Esq. of Beddington, by Philippa, dau. of Nicholas Carew, Esq. of Beddington. Mr. Gee assumed the surname and arms of CAREW, but d. unm. in 1816, bequeathing the property to his brother William's widow, Mrs. Anne-Paston Gee, who d. in 1828, and by her will devised Beddington, &c., to

ADMIRAL SIR BENJAMIN HALLOWELL, who assumed the surname of CAREW; and dying in 1836, was s. by his son, the present CAPT. CAREW, R.N. of Beddington.

Arms—Or, three lioncels, passant, in pale, sa.
Seat—Beddington, near Croydon.

CAREY OF CAREYSVILLE.

CAREY, EDWARD, Esq. of Careysville, co. Cork, m. 1 Sept. 1826, Elizabeth-Margaret, dau. of William Cooke-Collis, Esq. of Castle Cooke, co. Cork, and has issue.

Lineage.—PETER CAREY (stated to have been a son of Thomas Carey, of Carey, co. Devon) went to Ireland and m. Sarah Graham, by whom he was father of

PETER CAREY, of Ballymacpatrick, *alias* Careysville, who m. Elizabeth Greene, and had, besides three daus. (Elizabeth, m. to Power; Anna, m. to Lane; and Katherine, m. to Fenlon), and four sons, who d. s. p., viz., Peter, Thomas, Roger, and George, another son,

JOHN CAREY, of Careysville, who m. in 1737, Anna, dau. of Thomas Maunsell, Esq., and had issue, PETER, of whom presently; John, m. a dau. of Yielding, Esq.; Richard, m. a dau. of Ball; Langor, d. s. p.; Anna, m. to Croly; and Eliza, m. to Power. The eldest son,

PETER CAREY, of Careysville, m. Anna, dau. of Lawton, Esq., and was father (besides two daus., Jane, m. to William Collis; and Anna, m. to the Rev. Alexander Grant) of a son,

PETER CAREY, Esq., of Careysville, who m. 1st, Elizabeth, dau. of John Kelley, Esq. of co. Waterford; and 2ndly, Sarah Moore. By the former he had issue,

Peter, m. Anne Clarke.
Richard, in holy orders, M.A., prebendary of Lismore, and d. in 1820, leaving, by Elizabeth Labarte his wife, a son, the Rev. Robert Carey, prebendary of Lismore.
Langor, m. Margaret Hunter.
EDWARD, now of Careysville, by his father's will.
Sarah.

Seat—Careysville, co. Cork.

CAREY OF ROZEL.

CAREY, THOMAS, Esq. of Rozel, Guernsey, b. 31 Oct. 1780; m. 1st, 7 March, 1803, Mary, dau. of John Le Mesurier, Esq., governor of the island of Alderney, and by her (who d. in 1815) had issue,

I. ALBERT, m. 1st, Leonora, dau. of Col. Cardew, royal engineers; and 2ndly, Frances-Elizabeth-Henrietta, eldest dau. of John Brenton, Esq., son of Judge Brenton, of Halifax, Nova Scotia: by the former he has issue a son, Falkland.
II. Edward, m. Margaret, dau. of Thomas Maingay, Esq. of Guernsey, and has issue.
III. Robert-Gledstanes, m. Emma, dau. of the Rev. Thomas Brock, rector of St. Peter's-in-the-Wood, Guernsey, and has issue.
I. Harriet-Dobree, m. to Col. White, of the 70th regt.
II. Amelia, m. to Ernest le Pelley, Lord of the island of Sark.

He m. 2ndly, Barbara, dau. of Colonel Jackson, of Enniscoe, co. Mayo, M.P., and by her has issue,

---

dau. of Charles Price, Esq., and had issue seven sons and three daus., viz., 1 Hanmer-George; 2 William-Henry, late capt. 3rd dragoon-guards, who m. Emma, dau. of Major Van Cortlandt, and has issue; 3 Charles-Thornhill, 11th light-dragoons, d. in 1839; Frederick-Herbert, H.M.'s vice-consul at Tripoli; 5 Osman, of the 77th regt.; 6 Henry; 1 Jane, m. to Thomas Wood, Esq., H.M.'s vice-consul at Bengazi; 2 Emma, m. to Major Gordon Laing, and is deceased; and 3 Louisa.
IV. Thornhill Warrington, late capt. 8th light-dragoons; who has one son, Strudwick, in holy orders.

I. George-Jackson, Cape Mounted Rifles.

II. Adolphus-Frederic, M.A., in holy orders; *m.* 10 Sept. 1846, Harriet-Mary, dau. of Admiral Sir Jahleel Brenton, Bart., and has issue, 1 Jahleel-Brenton, *b.* 18 July, 1847; Reginald-Orme-Brenton, *b.* 22 Dec. 1848; and 3 Cranstoun-Adolphus-Brenton, *b.* 3 June, 1852.

III. Thomas-Augustus, E. I. Co.'s service.

IV. John-James.

Lineage.—The CAREYS *of Guernsey* have for centuries held a distinguished position in that island, and filled its chief local offices. Their late representative,

ISAAC CAREY, Esq. of Hauteville, Guernsey, son of THOMAS CAREY, Esq. of that island, *m.* Margaret, dau. of Elisha Tupper, Esq. of Guernsey, and had issue,

THOMAS, now of Rozel.
John, of Castle Carey, Guernsey, *b.* 18 April, 1786; *m.* 3 March, 1819, Matilda, dau. of Carteret Priaulx, Esq., and has issue, Carteret-Priaulx, Frederick-Augustus, Osmond, Le Marchant-John, and Elizabeth-Dobree.
Tupper, of Summerland, Guernsey, *m.* Anne, dau. of John Le Mesurier, Esq., and has issue, Tupper, Charles, and Augusta.
De Vic, of Le Vallon, Guernsey, *m.* Fanny, dau. of Thomas Priaulx, Esq., and has issue.
Saumarez, *m.* Elisabeth, dau. of Thomas-Godfrey Dobree, Esq., and has issue. Frederick-Charles.
Havilland, *m.* Augusta, dau. of Thomas-Godfrey Dobree, Esq., and has issue.
Adolphus, *m.* Fanny, dau. of Robert Walters, Esq., M.D.; and *d.* leaving a dau., Fanny.
Henrietta-Tupper, *m.* to her cousin, John Carey, Esq., M.D.
Elizabeth-Dobree, *m.* to Albert Forster, Esq.
Maria, *m.* to the Rev. John-Tupper Connell.

Arms—Arg., on a bend, sa., three roses, of the field.
Crest—A swan, ppr.
Seat—Rozel, island of Guernsey.

CARLEILL OF SEWERBY.

CARLEILL, WILLIAM, Esq. of Sewerby, co. York, D.L., *b.* in 1768; *m.* 18 June, 1788, Eleanor, dau. of William Greene, Esq. of York, and by her (who *d.* 14 June, 1818) had issue,

I. Randolph, *b.* at Brosterfield, 17 Oct. 1794; buried at Longstone, 20 Sept. 1814.

I. Katharine. II. Alicia-Maria, *d.* young.
III. Eleanor, *d.* in 1814. IV. Martha, *d.* in 1830.
V. Anne. VI. Elizabeth. VII. Maria.

Major Carleill, who was only surviving son of Randolph Carleill, Esq. of Brosterfield, co. Derby, D.L., by Eleanor his wife, dau. of Smithson Greene, Esq. of Thundercliffe Grange, represented the ancient family of CARLEILL *of Sewerby*. He *d.* in Aug. 1843, leaving his daus. his co-heirs.

Arms—Arg., on a chevron, sa., between three Cornish choughs, ppr., beaked and legged, gu., as many mullets of six points, or.
Crest—A Moor's head in profile, couped at the shoulders, ppr.
Seat—Longstone Hall, Derbyshire.

CARLETON OF MARKET HILL.

L'ESTRANGE-CARLETON, GEORGE, Esq. of Market Hill, co. Fermanagh, *b.* in 1811.

Lineage.—CHRISTOPHER CARLETON, Esq. of Market Hill, co. Fermanagh, 2nd son of Lancelot Carleton, Esq. of Rossfad, near Enniskillen, who was slain in the service of CHARLES I., and grandson of Lancelot Carleton, Esq. of Brampton Foot, in Cumberland, *m.* Anne, dau. and heir of the Rev. George Hamilton; and dying in 1716, left three sons, ALEXANDER, a magistrate for Meath, who *d. s. p.* in 1745; GEORGE, of whose line we have to treat; and Lancelot, A.M., father of Alexander Carleton, banker of London. The 2nd son,

GEORGE CARLETON, Esq. of Market Hill, high-sheriff of the co. of Monaghan, *m.* Catherine, dau. of John Creighton, Esq., and was father of

CHRISTOPHER CARLETON, Esq. of Market Hill, who *m.* Henrietta-Maria, dau. of Col. Creighton, and had three daus., of whom MARY, *m.* in 1765, HENRY-PEISLEY L'ESTRANGE, of Moystown, King's Co., Esq., and had issue: the 2nd son,

CHRISTOPHER L'ESTRANGE, Esq., assumed the surname and arms of CARLETON at the decease of his mother in 1830, and became of Market Hill. He was *b.* in Feb. 1776; and *m.* 8 May, 1808, Jane, dau. of Col. Jackson, M.P. of Enniscoe, co. Mayo, and had issue,

HENRY, *d. unm.* 31 Oct. 1839.
GEORGE L'ESTRANGE-CARLETON, now of Market Hill.
Christopher-Carleton L'Estrange, *m.* 19 Feb. 1852, Charlotte, youngest dau. of Arthur Cooper, Esq. of Cooper's Hill, co. Sligo.
William-Jackson L'Estrange.
Guy-James L'Estrange, in holy orders.
Mary, *m.* 10 Aug. 1848, to John George, Esq., M.P., of Cahore House, co. Wexford.
Janette, 20 Sept. 1837, William Orme, Esq. of Owenmor, co. Mayo; and *d.* 30 Aug. 1850.
Elizabeth-Henrietta, *d.* 7 Oct. 1835.
Alice.
Louisa, *m.* 13 Sept. 1842, to William-Digges La Touche, Esq. of Stephen's Green.
Sidney-Fanny, *m.* 16 May, 1843, to Robert Orme, Esq. of Mountanvil, co. Dublin.
Sarah, *d. unm.* 8 April, 1838.

Major Carleton, who served as high-sheriff of Fermanagh in 1811, *d.* in Sept. 1843.

Arms—Erm.; on a bend, sa., three pheons, arg.
Crest—A dexter arm, embowed, holding an arrow, ppr., the arm naked to the elbow, the shirt folded above it, arg., and vested above, gu.
Seat—Market Hill, co. Fermanagh.

CARLYON OF TREGREHAN.

CARLYON, THOMAS-TRISTREM-SPRY, Esq. of Tregrehan, co. Cornwall, and of Greenaway, co. Devon, Esq., B.A., major 3rd dragoon-guards, *b.* 6 April, 1822.

Lineage.—"This old and respectable family," says one of the Cornish historians, "has principally resided, for upwards of three centuries, in the parishes of St. Austell and St. Blazey. The surname of Carlyon, in connexion with Cornwall, is derived from very remote antiquity; for, besides the Barton of Carlyon, near Truro, it is on record that a seaport town of the name was formerly in existence on the north-west coast of the county." The Carlyons represent a branch of the great house of Tredenham, eminent in Cornwall from the time of the early Plantagenets.

PHILIP CARLYON, of Tregrehan, Esq., son and heir of Thomas Carlyon, Esq. of Tregrehan, by Elizabeth his wife, dau. and co-heir of Philip Hawkins, Esq. of Pennans, and Elizabeth Scobell his wife, whose mother, Mary, was 2nd dau. and co-heir of Sir Joseph Tredenham, Knt. of Tregonan, governor of St. Maw's, *m.* Elizabeth, only child of the Rev. Samuel Trewbody, of Boscundle, and niece of Edward-Craggs, the 1st Lord Eliot, of Port Eliot. By this lady he had a son and heir,

EDWARD-TREWBODY CARLYON, of Tregrehan, Esq., at whose decease, *s. p.*, the estates devolved upon (the eldest son of his uncle, the Rev. Thomas Carlyon, of St. Just, in Roseland, by Anne his wife, dau. and co-heir of William Gwavas, of Penzance, Esq.) his first-cousin,

THOMAS CARLYON, of Tregrehan, Esq. high-sheriff of Cornwall in 1802; who *m.* his cousin, Mary, only dau. and heir of William Carlyon, Esq. of St. Austell, by Elizabeth his wife, dau. and co-heir of the Rev. John Pomeroy, of St. Ewe, by Thomazina Hooker his wife, great-niece of the celebrated divine, Richard Hooker. By this lady (who *d.* 13 Jan. 1821), Mr. Carlyon had issue, WILLIAM, his heir; EDWARD, successor to his brother; Thomas, *d.* young; Mary, *m.* to Capt. Collins, R.N., of Trewardale; Eliza, wife of Clement Carlyon, M.D. of Truro; and Harriet. He *d.* 16 Dec. 1830. He was *s.* by his elder son,

WILLIAM CARLYON, of Tregrehan, Esq., barrister-at-law; *b.* 7 Jan. 1781; *d. unm.* 27 May, 1841, and was *s.* by his brother,

EDWARD CARLYON, Esq. of Tregrehan and Greenaway, J.P. and D.C., major-general in the army; *b.* in 1783; who *m.* in 1820, Anna-Maria, elder dau. of Admiral Spry, of Place and Tregolls, co. Cornwall, and by her (who *d.* 13 June, 1854) had issue,

THOMAS-TRISTREM-SPRY, now of Tregrehan.
Edward-Augustus, M.A., barrister-at-law; *b.* 3 June, 1823.
George-Gwavas, capt. 1st royal regt. of foot; *b.* 21 July, 1824.
Richard-Hawkins, lieut. R.A.; *d.* 27 April, 1845.
Samuel-Alfred, *d.* 14 Aug. 1830.
William-Pomeroy, *d.* in 1853.
Horatio, *b.* 12 May, 1833.
Arthur-Hooker, *b.* 10 March, 1835.
Tredenham-Fitzherbert, *b.* 3 July, 1841.
Anna-Maria, *m.* to Edward Coode, Esq., J.P., of Trevor Cottage, St. Austell.

Major-Gen. Carlyon *d.* 4 July, 1854.

Arms—Sa., a plate between three castles, arg., each charged with a cross-crosslet, gu.

N 2

Crest—A demi-lion, rampant, gu., ducally crowned, or, collared, arg., holding between his paws a bezant.
Motto—Turris tutissima virtus.
Seat—Tregrehan, St. Austell, Cornwall.

CARNE OF NASH.

NICHOLL-CARNE, ROBERT-CHARLES, Esq. of Nash, co. Glamorgan, J.P. and D.L., constable of the Castle of St. Quintin, barrister-at-law, *b.* 27 April, 1806; *m.* 15 May, 1838, Sarah-Jane, dau. and co-heir of the Rev. Nathaniel Poyntz, M.A., of Longworth, Berks, of the ancient family of POYNTZ *of Iron Acton*, co. Gloucester.

Lineage.—The ancient family of CARNE *of Nash* is deduced in a direct and unbroken line from YNYR, King of Gwent, who *s.* his brother, Ithel, slain in 846. His great-great-grandson,

THOMAS O'R GARNE, son of Iddyn, King of Gwent, was brought up at Pencarne, whence he was named Carne, which has continued the surname of the family. He was father of

SIR DEVEREUX CARNE, Knt., called in some pedigrees SIR DYFRYG CARNE, whose great-grandson, WILLIAM CARNE, *m.* Margaret, dau. and heir of Owen ap Cradock ap Justin, and was father of SIR JOHN CARNE, Knt., lord of Nether Gwent, who, by Joan his wife, dau. and heir of Sir Thomas Moore, Knt., was father of THOMAS CARNE, Esq., whose son (by Mabel his wife, dau. of Howel ap Jorweth), JOHN CARNE, Esq., *m.* Elizabeth, dau. and heir of Sir Nicholas Poyntz, Knt., and was father of

HOWELL CARNE, of Cowbridge, who became seated at Nash, by marrying Tibet, dau. and heir of Alexander Giles, of that place, a younger son of the GILES's *of Gileston*, Glamorgan. Their son,

JOHN CARNE, of Nash, *m.* Isabel, dau. of Howell Gwylym Jenkin, Esq. of Berth hir ap Thomas, of Monmouthshire, and had a son and heir,

HOWELL CARNE, of Nash, living 9th HENRY VIII., *m.* Cecil, dau. and heir of William Kemeys, of Newport, and had, with younger children, RICHARD, of Nash, of whom hereafter; and Edward (Sir), Knt., ancestor of the distinguished family of CARNE *of Ewenny*. The eldest son,

RICHARD CARNE, Esq. of Nash, *m.* 1st, a dau. of Rees Mansel, Esq. of Oxwich, S.P., and 2ndly, Joan, dau. and heir of Jenkin ap Edward Dalton or Dalden, Esq. of Penmark, by whom he left, with three daus., two sons,

I. JOHN, of Nash, sheriff of Glamorgan in 1561, *m.* Margaret, dau. of Sir John Ragland, of Carnlloyd, in Lancarvan, by Eleanor his wife, dau. of Sir William Courtenay, and had seven daus. His widow *m.* John Sheppard, Esq. of Aleston, Wilts, and afterwards Richard Bassett, Esq. of Beaupré. The daus. were,
1 Mary, *m.* Edward Prichard, Esq. of Lancaiach, sheriff of Glamorgan in 1599.
2 Elizabeth, *m.* 1st, James Matthews, Esq. of Roose; 2ndly, Watkin Lougher, Esq. of Tytheegston.
3 Cicely, *m.* Giles Kemys, Esq. of Newport.
4 Barbara, *m.* 1st, James, 2nd son of James Turberville, Esq. of Sutton in Landow, and 2ndly, to Thomas Griffiths.
5 Jane, *m.* William Griffith, of Lanveythin.
6 Catherine, *m.* Edward Bassett, Esq. of Fishwear, in St. Mary's Church, heir of Bewper.
7 Margaret.
II. WILLIAM, of whom hereafter.

The 2nd son,

WILLIAM CARNE, Esq. of Nash (successor to his brother), *m.* Elizabeth, dau. and heir of William Vann, Esq. of Marcross and Lantwit, by Catherine his wife, dau. of Sir George Mathews, of Radyr, and was father of

SIR EDWARD CARNE, Knt. of Nash, receiver-general of South Wales, and one of the four tellers of the Exchequer, *m.* Mary, dau. of Sir Edward Mansel, of Margam, by Lady Jane his wife, dau. of Henry, Earl of Worcester, and left at his decease a son and successor,

WILLIAM CARNE, Esq. of Nash, who *m.* Jane, dau. and heir of William Thomas, Esq. of Llanmihangle, by Eleanor his wife, dau. of Sir John Carne, of Ewenny, and had, with other children, a son and successor,

THOMAS CARNE, Esq. of Nash, sheriff of Glamorgan in 1690, *m.* in 1652, Jane, dau. of Sir Edward Stradling, Bart. of St. Donat's Castle, by Mary his wife, dau. of Sir Thomas Mansel, of Margam, and was *s.* by his son,

THOMAS CARNE, Esq. of Nash, who went to Ireland in his father's lifetime, and *d.* there. He *m.* in 1675, Catherine, dau. and heir of William Bassett, Esq. of Welsh St. Donats, and was father of

EDWARD CARNE, Esq. of Nash, who *m.* Grace, dau. of William Mathew, Esq. of Aberamon and Roose, sheriff of Glamorgan in 1693, descended from Sir David ap Mathew, standard-bearer to EDWARD II., and dying 28 Jan. 1713, was buried at Cowbridge, and *s.* by his son,

JOHN CARNE, Esq. of Nash, and of Marcham, Berks, sheriff of Glamorganshire in 1731, who *m.* in 1723, Elizabeth, dau. and co-heir of Charles Loder, Esq. of Hinton, Berks, and had issue,

JOHN, his heir.
Edward, Fellow of Jesus College, Oxford, instituted to the rectory of Marcross in 1770, incumbent of Holyhead, and prebendary of Landaff, *d.* at Oxford, 28 Sept. 1787, aged 48.
CHARLES-LODER, capt. R.N., *b.* 25 Sept. 1742, *m.* Elizabeth Robinson, widow, dau. of the Rev. Rees Davies, of Lanmaes, and had two daus., ELIZABETH, *m.* 29 April, 1800, to the Rev. Robert Nicholl, M.A. of Dimlands; ELEANOR, *d. unm.* 29 May, 1822.
Catherine, *m.* to the Rev. Richard-Vaughan Norman, and *d. s. p.*
Eleanor, *m.* in 1767, George Kemeys, Esq. of Newport, and *d. s. p.* in 1803.
Mary, *m.* to her cousin, the Rev. John Loder, of Hinton, Berks, and had one dau., *m.* to the Rev. Robert Symonds, of Herefordshire.

The eldest son,

THE REV. JOHN CARNE, of Nash, rector of Plumtree, Notts, and prebendary of Landaff, *m.* his cousin Eleanor, dau. of Richard Carne, and *d.* at Nash, 1 Oct. 1798, leaving an only dau. and heiress, ELEANOR CARNE, of Nash, who *m.* in 1798, Thomas Markham, Esq. of Cheltenham, but *d. s. p.* 10 Oct. 1842, when the estates devolved, under the entail, on

THE REV. ROBERT CARNE, of Dimlands, in right of his wife Elizabeth. This gentleman, *b.* 13 April, 1763, was son of Whitlock Nicholl, Esq. of The Ham, co. Glamorgan, and assumed, together with his sons, by royal license, 16 Dec. 1842, the surname of CARNE; *m.* 1st, 7 Aug. 1792, Mary, dau. of Daniel Woodward, Esq., and niece of Richard Huntley, of Boxwell Court, co. Gloucester, and by her (who *d.* 1 April, 1799), had one child, who *d.* in infancy. He *m.* 2ndly, 29 April, 1800, Elizabeth, dau. and heir of Capt. Charles-Loder Carne, and eventually heiress to her uncle, the late Rev. John Carne, of Nash, and by her had issue,

ROBERT-CHARLES, now of Nash.
JOHN-WHITLOCK, of Dimland Castle.
Emma-Anne, *m.* 8 Oct. 1833, to Evan Wilkins, Esq. of Llantwitt Major, and has two daus., Emma-Janetta and Ellen.
Anna-Maria, *m.* 17 April, 1833, to Col. Robert-K. Dawson, Royal Engineers, one of the Tithe Commissioners for England and Wales. She *d.* 27 Sept. 1837, leaving issue, Robert-Nicholl and Ellen-Jane.
Ellen-Louisa, *m.* in 1843, the Rev. John Williams, rector of Marcross, and *d.* in 1847, leaving Charles-Carne and Mary-Frances.
Frances-Susanna, *d. unm.* 24 April, 1839.

Arms—Gu., a pelican on her nest, with wings displayed, or, feeding her young and vulning herself, ppr.
Crests—A pelican, displayed, with two heads, sa., issuing from a ducal coronet, ppr.
Mottoes—Above the shield, "En toute loyale;" under the arms, "Fy ngobaith sydd yn nuw."
Seat—Nash Manor House, co. Glamorgan.

CARNE OF DIMLAND CASTLE.

NICHOLL-CARNE, JOHN-WHITLOCK, Esq., D.C.L. and M.A., of Dimland Castle, Glamorganshire, J.P. and D.L., barrister-at-law, *b.* 17 April, 1816; *m.* 10 April, 1844, Mary-Jane, only dau. of Peter-Whitfield Brancker, Esq. of Wavertree, Lancashire, by Elizabeth his wife, dau. and heiress of John Houghton, Esq. of that place, and has issue,

I. EDWARD-STRADLING-NICHOLL, *b.* 8 Sept. 1849.
II. John-Devereux-Vann-Loder, *b.* 20 April, 1854.
I. Elizabeth-Mary. II. Grace-Mansel-Carne.
III. Blanch-Elinor. IV. Eva-Loder-Brancker.

John Nicholl-Carne is 2nd son of the late Rev. Robert Carne, of Nash and Dimland Castle, by Elizabeth his wife, dau. and heir of Captain Charles Loder Carne.

Arms, &c.—See CARNE *of Nash*.
Seat—Dimland Castle, Cowbridge.

CARNEGIE OF BOYSACK AND SPYNIE.

See LINDSAY-CARNEGIE.

CARPENTER OF MOUNT TAVY.

CARPENTER, JOHN, Esq. of Mount Tavy, co. Devon, b. 28 Feb. 1839; s. his father, 16 May, 1842.

Lineage.—JOHN CARPENTER, Esq., who m. Mary, sister of William Spry, of Tavistock, had (with four daus., viz., Hannah, m. to John Bolt, Esq.; Mary, m. to the Rev. C. Porter; Deborah; and Catherine) six sons,

John, father of Mrs. Hale, of Hingston House.
Nathaniel, who had a son, Coryton; and two daus., one m. to Admiral Bodger, the other to Mr. Rowe, of Launceston.
Samuel, of Launceston, who m. Elizabeth Hodge, and had, with two daus., four sons, 1 John, whose son, John, an officer in the army, m. in 1797, Teresa, dau. of George-Fieski Heneage, Esq. of Hainton, co. Lincoln, and has issue; 2 Charles, of Moditonham; 3 James, admiral, R.N., m. and had issue; 4 Samuel, barrister-at-law, d. in 1815, leaving issue.
Joseph, father of the Rev. William Carpenter.
BENJAMIN, of whom presently.
Philip.

The 5th son,

BENJAMIN CARPENTER, Esq., m. Patience Edgecumbe, and was father of

JOHN CARPENTER, Esq., who m. Christian Phillipps, and had issue, JOHN-PHILLIPPS, his heir; Benjamin-Edgecumbe; Charles-Coryton; George; Elizabeth-Pomeroy; Patience; and Christian. The eldest son,

JOHN-PHILLIPPS CARPENTER, Esq. of Mount Tavy, co. Devon, m. Elizabeth Stubling, and d. in 1812, leaving (with a dau., Patience-Christian, m. 24 Aug. 1807, to Sir William-L.-Salusbury Trelawny, Bart. of Trelawny,) two sons, JOHN, his heir; and Jonathan-Phillipps, in holy orders, who m. 16 April, 1827, Harriett, eldest dau. of the Rev. William Garnier, and d. 26 Aug. 1841. The elder son,

JOHN CARPENTER, Esq. of Mount Tavy, J.P., b. 30 Dec. 1796, m. 19 July, 1828, Lucy, 4th dau. of the Rev. William and Lady Harriett Garnier, of Hampshire, and d. 16 May, 1842, leaving (with three daus., Elizabeth-Harriet, m. to the Rev. H. M. Sims, rector of Hinderwell, co. York; Lucy, m. to Henry Clarke, Esq. of Efford Manor, co., Devon; and Anne) an only son, the present JOHN CARPENTER, Esq. of Mount Tavy.

Motto—Spernit pericula virtus.
Seat—Mount Tavy, co. Devon.

CARROLL OF BALLYNURE.

CARROLL, HENRY, Esq. of Ballynure, co. Wicklow, J.P. and D.L., high-sheriff in 1826, b. 22 Sept. 1799; m. 3 Aug. 1822, Catherine, dau. of David Mitchell, Esq. of the island of Jamaica.

Lineage.—JAMES CARROLL, Esq., son of James Carroll, Esq., m. Miss Bagenal, sister of Beauchamp Bagenal, of Dunleckney and Bagenalstown, co. Carlow, Esq., and was father of

WALTER-BAGENAL CARROLL, Esq. of Ballynure, who m. in 1796, Charity, dau. of Richard Rice, of Mount Rice, co. Kildare, Esq., and dying 19 Nov. 1801, was s. by his only son, the present HENRY CARROLL, Esq. of Ballynure.

Arms—Arg., two lions, combatant, gu., supporting a sword, of the first, hilted and pommelled, or.
Crest—On the stump of an oak, sprouting new branches, ppr., a hawk, of the last, belled, or.
Motto—In fide et in bello forte.
Seat—Ballynure, co. Wicklow.

CARTER OF ERRIS.

CARTER, WILLIAM-HENRY, Esq. of Erris, co. Mayo, formerly of Castle Martin, co. Kildare, b. 18 Dec. 1783; m. 28 June, 1809, Elizabeth, 3rd dau. of Francis Brooke, Esq., and sister of Sir Henry Brooke, Bart. of Colebrooke, co. Fermanagh, and by her (who d. 21 March, 1820) has issue,

I. THOMAS-SHAEN, b. 10 Sept. 1813, m. 21 July, 1842, Maria-Susan, only surviving child and heiress of John-Henry Tilson, of Watlington Park, Oxon, Esq. and has issue,
1 HENRY-TILSON-SHAEN, b. 21 June, 1845.
2 George-Tilson-Shaen, b. 4 March, 1847.
3 Thomas-Tilson-Shaen, b. 16 June, 1848.
4 Arthur-Tilson-Shaen, b. 14 Sept. 1851.
5 Francis-Tilson-Shaen, b. 24 Sept. 1852.
1 Augusta-Susanna-Shaen.
2 Elizabeth-Sophia-Shaen.

I. Susanna, m. 26 Oct. 1846, to Francis-Sedleir Prittie, Esq., formerly a captain in the army, 3rd son of the Hon. Francis-Aldborough Prittie, only brother of Henry, 2nd Lord Dunalley, and has issue.

Mr. Carter m. 2ndly, 10 June, 1846, Frances, 2nd dau. of Richard, late Bishop of Waterford and Lismore, and sister of Robert, 5th Earl of Mayo. Mr. Carter was a magistrate of Kildare for thirty-five years, and deputy-lieutenant, and served as high-sheriff for that county in 1817.

Lineage.—THOMAS CARTER, of Robertstown, co. Meath, Esq., a gentleman whose services to his country at the Revolution were very considerable, for he not only served King WILLIAM at the battle of the Boyne, but secured divers useful books and writings belonging to King JAMES and his secretaries; m. twice: by his 1st wife he was father of the RT. HON. THOMAS CARTER. Mr. Carter m. 2ndly, 2 Aug. 1702, Isabella, dau. of Matthew, 2nd son of Sir Mathew Boynton, of Barmeston, in Yorkshire, and widow of Wentworth, 4th Earl of Roscommon (the poet), but by her he had no issue. His son,

THE RT. HON. THOMAS CARTER, Master of the Rolls, Secretary of State, and P.C., of Robertstown and Rathnally, co. Meath, m. 1719, Mary, dau. and co-heiress (with her sister, the Viscountess Jocelyn) of Thomas Claxton, Esq. of Dublin, and had issue,

THOMAS, M.P. for Old Leighlin, m. to Anna-Maria, sister of Sir George Armytage, of Kirklees, co. York, and by her (who m. 2ndly, 18 Sept. 1766, John Nicholson, Esq. of Balrath, co. Meath) had issue one dau., MARY, m. to Skeffington Thompson, Esq. of the co. Meath.
HENRY-BOYLE, of whom presently.
Frances, m. 1st, 27 Feb. 1749, to the Rt. Rev. Dr. Philip Twysden, bishop of Raphoe, by whom she had issue an only dau., Frances, m. 4 March, 1770, to George-Bussey, 4th Earl of Jersey. Mrs. Twysden m. 2ndly, Gen. James Johnston, colonel of the Scots Greys.
Susan, m. 21 April, 1743, to Thomas Trotter, of Duleek, co. Louth, grandfather of Elizabeth, Marchioness of Thomond.
Mary, d. unm.

The 2nd son,

HENRY-BOYLE CARTER, Esq. (a capt. in Col. Irwin's regt.) of Castle Martin, m. 23 Feb. 1750, Susanna, dau. and coheiress (with her sister, Elizabeth, who m. 1 June, 1738, John Bingham, of Newbrook, grandfather of John Bingham, 1st Lord Clanmorris), of Sir Arthur Shaen, Bart. of Kilmore, co. Roscommon, and widow of James Wynne, Esq. of Haslewood, co. Sligo, and by her had issue,

THOMAS, his heir.
Arthur, col. in the 18th dragoons, d. unm.
Henry, capt. in the Scots Greys, d. s. p.
Mary, m. to John Kirwan, Esq. of Castle Hackett, co. Galway, and had issue.

The eldest son,

THOMAS CARTER, Esq. of Castle Martin, b. 20 May, 1753, m. in Jan. 1783, Catherine, dau. of the Hon. John Butler, brother of Humphrey, 1st Earl of Lanesborough, and had issue,

WILLIAM-HENRY, now of Erris.
John, an admiral R.N., m. Julia, dau. of M. Georges, Esq., and has issue.
Thomas, late a capt. in the royal artillery.
Margaret, m. to James Hamilton, Esq. of Ballymacoll, co. Meath, deceased, leaving issue.

Arms—Arg., two lions, combatant, sa., quartering SHAEN, viz., or, a lion, rampant, vert.
Crest—A talbot, passant, arg., on a mural crown, sa.
Motto—Sub libertate quietem.

CARTHEW OF WOODBRIDGE ABBEY.

CARTHEW, MORDEN, Esq. of Woodbridge Abbey, co. Suffolk, lieut.-col. of the 21st regt., Hon. E. I. Co.'s service, Madras, b. 25 Oct. 1804; m. 16 July, 1827, Jemima-Borland, dau. of John Ewart, Esq. of Edinburgh, and has,

I. MORDEN, b. 21 June, 1832, in the Madras army.
II. Charles-Alfred, b. 5 Sept. 1841.
III. Ewart, b. in 1846.
I. Margaret, m. to Lieutenant Rigg.
II. Emily-Jane. III. Fanny-Jemima. IV. Mary.

Lineage.—The family of Carthew (in Cornish, Cardu or Carthu) has given its name to three places in Cornwall—Carthew in Madron, Carthew in St. Issey, and Carthew in St. Austell; and when Norden wrote, was seated at Boskenna, in St. Burien.

RANULPHUS DE CARDU or CARTHU was a person in good consideration in Cornwall in the reign of EDWARD II. From him descended the CARTHEWS *of Cannalidgy*, Cornwall, of whom was

THOMAS CARTHEW, Esq., *b.* in April, 1657, who had Cannalidgy in the lifetime of his father, Thomas, and became an eminent serjeant-at-law. He died and was interred in the Temple Church, 12 Feb. 1704. He *m.* Mary, dau. and co-heiress of John Colby, Esq. of Banham, in Norfolk; Anne, the other dau., having *m.* his friend, Edward North, Esq. of Benacre, in Suffolk. By this lady, who *d.* 15 June, 1726, he left issue two sons, THOMAS, his heir; and John, one of his Majesty's carvers, of Bergh Apton, in Norfolk, *d. unm.* 23 Jan. 1770. The elder son,

THOMAS CARTHEW, Esq., J.P., of Benacre Hall and Woodbridge Abbey, *b.* 30 June, 1687, barrister-at-law, *m.* 1st, in 1710, Sarah, dau. of Sir Thomas Powys, Knt., judge of the Queen's Bench, by whom he had four daus.,

Anne, *m.* to John Norris, Esq. of Witton, by whom she was the mother of John Norris, Esq., founder of the Norrisian Professorship of Cambridge, whose only dau. and heiress *m.* to John, Baron Wodehouse, of Kimberly.
Mary, *m.* to Stephen Gardiner, Esq. of Norwich, by whom she had an only child, Mary, who *m.* Thomas Berney Bramston, Esq. of Skreens, in Essex.
Elizabeth, *d. unm.*
Sarah, *m.* to Henry Lossen, Gent.

His wife dying 17 Aug. 1727, was buried at Benacre, and Mr. Carthew *m.* 2ndly, Miss Elizabeth Mitchell, and by her (who survived, and *m.* 2ndly, the Rev. Thomas Morden) left at his decease, 20 March, 1741-2, a son, THOMAS, and four daus., of whom

Grace, *m.* 1st, to Lieut.-Col. Charles Owen, of Nash, in Pembrokeshire, by whom she had one son, Wyrriot Owen, who *d. s. p.;* 2ndly, Thomas Schreyr, Esq. of Jamaica.
Caroline, *m.* to Sampson Arnold, Esq. R.N.

THE REV. THOMAS CARTHEW, M.A., F.S.A., J.P. and D.L., of Woodbridge Abbey, rector of Little Bealings, only surviving son and heir, *b.* at Benacre, 4 Aug. 1732, sold Benacre to Thomas Gooch, Esq. He *m.* 1st, 31 Aug. 1754, Elizabeth, dau. and heir of the Rev. Thomas Morden, of Weston in Suffolk, rector of Cantley in Norfolk, younger son of William Morden, Esq. of Suffield, in Norfolk, by Judith, sister and co-heir of Harbord Harbord, Esq. of Gunton. By this lady, who *d.* 13 Dec. 1768, he had issue,

I. WILLIAM, of whom hereafter.
II. Morden, *b.* 27 Nov. 1760, rector of Frettenham-cum-Stanninghall, and vicar of Hoveton St. Peter and Hoveton St. John, which he exchanged for the vicarage of Mattishall, all in Norfolk, *m.* Emily, dau. of George-Tweed Pyke, Esq. of Baythorn Park, co. Essex, and *d.* 10 June, 1821, leaving two sons and seven daus. (his widow *d.* at Leamington Priors),
 1 MORDEN, now of Woodthorpe Abbey, as successor to his uncle.
 2 Edward, now of Guelph, Upper Canada, *m.* in 1847, Hannah, dau. of the late James Secord, Esq. of Queenston, and relict of Howley Williams, Esq., and has issue.
 1 Emily, *m.* to Walter James, Esq.
 2 Elizabeth, *m.* to James, eldest son of the Rev. J. Wright, rector of East Harling, co. Norfolk.
 3 Harriet, *m.* to Sir John Hammet, Knt., M.D., R.N., F.R.S.
 4 Anna, *m.* to Capt. George Gray, 21st regt., H.E.I.C.S.
 5 Caroline, *m.* to the Rev. John Wakefield.
 6 Louisa, *m.* to Capt. Rickards, 21st regt., H.E.I.C.S.
 7 Frances.
III. Thomas, *b.* 2 May, 1764, originally a first-lieutenant in the royal marines, took holy orders, and was, after his father's decease, instituted to the living of Woodbridge; he *d.* 17 Sept. 1831, leaving, by Anne his wife, dau. of Isaac Boggis, Esq. of Colchester, two sons and a dau.,
 1 Thomas, of Woodbridge, who *m.* 1st, Louisa, dau. of John Clarkson, Esq. of Woodbridge, who *d. s. p.;* 2ndly, his cousin Charlotte, dau. of the Rev. Harrison Shaw, by whom he left at his decease, in 1843, two sons.
 2 William-Morden, of High Hall, in Nettlestead, co. Suffolk.
 1 Anna, wife of Thomas Pytches, Esq., major of the East Suffolk militia.
IV. John, of Woodbridge, *b.* 28 April, 1766; *m.* Mary, dau. of the Rev. Christopher Jeffreson, rector of Tunstal, and *d.* 11 Sept. 1804. His widow afterwards *m.* Captain (afterwards Admiral) John-Fordyce Maples, R.N., C.B.
V. Edward, lieutenant R.N., *b.* 30 July, 1768; *d.* at sea 1800, *unm.*
I. Charlotte, *d. unm.* 1808.
II. Anna, *m.* 1784, to the Rev. William Collett, rector of Swanton Morley, and vicar of Holkham, Norfolk, both deceased; she, the survivor, *d.* 24 Dec. 1830, leaving issue.
III. Frances, *m.* 1790, to the Rev. Harrison Shaw, vicar of Bongate, Westmoreland, both deceased; she, the survivor, *d.* 12 March, 1835, leaving issue.

Mr. Carthew *m.* 2ndly, in 1770, Mary, dau. of Thomas Wall, Esq. of Aldborough, Suffolk, who *d.* in June, 1771, *s. p.*; and 3rdly, 19 May, 1774, Anne, dau. and co-heiress of Robert Denny, Esq. of Eye, co. Suffolk, by whom (who *d.* in childbed, Dec. 1785) he had issue,

I. George, a solicitor at Harleston, co. Norfolk; *b.* 9 Nov. 1777; *m.* 19 June, 1806, Elizabeth, only child of Peter Isaack, Gent. of Wighton, and had issue,
 1 George-Alfred, a solicitor at East Dereham, co. Norfolk.
 2 Robert-Isaack, *d. unm.* 19 June, 1831, aged 21.
 3 Charles, a midshipman of H.M.S. "Redwing," lost at sea in June, 1827, *unm.*
II. Robert, *b.* in 1780, was a captain in the royal artillery, and *d.* at sea, from exhaustion, after the battle of Corunna, in 1809, *unm.*
III. Charles, *b.* in 1781, major 39th regt., *d.* at Chatham in Jan. 1826, leaving, by Mary-Anne his wife, dau. of John-Southwell Brown, Esq. of Mount Brown, co. Limerick, a posthumous dau., Pleasance.
IV. Alfred, *b.* 1783; *d. unm.* at Bombay, in 1807.
I. Mary-Anne, *m.* to Charles Dashwood, Esq. of Beccles, co. Suffolk, and *d.* leaving issue.
II. Louisa, *m.* to the Rev. John-Drew Borton, rector of Blofield, co. Norfolk, both deceased, leaving issue.
III. Laura, *m.* to Searles Wade, of Ipswich, brewer, whom she survived, and has issue.
I. Emily, *m.* to John-Thomas Fuller, Esq. of Heathfield, co. Sussex, captain R.A., *d.* leaving issue.

Mr. Carthew *m.* 4thly, in 1788, Elizabeth, dau. of John Russell, Gent. of Ottley, co. Suffolk, who survived him, without issue. He *d.* 4 Jan. 1791, and was buried at Woodbridge. The eldest son,

WILLIAM CARTHEW, Esq. of Woodbridge Abbey, J.P. and D.L., *b.* 4 Nov. 1758, rear-admiral R.N., *m.* Pleasance, one of the three daus. and co-heirs of Graham-Thomas Myers, Esq., only brother of General Sir William Myers, Bart., K.C.B. He *d.* 31 July, 1827 (his widow, 27 Jan. 1830), without issue. At his death, his nephew, the present MORDEN CARTHEW, Esq., inherited Woodbridge Abbey.

Arms—1st and 4th, or, a chevron, sa., between three murrs, ppr., CARTHEW; quartering, 2nd, az., a chevron between three escallops, within a bordure, engrailed, or, for COLBY; 3rd, arg., a fleur-de-lis, gu., for MORDEN.
Crests—1st, a murr, ppr., ducally gorged, or, CARTHEW; 2nd, a sinister arm in armour, embowed and couped at the shoulder, grasping a broken sword, ppr., for COLBY.
Motto—Bedhoh fyr ha heb drok.
Seat—Woodbridge Abbey, Suffolk.

CARTWRIGHT OF AYNHOE.

CARTWRIGHT, WILLIAM-CORNWALLIS, Esq. of Aynhoe, co. Northampton, *b.* 24 Nov. 1825.

Lineage.—ROWLAND CARTWRIGHT (2nd son of Hugh Cartwright, living in the time of HENRY VII., and brother of William Cartwright, ancestor of the CARTWRIGHTS *of Norwell*, and of Edmund Cartwright, ancestor of the CARTWRIGHTS *of Ossington*, Notts) was father of

JOHN CARTWRIGHT, of Aston, co. Chester, who *m.* Eleanor, dau. of John Shobridge, of the same place, and was father of

RICHARD CARTWRIGHT, Esq. of the Inner Temple, who purchased the manor of Aynhoe. Mr. Cartwright *m.* Mary, 4th dau. of Sir John Egerton, Knt. of Egerton, in Cheshire, and dying 13 Jan. 1637-8, aged 74, was *s.* by his son,

JOHN CARTWRIGHT, Esq. of Aynhoe, a Parliamentarian, who *m.* Catherine, dau. of William Noy, Esq., attorney-general to King CHARLES I., and had an only son, William, of Bloxham, co. Oxford, *b.* in 1634, who *d.* in 1674, *v. p.*, leaving, by Anne, his 1st wife, dau. of Sir Roger Townshend, Bart., a dau., Mary, *m.* 1st, to Robert Fane, Esq., and 2ndly, to Fulk Grosvenor, Esq.; and by Ursula, his 2nd wife, dau. of Ferdinando, 2nd Lord Fairfax, of Cameron, a son, THOMAS, successor to his grandfather, and a dau., Rhoda, *m.* to Lord Henry Cavendish. Mr. Cartwright was sheriff of Oxfordshire in 1654 and in 1670. He *d.* 17 April, 1676, and was *s.* by his grandson,

THOMAS CARTWRIGHT, Esq. of Aynhoe, *b.* in 1671, M.P. for Northamptonshire, who *m.* 30 March, 1699, the Hon. Airmine Crewe, one of the daus. and co-heirs of Thomas, 2nd LORD CREWE, of Steno, and dying in 1747-8, left (with two daus., Armine, *m.* to William Ward, Esq. of York, and Ursula, *m.* to Sir Francis Skipwith, Bart.) a son and successor,

WILLIAM CARTWRIGHT, Esq. of Aynhoe, M.P. for the co. of Northampton from 1754 to 1768, who *m.* 1st, 16 June,

1726, Byzantia, youngest dau. of Ralph Lane, Esq. of Woodbury, in Cambridgeshire, and by her, who *d.* in June, 1738, had (with three daus., who all *d.* young and *unm.*) a son and heir, THOMAS. He *m.* 2ndly, 2 July, 1748, Elizabeth, 3rd dau. of Sir Clement-Cotterel Dormer, Knt. of Rowsham, in the co. of Oxford, and had, William, *b.* 1754, a general in the army, and colonel of the 1st dragoon-guards, *d. unm.* 1827; and Clement, *b.* 1761, fellow of All Souls College, Oxford, *d. unm.* 1828. Mr. Cartwright *d.* in London, 29 June, 1768, and was *s.* by his eldest son,

THOMAS CARTWRIGHT, Esq. of Aynhoe, *b.* at Woodbury Hall, 13 Jan. 1735-6; *m.* 6 April, 1765, Mary-Catherine, dau. of Major-General Thomas Desaguiliers, of Grace, in Essex, by whom (who *m.* 2ndly, 10 April, 1777, Sir Stephen Cotterel, of London) he left at his decease, 24 Aug. 1772 (with four daus., Byzantia, *m.* in 1792, to Sir William-Henry Clerke, Bart.; Mary, *m.* in 1796, to the Rev. Wollaston Pym, of Radwell, Herts; Elizabeth; and Charlotte, *m.* to Richard, 5th Viscount Chetwynd), an only son,

RALPH-WILLIAM CARTWRIGHT, Esq. of Aynhoe, M.P. for Northamptonshire, *b.* 30 March, 1771; *m.* 1st, 12 April, 1794, the Hon. Emma, dau. of Cornwallis, 1st Viscount Hawarden, and by her, who *d.* in 1808, had issue,

- THOMAS (Sir), minister plenipotentiary to the Diet of Frankfort, *b.* in 1795, *m.* in 1824, Maria-Elizabeth-Augusta, dau. of the Count von Sandisell, of Bavaria, and *d.* 17 April, 1850, leaving two sons, WILLIAM-CORNWALLIS, now of Aynhoe, and Thomas-Robert-Brook.
- William (Col.), *b.* 24 Feb. 1797, served in the Peninsula and at Waterloo: he *m.* 6 Aug. 1822, Mary-Anne, dau. and heiress of Henry Jones, Esq. of London, and has issue. His son, Capt. Aubrey-Agar Cartwright, of the 1st battalion of the Rifle Brigade, fell in action at the battle of Inkerman.
- Cornwallis-Richard, *b.* in 1801.
- Robert, *b.* in 1805, barrister-at-law, *m.* 2 March, 1842, to Catherine-Frances, eldest dau. of Andrew-Redmond Prior, Esq.
- Stephen-Ralph, *b.* in 1806, in holy orders, rector of Aynhoe.
- Emma, *d unm.* in Aug. 1827.
- Mary-Catherine, *m.* in 1827, to the Rev. Henry Gunning, son of the late Sir George-William Gunning, Bart.
- Sophia, *m.* in 1831, to William Willes, Esq. of Astrop House, Northamptonshire.

Mr. Cartwright *m.* 2ndly, 29 May, 1810, Julia-Frances, only dau. of the late Colonel Richard Aubrey, and had by her,

- Richard Aubrey, of Edgcott, *b.* in 1811, *m.* 19 Sept. 1848, Mary, eldest dau. of the Rt. Hon. Sir Thomas-Francis Freemantle, Bart. of Swanbourne.
- Henry, *b.* in 1814.
- Frederick-William, *b.* in 1818
- Julia. Frances-Eliza.

Mr. Cartwright was lieut.-col. of the Northamptonshire Yeomanry.

Arms—Erm., a fesse, between three fireballs, sa., issuing flames, ppr.
Crest—A wolf's head, erased, or, pierced through the neck with a spear, arg.
Seat—Aynhoe, Northamptonshire.

CARTWRIGHT OF NORWELL AND NORMANTON.

CARTWRIGHT, GEORGE, Esq., R.N., of Wyberton, co. Lincoln, now resident at Lyme Regis, in Dorsetshire, of which county he is a magistrate, *b.* 24 Jan. 1811; *m.* 3 Nov. 1836, Henrietta-Maria Powell, great-niece and heiress of General Henry-Watson Powell, Governor of Gibraltar.

Lineage.—The CARTWRIGHTS *of Norwell*, now represented by George Cartwright, of Wyberton, are the senior line of the family of Cartwright. WILLIAM CARTWRIGHT, Esq. of Marnham Hall, Notts, high-sheriff in 1742, was lineally descended from William, of Norwell, elder brother of Roland Cartwright, ancestor of the Aynhoe branch. Of his sons, the 3rd, JOHN, the well-known politician, MAJOR CARTWRIGHT, *d. s. p.* 23 Sept. 1824, aged 84; and the 4th, EDMUND, D.D., F.R.S., and F.R.L.S., was the inventor of the power-loom, of wool combing by machinery, &c.; he *m.* 1st, Alice, dau. and co-heir of Richard Whitaker, Esq. of Doncaster, and by her had issue, EDMUND, of whom presently; Mary, *m.* to H.-E. Strickland, Esq.; Elizabeth, *m.* to the Rev. John Penrose (this lady wrote, under the name of Markham, several elementary histories); Anne-Catherine, *d. unm.*; and Frances-Dorothy, author of *Major Cartwright's Life and Correspondence*. Dr. Cartwright *m.* 2ndly, Susanna, dau. of the Rev. Dr. Kearney, and *d.* 30 Oct. 1823. His son and heir,

THE REV. EDMUND CARTWRIGHT, M.A., F.A.S., rector of Earnley, vicar of Lyminster, and prebendary of Chichester, was the able author of the *History of the Rape of Bramber*. He *m.* 1st, in 1794, Sophia, only dau. of John Wombwell, Esq., which lady *d. s. p.* the next year; and 2ndly, Anne, dau. of the Rev. Edward-William Tredcroft, by whom he left at his decease, 18 March, 1833, three sons, viz., EDMUND-WILLIAM, capt. Bombay native infantry, *d. s. p.* in 1842; GEORGE, now of Wyberton; and John, lieut. R.N., *b.* 1820, *m.* 1852, Helena-Augusta, eldest dau. of Major Von Beveroudt, and has a son, George, *b.* 1854.

Arms—Erm., a fesse, gu., between three fire-balls, sa., issuing flames, ppr.
Crest—A wolf's head, erased, or, pierced through the neck with a spear, arg.
Motto—Defend the fold.

CARY OF TORR ABBEY.

CARY, ROBERT-SHEDDEN-SULYARDE, Esq. of Torr Abbey, co. Devon, *b.* 22 June, 1828.

Lineage.—The ancient family of CARY derives its surname from the manor of Cary, or Kari, as it is called in Domesday Book, lying in the parish of St. Giles-in-the-Heath, near Launceston. In the year 1198,

ADAM DE KARRY was lord of Castle Karry, in the co. of Somerset. His descendant,

SIR ROBERT CARY, Knt.* *m.* 1st, Elizabeth, dau. of Sir Philip Courtenay, of Powderham, in Devonshire, and 2ndly, Jane, dau. of Sir William Hanchford, Knt., and widow of Wadham. A proof of the great prowess in arms of this gallant knight is recorded in the following exploit:—"In the beginning of the reign of HENRY V., a certain knight-errant of Arragon, having passed through divers countries, and performed many feats of arms, to his high commendation, arrived here in England, where he challenged any man of his rank and quality to make tryal of his valor and skill in arms. This challenge Sir Robert Cary accepted, between whom a cruel encounter and a long and doubtful combat was waged, in Smithfield, London. But at length this noble champion vanquished the presumptuous Arragonois, for which King HENRY V. restored unto him good part of his father's lands, which, for his loyalty to King RICHARD II., he had been deprived of by King HENRY IV., and authorized him to bear the arms of the knight of Arragon, viz., 'In a field, silver, on a bend, sa., three white roses,' which the noble posterity of this gentleman continue to wear unto this day; for, according to the laws of heraldry, whosoever fairly in the field conquers his adversary, may justify the bearing of his arms." Sir Robert was *s.* at his decease by his son by his 1st marriage, with Elizabeth Courtenay,

SIR PHILIP CARY, Knt. of Cockington, co. Devon, who *m.* Christian, dau. and heir of William Orchard, of Orchard, in Somersetshire, by whom (who *m.* 2ndly, Walter Portman) he had a son and successor,

SIR WILLIAM CARY, Knt., who fell in the battle of Tewkesbury, *anno* 1471, fighting under the banner of Lancaster. He had *m.* 1st, Elizabeth, dau. of Sir William Paulet, of Hinton St. George, co. Somerset, and had a son, ROBERT, his heir. His 2nd wife was Alice, dau. of Sir Baldwin Fulford, of Fulford, co. Devon, Knt., and by her he was father of THOMAS, of Chilton Foliot, who *m.* Margaret, dau. and heir of Sir Robert Spencer, Knt., by Alianore, dau. and co-heir of Edmond Beaufort, Duke of Somerset, and had two sons, SIR JOHN CARY, ancestor of the Viscounts Falkland; and WILLIAM CARY, who *m.* Mary, sister of ANNE BOLEYNE, the unhappy consort of HENRY VIII., and had by her (who *m.* 2ndly, Sir William Stafford, Knt.) a son, HENRY CARY, created by his cousin, Queen ELIZABETH, Baron Hunsdon.† Sir William Cary was *s.* by his elder son,

ROBERT CARY, Esq. of Cockington, who *m.* 1st, Jane, dau. of Sir Nicholas Carew, Knt., and had two sons, JOHN, who *m.* Jane, dau. and heir of Edmund Derick, Esq. of Oakhampton, and had issue; and THOMAS, of Cockington. Robert Cary *m.* 2ndly, Agnes, dau. of Sir William Hody, Knt. of Pillesdon, co. Dorset, and had a son, William. He *m.* 3rdly, Margaret, dau. and heir of William Fulkeram, Esq. of Dartmouth, and had another son, Robert, upon whom he conferred Clovelly, in the north of Devon. The 2nd son of Robert Cary,

THOMAS CARY, Esq., inherited the lands of Cockington

* Sir Robert's brother was Bishop of Exeter.
† His 4th son, ROBERT CARY, was created EARL OF MONMOUTH.

and Chilson. He *m.* Mary, dau. of John Southcot, Esq. of Bovy Tracy, in Devonshire, and had issue,

I. GEORGE (Sir), his heir.
II. John, of Dudley, co. Stafford, *m.* a dau. of — Norton, and had issue,
 1 John, *m.* and left issue.
 2 EDWARD, of whom presently, as part inheritor of the property of his uncle, Sir George Cary, the lord-deputy.
 3 Thomas, of Moushall, co. Stafford, *m.* Martha, dau. of William Steward, of Rowley, in the same shire, and *d.* in 1644. He was father of
  John Cary, of Ditchley, in Oxfordshire, who *m.* Jane, dau. of Richard Nanfant, of the co. Gloucester, and dying in 1664, left several sons.
  Edward Cary, of Moushall.
 4 Edward, *d. s. p.*
 5 GEORGE, who inherited Cockington, and the remainder of his uncle the lord-deputy's estates, *m.* Elizabeth, dau. of Sir Edward Seymour, Bart. of Berry Pomeroy, co. Devon, and had (with three younger sons and a dau.) SIR HENRY CARY, Knt. This gentleman was sheriff of the co. of Devon in the 18th of CHARLES I., and during the civil wars devoted himself and his fortune to the services of that unhappy prince. Having thus consumed a considerable estate, when the royal cause fell he was forced to fly his native land. The house of Stuart was not, however, unmindful of such disinterested devotion, for when the Duke of Ormonde, in a succeeding reign, appeared off Torbay, he assured the family, on the part of his royal master, the CHEVALIER, of that prince's recognition of their great services, and of his wish to grant them high honours and honourable indemnification, in pledge of which he had sent them his father King JAMES II.'s picture, with that of his mother, the Queen, inclosed in a silver box. This memorial is now preserved at Follaton Park.
 6 Dudley, *m.* and had issue.

Thomas Cary was *s.* at his decease by his eldest son,

SIR GEORGE CARY, Knt. of Cockington, treasurer of Ireland, and afterwards lord-deputy. Sir George *m.* 1st, Wilmot, dau. and heir of John Gifford, Esq. of Yeo, in the co. of Devon, and had a dau., Anne, *m.* to Sir Richard Edgcomb, Knt. of Mount Edgcomb. He *m.* 2ndly, Lettice, eldest dau. of Robert, Lord Rich, 1st Earl of Warwick, but by her (who *m.* 2ndly, Sir Arthur Lake, Knt.) he had no children. Sir George *d.* in 1616, and was *s.* by his nephew,

SIR EDWARD CARY, Knt. of Marldon, co. Devon. He *m.* Margaret Blackhurst, of Lancashire, and had two sons and a dau., GEORGE (Sir), his heir; Thomas, of Stantor, co. Devon; and Anne, wife of Sir George Southcott. The elder son,

SIR GEORGE CARY, received the honour of knighthood from King CHARLES I., at Greenwich, 3 July, 1632. He *m.* 1st, Anne, dau. of Sir Charles Manners, Knt., by whom he had a son and dau., who both *d.* young; and 2ndly, a dau. of — Browne, of Hampshire, but had no issue. He *m.* 3rdly, Elizabeth, dau. of Thomas Wells, Esq. of Brambridge, co. Southampton, and had issue, EDWARD, his heir; George, living *unm.* in 1701; Christopher, living *s. p.* in 1701; John, who went to Portugal; Elizabeth, *m.* to Sir Thomas Manby, Knt. of Brentwood; Frances; Margery; and Constance, *m.* to George Blount, Esq. Sir George Cary, who purchased Torr Abbey from the Earl of Londonderry, *d.* 27 May, 1678, and was *s.* by his eldest son,

EDWARD CARY, Esq. of Torr Abbey, who *m.* Mary, 2nd dau. and co-heir of Richard Pelsont, Esq., by Anne his wife, relict of Thomas Savile, Earl of Sussex, and dau. of Christopher Villiers, 1st Earl of Anglesey. By this lady he had issue, 1 GEORGE, his heir; 2 William, who *m.* Miss Dorothy Rowe, and had (with a dau., Dorothy, wife of Edward Meynell, Esq. of Yarm and Kilvington) two sons, GEORGE, who *s.* to Torr Abbey, and EDWARD, father of GEORGE-STANLEY CARY, Esq. of Follaton Park; 3 Francis, who *d. unm.*; 1 Ann; 2 Mary; and 3 Winifred. Mr. Cary was *s.* at his decease by his eldest son,

GEORGE CARY, Esq. of Torr Abbey, *b.* in 1685, who *m.* Anne, dau. of Hugh, Lord Clifford; but *d.* 1 Oct. 1758, without issue, when the estates passed to the children of his brother William, George and Edward; by the elder of whom,

GEORGE CARY, Esq., he was *s.* at Torr Abbey. This gentleman *m.* Cecilia Fagniani, and had issue,

 GEORGE, his heir.
 JOHN, *b.* 17 Feb. 1770, who *m.* 1st, Sophia, dau. of Edward Sulyard, Esq., and *d.* 19 March, 1820, leaving issue, HENRY, heir to his uncle; Bernard; Lucius, lieut. in the Walmoden Cuirassiers, *m.* 8 Jan. 1839, Amelia, dau. of Count Starhemberg; Hugh; John; Sophia, *m.* to Charles Stonor, Esq.; Fanny; Susan; and Mary-Anne. Mr. John Cary *m.* 2ndly Miss Johnson, of the co. of Norfolk, and by her had one dau., Blanche.
 Mary, *m.* to J.-P. Chichester, Esq. of Arlington.
 Frances, *m.* in 1795, to Henry Stonor, Esq. of San Lucar, in Spain.

George Cary *m.* 2ndly, Frances Stonor, relict of Thomas Giffard, Esq. of Chillington, and had further issue,

 Mary-Anne, who *m.* 1st, John Dalton, Jun. Esq. of Thurnham Hall; 2ndly, Sir John - Hayford Thorold, Bart. of Marston; and 3rdly, Sir Charles Ogle, Bart. Her ladyship *d.* in 1842.
 Georgiana, *m.* to Francis Langan, Esq.

Mr. Cary *d.* in 1805, and was *s.* by his eldest son,

GEORGE CARY, Esq. of Torr Abbey, who *m.* Miss Franklin; but dying without issue, was *s.* by his nephew,

HENRY-GEORGE CARY, Esq. of Torr Abbey, *b.* 5 Oct. 1800; who *m.* in 1827, Emily-Munro, only child of Robert Shedden, Esq. of Brooklands, Hampshire, by Millicent his wife, dau. of the late Robert-Duncan Munro, Esq., E.I.C.S., and had issue,

 ROBERT-SHEDDEN-SULYARDE, his heir.
 Henry-Fraser-Lovat, *b.* 4 Nov. 1833, *d.* 25 Oct. 1838.
 Lionel-Stuart-Traquair-Munro.
 Millicent-Maria-Johnes, *m.* to John-Stuart Coxon, Esq. 3rd son of the late John-Stuart Coxon, Esq. of Fleek Priory, Kerry.
 Agatha-Edith-Dottin.
 Henrietta-Margaret-Emily, *d.* 7 March, 1842.

Mr. Cary *d.* 2 Sept. 1840.

Arms—Arg., on a bend, sa., three roses, of the first.
Crest—A swan, ppr.
Motto—Virtute excerptæ.
Seat—Torr Abbey, Torquay.

CARY OF FOLLATON PARK.

CARY, GEORGE-STANLEY, Esq. of Follaton Park, co. Devon, J.P. and D.L., *b.* in 1780; *m.* in 1821, Matilda, 2nd dau. of Sir Richard Bedingfeld, Bart. of Oxburgh Hall, co. Norfolk, by Charlotte-Georgiana his wife, only sister of George-William, Lord Stafford, and has issue,

I. STANLEY-EDWARD-GEORGE.
I. Camilla-Annabella. II. Charlotte-Matilda.
III. Isabella. IV. Helen.
V. Laura. VI. Adelaide. VII. Bertha.

Lineage.—This is the nearest collateral branch of the ancient family of CARY *of Torr Abbey*.

EDWARD CARY, Esq., 2nd son of William Cary, Esq., and grandson of Edward Cary, Esq. of Torr Abbey, purchased Follaton, co. Devon, and there seated himself. He *m.** Camilla-Annabella, eldest dau. of Gilbert-Fane Fleming,† Esq., by the Lady Camilla his wife, sister of Charles, 4th Earl of Tankerville, and had (with a younger son, Edward, and a dau., Camilla, who both *d. unm.*) a son and successor, the present GEORGE-STANLEY CARY, Esq., who, by his marriage with Matilda, dau. of Sir Richard Bedingfeld, has become connected with the noble Catholic families of Stafford, Petre, Clifford, Dillon, Kenmare, &c.

Arms—1st and 4th, arg., on a bend, sa., three roses of the field, for CARY; 2nd and 3rd, for FLEMING; gu., semée of crosses-fitchée, three crescents, or.
Crest—1st, for CARY, a swan, ppr.; 2nd, for FLEMING, a dexter hand in armour, holding a sword, all ppr.
Motto—Virtute excerptæ.
Seat—Follaton Park, near Totnes.

CARY OF WHITE CASTLE.

CARY, GEORGE, Esq. of White Castle, co. Donegal.

Lineage.—GEORGE CARY, Esq., recorder of Londonderry, and M.P. in 1613 (stated to have been son of Francis Cary, Esq., who was sixth son of Robert Cary, Esq. of Clovelly), had a grant of Red Castle (an Irish estate in the barony of Innishowen, co. Donegal) from Sir Arthur Chichester, Baron of Belfast, who was lord high treasurer of Ireland in 1618. This first George Cary, of Red Castle, *m.* Jane, dau. of Sir Tristram Beresford; and *d.* 22 April, 1640, having had, with four daus., five sons, 1 GEORGE, of Red Castle, *m.* Alice Vaughan, and *d.* in 1669, leaving a son, FRANCIS, of Red Castle; 2 EDWARD, of Dungiven; 3 Robert, of White Castle, *m.*, and had five sons and three daus.; he *d.* in 1681; 4 Tristram, lieut. in the army, *m.*

* Mr. Cary *m.* 2ndly, Miss Ferrall, sister of Roger Ferrall, Esq., but by her had no issue.

† Mr. Fane Fleming was son of the Hon. Gilbert Fleming, lieut.-gen. of the Leeward Islands. His 2nd dau. *m.* Sir John Brisco, Bart.

Eliza, dau. of Major Monkton, and had issue, five sons and three daus.; 5 Henry. The 2nd son,

EDWARD CARY, Esq. of Dungiven, m. Mrs. Brazier, widow of Paul Brazier, Esq., and dau. of Sir Tristram Beresford, and had three sons,

1 EDWARD, who m. Martha Mervin, of Trelick, and had issue, HENRY CARY, of Dungiven, M.P. for Coleraine, who m. Anne Hamilton, niece to Gen. Hamilton, of Walworth, co. Derry, and had five sons and three daus. The eldest son, the Right Hon. Edward Cary, M.P. for Dungiven, m. twice: 1st, Jane, dau. of Viscount Tyrone; and 2ndly, a Miss Gore, but had no issue. His four brothers, Frederick, Henry, George (in holy orders), and William, were called Cary Hamiltons, from their mother, and d. without issue. The eldest sister, Letitia Cary, m. William Blacker, Esq.; and the two younger, Martha and Anna, d. unm. Thus ended the eldest branch of the Dungiven Careys.

2 George. 3 TRISTRAM.

The youngest son,

TRISTRAM CARY, Esq., m. twice: 1st, Charity Staples, and had a son, GEORGE, of Turnaleague, from whom descended the CARYS *of Turnaleague*. Tristram m. 2ndly, Margaret Cunningham, by whom he had one son,

TRISTRAM CARY, Esq., who m. three times, but had issue only by his first wife, Miss Baird, viz., six sons and two daus. The 3rd son,

GEORGE CARY, Esq., purchased the property of White Castle from a descendant of Robert Cary, the 3rd son of the 1st George Cary, of Red Castle. He m. Anne-Lunell Grayson (widow of George Cary, of Red Castle), and had issue,

I. TRISTRAM, his heir.
II. Anthony-Greigson, in holy orders, m. Charlotte, 4th dau. of John Slacke, Esq. of Slackegrove, co. Monaghan, barrister-at-law, and has issue,
  1 George, in holy orders.
  2 John. 3 Tristram.
  4 Arthur. 5 Redcliffe.
  1 Charlotte. 2 Agnes-Gray.
I. Matilda, m. to J. Chambers, Esq.
II. Rosetta, m. to Thomas Kennedy, Esq.

The eldest son,

TRISTRAM CARY, Esq. of White Castle, b. Aug. 1786, m. Henrietta-Sophia, 2nd dau. of the late Col. Henry-John Kearney, of White Waltham, Berks, by Anne Banks his wife, dau. of the late Joseph Banks, Esq., chancellor of York; and d., leaving three children,

GEORGE, now of White Castle.
Annie.
Caroline, m. Alexander Curry, Esq. of Dublin, barrister-at-law, and has issue.

Arms—Arg., on a bend, sa., three roses, of the first.
Crest—A swan, ppr.
Motto—Sine maculâ.
Seat—White Castle, co. Donegal.

CASBORNE OF NEW HOUSE.

CASBORNE, THE REV. WALTER-JOHN-SPRING, of New House, Pakenham, co. Suffolk, J.P., b. in 1790; m. in 1826, Anne, eldest dau. of Capel Lofft, Esq. of Troston Hall.

Lineage.—THE REV. JOHN CASBORNE, rector of Elmswell, co. Suffolk, m. Mary, dau. and heiress of the Rev. John Barrett, D.D., rector of Hartest, in the same county, and was father of

THE REV. JOHN CASBORNE, who m. De la Riviere, dau. of the Rev. John Symonds, D.D., by Mary his wife, sister and co-heir of Sir William Spring, Bart. of Pakenham Hall (*see* BURKE'S *Extinct Baronetage*), and had, with a dau., who d. s. p., an only son,

THE REV. JOHN-SPRING CASBORNE, of New House, who m. in 1784, Frances, dau. of Edmund Rogers, Esq. of Walsham-le-Willows, co. Suffolk, and had (with six daus., viz., 1 Frances-Merelina; 2 Theresa-Rebecca, m. to the Rev. Joseph Haddock; 3 Annabelle; 4 Maria, m. to Captain William Baynes, E.I.Co.'s service; 5 Lucretia, m. to Edward Stanley, Esq., M.D.; 6 Mary-Delariviere; and two sons, Frederic-Jermyn, lieut. R.N., and Henry-Edmund, R.N., both of whom d. unm.) another son, the present REV. WALTER-JOHN-SPRING CASBORNE, of Newhouse. The Rev. John-Spring-Casborne d. in 1822.

Arms—Gu., a lion, passant, or, gorged with a ducal crown, of the first, between three annulets, of the second.
Crest—A lion, passant, or, gorged with a ducal coronet, gu.
Motto—Puro de fonte.
Seat—New House, Pakenham, near Bury St. Edmunds.

CASE OF PAPPLEWICK HALL.

CASE, JOHN-ASHTON, Esq. of Papplewick Hall, co. Notts, b. in 1804; m. in 1832, Caroline-Elizabeth, eldest dau. of Henry Walker, Esq. of Blythe Hall, co. Nottingham, and Clifton House, co. York, and has issue.

Lineage.—THOMAS CASE, Esq. of Liverpool, merchant, b. 15 March, 1731 (3rd son of Thomas Case, Esq. of Red Hazles, co. Lancaster, J.P., by Margaret his wife, dau. and co-heir of William Clayton, Esq. of Fulwood, and grandson of Jonathan Case, Esq., lineally descended from Richard Case, of Hayton), m. in 1775, Anna, 2nd dau. of John Ashton, Esq. of Woolton Hall, near Liverpool, and had issue,

THOMAS, his heir.
John-Ashton, b. 17 April, 1779, d. s. p. 20 Aug. 1836.

He d. in 1790, and was s. by his eldest son,

THOMAS CASE, Esq. of Thingwall Hall, co. Lancaster, J.P. and D.L., b. 4 Nov. 1777; m. 21 Dec. 1801, Jane-Sarah, eldest dau. and co-heiress of Edward Holt, Esq. of Ince Hall, near Wigan, co. Lancaster, and had issue,

JOHN-ASHTON.
Jane-Sarah, m. in 1837, to Marmaduke Middleton, 2nd son of M.-M. Middleton, Esq. of Leam, in Derbyshire.
Emma-Anna, m. in 1839, to Arthur, 4th son of William Le Blanc, Esq. of London.

Arms—Arg., on a bend, engrailed, gu., cotised, sa., three round buckles, or, quartering OGLE and CLAYTON.
Crest—A cubit arm, habited, erm., cuff, arg., holding in the hand, ppr., a round buckle, or.
Motto—Distantia jungit.
Seat—Papplewick Hall, Notts.

CASSAN OF SHEFFIELD.

CASSAN, MATTHEW-SHEFFIELD, Esq. of Sheffield House, Queen's County, b. 23 Dec. 1812; m. 1 May, 1843, and has surviving issue, by Phœbe-Louisa his wife,

I. FRANCIS-SEYMOUR-STUART, b. 12 July, 1848.
II. Henry-Erskine, b. 14 Sept. 1849.
III. Stephen-Sheffield, b. 29 Aug. 1851.
IV. Matthew-Sheffield, b. 14 Sept. 1852.

Lineage.—The family of Cassan, or De Cassagne, of French origin, was founded in Ireland by

STEPHEN CASSAN, a native of Montpelier, b. in 1659, who sought an asylum in Holland at the revocation of the edict of Nantes; and, in 1689, being then an officer in the Foreign Brigade, was engaged under the command of Schomberg, in Ireland, where he eventually settled. He m. *anno* 1692, Elizabeth, dau. and sole heir of Joseph Sheffield, Esq. of Navestock, in Essex, and of Cappoly, in the Queen's County, and had an only son,

MATTHEW CASSAN, Esq. of Cappoly, or Sheffield, in the Queen's County, b. in 1693. He likewise inherited Navestock, but sold that property. He built the present mansion at Sheffield. Mr. Cassan m. 1st, Ann, dau. of Jonathan Baldwin, Esq. of Summer Hill, Queen's County, and had (besides two daus., Eliza, m. to the Rev. George Cook; and Margaret, m. to Aaron-Crossley Seymour, Esq.) two sons,

STEPHEN, his heir.
Richard-Sheffield, barrister-at-law; b. 1729; m. Isabella, dau. of Alexander Hamilton, Esq. of Knock, co. Dublin, M.P., and left at his decease four daus., his co-heirs.

Mr. Cassan m. 2ndly, Christian, dau. of John Walsh, Esq. of Jamaica, and had by her,

Joseph, in holy orders, of Stradbally; b. in 1742; d. in 1830, aged 88, leaving issue.
John, a capt. in the army; d. in Aug. 1805, leaving issue.
Christiana, b. 12 March, 1743; m. to James Price, Esq. of Westfield, Queen's County; and d. in 1814, leaving issue.

The eldest son and heir,

STEPHEN CASSAN, Esq. of Sheffield, barrister-at-law, b. 22 May, 1824-5; high-sheriff of the Queen's County in 1763; m. 9 Dec. 1750, Alicia, relict of Benjamin Hunt, Esq., and dau. of William Mercer, Esq. of Fair Hill, co. of Louth. Mr. Cassan d. 26 April, 1773, aged 48; Mrs. Cassan 6 Feb. 1789. They had two sons and a dau., viz.,

I. MATHEW, his heir.
II. Stephen, barrister-at-law; b. 2 Jan. 1757; m. 4 March, 1786, Sarah, only dau. and eventual heir of Charles Mears, Esq., captain of the "Egmont"; and d. 26 Jan. 1794, leaving an only son,
  STEPHEN-HYDE, M.A., F.S.A., vicar of Bruton and of Wyke, co. Somerset; m. 27 Dec. 1820, Frances, 3rd dau. of

the Rev. William Ireland, M.A., vicar of Frome, and left at his decease, 19 July, 1841, one son and three daus.,

Algernon-William, b. 18 July, 1822.
Gertrude-Ann-Caley.
Frances-Alicia. Florence-Georgiana.

I. Alicia, m. the late Rev. George Howse, M.A., rector of Inch.

Mr. Cassan was s. at his decease by his elder son,

MATTHEW CASSAN, Esq. of Sheffield, b. in 1754; high-sheriff of the Queen's County in 1783, and major of the Queen's County militia; m. 1st, 13 May, 1776, Sarah, 3rd dau. of Col. Forde, of Seaforde, co. Down; and 2ndly, 15 Sept. 1819, Catherine, dau. of John Head, Esq. of Ashley Park, co. Tipperary, but left at his decease, 1 Nov. 1837, issue only by the 1st wife, one son,

STEPHEN-SHEFFIELD CASSAN, Esq. of Sheffield, J.P., barrister-at-law, b. 18 Oct. 1777; who m. 4 Aug. 1804, Anne-Elizabeth, dau. of Edward Laurenson, Esq. of Capponellan, co. Kilkenny, and had issue,

I. MATTHEW-SHEFFIELD, now of Sheffield.
II. Stephen-Sheffield. III. Edward.
IV. Arthur-Moore, 84th regt.
I. Sarah-Elizabeth. II. Mary-Ann.
III. Alicia. IV. Ann. V. Margaret.

Arms—Quarterly: 1st, arg., three oaks, eradicated, two and one, ppr., for CASSAN; 2nd, or, a fesse between six garbs, gu., for SHEFFIELD; 3rd, arg., two bars, in chief, three fleurs-de-lis, gu., for ST. LIZ; 4th, az., three bucks, tripping, or, for GREENE.
Crest—Issuant from an earl's coronet, ppr., a boar's head and neck, erased, or, langued, gu.
Motto—Juvant arva parentum.
Seat—Sheffield, near Maryborough.

CASS OF LITTLE GROVE.

CASS, FREDERICK, Esq. of Little Grove, East Barnet, Herts, J.P. and high-sheriff in 1844-5, m. Martha, eldest dau. of John-Dell Potter, Esq. of Ponder's End, and has issue,

I. FREDERICK-CHARLES, in holy orders, M.A., of Balliol College, Oxford.
II. Charles-William, M.A., in holy orders.
III. Arthur-Herbert, an officer 10th hussars.

Mr. Cass s. his father 29 Oct. 1819.

Lineage.—ROBERT CASSE, of Barmbie-on-the-Marsh, Howden, Yorkshire, bapt. 19 Dec. 1620 (descended from John Casse, living at the same place *temp.* HENRY VII.); m. 21 May, 1674, Elizabeth, sister and heir of William Sharpe, and was father of JOHN CASSE, of Sand Hall, near Howden, who d. in July, 1717, leaving, by Jane Sutton his wife, a son and heir, JOSEPH CASS, of Barmby, co. York, b. in Feb. 1710, who m. 25 Nov. 1740, Martha, dau. of William Hopper, of Bradley Hall, near Huddersfield, and by her (who d. 5 July, 1802) left at his decease, May, 1755, a son,

WILLIAM CASS, Esq. of Beaulieu Lodge, Winchmore Hill, Middlesex, b. 20 Feb. 1743; who m. Elizabeth, dau. of Evan Owen, Esq., and was father of the present FREDERICK CASS, Esq. of Little Grove.

Arms—Per chevron, or and erm., on a chevron, sa., between two eagles' heads, erased, gu., in chief, and a garb, of the first, in base; a harrow, gold, between two fountains.
Crest—An eagle's head, erased, gu., charged on the neck with a fountain; in the beak three ears of wheat, or.
Seat—Little Grove, East Barnet, Herts.

CASWALL OF ELM GROVE.

CASWALL, ALFRED, Esq. of Elm Grove, Binfield, Berks, a barrister of the Inner Temple, b. 9 Nov. 1811; m. 27 June, 1843, Mary-Elizabeth, dau. of James Powell, Esq. of Clapton House, Middlesex, and has had issue,

I. JAMES-CLARKE, b. 5 Nov. 1845.
II. Alfred-Clarke, b. 28 March, 1847; d. 2 June, 1852.
III. Walter-Randolph-Le Hardy, b. 19 Aug. 1853.
I. Anna-Maria. II. Katherine-Elizabeth.
III. Jane-Mary-Cotton. IV. Ellen.

Lineage.—This family is of considerable antiquity in Wales and the neighbouring county of Hereford.

SIR THOMAS CASWALL, a knight of the Holy Wars, was buried at Leominster. Long subsequently Sir George Caswall, who had very great estates in that neighbourhood, and represented Leominster in several parliaments, was implicated with Mr. Aislabie, chancellor of the exchequer, and others, in the South Sea Scheme; was fined to an enormous amount, and committed to the Tower, till, by the sale of his Herefordshire estates, he paid the charge imposed upon him—being upwards of a quarter of a million sterling. He left two sons, John and Timothy. John, the eldest, left one son, John, father of THE REV. ROBERT-CLARKE CASWALL, who m. Elizabeth-Clarke Pryor, (the sole representative in direct descent of the ancient family of Clarke, of whom Sir John Clarke, Banneret, in stricken field, took prisoner, *temp.* HENRY VIII., Louis d'Orleans, Duke de Longueville, and was rewarded by a grant of arms: a gold thumb-ring, given by the king, bearing the fleur-de-lis of France, is still in possession of the family), and one dau., Henrietta, m. to William Halhed, Esq., a director of the Bank of England. Timothy, the younger son of Sir George, left a son, George Caswall, of Sacombe Park, Herts, who d. leaving no male issue.

The old family estates were at Presteign, Eye, Kimbolton, Eynshaw, Berrington, Leominster, and other places in Herefordshire. Those of late date are at Burford and Alvescott, Oxfordshire, and Murly Manor, Hants.

The late

REV. ROBERT-CLARKE CASWALL, b. 17 Oct. 1768, m. Mary, dau. of John Burgess, Esq. of Brook House, Hants, and niece of Dr. Thomas Burgess, Lord Bishop of Salisbury, and had issue,

ALFRED, now of Elm Grove.
Henry, in holy orders; m. Mary, niece of Bishop Chase, of Ohio.
Edward, in holy orders, of Brazenose College, Oxon; m. Louisa-Stuart, only child of Major-Gen. Walker, of Whetleigh House, Somersetshire.
Thomas, of Clare Hall, Cambridge.
Frederick, settled in America.
Jane, m. the Rev. Henry Deane, of Gillingham, Dorsetshire; d. 2 Jan. 1847, leaving one son and two daus.
Maria, m. the Rev. B. C. Dowding, of Devizes.
Emma. Olivia-Mary.

Mr. Caswall d. 4 Sept. 1846.

Arms—Arg., three bars, gemelles, sa.
Crest—A dexter arm, couped at the shoulder, in mail, holding in the hand, ppr., a cross-crosslet, fitchée, or.
Motto—Non multa sed multum.
Seat—Elm Grove, Binfield.

CATHCART OF CARBISTON.

CATHCART, TAYLOR, Esq. of Carbiston, co. Ayr, and of Pitcairlie, co. Fife, m. in 1823, Frances, eldest dau. of George Marcy, of Geneva and Kepp, in Jamaica, and has issue,

I. JAMES. II. Robert. III. William-Taylor.
I. Frances.

Lineage.—The CATHCARTS *of Carbiston*, says Nisbet, are an "old branch of the family of Cathcart, as far back as the time of ROBERT III.;" but it would appear that a still greater antiquity can be claimed for them. They had a gift of the wardship of the lands of Carbiston, during the reign of DAVID II., in 1368.

JAMES CATHCART, of Carbiston, son of Francis, of Carbiston, and the lineal descendant of David Cathcart, of Duchray, 3rd son of John, Lord Cathcart, m. Magdalen, eldest dau. of Sir James Rochead, Bart. of Inverleith, by whom he had COL. JAMES CATHCART, and Capt. Thomas Cathcart, the latter of whom was killed in the Spanish wars. He was s. by his son,

COL. JAMES CATHCART, who, on his succession, became Col. James Rochead-Cathcart, of Inverleith and Carbiston. He d. unm., and was s. by his grand-nephew,

JAMES CATHCART, of Carbiston, who m. in 1764, Lucretia, eldest dau. of Robert Colquhoun, of St. Christopher's and Santa Cruz; and dying in 1795, was s. by his son,

JAMES CATHCART, major in the 19th dragoons, many years on active service in India. He d. unm. in 1810, and was s. by his brother,

ROBERT CATHCART, capt. in the royal navy, an officer of distinguished merit. In the memorable battle of the Nile, he served as fifth lieutenant in the "Bellerophon," and his captain having been wounded early in the action, and the four senior lieutenants killed, he had the glory of continuing the contest with the "L'Orient," till the latter blew up. In 1813, while in the "Alexandria," 32 guns, he gave chase for eighty hours (H.M. sloop "Spitfire," 18 guns, in company) to the American ship "President," 50 guns, Capt. Rogers—the latter only escaping by superiority of sailing. Capt. Cathcart m. in 1814, Catherine-Scrymgeour, dau. of Henry-Scrymgeour Wedderburn, of Wedderburn and Birkhill. He

d. in 1833, leaving no issue, and was s. by his brother, the present TAYLOR CATHCART, Esq. of Carbiston and Pitcairlie, many years resident in Jamaica.

Arms—Az., three cross-crosslets, fitchee, issuing out of as many crescents, arg., two and one; and in the collar point a man's heart ensigned with an imperial crown, ppr., as a maternal difference from other descendants of the family of CATHCART.

Crest—A hand issuing out of a wreath, holding up a crescent, arg.

Motto—I hope to speed.

Seat—Pitcairlie, Fifeshire.

CATHCART OF KNOCKDOLIAN.

CATHCART, ALEXANDER, Esq. of Knockdolian Castle, co. Ayr, b. 6 March, 1800; s. his brother in 1840; m. 13 July, 1841, Margaret, 4th dau. of James Murdoch, Esq.

Lineage.—JAMES CATHCART, of Barneill, 2nd son of John Cathcart, of Carleton, and grandson of Robert Cathcart, of Killochan, obtained a charter of the lands of Easter Barneill M'Lune from King JAMES, in 1601, and purchased the estate of Genoch, co. Wigton, about 1618. His grandson,

JOHN CATHCART, of Genoch and Knockdolian (son of Robert Cathcart, of Genoch, and grandson of John Cathcart, of Genoch, by Rosina his wife, dau. of Sir Peter Agnew, of Lochnaw), m. 9 June, 1719, Agnes, eldest dau. of Alexander Cochrane, of Craigmuir, nephew of the 1st Earl of Dundonald; and d. in 1779, leaving an only son,

ROBERT CATHCART, of Genoch and Knockdolian, b. in 1721; who m. 12 May, 1763, Marion, only dau. of John Buchan, of Letham, co. Haddington, by his wife, Elizabeth Hepburn, of Smeaton, and by her (who d. 10 Aug. 1819, aged 70), had issue. Mr. Cathcart d. in 1784, and was s. by his eldest son,

JOHN CATHCART, of Genoch and Knockdolian, an advocate at the Scottish bar, b. 14 May, 1768; who m. 17 June, 1795, Ann, eldest dau. of the Hon. Alexander Gordon, of Rockville, 3rd son of William, 2nd Lord Aberdeen, and by her (who d. 27 March, 1837) had issue, 1 ROBERT, his heir; 2 George, d. young in 1811; 3 ALEXANDER, now of Knockdolian; 1 Ann, m. in Nov. 1839, Samuel Berger, Esq., jun., of Homerton, Middlesex, and d. 29 Aug. 1852; 2 Marion, d. young in 1824. Mr. Cathcart d. at Genoch, 5 Oct. 1835, and was s. by his son,

ROBERT CATHCART, Esq. of Genoch and Knockdolian, in the E.I.Co's civil service, b. in 1797; who d. unm. at Agra, Bengal, 14 July, 1840, and was s. by his brother, the present ALEXANDER CATHCART, of Knockdolian.

Arms—Az., three cross-crosslets, fitchee, issuing out of as many crescents, arg.; in chief, a man's heart, gu., ensigned with an imperial crown, ppr.

Crest—A dexter hand, couped at the wrist, issuing out of a wreath, holding up a crescent, arg.

Motto—I hope to speed.

Seat—Knockdolian Castle, Ayrshire.

CATON OF BINBROOK.

CATON, THE REV. RICHARD-BEWLEY, of Binbrook, co. Lincoln, M.A., b. in 1774, formerly an officer in the 12th light dragoons, afterwards major in the 3rd Royal Lincoln militia; m. Eliza, youngest dau. of Redmond Power, Esq. of Whitefort, co. Tipperary, and has issue,

I. RICHARD-REDMOND, b. 21 Aug. 1806; m. 28 June, 1831, Anna-Maria, only dau. of the Rev. John Rideout, rector of Woodmancote, co. Sussex, and (by her, from whom he was divorced) has issue, Redmond-Rideout-Bewley, b. 1 October, 1833; Frances-Eliza; Georgiana-Maria; and Laura-Sophia.

II. Thruston-Bewley, m. in 1835, Marie-Louise-Esther, dau. of Colonel de St. Rose, late chef de l'état à Paris, and has issue.

I. Maria-Eliza, m. in 1831, Richard-Henry Kinchant, Esq. of Park Hall and Bishop's Castle, co. Salop, and has issue.

Lineage.—THRUSTON-JOHN CATON, Esq. of Thorpe Abbots, b. 15 Aug. 1745, (the son of Thomas Caton, Esq. of Thorpe Abbots, by Hannah his wife, dau. of John Thruston, Esq. of Weston Market, Suffolk), m. Margaret Hawkesmore, eldest dau. and co-heiress (with her sister Hannah, wife of John Tuffnell, Esq., and Mary, wife of George Meek, Esq.), of Richard Bewley, Esq. of Binbrook and Kirton, co. Lincoln, by whom (who m. 2ndly, Lieut.-Colonel Adams, 66th regt.) he had

RICHARD-BEWLEY, now of Binbrook.
Thomas-Mott, M.D., m. Eliza, dau. of Major Basil Wood, of Oxfordshire.
Harriet.
Eliza, m. to Benjamin Borrell, Esq. of Brigsley, Lincolnshire, and has issue.

Mr. Caton d. 13 June, 1782.

Arms—1st and 4th, party per fesse, gu. and az., two lynxes, or cats-o'-mountain, passant, arg., spotted, sa.; on a canton, or, a cross-crosslet, fitchee, of the fourth, for CATON; 2nd and 3rd, quarterly, gu. and vair, a bend, or, thereon an annulet and crescent, for CONSTABLE.

Crest—Out of an embattlement, ppr., charged with three cross-crosslets, fitchee, sa., a Saracen's head, quarter-faced, ppr., wreathed round the temples, or and gu.

Motto—Cautus metuit foveam lupus.

CATOR OF BECKINGHAM AND WOODBASTWICK.

CATOR, JOHN, Esq. of Beckingham Place, Kent, and Woodbastwick Hall, Norfolk, m. 25 Sept. 1806, and by his wife, Elizabeth-Louisa (who d. 11 Feb. 1847), has issue,

I. ALBEMARLE, b. 7 April, 1813, m. 22 April, 1834, Elizabeth-Margaret, eldest dau. of John Blakeney, Esq. of Abbert, co. Galway, and has issue;
   1 JOHN, b. 8 Feb. 1835.
   2 Albemarle, b. 6 April, 1836.
   3 William, b. 26 Aug. 1839.
   4 Bertie, b. 30 July, 1843.
   5 Edward, b. June, 1847.
   6 Robert, b. 3 April, 1851.
   1 Charlotte. 2 Elizabeth-Margaret. 3 Mary.

II. William-Thornhill, m. Miss Sayer.

I. Elizabeth-Diana, m. to D.-H. Kelly, Esq. of Castle Kelly, co. Galway.

II. Anne-Charlotte, m. to Capt. Drew.

Lineage.—The late JOSEPH CATOR, Esq., a merchant of high standing, s. to Beckenham and the other estates of his uncle, John Cator, Esq., in 1806. He m. at Calcutta, in 1780, Diana, sister of the late Admiral Sir Albemarle Bertie, Bt., K.C.B. (of the ducal family of Ancaster), and by her (who d. in 1829) left at his decease, in 1818, several children, of whom the eldest son is the present JOHN CATOR, Esq. of Beckenham; and the 4th, Rear-Admiral Bertie-Cornelius Cator.

Arms—Erm., on a pile, gu., a lion, passant-guardant, or.

Crest—A lion's head, erased, or, collared, with a bar gemelle, az.

Motto—Nihil sine labore.

Seat—Woodbastwick Hall, Norfolk.

CAULFIELD OF DRUMCAIRNE.

CAULFEILD, EDWARD-HOUSTON, Esq. of Drumcairne, co. Tyrone, J.P. and D.L., high-sheriff in 1838, b. 28 Feb. 1807; m. 26 April, 1828, Charlotte, 2nd dau. of Piers Geale, Esq. of Mountjoy Square, Dublin, and by her (who d. 11 Nov. 1840) has issue,

I. JAMES-ALFRED, lieut. 17th foot, b. 20 March, 1830.

II. Marcus-Piers-Francis, b. 3 Nov. 1840.

I. Charlotte-Harriet.

Lineage.—THE HON. AND REV. CHARLES CAULFEILD, bapt. 27 Dec. 1686, rector of Donoghenue, in the diocese of Armagh, 2nd son of William, 2nd Viscount Charlemont, m. Alice, dau. and co-heiress of John Houston, Esq. of Craigs, co. Antrim, and was father of

JAMES CAULFEILD, Esq. of Drumcairne, co. Tyrone, who m. Catherine Burgh, of Old Town, co. Kildare, aunt of the Dean of Cloyne, and was father of

JAMES CAULFEILD, Esq. of Drumcairne, who m. in 1806, Harriet, dau. of Sir Edward Crofton, M.P., and by her, who d. in 1837, had issue,

EDWARD-HOUSTON, now of Drumcairne.
William-Gorges Crofton, an officer in the 18th regt.; d. at Ceylon in 1839.
Harriet-Anna, m. to William French, Esq. of Rutland-square.

Arms—Barry of ten, arg. and gu., on a canton, of the second, a lion, passant-guardant, or.

Crest—A dragon's head, erased, gu., gorged with a bar gemelle, arg.

Motto—Deo duce, ferro comitante.

Seat—Drumcairne, Stewardstown, co. Tyrone.

CAULFEILD OF RAHEENDUFF.

CAULFEILD, EDWIN-TOBY, Esq. R.N. of Raheenduff, Queen's County, *b.* 14 Jan. 1793; *m.* 1st, Frances-Sally, dau. of the late Eyles Irwin, Esq. of co. Fermanagh, and by her (who *d.* 13 Nov. 1841) has issue,

I. HENRY-COPE, M.A., barrister-at-law, *m.* 20 April, 1847, Anne-Louisa, dau. of the late J.-R. Francklin, Esq.

I. Sophia-Frances-Anne.

II. Louisa-Lavinia, *m.* 3 Dec. 1850, to the Rev. Hans Atkinson, M.A.

He *m.* 2ndly, 9 May, 1846, Alicia-Almeria, youngest dau. of the late Gen. Sir David-Latimer-T. Widdrington, K.C.H., and widow of Capt. Henry Pooley, R.E., and has by her an only son,

I. Edwin-James-Stuart-Widdrington, *b.* 14 Jan. 1848.

Lineage.—THE HON. TOBY CAULFEILD, of Clone, co. Kilkenny, 3rd son of William, 5th Baron Charlemont, was father (with a dau. Edith, *m.* to William, Lord Castle Durrow) of several sons, all of whom *d. s. p.* excepting

COLONEL WILLIAM CAULFEILD, of Raheenduff, Queen's County, lieut.-governor of Fort George, N.B., who, with other issue, had two sons, WADE-TOBY, his heir, and John, Archdeacon of Kilmore. The former,

WADE-TOBY CAULFEILD, Esq. of Raheenduff, and Catcombe, co. Wilts, captain in the 3rd Dragoon-guards, *b.* in 1733, *m.* 1st, in 1765, Jessie, dau. of James, 3rd Lord Ruthven, and 2ndly, in 1786, Anne, sister of Sir Jonathan Cope, Bart. of Hanwell and Brewerne; by the latter (who *m.* 2ndly, Monsieur François le Chartier de Bolleville, and *d.* 7 July, 1852), he left at his decease in Aug. 1800,

EDWIN-TOBY, now of Raheenduff.
Edward-Warren, in holy orders, M.A.; *m.* 1st, Anne, dau. of the late John Pybus, Esq., and has, Edward-Wade, *b.* 15 Jan. 1829; Elizabeth-Ann, *m.* in 1851, to James-William Cottell, Esq., H.E.I.C.S.; Mary; Katherine-Arabella; and Ann-Pybus. He *m.* 2ndly, 20 Oct. 1842, Millicent, youngest dau. of Joseph Hellicar, Esq., and has by her a son, Francis-William, *b.* 29 Aug. 1843.
Emma-Ashwell, *m.* to Frederick William Campbell, Esq. of Barbreck, N.B.; and *d.* in 1817.
Sophia-Frances-Mary.

Arms, &c.—As the preceding.

CAULFEILD OF BLOOMFIELD.

CAULFEILD, LIEUT.-COL. JOHN, of Bloomfield, co. Westmeath, J.P. and D.L., high-sheriff of Roscommon in 1826, *b.* in 1793; *m.* in 1824, Anne-Lovell, dau. of James Bury, Esq. of St. Leonards Nazing, co. Herts, and has issue,

I. FRANCIS-WILLIAM, lieut. 44th regt., *b.* in 1826.
II. Robert, capt. 7th Madras cavalry, *b.* in 1829.
III. Henry, lieut. 1st Bengal fusiliers, *b.* in 1831.
IV. St. George, an officer Madras infantry, *b.* in 1837.
V. John, *b.* in 1839.
I. Anna-Julia, *m.* to Capt. Winter, Bengal army.
II. Fanny-Elizabeth, *m.* to Major Maydwell.
III. Christina, *m.* to Capt. W.-A. Mainwaring.
IV. Mary.
V. Lucy-Adela, *m.* July, 1854, to Capt. Charles-Yelverton Balguy, 42nd Highlanders.
VI. Augusta-Florence.

Lineage.—THE VENERABLE JOHN CAULFEILD, archdeacon of Kilmore, son of Colonel William Caulfeild, of Raheenduff, Queen's County, governor of Fort George, in Scotland, *m.* Euphemia Gordon, of Kenmure, co. Dumfries, and had issue, WILLIAM; Thomas-Gordon, commodore R.N., who *d.* in 1821, leaving, by Theodosia his wife, dau. of William Talbot, Esq., a son, the Rev. William Caulfeild, rector of Mullahiffe, and four daus.; John; George; Alexander; Robert, capt. R.N.; and James, major-general E.I.C.S. The eldest son,

LIEUT.-COLONEL WILLIAM CAULFEILD, of Benown, co. Athlone, *m.* 1st, in 1788, Lucy, dau. of James Sanderson, Esq., of Clover Hill, co. Cavan, and by her had issue,

JOHN, now of Bloomfield. William.
James, R.N., who *m.* 1st, in 1823, Augusta, dau. of Anna, Baroness Crofton, and has by her one son, William-Montgomerie-Stewart, *b.* 1825, *m.* 1847, Dora-Jane, dau. of William French, Esq. Mr. James Caulfeild *m.* 2ndly, Miss Emily French, by whom he has no issue.
Thomas-Gordon, in holy orders; who *m.* Eliza, dau. of John-Pratt Winter, Esq. of Agher.
Lucy, *m.* to Matthew Lyster, Esq.
Phemy, *m.* 1st, to Col. Vandeleur; and 2ndly, to J. Cary, Esq.
Grace, *m.* to Capt. Barry, of Kilbolane House, co. Cork.
Mary-Maud, *m.* 1st, to Robert Goff, Esq.; and 2ndly, to the Rev. Thomas Battersby.

Colonel Caulfeild *m.* 2ndly, Anna Baker, of Castle Bamford, but by her had no issue. He *d.* in 1831.

Arms, &c.—As CAULFEILD *of Drumcairne.*
Seat—Bloomfield, Mullingar.

CAULFEILD OF DONAMON CASTLE.

CAULFEILD, ST. GEORGE-FRANCIS, Esq. of Donamon Castle, co. Roscommon, *b.* 8 March, 1806; *m.* 17 Aug. 1830, Susan, sister of the present Lord Crofton, and has,

I. ST. GEORGE-FRANCIS-ROBERT, *b.* 20 April, 1831.
II. Alfred-Henry, *b.* 29 Dec. 1834.
I. Emily-Susan, *m.* 31 July, 1852, to Captain Henry Lowther, M.P.
II. Fanny-Florence.

Lineage.—THOMAS CAULFEILD, Esq. of Donamon, co. Roscommon, M.P., Master in Chancery (7th son of William, 2nd Baron Charlemont), *m.* in 1657, Anne, dau. of Charles, 2nd Viscount Moore, of Drogheda, and by her, who *d.* in 1672, had, I. WILLIAM, his heir; II. Toby, archdeacon of Killala, *m.* Anne, dau. of Adam O'Hara, Esq., and granddau. of Cain O'Hara, Esq. of Nymphsfield, and had, with other issue, Adam, in holy orders; and Richard, of Ardcree, co. Sligo, lieutenant in the navy, who *m.* and left issue; III. Mary, *m.* to Thomas Cuffe, Esq.; IV. Alice; and V. Sarah. Captain Caulfeild *d.* in 1690, and was *s.* by his eldest son,

WILLIAM CAULFEILD, Esq. of Donamon, H. M. first serjeant-at-law, and subsequently a justice of the King's Bench, from 1715 until 1734. He *m.* Lettice, 4th dau. of Sir Arthur Gore, of Newtown, co. Mayo, Bart., and by her had issue, I. Thomas, M.P., *d. unm.*, 1747; II. Toby, M.P., *d. unm.*, 1741; III. WILLIAM, of whom presently; IV. St. George, chief baron of the Exchequer, and afterwards chief justice of the King's Bench, and *d. unm.*, 1778; V. Robert, M.A., rector of Harristown, *m.*, and had issue; and I. Lettice, *m.* to Blayney Walcot Browne, Esq. The 3rd son,

WILLIAM CAULFEILD, Esq., *m.* Frances Gunter, and *d.* in 1745, leaving a son, GORE CAULFEILD, Esq. of Donamon, who was father of

COLONEL JOHN CAULFEILD, of Donamon, who *m.* Mary, dau. of Henry Irvine, Esq., younger brother of William Irvine, Esq. of Castle Irvine, M.P. for Fermanagh, and by her had a son,

ST. GEORGE CAULFEILD, Esq. of Donamon, who *m.* 2 April, 1802, Frances, dau. of Baroness Crofton, and had issue,

ST. GEORGE-FRANCIS, present representative.
Frances-Henrietta, *m.* 10 July, 1827, Frederick-Hamilton Cornewall, Esq. of Delbury Hall, co. Salop, eldest son of the late Dr. Cornewall, Bishop of Worcester.
Harriet, *m.* in Feb. 1830, to Le Comte Achille de la Marre.

Arms, Crest, and *Motto.*—Same as CAULFEILD *of Drumcairne.*
Seat—Donamon Castle, co. Roscommon.

CAY OF NORTH CHARLTON.

CAY, JOHN, Esq. of North Charlton Hall, co. Northumberland, F.R.S.E., sheriff of Linlithgowshire, *b.* 31 Aug. 1790; *m.* 1 June, 1819, Emily, dau. of the late William Bullock, Esq., secretary of the island of Jamaica, by whom (who *d.* 20 June, 1836) he has surviving issue,

I. JOHN. II. Robert. III. Edward.
IV. Thomas. V. Francis-Albert.
I. Emily. II. Elizabeth. III. Lucy.

Lineage.—The family of CAY (or, as the name was formerly spelt, KEY) is believed to have enjoyed very fair possessions in the Eastern Borders.

JABEZ CAY, M.D., son of Robert Key or Cay, of Newcastle, practised in Northumberland, and purchased a portion of the estate of North Charlton, in 1696. Dr. Cay, dying in 1702, *unm.*, left his share of the property to his brother,

JOHN CAY, Esq., who obtained also the remainder of the estate, and thus became of North Charlton. He *m.* Grace, dau. and co-heir of Henry Wolff, Esq. of Bridlington, and had issue,

ROBERT, his successor. Henry.
John, *b.* in 1700; who was appointed judge of the Marshalsea; *m.* Miss Boult, and had issue, 1 Henry-Boult,

who m. Miss Stawel Pigot, and left two daus., Frances, m. to Dr. Adams, rector of Halstead, in Essex; and Mary; 1 Grace, m. to John Adams, Esq.; and 2 Mary.

Mr. Cay was s. at his decease by his eldest son,

ROBERT CAY, Esq. of North Charlton and of the Lay-gate, Durham, b. in 1604. He m. Elizabeth, dau. of Reynold Hall, Esq. of Catcleugh, and had issue, JOHN, his successor; Reynold; Robert, a colonel in the E. I. Co.'s service, who d. of wounds received in action; Grace; and Gabriel. The eldest son,

JOHN CAY, Esq. m. Frances, dau. of Ralph Hodshon, Esq. of Lintz, and had a son and successor,

ROBERT-HODSHON CAY, Esq., b. 5 July, 1753, one of the Judges of the Consistorial Court, and Judge of the High Court of Admiralty in Scotland. He m. Elizabeth, dau. of John Liddell, Esq. of North Shields, and had surviving issue, I. JOHN, now of Charlton Hall; II. Albert; III. Robert-Dundas, who is m., and has four sons and one dau., I. Frances, m. to John-Clerk Maxwell, Esq. of Middlebie and Glenlair; and II. Jane.

Arms—Vert, a rose, arg., between two bars, or.
Crest—A royal eagle, gorged with a collar and banner, vert, bearing a rose, arg.
Motto—Sit sine spinâ. *Seat*—Charlton Hall.

CAYLEY OF WYDALE.

CAYLEY, EDWARD-STILLINGFLEET, Esq. of Wydale and Low Hall, co. York, M.P. for the North Riding, J.P. and D.L., b. 13 Aug. 1802; m. 30 Aug. 1823, Emma, 3rd dau. of Sir George Cayley, Bart., and by her (who d. 8 Aug. 1848) has issue,

I. EDWARD-STILLINGFLEET, b. 1st July, 1824.
II. George-John, b. 26 Jan. 1826.
III. Charles-Digby, b. March, 1827, R.N., d. 17 May, 1844.

Lineage.—ARTHUR CAYLEY, 2nd son of Sir William Cayley, 1st Baronet, of Brompton, co. York, m. Elizabeth, dau. of Thomas Shipton, Esq. of Low Hall, and was father of

ARTHUR CAYLEY, Esq. of Low Hall, co. York, who m. three times: 1st, Miss Noel, of the Gainsborough family; 2ndly, Miss Thompson, of Kilham; and 3rdly, Miss Judson. By the last only he had issue, viz., a son and heir,

THE REV. JOHN CAYLEY, of Low Hall, who m. Rebecca, dau. and co-heir of Alexander Nowell, Esq. of Rede, co. Lancaster, and had (with two daus., one of whom d. unm., and the other m. but had no issue) an only son,

THE REV. JOHN CAYLEY, of Low Hall, Brompton, who m. Frances, only dau. of Sir George Cayley, 4th Bart., by Philadelphia his wife, dau. of John Digby, Esq. of Mansfield Woodhouse (through this marriage, the present families of Cayley derive from Queen Adelicia, by her 2nd husband, William de Albini, and so, from CHARLEMAGNE), and had a dau., Philadelphia-Frances, and one son,

JOHN CAYLEY, Esq. of Low Hall, who m. 30 May, 1798, Elizabeth-Sarah Stillingfleet, great-granddau. of the celebrated Bishop Stillingfleet, and by that lady (who d. in 1807), left at his decease, 16 June, 1846, (with four daus., all of whom d. unm.) an only son, the present EDWARD-STILLINGFLEET CAYLEY, Esq., as above.

Arms—Quarterly: arg. and sa., on a bend, gu., three mullets, of the first.
Crest—A demi-lion, rampant, or, charged with a bend, gu., thereon three mullets, arg., in the paws a battle-axe, ppr.
Seats—Wydale House, near Scarborough; and Low Hall, Brompton, Yorkshire.

CHADWICK OF HEALEY, RIDWARE, AND NEW HALL.

CHADWICK, JOHN-DE HELEY-MAVESYN, Esq. of Healey, co. Lancaster, Ridware, co. Stafford, New Hall, co. Warwick, and Callow, co. Derby, b. 30 Dec. 1834.

Lineage.—JORDAN CHADWYK (younger brother of Henry de Chadwyk, of Chadwyk, co. Lancaster) m. Elianore, dau. of Christopher Kyrkeshagh, of Hundersfield, and by her was father of

JOHN CHADWYKE, who m. in 1483, Alice, eldest dau. and co-heir of Adam Okeden, of Heley, lineally descended from Adam de Okeden, who m. Havise, the heir of Thomas de Heley. John Chadwyck d. in 1498, leaving, with a younger son, James, a priest, his successor,

THOMAS CHADWYKE, of Heley, grandfather of

ROBERT CHADWYCKE, Esq. of Healey, who rebuilt with stone the old family mansion there. His grandson,

JOHN CHADWICKE, Esq. of Healey Hall, m. Katharine, only surviving dau. and heir of Lewis Chadwicke, Esq. of Mavesyn-Ridware, co. Stafford, colonel in the service of the Parliament, by Mary his wife, dau. and heir of Anthony Bagot, Esq. of Colton, which Lewis Chadwicke was eldest son of John Chadwicke, Esq., and Joyce his wife, dau. and co-heir of Thomas Cawarden, Esq. of Mavesyn-Ridware, sixth in descent from Sir John Cawarden, Knt., and Elizabeth his wife, dau. and co-heir of Sir Robert Mauveysin, Knt., lord of Mauvesyn-Ridware, *temp.* EDWARD III. By the heiress of Chadwicke of Mavesyn-Ridware (who m. 2ndly, in 1670, Jonathan Chadwicke, Esq. of Chadwicke, and 3rdly, George Halstead, Esq. of Manchester), Mr. Chadwicke of Healey had (with three daus., of whom the youngest, Mary, m. Robert Illingworth, Esq. of Huntsbank) five sons, viz.: 1 CHARLES, his heir; 2 John, M.A., vicar of Darenth, &c., co. Kent, father of CAPTAIN ROBERT CHADWICK, R.N. of Northfleet; 3 Jordan, of Oldham, who d. in 1728, leaving, by Jane his wife, relict of John Dearden, Esq., two sons, John and Richard; 4 Lewis, of Whitworth; 5 Robert, who d. unm. The eldest son,

CHARLES CHADWICK, Esq. of Healey and Ridware, bapt. 6th March, 1637, m. in 1665, Anne, only dau. of Valence Sacheverell, Esq. of New Hall, in Warwickshire, and of Callow, co. Derby, by Anne his wife, dau. of Sir George Devereux, Knt. of Sheldon Hall, and by her, who d. in 1689, he left at his decease, in 1697, a dau., Catherine, m. in 1696, to Ralph Floyer, Esq., and a son,

CHARLES CHADWICK, Esq. of Healey and Ridware, bapt. 22 Feb. 1675, who m. 1st, in 1699, Dorothy, dau. of Sir Thomas Dolman, Knt. of Shaw House, Berkshire, and had by her a son, CHARLES, his heir, and two daus., Mary, who d. unm. in 1770, and Dorothy, who inherited in 1779 the estates of Ridware, New Hall, and Callow, and d. unm. in 1784. Charles Chadwick m. 2ndly, 20 Nov. 1714, his cousin Mary, dau. of Robert Illingworth, Esq., and by her, who d. in 1737, had an only son, JOHN, of whom presently. Mr. Chadwick d. on Christmas-day, 1756, aged 82, and was s. by his son,

CHARLES CHADWICK, Esq. of Ridware, New Hall, and Callow, b. at Sutton, 1 Feb. 1706, who assumed, in compliance with the testamentary injunction of his great-uncle, George Sacheverell, Esq., the surname and arms of SACHEVERELL. He m. in 1741, Anna-Maria, eldest dau. and co-heir of William Brearley, Gent., of Handworth, but d. without issue, 31 July, 1779. His widow, surviving, succeeded to the large property of her only sister, Jane (who had m. 1st, Captain Clapton, and 2ndly, Walter Gough, Esq. of Perry Hall), and d. 12 Jan. 1795, aged 85. At the demise of Mr. (Chadwick) Sacheverell, the representation of the family devolved on his half-brother,

JOHN CHADWICK, Esq. of Healey Hall, J.P. and D.L., b. at Ridware, 22 Jan. 1720, lieut.-col. of the royal Lancashire militia. Colonel Chadwick m. in 1743, Susannah, youngest dau. of Robert Holt, Esq. of Shevington, and by her, who d. 19 Jan. 1765, he left at his decease, 23 Nov. 1800, a son and successor,

CHARLES CHADWICK, Esq. of Healey, Ridware, New Hall, and Callow, b. 2 Oct. 1753, m. in 1788, Frances, only surviving dau. and eventual heiress of Richard Green, Esq. of Leventhorp House, co. York, by Frances his wife, sister of Sir Henry Cavendish, Bart. of Doveridge, and dying in 1829, was s. by his only son,

HUGO-MAVESYN CHADWICK, Esq. of Mavesyn, Ridware, Healey, New Hall, and Callow, b. 28 Nov. 1793, who m. 13 June, 1826, Eliza-Catherine, youngest dau. of the late Lieut.-Gen. Chapman, R.A., and d. in 1854, leaving a son, the present JOHN-DE HELEY-MAVESYN CHADWICK, Esq. of Healey; and two daus., Elizabeth-Catherine, and Laura-Isabella-Louisa.

Arms—Gu., an inescutcheon within an orle of martlets, arg.
Crests—1st, a lily, arg., stalked and leaved, vert, for CHADWICK; 2nd, a talbot's head, gu., having the arms of Handsacre (erm., three cronels, gu.) on the collar, and pierced through the neck with an arrow.
Motto—Stans cum Rege.
Seats—Healey, Lancashire; New Hall, Warwickshire; and Ridware, Staffordshire.

CHADWICK OF HIGH-BANK.

CHADWICK, ROBERT, Esq. of High Bank, Prestwich, Lancashire, J.P., b. 16 Jan. 1797; m. 15 July, 1821, Elizabeth, dau. of John Kershaw, Esq. of Rochdale, and has issue,

I. JAMES, b. 15 July, 1824, m. 25 April, 1854, Laura-Janet-Emma, 3rd dau. of Charles Barnett, Esq. of Stratton Park, Bedfordshire.

II. Robert, b. 3 April, 1835, lieut. 14th light dragoons.
I. Eliza-Jane, d. young.
II. Mary, d. unm.
III. Eliza, m. 19 Sept. 1850, William-Henry, 6th son of Oswald Milne, Esq. of Prestwich Wood, Lancashire.
IV. Anne. V. Catharine-Anne.

Lineage.—James Chadwick, Esq. of Patricroft House, Eccles, m. 5 Jan. 1777, Mary, dau. of Thomas Chorlton, Esq. of The Weaste, and by her, who d. 8 Oct. 1839, had issue,

William, b. 25 Aug. 1780, m. Elizabeth-Anne, dau. of Thomas Wilkinson, Esq. of Leeds, and d. leaving one dau.
James, b. 9 Feb. 1794, m. Alice, dau. of Thomas Fogg, Esq. of Bolton, and d. without issue.
Robert, now of High Bank.
Mary, m. Thomas Salter, Esq., and d. leaving one dau.
Catherine-Chorlton, d. unm.
Anne, of Barton-on-Irwell.

Arms—Per pale, az. and gu.: an inescocheon, erm., within an orle of fleurs-de lis and martlets alternately, arg.
Crest—In front of a lily, stalked and leaved, ppr., a martlet, arg.
Motto—Deo fidens proficio.
Seat—High Bank, Prestwich.

CHADWICK OF PUDLESTON COURT.

Chadwick, Elias, Esq. of Pudleston Court, co. Hereford, late of Swinton Hall, co. Lancaster, Hon. A.M. Oxford and Cambridge, J.P. and D.L., b. 6 Jan. 1813; s. his father in Jan. 1834; m. 7 Aug. 1840, Ellen, dau. of Thomas Seddon, Esq. of Manchester.

Lineage.—This family springs originally from the hamlet of Chadwick, in the parish of Rochdale. William de Chadwyke, the first of the name on record, was born about the year 1355, as he was living in 1418, being then styled *senior*, and having a son, William, of age. His descendant,

John de Chadwyk, was ancestor of the Chadwickes *of Chadwick;* the Chadwickes *of Healey Hall*, Lancashire; the Chadwickes *of Mavesyn-Ridware;* and of

Elias Chadwick, Esq. of Wigan, son of Elias Chadwick, of Winstanley, who m. Ellen, dau. of James Strettell, of Swinton, co. Lancaster, Esq., and had issue,

I. Strettell, who m. Grace, widow of — Bolton, Esq., and is deceased.
II. Elias, of whom presently.
I. Margaret, m. Thomas Seddon, Esq. of Manchester, and had five sons and daus., viz.,
  1 James Seddon.
  2 Robert Seddon, who m. 1st, his cousin Mary, dau. of Strettell Seddon, Esq. of Darley, and 2ndly, Judith, dau. of R. Wetherell, Esq. of Liverpool.
  3 Strettell Seddon, who m. Mary, dau. of R. Wetherell, Esq., and has, Strettell, Sandford, Thomas, Robert, and James.
  1 Ellen Seddon, m. to her cousin, Elias Chadwick, Esq.
I. Ellen, m. to Jeremiah Royle, Esq. of Manchester, who is deceased.

The youngest son,

Elias Chadwick, of Swinton Hall, Esq., m. 14 Aug. 1806, Alice, dau. of Henry Arrowsmith, Esq. of Astley, in the same county, and by her (who is deceased) had issue,

I. Henry-Strettell, of the Inner Temple, barrister-at-law, b. 11 June, 1807, m. Miss Elizabeth Pearce, of Norwich, and has a son Harry, and a dau. Emily.
II. Elias, now of Pudleston Court.
I. Ellen, who m. the Rev. Samuel-Broomhead Ward, B.A., rector of Teffont Evias, Wilts, eldest son of Samuel-Broomhead Ward, Esq. of Mount Pleasant, in Yorkshire, and has issue,
  1 Samuel-Broomhead Ward.
  2 Henry-Chadwick Ward.
  3 Francis-William Ward.
  4 James-Rimington Ward.
  5 Charles-Godolphin Ward.
  1 Ellen-Sarah Ward.
  2 Isabella-Louisa Ward.
II. Elizabeth, d. unm. 24 Dec. 1832.
III. Fanny, m. Thomas-Archer Colt, Esq. M.D., 2nd son of the late Sir E.-V. Colt, Bart., and has, Edward-Harry-Dutton, Thomas-Archer, and Frances-Alice.

Mr. Chadwick d. 8 Feb. 1825.

Arms—Gu., an inescutcheon within an orle of martlets, arg., all within a bordure, engrailed, or, charged with crosses-crosslet.
Crest—In front of two crosses-crosslet fitchée, in saltier, the flower and stem of a white lily, slipped, ppr.
Motto—In candore decus.
Seat—Pudleston Court, Leominster.

CHADWICK OF DARESBURY HALL.

Chadwick, Samuel-Beckett, Esq. of Daresbury Hall, Preston Brook, co. Chester, b. 28 Jan. 1818; m. 6 April, 1843, Elizabeth, dau. of Philip Whiteway, Esq., J.P. of Runcorn, and has surviving issue,

I. Samuel-Beckett, b. 9 Oct. 1848.
II. Philip-Richard, b. 4 Oct. 1850.
I. Mary-Anne. II. Frances.
III. Elizabeth-Catherine.

Mr. Chadwick is son and heir of the late Samuel Chadwick, Esq., who purchased from the Rev. George Heron, in 1832, the manor and estate of Daresbury.

Arms—Gu., an inescutcheon, within an orle of martlets, arg.
Crest—A lily, arg., stalked and leaved, vert.
Motto—In candore decus.
Seat—Daresbury Hall, near Warrington.

CHALLEN OF SHERMANBURY PARK.

Challen, Stephen-Hasler, Esq. of Shermanbury Park, co. Sussex, m. Barbara, dau. and heir of William Chambers, Esq. of Seaford, and had issue,

I. Maria-Harriet. II. Barbara-Jane.
III. Caroline. IV. Emily.

Lineage.—John Challen, Esq., m. Cassandra, only dau. and heir of Henry Farncomb, of Shermanbury, and had issue,

John-Gratwick, his heir. Stephen-Hasler.
George, capt. N.I., who d. at Bombay in 1825.
Ann-Farncombe, d. unm. 3 Feb. 1839.
Augusta, m. to Capt. Robert-William Gillum.

The eldest son,

The Rev. Dr. John-Gratwick Challen, m. Sophia, dau. of John Diggins, Esq. of Chichester; but d. s. p. 6 Dec. 1835, and was s. by his brother, the present Stephen-Hasler Challen, Esq. of Shermanbury

Arms—Sa., a chevron, engrailed, or, between three cherubs' heads, of the second.
Crest—A demi-horse, saliant.
Motto—Gloria Deo.
Seat—Shermanbury Park, near Henfield.

CHALLONER OF PORTNALL.

Challoner-Bisse, Thomas-Chaloner, Esq. of Portnall Park, co. Surrey, lieut.-col. comm. 3rd royal Surrey militia, J.P. and D.L., high-sheriff in 1838, b. in Dec. 1789; m. in June, 1812, Anne, dau. of Nicholas-Loftus Tottenham, Esq., M.P. He s. his father, the Rev. Thomas Bisse, in 1828, and assumed the name of Challoner, by royal license, in 1829, in accordance with the terms of the will of his maternal great-aunt, Mrs. Challoner.

Lineage.—Thomas Bisse, Esq., nephew of Dr. Bisse, author of the *Beauties of Holiness*, and great-nephew to Dr. Bisse, founder of the library of Wadham College, Oxford, and benefactor to All Souls College, Oxford, was father of

The Rev. Thomas Bisse, who m. 1st, in 1787, Miss Katherine Townshend, who d. in 1815; and 2ndly, Miss Charlotte Price, by whom he had one son, b. in 1822. He d. in 1828, and was s. by the son of his first marriage, the present Thomas-Chaloner Bisse-Challoner, Esq. of Portnall Park.

Arms—Quarterly: 1st and 4th, for Challoner; 2nd and 3rd, for Bisse, sa., three escallops, in pale, arg., a canton, erm., and a crescent, for difference.
Crests—1st, for Challoner; 2nd, for Bisse, on a mount, vert, two snakes, or, interlaced, respecting each other.
Seat—Portnall Park, Virginia Water, co. Surrey.

CHALMERS OF ALDBAR CASTLE.

Chalmers, John-Inglis, Esq. of Aldbar Castle, Forfarshire, s. his brother in 1854.

Lineage.—As to the origin of the Chalmers in the north of Scotland, it is most probable that they are a branch of the clan Cameron, from the affinity of their arms; and besides, Sir George Mackenzie, in his genealogical manuscript of the families of Scotland, says, "One of the clan going to France, put his name in a Latin dress, by designing himself Camerario, which, in French, is "de la chambre," who, upon his return to Scotland, was, according to our dialect, called Chambers, which tradition (continues Sir George) is more confirmed by the fleur-de-lis carried in base in their arms, which addition their predecessor has no doubt got when in France for some meritorious action done there."

Derived from a branch of CHAMBERS *of Balnacraig*, was,

WILLIAM CHALMERS, Esq. of Albar, son of — Chalmers, of Aldbar, Esq., by his wife, the eldest dau. of — Forbes, of Foveran, Bart. He *m.* Cecilia, dau. of Elphinstone of Glack, Aberdeenshire, and had (with a dau., who *m.* Irvine of Inveramsay) a son,

PATRICK CHALMERS, Esq. of Aldbar, who, by his wife, Isabel Tindal, was father of

PATRICK CHALMERS, Esq. of Aldbar, who *m.* in 1801, Frances, eldest dau. of John Inglis, of Verehills, co. Lanark, a merchant in London, and an E. I. Director, by whom he had issue,

PATRICK, of Aldbar.	JOHN-INGLIS, now of Aldbar
Isabella.	Frances.
Margaret-Anne.	Euphemia, deceased.

He *d.* in 1826, and was *s.* by his son,

PATRICK CHALMERS, Esq. of Aldbar Castle, J.P. and D.L., formerly captain 3rd dragoon guards, and M.P. for Montrose, *b.* in 1802, who *d.* in 1854, and was *s.* by his brother, the present JOHN-INGLIS CHALMERS, Esq. of Aldbar Castle.

Arms—Arg., a demi-lion, rampant, issuing out of a fesse, gu., with a fleur-de-lis, in base, of the last.
Crest—An eagle rising, ppr.
Motto—Spero. *Seat*—Aldbar Castle, co. Forfar.

CHALONER OF GUISBOROUGH.

CHALONER, ROBERT, Esq. of Guisborough, co. York, *b.* 3 April, 1813; *s.* his father 7 Oct. 1842; *m.* 29 Feb. 1844, Laura-Mary, dau. of Sir Thomas Butler, Bart. of Garryhundon, which lady is deceased.

Lineage.—EDWARD CHALONER, D.D., one of the chaplains to CHARLES I., next brother of Sir William Chaloner, Bart. (*see* BURKE'S *Extinct Baronetage*), *m.* Elizabeth, dau. of Dr. Hovedon, prebendary of Canterbury; and *d.* in 1625, aged 35, leaving an only son and heir,

SIR EDWARD CHALONER, Knt., who *m.* Anne, dau. of Sir R. Ingoldsby, Knt. of Waldridge, Bucks, and was father of

WILLIAM CHALONER, Esq. of Guisborough, who *m.* Honora, eldest dau. of Sir David Foulis, Bart. of Ingleby Manor, and had issue. The eldest son,

EDWARD CHALONER, Esq. of Guisborough, *m.* Anne, dau. of Sir William Bowes, of Streatlam Castle, co. Durham, Knt.; and *d.* in 1737, leaving one son and heir,

WILLIAM CHALONER, Esq. of Guisborough, who *m.* Mary, dau. and heir of James Finny, Esq. of Finny Lane, co. Stafford, late of the city of Durham, and had two sons and four daus., viz., WILLIAM, his heir; Edward, a capt. in the army, who *d.* in 1807, of wounds received at the storming of Morne Fortuné, St. Lucia; Anne, *m.* in 1761, to Edward, 1st Lord Harewood; Mary, *m.* to General John Hale, governor of Londonderry; Elizabeth, who *d. unm.*; and Jane, wife of Sir Henry Wilson, Knt. The elder son,

WILLIAM CHALONER, Esq. of Guisborough, *m.* 8 Aug. 1771, Emma, dau. of William Harvey, Esq. of Chigwell, and sister of Admiral Sir Eliab Harvey, G.C.B., and left issue, ROBERT, his heir; Henry, in holy orders, *b.* in 1791, vicar of Alne, co. York; Anna-Maria, *m.* to John-William Bethell, Esq.; Elizabeth; Louisa; Charlotte, *m.* to Thomas-Barton Bowen, Esq., barrister-at-law, and one of the commissioners of the Court of Insolvency; and Williamina, *m.* to Alexander Wynch, Esq. The elder son,

ROBERT CHALONER, Esq. of Guisborough, *b.* 28 Sept. 1776, *m.* 24 Jan. 1805, Frances-Laura, dau. of Thomas, 1st Lord Dundas, and had issue, William, lost at sea, in going to join his regiment at Halifax, Nova Scotia; ROBERT, his heir; Thomas, lieut. R.N., *b.* 6 Feb. 1815; Margaret-Bruce, *m.* to William-Wentworth-Fitzwilliam Hume, Esq. of Humewood, co. Wicklow, and *d.* in 1840; Emma, *m.* to George Serjeantson, Esq. of Camphill; and Charlotte. Mr. Chaloner, who was a magistrate and deputy-lieutenant for Yorkshire, *d.* 7 Oct. 1842, and was *s.* by his son, the present ROBERT CHALONER, Esq. of Guisborough.

Arms—Sa., a chevron, between three cherubim, or.
Crest—A demi-seawolf, rampant, or.
Seat—Longhull, Guisborough, North Riding of Yorkshire.

CHALONER OF KINGSFORT.

CHALONER, RICHARD, Esq. of Kingsfort, co. Meath, J.P., *b.* 20 April, 1810; *m.* 12 Feb. 1835, Henrietta, 2nd dau. of Charles-Arthur Tisdall, Esq. of Charlesfort. This gentleman, 2nd son of Claude-William-Cole Hamilton, Esq. of Beltrim, co. Tyrone, by Nichola Sophia his wife, dau. and heir of Richard Chaloner, Esq. of Kingsfort, assumed the surname and arms of CHALONER, on inheriting the property of his mother's family.

Arms, &c.—See CHALONER *of Guisborough*.
Seat—Kingsfort, co. Meath.

CHAMBERLAYNE OF MAUGERSBURY.

CHAMBERLAYNE, JOSEPH-CHAMBERLAYNE, Esq. of Maugersbury House, co. Gloucester, *b.* 19 Dec. 1791; *m.* 26 Oct. 1824, Henrietta-Catherine, dau. of the Rev. Guy Fairfax (of the family of Lord Fairfax), and granddau. of the Rev. John Kearney, D.D., by his wife, Henrietta, dau. of the Hon. and Rev. Henry Brydges, brother of James, Duke of Chandos, and has had issue,

I. Henrietta-Catherine-Elizabeth, deceased.
II. Lavinia-Frances-Elizabeth.
III. Theophania-Caroline-Elizabeth, deceased.
IV. Blanche-Frances-Elizabeth.

Mr. Chamberlayne, lately an officer in the royal artillery, assumed, in compliance with his maternal uncle's will, the surname of CHAMBERLAYNE only, in lieu of his patronymic, Ackerley.

Lineage.—This family is descended from John, Count de Tankerville, of Tankerville Castle, in Normandy, who accompanied the CONQUEROR to England; and, on the subjugation of that country, returned to his extensive landed possessions in Normandy. This ancient family of the Tankervilles was nearly allied to the Montmorency branch of the royal house of France. JOHN, son of the Earl of Tankerville, being left in England, became lord-chamberlain to HENRY I., and was father of RICHARD, lord-chamberlain to King STEPHEN, who assumed the surname of CHAMBERLAYNE from his office, the sign-manual having been given as its warranty. He was father of WILLIAM CHAMBERLAYNE, Lord of North Ryston, chamberlain to HENRY II., who, having made prisoner Robert de Bellemont, Earl of Leicester, had permission, in 1174, from the king to quarter that nobleman's arms with his own. His grandson, SIR RICHARD CHAMBERLAYNE, *m.* Jane, dau. and heir of John Gatesden, and was grandfather of SIR JOHN CHAMBERLAYNE, distinguished in the martial reign of EDWARD III., who *m.* Jane, dau. and heir of John Mortein, son and heir of Sir John Mortein, by Joan his wife, dau. and heir of Richard Ekney, of Ekney, and was father of SIR RICHARD CHAMBERLAYNE, who *m.* Jane, dau. of Sir John Reynes, of Clifton Reynes, Knt., and had issue. The eldest son, SIR RICHARD, settled at Sherborn, co. Oxford, where his descendants continued until the time of JAMES I., when John, the last male of the branch, *d.*, leaving two daus. and co-heirs: the elder *m.* 1st, to Sir Thomas Gage, Bart., and 2ndly, to Sir William Goring, Bart.; and the younger, *m.* to Nevil, Lord Abergavenny. Sir Richard's younger son, JOHN CHAMBERLAYNE, Esq. of Hopton, co. Derby, was father of THOMAS, whose son, JOHN, *m.* a dau. of — Elton, and was *s.* by his son, JOHN, father, by Agnes Keynes his wife, of WILLIAM CHAMBERLAYNE, Esq., who *m.* Elizabeth Fleming, of Dartmouth, and had two sons; from the younger, William, descended the CHAMBERLAYNES *of Wickham*, Baronets, extinct in 1776. The elder son,

SIR THOMAS CHAMBERLAYNE, of Prestbury, co. Gloucester, ambassador to the court of Spain in the reigns of HENRY VIII., EDWARD VI., Queens MARY and ELIZABETH, *m.* thrice: 1st, Ann Van der Zenny, of the royal house of Nassau; 2ndly, Elizabeth, dau. of Sir John Luddington, and relict of — Machine, and from this marriage derive the Maugersbury branch; and 3rdly, Anne Kirkest, half-sister to Anthony Monk, of Devonshire, granddau. to the Duke of Albemarle, from whom descended the CHAMBERLAYNES *of Oddington*.

EDMUND CHAMBERLAYNE, Esq. of Maugersbury, co. Gloucester, 2nd son of Sir Thomas Chamberlayne, by his 2nd wife, became heir to his brother, Sir John, of Prestbury, who had *m.* Elizabeth, dau. of Thynne of Longleat, but *d. s. p.* Edmund *m.* 1st, Anne, relict of — Moreton, of Surrey; and 2ndly, Grace, dau. of John Strangeways, Esq. of Melbury, co. Dorset. He was high-sheriff of Gloucestershire, 39th ELIZABETH, and *d.* in 1634, when he was *s.* by his son by his second marriage,

John Chamberlayne, Esq. of Maugersbury House, eminent for his loyalty. He was sequestered in the Great Rebellion, and paid £1,246 for composition. He m. Elizabeth, dau. of Sir William Leigh, of Longborow; and dying in 1663, was s. by his son,

John Chamberlayne, Esq. of Maugersbury House, who m. Mary, dau. of Walter Savage, Esq. of Broadway, co. Worcester; and d. in 1691, when he was s. by his son,

Edmund Chamberlayne, Esq. of Maugersbury House, high-sheriff of Gloucestershire, 4th Queen Anne, who m. the Hon. Emma Brydges, sister of James, Duke of Chandos, and was father of

Edmund Chamberlayne, Esq. of Maugersbury, who m. Elizabeth, dau. and co-heir of Robert Atkyns, Esq., and had issue, John, his heir; and Charles, admiral R.N., who d. in 1810, leaving issue. The son and heir,

The Rev. John Chamberlayne, of Maugersbury House, m. Martha, dau. and co-heir of Henry Doughty, Esq. of Broadwell, co. Gloucester, and had a son and dau., twins, b. 19 May, 1766, viz., Edmund-John, his heir, and Elizabeth, who m. 16 Feb. 1791, John-Hawksey Ackerley, Esq., barrister-at-law, and had issue two sons, Joseph Chamberlayne, who inherited Maugersbury from his uncle, and is the present Joseph-Chamberlayne Chamberlayne, Esq.; and Charles-Henry; and two daus., the elder of whom m. Peter-Joseph Browne, Esq. of the family of the Marquis of Sligo: and the younger m. John-Crooke Freeman, Esq. of Crooke Hall, co. Lancaster. The only son of the Rev. John Chamberlayne,

Edmund-John Chamberlayne, Esq. of Maugersbury House, m. Cecil, dau. of the Hon. and Rev. Dr. Talbot, dean of Salisbury, and niece of Earl Talbot; and d. s. p. in Feb. 1831, leaving his estates to his twin sister's eldest son, the present Joseph-Chamberlayne Chamberlayne, Esq. of Maugersbury House.

Arms—Quarterly: 1st and 4th, gu., a chevron, between three escallops, arg.; 2nd and 3rd, gu., on a fesse, engrailed, arg., between three griffins' heads, erased, or, as many crosses patée-fitchée, sa.

Crests—1st, out of a ducal coronet, an ass's head; 2nd, a lion's head, erased, charged with three trefoils.

Motto—Virtute nihil invium.

Seat—Maugersbury House.

CHAMBERLAYNE OF STONEY THORPE.

Chamberlayne, Henry-Thomas, Esq. of Stoney Thorpe, co. Warwick, J.P., high-sheriff in 1836, b. 23 May, 1798; m. 6 Dec. 1824, Mary, only child of Edward Tomes, Esq. of Southam, and has issue,

i. William-Tankerville, b. 14 Nov. 1828.
ii. Edward-Tomes, b. 4 Feb. 1833.
iii. Stanes-Brocket-Henry, b. 8 Feb. 1843.
i. Emma-Caroline. ii. Ellen-Bridget.
iii. Thermuthes-Fauquier.

Lineage.—This is a branch of the distinguished family of Chamberlayne, which derived from the Norman Counts of Tankerville, and maintained for a long series of years a leading position in the various counties in which it was established. The chief line were the Chamberlaynes *of Sherborne*, in Oxfordshire, from which derived (through a younger son) the celebrated Sir Thomas Chamberlayne, of Prince Thorpe and Presbury, a distinguished diplomatist in the reigns of Henry VIII., Edward VI., Queen Mary, and Queen Elizabeth. The immediate ancestor of the family before us was,

Edward Chamberlayne, of Prince Thorpe, in the county of Warwick, Esq. His son was great-great-grandfather of

Stanes Chamberlayne, Esq. of Ryes, in Essex, only son of Richard Chamberlayne, Esq. of Princethorpe, by Sarah his wife, dau. and heir of Jeffery Stanes, Esq. of Ryes, Essex, m. in 1745, Miss Thermuthes Smith, of Hoddesdon, co. Herts, and had issue. The eldest son,

Stanes Chamberlayne, Esq. of Ryes, m. in 1780, Mary, dau. and heir of William Brockett, Esq. of Spains Hall, Essex, and had issue,

Stanes (now Brockett), of The Ryes, b. 9 April, 1782, m. Eliza, widow of William Woollett, Esq.
William, col. in the army, b. 12 Aug. 1788, who m. Sarah, 4th dau. of the Rev. John Preston, of Flasby Hall, co. York, and has two daus., Sarah-Anne-Olivia and Caroline-Mary.
John, in holy orders, rector of East Wick, co. Hants, b. 25 Aug. 1791.
Henry-Thomas, now of Stoney Thorpe.
Maria, m. to James Hamerton, Esq. of Hellifield Peel, co. York.
Sarah. Emma. Harriet-Alicia.

Arms—Quarterly: 1st and 4th, gu., an inescutcheon in an orle of mullets, arg.; 2nd and 3rd, gu., a chevron, between three escallops, or.

Crest—Out of a ducal coronet, or, an ass's head.

Motto—Prodesse quam conspici.

Seat—Stoney Thorpe, near Southam.

CHAMBERLAYNE OF CRANBURY PARK.

Chamberlayne, Thomas, Esq. of Cranbury Park, and Weston Grove, co. Hants, J.P. and D.L., high-sheriff in 1835, b. in 1805; m. in 1830, Amelia, dau. of the late Gen. Denzil Onslow, of Stoughton House, co. Huntingdon, and has issue,

i. Denzil-Thomas, b. in 1833.
ii. Tankerville, b. in 1840.
i. Amy-Sophia. ii. Francesca-Maria.

Mr. Chamberlayne s. the late Miss Charlotte Chamberlayne in 1831. He is only son of the late Rev. Thomas Chamberlayne,* rector and patron of Charlton, by Maria-Francesca, his 1st wife, dau. of Capt. Robert Walter, R.N., and grandson of the Rev. Thomas Chamberlayne, rector and patron of Charlton, by Catherine Crossweller his wife.

Arms—Gu., an inescutcheon, arg., within an orle of mullets, or.

Crest—Out of a ducal coronet, or., an ass's head, arg.

Motto—Mors potior macula.

Seats—Cranbury Park, near Winchester; and Weston Grove, near Southampton.

CHAMBERS OF FOX HALL.

Chambers, John, Esq. of Fox Hall, co. Donegal, J.P., b. 21 March, 1793; m. 14 July, 1826, Anne, eldest dau. of Charles Calhoun, Esq. of Letter-Kenny, and has issue,

i. Brooke-Rynd, b. 1834. ii. Charles-Patton, b. 1836.
iii. Daniel, b. 1842. iv. John, b. 1845.
v. William-Grove, b. 1848. vi. Henry-Ellison, b. 1850.
i. Anne-Henrietta.

Lineage.—This family claims to be a branch of the ancient Scottish house of Chambers or Chalmers.

Brooke Chambers, Esq. of Rock Hill, co. Donegal, J.P., m. in 1723, Letitia, dau. of Col. Daniel M'Naill, of Binion, and of Tynan, Argyllshire, N.B., and had (with three daus., Anne, Frances, and Isabella) a son,

Daniel Chambers, Esq. of Rock Hill, J.P., who m. in 1752, Isabella, only dau. of John Davis, Esq. of Errity and Cappagh, and Old Grange, co. Kilkenny, and had issue, Brooke, his heir; John; William; Catherine-Letitia-Isabella; and Susannah. The eldest son and heir,

Brooke Chambers, Esq. of Rock Hill, J.P., high-sheriff of Donegal in 1798, m. in 1789, Margaret, eldest dau. of Charles Colhoun, Esq. of Letterkenny, and granddau. of William Richardson, Esq. of Drum, co. Tyrone, and by her had issue,

Daniel, of Loughveagh, J.P. and D.L., high-sheriff in 1839, m. 1816, Elizabeth-Rebecca, only dau. of John-William Beyton, Esq., M.D., and d. s. p. 8 Oct. 1850.
Charles, b. in 1791, d. in the E.I.C.S. in 1815.
John, now of Fox Hall.
Jane-Mary, m. in 1816, to John-W. Patton, capt. E.I.C.S.
Isabella, m. in Jan. 1815, to Gen. Mossom Boyd, of the Bengal army.

Arms—Arg., a demi-lion, issuing from a fesse, gu., a fleur-de-lis, in base, of the last.

Crest—A falcon, close, belled, ppr.

Motto—Spero dum spiro.

Seat—Lougveagh, Church Hill, Letterkenny.

CHAMBRE OF HAWTHORN HILL.

Chambre, Meredith, Esq. of Hawthorn Hill, co. Armagh, J.P., b. 15 May, 1814; m. 4 April, 1843, Mabella, only dau. of Kenrick-Morris Jones, Esq. of Moneyglass House, co. Antrim, and has issue,

i. Hunt-Walsh, b. 1844.
ii. Kenrick-Hamilton, b. 1845.

* William Chamberlain, solicitor to the Treasury and to the Royal Mint, cousin of Thomas Chamberlayne, Esq. of Charlton, left one son and two daus., viz.,

William, of Weston Grove and Cranbury Park, Hants, M.P. for Southampton, who d. unm. 10 Dec. 1830.
Mary, who d. unm. Charlotte, who d. unm. in 1831.

III. Thomas-Morris-Hamilton-Jones, *b.* 1847.
I. Rebecca. II. Mabella.

Lineage.—This is a branch of the ancient Shropshire family of CHAMBRE *of Petton*.

HUNT-CALCOTT CHAMBRE, Esq. (eldest son of Capt. Calcott Chambré, of Wexford, by Mary his wife, dau. of Oliver Walsh, Esq. of Dollardstown, and grandson of Calcott Chambré, Esq. of Coolatrundle,) *m.* Anna-Maria, eldest dau. and co-heir of William Meredith, Esq., and had (with other children, who *d. unm.*, three daus., Ellinor, *m.* to George Daker, of Athy, co. Kildare, Esq.; Anne, *m.* to Lieut.-Col. William Conolly, 18th foot; and Henrietta, *m.* to Wm. Madden, Esq.) a son and successor,

MEREDITH-CALCOTT CHAMBRE, Esq. of Hawthorn Hill, who *m.* 30 July, 1785, Margaret, 2nd dau. and co-heir of George Falkner, co. Dublin, Esq., and had issue,

HUNT-WALSH, heir to his father.
William, major in the army, and senior capt. in 11th foot.
Maria, *m.* to the Rev. Robert Henry, rector of Joinsborough, co. Armagh.

Mr. Chambré *d.* 8 Feb. 1812, and was *s.* by his eldest son,

HUNT-WALSH CHAMBRE, Esq. of Hawthorn Hill, *b.* 9 Dec. 1787, *m.* 15 May, 1813, Rebecca, only dau. of William Upton, of Ballynabearney, co. Limerick, Esq., a branch of Lord Templetown's family, and had issue,

I. MEREDITH, now of Hawthorn Hill.
II. William, married. III. Hunt-Walsh. IV. John.
I. Catherine, *m.* to George-W. Leech, Esq. of Rathkeale.
II. Anna-Maria, *m.* to Charles Leech, Esq., barrister-at-law.
III. Rebecca.
IV. Margaret-Elizabeth, *m.* to Townley-William Hardman, Esq.
V. Olivia-Henrietta-Agnes, *m.* to Robert Crookshank, Esq.
VI. Mary-Frances.
VII. Jane-Hunt, *m.* to the Rev. Henry-Wray Young.

Mr. Chambré was captain in the Armagh Yeomanry, and a magistrate for the co. of Armagh, for which he served as high-sheriff.

Arms—Az., a dexter armed arm, embowed, or, the hand grasping the stalk of a red rose, slipped and leaved, ppr.
Crest—A greyhound's head, erased, arg., collared, az., therefrom a cord knotted, and terminated by a ring, or.
Motto—Tutamen pulchris.
Seat—Hawthorn Hill, near Newry, co. Armagh.

CHAMPERNOWNE OF DARTINGTON.

CHAMPERNOWNE, ARTHUR, Esq. of Dartington, co. Devon, *b.* 19 March, 1839.

Lineage.—The family of CHAMPERNOWNE, which, in splendour of descent, yields to few in the west of England, was originally called CAMPO ARNULPHI; and the first members sent to parliament by the co. of Cornwall were William de Campo-Arnulphi and Reginald Beville.

SIR ARTHUR CHAMPERNOWNE, living *temp.* HENRY VIII., 2nd son of Sir Philip Champernowne, Knt. of Modbury, by Katherine his wife, dau. of Sir Edmund Carew, exchanged, early in the reign of ELIZABETH, the lordship of Polsloe for that of Dartington, in the co. of Devon, and seated himself there, where his descendants have since remained. He *m.* Mary, dau. of Henry Norreys, father of Henry, Baron Norreys of Rycote, and widow of Sir George Carew, by whom he had (with a dau., Elizabeth, *m.* in 1576, to Sir Edward Seymour, Bart.) a son,

GAWEN CHAMPERNOWNE, Esq. of Dartington, in Devon, who *m.* the Lady Gabrielle, dau. of the Count Montgomerie, in France, and left (with several daus., one of whom *m.* Richard Hillersdon, of Membland, and another, Ursula, Sir Gerard Sams, of Essex) a son,

ARTHUR CHAMPERNOWNE, Esq. of Dartington, living in 1620, who *m.* Bridget, dau. of Thomas Fulford, Esq. of Fulford, in Devon, and was *s.* by his son,

ARTHUR CHAMPERNOWNE, Esq. of Dartington, living in 1678, who *m.* Margaret, dau. and eventually co-heir of Sir John Fowell, Bart. of Fowellscombe, M.P., colonel of foot in the service of the Parliament, and Governor of Totnes. By her Mr. Champernowne had eight sons. The eldest son,

RICHARD CHAMPERNOWNE, Esq. of Dartington, dying *unm.* in 1696, was *s.* by his brother,

ARTHUR CHAMPERNOWNE, Esq. of Dartington, who *m.* Elizabeth, 2nd dau. of Francis Courtenay, Esq., who *d.* in 1669, eldest son of Sir William Courtenay, of Powderham, and dying in 1717, left (with a dau., Elizabeth, wife of Gabriel Yard, Esq. of Stoke Gabriel) two sons: the younger Francis, rector of Dartington, *d. unm.*; the elder,

ARTHUR CHAMPERNOWNE, Esq. of Dartington, *m.* Jane, dau. of John Hollings, M.D., physician to GEORGE II., and dying in April, 1766, left an only dau. and heiress,

JANE CHAMPERNOWNE, of Dartington, who *m.* the Rev. Richard Harington, 2nd son of Sir James Harington, Bart., of Ridlington, and by that gentleman (who *m.* 2ndly, Miss Hussey, of Truro, and 3rdly, Elizabeth, dau. of Abraham Chambers, Esq. of Totteridge, and relict of William Hallett, Esq.) had a son and successor,

ARTHUR HARINGTON, Esq. of Dartington, who assumed the surname and arms of CHAMPERNOWNE. He *m.* in 1806, Louisa, dau. of John Buller, Esq. of Morval, in the co. of Devon, and had issue, HENRY, his heir; Richard, *m.* Elizabeth Keble, and has two sons and a dau.; John, *d.* in 1837; Jane, *m.* to the Rev. William Martin, late vicar of Staverton; Louisa; Caroline, *m.* to the Rev. Isaac Williams; and Maria, *m.* to Charles-Herbert Mallock, Esq. Mr. (Harington) Champernowne, M.P. for Saltash in 1806, and high-sheriff of Devon in 1811, *d.* in 1819, and was *s.* by his eldest son,

HENRY CHAMPERNOWNE, Esq. of Dartington, *b.* 14 Sept. 1815, who *m.* 24 April, 1838, Charlotte, dau. of Sir Antony Buller, and *d.* 24 May, 1851, leaving issue, ARTHUR, now of Dartington; Henry, *b.* 21 May, 1840, Walter, *b.* 3 Sept. 1848; Caroline; Elinor; and Margaret.

Arms—Gu., a saltier, vair, between twelve billets, or.
Crest—A swan, sitting, ppr., holding in the beak a horseshoe.
Seat—Dartington House, near Totnes.

CHAPLIN OF BLANKNEY.

CHAPLIN, CHARLES, Esq. of Blankney and Tathwell, co. Lincoln, J.P. and D.L., late M.P. for Lincolnshire, *b.* 21 April, 1786; *m.* 17 Sept., 1812, Caroline, dau. of the Hon. Henry Fane, of Fulbeck.

Lineage.—The family of Chaplin, long of high consideration in Lincolnshire, derives from

SIR FRANCIS CHAPLIN, alderman of London, lord mayor in 1677. He *m.* and had issue, JOHN, his heir; Charles; Robert (Sir) created a baronet, with limitation to his grand-nephew John; Anne; Elizabeth. The eldest son,

JOHN CHAPLIN, Esq., *b.* 29 Jan. 1657, *m.* Elizabeth, dau. of Sir John Hamby, of Tathwell, and by her had issue,

I. PORTER, who *m.* Anne Sherwin, and had issue,
1 JOHN (Sir), who *s.* his granduncle as 2nd bart.; his only child (a posthumous dau.) *m.* — Gregory, Esq. of Warwickshire.
1 Elizabeth, *m.* to Edward Ayscough, Esq. of Louth.
2 Anne, *m.* to William Vavasor, Esq. of Yorkshire.
3 Frances, *m.* to Charles Fitzwilliam, Esq. of Caistor.
II. Francis, *d.* in 1720.
III. John, *d.* in the West Indies.
IV. THOMAS, of whom we treat.
I. Anna, *m.* to Thomas Archer, Esq.

The youngest son,

THOMAS CHAPLIN, Esq., *m.* Diana, sister of Thomas, 1st Lord Archer, and had issue,

JOHN, of Blankney.
CHARLES (see CHAPLIN *of Tathwell Hall*).
Diana, *m.* to Lord George-Manners Sutton.

The son and heir,

JOHN CHAPLIN, Esq. of Blankney, *m.* 24 Nov. 1757, Lady Elizabeth Cecil, dau. of Brownlow, 8th Earl of Exeter, and left, with three daus., Elizabeth, Sophia, and Diana, an only surviving son,

CHARLES CHAPLIN, Esq. of Blankney, M.P. for Lincolnshire, *b.* in 1759, who *m.* in 1781, Elizabeth, only dau. and heiress of Robert Taylor, Esq., M.D., and had issue,

CHARLES, now of Blankney and Tathwell.
Henry, *b.* 8 June, 1789; *m.* 19 Aug. 1834, Caroline-Horatia, dau. of William Ellice, Esq., and has issue surviving, Charles, *b.* 16 May, 1836; Henry, *b.* 22 Dec. 1840; Edward, *b.* in 1842; and Harriett.
Thomas, *b.* 17 April, 1794; *m.* Mary-Millicent, dau. of William Reeve, Esq. of Leadenham, co. Lincoln.
Elizabeth, *m.* to Vere, 3rd son of the Hon. Henry Fane, 2nd son of Thomas, 8th Earl of Westmoreland.
Emma, *d.* in 1833.
Sophia, *m.* to J.-B. Praed, Esq. of Tyringham, Bucks.
Louisa, *m.* to the Rev. B.-G. Bridges.
Harriett, *m.* to Russell Ellice, Esq.
Charlotte, *d.* 3 Dec. 1819.

Arms—Erm., on a chief, indented, vert, three griffin's heads, erased, or.
Crest—A griffin's head, erased, or, gorged with a mural crown, vert.
Seats—Blankney, near Sleaford, and Tathwell, near Louth, co. Lincoln.

CHAPLIN OF TATHWELL HALL.

CHAPLIN, FREDERIC, Esq. of Tathwell Hall, co. Lincoln, *b.* in 1803; *m.* Jane, eldest dau. of James-B. Topham, Esq. of Candlesby, and has issue,

I. WILLIAM, b. 19 Feb. 1836.

II. Richard-Francis, b. 19 Oct. 1841.

III. Charles-Edward-Pulteney, b. 31 March, 1846.

I. Caroline-Georgiana.

Lineage.—This is the second branch of the CHAPLINS *of Blankney*.

CHARLES CHAPLIN, Esq. (2nd son of Thomas Chaplin, Esq. of Blankney, by Diana his wife, sister of Thomas, 1st Lord Archer,) b. 27 July, 1730, m. Elizabeth Thoroton, of Screveton, Notts, and had issue,

Charles, d. unm.
Thomas, of Riseholme, m. Elizabeth, dau. of Sir Godfrey Webster, Bart., and d. s. p.
ROBERT, in holy orders, m. Anne, dau. of Sir Richard Sutton, Bart., and d. 29 May, 1839, leaving three daus., Fanny, m. to the Rev. Henry Howson, of Southwell; Sophy, m. to the Rev. John Girardot; Georgiana, m. to the Rev. G. Barrow, of Southwell.
Francis, m. Elizabeth, dau. of John Chaplin, Esq. of Blankney, and d. s. p. 28 May, 1838.
George, d. unm. 4 May, 1835.
WILLIAM, in holy orders, of whom we treat.
Edward, in holy orders, rector of Blankney.
Charlotte, m. to Edward Harrison, M.D., of London.
Sophia, m. 1st, to John, eldest son of Sir R. Sutton, Bart.; and 2ndly, to Thomas Wright, Esq. of Upton.

The 6th son,

The Rev. WILLIAM CHAPLIN, m. Isabella, dau. of Sir Richard Sutton, Bart. of Norwood Park, and d. 11 Dec. 1835, having had issue,

William, b. in 1799; d. young.
Charles, in holy orders, b. in 1800; d. in 1832, unm.
Richard, b. in 1802; d. in 1840, unm.
FREDERIC, now of Tathwell Hall.
James-Pulteney, b. in 1807, married.
George-Ayscough, in holy orders.
Edward-John, in holy orders, fellow of Magdalen College, Oxford.
Battina-Mary-Elizabeth, m. to the Rev. Basil Berridge, and d. s. p. in 1826.

Arms—Erm., on a chief, indented, vert, three griffin's heads, erased, or.
Crest—A griffin's head, erased, or, murally gorged, vert.
Seat—Tathwell Hall, co. Lincoln.

CHAPMAN OF WHITBY STRAND.

CHAPMAN, THOMAS, Esq. of Whitby, co. York, J.P., F.R.S. and F.S.A., b. 21 June, 1798; m. 24 March, 1825, Maria-Louisa, youngest dau. of John Hanson, Esq. of The Rookery, Woodford, and of Great Bromley Hall, co. Essex, and has an only dau.,

ETHEL-MARIA.

Lineage.—"The Chapman family," says, Young, in his *History of Whitby*, "resided at Whitby, and in Yburn Dale, prior to the year 1400, as appears from the registers and rolls of Whitby Abbey. The late Sir Thomas Chapman, of Ireland, and Admiral Chapman, of Sweden, belonged to the family." "This family (we quote an old family MS.) was settled at or near Whitby, in the time of HENRY III., as appears by ancient records; and in the time of RICHARD II. some of them were prosecuted and imprisoned by the Abbot of Whitby, for maintaining their just rights and privileges, but were soon set at liberty by the abbot without paying any fees. They increased much in a century or two, and many of them were in the parliamentary army."

ROGER CHAPMAN and JOHN CHAPMAN were of Yburn, near Whitby, York, in 1381, from one of whom descended,

ABEL CHAPMAN, of Whitby, b. 22 Oct. 1694 (4th son of William Chapman and Mary his wife, dau. and heir of William Temple, Esq., grandson of Sir William Temple, provost of Trinity College, Dublin,) m. 1st, 25 Jan. 1720-1, Susannah, dau. of George Lotherington, Esq., by whom he had two daus., Elizabeth and Mary, both d. s. p. He m. 2ndly, 10 Jan. 1727-8, Elizabeth, dau. of John Walker, Esq. of Whitby, and by her (who d. 8 Nov. 1735) had issue, JOHN, of whom presently; William, b. 29 Oct. 1733, d. s. p. 8 March, 1755; Esther, m. 2 April, 1748, Isaac Stockton, Esq. of Hawsker Hall, co. York; Mary, d. in 1837. Mr. Chapman m. 3rdly, 8 April, 1745, Hannah, dau. and co-heiress of William Gaskin, Esq. of Whitby, and by that lady, who d. 30 April, 1795, had further issue,

I. Abel, of Woodford, co. Essex, an elder brother of the Trinity House, treasurer of St. Thomas's Hospital, &c., b. 2 May, 1752; m. 13 July, 1784, Rebecca, dau. of Daniel Bell, Esq., and Catherine his wife, dau. of David Barclay, Esq., and by her (who d. 17 May, 1828) had issue,

1 Abel, in holy orders, b. 6 June, 1789; m. 20 Sept. 1818, Anne, dau. of J. Hubbersty, Esq.
2 Daniel, b. in 1790; drowned at sea in 1811, s. p.
3 William, of Newcastle-on-Tyne, b. 28 June, 1792; m. 1 April, 1816, Jane, eldest dau. of Edward Chapman, Esq. of Whitby, by whom (who d. 18 March, 1826) he had issue, 1 Abel, b. 23 March, 1817, m. 10 June, 1846, Elizabeth, dau. of John-Gurney Fry, Esq. of Warley Lodge, Essex; 2 Edward-John, in holy orders, b. 22 April, 1819; 3 William-Daniel, b. 17 Jan. 1826; 1 Martha-Holt, m. 18 April, 1841, to Charles-Fawcett-Neville-Rolfe, Esq. of Sedgeford Hall, co. Norfolk; 2 Margaret-Rebecca.
4 Jonathan, b. 13 April, 1795, m. in Oct. 1819, Agatha, dau. of Jacob-Foster Reynolds, Esq., by Anne his wife, dau. of Robert Barclay, Esq. of Bury Hill, and by her (who d. 27 July, 1840) had issue, 1 Robert-Barclay, b. 21 Nov. 1829; 2 William-Henry, b. in Sept. 1831, d. in Oct. 1841; 3 Charles-Edward, b. 5 Nov. 1832; 4 Abel-Henry, b. 10 May, 1836; 1 Anna-Rebecca, m. 5 March, 1846, to Edmund, son of Sir John Pelly, Bart.; 2 Agatha-Elizabeth, m. 26 July, 1842, to Francis Bland, Esq.; 3 Catherine-Rachel; 4 Mary; 5 Emma; 6 Jane; 7 Louisa-Frances; 8 Ellen.
5 Alfred, b. 28 April, 1796, m. in July, 1824, Caroline, dau. of Sir Francis-Workman MacNaghten, Bart. of Beardville, co. Antrim, and has issue, 1 Alfred-Daniel, b. 22 Feb. 1827; 2 Francis-Stewart, b. in 1829; 3 Edmund-Henry, b. in 1831; 4 William-Hay, b. 23 Sept. 1832; 1 Letitia-Maria; 2 Caroline-Matilda; 3 Alicia-Hannah; 4 Eliza-Ellen.
6 Henry, b. 25 Aug. 1797, m. at Calcutta, 28 Nov. 1836, Priscilla-Susan, dau. of Edward Wakefield, Esq., and has surviving issue, 1 Henry Howard, b. 25 Jan. 1838; 2 Edward-Francis, b. in 1840; 3 Joseph-Gurney, b. 24 May, 1842; 1 Emily-Priscilla-Rebecca; 2 Hannah-Gascoigne.
7 David-Barclay, b. 28 Oct. 1799, m. 1st, Charlotte-Anne-Dorothea Ward, dau. of the Right Rev. William, Lord Bishop of Sodor and Man, and by her (who d. in Aug. 1828) has one son, David Ward, b. 23 March, 1828. He m. 2ndly, 17 Nov. 1829, Maria, dau. of the Rev. Robert Chatfield, D.D., rector of Chatteris, co. Cambridge, and by her has issue, 1 Arthur-George, b. 1 Nov. 1834; 2 Peter-Godfrey, b. in 1836; 3 Kyrle-Alfred, b. in 1838; 4 Frederick-Barclay, b. in 1840; 5 Horace-Edward, b. in 1842; 6 Spencer, b. 31 March, 1843; 1 Ellen-Maria; 2 Eugenia-Susannah.
8 Frederick, b. 1 Feb. 1801, m. in Sept. 1825, Arabella, youngest dau. of Peter Godfrey, Esq. of Old Hall, co. Suffolk, and Arabella his wife, dau. of Sir Joshua Rowley, Bart. of Tendring Park, Suffolk, and d. s. p. in 1838.
9 Edward, b. 26 Nov. 1804, m. in Nov. 1827, Mary-Jane, dau. of James Burnett, Esq., and has issue, George-Henry-James-Mowbray, b. in March, 1834; and Mary-Georgiana.
1 Hannah-Gaskin.
2 Catherine, m. 17 June, 1805, to Peter Godfrey, Esq. of Old Hall, co. Suffolk.
3 Emma, m. 26 April, 1814, to Abraham Rawlinson, Esq. of Fakenham, co. Norfolk.
4 Mary, m. in Feb. 1823, to George Hillhouse, of Combe House, co. Somerset, and d. in 1826. 5 Ellen.

I. Mary, m. 8 March, 1769, to John Walker, Esq. of Walls End, co. Northumberland.

II. Hannah, m. to Bartlett Gurney, Esq. of Coltishall, co. Norfolk, eldest son of John Gurney, Esq. of Norwich (see GURNEY *of Keswick*).

III. Jane, m. 6 Oct. 1784, to Joseph Gurney, Esq. of Lakenham Grove, near Norwich, 3rd son of John Gurney, Esq. of Keswick (*which see*).

Mr. Abel Chapman d. 13 Oct. 1777. His eldest son (of his 2nd marriage),

JOHN CHAPMAN, Esq. of Whitby, b. 27 May, 1732, m. 9 Jan. 1755, Jane, dau. of John Mellar, Esq., by Jane his wife, dau. and co-heiress of William Gaskin, Esq., and by her (who d. 31 Aug. 1801,) had issue,

I. Abel, of Stakesby Hall, co. York, b. 14 Nov. 1757, m. 1 Jan. 1788, Elizabeth, dau. of Wakefield Simpson, Esq., and has issue,

1 Wakefield-Simpson, b. 27 May, 1790, m. 1 Aug. 1814, his cousin, Dorothy, eldest dau. of Henry Simpson, Esq. of Meadow Field House, near Whitby, and has issue surviving, five daus., Elizabeth, m. to James Walker, Esq.; Hannah; Dorothy, m. to Henry Simpson, Esq. of Meadowfield House, near Whitby; Jane; and Mary.
2 John, b. 24 April, 1798, J.P. for the North Riding of Yorkshire. 1 Jane.

II. John, b. 4 July, 1759, d. s. p. 3 Sept. 1784.

III. William, b. 6 Sept. 1761, m. 10 Oct. 1782, Elizabeth, dau. of Joseph Anderson, Esq., and d. 2 March, 1840, having had issue by her (who d. in 1788),

1 John, b. 9 June, 1785, m. 22 Aug. 1809, Sarah Alderson, and d. 12 Aug. 1838, leaving issue, 1 John, of Whitby, b. 17 Feb. 1814, m. 5 Sept. 1837, Mary, dau. of Edward Chapman, Esq., and has issue three daus., Maria-Louisa, Harriet-Curtis, and Augusta-Mary; 2 Thomas-Hall, b. 9 Aug. 1816, m. 4 Aug. 1840, Ann, dau. of John Campion, Esq. of Whitby, and d. 10 March, 1846, leaving a son, John-Henry, b. 12 April, 1841, and a dau., Ada-Florence; 3 Henry, b. 1 Sept. 1820; 1 Mary-Anne, m.

14 Aug. 1841, to the Rev. Robert Gamson; 2 Elizabeth; 3 Hannah, m. 15 Feb. 1841, to Edward Thompson, Esq.
1 Hannah, m. to Benjamin Flounders, Esq. of Culmington, co. Salop, and of Yarm, co. York, and d. s. p. 6 Aug. 1814.
IV. Robert, b. 12 Oct. 1762, m. Susanna, dau. of Benjamin Bovill, Esq., and has (with two daus., Jane-Bovill, m. 1st, 23 Nov. 1824, to the Rev. Robert-Hopton Smith, and 2ndly, 11 Nov. 1841, to William Brown, Esq.; and Susan, m. 1st, 14 Aug. 1823, to Thomas Pugsley, Esq., and 2ndly, 1 May, 1838, to the Rev. John Corser), an only son, Benjamin, in holy orders, vicar of Leatherhead, Surrey, b. 10 July, 1798, m. 25 Sept. 1832, Laura-Maria, only dau. of Jonathan Wilson, Esq. of Tooting Common, and has issue, 1 Robert-Graham, b. in 1837; 2 Arthur-Drinkwater-Bethune, b. in 1838; 3 Henry-Mapleton, b. in 1841; 1 Laura-Mary-Anna; 2 Jane-Susan; 3 Agnes-Elizabeth; 4 Eleanor-Georgiana; 5 Emily-Augusta; 6 Edith-Jane; and 7 Margaret-Ann.
V. Henry, b. 17 March, 1764, d. unm. 23 Oct. 1808.
VI. Thomas, of Elsinore, kingdom of Denmark, b. 12 Feb. 1766, m. Ann, dau. of Edward Cleaver, Esq. of Nunnington Hall, co. York, and d. 26 March, 1844, having had, with three daus., Anne, Jane-Frances, and Arabella, five sons, 1 John, of Blackheath Park, Kent, b. in 1797, m. 21 Sept. 1831, Elizabeth Haddan, and by her (who d. 19 Aug. 1834) has a dau., Elizabeth; 2 Edward, d. unm. at Batavia; 3 William, b. 29 Oct. 1799; 4 Robert-Cleaver, b. 12 Jan. 1803; 5 Henry-Cleaver, of Liverpool, b. 3 Jan. 1805, m. 11 July, 1836, Sarah, dau. of James-M.-Taylor, Esq. of Westwood, co. Lancaster, and has issue, Thomas-Henry, b. 18 April, 1837; Arthur-Edward, b. 2 Oct. 1844; Mary-Anne-Taylor, Florence, Henrietta-Cleaver, Julia, and Jane-Gertrude; 5 Thomas, of Exeter Coll., Oxford, d. unm. in 1834.
VII. Jonathan, of Tooting Common, Surrey, b. 30 Sept. 1767, m. 27 April, 1790, Mary-Anne, dau. of Robert Taylor, Esq. of Tolmers, co. Herts, and d. 4 Nov. 1846, and was buried in the family vault at Sneaton, co. York.
VIII. EDWARD, of whom presently.
IX. Aaron, of Highbury Park, co. Middlesex, J.P., M.P. for the borough of Whitby, b. 13 Sept. 1771, m. 2 June, 1796, Elizabeth, dau. of Joseph Barker, Esq. of Whitby, and had (with two daus., Ann; and Jane Mellar, m. 29 April, 1841, to John Hubbersty Matthews, Esq. of Lincoln's-inn, barrister-at-law) four sons, viz., 1 Joseph Barker, b. 27 Feb. 1799, m. 12 June, 1832, Louisa-Agnes, eldest dau. of Thomas Simpson, Esq. of Platway, co. Devon, and has a son, Joseph-John, b. in 1837, and four daus., Elizabeth-Ann, Louisa-Agnes, Ellen-Maria, and Margaret-Jane; 2 John, b. 5 July, 1801, d. at Calcutta, 19 Nov. 1816; 3 Edward-Henry, of Harringay House, Middlesex, a director of the Bank of England, J.P. for Middlesex, b. 16 Jan. 1803, m. 28 April, 1829, Mary-Elizabeth, dau. of Lancelot Haslope, Esq. of Selly Hall, co. Worcester; 4 William-Robert, b. 21 May, 1806, m. 29 March, 1842, Caroline-Sarah, eldest dau. of John Fryer, Esq. of Chatteris, co. Cambridge, and has issue a son, William-Edward, b. 22 Feb. 1843.
X. Benjamin, b. 23 Oct. 1775, d. in Sept. 1779.
I. Elizabeth, m. to Thomas Hall, Esq. of Brixton Place, co. Surrey, d. s. p. 25 Dec. 1838.
II. Jane, m. 1st, 16 April, 1794, to Ingram Chapman, Esq. of Whitby, and 2ndly, 15 Jan. 1810, Euseby Cleaver, Esq. youngest son of Edward Cleaver, Esq. of Nunnington Hall, co. York.

Mr. John Chapman d. 5 Jan. 1822. His 8th son,

EDWARD CHAPMAN, Esq. of Whitby, J.P. and D.L., N. R. Yorkshire, b. 1 Sept. 1769, m. 21 April, 1794, Martha, eldest dau. and co-heiress of Thomas Holt, Esq. of Whitby, and Esther his wife, dau. and co-heiress of Isaac Stockton, Esq. of Hawsker Hall, co. York, and by her had issue,

THOMAS, now of Whitby.
John-Mellar, of Usworth Place, co. Durham, b. 21 June, 1805, m. 8 May, 1832, Caroline-Sarah, 3rd dau. of Samuel Walker Parker, Esq. of Scotts House, co. Durham, and has issue, Edward, b. 26 Feb. 1833; Henry-Parker, b. 4 March, 1836; Herbert, b. 31 July, 1837; Reginald-Temple, b. 8 Feb. 1841; Arthur-Gascoyne, b. 21 Feb. 1842; Catherine; Caroline; Theodosia; and Harriet-Adeline.
Edward-William, b. 9 Oct. 1815.
Jane, m. 1 April, 1816, to her cousin, William Chapman, Esq. of Newcastle-on-Tyne, and d. 18 March, 1826, having had issue.
Esther-Elizabeth, m. 6 Nov. 1834, to William-Clayton Walters, Esq. of Stella Hall, Durham, M.A., barrister-at-law.
Elizabeth, m. 17 Oct. 1822, to the Rev. Robert Taylor, M.A. rector of Clifton Camvile, co. Stafford.
Isabella-Margaret, d. 19 Aug. 1804.
Margaret, d. in 1822.
Mary, m. 5 Sept. 1837, to her cousin, John Chapman, Esq.

Mr. Edward Chapman d. 22 Jan. 1836.

Arms—Per chevron, erm. and gu., a crescent, counterchanged; in chief, three annulets, of the second.
Crest—Two spears' heads in saltier, in front of a dexter arm embowed in armour, the hand gauntleted, and grasping a broken tilting spear, ppr., enfiled with an annulet, or.
Motto—Crescit sub pondere virtus.
Residence—Whitby, co. York.

CHARLESWORTH OF CHAPELTHORPE HALL.

DODGSON-CHARLESWORTH, JOHN-CHARLESWORTH, Esq. of Stanley Hall and Chapelthorpe Hall, both in the West Riding of Yorkshire, J.P., *m.* Sarah, 2nd dau. of Walker Featherstonhaugh, Esq. of The Hermitage, co. Durham.

Arms—Erm., a chevron, sa., fretty, or, between, in chief, two eagles, displayed, sa., and in base a mascle, of the second.
Crest—A demi-eagle, sa., the wings elevated, fretty, or, in the beak a mascle, of the last.
Motto—Justitia et virtus.
Seats—Chapelthorpe Hall; and Stanley Hall, West Riding, Yorkshire.

CHARLTON OF HESLEYSIDE.

CHARLTON, WILLIAM-HENRY, Esq. of Hesleyside, co. Northumberland, *b.* in 1810; *m.* in 1839, Barbara, dau. of Michael Tasburgh, Esq. of Burghwallis, co. York, and has issue,

I. WILLIAM-OSWALD, b. in 1850.
II. Ernest-Lambert-Swinburne, b. in 1852.
I. Frances-Mary. II. Amy-Mildred-Mary.

Lineage.—The family of Charlton of Hesleyside descends from Adam de Charlton, lord of the manor of Charlton, in Tynedale, co. Northumberland, A.D. 1303.

WILLIAM CHARLTON, Esq. of Hesleyside, co. Northumberland, living at the survey of 1542, son of Edward Charlton, Esq. of Charlton Tower, in Tynedale, and of Hesleyside, had two sons, EDWARD CHARLTON, who left four daus., his co-heirs, and MATTHEW CHARLTON, Esq., whose son, WILLIAM CHARLTON, Esq. of Bellingham and Hesleyside, m. Jane, dau. of William Swinburne, Esq. of Capheaton, and left two sons; SIR EDWARD, the elder, and heir, was created a Baronet in 1645. The younger son,

WILLIAM CHARLTON, Esq. of Longlee, m. 1st, Jane, dau. of William Swinburne, Esq. of Capheaton, and had an only dau., a nun; and 2ndly, Elizabeth, dau. of Sir Philip Musgrave, Bart., by whom he was father of

WILLIAM CHARLTON, Esq. of York and Longlee, who purchased the whole of Hesleyside from the heirs of his uncle, Sir Edward Charlton. He m. his cousin, Elizabeth, eldest dau. and co-heir of that gentleman, and dying in 1682, left (with a dau., Margaret, *m.* in 1674, to Henry Dacre, Esq. of Lanercost Abbey) a son and successor,

EDWARD CHARLTON, Esq. of Hesleyside, who *m.* Margaret, dau. of Sir Francis Salkeld, Knt., and d. in 1710, leaving a dau., Anne, wife of Roger Meynell, Esq., and a son and heir,

WILLIAM CHARLTON, Esq. of Hesleyside, who m. Mary, dau. and co-heir of Roger Croft, of East Appleton, and was s. at his decease, in 1736, by his son,

EDWARD CHARLTON, Esq. of Hesleyside, who m. in 1746, Teresa, dau. of Sir John Swinburne, Bart. of Capheaton, and dying in 1767, left a son and successor,

WILLIAM CHARLTON, Esq. of Hesleyside, who m. Margaret, dau. of John Fenwicke, Esq. of Morpeth, by Mary his wife, dau. of John Thornton, Esq. of Netherwitton, and by her, who d. 12 March, 1833, he left at his decease, in 1797, an only child and heir,

WILLIAM-JOHN CHARLTON, Esq. of Hesleyside, b. in 1784, who m. in 1809, Katharine-Henrietta, dau. of Frances Cholmeley, Esq. of Brandsby, and by her (who d. in 1849), had,

WILLIAM-HENRY, now of Hesleyside.
Edward, M.D., m. in 1842, Eliza-Janet, dau. of James Kirsopp, Esq. of The Spital, co. Northumberland.
Francis.
Mary, m. in 1850, to the Marquis Giuseppe Pasqualino, of Palermo.
Katherine.

Mr. Charlton served as high-sheriff in 1837. He d. in 1846.

Arms—Or, a lion, rampant, gu.
Crest—A demi-lion, rampant.
Motto—Sans varier.
Seat—Hesleyside, co. Northumberland.

CHARLTON OF LUDFORD.

LECHMERE-CHARLTON, FRANCIS, Esq. of Ludford, co. Hereford, *b.* 19 Nov. 1790; *s.* to the estates and representation of the united families of Charlton and Lechmere, upon the demise of his brother. Mr.

Lechmere-Charlton is great grand-nephew and representative of Nicholas, Lord Lechmere, of Evesham.

Lineage.—ELIZABETH CHARLTON, dau. of Sir Blundel Charlton, Bart., m. Edmund Lechmere, Esq. of Hanley Castle, co. Worcester, M.P. for that shire, in 1734, and had a son and heir,

NICHOLAS LECHMERE, of Hanley Castle, b. in 1733, who s. to the Charlton estates upon the demise of his uncle, Sir Francis Charlton, in 1784, and assumed that additional surname. He m. Susanna, dau. of Jesson Case, Esq. of Powyck, and had issue, I. EDMUND, his heir; II. FRANCIS, now of Ludford; I. Emma, d. in 1809, unm. Mr. Lechmere Charlton was s. at his decease by his elder son,

EDMUND-LECHMERE CHARLTON, Esq., representative of the two families of Lechmere and Charlton, b. 20 Sept. 1789, M.P. for Ludlow, who d. unm., and was s. by his brother, FRANCIS.

Arms—Quarterly: 1st and 4th, or, a lion, rampant, gu., for CHARLTON; 2nd and 3rd, gu., a fesse between three pelicans, or, vulning their breasts, ppr., for LECHMERE.
Crests—A leopard's head, front-faced, gu., for CHARLTON. Out of a ducal coronet, a pelican, vulning herself, ppr.
Seat—Ludford, Herefordshire.

CHARLTON OF APLEY CASTLE.

CHARLTON, ST. JOHN-CHIVERTON, Esq. of Apley Castle, co. Salop, J.P., b. 29 May, 1799; m. 1st, 7 Sept. 1820, Jane-Sophia, only dau. of Thomas Meyrick, Esq. of Bush, co. Pembroke, and by her has issue,

I. ST. JOHN-WILLIAM. II. Thomas.
I. Catharine-Jane. II. Louisa-Catharine-Sophia.
III. Jane. IV. Lucy. V. Dorothea.

He m. 2ndly, 24 Feb. 1842, Anne, 3rd dau. of Philip Charlton, Esq. of Wytheford Hall, co. Salop.

Lineage.—SIR ALAN CHARLTON, Knt. of Apley Castle, younger brother of Sir John de Charlton, ancestor of the Barons Charlton, marrying Margery, the heiress of Hugh Fitz-Aer, acquired Witheford and Aston Aer. In the 5th EDWARD II. he was constituted governor of Montgomery and Wigmore Castles, and obtained permission from the king to embattle his own castle of Apley. His son and successor,

THOMAS CHARLTON, of Apley Castle, had an only dau.,

ANNE CHARLTON, sister and heir of Thomas Charlton, Esq. of Apley, m. WILLIAM KNIGHTLEY, Esq. of the Fawsley family, and had a son,

KNIGHTLEY CHARLTON, Esq. of Apley, father of

ROBERT CHARLTON, Esq. of Apley, sheriff of Shropshire in 1472, eighth in descent from whom was

FRANCIS CHARLTON, Esq. of Apley Castle, sheriff of Salop in 1665, who m. Dorothy, dau. and co-heir of Oliver, Lord St. John, and was, by her, great-grandfather of

ST. JOHN CHARLTON, Esq. of Apley Castle, b. in 1733, sheriff in 1757, J.P. and D.L., who d. in 1776, leaving by Mary Tampsit, of Goudhurst, his wife (who d. in 1767), three sons, ST. JOHN, his heir; WILLIAM, successor to his brother; and PHILIP, of Wytheford Hall, co. Salop, b. in 1767, who m. in 1796, Jane-Brady, dau. of the Hon. William Barnett, of Arcadia, Jamaica, and had issue, I. ST. JOHN, m. Julia, relict of William Ripley, Esq. of Liverpool; II. Philip; III. Andrew; IV. Henry; V. John-Kynaston; I. Jane-Eleanor, m. to Richard Houghton, Esq.; II. Alicia, m. to Thomas Parr, Esq. of Grappenhall, Hayes; III. Anne, m. to St. John-Chiverton Charlton, Esq. of Apley Castle; and IV. Frances. The elder son,

ST. JOHN CHARLTON, Esq. of Apley Castle, high-sheriff in 1790, m. Charlotte, dau. of James Payne, Esq. of Hayes, co. Surrey, and d. in 1802, leaving two daus. He was s. by his brother,

WILLIAM CHARLTON, Esq. of Apley Castle, high-sheriff in 1807, who m. in 1796, Catharine, relict of the late Dr. Thomason, of York, and had one son, ST. JOHN-CHIVERTON, now of Apley Castle, and three daus., Charlotte-Anne, m. to the Rev. Arthur-Charles Verelst, of Aston Hall, co. York; Elizabeth, m. to Harry Croft, Esq. of Stillington Hall, co. York; and Louisa, m. to William Garforth, Esq. of Wiggarthorpe, co. York. Mr. Charlton d. 14 Jan. 1838.

Arms—Or, a lion, rampant, gu.; a canton, sinister. Quarterly: 1st and 4th, gu., ten besants, four, three, two, and one, for ZOUCH; 2nd and 3rd, az., on a mount, vert, a lion, passant-guardant, or, for FITZ-AER.
Crest—Out of an eastern coronet, or, a tiger's he d and neck, affrontée, gu.
Seat—Apley Castle, co. Salop.

CHARLTON OF CHILWELL.

CHARLTON, THOMAS-BROUGHTON, Esq. of Chilwell Hall, co. Nottingham, J.P., b. 15 Aug. 1815; m. in 1843, dau. of John Walter, Esq. of Bearwood, Berks, and has issue,

I. NICHOLAS-JOHN, b. in 1847.
I. Catherine-Mary. II. Alice-Isabel.

Lineage.—From the beginning to the close of the fifteenth century, this family was resident in St. Austin's parish, Watling-street, London. Early in the following century they were in Sandiacre, co. Derby, and the earliest direct ancestor who can be authoritatively traced, is

THOMAS CHARLTON, of Sandiacre, Esq., b. about 1525, who d. in 1579. He was father of

THOMAS CHARLTON, Esq. of Sandiacre, b. in 1560, who m. Catherine Pym (whose family were then of Risley, co. Derby, and Chilwell, Notts, and were said to be related to the celebrated John Pym), and had issue eight sons and three daus.,

Michael, d. unm. in 1615; fellow of Trinity College, Cambridge.
NICHOLAS, heir to his father.
Thomas, of Risley and Breaston, m. Margaret Dalton, of Derby; d. in 1638, and was s. by his eldest son,
JOHN CHARLTON, of Breaston, who m. Margery, dau. of Christopher Pegge, of Rodsley, co. Derby; and d. in 1674, leaving, with other issue, his eldest son and heir,
THOMAS CHARLTON, of Breaston, who m. Mary, dau. of — Marshall, Esq. of Scaldwell, co. Leicester, and by her (who m. 2ndly, Mr. Bagguley) left at his decease, in 1687, an only son,
JOHN CHARLTON, of Breaston, Esq., who m. Dorothy, dau. of William Boothby, Esq. of Potters Marston, co. Leicester; and d. in 1739, aged 56, leaving, with other children, his eldest son,
THOMAS CHARLTON, of Breaston, Esq., successor to his relative in the Chilwell estate.
Edward, of Sandiacre, a commissioner under the Parliament for raising 516 men for the Derbyshire contingent; m. 1st, Amy, dau. of Robert Willmott, of Chaddesden; and 2ndly, Miss Hill; and d. in 1656.
Anne, m. 1st, to — Handley, Esq. of Wilford; and 2ndly, to — Hood, Esq. of Bardon Park, co. Leicester.

Thomas Charlton d. in 1631, and his eldest surviving son,

NICHOLAS CHARLTON, Esq. of Chilwell, m. 1st, Alice Handley, and 2ndly, Elizabeth Flackett, of Hunsden Grange, co. Derby. He d. in 1650, leaving (with three daus., Jane, m. to Philip Pendock, Esq. of Tollerton; Anne, m. to Ralph Edge, Esq. of Strelley; and Elizabeth, m. to George Pole, of Heage), three sons, Thomas, Nicholas, and Michael; the 2nd, who was of London, left two daus. and co-heirs, one, Catherine, m. in 1689, to William Wollaston, Esq. of Shenton, and the other, to Mr. Palmer, of Wanlip. The eldest son,

THOMAS CHARLTON, Esq. of Chilwell, high-sheriff of Notts, in 1666, m. Tabitha, heiress of William Nix, of Nottingham, Esq., and d. in 1690, aged 71, leaving numerous issue; his dau., Elizabeth, m. William Cartwright, of Normanton, ancestor of Major Cartwright, the reformer. The eldest son,

THOMAS CHARLTON, Esq. of Chilwell, m. 1st, Lucy, sole heiress of the ancient family of DANNETT *of Bruntingthorpe*, co. Leicester, which estate he inherited in right of his wife, and 2ndly, Mary Faun. He d. in 1701, and left (with a dau., Sarah, m. to Sir John Toppe, Bart.) two sons, the elder of whom,

THOMAS CHARLTON, Esq. of Chilwell, d. unm. the year he inherited, aged 29, the estates and representation devolving upon his brother,

NICHOLAS CHARLTON, Esq. of Chilwell, who also d. unm. in 1748, aged 55, and bequeathed his principal estates to his kinsman,

THOMAS CHARLTON, Esq. of Breaston and Chilwell, who m. Dorothy, dau. and heiress of G. Sharpe, Esq. of Beeston, formerly of Barnby in the Willows, Notts, and d. aged 77, in 1798, leaving an only son,

THOMAS CHARLTON, Esq. of Chilwell, for many years lieut.-col. of the Nottingham militia. He d. in 1808, aged 51, and was s. by his eldest son,

WILLIAM CHARLTON, Esq. of Chilwell, who m. Emma, dau. of the Rev. Peter Broughton, of Tunstall Hall, Salop, by whom he had issue,

THOMAS-BROUGHTON, present representative.
Welles, b. in 1819.
Caroline-Emma, m. in 1836, to the Rev. S. Fox, of Morley, co. Derby.

Mr. Charlton, who was high-sheriff of Notts in 1824, *d.* in 1831, aged 51.

Arms—Az., on a chevron, or, between three swans, arg., as many cinquefoils, gu.
Crest—A swan's head and neck, erased, arg., beaked, gu., gorged with a chaplet, vert.
Motto—Stabit conscius æqui.
Seat—Chilwell, Nottingham.

CHAUNCY OF LITTLE MUNDEN.

CHAUNCY, CHARLES-SNELL, Esq. of Munden Parva, co. Herts, *b.* 12 Jan. 1789, high-sheriff in 1841; *m.* 9 Aug. 1817, Elizabeth, dau. of Daniel Beale, Esq. of Fitzroy Square, London, and has an only dau.,

ELIZA-SNELL, *m.* 6 Dec. 1843, Henry-Edward Surtees, Esq., 2nd son of Robert Surtees, Esq. of Redworth, and has three daus., Elizabeth-Ellen; Caroline-Isabel; and Georgina-Mary.

Lineage.—GEORGE CHAUNCY, Esq. of Yardly, Bury, and New Place, Herts, sixth in descent from Sir William de Chauncy, Baron of Scirpenbeck, who derived from Chauncy de Chauncy, near Amiens, one of the companions in arms of the CONQUEROR, *m.* 1st, Jane, dau. and heir of John Cornwall, Esq. of Stebbing, co. Essex, by whom (who *d.* in 1582) he had, with other issue, a son and heir,

HENRY, whose son, HENRY CHAUNCY, Esq., was father of SIR HENRY CHAUNCY, author of the *Historical Antiquities of Hertfordshire;* who *d.* in 1719, leaving issue by his first and third wives. His son by the third, ARTHUR CHAUNCY, *b.* in 1690, *d.* in 1751, leaving a son, the REV. CHARLES CHAUNCY, rector of Ayot St. Peter, Herts, who *m.* in 1763, Susanna, dau. of Thomas Caton, Esq. of Thorp Abbots, co. Norfolk, and had a son, the REV. CHARLES CHAUNCY, vicar of Paul's Walden, who *m.* in 1806, Rebecca-Ann, dau. of Thomas Crawley, Esq. of Welwyn, and had issue a dau., Elizabeth, *m.* in 1808, to John-Montagu Poore, Esq. of Wedhampton.

George Chauncy *m.* 2ndly, Agnes, dau. of Edward Welch, of Great Wimondley, and widow of Edward Humberstone, by whom he left, at his decease, 1625, with other issue, a son,

CHARLES CHAUNCY, President of Hayward College, bapt. 5 Nov. 1592, who *m.* in 1630, Catherine, dau. of Robert Eyre, Esq. of Wilts, and dying in New England, 19 Feb. 1671-2, left (with a dau., Sarah, *m.* to the Rev. Mr. Buckley,) six sons, Isaac, *b.* in 1632, a physician, who *m.* and had issue; ICHABOD, of whom presently; Barnabas; Nathaniel, in holy orders, of Hatfield, New England, who *m.* and had issue; Elnathan; Israel, who *m.* and had issue. The 2nd son,

ICHABOD CHAUNCY, M.D., *d.* at Bristol in 1691, aged 56, leaving, by Mary King his wife, *inter alios,* a son,

CHARLES CHAUNCY, Esq., *b.* 14 March, 1673-4, who *m.* in 1708, Martha, dau. of Philip Brown, Esq. of New Buckenham, and had issue, CHARLES, M.D., F.R.S., F.S.A., who *d. s. p.* in 1777; NATHANIEL, of whom presently; PHILIP, who *d. s. p.* in 1783; and Martha, who *m.* William Snell, Esq. of London, merchant (and had issue, William Snell, of London, merchant, who took the name of CHAUNCY in 1780; CHARLES, of whom hereafter; and Nathaniel). The youngest son,

NATHANIEL CHAUNCY, Esq. *b.* in 1717, *m.* Mary Justice, and dying in 1790, left two daus., Charlotte-Maria, *m.* in 1779, to Thomas White, Esq., M.D., and AMELIA CHAUNCY, *b.* 28 Dec. 1758, who *m.* 15 Dec. 1781, her cousin, Charles Snell, Esq., who assumed the surname and arms of CHAUNCY in 1783, and had issue,

CHARLES-SNELL CHAUNCY, now of Little Munden.
Nathaniel-Snell Chauncy, *m.* 29 Aug. 1814, Anne-Oram, dau. of Col. John-Alexander Bannerman, H. E. I. C. S., and has issue.
Mary. Charlotte. Amelia. Jane.

Arms—Gu., a cross patonce, arg.; on a chief, az., a lion, passant, or.
Crest—Out of a ducal coronet, or, a griffin's head, gu., between two wings displayed, az., the inward parts of the wings, gu.
Seat—Dane End House, Little Munden, Herts.

CHAWNER OF NEWTON MANOR HOUSE.

CHAWNER, EDWARD-HORE, Esq. of Newton Manor House, co. Hants, capt. in the army, h.p. unattached, *b.* in 1802; *m.* in 1830, Miss Amelia Belstead, and has,

I. EDWARD-HENRY, lieut. 77th foot, *b.* in 1831.
II. Henry-Charles, *b.* in 1835.
I. Blanche. II. Constance. III. Florence.

Lineage.—JOHN CHAWNER, Esq. of Muselane, co. Derby, only son of John Chawner, Esq. of Muselane, *m.* Anne, dau., of Edmund Chaloner, Esq. of Marston Woodhouse, co. Derby, and was father of

THOMAS CHAWNER, Esq. of Muselane, co. Derby, *m.* in 1730, Sarah Emery, dau. of Robert Emery, Esq. of Doveridge, co. Derby, and had an only son,

HENRY CHAWNER, Esq. of Newton Manor House, J.P., *b.* 14 Nov. 1764, who *m.* 3 March, 1788, Mary, only dau. and heiress of Edward Hore, Esq., of Esher, Surrey, and by her (who *d.* in 1848,) had issue,

EDWARD-HORE, now of Newton Manor House.
CHARLES-FOX, rector of Blechingly, co. Surrey; *m.* in 1825, Marian, youngest dau. of the Rev. Dr. Richardson, rector of Dunmow, Essex.
Caroline, *m.* 1827, to Thomas Kerslake, Esq., J.P. and D.L., of Barmer, near Fakenham, co. Norfolk.
Louisa, *m.* 1832, Robert-Henry Payne, Esq. of Borndean House, Hants, 2nd son of the late Sir Peter Payne, Bart. of Blunham House, Beds, M.P.

Mr. Chawner *d* in 1851.

Arms—Sa., a chevron, between three cherubims' heads, or.
Crest—A sea-wolf's head, erased, sa.
Motto—Nil desperandum.
Seat—Newton Manor House, near Alton, co. Hants.

CHEESE OF HUNTINGTON.

CHEESE, JAMES, Esq. of Huntington Court, co. Hereford, J.P. and D.L., high-sheriff in 1852, *b.* 2 Oct. 1798; *m.* 31 Oct. 1821, Anne-Bisse, only surviving child of John Cowper, Esq. of Bristol, and has an only child,

ANNE COWPER, *m.* in 1853, to Thomas Lloyd, Esq., eldest son of Eyre Lloyd, Esq. of Prospect, co. Limerick.

Lineage.—EDMUND CHEESE, Esq. of Ridgebourne House, Kington, eldest son of Edmund Cheese, Esq., and grandson of Edmund Cheese, Esq. of Herefordshire, *m.* in 1792, Mary, dau. and heiress of James Watkins, Esq., descended from the family of WATKINS *of Breconshire,* and had (with two daus., Mary, *m.* to William Baynton, Esq. of Bristol; and Ann, who *d. unm.* in 1833) three sons, the only survivor of whom is the present JAMES CHEESE, Esq. of Huntington. The other two sons were EDMUND-WATKINS CHEESE, Esq., J.P. and D.L. of Ridgebourne, who *d. unm.* in 1837, and JOHN-HARRIS CHEESE, Esq., who *d. unm.* in 1832.

Arms—Az., a lion, rampant, or, quartering, gu., a chevron, between three spear-heads, embrued, arg.
Crest—A lion's head, erased, or.
Motto—Omnia fert ætas.
Seat—Huntington Court, near Kington, co. Hereford.

CHEEVERS OF KILLYAN HOUSE.

CHEEVERS, JOHN, Esq. of Killyan House, co. Galway, J.P. and D.L., high-sheriff in 1836-7, *b.* 16 May, 1790; *m.* 20 Dec. 1822, Elenor, eldest dau. of the late John MacDonnell, Esq. of Caranacon, co. Mayo, and has issue,

I. MICHAEL, *b.* in Oct. 1825.
II. Christopher, of Lincoln's Inn, barrister-at-law.
III. Joseph, who has assumed the additional surname of MACDONNELL, pursuant to his maternal uncle's will.
IV. Patrick-Edward. V. Hyacinth.
I. Maria.

Lineage.—The family of Cheevers was established in England by a Norman knight in the army of the CONQUEROR, and in Ireland by Sir William Chevre, one of the companions of Strongbow. Of his descendants, the senior line was that seated at Ballyhaly, co. Wexford. The estate of Macetown, in the co. of Meath, was acquired by the marriage of Sir Christopher Chevers, of Ballyhaly, with Anne Plunkett, an heiress. Sir Christopher was direct ancestor of JOHN CHEEVERS, of Macetown, who was dispossessed by CROMWELL, and transplanted to Connaught. He *m.* for his 2nd wife, Jane, dau. of Edward Sutton, Esq., and had several sons and daus.; of the former were 1 EDWARD, created a peer, as VISCOUNT MOUNT LEINSTER and *Baron of Bannow,* who adhered to the cause of JAMES II, and followed his majesty into exile; he *m.* Ann, sister of Patrick Sarsfield, Earl of Lucan, but *d. s. p.*; 2 Andrew, whose male line became extinct; and 3 JOHN. This last-named

JOHN CHEEVERS, Esq. (brother of Edward, Viscount Mount Leinster), *m.* Ellis, dau. of Edward Geoghegan, Esq. of Castletown, co. Westmeath (whose mother was dau. of Mathias, Lord Trimlestown), and by her (who *d.* 31 April, 1739) had (with a dau. *m.* to Richard, son of Sir John Burke, Bart. of Glynsk), four sons, viz., MICHAEL, of whom presently; Edward; Christopher; and Mathias, lieut.-col. in the Spanish service, and a Knight of San Fernando. The eldest son,

MICHAEL CHEEVERS, Esq. of Killyan, co. Galway, m. a dau. of O'Flyn of Furbough, co. Galway, by his wife, a dau. of Sir Edmund Burke, Bart. of Glynsk, and had issue, John, d. s. p.; Christopher, m. the Hon. Miss Nugent, and d. s. p.; HYACINTH, of whom presently; and a dau., m. to Michael Blake, Esq. of Kiltulla Castle, co. Galway. The youngest son,

HYACINTH CHEEVERS, Esq. of Killyan, m. about 1782, Mary, dau. of the late Patrick Lynch, Esq. of Cottage, co. Galway, and had issue,

JOHN, now of Killyan House. Christopher.
Patrick, m. Eleanor Cashell, and has a dau.
Mary, m. to Michael-R. Plunket, Esq., an officer in the army, and deceased.
Eliza, m. to James D'Arcy, Esq. of New Forest, co. Galway, and Rockvale, co. Clare.

Arms—Gu., three goats, two and one, saliant, arg.
Crest—A demi-goat, arg., as in the arms, collared, gu., armed and unguled, or.
Motto—En Dieu est ma foi.
Seat—Killyan House, co. Galway.

CHENEY OF BADGER HALL.

CHENEY, ROBERT-HENRY, Esq. of Badger Hall, co. Salop, b. in 1801; s. to his brother in 1820.

Lineage.—This is a branch of the great family of CHENEY (or CHEYNE) *of Sherland*, in the Isle of Sheppey, founded by Ralph de Caineto, one of the companions in arms of the CONQUEROR. From a scion of this ancient house, of which was SIR JOHN CHENEY, K.G., created BARON CHENEY by HENRY VII., for his service at Bosworth, descended

ROBERT CHENEY, Esq. of Meynell Langley, co. Derby, son of Edward Cheney, of Yoxall, co. Stafford, Esq., and his wife, a dau. of — Browne, Esq. of Burton-upon-Trent. He entered the army early in life, and served in the Blues, under the Marquis of Granby. He was severely wounded in the head at the battle of Dettingen, and quitted the service on his marrying Dorothy Cheshyre, an heiress, and relict of — Peach, Esq., who d. soon after giving birth to an only child, ROBERT, of whom presently.

He m. 2ndly, Bridget Leacroft, of Wirksworth, co. Derby, by whom he had (with daus.) several sons, the eldest of whom, Edward Cheney, of Goddesby, co. Leicester, m. Elizabeth Ayre, by whom he had issue a son and a dau. Mr. Cheney served the office of high-sheriff for the co. of Derby in 1765. His eldest son,

ROBERT CHENEY, Esq., a general in the army, d. at the age of 54, leaving issue by his wife, Harriet, youngest dau. of Ralph Carr, Esq. of Dunston Hill, co. Durham, whom he m. in 1799, three sons and two daus, viz.,

ROBERT-HENRY, now of Badger Hall.
Edward, a captain in the army, unattached.
Ralph, an officer in the 71st regiment.
Frederica, m. to Capel Cure, Esq. of Blake Hall, co. Essex.
Harriet-Margaret.

Arms—Az., six lions, rampant, arg.; a canton, erm.
Crest—A bull's scalp, arg.
Motto—Fato prudentia major.
Seat—Badger Hall, Shiffnal.

CHERRY OF BUCKLAND.

CHERRY, WILLIAM-GEORGE, Esq. of Buckland, co. Hereford, J.P., b. 13 Sept. 1777; m. 17 March, 1817, Eleanora, dau. of James-Sackville-Tufton Phelp, Esq. of Coston, co. Leicester, and has issue,

I. Rosa-Edwyna, m. 1 May, 1839, to Capt. William-Thomas-Rowland Powell, eldest son of the late William-Edward Powell, Esq. of Nanteos, M.P., and lord-lieutenant of Cardiganshire.
II. Williama-Emma, m. 16 May, 1844, Weston Cracroft, Esq. (now Amcotts,) of Hackthorn, co. Lincoln.

Lineage.—The family of Cherry, formerly of Shottesbrooke, or more properly, as of old, Cherrie, of which there are several branches remaining, is of Norman origin, being, it is said, descended on the male side from the De Cheries, Seigneurs de Branvel, Villamara, Beauval, and Villencourt, &c., in Normandy, and on the female, from the Bretons, both families recognised in all the earlier "Recherches," or Visitations, as of the noblesse of Normandy. A branch of the Cheries at an early period embraced the Huguenot doctrine, and in consequence of the religious persecutions carried on against that party, migrated and settled in England, where they afterwards became possessed of considerable estates.

The great-grandfather of the present W.-G. Cherry, Esq. of Buckland, GEORGE CHERRY, Esq., by Elizabeth his wife, was father of

WILLIAM CHERRY, Esq., b. 1698-9, d. 1776, aged 76. He m. Mary-Ann, dau. of Peter Breton, Esq., of an old and noble Norman family, and had issue, WILLIAM, d. unm.; George, m. Susan Curteis; PETER, of whom presently; Susannah, m. to Hector Rose, Esq.; Mary-Ann, d. unm.; Elizabeth, d. unm. The youngest son,

PETER CHERRY, Esq., m. in 1770, Elizabeth, youngest dau. of George Becher, Esq., and by her (who d. in 1818) left at his decease in 1818,

WILLIAM-GEORGE, now of Buckland.
John-Peter, b. in 1780.
Elizabeth, d. unm. in 1835.

Arms—Arg., a fesse, engrailed, between three annulets, gu.
Crest—A demi-lion, rampant, holding between his paws an annulet.
Motto—Chéris l'espoir.
Seat—Buckland, co. Hereford.

CHERRY OF DENFORD.

CHERRY, GEORGE-CHARLES, Esq. of Denford, co. Berks, b. in 1822.

Lineage.—GEORGE CHERRY, Esq., for many years Chairman of the Victualling Board, m. Sarah, dau. of Henry Curtis, Esq. of Chatham, co. Kent, and had issue,

I. GEORGE-FREDERICK, his heir.
II. John Hector, who d. in 1803, leaving, by Catherine his wife, dau. of William Stratton, Esq., four sons and three daus., viz.,
 1 George-Frederick, who m. 1st, Mrs. Irvin; and 2ndly, Miss Charlotte Hughes, by the latter of whom he had a son, John-William.
 2 John-Hector, d. unm. in 1824.
 3 Henry-Curtis, m. Anne-Alicia, dau. of Major-General Sir John Cameron, K.C.B., and has issue.
 4 Alexander-Inglis, m. in 1827, Georgiana, dau. of Evelyn Gascoigne, Esq., and has issue.
 1 Maria, m. 1814, to Sir James Sutherland.
 2 Kitty-Rosanna.
 3 Charlotte-Cornish, m. 1816, to Solomon Nicholls, Esq.
III. James-Curtis, d. unm. in 1770.
IV. William, d. unm. in 1788.
V. Peter, m. Mary, dau. of Francis Robson, Esq., and had issue.
I. Susan-Mary, m. in 1791, to the Rev. Charles Proby.
II. Elizabeth-Anne, d. unm.
III. Rosanna, m. 1st, to Thomas Blackford, Esq.; and 2ndly, to Henry Sawbridge, Esq.
IV. Mary-Anne, m. to George Rose, Esq.
V. Elizabeth-Curtis, m. to John Gosling, Esq.

The eldest son,

GEORGE-FREDERICK CHERRY, Esq. of Denford, m. Martha-Maria, dau. of Henry Paul, Esq., and dying in 1799, was s. by his only son,

GEORGE-HENRY CHERRY, Esq. of Denford, b. in Aug. 1793, J.P. and D.L., high-sheriff of Berks in 1829, m. 9 Sept. 1819, Charlotte, 2nd dau. of Charles Drake Garrard, Esq. of Lamer, co. Herts, and has issue,

GEORGE-CHARLES, now of Denford.
Apsley, b. in 1832.
Maria-Anne, m. in 1850, to the Rev. John Butler, rector of Inkpen, co. Berks, eldest son of John Butler, Esq. of Kirby House, Berks.
Caroline-Charlotta, d. unm. 1858.
Emily-Jane, m. in 1858, to John Smith, Esq. of Hollyfield, co. Warwick.
Amy-Elizabeth, m. in 1850, to Col. M.-C.-Downes St. Quintin, late of the 17th lancers, 2nd son of the late William St. Quintin, Esq. of Scampston Hall, co. York.
Louisa-Rosanna. Rachel-Mary.

Mr. Cherry d. in 1848.

Arms—Arg., on a fesse, engrailed, between three annulets, gu., a fleur-de-lis, or.
Crest—A demi-lion, arg., holding out in the paw a gem-ring, or, enriched with a precious stone, ppr., the collet in pale.
Motto—Chéris l'espoir.
Seat—Denford, co. Berks.

CHESTER OF BUSH HALL.

CHESTER, CHARLES, Esq., H.E.I.C.S., present representative of the CHESTERS *of Cockenhatch*, b. 19 Aug. 1803; m. Margaret Faithfull.

Lineage.—The CHESTERS enjoyed, at a very remote period, large possessions in Derbyshire, and represented the town of Derby in parliament *temp.* EDWARD II. and EDWARD III. Their Derbyshire estates* were, however, expended in supporting the claim of the Earl of Richmond (HENRY VII.) to the crown,

SIR ROBERT CHESTER,† only son of the Lancastrian, one of the gentlemen of the privy chamber to King HENRY VIII., obtained from that monarch a grant, by charter, of the monastery of Royston, with the lands and manors thereunto belonging, in the counties of Hertford and Cambridge. Sir Robert, who was knighted at Wilton by EDWARD VI. in 1552, *m.* Katherine, dau. of Christopher Throckmorton, Esq. of Coorse Court, Gloucestershire, and had (with other issue, whence the CHESTERS *of Gloucestershire*) a son and successor,

EDWARD CHESTER, Esq. of Royston, who *m.* Katherine, dau. and heir of Sir James Granado, Knt., equerry to HENRY VIII., and had (with a dau., Mary, *m.* to Edward Thornborough, Esq. of Chaddesden, Bucks) a son and successor,

SIR ROBERT CHESTER, of Royston and Cockenhatch, who, entertaining King JAMES I. in the king's progress from Scotland, received the honour of knighthood, 1603. He *m.* Anne, dau. of Sir Arthur Capel, Knt. of Haddam Hall, by Mary his wife, dau. of John, Lord Grey of Pargo, and had, EDWARD, his heir; Granado, and Robert, both doctors in divinity; John, *b.* in 1607; Henry, a colonel in the army; Katharine, *m.* to Sir Thomas Nightingale, Bart.; Anne, *m.* in 1621, to Edward Radcliffe, Esq. of Hitchin; Theodosia, *m.* 1st, to Robert Nightingale, Esq. of Newport, and 2ndly, to Sir Francis Theobald, Knt.; Elizabeth, *m.* to Samuel Hinton, D.C.L., of Lichfield; and Frances, *m.* to George Pigot, Esq. of Abingdon. Sir Robert was *s.* by his eldest son,

SIR EDWARD CHESTER, of Royston and Cockenhatch, who was knighted in 1642. He *m.* 1st, Katherine, dau. of John Stone, Esq. of Bradfield Grange, Herts, serjeant-at-law, and had, John, who predeceased his father, leaving issue, whose descendants alienated the Royston property; Anne, *m.* 1st, to Robert Eade, M.D., and 2ndly, to Henry Hoogan, M.D.; and Cecilia, *m.* to Thomas Turner, Esq. of Walden. Sir Edward *m.* 2ndly, Anne, dau. and heir of Sir Peter Saltonstall, Knt. of Barkway, co. Herts; and dying in 1664, left by her a son,

EDWARD CHESTER, Esq. of Barkway and Cockenhatch, sheriff of Herts in 1666, who *m.* Judith, dau. and heir of Edward Wright, Esq. of Finley, in Nottinghamshire, and had (with four daus.) two sons, viz., Robert, who alienated all the remaining estates: he *m.* twice, and left several children by his 2nd wife; and Peter, of whom presently. Edward Chester, of Barkway, *d.* 21 May, 1718. His younger son,

THE REV. PETER CHESTER, D.D., rector of Heydon, in Essex, bapt. at Barkway, 10 July, 1678; *m.* Sarah, 2nd dau. of Richard Webb, Esq. of Cavenham, in Suffolk, and left at his decease, in 1728, with other issue, a son,

ROBERT CHESTER, Esq. of the Middle Temple, who *m.* Harriot, dau. and co-heir of Charles-Adelmare Cæsar, Esq.,‡ and had issue,

ROBERT (Sir), his heir.
Charles, *b.* 31 Dec. 1768, in holy orders, chaplain to the Earl of Hardwicke, *m.* Catherine, dau. of the Rev. John Roberts, archdeacon of Merioneth, and has issue.
Harry, *b.* 10 Aug. 1770, of the Coldstream-guards, a major-general in the army, *m.* Harriot, youngest dau. of Gen. Sir Henry Clinton, K.B., and *d.* 26 June, 1821, leaving issue.
Jane.
Harriott, *m.* to the Rev. Thomas-Ellis Owen, rector of Llandyfrydog, in Anglesea, and left issue.
Sarah, *d. unm.* 5 Dec. 1787.
Catherine, *m.* 11 Oct. 1792, to the Rev. John-Strange Dandridge, rector of Rousham, Oxfordshire, and of Syresham, Northamptonshire, and *d.* 7 April, 1825, leaving issue.

Mr. Chester was *s.* at his decease by his eldest son,

SIR ROBERT CHESTER, Knt. of Bush Hall, Herts, *b.* 5 Jan. 1768; *m.* 10 Oct. 1797, Eliza, 3rd dau. of John Ford, Esq. of The Chauntry, near Ipswich, and had issue,

ROBERT, *b.* 6 Oct. 1800, *d. unm.* 20 Sept. 1822.
CHARLES, present representative.
Harry, J.P. for Middlesex, *b.* 1 Oct. 1806, *m.* 2 Sept. 1837, Anna-Maria, only child of the late Robert Isherwood, Esq. of Highgate, and has issue, Harry-Robert, *b.* in 1840; Robert-Mervyn, *b.* in 1843; Dulcibella-Fanny-Sophia; and Caroline-Mary.
Eliza, *m.* in 1819, to Sir John-Eardley Eardley-Wilmot, Bt.
Harriott-Cæsar, *d. unm.* 6 Jan. 1821.
Dulcibella, *m.* to the Rev. Charles Childers.

Sir Robert Chester, J.P. and D.L., formerly lieut.-colonel of the Hertfordshire militia, was master of the ceremonies under GEORGE III., GEORGE IV., WILLIAM IV., and Queen VICTORIA.

Arms—Erm., on a chief, sa., a griffin, passant, arg.
Crest—A demi-griffin, rampant, erm.; beak, tongue, talons, and eyes, ppr.
Motto—Vincit qui patitur.

CHESTER OF CHICHELEY HALL.

CHESTER, THE REV. ANTHONY, of Chicheley Hall, co. Bucks, J.P., *b.* Feb. 1800; *m.* in 1834, Henrietta, only child of the late William Brown, Esq. of Lisbon, and has one dau.,

HENRIETTA-MARY.

Lineage.—CHARLES BAGOT, Esq., 2nd son of Sir Walter-Wagstaffe Bagot, LL.D., and next brother of William, 1st Lord Bagot, *b.* 1 Sept. 1730, assumed the name and arms of CHESTER, in compliance with the will of his first-cousin, Sir Charles-Bagot Chester, Bart. of Chicheley. (*See* BURKE'S *Extinct Baronetage.*) He *m.* in 1765, Catherine, dau. of the Hon. Heneage Legge, Baron of the Exchequer, and left at his decease, in 1792, fourteen children, viz.,

CHARLES, his heir.
Anthony, capt. 18th infantry, killed in Egypt, March, 1801, leaving by Anne-Eliza his wife (*m.* in 1799), dau. of Hamlet Obins, Esq. of Castle Obins, co. Armagh, an only son, ANTHONY, successor to his uncle.
William, in holy orders, *b.* 27 May, 1775, *m.* in 1810, Elizabeth, dau. of Lord Berners, *d.* in 1838, leaving issue.
John, *b.* 3 Aug. 1779, a col. in the army, *m.* Sophia-Elizabeth, dau. of Charles Stewart, Esq., and has issue, John, Heneage, Sophia, Mary, Barbara, &c.
Henry, deceased.
George, *m.* Miss Butler, *d.* in 1833.
Catharine, deceased. Louisa, deceased.
Barbara, *m.* to John Drummond, Esq., and is deceased.
Frances, *m.* to T.-R.-G. Braddyll, Esq.
Anne, deceased.
Mary, *m.* to Robert, 2nd Earl of Liverpool.
Elizabeth. Harriet, *m.* to A.-B.-St. Leger, Esq.

The elder son,

CHARLES CHESTER, Esq. of Chicheley, *d. unm.* 11 June, 1838, when he was *s.* by his nephew, the present REV. ANTHONY CHESTER, of Chicheley.

Arms—Per pale, arg. and sa., a chevron, engrailed, between three ram's heads, erased (attired, or), all counterchanged, for CHESTER; quartering BAGOT.
Crest—A ram's head, couped, arg., attired, or.
Seat—Chicheley Hall, co. Bucks.

CHETWODE OF WOODBROOK.

WILMOT-CHETWODE, EDWARD, Esq. of Woodbrook, Queen's County, J.P., *b.* 4 Feb. 1801; *m.* 29 April, 1830, Lady Jean-Janet Erskine, younger dau. of John-Thomas, late Earl of Mar, and has issue,

I. KNIGHTLEY-JONATHAN, *b.* 31 May, 1831.
II. Edward-Robert-Erskine, *b.* 24 Sept. 1852.
I. Alice-Margaret-Agnes. II. Fanny-Elizabeth-Isabella.
III. Janet-Philadelphia.

Mr. Wilmot-Chetwode assumed by royal license, in 1839, the surname and arms of CHETWODE, in addition to his patronymic, WILMOT.

Lineage.—RICHARD CHETWODE, Esq. (3rd son of Roger Chetwode, Esq. of Oakley, by Ellen Masterson his wife), *m.* Agnes, only dau. and heiress of Anthony Wodehull, Esq., 8th and last male descendant of Thomas de Wahull, who was summoned to parliament as BARON WAHULL, 26 Jan. 1297, 25th EDWARD I., and by her (who *m.* 2ndly, Sir George Calveley, Knt.) left an only son,

* When the family left Derbyshire, a branch settled in London, and another at Bristol, but both have long since become extinct. A family of Chester, deriving from a common ancestor with the Hertfordshire house, seated itself at Chicheley, co. Buckingham, but expired in the male line in 1755, the estates passing by a female heir to the family of Bagot (*see* CHESTER *of Chicheley*).

† From an uncle of this Sir Robert, a younger brother of his father, descended the CHESTERS *of Leicestershire.*

‡ Lineally descended from Peter-Maria Adelmare, of Treviso, and his wife, Paola, dau. and co-heir of John de Paolo Cæsarino. Their grandson, SIR JULIUS CÆSAR, was Master of the Rolls in 1610; he *m.* twice, and was direct ancestor of Charles-Adelmare Cæsar, Esq., who *m.* Jane, only child and heir of Henry Long, of Bayford Place, Herts, and left at his decease (in battle, being an officer of cavalry) two daus, viz.,

JANE, *m.* 1st, to Sir Charles-Cottrell Dormer, Knt.; and 2ndly, General the Hon. John Parker.
HARRIOT, *m.* to ROBERT CHESTER, Esq.

SIR RICHARD CHETWODE, who preferred a claim, *temp.* JAMES I., to the barony of Wahull. He *m.* twice, but had issue only by his 1st wife, Jane, dau. and co-heir of Sir William Drury, Knt., viz., William, who *d.* in the lifetime of his father; and RICHARD, who also predeceased his father, leaving, by Anne his wife, dau. and co-heir of Sir Valentine Knightley, a son, VALENTINE CHETWOOD, who *m.* Mary, dau. and co-heir of Francis Shute, Esq. of Upton, co. Leicester, and had two sons, KNIGHTLEY CHETWOOD, dean of Gloucester, whose son and dau. both *d. unm.*; and the REV. JOHN CHETWOOD, D.D., father of

KNIGHTLEY CHETWOOD, Esq. of Woodbrook, who *m.* in 1700, Hester, dau. and heir of Richard Brooking, Esq. of Totnes, co. Devon, and had issue,

VALENTINE, his heir.
Crewe, who *m.* Anna-Maria, dau. of Allan Holford, co. Chester, and relict of Ralph Sneyd, Esq. of Keele, co. Stafford, and had, with two daus., one son,
John, in holy orders, of Glanmire, co. Cork, who *m.* Elizabeth, dau. of William Hamilton, Esq., and had a son, John, captain in the 33rd regt. (who *m.* Eliza, dau. of G. Patton, Esq., governor of St. Helena, and *d.* leaving an only dau., Eliza-Constance, wife of Peter Aiken, Esq. of Clifton), and several daus., the eldest of whom, ELIZABETH-HESTER, *m.* 23 Sept. 1798, ROBERT-ROGERS-WILMOT, elder son and heir of Edward Wilmot, Esq., by Martha his wife, dau. and co-heir of Charles Moore, Esq. of Lisapooka, and grandson of Robert Wilmot, elder brother of Dr. Ryder Wilmot, archbishop of Tuam, and had issue,
EDWARD, the present EDWARD WILMOT-CHETWODE, Esq. of Woodbrook.
Emily-Margaret, *m.* William Brooke, Esq., and *d.* in 1850.

The elder son,

VALENTINE-KNIGHTLEY CHETWOOD, Esq. of Woodbrook, *m.* Henrietta-Maria, dau. of Sir Jonathan Cope, of Brewerne, co. Oxford, Bart., aunt to Arabella, Duchess of Dorset and Countess of Whitworth, and was father of

JONATHAN CHETWOOD, Esq. of Woodbrook, *b.* 31 May, 1757, high-sheriff of the Queen's County in 1781; who *m.* Margaret, dau. and co-heir of Lawrence Clutterbuck, Esq. of Derrylusken, co. Tipperary; and *d. s. p.* 11 May, 1839, when his estates devolved upon his kinsman, the present EDWARD WILMOT-CHETWODE.

Arms—Quarterly: 1st and 4th, arg. and gu., four crosses-formée, counterchanged, an annulet, az., for difference, for CHETWODE; 2nd and 3rd, sa., on a fesse, or, between three eagle's heads, erased, arg., three escallops, gu., a mullet, for WILMOT; 4th, vert, a lion, rampant, in chief, three estoiles, or, for O'MORE or MOORE.
Crests—1st, out of a ducal coronet, or, a demi-lion, rampant, gu., for CHETWODE; 3rd, an eagle's head, erased, sa., in the mouth an escallop, gu., for WILMOT.
Supporters—Two man-tigers, rampant-guardant, arg.
Motto—Corona mea Christus.
Seat—Woodbrooke, Portarlington, Queen's County.

CHICHESTER OF HALL.

CHICHESTER, ROBERT, Esq. of Hall, co. Devon, J.P., *b.* 13 March, 1804; *m.* in Dec. 1826, Clarentia, only child of the late Lieut.-Col. Mason, of Chichester, co. Sussex, and has issue,

I. CHARLES, *b.* 4 Feb. 1828.
II. William-Henry, *b.* 8 Sept. 1831.
III. Edmond-Hall, *b.* 30 Sept. 1834.
IV. Hugh, *b.* 22 Sept. 1836.
V. Richard, *b.* 19 July, 1838.
I. Ann. II. Clarentia.
III. Gertrude. IV. Elizabeth.

Lineage.—This is the senior of the numerous branches of the CHICHESTERS *of Raleigh*, Baronets, derived from RICHARD, 3rd son of Richard Chichester, Esq. of Raleigh, *temp.* HENRY VI., by Margaret his wife, dau. and heir of Nicholas Keynes, of Winkleigh Keynes. This Richard *m.* *temp.* EDWARD IV., Thomasyne, dau. and heir of Symon Halle, of Halle, who thereupon settled that estate and his other possessions upon them. The issue of this marriage was an only son, JAMES CHICHESTER, Esq. of Hall, grandfather of

JOHN CHICHESTER, Esq. of Hall, who *m.* Elizabeth, eldest dau. and co-heir of John Marwood, Esq. of Westcote in Marwood, co. Devon, and by her had, with other issue, two sons, JOHN and HUGH: the elder, JOHN, was father of

SIR JOHN CHICHESTER, Knt. of Hall, *b.* 10 Dec. 1598, knighted by CHARLES I., 17 Sept. 1625, whose last surviving son,

FRANCIS CHICHESTER, Esq. of Hall, LL.B., *b.* 1 June, 1698; *d. s. p.* 27 Aug. 1698, when the estates reverted to his cousin,

ARTHUR CHICHESTER, Esq. of Stowford and Hall, derived from Hugh, 2nd son of John Chichester, of Hall, by Elizabeth Marwood his wife. He *d.* 5 Feb. 1737, leaving, by Jane Harris his 1st wife,

ARTHUR CHICHESTER, Esq. of Hall, *b.* 24 Aug. 1698; who *m.* in 1719, Katherine, only child of the Rev. Charles Harward; and dying 26 June, 1725, was *s.* by his son,

CHARLES CHICHESTER, Esq. of Hall, *b.* 31 Jan. 1722; who *m.* 13 April, 1748, Amy, dau. of Robert Incledon, Esq. of Pilton, co. Devon, and had issue, CHARLES, his heir; Robert, in holy orders, vicar of Chittlehampton, who *m.* Sarah, dau. of Lewis Cossey, Esq. of Atherington, and had issue; Penelope, *d. unm.*; Jane, *m.* to Admiral Bury, of Cellaton and Denington, co. Devon; Amy. He was *s.* at his decease, 22 Jan. 1798, by his eldest son,

CHARLES CHICHESTER, Esq. of Hall, *b.* 18 Jan. 1749; who *m.* 13 Aug. 1799, Henrietta, dau. of P.-R. Webber, Esq. of Buckland House, co. Devon, by Mary his wife, dau. and co-heiress of John Incledon, Esq. of Buckland, and had issue,

ROBERT, present representative.
Henry, *b.* 5 July, 1816.
Ann, *m.* in 1830, to the Rev. Thomas Hulton, rector of Gaywood, co. Norfolk. She *d.* in 1834.
Jane, *m.* in May, 1828, to the Rev. John Landon, vicar of Braunton, co. Devon, eldest son of the late Dean of Exeter.
Henrietta, *m.* in 1832, to Charles Henry Webber, Esq. of Buckland House, co. Devon.

Mr. Chichester *d.* 22 May, 1835.

Arms—Chequy, or and gu., a chief, vairé.
Crest—A heron rising with an eel in its beak, ppr.
Motto—Ferme en foy.
Seats—Hall and Pill House, near Barnstable, co. Devon.

CHICHESTER OF CALVERLEIGH.

(*See* CHICHESTER-NAGLE.)

CHILDE OF KINLET.

CHILDE, WILLIAM-LACON, Esq. of Kinlet, co. Salop, J.P. and D.L., high-sheriff in 1828, and formerly M.P. for Wenlock, *b.* 3 Jan. 1786; *m.* 18 Aug. 1807, Harriet, 2nd dau. of the late William Cludde, Esq. of Orleton, and has issue,

I. WILLIAM-LACON, *b.* 6 June, 1810, *m.* Barbara-Denise, 5th dau. of the late Thomas Giffard, Esq. of Chillington, and by her, who *d.* 4 Sept. 1841, he has one son.
II. Jonathan, *b.* 8 Oct. 1811.
III. Charles-Orlando, *b.* 27 Dec. 1812, assumed by royal license, 2 July, 1849, the additional surname and arms of PEMBERTON, in compliance with the testamentary injunction of the Rev Robert-Norgrave Pemberton, of Millichope Park, co. Salop.
IV. Edward-George, *b.* 28 Dec. 1818.
V. Arthur, *b.* 2 April, 1820.
I. Harriet. II. Anna-Maria.
III. Catherine. IV. Lucy. V. Mary.

Lineage.—The family of BALDWIN, which eventually assumed the name of CHILDE, through an heiress, is stated, from strong presumptive testimony, by Blakeway, in his *Sheriffs of Shropshire*, to derive from BAWDEWYN, a Norman on the Roll of Battle Abbey; and it appears that the Baldwyns at a very remote period were seated at Diddlebury, more recently Delbury, in Coverdale, Salop. The lineal male descendant of this ancient house,

SIR SAMUEL BALDWYN, *b.* in 1618 (son of Charles Baldwin, Esq., M.P., a steady royalist, and nephew of Thomas Bawdewin, of Diddlebury, who suffered imprisonment in the Tower of London, *temp.* ELIZABETH), was a barrister-at-law, and one of the King's serjeants in 1672. He *d.* in 1683, and was buried in the Temple Church, being styled on his monument, "of Stoke Castle." Sir Samuel's eldest surviving son,

CHARLES BALDWYN, Esq. of Elsich and Stoke Castle, *m.* Elizabeth, dau. and heir of Nicholas Acton, Esq., by Mary his wife, sister and co-heir of Edwin Skrymsher, Esq. of Aqualate, and was grandfather of

CHARLES BALDWYN, Esq. of Aqualate, M.P. for Shropshire (grandson of Charles Baldwin, Esq., by Elizabeth Allgood his wife). He m. Catherine, elder dau. and co-heir of William-Lacon Childe,* Esq. of Kinlet, by Catherine his wife, dau. of Samuel Pytts, Esq. of Kyre, and had, with a dau., Catherine, two sons, Charles (the younger), who d. in 1811, and the elder, his successor,

William Baldwyn, Esq., who assumed the surname and arms of Childe only. He m. 20 Nov. 1775, Annabella, 2nd dau. of Sir Charlton Leighton, Bart., and by her, who d. 21 Jan. 1816, had

William-Lacon, now of Kinlet.
Annabella, who m. Samuel-Richard Alleyne, Esq.

Mr. Childe d. 3 Feb. 1824.

Arms—Gu., a chevron, erm., between three eagles, close, arg.
Crest—An eagle, with wings expanded, arg., enveloped round the neck with a snake, ppr.
Seats—Kinlet Hall, Shropshire; and Kyre House, Worcestershire.

CHILD OF BIGELLY HOUSE.

Child, James-Mark, Esq. of Bigelly House, co. Pembroke, J.P. and D.L., b. 14 Feb. 1794; m. 1st, 29 May, 1816, Elizabeth, dau. and co-heiress of Richard-Stedman Davies, Esq. of Dolgaer, co. Brecon, which lady d. s. p. 9 May, 1822. He m. 2ndly, 9 Oct. 1824, Emma-Elizabeth-Townshend, 2nd dau. of Hugh Webb Bowen, Esq. of Camrose House, and has by her an only son,

James-Mark-Philipps, b. 26 Sept. 1825, m. in 1843, Elizabeth, youngest dau. of William Challoner, Esq. of Richmond, Surrey.

Lineage.—John Child, Esq., stated to have been brother of Lord Castlemaine, m. Sophia, dau. of Thomas Laugharne, Esq. of Bigelly House, co. Pembroke, and left, with a dau. Ann, a son,

John Child, Esq. of Bigelly, who m. Catherine, dau. of Richard Poyer, Esq. of Pembrokeshire, and was s. by his son,

James Child, Esq. of Bigelly, who m. Margaret, eldest dau. of the Rev. Theophilus Rice, of Carmarthenshire, and had four sons and two daus. The eldest son,

James Child, Esq. of Bigelly, who s. his father, m. 1st, Maria-Philippa-Artemisia, only dau. of Bulkeley Philipps, Esq. of Pembroke, and niece of Sir John Philipps, Bart. of Picton Castle, by whom he had an only dau.,

Maria-Philippa-Artemesia, m. to John Grant, Esq., and was mother of the present Sir Richard-Bulkeley-Philipps Philipps, Bart.

Mr. Child m. 2ndly, Sarah, 3rd dau. of Mark Davis, Esq. of North Wraxall, in Wiltshire, and left by her, at his decease, 14 Feb. 1815, an only son, the present James-Mark Child, Esq. of Bigelly.

Arms—Gu., a chevron, erm., between three eagles, close.
Crest—An eagle, with wings expanded, arg., having its neck enveloped with a snake, its tail waved over the back, all ppr.
Motto—Imitari quam invidere.
Seats—Bigelly House and Bonvilles Court Tower, co. Pembroke.

CHILD OF NEWFIELD.

Child, Smith, Esq. of Newfield, co. Stafford, J.P. and M.P. for that shire, b. 5 March, 1808; m. 28 Jan. 1835, Sarah, dau. and heir of the late Richard-Clarke Hill, Esq. of Stallington Hall, co. Stafford, and has issue,

I. Smith-Hill, b. in 1837.
II. John-George, b. in 1847.
I. Elizabeth-Sarah.

Lineage.—Smith Child, Admiral of the Blue, son of Smithe Child, Esq., by Mary his wife, dau. of Randle Baddeley, Esq. of Newfield, and grandson of Smithe Child, Esq., whose father, Smithe Childe, migrated from Shropshire to Staffordshire, in 1657, s. to the Newfield and other estates upon the death of his maternal uncle, Thomas Baddeley, of Newfield, Esq. He m. in 1763, Margaret, only child and heiress of T. Roylance, Esq. and d. in 1813, when he was s. by his grandson, the present Smith Child, of Rownall Hall, Esq., son of the late John-George Child, Esq., and Elizabeth his wife, dau. of T. Parsons, Esq. of Massachusetts, United States.

Arms—Gu., a chevron, erm., between three eagles, close, arg.
Crest—An eagle, arg., wings expanded, entwined by a snake attacking the wing.
Motto—Imitari quam invidere.
Seats—Rownall Hall and Stallington Hall, both in co. Stafford.

CHILDERS OF CANTLEY.

Walbanke-Childers, John, Esq. of Cantley, co. York, J.P., formerly M.P. for Cambridgeshire, b. 27 May, 1798; m. 29 March, 1824, Anne, only dau. of Sir Francis-Lindley Wood, Bart. of Hickleton, and has issue,

I. Rowland-Francis, b. 26 Sept. 1830, m. 17 May, 1858, Susan-Anne, youngest dau. of General Bourchier, of Lavant House, Chichester.
I. Charlotte-Anne, m. 10 Dec. 1850, to Henry-Wollaston Blake, Esq., son of William Blake, Esq., of Danesbury, Herts.
II. Lucy.

Lineage.—Childers Walbanke, Esq. (son of William Walbanke, Esq. of Kirkbridge, co. York, by Mildred his wife, eldest dau. and heir of Leonard Childers, Esq. of Carr House, co. York, great-grandson of Hugh Childers, Esq. of Carr House, mayor of Doncaster in 1604), assumed the additional surname and arms of Childers. He m. 1st, Mary, dau. of John Thompson, Esq. of Kirby Hall, by whom (who d. in 1773) he had issue,

John, his heir.
Leonard, of Doncaster, m. Sarah-Anne, dau. of Sir Charles Kent, Bart., and dying 24 Jan. 1826, aged 57, left, 1 Charles-Henry, 2 George-Leonard, 3 Edward, 4 Frederick, 1 Mary-Anne, 2 Louisa, 3 Frances, 4 Sophia-Charlotte, and 5 Maria.
William, in holy orders, M.A., rector of Beeford, vicar of Cantley, and prebendary of Ely, d. 8 Feb. 1833.
Maria, d. young.

Mr. Walbanke-Childers m. 2ndly, Sarah, dau. of the Rev. Mr. Fowler, of Shropshire, and had,

Michael, an officer in the army.
Harriet, m. to the Rev. R. Thompson, of Askham Brian.
Anna-Mildreda, m. to Richard Bell, Esq. of Newcastle.
Eliza-Diana, m. to Edward Radford, Esq.

Mr. Childers was s. at his decease, 16 June, 1802, by his eldest son,

John Walbanke-Childers, Esq. of Cantley, col. 11th light dragoons, who m. in March, 1797, Selina, 3rd dau. and co-heir of Sampson, Lord Eardley, and had issue,

John, now of Cantley.
Eardley, in holy orders, m. his cousin, Maria-Charlotte, eldest dau. of Sir Culling Smith, Bart., and d. at Nice in 1830.
William, capt. in the 42nd regt., m. 16 Aug. 1826, Mary-Elizabeth, relict of Robert Hume, Esq., and has issue. His son, Captain Spencer Childers, royal artillery, was killed in the trenches before Sebastopol, 23 Oct. 1854.
Leonard, deceased.
Charles, in holy orders, vicar of Cantley.
Selina, m. to George Burroughs, Esq., Royal Artillery, and d. at Gibraltar.
Charlotte-Anne, d. in Oct. 1828. Joanna-Maria.

Col. Childers d. 1 March, 1812.

Arms—Arg., a cross-humettée, between four round buckles, gules.
Crest—A dexter-hand, grasping a round buckle.
Seat—Cantley, near Doncaster.

CHISHOLM.

The Chisholm. Duncan-Macdonell Chisholm, of Erchless Castle, co. Inverness, b. 5 Aug. 1811, inherited the estates of his family and the chiefship of his clan, on the decease of his brother, 8 Sept. 1838.

Lineage.—The antiquity of the Chisholms in the Highlands of Scotland appears established beyond disputation. The reputed founder of the clan, Harald, is stated, in the *History of Shetland and Orkney*, to have been of the royal stock of Norway. Sir Robert Gordon calls this chief Harald Chisholm, and however he acquired the surname, it is clearly the tradition that he bore it. The Chisholms of

* Mr. Childe was son of Thomas Childe, Esq. of Kinlet, sheriff of Salop in 1705, who was son of Sir William Childe, Knt., LL.D., master in Chancery, by Anne his wife, only dau. and heir of Rowland Lacon, Esq. of Kinlet, who was great-grandson of Richard Laken, Esq. of Willey, by Agnes his wife, dau. of Sir John Blount, Knt. of Kinlet.

the North are known in their vernacular tongue by the appellation *An Siosalach*, "THE CHISHOLM," emphatically as the chief.

SIR ROBERT CHISHOLM, who became possessed of Quarrelwood, in right of his mother, the dau. and heir of Sir Robert Lauder, of Quarrelwood, acquired the office of constable of Urquhart Castle. He received the honour of knighthood, and was taken prisoner, with King DAVID, at the battle of Redhills, 17 Oct. 1346. He was ransomed, or otherwise obtained his liberty, and lived many years after. Sir Robert Chisholm left (with a dau., Janet, *m.* to Hugh Rose, 5th laird of Kilravoch, who received the lands of Cantra and others in Strathnairn as her tocher) an only son and heir,

SIR ROBERT DE CHISHOLM, styled "of Comar," living about the year 1380, who had two sons. The elder,

JOHN CHISHOLM, was Treasurer of Moray, and is officially called "Dominus et Venerabilis Vir." He was father of an only dau. and heir, MORELLA, *m.* to Alexander Sutherland, baron of Duffus. The Chisholm's brother and heir male,

ALEXANDER DE CHISHOLM, also styled of Comar, *m.* Margaret, dau. of Lachlan Macintosh, of that ilk, about 1400, and was father of THOMAS DE CHISHOLM, whose son, ALEXANDER DE CHISHOLM, had (with two daus., one *m.* to Ewen Maclean, of Ardgour, and the other to Farquhar Farquharson, of Invercauld), a son, UALAN, or WILAND DE CHISHOLM, of Comar, who lived about the year 1513, and was father of JOHN CHISHOLM, of Comar, A.D. 1538, whose son, ALEXANDER CHISHOLM, *s.* in 1555. He *m.* Janet, dau. of Kenneth Mackenzie, 10th baron of Kintail, and had two sons, THOMAS, who *d. s. p.*, and JOHN, who *s.* his brother in 1590, and *m.* the eldest dau. of Mackenzie of Coul, by whom he was father of ALEXANDER CHISHOLM, infeft in 1630, whose son, by his wife, a dau. of Alexander Mackenzie, of Gairloch, was ALEXANDER CHISHOLM, who *s.* in 1677. He *m.* a dau. of Roderick Mackenzie, of Applecross, and left (with a dau., Jean, wife of Sir Kenneth Mackenzie, of Coul) a son and heir,

JOHN CHISHOLM, "The Chisholm," living at the close of the 17th century, who *m.* Jean, 3rd dau. of Sir Thomas Mackenzie, of Findon, and received a fortune with her in money, her eldest sister, as heiress, carrying the lands to her husband, Sir Kenneth Mackenzie, of Scatwell. He was *s.* by his only son,

THE CHISHOLM, RODERICK, who *m.* 1st, Elizabeth, dau. of Duncan Macdonell, of Glengarry, by whom he had five sons, viz., 1 ALEXANDER, his heir; 2 James, major in the 92nd Highlanders, *d. unm.* in 1789; 3 William, provost of Inverness, *d.* in 1807, leaving two sons, Colin and Alexander, who both *d. s. p. m.*; 4 John, a captain in the army, *d. unm.*; 5 Colin, a colonel in the army of Prince CHARLES, fell at Culloden, *s. p.* The chief *m.* 2ndly, Isabel, 2nd dau. of Sir Kenneth Mackenzie, of Scatwell, and had by her a dau., *m.* to Fraser of Culduthel. The Chisholm, with his clan, joined the Chevalier St. George in 1715, and Prince Charles in 1745. He *d.* in 1785, and was *s.* by his son,

THE CHISHOLM, ALEXANDER, who *m.* 1st, a dau. of Mackenzie of Applecross, and had two sons and two daus., viz., 1 Duncan, captain in the 71st, who *d.* 23 Oct. 1782, *unm.*; 2 ALEXANDER, who *s.* his father. The elder dau., Margaret, *m.* Fraser of Dunballoch; the younger, Mackenzie of Scotsburn. The chief *m.* 2ndly, Margaret, dau. of Mackenzie of Allangrange, and by her had a numerous family; of these, three sons and three daus. survived him. The eldest, Mary, *m.* William Robertson, of Kindeace, and left issue; the 2nd *m.* General John Mackenzie; the 3rd is *unm.* Two of the sons *d.* abroad, and the youngest became eventually chief. The Chisholm was *s.* by his eldest surviving son,

THE CHISHOLM, ALEXANDER, who *m.* Elizabeth, dau. of Doctor Wilson, of Edinburgh, and dying 7 Feb. 1793, aged 44, left an only child, MARY, who *m.* James Gooden, Esq., merchant of London, the estates and chieftainship devolving upon his youngest and only surviving half-brother,

THE CHISHOLM, WILLIAM, who *m.* 13 March, 1795, Eliza, eldest dau. of Duncan Macdonell, of Glengarry, by whom (who *m.* 2ndly, in 1819, Sir Thomas Ramsay, of Balmain, Bart.) he had issue,

ALEXANDER-WILLIAM, his heir, *b.* in 1810.
DUNCAN-MACDONELL, who *s.* his brother.
Jemima, *m.* 1 Aug. 1843, to Edmund Batten, Esq., barrister-at-law.

The chief *d.* 21 March, 1817, and was *s.* by his elder son,

THE CHISHOLM, ALEXANDER. This estimable chieftain, M.P. for Inverness-shire, *d.* prematurely, 8 Sept. 1838, *unm.*, and was *s.* by his brother, DUNCAN-MACDONELL CHISHOLM, The Chisholm.

Arms—Gu., a boar's head, erased, or.
Crest—A dexter hand holding a dagger, erect, ppr.; on the point a boar's head, couped, gu.
Supporters—Two naked men, wreathed about the loins, with clubs over their shoulders, ppr.
Mottoes—"Vi aut virtute;" and above the crest, "Feros ferio."
Seat—Erchless Castle, co. Inverness.

CHOLMLEY OF WHITBY AND HOWSHAM.

CHOLMLEY, GEORGE, Esq. of Whitby and Howsham, co. York, *s.* his father in 1809; *m.* in 1824, Hannah, dau. of John-Robinson Foulis, Esq. of Buckton.

Lineage.—This is a branch of the ancient Cheshire stock of Cholmondeley, springing from ROBERT, younger son of Hugh de Cholmondeley, deputy-serjeant of Cheshire, *temp.* EDWARD I. His great-great-grandson, SIR RICHARD CHOLMLEY, Knt. of Roxby, purchased in 1541, a lease for twenty-one years, of the abbey lands of Whitby, and subsequently obtained a grant of all the possessions of the monastery there. This gallant soldier, who was knighted at Leith, in 1544, *m.* 1st, Margaret, dau. of Lord Conyers, and had by her, with three daus., as many sons, viz., FRANCIS, his heir; ROGER, ancestor of the CHOLMELEYS *of Brandsby;* and Richard. He *m.* 2ndly, Lady Katharine Clifford, dau. of Henry, 1st Earl of Cumberland, and widow of John, Lord Scrope of Bolton, by whom he had a son, HENRY, successor to his brother Francis. Sir Richard's eldest son, SIR FRANCIS CHOLMLEY, Knt. of Whitby, *d. s. p.* in 1579, and was *s.*, under the entail of his father's will, by his youngest brother, SIR HENRY CHOLMLEY, Knt. of Whitby and Roxby, father of SIR RICHARD CHOLMLEY, Knt. of Whitby, M.P. for Scarborough in 1620, who *m.* twice. By his 2nd wife he was father of the gallant Cavalier commander, SIR RICHARD CHOLMLEY, Knt. of Gromont, slain at the siege of Lyme; and by his 1st wife had a son, SIR HUGH CHOLMLEY, of Whitby, equally distinguished in the royal cause, who was created a Baronet in 1641. He *d.* in 1657, leaving by Elizabeth his wife, dau. of Sir William Twisden, Bart., two sons, of whom the younger, SIR HUGH CHOLMLEY, *s.* his nephew as 4th Bart. He *m.* in 1666, Lady Ann Compton, and dying in 1688, left an only dau. and heir,

MARY CHOLMLEY, of Whitby, *b.* in 1667, who *m.* Nathaniel Cholmley, Esq. of London, and had a son,

HUGH CHOLMLEY, Esq. of Whitby, *b.* in 1684, M.P. for Hedon, high-sheriff of Yorkshire in 1724, and surveyor-general of the crown lands. He *m.* in 1716, Catherine, only dau. and eventual heir of Sir John Wentworth, Bart. of Elmsall and Howsham, and dying in 1755, left, with other issue, a son and successor,

NATHANIEL CHOLMLEY, Esq. of Whitby and Howsham, M.P., who *m.* 1st, in 1750, Catherine, dau. of Sir Rowland Winn, Bart. of Nostel, and had by her two daus., CATHERINE, of whom presently, and Mary, wife of Abraham Grimes, Esq. He *m.* 2ndly, Henrietta-Catherine, dau. of Stephen Croft, Esq. of Stillington, and 3rdly, Anne-Jesse, 3rd dau. of Leonard Smelt, Esq. of Langton. By the 2nd wife he had Henrietta, *m.* to Sir William Strickland, Bart., and Anne-Elizabeth, *m.* to Constantine-John, Lord Mulgrave. The eldest dau. and heiress,

CATHERINE CHOLMLEY, of Whitby and Howsham, *m.* in 1774, Henry-Hopkins Fane, Esq., who assumed the surname of CHOLMLEY, and *d.* in 1809, leaving (with five daus., Catherine-Jesse, *m.* to Charles-Edward Repington, Esq. of Amington; Louisa, *m.* to the Rev. Thomas-Cutler Rudston Read, of Sand Hutton; Mary, Charlotte, and Amelia-Elizabeth) a son and successor, the present GEORGE CHOLMLEY, Esq. of Whitby and Howsham.

Arms—Gu., two helmets, in chief, arg., and a garb, in base, or.
Crest—A demi-griffin, segreant, sa., beaked, or, holding a helmet of the arms.
Seats—Whitby Abbey and Howsham, co. York.

CHOLMELEY OF BRANDSBY.

CHOLMELEY, FRANCIS, Esq. of Brandsby Hall, co. York, *b.* 25 Nov. 1810; *m.* 22 Feb. 1838, Harriet, youngest dau. of Charles-Gregory Fairfax, Esq. of Gilling Castle, co. York.

Lineage.—This is the senior line of the eminent Yorkshire family of CHOLMLEY.

SIR RICHARD CHOLMELEY, of Roxby, a distinguished

soldier under the Earl of Hertford, received the honour of knighthood, at Leith, in 1544. By Margaret, his 1st wife, dau. of the Lord Conyers, he had (with three daus.) three sons, FRANCIS, of Whitby, who *d. s. p.* in 1579; ROGER, of whom presently; and Richard. By Lady Katharine Clifford, his 2nd wife, Sir Richard left a son, HENRY (Sir), Knt. of Whitby and Roxby, ancestor of the CHOLMLEYS *of Whitby and Howsham*. The 2nd son of the 1st marriage,

ROGER CHOLMELEY, Esq., *m.* a dau. of a gentleman named Dallrivers, and was ancestor of the CHOLMELEYS *of Brandsby*, whose representative,

THOMAS CHOLMELEY, Esq. of Brandsby, *m.* Ann, dau. of Robert Plompton, of Plompton, co. York, and had issue three sons, I. THOMAS, his heir, *m.* Eliza, dau. of Thomas Walton, Esq. of Windermere, co. Lancaster, and *d.* in 1742; II. FRANCIS, of whom presently; III. Robert, *d. unm.*; and ten daus., I. Ann, *m.* to Thomas Mitchell, Esq. of Angram; II. Lucy, *m.* to William Stubbs, Esq.; III. Catherine; IV. Margaret; V. Jane; VI. Mary; VII. Ursula; VIII. Elizabeth; IX. Barbara; X. Alathea. The 2nd son,

FRANCIS CHOLMELEY, Esq. of Brandsby, *b.* 11 March, 1704, *s.* his elder brother in 1742. He *m.* Mary, dau. of Edward Ferrers, Esq. of Baddesley Clinton, co. Warwick, and relict of Thomas Berkeley, Esq. of Spetchley, co. Worcester, and by her, who *d.* in 1767, had (with three daus., two of whom *d.* young, and the third *unm.*) an only son and heir,

FRANCIS CHOLMELEY, Esq. of Brandsby, *b.* 8 May, 1750, who *m.* in 1792, Teresa-Ann, dau. of Sir Henry Englefield, Bart. of White Knights, co. Berks, and by her, who *d.* in 1810, left at his decease, 27 Jan. 1808,

FRANCIS, his heir.
Anne, *m.* in 1814, to Jarrard-Edward Strickland, Esq., and *d.* 15 Jan. 1829.
Mary-Catherine, *m.* in 1816, to John Wright, jun. Esq. of Kelvedon Hall, Essex, who *d.* in 1822.
Katherine-Henrietta, *m.* in 1809, to William-John Charlton, Esq. of Hesleyside, co. Northumberland.
Harriet, *d. unm.* in 1813.

The son and heir,

FRANCIS CHOLMELEY, Esq. of Brandsby, J.P. and D.L., *b.* 9 June, 1783, *m.* 22 Aug. 1809, Barbara, 5th dau. of Henry Darell, Esq. of Calehill, Kent, and had issue,

FRANCIS, now of Brandsby.
Henry-Philip, *b.* 12 June, 1818.
Hugh-Edward, *b.* 2 June, 1822.
Thomas-Charles, *b.* 5 Dec. 1825.
Barbara, *m.* 2 Jan. 1834, to William Plowden, Esq. of Plowden, Salop.
Teresa-Mary. Mary.
Eleanor. Margaret.

Arms—Gu., two helmets, in chief, ppr., garnished, or; in base, a garb, of the last.
Crest—A demi-griffin, segreant, sa., beaked, or, holding a helmet of the arms.
Seat—Brandsby, Yorkshire.

CHOWNE OF WHEATLEIGH LODGE.

CHOWNE, THE REV. JAMES-HENRY, M.A. of Wheatleigh Lodge, Taunton, in the co. of Somerset, formerly an officer in the military service of the E.I. Company, on their Bengal establishment, only surviving son of the late James Tilson, Esq. of Goring, co. Oxford, assumed, by royal license, the surname of CHOWNE only, on the demise of the late General Christopher Chowne, in 1835, in compliance with the will of Mary, late Countess De Bruhl. He *m.* in 1835, Mary-Maynard, eldest dau. of William Braddon, Esq. of Blacklands, co. Devon, and has issue. Both the families of Tilson and Chowne are ancient, the former tracing, in Ireland, to remote antiquity; the latter name is borne upon the roll of Battle Abbey, the first of the family having come over from La Vendée with the Norman Conqueror.

Arms—Quarterly, 1st and 4th, sa., three thatcher's hooks, in pale, arg., 2nd and 3rd, or, on a bend, cotised, between two garbs, sa., a mitre, of the field; on a canton, gu., a rose, arg.
Crests—1st, a cubit arm erect in armour, holding in the gauntlet, ppr., a broad arrow, sa., feathered, arg., for CHOWNE. 2nd, a dexter arm, embowed, habited, arg., charged on the elbow with a garb, sa., grasping in the hand ppr., a crozier, gu., ferruled, or, for TILSON.
Motto—Fugit irreparabile tempus.
Seat—Wheatleigh Lodge, Taunton.

CHRISTIAN OF EWANRIGG HALL.

CHRISTIAN, JOHN, Esq., M.A., of Ewanrigg Hall, co. Cumberland, and Milntown, Isle of Man, barrister-at-law, J.P., and chief judge of the Isle of Man, *b.* 12 July, 1776; *m.* 28 April, 1807, Susanna, dau. of Lewis-Robert Allen, Esq. of Bath, and has issue,

I. John-Allen, *b.* 28 Feb. 1809, *d. unm.* 3 June, 1828.
II. HENRY-TAUBMAN, *b.* 29 Jan. 1810.
III. Robert, *b.* 30 Aug. 1812, *d.* 1813.
IV. William-Bell, in holy orders, *b.* 17 Aug. 1815, *m.* Charlotte-Elizabeth, dau. of Thomas Brine, Esq. of the Isle of Man, and has issue, Annie-Louisa and Charlotte-Isabella.
V. Charles-Craik, *b.* 28 March, 1821, *d.* in 1838.
I. Susan-Curwen, *m.* to Augustus-William Hillary, only son of Sir William Hillary, Bart.
II. Margaret, *m.* to Thomas Underwood, Esq. M.D.
III. Isabella-Anne.
IV. Louisa-Dorothy, *m.* to the Rev. John-William Molyneux.

Lineage.—The first ancestor of the family on record was a member of the House of Keys, in the Isle of Man, at the Tynwald Court held in that island in 1422. The manorial records previous to that year were all destroyed, and, in consequence, the pedigree cannot be traced further back. It is registered in the College of Arms, Book vii., D. 14, p. 170.

The first who settled at Ewanrigg was

EWAN CHRISTIAN, Esq. of Milntown, barrister-at-law, eldest son of Edward Christian, Esq. of Milntown, Demster of the Isle of Man, by Dorothy his wife, sister of Edward Wilson, Esq. of Dallam Tower, and grandson, by Margaret his wife, dau. of John Parker, Esq. of Bradkirk, co. Lancaster, of John Christian, Esq. of Milntown, living in 1643, who was son of Ewan Christian, Esq. of Milntown, made Demster of the Isle of Man in 1605, and grandson of William M'Christen, of Milntown, seventh in lineal descent from William M'Christen, a member of the House of Keys in 1422. Ewan Christian (the first settler at Ewanrigg) *m.* in 1677, Mary, eldest dau. of John Caine, Esq., and dying in 1719, was *s.* by his eldest surviving son,

JOHN-CHRISTIAN, Esq. of Milntown and Ewanrigg, *b.* in 1688, who *m.* 14 May, 1717, Bridget, eldest dau. of Humphrey Senhouse, Esq. of Nether Hall, or Ellenborough, co. Cumberland, and by her, who *d.* in 1749, had seven sons and four daus.; of the latter, MARY *m.* Edward Law, Bishop of Carlisle, and was mother of Edward Law, Baron Ellenborough. Mr. Christian *d.* 20 Sept. 1745, and was *s.* by his son,

JOHN CHRISTIAN, Esq. of Milntown and of Ewanrigg Hall, *b.* 5 Oct. 1719, high-sheriff of Cumberland in 1766; *m.* Jane, eldest dau. of Eldred Curwen, Esq. of Workington Hall, co. Cumberland, and by her (who *d.* in 1762), had two sons, JOHN, his heir, and Henry, *b.* in 1761, and six daus., viz., Bridget; Julia, *m.* in 1769, to Edward Stanley, Esq. of Workington; Jane, *m.* to W. Blamire, Esq.; Frances, *m.* to Edward Christian, Esq. of Brancaster, Norfolk; Dorothy, *m.* in 1774, to John Taubman, Esq. of Nunnery, Isle of Man; and Mary. He *d.* in 1757, and was *s.* by his eldest son,

JOHN CHRISTIAN, Esq. of Milntown and Ewanrigg Hall, who *m.* 1st, 10 Sept. 1775, Margaret, dau. of John Taubman, Esq. of the Isle of Man, and by her (who *d.* in 1778), had one son, JOHN, now of Ewanrigg. He *m.* 2ndly, 5 Oct. 1782, Isabella, dau. and sole heir of Henry Curwen, Esq., M.P., of Workington Hall, co. Cumberland, and had by her four sons and three daus. (*See* CURWEN *of Workington.*) Mr. Christian, who was for many years M.P. for Cumberland, assumed the surname of CURWEN. He *d.* 13 Dec. 1829, when he was *s.* by his son by his first marriage, the present JOHN CHRISTIAN, Esq. Ewanrigg Hall and Milntown.

Arms—Az., a demi-mascle, between three covered cups, or.
Crest—An unicorn's head, erased, arg., armed, and gorged with a collar, invecked, or.
Motto—Salus per Christum.
Seats—Ewanrigg Hall, co. Cumberland; and Milntown, Isle of Man.

CHRISTIE OF DURIE.

CHRISTIE, CHARLES-MAITLAND, Esq. of Durie, co. Fife, J.P. and D.L., *b.* 31 Dec. 1785; *m.* 1st, in Nov. 1815, Mary Butler, eldest dau. of the Hon. Robert

Lindsay, brother of the Earl of Balcarres, and by her has issue,

I. JAMES.
II. Robert. III. Charles-Maitland.
IV. Alexander, V. Peter-John.
VI. Hugh-Lindsay, lieut. 10th Madras N. I.
VII. Napier.
I. Elizabeth.
II. Mary, m. in Jan. 1845, to Francis-Brown Douglas, Esq., advocate.
III. Anne. IV. Margaret.

He m. 2ndly, 2 April, 1830, Elizabeth, 4th dau. of Alexander Pringle, Esq. of Yair, and by her has,

I. William. II. David. III. Benjamin.
I. Susan. II. Agnes. III. Jane.

Lineage.—THOMAS CHRISTIE, Esq., son of JAMES CHRISTIE, Esq., and Margaret Walker, his wife, m. Mary Watson, and was father of

JAMES CHRISTIE, Esq. of Durie, who m. 1st, Miss Milligan, and by her had a son,

Thomas, who m. and has issue surviving,
James. Edmund.
Mary. Susan. Anne-Caroline.

He m. 2ndly, in 1783, Mary Turner, eldest dau. of the Hon. Charles Maitland, 2nd son of Charles, 6th Earl of Lauderdale, and by her had

CHARLES-MAITLAND, of Durie.
James, m., and has surviving issue, Robert, and Jane.
Robert, m. Miss Stark, and has issue three sons and a dau.
William, m. Miss Burchell, and has two sons and six daus.
Mary, m. to Alexander Smith, Esq.
Isabella, m. to the Rev. William Fortescue.
Margaret, m. to John-Irvine Boswell, Esq. of Kingcausie and Balmuto.
Erskine, m. to Mathew Fortescue, Esq., nephew of Earl Fortescue.
Anne.

Mr. Christie d. in 1808.

Arms—Or, a saltier, cantoned, between two stars, in the flanks, sa.; in chief, a demi-lion, couped at the joints, gu., and in base, a cross-patée, of the last.
Crest—A dexter hand, holding a missive letter, ppr.
Motto—Pro rege.
Seat—Durie, co. Fife.

CHRISTMAS OF WHITFIELD.

CHRISTMAS, WILLIAM, Esq. of Whitfield, co. Waterford, J.P., and D.L. for that shire, m. Miss Wynneatt, of co. Gloucester. Mr. Christmas has sat in parliament for the co. of Waterford, and served as high-sheriff for the county.

Seat—Whitfield, Waterford.

CHRISTOPHER OF BLOXHOLM.

CHRISTOPHER, THE RT. HON. ROBERT-ADAM, of Bloxholm Hall, co. Lincoln, J.P., M.P. for the northern division of that shire, b. 9 Feb. 1804; m. 28 Jan. 1828, Lady Mary Bruce, eldest dau. of the late Earl of Elgin, and has an only dau. Mr. Christopher, whose patronymic was DUNDAS, assumed his present surname in compliance with the will of the late George Manners, Esq. of Bloxham, whose estates he became possessed of in right of his wife.

Lineage.—PHILIP DUNDAS, Esq., Governor of the Prince of Wales Island, 4th son (by Grace his 2nd wife, dau. of William Grant, Lord Prestongrange) of Robert Dundas, Esq. of Arniston, Lord President of the Court of Session, elder brother of Henry, 1st Viscount Melville, m. in 1803, Margaret, sister of Sir David Wedderburne, Bart., and d. in 1807, leaving two sons, ROBERT-ADAM, who assumed the surname of CHRISTOPHER, and is now of Bloxholm; and Philip, colonel in the army.

Arms—Arg., a chevron, sa. between three fir-cones, ppr., a chief.
Crest—An arm embowed, vested, holding a fir-branch,
Motto—Essayez.
Seat—Bloxholm Hall, Sleaford.

CHRISTY OF APULDREFIELD.

CHRISTY, JOHN, Esq. of Apuldrefield, co. Kent, b. 19 June, 1781; m. 20 Oct. 1812, Sarah, 2nd dau. of the late Abraham De Horne, Esq. of Surrey Square (*see family of* DE HORNE), and has had issue,

I. JOHN-DE HORNE, of Cudham Lodge, Kent, b. 25 Aug. 1814, m. 21 July, 1842, Ann, dau. of Mr. Robert Kidder, of Westerham, and d. 1 Aug. 1850, leaving two sons and two daus.
II. Alfred, b. 14 Jan. 1818.
III. George, b. 11 April, 1819.
IV. Edward, of Farringdon, Berks, b. 6 June, 1820; m. 31 Aug. 1847, Julia-Shears, dau. of Charles Spurrell, Esq. of Hill House, Dartford, and d. s. p. 4 May, 1850.
V. Frederick-Collier, of Melbourne, Australia, b. 9 Sept. 1822.
VI. Arthur-De Horne, b. 6 Aug. 1828.
VII. Albert, Lieut. 10th Madras N.I., b. 21 March, 1830.
I. Emma-Catherine-Collier, m. 2 Feb. 1836, George-Steinman Steinman, Esq., F.S.A., of Priory Lodge, Peckham, Surrey, and has issue.

Lineage.—ALEXANDER CHRISTY, of Aberdeen, b. in Scotland, in 1642, passed over into Ireland. and residing at Moyallan, co. Down, d. there, 29 April, 1722, leaving (with a dau., Sarah, m. to Samuel Morton, Esq. of Kilmore, co. Armagh) a son,

JOHN CHRISTY, of Moyallan, b. 10 Sept. 1673, who m. Mary Hill, of Magheramesko, and d. in May, 1768, leaving issue,

I. Alexander, b. 4 Jan.1699, who went into Scotland, and after residing some time at Ormiston, co. Edinburgh, removed in 1736 to Perth. He m. Anne, dau. of George Huntingdon, M.D., but d. s. p. in 1764.
II. Joseph, b. 29 March, 1703, m. 18 April, 1733, Patience, dau. of John Chambers, Esq. of Lurgan, and d. in 1755, leaving a dau., Mary, m. to Archibald Horn, Esq.
III. JOHN, of whom presently.
IV. James, of Lower Stramore, in Moyallan, b. 29 March, 1708, m. 4 July, 1733, Margaret, dau. of John Morton, Esq., and had issue,
1 John, b. 19 June, 1735, m. 15 April, 1759, Deborah, dau. of Joseph Thompson, Esq. of Castletown, and d. 13 Aug. 1771, leaving issue, a son and successor, JAMES, of Lower Stramore, b. 17 Dec. 1762, who m. 22 Nov. 1785, Mary, dau. of Thomas Mark, Esq. of Limerick, and d. 5 Jan. 1820, leaving, with other issue, a son and heir, JOHN, of Lower Stramore, b. 6 July, 1789, who m. Sarah, dau. of John Lecky, Esq. of Ballykealy, co. Carlow, and d. 4 April, 1848, leaving, John Lecky, of Cincinnati, b. 25 May, 1830, and other issue.
2 James, of Lurgan, m. 1 Dec. 1768, Lucia, dau. of Archibald Shaw, Esq., and d. s. p. 26 Aug. 1798.
1 Mary, b. 31 Jan. 1734, m. 29 April, 1758, Thomas Dawson, Esq., and d. 22 Jan. 1785. Mr. Dawson d. 15 Jan. 1735.
2 Margaret, b. 18 Oct. 1737, m. 29 Sept. 1756, Thomas Linton, Esq., and had issue.
3 Sarah, b. 20 Aug. 1740, m. her cousin, John Christy, and had issue.
V. Thomas, b. 22 Jan. 1711, of Moyallan, m. 1st, 6 March, 1739-40, Mary, dau. of John Bramery, Esq., and 2ndly, Mary Nicholson, and d. 28 April, 1780, having had issue, by his first wife,
1 John, drowned 27 Oct. 1758, s. p.
1 Hannah, b. 3 May, 1748, m. 18 Dec. 1766, John Wakefield, Esq., and d. 14 July, 1779, leaving issue, Thomas-Christy Wakefield, Esq. of Moyallan.
2 Mary, b. 9 Jan. 1783, m. 27 Oct. 1771, Joseph Phelps, Esq.

The 3rd son,

JOHN CHRISTY, Esq., passed over to Scotland, and built Ormiston Lodge, co. Edinburgh. He was b. 29 June, 1707, and m. Mary, dau. of William Miller, Esq. of Craigentinnie, co. Edinburgh, and aunt to William-Henry Miller, Esq., F.S.A., of Brittwell House, Bucks, sometime M.P. for Newcastle-under-Lyme, and d. in 1761, leaving issue,

I. John, who d. young.
II. William, who sold Ormiston Lodge, 24 Feb. 1764, m. 1st, Jane Erskine, and 2ndly, Alison Dunn, and d. in 1814, leaving issue.
III. Hill, lieut. 61st foot, b. in 1741, m. 1769, Helen, dau. of Archibald Cuthbertson, M.D., and d. 18 May, 1819, leaving issue,
1 Archibald, d. s. p.
2 John, of Fort Union, Adare, near Limerick, m. Eliza, dau. of Luke Mullock, of Limerick, and has issue, Mathew, Luke, John-Hill, Helen, and Anne.
3 Mathew, M.D., surgeon E. I. C. S., m. Esther Miller (who m. 2ndly, Major Mungo Campbell); and d. in India, leaving issue, Ann, m. to the Rev. James-Charles Thompson.
1 Agnes, m. William Ramage, Esq., capt. R.N., and had issue.
IV. John, of Kircassock, co. Down, m. 28 Nov. 1766, Sarah, dau. of James Christy, Esq., of Lower Stramore, and had issue,

1 John, *d.* at Nantucket, North America.
2 James, of Kircassock, *m.* Anne, dau. of Joseph Murphy, Esq., and has surviving issue, Mary-Anne, *m.* in 1821, to Richard Tighe, Esq., barrister-at-law; Charlotte; and Eliza, *m.* 19 July, 1848, to Jonathan-Joseph Richardson, Esq. of The Island, Lisburn, co. Antrim, M.P.
1 Margaret.

V. MILLER, of whom presently.
I. Ann, who *d.* young.
II. Euphemia, *m.* William Miller, Esq. of Edinburgh.
III. Ann, *d. unm.* 1788.
IV. Margaret, *b.* in 1750, *m.* in 1768, Alexander Sinclair, Esq. of Brabster Doran, in Bower, Caithnesshire, and had issue.
V. Mary, *b.* in 1755, *m.* 1st, in 1775, John Dollin, of London, and 2ndly, Thomas Jeffrys, Esq. of London.

The 5th son,

MILLER CHRISTY, Esq., *b.* in 1748, resided at Stockwell, Surrey. He *m.* 29 Sept. 1773, Ann, dau. of William Rice, of Manuden, Essex, and *d.* 12 June, 1820, leaving issue,

I. Thomas, of Brooklands, Essex, lord of the manor of Black Notley, *b.* 25 Sept. 1776, *m.* Rebecca, dau. of Samuel Hewlings, Esq. of Reading, and by her (who *d.* 14 Jan. 1837) left issue at his decease, 14 June, 1846,
1 Thomas, of Brooklands, *m.* in 1829, Jane, dau. of Thomas-Christy Wakefield, Esq. of Moyallen House, Moyallan, and has issue, Thomas, of Shanghai, *b.* 9 Dec. 1831; Wakefield, *b.* 6 Dec. 1834; Stephen, *b.* 13 Dec. 1840; Louisa; and Ellen-Sophia.
2 Samuel, M.P. for Newcastle-under-Lyme, *m.* 20 April, 1842, Mary, dau. of Thomas Hardcastle, of Firwood, near Bolton-le-Moors, and has, William-Henry-Archibald, *b.* 16 Nov. 1850.
1 Rachael, lady of the manor of Black Notley, *m.* 7 Oct. 1824, Daniel-Bell Hanbury, Esq. of Lambeth, and has issue.
2 Charlotte, *m.* in 1832, Edmund Ashworth, Esq., J.P., of Egerton Hall, Turton, Lancashire, and has issue.
3 Anne, *m.* in 1836, to Thomas Ashworth, Esq. of Poynton, co. Chester, and *d.* in 1838, *s. p.*
II. William-Miller, of The Woodbines, Kingston, Surrey, *b.* 12 Jan. 1778, *m.* Ann, dau. of John Fell, Esq. of Peckham, and has issue.
1 William, F.L.S., F.Z.S., &c., *d.* 24 July, 1839.
2 Henry, of Stockwell. 3 John-Fell, *d.* 1851.
4 Alexander, of Fairfield in Droylsden, co. Lancashire.
5 Richard, of Fairfield.
6 Joseph-Fell, of Clapham, co. Surrey, *m.* 28 June, 1854, Lilias, dau. of James Dowie, Esq. of Chesnut Grove, Kingston.
7 Edmund, of Stockport, co. Chester.
1 Mary-Anne. 2 Elizabeth.
3 Rebecca, *m.* 10 May, 1848, to Alfred Darby, Esq. of Stanley Hall, Astley's Abbots, co. Salop.
III. JOHN, of Apuldrefeild Manor.
IV. Joseph, of Maidstone, Kent, *m.* in 1822, Elizabeth, dau. of Joseph Johnson, Esq. of Pontefract.
V. James, of Brownings, in Broomfield, *m.* 2 June, 1812, Charlotte, youngest dau. of John Fell, Esq. of Peckham Rye, and has, 1 James, of Boynton Hall, Essex, who *m.* in 1842, Elizabeth, dau. of Wm.-Cruttenden Marten, Esq. of Lewes, and has, James, Wilfred, Alice, Charlotte-Mary, Anna-Louisa, and Ada; 2 Robert; 3 David, of Patching Hall, Broomfield, *b.* 22 July, 1823; 4 Fell; 1 Mary, *m.* in 1837, to Joseph Smith, Esq. of Patterswick Hall, Essex; 2 Sophia, *m.* in 1839, to William Marriage, Esq. of Springfield; 3 Caroline; 4 Ellen-Jane.
I. Anne, *m.* Alexander Cruickshank, of Laureston Lane, Edinburgh (who had before *m.* her cousin), and *d.* 31 Dec. 1836, leaving issue.

Arms—Or, on a saltier, invecked, sable, between four mullets, pierced, az., a saltier, erm.
Crest—A mount, vert., thereon the stump of a holly tree, sprouting, between four branches of fern, all ppr.
Motto—Sic viresco.
Seat—Apuldrefeild Manor, Cudham, Kent.

CHUTE OF THE VINE.

WIGGETT-CHUTE, WILLIAM-LYDE, Esq. of The Vine, co. Hants, and of Pickenham Hall, in Norfolk, J.P. and D.L., high-sheriff in 1832, and formerly M.P. for Norfolk, *b.* 16 June, 1800; *m.* 1 June, 1837, Martha, dau. of Theophilus-Russell Buckworth, Esq. of Cockley-Cley Hall, co. Norfolk, and has issue,

I. CHALONER-WILLIAM, *b.* 1 Aug. 1838.
II. Devereux-Wiggett, *b.* 20 Dec. 1839.
III. Charles-Thomas, *b.* 17 Aug. 1841.
IV. Edward-Russell, *b.* 11 July, 1846.
V. Theophilus-Dacre, *b.* 10 June, 1852.
I. Elizabeth-Martha. II. Emmeline-Mary.
III. Georgina-Fanny. IV. Mary-Esther.

This gentleman, whose patronymic is WIGGETT, assumed, by royal license, in 1827, on succeeding to the estates of the Rev. Thomas-Vere Chute, the additional surname and arms of that family.

Lineage.—The CHUTES were of long standing in the counties of Kent and Somerset, where they were originally settled. They were lords of the manor of Taunton, until about the year 1500, when Edmund Chute sold the manor to Lord Denham. The Kentish branch of the family expired in 1700, on the death of Sir George Chute, Bart.

CHALLONER CHUTE, Esq., son and heir of Charles Chute, Esq. of the Middle Temple, by Ursula his wife, dau. of John Challoner, Esq. of Fulham, purchased from Lord Sandys, in 1653, the estate of The Vine, co. Hants. He *m.* 1st, Ann, dau. and co-heir of Sir John Skory, Knt. and had a son, CHALLONER, his heir, and two daus., Anne and Cecilia. He *m.* 2ndly, Dorothy, Lady Dacre, dau. of Lord North, but had no further issue. Mr. Challoner Chute *d.* in 1659, then Speaker of the House of Commons to RICHARD CROMWELL'S Parliament, an arduous office, which he filled to the great satisfaction of all parties. His great-grandson,

JOHN CHUTE, Esq. of The Vine, *d. unm.* in 1776, when this branch of the family became extinct in the male line, but the possessions devolved on

THOMAS LOBB, Esq. of Pickenham Hall, in Norfolk, son of Elizabeth Chute (granddau. of CHALLONER CHUTE, Esq. of The Vine), by Thomas Lobb, Esq. This gentleman assumed the surname and arms of CHUTE. He *m.* Ann-Rachel, dau. of WILLIAM WIGGETT, Esq., and had, (with other children, who *d. unm.*) WILLIAM; THOMAS-VERE; Anne-Rachel, *m.* to Sir William Hicks, Bart.; and Mary, *m.* to Wither Branston, Esq. of Oakley Hall, Hants, and *d. s. p.* Mr. Lobb Chute *d.* in 1791, and was *s.* by his eldest surviving son,

WILLIAM-JOHN CHUTE, Esq. of The Vine and Pickenham Hall, M.P. for Hants, who *m.* Elizabeth, dau. and co-heiress of Joshua Smith, Esq. of Stoke Park, Wilts, but dying *s. p.* in 1824, was *s.* by his brother,

THE REV. THOMAS-VERE CHUTE, of The Vine and Pickenham Hall, rector of South Pickenham and Moulton St. Michael's, co. Norfolk, at whose decease *unm.*, in 1827, the estates devolved on WILLIAM-LYDE WIGGETT, Esq., who assuming, on inheriting, the surname and arms of CHUTE, is the present WILLIAM-LYDE WIGGETT-CHUTE, Esq. of The Vine and Pickenham Hall.

Arms—Quarterly: 1st and 4th, gu., three swords, barways, the points towards the dexter, ppr., pommels and hilts, or, for CHUTE; 2nd and 3rd, erm., three mullets, two and one, az., pierced, gu.; on a chief, wavy, sa., a dove, regardant, ppr., for WIGGETT.
Crests—1st, a dexter cubit arm, in armour, the hand in a gauntlet, grasping a broken sword in bend sinister, ppr., pommel and hilt, or, for CHUTE; 2nd, a griphon's head, couped, sa., holding in the beak an ear of wheat, ppr., between two wings, arg., each charged with a mullet, gu., for WIGGETT.
Motto—Fortune de guerre.
Seat—The Vine, in Hampshire.

Family of Wiggett.

WILLIAM WIGGETT, Esq. of Geist, descended from an old Norfolk family, *m.* in 1616, Anne Sherringham, and had issue,

I. WILLIAM, who *m.* Elizabeth, dau. of Edward Davy, Esq., and had an only dau., ANN-RACHAEL, who *m.* THOMAS LOBB CHUTE, Esq., and had, with other issue, a son, the REV. THOMAS-VERE CHUTE, at whose decease, *unm.*, in 1827, the estates of the Chutes devolved on W.-L. WIGGETT, Esq., their present possessor.
II. JAMES, who *m.* Frances, dau. and co-heir of — Mackarell, Esq., and had, with three daus., a son,
THE REV. JAMES WIGGETT, rector of Crudwell and Hankerton, in Wilts, who *m.* 1st, in 1791, Rachel, dau. and heiress of Samuel Lyde, Esq. of Ayott, Herts, by whom (who *d.* in 1802) he had surviving issue,
1 JAMES-SAMUEL, in holy orders, rector of Moulton, in Norfolk, *b.* 12 July, 1797, *m.* Mary-Ann, dau. of Allan Thompson, Esq., and has two sons, Allan and William.
2 WILLIAM-LYDE, the present MR WIGGETT CHUTE.
1 Anna-Maria, *m.* Roger-P. Western, Esq., and *d.* 1858.
2 Frances-Rachel, *m.* to Admiral Colquitt.
3 Caroline, *m.* to Thomas Workman, Esq.
Mr. Wiggett (the rector of Crudwell) *m.* 2ndly, and had another son, Edward-Humphrys, *b.* in 1817, *m.* 1852, Margaret Wade.

CHUTE OF CHUTE HALL.

CHUTE, RICHARD, Esq. of Tullygaron (or Chute Hall), co. Kerry, J.P., *b.* 22 May, 1811; *m.* 1st,

18 Oct. 1836, Theodora, dau. and heir of Arthur Blennerhassett, Esq. of Blennerville, by Helen-Jane his wife, dau. of Thomas, Lord Ventry, and grand-dau. of Sir Rowland Blennerhassett, Bart. of Blennerville, and by her has issue,

I. FRANCIS-BLENNERHASSETT, b. 18 Sept. 1837.
II. Arthur-Rowland, b. 20 Dec. 1838.
I. Melicent-Agnes. II. Helena-Jane.

Mr. Chute m. 2ndly, 3 March, 1847, Rose, dau. of the present Lord Ventry, and by her has,

I. Thomas-Aremberg, b. 14 Oct. 1848.
II. Mary-Anne.

Lineage.—The CHUTES *of Chute Hall* derive from that branch of the ancient family of Chute which was seated in the county of Kent.

The first who settled in Ireland,

GEORGE CHUTE, a military officer, went into that kingdom during the rebellion of Desmond, and obtained grants of land near Dingle, and in the county of Limerick, which were soon, however, alienated. He m. an Evans, of the county of Cork, and had a son,

DANIEL CHUTE, who acquired, in marriage with a dau. of McElligott, the lands of Tulligaron (subsequently called Chute Hall), which was afterwards (with others since disposed of) confirmed by patent, in 1630, under which they are now held. He left (with a dau., m. to — Crosbie, Esq.) a son and successor,

RICHARD CHUTE, Esq. of Tulligaron, co. Kerry, who m. a dau. of Crosbie of Tubrid, and was s. by his son,

EUSEBIUS CHUTE, Esq. of Tulligaron, who m. Mary, sister of Mr. Justice Bernard, of the court of Common Pleas in Ireland, ancestor of the Earls of Bandon. By this lady he had issue, I. RICHARD, his heir; II. Francis, who died collector of Tralee, s. p.; III. Pierce, ancestor of the CHUTES *of Tralee;* and IV. Arthur, in holy orders, who d. unm. The eldest son,

RICHARD CHUTE, Esq. of Tulligaron, m. Charity, dau. of John Herbert, Esq. of Castle Island, co. Kerry, and had issue, I. FRANCIS, his heir; II. Richard, of Roxborough, in Kerry; I. Margaret, m. to George Rowan, Esq. of Bahtarmy; II. Agnes, m. to John Sealy, Esq. of Maglass; III. Catherine, m. to Cornelius M'Gillicuddy (M'Gillicuddy of The Reeks). Mr. Chute was s. at his decease by his eldest son,

FRANCIS CHUTE, Esq. of Tulligaron, or Chute Hall, who m. in 1761, Ruth, dau. of Sir Riggs Falkiner, Bart. of Anne Mount, co. Cork, and had issue,

I. RICHARD, his heir.
II. Falkiner, captain in the 22nd regiment of light dragoons, who m. Anne, dau. of Captain Goddard, of the Queen's County, and left at his decease an only dau., Catherine, m. to William Cooke, Esq. of Retreat, near Athlone.
III. Caleb, captain in the 69th foot, who m. Elizabeth, dau. of Theophilus Yielding, Esq. of Cahir Anne, co. Kerry.
IV. Francis-Bernard, who m. Jane, dau. of John Rowan, Esq. of Castle Gregory, and has issue,
 1 Francis-Bernard.
 1 Elizabeth.
V. Arthur, who m. Frances, dau. of John Lindsey, Esq. of Lindville, Cork, and has issue,
 1 Francis, in holy orders.
 2 John, also in holy orders.
 1 Frances. 2 Ruth. 3 Anne.
I. Margaret, m. to Thomas-William Sandes, Esq. of Sallowglin, co. Kerry.
II. Ruth, m. to the late Thomas Elliot, Esq. of Garrynthenavally, in Kerry.

Mr. Chute d. in 1782, and was s. by his eldest son,

RICHARD CHUTE, Esq. of Chute Hall, b. in 1763, high-sheriff of the county of Kerry in 1786, m. 1st, in 1785, Agnes, dau. of Rowland Bateman, Esq. of Oak Park, and had by her,

FRANCIS, his heir.
Rowland, of Leebrooke, near Tralee, formerly captain in the 58th regiment, m. Frances, dau. of James Crosbie, Esq. of Ballyheigue Castle, formerly M.P. for the co. of Kerry, and has two sons and two daus.
Lætitia, m. to William Raymond, Esq. of Dromin, co. Kerry.
Ruth, m. to William Cooke, Esq. of The Cottage, near Athlone.
Agnes, m. to Richard Mason, Esq. of Cappanshane, co. Limerick, and is deceased.

Mr. Chute m. 2ndly, in 1798, Elizabeth, dau. of the Rev. Dr. William Maunsell, D.D. of the city of Limerick, and by her had two sons and three daus.,

William-Maunsell, m. the dau. of the Rev. Mr. Nash, of Ballycarthy, near Tralee, and has issue.
Richard, M.D., of Tralee, m. Miss Elizabeth Rowan, of Bahtamy, and has issue.
Elizabeth, m. to the Rev. Robert Wade, of Tralee.
Dorothea, m. to William Neligan, Esq. of Tralee, and is deceased.
Margaret.

The eldest son,

FRANCIS CHUTE, Esq. of Chute Hall, m. 1st, 18 Feb. 1810, Mary-Anne, dau. of Trevor Bomford, Esq. of Dublin, and by her had issue,

RICHARD, now of Chute Hall.
Trevor, lieut.-col. 70th regt.
Rowland, deceased.
Mary, m. to — Harnett, Esq.

Mr. Chute m. 2ndly, Arabella, dau. of the Rev. Maynard Denny, of Churchill, brother of Sir Barry Denny, Bart. of Tralee, M.P. for the co. of Kerry, and by that lady had,

Arthur.
Penelope. Arabella.

He d. 12 Aug. 1849.

Arms—Gu., semée of mullets, or, three swords, barways, ppr., the middlemost encountering the other two; a canton, per fesse, arg. and vert, thereon a lion passant.

Crest—A dexter cubit arm in armour, the hand on a gauntlet grasping a broken sword, in bend sinister, ppr., pommel and hilt, or.

Motto—Fortune de guerre.

Seat—Chute Hall, co. Kerry.

CLAPHAM OF BURLEY GRANGE.

CLAPHAM, JOHN-PEELE, Esq. of Burley Grange, co. York, J.P., b. 7 July, 1801; m. 11 April, 1827, Mary-Anne, dau. of John Clapham, Esq. of Leeds, and has issue,

I. WILLIAM-HENRY. II. John-Arthur.
I. Mary. II. Emma.

Lineage.—JOHN CLAPHAM, Esq., by Martha his wife, was father of JOHN CLAPHAM, who, by Hannah his wife, had issue, William; John; Samuel; Hannah; Elizabeth; Mary; and Martha. Of these,

WILLIAM CLAPHAM, Esq., m. 1 Oct. 1798, Anne, dau. of John Peele, Esq. of London, and had an only surviving son, the present JOHN-PEELE CLAPHAM, Esq. of Burley Grange, co. York.

Arms—Arg., on a bend, az., six fleurs-de-lis, two, two, and two.

Crest—A lion, rampant.

Motto—Post est occasio calva.

Seat—Burley Grange, near Otley, co. York.

CLARK OF BELFORD HALL.

CLARK, THE REV. JOHN-DIXON, M.A. of Belford Hall, co. Northumberland, J.P. and D.L., b. 16 Jan. 1812; m. 8 June, 1843, Ann, 2nd dau. of Addison Fenwick, Esq. of Pallion and Bishopwearmouth, and by her (who d. in 1847) has one dau.,

ANNE-ELIZABETH.

Lineage.—WILLIAM CLARK, Esq. of Belford Hall and Benton House, co. Northumberland, b. in 1766 (son of William Clark, late of Tynemouth, and grandson of William Clark, whose family were settled near Alnwick for a series of years), was lieut.-col. commanding the North local regiment of Militia, a deputy-lieutenant and a deputy vice-admiral, and served as high-sheriff of Northumberland in 1820. He m. 1st, in 1794, Ann, dau. of James Hutchinson, Esq. of Tynemouth, by whom (who d. in 1802) he had three daus., viz., Anne-Elizabeth; Mary-Elizabeth, m. in 1822, to the Rev. W.-C. King, of Lowestoft; and Elizabeth-Sarah. He m. 2ndly, in 1806, Mary, dau. of William Brown, Esq. of Long Benton, and by her (who d. in 1814) had issue, WILLIAM-BROWN, his heir; JOHN-DIXON, now of Belford Hall; Jane-Margaret, m. 2 July, 1833, to the Rev. William Atkinson, M.A. He m. 3rdly, Margaret, eldest dau. of George Selby, Esq. of Twizell House, in Northumberland. Mr. Clark d. in 1837, and was s. by his elder son,

WILLIAM-BROWN CLARK, Esq., M.A., of Belford Hall, b. 12 Nov. 1807, barrister-at-law, J.P., who m. 11 June, 1833, Eleanor, eldest dau. of Addison Fenwick, Esq. of Pallion, and Bishop Wearmouth, co. Durham, and had issue, Emily-Anne and Julia-Mary. Mr. Clark d. 9 Nov. 1840.

Arms—Erm., on a chevron, embattled-counter-embattled, between three dragons' heads, erased, az., a chaplet between two roses, or.

Crest—A dragon's head, erased, az., guttée d'or, with a collar, embattled-counter-embattled, and charged on the neck with three amulets, interlaced, gold.

Motto—Fortitudo.

Seat—Belford Hall, Northumberland.

CLARK OF BUCKLAND TOUSSAINTS.

CLARK, WILLIAM-JOHN, Esq. of Buckland Toussaints, co. Devon, J.P. and D.L., high-sheriff in 1843, *b.* 16 April, 1793; *m.* 1st, 8 June, 1815, Mary, 2nd dau. of John Smith, Esq. of Sumner Castle, co. Lancaster, by Mary his wife, dau. of Edmund Smith, Esq. of Sparth Hall, in the same county, and has by her,

I. WILLIAM-IRVING SMITH, *b.* 6 March, 1816, *m.* 21 March, 1844, Mariane, eldest dau. of Sir Robert-William Newman, Bart., and has issue.

II. Mary.

Mr. Clark *m.* 2ndly, 28 March, 1826, Matilda, 5th dau. of Paul-Treby Treby, Esq. of Goodamoor, co. Devon, by Lætitia-Anne his wife, only dau. of Sir William Trelawny, of Trelawny, co. Cornwall, Bart., governor of Jamaica, and by her has issue,

I. Lewis-Trelawney, first-lieut. 21st Royal N.B. fusiliers, *b.* 14 Jan. 1828.

II. George-Ourry, of Pemb. Col. Oxford, *b.* 9 Oct. 1831.

III. Edward-Hele, *b.* 23 May, 1833.

IV. Ernest-Leith, *d.* 1 March, 1849.

V. Norman-Leith-Hay, *b.* 11 April, 1845.

I. Katherine-Treby. II. Caroline-Maud.

III. Barbara-Treby.

Lineage.—This family, originally from the northern counties, settled in the parishes of South Huish and Honiton-Clyst, co. Devon, in the year 1630, when we find STEPHEN and OTHO CLARKE residing on Sampton and Clarke's Land, in the county aforesaid. Stephen Clarke, Gentleman, *m.* in 1664, Christian Chresham, and had issue, William, Mary, Joan, Edward-Nosworthy, Thomas, and James: the two latter were buried in Honiton-Clyst, in the years 1688 and 1689, and

EDWARD-NOSWORTHY CLARKE, Gentleman, the 2nd son, *m.* in 1701, Joan Harris, from whom descended

WILLIAM CLARKE, Esq., who *m.* Mary Jervis, and was buried 1767, aged 74: the issue of this marriage was WILLIAM. This

WILLIAM CLARK (by whom the name was first so spelt, for what reason there is no record), of Efford Manor, co. Devon, *m.* Margaret Smith, dau. of James Pett, Gentleman, and Anne Maye his wife, and had issue,

WILLIAM, of whom presently; Mary, *m.* 25 Feb. 1754, to Courtney O'Connell, Esq.; and Elizabeth, who *m.* Philip Langmead, Esq. of Houghton, late M.P. for Plymouth, and had, Mary, wife of William Clark, of Buckland Toussaints and Efford Manor; and Elizabeth, wife of George Byng, Viscount Torrington.

The son and heir,

WILLIAM CLARK, Esq. of Buckland Toussaints and Efford Manor, *m.* 18 Dec. 1786, Mary, dau. of Philip Langmead, Esq. of Houghton, co. Devon, M.P. for Plymouth, and had,

I. WILLIAM-JOHN, now of Buckland Toussaints.

II. Erving, of Efford Manor, co. Devon, Esq., *m.* 1822, Anne-Lætitia, 3rd dau. of Paul-Treby Treby, of Goodamore and Plymton House, Esq., and had issue,

1 Irving-Frederick, who *d.* in the year 1850.

2 Henry, *m.* Lucy, 2nd dau. of the late John Carpenter, of Mount Tavy, co. of Devon, Esq., and granddau. of Mr. and Lady Harriett Garnier, of Rooksbury Park, Hants.

3 Paul-Francis. 4 Reginald-Treby, R.N.

5 Charles-Ourry.

1 Cordelia-Lucy, *m.* in 1854, to Henry-Charles Lopes, Esq., barrister-at-law, 3rd son of the late Sir Ralph Lopes, Bart.

2 Florence, *m.* 10 March, 1854, Sir William-Norris Young, of Marlow Park, co. Bucks, Bart., an officer 23rd Royal Welch Fusiliers, who fell at the battle of the Alma.

3 Lætitia-Anne, *m.* 16 July, 1853, the Hon. Leonard-Allen Addington, R.A., 2nd son of Viscount Sidmouth.

4 Marian-Erving, *d.* in 1842.

I. Mary-Margaret, *m.* to Sir Andrew Leith-Hay, of Leith Hall and Rannes, K.C.H., formerly M.P. for Elgin.

Arms—Erm., a lion, rampant; az., on a chief, sa., a leopard's face, arg., between two cross-crosslets, or; quartered with, az., three escallops, arg. between two flaunches, or.

Crest—A demi-lion, gu., collared, or; on the shoulder an estoile, arg., in the paw a baton, sa.

Motto—Victor mortalis est.

Seat—Buckland Toussaints, Kingsbridge, co. Devon.

CLARKE OF WELTON PLACE.

CLARKE, RICHARD-TREVOR, Esq. of Welton Place, co. Northampton, *b.* 29 Aug. 1813; *m.* 18 Nov. 1847, Fanny-Hyde, eldest dau. of Sir William Pearson, F.R.S.

Lineage.—This is the principal remaining branch, in Northamptonshire, of a distinguished and extensive family, whose name has been spelt indifferently, Clerke, Clerk, and Clarke.

The first of the CLARKES *of Welton* who made his residence there, was THOMAS CLARKE, Esq., about 1590. He was also possessed of property, and the manors of Daventry and Drayton, which still remain in the possession of the present representative of the family of Welton Place.

JOHN PLOMER, Esq., elder brother of Sir Wm. Plomer, lord mayor of London in 1781, and son of John Plomer, Esq. of Stone, by Frances his wife, only dau. of William Adams, Esq. of Welton, and Mary his wife, dau. of JOHN CLARKE, Esq. of Drayton, assumed, by act of parliament, 15 GEORGE III., in compliance with the testamentary injunction of his grand-uncle, Richard Clarke, Esq. of Norfolk, the surname and arms of CLARKE. He purchased Welton Manor in 1804, and was sheriff of Northamptonshire in 1778. He *m.* Mary, dau. and heir of Nicholas Child, Gent. of London, and by her, who *d.* 25 Dec. 1816, aged 73 had (with three daus., Anne-Frances, *m.* in 1806, to the Rev. Thomas Pettat; Mary; and Helen-Amelia, *m.* to the Rev. Thomas Smith, of Calthorpe, Leicestershire) two sons, in succession his heirs. Mr. Plomer Clarke *d.* 9 Jan. 1805, aged 61, and was *s.* by his son,

JOHN-PLOMER CLARKE, Esq. of Welton Place, bapt. 26 Aug. 1776, lieut.-colonel commanding the Western regiment of Northamptonshire local militia in 1813; high-sheriff in 1814, and verderer of Rockingham Forest. He *m.* 16 April, 1806, Anna-Maria-Charlotte, eldest dau. of Sir John Nelthorp, Bart. of Scawby, co. Lincoln, but dying *s. p.* 23 March, 1826, aged 50, was *s.* by his brother,

RICHARD CLARKE, Esq. of Welton Place, an officer in the 3rd Dragoon-guards, bapt. 31 Dec. 1777, who *m.* 21 Aug. 1806, Philippa, dau. and heir of the Rev. George Tymms, M.A., rector of Harpole, and vicar of Dallington, and had (with two daus., Caroline-Charlotte and Mary Susan) three sons, viz.,

RICHARD-TREVOR, now of Welton Place.

John-Alexander, of Trinity College, Oxford, in holy orders, *b.* 17 Sept. 1814.

George-Henry, R.N., *b.* 20 May, 1816, *m.* 28 May, 1846, Elizabeth-M., dau. of John Darcy, Esq. of Clifden Castle and Kiltulla, and has a son and heir, George-Darcy, *b.* 8 Mary, 1847.

Mr. Clarke *d.* 16 Dec. 1829.

Arms—Arg., on bend, gu., between three torteaux, as many swans, arg.

Crest—A swan, rising, arg., ducally gorged and chained, or.

Motto—Erectus non elatus.

Seat—Welton Place.

CLARKE OF COMRIE CASTLE.

See CLARKE-WARDLAW.

CLARKE OF HANDSWORTH.

CLARKE, NATHANIEL-RICHARD, of Handsworth, co. Stafford, M.A., serjeant-at-law, *m.* in 1814, Anna-Maria Fuhrmann, eldest dau. and co-heir of Thomas Garnett, of Nantwich, co. Chester, Esq., by his wife, a dau. and co-heir of the Rev. Edward Harwood, vicar of Shenstone, co. Stafford, and has issue,

I. Nathaniel-Garnett, Gisborne scholar of St. Peter's College, Cambridge, *b.* 14 Feb. 1818, *d.* 5 July, 1839.

II. CHARLES-HARWOOD, B.A., F.S.A., *b.* 8 July, 1820.

III. Henry-James, in holy orders, *b.* 9 Aug. 1823.

IV. Frederic-Fuhrmann, *b.* 8 Aug. 1825, *m.* 17 Oct. 1850, Lucy-Annette, 2nd dau. of Francis Boott, Esq., M.D., by Mary his wife, dau. and co-heir of John Hardcastle, of Derby, Esq., and has issue,

1 Lucy-Constance. 2 Annette-Mary.

v. Edward-Trevisa, b. 27 Sept. 1827, d. 7 Feb. 1828.
vi. Herbert-Stephenson, b. 28 July, 1829, d. 28 April, 1831.
i. Mary-Constance. ii. Isabel-Maria.

Mr. Clarke is of the Middle Temple, serjeant-at-law, a judge of the county courts for the counties of Stafford and Worcester, recorder of Lincoln, Northampton, Newark, and Walsall, in the commission of the peace, as also deputy-lieutenant for the counties of Stafford, Derby, and Warwick, lieut.-col. of the 5th Warwickshire local militia, and formerly fellow of Christ College, Cambridge. He s. his father in 1833.

Lineage.—The family of Clarke was settled at Leadenham, co. Lincoln, at the time of the visitation of that county, 1562, in which their pedigree is entered.

Richard Clarke, of co. Lincoln, Esq., m. Ruth, dau. of John Coulson, Esq. Their son and heir,

Richard Clarke, Esq., was of Norwich, for which city he served the office of sheriff, and had issue by his wife Francis, dau. of Nathaniel Gooding, capt. R.N., a son,

Nathaniel-Gooding Clarke, of Handsworth, co. Stafford, Esq. This gentleman, b. 1756, was one of His Majesty's counsel, and held the now abolished office of chief-justice of Brecon and Carmarthen, South Wales. He m. 17 Feb. 1783, Constance-Elizabeth, dau. and sole heir of Anthony Stephenson, of co. Derby, Esq. (and relict of James Shuttleworth Holden of Aston, in the same co., Esq.); by her, who d. 1839, he had issue,

i. Nathaniel-Richard, his heir.
ii. Francis, d. 17 Aug. 1795.
iii. Charles, of Matlock, co. Derby, J.P. and D.L., m. 1821, Anne, youngest dau. and co-heir of Adam Wolley, of Matlock, Esq.
iv. Anthony-James, in holy orders, rector of Porlock, co. Somerset, m. Elizabeth, dau. of George Langton, of Langton Hall, co. Lincoln, Esq., and d. 1839. By his wife, who d. 1850, he had issue,
1 James-Langton, b. 17 Sept. 1833, scholar of Durham College.
2 Bennet-Charles-Stephenson, b. 9 June, 1838, H.E.I.C. navy.
1 Fanny-Jane.
i. Constance-Frances, d. 1801.
ii. Clara, d. 8 July, 1848.

Mr. Clarke d. 24 July, 1833.

Arms—Erm., on a fesse, gu., three bezants; on a canton of the second, a buck's head, caboshed, arg., attired, or.
Crest—A wing, or.
Seat—Handsworth, co. Stafford.

CLARKE OF BRIDWELL.

Clarke, Richard-Hall, Esq. of Bridwell House, co. Devon, b. 24 Oct. 1818.

Lineage.—This family has been seated at Bridwell for upwards of two centuries. The late

John-Were Clarke, Esq. of Bridwell and Burrington, J.P. and D.L., b. 20 Sept. 1784, and his sister, Mary-Ann, wife of William Welsford, Esq. of Exeter, were the only children of the late Richard-Hall Clarke, Esq., by Mary his wife, only dau. and heiress of Thomas Were, Esq. of Burrington, and grandchildren of Richard Clarke, Esq., and Mary Rowe, of Spencecombe, his wife, which Richard was son of Richard Clarke, Esq. of Bridwell. Mr. Clarke m. 10 Sept. 1810, Frances, dau. of the late Sir Thomas Carew, of Haccombe, co. Devon, Bart., and had issue,

i. Richard-Hall, now of Bridwell.
ii. Thomas.
i. Mary-Were. ii. Jane.
iii. Agnes, m. to R.-Frederick Pratt, Esq. of Hollington, Sussex.
iv. Marcella, m. to Richard Roope, Esq., barrister-at-law.
v. Laura-Catherine. vi. Florence-Smalwood.
vii. Frances, m. to the Rev. Arthur Dene, vicar of Rattery, co. Devon.
viii. Eliza-Were, m. to Timothy Featherstonhaugh, Esq. of Kirkoswald, co. Cumberland.

Arms—Arg., on a bend, gu., between three pellets, as many swans, ppr.
Crest—A lark rising, holding in the beak an ear of wheat, ppr.
Motto—Carpe diem.
Seat—Bridwell, near Collumpton, co. Devon.

CLARKE OF KNEDLINGTON MANOR.

Clarke, Thomas, Esq. of Knedlington Manor, East Riding of Yorkshire, M.A., barrister-at law, J.P. and D.L., b. 4 Nov. 1796; m. 10 Aug. 1825, Sarah, eldest dau. of the Rev. Eric Rudd, of Thorne, co. York (who is heir general and claimant of the barony of Duffus), and has issue,

i. Eric-William, M.A., St. John's College, Cambridge, b. 28 April, 1826.
ii. Elmer, b. 5 April, 1827; d. 10 May, 1846.
iii. John-Sutherland, M.A., St. John's College, Cambridge, b. 3 May, 1828.
iv. Thomas-St. Clair, B.A., St. John's College, Cambridge, b. 3 Feb. 1831.

Lineage.—William Clarke, Esq., b. 10 Sept. 1700, eldest son of Roger Clarke, the younger, of Hensal, West Riding, co. York, m. Mary, dau. of William Bramham, of Bowthorpe, and had issue, Thomas, of whom presently; John, of Pricket Hill, d. in 1822, s. p., leaving his great-nephew and heir-at-law, Thomas Clarke, now of Knedlington, his devisee and executor. The elder son,

Thomas Clarke, Esq. of Knedlington, m. in June, 1761, Grace, dau. of William Johnson, of Hooke, co. York, and had two sons, John, who d. s. p. in March, 1783, and William. The 2nd,

William Clarke, Esq. of Knedlington, m. 21 Dec. 1795, Jane, only child of George Elmer, Esq. of Bubwith, co. York, by Jane his wife, dau. of John Maram, Esq. of Wressell, co. York. Mr. Clarke d. in Jan. 1822, and was s. by his only son, the present Thomas Clarke, Esq. of Knedlington. Mrs. Clarke m. 2ndly, 13 Oct. 1823, the Rev. Ralph Spofforth, M.A., vicar of Howden, who d. in June, 1824.

Arms—Arg., on a chevron, gu., between three wolves' heads, erased, az., three roses, of the first; on a canton, sa., a lion's head, erased, or.
Crest—On a chapeau, az., turned up, erm., two wings expanded, out of a ducal coronet; between the wings the words "Elmer," in Saxon characters.
Motto—The time wille come.
Seat—Knedlington Manor, near Howden, East Riding, co. York.

CLARKE OF SWAKELEYS.

Clarke, Thomas-Truesdale, Esq., J.P., of Swakeleys, co. Middlesex, b. 29 Oct. 1802; m. 9 May, 1826, Jane-Selina, eldest dau. of the Hon. and Rev. William-Robert Capel, vicar of Watford, Herts, 4th son of William-Anne, 4th Earl of Essex, and has issue,

i. William-Capel, an officer 23rd R. W. fusiliers; b. 8 April, 1832.
i. Louisa-Jane-Selina, m. 19 June, 1851, to Comm. Thomas Cochran, R.N.
ii. Helen.
iii. Marion-Georgina, d. 16 Dec. 1852.

Lineage.—The Rev. Thomas Clarke, rector of Ickenham, by his 2nd wife, Frances Truesdale, had two sons, John, the younger, barrister-at-law, and

Thomas-Truesdale Clarke, Esq. of Swakeleys, who m. in 1801, Louisa-Anne, dau. of Charles Hawkins, Esq., and had issue,

Thomas-Truesdale, now of Swakeleys.
Henry-Bridges, m. Sophia, dau. of the Rev. Sir George Stracey, Bart.
Algernon-Adair, d. 16 Feb. 1853.
Caroline.

Crest—A peacock's head, erased, ppr.; in the beak a trefoil, slipped, vert.
Motto—Noli altum sapere.
Seat—Swakeleys, near Uxbridge.

CLARKE OF HYDE HALL.

Clarke, Edward-Hyde, Esq. of Hyde Hall, in Cheshire, b. in 1796; m. 19 Oct. 1825, his cousin, Georgiana O'Moran, grand-niece of Dorothy, Countess of Macclesfield.

Lineage.—George Clarke, lieut.-governor of the province of New York, son of George Clarke, Esq. of Swanswick, in Somersetshire, m. Anne, dau. and eventual heiress of EDWARD HYDE, Esq.* of Hyde Hall, co. Chester, and left (with four daus., Elizabeth, m. to Capt. Cock; Anne, m. to Joshua Horton, Esq.; Penelope, d. unm.; and Mary, m. to Ballard Beckford, Esq.) three sons, of whom the eldest,

GEORGE CLARKE, Esq. of Swanswick and Hyde, secretary of New York, d. s. p. 11 Nov. 1777, and was s. by his nephew,

GEORGE-HYDE CLARKE, Esq. of Hyde (son of Edward Clarke and Elizabeth his wife, widow of Philip Haughton, Esq., and dau. of — Guthrie, of Jamaica), who m. Catherine Hussey, of Ireland, and had issue, GEORGE, his heir; and Edward, of Swanswick, who m. Anne-Margaret, dau. of Gen. Prevost. Mr. Clarke was s. at his decease by his elder son,

GEORGE CLARKE, Esq. of Hyde Hall, who m. in 1798, Eliza, dau. of Gen. George Rochfort, first-cousin of the last Earl of Belvedere, and had issue, George-Hyde, d. unm. in 1822; EDWARD-HYDE, present possessor; George-Rochfort, m. 9 July, 1830, Elizabeth, eldest dau. of the late Rev. Henry Byron, grandson of William, 3rd Lord Byron; Katherine; and Elizabeth.

Arms—Quarterly: 1st and 4th, az., three escallops, in pale, or, between two flaunches, erm.; 2nd and 3rd, az., a chevron between three losenges, or.

Crests—1st, a pheon, ppr.; 2nd, an eagle, with wings expanded, sa., beaked and membered, or.

Seats—Hyde Hall, Cheshire; and Tickford Park, Bucks.

CLAVERING OF CALLALY.

CLAVERING, EDWARD-JOHN, Esq. of Callaly Castle, co. Northumberland, m. 3 July, 1838, Jane, only child of John Carr, of Bondgate Hall, and of Broxfield, in the same county, and has a dau.,

AUGUSTA-LUCY.

Lineage.—This family, from which sprang the Vescis, Lords of Alnwick, the Lacis, Earls of Lincoln, the Eures, Lords Eure, in the male line; and the Altons, and many other eminent houses, in the female, entered England under the banner of the CONQUEROR; and the gift of numerous estates marked the services which they subsequently rendered to his cause. The family is a scion of the great house of De Burgh, and it originally bore that surname; but from the time of HENRY I. until that of EDWARD I., when commanded to take the designation of CLAVERING, from an estate in Essex, the head of the family assumed for surname the Christian name of his father, with the addition of FITZ.

SIR ALAN DE CLAVERING, 2nd son of Robert FitzRoger, 5th Lord of Warkworth, co. Northumberland, summoned to parliament as a Baron in 1295 (see BURKE'S *Extinct Peerage*), obtained from his father the estate of Callaly. He m. Isabella, dau. of Sir William Riddel, and was father of

WILLIAM DE CLAVERING, ancestor of the great house of CLAVERING *of Callaly*, and its derivative branches CLAVERING *of Axwell*, CLAVERING *of Berrington*, CLAVERING *of Learchild*, and CLAVERING *of Tilmouth*. At the period of the great civil war,

SIR JOHN CLAVERING, Knt. of Callaly, was a stanch royalist, and d. a prisoner in London. His eldest, Sir Robert Clavering, Knight-Banneret, a colonel in the royal army, d. unm. From his 2nd, RALPH, the 3rd in descent,

RALPH CLAVERING, Esq. of Callaly, b. 27 June, 1727; m. 1st, Eliza, dau. of James Egan, Esq., but had no issue. He m. 2ndly, Frances, dau. of John Lynch, Esq., and had a son, JOHN-ALOYSIUS, his successor. He m. 3rdly, in 1767, Mary, dau. of Edward Walsh, Esq., and had issue, EDWARD, successor to his brother; Lucy, m. 1st, to John Stapleton, Esq. of Clints, in Yorkshire, and 2ndly, to J. Paston, Esq. of Norfolk; Frances, m. to Henry Robinson, Esq.; Anne; Ellen; and Eliza. Mr. Clavering was s. in 1788, by his eldest son,

JOHN-ALOYSIUS CLAVERING, Esq. of Callaly, b. in 1765, who m. 1st, Christina, dau. of Sir Edward Swynburne, Bart.; and 2ndly, in 1820, Catherine, dau. of Thomas Selby, Esq. of Biddleston, in Northumberland; but d. s. p. 1 Dec. 1826, when the estates passed to his half-brother,

EDWARD CLAVERING, Esq. of Callaly, who m. 10 Oct. 1803, Mary, dau. of J.-O. Byrne, Esq., and had two sons, EDWARD-JOHN, of Callaly, and Augustus.

Arms—Quarterly: or and gu., over all a bend, sa.

Crest—A cherub's head, with wings erect.

Motto—Ad coelos volans.

Seat—Callaly Castle.

CLAYTON OF HEDGERLEY PARK.

CLAYTON, RICE-RICHARD, Esq. of Hedgerley Park, co. Bucks, J.P. and D.L., high-sheriff in 1838, b. in 1798; m. in 1832, Maria-Æmilia, 2nd dau. of Gen. Sir George Nugent, Bart., G.C.B., of Westhorpe House, Great Marlow, and has issue,

I. RICHARD-NUGENT, b. in 1833.
II. George-Augustus, b. in 1840.
I. Maria-Augusta.

Mr. Clayton is 4th son of the late Sir William Clayton, of Marden Park, co. Surrey, Bart.

Arms—Arg., a cross, sa., between four pellets.

Crest—A leopard's gamb, erased and erect, arg., grasping a pellet.

Mottoes—"Virtus in actione consistit;" and "Quid leone fortius?"

Seat—Hedgerley Park, Bucks.

CLAYTON OF ADLINGTON.

BROWNE-CLAYTON, RICHARD-CLAYTON, Esq. of Adlington Hall, co. Lancaster, and of Carrigbyrne, co. Wexford, J.P., b. 12 Nov. 1807; m. 5 Jan. 1830, Catherine-Jane, only dau. of the Rev. Robert Dobson, and has issue,

I. ROBERT-JOHN, b. 26 Aug. 1834, an officer in the army.
I. Henrietta. II. Catherine-Annette.
III. Emma. IV. Mary-Edith.

Lineage.—The first ancestor of this family was ROBERT DE CLAYTON, who came to England with the CONQUEROR, and had the manor of Clayton conferred upon him for his military services, which estate gave the name to the family, and remained in their possession until conveyed by the sole heiress, DOROTHY, sister of Richard Clayton, Esq., who d. s. p., to her husband, GEORGE LEYCESTER, Esq. of Toft, co. Chester. A junior branch was established at Fulwood, co. Lancaster, by

THOMAS CLAYTON, Esq., who had those estates settled upon him. He m. Anne, dau. of Robert Blundell, Esq. of Ince, and had issue,

ROBERT, of Fulwood, who m. Eleanor, dau. of John Atherton, Esq. of Busie, and had four sons and four daus. THOMAS CLAYTON, D.D., the eldest son, became eventually Bishop of Clogher.
THOMAS.
Anne.

The 2nd son,

THOMAS CLAYTON, Esq., b. in 1630, purchased the estates of Worthington and Adlington. He m. Anne, dau. of John Atherton, Esq. of Busie, and was great-grandfather of

RICHARD CLAYTON, Esq. of Adlington, created a Baronet, 3 May, 1774. He m. Anne, dau. of Charles White, Esq. of Manchester, by whom he had an only dau. and heiress,

HENRIETTA CLAYTON, of Adlington, who m. 1 Dec. 1808, GENERAL ROBERT BROWNE, of the 12th light dragoons (see BROWNE *of Browneshill*), who assumed, in 1829, upon coming into possession of Adlington, the surname and arms of CLAYTON, and had issue,

RICHARD-CLAYTON, of Adlington.
Eleanor, m. in 1835, the Rev James Daubeny, and has issue.

General Browne Clayton d. in 1845.

Arms—Quarterly: 1st and 4th, CLAYTON, arg., a cross, engrailed, sa., between four torteaux; 2nd and 3rd, BROWNE, gu., a chevron between three lions' gambs, erased and erect, arg.; on a chief of the second, an eagle displayed, sa., armed and crowned, or.

Crests—1st, a dexter armed embowed, the hand grasping a dagger, the point to the dexter, all arg., for CLAYTON; 2nd, the eagle of Sicily displayed, with two heads, sa., for BROWNE.

Motto—Probitatem quam divitias.

Seats—Adlington Hall, Wigan; and Carrigbyrne Lodge, New Ross, co. Wexford.

* Only son of Robert Hyde, Esq. of Norbury and Hyde Hall, the direct descendant of Sir Robert Hyde, Knt., living in the time of HENRY III., lord of Hyde and Newton in Cheshire, of Shalcross in Derbyshire, and Haighton in the co. of Lancaster.

CLAYTON OF ENFIELD OLD PARK.

CLAYTON, THE REV. JOHN-HENRY, Esq. of Enfield Old Park, co. Middlesex, *b.* 8 June, 1809, in holy orders, rector of Farnborough, Hants; *m.* 19 April, 1838, Jane-Bunn, youngest dau. of George Sheppard, Esq. of Fromefield House, co. Somerset, and has issue,

I. JOHN-ERNEST, *b.* 29 Dec. 1841.
II. Charles-Cecil, *b.* 10 Nov. 1843.
III. Reginald-Byard-Buchanan, *b.* 16 July, 1845.
IV. Sidney-Stuart, *b.* 16 March, 1851.
V. Horace-Evelyn, *b.* 8 April, 1853.
I. Janet-Stuart. II. Maud-Lindsay.

Lineage.—This family was originally from Yorkshire. About 1650, JOHN CLAYTON settled in London as a merchant, and resided at Forty Hill, Enfield. By his wife, Mary Whiston, he had an only son,

SAMUEL CLAYTON, Esq., *b.* in 1690, who *m.* in 1724, Elizabeth, youngest dau. of Sir James Collet, Knt. of London, and resided at Forty Hill until 1735, when he purchased Enfield Old Park, a royal demesne in the time of ELIZABETH, near the Palace at Enfield. Mr. Clayton *d.* 27 July, 1749, leaving four children surviving, viz.,

I. SAMUEL, his heir.
II. John, *b.* 6 June, 1728, *m.* 6 March, 1776, Anne Skerret, and *d.* 28 June, 1800, leaving surviving issue,
 1 JOHN, successor to his uncle.
 2 Samuel, *b.* 18 Aug. 1780, *m.* 5 July, 1808, Mary Wyatt, of Hartlip, Kent, and has issue one dau.
 1 Anne, *m.* 16 Dec. 1801, to Henry Sawyer, Esq. of Enfield, and has issue.
III. Nicholas, *b.* 10 Dec. 1730, in holy orders, D.D., *m.* Dorothy Nicholson, of Liverpool, and *d. s. p.* 20 May, 1797.
I. Elizabeth, *m.* to the Rev. T. Laugher, and *d. s. p.* 24 May, 1784.

The eldest son,

SAMUEL CLAYTON, Esq. of Enfield Old Park, *b.* 23 Feb. 1727, *d. unm.* 8 July, 1800, when the estate devolved upon his brother John's eldest son,

JOHN CLAYTON, Esq. of Bath, *b.* 7 April, 1777; *m.* 11 Dec. 1806, Jane, 3rd dau. of Charles Buchanan, Esq. of Burton-on-Trent, and had issue,

JOHN-HENRY, present representative.
William-Ashley, *b.* 8 Oct. 1815, Helen, dau. of the Rev. John P. Stubbs, vicar of Market Drayton, co. Salop, and has issue.
Elizabeth-Jane, *m.* 8 Jan. 1835, to Col. Thomas Reed, C.B., aide-de-camp to the Queen, and has issue.
Arabella.
Emily-Mary, *m.* 8 Jan. 1835, to the Rev. James Bliss, M.A., *d. s. p.* 18 Nov. same year.
Mary-Anne, *m.* 18 April, 1838, to the Rev. C. E. Armstrong, M.A., Master of Hemsworth Hospital, and perpetual curate of Frickley cum Clayton, co. York, and nephew of Sir Francis-L. Wood, Bart.

Mr. Clayton *m.* 2ndly, Anna-Maria, dau. of the Rev. John Hubbard, of Little Horsford, Sussex, and *d.* 22 Jan. 1854.

Arms—Arg., a saltier between four martlets, gu.
Crest—A dove with an olive branch, all ppr.
Motto—Quod sors fert, ferimus.

CLELAND OF RATH-GAEL.

ROSE-CLELAND, JAMES-BLACKWOOD, Esq. of Rath-Gael House, co. Down, *b.* 30 Jan. 1835.

Lineage.—The family of Cleland is of great antiquity in Scotland. Their coat of arms, tradition states, was acquired by their being hereditary foresters to the ancient Earls of Douglas.

The first of the family of whom there is any record was ALEXANDER CLELAND (or Kneland) of that ilk, in the county of Lanark. He was living in the reign of King ALEXANDER III., and *m.* Margaret, dau. of Adam Wallace, of Riccarton, and sister of Sir Malcolm Wallace, the father of Sir William Wallace. He was ancestor of the Clelands of that ilk, and of several families of the same surname.

ALEXANDER CLELAND, the 12th Cleland of that ilk, *m.* Mary, sister of John Hamilton, 1st Lord Bargany. By her he had several sons, the eldest of whom sold the lands of Cleland to a cousin of his own name.

JOHN CLELAND, of Laird Braes, in the parish of Eeswalt, was either the 2nd or 3rd son of this Alexander Cleland, and was *b.* about the year 1623. He *m.* about the year 1651, Katharine Ross, descended from the ROSSES *of Henning*, and *d.* in 1683, leaving a son and successor,

JAMES CLELAND, of Laird Braes, *b.* in 1652, *m.* in 1690, Agnes Innes, descended from the INNESES *of Benwall*; she *d.* in 1711, and he *d.* in 1717, leaving issue. The son and heir,

JOHN CLELAND, of Whithorn, in Wigtonshire, Scotland, was appointed factor to James, 5th Earl of Galloway, and in 1731, *m.* Margaret Murdoch, only child of Murdoch, provost of Whithorn, descended from the MURDOCHS *of Cumloddan*; she was *b.* in 1701, and *d.* 21 Sept. 1747; he *d.* 10 Aug. 1747, leaving issue by her,

JAMES, *b.* 4 May, 1736 (of whom hereafter).
Agnes, *b.* 4 Sept. 1740, *m.* 1st, at Fort St. David's, in the East Indies, 5 June, 1766, to Lieut. Richard Rose, H.E.I.C.S., who *d.* at Trichinopoly, 7 June, 1768, of wounds received at the siege of Altoor, by whom she had an only child,
 JAMES-DOWSETT ROSE, who afterwards assumed the additional surname of CLELAND, *b.* 24 March, 1767.
She *m.* 2ndly, in 1774, William Nicholson, Esq. of Ballow House, and *d.* 11 July, 1775 (and was buried at Bangor, Ireland), without having issue by him.

The son and successor,

JAMES CLELAND, Esq. of Newtown Ards, co. Down, Ireland, *m.* in 1770, Sarah, only child of Capt. Patrick Baird, (brother of William Baird, of Newbyth, and James Baird, Esq. of London, and uncle to General Sir David Baird.) He *d.* at Newtown Ards, 14 May, 1777, *s. p.*; will dated 5 May, 1775. His widow *d.* and was buried at Abingdon, Berks, 7 Dec. 1787; will dated 23 Nov. 1787. Mr. Cleland was *s.* by his nephew,

JAMES-DOWSETT ROSE CLELAND, Esq. of Rath-Gael, *b.* 24 March, 1767, J.P. and D.L., served as high-sheriff 1805. He *m.* 1st, 14 Aug. 1790, Sarah, only child of William-Eaton Andrews, Esq. of London, and by that lady, who *d.* 2 Oct. 1830, had a son and dau., viz.,

WILLIAM-NICHOLSON, *b.* 18 June, 1794, *d.* 20 Nov. 1794.
Elizabeth-Hawkins, *m.* 8 Sept. 1829, Fortescue Gregg, Esq. of Knockcairn, co. Antrim.

He *m.* 2ndly, 10 Dec. 1832, Elizabeth, eldest dau. of William Steele-Nicholson, Esq. of Ballow House, and by her had,

JAMES-BLACKWOOD, now of Rath-Gael.
Richard, *b.* 1 May, 1836.
Edward-Allen, *b.* 21 Jan. 1840.
Henry-Somerville, *b.* 4 Nov. 1843.
Agnes-Elizabeth. Isabel-Hamilton. Margaret-Sabina.

Mr. Rose-Cleland *d.* 25 Sept. 1852.

Arms—Az., a hare, salient, arg., with a hunting horn round its neck, vert, garnished gu., for CLELAND, quartering ALLEN, BENNET, MURDOCH, and CLELAND.
Crests—A hawk on a left-hand glove, ppr., for CLELAND. A rose, gu., seeded and slipped, ppr., between two wings, erm., for ROSE.
Mottoes—"For sport," and "Je pense à qui pense plus."
Seat—Rath-Gael House, Bangor, in the co. of Down.

CLEMENTS OF ASHFIELD.

CLEMENTS, HENRY-THEOPHILUS, Esq. of Ashfield Lodge, co. Cavan, *b.* 24 July, 1820.

Lineage.—THE RIGHT HON. HENRY-THEOPHILUS CLEMENTS, lieut.-col. of the 69th regt., and M.P., 2nd son of the Right Hon. Nathaniel Clements, M.P., teller of the Exchequer, and brother of ROBERT CLEMENTS, created LORD LEITRIM in 1783; *m.* 1st, in 1770, Mary, dau. and heir of Gen. Webb, by whom he had issue,

Robert-William, *b.* in 1783, deceased.
Theophilus, *b.* in 1785, deceased.
John-Marcus, *b.* 4 May, 1789; *m.* Catherine, dau. of Godfrey Wentworth, Esq., and had issue, a son, *d.* young; John-Marcus, *b.* 27 July, 1826; and Henry-John-George, *b.* in Nov. 1829.
Harriet, *m.* to William Hoader, Esq.
Maria, *m.* to the Very Rev. Dean Keating.

Col. Clements *m.* 2ndly, in 1778, Catherine, eldest dau. of the Right Hon. John Beresford, 2nd son of Sir Marcus Beresford, created Earl of Tyrone in 1746, and brother to the 1st Marquis of Waterford. By this lady (who *d.* 7 Jan. 1836) he left at his decease, in 1795, an only dau., Selina, *m.* in 1808, to William-M.-S. Milner, Esq., eldest son and heir of the late Sir William Milner, Bart., and a son,

HENRY-JOHN CLEMENTS, Esq. of Ashfield, co. Cavan, J.P. and D.L., high-sheriff in 1803, M.P. for Leitrim, and afterwards for co. Cavan, colonel of the Leitrim militia; *b.* 16 July, 1781; who *m.* 11 Dec. 1811, Louisa, 2nd dau. of James Stewart, Esq. of Killymoon, co. Tyrone, and had issue,

I. HENRY-THEOPHILUS, now of Ashfield.
I. Elizabeth-Catherine-Henrietta, *d.* in 1827.
II. Selina. III. Louisa. IV. Mary-Isabella.
V. Catherine, *d.* in Sept. 1830.

Arms—Arg., two bendlets, wavy, sa.; on a chief, gu., three bezants.
Crest—A hawk, statant, ppr.
Motto—Patriis virtutibus.
Seat—Ashfield Lodge, co. Cavan.

CLEMENTS OF RATHKENNY.

CLEMENTS, THEOPHILUS, Esq. of Rathkenny, co. Cavan, J.P., *b.* in 1830.

Lineage.—ROBERT CLEMENTS, Esq., M.P. for Carrickfergus in 1692, possessed large estates in Down and Cavan. In 1689 he was attainted, but on the accession of WILLIAM III. was restored to his estates in Cavan, and appointed deputy vice-treasurer of Ireland. He *m.* Miss Sandford, of the Castlerea family, and had issue, 1 THEOPHILUS (the Rt. Hon.) *d. s. p.*; 2 ROBERT; and 3 NATHANIEL, father of the 1st Lord Leitrim. The 2nd son, ROBERT CLEMENTS, Esq., M.P. for Newry in 1715, *d.* in 1722, leaving a son, THEOPHILUS CLEMENTS, Esq. of Rathkenny, co. Cavan, whose dau. and heiress, ANNE, *m.* Edward Lucas, Esq., 2nd son of Francis Lucas, Esq. of Castle Shane, co. Monaghan, and was mother of

THEOPHILUS EDWARD LUCAS, Esq., who assumed the surname and arms of CLEMENTS, under the will of his maternal grandfather. He *m.* in 1829, Elizabeth-Beatrice, dau. of the Rev. Shuckburgh Whitney Upton, and *d.* in 1852, leaving issue, 1 THEOPHILUS, now of Rathkenny; 2 Henry-Upton; 3 Charles-John-Fulk; 1 Isabella-Margaret; 2 Harriet-Olivia.

Arms—Arg., two bendlets, wavy, sa.; on a chief, gu., three bezants.
Crest—A hawk, statant, ppr.
Seat—Rathkenny, co. Cavan.

CLEVLAND OF TAPELEY PARK.

CLEVLAND, ARCHIBALD, Esq., 17th lancers, *b.* 10 May, 1833; *s.* his father, Augustus Clevland, Esq., lieut.-col. of the North Devon militia, 5 July, 1849; fell in action in Turkey, 1854.

Lineage.—This is a family of great antiquity in Scotland, and claims descent from the CLEULANDS (or CLELANDS) *of Faskine*, co. Lanarkshire, which branch separated from the parent stem in the reign of ALEXANDER III.

WILLIAM CLEVLAND, the first of that family settled in Devonshire, was the eldest son of Archibald Cleuland of Knowhoblehill, in the co. of Lanarkshire. He was a distinguished commander in the royal navy, and was in every brave and memorable action in the reigns of King WILLIAM, Queen ANNE, and GEORGE I. He received in the year 1702, the freedom of the city of Edinburgh, and of Hamilton, in Lanarkshire, and as a reward for his long and faithful services was appointed commissioner of the royal navy. He *m.* 1704, Anne, dau. of John Davie, Esq. of Orleigh, co. Devon, by whom he had,

JOHN, *b.* 1706.
William, *b.* 1712, *d.* young.
Archibald, *b.* 1714, drowned on the bar of Salline by the upsetting of the boat on going ashore.
William, *b.* 1720, *d.* young.
Anne. Katherine, *d.* young.
Julianna, *m.* Louis Guiquer, of Geneva.
Penelope, *m.* Admiral John Towry.

William Clevland *d.* 1715, and was *s.* by his son,

JOHN CLEVLAND, Esq., M.P. for Saltash, and secretary to the Admiralty: he *m.* 1st, Elizabeth, dau. and co-heiress of Sir Cæsar Child, Bart. of Woodford, co. Essex, by whom he had issue,

William, *b.* 1732, *d.* young. JOHN, *b.* 1734.
Archibald, *b.* 1738, captain R.N., *d.* 1765, *unm.*
Hester, *m.* William-Saltren Willett, of Porthill, co. Devon, captain R.N.
Anne, *d.* young. Elizabeth, *m.* John Ibbetson, Esq.

He *m.* 2ndly, Sarah Shuckburgh, dau. of Charles Shuckburgh, Esq. of Longborow, co. Gloucestershire, and sister to Sir Charles Shuckburgh, Bart., and had issue,

George, *b.* 1749, *d.* 1765.
Augustus, *b.* 1754, appointed chief of Boglebore in 1778, *d.* 1784.
Selina-Shore, *m.* John Udney, Esq.
Matilda-Shore, *m.* the Baron de Pragena, of Switzerland.

John Clevland *d.* 1763, and was *s.* by his son,

JOHN CLEVLAND, Esq., M.P. for Barnstaple for seven parliaments, and a director of Greenwich hospital: he *m.* Elizabeth, dau. and heiress of Richard Stevens, Esq. of Winscott, co. Devon, and *d.* without issue 1817, and was *s.* by his great-nephew,

AUGUSTUS-SALTREN WILLETT, Esq. of the 6th or Inniskilling dragoons, in which regiment he served at the battle of Waterloo. This gentleman assumed by sign-manual, in compliance with the testamentary injunction of his great-uncle John Clevland, Esq., the surname and arms of CLEVLAND only. He *m.* June, 1830, Margaret-Caroline, eldest dau. of John-Palmer Chichester, Esq. of Arlington Court, co. Devon, and sister to the late Sir John-Palmer Bruce-Chichester, Bart., by Agnes, eldest dau. of James Hamilton, Esq. of Bangour and Ninewar, N. B., by whom he had,

ARCHIBALD, present representative.
Agnes-Hamilton. Caroline-Chichester.

Arms—A hare, salient, arg., with a hunting horn round its neck, garnished, gu.
Crest—A hand with a sword, hilted and pommelled, or.
Motto—Fortuna audaces juvat.
Seat—Tapely Park, co. Devon.

CLIFFE OF BELLEVUE.

CLIFFE, ANTHONY, Esq. of Bellevue, co. Wexford, high-sheriff in 1823, *b.* 10 March, 1800; *m.* 23 June, 1821, Isabella-Frances, dau. of Charles-Powell Leslie, Esq. of Glaslough, co. Monaghan, M.P., and has had,

I. ANTHONY-JOHN, D.L., *b.* Oct. 1822.
II. Charles-Henry, late an officer 58th foot; *b.* June, 1826.
III. Edward, an officer in the army; *b.* April, 1830.
I. Marianne-Jane-Place. II. Frances-Harriet.
III. Isabella-Catherine. IV. Emily-Cecilia.
V. Jane-Elizabeth. VI. Eleanor-Barbara.

Lineage.—ANTHONY CLIFFE, Esq. of the city of Westminster, *m.* a dau. of — Yeats, Esq., and was father of

JOHN CLIFFE, citizen of Westminster, who went to Ireland as secretary at war to the army sent by the Parliament, under the command of CROMWELL, in 1649; and acquired grants of land in the counties of Wexford and Meath. He *m.* Eleanor, 5th dau. of Nicholas Loftus, Esq. of Fethard, co. Wexford, grandfather of the 1st Lord Loftus, of Loftus Hall, and by her (who was *b.* 1 Dec. 1641, and *d.* 3 Sept. 1700) had issue,

I. JOHN, his heir.
II. Anthony, of Dungulph Castle, co. Wexford, *b.* 3 July, 1662, one of the commissioners for raising money by loan for WILLIAM III., in 1695 and 1698.
III. Nicholas, *b.* 22 Jan. 1664.
IV. Loftus, *b.* 16 March, 1665, of Blarney, in the co. Cork; who *m.* Elizabeth, dau. of Sir James Jefferies, of the famous Blarney Castle. His will is dated 6 March, 1722, and was proved in Dublin, in 1728. He left a dau.,
  Eleanor, heir to her brother, Loftus Cliffe, killed at Fontenoy; *m.* in 1745, to Richard Symes, Esq. of Ballyarthur, co. Wicklow.
V. Robert, *b.* 3 Aug. 1669; and *d. s. p.*
VI. Henry, of Sutton, co. Surrey, *b.* 16 Oct. 1671; *m.* Barbara, only dau. of Jane, Countess of Donegal, widow of Arthur, 2nd earl, by her second marriage with Richard Rooth, Esq., and had issue (with three daus., Jane, *m.* to John Cliffe, of New Ross; Mary; and Margaret) two sons, the elder, Richard, *d. unm.*; the second, Henry, *m.* and had one dau.,
  Margaretta-Eleanora, who *m.* Thomas Hatch, Esq of Surrey, and had one son, the Rev. Thomas Hatch, vicar of Walton-upon-Thames, and two daus.
I. Elizabeth, *b.* 30 Dec. 1667; *m.* John Tench, Esq. of Mullenderry, co. Wexford, 2nd son of John Tench.
II. Margaret, *b.* 28 Oct. 1670; *m.* (license dated 6 Sept. 1699) the Rev. Thomas Bunbury, of Baleaker, son of the Rev. Thomas Bunbury, of Baleaker, by Anne, co-heir of — Code, Esq. of Castletown, co. Wexford, and had one dau., Anne, who *m.* Colonel Philip Savage, of Kilgibbon, co. Wexford.
III. Eleanor, *b.* 16 Dec. 1674.
IV. Jane, *b.* 16 June, 1682; *m.* Richard Vigors, Esq. of Old Leighlin, co. Carlow, nephew of the Right Rev. Dr. Bartholomew Vigors, Bishop of Ferns, and had issue, with three sons, one dau., Eleanor, who *m.* her cousin, William Cliffe, of New Ross.
V. Anne, *b.* 2 Dec. 1683.

Mr. Cliffe was M.P. for the borough of Taghmon in 1661, and was appointed high-sheriff for the co. of Wexford, 9 Dec. 1680. His will is dated 18 April, 1691, and was proved in Dublin in the same year. He was *s.* by his eldest son,

JOHN CLIFFE, Esq. of Malrankan Hall, Dungulph Castle, and New Ross, b. 3 May, 1661; m. in 1694, Barbara, eldest dau. and eventual heir of William Carr, Esq. of the city of Cork, and had issue,

I. JOHN, his heir.
II. William, of New Ross, b. 5 April, 1701; who m. his cousin, Eleanor, dau. of Richard Vigors, Esq., of Old Leighlin, co. Carlow, and had issue seven sons, who all d. unm. except
The Rev. John Cliffe, of New Ross, b. 1736; who m. Sarah, dau. and co-heir of Richard Wilson, Esq.; and dying there 14 Feb. 1816, left issue, one son and two daus., viz.,
1 John, who was lost on his passage from Bristol to Waterford in 1817, unm.
1 Sarah, m. in March, 1803, Henry-Loftus Tottenham, Esq. of Macmurrough, co. Wexford; and d. 12 Dec. 1839.
2 Anne, m. in Sept. 1810, the Rev. Thomas-Mercer Vigors, of Burgage, co. Carlow.
William Cliffe d. intestate in 1746.
III. Anthony, b. 30 March, 1703, a major in the army.
IV. Edward, b. 26 Aug. 1705, supposed to have died a child.
V. George, b. 27 May, 1707.
VI. Edward, b. 30 July, 1709.
VII. Loftus, b. Dec. 1710. He was a captain at the battle of Minden on the 1st of Aug. 1759, when he was severely wounded, after which he was promoted to a majority in an invalid corps; and d. in 1766. He m. Anne, dau. of William Hore, Esq. of Harperstown, co. Wexford, which lady, having survived him many years, d. at Wexford in March, 1814, aged 83, and was buried at the family burying-place in New Ross, having had issue, one son and three daus., viz.,
1 Walter Cliffe, b. 4 Feb. 1757; m. Harriet, dau of Gen. Sir Anthony Farrington, Bart., and having attained to the rank of lieut.-general, d. July, 1816, leaving an only child,
The Rev. Loftus-Anthony Cliffe, of Osborne Place, Wilton, Taunton, Somersetshire, b. 12 Sept. 1795; m. 1 Aug. 1821, Salome, dau. of John Capon, Esq. of Taunton, and has an only dau.,
Harriet-Salome, m. in July, 1844, to Arthur Kinglake, Esq. of Taunton.
1 Dorothy, b. 2 Jan. 1756; m. John Harvey, Esq. of Killiane Castle, co. Wexford; and d. in 1813, leaving issue.
2 Barbara, b. 6 Dec. 1762; m. at Wexford, 22 Oct. 1784, John Stanford, Esq. of Corn, co. Cavan, a barrister. She d. in 1815.
3 Anne, b. 2 Feb. 1764; m. 1 May, 1783, the Rev. Roger Owen, rector of Camolin, co. Wexford, and d. leaving issue.
VIII. Henry, b. 17 March, 1711, supposed to have died a child.
IX. Henry, b. 16 Dec. 1714.
I. Eleanor, b. 16 July, 1695; m. Charles Tottenham, Esq. of Tottenham Green. She was buried 7 June, 1747.
II. Barbara, b. 27 Oct. 1697; m. Arthur Gifford, Esq. of Aherne, co. Cork, and had issue,
Catherine, sole heir, who m. 10 May, 1764, the Hon. William Brabazon, 2nd son of Edward, 7th Earl of Meath, and had issue,
III. Anne, b. 11 Jan. 1698.
IV. Elizabeth, b. 27 Feb. 1699.
V. Mary, b. in May, 1704; m. John Leigh, Esq. of Rosegarland, co. Wexford, and had a son and a dau., viz.,
Robert-Leigh, who m. Annabella, dau. of Robert Leslie, Esq. of Glaslough.
Grace-Leigh, m. 20 May, 1758, to Anthony, 8th Earl of Meath.

Mr. Cliffe was one of the commissioners for raising money by loan for WILLIAM III., in the co. of Wexford, in 1695 and 1698, and was M.P. for the borough of Bannow from 1692 to 1715. His wife's will was proved in Dublin in 1735, and his own will was proved in the same place, 1728. He was s. by his eldest son,

JOHN CLIFFE, Esq. of New Ross, b. Aug. 1696, who m. 9 Jan. 1727-8, Jane, eldest dau. of his cousin, Henry Cliffe, of Sutton, co. Surrey (to whose will he took out administration) and had issue,

I. JOHN, his heir.
II. ANTHONY, who succeeded his brother John.
III. Edward-Lard, of co. Carlow, clerk (will proved in Dublin in 1782); d. s. p.
I. Barbara, b. 18 Jan. 1728-9, d. unm.
II. Jane, b. 10 Oct. 1730; m. 1st, the Rev. Joshua Tench, of Bryanstown, and had issue, a son, d. young; Jane, d. unm.; and Marianne, who m. Charles-Powell Leslie, Esq. of Glaslough, who had, with other issue,
Isabella-Frances, wife of the present ANTHONY CLIFFE, of Bellevue.
She m. 2ndly, Charles Tottenham, Esq., but had no issue by him. She d. 11 Jan. 1797.
III. Mary, b. 15 Nov. 1735, d. a child.
IV. Mary, b 2 Feb. 1740; d. unm. in 1834, at Bath.
V. Henrietta, b. in July, 1748; d. unm. in 1821, at Bath.

Mr. Cliffe's will is dated 24 May, 1757, and was proved in Dublin in 1761. He was s. by his eldest son,

JOHN CLIFFE, Esq. of New Ross, of which he was Recorder, b. 31 Aug. 1733. He d. unm. and intestate in 1795, and was s. by his brother,

ANTHONY CLIFFE, Esq. of New Ross, b. 11 Oct. 1734; capt. 4th Horse, 1 Oct. 1766, and a major in the army; m. in 1795, Frances, 2nd dau. of Col. Joseph Deane, of Terenure, co. Dublin, and left at his decease, in 1803 (with two daus., Jane-Catherine, m. Robert-Shapland, Baron Carew, of Castleborough, co. Wexford; and Cecilia-Frances, m. to Robert Daniell, Esq. of New Forest, co. Westmeath), an only surviving son, the present ANTHONY CLIFFE, Esq. of Bellevue.

Arms—Erm., on a fesse, between three wolves' heads, erased, sa., a trefoil between two mullets, or.
Crest—A wolf's head, erased, quarterly, per pale, indented, or and sa.
Motto—In cruce glorior.
Seat—Bellevue, on the Slaney.

CLIFFORD OF FRAMPTON.

CLIFFORD, HENRY-CLIFFORD, Esq. of Frampton, co. Gloucester, b. in 1785; m. 28 April, 1808, Elizabeth, only child of John Wallington, Esq. of Peers Court, co. Gloucester, and by her (who d. in 1838) had issue,

I. HENRY-JOHN, b. 21 Sept. 1810, m. 19 July, 1838, Marianne, dau. of the Rev. James Phelps, rector of Brimpsfield, co. Gloucester, and has issue.
II. Walter-Charles, d. under age.
III. William, d. an infant.
IV. Edmund, b. 26 July, 1821.
V. Frederick, b. 11 April, 1823.
VI. John, b. 20 Oct. 1824.
I. Elizabeth. II. Mary-Anne. III. Charlotte.
IV. Catherine. V. Constance.

Lineage.—MARY CLIFFORD, eldest dau. and co-heir of John Clifford, Esq. of Frampton, the representative of the Frampton branch of the illustrious house of Clifford, m. Nathaniel Clutterbuck, Esq. of Nast End, in the parish of Eastington, co. Gloucester, and d. 7 Oct. 1680, leaving a son and successor,

WILLIAM CLUTTERBUCK, Esq. of Frampton, who m. 1st, Sarah, dau. of John Wade, Esq., by whom he had no issue to survive him; and 2ndly, Abigail, dau. of William Clutterbuck, Esq. of Mill End, by whom he left at his decease, two sons, who d. unm., and two daus. The only surviving dau.,

CATHERINE CLUTTERBUCK, heiress to her brothers, m. William Bell, Esq. of Gloucester and Sainthurst, and left two daus. and co-heirs, viz.,

ELIZABETH BELL, who m. Edmund Phillipps, Esq. of Putley, co. Hereford, and d. a widow, without issue, 16 Jan. 1801.
ANNE BELL, who m. Nathaniel Winchcombe, Esq.

The younger dau.,

ANNE BELL, who m. Nathaniel Winchcombe, Esq., and d. 7 Aug. 1757, left, by him (who d. 22 Oct. 1766), an only son,

NATHANIEL WINCHCOMBE, Esq. of Frampton, b. in 1757, who assumed by royal license, 31 Oct. 1801, the surname and arms of CLIFFORD. He m. in 1782, Mary, dau. and heir of Daniel Packer, Esq. of Painswick, co. Gloucester, and had issue,

HENRY-CLIFFORD, his heir.
Catherine-Elizabeth.
Maria, m. in 1806, to the Rev. Powell-Colchester Guise, rector of Craike, co. Durham.
Charlotte-Anne, m. in 1813, to Purnell-Bransby Purnell, Esq. of Stancombe Park, co. Gloucester.
Rosamond.

Mr. Clifford d. 16 Sept. 1817, and was s. by his son, HENRY-CLIFFORD CLIFFORD, Esq. of Frampton.

Arms—Chequy, az. and or; on a bend, gu., three lions, passant, of the second.
Crest—A hand, ppr., holding a fleur-de-lis, or.
Motto—Dulcis amor patriæ.
Seat—Frampton Court, co. Gloucester.

CLIFFORD OF PERRISTONE.

CLIFFORD, HENRY-MORGAN, Esq. of Perristone, co. Hereford, and of Llantilio, co. Monmouth, J.P.

and D.L., lieut.-col. Monmouthshire militia, M.P., b. in 1806; m. 12 Aug. 1834, Catherine-Harriett, only dau. of Joseph Yorke, Esq. of Forthampton Court, co. Gloucester (eldest son of James, Bishop of Ely, and grandson of Lord Chancellor Hardwicke), by Catherine his wife, eldest dau. of James Cocks, Esq., and niece to Charles, 1st Lord Somers, and by this lady has issue,

HENRY-SOMERS-MORGAN, b. in 1836.
Marian.

Lineage.—This is a branch of the ancient family of MORGAN *of Tredegar*, settled for some centuries at Hurst, co. Gloucester, which property still remains in the possession of the present representative, who is likewise, through his great-great-grandmother, representative of the old family of PROBERT *of the Argoed and Panglass*, co. Monmouth, the last male heir of which, Col. Probert, d. in 1727. The surname of CLIFFORD was assumed in 1760, in compliance with the will of Thomas Clifford, Esq., son of a sister of Col. Probert, by the late WILLIAM MORGAN CLIFFORD, Esq., son of Richard Morgan, by his wife Abigail Phelps. He m. Eliza-Maria, eldest dau. of Richard Lewis, Esq. of Llantilio, co. Monmouth, and had a son,

MORGAN CLIFFORD, Esq. of Perristone, who m. Sophia, 2nd dau. of the late Jonathan Willington, Esq. of Rapla, co. Tipperary, and by her was father of the present HENRY MORGAN CLIFFORD, Esq. of Perrristone.

Arms—Quarterly: 1st and 4th, chequy, or and az., a fesse, gu., for CLIFFORD; 2nd, or, a griffin, segreant, sa., for MORGAN *of Tredegar;* 3rd, per pale, sa. and az., three fleurs-de-lis, arg., for PROBERT.
Crest—A griffin, segreant, sa.
Motto—Semper paratus.
Seats—Perristone, near Ross; and Llantilio, co. Monmouth.

CLIFFORD OF CASTLE ANNESLEY.

CLIFFORD, EDWARD, Esq. of Castle Annesley, co. Wexford, b. 5 Oct. 1798; m. 13 May, 1827, Barbara, dau. of William Hodges, Esq. of Dublin, and has issue,

I. EDWARD-JOHN, b. 25 March, 1828.
I. Catherine. II. Sarah.
III. Barbara. IV. Isabella.

Lineage.—ROBERT CLIFFORD, of Dublin, 3rd son of Robert Clifford, by Anne his wife, sister and co-heir of William Knight, of Dublin, m. in 1680, Mary, dau. and co-heir of Joseph Miller, Esq. of Rosgarland, co. Wexford, by whom the Castle Annesley estate came into the family, and had issue, I. MILLER, his heir; II. Robert, of Wexford, who m. 1 Aug. 1715, Mary, dau. of Highgate Boyd, Esq. of Roslare, co. Wexford, and had issue nine sons and four daus.; and I. Mary, (Mrs. Hatton.) Robert Clifford, of Dublin, was s. by his eldest son,

MILLER CLIFFORD, Esq. of Castlestingly, or Castle Annesley, co. Wexford, who had by Rachel his wife, an only son,

JOHN CLIFFORD, Esq. of Castle Annesley, father of

WILLIAM CLIFFORD, Esq. of Castle Annesley, who m. Mary Holmes, an English lady, and had issue,

I. William, who m. Mary Hatton, and dying in the lifetime of his father, left issue an only child,
Mary, who m. Mr. Blayney.
II. JOHN, his heir.
I. Alice, m. John Lyndon, Esq. of Tomduff, co. Wexford.
II. Elizabeth.
III. Mary, m. the Rev. Robert Burrowes, rector of Kilmuckridge, co. Wexford: he was killed by the rebels in 1798.

William Clifford's will is dated 1 July, 1785, and was proved the 21st of the same month; he was s. by his 2nd son,

JOHN CLIFFORD, Esq. of Castle Annesley, who m. Catharine, dau. and co-heir of Maurice-Howling Darcy, Esq. of Cooleur, co. Wexford, and left issue,

I. EDWARD, now of Castle Annesley.
II. Thomas.
I. Eleanor, m. to Josiah Martin, Esq. of Ballingale, co. Wexford.
II. Marianne. III. Barbara.

John Clifford d. in 1820.

Arms—Chequy, or and az., a fesse, gu. charged with three lions, passant, of the first.
Crest—A hand, fessewise, ppr., holding a fleur-de-lis.
Motto—Dulcis amor patriæ.
Seat—Ashfield, near Wexford; and Castle Annesley.

CLIFTON OF CLIFTON AND LYTHAM.

CLIFTON, JOHN-TALBOT, Esq. of Clifton, and Lytham, co. Lancaster, b. 5 March, 1819; m. 22 April, 1844, Eleanor-Cecily, dau. of the Hon. Col. Lowther, M.P., and has issue,

THOMAS-HENRY, b. 3 March, 1845.

Lineage.—The precise period when the first ancestor of Clifton seated himself at Clifton, cannot be ascertained. The most probable conjecture is, that either Roger de Poictou, or Herveus, the great grantees of the crown, bestowed part of their vast possessions upon their officers and followers, to be holden of them, or of their superior lords. One of these officers may reasonably be presumed to have seated himself at Clifton, and in conformity to the almost invariable practice of those times acquired his patronymic of Clifton, from the place of his residence. The first person whose name occurs on authentic record is

WILLIAM DE CLIFTON, who held ten carucates of land in the hundred of Amounderness, in the 42nd HENRY III. A.D. 1257. From him lineally derived, 6th in descent,

THOMAS CLIFTON, who was in the retinue which accompanied HENRY V. into France, in 1415. He d. in 1442, leaving by his wife Agnes, dau. of Sir Richard Molyneux, of Sefton, Knt., a son, his successor, RICHARD CLIFTON, of Rawcliffe, co. Lancaster, direct ancestor of

THOMAS CLIFTON, Esq. of Westby, who m. Anne, dau. and co-heir of Sir Cuthbert Halsall, of Halsall and Clifton (representative of Elizabeth, heiress of Cuthbert Clifton, of Clifton), and thus the latter estate became again the possession of the Cliftons. Mr. Clifton d. 15 Dec. 1657, and was s. by his eldest son,

CUTHBERT CLIFTON, Esq. of Westby and Clifton, who m. in 1641, Margaret, dau. and sole heir of George Ireland, Esq. of Southworth, co. Lancaster, but dying without issue, was s. by his brother,

SIR THOMAS CLIFTON, b. 7 July, 1628, created a Baronet, in 1642. He m. 1st, Bridget, dau. of Sir George Heneage, of Hainton, co. Lincoln, by whom he had several children, who all d. young, except Mary, who m. Thomas, 6th Lord Petre. Sir Thomas m. 2ndly, Bridget, dau. of Sir Edward Hussey, Knt. of Hunnington, co. Lincoln, by whom he had a dau., Bridget, m. to Sir Francis Andrews, of Denton, co. Northampton. Sir Thomas Clifton, with Lord Molyneux, and several other Catholic gentlemen of rank, were unjustly accused of treason, in 1689, and all acquitted. He d. 13 Nov. 1694, when the baronetcy became extinct, and the estates devolved on (the son of his brother John) his nephew,

THOMAS CLIFTON, Esq., who m. Eleanora-Alathea, dau. of Richard Walmsley, Esq. of Dunkenhalgh, co. Lancaster, and dying in 1720, was s. by his son,

THOMAS CLIFTON, Esq. of Clifton, Westby, and Lytham, b. in 1696, who m. Mary, dau. of Richard, 5th Viscount Molyneux, by whom (who m. 2ndly, 8 Feb. 1752, William Anderton, Esq. of Euxton Hall, co. Lancaster) he left at his decease, 16 Dec. 1734, a son,

THOMAS CLIFTON, Esq. of Clifton, Westby, and Lytham, b. in 1728, who m. three wives, but left surviving issue by his 3rd wife only, Lady Jane Bertie, dau. of Willoughby, 3rd Earl of Abingdon, viz.,

JOHN, his successor.
Eleanora, m. Thomas Scarisbrick-Ecclestone, Esq. of Scarisbrick and Ecclestone, living a widow, May, 1838.
Catherine, m. 29 May, 1789, to John Talbot, Esq., brother of Charles, 16th Earl of Shrewsbury, and d. May, 1791.
Sophia.

Mr. Clifton, who built Lytham Hall, d. 11 May, 1783, and was s. by his eldest son,

JOHN CLIFTON, Esq. of Clifton, Westby, and Lytham, b. in 1764, who m. in 1785, Elizabeth, dau. of Thomas Riddell, Esq. of Felton Park and Swinburne Castle, co. Northumberland, by whom, who d. 19 Nov. 1825, he had issue,

I. THOMAS, his heir.
II. John, b. 1790, of Lincoln's Inn, m. 23 April, 1817, Maria, youngest dau. of John Trafford, Esq. of Trafford, co. Lancaster, and has issue, Cuthbert-William, John, and Edmund.
III. William, b. in 1791.
IV. Edward, b. in 1794, served in the Coldstream-guards in Spain and France, under the Duke of Wellington, 1814, m. 15 Jan. 1819, to Eliza, 3rd dau. of Thomas-S. Ecclestone and Eleanora Clifton, and has issue, Thomas; William; Harriet; and Edward-Gerard.
V. Charles, b. 5 July, 1796, d. Dec. 1825.
VI. Elizabeth, m. in Aug. 14, at Marylebone Church, London, to Charles-Thomas Conolly, Esq. of Midford Castle, co. Somerset.
VII. Mary, d. 5 July, 1808. VIII. Harriet.

Mr. Clifton d. 28 March, 1832, and was s. by his eldest son,

THOMAS CLIFTON, Esq. of Clifton, and Lytham, J.P. and D.L., b. 29 Jan. 1788, who m. 17 March, 1817, Hetty, dau. of Peregrine Treves, Esq., postmaster-general of Calcutta, and relict of David Campbell, of Kildaloig, in Argyllshire, North Britain, and has issue,

I. JOHN-TALBOT, now of Lytham.
II. Thomas-Henry, b. May, 1820, capt. 7th dragoon-guards.
III. Charles-Frederick, b. June, 1822, m. 30 April, 1853, Lady Edith-Maud Rawdon-Hastings, eldest dau. of George-Augustus-Francis, 2nd Marquess of Hastings.
IV. Edward-Arthur, b. in 1825, d. in 1850.
V. Augustus-Wykeham, rifle brigade, b. in 1829.

Arms—Sa., on a bend, arg., three mullets, gu.
Crest—A dexter arm, embowed in armour, holding a sword, ppr. *Motto*—Mortem aut triumphum.
Seats—Clifton and Lytham Hall.

CLIVE OF WHITFIELD.

CLIVE, THE REV. ARCHER, of Whitfield, co. Hereford, J.P. and D.L., rector of Solihull, co. Warwick, b. 16 March, 1800; m. 10 Nov. 1840, Caroline, dau. and co-heir of Edmund-Meysey Wigley, Esq. of Shakenhurst, co. Worcester, and has issue,

CHARLES-MEYSEY-BOLTON, b. 30 Jan. 1842.
Alice.

Lineage.—THE REV. BENJAMIN CLIVE, vicar of Duffield, co. Derby (youngest brother of Richard, of Styche, father of Robert, 1st Lord Clive), m. Miss Floyer, and was father of

GEORGE CLIVE, Esq. of Whitfield, who m. Sydney Bolton, of Louth, Ireland, and had issue, EDWARD-BOLTON; Theophilus; Henry; and Louisa, m to Frederick Keppel, Esq. of Lexham Hall, Norfolk. The eldest son,

EDWARD-BOLTON CLIVE, Esq. of Whitfield, m. in Nov. 1790, the Hon. Harriet Archer, 4th dau. and co-heir of Andrew, last Baron Archer of Umberslade, co. Warwick, and had issue,

Edward, colonel in the Grenadier-guards, b. in Nov. 1793, d. unm. 14 April, 1845.
ARCHER, successor to his father, now of Whitfield.
George, m. Miss Farquhar, dau. of Sir Thos. Farquhar, Bart., and had, Edward-Henry, Archer, and Harriet-Sybilla.
Harriet-Maria, m. to the Rev. H. Wetherell, archdeacon of Hereford.

Mr. Clive d. in July, 1845.

Arms—Arg., on a fesse, sa., three mullets, or.
Crest—A griffin, passant, arg., ducally gorged, gu.
Motto—Audacter et sincerè.
Seat—Whitfield, Herefordshire.

CLOSE OF ELM PARK, NOW OF DRUMBANAGHER.

CLOSE, MAXWELL, Esq. of Drumbanagher, co. Armagh, J.P. and D.L., high-sheriff in 1818, colonel in the army, b. 14 March, 1783; m. 14 March, 1820, Anna-Elizabeth, sister of Charles Brownlow, Lord Lurgan, and has issue,

I. MAXWELL-CHARLES, b. 25 June, 1827, m. 23 Nov. 1852, Catherine-Deborah-Agnes, dau. of Henry-Samuel Close, Esq. of Newtown Park, co. Dublin, and has a son, MAXWELL-ARCHIBALD, b. 5 Oct. 1853.
II. Barry, b. 22 June, 1833.

Lineage.—RICHARD CLOSE, the first of the family who settled in Ireland, was the younger son of a respectable house in Yorkshire, and held a commission in the army, sent from England, in the reign of CHARLES I., into that kingdom, A.D. 1640, where he remained after the termination of the civil wars, and became one of the lords of the soil, as we find him seised of four tates, or townlands, in the county of Monaghan, *temp.* CHARLES II. After the Restoration he fixed himself at Lisnegarvey (now Lisburn), co. Antrim, where a Protestant colony had been located under the protection of the then Lord Conway. There he lived and died, leaving a son and heir,

RICHARD CLOSE, Esq., who inherited the Monaghan estates. He m. the sister of Samuel Waring, Esq. of Waringstown, co. Down, M.P. for Hillsborough, and left at his decease (with three daus., the eldest m. to the Rev. Dean Welch; the second to — Jones, Esq.; and the third to John Peirse, Esq.) five sons. The 2nd son (in whose descendant the representation of the Close family is now vested),

THE REV. SAMUEL CLOSE, rector of Donaghhenry, Stewardstown, co. Tyrone, m. Catherine, dau. of Captain James Butler, of Ringhaddy, in Downshire, by Dame Margaret Maxwell, of Mullatinny (now Elm Park), co. Armagh, relict of Sir Robert Maxwell, Bart. of Ballycastle, co. Derry. This Dame Margaret Maxwell was the dau. and heiress of Henry Maxwell, Esq. of Mullatinny, who was the son of James Maxwell, the 3rd son of Robert Maxwell, dean of Armagh (a younger son of the house of Calderwood, in Scotland), who, after building the house of Mullatinny, in 1626, was murdered in 1641, by Sir Phelim O'Neill, at College Hall, the seat of his elder brother, Dr. Robert Maxwell, afterwards Bishop of Kilmore, and founder of the Farnham family. Captain James Butler, who was of the Ormonde branch of the Butlers, resided with the Lady Maxwell his wife, at Mullatinny, and d. there, having first bequeathed, by his will, made in 1713, his own estates to James Butler, Esq., his eldest son by a former wife, and the estate of Ballycastle, co. Derry, which he enjoyed in right of Lady Maxwell his wife, to whom it had been bequeathed by her 1st husband, Sir Robert Maxwell, to his dau. Catherine, after the death of her mother, by whom it was afterwards settled on the Rev. Samuel Close and his issue, on the marriage of that gentleman with Catherine Butler, her dau.; but they both d. before her at Mullatinny, leaving (with four daus., namely, I. Margaret, m. to Captain Charles Woolly; II. Mary, d. unm.; III. Catherine, d. unm.; and IV. Elizabeth, m. to Peter Gervais, Esq.) a son and successor,

MAXWELL CLOSE, Esq., who s. his grandmother, Lady Maxwell, who d. in 1758, in the possession of Elm Park, and the lands settled upon him. He m. in 1748, Mary, eldest dau. of Captain Robert Maxwell, of Fellows Hall, co. Armagh, brother of John, Lord Farnham, and had issue,

I. SAMUEL, his heir. II. Robert, d. unm.
III. Barry, b. in Dec. 1756, a major-general E.I.C.S., who was created a Bart. in 1812. This highly distinguished officer d. s. p. in April, 1813, when the title expired.
IV. Farnham, d. in the island of Guadaloupe, in 1794, lieut.-col. of the 65th regt., unm.
I. Grace, b. in Jan. 1750, m. to the Rev. Dr. St. John Blacker.
II. Catharine, b. in Nov. 1753, m. to Arthur Noble, Esq.
III. Margaret. IV. Mary. V. Elizabeth.

Mr. Close d. in 1793, was buried at Tynan, and s. by his eldest son,

THE REV. SAMUEL CLOSE, of Elm Park, rector of Keady, co. Armagh, and of Drakestown, in Meath. He m. 1782, Deborah, dau. of the Rev. Arthur de Robillard Champagné, dean of Clonmacnoise, son of Major Josias de Robillard Champagné, by the Lady Jane Forbes his wife, dau. of Arthur, Earl of Granard, and had four sons and three daus., viz.,

I. MAXWELL, his heir, now of Drumbanagher.
II. Robert, a major in the E.I.C.S., who m. Caroline, sister of the late Sir Thomas Palmer, Bart. of Northamptonshire, and has issue.
III. Henry-Samuel, m. Jane, dau. of the Rev. Holt Waring, of Waringstown, co. Down, and has issue.
IV. John-Forbes, in holy orders, rector of Kilkeel, in Downshire, who m. Mary, youngest dau. of Charles Brownlow, Esq. of Lurgan, and has issue.
I. Mary, m. to Sir Justinian Isham, Bart. of Lamport, co. Northampton, and has issue.
II. Jane, m. to Captain Chidley Coote, brother of Sir Charles-Henry Coote, Bart. of Ballyfin, in the Queen's County, and has issue.
III. Harriett, m. to the Rev. Ralph Coote, youngest brother of Sir C.-H. Coote, Bart.

Mr. Close d. in 1817.

Arms—Az., on a chevron arg., between three mullets, or, two bugle-horns, ppr., stringed, gu., with a stirrup-iron in the centre, ppr., quartering BUTLER.
Crest—A demi-lion, vert, holding a battle-axe, or, headed, arg.
Mottoes—"Fortis et fidelis," for CLOSE. "Sine cruce, sine luce," for MAXWELL.
Seat—Drumbanagher, near Newry.

CLOUGH OF PLAS-CLOUGH.

CLOUGH, HARRIETT-ELLEN, heiress of Plâs-Clough, co. Denbigh, m. the Rev. John-Williams Ellis, eldest son of the Rev. T. Ellis, M.A., of Glasfryn, and has issue.

Lineage.—This family, as its name and arms imply, is of Norman origin, and deduces from the Seigneurs de Rohan, in the Dukedom. Its first settlement in England appears by an ancient deed from Whalley Chartulary, bearing date in 1315, to have been in the northern counties. In Wales, the first settler on record was,

Richard Clough, commonly called *Hen*, or *The Old*, from having lived during the reigns of Henry VII. and VIII., of Edward VI., and of the Queens Mary and Elizabeth. In the *Harleian MSS.*, fol. 1971, entitled *N. Wales Ped.*, it is stated that he *m.* in the time of Henry VIII., and settled on Lleweni Green, near Denbigh. He had five sons and one dau. The 5th son,

Sir Richard Clough, Knt., became an eminent merchant, and was partner of the celebrated Sir Thomas Gresham, who, at Sir Richard's suggestion, erected the Royal Exchange. Sir Richard built, in the year 1567, on his paternal estate, the mansion of Plâs Clough, which is still in the possession of his lineal descendants. By his first wife he had a son and heir, Richard. He *m.* 2ndly, Catherine, widow of John Salusbury, Esq., son and heir of Sir John Salusbury, of Lleweni, Knt., and dau. and heir of Tudor ap Robert Vychan, of Berain (who *m.* 3rdly, Maurice Wynn, of Gwydyr, co. Carnarvon, Esq.; and 4thly, Edward Thelwall, of Plas-y-Ward, co. Denbigh, Esq.) Sir Richard had two daus.,

Mary, *m.* to William Wynn, Esq. of Melai, co. Denbigh, to whom Sir Richard gave Maynan Abbey, in Carnarvonshire, now in possession of her descendant, Spencer, 3rd Baron Newborough.

Katherine, *m.* to Roger Salusbury, D.C.L. of Jesus Coll., Oxford, younger son of Sir John Salusbury, Knt. of Lleweni.

From Sir Richard's son, Richard Clough, Esq. of Plâs Clough, the 4th in descent was,

Hugh Clough, Esq. of Plâs Clough, *b.* in 1709, high-sheriff for Denbighshire, *m.* Catherine, dau. and heir of Henry Powell, Esq. of Glanywern, co. Denbigh, and had,

I. Hugh, *b.* in 1746, Fellow of King's Coll., Cambridge, *d* young.
II. Richard, heir to his father.
III. Thomas, *b.* in 1756, M.A., rector of Denbigh and canon of St. Asaph, *m.* Dorothea, eldest dau. of John Lloyd, Esq. of Havodûnas, Denbighshire. By this lady, who *d.* in 1814, he left,
  1 Thomas-Hugh, *m.* Caroline, dau. of R. Price, Esq. of Rhiwlas, co. Merioneth.
  2 Howel-Powel, *m.* Barbara, dau. of — Westrop, Esq. of Limerick.
  1 Dorothea-Catherine, *m.* to the Rev. Richard Howard, D.D., canon of Bangor, and rector of Denbigh.
  2 Eliza, *m.* Charles-Gethin Kenrick, Esq.
  3 Mary-Anne.
IV. Roger, *b.* in 1759, some time of Bathafern Park, co. Denbigh, canon of St. Asaph, and rector of Lausannon, in Denbighshire, *m.* Anne-Jemima, eldest dau. and co-heir of James Butler, Esq. of Warminghurst Park, co. Sussex, and had issue by her, who *d.* in 1812,
  1 Roger-Butler, in holy orders, *b.* in 1782, M.A., vicar of Corwen, *m.* Amelia-Maria, dau. of R. Price, Esq. of Rhiwlas, co. Merioneth, and *d.* in 1830, having had two daus.,
    Amelia-Jemima, *m.* to Walter-Powel Jones, Esq. of Cefn Rûg, and has issue.
    Catherine-Elina, *d.* in 1827.
  2 James-Butler, *b.* in 1784, *m.* Anne, dau. of I. Perfect, Esq. of Pontefract, and has three sons and one dau.
  3 Henry-Butler, *b.* in 1789, capt. 17th native infantry, *d.* at Calcutta, in 1828.
  4 Charles-Butler, *b.* in 1793, M.A., rector of Llanferras, in Denbighshire, and vicar of Mold, Flintshire, *m.* Margaret Sydney, dau. of Edward Jones, Esq. of Weprè Hall, in the latter county.
  5 Frederick-Butler, *b.* in 1795, recorder of Ruthin, *m.* Elizabeth-Butler, dau. of the Rev. George Marshall, of Horsham, in Sussex, and *d.* in 1826, leaving a dau.
  6 Alfred-Butler, *b.* in 1796, S.T.B., rector of Braunston, *m.* 28 Oct. 1839, Sarah, dau. of R.-H. Lamb, Esq. of Bragborough House, co. Northampton.
  1 Ann-Jemima.
  2 Catherine, *m.* in 1836, to Richard-Butler Clough, Esq.
  3 Martha-Matilda. 4 Anna-Maria.
I. Margaret, *b.* in 1742, *m.* John Foulkes, Esq. of Eriviatt, co. Denbigh.

Hugh Clough was *s.* by his son,

Richard Clough, Esq. of Plâs Clough and Glanywern, *b.* in 1753, who *m.* Patty, 2nd dau. and co-heir of James Butler, Esq. of Warminghurst Park, in Sussex, and had issue,

Richard-Butler, his heir.
Hugh-Powel, *b.* in 1783, and *d.* at Gibraltar, in 1805.
James-Henry, *b.* in 1784, *m.* 1st, Harriett, 2nd dau. of Joseph Parr, Esq. of Firgrove, in Lancashire, and had by her one dau.,
  Harriett-Ellen, heiress of Plâs Clough, wife of the Rev. J.-W. Ellis.
He *m.* 2ndly, Anne, dau. of — Stone, Esq. of Rolleston Park, in Stafford.

Mr. Clough, who served the office of sheriff for Denbighshire in 1782, *d.* in 1784, and was *s.* by his eldest son,

Richard-Butler Clough, Esq. of Plâs Clough and Minydon, J.P. and D.L., *b.* 22 Dec. 1781, *m.* in 1836, his cousin Catherine, 2nd dau. of the Rev. Roger Clough, M.A., and *d. s. p.*

Arms—Quarterly: 1st and 4th, az., a greyhound's head, couped, arg., between three mascles, of the last, for Clough; 2nd and 3rd, or, a lion, passant, az., crowned; on a chief, the red cross between four cross-crosslets, gu., and on each side a sword, arg., handled, or, (augmentation coat given to Sir Richard Clough).

Crest—A demi-lion, rampant, az., holding in the dexter paw a sword, arg., handled, or, for Clough.

Motto—Sine maculâ macla.

Seat—Plâs-Clough.

CLOWES OF DELAFORD.

Clowes, Charles, Esq. of Delaford Park, co. Bucks, J.P. and D.L., high-sheriff in 1832, *b.* 25 Jan. 1785; *m.* 4 Oct. 1831, at St. James's Church, London, Mary-Anne, dau. of Samuel Parker, Esq. of Treleigh House, co. Cornwall, and has issue,

I. Mary-Anne. II. Frances-Daniell.
III. Isabella-Dorothy-Montague.

Lineage.—This family, of Cheshire extraction, possessed (besides lands in Staffordshire) property and a residence in the neighbourhood of Macclesfield, from the reign of Henry VII. A portion of their property in Cheshire, where they resided in the reign of Henry VIII. to that of Charles II. was called Whiteley, and situated about six miles from Macclesfield, in the township of Wincle, on the river Dane, which divides Cheshire from Derbyshire.

In the reign of Charles II. this family acquired by marriage an estate called Langley, also a few miles from Macclesfield, in the township of Sutton, on which they resided for several generations.

The 11th in descent from Clowes of Sutton, near Macclesfield, living in 1509, was

Robert Clowes, of Langley and Whiteley, *b.* 21 Aug. 1717, who *m.* 27 Aug. 1741, Dorothea, dau. and co-heir of John Daniell, Esq. of Daresbury, Cheshire, but dying without male issue, was *s.* by his brother,

William Clowes, Esq., afterwards of Langley and Whiteley, J.P. and D.L., *b.* 18 July, 1722, who *m.* 18 April, 1745, Frances, 2nd dau. and co-heir of John Daniell, Esq. of Daresbury, and *d.* 27 Sept. 1785, leaving a son and heir,

Charles Clowes, Esq. of Langley Hall, Cheshire, and Delaford, Bucks, J.P. and D.L., *b.* 28 Sept. 1747, who *m.* in 1780, Anne, dau. and co-heir of Edmond Dawson, Esq. of Warton, co. Lancaster, and had issue,

Charles, now of Delaford.
Edmund, of Warton, in Lancashire.
Robert, in holy orders, vicar of Nether Knutsford, in Cheshire, *m.* Catherine, only child of the Rev. Thomas Jee, vicar of Thaxted, Essex, by Catherine his wife, only dau. of Sir Peter Leicester, Bart. of Tabley, and relict of the Rev. Christopher Atkinson, and has issue.
John-Ellis, of the Inner Temple, and of Brunswick Square, London, *m.* Sophia-Ann, only surviving child of John-B.-B. Cobb, Esq. of Percy Street, and the India House, and has issue.
William, of the Middle Temple, and of Bedford Place, London, barrister-at-law, *m.* Ann, eldest dau. of John Legh, Esq of Norbury, Booth's Hall, Cheshire, and has issue.
Frances, *m.* to Maurice Swabey, Esq. of Lincoln's Inn, barrister-at-law, of Langley Marish, Bucks.

Mr. Clowes, who served as sheriff of Bucks in 1794, *d.* in Oct. 1818.

Arms—Vert, on a chevron between three unicorns' heads, erased, or, three crescents, gu.

Crest—A demi-lion, vert, crowned, or, supporting a battle-axe, arg., the staff, gold.

Seat—Delaford Park, Bucks.

CLUDDE OF ORLETON.

Cludde, Anna-Maria, of Orleton, co. Salop, *b.* 9 Sept. 1830; *m.* 22 June, 1854, the Hon. Robert-Charles Herbert, 4th son of the late Earl of Powis, K.G.

Lineage.—The Cluddes or Cluyddes claim Saxon origin, and at a very remote period possessed property in Shropshire. In the reign of Henry I. they were seated on the lands of Cluddeley, and in the third year of Edward III. they acquired, in marriage with the heiress of Orleton, that estate, which has ever since remained their principal residence.

William Cludde, Esq. of Orleton, was ancestor in the fourth degree of

Edward Cludde, Esq. of Orleton, who *m.* Anne, coheiress of William Beyst, Esq., and had two sons, Thomas and Charles; by the elder of whom,

Thomas Cludde, Esq. of Orleton, he was succeeded. This gentleman *m.* in 1591, the only child and heiress of John Coston, Esq. of Coston, by whom he left an only dau.,

Beatrice, heiress of Coston, *m.* to Coningsby Freeman, Esq. of Neen Solers.

Mr. Cludde, who is said to have served with reputation in Ireland, and to have been offered the honour of knighthood, was *s.* at Orleton by his brother,

Colonel Charles Cludde, of the Guards, who fell at the battle of Landen in 1693, leaving by Beatrice his wife, dau. of Wrottesley Prince, Esq., and relict of Robert Bretton, Esq., a son and successor,

William Cludde, Esq. of Orleton, high sheriff of Shropshire in 1723, who *m.* Martha, dau. and heir of Peter Langley, Esq. of Burcott, by whom he left with (two daus.) an only surviving son,

Edward Cludde, Esq. of Orleton, who *d. unm.*, and was *s.* by his nephew,

William Pemberton, Esq. of Wrockwardine (eldest son of Edward Pemberton, Esq. of Wrockwardine, by Martha his wife, sister of Edward Cludde, Esq. of Orleton.) Mr. Pemberton assumed by act of parliament the surname and arms of Cludde only, and was sheriff of Shropshire in 1814. He *m.* in 1781, Anna-Maria, dau. of Edward Jeffreys, Esq. of Shrewsbury, and *d.* 25 Aug. 1829, having had issue, Edward, his heir; William, capt. of dragoons, *d.* in 1809; Anna-Maria; and Harriett, *m.* in 1807, to William-Lacon Childe, Esq. of Kinlet. Colonel Cludde, who united in his person the representation of the very ancient families of Cludde, Orleton, and Pemberton, was *s.* by his son,

Edward Cludde, Esq. of Orleton and Wrockwardine, who *m.* 6 May, 1828, Catherine-Harriett, only dau. of Lieut.-Gen. Sir William Cockburn, Bart. of Cockburn and Reysland, and left, at his decease, an only dau. and heir, the present proprietrix of Orleton.

Arms—Erm., a fret, sa.

Crest—An eagle with wings expanded, ppr., preying on a coney, arg. *Seat*—Orleton, Shropshire.

CLUTTERBUCK OF WARKWORTH.

Clutterbuck, John, Esq. of Warkworth, co. Northumberland, *b.* 5 Sept. 1784, J.P., formerly major in the army; *m.* 31 Oct. 1821, Mary Anne, youngest dau. of the Hon. Thomas Lyon, of Hetton House, Durham, 3rd son of Thomas, 8th Earl of Strathmore, and has issue,

I. John-Lyon, *b.* 18 Feb. 1824; capt. 37th regt.
II. Thomas, *b.* 11 Dec. 1826.
III. Charles-Henry, lieut. R.N.
I. Mary.
II. Frances-Anne, *m.* 19 Aug. 1845, to Robert, eldest son of Robert Fellowes, Esq. of Shottisham Park, Norfolk.
III. Susan-Harriet.
IV. Charlotte-Eliza.

Lineage.—John Clutterbuck, Esq., 2nd son of Richard Clutterbuck, Esq. of Mill End, co. Gloucester, and nephew of Josias Clutterbuck, of Bristol, whose eldest son, Sir Thomas Clutterbuck, was consul at Leghorn, and was named among the intended knights of the Royal Oak, settled as a merchant at Newcastle-upon-Tyne. He *m.* 1st, Miss Priscilla Place, of that town, and had one dau., Hannah, *m.* to William Wharton, Esq. of Hertford, in Northumberland. He *m.* 2ndly, Miss Anne Collier, by whom he had another dau., Anne, *m.* to John Simpson, Esq., high-sheriff for Northumberland. Mr. Clutterbuck *m.* 3rdly; and dying in 1717, left a son and successor,

Richard Clutterbuck, Esq. of Warkworth, in Northumberland, living in 1781, who *m.* Margaret, dau. of George Ord, Esq. of Longridge, in Durham, and left (with three daus., one of whom, Elizabeth, *m.* in Feb. 1770, the Rev. Thomas Bates) a son and heir,

John Clutterbuck, Esq. of Warkworth, J.P., who *m.* 17 Feb. 1776, Anne, dau. of Capt. Lyon, Esq. of East Thetford, and had issue, John, of Warkworth; Anne; Margaret; Eliza-Maria, *m.* in 1822, to the Rev. T.-C. Winscom; Susanne, *m.* to Francis Forster, Esq. of Buston Vale. Mr. Clutterbuck *d.* 19 Nov. 1832.

Arms—Az., a lion, rampant, arg.; in chief, three escallop shells, of the second.

Crest—A buck, statant, arg., between two laurel branches, ppr.

Seat—Warkworth, co. Northumberland.

CLUTTERBUCK OF NEW ARK PARK.

Clutterbuck, Lewis, Esq. of New Ark Park, co. Gloucester, *b.* 14 Jan. 1794; *m.* 16 Dec. 1819, Sarah, dau. of the late William Balfour, Esq. of Jamaica, and has had,

I. Lewis-Balfour, in holy orders, rector of Doynton, *b.* 14 April, 1822.
II. James-Edmund, *b.* 28 May, 1823.
III. William, *b.* 20 Jan. 1825.
IV. Charles-Francis, *b.* 6 March, 1826.
V. John-Balfour, *b.* 4 July, 1831.
I. Sarah-Catherine.
II. Eleanor-Isabella.

Lineage.—This family, which has been for many generations of consideration and fortune, came to England from the Low Countries at the time of the Duke of Alva's persecutions. In 1586, Thomas Cloerterbooke was sheriff of Gloucester. The late James Clutterbuck, Esq., M.P. for Cirencester, the friend of David Garrick, possessed large estates in the counties of Surrey, Wilts, Somerset, and Gloucester.

John Clutterbuck, Esq., brother of Richard Clutterbuck, ancestor of the Cliffords *of Frampton*, and son of William Clutterbuck, of King's Stanley, *m.* Elinor-Henriette Tollemache, and by her (who *d.* in 1616) was father of Thomas, whose son, Jasper, had by Catharine Nash his wife, William Clutterbuck, who *m.* Barbara, dau. of Thomas Hawley, Esq., and was *s.* by his son, Edmund, father of Edmund, of Hyde, *b.* in 1763, who *m.* Penelope Smith, and had a son, Lewis, of Widcombe and Claverton, Bath, who *m.* Elizabeth Price, and had, with other issue, a son,

Rev. Lewis Clutterbuck, rector and patron of Ozleworth, J.P., *m.* 1st, 20 July, 1790, Catherine, dau. of Thomas Partridge, Esq., and on the maternal side descended from the ancient family of the Estburys *of Hawkesbury*, in Gloucestershire, by whom he had issue, Lewis, his heir, now of New Ark Park. Mr. Clutterbuck *m.* 2ndly, in 1809, Frances Elton, and by her (who *d.* in 1836) had a dau., Sarah-Frances, *m.* in 1842, to Thomas-D. Bayly, Esq. Mr. Clutterbuck *d.* 7 Aug. 1820.

Arms—Az., a lion, rampant, arg.; in chief, three escallops, of the second.

Crest—A buck, statant, arg., between two laurel-branches, ppr.

Seat—New Ark Park, co. Gloucester.

CLUTTON OF CHORLTON HALL.

Clutton, Thomas-Charlton, Esq. of Chorlton Hall, co. Chester, J.P. and D.L., *b.* in 1785, and *m.* in 1833, Miss Frances Lewis.

Lineage.—Roger Clutton, Esq. of Chorlton, living *temp.* Henry VIII. (3rd son of Owen Clutton, Esq. of Courthin, by Margery his wife, dau. of Humphrey Wilbraham, of Burham, and great-grandson of Hugh Clutton, Esq., by Elizabeth his wife, dau. of Richard Caldecote, Esq. of Caldecote, which Hugh was eighth in direct descent from Roger de Clutton, living *temp.* Henry III. (*see* Clutton-Brock *of Pensax*), *m.* Anne, dau. and heir of John Aldersey, Esq. of Chorlton, and was father of

Thomas Clutton, Esq. of Chorlton, living 1594 and 1609, who *m.* Alice, dau. and heir of John Heath, Esq. of Overton, and with two sons, who *d.* in infancy, had three other sons and three daus., viz., Raffe, of whom presently; Roger; Owen, of Chorlton, *m.* Anne, dau. of Richard Yardley, Esq. of Chorlton, and was buried 20 Nov. 1648; Anne; Elizabeth; and Dorothea. The eldest surviving son,

Raffe Clutton, Esq. of Overton and Kiddington, *m.* and *d.* in 1677, leaving two sons, Richard, the younger, *m.* a dau. of Leche of Malpas; and his heir,

Owen Clutton, Esq. of Kiddington, who *d.* in 1735, leaving, with other issue, two sons, Owen, his heir, and Ralph, rector of Horsted Keynes, Sussex. The elder son,

Owen Clutton, Esq. of Duckington and Chorlton, *m.* Alice, dau. of — Piggott, Esq. of Harthill, co. Chester, and had issue,

I. Richard, his heir.
II. Owen; III. John; IV. Ralph, all *d. s. p.*
V. George, *m.*, and left issue at his death, in 1781, Thomas-Charlton, successor to his uncle, and now of

Chorlton; George-Edward, *d. s. p.* in 1820; and Alice, *m.* to Roger Dutton, Esq. of Grafton, co. Chester.

VI. Thomas, *m.* Katherine, dau. and heir of — Knapp, Esq. of Oxfordshire; and *d.* in 1791.

The eldest son,

RICHARD CLUTTON, Esq. of Chorlton, *m.* Miss Benyon, and *d. s. p.* in 1790, aged 75, when he was *s.* by his nephew, the present THOMAS-CHARLTON CLUTTON, Esq. of Chorlton.

Arms—Arg., a chevron, erm., cotised, sa., between three annulets, gu.
Crest—A cock, or.
Seat—Chorlton Hall, Malpas, co. Chester.

CLUTTON-BROCK.

(*See* BROCK *of Pensax*).

COBBE OF NEWBRIDGE.

COBBE, CHARLES, Esq. of Newbridge, co. Dublin, J.P. and D.L., high-sheriff in 1821, *b.* 1781; *m.* in 1809, Frances, only dau. of Thomas Conway, Esq. of Morden Park, Surrey, and by her (who *d.* in 1847) has,

I. CHARLES, *b.* 1811, D.L., high-sheriff for co. Dublin, 1841; *m.* 1839, Louisa-Caroline, dau. of George-F. Brooke, Esq. of Somerton, co. Dublin.
II. Thomas, barrister-at-law, *b.* 1818.
III. William, *b.* 1816; *m.* Clara, dau. of J. Nottidge, Esq. of Rose Hill, Suffolk.
IV. Henry, in holy orders, M.A., perpetual curate of Grange, Armagh; *b.* 1817.
V. Frances-Power.

Lineage.—WILLIAM COBBE, of Steventon, Hants, *b. circa* 1450, was father of

JOHN COBBE, of Swaraton (now The Grange), who *m.* Amy Barnes, and had a son,

THOMAS COBBE, of Swaraton, *b. circa* 1510, still living at the time of the Visitation of Hampshire in 1575, when he received from Robert Cooke (Clarenceux) a ratification of the "armes and chriests of his auncestors," now in the possession of Mr. Cobbe. By his 2nd wife, Agnes, dau. of John Hunt, Thomas Cobbe was father of Richard, B.D., fellow and vice-president of Corpus Christi College, Oxon, and one of its earliest benefactors; also of two other sons, joint possessors of the estate of Nottington, adjoining Swaraton. By his 1st wife, Margaret, dau. of Edward Beronsaw, Esq., Thomas Cobb had, with other issue,

MICHAEL COBBE, of Swaraton, *b.* 1547; *d.* 40th ELIZABETH. He *m.* Joan, eldest dau. and heiress of George Welborne, Esq. of Allington, Dorset, and had issue. The eldest son,

THOMAS COBBE, of Swaraton, *b.* 1575; capt. of a foot company, 1634; *m.* Catherine, dau. of the Ven. Owen Owen, archdeacon of Anglesey, and rector of Burton-Latymer, sister of John Owen, Bishop of St. Asaph. By her he had, Michael (*m.* Anne, dau. of Arthur Broomfield, of Tichfield, M.P., had issue, Arthur and Lucy); and

RICHARD COBBE, *b.* 1607; member for Hants in the Cromwellian parliament of 1656, and still living in 1666, when he presented to Corpus Christi College, Oxon (of which he was gentleman commoner) a tankard, now preserved there, bearing his own arms and those of his wife, Honor Norton, 2nd dau. and co-heir of Sir Richard Norton, of Rotherfield, 2nd bart.

THOMAS COBBE, son of this Richard and Honor his wife, *m.* Veriana, dau. of James Chaloner, M.P. during the Long Parliament, son of Sir Thomas Chaloner, governor of Prince HENRY, and grandson of Sir Thomas, ambassador from Queen ELIZABETH to CHARLES V. James Chaloner *m.* Ursula, dau. of Sir Philip Fairfax, of Steeton; and there is still preserved at Newbridge his original correspondence with his cousin, Thomas, 3rd Lord Fairfax, the parliamentary general. By Veriana Chaloner, Thomas Cobbe (whose picture by Lely is at Newbridge) was father of

I. Richard-Chaloner, colonel of militia, *m.* Mary, dau. of F. Godolphin, Esq., governor of Scilly, and was father of Richard, D.D., rector of Finglas, father of Richard-Chaloner Cobbe, D.D., rector of Little Marlow, Bucks, father (with other children, *d. v. p.*) of Frances, *m.* to Hans Francis, 11th Earl of Huntingdon, and had issue, Francis, 12th Earl of Huntingdon.
II. William, captain, *d. s. p.* 1749.
III. CHARLES.

The youngest son,

CHARLES COBBE, *b.* 1686; Archbishop of Dublin; *m.* Dorothea, dau. of the Right Hon. Sir Richard Levinge, Bart., Speaker of the House of Commons, and Chief Justice of Common Pleas in Ireland, widow of Sir John Rawdon, Bart. of Moira. The Archbishop built Newbridge House about 1737, and *d.* 1765, leaving one surviving son,

THOMAS COBBE, of Newbridge, *b.* 1733; M.P. and colonel of militia; *m.* 1751, Lady Eliza Beresford, dau. of Marcus, 1st Earl of Tyrone, and sister of George, Marquess of Waterford. By her he had issue, two daus., Catherine, *m.* the Hon. Henry Pelham (and had issue, Catherine, and Frances, *m.* to Capt. Murray); and Elizabeth-Dorothea, *m.* Sir Henry Tuite, Bart., *d. s. p.* 1850, and one son,

CHARLES COBBE, Esq. of Newbridge, *b.* 1756, *d. v. p.* 1798. He *m.* Anne-Power Trench, sister of William, 1st Earl of Clancarty, and by her (who *d.* 1835) had five sons,

CHARLES, now of Newbridge.
George, col. R.A., *b.* 1782, *m.* Amelia, dau. of the Rev. Royston Barton, and has issue, 1 Charles-Henry, capt. H.E.I.C.S., *m.*, and has issue; 2 Thomas-Monk; 1 Frances, *m.* to Dawson Littledale, Esq., and has issue; 2 Anna; 3 Linda, *m.* to Thomas Thompson, Esq., and has issue.
Henry, vicar of Templeton, *d. s. p.* 1823.
Thomas-Alexander, colonel H.E.I.C.S; *b.* 1788; *d.* 1836; *m.* Nuzzeer Begum, dau. of Azeeze Khan, of Cashmere, and had issue, 1 Henry-Clermont, lieut.-colonel; 2 Charles-Augustus, capt. 3rd regt.; 3 William, *d. s. p.*; 4 Francis-Hastings, H.E.I.C.S.; 5 Alexander-Hugh, captain 37th regt.; 1 Azélie; 2 Florence, *m.* 1st, to John Ensor, Esq. of Rollesby, and has issue; 2ndly, to Chardin Wroughton, Esq., and has issue; 3 Laura, *m.* to John Locke, Esq., and has issue; 4 Sophia; 5 Eliza.
William-Power, capt. R.N., *b.* 1790, *m.* Elizabeth-Bridget, dau. of Richard Sharkey, Esq., barrister-at-law, and dying 1831, left issue, 1 Charles-Power, 8th regiment.; 2 William-Power, vicar of Guilecagh; 1 Jane-Power; 2 Flora-Power: Elizabeth-Dorothea.

Arms—Quarterly: 1st, for COBBE (modern), gu., a fesse, arg.; in chief, two swans, ppr. 2nd, for WELBORNE *of Allington*, az., in fesse, three lozenges, sa., charged with fountains, between three goats' heads, gu., collared and attired, or. 3rd, for NORTON *of Rotherfield*, vert, a lion, rampant, or. 4th, for COBBE (ancient), gu., a fesse, or; in chief, two swans, ppr.
Crest—Out of a ducal coronet, gu., a pelican's head and neck vulning itself, ppr.
Motto—"Moriens cano." Over the crest, "In sanguine vita."
Seat—Newbridge, co. Dublin.

CODDINGTON OF OLDBRIDGE.

CODDINGTON, HENRY-BARRY, Esq. of Oldbridge, co. Meath, J.P., high-sheriff in 1843, *b.* 22 May, 1802; *m.* 26 Sept. 1827, Maria, eldest dau. of William Sharman-Crawford, Esq. of Crawfordsburn, co. Down, and by her (who is deceased) has issue,

I. JOHN-NICHOLAS, *b.* 24 June, 1828.
II. William-Henry, *b.* 19 June, 1833.
III. Henry-Joshua, *b.* 31 Aug. 1836.
IV. Fitzherbert, *b.* 22 May, 1838.
V. Arthur-Blany, *b.* 20 Feb. 1840.
VI. Lathum-Dixie.
I. Letitia-Mabella. II. Maria-Anna.

Lineage.—DIXIE CODDINGTON, the first of the family in Ireland, went from Cheshire in 1656.

DIXIE CODDINGTON, of Holmpatrick (probably son to the former), had two sons, John; and Nicholas, who *m.* Miss Stearne, and had one dau., Anne, *m.* to Dixie Coddington, Esq.

NICHOLAS CODDINGTON, the 2nd son, *m.* Miss Dixie, and had issue, Dixie, and Henry; and one dau., Elizabeth.

DIXIE CODDINGTON, eldest son, *b.* in 1665, and *m.* his cousin, Anne Coddington, and had issue, JOHN; NICHOLAS; Dixie, *m.* Hannah Waller, of Allenstown, and had issue; Henry, *d. unm.*; William, *m.* Miss Bellingham, and had issue; Elizabeth, *m.* to John Lyster, Esq. of Rocksavage; and Jane, *m.* to Ralph Blundell.

JOHN CODDINGTON, eldest son of Dixie and Anne, *m.* Frances Osborne, by whom he got a large fortune, particularly Oldbridge, rendered famous by the battle of the Boyne, 1 July, 1690. They had but one child, John, a most accomplished young man, who was drowned in the River Boyne in 1730, the day previous to his attaining his majority.

NICHOLAS CODDINGTON, Esq., 2nd son of Dixie and Anne Coddington, *m.* Mary Tenisson, sister of Judge Tenisson, of Dunbar, co. Louth, and had issue, 1 Dixie, of Oldbridge, *m.* Catherine Burgh, and *d. s. p.*; HENRY, of whom presently; 1 Elizabeth, *m.* to Robert Hart, Esq.; 2 Frideswide, *m.* to Thomas L'Estrange, Esq.; 3 Mary, *m.* to Gore Ellis,

Esq.; 4 Dorothea, m. to the Very Rev. Archdeacon Montgomery; 5 Jane, m. to the Rev. Dr. Norris; 6 Frances, m. Hercules Ellis, Esq. The 2nd son,

HENRY CODDINGTON, Esq. of Oldbridge, M.P. in 1763, Elizabeth, dau. of Latham Blacker, Esq. of Rathescar, co. Louth, and had issue,

NICHOLAS, his heir.
Henry, m. Eleanor Hamilton, of Browne Hall, co. Donegal, and d., leaving three daus., one of whom is m. to the Rev. Thomas Lindesay, rector of Upper Cumber, co. Londonderry.
Latham, M.A., in holy orders, rector of Timolin, co. Kildare; m. Anne, dau. of Col. Bellingham, of Ardah, co. Louth, and has had, with other issue, Henry, in holy orders, and John-George, of Ravensdale, co. Louth.
Thomas, d. unm.
Martha, m. Philip Pendleton, Esq. of Moortown, Meath, and left issue.
Elizabeth, m. to Edward Winder, Esq., and has issue.
Anne, m. to Edward-Augustus Waller, Esq., and d. leaving issue.
Mary-Jane, m. to George Lendrum, Esq. of Jamestown, co. Fermanagh, and d. leaving issue.

The elder son,

NICHOLAS CODDINGTON, Esq. of Oldbridge, m. in July, 1793, Letitia, dau. of Gaynor Barry, Esq. of Beau, co. Dublin, and had issue,

HENRY-BARRY, now of Oldbridge.
Joshua-William, captain R.E.; m. in 1840, Agnes, dau. of Col. Emmett, royal engineers; and d. in 1853, leaving issue, Charles-Edward, and Edward-Fitzherbert.
Fitzherbert-Nicholas, major in the army; m. in 1841, Jane, dau. of Col. Trelawny, governor of St. Helena; and d. in 1853, leaving issue, Fitzherbert-Henry, Charles-Hamlyn, and Blanche Martha.
Anne-Elizabeth, m. to Fitzherbert Ruxton, Esq. of Ardee House, co. Louth, and has issue.
Letitia-Mary.

Upon the decease of Mr. Coddington, 31 Aug. 1837, aged 72, he was s. by his eldest son, the present HENRY-BARRY CODDINGTON, Esq. of Oldbridge.

Arms—Arg., a cross, sa., fretty, of the first, between four trefoils.
Crest—A wolf's head, erased, or.
Mottoes—"Nil desperandum," or "Nec metuas nec optes."
Seat—Oldbridge, co. Meath.

CODRINGTON OF WROUGHTON.

CODRINGTON, WILLIAM-WYNDHAM, Esq. of Wroughton, co. Wilts, b. 25 June, 1825; m. 21 June, 1854, Cecilia-Charlotte, dau. of the late Frederick Webb, Esq. of Westwick, Durham.

Lineage.—This is the older branch of the very ancient Gloucestershire family of Codrington, from which descend the existing Baronets of the name.

JOHN DE CODRINGTON, grandson of Geoffrey Codrington, was standard-bearer to HENRY V., in the French wars of that monarch, *anno* 1415. He purchased the manor of Wapeley in 1455, and living to the advanced age of 112, d. in the year 1475. His great-grandson,

SIMON CODRINGTON, m. Agnes, dau. and heiress of Richard Seacole, of Didmartin, and was s. by his son,

ROBERT CODRINGTON, father, by Anne Stubbs, of two sons, viz., CHRISTOPHER, the younger, ancestor of the Baronets Codrington, of Dodington; and his heir, in 1618,

JOHN CODRINGTON, Esq. of Didmarton, high-sheriff of Gloucestershire, in 1633. Fourth in descent from this John was

WILLIAM CODRINGTON, Esq. of Wroughton, co. Wilts, who m. Mary, dau. of John Lewsley, Esq., and had issue,

WILLIAM, his heir.
John-Lewsley, of Woodhouse, co. Gloucester, b. in 1793; m. Laura-Mary Charlton; d. s. p. in 1837.
Oliver-Calley, of Dean House, Hants.
Thomas-Stretton, in holy orders, vicar of Wroughton; m. Miss White; and d. in Dec. 1839, leaving six sons.
Robert, d. unm. Feb. 1835.
Ellinor, m. to the Rev. Edmond-Leigh Bennett, rector of Lechlade, co. Gloucester; d. July, 1842, leaving two sons.

Mr. Codrington was s. by his son,

WILLIAM CODRINGTON, Esq. of Wroughton, b. in April, 1790; m. 10 June, 1824, Letitia, dau. of William Wyndham, of Dinton, co. Wilts, Esq., and by her (who d. 28 Nov. 1845) had issue,

WILLIAM-WYNDHAM, his heir, now of Wroughton.
Charles, b. 18 June, 1827. John, b. 17 Jan. 1829.
Robert, b. 23 Jan. 1831. Alexander, b. 3 July, 1832.
George, b. 8 Jan. 1834.
Letitia-Mary. Marian.

Mr. Codrington d. 11 April, 1842.

Arms—Arg., a fesse, embattled-counter-embattled, sa., fretty, gu., between three lioncels, passant, of the third.
Crest—A dragon's head, gu., issuing from a ducal coronet, between two dragon's wings, chequy, or and az.
Motto—Immersabilis est vera virtus.
Seat—Wroughton, Swindon, Wilts.

COFFIN OF PORTLEDGE.

PINE-COFFIN, THE REV. JOHN-THOMAS, of Portledge, co. Devon, prebendary of Exeter, b. 8 Jan. 1800; m. 1st, June, 1838, Frances, dau. of the late William Speke, Esq. of Jordans, and by her (who d. 30 March, 1845) has,

I. JOHN-RICHARD, b. June, 1842.
II. Edward, b. July, 1843.
I. Frances. II. Henrietta-Isabella.

Mr. Pine-Coffin m. 2ndly, Oct. 1848, Charlotte, dau. of the late Samuel Chandler, Esq. of Bath.

Lineage.—The Coffins possessed the manor of Alwington, in which parish Portledge is situated, as early as the time of WILLIAM the Conqueror.

The authorities who have written respecting the co. of Devon make honourable mention of SIR ELIAS COFFIN, Knt. of Clist and Ingarby, in the days of King JOHN; of SIR RICHARD COFFIN, of Alwington, *temp.* HENRY II.; of SIR JEFFREY COFFIN, of Coombe Coffin, under HENRY III.; and of other knights, descendants of these, during successive reigns, till the time of HENRY VIII., when we find SIR WILLIAM COFFIN sheriff of Devonshire, and, being highly preferred at court, master of the horse at the coronation of Anne Boleyn, a gentleman of the privy chamber, and afterwards one of the eighteen assistants of King HENRY VIII., at the tournament of Guienne, in France, A.D. 1519. This Sir William Coffin was also high steward of the manor and liberties of Stanton, co. Hertford. At his death, he humbly bequeathed to his great master, HENRY VIII., with whom he was in especial grace and favour, all his hawks, his best horses, and a cart; and leaving no issue, he conveyed the manor of East Higgington, in the parish of Be ryn Arbor, with all his other estates in the co. of Devon, to his eldest brother's son, RICHARD COFFIN, Esq. of Portledge. The last male descendant,

RICHARD COFFIN, Esq. of Portledge, d. unm. 9 Dec. 1766, aged 84, and willed his estates to nephews, Robert Bennett, and his elder brother Richard Bennett, sons of his sister, Honour Bennet, with remainder to his great-nephew, John Pine, Esq. of East Downe, and heirs male. Eventually, the estate went, at the death of Richard Bennett Coffin, according to the entail, to

THE REV. JOHN PINE,* of East Down (son and heir of John Pine, Esq., and grandson of Edward Pine, Esq. of East Down, by Dorothy his wife, dau. of Richard Coffin, of Portledge). He was b. in 1736, and assumed, in 1797, by royal license, the additional surname and arms of COFFIN. He m. 3 Dec. 1765, Grace, dau. of James Rowe, Esq. of Alverdiscott, in Devon, and had issue,

I. RICHARD, his heir.
II. Charles, in holy orders, rector of East Down, b. 3 Nov. 1771; m. Charlotte, dau. of Samuel Knight, Esq. of Milton, co. Cambridge, by whom he has issue, Charles-John-Samuel, and eight daus., Mary-Anne-Elizabeth; Charlotte-Philippa; Lucy-Judith, m. to the Rev Robert-G. Rogers, rector of Yarlington; Emily-Grace; Caroline-Emma; Elizabeth-Fanny; Septimia; Octavia.
III. James-William, b. 23 Sept. 1773; d. unm. at Jamaica, in April, 1792.
IV. John, b. 16 March, 1778; a major-general in the army, C.B.; who m. 13 April, 1820, Maria, eldest dau. of George Monkland, Esq. late of Belmont, Bath; but d. s. p. 10 Feb. 1830.
V. Edward (Sir) Knt., b. 20 Oct. 1784, a commissary-general.
I. Mary-Anne.

The Rev. John-Pine Coffin d. at Bath, in April, 1824, and was s. by his eldest son and heir,

RICHARD PINE COFFIN, Esq. of East Down and Portledge, b. 6 March, 1770; m. 28 Oct. 1797, Henrietta, dau. of the Rev. Thomas Kitson, of Shiphay, co. Devon, and by her had issue,

RICHARD, his successor, d. unm. 1837.
JOHN-THOMAS, successor to his brother, and present representative.

* Lineally descended from the marriage of Oliver Pine, of Hame, co. Cornwall, living in 1296, with Elinor, dau. and heir of Philip le Downe, of East Downe.

Henrietta, *d. unm.* in May, 1837.
Mary-Anne.

Mr. Pine Coffin *d.* 6 Oct. 1833.

Arms—Az., semée of crosses-crosslet, or, three bezants.
Crest—1st, a martlet, az., charged on the breast with two bezants; 2nd, a pine-tree, ppr.
Motto for PINE—In tempestate floresco.
Seat—Portledge, near Bideford, co. Devon.

COHAM OF COHAM.

COHAM, WILLIAM-HOLLAND-BICKFORD, Esq. of Coham and Dunsland, co. Devon, J.P., *b.* 28 July, 1828.

Lineage.—In passing by the banks of the River Torridge, towards the parish of Black Torrington, Devon, the dwelling of Coham, with owners of its own name, comes in view. It is not known when its possessors did not dwell there, they having possessed it from time immemorial. The name denotes Saxon origin—*ham*, a Saxon word, signifying "a home" or "dwelling-place," surrounded by wood, water, and fields, just as Coham is situated; but the family can only *prove* their home at this place from the year 1547, and this proof from the aid of the Black Torrington parish register, where the following entry may be seen: "Margaret, daugter of Stephen Coham, gentleman, of Coham, was baptized April 4th, 1547," and this extract is from the earliest register extant in the parish-chest. We find this Stephen Coham succeeded by Stephen Coham, the father of Lewis Coham, of Coham, Esq., living in the beginning of the seventeenth century. To this gentleman succeeded

LEWIS COHAM, Esq. of Coham, who *m.* 22 Dec. 1669, Mary, the sister of John Arscott, Esq. of Totcott, near Holsworthy (who succeeded the John Arscott who *m.* Gertrude, the dau. of Sir Shilston Calmady, but left no family), by whom he had three sons and two daus.,

I. STEPHEN, his heir.
II. John, who settled at Bovacott, in the parish of Bradford. He *m.* Margaret, the 2nd dau. and co-heiress of William Holland, Esq. of Upcott-Avenel, in the parish of Sheepwash, and of Thorne, in the parishes of Holsworthy and Pyworthy, by whom he had three sons, Stephen, who lived and *d.* at Bovacott, *unm.*; William, who lived at a house in the town of Holsworthy, called The Croft, where he *d. unm.*; Arthur, in holy orders, archdeacon of Wilts, &c., *m.* Grace, dau. of George-Plunkett Woodruffe, Esq. of the Manor House, of Chiswick, by whom he had two sons and two daus., all of them married.
III. Arthur, who *m.* a dau. of Burdon of Burdon, and settled at Holsworthy, where this branch of the family continue to reside.
I. Mary, *m.* to the Rev. Benoni Bampfylde (rector of Black Torrington), of Poltimore.
II. Gertrude, *m.* to Clement Gay, Esq. (related to Gay the poet).

The eldest son,

STEPHEN COHAM, Esq. of Coham, *m.* in the 5th of Queen ANNE, Mary, dau. and co-heiress of William Holland, Esq. of Upcott Avenel, in Devon (lineally descended from JOHN, 4th son of Robert, Lord Holland, by Maude his wife, one of the daus. and co-heiresses of Alan le Zouch, of Ashby), and thus acquired that estate. About this time the mansion house of Coham was destroyed by fire, and the family, in consequence, removed to their seat at Upcott Avenel. By the heiress of Holland, Mr. Coham had two sons,

I. LEWIS, his heir.
II. Holland, in holy orders, rector of North Lewe, Devon, who *m.* Christian, dau. of the Rev. James Silke, of Bedminster, of an ancient family there settled, and had issue,
1 STEPHEN, successor to his uncle.
2 WILLIAM-HOLLAND, heir to his brother.

The elder son,

LEWIS COHAM, Esq. of Upcott Avenel, rebuilt the mansion of Coham. He *m.* Lucretia, dau. and co-heiress of — Barnfield, Esq. of Mambury and Great Torrington, Devon; but dying without issue, in 1778, was *s.* by his nephew,

STEPHEN COHAM, Esq. of Coham and Upcott Avenel, at whose decease, *unm.*, in 1786, the representation and possessions of the family devolved upon his brother,

THE REV. WILLIAM-HOLLAND COHAM, of Coham and Upcott Avenel. This gentleman *m.* 29 Nov. 1790, Mary, dau. and eventually sole heiress of George Bickford, Esq. of Dunsland and Arscott, both in the co. of Devon, representative of the ancient family of ARSCOTT *of Arscott and Dunsland*, co. Devon, and by her (who *d.* 4 Feb. 1839) had issue,

WILLIAM-BICKFORD, his heir.
George-Lewis, of Upcott Avenel, co. Devon, J.P. and D.L.
Holland, J.P. for Devonshire.
Mary-Anne. Christiana.

Mr. Coham *d.* 15 March, 1825, and was *s.* by his eldest son,

THE REV. WILLIAM-BICKFORD COHAM, of Coham and Dunsland, who *m.* 17 April. 1827, Augusta-Mary, eldest dau. of the late Joseph Davie Bassett, Esq. of Heanton Court and Watermouth (whose great-grandmother, Elinor Courtenay, was eldest dau. of Sir William Courtenay, by the Lady Anne Bertie his wife), and had issue, WILLIAM-HOLLAND-BICKFORD, now of Coham and Dunsland; Arscott-Bickford-Courtenay, *b.* 29 April, 1832; Mary-Bassett-Elinor, *m.* 17 Aug. 1852, to William Parr, Esq. of Fernside, Bournemouth, Dorset; and Augusta-Christiana-Davie. Mr. Coham *d.* 2 July, 1843.

Arms—Per chevron, engrailed, gu. and erm.; in chief, five fleurs-de-lis, three and two, and in base, a lion, rampant, or.
Crest—In front of a plume of five feathers, arg., two crosscrosslets, fitchée, in saltire, az.
Motto—Fuimus, et sub Deo erimus.
Seats—Coham (anciently spelt Cohame), in the parish of Black Torrington; Dunsland, in the parish of Bradford, co. Devon; and Trevedoe Manor.

COKE OF TRUSLEY.

COKE, D'EWES, Esq. of Brookhill Hall, co. Derby, J.P. and D.L., *b.* 22 Dec. 1774; *m.* 2 Nov. 1797, Harriet, dau. of Thomas Wright, Esq. of Mapperley Hall, Notts, and has issue,

I. FRANCIS-LILLYMAN-D'EWES, *b.* 4 June, 1804, B.A.
II. William-Sacheverell, J.P., *b.* 31 Aug. 1805, late lieut. 89th regt., *m.* 21 Nov. 1837, Sarah-Gift, dau. of John Deane, Esq., and has issue, Mary; Alice; and Harriet.
III. Edward-Thomas, J.P., *b.* 4 Jan. 1807, late a captain in the 69th regt., and now major in the Derbyshire militia, *m.* 6 Aug. 1835, Diana, 2nd dau. of the late Rev. John-Talbot Crosbie, of Ardfert Abbey, co. of Kerry, Ireland, and has issue, John-Talbot, *b.* 9 Aug. 1841; Jane-Susanna; Diana; and Gertrude-Alice.
IV. John-Henry, *b.* 12 Dec. 1811, B.A., in holy orders.
V. Richard-George, *b.* 12 Feb. 1813, settled in New South Wales in 1835.
I. Harriet-Frances. II. Elizabeth-Anne.
III. Sarah-Sophia, *m.* 22 June, 1827, to George Robinson, Esq. lieut. R.N., and has issue.
IV. Mary-Agnes, *m.* 9 March, 1830, to Arthur Burnell, Esq., and has issue.
V. Emma-Isabella, *m.* 16 Aug. 1782, to James Salmond, Esq., captain 2nd dragoon-guards, and has issue.

Lineage.—This ancient and respectable family, which can trace its descent in a direct male line for upwards of five hundred years, settled at Trusley, in the co. of Derby, in the early part of the reign of EDWARD III., at which time

HUGH, son of Robert Coke, *m.* Agnes, dau. and sole heir of Robert Owen, of Marchington Woodhouse, in the co. of Stafford. His descendant,

RICHARD COKE, *m.* Mary, dau. and heir of Thomas Sacheverell, of Kirkby, in the co. of Nottingham, and *d.* in 1582, leaving (with a dau., Dorothy, *m.* to Valentine Carey, D.D., Bishop of Exeter) five sons, viz., I. FRANCIS (Sir), his heir; II. John (Sir), principal secretary of state for upwards of twenty years to CHARLES I., ancestor of the COKES *of Melbourne*; III. Thomas, *d.* at Padua, 1623, *s. p.*; IV. Philip, Fellow of Trinity Coll. Cambridge, and *d.* there; V. George, D.D., consecrated, in 1633, Bishop of Bristol, and in 1636 translated to Hereford. He *m.* Jane, dau. of William, son of Sir Clement Heigham, of Suffolk, and dying in 1646, left issue, 1 Richard, B.D., of Suckley, co. Worcester, whose only son, HEIGHAM, was father, by Elizabeth, his 2nd wife, dau. of Sir Willoughby D'Ewes, of a son, D'EWES COKE, who *m.* Frances Coke, of Trusley; 2 John, prebendary of Moreton Magna; 3 William, of Quistmoor, co. Hereford, ancestor of the COKES *of Lower Moor*; 4 Thomas, *d. s. p.*; 5 Robert, was killed in action at Nieuport, *temp.* ELIZABETH. The eldest son,

SIR FRANCIS COKE, of Trusley, *m.* 1st, Frances, dau. of Denzell Holles, son and heir of Sir William Holles. He *m.* 2ndly, Elizabeth, dau. of George Curzon, of Croxhall, in the co. of Derby, and relict of Thomas Leigh, of Egington. He *d.* in 1639, at the age of 73, leaving (with four daus., I. Eleanor, *d. unm.*; II. Susanna, *m.* to Roger Bates, D.D.; III. Elizabeth, *m.* to Percival Willoughby, M.D., son of Sir

Percival Willoughby, of Wollaton, co. of Nottingham, and IV. Anne, m. to John Mundy, of Markeaton, co. Derby) three sons, I. WILLIAM, his heir; II. Gilbert, captain serving in the army in Holland, father of a dau. and heir, Frances, wife of William Mundy, Esq. of Darley; and, III. Francis, Archdeacon of Stafford. The eldest son,

WILLIAM COKE, Esq. of Trusley, m. 1st, Maude, dau. and co-heiress of Henry Beresford, of Alsop-in-the-Dale, in the co. of Derby, had (with four daus., I. Elizabeth, m. to Thomas Sherman, London; II. Mary, m. to John Fitzherbert, of Somersall, co. Derby; III. Alice, m. to William Harpur, of Bilson, in the co. of Derby, son to Sir Henry Harpur, Bart. of Calke; and IV. Isabel, d. young) four sons, who all d. s. p. except the eldest. Mr. Coke's 2nd wife, who d. without issue, was Dorothy, dau. of Francis Saunders, of Shankton, in Northamptonshire. He d. in 1641, and was s. by his eldest son,

RICHARD COKE, Esq. of Trusley, one of the intended knights of the Royal Oak, who m. Catherine, dau. of Robert Charlton, of Whitton, in Shropshire, sister to Sir Job Charlton, Speaker of the House of Commons, and d. 12 March, 1664, leaving, with daus., who d. unm. I. ROBERT, his heir; I. Anne, m. to Paul Ballidon, of Derby, whose dau., Catherine, was m. to William Coke, of Trusley, of whom presently; II. Susanna, m. to Edward Wilmot, of Spondon, co. Derby, barrister-at-law, son of Edward Wilmot, D.D., and had issue, Robert-Wilmot, who rebuilt the family seat at Chaddesden; Edward-Wilmot, m. to Catherine-Cassandra-Isabella Coke, of whom presently; and Richard-Wilmot, m. to Henrietta, dau. of William Cavendish, of Doveridge, co. Derby; III. Elizabeth, m. to John Ward, rector of Mickleover, near Derby; V. Matilda, m. to Thomas Bull, and d. in 1719. The son and successor,

ROBERT COKE, Esq. of Trusley, m. Elizabeth, dau. of Anthony Samwell, 4th son of Sir William Samwell, Bart. of the co. of Northampton, auditor to Queen ELIZABETH, and d. 22 Jan. 1713, aged 67, leaving, with other issue, I. WILLIAM, his heir; II. Thomas, B.D., rector of Trusley, whose male line became extinct with his grandson, Daniel-Parker Coke, M.P. for Nottingham, in 1825; III. John, M.D., d. 18 Nov. 1720, s. p.; IV. Richard, m. Elizabeth, dau. of Thomas Robie, of Donnington, co. Leicester, and had issue, of which the 2nd son, John, emigrated to Virginia. The eldest son,

WILLIAM COKE, Esq. of Trusley, m. Catherine, dau. of Paul Ballidon, Esq. of Derby, and dying 20 Jan. 1718, aged 39, without male issue, the elder branch of the family became extinct. Of his daus.,

I. CATHERINE-CASSANDRA-ISABELLA, m. her cousin, Edward Wilmot, of Spondon, barrister-at-law, and had a son and heir, Francis-Ballidon Wilmot, who m. Elizabeth, dau. of Richard Wilmot, of Derby, by Henrietta, dau. of William Cavendish, and left issue one son and one dau., viz., Francis, rector of Trusley and Pinxton, who dying 21 April, 1818, unm., the Trusley and Spondon properties devolved upon his only sister and heir, Susanna, m. to John Coke, of Debdale, co. Nottingham, of whom presently. II. FRANCES.

The 2nd dau. and co-heir,

FRANCES COKE, m. in 1720, D'EWES COKE, Esq. of Suckley, son of Heigham Coke, descended from the Bishop of Hereford. She d. leaving issue three sons, of whom the only survivor was GEORGE, of whom presently. Mr. D'Ewes Coke m. 2ndly, Catherine, dau. of Francis Hurt, of Alderwasley, co. Derby, by whom he had two sons, who d. s. p., and three daus. He d. in 1751, and was s. by his son,

GEORGE COKE, Esq., for some time an officer of dragoons, who m. Elizabeth, dau. of the Rev. Seth Ellis, of Brampton, co. Derby, and d. 17 Nov. 1759, leaving one son,

THE REV. D'EWES COKE, rector of Pinxton and South Normanton, co. Derby, who m. Hannah, dau. and heiress of George Heywood, of Brimington, co. Derby, and by her (who d. in 1818) had issue,

I. D'EWES, now of Brookhill.
II. William (Sir), one of the judges in the Supreme Court of Ceylon, d. at Trincomalee, 1 Sept. 1818, aged 42.
III. John, J.P. and D.L., high-sheriff for the co. Nottingham in 1830, m. in 1806, Susanna, only dau and heiress of Francis-Ballidon Wilmot, of Spondon and Trusley. Mr. Coke d. without surviving issue, 14 Sept. 1841, bequeathing his estates to his nephew, Edward-Thomas Coke, Esq.
I. Hannah, m. to Rev. Ellis Williams, rector of Pinxton, d. in 1833, s. p.

The Rev. D'Ewes Coke d. at Bath, 12 April, 1811.

Arms—Gu., three crescents, and a canton, or.
Crest—The sun in splendour, or.
Motto—Non aliunde pendere.
Seat—Brookhill Hall, Notts.

COKE OF LOWER MOOR.

COKE, THE REV. GEORGE, of Lower Moor House, co. Hereford, b. 8 Jan. 1797, rector of Aylton, in that shire; m. 21 Dec. 1825, Anne-Elizabeth, sister of the Rev. Francis Hodgson, late Provost of Eton, and only dau. of the Rev. James Hodgson, rector of Barwick, co. York, and by her (who d. in 1831) has issue,

I. GEORGE-FRANCIS, b. 15 Jan. 1830.
I. Anne-Elizabeth, m. 8 Aug. 1849, to the Rev. Henry-John Potts.
II. Lucy-Elizabeth-Hodgson.

Mr. Coke, who is a magistrate for Herefordshire, s. his father in 1831.

Lineage.—FRANCIS COKE, of Quistmoor and Lower Moor (the son of William, the vicar of Bosbury: *see* COKE *of Trusley*), m. Lucy, dau. of Thomas Coucher, of Parton, co. Hereford, and had issue by her one son and three daus. She d. in 1692; and he m. 2ndly, in 1725, Barbara Harper, widow, by whom he had no issue. Dying in June, 1750, at the age of 90, he was s. by his only son,

GEORGE COKE, who m. Elizabeth, dau. of Richard Bytheway, of the ancient family residing at Leintwardine, co. Hereford. He left at his decease (his widow dying 1 Sept. 1781, at the advanced age of 96) a son and successor,

RICHARD COKE, vicar of Eardisley, J.P., m. Jane, dau. of Jeremiah Griffiths, rector of Diserth, and dying 27 Dec. 1798, aged 75, left with three daus. (I. Elizabeth; II. Jane, m. to the Rev. James Hodgson, M.A. of Christchurch College, Oxford, and of Humber, co. Hereford; and III. Lucy), a son and successor,

THE REV. FRANCIS COKE, M.A., J.P., rector of Gladestry, co. Radnor, vicar of Sellack and Caple, co. Hereford, and prebendary of Hereford. He m. in 1791, Anne, dau. of Robert Whitcombe, Esq. of Kington, and d. in 1831, leaving

I. GEORGE, now of Lower Moor.
II. Robert, b. 2 Sept. 1801, m. in 1832, Isabella, only dau. of Walter Hill, Esq., formerly of Rocklands, co. Hereford.
III. William, B.A. of Trinity College, Cambridge, b. 2 Nov. 1803, perpetual curate of the parishes of Marstow and Pencoyd, co. Hereford.
IV. John, b. 17 Nov. 1806, major H.E.I.C.S.
I. Anne, m. in 1823, to Sir William-Sarsfield-Rossiter Cockburn, Bart.
II. Jane. III. Lucy, d. 21 Oct. 1841.

Arms, Crest, &c., as COKE *of Trusley*.
Seat—Lower Moor House, co. Hereford.

COKER OF BICESTER.

COKER, LEWIS, Esq. of Bicester, co. Oxford, J.P. and D.L., late major 29th regt., b. 24 July, 1820; m. 23 March, 1848, Caroline-Agnes, dau. of the late James Pitman, Esq. of Dunchideock House, co. Devon, and has issue,

I. LEWIS-EDMUND, b. 24 March, 1850.
I. Caroline-Charlotte. II. Isabella-Aubrey.
II. Florence-Wrey.

Lineage.—This ancient family dwelt in former ages at Coker, in Somersetshire, to which place they were beholden for their name.

ROBERT DE COCRE, the first of this line, was witness to a charter of Robert de Mandeville (*temp.* EDWARD I., A.D. 1272) concerning land at East Cocre.

JOHN COKER, b. in 1523 (2nd son, Robert Coker, of Mapouder, Dorsetshire, by Alice his wife, dau. of Robert Turges, of Melcombe Turges), purchased, in 1554, the manor of Nun's Place, or King's End, Bicester, co. Oxford, and became the founder of the Oxfordshire branch of the family. He d. in 1606, and was s. by his son,

CADWALLADER COKER, Esq. of Bicester, b. 1573, who dying in 1653, was s. by his son,

JOHN COKER, Esq. of Bicester, b. 1623, who d. in 1730, at the advanced age of 102 years, and was s. by his youngest and only surviving son,

THE REV. JOHN COKER, a canon of Salisbury Cathedral. He was b. in 1660, and dying in 1740, was s. by his sons,

JOHN COKER, b. in 1698, high-sheriff for the co. Oxford in 1750, who d. in 1766, and

THOMAS COKER, b. in 1705, d. 1799. On the death of Thomas, in 1799, the estate devolved upon

JOHN COKER (the eldest son of Cadwallader Coker, 3rd brother of the aforesaid John and Thomas, who had deceased in 1780, having m. Catherine, dau. of J. Savary, Esq. of

Marlborough). He *m.* in 1792, the Hon. Charlotte Marsham, youngest dau. of Robert, Lord Romney, by whom he had issue one dau., Charlotte-Priscilla, who *m.* in 1826, John Adams, serjeant-at-law, and assistant judge of the Middlesex sessions (*See* ADAMS *of Ansty Hall*). Mr. Coker was a fellow of New College, and, in 1798, was unanimously chosen colonel of the Oxford University Volunteers, and filled the office of chairman of the Oxfordshire Quarter Sessions from the year 1809 until his decease in January, 1819, when he was *s.* by his nephew,

THOMAS-LEWIS COKER, the eldest son of Cadwallader Coker, Esq., barrister-at-law (the 3rd son of the last-named Cadwallader), who *m.* Miss Clutterbuck. The said Thomas-Lewis was *b.* in 1791, and entering the army in 1808, served with distinction in Spain during the whole Peninsular war in the 29th regiment, and afterwards in America and Belgium. He left the army in 1819, and *m.* 28 July, 1819, Charlotte Aubrey, youngest dau. the late Lieut.-Col. Aubrey, by whom he had issue,

LEWIS, late major in the 29th regiment, and present possessor.
John, *b.* 28 July, 1521, in holy orders, and fellow of New College, Oxford.
Cadwallader, *b.* 27 Nov. 1824, in holy orders, *m.* 26 Aug 1852, Emily-Harriet, dau. of J. Gould, Esq. of Knapp, Devon, and has issue. Marianne-Charlotte.
Charlotte-Lydia, *m.* 18 Jan. 1855, to the Rev. Bolton Waller Johnstone, incumbent of Farndon, Cheshire.
Fanny, *m.* 30 Aug. 1849, to the Rev. Bulkeley-Owen Jones, M.A., and has issue, Fanny-Bulkeley.

He *d.* 6 Jan. 1849, and was *s.* by his eldest son.

Arms—Arg., on a bend, gu., three leopards' faces, or; in chief, a crescent, for difference.
Crest—A Moor's head, side-faced, wreathed, arg. and gu.
Motto—Fiat justitia.
Seat—Bicester House, Oxfordshire.

COLCLOUGH OF TINTERNE ABBEY.

COLCLOUGH, JOHN-THOMAS-ROSSBOROUGH, Esq. of Tinterne Abbey, co. Wexford, *m.* 12 Jan. 1848, Mary-Grey-Wentworth, dau. and heir of Cæsar Colclough, Esq., chief-justice of Prince Edward's Island, and of Newfoundland, and assumed, in consequence of succeeding, through his wife, to the estates of the late Cæsar Colclough, Esq., the surname and arms of COLCLOUGH, by royal license, 3 June, 1853. He has issue.

Lineage.—The Visitation of Staffordshire shews this family to have been of consideration in that county before it became eminent in Ireland.

RICHARD COLCLOUGH, living 40th EDWARD III., had issue, three sons. The eldest,

HUGH COLCLOUGH, granted Blurton and Cockenidge to his son (48th EDWARD III.), by name

RICHARD COLCLOUGH, who lived in 7th HENRY V., and *m.* Elizabeth, dau. of John Delves.

JOHN COLCLOUGH, whose relationship to the above is not given, had a son and heir,

THOMAS COLCLOUGH, living 11th and 22nd HENRY VI., who had

RICHARD COLCLOUGH, mayor of Newcastle-under-Lyne, *anno* 18th EDWARD IV., who *m.* Blanche, dau. of William Davenport, of Davenport, Cheshire, Esq., and had a son,

JOHN COLCLOUGH, of Blurton, Staffordshire, 1st EDWD. V. He *m.* Agnes, dau. and heir of Lockwood, and left two sons,

RICHARD, his heir.
Thomas, who had Delfe House, *alias* High Haugh, by gift of his father, dated 19th February, 14th HENRY VIII.

The elder,

RICHARD COLCLOUGH, Esq. of Wolstanton, or Yolverton, in Staffordshire, *m.* Eleanor, dau. of Sir John Draycote, of Payneeley, Knt., by whom he had issue.

ANTHONY COLCLOUGH, Esq. of Blorton, Staffordshire, in 1566, son and successor, was captain of the band of pensioners to Queen ELIZABETH, and was granted the abbey and lands of Tinterne, in the co. Wexford. He came first into Ireland in the year 1542, and was knighted by the lord justice of that kingdom 7 Sept. 1569. Sir Anthony *d.* 9 Dec. 1584. His wife was Clare, dau. of Thomas Agard, Esq., and by her, who *m.* 2ndly, Sir Thomas Williams, Knt., who *d.* a prisoner in the Tower of London, Sir Anthony had issue, seven sons and four daus. The eldest surviving son,

SIR THOMAS COLCLOUGH, Knt. of Tinterne Abbey, Wexford, *b.* 1564. He *m.* Martha, 4th dau. of Adam Loftus, archbishop of Dublin, and by her, who *d.* 19 March, 1609, he had issue,

I. ADAM (Sir), Bart. of Tinterne Abbey, *b.* 1600, created a BARONET in 1628: he *m.* Alice, dau. of Sir Robert Rich, Knt., a Master in Chancery in England, and dying 4 April, 1634, left issue,

CÆSAR (Sir), his heir.
Anthony, of Rathlin, co. Wexford, a member of the supreme council at Kilkenny in 1642, *m.* Ismay Browne, of Mulrankan Hall, co. Wexford.

The eldest son,

SIR CÆSAR COLCLOUGH, 2nd Bart. of Tinterne Abbey, *b.* 1624, *m.* Frances, dau. of Sir William Clarke, Bart., of Thame Oxfordshire, who *d.* before him. He *d.* 22 June, 1684, having had a son and dau., viz.,

CÆSAR (Sir).
Margaret, who became heiress to her brother. She *m.* 1st, Robert Leigh, Esq. of Rosgarland, co. Wexford, who took the name of COLCLOUGH; and 2ndly, John Pigot, Esq. of Kilfinny, Limerick, who also assumed the name of COLCLOUGH. She *d.* in 1722, leaving an only child, Elizabeth, *m.* in 1695, to Richard Warburton, Esq. of Garryhinch, and was *s.* in the manor of Tinterne by her heir-at-law, Colonel CÆSAR COLCLOUGH, of Duffry Hall.

Sir Cæsar *d.* 22 June, 1684, and was *s.* by his only son,

SIR CÆSAR COLCLOUGH, 3rd Bart. of Tinterne Abbey, deputy-lieut.-governor of the co. of Kilkenny, at whose decease (22 Sept. 1687) the Baronetcy became EXTINCT.

II. Thomas, *d.* before March, 1609.
III. John, *m.* Catherine, dau. of Walter, son and heir of Richard Synnott, Esq. of Ballybrennan, and Rosgarland Hall, M.P. for the co. of Wexford in 1559, by whom he had,

Mary, *m.* James Butler, Esq. of Clough, in the co. of Wexford.
Martha, *m.* Thomas Cullen, Esq. of Cullenstown, in the co. of Wexford.
Clara, a nun.

IV. Richard. V. Leonard.
I. Anne, *m.* Nicholas, grandson and heir of Sir Nicholas Bagenal, Knt. of Dunleckny, in the co. of Carlow; 2ndly, Sir Thomas Butler, Bart. of Garryhundon, or Clough-grenane.
II. Jane, *m.* John Wogan, Esq. of Weston, in Pembrokeshire.
III. Martha, *m.* John Piggott, of The Desert, Queen's County, Esq., eldest son of Sir Robert Piggott, Knt.
IV. Mary, *m.* Sir Nicholas Walsh, Knt., jun., of Ballycarrigmore, co. Waterford.
V. Eleanor, *m.* Bryan Kavanagh, Esq. of Polemonty and Borris, co. Carlow, chief of his nation.

Sir Thomas *m.* 2ndly, Elinor, 2nd dau. of Dudley Bagenal, Esq. of Dunleckny, co. of Carlow, 2nd son of Sir Nicholas Bagenal, Knt. of Newry, marshal of Queen ELIZABETH'S armies in Ireland. She *m.* again (as 3rd wife), Luke Plunkett, 1st Earl of Fingall, and Nov. 1632. Sir Thomas Colclough *d.* 23 Aug. 1624, and was buried at Tinterne Abbey, leaving by his 2nd wife,

I. DUDLEY (Sir), of whom presently.
II. Anthony, *m.* Mary, dau. of William Esmonde, Esq. of Johnstown Castle, co. Wexford, knight of the shire for that county in 1634, by whom he had,

Adam, of Gray's Inn, London, *m.* Mary, dau. of Colonel Blague, groom of the chamber to CHARLES II. She was maid of honour to the Duchess of York, and the lady celebrated by Grammont, for "ses paupières blondes."
Cæsar, of Rosgarland, which he rented from the Leigh family, its possessors since the restoration of CHARLES II. Mr. Colclough's will, dated 24 April, 1724, was proved 1726.

III. John, living 1642.
I. Mabel, *d.* young.

DUDLEY COLCLOUGH, Esq. of Mochary, co. Wexford, eldest son of Sir Thomas Colclough, Knt. of Tinterne Abbey, by Elinor his 2nd wife, *m.* Catherine, dau. of Patrick Esmond, Esq. of Johnstown, co. Wexford, and had a son and successor,

PATRICK COLCLOUGH, Esq. of Mochary, who *m.* Catherine, dau. of Walter Bagenal, Esq. of Dunkleckny, co. Carlow, and was father of

DUDLEY COLCLOUGH, Esq. of Mochary, who *m.* Mary, dau. of the Hon. Francis Barnewall, 4th son of Nicholas, Viscount Kingsland, and had, with other issue, a son and successor,

CÆSAR COLCLOUGH, Esq. of Mochary, *b.* in 1694, who *s.* to Tinterne Abbey by entail. He *m.* 1st, in 1718, Frances, dau. of Sir Thos. Vesey, Bart., bishop of Ossory, and had by her issue, who *d.* young. He *m.* 2ndly, in 1721, Henrietta, dau. of Agmondisham Vesey, Esq. of Lucan, co. Dublin, and by her, who *d.* in 1771, had issue,

I. VESEY, his heir.
II. Agmondisham-Vesey, captain in the army, *d. unm.* 1758.

III. Adam, of Cloghjordan and Duffery Hall, co. Wexford, J.P., m. Mary-Anne, dau. of John Byrne, Esq. of Cabinteely, co. Dublin, and left issue,
Cæsar, barrister-at-law, chief-justice of Prince Edward's Island and of Newfoundland, m. 27 Oct. 1804, Susan, dau. of James Leech, Esq. of St. James's, and d. 10 Feb. 1822, leaving issue, Louisa-Ponsonby, who d. unm. 25 May, 1833, and Mary-Grey-Wentworth, m. 12 Jan. 1848, to JOHN-THOMAS ROSSBOROUGH, Esq., the present proprietor of Tinterne Abbey.
Dudley, in holy orders, m. Mary Gaven, and had issue, Cæsar and Agmondisham.
Patrick-Sarsfield, of Annville, co. Carlow, m. Margaret, dau. of Patrick Colclough, Esq., and had Patrick-Sarsfield, of Woodbrook, co. Wexford, and other issue,
IV. Adam, Bart., d. s. p.

Cæsar Colclough, colonel in the army, and M.P. for the co. of Wexford, 1726, d. 15 April, 1766, and was s. by his son,

VESEY COLCLOUGH, Esq. of Mochary, who d. 31 Jan. 1744-5, leaving by Mary his wife, dau. of Sir John Bingham, Bart. of Castlebar, and widow of Hugh Montgomery, Esq., a son and heir,

VESEY COLCLOUGH, Esq. of Tinterne Abbey, M.P., co. Wexford, b. 2 July, 1745, who m. 2 Aug. 1765, Catharine, dau. of John Grogan, Esq. of Johnstown, co. Wexford, and had issue,

CÆSAR, his heir.
John, killed in a duel, 1807, unm., M.P. for co. Wexford.
Vesey, d. young.

Vesey Colclough d. 8 July, 1794, and was s. by his son,

CÆSAR COLCLOUGH, Esq. of Tinterne Abbey, M.P., co. Wexford, who m. 3 Nov. 1818, Jane, dau. of John Kirwan, Esq., and by her (who m. 2ndly, Thomas Boyce, Esq. of Bannow) had no issue. He d. in 1842.

Arms—Arg., five eaglets displayed in cross, sa., quartering, for ROSSBOROUGH, az., on a chevron, or, three roses, gu.
Crest—For COLCLOUGH, a demi-eagle, displayed, sa., gorged with a ducal coronet, or.; for ROSSBOROUGH; on a dexter hand in fesse, a dove, close, with a branch of olive in his beak, all ppr.
Seat—Tinterne Abbey, co. Wexford.

COLDHAM OF ANMER HALL.

COLDHAM, HENRY-WALTER, Esq. of Anmer Hall, co. Norfolk, J.P. and D.L., b. 14 Oct. 1787; m. 6 Nov. 1834, Maria, 2nd dau. of E.-R. Pratt, Esq. of Ryston, and has issue surviving,

I. HENRY-JAMES, b. 9 Dec. 1839.
I. Maria-Elizabeth. II. Lucy-Harriet.

Lineage.—The COLDHAMS *of Anmer* are, most likely, from the exact similitude of arms they bear, descended from the COLDHAMS *of Midhurst*, Sussex, whose pedigree is to be found in the Visitation of that county.

JOHN COLDHAM, Esq. of Anmer, son of JAMES COLDHAM, who was the first that presented to the living of Anmer, A.D. 1704, m. Rachel, dau. of the Rev. William Houghton, of Anmer, and was father of

JOHN COLDHAM, Esq. of Anmer, who m. Elizabeth Hales, and had a son and heir,

JAMES COLDHAM, Esq. of Anmer, b. in 1759, who m. 1 March, 1783, Elizabeth, dau. of Walter Wright, Esq. of Bury St. Edmunds, and had issue,

I. HENRY-WALTER, present representative.
II. John, b. 22 March, 1790, m. 1st, in Aug. 1816, Anna, eldest dau. of Charles Blackley, Esq., by whom he had five sons and five daus. He m. 2ndly, Catherine, dau. of the Rev. E. North.
III. George, b. 1 April, 1804, in holy orders, rector of Gaytonthorpe, m. 2 Jan. 1832, Mary-Anna, eldest dau. of Sir Charles-M. Clarke, Bart. of Dunham Lodge, co. Norfolk, and has issue, a son and three daus.
I. Elizabeth.
II. Harriet, m. 28 May, 1816, to the Rev. George Mason, of Notts, and has three sons and two daus.

Arms—Az., a mullet, arg., pierced, gu.
Crest—A griffin's head, couped, pierced through by an arrow.
Motto—In cœlo quies.
Seat—Anmer Hall, near Lynn, co. Norfolk.

COLE OF TWICKENHAM.

COLE, EDWARD-HENRY, Esq. of Twickenham, co. Middlesex, and Stoke Lyne, co. Oxford, m. Mary-Letitia, dau. of Henry Brooke, late Lord Congleton, and widow of Lord Henry-Seymour Moore, who d. in 1825. By her Mr. Cole has,

I. EDWARD; and other issue.

Lineage.—The Cole family has been seated at Twickenham, in Middlesex, for several generations, and may be found in the church registers as early as 1584. Previous to the usurpation of CROMWELL, the Coles possessed nearly the whole place; and there is a fine monument of them in Petersham Church, erected in 1624.

One branch of the family was elevated to the rank of Baronet, in 1640.

The late THOMAS-REA COLE, Esq., major 98th regiment, eldest son of Stephen Cole, Esq. of Twickenham, by Frances his wife, dau. of William Laremar, of Knightsbridge, m. in 1764, Isabella, eldest dau. of Sir Henry Ibbotson, Bart., and s. in her right, to the estates in Oxfordshire, of Alice, Countess of Shipbrook, only dau. of Samuel Ibbetson, Esq. of Denton Park, elder brother of Sir Henry. Major Cole had issue,

STEPHEN-THOMAS, his heir.
Henry, father of OWEN-BLAYNEY COLE, Esq. of Brandrum, co. Monaghan.
Harriet, m. to Captain William Tudor.

Major Cole d. in 1807, and was s. by his son,

STEPHEN-THOMAS COLE, Esq. of Stoke Lyne, co. Oxford, and Twickenham, co. Middlesex, b. 26 April, 1765, m. 15 Jan. 1795, Lady Elizabeth-Henrietta Stanley, 2nd dau. of Edward, 12th Earl of Derby, and had issue,

EDWARD, now of Twickenham.
George-Beauchamp, deputy-lieut. for Middlesex, m. Julia, dau. of Col. Espinasse.
Mowbray, an officer in the army, settled at the Cape, m. a German lady of rank, and has issue.
Burton-Stanley.
Elizabeth, m. to Frederick Lee, Esq.
Catherine, m. 16 March, 1837, to Walter Frederick Campbell, of Islay, Esq., M.P.

Mr. Cole d. 6 April, 1835.

Arms—Arg., a bull, passant, gu., armed, or, within a bordure, sa., bezantée.
Crest—A demi-gryphon, holding an arrow, headed, or, and feathered, arg.
Motto—Deum cole, regem serva.
Seat—Twickenham, Middlesex.

COLE OF BRANDRUM.

COLE, OWEN-BLAYNEY, Esq. of Brandrum, co. Monaghan, D.L., m. 25 Aug. 1834, Lady Frances-Isabella Monck, 2nd dau. of Henry Stanley, late Earl of Rathdowne, and has issue,

I. FRANCIS-BURTON-OWEN, b. 1 May, 1838.
I. Frances-Elizabeth-Owen.
II. Henrietta-Stanley-Owen.

This gentleman and his sisters, Eliza-Ibbetson, wife of J. Metge, Esq. of Athlumny, co. Meath, and Henrietta-Isabella, wife of the Rev. John Finlay, are the children of the late Henry Cole, Esq., and Jane-Elizabeth his wife, 3rd dau. and co-heir of John Owen, Esq. of Raconnell, co. Monaghan, the descendant of Nicholas Owen, of Reswasta, co. Montgomery.

For COLE lineage, see COLE *of Twickenham*.

Arms—Arg., within a bordure, sa., bezantée, a bull, gu.; and for augmentation, on a canton, erm., a nag's head, ppr., over which, on a chief, or, three estoiles, arg.
Crest—A demi-dragon, vert, bearing in its dexter paw a javelin, armed, or, feathered, arg.
Motto—Deum cole, regem serva.
Seat—Brandrum, co. Monaghan.

COLE OF HOLYBOURN.

COLE, ROBERT, Esq. of Holybourn Lodge, Hants, J.P. and D.L., F.L.S., m. in 1817, Maria, dau. and heir of Henry Wilding, Esq.

Lineage.—This family claims descent from the very ancient house of COLLE or COLE *of Shrewsbury*, there settled *temp.* King STEPHEN. Nicholas Colle appears on the roll of the guild of Shrewsbury, 1209, and his descendant Thomas Cole sat in parliament as M.P. for that town in 1337 and 1341. In 17 HENRY VIII., WILLIAM COLE, Esq. of Shrewsbury, is included among the "lords, knights, esquires, and gentlemen, resydent in the county of Salop." His son, EDMUND COLE, Esq. M.P., and four times bailiff for Shrewsbury, bore a coat of arms of eight quarterings.

ROBERT COLE, b. in 1715, a lineal descendant of this old and influential Shrewsbury family, settled in the Isle of Wight, and purchased the Rue Street estate, in the parish of Northwood: he m. 26 Feb. 1754, Mary Packford, and d. 27 Dec. 1786, leaving issue:

I. ROBERT, of Newport, Isle of Wight, banker, capt. of the Niton Infantry, *m.* Elizabeth, dau. of Henry Dennett, Esq., of Newport, and *d.* 14 Sept. 1818, leaving four sons and seven daus.; of the daus., the eldest, Eliza, *m.* Chas. Jolliffe, Esq., the 2nd, Mary, Lieut. Jenour; the 3rd, Jane, James Harvey, Esq., the 5th, Amelia, Capt. Hyde; and the 7th, Louisa, W. Hall, M.D., of Wareham: the sons were ROBERT; Henry, H.E.I.C.S.; William, lieut. 67th regt., *d.* 1833; and James-George, also deceased. The eldest, ROBERT COLE, Esq., lieut.-col. in the army, *m.* Mary-Eden, dau. of G.-R.-P. Jarvis, Esq., of Doddington Hall, co. Lincoln, and has surviving issue, ROBERT-EDEN-GEORGE, of University College, Oxford, *b.* 1831, William Gordon; and Anne-Henrietta.

II. William, of Rue Street, *m.* Margaret, dau. and heir of Cornelius Cornock, Esq., of Pembrokeshire, and *d.* in 1801, leaving three sons,

1 CORNELIUS CORNOCK, of Pembrokeshire, *m.* Charlotte, dau. of Henry Roach, Esq. of Ridway, and has five sons and three daus., viz., Cornelius-Cornock; John-Jones, H.E.I.C.S., *m.* Judith-Marcella, dau. of Capt. Fraser, and has issue; Henry, *m.* Ellen, dau. of Capt. Charles Copp, H.E.I.C.S., and has issue; William; Robert-Octavius; Margaret; Charlotte; Maria, *m.* to Charles, son of William-Dutton Pollard, Esq. of Castle Pollard.

2 William, now of Pembrokeshire.

3 ROBERT, now of Holybourn Lodge.

III. James, of Chiverton, lieut. of the West Medina troop of cavalry, *b.* 1768, *m.* Sarah, dau. of Henry Dennett, Esq. of Newport, and *d.* 23 Jan. 1816, leaving issue,

1 James, of Tapnell, *m.* Louisa, 3rd dau. of Brown Hearne, Esq. of Fulford, and *d.* 6 June, 1831, leaving James (*m.* and has issue); Henry-Hearne, of the United States; William; and Mary.

2 Henry-Dennett, of Carisbrooke, *b.* 14 Jan. 1797, *m.* Anne, 2nd dau. of Brown Hearne, Esq. of Fulford, and had issue two surviving daus., Anne and Eliza-Sarah; and sons, viz.,

HENRY-DENNETT, of Bucknowle House, Dorset, *b.* 27 Oct. 1820, *m.* 20 Oct. 1847, Emma-Maria, dau. of John Cooke, Esq. of Bellcroft House, Isle of Wight, and has issue.

Alfred, *b.* 9 Dec. 1824.

Constantine, *b.* 30 Dec. 1825, *m.* 10 June, 1850, Sarah-Anne-Catherine, dau. of Colonel Charles-Fitzgerald Mackenzie, 60th royal rifles, and niece of the late Sir Colin Mackenzie, Bart.

James-William, of the United States, *b.* 1827.

Charles-Newnham, *b.* 24 June, 1828.

Clarence-Hearne, physician, United States, *d. s. p.* 15 Jan. 1852.

Septimus, *b.* 1832. Octavus-Dennett, *d.* 1844.

John-Arnold, *b.* 1838.

1 Mary-Anne, *m.* to John Arnold, Esq. of Rushville, Indiana.

I. Elizabeth, *m.* 1st, to Patrick Barry, and 2ndly, to Osmond Johnson, Esq.

II. Mary, *m.* Thomas Glud, Esq. of Priory, Isle of Wight, and had issue, Thomas; Mary, *m.* to Edward Roberts, Esq.; Fanny, *m.* to Malcolm Mac Gregor, H.B.M. consul at Panama; and Anne, *m.* to Charles-Cornwall-Cecil Worsley, Esq.

III. Anne, *m.* to James Cantelo, Esq., and had two daus., Jane, *m.* to Captain Roberts; and Amelia, *m.* to Major-Gen. George-Stracey Smyth, lieut.-governor of New Brunswick.

IV. Grace, *m.* to Mc Arthur, Esq.

Arms—Arg., a chevron, gu., between three scorpions reversed, sa.

Crest—A naked arm holding a scorpion, ppr., armed, or.

Motto—"Deum cole, regem serva," or "Esto quod esse videris."

Seat—Holybourn Lodge, Alton.

COLE OF MARAZION.

COLE, FRANCIS-SEWELL, Esq. of Childown, Chertsey, co. Surrey, *b.* 15 Oct. 1817.

Lineage.—This family has been long settled in the counties of Devon and Cornwall. Of the Cornish branch of the family were Catherine, *m.* 9 March, 1671, to William Davies, Esq. of Boswergy, in St. Erth (his 1st wife), and HUMPHREY COLE, of Perran, who was father of Philippa, who *d.* in 1730, and of

FRANCIS COLE, who *m.* Hester, dau. of William Davis, Esq. of Boswergy in St. Erth, by his wife, Catherine, dau. of Humphrey Noye, of Carnanton, and Hester his wife, sister of Lord Sandys of The Vine, and a descendant of Thomas, father of Henry Chichele, founder of All Souls' College, Oxon. Francis Cole *d.* in June, 1769, leaving a son,

HUMPHREY COLE, *m.* in 1754, Phillis, dau. of Francis Maugham, Esq. She *d.* in 1800, aged 67. He *d.* in 1777, aged 42, leaving eleven children, I. Humphrey, major in the army, *d.* in Jamaica, aged 40; II. John, D.D., rector of Exeter College, Oxford, and vice-chancellor of that University, *d. unm.* aged 63, in 1819; III. FRANCIS; IV. Henry, *d.* in 1826, aged 46; V. Samuel, D.D., senior chaplain of Greenwich Hospital, *d.* in 1838, aged 71, leaving issue, by his wife, Jane, dau. of John Griffith, Esq., a judge in India, an only child, John-Griffith Cole, Esq.; VI. Christopher, (Sir), post-captain R.N., colonel of royal marines, K.C.B., and M.P. for Glamorganshire, *m.* Mary, dau. of Henry, 2nd Earl of Ilchester, and widow of T.-M. Talbot, Esq. of Margam. Sir C. Cole distinguished himself by the capture of Banda, and *d.* without issue, in 1836, aged 68; I. Philippa, *d. unm.* in 1824, aged 70; II. Amy, *m.* Major Creswell, of the royal marines, and *d.* in 1807, aged 45, leaving an only child, John, R.N.; III. Catherine, *d.* in 1845, aged 72, *unm.*; IV. Frances, *m.* to Peter Boover, Esq., post-captain R.N., *d.* in 1811, aged 46; V. Harriett, *d. unm.* in 1807, aged 31. The 3rd son,

FRANCIS COLE, captain R.N., *m.* Honor, dau. of John Keir, Esq., of the family of KEIR *of Kindrogan*, in Perthshire, *d.* in 1798, aged 38, leaving issue, I. FRANCIS-HAWKINS; I. Honor, *m.* to William Cornish, Esq. of Marazion; II. Mary-Ellis, *m.* to J.-A. Stevens, Esq., post-captain R.N. The son and heir,

THE REV. FRANCIS-HAWKINS COLE, *m.* Elizabeth Blake, dau. of Thomas-Bailey-Heath Sewell, by his wife Elizabeth, eldest dau. and co-heiress of Thomas, Earl of Louth, and 24th Baron Athenry, Premier Baron of Ireland. By his wife, who *d.* in 1828, the Rev. F.-H. Cole has two children,

FRANCIS-SEWELL, now of Childown.

Louisa, *m.* in 1841, to Luther Watson, Esq. of Calgarth, Westmorland, grandson of Dr. Watson, Bishop of Llandaff, and has issue, four daus.

The Rev. F.-H. Cole *m.* 2ndly, in 1831, Elizabeth, dau. of the late James Ewing, Esq., by whom he had no issue.

Arms—Erm., a bull, passant, sa., thereon three annulets, or, within a bordure of the second, charged with annulets and bezants, of the third.

Crest—A semi-dragon, with a dart in hand.

Motto—Deum cole, regem serva.

Seat—Childown, Chertsey.

COLES OF DITCHAM.

COLES, THE REV. JOHN, of Ditcham Park, in the cos. of Hants and Sussex, J.P., *m.* 1st, Marianne-Goodhead, dau. of Captain Rogers, R.N.; and 2ndly, Lucy, relict of Robert-James Harrison, Esq., captain in the Royal Horse-guards Blue. By his 1st wife (who *d.* in 1832) he has issue,

I. JOSIAS-ROGERS-JOHN.

II. Henry-Thomas. III. Cowper-Phipps.

IV. Richard-George, *m.* Fanny, dau. of John Morris, Esq. of Halifax, Nova Scotia.

I. Marianne, who *d.* in 1840.

II. Augusta, *d.* 1847.

III. Emily-Frances, *m.* to Geoffrey-Phipps Hornby, Esq., captain R.N., son of Admiral Sir Phipps Hornby, K.C.B., of Little Green, Sussex.

Lineage.—The grant of the estate of Ditcham, was in the 35th of HENRY VIII., to John Cowper, and Margaret his wife. In 1550, Major Cowper, one of his descendants, was slain in the service of CHARLES I., at Winchester.

WALTER COLES, of Polborough, Esq., *m.* Catherine Cowper, 2nd dau. of Richard and Joan Cowper, and left a son,

JOHN COLES, in whom the families of Cowper and Coles were united, and who *s.* to the estates of Richard Cowper, the last male heir of the Cowpers, who *d.* in 1767. He left issue, Frances-Elizabeth-Catherine; and

CHARLES COLES, who *s.* to the estates on the death of his father. He *m.* Frances-Elizabeth, dau. of Richard Barwell, of Chartrey Abbey, Surrey, Esq., and left issue,

CHARLES-BARWELL.

JOHN, the present possessor of Ditcham Park.

William-Cowper, colonel in the army, *m.* Anne, dau. of G.-S. Butler, Esq.

Frances-Elizabeth, *m.* to Colonel Tadd.

Seat—Ditcham Park.

COLES OF PARROCKS LODGE.

COLES, JAMES-BENJAMIN, Esq. of Parrocks Lodge, co. Somerset, J.P. and D.L., *b.* 28 Sept. 1784; *m.*

5 May, 1807, Mary, 2nd dau. of William Weekes, Esq. of Taunton, and has issue,

I. JAMES-STRATTON, J.P., in holy orders, rector of Shipton Beauchamp, co. Somerset.
II. William-Gale.
I. Mary-Weekes, m. 22 July, 1828, to the Rev. Hugh Speke, M.A., of Wakehill, Somerset.
II. Sarah-Frances, m. 25 Feb. 1834, to Cornish Henley, Esq. III. Hester-Elizabeth.

Lineage.—HENRY COLES, Esq., son of Nicholas Coles, Esq., by Bridget his wife, was, by Margaret his wife, father of another

HENRY COLES, Esq., who m. in 1714, Honour, dau. of the Rev. Avery Thompson, rector of Steeple Ashton, and by her (who m. 2ndly, John Cook, Esq. of Trowbridge) had two sons, JAMES and Henry, and a dau., Margaret. The elder son,

JAMES COLES, Esq., m. 7 June, 1744, Hester, dau. of Edward Shrapnell, Esq., and had, with a dau., Hester, three sons, JAMES, John, and Richard, of whom

JAMES COLES, Esq., m. 24 Aug. 1779, Elizabeth, dau. of Thomas Stratten, Esq. of The Grove, Hackney, co. Middlesex, by whom he had issue, JAMES-BENJAMIN, now of Parrocks Lodge.

Arms—Arg., a bull, gu., within a bordure, sa., bezantée.
Crest—Out of a ducal coronet, or, a demi-dragon, vert, holding an arrow of the first, headed and feathered, arg.
Motto—Nemo sibi nascitur.
Seat—Parrock's Lodge, co. Somerset.

COLGRAVE OF DOWNSELL HALL.

COLGRAVE, WILLIAM, Esq. of Downsell Hall and Cann Hall, co. Essex, and of Bracebridge and Mere Hall, co. Lincoln, formerly a major in the army, b. 24 Feb. 1788; m. 12 June, 1810, Catherine-Anne-Sarah, eldest dau. of the late General John Fraser, G.C.H., colonel of the Royal York Rangers, and has,

I. JOHN-WILLIAM-MANBY, b. 20 Oct. 1811; m. 28 Sept. 1835, Louisa-Maria, only dau. of the late — Isaac, Esq., and has issue.
II. William-Manby, b. 29 March, 1819; m. 4 Aug. 1841, Eleanor, 2nd dau. of the late Charles Walmesley, Esq. of Westwood House, co. Lancaster, and has issue.
III. Francis-Edward, b. 23 Sept. 1824; m. 15 July, 1847, Mary-Elizabeth, eldest dau. of Robert-Bruce Chichester, Esq.
I. Everilda-Henrietta.
II. Catherine-Frances-Eleanora.
III. Isabella-Frances-Sarah, m. 11 June, 1838, to Eben-William, only surviving son of Francis Robertson, Esq. of Chilcote, co. Derby.

Major Colgrave assumed, by royal license, 16 Feb. 1819, in pursuance of the will of his great-uncle, William Colgrave, Esq., his present surname, in lieu of his patronymic, MANBY.

Lineage.—SIR WILLIAM MANBY, Knt., living *temp.* EDWARD III. (son of ROBERT MANBY, by his wife, the dau. of Sir John Gastinbridge, Knt., grandson of JOHN DE MANBY, and his wife, the dau. of Sir John Boys, Knt., and grandson of PETRONELLUS DE MANBY, Lord of Manby, co. Lincoln), m. Alice, dau. and heir of Alan Malkake, Lord of Elsham, co. Lincoln, and by her was lineal ancestor of the distinguished family of MANBY *of Lincolnshire.*

ROBERT MANBY, of Walmsgate and Wragby, co. Lincoln, entered his pedigree at the Visitation in 1634. His son,

THOMAS MANBY, Esq., sometime of Lincoln's Inn, purchased the manor and estate of Downsell Hall, in the parish of South Weald, co. Essex, 10 Oct. 1660, and was father of

SIR THOMAS MANBY, Knt. of Downsell Hall, knighted at Whitehall, 25 May, 1686, high-sheriff of Essex in 1688; who m. 1st, 1683, Juliana, dau. and co-heir of Sir George Selby, Bart. of White House, co. Durham, and of Dawley, co. Middlesex, and by her had, FRANCIS, his heir, of whom presently. He m. 2ndly, 1694, Elizabeth, dau. of Sir George Cary, Knt. of Torr Abbey, co. Devon, and by her (who was buried 24 May, 1726) had two sons, Robert, of Lincoln's Inn, m. Mary Cary, and d. s. p. in 1737; and Edward. Sir Thomas d. 21 Aug. 1729, aged 75, and was s. by his eldest son,

FRANCIS MANBY, Esq. of Downsell Hall, b. about 1684; who m. 1728, Anne Hickins, and by her (who d. 16 Feb. 1757) had issue, 1 FRANCIS, his heir; 2 THOMAS, successor to his brother; 1 Frances, m. to John Petre, Esq. of Bell House, co. Essex; 2 Catherine; 3 Anne, d. unm.; 4 Mary, m. 31 Aug. 1762, to William Colgrave, of Cann Hall, co. Essex, who d. 27 April, 1798: she d. s. p. 4 Feb. 1810. Mr. Manby d. 14 June, 1755, and was s. by his eldest son,

FRANCIS MANBY, Esq. of Downsell Hall, b. in 1732; who m. in 1761, Mary, dau. of Anthony Wright, Esq., banker; but dying without surviving issue, 2 March, 1780, was s. by his brother,

THOMAS MANBY, Esq. of Downsell Hall, who m. Anne, dau. of William Colgrave, Esq. of Cann Hall, and sister of William Colgrave and Robert Colgrave, Esqs. of Cann Hall, who d. s. p. 1801. By this lady Mr. Manby had issue,

I. JOHN, his heir.
II. Francis, who m. Isabella, dau. of Thomas Hurnall, Esq. of London, and d. 13 Dec. 1794, having had by her (who m. 2ndly, — Gawthorpe, of Hull),
  1 WILLIAM, successor to his uncle, and present representative.
  2 Richard, d. an infant.
  1 Bridget, m. in 1818, to John Davies, Esq. of Berbice.
I. Catherine, m. 16 Aug. 1795, to Richard Walmesley, Esq.
II. Frances, m. 1st, 6 Feb. 1797, to Mark-Anthony Browne, last Viscount Montague; and 2ndly, to Henry Slaughter, Esq. of Kingsdown, near Bristol.
III. Anne, m. April, 1799, to Philip Hughes, Esq., lieut.-col. royal engineers.

Mr. Manby d. in 1786, and was s. by his elder son,

JOHN MANBY, Esq. of Downsell Hall, who m. Harriott-Maria Cliff, of Brigg, co. Lincoln; but d. s. p. 5 Jan. 1819, and was s. by his nephew, WILLIAM, who is the present WILLIAM COLGRAVE, Esq. of Downsell Hall and Cann Hall.

Arms—COLGRAVE and MANBY, quarterly.
Seats—Downsell Hall, and Cann Hall, co. Essex.

COLLING OF RED HALL.

COLLING, ROBERT, Esq. of Red Hall, co. Durham, J.P., major North York rifle regiment of militia, b. 7 July, 1789; m. 25 Oct. 1825, Elizabeth, dau. of the late Lieut.-Col. Gordon Skelly, of Pilmore House, co. Durham.

Lineage.—MAJOR COLLING, the eldest son, by Margaret Hutton his wife, of the late Robert Colling, Esq. of Red Hall, who d. 23 July, 1824, descends paternally, through a series of ancestors bearing the Christian name of Robert, from Robert Colling, Esq., who purchased, in 1698, the estate of Red Hall, previously the property of the Lambtons, Chaytors, and Killinghalls. Maternally, Major Colling claims descent from the ancient Sovereigns of Wales. He has two surviving brothers and two sisters, viz.,

JOHN, b. 3 Dec. 1797; m. 10 May, 1831, Elizabeth, only dau. of Ambrose Weston, Esq. of London, and has three sons and one dau.
THOMAS, b. 25 May, 1802.
Margaret. Elizabeth.

Arms—Per pale, vert and gu., a griffin, segreant, or.
Seat—Red Hall, near Darlington.

COLLINGS OF GUERNSEY.

COLLINGS, BONAMY, Esq. of Guernsey, b. 30 Aug. 1814; m. 13 Aug. 1850, Elizabeth-Durell, dau. of Charles d'Auvergne, Esq., and has issue,

I. JOHN-BONAMY, b. 30 July, 1851.
II. Charles-d'Auvergne, b. 12 Sept. 1852.

Lineage.—EDWARD COLLINGS, elder son of Thomas Collings, of Ansford, co. Somerset, and of Jersey, b. in 1712, settled in Guernsey; m. Ann, dau. of Andrew Smith, Esq. of Limerick, Ireland, and had (with two daus, Ann, b. in 1742, m. to Nicholas Corbin, Esq.; and Sarah, b. in 1749, who m. John Lukis, Esq. of The Grange, and d. in 1816) two sons, Edward, b. in 1740, who m. Ann Barbier, and had issue; and

JOHN COLLINGS, b. in 1745; who m. Margaret, dau. of Philip Mauger, of Saints, in the island of Guernsey, descended from Jacques Mauger, who obtained from King HENRY V. the distinguished honour of adding to his family arms the cross of St. George. The said John had issue, viz.,

I. JOHN, b. 1777; m. 20 Nov. 1810, Mary Bonamy; colonel of the royal artillery, Guernsey Militia; and 11 Oct. 1841, leaving,
  1 BONAMY, present head of the family.
  2 Alfred-Smith, a jurat of the Royal Court; b. in 1816; who m. 16 Aug. 1844, Matilda-Lukis, dau. of Joseph Collings, Esq., and has issue.

3 Peter-Bonamy, *b.* in 1821; M.A., in holy orders; *m.* 16 Nov. 1852, Elizabeth-Jane, only dau. of John Jackson Bird, Esq. of Boughton Monchelsea, Kent.

1 Eliza-Margaret, *b.* in 1812; *d.* in 1832.

II. William (Sir), Knt., *b.* 20 May, 1781; *m.* 1811, Margaret, dau. of John Lukis, Esq. of The Grange, in the island of Guernsey, is a colonel of the Royal Guernsey Militia. In 1822, he was appointed a jurat of the royal court, and received the honour of knighthood, 2 May, 1838.

III. Elias, *b.* in 1782; *m.* Euphemia Arsandeau, of Pondicherry, E. I.; captain in the 8th regt. native infantry, H.E.I.Co.'s service; and *d.* at Hyberabad, 1818, leaving issue.

IV. Joseph, *b.* in 1784; *m.* Elizabeth, dau. of Elias Collings, Esq., the only surviving lineal descendant of the Jersey branch; attained the rank of lieut.-col. of the Royal Guernsey Militia, and became vice-consul in the islands of Guernsey and Jersey to H. M. the Emperor of all the Russias. He had issue, viz.,

1 Joseph, *b.* in 1808; a capt. in the Royal Guernsey Militia; *m.* to Catherine-Lukis, dau. of Rear-Admiral Sir Thomas Mansell, R.N. and K.C.H., and has issue.

2 Mauger-Smith, *b.* in 1809, settled at Rio de Janeiro.

3 Augustus-William, *b.* in 1812, was assistant-surgeon in the H.E.I.Co.'s service; *d.* at Moulmein in 1838.

4 Adolphus, *b.* in 1815, Esq.; M.D., staff-sugeon in the island of Barbadoes; *m.* Georgiana, dau. of the Hon. John-Henry Nurse, M.C. of the island of Barbadoes.

5 Charles, *b.* in 1816; *d.* in 1817.

6 John-Elias, *b.* in 1821; a captain in Her Majesty's 23rd regt. of foot.

7 Thomas-Allaire, *b.* in 1824; *d.* in 1834.

1 Elizabeth, *b.* in 1811.

2 Rosalie-Bradley, *b.* in 1812; *m.* Mark-Anthony-Bazille Corbin, Esq., surgeon, and has issue.

3 Margaret-Mauger, *b.* in 1818; *m.* Thomas Nurse, Esq., M.D., son of the Hon. John-Henry Nurse, of Ashbury, M.C. of the island of Barbadoes, and has issue,

4 Louisa, *b.* in 1819; *m.* to Charles Anson, Esq. principal officer of customs at Guernsey, son of the late Edward Anson, Esq. of Bentley Hall, Staffordshire, and has issue.

5 Matilda-Lukis, *b.* in 1822; *m.* to Alfred-Smith Collings, son of John (before mentioned), Esq., a capt. in the Royal Guernsey Militia, and has issue.

6 Ellen-Marian, *b.* in 1827.

V. Thomas-Guerin, *b.* in 1786; *m.* Mary, dau. of John Allaire, Esq. of Mount Durant, in the island of Guernsey; and *d.* in 1832: had issue, viz.,

1 William-Thomas, *b.* in 1823; B.A., Trinity College, Cambridge, F. G. S.; *m.* Louisa-Elizabeth, dau. of Frederick-Corbin Lukis, Esq. of The Grange, in the island of Guernsey, and has issue.

2 Mary-Ann, *b.* in 1811; *m.* to Henry Tupper, Esq. of The Cotils, in the island of Guernsey, lieut.-col. of the 2nd regt. of Royal Guernsey Militia, and an advocate of the Royal Court, and has issue.

2 Amelia, *b.* in 1815; *m.* to Frederick-Collings Lukis, Esq., M.D., and has issue.

3 Ann-Sophia, *b.* in 1819; *d.* in 1830.

4 Catherine-Ann-Allaire, *b.* in 1826; *m.* to the Rev. Richard Ozanne, M.A. of Pembroke College, Oxford, and has issue.

I. Ann, *b.* in 1773; *m.* to Peter Grut, Esq.; and *d.* in 1811, and had issue.

II. Caroline, *b.* in 1775; *m.* to Daniel Naftel, Esq. of The Vrangue, in the island of Guernsey, and has issue.

III. Margaret-Sarah, *b.* in 1780; *m.* to Hilary Carré, Esq. of Valnor, a jurat of the royal court of Guernsey.

IV. Mary-Ann, *b.* in 1788; *m.* to Elias Guerin, Esq. of Mount Durant, and has issue.

V. Elizabeth, *b.* in 1791; *m.* to Frederick-Corbin Lukis, Esq. of The Grange, in the island of Guernsey, and has issue.

Arms—Az., between three fleurs-de-lis, two and one, or, a gryphon, segreant, holding between the claws an escutcheon, arg., the latter charged with an anchor, erect, sa.

Crest—A horse's head, issuant, arg., bridled and charged on the neck with three fleurs-de-lis, one and two, az.

Motto—Fidelis in omnibus.

Residence—Guernsey.

COLLINGWOOD OF CHIRTON AND LILBURN TOWER.

COLLINGWOOD, EDWARD-JOHN, Esq. of Chirton and Lilburn Tower, co. Northumberland, *b.* 4 Feb. 1815; *m.* 23 Aug. 1842, Anna, 2nd dau. of the late Arthur Burdett, Esq. of the co. Tipperary, and has issue,

I. EDWARD-JOHN, *b.* 20 Dec. 1843.

II. Arthur-Burdett, *b.* 2 April, 1847.

III. Cuthbert-George, *b.* 29 Nov. 1848.

I. Anna-Elizabeth. II. Adelaide-Mary.

Lineage.—The ancient Northumbrian family of COLLINGWOOD was seated at Eslington, in that co., in the early part of the reign of HENRY VIII.

JOHN COLLINGWOOD, Esq. of Chirton, brother of the gallant naval commander, Cuthbert, Lord Collingwood, and 5th in descent from Cuthbert Collingwood, 3rd son of Sir Cuthbert Collingwood, of Dalden and Eslington, by Dorothy his wife, dau. of Sir George Bowes, of Streatlam, *m.* Sarah, dau. of Thomas Fenwick, Esq. of Earsdon, and left at his decease (with two daus., Ann, *m.* to the Rev. Christopher Reed, vicar of Tynemouth; and Mary, *m.* to Frederick-John-Woodley Collingwood, Esq. of Glanton Pyke), a son and successor, the present EDWARD-JOHN COLLINGWOOD, of Chirton and Lilburn Tower, Esq.

Arms—Arg., a chevron, sa., between three stag's heads, erased, of the second.

Crest—A stag at gaze, in a holly-bush, ppr.

Motto—Ferar unus et idem.

Seats—Chirton, and Lilburn Tower, co. Northumberland.

COLLINGWOOD OF DISSINGTON.

COLLINGWOOD, EDWARD, Esq. of Dissington, co. Northumberland, *b.* 30 Oct. 1791; *m.* 9 Sept. 1820, Arabella, dau. of General John Calcraft, and by her (who *d.* 31 May, 1840) has issue,

I. EDWARD, *b.* 22 July, 1823, *m.* Fanny, dau. of Colonel Maxwell.

II. Cecil. I. Arabella.

This gentleman, who is second surviving son of the late WALTER SPENCER-STANHOPE, Esq. of Cannon Hall, co. York, by Mary-Winifred his wife, dau. of Thomas-Babington Pulleine, Esq. of Carlton Hall, and Winifred his wife, dau. of Edward Collingwood, Esq. of Byker and Dissington, assumed by letters-patent, in compliance with the testamentary injunction of his great-uncle, EDWARD COLLINGWOOD, Esq., the surname and arms of COLLINGWOOD only.

Arms, Crest, and Motto—Same as COLLINGWOOD *of Chirton and Lilburn Tower.*

Seat—Dissington Hall, ten miles north-west of Newcastle-upon-Tyne.

COLLINGWOOD OF CORNHILL HOUSE.

COLLINGWOOD, JOHN, Esq., late of Lilburn Tower, co. Northumberland, and now of Cornhill House, co. Durham, *b.* 25 Dec. 1826; *s.* his father 14 April, 1840.

Lineage.—This is another branch of the Northumberland Collingwoods.

JOHN COLLINGWOOD, Esq. of Lilburn Tower, co. Northumberland, and Cornhill House, North Durham, son of Henry Collingwood, Esq. of Westerhaugh, *m.* a lady named Cornthwaite, and had two sons, HENRY, his heir; and John, *b.* in 1758; and four daus., Ann; Judith; Mary; and Elizabeth. The eldest son,

HENRY COLLINGWOOD, Esq. of Lilburn Tower and Cornhill House, *b.* 20 July, 1757, *m.* 1st, Margaret Mills, of Glanton, 2ndly, Dorothy Wilkinson, of Coxhoe, and 3rdly, Mary-Anne, younger dau. of the Rev. Samuel Watson, D.D. of Rothbury, by the last of whom (who *d.* 17 Feb. 1852), he had issue,

HENRY-JOHN-WILLIAM, his heir.

Frederick-John-Woodley, of Glanton Pyke, co. Northumberland, J.P. and D.L., *b.* 20 Nov. 1805, *m.* 4 Dec. 1838, Mary, 2nd dau. of the late John Collingwood, Esq. of Chirton House.

Judith.

Margaret, *m.* to Charles Fenwick, Esq. of Earsdon.

Harriet, *m.* to George-Thomas Leaton, Esq. of Whickham.

Mary-Anne, *m.* in 1830, to James Vibart, Esq., lieut. R.N.

Mr. Collingwood *d.* 20 July, 1827, and was *s.* by his eldest son,

HENRY-JOHN-WILLIAM COLLINGWOOD, Esq. of Lilburn Tower and Cornhill House, who *m.* in 1825, Frances, dau. of Thomas Haggerston, Esq. of Ellingham, and dying 14 April, 1840, left issue,

JOHN, now of Cornhill.

William-Pole, *b.* 2 Nov. 1829, capt. 21st R.N.B. fusiliers.

Thomas-Haggerston, *b.* 12 May, 1831, lieut. R.N.

Clennell, royal artillery, *b.* 16 Feb. 1836.

Frederick, *b.* 17 Nov. 1837, R.N.

Henry, *b.* 7 Dec. 1839.

Frances, *m.* 22 July, 1851, to George-Caldwell Dickins, Esq., capt. 46th regt.

Mary-Anne. Winifred.

Mr. Collingwood was *s.* at his decease by his son, the

present JOHN COLLINGWOOD, Esq. of Cornhill House. Lilburn Tower was sold by the trustees in 1842, to Edward Collingwood, Esq. of Chirton.

Arms, &c.—As COLLINGWOOD *of Chirton*.
Seat—Cornhill House, North Durham.

COLLINS OF WALFORD.

COLLINS, JOHN-STRATFORD, Esq. of Walford, co. Hereford, *m.* Edith, dau. of Philip Jones, Esq. of The Cleeve, co. Hereford, by Anne his wife, dau. of William Hutcheson, Esq. of Clifton, co. Gloucester, by Sarah his wife, only child of Robert Kyrle, Esq., son and heir of Vandervert Kyrle, devisee of John Kyrle, Pope's "Man of Ross." By this lady, Mr. Collins has issue,

I. JOHN-STRATFORD, barrister-at-law and J.P., *m.* Ellen, only surviving dau. of John Lloyd, Esq. of Lloydsboro', Ireland, and by her (who *d.* Nov. 1852), he has issue, John-Stratford; Amy-Stratford; and Ellen-Edith-Lloyd.
II. William-Hutcheson, of Cabberly House, co. Hereford, an officer in the Herefordshire militia, *m.* Laura-Elizabeth, eldest dau. of the late John Hancocks, Esq. of Wolverley Court, co. Worcester.
III. Nathaniel-Kyrle-Collins.
I. Edith-Alicia. II. Sarah.
III. Anne-Jones. IV. Katherine.

Lineage.—The family of Collins is one of great antiquity in the cos. of Hereford and Salop. The Collins' were landed proprietors at the time of the general survey of 1066. William Collins was member for Hereford, in the 36th parliament of King EDWARD III.; and again, in the 39th, 40th, 43rd, 45th, and 46th parliaments in the same reign, he represented the city of Hereford. The representative and head of the family is returned in the list of principal inhabitants for the co. of Hereford, by the commissioners appointed 12th HENRY VI.

This pedigree is given in the visitations of Hereford and Salop, commencing with Sir Peter Collins, Knt. of Church Stretton, whose son and heir, Adam Collins, was father of Geoffrey Collins, who *m.* Anne, dau. of Bowdler of Hope Bowdler, who was father of William Collins, who *m.* Eliza, dau. of Acton of Acton Scott, co. Salop, and had two sons, Roger Collins; and JOHN COLLINS, of whose line we treat. The 2nd son,

JOHN COLLINS, *m.* a dau. of Roberts of Staunton Lacy, and was father of HENRY COLLINS, whose son by his wife, a dau. of Mynde of Mynde Town, co. Salop, GEOFFREY COLLINS, *m.* a dau. of Hockleton of Hockleton, and was father of

ABRAHAM COLLINS, who *m.* Maria, dau. and heir of William Collins, of Inchcombe, and had John Collins, who left by Anna, dau. of Windsbury of Windsbury, a son,

RICHARD COLLINS, of Woodhide, co. Hereford, who *m.* Jane, dau. of John Parker, of Netherwood, and had a son and heir,

RICHARD COLLINS, of Woodhide, who *m.* Jane, dau. of Thomas Gam, and had issue three sons, THOMAS, of Woodhide; JOHN, of whose line we treat; Roger, who was father of Roger Collins, of Stapleton, co. Hereford, and ancestor of that branch of the family. The 2nd son,

JOHN COLLINS, of Dovehill, co. Hereford, *m.* Alice, dau. of Thomas Barrowe, and was father of HENRY COLLINS, who *m.* Anne, dau. of Thomas Masson, and had, besides three younger sons, George Collins, Henry Collins, and John Collins, an eldest son and heir,

RICHARD COLLINS, Esq. of Upton, co. Hereford, usher of the chamber, 1623, who had a confirmation of his arms by Camden, Clarenceux, Oct. 1612. He *m.* Alicia, dau. and heir of William Downman, Esq. of Upton Bishop, and was father of

RICHARD COLLINS, Esq. of Upton, co. Hereford, who *m.* Elizabeth, dau. and heir of James Creswell, of Crawley, co. Surrey, by Elizabeth, dau. and heir of Alexander Browne, 4th son of Magens Browne, of Brichwoth, and had, with two daus., Elizabeth and Alice, a son,

JAMES COLLINS, Esq. of Upton, co. Hereford, who *m.* Catherine, dau. of James Skinner, Esq. of Ledbury, co. Hereford, and dying, left issue, a son,

WILLIAM COLLINS, Esq. of Upton, co Hereford, captain in the trained bands, who *m.* Sept. 1680, Mary, dau. and heiress of Robert Stratford, Esq. of Walford, co. Hereford, great-grandson of Ferdinando Stratford, of Walford, by Ursula his wife, dau. and co-heir of John Hereford, of Sufton, co. Hereford, and Blanche his wife, dau. of Thomas Kyrle, of Walford Court. He was buried at Upton, 10 Jan. 1717, and left at his decease a son and heir,

JAMES COLLINS, Esq. of Walford, co. Hereford, *m.* in London, Aug. 1726, Elianor, dau. of John Stacy, Esq. of London. He *d.* and was buried at Walford, 7th June, 1765, and left issue a son and heir,

JOHN-STRATFORD COLLINS, Esq. of Walford, *b.* Dec. 1730, high-sheriff for the co. of Hereford 1774, *m.* in 1758, Alice, only child of John Furney, Esq. of Perristone, co. Hereford, and *d.* Aug. 1780, leaving issue, JOHN-STRATFORD, his heir; Ferdinando-Stratford, R.N.; Alicia, *m.* the Rev. John-Howton Beeston, vicar of Walford, and left issue. The elder son,

JOHN-STRATFORD COLLINS, Esq. of Walford, *m.* Mary, dau. of James Davis, Esq. of Ross, co. Hereford, and left issue, four daus. and three sons, viz:

JOHN-STRATFORD, present representative.
Ferdinando-Stratford, deceased, who *m.* Frances, dau. of John Morris, Esq. of Leominster, by Anne, dau. of Thomas-Legge Berbee, Esq. of Willey Court, co. Hereford.
James, of Woolhope, *m.* Eliza, dau. and heir of Henry-William Gwillim, Esq., deceased, of Brainge Court, co. Hereford.

Mr. Collins *d.* in 1809.

Arms—Vert, a griffin, segreant, and a crescent, or.
Crest—A dexter-arm, embowed, habited, arg., the hand, ppr., holding a scimitar, or.
Seat—Wythall, Walford, co. Hereford.

COLLINS OF BETTERTON.

COLLINS, THE REV. JOHN-FERDINANDO, of Betterton, co. Berks, *b.* 15 Oct. 1812; *m.* 30 Sept. 1836, Sarah, dau. of John Hawthorn, Esq. of Glenluce, co. Wigton, and late of Jamaica, and has issue,

I. JOHN-FERDINANDO, *b.* 12 July, 1837.
II. Henry, *b.* 31 Aug. 1838.
III. Charles, *b.* 23 Sept. 1839.
IV. Robert-Hawthorn, *b.* 3 Aug. 1841.
V. Arthur, *b.* 26 June, 1845.
VI. Francis, *b.* 20 April, 1851.
I. Emily-Jane. II. Fanny-Katharine.

Lineage.—This family have possessed the lands of Betterton, descending from sire to son, since the time of HENRY VI.

CHARLES COLLINS, of Pembroke College, Oxford, and of the Middle Temple, *b.* 13 June, 1686, lineally descended from Thomas Collins, of Betterton, *temp.* HENRY VI., *m.* 1st, Anne, eldest dau. of John Head, Esq. of Hodcut, Berks, and left by her two daus., Charlotte, wife of John Saunders, Esq. of Woolston, and Frances, of Richard Hartend, Esq., with four sons who *d.* before him *s. p.* He *m.* 2ndly, Elizabeth Coghill, of Bletchington, without issue; and 3rdly, Anne, eldest dau. of Ferdinando White, Esq. of Fryers Court, in the co. of Berks, and by her had his successor,

FERDINANDO COLLINS, Esq., M.A., *m.* Katherine Boots, of Deucies, of Berks, and had (with a son, Ferdinando, who *d. s. p.*, and two daus., Anne, *m.* to Francis-Brownswood Bullock, Esq., and Katharine, *m.* to Isaac Pickering, Esq. of Foxlease, Hants) a son and successor,

THE REV. JOHN COLLINS, of Betterton, vicar of Cheshunt, *b.* 6 July, 1758, *m.* Martha, dau. of James Smith, Esq. of Rotterdam and Hammersmith, and had, JOHN-FERDINANDO, now of Betterton; Katharine, *m.* to the Rev. Giles Daubeney; Anna-Maria, *m.* to the Rev. Benjamin Morland. Mr. Collins *d.* 17 March, 1826.

Arms—Vert, a griffin, passant, or; a chief, erm.
Crest—A griffin's head, erased, vert, crowned, or.
Motto—Per callem collem.
Seat—Betterton House, Wantage.

COLLINS OF TRUTHAN.

COLLINS, EDWARD, Esq. of Truthan and Newton-Ferrers, co. Cornwall, J.P. and D.L., high-sheriff in 1830, *b.* 7 Sept. 1782; *m.* 8 Nov. 1831, Elizabeth, 2nd dau. of Francis Drake, Esq., late minister-plenipotentiary at Munich, by Eliza-Anne his wife, only dau. of Sir Herbert Mackworth, Bart., and has issue,

I. EDWARD, *b.* 2 Dec. 1833.
II. Charles, *b.* 3 May, 1835.
III. Digby, *b.* 7 Sept. 1836.

Lineage.—The family of Collins is of very ancient standing in Cornwall. In the 1st of EDWARD II., John Collins represented Launceston in parliament, and in the 11th and 15th RICHARD II. was sheriff of the county. The great-grandfather of the present proprietor of Truthan,

JOHN COLLINS, Esq. of Treworgan, high-sheriff of Cornwall in 1726, m. Mary May, and had, with daus., two sons, EDWARD, and John. The younger,

THE REV. JOHN COLLINS, m. 1st, Mary, eldest dau. of Francis Bassett, Esq. of Tehidy Park, by whom he had a son, JOHN BASSETT. He m. 2ndly, Constance, dau. and heiress of Paul Mitchell, Esq., by whom he had a son, EDWARD, of whom presently; and 3rdly, Anne Williams, by whom he also had issue, Charles, who d. unm., Jeremiah, in holy orders, and Anne, who d. unm. The only son of the 2nd marriage,

EDWARD COLLINS, Esq. of Truthan, co. Cornwall, b. 21 April, 1747, high-sheriff of Cornwall in 1801, m. 7 March, 1779, Mary, only dau. of the Rev. Richard Thomas, and sole heiress of her uncle, Richard Thomas, Esq. of Tretheake, and d. 13 Sept. 1827, having had issue by her (who d. 9 Dec. 1831), EDWARD, now of Truthan; Clement, b. 17 Dec. 1784, d. 11 Feb. 1789; and Mary, who d. unm. 2 Oct. 1837. Mr. Collins d. 13 Sept. 1827.

Arms—Sa., a chevron, arg., gutté-de-sang, between three doves, ppr.
Crest—A dove, with wings expanded, ppr.
Motto—Volabo et requiescam.
Seats—Truthan, near Truro; and Newton Park, near Callington.

COLLIS OF CASTLE COOKE.

COOKE-COLLIS, WILLIAM, Esq. of Castle Cooke, co. Cork, J.P., b. 30 Jan. 1783; m. 28 June, 1808, Elizabeth-Geraldine, eldest dau. of Maurice-Uniacke Atkin, Esq. of Leadington, co. Cork, and has issue,

I. WILLIAM-COOKE, J.P., b. 19 May, 1809; m. Sarah, eldest surviving dau. of John Hyde, Esq. of Castle Hyde, co. Cork.
II. Maurice-Atkin, in holy orders; b. 24 March, 1812; m. 27 June, 1839, Anne, eldest dau. of the Rev. John Talbot, 2nd son of William Talbot, of Mount Talbot, co. Roscommon, Esq., and the Lady Anne, eldest dau. of William, 1st Earl of Glandore, and has issue.
III. John-Thomas, b. in Oct. 1818.
I. Elizabeth-Margaret, m. 1 Sept. 1846, to Edward Carey, Esq. of Careysville, co. Cork.
II. Jane-Leslie, m. to Richard-Jasper-Alexander Grant, Esq. of Kilmurry, co. Cork.

Lineage.—THOMAS COOKE, of the city of London, a wealthy merchant, purchased, about 1670, large tracts of land in Ireland, which he bequeathed to his only son,

PETER COOKE, Esq. of Castle Cooke, co. Cork, who m. 23 April, 1696, Elizabeth Mitchell, and by her had two sons and one dau. The elder son,

THOMAS COOKE, Esq. of Castle Cooke, m. Dorothea Addis, and by her left three daus., Elizabeth, m. to Sir Thomas Blackhall, and d. without leaving issue; Martha, eventual heiress, m. to her cousin, WILLIAM COLLIS; and Anne. Thomas was s. by his brother,

ZACHARY COOKE, of Castle Cooke, who d. unm., and was s. by his niece,

MARTHA COOKE, who had m. her cousin, the Rev. William Collis, rector of Church Hill and Kilgobben, co. Kerry, son of John Collis, Esq. of Cork, by Elizabeth his wife, only dau. of Peter Cooke, of Castle Cooke, and had issue, ZACHARY, his heir; William, of Richmond, co. Waterford, barrister-at-law, m. Jane, eldest dau. of Peter Carey, Esq. of Careysville, co. Cork; Martha, d. unm. The elder son,

THE REV. ZACHARY-COOKE COLLIS, archdeacon of Cloyne, s. to the Castle Cooke estate, and assumed the additional surname and arms of COOKE. He m. in 1782, Jane, dau. of Charles Leslie, Esq., M.D. of the city of Cork, by Anne his wife, dau. of Alderman Lawton, of the same city, and had issue, WILLIAM, of Castle Cooke; Anne-Leslie, m. to Thomas Perrott, Esq. of Upland, co. Cork; Mary-Peacock, m. to David Barry, Esq., M.D. of Fermoy; Sarah-Hyde, m. to John Perrott, Esq. of Limerick.

Arms—Arg., on a chevron, between three lions' heads, erased, sa., three cinquefoils, of the first, quartering COOKE.
Crest—A sea-pie, standing on and pecking at a small fish.
Motto—Mens conscia recti.
Seat—Castle Cooke, Kilworth, co. Cork.

COLLIS OF LISMORE.

COLLIS, WILLIAM, Esq. of Lismore, co. Kerry, m. in 1806, his cousin Catherine, eldest dau. of the Rev. Samuel Collis, of Fort William, and has issue,

I. EDMUND, b. in 1810.
II. Samuel. III. William. IV. Richard.
I. Charity, m. Richard de Moleyns, Esq.
II. Anna. III. Frances. IV. Catherine.

Captain Collis has served as high-sheriff for co. Kerry.

Lineage.—WILLIAM COLLIS, an officer in Hierome Sankey's regiment of horse in CROMWELL'S army, left a son,

JOHN COLLIS, Esq., who m. Mary, dau. of Philip Corridon, of Kilmackada, co. Kerry, and had, besides a dau., Margaret, who m. Maurice Stock, a son,

WILLIAM COLLIS, Esq. of Lisodoge, co. Kerry, who m. 1st, in 1685, Martha Mullins, of Ballingolin (now Burnham), near Dingle, and by her had a son, WILLIAM, of whom presently. He m. 2ndly, in 1698, Mary, dau. of Dr. Benjamin Cross, rector of Christ Church, Cork, by Ann his wife, dau. of Dean John Eveleigh, of Bandon, and Mildred Caldwall his wife, and by her had issue,

I. John, m. Elizabeth Cooke, and was ancestor of the Castle Cooke branch.
II. Thomas, in holy orders; m. Avis Blennerhasset (of the family of Ballyseedy), and left issue a dau., Jane, m. to Frederick Mullins, eldest brother of Thomas, 1st Lord Ventry, but d. s. p.
III. EDWARD, who s. his half-brother, and of whom hereafter.
IV. Robert, m. 1st, 1729, Elizabeth, dau. of Edward Day, Esq. of Tralee; and 2ndly, in 1748, Mary Fitzgerald, dau. of Maurice, Knight of Kerry, and by the latter only left issue, a son,
   John, who m. Margaret, dau. of the Rev. John Day, of Loheroannon, co. Kerry, by Lucy his wife, dau. of Maurice Fitzgerald, Knight of Kerry, and, by her, left three sons,
   1 John-Day, d. s. p.
   2 Robert, in holy orders; b. Miss Burke, of Galway, and has issue a son, John-Day, in holy orders.
   3 Maurice, of Dublin, an eminent surgeon; m. Frances, sister of the Rev. Edward Herbert, of Kilpeaton, co. Limerick.

The son of the first marriage,

THE REV. WILLIAM COLLIS, rector of Churchill, acquired estates in Kerry by purchase, and was the devisee of others from distant relatives. He m. Isabella Galwey, of the family of GALWEY *of Carberry*; and d. s. p. in 1750, leaving all his estates to his half-brother,

EDWARD COLLIS, Esq. of Barrow, who m. 1726, Ellen, dau. of Christopher Hilliard, Esq. of Ballygarron, by whom he had several children. He was s. by his eldest son,

WILLIAM COLLIS, Esq. of Lismore, who m. 1756, Catharine, dau. of Samuel Sealy, Esq. of Maugh, co. Kerry, and by her left issue,

EDWARD, his heir.
SAMUEL, of Fort William (*see that branch*).
Maurice, capt. Royal Kerry Militia; m. Frances Scally, and had issue.

The eldest son,

EDWARD COLLIS, Esq. of Lismore, m. Charity, dau. of Cornelius M'Gillycuddy, of The Reeks, and left at his decease a son, the present WILLIAM COLLIS, Esq. of Lismore, and two daus., Arabella, m. to David Fitzgerald, Esq.; and Margaret, m. to Francis Twiss, Esq.

Seat—Lismore, near Tralee.

COLLIS OF FORT WILLIAM.

COLLIS, ROBERT, Esq. of Fort William, co. Kerry, b. 25 Oct. 1832.

Lineage.—THE REV. SAMUEL COLLIS, of Fort William, 2nd son of WILLIAM COLLIS, Esq. of Lismore, by Catharine Sealy his wife, m. Anna, dau. of Edward Rae, Esq. of Keel, co. Kerry, by Anna his wife, dau. and co-heir of Robert Langford, Esq. of Gardensfield, co. Limerick, and Anna Meredith, of Dixgrove, co. Kerry, and by her left issue, 1 WILLIAM, his heir; 2 Samuel, of The Spa, Tralee, lieut. R.N., m. Charity, dau. of Dr. Lyne, of Tralee; 2 Catharine, m. to her cousin, William Collis, Esq. of Lismore; 2 Ellen, m. to Francis-Edward Collingwood, capt. R.N.; 3 Margaret, m. to Augustus-Richard Yielding, Esq. of Bally MacThomas and Cloughers; and 4 Anna-Priscilla. The elder son,

WILLIAM COLLIS, Esq. of Fort William, capt. and adjutant of the Royal Kerry Militia, m. 1st, in 1814, Debora, eldest dau. of William-John Crumpe, Esq., M.D., of Tralee, and by her had, WILLIAM, his heir; Anna-Hobarton; Debora, m. William-Samuel Sealy, Esq. of Maugh, co. Kerry; Aphra, m. Thomas-Barry Hurly, solicitor. Mr. Collis m. 2ndly, in 1830, Louisa-E., dau. of Dr. Burke, R.N., co. Wexford, and by her had a son, ROBERT, present representative. He d. in 1834, and was s. by his elder son,

WILLIAM COLLIS, Esq. of Fort William, who d. s. p. in 1842, when the representation devolved on his half-brother, the present ROBERT COLLIS, Esq. of Fort William.

Seat—Fort William, co. Kerry.

COLLYER OF HACKFORD HALL.

COLLYER, THE VEN. JOHN-BEDINGFELD, M.A. of Hackford Hall, co. Norfolk, archdeacon of Norwich, J.P. and D.L., b. 26 Jan. 1777; m. 18 March, 1800, Catherine, dau. of William Alexander, Esq., formerly of the city of London (elder brother of James, 1st earl of Caledon), and grand-dau., through her mother, of Dr. M. Monsey, formerly physician to Chelsea Hospital, to whose estate in Hackford, and adjoining parishes and manors in Whitwell, Norfolk, she s. by his will. By this lady, who d. 17 March, 1853, the Archdeacon has issue,

I. JOHN, barrister-at-law; b. 15 July, 1801; m. in March, 1837, Georgina-Frances-Amy, eldest dau. of Sir William Johnston, Bart. of that ilk.

II. Robert, in holy orders, rector of Warham All Saints, and Warham St. Mary; b. 8 May, 1804.

III. George, d. 27 June, 1832.

I. Catherine. II. Mary.

III. Charlotte, m. in Aug. 1829, to Joseph-Hemington Harris, D.D.; and d. leaving issue.

IV. Elizabeth. V. Rebecca, deceased.

Lineage.—THE REV. DANIEL COLLYER, of Wroxham Hall and Necton Lodge, elder son of Daniel Collyer, Esq. of Wroxham Hall, and of the city of London, and director of the Royal African Society, who was 2nd son of Daniel Collyer, of the city of London, merchant, m. in 1774, Catherine, dau. and co-heiress of John Bedingfeld,* Esq., formerly of Beeston St. Andrew, and of Caister, co. Norfolk, and had,

I. DANIEL, who m. 1st, in 1807, Sarah, dau. of Alexander, 3rd Earl of Fife, by whom (who d. in 1811) he had an only son, James, d. an infant. He m. 2ndly, Elizabeth, dau. of John Chancellor, Esq. of Shield Hill, co. Lanark, and had a son and heir, GEORGE-CHANCELLOR, E.I.C.S., and other issue.

II. JOHN-BEDINGFELD, now of Hackford Hall.

III. William, lieut.-col. E.I.C.S., of Gimingham, Norfolk, a magistrate for Norfolk and Norwich. He m. Harriet, dau. of the Rev. Charles Collyer, of Gunthorpe Hall, by Sarah his wife, dau. of Edward-Roger Pratt, Esq. of Ryston.

IV. George, capt. in the royal engineers, fell at the attack on St. Sebastian, in 1813, unm.

I. Catherine, d. unm.

Arms—Arg., a chevron, between three unicorns' heads, couped, gu.
Crest—A unicorn's head, ppr.
Motto—Avance.
Seat—Hackford Hall, Norfolk.

COLMORE OF MOOR END.

CREGOE-COLMORE, COLMORE-FRIND, Esq. of Moor End, Charlton Kings, co. Gloucester, b. 12 March, 1827; m. 18 July, 1850, Mary, only dau. of the Rev. Edward-Pryce Owen, of Bettwys Hall, co. Montgomery, and has had issue,

Henry-Owen-Garland, d. an infant.
Mary-Harriet-Frances.

Lineage.—FRIND CREGOE, Esq. of Moor End, a younger son of Edward Cregoe, Esq. of Trewithian, Cornwall, by Mary his wife, dau. of Matthew Garland, Esq., assumed the additional surname of COLMORE. He m. 20 Sept. 1818, Elizabeth-Sarah Roberts, and had issue,

Colmore-Prescoed, d. 14 April, 1826.
COLMORE-FRIND, now of Moor End.
Marianne-Colmore, m. 15 April, 1838, to W.-A.-Burlton Bennett, Esq.
Emma, d. 15 Oct. 1830.
Maria-Prescoed, d. 24 June, 1833.
Harriet, m. 20 July, 1842, Irwin Grant de Longueville.
Elizabeth-Charlotte, m. 1st, 12 May, 1846, to Capt. William-Beaumain Knipe, 5th dragoon-guards; and 2ndly, to Coplestone-Lopes Radcliffe, Esq., 2nd son of the Rev. Walter Radcliffe, Warleigh, Plymouth.

Mr. Cregoe Colmore d. 12 Oct. 1839.

Arms—Quarterly: 1st and 4th, per chevron, gu., and az., nine billets, three, three, and three, arg., and three crescents, two and one, erminois; 2nd and 3rd, az., on a chevron, or, between three falcons, volant, as many plates.
Crest—Out of a crescent, or, a blackamoor's head in profile, wreathed about the temples, or and gu.
Seat—Moor End, Cheltenham.

COLQUHOUN OF KILLERMONT.

COLQUHOUN, JOHN-CAMPBELL, Esq. of Killermont, co. Dumbarton, J.P., and formerly M.P. for Dumbartonshire, and afterwards for Kilmarnock, b. 23 Jan. 1803; m. 10 Sept. 1827, the Hon. Henrietta-Maria Powys, eldest dau. of the 2nd Lord Lilford, and has issue,

I. ARCHIBALD-CAMPBELL, b. 25 July, 1828.
II. John-Erskine, b. 15 June, 1831.

Lineage.—This is a scion of the Comstroden branch of the ancient Scottish line of COLQUHOUN *of Luss*, derived in direct descent from a younger son of ROBERT COLQUHOUN, of Comstroden, living in 1540. The late

RIGHT HON. ARCHIBALD CAMPBELL, Lord Advocate, and subsequently Lord Clerk Register of Scotland, son of John Coates, Esq., Lord Provost of Glasgow in 1784, who assumed the surname of CAMPBELL on succeeding to the property of Clathick, m. in 1796, Mary-Anne, dau. of the Rev. William Erskine, Episcopalian clergyman in Muthel, co. Perth, and had issue,

JOHN-CAMPBELL, now of Killermont and Garscadden.
William-Lawrence, of Clathick, co. Perth, b. 4 March, 1810; m. Miss Locke, and has issue.
Mary-Anne, m. in 1819, to Walter Long, Esq. of Rood Ashton, co. Wilts.
Elizabeth-Margaret, m. to the Rev. E. Boyle.

The Right Hon. Archibald Campbell, who took the name of COLQUHOUN on succeeding to the estate of Garscadden, on the extinction of the family of Colquhoun of that place, a cadet of Luss, d. in 1820.

Arms—Arg., a saltier, engrailed, sa., thereon, for difference, a buckle, or; in base, an anchor, ppr., all within a bordure, of the second, charged with eight roses.
Crest—A stag's head, erased, ppr.
Motto—If I can.
Seat—Killermont, near Glasgow.

COLSTON OF ROUNDWAY PARK.

COLSTON, EDWARD, Esq. of Filkins Hall, co. Oxford, and of Roundway Park, Wilts, an officer in the King's Hussars, b. in 1822; m. 20 June, 1848, Louisa-Ruperta, dau. of the Rev. Edward Murray, 2nd son of Lord George Murray, bishop of St. David's, 2nd son of James, Duke of Atholl, and has issue,

I. EDWARD-GLOUCESTER-MURRAY, b. 15 April, 1849.
I. Amy-Ruperta. II. Lilian-Anne.

Lineage.—This family claims descent by a long line of ancestry from ROBERT DE COLSTON, of Colston Hall, in the co. of Lincoln, living at the time of the Conquest.

THE REV. ALEXANDER COLSTON, of Filkins Hall, rector of Broadwell and Henbury, A.D. 1744, son and heir of Alexander Ready, Esq. (afterwards Colston), of the Inner Temple, by Sophia his wife, dau. and co-heir of Thomas Edwards, Esq. of Filkins Hall, co. Oxford, and Mary his wife, only dau. and heir of Sir William Hayman, of Bristol, who m. in 1670, Mary, only surviving sister and heir of EDWARD COLSTON, of Bristol, the philanthropist, m. 1st, Louisa-Minshull, dau. of Paul-George Elers, Esq. of Black Bourton, Wilts, by Mary his wife, dau. and heir of Anthony

* Mr. Bedingfeld served the office of sheriff of Norfolk in 1728. He was son of William Bedingfeld, grandson of Henry Bedingfeld, and great-grandson of Francis Bedingfeld, who was son of Henry Bedingfeld, of Sturston, co. Norfolk, fifth son of Sir Henry Bedingfeld, Bart. of Oxborough.

Mr. Bedingfeld m. 1st, a dau. of — Kendal, Esq., by whom he had a dau., Judith, wife of Sir John Rous, Bart., and mother of John, 1st Earl of Stradbroke; and 2ndly, Phœbe, dau. of James Gibson, Esq. of Norwich, by whom he had two daus., the elder m. to the Rev. DANIEL COLLYER, of Wroxham Hall, and the younger m. to the Rev. George Preston, of Standfield Hall, Norfolk.

Hungerford, Esq., a lineal descendant of the great baronial family of Hungerford, and by her had issue,

I. EDWARD-FRANCIS.
II. Alexander, lieut.-col. in the army, of Belvedere, Malvern; m. Ann, dau. of John Warrington, Esq.
III. Thomas-Edward, m. 1st, Miss Ann Morris; and 2ndly, Miss Henrietta Tinney, and has issue, a son, John.
IV. William-Hungerford, D.D., rector of West Lydford; who m. 1st, Margaret, dau. of Crisp Molyneux, Esq., M.P.; 2ndly, Mary, dau. of John Morris, Esq. of Ampthill, Beds; and 3rdly, Mary-Anne Heath, youngest dau. of the Rev. John Brice, rector of Asholt, co. Somerset. By his 1st and 3rd wives, Dr. Colston has no issue, but by his 2nd he has one son and one dau.,
1 William-Hungerford-Morris, fellow of New College, Oxford.
1 Georgiana-Sophia.
I. Louisa-Minshull, m. to the Rev. Robert-Parker Bell.
II. Sophia, d. in infancy.
III. Mary, m. 7 Oct. 1801, to the Hon. and Rev. George Browne, 3rd son of the 1st Lord Kilmaine.

The Rev. Alexander Colston m. 2ndly, Susannah, dau. of the Rev. Mr. Hook, of Gloucester, but had no further issue. His eldest son,

EDWARD-FRANCIS COLSTON, Esq. of Filkins Hall, m. 1st, in 1792, Arabella, dau. of Michael Clayfield, Esq. of Bristol, and by her (who d. 24 Feb. 1812) had issue,

EDWARD-FRANCIS, his heir.
William, who m. Julia, eldest dau. of Dr. Felix, and sister of Col. Felix, and has a dau., Julia.
Sophia, deceased.
Arabella, m. to the Rev. John Rathbone; and d. in Sept. 1829.
Frances-Louisa, m. to Richard Dutton, Esq. of London.
Louisa-Mary, m. to Morris, 2nd son of John-Izard Pryor, Esq. of Clay Hall, Herts, and has issue, Louisa.

Mr. Colston m. 2ndly, 18 Oct. 1814, Harriet, dau. of Robert Davies, Esq. of Farthingville, co. Cork. His eldest son,

EDWARD-FRANCIS COLSTON, Esq. of Filkins Hall, Oxfordshire, and of Roundway Park, Wilts, b. 15 April, 1795; m. 1 Nov. 1819, Marianne, only dau. and heiress of William Jenkins, Esq. of Shepton Mallet; and d. in April, 1847, leaving issue,

EDWARD, present representative.
William-Jenkins-Craig, b. in 1824.
Samuel-Hunt, b. in 1825.
Arabella-Sarah.

Arms—Arg., between two dolphins, haurient, respecting each other, an anchor, all ppr.
Crest—A dolphin, embowed, ppr.
Motto—Go and do thou likewise.
Seats—Roundway Park, Wilts; and Filkins Hall, Oxon.

COLT OF GARTSHERRIE.

COLT, JOHN-HAMILTON, Esq. of Gartsherrie, co. Lanark, b. 19 Aug. 1811; m. 13 May, 1834, Jane, 2nd dau. of George-Cole Bainbridge, Esq. of Gattonside House, co. Roxburgh, and has issue,

I. OLIVER, m. 12 May, 1835.
II. George-Frederick-Russell, b. 14 Jan. 1837.
III. John-Hamilton, b. 1 Aug. 1840.
I. Jane-Osborne. II. Grace-Dundas.

Lineage.—This family was established in Scotland by BLAIS COULT, who fled from France during the persecution of the Huguenots, and, coming to St. Andrews, became a professor in the college. He was father of OLIVER COLT, Esq., a lawyer, living *temp.* Queen MARY, whose son, ADAM COLT, living *temp.* JAMES VI., minister of Inveresk for upwards of fifty years, was direct ancestor of

JOHN-HAMILTON COLT, Esq. of Inveresk and Gartsherrie, b. 12 May, 1789 (son and heir of Robert Colt, Esq. of Auldhame, Inveresk, and Gartsherrie, by Grace his wife, dau. of Robert Dundas, of Arniston, Lord President of the Court of Session, and grandson of Oliver Colt, Esq. of Auldhame and Inveresk, by Helen his wife, dau. of Robert, 7th Lord Blantyre). He m. 27 Sept. 1809, Sarah, youngest dau. of Joseph Mannering, Esq., and had issue,

JOHN-HAMILTON, present representative.
Frederick-Montague, b. 7 Nov. 1817; d. 25 June, 1838.
Charles-Russell, b. 18 May, 1822.
Helen-Stuart, m. 7 July, 1831, to Capt. William Osborne, 71st regiment.
Harriet-Matilda, d. 14 March, 1829.
Charlotte-Frances, d. 11 Nov. 1825.
Caroline-Augusta. Catherine-Melville.

Mr. Colt d. 10 Sept. 1840.

Arms—Arg., a stag's head, erased, gu.; between the attires, a pheon, az.
Crest—A dexter naked arm, embowed, holding in the hand an arrow, in bend sinister, ppr.
Motto—Transfigam.
Seat—Gartsherrie, co. Lanark.

COLTHURST OF DRIPSEY CASTLE.

COLTHURST, JOHN-HENRY, Esq. of Dripsey Castle, co. Cork, b. 3 May, 1808.

Lineage.—JOHN COLTHURST, of Dripsey Castle, co. Cork (son, by Elizabeth Russell his wife, of James Colthurst, Esq. of Knockannauff, brother of Sir John-Conway Colthurst, 1st Bart. of Ardrum), m. Jane, dau. of John Bowen, Esq. of Oakgrove, co. Cork, and had issue,

JAMES-BOWEN, his heir.
James, m. Esther, sister of the present Sir Augustus Warren, Bart., by whom he has issue.
Nicholas, m. twice; but had no issue.
Wallis, d. young.
Charles, now of Clonmoyle, co. Cork, m. Lavinia, dau. of Robert-Warren Gumbleton, Esq. of Castleview, and has issue.
Catherine, wife of John Pyne, Esq.
Jane, wife of — Bustead, Esq.

The eldest son,

JOHN-BOWEN COLTHURST, Esq. of Dripsey Castle, major in the army, m. Margaret, dau. of — Billinghurst, Esq., by whom he had issue, JOHN-HENRY, now of Dripsey Castle; Richardson, killed in India; George-Charles-Edward; Joseph; and Peggy, m. in Oct. 1853, to Alfred Greer, Esq. of Dripsey House.

Arms—Arg., on a fesse, between three colts, courant, sa., as many trefoils, slipped, or.
Crest—A colt, statant, sa.
Seat—Dripsey Castle, near Coachford.

COLVILE OF LULLINGTON.

COLVILE, CHARLES-ROBERT, Esq. of Lullington, co. Derby, b. 30 March, 1815; m. in 1850, Katherine-Sarah-Georgina, dau. of John Russell, Esq., R.N., by his wife, the Baroness de Clifford, and has issue,

HENRY-EDWARD, b. 10 July, 1852.

Lineage.—The family of Colvile is one of the most distinguished and ancient in Cambridgeshire. The original ancestor, GILBERT DE COLAVILLA, DE COLVILE, or COLVYLE, came from Normandy with WILLIAM the Conqueror. The name was derived from a castle on a hill, *col-vile* (*vile*, in ancient French, was *castle*; towns were the dependents of castles). There is a town in Normandy still called Colvile.

ROBERT DE COLVILE occurs in the time of HENRY I. He bore for his arms a cross-fleury, gu., on a field, arg. He left issue, 1 GILBERT, ancestor of the COLVILES *of Newton Colvile*; 2 PHILIP, of Stanton, who went into Scotland, and became ancestor of the noble family of COLVILE *of Culross*; 3 Robert, whose descendants were ennobled by CHARLES I. The eldest son,

GILBERT DE COLVILE, living *temp.* STEPHEN and HENRY II., was ancestor of

SIR WILLIAM COLVILE, of Newton Colvile, one of the intended knights of the Royal Oak, was a devoted supporter of the royal cause. He m. Anne, dau. of Sir Richard Stone, of Stukeley, Hunts, and widow of Anthony Goldsborough, Esq.; but d. without male issue, 13 July, 1680, and was s. by his nephew (the eldest son of his brother, Jeffrey),

RICHARD COLVILE, Esq. of Newton, who m. Francis, dau. of Thomas Carter, Esq. of York; and d. in 1666, leaving a son and successor,

ROBERT COLVILE, Esq. of Newton Colvile, who m. 1st, Anne, dau. of William Whiting, Esq.; and 2ndly, a dau. of David Waite, Esq. of Wisbeach, and left issue,

RICHARD COLVILE, Esq. of Newton Colvile, who m. Elizabeth, dau. of Nathaniel Acton, Esq. of Bramford Hall, Suffolk, and had issue, with two daus., the younger m. to the Rev. Dr. Gee,

I. ROBERT, his heir.
II. Nathaniel, D.D. of St. Mary Hall, Oxford, rector of Lowshall, Suffolk; m. 13 Sept. 1794, Amy-Letitia, dau. of the Rev. Thomas Purvis, rector of Melton, in Suffolk, and has had issue,
1 Nathaniel, M.A., m. Emma, youngest dau. of the late Christopher-Barton Metcalfe, Esq. of West Ham, Essex, and Hawstead, Suffolk. She d. 14 Feb. 1840.

2 William, M.A., *m.* Margaret-Augusta, dau. of General Kelso, and granddau. of John Kelso, Esq. of Dalkeith, in Ayrshire.
1 Fanny.
2 Amy-Lætitia, *m.* 11 Sept. 1820, Capt. Barrington Purvis, R.N., by whom (who *d.* 4 April, 1822) she had issue one dau., Philippe, who *m.* 1841, Capt. William Kelso, late of the 72nd Highlanders.

The elder son,

ROBERT COLVILE, Esq. of Newton Colvile, *b.* 3 Sept. 1763, sold the manor of Newton in 1792. He *m.* Amelia, eldest dau. of Sir Charles Asgill, Bart., and had issue,

I. CHARLES-HENRY (Sir), his heir.
II. Frederick-Charles-Acton, late capt. 3rd foot-guards, and aide-de-camp to Lord Lynedoch; *m.* 2 July, 1817, Mary, sister to Chandos, Lord Leigh, and granddau. of Thomas, 10th Lord Saye and Sele, and has had issue, Frederick-Leigh, M.A., vicar of Leek Wooton, co. Warwick, *b.* 4 June, 1818; Henry-Chandos, *b.* in 1822, *d.* in 1840; Graham, an officer in the 43rd regt., *b.* in 1824; George-Twisleton, R.N.; Fiennes-Middleton, *b.* in 1832; Emily, *d.* in 1837; Maria, *d.* in 1838; and Isabel.
III. Augustus-Asgill, M.A., rector of Great and Little Livermere, co. Suffolk; *m.* 1st, Maria, dau. of Edmund Broderip, Esq. of Bath, and by her (who *d.* 15 Jan. 1835) he has issue, Robert-Acton and Amelia. He *m.* 2ndly, at Paris, in 1839, Miss Hemings, and has issue, Eleanora, and Augustus-Henry-Asgill.
IV. Henry-Robert, lieut.-col. Scots fusilier-guards; *m.* in 1836, Julia, eldest sister of Chandos, Lord Leigh.

Mr. Colvile *d.* 24 Sept. 1799, and was *s.* by his son,

SIR CHARLES-HENRY COLVILE, Knt., who was high-sheriff for Derbyshire in the year 1831. He *m.* Hariot-Anne, dau. of Thomas-Porter Bonnel, Esq., heiress to the families of Porter and Coape, by Anne, dau. of Joseph Bradshawe, Esq. of Barton Hall, Derbyshire. By this marriage he became possessed of Duffield Hall, Derbyshire. He *d.* at Stutgardt, in the kingdom of Wirtemburg, 28 Sept. 1833, Lady Colvile surviving him only fifteen months, dying at Nice, 11 Dec. 1834, at which respective places they were severally interred. They left issue,

CHARLES-ROBERT, now of Duffield Hall and Lullington.
Anne-Amelia, *m.* to the Rev. Samuel Bradshaw, of Basford Hall, co. Stafford.
Constance-Hariot, *m.* to the Rev. Hayter-George Hames rector of Chagford, Devon.

Arms—Az., a lion, rampant, or; a label of five points, gu., the whole width of the shield.
Crest—On a chapeau, gu., turned up, erm., a lion, statant, tail extended, arg., gorged with a label of three points, of the first.
Motto—Persevere.
Seat—Lullington, Burton-on-Trent.

COMER OF FITZHEAD.

COMER, THOMAS, Esq. of Fitzhead, co. Somerset, *b.* 3 Sept. 1790; *m.* in 1813, Susanna, eldest dau. of the late Robert Baker, Esq. of Halse and Broadway, co. Somerset (by Sarah his wife, eldest dau. of Henry Spurway, Esq. of The Fort, in Milverton), and has had issue,

I. THOMAS, *b.* in 1813, *m.* in 1844, Carmela-Theresia-Vincenta-Anna, eldest dau. of Lewis Barbar, Esq. of Malta, and has two sons and one dau.,
1 Charles-William, *b.* in 1848.
2 Walter-Frederick-Bluett, *b.* in 1850.
1 Carmela-Mary, *b.* in 1851.
II. John-Bluett, *b.* in 1815, and *d.* *unm.* in 1835.
III. Robert-Baker, *b.* in 1821.
I. Mary. II. Susan.

Lineage.—The family of Comer have been settled in Somersetshire for many generations. John Comer, who held lands there in Wynsford, had other lands situate in Ashe or Aishe, conveyed to him and his wife Christian, *temp.* ELIZABETH. The present Thomas Comer, Esq. of Fitzhead, who is son of Thomas Comer, Esq. of Fitzhead, by Mary his wife, dau. of John Harecombe, Esq., and Mary Arscott his wife, descends in the 3rd degree from John Comer, Esq. of Milverton, and Jane his wife, dau. of John Bluett, Esq.

Arms—Vert, on a fesse, between three eagles, displayed, or, as many keys, wards upwards, sa.
Crest—A squirrel, sejant, ppr., collared, dancetté, and line reflexed over the back, or, and holding in the paws a key, as in the arms.
Motto—Persevere.

COMMERELL OF STROOD.

COMMERELL, JOHN, Esq. of Strood, co. Sussex, *b.* in 1796; *m.* 17 July, 1822, Sophia, dau. of William Bosanquet, Esq. of Harley Street, London, and has issue,

I. WILLIAM-AUGUSTUS, *b.* 1 Oct. 1828.
II. John-Edmund, *b.* 15 Jan. 1829.
I. Henrietta-Sophia.

Lineage.—FREDERICK-WILLIAM COMMERELL, son of WILLIAM-FREDERICK COMMERELL, of Heilbronn, in Suabia, came from that imperial German town to England in 1732, and was naturalised by letters-patent, in 1752. He *m.* in 1749, Catherine, dau. of Thomas Elton, Esq. of Little Gaddesden, co. Herts, and *d.* at Hanwell, Middlesex, in 1798, leaving an only son,

JOHN-WILLIAM COMMERELL, Esq. of Strood, near Horsham, co. Sussex, high-sheriff of that co. in 1808, who *m.* 2 Nov. 1786, Mary, dau. of Jacob Bosanquet, Esq. of London, and had issue,

JOHN, now of Strood.
Maria-Susannah, *m.* 20 July, 1821, to Capt. Robert-Melville-Grindlay, E.I.C.S. Eliza-Christina.

Arms—Gu., a dexter arm, embowed, couped below the shoulder, holding in the hand a branch of laurel, all ppr.
Crest—A dexter arm, holding a laurel-branch, as in the arms.
Seat—Strood, near Horsham, co. Sussex.

COMPTON OF THE MANOR HOUSE.

COMPTON, HENRY-COMBE, Esq. of The Manor House, Minestead, Hants, *b.* 6 Jan. 1789; *m.* 16 Jan. 1810, Charlotte, 2nd dau. of William Mills, Esq. of Bisterne, Hants, and by her, who *d.* March 23, 1854, has issue,

I. HENRY, *b.* 28 Sept. 1813.
II. John, in holy orders, *b.* 21 March, 1817, rector of Minestead.
III. Berdmore, in holy orders, *b.* 14 July, 1820, *m.* Agnes, 5th dau. of Mortimer Drummond, Esq.
IV. Charles-Talbot, *b.* 8 Dec. 1821.
V. Paulet-Mildmay, *b.* 24 Feb. 1823, *m.* Mary-Catherine, 2nd dau. of Henry Weyland, Esq.
VI. Francis, *b.* 20 Nov. 1824, barrister-at-law.
VII. Berkeley-Drummond, *d.* 22 May, 1851.
VIII. Digby, *b.* 18 Jan. 1830.
I. Catherine, *m.* 28 April, 1838, to Capt. Aitchison, R.N.
II. Selina-Maria.

Mr. Compton, who is son of the late John Compton, Esq., by Catherine his wife, eldest dau. of the Rev. John Richards, of Longbredy, co. Dorset, and grandson of Henry Compton, Esq., by Lucretia Mills his wife, represented the southern division of Hampshire in parliament. He has had one brother, the Rev. John-Combe Compton, *b.* 9 June, 1793, rector of Minestead, who *d.* 25 April, 1835; and three sisters, Lucretia-Catherine, Mary, and Charlotte, *m.* to the Rev. Francis Dyson, rector of Tedworth.

Arms—Sa., a lion, passant-guardant, or, between three helmets, arg.
Crest—A demi-dragon, erased, wings elevated, the body encircled with a ducal coronet.
Seat—The Manor House, Minestead.

COMYN OF WOODSTOCK AND KILCORNEY.

COMYN, FRANCIS, Esq. of Woodstock, co. Galway, and of Kilcorney, co. Clare, J.P., *b.* 3 Oct. 1801; *m.* 28 April, 1834, Honoria, dau. of Edward-James Beytagh, Esq. of Cappagh, co. Galway, by the Hon. Sarah ffrench his wife, dau. of Thomas, Lord ffrench, and has issue,

I. FRANCIS-LORENZO, a lieut. in the co. of Galway militia, *b.* 12 Nov. 1835.
II. Sarsfield-John, *b.* 6 Feb. 1837.
III. Charles-Edward-ffrench, *b.* 2 April, 1844.
IV. William-Alfred, *b.* 25 Jan. 1846.
V. George-Patrick, *b.* 17 March, 1848.
VI. Harry-Edward-Beytagh, *b.* Oct. 1850.
I. Rosa-Selina-Margaret.
II. Laura-Mary-Honoria.

Lineage.—This family of Comyn, claiming to be originally a scion of the great Scottish house of COMYN of

Badenoch, in which vested the office of Justiciary of Scotland, and on which was conferred the Earldom of Buchan, has been established in Ireland for many centuries. At an early period after their settlement in that kingdom, we find the Comyns resident at Comyns Castle, in St. Mary's parish, Limerick, of which city a member of the family filled the chief civic office so far back as the reign of HENRY IV. From Limerick, the Comyns passed into Clare, and became possessed of considerable landed property in that county. From Sir William Comyn, Knt. of Limerick, living *circa* 1440, great-grandson of Sir Laurence Comyn, Knt., lineally descended the COMYNS *of Corcomroe*, of whom a pedigree was registered in the office of Ulster King of Arms in the year 1748; and the COMYNS *of Kilcorney*, of whom we are about to treat.

GEORGE COMYN, the immediate ancestor of the Woodstock family, was protected from forfeiture in the Great Civil War through the intervention of his cousin, Sir Hardress Waller, the Parliamentarian. His son,

JOHN COMYN, Esq., *m.* Margaret, dau. and co-heir of Thomas Comyn, Esq. of Moynoe, by Joan his wife, dau. of Sir Dominick Fannin, granddau. of Sir Dominick Arthur, and widow of Sir Dominick White, which Joan got from CROMWELL a grant of Kilcorney, co. Clare. By Margaret his wife, John Comyn had a son,

DAVID COMYN, Esq. of Kilcorney, who *m.* Elizabeth, sister of John Davorne, Esq. of the co. Clare, and had issue, Laurence; and George, M.D., physician to LOUIS XVI. The elder son, LAURENCE COMYN, Esq. of Kilcorney, *m.* Julian-Maria, dau. of Peter Martyn, Esq. of Coole, co. Galway, and was *s.* by his son,

DAVID COMYN, Esq. of Kilcorney, who *m.* Dora, dau. of William Macnamara, Esq. of Doolen, co. Clare, by Catharine his wife, dau. and heir of Francis Sarsfield, Esq., and had issue, 1 LAURENCE, his heir; and 2 William, whose son, Laurence Comyn, Esq. of Moyne, co. Clare, left a son, Nicholas, who *d. s. p.*, and two daus., the elder *m.* to Thomas Browne, Esq. of Newgrove, co. Clare; and the younger, Bridget, to Andrew Stackpole, Esq. of Castle Lodge, co. Clare. The son and heir,

LAURENCE COMYN, Esq. of Kilcorney, *m.* Jane, dau. of Nicholas Lynch, Esq. of Barna, co. Galway, and left at his decease, 1820, with junior issue, FRANCIS, now of Woodstock; and Sarsfield-Peter, of The Farm, near Galway.

Arms—The same as COMYN *of Badenoch*: Gu., three garbs, arg.
Crest—A demi-lion, gu., crowned, or, supporting an Irish harp, ppr.
Seat—Woodstock, co. Galway.

CONCANON OF CARROWNACREGGY.

CONCANON, EDMOND-JOHN, Esq. of Waterloo, co. Galway, late of Carrownacreggy, in that county, lineal male descendant of the old and distinguished Irish house of O'Concanon, *b.* 29 Jan. 1792; *m.* in 1815, Jane, dau. of John Blake, Esq., J.P., of Belmont House, co. Galway, an officer in the 13th dragoons, by Sarah his wife, dau. of the Right Hon. James Cuff, of Ballinrobe, M.P. for Mayo, sister and eventual co-heiress of James Cuff, Lord Tyrawley, and niece of Arthur, Earl of Arran. Jane Blake (Mrs. Concanon) derived, through the noble lines of Cuff, Aungier, Fitzgerald, Grey, Neville, and Holland, from Edmund Plantagenet, surnamed of Woodstock, son of King EDWARD I. (*See* BURKE'S *Royal Families*, vol. ii., ped. clviii). By her, who *d.* 26 March, 1854, Mr. Concanon has had issue,

I. HENRY, B.A. of Lincoln's Inn, barrister-at-law, *m.* 25 Nov. 1854, the Countess Maria-Aurora-Arabella de Lusi, dau. of the late Count de Lusi, by Maria his wife, dau. of Sir Duke Gifford, Bart. and Maria his wife, afterwards Marchioness of Lansdowne.
II. John, accidentally drowned at the Dargle, co. Wicklow, 15 June, 1847.
III. Edmond, *m.* Kate, eldest dau. of Charles Parsons, Esq., and has, Edmond-John, and other issue.
IV. James-Blake.
V. Anthony, an officer 3rd W. I. regt., *d. unm.* 25 Feb. 1838.
VI. George-Blake, in holy orders, B.A., deputation secretary to the Irish Society, *m.* Georgina-Harriette, 2nd dau. of Capt. Pollock, R.M., late of Castle Wilder, co. Longford, and has a son, William-Augustus, and a dau.

I. Sarah, *m.* to Edward Rochfort, Esq.
II. Anna, who *d. unm.*
III. Rachel-Mary.

Lineage.—The ancient Milesian family of O'Concanon derives its descent from Dermot, brother of Murias, 29th king of Connaught, in the 9th century, A.D. 815, whose grandson, Connor, king of Connaught, was ancestor of the O'CONOR DON (*see that family*). The celebrated Cathal Crovedearg O'Conor, King of Connaught, was fostered by Teige O'Concanon, at Hy-Diarmada, the ancient patrimony of the O'Concanons, in the county of Galway.

Frequent and honourable mention of the name occurs in the annals of Ireland, particularly in those of the Four Masters. At the great battle of Ceiscorainn, fought A.D. 971, Murcentach O'Concanon was slain; in 1168, Hugh O'Concanon, Lord of Ui Diarmada, a Religious, died at Clonmacnoise on the Shannon; and in 1478, Thomas O'Concanon, Lord of Ui or Hy Diarmada, was slain in a family feud. In 1585, Moriartach O'Concanon, otherwise styled "The O'Concanon," chief of his name, was one of the contracting parties in the Indentures of Composition for the county of Galway, entered into between the chieftains and gentry of Galway and Sir John Perrott, lord deputy of Ireland. During succeeding years, several members of the Concanon family obtained grants of lands in the county of Galway, and among others, Melaghlin and Edmond O'Concanon, of Moylagh, and William and John O'Concanon, of Coolowe. A lineal male descendant of this old and distinguished family,

EDMOND CONCANON, Esq. of Carrownacreggy, co. Galway (son and heir of John Concanon, Esq. of Carrownacreggy, and grandson of Edmond Concanon, Esq. of Carrownacreggy, to whose mother, Sisby O'Concanon, *née* Bourke, King CHARLES II., by patent bearing date 21 March, 1678, granted the lands of Carrownacreggy), *m.* in 1745, Elinor, dau. of Thomas Cuniffe, Esq. of Ardroe, co. Galway; and *d.* in 1770, leaving a son and successor,

HENRY CONCANON, Esq. of Carrownacreggy, who *m.* Rachel, dau. of John Marshall, Esq. of Ballygaddy, co. Galway, and by that lady, who *d.* in Dec. 1847, had issue,

I. EDMOND-JOHN, present representative.
II. James-Henry, who *m.* Olivia, dau. of Neptune Lynch, Esq. of Wood Park, co. Roscommon, and *d.* leaving issue.
I. Elinor, *m.* to Owen Lynch, Esq. of Wood Park, co. Roscommon.
II. Celia, *m.* to Dominick Bodkin, Esq. of Trasterna, co. Galway.

Mr. Concanon *d.* 11 Dec. 1810.

Arms—Arg., on a mount, vert, an oak tree, ppr., perched thereon a falcon, also ppr., belled, or; between, in base, two cross-crosslets, fitchée, gu.
Crest—An elephant, statant, ppr., tusked, or.
Motto—Coñ gan an: *i. e.*, Sagesse sans tache.
Seat—Waterloo, Glantane, co. Galway; formerly Carrownacreggy, in the same county.

CONGREVE OF CONGREVE.

CONGREVE, WILLIAM, Esq. of Congreve, co. Stafford, *b.* 2 March, 1777; *m.* 11 July, 1799, Mary-Mackintosh-Hurst, 2nd dau. and co-heiress of the late Sir William Pepperell, Bart. She *d.* 3 Feb. 1839.

Lineage.—This family, one of the most eminent in the co. Stafford, was settled at Congreve soon after the Conquest.

RICHARD CONGREVE, Esq. of Congreve and Stretton, (lineally descended from Galfrid de Congreve, who acquired, *temp.* EDWARD II., the manor of Stretton, in marriage with Catherine, heiress of William le Schampion), was one of the thirteen Staffordshire gentlemen upon whom King CHARLES II. intended to have conferred the order of the Royal Oak. He *m.* Anne, dau. of Sir Thomas Fitz-Herbert, of Norbury, son of Sir Anthony Fitz-Herbert, the eminent judge, and had two sons, JOHN, his successor; and William, a col. in the army, father of WILLIAM CONGREVE, the dramatist, *b.* in 1672; *d.* in 1728. Mr. Congreve was *s.* by his elder son,

JOHN CONGREVE, Esq. of Congreve and Stretton, *b.* 18 June, 1686, whose grandson,

THE REV. RICHARD CONGREVE, of Congreve, son of John Congreve, Esq. of Congreve and Stretton, *m.* Martha, dau. and heiress of John Jones, Esq. of Fynnant, co. Montgomery, and had issue,

William, present proprietor.
Richard, of Burton, co. Chester, *b.* 2 Aug. 1778, who *m.* Mary-Anne, dau. of George Birch, Esq. of Hampstead Hall, in Staffordshire, and has a numerous family.
Marianne, of Iswyd Park, Flintshire.

Mr. Congreve *d.* 27 July, 1782.

Arms—Sa., a chevron between three battle-axes, arg.
Crest—A falcon rising, wings expanded.
Motto—Non moritur cujus fama vivit.

CONGREVE OF MOUNT CONGREVE.

Congreve, John, Esq. of Mount Congreve, co. Waterford, D.L. for that county, *m.* in 1827, Harriet, eldest dau. of the 2nd Lord Clonbrock, and has issue.

Seat—Mount Congreve, Kilmeadan.

CONNELLAN OF COOLMORE.

Connellan, Peter, Esq. of Coolmore, co. Kilkenny, *b.* 3 Feb. 1806; a magistrate and deputy-lieut., and high-sheriff of the county in 1836; *m.* 25 July, 1844, Anne-Maria, 2nd dau. of the Rev. Sir Hercules-Richard Langrishe, Bart. of Knocktopher Abbey, co. Kilkenny, by whom he has,

I James-Fitzwalter-Hercules-Henry, *b.* 20 Aug 1849.
I. Maria-Isabella. II. Harriet-Charlotte.
III. Fanny-Rose. IV. Georgina-Jane.
V. Eliza-Mary.

Lineage.—The family of Connellan, or O'Connellan, as it was originally written, is of ancient Milesian extraction, and in Comerford's *History of Ireland*, is deduced from the great family of O'Neill, on the authority of the Psalters of Tara and Cashel, the great sources of Irish genealogy. This descent is further confirmed by a very ancient Irish manuscript, (in the possession of the late Sir William Betham) in which the family of O'Connellan is made one of the branches from Niall *of the Nine Hostages*. From Hardiman's *Ancient Irish Deeds, No. XIV.*, it would appear that the family was seated in the co. Limerick in the middle of the 14th century, as we find that tribute of wheat and money was levied yearly off the lands of Lis-Connellan, proving the location of a family of consequence there, and giving name to the place; and in the same work is found (*No. XXVIII.*) that Siacus O'Connellan, in the same county, was witness to certain covenants in 1573. It is probable that their possessions in that county were lost by confiscation, as from this period we find mention of the family principally in Connaught, where they became seised of a part of the forfeited Clanricarde estates. As appears from public records in the Record Tower of Dublin Castle: "Donough O'Conolane, son of Shane O'Conolane, had a grant from the crown of an eighth part of the lower quarter of the lands of Rahassan, co. Galway, in 1619; William-Nevagh O'Conolane, of Rahassan, had a grant from the crown, 27 March, 1619, of half the Cartrons of Cahiroane and Pole Idownine, and three-sixteenths of the lower quarter of Rahassan; and Gilpatrick O'Conellan, in the same year, had a grant from the crown of the other half of the Cartrons of Cahiroane and Pole Idownine, in the barony of Kiltaragh, and co. Galway." Descended from this latter, was James Connellan, *b.* early in the 17th century, who *m.* Miss Graham, of the Montrose family, and was father of

Martin Connellan, *b.* in 1688, who *m.* Miss Butler, descended from a branch of the Ormonde family, and by her had six sons, all of whom *d.* without legitimate male issue, except the youngest,

Peter Connellan, *b.* in 1745, who *m.* Miss Galhie, a lady of French extraction, and by her (who *d.* in 1786,) had one dau., Anne, wife of Pierce Blake, Esq. of Holly Park, co. Galway, brother of the Right Hon. Anthony-Richard Blake, chief remembrancer of Ireland, and one son,

Peter, *b.* 7 July, 1782, who *m.* in March, 1805, Harriet, dau. of James Corry, Esq., clerk of the journals of the Irish House of Commons, and predeceasing his father, 11 Nov. 1806, left two sons,
Peter, successor to his grandfather.
James-Corry (posthumous), *b.* 13 Jan. 1807, M.A. of Oriel College, Oxford, and barrister-at-law. Mr. Corry Connellan has been for some years in the public service, having filled the office of Chancellor's secretary during the tenure of the Great Seal of Ireland by Lords Plunket and Campbell; of private secretary to their Excellencies the Earls of Bessborough and Clarendon, K.G., during their viceroyalties; and of inspector-general of prisons.

Mr. Connellan *d.* in 1820, aged 75, and was *s.* by his grandson, the present Peter Connellan, Esq., of Coolmore.

Arms—Per fesse, az. and vert, a fesse, or, between a pelican, arg., vulned, gu., in chief, and a land-tortoise, passant, of the third, in base.
Crest—An owl perched on the stump of an oak-tree, ppr.
Motto—Inter utrumque. Over the crest:—Sape et tace.
Seat—Coolmore, Thomastown, co. Kilkenny.

CONNER OF MANCH.

Conner, Daniel, Esq. of Manch House, co. Cork, J.P., *b.* 13 Feb. 1798; *m.* 4 June, 1822, Elizabeth, dau. of the Rev. Mountifort Longfield, of Church Hill, co. Cork, and has issue,

I. Daniel, *b.* 25 Feb. 1823, *m.* 6 Jan. 1848, Patience, dau. of Henry Longfield, Esq. of Waterloo, co. Cork, and has three daus., and one son, *b.* 11 April, 1853.
II. Mountifort-Longfield, *b.* 18 Sept. 1824, *m.* 4 Dec. 1849, Anna, dau. of the Rev. G. Smith.
I. Grace-Elizabeth, *m.* 28 June, 1851, to the Rev. R.-M. Conner, F.T.C.D.
II. Mary-Elizabeth, *m.* 17 June, 1852, to the Rev. Edward Lysaght.
III. Elizabeth-Jane. IV. Louisa-Sophia.
V. Charlotte-Alicia.

Lineage.—Daniel Conner, of Bandon, merchant, descended from an ancient Munster family, realized a large fortune, which he invested in the purchase of estates, principally situate in the co. of Cork. He *m.* and had issue, I. Daniel, of Bandon, merchant, who *d.* in 1737; II. William, of whom hereafter; III. George, of Ballybricken, who left a dau., Mary-Anne, *m.* in 1778, John Lysaght, 2nd Lord Lisle; and a son, the ancestor of the present Daniel Conner, Esq., J.P., of Ballybricken; I. Jane, who *m.* Mr. Lapp, of Cork, merchant; II. Mary, *m.* to — Thomas, Esq. of Everton, co. Carlow; III. Hannah, *m.* to — Delahoyde, Esq.; and IV. Elizabeth, *m.* to Richard Gumbleton, Esq. of Castle Richard, co. Waterford. The 2nd son,

William Conner, Esq. of Connerville, co. Cork, M.P. for Bandon in 1765, *m.* in 1721, Anne, dau. of Roger Bernard, Esq. of Palace Anne, co. Cork. His 4th son,

Roger Conner, of Connerville, *m.* Anne Longfield, sister of the Right Hon. Lord Longueville, and by that lady had issue,

Daniel, *b.* in 1754.
William, who *m.*, and left issue.
Robert-Longfield, of Fort Robert, co. Cork, who *m.* Miss Madras, and left issue, three daus.
Roger, of Connerville, *b.* in 1763, who *m.* 1st, Louisa, dau. of Col. Strachan, by whom he had issue, Roderick, now settled in Van Diemen's Land; and Louisa, who *d. unm.* He *m.* 2ndly, Wilhelmina, dau. of — Bowen, Esq. of Bowenscourt, co. Cork, by whom he had issue, Arthur, who *m.* his cousin, Mary Connor, of Fort Robert; Feargus-Edward, *b.* in 1796, M.P. for co. Cork in 1832, and for Nottingham in 1847; Francis-Burdett, an officer in the Bolivian army; George-Roger, who *m.* his cousin, Elizabeth Conner, of Fort Robert; besides daus.
Arthur, *b.* in 1765, *m.* a dau. of M. de Condorcet, by whom he left issue: he was representative in parliament for the borough of Philipstown.

The eldest son,

Daniel Conner, of Orme-square, Bayswater, London, *b.* in 1754, *m.* 5 Feb. 1789, Mary, dau. of the Rev. Arthur Hyde, by whom he left at his decease in 1846, several daus., and an only son, the present Daniel Conner, Esq. of Manch House.

Arms—Vert, a lion, rampant, double-queued, or.
Crest—A dexter arm, embowed, in armour, ppr., garnished, or, the hand grasping a short sword, ppr., the hilt and pommel, of the last.
Motto—Min, sicker, reag.
Seat—Manch House, near Dunmanway, co. Cork.

CONOLLY OF CASTLETOWN.

Conolly, Thomas, Esq. of Castletown, co. Kildare, and of Cliff, co. Donegal, M.P., *b.* in 1823.

Lineage.—*See* Burke's *Peerage*—Longford. The late Edward-Michael Conolly, Esq. of Castletown and Cliff, lieut.-colonel Donegal militia, and M.P. for the co. of Donegal, *b.* 24 Aug. 1786 (eldest son and heir of Admiral the Hon. Sir Thomas Pakenham, G.C.B., by Louisa-Augusta his wife, dau. of the Right Hon. John Staples, M.P., and

Harriet his wife, dau. of the Right Hon. William Conolly,* by the Lady Anne Wentworth his wife), s. to the estates of his grand-uncle the Right Hon. Thomas Conolly, at the decease of that gentleman's widow in 1821, and thereupon took the surname and arms of CONOLLY. He m. 20 May, 1819, Catherine-Jane, dau. of Chambre-Brabazon Ponsonby-Barker, Esq., by the Lady Henrietta Taylour his wife, dau. of Thomas, Earl of Bective, and has issue,

I. THOMAS, b. in 1823.
II. Chambre-Brabazon, d. in 1835.
III. Edward-Frederick.
IV. Arthur-Wellesley, capt. 30th foot, killed in the Crimea.
V. John-Augustus, capt. Coldstream-guards, so gallantly distinguished in the Crimea.
I. Louisa-Augusta, m. to the late Lord Langford, and was accidentally drowned, 4 Nov. 1853.
II. Harriet.
III. Mary-Margaret, m. 6 June, 1854, to Henry Bruen, Esq. of Oak Park, co. Carlow.
IV. Fanny.

Arms—Arg., on a saltier, sa., five escallops, of the field.
Crest—A cubit arm, erect, vested, gu., cuff, arg., holding in the hand an annulet, arg.
Motto—En Dieu est tout.
Seats—Castletown, Celbridge; and Cliff, Ballyshannon.

CONOLLY OF MIDFORD CASTLE.

CONOLLY, CHARLES-JOHN-THOMAS, Esq. of Midford Castle, co. Somerset, b. 12 Sept. 1818; m. 15 Sept. 1840, Louisa-Margaret-Catherine-Brancaccio, only dau. of the late Prince Ruffano, chamberlain to FERDINAND, king of Naples.

Lineage.—This family claims to be a branch of that of Castletown. The late

CHARLES-THOMAS CONOLLY, Esq. of Midford Castle, b. 14 March, 1791 (only son of Charles Conolly, Esq., by Maria-Rebecca his wife, dau. of Thomas Bourke, Esq., and great-grandson of Thomas Conolly, Esq.), m. 1st, 23 Aug. 1814, Elizabeth, dau. of John Clifton, Esq. of Lytham Hall, co. Lancaster, and 2ndly, 8 Oct. 1828, Jane, dau. of Philip Lawless, Esq. of Dublin. By the former he left at his decease, 13 Feb. 1850, an only child, CHARLES-JOHN, now of Midford Castle.

Arms—Arg., on a saltier sa., five escallops, of the field.
Crest—A cubit-arm, erect, vested, sa., cuffs, arg., holding in the hand a wreath, or, and three rogets, as.
Motto—En Dieu est tout.
Seat—Midford Castle, near Bath, co. Somerset.

CONWY OF BODRHYDDAN.

CONWY, WILLIAM-SHIPLEY, Esq. of Bodrhyddan, co. Flint, b. 14 Aug. 1807; D.L. and high-sheriff for Flintshire in 1840.

Lineage.—The distinguished race of the Conwys† have been seated at Prestatyn and Bodrhyddan since the time of EDWARD I. They derive their descent from SIR HUGH CONWY, son of old Sir John Coniers, of Richmond, in Yorkshire, brother to Ievan, Lord Coniers. For details of the lineage see BURKE's *Extinct Baronetage*.

SIR JOHN CONWY, the 2nd and last Baronet, M.P., d. in 1721. He m. twice: his 1st wife was Margaretta-Theophila, dau. of John Digby, of Goathurst, son of the celebrated Sir Kenelm Digby; by her he had (with a dau., Maria-Margaretta, m. to Sir Thomas Longueville, Bart.) one son, Harry, who m. Honora, dau. of Edward Ravenscroft, of Broadlane, Hawarden. He, dying in the lifetime of his father, left one only child, Honora, who m. Sir John Glynne, of Hawarden Castle, ancestor of the present Sir Stephen-Richard Glynne, Bart. Honora was ten years old when her grandfather d., in 1721. Sir John Conwy m. 2ndly, Penelope, dau. of Mr. Grenville, of Wootton, in Buckinghamshire. By her he had two daus.: one never married; the eldest,

PENELOPE CONWY, m. James-Russell Stapleton, Esq., a col. in the Guards, 2nd son of Sir William Stapleton, Bart., and had four daus., co-heiresses. The eldest dau.,

PENELOPE YONGE, wife of Ellis Yonge, Esq. of Bryn Yorcin, d. in 1783, leaving two daus., and co-heirs. The younger, Barbara, d. unm. in 1837; the elder,

PENELOPE YONGE, m. the VERY REV. WILLIAM-DAVIES SHIPLEY, Dean of St. Asaph, only son (by Anna-Maria his wife, dau. and co-heir of the Hon. and Rev. George Mordaunt) of Jonathan Shipley, Bishop of St. Asaph. Mrs. Shipley d. 5 Nov. 1789, aged 31, leaving five sons and three daus.,

I. WILLIAM SHIPLEY, lieut.-col. in the army, M.P. for the Flint boroughs, m. in 1806, Charlotte, sister of the late Sir Watkin Williams-Wynn, Bart. of Wynnstay, and dying s. p. in 1819, left issue,
  1 WILLIAM, now of Bodrhyddan, who assumed the surname of CONWY.
  1 Charlotte, m. to the Hon. Richard Rowley.
II. Mordaunt Shipley, d. s. p. in 1807.
III. Robert-John Shipley, royal engineers, d. unm.
IV. Conwy Shipley, capt. R.N., killed in 1808.
V. Charles Shipley, in holy orders, of Twyford House, Hants, rector of Mappowder, co. Dorset, b. in 1783, m. in 1821, Charlotte, dau. of Robert Orby Sloper, Esq. of Woodhay, Berks, and has issue.
I. Penelope, m. to Pelham Warren, M.D. of London.
II. Anna-Maria, m. to Col. Charles-Armand Dashwood.
III. Emily, m. to Reginald Heber, Bishop of Calcutta.

The Dean of St. Asaph d. in 1826.

Arms—CONWY and SHIPLEY, quarterly.
Crest—A Moor's head in profile, couped, ppr., wreathed about the temples, arg. and az.
Motto—Fide et amore.
Seat—Bodrhyddan, near Rhyl.

CONYNGHAM OF SPRING HILL.

CONYNGHAM, WILLIAM-LENOX, Esq. of Spring Hill, co. Londonderry, J.P. and D.L., high-sheriff of Tyrone in 1818, and of Londonderry in 1828, b. 9 Jan. 1792; m. 7 June, 1819, Charlotte-Melosina, dau. of the late Right Hon. John Staples, of Lisson, and has issue,

I. WILLIAM-FITZWILLIAM, b. 25 April, 1824.
II. John-Staples-Molesworth, b. 9 Jan. 1831.
I. Harriett-Rebecca-Frances.
II. Jane-Hamilton. III. Charlotte-Melosina.

Lineage.—The family of Conyngham settled at Spring Hill in 1658, and the family of Lenox, in Londonderry, *temp.* JAMES I.

CLOTWORTHY LENOX, Esq. of the city of Derry, 2nd son of John Lenox, Esq., by Rebecca Upton his wife, and grandson of James Lenox, M.P. for Derry, who was distinguished at the siege of that city, m. 13 June, 1745, Anne, dau. of George Conyngham, of Spring Hill, Esq., and by her had, with other issue, a son,

GEORGE LENOX, Esq., who assumed the name and arms of CONYNGHAM. He m. 1st, 11 April, 1779, Jane, eldest dau. of Jane Conyngham, by her 1st marriage, with John Hamilton, Esq. of Castlefin, and by her, who d. 20 Feb. 1793, had an only son,

WILLIAM LENOX, now of Spring Hill.

Mr. Lenox Conyngham m. 2ndly, 5 April, 1794, Olivia, 4th dau. of William Irvine, Esq. of Castle Irvine, co. Fermanagh, and by her had issue,

George, chief clerk in the Secretary of State's office for Foreign Affairs, m. Elizabeth, only child of Robert Holmes, Esq. of the city of Dublin, barrister-at-law, and has issue one son and one dau., Mary-Anne-Grace-Louisa, m. 20 Aug. 1851, to Hayes, Viscount Doneraile.
Sophia, m. to the Hon. A.-G. Stuart, of the co. Tyrone.
Anna, m. to C.-A. Nicholson, Esq. of Balrath, co. Meath.
Harriett, m. to Capt. Joseph Postlock, royal engineers.
Eliza.

Arms—CONYNGHAM and LENOX, quarterly.
Crest—1st, A unicorn's head, couped, arg., maned and horned, or, for CONYNGHAM; 2nd, LENOX.
Motto—Over, fork over.
Seat—Spring Hill, co. Londonderry.

COOKE OF OWSTON AND GWYSANEY.

COOKE, PHILIP-BRYAN-DAVIES, Esq. of Owston, co. York, and Gwysaney, co. Flint, b. 2 March, 1832.

Lineage.—HENRY COOKE, Esq., 2nd son of Sir Henry Cooke, 2nd baronet of Wheatley, purchased from the family of Adams, the lands of Owston, in the co. of York, and there seated himself. He m. Anne, dau. and co-heir of the Rev. Ralph Eaton, rector of Darfield, and dying in in 1717, was s. by his son,

BRIAN COOKE, Esq. of Owston, recorder of Doncaster,

* The Right Hon. William Conolly was nephew of the Right Hon. William Conolly, Speaker of the House of Commons in Ireland, *temp.* Queen ANNE.

† Edward Conway, created BARON CONWAY and EARL OF CONWAY, was one of this family. He dying s. p., left his estates, his names, and arms, to Francis Seymour, who was, in 1702, created a Peer of England, by the title of Baron Conway, and became founder of the Hertford family.

at whose decease, unm. in 1754, aged 52, the estates devolved upon his brother,

ANTHONY COOKE, Esq. of Owston, b. in 1710, who m. Mary, dau. of Anthony Eyre, Esq. of Adwickle Street, and d. in 1761, leaving, with a dau. Anne, wife of St. Andrew Wards, Esq. of Hooton Pagnel, a son and heir,

BRYAN COOKE, Esq. of Owston, col. of the 3rd West York militia, and M.P. for Malton, who m. 1st, Frances, dau. and heir of Philip Puleston, Esq. of Hafodywern, in the co. of Denbigh, by Mary his wife, dau. and co-heir of John Davies, Esq. of Llanerch and Gwysaney,* who d. 1 Jan. 1818, and by her had issue,

PHILIP-DAVIES, his heir.
Robert-Bryan, in holy orders, b. 29 Aug. 1800, m. in 1825, Emily-Carterett, youngest dau. of Philip Smith Webb, Esq. of Milford House, Surrey, and has issue.
Anthony-Henry, b. 16 Aug. 1801, d. on board the "Liffey," at Trincomalee, 11 Feb. 1823.
William-Bryan, an officer in the army.
Mary-Frances, m. in 1818, to the Rev. William Margesson.

Col. Cooke m. 2ndly, Charlotte, dau. of Sir George Cooke, Bart. of Wheatley, but had no further issue. He d. 8 Nov. 1820, and was s. by his eldest son,

PHILIP-DAVIES COOKE, Esq. of Owston and Gwysaney, J.P. and D.L., F.L.S., F.H.S., F.G.S., and F.Z.S., b. 11 Aug. 1793; m. 8 Dec. 1829, Helena-Caroline, eldest dau. of George, 3rd Earl of Kingston, and had issue,

PHILIP-BRYAN-DAVIES, now of Owston and Gwysaney.
Bryan-George-Davies, b. 3 Jan. 1835.
George-Robert-Davies, b. 29 May, 1836.
James-Robert-Davies, b. 4 July, 1837.
Adelaide-Flora-Frances.

Arms—Or, a chevron, gu., between two lions passant-guardant, sa.
Crest—Out of a mural crown, arg., a demi-lion, guardant, sa., ducally gorged, or.
Seats—Owston, Doncaster; and Gwysaney, Flintshire.

COOKE OF KYLTINAN CASTLE.

COOKE, ROBERT, Esq. of Kyltinan Castle, co. Tipperary, J.P., m. Hannah, dau. of the late Sir Richard-Wheeler Cuffe, Bart. of Leyrath, co. Kilkenny, and has issue,

ROBERT, who m. Jane, sister of John Congreve, Esq. of Mount Congreve, co. Waterford, and d., leaving issue.
Anne.

Lineage.—EDWARD COOKE, 2nd son of PETER COOKE, and brother of THOMAS COOKE, was father of

JOHN COOKE, Esq., one of the commissioners named in the statutes 9 WILL. III., c. 8, and 10 WILL. III., c. 8, for assessing the land and poll taxes in the co. Tipperary. His son and heir,

ROBERT COOKE, Esq. of Kyltinan Castle, was father, by his wife, a sister of Field-Marshal Wade, of the co. Cork, of

EDWARD COOKE, Esq. of Kyltinan Castle, who by his wife, Abygaile Green, of Greenville, co. Waterford, left a son and successor, ROBERT COOKE, Esq. of Kyltinan Castle, and a dau., Frances, who m. Lieut.-Colonel John Jackson Glover, of the 11th infantry and colonel-commandant of the Bath Loyal Volunteers, and d. his widow at Bath, 27 Feb. 1847.

Arms—Party per pale, gu. and az., three eaglets, displayed, arg.
Crest—On a chapeau, gu., turned up erm., an ostrich, ppr., holding in its bill a horse-shoe, or.
Motto—Virtus ardua petit.
Seat—Kyltinan Castle, co. Tipperary.

COOKE OF CORDANGAN.

COOKE, JOSEPH, Esq. of Cordangan, co. Tipperary, b. 8 Oct. 1787; m. 18 May, 1813, Jane-Scott, dau. of Thomas Rodie, Esq. of Liverpool, and has issue,

I. JOHN, b. 8 May, 1820, in holy orders, a graduate of Oxford, m. 29 April, 1847, Ellen-Durham, dau. of the late Sir Joseph Huddart, Knt.
II. Thomas-Rodie, b. 9 Feb. 1823.
III. Joseph-Henry, b. 27 April, 1826.
I. Elizabeth-Matilda. II. Mary-Jane.

Mr. Cooke is a magistrate and deputy-lieutenant for the co. of Tipperary.

Lineage.—PETER COOKE, Esq., youngest son of Peter Cooke, and brother of the ancestor of the Kyltinan family, d. at Knockgraffon, co. Tipperary, and devised his property to his son and successor,

JOSEPH COOKE, Esq. of Arraglin, b. 11 Nov. 1669, who m. twice; by his 1st wife, he was father of JOHN, of Cordangan; and by the 2nd, Anne Boyce, he had three sons,

JOSEPH, of Gurrangreny.
Samuel, of Clanamicken, co. Tipperary.
Peter, who was in holy orders, and the first chaplain appointed under Stella's will to Madam Stephen's Hospital: he held the situation for fifty-three years, and was the intimate friend of the celebrated Dean Swift. By his wife, Anne, sister of Rev. William Shewbridge, rector of Portumna, he was father of Hannah, wife to her cousin Capt. William Shewbridge, of Heathlawn, co. Galway, whose only dau. Sydney, m. Dr. John Connor, of Dublin, and had issue by him several sons, two of whom d. abroad in the army, and two were drowned accidentally in the Shannon in 1820. Peter Cooke had also another dau., who d. unm.; and his 3rd dau. was m. to a Mr. Smith. Many of Dean Swift's letters were formerly in the possession of Mrs. Connor, of Dublin.

Joseph Cooke d. at Arraglin, and was s. by his son,

JOHN COOKE, Esq. of Cordangan, an alderman of Youghal, m. Elizabeth Hobbs, and left (with a son, Samuel, barrister-at-law, who d. unm., and two daus., Elizabeth, wife of David Courtney, Esq., co. Mayo, and Anne, wife of John Waters, Esq.) a son,

JOSEPH COOKE, Esq. of Cordangan, who m. Anne Garnot, and had issue,

JOHN, his heir.
Elizabeth, m. to the Rev. Robert-Carew Armstrong, of Moycliffe, co. Tipperary.
Mary, m. to John Orpen, Esq. of Flintfield, co. Kerry.

The son and heir,

JOHN COOKE, Esq. of Cordangan, barrister-at-law, J.P. and deputy-governor of the co. Tipperary, m. 10 March, 1783, Mary, dau. of Nicholas Taylor, Esq. of the island of Antigua, and had issue,

JOSEPH, now of Cordangan.
Margaret, m. to Michael Bevan, Esq. of Cammas, co. Limerick.

Arms—Arg., a lion, passant, in bend, between two cotises, gu.; on a chief, az., two estoiles, or.
Crest—A demi-lion, rampant, gu., holding between his paws a mullet, or.
Motto—Tu ne cede malis, sed contra audentior ito.
Seat—Cordangan.

COOKE OF RETREAT.

COOKE, WILLIAM, Esq. of Retreat, co. Westmeath, J.P., b. 23 Jan. 1793; m. 1st, in 1815, Catherine, only child of Falkiner Chute, Esq., capt. 6th dragoon-guards; and 2ndly, Ruth, 2nd dau. of Richard Chute, Esq. of Chute Hall, co. Kerry, and has had issue,

I. Thomas-Wyndham, b. in 1821, d. in 1840.
II. FALKINER, of the Lissavolan, near Athlone, b. in 1823.
III. William, b. in 1826. IV. Henry, b. in 1831.
V. John, b. in 1832. VI. Francis, b. in 1833.
I. Anne-Elizabeth, d. in 1839.
II. Kate, m. to her cousin, Edward Daly, Esq. of Mornington, co. Westmeath.

Lineage.—In the reign of ELIZABETH, three brothers of the Norfolk branch came in her army to Ireland, and obtained grants of lands in co. Cork. From one of them descended John or Thomas Cooke, who had five sons: Peter, who was of Ballyshiane, co. Tipperary, was ancestor to the families of Castle Cooke, co. Cork; Cappoquin, co. Waterford; and Kiltinan Castle and Cordangan, co. Tipperary. John, a younger brother of Peter, m. a dau. of Barry of Tinnscart, whose ancestor, Robert, a cadet of the Lord Barry's family, built the castle of Ballycclough, near Mallow. The issue of this marriage were several children, one of whom,

THOMAS COOKE, Esq., entered the army early in life, and in 1742 acquired the lands of Retreat. He m. 1st, Jane, dau. of William Horsburgh, Esq. of Dalkeith, N.B.; and

* The DAVIES'S of Gwysaney yield to few families of the Principality in lineage, alliances, station, and possessions. In common with its derivative branches, the DAVIES'S of Eltham House, Kent (represented by OWEN DAVIES, Esq.), DAVIES'S of Marrington Hall; EYTONS of Leeswood; and PARRYS of Plas Newydd and Warfield, the House of Gwysaney traces its immediate descent from CYNRIC EFELL, Lord of Eglwys Egle, younger son of Madoc ap Meredith, last sovereign of the Royal Dynasty of Powys, 8th in descent from, and representative of, Mervyn, King of Powys, 3rd son of Rhodri Mawr, King of Wales, who ascended the throne A.D. 843. (For lineage, see DAVIES of Marrington.)

2ndly, Anne, 3rd dau. of — Parker, Esq. of Dowdstown, co. Kildare, and had a son and successor,

THOMAS COOKE, Esq. of Retreat, who m. in 1790, Elizabeth, only dau. of William Dawson, Esq. of Nohaville, co. Westmeath, and had issue,

THOMAS, lieut. 9th regt., d. in 1811.
WILLIAM, now of Retreat. John, d. in 1818.
Jane, d. unm.
Kate, m. in 1816, to Owen Daly, Esq. of Mornington, co. Westmeath.

Arms—Per pale, gu. and az., three eaglets, displayed, arg.
Crest—An ostrich, ppr., on a cap of maintenance, turned up, erm., holding in its bill a horse-shoe, or.
Motto—Nihil haberi sine labore.
Seat—Retreat, near Athlone.

COOKES OF BENTLEY.

COOKES, THOMAS-HENRY, Esq. of Bentley, co. Worcester, J.P. and D.L., formerly M.P. for East Worcestershire, b. 25 Oct. 1804.

Lineage.—This family came into England with the CONQUEROR, and has been for centuries seated in the highest respectability in the co. of Worcester. The senior line obtained a Baronetcy.

SIR THOMAS COOKE, 2nd baronet, of Norgrove, Founder of Worcester College, Oxford, d. without issue about 1701, when the Baronetcy became EXTINCT.

HENRY COOKES, Esq. of Barbon, in Worcestershire, bapt. 29 Sept. 1625, 2nd son of Edward Cookes, of Bentley Pauncefort, Esq., J.P., and brother of Sir William Cookes, 1st Bart., m. Mary, dau. of Richard Stanley, Esq. of Stoke Prior, and dying about the year 1678, was s. by his eldest surviving son,

JOHN COOKES, of London, bapt. 4 Aug. 1658, who m. 1st, Elizabeth, dau. of John Knap, of London, merchant, which lady d. in childbed, 28 Feb. 1683; and 2ndly, 11 Feb. 1685, Elizabeth, eldest dau. of Sir William Russell, Knt. of London, by whom, who d. in 1734, he had, with other children,

HENRY COOKES, Esq., b. 26 April, 1702, m. at Abbeville, in France, in 1720, Jane, dau. of Robert Magraith, Esq. of Lockloker Castle, co. Tipperary, and by her, who d. in 1765, had, with other children, who d. young, a son,

THE REV. THOMAS COOKES, rector of Notgrove, in Gloucestershire, b. 2 April, 1735, who m. in 1765, Anne, only dau. and heir of John Denham, Esq. of Welling, in Kent, and had issue, George, b. in 1767, d. in 1795; Thomas, b. in 1769, d. in 1774; Henry, b. in 1773, captain in the Romney Fencibles, was killed at Kilcullen, near Harristown, in Kildare, in an action with the Irish rebels; Thomas-Secundus, b. in 1775, lieut. in his Majesty's ship "Marlborough," d. and was buried at Carmarthen; DENHAM-JAMES-JOSEPH, of whom presently; Charles-Burrell, b. in 1786, m. in 1818, Mary-Anne, dau. of Thomas Hayes, Esq. of Bath; and Alice-Maria, m. to Col. William M'Clary, of Minerabin, in the co. of Caermarthen. The 5th son,

THE REV. DENHAM-JAMES-JOSEPH COOKES, b. at Herne, in Kent, 12 March, 1777, was rector of Stanford, and vicar of Clifton-on-Terne, in Worcestershire. He m. 29 Aug. 1803, Maria-Henrietta, dau. of Charles-Johnstone, Esq., 2nd son of the Marchioness of Annandale, by her second husband, Col. Johnstone, and had issue,

THOMAS-HENRY, now of Bentley.
Denham-Charles-Johnstone, b. 19 Nov. 1810.
Henry-Winford, b. 15 Nov. 1812.
John-Russell, b. 21 Sept. 1814.
William-Russell, b. 9 Aug. 1822.
Anna-Almeria-M'Clary. Georgiana-Maria, d. in 1832.
Henrietta. Louisa-Laura.

Mr. Cookes d. 23 May, 1829.

Arms—Arg., six martlets, gu., three, two, and one, between two chevrons, of the second.
Crest—An arm, armed with a short sword, issuing from a mural crown.
Motto—Deo, Regi, Vicino.
Seat—Bentley, Worcestershire.

COOKSON OF WHITEHILL.

COOKSON, JOHN, Esq. of Whitehill, co. Durham, D.L., b. 9 March, 1773.

Lineage.—This family came originally from Settle, in Yorkshire, where it held the same paternal inheritance for upwards of three hundred years, by the alternate names of Brian and Robert. (See pedigree of COOKSON, in Thoresby's *History of Leeds*.)

WILLIAM COOKSON, the immediate ancestor of the COOKSONS *of Whitehill*, had two sons, ISAAC, of whom presently, and William, whose son,

CHRISTOPHER, assumed the surname of CRACKENTHORPE. The elder son,

ISAAC COOKSON, of Newcastle-upon-Tyne, merchant adventurer, purchased considerable property, and erected a spacious mansion. He was interred in St. Nicholas Church, in that town, where also lie the remains of Hannah his wife, and was s. by his only son,

JOHN COOKSON, Esq., who purchased, in 1745, the estate of Whitehill, co. Durham. He m. Elizabeth, eldest dau. and co-heir of Thomas Ludwidge, Esq. of Whitehaven, and had issue, ISAAC, his heir; John, barrister-at-law, who m. Hannah-Jane, dau. and co-heiress of William Reed, Esq. of Halliwell, in Durham; Thomas, d. young; Joseph, capt. in the life-guards; Elizabeth, m. to Samuel Castell, Esq. of Wimbledon, Surrey; Hannah-Jane, m. to Richard Ellison, Esq. of Sudbrooke Holme, co. Lincoln, M.P.; Sarah. John Cookson d. in Dec. 1783, and was s. by his eldest son,

ISAAC COOKSON, Esq. of Whitehill, b. in 1745, who m. in 1772, Margaret, dau. of James Wilkinson, Esq. of Newcastle-upon-Tyne, by Bridget Blencowe, of Blencowe Hall, in Cumberland, and had seven sons and three daus., viz.,

I. JOHN, now of Whitehill.
II. James, col. in the army, b. in 1775, m. Marianne, dau. of David Stephenson, Esq. of Newcastle-upon-Tyne, and d. in 1841, leaving issue,
1 James. 2 William. 3 Christopher.
1 Emma-Donna, d. in 1842.
2 Marianne.
III. ISAAC, of Meldon Park. (*See that family.*)
IV. Thomas, of Hermitage, co. Durham, b. in 1779, m. Elizabeth, only dau. of Edward Selby, Esq. of Earle, in Northumberland, and has two sons and two daus., viz.,
1 Isaac-Thomas. 2 Charles-Edward.
1 Elizabeth-Jane.
2 Matilda, m. to Richard-Pierse Butler, Esq., eldest son of Sir Thomas Butler, Bart. of Garryhundon.
V. Christopher, barrister-at-law, recorder of Berwick-upon-Tweed, and of Newcastle-upon-Tyne, d. 10 May, 1832.
VI. Joseph, b. in 1782, m. Elizabeth, 2nd dau. of William Elton, Esq. of Clifton, co. Gloucester.
VII. Septimus, d. at Clifton in 1828.
I. Elizabeth, m. to Robert Surtees, Esq. of Redworth House, co. Durham, and has issue.
II. Emma-Donna, m. to Robert Bell, Esq. of Fenham, in Northumberland, formerly a lieut.-col. in the army.
III. Caroline, d. young.

Mr. Cookson d. in 1831.

Arms—Party per pale, arg. and gu., two armed legs, couped and counterchanged.
Crest—A demi-lion, rampant, bearing a ragged staff, ppr.
Motto—Nil desperandum.
Seat—Whitehill.

COOKSON OF MELDON PARK.

COOKSON, JOHN, Esq. of Meldon Park, co. Northumberland, b. 11 Sept. 1808; m. 11 April, 1837, Sarah, eldest dau. of the late Sir M.-W. Ridley, Bart., of Blagdon, and has issue,

I. JOHN-BLENCOWE, b. 19 July, 1843.
II. Charles-George, b. 30 Oct. 1848.
I. Jane-Lutwidge. II. Sarah-Elizabeth.
III. Laura.

Lineage.—ISAAC COOKSON, J.P., high-sheriff for Northumberland in 1838, b. in 1776, 3rd son of the late Isaac Cookson, Esq. of Whitehill, co. Durham, m. in 1805, Jane, only child of the late Edward Cooke, Esq. of Togston, and had issue,

JOHN, now of Meldon.
Edward, in holy orders, b. in 1810, m. in 1833, Sabina-Eleanor, dau. of the late G. Strickland, Esq. of Newton, and granddau. of Sir William Strickland, Bart., and has issue, Alfred; Georgiana; and Jane.
William-Isaac, b. in 1812, m. in July, 1839, Jane-Anne, 2nd dau. of William Cuthbert, Esq. of Beaufront, co. Northumberland, and has issue, Bryon; and Norman-Charles.
Arthur-James, b. in 1813, d. in 1841.
Isaac, b. in 1817, d. young.
Elizabeth.
Emma-Donna, m. in 1836, to the Rev. John Shadwell, 2nd son of Sir Lancelot Shadwell, Vice-Chancellor of England, and has issue.
Fanny-Isabella, d. in 1835.
Sarah-Jane, m. 1st, 12 Sept. 1839, Sidney-Robert Streatfeild, Esq., major 52nd regiment; and 2ndly, Captain H. Cust.

Mary, *m.* in 1840, to William Cuthbert, Esq., eldest son of W. Cuthbert, Esq. of Beaufront, and has issue.
Emily-Lutwidge, *m.* to Count Mox de Lerchenfeld, of Munich.

Arms, &c.—As COOKSON *of Whitehill.*
Seat—Meldon Park, co. Northumberland.

COOPER OF MARKREE CASTLE.

COOPER, EDWARD-JOSHUA, Esq. of Markree Castle, co. Sligo, formerly M.P. for that county, *m.* 1st, Sophia, 3rd dau. of Henry-Peisley L'Estrange, Esq. of Moystown, King's County, which lady *d.* the year after her marriage; and 2ndly, Sarah-Francis, dau. of the late Owen Wynne, Esq., M.P., of Haslewood.

Lineage.—The family of Cooper has been long seated at Markree Castle, and has enjoyed for a considerable period a leading influence in the county of Sligo. The late

RIGHT HON. JOSHUA COOPER, M.P. for the co of Sligo, was son of Joshua Cooper, Esq. of Markree, M.P. for Sligo, by Mary his wife, dau. of Richard Bingham, Esq. of Newbrook, co. Mayo, grandson of Arthur Cooper, Esq. of Markree, by Mary his wife, sister of John, Viscount Allen), and great-grandson of Cornet Edward Cooper, who purchased the estate of Markree, and *d.* in 1680. He *m.* 1758, Alicia, dau. and heir of Edward Synge, D.D., bishop of Elphin, and by her (who was *b.* in 1723) had issue,

JOSHUA-EDWARD, of Markree Castle, col. of the Sligo militia, and M.P. for the co. of Sligo before and after the Union, *d. s. p.* 8 June, 1837.
EDWARD-SYNGE, M.P. for the co. of Sligo, who *m.* Anne, dau. of Harry Verelst, Esq., and had two sons, EDWARD-JOSHUA, now of Markree Castle; and Richard-Wordsworth, of Dunboden Park, co. Westmeath, who *m.* in 1826, Emelia-Elenor, dau. of Lodge, Viscount Frankfort de Montmorency, and *d.* 3 March, 1850, leaving issue, EDWARD-HENRY, capt. 7th hussars; Joshua-Harry; Richard-Augustus; William-Synge; Emelia-Anne; Catherine-Elizabeth; and Frances-Louisa.

Arms—As., on a chevron, between three cinquefoils, or, two lions, passant-respectant, sa.
Motto—Deo, patriâ, rege.
Seat—Markree Castle, co. Sligo.

COOPER OF COOPER'S HILL.

COOPER, CHARLES-WILLIAM, Esq. of Cooper's Hill, co. Sligo, J.P. and D.L., *b.* 30th Oct. 1817. Mr. Cooper is son of Arthur-Brooke Cooper, Esq. of Cooper's Hill, by Jane-Frances O'Hara his wife, and grandson of Arthur Cooper, Esq. of Cooper's Hill, by Sarah Carleton his wife. Mr. Arthur-Brooke Cooper has had, besides the present Charles-William Cooper, Esq., another son, Arthur, who *m.* 24 Nov. 1843, Elizabeth Turlock, and *d.* 12 June, 1845; and four daus., viz., Jane-Henrietta, *m.* 19 Feb. 1850, to Capt. Alexander McKinstry, of the 17th regt.; Charlotte-Annie, *m.* 19 Feb. 1852, to Christopher-Carleton L'Estrange, Esq.; Margaret; and Mary.

Motto—Vincit amor patriæ.
Seat—Cooper's Hill, Collooney.

COOPER OF TODDINGTON MANOR.

COOPER, WILLIAM-DODGE-COOPER, Esq., J.P. and D.L., high-sheriff of Bedfordshire in 1829, *m.* Elizabeth, dau. and heiress of John Cooper, Esq. of Toddington Park, co. Bedford, and of Park House, Highgate, Middlesex, and dropping his paternal surname of HEAP, assumed, by sign-manual, in 1819, the name and arms of COOPER. Mr. Cooper has issue,

I. WILLIAM-COOPER, *m.* 26 April, 1831, Laura-Georgiana, dau. of Capt. Ellis, and has a son,
1 William-Smith-Cowper, *b.* in 1832.
II. James-Lindsay, *m.* Rebecca, dau. of John Singleton, Esq. of Givendale House, co. York.
I. Jane-Cooper.
II. Elizabeth-Cooper, *m.* 27 May, 1827, Count Alexandre-Charles-Joseph Vander Burch, eldest son of the Count Vander Burch, of Escanassines, in the Netherlands, and has two sons and a dau., viz.,
1 Guillaume-Alexandre-Felix-Charles.
2 Arthur-Louis-Alexandre-Charles-Joseph.
1 Marie-Charlotte-Elizabeth, *m.* to Charles, Marquis de Froissart Broissia, and has a dau., Jeanne.

III. Amelia-Cooper.
IV. Caroline-Cooper.
V. Lucy-Cooper, *m.* 14 July, 1842, to Sir Henry Robinson, Esq. of Knapton House, co. Norfolk, and has issue,
1 Henry.
1 Constance-Amelia.
2 Elizabeth-Caroline.
3 Lucy-Henrietta-Maria.
4 Another dau.

Lineage.—This family resided originally for many years in Sussex, and the branch of which we are about to treat was dwelling at Bosden, co. Chester, about the year 1377. The inscription upon the gravestone, in the middle aisle, approaching the pulpit, in Stockport Church, bears the names of "Thomas Cowper, de Bosden, February 13, 1411—and, Thomas Cowper, ye son, October 8, 1471."

JOHN COWPER, Esq., baptized 11 March, 1598 (son and heir of John Cowper of Bosden, the staunch loyalist, *temp.* CHARLES I.), *m.* 14 Feb. 1631, Mary, dau. and heiress of W.-R. Handford, Esq. of Handford Hall, co. Chester, and dying in 1700, was *s.* by his son,

JOHN COWPER, Esq. of Bosden, who *m.* in 1658, Sarah, dau. and heir of Walter Copestick, Esq. of Langley Park, in Derbyshire, and had issue,

I. JOHN, who *m.* in 1721, Hannah, only dau. and heiress of Thomas Strettell, Esq. of Ashton, and dying before his father, in 1728, left two sons and a dau., viz.,
1 JOHN, who *s.* his grandfather at Bosden, and altered the spelling of the name to that now used. He *m.* in 1744, Anne, dau. of the Rev. William Dodge, of Sowerby, in Yorkshire, and his dau., ANNE COOPER, marrying the Rev. John Heap, of Birdham, Sussex, was mother of the present WILLIAM-DODGE-COOPER (*late* HEAP) COOPER, Esq.
2 THOMAS, of whom presently.
1 Sarah, *m.* to Joshua Roylance, Esq.
I. Elizabeth, *m.* to William Dale, Esq. of Handford, and had two daus., viz., Elizabeth Dale, *m.* to William Warren, Esq. of the WARRENS *of Poynton;* and Bridgett Dale, *m.* to Henry Leigh, Esq.
II. Hannah, *m.* to Sir Thomas Banastre, and had a dau., Hannah, *m.* to John Ashley, Esq.

Mr. Cowper *d.* 6 Oct. 1728, and was *s.* by his elder grandson, John Cooper, Esq. His younger grandson,

THOMAS COOPER, Esq., *m.* 18 June, 1749, Sarah, dau. and heir of William Paulden, Esq. of Timperley, and had twelve children, eight sons and four daus., ten of whom died infants; the youngest dau., Sarah, *d.* in 1785. The only surviving son,

JOHN COOPER, Esq., *b.* 16 Jan. 1759, *m.* Jane, dau. of William Gidden (or, as anciently spelt, Gideon), Esq., and had an only dau. and heiress,

ELIZABETH COOPER, who *m.* her cousin, William-Dodge-Cooper Heap, Esq., who in consequence changed his surname to COOPER, and is the present proprietor of Toddington Park, Bedfordshire, and of Park House, Middlesex.

Mr. Cooper served the office of sheriff for the co. of Bedford in 1812, and was *s.* at his decease, in 1824, by his son-in-law, the present WILLIAM-DODGE-COOPER COOPER, Esq.

Arms—Gu., on a chevron, between three lions, passant, arg., each holding a battle-axe in his fore paw, or, three lozenges, sa.: on a chief, engrailed, gold, a lozenge of the field, between two martlets, of the fourth; an escutcheon of pretence, quarterly, gu. and az.; on a chevron, erm., between three lions, passant, or, as many lozenges, voided, of the first.
Crest—On a gazon, vert, a lion, sejant, or and erminois, holding in his dexter paw a battle-axe, and in the sinister a tilting-spear, all ppr.
Motto—Tuum est.
Seats—Toddington Manor, Bedfordshire; Park House, Middlesex.

COOPER OF FAILFORD.

COOPER, WILLIAM, Esq. of Failford, co. Ayr, and Solsgirth, co. Dumbarton, *m.* 1st, in 1835, Isabella, dau. of Robert Clarke, Esq. of Comrie Castle, co. Perth, which lady *d. s. p.* in 1841; and 2ndly, in 1845, Margaret, eldest surviving dau. of the Rev. Dr. Hill, professor of divinity in the University of Glasgow, by Margaret his wife, only dau. of Major Crawfurd, of Newfield, Ayrshire; by her he has issue,

I. WILLIAM-SAMUEL.
II. Alexander-Hill.
I. Margaret-Crawfurd.
II. Janet-Ritchie.

Lineage.—The surname of this family was originally written Couper, or Cowper. It is stated by Playfair, in his *Baronetage,* to be nearly as old, in Scotland, as the time of Malcolm Canmore. Sir George Mackenzie, in his *Science of*

Heraldry, 1680, says, that the arms of the Cowpers "signify their descent from France, and from Bretagne, in that kingdom." They anciently bore fleurs-de-lis and ermine in one shield, although subsequently the fleurs-de-lis were changed to slips of laurel, as appears from *Nisbet's Heraldry.* The Coupers appear as landholders, in various counties, at an early date. The principal family of the name was COUPER *of Gogar*, in Mid-Lothian, of whom the Lyon Register, and Playfair, both state that their first ancestor on record was Simon Couper, one of the Barons of Scotland, who was compelled to swear fealty to EDWARD I., in the year 1296, and whose name accordingly appears on the Ragman Roll. This family was raised to the baronetage of Nova Scotia, in 1638, in the person of John Couper, or Cowper, of Gogar, who was killed in 1640, along with the Earl of Haddington and many gentlemen, in the blowing-up of Dunglass Castle, when that fortress was held by the Scotch army. From William Cowper, the 3rd son of the 1st baronet, the family now settled in Ayrshire claim descent.

WILLIAM COUPER, or COWPER, *b.* 1629, was an officer of dragoons during the civil war. He *m.* Christian Scot, and settled in the co. Dumbarton. He had, with other issue,

JOHN COUPER, or COWPER, who resided at the Tower of Banbeath, co. Dumbarton; he *m.* Christian Grey, in 1676, and *d.* in 1687. His son and successor,

JOHN COUPER, *b.* 1677, also resided at the Tower of Banbeath; he *m.* Margaret Thom, in 1708, and had a numerous issue.

THE REVEREND JOHN COUPER, the eldest son, was settled as a clergyman in the co. Lincoln. He changed his name to COOPER, and *d. unm.* at Glasgow, in 1789, when the representation of the family devolved on his brother,

WILLIAM COUPER, of Smeithston and Failford, who also changed his name to COOPER, which name he entailed upon his successors along with his estates. He *m.* in 1754, Mary, eldest dau. of Hugh Stewart, Esq., and by her, who *d.* 1768, had issue,

I. William, *b.* 1761, *d.* 1768.
II. ALEXANDER, *b.* 1765, of whom afterwards.
III. SAMUEL, *b.* 1768, of whom afterwards.
I. Cecilia, *b.* 1757, *m.* Lieutenant-General David Shank, an officer who highly distinguished himself in the American war. She *d.* in 1842.
Also three daus., of whom two *d.* in infancy, and the other *unm.*

William Cooper *d.* in 1793, and was *s.* by his eldest surviving son,

ALEXANDER COOPER, of Failford, who held a commission in the army, and served abroad. He was afterwards appointed captain commandant of the Mauchline Volunteers, lieutenant-colonel of the 2nd regiment of Ayrshire local militia, and a deputy-lieutenant for the co. Ayr. He *d. unm.* in 1829, and was *s.* by his brother,

SAMUEL COOPER, of Failford, and of Ballindalloch, co. Stirling; who *m.* in 1795, Janet, dau. and heiress of Henry Ritchie, Esq., of the family of Craigton, by Esther Craufurd, representative of the CRAUFURDS *of Balshagray and Scotstoun*, a family possessed of valuable estates in the cos. of Lanark and Renfrew, and descended from the very ancient house of Craufurdland, in the co. of Ayr. Soon after his marriage, Samuel Cooper acquired the barony of Ballindalloch, in the co. of Stirling. He was lieutenant-colonel of the western battalion of Stirlingshire local militia, and a deputy-lieutenant for that co. He *d.* in 1842, leaving issue,

I. WILLIAM, now of Failford.
II. Henry-Ritchie, of Ballindalloch, *m.* Mary-Jones, dau. of Gerald Butler, Esq. of the co. Wexford, and has issue.
I. Janet-Craufurd, *m.* William Wallace, Esq. of Busbie, co. Ayr, and has issue.
II. Mary.
III. Cecilia, *m.* Robert Struthers, Esq., and *d.* in 1841, leaving issue.
IV. Henrietta, *m.* John Crooks, Esq. of Levan, co. Renfrew.
V. Frances, *m.* Herbert Buchanan, Esq., son of Herbert Buchanan, Esq. of Arden, co. Dumbarton, and *d.* in 1843, leaving issue.
VI. Anne, *m.* George-Ross Wilsone, Esq., and has issue.
VII. Ellenor, *m.* Thomas-Gray Scott, Esq., and has issue.
VIII. Esther-Ritchie, *m.* Alexander-Graham Dunlop, Esq., and *d.* in 1844, leaving one son who *d.* same year.

Arms—Quarterly, 1st, arg., on a bend engrailed, between two lions rampant, gu., three crescents, of the field, all within a bordure chequy arg. and az., for COOPER; 2nd and 3rd, quartered, first and fourth, arg., on a chief, gu., three lions' heads, erased, of the first, all within a bordure, erm., for RITCHIE; 2nd and 3rd, gu., a fess, erm., and in chief a mullet, of the last, for CRAUFURD; 4th, arg., a chevron, gu., surmounted of another, erm., betwixt three laurel-slips vert, all within a bordure, chequy, as the former, for COUPER or COWPER.
Crests—On the dexter side, issuant out of a wreath, arg. and gu., a dexter hand, holding a garland of laurel, both ppr., and over the same, the motto, "Virtute;" and on the sinister, upon a wreath, arg. and az., an oak tree, with a branch borne down by a weight, both ppr.; and over the same, the motto, "Resurgo."
Seat—Smithstone House, Ayrshire.

COORE OF SCRUTON HALL.

COORE, HENRY, Esq. of Scruton Hall, co. York, *b.* 18 Jan. 1820, *m.* 4 July, 1841, Augusta-Caroline, dau. of Mark Milbank, Esq. of Thorp Perrow, by the Lady Augusta his wife, and has issue,

I. HENRY-MILBANK, *b.* 4 June.
II. Alfred-Thomas, *b.* 3 Sept. 1846.
III. Augustus-Lechmere, *b.* 18 May, 1847.
I. Louisa. II. Caroline-Augusta.

Lineage.—The family of Gale, now merged in that of COORE, was of importance in the North and East Ridings of Yorkshire, early in the 16th century.

JAMES GALE, the first named in the pedigree, was seated at Thirntoft, near Scruton, in the hundred of East Gilling and North Riding, *anno* 1523. His son and heir,

OLIVER GALE, of Thirntoft, *m.* Ellen Marshall, of Richmond, and had, with another son, James, who *m.* and resided some time in Spain,*

GEORGE GALE, Esq. lord-mayor of York, in 1534 and 1546, ancestor of the GALES *of Scruton.*

The late LIEUT.-COL. FOSTER-LECHMERE COORE, of Firby, N.R., Yorkshire, eldest son of John Coore, Esq., and Ann Lechmere his wife, *s.* in 1821, his uncle, Colonel Thomas Coore, whose father, Foster, was son of Alderman Thomas Coore, of Liverpool, *m.* in 1816, HARRIET-GALE, of Scruton, eldest dau. and heiress of Henry Gale, Esq. of Scruton, eldest son of Roger-Henry Gale, Esq. of Scruton, by Catherine his wife, dau. of Christopher Crowe, Esq. of Kiplin, and grandson of Roger Gale, of Scruton, M.P., the well-known author of the *Registrum Honoris de Richmond*, 1st Vice-President of the Society of Antiquaries, and by her (who *d.* 15 Dec. 1839), left at his decease, in 1837 (with four daus., Mary, *m.* to Colonel Wade; Sophia; Augusta, *m.* to Capt. Frederick-Gordon Christie; and Charlotte, *m.* to Capt. Samuel Stovin Hood Inglefield), one son, the present HENRY COORE, Esq. of Scruton.

Arms—Az., on a fesse, between three saltiers, arg., as many lions' heads, erased, of the field, langued, gu.
Crest—An unicorn's head, or.
Motto—Qui semina vertù raccoglia fama.
Seat—Scruton Hall, Bedale.

COOTE OF MOUNT COOTE.

COOTE, CHARLES-CHIDLEY, Esq. of Mount Coote, co. Limerick, *s.* his father 11 July, 1843. Mr. Coote of Mount Coote is, through the Meath family, the representative of Sir Lewis Clifford, K.G., *temp.* HENRY IV., younger son of Roger, Lord Clifford, and one of the co-heirs of Sir Arnold Savage, Speaker of the House of Commons about the same time.

Lineage.—SIR PHILIPS COOTE, Knt. of Mount Coote, co. Limerick, bapt. 10 March, 1658 (son of Col. Chidley Coote, of Killester, younger brother of Charles, 1st Earl of Mountrath), fought for WILLIAM at the Boyne. He *m.* 1st, Jane, dau. of Dr. Henry Jones, bishop of Meath, by whom he had an only child, Anne, who *d.* young; and 2ndly, Lady Elizabeth Brabazon, elder dau. and co-heir of William, 3rd earl of Meath, by whom (who, through her mother, Elizabeth, dau. of Francis, Lord Dacre of the South, derived from the Plantagenets) he was father of CHARLES COOTE, Esq., who *m.* Katherine, dau. of Sir Robert Newcomen, Bart., by Lady Mary Chichester his wife, dau. of Arthur, 2nd Earl of Donegal, and dying in 1761, was *s.* by his son,

CHIDLEY COOTE, Esq. of Mount Coote, who *m.* Jane, dau. of Sir Ralph Gore, Bart., Speaker of the Irish House of Commons, and left at his decease, 24 Feb. 1764 (with a dau., Elizabeth, wife of James King, Esq. of Gola, Fermanagh), a son,

* He subsequently settled in Ireland, whence his descendants, during the rebellion there, transplanted themselves to Whitehaven. From this branch descends LIEUT.-COL. GALE BRADDYLL, late of Conishead Priory.

CHARLES COOTE, Esq., who m. Elizabeth, dau. and co-heir of Philip Oliver, of Altamira, Esq., M.P., 2nd son of Robert Oliver, Esq. of Castle Oliver, and by her had,

CHIDLEY, of Mount Coote.
Charles-Philip, m. Anne, dau. of Charles Atkinson, Esq. of Rehins, co. Mayo, and left issue.
Elizabeth, m. to Major Caleb Barnes, of the co. of Meath.

The eldest son,

CHIDLEY COOTE, Esq. of Mount Coote, m. in July, 1797, Anne, dau. and co-heir of the Hon. William-Williams Hewett, and by her (who d. in 1842) had issue,

CHARLES CHIDLEY, now of Mount Coote.
Charles-William.
Charles-Eyre, m. a dau. of the late Major Crofton Croker, and has issue.
Charles-Philips, married.
Charles-John.
Charles-James, m. a dau. of Thomas-Stewart, of Limerick, and has a son, Charles.
Alicia, m. to John-Wingfield King, Esq., 2nd son of Lieut.-General the Hon. Sir Henry King, K.C.B.

Mr. Coote d. 11 July, 1843.

Arms—Arg., a chevron, between three coots, sa.
Crest—A coot, ppr.
Seat—Mount Coote, co. Limerick.

COPE OF DRUMMILLY.

COPE, ANNA GARLAND, of Drummilly, co. Armagh, m. 3 March, 1814, Nathaniel Garland, Esq. of Michaelstow Hall, co. Essex, and Woodcote Grove, co. Surrey, and by him (who is deceased) has issue,

I. EDGAR-WALTER GARLAND, Esq. of Michaelstow Hall, m. Amelia, 2nd dau. of Robert Robertson, Esq. of Auchleeks, co. Perth.
II. Nathaniel-Arthur Garland, in holy orders, of Nonington, co. Kent, m. Mary, eldest dau. of the Rev. Ferdinand Faithful, of Headleigh Rectory, co. Surrey, and has issue, Arthur Nathaniel.
III. Edward-Blake Garland.
IV. Trevor-Laurance Garland. V. James-George.
I. Arabella, m. to the Rev. George Burmester, of Little Oakley Rectory, co. Essex, and has issue.
II. Indiana-Elinor. III. Georgina-Catherine.
IV. Anna-Eliza.

Lineage.—This family derives from a branch of the ancient baronetical family of Cope.

WALTER COPE, Esq. of Drummilly, d. in 1660, leaving a son, WALTER, of whom presently, and five daus., all of whom d. unm., except the youngest, Abigail, who m. Archdeacon Meade, and had one dau., SARAH-ARABELLA-ABIGAIL, of whom hereafter. Mr. Cope was s. by his son,

THE RIGHT REV. DR. WALTER COPE, of Drummilly, Lord Bishop of Leighlin and Ferns, who m. a dau. of Sir Arthur Acheson, of Gosford, co. Armagh, but d. s. p., and was s. by his niece,

SARAH-ARABELLA-ABIGAIL MEADE, who assumed the surname of COPE. She m. Nicholas Archdale, Esq. of Castle Archdale, co. Fermanagh, and had issue (besides one dau., ANNA, who s. her brother) three sons, viz., Walter, d. unm.; Samuel-Walter, d. unm.; and

ARTHUR-WALTER COPE, Esq. of Drummilly, who m. Caroline Lester, and had one dau., Caroline-Arabella Archdale, who m. Francis-Wilson Heath, Esq. of New Grove, Lisburn. Mr. Cope d. 8 Nov. 1846, and was s., under the will of his grand-uncle, Dr. Walter Cope, by his sister, ANNA, the present proprietor of Drummilly.

Arms—On a chevron, between three roses, slipped and leaved, ppr., as many fleurs-de-lis.
Crest—A fleur-de-lis, or, with a dragon's head issuing from the top thereof, gu.
Motto—Æquo adeste animo.
Seat—Drummilly, Loughgall, co. Armagh.

COPE OF LOUGHGALL MANOR.

COPE, ROBERT-WRIGHT-COPE, Esq. of The Manor, Loughgall, co. Armagh, J.P. and D.L., b. 2 Feb. 1810; m. 6 June, 1848, Cecilia-Philippa, dau. of Capt. Shawe Taylor, of Castle Taylor, co. Galway, and has issue,

I. FRANCIS-ROBERT, b. 21 Nov. 1853.
I. Albinia-Elizabeth. II. Emma-Sophia.

Lineage.—The late RICHARD and MARY DOOLAN left two sons, ROBERT-WRIGHT-COPE, and Kendrick-Hugh, the elder of whom, Robert, took the name of COPE, in lieu of Doolan, in compliance with the will of his cousin, Arthur Cope (only son of Robert-Camden Cope), to whose estates he succeeded in 1844.

Arms—Quarterly: 1st and 4th, arg., on a chevron, az., between three roses, gu., stalked and leaved, vert, as many fleurs-de-lis, or; a mullet, of the second, for difference; 2nd and 3rd, arg., three crescents, in pale, az., between two pellets, in fesse.
Crest—1st, out of a fleur-de-lis, or, charged with a mullet, gu., a dragon's head, of the second; 2nd, on a chapeau, az., turned up, erm., a crescent, or, therefrom issuant a trefoil, slipped, vert.
Motto—Æquo adeste animo.
Seat—The Manor, Loughgall.

COPPINGER OF BALLYVOLANE.

COPPINGER, WILLIAM, Esq. of Ballyvolane and Barryscourt, co. Cork, s. his father 15 July, 1816.

Lineage.—So far back as the beginning of the fourteenth century, (*anno* 1319,) we find, by the municipal records of Cork, Stephen Coppinger, mayor of that city, about the period, in EDWARD II's reign, when the chief magistrate of London first adopted a similar designation. This Stephen Coppinger's relatives and descendants long continued to sustain their local influence, as appears by the frequency of the name in the civic annals of Cork, and to spread themselves as large proprietors over the adjoining county.

STEPHEN COPPINGER, Esq., son of Stephen Coppinger, Esq. of Ballyvolane, who d. in 1620), is described in his monumental inscription in Upper Shandon churchyard, as chief of his name. He m. Elizabeth (or Elice) Goold, and had issue, I. THOMAS, his heir; II. William, last Catholic sheriff of Cork in 1687, whose grandson, WILLIAM COPPINGER, founded a commercial establishment at Bordeaux. He had, with several other children, a son, WILLIAM COPPINGER, b. in 1735, who d. in 1802, leaving, with two daus., Adelaide, m. to Luke Callaghan, Esq. of Paris, banker, (who d. in 1832, leaving a son, Augustus Callaghan, and two daus.) and Emilie, a son, JAMES COPPINGER, of Paris, banker, who m. Mademoiselle Salle, and had issue; III. Henry, ances. or of General Joseph Coppinger, of the Spanish service, resident at the Havannah; IV. Matthew. Stephen Coppinger d. in 1678, and was s. by his eldest son,

THOMAS COPPINGER, Esq., who m. Ellen, dau. of Edward Galwey, Esq. of Lota, and had (with four daus., the eldest m. to Connor O'Brien, Esq.; the 2nd, to — Ronayne, Esq.; the 3rd, to — Nihil, Esq.; and the 4th, to Patrick Rochfort, Esq. of Cork) three sons, STEPHEN, his heir; Edward, captain in the service of JAMES II., killed in 1691, at Bottlehill, co. Cork; and John, of Granacloyne, ancestor of Thomas-Stephen Coppinger, Esq. of Midleton. The eldest son,

STEPHEN COPPINGER, Esq., m. at La Rochelle, in 1700, Johanna, dau. of Stephen Gould, Esq. of Cork, and had three sons, viz., I. JOHN, his heir; II. WILLIAM, eventual inheritor; III. Joseph, who m. Miss Arthur, of Limerick, and had (with four daus., two of whom were nuns; another was the wife of Daniel Cronin, Esq. of The Park, near Killarney, predecessor to the present proprietor; and the 4th m. Nicholas-Tuite Selby, Esq.) six sons, viz.,

I. Stephen, who m. Miss Gallwey, of Killarney.
II. William, Catholic Bishop of Cloyne.
III. Thomas, who d. s. p. in the West Indies.
IV. Peter, who m. for his 2nd wife, the dau. of Henry O'Brien, Esq. of Kilcor, by Miss Coppinger, aunt of the present Mr. Coppinger, of Barryscourt, and had a son, William-Henry Coppinger, Esq., who m. Elizabeth, 3rd dau. of Richard O'Byrne, Esq. of the ancient house of Cabinteely, and has issue.
V. Joseph, who d. at New York, without issue.
VI. John, d. at St. Croix, without issue.

The eldest son,

JOHN COPPINGER, Esq., m. 1st, Mary, elder dau. and coheir of Nicholas Blundell, Esq. of Crosby, in Lancashire, and by her had a son, who d. 1745. Mr. Coppinger m. 2ndly, the dau. and co-heir of Michael Moore, Esq. of Drogheda, and had an only dau., his successor,

MARIANA COPPINGER, who m. in 1767, Charles Howard, 11th Duke of Norfolk, but dying in childbed in 1769, her Grace was s. by her uncle,

WILLIAM COPPINGER, Esq. of Ballyvolane and Barryscourt, who m. his cousin, Elizabeth, dau. of John Galwey, Esq. of Lota, and had four daus., (of whom the eldest m. Cornelius O'Brin, Esq. of Kilcor; the 2nd, Mary, m. Dr. Callaghan, of Cork; and the youngest, Teresa, m. Pierce Power, Esq. of Clonmel,) and seven sons, viz.,

I. Stephen, who predeceased his father, unm.
II. WILLIAM, his heir.

III. John, *d. unm.*
IV. Thomas, *m.* Dorinda, dau. of Edmund Barry, Esq., and had, with other children, a son, Edmund, father of the present Thomas Coppinger, Esq. of Ropmore.
V. Richard, an officer in the Austrian service, under his friend, Gen. Lord Taaffe. He *d.* at Prague, issueless.
VI. Joseph, *m.* his cousin, Alicia, dau. of John Coppinger, Esq. of Gronacloyne, and was father of Joseph-William Coppinger, Esq., who *m.* Margaret, dau. of Henry O'Brien, Esq. of Kilcor.
VII. James, who *m.* his cousin, Alicia, dau. of William Coppinger, Esq. of Cork, and had issue. His eldest son, William, *m.* 1st, Ellen, dau. of Richard Moylan, Esq., and 2ndly, in Paris, Harriet, 2nd dau. of the Rev. James Saunders, rector of Sawtry. He has issue by both wives.

Mr. Coppinger was *s.* at his decease by his eldest surviving son,

WILLIAM COPPINGER, Esq. of Barryscourt, who *m.* Jane, dau. of Stanislaus, and sister of Donat M'Mahon, Esq. of Clenagh, in the co. of Clare. By this lady, who *d.* 31 Jan. 1833, he had, with several other children who predeceased him,

WILLIAM, now of Ballyvolane.
John M'Mahon, late of the 12th dragoons, who *d.* in London in 1829.
Elizabeth, *m.* to John O'Connell, Esq. of Grena.
Mary, *m.* to her cousin, James Blackney, Esq., eldest son of Walter Blackney, Esq., M.P., and *d.* in Sept. 1833.

Mr. Coppinger *d.* 15 July, 1816, aged 75.

Arms—Az., a bull's head, arg.
Crest—A demi-lion, rampant.
Motto—Virtute non vi. *Seat*—Barryscourt.

COPPINGER OF MIDLETON.

COPPINGER, THOMAS-STEPHEN, Esq. of Midleton, co. Cork, J.P., *b.* 6 Jan. 1800; *m.* 13 Feb. 1840, Annette, 4th dau. of Sir John Power, Bart., and has issue,

I. JOHN, *b.* May, 1841.
II. Thomas, *b.* 1843. III. Stephen, *b.* 1847.

Lineage.—This is a branch of the ancient family of COPPINGER *of Ballyvolane*. The late STEPHEN-J. COPPINGER, Esq. of Cork, and of Granacloyne, son of William Coppinger, Esq. of Granacloyne, by Mary Gould his wife, was lineally descended from John, of Granacloyne, 3rd son of Thomas Coppinger, Esq. of Ballyvolane (*see preceding pedigree*). He *m.* 1796, his cousin, Joanna Coppinger, of Rossmore, and had issue, THOMAS-STEPHEN, now of Midleton; Stephen-William, in holy orders of the Church of Rome, *d.* 1851; Joseph-William, of Dublin, *m.* and has issue; Edmund, *m.* and has issue; Dorinda, *m.* to John-M. Ashlin, Esq. of Rush Hill, co. Surrey; and Mary.

Arms, &c.—See COPPINGER *of Ballyvolane*.
Seat—Midleton, co. Cork.

COPPINGER OF CARHUE.

COPPINGER, STEPHEN, Esq. of Leemount, in the city of Cork, barrister-at-law, *b.* in 1791; *s.* his father in 1829; *m.* in 1834, Juliana-Maria-Josephina, only dau. of John Walsh, Esq. of Blarney Hill, near Cork, and has issue,

I. THOMAS-STEPHEN.
I. Stephanie. II. Mary-Anne. III. Margaret.

Lineage.—STEPHEN COPPINGER, mayor of Cork, *temp.* ELIZABETH, was grandfather of ALDERMAN JOHN COPPINGER, who served corporate office in 1610. His elder son,

THOMAS COPPINGER, purchased, 18 July, 1636, the estate of Carhue, in the barony of Muskerry, co. Cork. He *m.* in 1640, Miss Elizabeth Saarsfield, of Cork, and had issue,

STEPHEN COPPINGER, Esq. of Carhue, the elder son, *m.* in 1670, Katharine, dau. of Henry Hayes, Esq. of Cork, and was father of

THOMAS COPPINGER, Esq. of Carhue, who *m.* in 1710, Katharine, dau. of William O'Mahony, Esq. of Ballinamona Abbey, and had issue,

I. STEPHEN, his heir.
II. JOHN, *m.* Miss Rose Goold, and had issue two sons: the younger, Henry, was killed in a duel by William Penrose, Esq. of Shandangan; the elder, THOMAS-JOHN COPPINGER, Esq., *m.* Mary, dau. of James Gollock, Esq. of Forest, co. Cork, and had issue,
1 John-Rye, *m.* 1st, in 1810, Emily, dau. of Henry Leader, Esq. of Mount Leader; and 2ndly, Christabella, eldest dau. of Mathias Handley, Esq. of Mount Rivers, but had no issue.
2 Thomas, capt. 96th foot, wounded at Waterloo, *m.* the relict of Benjamin Friend, Esq. of Limerick, but had no issue.
3 Mary, *m.* James Thorne, Esq., a capt. in the 56th foot, and left issue, Henry, who, pursuant to the will of his uncle, John-Rye Coppinger, assumed his name, and is the present HENRY-THORNE COPPINGER, Esq. He *m.* Anne, only dau. of Roger O'Connor, Esq. of Fort Robert, co. Cork, and niece of Gen. Arthur O'Connor.
III. Thomas, *d.* at Gottenburgh.
I. Elizabeth, *m.* to Richard Hennesey, Esq. of Killavullen.
II. Margaret, *m.* her cousin, Robert O'Mahoney, of Ballinamona.

The eldest son,

STEPHEN COPPINGER, Esq. of Carhue, *m.* in 1743, Miss Mary Goold, of Ahaballoge, and had issue, THOMAS-STEPHEN, his heir; Elizabeth, *m.* Denis O'Leary, Esq., commonly called "The O'Leary." The only son,

THOMAS-STEPHEN COPPINGER, Esq. of Carhue, *m.* in 1786, Helena, dau. of Geoffrey-O. Hanlahan, Esq., and had issue,

I. STEPHEN, the present head of the family.
II. Thomas, of Sandy Hill, *m.* in 1824, Margaret, relict of David Barry, Esq. of Macroom, and dau. of Owen Madden, Esq. of Convoye House, and left issue, one son, THOMAS-STEPHEN, *b.* 1824, who succeeded him in 1837.
III. Richard, of Green Lodge, *m.* Anne, only dau. of Stephen M'Carthy, Esq. of Cork, and has issue,
1 Mary-Anne. 2 Margaret.
IV. Dominick, }
V. William, } *d. unm.*
I. Mary-Anne, }

Mr. Coppinger *d.* in 1829, and was *s.* by his eldest son, the present STEPHEN COPPINGER, Esq. of Leemount.

Arms—Az., a bull's head, arg.
Crest—A demi-lion, rampant.
Motto—Virtute non vi.
Seat—Carhue Hall and Leemount, co. Cork.

CORBALLY OF CORBALTON HALL.

CORBALLY, MATTHEW-ELIAS, Esq. of Corbalton Hall, co. Meath, J.P., high-sheriff in 1838, and M.P. for the co. Meath, *b.* in April, 1797; *m.* 17 June, 1842, Matilda, only dau. of Viscount Gormanstown, by Margaret his wife, dau. of Thomas Arthur, 2nd Viscount Southwell. Mr. Corbally is only son of the late Elias Corbally, of Corbalton, Esq. by Mary his wife, widow of Frederick Netterville, Esq. of Woodbrook, co. Galway. He has one sister, Louisa, *m.* in 1817, to the present Earl of Fingall.

Seat—Corbalton Hall, co. Meath.

CORBET OF SUNDORNE.

CORBET, ANDREW-WILLIAM, Esq. of Sundorne Castle, co. Salop, *b.* 22 Sept. 1801; *m.* 14 June, 1823, Mary-Emma, dau. of John Hill, Esq., and sister of Sir Rowland Hill, Bart. of Hawkestone.

Lineage.—This is a principal branch of the great Norman family, whose ancestor, ROGER CORBET, accompanied WILLIAM I. to the Conquest of England.

WILLIAM CORBET, the eldest son of Roger, was seated at Wattlesborough. His 2nd son,

SIR ROBERT CORBET, Knt., had for his inheritance the castle and estates of Caus, with a large portion of his father's domains. He was father of

ROBERT CORBET, also of Caus Castle, who accompanied RICHARD I. to the siege of Acre, and then bore for arms the two ravens, as now borne by all his descendants. From this Robert derived the CORBETS *of Legh-juxta-Caus*, for centuries one of the leading families in Shropshire. Their representative in the 18th century,

ANDREW CORBET, Esq. of Leigh and Adbright Hussey, succeeded in 1740, by the devise of his kinsman, Corbet Kynaston, Esq., to the Sundorne and other extensive estates in Shropshire. Dying *s. p.*, 15 April, 1741, he was *s.* by his brother,

JOHN CORBET, Esq. of Sundorne, Adbright Hussey, &c., who sold the ancient patrimony of Legh. He *m.* 1st, Frances, dau. of Robert Pigott, Esq. of Chetwynd, and 2ndly, Barbara-Letitia, dau. of John Mytton, Esq. of Halston. By the latter he had two sons, JOHN, his heir, and Andrew, a lieut.-col. in the army; and one dau., Mary-Elizabeth, *m.* to Sir John-Kynaston Powell, Bart. Mr. Corbet *d.* in 1759, and was *s.* by his son,

JOHN CORBET, Esq. of Sundorne, M.P. for Shrewsbury, from 1774 to 1780, and high-sheriff of Salop in 1793. He m. 1st, Emma-Elizabeth, dau. of Sir Charlton Leighton, Bart., and by her (who d. 19 Sept. 1797) had one son and one dau., viz., John-Kynaston, d. 23 April, 1806, aged 15; and Emma, m. to Sir Richard Puleston, Bart., 19 Feb. 1800. He m. 2ndly, Anne, 2nd dau. of the Rev. William Pigott, of Edgmond, in Salop, and had issue, ANDREW-WILLIAM, now of Sundorne; Dryden-Robert; Vincent; Kynaston; and Annabella. Mr. Corbet d. 19 May, 1817.

Arms—Or, two ravens, in pale, ppr.
Crest—An elephant-and-castle, ppr.
Motto—Deus pascit corvos.
Seat—Sundorne Castle, near Shrewsbury.

CORBETT OF ELSHAM AND DARNHALL.

CORBETT, THOMAS-GEORGE, Esq. of Elsham, co. Lincoln, and of Darnhall, in Cheshire, formerly M.P. for Lincolnshire, s. his father 3 Feb. 1832; m. 15 Dec. 1836, Lady Mary-N. Beauclerk, sister of the Duke of St. Albans, and has issue,

I. Eleanor-Blanche-Mary. II. Sybil-Elizabeth.

Lineage.—WILLIAM CORBETT, secretary to the Admiralty (son of Thomas Corbet, of Nash, co. Pembroke, and grandson of Robert, 2nd son of Sir Vincent Corbet, Knt. of Moreton Corbet), m. Eleanor, dau. and co-heir of Col. John Jones, of Nantoes, co. Cardigan, by whom he had three sons.

THOMAS CORBETT, Esq. of Darnhall, co. Chester, grandson of William, being son of his 3rd son, William, cashier of the navy, m. Elizabeth, only child and heir of Humphrey Edwin, Esq. of St. Albans, co. Herts, by Mary his wife, dau. of William Thompson, of Elsham, co. Lincoln, Esq., and had issue,

I. WILLIAM, his heir.
II Edwin, who m. Ann, dau. of the late John Blackburn, Esq. of Hale, M.P. for the county of Lancaster, and has issue, Edwin, and several other children.

Mr. Corbett d. 18 Dec. 1808, and was s. by his son,

WILLIAM CORBETT, Esq. of Darnhall, took the name and arms of THOMPSON, in addition to those of CORBETT, 20 July, 1810. He m. in 1794, Jane-Eleanor, eldest dau. of General Ainslie, and niece of the late Sir Robert Ainslie, Bart., ambassador to the Ottoman Porte, and by her had (with other issue), the present THOMAS-GEORGE CORBETT, Esq. of Elsham, who s. his father in the family estates, 3 Feb. 1832; Andrew-Robert, in holy orders, rector of South Willingham, Lancashire, who m. Marian, dau. of the late Sir Matthew-White Ridley, Bart., and has a son and two daus.; and Caroline-Arabella, m. to Major Philip Sandilands, royal horse-artillery.

Arms—Or, a raven, ppr.
Crest—An elephant-and-castle, ppr.
Motto—Deus pascit corvos.
Seats—Elsham, in the county of Lincoln; and Darnhall, in the county of Chester.

CORBETT OF LONGNOR AND LEIGHTON.

CORBETT, PANTON, Esq. of Longnor and Leighton, co. Salop, formerly M.P. for Shrewsbury.

Lineage.—This family of Corbett is a branch of the great Shropshire family of CORBETT (or CORBET) *of Moreton Corbet*.

SIR EDWARD CORBETT, of Longnor, and of Leighton, Knt., was created a Baronet in 1642. The senior branch of the line expired in 1774 with Sir Richard Corbett, Bt., whereupon the title devolved upon Charles Corbett, of London, great-grandson of Thomas, the 2nd son of the first Baronet; but the estates were devised by Sir Richard Corbett, in 1774, to his kinsman, Robert Flint, great-grandson (maternally) of Waties Corbett, the youngest brother of the said Thomas, and upon the death, without issue, of Robert Corbett, (Mr. Flint having taken that name,) descended to his nephew,

THE REV. JOSEPH PLYMLEY, archdeacon of Salop, only son and heir of Joseph Plymley, Esq., who d. in 1802, in his eighty-sixth year, by Diana his 1st wife, dau. of John Flint, Esq., and JANE his wife, dau. of Waties Corbett, Esq. of Elton. Archdeacon Plymley assumed the surname and arms of CORBETT in 1804. He m. twice: his 2nd wife, Matty, 3rd dau. of Dansey Dansey, Esq. of Brinsop, co. Hereford, d. in 1812, aged 40. He d. 22 June, 1838, aged 79, and was s. by his son, the present PANTON CORBETT, of Longnor and Leighton, Esq.

Arms—Or, two ravens, in pale, ppr., within a bordure engrailed, sa., bezantée.
Crest—A raven, ppr., with a holly-branch in its bill, vert, fructed, gu.
Seats—Longnor and Leighton, co. Salop.

CORBETT OF ADMINGTON HALL.

HOLLAND-CORBETT, CORBETT, Esq. of Admington Hall, co. Gloucester, J.P., b. in 1794; m. in 1829, Louisa, 7th dau. of the late John Elmslie, Esq. of London. This gentleman, son of Francis Holland, Esq. of Crossthorne, co. Worcester, by Anne his wife, dau. of Michael Corbett, Esq. of Quinton, co. Gloucester, assumed by letters-patent, 2 May, 1839, the additional surname and arms of CORBETT, on succeeding his maternal uncle, Michael Corbett, Esq., in the Admington Hall estate. He has one brother and five sisters, viz.,

I. Francis-Holland, Esq. of Crossthorne, near Pershore, co. Worcester, J.P., who m. Jane, eldest dau. of the late — Warry, Esq. of co. Somerset, and has issue two sons and a dau., viz.,
1 Francis-Dermock. 2 Corbett.
1 Jane-Corbett.

I. Maria-Corbett, m. to Frederick Vandeburgh, Esq., M.D., of Liverpool.
II. Mary-Anne.
III. Elizabeth, m. to — Addams, Esq. of co. Somerset.
IV. Susan, m. to J.-T. Addam, Esq. of Cheltenham.
V. Caroline, m. to Charles Best, Esq. of co. Worcester.

Arms—Arg., two ravens, in pale, sa., charged on the body with three ermine spots, two and one, or; a bordure, gu., bezantée.
Crest—A raven, sa., with three ermine spots, or; in the beak a sprig of holly.
Seat—Admington Hall, near Campden, co. Gloucester.

CORNEWALL OF DELBURY.

CORNEWALL, HERBERT, Esq. of Delbury, co. Salop, b. in 1794; m. Charlotte, 2nd dau. of General Lord Charles-Henry Somerset, governor of the Cape of Good Hope, by Elizabeth his wife, sister of the late Earl of Devon, and has,

I. HERBERT-SOMERSET-HAMILTON, b. at Quebec, 7 Dec. 1826, lieut. in the rifle brigade.
II. Frederic-Talbot, b. 2 Sept. 1828, ensign in the 12th regt. of Bombay native infantry.
I. Charlotte-Henrietta. II. Elizabeth. III. Cecil.

Lineage.—RICHARD, King of the Romans, and Earl of Cornwall and Poictou, 2nd son of JOHN, King of England, by his 3rd wife, Isabel, sister and heir of Aymer, Earl of Angoulême, m. Sauchia, 3rd dau. of Raymond, Earl of Provence, sister of Queen Eleanor, wife of HENRY III.; and by her had two sons, Edmund, Earl of Cornwall, who m. Margaret, dau. of Richard de Clare, Earl of Gloucester, and d. s. p. in 1300; and Richard de Cornewall, who was slain at the siege of Berwick in 1296. Richard, Earl of Cornwall and Poictou, d. at Berkhampstead in 1279, having had, besides, three natural children—viz., a dau. Isabella, m. to Maurice, Lord Berkeley, of Berkeley Castle, and two sons, RICHARD, ancestor of the family of the Cornewalls, Barons of Burford; and Walter. The elder son,

RICHARD DE CORNEWALL, had the manor of Thunnock, in Lincolnshire, from Edmund, Earl of Cornwall, 8th EDWARD I., *anno* 1280. He was ancestor of the Cornewalls, Barons of Burford, the senior line of which family is now represented by the heir-general, GEORGE-CORNEWALL LEGH, Esq. of High Legh, Cheshire.

SIR ROWLAND (or SIR RICHARD) CORNEWALL, of Berrington, co. Hereford (2nd son of Thomas Cornewall, Baron of Burford, by Elizabeth his wife, dau. and co-heir of Sir Rowland Lenthall, Knt. of Hampton Court, co. Hereford), was father of

SIR RICHARD CORNEWALL, Knt. of Berrington, who m. Jane, 2nd dau. and co-heir of Simon Milborne, Esq. of Tillington, co. Hereford, and had a son,

SIR GEORGE CORNEWALL, of Berrington, who m. Mary, sister of Edmond, Lord Chandos, and had a son and heir,

HUMPHREY CORNEWALL, Esq. of Berrington, who m. Elizabeth, dau. of John Bradshaw, Esq. of Presteign, co.

Radnor, and by her had issue. Mr. Cornewall served the office of high-sheriff for co. Hereford, 9th JAMES I. He d. in 1663, and was s. by his eldest son,

JOHN CORNEWALL, Esq. of Berrington, who m. Mary, dau. of William Barnaby, Esq. of The Hill, co. Worcester, and by her had issue, HUMPHREY, his heir; Coningsby, bapt. 31 May, 1620, and Edward (Colonel), of Moccas and Bredwardine Castle, ancestor of the CORNEWALLS *of Moccas*, Barts. The eldest son,

HUMPHREY CORNEWALL, Esq. of Berrington, b. in 1616, m. Anne Skinner, of Thornton College, co. Lincoln, and had issue. The eldest son,

ROBERT CORNEWALL, Esq. of Berrington and Ludlow, b. in 1646, m. Edith Cornwallis, of Abermarles, co. Carmarthen, and by her (who d. 15 July, 1696) had, with other issue, Charles, of Berrington, bapt. 9 Aug. 1669, vice-adm. R.N., father of JACOBS CORNEWALL, whose son, CHARLES-WALFRAN CORNEWALL, Speaker of the House of Commons, d. s. p. 1789. His 4th son,

THE REV. FREDERICK CORNEWALL, M.A. of St. John's College, Cambridge, was vicar of Bromfield forty-six years. He m. Elizabeth Trice, of co. Huntingdon, and d. in 1748, having had, besides a dau. Frances, and a son, Robert, who d. in 1705, another son,

FREDERICK CORNEWALL, Esq. of Delbury, capt. R.N., b. in 1706, who m. Mary, dau. of Francis Herbert, Esq. of Ludlow (first-cousin to the 1st Earl of Powis), of Oakley Park. By this lady, Capt. Cornewall (whose will was proved 19 Nov. 1788) had two sons, Frederick, M.P. for Ludlow, who d. s. p. in 1783, and

THE REV. FOLLIOT-HERBERT-WALKER CORNEWALL, D.D., successively Bishop of Bristol, Hereford, and Worcester. He m. Anne, dau. of the Hon. George Hamilton, youngest son of James, Earl of Abercorn, and by her (who d. 25 Dec. 1795) had issue,

- I. Frederick-Hamilton, of Delbury, bapt. there 15 Oct. 1791, who m. Fanny-Harriet, eldest dau. of St. George Caulfeild, Esq. of Donamon Castle, co. Roscommon, by Frances his wife (dau. of Sir Edward Crofton, Bart., and Baroness of Crofton in her own right), and by her had two daus.,
  - 1 Henrietta, m. to the Hon. Spencer Lyttelton, son of William, 3rd Baron Lyttelton, by the Lady Sarah Spencer, his wife, dau. of George, 1st Earl Spencer.
  - 2 Mary-Fanny.
- II. HERBERT, now of Delbury.

Dr. Cornewall d. at Hartlebury, 5 Sept. 1831, aged 77.

Arms—Arg., a lion, rampant, gu., ducally crowned, or, within a borbure, engrailed, sa., bezantée.
Seat—Delbury, near Ludlow.

CORNISH OF BLACK HALL.

CORNISH, JAMES, Esq. of Black Hall, co. Devon, b. 25 Aug. 1792; m. 25 Aug. 1840, Elizabeth-Anne, dau. of Capt. Robert Hall, R.M., by Elizabeth-Anne Churchill his wife, a co-heiress of Peter Churchill, Esq. of Dawlish, J.P. for Devon, and has had issue,

- I. JAMES-HUBERT, b. 13 Oct. 1847, d. 30 Nov. 1849.
- I. Elizabeth-Anne. II. Esther-Priscilla.

Lineage.—The late JAMES CORNISH, Esq. of Black Hall (eldest son of James Cornish,* M.D. of Totnes, eldest son of James Cornish, Esq. of Teignmouth, by Margaret his wife, dau. of the Rev. William Floyer, a descendant of Nicholas Wadham, founder of Wadham College, Oxford), d. at Black Hall, 6 Oct. 1837, and was buried at North Huish, Devon. By Priscilla his wife, who d. 13 April, 1833, he had issue,

JAMES, now of Black Hall.
William-Floyer, of the Inner Temple, barrister-at-law, d. 26 Aug. 1830, aged 29.
Esther, of Blackmore Hall, Sidmouth.
Sarah, of Blackmore Hall, d. unm.
Charlotte, d. unm.
Elizabeth-Rhodes, wife of Charles-John Cornish, Esq. of Salcombe House, Devon, d. there, 5 Nov. 1853.

Arms—Sa., a chevron, embattled, or, between three roses, arg.
Crest—A Cornish chough, ppr.
Seat—Black Hall, Joybridge.

CORNISH OF MARAZION.

CORNISH, WILLIAM, Esq. of Marazion, co. Cornwall, J.P. and D.L., b. 1783; m. in 1808, Honor, dau. of Francis Cole, Esq., post-captain R.N., and niece of Sir Christopher Cole, K.C.B., and has issue,

- I. WILLIAM. II. John.
- III. Francis, 97th regt. IV. Charles.
- V. Edward.
- I. Jane, m. to James Clayton, Esq., lieut. R.N.
- II. Harriet-Cole, m. to Walter Lindesay, Esq. of Dublin, barrister-at-law.
- III. Honor-Cole, m. to George Gahan, Esq., lieut. R.N.
- IV. Frances, m. to William Carne, Esq. of Penzance.
- V. Philippa. VI. Elizabeth.

Mr. Cornish is only surviving son of William Cornish, Esq., by Jane his wife, dau. of Thomas-Saunders Allen, Esq., and grandson, by Frances James his wife, of William Cornish, Esq., son of William Cornish, Esq.

Arms—Sa., a chevron, embattled, or, between three roses, arg.
Crest—A Cornish chough, sa., wings endorsed, beaked and legged, gu., standing on a branch of olive, ppr.
Seat—Marazion, co. Cornwall.

CORNOCK OF CROMWELLSFORT.

CORNOCK, ISAAC, Esq. of Cromwellsfort, co. Wexford, an officer 14th light dragoons.

Lineage.—ISAAC CORNOCK, Esq. of Cork, only son of Jacob Cornock, who went in CROMWELL'S army to Ireland, and grandson of Col. Isaac Cornock, slain at Naseby, 1645, m. 22 June, 1686, Hannah, only child of the above-named Lieut.-Colonel Corbett, by whom he acquired the grants made to her father, in the vicinity of Ferns, co. Wexford, where he resided. Isaac Cornock's will was proved in Dublin in 1691, and he was s. by his only son,

ISAAC CORNOCK, Esq. of the city of Cork, b. in 1687, who m. 23 Sept. 1708, Mary, dau. of Joseph Jervoice, Esq. of Brade, co. Cork. His will was proved in Dublin, in 1726. His only son,

ZACHARIAH CORNOCK, Esq. of Kilcassane, co. Wexford, b. 1709, m. Frances, dau. of the Rev. Bartholomew Thomas, rector of Ferns, co. Wexford, and d 31 Dec. 1740. His only son,

CAPTAIN ISAAC CORNOCK, b. Aug. 1739, m. 10 Oct. 1764, Sarah, dau. of Francis Wheeler, of Motabeg, co. Wexford, great-grandson of Col. Francis Wheeler, of Cromwell's army, and by her (who d. 2 Aug. 1779) had issue,

ZACHARIAH, his heir.
Frances, b. Aug. 1765, d. unm. 26 March, 1783.
Mary, b. 7 May, 1771, m. 5 March, 1789, John Hawkes, Esq. of Grange, co. Cork, and had issue.

Captain Isaac Cornock d. 30 Nov. 1808, and was s. by his only son,

THE REV. ZACHARIAH CORNOCK, of Cromwellsfort, J.P., b. 3 March, 1770, who m. 17 Feb. 1815, Charlotte, dau. of Thomas Burgh, Esq. of Bert, co. Kildare, and sister of the present Lord Downes, and by her (who d. 1 Sept. 1827) has issue,

ISAAC, lieut. 14th light dragoons.
Thomas-Burgh, d. 2 June, 1829.
Zachariah-Burgh.

Seat—Cromwellsfort, near Wexford.

CORRANCE OF PARHAM HALL.

CORRANCE, FREDERICK, Esq. of Parham Hall, co. Suffolk, m. 27 Sept. 1819, Frances-Anne, 3rd dau. of William Woodley, Esq., governor of Berbice, and has issue,

- I. FREDERICK-SNOWDEN, late of the 11th Hussars, b. 17 Jan. 1822.
- II. Charles-Thomas, in holy orders, b. 7 March, 1823.
- III. Henry-William, b. 30 April, 1828.
- IV. George-Edward, an officer 76th regt., b. 9 April, 1830.
- I. Frances-Anne, d. 2 June, 1836.
- II. Louisa-Jane.

Mr. Corrance assumed, 16 May, 1837, the surname of CORRANCE, in lieu of his patronymic, White.

Lineage.—SNOWDEN WHITE, Esq., M.D. of Nottingham, eldest son and heir of Snowden White, Esq. of Newton Flottman, co. Norfolk, by Elizabeth his wife, dau. of Dr. Latham, of Derbyshire, and grandson of Samuel White, Esq. of St. Ives, who was a younger son of Thomas White,

* James Cornish's only sister, Charlotte, m. 1786, John, 1st Lord Teignmouth.

Esq. of Pirton, co. Herts, an officer in the parliamentary army, m. in 1782, his cousin, MARY CORRANCE, dau. and co-heir of MAJOR JOHN CORRANCE, a distinguished officer at Dettingen, Fontenoy, and Culloden, son of Richard Corrance, 2nd son of John Corrance, of Rendlesham, whose ancestor was Allen Urren, *alias* Corrance, citizen of London, to whom arms were granted, 27 Feb. 1619. By this lady he left at his decease, in 1797, an only son and heir, FREDERICK, who is the present representative, having *s.* his mother, and assumed the surname of CORRANCE.

Arms—Arg., on a chevron, between three ravens, sa., three leopards' faces, or.
Crest—A raven holding with his dexter claw an escutcheon, sa., charged with a leopard's face, or.
Seat—Parham Hall. *Residence*—Loudham Hall, both in co. Suffolk.

CORRY OF NEWRY.

CORRY, ISAAC, Esq. of Abbey Yard, Newry, co. Down, J.P. and D.L., *b.* 8 May, 1810; *m.* Jan. 1840, Ellis, 2nd dau. of Henry Ryan, Esq. of Kilfera, Kilkenny, and has issue,

I. TREVOR, *b.* 6 Jan. 1846.
I. Ellis-Louisa. II. Anne-Adelaide.
III. Lara. IV. Charlotte.
V. Frances.

Lineage.—The late TREVOR CORRY, Esq. of Newry, *m.* July, 1809, Anne, eldest dau. of the late Savage Hall, Esq. of Narrow Water, co. Down, and by her (who *d.* 24 April, 1852) had issue,

ISAAC, now of Abbey Yard, Newry.
Savage-Hall, lieut. 17th regt., *d.* in India.
Edward-Smyth. Trevor, *d.* 1852.
Mary-Catherine, *d.* in 1818.
Louisa-Barbara, *m.* to Capt. G.-T. Evans (74th regt.), of Ashhill Towers, co. Limerick.
Mary-Steuart, *m.* to the Rev. J.-C. Quinn, of Beech Hill, co. Down.

Mr. Corry *d.* 22 July, 1838.

Arms—Sa., on a chevron, or, between three dragons' heads erased, three estoiles.
Crest—Out of a ducal coronet, a dragon's head, between two wings.
Motto—Gripe fast.
Seat—Abbey Yard, Newry.

CORSELLIS OF WYVENHOE HALL.

CORSELLIS, NICHOLAS-CÆSAR, Esq. of Wyvenhoe Hall, Essex.

The estate of Wyvenhoe was acquired by the family of Corsellis, by purchase, about the time of the Restoration, from the Townshends, who had bought it from Edward De Vere, 17th Earl of Oxford.

Seat—Wyvenhoe Hall, near Colchester.

CORYTON OF PENTILLIE CASTLE.

CORYTON, AUGUSTUS, Esq. of Pentillie Castle, co. Cornwall, *b.* 30 Jan. 1809.

Lineage.—ELIZABETH CORYTON (elder dau. and eventual co-heir of Sir John Coryton, 1st Bart. of Coryton and Newton Ferrars), inherited, as co-heir with her sister Anne, wife of John Peter, Esq., the representation of the ancient family of Coryton. She *m.* William Goodall, Esq. of Fowey, and had a son and successor,

JOHN GOODALL, Esq., whose son and heir,

PETER GOODALL, Esq., assumed the surname and arms of CORYTON. He was *s.* at his decease, in 1756, by his son,

JOHN CORYTON, Esq., who *m.* Mary-Jemima, only dau. and heiress of James Tillie, Esq. of Pentillie Castle, and was *s.* by his son,

JOHN-TILLIE CORYTON, Esq. of Pentillie Castle, *b.* 4 April, 1773, *m.* 15 Aug. 1803, Elizabeth, 2nd dau. of Admiral the Hon. John-Leveson Gower, and had issue,

WILLIAM, *b.* 17 Feb. 1807, *m.* Harriet-Sophia, dau. of Montagu-Edmund Parkes, Esq., and *d.* 17 May, 1836. His widow *m.* 2ndly, in 1842, Edmund, Earl of Morley.
AUGUSTUS, now of Pentillie.
Henry, *b.* 28 March, 1810.
Granville, in holy orders, *m.* Oct. 1845, Jessie, dau. of F. King, Esq., *b.* 30 May, 1816.
George Edward, *b.* 1 Feb. 1819, *m.* Louisa, dau. of the Rev. Charles Phillott, rector of Frome, and has issue.
Frederick, *b.* 4 March, 1824, *d.* 1 March, 1830.
Jemima, *d.* 10 Sept. 1853.
Mary-Anne, *d.* 4 May, 1848.
Charlotte. Elizabeth.

Mr. Coryton *d.* Sept. 1843.

Arms—Arg., a saltier, sa.
Crest—A lion, passant, gu.
Seat—Pentillie Castle, Cornwall.

COSBY OF STRADBALLY.

COSBY, ROBERT, Esq. of Stradbally Hall, Queen's County.

Lineage.—The family of Cosby is of Saxon origin, and is stated to have possessed the lordship of Cosby, co. Leicester, previously to the Norman Conquest. It first became settled in Ireland *temp.* Queen MARY.

FRANCIS COSBIE, the patriarch of the family in Ireland, a man famed for personal courage as well as civil and military talents, became an active defender of the Pale, and was appointed, 14 Feb. 1558, General of the Kerne, a post of great importance in those times. Francis Cosbie had, ALEXANDER, inheritor of the estates; Henry, who *d.* before his father settled in Ireland; Arnold, who served under Robert, Earl of Leicester, with great reputation in the Low Countries, *anno* 1586, with the celebrated Sir Philip Sidney, and was at the battle of Zutphen; Catherine, *m.* to Archibald Moor, Esq., but *d.* issueless. Francis Cosbie eventually fell at the battle of Glendalough, at the head of the Kerne, whom he valiantly led to the charge, although then seventy years of age. He was *s.* by his eldest son,

ALEXANDER COSBIE, Esq. of Stradbally Abbey, who seems to have been engaged during the whole of his time in warfare with the O'Mores. He *m.* DORCAS, dau. of WILLIAM SYDNEY,* Esq. of Otford, in Kent, and had fifteen children. This lady, who had been one of the maids of honour to Queen ELIZABETH, obtained, through her influential connexions at Court, grants in Ireland (in Leix) so extensive that, at one period, the family were the territorial lords of more than a moiety of the Queen's County. The issue of Alexander Cosby and Dorcas Sydney were,

FRANCIS, *b.* 1 Jan. 1751, captain of the Kerne, who fell immediately after his father, at the battle of Stradbally Bridge, on 19 May, 1590, leaving by his wife, Hellen Harpole (who *m.* 2ndly, Sir Thomas Loftus, of Killian, in the King's County), an infant child, WILLIAM, *b.* in 1596, who *s.* him.
RICHARD, successor to his nephew.
Charles, *b.* 12 Sept. 1585, *m.* a dau. of the Loftus family.
Arnold, *b.* 20 June, 1591, settled in the co. Cavan, and planted a branch of the family there.
Mable, *b.* 12 Aug. 1598, *m.* to George Harpole, Esq. of Shrule, in the Queen's County, and *d.* in 1632, leaving issue.
Rose, *b.* in the Queen's house, at Otford, in Kent, 20 Nov. 1582, said to have *m.* a Lord Howth.

Alexander Cosby, who was slain in a battle with the O'Mores, was *s.*, although for a few minutes only, by his eldest son,

FRANCIS COSBY, Esq. of Stradbally Abbey, who being slain, as stated above, never enjoyed the inheritance, but left it to his infant child,

WILLIAM COSBY, Esq. of Stradbally Abbey, who *d.* young, when the estates reverted to his uncle,

RICHARD COSBY, Esq., who thus became of Stradbally Abbey, and was Captain of the Kerne. He entirely defeated the O'Mores, and avenged his father's and brother's deaths. By Elizabeth his wife, dau. of Sir Robert Pigot, of Dysert, Captain Cosby had, with a dau., Dorcas, *m.* to William Loftus, Esq. of Ballymann, four sons, of whom the eldest, ALEXANDER, was his heir; and the 2nd, Francis, M.P., *b.* in 1612, *m.* Anne, dau. of Sir Thomas Loftus, of Killyan, and had issue, 1 ALEXANDER, successor to his uncle; 2 THOMAS, of Vicarstown, who *m.* Anne, dau. of Sir William Smith, and *d.* in 1713 (his great-grandson, THOMAS COSBY, of Vicarstown, eventually inherited Stradbally); and 3 Sydney, of Ballymanus, who *d.* in 1716, leaving issue. Richard Cosby was *s.* by his eldest son,

ALEXANDER COSBY, Esq. of Stradbally, *b.* 8 Feb. 1610, who *m.* Anne, dau. of Sir Francis Slingsby, Knt. of Kilmore, co. Cork, but, dying without issue, was *s.* by his nephew,

* Grand-nephew of William Sydney, Lord of Cranleigh.

Alexander Cosby, Esq. of Stradbally Hall, who m. Elizabeth, dau. of Henry L'Estrange, Esq. of Moystown, King's County, by whom (who d. in 1692) he had issue,

I. Dudley, his heir.
II. Henry, capt. of foot, d. in Spain, in 1715. He had m. a Miss Higgins.
III. Thomas, major of foot, m. Jane, dau. of Henry Loftus, Esq., and sister of Nicholas, Viscount Loftus, of Ely, by whom he had two daus.,
1 Anne, m. to Charles Davis, Esq. 2 Jane.
IV. Loftus, capt. of foot, d. at Marseilles, 3 Jan. 1726.
V. Alexander, lieut.-col. in the army, and lieut.-governor of Nova Scotia, where he d. 26 Dec. 1743, leaving, by Anne his wife, dau. of Alexander Winnard, Esq. of Annapolis, two sons and two daus., viz.,
1 William, a capt. in the army, d. of the small-pox, at Windsor, in 1748.
2 Phillips, who eventually inherited Stradbally.
1 Elizabeth, m. to Capt. Foye.
2 Mary, m. to Capt. Charles Cotterell.
VI. William, a brigadier-general in the army, col. of the Royal Irish, Governor of New York and the Jerseys, equerry to the Queen, &c., m. Grace, sister of George Montague, Earl of Halifax, K.B., and left by that lady (who d. 25 Dec. 1767), at his decease, 10 March, 1736, the following issue,
1 William, an officer in the army.
2 Henry, R.N., d. in 1753.
1 Elizabeth, m. to Lord Augustus Fitzroy, 2nd son of Charles, Duke of Grafton.
2 Grace, m. to — Murray, Esq. of New York.
I. Anne, m. to William Wall, Esq. of Coolnamuck, co. Waterford.
II. Elizabeth, m. to Lieut.-Gen. Richard Phillips, Governor of Nova Scotia.
III. Jane, b. in 1661.
IV. Dorcas, m. to — Forbes, Esq.
V. Celia, m. to William Weldon, Esq. of Rosscumro, in the King's County.

Alexander Cosby d. in 1694, and was s. by his eldest son,

Dudley Cosby, Esq. of Stradbally Hall, lieut.-col. in the army, and M.P. for the Queen's County. He m. Sarah, dau. of Periam Pole,* Esq. of Ballyfin, in that shire, and had, Pole, his heir; and Sarah, m. to Robert Meredith, Esq. of Shrowland, in Kildare. Colonel Cosby d. 24 May, 1729, and was s. by his son,

Pole Cosby, Esq. of Stradbally Hall, who m. Mary, dau. and co-heir of Henry Dodwell, Esq. of Manor Dodwell, co. Roscommon, and by her (who d. 9 Jan. 1742) left at his decease, 20 May, 1766, (with a dau. Sarah, b. in 1730, m. 1st, to the Right Hon. Arthur Upton, of Castle Upton, and 2ndly, to Robert, Earl of Farnham), a son and successor,

Dudley-Alexander-Sydney Cosby, Esq. of Stradbally Hall, created, in 1768, a peer of Ireland, as *Baron Sydney, of Leix*, in the Queen's County. His lordship was minister plenipotentiary to the court of Denmark. He m. in Dec. 1773, the Lady Isabella St. Lawrence, dau. of Thomas, 1st Earl of Howth, but d. in the ensuing month, 17 Jan. 1774, without issue. His peerage became, of course, extinct, while the inheritance reverted to his lordship's cousin,

Phillips Cosby, Esq., admiral of the White. He m. in August, 1792, Eliza, dau. of W. Gunthorpe, Esq., and sister of W. Gunthorpe, Esq. of Southampton, but having no issue, was s. at his decease by his kinsman,

Thomas Cosby, Esq. of Vicarstown. He m. Miss Johnstone, an heiress of the Annandale family, and dying 10 Dec. 1788, was s. by his only surviving child,

Thomas Cosby, Esq. of Stradbally Hall, Governor of the Queen's County, who m. in 1802, Charlotte-Elizabeth, dau. of the Right Hon. Thomas Kelly, lord chief-justice of the Court of Common Pleas in Ireland, and had issue,

I. Thomas-Phillips, of Stradbally.
II. William, in holy orders, m. Miss Jephson, niece of Lord Dunalley, and has one son, Thomas.
III. Sydney, m. in 1834, Emily, elder dau. and co-heir of Robert Ashworth, Esq., and d. in 1840, leaving a son, Robert, and two daus.,
IV. Wellesley-Pole, m. in 1841, Marie, 2nd dau. and co-heir of Robert Ashworth, Esq., and d. s. p. in 1842.
I. Frances-Elizabeth, m. in 1837, to Horace Rochfort, Esq. of Clogrenane Castle, co. Carlow, and d. in 1841, leaving issue.
II. Harriett-Georgiana, m. to Frederick, Lord Ashtown.

Mr. Cosby, who served the office of high-sheriff of the Queen's County, d. 22 Jan. 1832, and was s. by his son,

Thomas-Phillips Cosby, Esq. of Stradbally Hall, J.P. and D.L., b. 20 Sept. 1803, high-sheriff in 1834, capt. royal regt. horse guards, at whose decease the property devolved on his nephew, Robert Cosby, Esq., now of Stradbally.

* By Anne his wife, dau. of Henry Colley, Esq. of Castle Carbery, in Kildare.

Arms—Cosby and Sydney, quarterly.
Crest—A griffin, his wings erect, gu., supporting a standard, the head broken off, or.
Motto—Audaces fortuna juvat.
Seat—Stradbally Hall.

COTES OF WOODCOTE.

Cotes, John, Esq. of Woodcote, co. Salop, J.P. and D.L., b. in 1802, high-sheriff of Shropshire in 1826; m. 5 Sept. 1839, Lady Louisa-Harriet Jenkinson, youngest dau. of Charles-Cecil, last Earl of Liverpool, and has issue,

Victoria, for whom Her Majesty stood sponsor.

Mr. Cotes represented North Salop in parliament in 1834.

Lineage.—The family of Cotes have been possessed of extensive landed property in the counties of Stafford and Salop from a very remote period. The first of the family on record as seated at Woodcote is

Humphrey Cotes, Esq. of Cotes and Woodcote, tenth in lineal descent from Ricardus de Cotes, and son and heir of Sir Thomas Cotes. He m. Johanna, dau. and heir of Thomas de Daventry, and was father of

John Cotes, Esq. of Cotes and Woodcote, high-sheriff of the county of Stafford, 35th Henry VI., who m. Elizabeth, 2nd dau. and co-heiress of Thomas Downton, Esq., and had issue, Humphrey, of Cotes and Woodcote, father of

John Cotes, Esq. of Cotes and Woodcote, who m. Ellen, dau. of Richard Littleton, Esq. of Pillaton Hall, co. Stafford, 2nd son of the eminent lawyer, Sir Thomas Littleton, Knt., K.B., judge of the Common Pleas, and author of the *Treatise on Tenures*; and by that lady had issue, of which the eldest son,

John Cotes, Esq. of Woodcote, living 1574, was great-great-grandfather of

John Cotes, Esq. of Woodcote (son of Charles Cotes, Esq. of Woodcote, and Lettice his wife, only dau. of Kildare, 2nd Lord Digby). He m. Dorothy, dau. of Robert, Earl Ferrers, and had issue,

Shirley, in holy orders, who predeceased his father, leaving a son, John, successor to his grandfather.
James, col. in the army, m. Frances, youngest dau. of William, 5th Lord Digby.
Washington, LL.D., dean of Lismore, and chaplain to the Lord Lieutenant of Ireland, m. 1st, in 1720, Miss Corbet; and 2ndly, 5 June, 1750, Mrs. Holland, of Shrewsbury.
Digby, in holy orders, Vice-Chancellor of Oxford in 1738, m. and had issue, Digby, b. in 1714, M.A., and principal of Magdalen Hall, and upwards of 52 years rector of Dore, and vicar of Bromyard, co. Hereford. He d. 4 March, 1793, leaving issue, Marianne, m. 31 July, 1767, to the Rev. James Halifax, D.D.; and Charlotte-Anne, m. to John Meysey, Esq. of Oxford, and d. 29 Oct. 1795.
Dorothy, m. to the Rev. William Pigott, rector of Edgmond and Chetwynd, Salop.
Mary, m. to Wriothesley, son of William, 5th Lord Digby.

The grandson,

John Cotes, Esq. of Woodcote, M.P. for Wigan and for the county of Salop in several parliaments, m. 19 Oct. 1777, Lucy, 2nd dau. of William, 1st Viscount Courtenay, and had (with two daus., Charlotte, maid of honour to H.R.H. the Princess Charlotte; and Mary, also in the Princess's household) two sons, James, the younger, capt. R.N., d. 27 June, 1802; and

John Cotes, Esq. of Woodcote, some years M.P. for co. Salop, who m. 2 May, 1794, Lady Maria Grey, 2nd dau. of George-Harry, 5th Earl of Stamford and Warrington, and had issue,

John, present representative.
Charles-George, in holy orders, rector of Staunton and Quinton, co. Wilts, m. 4 April, 1837, Fanny-Henrietta, dau. of General Sir George Pigot, Bart.
Henrietta-Louisa, m. 5 May 1836, to the Rev. William Cafield, M.A.

Mr. Cotes d. 24 Aug. 1821.

Arms—Quarterly: 1st and 4th, erm.; 2nd and 3rd, paly of six, or and gu.
Crest—A cock, ppr., combed, wattled, and legged, or.
Seat—Woodcote, co. Salop.

COTTON OF ETWALL.

Cotton, The Rev. Charles-Evelyn, of Etwall Hall, co. Derby, patron and rector of Dalbury, in that shire, and lord of the manors of Etwall, Burnaston, and Dalbury, *b.* 14 Sept. 1782; *m.* 3 March, 1828, Frances-Maria, dau. of Francis Bradshaw, Esq. of Barton Hall, co. Derby, and has issue,

I. ROWLAND-HUGH, *b.* 13 Jan. 1833.
I. Elizabeth-Emma. II. Agnes-Maria.
III. Harriet-Bertha. IV. Marian-Frances.

Lineage.—This ancient family can be authentically traced from the reign of King HENRY II., when SIR HUGH COTTON, Knt., was of Cotton, in the co. Salop. By Elizabeth his wife, dau. and heir of Hamon Titley, of Titley, he had three sons, HUGH (Sir), knight of St. John; ALLEN, of whose descendants we treat; and William, dean of Worcester. The 2nd son,

ALLEN COTTON, brother and heir of Sir Hugh, *m.* Margaret, dau of Roger Acton, and was father of

HUGH COTTON, of Cotton, who *m.* Isabel, dau. and heir of Thomas Heyton, and had two sons, I. NICHOLAS, of Cotton, whose dau. and heiress Ellen, *m.* Robert de Lacon; and II. HUGH, living *temp.* EDWARD III., whose grandson, ROGER COTTON (son of Richard), *m.* Ellen, dau. and co-heir of John Gremyson, of Alkington, and was father of

WILLIAM COTTON, of Alkington, *temp.* HENRY VI. His son and heir,

JOHN COTTON, of Alkington, 23rd EDWARD IV., had, by Catherine his wife, dau. of Thomas Constantine, of Doddington, three sons, THOMAS, his heir; William, alderman of Coventry; and Richard (Sir), priest. The eldest,

THOMAS COTTON, Esq. of Alkington, *temp.* HENRY VII., *m.* Alice, dau. and co-heir of Ralph Johnstone, of Whitchurch, and had issue, I. RALPH, his heir; II. John, who *m.* Beatrice Whitfield, and had four sons; III. Roger, *m.* Dorothy, dau. of William Herring, of Coventry, and had issue; IV. William, whose dau. and heiress Margaret, *m.* Randal Taylor, of Whitchurch. The eldest son,

RALPH COTTON, Esq. of Alkington, *m.* Jane, dau. and co-heir of John Smith, and had issue, I. JOHN, *m.* Jane, dau. of John Dod, Esq. of Cloverly, but *d. s. p.* 1606; II. Thomas, *d. s. p.*; III. WILLIAM, of whom we treat; IV. Randal, captain in the army, *d. s. p.*; V. Roger; VI. Allen (Sir), Knt.; and several daus. The 3rd son,

WILLIAM COTTON, Esq. alderman of London, *m.* Jane, dau. and co-heir of William Shabery, and was *s.* by his eldest son,

SIR ROWLAND COTTON, Knt. of Alkington, who *m.* 1st, Frances, eldest dau. of Robert, Viscount Kilmorey, and 2ndly, Joyce, dau. and heir of Sir R. Walsh, of Shelsey, but *d. s. p.* in 1634, and was *s.* by his brother,

WILLIAM COTTON, Esq. of Alkington, who *m.* twice, but left issue only by his 2nd wife, Ann, dau. of Philip Draul, Esq. of Sedshall, co. Stafford. His eldest son and heir,

WILLIAM COTTON, Esq. of Alkington and Bellaport, was living at the period of the great civil war. There is still preserved at Etwall Hall, a portrait of this William Cotton, of Bellaport, as well as the following order of Prince Rupert:—

"Wee doe hereby strictly charge and command all and every of you whom it may or shall concern, that imediately upon your sight or knowledge hereof, you doe no manner of injury, hurte, violence or damage, to William Cotton, of Bellaport, in the county of Salop, Esq., in his person, goodes, family, halls, &c., or chattells whatsoever, here or elswhere remaining. As you will answere for contrary att your uttmost perrills. Given at Salop, this eleventh of May, 1644. RUPERT."

"To all commanders and officers
and soldiers whatsoever, or anyways
belonging to His Majesty's armye."

William Cotton *m.* 1st, Joyce, 2nd dau. of Sir Thomas Bromley, Knt., and 2ndly, Dorothy, dau. of John Whetnall, Esq. of Hanklow, co. Chester, and was *s.* by his eldest son,

RALPH COTTON, Esq. of Bellaport, who *m.* Abigail, dau. of Sir Thomas Abney, Knt. of Willesley, co. Derby, and *d.* 28 Aug. 1663, leaving a son and successor,

ROWLAND COTTON, Esq. of Bellaport, who *m.* Mary, dau. and co-heir (with her sister who *m.* Humphrey Chetham, Esq., and *d. s. p.*) of Sir Samuel Sleigh, Knt. of Etwall, and had issue, WILLIAM, his heir; Mary, *m.* to Henry Eyre, Esq.; Elizabeth-Abigail, *m.* to Sir Lynch-Salusbury Cotton, Bart. of Combermere, co. Chester, the descendant of the younger branch of the COTTONS *of Cotton*, and Katherine, *m.* to Robert, Earl Ferrers. Rowland Cotton *d.* 1753, and was *s.* by his son,

WILLIAM COTTON, Esq. of Bellaport and Etwall, *b.* Nov. 1700, who *m.* 14 June, 1742, Rebecca, dau. of Daniel Webster, and *d.* Jan. 1776, leaving issue, of which the son and heir,

WILLIAM COTTON, Esq. of Etwall Hall, co. Derby, bapt. 27 Jan. 1740, *d. unm.* 4 Nov. 1819. His sister and co-heir,

ELIZABETH COTTON, bapt. 26 Aug. 1748, the relict of Joseph Green, Esq. of Hall Green, co. Worcester, and Portugal House, Birmingham, assumed by royal license, bearing date 14 Jan. following, for herself and her issue, the surname and arms of COTTON only. She *d.* in 1833, leaving issue,

EDWIN-ROWLAND-JOSEPH.
CHARLES-EVELYN, now of Etwall Hall.
Rebecca-Maria, *m.* to J.-S. Stovin, Esq. of Cheltenham.
Eliza-Catherine, *m.* to Admiral Clement Sneyd, of Huntley Hall, co. Stafford.
Emma-Cotton.

The eldest son,

EDWIN-ROWLAND COTTON, Esq. of Etwall Hall, a major-general in the army, who *m.* Frances-Hester, 2nd dau. of the Very Rev. George Cotton, dean of Chester, and *d. s. p.*, when he was *s.* by his brother, the present head of the family.

Arms—Azure, a chevron, between three Hanks of Cotton, argent.

Crest—A falcon, ppr., beaked, legged, and belled, or, the dexter claw supporting a belt, also ppr., buckle, gold.

Motto—In utraque fortunâ paratus.

Seat—Etwall Hall, co. Derby, a very fine old baronial mansion in high preservation, containing a great number of ancient family pictures.

COTTRELL OF HADLEY.

COTTRELL, CHARLES-HERBERT, Esq. of Hadley, co. Middlesex, J.P., *b.* 27 Nov. 1806, M.A. Pembroke College, Cambridge.

Lineage.—COLONEL JOHN COTTRELL, eldest son of Sir Charles-Ludowicke Cottrell, Knt., Master of the Ceremonies (*see* COTTRELL-DORMER), by Elizabeth his 2nd wife, only dau. of Chaloner Chute, Esq. of The Vine, *m.* in Ireland, Miss Martha Orr, of Londonderry, and by her, who *d.* in 1778, had issue, two sons and two daus. Col. Cottrell *d.* in Oct. 1746, and was *s.* by his son,

CHARLES-JEFFREYS COTTRELL, *b.* in Dublin, in 1739, who, on selling out of the army, took holy orders, and *m.* in 1763, Miss Fanny Smith, of Hadley, in Middlesex, sister of Sir Culling Smith, Bart., by whom, who *d.* in 1811, he had issue,

I. CHARLES, his heir.
II. John, an officer in the E.I.C.S., *d. unm.* in Jan. 1766.
III. Clement, M.A., rector of North Waltham, Hants, *m.* Georgiana, dau. of the late John Adams, Esq. of Peterwell, formerly M.P. for Cardigan, and dying 26 July, 1814, left issue,
  1 CHARLES-HERBERT, successor to his uncle.
  2 Clement-Chute, an officer in the E.I.C.S., *b.* 29 Feb. 1808, *m.* Miss Gorman, and by her (who *d.* in 1854) has three sons and one dau.
  3 Lucius-Frederick, also an officer in the E.I.C.S., *b.* in 1800, *m.* in 1832, Euphemia-Eliza, dau. of Francis Robertson, Esq. of Chilcott, Derbyshire, and *d.* at Pisa, in 1836, *s. p.*
  4 Henry, formerly in the R.N., and afterwards resident chamberlain of the Duke of Lucca, *b.* in 1811, created Count in Tuscany, *m.* Sophia, youngest dau. of the late C.-A. Tulk, Esq., M.P., and has a son, *b.* 1 Aug. 1851.
  5 George-Edward, *b.* in 1812, barrister-at-law, *m.* Emily, eldest dau. of E. Stephenson, Esq., and has two sons.
  1 Georgiana-Clementina, *m.* in 1839, to the Rev. John Sloper, of West Woodhay House, Berks.
IV. Frederick, capt. R.N., *d.* in the West Indies in 1811, *unm.*
I. Frances, *m.* to the Rev. Mr. Evans.
II. Isabella. III. Harriet.
IV. Anna-Frederica, *d. unm.* in 1818.
V. Sophia, *m.* to the Rev. G. Lefroy, of Ewshot House, Surrey.

Mr. Cottrell *d.* 25 Jan. 1819, and was *s.* by his son,

CHARLES COTTRELL, Esq. of Hadley, in Middlesex, who *d. unm.* 25 Feb. 1829, aged 62, and was *s.* by his nephew, the present CHARLES-HERBERT COTTRELL, Esq. of Hadley.

Arms—Arg., a bond between three escallops, sa.
Crest—A talbot's head, sa., collared and lined, or; the collar charged with three escallops.
Motto—Nec temere nec timide.
Seat—Hadley, near Barnet.

COULSON OF BLENKINSOPP.

COULSON, JOHN-BLENKINSOPP, Esq. of Blenkinsopp Castle, in Northumberland, lieut. col. of the militia, J.P. and D.L., *b.* 8 May, 1779; *m.* 22 June, 1796, Alicia-Frances-Forth, dau. of the Rev. Gustavus

Hamilton, son of the Hon. Henry Hamilton, 3rd son of Gen. Gustavus Hamilton, Viscount Boyne, and has issue,

I. JOHN-BLENKINSOPP, capt. in the grenadier-guards, and D.L., *b.* 7 Aug. 1799, *m.* 1st, 8 Dec. 1829, Juliana-Elizabeth, only child of the Rev. Edward Dawkins, of Portman-square, and granddau. of James Dawkins, Esq. of Standlynch, by the Lady Juliana Collyear his wife, dau. of Charles, 2nd Earl of Portmore. Mrs. Coulson dying in childbirth, 27 Aug. 1831, Mr. Coulson *m.* 2ndly, 4 June, 1834, the Hon. Mary-Anne, eldest dau. of George, present Lord Byron, and by her has issue,

1 JOHN-BYRON-BLENKINSOPP.
2 Gustavus-George Blenkinsopp.
3 Robert-Harry-Blenkinsopp.
4 George-Bell. 5 William-Lisle. 6 Arthur.

II. Gustavus-Hamilton, captain R.N., *b.* 7 Jan. 1801.
III. Robert-Blenkinsopp, captain in the grenadier-guards.
I. Mary-Alicia. II. Arabella-Frances.

Lineage.—The Blenkinsopps, whom Camden styles "a right ancient and generous family," have resided at Blenkinsopp Castle for many centuries. In the time of EDWARD I., the castle and manor was held by Ranulphus de Blenkinsopp; in the reign of EDWARD III., by Thomas de Blenkinsopp; and in that of ELIZABETH, by William Blenkinsopp.

THOMAS BLENKINSOPP, Esq. of Blenkinsopp Castle, representative of this ancient house, *temp.* GEORGE I., *m.* Frances, dau. of Turville, Esq. of Newhall Park, co. Leicester, and had an only dau. and heiress,

JANE BLENKINSOPP, who *m.* in 1727, WILLIAM COULSON, Esq. of Jesmond House, co. Northumberland, *b.* in 1692, son and heir of John Coulson, Esq. of Jesmond House, by Elizabeth, dau. of Robert Bromley, Esq., descended from the famous Sir John Bromley, who lived in the time of HENRY V. The heiress of Blenkinsopp had issue. The eldest son,

JOHN-BLENKINSOPP COULSON, Esq., *b.* 7 May, 1729, of Blenkinsopp Castle, in right of his mother, and of Jesmond, *s.* his father, in 1750, but *d. unm.* in 1788, when the estates devolved on his brother,

WILLIAM COULSON, Esq. of Blenkinsopp Castle and of Jesmond, *b.* in 1737, who *m.* in 1772, Mary, dau. of John Lisle, Esq. of Felton and Elyhaugh, lineally descended from William de Insula, and had issue,

JOHN-BLENKINSOPP, his heir.
Robert-Lisle, *b.* in Oct. 1780, capt. R.N., *m.* in 1815, Miss Veitch, of Houndwood, in Berwickshire, and *d.* in 1822, leaving three daus., viz., Sarah, Mary, and Elizabeth.
William, *b.* 14 Feb. 1786.
Jane, *m.* to Captain Quin, of the 55th regt., and *d.* in 1798, without issue.
Margaret. Mary, *d.* young, in Oct. 1778.

Mr. Coulson *d.* in May, 1789, and was *s.* by his eldest son, the present JOHN-BLENKINSOPP COULSON, Esq. of Blenkinsopp Castle.

Arms—Quarterly: COULSON and BLENKINSOPP.
Crest—A pelican feeding her young.
Motto—Je mourrai pour ceux que j'aime.
Seat—Blenkinsopp Castle, Northumberland.

COULTHART OF COULTHART AND COLLYN.

COULTHART, JOHN, Esq. of Coulthart, co. Wigtown, Collyn, co. Dumfries, and Croft House, Ashton-under-Lyne, co. Lancaster, *s.* his father, 7 Oct. 1847, as chief of the name COULTHART.

Lineage.—The Coultharts are of the highest antiquity in the south of Scotland.

SIR ROGER DE COULTHART, chief of Coulthart, co. Wigtoun, and of Largmore, in the stewartry of Kirkcudbright (son of Gilbert de Coulthart, who *d.* in 1391), *m.* Margery, dau. and co-heiress of Sir John the Ross, of Renfrew, Knt., and maternally co-heiress of Macknyghte of Macknyghte, and Glendonyn of that ilk. By that heiress, Sir Roger had issue. Sir Roger distinguished himself at the battle of Aberbrothok, 13 Jan. 1445-6, and fell at the siege of Roxburgh Castle, 17 Sept. 1460. He was *s.* by his son,

SIR ROGER DE COULTHART, of Coulthart and Largmore. He *m.* Anne, dau. and co-heiress of Sir Richard Carmichael, of Carspherne, and had issue. Sir Roger was killed at Bannockburn, 11 June, 1488. His successor was his eldest son,

RICHARD DE COULTHART, who fell at Flodden, 9 Sept. 1513, leaving, by Matilda his wife, dau. of David Betoun, of Creech, a large family of children, the eldest of whom was

CUTHBERT DE COULTHART, *m.* Lady Elizabeth Hay, dau. of George, 7th Earl of Errol, and dying at Solway Moss, in 1542, was *s.* by his eldest son,

JOHN COULTHART, of Coulthart and Largmore, who *m.* Helen, dau. and eventually co-heiress of John Forbes, of Pitscottie, by whom he had issue. The eldest son,

WILLIAM COULTHART, of Coulthart and Largmore, *m.* in 1624, Mary, dau. and co-heiress of Richard Mackenzie, of Craighall, and niece of Gavin Hamilton, D.D., sometime Bishop of Galloway. By this lady he had issue. Mr. Coulthart, of Coulthart, *d.* 20 Feb. 1653, and was *s.* by his son,

JOHN COULTHART, Esq. of Coulthart and Largmore, who. *m.* in 1658, Janet, 3rd dau. of James Douglas, Esq. of Dee House, and by her (who *d.* 24 June, 1692) had issue. The Chief *d.* 11 Sept. 1690, and was *s.* by his son,

RICHARD COULTHART, Esq. of Coulthart and Largmore, who *m.* in 1698, Jean, dau. and heiress of William Gordon, Esq. of Sorbie, by whom he left, at his death, in 1717, an only son,

JAMES COULTHART, Esq. of Coulthart and Largmore, *b.* in 1702, *m.* in 1734, Grizel, dau. of M'Turk, Esq. of The Glenkens, Kirkcudbright, and by her (who *d.* 14 Jan. 1765) left at his decease, 8 May, 1785, his eldest son,

WILLIAM COULTHART, Esq. of Coulthart and Largmore, *b.* 6 Jan. 1739, *m.* 6 Oct. 1766, Janet, eldest dau. of John M'Naught, Esq. of Milltown, co. Kirkcudbright, by whom (who *d.* at Collyn House, 18 May, 1832) he had issue. Mr. Coulthart removed from Largmore to Collyn, co. Dumfries. He *d.* 15 Feb. 1807, aged 68 years, and was *s.* by his only surviving son,

WILLIAM COULTHART, Esq. of Coulthart, co. Wigtoun, and of Collyn, co. Dumfries, *b.* 21 March, 1774, who *m.* 3 Sept. 1801, Helen, 2nd dau. of the late John Ross, Esq. of Dalton, co. Dumfries, a collateral descendant of the noble family of Ross *of Halkhead*, and dying 7 Oct. 1847, left a son, JOHN, the present representative, and a dau., Margaret, *m.* 25 March, 1838, James Macguffie, Esq. of Crossmichael, co. Kirkcudbright, and has issue.

Arms—Arg., a fesse between two colts in chief and one in base, courant.
Supporters—On the dexter, a war-horse, arg., completely armed for the field, ppr., garnished, or; on the sinister, a stag, of the second, attired and ducally gorged, of the third.
Crest—A war-horse's head and neck couped, arg., armed and bridled, ppr., garnished, or.
Motto—Virtute non verbis.
Seats—Collyn House, near Dumfries; and Croft House, Ashton-under-Lyne.

COURTENAY OF BALLYEDMOND.

COURTENAY, GEORGE, Esq. of Ballyedmond, co. Cork, *b.* in 1822.

Lineage.—JOHN COURTENAY, a son of George Courtenay, *m.* Anne, dau. of Browne, Esq. of Ballyedmond, and left by her two sons, Thomas, the younger, and

GEORGE COURTENAY, Esq., who *m.* Anne, eldest dau. of Leonard Ashe, Esq. of Drishane, co. Cork, and by her, who *d.* in 1823, had (with other issue, deceased) a son and heir,

ROBERT COURTENAY, Esq. of Ballyedmond, J.P., who *m.* in 1790, Catherine, 2nd dau. of John Nash, Esq. of Ballyheen, co. Cork, and by her (who *d.* in 1799) had issue,

I. GEORGE, *b.* 1795, high-sheriff of the co. of Cork in 1826, *m.* in 1814, Caroline-Augusta, eldest dau. of James-Hugh-Smith Barry, Esq. of Foaty Island, co. Cork, and *d.* in 1837, leaving issue,

GEORGE, now of Ballyedmond.
John, *b.* in 1824.
Caroline-Augusta, *m.* in 1840, to Mountifort Longfield, eldest son of the Rev. Robert Longfield, of Castle Mary, co. Cork.

II. John, of Ballymagooly, co. Cork, *b.* in 1798.
I. Anne, *m.* in 1811, to Simon Dring, Esq. of Rockgrove, co. Cork, and *d. s. p.* in 1812.
II. Eliza-Mary, *m.* in 1814, to John-Smith Barry, of Foaty Island, and of Marbury Hall, co. Chester, *d.* in 1828.
III. Catherine-Mary, *d. unm.* in 1813.

Arms—Or, three torteaux.
Crest—Out of a ducal coronet, or, a plume of seven ostrich feathers, four and three, arg.
Seat—Ballyedmond, co. Cork.

COX OF BALLYNOE.

COX, WILLIAM, Esq. of Ballynoe, co. Limerick, J.P., b. 22 Jan. 1799; m. 8 June, 1826, Elizabeth, dau. of John-Ormsby Vandeleur, Esq., lieut.-col. in the army, and has,

I. WILLIAM, b. 11 Feb. 1837.
II. Ormsby, b. 6 March, 1838.
I. Rosetta. II. Mary.
III. Elizabeth. IV. Frances.

Lineage.—ROBERT COX, Esq., who had a grant of the lands of Ballynoe, &c., in the co. of Limerick, by patent dated the 28 Sept. 1637, m. Mary, dau. of the Right Hon. Sir Thomas Standish, of Bruffe, co. Limerick, and sister and co-heir of Edward Standish, Esq. of Bruffe, and left a son and successor,

WILLIAM COX, Esq. of Ballynoe, one of the grand juries for the co. Limerick, which addressed King CHARLES II. in 1682 and 1683. He m. and had, with a dau. Frances, wife of Humphrey Massey, Esq., major in the army, two sons, SAMPSON, his heir, and Robert, whose son Robert, of Plymouth, co. Devon, m. Miss Hutchinson, and had issue. The elder son,

SAMPSON COX, Esq. of Ballynoe, m. Constantia, dau. of the Right Hon. William Fitzmaurice, Baron of Kerry and Lixnaw, and relict of John Odell, Esq. of Ballingarry; and had, with five daus., of whom the 4th, Margery, m. John Gabbett, Esq. of Limerick, and the 5th, Catharine, Jeremiah Jackson, Esq. of Fanningstown, five sons, of whom the eldest survivor,

WILLIAM COX, Esq. of Ballynoe, bapt. 20 Jan. 1703, m. 18 March, 1727, Margaret, dau. of Hugh Hutchinson, Esq. of Bantry, and d. in Oct. 1762, leaving issue, HUGH, his heir; Emanuel; Samuel; Robert, a military officer; William, R.N.; Constantia, m. to Richard Stephenson; Frances, m. to Samuel Adams, of the co. Cork; and Deborah, m. to Richard Lane, Esq. of Ballyscanlan, co. Limerick. The eldest son,

HUGH COX, Esq. of Ballynoe, bapt. 31 Dec. 1730, m. 1757, Elizabeth, dau. and co-heir of John Vowell, Esq. of Springfort, and had issue, I. Vowell, of Ballynoe, whose only child, Anne, was wife of Patrick O'Kelly, Esq. of the co. Clare; II. WILLIAM; III. Hugh, of Knockloogh, co. Cork, m. Anstace, dau. of John Spread, Esq. of Forest, co. Cork, and d. in 1821, leaving issue; IV. John, m. Catherine Scanlan, and had, John, and other issue; V. Sampson, paymaster, 8th foot; VI. Robert, d. unm.; and three daus. who d. unm. Mr. Cox d. in 1783; his 2nd son,

WILLIAM COX, Esq. of Ballynoe, heir to his brother, b. 1765, m. 27 June, 1796, Mary, dau. of Michael Scanlan, Esq. of Ballinaha, co. Limerick, and d. 20 Oct. 1810, leaving, with three daus., Mary, wife of John-Edward Langford, Esq. of Stonehall, co. Limerick; Aphrasia, wife of John White, Esq. of Dublin; and Elizabeth, wife of Edward-John Croker, Esq. of Grange Hill, co. Limerick; an only son, the present WILLIAM COX, Esq. of Ballynoe.

Arms—Arg., three bars, gu.; on a canton, az., a lion's head erased, or.

Crest—An antelope's head erased, sa., attired, or, transfixed through the neck with a broken spear, ppr.

Motto—Fortiter et fideliter.

Seat—Ballynoe, co. Limerick.

COX OF COOLCLIFFE.

COX, COL. SIR WILLIAM, of Coolcliffe, co. Wexford, K.T.S., J.P. and D.L., high-sheriff of the King's County in 1825, b. 5 Dec. 1776; m. 27 June, 1820, Anna, youngest dau. of the late Robert Hickson, Esq. of The Grove, co. Kerry, and has issue,

I. JOHN-WILLIAM, b. 19 May, 1821, m. 1 Jan. 1850, Emma, dau. of Capt. Charles Griffin, R.N., and has surviving issue, Annie-Georgiana and Dorothea-Kate-Macdonald.
II. Robert-Allan, b. 16 Oct. 1823.
III. James-Ponsonby, b. 5 June, 1830.
IV. William-Edward, b. 23 July, 1835.
I. Sarah-Julia.
II. Anne-Elizabeth, m. 23 Aug. 1849, to the Rev. A.-Betlesworth Perry.

Lineage.—JOHN COX, Esq., son of JOHN COX, Esq., by Elizabeth his wife, daughter of Joshua Tench, Esq. of Bryanstown, co. Wexford, m. Mary, dau. of William Hore, Esq. of Harperstown, in the same county, and by her had four sons, viz., JOHN, his heir; William-Allan; Ponsonby; and Walter, who all three d. unm.; and three daus. The eldest son,

JOHN COX, Esq. of Coolcliffe, b. 12 March, 1749, m. in 1773, Sarah, dau. of the late Richard Donovan, Esq. of Clonmore, co. Wexford, and had issue seven sons (five d. unm.; the youngest, Thomas, roy. art., m. Catherine, dau. of the late Dr. Hamilton, of Castlebar) and two daus.; Sarah, m. to Sir Aretas-Wm. Young, and d. leaving issue; and Mary, m. to the late Rev. William Sutton, of Long Grage, co. Wexford, and d. 1854, leaving issue. Mr. Cox d. in 1793, and was s. by his eldest surviving son,

RICHARD COX, Esq., who d. unm. in 1796, when the representation devolved upon his next brother, the present COLONEL SIR WILLIAM COX, Knt

Arms—Or, three bars, az., on a canton, gu., a lion's head, erased, arg.

Crest—A goat's head, erased, sa.

Motto—Fide et fortitudine.

Seat—Coolcliffe, co. Wexford.

COXWELL OF ABLINGTON.

(*See* COXWELL-ROGERS *of Dowdeswell.*)

COX OF BROXWOOD AND EATON BISHOP.

COX, RICHARD-SNEAD, Esq. of Broxwood and Eaton Bishop, co. Hereford, and Souldern, co. Oxford, b. 14 Sept. 1820; m. 24 Nov. 1853, Maria-Teresa, dau. of George Weld, Esq. of Leagram Hall, co. Lancaster.

Lineage.—This ancient family claims to derive its descent from CLEMENT COX, whose son was raised to the dignity of an Earl by King EDWARD the Confessor. Passing over the earlier line of ancestors, the Lords of Broxwood, mostly of knightly degree, which our limits preclude our detailing, we come to

RICHARD COX, 2nd son of Sir Richard Cox, of Kingsberry, co. Hertford, and the lineal descendant of Sir Edmund Cox, of Broxwood, one of the heroes of Poictiers. He became heir to his cousin, Richard Cox, of Herefordshire, and served as high-sheriff, 13 JAMES I. At the outbreak of the Civil War, he sided with the King, and after much service in the royal cause, died from a wound received at Naseby. On his monument, a Latin inscription stiles him "twenty-fourth titular Earl Cox." By Mary his wife, dau. of John Brent, of Gloucestershire, he left, with four daus., five sons, viz.

GABRIEL.
Richard, a priest. JOHN.
Daniel, an eminent physician, buried in Westminster Abbey.
Edward, a Welsh judge.

The eldest son, Gabriel, a gentleman of the band of pensioners, left at his decease three daus., of whom the eldest, Octavia, was the wife of Col. Monson. The 3rd son,

SIR JOHN COX, Knt., a naval captain under Prince Rupert and the Duke of York, was killed in one of the sea fights with the Dutch. He m. the dau. of Samuel Delahay, and left, with three daus., an only son,

GABRIEL COX, Esq. of Farmingham Lodge, Kent, who m. Elizabeth, dau. of Richard Sneade, Esq. of Eaton Bishop, co. Hereford, by Elizabeth Napier his wife, and dying at St. Germains, in France, left issue, besides three daus., five sons, viz.,

SAMUEL, his heir.
Richard, d. unm.
Gabriel-Sneade, of Eaton Bishop, m. Elizabeth, dau. and heir of William Hodges, Gent., of Dimock, and had three daus., of whom the eldest, Elizabeth, m. John Witherston, Esq.
Edmund, a monk.
Ralph, who left no surviving issue.

The eldest son,

SAMUEL COX, Esq. of Souldern, co. Oxford, d. at Farmingham Lodge, leaving, by Alicia his wife, dau. of Richard Kilbye, Gent. of Souldern, two sons and three daus., of whom the 2nd, Elizabeth, m. the Rev. Walter Saunders, and Alicia, the youngest, m. William Bund, Esq. of Wick. The elder son, Samuel, d. unm. 1781, aged 80; the younger,

GABRIEL COX, Esq. of Highgate, Middlesex, m. the dau. of Mr. Richard Walker, of Brailes, co. Warwick, and had issue,

Robert-Kilbye, who d. 1 Feb. 1829, aged 84, leaving by his wife Elizabeth Linnell, Samuel, who m. his cousin, Elizabeth Cox, but d. s. p., 18 April, 1851; Robert, who d. s. p., 12 Feb. 1833; Alicia, d. unm., 1838; and Mary-Anne.
SAMUEL.
Mary. Helen.

The 2nd son,

Samuel Cox, of Eaton Bishop, to which es ate he succeeded at the death of Mrs. Witherston, in 1782, d. 21 Jan. 1840, aged 93. He had, by his wife Sarah, dau. of George Duncumb, Esq., one son,

Samuel Cox, M.D., who m. 31 Dec. 1800, Anne, only child of Major Murdoch McLean, of Kingorloch, Argyllshire, and by her, who d. 17 May, 1844, aged 68, had issue,

Robert-Kilbye, b. 27 Feb. 1803, d. unm., 13 July, 1822.
George-Duncumb, M.D., b. 1808, d. unm., 31 Oct. 1840.
Victor-Samuel, b. 1819, d. the same year.
Richard-Snead, his heir, now of Eaton Bishop.
Elizabeth-Mary, m. to her cousin, Samuel Cox, Esq., d. without issue, 18 Oct. 1828.
Clementina, a nun at Le Mans, in France.
Alicia, a Benedictine nun at St. Benedict's Priory, Staffordshire.
Anne-Helen, m. John-Thomas Dolman, Esq., of Pocklington, and has issue, Louis-Marmaduke, George, and Mary-Helen.
Euphemia, d. unm., 4 Sept. 1842.
Mary-Anne, d. unm., 12 Aug. 1850.
Sarah, d. unm., 5 July, 1844.

Dr. Cox d. 4 March, 1851, aged 74.

Arms—Or, three bars, az.; on a canton, arg., a lion's head erased, gu.
Crest—An antelope's head, erased, ppr., pierced through the neck by a spear.
Seats—Broxwood and Eaton Bishop, co. Hereford.

COYNEY OF WESTON COYNEY.

Coyney, Charles, Esq. of Weston Coyney, co. Stafford, b. 23 Jan. 1801, major King's Own Stafford rifle militia; m. 4 Dec. 1838, Sophia-Henrietta, dau. of Captain Rowland Mainwaring, R.N., of Whitmore Hall, co. Stafford, and has a son and heir,

Walter-Mainwaring, b. 18 Sept. 1839.

Lineage.—The family of Coyney has been seated at Weston Coyney, in the parish of Caverswall, since the time of Henry III., when John, the son of Alan (Fitzalan, Lord of Oswestry, ancestor of the Earls of Arundel), who d. in the twenty-fourth of that reign, *anno* 1240, granted by his charter, *sans date*, to Walter Coyne, the manor of Weston-subter-Kiversmond, in the parish of Caverswall, called Weston Coyney, in the co. of Stafford, subject to the chief rent of half a mark of silver.

Sampson Coyney, Esq., representative of the family at the commencement of the 17th century, m. in 1633, Anne, dau. and co-heir of Philip Draycot, Esq. of Draycot, in Staffordshire, by whom (who d. in 1691) he had five sons and one dau.; the fifth son, Mark, who d. in 1695, left John, of whom presently, and Catherine, wife of Anthony Hill, Esq. of Pepperhill, and grandmother of the late Walter-William Hill Coyney, Esq. Sampson Coyney d. 2 March, 1653, and was s. by his son,

John Coyney, Esq., b. in 1637, who m. in Oct. 1661, Ellen, dau. and co-heir of John Dawes, Esq. of Caughley, in Shropshire, and by her (who m. 2ndly, William Parker, Esq. of Park Hall) he had (with a dau. Ellen) a son and successor,

Sampson Coyney, Esq., b. in 1662: the last male heir dying unm. 1 May, 1693, he devised his estates to his sister,

Ellen Coyney, who m. in Sept. 1694, William Gower, Esq. of Colmers and Queenhill, co. Worcester, by whom (who d. 1 June, 1736) she had an only son,

William Gower, Esq., in right of his mother, lord of Weston Coyney. This gentleman was unfairly killed in a duel at a tavern in Drury Lane, Feb. 1725, by Major Oneby. William Gower, by his will of 10 Aug. 1721, bequeathed Weston Coyney to his father for life, with remainder to the heir male of the family,

John Coyney, Esq., grandson of Sampson Coyney, by Ann Draycot. He d. in 1732, before William Gower the elder, and left issue, by Ann his wife, three sons and two daus. The eldest son,

Edward Coyney, Esq., at the decease of William Gower, 1 June, 1736, entered into possession of the Weston Coyney estates. He m. in July, 1768, Mary, dau. of Matthew Smith, Esq., and by that lady (who m. 2ndly, in Oct. 1778, Michael Jones, Esq. of Lancaster, and d. in Nov. 1814) left at his demise, 2 May, 1772, an only dau. and heiress,

Mary-Catharine, lady of the manor of Weston Coyney, who m. 18 Aug. 1758, her cousin, Walter-William Hill, Esq., and had surviving issue,

Charles, now of Weston Coyney.
Thomas-Edward, b. 2 Aug. 1810, m. Florence, dau. of Chas. Mason, Esq.
Mary, m. to George-Lambert Clifford, Esq., youngest son of the Hon. Thomas-Clifford, of Tixal, in the co. of Stafford.
Elizabeth-Mary, m. to John Vanzeller, Esq., of Liverpool, and is deceased.
Anne-Mary, m. at Paris, 8 Feb, 1833, to Monsieur Hippolyte de Pilliet, col. in the French service.

This gentleman assumed on his marriage, by sign-manual, in pursuance of the testamentary injunction of Edward Coyney, Esq., the surname and arms of Coyney. Mr. Coyney was lieut.-col. of the Staffordshire militia, and a magistrate and deputy-lieutenant for the county. He d. 29 Aug. 1844.

Arms—Or, on a bend, sa., three trefoils, slipped, arg.
Crest—A cubit arm, erect, vested, sa., slashed and cuffed, or, holding in the hand, ppr., a faulchion, arg., embrued with blood in three places, hilt and pommel, gold.
Motto—Fide, sed cui vide.
Seat—Weston Coyney, Cheadle, Staffordshire.

CRACKANTHORPE OF NEWBIGGIN.

Crackanthorpe, William, Esq. of Newbiggin Hall, Westmoreland, J.P., high-sheriff of Cumberland in 1826, b. 25 Feb. 1790.

Lineage.—This is an ancient Westmoreland family, branches of which have occasionally been settled in Cumberland. Crackanthorpe of Cockermouth was high-sheriff, *temp.* Henry VI.

William Cookson, Esq., 2nd son of William Cookson, and younger brother of Isaac Cookson, whose son, John, purchased the estate of Whitehill, co. Durham, m. Miss Crackanthorpe, of Newbiggin, sister and heir of James Crackenthorpe, Esq. of Newbiggin, the last male representative; and with a younger son, William, D.D., dean of Windsor, was father of

Christopher-Crackanthorpe Cookson, who s. to Newbiggin on the death of his uncle, James Crackanthorpe, and thereupon assumed the additional surname and arms of Crackanthorpe. He m. Charlotte Cust, and dying in 1800, left (with two daus., Charlotte and Sarah,) an only son, the present William Crackanthorpe, Esq. of Newbiggin.

Arms—Or, a chevron, between three mullets, pierced, az.
Crest—A holly tree, ppr.
Seat—Newbiggin Hall, Westmoreland.

CRACROFT, NOW AMCOTTS, OF HACKTHORN.

Amcotts, Robert, Esq. of Hackthorn, co. Lincoln, J.P. and D.L., b. 25 Jan. 1783; m. 14 June, 1814, Augusta, 2nd dau. of the late Sir John Ingilby, Bart. of Ripley, co. York, by Elizabeth his wife, dau. and heir of Sir Wharton Amcotts, Bart., and has issue,

I. Weston, b. 9 March, 1815, m. Williams-Emma, 2nd dau. of W.-G. Cherry, Esq. of Buckland, co. Hereford.
II. Peter, comm. R.N., b. 15 March, 1816, m. Caroline, dau. of Sir Samuel Scott, Bart.
III. Robert-Wentworth, b. 15 June, 1826, in holy orders, rector of Harrington and Brinkhill, co. Lincoln.
I. Frances-Amcotts, m. in 1841, to the Rev. Edwin Jarvis, 5th son of Colonel Jarvis, of Doddington Hall, co. Lincoln.
II. Augusta, m. in 1840, to the Rev. Charles Jarvis, 2nd son of Lieut.-Col. Jarvis, of Doddington Hall.
III. Louisa, m. to Gervais-Waldo Sibthorp, Esq., eldest son of Colonel Sibthorp, M.P.
IV. Constance-Elizabeth.

Colonel Cracroft assumed the surname and arms of Amcotts, by royal license, 11 July, 1854.

Lineage.—The family of Cracroft has been resident at Hackthorn for many centuries, and its pedigree can be traced from the time of Henry III. William Cracroft, son of Stephen de Cracroft, and grandson of Walter de Cracroft, was lord of the manor of Cracroft, co. Lincoln, A.D. 1284. The great-grandfather of the present representative,

Robert Cracroft, Esq. of Hackthorn, b. in 1677, m. Grace, dau. of the Rev. J. Baxter, of Lincoln Cathedral, and dying in 1712, left issue, Robert, John, Edward, Thomas, Elizabeth, and Grace. Of these, the elder son,

Robert Cracroft, Esq. of Hackthorn, b. in 1702, m. 1st, Anne, dau. and heir of M. Brown, Esq., of Louth, and by her, who d. in 1738, had three daus., Anne, Grace, and

Mary. He *m.* 2ndly, Rebecca Waldgrave, niece of the Rev. B. Wilson, of West Keal Hall, co. Lincoln, and had issue, Robert-Wilson, *d. unm.*; JOHN, his successor; Thomas, Edward, Bernard, Charles, Francis, William, and Edmund, and a dau., Elizabeth-Clementina. The eldest surviving son,

JOHN CRACROFT, Esq., of Hackthorn, *b.* in 1748, *m.* Penelope-Anne, dau. of the Rev. Charles Fleetwood Weston, of Somerby Mall, co. Lincoln, rector of Therfield, Herts, and prebendary of Durham, and had issue,

- ROBERT, present representative.
- John, in holy orders, *b.* in 1784, was twice married: 1st, to Eliza, dau. of Charles Lewis, Esq. of Totteridge, Herts, by whom he had issue, Eliza, *m.* to the Rev. J.-T. Maine; and 2ndly, to Jane, dau. of H. Brown, Esq., Minster Yard, Lincoln, and *d.* 21 Sept. 1842, having had issue by his 2nd wife also, viz., John, Robert, and Bernard, and two daus., Emily and Jane.
- Penelope-Anne. Lucy.
- Emily, *d. unm.* in 1828.
- Arabella, *m.* to Matthew Lister, Esq., eldest son of Matthew-B. Lister, Esq., of Burwell Park, co. Lincoln.

Arms—Vert, on a bend dancetté, arg., three martlets, sa.
Crest—A stork, ppr., supporting with his dexter foot a battle-axe, staff, or, headed, arg.
Seat—Hackthorn, co. Lincoln.

CRANSTOUN OF COREHOUSE.

EDMONDSTOUNE-CRANSTOUN, MARIA, of Corehouse, co. Lanark, dau. of William Cuninghame, of Lainshaw, co. Ayr, *s.* in 1850, to the estate of Corehouse, by deed of entail made by her maternal uncle, George Cranstoun, Esq. of Corehouse, and assumed thereon the name of EDMONDSTOUNE-CRANSTOUN.

Lineage.—GEORGE CRANSTOUN, youngest son of William, 5th Lord Cranstoun, by Lady Jane Kerr his wife, dau. of William, 2nd Marquess of Lothian, and granddau. of Archibald, 9th Earl of Argyll, beheaded 1685, *m.* Maria, dau. of John Brisbane, of Brisbane (by Isabella his wife, dau. and co-heiress of Sir Thomas Nicholson, of Kemries, Bart., and sister of Margaret, Marchioness of Lothian, and of Mary, wife of the Hon. Mr. Boyd, brother to the Earl of Kilmarnock, beheaded 1745-6) and had issue,

- Henry-Kerr, *m.* Mary-Anne, eldest dau. and co-heiress of Sir John Whiteford, of Whiteford, Bart.
- George, called to the bar in Scotland, and appointed a judge in the Court of Session, 1826, *d. unm.* 1850.
- Margaret-Nicholson, *m.* to William Cunninghame, of Lainshaw, and had (with other issue—*See* CUNINGHAME *of Lainshaw*) a dau., MARIA, now of Corehouse.
- Jane-Anne, *m.* to Wenceslaus, Count von Purgstall, Count of the Holy Roman Empire, and chamberlain to the Emperor of Austria; and had issue, Wenceslaus, Count von Purgstall, *d. unm.*, 1817; and a dau., *d.* an infant.
- Helen D'Arcy, *m.* Dugald Stewart, of Catrine, and had issue.

Family of Edmondstoune.

This ancient family dates their establishment in North Britain, from the latter end of the 11th century. Edmundus, traditionally a younger son of Count Egmont, of Flanders, one of the numerous foreigners who attended Margaret, dau. of EDGAR ATHELING, into Scotland, in 1070, rose to great distinction. He and his descendants obtained numerous grants of land in various parts of the country, and one of them married the Princess Isabel Steuart, dau. of ROBERT II; and their son, his cousin-german Mary, dau. of ROBERT III. From the former marriage was derived the chief branch of the family: the EDMONDSTOUNS *of Ednam*, in the co. Roxburgh, and subsequently of Corehouse, co. Lanark. On the death of the last representative of the elder branch, George Cranstoun, son of the Hon. George Cranstoun, succeeded by will to the property of Corehouse.

Arms—Quarterly: 1st and 4th, gu., three cranes, close, ppr.; 2nd and 3rd, or, three crescents, gu.
Seat—Corehouse, Lanarkshire.

CRA'STER OF CRA'STER TOWER.

WOOD-CRA'STER, THOMAS, Esq. of Cra'ster Tower, co. Northumberland, J.P. and D.L., *b.* 21 Aug. 1786; *m.* 21 Aug. 1820, Margaret-Eleanor, dau. of John Longfield, Esq. of Longueville, co. Cork, and has issue,

- I. JOHN, *b.* 6 Sept. 1823.
- II. Edmund, *b.* 14 Sept. 1824.
- III. Shafto, *b.* 22 May, 1826.
- IV. Richard-Longfield, *b.* 19 July, 1828.
- V. George-Ayton, *b.* 9 June, 1830.
- VI. Thomas-Henry, *b.* 4 Aug. 1834.
- VII. William-Robert, *b.* 26 Sept. 1836.
- VIII. Henry, *b.* 10 Dec. 1840.
- I. Eleanor-Ann. II. Ann.
- III. Elizabeth-Hamar-Isabel.

Mr. Wood-Cra'ster assumed, by royal sign-manual, the surname of CRA'STER,* on succeeding, by the will of George Cra'ster, of Cra'ster, to the estates of that family.

Lineage.—This was the principal family, and is the only one remaining which held by military tenure under the Barony of Visconti. The manor of Crawcestre, or Craucestre, now written Craster, formed part of the barony of Emildon, which was granted to the House of Visconti by King HENRY I., to be holden by three knight's fees; but since the forfeiture, after the battle of Evesham, of Simon de Montfort, Earl of Leicester, who had obtained the barony from Ranetta, dau. and heir of John le Visconti, the manor of Crancestre has ever been separated, and held of the crown *in capite*.

In a return of the knights' fees in the co. of Northumberland, supposed to be made in the 6th year of King JOHN, WILLIAM DE CRAUCESTRE is there returned as lord of the manor of Craucestre, which he then held by half a knight's fee of ancient feoffment, by which it appears that this family had been possessed of that manor in the time of King HENRY I.

SIR RICHARD DE CRAUCESTRE, lord of the manor of Craucestre, was knighted by EDWARD I., in the Scotch wars, and

SIR EDMUND DE CRAUCESTRE, who served both in the wars of France and Scotland, was knighted for his services therein by EDWARD III.

JOHN CRA'STER, Esq. of Cra'ster (grandson of Lieut.-Col. William Cra'ster, of Cra'ster, who defended Morpeth Castle for CHARLES I, and the lineal male representative of the CRA'STERS *of Craster*), *m.* Mary, dau. of John Ayton, Esq. of West Herrington, co. Durham, and had issue three sons and three daus.

- I. JOHN, his heir.
- II. William; and III. Bertram; both *d. s. p.*
- I. Isabel, *m.* to John Mylott, Esq. of Whithill, co. Durham, and *d. s. p.*
- II. Elizabeth, *m.* 1st, to Christopher Blackett, Esq. of Newham, and 2ndly, to John Watson, Esq. of Goswick; by the latter only she had issue, a dau., who *m.* John Askew, Esq. of Pallinsburn.
- III. Anne, *m.* Thomas Wood, Esq. of Beadnel, and had (with two daus., Catherine and Elizabeth, and a son, Thomas) an elder son, John Wood, Esq., who *m.* 4 Sept 1781, Anne, 2nd dau. of Daniel Cra'ster, Esq. of Cra'ster, and had issue,
  - 1 THOMAS WOOD-CRA'STER, the present representative of the family.
  - 2 John-Ayton Wood, in holy orders, *m.* Margaret, dau. of Ralph Compton, Esq. of Melkington, and *d.* 30 Jan. 1853, leaving three sons and three daus.
  - Annabel; Maria-Catherine; Elizabeth; and Barbara-Jane; all four *d. unm.*

The eldest son,

JOHN CRA'STER, of Cra'ster, barrister-at-law, *m.* Catherine, dau. of Col. Henry Villiers, Governor of Tinmouth Castle, and son of Sir Edward Villiers, Knt., Marshal of England, the youngest son of Edward, Viscount Grandison, and *d.* in 1764, having had several children, all of whom *d.* young, except his 3rd son,

GEORGE CRA'STER, Esq. of Cra'ster, an officer in the 2nd troop of horse-grenadier-guards, who *m.* Olivia Sharp, and *d.* in 1772, without issue, when the estates, in accordance with the will of John Cra'ster, of Cra'ster, devolved upon his kinsman,

DANIEL CRA'STER, Esq. of Cra'ster, great-grandson of Daniel, 3rd son of Col. William Cra'ster, of Cra'ster, the cavalier. This Daniel *m.* and had five sons, all of whom *d. s. p.*, except the 3rd, SHAFTO, and four daus. He *d.* in 1784, and was *s.* by his eldest surviving son,

SHAFTO CRA'STER, Esq. of Cra'ster, high-sheriff in 1803, who *m.* Isabel, dau. of James Atkinson, Esq. of Newcastle-on-Tyne, by whom he left an only dau, at his decease in 1837, whereupon the estates devolved, by virtue of the will

* Mr. Wood Cra'ster's children retain the surname of Cra'ster only.

of George Cra'ster, Esq., on THOMAS WOOD, Esq., who assumed the surname and arms of CRA'STER, and is the present possessor.

Arms—Quarterly: 1st and 4th, quarterly, or and gu., in the 1st quarter, a raven, ppr., for CRA'STER; 2nd and 3rd, az., on a bend, arg., three fleurs-de-lis, sa., each charged with as many bezants, for WOOD.

Crests—1st, a raven, ppr., charged on the breast with an escallop, or, for CRA'STER; 2nd, a wolf's head, sa., erased, or, gorged with a collar, of the last, charged with three annulets, gu., for WOOD.

Seat—Cra'ster Tower, near Alnwick, co. Northumberland.

CRAUFUIRD OF BAIDLAND, NOW OF ARDMILLAN.

CRAUFUIRD, THOMAS-MACMIKEN, Esq. of Grange House, co. Ayr, *b.* 12 Aug. 1814; *m.* 13 June, 1843, Elizabeth-Fraser, 2nd dau. of David Steuart-Galbraith, Esq. of Machrehanish and Dromore, co. Argyle, and has a son and heir,

ARCHIBALD-HEW, *b.* 16 July, 1844.

Lineage.—ANDREW CRAUFUIRD, of Baidland (lineally derived from a younger brother of Sir Reginald Craufurd, of Loudoun, sheriff of Ayrshire in 1296), *m.* Jean, eldest dau. of Sir James Lockhart, of Lee, and was father of

DAVID CRAUFUIRD, of Baidland, who had a son, PATRICK, and a dau., Margaret, *m.* in 1617, to James Boyle, Esq. of Hawkshill, ancestor of the Boyles, Earls of Glasgow. The son,

PATRICK CRAUFUIRD, of Baidland, retoured in 1611, was father of

WILLIAM CRAUFUIRD, of Baidland, who had (besides a dau., Isabel, *m.* to James Craufurd, Esq. of Jordan Hill, ancestor, by her, of Sir Robert Craufurd-Pollock, Bart.) a son and successor,

JAMES CRAUFUIRD, of Baidland, who *m.* one of the daus. and co-heirs of Hugh Kennedy, Esq. of Ardmillan, by Margaret his wife, dau. of John Blair, of Blair, and, by her, (with whom he eventually acquired the estate of Ardmillan) had numerous issue; of whom were WILLIAM, his heir; James, ancestor of the CRAWFURDS *of Sussex*; a dau. *m.* to David Craufurd, of Drumsoy. The eldest son,

WILLIAM CRAUFUIRD, of Ardmillan, distinguished for his defence of the fortress of the Bass, in the Frith of Forth, against King WILLIAM, in 1691. He *m.* Margaret, dau. of Kennedy of Baltersane, and predeceased his father, leaving an eldest son,

ARCHIBALD CRAUFUIRD, of Ardmillan, who *m.* Marion Hay, a descendant of one of the branches of the Tweeddale family, and by her had two sons,

I. ARCHIBALD, of whom presently.
II. Thomas, an officer in the army, who purchased Ardmillan from his elder brother, *m.* 1st, Anne, dau. of John Taylor, Esq. of East Sheen, co. Surrey; and 2ndly, Jane, dau. of the Rev. Hugh Hamilton, of Girvan, and *d.* in 1793, having had issue by the former lady, viz.,
   1 ARCHIBALD-CLIFFORD-BLACKWELL CRAUFUIRD, major in the army, now of Ardmillan, *m.* Jane, dau. of Dr. Leslie, and has issue.
   1 Margaret, *m.* to her cousin, Archibald Craufuird, Esq. of Ardmillan.
   2 Anne, *m.* to MacMiken of Grange.

The elder son,

ARCHIBALD CRAUFUIRD, of Ardmillan, *m.* Anne, dau. of Robert Kennedy, Esq. of Liverpool, and dying in 1784, was *s.* by his eldest son,

ARCHIBALD CRAUFUIRD, Esq. of Ardmillan, who *m.* his cousin, Margaret, dau. of Thomas Craufuird, Esq., and dying 16 May, 1824, left the present THOMAS-MACMIKEN CRAUFUIRD, of Grange; Hamilton-Cathcart, now in America; Margaret, *m.* to William Sterndale, Esq.; Marion; and Anne, *m.* to Graham Hutcheson, Esq.

Arms—Quarterly: 1st and 4th, gu., on a fesse, erm., between three mullets, arg., two crescents, interlaced, of the field, for CRAUFUIRD; 2nd and 3rd, arg., a chevron, gu., between three cross-crosslets, fitchée, sa., for KENNEDY.

Crest—A game-hawk, hooded and belled, ppr.

Motto—Durum patientiâ frango.

Seat—Grange House, Maybole, co. Ayr.

CRAUFURD OF CRAUFURDLAND.

HOWISON-CRAUFURD, WILLIAM, Esq. of Craufurdland, co. Ayr, and of Braehead, Mid-Lothian, J.P. and D.L., *b.* 29 Nov. 1781; *m.* 14 June, 1808, Jane-Esther, only dau. of James Whyte, Esq. of Newmains, and has issue,

I. JOHN-REGINALD, *b.* 30 Aug. 1811; *m.* April, 1847, Mary-Dundas, dau. of John Hamilton, Esq. of Sundrum, co. Ayr.
I. Elizabeth-Constantia, *m.* to James-Ogilvy Fairlie, Esq. of Coodham, co. Ayr.

Lineage.—JOHN CRAUFURD, 3rd son of Sir Reginald de Craufurd, sheriff of Ayrshire, by MARGARET DE LOUDOUN his wife, obtained broad lands from his father, in Clydesdale, and in right of his wife became chief proprietor of the barony. This John conferred Ardoch, or Craufurdland, in Ayrshire, upon his 2nd son,

JOHN CRAUFURD, who lived in the time of ALEXANDER II., and was *s.* by his son,

JOHN CRAUFURD, of Craufurdland, father of

JAMES CRAUFURD, of Craufurdland, who fought under WALLACE, and assisted at the election of that illustrious chief to the wardenship of Scotland, at the Forest Kirk, in the shire of Selkirk, *anno* 1297. He was grandfather of

JOHN CRAUFURD, who obtained from King ROBERT III. a charter of confirmation of the lands of Ardoch, or Craufurdland, dated at Dundonald, in 1391. This laird had, with other children, WILLIAM (Sir), his heir; and John, who became Laird of Giffordland, and was ancestor of the CRAUFURDS *of Birkheid*. The eldest surviving son,

SIR WILLIAM CRAUFURD, of Craufurdland, distinguished himself in arms, and had the honour of knighthood from JAMES I. In 1423, he received a severe wound at the siege of Crevelt, in France, and the next year we find him amongst the prisoners released with the Scottish king. His lineal descendant,

JOHN CRAUFURD, of Craufurdland, *m.* 1st, in 1719, Robina, dau. and heiress of John Walkinshaw of that ilk, and in consequence assumed the additional surname and arms of the family. By this lady he had one son only to survive, JOHN. He *m.* 2ndly, Elenora, dau. of Sir Thomas Nicolson, of Carnock, and widow of the Hon. Thomas Boyd. He *d.* 10 Jan. 1763, and was *s.* by his only child,

LIEUT.-COL. JOHN-WALKINSHAW CRAUFURD, of Craufurdland, appointed in Aug. 1761, falconer to the king for Scotland. He shared in the victory of Dettingen, and distinguished himself in the hard-fought field of Fontenoy. Col. Craufurd *d.* at Edinburgh, *unm.*, in Feb. 1793, aged 72, settling his estate, by deed made on his death-bed, upon Thomas Coutts, Esq. of London, banker. That instrument was, however, disputed by his aunt and next heir,

ELIZABETH CRAUFURD, who instituted an action of reduction, and after protracted litigation, carried on by herself and her successor, the deed was eventually reduced by a decree of the House of Lords, in 1806, and the ancient estates came back to the rightful heirs. Miss Crawfurd had *m.* 1st, William Fairlie, of that ilk, by whom she had one dau., who *d.* in infancy. She *m.* 2ndly, 3 June, 1744, John Howison, Esq. of Braehead, in Mid-Lothian, descended from John-Howison Burgen, of Edinburgh, in 1450, and dying in 1802, aged 97, was *s.* by her only surviving child,

ELIZABETH HOWISON-CRAUFURD, of Braehead, and, by the decree of the House of Lords, of Craufurdland. This lady *m.* in 1777, the Rev. James Moody, who assumed the additional surnames of HOWISON and CRAUFURD, and by whom (who *d.* in 1831) she left at her decease, 1 April, 1823, a dau., Isabella, *m.* to William Keith, Esq., brother of Sir Alexander Keith, of Ravelston and Dunnottar, and an only surviving son, the present WILLIAM HOWISON-CRAUFURD, Esq. of Craufurdland and Braehead.

Arms—Quarterly: CRAUFURD and HOWISON.

Crests—CRAUFURD: a marble pillar, supporting a man's heart, ppr. HOWISON: a dexter hand, erect, couped at the wrist.

Supporters—Two husbandmen in the dress of the 14th century; one holding a flail, the other a bason and napkin.

Mottoes—CRAUFURD: Stant innixa Deo. HOWISON: Sursum corda.

Seats—Craufurdland Castle, near Kilmarnock, Ayrshire; and Braehead, in Mid-Lothian.

CRAUFURD OF AUCHINAMES.

CRAUFURD, JOHN, Esq. of Auchinames and Crosbie, co. Ayr, J.P. and D.L., *b.* 4 Jan. 1780; *m.* 16 Aug. 1814, Sophia-Marianna, dau. of Major-Gen. Horace Churchill, and great-granddau. of Sir Robert Walpole, and has issue,

I. EDWARD-HENRY-JOHN, M.P. for Ayr, M.A., barrister-at-law, *b.* in 1816.
II. Frederick-Augustus-Buchanan, *b.* in 1823.

III. Robert-Emilius-Fazakerley, *b.* in 1824.
IV. George-Ponsonby, *b.* in 1826.
I. Katherine-Horatia. II. Georgiana-Janet.

Lineage.—This branch of the great house of Craufurd derives from DUNCAN CRAUFURD, of Camlarg, 3rd son of David Craufurd, of Kerse, who appears to have had (living in the reign of JAMES IV.) an only dau.,

MARGARET CRAUFURD, who *m.* John Craufurd, of Drongan. The direct male descendant,

DAVID CRAUFURD, of Drumsoy, historiographer for Scotland to Queen ANNE, a gentleman of literary abilities, distinguished, amongst other works, by an historical defence of MARY Queen of Scots, *d.* in 1710, leaving an only dau. and heiress,

EMILIA CRAUFURD, of Drumsoy, who *d. unm.* in 1731, when the representation of the family reverted to her grand-uncle,

PATRICK CRAUFURD, of Drumsoy, who had previously acquired the estate by purchase. He *m.* 1st, a dau. of Gordon of Turnberry, and had one son and two daus, viz.,

THOMAS, who *d.* at Paris, in 1724, being at the time envoy-extraordinary from the court of St. James's to that of Versailles.
Robert, *d. unm.*
Anne, *m.* to William Hogg, merchant at Edinburgh.
Margaret, *m.* to John Cochrane, of Ravelrig.

He *m.* 2ndly, Jane, dau. of Archibald Craufurd, of Auchinames, and by her had seven sons, viz.,

I. PATRICK, his successor.
II. GEORGE, lieut.-col. 53rd regt., *m.* Anne, dau. of Edward Randal, Esq. of Salisbury, and had (with a dau., Mary, the wife of Thomas Gilbert, Esq., M.P.) a son and successor, at his decease, in 1758,

PATRICK-GEORGE, who *m.* Jane, dau. of Lieut.-Colonel Donald Macdonald, of the 84th regt., brigadier-general in America, and by her (who *d.* in July, 1811) had, with two daus., Margaret-Randal and Catherine-Mary, four sons, viz.,
George, who *d. unm.*
JOHN, present representative.
Donald, capt. royal artillery, *d. unm.* in Oct. 1819. This officer was wounded at Waterloo.
Patrick-George, *d.* in 1804.

III. Ronald, of Restalrig, writer to the signet, *m.* in 1743, Catherine, dau. of John Forbes, of Newhall, by whom he had a son, Patrick, who *d. unm.*, and three daus, viz.,

1 Margaret, who *m.* Patrick, 5th Earl of Dumfries, and had an only child, the LADY ELIZABETH PENELOPE CRICHTON, who *m.* John, Viscount Mountstuart.
2 Jane, *m.* to William Berry, nephew and heir-presumptive of Ferguson of Rait.
3 Annabella, *m.* to William Fullerton, of Rosemount, whom she survived.

IV. James, an eminent merchant in Holland, *m.* Elizabeth, dau. of — Andrews, Esq. of Rotterdam, and had issue,

1 Patrick, appointed, in 1760, conservator of Scots' privileges in Holland.
2 James.
3 George, who, with Patrick, succeeded to his father's commercial establishment.
4 Ronald, a merchant in Glasgow, of the house of Spiers and Co.
1 Margaret, *m.* to Macleod of Geanies.

V. Hugh, a merchant in the East Indies, where he *d. unm.*
VI. Alexander, an officer in the army, *d.* in Lord Cathcart's expedition to Carthagena, in 1741.
VII. John, an officer in the army, who attained the rank of lieutenant-general, and died Governor of Minorca, *unm.*

Patrick Craufurd, of Drumsoy and Auchinames, *d.* in 1733, and was *s.* by his eldest surviving son,

PATRICK CRAUFURD, of Drumsoy, Auchinames, &c., M.P. for the co. of Edinburgh in 1741 and 1747, and for Renfrewshire in 1761. He *m.* 1st, Elizabeth, dau. and co-heir of George Middleton, Esq., a banker in London, and had two sons, JOHN, his heir; and James, col. in the Guards, and governor of Bermuda, *d. s. p.* in 1811. The laird *m.* 2ndly, Sarah, dau. of Lord Sempill, by whom he had a dau., Sarah, who *d. unm.* in 1796. He *d.* in 1778, and was *s.* by his older son,

JOHN CRAUFURD, of Drumsoy and Auchinames, M.P. for Old Sarum in 1768, and afterwards for co. Renfrew in Oct. 1774. This gentleman, who was the associate and friend of Charles-James Fox, *d. unm.* in 1814, and was *s.* by his cousin, JOHN CRAUFURD, Esq. of Auchinames and Crosbie.

Arms—Quarterly: 1st and 4th, gu., a fesse, erm.; 2nd, a stag's head, erased, gu.; 3rd, arg., two spears in saltier, between four spots of ermine.

Crests—A stag's head, erased, gu., between the attires a cross-crosslet fitchée; 2nd, a phœnix, ppr., rising from the flames.

Mottoes—"Tutum te robore reddam." And "God shew the right."

Seat—Crosbie Castle, Ayrshire.

CRAVEN OF RICHARDSTOWN.

CRAVEN, CHARLES-COOLEY, Esq. of Richardstown, co. Louth, late captain 72nd Highlanders, *m.* Augusta, youngest dau. of the late Col. George Dacre, of Marwell, Hants, of the family of the Dacres of the North, and has issue,

I. CHARLES-DACRE. II. Dacre.
I. Augusta.

Lineage.—This family claims to be a branch of Sir William Craven's, who was lord-mayor of London in 1610-11, and father of the celebrated William, 1st Earl of Craven.

CHARLES CRAVEN, Esq., *b.* 24 Oct. 1718 (2nd son of Charles Craven, Esq., by Anne his wife, sister and co-heir of Captain John Dobbyn, of Drumcashel, co. Louth, and grandson of Loven Craven, an officer in the army of WILLIAM III., who fell at the battle of Aughrim, in 1691), served in Germany from 1741 to 1743; in Scotland in 1745, under the Duke of Cumberland; at Gibraltar, and America. He *m.* 19 Aug. 1766, Eleanor, dau. and co-heir of Thomas Cooley, Esq. of Dublin, barrister-at-law, and M.P. for Gorey, by Sarah his wife, dau. of Abel Ram, Esq. of Ramsfort, co. Wexford, M.P., and J.P., and, by her (who *d.* 10 March, 1825) had issue,

CHARLES, his heir.
Thomas, of Drumcashel, co. Louth, *b.* 27 Sept. 1773, *m.* 12 Feb. 1798, Anne, youngest dau. of Richard, 4th Viscount Boyne, and *d.* in 1838, having had by this lady, who predeceased him, in 1828, a son, Thomas, drowned at Dundalk, in 1828, and six daus.
Abel, lieut. in the army, *d.* in 1830.
Sarah-Rebecca, *m.* 20 Feb. 1796, the Rev. Francis Thomas, of Tullabrin, co. Kilkenny, who *d.* leaving issue.
Catherine, *m.* Alexander Humfrey, Esq. of Dublin, who *d.* in 1845, leaving issue

Major Craven, who served as high-sheriff of Louth, *d.* in April, 1784, and was *s.* by his son,

CHARLES CRAVEN, Esq. of Richardstown, a general in the army, *b.* 15 Dec. 1769, a distinguished officer; he *m.* in 1798, Alice, dau. of John Randall, Esq., and left at his decease a son and heir, the present CHARLES-COOLEY CRAVEN, Esq.

Arms—Quarterly: 1st and 4th, a fesse, engrailed, between four cross-crosslets, fitchée, and two fleurs-de-lis, for CRAVEN; 2nd and 3rd, az., a chevron between three annulets, two and one, or, for DOBBYN.

Crest—On a chapeau, gu., turned up, erm., a gryphon, statant, sa., wings addorsed, beaked and semeé of fleurs-de-lis, or.

Motto—Fortitudine crevi.

CRAVEN OF BROCK HAMPTON PARK.

CRAVEN, FULWAR, Esq. of Brock Hampton Park, co. Gloucester, and Draycott Fitzpaine, Wilts, *b.* 25 June, 1782; *m.* 26 Nov. 1809, Laura, 2nd dau. of George Vansittart, Esq. of Bisham Abbey, M.P. for Berks, and has had issue,

I. Fulwar, an officer in the army, *b.* 12 Sept. 1810, *d.* 4 April, 1837, leaving one dau.
II. GEORGE-VANSITTART, *b.* 15 Oct. 1812.
III. William-East-Edward, *b.* 24 Oct. 1815.
I. Georgina-Maria, *m.* in 1841, to Goodwin-Charles Colquitt, Esq.

Lineage.—CHARLES CRAVEN, Esq., youngest brother of William, 2nd Lord Craven, was constituted Governor of Carolina, in the reign of Queen ANNE. He *m.* Elizabeth Staples, by whom (who *m.* after his decease, Jemmit Raymond, Esq. of Berkshire) he left at his death, in 1754, an only surviving son,

REV. JOHN CRAVEN, of Chilton House, co. Wilts, who *m.* Catherine, dau. of James Hughes, Esq. of Litcomb, in the co. of Berks, and had surviving issue,

I. FULWAR, present proprietor.
II. Charles-John, *m.* 28 Oct. 1817, Penelope, dau. of Edward Wheeler, Esq., and has issue,

CHARLES, *b.* 2 Aug. 1818, 2nd dragoons.
Charlotte-Penelope. Cecilia-Catherine.

I. Charlotte-Elizabeth, *m.* in 1819, to Sir John-Walter Pollen, Bart., M.P.

Arms—Arg., a fesse between six cross-crosslets fitchée, gu.
Crest—On a chapeau, gu., turned up, erm., a gryphon, statant, of the 2nd, beaked, or.
Motto—Virtus in actione consistit.
Seat—Breck Hampton Park, near Cheltenham.

CRAWFORD OF CRAWFORDSBURN.

Sharman-Crawford, William, Esq. of Crawfordsburn, co. Down, and Stalleen, co. Meath, J.P., *m.* in 1805, Mabel-Fridiswid, dau. of John Crawford, Esq. of Crawfurdsburn, co. Down, and has issue,

i. John. ii. Arthur. iii. James.
iv. Frederick. v. Charles.
vi. William. vii. Henry.
i. Maria, *m.* to Henry Coddington, Esq. of Oldbridge, co. Meath.
ii. Arminella. iii. Mable. iv. Eleanor.

Mr. Sharman-Crawford assumed the latter surname, in addition to his paternal one of Sharman, by royal license, in compliance with the will of the late John Crawford, Esq. He served as high-sheriff for the co. Down in 1811, was M.P. for the borough of Dundalk from 1834 till the dissolution, 1837, and subsequently sat for Rochdale.

Arms—Quarterly: 1st and 4th, gu., on a fesse, erm., between three mullets, arg., two crescent, interlaced, of the field, for Crawford; 2nd, or, a dove, wings expanded, with an olive-branch in its mouth; 3rd, gu., a lion, rampant, arg.
Motto—Durum patientiâ frango.
Seats—Crawfordsburn, co. Down; and Stalleen, co. Meath.

CRAWFURD OF MILTON.

Stirling-Crawfurd, William-Stuart, Esq. of Milton, co. Lanark, *b.* 29 Nov. 1819. In descent from Jean Stuart, his grandmother, Mr. Crawfurd succeeded to the estate of Milton, and took the name of Crawfurd, in terms of the entail executed by John Crawfurd, Esq., in 1706; while his brother, Captain Stuart, succeeded, as 2nd son, to the estate of Castlemilk, and took the name of Stuart, in terms of the entail of that estate, executed by Sir John Stuart.

Lineage.—The late Capt. William Stirling, 1st dragoon-guards, was son of the late William Stirling, Esq. of Kier, by his 2nd wife, Jean Stuart, dau. of Sir John Stuart, of Castlemilk. He *m.* 1st, 13 March, 1818, Mary, dau. of John Anderson, Esq., and by her, who *d.* 17 Dec. 1819, had an only child, the present William-Stuart-Stirling Crawfurd, of Milton. He *m.* 2ndly, Ann-Charlotte, dau. of Sir Alexander-Gibson Maitland, Bart. of Clifton Hall, and had by her, Capt. James-Stirling-Stuart, of Castlemilk, co. Lanark, who *m.* Miss Harriet Fortescue, of Dublin, and has issue; and a dau. Helen, *m.* to Henry Everard, Esq. of Langton Hall.

Arms—Gu., a fesse, erm., between three mullets, arg., within a bordure of the last.
Crest—A crescent, arg.

CRAWFURD OF SAINT HILL.

Crawfurd, Robert, Esq. of Saint Hill, co. Sussex, J.P., *b.* 13 July, 1801; *m.* 2nd March, 1824, Patty, 3rd dau. of James Stutter, Esq. of Higham Hall, co. Suffolk, and by her (who *d.* 30 June, 1852) has issue,

i. Robert-Henry-Payne, capt. 90th light infantry, *b.* 2 Feb. 1825.
ii. Charles-Walter-Payne, in holy orders, *b.* 14 March, 1826, *m.* in 1853, Mary, dau. of Dr. Ogle, Regius Professor of physic in the University of Oxford.

Lineage.—Gibbs Crawfurd, Esq., son of John Crawfurd, Esq., and Elizabeth Gibbs his wife, M.P. for Queenborough, *m.* Anne Payne, and was father of

Charles-Payne Crawfurd, Esq. of Saint Hill, who *m.* 5 June, 1800, Arabella, eldest dau. of the Rev. Narcissus-Charles Proby, rector of Stratford St. Mary, co. Suffolk, and dying in 1814, was *s.* by his only son, Robert Crawfurd, Esq., now of Saint Hill.

Arms—Gu., on a fesse, erm., between three mullets, arg., two crescents, entwined, of the field.
Crest—A hawk, hooded and belled, ppr.
Motto—Durum patentiâ frango.
Seat—Saint Hill, East Grinsted, co. Sussex.

CREAGH OF BALLY ANDREW.

Creagh, John-Bagwell, Esq. of Bally Andrew, co. Cork, *b.* in 1828.

Lineage.—This very ancient Irish family claim to be a branch of the "Hy Niall" race, descended from Eogan, son of Niall *of the Nine Hostages*, from whom sprang many illustrious families of the ancient Irish; amongst others, that of O'Niall, always kings of Tyrone, and sometimes monarchs of Ireland: even so late as the reign of Elizabeth, O'Niall was obeyed as monarch by his own sept. Collateral with the family of The O'Niall of Ulster, Chief of Tyrone, was O'Craoibhe, Creavh, or Creagh, as it has been written for centuries. Some writers, and the tradition in the family, account for the change of name from O'Niall to Creagh, as follows:—"One of the princes of the Hy Niall dynasty led his clan from Ulster to the assistance of Limerick, against the Danes, and they being expelled therefrom, through his timely aid, the citizens placed green boughs in the headstalls of their deliverers' horses; thence the chief was named O'Niall *na Creavh*, signifying, "O'Niall of the Green Branch." In commemoration of this event, the family crest has since been the head of a war-horse, bearing a laurel branch in the headstall of his bridle. We find the family settled in Limerick and its neighbourhood in the beginning of the 13th century, and Mr. Creagh possesses property in that city, part of the estates of O'Niall of the Branches, granted to him by the grateful citizens, which was never forfeited, paying neither quit nor crown-rent, his title being antiquity of possession.

That branch of the descendants of the Hy Niall prince now before us, was settled in the city of Cork, in or previous to the time of Edward III., where they continued to reside, having attained great opulence as merchants, and intermarried with the leading families within the city, until expelled therefrom (with the other ancient Irish inhabitants) about the year 1644, when they lost their great wealth, and a few of the family returning after the troubles, others settled in the county.

John Creagh, the earliest settler in Cork of whom anything has been ascertained, left a son, William Creagh, father of John Creagh, *temp.* Richard II., or Edward III. He *m.* a dau. of the family of Wynchedon, and dying about 1430, left a son, Stephen Creagh, *temp.* Henry V. and Henry VI., *d.* in that of Edward IV., about the year 1466, leaving, by Joan Skiddy, a son,

William Creagh, who *m.* Jane Galway, and dying about 1521, left a son, Christopher Creagh, *b.* in 1486 or 1487, and living 8th Elizabeth, was mayor of Cork in 1541, and a man of great influence and power amongst the native Irish. He was appointed, in conjunction with the Earl of Desmond, the Bishops of Cork, Ross, and Waterford, and others, by the then lord-deputy, Sir Anthony St. Leger, and the privy council, judges and arbitrators in Munster, to hear and determine all controversies amongst the natives for the future, instead of their Irish Brehons. He *m.* Mary, dau. of Dominick Roche (of the family of the Lords Roche, or De la Rupe, of Fermoy), and was *s.* by his son,

John Creagh, who *m.* (articles dated 15 May, 1557) Mary, dau. of Michael, and granddau. of John Waters (an eminent citizen of Cork, who was executed for aiding Perkin Warbeck, in 1492), and *d.* about 1601, leaving issue, Christopher, who *d.* before his father; John. The 2nd son,

John Creagh, *b.* in 1561, *m.* Margaret, dau. of George Archdeken, and dying 2 May, 1614, left issue,

Christopher, *d. s. p.*
William, of whom presently.
Michael, *m.* the dau. of O'Driscol, and had issue, one son, Michael (Sir), lord-mayor of Dublin in 1688, and a colonel in the service of James II., whom he faithfully served. He left no descendants.
John, was of Ballyvolane, in the co. Clare, and a colonel in the army of the confederated Catholics in 1642. He *m.* a Lysaght, of that shire, and left issue, one dau.,
Christian, *m.* to Philip Stackpoole, Esq.

The 2nd son,

William Creagh, *b.* in 1594, *m.* Ellen, dau. of Roche Fitz Richard, of Poulnalong Castle, between Bandon and Kingsale, and *d.* before 1670, leaving issue, i. John, of whom presently; ii. Pierce, *m.* Mary Price, and had issue, a son Christopher, m. Jane Galway, and left three sons, 1 John, of Ballybunnion, co. Kerry; 2 William, d. s. p.; 3 Patrick, m. Elizabeth Cooke, and left issue, Anne, m. Denis Moylan, of the city of Cork, and had a son, Denis-Creagh Moylan; Elizabeth, m. in 1786, Major Daniel Mahony, of Dunlogh Castle, in the co. Kerry. The eldest son of William Creagh and Ellen Roche,

JOHN CREAGH, b. in 1631, m. Julia, or Giles Verdon. John Creagh was one of those denominated "ancient Irish inhabitants," and, when a boy, was with his father, William, expelled the city, to which he never returned, but d. and was buried at Clonfert, near Newmarket, co. Cork. He left issue, I. JOHN, of whom presently; II. William, m. Catherine Rice, of the co. Kerry, and left Michael, m. Joanna, dau. of Charles McCarthy, of Stonefield, co. Cork, and had a son, William, of Oldtown, near Doneraile, in the county, who m. in 1770, Sarah Nagle, of Annakissy, in the same shire, and left issue; III. Stephen, d. without issue; IV. Dominick, m. Margaret Barratt, and settled in Kerry. He left a son, Francis, m. Jane Mason, who left (with a younger son, Francis) a son, John, m. Anne Carey, and, left, with a younger son, Moncton, an elder son, Francis, m. Martha Mason, of Ahamore, co. Kerry, and left issue, John, now of Dromartin, co. Kerry. The eldest son of John Creagh and Julia or Giles Verdon,

JOHN CREAGH, Esq., b. in 1667, was of Kilowen, co. Cork. He m. in 1695, Ellinor, dau. of Col. John Barrat, of Castlemore: by her (who, with her husband, lies buried at Clonfert, near Newmarket, in his father's tomb) he had issue, six sons and one dau.,

I. RICHARD, m. Mary Armstead, and left issue,

1 William, m. in 1786, Rebecca Morris, co-heiress (with her sisters, Sarah, m. to William Raymond, of Dromin, co. Kerry; and Catharine, who d. unm.) of Daniel-Theophilus Morris, Esq. of Ballingown, co. Kerry, and left one dau.

Sarah, m. Ezekiel-Tidd Abbott, Esq., and has issue,

Sarah, who m. the Right Hon. John Philpot Curran, Master of the Rolls in Ireland, and d. 18 Nov. 1844, aged 89.

II. John, of Creagh Castle, co. Cork, m. 1st, Mary Ruddock, of Wallstown, near Doneraile, and had issue,

Catharine, m. to William Stawell, Esq. of Kilbrack, and d. without issue.

Mr. Creagh m. 2ndly, Judith, dau. of Beverly Usher, of Cappagh, co. Waterford, widow of Edmond Shouldham, of Dunmanway, and left a dau.,

Mary, m. to Kilner Brasier, of Lizard, co. Limerick, and by him was mother of the present GEORGE-WASHINGTON BRASIER-CREAGH, of Creagh Castle (*See that family*).

III. Stephen, of Kilowen, m. Ellen Leyne, but had no issue.

IV. William, who was an officer in the Austrian service, and d. abroad. Mr. Creagh was "out" in 1745 with Prince Charles, the young Chevalier.

V. James, d. s. p.

VI. MICHAEL, of whom hereafter.

I. Catharine, m. to James Stackpoole, in the same service with her brother William, and both d. abroad without issue.

The 6th and youngest son,

MICHAEL CREAGH, Esq., b. in 1706, became of Laurentinum, co. Cork. He m. 1741, Catherine Parker, of the family of Inchigaggin, and by her had one son, John, d. young. Mr. Creagh m. 2ndly, Mary Gethin, sister and heiress of Captain Richard Gethin, killed in 1759, at the surprise of General Braddock, in North America. Miss Gethin was the dau., by Anne Clayton,* of Arthur Gethin, eldest son of Randolph Gethin, by Mary St. Leger, dau. of Col. John St. Leger (ancestor of the Lords Doneraile), and Mary, dau. of Arthur Chichester, 1st Earl of Donegal. By his 2nd marriage, Mr. Creagh left issue,

I. ARTHUR-GETHIN, of whom hereafter.

II. Richard-Gethin, d. unm.

I. Mary-Anne, who m. John, eldest son of Stephen Creagh, of Reens, co. Limerick, representing an ancient branch of the family, and had, with other issue, a son, Michael.

II. Theodosia, m. Major Eyre Coote, of the family of Mountrath, and had issue.

Mr. Creagh d. 11 Nov. 1781, and was buried with his wives, at Doneraile, and was s. by his eldest son surviving,

ARTHUR-GETHIN CREAGH, Esq. of Laurentinum, b. in Nov. 1746, m. (settlement dated 23 March, 1770) Isabella, dau. of William Bagwel, Esq., M.P. for Clonmel, by Jane his wife, dau. of Alderman John Harper, of the city of Cork, and Isabella Knapp his wife, and d. 13 May, 1833, having had issue,

I. MICHAEL, of Laurentinum, b. 25 March, 1771, m. in June, 1796, Sarah Dobson, dau. of Shapland Carew, Esq. of Castleboro', co. Wexford, and aunt to the 1st Lord Carew; and left, at his decease, 17 Oct. 1845, an only child,

ISABELLA-CAREW, m. John Singleton, Esq. of Quinville, co. Clare, and has, with other issue, a son and heir, Michael Creagh-Singleton, Esq., of the 10th foot.

II. JOHN-BAGWELL, of whom presently.

III. Arthur-Gethin, of Doneraile, b. in 1780, m. in 1810, Eliza, only dau. of Admiral Henry Evans, Esq. of Oldtown, Doneraile, but has no issue.

IV. William, lieut., cavalry, E. I. Co.'s service, b. in 1782; d. of fatigue after a series of engagements with the forces under Holkar.

V. Benjamin Bousfield, of Doneraile, b. 1784, m. Margaret Morris, and d. 12 May, 1846, leaving issue,

1 Arthur-Gethin. 2 Benjamin. 3 John-Merrick.
1 Isabella. 2 Dorcas.

I. Mary, m. to Thady McNamara, Esq. of Ayle, co. Clare, and survives, his widow, but has no issue.

II. Jane, m. Capt. Taylor, maternally descended from the celebrated Scottish Reformer, John Knox, and left issue.

III. Isabella, m. Arthur Shawe, late lieut.-col. in the 87th foot, and has issue.

IV. Dorcas, m. James Norcott, Esq. of Springfield, co. and has issue.

V. Emily, m. Ion Studdert, Esq. of Elm Hill, co. Limerick, (*see* STUDDERT *of Bunratty*), and has issue.

The 2nd son,

THE REV. JOHN-BAGWELL CREAGH, of Bally Andrew, co. Cork, vicar of Carrig, and rector of Rincurran, in the same shire, b. 26 Dec. 1772, m. (settlement dated 28 July, 1797) Gertrude, dau. of John Miller, Esq. of Toonaghmore, co. Clare, and by her (who d. 11 March, 1844, aged 63) had issue, seven sons and five daus.,

I. ARTHUR-GETHIN, his heir.

II. John, b. in 1802, m. in 1831, Mary, dau. of St. John Galway, Esq. of Mallow, co. Cork, representative of an ancient family of Carberry, of that name, and d. 9 March, 1841, leaving a son,

Arthur-Gethin, b. in 1836.

III. Thomas-Miller, b. in 1803, lieut. and paymaster of the 52nd foot, m. in 1843, Eliza Hewitt, of Giancoole, co. Cork.

IV. Michael, b. in July, 1811, m. 24 May, 1843, Louisa-Emma, dau. of James-Dominick Burke, of Becan, co. Mayo, surgeon in the royal navy, by his wife Louisa Collingwood, granddau. of Edward Collingwood, of the family of Chirton, in Northumberland, who accompanied Lord Anson in his celebrated voyage, and was uncle to Cuthbert, Lord Collingwood; and has,

1 John, b. 23 Feb. 1844.
2 Michael-Clayton, b. 25 May, 1845.
3 Randolph-Gethin, b. 25 March, 1847.
4 Arthur-Gethin, b. 31 July, 1850.
1 Gertrude-Olivia. 2 Louisa, deceased.

V. Richard-Gethin, b. in June, 1813, m. in 1842, Isabella Mellifont, and has issue,

1 John, b. in 1843.
2 Richard-Gethin, b. in 1845.
1 Gertrude-Miller. 2 Isabella-Gethin.

VI. William, d. an infant.

VII. Benjamin-Bousfield.

I. Isabella-Gethin, m. William Davis, Esq., M.D., and has issue.

II. Rebecca, m. Arthur Murphy, of Oulartleigh, co. Wexford, and has a son.

III. Eliza, m. John Stevens, Esq., M.D., of St. Keverne, Cornwall, and has issue.

The Rev. John-Bagwell Creagh d. 12 Feb. 1846, and was s. by his son,

ARTHUR-GETHIN CREAGH, Esq. of Bally Andrew, b. in 1799, m. in 1827, his cousin Mary, only dau. and heir of James McGhie, Esq. of Caharan, co. Clare, by Bridget his wife, dau. of John Miller, of Toonaghmore, in that co., and had issue,

I. JOHN-BAGWELL, now of Bally Andrew.

II. Arthur-Gethin, b. 1830.

III. Thomas-Miller, b. 1838. IV. Michael, deceased.

I. Rebecca-Victoria.

Mr. Creagh d. 25 Feb. 1849.

Arms—Arg., a chevron, gu., between three laurel-leaves, vert; on a chief, az., as many bezants.

Crest—A horse's head fully caparisoned, with a laurel branch in the headstall of the bridle.

Motto—Virtute et numine.

Seat—Bally Andrew, co. Cork.

* Anne Clayton was dau. of Courthorpe Clayton, of Annabella, near Mallow, and granddau. of Col. Randolph Clayton, by Judith Perceval his wife, dau. of Sir Philip Perceval, great-grandfather of John, 1st Earl of Egmont.

CREAGH OF DANGAN.

CREAGH, CORNELIUS, Esq. of Dangan, co. Clare, became representative of the family, on the death of his brother, and is married.

Lineage.—PIERSE CREAGH, Esq. of Adare, mayor of Limerick in 1651, son and heir of Pierse Creagh, Esq. of Adare, M.P. for the city of Limerick in 1639, was deprived of his estate of Adare for having corresponded with the Duke of Ormonde, and forced to take refuge on the Continent, where he remained in the service of the French King until the Restoration, when he returned, and applied to the Court of Claims for a restitution of his estates, which had been parcelled out amorg CROMWELL's officers and soldiers. In this he was unsuccessful, but through the interest of the Duke of Ormonde, King CHARLES II. granted, by patent enrolled 10 Oct. 1666, to him and his heirs, the castle, town, and lands of Dangan, &c., all in the county of Clare, which lands were further secured to him by the 17th and 18th CHARLES II., and were erected into a manor, with divers manorial rights and privileges. This Pierse Creagh *m.* in 1639, M. MacNamara, of Creattalough, or Cratloe Castle, co. Clare, and *d.* in 1670, at his Castle of Dangan. He was *s.* by his son,

SIMON CREAGH, Esq. of Dangan, who *m.* Mary MacMahon, of the Castle of Clenagh, and was father of

PIERSE CREAGH, Esq. of Dangan, who *m.* Elizabeth, dau. of George Matthew, Esq. of Thomastown, co. Tipperary, and aunt to the 1st Lord Llandaff, and had issue a son and dau., PIERSE, his heir; and Elizabeth, *m.* to Davoren of Lisdoonvarna. Mr. Pierse Creagh was *s.* by his son,

PIERSE CREAGH, Esq. of Dangan, who *m.* thrice: 1st, in 1738, Catherine, dau. of Valentine Quin, of Adare, and aunt to the 1st Earl of Dunraven and Mountearl, but had no surviving issue; 2ndly, in 1755, Gertrude Maghlin, of Brickhill, and by her had a son, ROBERT, his heir, of whom presently; and 3rdly, in 1759, Lavinia, dau. of Richard Pennefather, of Newpark, and aunt of the present chief justice of Ireland and Baron Pennefather, and by this lady had two sons and a dau.,

Richard, *m.* Christina O'Callaghan, of Maryfort, and *d.* in 1836, leaving two sons, RICHARD, and CORNELIUS, now of Dangan.
Simon, *m.* his cousin Dora, dau. of B. MacNamara, Esq., by Elizabeth his wife, dau. of Davoren of Lisdoonvarna, and *d.* in 1815, leaving four sons, 1 Pierse, *m.* in 1836, Belinda, dau. of Walter Butler, Esq. of Bunnahow, co. Clare, and has a son, Simon, *b.* May, 1842; Walter; and two daus., Henrietta and Belinda; 2 Simon; 3 MacNamara, deceased; and 4 Richard.
Charity, *m.* to Gerald Carrick, Esq.

Mr. Creagh *d.* in 1780, when he was *s.* by his eldest son,

ROBERT CREAGH, Esq. of Dangan, who became a lunatic in 1792, when his property was vested in the Court of Chancery. He *d. s. p.* in 1842, when the representation devolved upon his nephew, RICHARD, to whom *s.* his brother CORNELIUS, now of Dangan.

Arms—Arg., three laurel-branches, ppr.; on a chief, az., as many besants.
Crest—A horse's head, fully caparisoned, with a laurel-branch in the headstall of the bridle.
Motto—Virtute et numine.
Seat—Dangan, co. Clare.

CREAGH OF CREAGH CASTLE.

BRASIER-CREAGH, GEORGE-WASHINGTON, Esq. of Creagh Castle, co. Cork, *b.* 8 April, 1797; *m.* 30 July, 1822, Anne-Catherine, dau. of the Rev. Bartholomew Pack, rector of Etta, and has issue,

I. WILLIAM-JOHNSON. II. John, R.N.
III George-Washington, *m.* Averina, dau. of Capt. Sherlock, late of the 69th regt.
IV. Richard-Bartholomew, R.N.
V. Kilner-Augustus-Arthur.
I. Catherine, *m.* to Capt. Robert-B. Stowards, of the 8th regt.
II. Lucy-Susan. III. Anna-Frances.

Mr. Creagh has served as high-sheriff of the county of Cork, and was mayor of Limerick in 1809. He is son of the late KILNER BRASIER, Esq., by Mary his wife, dau. and heiress of JOHN CREAGH, of Creagh Castle, and grandson of Brooke Brasier, Esq. of Lizard, co. Limerick. His eldest brother, BROOKE BRASIER, Esq., *m.* Ellen, dau. and co-heiress of Henry Mitchell, Esq. of Mitchellsfort, co. Cork, and left issue, 1 KILNER BRASIER, Esq., now of Bally Ellis, co. Cork, who *m.* his cousin, Mary Griffin; 2 Henry, who has assumed the surname of MITCHELL: 3 Brooke; 4 John; 5 Gryce-Smyth; 1 Ellen, *m.* to Wm. Quin, Esq.; 2 Mary, *m.* to John Smyth, Esq.; and 3 Catherine, *m.* to Sir Richard de Burgho, Bart. Mr. Brasier-Creagh's sisters are, 1 Catherine, *m.* 1st, to John Mathias, Esq. of Langwaron, co. Pembroke, and 2ndly, to the Rev. Wm. Bourne, rector of Rathargan, co. Kildare; 2 Judith, *m.* to Thomas-F. Wilkinson, Esq., Alderman of Limerick; 3 Emma, *m.* to James Griffin, Esq.: 4 Mary, *m.* to Attiwell Wood, Esq.; 5 Lucy, *m.* 1st, to Charles Bell, Esq., and 2ndly, to Bertram Jarves, Esq. of Antigua.

Lineage.—The family of Brasier was established in Ireland by PAUL BRASIER, an officer of CROMWELL's army. His son, COL. KILNER BRASIER, of Bigley, co. Donegal, M.P., who *m.* Anne, dau. of Sir Henry Brooke, Knt., was great-grandfather of KILNER BRASIER, who *m.* Mary Creagh.

Arms and *Crest*—As CREAGH *of Ballyandrew*.
Motto—Virtute et numine.
Seat—Creagh Castle, near Doneraile.

CREAN OF BALLENVILLA.

CREAN, AUGUSTUS-FRANCIS, Esq. of Ballenvilla, co. Mayo, J.P., *b.* 31 May, 1817; *m.* 2 June, 1844, Mary, dau. of the late Arthur-Henry Lynch, Esq. of Petersburgh Castle, co. Galway, by Frances his wife, dau. of Isidore Blake, Esq. of Tower Hill, and has issue,

I. ARTHUR-LYNCH, *b.* June, 1845.
II. Joseph, *b.* March, 1847.
III. Charles, *b.* April, 1848.
I. Frances. II. Mary.

Lineage.—This family, one of great antiquity, is lineally descended from the O'Creans of Sligo, whose estates in that county were confiscated on account of the active part they toon in the Rebellion. A scion of this ancient stock settled, afterwards, at Ballenvilla, co. Mayo, and there the family has remained for more than two centuries. The late

JOSEPH-A. CREAN, Esq. of Ballenvilla, son and heir of Austin Crean, Esq. of the same place, by Eliza Ffrench his wife, *m.* in Aug. 1816, Maria Coghlan, and *d.* in 1852, leaving (with a dau., Josephine-Anne) a son and heir, the present AUGUSTUS-FRANCIS CREAN, Esq. of Ballenvilla.

Seat—Ballenvilla, co. Mayo.

CREGOE OF TREWITHIAN.

CREGOE, MATTHEW-GARLAND, Esq. of Trewithian, co. Cornwall, J.P., *b.* 12 Nov. 1776; *m.* 4 Aug. 1803, Anne-Coryton, eldest dau. of Admiral Arthur Kempe, of Polsac, in the same county, by Ann Coryton his wife, and has issue,

I. JOHN-GARLAND, *b.* 5 April, 1810, *m.* in May, 1841, Cornelia Powne, eldest dau. of Major William-Slade Gully, of Trevenen, co. Cornwall.
I. Letitia-Maria. II. Laura-Elizabeth-Ann.
III. Elizabeth-Courtenay, *m.* in March, 1851, to George Beauchant, Esq.

Lineage.—EDWARD CREGOE, Esq., only son of STEPHEN CREGOE, Esq., by Abigail his wife, dau. of Edward Hobbs, Esq. of Gervans, *m.* Sarah Foote, and, with two other sons, was father of

EDWARD CREGOE, Esq., who *m.* Mary, dau. of the Rev. John Pomeroy, of the parish of St. Ewe, and had, with a younger son, John, an elder son and heir,

EDWARD CREGOE, Esq. of Trewithian, who *m.* in 1775, Mary, only child and heiress of Matthew Garland, Esq. of Chivelstone, Devonshire, and dying in July, 1799, left issue,

MATTHEW-GARLAND, now of Trewithian.
Edward, *d. unm.*
Frind, who assumed the additional surname of Colmore, in 1834, and *d.* in 1839 (*see* COLMORE *of Moor End*).
Mary, *d. unm.*
Harriet, *m.* to the Rev. Charles Lyne, and is deceased.
Celia.

Arms—Az., on a chevron, or, between three falcons, volant, as many plates.
Crest—An arm embowed in armour, cut off below the wrist, and dropping blood; in the hand an arrow.
Motto—Fortuna audaces juvat, timidosque repellit.
Seat—Trewithian, in the parish of Gerrans, co. Cornwall.

CREE OF OWER MOIGNE.

CREE, THE REV. JOHN-ROBERT, of Ower Moigne, co. Dorset.

Lineage.—The late JOHN CREE, Esq. of Ower Moigne, co. Dorset, J.P. and D.L., *b.* in 1780, son of the late Terence M'Mahon, Esq. of Cullenswood, co. Dublin, and Rachel his wife, co-heiress of George Longworth, Esq. of Craggan House, near Athlone, Ireland, assumed, by royal license, in 1814, the surname and arms of CREE, in lieu of his paternal ones, in compliance with the will of his uncle, John Cree, Esq. of Thornhill House, co. Dorset, whom he succeeded. He *m.* in 1806, Anne, 3rd dau. of Robert Strickland, Esq. of Dorchester, and has issue surviving,

JOHN-ROBERT, rector of Ower Moigne, near Dorchester.
James, in holy orders, vicar of Chaldon, near Dorchester.
Georgiana.

Mr. Cree *d.* 3 July, 1853.

Seat—Ower Moigne, near Dorchester.

CRESSWELL OF CRESSWELL.

BAKER-CRESSWELL, ADDISON-JOHN, Esq. of Cresswell, co. Northumberland, *b.* 1 Oct. 1788, M.P. for Northumberland, high-sheriff in 1821; *m.* 25 June, 1818, Elizabeth-Mary, dau. of Gilfrid-Lawson Reed, Esq. of Campion Hill, and cousin and heir of John Baker, Esq. of Hinton, in Gloucestershire, and of Grosvenor Street, London, by whom he has issue,

I. OSWIN-ADDISON, *b.* 10 April, 1819, *m.* 1 Aug. 1843, Anne-Seymour, eldest dau. of Sir William Gordon-Cumming, Bart. of Altyre and Gordonstoun.
II. Francis-John, *b.* 20 Feb. 1822, and *d.* 20 March, 1827.
III. William-Gilfrid, *b.* 21 March, 1825, *m.* Adelaide-Eliza, 2nd dau. of Sir W. Gordon-Cumming, Bart.
IV. Henry-Robert, *b.* 22 Aug. 1829.
I. Anna-Fanny. II. Elizabeth-Jane-Isabella.

Lineage.—This family has been seated from an early era in the North of England, Robert de Cresswell having been (according to a MS. taken from old writings) in possession of the estate so far back as the reign of RICHARD I. From

SIR ROBERT DE CRESSWELL, Knt., living in 1240, 1246, 1249, and 1256, lineally derived

JOHN CRESSWELL, Esq. of Cresswell, who sold his estate at Long Framlington. He *m.* Catherine, dau. of John Dyer, Esq. of Aberglasyn, in Wales, and dying 10 Jan. 1781, left two twin daus., his co-heirs, viz.,

FRANCES-DOROTHEA, of whom presently.
CATHERINE-GRACE, who *m.* Birnie Brown, Esq., and had issue, James, Birnie, Walter, William; Elizabeth-Addison, *m.* to James Terranean, Esq., H.I.C.C.S.; Alicia, and Arminia.

The elder dau. and co-heir,

FRANCES-DOROTHEA CRESSWELL, *m.* FRANCIS EASTERBY, Esq. of Blackheath, who purchased the other co-heir's moiety of CRESSWELL, assumed the surname of CRESSWELL, and had issue,

I. ADDISON-JOHN, the present Mr. CRESSWELL, of Creswell.
II. Francis, who *m.* Rachel-Elizabeth, dau. of Joseph Fry, Esq., by Elizabeth his wife, dau. of John Gurney, Esq. of Earlham, co. Norfolk, and had issue,
  1 FRANCIS-JOSEPH, *m.* Aug. 1850, Charlotte-Frances-Georgina, eldest dau. of Lord Calthorpe and the Lady Charlotte-Sophia his wife, eldest dau. of the 6th Duke of Beaufort.
  2 Addison-John.
  3 Samuel-Gurney, of the Royal Navy: he having returned to England, 6 Oct. 1853, the bearer of dispatches from Capt. McClure, of H.M.S. "Investigator," is the first person to have accomplished the North-West Passage.
  4 William-Edward. 5 Gerard-Oswin. 6 Oswald.
  1 Harriet-Frances-Elizabeth, *d.* young.
III. William.
IV. Cresswell (Sir), Knt., one of the Judges of the Court of Common Pleas.
V. Oswald-Joseph, in holy orders, vicar of Sealan.
I. Elizabeth, *d.* in 1827. II. Frances.
III. Jane-Catherine, *d.* in 1828.

Arms—Quarterly: CRESSWELL and BAKER: and on an escutcheon of pretence, BAKER and REED, quarterly.
Crests—1st, on a mount, vert, a torteau, charged with a squirrel, sejant, arg., for CRESSWELL; 2nd, a goat's head, erased, arg., armed and crined, or, gorged with a collar, gemelle, and charged on the neck with a saltier, gu., for BAKER.
Motto—Cressa ne careat.
Seat—Cresswell.

CRESWELL OF PINKNEY PARK.

CRESWELL, WILLIAM-HENRY, Esq. of Pinkney Park, co. Wilts, and Sidbury, co. Salop, *b.* 14 Oct. 1817; *m.* 21 Sept. 1841, Elizabeth, only dau. of the late Thomas Mawson, Esq. of Ardwick Green, Manchester, and has issue,

I. CHARLES-RICHARD-ESTCOURT, *b.* 24 Oct. 1842.
II. Henry-Thomas, *b.* 13 Dec. 1848.
I. Catherine-Purslow. II. Elizabeth-Sackville.

Lineage.—The family of Creswell, which has been in possession of considerable estates in the county of Salop for upwards of two centuries, was anciently seated at Barnehurst, in the parish of Tettenhall, co. Stafford, where it had a fine old manor house, and enjoyed an extensive property. The only vestige of the ancient mansion now left, is a square ivy-grown tower and gateway, which remain a pleasing relic of the architecture of olden times. The Creswells appear to have been established in Staffordshire from a very early period, and to have ever maintained a high position among its great landed proprietors. Shaw, in his *History and Antiquities of Shropshire*, observes, that there was an estate called after their name near Stafford, where a branch of the family resided, and whence he considers that they originally sprung.

RICHARD CRESWELL, Esq. of Barnehurst, *b.* 6 April, 1620, son and heir of Richard Creswell, Esq. of Barnehurst, by Margery his wife, dau. and heir of Reginald Fowke, Esq. of Gunston, and 4th in descent from Thomas Creswell, Esq. of Barnehurst, *m.* 26 Jan. 1657, Anne, dau. of George Lea, Esq. of Lea, co. Hereford, and half-sister and devisee of Rowland Purslow, Esq. of Sidbury, and by her acquired that estate. Mr. Creswell served the office of high-sheriff for Salop in 1670, and was a staunch royalist during the Civil Wars. He *d.* in 1704, and was *s.* by his only surviving son,

RICHARD CRESWELL, Esq. of Sidbury and Barnehurst, M.P. for Bridgenorth in 1710, and high-sheriff of Salop in the following year. He *m.* Margaret, dau. of Edward Moreton, of Moreton, co. Stafford, Esq., and sister of Matthew, 1st Lord Ducie, by whom he had, with a dau., Elizabeth, *m.* to Gervase Scrope, Esq. of Cockerington, co. Lincoln, a son and heir,

RICHARD CRESWELL, Esq. of Sidbury, who *m.* Elizabeth, dau. and eventually heir of Sir Thomas Estcourt, Knt. of Pinkney, and had two sons, THOMAS, his heir; Richard, who *m.* and had a dau., Mary, to William Long, Esq. of Bainton, Wilts. The eldest son,

THOMAS-ESTCOURT CRESWELL, Esq. of Pinkney Park and Sidbury, M.P. for Wotton Bassett, *m.* Anne, sole dau. and heir of Edmond Warneford, Esq. (by Elizabeth his wife, only dau. aud heiress of Henry Sackville, Esq. of Bibury), and *d.* 14 Nov. 1788, leaving (with a dau., Frances, *m.* 30 Sept. 1790, to Dr. Hall, of Lewisham, Kent) a son and successor,

THOMAS-ESTCOURT CRESWELL, Esq. of Pinkney Park, Sidbury, and Bibury, many years M.P. for Cirencester, who *m.* 1st, Mary, only dau. and heiress of Samuel Wotton, Esq. of Speechwick Park, Devon, and by her had an only child, *m.* 23 Sept. 1802, to the Rev. Thomas Fry, M.A., vicar of Radley, Berks. Mr. Creswell *m.* 2ndly, Miss Gregory, of Sherston, Wilts, and by her had issue,

RICHARD-ESTCOURT, his heir.
Henry, in holy orders, vicar of Creech St. Michael, Taunton, co. Somerset, *m.*, and had, with other issue, Mary-Sophia, *m.* 16 Aug. 1838, to H.-M. Daniel, Esq. of Worcester.
Sackville, in holy orders, vicar of Bibury.
Estcourt, *d. unm.* Edmund.

He *d.* 4 July, 1823, and was *s.* by his eldest son,

RICHARD-ESTCOURT CRESWELL, Esq. of Pinkney Park, Sidbury, and of Bibury, formerly M.P. for Cirencester. He *m.* in May, 1803, Elizabeth, youngest dau. of the Rev. Charles Coxwell, of Ablington, co. Gloucester, and had issue,

Richard-Estcourt, *m.* 18 Dec. 1826, Mary-Anne-Lawrence, eldest dau. of the Rev. R.-L. Townshend, D.D., and *d. s. p.* 5 April, 1837.
Charles-Attwell, *d.* abroad, 31 March, 1819.

Thomas-Estcourt-Moreton-Corbett, *d. unm.* 28 Dec. 1836.
Warneford-Sackville, drowned at Chester, in June, 1835.
WILLIAM-HENRY, present representative.
George-Wotton, *d.* young.
Elizabeth-Mary, *m.* to her cousin, Charles-Rogers Coxwell, Esq., 3rd son of the Rev. Charles Coxwell, of Ablington, rector of Dowdeswell, co. Gloucester.
Anne, *m.* in 1830, to Francis-Kirkham Fowell, Esq., 2nd son of the late Rev. John-Digby Fowell, of Blackhall and Diptford, Devon.
Eleanor-Frances, *m.* 25 July, 1839, to George-Lewis Cooper, Esq. of Torrington-square, London, 2nd son of the late Hon. Sir George Cooper, judge at Madras.
Barbara-Jane, *m.* to William-Doidge Taunton, Esq.
Emma, *m.* 11 Sept. 1832, to the Rev. John Thompson.
Catherine-Margaret, *m.* 30 Aug. 1842, to George-Thomas Ellison, Esq. of Lincoln's Inn.

Mr. Creswell *d.* in France, in March, 1841.

Arms—Gu., three plates, each charged with a squirrel, sejant, of the field.
Crest—A Saracen's head, ppr., wreathed about the temples, vert and arg.
Motto—Aut nunquam tentes aut perfice.
Seat—Pinkney Park, Wilts; and Sidbury, co. Salop.

CRESWELL OF RAVENSTONE.

CRESWELL, ROBERT-GREEN, Esq. of Ravenstone, in the cos. of Leicester and Derby, J.P., *b.* 18 Feb. 1778.

Lineage.—The CRESWELLS have been resident landholders at Ravenstone from a remote period, as their title-deeds and family records clearly prove.

ROBERT CRESWELL, who was living at Ravenstone during the time of the civil war, purchased property there in 1645 and 1650. He was father of

RICHARD CRESWELL, who *m.* Mary Lawrence, a dau. of an ancient family of that name in Sutton Bonington, co. Nottingham. He *d.* 29 March, 1734, aged 65, and was buried at Ravenstone. His son and successor,

ROBERT CRESWELL, *m.* in 1725, Catherine, dau. of Matthew White, of Great Appleby, Gent., and *d.* 30 June, 1747, aged 43, and was buried at Ravenstone. He left issue,

RICHARD, his heir.
Mary, *d. unm.* in 1777. Catherine, *d. unm.* in 1797.
Elizabeth, *m.* to Thomas Sperry, and had issue.

RICHARD CRESWELL, the only son, succeeded to the whole of the landed property of his father and mother. He *m.* Elizabeth, dau. of Ambrose Salisbury, by whom he had issue,

ROBERT, his successor.
Richard, who *d. unm.* 29 Nov. 1830.
Elizabeth, *m.* to John Eames, and had issue.
Catherine, *m.* to John Mills, and had issue.

Mr. Creswell *d.* 26 June, 1768, and was buried at Ravenstone. His widow *d.* in Jan. 1807. The elder son,

ROBERT CRESWELL, Esq. of Ravenstone, *m.* twice; 1st, 18 May, 1777, Ann, 3rd dau. of Robert Green, Esq. of Normanton-on-the-Heath, co. Leicester, and Margery his wife, by whom he had two sons and three daus.,

I. ROBERT-GREEN, now of Ravenstone.
II. Richard-Edward, *b.* 1779, *m.* 1810, Alice, dau. of Henry Chapman, Esq. of Neasham, co. Durham, and has issue,
1 Richard-Henry, in holy orders, *m.* in 1835, Ann, dau. of Valentine Green, Esq. of Normanton.
2 Robert. 3 Edward.
4 Mary-Ann. 2 Elizabeth-Martha-Caroline.
I. Mary-Anne, *m.* to William Hall, Esq of Cotes, co. Leicester, now of Knutsford, Cheshire.
II. Elizabeth, *m.* to the Rev. John Oliver, rector of Swepstone.
III. Catherine, *d. unm.*

By his 2nd marriage Mr. Creswell had one son,

I. Creswell-Creswell.

Mr. Creswell *d.* in Feb. 1825.

Seat—Ravenstone.

CREYKE OF MARTON.

CREYKE, RALPH, Esq. of Marton, in the East Riding, and of Rawcliffe, in the West Riding of the county of York, *b.* 6 Sept. 1813; *m.* 27 Aug. 1846, Louisa-Frances, youngest dau. of Colonel Croft, of Stillington Hall, Yorkshire, and has issue,

I. RALPH, *b.* 5 Sept. 1849.
I. Everilda-Elizabeth. II. Catherine-Harriet.

Lineage.—The family of CREYKE is of ancient date in the East Riding of the co. York. The first on record is Sir Walter de Creyke, Knt., who was appointed Governor of Berwick in 1340, after Sir Richard Talbot, by EDWARD III. In 1358, John de Creyke represented York in a parliament held in that city, and Robert de Creyke was bailiff of the same place in 1379. The representative of the family in the 17th century,

GREGORY CREYKE, Esq. of Marton (son of Ralph Creyke, of Marton, by Katherine his wife, dau. of Thomas Crathorne, of Crathorne, lineally derived from Anne Plantagenet, sister of King EDWARD IV., *see* BURKE'S *Royal Families*), suffered severely for his devoted attachment to CHARLES I., and compounded heavily for his estates. He *m.* Ursula, dau. of Sir John Legard, Knt. of Ganton, by Elizabeth his wife, dau. of Sir John Mallory, Knt. of Studley, and had issue, ten sons and four daus. The 3rd but eldest surviving son,

GREGORY CREYKE, Esq. of Marton, *b.* 9 April, 1631, *m.* in 1672, Amie, dau. of Randolph Carliel, of Sewerby, and had a son,

RALPH CREYKE, Esq. of Marton, who *m.* 1 Aug. 1700, Priscilla, dau. of William Bower, Esq. of Bridlington, and had (with two daus.) two sons, viz.,

I. RALPH, his heir.
II. John, of Burleigh-on-the-Hill, in Rutlandshire, in holy orders, *b.* 29 April, 1713, *m.* Catherine, dau. of John Austen, Esq. of Adisham, in Kent, and had issue, 1 RALPH, successor to his uncle; 2 Richard, *b.* 8 Aug. 1746, capt. R.N., commissioner of the Victualling Office, and governor of the Royal Naval Hospital, Plymouth, *m.* Anne-Leming, eldest dau. of George Adey, Esq. of London, and *d.* 8 Dec. 1826, having had issue, George-Adey, capt. R.N., *d. s. p.*; Richard, capt. R.N., *m.* in 1818, Harriet-Elizabeth, dau. of the Rev. James Furneaux, of Swilly, in Devonshire, and has surviving issue, Richard-Henry-Adey, *b.* 31 Aug. 1822, Anne-Elizabeth-Harriet; 3 Stephen, in holy orders, who *m.* 6 Sept. 1823, Sarah, dau. of Col. George Hotham, and has three sons and three daus., viz., Walter-Pennington, in holy orders, private chaplain to H. E. the Lord Lieutenant of Ireland, Archdeacon, *b.* 17 Oct. 1828; Alexander-Stephen, *b.* 2 Feb. 1830; Alfred-Richard, *b.* 1 Sept. 1831; Caroline-Julia; Diana-Jane; Gertrude-Hotham; Anna; 3 Priscilla, *m.* to William Lynes, Esq. of London.

The elder son,

RALPH CREYKE, Esq. of Marton, *b.* 5 Oct. 1702, *d. s. p.* in Jan. 1759, and was *s.* by his nephew,

RALPH CREYKE, Esq. of Marton, *b.* 6 July, 1745, who *m.* 6 Feb. 1772, Jane, 5th dau. of Richard Langley, Esq. of Wykeham Abbey, by Elizabeth his wife, elder dau. and co-heir (with her sister, Judith, wife of John Twistleton, Esq. of Drax) of Boynton Boynton, Esq. of Rawcliffe, in the West Riding, who *d.* 31 Dec. 1794, he had (with seven daus., viz., Everilda; Catherine, *d.* 7 Sept. 1824; Frances, *m.* 1797, to Digby Legard, Esq., 5th son of Sir Digby Legard, Bart. of Ganton; Jane; Agnes, *m.* to Archdeacon Wrangham; Elizabeth; and Anne) two sons, RALPH, his heir, and Gregory, R.N., *d.* in 1795. Mr. Creyke *d.* 24 May, 1826, and was *s.* by his elder son,

RALPH CREYKE, Esq. of Marton and Rawcliffe, *b.* 11 April, 1776, who *m.* 14 Nov. 1807, Frances, eldest dau. of Robert Dennison, Esq. of Kilnwick Percy, and had by her (who *d.* in 1840) issue, viz., RALPH, of Marton and Rawcliffe; Richard-Boynton; Robert-Gregory; Frances; Mary-Anne-Elizabeth; and Emma-Jane, *m.* 20 June, 1843, to Charles-Granby Burke, Esq., 2nd son of the late Sir John Burke, Bart., of Marble Hill, co. Galway. Mr. Creyke *d.* 7 June, 1828.

Arms—Per fesse, arg. and sa., a pale and three ravens (called *creykes* in the old language of Yorkshire), counter-changed.
Crest—On a garb, or, a raven, ppr.
Seats—Marton, in the East, and Rawcliffe, in the West Riding of Yorkshire.

CRICHTON OF RANKEILOUR.

MAITLAND-MAKGILL-CRICHTON, CHARLES-JULIAN, Esq. of Rankeilour, co. Fife, *b.* 15 May, 1828.

Lineage.—The family of Crichton is one of the oldest and most distinguished in Scotland.

THE HON. JANET CRICHTON, dau. of James Crichton, Viscount Frendraught, by Janet, his 1st wife, dau. of Alexander, 1st Earl of Leven, *m.* in 1665, SIR JAMES MAKGILL, of Rankeilour, eldest son and heir of David Makgill, Esq., of Rankeilour, and was mother of an only son,

DAVID MAKGILL, of Rankeilour, who *m.* 10 Feb. 1698, Janet, dau. of John Craig, of Ramornie, and sister of Robert Craig (*alias* Heriot) of Ramornie, and by her (who survived him) had a son, JAMES, and two daus., viz., CATHERINE, *s.* her brother; and ISABELLA, *s.* her sister. The son,

JAMES MAKGILL, of Rankeilour, designated also Viscount Oxford, having claimed that dignity in 1733–4, *m.* 20 Jan. 1720, Jane, 2nd dau. of Sir Robert Anstruther, of Balcaskie, and dying without issue before 24 July, 1765, was *s.* by his sister,

CATHERINE MAKGILL, of Rankeilour, who *m.* Alexander Chrystie, Esq. of Edinburgh, and dying without issue before 11 April, 1776, was *s.* by her sister,

ISABELLA MAKGILL, of Rankeilour, who *m.* the Rev. William Dick, minister of Cupar, and had an only son, James, of Colluthie, an ensign in the army, predeceased his mother, before 20 Sept. 1768, leaving a dau., MARGARET, who *s.* her grandmother. Mrs. Dick was *s.* by her granddaughter,

MARGARET DICK, of Rankeilour, who *m.* the Hon. Captain Frederick Maitland, R.N., 6th son of the 6th Earl of Lauderdale, and assumed the surname of MAKGILL; and by him, who predeceased her, had issue,

I. Charles, the younger, of Rankeilour, *m.* 26 Aug. 1794, Mary, dau. of David Johnston, Esq. of Lathrisk, and by her (who *d.* 11 June, 1824) had,
  1 DAVID MAITLAND-MAKGILL, of Rankeilour.
  2 James, of Rossie, co. Fife, commander R.N., *b.* 18 April, 1806, *m.* 1st, Emma Willing, and 2ndly, in Aug. 1840, Frances-Harriet, dau. of Richard-Samuel Short, Esq.
  3 Charles, *b.* 31 May, 1807.
  4 Lewis, commander R.N., *b.* 12 April, 1811, *m.* in Dec. 1841, Henrietta, dau. of the late Sir John Newbolt, Chief Justice at Madras, and has issue.
  5 Henry, *b.* 13 April, 1813, *m.* 15 Feb. 1838, Anna, dau. of John Stirling, Esq.
  1 Mary, *m.* to Dr. George Govan, E. I. Co.'s service.
  2 Margaret-Louisa, *m.* to Frederick-L. Roy, Esq. of Newthorn, co. Roxburgh.
  3 Elizabeth, *m.* to Alexander Meldrum, Esq. of Kincaple, co. Fife.
II. James-Heriot, of Ramornie, co. Fife. See HERIOT *of Ramornie.*
III. Frederick-Lewis (Sir), Rear-Admiral R.N., K.C.B., *b.* in 1776, *m* in April, 1804, Catherine, 3rd dau. of Daniel Connor, Esq. of Ballybricken, co. Cork, *d.* in command in the Indian Seas, 30 Nov. 1832, *s. p.*
I. Mary-Turner, *m.* 5 April, 1793, to Henry-Scrymgeour Wedderburn, Esq. of Wedderburn, co. Forfar, who *d.* in Jan. 1842.
II. Elizabeth.
III. Isabella, *m.* 8 July, 1794, to William Roy, Esq. of Newthorn, co. Roxburgh, who *d.* in 1825.

Mrs. Maitland-Makgill *d.* in 1827, and was *s.* by her grandson,

DAVID MAITLAND-MAKGILL-CRICHTON, Esq. of Rankeilour, *b.* 4 March, 1801, who was served heir of line in general to James Crichton, 1st Viscount Frendraught, in June, 1839. He *m.* 1st, 7 Aug. 1827, Eleanor-Julian, 2nd dau. of the late Thomas Hog, Esq. of Newliston, and by her (who *d.* in 1833) had issue,

CHARLES-JULIAN, now of Rankeilour.
Thomas-Hog, *b.* 16 June, 1830.
Mary-Stuart, *m.* in 1849, to Philip Somerville, Esq. commander R.N.
Eleanor-Julian-Hog.

He *m.* 2ndly, 2 Dec. 1834, Esther, dau. of the late Dr. Andrew Coventry, of Chanwell, and by her had issue,

David, *b.* 20 Aug. 1841.
Andrew, *b.* 20 June, 1846.
Martha-Cunningham. Esther-Frederica.
Janet-Cunninghame.

Arms—CRICHTON, MAKGILL, and MAITLAND, quartered.
Crests—A lion, sejant, affronté, gu., ducally crowned, holding in the dexter paw a sword, ppr., pommel and hilt, or, in the sinister a fleur-de-lis, az., for MAITLAND. A dragon's head, erased, spouting fire, ppr., for CRICHTON. A phœnix, in flames, ppr.
Supporters—Two lions, az., armed and crowned, or.
Motto—Sine fine.
Seats—Rankeilour, and Barham Cottage, co. Fife.

CROFT OF STILLINGTON HALL.

CROFT, HARRY, Esq. of Stillington Hall, co. York, *b.* 9 May, 1775; *m.* 20 June, 1822, Elizabeth, 2nd dau. of William Charlton, Esq. of Apley Castle, co. Salop, and has issue,

I. HARRY. II. Stephen.
I. Elizabeth-Catherine. II. Louisa-Frances.

Mr. Croft *s.* his father, the late Stephen Croft, Esq., in Aug. 1813. He is a colonel in the army, and a magistrate and deputy-lieutenant of the county.

Lineage.—This family derives from a common ancestor with the ancient house of CROFT *of Croft Castle*, co. Hereford. Its immediate progenitor,

HENRY CROFT, Esq. of East Witton, North Riding of Yorkshire (descended out of Lancashire), was father of

CHRISTOPHER CROFT, Esq. of East Witton, styled of Cottescue Park, co. York, in 1611, whose son,

SIR CHRISTOPHER CROFT, lord-mayor of York in 1629 and 1641, was knighted by CHARLES I., upon entertaining that monarch and suite at his house, the 20th Nov. in the last mentioned year. Sir Christopher *d.* 5 July, 1649; his only surviving son and heir,

THOMAS CROFT, Esq. of Stillington, bapt. 22 Dec. 1619, *m.* 26 May, 1640, Olive, dau. and heir of John Dunstey, Esq. of Bramhope, and *d.* in 1654, having had, with other issue, two sons, JOHN, his heir; and THOMAS, successor to his brother. The former,

JOHN CROFT, Esq. of Stillington, *m.* in Jan. 1673, Anne, 2nd dau. of Lionel Copley, Esq. of Wadsworth, by whom he had an only child, Olive, who *d.* in her infancy in June, 1675. He *d.* in 1677, and was *s.* by his brother,

THOMAS CROFT, Esq. of Stillington, who *m.* 11 May, 1681, Frances, dau. of Sir Stephen Thompson, Knt., by whom he had numerous issue. He *d.* in 1711, and was *s.* by his elder son,

STEPHEN CROFT, Esq. of Stillington, bapt. 14 Nov. 1683, who *m.* in 1711, Elizabeth, dau. of Sir Edmund Anderson, Bart. of Broughton, co. Lincoln, and *d.* in 1733, leaving three sons,

STEPHEN, his heir, of whom presently.
THOMAS, *b.* 15 Oct. 1717, grandfather of the present SIR JOHN CROFT, Bart. of Cowling Hall, co. York.
John, of York, *b.* 28 Feb. 1732, sheriff of York in 1773, *m.* 6 June, 1774, Judith, dau. of Francis Bacon, Esq. senior alderman of York, and had issue two sons, Francis, *b.* 5 Dec. 1776, and John, *d.* at York, 14 May, 1786, aged eleven.

The eldest son,

STEPHEN CROFT, Esq. of Stillington, *b.* in London, 8 Dec. 1712, *m.* Henrietta, dau. of Henry Thompson, Esq. of Kirby Hall, and by her, who *d.* in 1772, left at his decease, 12 Sept. 1798, two sons and one dau., viz.,

STEPHEN, his heir.
Robert-Nicholas, *b.* 8 June, 1754, in holy orders, prebendary of Botevant, and canon-residentiary of St. Peter's Cathedral at York. He *m.* Elizabeth, 3rd dau. and coheir of George-Wanley Bowes, Esq. of Hanwell, co. Middlesex, and, with other issue, was father of the Ven. James Croft, the present Archdeacon of Canterbury.
Frances.
Henrietta-Catherine, *m.* to N. Cholmley, Esq. of Whitby and Howsham.

The elder son and heir,

STEPHEN CROFT, Esq. of Stillington, *m.* in 1764, Frances Clarke, of Askham Bryan, co. York, and had issue,

HARRY, his heir and present representative.
William, rear-admiral R.N., *m.* Harriet, dau. of Hall Plumer, Esq. of Bilton Hall, co. York, and niece of Sir Thomas Plumer, Master of the Rolls, and had issue four sons and six daus.
Sarah.
Lucy, *m.* to George Anderson, Esq. of Newcastle-on-Tyne.

Mr. Croft *d.* in Aug. 1813, and was *s.* by his eldest son, the present COLONEL HARRY CROFT, of Stillington.

Arms—Quarterly, indented, erminois and gu.; in the first quarter a lion, passant-guardant, of the second.
Crest—A lion, passant-guardant, per pale indented, gu. and erminois, the dexter fore-paw resting on a shield; quarterly indented, as in the arms.
Motto—Esse quam videri.
Seat—Stillington Hall, co. York.

CROFT OF GREENHAM LODGE.

CROFT, ARCHER-JAMES, Esq. of Greenham Lodge, co. Berks, *b.* 13 Feb. 1790; *m.* 1st, 14 March, 1811, Frances-Charlotte, eldest dau. of Harry Mount, Esq. of Wasing, and Frances-Dorothea his wife, and by her had issue,

I. Frances-Charlotte, *m.* in 1830, the Chevalier da Silveira.
II. Charlotte-Elizabeth, *d.* young.

Mr. Croft *m.* 2ndly, 13 Nov. 1834, Elizabeth, eldest dau. of Henry-Boyle Deane, Esq., and by her has issue,

I. Archer-Bernard, *b.* 12 Aug. 1838.
II. James-Henry-Herbert, *b.* 14 May, 1840.
I. Elizabeth-Charlotte. II. Charlotte-Susanna.

Lineage.—The family of Croft, which is of Saxon origin, settled in Herefordshire at a very remote period. Camden, in his description of that county, says: "Not far off [from Richard's Castle] stands Croft Castle, belonging to the very ancient and knightly family of the Crofts;" and in *Domesday Book*, Bernard de Croft is mentioned as holding the lands of Croft, which his descendants inherited until the close of the 18th century.

Charlotte-Elizabeth Croft, eldest dau. and co-heir of Sir Archer Croft, Bart. of Croft Castle, co. Hereford, by Elizabeth-Charlotta his wife, dau. of Ashley Cowper, Esq. *m.* in 1778, James Woodcock, Esq. of Berkhampstead, and that gentleman assumed, in consequence, the surname and arms of Croft, by royal license, in 1792. The issue of the alliance were four sons and six daus., viz.,

Archer-James, the present representative.
James-William, *b.* in 1792; *m.* in 1818, Anna-Eliza, dau. of Sir Edward-Hyde East, Bart., and had an only son, Edward Nugent, deceased.
John-Thomas, major 34th nat. inf. E. I., *b.* in 1794.
Ashley-Cowper, *b.* in 1800; *m.* Anne, dau. of Mr. Charles Bellinger, but *d. s. p.* 28 May, 1883.
Charlotte-Harriet, *d.* young.
Harriet-Dorothea.
Charlotte-Elizabeth, *m.* in 1809, to the Hon. and Right Rev. Edward Grey, Bishop of Hereford, youngest son of Earl Grey, and is deceased.
Theodora-Mary. Margaret-Frances, deceased.
Fanny, *m.* to William Critchell, Esq. R.N.

Mr. Croft *d.* in Jan. 1829, and was buried at Greenham Chapel.

Arms—Quarterly: per fesse indented, az. and arg.; in the first quarter, a lion, passant-guardant, or.
Crest—A wyvern, sa., vulned in the side, gu. (Prior to 1520, the crest borne by the family was a lion, passant-guardant, arg.)
Motto—Esse quam videri.
Seat—Greenham Lodge, Berks.

CROFTS OF VELVETSTOWN.

Crofts, The Rev. William, Esq. of Velvetstown, co. Cork, *b.* 19 Aug. 1791.

Lineage.—This family, as well as that of Churchtown, derives from a common ancestor with the ancient English house of Crofts *of Westow and Saxham*, co. Suffolk, of which was William, Lord Crofts, so created 10 Charles II. The immediate ancestor of the Irish branch had two sons, one the progenitor of the Crofts *of Velvetstown*, the other of the Crofts *of Churchtown*, but the seniority of these sons has not been ascertained. The former,

George Crofts, Esq. of Velvetstown, co. Cork, had (with several daus., of whom Mary *m.* William Dunscombe, Esq. of Mount Desert) three sons, Christopher, of Velvetstown, *d. unm.*; George, of whom we have to treat; and William. The 2nd son,

George Crofts, Esq. of Velvetstown and Cahircalla, co. Clare, whose will is dated 24 March, 1718, *m.* a dau. of — Freeman, Esq. of Cahirmee, co. Cork, and had (with two daus., Elizabeth, *m.* in 1703, to Jacob Ringrose, Esq.; and Anne, *m.* to George Redman, Esq.) two sons, of whom the elder,

Christopher Crofts, Esq. of Velvetstown, *b.* in 1694, *m.* 1st, Mary, dau. of Peter Graham, Esq. of Dromore and of Conveymore, both in the co. of Cork, and had issue,

George, of Stream Hill, co. Cork, *b.* in 1724, *m.* Mary, dau. of Cornelius Holmes, Esq. of Shinnanah, in the same co., and *d.* in 1801, leaving (with five daus., Catherine; Margaret, *m.* to Lewis Smith, Esq.; Susan, wife of Robert Philpot, Esq. of Newmarket, co. Cork; Mary, wife of Roger Atkins, Esq. of Roseagh; and Eleanor) a son and heir, Christopher, of Stream Hill, *b.* in 1737, who *m.* 1st, Christian, dau. of Charles Creed, Esq. of Ballynanty, co. Limerick, and by her had three daus., 1 Christian, *m.* to — Goold; 2 Mary, *m.* to Henry Lee, Esq. of Barna, co. Tipperary; and 3 Anne. He *m.* 2ndly, Anne, dau. of Richard Crone, Esq. of Ballydineen, co. Cork, and *d.* 10 Nov. 1837, aged 90, leaving by this latter lady, with other children, a son and heir, George Crofts, Esq. of Stream Hill, who is married, and has issue.
William, of Velvetstown, of whom presently.
Christopher.
Mary, *m.* to John Bond, Esq. of Ballynahilish, co. Cork.
Catherine, *m.* to John Wilkinson, Esq. of Johnstown, co. Cork.

Mr. Crofts *m.* 2ndly, Mary, dau. of William Austen, Esq. of co. Cork, and by her had one dau., who *d.* young. He *d.* 9 July, 1757; his 2nd son,

William Crofts, Esq. of Velvetstown, *b.* in 1726, *m.* 1754, Elizabeth, dau. of John Beere, Esq. of Gurteen, co. Cork, and by her (who *d.* aged 86, in 1813) left at his decease, in 1784, seven sons and four daus., of whom were,

I. Christopher, his heir.
II. George, *b.* 23 Oct. 1763, *m.* 1st, Jane, dau. of Robert Johnson, Esq. of Cork, and had a son, William, deceased. He *m.* 2ndly, Sarah, relict of Humphries Manders, Esq., and by her had a dau., *m.* to William-Prittie Harris, Esq. of Lakeview, co. Cork.
III. William, of Danesfort, co. Cork, *b.* 1 Aug. 1765, *m.* Catherine-Anne, dau. of Bartholomew Gibbins, Esq. of Gibbins Grove, in the same co., and *d.* 20 Dec. 1801, having had a son, William, who *d.* young, and four daus., co-heiresses, viz., 1 Elizabeth, *m.* to the Rev. John Beasley, and had issue three daus., Anne, Jane, and Elizabeth; 2 Anne, *m.* to the Rev. Arthur-Bernard Baldwin, vicar of Raghan, co. Cork; 3 Jane, *m.* to George-Sackville Cotter, Esq., capt. in the 69th regt., nephew of the late Sir James-L. Cotter, Bart.; 4 Wilhelmina, *m.* to John Wrixon, Esq., Jun., of Sommerville, co. Cork.
IV. James, *b.* 31 July, 1766, *m.* Jane, dau. of Aylmer Allen, Esq. of Woodview, co. Cork, and had issue, William, M.D., deceased; Aylmer; James-Nelson, *m.* Dora, relict of Patrick Brown, Esq. of Foxhall; George; Elizabeth; Mary-Anne, *m.* to Benjamin Sweete, Esq. of Ballynascarty; Anne; and Jane.
V. Richard, *b.* 7 June, 1767, *m.* Sarah, sister of Carden Terry, Esq., and *d.* 5 June, 1823, leaving, 1 William, *m.* Marian, eldest dau. of Richard-Giffard Campion, Esq. of Bushy Park, and has issue five daus., Mary, Sarah, Martha, Wilhelmina, and Catherine; 2 Carden-Terry, *m.* his cousin, Ruth, dau. of Christopher Crofts, Esq. of Velvetstown, and has issue, Richard and Christopher, and Mary; 3 Richard, *d. unm.*; 1 Catherine, *m.* to Carden-S. Williams; 2 Eliza, *m.* to John Williams; and 3 Sarah.
VI. Robert, *b.* 10 March, 1769, *m.* Mary, dau. of Thomas Nash, Esq. of Rockfield, co. Cork, and *d.* 21 May, 1818, having had issue.
VII. Charles, *b.* 18 April, 1770, *d. unm.*
I. Ruth, *m.* to Michael Busteed, Esq., mayor of Cork in 1801.
II. Mary, *m.* to her cousin, William Fitzgerald, Esq. of co. Clare.
III. Catherine, *m.* to Charles O'Keefe, Esq. of Mount Keefe, co. Cork.
IV. Elizabeth, *m.* to Robert Kean, Esq. of Hermitage, co. Clare.

The eldest son and heir,

Christopher Crofts, Esq. of Velvetstown, *b.* 5 March, 1755, *m.* in 1782, Mary, dau. of Thomas Lucas, Esq. of Richfordstown, co. Cork, by Dorothy his wife, dau. of Thomas Evans, Esq. of Miltown Castle, co. Limerick, and by her, who *d.* 1 June, 1838, aged 80, had issue,

Thomas-Lucas, of Velvetstown, *d. unm.* in 1851.
William, in holy orders, now of Velvetstown.
Christopher, *b.* 3 Nov. 1792, *m.* in 1824, Alice, dau. of Richard Nason, Esq. of Bettyville, co. Cork, and has issue, Christopher and Richard-Nason, and a dau.
Dorah, *m.* to Henry Langley, Esq. of Ballyellis, co. Cork.
Elizabeth, *m.* to John Nash, Esq. of Rockfield, co. Cork.
Ruth, *m.* to her cousin, Carden-S. Crofts, Esq.

Mr. Christopher Crofts *d.* 21 June, 1811.

Arms—Or, three bull's heads, caboссed, sa.
Crest—A bull's head, cabossed, sa.
Motto—Virtute et fidelitate.
Seat—Velvetstown, co. Cork.

CROFTS OF CHURCHTOWN.

Crofts, Freeman, Esq. of Cloheen House, co. Cork, J.P., barrister-at-law, *b.* 3 July, 1816; *m.* 24 Dec. 1851, Ellen, youngest dau. of the late Joseph Deane-Freeman, Esq. of Castle Cor, co. Cork, and has a son,

Freeman-Wills, *b.* 11 April, 1853.

Lineage.—The first immediate ancestor of the Churchtown branch of the Crofts was a brother of George Crofts, of Velvetstown, but whether older or younger has not been ascertained. His eldest son,

George Crofts, Esq. of Churchtown, M.P. for Charleville, *d.* in 1698, leaving, by Sarah his wife, a son and heir,

George Crofts, Esq. of Churchtown, high-sheriff in 1712, who *m.* Mary, dau. and eventual co-heir of Thomas Wills, Esq. of Wills Grove, and *d.* in 1741, leaving issue. The eldest son,

George Crofts, Esq. of Churchtown, a capt. in Colonel Hargrave's regiment, *d. unm.*, and was *s.* by his only surviving brother,

Wills Crofts, Esq. of Churchtown, J.P., *b.* 24 Dec. 1718, who *m.* in 1743, Eleanor, dau. of Robert Freeman, Esq. of Ballinguile, co. Cork, son of William Freeman, Esq. of Castle Cor, and by her, who *d.* in 1792, had issue,

I. George, his heir.
II. Freeman, in holy orders, *b.* 11 Aug. 1748, *m.* in Aug. 1781, Anna, eldest dau. of John Spread, Esq. of Forrest, co. Cork, and by her, who *d.* in 1827, had issue,
  1 Freeman-Wills, now of Churchtown.
  2 John-Spread, lieut. in the 87th regt., *b.* 1790, *d.* at Trinidad, 1807.
  3 George, in holy orders, *m.* Elizabeth, eldest surviving dau. of the Rev. Mathew Purcell, rector of Burton, co. Cork.
  1 Anastasia-Earbury, *d.* young.
  2 Hannah, *d.* young, in 1800. 3 Elena, *d. unm.*
  4 Alicia, *m.* in 1818, to Thomas Milward, Esq., and *d.* in 1832, leaving a dau., *m.* in 1839, to George Wood, Esq., barrister-at-law.
III. Wills, *b.* in 1750, a capt. in the 84th regt. He *m.* Mary, dau. of Richard Gason, Esq. of Killeshallagh, co. Tipperary, and left an only dau. and heiress, Mary, *m.* in 1805, to John Bennett, Esq., eldest son of the Right Hon. Judge Bennett.
I. Alicia, *m.* in 1770, to Richard Gason, Esq. of Richmond, co. Tipperary.

The eldest son and heir,

George Crofts, Esq. of Churchtown, *b.* 22 April, 1745, *m.* Mary, eldest dau. of Francis Greene, Esq. of Greenmount, co. Limerick, and by her, who *d.* in 1787, left at his decease, in 1801, an only son and heir,

Wills-George Crofts, Esq. of Churchtown, of St. John's College, Cambridge, barrister-at-law, and high-sheriff of co. Cork in 1822, *d. unm.* 10 Nov. 1826, and was *s.* by his first-cousin,

The Rev. Freeman-Wills Crofts, of Churchtown, *b.* 22 Sept. 1785, *m.* 1st, 26 May, 1810, Mary-Marten, eldest dau. of the Rev. William Gorman, by Elizabeth his wife, sister of Charles-Kendal Bushe, lord chief justice of the Queen's Bench in Ireland, and by her (who *d.* 16 June, 1823) had issue,

Freeman, present representative.
Wills-George, *b.* 17 April, 1818, *m.* Feb. 1843, Elizabeth, only dau. of James-Grove White, Esq. of Kilburn, co. Cork, and has issue.
William-Fortescue, *b.* 28 April, 1822.
Anne-Spread.
Catherine-Doyle, *m.* Oct. 1845, to Richard Gason, Esq. of Richmond, co. Tipperary.
Maria-Marten, *m.* in May, 1853, to Justin Deane-Freeman, Esq., 5th son of the late Joseph Deane-Freeman, Esq. of Castle Cor.

The Rev. Freeman-Wills Crofts *m.* 2ndly, Jane-Hannah, relict of William Jameson, Esq., and dau. of the late Henry Milward, Esq., but by her (who *d.* 31 May, 1854) had no issue. He *d.* 9 Aug. 1849.

Arms, Crest, and *Motto*—As Crofts *of Velvetstown.*
Seat—Cloheen House, co. Cork.

CROFTON OF LAKEFIELD.

Crofton, Duke, Esq. of Lakefield, co. Leitrim, *s.* his father 10 Dec. 1845.

Lineage.—Duke Crofton, Esq. of Lakefield, co. Leitrim, who *m.* twice: 1st, Mary Crofton; and 2ndly, Maria, youngest dau. of the late James Webster, Esq. of Longford, left, with a dau., Susan, *m.* to the Rev. Henry Crofton, 2nd son of the late Sir Morgan Crofton, Bart., a son,

Duke Crofton, Esq. of Lakefield, J.P. and D.L., high-sheriff in 1800, *b.* 13 Nov. 1768, and *m.* 18 Aug. 1808, Alicia, eldest dau. of the late William Jones, Esq. of Belleville, co. Westmeath, by whom he had issue,

Duke, now of Lakefield.
William, M.D., *m.* 31 March, 1848, Fanny-E., only dau. of Capt. Dunn, R.N. of Cheltenham.
John, in holy orders, *m.* 1st, July, 1843, Anne Newcomen, youngest dau. of the late Berry Norris, Esq. of Mohill, co. Leitrim.
Richard-Henry, capt. royal artillery, *m.* 22 June, 1848, Fanny-M., 2nd dau. of the late Arthur-Cuthbert Marsh, Esq. of Eastbury, Herts.
Henry-Robert, capt. R.N., *m.* 13 April, 1850, Bessie, dau. of Dr. Singer, Bishop of Meath.
Travers, capt. 52nd Madras native infantry, *m.* 7 April, 1850, Annie-E., eldest dau. of the late James Singer, Esq. M.D.
Gustavus-St.John, royal engineers.

Mary, *m.* 30 Sept. 1846, to Charles Stanhope, youngest son of the late Rev. Henry Crofton.
Alicia-Maria.

Arms—Per pale, indented, or and az., a lion, passant-guardant, counterchanged.
Crest—Seven stalks of wheat on one stalk, ppr.
Motto—Dat Deus incrementum.
Seat—Lakefield, co. Leitrim.

CROKE OF STUDLEY.

Croke, George, Esq. of Studley Priory, co. Oxford, *s.* his father 27 Dec. 1842.

Lineage.—The surname of this family was originally Le Blount, and Sir Alexander Croke claimed, in his *History of the Blounts*, to be representative of the senior branch of that ancient house, which had its own origin from the Blondi, or Brondi, of Italy.

James Croke *alias* Le Blount (son of Nicholas Le Blount, who changed his name to Croke to avoid state persecution), was fourth in descent from Sir Ralph Blount, elder brother of Sir William Le Blount, ancestor of the Blounts *of Sodington.* From him sprang the Crokes *of Chilton*, so distinguished in our legal annals, and the Crokes *of Studley Priory.* The late

Sir Alexander Croke, Knt., of Studley Priory, *b.* 22 July, 1758 (son of Alexander Croke, Esq. of Studley, and great-grandson of the Rev. Alexander Croke, M.A. of Wadham College, Oxford, the friend and companion of Creech the poet, 4th in descent from Sir John Croke, of Chilton), was called to the bar, and became judge of one of the Vice-Admiralty Courts in North America. In 1823 he was elected a bencher of the Inner Temple, and appointed, in 1829, treasurer of that society. He *m.* in 1796, Miss Alice Blake, and had issue, I. Alexander, *b.* in 1798, *d.* in 1818; II. George, present representative; III. Wentworth, *d. unm.* 12 Sept. 1837; IV. John; and V. Alexander; I. Adelaide; II. Jane-Sarah-Elizabeth, *m.* 28 Dec. 1826, to her cousin, Sir Charles Wetherell, Knt., then attorney-general, and *d.* without surviving issue, 21 April, 1831; III. Anna-Philippa.

Arms—Gu., a fesse between six martlets, arg.
Crest—Two swans' necks, indorsed and interlaced, issuing out of a crescent, all arg., and holding in their beaks an annulet, gu.
Seat—Studley Priory, Oxon.

CROKER OF BALLYNAGARDE.

Croker, John, Esq. of Ballynagarde and Raleighstown, co. Limerick, J.P., high-sheriff in 1832, *b.* 4 Oct. 1784; *m.* 14 Sept. 1810, Catherine-Adeline, youngest dau. of Col. Bagwell, of Marlfield, co. Tipperary, M.P., and has issue,

I. Edward, *b.* 31 Aug. 1812, late capt. in the 17th Lancers, *m.* 17 May, 1841, the Lady Georgiana-Ellen, 6th dau. of the Earl of Rathdowne, and has issue, John, *b.* 16 March, 1842; Henry-Stanley; Frederick-Albert; Edward-William; Courtenay-Le Poer-Trench; Frances; Alice; and Georgiana.
I. Marianne-Margaret. II. Margaret-Anne.
III. Catherine-Adeline-Bagwell, *d.* young.
IV. Henrietta, *m.* to Frederick-John Partridge, Esq., R.N., son of John Partridge, Esq. of Bishop Wood, co. Hereford.
V. Janet, *m.* to Francis Walsh, Esq., son of George Walsh, Esq. of Lisbon.

Lineage.—This is a branch of the house of Crocker (or Crocker) *of Lineham*, co. Devon, a family so ancient that an old proverbial distich records that,

"Croker, Crewys, and Coplestone,
When the Conqueror came, were at home."

Thomas Croker, of Trevillas, in Cornwall, 2nd son of the 8th John Croker, of Lineham, obtained, about the year 1600, the estate of Ballyanker, co. Waterford; and while his eldest son remained at Trevillas, his younger sons, to the number of three or four, migrated to Ireland. They were all probably soldiers; two of them, at least, were so, and distinguished themselves by the extraordinary and almost romantic capture of the city of Waterford in 1650. One of the brothers was killed in the assault; the other, Hugh, after a long course of military service, settled at Ballyanker, and *d.* in 1663; his present representative is Edward Croker, Esq. of Lisnabin, co. Cork. Another of the brothers, Edward Croker, who was murdered in the Irish rebellion of 1641, was ancestor of the respectable and influential family of CROKER *of Ballynagarde*, and of a numerous branch settled in Dublin, to which belonged ANNE, dau. and heir of Thomas Croker, and wife of Sir Edward Crofton, Bart., created in 1797 BARONESS CROFTON in her own right; and the late THOMAS-CROFTON CROKER, Esq., F.S.A.

The great-grandfather of the present representative of the Ballynagarde family,

EDWARD CROKER, Esq. of Rawleighstown, *m.* Elizabeth, eldest dau. of Henry Prittie, Esq. of Dunalley Castle, co. Tipperary, who *d.* in 1738, and was father of

JOHN CROKER, Esq. of Ballynagarde, co. Limerick, who *m.* Mary, dau. of Richard Pennefather, Esq. of New Park, M.P. for the co. of Tipperary in 1738, and had issue, EDWARD, his heir; Henry; John, a general in the army; Richard-William; Charity, *m.* to John Grady, Esq. of Cahir, co. Limerick; Eliza, *m.* to E. Croker, Esq. of Grange Hill; and Sally, *m.* to L. Sandes, Esq. of the Queen's County. The elder son,

EDWARD CROKER, Esq. of Ballynagarde, *m.* in 1783, Margaret-Anne, youngest dau. of Richard Hare, Esq., and sister to William, 1st Earl of Listowel, and had issue,

JOHN, now of Ballynagarde, as above.
Richard-Hare, col. in the army, *m.* Miss Haigh, of Whitwell, co. York, and *d.* 15 Jan. 1854, leaving issue.
Edward, in holy orders, *m.* Miss Lascelles, and has issue.
William, col. in the army, C.B., *m.* Miss Stokes, of Madras, and *d.* 12 Sept. 1852, leaving issue.
Henry, *m.* Miss O'Grady, of Linfield, and has issue.
Charles, commander R.N., *m.* Miss Crowe, and has issue.
Robert, *m.* Miss O'Grady, of The Grange, and *d.* in May, 1848, leaving issue.
Albert, commander R.N., *d.* in 1826, *unm.*
Thomas, in holy orders, *m.* Miss E. Haigh, of Whitwell, and has issue.
Margaret, *m.* to the Very Rev. Richard Bagwell, of Marlfield, Dean of Clogher.
Sarah, *m.* to Major George Gough, eldest son of Colonel Gough, of Woodstown, co. Limerick, brother of Gen. Lord Gough, G.C.B.

Arms—Arg., a chevron, engrailed, gu., between three ravens, ppr.
Crest—A drinking-cup, or, with three fleur-de-lis, ppr., above it, and on the centre, a rose, gu.
Motto—Deus alit eos.
Seat—Ballynagarde, co. Limerick.

CROKER OF WEST MOLESEY.

CROKER, THE RIGHT HON. JOHN-WILSON, P.C., LL.D., F.A.S., of West Molesey, co. Surrey, *b.* 20 Dec. 1780; *m.* 22 May, 1806, Rosamond, eldest dau. of William Pennell, Esq., his Majesty's consul-general at Rio Janeiro, by whom he had a son, who *d.* 15 May, 1820, aged 4 years. Mr. Croker entered Trinity College, Dublin, as a fellow commoner, Nov. 1796, and graduated A.B. in 1800, and LL.D. in 1807. He sat in parliament from 1807 to 1832, and filled the office of secretary to the Admiralty from 1809 to 1830. He is eminently distinguished as a political writer.

Lineage.—WALTER CROKER, Esq. of Tallow, the grandson of Hugh Croker, the captor of Waterford (*see* CROKER *of Ballynagarde*), had, by the dau. of Reginald Bray, an only son,

JOHN CROKER, Esq. of Tallow, who was *b.* 1695, and *d.* in 1743, leaving three sons, Walter, of Tallow; John, of Airhill; and William, of Johnstown. John left male issue, but William left an only dau. and heiress, who *m.* the Hon. Frederick Mullins, son of the 1st Lord Ventry, and by him has issue, Frederick-William De Moleyns, late M.P. for Kerry.

WALTER CROKER, Esq., the eldest son of John, of Tallow, was *b.* in 1728, and *d.* in 1789, leaving, by his wife Sarah, dau. of Edward Devereux, Esq., one son,

JOHN CROKER, Esq., surveyor-general of Ireland, who was *b.* in 1743, and *d.* 29 April, 1814. He was a man of great abilities and most amiable manners, an able and upright public servant, and in private life universally respected and beloved. He *m.* 1st, Catherine Walstead, by whom he had surviving issue,

WALTER, who *d.* in 1807, leaving two daus., CATHERINE, the wife of William Pennell, jun., Esq.; and MARGARET, the wife of Lovell Pennell, Esq. These ladies both have issue.
Catherine, *m.* to William Miller, Esq. of Londonderry, and has issue.

Mr. Croker *m.* 2ndly, in 1779, Hester, only dau. of the Rev. Richard Rathborne, and granddau. of Admiral Wilson, by whom he had two surviving children, the present RIGHT HON. JOHN-WILSON CROKER, and Sarah, who *m.* in 1815, the Very Rev. J.-T. Bond, dean of Ross, and *d.* in 1820. The Surveyor General *d.* 29 April, 1814, at the age of 73.

Arms—Arg., a chevron, engrailed, gu., between three ravens, ppr., quartering the arms of CHURCHILL.
Crest—A drinking-cup, or, with three fleurs-de-lis, ppr., above it, and on the centre a rose.
Mottoes—Deus alit eos; and, J'ay ma foi tenu à ma puissance.
Seats—West Molesey, Surrey, and Alverbank, Gosport.

CROMMELIN OF CARROWDORE CASTLE.

DE LA CHEROIS-CROMMELIN, NICHOLAS, Esq. of Carrowdore Castle, co. Down, J.P. and D.L., *b.* 10 June, 1783; *m.* 17 Dec. 1810, Elizabeth, 2nd dau. of William, 2nd Lord Ventry, and has had by her (who *d.* 12 April, 1820) three sons and four daus., viz.,

I. SAMUEL-ARTHUR-HILL, *m.* 30 Oct. 1845, Anna-Maria, only dau. of John-Graves Thompson, Esq. of the co. Tyrone.
II. Nicholas, *b.* 7 March, 1819, *m.* 8 Jan. 1851, Annie, 2nd dau. of Andrew Mullholland, Esq. of Springvale, co. Down.
III. William-Thomas, in holy orders, vicar of Comber, co. co. Down, *b.* 14 Feb. 1820.
I. Anna-Sarah. II. Maria-Matilda.
III. Clara-Susanne, *d.* young.
IV. Elizabeth-Emily, *m.* 12 July, 1840, to John-Robert Irwin, Esq. of Carnagh, co. Armagh.

Mr. De la Cherois-Crommelin served as high-sheriff of Down in 1821, and for Antrim in 1830.

Lineage.—The CROMMELINS are of French origin, and were possessed of considerable property at Armancour, a village near St Quentin, near Picardy, when the revocation of the Edict of Nantes compelled them, being protestants, to leave their native country.

SAMUEL CROMMELIN, from whom the Irish branch is descended, took refuge in Holland, where he *d.*, leaving issue six children, LOUIS, Samuel, Alexander, William, Magdalene, and Mary. In the year 1698, the family was induced, by King WILLIAM III. of England, to go over to Ireland, where they finally settled at Lisburn, in the co. Antrim, bringing with them a number of tradesmen, and a capital of 20,000*l.*, with which they established the linen manufacture, which was adopted by the natives, and has flourished ever since. In consideration of Louis Crommelin having spent 10,000*l* on its establishment, King WILLIAM, who was much interested in its success, and during his life granted 5*l.* for every loom, conferred on him a pension of 200*l.* a year for the life of his son, who, however, *d.* only three months after, when it was discontinued. Samuel's children were,

I. LOUIS, who *m.* Miss Crommelin, and had issue, Louis, *d. unm.*; and Magdeline, *m.* Captain de Berniere.
II. Samuel, *m.* Miss Bellecastle, dau. of General Bellecastle, and had issue,
  1 Samuel-Louis, who *m.* 1st, Mademoiselle Gilliotte, and 2ndly, Harriet Mangen, by whom he had eight children, Abraham, who *m.* 1st, Catherine Laurent, and 2ndly, Anna Carden, and *d.* leaving no issue; Samuel; Mary; Harriet; Jane; Anna; Magdeline; who all *d. unm.*; and Alexander, who *m.* Miss Neland, and had two daus., Mary, *m.* Daniel de la Cherois, Esq. of Donaghadee, co. Down; and Jane, *m.* R. Hamond, Esq.
  2 Daniel, *m.* Madelaine, only dau. of Major de la Cherois, by whom he had three sons, Nicholas, *d. unm.*; Daniel, *d. unm.*; and De la Cherois, who *m.* Elizabeth, dau. of — Piers, Esq., and had a dau., Mary-Angelica, who *m.* the Rev. Dr. Francis Hutcheson, and was mother of Elizabeth, *m.* to George Leslie, Esq., brother of James Leslie, Esq. of Leslie Hill, co. Antrim.
  3 James, who *m.* Mademoiselle Gilliotte, and *d. s. p.*
  4 John, who *m.* Mademoiselle de Blaquiere, and had issue, Isaac, who *m.* in Holland.
III. Alexander, who *m.* Mademoiselle Lavalade, and had a son, Charles, who *d. unm.*, and a dau. Magdeline, *m.* to the Rev. Archdeacon Hutcheson, by who he had, Samuel; Frances, *m.* to D. Browne, Esq.; and Matilda, *m.* to R. Smythe, of Drumcree, co. Westmeath.
IV. William, *m.* Miss Butler, of the Ormonde family, and had a son, Louis, *d. unm.*, and a dau., Maryanne.
V. Magdeline, *m.* Paul Mangen, Esq.
VI. MARY, *m.* to Major de la Cherois (*see* DE LA CHEROIS *of Donaghadee.*)

The younger dau., MARY, wife of Major de la Cherois, had a son,

SAMUEL DE LA CHEROIS, whose 4th son,

SAMUEL DE LA CHEROIS, Esq., *b* in 1744, assumed, in compliance with the will of his cousin, Nicholas Crommelin, Esq. of Lisburne, the additional surname of CROMMELIN. He *m.* 16 April, 1776, Maria, only dau. of the Rev. Dr. Thomas Dobbs, fellow of Trinity Coll., Dublin (brother of Conway Dobbs, Esq. of Castle Dobbs, co. Antrim, Governor of North Carolina), by Mary his wife, dau. of J. Young, Esq. of Lisanae, in Tyrone, and had issue,

NICHOLAS, now of Carrowdore Castle.
Richard, brigade-major to the forces in the island of Curacoa, *d.* there *unm.* 1810.
Mary, *d. unm.* 1842.
Sarah, *m.* in 1807, to William Irwin, Esq. of Mount Irwin, co. Armagh.
Anne, *m.* in 1798, to Henry Purdon, M.D. of Rathwire, in Westmeath.
Harriet-Judith, *m.* in 1808, to Henry-Aldborough Head, Esq., lieut.-col. 7th dragoon-guards, 2nd son of Michael Head, Esq. of Derry Castle, co. Tipperary.
Jane-Suzanna, *m.* in 1817, to Thomas-Richard Bruce, Esq., R.N., 2nd son of the late Edward Bruce, Esq. of Kilroot, in Antrim.

Mr. De la Cherois-Crommelin *d.* in 1816.

Arms—Quarterly: 1st and 4th az., on a chevron, between three martlets, arg., a trefoil, slipped, vert, for CROMMELIN; 2nd and 3rd, gu., a chevron between three mullets, in chief, or, and in base an anchor, arg., for DE LA CHEROIS.
Crest—For CROMMELIN, out of a ducal coronet, or, a swan rising, ppr.; and for DE LA CHEROIS, an anchor, az.
Supporters—Two griffins regardant, gu., guttée d'or.
Motto—Fac et spera.
Seat—Carrowdore Castle, Downshire.

CROMPTON OF DUFFIELD HALL.

CROMPTON, JOHN-BELL, Esq. of Duffield Hall, co. Derby, J.P. and D.L., *b.* 12 Jan. 1785; *m.* 8 Sept. 1810, Jane, 3rd dau. of Edward-Sacheverell Sitwell, Esq. of Stainsby, and by her (who *d.* 17 Dec. 1852) had a dau.,

JANE, *m.* 3 July, 1834, to Lorenzo-Kirkpatrick Hall, Esq. nephew of J.-K. Hall, Esq. of Holly Bush, in Staffordshire, and *d.* 28 Jan. 1835.

Lineage.—SAMUEL CROMPTON, Esq. of Derby, an eminent banker, (eldest son of Abraham Crompton, who settled at Derby, brother of Abraham and John Crompton, of Chorley,* and grandson of the Rev. John Crompton, M.A., who *d.* in 1669), *m.* 3 April, 1710, Anne, dau. of William Rodes, Esq. of Long Houghton Hall, co. York, and had by her (who *d.* 16 May, 1724) three sons and one dau., viz.,

I. SAMUEL, his heir.
II. John, of Derby.
III. Joshua, of Derby, who *m.* in 1758, the dau. and heiress of the Rev. Thomas Colthurst, presbyterian minister at Chester, and had issue,
  1 Thomas, *d. s. p.*, aged 22.
  2 Peter, M D., of Eaton House, near Liverpool, *m.* his cousin Mary, dau. of John Crompton, Esq. of Chorley, and had issue, Edward and Henry, who both are *unm.*; Charles (Sir), one of the Judges of the Court of Queen's Bench, *b.* in 1797, *m.* in 1832, the 4th dau. of Thomas Fletcher, Esq. of Liverpool, and has issue; Albert, barrister-at-law, *d. unm.* in 1841; Stamford, deceased; Caroline, *m.* to Robert Hutton, Esq. of Putney Park, late M.P. for Dublin; and Emma.
I. Rebecca, buried at Duffield, 15 March, 1788, aged 67.

Mr. Crompton *d.* in 1757, and was *s.* by his eldest son,

SAMUEL CROMPTON, Esq., mayor of Derby, in 1758 and 1767, and in 1768 high-sheriff of the county, for which he was during many years receiver-general. He *m.* at Osmaston, 8 May, 1744, Elizabeth, only dau. of Samuel Fox, Esq., and by her (who *d.* 29 April, 1789, aged 71), had four sons and one dau. viz.,

I. SAMUEL, of Woodend, father of the late SIR SAMUEL CROMPTON, Bart.
II. JOHN, of whom presently.
III. Joshua, of York, father of WILLIAM-ROOKES CROMPTON-STANSFIELD, Esq. of Esholt Hall, co. York. (*Refer to that family.*)
IV. Gilbert, also of York, *b.* in 1755, who *m.* Eliza, dau. of the Rev. George Johnson, rector of Loftus, in the North Riding of Yorkshire, and vicar of Norton, co. Durham, and had issue,
  1 Samuel-Gilbert, in holy orders, *m.* Clara, daughter of Richard Down, Esq. of Halliwick Manor House, Middlesex, by Rose his wife, dau. and heir of Henry Neale, Esq., and has issue.
  2 George, captain 40th regiment, *d.* in the West Indies, Jan. 1815.
  3 Robert, a naval officer.
  4 William, in the army.
  1 Anne.
I. Elizabeth.

The second son,

JOHN CROMPTON, Esq. of The Lilies, Duffield, Derbyshire, mayor of Derby five times from 1792 to 1826, and high-sheriff of the county in 1810. He acted for a long time as receiver-general, and as a justice of the peace. He *m.* in 1784, Eliza, only dau. of Archibald Bell, Esq. of Manchester, and by her (who *d.* in March, 1807) had issue,

I. JOHN-BELL, of Duffield Hall.
II. Gilbert, of Durant Hall, Chesterfield, J.P. and D.L., *b.* Sept. 1786, *m.* in 1817, Deborah-Catharine, dau. of the Rev. George Bossley, vicar of Chesterfield, and had issue,
  1 John-Gilbert, *b.* 1820, *m.* 1852, Millicent-Ursula, dau. of Henry Smedley, Esq. barrister-at-law, and has issue.
  2 George.
  1 Deborah-Sarah, *m.* in 1845, to the Rev. A. C. Bromehead.
  2 Mary-Anne.
I. Elizabeth, *m.* in Dec. 1810, Thomas Kirkpatrick Hall, Esq. of Holly Bush, in Staffordshire, and *d.* in 1836.
II. Sarah-Maria, *m.* in Oct. 1827, to the Rev. Charles-Robert Hope.

Mr. Crompton *d.* in 1834.

Arms—Vert, on a bend, arg., double-cotised, erm., between two covered cups, or, a lion, passant, gu.; on a chief, az., three pheons, or.
Crest—A demi-horse, rampant, vulned in the breast by an arrow, or, shafted and feathered, arg.
Seat—Duffield Hall, Derby.

CROMWELL OF CHESHUNT PARK.

Representative of the Protector.

CROMWELL, ELIZABETH-OLIVERIA, of Cheshunt Park, co. Herts, *b.* 8 June, 1777; *m.* 18 June, 1801, Thomas-Artemidorus Russell, Esq. (son of John Russell, of Thruxton's Court, co. Hereford), and had issue,

I. Antemidorus-Cromwell Russell, *b.* 20 Aug. 1803, *m.* 4 Oct. 1825, Averilla Armstrong, and *d.*, leaving a dau.
II. JOHN-HENRY-CROMWELL RUSSELL, of Sittingbourne, *b.* 29 Aug. 1807; *m.* 14 Aug. 1832, Eliza, only dau. of Morris Lievesley, Esq.
III. Thomas-Artemidorus Russell, *b.* 25 Oct. 1810.
IV. Charles-William-Cromwell Russell, *b.* 18 May, 1814.
I. Elizabeth-Oliveria Russell, *m.* 17 Nov. 1823, to Frederick-Joseph, only son of Frederick Prescott, Esq. of Theobalds Grove, Herts.
II. Mary-Esther Russell, *m.* 14 Aug. 1832, to Lieutenant-General George-Andrew Armstrong, who *d.* in 1834.
III. Letitia-Cromwell Russell, *m.* 4 Nov. 1847, to Frederick Whitfield, Esq.
IV. Emma-Bridget Russell, *m.* 2 June, 1834, to Capt. Warner.

Mrs. Russell *s.* her father, Oliver Cromwell, Esq., 18 June, 1821, and became representative of the family of CROMWELL.

Lineage.—The family of the PROTECTOR, which arose in Wales, and was deemed illustrious by the genealogists of the Principality, bore the surname of CROMWELL by assumption only, its patronymic, WILLIAMS, having been abandoned at the special desire of King HENRY VIII.

SIR RICHARD WILLIAMS, eldest son of Morgan Williams (of ancient Welsh descent), by his wife, a sister of Thomas Cromwell, Earl of Essex, assumed, at the desire of HENRY VIII., the surname of his uncle, CROMWELL, and through the influence of that once powerful relative, himself and his family obtained wealth and station. Sir Richard Cromwell served the office of sheriff for the counties of Cambridge and Huntingdon, in 1541, and was member for the latter shire in the parliament which began 16 Jan. 1542. He *m.* in 1518, Frances, dau. and co-heir of the then lord-mayor of London, Sir Thomas Murfyn, of Ely, and had two sons, of whom the elder,

SIR HENRY CROMWELL, of Hinchinbrooke, received the honour of knighthood from Queen ELIZABETH, in 1563, and the same year was returned to parliament by the co. of

* Of the Chorley branch of the family was Hannah, eldest daughter of John Crompton, of Chorley Hall, Esq., who *m.* Thomas Stamford, Esq. of Derby, and had two daughters, of whom Elisabeth *m.* James Caldwell, of Linley Wood, Esq. (*See* CALDWELL *of Linley Wood.*)

Huntingdon. He was sheriff for the shires of Huntingdon and Cambridge in the 7th, 13th, 22nd, and 34th of ELIZABETH. Sir Henry m. twice, but had issue only by Joan, dau. of Sir Ralph Warren, Knt., his 1st wife, namely, 1 OLIVER (SIR), K.B., who inherited Hinchinbrooke at his father's decease, in 1603; 2 ROBERT, of whom presently; 3 Henry of Upwood; 4 Richard; 5 Philip (Sir), of Biginhome, m. Mary, dau. of Sir Henry Tounsend, chief-justice of Chester; 6 Ralph; 1 Joan, m. to Sir Frances Barington, Bart.; 2 Elizabeth, m. to William Hampden, Esq. of Great Hampden, and by him was mother of JOHN HAMPDEN, the patriot; 3 Frances, m. to Richard Whalley, Esq. of Kirkston; 4 Mary, m. to Sir William Dunch, of Little Wittenham; 5 Dorothy, m. to Sir Thomas Fleming, son of the Lord Chief-Justice. The second son,

ROBERT CROMWELL, settled in the town of Huntingdon, and became a brewer there. He m. Elizabeth, dau. of William Stewart, Esq. of Ely, and widow of William Lynn, Esq., and had surviving issue,

OLIVER, his successor,
Catherine, m. 1st, to Capt. Roger Whitstone, and 2ndly, to Colonel John Jones.
Margaret, m. to Colonel Valentine Waughton.
Anne, m. to John Sewster, Esq. of Wistow.
Jane, m. to John Desbrow, Esq.
Robina, m. 1st, to Doctor Peter French, canon of Christ Church, Oxford (by whom she had an only dau. Elizabeth, wife of John Tillotson, Archbishop of Canterbury), and 2ndly, to Dr. John Wilkins, Bishop of Chester.

Robert Cromwell, who sat in parliament for the borough of Huntingdon, d. in 1617, leaving his son,

OLIVER CROMWELL, then a youth of 18, having been born in the parish of St. John, Huntingdon, on the 25th April, 1599. He m. on the 20th Aug. 1620, ELIZABETH BOURCHIER, dau. of Sir James Bourchier, of Fitsted, in Essex, and had by that lady nine children, of whom survived infancy,

I. ROBERT, b. in 1621, d. unm. before his father.
II. OLIVER, b. in 1622, killed in 1648, fighting under the parliamentary banner.
III. RICHARD, who s. his father in the PROTECTORATE, m. Dorothy, dau. of Richard Major, Esq. of Hursley, in Hants, and left surviving issue,
1 Elizabeth, who d. unm. in 1731.
2 Anne, m. to Thomas Gibson, M.D., physician-general to the army, and d. s. p. in 1727.
3 Dorothy, m. to John Mortimer, Esq. of the county of Somerset, and d. in 1681.
IV. HENRY, of whom presently.
I. BRIDGET, m. 1st, in 1746-7, to Lieut.-Gen. Henry Ireton, Lord-Deputy of Ireland, and m. 2ndly, General Charles Fleetwood, also Lord-Deputy of Ireland, and d. in 1681.
II. ELIZABETH, m. in 1645-6, to John Claypole, Esq. of Norborough, co. Northampton, master of the horse to the Protector, and d. in 1658.
III. MARY, m. in 1657, to Thomas Belasyse, Viscount (afterwards Earl of) Fauconberg, and d. s. p. in 1712-13.
IV. FRANCES, m. 1st, in 1657, to the Hon. Robert Rich, grandson of Robert, Earl of Warwick, and 2ndly, to Sir John Russell, Bart. of Chippenham, in Cambridgeshire. Her ladyship d. in 1720-1.

Cromwell, after a series of military triumphs, was declared LORD PROTECTOR on the 12th December, 1653, and inaugurated on the 16th of the same month. He d. at Whitehall, on the 3rd Sept. 1658, and was publicly interred, with regal pomp, in HENRY VII.'s chapel, on the 23rd Nov. following. His 4th son,

HENRY CROMWELL, b. 20 Jan. 1627-8, was lord-deputy of Ireland. He m. in 1655, Elizabeth, eldest dau. of Sir Francis Russell, Bart. of Chippenham, and had issue,

OLIVER, b. in 1656. HENRY, b. in 1658.
Francis, b. in 1663, d. unm. in 1719.
Richard, b. in 1665, d. unm. in 1686.
William, b. in 1667, d. unm. in 1691.
Elizabeth, m. to William Russell, Esq. of Fordham, and d. in 1711. The lineal descendant and representative of this marriage is the present WILLIAM-ANDREW DYER, Esq., eldest son of the late William Dyer, Esq., a magistrate for Essex, by Rebecca his wife, dau. of Thomas Russell, Esq.

Henry Cromwell d. in 1673, and was s. at Spinney Abbey by his eldest son,

OLIVER CROMWELL, Esq. of Spinney Abbey, co. Cambridge, who was s. at his decease by his next brother,

HENRY CROMWELL, Esq., who disposed of the estate at Spinney Abbey, and entered the army: he became a major of foot. His death occurred in 1711. He had m. Hannah, eldest dau. of Benjamin Hewling, a Turkey merchant, and left five sons and two daus. The 4th son,

THOMAS CROMWELL, Esq., b. in 1699, wedded 1st, Miss Frances Tidman, and had surviving issue, Henry, who d. unm. in 1771; Anne, m. to John Field, of London. Mr. Cromwell m. 2ndly, Mary, dau. of Nicholas Skinner, Esq. merchant of London, and had two other sons and two daus., viz.,

OLIVER, his successor.
Thomas, lieut. in the E.I.C.S., d. in India, in 1771, unm.
Elizabeth; Susannah; both d. unm.

The elder son of the second marriage,

OLIVER CROMWELD, Esq., s. to the estate at Theobalds, under the will of his cousins, Elizabeth, Anne, and Dorothy, daus. of Richard Cromwell, Esq. He m. in 1771, Mary, dau. and co-heir of Morgan Morse, Esq., and had a son and dau., viz.,

OLIVER, who d. in his father's lifetime.
ELIZABETH-OLIVERIA (Mrs. Russell), of Cheshunt Park.

Mr. Cromwell d. in 1821.

Arms—Sa., a lion, rampant, arg.
Crest—A demi-lion, rampant, arg., in his dexter gamb a gem ring, or.
Motto—Pax quæritur bello.
Seat—Cheshunt Park.

CROSBIE OF BALLYHEIGUE.

CROSBIE, JAMES, Esq. of Ballyheigue Castle, co. Kerry, b. 11 Dec. 1832.

Lineage.—THOMAS CROSBIE, Esq. of Ballyheigue, M.P. for Kerry in 1709 (eldest son, by his 3rd wife, Elizabeth, eldest dau. and co-heir of William Hamilton, Esq., and relict of — Johnson, Esq., of SIR THOMAS CROSBIE, Knt. whose son and heir (by his 1st marriage), David, was ancestor of the Earls of Glandore), m. in 1711, Lady Margaret Barry, dau. of Richard, 2nd Earl of Barrymore, and left at his decease (will proved 12 May, 1731), with two daus., viz., Anne-Dorothy, m. to William Carrigue, Esq. of Glandyne, co. Clare; and Harriot-Jane, wife of Col. Launcelot Crosbie, of Tubrid, co. Kerry, a son and heir,

JAMES CROSBIE, Esq. of Ballyheigue, who m. his cousin, Mary, dau. of Pierce Crosbie, Esq. of Rusheen, and d. in March, 1761, leaving (with a dau., Henrietta-Elizabeth-Anne) two sons, James, the younger; and

PIERCE CROSBIE, Esq. of Ballyheigue, who m. Frances, dau. of Rowland Bateman, Esq. of Oak Park, and had, with daus., two sons, of whom the elder,

COLONEL CROSBIE, of Ballyheigue, m. his cousin, Elizabeth, dau. of Rowland Bateman, Esq., and left a son,

JAMES CROSBIE, Esq. of Ballyheigue, M.P. for the co. of Kerry, colonel-commandant of the militia, and custos rotulorum, father of

PIERSE CROSBIE, Esq. of Ballyheigue, who m. 1st, Miss Sandes, dau. of Thomas Sandes, Esq. of Sallow Glen, co. Kerry, by whom he had, with one dau., a son, JAMES, now of Ballyheigue. He m. 2ndly, Miss Wren, of Littur, co. Kerry, and had issue by her. He d. about the year 1849.

Arms—Arg., a lion, rampant, sa.; in chief, two dexter hands, couped and erect, gu.
Crest—Three swords, two in saltier, the points in base, the third in pale, point upwards, environed with a snake.
Seat—Ballyheigue Castle, co. Kerry.

CROSBIE OF ARDFERT ABBEY.

CROSBIE, WILLIAM-TALBOT, Esq. of Ardfert Abbey, co. Kerry, b. 19 March, 1817; m. 1st, 29 July, 1839, Susan-Anne, 3rd dau. of the Hon. Lindsey-M.-Peter Burrell, 2nd brother of the present Lord Willoughby d'Eresby (which lady d. in 1850); and 2ndly, 28 July, 1853, Emma, 2nd dau. of the Honble. Lindsey-M.-P. Burrell.

Lineage.—THE REV. JOHN TALBOT, son of William Talbot, Esq. of Mount Talbot, co. Roscommon, by Anne his wife, dau. of William Crosbie, 1st Earl of Glandore, took the name and arms of CROSBIE, pursuant to the will of his uncle, John, last Earl of Glandore, 14 February, 1816. He m. in Sept. 1811, Jane, dau. of T. Lloyd, Esq., by whom he had issue,

WILLIAM, now of Ardfert Abbey.
John, b. in Oct. 1818. In the 35th Royal Sussex regt.
Anne, m. 27 June, 1839, to the Rev. Maurice Atkin Collis, 2nd son of William Collis, Esq. of Castle Cooke, co. Cork.
Diana, m. 6 Aug. 1835, to Edward-Thomas Coke, Esq. of Brimington Hill, co. Derby, 3rd son of D'Ewes Coke, Esq. of Brook Hill, in the same county.

The Rev. John Talbot-Crosbie d. in Jan. 1818.

Arms—Quarterly: CROSBIE and TALBOT.
Crest—Three swords, two in saltier, the points in base, the third in pale, point upwards, encircled by a snake, all ppr.
Motto—Indignante invidia florebit justus.
Seat—Ardfert Abbey, co. Kerry.

CROSSE OF SHAW HILL.

CROSSE, THOMAS-BRIGHT, Esq. of Shaw Hill, co. Lancaster, J.P. and D.L., high-sheriff in 1837, at one time M.P. for Wigan, *m.* 6 May, 1828, Anne-Mary Crosse, 2nd dau. of Richard Crosse, Esq. of Shaw Hill, co. Lancaster (afterwards Legh, of Adlington, co. Chester), and by her, upon whom her father entailed his Lancashire estates of Shaw Hill, Chorley, and Liverpool, in remainder after the death of his 2nd son, Richard-Townley Crosse, he has had issue,

I. THOMAS-RICHARD. II. Charles-Kenrick.
III. John-Legh, deceased.
IV. Henry-Townley, deceased.
V. Hugh-Banastre. VI. Robert-Legh.
I. Harriet-Anne. II. Anne-Mary.
III. Caroline-Susan.

This gentleman, whose patronymic is IKIN, assumed his present surname and arms of CROSSE, by sign-manual, 8 Sept. 1828.

Lineage.—The family of De la Croys, De Cruce, Del Crosse, Crosse, as the name is variously spelt in ancient deeds—was originally seated at Wygan, co. Lancaster, in the reign of EDWARD I., and about the year 1350 were settled at Crosse Hall, in Liverpool, and subsequently obtained estates in Chorley, also denominated Cross Hall. The first we find on record in the extensive collection of charters among the muniments preserved at Shaw Hill, is RICHARD DE LA CROYZ, living in the reign of EDWARD I., about 1272. ADAM DE CRUCE, "son of Richard De la Croyz," is mentioned in a deed, sans date, but about the year 1299, by which he bestowed lands in Wygan upon his daughter, Elena. He had another dau., Margaret, and was succeeded by his son, JOHN DE CRUCE, who by deed, 27 EDWARD I., A.D. 1299, confirms his father's gift of lands to his sister, Elena, in free marriage with Alan, the son of Walter de Wygan. He was living in 1325, and had issue, Thurstan; William; and Matilda, wife of Henry Banastre, upon whom, 13 January (18th EDWARD II.) A.D. 1324, he entailed his estates on failure of issue of his sons, Thurstan and William. From

THURSTAN DE CRUCE, descended the family of CROSSE *of Crosse Hall*, the representative of which was

JOHN CROSSE, of Crosse Hall, in Chorley, and Cross Hall, in Liverpool. In 1588, his name appears among the "gentlemen of the best callinge in the county of Lancaster, whereof choyse ys to be made of certen number, to send unto her Majestie money upon private seale." He was buried at Chorley, 6 Sept. 1612. By his wife Alice, dau. of John More, of Bank Hall, he had a dau., Elizabeth, *m.* to William Chorley, of Chorley, and a son and successor,

RICHARD CROSSE, from whom derived, 7th in descent,

RICHARD CROSSE, Esq. of Shaw Hill (son of Thomas Crosse, Esq. of Crosse Hall and Shawe Hill, and grandson of Richard Crosse, Esq., by Anne his wife, dau. and co-heir of Robert Legh, 2nd son of Thomas Legh, Esq. of Adlington, co. Chester), who *s.* in 1806 to the estates of his cousin, Charles Legh, Esq. of Adlington, co. Chester, and assumed in consequence the name and arms of LEGH. He served as sheriff of Lancashire in 1807. He *m.* in Sept. 1787, Anne, only surviving dau. of Robert Parker, of Cuerden, co. Lancaster, and by her (who *d.* 17 Dec. 1807, aged 39) he left at his decease, 11 Aug. 1822,

THOMAS LEGH, who *s.* to the estates of Adlington, co. Chester, and was father of CHARLES-RICHARD-BANASTRE LEGH, Esq., their present proprietor. (*See* LEGH *of Adlington.*)
Richard-Townley Crosse, *b.* 6 Dec. 1794; *d. unm.* 27 Feb. 1825.
Sarah-Crosse, *m.* 16 Sept. 1823, the Rev. Thomas Clarke, eldest son of Henry Clarke, of Liverpool, and of Belmont, co. Chester; he *d.* Dec. 1837, without issue.
ANNE-MARY, upon whom her father settled his paternal Lancashire estates of Shaw Hill, Chorley, and Liverpool. She *m.* THOMAS-BRIGHT IKIN, Esq., as above.
Jane Legh.

Arms—Quarterly: gu. and or, in 1st and 4th, a cross-potent, arg.; and for difference, a canton, erm., impaling the same arms, without the canton.
Crest—On a wreath of the colours, a stork, ppr.; in its beak a cross-potent, fitchée, arg., and for difference, charged with an escallop shell.
Motto—Sub cruce salus.
Seat—Shaw Hill, Chorley.

CROSSE OF BROOMFIELD.

CROSSE, ANDREW, Esq. of Fynecourt House, Broomfield, co. Somerset, J.P., *b.* 17 June, 1784; *m.* 1st, May, 1809, Mary-Anne, eldest dau. of Captain John Hamilton, 61st regt., of Garrison, near Ballyshannon, co. Fermanagh, and by her has issue,

I. JOHN.
II. Robert, in holy orders, *m.* Eliza-Mary, dau. of Charles Mackenzie, Esq., Bengal civil service, and has issue, John-Richard-Davey-Hamilton; Matilda-Mary-Anne; Isabella-Frances; and Alice-Caroline.
I. Isabella, married.

He *m.* 2ndly, in 1850, Cornelia-Augusta-Hewitt, dau. of Capt. Berkeley, of Exeter, and by her has issue,

I. Andrew-Frederick, *b.* in 1852.
II. Landor-Richard, *b.* in 1854.

Lineage.—The family of Crosse is of considerable antiquity, and has been seated at Fynecourt House, Broomfield, since the year 1629.

In 1602, William Camden, Clarenceux, designed a crest to the "ancient arms of Sir Robert Crosse, Knt., a son of William Crosse, of Charlenge, co. Somerset, descended of a house long time bearing arms." The grandfather of the present Andrew Crosse, Esq.,

THE REV. RICHARD CROSSE, vicar of Cannington, co. Somerset, younger brother of ANDREW CROSSE, Esq. of Broomfield, who made an entail of the estate on the present Mr. Crosse, was father of

RICHARD CROSSE, Esq. of Fynecourt House, Broomfield, J.P. and high-sheriff of co. Somerset, who *m.* 1st, a Swiss lady, by whom he had a dau., Louisa, *m.* to Joseph Porter, Esq. He *m.* 2ndly, Susanna, only dau. of Jasper Porter, Esq. of Bloxhold, co. Somerset, and by her had issue,

ANDREW, his heir. Richard, *d. s. p.*
Louisa-Porter.

Mr. Crosse *d.* in 1800, and was *s.* by his son, the present ANDREW CROSSE, Esq.

Arms—Quarterly: Arg. and gu., in the first quarter, a cross-crosslet, of the second.
Crest—A cross patée-fitchée, gu., between two wings, arg., each charged with a cross-crosslet, of the first.
Motto—Se inserit astris.
Seat—Fynecourt House, Broomfield, near Taunton.

JOHN CROSSE, Esq. of Thurloxton, co. Somerset, brother of the Rev. Richard Crosse, of Broomfield, was father of

THOMAS CROSSE, Esq. of Bovey Hall, co. Somerset, who *m.* Mary, sister of Sir Aretas Young, governor of Prince Edward's Island, and was father of

THOMAS CROSSE, Esq. of Hayes, co. Kent, who *m.* Mary-Anne, dau. of William Gordon, Esq., and had issue,

I. THOMAS-FRANCIS.
II. Aretas-Young. III. Arthur-Charles.
I. Mary-Anne, *m.* to James Parker, Esq.

CROSSLEY OF SCAITCLIFFE.

CROSSLEY, JOHN, Esq. of Scaitcliffe, co. Lancaster, M.A., barrister-at-law, J.P. and D.L., *b.* 20 March, 1807; *m.* 27 Sept. 1834, Mary, only dau. of Thomas Ramsbotham, Esq. of Centre Vale, Todmorden.

Lineage.—"Two only of the old families in the parish of Rochdale," says Dr. Whitaker, "now remain—namely, the ENTWISLES *of Foxholes*, and the CROSSLEYS *of Scaitcliffe*, formerly called CROSSLEGH, near Todmorden, who have been seated at that place from an era which cannot be ascertained."

JOHN DEL CROSLEGH, son of Adam del Crosiegh, of Todmaredene, by Matilda his wife, was living 38th EDWARD III., A.D. 1365. He *m.* Johanna, and left a son and successor,

WILLIAM DEL CROSLEGH, who was living in 1411, as appears by deed dated at Todmorden, on Monday next after the feast of St. Andrew the Apostle. He was ancestor of

John Crosleyr, of Scaytcliffe, who adhered during the civil wars to King Charles, and fought under the royal banner at Marston Moor. His sword is still preserved in the Scaitcliffe armory. His son,

John Crosley, Esq. of Scaytcliffe, who m. in 1640, a dau. of Cæsar Jackson, of Worsthorn, had issue, Anthony, his heir; Abraham, whose son, Aaron Crosley, Esq., m. Mademoiselle Paracheau, and was father of Frances Crosley, m. to John Seymour, Esq., by whom she was great-grandmother of Aaron Crossley-Seymour, Esq. of Castletown House, Queen's County; Luke; and Anne. The eldest son,

Anthony Crosley, Esq. of Scaytcliffe, who rebuilt the south front of Scaytcliffe House in 1666, d. in 1707. His great-grandson,

John Crossley, Esq. of Scaitcliffe and Walsden, co. Lancaster, b. 14 June, 1737 (son of Anthony, and grandson of John Crossley, both of Scaitcliffe), m. 10 July, 1759, Mary, elder dau. of Thomas Foster, Gent. of Foster Mill, co. York, and had two sons, Anthony and John. John Crossley d. at Scaitcliffe, 29 Sept. 1799, aged 62 years, and was s. by his elder son,

Anthony Crossley, Esq. of Scaitcliffe, who had purchased, in 1795, the estate of Todmorden Hall, with the ancient structure for his family residence. He m. 19 Aug. 1783, Betty, elder dau. of Abraham Gibson, Esq. of Briggroyd, co. York, and had an only dau.,

Anne, of Todmorden Hall, co. Lancaster, m. 17 Sept. 1801, to James-Joseph-Hague Taylor, Esq., and was mother of James Taylor, Esq., now of Todmorden Hall.

Mr. Crossley d. 1 June, 1810, aged 48 years, and was s. in the representation of the family by his brother,

John Crossley, Esq., F.S.A., J.P. and D.L., b. 23 May, 1778, who had purchased from his brother, 16 March, 1802, the estate of Scaitcliffe. He m. 20 May, 1800, Sarah, only dau. and heiress of John Lockwood, Esq. of Ewood, co. York, and had one son and two daus., viz.,

John, now of Scaitcliffe.
Mary, m. 18 Aug. 1827, to William Hepworth, Esq., J.P. and D.L., of Pontefract.
Matilda, m. 9 May, 1832, Christopher-Edward Dampier, Esq., and has issue, Croslegh, Harry-Edward, Mary-Elizabeth, and Matilda-Catherine.

Mr. Crossley d. 11 Dec. 1830.

Arms—Per chevron, or and vert; in chief, a tau, between two crosses-patonce, fitchée, gu.; in base a hind, trippant, arg., charged on the neck with a tau, of the third.
Crest—A hind's head, couped, ppr., charged on the neck with a tau, and holding in the mouth a cross-patonce, fitchée, gu.
Motto—Credo et amo.
Seat—Scaitcliffe, Todmorden, Lancashire.

CROWE OF THE ABBEY.

Crowe, Wainright, Esq. of The Abbey, Ennis, co. Clare, J.P., b. 29 Dec. 1817. Mr. Crowe is son of the late Thomas Crowe, Esq. of Ennis, J.P., and Ellen his wife, and grandson of Thomas Crowe, Esq. of Ennis, whose dau., Anne, relict of William Arthur, Esq., m. Sir Henry Marsh, Bart. of Dublin. Mr. Wainright Crowe has one brother and four sisters, viz.,

I. Thomas Crowe, Esq., jun., a magistrate for the co. of Clare, m. Miss Hume, of Humewood, co. Wicklow.
I. Eliza, m. to William Kean, Esq.
II. Ellen, m. to Joseph Tabuteau, Esq., R.M., Waterford.
III. Anne, m. to Thomas Kean, Esq.
IV. Matilda, m. to James Johnston, Esq. of Kincardine.

Seat—The Abbey, Ennis.

CRUTCHLEY OF SUNNINGHILL PARK.

Crutchley, George-Henry, Esq. of Sunninghill Park, co. Berks, J.P. and D.L., high-sheriff in 1807, m. 14 April, 1806, Juliana, eldest dau. of Sir William Burrell, Bart., and has issue,

I. Percy-Henry, b. in Dec. 1807.
II. Charles, b. April, 1810, a captain in the 23rd foot.
I. Elizabeth. II. Caroline.

Mr. Crutchley, whose patronymic was Duffield, assumed the surname and arms of Crutchley only, by royal license, in 1806.

Lineage.—Alice Crutchley (only dau. of Jeremiah Crutchley, Esq., by Alice Jackson his wife), b. in July, 1751, m. in 1767, Michael Duffield, Esq., and dying in 1833, left issue,

I. George-Henry, of Sunninghill.
II. Thomas, M.P. for Abingdon, m. 1st, in 1810, Emily, only child of George Elwes, Esq., of Marcham Park, Berks, and has issue, viz.,
1 George, d. in Jan. 1833.
2 Henry. 3 Charles.
1 Caroline, m. to Edwin-Martin Atkins, Esq. of Kingston Lisle, Berks.
2 Maria, m. to Head-Pottinger Best, Esq.
3 Anna, m. to John-S. Phillips, Esq. of Culham, co. Oxford.
4 Susan, d. in May 1841. 5 Elizabeth.
He m. 2ndly, in 1838, Augusta, 2nd dau. of Col. Rushbrooke, M.P. for West Suffolk, and has issue,
1 Thomas.
1 Augusta. 2 Mary.
I. Alicia-Julia. II. Maria. III. Matilda.
IV. Anna-Maria. V. Jane-Hester.

Arms—Arg., a chevron, gu., cotised, az., between three torteaux, each encircled by two branches of oak, ppr.
Crest—On a mount, vert, a talbot, sejant, arg., collared and line reflexed over the back, or; the dexter fore-paw on a torteau.
Seat—Sunninghill Park, co. Berks.

CUBITT OF CATFIELD HALL.

Cubitt, George, Esq. of Catfield Hall, co. Norfolk, J.P. and D.L., m. 1st, Mary, dau. of the Rev. C. Finley; and 2ndly, Frances, dau. of the Rev. Henry Parish, and has issue,

I. Thomas, lieut.-colonel royal artillery, m. Annette, dau. of General Sir John Campbell.
II. William, major Bengal native infantry.
III. Henry, captain royal artillery, m. 1st, Mary, dau. of Robert Mangles, Esq., and 2ndly, Mary, dau. of Robert Fellows, Esq. of Shottisham, co. Norfolk.
IV. Charles.
V. Benjamin-Lucas, in holy orders, m. Emma, sister of Sir Francis Lyttleton-Holyoake Goodricke, Bart.
VI. Edward, lieutenant 71st foot.
I. Charlotte, m. to the Rev. Thomas Wright, of Kilverston, Norfolk.
II. Ann-Elizabeth, m. to Col. Story, royal artillery.
III. Mary, m. to J. Meggison, Esq. of Northumberland.
IV. Fanny. V. Agnes.
VI. Marianne, m. to the Rev. R. Johnson, rector of Lavenham, Suffolk.

Lineage.—The family of Cubitt has been settled in the county of Norfolk from a very early period, mention being made by Bloomfield, in his history of that county, of a person of that name having been one of the ringleaders who were selected by the Commons to go to the King, on the rebellion of Wat Tyler having extended to Norfolk, *temp.* Richard II., but they were beheaded on the way. In 1487, Robert Cubitt was abbot of St. Bennet's, at Holme. The family subsequently settled at Yarmouth, of which borough Benedict Cubitt, son of Robert Cubitt, was mayor in 1566, and was father of Thomas Cubitt, of Southrepps, Norfolk, whose son (by Diana his wife, dau. of John Housegoe, Esq. of Lynn),

John Cubitt, Esq., was mayor of Great Yarmouth in 1664, and settled at Hickling. He m. Elizabeth, dau. and sole heiress of William Lynn, Esq., lord of the manor of Bintree, Norfolk, and had issue, John; Benjamin; and Mary. The 2nd son,

Benjamin Cubitt, Esq., was father of two sons, Benjamin, and Thomas. The younger was grandfather of the present Edward-George Cubitt, Esq. of Honing Hall, and the elder,

Benjamin Cubitt, Esq. of Catfield Hall, had a son and successor, the present George Cubitt, Esq. of Catfield.

Arms—Sa., a bow and arrow, arg.
Arms—An arm in armour, holding an arrow, fesseways, ppr.
Seat—Catfield, Norfolk.

CUBITT OF HONING HALL.

Cubitt, Edward-George, Esq. of Honing Hall, co. Norfolk, late of the Enniskillen dragoons, J.P. and D.L., b. 10 March, 1795.

Lineage.—Thomas Cubitt, Esq. of Honing Hall, J.P. and D.L., b. 1 Jan. 1760, son and heir of Thomas Cubitt, Esq. of Honing Hall, by Mary his wife, dau. of the Rev. J. Smith, of East Dereham, Norfolk, m. 18 July, 1785, Catharine, dau. of Henry Spencer, Esq. of Dulwich, a branch of the Spencers *of Althorpe*, and has issue,

Edward-George, now of Honing Hall.
Francis-William, rector of Fritton, Suffolk, J.P., *b.* 7 April, 1799, *m.* Jane-Mary, dau. of the Rev. H.-N. Astley, son of the late Sir E. Astley, Bart., and uncle to Lord Hastings, and has issue, Frank-Astley, Spencer, Lucy, Jane, Sophia, and Georgina.
Marianne, *m.* to the Rev. J. Taylor, rector of Hainford, Norfolk, and Diptford, Devon.
Sophia, *m.* to the Rev. H. Evans, rector of Lyng and Swanton Abbots, Norfolk.
Maria-Emily, *m.* to Thomas-Jex Blake, Esq. of Doctors' Commons.

Arms, &c.—As Cubitt *of Catfield Hall.*
Seat—Honing Hall, near North Walsham.

CULLEN OF GLENADE.

Cullen, Cairncross-Thomas, Esq. of Glenade, co. Leitrim, J.P. and D.L., high-sheriff in 1825, *b.* 20 Jan. 1802; *m.* 12 Feb. 1830, Jane-Eleanor, dau. of Henry Palmer, Esq., and has issue,

I. Cairncross-Palmer, *b.* 22 March, 1835.
I. Hester-Jane. II. Catherine-Susannah.
III. Marguerite-Victoria. IV. Ethel-Henrietta.
V. Elizabeth-Constance. VI. Gertrude-Marion.

Lineage.—Patrick Cullen, Esq., of an ancient Scottish descent, accompanied Sir Frederick Hamilton to Ireland, 16 Charles I., and founded the family of Cullen *of Skreeney.* The great-grandfather of the present representative,

Patrick Cullen, Esq. of Skreeney, *m.* Isabella, dau. of Cairncross Nesbitt, Esq. of Aughamore, co. Roscommon, and had issue, Patrick, who *m.* Judith, dau. of Owen Wynne, Esq. of Hazelwood, co. Sligo; Cairncross, of whom presently; James, who *m.* Elizabeth, dau. of Samuel Adams, Esq. of the co. of Cavan; John, who *m.* Margaret, another dau. of Samuel Adams, Esq.; Francis, major of carbineers, who *d. unm.*; Henry, captain of the Leitrim militia, who *d. unm.*; Isabella, *m.* to Francis Isdell, Esq. of Rockbrook, co. Westmeath; Margaret, *m.* to the Rev. Whitnell Sneyd; and Elizabeth, *m.* to — L'Estrange, Esq. of the co. of Westmeath. The 2nd son,

The Rev. Cairncross Cullen, rector of Manor Hamilton, *m.* Elizabeth, dau. and co-heir of James Soden, Esq. of Grange, co. Sligo, and had issue,

Cairncross, his heir.
John-James, of Skreeny, J.P., lieut.-col. of the Leitrim militia, *m.* Bridget, dau. of Daniel Finucane, Esq. of Stamer Park, co. Clare, and has issue.
Henry-Francis, *m.* Hester, dau. of John Dickson, Esq. of Woodville, co. Leitrim, barrister-at-law.
Catherine, *m.* to Henry Palmer, Esq. capt. in the Prince of Wales's Fencibles.
Jane-Elizabeth, *m.* to George Gledstanes, Esq. co. Tyrone.
Eliza-Melvina, *m.* 1st, to Major Jones, 25th light dragoons, and 2ndly, to Lieut.-Col. Campbell, 9th royal lancers.

The eldest son,

Cairncross Cullen, Esq. of Glenade, *m.* 10 April, 1800, Hester, dau. of Major Dickson, of Woodville, co. Leitrim, M.P. for Ballyshannon; and had, by her, who *m.* 2ndly, the Rev. Herbert-Mandeville Nash, an only son, the present Cairncross-Thomas Cullen, Esq. of Glenade.

Arms—Or, two lions, rampant-combatant.
Crest—A pelican in her nest, feeding her young, ppr.
Motto—Carpe diem.
Seat—Glenade, Manor Hamilton.

CULLEY OF FOWBERRY TOWER.

Culley, George, Esq. of Fowberry Tower, co. Northumberland, *b.* 26 Jan. 1834.

Lineage.—Matthew Culley, Esq. of Denton, bapt. 28 Sept. 1697 (son of John Culley, Gent. of Beaumont Hill, and grandson of Matthew Culley, of Beaumont Hill, whose father was John Culley, of the same place), *m.* Eleanor, dau. of Edward Surtees, Esq. of Mainsforth, co. Durham, and had, with numerous other children, who *d. unm.*, three sons, Matthew, of Coupland Castle, who *m.* Miss Elizabeth Bates, and had a son, Matthew, of Coupland Castle; George; and James, who left an only dau. and heir. The 2nd son,

George Culley, Esq. of Fowberry Tower, *m.* in 1777, Jane, dau. of Walter Atkinson, Esq., by whom he left at his decease in 1813 (with one dau., Eleanor, *m.* to James Darling, Esq.) a son,

Matthew Culley, Esq. of Fowberry Tower, *b.* 15 Feb. 1778, J.P., who *d.* in 1849, and was *s.* by his nephew (the only son of James Darling and Eleanor Culley),

George Darling, Esq. of Fowberry Tower, who was killed by a fall from his horse, 29 Feb. 1850. He *m.* 5 July, 1831, Helen, dau. of Capt. Thomas Masson, royal artillery, and had issue,

George, who has taken the name of Culley, and is now of Fowberry Tower.
James.
William, *b.* 7 June, 1838, *d.* 17 May, 1841.
Matthew-Thomas, *b.* 10 March, 1840.
Thomas-William, *b.* 3 Dec. 1847.
Isabella-Eleanor. Eleanor-Jane.
Rose-Helen, *d.* 24 Jan. 1852.

Arms—Per pale, indented, az. and sa., on a chevron, engrailed, erm., between three talbots' heads, erased, or, as many roses, gu., barbed and seeded, ppr.
Crest—In front of an oak-tree, ppr., a talbot, statant, per pale, az. and or, gorged with a collar gemelle, arg., and holding in the mouth a lily, slipped, ppr.
Motto—Amicos semper amat.
Seat—Fowberry Tower, near Wooler.

CUNINGHAME OF LAINSHAW.

Cuninghame, John, Esq. of Lainshaw, co. Ayr, and Hensol, Kirkcudbright, *b.* 13 Feb. 1796, *m.* 26 March, 1831, Eliza-Mary, dau. of Capt. Upton, R.N., and has issue,

I. John-William-Herbert, *b.* 18 Dec. 1834.
II. Richard-Barrè-Dunning, *b.* 27 May, 1836.
III. George-Wenceslaus, *b.* 12 Nov. 1837.
IV. Charles-Edward-Harris, *b.* 11 June, 1841.
I. Eliza-Anne. II. Margaret-Mary.

Lineage.—The Cuninghames *of Lainshaw* are a branch of the Caprington family.

William Cuninghame, of Brighouse (son of Alexander Cuninghame, by Barbara Hay his wife, granddau. of Andrew Hay, of Craignethan), purchased the estate of Lainshaw in 1779, and *d.* in April, 1799. By his 2nd wife, Elizabeth, 2nd dau. of James Campbell, Esq. of Glasgow, he had an only son, William, his heir; and by his 3rd wife, Margaret Nicholson, eldest dau. of the Hon. George Cranstoun, he left issue,

John, now of Lainshaw.
Margaret, *d.* an infant.
Maria, now of Corehouse.
Margaret-Nicholson.
Anne-Selby, *m.* Richard-Barrè Dunning, 2nd Lord Ashburton, and *d.* 1835, leaving no issue.
D'Arcy-Maxwell, } *d. unm.*
Louisa, }
Isabella, *m.* Roderick Macleod, of Cadboll, Esq.; lord-lieutenant and M.P. for the co. of Ross.

The only son of the 2nd marriage,

William Cuninghame, Esq. of Lainshaw, H.E.I.C. civil service, who was well known as a writer on Prophecy and Scriptural Chronology, *d. unm.* in Nov. 1849, and was *s.* by his half-brother, the present John Cuninghame, Esq. of Lainshaw.

Arms—Arg., a shakefork, sa., within a bordure, erm.
Crest—A dexter hand, holding a plumb-rule, ppr.
Motto—Over, fork over.
Seat—Lainshaw, co. Ayr.

CUNINGHAME OF CADDELL AND THORNTON.

Cuninghame, Archibald, Esq. of Caddell and Thornton, co. Ayr.

Lineage.—John Cuninghame, of Glengarnock, the most ancient cadet of the family of Glencairn, had two sons, William Cuninghame; and

John Cuninghame, of Caddell, living in 1572. From him we pass to

John Cuninghame, of Caddell, who *m.* 1st, in 1699, Margaret, eldest dau. of Sir Archibald Muir, Knt. of Thornton, lord-provost of Edinburgh, and had issue,

Archibald, his heir.
John, some time a merchant in Lisbon, who purchased the lands of Carmelbank, adjacent to those of Thornton, in Ayrshire. His eldest son, John, now possesses the estate.
Jane, *m.* to Thomas Boyd, of Pitcon.
Helen, who *d. unm.*
Margaret, *m.* to Archibald Crawford, of Cartsburn.

The laird *m.* 2ndly, a dau. of Stevenson of Mountgreen, and had by her sixteen children. He *d.* in 1753, and was *s.* by his son,

Archibald Cuninghame, of Caddell and Thornton, then

a captain in Boscawen's regiment of foot. This gentleman m. in 1754, Christian, eldest dau. of Andrew Macredie, Esq. of Pierceton, and had, with three daus., all deceased, three sons, 1 JOHN, his heir; 2 Andrew, capt. in the 48th regt., severely wounded at the taking of Martinique, in 1794: he d. at Thornton in 1798; and 3 Archibald, capt. in the 51st regiment, in which he served at Minorca, and was present when the island was captured by the Spaniards in 1782. He m. in 1785, Mary, dau. of John Wallace, Esq. of Kelly, but d. s. p. in 1799. Capt. Cuninghame d. in 1778, and was s. by his eldest son,

LIEUT.-COL. JOHN CUNINGHAME, of Caddell and Thornton, J.P. and D.L., lieut.-col. in the army, b. 21 Oct. 1756, m. 13 Aug. 1804, Sarah, only child of Major Pebbles, late of the 42nd regt., by Anna his wife, eldest dau. of Charles Hamilton, Esq. of Craighlaw, and has issue,

ARCHIBALD. John.
Christiana. Sarah. Helen.
Margaret. Catherine.

Arms—Arg., a shakefork, sa., charged with a cinquefoil, for GLENGARNOCK.
Crest—A unicorn's head, erect, couped.
Motto—Over fork over.
Seat—Thornton House.

CURE OF BLAKE HALL.

CURE, CAPEL, Esq. of Blake Hall, co. Essex, J.P. and D.L., high-sheriff in 1830, b. 9 Jan. 1800; m. 27 Feb. 1822, Frederica, eldest dau. of Gen. Robert Cheney, of Langley, co. Derby, by whom he has, with two daus., four sons, viz.,

I. ROBERT, b. 1 Jan. 1823, m. 9 Jan. 1850, Sarah-Jane, dau. of Dr. Murray, Bishop of Rochester.
II. Alfred, b. Dec. 1826.
III. Edward, b. 6 Nov. 1828.
IV. Lawrence-George, b. 22 Aug. 1833.

Mr. Cure s. his father in Jan. 1820.

His father, the late CAPEL CURE, Esq. of Black Hall, co. Essex, m. Joanna, dau. of — Coope, Esq. of Oxton, Notts, and d. in 1820. Mr. Cure's sisters are, Joanna-Freeman, m. to John-Burton Philips, Esq. of Heath House, co. Stafford; and Mary-Caroline, m. to William Hibbert, Esq.

Arms—Gu., a chevron, arg., between two roses, in chief, or, and in base a fleur-de-lis, of the second.
Crest—Out of a ducal coronet, arg., a griffin's head, and wings expanded, of the same, charged on the neck with a rose, gu.
Motto—Fais que doit, arrive qui pourra.
Seat—Blake Hall, near Ongar.

CURRER OF KILDWICK.

RICHARDSON-CURRER, FRANCES-MARY, of Kildwick, co. York, s. her father in 1784, and is representative of the ancient families of CURRER *of Kildwick* and RICHARDSON *of Bierley*.

Lineage.—The Currers have been seated at Kildwick, in Yorkshire, for nearly three centuries.

HENRY CURRER, Esq. of Kildwick, son of Hugh, of Kildwick, and 5th in descent from Hugh, of Kildwick, who m. Anne Knowles; b. 25 July, 1651, m. 1st, Margaret, dau. of Abraham Fothergill, Esq. of London, and by her, who d. in 1697, had (with three younger daus.),

I. HAWORTH, his heir.
I. Ann, m. Benjamin Ferrand, Esq. of St. Ives, and d. s. p.
II. DOROTHY, b. in 1687, who m. RICHARD RICHARDSON, M.D. of Bierley, and d. in 1763, leaving issue,
 1 RICHARD RICHARDSON, Esq. of Bierley, lord of the manor of Okenshaw and Cleck Heaton, a magistrate and deputy-lieut. for the West Riding, b. in 1708, who m. in 1750, Dorothy, only dau. and heir of William Smallshaw, Esq. of Bolton-in-the-Moors, by Mary his wife, dau. of John Starkie, Esq. of Huntroyde, but d. s. p. in 1781.
 2 William Richardson, M.D. of Ripon, b. in 1709, and d. unm. in 1783.
 3 Henry Richardson, A.M., rector of Thornton-in-Craven, b. in 1710, m. in 1747, Mary, dau. of Benjamin Dawson, Esq. of Oldham, merchant, and d. in 1778, leaving two sons and two daus., viz.,
  Richard Richardson, b. 19 Jan. 1755, d. unm. at Lisbon, 24 May, 1782.
  HENRY RICHARDSON, in holy orders, of whom hereafter, as successor to his uncle John, in the Currer estates.
  Dorothy Richardson, of Gargrave.
  Mary Richardson, b. in 1752, who m. in 1775, the Rev. William Roundell, of Gledstone, and had issue.
 4 JOHN RICHARDSON, of whom presently, as successor to his cousin, SARAH CURRER.
 5 Thomas Richardson, b. in 1724, d. unm. in 1763.
 1 Dorothy Richardson, b. in 1712, m. in 1730, Sir John-Lister Kaye, Bart, of Denby Grange, co. York, and d. in 1772, leaving issue.
 2 Margaret Richardson, d. unm. in 1764.

Henry Currer, of Kildwick, m. 2ndly, Mary, dau. of Edmund Watson, Esq. of East Hage, in the co. of York, and widow of Thomas Yarborough, Esq. of Campsall, but had no issue. He d. 19 Jan. 1723, and lies interred at Kildwick. He was s. by his only son,

HAWORTH CURRER, Esq. of Kildwick, b. 26 Jan. 1690, who m. 5 July, 1722, Sarah, 4th dau. of Tobias Harvey, Esq. of Womersley, and by her, who d. in 1766, had one son and one dau., HENRY and SARAH. He d. 13 April, 1744, and was s. by his son,

HENRY CURRER, Esq. of Kildwick, b. in 1728, who m. in 1756, Mary, dau. and co-heir of Richardson Ferrand, Esq. of Harden, but d. s. p. 10 March, in the same year. His widow m. 2ndly, Peter Bell, Esq., 2nd son of Ralph Bell, Esq. of Thirsk. Mr. Currer was s. in his estates by his sister,

SARAH CURRER, of Kildwick, b. in 1729, who d. unm. at Widcombe, near Bath, in 1759. She was s. by (the 4th son of her aunt, Dorothy Currer, by her husband, Richard Richardson, Esq. of Bierley) her first-cousin,

JOHN RICHARDSON, Esq., J.P. and D.L., who then became of Kildwick, and assumed the surname and arms of CURRER. He d. unm. 22 June, 1784, and was s. by his nephew,

THE REV. HENRY RICHARDSON, A.M., b. 9 Dec. 1758, rector of Thornton-in-Craven, who assumed a short time before his death, on inheriting the Kildwick estates, the surname and arms of CURRER. He m. in 1783, Margaret-Clive, only dau. of Matthew Wilson, Esq. of Eshton, by Frances his wife, dau. of Richard Clive, Esq. of Stych, in Shropshire, and by her (who m. 2ndly, her cousin, Matthew Wilson, Esq. 2nd son of the Rev. Henry Wilson) had an only dau. and heiress,

FRANCES-MARY, now representative of the ancient families of Richardson and Currer.

Mr. Richardson-Currer d. 10 Nov. 1784.

Arms—CURRER and RICHARDSON, quarterly.
Seat—Eshton Hall, Gargrave, Yorkshire.

CURRER OF CLIFTON HOUSE.

See ROUNDELL OF GLEDSTONE.

CURRIE OF BUSH HILL.

CURRIE, ISAAC GEORGE, Esq. of Bush Hill, co. Middlesex, b. in 1792; m. May, 1847, Mary, widow of Colonel Hay.

Lineage.—This family, settled at Dunse, co. Berwick, in 1571, derived from CUTHBERT CURRIE, a cadet of the family of that ilk, in Annandale, Dumfriesshire. For full details of lineage, see BURKE'S *Peerage and Baronetage*. The late

WILLIAM CURRIE, Esq., b. in 1718, banker of London, son of Mark Currie, and Magdalen Anderson his wife, m. 1753, Madeleine, dau. of Isaac Lefevre, Esq., great-grandfather of the Rt. Hon. C.-S. Lefevre, and had issue,

I. WILLIAM, of East Horsley Park, Surrey, M.P., who m. 1795, Percy, dau. of Francis Gore, Esq., and d. in 1829, leaving issue,
 1 William, of East Horsley, b. 1797.
 2 Henry, b. 1798, m. Emma, dau. of Col. Knox, and has issue.
 3 Francis-Gore.
 4 Horace-Gore, in holy orders, who m. Charlotte, dau. of Viscount Sidmouth.
 5 Blackwood-Gore, b. 1808, m. 1829, Laura Gossett, and d. in 1834, leaving issue.
 1 Percy, m. to the Hon. and Rev. Horace Powys.
 2 Harriet, m. to Robert Webb, Esq. of Milford House, Surrey.
II. Mark, father of the present SIR FREDERICK CURRIE, Bart., and other issue (see *Baronetage*).
III. ISAAC, of Bush Hill.
IV. John, of Essendon, Herts, who m. Isabella, dau. of Robert Parnther, Esq., and d. in 1829, leaving a son, John, at one time M.P. for Hertford, and two daus.
V. Leonard, who m. Dorothy, dau. of John Close, Esq. of Easby, co. York, and had, Leonard, and other issue.
I. Magdalen, d. unm.
II. Mary, m. to the Rev. John Chandler.

The 3rd son,

ISAAC CURRIE, Esq. of Bush Hill, co. Middlesex, b. 13 March, 1760, m. 2 April, 1789, Mary-Anne, eldest dau. of William Raikes, of Valentines, co. Essex, Esq. (see RAIKES of Yorkshire), who d. July, 1834, and has issue,

I. ISAAC-GEORGE, b. in 1792.
II. Raikes, M.P. for Northampton since 1837, J.P. and D.L., b. in 1801, m. in 1825, the Hon. Laura-Sophia, eldest dau. of John, 2nd Lord Wodehouse, and has issue,
 1 GEORGE-WODEHOUSE, b. 13 April, 1826, m. 1850, Miss Vernon Smith, only dau. of the Rt. Hon. R.-Vernon Smith.
 2 Bertram-Wodehouse, b. 25 Nov. 1827.
 3 Maynard-Wodehouse, b. 25 Feb. 1829.
 4 Philip-Henry-Wodehouse, b. 13 Oct. 1834.
 1 Mary-Sophia. 2 Edith-Harriet-Sophia.
I. Marianne, m. Nov. 1814, George Raikes, Esq., since deceased.
II. Emma.
III. Louisa, m. in 1847, to the Rev. G.-B. Fisher, rector of Basildon.
IV. Georgina.

Arms—Gu., a saltier, arg.; in chief, a rose, of the second, barbed and seeded, ppr.
Crest—A cock, gu.
Seat—Bush Hill, co. Middlesex.

CURTEIS OF WINDMILL HILL.

CURTEIS, HERBERT-MASCALL, Esq. of Windmill Hill, co. Sussex, late M.P. for Rye, b. 8 Jan. 1823; m. 15 June, 1848, Paulina, dau. of Sir Godfrey-J. Thomas, Bart. of Bodiam, and has issue,

I. HERBERT, b. in 1849.
II. Robert-Mascall, b. 1851
I. Caroline. II. Paulina.

Lineage.—STEPHEN CURTEIS, of Appledore, in the co. of Kent, descended from an ancient family resident in that shire, was great-grandfather of

THOMAS CURTEIS, of Appledore, living in 1527, who m. Joane, dau. and co-heir of Edward Twaights, warden of the Cinque Ports, and was s. by his son,

WILLIAM CURTEIS, of Tenterden, in Kent, who m. 1st, Joan Bunting, and had issue,

William, bailiff of Tenterden, in 1591, from whom lineally descend the REV. THOMAS-SACKVILLE CURTEIS, rector of Sevenoaks, and his cousin, the REV. THOMAS CURTEIS, of Sevenoaks, A.M., J.P.
THOMAS, mayor of Tenterden, in 1606.

He m. 2ndly, Joan Pattenden, and had, with three daus., two sons, viz.,

George, of Chart Sutton, who was sheriff of Kent in 1651. From him derived the CURTEISES *of Otterden Place*.
STEPHEN.

Mr. Curteis's 2nd son by his 2nd marriage,

STEPHEN CURTEIS, Esq., mayor of Tenterden in 1622, m. Elizabeth, dau. and heiress of Edward Short, Esq. of Heronden, and dying in 1654, was s. by his son,

SAMUEL CURTEIS, Esq. of Tenterden, who m. Martha, dau. and co-heir of John Porter, Esq. of Fairlawn, and was father of

EDWARD CURTEIS, Esq., mayor of Tenterden in 1663, whose son,

JEREMY CURTEIS, Esq., mayor of Tenterden in 1696, m. Sarah, dau. of Edward Wilmshurst, Esq. of Cadborough, in the co. of Sussex, and dying in 1725, left issue. The 3rd son,

EDWARD CURTEIS, Esq. of Tenterden, m. Sarah, dau. of Richard Beale, Esq. of Biddenden, and had issue, Jeremiah, his heir; Richard, of Tenterden; William; and three daus. He d. in 1777, and was s. by his eldest son,

JEREMIAH CURTEIS, Esq. of Rye and Tenterden, m. Jane, dau. and co-heir of Scarlee Giles, Esq. of Biddenden, and had issue, EDWARD-JEREMIAH, his heir; Martha, m. to Robert Mascall, Esq. of Ashford; Anne, m. to Samuel-Russell Collett, Esq. of Worcester; Jane, d. unm.; Catharine-Sarah, m. to John Luxford, Esq. of Higham. Mr. Curteis d. 31 Dec. 1806, and was s. by his only son,

EDWARD-JEREMIAH CURTEIS, Esq. of Windmill Hill, b. 6 July, 1762, elected M.P. for Sussex in 1820 and 1826. He m. 14 April, 1789, Mary, only dau. and heir of the Rev. Stephen Barrett, rector of Hethfield, Kent, the last male descendant of the ancient family of BARRETT *of the Bent*, Kildwick, Yorkshire, and by her, who d. 14 May, 1841, aged 76, had issue,

HERBERT-BARRETT, his heir.
Edward-Barrett, major 7th dragoon-guards, and M.P. for Rye in 1832 and 1834, m. 1st, 9 March, 1837, Charlotte-Lydia, youngest dau. of Thomas-Law Hodges, Esq. of Hempstead, M.P. for West Kent, which lady d. in child-birth, 8 June, 1838, leaving a son, Edward-Barrett Hodges. Major Curteis m. 2ndly, 15 Sept 1841, Frances, dau. of the late William Kenrick, Esq. of Broome, co. Surrey, and has by her, Anne-Mary; Frances; Elizabeth; Anne; and Jane.
Reginald, capt. 1st royal dragoons, m. 2 Oct. 1838, Frances-Mary, eldest dau. of Lawrence Reynolds, Esq. of Paxton Hall, co. Huntingdon, and d. 28 Jan. 1847, leaving issue, Reginald-Lawrence-Herbert, b. 3 Jan. 1843; Mary-Frances; and Mary-Frances-Ida.
Mary-Barrett, m. to Stewart-Boone Inglis, and d. in 1813.
Jane-Anne-Elizabeth, d. unm. in 1890.
Laura-Charlotte, m. to William-Henry Darby, Esq. of Leap Castle, King's County.
Anne-Katharine, m. to Lieut.-Col. Charles-William Elwood, of Clayton Priory, Sussex.
Caroline-Elinor, m. to John Graham, Esq of The Elms, Eastbourne, Sussex.
Elizabeth-Julia, m. to Howard Elphinstone, Esq., only son of Major-Gen. Sir Howard Elphinstone, Bart.

Mr. Curteis d. in 1835, and was s. by his son,

HERBERT-BARRETT CURTEIS, Esq. of Windmill Hill, M.P. for Sussex, b. 19 June, 1793, who m. 28 June, 1821, his cousin, Caroline-Sarah, dau. and co-heir of Robert Mascall, Esq. of Peasmarsh Place, in Sussex, and Ashford, in Kent, by whom (who d. in May, 1825) he left at his decease, 13 Dec. 1847, an only son, HERBERT-MASCALL, now of Windmill Hill.

Arms—Arg., a chevron, sa., between three bulls' heads, caboshed, gu. (see BURKE's *General Armory*).
Crest—A unicorn, passant, or, between four trees, ppr
Seats—Windmill Hill and Great Knello, Sussex.

CURTIS OF EAST CLIFFE.

CURTIS, FRANCIS-SAVAGE, Esq. of East Cliffe House, co. Devon, J.P. and D.L., b. 8 July, 1836.

Lineage.—The late GEORGE-SAVAGE CURTIS, Esq. of East Cliffe House, Devon, J.P. and D.L., b. 11 Feb. 1801, the only child of Liscombe-John Curtis, Esq., by his wife, Anna-Maria Savage, m. 31 Aug. 1826, Emma, 2nd dau. of Sir William Curtis, Bart. of Culland's Grove, co. Middlesex, and has issue,

FRANCIS-GEORGE-SAVAGE, now of East Cliffe House.
Selina-Emma. Susan. Ellen.
Amelia-Charlotte. Charlotte.

Mr. Curtis d. in 184 . His widow m. 2ndly, 1848, William Winthrop, Esq. of Massachusetts.

Arms—Erm., a chevron, sa., between three fleurs-de-lis, or.
Crest—An arm embowed, habited in mail, holding in the hand, ppr., a scimitar, arg., hilt and pommel, or. (*Another Crest*—An arm, erect, habited in mail, holding in the hand a sword, all ppr., hilt and pommel, or.)
Motto—Velle bene facere.
Seat—East Cliffe House, Teignmouth, co. Devon.

CURWEN OF WORKINGTON HALL.

CURWEN, HENRY, Esq. of Workington Hall, co. Cumberland, J.P. and D.L., b. 5 Dec. 1783; m. 11 Oct. 1804, Jane, dau. of Edward Stanley, Esq. of Whitehaven, and has issue,

I. JOHN.
II. Edward-Stanley, m. 22 Jan. 1838, Frances, dau. of Edward Jesse, Esq. of Hampton Court, in Middlesex.
III. Henry, of Trinity College, Cambridge.
IV. Charles. V. William.
I. Isabella, m. to the Rev. John Wordsworth, rector of Moresby, in Cumberland.
II. Julia. III. Jane.

Lineage.—"Workington (says Camden) is now the the seat of the ancient knightly family of the CURWENS, descended from Gospatric, Earl of Northumberland, who took that name by covenant from Culwen, a family of Galloway, the heir whereof they had married. They have a stately castlelike seat; and from this family (increaseth vanity) I myself am descended by the mother's side." To

GOSPATRIC, son of Orme, and great-grandson of Eldred, 2nd feudal Lord of Kendal, Alan, 2nd Lord of Allandale, his cousin-german, gave High Ireby, which remained vested in a younger branch of the Curwens, which terminated in female heirs. This Gospatric was the first of the family who was Lord of Workington, having exchanged with his cousin,

William de Lancaster, the lordship of Middleton, in Westmoreland, for the lands of Lamplugh and Workington, in Cumberland. Gospatric had (with four younger sons, Gilbert; Adam; Orme; and Alexander) his successor,

THOMAS, called after the fashion of those times, "son of Gospatric." To this Thomas, one Rowland, son of Ughtred, son of Fergus, gave the lordship of Curwen, in Galloway. He d. 7 Dec. 1152. To his 2nd son, Patric, he had given, while his eldest son was living, the lordship of Culwen, in Galloway, and the said Patric assuming his surname therefrom, became

PATRIC DE CULWEN, ancestor of the great family of CURWEN.

SIR CHRISTOPHER DE CULWEN, of Workington, like his father, represented his native county in several parliaments. He was sheriff of the same shire in the 2nd and 12th of HENRY VI. by the name of CULWEN, and in the 6th of the same reign by that of CURWEN, to which latter cognomen the family has ever since adhered. Sir Christopher's great-great-grandson,

SIR HENRY CURWEN, of Workington, had the honour of affording an asylum in his mansion-house to the Queen of Scotland, MARY STUART, when that princess sought the protection of England. Sir Henry, who represented Cumberland in parliament, in the 6th of EDWARD VI. and 1st ELIZABETH, was s. at his decease in the 35th of the latter reign, by his eldest son,

SIR NICHOLAS CURWEN, of Workington, M.P. for Cumberland, father of

SIR HENRY CURWEN, of Workington, M.P. for Cumberland in the 18th of JAMES I. His eldest son,

SIR PATRIC CURWEN, of Workington, M.P. for Cumberland, was created a Baronet in 1696, but d. issueless, in 1664, when the title became extinct, while the estates devolved upon his brother,

THOMAS CURWEN, Esq. of Workington, at whose decease, unm., 25th CHARLES II., the estates passed to his half-brother,

ELDRED CURWEN, Esq. of Workington, who d. the next year, and was s. by his son,

HENRY CURWEN, Esq. of Workington. He dying without issue, his branch of the family expired, when the estates and representation reverted to his cousin (the great-grandson of Sir Henry Curwen (Mary Stuart's host) by his 2nd wife, Jane Crosby),

ELDRED CURWEN, Esq., who thus became of Workington. Mr. Curwen served the office of sheriff for Cumberland in the 3rd of GEORGE II., and represented Cockermouth in parliament. He d. in the 18th year of the same reign, and was s. by his son,

HENRY CURWEN, Esq. of Workington, M.P. for Carlisle in 1762, and for Cumberland in 1768. Mr. Curwen m. the dau. of William Gale, Esq. of Whitehaven, and had an only dau. and heiress,

ISABELLA CURWEN, who m. JOHN CHRISTIAN, Esq of Ewanrigg Hall, and conveying to him the lands of the Curwens, he assumed, in 1790, their surname and arms, and thus became

JOHN-CHRISTIAN CURWEN, Esq. of Workington. Mr. Christian had been m. previously to Miss Taubman, of the Isle of Man, who left at her decease an only son, JOHN CHRISTIAN, Esq. of Ewanrigg Hall, one of the Dempsters of that island. (*See family of* CHRISTIAN). By the heiress of the Curwens (his 2nd wife) he had issue,

- HENRY, present possessor of Workington.
- William, in holy orders, rector of Harrington, in Cumberland, now deceased.
- Edward, of Belle Grange, co. Lancaster.
- John, in holy orders, rector of Harrington, d. 25 Feb. 1846, aged 46.
- Bridget, m. to Charles Walker, Esq. of Ashford Court, co. Salop.
- Christiana-Frances, of Uppington, in Shropshire.

Mr. Curwen served the office of sheriff for Cumberland in 1784, and was knight of the shire for Cumberland. He d. in 1828.

Arms—Arg., fretty, gu., a chief, az.
Crest—A unicorn's head, erased, arg., armed, or.
Motto—Si je n'estoy.
Seats—Workington, in Cumberland, and Belle Isle, in Windermere, Westmoreland.

CURZON OF BREEDON.

CURZON, JOHN, Esq. of Breedon, co. Leicester, b. 8 Aug. 1777; m. Rosamond-Martha, dau. of the Rev. Charles-Stead Hope, and has issue,

- I. JOHN, b. 16 Sept. 1828, d. 3 July, 1840.
- II. NATHANIEL-CHARLES, b. 26 Nov. 1829, m. Emily-Frances-Anne, youngest dau. of the Rev. German Buckston, of Sutton, co. Derby.
- III. Richard, b. 19 Nov. 1833.
- IV. William, b. 14 March, 1836.
- V. Robert, b. 3 May, 1841.
- I. Anne-Rosamond.

Lineage.—RICHARD CURZON, of Breedon, co. Leicester, b. 6 March, 1599, 2nd son of John Curzon, of Kedleston, Esq., ancestor of the Lords Scarsdale, left a son,

JOHN CURZON, Esq. of Breedon, whose son, by Mary, his wife, dau. of Rowland Lilley, Esq., was

THE REV. JOHN CURZON, rector of Kedleston, who m. Anne Toone, and d. in 1789, leaving a son,

NATHANIEL CURZON, Esq. of Breedon, who m. Anne, dau. and co-heir of John ffarnell, Gent. of Overseal, and d. 30 March, 1787, aged 51, leaving a son and successor, the present JOHN CURZON, Esq. of Breedon.

Arms—Arg., on a bend, sa., three popinjays, or, collared, gu.
Crest—A popinjay rising, or, collared, gu.
Motto—Recte et suaviter.
Seat—Breedon, co. Leicester.

CUSACK OF GERARDSTOWN AND CLONARD.

CUSACK, JAMES-WILLIAM, Esq., M.D., of Feltrim, co. Dublin, m. in April, 1818, Elizabeth-Frances, eldest dau. and co-heir of Joseph Bernard, Esq. of Greenhills, King's County, and granddau. of John Bernard, of Straw Hill, co. Carlow, and Elizabeth his wife, dau. and co-heir of Sir Gilbert Pickering, Bart. of Nova Scotia, and has issue by her (who d. 4 Sept. 1837),

- I. HENRY-THOMAS, barrister-at-law, b. 20 Oct. 1820, m. in 1854, Sophia, dau. of the late William Tanner, Esq. of Blackland House, and has issue.
- II. Ralph-Smith, barrister-at-law, b. 16 Nov. 1821, m. 23 April, 1850, Elizabeth, 2nd dau. of Richard Barker, Esq. of Stirling, co. Dublin, and has issue.
- III. James-William, M.D., b. 6 Aug 1824, m. 12 July, 1849, Sarah, 3rd dau. of the late William Tanner, Esq. of Blackland House, and has issue.
- IV. Thomas-Bernard, b. 11 Dec. 1831, m. Miss Tanner.
- I. Mary-Anne, m. 7 May, 1845, Robert-H. Tilly, Esq. of Tolerton Park, Carlow.
- II. Elizabeth-Jane, m. 7 May, 1850, Samuel-George Wilmot, Esq., M.D., of Dublin.

Mr. Cusack m. 2ndly, 10 Sept. 1838, Frances-Rothwell, relict of Richard Rothwell, Esq. of Hurlestown, co. Meath, and dau. of the Rev. S. Radcliffe. Mr. Cusack is president of the Royal College of Surgeons in Ireland, and 24th in descent of the CUSACKS *of Gerardstown*.

Lineage.—Two early descents are given by different writers, of this family, one deducing the line from the Sieurs de Cusac, who are stated to have been one of the most ancient and illustrious families in Guienne at the end of the 9th century, and where there are several towns of the name; a member of which family is said to have come over to England with WILLIAM the Conqueror, his descendants afterwards going to Ireland with King JOHN. The name was certainly in good repute several centuries afterwards in France, for we find Charles Cusake summoned to a conference of the three estates of the realm, by the Duke of Normandy, to take measures for the release of JOHN, King of France, taken prisoner at Poictiers, and mentioned as one "who bore the principal rule in the city [Rouen], and a leader in all discussions of the estates," at which conference he made so bold a speech against the king's officer, that he was imprisoned; and in the year 1451, le Sieur de Cusac, one of the generals in the army of Count Gaston de Foix, besieged Bayonne, and was made a knight for his valour by the count. The other descent is given by several old Irish writers, who deduce it from Olioll Olium, King of Munster, who d. A.D. 234; eleventh in descent from whom was Isog, ancestor of the Clan Isog, or Clan Cusack, of Clare, where they held, at a very early date, large possessions as a sept of the Macnamaras, in a very early rental of which family is given the number of silver ounces paid by the Clan Cusack as tribute, and where the name exists to this day. The Macnamaras bear, also, the same crest as the Cusacks. The name was spelt in several different ways, Cusac, Cusak, Cusacke, Cusack, Cusake, Cusacque, Cussac, Cussack, Cuisac, Cuysac. Without entering into the merits of the two descents, we will begin with

GEOFFREY DE CUSAC, living at the time of the invasion of Ireland: his name appears in the early charters of St. Mary's Abbey, Dublin, relative to various disputes concerning tithes, and again as a donor of vestments to the altar of the abbey.

GEOFFRY DE CUSACK, Lord of Killeen, Gerardstown, Folystown, Clonard, &c., held under Hugh de Lacy, in Meath, and Tyrawley, in Counaught. He *m.* the dau. and heir of Adam Petit, and had with her the manors of Clonry and Gonock, in frank-marriage. He was summoned to the first parliament held in Ireland, in 1295; he left issue,

I. ADAM, Lord of Killeen, his heir, surnamed *Ciosogach*, or "Head of the Cusacks." His granddau. and heir, Margery, marrying Richard Tuite, Knt., conveyed Killeen to her husband. She had an only dau. and heir, Joan, Lady of Killeen, who *m.* Walter Cusack, a cadet of Gerardstown; and their granddau. and heir, Joan, marrying Sir Christopher Plunket, conveyed to him Killeen Castle, which is still possessed by the Earls of Fingal, Viscounts Killeen.

II. ANDREW, Lord of Gerardstown.

III. Nicholas, who *d.* in 1299, twenty years Bishop of Kildare.

IV. Geoffrey, *d.* in 1300, Bishop of Meath.

V. William, ancestor of the line of Cussington.

The second son,

SIR ANDREW CUSACK, who inherited Gerardstown, *d.* in the year 1295, leaving issue, JOHN (Sir), his heir; Simon (Sir); WALTER (Sir), living in 1290 and 1299, who *m.* Maud, co-heir, with her sister, Isabella, Lady Howth, of William Pilate, of Pilatestown, and was ancestor of the CUSACKS, Lords of Culmolyn, Dangan, and Dunsaney. The eldest son was

SIR JOHN CUSACK, 2nd Lord of Gerardstown, &c. He and his brothers participated in the battle of Dundalk, where Edward Bruce was defeated and slain, and where Sir John and his brothers, Simon and Walter, were made knights on the field for their distinguished valour. From Sir John descended the subsequent Cusacks, Lords of Gerardstown, one of the most eminent families in Ireland.

ROBERT CUSACK, 14th Lord of Gerardstown, *m.* 1st, Margaret Porter, of Kingstown, co. Meath, and had issue by her, an only son, James, who predeceased him, leaving issue, by Margaret Bermingham, his wife, one son, heir to his grandfather; he *m.* 2ndly, Margaret, dau. of Oliver, Lord Louth, and had issue by her (who *m.* 2ndly, William Dillon). Robert Cusack *d.* 28 April, 1632 (will dated 1632), and lies buried under a tomb, with his wives and son James, in Killeen Church. He left surviving issue by his 2nd wife,

THOMAS, to whom his father gave Staffordstown estate. He *m.* Cecilia, dau. of Edward Cusack, of Lismullen, and Lucinda his wife, sister of R. Talbot, Duke of Tyrconnell. He became eventually representative of the Lismullen branch, and one of the heirs-general to the duke. His granddau. and eventual heir carried the representation to her husband, James Cusack.

Christopher. Patrick. Adam.

And several daus.

PATRICK CUSACK *s.* his grandfather Robert, in 1632, and was then aged 20 years. He *d.* leaving issue by Catherine, dau. and heir of David Sutton and his wife Catherine, dau. and co-heir of Patrick, 3rd Lord Louth, a son,

JAMES CUSACK, captain in the navy, who settled at Clonard, one of the ancient places of his family. He *m.* Alison, sole heir of John Golding, and Alison his wife, dau. of Edward, 18th Baron Howth, who, on the decease of her brother, Richard, 19th lord, became co-heir to the lineal heirship of whatever honours accrued to the family of Howth by the marriage of Robert St. Lawrence, with Joan, one of the co-heirs of Prince Edward, Duke of Somerset, Marquess of Dorset, by the Princess Elenora, co-heir of the Earl of Warwick. He left issue,

ATHANASIUS CUSACK, of Clonard, his heir, who made his will in 1679, leaving issue, by Bridget his wife, dau. and heir of Patrick, son of Francis Barnewall, of Beggstown, son of Nicholas, Lord Kingsland, a son and successor,

JAMES CUSACK, of Clonard, *b.* in 1656, an officer in King JAMES II.'s army at the battle of the Boyne. He *d.* 13 Aug. 1722, having made his will in 1720, leaving issue, by Catherine his wife, dau. and eventual heir of Robert Cusack, of Staffordstown, ATHANASIUS, his heir; HENRY, who had Clonard; and Margery, *m.* 1st, to Christopher Willson, Esq. of Moyaugher, and 2ndly, to John Martley, Esq. of Newtown Ballyfallin. The elder son,

ATHANASIUS CUSACK, inherited his father's lease of Moyaugher. He *m.* 3 July, 1707, Catherine Lloyd, niece of John Martley, Esq. of Newtown Ballyfallin, and left, with several daus., two sons, James, who *d. s. p.* in 1776, and HENRY CUSACK, Esq. of Moyaugher and Girley, *d.* 6 May, 1792, leaving issue, by his wife, Esther, dau. of Thomas Chamney, Esq. of Platten.

ATHANASIUS, his heir.

James, of Jamestown, *m.* Eliza Jones, and *d.* intestate 1790.

John.

Thomas, *d.* off Halifax, signal-lieut. to Sir John Collier.

Patrick. William-Graves.

Margaret, twin with John, *d.* 1809.

Catherine. Catherine-Esther.

The eldest son,

ATHANASIUS CUSACK, Esq. of Laragh, co Kildare, Moyaugher, and Girley, *b.* 11 May, 1749, *d.* in 1813, aged 64, and was buried in St. Thomas's, Dublin. He *m.* 1st, in 1778, Mary-Ann, only dau. of Edward Rotherham, Esq. of Crossdrum, and by her had issue,

HENRY, of Girley, who *m.* Anne, dau. of Richard Rothwell, of Barford, co. Meath, by his wife Anne, a dau. and coheir with her sister, Lady Chapman, of George Lowther, of Hurlestown, and *d.* in 1817, leaving issue, two daus., Mary, *m.* in 1836, to Charles-Cutliffe Drake, of Devonshire; and Anne.

Edward, in holy orders, *m.* Alicia, dau. of — Wolfe, Esq. of co. Kildare, but had no issue.

JAMES-WILLIAM, now of Feltrim, present heir-male.

George, now of Moyaugher, a magistrate for Meath, *b.* 6 May, 1790.

Elizabeth, *m.* to Alexander Battersby, Esq. of Daffsy Lodge, co. Kildare.

Mr. Cusack *m.* 2ndly, 1794, Katherine-Frances, dau. of Samuel Forster, of Kilmury, co. Meath, and relict of Thomas Chamney, Esq., and had issue by her,

Samuel, M.D., who *m.* Sarah, dau. of Johnston Stoney, Esq. of Oakley Park, co. Tipperary, and left issue, Samuel and Margaret.

Frances, *m.* to Capt. John Kelly.

Alicia, *m.* to Robert Warren, Esq. of Killiney Castle, co. Dublin. (*See family of* WARREN.)

Arms—Per pale, or and arg., a fesse, counterchanged.

Crest—A mermaid, sa., holding in the dexter hand a sword; sinister, a sceptre.

Mottoes—"Ave Maria, plena gratia!" and, "En Dieu est mon espoir."

CUSTANCE OF WESTON.

CUSTANCE, HAMBLETON-FRANCIS, Esq. of Weston House, co. Norfolk, *b.* 8 Nov. 1809; *m.* 29 Oct. 1841, Frances, widow of the Rev. Henry-Walpole Nevill, and youngest dau. of Sir Edmund Bacon, Bart., and has issue,

I. FREDERIC-HAMBLETON, *b.* 3 Dec. 1844.

II. Adeline-Maria.

Lineage.—JOHN CUSTANCE, an eminent merchant and alderman of Norwich (son of, William Custance, Esq. *b.* in 1632, and grandson, by Cicely his wife, dau. of Richard Atthill, Esq. of Cawston, of William Custance, Esq., who was great-grandson of Robert Custance, a large landed proprietor of Norfolk, who *d.* in 1549), purchased the Weston estates in 1726. He *m.* Sarah, dau. and co-heiress of John Hambleton, Esq. of Banham, in Norfolk, by whom (who *d.* 22 Nov. 1756), he had (with a dau., Sarah, *m.* in 1736, to Anthony Norris, Esq. of Barton Turf, in the same county) an only son and successor, at his decease, 31 May, 1752,

HAMBLETON CUSTANCE, Esq. of Weston, *b.* in 1715, *m.* Susannah, dau. and heir of John Press, alderman of Norwich, by whom (who *d.* in 1761) he had, JOHN, his heir; and Susanna, *m.* to Sir Thomas Durrant, Bart. of Scottow. Mr. Custance, who was high-sheriff in 1753, *d.* 15 April, 1757, and was *s.* by his son,

JOHN CUSTANCE, Esq. of Weston, *b.* in 1749, who *m.* Frances, 2nd dau. of Sir William-Beauchamp Proctor, Bart. of Langley Park, and had issue,

HAMBLETON-THOMAS, his heir.

George, lieutenant-colonel E.I.C.S., *d. unm.* in 1814.

William, *b.* 18 Sept. 1781.

John, in holy orders, rector of Blickling and Erpingham, *b.* 6 May, 1787.

Neville, a captain in the army, *b.* 23 Feb. 1790, *m.* in 1834, Frances, eldest dau. of Charles Weston, Esq. of Thorpe, near Norwich, and has issue two sons.

Frances-Anne, *m.* to Robert Marsham, Esq. of Stratton Strawless.

Emily, *m.* to the Rev. B. Edwards, rector of Ashill.

Charlotte, *d.* young.

Mr. Custance, who was a gentleman of the Privy Chamber, *d.* 18 Aug. 1822, and was *s.* by his eldest son,

HAMBLETON-THOMAS CUSTANCE, Esq. of Weston, *b.* 12 Feb.

1779, J.P. and D L., who *m.* 11 Feb. 1809, Mary, only child of the late Miles Bower, Esq., and niece of John Bower-Jodrell, Esq. of Henbury Hall, in Cheshire, by whom (who *d.* 6 Jan. 1851) he had issue,

HAMBLETON-FRANCIS, now of Weston.
William-Neville, *b.* 24 Oct. 1811, an officer in the army, *m.* 1st, 6 June, 1837, Jane, 2nd dau. of Colonel Campbell, K.H., of the 95th regiment, and had issue a dau. He *m.* 2ndly, Mary, dau. of Thomas Meggison, Esq. of Walton, Northumberland, and has by her two sons and three daus.
Emily-Susanna, *d.* 12 Feb. 1837.

Arms—Or, an eagle displayed, gu., charged on the breast with a star of six points, of the first, quartering, az., on a bend, erm., three legs, couped at the thigh, or, for HAMBLETON.
Crest—A demi-eagle displayed, as in the arms.
Motto—Appetitus rationi pareat.
Seat—Weston House, near Norwich.

CUTLER, FORMERLY OF YORKSHIRE.

CUTLER, JOHN, Esq. of Sidmouth, co. Devon, *b.* 20 Feb. 1789; *m.* 15 Feb. 1827, Caroline, 2nd dau. of Thomas Cotton, Esq. of London, and has issue,

I. HENRY-JOHN, *b.* 29 Aug. 1829.
II. Egerton-Cotton, *b.* 10 Aug. 1832.
I. Catherine-Emma.

Lineage.—The first authenticated ancestor of this family, JOHN CUTLER, resided at Wortley, in Yorkshire, with his kinsman, Sir Nicholas Wortley, and was standard-bearer in the wars of the Roses.

SIR THOMAS CUTLER, of Lechdale, in Gloucestershire, knighted at Whitehall, 25 Feb. 1681 (2nd son of Sir Gervase Cutler, of Stainbrough, by his wife Lady Magdalen Egerton), served as captain in the Duke of York's regiment, and was for four years and a half under the Duke of Luxembourg, the Prince of Condé, and Marshal Turenne, in the French service. He *m.* Susannah, dau. of Thomas Cook, Esq. of Stanton, Worcestershire, and widow, 1st, of Laurence Bathurst, Esq. of Lechlade, and, 2ndly, of Sir John Fettiplace, Bart. of Childrey. By this lady he had a son and heir,

THE REV. SIR EGERTON CUTLER, *b.* 20 July, 1678, chaplain to the Duke of Marlborough, in Flanders. He *m.* Mary Lipton, of the city of Oxford, and by her, who *d.* in the Low Countries about the year 1710, had a son and heir.

EGERTON CUTLER, Esq., to whom Henry Cutler, Esq., his cousin, only son of his uncle, Sir Gervase, left his estate, was sometime of the parish of St. George in the East, and *d.* about the year 1741, on shipboard, in the river Gambia, in Africa. He *m.* Grace, dau. of John Fenwick, Esq. of London, and had issue. The second son,

HENRY CUTLER, Esq., sometime of Wakefield, and afterwards of Barnsley, *m.* Eleanor, dau. of Gervase Becket, Esq., of the latter place, and by her, who *d.* 10 Dec. 1776, aged 46, had issue, HENRY, his heir; John, from whom CUTLER *of Upton*; Egerton, *d. unm.*; and Thomas, who *d.* in 1775. Mr. Cutler *d.* at Barnsley, in Oct. 1764, aged about 37, and was *s.* by his eldest son,

HENRY CUTLER, Esq. of Sidmouth, co. Devon, *b.* 9 April, 1752, who *m.* 1st, Katherine, 2nd dau. of John Olive, Esq. of Oporto, and by her, who (*d.* at Exeter, 3 Nov. 1816, had issue,

JOHN, now of Sidmouth.
Charles, *b.* 25 Jan. 1790, *m.* at Calcutta, 28 June, 1817, Maria-Jane, eldest dau. of Joseph Marechaux, Esq.
Egerton, *b.* 24 June, 1791, *m.* at Stamford, 12 April, 1814, Mary-Anne, yonngest dau. of Jeremiah Belgrave, Esq., and *d.* 7 March, 1833, *s. p.*
Catherine. Elizabeth. Eleanor.

Mr. Cutler *m.* 2ndly, Albinia, dau. of Robert Raikes, Esq., and widow of John Birch, Esq., but by her had no issue. He *d.* 2 Jan. 1835.

Arms—Az., three dragon or wyverns' heads, erased, within a bordure, or.
Crest—A wyvern's head, erased, or, ducally collared, az.
Seat—Sidmouth, Devon.

CUTLER OF UPTON.

CUTLER, GEORGE-HENRY, Esq. of Upton, co. Devon, J.P., *s.* his father in 1799.

Lineage.—JOHN CUTLER, Esq. of Upton, in Devon, J.P., 2nd son of Henry Cutler, Esq. of Barnsley, by Eleanor his wife, dau. of Gervase Beckett, Esq. of the same place, *m.* 29 March, 1783, Sarah, dau. of George Olive, Esq. of that town, and had issue,

GEORGE-HENRY, now of Upton. Frank.
Wingfield. Olive. Beckett.
Sarah-Ellison, *m.* to the Rev. Thomas Blackhall, vicar of Tardebig, Worcestershire, and *d.* leaving two children.
Eleanor, *m.* to the Rev. Robert Holdsworth, vicar of Brixham and of Townstall, Devon, and has issue.

Mr. Cutler *d.* in July, 1799.

Arms and *Crest*—As preceding article.
Seat—Upton, Torbay.

D'AETH OF KNOWLTON COURT.

HUGHES-D'AETH, GEORGE-WILLIAM, Esq. of Knowlton Court, in Kent, Rear-Admiral, R.N., *m.* 1816, Harriet, dau. of the late Sir Edward Knatchbull, Bart. of Mersham Hatch, and has issue,

I. NARBOROUGH. II. Edward-Henry.
III. George-Wyndham. IV. Charles.
I. Harriet. II. Frances. III. Elizabeth.

This family, which derives its surname from Aeth, in Flanders, is of ancient standing in the co. of Kent. Its representative,

SIR THOMAS D'AETH, who was created a BARONET 16 July, 1716, *m.* 1st, Elizabeth, sole heiress of her brother, Sir John Narborough, of Knowlton Court, Bart., who was unfortunately cast away, with his father-in-law, Sir Cloudesley Shovel, on the rocks of Scilly, 22 Oct. 1707. By the heiress of Knowlton Sir Thomas D'Aeth had,

I. NARBOROUGH, his heir, 2nd Bart., whose only child, SIR NARBOROUGH D'AETH, 3rd Bart., *d. unm.* in April, 1808, when the estates devolved in his cousin, GEORGE-WILLIAM HUGHES, the present REAR-ADMIRAL D'AETH.
II. Thomas.
I. Elizabeth, who *m.* in 1740, the Hon. and Rev. Godfrey Dawney, and *d. s. p.*
II. Elhanna, *m.* to Capt. Fitzgerald, of the French service, and *d. s. p.*
III. Sophia, *m.* in 1749, William Champneys, Esq. of Vintners, in Kent, but *d.* without issue, in 1772.
IV. Bethia, *m.* 1st, to Herbert Palmer, Esq. of Wingham, in Kent, and 2ndly, to John Cosnan, Esq. She *d. s. p.*
V. HARRIET, *m.* Josiah Hardy, Esq. consul at Cadiz, and had five daus. namely,
  1 HARRIET HARDY, who became the 2nd wife of William Hughes, Esq. of Betshanger, in Kent, son of Thomas Hughes, M.D. of Oxford, by Mary his wife, only child and heiress of William Smith, Esq. of Eltham, and grandson of John Hughes, Esq. of Newbery, co. Berks, and by him, who *d.* in April. 1786, had (with three daus., Harriet Hughes, *m.* to George-Leonard Austen, Esq. of Sevenoaks, in Kent; Louisa Hughes; and Charlotte Hughes, *d. unm.*) one son, GEORGE-WILLIAM HUGHES, the present REAR-ADMIRAL D'AETH, of Knowlton.
  2 Elizabeth-Sophia Hardy, *m.* to Edward Markland, Esq. of Leeds.
  3 Priscilla Hardy, *m.* to John Godby, Esq. of Greenwich.
  4 Louisa Hardy, *m.* to John Cooke, Esq., captain of the "Bellerophon," killed at Trafalgar.
  5 Charlotte Hardy, *m.* to Lieut.-Colonel George-John Hamilton, R.A.

Sir Thomas D'Aeth *m.* 2ndly, Jane, dau. of Walter Williams, Esq. of Dingestow, in the co. of Monmouth, and had by her one son, Francis, in holy orders, rector of Knowlton, who *d. unm.* in 1784. Sir Thomas was chosen member of parliament for Canterbury in 1708, and for Sandwich in 1714. He *d.* 4 Jan. 1745.

Arms—Quarterly: 1st and 4th, sa., a griffin, passant, or, between three crescents, arg.; 2nd and 3rd, sa., a chevron, between three fleurs-de-lis, arg.
Crest—A griffin's head, erased, or, in the mouth a trefoil, slipped, vert.
Seat—Knowlton Court, co. Kent.

DALE OF GLANVILLE'S WOOTTON.

DALE, JAMES-CHARLES, Esq., M.A., of Glanville's Wootton, and Newton Montague, co. Dorset, *b.* 13 Dec. 1791, high-sheriff of Dorsetshire in 1843; *m.* 28 Dec. 1848, Marianne-Lucy, dau. of Henry Wylde, Esq., and by her (who is a descendant of Robert de Eglesfield, founder of Queen's College, Oxford) has issue,

I. CHARLES-WILLIAM, *b.* 15 May, 1851.
II. Edward-Robert, *b.* 29 Jan. 1853.

Lineage.—THOMAS DALE, Esq. of Purewell, Christchurch, co. Southampton, a younger son of William Dale, Esq. of Chewton House, co. Hants, *m.* Anne Lapthorne, of Plymouth (her sister, Martha Lapthorne, *m.* Captain Pelly, of Upton, Essex), and had issue four sons and four daus. Of the former, the only one who survived his father was

James Dale, Esq. of Blandford, who was b. in Dec. 1722, entered the navy at an early age, and subsequently was in the East India service. Captain Dale, after his retirement from sea, purchased the residence at Blandford in 1763, and served as high-sheriff of Dorsetshire in 1770. He m. Elizabeth, dau. of John Ganett, Esq. of Blandford and of Woolland. He d. in 1794, having purchased, in 1767, from Edmund Walter, Esq. of Stoilbridge, the estate of Glanville's Wootton, and settled it in the following year upon his eldest son,

James Dale, Esq. of Glanville's Wootton, co. Dorset, b. 16 Feb. 1765, who m. in 1788, Mary-Kellaway, dau. of Stephen Barton, Esq., and had issue,

James-Charles, of Glanville's Wootton.
Mary, m. Henry Meggs, Esq., and d. 1 Jan. 1822.

Mr. Dale d. 21 July, 1835.

Arms—Az., three bugle-horns.
Crest—A garb, ppr.
Seats—Glanville's Wootton, and Newton-Montague (once the property of John, 1st Duke of Marlborough), co. Dorset.

DALE OF ASHBORNE.

Dale, Helen-Katharine, and Frances-Elizabeth, succeeded their brother, Robert Dale, Esq., in 1853. Helen-Katharine, the eldest sister, m. 28 Dec. 1829, John-J. Shuttleworth, Esq. of Hodsack Park, co. Nottingham, and has had issue,

I. George-Joseph, d. 22 Dec. 1842.
I. Mary-Katharine-Frances.

Lineage.—This family is of great antiquity in the county of Derby. Fragments of old manuscripts in the possession of the family mention "Sir Thomas Dale, lord-justice of Ireland in 1365," "In ye 3 or 4 of Philip and Mary, Wal. de Dale, Dr. of Civil Law, Mr. of ye Court of Requests," "Mestre Henri de Dale lent to ye king 300 marks," "Walter de la Dale" (14 Rich. II.), "Willus atte Dale, de Derby" (15 Rich. II.)

Robert Dale, Esq. of Flagg, co. Derby, entered his pedigree at the Herald's Visitation of that county in 1634. He m. Margery, dau. of Thomas Chadwick, Esq. of Fairfield Head, co. Stafford, and d. in 1642, leaving (with three daus.) three sons, viz., 1 Thurstan, d. unm.; 2 Richard, who m. Mary, dau. of William Baker, of Ashover and Sheldon, and d. in 1642, leaving a son, George, of Flagg, who m. Millicent, dau. of Robert Dakayne, of Prestcliff, co. Derby, and had, with a dau. Anne, wife of Sir William Bowyer, Bart., two sons, Thurstan, who d. unm.; and Robert, of Flagg, whose dau. Millicent, m. Thomas Powell, Esq. of Parke, in Salop, who survived her, and sold the Flagg estate to Thomas Bagshaw, Esq. of Ridge; 3 Thomas. The 3rd son,

Thomas Dale, Esq. of Parwich, co. Derby, b. in 1603, m. Mary, dau. of Thomas Piatts, of Flagg, and had two sons and two daus. The elder son,

Robert Dale, Esq. of Parwich, m. 1st, Alice, dau. of German Buxton, Esq. of Brassington, co. Derby, and 2ndly, Anne, dau. of George Milward, of Alsop, in the same county. By the former he had two sons and as many daus., viz., Thurstan, his heir; Robert, aged 40 in 1710, being then unm.; Margaret, m. to the Rev. Luke Flint, M.A. of Somersall, in Staffordshire; Mary, living unm. in 1710. Mr. Dale was 68 years of age in 1710, and was s. by his eldest son,

Thurstan Dale, Esq. of Bakewell and Ashborne, co. Derby, b. in 1668, m. 1st, Dorothy, dau. of John Hayne, Esq. of Ashborne, and heir of her mother, Dorothy, dau. and heiress of James Bullock, Esq. of Brampton, and had issue three sons, Robert, his heir; John, buried at Bakewell, 1752; Thurstan, b. in 1797. He m. 2ndly, Troth, dau. of — Sleigh, of Ashborne, and widow of Charles Grammar, Esq. of the same place, but by her had no issue. He was s. by his eldest son,

Robert Dale, Esq. of Ashborne, J.P., b. in 1693, m. Tryphena, dau. of Charles Grammer, Esq. of the same place, and had two sons, Thurstan, his heir; Robert, d. unm. 20 May, 1795. Mr. Dale d. 1765, and was s. by his son,

Thurstan Dale, Esq. of Ashborne. m. Elizabeth, dau. of Isaac Burrows, Esq. of Castlefield, co. Derby, by his 2nd wife, Honora Burton, who was directly descended from King Edward III., and by her, who was buried 15 March, 1781, left, at his decease in July, 1761, a son and successor,

Robert Dale, Esq. of Ashborne, high-sheriff for the co. of Derby in 1786, deputy-lieutenant of the same county, and commandant of the late corps of Ashborne Volunteer Infantry, m. 2 May, 1773, Katharine, eldest dau. of Richard Dyott, Esq. of Freeford, co. Stafford, great-grandson of Richard Dyott, Esq. of Freeford, by Katharine his wife, dau. of Thomas Gresley, Esq. eldest son of Sir Thomas Gresley, Bart. of Drakelow, by Susan his wife, dau. of Sir Humphrey Ferrers, Knt. descended from King Edward I., and by her, who d. 6 July, 1831, had issue.

Robert, lieutenant-colonel in the army, commanded the 93rd Higlanders at the battle of New Orleans, in 1815, where he fell at the head of his regiment. He m. Harriet, dau. of Lieut.-Colonel Bainbrigge, but d. without issue.
Thurstan, heir to his father, major in the army.
Richard, lieutenant of the 9th foot, who was on active service during the whole of the Peninsular War, d. in camp, near Paris, Sept. 1815.
Katharine, m. to Joseph Dalby, Esq. of Leicester.
Elizabeth. Anne, d. young. Mary-Frances.

Mr. Dale d. 3 Jan. 1835, and was s. by his eldest surviving son,

Thurstan Dale, Esq. of Ashborne, major of the 4th, or King's Own, regiment of foot, who was taken prisoner by the French in 1797. The following year he succeeded in making his escape from the prison of Orleans, together with two other officers of the King's Own. He was likewise with the army in Holland, and finally on the Staff, and aide-de-camp to General Dyott. He m. 28 March, 1800, Helen, dau. of Thomas Matthews, Esq. of Drogheda, and sister to Colonel James de MacMahon, of the Château de Caumont, near Toulouse, who, on entering the Spanish service, resumed the family name of MacMahon. Major Dale d. 6 July, 1850, leaving issue,

Thurstan, heir to his father, B.A. of the Inner Temple.
Robert, a lieutenant in the army.
Helen-Katharine, m. to John-J. Shuttleworth, Esq. of Hodsack Park, co. Nottingham.
Frances-Elizabeth.
Katharine-Amelia, m. to Edward Chaloner, Esq. of Goldthorpe Grange, co. Nottingham, and d. 19 May, 1840, leaving three daus., Helen-Mary; Henrietta-Mary; and Katharine-Flora.

Thurstan Dale, Esq. of Ashborne, B.A. of the Inner Temple, s. his father, d. 14 Dec. 1851, and was s. by his brother,

Robert Dale, Esq. of Ashborne, a lieutenant in the 63rd regiment of foot, who was sent out, in Feb. 1829, with a detachment of his regiment, to the Swan River Settlement, Western Australia. His public services were most invaluable and important to the new colony; he explored the interior of the country to the eastward of the Darling range of mountains, and discovered the great grazing district. On this expedition he discovered the Avon river, the Dyott range (so called in compliment to General Dyott, the colonel of his regiment), and Mount Bakewell, the highest of these. Mount Dale, lying between the Swan and the Avon, was named by Governor Sir James Stirling, after the discoverer. Two government grants of above 2000 acres each, and free from all location-duties, were given to Lieutenant Dale by the governor, in acknowledgment of his services. He left the army in 1832, d. at Bath, 20 July, 1853, and was buried in the Catholic Church of St. John the Evangelist, in that city. Mr. Dale was s. by his sisters, Helen-Katharine and Frances-Elizabeth.

Arms—Paly of six, gu. and arg., a bend, erm.; on a chief, az., three garbs, or.
Crest—A mount, vert, thereon three Danish battle-axes, one in pale, and two in saltier, ppr., the staves, az., encompassed by a chaplet of roses, alternately gu. and az., banded by a riband, or.
Motto—Non arbitrio popularis auræ.
Seat—Ashbourn.

DALISON OF HAMPTONS.

Dalison, Maximilian-Dudley-Digges, Esq. of Hamptons, co. Kent, J.P. and D.L., major West Kent militia, b. 3 Sept. 1792; m. 8 May, 1819, Anne-Maria, 3rd dau. of Sir John-Gregory Shaw, Bart. of Kenward, Kent, and has issue,

I. Maximilian-Hammond, b. 13 May, 1820, m. 10 July, 1845, Matilda, 2nd dau. of the Rev. Robert Alexander, and has issue, Maximilian-Dudley-Digges, b. 5 Feb. 1852; Matilda-Theodosia; and Dorothea-Caroline.
II. John-Beauvoir, b. 28 Feb. 1822, in holy orders, m. Harriet-Augusta, dau. of Capt. C. Shaw, R.N., and has issue.
III. William-Stanley, b. 25 April, 1828.
IV. Francis-Shaw, b. 8 April, 1831, lieut. R.N.
V. Charles-Burrell, b. 19 Feb. 1835.

I. Anna-Maria-Julia, m. 13 May, 1845, to James, 2nd son of James Alexander, Esq. of Somerhill.
II. Caroline-Mary.
III. Emma, m. 13 May, 1845, to the Rev. R. Pulteney.
IV. Georgiana, m. 12 Aug. 1851, to Charles-Watson Townley, eldest son of R.-G. Townley, Esq. of Fulbourn, co. Cambridge.
V. Louisa.

Mr. Dalison, who is 2nd son of the late William Hammond, Esq. of St. Alban's Court, co. Kent, by Elizabeth his wife, eldest dau. and co-heiress of the Rev. Osmund Beauvoir, D.D., assumed, by letters-patent, dated 10 March, 1819, the surname of DALISON only, upon inheriting, under the will of the late Frances-Isabella Master, widow of W.-D. Master, Esq. of Yotes Court, Kent, the estates in Kent and Lincolnshire of the ancient family of DALISON *of Hamptons*.

Lineage.—The family of Dalison is stated to derive from William D'Alençon, one of the companions in arms of the CONQUEROR. The representative of the family in the 16th century,

WILLIAM DALYSON, Esq. of Laughton, co. Lincoln, son of William Dalison, and grandson of William Dalyson, by his wife, a dau. of John Vavasour, of Spaldington, was sheriff and escheator of that county. He d. 18 Dec. 1546, leaving, by his wife, a dau. of George Wastneys, Esq. of Haddon, Notts, with three daus., two sons, viz.,

GEORGE, of Laughton, grandfather of SIR ROGER DALISON, of Laughton, lieutenant-general of the Ordnance, who was created a BARONET in 1611. His son and successor, SIR THOMAS DALISON, 2nd Baronet, fell, gallantly fighting under the royal banner, at Naseby, in 1645, when the title became EXTINCT.
WILLIAM, M.P. for Lincolnshire, one of the judges of the Court of King's Bench, ancestor of the Kentish family, of which M.-D.-D. Dalison, Esq., now of Hamptons, is a descendant, being 7th in a direct line from Sir Maximilian Dalison, of Halling, grandson of the judge.

Arms—Gu., three crescents, or; a canton, erm.
Crest—A man, completely accoutred in armour, ppr., holding in his dexter hand a battle-axe, arg., handle, gu.
Motto—D'accomplir Agincourt.
Seat—Hamptons, near Tonbridge.

DALTON OF SLENINGFORD.

DALTON, JOHN, Esq. of Sleningford, co. Yorkshire, and of Fillingham Castle, co. Lincoln, late a captain in the army; m. Elizabeth, only dau. of Richard Lodge, Esq. of Leeds, and has issue.

Lineage.—The family of DALTON is proved by Dugdale's Visitation (1666) to have been settled at Kingston-upon-Hull many years prior to going into Richmondshire.

SIR WILLIAM DALTON, Knt. of York, one of the King's council for the northern parts, son of Thomas Dalton, of Sutton in Holdernesse, by Anne his wife, dau. of Sir Robert Tyrwhitt, of Kettelby, filled the office of recorder of York and Hull, and was subsequently appointed by JAMES I., attorney-general to the court at York, receiving at the same time, the honour of knighthood. Sir William d. in 1649. His son and heir,

JOHN DALTON, Esq. of Hawkeswell, who m Dorothy, dau. of Sir Conyers Darcy, Lord Darcy, served as lieut.-col. to his brother-in-law, the Lord Darcy, and was mortally wounded on passing the bridge of Burton-upon-Trent, while conducting the Queen from Burlington to Oxford. His eldest son was Sir William Dalton, of Hawkeswell: his 2nd,

THOMAS DALTON, Esq. of Bedale, who m. Anne, dau. of Sir Marmaduke Wyvill, Bart. of Constable Burton, was great-grandfather of

JOHN DALTON, Esq., who acquired very high reputation in the E. I. Co.'s service. He m. Isabella, 2nd dau. of Sir John Wray, Bart., by whom (who d. 29 May, 1780) he left at his decease, in July, 1811, three sons and two daus., viz.,

THOMAS, who assumed, in 1807, the surname of NORCLIFFE (*see that family.*)
JOHN, who inherited Sleningford.
James, in holy orders, rector of Croft, in Yorkshire, who m. Maria, dau. of the Rev. E. Gibson, of Bishop's Stortford, in Essex, and has issue.
Frances-Elizabeth, m. to William Garforth, Esq. of Wiganthorpe.
Isabella, m. to George Baker, Esq. of Elemore, in Durham.

Mr. Dalton, who purchased Sleningford from Sir Cecil Wray, Bart., was s. therein by his 2nd son,

JOHN DALTON, Esq. of Sleningford, co. York, and Fillingham Castle, co. Lincoln, a lieut.-col. in the army, who m. 10 March, 1783, Susanna, eldest dau. of General Robert Prescott, of Rose Green, co. Sussex, and had issue,

JOHN, now of Sleningford.
James-Robert, commander in the royal navy.
Charles, royal artillery, m. in Feb. 1832, Mary, dau. of Dr. Duncan, M.D.
George, royal engineers, m. in Aug. 1829, Euphemia Caulfield, dau. of Thomas Hannington, Esq. of Dungannon Castle, Derry, Ireland.
William-Serjeantson, an officer in the army, m. in Jan. 1830, Laura, dau. of Captain King, R.N.
Susanna-Isabella, m. in 1805, to Lieut.-General Sir James-Charles Dalbiac, and has issue, an only child, Susannah-Stephania, m. 29 Dec. 1836, to the Duke of Roxburghe.
Frances-Elizabeth, m. to the Rev. John-Walker Harrison, of Norton-le-Clay, in the county of York, and has issue.
Maria-Catherine, m. to George Cleghorne, Esq. of The Weens, in Roxburghshire, and has issue.
Albinia.
Madelina-Agnes, m. in Oct. 1830, to the Rev. Cecil-Wray Dalton.

Col. Dalton d. 29 Sept. 1841.

Arms—Az., semée of cross-crosslets, arg., a lion, rampant-guardant, of the second; a chief, nebulée, arg. and sa.
Crest—A wyvern's head, displayed, vert, the sides of the wings, or, gorged with a collar.
Seats—Sleningford, near Ripon; Fillingham Castle, ten miles north of Lincoln.

DALTON OF THURNHAM.

THE representation of this ancient family at present vests in the two surviving daus. and co-heirs of the late JOHN DALTON, Esq. of Thurnham Hall; viz., LUCY, wife of JOSEPH BUSHELL, Esq., barrister-at-law, and ELIZABETH.

Lineage.—SIR JOHN DALTON, Knt., son of Sir Robert de Dalton, living in the reign of EDWARD III., d. in 1369, seised of the manors of Bispham, Dalton Hall, and other lands in the county of Lancaster. He was direct ancestor of

ROBERT DALTON, Esq. of Bispham and Pilling, who acquired by purchase, in 1556, the manor and estate of Thurnham.

THOMAS DALTON, Esq. of Thurnham, an enterprising cavalier, raised, at his own expense, a regiment of horse, to support the cause of royalty. After rendering many very essential services to his ill-fated sovereign, he was at length so desperately wounded at the second battle of Newbury, as to survive but a very short period that unhappy conflict. His granddau. and co-heir,

ELIZABETH DALTON, eldest dau. of ROBERT DALTON, Esq. of Thurnham, by Elisabeth Horner his wife, s. to the estates of Thurnham, Cockersand, &c., co. Lancaster. She m. WILLIAM HOGHTON, Esq. of Park Hall, derived from Richard Hoghton, Esq. of Park Hall, 3rd son of Sir Richard Hoghton, of Hoghton Tower, co. Lancaster, and was s. at her decease, in 1710, by her eldest son,

JOHN HOGHTON, Esq., who assumed the surname of DALTON. He m. Frances, dau. of Sir Piers Mostyn, Bart. of Talacre, and was s. by his son,

ROBERT DALTON, Esq. of Thurnham, who m. 1st, Miss Butler, and had a son JOHN, his heir. He m. 2ndly, Bridget, dau. of Thomas More, Esq. of Barnborough, and by her had a son, William, and a dau., Anne, m. to Sir James Fitzgerald, Bart. of Castle Ishen. The eldest son,

JOHN DALTON, Esq. of Thurham Hall, m. Mary, dau. of Sir Thomas-Rookwood Gage, Bart. of Hengrave, and by her, who d. in 1819, had issue,

JOHN, who m. Mary-Anne, dau. of George Cary, Esq. of Torr Abbey, co. Devon, but d. s. p. His widow, who m. 2ndly, Sir John-Hayford Thorold, Bart., and 3rdly, Sir Charles Ogle, Bart., d. in 1842.
Mary, d. unm.
LUCY, co-heiress, m. in 1816, to Joseph Bushell, Esq., barrister-at-law, of Meyerscough Cottage, co. Lancaster.
ELIZABETH, co-heiress.
Bridget; Charlotte; who both d. unm.

Arms—Az., semée of cross-crosslets, arg., a lion, rampant-guardant, of the last.
Crest—A dragon's head, vert, between two dragons' wings, or.
Seat—Thurnham Hall, Lancashire.

DALTON OF DUNKIRK MANOR HOUSE.

DALTON, EDWARD, Esq., D.C.L., F.S.A., of Dunkirk Manor House, Minchinhampton, co. Gloucester, barrister-at-law, *b.* 22 May, 1787; *m.* 24 Nov. 1831, Elizabeth-Head, only dau. of Nathaniel Lloyd, Esq. of Uley, co. Gloucester, and has an only surviving child,

ELIZABETH-HEAD.

Lineage.—This is a branch of the family of the name of Thurnham Hall, Lancashire, resident for many generations at Curbridge, in the parish of Witney, Oxfordshire, whence Walter Dalton, with his sons, joined his chief, Colonel Thomas Dalton, who raised a regiment to assist King CHARLES I., as recorded by Lloyd, and other historians. They suffered severely at Newbury, in 1644. Colonel Dalton died of his wounds, at Marlborough, and Walter Dalton, the younger, escaped wounded into Wales, where he purchased lands near Kidwelly, still in possession of the family. He left issue,

JAMES DALTON, Esq., barrister-at-law, resident at Pembrey, near Kidwelly, where he *d.* 5 May, 1721, aged 71.*

JOHN DALTON, Esq., his eldest son, receiver for the Duchy of Lancaster, *m.* Mary, dau. and co-heir of Howel Powel, Esq. of Host House, and dying 22 Feb. 1724, left issue. The son and heir,

THE REV. JAMES DALTON, A.M., *b.* 23 June, 1718, rector of Stanmore, Middlesex, *d.* in 1788. He *m.* 1st, Grace, dau. of William Ellis, Esq. of St. Julians, and had by her a son, James, a district judge in the East Indies, where he *d. s. p.*, and a dau., Sarah, wife of Wm. Covell, Esq. He *m.* 2ndly, Mary-Box, co-heiress of John Woodward, Esq. of Butler's Merston, Warwickshire, and by her (who *d.* 15 Dec. 1790) had two sons, of whom the elder,

JOHN DALTON, Esq., Hon. E. I. Company's civil service at Bombay, *m.* Elizabeth, sister of James Forbes, Esq., F.R.S., author of *Oriental Memoirs, &c.*, and *d.* in 1785, *s. p.* His brother and heir,

WILLIAM-EDWARD DALTON, Esq., *m.* Anne, dau. of Captain Covell, descended from the "judicious" Hooker. He *d.* 5 Dec. 1797, having had four daus., Mary, *m.* to William Allies, Esq.; Anne, *m.* to Edwin Allies; Eliza, *m.* to John Budden, Esq.; and Sarah; and four sons, viz.,

JOHN, *b.* 25 Aug. 1780, of Stanmore, and the Priory House, Peckham, Surrey, *m.* 1st, Hannah, only dau. of James Neale, Esq., by whom he had issue two daus., Eliza and Hannah, and seven sons, viz., 1 James-Edwards, A.M., in holy orders, *b.* 4 May, 1807, wrangler in 1829, fellow of Queen's College, Cambridge; 2 John-Neale, A.M., in holy orders, of Caius College, Cambridge, *b.* 27 July, 1808, wrangler in 1834; 3 William-Henry, *b.* 24 Oct. 1809; 4 Samuel-Neale, A.M., of Caius College, Cambridge, in holy orders, *b.* 30 Dec. 1813, wrangler in 1837; 5 Edward, *b.* 22 April, 1815; 6 Benjamin-Neale, *b.* 11 Aug. 1816; and, 7 Herbert, *b.* 9 April, 1821. He *m.* 2ndly, in 1823, Catharine, only dau. of Thomas Chambers, Esq., but had no issue by her.

James-Forbes, *b.* 25 April, 1785, of Hornsey, Middlesex.

EDWARD, D.C.L., F.S.A., of Dunkirk Manor House.

Arthur, of Swansea, *b.* 20 March, 1794, *m.* his third-cousin, Mary, only dau. of Thomas Dalton, Esq. of Cardiff, and has issue, Arthur; Thomas-Masters; and Mary.

Arms—Az., semée of cross-crosslets, a lion, rampant-guardant, arg.

Crest—A gryphon or demi-dragon, issuant, vert, wings ouvert.

Motto—Inter cruces triumphans in cruce.

Seat—Dunkirk House, near Minchinhampton, in the co. Gloucester.

DALWAY OF BELLA HILL.

DALWAY, MARRIOTT, Esq. of Bella Hill, M.A., co. Antrim, *b.* 8 April, 1798; *m.* 29 June, 1827, Euphemia, dau. of Thomas Henry, Esq. of Castle Dawson, co. Londonderry, and has issue,

I. MARRIOTT-ROBERT, *b.* 17 Nov. 1832.

I. Euphemia, *m.* 4 Aug. 1853, the Rev. Alfred-T. Lee, youngest son of Sir J.-Theophilus Lee, of Lamister Hall, Torquay, and has issue, a son, Marriott-Dalway, *b.* 17 May, 1854.

Mr. Dalway was four times high-sheriff for the county of the town of Carrickfergus, and has been mayor of that borough since 1838.

Lineage.—The first of this family who settled in Ireland was JOHN DALLWAYE, who went over from Devonshire in 1573, a cornet in the army of Queen ELIZABETH, under Walter Devereux, Earl of Essex. He *m.* Jane O'Bryne, granddau. of Hugh O'Neill, Earl of Tyrone, and related by the mother to Shane MacBryan O'Neill, of the Lower Clandeboye. He obtained from Shane MacBryan O'Neill a grant of the greater part of the Tough of Bradenisland or Braidisland, and the lands of Kilroot. On O'Neill's death, in 1595, his lands became forfeited to the Crown; but on 8 Oct. 1603, John Dallwaye, then constable of Carrickfergus Castle, obtained from King JAMES I. a grant for ever of "the barony of Braidiland, at the rent of xiii Engl. to hold for ever in free and common soccage, as of the Castle of Carrickfergus." These lands, together with those purchased from James Hamilton, Lord Clandeboye, were on 8 July, 1608, erected by letters-patent into the manor of Dallwaye. John Dallwaye was mayor of Carrickfergus in 1592 and 1600, and in 1613 was M.P. for Bangor in the Irish Parliament; by his marriage with Jane O'Bryne, he had an only child, Margaret, who was *m.* about 1603, to John Dobbs, who became possessed of the lands of Castle Dobbs and Ballymure (*see* DOBBS *of Castle Dobbs*). On his death, about 1618, he was *s.* by his nephew,

JOHN DALLWAY the elder son of his brother Giles (he had a younger brother also named John, who was captain in the army, and high-sheriff of the co. Antrim in 1636). He *m.* a dau. of William Edmonstone, of Red Hale, co. Antrim, and by her had issue, ALEXANDER, his heir; Robert; John; Archibald; Henry; Helen, *m.* 1st, Andrew Clements, Esq. of Carrickfergus, and 2ndly, Col. James Wallace. John Dalway was mayor of Carrickfergus in 1660 and 1661. He *d.* in 1665, and was *s.* by his eldest son,

ALEXANDER DALWAY, who *m.* Anne, dau. of John Parks, Esq. of Carrickfergus: she survived him, and *m.* 2ndly, James Shaw, Esq. of Dunnathie. By his marriage with Anne Parks, Alexander had issue, JOHN, his heir; Robert, *m.* Lettice, dau. of Capt. John Dalway, and *d. s. p.* 1698; Elinor, *m.* to Henry Clements, Esq. of Mullakinhill, co. Antrim (who was high-sheriff for the county in 1707), she *d.* 1696; Mary, *m.* Anthony Kerr, Esq.; Jane. Alexander Dalway was high-sheriff of co. Antrim in 1662. He *d.* in 1668, and was *s.* by his eldest son,

JOHN DALWAY, who *d. s. p.* 1687, and left his estates to his uncle,

COL. ROBERT DALWAY, who *m.* Mary, dau. of Sir John William, Bart., co. Kent, and widow of Charles, 1st Lord Shelburne, and by her (who *d.* in 1760) had issue, ALEXANDER, his heir; Henry; John; Anne; Elinor, *m.* Andrew Stewart, Esq. of Castle Stuart. Col. Robert Dalway was, in 1695, M.P. for Antrim. He was *s.* by his eldest son,

ALEXANDER DALWAY, Esq., who *m.* 27 Sept. 1695, Anna-Helena, dau. of Archibald Edmonstone, Esq. of Red Hall, and by her had issue, ROBERT, his heir; Archibald; Alexander; Elizabeth, *m.* James Macartney, Esq.; Anne, *m.* 1st, Arthur Maxwell, Esq. of Drumbeg, co. Down, 2ndly, Rev. Samuel Halliday, of Belfast; Helena; Emily; Lettice, *m.* John Hamilton, of Ballybogh, co. Cavan. Alexander Dalway was, in 1715, M.P. for Carrickfergus; he *d.* in 1718, and was *s.* by his eldest son,

ROBERT DALWAY, who *m.* 21 Jan. 1718, Mary, dau. of Joseph Marriott, Esq. of Dublin, and 2ndly, Jane Steele, of Craigs Castle, Ballymena: by his 1st wife he had issue,

Robert, *b.* 5 Aug. 1723, *d.* young.

MARRIOTT, his heir.

Mehetabella, *m.* Noah Webb, Esq. of Dunshogklin, co. Meath, and had issue a son, NOAH, of whom presently.

Ann, *d. unm.*

Eleanor, *d.* 1791, *unm.*

Mary, *d.* Oct. 1795.

Robert Dalway, in 1721, was M.P. for Newry, and in 1740 was high-sheriff for the co. of Dublin. He *d.* in 1761, and was *s.* by his son,

MARRIOTT DALWAY, in 1761 was M.P. for Carrickfergus, and in 1784 colonel of the volunteer battalion raised by himself. He *d. s. p.* 8 April, 1795, leaving his estates to his nephew, Noah Webb, who in accordance with the will of his uncle assumed the name and arms of DALWAY. This

---

* EDWARD DALTON, 5th son of James Dalton, Esq., by Joyce Vaughan his wife, was Collector at Llanelly. He *m.* Elizabeth, dau. of John Bevan, Esq. of Penecoyd, and had,

JOHN, *b.* in 1706, whose son, EDWARD DALTON, *m.* his cousin Ayliffe, dau. of James-Ormonde Dalton, Esq., and had, with three daus., two sons: the younger, John, lieut. E I.C.S., was killed at Assaye; the elder JAMES DALTON, Esq. (medical service, E.I.), *m.* Augusta Ritso, and *d.* in 1823, leaving issue, Henry-Augustus, *b.* in 1808; Hawkins-Augustus, *b.* in 1813; Charlotte-Augusta; and Carolina-Georgiana, *m.* to Daniel Prytherch, Esq. of Abergole, co. Carmarthen.

NOAH DALWAY, Esq. m. in 1795, Ellen, dau. of Archdeacon Conway Benning, and had issue,

MARRIOTT, his heir.
Noah, lieut. R.N., b. 30 April, 1799, m. 1828, Emily Gibbon, and has issue two sons and four daus.
John-Benning, b. 8 Dec. 1802, capt. 2nd Queen's, d. s. p.
Henry, b. 14 Dec. 1803.
George-Montague, b. 1810.
Ann, m. 1st, to Gilbert McIlveen, Esq; and 2ndly, to George-W. Braddell, Esq.
Mary-Margaret, m. to Joseph Barns, Esq., capt. R.A., and has issue.
Ellen, m. to Peter Kirk, Esq., late M.P. for Carrickfergus, and has issue, William Kirk, high-sheriff for Carrickfergus for 1854; Charles Kirk, lieut. 1st-foot; Ellen Kirk; Anne Kirk; and Maria Kirk.
Millicent-Jane, m. 1st, to Thomas Millar, Esq. of Carrickfergus, and has issue, Millicent Millar; Ann Millar; and Ellen Millar. She m. 2ndly, Philip Fletcher, Esq., capt. H.E.I.C.S.
Jane, m. to Duncan-Davys Wilson, Esq., and has issue, William-Duncan Wilson; Sophia Wilson; Ellen Wilson.
Lucy, m. to Henry Baldwin, Esq., and had issue a son, d. in 1832.
Mehetabella, d. 22 April, 1815.

Mr. Noah Dalway was mayor of Carrickfergus in 1806, 1809, 1811, 1816, and was M.P. for that borough in 1799 and 1801, and was the first member for that town to the Imperial Parliament. He was also a commander R.N. He d. in 1820, and was s. by his eldest son, MARRIOTT, the present possessor of Bella Hill.

Arms—Arg., two lions in chief, counter-passant, and one in base, passant, all guardant, gu., armed and langued, az.
Crest—A demi-lion, rampant, holding in his paw a staff, erect, ppr.; on a banner appendant thereto, and flotant to the sinister, arg., a saltier, of the first.
Motto—Esto quod audes.
Seat—Bella Hill, Carrickfergus.

DALY OF CASTLE DALY.

DALY, JAMES, Esq. of Castle Daly, co. Galway, b. in March, 1808; m. Margaret, eldest dau. of the late Hubert Dolphin, Esq. of Turoe, co. Galway, and has, with other issue, an eldest son,

PETER-HUBERT, b. in Nov. 1838.

Mr. Daly is son of Peter Daly, Esq., by Louisa his wife, dau. of Christopher MacEvoy, Esq., and Mary-Lowe his wife.

Seat—Castle Daly, Loughrea.

DALY OF COOLINEY.

DALY, JAMES, Esq. of Cooliney, co. Galway, b. 9 March, 1826; m. 17 Jan. 1854, Margaret, 2nd dau. of the late Charles-Edward Kennedy, Esq. of Peamount, co. Dublin. This gentleman is eldest son of the late Henry-De Burgh Daly, Esq. of Lurgan, co. Galway (who d. 8 Nov. 1838), by Margaret Coghlan his wife, and grandson of Arthur Daly, Esq., by Jane Gore his wife. He has two brothers and as many sisters, viz.,

Henry-Michael, m. 2 April, 1851, Elizabeth, dau. of the Rev. Thomas Caddy.
Denis-Bowes.
Maria-Jane. Anna-Margaret.

Motto—Deo et regi fidelis.
Seat—Cooliney, co. Galway.

DAMES OF GREENHILL.

LONGWORTH-DAMES, FRANCIS, Esq. of Greenhill, King's County, J.P. and D.L., high-sheriff in 1832, m. 1st, 1 June, 1830, Anna, youngest dau. of the Rev. Travers Hume, D.D., by Elizabeth Balaguier his wife, niece and heiress of Earl Macartney, and by her (who d. in 1835) had issue,

I. THOMAS, b. 12 March, 1831.
II. Francis-Travers, b. 26 April, 1834.
I. Elizabeth, d. in 1835.

He m. 2ndly, 13 Aug. 1839, Elizabeth-Selina, youngest dau. of the late Ralph Smyth, Esq. of Gaybrook, co. Westmeath, by Hannah-Maria his wife, 2nd dau. of Sir Robert Staples, Bart. of Durrow, Queen's County, and by her has issue,

I. Ralph, b. in 1840, d. 1841.
II. Robert-Staples, b. in 1841.
I. Mary-Jane.

Lineage.—THOMAS LONGWORTH, Esq., 3rd son of Francis Longworth, Esq. of Craggan Castle, co. Westmeath, by Elizabeth his wife, dau. and co-heir of Thomas Dames, Esq. of Rathmoyle, King's Co., assumed the additional surname and arms of DAMES, as heir of his maternal grandfather, Thomas Dames, Esq. of Rathmoyle. He m. Jane, youngest dau. of Maunsell Burke, Esq., son of Anthony Burke, Esq. of Springfield, co. Galway, and by her had issue,

FRANCIS, now of Greenhill.
John-Maunsell, m. Julia, dau. of — Ombler, Esq. of Parlington, co. York.
Thomas, capt. 1st dragoon-guards, d. in 1845.
John, banker in Devonshire.
Arthur, vicar of Kenton, co. Devon.
William, colonel 37th regt., m. Christina, dau. of Smith, Esq. of Toronto, Canada.
George, capt. 66th regt., m. Emma, dau. of John Kemble, Esq. of Quebec.
Jane, m. to Hugh Hammill, Esq. of Hartfield, co. Dublin.
Eliza, d. unm. in 1835.
Maria, m. to Robert-Fleetwood Rynd, Esq. of Ryndville, co. Meath.

Arms—Quarterly: 1st and 4th, arg., three wolves' heads, erased, gu.; 2nd and 3rd, az., three mullets, pierced, or.
Crest—A mullet, pierced, or, and a talbot's head, erased.
Motto—Virtute et prudentiâ.
Seat—Greenhill, Edenderry, King's County.

DANE OF KILLYHERLIN.

DANE, PAUL, Esq. of Killyherlin, co. Fermanagh, b. 5 July, 1810.

Lineage.—JOHN DANE, Esq. of Killyherlin, captain in the army, son of PAUL DANE, provost of Enniskillen in 1688, m. Elizabeth, dau. of James Auchinleck, Esq. of Kilyreagh, co. Fermanagh, and was father of

PAUL DANE, Esq. of Killyherlin, who m. Margaret Swords, and was s. by his son,

RICHARD DANE, Esq. of Killyherlin, D.L. and J.P., many years provost of Belturbet, co. Cavan, b. 10 Feb. 1771, who m. 12 Aug. 1809, Anna, dau. of the Rev. Alexander Auchinleck, rector of Rossony, co. Fermanagh, and had issue,

PAUL, now of Killyherlin.
Samuel-Lowry-Corry, deceased.
Richard-Martin, of the 29th regt.
William-Auchinleck. Daniel-Auchinleck, deceased.
Armar-Lowry-Corry, deceased.
Eldon, deceased. John.
Juliana, wife of William-Acheson O'Brien, Esq. of Drumsalla, co. Leitrim.
Anna-Maria. Henrietta.
Margaret-Elizabeth. Emily, deceased.

Mr. Dane d. 29 Jan. 1842.

Arms—Sa., a serpent, entwined and erect, arg.
Crest,—A demi-lizard, issuing from a ducal coronet.
Motto—Forti et fideli nihil difficile.
Seat—Killyherlin, co. Fermanagh.

DANIELL OF NEW FOREST.

DANIELL, ROBERT, Esq. of New Forest, co. Westmeath, b. 12 June, 1830.

Lineage.—This is a branch of the very ancient Cheshire family of DANIELL *of Daresbury*.

MICHAEL DANIELL, Esq. (whose father m. the heiress of John Wade, Esq. of Clonabraney, co. Meath (*see* WADE *of Clonabraney*), was a descendant of this old Cheshire race. He m. Margaret, dau. of Samuel Woodward, Esq. of Woodville, co. Meath, and had two sons, JOHN DANIELL, Esq. of Bellevue, co. Meath, capt. 17th Lancers, who d. 15 May, 1846, and

HENRY DANIELL, Esq. of New Forest, J.P. for the counties of Meath and Westmeath, who served as high-sheriff of the latter in 1808. He was b. in Sept. 1767, and m. 15 Aug. 1794, Isabella, 2nd dau. of Robert Tighe, Esq. of South Hill, co. Westmeath, M.P. for Carrick, by Isabella his wife, sister of Sir Gilbert King, of Charleston, co. Roscommon, and had issue,

I. ROBERT, J.P. and D.L., b. 27 Sept. 1796, m. 21 July, 1827, Cecilia-Frances, 2nd dau. of Major Cliffe, of Bellevue, co. Wexford, and d. 6 Aug. 1841, leaving issue,

T

ROBERT-GEORGE, now of New Forest.
2 Anthony-John, b. 16 March, 1833.
1 Frances. 2 Isabella-Jane. 3 Henrietta-Cecilia.

II. George, capt. R.N., J.P., b. 31 Aug. 1797, m. 23 June, 1842, Alicia-Katherine, eldest dau. of the Rt. Hon. Francis Blackburne, late lord-chancellor of Ireland, and has issue.
III. Henry, in holy orders, rector of Portnashangan, co. Westmeath, b. 28 July, 1801, d. unm. 29 March, 1836.
IV. John-Michael, lieut. 26th regt., b. 19 Oct. 1815, d. unm. at Chusan, 27 Nov. 1840.
I. Isabella-Margaret, m. 23 May, 1821, to William-Hamilton Smyth, Esq. of Drum House, co. Down, son, by his 2nd marriage, of William Smyth, Esq. of Drumcree, M.P. for the co. of Westmeath.
II. Frances-Louisa, d. unm. 24 Feb. 1826.

Mr. Daniell was s. at his decease, by his grandson, the present ROBERT-GEORGE DANIELL, Esq. of New Forest.

Arms—Arg., a pale fusilly, sa.: a crescent, gu.
Crest—An unicorn's head, erased, armed and crined, or, charged with a crescent, gu.
Motto—Pro fide et patria.
Seat—New Forest, Tyrrel's Pass, Westmeath.

DANSEY OF EASTON.

DANSEY, DANSEY-RICHARD, Esq. of Easton Court, co. Hereford, J.P., m. in 1814, Frances-Elizabeth, dau. and co-heir of the Rev. James Ingram, of Burford, co. Salop, and has issue,

I. RICHARD-INGRAM, m. in 1844, Annabella-Caroline, dau. of Robert-Bell Price, of Bitterley, co. Salop, and has issue, Richard-Ingram and Henry-Barwell.
II. Roger-Delamere, E.I.C.S.
I. Frances-Milborough, m. to Richard Green, Esq. of Frydd House, co. Radnor.
II. Constance-Elizabeth, m. to Richard-Douglas Gough, Esq. of Ynisecdwyn, co. Brecon.

Lineage.—The Danseys, originally Daunteseys, rank with the most ancient families in Herefordshire. Their original place of residence was in Wilts, in which shire Camden records that William Dauntesey held lands by knight's service, 7 HENRY III. The same antiquary also mentions that Richard Dauntesey was possessed of estates, both in Wiltshire and Herefordshire, in the reign of EDWARD I. The last direct male representative of the Herefordshire line was

RICHARD DANSEY, Esq., a colonel in the army, distinguished for his services in Spain under Lord Peterborough, d. unm. in 1740, having bequeathed his estate to (the 2nd son of his sister Deborah, the wife of Edward Collins, of Acton Burnell) his nephew,

WILLIAM COLLINS, Esq., who assumed, in consequence, the surname and arms of DANSEY. He m. Harriet, dau. of John Sawyer, Esq. of Haywood, co. Berks, but dying s. p. in 1775, was s. by (the son of his brother Edward) his nephew,

DANSEY COLLINS, Esq. of Easton Court, who assumed the surname and arms of DANSEY. He m. Ellen, dau. of R. Sutton, Esq. of Cheshire, and had issue,

Dansey, major in the Worcester militia, m. Miss Frances Warren, and left two daus., his co-heirs.
RICHARD, of whom presently.
Ellen, m. 1st, to George Pardoe, Esq. of Nash Court, co. Salop, and 2ndly, to the Rev. Thomas Rocke, of Tenbury.
Betsy, d. unm.
Martha, m. the Ven. Joseph Corbett, of Longnor, co. Salop, and d. in 1812, aged 40, leaving issue.
Nancy, d. unm.
Mary, m. to Henry Johnson, Esq. of Frankwell, co. Salop, and had numerous issue.

The 2nd son,

RICHARD DANSEY, Esq. of Easton Court, m. in 1788, Miss Emma Johnson, and left, with other issue, a son and heir, DANSEY-RICHARD DANSEY, Esq., the present representative of the family.

Arms—Barry-wavy of six, arg. and gu.
Crest—A lion's head, erased, arg., collared, gu.
Seat—Easton Court, co. Hereford.

DARBY OF LEAP CASTLE.

DARBY, WILLIAM-HENRY, Esq. of Leap Castle, King's County, m. Laura-Charlotte, dau. of the late Edward-Jeremiah Curteis, Esq. of Windmill Hill, co. Sussex, and by her (who d. 27 March, 1847) has issue,

I. JONATHAN, b. 25 June, 1828, m. 7 Sept. 1853, his cousin Caroline-Curteis Graham.
I. Mary-Charlotte.

Lineage.—The family of Darby has long been seated at Leap Castle, in the King's County.

JOHN DARBY, Esq. of Leap Castle and of Markley, co. Sussex, brother of the late Admiral Darby, and of General Darby, married, and had issue, WILLIAM-HENRY, now of Leap Castle; and GEORGE, barrister-at-law, of Markley, M.P. for East Sussex.

Seat—Leap Castle, King's County.

DARBY OF STOKE COURT.

DARBY, ABRAHAM, Esq. of Stoke Court, Bucks, J.P. and D.L., high-sheriff in 1853, b. 30 March, 1804; m. 8 Aug. 1839, Matilda-Frances, eldest dau. and co-heir of the late Francis Darby, Esq. of Sunniside House, Colebrookdale.

Lineage.—This family has resided at Colebrookdale for many generations, and has acquired, by purchase, estates in that vicinity.

ABRAHAM DARBY, b. 3 March, 1711, son of Abraham, living at Colebrookdale, 1697, m. 1st, Miss Margaret Smith, and had by her one dau., Hannah, m. to Richard Reynolds, Esq. of the city of Bristol. Mr. Darby m. 2ndly, Abiah, widow of — Sinclair, and youngest child of Samuel Maude, Esq. of Sunderland, and had two sons and two daus.,

I. ABRAHAM, of Colebrookdale, b. 24 April, 1750, m. Rebecca, dau. of Francis Smith, Esq. of Doncaster, and had issue,
1 FRANCIS, his heir, of Sunniside House, Colebrookdale, b. 5 April, 1783, m. 16 June, 1808, Hannah, only child of John Grant, Esq. of Leighton Buzzard, Beds, and left two daus., his co-heirs, Matilda-Frances, wife of Abraham Darby, Esq. of Stoke Court; and Adelaide-Anne.
2 Richard, b. 1 Jan. 1788, m. Maria, only child of the late John Sorton, Esq. of Chester, and has issue.
1 Anne, m. to Barnard Dickinson, Esq., and has issue.
2 Hannah, m. to William Tothill, Esq. of Redland, near Bristol, and has issue.
II. SAMUEL, of whom presently.
I. Mary, m. to Joseph Rathbone, Esq. of Liverpool, and d. s. p.
II. Sarah, d. unm.

The 2nd son,

SAMUEL DARBY, b. 10 Jan. 1755, m. in 1776, Deborah, dau. of John Barnard, Esq. of Sheffield, and d. 1 Sept. 1796, leaving two sons,

I. SAMUEL, who m. Frances-Anna, dau. of John Williames, Esq. of Welch Pool, co. Montgomery, and d. 1 Feb. 1808, leaving an only dau. and heiress, MARY, m. 6 Dec. 1825, to the Rev. Edward-Pryce Owen, M.A., vicar of Wellington, and rector of Eyton, in Salop, only son of the late Archdeacon Owen, of Shrewsbury.
II. EDMUND, of whose line we treat.

The 2nd son,

EDMUND DARBY, b. 22 April, 1782, m. 1803, Lucy, dau. of John Burlingham, Esq. of Catherine Hill, Worcester, and d. 29 March, 1810, leaving with two daus., two sons,

I. ABRAHAM, now of Stoke Court.
II. Alfred, of Stanley Hall, b. 1807, m. April, 1848, Rebecca, dau. of William Christy, Esq., and d. 14 April, 1852, leaving a son, Alfred-Edmund-William, b. 7 Sept. 1850, and two daus., Alice-Mary and Alfrida-Darby.

Arms—Per chevron battelly, az. and erminois, three eagles displayed, two and one, each charged on the breast with an escallop, all counterchanged.
Crest—In front of two crosses-crosslet fitchée, in saltier, sa., a demi-eagle displayed, couped, erminois, wings, az., charged on the breast with an escallop, of the last.
Motto—Utcunque placuerit Deo.
Seat—Stoke Court, Bucks.

D'ARCY OF HYDE PARK.

D'ARCY, GEORGE-JAMES-NORMAN, Esq. of Hyde Park, co. Westmeath, J.P., b. in 1820.

Lineage.—The family of DE ARCY ranks with the most eminent established in England by the Norman Conquest; and amongst the peerages of past times, there are two Baronies in Abeyance, one Forfeited Barony, and three Extinct Baronies, all of which had been conferred upon members of the house of D'Arcy, besides the extinct Earldom of Holderness. The D'ARCYS *of Hyde Park* are the chief and eldest existent line of this ancient and distinguished family.

NORMAN D'ARCY, Lord of Nocton, *temp. Conquest*, living in 1092, was father of ROBERT D'ARCY, of Nocton, who d. 9 HENRY II., and was s. by his son, THOMAS D'ARCY, Baron of Nocton, who m. Alice, dau. of Ralph Deincourt, and dying 27 HENRY II, left a son and successor, THOMAS D'ARCY, Baron of Nocton, 6 RICHARD I. and 5 JOHN, father of NORMAN D'ARCY, Baron of Nocton, in arms against King JOHN. His son and heir, PHILIP D'ARCY, Baron of Nocton, m. Isabel, sister and eventually co-heir of Roger Bertram, Baron of Mitford, and was father of NORMAN D'ARCY, Baron of Nocton, summoned to parliament 49 HENRY III., and 22 EDWARD I., who had three sons, PHILIP, Baron of Nocton, summoned to parliament from 28 EDWARD I. to 34 EDWARD I.; John (Sir), of whose line we treat; and Robert, Lord of Stallingborough, co. Lincoln. The 2nd son,

SIR JOHN D'ARCY, Knt., called *Le Cosin*, 13 EDW. II., sheriff of Nottingham and Derby, 16 EDWARD II., lord-justice of Ireland, called *Le Neveu*, 2 EDWARD III., and finally styled *Le Père*, was one of the heroes of Crecy. To him and his heirs-male the manors of Rathwire and Lynn, with knights' fees and advowsons of churches, were granted. He m. 1st, Emeline, dau. and heir of Walter Heron, Esq. of Haddesdon, and had by her a son,

JOHN, Baron of Knayth, Constable of the Tower of London for life, ancestor of the D'Arcys, Barons D'Arcy and Meynell, and the Earls of Holderness, now represented by the Duke of Leeds.

Sir John D'Arcy m. 2ndly, Joane, dau. of Richard de Burgh, Earl of Ulster, and widow of Thomas FitzJohn, Earl of Kildare, and had by her a son,

WILLIAM D'ARCY, Esq. of Plattyn, co. Meath, who m. Catharine, dau. of Sir Robert Fitzgerald, of Alen, co. Kildare, and was ancestor of the distinguished family of D'ARCY *of Platyn*, the main stem from which have branched D'ARCY *of Hyde Park*, D'ARCY *of Kiltulla and Clifden*, D'ARCY *of New Forest, &c.*

THOMAS D'ARCY, Esq. of Dunmow, co. Meath, 2nd son of George D'Arcy of Platyn, by Jane his wife, dau. and heir of Tuite M'Riccard of Sonagh, and younger brother of Sir William D'Arcy of Platyn, whose male issue became extinct, m. Margaret, dau. of Richard Kiltole, and was father of JOHN D'ARCY, Esq. of Dunmow, whose son and heir, WILLIAM D'ARCY, Esq. of Dunmow, m. Margaret Brandon, niece of Thomas Brandon, Esq. of Dundalk, and had a son, THOMAS D'ARCY, of Dunmow, aged 28 in 1639, who m. Alicia Nugent, of New Haggard, and was father of GEORGE D'ARCY, Esq. of Dunmow, declared an innocent Papist, 20 Aug. 1663, who, by Alice his wife, dau. of Thomas Nugent, Esq. of Clonlost, co. Westmeath, had a son, THOMAS, of Lisnabin, co. Westmeath, who predeceased his father, leaving, by Jane his wife, dau. of Bellew of Bellewstown, co. Meath, a son, and successor to his grandfather, viz.,

JOHN D'ARCY, Esq. of Dunmow, who m. 1727, Elizabeth, dau. and co-heiress of Thomas Judge, Esq. of Grangebeg, co. Westmeath, and by her (who d. in 1773) had

JUDGE, of Dunmow and Grangebeg, who d. in 1766, leaving by Elizabeth Nugent his wife, an only dau. and heiress, ELIZA, who m. Col. Gorges-Marcus Irvine, of Castle Irvine, co. Fermanagh.
JAMES, of whom we treat.

This

JAMES D'ARCY, Esq. of Hyde Park, co. Westmeath, b. in 1740, m. in 1766, Martha, dau. and heir of William Grierson, Esq. of Deanstown, co. Dublin, and had issue,

JOHN, his heir.
Joshua, in holy orders, rector of Killalon, in the diocese of Meath, m. in 1811, Sarah, dau. of the late Capt. Fleming, of the co. Kildare, and has issue six sons and three daus., of whom the eldest is JOHN-SAMUEL D'ARCY, Esq. of Bagatelle, co. Westmeath, who m. in 1834, Louisa, only dau. of William Handcock, Esq., by Anne his wife, dau. of John Henry, Esq. of Carrintrilly, co. Galway, and has issue two sons and two daus.
Thomas, deceased, was a major in the army, and at his death inspector-general of police in Ulster. He m. Eliza, dau. of Capt. Buchanan, and has left two sons and three daus.; the eldest son, William-James, is at the Irish bar.
Eliza, m. to the late Major Sirr, of the city of Dublin, and has two sons (Joseph Darcy Sirr, rector of Kilcolman, and Henry-Charles Sirr, at the English bar,) and two daus.
Alice.
Martha, relict of F. Handy, Esq.
Frances, m. to Joseph Fox, Esq. Doolistown, co. Meath, and has issue three daus.
Harriett, m. to James Fox, Esq. of Galtrim, co. Meath, and has issue, three sons and three daus.

Mr. D'Arcy d. in 1803, and was s. by his eldest son,

JOHN D'ARCY, Esq. of Hyde Park, b. in 1767, J.P., who m. 1st, in 1801, Emily, dau. of Thomas Purdon, Esq. of Huntingdon, co. Westmeath, which lady d. s. p. in 1802; and 2ndly, in 1817, Mary-Anne, dau. and co-heir of Thomas Cary, Esq. of Dublin, by whom he had surviving issue,

GEORGE-JAMES-NORMAN, now of Hyde Park.
Thomas-Lavallin, of Kilylass, co. Kildare, b. in 1821, m. 1845, Maria-Louisa, youngest dau. of James Fox, Esq. of Galtrim, co. Meath.
John-Charles, of Rehoboth, co. Dublin, b. 1828, m. 1852, Henrietta-Anne, eldest dau. of Thomas Brierly, Esq. of Dublin.
Anthony-Ralph, b. 1832.
Martha-Emily. Frances-Louisa.
Phœbe-Sophia.

Mr. D'Arcy d. in 1846.

Arms—Az., three cinquefoils and semée of cross-crosslets arg.
Crest—A bull, sa., armed, or, on a cap of maintenance.
Supporters—Dexter, a tiger, ppr.; sinister, a bull, sa., armed, or.
Motto—Un Dieu, un Roi.
Seat—Hyde Park, Kinnegad, co. Westmeath.

D'ARCY OF NEW FOREST.

D'ARCY, RICHARD, Esq. of New Forest, co. Galway, and Fisher Hill, co. Mayo, b. 20 April, 1829, s. his father 8 April, 1851. Mr. D'Arcy is a justice of the peace for the county of Galway.

Lineage.—NICHOLAS D'ARCY, Esq., a captain of horse, 2nd son of D'Arcy of Platyn, m. Jane, dau. and heir of O'Duraghy of Partry, co. Mayo, and was s. by his son,

THOMAS D'ARCY, Esq., who made a settlement, dated A.D. 1484. He was father of

CONYERS D'ARCY, Esq., who m. Christian, dau. of Richard Blake, Esq., and was s. by his son,

NICHOLAS D'ARCY, Esq. of Kiltullagh, co. Galway, father of two sons, JAMES, his heir; and Richard, whose only dau. m. Robert Blake, Esq. of Ardfry. The elder son,

JAMES D'ARCY, Esq. of Kiltullagh, surnamed *Riveagh*, "the Swarthy," was made vice-president of Connaught by Queen ELIZABETH. He was likewise chief magistrate of Galway, where, in the Franciscan Abbey, is a monument to his memory. He d. in 1603, leaving a dau., Anastace, wife of Sir Dominick Browne, ancestor, by her, of Lord Oranmore, and seven sons, viz.,

Nicholas, whose two sons, James and Dominick, d. s. p.
MARTIN, of whom we treat.
James, ancestor of the D'ARCYS *of Gorteen*, co. Mayo, the D'ARCYS *of Ballybocock*, in the same county, and the D'ARCYS *of Hounswood and Tuam*.
Anthony, ancestor of the D'ARCYS *of Brest*, in France.
Mark. Andrew.
Patrick, ancestor of the D'ARCYS *of Kiltullagh and Clifden*.

The 2nd son,

MARTIN D'ARCY, Esq., high-sheriff of the county of Galway, suffered much persecution from Wentworth, Earl of Strafford, and d. in prison in Dublin, 3 Jan. 1636. He m. Christick, dau. of Richard Martin, alderman of Galway, and had an eldest son and heir,

RICHARD D'ARCY, Esq., who m. Mary, dau. of Nicholas Browne, of Galway, and was father of

MARTIN D'ARCY, Esq. of Clonuane, co. Clare, who m. 20 May, 1653, Catherine, dau. of Sir Richard Blake, Bart. of Ardfry, and d. 17 Oct. 1690, leaving issue, Richard, of Clonuane, who m. Catherine, dau. of Major Peter Blake, of Moorfield, and d. 16 Dec. 1727; and

DOMINICK D'ARCY, Esq. of Rockvale, co. Clare, who m. Elizabeth, dau. of James Butler, Esq. of Doon, in the same county, and had three sons, Richard; James, who d. s. p.; and DOMINICK; and a dau., m. to M. Hogan, Esq. of Cross. The younger son,

DOMINICK D'ARCY, Esq. of Clonuane, near Rockvale, m. Bridget, dau. of Stephen Blake, Esq. of Moorfield, co. Galway, and had issue, RICHARD, his heir; James, barrister-at-law, d. unm. in 1790; and Mary-Anne, m. to Christopher O'Brien, Esq. of Ennistymon, co. Clare. The elder son and heir,

RICHARD D'ARCY, Esq. of Rockvale, m. 30 Nov. 1783, Mary, dau. of John Blake, Esq. of the city of Dublin, (a younger brother of Maurice Blake, Esq. of Tower Hill, co. Galway,) and by her had three sons,

DOMINICK, b. 1784, capt. 47th regt., d. s. p. in 1811.
John, d. s. p. 1822.
JAMES, of whom presently.
Richard, d. an infant.
Isidore, b. 1789, an officer 56th regt., d. s. p. 8 Dec. 1850, at Clonuane or Rockvale.
MARTIN, of Wellfort, co. Galway, b. in 1791, m. 17 June, 1817, Henrietta, dau. of Dominick Beytagh, Esq. of Cappagh House, in the same county, and dying in 1844, left issue, I. Richard; II. Dominick; III. John; IV. James; and I. Mary.

The 3rd son,

JAMES D'ARCY, Esq. of New Forest, J.P., *b.* 10 Feb. 1787, *m.* 20 Sept. 1827, Elizabeth, dau. of Hyacinth Cheevers, Esq. of Killyon, and *d.* 8 April, 1851, leaving issue,

RICHARD, now of New Forest.
Hyacinth, *b.* 26 Feb. 1830.
Mary. Elizabeth.

Arms—Az., semée of cross-crosslets and three cinquefoils, arg.
Crest—On a chapeau, gu., turned up, erm., a bull, sa., armed, or.
Motto—Un Dieu, un Roi.
Seat—New Forest, co. Galway.

D'ARCY OF KILTULLAGH AND CLIFDEN.

D'ARCY, THE REV. HYACINTH, rector and vicar of Omey, Ballindoon, and Moyrus, co. Galway, formerly of Kiltullagh House and Clifden Castle, in that county, *b.* 27 July, 1806; *m.* 8 June, 1852, Fanny, 2nd dau. of John Bellingham, Esq. of Castle Bellingham, which lady *d.* 26 June, 1854.

Lineage.—PATRICK D'ARCY, Esq. of Kiltulla, youngest son of James D'Arcy *Riveagh* (see D'ARCY *of New Forest*), *b.* in 1598, an active member of the House of Commons, in the parliament assembled at Dublin in 1640, *d.* in Dublin, *anno* 1668, leaving, by his wife Elizabeth, dau. of Sir Peter French, an only son,

JAMES D'ARCY, Esq. of Kiltulla, who *m.* Frances Trushot, a lady of Brittany, whose father was captain of a man-of-war in the service of LOUIS XIII., and her mother Anne Keating (his wife), was maid of honour to HENRIETTA-MARIA, Queen Consort of CHARLES I. By this lady, Mr. D'Arcy, who *d.* in 1692, had (with four daus., Anne, *m.* to Charles Daly, Esq. of Culla; Frances, *m.* 1st, to Capt. Ulick Burke, and 2ndly, to Lieut. Francis Darcy; Bridget, *m.* to Counsellor Dillon; and Clare) a son and heir,

HAYCINTH D'ARCY, of Kiltullagh, a captain in the army, *b.* in 1665, who *m.* Catherine, dau. of John D'Arcy, Esq. of Gorteen, co. Mayo, and had issue, nine sons and three daus. Capt. Haycinth D'Arcy *d.* 1743: his 2nd son (the eldest, Patrick, *d. s. p.*),

JOHN D'ARCY, Esq., *m.* Jane, dau. of Sir Robert Lynch, Bart. of Castle Carra, and was father of

JOHN D'ARCY, Esq., who *m.* in 1752, Catherine, dau. of Col. Isidore Lynch, of Drincong Castle, and had, with one dau. (Jane, *m.* 1st, to her kinsman, M. le Comte d'Arcy, lieut.-general of the armies of the King of France, grand cordon of St. Louis, 1st aide-de-camp to LOUIS XVI., and member of the Academy of Science, and 2ndly, to Matthew Talbot, Esq. of Castle Talbot, co. Wexford) one son,

HAYCINTH D'ARCY, Esq. of Kiltullagh, who *m.* 1st, Mary, dau. of F. Blake, Esq. of Bahara, co. Roscommon, by whom he had no issue, and 2ndly, in 1784, Julia, dau. of Mark Lynch, Esq. of Barna, co. Galway, by whom he had one dau., who *d. unm.*, and two sons, JOHN, his heir; and Mark. The elder son,

JOHN D'ARCY, Esq. of Kiltullagh and Clifden Castle, J.P., *b.* 26 Nov. 1785, served as high sheriff of the county of Galway, in 1811. He *m.* 1st, 4 June, 1804, Frances, dau. of Andrew Blake, Esq. of Castle Grove, and niece of the late Viscount Netterville, by whom (who *d.* 15 April, 1815) he had issue,

I. HAYCINTH, present representative.
II. JOHN-TALBOT, of Castle Park, co. Roscommon, J.P., *b.* 24 June, 1810, *m.* 22 Feb. 1846, Jane, dau. and co-heir of Daniel Kelly, Esq. of Cargins, co. Roscommon, by Mary his wife, sister of Lord De Freyne, and has issue,
  1 John-Lionel, *b.* 21 Dec. 1847.
  2 Alfred-De Freyne, *b.* 11 Feb. 1849.
III. Patrick.
IV. James, *m.* Mary, 2nd dau. of Capt. John Andrews, R.N.
I. Isabella.
II. Julia, *m.* to the late Richard Levingston, Esq. of Westport.

He *m.* 2ndly, 3 March, 1821, Louisa-Bagot, dau. of the late Walter Sneyd, Esq. of Keele Hall, in Staffordshire, and had by her,

I. Edmund. II. Henry.
III. William. IV. Norman.
I. Elizabeth, *m.* to George Clarke, Esq., commander, R.N.
II. Louisa, *m.* to Sydney Smith, Esq.

Arms—Az., semée of cross-crosslets, and three cinquefoils, arg.
Crest—A spear, broken in three pieces, or, headed, arg., and banded together in the middle by a riband, gu.
Motto—Un Dieu, un Roi.

DARELL OF CALEHILL.

DARELL, HENRY-JOHN, Esq. of Calehill, in Kent, *b.* 25 June, 1819.

Lineage.—The family of Dayrell or Darell was established in England by one of the companions in arms of the CONQUEROR, and the name of its founder appears on the roll of Battle Abbey. Numerous divergent branches were planted in various counties, and for centuries flourished in all; the principal were those of Calehill and Scotney, in Kent; of Sesay, in Yorkshire; of Littlecote, in Wilts; of Pageham, in Sussex; and of Trewornan, in Cornwall.

From WILLIAM DARELL, of Sesay, co. York, 7th from William Darell, of Sesay, living *temp.* King JOHN, descended

SIR JOHN DARELL, Knt. of Calehill (grandson of Sir James Darell, Knt. of Calehill, governor of Guisnes and Hames Castle, near Calais). He *m.* Anne, dau. and co-heir of Robert Horne, Bishop of Winchester, and had eleven sons and five daus., of whom the eldest son, SIR ROBERT, of Calehill, whose male line became extinct, and the 2nd, NATHANIEL, Governor of Guersey, was father of Nathaniel, Governor of Sheerness, whose son,

JOHN DARELL, Esq. of Calehill, *m.* Olivia, 2nd dau. of Philip Smith, Viscount Strangford, and had, with junior issue,

PHILIP, his successor,
George, who *s.* to the estate of Scotney, in 1720, upon the failure of male issue in that branch.
James, in holy orders.

The eldest son and heir,

PHILIP DARELL, Esq. of Calehill, *m.* Mary, dau. of Robert Constantine, Esq., and had issue: the son and heir,

HENRY DARELL, Esq. of Calehill, *m.* Elizabeth, 2nd dau. of Sir Thomas Gage, Bart., and had issue,

Henry, *d. unm.* in 1802, at Bengal.
EDWARD, his successor. Philip, *d. unm.* in 1813.
Mary.
Lucy, *m.* to Sir Edward Hales, Bart., who *d. s. p.* in 1829.
Catherine, *d. unm.*
Elizabeth, *m.* to John-Linch French, Esq.
Barbara, *m.* to Francis Cholmeley, Esq. of Brandsby.
Margaret.

Mr. Darell was *s.* by his eldest surviving son,

EDWARD DARELL, Esq. of Calehill, Kent, *m.* 10 Feb. 1810, Mary-Anne, dau. and heir of Thomas Bullock, Esq. of Muscoats, in the co. of York, and had issue,

EDWARD-HENRY, *m.* 24 April, 1837, Lucy Wright, and *d.* 4 Sept. 1846, leaving an only child, Henrietta.
PHILIP-JOHN, *b.* 28 Jan. 1817, was of Calehill, *d. unm.* 1855.
HENRY-JOHN, now of Calehill.
James-Stephen, *b.* 10 Dec. 1820, *d. unm.* 1850.
William, *b.* 6 Jan. 1823, *d. unm.* 1846.
Robert, *b.* 27 March, 1824.
Mary-Anne. Olivia-Lucy.

Mr. Darell *d.* 18 Jan. 1851.

Arms—Az., a lion, rampant, or, ducally crowned, arg.
Crest—Out of a ducal coronet, or, a Saracen's head, couped below the shoulders, ppr., wreathed about the temples, arg. and az.; on his head a cap, of the last, fretty, arg., turned up, erm.
Motto—True to you. *Seat*—Calehill, Kent.

DARLEY OF ALDBY PARK.

DARLEY, HENRY-BREWSTER, Esq. of Aldby Park, co. York, J.P., *b.* 26 Nov. 1809; *m.* 5 March, 1832, Harriet-Louisa, youngest dau. of Harrington Hudson, Esq. of Bessingby, East Riding, co. York, by the Lady Anne his wife, and has issue,

I. HENRY, *b.* 9 Sept. 1839.
II. Cecil-Harrington, *b.* 6 Dec. 1841.
III. James-Vere, *b.* 4 Sept. 1847.
IV. Bertram, *b.* 4 Nov. 1850.
V. Edmond-Oswald, *b.* 19 Oct. 1854.
I. Ann. II. Adelaide. III. Harriet-Louisa.

Lineage.—This very ancient family, originally D'Erlé, was established in England at the Conquest. The great-grandfather of the present representative,

HENRY-BREWSTER DARLEY, Esq. of Aldby Park, son of Henry Brewster and Jane Darley, *m.* 1st, Elizabeth, eldest dau. of Sir Charles Anderson, Bart. of Broughton, co. Lincoln, who *d.* in 1765, and had by her a son, John, who *d.* young. He *m.* 2ndly, the dau. of Henry Wilks, Esq., and had by her two daus. and one son,

HENRY DARLEY, Esq. of Aldby Park, who *m.* Elizabeth, dau. of R. Lewis, Esq. of Glamorganshire, and dying in 1810, left a son,

HENRY DARLEY, of Aldby Park, Esq., J.P. and D.L., high-sheriff 1827, b. 17 Aug. 1777, m. 23 June, 1808, Mary-Ann, dau. of S. Martin, Esq. of Newington, Surrey, and had issue,

Henry-Brewster, now of Aldby.
Charles-Albert, b. 17 June, 1811, m. Aug. 1836, Marianne, youngest dau. of the Rev. William Nesfield, rector of Brancepeth, and has issue.
Alfred-Horatio, b. 25 Jan. 1813, m. Elizabeth, 3rd dau. of Col. Clervaux Chaytor, of Spennithorne, North Riding, co. York, and has issue.
Helen, m. Nov. 1837, to George Bridge, Esq., capt. 3rd foot.
Arabella-Sophia, m. 1839, to Christopher-C. Chaytor, Esq. of Spennithorne, co. York.

Arms—Gu., six fleurs-de-lis, arg., three, two, and one, within a bordure, erm.
Crest—A horse's head, couped, gu., accoutred in armour and bridled, or.
Motto—Vivitur ingenio.
Seat—Aldby Park, and Spaunton Lodge, Yorkshire.

DARROCH OF GOUROCK.

DARROCH, DUNCAN, Esq. of Gourock, co. Renfrew, b. 19 Feb. 1800; m. 31 July, 1821, Susan, dau. of Charles-Stewart Parker, merchant, of Glasgow, and has issue,

I. DUNCAN, b. 15 March, 1836.
II. Charles-Stewart-Parker, b. 29 Jan. 1843.
III. George-Edward, b. 22 April, 1846.
I. Eliza-Cotter. II. Margaret-Parker.
III. Caroline-Anne, m. to Richard Birley Baxendale, Esq. son of Joseph Baxendale, Esq. of Woodside, Whetstone, Middlesex.
IV. Susan-Louisa. V. Mary-Babington.

Lineage.—The estate and barony of Gourock was purchased from the STEWARTS *of Castlemilk*, in 1784, by

DUNCAN DARROCH, Esq. (who d. in 1823), on his return from Jamaica. His son,

DUNCAN DARROCH, Esq. of Gourock, a general in the army, m. in March, 1799, Elizabeth Cotten, dau. of Rev. George-Sackville Cotten, M.A., and by her (who d. 16 Dec. 1834) left at his decease, 16 Feb. 1847,

DUNCAN, present representative.
George-Sackville, b. 15 June, 1801, d. 14 Aug. 1802.
Donald-Malcolm, b. 21 Aug. 1805, d. May, 1806.
Donald-George-Angus, b. 17 Sept. 1814, major in Her Majesty's service, m. Eliza, dau. of Major Scott.
Elizabeth-Arabella, m. William-Wright Swain, major in Her Majesty's service.
Margaret-Janetta-Louisa, m. George Rainy, Esq. of Raasay, and d. 17 Nov. 1854.

Arms—Arg., a three-masted ship under full sail, in a sea, all ppr., between three oak-trees.
Crest—A demi-negro, in his dexter hand a dagger, ppr., and in an escrol above the crest this motto, "Be watchful."
Supporters—Two alligators, ppr.
Motto—Be watchful.
Seat—Gourock, co. Renfrew.

DARWIN OF BREADSALL PRIORY.

DARWIN, SIR FRANCIS-SACHEVEREL, of Breadsall Priory, co. Derby, b. in 1786; m. in 1815, Jane-Harriet, dau. of the late John Ryle, Esq. of Park House, Macclesfield, by whom he has issue,

I. REGINALD, b. in 1818, m. in 1842, Mary, dau. of J.-B. Sanders, Esq. of Exeter.
II. Edward-Levett, b. 13 April, 1821, m. in 1850, Harriet, dau. of F. Jessop, Esq. of Derby.
III. John-Robert, b. 1835.
I. Mary-Jane, m. in 1840, to Charles-Carill Worsley, Esq.
II. Emma-Elizabeth, m. in 1841, to Edward-Woollet Wilmot, Esq.
III. Frances-Sarah, m. 1st, in 1847, to the Rev. Gustavus Barton, who d. in 1848, and 2ndly, in 1850, to Marcus Huish, Esq.
IV. Georgiana-Elizabeth. V. Violetta-Harriette.
VI. Anne-Eliza-Thomasine. VII. Millicent-Susan.

Lineage.—ERASMUS DARWIN, of Derby, M.D., F.R.S., afterwards of Breadsall Priory, b. 12 Dec. 1731, the well-known poet, author of *The Botanic Garden*, *The Loves of the Plants*, &c. (3rd son of Robert Darwin, Esq. of Elston, Notts), m. 1st, Mary, dau. of Charles Howard, Esq. of Lichfield, by whom he had issue,

Robert-Waring, M.D. of Shrewsbury, b. in 1766, m. Susannah, dau. of Josiah Wedgwood, Esq. of Etruria, co. Stafford, and had issue.
Charles, of Christ Church College, Oxford, who d. in 1778.

Dr. Darwin m. 2ndly, in 1781, Elizabeth, widow of Col. Edward-Sacheverel Chandos-Pole, of Radborne, and by that lady had issue,

Edward, of Mackworth, b. in 1782, d. unm. 30 July, 1829.
FRANCIS-SACHEVEREL, now of Breadsall Priory.
John, in holy orders, b. in 1787, rector of Elston, Notts, d. unm. 1818.
Frances-Anne-Violetta, m. 30 March, 1807, to Samuel-Tertius Galton, Esq. of Duddeston House, co. Warwick.
Emma, d. unm. 1818.
Harriette, m. to Thomas-James Maling, Esq., capt. R.N., and d. 5 Aug. 1825.

Dr. Darwin d. 18 April, 1802.

Arms—Arg., on a bend, gu., cotised, vert, three escallops, or.
Crest—A demi-griffin, segreant, vert, holding in the claws an escallop, or.
Seat—Breadsall Priory, co. Derby.

DARWIN OF ELSTON HALL.

DARWIN, FRANCIS, Esq. of Elston Hall, co. Nottingham, J.P. and D.L., b. in 1825; m. in 1849, Charlotte-Maria-Cooper Darwin, eldest dau. and heiress of William-Brown Darwin, Esq. of Elston, and has issue,

I. FRANCIS-ALVEY, b. in 1850.
II. Gerard-Lascelles, b. in 1852.
I. Charlotte-Elizabeth-Ann.

This gentleman, 3rd son of William Rhodes, Esq. of Bramhope Hall, co. York, assumed, by royal license, 21 Feb. 1850, the surname and arms of DARWIN, in compliance with the testamentary injunction of Robert-Alvey Darwin, Esq. of Elston.

Lineage.—The family of DARWIN came originally from Cleatham, co. Lincoln.

ROBERT DARWIN, Esq. of Elston, Notts, barrister-at-law, b. in 1682, m. Elizabeth, dau. of John Hill, Esq. of Sleaford, co. Lincoln, and d. in 1754, leaving a dau., Elizabeth, b. in 1725, m. to the Rev. Thomas Hall, of Westborough; and three sons, Robert-Waring, b. in 1726, d. 1816; WILLIAM-ALVEY, of whom we treat; and Erasmus, M.D., the poet, (see DARWIN *of Breadsall Priory*). The 2nd son,

WILLIAM-ALVEY DARWIN, Esq. of Elston, b. in 1727, m. in 1772, Jane, dau. of William Brown, Esq. of Balderton, Notts, and d. in 1783, leaving a son and successor,

WILLIAM-BROWN DARWIN, Esq. of Elston, who m. in 1817, Elizabeth St. Croix, and d. in 1841, leaving issue,

ROBERT-ALVEY, of Elston Hall, d. unm. 1847.
CHARLOTTE-MARIA-COOPER, wife of Francis Rhodes, (now DARWIN), Esq., of Elston Hall.
Sarah-Gay-Forbes, m. in 1848, to Edward Noel, Esq. capt. 31st regt.

Arms—Quarterly; 1st and 4th, erm., a leopard's face, jessant de lis, between two escallops, all within two bendlets, gu.; in chief, a cross-patée, also gu.; 2nd and 3rd, per pale, arg. and az., on a bend, nebuly, a lion, passant-guardant, between two acorns, slipped, all counterchanged.
Crests—1st, a demi-griffin, sa., semée of mascles, or, charged on the shoulder with a cross-patée, gold, resting the sinister claw on a shield, arg., charged with a leopard's face, jessant de lis, gu. 2nd, a cubit arm, erect, vested, bendy of six, arg. and az., cuff, gu., the hand holding in saltier an oak-branch and vine-branch, both fructed, ppr.
Seat—Elston Hall, Notts.

DASHWOOD OF STANFORD PARK.

DASHWOOD, THE REV. SAMUEL-VERE, of Stanford Park, Notts, b. 3 Nov. 1804; m. 1st, 24 Oct. 1828, Caroline, dau. of Philip Hamond, Esq. of Westacre, Norfolk, and has by her,

I. CHARLES-LEWES, b. 8 May, 1833.
II. Richard-Lewes, b. 18 Feb. 1837.
III. Robert-Lewes, b. 9 Feb. 1840.
I. Caroline-Maria, m. to the Rev. Richard Surtees.
II. Matilda-Katherine, m. to the Rev. Charles Snell.
III. Sophy-Diana. IV. Lydia-Charlotte.

Mr. Dashwood m. 2ndly, 25 Jan. 1844, Edith, dau. of Colonel Hawkshaw, of Clifton, near Bristol, and has by her,

I. Edward-Vere, b. 25 June, 1846.
II. Samuel-Francis, b. 3 April, 1848.
III. Frederick, b. 10 Oct. 1849.
I. Edith-Helen. II. Alice.

Lineage.—The lordship of Stanford was granted by King PHILIP and Queen MARY, to Robert Raynes, Her Majesty's goldsmith, and by Raynes's descendants was alienated to Thomas Lewes, Esq., alderman of London (of ancient Welsh ancestry), from whose family it passed, by marriage, to that of Dashwood, a branch of the DASHWOODS *of Oxfordshire and Bucks*. The grandfather of the present proprietor,

CHARLES-VERE DASHWOOD, Esq. of Stanford, sprung from the marriage of Richard Dashwood, Esq. of Leadwell, Oxon, 3rd son of Sir Robert Dashwood, Bart., with Elizabeth, dau. of Thos. Lewes, Esq., rebuilt the Hall in 1771. He *m.* in 1765, Diana Dashwood, and *d.* in June, 1821, leaving a son and successor,

SAMUEL-FRANCIS DASHWOOD, Esq. of Stanford, who *m.* in May, 1803, Lydia-Boughton Lister, and by her, who *d.* 25 March, 1850, had issue,

SAMUEL-VERE, now of Stanford Park.
Lydia, *m.* to Major Birch, of Clare, Hants.
Sophia, *m.* to the Rev. Banks Wright, of Shelton Hall, Notts.
Maria.

Mr. Dashwood *d.* 10 Sept. 1826.

Arms—Arg., on a fesse, between four barrulets, gu., three griffins' heads, erased, of the first; quartering LEWES.
Crest—A griffin's head, erased, erm.
Seat—Stanford Park, Loughborough.

DAUBENEY OF COTE.

DAUBENEY, GEORGE-MATTHEWS, Esq. of Cote, co. Gloucester, barrister-at-law, *b.* 9 July, 1800; *m.* 28 May, 1830, Elizabeth, dau. of Humphrey Creswicke, Esq. of Hanham Court, co. Gloucester, and has issue,

I. GEORGE-ROBERT-HENRY, *b.* 28 July, 1840.
II. Giles, *b.* 14 Dec. 1841.
III. Henry-Elias, *b.* 19 Jan. 1848.
I. Rebecca-Georgina. II. Mary-Elizabeth.
III. Blanche. IV. Frances-Amelia.
V. Elizabeth. VI. Jane. VII. Cecilia.
VIII. Alice. IX. Adelinda-Georgina.

Lineage.—GEORGE DAUBENEY, Esq. of the city of Bristol (son and heir of Andrew Daubeney, 2nd son of George Daubeney, Esq. of Gorwell, co. Somerset, who claimed descent from a branch of the ennobled house of D'Aubeney), *m.* Jane Lloyd, and *d.* 28 Feb. 1740, leaving three sons,

I. GEORGE, his heir.
II. Andrew, of Bristol, who *m.* Miss Mary Drewett, of Bath Easton, Somersetshire, and had issue,
1 Andrew, in holy orders, rector of Publow, co. Somerset, who *m.* Elizabeth, dau. of George Daubeney, Esq., M.P. of Redland, and had issue, Alfred-Andrew, in holy orders; James, in holy orders; Edmund; Frederick; Mary; Elizabeth; Jane.
2 Giles, of Cirencester, Gloucestershire, *b.* in 1770, *m.* in 1795, Elizabeth, dau. of John Gunning, Esq. surgeon-general to the army, *temp.* GEORGE III., and had with three younger sons, Andrew, Edward, John, all deceased), Giles, *b.* 26 Jan. 1796, rector of Lydiard Tregoze, Wilts, J.P., *m.* 7 June, 1819, Katharine, eldest dau. of the Rev. John Collins, of Betterton, Berks, and has surviving issue, two daus., Amelia, *m.* to the Rev. Henry Drury, vicar of Bremhill, Wilts, and Ellen-Katharine.
1 Helena, *m.* to the Rev. James Daubeney, rector of Stratton, Gloucestershire.
2 Anne, *m.* to Joseph Pitt, Esq. of Eastcourt, Wilts.
III. Giles, *d. s. p.*

The eldest son,

GEORGE DAUBENEY, Esq. of Bristol, *m.* 30 Aug. 1741, Miss Mary Jones, and had,

I. GEORGE, his heir.
II Charles, archdeacon of Sarum, and rector of North Bradley, Wilts, *m.* Elizabeth, dau. of William-G. Barnston, Esq. of Chester, and had,
1 Charles, who died in youth.
2 George-William, in holy orders, *m.* Miss Crawley, and has a dau., Elizabeth, *m.* 9 June, 1836, to Martin-Hyde, only son of Sir Thomas-Crawley Boevey, Bart.
3 Henry-Charles, *m.* Miss Haines.
1 Elizabeth, *m.* Col. Daubeney.
2 Mary, *m.* Rev. T. Tudball.
III. John, of the city of Bristol, *m.* 4 Feb. 1773, Miss Ann Brown, maternally descended from the Hungerfords, and had issue,
1 John, doctor of civil law, *m.* in April, 1808, Miss Fortune.
2 Francis-Hungerford, in holy orders, rector of Benwell, in Norfolk, and of Tydd St. Giles, Cambridgeshire, *m.* in 1808, Elizabeth, only dau. of the Rev. John Jones, and niece of the late Dr. Sparke, Bishop of Ely, by whom he has issue, Henry-Jones, in holy orders; Francis; Edward; Henrietta-Eliza; Mary-Sparke, *m.* 13 Aug. 1839, to George Bramwell, Esq.; and Harriet.
3 Henry, a major-gen. in the army, J.P., *m.* 22 Sept. 1808, Elizabeth, eldest dau. of the late Archdeacon Daubeney, and has surviving issue, Henry-Charles-Barnston, captain in the army; Henry-William-Bowles, in holy orders; Frederick-Sikes; Elizabeth-Sophia; and Maria-Barnston.
4 Thomas, captain H.E.I.C.S., *d.* in India, in 1820.
5 William, *d.* young.
1 Marianne, *m.* Frederick Jones.
2 Fanny. 3 Charlotte-Sophia. 4 Harriett.
IV. James, rector of Stratton, Gloucestershire, *m.* Helena, 3rd dau. of Andrew Daubeney, Esq. of Bristol, and had issue,
1 Edward-Daubeney, rector of Garlington, Gloucestershire, *m.* Miss Croome, of Cirencester.
2 Charles, doctor of medicine, professor of chemistry at the university of Oxford; *unm.*
1 Mary.
2 Caroline, *m.* Rev. Henry Richards, of Horfield, Gloucestershire.

The eldest son,

GEORGE DAUBENEY, Esq. of Redland, in Gloucestershire, J.P., bapt. 21 Sept. 1742, M.P. Bristol, *m.* Miss Martha Baker, and had issue,

GEORGE, his heir. Frederick, *d. unm.*
Maria, *m.* in Sept, 1799, to William Dymock, Esq., and has left issue two sons, William-George and Frederick.
Martha.
Elizabeth-Innes, *m.* to the Rev. Andrew Daubeney, rector of Publow.
Joanna, *m.* in 1807, to Edward Sampson, Esq. of Henbury.
Caroline, *d. unm.*

Mr. Daubeney *d.* in 1806, and was *s.* by his son,

GEORGE DAUBENEY, Esq. of Cote, *b.* 30 Jan. 1775, who *m.* 1st, in 1799, Mary, dau. and heir of D. Matthews, Esq. of Buscot, and had by her two sons, GEORGE-MATTHEWS, present representative, and Robert-Henry, *b.* 5 Sept. 1801, *m.* Margaret Croome. Mr. Daubeney *m.* 2ndly, Miss Anne Drewett, of Colerne, Wilts, and had by her two sons, Arthur-Frederick, *b.* in 1808, and Joseph-Walters, *b.* in 1810. He *d.* 29 March, 1851.

Arms—Gu., four lozenges, in fesse, arg.
Crest—A pair of wings, sa.
Seat—Cote, near Bristol.

DAUNT OF OWLPEN AND GORTIGRENANE.

DAUNT, MARY, of Owlpen, co. Gloucester, and Gortigrenane, co. Cork, *m.* in July, 1815, THOMAS-ANTHONY STOUGHTON, Esq. of Ballyhorgan, co. Kerry, and has issue,

I. THOMAS-ANTHONY. II. Charles-William.

Lineage.—Several writers on heraldry identify the name of DAUNT with that of DAUNTRE, which occurs on the roll of Battel Abbey.

From SIMON DAUNT, living in co. Gloucester, *circiter* A.D. 1380, the 3rd in descent,

JOHN DAUNT, *m.* Anne, dau. of Sir Robert Stawell, Knt. of Cotherston, co. Somerset, ancestor of the Lords Stawell of Somerton. In 1471, Prince EDWARD, son of King HENRY VI, addressed to him a letter soliciting aid against "the king's great rebel, Edward, Earl of March." He was great-great-grandfather of

THOMAS DAUNT, lord of the manor of Owlpen in 1608, who also acquired the lands of Tracton Abbey, co. Cork, by lease; and the estate of Gortigrenane, in the same county, by purchase, from Sir Warham St. Leger, in 1595. He *m.* Mary, dau. of Bryan Jones, of Glamorganshire, and dying in 1620, was *s.* by his son,

THOMAS DAUNT, of Owlpen and Gortigrenane, who *m.* Katherine, dau. of John Clayton, Esq. of Chester, by whom he had issue, I. Thomas, who *m.* Eliza, dau. of Sir Gabriel Lowe, Knt. of Newark, but left no male issue; II. Achilles, who *s.* to Owlpen, but never married; III. John, who *d.* a minor; IV. GEORGE; I. Frances, wife of Henry Trye, Esq. of Hardwicke, co. Gloucester; and II. Catherine, wife of Sir Peter Courthope, Knt. of Courtstown, M.P. for the co. of Cork in 1661. He *d.* in 1670, and was *s.* in Gortigrenane by his 4th son,

GEORGE DAUNT, of Nohoval and Gortigrenane, co. Cork. He *m.* Martha, dau. of Major Turner, of Bandonbridge, co. Cork, by whom he had issue, I. THOMAS; and, II. HENRY, of Knocknamana, co. Cork, of whom hereafter. He *d.* in 1697, and was *s.* by his eldest son,

THOMAS DAUNT, of Owlpen and Gortigrenane, who *m.* in

1697, Elizabeth, dau. of the Rev. George Synge, and grand-dau. of the Right Hon. and Right Rev. George Synge (*alias* Millington), Lord Bishop of Cloyne. By her he had issue, I. THOMAS, a twin; II. ACHILLES, a twin; III. Kingscote; I. Martha, wife of Richard Bourne, Esq. of Burren, co. Cork; II. Hannah, wife of her cousin, George Daunt, of the city of Dublin, surgeon; and, III. Elizabeth. He *d.* in 1745, and was *s.* 1st, by his eldest son, THOMAS, failing whom, without issue, the representation devolved upon the 2nd twin,

ACHILLES DAUNT, of Owlpen and Gortigrenane, who *m.* in 1742, his cousin Anne, dau. of Henry Daunt, Esq. of Knocknamana, co. Cork, by whom he had issue,

THOMAS DAUNT, of Owlpen and Gortigrenane, *b.* in 1755, who *m.* Mary, dau. of George Baker, Esq. of Cork, and dying without male issue, in 1803, his estates devolved on his dau. and sole heiress, MARY DAUNT, of Owlpen and Gortigrenane, who *m.* in 1815, Thomas-Anthony Stoughton, Esq. of Ballyhorgan, co. Kerry.

Arms—Quarterly: 1st and 4th, arg., a chevron, sa., between three choughs' heads, erased, of the second, beaked, gu.; 2nd and 3rd, sa., a chevron, arg., between three owls, ppr., for the name of OWLPEN.
Ancient Arms—Sa., three beacons, with ladders, or, fired gu., for DAUNTRE.
Crest—A hutchet, or bugle-horn, stringed, sa.
Motto—Vigilo et spero.
Seats—Owlpen, near Dursley, Gloucestershire; and Gortigrenane, near Carrigaline, co. Cork.

DAUNT OF FAHALEA.

DAUNT, THOMAS-ACHILLES, Esq. of Fahalea, co. Cork, *b.* in 1780; *m.* in 1806, Mary, dau. of — Coghlan, by whom he has, with other issue, a son and heir,

GEORGE, who is *m.*, and has issue.

Lineage.—HENRY DAUNT, of Knocknamana, 2nd son of George Daunt, of Nohoval and Gortigrenane, by Martha Turner his wife, *m.* 1st, in 1698, Catherine, dau. of — Roe, Esq. of Clonteede; and 2ndly, in 1706, Anne, dau. of Thomas Knolles, Esq. of Killeighy, co. Cork. By her he had, I. THOMAS, his heir; II. GEORGE, of the city of Dublin, surgeon, who *m.* his cousin, Anne Daunt, of Owlpen and Gortigrenane, by whom he had issue, Anne; Mildred, wife of Thomas Pleasants, Esq., barrister-at-law; and Hannah, wife of Thomas-Knox Grogan, Esq. of Johnstown Castle, co. Wexford; III. HENRY, of Dublin, who *m.* Mary, dau. of Robert O'Callaghan, Esq. of Clonmeen; IV. ACHILLES, of Newborough, co. Cork, in holy orders, *b.* in 1713, *m.* in 1747, Frances, dau. of Philip French, Esq. of Rath, co. Cork, and had (with four daus., Anne, Frances, Elizabeth, and Harriet) three sons, Henry; Thomas; and George; of whom the youngest, the Rev. George Daunt, of Newborough, *b.* in 1754, *m.* in 1786, Helena, dau. of the Rev. Arthur Herbert, rector of Castle Island, co. Kerry, and *d.* in 1819, leaving two sons and three daus., viz., GEORGE-ACHILLES, now of Newborough, Arthur-Henry, Mary-Townsend, Frances-Anne, and Helena-Susanna-Amelia; V. HUNGERFORD; and I. Anne, wife of her cousin, Achilles Daunt, Esq. of Owlpen and Gortigrenane. The eldest son of Henry Daunt's marriage with Miss Knolles, was,

THE REV. THOMAS DAUNT, of Fahalea, co. Cork, *b.* in 1707, who *m.* in 1755, Lettice, dau. of John Digby, Esq. of Landanstown, co. Kildare, high-sheriff of Kildare in 1732, and member in the Irish parliament for the town of Kildare in 1731. By her he had issue, several children, and dying in 1779, was *s.* by his eldest son,

THOMAS DAUNT, of Fahalea, *b.* in 1758, who *m.* 1st, his cousin, Frances, dau. of the Rev. Achilles Daunt, of Newborough; and 2ndly, Helena, dau. of — Scott, Esq. He *d.* in 1837, leaving, amongst other issue by his 1st wife, the present THOMAS-ACHILLES DAUNT, Esq. of Fahalea, co. Cork.

Arms, Crest, and *Motto*—same as those of DAUNT *of Owlpen*.
Seat—Fahalea, co. Cork.

DAUNT OF NEWBOROUGH.

DAUNT, GEORGE-ACHILLES, Esq. of Newborough, co. Cork, *b.* 14 June, 1790; *s.* his father, the Rev. George Daunt, in 1819, and is a magistrate for the co. of Cork.

DAU

For LINEAGE, &c., *see preceding family*.

Arms, Crest, and *Motto*—same as DAUNT *of Owlpen*.
Seat—Newborough, co. Cork.

DAUNT OF SLIEVERON.

DAUNT, GEORGE, Esq. of Slieveron, co. Cork, *b.* in 1792; *s.* his father, the late George Daunt, M.D., of Cork.

Lineage.—HENRY DAUNT, Esq. of Knocknamana and Fahalea (*see* DAUNT *of Fahalea*), had, amongst other issue, by his 2nd wife, Anne, dau. of Thomas Knolles, Esq. of Killeighy, HUNGERFORD, of the city of Cork, *b.* in 1718; Boyle, *b.* in 1725, *d.* in 1742; and three daus., Martha; Anne; and Lydia. The son and heir,

HUNGERFORD DAUNT, *m.* Joyce, dau. of Jonas Travers, Esq. of Butlerstown, co. Cork, by whom he had issue, GEORGE, and an only dau., Anne, who *d. unm.* His son,

GEORGE DAUNT, of the city of Cork, M.D., was *b.* in 1755, and *m.* his cousin, Mary, dau. of Thomas Daunt, Esq. of Fahalea, by whom he had issue, GEORGE DAUNT, Esq., now of Slieveron, near Carrigaline, co. Cork; and four daus., Mary; Catherine; Eliza, wife of Thomas Hungerford, Esq.; and Joyce, wife of Abel Harris, Esq.

Arms, Crest, and *Motto*—same as DAUNT *of Owlpen*.
Seat—Slieveron, co. Cork.

DAUNT OF TRACTON ABBEY.

DAUNT, ACHILLES, Esq. of Tracton Abbey, co. Cork, J.P., *m.* Mary, third dau. of John-Isaac Heard, Esq., M.P. for Kinsale, and high-sheriff of the co. Cork in 1839, by whom he has (with other issue) a son,

ACHILLES.

Lineage.—THOMAS DAUNT, of Owlpen, *m.* (see DAUNT *of Owlpen*) Alice, dau. of William Throckmorton, Esq. of Tortworth, co. Gloucester, by whom he had (amongst other issue), Thomas, the acquisitor of Tracton Abbey by lease, and of Gortigrenane, by purchase, in 1595; and a 4th son,

WILLIAM DAUNT, who *m.* Mary, dau. of Thomas Hutton, Esq. of Hutton, co. York, by whom he had issue, WILLIAM; and Thomas, who *m.* Susan, dau. of — Curle. He was *s.* by his eldest son,

WILLIAM DAUNT, who *m.* Mary, dau. of Isham Nowell, Esq. At this time we find, in the MS. depositions preserved in Trinity College, Dublin, a claim made on the government, in 1642, by James Daunt, Esq., described as "late of Tracton Abbey," for £622, on account of losses sustained in the civil war of the preceding year.

WILLIAM DAUNT, of Tracton Abbey, *m.* Jane, dau. of John Dolbear, Esq. of Cork, by whom he had (with other issue), ACHILLES, his successor in Tracton; and FRANCIS, of whom hereafter. Dying in 1676, he was *s.* by his 2nd son,

ACHILLES DAUNT, of Tracton Abbey, who *m.* 1st, in 1667, Elizabeth, dau. of Thomas Hungerford, Esq. of Inchidony, co. Cork, by whom he had issue, I. Thomas, who *m.* in 1692, Jane, dau. of — Saunders, and to whom his father gave the lands of Kilpatrick, co. Cork; II. WILLIAM; I. Margaret; II. Susanna; and III. Angel. He *m.* 2ndly, Margaret, dau. of Shuler, and widow of Thomas Herrick, Esq. of Shippool, co. Cork, by whom he had issue; III. John; and IV. Richard. He *d.* in 1711, and was *s.* in Tracton Abbey by his 2nd son,

WILLIAM DAUNT, of Tracton Abbey, who *m.* 1st, in 1700, Mary, dau. of William Bayly, by whom he had issue, I. ACHILLES; II. William, who *m.* in 1739, Barbara, dau. of — Busteed, Esq.; III. Bayly; IV. George; V. James; and VI. Swithin, besides daus. He was *s.* by his eldst son,

ACHILLES DAUNT, of Tracton Abbey, who *m.* in 1727, Elizabeth, dau. of Edward Bullen, Esq. of Oldhead, near Kinsale, by whom he had issue, WILLIAM; and Edward. He was *s.* by his eldest son,

WILLIAM DAUNT, who *m.* in 1753, Anne, dau. of Thomas Austin, and was grandfather of the present ACHILLES DAUNT, Esq. of Tracton Abbey.

Arms, Crest, and *Motto*—same as DAUNT *of Owlpen*.
Seat—Tracton Abbey, co. Cork.

DAUNT OF KILCASCAN.

DAUNT, WILLIAM-JOSEPH-O'NEILL, Esq. of Kilcascan, co. Cork, M.P. in 1833 for the borough of Mallow, m. in 1839, Miss Ellen Hickey, and has issue,

I. ACHILLES-THOMAS, b. 1849.
I. Alice-Iamena.

Lineage. — WILLIAM DAUNT, of Tracton Abbey (*see preceding family*), d. in 1676, leaving a 3rd son,

FRANCIS DAUNT, of Knockatour, co. Cork, who m. in 1667, Mary, dau. of George Wood, Gent. of Ballymoney, same co., by whom he had issue; George, of Knockatour, who m. in 1692, Dorothy, dau. of Thomas Knolles, Esq. of Killeighy, co. Cork, by whom he had issue; WILLIAM; Francis, who m. in 1700, Mary, dau. of — Austin, Esq., by whom he had, with other issue, Samuel Daunt, of Knocknasillagh, high-sheriff of the co. Cork, in 1749. His 2nd son,

WILLIAM DAUNT, of Kilcascan, m. in 1697, Rachel, dau. of Thomas Knolles, Esq. of Killeighy, by whom he had (besides other issue), JOSEPH; and Francis, who d. s. p. He acquired Kilcascan in 1712, and dying in 1760, was s. by his eldest son,

JOSEPH DAUNT, of Kilcascan, b. in 1702. He m. in 1729, Sarah, dau. of John Rashleigh, Esq. of Cloncoose and Ballinadee, co. Cork, by whom he had (besides daus.), WILLIAM, b. in 1750. He d. in 1783, and was s. by his only son,

WILLIAM DAUNT, of Kilcascan, who m. in 1775, Jane, dau. of Richard Gumbleton, Esq. of Castle Richard, co. Waterford, and uterine niece of William Conner, Esq. of Connerville, co. Cork, by whom he had issue, I. JOSEPH; II. Richard-Gumbleton, a captain in the 90th regt., who m. 1st, Anne, dau. of the Rev. John Dixon, vicar of Humbleton, co. York, by whom he had issue, Richard-Gumbleton; Harold; and a dau.; and 2ndly, his cousin Margaret, dau. of Robert-Warren Gumbleton, Esq. of Castleview, co. Cork; III. Robert-Gumbleton, a lieut. in the 62nd regt., who m. Miss Harris, of Cork, by whom he had issue. Dying in 1809, William Daunt was s. by his eldest son,

JOSEPH DAUNT, of Kilcascan, b. in 1779. He m. 1st, in 1806, Jane, dau. of the Rev. Thomas Wilson, D.D., rector of Ardstraw, co. Tyrone, and niece of John Wilson, Esq., Governor of Minorca, by whom he had issue, WILLIAM-JOSEPH-O'NEILL; Thomas-Wilson, who d. in 1854; Henry, who d. in infancy; Catherine-Elizabeth; and Lavinia-Isabella. His 1st wife dying in 1816, he m. 2ndly, in 1822, his cousin Jane, dau. of Robert-Warren Gumbleton, Esq., by whom he had issue, a dau., Margaret-Alice, b. in 1826. Dying in 1826, he was s. by his eldest son, the present WILLIAM-JOSEPH-O'NEILL DAUNT, Esq. of Kilcascan.

Arms, Crest, and *Motto*—same as DAUNT *of Owlpen.*
Seat—Kilcascan, near Dunmanway, co. Cork.

DAVENPORT OF CAPESTHORNE.

DAVENPORT, ARTHUR-HENRY, Esq. of Capesthorne, co. Chester, an officer 1st life guards, b. 9 June, 1832.

Lineage.—The Davenports descended from Ormus de Davenport, living *temp.* CONQUESTORIS.

From NICHOLAS DAVENPORT de Woodford (3rd son of Sir John Davenport, of Weltrough and Henbury, Knt., justice of Lancaster, 7th RICHARD II., and 9th in descent from Ormus the Norman), living 44th EDWARD III., lineally derived

CHRISTOPHER DAVENPORT, Esq. of Woodford, 1556, grandson and heir of John Davenport, Esq. of Woodford. His eldest son by his 1st wife, Jane, dau. of Richard Gerard, Esq. of Crewood,

WILLIAM DAVENPORT, Esq. of Woodford, who d. in 1632, had by his 1st wife, Dorothy, dau. of Robert Hyde, Esq. of Norbury, with other children, an elder son and heir,

JOHN DAVENPORT, Esq. of Woodford, who m. in 1594, Mary, dau. of Hugh Bromley, Esq., and d. in 1653. His great-grandson,

JOHN DAVENPORT, Esq. of Woodford, major of the Cheshire force raised at Nantwich in 1689, m. Anne, dau. and coheiress of John Davenport, Esq. of Davenport, and d. s. p. 4 Feb. 1733, when he was s. by his brother,

MONK DAVENPORT, Esq. of Woodford, who m. Elizabeth, dau. of John Davies, Esq. of Manley, co. Chester, and by her, who d. 24 Feb. 1735, had, with other issue,

DAVIES DAVENPORT, of Woodford and Marton, barrister-at-law, of the Inner Temple, London, b. in 1696, m. in 1721, Mary, dau. and sole heiress of John Ward, Esq. of Capesthorne, and d. leaving, with other issue, DAVIES, his heir; Charles, b. 7 April, 1835, rector of Brereton; Thomas (Sir), of Hendon, Knt., m. Jane, dau. of John Seal, Esq. The eldest son and heir,

DAVIES DAVENPORT, Esq. of Woodford, Marton, and Capesthorne, barrister-at-law, of the Inner Temple, b. 20 Oct. 1723, m. Phœbe, dau. and co-heir of Richard Davenport, Esq. of Calveley (descended from the marriage of Arthur, a younger son of Sir Ralph Davenport, of Davenport, with the heiress of Calveley of Calveley), and left, with a dau. (Phœbe, wife of Eusebius Horton, Esq. of Catton, co. Derby, and mother of a dau., Anne, m. to the Right Hon. Sir Robert Wilmot, Bart., who thereupon assumed the surname of Horton), a son and heir,

DAVIES DAVENPORT, Esq, of Woodford, Marton, Calveley, and Capesthorne, high-sheriff of Cheshire in 1783, and M.P. for that county from 1806 until 1830, when he retired. He was b. 29 Aug. 1757, and m. Charlotte, dau. of Ralph Sneyd, Esq. of Keel, co. Stafford, by whom he had,

EDWARD-DAVIES, present representative.
Henry, major in the 87th regiment, lieut.-col. in the army, d. in 1833.
Walter, in holy orders, who has assumed the additional surname of BROMLEY. He m. 1st, in July, 1818, Caroline-Barbara, dau. of Archdeacon Gooch, and niece to Sir Thomas Gooch, Bart., and 2ndly, 22 Feb. 1829, the Lady Louisa Dawson, sister of the Earl of Portarlington.
Harriet-Katherine, m. to the Hon. Sir John Williams, Knt., Judge of the Queen's Bench.

Mr. Davenport d. 5 Feb. 1837, when he was s. by his eldest son,

EDWARD-DAVIES DAVENPORT, Esq. of Capesthorne, co. Chester, and Court Garden, Bucks, b. 27 April, 1778, who m. 30 Nov. 1830, Caroline-Anne, dau. of Richard Hurt, Esq. of Wirksworth, co. Derby, and d. in 1847, leaving a son and heir, the present ARTHUR-HENRY DAVENPORT, Esq. of Capesthorne.

Arms—Arg., a chevron, between three crosses-crosslet, fitchée, sa.
Crest—A man's head, couped at the shoulders, and in profile, ppr.; round the neck a halter, or.
Seats—Calveley Hall, and Capesthorne, co. Chester; and Court Garden, Bucks.

DAVENPORT OF DAVENPORT.

DAVENPORT, WILLIAM-SHARINGTON, Esq. of Davenport, co. Salop, J.P., b. 30 July, 1808; m. 22 Dec. 1835, Catherine-Louisa, only dau. of Samuel-Peter Marindin, Esq. of Chesterton, co. Salop, and has issue,

I. WILLIAM-BROMLEY, b. 14 Oct. 1836.
II. Edmund-Henry, b. 19 Aug. 1839.
III. Vivian, b. 31 Jan. 1848.
IV. Charles-Talbot, b. 16 Oct. 1848.
I. Louisa-Marindin, d. 16 May, 1853.

Lineage.—The pedigree of this family is authentically deduced in an unbroken male line, from ORMUS DE DAVENPORT, living *temp.* WILLIAM the Conqueror.

THOMAS DAVENPORT, Esq., living 14th HENRY VII., 2nd son of SIR RALPH DAVENPORT, of Davenport in Cheshire, Knt., and the lineal descendant of Ormus, m. Alice, sole dau. and heir of Robert Hanford, Esq. of Chorley. He was father of ROBERT DAVENPORT, Esq. of Chorley, who m. Anne, dau. of Bellot of Bellott, co. Chester, and had a son and heir,

WILLIAM DAVENPORT, Esq. of Chorley, who m. Grace, dau. of Fowke Dutton, Esq. of Dutton, co. Chester, and was father of HENRY DAVENPORT, Esq. of Chorley, who m. Jane, dau. of William Leicester, Esq. of Toft. His son,

WILLIAM DAVENPORT, Esq., sold the estate of Chorley, and seated himself at Hollon, co. Salop, which estate he acquired by his marriage with Jane, dau. and heir of Francis Bromley, Esq. of Hollon, co. Salop, son and heir of Sir George Bromley, Knt. He was s. by his eldest son,

HENRY DAVENPORT, Esq. of Hollon, who m. Lettice, dau. and heir of Thomas Maddocks, Esq. of Bridgnorth, and d. in Feb. 1664, leaving an only surviving son,

HENRY DAVENPORT, Esq., who m. 22 Oct. 1665, Elizabeth, dau. of Sharington Talbot, Esq. of Lacock, co. Wilts, and d. in July, 1698, leaving (with other daus., who d. unm.), a dau., Mary, m. 1st, to the Rev. William Hallifax, D.D., who d. in 1720, and 2ndly, to the Rev. Prideaux Sutton, of Bredon, co. Worcester; and two sons, Sharington, the elder, a major-general in the army, who d. unm. in Ireland, 5 July, 1719; and

HENRY DAVENPORT, Esq., bapt. 26 Feb. 1677-8, who m.

1st, Mary-Lucy, dau. of Daniel Charden, Esq., and [illegible] her a son, SHARINGTON, of whom presently; and two [illegible] Mary-Elizabeth, *m.* to John Mytton Esq. of Halston, [illegible] Mary-Luce, *d. unm.* Mr. Davenport *m.* 2ndly, Barbara, 2nd dau. of Sir John Ivory, of Ireland, by Anne his wife, dau. of Sir John Talbot, of Lacock, co. Wilts, and by her, who *d.* in 1748. left at his decease, in 1731, a son, William, in holy orders, D.D., rector of Breedon, who *m.* Mary, dau. of John-Ivory Talbot, of Lacock, and had issue. The only son of the 1st marriage,

SHARINGTON DAVENPORT, Esq., *m.* Gratiana Rodd, of Hereford, and *d.* in 1744, leaving with other surviving issue,

- Daniel-Chardin, *m.* Jane Blockley, and *d.* in 1778.
- Sharington, baptised 11 June, 1871, *m.* a dau. of Major Farhington.
- WILLIAM-YELVERTON, of whom presently.
- Edward, in holy orders, vicar of Worfield, *b.* 19 Jan. 1754, *m.* in 1776, Catherine, dau. of the Rev. Edmund Taylor, of Worcester, and afterwards of Grappenhal, co. Chester, and had issue, EDMUND-SHARINGTON, of whom presently, as successor to his uncle; Harry-Chardin, *b.* 4 Dec. 1781, deceased; William-Yelverton, *b.* in 1780; Edward-Ormus, *b.* 1 March, 1785, *d.* in the East Indies; Catherine-Gratiana; Myra; Anne; Mary, *m.* to Alexander White, Esq. of Scotland; Bertha, *m.* to James Milman Caley, Esq.; Arabella; and Barbara-Juliana.

The 3rd son,

WILLIAM-YELVERTON DAVENPORT, Esq. of Davenport, co. Salop, *b.* 19 Feb. 1750, *m.* Jane-Elizabeth, dau. of Crawley, Esq. of Bath, and relict of — Blythe, Esq., and *d. s. p.* in Feb. 1834, when he was *s.* by his nephew,

THE REV. EDMUND-SHARINGTON DAVENPORT, of Davenport, vicar of Worfield, *b.* 18 May, 1778, who *m.* 7 Aug. 1806, Elizabeth, dau. of Joseph Tongue, Esq. of Hollon, and by her (who *d.* 21 Sept. 1850) had issue,

- WILLIAM-SHARINGTON, now of Davenport.
- Joseph-Tongue, *b.* 25 Aug. 1813, *m.* Emily Leicester.
- Edward-Montague, *b.* 13 April, 1817.
- Edmund-Sharington, *b.* 28 June, 1821, *m.* Mary Moss.
- Daniel-Decimus-Tongue, *b.* 3 Nov. 1828.
- Barbara-Anne, *m.* to the Rev. Cornelius-F. Broadbent, M.A.
- Catherine-Gratiana, *m.* to Octavius-E. Johnson, Esq.
- Elizabeth, *m.* to George Nicholas, Esq.
- Harriet-Juliana, *m.* to Edward Owen, Esq., lieut. R.N.
- Lucy-Susanna.

The Rev. Mr. Davenport *d.* 27 Feb. 1842.

Arms—Arg., a chevron between three cross-crosslets, fitchée, sa.
Crest—A man's head, couped at the shoulders, and side-faced, ppr., with a rope round the neck, or.
Motto—Audaces fortuna juvat.
Seat—Davenport, co. Salop.

DAVENPORT OF BRAMALL HALL.

DAVENPORT, WILLIAM-DAVENPORT, Esq. of Bramall Hall, co. Chester, lieut.-col. commanding 2nd regt. royal Cheshire militia, J.P. and D.L., *b.* 15 Sept. 1811; *m.* 1st, 14 Nov. 1833, Camilla, dau. of V. Gatt, Esq., and by her, who *d.* in 1845, has one dau.,

Maria-Dorothea.

He *m.* 2ndly, 24 Oct. 1850, Diana-Elizabeth, dau. of John Handley, Esq., banker, of Nottinghamshire, and by her has a son,

JOHN-WILLIAM-HANDLEY, *b.* 19 Oct. 1851.

Colonel Davenport served in the army from 1826 to 1847.

Lineage.—REAR-ADMIRAL SIR SALUSBURY HUMPHREYS, K.C.H., C.B. of Weedon Lodge, Bucks (*see family of* HUMPHREYS), *m.* for his 2nd wife, in 1810, MARIA, dau. and heir of WILLIAM DAVENPORT, Esq. of Bramall Hall, co. Chester, and assumed in consequence the surname and arms of DAVENPORT. By the heiress of Bramall, he left, at his decease in 1845,

- WILLIAM-DAVENPORT, now of Bramall Hall.
- Trevor, capt. in the army, *b.* 29 July, 1814, *m.* 1 July, 1837, Frances, dau. of the late Chief-Justice Sewell, of Quebec, and has issue.
- Henry-Wayet, lieut. 39th regt. *m.* 23 June, 1843, Catherine, eldest dau. of Capt. John Durie, *d.* in India, 1845.
- John-Salusbury, *b.* 24 June, 1817, *m.* Anne, dau. of Sir Allan McNab.
- Charles-Edgecumbe, an officer in the army, *b.* 26 Dec. 1819, *m.* Emma, dau. of the Very Rev. Dr. Webber, dean of Ripon.
- Emily, *m.* 1841, to the Rev. Arthur Douglas.
- Julia, *m.* 1842, to Henry Crookenden, Esq., M.D.

Arms and *Crest*—*See* DAVENPORT *of Capesthorne.*
Seat—Bramall Hall, Stockport, Cheshire.

DAVEY OF REDRUTH.

DAVEY, STEPHEN, Esq. of Redruth, co. Cornwall, J.P. and D.L., *m.* 12 May, 1838, Charlotte, dau. (by Elizabeth Lyon his wife, a descendant of the Strathmore family) of the Rev. William Horton, 3rd son of Joshua Horton, of Howroyde, co. York, who was next brother of Sir William Horton, 1st Bart. of Chadderton, and has issue,

I. WILLIAM-HORTON.
I. Elizabeth-Maria. II. Charlotte-Mary-Horton.

Mr. Davey is eldest son and heir of the late William Davey, Esq. of Redruth, in which parish the family has been settled for several generations.

Arms—Arg., on a chevron, az., between two mullets, pierced, in chief, and a lion, passant, in base, gu., three cinquefoils, or.
Crest—A mount, vert, thereon an eagle, rising, az., charged on the wing with a cinquefoil, or, holding in the dexter claw a staff, sa., therefrom flowing a pendant, gu.
Motto—E perseverantiâ honor.
Seat—Redruth, Cornwall.

DAVIDSON OF CANTRAY.

DAVIDSON, HUGH-COCHRANE, Esq. of Cantray, co. Inverness, J.P. and D.L., *b.* 20 April, 1809; *m.* 19 Aug. 1830, Maria, 3rd dau. of Col. Grogan, of co. Meath, and has issue,

I. HUGH-GROGAN, *b.* 18 Dec. 1833.
II. Cuthbert-John, *b.* 18 Aug. 1839.
I. Margaret. II. Catherine-Jane.
III. Frances-Harriet. IV. Maria-Anne-Elizabeth-Brodie.

Lineage.—The late SIR DAVID DAVIDSON, of Cantray, only son of DAVID DAVIDSON, Esq., and his wife, Mary Cuthbert, of Castle Hill, co. Inverness, *m.* 12 Dec. 1804, Margaret Rose, of the family of Kilravock, and had issue,

- HUGH-COCHRANE, his heir, now of Cantray.
- Cuthbert, *b.* 24 May, 1810, *m.* the dau. of — Mainwaring, Esq., Bengal civil service, and has issue, one son and one dau.
- Frances-Russell, *b.* 24 May, 1810, Bengal civil service.
- Margaret, *m.* to Sir Robert Grant, late governor of Bombay, brother of Lord Glenelg.

Arms—Az., on a fesse, between three pheons, arg., a buck, couchant, gu.
Crest—A youth from the middle, holding in the dexter hand a man's heart, all ppr.
Motto—Sapienter si sincerè.
Seat—Cantray, Nairn.

DAVIDSON OF INCHMARLO.

DAVIDSON, PATRICK, Esq. of Inchmarlo, co. Kincardine, D.L., *b.* 29 Oct. 1809; *m.* 2 Aug. 1836, Mary-Anne, eldest dau. of William Leslie, Esq. of Warthill (*see that family*), and has issue,

I. DUNCAN, *b.* 5 Aug. 1843.
II. William-Leslie, *b.* 31 Jan. 1850.
I. Jane-Anne. II. Frances-Mary.
III. Katharine-Helen. IV. Mary-Margaret.
V. Matilda-Rose.

Mr. Davidson is Professor of Civil Law in the University and King's College of Aberdeen.

Lineage.—A branch of the Douglas family, for nearly four centuries, possessed large estates in Kincardine district, including, besides Inchmarlo and Dalkaikie, the now separate properties of Tillywhilly, Kincardine, &c.

The Douglases sold off all their lands on the Deeside about 1819, in which year the estates of Inchmarlo and Dalkaikie, or Tillishaikie, were acquired by Walter-S. Davidson, Esq., and in 1838 were purchased by the late Duncan Davidson, Esq. of Tilliekelty and Desswood, father of the present possessor, whose grandfather,

JOHN DAVIDSON, Esq. of Tillichetly and Desswood, *m.* in 1770, Anne-Farquharson, dau. of Harry-Farquharson Indego, and by her (who *d.* 22 May, 1812,) left, at his decease, 31 March, 1802, an eldest son and heir,

DUNCAN DAVIDSON, Esq. of Tillichetly and Desswood, D.L., who purchased the estate of Inchmarlo, in 1838. He *m.* 28 June, 1804, Frances-Mary, dau. of Patrick Pirie, Esq. of Aberdeen, by whom he had issue,

- PATRICK, now of Inchmarlo.
- Duncan, of Tillichetly, co. Aberdeen, H.E.I.C.C.S., post-

master-general, Bombay, m. in 1842, Katherine-Frances, dau. of Charles Gordon, Esq. of Abergeldie, co. Aberdeen.
Charles-Forbes, of Edinburgh.
James, of London.
Alexander, of Desswood, co. Aberdeen.
Margaret-Jane, m. 5 Aug. 1850, to Arthur Fraser, Esq. of London, son of the late Alexander Fraser, Esq. of Aberdeen.
Anne. Williamina.

Mr. Davidson d. 8 Dec. 1849, and was s. by his eldest son.

Arms—Az., on a fesse, between three pheons, or, a stag couchant, gu., attired with ten tynes, or.
Crest—A youth from the middle, holding in dexter hand a man's heart, all ppr.
Motto—Sapienter si sincerè.
Seat—Inchmario, co. Kincardine.

DAVIES OF MARRINGTON HALL.

DAVIES, JOHN, Esq. of Marrington Hall, co. Salop, b. 14 March, 1821; s. his father in June, 1842.

Lineage.—CYNRIC EFELL, the elder of the twin sons of Madoc ap Meredith, Prince of Powys, on the decease of his father, succeeded to the lordship of Eglwys Egle, a division of the lordship of Bromfield. His eldest son,

LLEWELYN AP CYNRIC EFELL, a noble of Molesdale, m. Efa, dau. of Bleddyn ap Gwion, Lord of Uwch Aled, in Denbighland, and was ancestor of the house of GWYSANEY, for ages one of the most distinguished in the county of Flint.

GRIFFITH AP LLEWELLYN, eldest son of Llewellyn, and grandson of Cynric Efell, the founder of this line, m. and had issue.

JOHN AP DAVID, of Gwysaney, who first assumed the name of DAVIES, was 14th in descent from CYNRIC EFELL. He m. Jane, widow of Richard Mostyn, and dau. of Thomas Salusbury, of Leadbroke, and had issue,

I. ROBERT, of Gwysaney, living 20 April, 1581, great-grandfather of

MUTTON DAVIES, of Gwysaney, and high-sheriff of Flintshire in 1670, who s. to the estate of Llanerch in right of his mother, Anne, dau. and co-heir of Sir Peter Mutton, chief-justice of North Wales. He m. Elizabeth, only dau. of Sir Thomas Wilbraham, of Woodhey, co. Chester, Bart., and by her had issue,

1 ROBERT DAVIES, Esq. of Gwysaney and Llanerch Park, high-sheriff for Flintshire in 1704. He m. Letitia, sister of John Vaughan, 1st Viscount Lisburne, and had issue, ROBERT, his heir, of Gwysaney and Llanerch Park, ancestor of the DAVIES's *of Gwysaney and Llanerch*, now represented by PHILIP BRYAN DAVIES COOKE, Esq. of Owston and Gwysaney.
2 THOMAS, m. in 1687, Margaret, dau. of Owen Madoc, Gent., and d. in 1697, leaving a son and heir,

THE REV. OWEN DAVIES, b. in 1689, who m. in 1714, Jane, dau. of William Lloyd, Esq., and d. in 1766, leaving an only son,
OWEN DAVIES, Esq., b. in 1715, who m. 9 Sept. 1856, Sarah, dau. of James Stockell, Gent. of Westbury, co. Salop, and d. in 1805, leaving a son and successor,
THOMAS DAVIES, Esq., seated at Trefynant, co. Denbigh. He was b. 8 Nov. 1757, and m. Margaret, dau. of John Peploe, Esq. of Peploe, co. Salop, by Elizabeth his wife, dau. of Edward Hill, Esq. of the last-named shire, and by her (who d. 24 Jan. 1809, aged 49) had issue,

THOMAS, lieutenant of engineers, E.I.C.S., a very distinguished officer, b. 7 Nov. 1789, killed in action on the night of the 18th May, 1818, at Malegaume, in India, commanding engineer of the army of the Dekkan.
OWEN, sometime resident at Chilwell Hall, Notts, and subsequently at Eton House, co. Kent, b. 4 Nov. 1796; m. 4 Nov. 1826, Frederica-Wilhelmina, dau. of Samuel-Cutler Hooley, Esq. (who d. in his father's lifetime), only son of James Hooley, Esq. of Woodthorpe, co. Nottingham, a deputy-lieut. of that shire, and major of the Nottingham volunteers. By this lady he has had issue, OWEN, an officer in the army, b. 1 March, 1831; Thomas, b. 2 Feb. 1833; Margaret, m. 11 July, 1850, to Michael-Joseph-Charles Ripport, Avocat attaché à la Cour de Cassation; Mary-Hooley, also m. in France; and Frederica, d. 1 March, 1846.
Elizabeth, m. 27 March, 1800, to William Hughes, Esq. of Pen-y-clawdd, co. Denbigh.

3 Roger, buried at Mold, 30 March, 1677.
4 John, D.D., rector of Kingsland, co. Hereford, precentor of St. David's, and prebendary of Hereford and St. Asaph.
5 Richard, vicar of Rhuabon, co. Denbigh.
1 Anne.
2 Mary, m. to the Rev. Thomas Holland, of Berow, co. Anglesey.
3 Elizabeth.
4 Katherine, 2nd wife of Sir William Williams, Bart., M.P.

II. JOHN, of whom we treat.
I. Catherine, m. to Edward Morgan, Esq. of Golden Grove, co. Flint.

The 2nd son,

JOHN DAVIES, Esq., living in 1578, m. twice, and was father of

JOHN DAVIES, Esq., who m. the dau. and heir of Davies of Peniarth, in the co. of Montgomery, and was s. by his son,

RICHARD DAVIES, Esq. of Peniarth, in Montgomeryshire, living in 1645. He m. Anne, dau. of Henry Lloyd, Gent., and had a son and heir,

RICHARD DAVIES, Esq. of Peniarth, in 1698, whose son, by Mary, his wife, eldest dau. of John Downes, Esq. of Marrington,

JOHN DAVIES, Esq. of Peniarth and Marrington, m. Margaret, dau. and co-heiress of Richard Mathews, Esq. of Penybryn, Llanyblodwel, Shropshire, and dying 24 Aug. 1772, was s. by his elder son,

JOHN DAVIES, Esq. of Marrington and Peniarth, at whose decease, s. p. in 1792, aged 64, the representation of the family devolved on his brother,

WILLIAM DAVIES, Esq. of Brompton, co. Salop, who m. Sarah, dau. of Benjamin Pool, and by her (who d. in 1827, aged 75) had two sons and three daus.,

JOHN, his heir.
Richard-John, in holy orders, of Brompton, in Salop, rector of Aberhafesp, co. Montgomery.
Ann. Sarah. Margaret.

Mr. Davies d. in 1806, and was s. by his eldest son,

JOHN DAVIES, of Marrington Hall, Esq., J.P. and D.L., lieut.-col. royal Montgomery light infantry militia, b. 12 Jan. 1770, m. in Feb. 1805, Charlotte, 3rd dau. of Peter Butt, Esq. of Deptford, and dying in June, 1842, left a dau. (Charlotte, m. John-Glynn Mytton, Esq. of Penylan, co. Montgomery, and d. leaving issue), and a son, JOHN, the present inheritor of the estate.

Arms—Quarterly: 1st and 4th, gu., on a bend, arg., a lion, passant, sa., for DAVIES *of Gwysaney*; 2nd, arg., a lion, rampant, sa., armed and langued, gu. (the Black Lion of Powys) for Madoc ap Meredith, last Prince of Powys; 3rd, or, a lion, rampant, gu., armed and langued, of the first, for Bleddyn ap Cynfyn, King of Powys.
Crest—A lion's head, couped quarterly, arg. and sa., as granted to Robert Davies, Esq. of Gwysaney, 20 April, 1581, when the arms were confirmed.
Motto—Heb Dhuw heb ddym Dhuw a digon.
Seat—Marrington Hall, co. Salop.

DAVIES OF MOOR COURT.

DAVIES, JAMES, Esq. of Moor Court, co. Hereford, J.P. and D.L., m. 18 April, 1804, Marianne, 3rd dau. of John Lewis, Esq. of Harpton Court, co. Radnor, and sister of the Right Hon. Sir Thomas-Frankland Lewis, Bart., but by her (who d. 30 April, 1845) has no issue. Mr. Davies, of Moor Court, is son of the late William Davies, Esq. of Bwynllys Castle, co. Brecon, by Esther his wife, dau. and eventual heir of Hugh Powell, a lineal descendant of Lewis ap Howel ap Lewis, of Cwmclyn, living in 1592. Through his great-grandmother, Anne, dau. of William Lloyd, and wife of William Davies, Esq. of Noyadd, Llandewyrcwm, Breconshire, he lineally derives from Thomas Lloyd, lord-lieut. of Breconshire, temp. HENRY VII., whose eldest son, John Lloyd, of Towy, lies buried in Builth Church.

Arms—Quarterly: 1st and 4th, gu., a griffin, segreant, or, for DAVIES; 2nd and 3rd, arg., a lion, rampant, sa.; over all a fesse, engrailed, gu. for POWELL.
Crest—A griffin, segreant, or.

DAVIES OF ALLTYR ODIN.

LLOYD-DAVIES, JOHN, Esq. of Alltyr Odin and Blaendyffryn, co. Cardigan, and Healddû, co. Carmarthen, M.P., J.P., and D.L., high-sheriff of Cardiganshire in 1845, b. 1 Nov. 1801; m. 30 June, 1825, Anne, only surviving child of John Lloyd, Esq. (2nd son of David Lloyd, Esq. of Alltyr Odin) and Elizabeth Lloyd, only child of Philip Lloyd, Esq. of Healddû, and had an only child, Arthur-Lloyd Davies, *b.* 6 Jan. 1827, who, on attaining his majority, took by royal license the surname of Lloyd, in addition to that of Davies, in compliance with the provisions of his maternal uncle's will; he *m.* 11 Dec. 1849, and *d.* 27 July, 1852, leaving a son, John Davies-Lloyd, *b.* 30 Oct. 1850, and a dau., Anne-Justina Davies-Lloyd.

Lineage.—Mr. Lloyd Davies was the sole representative of the houses of Castle Howell and Alltyr Odin, and lineally descended from David ap Llewellyn Llwyd, of Castle Howell, Esq., who was the first knight of the shire in the county of Cardigan, in the reign of Henry VIII.; and descended in a right line from Cadivor ap Dinawal, a man of great valour and conduct, who having taken the castle of Cardigan from the Earl of Clare and the Flemings, by escalade, was honoured by his prince, the great Lord Rhys, for that service, with these arms, viz.; Sa., a spear's head, embrued, between three scaling-ladders, arg.; on a chief, gu., a castle triple-towered, of the second. He was also rewarded with divers territories, and entitled Lord of Castle Howell, Pantstrimon, and Gilfachwen. He *m.* Catherine, dau. of the said Lord Rhys, Prince of South Wales.

Arms—Per chevron, arg. and sa., in chief two antelopes' heads erased, of the second; in base a mullet, of the first.
Crest—A demi-antelope, sa., semé of mullets, arg. holding between the legs a cross-crosslet, sa.
Motto—Bydd gyfiawn, bydd 'lwyddiannus: Be just, be prosperous.
Seat—Blaendyffryn, co. Cardigan.

DAVIES OF PENTRE.

Davies, David-Arthur-Saunders, Esq. of Pentre, co. Pembroke, J.P. and D.L., M.P. for Carmarthenshire, *b.* 9 June, 1792; *m.* 31 July, 1826, Elizabeth-Maria, only dau. of Col. Owen Philipps, of Williamston, co. Pembroke, and has issue,

I. Arthur-Henry-Saunders, *b.* 22 April, 1832.
II. Owen-Gwyn-Saunders, *b.* 14 May, 1834.
III. Henry-David-Saunders, *b.* 6 Jan. 1836.
I. Susan-Maria-Anne. II. Agnes-Elizabeth.

Lineage.—The Davies's were resident for several generations at Llandovery, where they were of much influence and respected. Evans Davies, one of this family, commanded a troop of cavalry in the wars under John, Duke of Marlborough, *temp.* Queen Anne.

Arthur Davies, of Llandovery, son of Rhys Davies, *m.* Anne, dau. and heiress of Jenkin Morgan, of Cathelid, co. Glamorgan, and was father of

David Davies, who *m.* Susannah, 2nd and only surviving dau. and heiress of Erasmus Saunders, Esq. of Pentre, by Jane his wife, dau and heiress of Richard Philips, Esq. of Dolhaida Issa, co. Carmarthen, and Moel Ifor, co. Cardigan, and granddau. of David Saunders, Esq., by his wife, Susan Morgan, of Blanhylan; and by this lady, who *d.* in 1823, had issue,

David-Arthur-Saunders, now of Pentre.
Jane-Anne-Bridget, *m.* to the Rev. Augustus Brigstocke, 3rd son of William-Owen Brigstocke, Esq. of Blaenpant, co. Cardigan, and had issue, one son, William-Owen Brigstocke.
Catherine-Angharad, *m.* to William-Webley Parry, only son of Admiral Webley Parry, of Noyadd Trefawr, co. Cardigan, and has issue.

Arms—Quarterly: 1st and 4th, sa., a wolf, salient, arg., for Davies; 2nd and 3rd, sa., a chevron, or, between three eagles' heads, erased, arg., for Saunders.
Crests—1st, a wolf, salient, arg., for Davies; 2nd, a demi-bull, salient, couped at the loins, arg., for Saunders.
Motto—Solem ferre possum.
Seat—Pentre, co. Pembroke.

BOWEN-DAVIES OF MAES-Y-CRYGIE.

Bowen-Davies, David-Thomas, Esq. of Maes-y-Crygie, co. Carmarthen, and Glanrhocca, co. Cardigan, J.P. and D.L., *b.* 26 Nov. 1792; *s.* his mother in 1828.

Lineage.—This family, with many others in the Principality, derives from Cadivor ap Dinawal, Lord of Castel Hywel. The Glaurhocca estate has descended from father to son, David and Jenkin, for upwards of three hundred years.

Jenkin Davies, Esq. of Glanrhocca, co. Cardigan, son of David Davies, Esq., and grandson of Jenkin Davies, Esq., *m.* Sarah, dau. of John Bowen, Esq. (youngest son of Daniel Bowen, Esq. of Waun-Ifor), by his wife, Margaret, dau. of Thomas Thomas, of Maes-y-Crygie, and Sarah his wife, dau. and co-heir of John Lewes, of Gernos, co. Cardigan, a descendant of one of the partisans of the Earl of Richmond, afterwards Henry VII., and by her had issue,

David-Thomas-Bowen, of Maes-y-Crygie.
John-Bowen, *d. s. p.*
Margaretta-Bowen.

Mr. Davies *d.* in 1828.

Arms—Quarterly: 1st, sa., a spear's head, arg., imbrued, gu., between three scaling-ladders (two and one), of the second; on a chief, gu., a castle, triple-towered, ppr.; 2nd, gu., a lion, rampant-regardant, or; 3rd, arg., three boars' heads (two and one), couped, sa.; 4th, gu., three snakes, nowed, as.
Crest—An eagle, displayed.
Motto—Virtus sine dolo.
Seat—Maes-y-Crygie, co. Carmarthen.

DAVY OF INGOLDSTHORPE.

Davy, John, Esq. of Ingoldsthorpe, co. Norfolk, captain R.N., J.P., *b.* 5 June, 1789; *m.* in Feb. 1832, Catharine, eldest dau. of the late Richard Day, Esq. of Yoxford, Suffolk, and has issue,

I. John-William, *b.* in Jan. 1836.
I. Jane-Amelia. II. Mary-Anne. III. Emma.

Lineage.—William Davy, son of John Davy, had four sons, by Jane his wife, viz., William, of whom presently; John, *d. s. p.* in 1811; Augustine, *d. s. p.* in 1827; and Martin, D.D., master of Caius College, Cambridge, *d. s. p.* in May, 1839. The eldest son,

William Davy, Esq., *m.* his first-cousin, Elizabeth, dau. of Edward Davy, Esq. of Milsham, co. Norfolk, by Mary his wife, and had issue,

John, now of Ingoldsthorpe.
William, an officer in the army, was drowned at St. Helena, in Dec. 1818, *s. p.*
Edward, in holy orders, *d. s. p.* 1803.
Henry, in the royal engineers, killed at Corunna, with Sir John Moore, in Jan. 1809, *s. p.*
Martin, fellow of St. Mary's Coll., Oxon, *d. s. p.* in 1834.
Elizabeth, *d. unm.* in 1835.
Mariane, *m.* to the Rev. J. Brett.
Emily. Lucy-Jane.

Mr. Davy *d.* in 1824.

Arms—Sa., a chevron engrailed, erm., between three annulets, arg.
Crest—Out of a ducal coronet, or, an elephant's head, sa., armed, arg.; in the front of the coronet, a ring, thereto a line and ring, gold, turned over the trunk.
Seat—Ingoldsthorpe, co. Norfolk.

DAVY.

Davy, John, M.D., F.R.S. London and Edinburgh, &c., inspector-general of army hospitals, a magistrate for the county of Westmoreland, brother of the late Sir Humphrey Davy, Bart., president of the Royal Society; *m.* Margaret, dau. of the late Archibald Fletcher, Esq., advocate, Edinburgh.

Residence—Lesketh How, near Ambleside, Westmoreland.

DAWE, OR DAWES, OF DITCHEAT.

Dawe, Hill, Esq. of Ditcheat, in Somersetshire, J.P., *b.* 16 Dec. 1771.

Lineage.—This family, which settled at Ditcheat in 1669, having bought the manor and advowson of the parish church, which were part of the property of Lord Hopton, is a scion of the Dawes *of Dorsetshire*, of the time of Edward IV.

Edmund Dawe, son of Edmund Dawe, of Ditcheat, *s.* his father in 1695. He *m.* Martha, dau. of Jonathan Hill, Esq. of Cholderton, Wilts, high-sheriff for that county in 1689, and had issue,

Hill, *b.* 26 April, 1704, his heir.
Edmund, *b.* 5 June, 1706, of Nether Stowey, *m.* Anne Webber, of Bromefield, Somerset, and had issue several children, who all *d. s. p.*, except Hill, who became a surgeon at Bridgewater, and *m.* Miss Mary Coles, by

whom he had one dau., Mary-Anne, who *m.* in 1800, James-Anthony Wickham, Esq. of North Hill House, Frome.

Elizabeth, *b.* 17 Oct. 1702.

Edmund Dawe *d.* and was buried at Ditcheat, 10 Sept. 1708. His widow Martha remarried, 1st, George Vince, surgeon, of Marlborough; 2ndly, Henry Hale, M.D. of Salisbury, and left issue by both. His son and heir,

Hill Dawe, Esq. of Ditcheat, J.P., *s.* his father in 1708. He *m.* Susannah, dau. of Andrew Moore, Esq. of North Newton, high-sheriff for Somersetshire in 1725, and had issue. Hill Dawe *d.* 25 June, 1769. His son and successor,

Hill Dawe, Esq. of Ditcheat, capt. in the Somerset militia, *m.* Miss Mary Muns, of Wells, by whom he had,

I. Hill, his heir, now of Ditcheat.

II. Andrew-Moore, *b.* in 1778, paymaster to the 53rd regiment of foot, *m.* Anne, dau. of Richard Hare, Esq. of Bath, and has issue,

1 Henry-Andrew, *b.* in 1809, who *m.* Catharine, dau. of the Rev. Mr. Murray, minister of Dysart, Fifeshire, Scotland.

2 Hill-Richard, *b.* in 1810.

III. George-Selwyn, *b.* in 1784.

IV. Charles, *b.* in 1789, captain in the 46th regiment of foot, *m.* in 1833, Sophia, dau. of the Rev. William Leir, rector of Ditcheat, and has issue, three children, Charles-Richard, William-Hill, and Sophia-Nina.

I. Susannah. II. Charlotte.

III. Elizabeth, *m.* William Jeffreys, Gent.

Arms—Arg., on a pile, gu., a chevron between three crosses-crosslet, arg.
Crest—A lion's gamb, erased, arg., holding a fleur-de-lis, or.
Seat—Ditcheat House.

DAWSON OF OSGODBY HALL AND ARBORFIELD.

Dawson, George-Pelsant, Esq. of Osgodby Hall, co. York, J.P. and D.L., barrister-at-law, *b.* 22 July, 1802; *m.* Susan-Jane, dau. of Henry Dod, Esq. of Burnham, and has issue,

I. George. II. Pelsant. III. Charlton.
IV. Edward-Conyers. V. Henry.
I. Elmira, *m.* to Robert-Bligh Sinclair, Esq., late capt. 42nd Highlanders.
II. Fanny. III. Blanche.

Lineage.—Bertram Dawson (the 7th in lineal descent from Archibald Dawson, of Greystock, in Cumberland, by his wife, the dau. of Thomas Nevile, of Hornby Castle) is recorded as having been with Edward *the Black Prince* in France; he *m.* a dau. of Edmund Clare, and had issue,

Simon Dawson, who *m.* the dau. of Adam of Dalstone, and had issue,

Sir Roger Dawson, Knt. of Dalstone, who *m.* a dau. of Sir Simon Montford, Knt., and was father of

Bertram Dawson, who *m.* a dau. of Lewis of Marr, and had eleven sons. Gilbert, 9th son, was ancestor of the Dawsons *of Agerley*. The 4th son,

Richard Dawson, Esq. of Heworth, co. York, and West Ham, co. Essex, living in 1588, *m.* Judith, dau. of Conyers of Boulby, co. York, and had (besides two daus., Anne, *m.* to Henry Tankred, Esq., son of Ralph Tankred, Esq. of Arden; and Edith, *m.* in 1562, to William Newby, Esq.; and other issue) a son and heir,

Richard Dawson, Esq. of Heworth, who purchased the manor of Farlington, &c., from John Boucher, Esq. He *m.* Maria, dau. of Thomas Thwenge, Esq. of Heworth, and had issue. Mr. Dawson *d.* in 1602, and was *s.* by his eldest son,

William Dawson, Esq., lord of the manor, and patron of Farlington. He *m.* in 1627, Mary, dau. of — Agar, Esq. of Stockton, near York, and at his decease *s. p.* was *s.* by (the son of his brother Richard) his nephew,

William Dawson, Esq. of Heworth and Farlington, who *m.* Elizabeth, dau. of Robert Gere, Esq. of Great Barough, by Frances his wife, dau. of Isaac Mountagne, Esq. of Weston, and *d.* 1681, having had issue. The eldest son,

William Dawson, Esq. of Heworth and North Ferriby, *b.* 1662, had by his 1st wife, Agnes, dau. of Sir William Lowther, Knt., several children, of whom the 2nd son,

George Dawson, Esq. of North Ferriby, major in the army, bapt. 13 March, 1689, *m.* 1719, Dorothy, dau. of John Heaton, Esq. of Firby, and was father of

George Dawson, Esq. of Ackworth Park and Osgodby Hall, co. York, governor of Masulipatam, and 2nd member of council at Madras. He *m.* twice, and by his 1st wife, Isabell, dau. of Francis Charlton, Esq. of Salop, he left at his decease, 25 Aug. 1812, a son,

George Dawson, Esq. of Osgodby Hall, lieut. 1st Royals, major in the North York militia, and deputy-lieutenant, who *m.* Elmira, dau. of John Reeves, Esq. of Arborfield House, Berks, and sister and heir of Pelsant Reeves, Esq., capt. 1st Royals, who was killed at Toulon; and by this lady (who *d.* 28 Dec. 1848) had issue,

George-Pelsant, his heir, and present representative.

Elmira-Catherine-Philadelphia, *m.* to Capt. William Mallet, 46th regt.

Isabel, *m.* to the Rev. Henry Cary, M.A.

Mr. Dawson *d.* 1 May, 1832, aged 69.

Arms—Erm., on a canton, az., a stag, lodged, or.
Crest—On a mount, vert, a hound, statant, proper.
Seat—Osgodby Hall, near Selby, Yorkshire.

DAWSON OF LANGCLIFFE AND HORNBY CASTLE.

Dawson, Pudsey, Esq. of Hornby Castle, co. Lancaster, of Langcliffe and Great Stainforth, in the West Riding of Yorkshire, J.P. and D.L., high-sheriff of Lancashire in 1845, *b.* 2 Oct. 1778; *m.* 1st, 19 Sept. 1808, Sarah, eldest dau. of George Bigland, Esq. of Bigland Hall, and by her (who *d.* in Dec. 1816) had a son,

Hugh-Pudsey, B.A. Oxford; *d.* at Madeira, 30 June, 1831, aged 22, *unm.*

He *m.* 2ndly, 9 May, 1821, Jane-Constantine, 2nd dau. and co-heir of the Rev. Richard Dawson, of Halton Gill, and rector of Bolton-by-Bowland, Yorkshire. Mr. Dawson *s.* to the Hornby Castle property under the will of his kinsman, the late Admiral Sandford Tatham, who *d.* 24 Jan. 1840.

Lineage.—The Dawsons *of Halton Gill* in the parish of Arncliffe, and Langcliffe Hall in the parish of Giggleswick, both in the West Riding of Yorkshire, have been of highly respectable descent, and seated at the former place for many generations.

Josias Dawson, Esq., the eldest son of Christopher Dawson, Esq. of Halton Gill, upon his marriage in 1646, with Mary, only dau. of William Foster, removed to Langcliffe Hall. His eldest son,

Christopher Dawson, Esq. of Langcliffe Hall, *m.* 27 May, 1673, Margaret, 3rd dau. of Sir Thomas Craven, of Appletrewick in Craven, co. York, and left two sons: Josias, who *d. unm.* aged 16; and

William Dawson, Esq. of Langcliffe Hall, J.P., a major in the Yorkshire militia, who *m.* 1st, Jane Pudsey, eventually the sole heiress of her father, and brother, Ambrose Pudsey, of Bolton Hall, in Craven,* and by her had two sons,

---

* Oughtred de Bolton, living *temp.* Henry I., held among other possessions the manor of Bolton-by-Bowland. Seventh in descent from him was Richard de Bolton, bow-bearer of the Forest of Bowland, upon whose death, without issue, *temp.* Edward I., the manor of Bolton devolved upon his nephew, John de Pudsey, son and heir of his eldest sister and co-heiress, Catherine, by her husband Simon de Pudsey, living *temp.* Edward II. John de Pudsey's son and heir, Henry Pudsey, Esq. of Bolton Hall, *m.* Elizabeth, dau. and heir of John Layton, of Barforth, and was father of Sir John Pudsey, Knt., Lord of Bolton, 3 Henry IV., who *m.* Margaret, dau. of Sir William Eure, Knt., by Maud his wife, dau. of Lord Fitz-Hugh, and had a son, Sir Ralph Pudsey, Knt, Lord of Bolton 31 Henry VI., who concealed his royal master for several weeks at Bolton Hall, after the fatal battle of Hexham; whose son and heir, by his 1st wife, Margaret, dau. of Sir Thomas Tunstal, Knt. of Scargill, Sir John Pudsey, Knt., of Bolton, *m.* Grace, dau. of Lawrence Hamerton, Esq. of Hamerton, and was father of Henry Pudsey, Knt. of Bolton, who *d.* in 1520, leaving by Margaret his 1st wife, dau. of Sir John Conyers, Knt. of Hornby Castle, in Yorkshire, an eldest son and heir, Thomas Pudsey, Esq. of Bolton and Barforth, who *m. temp.* Henry VII., Margaret, dau. and co-heir of Roger Pilkington, of Pilkington, co. Lancaster, and was *s.* by his eldest son, Henry Pudsey, Esq. of Bolton and Barforth, who *d.* 8 Dec., 34 Henry VIII. (1542), leaving by his 1st wife, Joan, dau. of Sir Ralph Eure, Knt., an eldest son and heir,

Thomas Pudsey, Esq. of Barforth and Bolton (to whom [who lay with the army of reserve] the Earl of Surrey, on the march of the English army to Flodden Field, of which he held the command, addressed an important letter from Newcastle, the last day of May, 1513, which is still in the possession of Mr. Pudsey Dawson). He *m.* Elizabeth, dau. of Lord Scrope, of Bolton and Masham, and was father of William Pudsey, Esq. of Bolton, living 19 Elizabeth, who left, by his 1st wife, Elizabeth Banister, an eldest son,

CHRISTOPHER, who *s.* to the estates at Bolton, &c., on the death of his maternal uncle, Ambrose Pudsey, Esq., and *d. unm.* in 1786, aged 81, and was *s.* by his brother,
AMBROSE, heir to his brother and father, and of whom presently.

Major Dawson *m.* 2ndly, Elizabeth Marsden, dau. of Henry Marsden, of Gisburne Hall, co. York, and Wennington, co. Lancaster, first-cousin of his 1st wife. By this marriage he had a son and a dau., from whom are descended the DAWSONS *of St. Leonard's Hill*, co. Berks, and the COOKSONS *of Leeds*. Major Dawson was the personal friend of Sir Isaac Newton, who paid him frequent visits at Langcliffe. His 2nd son,

AMBROSE DAWSON, Esq. of Langcliffe Hall, and of Bolton, *m.* in 1742, Mary, dau. of Richard Aston, Esq., and sister of Sir Willoughby Aston, Bart., and to Sir Richard Aston, judge of the Court of Queen's Bench, and by her had issue,

PUDSEY, his heir.
William, *m.* Eleanor Lee, and had issue, four sons and three daus.
Richard, *m.* Elizabeth Crosbie, and had issue, two sons and three daus.
Mary, *m.* to William Crosbie, Esq.
Jane, *d. unm.*
Elizabeth, *m.* to Col. Charles Rooke.

Mr. Dawson, an eminent physician in London, *d.* in Dec. 1794, aged 88, and was *s.* by his son,

PUDSEY DAWSON, Esq. of Langcliffe Hall, and of Bolton Hall, *b.* 16 Feb. 1752; who *m.* Miss Elizabeth-Anne Scott, dau. of James Scott, Esq. of Amsterdam (who *d.* 2 Feb. 1837, aged 86), and had issue,

PUDSEY, present representative.
William, post-capt. R.N.; *d.* at Madras, in 1811, *s. p.*, aged 28.
Richard, *m.* in 1818, Mary-Ann Perkin, and has issue, a son, RICHARD-PUDSEY; and a dau., Mary, *m.* to Henry-R. Hoskins, Esq., and has four sons.
Ambrose, B.D., senior fellow of Brazennose.
Henry, capt. 52nd light infantry, killed in Spain, 17 Nov. 1812, in his 24th year, *unm.*
Charles, lieut. in the same regt., *d.* in his 23rd year, *unm.*
Edward, *m.* Eliza Liot, and *d.* in Jan. 1843, at Bermuda, aged 46, leaving one dau., Elizabeth-Anne Pudsey.
Mary, *m.* in 1809, to Anthony Littledale, Esq. of Liverpool, and has issue.
Jane, *m.* in 1832, to the Rev. John Jennings, canon of Westminster and rector of St. John, and *d.* in childbirth the following year, leaving a son, Ambrose-Dawson Jennings.

Mr. Pudsey Dawson, mayor of Liverpool in 1799 and 1800, and one of the founders there of a school for the indigent blind, *d.* 19 April, 1816.

Arms—Quarterly of eight, I. DAWSON, II. PUDSEY, III. BOLTON, IV. LATON, V. STRABOLGI, VI. PILKINGTON, VII. SCROPE, VIII. SANDFORD.
Crests—A tabby cat's head, guardant, erased, a rat in the mouth, fesseways, gorged with a mural crown, or, for DAWSON; a stag, lodged, ppr., for PUDSEY.
Motto—Penser peu de soi.
Seat—Hornby Castle, co. Lancaster.

DAWSON OF EDWARDSTON HALL.

DAWSON, CHARLES, Esq. of Edwardston Hall, co. Suffolk, J.P. and D.L., *b.* 30 Dec. 1776.

Lineage.—THOMAS DAWSON, Esq. of Edwardston Hall, co. Suffolk, son of Thomas Dawson, Esq. and Eleanor Porster his wife, *m.* in 1775, Anne, only child of Thomas Manning, Esq. and Grace his wife, only child of Lieut.-Col. Norris, and had issue,

CHARLES, now of Edwardston Hall.
George-Augustus, in holy orders, *m.* Louisa, one of the daus. and co-heiresses of the late Sir Thomas Pilkington, Bart. of Chevet, co. York, and has issue, Thomas-Pilkington; and Gertrude.
Anne-Lovell, *m.* to the late William Shepherd, Esq. of Bradbourne, co. Kent, since deceased, leaving issue, Anne-Maria, *m.* to Richard Magenis, Esq. of the county of Antrim; Emily-Louise, present Countess of Belmore.

AMBROSE PUDSEY, Esq. of Bolton, father, by his 1st wife, Bridget, dau. of Sir Richard Sandford, Knt. of Howgill Castle, co. Westmoreland, of AMBROSE PUDSEY, Esq. of Bolton, colonel of a regiment of foot, who *m.* Jane, dau. of Sir Thomas Davison, Bart. of Blakiston, co. Durham, and was father of AMBROSE PUDSEY, Esq. of Bolton, who *m.* Elizabeth, dau. of Henry Marsden, Esq. of Gisburne Hall, co. York, and of Wennington, co. Lancaster, and had, with other issue, who *d.* in infancy, a dau. Jane, *m.* in 1705, to William Dawson, Esq. of Langcliffe, as above; and Bridget, who *d.* aged 80, *unm.*, devising her property to her nephews, Christopher and Ambrose Dawson.

Arms—Az., a chevron, erm., between three arrows, or, feathered and barbed, arg.; on a chief of the last, three Cornish choughs, ppr.; a canton, gu., charged with a mullet, gold.
Crest—A tabby cat's head, guardant, erased; in the mouth a rat, ppr.
Motto—Vitæ via virtus.
Seat—Edwardston Hall, co. Suffolk.

DAWSON OF CASTLE-DAWSON.

DAWSON, THE RIGHT HON. GEORGE-ROBERT, of Castle-Dawson, co. Londonderry, *b.* 24 Dec. 1790; *m.* 8 Jan. 1816, Mary, dau. of Sir Robert Peel, 1st Bart. of Drayton Manor, co. Stafford, and by her (who *d.* 15 Jan. 1848) has issue,

I. ROBERT-PEEL, *b.* 2 June, 1818, J.P. and D.L., *m.* 8 May, 1848, Mary-Elizabeth, eldest dau. of Charles Brownlow, 1st Lord Lurgan, and has a dau., Mary.
II. George-Beresford, *b.* 18 June, 1819.
III. Henry, in holy orders, rector of Great Munden, Herts, *b.* 27 Jan. 1821, *m.* 21 Sept. 1848, Anne, 2nd dau. of the Hon. Baron Dimsdale, of Camfield Place, Herts.
IV. Francis-Alexander, *b.* 26 April, 1823, *m.* 9 May, 1854, Caroline-Agnes, dau. of Jonah Harrop, Esq. of Bardsley House, Ashton-under-Lyne.
V. Frederick, *b.* 11 July, 1824.

This gentleman represented the county of Londonderry in parliament from 1815 to 1830, and subsequently the borough of Harwich. He was appointed Under Secretary of State for the Home Department in Jan. 1823; Secretary to the Treasury in Jan. 1828; sworn a Privy Councillor in Nov. 1830; and made Secretary to the Admiralty in Dec. 1834, which office he resigned in 1835. He is now Deputy-Chairman of the Board of Customs.

Lineage.—The Dawson family went to Ireland in 1601, from Temple Sowerby, Westmoreland.

THOMAS DAWSON, who purchased the lands at Castle-Dawson, co. Londonderry, in the 8th year of CHARLES I.'s reign (1633), from George and Dudley Philips, had a son and successor,

THOMAS DAWSON, commissary of the musters of the army in Ireland, *d.* in 1683, and was *s.* by his son,

THOMAS DAWSON, Esq. of Castle-Dawson, M.P. for Antrim, who *m.* Arabella Upton, of Castle Upton, co. Antrim, and dying in 1695, was *s.* by his brother,

JOSHUA DAWSON, Esq. of Castle-Dawson, M.P. for Wicklow, and chief secretary for Ireland to the Lords Justices, in 1710. He *d.* 1727, leaving, with other issue, two sons and a dau., namely,

I. ARTHUR, his heir.
II. William, who *m.* Sarah Newcomen, widow of Colonel Dawson, of the county of Tipperary, and had issue,
 1 ARTHUR, successor to his uncle.
 2 Sarah, *m.* to Thomas Newenham, Esq. of Coolmore, co. Cork,
I. Mary, *m.* to the Hon. Henry Hamilton, M.P.

The elder son,

ARTHUR DAWSON, Esq. of Castle-Dawson, M.P. for the county of Londonderry, one of the barons of the Exchequer, 1742. He *m.* Jane Neill, of Shane's Castle, and, dying in 1775, was *s.* by his nephew,

ARTHUR DAWSON, Esq. of Castle-Dawson, M.P., *b.* 1745, who *m.* in 1775, Catherine, dau. of George Paul and Lady Araminta Monck, and by her (who *d.* 20 May, 1838), had issue,

GEORGE-ROBERT, now of Castle-Dawson.
Henry-Richard, dean of St. Patrick's, Dublin, who *m.* Frances Heseltine.
Araminta.
Maria, *m.* to Henry Kemmis, Esq. of Dublin.
Louisa.
Isabella, *m.* to Richard Cane, Esq. of Dublin.

Mr. Dawson *d.* 6 Dec. 1822.

Arms—Az., on a bend, or, three martlets, gu.
Crest—An estoile of six points, or.
Motto—Toujours propice.
Seat—Castle Dawson, co. Londonderry.

DAY OF KERRY.

DAY, THE REV. EDWARD, of Beaufort, co. Kerry, rector of St. John's, Sligo, *m.* in June, 1825, Anne, dau. of Richard Holmes, Esq. of the city of Dublin, and has issue,

I. EDWARD, b. 12 May, 1826. II. Arthur.
III. Richard. IV. John. V. William.
I. Elizabeth, m. 24 Dec. 1844, to Thomas-Yates Ridley, Esq. of Heysham, Lancashire.
II. Harriett. III. Lucy.

Lineage.—The DAYS *of Kerry* are a branch of a very ancient and widely-spreading family in the sister kingdom, and are very numerous in Norfolk and Suffolk. They claim descent from Geoffrey D'Eye, a follower of the Norman conqueror, who received a large grant of lands in Suffolk, afterwards erected into a manor, part of which now forms the parish of D'Eye.

At what period precisely the branch before us settled in Kerry has not been ascertained, but the first of the family, of whom anything is known, was

JONATHAN DAY, living in the year 1654, whose son,

NATHANIEL DAY, a member of the society of Friends, m. Mary Kitchener, an English lady, and left two sons,

EDWARD, of whom presently.
Nathaniel, a confidential agent of the house of Stuart in this country. Mr. Day suffered death in June, 1713, for enlisting men and collecting arms for the Pretender.

The eldest son,

EDWARD DAY, of Tralee, m. in 1697, Ellen, dau. of Philip Quarry, of Cork, and left two sons and two daus., viz.,

I. JOHN, of whom hereafter.
II. Edward, in holy orders, m. Mary, dau. of John Rowan, Esq. of Castle Gregory, granddau. of Dean John Leslie, famed for his loyal services in 1688, and left issue,
 1 James, in holy orders, rector of Tralee, and vicar-general of the diocese of Ardfert and Aghadoe, m. Margaret, dau. of M'Gillycuddy of The Reeks, and left issue,
  Edward, in holy orders, rector of Kilgobbin, who m. Deborah, dau. of John Curry, Esq., and has issue, James; John, lieut. H. E. I. Co.'s service; Richard; Edward; Robert; Leslie; Margaret; Deborah, m. to James-John Hickson, of Hilville; Betsey; Agnes; Lucy; and Sarah.
  Richard. John-Sealy, capt. 87th regt., dec.
  James-Leslie, major in the Bengal army, deceased.
  Agnes.
  Sarah, m. to John-James Hickson.
  Alicia, m. to James Morphy, Esq. Lucy.
 2 Edward, in holy orders, d. unm.
 1 Sarah, m. to John Rae, Esq. of Derrymore.
I. Ellen, m. Giles Rae, of Derrymore, co. Kerry, and had issue.
II. Elizabeth, m. to Robert Collis, Esq.

The eldest son,

THE REV. JOHN DAY, m. in 1737, Lucy-Fitzgerald, dau. of Maurice Knight, of Kerry, by Elizabeth Crosbie, sister of Maurice, 1st Lord Brandon, and had issue,

I. EDWARD, of whom hereafter.
II. John, mayor of Cork in 1806, m. Margaret Hewson, and left issue,
 1 John, in holy orders, rector of Kiltullagh, co. Kerry, m. Arabella, dau. of Sir William Godfrey, Bart., and had issue,
  John, in holy orders, rector of Valentia, m. his cousin, Eleanor, dau. of Sir John Godfrey, and has issue.
  Edward, in the H. E. I. Co.'s service.
  Robert, m. Miss Alicia Thompson, of Dublin.
  William, in holy orders.
  Maurice, in holy orders.
  Agnes, m. James Butler, of Waterville, in Kerry, and d. leaving issue, James; John; Arabella; and Belinda.
  Margaret, m. to Capt. Roderick Mackenzie, brother of Sir Francis Mackenzie, of Gairloch, N.B.
  Ellen. Arabella.
 2 Edward, lieut.-colonel in the H. E. I. Co.'s service, m. Mary, dau. of Patrick Trant, of Dingle, and has issue.
 1 Elizabeth, m. to Oliver Stokes, Esq.
 2 Margaret, m. to John-Fitzgerald Collis.
 3 Lucy, d. unm. 4 Catherine, d. unm.
III. Robert, an eminent lawyer, M.P. for Ardfert, in the Irish parliament, and one of the justices of the Court of King's Bench, in Ireland, m. in Aug. 1774, Mary Potts, of the city of London. Judge Day d. at an advanced age, in 1841, having had one dau.,
  ELIZABETH, who m. in 1795, Sir Edward Denny, Bart., of Tralee, and left issue.
I. Catherine, m. Thomas Franks, Esq., and left issue.

The eldest son,

THE REV. EDWARD DAY, of Beaufort, co. Kerry, archdeacon of the diocese of Ardfert and Aghadoe, m. in Aug. 1769, Barbara Forward, and left issue,

EDWARD, of whom presently.
Robert, of Logheroannon, in Kerry, barrister-at-law, m. in July, 1808, Christian, dau. of William Marshall, of Dublin, and has issue, William, who m. Mary, dau. of Alexander Elliott, of Killscrim, in Kerry.
Margaret, m. in Oct. 1790, John Mahony, Esq. of Dromore Castle, and by him left, with other issue, a son, the Rev. Denis Mahony, of Dromore Castle.
Lucy, m. the Rev. William Godfrey, rector of Kenmare, and brother of Sir John Godfrey, Bart., and has issue.
Barbara, d. unm.

The elder son,

THE REV. EDWARD DAY, of Beaufort, m. in April, 1802, Harriett, eldest dau. and co-heiress of John Rowan, Esq. of Castle Gregory, co. Kerry, and had issue, EDWARD, present representative; Robert, d. unm.; Elizabeth, m. to the Rev. George Brown; Barbara, d. unm.

Arms—Per chevron, arg. and az., three mullets, counter-changed.
Crest—Two hands clasping each other, couped at the wrist, and conjoined to a pair of wings, ppr.
Motto—Sic itur ad astra.
Seat—Beaufort, Killarney.
Residence—St. John's, Sligo.

DAYMAN OF MAMBURY.

DAYMAN, JOHN, Esq. of Mambury, co. Devon, b. 24 Nov. 1778; m. 1st, in 1801, Jane, only dau. of Nicholas-Donithorne Arthur, Esq. of St. Columb-Major, Cornwall; and 2ndly, Mary, 3rd dau. of William Harrison, Esq. of Leytonstone, Essex. By the former (who d. 28 Jan. 1841) he has issue,

I. JOHN, M.A. in holy orders, rector of Skelton, Cumberland, m. 15 Oct. 1831, Levina-Elizabeth, eldest dau. of Captain Angelo *alias* Tremamondo, and has, Arthur-Edward, and Levina-Beatrice.
II. Charles-Orchard, M.A., scholar of St. John's Coll., Cambridge, Revising Barrister for South Wilts.
III. Edward-Arthur, B.D., in holy orders, rector of Shillingstone, Dorset, m. 7 July, 1842, Ellen-Maria, eldest dau. of Wm. Dunsford, Esq. of Ashley Court, near Tiverton, by Emelia his wife, dau. and co-heir of John Halsey, Governor of Surat, and has issue, Edward-Arthur; Walter-Wythers; William-Hankford; Francis-Stanbury; Helen-Halsey; and Alice-Mary.
IV. Henry, of Brooklands, Milbrook, co. Hants, m. 4 March, 1840, Elizabeth-Adams, eldest dau. of J.-W. Chadwick, Esq. of Long Ashton.
V. Phillipps-Donithorne, M.A., in holy orders, vicar of Poundstock, Cornwall, m. 1840, Elizabeth, dau. of Mr. Gamond, of Herefordshire, and has, Phillips-Donithorne; Barnfield; Jane; Sybylla; and Mary-Coryndon.
I. Mary-Jane.
II. Lucretia, m. 21 Sept. 1837, to the Rev. Carrington Ley, M.A., vicar of Bere Regis, and has issue.
III. Caroline.

Lineage.—This family, the name of which has been spelt in a variety of ways at different times,* is descended from a family which took its origin and name from the town of Dinan in Britany. The first we hear of is Ammon or Hamon, Vicomte de Dinan, who lived about A.D. 970, from whom, according to Augustin du Pas, descended four noble families of France; viz.: 1st, the Vicomtes de Dinan, which branched off into England, of whom presently; 2ndly, the Lords of Combowe; 3rdly, the Vicomtes de Dinan, lords of Beaumanoir and Montafilant, a branch which, after giving a Grand Butler to France in the person of Jacques de Dinan, A.D. 1427, ended in his dau. Françoise, who, though thrice married, appears to have died s. p. Jan. 3rd, 1493, just when the noble branch in England ceased also in the male line, and the humbler descendants began to emerge; and 4thly, the Vicomtes de la Bellière: whilst from the 5th, but illegitimate, son of the above-named Ammon, called Salomon, Lord of Guarplic, descended lineally, according to the same authority, the celebrated Bertrand du Guesclin, Constable of France and Castile.

Bertrand, Vicomte de Dinan, grandson of the above mentioned Ammon, followed the CONQUEROR to England, and was rewarded by him with manors and lands, especially at Hartland, in Devonshire, of which place his descendants were lords for many generations, and great benefactors to

* As Dinan, Dynaunt, Dynam, Dynham, Dymant, Dimonde, Deimond, Dyamond, Deyman, &c. In the Heralds' Visitation, 1620, it is spelt DYAMOND, but DEYMAN in the index of the same, which latter is the one adopted in the parochial registers of the same date, and in most of the old family deeds and documents.

the abbey founded there by Githa, mother of King HAROLD, in honour of St. Neelda. This branch became extinct in the male line by the death of John, Baron Dynham, K.G. in 1509, *s. p. l.*, and his four sisters became co-heiresses. But a younger branch, descended from a younger son of Geffry de Dynan, who *d.* 5 EDWARD I. (1276), remained for many generations at Hartland and the neighbourhood, holding leases of lands under the abbey. Between the reigns of HENRY VI. and HENRY VII., family tradition says that two of the sons of John Dynant or Dymant, of Hartland, migrated to Barnstaple* and Tiverton in Devonshire, where they engaged in the trade of those towns, and became manufacturers of serges or kerseys, maintaining at the same time their connexion with the parent stock by purchasing, through the wool-staplers, the raw material of their trade, the wool grown by their relatives of the same name who remained on the land. Their names often occur in the annals of both the above named towns, as members of the respective corporations, or filling municipal offices; and at Tiverton† they suffered severely during the Great Rebellion, both in property and person, for their loyalty. Both these branches, it is believed, have been extinct in the male line for some generations; that at Barnstaple, after an heiress had married into the Cholwell family about 1607, and another into that of Burgoyne, ended probably towards the close of the 17th century; and that at Tiverton, it is supposed, either in the person of "the Rev. Dr. Deyman, 40 years master of Uffculme school, in Devonshire, who died Feb. 23rd, 1739," but whose descendants in the female line are still to be found; or in an old gentleman of the name, who is said to have died at Tiverton about 1780, leaving no relatives.

Of the original family which continued at Hartland, and the neighbouring parishes of Morwenston and Kilkhampton, two branches still remain. One has possessed and resided on a small estate called Breadon, in Pancras-Wike parish, co. Devon, for 250 years; the other was settled at a still earlier date at Flexbury, and afterwards at Maer, in Poughill parish, co. Cornwall, and is now represented by JOHN DAYMAN, Esq. of Mambury, co. Devon.

JOHN DEYMAN, of Flexbury, *b.* 8 Aug. 1691 (the eldest son and heir of John Deyman, of Flexbury, and grandson of Richard Deyman, of Flexbury, who was 5th in descent from Richard Deyman, of Fillam in Hartland, Devon, and 12th from Geffry de Dynan, *temp.* EDWARD I.), *m.* 1 March, 1715, Thomasine, dau. of Daniel Dennis, Gent. of Poughill, and *d.* in 1741, leaving a son and heir,

JOHN DAYMAN, of Flexbury, *b.* 15 Dec. 1717, who *m.* 21 Dec. 1748, Barbara, only dau. of the Rev. Charles Orchard, rector of Coryton, and dying 17 April, 1793, was *s.* by his eldest son,

JOHN DAYMAN, Esq. of Maer and Flexbury, *b.* 17 Oct. 1753, who *m.* Mary, eldest dau. (by Eulalia his wife, dau. and heir of Abraham Barnfield, of Mambury) of Joseph Phillipps, Esq. of Maer, sister and co-heir of the Rev. John Phillipps, M.A. of Mambury, Devon, granddau. of Samuel Phillipps, Esq. of Maer, high-sheriff of Cornwall, 1727, by Bridget his wife, dau. and co-heir of Thomas Coryndon, Esq. of Redstone, who was grandson of Thomas Coryndon, Esq. of Bratton, and Dorothy his wife, dau. of William Langford, of the same place, whose ancestor Roger de Langford, was sheriff of Cornwall, 10 HENRY III. By the co-heiress of Phillipps, Mr. Dayman left at his decease, 31 May, 1786,

JOHN, now of Mambury.
Charles, M.A. vicar of Great Tew, Oxfordshire, *b.* 18 Sept. 1786, *m.* Flavie Restitude, only dau. and heir of M. Delmaire, of Lillers, Pas de Calais, and *d.* 1847, leaving surviving issue, Joseph, lieut. R.N.; Gordon, of Oxford; Alfred-Jeken, B.A. in holy orders; Flavia; and Helen.
Mary.
Lucretia, *m.* 5 May, 1807, Richard-Martyn Braddon, Esq., and has, Charles, M.R.C.S.; and William.

Arms—Gu., four fusils in fesse, erm.
Crest—Sa., a demi-lion, rampant, ducally gorged and chained, or.
Motto—Toujours prest.
Seat—Mambury, Devon.

---

* Barnstaple, 1 ELIZ., 1559:—
"This Invent. mad. the iiii. of October, and in the fyurste year of the raigne of our Sov. Lady ELIZABETH, by the grace of God, Queen of England, France, and Yrland, &c., by Nicholas Wychalse and John Peard, Wardens, Hugh Brasiers, Willm. Dakyns, JOHN DEYMAN, and Richd. Witherege, Syd-men, &c."—*MS. of Church furniture, penes Barn. Corporation.*

† John Deyman, Gent., with his son, were among the prisoners taken in Tiverton Castle by the parliamentary army under Fairfax, Oct. 18th, 1645. William Deyman, Gent., was "committed as prisoner upon the late insurrection" in 1654; and in 1655 John Deyman was turned out of the corporation upon political grounds.—*History of Tiverton*, by Lt.-Col. Harding, F.G.S., 1845, Vol. i. pp. 77–8; see also Vol. ii. pp. 3, 34, 68, &c.
A grant of arms was confirmed to John Deyman of Tiverton, and in *Harl. MSS.* 1080, is given a pedigree of this branch.

DAYRELL OF LILLINGSTON DAYRELL.

DAYRELL, EDMUND-FRANCIS, Esq. of Lillingston Dayrell, co. Buckingham, *s.* his kinsman, the late Capt. Dayrell.

Lineage.—The DAYRELLS *of Lillingston Dayrell* derive from a common ancestor with the DARELLS *of Calehill*, and possess their lands from the Conquest.

RALPH DAIRELL, of Lillingston Dairell and Hanworth, living in 10th HENRY III., descended from Richard Dayrell, who was seised in fee of a messuage in Lillingston Dayrell, *temp.* RICHARD I., *m.* Juliana de Barré, an heiress, and was *s.* by his eldest son,

HENRY DAYRELL, of Hanworth and Lillingston, who flourished in the reigns of HENRY III. and EDWARD I. By his 2nd wife, Alicia, whose mother Christian was dau. and heiress of Alexander Hampden, he appears to have had no issue. By his 1st, Johanna, dau. and co-heir of Roger de Samford, and first-cousin to Alicia de Samford, wife of Robert de Vere, Earl of Oxford, he had a dau. Emma, *m.* to Richard de Grusset; and a son,

SIR RALPH DAIRELL, of Lillington Dairell, alive in 1282, ancestor of the distinguished family of DAYRELL *of Lillingston Dayrell.*

PAUL DAYRELL, Esq. of Lillingston Dayrell, sheriff of Buckinghamshire in the 5th and and 22nd of ELIZABETH, eldest son and heir of Paul Dairell, Esq. of Lillingston Dairell, *temp.* HENRY VIII., and brother of Frances Dayrell, Esq. of Lamport, *m.* Frances, dau. of William Saunders, Esq. of Welford, and had issue, THOMAS, his heir; FRANCIS, ancestor of the DAYRELLS *of Shudy Camps*, in Cambridgeshire (*see that family*); and other issue. Paul Dayrell *d.* in 1606, and was *s.* by his son,

SIR THOMAS DAYRELL, Knt., of Lillingston Dayrell, who *m.* Margery, dau. and co-heir of Robert Horne, Bishop of Winchester, and was direct ancestor of

THE REV. RICHARD DAYRELL, D.D., *b.* in 1720, who *m.* Anne, dau. of Sir John Langham, Bart. of Cottesbrooke, Notts, and niece to Richard, Viscount Cobham, and had by her, who *d.* in 1730,

RICHARD, his heir.
PAUL, successor to his brother.
Henry, capt. R.N., *b.* in June, 1746. *m.* in 1776, Mary-Martha-Penelope, eldest dau. of John Miller, Gent. of Buckingham, and had (with two daus., Anna-Maria, wife of the Rev. John-Theodore-Archibald Reed; and Frances-Langham, wife of William Reed) RICHARD, successor to his uncle Paul.
John-Langham, *b.* 2 July, 1756, in holy orders, rector of Lillingstone Dayrell. *m.* 1st, Mary, dau. of William Wilson, Gent., and 2ndly, Frances, only child and heiress of the Rev. Mr. Knight, rector of Lillingston Lovel, Oxon.

Dr. Dayrell *d.* 14 April, 1767, *æt.* 47, and was *s.* by his son,

RICHARD DAYRELL, Esq. of Lillingston Dayrell, a captain in the 10th dragoons, who entailed the family estates on his brothers and their heirs male, with remainder, in default of such issue, on the DAYRELLS *of Lamport.* Captain Dayrell, who served the office of sheriff, *d.* in 1800, *unm.*, and was *s.* by his brother,

PAUL DAYRELL, Esq. of Lillingston Dayrell, *b.* in June, 1746, a capt. in the 52nd regiment, who resided in America, where he *m.*, and *d.* without issue, 1803, when the estates and representation of the family devolved on his nephew,

RICHARD DAYRELL, Esq. of Lillingston Dayrell, capt. in the army, *b.* 1 April, 1779, who served as high sheriff of Bucks in 1808. He *m.* 1st, 1802, Ann, only child of Gabriel Parker, and 2ndly, 1807, Frances-Elizabeth, eldest dau. of John Dax, Esq., Master of the Exchequer Office of Pleas, but *d. s. p.*, when he was *s.* by his kinsman, the present EDMUND-FRANCIS DAYRELL, Esq. of Lillingston Dayrell.

Arms—Quarterly: 1st and 4th, az., a lion, rampant, or, crowned, arg.; 2nd and 3rd, arg., three bars, sa., charged with six cinquefoils, of the first.
Crest—A goat's head, erased, ppr.
Motto—Securè vivere mors est.
Seat—Lillingston Dayrell, Buckingham.

DAYRELL OF SHUDY CAMPS.

DAYRELL, THE REV. THOMAS, Esq. of Shudy Camps Park, Cambridgeshire, rector of Marston, co. York, J.P. and D.L., b. 28 May, 1802, m. 9 June, 1828, Maria, dau. of the Rev. Richard Hawksworth, by Isabella his wife, dau. of Sir Richard Pilkington, Bart., and has issue,

I. MARMADUKE-FRANCIS, b. 4 Jan. 1834.
II. Charles-Lionel, b. 8 Jan. 1836.
III. Thomas, b. 1 May, 1838. IV. Richard, b. 8 June, 1841.
I. Mildred-Maria. II. Isabel-Jane.
III. Mary-Anne. IV. Caroline-Charlotte.
V. Florence. VI. Emily-Elizabeth.

Lineage.—This is a branch of the DAYRELLS *of Lillingston Dayrell.*

FRANCIS DAYRELL, Esq., 2nd son of Paul Dayrell, Esq. of Lillingston, sheriff of Buckinghamshire in 1579, m. Barbara, dau. of Anthony Powell, Esq. of Gloucestershire, and dying 29 Jan. 1614, was s. by his only son,

SIR THOMAS DAYRELL, Knt., who seated himself at Shudy Camps, co. Cambridge, and it is recorded in his monumental inscription, that "he was eminent for his loyalty and services to their Majesties CHARLES I. and II. in the civil wars." He m. Sarah, dau. and co-heir of Sir Hugh Windham, Bart. of Pilsden Court, co. Dorset, and had FRANCIS (Sir); Marmaduke (Sir); and Sarah, wife of Francis Windham, Esq., only son of Sir George Windham. He d. in 1669, and was s. by his son,

SIR FRANCIS DAYRELL, Knt. of Shudy Camps, who m. Elizabeth, dau. and co-heir of Edward Lewis, Esq. of The Van, co. Glamorgan, but dying without issue, in 1675, was s. by his brother,

SIR MARMADUKE DAYRELL, of Shudy Camps, who m. 1st, Mary, only dau. of Sir Justinian Isham, Bart. of Lamport, Notts, but had no issue; and 2ndly, Mary, dau. and heir of William Glascock, Esq. of Farnham, in Essex, by whom he left at his decease, in 1712, a son,

FRANCIS DAYRELL, Esq. of Shudy Camps, who m. Elizabeth, dau. of Peter Witchcomb, Esq. of Braxted Lodge, Essex, and one of the co-heirs of Sir Brownlow Sherrard, Bart. of Lobthorp, in Lincolnshire, and had a son,

MARMADUKE DAYRELL, Esq. of Shudy Camps, living in 1784, who m. Henrietta, dau. of Warner Tempest, Esq. of the island of Antigua, and had (with three daus., all now deceased, except the youngest, Maria) a son and successor,

MARMADUKE DAYRELL, Esq. of Shudy Camps, who m. in 1797, Mildred-Rebecca, dau. of the late Sir Robert Lawley, Bart., and sister to Lord Wenlock, by whom he had,

FRANCIS, capt. in the army, b. 18 July, 1798, d. unm.
Thomas, now of Shudy Camps Park.
Robert, in holy orders m. Elizabeth, sister of Sir Thomas-Fletcher-Fenton Boughey, Bart.
Jane-Elizabeth, m. to the Rev. Fitzgerald Wintour, of Barton, co. Nottingham, and has two sons and two daus.

Mr. Dayrell d. in Aug. 1821.

Arms—Az., a lion, rampant, or, crowned, arg., armed and langued, gu.
Crest—Out of a ducal coronet, a goat's head, erased, ppr.
Motto—Virtus mille scuta.
Seat—Shudy Camps Park, Linton.

DEANE OF BERKELEY FOREST.

DEANE, JOHN-ST. GEORGE, Esq. of Berkeley Forest, co. Wexford, b. in 1803; m. 1st, in 1847, Grace-Wandesford, 4th dau. of the late Thomas Kavanagh, Esq. of Borris House, co. Carlow, by the Lady Elizabeth Butler, his 1st wife, which lady d. s. p. at Rome in 1848; and 2ndly, in 1850, Catherine, only dau. of John Gordon, Esq. of Aikenhead House, Glasgow.

Lineage.—JOHN-BERKELEY DEANE, Esq. of Berkeley Forest, eldest son of Joseph Deane, Esq. of Terrenure and Cromlin, co. Dublin, M.P. co. Dublin, by his 3rd wife, the dau. of Col. Green, of Greenville (*see* DEANE-FREEMAN), m. 1800, Miss Knudson, dau. of General Knudson, E.I.C.S., and d. 1837, leaving issue,

JOHN-ST. GEORGE, of Berkeley Forest.
George, m. 1842, Isabella, sister of James-L. Wise, Esq., and has issue.
William, lieut. R.N., m. Caroline Nixon, of Brownsbarn, and d. in 1745.
Cecilia. Frances.
Elizabeth, m. 1846, James-Lawrence Wise, Esq., grandson of Sir James Cotter, Bart., and has issue.

Arms—Arg., on a chevron, gu., between three Cornish choughs, sa., beaked and legged, gu., as many crosses-patée, of the field.
Crest—A tortoise, displayed, ppr.
Motto—Ferendo, non feriendo.
Seat—Berkeley Forest, New Ross.

DEARDEN OF ROCHDALE MANOR.

DEARDEN, JAMES, Esq. of Rochdale Manor, co. Lancaster, J.P., barrister-at-law, F.S.A., b. 30 July, 1798; m. 4 Nov. 1829, Jane, eldest dau. of the Rev. William Griffith, M.A., rector of Llanwrog, in Carnarvonshire, and sister and co-heir of William Griffith, Esq., and has issue,

I. JAMES, b. 23 Aug. 1839.
II. William-Griffith, b. 6 Nov. 1841, d. 11 Sept. 1842.
I. Frances-Sydney, d. 1847. II. Jane-Elizabeth.
III. Susanna-Ada, d. 1843. IV. Mary-Anne.

Lineage.—The ancient and modern pronunciation of the name of this family, by the natives of Lancashire, is DU-ER-DEN; and JACOB, in his *Law Dictionary*, interprets it, "a thicket of wood in a valley," giving Cowel as his authority.

ELIAS DE DUERDEN occurs as a party to a bond between himself and Thomas Haworth de Haworth, in the parish of Rochdale, senior, dated 10 July, 23rd HENRY VI. He was the lineal ancestor of

OTTIWELL DUERDEN, of Whitfield, in the parish of Rochdale, whose descendant,

JAMES DEARDEN, Esq., b. 25 Dec. 1597 (2nd son of Richard, of Whitfield and Handle Hall), made considerable additions to the family estates. This gentleman, a stanch royalist, m. Jane, dau. of Robert Newall, of Town House, in the parish of Rochdale, Gent., and dying 30 June, 1672, left, with other issue, a son and heir,

JOHN DEARDEN, Esq. of Handle Hall and Whitfield, b. 21 Oct. 1655, who m. in 1677, Jane, only child of Richard Ingham, Esq. of Cleggs Wood, co. Lancaster, by Ann his wife, sister and heir of John Belfield, Esq. of Cleggs Wood, and by her (who m. 2ndly, Jordan Chadwick, Esq.) left at his decease, 31 Dec. 1683 (with two daus.), one son,

JAMES DEARDEN, Esq. of Handle and Cinderhill, co. Lancaster, b. 27 April, 1682, who m. 1st, in 1705, Margaret, dau. of the Rev. Joshua Dixon, M.A., incumbent of Ringley, and 2ndly, Mrs. Elizabeth Fallows. By the former, he left at his demise, 9 June, 1749, five sons, of whom the eldest,

JOHN DEARDEN, Esq. of Cinderhill, b. 7 Feb. 1706, m. 18 Sept. 1735, Miss Mary Greaves, of Outwood, Prestwich, and dying 16 May, 1774, left a son,

JAMES DEARDEN, Esq. of Cinderhill, b. 16 March, 1739, who m. 10 Dec. 1773, Alice, dau. of Mr. Walworth, of Eccles, and by her (who m. 2ndly, in 1792, Mr. Thomas Worsley), he left at his decease, 4 June, 1791, four sons, James; Simon; Joshua; and Ralph; who all d. s. p. except the eldest,

JAMES DEARDEN, Esq. of Handle Hall, and of The Orchard, lord of the manors of Rochdale, co. Lancaster, and of West Scrafton, co. York, b. 21 July, 1774, who m. 7 Sept. 1797, Frances, dau. of Thomas Ferrand, Esq. of Thornhill, co. York, by his 2nd wife, Susannah, dau. and co-heiress of Robert Royds, Esq. of Higher Town House, Lancashire, and had,

JAMES, now of Rochdale Manor.
Thomas-Ferrand, b. 28 Feb. 1801, m. in 1835, Emma, eldest dau. of the Rev. William Hodgson.
Henry, b. 24 June, 1805, m. 1 July, 1837, Julia, dau. of Joseph Aston, Esq. of Castleton Hall near Rochdale, and has issue, Charles-Ferrand, and Edith.
Peregrine-Royds, b. 20 June, 1811, m. 28 June, 1838, Sarah, dau. of George Walkden, Esq. of Mansfield, and has issue. Elizabeth.
Susannah, m. 7 July, 1835, to Robert-Joseph Monypenny, Esq. of Maytham Hall, Rolvenden, Kent.

Mr. Dearden d. 21 Sept. 1828.

Arms—Arg., an inescutcheon, within an orle of martlets, sa.; as depicted in Trinity Chapel, in Rochdale Church, the family burial-place.
Crest—A stag, trippant-regardant.
Motto—Dum spiro spero.
Seat—Rochdale Manor, Lancashire.

DEASE OF TURBOTSTON.

DEASE, JAMES-ARTHUR, Esq. of Turbotston, co. Meath, b. in 1826; m. in 1853, Charlotte, eldest dau. of Edmund Jerningham, Esq., by Matilda Waterton his wife.

Lineage.—The family of Dease, formerly spelt Deece, is one of the oldest in Westmeath. The list of forfeited estates in that county shews that the Deases are the sole present occupiers, who held property in 1641, in the district where they still reside. In a manuscript of the time of HENRY VIII. occurs among the gentry of Meath the name of "Richard Dees of Turbottstown;" and in the *Magnā Panellā* of Westmeath, of 1703, that of "Jacobus Dease de Turbottstown."

GERALD-RICHARD DEASE, Esq. of Turbotston, who m. in 1740, Susan, dau. and co-heir of Oliver Plunkett, Esq. of Bathmore Castle, co. Meath, was father of

JAMES DEASE, Esq. of Turbotston, who m. in 1788, Lady Theresa Plunkett, only dau. of Arthur-James, 7th Earl of Fingall, and by her had issue,

GERALD, his heir.
William-Henry, of Rath House, Queen's County, m. Frances, only dau. and heir of H. De Friese, Esq.
Mary, d. in 1851. Theresa, d. in 1852.
Charlotte.

The elder son,

GERALD DEASE, Esq. of Turbotston, b. in 1790, m. in 1820, Elizabeth, dau. (and co-heir with her sisters, Bridget, who d. unm., 1832; Ellen, wife of J.-J. Bagot, Esq. of Castle Bagot; Marcella, a nun; and Catherine, late Countess of Kenmare) of Edmund O'Callaghan, Esq. of Kilgory, co. Clare, and by her (who d. in 1846) had issue,

JAMES-ARTHUR, his heir.
Edmund-Gerald, b. in 1829.
Gerald-Richard, b. in 1831.

Mr. Dease d. in 1854.

Arms—Arg., a lion, rampant, gu.
Crest—A lion, rampant, holding a drawn dagger.
Motto—Toujours prêt.
Seat—Turbotston, co. Westmeath.

O'REILLY-DEASE OF CHARLEVILLE.

O'REILLY-DEASE, ANNA-MARIA, of Charleville, co. Louth, m. 12 April, 1814, RICHARD DEASE, Esq., M.D., of Lisney, co. Cavan, and of the city of Dublin, and has had issue, two daus., Anna-Maria and Matilda-Mary-Richarda, both deceased, and one surviving son,

MATTHEW-O'REILLY DEASE, J.P. and D.L., b. in 1819.

This lady is the only surviving child of the late Matthew O'Reilly, Esq. of Thomastown, co. Louth, by Anna-Maria, his 1st wife, dau. of John O'Connor, Esq. of Dublin (*see* O'REILLY *of Knock Abbey Castle*).

Lineage—The family of Dease, of Milesian origin, was, at the period of CROMWELL's invasion, seated at Kilrue, co. Meath, whence

WILLIAM DEASE, colonel in King CHARLES's army, having been, with other royalists, deprived of his estate, retired to Lisney, co. Cavan. Of his sons, the 2nd, Michael, a count of the Russian empire, and one of the Empress CATHERINE's physicians, d. unm., and the eldest,

RICHARD DEASE, Esq. of Lisney, m. Anne, dau. of John Johnson, Esq. of Warrenstown, co. Meath, and had issue, John Dease, deputy-governor of Upper Canada, who d. unm., and

WILLIAM DEASE, Esq., an eminent physician, of the city of Dublin, who m. Elizabeth, only child of Sir Richard Dowdall, of Athlumney, co. Meath, and left a son,

RICHARD DEASE, Esq. of Lisney, co. Cavan, and of the city of Dublin, M.D., who m. 12 April, 1814, Anna-Maria, dau. of Matthew O'Reilly, Esq. of Thomastown (by his 1st wife, Anna-Maria, dau. of John O'Conor, Esq.), which lady became heiress by the whole blood, to her brothers, Matthew and John O'Reilly, and is the present Mrs. O'Reilly-Dease, of Charleville.

Seat—Charleville, co. Louth.

DE BURGH OF WEST DRAYTON.

DE BURGH, HUBERT, Esq. of West Drayton, co. Middlesex, J.P. and D.L., b. 15 Nov. 1799; m. 6 Sept. 1827, Marianne, 6th dau. of Admiral and Lady Elizabeth Tollemache, and had issue,

Selina-Constance, m. in 1851, to the present Baron Ward, and d. 14 Nov. same year.

Mr. De Burgh is one of the co-heirs to the Barony of Burg, or Borough, of Gainsborough.

Lineage.—THE HON. FRANCES BURGH, sister and co-heir of Robert, 7th Lord Burgh, or Borough, of Gainsborough, m. FRANCIS COPPINGER, Esq., 2nd son of Thomas Coppinger, Esq. of Stoke, co. Kent, by Frances his wife, only dau. of William Brooke, Baron Cobham, K.G., and had (with other issue, who d. s. p.) a dau., Lettice, m. to Sir William Hooker, and a son,

NICHOLAS COPPINGER, Esq., great-grandfather of

FYSH COPPINGER, Esq. of West Drayton, Middlesex, who m. Easter, dau. of Cornelius Burgh, Esq. of Scarborough, and assumed, by sign-manual, in 1790, the surname and arms of DE BURGH, in consequence of his descent from the Hon. Frances Burgh, one of the co-heirs to the Barony of Burgh. His only dau. and eventual heiress,

CATHERINE DE BURGH, m. 22 May, 1794, James-Godfrey Lill,* Esq. of Gaulstown, Westmeath (who took the name of DE BURGH), and dying in 1809, left issue,

HUBERT, her heir, now of West Drayton.
Robert-Lill, in holy orders.
Catherine-Alicia, m. to Charles Tyrwhitt-Jones, Esq., only brother of Sir Thomas-John Tyrwhitt-Jones, Bart.

Arms—Az., three fleurs-de-lis, erm.
Crest—A dexter arm, embowed in armour, couped at the shoulder, gauntlet open, exposing the hand, ppr., stringed as a bugle-horn, az., tassels, gold.
Motto—Nec parvis sisto.
Seat—Manor House, West Drayton.

DEEDES OF SANDLING PARK.

DEEDES, WILLIAM, Esq. of Sandling Park, co. Kent, J.P. and D.L., M.P., b. 17 Oct. 1796; m. 30 May, 1833, Emily-Octavia, dau. of Edward Taylor, Esq., late of Bifrons, co. Kent, and niece to the late Sir Herbert Taylor, G.C.B., and has issue,

I. WILLIAM, b. 11 Oct. 1834.
II. Herbert-George, b. 28 Sept. 1836.
I. Louisa. II. Emily. III. Mary.

Lineage.—WILLIAM DEEDES, M.D. of Canterbury (son of Julius Deedes, Esq. of Hythe, M.P., grandson of William Deedes, Esq. of Hythe, who d. in 1653, and great-great-grandson of Thomas Deedes, by Elizabeth his wife, sister of Robert Glover, Somerset herald) m. Mary, dau. and co-heir of the Rev. Henry Gregory, of Middleton Stoney, and had, with a dau., Mary, wife of Elias Sydal, bishop of Gloucester, a son,

THE REV. JULIUS DEEDES, A.M., b. in 1693, prebendary of Canterbury, and rector of Great Mongeham and Dimchurch, in Kent, who m. Dorothy, relict of the Rev. Richard Ibbetson, D.D., and eldest dau. of Nathaniel Denew, Esq. of St. Stephen's, by Dorothy his wife, dau. of Sir Abraham Jacob, and left at his decease, with a dau., Dorothy, m. to Sir John Filmer, of East Sutton, 4th Bart., a son,

WILLIAM DEEDES, Esq. of St. Stephen's, Canterbury, and Hythe, co. Kent, chairman of quarter sessions for East Kent, who m. in 1758, Mary, dau. of Thomas Bramston, Esq. of Skreens, co. Essex, and had, with a younger son, John, and two daus., Mary and Caroline, an elder son and heir,

WILLIAM DEEDES, Esq. of Sandling, M.P. for Hythe. He m. 27 Dec. 1791, Sophia, 2nd dau. of Sir Brook Bridges, Bart., and had issue,

WILLIAM, now of Sandling.
Julius, in holy orders, rector of Wittersham, Kent, b. in 1798, m. in 1829, Henrietta-Charlotte, dau. of the late Edward Dering, Esq., and sister of the present Sir Edward-Cholmeley Dering, Bart.
Henry, b. in 1800, major in the army.
Edward, b. in 1801, in the Hon. E. I. C. civil service.
John, b. in 1803, barrister-at-law.
George, b. in 1806, major in the army.
Charles, b. in 1808, rector of West Carmel, co. Somerset. m. 29 Nov. 1843, Letitia-Anne, eldest dau. of the Hon. Pleydell Bouverie.
Robert, b. in 1809, settled in Canada.
Lewis, b. in 1811, rector of Bramfield, m. in 1839, Augusta, dau. of the late George Smith, Esq.
Edmund, b. in 1812, settled in Canada.
Sophia and Mary, both d. unm.
Fanny, m. to Charles Andrew, son of the late Archdeacon Andrew.
Isabella, m. to George Warry, Esq. of Shapwick, co. Somerset.
Marianne, m. to the Rev. Gordon-F. Deedes, vicar of Netherbury, Dorset.

* JAMES GODFREY (LILL) DE BURGH, Esq., m. 2ndly, in 1818, Mrs. Eliza Hayne, of Ashbourne, co. Derby; and by that lady left, at his decease, 7 March, 1832, two sons, James-Godfrey, and Hubert-Lill.

Arms—Per fesse, nebulée, gu. and arg., three martlets, counterchanged.
Crest—An eagle's head, erased, per fesse, nebulée, gu. and arg., between two wings, expanded, sa.
Motto—Facta non verba.
Seat—Sandling Park, near Hythe, co. Kent.

DE HAVILLAND.—*See* HAVILLAND.

DE HORNE OF STANWAY HALL.

DE HORNE, GEORGE, Esq. of Stanway Hall, co. Essex, *b.* 27 Jan. 1788.

Lineage.—This is one of the families which were driven out of Flanders, in the reign of ELIZABETH, by the persecution attending their religion.

OLIVER DE HORNE, of Nieuw Kirke, near Ipres, Flanders, came over to England with his wife in the reign of JAMES I., and settled at Norwich. By Jocamina Neuville (whose family had been, in 1571, driven out of Flanders by the persecution of the Duke of Alva, and were settled at Colchester, and who afterwards *m.* a Walloon at Norwich) he had an only son,

ABRAHAM DE HORNE, of Colchester, Essex, *b.* in 1597, *m.* 1627, Mercy, dau. of William Rush, of the same place (ancestor of the late Sir William-Beaumaris Rush, Knt., sheriff of Suffolk, 1800), by whom he had, with several other children, who *d.* young, a son,

GEORGE DE HORNE, of Colchester, who *m.* 1661, Priscilla, dau. of John Bundock, of Brook House, near Tay Hall, Mark's Tay, Essex, who remarried Joseph Flowers, and *d.* 7 Sept. 1719. Mr. De Horne *d.* 1665 (*v. p.*), and, like his grandfather, Oliver, of the plague. He had issue Abraham, who *d.* an infant, and

GEORGE DE HORNE, of Colchester, *b.* in 1662, who removed to Ratcliffe, where he *d.* 12 Jan. 1728-9. He *m.* 6 Feb. 1684-5, Elizabeth, dau. of William Norrish, of Taunton, Somerset, who *d.* 3 Dec. 1736. Their issue was, George, of Ratcliffe, *d. s. p.* in 1718; ABRAHAM, of whom presently; Richards, *d. unm.* in 1725; Elizabeth, *d. unm.* in 1718; Hannah, *m.* in 1716, to Joseph Besse, of Colchester; Priscilla, *m.* in 1732, to John Dyson, of Rotherhithe; and Sarah, who *d. unm.* in 1732. The 2nd son,

ABRAHAM DE HORNE, of Ratcliffe, *b.* 8 Feb. 1695-6, *m.* 31 May, 1722, Mary, dau. and heir of John Cook, of Stair Stile, Halsted, Essex, and by her (who *d.* 21 Jan. 1770) had, with other children, who *d.* young,

GEORGE, of whom presently.
John, *b.* 16 Sept. 1736, *d.* 2 June, 1769, *s. p.*
Mary, *b.* 29 April, 1739, *m.* 1 Nov. 1770, John Scott, Esq. of Amwell, Herts (the poet), who *d.* 12 Dec. 1783, and had an only child,
Maria-De Horne Scott, *m.* 13 Dec. 1798, Joseph Hooper, Esq., who *d.* 6 May, 1815. Mrs. Hooper is now residing on her estate at Amwell.

Mr. De Horne *d.* 19 Nov. 1772. His eldest son,

GEORGE DE HORNE, Esq. of Stanway Hall (by purchase), *b.* 12 Oct. 1728, *m.* 17 Jan. 1760, Sarah, dau. and heir of William Blewett, Esq. of Romford, and *d.* Nov 1789, leaving issue,

I. ABRAHAM, of Surrey-square, *b.* 2 Jan. 1762, *d.* 17 July, 1830, *m.* 19 Oct. 1786, Mary, dau. and sole heir of Benjamin Collier, Esq. of the Victualling Office, Deptford, who *d.* 25 Nov. 1823, and by whom he had issue,
1 GEORGE, now of Stanway Hall.
2 Benjamin-Collier, of Farringdon, Berks, *b.* 1 Dec. 1790, *m.* 23 Feb. 1814, Mary, dau. of Thomas Huntley, Esq. of Burford, Oxon, and has a dau., Katherine-Collier, *m.* in 1841, George Bevington, Esq. of Camberwell, Surrey.
3 John, of Camberwell, *d.* 23 June, 1821, *s. p.*, having *m.* 27 Oct. 1819, Sarah, dau. and co-heir of Thomas Manning, Esq. of Poole, Dorset, who *m.* 2ndly, Henry Festing, Esq. of The Elms, Parkstone, Dorset, a captain in the Royal Artillery, and magistrate for the borough of Poole (elder brother of Rear-Admiral Robert Festing, R.N., C.B.), who *d.* in 1838.
4 Abraham, of Lexden, Essex, *b.* 8 May, 1796, *m.* 1st, 6 Nov. 1813, Mary, dau. of Josiah Wild, Esq. of Camberwell, who *d.* 16 Nov. 1827, and by whom he has had issue, John-Wild, of Adelaide, New South Wales (*m.* 22 March, 1838, Maria Gotsall, and has issue); George, *d.* in 1847; Abraham, *d.* 2 Jan. 1836; Thomas, *b.* 3 Feb. 1824; Emily, *m.* in 1834, to Henry-Waddilowe Best, Esq. of Thetford, Norfolk; Louisa, *m.* in 1844, to Alexander Bevington, Esq. of Clapham; and Mary, *m.* in 1848, to Dennis-De Berdt Hovell, Esq. of Lower Clapton. He *m.* 2ndly, 21 June, 1835, Eliza, dau. of William-Henry Butler, Esq., by whom he has had issue, Abraham, *b.* in 1846; William-Henry, *b.* in 1850; Stewart, *b.* in 1852; Eliza-Emmeline; Ada; Rosalind; and Katharine.

1 Katherine, *m.* 15 Oct. 1807, to Alfred Smith, Esq. of Earls Colne, Essex, and dying 5 Aug. 1847, left issue.
2 Sarah, *m.* 20 Oct. 1812, to John Christy, Esq., and has issue.
3 Mary.
II. JOHN, of Stanway Hall, *b.* 1 May, 1771, *m.* 27 Oct. 1801, Sarah Sheppard, dau. of Jacob Bell, Esq. of Plaistow, but *d. s. p.* 4 Jan. 1845.
I. Mary, *b.* 1 July, 1773, *m.* 26 April, 1798, Robert Brightwen, Esq. of Colchester, by whom she has issue.
II. Sarah, *b.* 22 Sept. 1775, *d.* in 1840, *m.* 29 March, 1789, John Vaizey, Esq. of Stair Stile, a magistrate for the county of Essex, who *d.* 23 Aug. 1831, leaving issue.

Arms—Or, three bugle-horns, gu., mouthed and ringed, arg., the mouths to the sinister.
Crest—A cap, round at top, erm., bordered with the eyes of peacock's feathers, ppr.
Seat—Stanway Hall, Stanway, Essex.

DE LA CHEROIS OF DONAGHADEE.

DE LA CHEROIS, DANIEL, Esq. of Donaghadee, co. Down, J.P. and D.L., high-sheriff in 1829, *b.* 1 Dec. 1783.

Lineage.—The family of De la Cherois descends from the younger branch of an ancient and noble house in France, formerly resident at Cheros or Cherois, a small town near Sens, in the province of Champagne, whence the name is derived.

The revocation of the Edict of Nantes, in the year 1685, compelled the De la Cherois', being Protestants, to emigrate from their native country.

In the year 1641,

CAPTAIN SAMUEL DE LA CHEROIS (ancestor of the branch of the family settled in Ireland) served in the war undertaken by Cardinal Richelieu against the House of Austria. He left three sons, NICHOLAS, appointed a lieutenant of fusiliers by LOUIS XIV. in 1675, and promoted to the rank of captain in 1677; Daniel, and Bourjonval, both appointed lieutenants in their brother's company in 1677. In the year 1685, these three brothers fled to Holland, where they were received with great kindness by the Stadtholder, into whose service they entered, obtaining commissions in the Dutch army of the same rank as those they had held in that of France. In 1689, WILLIAM, Prince of Orange, being called to the throne of Great Britain, formed two regiments of the French Huguenots, of which Nicholas De la Cherois was appointed major, Daniel captain, and Bourjonval lieutenant in the first, commanded by the Comte de Marton. They accompanied King WILLIAM to Ireland in 1690, and finally settled there. The eldest,

MAJOR NICHOLAS DE LA CHEROIS, distinguished himself at the battle of the Boyne, and afterwards performed a very gallant action, making fifteen hundred men lay down their arms with only a subaltern's guard, for which he was presented by the government with fifteen hundred crowns and a lieutenant-coloneloy. He *m.* Mary, dau. of Samuel Crommelin, and left a dau., Madelaine, wife of Daniel Crommelin, Esq. of Lisburn, and a son,

SAMUEL DE LA CHEROIS, who *m.* Mademoiselle Sarah Cormière, and had issue,

DANIEL, his heir.
Nicholas, captain in the army, *d. s. p.* in 1829.
Samuel, who assumed the surname of CROMMELIN (*see* CROMMELIN *of Carrowdore*).
Judith, *m.* to John Smythe, Esq.

The eldest son,

DANIEL DE LA CHEROIS, Esq. of Donaghadee, *m.* 13 Feb. 1782, Mary, dau. of Alexander Crommelin, Esq., and by her had issue,

DANIEL, now of Donaghadee.
Samuel-Lewis, *m.* in 1820, Mary, dau. of John Roland, and *d.* in 1836, having had issue, Nicholas, Daniel, Samuel, Lewis, Alexander, and Jane.
Nicholas, ensign 47th regt., killed in Spain, at Barossa, in 1811.
Mary.

Arms—Gu., a chevron, or, between three mullets, arg., in chief, and an anchor, ppr., in base.
Crest—An anchor, erect, ppr.
Motto—Fac et spera.
Seat—Donaghadee.

DELAP OF MONELLAN.

DELAP, THE REV. ROBERT, of Monellan, co. Donegal, *b.* in 1802; *m.* 16 Nov. 1834, Isabella, dau. and co-heir of Sir James Galbraith, Bart., and has issue,

I. James-Bogles, b. 8 Jan. 1847.
I. Susan-Dorothea.

Lineage.—Samuel Delap, Esq. of Ramelton, co. Donegal, treasurer of that county (descended, according to Robertson's *Ayrshire Families*, from Allan Dunlop, provost of Irvine in 1625), m. Anne, dau. of Captain Drummond, R.N., and was father of

Robert Delap, Esq., who m. about 1776, Mary-Anne, only child and heiress of James Bogle, Esq. of Monellan, and had issue,

Samuel-Francis, his heir.
James-Bogle, of Stoke Park, Surrey, J.-P. and D.-L., lieut.-col. of the 1st regiment of Surrey militia, b. 24 June, 1779, m. in 1809, Harriet, eldest dau. and co-heiress (with her sister, Susan-Eliza, m. to the Hon. Col. Crawley Onslow, 2nd son of the Earl of Onslow) of Nathaniel Hillier, Esq. of Stoke Park.
William-Drummond, of Monsterboyce, co. Louth, m. Catherine, dau. of the Rev. Dr. Foster, Lord Bishop of Clogher, and has issue, Robert Foster, m. to the Hon. Anna Skeffington, dau. of Viscount Ferrard, and had issue, two daus.

The eldest son,

Samuel-Francis Delap, Esq. of Monellan, J.P. and D.L., b. in 1777, m. in 1800, Susan, dau. of the Hon. John Bennett, Judge of the Queen's Bench in Ireland, and has had issue,

Robert, now of Monellan.
John, in holy orders, m. Mary-Anne-Sarah, only dau. of Robert Saunderson, of Drumkeen, Esq., co. Cavan, d. s. p. in 1841.
Jane. Mary-Anne.

Arms—Gu., on a pile, arg., an eagle displayed, of the field.
Crest—A dexter arm in armour, grasping a sword, combined with an arm sinister, holding a rose, sprig and bud, ppr.
Mottoes—(above the crest) "Merito." (under the arms) "E spinis."
Seat—Monellan, co. Donegal.

DE MONTMORENCY OF CASTLE MORRES.

De Montmorency, Harvey, Esq. of Castle Morres, co. Kilkenny, b. Sept. 1782; m. July, 1811, Rose, dau. of John Kearney, late bishop of Ossory, and had issue,

I. John, m. 1838, the Hon. Henrietta O'Grady, dau. of the 1st Viscount Guillamore, and has issue.
II. Joseph, capt. 59th regt.
III. Harvey-Mervyn, m. Aug. 1853, Louisa, 2nd dau. of the late Wm.-Morris Reade, Esq. of Rossenara, co. Kilkenny, and has issue.
I. Anne, m. John-Congreve Fleming, Esq. and has issue.
II. Letitia, m. John Armstrong, Esq. of Graigaverne, Queen's Co., and has issue.
III. Rose, d. unm.
IV. Elizabeth, m. to Wm.-Jacob Blacker, Esq. of Woodbrook, co. Wexford.
V. Sarah, m. to Thos.-R. Browne, Esq. of Aughentaine, co. Tyrone, and has issue.
VI. Fanny.

Major De Montmorency, who is 3rd son of the late Rev. Joseph Pratt, of Cabra Castle, co. Cavan, by the Hon. Sarah de Montmorency his wife, dau. of Harvey, Viscount Mountmorres, of Castle Morres, s. to the estates of his mother's family, and assumed the surname and arms of De Montmorency.

Arms—Arg., a cross, gu., between four eagles displayed, sa.
Crest—A peacock in his pride, ppr.
Motto—Dieu ayde.
Seat—Castle Morres, co. Kilkenny.

DEMPSTER OF SKIBO CASTLE.

Dempster, George, Esq. of Skibo Castle, co. Sutherland, J.P. and D.L., b. 26 Feb. 1804; m. 8 May, 1827, Joanna-Hamilton, 7th dau. of the Right Hon. Robert Dundas, of Arniston.

Lineage.—The surname of Dempster, which is of great antiquity in Scotland, was assumed from the honourable office of Dempster of Parliament, long heritably enjoyed by the family.

George Dempster, Esq. of Dunnichen (descended from James, 2nd son of James Dempster, of Muresk, living in 1574, which James, of Muresk, was representative of David Dempster, of Auchterless and Caroistown, *temp.* David Bruce), was father of

John-Hamilton Dempster, Esq. of Skibo, who m. Miss Thompson, by whom he had one dau. and heiress, Harriett, of whom presently. He m. 2ndly, Jean, dau. of Charles Ferguson, Esq., and sister of Sir James Ferguson, Bart. of Kilkerran, co. Ayr, and by her had one son, George, who d. young, in 1800. Mr. Dempster was s. at his decease by his only surviving child and heiress,

Harriet Dempster, of Dunnichen and Skibo, b. 6 Jan. 1786, who m. in 1801, William Soper, Esq. of the E. I. C. civil service, who assumed, by royal license, the surname of Dempster, in compliance with the entail of the estates. Mrs. Dempster d. 16 Oct. 1810, leaving issue,

George, now of Skibo.
Ellen, m. in 1828, to Col. Henry White, M.P., lord-lieut. of the county of Longford, and has issue.
Harriet, m. in 1831, to Robert Browne, Esq., cousin of the Marquess of Sligo, and has issue.
Charlotte, m. in 1830, to James-Whitehed-Hawkins Dempster, Esq. of Dunnichen, co. Forfar, and d. in 1842.
Rose, m. in 1832, to the Rev. R.-M. Bonnor, vicar of Rhuabon, Wales.

Arms—Gu., a sword, arg., hilted and pommelled, or, bendwise, surmounted by a fesse, of the last, all within a bordure per pale, of the second and sa.
Crest—A leg-bone and palm-branch, in saltier, ppr.
Motto—Mors aut vita decora.
Seat—Skibo Castle, by Dornoch, co. Sutherland, N.B.

DENISON OF OSSINGTON.

Denison, John-Evelyn, Esq., M.A., of Ossington Hall, co. Notts, M.P., J.P. and D.L., b. 27 Jan. 1800; m. 14 July, 1827, Lady Charlotte Bentinck, 3rd dau. of the Duke of Portland. Mr. Denison, M.P. for Newcastle-under-Lyme in 1823, sat for Hastings in the next parliament, and in 1831 was chosen for Liverpool and Notts, for the latter of which he made his election to serve; after the division of the county, he represented the southern district in two parliaments; and in 1841, 1847, and 1853, was returned for Malton. He was Lord of the Admiralty in Mr. Canning's administration.

Lineage.—This family is of Yorkshire origin. William Denison, an eminent merchant of Leeds, purchased the manor of Ossington, Notts, in 1753, and served as high-sheriff of that county in 1779. He d. in 1782, and was s. in his estates in the counties of Nottingham, York, Lincoln, and Durham, by his brother Robert, who d. in 1785, and was s. by his nephew, John Wilkinson, Esq., who took the name and arms of Denison. He became of Ossington, and was M.P. for Chichester and afterwards for Minehead. He m. 1st, a dau. of J. Horlock, Esq. of Ashwick, and had by her two sons, who d. young, and a dau. Charlotte, wife of the Right Hon. C. Manners-Sutton, speaker of the House of Commons, afterwards Viscount Canterbury. He m. 2ndly, Charlotte, 2nd dau. of Samuel Estwick, Esq., M.P., and d. 6 May, 1820, having had issue,

John-Evelyn, now of Ossington.
Edward (Right Rev.), D.D. (1st class degree, Univ. Oxon), b. 13 May, 1801, consecrated Bishop of Salisbury in 1837, m. 1st, 27 June, 1839, Louisa-Maria, 2nd dau. of the late Henry-Ker Seymer, Esq. of Hanford House, co. Dorset, and by her (who d. 22 Sept. 1841) had a surviving dau., Louisa. He m. 2ndly, Clementina-Baillie Hamilton, and d. 6 March, 1854.
William-Thomas (Sir), Knt., capt. royal engineers, Governor-General of the Australian colonies.
George-Anthony, in holy orders, M.A. (1st class degree, Univ. Oxon), archdeacon of Taunton, b. 11 Dec. 1805, m. 4 Sept. 1838, Georgiana, eldest dau. of J.-W. Henley, Esq. of Waterpery, Oxon.
Henry (double 1st class, Univ. Oxon), fellow of All Souls, M.A., and barrister-at-law, b. 2 June, 1810.
Stephen-Charles (1st class, Univ. Oxon), M.A., barrister-at-law, b. 2 July, 1811, m. Susan, dau. of the Rev. F. Fellowes.
Frank, lieut. R.N., d. 1843.
Robert-Alfred, b. Aug. 1816.
Charles-Albert, capt. 52nd regt., b. in 1819.
Julia-Grace, m. to the Rev. C. Desvoeux.
Henrietta, m. in 1840, to J.-H. Jacob, Esq.
Charlotte, m. to Robert-Joseph Phillimore, Esq., M.P.

Arms—Arg., on a bend, between an unicorn's head, erased, in chief, and a cross-crosslet, fitchée, in base, sa., three besants.
Crest—A sinister cubit arm, in bend dexter, vested, vert, cuff, erm., charged with a cross-crosslet on the hand, ppr., pointing with the fore-finger to an estoile.
Seat—Ossington Hall, Notts.

DENISON OF GRIMTHORPE.

DENISON, EDMUND, Esq. of Grimthorpe, East Riding co. York, M.P., J.P. and D.L., *b.* 29 Jan. 1787; *m.* 14 Dec. 1814, Maria, dau. of William Beverley, Esq. of Beverley, and great-niece of the wife of Sir Thomas Denison, Knt., judge of the Common Pleas, and by her has issue,

I. EDMUND-BECKETT, *b.* 12 May, 1816, of Lincoln's Inn, Queen's Counsel, *m.* 7 Oct. 1845, Fanny-Catharine, 2nd dau. of the Rt. Rev. John Lonsdale, Bishop of Lichfield.
II. Christopher-Beckett, *b.* 9 May, 1825, E. I. C. Civil service.
III. William-Beckett, *b.* 6 Sept. 1826.
I. Mary, *m.* 21 June, 1837, to Charles-Wilson Faber, Esq.
II. Elizabeth, *m.* 25 March, 1841, to William Bethell, Esq. of Rise Park, co. York.
III. Sophia, *m.* 19 Aug. 1847, to the Rev. T.-B. Paget, vicar of Welton.
IV. Augusta.

Mr. Denison, who is 5th son of the late Sir John Beckett, of Leeds, Bart., and brother of the late Right Hon. Sir John Beckett, Bart. of Somerby Park, co. Lincoln, assumed the surname and arms of DENISON, by royal license, 8 Sept. 1816.

Arms—Quarterly: 1st and 4th, arg., on a bend, between an unicorn's head, erased, in chief, and a cross-crosslet in base, sa., three bezants, for DENISON; 2nd and 3rd, gu., a fesse between three boars' heads, couped, erminois, an annulet for difference, for BECKETT.
Crest—A sinister cubit arm, in bend dexter, vested, vert, cuff, erm., charged with a cross-crosslet, the fore-finger pointing to an estoile, radiated gold, for DENISON; a boar's head, couped, or, pierced by a cross patee-fitchée, erect, sa., for BECKETT.
Motto—Prodesse civibus.
Seat—Binbrook, co. Lincoln.

DENNE OF LYDD.

DENNE, DAVID, Esq., M.A., of Lydd, co. Kent, J.P. and D.L., *b.* 6 April, 1798; *m.* 21 Oct. 1826, Louisa-Ann, dau. of the Rev. Thomas Cobb, M.A., rector of Ightham and vicar of Sittingbourn, co. Kent, and canon of Chichester, and has issue,

I. THOMAS-PLANTA, late of H. M.'s 10th foot, *b.* 28 May, 1829.
II. Lambert-Henry, lieut. royal artillery, *b.* 21 Jan. 1831.
III. Edward-William, *b.* 17 Nov. 1833.
IV. Robert-Alured, R.N., *b.* 15 Sept. 1838.
I. Louisa-Katharine. II. Katharine-Elizabeth.

Lineage.—The Dennes were established in Kent, antecedently to the Conquest, by a Norman, ROBERT DE DENE, who held large estates in Sussex and Kent, as well as in the Duchy, and was *Pincerna* or Butler to EDWARD the Confessor. His son and heir,

ROBERT DE DENE, was father of

RALPH DE DENE, living in the time of WILLIAM the Conqueror, lord of Buckhurst, in Sussex, who *m.* Sybella, sister of Robert de Gatton, and had a son, ROBERT, his heir; and a dau. Ela, *m.* to Sir Jordan Sackville, ancestor of the Dukes of Dorset. This Ralph de Dene, who possessed large estates in Kent and Sussex, founded Otteham Abbey, for monks of the Premonstratensian order. His great-grandson,

SIR ALURED DE DENE, of Denn Hill, a person of great learning, seneschal of the Priory of Canterbury, and escheator of Kent, *anno* 1234, was great-great-grandfather of

SIR WILLIAM DENNE, Knt. of Denne Hill, M.P. for the city of Canterbury 19th EDWARD II., and for the co. of Kent in the 14th of the following reign. From him descended the families of DENNE *of Denne Hill, of Kingston, of Littlebourne, of Patricksbourne Court, and Lydd.*

THOMAS DENNE, Esq. of Lydd, *b.* in Feb. 1701, son of David, of Bishopsbourne, and grandson of John, of Patricksbourne Court, *m.* in 1741, Sarah, dau. and co-heir of Thomas Greenland, Esq. of Lydd, and had five sons and two daus., viz.,

I. JOHN, of Bath, *b.* in 1748, *m.* Miss Anna-Maria Heblewhite, and *d.* in 1828, *s. p.*
II. RICHARD, of Winchelsea, *m.* in 1783, Mary, dau. of William Steer, Esq. of Northampton, by Anne his wife, dau. of the Very Rev. William Rastall, D.D., Dean of Southwell, a lineal descendant of Chief Justice Rastall, and dying in Jan. 1819, left issue,

1 WILLIAM-JOHN, of Winchelsea, *b.* 1788, *m.* 1817, Mary-Jane, dau. of Major Alexander Orme, E.I.C.S., and has an only child, Mary-Jane.
2 Richard-Greenland, of the Inner Temple, barrister-at-law.
1 Anna-Maria, of Broadstairs.
2 Frances, *m.* to Captain Ernest-Christian Welford, of the royal engineers.
3 Mary-Jane, *m.* to Sir Robert-William Newman, Bart. of Mamhead, in Devon, late M.P. for Exeter.

III. DAVID, of Lydd.
IV. Thomas, who *d. unm.* in 1783, aged 27.
V. William, in the army, *d. unm.* in 1783, aged 21.
I. Sarah, *m.* to John Porker, Esq. of Muswell Hill, a banker in London, and dying in 1808, left issue, John Porker, of London; Mary Porker, *m.* to Sir John Peter; Elizabeth Porker, *m.* to General George Cookson, R.A.; Caroline Porker, *m.* to James Atkinson, Esq. of Russell Square, and *d.* in 1810; and Emily Porker, *m.* to General Sir Alexander Bryce, R.E.
II. Elizabeth, *m.* to Richard Ruck, Esq. of Gravesend, and *d. s. p.*

Mr. Denne *d.* in 1777. His 3rd son,

DAVID DENNE, of Lydd, Esq. *m.* 27 March, 1788, Katherine, dau. of Robert Cobb, Esq. of Lydd, and had issue,

DAVID, now of Lydd.
Thomas, *m.* 1st, Jane Duff, dau. of John Falconer, Esq., British Consul at Leghorn; and 2ndly, Mary-Ann Laidlaw.
Elizabeth, *m.* to the Rev. William Vallance, M.A., rector of Southchurch, Essex.
Katharine, *d.* 1846.
Cecilia, *m.* to the Rev. Edward-Robert Nares, rector of Newchurch.
Mary-Julia.

Mr. Denne *d.* in Feb. 1819, aged 67.

Arms—Az., three bars, erm.; in chief, as many fleurs-de-lis, or.
Crest—On a chapeau, vert, turned up, erm., a demi-peacock, wings expanded and elevated, ppr.
Seat—Lydd, near New Romney, co. Kent.

DENNIS OF FORT GRANITE.

DENNIS, THOMAS-STRATFORD, Esq. of Fort Granite, co. Wicklow, J.P., *b.* 12 June, 1782; *m.* 30 Jan. 1810, his cousin, Katherine-Martha-Maria, eldest dau. of Morley Saunders, Esq. of Saunders Grove, co. Wicklow, niece to the Earl of Aldborough, and granddau. to Lady Martha Saunders, and by her (who *d.* in July, 1825) had issue,

I. MEADE-CAULFEILD, A.M., J.P., *b.* in 1810, *m.* Margaret-Catherine, eldest dau. of the late Major Crosbie, and granddau. of the late Col. Crosbie, of Ballyheige Castle, M.P.
II. Morley-Stratford-Tynte, A.M., *b.* in 1811, major 76th foot.
III. John-Fitz-Thomas, *b.* in 1817, major 95th foot, *m.* 24 May, 1854, Jane, only dau. of Jebb Brown, M.D., staff-surgeon.
IV. James-Benjamin, *b.* in 1818, capt. royal artillery.
V. Robert-William, barrister-at-law, *b.* in 1823.
VI. Edward-Albert, J.P., *b.* in 1824.
I. Katherine-Sophia, *m.* to the Rev. Solomon Donovan, rector of Kilpipe, brother of the late Richard Donovan, Esq. of Ballymore.
II. Ellen-Louisa.

Lineage.—THE RIGHT HON. JAMES DENNIS, Lord Chief Baron of the the Exchequer in Ireland, was raised to the peerage of that kingdom as BARON TRACTON, *of Tracton Abbey*, co. Cork, 13 Dec. 1780. His lordship *d.* suddenly in 1782, *s. p.*, when the title expired. His estates in the co. of Kerry he bequeathed to his eldest nephew and heir-at-law, the Rev. Meade Swift, and those in the counties of Cork and Dublin to his other nephew, John Swift, subject to a jointure of £1800 per annum to Lady Tracton, and on condition that they and their heirs should take the name and arms of DENNIS. His lordship's only sister, FRANCES, *m.* THOMAS SWIFT, Esq. of Lynn, co. Westmeath, descended from a branch of the Carlingford family, and had two sons,

I. MEADE, of whom presently.
II. John, barrister-at-law, who assumed the surname of DENNIS. He *m.* Emily, dau. of Robert Hamilton, Esq., and *d.* at Sidmouth, in 1830, leaving issue,

1 JAMES DENNIS, Esq. barrister-at-law.
2 Robert Dennis, E.I.C.S.
1 Mary Dennis.

The elder son,

THE REV. MEADE SWIFT, co-heir, with his younger brother,

John, to his maternal uncle, Baron Tracton, assumed the surname and arms of DENNIS only. He m. Delia-Sophia, 2nd dau. of Morley Saunders, Esq. of Saunders Grove, co. Wicklow, by Martha his wife, dau. of John, 1st Earl of Aldborough, and by her had issue,

I. THOMAS-STRATFORD DENNIS, now of Fort Granite.
II. Meade-Paul, in holy orders, m. Mary-Anne, dau. of Coane, Esq. of the co. Fermanagh.
III. James-Aldborough, m. Caroline Wynne, dau. and co-heir of the late Col. Topp, of Lancashire.
IV. John, M.D., m. Elizabeth Manders.
V. George-Morley, in holy orders, m. Elizabeth, dau. and co-heir of the late — Maguire, Esq., J.P. co. Cavan.
I. Martha-Sophia. II. Frances-Maria, deceased.
III. Anne. IV. Louisa. V. Eliza.

Mr. Dennis was s. at his decease by his son, the present THOMAS-STRATFORD DENNIS, Esq. of Fort Granite.

Arms—Gu., on a chevron, between three fleurs-de-lis, or, as many annulets, of the first; a canton, chequy, of the second and az.
Crest—A castle with two towers, ppr., from each tower a banner floating, gu.
Motto—Suaviter sed fortiter.
Seat—Fort Granite, near Baltinglass, co. Wicklow.

DENNISTOUN OF DENNISTOUN.

DENNISTOUN, JAMES, Esq. of Dennistoun, b. in 1803, J.P. and D.L., member of the faculty of Advocates; s. his father, 1 June, 1834; m. in 1835, Isabella-Katharina, eldest dau. of the Hon. James Wolfe Murray, of Cringletie, one of the Senators of the College of Justice in Scotland. Mr. Dennistoun having, in 1836, sold his estates of Colgrain, Camis Eskan, and Kirkmichael Stirling, in Dumbartonshire, acquired a portion of the original family barony of Denzielstoun, in Renfrewshire. He was author of *Memoirs of the Dukes of Urbino, Memoirs of Sir Robert Strange*, and other works.

Lineage.—All the peerage writers and genealogical antiquaries of Scotland are agreed that this ancient family ranks with the most eminent in the western districts of that kingdom. It appears from a charter of MALCOLM IV., who d. in 1165, that the Dennistouns held lands on the Gryfe, in Renfrewshire. Here, it would seem, that one DANZIEL, or DANIEL, probably of Norman extraction, settled himself, and, calling the estate DANZIELSTOUN, assumed therefrom his surname.

SIR HUGH DE DANZIELSTOUN, of that ilk, accorded a reluctant submission to the victorious EDWARD I. in 1296. He had issue,

JOHN (Sir), his successor.
JOANNA, or Janet, who m. Sir Adam More, of Rowallan, and was mother of ELIZABETH MORE, whose marriage with King ROBERT II. became a fruitful ground of controversy among historians. From this union, in 1347, sprang the long line of the STUART monarchs, through whom the Imperial crown has passed to the reigning dynasty. In reference to this circumstance, the proud proverb has been preserved by the Dennistouns, "Kings came of us, not we of Kings."

Sir Hugh was s. by his son,

SIR JOHN DE DANZIELSTOUN, of that ilk, who, during the reign of DAVID II. was the constant associate in arms of his illustrious father-in-law, the Earl of Wigton, and of the brave Sir Robert Erskine. Offices of high trust were conferred upon him, and the accession of his relation, ROBERT II., was followed by new honours, and by grants of many splendid baronies in various counties. He was for many years high-sheriff of Dumbartonshire, and governor of Dumbarton Castle, the strongest fortress in the kingdom, and was one of the lords of parliament who concurred in the settlement of the crown upon the descendants of his niece, Elizabeth More. He m. Mary, dau. of Malcolm, 1st Earl of Wigton, who is lineally represented by the heir of this marriage, and had (with one dau., Janet, wife of Sir Adam Mure, of Rowallan) five sons, ROBERT, his heir; Walter, a bold and turbulent churchman, made Bishop of St. Andrews by ROBERT III.; WILLIAM (Sir), of Colgrain; Hugh; and Malcolm. The eldest son and heir,

SIR ROBERT DE DANZIELSTOUN, of that ilk, successor to his father as keeper of the Castle of Dumbarton, was one of the youths selected from the chief families in Scotland, in 1357, as hostages for the ransom of King DAVID II.; and, in 1370, was commissioner for a treaty of peace with England. His daus and co-heirs were

MARGARET, m. to Sir William Cunninghame, of Kilmaurs; hence sprang the Earls of Glencairn.
ELIZABETH, m. to Sir Robert Maxwell, of Calderwood; and from her sprang the Baronets of Calderwood and Pollock, and the Lords Farnham.

After the decease of Sir Robert, the male line of the family was carried on through his brother,

SIR WILLIAM DE DANZIELSTOUN, of Colgrain, co. Dumbarton, which estate, and that of Camis Eskan, in the same shire, he acquired before 1377, and had several other grants from the crown. His direct descendant,

ROBERT DANZIELSTOUN, of Colgrain, m. Katharine, dau. of David Semple, of Noblestoun, by Marion, dau. of Sir William Edmenston, of Duntreath, through whom she had at least three separate royal descents, from Kings ROBERT II., ROBERT III., and JAMES II. They left, with other issue, ROBERT, heir; and JOHN, living in 1560, father, by his wife Euphemia Bontyne, of WALTER DANZIELSTOUN, who, like his predecessor, resided at Colgrain. He d. in 1618, leaving, with several younger children, JOHN DENNISTOUN, who, by Margaret, dau. and eventual heiress of the ancient family of SPREULL *of Dalchurne*, had a son, ARCHIBALD DENNISTOUN, of Dalchurne, minister of Campsie, who m. 1st, Jane, dau. of Humphry Noble, of Farme and Ardardan, and 2ndly, Katharine, dau. of James Stirling, of Auchyle. By the former he had a son, WILLIAM, of whom in the sequel, as heir-male of the family, and husband of the heiress of Colgrain. The son and heir,

ROBERT DANZIELSTOUN, of Colgrain, m. Margret, dau. of John Hamilton, of Ferguslie, and, among other children, who left no issue, had Elizabeth, the wife of John Colquhoun, of Camstraddan; Catherine, m. to John Macgregor, of Ardenconnal; and his successor,

JAMES DENNISTOUN, of Colgrain, who impaired and involved the family inheritance to a considerable extent. His son and heir,

WALTER DENNISTOUN, of Colgrain, m. 1st, Sarah, dau. of Sir Patrick Houston, of Houston, by the Lady Janet Cunninghame, and 2ndly, Grace, dau. of John Brisbane, of Brisbane; by the former he had James, who d. unm., and an elder son, his successor,

JOHN DENNISTOUN, of Colgrain, who, during the wars of the Commonwealth, continued a zealous and steady adherent of the royal cause, and ultimately crowned his exertions by the sacrifice of his life. After a short but romantic campaign, the little army assembled under the Earl of Glencairn was disbanded in the next autumn, when John Dennistoun was specially included in the treaty of surrender, and his real and personal estates were exempted from attainder. This benefit he did not long enjoy, but died in the ensuing year, after lingering sufferings from a wound received in the Highland expedition. He m. Jean, dau. of William Semple, of Fulwood, and had three daus., viz.,

MARGARET, who s. to the estates in virtue of an entail made by her father, under condition of marrying the heir male of the family.
Jean.
Janet, m. to William Semple, of Fulwood.

On the decease of Colonel Dennistoun, the male representation devolved upon the elder son and heir of Mr. Archibald Dennistoun, of Dalchurne, minister of Campsie,

WILLIAM DENNISTOUN, who, under the settlement of Colonel Dennistoun, became the husband of his eldest dau., Margaret, heiress of Colgrain. Of sixteen children, one only survived their parents, viz.,

JOHN DENNISTOUN, of Colgrain, who freed the property from debt, and by Jane, heiress of Moses Buchanan, of Glins, had, besides several daus.,

JAMES DENNISTOUN, of Colgrain. This laird m. 1st, Janet, dau. of John Baird, of Craigtown, and by her left, JAMES, his successor, and Jean, m. to Andrew Buchanan, of Ardinconnal. He m. 2ndly, Mary, dau. of John Lyon, of Parklee, and had three other children, viz.,

I. ROBERT, m. to Anne-Penelope, dau. of Archibald Campbell, of Jura, and had issue.
II. RICHARD, who purchased Kelvin Grove, co. Lanark. He m. Christian, dau. of James Alston, merchant in Glasgow, heir to the estate of Westerton, co. Dumbarton, and dying in May, 1834, left surviving issue,
1 RICHARD, formerly of Kelvin Grove, Glasgow, now resident at Pinnacle Hill, near Kelso, b. 7 March, 1797, m. 21 March, 1839, Frances-Elizabeth, youngest dau. of Thomas-Rishton Satterthwaite, Esq. of Lancaster, and has issue, Richard-Campbell, b. 24 Aug. 1841; and Francis-Douglas, 8 Jan. 1848.
2 William, d. unm.
1 Isabella, m. to the late Colin Campbell, Esq., of Jura, and has issue.

2 Mary, m. to the late Archibald Buchanan, Esq. of Auchentorlie, co. Dumbarton, and has issue.
I. Mary, m. to John Alston, of Westerton, and has issue.

Colgrain d. in 1796, and was s. by his eldest son,

James Dennistoun, of Colgrain, convener of the county of Dumbarton for nearly 30 years; during a great part of the time he held the appointment of vice-lieutenant, and commanded the regiment of local militia of that shire. By Margaret, his 1st wife, dau. of James Donald, of Geilstoun, he left James, his heir; and by Margaret, his 2nd wife, dau. of Allan Dreghorn, of Blochairn, he left four daus., co-heirs to their mother's large fortune, viz.,

Isabella-Bryson, m. to Gabriel-Hamilton Dundas, of Westburn and Duddingstoun, and has issue.
Janet-Baird, m. to Hugh Maclean, of Coll, and has issue.
Elizabeth-Dreghorn, m. 22 Feb. 1815, to Sir Duncan Campbell, Bart. of Barcaldine, and has issue.
Mary-Lyon, m. to Sir William Baillie, Bart. of Polkemmet, and has issue.

He was s. at his decease, in 1816, by his only son,

James Dennistoun, of Dennistoun, who inherited the estates of Colgrain and Camis Eskan; and in 1828, on production of the most satisfactory evidence of his descent, obtained from the Lord Lyon of Scotland authority to bear the arms and style proper to the baronial house of De Danzielstoun *of that ilk*. By that Mary-Ramsay his wife, dau. of George Oswald, of Auchencruive and Scotstoun, he had issue,

James, his heir.
George, a merchant in Glasgow, m. Margaret-Helen, dau. of Henry Wallis, Esq. of Maryborough, co. Cork, and left a son, James-Wallis, R.N.
Richard, d. unm. 1829.
Robert, barrister at Peterborough, Canada West, m. Maxwell, dau. of Major Hamilton, and has, James-Frederick, and other issue.
Alexander.
Margaret.
Isabella, m. to the Rev. John Wilson, D.D.
Mary. Elizabeth. Camilla.
Janet, m. William-Gillespie Mitchell, Esq of Carwood, and left issue.

Mr. Dennistoun d. 1st June, 1834, and was s. by his eldest son, the late James Dennistoun, of Dennistoun.

Arms—Arg., a bend, sa.
Crest—A dexter arm in pale, ppr., clothed, gu., holding an antique shield, sa., charged with a mullet, or.
Supporters—On the dexter, a lion, rampant, gu., armed and langued, az.; on the sinister, an antelope, arg., armed, az., hoofed, or.
Motto—Adversa virtute repello.

*** The English families of Denison are said to be sprung from a cadet of this ancient house, who went from Scotland in the Great Rebellion, and fought at Marston Moor.

DENT OF RIBSTON HALL.

Dent, Joseph, Esq. of Ribston Hall, co. York, and Winterton, co. Lincoln, J.P., b. 1 May, 1791; m. 13 June, 1825, Martha, dau. of Mr. Joseph Birley, and has issue,

I. John-Dent, b. 11 June, 1826.
II. Joseph-Jonathan-Dent, b. 8 July, 1830.
III. William-Dent, b. 13 March, 1832.
IV. Henry-Francis-Dent, b. 2 June, 1839.
I. Ellen-Isabel.

Mr. Dent, who is eldest son of Robert Tricket, of Hillfoot, near Sheffield, by Catherine his wife, sister of Jonathan Dent, Esq., on inheriting the estates of his maternal uncle, Jonathan Dent, Esq. of Winterton, co. Lincoln, assumed, in compliance with that gentleman's will, the surname of Dent, in lieu of his patronymic, by royal license, dated 11 Sept. 1834.

Arms—Arg., on a bend, between two cotises, engrailed, sa., three lozenges, erm., quartering, az., three cranes, arg.; on a chief, or, two roses, gu.
Crests—1st, a demi-tiger, sa., collared, arg., resting the sinister paw on a lozenge, erm.; 2nd, on a mount, a crane, in the beak a rose, slipped, and resting the claw on a serpent, nowed, all ppr.
Motto—Patientiâ et perseverantiâ.
Seats—Ribston Hall, co. York; and Winterton, co. Lincoln.

DENT OF SUDELEY CASTLE.

Dent, John, Esq. of Sudeley Castle, co. Gloucester, b. in 1777, J.P., high-sheriff of Worcestershire in 1849-50.

Lineage.—John Dent, of Worcester, merchant, b. in 1751, son of Lawrence Dent, of Yarm, co. York, merchant, m. about 1775, Elizabeth Davis, and by her, who d. in 1819, had issue,

I. John, now of Sudeley Castle.
II. Thomas, m. 1819, Mary, dau. of Martin Coucher, Esq. of Woodmanton, co. Worcester, and dying 1824, left issue,
1 John-Coucher, of Severn Bank, co. Worcester, barrister-at-law, m. 1817, Emma, eldest dau. of John Brocklehurst, Esq., M.P., of Hardsfield House, Macclesfield.
2 Martin.
1 Elizabeth-Anne, d. in infancy.
III. William, b. 1784, J.P., high-sheriff of Gloucestershire, 1851-52, d. unm. 1854.
IV. Benjamin, b. 1786, M.A., Worcester Coll., Oxford, rector of Winford, co. Somerset, d. 1850.
I. Margaret, m. to John Mann, Esq. of Worcester.
II. Elizabeth, m. to Cuthbert Woodcock, Esq. of Stockwell, Surrey.

Mr. Dent d. 1811.

Arms—Erm., on a bend, nebuly, az., three lozenges, of the field.
Crest—An heraldic tiger's head, erased, erm., semée of lozenges, az., flames issuing from the mouth, ppr.
Motto—Concordia et industria.
Seat—Sudeley Castle, co. Gloucester.

DENT OF SHORTFLATT TOWER.

Dent, William-Dent, Esq. of Shortflatt Tower, co. Northumberland, formerly lieut. R.N., and now J.P., b. 18 April, 1796; m. 12 May, 1840, Ellen-Mary, dau. of Andrew-Seton Karr, Esq. of Kippilaw, co. Roxburgh, and has issue,

I. William-Seton, b. 16 April, 1841.
I. Ellen. II. Catherine-Anne. III. Alicia.
IV. Jane-Sarah. V. Georgiana.

Mr. Dent assumed his present surname, in lieu of his patronymic, Hedley, on succeeding to the property of his great-uncle, John Dent, Esq. of Shortflatt Tower.

Lineage. — William Hedley, Esq., son of William Hedley, Esq., by his wife, a dau. of the Johnstone family, claiming descent in the female line from the noble house of Annandale, m. Anne, dau. of William Dent, Esq., brother of John Dent, Esq. of Shortflatt Tower, and was father of

Matthew Hedley, Esq., who m. in 1792, Jane Charlton, of the family of the Charltons *of Lee Hall*, co. Northumberland, and great-niece of Sir William Loraine, of Kirke-Harle. He d. during his shrievalty of Newcastle-upon-Tyne, in 1802, leaving, with a dau. Jane, an only son, the present William-Dent Dent, Esq. of Shortflatt Tower.

Arms—Quarterly: 1st and 4th, or, on a bend, per bend, gu. and sa., three fusils, conjoined, of the field, for Dent; 2nd and 3rd, gu., two chevronels, or, between three hawks, belled, arg., for Hedley.
Crests—For Dent, a panther's head, affrontée; and for Hedley, a swallow rising out of clouds.
Seat—Shortflatt Tower, co. Northumberland.

DERING OF LOCKLEYS.

Dering, Robert, Esq. of Lockleys, co. Herts, J.P., formerly an officer in the rifle brigade, m. 4 June, 1829, Letitia, 2nd dau. of Sir George Shee, Bart. of Dunmore, co. Galway, and has issue one son,

George-Edward, b. 15 Jan. 1831.

Mr. Dering, 2nd son of George Dering, Esq., youngest son of Sir Edward Dering, Bart. of Surrenden-Dering, in Kent, s. to Lockleys, in right of his wife, in 1838.

Arms—Quarterly: 1st and 4th, or, a fesse, az., in chief, three torteaux; 2nd and 3rd, or, a saltier, sa.
Crest—On a ducal coronet, or, a horse, passant, sa., maned, or.
Motto—Terrere nolo, timere nescio.
Seat—Lockleys, Herts.

DE RINZY OF CLOBEMON HALL.

De Rinzy, Matthew-Scanderbeg, Esq. of Clobemon Hall, co. Wexford, b. 9 Dec. 1836.

Lineage.—The estate of Clobemon, co. Wexford, was granted by King Charles I., to the direct ancestor of the family, SIR MATTHEW DE RENZY, Knt., who is stated, in his monumental inscription, to have been born at Cullen, in Germany, and to have descended from George Castriota, the famous SCANDERBEG. The grandfather of the present representative,

THOMAS DE RINZY, Esq., son of Mathew de Rinzy, Esq., and his wife, Eleanor, only dau. of the Rev. James Kennelly, co. Kildare, *m.* Elizabeth, only dau. of Mathew White, of Scarnagh, co. Wexford, Esq., and was father of

MATHEW DE RINZY, Esq., who *m.* in Dec. 1784, Frances, 2nd dau. of Solomon Richards, of Selsborough, co. Wexford, Esq., and had issue,

THOMAS, his heir.
Bartholomew, a major in the 11th foot, *m.* Sarah, eldest dau. of Lieut.-General Nelson, of Devonport.
William-Richards.
Frances-Richards. Catherine-Vigors.

Mr. De Rinzy *d.* in Nov. 1795, and was *s.* by his eldest son,

THOMAS DE RINZY, of Clobemon Hall, Esq., *b.* 6 Nov. 1785, J.P. and D.L., high-sheriff of the co. of Wexford in 1809, who *m.* 7 March, 1808, Catherine, only child of James White, of Middletown, co. Wexford, Esq., and granddau. of John Grogan, of Johnstown Castle, co. Wexford, Esq., and had issue,

I. MATHEW, J.P., of Clobemon Hall, *b.* 1 Feb. 1809, *m.* 25 Feb. 1835, Jane-Richards, youngest dau. of the late John-Harward Jessop, of Doory Hall, co. Longford, Esq., and granddau. of Sir Frederick Flood, Bart., and left issue,
1 MATTHEW-SCANDERBEG, now of Clobemon Hall.
2 Thomas-Jessop, *b.* 1 Feb. 1837.
3 Frederick-Cavendish, *b.* 7 Sept. 1839.
4 James-Harward, *b.* 14 Sept. 1844.
1 Frances-Catherine.
II. George-Augustus-Frederick, an officer in the royal artillery.
III. Thomas-Richards, an officer in the 83rd foot, *d. unm.* in 1848.
I. Anna-Richards, *m.* 13 Sept. 1841, to William-De Courcy O'Grady, Esq., eldest son of the O'Grady of Kilballyowen.

Arms—Quarterly: 1st and 4th, a buck springing, or; 2nd and 3rd, az., a cross, arg., charged with five escallops, gu., within a bordure, or.
Crest—A naked sword, erect, ppr., hilted, or.
Motto—Facta non verba.
Seat—Clobemon Hall, co. Wexford.

DE TEISSIER OF WOODCOTE PARK.

DE TEISSIER, JAMES, of Woodcote Park, co. Surrey, Baron de Teissier of France, J.P. and D.L., *b.* 1794; *m.* in 1814, Henrietta, dau. of Henry-Poyntz Lane, Esq. of Alresford, Hants, and Worthing, Sussex, and has issue,

I. JAMES-FITZHERBERT, *b.* Nov. 1816.
II. Philip-Antoine, *b.* June, 1819.
III. Henry-Price, *b.* June, 1820.
IV. George-Frederick, *b.* Oct. 1821.
V. Lewis-Minet, *b.* Aug. 1823.

The title of Baron was assumed in 1819, with the permission of the Prince Regent, and at the desire of Louis XVIII. of France.

Lineage.—HONORE TEISSERI, a noble, *d.* at Nice, 1480, leaving two sons, LOUIS, justiciary of Nice in 1537, and GIOVAN, who *m.* Jeanne de Grivandé, and was father of HUGH, justiciary of Nice, 1570, who *m.* Gabrielle de Morthier, and had a son, ETIENNE, who settled in France, as receiver-general of the province of Languedoc. He *m.* Anne de Robert, and was father of ANTOINE, whose son, by his wife Madame de Pierre, ETIENNE, *m.* Claudine, granddau. of Charles Louis, Baron de Lonbens, by his wife, Rose de Hautefort de St. Chamans, and had a son, JAMES, *b.* 1667, who *m.* 9 July, 1728, Charlotte, dau. of Antoine de Lonbens, and by her, who *d.* in 1774, had a son,

LEWIS DE TEISSIER, of Woodcote Park, Surrey, who *m.* May, 1780, Mary, dau. of dau. of Capt. James Gardner, by Mary his wife, heiress of William Price, Esq. of Imley Park, co. Northampton, and *d.* in Oct. 1811, leaving the present BARON DE TEISSIER; another son, Lewis, who *m.* Harriet, dau. of W. Price, Esq. of Rhiwlas Park, co. Merioneth; and a dau., Mary-D'Yranda, *m.* to Admiral Prevost, R.N., brother of the late Gen. Sir G. Prevost, Bart.

Arms—Or, on a mount, a boar, sa.; a chief, gu., thereon a crescent, between two estoiles, arg.
Supporters—Two greyhounds.
Seat—Woodcote Park, Epsom.

DE RODES.—*See* RODES.

DEVENISH OF MOUNT PLEASANT.

DEVENISH, JOHN, Esq. of Mount Pleasant, co. Roscommon, *b.* 22 June, 1814; *m.* 20 Sept. 1838, Susan, dau. of Michael Fox, Esq. of Stephen's Green, Dublin, by Susan his wife, dau. of Robert Jones Lloyd, Esq., and has issue,

I. WILLIAM, *b.* 24 Oct. 1840.
II. Michael, *b.* 24 Feb. 1842.
III. John-Lloyd, *b.* 2 Dec. 1848.
IV. Robert-Jones-Sylvester, *b.* 6 Dec. 1856.
I. Susan. II. Jane-Sophia-Moore.
III. Anne-Sarah.

Lineage.—It is said that the original appellation of this family was Sutton, and that the present name, corrupted from the Saxon, and signifying "deep waters," was given to an ancestor, who, in some of the early civil wars, retired to an island at the confluence of the Isis and Thames. Be this as it may, their descent is claimed from

SIR JOHN DEVENISH, of Hellenleagh, *circa* 1399, who *m.* Elizabeth, sole dau. of Lord Hoo. In less than two centuries after,

EDMOND DEVENISH, *m.* Anne, dau. of Sir Rowland Pentony, and went to Ireland *temp.* HENRY VIII. From him sprang the Irish family. His descendant,

GEORGE DEVENISH, built The Court, at Athlone (called Court Devenish so late as 1791), and settled there. He *m.* Celia, dau. of Thomas Fitzgerald, Esq., and was *s.* by his son,

CHRISTOPHER DEVENISH, who settled at Carrowclogher, co. Roscommon. He *m.* Susan, dau. of John Hinde, of Castlemine, in the same county, Esq., by Mary his wife, dau. of Judge Jones, of Athlone, and had issue,

WILLIAM, his heir. Christopher, of Collierstown.
Sylvester, who had the Athlone estate, and *m.* Mary, dau. of Martin Dillon, of Clonbrock, co. Galway, Esq.
Alicia. Cecilia.

WILLIAM DEVENISH, Esq., eldest son and heir, *m.* Deborah Blackburne, and had issue, Christopher, WILLIAM, George, Elizabeth, and Susannah. The 2nd son,

WILLIAM DEVENISH, Esq. of Rush Hill, co. Roscommon, *m.* Anne, dau. of F. Fetherstone, of Whiterock, co. Longford, Esq., and had issue,

GEORGE, his heir. Christopher. John.
Susan, *m.* in 1786, to Robert-Jones Lloyd, of Ardnagovan, co. Roscommon, Esq.

The eldest son,

GEORGE DEVENISH, Esq. of Mount Pleasant, *m.* in 1772, Sarah, dau. of Godfrey Hemsworth, Esq. of the co. of Tipperary, and *d.* in 1829, leaving issue,

WILLIAM, his heir. Godfrey, in the artillery.
George. John.
ROBERT, of Rushhill. Christopher.
Anna-Maria. Sarah. Abigail. Susanna.

The eldest son,

WILLIAM DEVENISH, Esq. of Mount Pleasant, co. Roscommon, *b.* in 1780, *m.* Hannah, dau. of John Lloyd, of Denzille Street, Dublin, and of Cloonfinlough House, co. Roscommon, and had issue,

JOHN, now of Mount Pleasant. William.
Robert, of Cloonfinlough House.
Anna.
Sarah, *m.* to William-Lloyd O'Brien, of Mount Francis, co. Roscommon, Esq.
Hannah.
Jane, *m.* to William Mahon, 2nd son of Bartholomew Mahon, Esq. of Clonfree.
Susan.

Mr. Devenish *d.* Nov. 1838.

Arms—Sa., a sheldrake, arg., collared, or; on a chief, of the second, two sheldrakes, of the first, collared, gold.
Crest—A sheldrake, with spread wings, arg., collared, or.
Motto—Spero, et captivus nitor.
Seat—Mount Pleasant, co. Roscommon.

DEVENISH OF RUSHHILL.

DEVENISH, ROBERT, Esq. of Rushhill, co. Roscommon, *b.* 12 Dec. 1785; *m.* 21 Feb. 1816, Theodosia, youngest dau. of the Rev. Luke Mahon, of Strokestown House, and has issue,

I. GEORGE-DOMINICK, *b.* 2 Dec. 1822, *m.* 6 May, 1852, Anne, youngest dau. of Maurice Knox, Esq.

II. John, *b.* 4 Feb. 1833.

I. Sally, *m.* 6 Dec. 1837, to Thomas Morton, Esq. of Ruacon.

II. Anne, *m.* 19 Dec. 1849, to William Lloyd, Esq. of Rockville.

Mr. Devenish of Rushhill is 5th son of the late George Devenish, Esq. of Mount Pleasant, by Sarah Hemsworth his wife.

Arms, &c.—Same as DEVENISH *of Mount Pleasant.*
Seat—Rushhill, Drumsna.

DE WINTON OF GLAMORGANSHIRE.

DE WINTON, WALTER-THOMPSON, Esq. of Clifton, co. Gloucester, *s.* his father 19 Nov. 1852.

Lineage.—Some ancient deeds relating to the lordships of Lanquian, Lanblythyan, and Landough, in the neighbourhood of Cowbridge, co. Glamorgan, which were held by the ancestors of this family under the names of DE WINTONA, DE WINCESTRIA, and WYLCOLYNA *aut* WYLKLYN, are still in the possession of the family, bearing date so far back as the year 1327, and others, which continue, through successive reigns, to establish the family under the appellation of Wilkins in the same neighbourhood, in the enjoyment of property of considerable extent, down to the year 1750.

ROBERT DE WINTONA, or WINCESTRIA, came into Glamorganshire with Robert Fitzhamon: he was lord of the manor of Lanquian, near Cowbridge, and built a castle there, the ruins of which are still extant; the valley underneath is called Pant Wilkyn (Wilkin's Vale) to this day. From Robert lineally descended

THE REV. THOMAS WILKINS, LL.B., rector of Llanmaes and St. Mary Church, and prebendary of Llandaff, who *m.* Jane, dau. of Thomas Carne, of Nash, by Jane his wife, dau. of Sir Edward Stradling, Bart. of St. Donat's Castle, and left at his decease, in 1698, two sons, THOMAS, and Roger, who *m.* Elizabeth, dau. of Thomas Lewis, Esq. of Llanishen, and had a dau., Jane. The elder son,

THOMAS WILKINS, prothonotary on the Brecon Circuit, *m.* 1st, Anne, dau. of Richard Cann, Esq., brother of Sir Robert Cann, Bart. of Compton, in Gloucestershire, and had issue, CANN, his heir. He *m.* 2ndly, Anne, dau. of Meredith Bowen, Esq. of Lanwerne, in Breconshire, and had by her one son, JOHN (*see* DE WINTON *of Maesllwch* and *of Maesderwen*). He was *s.* by his son,

CANN WILKINS, Esq., *b.* 31 Oct. 1702, who *m.* Mary, dau. of Mrs. Anne Morgan, widow of Thomas Morgan, Esq. of St. George's, in the co. of Somerset, and had issue,

THOMAS, J.P., high-sheriff of Somersetshire in 1787, assumed the surname and arms of MORGAN. He *m.* 1st, Elizabeth, dau. of Ebenezer Mussell, Esq., by Elizabeth his wife, dau. of Sir John Davie, Bart. of Crediton, in Devonshire, and by her had one dau., Elizabeth, *m.* to Eli Bates, Esq. He *m.* 2ndly, Mary, dau. of John Thompson, Esq. of the city of Waterford, and had a dau., Mary-Anne, who *m.* Thomas-Edward Thomas, Esq. of Swansea, and has a son, Iltid Thomas.

Richard, vicar of St. George's, *m.* Cordelia, dau. of the Rev. Conyers Place, of Marnhall, in Dorsetshire, and had a son, Cann, who *d.* young.

GEORGE.

The 3rd son,

THE REV. GEORGE WILKINS, rector of St. Michael's, Bristol, *b.* in 1743, *m.* 1st, Mary, dau. of John Dinwiddie, Esq.; 2ndly, Johanna, dau. of John Wilkins, Esq. of The Priory, co. Brecon, by whom he had one dau., *m.* to John-Parry Wilkins, Esq.; and 3rdly, Anne, dau. of John Thompson, Esq. of Waterford, by whom (who *d.* in 1791) he had four sons and one dau, viz.,

CANN, his heir.

George, late captain 39th regiment, in the commission of the peace for Somersetshire, *m.* Emma-Juliana, 4th dau. of the late George Robinson, Esq. of Queen Square, Bath, and Rose Hill, Tunbridge Wells, Kent, and has issue, Frederica-Isabella, and George Jean de Winton, an officer in the 99th regiment.

Thomas, lieut. R.N., deceased, *m.* Miss Lynch, and had one dau., Mary-Anne-Morgan, *m.* in 1840, to the Baron William de Ludwigsdorff, of Deutsch-Altenburg, in Lower Austria.

William, late major in the light cavalry on the Bombay establishment.

Harriett, deceased, *m.* 1st, to William Jeffreys, Esq. of Swansea, and 2ndly, to George Bird, Esq. of the same place.

Mr. Wilkins was *s.* at his decease by his eldest son,

CANN DE WINTON, Esq. of Clifton, J.P. and D.L., who resumed, together with the rest of the family, by sign-manual, 1839, their ancient surname of DE WINTON. He *m.* Mary, dau. of Thomas Evans, Esq. of Berthlyd, and widow of William Williams, Esq. of Pwlly Pant, and by her (who *d.* 8 Sept. 1840) had issue,

WALTER-THOMPSON, present representative of the family.
Herbert-William, M.A., St. John's Coll., Camb.
Robert-Henry, late capt. H. M. 99th regt., *m.* and has issue.
Charlotte-Augusta.

Arms—Per pale, or and arg., a wyvern, vert.
Crest—A wyvern, ppr.
Motto—Syn ar dy Hûn.
Residence—Clifton.

DE WINTON OF MAESLLWCH CASTLE.

DE WINTON, WALTER, Esq. of Maesllwch Castle, co. Radnor, *b.* 30 Nov. 1832.

Lineage.—JOHN WILKINS, Esq., *b.* 13 Nov. 1713, only son of Thomas Wilkins, Esq., the prothonotary, by Anne Bowen, his 2nd wife, *m.* Sibil, dau. of Walter Jeffreys, Esq. of The Priory, co. Brecon, and had issue,

I. THOMAS, *m.* Elizabeth, dau. of the Rev. William Games, rector of Llandoffy, and had one son,

JOHN, who *m.* Miss Williams, of Brecon.

II. WALTER, of whom presently.
III. John, in holy orders, who *d. unm.*
IV. JEFFREYS. (*See* DE WINTON *of Maesderwen.*)
V. William, prothonotary, *d. unm.*
I. Anne, *m.* to John Maybery, Esq.
II. Magdalen, *m.* to Robert Corne, Esq.
III. Jane, who *m.* Meredith-Herbert James, Esq., and *d.s.p.*
IV. Johanna, *m.* to the Rev. George Wilkins.
V. Elizabeth, *m.* to Samuel Price, Esq. VI. Frances.

Mr. Wilkins *d.* in 1784. His 2nd son,

WALTER WILKINS, Esq., M.P., who represented the co. of Radnor in parliament for 36 years, *m.* 24 Feb. 1777, Catherine, dau. of Samuel Hayward, Esq. of Walsworth Hall, co. Gloucester, and left, with a dau., Augusta-Frances, now deceased, a son and successor,

WALTER WILKINS, Esq., M.P. of Maesllwch Castle, co. Radnor, who *m.* in March, 1806, the Hon. Catherine-Eliza Devereux, 3rd dau. of Henry, Viscount Hereford, and by her (who *m.* 2ndly, W.-R. Stretton, Esq.) had issue,

WALTER, his heir.
Katherine-Augusta-Marrianna, *m.* 10 Aug. 1830, to William Vann, Esq.
Mary-Anne-Eliza, *m.* to William Meyrick, Esq., barrister-at-law.
Georgiana-Frances, *m.* 7 Dec. 1830, to Charles Stretton, Esq. of Llangoed Castle, co. Brecon.

Mr. Wilkins *d.* 1 May, 1830, and was *s.* by his son,

WALTER WILKINS, Esq. of Maesllwch Castle, M.P. for Radnorshire, *b.* 13 Oct. 1809, who resumed, in 1839, the ancient surname of DE WINTON. He *m.* 14 Feb. 1831, Julia-Cecilia, 2nd dau. of the Rev. Richard-John Collinson, rector of Gateshead, co. Durham, and dying in May, 1840, left issue, WALTER, now of Maesllwch Castle; Francis-Walter; and Emily-Gwenlyan.

Arms—Per pale, or and arg., a griffin, vert, between two spear heads, sa.
Crests—1st, a wyvern's head, erased, vert, collared, arg., the collar embattled-counter-embattled; 2nd, a demi-lion, rampant, issuing from a mural crown, holding in his paws a rose-branch, and charged on the shoulder with a full-blown rose.
Motto—Syn ar dy Hûn.
Seat—Maesllwch Castle, co. Radnor.

DE WINTON OF MAESDERWEN.

DE WINTON, JOHN-PARRY, Esq. of Maesderwen House, co. Brecon, J.P. and D.L., high-sheriff in 1829-30, *b.* 21 July, 1778; *m.* 1st, 10 Oct. 1803, Jane, dau. of the late Rev. George Wilkins, of Weston, in Somersetshire, but by her (who *d.* in Aug. 1810) has no issue. He *m.* 2ndly, 1 Jan. 1812, Charlotte-Eliza, 3rd dau. of the Rev. William Davies, rector of Newport-Pagnel, Bucks, and of Llangorse, co. Brecon, by whom (who *d.* 26 Feb. 1826) he has issue,

I. JOHN-JEFFREYS, *b.* 28 Aug. 1813, *m.* Miss Emma Phillips, of Carmarthen, and has a son, Parry, and a dau., Emma.

II. Richard-Davies, *b.* 11 March, 1821, late of the 52nd regiment.

III. William, *b.* 8 Feb. 1823.

IV. Henry, *b.* 13 Feb. 1826.
I. Mary-Catherine.
II. Charlotte-Anna, *m.* to W. Elmslie, Esq., and has a son, William, and a dau., Charlotte.
III. Catherine-Rebecca.

Mr. De Winton *m.* 3rdly, 5 March, 1828, Harriet, 3rd dau. of the late Rev. Edward Powys, of Westwood, Staffordshire, and has a dau.,

I. Emily-Catherine-Powys.

Lineage.—JEFFREYS WILKINS, Esq. of The Priory, near Brecon (4th son of John Wilkins, Esq., *see* DE WINTON *of Maesllwch*), *m.* Catherine, 4th dau. of the late Rev. Gregory Parry, of Llandevaylog, co. Brecon, prebendary of Worcester, and had issue,

I. JOHN-PARRY, now of Maesderwen.
II. Jeffreys, of the Isle of Wight, *m.* Hannah Lel, and has issue.
III. Walter, in holy orders, of Hay Castle, Breconshire, *m.* Chiappini, sister of the Dowager Baroness Newborough, and has had four sons and two daus., viz.,
  1 Thomas, royal artillery.
  2 Walter, an officer, 2nd life-guards, *d. unm.* in 1842, deeply lamented.
  2 Charles, an officer 16th foot. 4 Henry.
  1 Frances-Maria, *m.* to Spencer-Bulkeley, 3rd Lord Newborough.
  2 Catherine.
IV. Richard, *m.* Angelina, dau. of Thomas Green, Esq., late M.P. for Arundel, and *d. s. p.*
V. Edward, *d. unm.* in Canada.
I. Elizabeth, *m.* to John Jones, Esq., late of Skethrog House, co. Brecon.
II. Catherine, *m.* to Captain William Murray.

Mr. Wilkins *d.* 21 Jan. 1819.

Arms, Crest, and *Motto*—See DE WINTON *of Clifton.*
Seat—Maesderwen House, near Brecon.

D'EYNCOURT OF BAYONS MANOR.

See TENNYSON-D'EYNCOURT.

DICK OF LAYER TOWER.

DICK, QUINTIN, Esq. of Layer Tower, co. Essex, lieut.-col. West Essex militia, and formerly M.P. for Maldon, *b.* 1780.

Lineage.—ROBERT DICK, of Garry, co. Antrim, *b.* about 1650, son or grandson of Robert Dick, a Scotchman, who had a grant of the lands of Dunovan, from Randall, Earl of Antrim, was father of two sons, I. QUINTIN, of Garry, co. Antrim, *b.* 1680, *d.* 1768, leaving a son, QUINTIN, of Ballymoney, *b.* 1711, who *m.* Elizabeth, dau. of John Campbell, Esq. and *d.* 1791, leaving Quintin, of Rosgarland, co. Derry; Hugh, of the co. Tyrone; and three younger sons, who settled in America; and II. JOHN, who *m.* Anne, dau. of William Adair, and was father of QUINTIN DICK, of Nenagh, co. Tipperary, who *m.* Anne, sister of Hugh Ker, merchant of Dublin, and had, with other issue, a son,

SAMUEL DICK, Esq. of Dublin, who *m.* 16 Nov. 1773, Charlotte, dau. of Nicholas Foster, Esq. of Tullaghan, co. Monaghan, and *d.* 17 Jan. 1802, leaving, with a dau., Charlotte-Anne, wife of William-Hoare Hume, Esq. of Humewood, co. Wicklow, M.P., three sons, of whom the only survivor is the present QUINTIN DICK, Esq. of Layer Tower.

Arms—Gu., a sword, erect, arg., pommel and hilt, gold; in chief, two mullets, or.
Crest—A cat, sejant.
Motto—Semper fidelis.
Seat—Layer Tower, Essex.

DICKIN OF LOPPINGTON.

DICKIN, THOMAS, Esq. of Loppington House, co. Salop, J.P. and D.L., formerly major Shropshire militia, *b.* Oct. 1781; *m.* 11 Oct. 1827, Jane, 4th dau. of the Hon. Edward Massy, 2nd son of Hugh, 2nd Lord Massy of Duntrileague, in Ireland, and has issue,

I. THOMAS-ACHERLEY-MASSY, *b.* 3 Dec. 1836.
II. Edward-Thomas-Massy, *b.* 22 Sept. 1842.
III. John-Lloyd, *b.* 4 Feb. 1845.
I. Catherine-Massy. II. Sarah.
III. Eleanor-Vickers. IV. Jane-Louisa.
V. Sophia-Anna, *d.* 21 April, 1835.
VI. Thomasine-Jannette, *d.* 17 Feb. 1845.

Lineage.—NICHOLAS DICKIN, of Loppington, co. Salop, Gent., *d.* in 1655, leaving by Anne his wife, who was buried at Loppington in 1662, a son, JOHN DICKIN, *b.* 14 Nov. 1659, who was interred at Loppington, 15 April, 1698, leaving a son, THOMAS DICKIN, of Loppington, Gent., who *m.* twice; by his 1st wife, Jane, he had a son, John, who *d.* in 1702; and by his 2nd, Sarah, he had another son, THOMAS DICKIN, of Loppington, who *d.* in 1729, leaving, by Sarah his wife, two sons, JOHN DICKIN, of Loppington, father of John Dickin, Esq. of Loppington, whose son, John Dickin, Esq. of Elm Grove, co. Devon, *m.* Miss Pleydell, of Somersetshire; and

THOMAS DICKIN, Esq. of Aston Hall, who *m.* 19 Feb. 1751, Anne Groome, widow, dau. of John Birch, Esq. of Lee, and had a son and heir,

THOMAS DICKIN, Esq. of Wem, high-sheriff of Shropshire in 1799, who *m.* Sarah, dau. of Roger Acherley, Esq. of The Cross, in the parish of Ellesmere, and co-heir (with her sisters, Mrs. Lloyd and Mrs. Philips) of her only brother, Edward Acherley, Esq. of The Cross. By this lady he had issue,

THOMAS, now of Loppington.
Roger-Spencer, of Broughton Villa, *m.* Jane, dau. of the late Rev. Richard Parkes, vicar of Loppington, and has issue.
Sarah, *m.* to the Rev. Corbett Brown, rector of Withington and Upton Magna, co. Salop, and *d.* leaving issue.
Anne, *d. unm.*
Dorothy, *m.* to John Walford, of Wem, Esq., and *d.* leaving issue.
Maria, *m.* to Captain Edward Cowley, and *d.* leaving issue.
Elizabeth, *d. unm.*

Mr. Dickin *d.* in 1805.

Arms—Erm., on a cross-flory, sa., a leopard's face, or.
Crest—A lion, sejant, or, holding in the dexter paw a cross-crosslet, or.
Motto—Vincit veritas.
Seat—Loppington House, co. Salop.

DICKINS OF SUSSEX.

SCRASE-DICKINS, CHARLES, Esq. of Coolhurst, co. Sussex, J.P. and D.L., *b.* 15 Sept. 1794; *m.* 18 Feb. 1829, Lady Frances-Elizabeth Compton, dau. of Charles, 1st Marquess of Northampton, and has issue,

I. CHARLES-SPENCER, *b.* 5 Feb. 1830.
II. Compton-Alwyne, lieut. 38th regt., *b.* 8 May, 1831.
III. William-Drummond, lieut. 20th regt., *b.* 29 May, 1832.

Lineage.—The family of Dickins was settled at Broadway, in Worcestershire, at an early period, and in the reign of CHARLES II. Thomas Dickins was a bencher and treasurer of the Inner Temple. He left an only dau. who *d. unm.* and bequeathed her property between Ambrose Dickins, Esq., father of the late Mr. Dickins, of Wollaston, and Anthony Dickins, who *m.* the heiress of Scrase.

ANTHONY DICKINS, Esq. of Broadway, in Worcestershire, son of William Dickins, was bapt. at Broadway, 19 Sept. 1624, and *m.* Margaret, dau. and heir of Edward Times, Esq. of Chevrington, in the co. of Warwick, by whom he left two sons, of whom the elder,

TIMES DICKINS, Esq. of London, bapt. at Broadway, 12 March, 1669, *d. s. p.* before 1707, and was *s.* by his brother,

WILLIAM DICKINS, Esq. of Chevrington, co. Warwick, bapt. at Broadway, 10 Aug. 1659, who was father of

ANTHONY DICKINS, Esq., whose son,

WILLIAM DICKINS, Esq. of Chevrington, bapt. at Broadway, 22 Jan. 1715, *m.* and had a son,

ANTHONY DICKINS, Esq. bapt. at Broadway, 6 Oct. 1734, prothonotary of the court of Common Pleas, who *m.* Sally, dau. and co-heir of Charles Scrase, Esq. of Brighton (lineally descended from Tuppin Scrase, Esq. of Bletchington, to whom Sir William Segar, Garter, granted in 1616, a crest for his arms. The family of Scrase, originally of Danish extraction, held lands in Sussex before and at the period of the Norman Conquest, as appears by the General Survey). Of this marriage there was issue,

I. CHARLES, his heir.
II. William, who *m.* Miss Bennett, dau. of — Bennett, Esq. of Thorpe, in Surrey, and had issue,
  1 William, of Chevrington, in Warwickshire, who *m.* Lucy, dau. of Sir James Allan Park.
  1 Mary, *m.* to the eldest son of Sir James-Allan Park.
  2 Sophy. 3 Harriet.

III. Thomas, who *m.* Louisa, dau. of — Hinde, Esq. of Longham Park, in Essex, but had no issue.
I. Sarah, *m.* to T. Sawyer, Esq. of Heywood Lodge, Berks, and had issue.

The eldest son,

CHARLES DICKINS, Esq., assumed the additional surname and arms of SCRASE, upon the demise of his maternal grandfather in 1792, and on the 5th May, in that year, *m.* Elizabeth, dau. of John Devall, Esq. of London, by whom he left, at his decease, 11 Oct. 1833, an only child, the present CHARLES SCRASE-DICKINS, Esq.

Arms—Quarterly: 1st and 4th, erm., on a cross-flory, sa., a leopard's face, or; 2nd and 3rd, az., a dolphin, naiant, arg., fins, or, between three escallops, of the last.
Crests—1st, a lion, sejant, sa., holding a cross-flory, or; 2nd, on the stump of a tree, entwined by a serpent, ppr., a falcon, volant, also ppr., beaked, membered, and belled, or.
Seat—Coolhurst, Horsham.

DICKINS OF WOLLASTON.

DICKINS, THE REV. WATSON-WILLIAM, M.A., prebendary of Lichfield, and rector of Addisham-cum-Staple, Kent, *b.* 1790; *m.* 1818, Mary, 2nd dau. of Sir Edward Knatchbull, 8th Bart., of Mersham Hatch, Kent (by his 2nd wife, Frances, dau. of Col. John Graham, lieut.-governor of Georgia, a collateral branch of the Montrose family: Mrs. Graham's immediate ancestor was Richard, Baron of Glendarlosh, who *m.* Elizabeth Heriot, dau. of James Heriot, jeweller to CHARLES I.) By this lady he has issue,

I. FRANCIS.
II. George-Caldwell, capt. in the 46th regt., *m.* 22 July, 1851, Fanny, dau. of H. Collingwood, Esq. of Cornhill House, co. Northumberland, and has issue, William-Henry-Collingwood, *b.* 25 May, 1852.
I. Eliza-Anne, *m.* 1849, Henry Pole, Esq., only son of the Rev. H. Pole, of Waltham Place, Berks.
II. Mary-Isabella. III. Laura. IV. Frances-Diana.

Lineage.—This ancient family is of the same origin as that of Scrase-Dickins, and dates back to the time of King EDWARD IV. The immediate ancestor of this branch was

AMBROSE DICKINS, Esq., serjeant-surgeon* to Queen ANNE, and also to Kings GEORGE I. and II.: he *m.* and had issue,

I. AMBROSE, his heir.
II. George, in holy orders, rector of Baine, Essex, *m.* and had issue,
  1 Ambrose, who *m.* and had a son, Ambrose, who *d.* young.
  2 George.
  1 Anne, *m.* Major Green, and *d. s. p.*
I. Ann, *d. unm.* II. Elizabeth, *d. unm.*
III. Catharine, *m.* Mr. Sparkes.

Mr. Dickins, the serjeant-surgeon, was *s.* by his eldest son,

AMBROSE DICKINS, Esq. of Wollaston, co. Northampton, who *m.* Mary, dau. of Sir William Abdy, 4th baronet, and had a dau., Mary, who *d. unm.*, and a son,

FRANCIS DICKINS, Esq. of Wollaston and Branches Park, Suffolk, *m.* 21 April, 1778, Diana, dau. of Lord George Manners-Sutton, son of John, 3rd Duke of Rutland, and sister to Charles, Lord Archbishop of Canterbury (whose son was created Viscount Canterbury, and was for many years speaker of the House of Commons), and of Thomas Manners, lord-chancellor of Ireland, created Baron Manners. By her he had issue,

I Francis-George, capt. R.N., *d. unm.*
II. Frederick-John, major in the 12th lancers, killed at the battle of Salamanca, in 1812, *unm.*
III. WATSON-WILLIAM, who *s.* his father.
I Maria-Isabella, *m.* Dec. 1804, the last Earl Cornwallis, and *d.* 1823, leaving issue,
  1 Charles-James, Viscount Brome, *b.* 1813, and *d. unm.* 1835.
  1 Jemima-Isabella, *m.* to Charles Wykeham-Martin, Esq. of Leeds Castle, Kent, and *d.* 1836, leaving issue, three sons and one dau.
II. Frances-Diana-Katharine, *d. unm.*

Mr. Dickins *d.* at Wollaston, in 1834, aged 85, and was *s.* by his only surviving son, WATSON-WILLIAM, present proprietor.

* The serjeant-surgeon had two younger brothers, Dr. Francis Dickins, fellow of Trinity Hall, Cambridge, and professor of civil law; and Dr. George Dickins, M.D., of Liverpool, *m.* and had a dau., Eleanor, who *m.* 1757, Lewis Buckle, Esq. of Borden in East Meon, Hants, and *d.* 1811.

Arms—Erm., on a cross-flory, sa., a leopard's face, or.
Crest—A lion, sejant, or, holding a cross-flory, sa.
Motto—In hoc signo vinces.

DICKINSON OF FARLEY HILL.

DICKINSON, CATHERINE, widow of the late Charles Dickinson, Esq. of Farley Hill, co. Berks, who *d.* in 1826, and dau. of Thomas Allingham, Esq. of the city of London, is a descendant of the ancient family of CHEKE *of Motstone*. By her late husband, she has one dau. and heiress,

FRANCES, *m.* 8 Oct. 1838, to John-Edward Geils, Esq. of Dumbuck, co. Dumbarton.

Lineage.—The late THOMAS ALLINGHAM, Esq. of the city of London, descended from the very ancient family of that name, *m.* Mary, 2nd dau. and co-heir of John Taylor, Esq. of Furzeyhurst, Isle of Wight, eldest son and heir of Richard Taylor, M.D., of Newport, by Grace Cheke his wife, descended from Sir John Cheke, Knt., one of the clerks of the council, *temp.* Queen ELIZABETH, and *d.* in 1803, having had by him (who *d.* in 1827) issue,

John-Till, *d. unm.* Charles.
Thomas, *d. unm.* Edward, lieut. E.I.C.S.
Maria, *m.* to Samuel Ricketts, of Surinam, and *d.* in April, 1811.
CATHERINE, widow of Charles Dickinson, Esq. of Farley House, Berks.
Emma, *m.* to George Magnus, Esq. of Twickenham.
Fanny, *m.* to Thomas Wilson, Esq.

Arms—Or, a bend, engrailed, between two lions, rampant, gu., impaling the arms of ALLINGHAM, CHEKE, &c.

DICKINSON OF KING WESTON.

DICKINSON, FRANCES-HENRY, Esq. of King Weston, co. Somerset, J.P. and D.L., high-sheriff in 1853, *b.* 6 Jan. 1813; *m.* 8 Sept. 1835, Caroline, dau. of Gen. Thomas Carey, by Caroline his wife, dau. of Samuel Smith, Esq. of Woodhall Park, Herts, and has issue,

I. WILLIAM, *b.* 20 Aug. 1839.
II. Reginald, *b.* 27 Jan. 1841.
III. Arthur, *b.* 18 Jan. 1847.
IV. Edmund, *b.* 27 June, 1850.
V. Carey, *b.* 18 Aug. 1851.
I. Sophia-Caroline. II. Frances-Gertrude.
III. Lucy-Philippa-Mary. IV. Mary.

Lineage.—The earliest particulars are given in Thoresby's *Ducatus Leudiensis*. THE REV. WILLIAM DICKINSON, B.D., rector of Appleton and Besselsleigh, near Oxford, *m.* Mary, dau. of Edmund Colepepper, Esq. of Hallingbourne, Kent, and had, with other issue, two sons, EDMUND, M.D., physician to King CHARLES II., *d.* 19 April, 1707, aged 83, leaving an only dau., Elizabeth, *m.* 1st, to Sir G. Shires, and 2ndly, to Baron Blomberg; and FRANCIS. This

FRANCIS DICKINSON, Esq. of Barton, Jamaica, *b.* 1632, *m.* 1662, Margaret, dau. of Stephen Crook; and dying 28 Nov. 1704, left, with other issue, a son,

CALEB DICKINSON, Esq. of Monks, Wilts, *b.* 1670, who *m.* Sarah, dau. of Richard Vickris, Esq. of Chew Magna, and *d.* 3 Nov. 1728, leaving issue, EZEKIEL, of Monks, *m.* Frances, dau. of Thomas Barnard, of London, and was father of Barnard, who *d. s. p.* 1832; CALEB; Vickers, father of Charles Dickenson, Esq., who *m.* Catherine Allingham; Margaret, *m.* 1st, to G. Oldner, Esq., and 2ndly, to Gabriel Goldney; Mary, *m.* to Truman Harford, Esq. of Bristol. The 2nd son,

CALEB DICKINSON, Esq. of Bristol, merchant, *d.* in 1783, leaving, by Sarah his wife, a son and heir,

WILLIAM DICKINSON, Esq., *b.* in 1735, three times M.P. for Somersetshire, who *m.* Philippa, dau. of Stephen Fuller, Esq. of Brightling, Sussex, and *d.* in April, 1806, leaving a dau. Frances, *m.* 1801, to John-F. Pinney, Esq. of Somerton Erleigh, and a son,

WILLIAM DICKINSON, Esq. of King Weston, *b.* 1 Nov. 1771, member for Somersetshire in seven successive parliaments, who *m.* 1803, Sophia, dau. of S. Smith, Esq. of Woodhall Park, Herts, and by her, who *d.* in 1844, had issue,

FRANCIS-HENRY, now of King Weston.
Edmund-Henry, *b.* 30 June, 1821.
Sophia-Gertrude, *m.* to the Rev. J.-S.-H. Horner, of Mells Park, co. Somerset.
Caroline, *m.* to W.-Bence Jones, Esq., of Lisselan, co. Cork.

Arms—Or, a bend, engrailed, between two lions, rampant, gu.
Seat—King Weston, Somerton.

DICKINSON OF ABBOT'S HILL.

DICKINSON, JOHN, Esq. of Abbot's Hill, Abbot's Langley, Herts, F.R.S., J.P., *b.* 1782; *m.* 1810, Ann, 2nd dau. of Harry Grover, Esq. of The Bury, Hemel Hempsted, and has issue,

I. JOHN, *b.* 1815.
I. Frances-Elizabeth, *m.* to Frederick-Pratt Barlow, Esq.
II. Harriet-Ann, *m.* John Evans, Esq.

Lineage.—CAPTAIN JOHN DICKINSON, R.N., an elder brother of the Trinity House, who was from Northumberland, lost all his books and papers, and a great deal of property, in the earthquake of Lisbon. He *m.* in 1749, Anne More, and *d.* in 1781, leaving a son,

CAPTAIN THOMAS DICKINSON, R.N., who obtained in 1782, the post of superintendant of shipping to the Board of Ordinance, which he retained till after the termination of the last French war. He *m.* 1781, Frances de Brissac, a descendant of the ancient family of COSSE DE BRISSAC, and by her (who *d.* in 1854) left at his decease, in 1828, a son, the present JOHN DICKINSON, Esq. of Abbot's Hill.

Arms—Quarterly: 1st and 4th, gu., a fesse, erm., between two lions, passant, or; for DICKINSON: 2nd and 3rd, sa., three closets, the lower side indented, or; for COSSE DE BRISSAC.
Crest—Out of clouds, ppr., a cubit arm, erect, of the last, holding a branch of laurel, vert.
Seat—Abbot's Hill, Hemel Hempsted.

DICKSON OF CO. LIMERICK.

DICKSON, SAMUEL-AUCHMUTY, Esq. of Beenham House, Berks, and of Clonleharde, co. Limerick, J.P. and D.L., lieutenant-colonel of the county of Limerick militia, *b.* 18 March, 1817; *m.* 5 June, 1847, Maria-Theresa, dau. of N. Saunders, Esq.

Lineage.—This family is derived from the Berwickshire Dicksons.

STEPHEN DICKSON, Esq., son of RICHARD DICKSON, Esq. of Ballyhonogue, co. Limerick, *m.* Mary Lane (whose mother was dau. and co-heir of Jeremiah Hayes, Esq. of Cahir Guillamore, by his wife, Honora Quard, from whom also derive, through the female line, Lords Clare and Guillamore, and the Farrells and Blennerhassetts), and by her had issue,

RICHARD, who inherited the family estates, and left a son, STEPHEN, who *d.* leaving two daus.
John, of Liverpool, an eminent merchant, left an only surviving dau., who *m.* James Cooper, Esq. of co. Limerick, and *d. s. p.*
Stephen, barrister-at-law, *m.*, and left several sons and daus., all deceased but Arthur, living in France.
Patrick, *d. s. p.*
Daniel, merchant in Limerick, left one son.
SAMUEL, of whom we treat.

The youngest son,

SAMUEL DICKSON, Esq. of Ballynaguile, *m.* 1st, Miss Farrell, of co. Limerick, and had by her one dau., *m.* to the late Richard Power, Esq. of Monroe, co. Tipperary. He *m.* 2ndly, Mary, dau. of John Norris, Esq., formerly of the city of Limerick, and by her had issue,

I. STEPHEN, barrister-at-law, and commissioner of bankrupts, J.P. and D.L., high-sheriff for co. Limerick in 1809. He *d. unm.* in 1839, leaving very large estates.
II. JOHN, of Clonshire, J.P. and D.L.; *b.* in June, 1778; lieut.-col. of the co. of Limerick militia; *d. unm.*
III. Samuel, J.P., high-sheriff in 1829.
IV. Richard, in holy orders, rector of Kilkeidy, co. Limerick, *m.* Anne, eldest dau. of the late Sir James Chatterton, Bart., and has issue two sons and two daus.
V. William, C.B., a major-general in the E.I.C.S., of Beenham House, Reading, Berks, *m.* Harriet, second dau. of Major-General Sir Thomas Dallas, G.C.B., and had issue,
1 SAMUEL-AUCHMUTY, now of Beenham House and Clonleharde.
2 William-Thomas, major 16th lancers.
1 Mary-Eleanor.
2 Harriet-Eliza, *m.* to John Neeld, Esq., M.P.
3 Fanny-Charlotte, *m.* to the Hon. Frederick-Mortimer-Sackville West, son of the Earl of De La Warr.
VI. Arthur, who *d. unm.*
I. Mary, *m.* to the late Right Hon. and Right Rev. Stephen, Bishop of Cashel.

II. Anne, *m.* to G.-W. Biggs, Esq., of Bellevue, co. Tipperary.
III. Catherine, *m.* in 1811, to Sir Robert Bateson, of Belvoir Park, co. Down, Bart., and M.P. for co. Londonderry.
IV. Eliza.

Arms—Az., a crescent between three mullets, arg.; on a chief, or, as many pallets, gu.
Crest—Out of battlements, a naked arm, embowed, holding a sword, in bend, all ppr.
Motto—Fortes fortuna juvat.
Seats—Beenham House, Berks; and Clonleharde, co. Limerick.

DICKSON OF BALLYFREE.

DICKSON, JOSEPH, Esq. of Ballyfree, co. Wicklow, J.P., *b.* 24 Sept. 1776; *m.* 13 May, 1803, Ann, dau. and co-heir of the late Patrick Smyth, Esq. of Bailieborough, co. Cavan, and has a son and heir,

ROBERT-SMYTH, barrister-at-law, *m.* Sarah-Ann, dau. of his uncle, Thomas Dickson, Esq., and sister of Mrs. Hamilton, of Castle Hamilton, co. Cavan.

Seat—Ballyfree, co. Wicklow.

DICKSON OF WOODVILLE.

DICKSON, JOHN-REYNOLDS, Esq. of Woodville and Dungarberry, co. Leitrim, J.P., *b.* 15 Aug. 1810; *m.* 29 April, 1837, Clara, dau. of Captain Skene, R.N., of Lethenty, co. Aberdeen, and has issue,

I. JOHN-WILLIAM, *b.* 19 Nov. 1842.
II. Thomas-Hyacinth, *b.* 11 Sept. 1844.
I. Ida-Frances. II. Mary-Elizabeth.
III. Clara-Hester. IV. Edith-Grace.

Lineage.—The late JOHN DICKSON, Esq. of Woodville, *m.* 18 April, 1806, Mary-Louisa Bodkin, Esq. of Thomastown, co. Galway, and *d.* in Jan. 1821, leaving, besides the present JOHN-REYNOLDS DICKSON, Esq. of Woodville and Dungarberry, four other sons, and three daus., viz.,

Hyacinth.
Robert, *m.* Mrs. Green. Alexander.
Joseph-William, in holy orders, *m.* Louisa-H. Frazer.
Hester, *m.* to Capt. Henry Cullen.
Belinda-Mary, *m.* to R. Hordman, Esq., M.D.
Mary-Belinda, *m.* to William Newcombe, Esq.

Seats—Woodville and Dungarberry, co. Leitrim.

DIGBY OF OSBERTSTOWN.

DIGBY, SIMON, Esq. of Osbertstown, co. Kildare, *b.* 11 Nov. 1797; *m.* 7 Jan. 1830, Elizabeth-Anne-Ella, only dau. of John Morse, Esq. of Abbott's Wotton, co. Dorset, and late of Sprowston Hall, Norfolk, by Elizabeth-Anne his wife, dau. of Gen. Hall, of Wratting Park, co. Cambridge, and Elizabeth his wife, dau. and eventual heir of John Carter, Esq. of Weston Colville, by Elizabeth his wife, dau. and co-heir of Maurice-Thompson, Lord Haversham, and has issue,

I. KENELM-ROY. II. Essex.
I. Ella-Geraldine. II. Gertrude-Simonetta.
III. Mabel.

Lineage.—THE REV. BENJAMIN DIGBY, prebendary and rector of Geashill, in the King's County, 3rd son of Simon Digby, Lord Bishop of Elphin, and brother of John Digby, Esq. of Landenstown, M.P., was grandson of Essex Digby, Bishop of Dromore, brother of Robert, 1st Lord Digby, *m.* 26 Sept. 1734, Mary, dau. and heir of Lewis Jones, Esq. of Osbertstown, in the co. of Kildare, descended from the Right Hon. Sir Theophilus Jones, son of the Bishop of Killaloe, and brother of the Bishops of Meath and Kildare. By this lady he left at his decease, in May, 1769, a dau., Mary, *m.* to the Very Rev. William Digby, dean of Clonfert, and several sons, of whom the eldest,

THE REV. SIMON DIGBY, of Osbertstown, in Kildare, *m.* Elizabeth, dau of the Rev. Jeremy Marsh, D.D., grandson of Francis Marsh, Archbishop of Dublin, by Mary his wife, dau. and co-heir of Jeremy Taylor, Esq., Bishop of Down and Connor, and left at his decease, in 1824, *inter alios*, a dau., Jane, *m.* to Charles Annesley, Esq. of Ballisax, in the co. of Kildare; and a son and heir,

THE REV. JOHN DIGBY, of Osberstown and of New Park, co. Meath, who *m.* 1st, in 1796, Elizabeth, dau. and co-heir of Edward Borr, Esq. of Spring Park, in the latter shire, and by her, who *d.* in 1806, had issue,

SIMON, his heir, now of Osbertstown.
Edward, lieut. R.N., *m.* Sarah, dau. of — Crawford, Esq. of Orangefield, in Downshire, and has issue,
John-Charles, *m.* Marianne, dau. of — Church, Esq. of Listowel, co. Kerry, and *d.* in Sept. 1836.
George, in holy orders, *m.* Juliana, dau. of — Chorley, Esq. of Leeds.
Alfred, *m.* Margaretta, dau. of — Busby, Esq. of Montreal, Upper Canada.

Mr. Digby *m.* 2ndly, in 1818, Miss Borr, dau. of Christopher Borr, Esq. of Ballendoolan, in the co. of Kildare, and had also issue by her.

Arms—Az., a fleur-de-lis, arg.
Crest—An ostrich, arg., holding in the beak a horseshoe, or.
Motto—Deo non fortunâ.
Seat—Osbertstown, in Kildare.
Residence—Cranhill House, Bath.

DILLWYN OF SKETTY HALL.

DILLWYN, LEWIS-WESTON, Esq. of Burroughs Lodge, and Sketty Hall, co. Glamorgan, F.R.S., J.P. and D.L., high-sheriff in 1818, and M.P. for Glamorganshire in 1832, *b.* 21 Aug. 1778; *m.* 18 July, 1807, Mary, dau. of the late John Llewelyn, of Penllergare and Ynys-y-gerwn, co. Glamorgan, Esq., and has surviving issue,

I. JOHN, of Penllergare, who has assumed the additional surname of LLEWELYN, *b.* 12 Jan. 1810, *m.* 18 June, 1833, Emma-Thomasina, sister of C.R.M. Talbot, Esq., M.P. for Glamorganshire.
II. Lewis-Llewelyn, of Hendrefoilan, co. Glamorgan, *b.* 19 May, 1814, *m.* Aug. 1838, Elizabeth, dau. and heir of Sir Henry-Thomas De la Beche, C.B., and has issue, Henry-De la Beche, *b.* May, 1843, and three daus., Mary-De la Beche; Elizabeth-Amy; and Sarah-Llewelyn.
I. Fanny-Llewelyn, *m.* in 1836, to Matthew Moggridge, Esq.
II. Mary.

Lineage.—By a pedigree preserved in the Harleian Collection, No. 6831, this family is traced from Sir John Dilwyn, of Dilwyn, co. Hereford. Towards the close of the 17th century, most of the descendants of

JEFFREYS DILWYN, of Langorse, adopted the Welsh custom by taking the surname of JEFFREYS; and about the year 1699,

WILLIAM DILWYN emigrated from Breconshire, with his friend, Governor Penn, to Philadelphia. He was father of

JOHN DILWYN, of Philadelphia, Esq., who *m.* Susanna, dau. and heiress of George Painter, of Haverford, in Pennsylvania, and formerly of Broomhill, in the parish of Dale, co. Pembroke, and had a son,

WILLIAM DILLWYN, Esq. of Higham Lodge, Walthamstow, co. Essex, who *m.* in Nov. 1777, Sarah, dau. and heiress of Lewis Weston, of High Hall, in the same co., Esq., and *d.* in Sept. 1824, aged 81, leaving a son and successor, LEWIS-WESTON DILLWYN, Esq. of Burroughs Lodge and Sketty Hall.

Arms—Gu., on a chevron, arg., three trefoils, slipped, of the first.
Crest—A stag's head, couped, ppr.
Motto—Craignez honte.
Seats—Burroughs Lodge, and Sketty Hall, near Swansea.

DIMSDALE OF ESSENDEN PLACE.

DIMSDALE, CHARLES-JOHN, Esq. of Essenden Place, Herts, *b.* 12 Feb. 1801; *m.* 16 Nov. 1826, Jemima, dau. of the Rev. Henry-Anthony Pye, late prebendary of Worcester, and has issue,

I. ROBERT, *b.* 4 July, 1828, *m.* 1 Nov. 1853, Cecilia-Jane, eldest dau. of the Rev. Marcus-Richard Southwell, vicar of St. Stephen's, St. Albans, and has issue.

Mr. Dimsdale of Essenden is younger brother of the present Hon. Baron Dimsdale, of the Russian empire (see BURKE'S *Peerage and Baronetage*), and 2nd son of the late Baron Robert Dimsdale, by Finetta his wife, eldest dau. of Charles Pye, Esq. of Wadley House, Berks.

Arms—Arg., on a fesse, dancettée, az., between three mullets, sa., as many bezants; on an escutcheon, or, an eagle's dexter wing, sa.
Crest—Out of a baron's coronet, a griffin's head, erm.
Seat—Essenden Place, Herts.

DINSDALE OF NEWSHAM PARK.

MOSES-DINSDALE, ROBERT, Esq. of Newsham Park, co. Durham, *b.* 15 Sept. 1778, J.P. and D.L. This gentleman assumed the surname of DINSDALE, in lieu of his patronymic, Moses, on succeeding to the property of the DINSDALES *of Newsham*, co. Durham, who were freeholders there before 1680.

DIROM OF MOUNT ANNAN.

DIROM, JOHN-PASLEY, Esq. of Mount Annan, co. Dumfries, J.P. and D.L., lieut.-col., late of the Grenadier-guards, *b.* 6 Nov. 1794, widower, without children.

Lineage.—LIEUT.-GENERAL ALEXANDER DIROM, son of Alexander Dirom, Esq. of Muiresk, in Banffshire, by Ann Fotheringham his wife, *m.* in 1793, Magdalen, dau. of Robert Pasley, Esq. of Mount Annan, by Christina Pringle his wife, and *d.* in Oct. 1830, leaving issue,

JOHN-PASLEY, now of Mount Annan.
Alexander, capt. 8th infantry, *d.* 1837, leaving two sons and four daus.
Robert, merchant of Liverpool, *m.* and has one son and one dau.
William, Bengal civil service, *m.* and has one dau.
James, commander, R.N.
Leonora. Anna, *m.* to the Rev. Dr. Muir.

Arms—Quarterly: 1st, or, a stag's head, erased, gu.; 2nd, erm., three bars, gu.; 3rd, gu. three swords, paleways, in fesse, hilted, or, on the point of each a dragon's head, couped, close, of the last; 4th, az., a griffin, segreant, or.
Crest—A stag's head.
Seat—Mount Annan, co. Dumfries.

DISNEY OF THE HYDE.

DISNEY, JOHN, Esq. of The Hyde, co. Essex, F.R.S., *b.* 29 May, 1779, barrister-at-law; *m.* 22 Sept. 1802, his first-cousin, Sophia, younger dau. and coheir of Lewis Disney-Ffytche, Esq. of Swinderby, co. Lincoln, and of Danbury Place, Essex, and has issue,

I. EDGAR, *b.* 22 Dec. 1810, *m.* Barbara, youngest dau. of the late Lewis-William Brouncker, Esq. of Boveridge, co. Dorset, and has a son and heir,
Edgar, *b.* in July, 1835.
I. Sophia, *m.* to William, eldest son of the Rev. William Jesse, vicar of Margaretting, Essex.

Lineage.—The family of DISNEY, anciently written DE ISNEY and D'EISNEY, and deriving its patronymic from Isigny, a bourg near Bayeux, in Normandy, came into England at the Conquest, as attested by the different copies of the Battle Abbey Roll. Leland, in his *Itinerary*, p. 29, in enumerating the gentry of the Kestevin division of Lincolnshire, mentions "Disney, *alias* De Iseney; he dwelleth at Diseney, and of his name and line be gentilmen of Fraunce. Aiteshara Priory, by Thorney Courtoise, was of the Diseneys' foundation, and there were divers of them buryed, and likewise at Diseney."

LAMBERT DE ISNEY, of Norton D'Isney, co. Lincoln, was ancestor of the DISNEYS *of Norton D'Isney*, a knightly race of high station and influence, intermarrying with the Lords Bardolph, Grey de Ruthyn, the Feltons, Nevils, Skipwiths, Ormesbys, Dives, Husseys, &c., many of their wives being heiresses. Twentieth in direct descent from this Lambert was

SIR HENRY D'ISNEY, of Norton D'Isney, *b.* 1 March, 1569, knighted at Whitehall, 23 July, 1603, and buried at Norton, 11 Oct. 1641. He *m.* 1st, Barbara, dau. of John Thornhaugh, Esq. of Fenton, Notts, and had (with a dau. Anne, wife of John Williamson, Esq. of Burton) a son and heir, WILLIAM, of Norton D'Isney, *d.* in 1656. His male line terminated with William Disney, of Norton D'Isney, who *d.* in 1722, and his brother, the Rev. Richard Disney, rector of Bloxham: the latter had three daus., ANNE, by his marriage with Rebecca, dau. of the Rev. Henry Wych, of Sutton; and by his 2nd wife, Bridget, dau. of Eakins Lenton, Esq. of Wigloft, Lincoln, BRIDGET, and ANNE, the latter wife of Timothy Boole, Esq. of Navenby, and 2ndly, of John Gilman, Esq. of Cunwick, both in Lincolnshire. Sir Henry

D'Isney *m.* 2ndly, Eleanor, dau. of Thomas Grey, Esq. of Langley, co. Leicester, by whom he had two other sons, viz., JOHN, of whom presently; Thomas, in holy orders, rector of Stoke Hammond, Bucks. Sir Henry's 2nd son,

JOHN D'ISNEY, Esq. of Swinderby, co. Lincoln, *b.* 30 Nov. 1603, *m.* 25 Jan. 1636, Barbara, dau. of Gervase Lee, Esq. of Norwell Hall, Notts, and had two sons, GERVASE and DANIEL. He *d.* 10 Jan. 1680–1, and was *s.* by his elder son,

GERVASE DISNEY, Esq. of Swinderby, who *d. s. p.* 3 April, 1691, and was *s.* by his brother,

DANIEL DISNEY, Esq. of Lincoln, who *m.* in 1674, Catherine, youngest dau. and co-heir of Henry-Fynes Clinton, Esq. of Kirksted, in Lincolnshire, grandson of Henry, 2nd Earl of Lincoln, by whom he had a son, JOHN, in holy orders, *b.* 26 Dec. 1677, *d.* in the lifetime of his father, 3 Feb. 1729–30, leaving, by Mary his wife, dau. of William Woolhouse, M.D., of North Muskham, Notts, six sons and three daus., of whom JOHN inherited; Henry, was a physician at Newcastle, and his son, Henry-Woolhouse Disney, assumed, on inheriting an estate, the name of ROEBUCK; Gervase, of Pontefract, left daus. Mr. Disney *d.* 29 Aug. 1734, and was *s.* by his grandson,

JOHN DISNEY, Esq. of Swinderby, and of the city of Lincoln, *b.* 3 April, 1700, sheriff for Nottinghamshire the year before the death of his grandfather, *m.* 29 Dec. 1730, Frances, youngest dau. of George Cartwright, Esq. of Ossington, Notts, by whom (who *d.* 5 Jan. 1791) he had issue,

I. LEWIS, who inherited Swinderby, *b.* 9 Oct. 1738, *m.* 16 Sept. 1775, ELIZABETH, only dau. and heir of William Ffytche, Esq., Governor of Bengal, and heir likewise of her uncle, Thomas Ffytche, Esq. of Danbury Place, co. Essex, in consequence of which he assumed, by sign-manual, 27 Sept. 1775, the additional surname and arms of Ffytche, and became LEWIS DISNEY-FFYTCHE, Esq. of Swinderby, Lincolnshire, and of Danbury Place, in Essex. He *d.* 22 Sept. 1822, leaving two daus., his co-heirs, viz.,
  1 FRANCES-ELIZABETH, *b.* 29 Aug. 1776, *m.* to Sir William Hillary, Bart.
  2 SOPHIA, *m.* to her cousin-german, the present JOHN DISNEY, Esq. of The Hyde.

II. Frederick, a major in the army, *b.* 12 Oct. 1741, *d. unm.* at Lincoln, 13 June, 1788.

III. JOHN, in holy orders.

I. Mary, *m.* 1st, in 1753, to Edmund Turnor, Esq. of Stoke Rochford, and 2ndly, to Murray, Esq., and *d.* in Nov. 1839.

Mr. Disney *d.* 26 Jan. 1771, and was *s.* by his eldest son and heir, LEWIS DISNEY, Esq., whose line terminated as stated above. His youngest son,

THE REV. JOHN DISNEY, of The Hyde, D.D., sometime rector of Panton, and rector of Swinderby, co. Lincoln, *b.* 17 Sept. 1746, *m.* 17 Nov. 1774, Jane, eldest dau. of the Rev. Francis Blackburne, A.M., rector of Richmond, Yorkshire, and archdeacon of Cleveland, by whom he had,

JOHN, now of The Hyde.
Algernon, *b.* at Flintham Hill, 1 June, 1780.
Frances-Mary, *b.* 7 Aug. 1775.

Mr. Disney *d.* 26 Dec. 1816.

Arms—Arg., on a fesse, gu., three fleurs-de-lis, or.
Crest—A lion, passant-guardant, gu.
Seat—The Hyde, near Ingatestone, Essex.

Disney of the co. Meath.

A branch of the DISNEYS *of Norton D'Isney* was established in Ireland by THOMAS DISNEY, an officer in WILLIAM III.'s army, who was appointed collector of Galway. His son,

THE REV. BRABAZON DISNEY, D.D., Regius Professor in Trinity College, Dublin, and rector of Kilmore, in the diocese of Armagh, *m.* in 1761, Patience, dau. of H.-M. Ogle, Esq., M.P. for Drogheda, and had three sons, William, of Somerset, co. Dublin; Brabazon, of Slane, co. Meath, in holy orders; and THOMAS, of Rock Lodge. The 3rd son,

THOMAS DISNEY, Esq. of Rock Lodge, co. Meath, an officer in the army, *m.* in 1791, Anne-Eliza, only dau. of William-John Purdon, Esq. by Jane Coote his wife, of the Mountrath family, and had issue,

BRABAZON, lieut.-col., formerly of the 7th fusiliers, *d. s. p.* in 1833.
William-John, R.N., killed on board H.M.S. "La Hogue," by an accident.
Thomas, barrister-at-law.
Robert-Anthony, of Dublin.
Edward-Ogle, in holy orders.
Henry-Purdon, in holy orders. James, in holy orders.
Lambert, *b.* in 1809, *m.* in 1835, Anna-Henrietta, dau. of William Battersby, Esq., and has issue, Thomas-William, *b.* in 1836; Lambert-John, *b.* in 1841; and Caroline-Frances.

Jane, *m.* in 1813, to John Barlow, Esq. of the co. of Dublin.
Anna, *m.* to the Rev. J. Disney, of Slane, co. Meath.
Catherine, *m.* the Rev. Wm. Barlow.
Caroline, *d. unm.* in 1839.
Louisa, *m.* to the Rev. Henry-T. Hobson.

DIXON OF ASTLE HALL.

DIXON, JOHN, Esq. of Astle Hall, co. Chester, *b.* 13 Feb. 1799, a captain in the army; *m.* 14 May, 1840, Sophia, dau. of the late T.-W. Tatton, Esq. of Wythenshawe, and has issue,

I. GEORGE, *b.* 23 May, 1842.
II John-Wykeham, *b.* 1 May, 1845.
III. Charles-Egerton, *b.* 12 Dec. 1848.
IV. Henry-Grey, *b.* 14 Aug. 1850.
V. Frederick-Parker, *b.* 17 Aug. 1852.
VI. William-Arthur-Tatton, *b.* 13 Feb. 1854.
I. Anna-Louisa. II. Sophia-Lydia.
III. Jessie-Maria.

Captain Dixon *s.* his brother, the late Henry Dixon, Esq., 3 Aug. 1838.

Lineage.—From WILLIAM DIXON, of Heaton Royds, living in 1564, lineally descended

JEREMIAH DIXON, Esq., F.R.S., who purchased, in 1764, the estate of Gledhow, from the Wilson family; in 1765, the manor of Chapel Allerton, from Mr. Kellingback; and in 1771, the estates of Lady Dawes and her son. He was son and heir of John Dixon, of Leeds, merchant, by Frances his wife, dau. of Thomas Gower, Esq. of Hutton, grandson of Edward Gower, younger brother of Sir Thos. Gower, Bt. He *m.* Mary, dau. of the Rev. Henry Wickham, rector of Guiseley, and had, with daus., three sons, viz.,

JOHN, his heir.
Jeremiah, mayor of Leeds in 1784, *m.* Mary, dau. of John Smeaton, Esq., who built the Eddystone lighthouse.
Henry, of Brookefarm, near Liverpool, *m.* Catherina-Towneley Plumbe, dau. of Thomas Plumbe, Esq., and sister of Colonel Plumbe Tempest, of Tong Hall, in Yorkshire, by whom (who *d.* in 1819) he had a large family.

Mr. Dixon *d.* 7 June, 1782, aged 56, and was *s.* by his son,

JOHN DIXON, Esq. of Gledhow, J.P. and D.L., *b.* 27 June, 1753, colonel of the 1st West York militia, who *m.* 18 July, 1784, Lydia, dau. of the Rev. T. Parker, of Astle, co. Chester, and had issue,

HENRY, his heir.
JOHN, present representative.
George, late capt. in the 3rd guards, *b.* 5 Aug. 1801, *m.* Miss M.-F. Biddulph, who is deceased.
Lydia. Mary, *m.* to George Stone, Esq.
Jane, *m.* to Capt. Charles Loftus, son of the late General Loftus.
Anne, *m.* James Kinnersley, Esq. of Clough Hall, Staffordshire, and is deceased.

Colonel Dixon *d.* 18 April, 1824, and was *s.* by his son,

HENRY DIXON, Esq. of Gledhow, *b.* 19 Nov. 1794, who *m.* 24 Dec. 1829, Emma-Matilda, niece of Sir Robert Wilmot, of Chaddesden, near Derby, and *d. s. p.* 3 Aug. 1838, when he was *s.* by his next brother, the present JOHN DIXON, Esq. of Astle.

Arms—Gu., a fleur-de-lis, or; a chief, ermine.
Crest—A demi-lion, rampant, arg.
Estates—In the counties of York and Chester.
Seat—Astle Hall, near Knutsford.

DIXON OF PAGE HALL.

DIXON, WILLIAM-FREDERICK, Esq. of Page Hall, co. York, J.P., *b.* 13 June, 1802; *m.* 2 Sept. 1824, Anne, dau. of Benjamin and Elizabeth Newton, of Sheffield, and has issue,

I. WILLIAM-FREDERICK, *b.* 13 June, 1825, of Birley House, co. York.
I. Ann-Elizabeth. II. Jane-Newton.
III. Helen. IV. Mary-Susanna.
V. Margaret-Newton. VI. Sarah-Sophia.
VII. Fanny. VIII. Lucy.

Lineage.—JAMES DIXON, Esq. son of Samuel Dixon, *b.* 27 Oct. 1737, *m.* 26 Aug. 1764, Hannah Eatherley, and was father of

JAMES DIXON, Esq., *b.* 27 Jan. 1776, who *m.* 1st, 25 Dec. 1797, Hannah Cooper, and by her (who *d.* in March, 1806) had, besides two other children who *d.* young, an only surviving son,

WILLIAM-FREDERICK, now of Page Hall.

Mr. Dixon m. 2ndly, 28 Nov. 1806, Anne, dau. of Thomas Nowell, Esq., and by her had,

James-Willis, m. in 1836.
Henry-Isaac, m. 8 Aug. 1850, Anne Woolhouse.
Anne-Nowill, m. 1 Feb. 1828, to William Faucitt.
Eliza, m. to Edmund Menlove.

Arms—(granted to James Dixon, of Page Hall, in 1849) Per pale, sa. and gu., a bend between two roundles, arg.; on a chief, of the last, a rose between two roundles, gu.
Crest—An arm, embowed, habited, ppr., cuffed, arg., charged with five pallets, the hand, ppr., holding a wreath.
Motto—Fide et constantia.
Seat—Page Hall, Sheffield, co. York.

DIXON OF UNTHANK HALL.

DIXON, DIXON, Esq. of Unthank Hall, Northumberland, J.P. and D.L., *b.* 19 July, 1776; *m.* 28 Nov. 1816, Elizabeth, eldest dau. of William Smith, Esq. of Togston. Mr. Dixon, eldest son of the late William Brown, Esq., by Margaret his wife, dau. of William Dixon, Esq. of Hawkwell, assumed the surname of DIXON, at the decease of Colonel Dixon, royal artillery, and in compliance with the testamentary injunction of William Dixon, Esq. of Gower Street, Bedford Square. He served the office of sheriff for Newcastle-upon-Tyne in 1802, and for Northumberland in 1827.

Arms—
Motto—Suivez raison.
Seat—Unthank Hall, Haltwhistle.

DIXON OF KNELLS.

DIXON, JOHN, Esq. of Knells, co. Cumberland, J.P., high-sheriff in 1838, and mayor of Carlisle in 1839 and 1840, *b.* 26 Oct. 1785; *m.* 22 Nov. 1814, Mary-Tirzah, dau. of the late Captain Stordy, 31st regt., and has had issue,

I. PETER-JAMES.
II. Robert-Stordy, 9th Lancers.
III. Richard-Ferguson, *d.* 3 Nov. 1840.
IV. George-Hodgson. V. William-Giles, *d.* in 1830.
I. Mary-Sarah, *d.* 9 Feb. 1821.
II. Sarah, *m.* to Charles-William Thompson, son of Col. T.-Perronett Thompson.
III. Jane-Eleanor, *m.* to James-Robert Grant, son of Sir James Grant.
IV. Mary-Tirzah, *d.* in April, 1827.
V. Elizabeth, *d.* in 1824.
VI. Henrietta. VII. Maria-Rebecca, *d.* in 1832.

Lineage.—PETER DIXON, Esq., son of John, and grandson of Christopher, of Edmond Castle, *m.* 2 Sept. 1783, Mary, dau. of Richard Ferguson, Esq. of Carlisle, and had issue,

JOHN, now of Knells, as above.
Richard-Ferguson, deceased.
Peter, *m.* Sarah-Rebecca, dau. of Lieut.-General Clarke, E.I.C.S., and has issue, Peter-Sydenham; Henry-Hall; F.-Clarke; John; Joseph; Edward; Sarah-Rebecca; Augusta-Jane; and Catherine-Anne.
George, *m.* Mary, youngest dau. of the Rev. Jonathan Boucher, vicar of Epsom, Surrey.
Robert, deceased.
Joseph, *m.* Ann, dau. of Wilson Perry, Esq. of Whitehaven, and has issue, Peter-Wilson, and Joseph.
Frances, *d. unm.* in 1818. Mary, *d. unm.* in 1832.

Arms—Az., a dove, statant, ppr.; in chief, two bees, volant, or; a chief, of the last, thereon three pallets, gu.
Crest—In front of an anchor, in bend sinister, sa., a dexter cubit arm erect, ppr., in the hand an olive-branch, also ppr.
Motto—Peace.
Seat—Knells, near Carlisle.

DIXON OF HOLTON.

DIXON, THOMAS-JOHN, Esq. of Holton, co. Lincoln, *b.* 2 June, 1785; *m.* 10 July, 1827, Mary-Ann, dau. of Richard Roadley, Esq. This gentleman, who is in the commission of the peace, and a deputy-lieut. for Lincolnshire, is son of the late William Dixon, Esq., by Amelia-Margaret Parkinson his wife, grandson of Thomas Dixon, Esq., by Martha his wife, and great-grandson of William Dixon, Esq., by Rachael his wife.

Seat—Holton, near Caister.

DOBBS OF CASTLE DOBBS.

DOBBS, CONWAY-RICHARD, Esq. of Castle Dobbs, co. Antrim, *b.* 1796; *m.* 26 Aug. 1826, Charlotte-Maria, dau. and co-heiress of William Sinclair, Esq. of Fort William, co. Antrim, and has had issue,

I. Richard-Archibald-Conway, *d.* 24 Feb. 1853, aged 10.
II. MONTAGU-WILLIAM-EDWARD, *b.* 28 Sept. 1844.
I. Olivia-Nichola, *m.* in Nov. 1854, to James-Macaulay Higginson, C.B., Governor of Mauritius.
II. Frances-Millicent. III. Charlotte-Louisa-Mary.
IV. Hester-Alice-Caroline, *m.* 6 April, 1853, to Gerald-George, only son of Sir G.-G. Aylmer, Bart., of Donadea Castle, co. Kildare.
V. Harriet-Sydney, *m.* 28 Aug. 1850, to George, Duke of Manchester.
VI. Nichola-Susan. VII. Millicent-Georgina-Montagu.

Lineage.—This family was established in Ireland by JOHN DOBBS, who accompanied Sir Henry Dockwra to that country in 1596, and was subsequently his deputy as treasurer for Ulster. This John Dobbs, who is stated to have been grandson of Sir Richard Dobbs, lord-mayor of London in 1551, *m.* Margaret, only child of John Dalway, of Ballyhill, and had by her two sons, Foulk, who was lost with his father, in returning from England, and HERCULES DOBBS, who *s.* to his father's property. He *m.* Magdalen West, of Ballydugan, co. Down, and left an only son,

RICHARD DOBBS, high-sheriff of the county of Antrim in 1664, who *m.* in 1655, Dorothy, dau. of Brien Williams, Esq. of Clints Hall, co. York, and by her (with three daus., Elizabeth, *m.* to Jackson, Esq.; Margaret, *m.* to Francis Dobbs, Esq.; and Mary) had two sons, John, who was designed for the church, but joining the society of Quakers, was disinherited by his father; and RICHARD, successor to his father. Mr. Dobbs *d.* in 1701, leaving his estate to his younger son,

RICHARD DOBBS, Esq. of Castletown, *b.* in 1660, who *m.* 1st, Mary, dau. of Archibald Stewart, of Ballintoy, and had (with two daus., Jane, *m.* to Edward Brice, of Kilroot; and Elizabeth, *d. unm.*) three sons, 1 ARTHUR, his heir; 2 Richard, for many years an officer in the navy, subsequently entered Trinity College, Dublin, and obtained a fellowship; he *m.* a dau. of William Young, and relict of Cornet M'Manus. From this marriage descended the late Rev. Richard Dobbs, dean of Connor, and Francis Dobbs, Esq., barrister-at-law, M.P. in the Irish parliament for Charlemont, who *m.* 17 July, 1773, Jane Stewart, of Ballintoy. And 3 Marmaduke. He *m.* 2ndly, Margaret Clugston, of Belfast, and by her had three daus., Margaret, *m.* 7 July, 1729, to George Spaight; Mary, *m.* to Andrew Boyd, Esq. of Ballymoney; and Ann-Helena, *m.* to William Ker, Esq. of Ballymena. This gentleman was one of those who signed the Antrim Association in 1688, for which he was attainted by King JAMES' parliament the following year. He was high-sheriff of the county of Antrim in 1694, and *d.* in 1711. His eldest son and heir,

ARTHUR DOBBS, Esq., *b.* 2 April, 1689, high-sheriff of the county of Antrim in 1720, and for many years M.P. for Carrickfergus, *m.* Anne, dau. and heir of Captain Osborne, of Timahoe, co. Kildare, and relict of Captain Norbury, by whom he had issue,

CONWAY-RICHARD, his heir.
Edward-Brice. Francis.
Mary, *m.* to Dean Ryder.

Mr. Dobbs, who was appointed engineer and surveyor-general of Ireland by Sir Robert Walpole, was, in 1753, sent out as Governor of North Carolina, where he acquired large possessions. He was *s.* by his eldest son,

CONWAY-RICHARD DOBBS, Esq. of Castle Dobbs, M.P. for Carrickfergus, and high-sheriff of the county of Antrim in 1752, who *m.* 1st, Anne, dau. of Alexander Stewart, of Ballintoy, and by her (who *d.* 19 Feb. 1765) had issue, RICHARD, his heir. He *m.* 2ndly, Charity, dau. of Robert Burrowes, Esq. of Kildare, and widow of Stephen Rice, of Mount Rice, in the same county, by Mary his wife, dau. of John O'Neill, Esq. of Shanes Castle, co. Antrim, and by her had issue,

Edward-Brice, capt. in the army, and twice mayor of Carrickfergus, *d.* at Castle Dobbs, Feb. 1803.
Robert, in holy orders, *m.* in 1798, W. Bristow, dau. of the Rev. William Bristow, vicar of Belfast, and *d.* 9 Dec. 1809, aged 38, leaving issue one son, William-Cary Dobbs, who *m.* Eleanor, eldest dau. of the late Henry Westropp, Esq. of Richmond, co. Limerick, and four daus., viz., Rose, wife of William-Maunsell Reeves, of Vostersberg, co. Cork; Charity, *m.* to John M'Donnell, Esq., M.D., of the city of

Dublin; Frances-Ann, m. to Richard Ellis, eldest son of the late Richard Ellis, Esq., Master in Chancery; and Mary, m. to Richard Reeves, Esq. of the city of Dublin. Frances, m. to Edward Gayer, Esq.

Mr. Dobbs d. in Belfast, 11 April, 1811, and was s. by his eldest son,

RICHARD DOBBS, Esq. of Castle Dobbs, who m. in 1792, Nichola, dau. of Michael Obins, Esq. of Portadown, by Nichola his wife, 2nd dau. of Richard, 1st Viscount Gosford, and by her had issue, 1 CONWAY-RICHARD, present representative; 2 Archibald-Edward (m. in India, Miss Chapman, and d. April, 1838, leaving one son, Archibald-Edward); 3 Acheson; 1 Nichola; 2 Frances, deceased; and 3 Olivia, also deceased. Mr. Dobbs d. in Feb. 1840, aged 87.

Arms—Quarterly: 1st and 4th, per pale, sa. and arg., a chevron, engrailed, between three unicorns' heads, erased, all counterchanged, for DOBBS; 2nd, sa., three lions, passant-guardant (the two in chief, rencontrant), or, for DALWAY; 3rd, per cross, erm. and sa., a cross, or, for OSBORNE.
Crest—A unicorn's head, erased, arg.
Motto—Amor Dei et proximi summa beatitudo.
Seat—Castle Dobbs, co. Antrim.

DOD OF EDGE.

DOD, CHARLOTTE, of Edge Hall, co. Chester, s. her father in 1829; m. 20 Feb. 1834, the Rev. Joseph-Yates Cookson, son of the late Lieut.-Gen. Charles-Norris Cookson, of Kenton House, Devon. Mr. Cookson, on his marriage, took by royal license the surname of DOD.

Lineage.—HOVA, son of Cadwgan Dot, the founder of this family, about the time of HENRY II., having m. the dau. and heir of the lord of Edge, in Cheshire, obtained one-fourth of that manor, and settled there. The name of this feudal lord is not ascertained, but the presumption is that he was the son of Edwin, a Saxon thane, who was allowed, after the Norman Conquest, to retain possession of his lands at Edge, in Cheshire.

HOVA DOD had two sons; the younger, John, of Smith's Pentrey, in Broxton, m. Margery, dau. of Hugh Le Byrd, of Broxton; and the elder,

THOMAS DOD, of Edge, temp. EDWARD III., m. Mabell, dau. of David Mere, and had two sons, viz., THOMAS, his heir; and JOHN, ancestor of the DODS of *Cloverley*. The elder son,

THOMAS DOD, of Edge, m. Mary, or Matilda, dau. of David Bird, of Broxton, and left a son and successor,

DAVID DOD, of Edge, who m. Cecilia, dau. and co-heir of William de Bickerton, and was father of

SIR ANTHONY DOD, of Edge, knighted by King HENRY on the field of Agincourt. He d. on his return homewards, and was interred in the cathedral of Canterbury. His son and heir,

DAVID DOD, of Edge, was one of the Cheshire gentlemen who signed the supplication to HENRY VI. respecting the liberties of the Palatinate. His direct male descendant,

SIR EDWARD DOD, Baron of the Exchequer of Chester, m. Margaret, dau. and eventual heir of Roger Mainwaring, Esq. of Nantwich, and was great-great-grandfather of

THOMAS DOD, Esq. of Edge, bapt. 5 July, 1688, who m. at Chester cathedral, 28 June, 1748, Rebecca, dau. of Crewe of Crewe, and of Holt, in the co. of Denbigh; and by her, who d. 26 June, 1778, had THOMAS-CREWE, his heir; William; Rebecca, wife of William-Mostyn Owen, Esq. of Woodhouse, Salop; and Anne-Sobieski, of Robert-Watkin Wynne, Esq. of Plas Newydd, Denbighshire. Mr. Dod d. 30 Dec. 1759, and was s. by his son,

THOMAS-CREWE DOD, Esq. of Edge, bapt. at Malpas, 11 July, 1754, who m. 20 Sept. 1786, Anne, 4th dau. of Ralph Sneyd, Esq. of Keele, co. Stafford, and had issue,

John-Anthony, b. in 1798, d. unm. in India, in 1821.
CHARLOTTE, heir to her father. Anne.
Frances-Rosamond, m. to the Rev. P. Parker.
Soby-Rebecca, m. to H.-R. Sneyd, Esq.

Mr. Dod d. in 1827, and was s. by his eldest dau., CHARLOTTE.

Arms—Arg., on a fesse, gu., between two cotises, wavy, sa., three crescents, or.
Crest—A serpent, vert, issuing from and piercing a garb, or.
Motto—In copia cautus.
Seat—Edge Hall, Cheshire.

DOD OF CLOVERLEY.

DOD, JOHN-WHITEHALL, Esq. of Cloverley, co. Salop, M.P., b. 17 Sept. 1797; m. 1st, 18 Nov. 1822, Elizabeth, dau. of the Rev. George Allanson, and by her (who d. 22 April, 1837) has an only son,

WHITEHALL, b. 2 Sept. 1823, m. 24 Aug. 1852, Emma-Matilda, dau. of Lieut.-Gen. Sir Henry-M. Vavasour, Bart.

Mr. Dod m. 2ndly, 1 July, 1841, Anne-Caroline, dau. of the Venerable Archdeacon Wrangham.

Lineage.—This is a branch of DOD *of Edge*.

THOMAS DOD, of Edge, living in the time of EDWARD III., m. Mabel, dau. of David Mere, and had THOMAS, his heir; and JOHN. The younger son,

JOHN DOD, living temp. RICHARD II., m. Johanna, dau and heir of John Warren, of Ightfield, Salop, and was s. by his son,

HUGO DOD, who m. Agnes, dau. and co-heir of Roger de Cloverley. This Hugo was living in the 14th of HENRY IV., and was s. at his decease by his son,

WILLIAM DOD, of Cloverley or Calverhall, living in the 33rd of HENRY VI., father of

JOHN DOD, of Calverhall, who m. Matilda, dau. of Ludovico Eyton, of Eyton, in Shropshire, and was s. by his son,

JOHN DOD, Esq. of Calverhall, living in the 15th of HENRY VII., who m. 1st, Alicia, dau. of Robert Aston, Esq. of Tixhall, co. Stafford, and had an only son, JOHN, his successor. He m. 2ndly, Elizabeth Egerton, and by her had several daus. He was s. at his decease by his son,

JOHN DOD, Esq. of Calverhall, who m. Margaret, dau. of John Mainwaring, Esq. of Ightfield, and had issue, Richard, who d. s. p. in 1616; Robert, who m. Catherine, dau. of John Norwich, of Brampton, and had a son, CHARLES, inheritor after his grandfather; and Jane, wife of J.-Cotton Atkinson, Esq. of Shropshire. Mr. Dod d. in the 21st of ELIZABETH, and the representation of the family devolved eventually upon (the son of his 2nd son) his grandson,

CHARLES DOD, Esq. of Calverhall. This gentleman m. Catherine, dau. of Robert Lee, Esq. of Brinfield, Berks, and had a numerous family, of whom,

I. ROBERT, inherited the estates.
II. Charles, living in Ireland in 1687, m. Elizabeth, dau. of John King, Esq., son of John, bishop of Elphin, and had two sons and a dau., viz.,
 1 JAMES, who m. in Ireland, and left a son,
  JOHN DOD, of whom hereafter, as inheritor of the estates from his kinswoman, CATHERINE KERR.
 2 John, who also m. in Ireland, and left a son and dau., namely,
  Charles, of Kingsfort, co. Sligo, in holy orders, m. Helen, dau. of the Rev. Roger Ford, and had issue,
   John, who d. s. p.
   Oliver, in holy orders, whose sons, Charles, Thomas, and (Rev.) Isaac, d. unm., and whose other son, Captain Roger, m. and d. s. p.
   Roger, vicar of Drumlease, b. in 1732, m. 1st, Sarah King, s. p., and 2ndly, 28 March, 1792, Margaret,* dau. of Matthew Phibbs, Esq. of Spurtown, and had an only son,
    Charles-Roger, of London, b. 8 May, 1793, m. 20 Oct. 1814, Jane-Elizabeth, eldest dau. of John Baldwin, Esq. of Cork, and d. in 1855, leaving issue, Robert-Phipps, associate of King's College, London; and Margaret-Jane.
   Josiah, d. unm.
   Thomas, d. unm.
  Judith Dod, who m. her cousin, John Dod, the eventual representative of the family.
III. John, m. Elizabeth, dau. of Rodulph Allen, Esq. of the county of Chester, and d. in 1680.
IV. George, m. Margaret, dau. of Sir William Dugdale, Knt., Garter king-of-arms, the celebrated genealogist.
V. William, m. Elizabeth, dau. of J. Coppinger, Esq.
VI. Philip, m. Anna Bowen.

Charles Dod was s. at his decease, in 1658, by his eldest son,

ROBERT DOD, Esq. of Calverhall, who m. Lucy, dau. of Humphrey Frodsham, Esq., and relict of Thomas Greaves, Esq., and left surviving issue, CATHERINE, wife of the Hon. William Kerr; and Mary, of Admiral Sir David Mitchel. Mr. Dod d. in May, 1686, and was s. by his elder surviving dau.,

CATHERINE, wife of the Hon. William Kerr, at whose decease the family estates devolved upon her kinsman,

JOHN DOD, Esq. (grandson of Charles Dod, who settled in Ireland, and his wife Elizabeth King), who m. his cousin,

* This lady was sister to Doctor Phibbs, senior fellow of Trinity Coll., Dublin, aunt to William Holmes, formerly M.P. of Grafton Street, London, and cousin to the Right Hon. Isaac Barré.

Judeth, dau. of his uncle, John Dod, and had two sons, ROBERT, his heir; and John, who left issue by his wife, a dau. of Charles Sandford, Esq. Mr. Dod *d.* in 1776, and was *s.* by his elder son,

ROBERT DOD, Esq. of Cloverley, *b.* in 1724, *m.* Mary, dau. of Broughton Whitehall, Esq. of Broughton, in the co. of Flint, and had several children. He *d.* in 1801, and was *s.* by his elder son,

JOHN DOD, Esq. of Cloverley, *b.* in 1753, who *m.* 1st, in 1775, Anne, dau. of Thomas Pares, Esq. of Leicester, and had one dau. to survive, Mary-Anne, who *m.* Samuel Miles, Esq. of Narborough, in Leicestershire, and *d.* 6 April, 1846. He *m.* 2ndly, 22 Dec. 1791, Eleanor, dau. and co-heir of John Woodyeare, Esq. of Crookhill, co. York, and had by her (who *d.* 23 Sept. 1804) JOHN-WHITEHALL, M.P. now of Cloverley; Charles-Broughton, who *d.* in 1825; and Eleanor. Mr. Dod *d.* in 1805.

Arms—Arg., a fesse, gu. between two cotises, wavy, sa.
Crest—A serpent, vert, issuing from and piercing a garb, or.
Seat—Cloverley, Shropshire.

DODWELL OF GLENMORE.

DODWELL, JAMES-CROFTON, Esq. of Shankill House, co. Dublin, and Glenmore, co. Sligo, J.P., *b.* 6 Sept. 1804; *m.* 2 Sept. 1830, Jane-Isabella, dau. of J.-V. Fowler, Esq. of Shankill House, co. Dublin, by Jane his wife, dau. of Matthew Bussy, Esq. of Carn, and has issue,

I. ROGER, *b.* 20 Dec. 1831, *m.* 23 Dec. 1852, Letitia-C., dau. of Villiers-Bussy Fowler, Esq.

I. Jane-Bussy. II. Marianne.

III. Catherine-Crofton.

Lineage.—The Dodwell family settled at Tanragoe, co. Sligo, about the year 1590. GEORGE DODWELL, the first settler, *m.* the dau. of Col. Watson, of Knocknarea. His eldest son, George, and his kinsman, Watson, being drowned on a sea-party of pleasure, near Tanragoe, Col. Watson's estate was inherited by his kinsman, Col. Smith, and Dodwell's fell to his 2nd son, EDWARD, whose son, EDWARD, *m.* the dau. of Jones of Banada, and by her was father of ROGER; Edward;* Michael; and James. ROGER DODWELL, the eldest son, was *m.* to Elizabeth Ormsby, of Rathlee, co. Sligo, and had one son,

MATTHEW DODWELL, Esq. of Tanragoe, *b.* 1744, who *m.* 1770, Catherine, sister of Malby Crofton, Esq. of Longford House, co. Sligo, and *d.* in 1811, leaving a son,

ROGER DODWELL, Esq. of Rathdooney, *b.* 1773, who *m.* 26 June, 1796, Jane, dau. of Humphrey Thomson, Esq. of Rathdooney, by Mary Dodwell his wife, and *d.* 1826, leaving issue,

JAMES-CROFTON, now of Glenmore.
Humphrey, *d.* 1810. Roger, *d.* 1832.
Mary-Anne, *m.* to Ormsby Rutledge, Esq. of Greenwood Cottage, co. Sligo.
Catherine-Crofton.
Isabella-Thomson, *m.* to John-K. Thompson, Esq. of Andrewsna, co. Sligo.

Arms—Arg., two bars, per pale, az. and gu.; in chief, three pellets.
Crest—A demi-lion, arg., pellettée, armed and langued, az.
Seats—Shankill House, co. Dublin; Glenmore, co. Sligo.

DOHERTY, OR O'DOCHERTY, OF INISHOWEN.

Lineage.—The surname of O'Docharty, or Doherty, is derived from DOCHARTACH, Lord and Prince of Inishowen, co. Donegal, son and heir of MAONGAL, of Inishowen, and grandson of FIANAN, Lord of Inishowen, who was 3rd son of CEAN FAOLA, Prince of Tire Connell, now the county of Donegal, and 12th in lineal descent from Conal Gulban, 7th son of NIAL *the Great*, also called NIALL *of the Nine Hostages*. This Dochartach was direct ancestor of the O'Docherty's, chiefs of Inishowen, whose representative

SIR JOHN MOR O'DOCHERTY, of Inishowen, submitted to the English, and was knighted, 3 Dec. 1541, by Sir Arthur

* EDWARD DODWELL, of Chaffpool, the 2nd son of Edward, of Tanragoe, and Miss Jones, of Banada, *m.* Barbara Birne, of Cregg, co. Sligo, and was father of George (who was high-sheriff, and obtained the freedom of every port in the British dominions, for some plans he drew of Dublin and other harbours): he *d.* without issue. Their eldest dau. was *m.* to Humphrey Thompson, of Rathdooney, and their dau., Jane, was *m.* to Roger Dodwell, who was father to the present James-Crofton Dodwell.

St. Leger, lord-deputy. He *d.* in 1566, leaving, by Rose his wife, dau. of Manus O'Donnell, lord of Tirconnell, an eldest son and heir,

SIR JOHN OGE O'DOCHERTY, Knt., lord and chief of Inishowen, knighted in May, 1585, who *m.* Elizabeth, eldest dau. of Sir Owen MacToole MacSwing, Knt., and had issue,

Cahir (Sir), Knt., Lord of Inishowen, engaged in the civil strifes of the time, and eventually defeated and slain by the English, in 1610, having had no issue by his wife, the Hon. Mary, dau. of Christopher, 4th Lord Gormanston.
JOHN, of whose line we treat. Rorie.
Rose, *m.* 1st, to the Hon. Caffar O'Donnell, of Caffarconce, co. Donegal, nephew of the 1st Earl of Tyrconnell, and 2ndly, to Eugene O'Neill, general and commander-in-chief of the Irish army in 1641.
Margaret, *m.* to Hugh Oge O'Hanlon.

The 2nd son,

JOHN O'DOCHERTY, of Londonderry, *m.* in 1602, Elizabeth, eldest dau. of Patrick O'Cahane, Esq. of Londonderry, and had issue,

I. John, of Derry, who, by Rose his wife, had two daus. and co-heirs, viz., Rose, *m.* to Roger Lyndon, of Carrickfergus, co. Antrim; and Eleanor, *m.* to Sir William Brownlow, ancestor of Baron Lurgan.

II. Eugene, or Owen, *m.* Mary, 4th dau. of Shane O'Rourke, Esq. of Clonoorrick, co. Leitrim, and *d.* in 1643, and had issue,

1 Cahir, *d.* in 1714, aged 74, having had, by Bridget his wife, dau. of Miles O'Reilly, Esq. of Drum, co Cavan, besides a dau., Mary, and an elder son, Cahir, who *d. s. p.*, another son, Eugene, who *m.* Margaret, dau. of Henry O'Cassidy, Esq. of Louth, M.D., and was father of John O'Docherty, Esq. of Newtown, co. Leitrim, who *m.* Margaret, dau. of Richard O'Kelly, Esq. of co. Cavan, and *d.* in 1762, leaving two sons,
[illegible] of Baillieborough, co. Cavan, who *m.* Jane, 2nd
Owen, [illegible] James Browne, Esq. of Graignes, co. Kildare,
dau. of [illegible] his decease (his will was dated 6 Feb.
and left [illegible]roved 27 Nov. 1790) three sons, Henry;
1783, and p[illegible]nton-Dillon, whose line is extinct.
John; and C[illegible]ders, D.D., Catholic rector of Trim,
Henry, in holy o[illegible] appointed guardian to his nephews,
and vicar-general, [illegible]n into Spain in 1790.
and retired with the[illegible] *m.* Ellen, dau. of Terence

2 Eugene, of Inishowen[illegible]arrick, co. Donegal, and had
MacSwing, Esq. of Rindu[illegible] heir,
(with other issue) a son an[illegible]acdonnell his wife, was
EDMOND, who, by Rose M[illegible] Esq., *b.* in 1725, who *m.*
father of Anthony Doherty, [illegible]onderry, and sister of
Eleanor Macdonagh, of Lond[illegible] had a son, Edward,
Peter Macdonagh, Esq., and [illegible]e, was father of the
who, by Isabella Walker his wi[illegible]ity of Dublin, Q.C.,
late JAMES DOHERTY, Esq. of the [illegible]oyce, Esq. of co.
who *m.* Eliza, dau. of Edward J[illegible] when this branch
Galway, and *d. s. p.* in Dec. 1852, [illegible]
became extinct.

III. WILLIAM, of whom we treat.

The 3rd son, [illegible] *m.* Mary, 2nd
WILLIAM O'DOCHERTY, Esq. of Inishowen, [illegible] an only son
dau. of Hugh Oge O'Hanlon, and was father o[illegible]
and heir, [illegible]owen, who
JOHN O'DOCHERTY, Esq., sometime of Inish[illegible] Tipperary.
was the first to establish the family in the co. of [illegible]ew Place,
He *m.* Sidney, dau. of William Lathum, Esq. of N[illegible]e of the
co. Donegal, and sister of Barbara Lathum, wi[illegible] Cloyne,
Right Rev. Edward Synge, D.D., bishop of Cork, [illegible]orth of
and Ross, and *d.* in 1679, while on a visit to the [illegible]
Ireland, having had issue, [illegible]dral of
John, in holy orders, M.A., precentor of the cathe[illegible]proved
Cashel, *d. unm.*; his will, dated 5 May, 1714, was [illegible]
at Cashel 26 July, 1715. [illegible]hard-
Lathum, of Dublin, *m.* Maria, dau. of Archibald Ri[illegible]
son, Esq., and had a son, Richardson, who *d. unm.*
JAMES, of whose line we treat.
Dise-Synge. Sydney. Samue[illegible]
Bridget, *m.* to Michel Symes, Esq. of Wexford.
Barbara, *m.* to James Hawkins, Esq. of Dublin.
Anne, *m.* to — Wilson, Esq. [illegible]ber

John O'Docherty's widow dropt the O', and educated [illegible]he children in the principles of the Church of England. [illegible]
3rd son, [illegible]by
JAMES DOHERTY, Esq. of Oldtown, co. Tipperary, had [illegible]s,
Frances his wife, dau. of George Mathew, Esq. of Thurl[illegible]
co. Tipperary, ancestor of the Earls of Llandaff,

I. JAMES, of whom presently.

II. Nicholas, of Outrath, co. Tipperary, whose will wa[illegible] proved 12 Feb. 1765. He *m.* and had issue,

1 Edward, *d. s. p.*, *v. p.*

2 John, of Outrath, *m.* a dau. of James Murrough, Es[illegible] of Kilworth, co. Cork, and had three sons, viz., Edmun[illegible] of Outrath, and afterwards of Long Orchard, co. Ti[illegible]perary; John, of Outrath, and now of Cashel, capt.

the army, m. Miss Lynch, of Galway; and Nicholas, of Ballydruid, co. Tipperary, who m. Margaret, dau. of Robert Keatinge, Esq. of Ballydruid, and has issue,

Nicholas, of Lough Kent, co. Tipperary.
Robert, of Ballydruid.
Anne, m. 1st, to Denis-James O'Meagher, Esq. of Kilmoyler, co Tipperary, and 2ndly, to John Grogan, Esq. of Limerick.
Charlotte.
Maria, m. in 1838, to Christopher Shea, Esq of Cappoquin, co. Waterford, M.D.

3 Thomas, of Moortown, co. Tipperary, m. Mary, dau. of John Cullen, Esq. of Boulick, co. Tipperary, and had issue, William, of Lisbon, d. s. p.; Nicholas, capt. in the Austrian service, d. s. p.; two other sons, and three daus., Bridget; Alice, m. to John Lalor, Esq. of Long Orchard, co. Tipperary; and Margaret.

I. Bridget, m. to James Lalor, Esq. of Thurles.

The eldest son and heir,

James Doherty, Esq. of Kedragh, co. Tipperary, m. Honora, dau. of Theobald Butler, Esq. of Grange, and of Ballycarron, co. Tipperary, and had issue,

I. Richard, his heir. II. Charles, of Kedragh, d. s. p.
III. Edmund, of Mount Bruis, co. Tipperary, m. a dau. of Charles Magrath, Esq. of Limerick, and had issue,

1 Charles, of Killemley, co. Tipperary, lieut. 32nd regt., m. Catherine, dau. of Edward Quinlan, Esq. of Tipperary, but d. s. p.
1 Mary, m. to Henry Bowen, Esq. of Bowen's Court, co. Cork.
Three other daus.

The eldest son and heir,

Richard Doherty, Esq. of Suirbank, and sometime of Kedragh, m. Catherine, dau. of Leonard Keatinge, Esq. of Knockagh, co. Tipperary, and had issue,

James, of Kedragh, m. Rebecca, dau. of Richard Lockwood, Esq. of Indaville, Cashel, co. Tipperary, and d. in 1819, having had issue, James, d. s. p., v. p.; Richard, d. unm., v. p.; and Catherine, m. to Richard, son of Edward Waller, Esq. of Castle Waller, co. Limerick.
Richard, lieut.-col. 18th Royal Irish regt. of foot, m. in 1792, Dorothea, dau. of James Dennahy, Esq. of Cork, and had an only child, Caroline, who d. unm.
Leonard, of whom presently.
John, capt. 19th regt., lost at sea, unm.
Charles, an officer in the army, killed in action, in America, s. p.
Edward, lieut. in the army, d. s. p.
Margaret, m. 14 July, 1779, to William Carroll, Esq. of Cahir, co. Tipperary, M.D.
Mary, m. to James Butler, Esq. of Kilcommon.
Honora, and Catherine, } d. unm.

The 3rd son,

Leonard Doherty, Esq. of Coolmoyne, co. Tipperary, m. Anne, dau. of Roger Scully, Esq. of Cashel, and by her (who d. in June, 1836) had issue,

Richard (Sir), Knt., major-gen. in the army, late inspecting Field-officer of the London district, and superintendent of the recruiting department, and now commanding the troops on the Jamaica station, present representative of the family, m. 8 July, 1845, Rachel-Sophia, dau. of Jonathan-Anderson Ludford, Esq., M.D., of Warwick Park, Jamaica (of the ancient Warwickshire family of Ludford), and relict of Gilbert Munro, Esq. of the island of St. Vincent. Lady Doherty d. deeply lamented, in Feb. 1853.
Roger, d. young. Leonard, of Dublin, d. s. p. in 1827.
Theobald, capt. 40th regt., served in the Peninsular war, m. Margaret, dau. of William Carroll, Esq. of Cahir, M.D.
Charles, d. unm. in 1820.
Anne. Mary.

Mr. Doherty d. at Cashel in April, 1833.

Arms—Quarterly: 1st and 4th, arg., a stag at full speed, gu.; on a chief, vert, three mullets, of the first; 2nd and 3rd, arg., a chevron, engrailed, between three trefoils, vert.
Crests—1st, a greyhound, courant, holding in the mouth a coney, all ppr.; 2nd, a naked hand, couped at the wrist, holding a sword, ppr., hilt and pommel, or.

DOLLING OF MAGHERALIN.

Dolling, Robert-Holbeach, Esq. of Magheralin, co. Down, J.P., barrister-at-law, b. 13 Feb. 1809; m. 22 Jan. 1842, Eliza, 3rd dau. of the late Josias-Du Pré Alexander, Esq., M.P., nephew of James, Earl of Caledon, and has issue,

I. Robert-William-Rattcliffe, b. 10 Feb. 1851.
I. Mary-Emma-Rattcliffe. II. Elise-Ann-Rattcliffe.
III. Adelaide-Harriet-Rattcliffe.
IV. Geraldine-Bouverie-Rattcliffe.
V. Nina-Caroline-Rattcliffe.
VI. Josephine-Maud-Rattcliffe.
VII. Ulrica-Douglass-Rattcliffe.

Lineage.—This family is of ancient French extraction. About the year 1580, a younger son of the Count Dolling, of the village of Dolling, near Toulouse, having embraced Huguenot opinions, is stated to have fled to England, and settled in the Isle of Purbeck, where he was living in 1613. His descendant,

Robert Dolling, Esq., left the Isle of Purbeck, and established himself in London. By Mary his wife he had an only son,

James Dolling, Esq. of London, who m. Mary, only child and heiress of the Hon. J. Ratcliffe, of Stockport, co. Chester, and Hatton Garden, London, cousin-german of the ill-fated Earl of Derwentwater, and left, with one dau., Mary-Ratcliffe, an only son,

The Rev. Robert-Ratcliffe Dolling, rector of Tilsey, Surrey, vicar of Aldenham, Herts, and rector of Bolnhurst, Bedfordshire, J.P. for Herts, who m. Mary, dau. of Paul Saunders, Esq. (which lady m. 2ndly, in 1815, Sir R. Dundas, a Swedish nobleman), and had issue,

Boughey-William, late of Magheralin.
John, d. at Westminster College.
Robert, d. young.
James-Adams, capt. in the 58th foot, killed in Egypt, leaving by his wife, Frances, dau. of the Rev. Dr. Bond, a son, Robert-James, in holy orders.
Mary, m. to Thomas Tomkinson, Esq., and has issue.

The eldest son,

The Rev. Boughey-William Dolling, of Magheralin, co. Down, b. 3 June, 1782; m. 28 July, 1806, Mary, dau. of John Short, Esq., and had issue,

Robert-Holbeach, now of Magheralin.
Mary-Ratcliffe, m. to James-Thomas Bolton, Esq. of The Elms.
Emily-Jane-Saunders, m. to the Rev. Thomas Hassard, Montgomery.

The Rev. Mr. Dolling was formerly fellow of Exeter College, Oxford, and rector of Magheralin, and precentor of Dromore. He d. 18 Jan. 1853.

Seat—Edenmore, Magheralin, co. Down.

DOLPHIN OF TUROE.

Dolphin, Oliver, Esq. of Turoe, co. Galway, b. in 1805; m. 13 April, 1842, Mary, dau. of Andrew Browne, Esq. of Movilla, co. Galway, by his wife Mary, sister of Maurice Blake, Esq. of Ballinafad, co. Mayo, and has,

I. Andrew, b. in 1846.
II. Oliver, b. in 1850. III. Hubert-Peter, b. in 1853.
I. Mary. II. Monica. III. Henrietta.

Lineage.—A baron of this name, who accompanied William the Conqueror to England, got possession of the district on which Carlisle now stands. William the Conqueror, on his return from the invasion of Scotland, liking the situation, ordered his barons to fortify it, which was accordingly done. It appears that the succeeding monarch, William II., was so pleased with the situation, that he expelled Dolphin, then lord of the district (1092), peopled it with a colony from the south of England, and built a castle for their protection. One of the grandsons of the expelled Dolphin is stated to have gone to Ireland, and to have been amongst the first of the Anglo-Norman invaders who settled in Connaught; certain it is that by ancient records, and other authorities, we find that the Dolphins have continued to reside in the immediate vicinity of their present seat, Turoe, for nearly six hundred years. To Thomas Dolphin, the son of John of Goulbully (which adjoins Turoe), were granted the customs of Galway, by letters-patent from Edward II., bearing date 4th May, 1307. The Dolphin family suffered much, in 1466, by the war between Mac William Bourke FitzRickard, &c., and Clanricarde. It is stated in the annals of Ireland, that Mac William Bourke FitzRickard, and his allies, laid waste the country as far as Loughrea, and on their return, entered the parishes of the Dolphins, burning and destroying everything that came within their reach, particularly about Tulluban, which then belonged to the Dolphin family.

In 1585, Redmond Dolphin, of Rathreddy, as chief of his name, entered, with other chieftains of Connaught, into a composition with Sir John Perrot, on the part of Queen Elizabeth, for his property and that of other members of his family.

X

By an inquisition taken on the 16th September, 1617, it was found that the following members of the Dolphin family were seised in fee of their respective demesnes and other lands, viz.: Redmond Dolphin, of Bathreddy; James Dolphin, of Shanvallynamigardagh; William Reagh Dolphin, of Caherduff; Redmond Dolphin FitzPatrick, of Carinarged; Redmond-Oge Dolphin, of Bruckloonmore; William-Oge Dolphin, of Turoe, was seised in fee of Turoe and other lands; and Walter and Edmond were seised in fee of half cartrons, in Turoe. By letters-patent, dated at Dublin, 27th March, 1619, all the several lands above recited were granted to said several proprietors and to their heirs, to hold the same, as of his Majesty's castle of Athlone, by knight's service.

During the Civil Wars, the Dolphins, in common with most of the Roman Catholic families in Connaught, sustained great losses by confiscations and forfeitures, which caused many members of the family to emigrate; however,

HUBERT DOLPHIN, living at Goulbully in 1691, preferred remaining in his native country, in the hope of preserving some of their property; he *m.* 1st, Sarah-M. Burke, of Derryhoyle, by whom he had,

JOHN, his heir.
Thomas, a clergyman at Esker convent.
Celia, *m.* to — McHugo, of Ballybrodough.

Mr. Hubert Dolphin *m.* 2ndly, Miss Deane, by whom he had,

Dominick, *m.* Miss Daly, of Benmore.
Alban, who *m.* and left a family.

The elder son and successor,

JOHN DOLPHIN, Esq. of Goulbully and Turoe, *m.* Mary Geoghegan, of Westmeath, and had issue,

HUBERT, his heir. Henry.
John, a clergyman at Esker.
Sarah, *m.* to M. Lennon.
Helen, *m.* to Rickard Burke, of Arranvilla.

The eldest son,

HUBERT DOLPHIN, Esq., *m.* Helen, dau. of Martin of Raheen, of the Tullira family, and had issue,

I. JOHN, his heir.
II. Oliver, of Loughrea, *m.* in 1770, Margaret-Helen, dau. of Lewis Collin, of Dublin, and *d.* in 1805, leaving four sons,
 1 HUBERT-THOMAS, his heir, of whom hereafter, as successor to his uncle.
 2 Anthony, *d. unm.*
 3 Paul, of Loughrea, *m.* Miss Burke, of Spring Garden.
 4 Henry, of Loughrea, *m.* 1st, a dau. of Pierce Blake, Esq. of Holly Park, co. Galway, and 2ndly, Miss Skerett, of the Ballinduff family; by the former he had issue, Pierce, his heir; Anthony; and Anne.
III. Henry, *d. unm.*
IV. Thomas, who entered the Spanish service, and *m.* a Mexican lady.
I. Margaret, *m.* to Dominick Burke, Esq. of Killymor Castle.

The eldest son,

JOHN DOLPHIN, Esq. of Turoe, *m.* Eleanor, dau. of John Burke, of St. Clerans, and had daughters only,

Jane, a nun in the convent of Loughrea.
Margaret, *m.* in 1790, to John Browne, Esq. of Moyne, and was mother of the present Michael-J. Browne, Esq. of Moyne; Anne Browne; and the late Lady ffrench.
Anne, a nun in the convent of Loughrea.
Celia, *m.* to John McDonnell, of Carnacon, and was mother of the late Joseph McDonnell; the present Mrs. Cheevers, of Killyan; and Mrs. O'Connor, of Miltown.
Eleanor, *m.* to the late Thomas Redington, of Ryehill, and was mother of the present Mrs. Roche, of Ryehill; Mrs. Bodkin, of Annagh; Miss Redington, a nun in Loughrea; and the late Mrs. Balfe, of South Park.
Sally, *m.* to Michael Balfe, Esq. of South Park, and had an only child, the wife of J.-J. Murphy, Esq., a Master in Chancery.
Elizabeth, *m.* to Edmond Balfe, of Marlborough-street; mother of the present Nicholas Balfe, Esq.; Mrs. Netterville; and the late Mrs. Veitch.

Mr. John Dolphin dying without male issue, was *s.* by his nephew,

HUBERT-THOMAS DOLPHIN, Esq. of Turoe. He *m.* in 1804, Mary, dau. of Peter Grehan, Esq. of Dublin, by his wife Mary, dau. of Stephen Roche, Esq. of Limerick and of Granagh Castle, co. Kilkenny, and had,

OLIVER, his heir and present proprietor.
Peter-Hubert, who *m.* in 1852, Antoinette, dau. of Peter McEvoy, Esq. of Great Cumberland Place, and Wimbledon, Surrey.
Margaret, *m.* to James Daly, Esq. of Castle Daly, in the county Galway, a magistrate for that county, for which he was high-sheriff in 1853.
Annastasia and Lucy, both nuns in the Carmelite convent of Loughrea.
Anne, *m.* to Peter Daly, Esq. of Daly's Grove, in the county Galway, a magistrate for that county, and brother to James Daly, of Castle Daly, Esq.
Helen, a nun in Westport. Lucy, a nun. Monica.

Mr. Dolphin *d.* in 1829.

Arms—Az., three dolphins, naiant, ppr.
Crest—A dolphin, salient, ppr.
Motto—Firmum in vita nihil.
Seat—Turoe, Loughrea, co. Galway.

DOLPHIN OF CORR.

DOLPHIN, EMILY-FRANCES-HESTER, of Corr, co. Galway, *s.* at the decease of her father, May, 1854.

Lineage.—This is another line of the Dolphin family, claiming to be the chief.

REDMOND DOLPHIN, brother of William Dolphin, of Turoe, co. Galway, was father of

REDMOND OGE, of Bruckloonmore, who was confirmed in the possession of his property by patents from JAMES I., 27 March, 1619. His property was confiscated. Redmond's grandson,

REDMOND DOLPHIN, of Creggan (the old name of Corr), living there in 1691 and subsequently, was father of

REDMOND DOLPHIN, of Corr, who was *s.* by his eldest son,

REDMOND DOLPHIN, of Corr, J.P., who filled the office of high-sheriff in 1783: he *m.* Miss French, of Rahmore, and had issue,

I. REDMOND, his heir.
II. Henry, lieut.-col. of the 6th West India regt., *m.* and had issue,
 1 Henry, *d.* at about 21 years of age.
 1 Charlotte, *m.* the Rev. Samuel Medlicott, rector of Loughrea, co. Galway, and has issue several children.
 2 Eliza, *m.* to the Rev. Thomas Kearns.
 3 Anna, *d.* young. 4 Jane.
III. John, *d. unm.*
IV. Thomas, an officer, *d.* of his wounds in the West Indies.
I. Jane, *m.* to Mr. Kelly, of Lisduff.
II. Ellen, *d. unm.*
III. Mary, *m.* to Mr. Banfield.
IV. Fanny, *m.* to — Magee, a lieut. in 6th West India regt.

The eldest son,

REDMOND DOLPHIN, Esq. of Corr, J.P., capt. in the Galway militia, *m.* Dec. 1778, Mabel, dau. of Anthony Donelan, of Hillswood, co. Galway. Captain Dolphin *d.* 8 Feb. 1813, having had issue,

I. REDMOND, his heir.
II. John, *d. unm.*
III. Gregory, a lieut. in the 74th regt., was with that distinguished corps through the Peninsular war: he *d. unm.* at Portumna, 16 June, 1833.
I. Clarinda, *m.* 27 July, 1820, Peter Burke, Esq. of Elm Hall, co. Tipperary, a magistrate for that and the King's County.
II. Jane, *m.* John Monahan, Esq. of Portumna, uncle to the Right Hon. James-Henry Monahan, chief-justice of the Common Pleas in Ireland, and had issue.

The eldest son,

REDMOND DOLPHIN, Esq. of Corr, capt. in the Galway militia, *m.* Elizabeth, dau. of — Conolly, Esq. of Shannon Hill, co. Galway, and left at his decease surviving issue, a dau., Elizabeth, *d.* in 1838, and a son,

REDMOND-PATRICK DOLPHIN, Esq. of Corr, J.P., capt. in the Galway militia, who *m.* Frances, dau. of Francis-Blake Foster, Esq. of Ashfield, co. Galway, by Rose his wife, dau. of Thomas, 2nd Lord ffrench, and left at his decease, May, 1854, an only child and heiress, EMILY-FRANCES-HESTER, now of Corr.

Arms, &c.—See DOLPHIN *of Turoe.*
Seat—Corr, co. Galway.

DOMVILLE OF LYMME HALL.

TAYLOR-DOMVILLE, MASCIE-DOMVILLE, Esq. of Lymme Hall, and Moss Hall, co. Chester, *b.* 13 July, 1815; lately an officer in the 68th light infantry.

Lineage.—HENRY TAYLOR, Esq., mayor of Liverpool in 1720, *m.* Anne, dau. (by Ursula his wife, dau. and coheiress of William Domville,* Esq. of Lymme Hall) of Wil-

* Two branches of the family of Domville were settled in Cheshire, the elder at Oxton, from the Conquest to the time of its termination in females, who carried the estate, through the families of Troutbeck and Hulse, into that of the Earls of Shrewsbury. The younger branch of the Domvilles was that of Lymme Hall.

liam Massey, or Mascie, Esq., 7th son of Richard Massey, or Mascie, Esq. of Sele, and Barbara his wife, dau. of Robert, 2nd son of J. Gleave, Esq. of High Legh, and grandson of James Massey, Esq. of Sele (who d. in 1649), by Mary his wife, dau. of Sir George Leycester, Knt., of Toft. By this lady Henry Taylor had two sons,

William, who m. Mrs. Hicks, and had a son, Mascie, of Lymme Hall, who m. Ann Mainwaring, of Bromborough, and d. s. p.
ROBERT, of whom we treat.

The latter,

ROBERT TAYLOR, Esq. of Chester, m. Ann Tagg, and was father of

THOMAS TAYLOR, Esq. of Lymme Hall, who m. Mary, dau. of Samuel Jackson, Esq. of Ash, Salop, and d. 27 Jan. 1814, aged 70, having had issue,

Robert, m. Jane Foulkes, of Mertyn, and had a dau., Elizabeth, m. to George Johnson, Esq.
MASCIE-DOMVILLE, of whom presently.
Mary, m. to Sir Andrew Corbett, Bart. of Acton Reynold, co. Salop.
Elizabeth, m. to the Rev. William Molyneux, M.A., of Hawkley Hall.

The younger son,

THE REV. MASCIE-DOMVILLE TAYLOR, m. 1st, Diana, dau. of John Houghton, Esq. of Wavertree, co. Lancaster, and by her (who d. 16 Aug. 1824) had issue,

MASCIE-DOMVILLE, present head of the family.
Thomas-John Domville, b. 10 April, 1817.
Robert-Mascie, late an officer in the 28th regt., b. 12 Oct. 1818, m. and has issue.
Diana-Anne, m. to the Rev. Philip Wynter, D.D., principal of St. John's College, Oxford.

Mr. Taylor m. 2ndly, Patty-Jemima, dau. of John Foulkes, Esq. of Eryviatt, co. Denbigh, and by her had a son,

Henry-John, b. 10 April, 1827.

Mr. Taylor d. 9 Oct. 1845.

Arms—Az., a saltier, voided, between four stag's heads, caboshed, or.
Crest—A buck's head, caboshed, ppr.
Seat—Lymme Hall, Cheshire.

DONELAN OF HILLSWOOD.

DONELAN, EDMOND-HYACINTH, Esq. of Hillswood, co. Galway, b. 14 Dec. 1804; m. 18 Feb. 1841, Maria-Theresa, only dau. of Denis Clarke, Esq. of Larch Hill, co. Galway.

Lineage.—This family, one of the most ancient in Ireland, derives from CAHAL (Charles), 2nd son of Morough Molathan, a celebrated prince of the House of Heremon, and King of Connaught, whose eldest son, Enragh, was progenitor of the O'CONORS-DON, which Cahal, at his father's death, in 701, had very large possessions in the counties of Roscommon and Galway, and was father of Arilgeal, King of Connaught, a descendant of whom, about 936, built a castle at Ballydonelan, called The Black Castle, part of which still remains. It was destroyed by fire, according to tradition, in the beginning of the 15th century, and in 1412, another castle was erected near the ruins by TULLY O'DONELAN, as appears by an inscription in the building. Lineally descended from this Tully was,

JOHN O'DONELAN, of Ballydonelan, son of Col. Melaghlin O'Donelan, wounded at the battle of Aughrim, and 5th in descent from Nehemias O'Donelan, styled Archbishop of Tuam, though never in holy orders. He m. Mary, dau. of Charles Daly, Esq. of Calla, and niece of the Right Hon. Denis Daly, of Dunsandle, a judge in the reigns of JAMES II. and WILLIAM III., by whom he had a numerous family, of whom only four sons and four daus. survived him at his decease, 10 Dec. 1748, viz.,

I. Malachy, of Ballydonelan, m. Mary, only child of Thomas-Power Daly, Esq. of Dunsandle, and, with two daus. (viz., Mable, m. to William Burke, Esq. of Ballydugan; and Anne, m. to Col. Denis Daly, of Raford, nephew to the Earl of Clanricarde), had one son,

JOHN DONELAN, of Ballydonelan, who m. Mable, eldest dau. of Matthew Hore, Esq of Shandon. and of Aghrahane, co. Galway, and left at his decease, in 1772,

MALACHY, his heir.
Matthew, who m. Maria, dau. of John Fallon, Esq. of Cloona, and was father of Malachy, who m. his cousin, Charlotte, dau. of Malachy Donelan, Esq. of Ballydonelan, and has issue.
Frances, m. 18 Dec. 1785, to Arthur-James, 8th Earl of Fingall.

The elder son,

MALACHY DONELAN, of Ballydonelan, m. Frances, eldest dau. of Sir Patrick Bellew, Bart. of Barmeath, and d. in Feb. 1830, leaving issue, viz.,

ARTHUR.
Mable, m. in 1811, to Anthony-Strong Hussey, Esq. of Westown, co. Dublin, and since deceased.
Maria. Frances.
Anne, m. to Lloyd-H. O'Reilly, of Lodge, co. Westmeath.
Charlotte, m. to her cousin, Malachy Donelan, son of Mathew Donelan, Esq., and since deceased.

II. Anthony, of Calla.
III. EDMOND, of Hillswood. IV. Charles.
I. Mable, wife of James French, Esq. of Duras.
II. Frances, wife of Oliver Martyn, Esq. of Tullyra.
III. Mary, a nun. IV. Anne, d. unm.

The 3rd son,

EDMOND DONELAN, Esq. of Hillswood, m. Margaret, dau. of James Hosier, Esq. of Holliwell, co. Galway, and was father of

HAYCINTH-EDWARD DONELAN, Esq. of Hillswood, who left by his wife, Honoria, dau. of James Meakle, Esq. of Currendoe, a son, the present EDMOND-HAYCINTH DONELAN, Esq., and two daus., Margaret, m. to Richard Golding, Esq. of Shrule, co. Mayo; and Belinda, a nun of the Presentation Convent, Galway.

Arms—Arg., a tree, thereto a slave tied, ppr.
Crest—A lion, rampant.
Motto—Omni violentia major.
Seat—Ballydonelan.

DONELAN OF SYLANE AND ST. PETER'S WELL.

DONELAN, THOMAS-O'CONOR, Esq. of Sylane, co. Galway, J.P., b. 12 Dec. 1812; m. 27 Oct. 1851, Elizabeth, eldest dau. of Joseph Burke, Esq. of Ower, co. Galway, and has issue,

DERMOT-O'CONOR, b. 6 March, 1853.

Lineage.—SIR JAMES DONELAN, lord-chief-justice of the Common Pleas in Ireland, 2nd son of Nehemiah O'Donelan, of Ballydonelan, by his wife, Elizabeth O'Donel, grand-dau. of O'Donel, Earl of Tyrconnel, d. in 1640, seised of St. Peter's Well, and several other denominations of the Donelan property, which had been given to him by his father. He m. the dau. of Browne of Coolarn, and had a son,

LOUGHLIN DONELAN, of St. Peter's Well, m. Mary, dau. of Walter Browne, Esq. of Galway. To this gentleman the above lands were regranted by CHARLES II. He d. in 1670, and was s. by his son,

NEHEMIAH DONELAN, of St. Peter's Well and Galway. Mr. Donelan, together with Sir Henry Belasyse, was in 1692 elected to represent in parliament the town of Galway, of which he was Recorder. He d. in 1699, leaving, by his wife, Margaret, dau. of Arthur French, Esq. of Tyrone, formerly mayor of Galway, together with two daus., a son,

NEHEMIAH DONELAN, of St. Peter's Well. This gentleman m. Sarah, 2nd dau. of Walter Taylor, Esq. of Castletaylor (ancestor of the late Gen. Sir John Taylor, of Castletaylor), by whom he left at his decease, in 1731 (with a dau., Sarah, who d. unm.), one son,

NEHEMIAH DONELAN, of St. Peter's Well, who, by his wife Marcia (dau. of Croadail Shawe, of Galway, Esq., and grand-dau. of Col. Shawe, who at the battle of Aughrim commanded the Enniskilling dragoons, under the banner of King WILLIAM III.), left issue at his death, in 1771, NEHEMIAH, his heir; John, d. s. p. in the East Indies; THOMAS, of whom presently; Robert, d. s. p.; and Rebecca, m. to Thomas Kirwan, Esq. of Blindwell.

THOMAS DONELAN, 3rd son of Nehemiah Donelan, m. in 1771, Mabel, dau. and heiress of Dermot O'Conor, Esq. of Sylane, descended from Loughlin O'Conor, a 2nd son of the ancient Irish chieftain O'Conor Sligo, by his wife, Mabel, 2nd dau. of Edward O'Flynn, Esq. of Furlough. Thomas d. in 1816, leaving, by his wife aforesaid, issue,

Nehemiah, d. s. p.
DERMOT, of whom presently. Edmond, d. s. p.
Marcia, m. 1st, John Joyce, of Oxford, co. Mayo, Esq.; 2ndly, Richard Rawson, Esq. of Baltinglass, and Kildare-street, Dublin.
Belinda, a nun.
Alice, m. Miles Burke, Esq., M.D., of the Ower family.
Margaret, m. her cousin, John Donelan, lieut. 66th regt.

DERMOT DONELAN, Esq. of Sylane, s. his father. This gentleman, on the death of his cousin, Nehemiah Donelan, of St. Peter's Well, in 1840, *s.* to the estate, and became representative of this branch of the ancient Irish family of the O'DONELANS, of which the O'DONELANS *of Ballydonelan* are the main stem. He *d.* 11 April, 1852, leaving, by his wife Maria, 2nd dau. of William Keary, Esq. of Clough, and sister of the Rev. William Keary, vicar of Mornington, formerly captain 5th dragoon-guards, two sons and two daus.,

THOMAS-O'CONOR, now of Sylane.
William-Edmond, M.D.
Elizabeth. Belinda.

Seat—Sylane, near Tuam, co. Galway.
Arms, Crest, Motto—Same as DONELAN *of Ballydonelan.*

DONELAN OF KILLAGH.

DONELAN, STEPHEN-JOSEPH, Esq. of Killagh, co. Galway, J.P., *b.* 8 March, 1789; *m.* 1 Dec. 1826, Evelina, 5th dau. of Robert French, Esq. of Monivea Castle, and has issue,

I. STEPHEN-JOSEPH, *b.* in April, 1830.
II. Joseph-Arthur, *b.* in 1833. III. Robert, *b.* in 1834.
IV. Richard, *b.* in 1837. V. Charles, *b.* in 1839.
I. Eliza-Ellis. II. Louisa.
III. Evelina. IV. Mary-Ellis.

Lineage.—WILLIAM DONELAN, Esq. of Killagh, co. Galway, descended from the DONELANS *of Ballydonelan*, *m.* Mary, dau. of Dominick Daly, Esq. of Benmore, and was father of

STEPHEN DONELAN, Esq. of Killagh, who *m.* Elizabeth, only dau. of Hugh Kelly, Esq. of Ballyforan, and *d.* in 1794, aged 80, leaving an only son,

JOSEPH DONELAN, Esq., who *m.* 1780, Ellis, dau. of Charles Lambert, Esq. of Creggclare, by Margaret his wife, dau. of Dominick Browne, Esq. of Castle McGarrett, and aunt of the present Lord Oranmore; and by her, who *d.* in Aug. 1823, had issue,

STEPHEN-JOSEPH, now of Killagh.
Eliza, *m.* in 1803, to Sir Valentine Blake, Bart. of Menlough, and *d.* 8 May, 1835.
Elly.

Arms, Crest, and *Motto*—Same as DONELAN *of Hillswood.*
Seat—Killagh, Kilconnell.

DONOVAN OF BALLYMORE.

DONOVAN, RICHARD, Esq. of Ballymore, co. Wexford, J.P., *b.* 17 Oct. 1819.

Lineage.—RICKARD DONOVAN, Esq. of Clonmore, co. Wexford, the first certain ancestor of this line, *m.* 1st, Bridget, sister of Thomas Kieran, of Dublin, and had (with three daus., the eldest *m.* to Gough of Ballyorel; the 2nd to King; and the 3rd, Elizabeth, to the Rev. Michael Mosse) four sons, viz.,

I. MORTAGH, his heir.
II. Cornelius, of Clonmore, who *m.* 1st, Bridget, dau. of Abraham Hughes, Esq. of Ballytrent, co. Wexford, and had issue,
 1 Abraham, a physician in Enniscorthy, *d. s. p.*
 2 Rickard, of Clonmore, who *m.* Winifred, dau. of Henry Milward, Esq. of Ballyharron, co. Wexford, and had issue five daus., Eliza, *m.* to Cadwallader Edwards, Esq. of Ballyhire, co. Wexford; Sarah, *m.* to John Cox, Esq. of Coolcliffe, co. Wexford; Winifred, *m.* to the Rev. Joseph Miller, of New Ross, as his 2nd wife; Lucy, *m.* to John Glascott, Esq. of Alderton, co. Wexford; and Julia, *m.* to Richard-Newton King, Esq. of Mackmine, co. Wexford.
 Cornelius Donovan *m.* 2ndly, Mary, dau. of John Harvey, Esq. of Killiane Castle, same county, and had issue,
 1 John. 2 Cornelius.
 1 Elizabeth.
 2 Juliana, *m.* to Cornelius Fitzpatrick, ensign in the Wexford militia.
III. Rickard, *m.* Miss Nixon, and had issue, 1 George; 2 Cornelius, a capt. in the dragoons. He resided at Camolin Park, and left a dau., Mary, *m.* to Robert Blayney, of Camolin; 3 Richard; 4 Rickard; 5 Denn-Nixon; and 1 Juliana, *m.* 1st, 15 Sept. 1741, to Richard, 6th Earl of Anglesey; 2ndly, to Matthew Talbot, Esq. of Castle Talbot, co. Wexford.
IV. Thomas, *m.*, and left issue a son, Mortagh.
V. Richard.

Rickard Donovan *m.* 2ndly, Julian Carew, by whom it does not appear there was issue. His eldest son,

MORTAGH DONOVAN, Esq. of Ballymore, *m.* in 1696, Lucy Archer, and had two sons, Richard and Henry. He *m.* 2ndly, 1704, Anna, 3rd dau. of Robert Carew, Esq. of Castletown, co. Waterford, and had issue two sons, Robert being one of them; and three daus., of whom Catherine *m.* Rev. S. Hayden, rector of Ferns, killed by the rebels at Enniscorthy, in 1798. Mr. Donovan *d.* in 1712, and was *s.* by his eldest son,

RICHARD DONOVAN, Esq. of Ballymore, *b.* 20 May, 1697, who *m.* Elizabeth, dau. of Edward Rogers, Esq. of Bessmount, co. Wexford, and had issue,

EDWARD, his heir.
Lucy, *m.* to Gilfred Lawson, eldest son of Sir Wilfred Lawson, Bart. of Brayton House, Cumberland, who *d.* before his father.
Mary, *d. unm.*, will proved 1805.
Frances, *m.* to Charles Hill, Esq. of St. John's, co. Wexford.
Henrietta, *d. unm.*, will proved 1795.

Richard Donovan's only son,

EDWARD DONOVAN, Esq. of Ballymore, barrister-at-law, who *m.* 1747, Mary, dau. of Capt. John Broughton, of Maidstone, co. Kent, and had issue,

RICHARD, his heir.
Robert, of Dublin, *d. unm.*, 1828.
George, went to America, *m.* Miss Devereux, of Wexford, and had issue.
John, attorney-gen. for Sierra Leone, *d. unm.* in 1817.
William, of Dublin, lieut. R.N., *d. unm.* in 1814.
Edward, in holy orders, of Ballymore, co. Westmeath, *d. unm.* in 1827.
Mary, of Dublin, *d. unm.* 1824.
Eliza, *d. unm.* Feb. 1831.
Julia, *m.* to Robert Verner, Esq. of Dublin, and dying March, 1840, had issue.
Lucy, *m.* to James Barker, Esq. of Dublin.
Caroline, *d. unm.*

Edward Donovan *d.* 16 April, 1773, and was *s.* by his eldest son,

RICHARD DONOVAN, Esq. of Ballymore, J.P., who *m.* 28 June, 1780, Anne, dau. of Goddard Richards, Esq. of The Grange, co. Wexford, and had issue,

I. RICHARD, his heir, now of Ballymore.
II. Goddard-Edward, capt. 83rd regt., *d. unm.* at the Cape of Good Hope, in 1803.
III. Robert, *m.* Mary, dau. of Major Joseph Taylor, H.E.I.C., and had issue,
 1 Richard-Edward. 2 Robert.
 3 Henry. 4 Edwin. 5 Albert-William.
 1 Harrietta-Ann, *m.* in 1837, to James M'Kenny, Esq., Dublin, and *d.* 1852.
 2 Laura. 3 Mary-Medora.
IV. John, *d. unm.* in 1829.
V. George, *d.* July, 1848.
VI. William, of Enniscorthy, *m.* Elizabeth, dau. of Capt. John Dallas, of Portarlington. She *d.* leaving issue,
 William-John.
VII. Henry, lieut. R.N., *d. unm.* in 1824.
VIII. Solomon, in holy orders, *m.* 18 Sept. 1848, Katherine-Sophia, dau. of Thomas-Stratford Dennis, Esq. of Fort Granite.
XI. Arthur, *d.* young.
I. Anne, *m.* to Solomon Speer, Esq. of Granitefield, co. Tyrone, barrister-at-law, and has issue,
II. Catharine, *d. unm.* 24 Jan. 1837.
III. Mary, *m.* to John Glascott, Esq. of Killowen, co. Wexford, barrister-at-law, and has issue.
IV. Eliza, *m.* to William-Russell Farmar, Esq. of Bloomfield, co. Wexford, and has issue.
V. Sarah-Caroline.

Richard Donovan *d.* 9 Jan. 1816, and was *s.* by his eldest son,

RICHARD DONOVAN, Esq. of Ballymore, *b.* 21 April, 1781, high-sheriff for co. Wexford, 1819, who *m.* 18 Oct. 1816, Frances, eldest dau. of Edward Westby, Esq. of High Park, co. Wicklow, and by her (who *d.* 29 March, 1853) had issue,

RICHARD, now of Ballymore.
Edward-Westby, *b.* 6 Sept. 1821, capt. 33rd regt.
Henry-George, *b.* 2 Feb. 1826.
Robert, *b.* 5 April, 1829.
Phœbe. Frances. Anne, *d.* 1847.

Arms—Arg., issuing from the sinister side of the shield, a cubit dexter arm, vested, gu., cuffed, az., the hand, ppr., grasping an old Irish sword, the blade entwined with a serpent, ppr.
Crest—A falcon alighting.
Mottoes—"Adjuvante Deo in hostes;" also, "Vir super hostes:"—Irish, "Gilloa eirh a nauidh a boo."
Seat—Ballymore, near Camolin, co. Wexford.

DONOVAN OF FRAMFIELD PLACE.

DONOVAN, ALEXANDER, Esq. of Framfield Place, Sussex, *b.* in June, 1819; *m.* 13 April, 1847, Ellen Poulett, dau. of John-Poulett Thompson, Esq. of Roehampton, and has issue, Geraldine, and Ada.

Lineage.—JAMES DONOVAN, Esq. of Chillowes Park, Surrey, claiming descent from Captain Donovan, an officer in the army of CROMWELL, in Ireland, said to have been Milesian, *m.* in 1772, Miss Margaret Moore, of Dublin, and had issue,

ALEXANDER.
James, of Buckram Hill, Sussex, who *m.* Miss Thompson, eldest dau. of George Thompson, Esq. of Dublin, and had a son, James Thompson, who *m.* 14 Dec. 1852, Anne, dau. of George Braddell, Esq. of Prospect.
Mary, *m.* to George Braddell, Esq. of Prospect, co. Wexford.

Mr. Donovan *d.* in 1831, and was *s.* by his eldest son,

ALEXANDER DONOVAN, Esq. of Framfield Place, *b.* 25 Oct. 1778, who served the office of sheriff for Sussex in 1832, *m.* 1st, Miss Anne Foster, and has issue,

HENRY.
Anne, *m.* to T. Braddell, Esq. of Prospect, co. Wexford.
Louisa, *m.* to R. Stone, Esq. of Gale House, Sussex.

He *m.* 2ndly, Eliza, dau. of Charles Mellish, Esq. of Blythe, in Nottinghamshire, and 3rdly, in May, 1817, Caroline, 2nd dau. of Joshua, 1st Lord Huntingfield. By the last lady (who *d.* in June, 1836) he has

ALEXANDER, now of Framfield Place.
Caroline, *m.* 16 Aug. 1838, to George Hankey, Esq. of Beckenham, Kent.
Maria, *m.* to Revel Braddell, Esq. of Raheengraney, co. Carlow.

Mr. Donovan *d.* 4 Sept. 1846.

Arms—Arg., an arm lying fessewise, couped at the elbow, and holding a sword erect, entwined round the blade a serpent, all ppr.
Crest—A hawk, wings displayed, ppr.
Motto—Adjuvante Deo in hostes.
Seats—Framfield Park, Sussex; and Chillowes Park, Surrey.

DORMER OF ROUSHAM.

COTTRELL-DORMER, CHARLES, Esq. of Rousham Hall, co. Oxford, *b.* in 1801; *m.* in 1826, Frances-Elizabeth, eldest dau. of William Strickland, Esq., and has issue.

Lineage.—SIR CLEMENT COTTERELL, *b.* at Wylsford, in the co. of Lincoln, in 1585, was for twenty years groom-porter to King JAMES I. His son,

SIR CHARLES COTTERELL, *b.* in 1615, the translator of *Cassandra*, the famed romance, was also principally concerned in the translation of *Davila's History of the Civil Wars*, from the Italian, and several pieces of note in the Spanish language. In 1641, he succeeded Sir John Finet as Master of the Ceremonies, and during the Interregnum was steward to the Queen of Bohemia. At the Restoration he returned to England; in 1661, was elected M.P. for Cardigan; in 1663, sent ambassador to the court of Brussels; and in 1670, made Master of the Requests. Sir Charles *m.* the dau. of Edward West, Esq. of Marsworth, Bucks, and had two sons and three daus. The 2nd son,

SIR CHARLES-LUDOWICKE COTTRELL, Knt., *s.* his father in 1686, as Master of the Ceremonies. He *m.* 1st, Eliza, dau. and co-heir of Nicholas Burwell, Esq. of Gray's Inn, and had by her, with other issue, who *d.* young, a son, CLEMENT (Sir), Knt., his heir. Sir Charles *m.* 2ndly, Elizabeth, only dau. of Chaloner Chute, Esq., and had by her three sons, JOHN, ancestor of COTTRELL *of Hadley* (*which see*); Stephen, LL.D., father of Sir Stephen Cottrell, Master of the Ceremonies, who *d. s. p.*; and William, D.D., Bishop of Leighlin and Ferns, who *d. unm.* in 1744. The eldest son,

SIR CLEMENT COTTRELL, Knt., Master of the Ceremonies, assumed, upon the demise of his cousin, General Dormer (son of his aunt, Anne Cottrell), the additional surname of DORMER. He *d.* in 1758, leaving, by his wife, the only dau. and heiress of — Sherburne, Esq. (with five daus., of whom Elizabeth *m.* in 1748, William Cartwright, Esq. of Aynhoe), two sons, CHARLES, his heir; and Robert, capt. of Marines, lost on board the "Victory," in 1774. The elder son,

SIR CHARLES COTTRELL-DORMER, Knt. of Rousham, Master of the Ceremonies, *m.* Jane, dau. and co-heir of Charles-Adelmare Cæsar, Esq., and dying in 1779, left by her, who *m.* 2ndly, Lieut.-General the Hon. George Parker, a son and successor,

SIR CLEMENT COTTRELL-DORMER, Knt. of Rousham, Master of the Ceremonies, who *m.* 1st, in 1783, Miss Heylin, and had by her two daus., Jane, *m.* in 1821, to Finch Mason, Esq.; and Elizabeth. Sir Clement Dormer *m.* 2ndly, Miss Robinson, and dying in 1808, left by her a son and successor, the present CHARLES COTTRELL-DORMER, Esq. of Rousham.

Arms—DORMER and COTTRELL, quarterly.
Crests—1st, DORMER; 2nd, COTTRELL.
Seat—Rousham, co. Oxford.

DORRIEN OF HARESFOOT.

SMITH-DORRIEN, ROBERT-ALGERNON, Esq. of Haresfoot, co. Herts, late capt. 16th Lancers, *b.* 2 Oct. 1814; *m.* 26 March, 1845, Mary-Anne, dau. of the late Thomas Driver, Esq., M.D., by Mary his wife, 2nd dau. of the late Thomas Dorrien, Esq. of Haresfoot, and has issue,

I. THOMAS-ALGERNON, *b.* 7 Feb. 1846.
II. Henry-Theophilus, *b.* 8 May, 1850.
III. Walter-Montgomery, *b.* 13 June, 1851.
I. Frances-Ann-Isabella.
II. Marian. III. Amy. IV. Edith.

Capt. Smith-Dorrien is youngest son of the late James Smith, Esq. of Ashlyns Hall, and brother of the present Augustus Smith, Esq. He assumed, in 1845, by royal license, the additional surname and arms of DORRIEN.

Arms—1st and 4th, DORRIEN: arg., issuant from a mount in base, three trefoils, vert; in chief a ring, gu., gem, arg. 2nd and 3rd, SMITH; or, a chevron, cotised, sa., between three demi-griffins, couped, of the last, the two in chief respecting each other.
Crests—DORRIEN: issuant from the battlements of a tower, arg., a dexter arm, erect, ppr., holding three trefoils, as in the arms of SMITH: an elephant's head erased, or, charged on the neck with three fleurs-de-lis, sa.
Motto—Preignes haleine, tire fort.
Seat—Haresfoot, Berkhampstead.

DOUCE OF WEST MALLING, NOW OF DEBTLING.

DOUCE, AUGUSTUS-THOMAS, Esq. of Debtling, co. Kent, J.P. and D.L., *b.* in Sept. 1779.

Lineage.—THOMAS DOUCE, Esq. of the Six Clerks' Office (descended from a respectable family in Hampshire, of which county Sir Francis Douce served as high-sheriff 4th CHARLES II.), *m.*, and left with other children, at his decease, in 1799, THOMAS-AUGUSTUS, his heir; FRANCIS, F.S.A., the well-known antiquary, who *d. s. p.* 30 March, 1834, aged 77; and William, of Bath, who left issue. The eldest son,

THOMAS-AUGUSTUS DOUCE, Esq., *m.* Margaret, dau. and eventually sole heir of Benjamin Hubble, Esq. of West Malling, co. Kent, and granddau. of John Savage, Esq. of Brighton, high-sheriff of Kent in 1726, who was son, by Anne Alchorne his wife, of John Savage, Esq. of Lincoln's Inn, descended from the SAVAGES *of Rock Savage*, and by this lady had issue,

Francis-Hubble, *d. s. p.*
THOMAS-AUGUSTUS, now of Debtling.
William-Henry, *m.* 1st, Jane, dau. of Col. Downman, and 2ndly, Emily, dau. of Edward Penfold, Esq. of Loose, and had issue, by the first, a dau.; by the latter, four sons and three daus.
Charles-Benjamin, *d. s. p.*
George-Frederick. Augustus-Edmund.
Sophia-Margaret, *m.* to John Dudlow, Esq. of West Malling.
Harriet-Elizabeth. Frances-Catherine.

Arms—Or, a chevron, chequy, arg. and az., between three greyhounds, courant, sa.
Crest—An antelope's head, per pale, arg. and sa.
Motto—Celer et vigilans.
Seat—Debtling, co. Kent.

DOUGHTY OF THEBERTON HALL.

DOUGHTY, HENRY-MONTAGU, Esq. of Theberton Hall, co. Suffolk, *b.* 15 March, 1841.

Lineage.—GEORGE DOUGHTY, Esq. of Leiston, and subsequently of Theberton Hall, of Suffolk (son and heir of Samuel-Park Doughty, Esq. of Martlesham, and grandson of the Rev. George Doughty, rector of Martlesham), was high-sheriff for that county in 1793. He m. Anne, dau. and heir of John Goodwin, Esq. of Martlesham Hall, and dying 21 Aug. 1798, was s. by his son,

THE REV. GEORGE-CLARKE DOUGHTY, of Theberton Hall, vicar of Hoxne, rector of Denham and of Martlesham, in Suffolk, bapt. 7 Sept. 1768, m. 4 July, 1796, Catharine, only dau. and heiress of Ezekiel Revett, Esq. of Hoxne, and by her, who d. in 1804, aged 28, had two sons and three daus., viz.,

CHARLES-MONTAGU, his heir, of Theberton Hall.
Frederick-Goodwin, b. 17 Oct. 1800, of Martlesham, in Suffolk, m. 21 Aug. 1833, Beatrice, dau. and co-heiress of rear-admiral Sir Charles Cunningham, of Oak Lawn, Hoxne, Suffolk, and has issue.
Mary-Anne.
Harriet, m. in 1827, to the Rev. Thomas D'Eye Betts, of Wortham, in Suffolk
Catherine-Helen, d. unm., 4 Jan. 1840.

Mr. Doughty d. 22 April, 1832, and was s. by his son,

THE REV. CHARLES-MONTAGU DOUGHTY, of Theberton Hall, b. 23 July, 1798, who m. 29 Jan. 1840, Frederica, 3rd dau. of the Hon. and Rev. Frederick Hotham, rector of Donnington, and d. 23 April, 1850, leaving issue, HENRY-MONTAGU, now of Theberton; and Charles-Montagu, b. 19 Aug. 1843.

Arms—Arg., two bars between three mullets, sa.
Crest—A mullet, sa.
Motto—Palma non sine pulvere.
Seat—Theberton Hall, Suffolk.

DOUGLAS OF DERVOCK.

DOUGLAS, CHARLES, Esq. of Dervock, co. Antrim, J.P., b. 25 Nov. 1791; m. 25 May, 1827, Frances-Higginson, dau. of Archer Bayley, Esq. (great-grandson of John Bayley, Esq. of Debsborough, co. Tipperary, by Deborah Foley his wife), and has issue,

I. CHARLES-EDWARD, b. 3 June, 1830.
II. Richard-Magenis, b. 1 Jan. 1832.
III. James, b. 7 Sept. 1836.
I. Grace-Gamble.
II. Fanny-Allen, m. 24 Aug. 1854, to Richard-William Bagley, Esq.
III. Eleanor-Macartney. IV. Letitia-Bayly.
V. Charlotte. VI. Millicent-Mary.

Lineage.—This family and that of DOUGLASS *of Grace Hall*, descend from a common Scottish ancestor, who accompanied WILLIAM III. to Ireland.

THE REV. CHARLES DOUGLAS, prebendary of Connor, who was great-grandson of the original settler in Ireland, m. Feb. 1787, Grace Gamble, and by her (who d. 25 Jan. 1818) had issue,

CHARLES, now of Dervock.
William-Traill, lieut. royal marines, d. 20 June, 1815.
Edmond-Alexander, resident magistrate, m. Anne, dau. of Samuel Allen, Esq. and d. at Ballinasloe, 20 March, 1846.
Charlotte.

Mr. Douglas d. 30 June, 1833.

Arms, &c.—See DOUGLASS *of Grace Hall*.
Seat—Dervock, co. Antrim.

DOUGLASS OF GRACE HALL.

DOUGLASS, CHARLES-MATHEW, Esq. of Grace Hall, co. Down, J.P. and D.L., high-sheriff in 1836.

Lineage.—This family was originally of Scottish descent.

ROBERT DOUGLASS, Esq., b. in 1665, son of Robert Douglass, of the co. of Down, by Elizabeth Henderson his wife, was a lieut. in the army of King WILLIAM III. at the battle of the Boyne. He was thrice married: 1st, to Miss Elliott; 2ndly, to Miss Whitney; and 3rdly, to Miss Usher; and d. in Jan. 1733, when he was s. by his son,

CHARLES DOUGLASS, Esq., who m. 1st, Grace, dau. of Richard Waring, Esq. of Waringstown, co. Down, but had no issue. He m. 2ndly, in 1758, Theodosia, dau. of George St. George, Esq. of Woodsgift, co. Kilkenny, who was created a Baronet in 1766, and by her had issue, THOMAS; George; and Robert; Elizabeth, and Ellen. The eldest son,

THOMAS DOUGLASS, Esq. of Grace Hall, m. in 1786, Elizabeth, dau. of Mathew Forde, Esq. of Seaforde, co. Down, and Coolgreaney, co. Wexford, by Elizabeth his wife, sister to Viscount Northland, and had issue,

CHARLES-MATHEW, his successor and present representative.

Elizabeth, m. to the Rev. Samuel Blacker, of Elm Park, co. Armagh.
Theodosia, m. to the Rev. William-Brownlow Forde, of Seaford, co. Down.
Charity. Anna.

Arms—Arg., a human heart, gu., ensigned with an imperial crown, ppr.; on a chief, az., three stars, of the first.
Crest—A dexter cubit arm, erect, grasping in the hand a human heart, all ppr.
Motto—Forward.
Seat—Grace Hall, co. Down.

DOUGLAS OF MOUNTAIN LODGE.

DOUGLAS, JOHN, Esq. of Mountain Lodge, co. Armagh, J.P., b. 10 April, 1825; m. 3 Feb. 1849, Jemima, dau. of Harry Bellhouse, Esq., son of the late David Bellhouse, of Manchester, and has issue,

I. HARRY-WILLIAM, b. 14 Nov. 1852.
II. Hugh-G., b. 12 July, 1854.
I. Lucy-Elizabeth.

Mr. Douglas, of Mountain Lodge, is son of the late William Douglas, Esq. of the same place, by Elizabeth his wife; he has one brother, Alexander, and one sister, Catherine-Ann, wife of James Morrisson, Esq.

Seat—Mountain Lodge, Keady.

DOWDALL OF IRELAND.

DOWDALL, THE REV. LAUNCELOT, A.M., vicar of St. Andrew's, *alias* Ballyhalbert, co. Down, m. in April, 1846, Maria, 4th dau. of John Downing, Esq. of Rowesgift, formerly judge of the Supreme Court of the Kandian Provinces, and niece of George-Alexander-Downing Fullerton, Esq. of Ballintoy Castle, co. Antrim, and of Tockington, co. Gloucester.

Lineage.—This family is of considerable antiquity: in the year 1435, we find ROBERT DOWDALL, Esq., serjeant-at-law, afterwards created chief-justice of the Common Pleas, by patent, bearing date 1446 (24th HENRY VI). To Sir Robert s. his son, SIR THOMAS DOWDALL, who m. Elizabeth, widow of James, 3rd Baron of Delvin, dau. and coheir of Sir Robert Hollywood, of Tartayne, or Artaine, co. Dublin, by his wife Elizabeth, dau. of Christopher, 3rd Lord Killeen, and by her had issue an only child, Eleanour, m. to John Nangle, styled Baron of Navan, whom she survived, and m. 2ndly, William, 2nd Viscount Gormanston.

In the year 1450, we find SIR JOHN DOWDALL, of Newtown and Termonfeichan, in possession of Artaine. He m Maud, dau. of Jenico D'Artois, who survived him, and m. 2ndly, Sir Rowland Eustace, of Harristown, co. Kildare, Baron of Portlester, and lord-chancellor and treasurer.

To Sir John Dowdall s. SIR THOMAS DOWDALL, created Master of the Rolls, by patent, bearing date 1478.

SIR WILLIAM DOWDALL s. in the year 1510, and in his time flourished a distinguished member of the family, GEORGE DOWDALL, Primate of all Ireland and Metropolitan, appointed by HENRY VIII. to the see of Armagh, in the year 1543.

To Sir William s. SIR JOHN DOWDALL, and to him his son, SIR JOHN DOWDALL, b. about the year 1570.

At this period the younger branches of the family were in possession of the valuable estates of Moncktown or Mountown, Athlumey, and Brownstown, in the co. Meath, and of Termonfeichan and Artreston, in the co. Louth.

Sir John Dowdall, last mentioned, m. Elizabeth, dau. of Sir Thomas Southwell, of Polylong, co. Cork, and had issue by her several daus., but no sons. The eldest dau., Anne, m. her relative, John Southwell, Esq. of Rathkeale. The 2nd dau., Elizabeth, was m. to Sir Hardress Waller, of Castletown, co. Limerick. The youngest dau., Honor, was m. to her relative, Laurence, son and heir of Edward Dowdall, of Mountown aforesaid, by whom she had issue an only dau., Elizabeth.

EDWARD DOWDALL, of Mountown, whose son thus allied himself by marriage to his kinsman, Sir John Dowdall, m. Margaret, dau. of Henry Piers, Esq., grandson of Sir William Piers, Bart. of Tristernagh, co. Westmeath, and by her had issue several children (besides Laurence).

One of the sons, Launcelot, m. Mary, dau. of Archdeacon, and granddau. of Archbishop Launcelot, Bulkeley, appointed to the see of Dublin, 11 Aug. 1619. This prelate was the 6th son of Sir Richard Bulkeley, of Beaumaris and Cheadle.

The issue of the marriage of Launcelot Dowdall and Mary Bulkeley were two sons, Bulkeley, who *d. unm.*; and Launcelot, who *m.*, but left no issue.

In the year 1789, Edward Dowdall, the then proprietor of the Mountown estate, by his will of that date, entailed this, among other properties, upon his five sons successively in tail male; remainder to his dau. and her issue; remainder to his own brother, Laurence, and his heirs for ever. These properties, however, were afterwards alienated by the eldest son, and are no longer in the possession of the Dowdall family.

Launcelot Dowdall, the eldest son of the vendor, instituted a suit to set aside the sale, but by his death the suit abated, and was never afterwards revived. This Launcelot was in holy orders, and rector of Duleek, co. Meath. He *m.* Miss Blacker, and had issue two sons, Laurence, who settled in the north of Ireland; and Launcelot. The 2nd son,

Launcelot Dowdall, *m.* Anne, dau. of the Rev. John Gibson, prebendary in the cathedral of Armagh, by Elizabeth his wife, dau. of the Rev. Dr. Raymond, and had issue,

Launcelot, of whom presently.
John, *d. unm.* in 1834.
Elizabeth, who *m.* William Studdert, 3rd son of Maurice Studdert, Esq. of Elm Hill, co. Limerick, and *d.* in 1845, leaving issue.

The elder son,

The Rev. Launcelot Dowdall, D.D., became Principal of the Royal College of Dungannon. He *m.* Hannah-Cassandra, dau. of Richard Eaton, Esq. of the city of Dublin, and had issue,

Launcelot, A.M., now vicar of St. Andrew's, *alias* Ballyhalbert, co Down.
John, A.B., in holy orders, who settled in Somersetshire, and *d.* in 1844.
Lydia-Anne. Hannah-Maria-Cassandra, *d.* in 1847.

Arms—Gu. a fesse, between six martlets, arg.
Mottoes—"Nec male notus eques:" and "Decrevi."
Seat—Avonrath.

DOWDESWELL OF PULL COURT.

Dowdeswell, William, Esq. of Pull Court, co. Worcester, *b.* Oct. 1804; formerly M.P. for Tewkesbury; *m.* 17 March, 1839, Amelia-Letitia, youngest dau. of the late Robert Graham, Esq. of Cossington House, co. Somerset, and has issue,

I. William-Edward, *b.* June, 1841.
II. Edmund-Richard, *b.* 1845.
III. Arthur-Christopher, *b.* 1846.

Lineage.—William Dowdeswell, Esq. of Pull Court, M.P., sheriff of Worcestershire in 1726, was elder son of Richard Dowdeswell, Esq. M.P., by Elizabeth his wife, dau. of Sir Edward Winnington, Bart., and great-grandson of Richard Dowdeswell, the cavalier, M.P. for Tewkesbury after the Restoration, whose father, Roger, of New Inn, obtained the manor of Pull, and *d.* 1633. William Dowdeswell *m.* 1st, in 1711, the Hon. Catherine Cockayne, dau. of Lord Cullen, by whom (who *d.* in 1716) he had an only surviving dau., Frances, *m.* to William Basil, Esq. He *m.* 2ndly, in 1719, Anne, dau. of Anthony Hammond, Esq., the elegiac poet, and great-granddau. of Sir Dudley Digges, Bart., M.P. By this lady he had issue, William, his heir; and George, M.D. (*See* Dowdeswell *of Redmarley*.) He *d.* in 1728, and was *s.* by his eldest son,

The Right Hon. William Dowdeswell, of Pull Court, M.P. for Worcestershire, one of the leading statesmen of his day, who filled the office of Chancellor of the Exchequer in the short-lived administration of the Marquess of Rockingham, in 1765. He *m.* in 1747, Bridget, youngest dau. of Sir William Codrington, Bart., and had issue. The Right Hon. gentleman *d.* in 1775, and was *s.* by his eldest son,

Thomas Dowdeswell, Esq. of Pull Court, who *m.* in 1798, Magdalena, 2nd dau. of Sir Thomas Pasley, Bart., but *d.* issueless, in 1811, when the estates devolved upon his next brother,

William Dowdeswell, Esq. of Pull Court, general in His Majesty's service, and M.P. for Tewkesbury from 1792 to 1796. He *d.* 1 Dec. 1828, *unm.*, when his Lancashire estates devolved upon his next brother, Edward-Christopher Dowdeswell, D.D., canon of Christ Church, Oxford; while those in the counties of Worcester and Gloucester passed to his youngest brother,

John-Edmund Dowdeswell, Esq. of Pull Court, a Master in Chancery, and formerly M.P. for Tewkesbury, who *m.* Miss Carolina Brietzcka, and left issue, William, now of Pull Court; John-Christopher; and Catharine, *m.* 10 Jan. 1833, to R.-B. Berens, Esq. of Lincoln's Inn.

Arms—Arg., a fesse wavy, between six billets, sa.
Seat—Pull Court.

DOWDESWELL OF REDMARLEY.

Dowdeswell, George, Esq. of Down House, Redmarley, Worcestershire, *m.* Miss Mary-Anne-Rose Egerton, and had two sons, viz.,

I. George-Francis. II. William-Tombella.

Mr. Dowdeswell went in early life to the East Indies, in the Company's civil service, in which he rose to the elevated situation of a member of the Supreme Council, and was for some months, during the absence of the governor-general from Calcutta, deputy-governor of Fort William, and vice-president in council.

Lineage.—George Dowdeswell, M.D., 2nd son of William Dowdeswell, Esq. of Pull Court, by Anne Hammond his wife, *m.* in 1760, Elizabeth, dau. of Richard Buckle, Esq. of Chaceley, and had a dau., Frances; and three sons, William; Charles, in holy orders, vicar of Bewley, co. Worcester, *d.* 27 June, 1839; and George; of whom the youngest was the late George Dowdeswell, Esq. of Down House, Redmarley.

Arms—As the preceding.
Seat—Down House, Redmarley.

DOYNE OF WELLS.

Doyne, Robert-Stephen, Esq. of Wells, co. Wexford, J.P., *b.* 23 Feb. 1806; *m.* 12 July, 1834, Sarah-Emily, dau. of Joseph Pratt, Esq. of Cabra Castle, co. Cavan, and has issue,

I. Charles-Mervyn, *b.* 27 Sept. 1839.
II. James-Walter-Chaloner, *b.* 27 April, 1851.
I. Jemima-Elizabeth.
II. Annette-Louisa.
III. Roberta-Frances-Mary.

Lineage.—Robert Doyne, Esq., *b.* about 1654-5, descended from O'Doyne *of Castlebracke* (*Harl. MSS.*, 1425), was made chief baron of the Exchequer of Ireland, by patent, dated 7 June, 1695, and chief-justice of the Common Pleas, by patent, dated 1 Feb. 1703. He *m.* 1683-4, Jane-Saunders, widow, dau. of Henry Whitfield, Esq. of Dublin, *d.* 28 Feb. 1732-3, and was *s.* by his eldest son,

Philip Doyne, Esq. of Wells, co. Wexford, who *m.* 1st, 10 Aug. 1704, Mary, dau. of Benjamin Burton, Esq. of Dublin, alderman of that city, and had issue, Robert, his heir. He *m.* 2ndly, 22 Feb. 1709, Frances South, and had further issue,

I John, *b.* 22 Feb. 1710, a lieut. in the army, 1733, *m.* Jane, dau. of Robert Ross, Esq. of Rosstrevor, co. Down, and had issue, Jane, bapt. 13 July, 1735.
II. Charles, D.D., dean of Leighlin, rector of Carlow, *b.* 3 Feb. 1711, *m.* 1st, 2 July, 1743, Anna-Maria, dau. of — Bury, Esq., and by her had issue,
1 Bury; will dated 12 Dec. 1772, and proved in 1773.
2 Philip, who *m.* Jane, dau. of John Vigors, Esq., and had issue,
Philip, of Dublin. Richard.
John (The Rev.), *b.* 3 April, 1791, *m.* 29 Oct. 1819, Ellen, dau. of Thomas Armstrong, Esq. of Farney Castle, co. Tipperary, by Sophia, dau. of Richard Vandeleur, Esq. of Kilrush, in the co. Clare, and had issue,
Philip-John, *b.* 3 Aug. 1820.
William-Thomas, *b.* 15 April, 1823.
Richard-Vigors, *b.* 19 Oct. 1824.
Charles-Armstrong, *b.* 18 Feb. 1826.
Henry-Archdall, *b.* 25 Oct. 1833.
Sophia-Anne.
Frances-Elizabeth.
Anne. Jane, *m.* to Henry Archdall.
3 Charles-Powlett, Esq. of Portarlington, Queen's County, *m.* Eliza-Jane, dau. of William Vicars, Esq. of Ballynakillbeg, co. Carlow, and had issue,
Charles-William (The Rev.), rector of Fethard, co. Wexford, who *m.* Charlotte, dau. of Thomas Stannus, Esq. of Portarlington, and has issue.
Philip-Walter, in holy orders, *m.* 1849, Emily-Sophia,

dau. of John-Goddard Richards, Esq. of Ardemine.
Charles, *d. unm.* 1853.
Elizabeth, *m.* Henry Newton, Esq. of Mount Leinster House, co. Carlow.
Charlotte. Sophia.
Philip, *m.* Catherine Botham, of Berkshire, and has one dau.
Bury, *b.* 1794, J.P. and D.L., of Weltham Grove, Berks, *m.* 1828, Caroline-Mary-Anne, dau. and co-heir of Col. Kearney, of White Waltham, Berkshire.
Robert, of Borris, co. Carlow, *m.* Bella-Mira, dau. of Valentine Munbee, Esq. of Horinger Hall, Suffolk, and had issue, Jane-Elizabeth.
Anne, wife of Robert White, Esq. of Old Park, Rathdowney, in the Queen's County.
Elizabeth.
Henrietta, wife of William Hamilton, of Montrath, Esq.
Frances-Georgiana, *d. s. p.*

The Very Rev. Charles Doyne *m.* 2ndly, 7 March, 1763, Mary, dau. of the Rev. Nicholas Millay, and relict of Wesley Harman, Esq., but had no further issue. His will is dated 28 June, 1769, proved 11 June, 1777. His wife's will, dated 11 Aug. 1784, proved 31 May, 1791.

I. Henrietta, *b.* 3 Dec. 1709.

Philip Doyne *m.* 3rdly, Elizabeth, dau. of James Stopford, Esq., father to the 1st Earl of Courtown, and had other issue. He *d.* 1753, and was *s.* by his eldest son,

Robert Doyne, Esq. of Wells, co. Wexford, *b.* 2 Jan. 1705, M.P., co. Wexford, *m.* 1 July, 1731, Deborah, dau. of Francis Annesley, Esq. of Ballyshannon, co. Kildare, and had issue. Robert Doyne *d.* 19 Aug. 1754, and was *s.* by his eldest son,

Philip Doyne, Esq. of Wells, *b.* 20 March, 1733, who *m.* 29 Aug. 1757, Lady Joanna Gore, dau. of Arthur, 1st Earl of Arran, by Jane, dau. of Richard Saunders, Esq. of Saunders Court, but *d.* without issue, 11 March, 1765, and his widow remarried Michael Daly, Esq. of Mount Pleasant, co. Galway. He was *s.* by his next brother,

Robert Doyne, Esq. of Wells, *b.* 11 Nov. 1738, *m.* 1777, Mary, dau. of Humphrey Ram, Esq. of Ramsfort, co. Wexford (she *d.* 1826), and dying in 1791, left (with daus., of whom Elizabeth, *m.* John Dwyer, Esq.; and Frances, *m.* St. George Irvine, Esq. of Ballynahown) an only son,

Robert Doyne, Esq. of Wells, *b.* 2 March, 1782, J.P. and D.L., who served as high-sheriff for the cos. of Wexford and Carlow. He *m.* 2 July, 1805, Annette-Constantia, dau. of the Right Hon. John Beresford, brother of George-De la Poer, Earl of Tyrone, and 1st Marquess of Waterford, relict of Robert Uniacke, Esq. of Woodhouse, co. Waterford, and had issue,

Robert-Stephen, now of Wells.
Charles-Henry, *b.* in Aug. 1809, lieut. 87th regt., *m.* Georgiana, dau. of — Kennedy, Esq.
Mary-Annette.
Annette-Constantia, *d.* Sept. 1819.

Arms—Quarterly: 1st and 4th, gu., a fesse dancettée, between three escallops, arg., for Doyne; 2nd and 3rd, az., an eagle displayed, or, for O'Doyne. The latter was certified the 6th day of March, 1606, as the arms of the ancient family of O'Duinne *of Oregan*, in Ireland, by Daniel Molyneux, Ulster King of Arms.
Crests—A demi-eagle rising, ppr., for Doyne; a holly-bush, ppr., in front thereof a lizard, passant, or, for O'Doyne.
Motto—Mullac a boo:—*i. e.* Victory for the Duns, or the inhabitants of the hills.
Seat—Wells, near Oulart, co. Wexford.

DRAKE OF ASHE.

Drake, Charles-Cutcliffe, Esq. of Springfield, co. Devon, *b.* 29 Sept. 1808; *m.* in 1836, Mary, elder dau. and co-heir of Henry Cusack, Esq. of Girley, co. Meath, by whom he has issue,

I. Charles-Henry, *b.* 4 June, 1840.
II. John-Rothwell, *b.* in 1842.
I. Dorothy-Mervin. II. Anne-Frances.

Lineage.—This family is of considerable antiquity in the county of Devon. Sir William Pole makes mention of Roger le Drak, who, in 31st Edward I. (1303), held Hurnford, cum terra de la Wood, of Dertington, at half a knight's fee; and prior to that, of others of the family who were possessed of several lands in the county.

John Drake, Esq. of Exmouth, co. Devon, described as "a man of great estate, and a name of no less antiquity," *m. temp.* Henry V., Christiana, elder dau. and co-heir of John Billet, Esq. of Ashe, by which alliance the estate of Ashe, in the parish of Musbury, accrued to the Drake family. He was *s.* by his son and heir,

John Drake, Esq., who was of Otterton, in the hundred of East Budleigh, and *m.* Christiana, dau. and heiress of John Antage, Esq. His son,

John Drake, was also of Otterton, and *m.* a dau. of John Cruwys, Esq., the then representative of the ancient house of Cruwys *of Cruwys Morchard.*

John Drake, Esq., the 4th of that name, of Otterton, by his wife, Agneta, dau. of John Koloway, Esq., had issue, John, his heir; Richard; Robert; and Thomas, Esq. of Hortford, co. Devon, *m.* Ellen, dau. of Bennett Hilton, of South Awtry, co. Devon, and had issue three sons and two daus.

John Drake, the eldest son and heir, was of Exmouth and Ashe. He *m.* Margaret, dau. and heiress of John Cole, Esq. of Rill, in the parish of Withecombe Raleigh, co. Devon. He *d.* leaving issue three sons, John, of whom presently; John (a 2nd son of the same name), who is mentioned by Sir William Poole to have been "a great merchant-man; Gilbert, of Spratshays, co. Devon. The eldest son,

John Drake, Esq. of Ashe, who *s.* his father in the representation of the family, *m.* (26th Henry VIII.), Amye, dau. of Roger Grenville, Esq. of Stowe, co. Cornwall, and had issue,

I. Bernard, his heir.
II. Robert, of Wiscomb Park, in the parish of South Legh, *m.* Elizabeth, dau. of Humphrey Prideaux, Esq. of Theoborough, and had issue seven sons and three daus.
  1 William, Esq. of Wiscomb, *m.* Philippa, dau. of Sir Robert Denys, Knt. of Halicomb, and had issue.
  2 Bernard. 3 John, *m.*, and had issue.
  4 Robert, } both in the army, and killed at the defence
  5 Henry, } of Ostend, in the prime of their age, *s. p.*
  6 Nicholas, *m.* Katherine, dau. of William Tottle, and relict of — Kingley.
  7 Humphrey.
  1 Gertrude, *m.* to Henry Honychurch, of Awn Gifford.
  2 Amye, *m.* — Poole, of Nottingham.
  3 Ursula, *unm.*
III. Richard, equerry to Queen Elizabeth, *m.* Ursula, dau. of Sir William Stafford, Knt., and from whom the Drakes *of Shardeloes.*

Mr. Drake, who served the office of sheriff for the county of Devon, 4th Elizabeth, *d.* 4 Oct. 1558, and was *s.* by his son,

Sir Bernard Drake, Knt., who was of Ashe and Mount Drake, a mansion he had built in the same parish, was knighted by Queen Elizabeth, at Greenwich, 9 Jan. 1585, and in the same year died, and was buried in Musbury church, where his effigy still remains. He *m.* Gertrude, dau. of Bartholomew Fortescue, of Filleigh, co. Devon (ancestors of the Earls Fortescue), and by her, who survived him, left,

John, his heir.
Margaret, *m.* to John Sherman, of Ottery St. Mary, and whose dau., Alice, *m.* Richard Perceval, Esq., ancestor of the Earls of Egmont.

John Drake, of Ashe and Mount Drake, son and heir, *m.* Dorothy, dau. of William Button, Esq. of Alton, co. Wilts, and had issue,

John, of whom hereafter.
William, of Yardbury, *m.* Margaret, sole dau. and heir of William Westover, of Yardbury in the parish of Collyton, co. Devon, and *d. circa* 1639, leaving issue, from whom descended Francis Drake, Esq. of Wells, co. Somerset, J.P. and D.L., *b.* in 1764, who entered the army at an early age, and was subsequently employed in many important diplomatic missions to foreign courts. He *d.* in 1821, leaving, by his wife, Eliza-Anne, dau. of Sir Herbert Mackworth, of Gnoll Castle, co. Glamorgan, Bart., two sons and three daus. Charles-Digby-Mackworth Drake, the 2nd son, *b.* 1800, is in holy orders, rector of Hunshaw, co. Devon, *m.* in 1835, Arthurina, dau. of the Rev. John Dene, rector of Horwood, co. Devon, by whom he has issue.
Mary, who *m.* Sir Henry Rowswell, Knt.

Mr. Drake *d.* in 1628, and was *s.* by his eldest son,

Sir John Drake, Knt. of Ashe, who *m.* Helena, 2nd dau. of John, Baron Boteler, of Bramfield, co. Herts, by Elizabeth his wife, dau. of Sir George Villiers, Knt. of Blokesby, co. Leicester, and half-sister to George, Duke of Buckingham. Lady Drake was co-heir of her brother, William, 2nd and last Baron Boteler, who *d. s. p.* The issue of this marriage were,

Sir John Drake, of Ashe, Knt., eldest son and heir, who was created a Baronet, 31 Aug. 1660. He *m.*, and had issue, but this branch of the family became extinct on the

death of Sir William Drake, the 6th and last Baronet, 21 Oct. 1733. (*Vide* BURKE'S *Extinct Baronetage*.)
George, *d. unm.* in 1664.
Thomas, *d.* in Ireland, *s. p.*, 1659.
HENRY, of whom hereafter.
Dorothy, *m.* to William Yardley, Esq.
Mary, *d. unm.*
Eleanor, *m.* to John Briscoe, Esq. of Cumberland.
Elizabeth, *m.* to Sir Winston Churchill, Knt., M.P., by whom she was mother of the celebrated John Churchill, Duke of Marlborough, who was *b.* at Ashe, whilst his mother was on a visit to her father there, in 1650.

HENRY DRAKE, Esq., the 4th son, but whose descendants eventually became, on the death of the last baronet, the representatives of the family, settled at Barnstaple, co. Devon, for which borough he, in 1679, served the office of mayor. He was twice married. By his 1st wife he had one child, who *d.* young; and by his 2nd, Anne, dau. of — Yeo, whom he *m.* in 1682, he had issue one son, who, on his death, in 1688, succeeded him. This

JOHN DRAKE, Esq. of Barnstaple, *b.* in 1682, *m.* in 1706, Christian, dau. and co-heiress of Robert Hacche, Esq. of Sitterleigh Park, by whom he left two sons,

HENRY, the elder, *m.* Mary, dau. of John Tucker, Esq., R.N., and had issue.
JOHN.

JOHN DRAKE, the 2nd son, of Barnstaple, *b.* in 1710, *m.* in 1773, Anne, dau. of the Rev. Mr. Gregory, and *d.* in 1770, leaving two children, Joan, who *m.* George Edwards, Esq., R.N., and

HENRY DRAKE, Esq. of Barnstaple, only son and heir, *b.* 1745, *d.* Feb. 1806, having *m.* in 1771, Ann, dau. of Richard Hammett, Esq. of Kennerland, in the parish of Clovelly, and sister to Sir James Hamlyn, of Clovelly Court, co. Devon, Bart., by whom he had issue,

I. ZACHARY-HAMMETT DRAKE, Esq. of Springfield, magistrate and deputy-lieut. for the cos. of Devon and Cornwall, *b.* 5 Sept. 1777, *d.* 11 March, 1847, having *m.* 6 Oct. 1803, Frances, eldest dau. of Charles-Newell Cutcliffe, Esq. of Marwood Hill, and co-heir of her brother, Colonel Cutcliffe, of Webbery, co. Devon, and by her, who survived, had issue,
  1 Zachary-Hammett, in holy orders, rector of Clovelly, co. Devon, *b.* 14 Feb. 1805, *m.* 1831, Eleanor Penrose, only dau. of Admiral Sir Samuel Pym, K.C.B., by whom he has surviving issue, John-Mervin-Cutcliffe, *b.* 6 Nov. 1838, lieut. R.N.
  2 CHARLES-CUTCLIFFE DRAKE, now of Springfield, as above.
  1 Francis-Mervin, *m.* 3 July, 1838, Captain John Graham, 55th B.N.I., and *d.* at Dacca, 19 Oct. 1845, without leaving issue.
II. John, *d.* April, 1799, *unm.*
III. Henry, *b.* 22 June, 1781, *m.*, and has surviving issue, three daus.
IV. Richard, *b.* in Feb. 1786, and *d.* in 1853.
V. WILLIAM DRAKE, *b.* 27 July, 1787, *m.* in 1816, Frances, dau. of Robert Lincoln, Esq., and *d.* 9 June, 1821, having had issue,
  1 WILLIAM-RICHARD DRAKE, Esq., F.S.A., of London, and The Lodge, Oatlands, co. Surrey, *b.* 25 Aug. 1817, *m.* 8 Aug. 1846, Katharine-Stewart-Forbes, dau. of the late Richard-Thomas Goodwin, Esq., formerly senior member of council at Bombay.
  2 Henry, *b.* in 1821.
  1 Frances-Ann.
I. Ann, *d.* 19 Oct. 1839, *unm.* II. Elizabeth.

Arms—Arg., a wyvern, wings displayed and tail nowed, gu.
Crests—1st, a dexter arm, erect, couped at the elbow, ppr., holding a battle-axe, sa., headed, arg.; 2nd, an eagle, displayed, gu.
Motto—Aquila non captat muscas.
Residence—Springfield, near Barnstaple.

TYRWHITT-DRAKE OF SHARDELOES.

TYRWHITT-DRAKE, THOMAS, Esq. of Shardeloes, co. Buckingham, of Stainfield Hall, Lincolnshire, and of St. Donat's Castle, Glamorganshire, *b.* 14 July, 1817; *m.* 8 Aug. 1843, Elizabeth-Julia, dau. of John Stratton, Esq., and widow of Col. Wedderburn, and has issue,

I. THOMAS-WILLIAM, *b.* 28 Nov. 1849.
II. William-Wykeham, *b.* 27 Sept. 1851.
I. Elizabeth-Caroline. II. Susan-Emily.
III. Florence-Georgina. IV. Julia-Diana.

Lineage.—RICHARD DRAKE, Esq., 3rd son of John Drake, Esq. of Ashe, by Amye his wife, dau. of Roger Grenville, Esq. of Stowe, was one of the equerries to Queen ELIZABETH. He *m.* Ursula, dau. of Sir William Stafford, Knt., and dying 11 July, 1603, was *s.* by his son,

FRANCIS DRAKE, Esq. of Esher, one of the gentlemen of the privy chamber in ordinary, who *m.* Joan, dau. of William Tothill, Esq. of Shardeloes, in the co. of Buckingham, and had issue, WILLIAM, his heir; John, who *d. unm.* in 1623; Francis, of Walton-on-Thames; and Joan. Mr. Drake *d.* 17 March, 1633, and was *s.* by his eldest son,

SIR WILLIAM DRAKE, of Shardeloes, *b.* in 1606, chirographer to the Court of Common Pleas, who was created a Baronet in 1641. He *d. unm.* in 1669, when the title became extinct, and the estates passed to his nephew,

SIR WILLIAM DRAKE, Knt., of Shardeloes, M.P. for the borough of Agmondesham, son of Francis Drake, of Walton-on-Thames, by Dorothy his 2nd wife, dau. of Sir William Spring, Bart. He *m.* Elizabeth, 2nd dau. and co-heiress of William Montague, Lord Chief Baron of the Exchequer, and *d.* in 1690, leaving a dau. Mary, *m.* to Sir John Tyrwhitt, Bart. of Stainfield, and a son,

MONTAGUE DRAKE, Esq. of Shardeloes, M.P. for Agmondesham, who *m* Jane, dau. and heiress of Sir John Garrard, Bart. of Lamer, and left at his decease, in 1698, with a dau. Mary, *m.* to Sir Edward Everard, Bart., a son, and heir,

MONTAGUE-GARRARD DRAKE, Esq. of Shardeloes, M.P. for Agmondesham in 1713, 1715, and 1727, and for the co. of Buckingham in 1722. He *m.* Isabella, dau. and heiress of Thomas Marshall, Esq., and dying in 1728, was *s.* by his elder surviving son,

WILLIAM DRAKE, Esq., LL.D., of Shardeloes, M.P. for Agmondesham from the year 1746 until his decease. He *m.* Elizabeth, dau. of John Raworth, Esq., by whom (who *d.* in 1757) he had, William, LL.D., M.P., *d. s. p.* in 1795; THOMAS, his heir; John, LL.D., rector of Agmondesham, *m.* Mary, eldest dau. and co-heir of the Rev. William Wickham, of Garsington; CHARLES, who took the name of Garrard (*see* GARRARD *of Lamer*); Elizabeth, *m.* to the Rev. Richard Frank, D.D.; and Isabel, *d. unm.* Mr. Drake *d.* 8 Aug. 1796, aged 72, and was *s.* by his eldest surviving son,

THOMAS DRAKE, Esq., LL.D., of Shardeloes, who had assumed, in 1776, the surname and arms of TYRWHITT, but upon inheriting the estates of his own family at the decease of his father, he resumed, in addition, his paternal name, and became Tyrwhitt-Drake. He *m.* 8 Aug. 1780, Anne, dau. and co-heiress of the Rev. William Wickham, of Garsington, in the co. of Oxford, and had issue,

THOMAS, his heir.
William, *m.* Emma, dau. of the late Joseph Halsey, Esq. of Gaddesden, Herts, and has issue.
John, in holy orders, rector of Amersham, *m.* 1st, Mary, 3rd dau. of Arthur Annesley, Esq. of Bletchingdon, in Oxfordshire, who *d.* in 1827. He *m.* 2ndly, Emily, 5th dau. of the late Charles Drake-Garrard, Esq. of Lamer Park, Herts, and has issue.
George, in holy orders, rector of Malpas, co. Chester, *m.* Jane, 2nd dau. of the late Joseph Halsey, Esq. of Gaddesden, and *d.* 6 March, 1840.
Frederick-William.
Mary-Frances.
Anne, *m.* to Hugh-Richard Hoare, Esq. of Lillingstone, Bucks.
Louisa-Isabella, *m.* to the Rev. John-Anthony Partridge, rector of Cranwich, co. Norfolk.

Mr. Tyrwhitt-Drake *d.* in 1810, and was *s.* by his eldest son,

THOMAS TYRWHITT-DRAKE, Esq. of Shardeloes, J.P. and D.L., high-sheriff of Bucks 1836, and for several years M.P. for Amersham, *b.* 16 March, 1783, *m.* in Oct. 1814, Barbara-Caroline, dau. of Arthur Annesley, Esq. of Bletchingdon Park, co. Oxford, and had issue,

I. THOMAS, now of Shardeloes.
II. John, *b.* in June, 1821, *m.* Emily, dau. of — Micklethwaite, Esq. of Taverham Hall, Norfolk.
III. Edward, *b.* in May, 1832. IV. George.
I. Barbara-Anne. II. Frances-Isabella.
III. Mary-Elizabeth.
IV. Augusta-Charlotte, *m.* Aug. 1853, to the Rev. James Dawkins.
V. Elizabeth-Catherine. VI. Susan-Louisa.
VII. Charlotte-Diana. VIII. Agnes-Agatha.

Mr. Tyrwhitt-Drake *d.* 21 March, 1852.

Arms—DRAKE and TYRWHITT, quarterly.
Crests—1st, DRAKE: 2nd, TYRWHITT.
Seat—Shardeloes, Amersham, Bucks.

DRAKE OF STOKESTOWN.

DEANE-DRAKE, JOHN, Esq. of Stokestown, co. Wexford, *b.* 1813; *m.* 1843, Emily-Letitia, dau. of

Thomas-Henry Watson, Esq. of Lumclone, co. Carlow, and has issue,

I. JOSEPH-EDWARD. II. Henry-Thomas.
III. John-Handfield.
I. Annette-Georgina. II. Sara-Cecilia.

Lineage.—JOSEPH DEANE, Esq., 2nd son of Joseph Deane, Esq. of Terrenure and Cromlin, co. Dublin, M.P., by Catherine his 3rd wife, dau. of Col. Green, of Greenville, m. in 1810, Sarah Drake, heiress of Stokestown, co. Wexford, and by her (who d. in 1854) left at his decease in 1850,

JOSEPH, now of Stokestown.
Joseph-William, of Longrange.
Sara-Urith, m. to Henry Roe, Esq. Juliana-Frances.

Arms—Quarterly: 1st and 4th, sa., a fesse, wavy, arg., between two stars of six points, or, for DRAKE; 2nd and 3rd, arg., on a chevron, gu., between two Cornish choughs, sa., beaked and legged, gu., as many crosses-patée, arg., for DEANE.

Crests—1st, a dexter arm, embowed, in armour, grasping a poleaxe, all ppr., DRAKE; 2nd, a tortoise displayed, ppr., DEANE.

Motto—Sic parvis magna.

Seat—Stokestown, co. Wexford.

DRAKE OF RORISTON.

DRAKE, COLUMBUS-PATRICK, Esq. of Roriston, co. Meath, representative of the ancient families of Drakestown and Drakerath, s. his father, 22 Feb. 1854.

Lineage.—This family, and those of Ashe and Shardeloes, derive from a common progenitor, but the settlement in Ireland must have taken place at a remote period, for we find Drake of Drakerath, a distinguished person in the annals of that kingdom under the Tudors and the Stuarts, CROMWELL, and WILLIAM.

The mansion of Drakerath was situated in the barony of Kells, in the co. of Meath (where the ruins still remain), and was erected by a member of the family of DRAKE *of Ashe*, in the co. of Devon, who acquired large estates in that part of Ireland, and settled there. Those estates continued vested in his descendants until the rebellion of 1641, when they were forfeited, but a small portion was subsequently restored by the Court of Claims in the beginning of CHARLES II.'s reign. A cadet of the family, Captain Peter Drake, a soldier of fortune, who followed the wars through all the fields of Europe in the beginning of the last century, published a very amusing detail of his adventures, which he begins with the situation of his house at the time of the Revolution. "I was born," he says, "12 Oct. 1671. My father's name was George; he was eldest son of William Drake, of Drakerath, and married Elizabeth, eldest dau. of Patrick Stanley, Esq. of Maristown, in the co. of Louth, and niece of John Stanley, Esq. of Finner, near Slane, in Meath. The family remained in peaceable possession of the estate from their first arrival until the war of 1641, when, with many more, they forfeited, and were driven to shift for themselves. At the beginning of CHARLES II.'s reign, there was a Court of Claims set on foot, by which a few of the proprietors were restored, and my father was of the number. He became, however, possessed only of a part, and was at the eve of being restored to the whole, when an order came from the king to dissolve the court, so that an end for that time was put to his hopes. My father had some time before this, with his family, settled in the co. of Kildare, having taken some lands from William, Lord Dungan (to whom he had the honour of being related), at Kildroughet, where he built a handsome seat. Here he continued until the Revolution, when his affairs took a new turn. Some time before, or about the beginning of the troubles, Lord Dungan was created Earl of Limerick, and, if I remember rightly, constituted governor of that city; thither his lordship repaired, taking my father with him, whom he soon after promoted. He was appointed one of the commissioners of the Customs, and chief comptroller of the Mint. As soon as King JAMES came to Dublin, and called a parliament, my father was put into the commission of the peace for the co. of Kildare, and declared himself a candidate for the borough of Navan. He was at the same time restored to the remainder of his estates, after which he returned to Limerick to fulfil his official duties. In June, 1690, he came to visit his family, and settle his affairs; but the loss of the battle of the Boyne (which happened July 1 following) obliged him with all expedition to move off with his family for Limerick, staying but one day after the battle to inter Lord Dungan, only son to the Earl of Limerick, who was that day killed by a cannon-ball, and brought to Castletown, the earl his father's seat. This melancholy affair being at an end, the next day we set forward on our journey. Arriving at Limerick, we found all hands employed in repairing the old, and throwing up new works for the defence of the place, which was soon after besieged; the particulars of which are so well known already, that it would be needless to descend to minute relation."

From the Irish records it appears that, in the 9th of RICHARD II., the king conceded to RICHARD DRAKE, of Drakestown, the office of high-sheriff of the co. of Meath; and that, in the 9th of HENRY V., the same appointment was granted to John Drake, of Drakestown, to be held during pleasure. Among the other early ancestry of the family, Catherine, sister and heiress of Nicholas Drake, of Drakerath, m. Richard Nugent, 2nd Baron of Delvin, living in 1428; and about the same period, Sir Christopher Barnewall, of Crickstown, lord high treasurer of Ireland, m. Matilda, dau. of the then Drake of Drakerath.

The immediate progenitor of the family before us,

COLUMBUS DRAKE, Esq. of Drakerath, in Meath, son of Patrick Drake, Esq., was b. in 1670, and m. in 1705, Anne, only dau. of Jennett, Esq. of Oldbridge, co. Louth, who was slain at the battle of the Boyne, in 1688, together with all his sons, except the youngest, then in infancy. This child and his sister, afterwards Mrs. Drake, were saved in a singular manner, by a faithful servant, who secreted them in baskets, and thus conveyed them across the river after the conflict. Mr. Drake left at his decease (with three daus., the eldest m. to William Cruise, Esq. of Mydoragh; the 2nd, to Curtis, Esq. of Mount Hanover; and the 3rd, who d. unm.) a son and successor,

PATRICK DRAKE, Esq. of Drakerath, b. in 1712, who m. in 1747, Frances, 3rd dau. of James O'Reilly, Esq. of Roriston, co. Meath, and had two sons and three daus., viz.,

COLUMBUS, his heir.
George, of Batterstown, b. in 1760, m. in 1796, Emily, dau. of John O'Reilly, Esq. of Rahattan, co. Wicklow, and had issue.
Catherine, m. in 1768, to George Dowdall, Esq. of Causestown.
Elizabeth, m. to Nicholas Browne, Esq.
Anne, b. in 1755, d. unm.

The elder son,

COLUMBUS DRAKE, Esq. of Roriston, b. in 1750, m. 18 Oct. 1777, Anne, only dau. of Christopher Barnewall, Esq. of Fyanstown Castle, in Meath, and had issue,

PATRICK, b. in 1782, d. in 1801.
CHRISTOPHER, successor to his father.
Cecilia, m. in 1796, to James-Archbold O'Reilly, Esq. of Rahattan, co. Wicklow, now deceased.
Frances, d. unm. in 1799. Anne.

Mr. Drake was s. at his decease by his only son,

CHRISTOPHER DRAKE, Esq. of Roriston, b. 4 June, 1790, m. 1st, Mary-Anne, dau. of Nicholas Gannon, Esq. of Ballyboy, co. Meath, and by that lady (deceased) had a son and dau., viz.,

COLUMBUS-PATRICK, now of Roriston.
Anne-Maria, d. young 1834.

He m. 2ndly, Mary, eldest dau. of the late Alexander Somers, Esq., and by her had issue,

Christopher-Somers, d. under age.
Alexander-Joseph.
Charles-William.
Catherine-Cecilia. Mary-Elizabeth, d. unm. 1852.

Arms—Arg., a wyvern, wings displayed and tail nowed, gu.

Crest—A wyvern, as in the arms.

Seat—Roriston, near Trim.

DRAX OF CHARBOROUGH.

SAWBRIDGE-ERLE-DRAX, JOHN-SAMUEL-WANLEY, Esq. of Charborough Park, co. Dorset, Olantigh, Kent, and Ellerton Abbey, co. York, M.P. for Wareham, b. 6 Oct. 1800; m. 1 May, 1827, Jane-Frances, only dau. of Richard Erle-Drax-Grosvenor, Esq., and has issue,

I. Maria-Caroline.
II. Sarah-Frances-Elizabeth, m. 14 Sept. 1853, to Capt. Francis-Augustus-Plunkett Burton, Coldstream guards, son of Rear-Admiral Ryder Burton, by Anna-Maria his wife, dau. of Randall Plunkett, 13th Lord Dunsany.

This gentleman, whose patronymic is SAWBRIDGE, s. to the estates in right of his wife, upon the demise of that lady's brother, Richard-Edward Erle-Drax, Esq., 13 Aug. 1828, and assumed, in consequence, the surnames and arms of ERLE-DRAX.

Lineage.—The Erles are of ancient and knightly descent. The first ancestor that occurs in the pedigree is Henry de Erle, lord of Newton, in Somersetshire, 35th HENRY III., but the family was long previously settled in that county. So far back as the 7th HENRY II., John de Erlegh paid five marks for the scutage of his lands at Beckington, in Somersetshire.

ELIZABETH ERNLE, of Charborough (only dau. and heiress of Sir Edward Ernle, Bart. of Maddington, Wilts, by Frances Erle, of Charborough, his wife, only dau. and heir of the famous GENERAL THOMAS ERLE, lieut.-gen of the ordnance, commander of the centre of the English army at the battle of Almanza, grandson and heir of SIR WALTER ERLE, of Charborough, the parliamentarian), m. HENRY DRAX,* Esq. of Ellerton Abbey, in Yorkshire, M.P. for Lyme Regis and Wareham, and secretary to Frederick, Prince of Wales; and by him, who d. in 1755, the heiress of Ernle and Erle left, at her decease, in 1759 (with five daus., Elizabeth, m. 1st, to Augustus, 4th Earl Berkeley, and 2ndly, to Robert, Viscount Clare; Mary, to John Durbin, Esq.; Harriot, m. to Sir William Hanham, Bart.; Susannah, m. 1st, to William Calcraft, Esq., and 2ndly, to John, Earl of Castlehaven; and Frances, who d. in 1751), three sons, of whom the eldest,

THOMAS ERLE-DRAX, Esq. of Charborough, m. Mary, dau. of Lord St. John, of Bletshoe, but d. without issue, in 1790, aged 67, when he was s. by his brother,

EDWARD DRAX, Esq. of Charborough, who m. 16 April, 1762, Mary, dau. of Awnsham Churchill, Esq. of Henbury, and had an only dau. and heiress,

SARAH-FRANCES DRAX, of Charborough, who m. 11 March, 1788, Richard Grosvenor, Esq., M.P. for West Looe, nephew of Richard, Earl Grosvenor, and that gentleman assumed, in consequence of his marriage, the surname and arms of ERLE-DRAX. The issue were one son and a dau., viz.,

RICHARD-EDWARD, the heir.
JANE FRANCES, successor to her brother.

Mr. Erle-Drax Grosvenor d. 8 Feb. 1819, aged 58, and his widow (the heiress of Charborough) 15 June, 1822. They were s. by their only son,

RICHARD-EDWARD ERLE-DRAX, Esq. of Charborough and Ellerton Abbey, d. unm. 13 Aug. 1828, and was s. by his sister,

JANE-FRANCES ERLE-DRAX, who had m. in the previous year, JOHN-SAMUEL-WANLEY SAWBRIDGE, Esq., and that gentleman having assumed the surname and arms of ERLE-DRAX, is the present possessor of Charborough Park, &c.

Arms—Quarterly: 1st, DRAX and ERLE, quarterly; quartering SAWBRIDGE.
Crests—1st, DRAX; 2nd, SAWBRIDGE.
Seats—Charborough Park, Wareham; Olantigh, Kent; Ellerton Abbey, Yorkshire.

DREWE OF THE GRANGE.

DREWE, EDWARD-SIMCOE, Esq. of The Grange, co. Devon, J.P. and D.L., high-sheriff in 1845, b. 20 Aug. 1805; m. 5 June, 1828, Jane-Susan-Adèle, dau. and heir of Jean-Gaspard Prevost, conseiller d'état in the republic of Geneva, and has issue,

I. FRANCIS-EDWARD, b. 24 Aug. 1830, lieut. 23rd Royal Welsh Fusiliers.
II. Edward, b. 26 Feb. 1834.
III. Albert-Cecil-Robert, b. 31 July, 1839.
I. Adèle-Caroline.
II. Alice-Fanny, m. 18 Sept. 1851, to the Hon. and Rev. John Gifford, vicar of Shalford, Surrey.

Lineage.—WILLIAM DREWE m. Joan, dau. and heir of John Prideaux, of Orcharton, in Devonshire, and co-heir of her mother, Agnes, or Amy, eldest dau. and co-heir of Robert French, Esq. of Hornford, by Anne, or Maud, dau. and heir of Robert Wynard, of Haccombe. His eldest son and heir,

WILLIAM DREWE, Esq. of Sharpham, was father of

HENRY DREWE, Esq., whose son and heir,

WILLIAM DREWE, Esq. dying 3 Sept. 1532, was s. by his son,

THOMAS DREWE, Esq. of Sharpham, b. in 1519, m. Elinora, dau. and co-heir of William, 2nd son of Roger Huckmore, of the co. of Devon, and left a son and heir,

EDWARD DREWE, Esq. of Sharpham, Killerton, and Broad Hembury, co. Devon, of the Inner Temple, barrister-at-law, recorder of the city of London 1584, and recorder of Exeter, serjeant-at-law and queen's serjeant, 38th ELIZABETH (1596). He m. Bridget, dau. of Fitzwilliams, of Lincolnshire, and dying in 1622, was s. by his eldest son,

SIR THOMAS DREWE, of The Grange, in Broadhembury, who received the honour of knighthood at the coronation of King CHARLES I., and was sheriff of this county in 10th JAMES I. Sir Thomas sold Killerton to Sir Arthur Acland, Bart., and erected the family seat on the site of an ancient grange of Donkeswell Abbey. He m. Elizabeth, dau. of Sir Edward Moore, of Odiham, Hants, and by her, who d. in 1635, had (with five daus., Elizabeth, Mary, Bridget, Jane, and Anne) two sons. Sir Thomas d. in 1651, and was s. by his elder son,

WILLIAM DREWE, Esq. of The Grange, b. in 1603. This gentleman m. no less than five times, but d. without male issue in 1654. His brother,

FRANCIS DREWE, Esq. of The Grange, b. in 1604, m. Mary, 2nd dau. of Richard Walrond, Esq. of Ilbrewers, and by her, who d. 14 Sept. 1699, left (with five daus., Susannah, m. to Andrew Davie, Esq. of Vaidhay; Mary, m. to William Bragge, of Sadborow; Bridget, m. 1st, to Francis Fulford, Esq. of Fulford, and 2ndly, to Bampfield Rodd, Esq. of Stoke; Elizabeth, m. to John Arundel, Esq. of Cornwall; and Margaret, m. to Charles Vaughan, Esq. of Ottery) three sons, THOMAS; FRANCIS; and EDWARD. The eldest,

THOMAS DREWE, Esq. of The Grange, b. in 1635, M.P. for Devon in 1699, m. in 1661, Margaret, dau. of Sir Peter Prideaux, Bart. of Netherton, and by that lady, who d. in 1695, had two daus., ELIZABETH, m. to Sir Charles Chichester, Bart. of Youlson; and MARGARET, m. to Charles Kellond, Esq. of Painsford, Devonshire. He d. 10 Aug. 1707, and was s. by his brother,

FRANCIS DREWE, Esq. of The Grange, b. in 1636, m. Miss Martha Webb, and by her, who d. in 1729, had four daus., the three youngest d. unm.; the eldest, ANNE, m. to — Thomas, Esq., auditor of the Imprest. Mr. Drewe d. 22 April, 1710, and was s. by his brother,

EDWARD DREWE, canon of Exeter, who m. Joan, dau. and co-heir of the Right Rev. Dr. Anthony Sparrow, bishop of Exeter, and by that lady, who d. in 1703, left at his decease, in 1714 (with two daus., Susan, m. 1st, to Thomas Ayloffe, LL.D., professor of civil law at Cambridge, and 2ndly, to John Bayley, of London; and Elizabeth, m. to Thomas Mitchell, Esq. of Exeter), an only son,

FRANCIS DREWE, Esq. of The Grange, b. in 1673, M.P. for Exeter in 1714, who sold the Sharpham estate in 1715, and d. in 1716. He m. Mary-Davie, dau. of Humphrey Bidgood, Esq. of Rockbeare, in Devon, and had issue, 1 FRANCIS, his heir; 2 Edward, of Starpoint and Exeter, whose dau. and eventual heir, JULIANA-DOROTHEA, m. Arthur Kelly, Esq. of Kelly; 1 Mary, b. 20 March, 1708, m. to Thomas Carew, Esq. of Crowcombe, co. Somerset, M.P. for Minehead; 2 Elizabeth, m. to Theophilus Blackall, D.D., Chancellor of Exeter, son of Bishop Blackall. Mr. Drewe was s. by his elder son,

FRANCIS DREWE, Esq. of The Grange, b. in 1712, sheriff of Devonshire in 1738, m. 1st, 21 Sept. 1737, Mary, dau. and heir of Thomas Rose, Esq. of Wootton Fitz-Paine, in the co. of Dorset, and by her had,

I. FRANCIS-ROSE, his successor.
II. THOMAS-ROSE, of Wootton Fitz-Paine, co. Dorset, inherited the paternal estates on the decease of his elder brother, in 1801.
III. Richard-Rose, b. 28 Dec. 1743, m. Hannah, dau. of — Spencer, Esq. of Dublin, and had an only child, Harriet, who d. 26 April, 1792. He d. 23 Jan. 1801.
IV. WILLIAM-ROSE, heir to his brother Thomas, in 1815.
V. JOHN-ROSE, successor to his brother William.
VI. Herman, in holy orders, rector of Wootton Fitz Paine, Dorsetshire, and Comb Raleigh, Devon, perpetual curate of Sheldon, b. 6 May, 1749, d. 19 April, 1817, m. Sarah-Mary, dau. of the Rev. William Hatherley, of Colyton, Devon, and had two daus., his co-heirs, viz.,
  1 SARAH-ELIZABETH, m. 9 June, 1800, to Edward-Wright Band, Esq. of Wookey House, Somerset.
  2 MARY, m. 30 Dec. 1801, to the Rev. Lewis Way.

Francis Drewe m. 2ndly, in 1753, Mary, dau. of Thomas Johnson, Esq. of London, and had by her,

I. Edward, in holy orders, rector of Willand, Devon, b. 27 Sept. 1756, m. in 1793, Caroline, dau. of John Allen,

* The family of Drax appears to have been anciently seated in the county of York. In 1647, Col. Drax, Col. Modiford, Col. Walrond, and other cavaliers, having converted their estates into money, and not being able to reside in England under the usurpation, retired to Barbadoes, where Colonel Drax acquired, in a few years, an estate of £8000 or £9000 per annum, and married the daughter of the Earl of Carlisle, then proprietor of the island.

Esq. of Cresselly, in Pembrokeshire, and dying 25 June, 1810, left by her (who *d.* in 1836) one son and three daus.,

1 EDWARD, heir to his uncle.
1 Marianne, *m.* to Algernon, 3rd son of Bennet Langton, Esq., and *d.* leaving a son, Bennet, deceased.
2 Harriett-Maria, *m.* 6 April, 1816, to Robert Gifford, Esq., who became subsequently Lord Chief Justice of the Common Pleas, and was created Baron Gifford.
3 Georgiana, *m.* to Sir Edward-H. Alderson, Baron of the Exchequer.
4 Charlotte, deceased.

II. Samuel, of London, *b.* 19 Nov. 1759, director, and at one time governor of the Bank of England, *m.* Selina Thackeray, and *d.* 3 Feb. 1837, leaving issue,

1 Frederick-William.
1 Emma, *m.* to her cousin, Francis, 3rd son of John-Fownes Luttrell, Esq., and has issue.
2 Augusta.
3 Fanny, *m.* 15 July, 1833, to the Rev. Thomas Marker, rector of Gittisham, and vicar of Farway, Devon.
4 Anna.

I. Mary, *m.* in 1782, to John-Fownes Luttrell, Esq. of Dunster Castle, co. Somerset, M.P., and had issue.
II. Catherine, *d. unm.* in 1772.
III. Charlotte, *m.* to Francis-Fownes Luttrell, Esq., commissioner of the Customs, 2nd son of Henry-Fownes Luttrell, Esq. of Dunster Castle.

Francis Drewe's eldest son,

FRANCIS-ROSE DREWE, Esq. of The Grange, *b.* 23 Sept. 1738, purchased Leyhill, in Payhembury, Devon, an ancient seat of the Willoughbys. He *d. s. p.* 29 April, 1801, and was *s.* by his brother,

THOMAS-ROSE DREWE, Esq. of Wootton Fitz-Paine, Dorsetshire, and afterwards of The Grange, Devonshire, *b.* 14 May, 1740, who *m.* Betty, dau. of Benjamin Incledon, Esq. of Pilton, in Devon, but dying *s. p.* 1 June, 1815, was *s.* by his brother,

WILLIAM-ROSE DREWE, Esq. of New Inn, London, and of The Grange, *b.* 10 July, 1745, at whose decease, in 1821, the estates devolved on his brother,

JOHN-ROSE DREWE, Esq. of The Grange, *b.* 6 June, 1747, who *m.* Dorothy, only dau. of the Rev. Charles Bidgood, of Rockbeare, and by her, who *d.* 11 Dec. 1834, had one son and one dau., viz.

Charles, who *d. unm.* in 1801.
Dorothy-Rose, *m.* to William Miles, Esq. of the life-guards.

Mr. Drewe *d.* 31 Aug. 1830, and was *s.* by his nephew, the present EDWARD DREWE, Esq. of The Grange.

Arms—Erm., a lion, passant, gu.
Crest—On a mount, vert, a roebuck, salient, or.
Seat—The Grange, near Honiton.

DREW OF THE STRAND HOUSE, YOUGHAL.

DREW, THE REV. PIERCE-WILLIAM, of The Strand House, Youghal, co. Cork, rector of Youghal, *b.* 13 March, 1799; *m.* Elizabeth, only dau. and heir of the late Thomas Oliver, Esq. of Wellington-place, Cork, and has had issue,

I. Thomas-Seward, deceased.
II. HENRY-BROUGHAM.
III. Pierce-William.
IV. Thomas-Seward, deceased.
V. Thomas-Seward.
VI. John-Francis-Fitz Drogo, deceased.

I. Matilda-Rowena.
II. Alicia, deceased.
III. Catherine, deceased.
IV. Elizabeth, deceased.
V. Mona-Brougham.
VI. Elizabeth-Oliver; and,
VII. Catherine-Henrietta-Lawton, twins.
VIII. Christina-Rebecca-Pomeroy.
IX. Agnes-Margaret-Naylor.

Mr. Drew is 4th son of the late JOHN DREW, Esq. of Meanus, Rockfield, and Listry, co. Kerry, and of Frogmore, near Youghal, co. Cork, eldest son of the late FRANCIS DREW, Esq., M.D., of Mocollop Castle, co. Waterford, who represented the Drew family in Ireland.

Lineage.—This is a junior branch of the Norman family of DREW *of Drewscliffe, Hayne, and Sharpham*, in Devon, descending from Richard, Duke of Normandy, the CONQUEROR's grandfather, and now represented in England by EDWARD-SIMCOE DREWE, Esq. of The Grange, co. Devon. The following is the preamble of the Drew pedigree, as arranged by Ulster King-of-arms (Betham), given under his official seal, and registered in his office of arms, in Dublin, viz.: "The pedigree of the ancient and knightly family of DREW of *Devonshire*, the lineal descendants of Drogo, or Dru, a noble Norman, son of Walter de Pons, and brother of Richard, ancestor of the Cliffords, who accompanied WILLIAM the Conqueror into England, and of the several branches," &c. This WALTER, or WILLIAM DE PONS, or PONCE, or POUS, was Earl of Arques and Thoulouse, and 3rd son of Richard, Duke of Normandy, grandfather of WILLIAM the Conqueror, and came to England with his victorious and royal nephew (*see* BURKE's *Peerage*, DE CLIFFORD). He had issue three sons, Walter, DREW, and Richard, of whom, RICHARD, the youngest, was father of Walter, surnamed De Clifford, from whom sprang the great and illustrious family of Clifford. DREW, the 2nd son, was, as Prince expresses himself, the "stirp" of the family of Drew, in Devon, where he had no less than seventy-three manors at the time of the Domesday survey.

THOMAS DREW, Esq. of Drewscliffe, Hayne, and Sharpham, who *m.* Eleonora, dau. and heir of William Huckmore, 2nd son of Roger Huckmore, Esq. of Buchite, co. Devon, had two sons, of whom

RICHARD DREW, Esq. of Drewscliffe and Hayne, was father of

JOHN DREW, Esq. of Drewscliffe and Hayne, who *m.* Joan Williams, of Ivesbridge, and had two sons, RICHARD, of Drewscliffe and Hayne, and FRANCIS, of whom we treat. The latter,

FRANCIS DREW, Esq. of Kilwinny, co. Waterford, and of Meanus, co. Kerry, went to Ireland, a captain in the army of Queen ELIZABETH, in or about the year 1598, being then a young man. He *m.* 1st, a dau. of Captain Hart, of co. Limerick; and 2ndly, Susanna, dau. of Leonard Knowel, Esq. of Ballygally, co. Waterford, and by the latter only (who survived him, and *m.* 2ndly, Col. J. Johnstone) had, with other issue, JOHN, of whom presently; BARRY, of Ballyduff, co. Waterford, and of Drewscourt, ancestor of the DREWS *of Drewsboro'* (*see that branch*). The eldest son and heir,

JOHN DREW, Esq. of Kilwinny and Meanus, *m.* 21 March, 1659, Margaret, dau. of the Very Rev. Robert Naylor, dean of Limerick, brother of Joan, mother of Richard Boyle, 1st Earl of Cork, and *d.* 30 May, 1672, leaving two sons and three daus., viz.,

I. FRANCIS, his heir.
II. John, of Ballinlough, co. Kilkenny, *m.* 1st, Sarah, dau. of Maunsell, Esq., by whom he had a son,

1 John, of Tercallen, co. Waterford, who *m.* Martha, dau. of Langley, Esq., and had, besides two daus. (Alice, *m.* to John Croker, Esq. of Glanbeg, co. Waterford; and Catharine, *m.* to Richard Medlicott, Esq. of Castle Lyons, co. Cork), and several sons who *d.* young, three other sons, viz., Francis, of Belloisle, *m.* Catherine, dau. of Burley, Esq., and *d.* in April, 1776; John, surgeon in the army; and Robert, capt. in the army, *d. unm.*

Mr. John Drew *m.* 2ndly, Catherine, dau. of William Heydon, Esq., and by her had (besides Catherine, *m.* to Robert Whitty, Esq., and *d.* in 1767; Susanna, *m.* to Thomas Smith, Esq. of Carrick, co. Tipperary; Jane; Margaret; and Rebecca) four sons, viz.,

1 Francis, of Ballinspellig, co. Waterford, *m.* Rebecca, dau. of Baines, Esq., and had two sons,

John, of Ballinspellig, *m.* Susanna, sister of Richard Gumbleton, Esq. of Castle Richard, and had two sons and three daus., viz., Francis, John-Gumbleton, Mary, Susannah, and Catherine.
George, of Ballybrittas, *m.* Susanna, dau. of John Drew, Esq., and by her (who *d.* in 1764) had a son, Francis, and three daus., Margaret, Rebecca, and Catherine.

2 William, *m.* Mary, dau. of Poe, Esq., and by her (who *m.* 2ndly, Dr Doherty) had issue,

John, *d. unm.*
Barry, of co. Kilkenny, *m.* a dau. of Paul, Esq.
Catherine, *m.* to the Rev. J. Hewson, of Suirville, co. Kilkenny.
Margaret, *m.* to Matthews, Esq. of Kilmacon, co. Kilkenny.

3 Barry, in holy orders.
4 James, *m.* a dau. of Conner, Esq.

I. Anne, *m.* to John Gibbins, Esq.
II. Bridget, *m.* to Langley, Esq.
III. Margaret.

The elder son and heir,

FRANCIS DREW, Esq. of Kilwinny and Meanus, *m.* 20 Dec. 1695, Rebecca, dau. and co heir of Samuel Pomeroy, Esq. of Pallace, co. Cork, and *d.* 2 Sept. 1734, leaving an only dau. and heiress,

MARGARET DREW, of Kilwinny and Meanus, *m.* 8 Jan. 1713, her kinsman, JOHN DREW, Esq. of Ballyduff House, co. Waterford, 2nd son of Barry Drew, Esq. of Drews Court, co. Limerick (*see* Drew *of Drewsboro'*), and by him (whose will is dated 24 Oct. 1747) had issue. The eldest son and heir,

Francis Drew, Esq., M.D., of Meanus, Listry, and Rockfield, co. Kerry, and Ballyduff House, Waterpark, and Mocollop Castle, co. Waterford, *m.* 1752, Arabella, dau. and co-heir of Colonel William Godfrey, of Bushfield (now Kilcoleman Abbey), co. Kerry, by Elizabeth his wife, dau. and co-heir of the Rev. Richard Downing, of Knockgrafton, co. Tipperary. By this lady, Dr. Drew had issue,

I. John, his heir.
II. Francis, of Mocollop Castle, *b.* in 1756, who *m.* Emilia, dau. of Boyd, Esq., and had issue,
  1 Francis, of Mocollop Castle, who *m.* a dau. of Ross, Esq., and relict of Evans, Esq., and had a son, Francis, an officer in the Scots Greys, *d. unm.* 1839; and a dau., Olivia, heiress of Mocollop Castle, *m.* James Barry, Esq. of Ballyclough, co. Cork.
  2 Tankerville, who *m.* Jane, dau. of John Elmore, Esq., and left issue, a son, Tankerville, and a dau., Helen.
  3 John, and 4 Samuel; both deceased.
  5 Henry. 5 James.
  1 Lucinda, 2 Emilia, and 3 Arabella; all deceased.
III. Barry, of Flower Hill, co. Waterford, *m.* Julia, dau. of the Rev. James Hewson, and had (besides a son, Francis, and two daus., Catherine; and Julia, deceased) an elder son and heir, Barry, of Flower Hill, who *m.* Jane, dau. of Arthur Baker, Esq. of Ballyheary House, co. Dublin, and has issue.
IV. William, *d. unm.*
V. Pascal-Paoli, M.D., *m.* Elizabeth Charteris, and had issue, William, M.D., deceased; Francis, M.D.; Edward, M.D.
I. Arabella, *m.* (settlement dated 28 Oct. 1784) to Peard-Harrison Peard, Esq. of Carrigeen, co. Cork.
II. Margaret, *m.* to Edward Heard, Esq. of Ballintober, co. Cork, major in the army.
III. Deborah, *m.* to the Rev. Pierce Power, of Affane, co. Waterford, and *d.* 26 Feb. 1844.

Dr. Drew *d.* 3 Sept. 1787, aged 79, and was *s.* by his eldest son.

John Drew, Esq. of Listry and Rockfield, co. Kerry, and of Frogmore, near Youghal, co. Cork, who *m.* in 1786, Alicia, eldest dau. of Pierce Power, Esq. of Affane, co. Waterford, by Elizabeth his wife, sole dau. and heir of Valentine Browning, Esq. of Affane, and Jane his wife, dau. of Samuel Hayman, Esq. of Clonpriest and Myrtle Grove, in Youghal, and by this lady (who *d.* 6 Dec. 1842) had issue,

Francis, his heir.
John, of Rockfield, co. Kerry, *m.* Helen, eldest dau. of John Elmore, Esq., and had, John, deceased; John-Henry; Helena; Alicia; Catherine, *m.* to Adam-Newman Perry, Esq. of the city of Cork.
Samuel-Browning, in holy orders, *m.* 1st, Mary, dau. of Col. Foot, of Millfort, co. Cork; and 2ndly, Anne, dau. of Richard-Townsend Herbert, Esq. of Cahernane, co. Kerry, and by the former had, Browning, an officer in the 14th regt. of foot; and Mary.
Pierce-William, in holy orders, now of The Strand House, rector of Youghal.
Arabella, *m.* to Walter Atkin, Esq. of Atkinville, co. Cork.
Elizabeth, *d. unm.*
Catherine, *d.* an infant.
Alicia, *m.* to Henry Lindsay, Esq. of Hayfield, co. Cork.

Mr. Drew *d.* 14 Dec. 1813, and was *s.* by his eldest son,

Francis Drew, Esq. of Meanus, co. Kerry, and Frogmore, near Youghal, who *m.* Jane, dau. of Thomas Garde, Esq. of Ballindinis, co. Cork, and *d.* in Dec. 1839, having had issue,

Francis. John.
Elizabeth. Deborah, deceased.
Rebecca. Louisa.

Arms—Erm., a lion passant, gu., langued and armed.
Crest—A bull's head, erased, sa., in his mouth three ears of wheat, or.
Motto—Drogo nomen et virtus arma dedit.
Seat—The Strand House, Youghal.

DREW OF DREWSBORO'.

Drew, Francis, Esq. of Drewsboro', co. Clare, *m.* 17 July, 1833, the Hon. Margaret-Everina Massy, dau. of Hugh, 3rd Lord Massy, and has issue.

Lineage.—Barry Drew, Esq. of Ballyduff, co. Waterford, and of Drews Court, co. Limerick, 2nd son of Francis Drew, Esq. of Kilwinny, co. Cork, and of Meanus, co. Kerry (*see preceding article*), was receiver to the estates of the Earl of Cork and Burlington, in the reign of James II. He *m.* 1st, a dau. of Sir Francis Foulkes, Knt. of Camphire, but by her had no issue; and 2ndly, Ruth, dau. of William Nettles, Esq. of Tourine, co. Waterford, by Mary his wife, sister of the celebrated Valentine Greatrakes, and had two sons,

Francis, his heir.
John, of Ballyduff House, who *m.* Margaret Drew, of Meanus. (*See preceding family.*)

The elder son,

Francis Drew, Esq. of Drews Court, co. Limerick, served as high-sheriff of that county in 1718. He *m.* Margaret, 2nd dau. and co-heir (by Avarina his wife, dau. and co-heir of Col. Purdon, of Ballyclogh, co. Cork, and Bell Kelly, co. Clare), of Col. Richard Ringrose, of Moynoe House, co. Clare, and had issue,

I. Francis, successor to his father at Drews Court, *m.* Susannah, dau. of John Bourke, Esq., and aunt of General Sir Richard Bourke, and *d. s. p.*
II. John, successor to his brother, *m.* a dau. of — Godfrey, Esq. of co. Kerry, and *d. s. p.*
III. Barry, of Drews Court, *m.* Mary, dau. of Odell Conyers, Esq. of Castletown Conyers, co. Limerick, and had one son and one dau., viz.,
  1 Francis, of Drews Court, *m.* Sarah, dau. and co-heir of Lloyd Langford, Esq. of the co. of Kerry, and *d. s. p.*
  1 Margaret, of Drews Court, heiress to her brother, *m.* to John-Cuffe Kelly, Esq., who *d. s. p.* She *d.* 15 March, 1845.
IV. Ringrose, of whom presently.
V. George-Purdon, of High Park, co. Dublin, one of the Six Clerks in Chancery in 1757. He *m.* Letitia, sister of Sir William Godfrey, Bart. of Bushfield, co. Kerry, and *d.* in 1785, aged 45, leaving issue,
  1 John-Godfrey, lieut.-col. in the army.
  2 George-Purdon, major 45th regt.
  3 Barry, capt. 45th regt.
  4 Francis, capt. 45th regt.
I. Alice, *m.* to Charles O'Neil, Esq. of Monkstown Castle, co. Dublin, barrister-at-law, M.P. for Cloghnakilty.
II. Jane, *m.* in 1775, to the Rev. Robert Nettles, rector of Ballinamona, near Mallow.
III. Ruth, *m.* to Joseph Hall, Esq. of Dublin, and had issue.
IV. Margaret, *m.* — Nash, Esq. of Briuny, co. Cork, and had issue.

The 4th son,

Ringrose Drew, of Skally, Coolrea, &c., and of Drewsboro', *m.* 6 Oct. 1750, his cousin, Jane, only dau. of James Molony, Esq. of Kiltanon, co. Clare, by Elizabeth Crossdaile his wife, and had issue. The eldest son and heir,

Francis Drew, Esq. of Drewsboro', high-sheriff of co. Clare in 1788, *m.* in 1782, Frances, dau. of John Odell, Esq. of Bealduroghy, co. Limerick, and had issue two sons, Ringrose, his heir; Francis, *m.*, but *d. s. p.*; and two daus., of whom one *m.* — Hewlett, Esq.; the other, — Brady, Esq. of Raheen, co. Clare. He was *s.* by his elder son,

Ringrose Drew, Esq. of Drewsboro', who *m.* Alicia, dau. of John Willington, Esq. of Castle Willington, co. Tipperary, and *d.* in 1834, leaving issue a son, Francis, now of Drewsboro', and three daus., of whom the 2nd, Alicia-Wellington, *m.* 23 July, 1836, the Rev. William Nisbet, M.A., of Agonilloe, co. Clare, and is since deceased; and the youngest *d. unm.*

Arms, Crest, and *Motto*—Same as Drew *of The Strand House*, but some different quarterings.
Seat—Drewsboro', co. Clare.

DRINKWATER OF IRWELL.

Drinkwater, Thomas, Esq. of Irwell House, co. Lancaster, J.P., *b.* 5 May, 1775; *m.* 9 Aug. 1813, Sarah, 4th surviving dau. of Nathan Hyde, Esq. of Ardwick, and has issue,

I. Fanny. II. Ellen.
III. Margaret. IV. Julia.

Lineage.—This branch of the ancient family of Drinkwater became seated at Irwell about the middle of the last century, at which period

Peter Drinkwater, Esq., son of Thomas Drinkwater, of Whalloy, purchased the estate. He *m.* 14 May, 1771, Margaret Bolton, of Preston, and had issue,

Thomas, now of Irwell.
John, of Sherborne, co. Warwick, who *m.* Ellen, 6th surviving dau. of Nathan Hyde, Esq. of Ardwick, in Lancashire, and has one dau., Sophia.
Margaret, *m.* to John-Pemberton Heywood, Esq. of Wakefield, barrister-at-law.
Eliza, *m.* to Colonel D'Aguilar, deputy-adjutant-general, Dublin.

Mr. Drinkwater *d.* 15 Nov. 1801.

Arms—Per pale, gu. and az., on a fesse, wavy, arg., three billets, of the second, between as many garbs, or.

Crest—Three ears of wheat, two in saltier, one in pale, or, encircled by a ducal coronet.

Motto—Ne quid nimis.

Seat—Irwell House.

DROUGHT OF LETTYBROOK.

DROUGHT, JOHN-HEAD, Esq. of Lettybrook, King's County, *b.* 20 Aug. 1790, J.P. and D.L., high-sheriff in 1821; *m.* 20 July, 1853, Frances, dau. of Henry Spunner, Esq. of Corolanty.

Lineage.—The first settler in Ireland, of this family, is presumed to have accompanied CROMWELL. He had three sons: William, of Killmagarvoge, co. Carlow; Thomas, of the same place, who *m.* Maria Peele, of Killenure; and the eldest,

RICHARD DROUGHT, Esq. of Cappogolan, King's County, who *m.* a dau. of John Baldwin, Esq. of Shinrone, in the same county, and had issue, 1 JOHN, his heir; 2 Arthur, of Heath, King's County; 3 Richard; 4 Robert, of Park, King's County, who was father of John Drought, Esq. of Ballyboy; and 5 Thomas, of Plunketstown, co. Kildare, who *m.* and had issue, William, of Commonstown, co. Kildare; John, father of John, of Dromore; and Anthony. The eldest son,

JOHN DROUGHT, Esq. of Cappogolan, *m.* Mary, dau. of Euseby Beasly, Esq., and had issue. The eldest son,

JOHN DROUGHT, Esq. of The Heath, King's County, *m.* Alice, dau. of Nathaniel Low, Esq. of Lowville, co. Galway, and had, with other issue,

THOMAS, of whom presently.
John, of Whigsboro' (*see* DROUGHT *of Whigsboro'*).
Euseby, *m.* Dorothy Elliot, and had two sons and two daus.
William-Beasley, capt. 12th dragoons.

The eldest son,

THOMAS DROUGHT, Esq. of Droughtville, *m.* Caroline, dau. of Warneford Armstrong, Esq. of Clara, King's County, and, with three daus., Alice, Caroline, and Mary, had two sons. The elder, THOMAS, of Droughtville, *b.* in 1758, *m.* Frances-Maria, dau. of the Hon. Col. Thomas Wallon, president of the council of Jamaica, and had issue, John, *b.* in Nov. 1780; James; Jane, wife of Captain Pigot; and Eliza, wife of William Hawkins, Esq., eldest son of the late Bishop of Raphoe. The younger,

JOHN-ARMSTRONG DROUGHT, Esq. of Lettybrook, *b.* about 1762, *m.* Letitia, dau. of John Head, Esq. of Ashley Park, co. Tipperary, by Phœbe his wife, sister of John, 1st Earl of Norbury, and had issue, JOHN-HEAD, now of Lettybrook; Michael-Head, barrister-at-law, who *m.* Anna, dau. of William Hutchinson, Esq. of Timoney Hall, co. Tipperary, and *d.* Nov. 1850; Thomas-Armstrong, colonel in the army; Phœbe, wife of Major-General Green Barry; Caroline, wife of Richard Millett, Esq. of Kyle, co. Tipperary; Letitia, wife of James-B. Elliott, Esq. of South Lodge, co. Tipperary, and *d.* 1839; Maria-Catherine, *d.* Nov. 1853; and Eliza-Barbara, who *d.* young. Mr. Drought *d.* in April, 1838.

Arms—Or, a chevron, between three wolves' heads, erased, sa.

Crest—A rainbow, ppr.

Motto—Semper sitiens.

Seat—Lettybrook, King's County.

DROUGHT OF WHIGSBORO'.

DROUGHT, JOHN-ALEXANDER, Esq. of Whigsboro', King's County, *b.* 19 Jan. 1808, J.P., capt. King's County militia, and captain in the army; *m.* 16 Jan. 1836, Caroline-Susanna, dau. of the late Lieut.-Col. John White, of the 80th regt., and has surviving issue,

I. JOHN-WILLIAM, *b.* 25 Sept. 1847.

I. Caroline-Jane-Isabella.
II. Anne-Perceval.
III. Alice-Elizabeth.
IV. Mary-Frances.
V. Georgiana-Letitia.
VI. Charlotte-Sarah-Carr.

Lineage.—THOMAS DROUGHT, Esq. of Whigsboro', *b.* in 1725, 2nd son of John Drought, Esq. of The Heath, by Alice Low his wife, *m.* Susanna, dau. of Adam Mitchell, Esq. of Rathgibbon, King's County, and widow of — Clarke, Esq., and had an only son and heir,

JOHN DROUGHT, Esq. of Whigsboro', *b.* in 1751, who *m.* 27 May, 1772, Isabella, dau. and co-heir of George Meares, Esq. of the city of Dublin, and by her (who *d.* in 1805), left at his decease, in 1814, issue,

JOHN, his heir.
George-Meares, of Willsborough, co. Wicklow, and of Bellomont, King's County, *m.* Jane, dau. of Thomas Acton, Esq. of West Aston, co. Wicklow, and has issue, Sidney, *b.* in March, 1806; and Isabella.
Francis.
Isabella, wife of Robert-James Enright Mooney, Esq. of Doone, King's County.
Susan, wife of Robert Lowther, Esq. of Moyclare, King's County.
Elizabeth, wife of Henry Spunner, Esq. of Corolanta, King's County.

The eldest son,

JOHN-THOMAS DROUGHT, Esq. of Whigsboro', *b.* 4 April, 1782, *m.* Oct. 1805, Anne-Carleton, sister of Col. Alexander Perceval, of Temple House, co. Sligo, and by her, who *d.* 5 May, 1841, had issue,

JOHN-ALEXANDER, now of Whigsboro'.
Philip-Francis, *m.* Miss Graves, co. Limerick.
George-Perceval, paymaster H.M. 62nd regt., *m.* Miss Rathborne.
Francis-Perceval, lieut. H.M. 53rd regt.
Isabella-Meares, *m.* to Major L'Estrange.

Mr. Drought *d.* 30 Nov. 1851.

Arms, &c.—*See* DROUGHT *of Lettybrook.*

Seat—Whigsboro', King's County.

DRUMMOND OF BLAIR DRUMMOND.

HOME-DRUMMOND, HENRY, Esq. of Blair Drummond, co. Perth, vice-lieutenant and M.P. for that shire, *b.* 28 July, 1783; *m.* 14 April, 1812, Christian, eldest dau. of Charles Moray, Esq. of Abercairny, co. Perth, and sister and heir of William Moray-Stirling, Esq., and has issue,

I. GEORGE, *b.* 1 March, 1813, M.A., of Christ Church, Oxford, *m.* in 1840, Mary, dau. of William Hay, Esq. of Dunse Castle, co. Berwick.

II. Charles, *b.* 17 April, 1816, late of 2nd life-guards; *m.* 11 Dec. 1845, Lady Anne-Georgina, youngest dau. of Charles, 5th Marquess of Queensberry, and has issue,
1 Henry-Edward, *b.* 15 Sept. 1846.
2 William-Augustus, *b.* 12 April, 1852.
1 Caroline-Frances.

I. Anne, *m.* in 1839, to George, Lord Glenlyon, now Duke of Atholl.

Lineage.—ALEXANDER HOME, of Manderston, 3rd son of Sir David Home, of Wedderburn, slain at Flodden, had two sons, 1 ALEXANDER, of Manderston, who commanded a body of horse at Langside—he was father of George, Earl of Dunbar; and 2 PATRICK, of Renton. This 2nd son,

PATRICK HOME, *m.* in 1558, Janet, dau. and heir of David Ellem, of Renton, and thereby acquired that estate. He was father of

ALEXANDER HOME, of Renton, whose son,

JOHN HOME, of Renton, had three sons, 1 Alexander (Sir), of Coldinghame, Bart., whose male line terminated with his grandson, Sir John Home, Bart., in 1788; 2 Patrick (Sir), of Renton, Bart., whose male line ended at the decease of his grandson, Sir James Home, Bart., in 1785; and 3 HENRY, of Kames. The youngest son,

HENRY HOME, of Kames, co. Berwick, was father of

GEORGE HOME, of Kames, whose son was the celebrated

HENRY HOME, of Kames, *b.* in 1696, who became a judge of session in 1752, and assumed the title of Lord Kames. Under this designation, he acquired great literary distinction by his *Elements of Criticism, Sketches of the History of Man, The Gentleman Farmer,* &c. Lord Kames *d.* in Dec. 1782. He *m.* Agatha, dau. of James Drummond, of Blair Drummond, co. Perth (descended from Walter Drummond, of Lederieff, 3rd son of Sir Walter Drummond, Knt. of Cargill and Stobhall, who *d.* in 1455), and by her (who *s.* to the estate of Blair Drummond, at the decease of her nephew, James, in 1766), had a son and successor,

GEORGE HOME-DRUMMOND, Esq. of Blair Drummond, who *m.* 11 Oct. 1782, Janet, dau. of John Jardine, D.D., a cadet of JARDINE *of Applegirth*, co. Dumfries, and by her (who *d.* 30 Jan. 1840) had issue,

HENRY, now of Blair Drummond.
John-George, of Abbotsgrange, *m.* 7 Jan. 1837, Mary, dau. of Archibald Drummond, of Rudgeway, a cadet of the family of Blair Drummond, and *d. s. p.* 5 Feb. 1848.
Agatha, of Abbotsgrange.

Mr. Home-Drummond *d.* 28 Oct. 1819.

Arms—Quarterly: DRUMMOND and HOME.

Seat—Blair Drummond, co. Perth.

DRUMMOND OF ALBURY PARK.

DRUMMOND, HENRY, Esq. of Albury Park, co. Surrey, F.R.S., J.P., and M.P. for West Surrey, *b.* 5 Dec. 1786; *m.* 23 June, 1807, Lady Henrietta Hay-Drummond, eldest dau. of Robert-Auriol, 9th Earl of Kinnoull, and has had issue,

I. Henry, *b.* 1811, *d.* 1827.
II. Malcolm, *b.* 1821, *d.* 1843.
III. Arthur-Henry, *b.* 1822, *d.* 1846.
I. Louisa, *m.* 26 May, 1845, to Lord Lovaine, eldest son of the Earl of Beverley.
II. Adelaide, *m.* 16 Sept. 1850, to Sir Thomas Rokewode Gage, Bart.

Lineage.—The Hon. Henry Drummond, 4th son of William, 4th Viscount Strathallan, was of The Grange, Hants, and Charing Cross, banker. He *m.* in 1761, Elizabeth, dau. of the Hon. Charles Compton, and *d.* in 1795, leaving issue,

I. Henry, banker, of the city of London, *m.* 13 Feb. 1786, Anne, dau. of Henry, 1st Viscount Melville (who was *m.* 2ndly, to James Strange, Esq.), and dying 4 July, 1794, left issue,
1 HENRY, now of Albury Park, Surrey, M.P., F.S.A.
2 Robert, *b.* 24 June, 1789, *d.* 17 June, 1811.
3 Spencer-Rodney, in holy orders, *b.* 17 Dec. 1790, *m.* 6 May, 1817, Caroline, only dau. of the late Montagu Montagu, Esq., and has an only dau., Caroline-Anne, *m.* 26 April, 1849, to the Rev. Henry-John Vernon.
1 Elizabeth, *m.* 1 Aug. 1815, to John Portal, Esq. of Freefolk, Hants.

Arms, &c.—As DRUMMOND *of Cadland.*
Seat—Albury Park, Guildford.

DRUMMOND OF CONCRAIG.

DRUMMOND, JOHN, Esq. of The Boyce, co. Gloucester, J.P., present head of the DRUMMONDS *of Concraig*, *b.* 5 Oct. 1793; *m.* 5 May, 1821, Georgiana-Augusta Finch, dau. of George, 8th Earl of Winchilsea, and has issue two daus.,

I. Georgiana-Matilda. II. Sophia-Annabella.

Mr. Drummond is a colonel in the army, and a magistrate for the county of Gloucester.

Lineage.—The DRUMMONDS *of Concraig* derive from SIR MAURICE DRUMMOND, of Concraig, 2nd son of Sir Malcolm Drummond, 10th Thane of Lennox, ancestor, by his eldest son, of the Drummonds, Earls and Dukes of Perth, and Earls of Melfort.

SIR JOHN DRUMMOND, 3rd Knight of Concraig, coroner and seneschal of Strathern, was involved in a serious contest with the Murray family, in vindication of his judicial authority, which led, in the sequel, to the death of the Earl of Strathern, by the hand of Sir John. The 2nd son of Sir John Drummond, 3rd knight of Concraig, JOHN DRUMMOND, to whom his father granted the lands of Lennoch, in Strathern, was ancestor of the DRUMMONDS *of Lennoch*, whose representative, in 1640,

JOHN DRUMMOND, 8th Baron of Lennoch, purchased from Sir George Hay, ancestor of the Earl of Kinnoull, the barony of Megginch. He *m.* Jean, dau. of Colin Campbell, of Aberuchill, uncle of John, Earl of Loudon, and by her was father of an only dau., Anne, *m.* in 1678, to Alexander Duncan, of Seaside, ancestor of the DUNCANS *of Lundie*; and of a son,

ADAM DRUMMOND, 9th Baron of Lennoch, and 2nd of Megginch, who was a privy councillor of Scotland, and, in 1695, one of the commissioners to inquire into the slaughter of the Macdonalds of Glencoe. He *m.* Alison, eldest dau. of John Hay, of Haystoun, descended from the Tweeddale family, and had issue. The elder son,

JOHN DRUMMOND, 10th of Lennoch, and 3rd of Megginch, M.P. for Perthshire in 1727, *m.* in 1712, Bethia, dau. of James Murray, Esq. of Deuchar, descended from the family of Philiphaugh, and had issue, of whom was

Adam, 11th of Lennoch, and 4th of Megginch, *b.* in 1713, capt. in the army. He served in the first American war, was M.P. for Lymington, for the Forfar burghs, and for Shaftesbury, and resided at Drummond Castle till the restoration of the estate. He *m.* in 1734, Lady Katharine Paulet, 2nd dau. of Henry, Duke of Bolton, but left no issue.
COLLIN, of whom presently.
Jean, *m.* 1st, to James, 2nd Duke of Atholl; and 2ndly, to Lord Adam Gordon, 6th son of the Duke of Gordon.

The only son to leave issue,

COLLIN DRUMMOND, Esq., *b.* in 1722, *m.* in 1753, Katherine, dau. of Oliphant of Rossie, and sister of the Countess of Hopetoun, and had issue,

I. JOHN, M.P., *b.* in 1754, 12th of Lennoch, and 5th of Megginch, sold the former patrimonial property, and, in 1795, disposed of Megginch to Robert, who entailed it on his next brother, Sir Adam Drummond, K.C.H.
II. Robert, capt. in the Hon. E. I. Co.'s marine, *b.* in 1759, *m.* in 1810, Mary, dau. of the Rev. Mr. Phillimore, and *d. s. p.* in 1815.
III. ADAM (Sir), of Megginch Castle.
IV. Gordon (Sir), *b.* in 1772, Gen., G.C.B., col. 49th regt., *m.* Margaret, dau. of W. Russell, Esq. of Brancepeth Castle, co. Durham, and had issue,
1 Gordon, capt. and lieut.-col. Coldstream-guards.
2 Russell, lieut. R.N., killed at Calloa Sanurica.
1 Eliza, *m.* in 1832, to the Earl of Effingham.
I. Elizabeth, *m.* in 1784, to Lord Hervey, capt. R.N., son of the Earl of Bristol, and *d.* in 1818.

The eldest son,

JOHN DRUMMOND, Esq., M.P., 12th of Lennoch, and 5th of Megginch, *m.* 1788, Lady Susan Fane, dau. of John, 9th Earl of Westmoreland, and by her (who *d.* in 1795) left at his decease, a dau., Susan, who *m.* in 1811, George Moore, Esq. of Appleby Hall, co. Leicester, and *d.* in 1813; and a son, the present JOHN DRUMMOND, Esq. of The Boyce.

Arms—Per fesse, wavy, or and gu.
Crest—Two arms drawing an arrow to the head, in a bow, ppr.
Supporters—Dexter, a naked savage, wreathed about the head and middle with oak-leaves, holding over his dexter shoulder a club, all ppr.; sinister, a knight, armed at all points, visor of his helmet up, a spear resting on his sinister arm, also ppr.
Motto—Marte et arte.
Seat—The Boyce, co. Gloucester.

DRUMMOND OF MEGGINCH CASTLE.

DRUMMOND, JOHN-MURRAY, Esq. of Megginch Castle, co. Perth, late of the Grenadier-guards, *b.* 10 April, 1803; *m.* 20 Nov. 1835, Frances-Jemima, 4th dau. of the late General Sir John Oswald, of Dunnikier, G.C.B., G.C.M.G., and has a dau., Mary.

Lineage.—SIR ADAM DRUMMOND, K.C.H., admiral R.N., of Megginch; *b.* in 1770, 3rd son of Colin Drummond, Esq., 11th of Lennoch, and 4th of Megginch, *m.* 28 May, 1801, Lady Charlotte Murray, eldest dau. of John, 4th Duke of Atholl, and widow of Sir John Menzies, Bart., and by her (who *d.* 31 May, 1832) had issue,

JOHN-MURRAY, now of Megginch.
Robert, in holy orders, vicar of Feering, Essex, *m.* 19 Jan. 1841, Hon. Charlotte-Olivia-Elizabeth, 2nd dau. of the late Col. Strutt and the Baroness Rayleigh, of Terling, co. Essex.
Adam-Augustus, major 11th regt. Bombay native infantry, *m.* in 1827, Miss Sandelia Symon, and has issue, James-Charles, *b.* in 1832 (deceased), and three daus.
James-Charles, lieut. 41st Bengal native infantry, *d.* in India, in 1827.
Charles-Gordon, Bengal civil service, *d.* in India, in 1831.
Henry-Maurice, late capt. 42nd Royal Highlanders, now major Royal Perthshire Rifles.
Jane-Catherine.

Arms, &c.—See preceding family.
Seat—Megginch Castle.

DRUMMOND OF CADLAND.

DRUMMOND, ANDREW-ROBERT, Esq. of Cadland, co. Hants, *b.* 28 July, 1794; *m.* 7 March, 1822, Lady Elizabeth-Frederica Manners, dau. of John-Henry, Duke of Rutland, and has issue,

I. ANDREW-JOHN, *b.* 13 May, 1823.
II. Edgar-Atheling, *b.* 21 Aug. 1825.
III. Alfred-Manners, lieut. rifle brigade, *b.* 26 Aug. 1829.
IV. Victor-Arthur-Wellington, *b.* 4 June, 1833.
V. Cecil-George-Assheton, *b.* 11 April, 1839.
I. Annabella-Mary-Elizabeth, *m.* 4 Dec. 1844, to Alexander-Dundas-Ross-Wishart-Baillie Cochrane, Esq.
II. Frederica-Mary-Adeliza, *m.* 8 Oct. 1846, to Richard-George Lumley, Esq.

Lineage.—ANDREW-BERKELEY DRUMMOND, Esq. of Cadland (eldest son of the Hon. Robert Drummond, 3rd son of William, 4th Viscount Strathallan, by Margaret his wife, dau. of William, Lord Nairne), *b.* Sept. 1755, *m.* 2 April, 1781, Lady Mary Perceval, dau. of John, 2nd Earl of Egmont, and had by her (who d. 10 Sept. 1839) two sons and two daus., viz.,

ANDREW-ROBERT, now of Cadland.
William-Charles, a lieut.-col. in the army, b. 14 July, 1796.
Mary, m. 18 Oct. 1830, to the Rev. Francis Fulford, D.D., Bishop of Montreal.
Catherine-Isabella, m. 27 March, 1826, to the Rev. Henry Perceval, son of the Right Hon. Spencer Perceval.

Mr. Drummond d. 27 Dec. 1833.

Arms—Quarterly: 1st and 4th, or, three bars, wavy, gu.: 2nd and 3rd, or, a lion's head, erased, within a double tressure, flory-counterflory, gu.
Crest—A goshawk, wings expanded, ppr.
Seat—Cadland, Hants.

DRUMMOND OF STANMORE.

DRUMMOND, GEORGE-HARLEY, Esq. of Stanmore, in Middlesex, at one time M.P. for Kincardineshire, b. 23 Nov. 1783; m. 9 Feb. 1801, Margaret, dau. of the late Alexander Munro, Esq. of Glasgow, and by her (who d. 23 July, 1858) has issue,

I. GEORGE, b. 12 Feb. 1802, m. 14 April, 1831, Marianne, 2nd dau. of the late Edward-Berkeley Portman, Esq. of Bryanston, in Dorsetshire, and by her (who d. 1 Dec. 1842) left at his decease, 5 Jan. 1851, 1 George-James, b. 22 June, 1835; 1 Mary-Margaret; 2 Lucy-Anne; 3 Beatrix-Sophia; and 4 Harriet-Ada.
II. Henry-Dundas, in the army, b. 17 Dec. 1812, m. 1 Dec. 1838, Sophia-Jane, only surviving dau. of the late Charles-C. Mackinnon, Esq.
I. Margaret, d. in 1838.

Lineage.—ANDREW DRUMMOND, Esq. (brother of William, 4th Viscount Strathallan), founder of the well-known banking-house of Drummond and Co., purchased the estate of Stanmore, in Middlesex, in 1729, and d. in 1769, aged 82, leaving, by Strachan his wife, a dau., Isabel, m. to Captain Peters; and a son,

JOHN DRUMMOND, Esq. of Stanmore, in Middlesex, M.P. for Thetford, who m. in 1744, Charlotte, dau. of Lord William Beauclerk, son of Charles, 1st Duke of St. Albans, and dying in 1774, left (with junior issue, for which see BURKE'S *Peerage*) a son and heir,

GEORGE DRUMMOND, Esq. of Stanmore, b. in 1758, who m. in 1779, Martha, dau. of the Right Hon. Thomas Harley, and had issue,

I. GEORGE-HARLEY, now of Stanmore.
II. Andrew-Mortimer, b. 9th Nov. 1786, m. 25 July, 1808, Lady Emily-Charlotte Percy, 4th dau. of Algernon, 1st Earl of Beverley, and has issue, 1 Mortimer-Percy, b. 7 Sept. 1816, m. 8 Oct. 1840, Jane, eldest dau. of James Drummond Nairne, Esq.; 1 Emily Susan; 2 Eleanor-Charlotte, m. 20 June, 1843, to George Wodehouse, Esq., comm. R.N.; 3 Julia-Frances; 4 Cecil-Elizabeth, m. 8 Jan. 1840, to the Rev. Heneage Drummond; 5 Agnes-Priscilla, m. 27 Feb. 1851, to the Rev. Berdmore Compton; 6 Susan-Caroline, m. 16 April, 1844, to Harvey Drummond, Esq.; 7 Marion.
I. Henrietta-Martha, m. 19 April, 1803, to Vice-Admiral Sir Charles Hamilton, Bart.

Mr. Drummond d. in 1789.

Arms and *Crest*—See DRUMMOND *of Cadland.*
Seat—Stanmore.

DRURY OF KNIGHTSTONE.

DRURY, THE REV. CHARLES, M.A., F.A.S., of Knightstone, co. Devon, prebendary of Hereford, and rector of the second portion of Pontesbury, Salop, b. 20 April, 1788.

Lineage.—This family is descended from the very ancient house of the DRURYS *of Suffolk*. The founder of it came into England with the CONQUEROR, as is recorded in the Battle Abbey Roll. He settled first at Thurston, and subsequently at Rougham, near Bury St. Edmunds, co. Suffolk, and his descendants continued in possession of that estate for about six hundred years or more.

From this house branched off the DRURYS *of Hawsted*, Suffolk, who built Drury House, in London, *temp.* ELIZABETH, the road leading to which has ever since retained the name of Drury-lane. It stood a little behind the site of the present Olympic theatre.

Of another branch of this family was SIR DRUE DRURY, who, together with Sir Amias Powlett, had, at one period, the custody of MARY Queen of Scots.

The immediate descent of DRURY *of Knightstone* is from JOHN DRURY, 3rd son of SIR ROBERT DRURY, of Rougham, Suffolk, b. *temp.* ELIZABETH. This gentleman became possessed of, and removed to, Leviate Hall, parish of Ashwyhen, near Lynn, in Norfolk, in the reign of JAMES I. His descendants, in the 3rd generation, alienated that property to the family of the Lord Keeper North. There is no trace that any of this branch of the Drurys again became possessors of landed estate, until the latter part of the last century, when

THE REV. JOSEPH DRURY, D.D., prebendary of Wells, purchased lands at Dawlish, in Devon, and built a seat thereon, called Cockwood House. Dr. Drury was for several years master of Harrow, but he relinquished that post in 1804. He m. in 1777, Louisa, dau. of Benjamin Heath, Esq., LL.D., of Exeter, author of many learned works, and had, with one dau., Louisa-Heath, m. to John Herman Merivale, Esq. of Benton Place, co. Devon (by whom she has numerous issue), three sons, the youngest and only surviving of whom is the present REV. CHARLES DRURY, M.A., of Knightstone. The two elder sons, Henry-Thomas-Joseph, and Benjamin-Heath, who are both deceased, married and left issue; the son of the eldest, the REV. HENRY DRURY, M.A., vicar of Bremhill, Wilts, being the present representative of the family. Mr. Drury d. 9 Jan. 1834.

Arms—Arg., on a chief, vert, two mullets pierced, or.
Crest—A greyhound, courant, ppr.
Motto—Non sine causâ.
Seat—Knightstone, near Ottery.

DUBERLEY OF GAINES HALL.

DUBERLY, JAMES, Esq. of Gaines Hall, co. Huntingdon, b. 9 Sept. 1788; served in the Peninsula and Flanders, in the 11th light dragoons; m. 21 Sept. 1837, Emily-Hannah, 3rd dau. of the late Hon. Col. William Grey, brother to Earl Grey, and has issue.

Lineage.—SIR JAMES DUBERLY, Knt. of Gaines Hall, co. Huntingdon, b. 21 Oct. 1758, purchased, in 1797, estates in the counties of Huntingdon, Bedford, Cambridge, and Norfolk. He m. 1st, 15 Nov. 1787, Miss Rebecca Howard, and had issue, JAMES, his heir; and Mary-Anne, d. 22 July, 1854. Sir James m. 2ndly, 17 Oct. 1805, Etheldred, elder dau. of Charles St. Barbe, Esq. of Lymington, Hants, and had issue, George, captain 64th regt., m. Miss Catherine Locke; Charles, in holy orders, m. Miss Fanny Potts; Henry, m. Miss Fanny Locke; and Etheldred, m. to Edward Vernon, Esq. of Shrawley, co. Worcester. He d. 26 May, 1832, and was s. by his eldest son, the present JAMES DUBERLY, Esq. of Gaines Hall.

Arms—Vert, on a fesse, or, between two garbs in chief, of the last, and a sickle in base, arg., handle, gold, an arrow, barwise, gu., headed and flighted, of the third, between two estoiles, az.
Crest—A dexter arm, embowed, ppr., holding in the hand three ears of wheat, or.
Motto—Res non verba.
Seat—Gaines Hall, St. Neot's, co. Huntingdon.

DU CANE OF BRAXTED.

DU CANE, CHARLES, Esq. of Braxted, Essex, J.P. and D.L., M.A. Exeter College, Oxford, b. in 1824.

Lineage.—This family is of noble French origin; the immediate ancestor of the English branch had settled in the Low Countries; another member of the family, Gabriel, Marquis du Quesne (grandson of the celebrated French Admiral Abraham du Quesne, to whom a statue has recently been erected at Dieppe, his native town), fled to this country on the revocation of the Edict of Nantes, and was father of the Rev. Thomas-Roger Du Quesne, prebendary of Ely, and vicar of East Tuddenham, Norfolk, who d. 1793, aged 76, s. p. The family is at present represented in France by the Vicomte du Quesne, capitaine de vaisseau.

JOHN DU QUESNE fled to England, out of Flanders, to avoid the Duke of Alva's persecutions, *circa* 1570. He left, by Judith his wife, a son,

JOHN DU QUESNE, b. in Canterbury, and bapt. 2 Aug. 1590. By Mary his wife, he left, with two daus., Mary, wife of James Houblon, Esq., and mother of Sir John Houblon; and Sarah, m. in 1636, to Isaac du Quesne, three sons, PETER; John; and Benjamin, of whom the eldest,

PETER DU QUESNE, *alias* DU CANE, settled in London, and was elected alderman, 1666. He m. Jane, dau. of Elias

Maurois, of Canterbury, by Elizabeth his wife, dau. of Lawrence Desbouverie, of Sandwich, and *d.* 7 Feb. 1671, leaving two daus., Jane, *m.* 26 Aug. 1661, to Sir Christopher Lethieulier, Knt.; and Elizabeth; and nine sons; the 2nd but eldest surviving,

PETER DU CANE, Esq., *m.* 6 Jan. 1675, Jane, eldest dau. of Richard Booth, and *d.* 16 Sept. 1714, leaving a son and successor,

RICHARD DU CANE, Esq., M.P. for Colchester, who *m.* Anne, only child of Nehemiah Lyde, lord of the manors of Great and Little Coggeshall, Essex, and dying 3 Oct. 1744, aged 63, was buried at Braxted. His son and successor,

PETER DU CANE, Esq. of Braxted Park, Essex, *b.* 22 April, 1713, served as high-sheriff 1745. He *m.* 27 March, 1735, Mary, only dau. of Henry Norris, Esq. of Hackney and Woodford, Middlesex, and dying 23 March, 1803, left issue,

I. PETER, his heir.
II. Henry, vicar of Coggeshall, Essex, *m.* Louisa, dau. of John-Charles Desmadryll, a collateral descendant of Oliver Cromwell, through the Disbrowes, and *d.* 12 Nov. 1812, aged 67, leaving issue,
  1 Henry, in holy orders, of The Grove, Witham, *b.* 1785, *m.* Mary Sowerby, and had surviving issue, Percy, *b.* 24 July, 1840; Emily, *m.*; Louisa; Charlotte; and Anna.
  2 Richard, *b.* 1788, major, 20th dragoons, *m.* Eliza, dau. of Thomas Ware, Esq. of Woodfort, co. Cork, and *d.* 4 Dec. 1833, leaving issue, Richard, *b.* 1819; Arthur, *b.* 1825; Robert, capt. 64th foot; Edmund-Frederick, royal engineers.
  3 Charles, *b.* 1789, capt. R.N., *m.* Frances, 2nd dau. of the Rev. Charles Prideaux-Brune, of Prideaux Place, co. Cornwall, and *d.* 17 Nov. 1850, leaving issue.
    CHARLES, now of Braxted Park.
    Francis, royal engineers, *b.* 1825.
    John, an officer in the Rifles, lost at sea on his way to the Cape, June, 1858.
    Alfred, *b.* 1834.
    Mary-Gertrude. Fanny. Bertha.
  1 Louisa. 2 Anna-Maria. 3 Sarah.
I. Mary, *d.* 12 Nov. 1812, aged 67.
II. Sarah, of The Grove, Witham, *d.* 13 Feb. 1830, aged 80.

The son and successor,

PETER DU CANE, Esq. of Braxted Park, *b.* 20 April, 1741, *m.* 22 Nov. 1769, Phœbe-Philips, eldest dau. of Edward Tredcroft, Esq. of The Manor House, Horsham, Sussex, and by her (who *d.* 28 Feb. 1831, aged 88) had issue,

PETER, his heir.
Mary, *m.* 22 Aug. 1794, Edmund, only son of William Smith, Esq. of Horsham Park and Woodbridge House, Guildford, and by him (who *d.* 29 Oct. 1845) left at her decease, 23 April, 1844, Percy, in holy orders, *m.* Mary Kenrick; Frederick, *m.* Isabella-O. James; William-Forster, J.P. and D.L. for Sussex, *m.* Lilla-Rosalie Greene; and Caroline, *m.* to J. Godman, Esq.
Charlotte-Phœbe, *m.* 4 Nov. 1803, Richard, 5th son of Randolph Marriott, Esq. of Leases Hall, Yorkshire, capt. H.E.I.C.S., but *d. s. p.* 15 April, 1854.

Mr. Du Cane *d.* 13 June, 1823, and was *s.* by his son,

PETER DU CANE, Esq. of Braxted Park, *b.* 19 Aug. 1778, high-sheriff of Essex 1826, who *d. s. p.* 23 May, 1841, and was buried at Braxted. The family estates are now possessed by his kinsman, CHARLES DU CANE, Esq. of Braxted Park, grandson of Mr. Peter Du Cane's uncle, the Rev. Henry Du Cane.

Arms—Arg., a lion, rampant, sa., ducally crowned, or; on a canton, az., a chevron, of the third, between two acorns, slipped and erect.
Crest—A demi-lion, rampant, sa., ducally crowned, or, supporting with the paws an anchor, erect, of the same.
Seat—Braxted Park, Essex.

DUCKETT OF DUCKETT'S GROVE.

DUCKETT, JOHN-DAWSON, Esq. of Duckett's Grove, co. Carlow, high-sheriff in 1819; *m.* 16 March, 1819, Sarah-Summers, dau. of William Hutchinson, Esq. of Timoney, co. Tipperary, and has issue,

I. WILLIAM. II. John-Dawson, *d.* young.
I. Eliza-Dawson, *d. unm.* II. Anna.
III. Sarah. IV. Victoria-Henrietta-Josephine.

Lineage.—The Ducketts of Fillingham in Lincolnshire, of Grayrigg, Heversham, and Morland in Westmoreland, of Flintham, Notts, of Hartham in Wiltshire, of Royden in Essex, of Newtown, co. Kildare, and of Duckett's Grove, co. Carlow, derive from a common ancestor in

RICHARD DUCKETT, lord of the manor of Fillingham in 1206, who was judge of the counties of Bedford, Buckingham, Cambridge, Huntingdon, Norfolk, Northampton, and Rutland, *temp.* HENRY III.

THOMAS DUCKETT, Esq., who first settled in Ireland, and purchased, in 1695, estates in the county of Carlow, from Thomas Crosthwaite, Esq. of Cockermouth, was son of James Duckett, Esq. of Grayrigg, by his 3rd wife, Elizabeth, dau. of Christopher Walker, Esq. He *m.* Judith, dau. and heir of Pierce De la Poer, Esq. of Killowen, co. Waterford, grandson of the Hon. Pierce De la Poer, of Killowen, brother of Richard, 1st Earl of Tyrone, and had an only son and successor,

THOMAS DUCKETT, Esq., who purchased Philipstown from the Earl of Ormond; his will was dated 18 Jan. 1732, and proved 13 May, 1735. By Elizabeth Stephens his wife, he had (with three daus., Elizabeth, *m.* to Thomas Russell, Esq. of Dublin; Anne, *m.* to James Hutchinson, Esq. of Knockballymagher; and Jane, *m.* to Thomas Sealy, Esq. of Waterford) a son and successor,

JOHN DUCKETT, Esq. of Philipstown and Newtown, co. Kildare, whose will, dated 13 April, 1733, was proved 17 May, 1738. He *m.* Jane, dau. of Thomas Devonsher Esq., by Sarah his wife, sister of Abraham Morris, Esq. of Cork, and has issue, 1 Thomas, of Newtown, who *d. unm.*; 2 William, of Philipstown, who *m.* Janet, dau. of Samuel Summers, Esq., but *d. s. p.*; 3 Abraham, of Ardnehue, co. Carlow, who *m.* Mary, dau. of Samuel Jessop, Esq., and had (with three sons, who *d. s. p.*) three daus., Jane, *m.* to Walter White, Esq.; Susanna, *d. unm.*; and Anne, *m.* to John Robertson, Esq.; 4 JONAS, of whom presently; 1 Sarah, *m.* to John Fuller, Esq. of Ballytore; 2 Elizabeth, *m.* to George Penrose, Esq. of Waterford; 3 Jane, wife of Thomas Irwin, Esq. of Cumberland. The 4th son,

JONAS DUCKETT, Esq. of Duckett's Grove, co. Carlow, whose will, dated 7 July, 1796, was proved 21 Dec. 1797, *m.* Hannah, dau. of William Alloway, Esq. of Dublin, and had issue,

WILLIAM, his heir. John, *d. s. p.*
Thomas, who *m.* Catherine, dau. of Arundel Madden, Esq. of Dublin, an had and only dau., HANNAH-THOMASINE, *m.* 1st, to the Rev. Samuel Madden, and 2ndly, to John Macdonnell, Esq. of New Hall, co. Clare.
Jonas, of Belle Vue, co. Kildare.
Frederick, *d. s. p.*
Mary-Alloway, *m.* to her cousin, Thomas Fuller, Esq.
Hannah, *m.* to Thomas Boake, Esq. of Boake Field, co. Kildare.
Jane, *m.* to James Hunt, Esq. of Dublin.

The eldest son,

WILLIAM DUCKETT, Esq. of Duckett's Grove, *m.* Elizabeth, dau. and co-heir of John-Dawson Coates, Esq. of Dawson Court, co. Dublin, banker in Dublin, and had issue,

JOHN-DAWSON, now of Duckett's Grove.
William, of Russellstown Park, co. Carlow, J.P., high-sheriff in 1825, *b.* Jan. 1797, *m.* Jan. 1843, Harriet-Isabella-Anne, only dau. of Colonel Charles-Edward Gordon, R.A., son of John Gordon, Esq. of Wardhouse and Kildrummie, co. Aberdeen; and by her (who *d.* 27 Nov. 1852) has issue, William-Gordon; Stewart-James-Charles; Charles-Edward-Henry; and Harriet Elinor-Alston.
Joseph-Fade. Thomas-Jonas, *d. unm.*
Elizabeth, *d.* young.
Elizabeth-Dawson, *m.* to William-Richard Steuart, Esq. of Steuart's Lodge, co. Carlow, high-sheriff in 1820.

Arms—Sa., a saltier, arg., charged with a crescent.
Crest—Out of a ducal coronet, or, a plume of five ostrich feathers, arg.
Motto—Spectemur agendo.
Seat—Duckett's Grove, Castledermot, co. Carlow.

DUCKWORTH OF OVER DARWEN AND MUSBURY.

DUCKWORTH, WILLIAM, Esq. of Beechwood, New Forest, co. Hants, J.P. for that county, *b.* 4 April, 1795; *m.* 1st, 3 Oct. 1825, Hester-Emily, dau. of Robert Philips, Esq. of The Park, Prestwich, Lancashire (who *d.* 25 Jan. 1834), and has issue,

I. George, *b.* 29 July, 1826, captain 5th dragoon-guards, *d.* 24 Aug. 1854, on board the "Bombay" transport, in Varna Bay.
II. WILLIAM-ARTHUR, *b.* 17 March, 1829.
III. Russell, *b.* 30 April, 1830.
IV. Herbert, *b.* 19 May, 1833.
I. Sarah-Emily.

Mr. Duckworth *m.* 2ndly, Margaret-Elizabeth, dau. of Samuel-Yate Benyon, Esq., K.C., and Vice-Chancellor of the county palatine of Lancaster.

Lineage.—This family has for several centuries held lands in Lancashire, the estate at Musbury, in the parish of Bury, having been granted to Mr. Duckworth's direct ancestor, Richard Duckeworth (before spelt "Dykewarde"), 30 HENRY VIII. (1538), on the dissolution of the monastery of Whalley. Mr. Duckworth's father, GEORGE DUCKWORTH, lord of the manor of Over Darwen, in the parish of Blackburn, *d.* 21 Nov. 1815, leaving also, Samuel Duckworth, who *d. unm.* 3 Dec. 1847, a barrister, and M.P. for Leicester when appointed a Master in Chancery, and two daus., Eliza-Duckworth, *unm.*, and Anna, *m.* to Sir Thomas Coltman, one of the justices of H.M. Court of Common Pleas.

Arms—Arg., a cross, pointed, sa., surmounted by a like cross, or; in chief, two gryphon's heads, erased, each surmounting four spear-heads, conjoined in saltier, ppr.
Crest—A gryphon's head, erased, and surmounting four spear-heads, conjoined as in the arms.
Residences—Beechwood, New Forest; and 38, Bryanston Square.

DUCKWORTH OF MOUNT ERRIS.

DUCKWORTH, JOHN, Esq. of Mount Erris, Boyle, co. Roscommon, J.P., captain Leitrim militia, *b.* 11 Jan. 1787; *m.* 30 Jan. 1810, Mary Smallman, and has issue,

I. WILLIAM, *b.* 10 Jan. 1822, *m.* 30 April, 1850, Maria-Henrietta, dau. of the Rev. Richard D'Olin, rector of Ballymore Eustace.
I. Jane, *m.* 4 Feb. 1839, to Arthur-John-Vesey-Lindsey Birchall, of Blackhurst House, Ireland.

Lineage.—RICHARD DUCKWORTH, Esq., served in the 60th regt. (which was formed out of the 2nd battalion of the 24th regt.), and was killed in action at the taking of Martinique, in .764, when his son, JOHN DUCKWORTH, was a child. That gentleman subsequently served in the same regiment, and was in several battles with it, particularly at the naval fight between Lord Rodney and Count de Grasse, in 1782; he died in the army. Captain John Duckworth *m.* March, 1786, Mary Williams, and *d.* in 1805, leaving one son, the present JOHN DUCKWORTH, Esq. of Mount Erris.

Seat—Mount Erris, Boyle.

DUFF OF HATTON.

DUFF, GARDEN, Esq. of Hatton and Balquholly, co. Aberdeen, J.P. and D.L., *b.* 29 Oct. 1779; *m.* 17 Sept. 1805, Louisa, eldest dau. of Sir Benjamin Dunbar, Bart. (afterwards 6th Baron Duffus), and by her had five sons and three daus.,

I. John, *b.* in 1807, *d.* in 1829.
II. BENJAMIN, *b.* 1808, *m.* 1832, Emma, dau. of Commissary-General Haines, and has issue one son and two daus.
III. Garden-William, *b.* in 1814, *m.* 1850, Douglas-Isabella-Maria, 3rd dau. of B.-C. Urquhart, Esq. of Meldrum and Byth, and has issue one son and two daus.
IV. Robert-George, *b.* in 1817, *m.* 1847, Mary, only child of W.-B. Astley, Esq. of Wellington Lodge, and has issue two sons and one dau.
V. James, *b.* May, 1820.
I. Jessie, *m.* in 1836, to Alexander Morison, Esq. of Bognie and Frendraught, co. Aberdeen.
II. Helen, *m.* in 1832, to James Buchan, Esq., of Auchmacoy, co. Aberdeen.
III. Louisa-Clementina.

Lineage.—ALEXANDER DUFF, of Hatton (son of Patrick Duff, of Craigstone, who was 3rd son of Alexander Duff, of Keithmore, and brother of William Duff, of Braco, father of William, 1st Earl of Fife), *m.* Katharine, 2nd dau. of Charles Hay, Esq. of Rannes, and *d.* in 1753, leaving a son and successor,

JOHN DUFF, Esq. of Hatton, who *m.* Helen, heiress of Patrick Duff, Esq. of Whitehills, and *d.* 2 Aug. 1787, leaving, with other issue, a son, the present GARDEN DUFF, Esq. of Hatton.

Arms—Vert, a fesse, dancettée, erm., between a hart's head, caboshed, in chief, and two escallops in base, or.
Crest—A demi-lion, rampant, with a dagger in dexter paw, ppr.
Motto—Virtute et operâ.
Seat—Hatton, co. Aberdeen.

DUFF OF ORTON.

DUFF, RICHARD-WHARTON, Esq. of Orton, co Moray, J.P. and D.L., *s.* to his maternal uncle, the Hon. Arthur Duff, 7th son of William, 1st Earl of Fife, who *d.* 26 April, 1805; *b.* 19 May, 1782; *m.* 16 Oct. 1809, the Lady Anne Duff, 2nd dau. of Alexander, 3rd Earl of Fife, and by her (who *d.* 24 Jan. 1829) has issue,

I. ALEXANDER-THOMAS, late capt. in 92nd Highlanders.
I. Sophia-Henrietta, *d.* 26 Jan. 1829.
II. Anne-Jane.
III. Jemima, *m.* Aug. 1841, to John-Robert Tod, Esq., W.S., and *d.* July, 1846, leaving a son and dau., John-Wharton, *b.* April, 1845; and Anne-Helen.

Lineage.—THOMAS WHARTON, Esq., one of H.M. Commissioners of Excise for Scotland, *b.* Oct. 1735, *m.* 1775, the Lady Sophia-Henrietta Duff, 5th dau. of William, 1st Earl of Fife, and *d.* in Feb. 1810, leaving surviving issue, Mary, *m.* 1811, to Daniel Buller, Esq.; and one son, the present ROBERT WHARTON-DUFF, Esq. of Orton.

Arms—DUFF and WHARTON, quarterly.
Seat—Orton.

DUFF OF FETTERESSO.

DUFF, ROBERT, Esq. of Fetteresso Castle, co. Kincardine, and Culter House, co. Aberdeen, J.P. and D.L.

Lineage.—ROBERT DUFF, Esq. of Logie and Fetteresso, son of Patrick Duff, Esq. of Craigston (who was 3rd son of Alexander Duff, of Keithmore, and brother of William Duff, of Braco, father of William, 1st Earl of Fife), entering the royal navy, attained the rank of admiral, and commanded at Gibraltar, in 1779. He *m.* in 1764, Lady Helen Duff, dau. of William, Earl of Fife, by whom he had three sons and one dau.,

ROBERT-WILLIAM, his heir.
Adam, sheriff of Forfarshire.
James-Alexander, lieut. 3rd foot-guards, *d. unm.* in 1800.
Jane, *m.* in 1791, to James Clerk, of Chesterhall, one of the Barons of the Court of Exchequer in Scotland.

Admiral Duff *d.* 6 June, 1787, and was *s.* by his son,

ROBERT-WILLIAM DUFF, Esq. of Fetteresso and Culter, lieut.-col. of the Forfarshire militia, who *m.* in 1789, Mary, only child of George Morison, Esq. of Haddo, by Jane his wife, eldest dau. of General James Abercromby, M.P. of Glasshaugh, and had issue,

ROBERT, now of Fetteresso.
Arthur, who bears the surname of ABERCROMBY, and is of Glasshaugh, Banffshire.
Adam, of Woodcott, co. Oxford, and Barmiskirk, co. Caithness, *b.* 1800, *m.* 1829, Eleanor, dau. of Capt. Thomas Fraser, royal engineers, of Woodcott, and had issue, Thomas-Fraser, *b.* 1830; Robert-William, *b.* 1831; George-Graham, *b.* 1835; Adam, *b.* 1839; Arthur, *b.* 1840; Mary-Abercrombie; Jane-Clerk; Eleanor-Traill.
Thomas-Abercromby, of Haddo, Banffshire.

Colonel Duff *d.* in March, 1834.

Arms—Vert, a fesse, dancetté, erm., between a buck's head, caboshed, in chief, and a mullet in base, or.
Crest—A demi-lion, rampant, gu., with a dagger in dexter paw, ppr.
Motto—Virtute et operâ.
Seats—Fetteresso Castle, Kincardineshire; and Culter House, Aberdeenshire.

DUGDALE OF MEREVALE.

DUGDALE, WILLIAM-STRATFORD, Esq. of Merevale Hall and Blyth Hall, co. Warwick, formerly M.P. for North Warwickshire, *b.* 1 April, 1800; *m.* 1 Mar. 1827, Harriet-Ella, dau. of the late Edward Berkeley Portman, Esq. of Bryanston, co. Dorset, and sister of Lord Portman, and has issue,

I. WILLIAM-STRATFORD, *b.* 7 May, 1828.
II. John-Stratford, *b.* 30 July, 1835.
III. Henry-Charles-Geast, *b.* 30 April, 1837.
I. Adelaide. II. Mary-Louisa.

Lineage.—RICHARD GEAST, Esq., barrister-at-law,

elder son and heir of Richard Geast,* Esq. of Handsworth, by Jane his wife, dau. and co-heir of William Dugdale, Esq. of Blythe Hall, son of Sir John Dugdale, and grandson of Sir William Dugdale, Knt., the celebrated antiquary and genealogist, inheriting, under the will of his uncle, the Dugdale estates, assumed, in 1799, the surname and arms of DUGDALE. He m. in 1767, Penelope-Bate, eldest dau. and co-heir (with Frances, wife of the late Joseph Cradock, Esq., F.S.A.) of Francis Stratford, Esq. of Merevale, by whom (who d. in 1819) he left at his decease, in 1806, one son and three daus., viz., DUGDALE-STRATFORD, his heir; Penelope, m. to Charles-James Packe, Esq. of Prestwold; Louisa-Anne, m. to William Dilke, Esq. of Maxstoke Castle, co. Warwick; and Emma. Mr. Dugdale was s. by his only son,

DUGDALE-STRATFORD DUGDALE, Esq. of Merevale Hall, co. Warwick, b. in 1773, M.P. for Warwickshire from 1802 to 1830, who m. 27 June, 1799, the Hon. Charlotte, dau. of Assheton, 1st Viscount Curzon (and aunt to the present Earl Howe), and by her, who d. 30 Dec. 1832, had an only son, WILLIAM-STRATFORD, now representative of the family. He m. 2ndly, 16 Sept. 1834, Mary-Elizabeth, sister of Wilbraham Tatton Egerton, Esq. of Tatton Park, co. Chester, and relict of the late Sir Mark-Masterman Sykes, Bart. Mr. Dugdale d. 5 Nov. 1836.

Arms—Quarterly: 1st and 4th, arg., a cross-moline, gu., in the 1st quarter, a torteau; 2nd and 3rd, arg., barry of ten, arg. and az., over all a lion, rampant, gu.
Crest—A griffin's head and wings, endorsed, or.
Motto—Pestis patriæ pigrities.
Seats—Merevale Hall, and Blythe Hall, both in Warwickshire.

DUKE OF LAKE.

DUKE, THE REV. EDWARD, of Lake House, co. Wilts, b. 6 Dec. 1814.

Lineage.—This, according to the Visitation made by the herald St. George, in 1623, is a branch of the ancient family of DUKE *of Power Hayes*, co. Devon.

JOHN DUKE, son of MICHAEL DUKE, a cadet of the Devonshire house, was father of GEORGE DUKE, Esq., who purchased, in 1578, the estate and manor of Lake, in Wiltshire. He m. Dorothy, dau. of Philip Poor, Esq., and had three sons, namely, JOHN, his heir; George; and Andrew, progenitor of the DUKES *of Bulford*. Mr. Duke d. in 1610, and was s. by his eldest son,

JOHN DUKE, Esq. of Lake, high-sheriff of the county of Wilts in 1640, who m. Maria, dau. of John Young, Esq. of Dunford, and had issue,

I. GEORGE, who d. v. p. in 1655, leaving, by Elizabeth his wife, dau. of Sir George Ayliffe, Knt. of Robson, two sons, JOHN, who predeceased his grandfather; and GEORGE, of whom presently.
II. John, of Sarson, in Hampshire, who had an only son, GEORGE, who m. Cecilia, dau. of Robert Newman, Esq. of Queen's Camel, and was s. by his son, JOHN, who m. Mary, dau. of the Very Rev. Dr. Harlow, dean of Chichester; and dying in 1743, was s. by his son, JOHN, who m. Miss Frances Bankes, and had surviving issue (Mrs. Duke d. in 1806), 1 GEORGE, lieut.-col. in the army, m. Emily, 3rd dau. of John Freeman, Esq. of Chute Lodge, by whom (who d. in 1819) he had no issue; 2 Charles, lieut. col. in the army, b. in 1769, m. in 1793, Miss Mary Nash, and left at his decease, in 1818, Edward, lieut. R.N., d. in 1825; WILLIAM-THOMAS, b. in 1801; Thomas, b. in 1804; Charles m. Miss Josephine-Isabella Douglas, and has issue two daus., viz., Selina-Mary, m. in 1833, to R.-Brownrigg Hodgson, Esq., youngest son of Lieut.-Gen. Hodgson; and Emma; 1 Frances; and 2 Selina.
III. Edward, of Winterborne-Stoke. This gentleman d. in 1705, and leaving no male issue, the estate of Scotland, in the parish of Winterborne, became vested in his grand-dau.,
   REBECCA DUKE, who m. in 1709, George Hely, Esq. of the co. Kilkenny, and the descendant of that marriage now enjoys the property.

Mr. Duke and his eldest son, George Duke, were involved, with Colonel John Penruddock, Hugh Grove, and several other eminent Royalists, in the unsuccessful attempt made in 1655 to restore the exiled monarch to the throne. The father, as stated above, outlived the son, and dying in 1671, was s. by his grandson,

GEORGE DUKE, Esq. of Lake, who m. Elizabeth, dau. of John Richards, Esq. of Heoverland, in the Isle of Wight, and had a son, ROBERT, his heir; with a dau., Susannah, the wife of John Worden, Esq. He d. in 1690, and was s. by his son,

ROBERT DUKE, Esq. of Lake. This gentleman m. in 1692, Jane, dau. of Thomas Freke, Esq. of Wyck, co. Dorset, and had, with other issue, ROBERT, his heir; and George, who m. Sarah, dau. of Edward Hanson, Esq. of Abingdon, and had, with other issue, a dau., Jane, m. to Captain Lawrence Boyd, R.N., and a son, EDWARD, of whom presently. Mr. Duke d. in 1725, and was s. by his eldest son,

ROBERT DUKE, Esq. of Lake, b. in 1696, who m. in 1723, Frances, dau. of Henry Blake, Esq. of Bristol, and dying in 1749, was s. by his son,

ROBERT DUKE, Esq. of Lake, who m. Jane, dau. of Jonathan Rashleigh, Esq. of Menabilly, in Cornwall, but d. s. p. in 1793, when the estates devolved on his widow for life, and the representation of the family passed to (the only surviving son of his uncle George) his cousin,

EDWARD DUKE, Esq., b. in 1731, who m. in 1771, Fanny, dau. of John Field, Esq. of Islington, and left (with six daus., Sarah; Jane, m. to John Westall, Esq., and d. in 1806; Mary; Lucy, m. to William Blandy, Esq.; Fanny; and Susannah, m. to James Prince, Esq.) an only surviving son,

THE REV. EDWARD DUKE, of Lake House, M.A., b. in 1779, m. in 1813, Harriet, dau. of Henry Hinxman, Esq. of Ivy Church House, Wilts, and had issue,

EDWARD, now of Lake House.
Henry-Hinxman, in holy orders, vicar of Westbury, Wilts.
Robert-Rashleigh, in holy orders, m. in 1850, Ellen-Savage, dau. of the Rev. C.-Savage Landor, of Colton, co. Stafford.
George-Frederick, lieut. H.E.I.C.S.
Harriet-Hinxman. Caroline.
Mary, m. to the Rev. William Bree.
Charlotte-Maria, m. to Captain Edward-Pellew-Hammett Ussher, R.M., son of the late Sir Thomas Ussher, K.C.H., C.B.

Mr. Duke d. in 1852.

Arms—Per fesse, arg. and az., three chaplets, two and one, counterchanged.
Crest—A demi-griffin, or, holding between the claws a chaplet, az.
Seat—Lake House, near Amesbury.

DUNCAN OF DAMSIDE.

BEVERIDGE-DUNCAN, JAMES, Esq. of Damside, co. Perth, J.P. and D.L., b. 2 Dec. 1792; m. 27 Oct. 1829, Miss Elizabeth-Fraser Ross, dau. of Mr. Robert Ross, and has one dau.,

ELIZABETH-FRASER.

Lineage. PATRICK DUNCAN, of Galloford or Galloflat, co. Perth (brother of Gilbert Duncan, of Seaside, of the family of Lundie), m. and had one son, PATRICK, and a dau., ELIZABETH, who m. JAMES BEVERIDGE, of Perth, son of William Beveridge, of Neat Hill, co. Fife, and grandson of James Beveridge, of Cash, co. Fife, and d. 9 Nov. 1792, leaving a son, James Beveridge, of Edinburgh, solicitor to the Post Office, b. 15 March, 1730, who m. 1756, Elizabeth, dau. and co-heir of William Duncan, of Perth, merchant, son of Gilbert Duncan, of Sea Side, and d. April, 1797, leaving two sons, JOHN BEVERIDGE, of whom presently; and William Beveridge, b. 16 Feb. 1763, who m. 1791, Barbara, dau. of James May, and d. in 1807, leaving issue. The son and heir of Patrick Duncan, of Galloford,

PATRICK DUNCAN, Esq. of Perth, d. 1788, leaving, by Barbara Barnard his wife, a son and heir,

PATRICK DUNCAN, Esq. of Damside, co. Perth, who m. 1786, Ann, dau. of William Mercer, Esq., and d. s. p. 28 Oct. 1798, when he was s. by his cousin,

JOHN BEVERIDGE, Esq. of Blackheath, Kent, b. 24 Nov. 1757, J.P. and D.L., chief of the name of Beveridge in Scotland, as confirmed to him, 1818, by the Lord Lyon Depute. In compliance with his cousin's will, Mr. Beveridge assumed the additional surname of DUNCAN, in 1798. He m. 5 Dec. 1785, Isabel, 3rd dau. and co-heir of Thomas Marshall, Esq., lord provost of Perth, by Isabel his wife, dau. and co-heir of William Duncan, of Perth, merchant, son of Gilbert of Seaside, and left issue, a son and heir, the present JAMES BEVERIDGE-DUNCAN, Esq., now of Damside; and one dau., Elizabeth Duncan, Viscountess Lake, widow of Warwick, last Viscount Lake.

Arms—DUNCAN and BEVERIDGE, quarterly.
Seat—Damside, co. Perth.

* Richard Geast was son, by Phœbe Downing his wife, of Nicholas Geast, Esq. of Handsworth, who was son of Richard Geast, Esq., and 6th in descent from John Geste, of Handsworth, who was admitted tenant of copyhold lands there, 12 HENRY VII., and whose grandson, Edmund Geast, was Lord Bishop of Salisbury.

DUNCOMBE OF BRICKHILL MANOR.

DUNCOMBE-PAUNCEFORT, PHILIP-DUNCOMBE, Esq. of Brickhill Manor, co. Buckingham, *m.* 1 May, 1844, Sophia-Caroline, youngest dau. of Colonel Maunsell, M.P., and has issue,

I. HENRY-PHILIP, *b.* 4 June, 1849.
I. Caroline-Alicia-Georgiana.
II. Isabel-Margaret-Cochrane.

Lineage.—This family of DUNCOMBE, which is of great antiquity in Buckinghamshire, became possessed of the manor and estate of Brickhill in 1527.

In the 11th JOHN, GEOFFREY DE PAUNCEFOTE, steward of the household to that monarch, *m.* Sybilla, dau. of William de Cantelupe. In the 33rd of the subsequent reign, RICHARD PAUNCEFORT had a grant of the manor of Hasfield, and, according to Camden, "built a fair house at this Hasfield, called Pauncefort Court, and his ancestors were possessed of fair lands there in the CONQUEROR'S time." By his wife Isabel, he had a son,

SIR GRIMBALD PAUNCEFORT, who *m.* Sybilla, dau. and heiress of the lord of the manor of Crickhowell, co. Brecon.

WALTER PAUNCEFORT, Esq. of Witham, co. Lincoln, son of Richard Pauncefort, Esq. of Hasfield, co. Gloucester, the lineal descendant of Sir Grimbald Pauncefort, *m.* Anne, dau. of John Yelverton, Esq. of Norfolk, and had, with a dau., Rachel, *m.* to Thomas, Earl of Kincardine, three sons, of whom the eldest was,

GRIMBALD PAUNCEFORT, Esq., receiver for the Duchy of Lancaster, who *m.* Anne, dau. of Sir Paul Tracy, Bart., of Stanway, in Gloucestershire, and had (with two other sons, Grimbald and Samuel (who both *d. unm.*) a successor,

TRACY PAUNCEFORT, Esq. of Witham, who *m.* Anne, dau. of George Billingsley, Esq. of Middlesex, and had two sons, TRACY, his heir; and Edward, who *m.* Rebecca, dau. of Samuel Moyer, Esq. The elder

TRACY PAUNCEFORT, Esq. of Witham, *m.* Jane, dau. of John Partherick, Esq. of Lincolnshire, and had a son and successor,

TRACY PAUNCEFORT, Esq. of Witham, who marrying Anne, sister of Lord Whitworth, had (with another son and dau., who both *d. unm.*) a successor,

EDWARD PAUNCEFORT, Esq. of Witham, who *m.* in 1737, Mary, only dau. and heir of William Dodd, Esq., co. Berks, and was *s.* at his decease by his only surviving son,

GEORGE PAUNCEFORT, Esq. of Witham, a major in the army, who *m.* 12 Jan. 1769, Henrietta, younger dau. and co-heir of James Digby, Esq. of Red Hall, in Bourne, co. Lincoln, younger son of Simon Digby, Esq. of North Luffenham, and left at his decease, 8 Oct. 1786, a son and heir,

PHILIP-DUNCOMBE PAUNCEFORT-DUNCOMBE, Esq. of Great Brickhill and Witham, *b.* 16 July, 1784, high-sheriff of Bucks, 1824, *m.* 5 Jan. 1818, the Lady Alicia Lambart, dau. of Richard, Earl of Cavan, by whom (who *d.* 3 April, 1818) he had issue,

PHILIP-DUNCOMBE, now of Brickhill Manor.
Honora-Henrietta, *m.* 1 Dec. 1835, to Charles-Bennett-Drake Garrard, Esq. of Lamer Park, co. Herts.
Henrietta-Philippa, *d.* in July, 1828.
Alicia, *d.* 2 April, 1817.

Mr. Duncombe *m.* 2ndly, 21 Aug. 1823, Sophia-Frances, youngest dau. of the late Sir William Foulis, Bart. of Ingleby Manor, co. York, and by her had, Mary-Venetia, *d.* in 1832, and Sophia. He *d.* 15 March, 1849.

Arms—Quarterly: 1st and 4th, per chevron, engrailed, gu. and arg., three talbots' heads, erased, counterchanged; on a chief, five fleurs-de-lis; 2nd, gu., three lions rampant, arg.; 3rd, az., a fleur-de-lis, arg.
Crests—1st, DUNCOMBE; 2nd, PAUNCEFORT.
Motto—Non fecimus ipsi.
Seat—Brickhill Manor, Bucks.

DUNDAS OF DUNDAS.

DUNDAS, JAMES, Esq. of Dundas, co. Linlithgow, *b.* 14 Jan. 1793; *m.* 20 July, 1813, the Hon. Mary-Tufton Duncan, dau. of the celebrated Admiral, Adam, 1st Viscount Duncan, and has issue,

I. GEORGE, *b.* 12 Nov. 1819.
II. Adam-Alexander, *b.* 22 Jan. 1822.
III. Henry-Robert, *b.* 4 Feb. 1823.
IV. Charles-Stirling, *b.* 9 Sept. 1824.
V. John-Dalrymple, *b.* 4 Feb. 1829.
VI. Frederick-H.-Fergusson, *b.* 26 March, 1832.

I. Henrietta Duncan.
II. Caroline-Stirling, *m.* 2 Aug. 1837, to the Hon. Henry-Amelius Coventry.
III. Catherine-Mary. IV. Mary-Jemima.
V. Anna-Maria, *m.* Sept. 1853, to Maitland Wardrop, Esq.

This gentleman was born Chief of Dundas, his father dying before his birth.

Lineage.—"The Dundases," says Lord Woodhouselee, in the *Transactions of the Royal Society*, "are descended of a family to which the historian and the genealogist have assigned an origin of high antiquity and splendour, but which has been still more remarkable for producing a series of men eminently distinguished for their public services in the highest offices in Scotland."

The DUNDASES are generally believed to have sprung from the DUNBARS, Earls of March, who derived themselves from the Saxon Princes of England.

COSPATRIC, 1st Earl of March, *d.* in 1139, leaving two sons, viz. Cospatric, the 2nd earl, and

UTHRED, living in the time of DAVID I., who obtained from Waldeve, his father's elder brother, the lands and barony of Dundas, in West Lothian. His son,

HELIAS, had a confirmation of the lands of Dundas, in the reign of King DAVID, and assumed therefrom, in conformity with the then prevailing custom, his name and designation, while to denote his alliance with the old Earls of March, he adopted for his armorial bearings the ensigns of those lords, differing, as a mark of cadency, in the colours only. He was *s.* in the beginning of the reign of WILLIAM *the Lion*, by his son,

SERLE DE DUNDAS, who is frequently mentioned in the affairs of Scotland, *temp.* King WILLIAM. He *d.* early in the next reign, and from him we pass over nine generations, amongst the chiefs of which find staunch adherents of Wallace and Bruce, to his descendant,

SIR ARCHIBALD DUNDAS, of Dundas. He was high in favour at Court, and had several confidential embassies entrusted to him. Some short period before the king's decease, Dundas received a letter from his Majesty, announcing the Royal intention of conferring upon him the Earldom of Forth, but the monarch's unexpected death in battle prevented the fulfilment of the promise. He *d.* within a short time afterwards, and was *s.* by his son,

SIR WILLIAM DUNDAS, of Dundas, served heir to his father in 1494. He *m.* Margaret, dau. of Archibald Wauchope, of Niddry, and had two sons, SIR JAMES, his heir; and William, ancestor of the DUNDASES *of Duddingston, &c.* The elder son,

SIR JAMES DUNDAS, of Dundas, had seisin of his estate 2 Oct. 1513. He *m.* Margaret Sandilands, of the house of Torpichen, and dying in 1553, left a son and heir,

GEORGE DUNDAS, of Dundas, who *m.* 1st, Margaret, dau. of David Boswell, of Balmuto, and had two sons, WALTER (Sir), and George. He *m.* 2ndly, Catharine, dau. of Laurence, 3rd Lord Oliphant, and had by her,

JAMES (Sir), of Arniston (*see that family*).
ROBERT.

The Laird of Dundas was *s.* by his eldest son,

SIR WALTER DUNDAS, of Dundas, knighted at the baptism of Prince Henry, who *m.* Janet, dau. of Sir Alexander Oliphant, of Kelly, and by her had daus. only. He *m.* 2ndly, Anne, dau. of Monteith of Carse, and had, GEORGE, his heir; William, ancestor of the DUNDASES *of Blair;* Walter, of the DUNDASES *of Magdalens*, now settled in Ireland; Alexander; Hugh; and Marian, wife of Blair of that ilk. He *d.* about the year 1634, and was *s.* by his eldest son,

GEORGE DUNDAS, of Dundas, who was served heir in 1636. This laird espoused the cause of the parliament in the Civil Wars. He *m.* Elisabeth, dau. of Sir Alexander Hamilton, of Innerwick, and had (with three daus.) 1 WALTER, his heir; 2 George, who *m.* Margaret, dau. of Hay of Monkton, and had, with other issue, GEORGE, who eventually inherited the chieftainship and estates; and James, ancestor of the present Robert Dundas, Esq. The laird lived several years after the Revolution, and was *s.* at his decease by his eldest son,

WALTER DUNDAS, Esq. of Dundas, who *m.* the Lady Christian Leslie, dau. of Alexander, 1st Earl of Leven, and had, RALPH; Walter, who *d. s. p.*; Agnes, wife of Sir John Foulis; Mary, of Sir Wm. Lockhart; and Barbara, of Alexander, Lord Raith. Dundas was *s.* by his elder son,

RALPH DUNDAS, Esq. of Dundas, living in 1680, who *m.* Elisabeth, dau. of William Sharp, Esq. of Houston, and had two sons, Thomas, and William, who both *d.* without issue, and thus terminated the male line of WALTER, eldest son of GEORGE DUNDAS, of Dundas, served heir in 1636; the chieftainship of the family devolved in consequence upon the grandson of the said George Dundas (the son of his 2nd son, George),

GEORGE DUNDAS, Esq., M.P. for Linlithgowshire, and master of the King's Works in Scotland. He *m.* Alison, dau. of General James Bruce, of Kennet, and was *s.* by his eldest son,

JAMES DUNDAS, Esq. of Dundas, who *m.* Jean-Maria, eldest dau. of William, Lord Forbes, and had (with four daus., Dorothea, wife of George Brown, Esq. of Elliston, co. Roxburgh; Alice, of Sir John Wedderburn; Barbara, of George Ogilvie, of Langley Park; and Elizabeth) an only son, his successor,

GEORGE DUNDAS, Esq. of Dundas, who *m.* 24 Nov. 1784, Christian, 2nd dau. of Sir William Stirling, Bart. of Ardoch, by whom (who *d.* 14 Sept. 1832) he left, JAMES, his heir; Christian, *m.* in 1804, to John Hamilton, Esq. of Sundrum; Maria, *m.* in 1813, to Robert Cunnyngham, Esq.; and Anne, *m.* in 1831, to Montgomerie Hamilton, Esq. The laird, who was a captain in the E. I. Co.'s service, and commander of the "Winterton" East Indiaman, was lost at the wreck of that ship off the coast of Madagascar, on the 22nd Aug. 1792. He was *s.* by his son, the present JAMES DUNDAS, Esq. of Dundas.

Arms—Arg., a lion, rampant, gu.
Crest—A lion's head, full-faced, looking through a bush of oak, ppr.
Supporters—Two lions, gu., and below the shield, for a compartment, a salamander in flames of fire, ppr.
Motto—Essayez.
Seat—Dundas Castle, near Queensferry.

DUNDAS OF ARNISTON.

DUNDAS, ROBERT, Esq. of Arniston, Mid-Lothian, *b.* 23 March, 1823; *m.* 25 Sept. 1845, Emily-Louisa-Diana, dau. of the Hon. James Knox, and has a dau., MARION.

Lineage.—SIR JAMES DUNDAS, of Arniston, 3rd son of George Dundas, Esq. of Dundas, by Catharine his 2nd wife, dau. of Lawrence, 3rd Lord Oliphant, was father of

SIR JAMES DUNDAS, of Arniston, M.P. for the co. of Edinburgh, who was appointed, in 1662, one of the senators of the College of Justice, and dying in 1679, left, by Marian his 1st wife, dau. of Robert, Lord Boyd, three daus. and one son, namely,

ROBERT DUNDAS, an eminent lawyer, appointed judge of the Court of Session in 1689, which office he filled for thirty-seven years. He *m.* Margaret, dau of Sir Robert Sinclair, of Stevenson, and left at his decease, in 1727, with other children, a son and successor,

ROBERT DUNDAS, Esq. of Arniston, *b.* 9 Sept. 1685, who was appointed solicitor-general in 1717, and lord advocate of Scotland in 1720. In 1722, he was returned to parliament for the co. of Edinburgh, and in 1737 raised to the bench, as one of the judges of session, when he assumed the titular designation of Lord Arniston. He subsequently, in 1748, succeeded the celebrated Duncan Forbes in the presidency of the court. His lordship *m.* 1st, Elizabeth, dau. of Robert Watson, Esq. of Muir House, by whom he had, with two daus., a son, ROBERT, his heir, of whom presently. Lord Arniston *m.* 2ndly, Anne, dau. of Sir Robert Gordon, Bart. of Invergordon, and by her was father of Henry, created Viscount Melville, 24 Dec. 1802. Lord Arniston *d.* in 1753, and was *s.* by his eldest son and heir,

ROBERT DUNDAS, Esq. of Arniston, lord president of the Court of Session, and M.P. for Mid-Lothian, who *m.* 1st, Henrietta, dau. of Sir James Carmichael, and had four daus., Elizabeth, *m.* to Sir John Lockhart Ross, Bart.; Henrietta, *m.* to Adam, 1st Viscount Duncan; Margaret, *m.* to General Scott, of Balcomie; Anne, *m.* to George Buchan, Esq. of Kello. He *m.* 2ndly, Jean, dau. of William Grant, Esq., Lord Prestongrange, and by her had,

ROBERT, his heir.
Francis, lieutenant-general and governor of Carrickfergus.
William, privy councillor.
Philip, governor of the Prince of Wales's Island, *m.* in 1803, Margaret, sister of Sir David Wedderburn, Bart., and *d.* in 1807, leaving issue.
Grizel, *m.* to Robert Colt, Esq.
Janet, *m.* 1st, to John Hamilton, Esq., and 2ndly, to George Dempster, Esq. of Skibo.

The eldest son and heir,

ROBERT DUNDAS, of Arniston, lord chief baron of the Court of Exchequer in Scotland, *m.* in 1787, the Hon. Elizabeth Dundas, eldest dau. of Henry, 1st Viscount Melville, and *d.* in 1819, leaving issue, ROBERT, his heir; Henry, capt. R.N.; William-Pitt; Anne, *m.* to J. Borthwick, Esq.; and Joanna, *m.* to G. Dempster, Esq. His eldest son and heir,

ROBERT DUNDAS, Esq. of Arniston, *m.* in 1822, Lillias-Calderwood Durham, of Largo and Polton, representative of the DURHAMS *of Largo*, and had issue, ROBERT, present representative; Thomas, capt. 12th foot, *b.* in 1825; William, *b.* in 1826; James-Durham, lieut. 60th Rifles, *b.* in 1835; Elizabeth; and Anne. Mr. Dundas *d.* in 1838.

Arms—Arg., a lion, rampant, gu., within a bordure, az.
Crest—A lion's head, affrontée, looking through an oak-bush, ppr.
Motto—Essayez.
Seat—Arniston, Mid-Lothian.

DUNDAS OF BARTON COURT.

WHITLEY-DEANS-DUNDAS, JAMES, Esq. of Barton Court, co. Berks, J.P. and D.L., vice-admiral R.N., *b.* 4 Dec. 1785; *m.* 1st, 28 April, 1808, his first-cousin, Janet, only dau. of the late Charles Dundas, Lord Amesbury, by Ann his wife, dau. and sole heir of Ralph Whitley, Esq. of Aston Hall. Flintshire, and by her (who *d.* 7 Dec. 1837, has had issue,

I. CHARLES-JAMES, late of the Coldstream-guards, *b.* 15 Jan. 1811, M.P. for the Flint district in 1838, *m.* 20 March, 1837, his cousin, Janet Lindsay, dau. of John Jardine, Esq., and granddau. of Bruce the traveller, and has issue, Charles-Amesbury, *b.* 30 Nov. 1845.
II. James, M.A., of Magdalen College, Cambridge, vicar of Kintbury.
I. Ann, *m.* to John-Archer Houblon, Esq. of Great Hallingbury, Essex.
II. Janet, *m.* to Henry Robarts, Esq.
III. Sophia, *m.* James-Coutts Crawford, Esq., and *d.* 1850, leaving issue.

Admiral Whitley-Deans-Dundas *m.* 2ndly, 3 Aug. 1847, Lady Emily Moreton, sister of the 1st Earl of Ducie. The Admiral (son of the late James Deans, Esq., M.D., of Calcutta, by Janet his wife, dau. of Thomas Dundas, Esq. of Fingask, M.P., descended from Alexander Dundas, of Fingask, eldest son of James Dundas, of Dundas, by his 2nd wife, Christian, dau. of John, Lord Innermeath and Lorn) assumed the surname and arms of DUNDAS by royal license. He was formerly M.P. for Greenwich, and a Lord of the Admiralty. In 1854 he was Commander-in-Chief of the British naval forces in the Black Sea.

Arms—Arg., a lion, rampant, gu., within a bordure, flory-counterflory, quarterly with WHITLEY and DEANS.
Crests—1st, for DUNDAS, a lion's head, full-faced, looking through a bush of oak, ppr.; 2nd, for WHITLEY, a stag's head, arg., attired, or, holding in its mouth the end of a scroll, bearing the motto, "Live to live."
Mottoes—"Essayez," for DUNDAS. "Arte vel Marte," for DEANS.
Seats—Barton Court, near Hungerford, Berks; and Aston Hall, Hawarden, Flintshire.

DUNDAS OF DUDDINGSTOUN.

HAMILTON-DUNDAS, GABRIEL, Esq. of Duddingstoun, in West Lothian, *s.* his father in 1820, and in 1833 became (at the death of Lady Mary Lindsay-Craufurd), along with the Earl of Glasgow, co-heir of line of the Earls of Crawfurd and Lindsay, and the Crawfurds Baronets, of Kilbirney; *m.* Isabella, eldest dau. of James Dennistoun, Esq. of Dennistoun and Colgrain, in Dumbartonshire, and had issue,

I. JOHN, *b.* in 1805, major in the army.
II. James, deceased. III. David, *d.* in 1833.
IV. Gabriel, major of hussars in the Austrian service.
V. Robert, deceased. VI. George.
I. Margaret. II. Grace, deceased. III. Jessie.
IV. Marion. V. Elizabeth.

Mr. Hamilton-Dundas was formerly an officer in the 3rd foot-guards.

Lineage.—WILLIAM DUNDAS, 2nd son of Sir William Dundas of that ilk, by Margaret Wauchope his wife, *m.* Marjory Lindsay, heiress of Duddingstoun. His son,

David Dundas, of Duddingstoun, m. Marjory, dau. of John Hamilton, of Orbieston, great-grandson of Gavin Hamilton, 4th son of Sir James Hamilton, Lord of Cadzow. By her he had two sons, James; and George, ancestor of Sir David Dundas, of Manor; and Dundas, of Richmond, Bart. The elder son,

James Dundas, of Duddingstoun, m. Isabella, dau. of William Maule (son of Thomas Maule, of Panmure, and uncle of Patrick, 1st Earl of Panmure), by Bethia his wife, dau. of Alexander Guthrie, of the family of Guthrie *of Guthrie*, by Janet, dau. of Henderson of Fordel. Duddingstoun was *s.* by his son,

George Dundas, of Duddingstoun, a parliamentarian in the civil wars *temp.* Charles I., and one of the Committee of Estates in 1649. In 1636, he m. Catherine, dau. of John Moneypenny, of Pitmilly, and *d.* in 1684, leaving, with other issue, a son and successor,

John Dundas, of Duddingstoun, *b.* 15 March, 1641, who m. 17 Feb. 1670, Anne, dau. of Sir David Carmichael, of Balmedie, and by her, who *d.* in 1711, had eight sons, of whom the eldest,

George Dundas, of Duddingstoun, m. Magdalen Lindsay-Craufurd, dau. of Patrick Lindsay-Craufurd, of Kilbirney, granddau. of John Lindsay, 15th Earl Craufurd and 1st Earl of Lindsay, niece to James and William, Dukes of Hamilton, sister to John Lindsay-Craufurd, Viscount Garnock, and to Margaret, Countess of Glasgow. By this lady he had, among other children, who left no issue,

John, his heir.
Agnes, wife of Gabriel Hamilton, of Westburn, a cadet of Hamilton of Torrance, and eventual inheritor of the estates.

The son and successor,

John Dundas, of Duddingstoun, m. Lady Margaret Hope, dau. to Charles, Earl of Hopetoun, by Lady Henrietta Johnstone, dau. of William, Marquis of Annandale; they had no issue; and on the death of John Dundas, the Duddingstoun estates passed for a few years to the heir male, David Dundas, of Newhalls, son of John, younger son of John Dundas, of Duddingstoun; but on his death, they reverted to the dau. of George Dundas and Magdalen Lindsay-Craufurd,

Agnes Dundas, of Duddingstoun, who m. Gabriel Hamilton, of Westburn, representative of Hamilton of Torrance, 2nd son of Thomas Hamilton, of Darngaber, 3rd son of Sir Thomas Hamilton, Lord of Cadzow, and had (with six daus., 1 Margaret, m. to Capt. Nasmyth, R.N.; 2 Graham-Christian; 3 Agnes; 4 Magdalen-Elizabeth; 5 Christian, wife of the Hon. Charles Napier, of Merchiston Hall; and 6 Mary-Anne, m. to Robert Gray, of Carntyne) seven sons, who all *d. unm.*, except the 6th son. Gabriel Hamilton, of Westburn, died many years before his wife, Agnes Dundas, who lived to a very advanced age, dying about the year 1798. During a long widowhood, she achieved the difficult task of restoring the dilapidated estates of her husband's family, and at the close of her life found herself seated with augmented wealth in the ancient halls of her youth, in which she was *s.* by her eldest surviving son,

John-Hamilton Dundas, of Duddingstoun and Westburn, *b.* in 1745, vice-lieutenant of the county of Linlithgow. He m. Grizzel, dau. of John Hamilton, of Barns, representative of the great Raploch branch of the house of Hamilton, descended from John, Lord of Cadzow. By her he had (with five daus., Marion; Agnes, wife of Cadell of Grange; Margaret; Magdalen-Elizabeth; and Eleanor) five sons, the four youngest of whom died before their father, all officers in the army, navy, or E.I.C. service. Mr. Hamilton-Dundas *d.* in 1820, and was *s.* by his only surviving son, the present Gabriel Hamilton-Dundas, Esq. of Duddingstoun.

Arms—Quarterly: 1st and 4th, arg., a lion, rampant, gu., langued, az., holding within his paws a man's heart, ppr., for Dundas *of Duddingstoun*: 2nd and 3rd gu., three cinquefoils, pierced, erm., within a bordure, potent and counterpotent, of the second and the first, for Hamilton *of Westburn*; quartering Lyndesay, Crawfurd, Dreghorn, &c.
Crest—1st, a hand, holding a mullet, az., for Dundas; 2nd, a hand, holding a spear, ppr., for Hamilton.
Mottoes—"Essayez," for Dundas. "Et arma et virtus," for Hamilton.

DUNDAS OF BLAIR CASTLE.

Dundas, Richard-Leslie, Esq. of Blair Castle, co. Perth, major in the army.

Lineage.—William Dundas, 2nd son of Sir Walter Dundas, of Dundas, m. Catherine, dau. of Murray of Henderland, and was *s.* by his elder son,

William Dundas, of Kincavel, who m. Margaret, dau. of Edmonston of Ednam, and had two daus., viz.,

Anne, m. to Lieut.-Col. Edmund Erskine, of Carnock.
Christian, m. to James, Earl of Bute.

William Dundas, leaving no male issue, was *s.* by his brother,

George Dundas, of Kincavel, who m. Helen, dau. of Adam Cooper, of Gogar, and had three sons, John, William, and James. The 2nd son,

William Dundas, m. Elizabeth, dau. of Richard Elphinstone, of Calder Hall, by Jean Bruce, heiress of Airth, only dau. of Alexander Bruce, son of Sir John Bruce, of Airth, representative of that distinguished branch of the great house of Bruce. Richard Elphinstone, of Calder Hall, was great-grandson of William Elphinstone, youngest son of Alexander, 2nd Lord Elphinstone. Mr. Dundas had eight sons and three daus. He joined the Chevalier in the rising of 1715, suffered imprisonment, and although eventually liberated by government, was forced to sell the estate of Airth. He purchased, subsequently, in the year 1720, the lands of Blair, in the co. of Perth. Mr. Dundas was *s.* at his decease by his eldest son,

Richard Dundas, of Blair Castle, who m. Margaret, dau. of Sir John Wedderburn, Bart. of Blackness, and had two sons, viz., Robert-Bruce, his heir, and John-Elphinstone, an officer in the E.I.C.S., killed at the battle of Tellicherry. Mr. Dundas *d.* 6 Oct. 1790, and was *s.* by his elder son,

Robert-Bruce Dundas, of Blair Castle, *b.* 6 Aug. 1754, m. Elizabeth, only child and heiress of Captain James-Drummond Spital,* younger, of Leuchet, in Fifeshire, by Miss Frances Innes, of the family of Innes *of that ilk*, and has had issue,

Richard-Leslie, now of Blair Castle.

Frances-Bruce.	Margaret-Elphinston.
Elizabeth-Vaneck.	Jane-De Viligas.

Arms—Arg., a lion, rampant, gu., with the mark of cadency.
Crest—A lion's head, full-faced, gu., looking through a bush of oak, ppr.
Motto—Essayez.
Seat—Blair Castle, near Culross.

DUNLOP OF DRUMHEAD.

Dunlop, Robert-Buchanan, Esq. of Drumhead, co. Dumbarton, *b.* 11 Oct. 1807; m. 20 July, 1837, Emma Smith, and by her (who *d.* 10 March, 1851) has had issue,

I. Robert, *b.* 27 May, 1838.
II. James, *b.* 19 Sept. 1840.
III. Charles-George, *b.* 2 Jan. 1843.
IV. Henry-Donald, *b.* 7 July, 1845.
V. Francis-Campbell, *b.* 20 Jan. 1847.
I. Elizabeth, *d.* 17 Dec. 1839.　II. Caroline-Annabella.
III. Frances-Harriett, *d.* 1845.　IV. Emma.

Lineage.—John Napier, of Kilmahew, the last representative in the male line of that ancient family, m. Lilias, dau. of Sir John Colquhoun, of that ilk and Luss, and of the Lady Lilias Graham his wife, sister of the great Marquess, and eldest dau. of the 4th Earl of Montrose. They had two daus., Margaret, m. 1st, to Sir Patrick Maxwell, of Newark, and 2ndly, to the Earl of Glencairn, but without issue by the latter; and Catherine, m. to Robert Campbell, of Northwoodside (2nd son of Colin Campbell, of Blythswood), whose only child, Lilias, m. James Dunlop, of Garnkirk, a branch of the family of Dunlop *of that ilk*. Their 2nd son, Robert Dunlop, of Househill, m. 1st, Jean Baird, dau. of Baird of Craigton, and his only child by her m. Robert Dinwiddie, of Germiston, and is now represented by William Lockhart, of Germiston, and Milton-Lockhart, for many years representative of the county of Lanark in parliament. Robert Dunlop m. 2ndly, Janet, dau. of Archibald Buchanan, of Drumhead, and Jean Buchanan, dau. of Gilbert Buchanan, of Bonkell, and Dorothea Napier, a descendant of the famous John Napier, of Murchiston, the inventor of logarithms. By this marriage, Robert Dunlop had,

I. James, of Househill, colonel of the Renfrewshire militia, who m. his cousin, Miss Buchanan, of the Bonkell family, and is now represented by four daus., one of whom, the 2nd, was m. to the late A.-D. Campbell, Esq. of Ash Craig, Ayrshire, but without issue.

* The mother of Captain James Drummond Spital was the Hon. Elizabeth Leslie, eldest dau. of Alexander, 4th Lord Lindores.

II. ROBERT-BUCHANAN,* of Drumhead, to which estate he *s.* as heir of entail, in right of his mother, on assuming the name and arms of that family. He was lieut.-col. of the London and Westminster light horse volunteers, raised at the time of Lord George Gordon's riots, and *m.* Frances, 7th dau. of Samuel Beachcroft, Esq. of Wickham Court, in the county of Kent, a merchant, and director of the Bank of England, and *d.* 15 Jan. 1837, having had, besides a dau. Elizabeth, three sons,

1 ROBERT-BUCHANAN DUNLOP, now of Drumhead.
2 James.
3 Charles, in holy orders, vicar of Henfield, Sussex, *d.* 4 Sept. 1851, leaving three sons and one dau. by his wife, Fanny, dau. of William Borrer, Esq. of Henfield, Sussex, viz., Charles-Seward, *b.* 24 Oct. 1840; Henry-Beachcroft, *b.* 27 Jan. 1842; William-Buchanan, *b.* 9 April, 1851; and Fanny-Elizabeth.

I. Lilias, *m.* to Robert Muirhead, of Croy, but without issue.
II. Dorothea, *m.* to Robert Findlay, of Easterhill (*see* FINDLAY *of Easterhill*).

In 1530, William Buchanan, of Boturich, *m.* Miss McAulay, granddau. of McAulay of Ardincapel, and as her marriage portion acquired the estate of Drumhead, at that time called "Blairhannachra McAulay." At a subsequent period, the estate of Boturich was exchanged with Haldane of Gleneagles for that of Blairhoish, sold by the grand-uncle of the present proprietor of Drumhead, who is the 11th in succession from the above William Buchanan, for whose descent from Buchanan of that ilk, and subsequent history of the Drumhead family, see Buchanan of Auchmar's history of the clan, published in 1723.

A brother of Archibald Buchanan, of Drumhead, acquired the estate of Sundon, in Bedfordshire, leaving two daus., one of whom was *m.* to Sir Walter Riddell, of that ilk, whose son, Sir John, succeeded to Sundon on adding BUCHANAN to his family name, and *m.* Lady Frances Marsham, dau. of the Earl of Romney, and is represented by his son, the present Sir Walter Buchanan-Riddell, Bart.

Arms—BUCHANAN and DUNLOP quarterly.
Crest and *Motto*—Par sit fortuna labori.
Present Residence—Drumhead, Dumbartonshire.

DUNNE OF BRITTAS.

DUNNE, FRANCIS-PLUNKETT, Esq. of Brittas, Queen's County, lieut.-col. in the army, D.L., and lieut.-col. Queen's County militia, M.P. for Portarlington.

Lineage.—The estate of Brittas has been, time immemorial, in the family of DUNNE. When required by King JAMES I, it was surrendered to the crown, and a grant retaken in fee, constituting it a manor subject to quit and crown rent. The grant was made to CHARLES DUNNE, Master in Chancery, and member for the College.

The great-grandfather of the present representative,

CHARLES DUNNE, Esq. of Brittas, who was killed at the battle of Aughrim, *m.* Alice, dau. of General Nugent, of the co. of Westmeath, slain at the siege of Derry, and had a son and successor,

EDWARD DUNNE, Esq. of Brittas, who *m.* Margaret Wyse, of the co. of Waterford, and was father of

FRANCIS DUNNE, Esq. of Brittas, who *m.* 10 Aug. 1760, Margaret Plunket, one of the co-heiresses of Nicholas Plunket, of Dunsoughly Castle, co. Dublin, Esq., and had issue,

EDWARD, his heir. Francis, a colonel in the army.
Nicholas, killed in the storming of Fort du Rhin, during the French revolutionary war.
Alice, *m.* to Henry Osborn, Esq. of Dardestown Castle, co. Meath, and since deceased.
Frances, *d. unm.* Catherine, *d. unm.*
Margaretta, *m.* to A. O'Farrel, Esq. of the co. of Kildare, and is deceased.

Mr. Dunne *d.* 20 Aug. 1771, and was *s.* by his son,

GENERAL EDWARD DUNNE, of Brittas, *b.* 14 Oct. 1763, *m.* 28 July, 1801, Frances White, of Bantry House, sister to the Earl of Bantry, and niece to Viscount Longueville, of Castle Mary, co. Cork, and had issue,

FRANCIS-PLUNKETT, now of Brittas.
Edward, barrister-at-law. Robert, in holy orders.
Richard, an officer in the army.
Charles, an officer in the army.
Frances-Jane.

* Robert-Buchanan Dunlop, of Drumhead, is the male representative of DUNLOP *of Garnkirk*, also, through the above-named females of Kilmahew and Northwoodside, of these two families.

Arms—Az., an eagle displayed, or.
Crest—On a mount, an oak-tree, in front thereof a nute, all ppr.
Motto—Mullher a boo.
Seat—Brittas, Clonaslee, Queen's Co.

DUNSCOMBE OF MOUNT DESERT.

DUNSCOMBE, NICHOLAS, Esq. of Mount Desert, co. Cork, J.P., *b.* 23 Aug. 1807; *m.* 2 April, 1839, Jane, 4th dau. of Robert Carr, Esq. of the city of Cork, and has issue,

I. GEORGE. II. Robert. III. Noble.
I. Jane.

Lineage.—The family of Dunscombe claim Saxon origin; their native county was Devonshire, where, in ages now forgotten, ere the Norman subjugated the Saxon, they gave name to Higher and Lower Dunscombe, and, in common with others of their race, suffered under Norman sway. It has been handed down in ancestral archives, that the progenitor of the first William Dunscombe, Esq., hereinafter mentioned, was engaged in the Crusade to Palestine as a knight's attendant.

As respects their standing in Ireland, Edward Dunscombe, Esq. resided at Saint Finbarry's, in the city of Cork, in 1590; and, beyond question, the family of Dunscombe is one of the oldest in that city, and with it the name is indelibly identified, for on Dunscombe's Marsh the greatest portion of the flat of the city has been built.

WILLIAM DUNSCOMBE, Esq. of London, *b.* in 1475, *d.* in 1540, leaving by his wife, named Clement, a son,

CAPTAIN CLEMENT DUNSCOMBE, who *d.* in 1590, leaving

EDWARD DUNSCOMBE, Esq., his son, then residing at Saint Finbarry's, in the city of Cork. He *m.* in London, Catherine, sister of the Rev. Henry Noble, afterwards of Urney, co. Tyrone, in Ireland, and *d.* in 1631, leaving, him surviving, a son,

COLONEL NOBLETT DUNSCOMBE, who *m.* Mary, dau. of Alderman Martell, of the city of Cork, and *d.* in 1651, leaving a son,

NOBLETT DUNSCOMBE, Esq., *b.* in 1628, who was mayor of Cork in 1665. He *m.* in 1652, Mary, sister of William Hull, Esq. of the city of Cork, niece to Sir William Hull, Knt. of Lemcon, co. Cork, and dau. of Henry Hull, of Clonakilty, co. Cork, by Hester, dau. of Humphrey Jobson, secretary to Charles Howard, Earl of Effingham, lord high-admiral of England, and *d.* in June, 1695, leaving one son, WILLIAM, of whom presently; and three daus., viz., Elizabeth, who, in 1673, *m.* Robert Rogers, Esq. of the city of Cork, and of Ashgrove, in that county, afterwards M.P. for the city of Cork, in 1692 and 1695; Mary, who in 1676, *m.* James Harlowyne, Esq. of the city of Cork; and he having *d.* in 1678, leaving no issue, she *m.* 2ndly, in 1680, John Hull, Esq. of The Little Island, co. Cork; and Sarah, who, in 1687, *m.* John Spread, Esq. The only son,

WILLIAM DUNSCOMBE, Esq., *b.* in 1660, *m.* twice: 1st, in Oct. 1682, Catherine, one of the three daus. of William Mead, Esq. of the city of Cork, and sister to Sir John Mead, Bart., and by her, who *d.* in Jan. 1692, he had (with four daus., viz., Mary, who *m.* John Carleton, Esq.; Elizabeth, who *m.* — Travers, Esq.; Ellinor, who *m.* Eleazar Masicke, Esq.; and Catherine, who *m.* Lionel Becher, Esq.) one son,

MEADE, *b.* in 1691, who *m.* in Nov. 1720, Elizabeth, eldest dau. of Dillon Newman, Esq. of the city of Cork. He contested the city of Cork in 1727, and petitioned against an undue return by the sheriff, but was defeated on it. He *d.* in 1729, leaving (with two daus., Mary and Catherine) two sons,

William, *b.* in 1721, *m.* in 1744, Mary-Anne, dau. of William Conner, Esq., and *d.* in Oct. 1751, without leaving issue.

Richard, *b.* in 1723, *m.* in 1746, Helena, dau. of Robert Atkins, Esq., alderman of the city of Cork, and *d.* in 1748, leaving one child, Richard, who *m.* in March, 1770, Jane, one of the daus. of Rowland Bateman, Esq. of Oak Park, co. Kerry, and *d.* in 1793, leaving (with six daus., viz., Eliza, who *m.* Captain Richard Carter; Helena, who *m.* her cousin, Robert-Parker Parker, Esq. of Inchigagin, near Cork; Sarah, who *m.* Capt. Joseph Beckett, R.N.; Jane, who *m.* Robert Allen, Esq., surgeon, R.N.; Mary, who *m.* James-Fitzgerald Massey, Esq. of the co. Limerick; and Anne, who *m.* William Russell, Esq. of Limerick,) three sons, Richard Meade, who *m.* in April, 1797, Avice-Elizabeth, the eldest dau. of Thomas Child, Esq. of Bandon, by whom he had two sons, both of whom *d. unm.*; Adam, a capt. in the 89th regt., *d.* of his wounds in the island of Ceylon, *unm.*; and Longfield, a midshipman, *d.* in the West Indies after battle, *unm.*

William Dunscombe m. 2ndly, in 1695, Mary, dau. of Alderman William Roberts, of the city of Cork. He d. in Sept. 1720, leaving issue, two sons and two daus., viz.,

Noblett, of Mount Desert, b. in 1699, who was high-sheriff of the co. of Cork in 1730, and represented Lismore in the Irish parliament, from 1727 to 1744. He m. Elizabeth, dau. of James Barry, Esq. of Rathcormac, and d. in May, 1745, leaving no issue.
George, of whom presently.
Helena, who m. Stephen Mazicke, Esq.
Henrietta, who m. Redmond Barry, Esq. of Ballyclough, co. Cork, and by him was mother of Mary Barry, who m. Richard-Aldworth St. Leger, Viscount Doneraile.

Mr. Dunscombe purchased the Mount Desert estate in 1703. His 3rd son,

George Dunscombe, Esq. of Mount Desert (it being entailed on him, on failure of male issue to his brother Noblett,) b. in May, 1712, s. his brother in 1745, though he did not reside at Mount Desert (but at Ballyally), his brother's widow doing so until her death, in Jan. 1772. He m. in Feb. 1738, Penelope, the 2nd and youngest dau. of Colonel Nicholas Colthurst, of Ballyally, co. Cork (grandson to Sir Nicholas Purdon, Knt. of Ballyclough, co. Cork), by Penelope his wife, the 2nd dau. of Sir John Topham, Knt. of Dublin, one of the Masters in Chancery in the reign of Charles II.: was a colonel, and also in the suite of his Royal Highness Frederick, Prince of Wales. He d. at Ballyally, the seat of his father-in-law, in Jan. 1752, leaving (with four daus., viz., Penelope, who, in May, 1760, m. John Carleton, Esq. of Woodside, co. Cork, only son and heir of Christopher Carleton, Esq. of the city of Cork; Mary, who, in July, 1769, m. Walter Atkin, Esq. of Leadington, co. Cork: she was his 2nd wife; Harriet, and Elizabeth, who both d. unm.) an only son and heir,

Nicholas Dunscombe, of Mount Desert, b. in 1741, high-sheriff of the co. Cork in 1765. He m. in May, 1764, Mary, the only child and heiress of Thomas Parker, Esq. of Inchigagin, near Cork, by Mary his wife, the eldest dau. of Swithin White, Esq. of the city of Cork, and had issue,

George, of whom presently.
Robert-Parker, who assumed the name and arms of Parker, in lieu of his patronymic, on succeeding to his mother's property. He m. 20 April, 1788, his cousin, Helena, one of the daus. of Richard Dunscombe, Esq., and Jane Bateman his wife, and d. in July, 1815, leaving several sons and three daus. (See Parker *of Inchigagin.*)
William, formerly a lieut. in the 12th light dragoons, d. in Feb. 1827, leaving no lawful issue.
Thomas, an alderman of the city of Cork, m. in Feb. 1798, Mary, the eldest dau. of Alderman Shaw, of the city of Cork, and d. in Dec. 1833, leaving issue: 1 Nicholas, in holy orders, chancellor of the diocese of Cork, and rector of St. Nicholas, in said chancellorship, city of Cork, b. 25 Dec. 1798, m. 3 Feb. 1844, his cousin, Penelope, youngest dau. of George Dunscombe, Esq. of Mount Desert; 2 John Shaw, b. in July, 1806, m. 1 Sept. 1830, Lucy, only child of Henry Orpen, Esq. of co. Kerry, d. 30 May, 1854; 3 Thomas-Shaw, b. 18 Feb. 1811, m. 24 July, 1850, Jane, the eldest dau. of William Gillespie, Esq.; and 4 Isabella.
Nicholas, in holy orders, rector of Kilcully, d. in Aug. 1838, unm.
Rowland, formerly a lieut. in the army, d. in April, 1835, leaving no lawful issue.
Parker, b. in 30 Nov. 1781, m. 6 Jan. 1803, Jane, the 3rd and youngest sister of William Waggett, Esq., recorder of Cork, and dau. of Christopher Waggett, Esq. of Kitsboro', near Cork, and d. 4 June, 1829, leaving issue,

Nicholas, b. 20 Oct. 1804, m. 23 July, 1830, at Caledon, co. Armagh, Anna-Matilda, the eldest dau. of Thomas Johnston, Esq. of Fort Johnston, co. Monaghan, by Martha his 1st wife, the eldest dau. of the Rev. Doctor Hingston, vicar-general of Cloyne, and has issue, Parker, b. 7 Feb. 1834; Nicholas, a lieut. in the 46th regt. of foot, b. 18 Jan. 1835; William-Waggett, b. 27 April, 1837; Henry, b. 5 June, 1839; George, b. 6 Dec. 1843; Clement, b. 27 March, 1846; and two daus., Martha, who, on 24 Dec. 1851, m. Rev. Walter Johnston (the eldest son of Henry-G. Johnston, Esq. of Fort Johnston, co. Monaghan,) her first-cousin; and Jane-Ellen Waggett.
Christopher-Waggett, b. 17 April, 1808, m. 6 July, 1830, Maria, only dau. of the Rev. Edward Batchelor, of Dublin, and d. 5 Feb. 1839, leaving issue, Parker, b. in Aug. 1831; Edward; Christopher; and two daus., Elizabeth and Jane.
Johanna-Waggett, m. 23 Dec. 1824, to the Rev. Dr. John Webb, LL.D., of The Hill, near Cork. He d. 9 Sept. 1842, leaving, him surviving, two sons, John M'Donnell, a capt. in the 4th royal Irish dragoon-guards, b. in Nov. 1825; and Randal, b. in Oct. 1832.

Mary, d. in July, 1827, unm. When Col. Moore, afterwards Sir John Moore, who fell at the memorable retreat on Corunna, was quartered in the south of Ireland, this lady was on the point of being united in marriage to him, but the prospect of his immediately going abroad prevented its taking place.
Penelope, who d. in 1816, unm.
Elizabeth, who m. in 1800, Abraham Lane, Esq., of the city of Cork, and sheriff of the same in 1798.

Mr. Dunscombe d. 15 March, 1793, (his mother, Penelope Dunscombe, d. in Jan. 1781,) and was s. by his eldest son,

George Dunscombe, Esq. of Mount Desert, b. 17 March, 1765, who was high-sheriff of the co. Cork, in 1789. He m. 25 Sept. 1806, Lydia, the 2nd dau. of Charles Denroche, Esq. of the city of Cork, by Anne Dorman his wife, and had issue one only son, Nicholas, his heir, and four daus., viz., Anne-Dorman, who m. 25 July, 1837, Benjamin Swete, Esq. of Greenville, co. Cork, only son and heir of the late Samuel Swete, Esq. of the same place; Mary-Parker; Lydia, who, 6 May, 1845, m. the Rev. Henry Gillman, 2nd son of the late Col. Gillman; and Penelope, who, 3 Feb. 1844, m. her cousin, the Rev. Nicholas Dunscombe, chancellor of the diocese of Cork, and rector of St. Nicholas, in the said chancellorship, city of Cork. Mr Dunscombe d. 3 March, 1835, (his widow Lydia Dunscombe, d. 25 Dec. 1842,) and was s. by his only son and heir, the present Nicholas Dunscombe, Esq. of Mount Desert, the representative of this ancient Saxon family.

Motto—Fidelitas vincit.
Seat—Mount Desert, co. Cork.

DUPPA OF HOLLINGBOURNE.

Duppa, Baldwin-Duppa, Esq. of Hollingbourne House, Kent, J.P. and D.L., b. in Nov. 1763; m. in 1800, Mary, dau. of Major-Gen. Gladwin, of Stubbing Court, co. Derby, and by her (who d. 28 June, 1837) had,

I. Baldwin-Francis, barrister-at-law, m. Catharine, dau. and co-heir of Philip Darell, Esq., brother to the late Henry Darell, Esq. of Calehill, in Kent, and left issue,

1 Baldwin Francis. 2 Brian-Philip-Darell. 3 Euston-Whitney. 1 Catharine-Mary. 2 Elenor-Henrietta. 3 Blanche-Florence.

II. Brian-Edward, B.A., m. Miss Long, dau. of W. Long, Esq., M.P., of Roodashton.
III. Henry-Clarke, of Malmaynes Hall, Kent, b. 6 April, 1805, m. 12 July, 1840, Julia-Anne, dau. of Col. Thorndyke, R.A., by Frances his wife, dau. of Col. Edmund Faunce.
IV. Charles-Berridge, m. 6 Dec. 1843, Ellen Pink, dau. of Major-General Faunce, C.B. of Bath.
V. George.
I. Mary-Dorothy, m. in 1840, to Edward-Barrell Faunce, Esq. of Sharsted, co. Kent.
II. Frances-Anne. III. Sarah-Charlotte.
IV. Harriet. V. Ellen.

Mr. Duppa d. 5 April, 1847.

Lineage.—The family of Duppa is one of considerable antiquity. Of its distinguished members were Bryan Duppa, bishop of Winchester; and Sir Thomas Duppa, Knt., usher of the Black Rod, *temp.* Charles II, James II, and William and Mary.

Baldwin Duppa, Esq. of Hollingbourne, barrister-at-law, high-sheriff of Kent in 1735, and one of its deputy-lieutenants, d. unm. 30 Nov. 1764, aged 82, and was buried in Hollingbourne church. By his will he devised his estates to his kinsman,

The Rev. Richard Hancorn (grandson of Richard Hancorn and Eleanor Duppa his wife), who assumed, by act of parliament, 5 George III., in compliance with a proviso in the bequest, the surname and arms of Duppa. He m. an heiress of the name of Baas, a lady of German extraction, but dying in 1790, was s. by his brother (who had previously changed his name from Hancorn),

Baldwin Duppa, Esq. This gentleman was shipwrecked in the "Ramillies," in 1760, on the Bolt Head, and was the only officer who, with twenty-five of the crew, escaped by leaping from the vessel upon the rocks. He m. in 1762, Miss Martha Geach, a lady of ancient descent in Cornwall, and had issue,

Baldwin-Duppa, his heir. Richard d. unm.
Martha, m. to William Higgins, Esq of Middlewood, in Herefordshire, and has issue, William; Robert; and Mary Anne.

Mr. Duppa d. in 1798, and was s. by his son, Baldwin-Duppa Duppa, Esq. of Hollingbourne.

Arms—Az., a lion's paw, erased, in fesse, between two bars of chain, or; on a canton, of the second, a rose, gu.
Crest—An arm in armour, holding a lion's paw, erased, or.
Seat—Hollingbourne House, near Maidstone.

DU PRE OF WILTON PARK.

Du Pre, James, Esq. of Wilton Park and Wooburn House, co. Bucks, *b.* 10 June, 1778; *m.* 18 May, 1801, Madelina, 2nd dau. of Sir William Maxwell, 4th Bart. of Monreith, co. Wigton, and has issue,

I. Caledon-George, M.P. for Bucks, *b.* 28 March, 1839, *m.* Louisa Cornwallis, 3rd dau. of the late Sir William Maxwell, 5th Baronet of Monreith, co. Wigton, and his issue, Georgiana-Louisa, and Emily-Madelina.
II. William-Maxwell, in holy orders, *m.* in June, 1837, Emily, 2nd dau. of Sir Thomas Baring, Bart. of Larkbeer, co. Devon, and has issue.
III. Charles-Lennox-Irby.
I. Catherine-Anne, *m.* to Pascoe-St. Leger Grenfell, Esq.
II. Mary-Louisa, *m.* to John Labouchere, Esq.
III. Emily-Madelina, *m.* to Lord William Montagu, son of the Duke of Manchester.
IV. Caroline-Adelaide, *m.* to the Rev. Spencer Thornton.
V. Gertrude-Frances. VI. Louisa-Frances.
VII. Fanny. VIII. Julia.

Mr. Du Pré, who *s.* to the Wilton Park estate upon the death of his mother, in 1800, is a magistrate and deputy-lieut. for Bucks, and served as high-sheriff in 1825.

Lineage.—The late Josias Du Pre, Esq. of Wilton Park, co. Bucks, Governor of Madras, *m.* in 1766, Rebecca, dau. of Nathaniel Alexander, Esq., and sister of James, 1st Earl of Caledon, by whom (who *d.* in 1800) he had (with five daus, Eliza, *m.* 1st, to Arthur Brice, Esq., and 2ndly, in 1803, to the Hon. and Rev. John Blackwood; Jane, *m.* to Wallop Brabazon, Esq. of Bath House, co. Louth; Charlotte, *m.* to Lieut.-Gen. O'Loghlin; Cornelia, *m.* to Edward Townsend, Esq of Wincham Hall; and Rebecca, *m.* to Sir Philip Grey Egerton, Bart.) a son and successor, the present James Du Pre, Esq. of Wilton Park.

Arms—Az., a chevron, or, between two mullets, in chief, and a lion, passant, in base, arg.; from the centre chief a pile issuant, of the second.
Crest—A lion, rampant, arg., resting the dexter hind paw on a fleur-de-lis, gu.
Seat—Wilton Park, Beaconsfield, Bucks.

DUTTON OF BURLAND.

Dutton, Joseph, Esq. of Burland Hall, co. Chester, *b.* 1768, the 18th in lineal descent from Odard, Lord of Dutton, and eldest heir male of William, Earl of Eu; *m.* Sarah, dau. of Robert Cawley, of Swandley, and has issue,

I. Thomas, *b.* 1796, *d. unm.* 16 June, 1849.
II. Robert, *m.* Ann, dau. of John Platt, Esq. of Holywell House, and has issue,
  John, *b.* 27 Jan. 1819.
  Thomas, *b.* 12 Dec. 1828, *m.* Emma, only child of George Allwood, Esq. of Brindley, and has a son, Hugh.
  Eliza. Mary.
III. Hugh, *b.* 1799. IV. John, *b.* 1804.
I. Mary, *m.* to Joseph Sutton, who *d.* 1820.
II. Eliza, *m.* to John Allwood, Esq.
III. Sarah. IV. Harriett.

Lineage.—The Duttons claim consanguinity with the ancient blood-royal of England, being descended from Rollo, the 1st Duke of Normandy, through William, Earl of Eu, who *m.* a niece of William the Conqueror.

Richard, Duke of Normandy (grandson of Rollo) surnamed *Sans-peur*, had issue (besides his son, Richard, who succeeded him; his dau., Emma, Queen of England; and other issue) two younger sons, Godfrey, and William. To Godfrey, his father gave the Earldoms of Eu and Brion. On his decease, the latter Earldom became the heritage of his posterity, branching out into the now-extinct house of the Earls of Clare and Pembroke, while William, the younger brother, succeeded him in the Earldom of Eu. He had, besides others, his successor, Robert, father of William, who *m.* a sister of Hugh Lupus, Earl of Avranches (afterwards Earl of Chester), named Jeanne, and niece of William the Conqueror.

There was issue of this marriage (besides William, successor in the Earldom of Eu, and another child), six sons, named Nigel, Geffry, Odard (or Huddard), Edard, Horswin, and Wlofaith; the six brothers accompanied their uncle, Hugh Lupus, into England, in the train of William the Conqueror, their great-uncle, and on the establishment of the Norman power, had various estates and honours conferred on them; Nigel was created Baron of Halton and Constable of Cheshire; Geffrey was Lord of Stopfort; Odard, Lord of Dutton; Edard, Lord of Haselwell; Horswin, Lord of Shrigley; and Wlofaith, Lord of Hatton. Odard, the 3rd son, was the ancestor of the Duttons *of Dutton*.

This Odard flourished during the reigns of William the Conqueror and William Rufus. "He," says Dr. Gower, "like his uncle, Hugh Lupus, had a sword of dignity," which in 1665, was in the possession of Eleanor, wife of Robert, 2nd Viscount Kilmorey (dau. and heir of Thomas Dutton, Esq. of Dutton, ancestors of the present Francis, Earl of Kilmorey; and had been preserved for many years as an heirloom, by the name of "Odard's Sword." Odard de Dutton, had a son, named Hugh Fitzodard, who flourished in the early part of the reign of Henry II.

Sir Peter Leycester, in his *Historical Antiquities of Cheshire*, has given us the pedigree of the Duttons *of Dutton*, which he says is faithfully collected from the evidences of that family, and other good records and deeds. He observes that the family is one of great worth, with almost a constant succession of knights.

Sir Thomas Dutton, of Dutton, Knt., son and heir of Sir Hugh Dutton, and Joane Holland his wife, was 6th in descent from Odard. He was made seneschal-governor and receiver of the castle and honour of Halton, in Cheshire, by William Clinton, Earl of Huntingdon. He *m.* Ellen, one of the daus. and heirs of Sir Peter Thornton, of Thornton, and had issue,

  Sir Peter Dutton, *d. s. p.* 35th Edward III.
  Thomas Dutton, *d. s. p.*
  Sir Lawrence Dutton, *d. s. p.* 1392.
  Edmund Dutton. Henry Dutton.
  William Dutton.

Edmund Dutton, the 4th son of Sir Thomas, *m.* Joan, dau. and heir of Henry Minshall, de Church Minshall, and had issue,

  Sir Peter Dutton, who became heir to his uncle, Sir Lawrence Dutton, of Dutton: he *d.* 1433. His last male heir, Lawrence, *d. s. p.* 1526.
  Hugh Dutton, of whom the Duttons *of Hatton*.
  Lawrence Dutton. Thomas Dutton.
  Agnes, *m.* William Leycester, of Nether Tabley, 22nd of Richard II (the immediate ancestor of the present George Warren, Baron De Tabley, 1855).
  Ellen.

Hugh Dutton, 2nd son of Edmund, *m.* Petronella, dau. of Ralph Vernon, of Hatton, in Cheshire, Esq., and had by her two sons, John, and Lawrence; of these the elder,

John Dutton, *m.* Margaret, dau. of Sir William Athurton, of Athurton, in Lancashire, Knt., by whom he had three sons,

I. Peter, living at Hatton, 1464. His descendant and eventual heiress, Elinor Dutton, *m.* Gilbert, 2nd Lord Gerard.
II. Richard. III. Geoffry.

Richard Dutton. 2nd son of John Dutton, of Hatton, had issue, Ralph Dutton, who had two sons, William and Richard. This Richard Dutton, who was an alderman and J.P. of the city of Chester, was removed by parliament for having been in arms against the Commonwealth:

William Dutton, eldest son and heir of Richard Dutton, lived at Chester, and had issue, by his wife Agnes, dau. of John Conway, of Flintshire, several children, whereof the 2nd son, Thomas, purchased the manor of Sherborne, in Gloucestershire; and from him descended Lucy, who *m.* Thomas Pope, Earl of Downe; and their only child, Lady Elizabeth, was the wife of Sir Francis-Henry Lee, of Ditchley; and from Thomas, the 2nd son of this William Dutton, of Chester, descended Sir Ralph Dutton, created a Baronet, 22 June, 1678, a title which expired with his son, Sir John Dutton. Sir Ralph's dau., Anne, *m.* James Naper, Esq., and their son, James, assumed the name of Dutton, and dying in 1776, left issue, James Dutton, M.P. for Gloucestershire, who was elevated to the peerage, 20 May, 1784, by the title of *Baron Sherborne*. Thomas Dutton, son of Hugh, eldest son of William Dutton, living at Dunham, near Chester, about 1660, had a son,

John Dutton, of Dunham, who *m.* Martha Breese, of Morley, in Little Barrow, co. Chester. John Dutton was buried at Thornton, 29 Jan. 1742, having had issue,

I. Thomas, of whom presently.
II. John, a merchant in the city of Chester, *m.* Miss Fair-

clough, and had issue, John, *d. unm.*; Charles, *m.* Miss Howard, and had issue an only son, John who *d. unm.* 1824; Esther, *m.* Dr. Jardine, of Liverpool; Elizabeth, *d. unm.*; and Mary, *m.* to her cousin, William Sefton, and *d. s. p.* 1846.

III. Robert, of Thornton Hall, who *m.* Mary Percival, and had issue, 1 Martha, *m.* — Whitley, of Alvanley, and *d.* leaving an only son, George Whitley, who *m.* Miss Greenall, sister of Gilbert Greenhall, Esq., M.P. for St. Helen's; 2 Anne, *m.* the Rev. Joseph Hodgkinson, D.D., rector of Dudcot, Berkshire, and *d. s. p.* 28 Jan. 1849; 3 Elizabeth, *m.* to John Reece, Esq. of Trafford, and *d.* leaving issue; 4 Thomas Dutton; 5 Robert Dutton, *m.* Mary, dau. of Charles Jones, Esq., of Stapleford Hall, and had issue, Elizabeth, who *m.* Richard Janion, of Rocksavage, Esq., and *d.* in 1852, leaving issue; 6 John Dutton, *m.* his cousin, Mary Sefton, and has issue Robert Dutton; 7 Mary.

I. Mary.

THOMAS DUTTON, the eldest son, *b.* in 1731, resided at Dunham, and had also a house at Pulford, co. Chester: he *m.* Mary dau. of — Reece, Esq. of Brereton Park, Tarvin, Chester, and *d.* in 1817, having had issue,

I. William, *d.* in 1819, *s. p.*
II. JOSEPH, present proprietor.
III. Robert, *d.* young.
I. Anne, *m.* Thomas Sefton, of Pickton, co. Chester, and *d.* in 1846, having had issue,

1 William Sefton, a merchant in the city of Chester, and sheriff in 1820: he *m.* his cousin, Mary Dutton, dau. of John Dutton, and *d.* in 1822, *s. p.*
2 Thomas Sefton, *d. unm.* 1846.
1 Mary, who *m.* her cousin, John Dutton.
2 Elizabeth, *m.* William Darlington, of Ivy Lodge, and of Marbury, in the co. of Chester, and *d.* in 1842, having had issue an only son,

JOHN DARLINGTON, *b.* 12 Jan. 1806, *m.* Elizabeth Turlay, and has issue, Henry-Cecil; Frederick-Arthur; Zoë; Warren · and other children.

3 Anne, *m.* to James Bickers.
4 Martha. 5 Hannah. 6 Catherine.

II. Martha.
III. Mary, *m.* to Richard Williams, of The Green Walls, Flintshire, and had, with other issue, a dau., who *m.* the Rev. Dr. Warren, father of SAMUEL WARREN, Queen's Counsel, recorder of Hull, F.R.S., D.C.L.
IV. Elizabeth, *m.* to Joseph Cheers.

JOSEPH DUTTON, the eldest surviving son, is the present representative of the Thornton branch of the DUTTONS *of Dutton.*

Arms—Quarterly: 1st and 4th, arg., 2nd and 3rd, gu.; a fret, or.
Crest—A plume of five ostrich feathers rising out of a ducal coronet, or; the feathers, arg., az., or, vert, and gu.
Motto—Servabo fidem.

DYKES OF DOVENBY.

BALLANTINE-DYKES, FRETCHEVILLE-LAWSON, Esq. of Ingwell, near Whitehaven, formerly M.P. for Cockermouth, *m.* 1844, Miss Gunson, eldest surviving dau. and co-heir of Joseph Gunson, Esq. of Ingwell, and has issue,

I. FRETCHEVILLE-BROUGHAM.
I. Mary-Frances. II. Adelina.
III. Eveline-Joyce. IV. Ida-Isabel.

Lineage.—This very ancient Cumberland family is said to have been located at Dykesfield, in that shire, prior to the Norman Conquest. The name "Del Dyke, or Dykes," is supposed to be derived from the Roman Wall, on the line of which Dykesfield (considered to be the site of a station) is situated.

WILLIAM DEL DYKES was grandfather of

ROBERT DEL DYKES, who granted lands at Burgh to William del Monkys, in a deed supposed to have been made in the time of HENRY III. The grandson of this Robert,

WILLIAM DEL DYKES, living in the reign of EDWARD II., *m.* Agnes, heiress of Sir Hugh Waverton, of Waverton, and had (with a dau. Agnes, the wife of J. de Ormby) a son and successor,

WILLIAM DEL DYKES, who flourished *temp.* EDWARD III, and was father of

WILLIAM DEL DYKES, who *m.* in the reign of RICHARD II, Jane, heiress of Sir H. Dystyngton, of Dystyngton, and was *s.* by his son,

WILLIAM DEL DYKES, living *temp.* HENRY IV., who *m.* Katherine Thwaites, of Thwaites, and left (with two daus., one *m.* to Nicholas Irton, of Irton, and the other, Isabel, *m.* to R. Brisco) a son and successor,

WILLIAM DEL DYKES, M.P. for the co. Cumberland, in the reign of HENRY VI. He *m.* Elizabeth, dau. of Sir William Leigh, Knt. of Isell (a descendant of Lucea, dau. of Hugh, Earl of Chester, whose mother was sister of WILLIAM the Conqueror). In the 9th of HENRY VI, he had a grant of lands at Wigton, from Henry, Earl of Northumberland. He was *s.* at his decease by his son,

WILLIAM DEL DYKES, who *m.* Christiana, dau. and co-heir of Sir Richard Salkeld, of Corby, a descendant and representative of Vaux of Tryermain, and was *s.* by his son,

THOMAS DYKES, Esq., who furnished horse in the border service, *temp.* HENRY VII. He *m.* Isabel, dau. and heiress of John Pennington, of Muncaster, and was father of a dau., Jane, *m.* to Richard Orfeur, and of a son,

LEONARD DYKES, Esq., who *m.* in 1541, Anne Layton, of Dalemain, and was *s.* by his son,

THOMAS DYKES, Esq., escheator of Westmoreland, *temp.* Queen ELIZABETH, who *m.* Jane, dau. of Lancelot Lancaster,* of Sockbridge, and was *s.* by his son,

LEONARD DYKES, Esq., who was sheriff for the co. of Cumberland, and, in the 19th CHARLES I, treasurer of the king's forces in that shire. He *m.* 1st, Anne, heiress of Radcliffe of Cockerton, and had, *inter alios*, Thomas, his successor. He *m.* 2ndly, Margaret Fretcheville, niece of Lord Fretcheville, of Staveley, and had a dau., Elizabeth, *m.* to Lawson Irton. Mr. Dykes was *s.* by his son,

THOMAS DYKES, who was distinguished by devotion to the cause of CHARLES I, and eventually fell into the hands of the parliamentarians, being discovered concealed amongst the branches of a mulberry tree in front of his house. Thence he was conveyed to Cockermouth, and there had an offer made to him, that his property should be restored, if he simply recanted. This proposition he met, however, with a decided negative, adding: "Prius frangitur quam flectitur," a sentiment since adopted as the family motto. This gallant cavalier *m.* 1st, Joyce Fretcheville, niece of Lord Fretcheville, of Staveley, and had issue,

LEONARD, his heir.
Joyce, *m.* to Thomas Curwen, Esq. of Workington.

He *m.* 2ndly, Margaret, heiress of Ralph Delavale, and had other issue. He was *s.* by his son,

LEONARD DYKES, Esq., who *m.* Grace Salkeld, and had,

FRETCHEVILLE, his successor.
Barbara, *m.* to J. Lathes, of Dalehead.

Mr. Dykes, who was sheriff of Cumberland twice in the reign of CHARLES II, was *s.* at his decease by his son,

FRETCHEVILLE DYKES, Esq., honourably mentioned by Camden, as a learned antiquary. He *m.* about the year 1697, Jane, eldest sister and heiress of Sir Gilfrid Lawson, of Brayton, and had (with a dau., Jane, *m.* to J. Ballantine, of Crookdale, and another son, Fretcheville, a captain in the navy and lost at sea) his successor,

LEONARD DYKES, Esq., who *m.* about the year 1728, Susanna, dau. of the Rev. Thomas Capstack, of Newburn, in Northumberland, by Hester his wife, granddau. of Sir John Lowther, and had

I. FRETCHEVILLE, of Warthole, who *m.* Mary, dau. of John Brougham, Esq. of Cockermouth, and sister and heir of P. Lamplugh, Esq. of Dovenby, and had an only dau.,

MARY, who inherited the property of her uncle, Peter-Lamplugh Brougham, Esq. of Dovenby, and *m.* her cousin, Joseph-Dykes Ballantine Dykes, Esq.

II. LAWSON.

The younger son,

LAWSON DYKES, Esq., who *m.* in 1765, Jane, dau. and heiress of John Ballantine, Esq. of Crookdale, and assumed, in consequence, the additional surname and arms of that family. He had issue,

JOSEPH, his successor.
Fretcheville, major-gen. in the E.I.Co.'s service
Mary, *m.* to James Spedding, Esq. of Summer Grove.

Mr. Dykes-Ballantine was *s.* at his decease by his elder son,

JOSEPH DYKES-BALLANTINE, Esq. of Dovenby Hall, in the co. of Cumberland, who *m.* Mary, dau. of Fretcheville Dykes, Esq. (by Mary, dau. of John Brougham, Esq. of Cockermouth, and sister and heiress of Peter Lamplugh-Brougham, Esq. of Scales), by whom he had issue,

FRETCHEVILLE-LAWSON, his heir.
Joseph, in holy orders, M A., a Fellow of Queen's College, Oxford, now rector of Headley, Hants.
Lamplugh-Brougham, a Fellow of Peter House, Cambridge, barrister-at-law.
Lawson-Peter, M.A., in holy orders, Fellow of Queen's College, Oxford.

---

* The Lancasters derive from John De Tailboys, brother of Fulke, Earl of Anjou.

Leonard-John, deceased.
James-William, collector of Salem, H.E.I.C.S.
Mary, *m.* 1st, in 1828, to John Marshall, Esq., son of John Marshall, Esq. of Headingley, by whom she had issue,
1 Reginald-Dykes. 2 Herbert-John. 3 Julian.
1 Janet-Mary. 2 Catherine-Alice.
Mrs. Marshall *m.* 2ndly, P. O'Callaghan, Esq. late 11th Hussars, and has by him a son, Desmond-Dykes-Tynte.
Jane-Christiana, *m.* in 1833, to Thomas Donnelly Esq. Major E.I.C.S., son of the late J. Donnelly, Esq. of Blackwatertown, and has an only child,
John-Frescheville-Dykes, Lieut. Royal Engineers.
Ellen, *m.* 1848, to James Walker, Esq. of Dalry House, co. Edinburgh, and has issue,
1 William-Frescheville. 2 Francis-Dyke.
1 Ellen-Mary.
Frances, *m.* to Edward Ormerod, Esq. of Seymore House, Old Trafford, co, Lancaster. Susan.

Mr. Ballantine, who assumed upon his marriage the additional surname of DYKES, was Sheriff of Cumberland in 1807. He *d.* in 1830, and was *s.* by his eldest son.

Arms—Or three cinquefoils, sa.
Crest—A lobster, vert.
Motto—Prius frangitur quam flectitur.
Seat—Dovenby Hall, Cumberland.

DYMOCK OF PENLEY HALL.

DYMOCK, EDWARD, Esq. of Penley Hall, co. Flint, and of Ellesmere, co. Salop, J.P. and D.L., *b.* 16 Dec. 1774; *m.* in 1 04, Mary, dau. of John Jones, Esq. of Coed-y-Glynn, co. Denbigh, and has issue,

I. EDWARD-HUMPHREY, in Holy Orders, *b.* in 1809.
II. John, *b.* in 1816.
III. Robert-Myddelton, *b.* in 1817.
IV. Thomas-Biddulph, *b.* in 1823.
I. Mary-Anne, *m.* in 1825, to Robert-Darwin Vaughton, Esq. of Whitchurch, in the co. of Salop.

Lineage.—This family descends from TUDOR TREVOR, Lord of Hereford and Whittington, Founder of the Tribe of the Marches. This chief had three sons, of whom the second,

LLYDOCK AP TUDOR TREVOR, Lord of both Maelors and Oswestry, *m.* Angharad, dau. of Iago ap Idwal, Prince of North Wales, A.D. 1021, and had a son and successor,

LLOWARCH GAM, a Nobleman in Maelor, father, by Lecky, his wife, dau. of Gwerystan ap Gwaethvoed Vawr, a Lord of Powys, of a son,

EDNYFED AP LLOWARCH, who *m.* Sionled, dau. and co-heir of Rhywalon ap Cynfyn, King of Powys, and was *s.* by his son,

RHYS AP EDNYFED (commonly called RHYS SAIS, from being bred among the English,) Lord of Oswestry, Whittington, and part of both Maelors, who *m.* Efa, dau. of Griffith ap Griffith, Prince of South Wales, and had issue,

I. TUDOR AP RHYS SAIS.
II. Elidyr ap Rhys Sais, Lord of Eyton, in Denbighland, ancestor of the EYTONS OF EYTON, SUTTONS OF SUTTON, and LEWIS'S OF GALTHROPE.
III. Iddon ap Rhys Sais, progenitor of the DAVIS'S OF DUDDLESTON, DAVIS'S OF MIDDLETON, and EDWARDES'S OF KILHENDRE, EDWARDES'S OF SHREWSBURY, BARTS., and VAUGHANS OF BURLTON.
I. Emory, *m.* Ednowain ap Ithal, of the Bryn in Powys.

The eldest son,

TUDOR AP RHYS SAIS, *m.* Jane, dau. of Rees Vychan ap Rees, ap Meredith, and had issue,

I. BLEDDYN AP TUDOR.
II. Grono ap Tudor, ancestor of the DAVIS'S OF DENBIGH.
III. Cyhelyn ap Tudor, from whom derived sixth in descent, Ieuaf ap Howell, whose dau. and heir,
Mawd, *m.* Tudor ap Griffith, Lord of Gwyddelwern, in Edeirnion, co. Merioneth, brother of OWEN GLENDOWER, and second son of Griffith, Lord of Glyndwrdwy, in Merioneth, Representative of the Sovereign Princes of Powys, North Wales, and South Wales, and was mother of a dau. and heir,
Lowrie, who *m.* Griffith ap Einion, of Cors-y-Gedol, co. Merioneth, and from this marriage derived, I. the VAUGHANS OF CORS-Y-GEDOL, II. YALES OF PLAS-YN-YALE, III. ROGERS'S OF BRYNTANGOR.

Tudor ap Rhys was *s.* by his eldest son,

BLEDDYN AP TUDOR, who *m.* Agnes, dau. of Llewellyn ap Iorwerth, ap Cadwgan, ap Elystan Glodrydd, Prince of Ferlys (*See* MORRIS OF THE HURST), and had three sons, I. OWEN; II. Madoc; III. Bleddyn. The eldest,

OWEN AP BLEDDYN, *m.* Efa, widow of Iorwerth ap Owain Brogyntyn, Lord of Edeirnion, Dinmael, and Abertanat, ancestor by her of the Hughes's of Gwerclas, Barons of Kymmer-yn-Edeirnion, and dau. and heir of Madoc, Lord of Mawddwy, in Merioneth, younger son of Gwenwynwyn, Prince of Powys, Wenwynwyn. By this lady he had issue,

I. Iorwerth Gam ap Owen, ancestor of the MOSTYNS OF MOSTYN, BARTS., MOSTYNS OF TALACRE, BARTS., MOSTYN, LORD VAUX, EDWARDES'S OF CHIRK, TREVORS OF BRYNKYNALLT, TREVORS OF TREVALLYN, and TREVORS-HAMPDEN, VISCOUNTS HAMPDEN,
II. THOMAS AP OWEN, progenitor of the line of which we have to treat.
III. Owen Vychan ap Owen, from whom derive the DYMOCKS OF PENLEY HALL.

The third son,

OWEN VYCHAN was great-grandfather of MADOC AP RIRID, who *m.* Margaret, dau. of Ithel Anwyl, a chieftain of Tegaing (as most of Flintshire was at that period called by the Welsh), and had a son and successor,

DAVID AP MADOC, who, according to the mode of address then used in Wales, was called "DAI MAIDOG," for David ap Madoc would thus be spoken, Dai being the diminutive of David. He *m.* Margaret, dau. and heir of Tudor ap Ririd, of Penley, by whom he acquired that estate, and had a son and heir,

DAVID AP DAI MADOC, whose name by mutation of address, was David Dai Madoc, that is David, the son of Dai (David) Madoc, and from the mode of expression then customary, David Dai Madoc became David Damoc or Dymock for it is written both ways in ancient manuscripts. Hence, forward Damoc or Dymock became the adopted surname of the family.

WILLIAM DYMOCK, Esq. of Willington Hall and Penley, living in the reign of ELIZABETH, was 6th in descent from David ap Dai Madoc. He *m.* Margaret, dau. of William Hanmer Esq. of Fens, and had, with four daus., two sons, HUMPHREY, of Willington, who *d.* in 1650, leaving with five daus., four sons, who all *d. s. p.*; and EDWARD. The younger son,

EDWARD DYMOCK, Esq. of Penley, *m.* Mary, dau. of John Davenport, Esq. and was father of

EDWARD DYMOCK, Esq. of Penley, who *m.* Mary, dau. of David Jones, Esq. of Oakenholt, and had (with a dau., Elizabeth, wife of Edward Morral, Esq. of Plâs Yolyn) three sons, EDWARD, his heir; John, who *d. s. p.*; and William, father of John, of Whitchurch, whose son, by Elizabeth his wife, was EDWARD DYMOCK, Esq. of whom presently, as inheritor of Penley. Mr. Dymock *d.* in 1705, was buried at Hanmer, and *s.* by his eldest son,

EDWARD DYMOCK, Esq. of Penley, who *d. unm.*, and left the Penley estate to his grand-nephew,

EDWARD DYMOCK, Esq. *b.* in 1730, who *m.* Elizabeth, dau. of Humphrey Brown, Esq. and had three sons, EDWARD; John; and William; by the eldest of whom,

EDWARD DYMOCK, Esq. of Penley, *b.* in 1752, he was *s.* in 1760. This gentleman *m.* 8 Jan. 1774, Mary, dau. of Edward Edwards, Esq. of Pentre Heylin, in the co. of Salop, and dying in 1784, left, with four daus., Christian; Elizabeth; Frances; and Anne; an only surviving son, EDWARD, now of Penley and Ellesmere.

Arms—Per bend sinister, erm. and erminois, a lion, rampant, langued and armed, gu.
Crest—An arm in armour, ppr., holding in the hand a spear, sa.
Motto—Pro rege et lege dimico.
Seat—Penley Hall.

DYNE OF GORE COURT.

BRADLEY DYNE, FRANCIS, Esq. of Gore Court, Kent, J.P. and D.L., High Sheriff in 1837, *b.* 28 Jan. 1790; *m.* in 1822, the Hon. Mary-Jane Harris, youngest dau. of Lord Harris, and has two sons.

I. FRANCIS-GEORGE, *b.* 21 June, 1823.
II. Musgrave-James, *b.* 16 Sept. 1827.

Lineage.—This family came over from Normandy with the CONQUEROR, and are so recorded in Battle Abbey Roll, and also, as holders of estate, in the first and subsequent surveys of Domesday. In these and all old records they are designated indiscriminately (as was also the river from which the invaders set sail from Normandy) "Dyne and Dyve," down to the time of the Usurpation, when they were enrolled at the Heralds' College under that double designation. The name, too, was still to be found at that period, and possibly at the present, in the *Nobiliare de Normandie*. After the first grants recorded in Domesday, they are found, within a century of the CONQUEST, in possession of lands, which same lands continued in the hands of the same family, down to the time of CROMWELL's rebellion, when the Parliament confiscated and sold that estate, together with others of the supporters of the Royal cause. In the time of RICHARD CŒUR DE LION, in consideration of services rendered to him, the DYNES received a remission of their *escuage*, or payment of the tax in lieu of military services formerly due upon their estates. In the reign of HENRY III., they are enumerated amongst the Barons, contending for the privileges sought to be wrested from them, one of them having fallen at the memorable battle of Evesham; and, as a proof that they were not of insignificant standing amongst the opposing barons, when the subjugation of HENRY was achieved, we find the Castle and Forest of Windsor allotted to Hugh de Dyne. At this period heraldic arms began to be used, when this family bore, as they have ever since done, as charges upon their shield, a fesse, either indented or barry, between three escallops. In the reign of EDWARD I., again, the infant grandson of Henry de Dyne, who was slain at Evesham, was taken, by Queen ELEANOR of Castile, into the Royal care and custody for education, thus securing this family to the Royal cause. They are found afterwards on the successful side, at that great crisis in the contest of the Roses, which terminated in the death of the "renowned Warwick," at Barnet, and the triumph of EDWARD IV. They were also considerable contributors to the estates of the Knights Hospitallers of St. John of Jerusalem, of which chivalrous institution, on three several occasions, their name appears in the list of Lords Priors.

HENRY DINE, Esq. who held lands by descent, in Bethersden, in Kent, *m.* in 1564, Elizabeth Longley, and was father of JAMES DYNE, Esq. whose son, JOHN DYNE, Esq. buried in the chancel at Bethersden, 1646, left by Margaret his wife, dau. of Baker of Ripplecourt, in Kent, a son and heir, JOHN DYNE, Esq. who *m.* Timothea, dau. and co-heir of Thomas Dyne, Esq. of Sussex, and had by her, who *d.* and was buried at Westfield, in 1682, with other issue, two sons, namely,

THOMAS, of Westfield and Lankhurst, whose son, EDWARD, of Lankhurst, *m.* Mary, dau. of William Fletcher, Esq. of Conghurst, in Sussex, and dying in 1732, left an only dau. and heiress, MARY FLETCHER, *m.* to Musgrave Briscoe, Esq.

HENRY, of whom presently.

The younger son,

HENRY DYNE, Esq. *m.* Elizabeth Crowhurst, niece of Francis Whitfield, Esq. of Thornehouse, in Bethersden, and *d.* in 1706, leaving a son,

JOHN DYNE, Esq. (buried at Bethersden in 1746), who *m.* Elizabeth Tylden, of Shadoxhurst, and had by her, who *d.* in 1776 (with other issue *d. s. p.*), three sons, I. JOHN, *b.* in 1725 (who had two sons, John, Capt. in the army; and Edward, who settled in Somersetshire); II. EDWARD; and III. William, who *m.* in 1758, Effield, dau. of James Chapman, Esq. and *d.* in 1800, leaving issue. The second son,

EDWARD DYNE, Esq. *b.* in 1727, *m.* Sept. 1755, Elizabeth, dau. of Andrew Hawes, Esq. and by her, who *d.* in 1793, left at his decease, in 1793, two sons, ANDREW HAWES, his heir; and Thomas, who *m.* Mary, dau. and co-heir of Peter Fountain, Esq. of London, and left one dau. The elder son,

ANDREW-HAWES DYNE, Esq. of Gore Court, in Kent, marrying in 1783, Frances, sister and heir of James Bradley, Esq. Secretary to the Board of Control, on its first formation, assumed, at Mr. Bradley's decease, by Sign Manual, in 1800, the surname of BRADLEY. By this lady he had issue, I. FRANCIS, his heir; II. James, capt. R.N., who *m.* Caroline, eldest dau. of Admiral Western, and *d.* in 1829; I. Frances-Rosilia, *m.* in 1805, to Henry Dickinson, Esq. E.I.Co.'s civil service; II. Elizabeth, *m.* 1st, to Michael Hoy, Esq. of Medenbury House, Hants, and 2ndly, to Capt. George Mainwaring, Royal Artillery; III. Margaret, *m.* to the Rev. Allen Morgan, of New Ross, co. Wexford. Mr. Dyne-Bradley *d.* in 1820, and was *s.* by his son, the present

FRANCIS BRADLEY-DYNE, Esq. of Gore Court, who has resumed by Royal Licence, the surname of DYNE.

Arms—Quarterly; 1st and 4th, arg., two bars gemelles between three escallops, gu., for DYNE; 2nd and 3rd, sa., a fesse engrailed, arg. in chief, a mullet between two crosses-formée-fitchée, all within a bordure, also engrailed, of the last, for BRADLEY.

Crests—1st and 2nd, an heraldic antelope's head, erased, armed, and maned, or, langued gu., for DYNE; a dexter arm, embowed, in armour, holding a battle-axe, all ppr. for BRADLEY.

Seat—Gore Court, near Sittingbourne.

DYOTT OF FREEFORD.

DYOTT, RICHARD, Esq. of Freeford, co. Stafford, late an officer in the Army, *b.* 26 May, 1808; *m.* 6 Dec. 1849, Ellen-Catherine, only dau. of Charles-Smith, Forster, Esq. of Lysways Hall, near Lichfield.

Lineage.—The estate of Freeford, in Staffordshire, came into the possession of the family of Dyott in the time of ELIZABETH.

Sir Gillbert Dethick, Garter King-of-arms, confirmed, on 20 Feb. 1562, by a patent now in the possession of Gen. Dyott, the ancient family arms of the Dyotts, with a crest, to

JOHN DYOTT, of Stichbrook and Lichfield. This John was grandfather of

ANTHONY DYOTT, Esq. of Lichfield, Barrister-at-law, Recorder of Tamworth, and M.P. for Lichfield. He *m.* Catherine, eldest dau. of John Harcourt, Esq. of Ronton Abbey, in Staffordshire, and by her, who *d.* in 1602, he had (with two daus., Mary, *m.* to Silas Taylor, Esq.; and Catherine) three sons, RICHARD (Sir), his heir; Robert, Rector of Darlaston; and JOHN, who was probably the Dyott whom Shakspeare mentions in the Second Part of King HENRY IV. (act iii. scene 2) Anthony Dyott was *s.* by his eldest son,

SIR RICHARD DYOTT, Knt. M.P. one of the Privy Council of King CHARLES I. in the Court held at York, High Steward of Lichfield, and Chancellor of the co. palatine of Durham, a stanch Royalist. He *m.* Dorothy, dau. and heir of Richard Dorrington, Esq. of Stafford, and had six sons; he *d.* 8 March, 1659, aged 69, and was *s.* by his eldest son,

ANTHONY DYOTT, Esq. of Freeford, barrister-at-law, major of a regiment of foot under the royal standard, and after the Restoration M.P. for Lichfield. He *m.* Barbara, dau. of James Ingram, Esq. but dying *s. p.*, was *s.* by his brother,

RICHARD DYOTT, Esq., captain of horse in the volunteers of Lichfield, under the standard of the King. At the battle of Edgehill, he accompanied the royal family to Holland, and returned some short time before the Restoration. By his 1st wife, Katharine, dau. of Thomas Gresley, Esq., son of Sir George Gresley, Bart. of Drakelow, he left at his decease, 1677, a son and successor,

RICHARD DYOTT, Esq. of Freeford, bapt. 22 May, 1667, M.P. for Lichfield from 1698 to 1714. He *m.* in 1685, Frances, eldest dau. of William Inge, Esq. of Thorpe Constantine, co. Stafford, and by her, who *d.* in 1702, left at his decease, in 1719, with four daus. (Frances, *m.* to Christopher Sanders, Esq. of Shareshill; Catherine, *m.* to Gervas Burton, Esq.; Dorothy; and Bridget, *m.* to Michael Rawlins, Esq. of The Friary) one son,

RICHARD DYOTT, Esq. of Freeford, bapt. 3 June, 1687, who *m.* Miss Mary Lane, by whom, who *d.* in 1739, he had (with a dau., Mary, who *m.* in 1760, Christopher Astley, Esq. of Tamhorn) a son,

RICHARD DYOTT, Esq. of Freeford, bapt. 14 May, 1723, who *m.* in 1751, Katharine, dau. of Thomas Herrick, Esq. of Leicester, and dying in 1787, left (with five daus., Katharine, *m.* to Robert Dale, Esq. of Ashbourn; Mary; Anne, *m.* to the Rev. William Southworth; Hannah, *m.* to the Rev. W. Lee; and Lucy, *m.* to the Rev. Mr. Burnaby, of Leicester) three sons, RICHARD, his heir; WILLIAM, successor to his brother; and John-Philip, of Lichfield. The eldest son,

RICHARD DYOTT, Esq. of Freeford, bapt. 29 Oct. 1754, High Sheriff for Staffordshire in 1798, and Recorder of Lichfield in 1805, *m.* in 1783, his first-cousin, Mary, dau. and heir of Christopher Astley, Esq. of Tamhorn, but dying issueless in 1813, was *s.* by his brother.

WILLIAM DYOTT, Esq. of Freeford, a general officer in the army, and colonel of the 63rd regt., *b.* 17 April, 1761; *m.* in Feb. 1806, Eleanor, dau. of Samuel Thompson, Esq. of Green Mount, co. Antrim, and has issue, RICHARD, now of Freeford; William-Herrick, in Holy Orders, *m.* Miss O'Brien, of Blatherwycke, co. Northampton; and Eleanor. General Dyott, who was a magistrate and deputy-lieutenant for the county of Stafford, *d.* 7 May, 1847.

Arms—Or, a tiger, passant, sa., armed and langued, gu.

Crest—A tiger, passant, arg., collared and chained, armed and langued.

Seat—Freeford Hall, near Lichfield.

EASTWOOD OF CASTLETOWN.

Eastwood, James, Esq. of Castletown Castle, co. Louth, J.P. and D.L., co. Armagh, barrister-at-law; high-sheriff 1833; *b.* 17 Aug. 1797; *m.* 25 Nov. 1831, Louisa-Catherine, 4th dau. of the late James Dawson, Esq. of Forkhill Lodge, co. Armagh.

Lineage.—This family was originally established in the county of Nottingham.

John Eastwood, Esq., grand-nephew of John Eastwood, lord mayor of Dublin in the reign of Charles II., *m.* Elizabeth Murphy, and had (with a son, Francis) another son,

John Eastwood, Esq. of Castletown, who *m.* Letitia Turner, and had issue,

Samuel, James, and George, all *d. unm.*
Charles, of whom presently.
Elizabeth, *m.* to Sir Barry-Colles Meredyth, Bart.
Anne, *m.* to Matthew Beresford Taylor, Esq.
Charlotte, *m.* to Lennox Bigger, Esq.

The only surviving son,

Charles Eastwood, Esq. of Castletown, *m.* 9 Nov. 1796, Elizabeth, dau. of Thomas Cavan, Esq. of Belfast, and had (with a younger son, Thomas, capt. in the 37th foot, who *d. unm.* 22 Nov. 1830) an elder son and heir, the present James Eastwood, Esq. of Castletown Castle.

Seat—Castletown Castle, co. Louth.

ECCLES OF CRONROE.

Eccles, Hugh, Esq. of Cronroe, co. Wicklow, *b.* in 1830; *s.* his father in 1837.

Lineage.—The surname of Eccles is local, and was assumed by the proprietors of the lands and barony of Eccles, in Dumfries-shire, as early as the period when surnames first became hereditary in Scotland. Eighth in descent from John de Eccles, a personage of rank in the reign of Alexander III., was

John Eccles, of Kildonan, co. Ayr, living in 1613, who *m.* Janet Cathcart, of the Carleton family, and had two sons, John and Gilbert. The elder, John Eccles, of Kildonan, a devoted Royalist, continued the senior line of the family at Kildonan, while the younger,

Gilbert Eccles, settled in Ireland, *temp.* Charles I., and became ancestor of the Eccles of that kingdom, of whom was

Sir John Eccles, Knt., collector of the port of Dublin, and lord-mayor of that city (in which, and in the county, he possessed a large property), in the year 1714. He *m.* Miss Elizabeth Best, of Hornby Castle, co. York, a near relative of Mrs. Jane Lane, who bore so conspicuous a part in preserving the life of King Charles II., and in assisting his escape after the battle of Worcester. By this lady Sir John left, besides daus., a son and successor,

Hugh Eccles, Esq. of Cronroe, co. Wicklow, who *m.* Elizabeth, only child of Isaac Ambrose, Esq., clerk of the House of Commons, in Ireland, by Mary his wife, only dau. of Isaac Holroyd, Esq. (great-grandfather of the 1st Earl of Sheffield), and had issue four sons, Isaac-Ambrose, his heir; John; Hugh; and William; and one dau., Mary. The eldest son,

Isaac-Ambrose Eccles, Esq. of Cronroe, a gentleman of distinguished literary attainments, *m.* Grace, eldest dau. of Thomas Ball, Esq. of Urker, co. Armagh, and of Sea Park, co. Wicklow, by Phillippa Usher his wife, and had issue, Isaac-Ambrose, his heir; Hugh, successor to his brother; Samuel, in holy orders, who *m.* Frances Kenna, widow of Dr. Andrews; Elizabeth; Grace; and Mary. The eldest son,

Isaac-Ambrose Eccles, Esq. of Cronroe, a magistrate of the county of Wicklow, who *d. unm.* in 1836, and was *s.* by his brother,

Hugh Eccles, Esq. of Cronroe, who *m.* Harriet-Anna, 3rd dau. of Sir Richard-Bligh St. George, Bart. of Woodsgift, co. Kilkenny, and was accidentally killed in 1837, leaving surviving issue, Hugh, now of Cronroe; Elizabeth; and Salisbury.

Arms—Arg., two halberts, crossing each other, saltierwise, az.
Crest—A broken halbert.
Motto—Se defendendo.
Seat—Cronroe, co. Wicklow.

ECHLIN OF ARDQUIN, AND FOR SOME TIME OF ECHLIN VILLE.

Echlin, The Rev. John-Robert, M.A., of Ardquin, co. Down, *b.* 15 July, 1811; *m.* 1st, 27 Sept. 1836, Jane, 3rd dau. of the late James Pedder, Esq. of Ashton Lodge, co. Lancaster, and by her (who *d.* 8 March, 1838) had an only son,

John-Pedder, *b.* 28 Nov. 1837; *d.* 16 Sept. 1838.

Mr. Echlin *m.* 2ndly, 26 Oct. 1841, Mary-Anne, dau. of the late Ford North, Esq. of The Oaks, Ambleside, co. Westmoreland, and has issue,

I. John-Godfrey, *b.* 14 April, 1843.
II. Frederic, *b.* 5 March, 1844.
III. Alfred-Ford, *b.* 27 Sept. 1849.
I. Edith-Althea.
II. Thomasine-Mary.

Lineage.—There is yet extant in M.S. an account compiled by George Crawfurd, Esq. (author of a *Peerage of Scotland*), who styles himself "antiquary and historiographer;" it bears date Glasgow, 13 August, 1747, and is entitled "Memoirs of the ancient familie of the Echlins of Pittadro, in the county of Fyfe, in Scotland, now transplanted to Ireland." Mr. Crawfurd therein states (giving his authorities) that the Echlin family are descended from one Philip le Brun, to whom "Rogerus de Mowbray, the great Baron of Dalmenie," &c. &c., granted a charter "de totis & integris terris de Echlin*, in constabulario de Linlithgow," &c., "to be held in fee and heritage of the granter." The charter, Mr. Crawfurd says, is not dated, "but must be in the beginning, if not sooner, of the reign of our victorious deliverer, King Robert the First." Mr. Crawfurd goes on to say, that "this Philip le Brun, who first got the lands of Echlin, assumed a sirname, as the ancient custom was, from his own estate, and became Echlin *of Echlin*, or Echlin of that ilk, and was the founder of the House of Pittadro, in the county of Fyfe, that continued so long a family of lustre and reputation. How they obtained the estate of Pittadro, whether by conquest or by marriage, not having seen the more ancient writts of the family, is more than I can say, and I don't offer a conjecture. After the family of Echlin of Echlin had fixed their residence att Pittadro, they parted with their ancient paternall estate to the family of Dundas, in the time of King James the First (of Scotland), and are vested in James Dundass, of that ilk, at his attainder, on the 9th February, 1449."

With reference to the situation of Pittadro, Mr. Crawfurd states that in his time the ruins of that "messuage" still remained, "situate below *Echin* Hill (sic), which they gave the name to, which is situate some miles westward to the royal burgh of Dunfermling, near to the House of Fordell, the seat of Sir Robert Henderson, Baronet, who is now the proprietor, I think, of the estate of Pittadro."

Somewhere in the latter part of the 15th century, there was a Sir John Echlin, whose dau. and co-heiress, Arabella, *m.* Sir Ninian Adaire, Laird of Kinhilt, in Galloway. In *Playfair's British Family Antiquity*, vol. ix., p. 372, note 6, this Sir John Echlin is stated to have been "of Piludra" (a mis-spelling for Pittadro), "in the shire of Fife." He belonged to the same family, there can be no doubt, with

William Echline, laird of Pittadro, in Fife, who (according to the memoir of 1747) was head and representative of the Echlin family in 1517. He *m.* Christian, dau. of Sir Alexander Innes, of Inverleith. Their son,

William Echlin, of Pittadro, *m.* Isobell (or Alyson, according to the memoir), dau. of Sir John Melvile, of that ilk, and of Raith, ancestor to the Earls of Leven and Melvile, and was father of

Andrew Echline, of Pittadro, the constable of Edinburgh Castle during the siege of 1573; (his brother, Patrick, was also of the garrison, according to Mr. Grant's "Memorials of Edinburgh Castle," p. 107). He *m.* Grizel, dau. of Robert Colvile, of Cliah, ancestor to the Lord Colvile, of Ochiltree, and had issue,

William, who *m.* Margaret, dau. of James Henderson, of Fordell, co. Fife, by whom he had issue, Henry Echline, who entered foreign service, and *d.* without issue.
Robert (Dr.), of whom presently.
David, who (Mr. Crawfurd states in his "Memorial") was physician to Anne of Denmark, consort to James VI. of

* In the modern maps of Scotland, there is a place called Echline (no doubt that alluded to by Mr. Crawfurd), about midway between Hopetoun and Dalmeny, and a mile to the southward of South Queensferry.

Scotland and I of England. Of these two last-mentioned brothers, Mr. Crawfurd says as follows:—"Both Dr. Robert Echlin, the bishop of Down and Conyr, and Dr. David Echlin, were eminently learned men. It is them the learned and ingenious Sir Robert Sibbald has in his view in the history of Fyfe. In a list of the learned men born in that shyre, he mentions the two Echlins Brothers."—(*Mr. Crawfurd's Memorial.*)

DR. ROBERT ECHLINE, on the death, without issue, of his nephew, Capt. Henry Echline, became the head and representative of the family. "In the year 1613, His Majestie King James the First of England," says Mr. Crawfurd, "calling to mind the memory and merit of the Laird of Pittadro, his father, and his long sufferings, was graciously pleased to promote Dr. Echlin to the bishoprick of Down and Conyr, in Ireland, the see being void by the death of his countryman, Dr. James Dundass." Bishop Echlin *m.* a dau. of George, Lord Seton, by whom he had issue,

JOHN, his heir, of whom presently.
Jane, who *m.* Henry Maxwell, Esq. of Finnebrogue.
Margaret, *m.* Dr. Robert Maxwell, bishop of Kilmore, ancestor to the Lords Farnham.

On Bishop Echlin's death, in 1633, he was *s.* by his eldest son,

JOHN ECHLIN, Esq. of Ardquin, co. Down. He *m.* the dau. of Sir Francis Stafford, of Mount Stafford, in the co. Antrim, and by her had issue,

ROBERT, his heir, of whom presently.
Francis (afterwards of Clonowen, co. Antrim), who inherited the estate of his uncle, Sir Edmond Stafford, of Mount Stafford (of "the far-descended Staffords, Barons of Stafford from the Conquest, and latterly Dukes of Buckingham"), whose name he took. Francis Echlin Stafford *m.* Sarah, dau. of Randal, Earl of Antrim. The present representative of this branch of the Echlin family is Arthur Willoughby Stafford, Esq.
Jane, who *m.* James Leslie.
———, who *m.* Robert Ward, the 2nd son of Nicholas Ward (ancestor of the Viscounts Bangor), and his wife Mary, who was dau. of Ralph Leycester, of Toft, in the co. of Chester. This Robert Ward was created a Baronet by CHARLES II., and survived his only son, Charles, who *m.* Catherine, dau. of Sir John Temple, but left no issue.

On the death of John Echlin of Ardquin, he was *s.* by his elder son,

ROBERT ECHLIN, also of Ardquin, who (about the year 1660) *m.* Mary, dau. of Dr. Henry Leslie, bishop of Meath (formerly of Down and Connor), and younger son of the Earl of Rothes. By her he had issue,

JOHN, his heir, of whom presently.
Henry (Sir), (created a Baronet in 1721), a Baron of the Court of Exchequer in Ireland, and founder of the Clonard and Rush branch of the Echlin family.
Robert, a lieut.-gen. in the army, and colonel of the Inniskillen dragoons. He *d.* without issue.

Robert Echlin of Ardquin was *s.* by his eldest son,

JOHN ECHLIN, also of Ardquin, who, in the year 1678, *m.* Hester, dau. of William Godfrey, of Coleraine, Esq., and had twenty sons and daus., amongst whom were,

I. CHARLES (their eldest son), who *m.* in 1709, Anne, dau. of Thomas Knox, of Dungannon, Esq., and Mary his wife, dau. of Robert Bruce, of Kilroot, in the co. Antrim, Esq. He left no issue.
II. ROBERT (Rev.), of whom presently.
III. Godfrey, of Marifield, who *m.* Anne, dau. of John Savage, of Ballyvarley, Esq., grandson of Rowland Savage, lord of the Little Ards. They had issue,
 1 Godfrey, also of Marifield, who, in the year 1756, *m.* Letitia, eldest dau. of George Macartney, of the co. Antrim, Esq., and sister of the late Earl Macartney ambassador-extraordinary to China, but left no issue.
 1 Anne, who (it is believed) *d. unm.*
IV. James, of Echlin Ville, who, in 1738, *m.* Mary-Ann Sampson, of Dublin. He *d.* in 1755,* leaving no issue.
I. Mary } II. Jane } who *d.* (it is supposed) *unm.*
III. Hester, who, on 29 June, 1722, *m.* Thomas Knox, of Ballycruly, co. Down, Esq. Their 2nd son, Thomas, became the 1st Viscount Northland.

* By his last will, dated 18 May, 1754, James Echlin left all his landed property, inclusive of Echlin Ville, to his nephews, John Echlin (eldest son of his brother, the Rev. Robert Echlin), and Godfrey Echlin (son of his brother Godfrey); and upon the death, without issue, of the said Godfrey, the entire property centered in John Echlin, of Thomastown, and his heirs. James Echlin left a legacy of £100 to his sister Elizabeth, wife of George Hamilton, Esq. of Tyrella; and in a codicil dated 7 June, 1755, he left a further legacy of the same amount to his "nephew, George Hamilton, jun., of Tyrella," whose present representative is George-Alexander Hamilton, Esq., M.P. for the University of Dublin.

IV. Elizabeth, who *m.* George Hamilton, of Tyrella, in the co. Down, Esq.
V. Rose, who *m.* Major North-Ludlow Bernard, of the co. Cork, and 3rd son of Judge Bernard, the ancestor of the Bandon family.

John Echlin of Ardquin *d.* about 1710, and was *s.* by his 2nd son,

THE REV. ROBERT ECHLIN, incumbent of Newtown Ards, co. Down. He *m.* in 1722, Jane, dau. of James Manson, of Tynan Abbey, co. Armagh, Esq., and with her sisters (of whom the eldest, Ellinor, *m.* the Rev. John Stronge, of Fair View, co. Armagh, ancestor to the present Sir James M. Stronge, Bart.; Mary, the 2nd, *m.* the Rev. Mr. Obins, of Portadown; and Sarah, the youngest, *m.* Dr. Irwin, a physician), his co-heiress. The Rev. Robert Echlin and Jane his wife had issue,

JOHN, his heir, of whom presently.
Charles, *d. unm.*
Hester, *m.* James Donaldson, of Castledillon, co. Armagh, Esq. They had issue a son, James (deaf and dumb), who *d.* at the Craven Hotel, London, in 1825; and a dau., Anne, who *m.* the Rev. Mr. Clewlow, but *d.* without issue.

On the death of the Rev. Robert Echlin, he was *s.* by his eldest son,

JOHN ECHLIN, of Thomastown, Ardquin, *b.* 1723, who, by Hester his wife, had issue,

CHARLES, *b.* in 1746; *m.* 1st, Miss Newburgh, of Ballyhaise, co. Cavan, by whom he had issue a son, who *d.* in infancy, through a fall from his nurse's arms; and a dau. Letitia, who *d.* young and *unm.*, 25 March, 1790. He *m.* 2ndly, Anne Graham, by whom he had issue three daus., Charlotte, who *d. unm.*; Hester-Letitia, who *d. unm.* 12 March, 1817, aged 18; and Anne-Jane, who *d.* (also *unm.*) 3 Sept. 1820, aged 20.
Robert, who *d.* (*unm.*) from a fall when hunting.
Godfrey, who *d. unm.*
JOHN, of whom presently.
James, who *d. unm.*
Jane, who *m.* George Matthews, of Spring Vale, co. Down, Esq., and *d.* leaving issue, 11 Jan. 1803. The present representative of this family is Edward-Ruthven Matthews, of Derryvunlam, co. Galway, Esq.

On the death of John Echlin of Thomastown, March 4, 1789, he was *s.* by his eldest son, CHARLES ECHLIN, who, along with his father's own property, inherited the estates of his grand-uncle, James Echlin, of Echlin Ville, who, as before mentioned, *d.* without issue in 1755; and upon Charles Echlin's death (without leaving issue male), on 22 Feb. 1817, he was *s.* by his only surviving brother,

JOHN ECHLIN, of Thomastown and Portaferry, bapt. in St. Mary's Church, Dublin, 28 March, 1757. He *m.* 8 Nov. 1786, Thomasine-Hannah, dau. of George Fleming, Esq. of Dublin (of the Slane family), by whom he had issue,

JOHN, his heir, *b.* 4 Oct. 1787, of whom presently.
Thomasine (who *m.* Thomas-R. Moore, Esq. of the co. Cavan), lately dec., and who had two sons and a dau., all dec.

John Echlin of Thomastown and Portaferry *d.* 25 Jan. 1825, and was *s.* by his only son,

JOHN ECHLIN, of Echlin Ville, who *m.* 3 Feb. 1809, Thomasine-Margaret, dau. of John Armstrong, of Dublin, Esq., and *d.* 14 April, 1842, having had issue,

John, *b.* 28 Jan. 1810; *d.* 4 March, same year.
JOHN-ROBERT, present representative.
George Fleming, *b.* 27 June, 1812; *m.* 15 Aug. 1842, Harriet-Georgina, only dau. of Col. Johnson, late of the 8th hussars, of Westfield, co. Dublin, and The Lodge, co. Donegal.
Charles.
Elizabeth.
Hester-Jane, *m.* to the Rev. Charles Ward, M.A.
Thomasine-Margaret, *m.* to John-Auchinleck Ward, Esq.
Jane. Margaretta-Watson-Jane-Colville.
Harriet.

Arms—1st and 4th, or, a galley, ppr.; 2nd and 3rd, or, a fesse, chequy, purp., and arg. in chief, a deer at full speed, pursued by a dog, all ppr.
Crest—A talbot passant, arg., spotted sable, langued gu.
Motto—Non sine præda.
Seat—The old family residence was at Ardquin, near Portaferry, co. Down, but it is now in ruins, and occupied by tenants.

ECKLEY OF CREDENHILL.

ECKLEY, THE REV. JOHN, of Credenhill Court, co. Hereford, *b.* 26 March, 1784; *m.* 31 July, 1807, Elizabeth, eldest dau. of Thomas Williams, Esq. of

Vellinnewydd, co. Brecknock, and has surviving issue,

I. JOHN-EDMUND, b. 5 May, 1808; m. 1838, Elizabeth, eldest dau. of William-Caldwell Brandrum, Esq. of London.
II. Edmund-Charles, b. 1822.
I. Elizabeth, m. to Thomas Lechmere, Esq., J.P., of Fownhope Court, co. Hereford.

Mr. Eckley is a magistrate of the county.

Lineage.—EDMUND ECKLEY, Esq., who served as high-sheriff of the co. of Hereford in 1742, m. Elizabeth, dau. of Thomas Powell, Esq. of Kinnaston, co. Hereford, and had issue two sons, viz., Edmund and RICHARD, and five daus., Elizabeth, Sarah, Jane, Margaret, and Eleanor. The 2nd son,

RICHARD ECKLEY, Esq., (who d. 1785,) m. Susannah Cooke, by whom he had John, Edmund, Susanah, and Martha. The eldest son,

JOHN ECKLEY, Esq. of Credenhill, co. Hereford, m. in 1775, Sarah Powell, and had, besides Richard, m. in 1800, to Anne-Maria, dau. of John Liotard, Esq. of Monmouth, and d. 7 Jan. 1807; and a dau., Sarah, m. in 1810, to William Palmer, Esq of Bolitree Castle, co. Hereford; another son, who is the present JOHN ECKLEY, Esq. of Credenhill.

Arms—Or, on a saltier, gu., a leopard's head, pierced by two swords, saltierwise, of the first.
Motto—Gesta verbis prævenient.
Seat—Credenhill, co. Hereford.

EDGAR OF THE RED HOUSE.

EDGAR, THE REV. JOHN-ROBERT-MATHEW, A.M., resident at Felixton House, co. Suffolk, b. 15 May, 1796; m. Elizabeth, 2nd dau. of the late Rev. Job Wallace.

Lineage.—The family of the Edgars were seated in the co. of Suffolk at a very early period. The following is from documents in the possession of the family:—

JOHN ÆDGAR, of Dunwich, co. Suffolk, seated himself at Glemham Magna, co. Suffolk, in 1237, and was s. by his son, THOMAS, in 1273. The line of Edgars of Ipswich follows in succession from WILLIAM EDGAR, of North Glemham, or Glemham Magna, who m. into the honourable and ancient family of Tollemache, of Framsden and Helmingham, by whom the said William, amongst other children, had a son, LIONEL. This William was the person who changed the arms of the family (which were, Gu., a chevron, or, between three leopards' faces, arg.), and took a new patent, *temp.* HENRY VIII, 1548 (Per chevron, or and az., in chief, two fleurs-de-lis of the second; in base, five lozenges, charged with an escallop, gu.) Lionel m. a dau. of — Cotton, Esq. of Earl Soham, co. Suffolk, and had by her one son, JOHN, who, at his father's death, lived in Framsden. He m. a dau. of Henry Peyto, Esq., and, with three daus., was father of one son, LIONEL, of Ipswich, who m. 1st, Elizabeth, dau. and heiress of William Morse, Esq. of Swilland, co. Suffolk, and had by her a dau., Mary, and a son, Lionel, who d. s. p. He m. 2ndly, Catherine, dau. and co-heiress of Thomas Glasscock, Esq. of Ipswich, and by her was father of

THOMAS EDGAR, Esq. of Ipswich, reader of Gray's Inn, 15 CHARLES II., and recorder of Ipswich, m. Mary, dau. and heiress of Philip Powle, Esq. of London; and d. 12 April, 1692, having had (besides other issue, who d. young) three sons,

I. THOMAS, of whom presently.
II. Robert, d. s. p.
III. Devereux, bapt. 30 Oct. 1651; m. 22 Sept. 1681, Temperance, only dau. of Robert Sparrowe, Esq. of Wickham Brook, co. Suffolk, had (besides two daus., Temperance and Mary-Devereux) a son,
    Robert-Devereux, who m. twice; by his 2nd wife, Elizabeth Harrington, an heiress, he had a son,
        Robert, High Sheriff of Suffolk 1747, who m. 1762, Susannah, only child of the Rev. Wm. Gery, prebendary, and had (with one son, who d. an infant) three daus., viz.,
            Susanna, m. to her kinsman, Mileson Edgar, Esq. of the Red House, Ipswich.
            Elizabeth, m. to Robert Herring, Esq. of Bracondale.
            Katherine, m. to Nicholas Starkie, Esq.
IV. Francis, d. unm.

The eldest son,

THOMAS EDGAR, Esq., m. Agatha, dau. and co-heir of Borodaile Mileson, Esq. of Norton, co. Suffolk; and d. in 1677, leaving by her (who m. 2ndly, John Brewes, Esq.) a son and a dau., viz., MILESON, of whom presently; and Agatha. The only surviving son,

MILESON EDGAR, Esq. of the Red House, m. Alice, dau. and sole heir of William Shawe, Esq. of St. Clement's, Ipswich, and by her (who m. 2ndly, Orlando Bridgman, Esq.) had a son; MILESON, and two daus, Alice, d. unm.; and Agatha, m. to Samuel Child, of London, banker. The son,

MILESON EDGAR, Esq., m. 1st, Ann, dau. of William Peck, Esq. of Sampford, Essex; and 2ndly, the only child and heiress of Thomas D'Eye, of Eye, co. Suffolk, and by the latter only had issue two sons, MILESON and Thomas, and three daus. The elder son

MILESON EDGAR, Esq., m. Elizabeth, only dau. of Richard Charlton, Esq. of London, and had issue, MILESON, his heir; John, in holy orders; Richard, capt. in the Scots fusiliers; Elizabeth, m. to John Willis, Esq.; Charlotte, m. to Gen. Hugonin. The eldest son and heir,

MILESON EDGAR, Esq. of the Red House, m. 16 Oct. 1783, Susannah, eldest dau. of Robert Edgar, Esq. of Wickham-Brook, co. Suffolk, and had issue,

MILESON-GERY, his heir.
JOHN-ROBERT-MATHEW, present representative.
Edward-Raikes, m. Mary, eldest dau. of Charles Collett, Esq., and has issue three sons and two daus.
Susanna, m. to M.-P. Manby, Esq. of Walsingham, co. Norfolk.

Mr. Edgar d. 16 June, 1830, and was s. by his eldest son,

REV. MILESON-GERY EDGAR, of the Red House, J.P., b. 19 Aug. 1784; who m. 1st, 19 Feb. 1818, Mary-Anne, eldest dau. of Nathaniel Brickwood, Esq. of Dulwich; and 2ndly, 26 March, 1840, Elizabeth Arkell, of London, great-great-granddaughter of Sir Mathew Hale. He d. 3 Aug. 1853 (his widow survives and resides at Red House), and was s. by his brother, the Rev. JOHN-ROBERT-MATHEW EDGAR.

Arms—Per chevron, or and az., in chief, two fleurs-de-lis, of the second, in base, five lozenges, of the first, each charged with an escallop, gu.
Crest—An ostrich's head, between two wings, expanded, or, each charged with as many bends, az., in the beak, a horse-shoe, arg.
Seat—The Red House, Ipswich.

EDGCUMBE OF EDGCUMBE HOUSE.

EDGCUMBE, RICHARD-DARKE, Esq. of Edgcumbe House, co. Devon, b. 4 June, 1811; m. 24 Aug. 1835, Louisa, dau. of Richard Marshall, Esq., M.D., of Totnes, and has issue,

I. PIERS, b. 19 April, 1844.
II. Richard-Wiseman, b. 23 Dec. 1853.
I. Ellen-Margaret, } both d. young in 1845.
II. Louisa, }
III. Eleanor. IV. Catherine.

Lineage.—The family of Edgcumbe has been settled in the parish of Milton Abbott, Devon, from a very early period, as appears, both from a deed in Norman French, having the words "de Eggecombe," and dated "in the twelfth year of the Conquest," and from an inscription over an old gateway in the family mansion, E.R. 1292, as well as from other documents now in the possession of the present proprietor, to whom the estate has descended in a direct line from that time. In one of these documents, dated the 17th of EDWARD II, certain lands there are described as "heretofore belonging to John de Eggecombe," &c. The precise time when the name first assumed its present mode of spelling is uncertain, but there is no doubt that Thomas Edgcumbe, of Edgcumbe, was buried in the church of Milton Abbott, on the 19th July, 1518, as shewn by a tablet in the south wall of that edifice.

RICHARD DE EGGECOMBE, living in 1292, had three sons, James, who d. unm.; RICHARD; and Reginald, who is styled "Clericus" in a deed dated 17th EDWARD II. The 2nd son, RICHARD, had two sons; JOHN, the elder, from whom is descended the present head of the family RICHARD DARKE EDGCUMBE, of Edgcumbe; and William, the younger, who m. 1353, Helena, dau. and heir of Ralph de Cotitcle, and was ancestor of the present Earl of Mount Edgcumbe.

The grandfather of the present representative,

RICHARD EDGCUMBE, of Edgcumbe, m. 28 April, 1757, Elizabeth, eldest dau and co-heir of Michael Goden, Esq. of Chatham; and d. 29 July, 1784, when he was s. by his son,

Pierce Edgcumbe, Esq. of Edgcumbe, who m. 18 Dec. 1798, Eleanor, dau. of Thomas Yorke, Esq. of Warbelton, co. Sussex, and by her (who survived him, and d. 8 Feb. 1846) had issue,

Richard-Darke, present representative.
Ellen-Susannah, m. to the Rev. George Rose.
Emma-Mary, m. 1st, to Peter Pilcher, Esq.; and 2ndly, to the Rev. Richard Martin.

Mr. Edgcumbe d. 17 April, 1834.

Arms—Gu., on a bend, ermines, cottised, or, three boars' heads, couped, arg.
Crest—A boar, passant, arg., with a chaplet of oak-leaves, fructed, ppr., round the neck.
Motto—Au plaisir fort de Dieu.
Seat—Edgcumbe House, Edgcumbe, near Tavistock, Devon.

EDGE OF STRELLEY HALL.

Edge, James-Thomas, Esq. of Strelley Hall, co. Nottingham, b. 14 Aug. 1827; assumed by royal sign-manual, 11 Oct. 1848, the surname of Edge only, and the arms of Edge, in compliance with the will of his maternal uncle, Thomas Webb Edge, Esq.

Lineage.—The Edges of Strelley descend from a younger branch of a family that was many years seated at Horton, co. Stafford.

Ralph Edge, Esq., m. Amye, dau. of Nicholas Charlton, Esq. of Chilwell, and was buried at Strelley, in 1681.

Richard Edge, Esq. of Strelley, was high-sheriff for co. Nottingham in 1709. His son,

Ralph Edge, of Strelley, left three daus., of whom Margaret m. John Webb, 2nd son of Thomas Webb, of Sherborne, co. Warwick, who served the office of high-sheriff of the said co. in 1722, as did his son, the said John Webb, in 1781. The issue of this marriage, Thomas Webb, afterwards

Thomas Webb-Edge, Esq. of Strelley Hall, b. 7 April, 1756; m. 24 May, 1785, Elizabeth, 5th dau. of Francis Hurt, Esq. of Alderwasley, co. Derby, assumed, in the year, 1776, in compliance with the will of his maternal grandfather, Ralph Edge, the surname and arms of Edge, which were confirmed to him and his issue by royal licence, dated 9 May, 1803. He served as high-sheriff for co. Nottingham in 1804; and d. 21 June, 1819, leaving issue two sons and two daus.,

I. Thomas Webb-Edge, of Strelley Hall, J.P., high-sheriff for co. Nottingham in 1838, major of the South Nottinghamshire yeomanry cavalry; b. 28 March, 1788; d. unm. 1844, aged 56.
II. John, in holy orders, M.A., rector of Strelly and Bilborough; b. 24 Nov. 1790; m. 11 Feb. 1824, Anne Neville, 4th dau. of Ichabod Wright, Esq. of Mapperley, co. Nottin ham, who survived him; and d. s. p. 30 April, 1842.
I. Elizabeth, m. 29 Aug. 1811, Thomas Moore 2nd son of George Moore, Esq. of Appleby Parva, co. Leicester; and d. at Appleby, 27 Nov. 1822, leaving issue one dau., Mary, m. to the Rev. James Holden, rector of Pleasley, co. Derby.
II. Mary-Margaret, m. 11 Oct. 1825, James Hurt, Esq. of Wirksworth, co. Derby, late a major in the 9th lancers, 2nd son of Francis Hurt, Esq. of Alderwasley. Their eldest son is the present James-Thomas Edge, Esq. of Strelley Hall.

Arms—Quarterly, 1st and 4th: Edge, viz., per fesse, sa. and gu., an eagle, displayed, arg., on a chief, or, a rose, between two amulets, of the 2nd; 2nd and 3rd, Hurt. Crest of Edge, viz., on a wreath of the colours a rein-deer's head, couped, ppr., collared and chained, or; crest of Hurt.
Motto—Semper fidelis.
Seat—Strelley Hall, Notts.

EDGELL OF STANDERWICK COURT.

Edgell, Harry-Edmund, Esq. of Standerwick Court, co. Somerset, capt. R.N., b. in 1809; J.P.; m. 1845, Caroline, youngest dau. of T. Rossiter, Esq., and has one dau.,

Fanny-Mary-Rose.

Lineage.—Chaffin Edgell, Esq., son of Harry Edgell, Esq., by Helen Chaffin, his wife, m. Lucretia-Eleanor Rishton, granddau. of Martin Folkes, Esq., President of the Royal Society, and had issue,

Harry-Folkes, his heir.
Martin-Folkes, captain in the army, deceased.
Richard, m. Jane, dau. of J. Griffiths, Esq., late stipendiary magistrate of Marlborough Street Police Office, and has issue.
Charles, major in the army, wounded at Waterloo, dec.
Edward, in holy orders, prebendary of Wells, rector of Rodden, m. and has issue: by his 1st he has two daus., by his second, Miss Wilson, he has Edward, rector of Bromham, Wilts; Henry, chaplain R.N.; Seymour, in holy orders; George, late capt. 7th R. Fusiliers; William, in holy orders, and Helen.
Beddison, captain in the army, deceased.
Lucretia, d. young.
Dorothy, m., 1st, to J. Jones, Esq., col. in the army, and, 2ndly, to Francis Bushe, Esq.; and
Helen, m. Col. Bonamy.

The eldest son,

Admiral Harry-Folkes-Edmund Edgell, of Standerwick Court, co. Somerset, J.P. and D.L., b. 13 Aug., 1767; m. in 1801, Mary, dau. of M. O'Keefe, Esq., and d. 14 June, 1846, leaving one son, the present Harry Edmund Edgell, Esq., capt. R.N.

Arms—Arg., on a chev., embattled, sa., betw. three cinquefoils, gu., as many bezants.
Crest—A falcon rising, belled, arg., guttée-de-sang, resting the dexter foot on an antique shield, of the first, charged with a cinquefoil, as in the arms.
Motto—Qui sera, sera.
Seat—Standerwick Court, co. Somerset.

EDGEWORTH OF EDGEWORTHSTOWN.

Edgeworth, Charles-Sneyd, Esq. of Edgeworthstown, co. Longford, b. 30 Oct. 1786; m. 2 Sept. 1813, Henrica, dau. of John Broadhurst, Esq. of Foston, co. Derby, which lady d. in 1846.

Lineage.—The Edgeworths, originally, it is said, established at Edgeworth, now called Edgeware, in Middlesex, settled in Ireland in the reign of Elizabeth, about the year 1583.

Two brothers, Edward and Francis Edgeworth, went to Ireland, probably under the patronage of Essex and Cecil, as those names have since continued in the family. The elder son,

The Right Rev. Edward Edgeworth, Bishop of Down and Connor in 1593, d. s. p., and was s. by his brother,

Francis Edgeworth, Clerk of the Hanaper in 1619, who m. Jane, dau. of Sir Edmond Tuite, Knt. of Sonna, in Westmeath, and had by her (who founded a religious house in Dublin) a son and heir,

Captain John Edgeworth, of Cranallagh Castle, co. Longford, who m. 1st, the dau. of Sir Hugh Cullum, of Derbyshire, by whom he had a son, John, his heir, and 2ndly, Mrs. Bridgman, widow of Edward Bridgman, Esq., brother to Sir Orlando Bridgman, the lord keeper, and went back with her to Ireland. He was s. by his son,

Sir John Edgeworth, knighted by Charles II., who m. the only dau. and heir of Edward Bridgman, Esq., acquired with her an estate in Lancashire, besides a considerable fortune in money, and had eight sons, of whom the eldest, Francis, s. to the paternal estate in Longford; the second, Robert, was ancestor of the Edgeworths of Kilshrewly; and the fifth, Essex, had a son, the celebrated Abbé Edgeworth, who styled himself, from the estate his branch of the family possessed, Monsieur de Firmont. The eldest,

Col. Francis Edgeworth, of Edgeworthstown, raised a regiment for William III. He m. successively several wives, one of whom, an English lady, was a widow Bradstone, who by her first husband had a dau., Miss Bradstone, wife of Mr. Pakenham, and mother of the first Lord Longford. By this lady Col. Edgeworth left a son and successor,

Richard Edgeworth, Esq., of Edgeworthstown, who m. in 1732, Rachel-Jane, dau. of Samuel Lovell, Esq., a Welsh judge, son of Sir Salathiel Lovell, Knt. of Harleston, co. Northampton, one of the barons of the Exchequer, and had two sons and two daus., viz.,

Thomas, who died before his father.
Richard Lovell, successor to his father.
Mary, m. to Francis Fox, Esq. of Fox Hall, co. Longford.
Margaret, m. to John Ruxton, Esq. of Black Castle, co. Meath.

Mr. Edgeworth, who served for five-and-twenty years in the Irish Parliament, and twice refused a proffered baronetcy, d. in his seventieth year, in 1769, and was s. by his son,

Richard-Lovell Edgeworth, Esq. of Edgeworthstown, b. at Bath in 1744, the late celebrated writer on Education and Inventions. This eminent person m. 1st, Anna-Maria, dau. of Paul Elers, Esq. of Black Bourton, in the co. of Oxford, and had by her one son and three daus.,

Richard, *b.* in May, 1765, *d.* in 1796.
MARIA, the distinguished authoress, so celebrated and so popular for her faithful delineations of the manners and customs of Ireland, *b.* 1 Jan. 1767, *d. unm.* 21 May, 1849.
Emmeline, *m.* in 1802, to John King, Esq., and has issue, Zoe and Psyche-Emmeline.
Anna-Maria, *m.* in 1794, to Dr. Beddoes, and *d.* in 1824, leaving Thomas-Lovell, Charles-Henry, Anna-Frances-Emily, and Mary-Eliza, who *d.* in 1833.

He *m.* 2ndly, in 1773, Honora, dau. of Edward Sneyd, Esq. of Lichfield, youngest son of Ralph Sneyd, Esq. of Bishton, in the co. of Stafford, and by her had issue,

LOVELL, who succeeded to the estates.
Honora, who *d.* in 1790.

He *m.* 3rdly, 25 Dec. 1780, Elizabeth, dau. of Edward Sneyd, Esq. of Lichfield, and had by her (who *d.* Nov. 1797) five sons and four daus., viz.,

Henry, *b.* 15 Sept. 1782, *d.* in 1813.
CHARLES-SNEYD, present representative.
William, *b.* 28 April, 1788, *d.* in 1 90.
Thomas-Day, *b.* 25 Oct 1789, *d.* in 1792.
William, *b.* 27 Jan. 1794, *d.* in 1829.
Elizabeth, *d.* in 1800. Charlotte, *d.* in 1807.
Sophia, *d.* in 1785.
Honora, *m.* 8 Nov. 1838, to Capt. Beaufort, R.N.

He *m.* 4thly, Frances-Anne, dau. of the Rev. Daniel Augustus Beaufort, and had by her two sons and four daus., namely,

Francis-Beaufort, *b.* 5 Oct. 1809, *m.* in 1831, Rosa-Florentina Eroles, and had issue a son, who *d.* in 1833; William, *b.* 12 May, 1835; and Maria: he *d.* 12 Oct. 1846.
Michael-Pakenham, *b.* 24 May, 1812; *m.* Feb. 1846, Christina, dau. of Dr. Hugh Macpherson, of Aberdeen.
Frances-Maria, *m.* in 1829 Lestock-P. Wilson, Esq. of London, and *d.* 5 Feb. 1848.
Harriet, *m.* in 1826, to the Very Rev. Richard Butler, dean of Clonmacnoise.
Sophia, *m.* in 1824, to Barry Fox, Esq., and has issue, Maxwell-William-Waller, Mary-Anne, and Charlotte.
Lucy-Jane, *m.* June, 1843, to the Rev. Thomas Romney Robinson, D.D.

Mr. Edgeworth *d.* 13 June, 1817, and was *s.* by his son,

LOVELL EDGEWORTH, Esq. of Edgeworthstown, J.P and D.L., high-sheriff co. Longford, 1819; *b.* 30 June, 1776. He *d. unm.* in Dec. 1841, and was *s.* by his brother.

Arms—Party per chev., gu. and or, three martlets, counterchanged
Crest—On a ducal coronet a pelican feeding her young, or.
Motto.—Constans contraria spernit.
Seat—Edgeworthstown, co. Longford.

EDGEWORTH OF KILSHREWLY.

EDGEWORTH, THOMAS-NEWCOMEN, Esq. of Kilshrewly, co. Longford, high-sheriff 1814-15, and for several years major royal Limerick county militia, *b.* 30 April, 1778; *m.* 1st, 1 Jan. 1806, Marian, only child of John Steele, Esq. of Carricklane, co. Armagh, by Catherine his wife, dau. of Robert Stuart, Esq. of Hanslong; and 2ndly, 14 April, 1834, Mary, dau. of Thomas Montgomery, Esq., of the city of Dublin. By the former (who *d.* in 1832) he has surviving issue,

I. JOHN-ESSEX-EDWARD, *b.* 25 Sept. 1814, *m.* 9 Dec. 1843, Elizabeth, only dau. of Lancelat Croasdaile, Esq. of Rynn, Queen's County, and has issue,
  1 THOMAS-NEWCOMEN, *b.* 24 Dec. 1850.
  2 Lancelot-Croasdaile-Agnew, *b.* 5 March, 1852.
  3 Edith-Marian-Susan.
II. George-Thomas-Henry, *b.* 4 Aug. 1816, *m.* 20 April, 1852, Amelia, only dau. of Col. James Considine, 10th regt., and has had issue,
  1 Richard Carmichael, *b.* 2 Feb. 1854, *d.* 4 Feb. 1855.
III. James-Bridgeman, *b.* 9 July, 1823.
I. Catherine-Jemima, *m.* to the Rev. Francis De Montmorency St. George, Rector of St. Paul's, Cork.
II. Cecilia, *m.* to James Johnstone, Esq. of Magheremena, co. Fermanagh.
III. Elizabeth.

Lineage.—ROBERT EDGEWORTH, Esq. (second son of Sir John Edgeworth, Knt.) *m.* Catherine, only child of Sir Edward Tyrrell, Bart. of Lynn, co. Westmeath, by Eleanor, his wife, dau. of Sir Dudley Loftus, Knt. of Killyan (and Cecilia, his wife, dau. of the learned Sir James Ware, auditor-general of Ireland). By this lady Mr. Edgeworth had issue, EDWARD, Packington, and other children. To the second son, Packington, Mr. Edgeworth, displeased at the marriage of his eldest son with a Catholic, left the estate of Sir Edward Tyrrell, which had been restored, and with Packington's descendants part of it still continues. The eldest son,

EDWARD EDGEWORTH, Esq. of Kilshrewly, inherited, under marriage settlement, the family estate. He *m.* in 1717, Mary, dau. of John Hussey, Esq. of Courtown, co Kildare, and had two sons, Robert and Newcomen. The elder *d. unm.* The younger,

NEWCOMEN EDGEWORTH, Esq. of Kilshrewly, *m.* 1st, Elizabeth, dau. of Col. Henry Edgeworth, of Lessord, co. Longford, which lady *d. s. p.*, and 2ndly, Mary, only dau. of Laurence Connell, Esq.* of St. Johnstown, in the same county, by whom (who *m.* 2ndly, 3 Dec. 1797, Capt. Francis Douglas, R.N.) he had issue,

ESSEX-AGNEW, his heir.
THOMAS-NEWCOMEN, successor to his brother.
James-Bridgeman, Lieut. Roy. Art.; retiring from that service he went to India, where he married and died, leaving three daughters.
Eliza, *d. unm.*

The eldest son,

ESSEX-AGNEW EDGEWORTH, Esq. of Kilshrewly, *d. unm.*, a lieut. in the 78th Regt., upon service under the late Duke of York, at Bergen-op-Zoom, in 1795, and was *s.* by his brother, the present THOMAS-NEWCOMEN EDGEWORTH, Esq. of Kilshrewly,

Arms, Crest, and *Motto*—See EDGEWORTH OF EDGEWORTHSTOWN.
Seat—Kilshrewly, in the county of Longford.

EDMANDS OF SUTTON.

EDMANDS, CHARLES-HENRY, Esq. of The Grange, Sutton, co. Surrey, and of Oakley Lodge, Chelsea, co. Middlesex, admitted a solicitor in 1847, but retired from practice in 1858; *b.* 19 July, 1820; *m.* 4 Aug. 1849, Arabella-Rose, dau. of the late Charles Ross, Esq. of Tain, co. Ross-shire, for ten years Inspector-General of Coasts and Harbours, and Commandant of the Flotilla in the island of Corfu, and has issue,

I. CHARLES-ADOLF, *b.* 13 June, 1853.
II. Henry, *b.* 13 Oct. 1854, *d.* 7 Nov. 1854.
I. Arabella-Rose. II. Margaret-Leonora.

Arms—Or, two cheveronells, between as many fleurs-de-lis in chief az., and a thistle slipped in base, ppr.
Crest—A griffin's head, erased, arg., holding in the beak a cross-crosslet fitchée, az., between two wings, also arg., each charged with a thistle, ppr.
Motto—Vincit veritas.
Residences—The Grange, Sutton, co. Surrey, and Oakley Lodge, Chelsea, co. Middlesex.

EDWARDS OF ARLESEY BURY.

EDWARDS, SAMUEL-BEDFORD, Esq. of Arlesey Bury, co. Bedford, J.P., high-sheriff in 1825; *b.* 27 Jan. 1799; *m.* 12 May, 1823, Sophia, eldest dau. of John Hubbard, Esq. of Forest House, co. Essex, and has issue,

SAMUEL-BEDFORD, *b.* 13 March, 1825.

Lineage.—The family of EDWARDS is noticed by Lysons as having existed at Arlesey, "upwards of a century;" but, in fact, it was settled in that parish in 1623, and was in Henlow at least as far back as 1499.

HENRY-EDWARDS, of Henlow, co. Bedford, *d.* in 1499, leaving, by Johanna, his wife, a dau., Agnes, *m.* to John Huckle, and a son, JOHN EDWARDS, *b.* about 1480, whose son, THOMAS EDWARDS, *b.* about 1500, at Henlow, had three sons, I. GEORGE; II. William, a monk; and III. Thomas, serjeant-at-arms to HENRY VIII., EDWARD VI., Queens MARY and ELIZABETH, and *d. s. p.* in 1576. The eldest son,

GEORGE EDWARDS, *b.* in 1520, was direct ancestor of,

RICHARD EDWARDS, Esq. of Arlesey, *b.* in 1663, *m.* 1st,

* By Mary, his wife, dau. of Capt. John Agnew, seventh son of Sir Stair Agnew, Bart. of Stranraer, in Scotland.

Frances Holgate, of London, by whom he had three daus., Frances, m. to Henry Wilson, Esq.; Elizabeth m. to John Hobbs, Esq. of Henlow; and Mary, m. to William Lowe, Esq. He m. 2ndly, Margaret Robinson, of London, and relict of John Coxe, Esq. of London, and by her had,

RICHARD, his heir.
Margaret, m. the Rev. William-Fuller Bedford, rector of Woolverton, co. Somerset, by whom she had two sons and a dau., viz.,

WILLIAM, who s. to Arlesey, on the death of his uncle, and assumed the surname of EDWARDS.
Samuel, d. s. p.
Mary, d. s. p.

Mr. Edwards d. in 1746, and was s. by his son,

RICHARD EDWARDS, Esq. of Arlesey, b. in 1717, m. in 1747, Mary, dau. and heiress of — Talman, Esq., and dying s. p. in 1789, was s. by his nephew,

WILLIAM BEDFORD, Esq, captain E. I. Co.'s service, who assumed by Royal licence, 20 Nov. 1792, the surname of EDWARDS. He m. Mary Crowther, and by her (who m. 2ndly, Thomas Innes, Esq., and d. in 1836) had, besides a son, Richard, and a dau., Mary-Margaret, both of whom d. in childhood, an only surviving son, the present SAMUEL-BEDFORD EDWARDS, Esq. of Arlesey Bury. Captain Edwards d. 27 Nov. 1800.

Arms—Per bend sinister, sa. and ermine, a lion rampant, or.

Crests—1st., The Prince of Wales's feathers, surmounted by a heron plume; 2nd., an esquire's helmet, ppr.

Seat—Arlesey Bury, co. Bedford.

EDWARDS OF ROBY HALL.

See EDWARDS-MOSS.

EDWARDS OF NANHORON.

EDWARDS, RICHARD-LLOYD, Esq. of Nanhoron, co. Carnarvon, J.P. and D.L., b. 9 April, 1806; m. 7 Nov. 1831, Mary, only dau. of John-Lloyd Wynne, Esq. of Coed Coch, co. Denbigh, and has issue,

I. RICHARD-LLOYD, b. 6 Aug. 1832, capt. 68th regt., killed before Sebastopol, 11 May, 1855.
II. Francis-William-Lloyd, b. 16 June, 1845.
I. Mary-Annabella-Lloyd.
II. Catherine-Agnes-Lloyd.
III. Margaret-Elizabeth-Lloyd.

Mr. Edwards has served as high-sheriff for the counties of Carnarvon, Anglesey, and Denbigh. He s. his father in July, 1830.

Lineage.—This ancient family is lineally descended from one of the royal tribes of Wales. Their immediate ancestors were Sir Griffith Lloyd and Sir Howel y Fwyallt, and Griffith ap Madoc of Nanhoron and Llwyndurus, co. Carnarvon, who served as high-sheriff of that county in 1555. The Nanhoron estate has devolved from father to son, almost uninterruptedly, down to the present time.

THE REV. WILLIAM EDWARDS, of Nanhoron, who m. Frances, dau of the Rev. William Williams, of Stoke, co. Salop, had with other issue,

TIMOTHY EDWARDS, Esq., capt. R.N., a very distinguished officer, who commanded at different periods the "Cornwall," "Valeur," "Volage," and "Wager." He m. Catherine, only dau. and heiress of John Browning, Esq. of Pullox Hill, co. Bedford, and had issue,

RICHARD, of whom presently.
John-Browning.
Catherine-Wakefield. Anne. Jane.

The eldest son,

RICHARD EDWARDS, Esq. of Nanhoron, col. Royal Carnarvon militia, m. 24 June, 1803, Annabella, only dau. and heiress of Richard Lloyd, Esq. of Bronhaulog, co. Denbigh, and had, (besides a son, who d. an infant,)

RICHARD-LLOYD, now of Nanhoron.
Annabella, m. to James Harden, Esq. of Harrybrook, co. Armagh.
Jane, m. to John Priestley, Esq. of Havod Gregog, co. Merioneth.
Catherine-Wynne.

Col. Edwards d. in July, 1830.

Motto—Dduw a diwedd da.
Seat—Nanhoron, co. Carnarvon.

EDWARDES OF RHYD-Y-GORS.

EDWARDES, DAVID-JOHN, Esq. of Rhyd-y-Gôrs, co. Carmarthen, late of the royal horse artillery; m. Caroline, 2nd dau. of John Forster, Esq. of Southend, Kent.

Lineage.—JOHN EDWARDES, of Rhyd-y-Gôrs, co. Carmarthen (descended through Grono Goch, Lord of Llangathan, Llewellyn, Lord of Buallt and Cadwgan, Lord of Radnor, from Ethelstan Glodrydd) m. and had two sons, David, who m. the dau. of Morgan Davies, Esq. of Cwm, co. Carmarthen, and d. s. p.; and

THOMAS EDWARDES, Esq. of Rhyd-y-Gôrs, who m. Lettice, dau. of John Lloyd, Esq. of Foesyblaiddiaid, co. Cardigan, and had issue,

DAVID, of whom presently.
John, who m. Miss Pusy, of Pusy Hall, Jamaica, and had issue a son, John-Pusy Edwardes, Esq.

The elder son,

DAVID EDWARDES, Esq., b. 1716, of Rhyd-y-Gôrs, admiral R.N., high-sheriff of co. Carmarthen in 1754, m. in 1748, Anne, dau. of Captain Blommart, descended from ancient family in the Netherlands, and had,

DAVID-JOHN, his heir.
Thomas, d. unm.
JOHN, of Gileston Manor, (*see* EDWARDES *of that place*.)
Lettice, Anne, and Martha, } d. unm.
Charlotte-Maria, m. 1st, to Cadwallader Brown, Esq. of Froodin, co. Carmarthen, and 2ndly, to the Rev. Edward Picton, A.M., younger brother of Lieut.-Gen. Sir Thomas Picton, G.C.B.
Isabella Margaretta, m. Lieut.-Gen. Archibald Campbell, and has issue, John, lieut.-col. in the army; and Isabella, m. Alderson Hodson, Esq.

The eldest son,

DAVID JOHN EDWARDES, Esq. of Rhyd-y-Gôrs, m. Elizabeth, 3rd dau. of John Jones, Esq. of Tyglin, co. Cardigan, and had two sons,

DAVID-JOHN, now of Rhyd-y-Gôrs.
Henry-Lewis, of Glanlery, co. Cardigan, J.P. and D.L., who has taken the additional surname of GWYNNE.

Arms—Quarterly: 1st, sa., a lion, rampant, within an orle of cinquefoils, or; 2nd, gu., a chev., or, between three bowens' knots; 3rd, sa., three bucks' heads, caboshed, arg.; 4th, chequy, or and sa, a fesse, arg.

Crest—A demi-lion, or, holding between the paws a bowens' knot.

Motto—Aspera ad virtutem est via.
Seat—Rhyd-y-Gôrs, co. Carmarthen.

EDWARDES OF GILESTON MANOR.

EDWARDES, THE REV. FREDERICK-FRANCIS, of Gileston Manor, co. Glamorgan, J.P., b. 5 Feb. 1801; m. 21 Aug. 1850, Susannah-Mary, youngest dau. of John Bevan, Esq. of Cowbridge, descended from the BEVANS *of Gelly-galed*, co. Glamorgan, by Susanna his wife, dau. of Whitlock Nicholl, Esq. of The Ham.

Lineage.—THE REV. JOHN EDWARDES, b. March 24, 1765, youngest son of David Edwardes, Esq. of Rhyd-y-Gôrs, co. Carmarthen, m. 1799, Margaret, only dau. and heiress of the Rev. William Willis, of Gileston Manor, co. Glamorgan, descended in the male line from the Willis's, Lords of the Manor of Fenny Compton, co. Warwick, and in the female from Dr. Beaw, Bishop of Llandaff, *temp.* CHARLES II., and Cecilia his wife, dau. of Charles, 8th Lord de Warr. By her (who d. in 1809) he had issue,

FREDERIC-FRANCIS, his heir, now of Gileston Manor.
Elizabeth, who m. in 1822, John Johnes, of Dalau Cothy, co. Carmarthen, and d. in 1848, leaving issue two daus.
Charlotte Anna, m. 1848 to Charles Cæsar, eldest son of Edward R. Cookman, Esq., of Monart House, co. Wexford; and Elizabeth.

The Rev. John Edwardes, d. in 1847.

Arms, &c., same as EDWARDES *of Rhyd-y-Gôrs*.
Seat—Gileston Manor, Glamorganshire.

EDWARDES OF SEALY HAM.

TUCKER-EDWARDES, WILLIAM, Esq. of Sealy Ham, co. Pembroke, b. in 1783; m. in 1807, Anna-Martha, 2nd dau. of J.-George Philipps, Esq. of Cwmgwilly, in Carmarthenshire, M.P., and has issue,

I. JOHN-OWEN, b. 19 Oct. 1808; m. 1849, Anna-Jane, only child of W. Jones, Esq. of Neeston, co. Pembroke.
II. William, b. 1810; d. 1855.
III Owen-John, b. June, 1815; m. 1845, Annie, 2nd dau. of G. Whittaker, Esq. of Barming, Kent.
IV. Thomas, b. 1816. V. Francis, b. 1824; d. 1851.
I. Mary, m. 1846, to Alfred Borradaile, Esq., colonel 4th Madras light cavalry.
II. Anna-Martha, m. 1847, to William Owen, Esq. of Tan-y-Gyrt, co. Denbigh.
III. Emma-Mary-Anne-Grace.

This gentleman inherited the TUCKER estates of Admiral Tucker. Mr. Edwardes, who is a magistrate and deputy-lieut. for the co. of Pembroke, served the office of high-sheriff for that shire in 1829.

Lineage.—TUDOR TREVOR (so called because born or nursed at Trevor), Lord of Hereford, Whittington, and both Maelors, was founder of the tribe of the Marches—an appellation derived from the numerous families seated in the *marches* of England and Wales, descended from him. Tudor Trevor's chief seat was Whittington Castle, of which he is said to have been the founder; and the Welsh heralds assign to him as ensigns, "Parted, per bend, sinister, ermine and ermines, over all a lion, rampant, or," which, as chief arms, or quartered, have been borne by all his descendants.

OWEN EDWARDES, Esq. of Trefgarne, co. Pembroke, lineally descended from TUDOR TREVOR, Lord of Hereford, m. about the middle of the 17th century, Damaris, dau. of James Perrott, Esq., Lord of Wellington, by Dorothy his wife, dau. of Sir Thomas Perrott, Bart., and the Lady Devereux his wife, sister of Robert, 2nd Earl of Essex, the ill-fated favourite of Queen ELIZABETH. By this lady Mr. Edwardes had issue,

JOHN, his heir.
Francis, ancestor of the LORDS KENSINGTON.

The eldest son and heir,

JOHN EDWARDES, Esq. of Trefgarne, m. in 1685, Frances, 4th and youngest dau. and co-heir of William Philipps, Esq. of Haythog, co. Pembroke, and had issue. The son and successor,

OWEN EDWARDES, Esq. of Trefgarne, m. in 1708, Jane, dau. and sole heiress of — Mortimer, Esq. of Lanmilo, co. Carmarthen, and had issue. Mr. Edwardes d. about 1740, and was s. by his eldest son,

ROWLAND EDWARDES, Esq. of Trefgarne, who m. Anne, dau. of George Harries, Esq. of Priskilly, co. Pembroke (who d. in 1732), by Margaret his wife, dau. of John Symmons, Esq. of Llanstinan, M.P. for Cardigan, and had issue,

JOHN-OWEN, his heir.
Rowland, a lieut.-col. in the army.
William-Mortimer, who m. Miss Tyson, and has issue, Rowland, Mortimer, and John.

Mr Edwardes d. in 1782, and was s. by his eldest son,

JOHN-OWEN EDWARDES, Esq. of Lanmilo, co. Carmarthen, who m. in 1777, Catherine, dau. and co-heir of John Tucker, Esq. of Sealyham, co. Pembroke, and had issue,

I. WILLIAM, his heir.
II. Thomas, formerly in the 23rd regt. of foot, aide-de-camp to Sir Thomas Picton during the latter part of the Peninsular War. This gentleman was severely wounded in the mouth at the siege of Badajos. He m. Miss Middleton.
I. Anne, m. to — George, Esq. II. Charlotte.
III. Jane, m. to — Shaw, Esq.

Mr. Edwardes d. in 1825, and was s. by his son, the present WILLIAM TUCKER-EDWARDES, Esq. of Sealyham.

Arms—Quarterly: 1st and 4th, az., a chevron, embattled and counter-embattled, or, between three sea-horses, naiant, arg.; 2nd and 3rd, erm., a lion, rampant, sa.
Crest—A bear's paw, holding a battle-axe, arg.
Mottoes—"Vigilate;" and "Gardez la foi."
Seat—Sealyham, near Haverfordwest.

EDWARDS OF PYE NEST.

EDWARDS, HENRY, Esq. of Pye Nest, co. York, J.P. and D.L., major of the 2nd West Yorkshire yeomanry, and M.P. for Halifax in 1847; b. July, 1812; m. April, 1838, Maria-Churchill, eldest dau. of Thomas Coster, Esq., formerly of Marchwood, near Southampton, and has several sons and daus.

Lineage.—JOHN EDWARDS, Esq., the descendant of a Warwickshire family, removed into Yorkshire A.D. 1749, and, having acquired, through his wife's family, the Lees of Skircoat, near Halifax, the estate of Pye Nest, built there the present mansion. He m. Miss Lees, and was father of

HENRY-LEES EDWARDS, Esq. of Pye Nest, who m. Lea, dau. of Joseph Priestley, Esq. of Whitewindows, descended from a very ancient family settled at Priestley and Sowerby, near Halifax, and had, with other issue, a son and heir, the present HENRY EDWARDS, Esq. of Pye Nest.

Arms—Az., a bend, cotised, arg., charged with three martlets, or.
Crest—A talbot, ppr., langued, gu., issuant from a marquess's coronet, or.
Motto—Omne bonum Dei donum.
Seat—Pye Nest, Halifax.

EDWARDS OF NESS STRANGE.

EDWARDS, GEORGE-ROWLAND, Esq. of Ness Strange, co. Salop, major H.E.I.C.S., b. 23 June, 1810; m. 11 March, 1847, Catherine-Jane, eldest dau. of Major-Gen. Edward Armstrong, H.E.I.C.S., and has issue,

I. JOHN, b. 30 July, 1850.
II. George-Rowland, b. 18 Feb. 1852.
III. James-Murray, b. 1 Jan. 1854.
I. Antoinette-Charlotte. II. Catherine.

Lineage.—EINION EFELL, living in 1182, Lord of Cynllaeth, Montgomeryshire, and of Llwynymaen, Salop, at the latter of which places he is said to have resided, m. Arddyn, dau. of Madoc Vychan ap Madoc, descended from Idnerth Benfras, Lord of Maesbrook, and was father of

RHUN AP INION EFELL, living in 1221, who m. Elizabeth, dau. of John, Lord Strange of Knockyn, and was s. by his son,

CYHELYN AP RHUN, of Lloran, in the lordship of Cynllaeth, who rebuilt, in 1230, the mansion-house of Lloran, as we learn from some Welsh verses, importing that the years from the incarnation of the Son of God were twelve hundred and three tens when Cyhelyn founded a huge and high house of wood and stone. "He erected," says the bard, "on the banks of Barrog, a house that will outstand the world. Let songs be sung to the amiable chief in the halls of Lloran." Cyhelyn m. Efa, dau. and heiress of Grono ap Cadwgan, Lord of Hen-Vache, in Llanrhaiadr-yn-Mochnant, Montgomeryshire, descended from Ririd, younger son of Bleddyn ap Cynfyn, King of Powys, and was father of

IEVAN AP CYHELYN, of Llwynymaen and Lloran, constable of Knockyn Castle, who, by Efa his wife, dau. of Adda ap Awr, of Trevor, had a son,

MADOC GOCH AP IEVAN, of Lloran, who m. Lleiki, dau. of Howel Goch ap Meredith Vychan, of Abertanat, in Shropshire, derived from Howel, son of Meredith ap Bleddyn, Prince of Powys, and had a son and successor,

MADOC KYFFIN AP MADOC GOCH, of Lloran and Garthervr, in Llanrhaiadr-yn-Mochnant. The surname of Kyffin, borne by Madoc, was derived from a locality of that name in the parish of Llangedwin, where he had been nursed, and was assumed to distinguish him from his father, Madoc, then living. Madoc Kyffin m. twice: 1st, Tangwystl, dau. of Ievan Voel ap Iorwerth, of Pengelly, descended from Aleth, Lord of Dyvet, by whom he had a son,

IEVAN GETHIN, of whom presently.

Madoc Kyffin m. 2ndly, a dau. of Griffith ap Rhys, great-grandson of Ririd Vlaidd, Lord of Penllyn, in Merioneth (*see* MYDDELTON OF GWAYNYNOG), and was, by her, father of David Vychan, ancestor of the VAUGHANS, EARLS OF CARBERY, VAUGHANS OF GOLDEN GROVE, KYFFINS OF MAENAN, &c. Madoc Kyffin was s. by the eldest son of his first marriage,

IEVAN GETHIN (*Terrible*) AP MADOC KYFFIN, of Lloran, Garthervr, and Moeliwrch. He m. twice: 1st, Margaret, dau. of Llewelyn ap Rotpert, descended from Ednowain Bendew, Lord of Tegaingl, in Flint, founder of the thirteen noble tribes of North Wales and Powys; and 2ndly, Margaret, dau. of Ievan ap Madoc ap Cadwgan Wenwys. By the latter he had a son,

MORRIS AP IEVAN GETHIN.

By his first marriage, Ievan Gethin ap Madoc Kyffin had issue,

GRIFFITH AP IEVAN GETHIN, of Lloran, ancestor of the MEREDITHS *of Abertanat*, co. Salop.
Iolyn ap Ievan Gethin.
IEVAN VYCHIN AP IEVAN GETHIN.

The 3rd son,

IEVAN VYCHAN AP IEVAN GETHIN, of Abertanat and Moeliwrch, was direct ancestor of

THOMAS AP LLEWELYN, of Cynllaeth, who resided in Llys Dynwallown. He *m.* Jane, dau. of Griffith Lloyd, Esq. of Ragad, co. Merioneth, and was father of

EDWARD THOMAS, Esq. of Trevonnen, who *m.* Margery, dau. of Thomas Wycherley, Esq. of Eyton, in the co. of Salop, and was *s.* by his son,

ROBERT EDWARDS, Esq. of Rhydycroesau, otherwise of Lledrode, co. Denbigh. This gentleman is the first of the family who assumed a distinct surname. He *m.* Anne, dau. and heir of Robert Kyffin, Gent. of Cynllaeth, and was *s.* by his eldest son,

JOHN EDWARDS, Esq., who purchased Ness Strange, in the co. of Salop. This gentleman was admitted, in 1666, to the freedom of Shrewsbury. He *m.* Dorothy, dau. of Thomas Barnes, Esq. of the Lowe, by whom (who *d.* in 1714) he had issue. Mr. Edwards *d.* in Feb. 1709-10, and was *s.* by his eldest son,

JOHN EDWARDS, Esq. of Great Ness, *alias* Ness Strange, in the co. of Salop, who *m.* 1st, Mary, dau. of Richard Muckleston, Esq. of Shrewsbury, brother of the Recorder of Oswestry; and 2ndly, Mary Corbet, a widow lady; by the former of whom (who *d.* 1 Jan. 1703) he had (with a dau., Mary, *m.* to the Rev. William Parry) a son and successor,

JOHN EDWARDS, Esq. of Great Ness, *alias* Ness Strange, *b.* 19 April, 1701; who *m.* 1st, in April, 1735, Margaret, dau. of Robert Lowndes, Esq. of Winslow, in the co. of Bucks, by Margaret his wife, dau. of Richard Atcherley, Esq. of Weston,* and had three sons,

ROWLAND, his heir.
John, twin with Rowland, *m.* and had issue. His son, JOHN EDWARDS, Esq. of Dolserey, co. Merioneth; *m.* Anne, younger dau. and co-heir of the late Edward Edwards, Esq. of Cerrig Llwydion, co. Denbigh, and had an only child, E.-Lloyd Edwards, Esq., who *m.* the eldest dau. of George-Edward-Beauchamp Proctor, Esq.
Thomas, *d. s. p.*

He *m.* 2ndly, in Dec. 1744, Mary, dau. of John Comberback, Esq., but by that lady (who *d.* 4 Feb. 1764) had no issue. Mr. Edwards *d.* 2 June, 1775, and was *s.* by his eldest son,

ROWLAND EDWARDS, Esq. of Ness Strange, *b.* Sept. 1738; who *m.* in April, 1765, Dorothy, dau. of John Scott, Esq. of Shrewsbury, and by her (who *d.* in 1781) had issue, JOHN, his heir; Lydia, who *d. unm.* in 1830; Mary, *d. unm.* in 1795; and Eliza. Mr. Edwards *d.* 31 May, 1796, and was *s.* by his only son,

JOHN EDWARDS, Esq. of Ness Strange, J.P. and D.L., *b.* 22 Sept. 1773; *m.* 2nd Dec. 1806, Charlotte-Margaret, dau. of the Rev. George Martin, vicar of Great Ness, by the Lady Mary Murray his wife, dau. of John, 3rd Duke of Atholl, and by her (who *d.* 15 Dec. 1849) had issue,

I. JOHN, *b.* 10 Dec. 1808; *d. unm.* 7 April, 1834.
II. GEORGE-ROWLAND, now of Ness Strange.
III. Rowland, *d. unm.* 22 Nov. 1854.
IV. James-Murray, *d.* 13 Feb. 1840.
I. Charlotte, *d.* an infant. II. Mary.
III. Charlotte, *d. unm.* 21 Sept. 1851.
IV. Margaret, *d. unm.* 18 Nov. 1529.
V. Georgiana, *m.* 20 Aug. 1846, to John Naylor, Esq.
VI. Eliza, *d.* 15 Nov. 1840. VII. Amelia-Murray.
VIII. Fanny, *d.* 19 Oct. 1853.

Mr. Edwards *d.* 26 July, 1850.

Arms—Per fesse, sa. and arg., a lion, rampant, counterchanged.
Crest—Within a wreath, a lion, rampant, as in the arms.
Seat—The Hall, Great Ness, near Shrewsbury.

EDWARDS OF OLD COURT.

EDWARDS, JOHN-KYNASTON, Esq. of Old Court, co. Wicklow, barrister-at-law, *b.* 12 Feb. 1819; *s.* his father 17 Feb. 1850.

Lineage.—RHODRI MAWR (Roderick the Great), who became king of all Wales, A.D. 843, left, with other issue, a younger son, TUDWAL, surnamed *Gloff*, or *the lame*, from a wound received in battle, 6th in descent from whom was HEDD MOLWYNOG, chief of the 9th noble tribe of North Wales and Powys (son of Greddf ap Tymyr ap Llewfrodedd Varfawg ap Alan ap Alser ap Tudwal); he was steward to his kinsman, David ap Owen Gwynedd, and "assisted that Prince to carry fire and sword through England, even to the walls of Coventry." He left three sons, Menter, Gwillonen, and GWRGAI, from the last of whom, 7th in descent, was DAVID (ap Meredydd ap Howel ap Bleddyn ap Gwion ap Rhadfach ap Aser ap Gwrgai): "he married an heiress in Brinpolin, in the parish of St. Asaph, next house to the Lord Bishop's," in which locality, in the township of Brinpolin, adjoining the bishop's palace, a property was in the possession of his descendants until about the year 1728, when it was disposed of by John Edwards, of Old Court.

THOMAS EDWARDS, of Llan Elwy, or St. Asaph, 8th in descent from David (and son of Edward ap Robert ap Edward ap Gryffyd ap Howel ap Bleddyn ap David), *m.* some years previously to 1639, Anne, dau. of Thomas Lloyd, of Berth, near Ruthin, co. Denbigh, who was descended, through Cyhelyn ap Tudor, from Tudor Trevor, Earl of Hereford, living A.D. 924: by her he left issue, RICHARD and Mary, the latter of whom was *m.* to — Woolhouse, and had issue. Thomas Edwards, *d.* 17 Dec. 1668, at Llandaff, in South Wales, where he was buried in the cathedral, and was *s.* by his son,

RICHARD EDWARDS, Esq. of Old Court, who had removed to Ireland; he *m.* 1stly, about the year 1656, Elizabeth, dau. and (by the death of her brother, Capt. Roger Kynaston, in 1657) heiress of Colonel John Kynaston, who, with his regiment of Welsh foot, landed in Ireland, 7 June, 1647, accompanying the Commissioners from the Parliament, who had come to treat with the Marquess of Ormond, Lord Lieutenant, for the surrender of Dublin, having for several years previously served in the wars of England, and in the expedition for reducing North Wales to the obedience of Parliament. Colonel Kynaston was 3rd son of Ralph Kynaston, B.D., chaplain to King JAMES I., and youngest son of Roger Kynaston, Esq. of Morton, co. Salop, who was younger brother of Edward Kynaston, Esq. (from whom descended the family of Kynaston, Barts.) and son of Humphrey Kynaston, Esq., who was son (by his wife Elizabeth, dau of Henry Grey,* Baron Powys, and Earl of Tankerville, in Normandy) of Sir Roger Kynaston, Knt. of Hordley, co. Salop, descended from Iorwerth Goch, younger son of Meredith ap Bleddyn, Prince of Powys (*see* MAINWARING *of Ottley*). Colonel Kynaston *d.* A.D. 1649, aged 39, and after his decease, in consideration of military pay due at his death, a grant of land, of which Old Court formed a portion, was made to his relict, Elizabeth, for the use of his family, and afterwards confirmed by patent, *temp.* CHARLES II., to his dau. and heiress, ELIZABETH, and her husband RICHARD EDWARDS.

The issue of Richard Edwards' first marriage was Richard; John Kynaston, *d. s. p.;* Thomas (who *m.* and had issue Richard, who *d. s. p.*); Anne, *m.* to Capt. Benjamin Hunt; and Mary, *m.* Richard Bourne. He *m.* 2ndly, Penelope, eldest dau. of Sir Robert Wolseley, Bart. of Wolseley, in Staffordshire, and relict of — Fountaine, Esq., but by her left no issue; he was dispossessed of Old Court by the partisans of King JAMES II., but reinstated after the battle of the Boyne. He *d.* in 1693, and was *s.* by his eldest son,

RICHARD EDWARDS, Esq. of Old Court, M.P. for Wicklow, *b.* 1659, and *m.* 1682, his stepmother's niece, Mary, 2nd dau. of Sir Charles Wolseley, Bart. of Wolseley, but dying without issue in 1722, he was *s.* by his only surviving brother,

JOHN EDWARDS, Esq. of Old Court, *b.* in 1665, who *m.* in 1697, Jane, eldest dau. of James Butler, Esq. of Rathelline, co. Carlow, by whom he had issue, (with others who died young) James; John, *d. unm.* in 1749; Mary, *m.* Joseph Bernard, Esq., of which marriage descended the family of BERNARD *of Castle Bernard*, King's Co.; Elizabeth, *m.* 25 Feb., 1727, Mark Whyte, Esq. (*see* WHYTE *of Newtown Manor*); Jane, *m.* John Hardy; and Grace, *m.* William Pleasants, Esq of Knockbeg, co. Carlow. He *d.* in 1728, and was *s.* by his son,

JAMES EDWARDS, Esq. of Old Court, *b. circa* 1706, who

---

* By Margaret his wife, dau. of Rowland Hill, Esq. of Hawkstone.

* Henry Grey, Earl of Tankerville, was in a female line descended from, and representative of, the Princes of Powys Wenwynwyn (*see* HUGHES *of Gwerclas*); he also derived from Gundred, dau. of WILLIAM the Conqueror, as well as from Joan Plantagenet, the Fair Maid of Kent, dau. and heiress of Edmund, Earl of Kent, son of EDWARD I., from whom Sir Roger Kynaston's descendants quarter the Plantagenet arms.

m. 29 Nov. 1750, Ann, 2nd dau. of Thomas Tenison, Esq., 3rd son of Richard Tenison, D.D., Bishop of Meath, and had,

I. JOHN, his heir.
II. James, capt. in the army, m. Charlotte, dau. of William Sturgeon, Esq., by his wife, the Lady Henrietta-Alicia Wentworth, dau. of the Marquess of Rockingham, by whom there were issue,
1 JAMES, of Ballyronan, co. Wicklow.
2 John, of Knockrobin, co. Wicklow.
3 Tenison, of the Inner Temple.
1 Henrietta-Alicia. 2 Anna-Charlotte.
3 Agnes-Elizabeth. 4 Maria.
5 Frances-Dorothea (dec.), m. to Marcus Maingay, Esq.
6 Elizabeth-Charlotte, m. to Francis Green, Esq.
III. Tenison, capt. in the army, m. Charity, dau. of John Barrington, Esq. of Castlewood, Queen's Co., by whom he left issue, Charity, m. Philip-Henry Crampton, Esq.; Annabella, m. Viscount Glentworth, by whom she is mother of the present Earl of Limerick.
I. Alicia, m. John Barrington, Esq. of Castlewood, Queen's County.

James Edwards d. in 1780, and was s. by his eldest son,

LIEUT.-COL. JOHN EDWARDS, of Old Court, b. in 1751, who m. in Jan. 1780, Charlotte, 5th dau. of John Wright, Esq. of Nottingham, and sister of John Wright, Esq. of Lenton Hall, Notts, by whom he left issue,

I. JAMES-KYNASTON. II. Richard, d. unm.
III. Wright, lieut. 58th regt., severely wounded at St. Sebastian, m. 1828, Sarah, widow of Capt. Jones, and has issue.
I. Anne, m. Henry-Eugene Perrin, Esq. of Dublin, d. leaving issue. II. Mary-Lucy.

He d. in 1832, and was s. by his eldest son,

JAMES-KYNASTON EDWARDS, Esq. of Old Court, major in the Wicklow militia, b. 12 Dec. 1780, m. 18 April, 1818, Emily, dau. of Henry Smith, Esq. of Beabeg, co. Meath, and had issue,

I. JOHN-KYNASTON, now of Old Court.
II. Henry-St.George, m. 5 Oct. 1854, Catherine, dau. of St. George Smith, Esq. of Greenhills, co. Louth, which lady d. in 1855.
III. James-Tenison.
I. Emily, m. the Rev. Richard Verschoyle, vicar of Carlingford, co. Louth.
II. Charlotte-Matilda. III. Elizabeth.

He d. 17 Feb. 1850, and was s. by his eldest son, the present JOHN-KYNASTON EDWARDS, Esq. of Old Court.

Arms—Those of Hedd Molwynog, (sa., a stag, passant, arg., attired and unguled, or), changed as to colours, viz.: vert, a stag passant, or, attired and unguled, arg.; with, as an augmentation, in 1683, on a chief, arg., three falcons, ppr.; quartering for KYNASTON, differenced with a crescent: quarterly: 1st and 4th, erm., a chevron, gu.; 2nd and 3rd, arg., a lion rampant, sa. (the Black Lion of Powys). Among the quarterings to which the family is entitled is that of PLANTAGENET.
Crests—A lion's head erased, ermines, between two palm-branches issuing out of a wreath, ppr., mantled, gu., doubled, arg., for EDWARDS; and an armed arm and hand, holding a sword within a sun, proper, for KYNASTON.
Mottoes—Heb Dduw heb ddim, Dduw a digon, *i. e.*, Everything with God, nothing without God, for EDWARDS; and Honor potestate honorantis for KYNASTON.
Seat—Old Court, co. Wicklow.

EGERTON OF TATTON PARK.

EGERTON, WILLIAM-TATTON, Esq. of Tatton Park, co. Chester, M.P. for Cheshire, b. 30 Dec. 1806; m. 18 Dec. 1830, Lady Charlotte-Elizabeth-Loftus, eldest dau. of the 2nd Marquess of Ely, and has,

I. WILBRAHAM, b. 19 Jan. 1832.
II. Alan-De-Tatton, b. 1846. III. Loftus-Charles, b. 1849.
I. Elizabeth-Anna-Maria-Barbara.
II. Alice-Mary. III. Emily-Marian.
IV. Beatrix-Lucia-Catherine.

Lineage.—SAMUEL EGERTON, Esq. of Tatton Park, b. 28 Dec. 1711 (son of John Egerton, Esq. of Tatton, by Elizabeth, his wife, dau. of Samuel Barbour, Esq., and grandson of the Honourable Thomas Egerton, of Tatton, 3rd son of John Egerton, 2nd Earl of Bridgewater), m. Beatrix, youngest dau. and co-heir of the Rev. John Copley, of Batley, rector of Elmley, in Yorkshire, and by her, who d. in April, 1755, had an only dau., Beatrix, who m. Daniel Wilson, Esq. of Dalham Tower, in Westmoreland, but predeceased her father, without surviving issue. Mr. Egerton d. himself 10 Feb. 1780, advanced in years, having been one of the representatives in that and the three preceding parliaments for the co. of Chester. He devised his estates with divers remainders in tail to his only sister,

HESTER EGERTON, who had m. in May, 1747, WILLIAM TATTON, Esq. of Withenshaw, but who, upon inheriting her brother's possessions, resumed, by sign-manual, 8 May, 1780, her maiden name. She d. the 9th of the following July, leaving a dau., Elizabeth Tatton, the wife of Sir Christopher Sykes, Bart. of Sledmere, M.P., and a son and successor,

WILLIAM-TATTON EGERTON, Esq. of Tatton and Withenshaw, b. 9 May, 1749. This gentleman represented the co. of Chester in Parliament. He m. thrice (*see Family of* TATTON), and dying in 1806, was s. in the Egerton estates by his eldest surviving son (by Mary, his 2nd wife, dau. of Richard Wilbraham Bootle, Esq.),

WILBRAHAM EGERTON, Esq. of Tatton, J.P. and D.L., M.P. for Cheshire, lieut.-col. of the yeomanry cavalry, lieut.-col. of the local militia, and high-sheriff in 1808, b. 1 Sept. 1781; m. 11 Jan, 1806, his first cousin, Elizabeth, 2nd dau. of Sir Christopher Sykes, Bart. of Sledmere House, Yorkshire, and by her (who d. 28 April, 1853), had issue,

WILLIAM-TATTON, now of Tatton.
Wilbraham, major 43rd Light Infantry, b. 31 May, 1808; d. 10 April, 1848.
Thomas, b. 16 Nov. 1809.
Mark, b. 27 Jan. 1815, and d. 28 Dec. 1831.
Edward-Christopher, M.P., b. 27 July, 1816; m. 1845, Lady Mary Pierrepont, dau. of Earl Manvers, and has issue.
Charles-Randle, b. 12 May, 1818.
Charlotte-Lucy-Beatrix.

Col. Egerton, d. 25 April, 1856.

Arms—Arg., a lion, rampant, gu., between three pheons, sa.
Crest—On a chapeau, gu., turned up, erm., a lion, rampant, gu., supporting a dart, argent.
Motto—Sic donec.
Seat—Tatton Park, near Knutsford.

ELD OF SEIGHFORD HALL.

ELD, FRANCIS, Esq. of Seighford Hall, co. Stafford, J.P. and D.L., b. 9 July, 1796; s. his father in 1855.

Lineage.—RICHARD ELDE, Esq. of Syford, co. Stafford, descended from the Eldes, of Boughton, co. Derby, treasurer and steward of the household to Walter, Earl of Essex, earl-marshal of Ireland, and paymaster of the Forces in Ulster, had a grant of arms for his services in Ireland, from Nicholas Narborne, Ulster king of arms, 16 QUEEN ELIZABETH, A.D. 1574. He m. Margaret, dau. of John Wrottesley, Esq., and Elizabeth, his wife, dau. of Thomas Astley, Esq. of Pateshall, and Mary, his wife, dau. of Sir Gilbert Talbot, and by this lady (who was buried 15 June, 1618) had a son, RICHARD, father, by Margaret, his wife, dau. of Sir Thomas Crompton, Knt. of Creswell Hall, co. Stafford, of FRANCIS ELDE, Esq. of Syford, whose eldest son, FRANCIS, had, by his 2nd wife, Mary, dau. of John Grove, Esq. of Rowley, a son,

JOHN ELDE, Esq. of Dorking, co. Surrey, who, at the death of his half-brother, Francis Elde, Esq. of Seighford, Master in Chancery, became possessed of Seighford, co. Stafford. He m. Catherine, dau. of Holbrooke, Esq., and widow of Rowland Cotton, Esq. of Etwall, and d. 16 April, 1796, aged 92, leaving a dau., Catherine, m. to Dr. Kirby, of Dorking, co. Surrey, and a son and heir,

FRANCIS ELD, Esq. of Seighford, b. in 1736, who was buried at Seighford, 17 July, 1817, aged 81, having had, by Elizabeth, his wife (who d. 8 Jan. 1833),

I. FRANCIS, his heir.
II. Richard, b. 9 Oct. 1778, d. in 1837.
III. John, b. 16 July, 1779, m. 17 Nov. 1807, the Hon. Louisa-Sarah-Sidney Smyth, dau. of Lionel, 7th Viscount Strangford, and dying Dec. 1855, leaving issue,
Lionel-Percy-Denham, b. 9 Dec. 1808, major H. E. I. Co.'s service.
IV. Stanton, b. 20 Jan. 1782, d. in Jan. 1800.
V. William, of Fradswell Hall, b. 26 Aug. 1783, m. Mary, dau. of William Keene, Esq. of Rowley, co. Stafford, and has,
Howard, bapt. 4 Jan. 1816.
VI. Charles-Howard, b. 20 April, 1785, d. 13 May, 1807.
VII. Thomas, b. in 1786, d. in 1844, leaving issue, Thomas and Rose.
I. Mary-Anne, m. to George Durant, Esq. of Tong Castle, and d. in 1829.
II. Elizabeth, m. to John Chambers, Esq. capt. in the 10th hussars.

The eldest son,

FRANCIS ELD, Esq. of Seighford Hall, J.P. and D.L., bapt.

20 June, 1778; high-sheriff 1821; *m.* Mary, dau. of John Mootham, Esq. of Percy-street, London; and *d.* 6 Jan. 1855, having had issue,

FRANCIS, now of Seighford Hall. George, *b.* 1798.
Frederick, col. in the army, *b.* 2 April, 1803; *m.* Annie, dau. of the late Dr. Middleton, of Cape Town, and has a dau., Cecilia-Frederica.
John, *d.* 14 Feb. 1830. Richard, *b.* 1806.
Edward, *b.* 1808.
Mary.
Charlotte, *m.* Lieut.-Col. Andrew-Hyacinth Kirwan, Esq., and has issue.
Caroline-Eliza, *m.* 16 Jan. 1850, to the Rev. Jos. Thompson, vicar of Seighford.

Arms—Arg., a chevron, between three partridges, close, ppr.
Crest—A falcon, rising, or, beaked, membered, jessed, and belted, gu, his mouth embrued, of the last.
Seat—Seighford Hall, near Stafford.

ELERS OF CHELSEA.

ELERS, THE REV. CAREW-THOMAS, B.D., rector and patron of Rishangles, Suffolk, and vicar of Bicken, hill, Warwickshire, *b.* 31 Dec. 1790; *m.* in 1821 Sarah, youngest dau. of Charles Palmer, Esq. of Coleshill, Warwickshire, and has issue,

I. CAREW-THOMAS, of the Middle Temple, *b.* in 1829.
II. Walter.
I. Sarah-Elizabeth. II. Charlotte. III. Louisa.

Lineage.—PETER ELERS, of the ancient baronial family of that name, migrated from Germany, and came over to this country at the time when GEORGE I. was called to the throne. His only son,

PETER ELERS, Esq., J.P. for Middlesex, who *m.* in 1715, Dorothy, younger dau. of Thomas Carew, Esq. of Carew Castle, Pembrokeshire, and sister of Thomas Carew, Esq. of Crowcombe Court, Somersetshire, settled at Chelsea, of which place he became a considerable proprietor. He was buried in the south cloisters of Westminster Abbey, in March, 1753, and his wife Dorothy in the same place some years previously. Of this marriage there was issue, a dau., Ann, *b.* in 1717, *m.* to William Poston, Esq., and *d. s. p.*, and an only son,

GEORGE ELERS, Esq. of Chelsea, and of the Middle Temple, *b.* in 1720, who *m.* Mary, dau. and sole heir of Peter Charon,* Esq. He *d.* 1784, and was buried at Chelsea, leaving issue,

CAREW, his heir.
Peter, rector and patron of Rishangles, Suffolk, rector of Addington, Kent, and domestic chaplain to his late Majesty, when Duke of Clarence: *d. unm.* in 1820, buried at Addington.
Charlotte, *b.* in 1761, *m.* John Peyto Shrubb, Esq., and *d.* in 1830, leaving issue.

The elder son,

CAREW ELERS, Esq., *b.* in 1755, *m.* Susanna, dau. and eventual heir of William Farrow, Esq. of Monkseleigh and Cockfield, Suffolk. He *d.* 1821, and was buried at Chelsea, leaving issue,

I. CAREW-THOMAS, the present head of the family.
II. William, of Oldbury, Kent, J.P. and D.L., who *m.* in 1828, Susanna, youngest dau. of John-Peyto Shrubb, Esq. of Meristwood, near Guildford, Surrey, and has issue,
  1 William-Shrubb. 2 Frederick-Wadham.
  3 Henry-Edward.
  1 Emily. 2 Isabella-Susannah.
  3 Augusta-Mary.
III. George, of Springfield Lodge, near Taunton, *b.* 9 Nov. 1808, *m.* 14 July, 1831, Emma, youngest dau. of John le Grice, Esq. of Bury St. Edmund's, and has issue,
  1 CHARLES-GEORGE, *b.* 9 Feb. 1838.
  1 Rosa. 2 Harriet. 3 Laura.
I. Elizabeth, *m.* to George-John Gibson, Esq. of Bradston Brook, Surrey, and Standgate Lodge, Sussex, and has issue,
  1 George.
II. Caroline. III. Sophia. IV. Mary.

Arms—A gyronny of twelve pieces, argent and gules, in the centre point an inescocheon, or.
Crest—An escocheon of the arms between two doves' wings, proper.
Motto—Gloria virtutis umbra.

* This French Protestant family sought refuge in England, in consequence of the revocation of the Edict of Nantz, and resided at Chelsea. They bore for armorial ensigns, argent, three stars, sable.

ELIOT, FORMERLY OF BUSBRIDGE.

ELIOT, THE REV. LAWRENCE-WILLIAM, rector of Peper Harow, co. Surrey, J.P. and D.L., *b.* 16 March, 1777; *m.* in 1811, Matilda-Elizabeth, dau. of Henry Halsey, Esq. of Henly Park, co. Surrey, and has issue surviving,

I. WILLIAM-LAWRENCE, in holy orders, *b.* 17 July, 1812, *m.* in 1842, Elizabeth, second dau. of C. Woodyer, Esq. of Guilford, Surrey.
II. George, *b.* 20 Nov. 1816, *m.* in 1842, Louisa, eldest dau. of M.-Waller Clifton, Esq. of Australind, F.R.S.
III. John, E.I.Co.'s Bengal Artillery. IV. Henry.
I. Matilda. II. Mary.

Lineage.—JOHN ELIOT, Esq. of Godalming, (great-grandson of Thomas Elyott, of Wonersh, filazer of the King's Bench for Surrey and Sussex, and clerk of the peace for the former in the reigns of HENRY VI. and EDWARD IV.,) purchased the estate of Busbridge, from James de Bushbridge, in the latter part of HENRY VIII.'s reign. From his son, LAWRENCE ELIOT, who accompanied Sir Francis Drake in his voyage round the world, and *d.* 7 Nov. 1582, derived the ELIOTS, *of Busbridge*, whose male representative,

THE REV. EDWARD ELIOT, rector of Hambledon (son of the Rev. Edward Eliot, of Dunsfold, and grandson of Sir William Eliot, of Busbridge), *m.* Mary Longhurst, relict of Thomas Chandler, Esq., and *d.* 7 Aug. 1790, aged fifty-nine, having had issue, with two sons, Edward and Thomas, who both *d. unm.*, another son, the present REV. LAWRENCE-WILLIAM ELIOT, and two daus., Catherine, and Maria, wife of Dollman.

Arms—Quarterly: 1st and 4th, az., a fesse, or; 2nd and 3rd, or, two bars, gu., and in chief, three crescents, of the field.
Crest—A griffin's head, couped, wings endorsed, sa., collared, arg.

ELLIOT OF BARLEY HOUSE.

ELLIOT, JOHN, Esq. of Barley House, Plymouth, lord of the manor of Leigham Egg Buckland, Devon, D.L.-colonel, retired list, Bengal army, *b.* 22 Jan. 1787; *m.* 9 Aug. 1832, Catharine-Charlotte, dau. of the late Andrew Tracy, Esq., and Sarah Moore his wife.

Lineage.—JAMES ELLIOT, Esq., son of James Elliot and Elizabeth Oldrieve, his wife, *m.* in May, 1782, Elizabeth Cole, and *d.* 30 March, 1831, leaving a son, the present Col. Elliot, of Barley House, and two daus., Sarah, *m.* to the late William Square, Esq., and Mary, *m.* to the late William Elliot, Esq. of Kingsbridge, Devon.

Seat—Barley House, Plymouth.

ELLIOT OF BINFIELD PARK.

ELLIOT, GEORGE-HENRY, Esq. of Binfield Park, Berks, and of Stonehouse, co. Gloucester, lieut.-col. Berks militia, J.P. and D.L., *b.* in 1789; *m.* 5 March, 1812, Mary-Josephine, dau. of Gen. Sir James Hay, colonel of the 2nd dragoon-guards, and has issue,

I. GEORGE-HENRY, capt. 2nd Dragoon-guards, *b.* 27 Feb. 1813.
I. Mary-Josephine. II. Louisa-Grace III. Caroline.

Lineage.—THE REV. GEORGE-HENRY GLASSE, A.M., rector of Hanwell, co. Middlesex, chaplain to the Duke of Cambridge, and a magistrate for Middlesex, *b.* 1 Sept. 1760 (son of the Rev. Samuel Glasse, D.D., rector of Hanwell, chaplain-in-ordinary to King GEORGE III., by Hannah, his wife, sister and co-heir of Giles Clutterbuck, Esq. of Mill End, co. Gloucester, and grandson of the Rev. Richard Glasse, A.M., vicar of Purton, Wilts, by Elizabeth, his wife, dau. of the Rev. Samuel Arnold), *m.* 1st, 24 Nov. 1783, Hannah, dau. of Thomas Fletcher, Esq. of Ealing, co. Middlesex, and by her, who *d.* at Clifton, 14 June, and was buried at Hanwell, 5 July, 1802, aged forty-two, had issue,

GEORGE-HENRY, his heir.
Arthur-Henry, in holy orders, chaplain to the Duke of Cambridge, *b.* 8 Aug., and bapt. at Hanwell, 27 Sept. 1798, died leaving, by Isabel-Caroline, his wife, a posthumous dau.,
  Caroline-Catharina, *b.* 16 Feb. 1841.
Caroline, *m.* at Hanwell, 11 May, 1805, to Thomas Hume, M.D., physician to the Forces.

Emma-Margaret, m. to Wm.-Papwell Brigstock, Esq. of Birdcombe Court, co. Somerset, late M.P. for the eastern division of that shire.
Ellen-Clara, m. to William Johnson, Esq., barrister-at-law, of Greig Avoren, Queen's County, eldest son of the Hon. Justice Johnson.
Mary-Louisa, who assumed the name of Shawe, by the King's letters-patent, m. to James Griffith, Esq.

Mr. Glasse m. 2ndly, 12 May, 1805, at Shorne, co. Kent, Harriet, dau. and heir of Thomas Wheeler, Esq. of Waterford, of the Royal Marines, by Susanna, his wife, dau. of John Hadden, Esq., captain in the same corps, and had by her (who m. 2ndly, Commodore Sir John-James-Gordon Bremer, K.C.B. and K.C.H., of the Priory, Compton Gifford, Devon,) one son,

Frederick-Henry-Hastings, capt. R.N., b. 11 April, and bapt. at Hanwell, 27 June, 1806.

Mr. Glasse d. 31 Oct. 1809, and was s. by his eldest son, who assumed the surname of Elliot and is the present George-Henry Elliot, Esq. of Binfield Park.

Arms of Elliot—Erm., a fesse, az., with two double cotties, indented, vert.
Arms of Glasse—Arg., a fleur-de-lis between three mullets, within a bordure, gu.
Crest of Elliot—An elephant's head, arg., erased, gu., about the neck two barrulets, invected, vert.
Crest of Glasse—A mermaid, holding a looking-glass and a comb in her hand, ppr.
Seat—Binfield Park, Berks.

ELLIS OF WYDDIAL HALL.

Ellis, Charles Heaton, Esq. of Wyddial Hall, Herts, b. 14 Aug. 1789; m. 30 Oct. 1819, Louisa, eldest dau. of Sir J.-H. Stracey, Bart., and has issue,

I. Charles-John, b. 11th April, 1830, in H. M.'s 9th Lancers.
II. Edward-Henry-Brabason, b. 19th May, 1834, of Exeter College, Oxford.
And several daughters.

Mr. Ellis was called to the bar in June, 1821.

Lineage.—The family of Ellis, of Alrhey, co. Flint, with its branches at the Wern and Pickill, is of great antiquity in North Wales, as appears by the Visitations in the Heralds' Office and the genealogy collected by Owen Salusbury, of Rûg, Esq., and Robert Davies, of Gwysaney, and continued to the year 1664, by John Salusbury de Erbystocke, Esq. A small portion of the old family estate is still in Mr. Ellis's possession, under different entails. The direct ancestor of the family was Tyngad (2nd son of Tudyr Trevor and Angharad, dau. of Howel Dha), who succeeded to the 3rd part of his father's estate, by the law of Gavel kind. His grandson, Kenrick (son of Rhiwallon), a nobleman in Bromfield and Lord of Whittington, m. Tuda, dau. of Ivor, Lord of Rhôs, and was slain in the defence of his country against the English, 5th Dec. 1073. Ednyved, his 2nd son, m. Gwladys, dau. of Aldred ap Grono, Lord of Englefield and of the 15 tribes or chief houses. His grandson, Ednyved, m. Jonet, dau. of Rys Vychan, Lord of South Wales. Their son, Llewellyn-Gôch, m. Lettice, dau. of Sir Richard Manley, Knt. Ierwerth, their great grandson, m. Jonet, dau. of Madoc Kynaston, of Kynaston and Caehowel, and was succeeded by

Morgan, of Alrhey, *temp.* Edward VI. Richard ap Howel, grandson of Morgan, m. Margaret, dau. of heir of Ellis, son of Ellis Eyton, of Rusbon, by Parnel, dau. of Sir William Bulkley, Knt. Ellis ap Richard, son and heir of Richard ap Howel, m. Jane, dau. of Sir Thomas Hanmer. Ralph Ellis, of Alrhey, their 5th son, m. Jane, dau. of S. Gryffith, of Overton, gent., and was succeeded by Thomas Ellis, who m. Jane, dau. of G. Salusbury, of Erbystock, by Mary, dau. of Thomas Grosvenor, son and heir of Sir Thomas Grosvenor, of Eaton, Knt. Andrew Ellis, only son of Thomas, m. Anne, dau. of Robert ap Richard, of Halkin, heir to his uncle, John, who died in 1654. John Ellis, 2nd son of Andrew, of Brasenose College, Oxford, m. Katherine, dau. of R. Kingsman, of Overton, in Wilts, and d. 9th July, 1740. Their son, John Ellis, b. Aug. 1686 O.S., Fellow of Brasenose College and D.D., m. Margretta, 2nd dau. of Thomas Phipps, Esq. of Heywood, Wilts, M.P. Dr. Ellis died 7th Oct. 1764 N.S. His youngest son, William, Governor of Patna, lost his life in the massacre there, 5th Oct. 1763. His eldest son, Brabazon, b. 12 Aug. 1723, and a dau., Catherine, who d. unmarried, survived him. Brabazon Ellis, d. at Wyddial, 28th Nov. 1780, leaving an only son, John-Thomas, and a dau., Elizabeth, m. to Samuel Elias Sawbridge, Esq. of Olantsigh, in Kent. John-Thomas Ellis, Esq., b. 28th Sept. 1756, High Sheriff for Herts, 1784, and a member of the 16th Parliament of Great Britain, m. Mary Anne, only dau. of John Heaton, Esq. of Bedfords, in Essex, and d. 6th Oct. 1836. His two eldest sons, John-Thomas and William-Fane, died in his lifetime, both in active military service, as well as his youngest son, Henry-Bennet, a midshipman in the Royal Navy. He left Charles-Heaton Ellis, Esq., now of Widdial Hall, his only surviving son, and a dau., Julia, m. to the Rev. Henry B. Thorold, grandson of Sir John Thorold, Bart.

Arms—Erm. a lion passant gardant gules.
Crest—Out of a ducal coronet, or, a lion's head gules crowned gold.
Motto—Fort et fidele.
Seat—Widdial Hall, Herts.

ELLIS-JERVOISE.

See Jervoise.

ELLIS OF GLASFRYN.

Ellis, The Rev. John-Williams, M.A., of Glasfryn, co. Carnarvon, J.P. and D.L., b. 21 Jan. 1808; m. 21 Feb. 1831, Harriet-Ellen, only child of J.-H. Clough, Esq., of the family of Clough *of Plâs Clough*, co. Denbigh, and has issue,

I. Thomas-Parr-Williams, b. 27 Jan. 1832.
II. John-Clough-Williams, b. 11 March, 1833.
I. Ellen-Augusta-Williams.

Lineage.—This family is entirely of Welsh extraction and traces its descent through many of the oldest Welsh families. The great grandfather of the present Mr. Ellis was prebendary of Llanfair, and married the sister of the Right Rev. Dr. Humphreys, Lord Bishop of Bangor, and had, with a dau., who d. young, a son,

The Venble. John Ellis, Archdeacon of Merioneth, a celebrated antiquary, the friend of Sir Joseph Banks and Dr. Solander. He was twice married: 1st, to Miss Lloyd, heiress of the Penrallt and Trallwyn estates, in Caernarvonshire; and 2ndly, Miss Williams. By the former he had issue, viz.,

John, d. unm.
Hugh, m. Miss Wright, dau. of J. Wright, Esq. of Thuntsford, and left issue, John, who took the surname of Lloyd, for the Trallwyn estate, m. Miss Jones, and had issue; and Frances, m. to the Rev. Harry Grey, nephew to the Rt. Hon. the Earl of Stamford and Warrington.
Thomas, of whom hereafter. Griffith, d. unm.
Richard, rector of Llawdwrog, m. Susan, eldest dau. and co-heir of Langford Meade, Esq.

The 3rd son,

The Rev. Thomas Ellis, was treasurer of Bangor Cathedral and rector of Llanfachreth, co. Anglesey. He m. in 1807, Miss Jane Bulgin, heiress of Brondanw, co. Merioneth, eldest dau. of J. Bulgin, Esq. of Bath, and by her (who d. July, 1849), left, at his decease, 15 Feb. 1833,

John-Williams, present representative.
Thomas-Roberts, in holy orders, b. 2 March, 1815.
Ellen-Frances. Sidney-Jane.
Catherine-Dorothy-Anne.

Arms—Arg., a mermaid, gu., crined, or, holding a mirror in her right hand and a comb in her left, gold; quartering, gyronny, erm., and ermines, a lion, rampt., or.
Crests—1st, a mermaid, as in the arms; 2nd, an arm, embowed, in armour, holding a broken spear-head, all ppr.
Motto—Wrth ein ffrwythau yn hadnabyddir. In English: Let us be seen by our actions.
Seat—Glasfryn, co. Carnarvon.

ELLISON OF HEBBURN.

Ellison, Cuthbert, Esq. of Hebburn, co. Durham, J.P. and D.L., high sheriff in 1808 and 1827, formerly M.P. for Newcastle-on-Tyne, b. 12 July, 1783; m. 21 July, 1804, Isabella-Grace, eldest dau. and co-heir of Henry Ibbetson, Esq. of St. Anthony's, co. Northumberland, and has issue,

I. Isabella-Caroline, m. in 1824, to George-John Lord Vernon, and has issue.
II. Henrietta, m. in Jan. 1824, to William-Henry Lambton, Esq. of Biddick Hall, co. Durham, next brother to John-George, first Earl of Durham.
III. Louisa, m. 8 April, 1829, to Viscount Stormont, eldest son of the Right Hon. the Earl of Mansfield, and d. in 1837.

IV. Laura-Jane, m. in 1838, to William, Lord Kensington.
V. Sarah-Caroline, m. to Sir Walter James, Bart.
I. Anne, d. young.

Lineage.—CUTHBERT ELLISON, of Newcastle-upon-Tyne, merchant adventurer, served the office of sheriff of Newcastle in 1544, and was mayor in 1549 and 1554. His great grandson,

ROBERT ELLISON, Esq., sheriff of Newcastle in 1646, and M.P., m. 1st, Elizabeth, dau. of Cuthbert Grey, Esq. of Newcastle, and of Backworth, co. Northumberland, by whom he had issue,

I. CUTHBERT, his heir.
II. Samuel, of Newcastle, d. in 1689, leaving issue.
III. Joseph, ancestor of ELLISON, of Lintz.
IV. Robert. V. John.
VI. Nathaniel, D.D., Prebendary of Durham, who d. in 1721, leaving (with seven daus.) three sons,
 1 John, vicar of Bedlington, m. and had issue.
 2 Robert, of Otterburn, m. and had issue.
 3 Nathaniel, A.M., Vicar of Kirk Whelpington.
I. Elizabeth, m. to William Fenwick, Esq. of Stanton.
II. Alice, m. to Henry Rawling, Esq.
III. Mary, m. to William Jennison, Esq.

He m. 2ndly, 27 July, 1672, Agnes, relict of James Briggs, of Newcastle, merchant, but had no further issue. His son and successor,

CUTHBERT ELLISON, Esq. of Hebburn, m. in 1663, Jane, dau. of William Carr, Esq. of Newcastle, and sister of Sir Ralph Carr, and was s. at his decease by his eldest son,

ROBERT ELLISON, Esq. of Hebburn, who m. in 1696, Elizabeth, dau. of Sir Henry Liddell, Bart. of Ravensworth Castle, and had issue, CUTHBERT, his heir; Henry, b. in 1699, (m. in 1729, Hannah, dau. and co-heir of William Coatsworth, Esq., and had issue, HENRY, of whom presently; Robert, d. unm.; Anne, m. to Ralph Bates, Esq.; Hannah, d. unm.; and Elizabeth, d. unm.); Robert, colonel, 44th regiment, d. s. p. in 1766; Catharine, m. to John Airey, Esq. of Newcastle; Jane, d. unm.; and Elizabeth, d. unm. The eldest son,

CUTHBERT ELLISON, Esq. of Hebburn, a general officer in the army, and M.P. for Shaftesbury, d. unm. 11 Oct. 1785, when the family possessions devolved upon his nephew,

HENRY ELLISON, Esq. of Hebburn, bapt. 9 Dec. 1734, who m. 15 May, 1779, Henrietta, dau. of John Isaacson, Esq., and had issue,

CUTHBERT, his heir.
Robert, Col. Grenadier Guards, m. the Hon. Mary Montague, dau. of the late Lord Rokeby, and d. 3 July, 1843, leaving one son.
Hannah, m. to John Carr, Esq. of Dunstan Hill, in Durham.
Henrietta, m. to George-Wm. Aylmer, Esq. of Mowden Hall, Essex.
Elizabeth, m. to Frederick-Edward Morrice, Esq. of Betshanger, in Kent.

Mr. Ellison d. in 1795.

Arms—Gu., a chevron, or, between three eagles' heads, erased, arg.
Seats—Hebburn Hall, co. Durham, and Juniper Hill, Surrey.

ELMHIRST OF ELMHIRST.

ELMHIRST, WILLIAM, Esq. of Round Green, co. York, b. 15 May, 1799; m. 9 March, 1825, Anna-Frances, dau. of William Walker, Esq., M.B., late of Swinnow Park, near Wetherby, co. York, and of Everley Lodge, near Barnet, by his wife, Elizabeth Pye, dau. of William Pye, an officer in the army, 7th son of Henry Pye, Esq. of Farringdon, co. Berks, and Elizabeth, dau. of Governor Saunders, and has,

I. WILLIAM, b. 1 Jan. 1827, M.A. in holy orders, m. 17 Aug. 1854, Ann-Elizabeth-Pasmore, dau. of William-Barnard Heaton, Esq. of Gainsborough, co. Lincoln.
II. Leonard, b. 3 Aug. 1829, d. 10 Jan. 1830.
III. James, now of Doncaster, b. 5 Sept. 1830.
IV. Robert, now of Liverpool, b. 20 Oct. 1835.
I. Anna-Frances, m. 21 Dec. 1852, to the Rev. John Newman, M.A. of Stainton Vicarage, near Doncaster, 2nd son of William Newman, Esq. of Darley Hall.
II. Elizabeth-Martha.

Lineage.—"Ouslethwaite, Houndhill, Elmhirst," says HUNTER, in his *History of Doncaster*, "have all been at different periods in the possession of one family, which has been seated in this valley from the earliest era to which we can usually ascend, when we find one Robert called de Elmhurst, that being then the place of his residence. Elmhurst is still the property of his descendant, William Elmhirst, Esq. of Round Green, and so is Ouslethwaite and Genne House, Ouslethwaite being a late purchase; but Houndhill passed at the beginning of the last century, by an heiress, to the Copleys of Nether Hall, near Doncaster.

The Elmhirsts have produced their own genealogist, in the person of Richard Elmhirst, of Houndhill, the head of the family in the 17th century. He was known to Dr. Johnson, who gives this account of him; "That he was a person of good judgment, and learned in the laws; he had the collection of the recusant's rents, payable to the crown, under the Earl of Strafford. It might have been added, that he was much employed by the Earl of Strafford in the administration of his private affairs. He was also employed under him, in the court of the lord president of the North, and was well esteemed by the neighbouring gentry. In the civil wars he fortified his house for the king, to defend himself from common plunderers, but yielded it to Sir Thomas Fairfax, who came in person to demand the surrender of it. Some of the soldiers would have killed him, but Sir Thomas, who had a kindness for him, prevented it. He got rich, and purchased considerable lands, of which the manor of Newton, on Derwent, for which he gave £650 to William Gower, Esq., appears to have been the chief. He stands in the Catalogue of Compounders for no less a sum than £566. By him was begun the family pedigree, which was continued by his son, a physician, who lived at Houndhill till the beginning of the last century."

The first ancestor from whom can be drawn a lineal descent, was "Robert de Elmehirst, who lived in the time of EDWARD I. and EDWARD II. The lineal descendant of ROBERT DE ELMEHIRST, *temp.* EDWARD I.

RICHARD ELMEHIRST, of Houndhill, eldest son and heir of Robert Elmehirst of Houndhill, was living at the close of the 16th century, and was much employed by Lord Strafford both respecting his own concerns, and in the collecting the recusants' rents, as well as in affairs connected with the presidency of the North; he was also employed by the second Earl of Strafford. He fortified his house at Houndhill at the time of the civil war. He m. 1st, in 1628, Margaret, dau. and co-heiress of Richard Micklethwaite, son of Elias Micklethwaite, of Swaithe Hall, in Worsbroughdale, and by her (who d. at York, 2 Oct. 1632) had issue,

Thomas, b. in 1631, and buried in 1632, at Worsbrough, where a brass plate, with a curious inscription, records his death.
Elizabeth, b. in 1629, and buried in 1638, at Worsbrough.

He m. 2ndly, Elisabeth, dau. of Thomas Waite, of Haxby, near York, and by her had issue,

II. RICHARD, bapt. 1 Jan. 1639, who lived at Houndhill. He recorded the pedigree at Dugdale's Visitation, in 1665; his will bears date, 12 Feb. 1673, and was proved 24 March, 1673. He m. Alice, dau. of Gervase Dickson, of Woodhall, Darfield, and by her (who d. in 1673) had issue,
 1 Joshua, b. in 1669, and d. 22 Aug. 1683, aged 14.
 1 Elizabeth, bapt. 2 Dec. 1662. She made over to her uncle, Dr. William Elmhirst, before her marriage, the ancient estates of Elmhirst and Genne House, whilst Houndhill went to her husband. At the time of Dugdale's Visitation, it is stated she was four years of age. She m. in 1684, John Copley, Esq. of Nether Hall, Doncaster, and left (with a dau., Anne, wife of George Healey, of Burringham, co. Lincoln) a son, Robert, who d. unm. in 1771, bequeathing Houndhill, and other estates, to Thomas Newby, who took the name of Copley.
 2 Eleanor, bapt. 16 June, 1665.
II. William, b. in 1645, was of Clare Hall, Cambridge, and took the degree of M.B. in 1670. He lived at Houndhill, and built Genne House, where he latterly lived. He practised his profession, and d. at Newark, 23 Dec. 1715, aged 71.
III Robert, bapt. 10 Aug. 1647.
IV. THOMAS, of whose line we treat.
I. Ellinor, b. in 1634, m. to Hastings Rasby, of Upper Hall, Kirksmeaton.
II. Mary, m. 1st, to Samuel Bridge of Boston, and 2ndly, to Samuel Saltonstall, of Rogerthorpe, co. York.
III. Rebecca.
IV. Elizabeth, bapt. 24 March, 1641; m. Edward Canby, of Fishlake.
V. Anne, m. in 1668, to Thomas Lambe, merchant, of Boston.

The youngest son,

THOMAS ELMHIRST, b. in 1649, d. 2 Feb. 1696, aged forty-seven, at Boston, co. Lincoln, of which town he was a merchant and alderman. He *m.* in 1685, Anne, dau. of Henry Boulton, of Langton, near Wragby, co. Lincoln, and by her (who was *b.* in 1661, and *d.* 23 Feb. 1693, aged thirty-two) he had issue,

I. WILLIAM, of Genne House and Elmhirst, from whom proceeds the Yorkshire branch, in Worsbroughdale.
II. Richard, *b.* in 1687, living in 1716, lost at sea, on a voyage from Virginia.
III. THOMAS, *b.* 6 Dec. 1692, ancestor of the ELMHIRSTS *of Lincolnshire (which see.)*
I. Elizabeth, *b.* 1 Oct. 1689, *m.* in 1724, at Lusby, to John Johnson, of Fulney Hall, near Spalding, co. Lincoln.
II. Anne, *b.* 17 Nov. 1690, *m.* to John Harrold, of Spilsby, co. Lincoln.
III. Helen, *b.* 7 Nov. 1691, *d.* 9 Feb. 1694.
IV. Grace, *b.* 17 Feb. 1693, *d.* 11 March, 1693.

The eldest son,

WILLIAM ELMHIRST, *b.* 8 Oct. 1686, commenced life as a merchant at Liverpool, but afterwards resided at Elmhirst, and in 1723 took up his abode at Genne House, both in Worsbroughdale. He was sole executor of his uncle, Dr. Elmhirst, M.B., from whom he received the estates of Elmhirst and Genne House, and other lands. Tradition says he lost most of his paternal property on his return from the East Indies. He *m.* at Silkstone, 18 March, 1715, Martha,* dau. and co-heiress of Robert Allot, of Lewdine, in Worsbroughdale, by his wife, Sarah Green, of Small Shaw, near Penistone; and by her (who was buried at Worsbrough, 25 March, 1740) had issue,

I. WILLIAM, his heir.
I. Sarah bapt. 9 Feb. 1716, *m.* 1st, to Robert Greaves, Esq. of Clayton Hall, in the parish of Darton, and 2ndly, to Joshua Littlewood, of Bilham.
II. Anne, bapt. 24 June, 1719, *m.* to John Cawood, of Robroyd. He *d.* 3 Nov. 1810, aged 89, *s. p.*
III. Martha, bapt. 14 July, 1726, *d. unm.*

Mr. Elmhirst *d.* in 1746, (his will bears date 5 July, 1742,) and was *s.* by his son,

WILLIAM ELMHIRST, Esq., bapt. at Worsbrough, 29 Dec. 1721, who resided first at Elmhirst, and afterwards at Genne House. He purchased Ouslethwaite of Mr. Hammersley. He *m.* 20 Oct. 1757, Elizabeth, dau. of John Wordsworth of Hermit Hill, Tankersley. By this lady (who *d.* May, 1804, aged sixty-six) he had issue. Mr. Elmhirst *d.* in July, 1773, having been killed by a fall from his horse, and was *s.* by his son,

WILLIAM ELMHIRST, Esq., D.L. bapt. at Worsbrough, 11 April, 1759, who greatly enlarged the house at Ouslethwaite, purchased by his father. He purchased Round Green and other lands, and had property bequeathed to him by his cousin Mordecai Cutts, at Thorne, Fishlake, Wroot, and Sykehouse. He *d.* at Usselby House, co. Lincoln, being then the residence of his relative, Colonel Elmhirst, 20 Sept. 1821, and was buried at Worsbrough, 27 Sept., aged sixty-three. His will bears date 31 Aug. 1817. He *m.* 9 Nov. 1790, Anne-Rachel, only dau. and heiress of Thomas Elmhirst, of Stixwould Abbey, co. Lincoln, by his wife Anne, only dau. and heiress of Theophilus Smith, of Wyham, co. Lincoln, and relict of Joseph Gace, of Rearsby Hall. By this lady (who was *b.* at Stixwould Abbey, 12 Oct. 1771) he had issue,

I. ROBERT, *b.* 10 Dec. 1794. He built the house at Round Green, where he resided. He *s.* his father in 1821, but *d.* 2 Dec. 1835, *unm.*, and was buried at Worsbrough, 9 Dec, 1835, leaving his brother, William, his successor, to whom he bequeathed the estates left him by his father.
II. WILLIAM, present representative of this ancient family.
III. Thomas, *b.* 24 Feb. 1801, who *d. unm.* at Ouslethwaite, 1 Feb. 1837, and was buried at Worsbrough, 7 Feb. He was a merchant, of Quebec, Canada West; his will bears date, 28 March, 1827.
IV. Richard, *b.* 18 Sept. bapt. 18 Sept 1803, of Caius College, Cambridge, M.B. in 1828, and M.D. in 1835; is now of Lincoln.
I. Anne. II. Elizabeth.

Arms—Barry, wavy, of six pieces, arg. and sable, a canton, paly, wavy, also of six pieces, arg. and sable.
Crest—A mount, vert, therefrom issuant rays of the sun, in front of a hurst of elm-trees, ppr.
Motto—In Domino confido.
Seat—Round Green, near Barnsley, co. York.

* Her sister, Anne, *m.* Thomas Potter, of Wetherby, co. York, and their dau., Martha, *m.* Thomas Walker, of Swinnow Park, near Wetherby, grandfather of Anna-Frances, wife of WILLIAM ELMHIRST, of Round Green, in Worsbroughdale, and Stainborough, the present representative of the family; Mary, the other dau., *m.* Bryan Greaves, of Clayton Hall, whose son, Robert, *m.* Sarah Elmhirst.

ELMHIRST OF WEST ASHBY.

ELMHIRST, WILLIAM, Esq. of West Ashby Grove, co. Lincoln, *b.* 25 Aug. 1802; *m.* Elizabeth, dau. and co-heir of John Yarburgh, Esq. of Frampton, co. Lincoln, and has issue,

I. WILLIAM-AUGUSTUS. II. John-Yarburgh. III. Harry
I. Elisabeth-Jane. II. Charlotte-Mary.

Lineage.—THOMAS ELMHIRST, Esq., *b.* 6 Dec. 1692 youngest son of Thomas Elmhirst, Esq. of Boston, by Anne, his wife, dau. of Henry Boulton, Esq. of Langton, (*see preceding family,*) resided at Stixwould Abbey. He *m.* Hannah, dau. of the Rev. John Marshall, vicar of Mumby, near Alford, and by her (who *d.* 9 Oct. 1764) he had issue,

THOMAS, capt. Royal North Lincoln militia, *b.* in May, 1728, resident at Stixwould Abbey, co. Lincoln, and afterwards at Swaithe, co. York. He *m.* 1st, Mary-Rachel, dau of Matthew Lister, Esq. of Burwell Park, co. Lincoln, but by her (who *d.* 9 March, 1767) he had no issue. He *m.* 2ndly, 16 Aug. 1770, Anne, relict of Joseph Gace, Esq. of Rearsby Hall, co. Lincoln, and only dau. and heir of Theophilus Smith, Esq. of Wyham, by Anne, his wife, dau. of John Uppleby, Esq. of Wootton. By this lady (who *d.* 16 March, 1826) Capt. Elmhirst left, at his decease, 2 Dec. 1792, an only surviving child,
ANNE-RACHEL, *m.* 9 Nov. 1790, to WILLIAM ELMHIRST, Esq. of Ouslethwaithe, Elmhirst, and Genne.
WILLIAM, of whom presently.
Anne, *b.* in Feb. 1730, *d.* in May, 1732.

The 2nd son,

WILLIAM ELMHIRST, Esq., *b.* 22 Sept. 1732, resided at Stainsbury House, co. Lincoln. He *m.* 7 Aug. 1761, Sarah, only dau. and heir of Richard Gilbert, Esq. of Leverton, near Boston, and by her (who *d.* 20 Dec. 1818) had, with other children, who *d.* young,

RICHARD, his heir.
Robert-Sampson, *b.* in April, 1776, *d.* in 1804, *s. p.*
Sarah.

Mr. Elmhirst *d.* at Enderby, 24 April, 1810, and was *s.* by his son,

RICHARD ELMHIRST, Esq. of West Abbey Grove J.P. and D.L. formerly Major of the North Lincoln militia, and Lieut.-Colonel-Commandant of the Lindsay Local militia, *b.* 16 Aug. 1771; *m.* Jane-Dorothea, dau. of Moses Benson, Esq. of Lutwyche Hall, co. Salop, and has issue,

WILLIAM, his heir. Moses.
Edward, in holy orders, rector of Shawell, co. Leicester, *m.* Sophia-Elizabeth, only dau. of the Rev. T.-H. Rawnsley, of Halton Holgate, co. Lincoln, and has, Edward-Pennell; Sophy-Jane; and Rosa-Mary.
George in holy orders, *d.* in Jan. 1848.
Charles, captain in the army.
Jane-Dorothea, *m.* to William Reader, Esq. of Baughurst House, Hants, and has issue.
Mary, *m.* Robert Luard, Esq, captain Royal horse-artillery, and *d.* in March, 1841, leaving issue.
Sarah.
Margaret, *m.* John Hassard Short, Esq. of Edlington Grove, co. Lincoln, and has issue.
Elizabeth-Anne, *m.* to Richard, second son of Sir Peter Pole, Bart, rector of Wolverton and Ewhurst, Hants.
Barbara, *m.* to Lawson Cape, Esq., M.D.

Arms, &c.—*See* ELMHIRST *of Elmhirst.*
Seat—West Ashby Grove, co Lincoln.

ELWES OF GREAT BILLING.

ELWES, CARY-CHARLES, Esq. of Great Billing, co. Northampton, J.P. and D.L., high-sheriff in 1853, *b.* 2 Nov. 1800; *m.* 17 Aug. 1826, Elinor, eldest dau. of Rear-Admiral Rye, of Culworth, and has issue,

I. VALENTINE-DUDLEY-HENRY-CARY. *b.* 26 Nov. 1832; served in the Caffre War in the 12th royal lancers, *m.* 28 April, 1856, Henrietta-Maria, 2nd dau. of Charles Lane, Esq., of Badgemore, co. Oxford.
I. Eleanora-Caroline-Arabella, *m.* March, 1847, to Captain FitzGerald, R.N., Governor of Western Australia.
II. Sophia-Dorothea. III. Marian-Georgiana.

Lineage.—The first recorded ancestor of this family, WILLIAM HELWISH, or ELWES, of Askham, co. York, *m.* the dau. of Livesey of Lancashire, and had, with two daus., four sons, namely, I. EDWARD, of Askham; II. John, of Worlaby, in Lincolnshire, father of SIR GERVASE ELWAIES, lieutenant of the Tower at the time SIR THOMAS OVERBURIE was murdered there; III. Thomas, of Hubblethorpe, in Lincolnshire; and IV. GEOFFREY. The youngest son,

GEOFFREY ELWES, an alderman of London, *m.* Elizabeth,

dau. of Robert Gabbott, and heir of her brother, Robert Gabbott, of London, merchant, and by her (who was buried at Woodford, in 1625) had, with other children, JEREMY, his heir; and John, an alderman of London, ancestor of ELWES of Stoke. Mr. Alderman Geoffrey Elwes was *s.* at his decease by his eldest son,

JEREMY ELWES, Esq. of Roxby, co. Lincoln, living in 1634, who *m.* Mary, dau. of James Morley, Esq., one of the six clerks in Chancery, and by her (who *d.* 4 Dec. 1667) had, with a younger son, James, and a dau., Mary, the wife of William Hale, Esq. of King's Walden, a son and heir,

JEREMY ELWES, Esq., who *m.* Frances, dau. and heiress of Robert Raworth, Esq. of Gray's Inn, by whom (who *d.* in 1678) he left at his decease, in the next year, two sons and two daus. The elder son,

JEREMY ELWES, Esq., *d.* without issue, in 1683, and was *s.* by his brother,

ROBERT ELWES, Esq. of Throcking, who erected the manor house there, "a curious and neat fabric, at a cost of 11,000*l*." This mansion was pulled down in 1743. Mr. Elwes *m.* 2 March, 1684-5, Elizabeth, dau. of Ralph Freman, Esq. of Aspeden, by Elizabeth his wife, the dau. of Sir John Aubrey, Bart. of Llanthrithed, in Glamorganshire, and had two sons, ROBERT, his heir; and Jeffrey (Sir), treasurer to Queen ANNE's bounty, bapt. 16 Jan. 1695-6, *m.* twice, but *d.* issueless, aged 81, in 1776. He *d.* 10 June, 1731 (Mrs. Elwes lived to the 22nd Jan. 1740-1), and was *s.* by his son,

ROBERT ELWES, Esq. of Throcking, who *m.* in 1717, Martha, dau. and heiress of Richard Cary, Esq. of Bedford Row, by whom (who *d.* at Chiswick, 25 March, 1768), he left at his decease, 17 Oct. 1752, an only child,

CARY ELWES, Esq. of Throcking, *b.* in London, 30 Jan. 1718; who *m.* 1st, in Sept. 1742, Hester, dau. of Henry Ewer, Esq. of Bushey Hall, Herts, and by her (who *d.* in 1770) had one son, CARY, *b.* 20 March, 1744-5, *d. unm.* in 1781. Mr. Elwes *m.* 2ndly, Miss Elizabeth Holgate, by whom (who *d.* 3 Feb. 1820) he had issue,

ROBERT-CARY, his heir.
Elizabeth, *m.* to the Rev. Robert-Cary Barnard, of Wethersfield, co. Suffolk; and *d.* 8 Jan. 1813.

Cary Elwes *d.* 22 Dec. 1782, and was *s.* by his only surviving son,

ROBERT-CARY ELWES, Esq. of Great Billing, co. Northampton, *b.* 28 July, 1772; who *m.* 1st, at Brocklesby, in Lincolnshire, 12 Oct. 1797, the Hon. Caroline Arabella Pelham, 2nd dau. of Charles, 1st Lord Yarborough, and sister of the present lord, by whom (who *d.* in July, 1812) he had issue,

CARY-CHARLES, now of Great Billing.
Dudley-Christopher-Cary, *b.* 19 March, 1804; *m.* at Culworth, 18 June, 1829, Sophia, 3rd dau. of Rear-Admiral Rye.
George-Cary, *b.* 3 Feb. 1806; *m.* in Dec. 1834, Arabella-Sophia, dau. of Thomas-Fieschi Heneage, Esq.
Henry-Robert-Harrington-Cary, *b.* 20 March, 1808; an officer in the army.
Caroline-Arabella-Elizabeth, *m.* 3 Feb. 1827, to the Rev. Charles-James Barnard, rector of Bigby and Roxby, co. Lincoln.
Sophia-Jane.

Mr. Elwes *m.* 2ndly, 22 Dec. 1814, Jane-Marianne, only dau. of the Rev. Richard Sykes, of Westella, near Hull, and by her had,

Lincoln-Cary, *b.* 12 Dec. 1816.
Frederick-Cary, *b.* 11 Nov. 1818.
Richard-James-Cary, *b.* 18 Sept. 1825.
Francis-Emilius-Cary, *b.* 23 Aug. 1828.

Mr. Elwes *d.* 10 Feb. 1852, and was *s.* by his eldest son, the present CARY-CHARLES ELWES, Esq., of Great Billing.

Arms—Or, a fesse, az., surmounted by a bend, gules, quartering GABBOTT and CARY.
Crest—Five arrows, or, feathered and headed, arg., entwined by a snake, ppr.
Seat—Great Billing, Northamptonshire, and Kemp Town, Brighton.

ELWES OF STOKE COLLEGE.

ELWES, JOHN-PAYNE, Esq. of Stoke College, co. Suffolk, J.P., *b.* 13 May, 1798; *m.* 17 July, 1824, Charlotte-Elizabeth, 4th dau. of Isaac Elton, Esq. of Stapleton House, co. Gloucester, and has issue,

I. JOHN-ELTON-HERVEY.
II. Frederick-George.
I. Charlotte-Elizabeth.
II. Isabella-Matilda.
III. Amey-Sophia.
IV. Emily-Martha.

Mr. Elwes was M.P. for North Essex in 1835, and high-sheriff in 1826.

Lineage.—SIR GERVASE ELWES, Knt. of Woodford, Essex, son of John Elwes, alderman of London, younger brother of Jeremy Elwes, Esq. of Roxby, co. Lincoln, *m.* Frances, 2nd dau. of Sir Robert Lee, Knt. of Billeslee, co. Warwick, and by her (who *m.* 2ndly, Sir Richard Everard, Bart. of Much Waltham) he had four sons and a dau. The eldest son and heir,

SIR GERVASE ELWES, of Stoke College, co. Suffolk, was created a BARONET by King CHARLES II., 22 June, 1660. He *m.* Amy, dau. of Dr. Trigge, of Highworth, in Wiltshire, and had three sons and five daus. Sir Gervaise, who represented the county of Suffolk in parliament, *d.* in May, 1705, and was *s.* by his grandson,

SIR HERVEY ELWES, 2nd baronet, M.P. for Sudbury, in the reign of Queen ANNE, who *d. unm.* 22 Oct. 1763, when his estates passed to (the son of his sister, Amy Meggot) his nephew,

JOHN ELWES, Esq., afterwards so well known as Elwes the miser, and so distinguished for integrity, generosity, and parsimony. He *d.* 26 Nov. 1789, when his landed property devolved on his grand-nephew and heir-at-law,

JOHN TIMMS, Esq., who assumed the surname and arms of HERVEY-ELWES. This gentleman was son of Lieut.-Col. Richard Timms, of the Royal Horse Guards, by Mary his wife, dau. of Thomas Hughes, Esq., M.D., and grandson of John Timms, Esq., by Anne his wife, dau. of Robert Meggot, Esq. of Southwark, and Amey his wife, sister of Sir Hervey Elwes, Bart. Mr. Hervey Elwes attained the rank of lieutenant-general in the army. He *m.* twice, and *d.* 29 Feb. 1824, leaving a son and successor, the present JOHN-PAYNE ELWES, Esq. of Stoke College.

Arms and *Crest*—as the preceding, without the quarterings.
Seat—Stoke College, near Clare, Suffolk.

ELWOOD OF CLAYTON PRIORY.

ELWOOD, COLONEL CHARLES-WILLIAM, of Clayton Priory, co. Sussex, J.P. and D.L., *b.* 18 May, 1781; *m.* 29 Jan. 1824, Anne-Katharine, 4th dau. of Edward-Jeremiah Curteis, Esq. of Windmill Hill, formerly M.P. for Sussex. Colonel Elwood attained his military rank in the E.I. Co.'s service.

Lineage.—This family is from the north of England, and was connected with that of the celebrated Quaker, Elwood, the friend of Milton. The late PEXALL ELWOOD, Esq., of Durham, who *m.* in 1780, Mary, dau of Captain Craig, R.N., by Jane Kennett his wife, had (with three daus., viz., Anne-Jane, *m.* 1st, to Captain Allen, of Pembroke, E.I. Co.'s service, and 2ndly, to the Rev. B.-J.-H. Cole, rector of Warbleton, co. Sussex: she *d.* in 1830; Jane, *m.* to Charles Ball, Esq. of Postford, Surrey; and Mary-Bovill, *m.* John Wise, Esq. of Maidstone, and *d.* June, 1854) an only son, the present COLONEL CHARLES-WILLIAM ELWOOD, of Clayton Priory.

Arms—Az., a chevron, arg., in chief, two mullets, or, in base, a buck's face, of the second, attired, of the third.
Crest—A dexter arm, embowed, in armour, the hand brandishing a pick-axe, all ppr.
Motto—Fide et sedulitate.
Seat—Clayton Priory, co. Sussex.

ELWOOD OF STRAND HILL.

ELWOOD, THOMAS, Esq. of Strand Hill, co. Mayo, *m.* in 1839, Catherine, dau. of Colonel Hearne, of the King's County, and has issue a son,

FRANCIS, *b.* in 1840.

Lineage.—WILLIAM ELWOOD, Esq. of Strand Hill, *m.* Miss Lindsay, of Hollymount, and had two sons, THOMAS, his heir; and Anthony, of Annefield, co. Mayo, who *m.* Miss Bowen, dau. and co-heir (with Mrs. Blake, of Windfield) of Christopher Bowen, Esq. of Annefield, and had issue, Christopher, deceased; and Anthony-Elwood Bowen, Esq. of Annefield, who *m.* Miss Blake, but has no issue. Mr. William Elwood's eldest son and heir,

THOMAS ELWOOD, Esq. of Strand Hill, *m.* Miss Lambert, and had issue, FRANCIS, his heir, Thomas, 3rd dragoon-guards, *d. unm.*; Rebecca, *m.* to Colonel Ormsby, of Ballinamore, co. Mayo; and Fanny, *m.* to the Hon. and Rev. Archdeacon Trench, brother to the Earl of Clancarty. The elder son,

Francis Elwood, Esq. of Strand Hill, m. Miss Ormsby, and by her (who m. 2ndly, George Ormsby, Esq. of Moate House, was father of two sons,

Thomas, his heir, present representative.
Ormsby, of Lough Mask Castle, co. Mayo, m. Miss Jones, and has issue.

Seat—Strand Hill, co. Mayo.

EMERSON OF ULVERSCROFT ABBEY.

Emerson, The Rev. Alexander-Lyon, of Ulverscroft Abbey, co. Leicester, and West Buckland, co. Somerset; *s.* his father 24 July, 1834; *m.* 1837, Julia, only surviving dau. of William Trenchard, Esq. of Taunton, and has issue,

I. Alexander. II. Charles-Edward.
III. Wharton-Amcotts. IV. Theodore-Bosville.
I. Mary-Alice.

Lineage.—One of the earliest records of this old Lincolnshire family is the will dated 7 May, 1567, of Edward, the son of George Emerson. He appears to have been father of three sons. The youngest,

Robert Emerson, of Glamford Briggs, co. Lincoln, *m.* Elinor Wainwright, and was father of

Alexander Emerson, Esq. of Caistor and Glamford Briggs, an eminent barrister, who *m.* in 1666, his cousin, Elizabeth, dau. and heir of Alexander Emerson, of Glamford Briggs, and had a numerous family; the eldest son of which was

Thomas Emerson, Esq. of Grimsby and Caistor, *b.* in 1628, who *m.* Mildred Saunderson, only dau. of George, 3rd Viscount Castleton, and dying in 1710, was *s.* by his son,

Alexander Emerson, Esq. of Caistor, *b.* in 1651, who *m.* Alice, sole heiress of George Wharton, Esq. of Retford, Notts, and had two sons, Thomas, who *d. s. p.*; and

Alexander Emerson, Esq. of Caistor, who *s.* under the will of G. Wharton, Esq., to the estate of West Retford, co. Nottingham. He *m.* Elizabeth, 2nd dau. and co-heiress of the Rev. Thomas Bosvile, rector of Ufford, co. Northampton, by Elizabeth his wife, sister and co-heir of John Bolle, of Thorpe Hall, co. Lincoln, and by this lady (who *m.* 2ndly, in 1745, the Rev. Stephen Ashton, vicar of Louth) had issue,

Wharton, (Sir), of East Retford, Notts, *b.* at Hackthorne, co. Lincoln, in Feb. 1739-40; *m.* 1st, 16 April, 1762, Anna-Maria, eldest dau. and co-heir of Vincent Amcotts, Esq. of Harrington and Aistrop, co. Lincoln, assumed in consequence the surname of Amcotts, and was created a Baronet in 1796. He had by her an only dau.,
Elizabeth, *m.* in 1788, to Sir John Ingilby, Bart. of Ripley.
Sir Wharton *m.* 2ndly, Amelia-Teresa Campbell, and by her had one dau.,
Sophia-Louisa, *m.* in 1826, to Matthew Wilson, Esq. of Eshton Hall, co. York.
Sir Wharton *d.* in 1808.
Alexander, of whom we treat.
Elizabeth, *m.* to Thomas Massingberd, Esq.

The 2nd son,

Alexander Emerson, Esq. of West Retford House, co. Notts, *b.* 1743; *m.* Susanna, 2nd dau. (and co-heiress, with her sister, Anne, wife of Major John Clutterbuck, Esq. of Warkworth, co. Northumberland) of Captain Patrick Lyon, of East Thetford, a descendant of the noble house of Strathmore, and left (with a dau., Harriet-Lyona, *m.* 1st, to Joseph Cavie, Esq., and 2ndly, to Colonel Campbell) a son and successor,

Alexander-Lyon Emerson, Esq., M.D., of West Retford House, Notts, and of Ulverscroft Abbey, co. Leicester, *b.* 10 May, 1770, who entered the army 5 March, 1795, and served throughout the campaigns in Holland, Egypt, Spain, Cape of Good Hope, &c. In 1817, he was one of the few promoted by the Prince Regent to the rank of deputy inspector of hospitals. Dr. Emerson *m.* Elizabeth, dau. of — Hunsdon, Esq. of Maldon, co. Essex, and has issue,

Alexander-Lyon, his heir.
William-Henry, of Cumberworth and Thorpe, co. Lincoln, an officer in the Cape mounted rifles. He entered the army, as ensign in the 10th foot, in 1842, and having obtained his lieutenancy in 1843, served through the campaign of the Sutledge, acting aide-de-camp to Brigadier Stracey, C.B., at Sobraon, and has received a medal and a clasp; *m.* in 1848, Flora-Brenda, dau. and co-heir of F.-D. Haynes, Esq. of Lonesome and Ashstead, co. Surrey, by Mary his wife, eldest surviving dau. of Sir Timothy Shelley, Bart. of Castle Goring.
Thomas-Wharton, of Cumberworth, co. Lincoln, and late of Pembroke College, Oxford, *m.* Mary, dau. of R. Corringham, Esq. of Misterton, Notts, and has a son.
Elizabeth, *m.* to Captain Tupman, R.N., of Reading, and *d.* in 1849, leaving three sons and one dau.
Julia. Isabella-Susanna. Anne-Louisa.

Dr. Emerson *d.* 24 July, 1834, was buried at Tunbridge Wells, and was *s.* by his eldest son, the present Rev. Alexander-Lyon Emerson, of Ulverscroft Abbey.

Seat—Ulverscroft Abbey, co. Leicester.

EMERY OF THE GRANGE, BANWELL.

Emery, George, Esq. of the Grange, Banwell, co. Somerset, a deputy-lieut. of that shire, and captain in the Dorset militia, *b.* in 1784; *m.* 1st, in 1805, Martha-Maria, dau. of John Marder, Esq., capt. R.N., and by her had issue,

I. Henderson-Finden, a magistrate for Somersetshire, *b.* in 1809.
II. Martha-Maria-Finden, *m.* to Herbert Williams, Esq. of Stinsford House, co. Dorset.

Mr. Emery *m.* 2ndly, in 1819, Leonora, dau. of Richard Bingham, Esq. of Bingham's Melcombe, colonel of the Dorset militia, but by her had no issue.

Lineage.—This family bears the arms that were confirmed or granted, 20 May, 1689, to Thomas Emery, of Little Badow, co. Essex, who came to England with William, Prince of Orange, 4 Nov. 1688, assisted at the coronation of that monarch the following year, and remained attached to his royal court for the remainder of his life. The late

John Emery, Esq., *m.* in 1772, Martha, dau. of Henry Gresley, Esq. of Bristol, (who claimed descent from the baronetical family of Gresley,) and had issue,

Henry-Gresley, M.D., inspector of military hospitals, deceased.
Thomas, capt. in the army, deceased.
George, now of the Grange.
Charles-Atwood, capt. Dorset militia.
Martha, *m.* to Charles Fowler, Esq.
Maria, *m.* to William Harrison, Esq.

Arms—Arg., three bars, nebulé, gu., in chief, as many torteaux.
Crest—A demi-horse, collared, issuing out of a mural crown.
Motto—Fidelis et suavis.
Seat—The Grange, Banwell, co. Somerset.

ENERY OF BALLYCONNELL.

Enery, William-Hamilton, Esq. of Ballyconnell House, co. Cavan, J.P. and D.L., *b.* 19 Sept. 1793; *m.* 9 Feb. 1839, Isabella-Alicia, dau. of Brook-Taylor Ottley, Esq. of Delaford, co. Dublin, and *d.* 20 Oct. 1854, leaving an only dau. and heir,

Constance-Isabella.

Mr. Enery served as high-sheriff in 1848.

Lineage.—The great-grandfather of the present representative of this respectable Irish family,

John Enery, Esq. of Bawnboy, co. Cavan, *m.* Rachel Holroyd, sister of Isaac Holroyd, Esq., father of John, first Lord Sheffield, and grandfather of the present peer, and by her was father of

John Enery, Esq. of Ballyconnell, who *m.* Margaret, dau. of Sir John-Charles Hamilton, Bart., and had (with two daus.) a son,

John Enery, Esq. of Ballyconnell, lieut.-col. Kilkenny Militia, who *m.* Sarah-Ainsworth Blunt, of Kilkenny, and had (with two sons, George and Joseph, both *d. unm.*), two other sons and two daus.,

William-Hamilton, of Ballyconnell House.
John, *m.* Miss Long, and *d.* leaving a son, Albert, dec.
Margaret-Rachel, *m.* to Major Arthur Helsham, of Kilkenny.
Sarah-Ainsworth, *m.* to Robert-William Story, capt. Royal Artillery.

Col. Enery *d.* 19 Sept. 1842.

Arms—Arg., an eagle, displayed.
Crest—A falcon, close, ppr.
Motto—Sans changer.
Seat—Ballyconnell House, Ballyconnell, co. Cavan.

ENNIS OF BALLINAHOWN.

ENNIS, JOHN, Esq. of Ballinahown, co. Westmeath, high-sheriff of that co. in 1837, and of the co. Dublin in 1849; m. in 1834, Anna-Maria, eldest dau. of David Henry, Esq., of the city of Dublin, and has issue,

I. JOHN-JAMES, b. in 1842.
I. Mary. II. Josephine. III. Elizabeth.

Mr. Ennis is Governor of the Bank of Ireland, and Chairman of the Midland Great Western Railway. He contested the county of Westmeath, unsuccessfully, in 1852, and the borough of Athlone in 1856.

Lineage.—The family of Ennis, originally from the county of Down, became established in the county of Meath a considerable time since. The late

ANDREW ENNIS, of Roebuck, Dublin, who was engaged extensively in commercial pursuits and realised a very large fortune, purchased, in 1800, the estate of Griffinstown, co. Westmeath, and subsequently made considerable additions to his landed property, by the acquisition of portions of the Rochfort and Malone estates, including Ballinahown, the seat of the Malones. Mr. Ennis married Miss M'Manus, and died in 1834, leaving issue,

JOHN, now of Ballinahown.
Ellen, m. Richard P. O'Reilly, Esq. of Dublin, and d. leaving issue.
Marianne, m. Edward Howley, Esq. of Belleek Castle, co Mayo, D L., and d. leaving issue.
Jane, m. Nicholas Balfe, Esq. of South Park, co. Roscommon, who d. 1856.
Alicia, m. John Reynolds Peyton, Esq., of Laheen, D.L., and d. leaving issue.

Town Residence—Merrion Square, Dublin.
Seat—Ballinahown, co. Westmeath.

ENSOR OF ROLLESBY HALL.

ENSOR, JOHN-MAPES-WEBB, Esq. of Rollesby Hall, co. Norfolk, lieut. 10th regt. of foot, b. 25 July, 1824.

Lineage.—THOMAS EDENSOR, Esq. of Cumberford, Staffordshire, m. Anne, sole dau. of Hopwas, of Hopwas, and was father of three sons, JOHN, his heir; Edward, of Pagets Bromley; and Humphrey: the eldest, JOHN EDENSORE, Esq. of Cumberford, m. the sole dau. and heir of Savage, and was father of THOMAS, of Cumberford, who m. Dorothea Cumberford, and was s. by his son, JOHN; GEORGE EDENSOR, b. in 1568, father, by his wife, E. Coleman, of JOHN EDENSOR, Esq. of Willencote, co. Warwick, who m. Henrietta Coleman, and their only son,

GEORGE ENSOR, Esq. of Willincote, m. Jane, dau. of Frances Saunders, Esq. of Swissin, co Northampton, and had one son,

EDWARD ENSOR, Esq. of Willincote, who m. Jane Darcy, and had issue,

JAMES, of Willencote, who m., and was father of Strong Ensor, who sold Willencote to Mr. Villers, of Atherston, and whose sole dau., Susan, m. — Paul, Esq.
JOB, whose line we treat of presently.
Edward, m., and had an only dau., Ann.

The 2nd son,

JOB ENSOR, Esq., m. Mary Hill, by whom he had, with a second son, George, (of Ardress, co. Armagh, who m. Sarah Clarke, and had issue two sons, I. George, who m. Ester Weld, of Dublin, and had issue two sons, George and Charles, and six daus.; and II. Col. Thomas, d. unm.,) an elder son,

JOHN ENSOR, Esq. of Dublin, who m. Elizabeth Sycan (born Waller), and left an only son,

JOHN ENSOR, Esq. of Rollesby Hall, J.P. and D.L. b. 4 Dec. 1773; m. 1st, 11 Aug. 1796, Amphillis, dau. and heir of Edmund Mapes, Esq. of Rollesby, and by her (who d. 28 April, 1830), had issue,

JOHN-MAPES, m. 8 Nov. 1823, Mary-Anne, dau. of Daniel Webb, Esq. of Worthing, co. Sussex, and d. in 1853, leaving issue two sons, JOHN-MAPES-WEBB, now of Rollesby Hall, and Charles-Peploe-Smith, with one dau., Mary-Anne.
Charles, Royal Eng., d. s. p.
Frederick, in holy orders, m. Mary-Anne Montague, of Ormsby, co. Norfolk, and has two daus., Louisa and Aurora.
Edmond, Clerk, m. Ellen Tompson, of Witchingham, co. Norfolk, and has issue.
Amphillis-Elizabeth-Anne.
Aurora-Sophia. Julia, deceased.
Anne-Georgiana-Matilda, deceased.

Mr. ENSOR m. 2ndly, in 1838, Florence-Agnes, dau. of Lieut.-Col. Cobbe, H.E.I.C.S., and has by her further issue, two daus.,

Florence-Georgiana. Elizabeth-Laura.

Arms—Quarterly: 1st and 4th, arg., a chev. between three horse-shoes, sa., for ENSOR; 2nd and 3rd, quarterly; 1st and 4th, sa., fesse, fusily, or, for MAPES; 3rd and 4th, barry nebulée of eight, or and sa., for BLUNT.
Crest—An unicorn's head, arg., horned and maned, or.
Seat—Rollesby Hall, co. Norfolk.

ENTWISLE OF FOXHOLES.

ENTWISLE, JOHN-SMITH, Esq. of Foxholes, and Castleton Hall, co. Lancaster, J.P. and D.L., b. 18 Sept. 1815; m. 18 May, 1843, Caroline, 2nd dau. of Robert-J.-J. Norreys, Esq. of Davy Hulme Hall, co. Lancaster, and has issue,

I. Caroline-Dorothea. Mary-Ellen.
III. Isabella-Margaret.

Mr. Entwisle was high-sheriff in 1849.

Lineage.—The family of Entwisle was long settled in the township of Entwisle, on the north-eastern extremity of the hundred of Salford; and Camden speaks of Entwisle Hall in his time as "a neat and elegant mansion," the residence of "noble proprietors of its own name." Of its distinguished members in early times was SIR BERTINE ENTWISELL, Knt., Viscount of Bricqbec, a gallant warrior of the martial times of HENRY V. and HENRY VI. He participated in the glory of Agincourt, and contributed by his valour to the conquest of France. Sir Bertine wedded Lucy, fifth dau. of Sir John Ashton, of Ashton, and relict of Sir Richard Byron, Knt., by whom he left a dau., Lucy, from whom the Northamptonshire Bradens descended.

ROBERT ENTWISLE, Esq. of Foxholes, b. in 1735, justice of the peace, d. unm. in 1787, when the estates passed to his kinsman,

JOHN MARKLAND, Esq., b. 21 Aug. 1744, son of John Markland, Esq. of Manchester, and grandson of John Markland, Esq. of Wigan, by Ellen Entwisle, his wife, whose father, Bertie Entwisle, vice-chancellor of the Duchy of Lancaster, was second son of JOHN ENTWISLE, Esq. of Foxholes, an utter barrister of the Middle Temple, living in 1665. Mr. Markland assumed, in consequence, the surname and arms of ENTWISLE. He m. 9 Oct. 1782, Ellen, dau. of Hugh Lyle, Esq. of Coleraine, and had issue,

JOHN, his heir.
Hugh, m. in 1824, Mary-Anne, dau. of T. Royds, Esq.
Robert, lieut.-col. of the Lancashire militia, b. in 1788.
Henry, d. unm. Philip-Bize, b. in 1790.
Bertin, b. in 1790, d leaving two daus.
Ellen, m. in 1804, to John-Gilbert Royds, Esq. of Brown Hill.
Elizabeth, m. in 1805, to Robert Peel, Esq. of Manchester.
Margaret. Mary, d. unm. in 1796.

The eldest son,

JOHN ENTWISLE, Esq. of Foxholes, M.P. for Rochdale, high-sheriff of Lancashire in 1824, b. 16 Aug. 1784, m. 14 May, 1812, Ellen, dau. and co-heir of Thomas Smith, Esq. of Castleton Hall, and dying 5 April, 1837, left (with two daus., Ellen-Matilda, m. to Sir Alexander Ramsay, Bt., and Augusta, m. 1842, to I. B. Mackinnon, Esq.), a son and heir, the present JOHN-SMITH ENTWISLE, Esq. of Foxholes.

Arms—Arg., on a bend, engrailed, sa., three mullets, of the first.
Crests—1st, a hand, fessewise, couped above the wrist, ppr., holding a fleur-de-lis, erect, or; 2nd, a dexter arm in armour, embowed, holding with the hand, by the hair, a Saracen's head, erased and affrontée, all ppr.
Motto—Par ce signe à Agincourt.
Seat—Foxholes.

ENYS OF ENYS.

ENYS, JOHN-SAMUEL, Esq. of Enys, co. Cornwall, J.P., high-sheriff in 1824, b. 21 Sept. 1796; m. 17 April, 1834, Catherine, eldest dau. of Davies Gilbert, Esq. of Tredrea and East Bourn.

Lineage.—This ancient family was seated at Enys in the time of EDWARD III., and from De Enys, the then proprietor, descended, in a direct male line,

LOUISA-ANNE ENYS (only dau. of Samuel Enys, Esq. of Enys, by Sarah, his wife, dau. of the Rev. Thomas Penrose, rector of Newbury; granddau. of John Enys, Esq. of Enys, by Lucy, his wife, dau. of Francis Bassett, Esq. of Tehidy, and great-granddau. of Samuel Enys, Esq. of Enys, by Dorothy, his wife, sister and co-heir of Sir William Willys, Bart. of Fen Ditton, co. Cambridge), became eventually heiress, in a direct line, of the family. She m. Samuel-Oliver Hunt, Esq. of Houndshill, Worcestershire, and had issue,

JOHN-SAMUEL, her heir.
Jane.
Frances-Anne, m. in 1828, to Otho Cooke, Esq.

Mrs. Hunt assumed, in 1813, her original family name of ENYS. Her only son is the present JOHN-SAMUEL ENYS, Esq. of Enys.

Arms—Quarterly: within a bordure, compony, or and sa., 1st and 4th, arg., three wyverns, volant, in pale, vert, a bordure, gu.; 2nd and 3rd, gu., on a fesse, embattled, counter-embattled, between three birds, arg., as many cinquefoils, sa.
Crest—Three white feathers, erect.
Motto—Serpentes velut et columbæ.
Seat—Enys, near Penryn.

ERLE-DRAX OF CHARBOROUGH.

See DRAX, p. 314.

ERRINGTON OF HIGH WARDEN.

ERRINGTON, JOHN, Esq. of High Warden, co. Northumberland, J.P. and D.L., *b.* 4 Oct. 1807; *m.* 1st, 24 Nov. 1836, Anne-Mary, 3rd dau. of Vincent-Henry Eyre, Esq. of Belgrave Square, London, and Highfield, co. Derby, and by her (who *d.* 22 Oct. 1842) had issue,

I. William-Valentine, *b.* 30 April, 1840; *d.* 9 March, 1852.
I. Anne-Lucy.

He *m.* 2ndly, 26 Oct. 1853, Caroline-Hope, eldest dau. of the Rev. William-J.-D. Waddilove, of Beacon Grange, Northumberland.

Lineage.—This family derives its name from Errington, a hamlet in the parish of St. John-Lee, and members of it were settled as freeholders in the contiguous parish of Warden at an early period. In 1206, Lord Adam de Tindale, Baron of Langley, had it entered upon the great Roll, that Elias of Erренton gave him thirty marks and a carucate of land in Alrewas. The Erringtons of Cockly Tower and Errington also resided at Wharnly, when they purchased that and other estates of Lord Burgh, in 1555.

About 1570-1580 lived NICHOLAS ERRINGTON, of Errington, who *m.* 1st, a dau. of Carnaby, of Beaufront; and 2ndly, Mary, dau. of Gavin Rutherford, Esq. from the 1st marriage sprang the family of Errington, of Beaufront; and from the 2nd, that of ERRINGTON OF WALWICK GRANGE.

WILLIAM ERRINGTON, Esq. of Walwick Grange, *s.* to the family estates of his grandfather, F. Errington, Esq., and of his kinsman, Edward Errington, of Walwick Grange. He was high-sheriff of Northumberland in 1738, and died while in that office (he was buried 9 March, 1738-9) having had, by Isabella his wife, dau. of John Bacon, Esq. of Staward (whom he *m.* 7 Oct. 1731; and who *m.* 2ndly, 2 Sept. 1740, the Rev. Richard Warge, vicar of Hartburn), two sons, Thomas, the elder, *b.* in 1732, *d.* the following year; and JOHN, his heir. The latter,

JOHN ERRINGTON, Esq. of Walwick Grange, and Chesters, built the mansion there. He *m.* 26 June, 1764, Mary, dau. of the Rev. Charles Stoddart, vicar of Chollerton; and *d.* in 1788 (buried 18 May), having had by her (who survived him, and was buried at Warden, 20 Jan. 1802) five sons and three daus., viz.,

WILLIAM, of whom hereafter.
Thomas, *b.* 5 Dec. 1766; *d. s. p.*
Charles, bapt. 13 July, 1770; a merchant in Newcastle; *m.* Isabella, dau. of the Rev. Thomas Bates, D.D., rector of Whalton; and *d.* at Lyons, in Aug. 1836, having had by her (who *d.* at Geneva, in 1828) an only child, Elizabeth.
John, bapt. in Feb. 1772; settled at Chester; *m.* and had issue one son, John, and two daus., Mary and Eleanor.
Ralph, bapt. 11 Dec. 1776; sometime in the Northumberland militia, also capt. in the 20th and 98th regiments. He afterwards entered into holy orders, and became curate of Ugham and of Widdrington. He *m.* Diana, dau. and co-heir of Cuthbert Watson, Esq. of Cowpen, and had issue five sons and eight daus., of whom Cuthbert-William, *d. unm.* in July, 1835; and Mary, *m.* 14 Oct. 1835, William Hogarth, Esq. of Clifton, co. Westmorland.
Anne, *m.* 17 June, 1784, the Rev. Oswald Head, vicar of Chollerton; who *d.* in 1820. She had issue.
Mary, *d. unm.* 9 July, 1829. Isabella.

The eldest son and heir,

WILLIAM ERRINGTON, Esq. of High Warden and Camden-place, Bath, barrister-at-law, *b.* 16 June, 1765, was, in 1796, of Headlam Hall, co. Durham. He *m.* Eleanor, dau. of Hugh O'Connor, of London, and by her (who *d.* Feb. 1842) left at his decease, Nov. 1826,

FREDERICK, his heir.
JOHN, successor to his brother, and present representative.
Eleanor, *d. unm.*
Mary, *d. unm.* in 1828.
Monica, *m.* in Sept 1838, to Valentine-O'Brien O'Connor, Esq. of Rockfield, near Dublin.

The elder son and heir,

FREDERICK ERRINGTON, Esq. of High Warden, *b.* in 1804; *d. unm.* 5 March, 1835, and was *s.* by his brother, the present JOHN ERRINGTON, Esq. of High Warden.

Arms—Arg., two bars, in chief, three escallops, az.
Crest—A cock, gu., combed and wattled, sa.
Seat—High Walden, near Hexham.

ESDAILE OF COTHELSTONE HOUSE.

ESDAILE, EDWARD-JEFFRIES, Esq. of Cothelstone House, co. Somerset, *b.* 6 April, 1785; *m.* 10 April, 1809, Eliza, only child of Clement Drake, Esq. of Taunton, and niece of the late Francis Drake, Esq., formerly minister-plenipotentiary at Munich, and has issue,

I. EDWARD-JEFFRIES, *b.* 28 June, 1813; *m.* 27 Sept. 1837, Ianthe, only child of the late Percy-Bysshe Shelley, Esq., by his first wife.
II. William-Clement-Drake, *b.* 14 Jan. 1820; *m.* 1846, Harriette, 2nd dau. of Cunliffe Lister-Kay, Esq., late M.P. for Bradford.
I. Emily-Frances, *m.* 31 Aug. 1847, to Plowden-Charles-Jennett Weston, Esq., only child of Marrion Weston, Esq. of Hagley, South Carolina, U.S.
II. Eliza-Drake, *m.* 9 March, 1837, to the Rev. W.-Wyndham Malet, son of the late Sir C.-W. Malet, Bart.

Mr. Esdaile, who is in the commission of the peace for Somersetshire, served the office of sheriff for that county in 1825.

Lineage.—At the revocation of the edict of Nantes, the ancestor of this family, descended from an honourable house, then represented by the Baron d'Estaile, being a Protestant, fled from France, and his property being confiscated in consequence, he lived and died in obscurity in England.

WILLIAM ESDAILE, Esq., an eminent banker in the city of London (3rd son of Sir James Esdaile, Knt. of Great Gains, Essex), *m.* Elizabeth, only child of Edward Jeffries, Esq., Treasurer of St. Thomas's Hospital, and *d.* 1837, having had two sons and four daus., viz.,

EDWARD-JEFFRIES, his heir.
Henry, *d. unm.*
Mary, *m.* to Dr. Richardson.
Louisa, *m.* to Robert Wirter, Esq.
Emma, *d. unm.*
Caroline, *m.* to Rees-Goring Thomas, Esq. of Llanon, in Carmarthenshire.

The elder son having inherited the estates of his maternal grandfather, Edward Jeffries, Esq., who *d.* 1814, is the present EDWARD JEFFRIES ESDAILE, Esq. of Cothelstone House.

Arms—Gu., a lion's head, erased, between three mullets, or.
Crest—A demi-lion, rampant, holding a mullet in his paws.
Seat—Cothelstone House, Taunton.

ESTCOURT OF ESTCOURT.

SOTHERON-ESTCOURT, THOMAS-HENRY-SUTTON, Esq. of Estcourt, co. Gloucester, and of Darrington Hall, co. York, J.P. and D.L., M.A. Oriel College, Oxford, and late M.P. for Devizes, *b.* 4 April, 1801; *m.* 21 Aug. 1830, Lucy-Sarah, only child of the late Frank Sotheron, Esq. of Kirklington, Notts, admiral of the Blue, and M.P. for Notts, and assumed,

17 July, 1839, the surname and arms of SOTHERON only. Subsequently, at the death of his father, he resumed his patronymic.

Lineage.—The family of ESTCOURT enjoys considerable estates and influence in the counties of Gloucester and Wilts, and the pedigree dates from Walter de la Estcourt, who died A.D. 1330, as appears by a deed still in the possession of the family. Since that time, the Estcourts have been seated on the same manor of Estcourt, near Tetbury.

MATTHEW ESTCOURT, Esq. of Cam, in Gloucestershire (great grandfather of the present proprietor), *m.* Esther Halling, and had, with four daus., as many sons, viz., Matthew, Thomas, Edward, and Edmund, all now deceased. The 2nd son,

THOMAS ESTCOURT, Esq., *m.* 6 Oct. 1774, the Hon. Jane Grimston, eldest dau. of James, second Viscount Grimston, by Mary, his wife, dau. of John-Askell Bucknall, Esq. of Oxney, in Hertfordshire, and had issue,

I. THOMAS-GRIMSTON-BUCKNALL, his heir.
II. Edmund-William, M.A., rector of Long Newnton, in Wiltshire, and of Shipton Moyne, Gloucestershire, *b.* 28 April, 1782; *m.* Bertha-Elizabeth, 2nd dau. of Thomas Wyatt, Esq. of Wargrave, in Berkshire, and has issue,
  1 Edward-Thomas.
  2 Edgar-Edmund.
  3 Matthew-Hale.
  4 Charles-Wyatt.
  5 Arthur-Harbottle.
  1 Mary-Jane.
I. Harriett-Jane-Bucknall, *d. unm.* 25 July, 1839.
II. Charlotte.

Mr. Estcourt *d.* 2 Dec. 1818, and was *s.* by his elder son,

THOMAS-GRIMSTON-BUCKNALL ESTCOURT, Esq., M.P., barrister-at-law, D.C.L. of Corpus Christi College, Oxford, and F.A.S., *b.* 3 Aug. 1775; *m.* 12 May, 1800, Eleanor 2nd dau. of James Sutton, Esq. of New Park, in Wiltshire, and had issue,

THOMAS-HENRY-SUTTON, now of Estcourt.
James-Bucknall, major-gen. in the army, and adjutant-gen. in the Crimea, *b.* 12 July, 1802, *m.* Caroline, dau. of the Right Hon. Reginald Pole-Carew, and *d.* 24 June, 1855.
Edmund-Hiley-Bucknall, M.A. of Merton College, Oxford, Rector of Eckington, *b.* 22 Nov. 1803, *m.* 15 April, 1830, Anne-Elizabeth, second dau. of Sir John-Lowther Johnstone, Bart. of Westerhall, in Dumfriesshire, and has three daus., viz., Charlotte-Eleanor, Jane, and Gertrude.
Walter-Grimston-Bucknall, comm. R.N., *b.* 16 May, 1807, *d.* on the coast of Africa 16 Sept. 1845.
William-John-Bucknall, B.A. in holy orders, *b.* 17 May, 1812, *m.* Mary, dau. of the Rev. John Drake.
Edward-Dugdale-Bucknall, barrister-at-law, *b.* 6 Feb. 1818.
Eleanor-Anne-Bucknall, *m.* to the Right Hon. H. Addington.
Georgiana-Charlotte, deceased.
Mary-Anne-Harriet-Bucknall.

Mr. Estcourt, a magistrate and deputy-lieutenant for the counties of Gloucester and Wilts, represented the borough of Devizes from Jan. 1805 to Feb. 1826, since which period he had a seat in parliament for the University of Oxford. He *d.* 26 July, 1853.

Arms—Erm., on a chief, indented, gu., three estoiles, or.
Crest—Out of a mural crown az., a demi-eagle with wings, displayed, ppr., beaked, or.
Seats—Estcourt, near Tetbury, and Darrington Hall, near Pontefract.

ETHELSTON OF WICKSTED HALL.

ETHELSTON, THE REV. CHARLES-WICKSTED, of co. Chester, Wicksted Hall, *m.* Anne, dau. and heir of Robert Peel, Esq. of Wallington Hall, co. Norfolk, brother of the 1st Sir Robert Peel, Bart., and has issue (*see* ETHELSTON-PEEL *of Bryn-y-pys*). Mr. Ethelston is a descendant of the ancient Saxon family of Ethelstone, which is traced in an ancient manuscript, No. 2042 Harleian MSS., British Museum, called "The Ethelestophylax," from the time of Athelstan. The estate of Wicksted Hall came to the family by the marriage of Mr. Ethelston's great-grandfather, SIMON ETHELSTON, Esq. of Malpas, with ELEANOR WICKSTED, heiress of that ancient family.

Arms—Az., on a pile between two cross crosslets in base, an eagle displayed purpure. Quartering; arg. on a bend, az. between three Cornish choughs, sa., beaked and legged gu., as many garbs, or, for WICKSTED.
Crest—A ram's head, couped, sa., charged with three cross-crosslets, or.
Motto—Dat et sumat Deus.
Seat—Wicksted Hall, Cheshire.

ETTRICK OF HIGH BARNES.

ETTRICK, ANTHONY, Esq. of High Barnes, co. Durham, J.P., *b.* 15 Sept. 1810; *s.* his father 18 Jan. 1847.

Lineage.—The first of this family on record,

ANTHONY ETTERICKE was of Barford or Berford, in the parish of Wimborn Minster, Dorset. He was born about the year 1504, and was captain of horse at the siege of Boulogne, when that place surrendered in 1544 to HENRY VIII. His grandson,

WILLIAM ETTRICKE, of Berford, *b.* in 1590, *m.* Anne, dau. of William Willis, of Pumphill, co. Dorset, and had (with two daus., one *m.* to —, Northover, of Somersetshire; the other to Sir William Cowthorp, of Ireland) three sons,

I. ANTHONY, of Holt Lodge, in the Forest, co. Dorset, an excellent antiquary and lawyer, *b.* in 1625, M.P. for Christchurch, Hants, in 1685, *m.* in 1650, Anne, dau. of the Rev. Edward Davenant, D.D. of Gillingham, co. Dorset, and grand-niece of John Davenant, Bishop of Salisbury, and had issue,
  1 WILLIAM, barrister-at-law, and M.P. for Christchurch from 1688 to 1714; *m.* 1st, Elizabeth, dau. of Sir Eden Bacon, Bart., by whom he had a dau., ELIZABETH, who *m.* Philip Boteler, Esq. of Woodhall, co. Herts, and 2ndly, Frances, dau. of Colonel Thomas Wyndham, of Witham, co. Somerset, by whom he had another dau., RACHEL, who *d. unm.* He *d.* 4 Dec. 1716.
  2 Edward *b.* in 1654, of London, *m.* and had issue long extinct.
II. Andrew, of Blandford Forum, or Sturminster, co. Dorset, *m.* Anne, dau. of Robert Barker, of Ashwell, in the same shire, and had two sons,
  Andrew and Robert, both in the royal navy, and both died issueless.
  He *d.* in 1679.
III. WALTER, of whose line we are about to treat.

William Ettricke *d.* in 1666. His younger son,

WALTER ETTRICKE, Esq. of Sunderland, *b.* 26 April, 1628, a zealous supporter of the royal cause. He was register of the Court of Admiralty in 1661. He *m.* in 1659, Margaret, dau. of William Sedgewick, Esq. of Elvet, co. Durham, and had six sons and five daus. He *d.* at Bath, 2 Aug. 1700, and was *s.* at High Barnes, by his second son,

ANTHONY ETTRICKE, Esq. of High Barnes, *b.* 16 Aug. 1663; *m.* 1st, Jane, dau. and heiress of Richard Starling, Esq., and great-niece of Sir Samuel Starling, Knt., alderman of London, by whom he had a dau., Elizabeth, *m.* 1st, to Musgrave Davison, Esq., and 2ndly, to Thomas Medlycott, Esq. of Venne, co. Somerset. He *m.* 2ndly, Elizabeth, dau. of Henry Coghill, Esq. of Aldenham, Herts. By this lady, who *m.* after his decease — Wittering, Esq., he had two sons and three daus. Anthony Ettricke *d.* in 1728, and was *s.* by his elder son,

WILLIAM ETTRICK, Esq. of High Barnes, *b.* 22 Dec. 1701, J.P. co. Durham, who *m.* in 1722, Isabella, dau. of William Langley, Esq. of Elwick, in Norfolk, grandson of Sir Roger Langley, Bart. of Sheriff Hutton Park, co. York, and had, with other issue,

WILLIAM, his heir.
Judith, *m.* 1st, to Mr. Woodward, of London, merchant, and 2ndly, to Hugh French, M.D.; *d.* in 1822.
Anne, *m.* to James Moor, Gent. of London, and *d.* 16 Sept. 1816.
Elizabeth, *m.* 1st to Edward Weddell, of Yarmouth, co. York, and 2ndly, to John Carter, Esq. of the same place.

William Ettrick *d.* in 1752, and was *s.* by his son,

WILLIAM ETTRICK, Esq. of High Barnes, *b.* in 1726, who *m.* in 1752, Catherine, dau. of Robert Wharton, Esq. of Old Park, co. Durham, and had by her (who *d.* in Nov. 1794) one son and one dau., viz.,

WILLIAM, his heir.
Catherine, *m.* William Budle, of Monkwearmouth and *d. s. p.* in 1821.

Mr. Ettrick *d.* 22 Feb. 1808, aged eighty-two, and was *s.* by his only son,

REV. WILLIAM ETTRICK, of High Barnes, *b.* 17 May, 1757, A.M., some time Fellow of University College, Oxford, rector of Toner's Piddle, and vicar of Aff Piddle, co. Dorset, *m.* Elizabeth, dau. of William Bishop, Esq. of Briants Piddle, and had issue,

WILLIAM, *b.* 3 July, 1801; *d.* Jan. 1838.
ANTHONY, now of High Barnes.
Walter, *b.* 24 Feb. 1812, *m.* Sophia-Cumberland, dau. of Capt. Edward Burt, R.N. of Bath, and has issue.
John, *b.* 18 April, 1814; *m.* 15 June, 1847, Sophia, dau. of the Rev. John-George Maddison, A.M. of Bath.
Elizabeth, *m.* to Lieut. Novosielski, R.N. of Bath.

Catherine, m. to Robert-Shank Atcheson, of Duke-street, Westminster.
Anne, b. 22 July, 1804, d. 20 May, 1818.
Isabella, m. in 1825, to Robert Horn, Esq. of Hunter's Hall, Bishopswearmouth.
Helen, m. 14 Aug. 1837, to Edward Webb, Esq. of Bath.
Mary, d. unm. 1 Aug. 1836.

Mr. Ettrick d. 18 Jan. 1847.

Arms—Arg., a lion rampant, and a chief, gu.
Crest—A demi-lion, rampant, gu., holding in the dexter paw a marshal's staff, sable, tipped at each end, or.
Seat—High Barnes.

EUSTACE OF BALTINGLASS.

EUSTACE, CHARLES-STANNARD, Esq. of Robertstown, co. Kildare, and Bally Doyle, co. Cork, heir male and recognized representative of the Viscounts Baltinglass, late a captain in the army; m. 8 April, 1843, Laura, dau. of Christopher-Thomas Tower, Esq. of Weald Hall, co. Essex, and by her (who d. in 1844) had one son, who d. in infancy. Captain Eustace s. his father 5 Jan. 1856.

In 1839, the late Rev. Charles Eustace having become male representative of the family, petitioned the crown that his right to the VISCOUNTCY of BALTINGLASS might be acknowledged: his petition was referred to the Attorney-General for Ireland, who, having investigated the case, made a report thereon to Government, concluding thus:—

"I am of opinion that the petitioner has shewn sufficient evidence of his right to the dignity of Viscount of Baltinglass, in case the attainder of James, the 3rd viscount, created by the act of Queen ELIZABETH, were reversed."

Lineage.—The family of Eustace, of ancient Norman descent, was established in Ireland by one of the companions in arms of HENRY II., by whom he was appointed governor of the county of Kildare. His descendant,

SIR ROWLAND EUSTACE, Knt. of Harristown, lord treasurer of Ireland, son of Sir Edward Eustace, Knt., lord deputy of Ireland to Richard, Duke of York, was created BARON PORTLESTER, in Meath, in 1454. He d. in 1496, and was s. by his nephew,

SIR THOMAS EUSTACE, Knt. of Harristown, created Baron of Kilcullen, co. Kildare, in 1541, and Viscount of Baltinglass, co. Wicklow, in 1542. His lordship made a settlement of all his estates upon the marriage of his son, SIR ROWLAND EUSTACE, 2nd Viscount, with Joan, dau. of James, Lord Dunboyne. The elder son of this marriage, JAMES EUSTACE, 3rd Viscount Baltinglass, having rebelled against the authority of Queen ELIZABETH, in 1558, by refusing to pay taxes unauthorized by the legislature, was attainted by an act of the parliament held in Ireland under the government of Sir John Perrott, in 1586, when the immense estates of the family were confiscated, and the title has since remained dormant. His lordship's brother, and eventual heir, the HON. WILLIAM EUSTACE (who had not been engaged in the rebellion), on the departure of Lord Baltinglass for Spain, retired with his family to England, and, in consequence of the edict of pardon and oblivion, published by King JAMES on his accession, together with the confirmatory acts of parliament of that and the subsequent reign, is recorded in the Heralds' College, London, as living as Viscount Baltinglass, in 1610. His only son by Margaret his wife, dau. of Ashe, of Great Forenass, co. Kildare, ROWLAND EUSTACE, m. Elizabeth Bigland, a Yorkshire lady, dau. of Mary Strickland, of Sizergh, one of "the Maries" residing with Mary Stuart at the time of her execution. By her he had two sons, of whom the elder, James, died in early youth, of the plague. The younger, RICHARD EUSTACE, became representative of the family. He served as Sovereign of Naas, and inherited the property of Ashe's Castle there, derived from his grandmother, Margaret Ashe. By Mary his wife, dau. of Sir William Forster, he was great-grandfather of

CHARLES EUSTACE, Esq. of Robertstown, co. Kildare, and of Corbally, Queen's County, a lieut.-general in the army, and member in the Irish parliament, only son of JOHN EUSTACE, Esq. of Naas, by Elizabeth his wife, dau. of Robert Greydon, Esq. of Russellstown. He m. in 1762, Alice, dau. of Oliver McCausland, Esq. of Stronorland, and had issue,

I. CHARLES, late representative, and male heir of the LORDS BALTINGLASS.
II. Oliver, cornet of horse, d. unm.
III. Henry, of Corbally, Queen's County, lieut.-general in the army, m. 1819, Henrietta, dau. of Peter, Count Dalton, and d. 5 Oct. 1844, leaving issue,
  1 Henry, of Corbally, Queen's County.
  2 Charles-Edward, late lieut. 46th regt.
  3 John-Rowland.
  1 Henrietta, d. young.
  2 Rosalie, m. 15 Aug. 1853, to the Marquis Ricci Paracciani of Rome.
IV. William-Cornwallis (Sir), lieut.-general in the army, K.C.H., C.B., of Sandford Hall, Essex, m. 1st, in 1809, Catherine-Frances, dau. of Lord Talbot of Malahide, by whom he has,
  1 Alexander-Talbot-Eustace-Malpas, m. Miss Georgiana Drummond, and has a son.
  1 Frances-Catherine-Elizabeth, m. 1st, in 1841, to Robert King, Esq. of Grosvenor Place; and 2ndly, to the Rev. Samuel Lloyd.
  2 Alicia Margaret-Maria, who d. unm. in 1840.

  Sir William m. 2ndly, Caroline-Margaret, dau. of John King, Esq., Under Secretary of State, and by her has two sons,
  1 John-Thomas. 2 Robert-Henry.

  He m. 3rdly, Emma, 2nd dau. and co-heir of Admiral Sir Eliab Harvey, of Chigwell, and has further issue one dau.,
  Emma-Louisa, m. to A. Miles Formby, Esq., late of the Carbineers.

  Sir William d. 9 Feb. 1855.
V. Alexander, captain of dragoons, killed at Vimiero.
VI. John Rowland (Sir), K.H., of Baltrasney, co. Kildare, major-gen. in the army, high-sheriff co. Kildare, 1848.
I. Elizabeth, m. to the Rev. Henry Johnson, of the family of Kilternon, co. Dublin.
II. Alicia, m. to Nicholas Barnewall, 14th Lord Trimlestown, but had no issue. She afterwards m. Lieut.-Gen. Sir Evan Lloyd, by whom she has a son and two daus. (*See* LLOYD *of Ferney Hall.*)
III. Mary-Anne, m. to Robert Shearman, Esq. of Grange, co. Kilkenny.

Lieut.-General Eustace d. in 1800, and was s. by his eldest son,

REV. CHARLES EUSTACE, of Robertstown, who m. in 1800, Cassandra, dau. and co-heir of John Stannard, Esq. of Bally Doyle, co. Cork, by whom he had,

CHARLES-STANNARD, now of Robertstown.
Alicia, m. to Robert Robertson, Esq. of Edinburgh.
Elizabeth, m. to Henry Leader, Esq. of Mount Leader, co. Cork.
Catherine, m. to H.-D. Arbuthnot, Esq., rear-adm. R.N.
Jane, m. to William-H. Connor, Esq., R.N., brother of Daniel Conner, Esq. of Ballybricken, co. Cork.

Arms—Or, a saltier, gu.
Crest—A stag, statant, between the horns a crucifix, all ppr.
Supporters—Two angels, ppr.
Motto—Cur me per sequeris?

EUSTACE OF CASTLEMORE.

EUSTACE, JAMES-HARDY, Esq. of Castlemore, co. Carlow, b. in 1787; m. March, 1826, Elizabeth Reed, and has one son,

I. HARDY, b. 13 Jan. 1827, m.

Captain Eustace, who s. his cousin 9 April, 1848, is a magistrate of the county of Carlow, and served the office of high-sheriff in 1835. He was formerly capt. 8th regt., and received a medal and clasp for services in the last war.

Lineage.—This family is a junior branch of the noble house of Baltinglass, deriving from Oliver Eustace, Esq., M.P. for Carlow, *temp* CHARLES I.; EDWARD EUSTACE, Esq. of Castlemore, living, at the close of the 17th century, m. (settl. dated 16 Feb. 1712) Bridget, dau. of Robert Longfield, Esq. of Kilbride, co. Meath, and had issue, JAMES, his heir; Robert, who m. Catherine Whelan (*see* EUSTACE *of Newstown*); William; Thomas; Maria, m. to Nathaniel Evans, Esq.; Anne, m. to Jacob Warren, Esq; and Bridget, m. to — M'Carthy, Esq. The eldest son and successor,

JAMES EUSTACE, Esq. of Castlemore, m. in 1743, Elizabeth only child and heir of John Hardy, Esq. of Kilballyhire, co. Carlow, and had issue,

I. EDWARD, his successor.
II. Hardy, of Kilballyhire, m. 1776, Susanna, dau. of Franks Bernard, Esq. and d. 22 Aug. 1820, having had,
  1. Hardy, of Hardy Mount, d. s. p.
  2. JAMES-HARDY, now of Castlemore.
  3. Thomas, d. 9 June, 1819.

1. Frances, m. to Oliver Moore, Esq.
2. Catherine, m. 1st to Francis Willet Hopkins Esq.; and, 2ndly, to Anthony Brabazon, Esq. of Mornington.
3. Elizabeth, m. 1803, James Eustace, Esq., J.P.
4. Bridget Longfield, m. to Edward Burton, Esq.
5. Susannah, m. to William Edmond Fitzgerald, Esq., late Major 82nd regt.

III. Elizabeth.

The eldest son and heir,

EDWARD EUSTACE, Esq. of Castlemore, m. 1765, Eleanor, dau. of Sir Richard Butler, Bart. of Ballintemple, co. Carlow, and by her had issue,

JAMES, his heir.
Richard, capt. in the 16th regt., d. in India, unm.
Nicholas, lieut.-col. of the 12th regt., d. unm. in India, in 1815.
Henrietta, m. to the Rev. John Digby, of Landenstown, co. Kildare.
Eleanor, m. to the Rev. J. McGhee. Dorothea.
Catharine, m. to Capt. William McPherson.
Alicia, d. unm. in 1840.
Melecina, m. to Thomas Talbot, Esq.

He d. 18 Oct. 1806, and was s. by his son,

MAJOR JAMES EUSTACE, of Castlemore, J.P., Major of the Roscommon militia, and high-sheriff of the co. of Carlow in 1813, b. in 1767; who m. 28 July, 1792, Margaret, dau. of J. Thewles, Esq. of Rookwood, co. Galway, and d. 9 April, 1848 (leaving a dau., Harriet), and was s. by his cousin, JAMES-HARDY EUSTACE, Esq. of Hardy Mount, the present proprietor of Castlemore.

Arms—Gu., a saltier, or.
Crest—A stag's head, caboshed, between the attires a crucifix, all ppr.
Motto—Soli Deo gloria.
Seat—Castlemore, co. Carlow.

EUSTACE OF NEWSTOWN.

EUSTACE, HARDY, Esq. of Newstown, co. Carlow, J.P., b. 8 Feb. 1812; m. 17 Aug. 1838, Bridget-Anne, only dau. of James Brown, Esq., late a major in the 103rd regt., by Catherine Swan his wife, and has issue,

I. JAMES, b. 29 June, 1839.
II. Robert, b. 17 July, 1840.
III. Edward, b. 23 Dec., 1841.
IV. Hardy, b. 2 Oct. 1843.
V. Thomas-Swan, b. 6 Jan., 1855.
I. Catherine-Elizabeth.
II. Elizabeth-Francis. III. Susanna.

Lineage.—JAMES EUSTACE, Esq., J.P., (son of Colonel Robert Eustace, by Catherine Whelan, his wife, and grandson of Edward Eustace, Esq. of Castlemore), m. 1803, Elizabeth, 3rd dau. of Major Eustace, J.P., of Kilballyhire, co. Carlow, and had issue,

HARDY.
Susanna, m. to Alexander Brenan, Esq., R.N.
Catherine, m. to the Rev. A.-A.-L.-D. Nickson.
Sarah.

Arms, Crest, and Motto, as the preceding family.
Seat—Newstown, co. Carlow.

EVANS OF TUDDENHAM.

EVANS, THOMAS-BROWNE, Esq. of North Tuddenham, co. Norfolk, and of Dean, Oxfordshire, b. 31 May, 1789; m. 4 July, 1814, Charlotte, dau. of Sir John Simeon, Bart., Senior Master of Chancery, of Grazeley, Berks, and has issue,

I. JOHN-ARTHUR, captain in the H.E.I. Co.'s service.
II. Francis-Edward, captain in H.M.'s 23rd Fusiliers.
III. Thomas-Henry, lieut. 4th light cavalry, Madras.
IV. Charles-Frederick, d. in July 1842.
V. Fitzwilliam. I. Harriett.
II. Charlotte. III. Louisa.
IV. Augusta. V. Mary.

Lineage.—The family of Evans is of Welsh extraction, and was originally seated in Carmarthenshire, whence a branch removed in the reign of JAMES I. to Ireland. Another scion,

THOMAS EVANS, settled at Bury St. Edmunds, Suffolk, about the year 1695. He m. in 1697, Hannah, dau. of Thomas Case, Gent. of Eton Bardolph, and was s. by his son,

THOMAS EVANS, Esq., barrister-at-law, and recorder of Bury St Edmunds, Suffolk. He m. in 1725, Mary, dau. of Edward Nightingale, Esq. of Kneesworth, Cambridgeshire, and had issue one son,

THOMAS EVANS, Esq., who m. Elizabeth, dau. and heiress of — Denny, Esq. of Eye, co. Suffolk, and left by her (who m. 2ndly, Edmund Jenny, Esq. of Bungay, Suffolk, a branch of the Jennys of Knodishall, Suffolk) a son and successor,

THOMAS-BROWNE EVANS, Esq., J.P. and D.L., who served as high-sheriff of Norfolk in 1795. He m. in 1787, Mary Hase, 4th dau. of Edward Hase, Esq., and Virtue his wife, of Sall House, co. Norfolk, and niece of Sir J. Lombe, Bart. of Great Melton, in the said county, and had issue,

I. THOMAS-BROWNE, now of Tuddenham.
II. Edward, in holy orders, rector of Eeswell, co. Suffolk, and of Eccles, co. Norfolk.
III. Henry, in holy orders, rector of Lyng and Swanton Abbotts, co. Norfolk, m. Sophia, dau. of Thomas Cubitt, Esq. of Honing Hall, Norfolk, and has issue,
1 Henry, in holy orders.
2 Thomas-Robert. 3 Edward. 4 Charles.
1 Catherine-Mary. 2 Mary-Jane.

Mr. Evans d. in 1827.

Arms—Arg., three boars' heads, couped, sa.
Seats—North Tuddenham, Norfolk; and Dean, co. Oxford.

EVANS OF EYTON.

EVANS, RICHARD-WEAVER, Esq. of Eyton Hall, co. Hereford, J.P. and D.L., s. his father in 1851; m. Eleanor, eldest dau. of the late Thos. Clutterbuck, Esq. of Bushey, Herts, and by her (who d. in 1833) has issue three sons,

I. RICHARD.
II. Henry-Charles. III. Edward-James.

Lineage.—WILLIAM EVANS, Esq. of Treveilir, sheriff in 1733, m. Margaret, eldest dau., by Dulcibella his wife, dau. of Henry Jones, Esq. of Llangard, of William Morgan, of Henblas, LL.B., chancellor of Bangor (3rd son of the Right Rev. Robert Morgan, bishop of Bangor in 1666, by Anne his wife, only child and heiress of William Lloyd, Esq. of Henblas, who was great-grandson of David ap Tydyr, of Sychnant, by Elizabeth his wife, dau. and heiress of Robert ap Ievan, of Henblas, co. Anglesey), and by this lady had issue,

CHARLES, of Treveiler and Henblas, high-sheriff 1752; who m. Elizabeth, dau. of Hugh Lewis, Esq. of Pont Newydd, and was father, with three sons, William, Charles, and John, all d. s. p., and two daus., Elizabeth and Mary, both d. unm., of another son, Hugh, who, by Elizabeth Furness his wife, had a son, the present Charles-Henry Evans, Esq. of Plas-Gwyn, Treveiler and Henblas, who m. Henrietta, dau. of the Very Rev. John Warren, late dean of Bangor, and had issue, Henry-John; Charles-Henry; and Henrietta-Dulcibella.
William, of Glenalow, who, by Jane his wife, had a son, William, who d. s. p.
RICHARD, of whom presently.
Dulcibella, m. to the Rev. H. Rowlands, grandson of the author of "Mona Antiqua," and had issue.

The youngest son,

THE REV. RICHARD EVANS, prebendary of Bangor, and rector of Kingsland, m. Jane, only dau. of the Rev. Robert Lloyd, of Cefn, by Susannah his wife, dau. of — Butler, Esq. of Llysvaen, co. Carnarvon (and granddau. of T. Lloyd, Esq. of Cefn, co. Denbigh, by Anne his wife, 2nd dau. of the Right Rev. Robert Morgan, bishop of Bangor, and Anne Lloyd his wife), and had issue,

Richard-Davies, d. in 1821. Robert, d. in infancy.
William, in holy orders, rector of Kingsland, and vicar of Vow Church, m. Margaret-Leaford, dau. of Anthony Goodwyn, Esq., M.D., of Wirksworth, co. Derby, and had issue, Richard-Davies, m. Caroline, dau. of the Rev. Robert-Fitzwilliam Hallifax, A.M., only son of Samuel Hallifax, Bishop of St. Asaph; William-Rowland; Margaret, m. to the Rev. Philip Whitcombe, and d. leaving issue; Jane, d. unm.
EDWARD, of Eyton Hall.

The Rev. Mr. Evans d. in 1797. His youngest son,

EDWARD EVANS, Esq. of Eyton Hall, J.P. and D.L., recorder of Leominster, m. Anne, dau. and heir of John Weaver, Esq. of Eyton, co. Hereford, and d. in 1851, leaving a dau., Jane, m. to the Rev. Edward-Richard Benyon, of Culford Hall, co. Suffolk, and two sons, RICHARD-WEAVER, now of Eyton Hall; and Edward-Charles, in holy orders, who m. Frances-Mary, dau. of Sir John Peyton, Bart., and has issue.

Seat—Eyton Hall, co. Hereford.

EVANS OF THE HILL COURT.

See POWER OF THE HILL COURT.

EVANS OF SUFTON COURT.

EVANS, THOMAS, of Sufton Court, co. Hereford, and of the city of Hereford, Esq., a D.L. for Herefordshire, *b.* 12 Mar. 1804; *m.* 1st, 23 Feb. 1830, Mary, only child and heiress of John Rogers, Esq., citizen and alderman of Hereford, and by her (who *d.* 29 Dec. 1849) had issue,

I. Charles-Rogers, *b.* 14 July, 1838; *d.* 27 Nov. 1839.
I. Elizabeth-Jane, *m.* 11 Sept. 1855, to the Rev. Henry Browne, M.A., rector of Eastham, co. Worcester.
II. Mary-Harriet, *d. unm.* 24 Jan. 1856.
III. Frances, *d.* young.
IV. Emily, *d.* young.
V. Sarah-Louisa.
VI. Bertha-Ellen, *d.* young.

He *m.* 2ndly, 16 Nov. 1852, Harriett, 5th, but 3rd surviving, dau. of Richard Webb, Esq. of Donnington Hall, co. Hereford, and has a dau.:

Harriett-Abiah.

Lineage.—The paternal ancestors of Mr. Evans are descended from an ancient family, proprietors of estates in Wales, and his maternal ancestors for several generations from ecclesiastics of the diocese and Cathedral Church of Hereford.

THE REV. MORGAN EVANS, B.C.L., *b.* 1664, was rector of Richards Castle, near Ludlow (1696), vicar of Weobly (1704), vicar of Newland with Coleford and Breaham, Gloucestershire (1710), prebendary of St. Dubritius, in Llandaff Cathedral (1713), and Chancellor of Llandaff (1718), was a magistrate for the county of Hereford, and *m.* Frances Sabine, dau. of William Sabine, Esq. of Kington, in 1694; and he (*M. E.*) was cousin and legatee named in the will of the Right Rev. John Tyler, D.D. (who was dean of Hereford (1692) and also (1706), bishop of Llandaff), and *d.* 20 March, 1736, having had issue,

John, *b.* 27 Sept. 1695; M.A., Fellow of Oriel College, Oxford, archdeacon of Llandaff. and one of the canons residentiary of Hereford Cathedral, prebendary of Warham, in the said cathedral, and rector of the 2nd portion in the Church of Bromyard, Hereford, named in the will of John Tyler, D.D., bishop of Llandaff; *d.* 23 March, 1748, and was *s.* by his son, John Evans, Clerk, M.A., prebendary of Nonnington, and canon-residentiary of Hereford Cathedral, vicar of Fownhope, co. Hereford, and vicar of Lidney, co. Gloucester, *b.* 2 Aug. 1725, and *d.* 6 April, 1783, and this, the eldest branch of the family, is now (1856) represented by THOMAS EVANS, Esq., M.D. of Gloucester.
Morgan, *d.* young.
Elizabeth, *m.* Rev. Thomas Hill, rector of Stanton, in the Forest of Dean.
Margaret, *m.* Rev. William Price, M.A., rector of Bishopstone, co. Glamorgan.
Frances, *m.* Rev. Joseph Guest, M.A., vicar of Stanton-upon-Arrow.
Sarah, *m.* Rev. Thomas Willym, M.A., rector of Eaton, bishop and prebendary of Hereford Cathedral, by whom she had issue, and is now represented by George Willym, Esq., M.A., of Eaton Bishop, co. Hereford.
Jane, *m.* Rev. Wm. Davies, M.A., rector of Stanton-upon-Wye.
Esther, *d. unm.*, ætat 17.

THOMAS, *b.* 1708, *d.* 27 March, 1767, was M.A. and prebendary of Hereford Cathedral, sometime vicar of Dilwyn, of King's Pyon, of Weobly, and of Bromyard, all in the co. of Hereford and also in the commission of the peace for the co. of Hereford, *m.* 25 Dec. 1732, his cousin, Jane Tyler (dau. of the Rev. William Tyler vicar of Dilwyn, and kinswoman of Robert Southey, poet laureate; also sister and legatee in the will of her brother, John Tyler, Esq. of Dilwyn, who was high-sheriff of Herefordshire in 1729), by whom she had issue. Elizabeth Tyler, another sister, *m.* the Rev. Lacon Lambe, vicar of Caerleon, co. Monmouth. John Evans, the youngest son of Thomas and Jane Evans, *b.* 18 May, 1743, *d.* 19 Feb. 1795, at Lucca, in Jamaica, and is now represented by Lieut. John Evans, R.N., of Bristol; and

THE REV. THOMAS EVANS, A.M., the eldest surviving son, *b.* 12 Sept. 1741, was vicar of King's Pyon, of Birley, and of Yasor, and rector of Bishopstone, co. Hereford, and also a magistrate of that county, and sometime of Watford, Herts, *m.* Feb. 1768. Sarah, only dau. and heir of Edward Finch, of Watford, Esq., who *d.* 20 Feb. 1816, and had issue, 1 THOMAS; 2 Edward, a captain in the army, *b.* 7 Feb. 1774, *d. unm.* 2 July, 1853; 3 John-Finch, *b.* 3 April, 1781; 1 Anne, *d.* unmarried 22 February, 1836; 2 Sarah; 3 Harriot, *m.* 29 May, 1813, Richard Underwood, 2nd son of the Rev. Richard Underwood, rector of St. John and St. Nicholas, Hereford, by whom she has issue two sons and a dau. The eldest son,

THOMAS EVANS, Esq., *b.* 25 April, 1772, *d.* 1 May, 1819, was treasurer of the co. of Hereford, *m.* 15 Oct. 1801, Mary-Frances, only dau. of the Rev. Thomas Watkins, clerk, of Pembroke College, Oxford, prebendary of Warham, in the Cathedral Church of Hereford, rector of Weston-under-Penyard, co. Hereford, whose only sister, Frances, *m.* the Rev. Thomas Ireland, D.D., prebendary of Wells, and rector of Christ Church, Bristol; a deputy-lieut. of the cos. of Somerset and Gloucester, and had issue one son, the Rev. Thomas-Rickards Ireland, since deceased. The Rev. Thomas Watkins and Mrs. Ireland were the only children of the Rev. Thomas Watkins, clerk, LL.B., of Brasenose College, Oxford, and successively rector of Knill, Byton, Tretyre, and Michaelchurch, and vicar of Dewsall, with the Chapel of Callow annexed, all in the co. of Hereford, *b.* 30 Sept. 1687, and *d.* 18 May, 1740, by Frances his wife, who he *m.* Oct. 1734; she was Frances Rickards, dau. of Peter Rickards,* Esq. of Enjobb or Evenjobb, co. Radnor; and the last-named Thomas Watkins, clerk, was only child of the Rev. Thomas Watkins, clerk, rector of Ashton, co. Hereford, to which he was instituted 19 May, 1677, and *m.* Ann, dau. of Richard Hoskins, Esq. of Aymestry, co. Hereford. The said Thomas and Mary-Frances Evans had issue,

THOMAS, present representative.
Edward, *b.* 23 Oct. 1805. *d. unm.* 3 May, 1856.
John, *b.* 7 April, 1807.
Morgan, *b.* 24 April, 1814.
Charles, *b.* 29 May, 1818; *m.* 8 Aug 1844, Henrietta, dau. of William Corles, Esq., a captain in the army.
Mary, *m.* 6 July, 1829, Thomas Jay, Esq. of Derndale, co. Hereford, deceased (who *s.* his father, Thomas Jay, Esq. of Derndale, high-sheriff of Herefordshire 1812), and has issue a son and a dau.
Harriett-Frances, *m.* 22 May, 1849, Rev. Edward Herbert, vicar of Killarney, co. Kerry, Ireland, son of Rev. John Herbert, vicar of Ledbury, co. Hereford.
Jane-Anne.
Sarah, *d.* young
Sarah-Emily.
Thomasine-Elizabeth, *m.* 15 June, 1852, the Rev. William-Henry Smythe, clerk, Market Bosworth, co. Leicester, only son of — Smythe, Esq., captain in the army.

Arms—Quarterly: 1st and 4th, per fesse, nebuly, ermine, and sable, three boars' heads, in chief, and one in base, erased, counterchanged, for EVANS; 2nd and 3rd, arg., two chevronels, and in chief three gryphons, passant, az., for FINCH.

Crest—Lion rampant, regardant, bendy of six, ermine and sable, supporting a tilting-spear, erect, ppr., enfiled, with a boars' head- erased, sa.

Motto—Libertas.

Residence—Sufton Court, Herefordshire.

EVANS OF ALLESTREE HALL.

EVANS, THOMAS-WILLIAM, Esq. of Allestree Hall, co. Derby, J.P. and D.L., *b.* 15 April, 1821; *m.* 21 May, 1846, Mary, eldest dau. of Thomas-John Gisborne, Esq. of Holm Hall, Bakewell.

---

* Mr. Evans is of founder's kin to All Souls, Oxford, and (through Sir Perceval Willoughby, after named,) is of royal descent from the Plantagenets.

Thus: Beatrice Chicheley, dau. of John Chicheley, Chamberlain of London, *b.* in 1425, *m.* to Sir Wm. Peche, Knt. of Lullingston, and had a dau. Elizabeth, wife of John Hart, Esq. of the Middle Temple, and mother of Sir Perceval Hart, of Lullingston, chief sewer and knight-harbinger to Henry VIII, who *m.* Frediswide, dau. and co heir of John Lord Bray, and had a daughter, Catherine, who was *m.* to Thomas Willoughby, Esq. of Blore Place, and left a son, Sir Perceval Willoughby, Knt.; father of Theodosia, wife of Rowland Mynors, Esq. of Treago, who *d.* 1651—

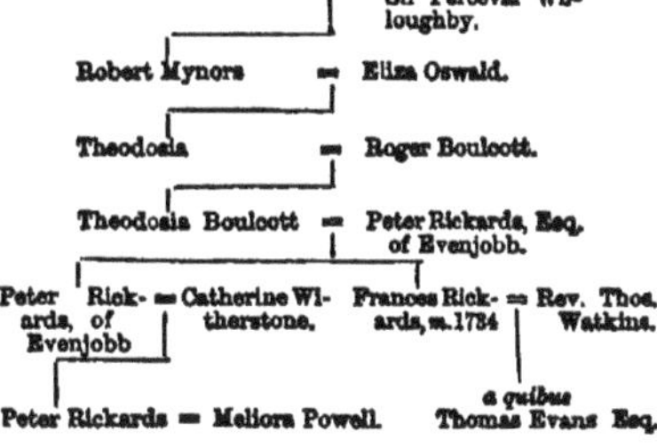

Lineage.—EDMUND EVANS, Esq. of Upper Bonsall, co. Derby, *b.* in 1690, *m.* Rebecca, dau. of Thomas Gell, Esq. of Middleton by Worksworth, and *d.* 25 Dec. 1746, leaving issue,

EDMUND, his heir, in holy orders, M.A., of Mayfield, co. Stafford, who *m.* Sarah, only dau. of William Greaves, Esq. of Mayfield Hall; and *d.* in 1790, leaving (with a dau., Elizabeth, *m.* to — Godwyn, Esq.) a son and heir, the REV. WILLIAM EVANS, of Mayfield, who *m.* Elizabeth, dau. and heir of John Spencer, Esq. of Wyaston, and had issue, a dau., Sarah, who *m.* William Greaves, Esq. of Mayfield Hall.
THOMAS, of whom presently.
George, of Cromford, who *m.* Anne, dau. of Peter Nightingale, Esq. of Lea; and *d.* 28 March, 1808, leaving a dau., Mary, *m.* to William Shore, Esq. of Tapton Hall, co. York.
Henry, of Caldwell, co. Derby, who *m.* Martha, dau. of George Wood, Esq. of Swanwick, and had a dau., Anne, *m.* to Edward Riley, Esq. of Bath.
Hannah, *m.* to the Rev. Anthony Carr, M.A., vicar of Alfreton and Snelston.

The 2nd son,

THOMAS EVANS, Esq. of Derby, for many years treasurer of the county, *m.* 1st, Sarah, dau. of William Evans, Esq. of Derby, and had issue,

WILLIAM, his heir, of whom presently.
Edmund, of Yeldersley House, who *m.* Dorothy, dau. of — Coles, Esq.; and *d.* 1 Oct. 1824, leaving two daus., Sarah, deceased; and Elizabeth, wife of John Harrison, Esq. of Snelston.
Sarah, *m.* to Charles Upton, Esq.; and *d.* 4 Dec. 1814.

Mr. Evans *m.* 2ndly, Barbara, dau. of — Stubbs, Esq. of Ranton Abbey, co. Stafford, and by her had further issue,

Walter, of Darley Abbey, lord of the manor of Alsop-le-Dale, founder of Darley Church and free schools; who *m.* Elizabeth, dau. of Jedediah Strutt, Esq., and widow of William Evans, Esq.
Barbara, *m.* to William Strutt, Esq., F.R.S.

The eldest son,

WILLIAM EVANS, Esq. of Darley, *m.* 1785, Elizabeth, dau. of Jedediah Strutt, Esq. of Belpar, and by her, who *m.* 2ndly, in 1798, Walter Evans, Esq. of Darley Abbey, and *d.* March, 1836, had issue,

WILLIAM, his heir.
George, *b.* 1789; *d.* 29 May, 1804.
Thomas, *b.* 1795; *d.* 4 April, 1797.
Elizabeth. Frances.
Ellen, *m.* 3 April, 1822, to the Rev. John-Edmund Carr, of St. John's College, Cambridge.

Mr. Evans *d.* 18 March, 1796, and was *s.* by his son,

WILLIAM EVANS, Esq. of Allestree Hall, co. Derby, J.P. and D.L., high-sheriff 1829, and formerly M.P., for 16 years, for that shire, *b.* 17 Jan. 1788; *m.* 31 July, 1820, Mary, dau. of the Rev. Thomas Gisborne, of Yoxall Lodge, co. Stafford, prebendary of Durham, and *d.* 8 April, 1856, leaving a son and heir, the present THOMAS-WILLIAM EVANS, Esq. of Allestree Hall.

Arms—Quarterly: 1st and 4th, gyronny of eight, arg. and vert, a lion, rampant, guardant, or, for EVANS; 2nd and 3rd, per bend, indented, arg. and gu., two lions' heads, erased, counterchanged, ducally crowned, or.
Crest—In a charger, a boar's head, erased, arg.
Seat—Allestree Hall, Derby.

EVANS OF PORTRANE.

EVANS, JOSHUA, Esq., one of the Commissioners of the Court of Bankruptcy, *s.* his brother 2 July, 1842; *m.* Eleanor, only child of Robert Harrison, Esq.

Lineage.—THE RIGHT HON. GEORGE EVANS, of Caherass and Bulgaden Hall, co. Limerick, M.P. (son and heir of Colonel George Evans, of Ballygrenane Castle, M.P., and grandson of John Evans, Esq., who settled in Ireland), *m.* 1679, Mary, dau. of John Eyre, Esq. of Eyre Court Castle, co. Galway, M.P., and *d.* 1720, having had, with seven daus., three sons, viz.,

I. GEORGE, created, *vitâ patris*, BARON CARBERY, with remainder to the male issue of his father: he *m.* in 1703, Anne, dau. and co-heir of William Stafford, Esq., of Blatherwyck, and *d.* 1749, leaving issue,
1 GEORGE, 2nd Lord Carbery, whose male line is EXTINCT.
2 John, of Bulgaden Hall, *m.* in 1741, Grace, only dau. and heir of Sir Ralph Freke, Bart., and left at his decease, in 1758 (with four daus., viz., 1 Grace, *m.* to R. Baldwin, Esq.; 2 Anne, *m.* to W. Putland, Esq., grandfather by her of Christie-Annette-Campbell, wife of Edward Hayward, Esq., barrister-at-law; 3 Catherine, *m.* to G. Putland, Esq.; and 4 Jane, *m.* to R. Grace, Esq.) five sons, of whom the 2nd, Sir John Evans Freke, Bart., was grandfather of the present Lord Carbery.

II. EYRE, of Portrane, of whom we treat.
III. Thomas, of Miltown Castle (*see* EVANS *of Ashhill Towers*).

The 2nd son,

EYRE EVANS, Esq. of Portrahern (now Portrane), M.P. for co. Limerick 1717, *m.* Sarah, 2nd dau. and co-heiress (with her sister, Mrs. Waller, of Castletown) of Thomas Dixon, Esq. of Ballylackin, co. Cork (by Elizabeth, only dau. and heiress of Edward Bolton, Esq. of Clonrushe, Queen's County), and had six sons, who all *d. s. p.* except the 4th; and three daus., of whom the youngest, Elizabeth, the wife of William Evans, Esq. of Ardreigh, co. Kildare, left issue. The 4th son,

HAMPDEN EVANS, Esq. of Portrane, an officer in the army, *s.* his eldest brother, George Evans, Esq., M.P. for the Queen's County. He *m.* Jan. 1769, Margaret, dau. of Joshua Davies, Esq., and had,

GEORGE, his heir. JOSHUA.
Eyre-Dixon, of Liverpool, *m.* and has issue.
Mary (widow of Gen. William Lawless, of the French service), *d.* Aug. 1854.
Anne-Dorothea, widow of her cousin, George Putland, Esq. of Bray Head, co. Wicklow, eldest son of the late George Putland, Esq., by Catherine, third dau. of the Hon. John Evans.
Sydney-Elizabeth, *m.* to the Rev. Thomas Acton, of West Acton, co. Wicklow, who *d.* 12 Aug. 1846.

Mr. Evans *d.* 22 April, 1820, and was *s.* by his eldest son,

THE RIGHT HON. GEORGE EVANS, of Portrane, M.P., co. Dublin, *m.* 21 Aug. 1805, Sophia, only dau. of the late Right Hon. Sir John Parnell, Bart. of Rathleague, Queen's County, sometime Chancellor of the Exchequer in Ireland, but had no issue. He *d.* 2 July, 1842.

Arms—Arg., three boars' heads couped, sable, quartering DIXON and BOLTON.
Crest—A demi-lion, rampant, regardant, or, holding between its paws a boar's head, couped, sa.
Seat—Portrane, near Swords, co. Dublin.

EVANS OF ASH HILL AND MILTOWN CASTLE.

EVANS, ELYSTAN-EYRE, Esq. of Ash Hill Towers, co. Limerick, *b.* 23 June, 1845; *s.* his grandfather.

Lineage.—This is a younger branch of the noble house of Carbery, originally of Welsh extraction, claiming descent from Elystan Glodrydd, Prince of Fferlys.

THOMAS EVANS, Esq. of Miltown Castle, co. Cork, M.P. for Castle Martyr, brother of George, 1st Lord Carbery, and 3rd son of the Right Hon. George Evans, of Caherass and Bulgaden Hall, co. Limerick, by Mary his wife, dau. of John Eyre, Esq. of Eyre Court Castle, co. Galway, M.P., *m.* in 1721, Mary, dau. of John Waller, Esq. of Castletown, co. Limerick, governor of Kinsale (grandson of Sir Hardress Waller, the celebrated parliamentary general) by whom (who *d.* at Timoleague, co. Cork, in 1762, aged 74) he had issue,

EYRE, his successor.
Thomas-Waller, in holy orders, rector of Dunmanway, co. Cork. (*See* D'ARCY EVANS *of Knockaderry.*)
John, an officer in the army, on active service during the American war, *m.* Catherine Gookin, widow of J. Harris, Esq., but *d.* without issue.
Mary, *m.* in 1753, to George Bruce, Esq., eldest son of the Very Rev. Jonathan Bruce, D.D., dean of Kilfenora, and *d.* in Feb. 1799.
Dorothy, *m.* to Thomas Lucas, Esq. of Richfordstown, co. Cork.

Mr. Evans *d.* 15 Sept. 1758, and was *s.* by his eldest son,

EYRE EVANS, Esq. of Miltown Castle. This gentleman *m.* 16 July, 1757, Mary, only child and sole heiress of Thomas Williams, Esq. of Ringawny, in the co. of Longford (only son of Major Charles Williams, the first of the family who settled in Ireland, by Mary Rose his wife, sister of the Right Hon. Henry Rose, lord chief justice of the King's Bench), and by her, who *d.* 29 Nov. 1825, aged 86, had issue,

Mary, *m.* 17 April, 1781, to her first cousin, the Rev. Jonathan Bruce, of Miltown, co. Cork, and *d.* 9 Feb. 1837.
Elizabeth, *d. unm.* in July, 1785.
Abigail, *m.* 6 July, 1796, to the Rev. William Stopford, of Abbeville, co. Cork, grandson of the Right Rev. James Stopford, D.D., Bishop of Cloyne, and Anne his wife, sister of the first Earl of Courtown: she *d.* 28 June, 1853.
Katherine, *m.* in 1792, to Thomas Lloyd, Esq. of Beechmount, M.P. co. Limerick: she *d.* 14 Feb. 1848.

Mr. Evans *d.* 5 April, 1773, leaving his wife *enceinte*, who gave birth, 28 May following, to an only son,

EYRE EVANS, Esq. of Miltown Castle and Ashhill Towers, *b.* 28 May, 1773; *m.* 20 March, 1805, Anna, eldest dau. of the late Robert Maunsell, Esq. of Limerick, formerly of Bumbo

House, in the East Indies, and member of the Supreme Council at Madras, and had issue,

I. EYRE, *b.* 5 May, 1806, *m.* at Genoa, 6 Dec. 1837, Hon. Sophia Crofton, sister of Edward, present Lord Crofton, and *d.* 17 July, 1852, leaving issue,
 1 ELYSTAN-EYRE, now of Ashhill Towers.
 2 St. George-Frederick-William, *b.* 28 Aug. 1847.
 1 Louisa-Charlotte-Georgiana.
 2 Anna-Caroline.
 3 Sophia-Helen-Augusta.

II. Robert-Maunsell, *b.* 4 May, 1808, in holy orders, *m.* 6 Feb. 1835, Deborah, 3rd dau. of William Casaubon Purdon, Esq. of Tinnerana, co. Clare.

III. George-Thomas, *b.* 17 Dec. 1809, late captain in the 74th regiment, *m.* 19 Jan. 1841, Louisa-Barbara, second dau. of Trevor Corry, Esq. of Newry, co Down, and has Eyre-Frederick-Fitz-George, *b.* 28 Feb. 1842, Trevor-Corry, and other issue.

IV. Thomas-Williams, *b.* 6 March, 1815, capt. 74th regt., *m.* 12 Aug. 1851, Helen-Elizabeth, 4th dau. and co-heir of the Rev. David Stewart Moncrieffe, rector of Loxton, co. Somerset, and has issue,
 1 Stewart-Eyre, *b.* 24 May, 1852.
 1 Annie-Moncrieffe.

V. John-Freke, *b.* 6 Feb. 1817, barrister-at-law, *m.* 27 May, 1851, Julia-Bruce, 2nd dau. and co-heir of the Rev. David Stewart Moncrieffe, and has a dau. Isabel-Freke.

VI. Henry-Frederick, late lieut. 21st Fusiliers, *b.* 12 April, 1821, *m.* 27 May, 1851, Sarah-Anne, youngest dau. and co-heir of the Rev. David Stewart Moncrieffe, and has
 1 Caroline-Susan-Moncrieffe. 2 Helen-Frederica.

I. Anna-Maria-Stone, *m.* 3 Feb. 1836, to the Rev. Robert-Hedges Maunsell Eyre, of Galway, eldest son of the late Richard and Lady Catherine Maunsell.

II. Caroline-Louisa, *m.* 6 April, 1841, to the Hon. James Ogilvie Grant, 2nd son of Francis-William, 6th Earl of Seafield.

III. Elizabeth.

Mr. Evans served as high-sheriff, co. Limerick, in 1810; he *d.* in 1855.

Arms—Quarterly: 1st and 4th, arg., three boars' heads, couped, sa., for EVANS; 2nd, gules, a lion, rampant, within a bordure, or, for WILLIAMS; 3rd, or, a lion, rampant, regardant, sa., for MORRICE.
Crest—A demi-lion regardant, or, holding between his paws a boar's head, couped, sa.
Motto—Libertas.
Seats—Ashhill Towers, near Kilmallock, co. Limerick; Miltown Castle, co. Cork.

EVANS OF KNOCKADERRY HOUSE.

D'ARCY-EVANS, THOMAS, Esq. of Knockaderry House, co. Limerick, J.P., *b.* 12 March, 1808; *m.* 21 May, 1835, Thomasina-Eliza, youngest dau. and co-heir of John-Boles Reeves, Esq. of Belfort, co. Cork, and has had issue,

I. Thomas *b.* 19 Feb. 1836; *d.* 25 July, 1855.
II. EYRE-GEORGE-ELYSTAN, *b.* 26 Feb. 1837.
I. Anna-Maria. II. Thomasina-Mary.
III. Catherine-Sophia.

Lineage.—THE REV. THOMAS-WALLER EVANS, rector of Dunmanway, co. Cork (2nd son of Thomas Evans, Esq. of Miltown Castle, M.P. for Castlemartyr, and brother of the 1st Lord Carbery, by Mary, dau. of John Waller, Esq. of Castletown, co. Limerick, governor of Kinsale, *temp.* Queen ANNE) *m.* 21 April 1768, Catherine, only dau and heir of James Conyers D'Arcy, Esq. of Knockaderry House, co. Limerick, by whom (who *d.* 13 April, 1804) he had issue,

 THOMAS, his heir.
 JAMES, successor to his brother.
 Eyre, *m* 10 May, 1821, Elizabeth, eldest dau. of Thomas Austin, Esq., and *d.* 14 Nov. 1847, leaving issue, Thomas (who *m.* his cousin Emily, dau. of James D'Arcy Evans, Esq.), Elizabeth, and Catherine.
 John, captain in the 24th regiment, killed at the battle of Talavera, 26 July, 1809.
 Elizabeth-Waller, *d. unm.* 28 June, 1845.
 Catherine, *m.* in July, 1800, Sampson Beamish, Esq. of Kilmaloda House, co. Cork, and *d.* 26 September, 1849.

Mr. Evans *d.* at Dunmanway, 24 Feb. 1797, and was *s.* by his eldest son,

THOMAS D'ARCY-EVANS Esq. of Knockaderry House, who *m.* in 1814, Brabazon, 2nd dau. of Richard Taylour, Esq. of Holly Park, co. Limerick, but had no issue. Mr. Evans, who assumed, upon inheriting the fortune of his maternal uncle Colonel James D'Arcy, the additional surname of D'ARCY, *d.* 10 Dec. 1833, and was *s.* by his brother,

JAMES-D'ARCY EVANS Esq. of Knockaderry House, *m.* 1st, May, 1800, Arabella, 3rd dau. of Col. Samuel Leake, of Rathkeale Abbey, co. Limerick, and by her (who *d.* 20 March, 1833) had issue,

 THOMAS-D'ARCY, now of Knockaderry House.
 James, killed by a fall from a pony, 10 March, 1823.
 John-D'Arcy, *b.* 29 September, 1817.
 Catherine, *m.* 6 July, 1832, Robert-Deane Hay, Esq., R.N.
 Elizabeth, *m.* 15 Aug. 1829, John-Evans Lucas, Esq., and *d.* 28 Dec. 1845.
 Emily-Mary, *m.* May, 1849, to her cousin, Rev. Thomas-Waller Evans.
 Mary-Anne, *m.* 12 Sep. 1835, to Thomas William Locke, Esq. of Castleview, co. Limerick.
 Arabella, *m.* 24 July, 1848, to William O'Hara, Esq.

Mr. Evans *m.* 2ndly, 2 Jan. 1834, Anne, widow of John Fitzgerald, Esq. He *d.* 7 March, 1848.

Arms—Same as EVANS *of Portrane*, quartering D'ARCY.
Crests—1st, EVANS; 2nd, D'ARCY, a spear broken in three pieces, or, two in saltire and one in pale, headed ppr., banded together at the middle by a ribbon.
Motto—Libertas.
Seat—Knockaderry House, near Newcastle, co. Limerick.

EVANS OF FARM HILL, ARDREIGH.

EVANS, GEORGE, Esq. of Farm Hill, Ardreigh, co. Kildare, J.P., *b.* 4 March, 1795; *m.* 25 Feb. 1819, Sophia, dau. of Richard Powell, Esq. of Stephen's Green, Dublin, by Mary Finnemore his wife, and has surviving issue,

I. RICHARD-POWELL, *b.* 11 May, 1830.
II. Eyre *b.* 12 Aug. 1833.
I. Margaret-Maria, *m.* John-Burrowes Gilsworth, Esq. of Wills Grove, co. Kildare.
II. Mary-Anne. III. Sophia.

Lineage.—WILLIAM EVANS, Esq. of Ardreigh, co. Kildare (son of Henry Evans Esq., who, upon his acquisition of the estate of Ardreigh, left the co. of Tipperary), *m.* (settlement dated 31 Dec. 1768) Elizabeth, dau. of Eyre Evans, Esq. of Portrane, co. Dublin, and left a son and successor,

GEORGE EVANS, Esq. of Ardreigh, who *m.* 25 May 1794, Margaret-Anne, dau. of George Harrisson, Esq. of Kilmullin, Queen's County, and *d.* 1819, having issue by his wife (who *d.* 1818),

 GEORGE.
 William-Henry, dec. Hampden, dec.
 Henry-Eyre, dec. Thomas, married.
 Mary-Frances, *m.* John Kinsly Tener, Esq.
 Anne-Dorcas, *m.* — Watson, Esq.
 Frances-Elizabeth, *m.* — Tener, Esq.
 Elizabeth.

Seat—Farm Hill (Ardreigh), Athy.

EVANS OF LOUGH PARK.

EVANS, NICHOLAS, Esq. of Lough Park, co. Westmeath, J.P., *b.* in 1795; *m.* 1819, Mary-Anne, dau. of Usher-P. Williamson, of Dromore, co. Cork, Esq., by his wife Anne, dau. of J. Lloyd, of Beechmount, co. Limerick, Esq., and has issue,

I. FRANCIS-HUGH, *b.* in 1821, late 1st royal regt. foot.
II. Usher-Williamson, M.D., *b.* in 1823.
III. Nicholas, *b.* in 1824; *m.* in 1851, Louisa-H., dau. of Rev. E. Batty.
IV. William, *b.* in 1829.
I. Anne. II. Frances-Jane. III. Maria.
IV. Marianne. V. Ellen. VI. Kate.

Lineage.—This family, and that of Lord Carbery, derive in direct descent from Elystan Gwdrydd.

HUGH EVANS, Esq. of Ballinrobe, co. Mayo, who *m.* Catherine Burrowes, *d.* 1717-18, and left issue,

 MICHAEL, of Ballinrobe, *d.* before 1729.
 Hugh, of Ballinrobe, *d.s.p.*
 FRANCIS, of whom we treat.

The 3rd son,

FRANCIS EVANS Esq. of Dublin *m.* 1st, 10 June, 1738, Martha, eldest dau. and co-heir of Joseph Sherwood, Esq. of Priors Wood, co. Dublin; and 2ndly, 1779 Christian Warren, widow, dau. of — Ogle, Esq., and *d.* 2 June, 1780, leaving issue,

I. NICHOLAS, his heir.
II. Francis, of New Forest, co Westmeath, colonel of volunteers in 1782; *m.* Alicia, dau. and co-heir of William Ogle, Esq. of Fatham Park, co. Down, and *d.* Oct. 1811, leaving an only child,
 FRANCIS, who *m.* 1st Harriet, dau. of John Locke, Esq. of Walthamstow; and 2ndly, Hannah-Anne, 2nd dau. of the late John Gardiner, Esq. of Farm Hill, co. Mayo, and had issue by the former, viz.—

1 Francis-Locke, *b.* 1812; *m.* in 1840, Anna-Maria, 3rd dau. of Thomas Stuart, Esq.
2 John-Ogle, *b.* 1814; *m.* 1837, Emily-Jane, eldest dau. of Thomas Stuart, Esq., and has issue.
1 Mary. 2 Alicia-Harriet. 3 Harriet.

I. Honora, *m.* to William Foster, Esq.
II. Anne, *d. unm.*

The elder son,

NICHOLAS EVANS, Esq. of Baymount and Prior's Wood, co. Dublin capt. 45th regt., who *m.* Mary-Anne eldest dau. of Vigors Thomas, Esq., by Mary his wife, eldest dau. and co-heir of John Gabbett, Esq., by Margery his wife, dau. of Sampson Cox, Esq. of Ballynoe, and had issue,

I. FRANCIS, his heir.
II. Nicholas, lieut. 41st regt., *d. unm. circa* 1796.
III. William, of Cheltenham, lieut.-col. 41st regiment; *m.* 20 Feb. 1819, Ann-Sarah, eldest dau. of William Sloane, Esq. of Tobago, by Ann his wife, 3rd dau. and co-heir of Henry Fisher, Esq., and *d.* 12 June, 1843, leaving issue,
1 Charles-Bidgood, *b.* 14 Feb. 1820.
2 William-Sloane, in holy orders, formerly incumbent of Holy Trinity, Barnstaple, *b.* 21 Aug. 1823; *m.* 21 Aug. 1847, Selina 2nd dau. of William Branscombe, Esq. of the co. of Devon, and has issue,
Helena-Gertrude-Vigors-Spenser.
Lucy-Georgiana-Sherwood.
Edith-Fitz-Maurice.
3 Henry-Hill, *b.* 1825; *d. unm.* 4 July, 1850.
1 Anne-Sloane, *m.* 12 Nov. 1842, to the Rev. Philip Thomas Drayton, B.A.

I. Martha, *m.* 1791, to Thomas Smith, Esq., M.D., of Maiden Hall, co. Kilkenny.
II. Mary-Anne, *m.* 1832, to John Francis Lane, Esq. of St. Annes, Enniscorthy.

The eldest son,

FRANCIS EVANS, Esq. of Prior's Wood, co. Dublin, and Robinstown, co. Westmeath, barrister-at-law, *m.* 1st, 1793, Anna, dau. of William Hickey, Esq.; and 2ndly, 1821, Frances, eldest dau. of Monsieur François Berthomé de la Mothe, of Nantes. By the former (who *d.* 21 May, 1815), he had issue,

I. NICHOLAS, now of Lough Park.
II. Francis, in holy orders, *b.* 1 Jan. 1803; *m.* Maria, dau. of the Rev. M. Lewis, of Taunton, co. Somerset, and has issue,
1 George-Mountain, *b.* 1 Feb. 1828.
2 Francis, *b.* 1829.
3 William-Berthomé, *b.* 1835.
4 Henry-James, *b.* 1837.
5 Lewis-Hamilton, *b.* 1841.
6 Another son, *b.* 1845.
1 Ann-Sophia. 2 Charlotte-Georgina.
3 Maria-Augusta. 4 Rosamond-Matilda.
5 Frances-Flora-Georgina.
III. William, lieut. 41st. regt., *d. unm.* 1831.
I. Mary-Anne.

Mr. Evans *d.* 20 May, 1834.

Arms, Crest, and Motto—Same as EVANS *of Portrane.*
Seat—Lough Park, co. Westmeath.

EVANS OF GORTMERRON HOUSE.

EVANS, EDWARD, Esq. of Gortmerron House, co. Tyrone, J.P., *b.* 31 May, 1762; *m.* 1789, Sarah-Maria, 2nd dau. of Thomas Kelly, Esq. of Dawson's Grove, co. Armagh, J.P., and has issue,

I. GEORGE, in holy orders, *m.* Elizabeth, dau. of William Murray, Esq., J.P., and has issue,
1 George. 2 Francis.
1 Sarah-Maria.
II. Thomas-Kelly J.P., *m.* Elizabeth, dau. of John Winder Esq., capt. royal artillery, and has issue four sons and seven daus., viz.,
1 Edward. 2 John-W.
3 Dawson-Kelly. 4 Arthur-Kelly.
1 Elizabeth. 2 Sarah.
3 Mary-Anne. 4 Alicia.
5 Letitia. 6 Jane.
7 Lucinda.
III. Robert, of Dungannon, J.P., *m.* Eleanor, dau. of George Stuart, Esq. of Dublin, surgeon-general.
IV. Edward, J.P.
I. Louisa-Jane, *m.* to Capt. A Stuart, 90th regt.
II. Priscilla, *m.* to D.-H. Sharrard, Esq. of Thorndale, co. Dublin.
III. Alicia, *m.* to the Rev. R.-W. Bland, of Abbeville, Belfast.
IV. Sarah-Maria, *m.* to John-Echlin Matthews, Esq. of White Abbey, co. Antrim, lieut.-col. Downshire militia deceased).

Lineage.—THOMAS EVANS, a Welsh gentleman, descended from Ethelystan Glodrydd, Prince of Ferlys North Wales was captain of a troop of horse in the English army, *temp.* CHARLES I. He served in Ireland in the rebellion of 1641, and obtained large grants of lands in the co. of Kilkenny, where he eventually settled at the end of the civil war, having also obtained estates in the Queen's County. He became an alderman of the city of Kilkenny, for which he served the office of mayor in the years 1658 1659, 1660, 1665, and 1668. He *m.* Katherine Weldon, and had issue, an only dau., Ellen, and two sons, viz.,

William, of Kilcreene, Kilkenny, created a Baronet by patent, dated 19 Feb. 1682. His dau. and eventual heiress, Catherine, *m.* Frances Morres, Esq. of Castle Morres.
EDWARD, of whose line we treat.

The latter,

EDWARD EVANS, Esq., elected sheriff of Kilkenny 25 July, 1665 commanded a troop in the Earl of Arran's Horse, at the battle of the Boyne. He *m.* and had issue,

Henry, of Belevans, co. Kilkenny, whose only son and heir, Joseph, of Belevans, was father of Joseph, of Belevans, who *d. unm.*, and left his large landed estates to found a charitable institution, now designated "Evan's Charity."
EDWARD, of whom we treat.

This

EDWARD EVANS, Esq. of Kilkenny *m.* 1st, Sarah Butler, of co. Tipperary, and by her had one son, Ambrose. He *m.* 2ndly Susanna Turvan, *alias* Lopdell, of co. Galway, and by her had a son,

THE REV. GEORGE EVANS, rector of Donaghmore, co. Tyrone, who *m.* Priscilla, dau. of Robert Armitage Esq. of Liverpool, and had,

Robert, in holy orders, who *m.* Emilia, dau. of the Rev. J. Forbes, and had by her a dau., Rebecca-Emilia, who *m.* Euseby-Stratford Kirwan, Esq. of Monkstown, co. Dublin, and *d. s. p.*
EDWARD, the present EDWARD EVANS, Esq. of Gortmerron.
Mary, *m.* to the Rev. Alexander-George Stuart, of Tullyniskan Glebe, co. Tyrone.

Arms—Ermine, three boars' heads, couped, in fesse, two and one, sa., langued, gu.
Crest—A demi-lion, rampant, regardant, erminois, holding between his paws a boar's head.
Motto—Libertas.
Seat—Gortmerron House, Dungannon, co. Tyrone.

EVELYN OF WOTTON AND ST. CLERE.

EVELYN, WILLIAM-JOHN, of Wotton, co. Surrey, and St. Clere, co. Kent, *b.* 27 July, 1822; *s.* his father 15 Feb. 1829.

Lineage.—This family flourished originally in the co. of Salop, at a place now called Evelyn, but formerly written Avelyn and Ivelyn. From Shropshire, it removed to Long Ditton, in Surrey; thence to Harrow-on-the-Hill co. Middlesex, *temp.* HENRY IV.; and to Kingston, in Surrey, in the reign of HENRY VIII.

RICHARD EVELYN (2nd son of George Evelyn, Esq. of Nutfield, M.P., by Frances, his 2nd wife, and grandson of Sir John Evelyn Knt. of Godstone, M.P., a distinguished parliamentarian whose father, John Evelyn, was uncle to JOHN EVELYN, the accomplished author of *Sylva*) was settled at Naas co. Kildare, Ireland, *m.* Jane Mead, and was father of an only son,

THE VERY REV. WILLIAM EVELYN, dean of Emley, in Ireland, who *m.* Margaret, dau. of Michael-Tankerville Chamberlain, Esq. of Chamberlain's Town, co. Meath, and *d.* in 1776, having had issue,

William, of Glanville, an officer in the army, killed in the American war. He was *unm.*
JOHN, his heir.
George, who *d.* about 1766, *unm.*

The dean's 2nd but only surviving son,

JOHN EVELYN, Esq., *s.* to the estate of Wotton co. Surrey, in 1817, under the will of Mary, Lady Evelyn, widow of Sir Frederick Evelyn, Bart. He *m.* 24 Nov. 1787, at Calcutta, Ann, dau. of Anthony Shee, Esq. of Castlebar, and sister of Sir George Shee, Bart., and had issue,

JOHN, *d.* an infant.
William, an officer in the army, lost in a transport-ship, in the Gulf of St. Lawrence, about the year 1808. He *d. unm.*
GEORGE, heir to his father.
Frances, who *m.* in 1822, Sir Charles Rowley, eldest son of Admiral Sir Charles Rowley, Bart., K.C.B., and *d.* at Florence, in 1834.

Mr. Evelyn *d.* in 1828, and was *s.* by his son,

GEORGE EVELYN, Esq. of Wotton. capt. 3rd regt. of guards, *b.* 16 Sept. 1791, who *m.* 12 July, 1821, Mary-Jane dau. of J.-H.-Massy Dawson, Esq. of Ballynacourte, M.P. for Clonmel, and had issue,

WILLIAM-JOHN, now of Wotton and St. Clere.
George-Palmer, an officer in the Rifle-brigade.
Charles-Francis, an officer in the navy.
Frederick-Massy. James,
Edmund-Boscawen.

Mr. Evelyn *d.* in 1829.

Arms—Az., a griffin, passant, or, a chief, of the last.
Crest—A griffin, passant, or, ducally gorged.
Motto—Durete.
Seats—Wotton, Surrey; and St. Clere, Kent.

EVERARD OF MIDDLETON.

EVERARD, EDWARD, Esq. of Middleton, co. Norfolk, *m.* 1 Jan. 1823, Anna-Theodora, dau. of St. Andrew St. John, LL.D., 4th son of the Hon. and Rev. St. Andrew St. John, D.D., 2nd son of the 10th Lord St. John, and has had issue,

I. Edward, who *d.* in infancy.
I. Georgina-Maria, *m.* 14 Aug. 1856, Thomas Hutton, major 4th light dragoons (*see* HUTTON *of Hutton Gate*).

Lineage.—The Everards are one of the oldest families in England, and their pedigree can be authentically deduced from the time of the early Plantagenets. Their chief seat was at Much Waltham, in Essex, but there were branches planted in several other places, in Berkshire, Bedfordshire, Staffordshire, Cambridgeshire, Kent Leicestershire Suffolk and Northamptonshire. In 1603, before the coronation of King JAMES I., Sir Anthony Everard of Much Waltham, received the honour of knighthood, and in twenty-five years after his nephew, Richard Everard, Esq. of the same place was created a Baronet of England. A direct descendant of this old stock

JAMES EVERARD, Esq. of Cambridge and Knapwell, *b.* about 1670, had, by Priscilla his wife, two sons, JAMES and William, and one dau. Priscilla. The elder son,

THE REV. JAMES EVERARD, Rector of Middleton and East Winch, *m.* Rebecca dau. of Edward Bodham, Esq. of King's Lynn by Frances Knight his wife, sister of John Knight, Esq., serjeant-surgeon to King CHARLES II. and by her (who became eventually co-heiress of Edward Bodham, Esq., her only brother) he left at his decease, in 1722, two sons, ROBERT EVERARD, of London, merchant, who *d. unm.* 1727, and

EDWARD EVERARD, Esq. of King's Lynn, whose Will, dated 26 Feb. 1766, was proved 31 March, 1769. He *m.* (settlement dated 6 Dec. 1735) Mary, dau. and co-heir of Benjamin Holley, Esq. of King's Lynn, Mayor thereof in 1707, by Alice his wife, dau. and heir of John Richard, Esq. of Terrington St. Clement's, and had issue,

I. BENJAMIN, *d. unm.* 4 July, 1755, aged 21.
II. EDWARD, of whom presently.
III. James, of Lynn; Will dated 28 Oct. 1772. He *m.* Miss Upwood, and *d.* 23 Feb. 1773, leaving a son,
JAMES, of Lowestoft, who *m.* Elizabeth, dau. of Henry-Prescott Blencowe, Esq. of Blencowe Hall, co. Cumberland, and left issue, James, R.N. drowned 1825; Mary, *m.* to Isaac Gaskarth; Eleanor, *m.* 1817 to Edward Proudfoot Montagu, Esq., lineally descended from the 1st Earl of Manchester; Fanny; Caroline; Louisa; and Anna.
I. Mary, of Bath, *d. unm.* 3 March, 1827.

The 2nd son,

EDWARD EVERARD Esq. of Lynn and Bath, *b.* in 1739 *m.* Mary, widow of P. Busham, Esq. and dau. of Samuel Browne, Esq. of King's Lynn, by Elizabeth his wife, dau. of Daniel Scarlett, and sister of Samuel Browne Esq. whose daus. and co-heirs were Pleasance, wife of Edward Roger Pratt, Esq. of Ryston; and Hester, wife of Sir Jacob Astley, Bart. By Mary his wife, who *d.* 1794, Edward Everard (who *d.* 1819) had issue,

I. EDWARD, his heir.
II. Daniel, of Burnham Thorpe and Stanhoe, *m.* Ann-Henrietta, dau. and co-heir of Rev. Henry-Handley Norris, of Hackney, and by her, who *d.* 1 May, 1841, had issue,
1 Henry, *d. unm.* 6 Aug. 1838.
2 William, in holy orders, *d. unm.* 1848.
3 Benjamin, an officer 16th lancers, *d.* at Poona, East Indies, 1827.
1 Ann, *m.* to William Taylor, Esq. of King's Lynn.
2 Caroline. 3 Grace.
III. Scarlett, of King's Lynn, *m.* Ann, dau. of Richard Salisbury, Esq. of Lancaster (descended from a common ancestor with the very ancient family of Salusbury of Lleweny), and sister of Grace, the wife of Thos. Philip Bagge, Esq. of Stradsett, father of William Bagge, Esq., M.P. for Norfolk, and by her (who *d.* 11 June, 1827) had,
1 Edward-Browne, in holy orders, rector of Burnham Thorpe, *m.* Sophia, dau. of Thomas-Coxhead Marsh, Esq. of Gaynes Park, Essex, and has issue.
2 Salisbury, in holy orders, vicar of Swaffham, *m.* Charlotte, dau. of the Rev. William Chester (nephew of the first Lord Bagot), by the Hon. Elizabeth Wilson his wife, dau. of Henry, late Lord Berners, and has issue.
3 Walling, captain in the army, late of the 60th rifles, and now gentleman of the bedchamber and assistant private secretary to H.E. the Earl of Carlisle, Lord-Lieutenant of Ireland.
I. Mary, *m.* to Edmund R. Elsden, Esq., died 1788.
II. Elizabeth, *m.* to Major Edward Batchellor, of the H.E.I.C. service, and *d.s.p.*
III. Rebecca, *m.* to Henry-Prescott Blencowe, Esq. of Blencowe, co. Cumberland, and *d.* 20 Oct. 1854, aged 88 (*see p.* 103).
IV. Sarah, *m.* in 1801, to the Rev. John Partridge, of Hockham, Norfolk, and dying in 1856, left two daus. Alice, wife of John Fry, Esq.; and Pleasance, of Frederick Ingle, Esq.
V. Pleasance, *m.* to John-Prescott Blencowe, Esq., 2nd son of H.-P. Blencowe, Esq. of Blencowe (*see p.* 103).

The eldest son,

EDWARD EVERARD Esq. of Middleton *m.* Dorothy, dau. of Edmund Elsden, Esq. of Lynn, by Elizabeth his wife, eldest dau. of Edmund Rolfe, Esq. of Heacham, co. Norfolk, and had issue,

EDWARD, now of Middleton.
William, *m.* Harriet, dau. of A Bowker, Esq. of Lynn, and has issue, Henry; Harriet; Eleanor; and Anna.
Benjamin, major 1st royal dragoons.
James-Elsden, of Congham, Norfolk, *m.* Isabella-Emma, dau. of Sir Peter Payne, Bart. of Bedfordshire, and has issue, Elsden; Constance; and Geraldine.
Dorothea, *m.* to Frederic Lane, Esq.
Mary, *m.* to William Lane, Esq., died 1853.
Elizabeth, *m.* to Lionel Self, Esq.
Catherine, *m.* to George Ogle, Esq., *d.* 1830; Maria, *d. unm.*
Henrietta, *m.* to Francis Hulton, Esq.

Mr. Everard, whose Will bears date 12 Aug. 1822, *d.* 7 Feb. 1829.

Arms—Arg., a fesse, wavy, between three estoiles, gu.
Crest—A man's head, couped at the shoulders, and capped, bendy, wavy of six, arg. and sa.
Motto—Say and do.
Seat—Middleton, Norfolk.

EWBANK OF EVERTON AND KIRTON DROVE.

EWBANK, WILLIAM-WITHERS, Esq., M.A., of Kirton Drove, co. Lincoln, incumbent of St. George's Church, Everton, co. Lancaster; *m.* in 1834, Justina-Elinor, dau. of the Hon. Sir George Cooper, Knt., one of the puisne judges of the Supreme Court of Judicature at Madras, by his wife Mary-Justina-Martha, dau. of John Lloyd, Esq. of Foes-y-Bleddial and Mabws, co. Cardigan, and Dale Castle, co. Pembroke, descended, on her mother's side, from Justina, only dau. of Sir Anthony Vandyke, Knt., by Maria his wife, dau. of John, 3rd Earl of Gowrie, and 6th Lord Ruthven.

Lineage.—ANDREW EWBANK, Esq., descended from the ancient family of that name in Durham and the north of Yorkshire, left issue a son,

GEORGE EWBANK Esq. of York, who *d.* 1737, leaving two sons, George and Andrew. George the eldest son, *d.* 1795, leaving no male issue. His dau. Elizabeth *m.* Richard Lodge, Esq., whose only dau. Elizabeth *m.* John Dalton, Esq. of Sleningford Hall and the Grange, co. York, and *d.* 1824, leaving a numerous family (*see* DALTON *of Sleningford*).

THE REV. ANDREW EWBANK, M.A., rector of Londesborough and Burgwallis, co. York, the second son, *m.* Jane, eldest dau. of the Rev. William Withers D.D., rector of Tankersley, co. York, and vicar of Higham-Ferrers, co. Northampton (descended from the ancient Lancashire family of that name), and *d.* 1822, leaving issue,

GEORGE, M.A., fellow and tutor of Trinity College, Cambridge, *d. unm.*
WILLIAM, of whom presently.
Henry, who *m.* Lydia-Ball, dau. of Jonathan Lucas, Esq. of The Grove, co. Surrey, and has issue, Henry, in holy orders; George-William-Withers; and several other children.
Dorothy-Cordelia, who *m.* the Rev. Edward-William

Stillingfleet, B.D. of Hotham, vicar of South Cave, co. York, and *d.* without issue.

Frances, who *m.* the Rev. George Briggs, of York, and *d.* leaving an only son, *George*, captain in the 1st Dragoon Guards, who *m.* Letitia, dau. of Smith Eggington, Esq., and has issue.

THE REV. WILLIAM EWBANK, M.A., rector of North Witham, co. Lincoln (the second son of Andrew) *m.* Theodosia, eldest dau. of Benjamin Cooper, Esq. of New Sleaford, co. Lincoln, sister to Sir John Hutton Cooper, Bart. (*see* BURKE'S *Extinct Baronetage*) and a descendant through her grandmother, Harriet Lawrence, of the ancient family of that name, of Ashton Hall co. Lancaster, and through her great grandmother, Elizabeth Cartwright, from the sister of Thomas Cranmer, archbishop of Canterbury. The Rev. William Ewbank *d.* 1840, leaving issue, by Theodosia his wife,

- WILLIAM, present representative.
- George, M.A., in holy orders, of Guilford, co. Surrey, who *m.* Elizabeth Bryan, dau. of Jonathan Lucas, Esq. of The Grove, and has issue, George Henry-Withers; Christopher-Cooper; William-Andrew; Thomas-Cranmer; and other children.
- Cooper, of Brompton, co. Middlesex, who *m.* Louis-Caroline-Maria Lloyd, second dau. of the Hon. Sir George Cooper, Knt. and has issue, George-Cooper-Lawrence; Alfred Lloyd-Vandyke; Withers-Stillingfleet; and other children.
- Henry, of Charleston, South Carolina, U.S., who *m.* Annie, dau. of Jonathan Lucas, Esq. of The Grove, and has issue, Harry Hutton, and other children.
- Harriet and Jane-Theodosia, *unm.*
- Agnes, who *m.* Rev. Henry Lister, M.A., and *d. s. p.*

Arms—Sa., three chevronels, interlaced in base, or., quartering WITHERS and COOPER.
Crest—Out of a ducal coronet, gu., a dragon's head, or.
Motto—Vincit veritas.

EYRE OF RAMPTON.

EYRE, THE REV. CHARLES-WASTENEYS, of Rampton, co. Nottingham, *b.* at Babworth, 7 March, 1802; *m.* in 1827, Lucy-Dorothea, dau. of John-Robinson Foulis, Esq. of Buckton, in Yorkshire, and has

- I. HENRY, lieutenant Rifle Brigade, *b.* 4 Feb. 1834.
- II. Arthur Stanhope, *b.* 3 Aug. 1840.
- I. Lucy-Harriet.

Lineage.—WILLIAM LE EYR, of Hope, in the co. of Derby *temp.* HENRY III. held lands of the king *in capite* by service of the custody of the Forest of High Peak and *d.* seised thereof before 4 Dec. 28 EDWARD I. He was direct ancestor of

GERVASE EYRE Esq. of Newbold and Keveton aged 26 years at his father Anthony's decease 31 April 17 ELIZABETH. He *m.* Mary 4th dau. of George Nevile, Esq. of Thorney in Nottinghamshire, by Barbara his wife one of the eight sisters and co-heirs of Sir George Mercy, Knt. Lord of Grove, and had issue,

- ANTHONY, his heir.
- Elizabeth, *m.* 1 Jan. 1594, to Thomas Riccard, Gent. of Hatfield, in Yorkshire.
- Barbara, *m.* to John Frecheville, 2nd son of Peter Frecheville, Esq. of Staveley, in Derbyshire.
- Jane, *m.* to Sir Hardolph Wasteneys, Bart. of Headon, co. Nottingham, and the great great great grandchild of this marriage, Judith Letitia Bury, *m.* in 1755, to ANTHONY EYRE, Esq. of Grove.

Gervase Eyre *d.* in 1626, and was *s.* by his son,

ANTHONY EYRE Esq. of Loughton en le Morthem, in the co. of York, and of Keveton in Derbyshire, aged nine in 1600, father by Anne Markham his 1st wife of

SIR GERVASE EYRE Knt. who was slain in defending Newark Castle for King CHARLES I. May 20th year of that reign. He *m.* 30 Nov. 1624, Elizabeth elder dau. and co-heir with her sister Barbara, wife of Thomas Brewile Esq. of [illegible] of John Babington, Esq. of Rampton in Nottinghamshire great-grandson of John Babington, Esq., by Saunchia his wife only dau. and heir of Richard Stanhope Esq. of Rampton, and had issue,

- ANTHONY his heir.
- Mary, *m.* to Sir John Newton, Bart. of Barrs Court, in Gloucestershire and of Thorpe, in Lincolnshire, and [illegible] issue.
- Anne.

Sir Gervase was *s.* at his decease (his widow *m.* William Moor, D.D.) by his son,

ANTHONY EYRE Esq. of Rampton, baptized 17 Sept. 1634, who *m.* 1st, 3 June, 1657, Lucy, dau. of Sir John Digby, of Mansfield Woodhouse, in the co. of Nottingham and by her, who *d.* in June, 1669, had an only dau. Elizabeth living under age and *unm.* in 1671. He *m.* 2ndly Elizabeth dau. of Sir John Packington, Bart. of Westwood in Worcestershire, by Dorothy his wife, dau. of Thomas Lord Coventry, and had issue, GERVASE his heir; Dorothy, *m.* in 1680, to John Bradshaw, Esq.; Mary; and Margaret. Anthony Eyre *d.* in 1671, and was *s.* by his son,

GERVASE EYRE Esq. of Rampton bapt. there 20 Aug. 1669, high-sheriff for Nottinghamshire and M.P., sometime resident at Sandbeck, in Yorkshire. He *m.* before 28 May, 1689, Catherine, only surviving dau. of Sir Henry Cooke, Bart. of Wheatley, and by her, who *d.* 7 Nov. 1704, had issue,

- ANTHONY, his heir.
- Henry, of Rowter, in Derbyshire, baptized at Rampton 22 Sept. 1693, high-sheriff of that county in 1723. He *m.* 1st, Elizabeth, dau. of Sir Willoughby Hickman, Bart. of Gainsborough, in Lincolnshire, and 2ndly, a dau. of Rowland Cotton, Esq. By the former he left an only dau. and heir,
  - ELIZABETH, *m.* to Clotworthy Skeffington, Earl of Massareene.
- George, sometime of West Retford, and afterwards of Doncaster, captain Royal horse-guards, *d.* without issue, 28 April, 1761.
- Gervase, *d. unm.* in 1741.
- Charles, of Doncaster, M.D., bapt. 18 Jan. 1699, *m.* Elizabeth, dau. of John Fountaine, Esq. of High Melton, in Yorkshire, and *d.* in 1763, leaving a son,
  - ANTHONY-FOUNTAINE, of Baronburgh, co. York, in holy orders, *m.* 1st, Susanna, youngest dau. of the Rev. Kenzie Prescott, D.D., master of Catherine Hall, Cambridge; and 2ndly, a dau. of the Rev. Godfrey Woolley, M.A., rector of Warmsworth and Thurnscoe. Mr. Anthony-Fountaine Eyre *d.* 14 Feb. 1794, leaving by his 1st wife a son, the Rev. Charles-Wolfe Eyre, and by his 2nd, another son, the Rev. Anthony-William Eyre, and a dau.

Gervase Eyre *d.* in London, 16 Feb. 1703, and was *s.* by his eldest son,

ANTHONY EYRE Esq. of Rampton, sometime of Adwick le Street and of Loughton, in Yorkshire who served the office of sheriff for Nottinghamshire in 1729. He *m.* 23 Dec. 1717 Margaret, 5th dau. of Charles Turner, Esq. of Kirk Leatham, co. York, and had issue,

- ANTHONY, his heir.
- Margaret, *b.* 5 Jan. 1718, *m.* in 1742, to Bache Thornhill, Esq. of Stainton, in Derbyshire.
- Katherine, *b.* 7 June, 1721, *m.* to Matthew Dodsworth, Esq. of Thornton Watlass, in Yorkshire.
- Elizabeth, *b.* 20 May, 1723, *m.* after 1759, to — Chambers, Esq. of Ripon, in Yorkshire.
- Diana, *b.* 26 July, 1725, *d. unm.*
- Mary, *b.* 21 Oct. 1726, *m.* 26 Oct. 1752, to Anthony Cooke, Esq. of Owston, in Yorkshire.

Anthony Eyre *d.* in 1748, and was *s.* by his son,

ANTHONY EYRE, Esq. of Grove co. Nottingham, and of Adwick le Street *b.* 9 Jan. 1727 who *m.* at Headon, in 1755, Judith-Lætitia only dau. and heir of John Bury, Esq. of Nottingham by Catherine Hutchinson his wife grandchild and heir of Sir Edmund Wasteneys Bart. and had by her, who *d.* in 1800 four sons and one dau., viz.,

- I. ANTHONY-HARDOLPH, his heir.
- II. John, in holy orders, *b.* 19 Feb. 1758, rector of Babworth, co. Nottingham, one of the canons residentiary of York, and archdeacon of Nottingham, *m.* 12 April, 1790, Charlotte, 3rd dau. of Sir George Armytage, Bart. of Kirklees, in Yorkshire, and had issue,
  - 1 John-Hardolph, *b.* 2 May, 1792, *m.* his first cousin, Henrietta, dau. of Col. Eyre, of Grove, but *d. s. p.* in 1827.
  - 2 CHARLES-WASTENEYS, present representative of the family.
  - 3 Anthony-Gervase, *b.* in Aug. 1812.
  - 1 Charlotte, *m.* to Henry Willoughby, Esq. of Birdsall House, co. York.
  - 2 Anna Maria, *d.* in 1828.
  - 3 Louisa-Henrietta, *d.* young.

  Archdeacon Eyre *d.* in March, 1830.
- III. Charles, in holy orders, sometime rector of Grove, *b.* 3 Jan. 1765, *d. unm.* 2 June, [illegible]
- IV. George, Sir, K.C.B., K.C.M.G., vice-admiral of the Red, *b.* 23 April, 1769, *m.* at Doncaster, 2 Nov. 1806, Georgiana, 3rd dau. of Sir George Cooke, Bart. of Wheatley, and dying in Sept. 1839, left with six issue,
  - 1 George-Hardolph, *b.* at [illegible], 29 Sept. 1801.
  - 2 William, Sir, K.C.B., lieutenant-col. in the army, *b.* at [illegible], 21 Oct. 1805, *m.* Georgiana, dau. of [illegible] Simpson, Esq.
- I. Judith, *m.* in 1778, to Robert-Auriol-Hay Drummond, afterwards Earl of Kinnoul, and *d. s. p.*

Anthony Eyre *d.* 14 Feb. 1788, and was *s.* by his son,

ANTHONY-HARDOLPH EYRE, Esq. of Grove, b. 8 March, 1757, lieut.-col. in the the army, and at one time colonel of the Nottinghamshire Yeomanry, member for the county and chairman of the Quarter Sessions at East Retford. He m. 20 Dec. 1783, Francisca-Alicia, 3rd dau. of Richard Wilbraham Bootle, Esq. of Latham Hall, in Lancashire, and sister to Lord Skelmersdale, by whom he had issue,

GERVASE-ANTHONY, b. 20 Oct. 1791, an officer in the 1st regt. of foot-guards, killed at the battle of Barossa, in Spain, March, 1811, unm.
MARY-LETITIA, m. at Grove, 23 Aug. 1804, to Charles-Herbert, Earl Manvers.
FRANCES, m. to Granville-Harcourt Vernon, Esq. M.P., son of the archbishop of York.
HENRIETTA, m. 1st, to her cousin, John-Hardolph Eyre, Esq.; and 2ndly, to Henry-Gally-Knight, Esq. of Firbeck Hall, in Yorkshire.

Col. Eyre d. in 1836, and was s. by his nephew, the present REV. CHARLES-WASTENEYS EYRE, of Rampton.

Arms—Arg., on a chev., sa., three quartrefoils, or.
Crest—A leg in armour, couped at the thigh, and spur.
Seat—Rampton.

EYRE OF WELFORD.

EYRE, CHARLES, Esq. of Welford, co. Berks, b. 13 Oct. 1806; m. in May, 1835, Mary-Anne, dau. of General Leyborne Popham, of Littlecote, Wilts, and has issue. This gentleman, whose patronymic is HOUBLON, assumed, in 1831, the surname and arms of EYRE, on succeeding his father, the late JOHN-ARCHER HOUBLON, Esq., in the Welford estates.

Lineage.—WILLIAM EYRE, Esq. of Gray's Inn, a scion of the EYRES *of Holme*, co. Derby, assumed the surname of ARCHER having m. Eleanor, dau. of Sir Walter Wrottesley, Bart. of Wrottesley, by Eleanor his wife sister and heir of JOHN ARCHER, Esq. of Welford, co. Berks. By this lady he had no issue, but by a 2nd wife, Susanna, sister and heir of Sir Michael Newton, Bart. of Barrs Court, he left two sons and two daus.,

JOHN, his heir.
Michael-Archer Newton, who d. s. p.
Susanna, m. in 1751, to Edward, 4th Earl of Oxford.
Catherine, m. to Peter Blundell, Esq.

The elder son and heir,

JOHN ARCHER Esq. of Welford, Berks, and Holme, co. Derby, m. Lady Mary Fitzwilliam, dau. of John, 2nd Earl Fitzwilliam, and by her (who d. in 1776) had a dau.,

SUSANNA ARCHER who m. JACOB HOUBLON Esq. (*see family of* HOUBLON) and had, with two daus., one son,

JOHN-ARCHER HOUBLON, Esq. of Hallingbury co. Essex, and Welford, Berks, who m. Mary-Ann dau. of Thomas Bramston, Esq. of Skreens, and had, with three daus., five sons, the eldest of whom is the present JOHN-ARCHER HOUBLON, Esq. of Hallingbury Place; and the 2nd, the present CHARLES EYRE, Esq. of Welford.

Arms, &c.—As EYRE *of Wiltshire*
Seat—Welford, Berks.

EYRE OF WILTSHIRE.

EYRE, HENRY-SAMUEL, Esq. of St. John's Wood, co. Middlesex, a colonel in the army, s. his father, as male representative of the ancient Wiltshire family of EYRE.

Lineage.—The old Wiltshire family of Eyre enjoyed, for several centuries, the highest distinction within its native county, and was of consideration in the state, most of its chiefs having had seats in parliament, and two of them, learned in the law, upon the bench—one as lord chief justice of the Common Pleas; a branch, too, which emigrated to Ireland, attained the peerage of that kingdom.

THOMAS EYRE Esq. of New Sarum, lineally descended from Humphrey le Heyr, of Bromham, Wilts, held lands in Wimborn, co. Dorset, 21st ELIZABETH m. Elizabeth, dau. of John Rogers, Esq. of Poole, and had issue, I. ROBERT, his heir; II. GILES of Brickworth in Wiltshire, from whom the family of the extinct LORD EYRE, of Ireland; III. Christopher, b. in 1578 founder of *Eyre's Hospital* in Sarum, d. s. p. 5 Jan. 1624; IV. Thomas, b. in 1580, mayor of Sarum in 1610, ancestor of the EYRES *of Box* who merged in the EYRES *of Botley Grange*; V. William, b. in 1585, barrister-at-law, bequeathed his estate of Bonhams to his great-nephew, Sir Samuel Eyre, and d. Nov. 1646; VI. John; I. Elizabeth, m. to Gilbert Tooker, Esq. of Madington, Wilts; II. Catherine, m. to Thomas Hooper, Esq. of Boveridge; III. Rebecca, m. to John Love, Esq. of Basing; IV. Anne, m. to John Swaine, of Gunvill Dorsetshire. Thomas Eyre d. in 1628, and was s. by his eldest son

ROBERT EYRE, Esq. of Chilhampton and Sarum, b. in 1569, barrister-at-law who m. Anne, dau. of the Right Rev. John Still, bishop of Bath and Wells (by Jane, dau. of Sir John Horner, of Cloford), and dying in Aug. 1638 left (with two daus., Blanche, m. to Thomas Pelham, of Compton Valence; and Catherine, m. to Charles Chauncey, of Herts) a son and successor,

ROBERT EYRE, Esq. of New Sarum and Chilhampton, b. in 1610, m. Anne, dau. of Sam. Aldersey, Esq. of London, descended from the family of Aldersey of Aldersey, in Cheshire, and had issue,

SAMUEL (Sir), his heir.
Margaret, m. to T. Hassell, Esq. of London.
Anne, m. to William Stear, Esq. of London.
Mary, m. to William Hitchcock, Esq. lord of the manor of Cowsfield, Wilts.

He d. in March, 1654, and was s. by his son,

SIR SAMUEL EYRE, Knt. of Newhouse and Chilhampton, bapt. 26 Dec. 1633, who inherited the estate of Bonhams from his great-uncle, William-Eyre, and purchased Newhouse from his cousin, William Eyre, in 1660. Sir Samuel was a lawyer of eminence and one of the puisne judges of the King's Bench, *temp.* WILLIAM III. He m. Martha 3rd dau. and co-heiress of Francis Lucy, Esq. (5th son of Sir Thomas Lucy, of Charlecote), by Elizabeth, dau. and heiress of Bevill Molesworth, Esq. of Hoddesdon, Herts, and acquired thereby the estate of Brightwalton, Berks. By her he had issue,

I. ROBERT (Sir), his heir.
II. Francis, D.D., Canon of Sarum, m. Ann, dau. of Alexander Hyde, D.D., Bishop of Sarum, and d. s. p. 28 Oct. 1738, aged sixty-eight.
III. Henry-Samuel, of St. John's Wood, Middlesex, d. s. p. in 1754, bequeathing his estates to his nephew, Walpole Eyre.
IV. KINGSMILL, treasurer of Chelsea College, m. Susanna, dau. of— Atkinson, Esq., and widow of Samuel Keylway, Esq., by whom he had,
  1 SAMUEL, of whom hereafter, as heir under the will of his cousin, ROBERT EYRE, Esq., of Newhouse.
  2 WALPOLE, of Burnham, Bucks, in whose heir the male line of the family continues: of this gentlemen in the sequel.
  1 Elizabeth, m. to Polydore, 4th son of John Plumptre, Esq. of Nottingham.
I. Martha, m. to Sir D. Bulkeley, of Burgate, Hants.
II. Lucy, m. to William Crey, Esq. of Horningham, Wilts, whose granddaughter, Elizabeth, dau. of Edmund Abbott, Esq., m. J. Wyche, Esq. of Sarum.

Sir Samuel d. 12 Sept. 1698 and was s. by his eldest son

THE RIGHT HON. SIR ROBERT EYRE, Knt., P.C., of Newhouse, b. in 1666, recorder of Salisbury in 1696, M.P. for that city in 1700, chancellor to the Prince of Wales (GEORGE II.), and eventually lord chief justice of the Court of Common Pleas. He m. Elizabeth dau. of Edward Rudge, Esq. of Warley Place, Essex, and had three sons and a dau., viz.,

ROBERT, his successor.
Samuel, D.D., d. s. p. 2 Dec. 1742.
Edward, Comptroller of Chelsea College, d. s. p. 29 June, 1750
Elizabeth, m. to Richard Lee, Esq. of Winslade, in Devonshire.

Chief Justice Eyre d. 28 Dec. 1735 was buried at St. Thomas's Sarum, and s. by his eldest son,

ROBERT EYRE, Esq. of New House, one of the commissioners of Excise, who m. Mary, dau. of Edward Fellowes, Esq. of Shottesham, and had an only son, Robert, who d. in his ninth year, 7 Feb. 1734. Mr. Eyre d. 15 Dec. 1752, bequeathing his estates, after the decease of his widow to whom he left a life interest, to his cousin Samuel, son of his uncle, Kingsmill Eyre; that lady d. 24 Oct. 1762 when

SAMUEL EYRE Esq., inherited, and became "of New House." He m. Stewart, dau. of John Russell, Esq., consul-general at Lisbon, and envoy to the Barbary Powers, and had two daus., viz.,

SUSANNAH-HARRIET, m. to William, son of Admiral Charles-Wager Purvis, of Darsham, in Suffolk, M.P. for Aldborough, which William assumed the surname of EYRE. His eldest dau. and co-heiress, HARRIET EYRE, m. to William-George Matcham, Esq., D.C.L., of Hoadlands, Sussex, eldest son of George Matcham, Esq. of Ashfold, by Catherine his wife, youngest sister of Lord Nelson, and had issue.
Charlotte-Louisa, m. to Alexander Popham, Esq. of Bagborough, co. Somerset, and had issue.

Mr. Eyre, who represented New Sarum in parliament, *d.* in Dec. 1794, and was buried at Exmouth, 2 Jan. 1795, when his estates passed to his elder dau. and the representation of the family devolved on his brother,

WALPOLE EYRE, Esq. of Burnham, Bucks, who *m.* in Nov. 1767, Miss Sarah Johnson, and had three sons, viz.,

HENRY-SAMUEL, his successor.
John-Thomas, *m.* Harriet-Margaret, dau. of — Ainslie, Esq., and had issue, Walpole-George, George-John, and Henrietta.
Walpole, *m.* Elizabeth, dau. of — Johnson, Esq., and had Henry-Samuel; Frederick-Edwin, *m.* 8 Aug. 1848, Eliza, youngest dau. of Thomas-Alexander Raynsford, Esq. of Devonshire Place; Elizabeth-Annabella; Alathea-Sarah-Henrietta; and Emma-Harriet.

Mr. Eyre *d.* and was *s.* by his eldest son, the present HENRY-SAMUEL EYRE Esq. of St. John's Wood.

Arms—Arg., on a chev., sa., three quartrefoils, or.
Crest—On a cap of maintenance a booted leg.
Motto—Virtus sola invicta.

EYRE OF EYRE COURT CASTLE.

EYRE, JOHN, Esq. of Eyre Court Castle, co. Galway, J.P.

Lineage.—JOHN EYRE, Esq., col. in the army (3rd son of Giles Eyre, Esq. of Brickworth, Wilts, by Jane his wife, dau. of Ambrose Snelgrove, of Redlynch), accompanied Gen. Ludlow into Ireland, and established himself at Eyre Court Castle, co. Galway. At the restoration, he was chosen M.P. for the county. He *m.* Mary, dau. of Philip Bygoe, Esq., high-sheriff of the King's County in 1662, and dying in 1685, left two sons,

I. JOHN, his heir.
II. Samuel, col. in the army, at Limerick in 1690, and M.P. for Galway; *m.* 1st Jane, dau. of Edward Eyre, Esq. of Galway, by whom he had a son, JOHN, ancestor of THOMAS-STRATFORD EYRE, Esq. of Eyreville, co. Galway. Colonel Samuel Eyre, *m.* 2ndly, Anne, 6th dau of Robert Stratford, Esq., of Baltinglass, co. Wicklow, M.P., and had issue,
1 Stratford, Governor of Galway, and Vice-Admiral of Munster, who died, leaving issue.
2 Thomas, a colonel in the army, M.P., and Master of the Ordnance in Ireland, *d. s. p.* in 1772.
1 Anne, *m.* in 1717, to Robert, only son of Richard Powell, Esq. of New Garden, co. Limerick, and was great-grandmother of Eyre-Burton Powell, Esq.
2 Mary, *m.* to Thomas Crossdale, Esq.

The eldest son,

JOHN EYRE, Esq. of Eyre Court Castle, *m.* Margery, dau. of Sir George Preston, of Craigmillar, in Mid-Lothian, niece of the Duchess of Ormonde, and had (with two daus. Mary, *m.* in 1679, to the Right Hon. George Evans, Esq. of Caheras; and Elizabeth, the wife of Richard Trench, Esq. of Garbally) two sons. The elder,

GEORGE EYRE, Esq. of Eyre Court Castle, *s.* his father in 1709. He *m.* Barbara, dau. of Lord Coningsby, but dying *s. p. m.** in 1711, the estates passed to his brother,

JOHN EYRE, Esq. of Eyre Court Castle who *m.* Rose, dau. of Lord Howth, and *d.* in 1741, leaving a son and successor,

JOHN EYRE Esq. of Eyre Court Castle, who *m.* Jane Waller, of Castle Waller, in the co. of Limerick, and dying in 1745 without issue (his only child, John, had predeceased him, in 1743), was *s.* by his brother,

THE VERY REV. GILES EYRE dean of Killaloe, who *m.* the dau. of Sir Richard Cox, and *d.* in 1757, leaving issue,

I. JOHN, his heir.
II. Richard, *m.* Anchoretta, dau. of John Eyre, Esq. of Eyreville, and dying in 1780, left four sons and one dau.
1 GILES, successor to his uncle.
2 John, killed at Margueritta.
3 Robert, in holy orders.
4 Samuel.
1 Jane-Blake.
III. Robert.

The Dean's eldest son,

JOHN EYRE, Esq. of Eyre Court Castle, was elevated to the Irish peerage in 1768, as Baron Eyre, of Eyre Court.† His lordship *m.* Eleanor, dau. of James Staunton, Esq. of Galway, and *d.* in 1792, leaving an only child,

Mary, *m.* to the Hon. Francis Caulfeild, and their dau., Eleanor Caulfeild, *m.* the Hon. William Howard, afterwards EARL OF WICKLOW.

Lord Eyre was *s.* at Eyre Court by his nephew,

GILES EYRE, Esq. of Eyre Court Castle, col. of the Galway militia, who *m.* 1st, in 1792, Ann, dau. of Michael Daly, Esq. of Mount Pleasant, and by her had issue,

JOHN, his heir.
Ann, *m.* to Walter Lambert, Esq. of Castle Lambert, co. Galway.
Jane, *m.* to the Rev. Samuel Roberts.
Ellinor, *m.* to Colonel Disney, E.I.C.S.

He *m.* 2ndly, in 1821, Sophia, dau. of Jonathan Walsh, Esq. of Walsh Park, co. Tipperary. He *d.* in 1829, and was *s.* by his son,

JOHN EYRE, Esq. of Eyre Court Castle, *b.* 15 May, 1794; *m.* 21 Aug. 1816, Mary, dau. of William Armit, Esq., and had issue,

I. JOHN, now of Eyre Court.
II. William-Armit.
III. Marmaduke.
I. Annastatia, *m.* to Henshaw Russell, Esq., capt. 97th regiment.
II. Charity.
III. Georgina-Ellinor.
IV. Diana.
V. Nance.
VI. Charlotte-Mary.
VII. Bessy-Armit.

Arms and Crest—As EYRE *of Wiltshire.*
Seat—Eyre Court Castle, co. Galway.

EYRE OF GALWAY.

EYRE-MAUNSELL, THE REV. ROBERT-HEDGES-EYRE, of Galway, *m.* 5 Feb. 1836, Anna-Maria, dau. of Eyre Evans, of Ashhill Towers, co. Limerick, and has issue,

I. EYRE-ORLANDO, *b.* in June, 1837.
II. Horatio-Hare, *b.* in 1838.
I. Anna.
II. Catharine, dec.

Mr. Maunsell-Eyre, who is eldest son (by Lady Catherine Hare, his wife, youngest dau. of William, Earl of Listowel) of the late Richard Maunsell, Esq., LL.D., barrister-at-law, 3rd son of the Rev. George Maunsell, D.D., Dean of Leighlin (*see* MAUNSELL *of Plassy*), by Helena his wife, dau. of Richard-Hedges Eyre, Esq. of Macroom Castle, and Mount Hedges, co. Cork, assumed his present surname of EYRE, in addition to his patronymic, in compliance with the will of his grand-uncle, Robert-Hedges Eyre, Esq., who *d. s. p.* in 1840, whose property he then became possessed of.

Lineage.—EDWARD EYRE, Esq., bapt. 28 Jan. 1626, 6th son of Giles Eyre, Esq of Brickworth, in Wiltshire, settled in Galway. He *d.* 14 April, 1683, leaving, by Jane his wife, a son,

EDWARD EYRE, Esq. of Galway, who *m.* Jane, dau. of Sir William Maynard, Bart. of Walthamstow, and *d.* 5 Nov. 1739, leaving three daus., I. Jane, who *m.* twice—1st, to Simon Purdon, Esq. of Tinnerana co. Clare; and 2ndly, Richard Fitzpatrick, Esq. of Galway mayor and M.P.—she *d.* without leaving issue; II. Mary, *m.* 1st, to Robert, son of Richard Hedges, Esq. of Macroom, co. Cork, and left one son, RICHARD eventual successor to his grandfather, and one dau., Frances, *m* to John Becher, Esq. of Hollybrook; Mary *m.* 2ndly, the Rev. Thomas Hemsworth, and had one dau., Jane; III. Elizabeth, *m.* to William Rowan, Esq., and had issue one dau., Jane, *m.* to George Hamilton, Esq. of Killeleagh Castle, co. Down, was mother of Archibald-Hamilton Rowan, Esq.; IV. Margaret, *m.* 1st, to Francis Annesley, Esq. of Ballysax, co. Kildare, and 2ndly, to Dominick Burke, Esq. of Galway, M.P.; she *d. s. p.* in 1787. Upon the death of the latter, the estates of her father, Edward Eyre Esq., vested in her nephew,

RICHARD HEDGES, Esq. of Mount Hedges, who thereupon assumed the surname of EYRE, in conformity with his grandfather's will. He *m.* Helena, dau. of Edward Herbert, Esq. of Muckross, co. Kerry and *d.* in 1780, leaving with two daus., viz., Frances-Jane, wife of Simon White, Esq., and mother of Richard, Earl of Bantry (*see Peerage*), and Helena, *m.* to the Rev. George Maunsell, D.D., dean of Leighlin, by whom she was grandmother of the present Rev. Robert-Hedges-Eyre Maunsell Eyre (*see* MAUNSELL *of Plassy*), two sons, EDWARD, the elder, who *d.* intestate and *s. p.* in 1808, and

ROBERT-HEDGES EYRE, who *d.* in 1840, without issue, when his Galway estates became vested in his grand-

* His daughter Frances *m.* William Jackson, Esq. of Coleraine.
† Cumberland, the dramatist, whose father was Bishop of Clonfert during Lord Eyre's lifetime, gives in his Memoirs a curious account of a visit he paid to his lordship's castle.

nephew, the Rev. Robert-Hedges-Eyre Maunsell, grandson of his sister, Helena, who has now assumed the additional surname and arms of Eyre. The Macroom property, the late Mr. Hedges Eyre devised to the Hon. William-Henry White; the Berehaven estate, to Lord Berehaven; and that in Tipperary, to Robert White, Esq. of Glengariff.

Arms—Quarterly: 1st and 4th, arg., on a chev., sa., three quartrefoils, or, for Eyre; 2nd and 3rd, arg., a chev. between three maunches, sa., for Maunsell.

Crests—of Eyre: On a cap of maintenance, a booted and armed leg, couped at the thigh, quarterly, arg. and sa., spur, or; for Maunsell, a falcon hawk, rising, wings expanded, ppr.

Mottoes—1st, Si je puis; 2nd, Honorantes me honorabo; and 3rd, Quid vult valde vult.

EYSTON OF EAST HENDRED.

Eyston, Charles, Esq. of East Hendred, co. Berks, J.P. and D.L., *b.* 17 May, 1790; high-sheriff in 1831; *m.* 7 May, 1814, Maria-Theresa, only dau. of Thomas-Peter Metcalfe, Esq. of Barnborough Hall, Yorkshire, and heiress of her brother, Thomas-Peter Metcalfe-More, Esq., who *d.* in 1838. By this lady (who *d.* 19 March, 1848), Mr. Eyston has issue,

- I. Charles-John.
- II. George-Basil, *m.* Maria-Theresa, youngest dau. of George-Thomas Whitgreave, Esq. of Moseley Hall, co. Stafford.
- III. Robert-Thomas.
- I. Mary-Anne, *m.* 1845, to Richard-Thomas Gillow, Esq. of Leighton Hall, co. Lancaster.
- II. Isabella-Jane. III. Frances-Teresa.
- IV. Catherine-Teresa.

Lineage.—The Eystons have enjoyed their Berkshire estates in the male line since the reign of Henry VI., but inherit them from families in whose possession they were at a much earlier period.

John Eyston (whose family had, for three generations before possessed a manor in Isleworth, in Middlesex, now belonging to the Duke of Northumberland), *m.* Isabel Stowe, heiress of East Hendred, only dau. and heir of John Stowe, Esq. of Burford, co. Oxford, by Maude his wife, only dau. and heir of William-Rawlin de Arches, grandson of William de Arches, M.P. for Berks in 1336, whose mother, Amicia, was dau. and heir of Richard de Turberville, of East Hendred. By Isabel his wife, John Eyston had a son and heir,

William Eyston, Esq. of East Hendred, living there in 1494 who was father of

Thomas Eyston, Esq. of East Hendred, who *m.* Elizabeth, dau. of Robert Hyde, Esq., and had a son, his successor,

John Eyston, Esq. of East Hendred, living in 1544, who *m.* Maud, dau. of Humphrey Tirrell, Esq. of Wanley, Essex, and was *s.* by his son,

John Eyston, Esq., *b.* in 1531, who *m.* 1st, Joan Clifford, but had no issue. He *m.* 2ndly, Jane, dau. and co-heir of Thomas Berington, of Streatly, co. Berks, and had several children, by the eldest of whom,

William Eyston, Esq., he was *s.* at his decease, in 1590. This g ntleman *m.* Mary, dau. and co-heir of James Thatcher Esq. of Priesthawes, Sussex, by whom he had fourteen children. Adhering to the tenets of the Roman catholic religion, Mr. Eyston had his lands repeatedly sequestered during the reign of Charles I. He *d.* in 1649, and was *s.* by his eldest son,

William Eyston, Esq., *b.* in 1611, who *m.* Eleanor, dau. of George Smith, Esq. of Ash, co. Durham, and had issue,

William, who was cast away in a vessel sailing between Marseilles and Leghorn, in the eighteenth year of his age.
George. John. Joseph.
Frances, an Augustine nun, at Paris.

This gentleman, a great sufferer during the Civil Wars, both on account of his religion and loyalty, *d.* 11 April, 1670, and was *s.* by his eldest surviving son,

George Eyston, Esq. of East Hendred. He *m.* in 1644, Anne, dau. of Robert Dormer, Esq. of Peterly, co. Bucks, by whom he had five sons, Charles, George, Robert, William, and John. Dying in 1691, he was *s.* by his eldest son,

Charles Eyston Esq. of East Hendred, who *m.* in 1692 Winifred-Dorothy, dau. of Basil Fitzherbert, Esq of Swinnerton, co. Stafford, and had ten ch ldren, viz., Charles his successor; Basil, *d. s. p.*; Thomas-John, who inherited the estates; William-George; Winifred-Anne; Frances; Jane; Mary; Anne-Catherine; and Catherine-Mary. This Charles Eyston was a diligent and curious antiquary, and a friend and correspondent of Thomas Hearne, of antiquarian celebrity, of Dr. Rawlinson, and of several other persons eminent in literary and scientific pursuits. He *d.* in 1721, and was *s.* by his eldest son,

Charles Eyston, Esq. of East Hendred, who *m.* Mary-Magdalen, dau. of Thomas Hawkyns, Esq. of Nash Court, co. Kent, but dying *s. p.*, in 1747, aged 41, was *s.* by his next surviving brother,

Thomas-John Eyston, Esq. of East Hendred, who *m.* Mary, dau. of George Bruning, Esq. of East Meon, Hampshire, of an ancient family in that county, and had (with three daus., Mary-Magdalen; Winifred, *m.* to Bryan Barrett, Esq. of Milton, co. Berks; and Mary, *m.* to the late Charles Butler, Esq. of Lincoln's Inn, an eminent lawyer, and king's counsel) five sons, Basil, John, William, George, and Matthew-Robert. Mr. Eyston *d.* in 1796, at the advanced age of 82 and was *s.* by his eldest son,

Basil Eyston, Esq. of East Hendred, *b.* in 1748, who *m.* Mary-Jane, dau. and heir of Richard Huddleston, Esq., a younger son of Richard Huddleston, Esq. of Sawston, and by her (who *d.* June, 1847) left at his decease, in 1817,

Charles, his heir, now of East Hendred.
Basil, *m.* Catherine Langford, and has issue.
George. Ferdinand. John.
Mary-Jane.

Arms—Sable, three lions rampant, or, two and one; quartering Stowe, Arches, Turbeville, Berington, Thatcher, Lawkener. (*See* Burke's *General Armory.*)

Crest—A lion, sejant, or.

Seat—East Hendred House, co. Berks.

EYTON OF EYTON.

Eyton, Thomas-Campbell, Esq. of Eyton, co. Salop, J.P. and D.L., *b.* 10 Sept. 1809; *m.* 13 May, 1835, Elizabeth-Frances, eldest dau. of Robert-Aglionby Slaney, Esq. of Walford Manor and Hatton, co. Salop, and has issue,

- I. Thomas-Slaney, *b.* 19 June, 1843.
- II. Robert-Henry, *b.* 7 Dec. 1845.
- III. William-Campbell, *b.* 15 Nov. 1848.
- I. Elizabeth-Charlotte. II. Rose-Mary.
- III. Frances-Julia. IV. Catherine-Anne.
- V. Mary-Elizabeth. VI. Alice-Emily.

Lineage.—The family of Eyton resided from a very early period at Eyton-on-the-Wyldmores, and are presumed, from their armorial bearings, to have been a younger branch, or, at least, early vassals, of Pantulf Baron of Wem, who was mesne Lord of Eyton at the time of the Domesday survey. The first name on the pedigree is Robert de Eyton, who witnessed a grant by Robert Corbet to the Abbey of Shrewsbury, together with William, Alan, and Hugh, sons of Hugh Pantulf, and granted himself to that religious house the lands of Butterey, *temp.* Henry II. Ninth in descent from Robert was John de Eyton, sheriff of Shropshire in 1394, whose brother Humphrey Eyton, Esq., Ranger of the Forest of Wrekin and Wildmore, was grandfather of Nicholas Eyton, Esq. of Eyton sheriff of Shropshire in 1440 and knight of the shire in 1449. He was father of Lewis Eyton, Esq. of Eyton, who *m.* Anne, dau. of Sir John Savage, Knt. of Cheshire, and was great-grandfather of Thomas Eyton, Esq. of Eyton, sheriff in 1567, who *m.* Alice, dau. of William Charlton, Esq. of Apley, and had three sons, I. Robert, who *m.* Anne, dau. of James Leveson, Esq., and had a son, Richard, who *d. s. p.*; II. William; and III Thomas, father of Sir Philip Eyton who *s.* his cousin, Richard, at Eyton, and was high-sheriff of Shropshire in 1633. He *m.* Mary, dau. of David Yale, chancellor of Chester, and had a son and successor, Sir Thomas Eyton, of Eyton, whose 2nd son,

The Rev. John Eyton, vicar of Wellington, *s.* to the family estates at the decease of his nephew, Sowdley Eyton. He *m.* Rachel, dau. of Thomas Acton, Esq. of Gatacre Park, co. Salop and by her (who *d.* in 1706) had issue, Thomas, of whom presently; Robert, *d.* in 1717; Sowdley, *d.* in 1719; Mabell, *m.* to George Whitmore, Esq. of London; and Margaret *d.* young. He *d.* in 1709, and was *s.* by his son,

Thomas Eyton, Esq. of Eyton, high-sheriff of Salop in 1741, who *m.* Ann, dau. of the Right Rev. Robert Butts, bishop of Ely, and by her (who *d.* in 1757) left at his decease, in 1776 (with two daus., viz., Anne, wife of Thomas Kynnersley, Esq. of Leighton; and Elizabeth, wife of

Richard Morrall, Esq. of Onslow, co. Salop) two sons, THOMAS; and Robert, who d. in 1772. The elder,

THOMAS EYTON, Esq. of Eyton, high-sheriff of Shropshire in 1779, m. in 1776, Mary, dau. of John Rocke, Esq. of Trefnanney, co. Montgomery, and by her (who d. 26 Jan. 1809) had issue,

I. THOMAS, his heir.
II. Robert, d. in 1780.
III. John, in holy orders, rector of Wellington, who m. Anna-Maria, sole dau. and heiress of Edmund-Joseph Plowden, Esq. of Plowden Hall, co. Salop, and by her (who d. 18 Oct. 1825) had issue,
1 John, d. in 1836. 2 Edmund-Thomas.
3 Walter-Nathaniel, d. 16 March, 1817.
4 Robert-William, in holy orders.
5 Henry, d. 30 Sept. 1841.
6 Joseph-Walter.
1 Mary, m. to William-Henry Perry, Esq.
2 Ann-Rose, m. to the Rev. Henry Beckwith.
3 Anna-Maria-Dorothea, m. to Richard Neave, Esq.
The Rev. John Eyton d. 10 Jan. 1823.

Mr. Eyton d. 22 Jan. 1816, and was s. by his eldest son,

THOMAS EYTON, Esq. of Eyton, J.P. and D.L., recorder of Wenlock, high-sheriff of Shropshire in 1840, b. 27 March, 1777; m. 8 Dec. 1808, Elizabeth eldest dau. of Major-General Donald Campbell, and by her (who d. 23 July, 1817) had issue,

THOMAS-CAMPBELL, now of Eyton.
Charles-James, d. 1854.
William-Archibald, formerly capt. 96th regt.

Mr. Eyton d. 18 Feb. 1855.

Arms—Quarterly: 1st and 4th, or, a fret, az.; 2nd and 3rd, gu., two bars, erm.
Crests—1st, a rein-deer's head, couped and attired, or, in his mouth an acorn slip, vert, fructed, of the first; 2nd, a Cornish chough's head, erased, sa., holding in its beak a trefoil, slipped; 3rd, a lion's head, arg., devouring a barrel or tun, or.
Seat—Eyton, co. Salop.

EYTON OF LEESWOOD.

EYTON, JOHN-WYNNE, Esq. of Leeswood, co. Flint, b. 12 May, 1786; m. Jane, dau. of Robert Lloyd, Esq. of Swanhill, co. Salop.

Lineage.—This is a younger branch of the Davies's of Gwysaney, representatives of CYNRIC EFELL LORD OF EGLWYS EGLE younger son of Madoc last Prince of Powys.

From the Lord of Eglwys-Egle derived, 4th in descent, MEILER AP GRONO, whose descendant

GRIFFITH AP NICHOLAS ap Dicus ap Grono ap Griffith Grach ap Meilir ap Grono, m. Margaret, dau. of John ap Ellis Eyton, of Rhuabon, co. Denbigh, a distinguished branch of the tribe of the Marches, established by Tudor Trevor, Lord of Hereford and Whittington. Of this marriage the elder son,

JOHN EYTON, had issue, by Catherine his wife, dau. of Ellis ap Tudyr, of Yale, several daus. and an only son,

JOHN EYTON, who m. Jane, dau. of John Lloyd, Esq. of Bodidris-yn-Yale, co. Denbigh, and sister of Sir Evan Lloyd, Knt. of Bodidris and was father of eight sons and three daus. From Ellis, one of the younger sons, derived the EYTONS *of Maes y Groes*, co. Flint, a younger son of which family Thomas Eyton, Esq. of Cilcain, was father of THOMAS EYTON, Esq. of Langynhafal co. Denbigh, who m. Alice Roberts, and had issue, I. Robert, in holy orders, d. unm.; II. Thomas, who m. Miss Pryse, of Caerwys, and was father of JOHN EYTON Esq., now of Llanerch-y-Mor; I. Elizabeth, m. in 1771, to the Rev. William Tooke, and had issue two sons, Thomas and William, and one dau. Elizabeth. The eldest son,

JOHN EYTON, Esq. of Leeswood, co. Flint m. 1st, Jane, dau. of David Jones, of Halkin, co. Flint; and 2ndly Jane, dau. of Edward Kynaston, of Pantybyrsley, relict of Philip Lloyd, of Hardwick. By his 1st lady he was father of four daus. and an only son,

JOHN EYTON, Esq. of Leeswood. He m. Susan, dau. and co-heir of Thomas Puleston, of Lightwood Green, and d. 19 March, 1600, having had issue (with a dau. Mary, wife of John Trevor, of Trevor Esq.) an only son,

JOHN EYTON, Esq. of Trimley, who wedded Dorothy dau. of William Herbert, of Kerry and Trefegiwys, both in the co. of Montgomery, and had issue,

John Eyton, Esq. of Leeswood, who m. Dorothea, dau. of Robert Davies, Esq. of Gwysaney, co. Flint, and widow of George Hope, Esq. of Brynne and Doddleston, co. Salop, and was father of a dau. who d. an infant in 1671.

THOMAS, continuer of the line. William.
Margaret.
Dorothy, m. Edward Lloyd, of Pentrehobyn, co. Flint.

The younger son,

THOMAS EYTON, Esq. of Trimley, m. Elizabeth, dau. of Sir Thomas Powell, Bart. of Horsley, co. Surrey, and had issue a son,

THOMAS EYTON, Esq., who m. Elizabeth, dau. of Robert Davies, Esq. of Gwysaney and Llanerch and had (with a son, THOMAS his heir, and other children, who d. unm.) a dau. Elizabeth, m. to Robert Wynne, Esq. of Garthewyn, and a son,

THE REV. JOHN EYTON, rector of Westbury co. Salop, who m. Penelope, only child of George Hope, Esq. of Hope, by Elizabeth Longueville his wife, and by her, who d. in 1800 left at his decease, with other issue, a son and successor,

HOPE EYTON Esq. of Leeswood, b. 19 Nov. 1754, who m. 10 Nov. 1783, Margaret, dau. of Robert Wynne, Esq. of Tower, co. Flint, and had issue,

JOHN-WYNNE, his heir. Thomas-Wynne.
Robert-Wynne, M.A., vicar of Llangollen, m. Charlotte, dau. of Thomas Griffith, Esq. of Rhual, co. Flint.
William-Wynne, R.N.
Charles-Watkin-Wynne, in holy orders.
Harriet. Louisa-Elizabeth.
Margaret-Letitia, d. unm. in 1808.

Mr. Eyton d. in 1824.

Arms—Az., on a bend, arg., a lion passant, sa.
Seat—Leeswood, Flintshire.

FAGAN OF FELTRIM.

FAGAN, WILLIAM-TRANT, Esq. of Feltrim, co. Cork, M.P., J.P., and D.L., b. 31 Jan. 1801; m. 21 June, 1827, Mary, dau. of Charles Addis, Esq. of London, by Rebecca Hornby his wife, and has issue,

I. CHARLES-ADDIS, b. 16 Aug. 1829.
II. William-Addis, b. 16 Dec. 1832.
III. Hornby, b. 7 May, 1838.
I. Mary, m. 1856 to Daniel Francis Leahy, Esq., son of the late Daniel Leahy, Esq., of Shannakiel House.

Lineage.—PATRICK O'HAGAN, alias FAGAN, second son of John O'Hagan, Baron of Tullagh-Og, in Tyrone, by Catherine, his wife, dau. of Hugh MacMahon, Baron of Furney, and second brother of Bryan More MacMahon, Dynast of Monaghan, accompanied his father, in 1180, in his expedition at the head of the forces of Tyrone, to the assistance of O'Melaghlin, Prince of Meath, in order to repel the encroachments of the English settlers in his principality. So soon as the object of the expedition was fulfilled, the troops returned to their respective homes; but Patrick O'Hagan remained in Meath, where he m. Dorothea, dau. of Cormac or Charles O'Melaghlin, son to the last reigning prince of that name, and acquired with her a large territory, which was confirmed to him by charter in 1210, by Walter de Lacy, Lord of Meath, in obedience to the command of King JOHN, then in Ireland. From that period Patrick assumed the English costume and an English name, and served his lord paramount with attachment and fidelity. In 1233, he accompanied William de Lacy on an incursion into O'Reilly's country, bordering on the province of Meath, and was slain, with William de Lacy, and others of the English and Irish chiefs. His son,

JOHN FAGAN, of Derry Fagan, Faganston, Monrath, &c., in Meath, also supported the English interest, until his death, in 1248. He m. Ann, dau. of Sir Alexander Plunkett, Knt., and was direct ancestor of the FAGANS *of Feltrim*, co. Dublin, a very influential and historic house.

RICHARD FAGAN, Esq. of Feltrim (son and heir of Christopher Fagan, of Feltrim, and Castle Fagan, and grandson of Richard Fagan, of Feltrim, who m. his cousin, Elinor, only dau. and heir of Thomas Fagan, Esq. of Castle Fagan), fought for King JAMES II. at Aughrim and Derry, and forfeited all his inheritance. His daus and co-heirs were Helen, wife of John Taylor, Esq. of Swords, and Mary, wife of John Eustace, of Clonfee Castle; and his sister, Elizabeth Fagan, was m. to George Hamilton, 4th Lord Strabane, by whom she was mother of the 4th and 5th EARLS OF ABERCORN.

JOHN FAGAN, Esq. (younger brother of Richard Fagan, Esq. of Feltrim, who m. the heiress of Castle Fagan, and 4th son of John Fagan, Esq. of Feltrim, by Alice his wife, dau. of Walter Segrave, Esq., Lord Mayor of Dublin), d. in 1683, having had three sons and one dau., viz.,

WILLIAM, his heir.
CHRISTOPHER, successor to his brother.
JAMES, lieut.-col. of Hamal's regiment in the Spanish service. He *m.* the heiress of the house of Turges, in the province of Lorraine, and was living, in 1722, at St. Martin's in that country.
Ellen, *m.* to Dominick Rice, Esq. of Ballymacdoyle, grandfather of James Rice, Count of the Holy Roman Empire.

The eldest son,

WILLIAM FAGAN, Esq., was surnamed the "Rich," from having acquired a very large fortune, which soon vanished through his attachment to King JAMES II. as well as his unbounded generosity to the chief officers of his army, as appears from the many bonds and notes still in the possession of the family. He *d. s. p.* bequeathing the residue of his property to his brother,

CHRISTOPHER FAGAN, Esq., captain in Browne of Kenmare's regiment of infantry, in the service of JAMES II. This gentleman, who was comprised in the capitulation of Limerick, purchased property in the co. of Kerry, and settled there. He *m.* after the Revolution, Mary, dau. of Patrick Nagle, Esq. of Ballinamona Castle, in the co. of Cork, by Catherine, his wife, dau of Hugh de Lacy, Esq. of Bruff, in Limerick, and was *s.* by his son,

PATRICK FAGAN, Esq. of Killarney, who *m.* in 1732, Christiana, dau. of Thomas Fitzmaurice, Esq. of Cossfoyle, in the co. of Kerry, by Mary his wife, dau. of Robert Rice, Esq. of Ballangolline, and had

I. CHRISTOPHER, *b.* in 1733, entered the French army in 1755, and became captain in Prince Soubise's dragoons, and had the cross of the royal military order of St. Louis. He *d.* in London, 6 Jan. 1816, aged eighty-three. This gentleman, for many years well known and highly esteemed in the English and French capitals as "the Chevalier de Fagan," *m.* Catherine, dau. of Joseph de Cortes, and had two sons,
  1 CHRISTOPHER, captain in Dillon's regiment of the Irish brigade, in the French service, and afterwards an officer in the British army, *d. unm.* in the West Indies.
  2 CHARLES, also captain in Dillon's regiment. He *m.* in 1788, Maria-Theresa-Pauline, Marchioness de Lawoestine, dau. of Maximilian, Marquis de Lawoestine, and de Becelaer, grandee of Spain of the first class. By Royal permision he assumed the title of Count de Fagan. Count Fagan *d.* 6 March, 1813, leaving issue,
    CHARLES-ANTOINE-EDWIN, Count de Fagan, a captain in the lancers of the gardes du corps to CHARLES X. He was killed by a fall from his carriage.
    Maria-Christiana-Pauline, chanoiness of the royal chapter of St. Anne de Bavaria.
    Maria-Theresa-Sophia, *m.* to Count Coronine, of Cronberg, chamberlain to his Majesty the Emperor of Austria, and grand cup-bearer to the Duke of Carniole.
II. STEPHEN, of whom presently.
III. Robert, of Philadelphia, who had three sons and a daughter. Of the former,
  CHRISTOPHER, major-gen. in the E. I. Co's service, *m.* 1st, his cousin, Mary-Eliza, dau. of John Fagan, Esq. of Kiltallagh, which lady *d. s. p.* at Calcutta, 10 Nov. 1805; 2ndly, Eliza Lawtre, of that city, by whom who *d.* 4 Jan. 1824, he had three sons and three daus.; and 3rdly, Maria, dau. of the Rev. Mr. Gibbon.
IV. Patrick, M.D. of Ross, in Wexford, *m.* Catherine Harper, of Ballingby.
V. Andrew, *d.* an officer in the Hon. E. I. Co's service.
VI. John, of Kittallah, co. Kerry, *m.* in 1772, Elizabeth, only dau. of George Hickson, Esq. of Tralee, by Mary, his wife, only dau. of Henry Gould, Esq., and niece of Dominick Trant, Esq of the city of Cork. By her he had issue,
  1 George-Hickson, *b.* 8 Nov. 1778, a highly distinguished officer, *m.* Harriet Lawtre, of Calcutta, and dying 25 May, 1821, left two sons and four daus., namely, Christopher-George, George-Hickson, and Elizabeth-Maria.
  2 Patrick-Charles, *b.* 17 March, 1780, lieut. E.I.C.S., *m.* Maria, dau. of the Rev. Dr. Slator, of Naas, co. Dublin, and had a dau. Eliza, *m.* to George Francs, Esq. of the Bengal civil service. Lieutenant Fagan *d.* at Patna, in the East Indies, 26 Oct. 1808.
  3 Christopher-Sullivan, C.B. colonel of a regiment of infantry in the Hon. E. I. Co.'s service, *b.* 22 March, 1781. Colonel Fagan *m.* 1st, Agnes dau. of Christopher Baldock, Esq. of the Island of Guernsey, by Catherine his wife, dau. of John Carey, Esq., and had by her four sons and six daus., viz.,
    George-Hickson, *b.* 18 Aug. 1810, an officer in the E.I.C.S.
    Christopher, *b.* 5 Nov. 1812, merchant and agent in Calcutta.
    John, *b.* 29 Oct. 1815, H.E.I.C.S.
    Robert-Charles Henry Baines, *b.* 14 May, 1823.
    Eliza, *m.* 4 Feb. 1831, General Sir J. W. Sleigh, K.C.B., and has issue.

    Mary, *m.* 27 Jan. 1836, to James Erskine, Esq. of the Bombay civil service.
    Catherine.
    Agnes-Cecilia-Adelaida. Carolina.
  Colonel Fagan *m.* 2ndly, Elizabeth-Jane, dau. of George Moule, Esq. of Melksham, Wilts, and had by her,
    William-Turton, *b.* 5 July, 1831.
    Frederick-Christopher, *b.* 9 March, 1836.
    Ellen-Georgiana-Elizabeth.
    Sarah-Christiana. Clementina-Marian.
  4 Robert, *b.* 21 July, 1783, entered the British service, and was wounded in the assault of Mona Fortuna, in the Island of Martinico, in 1802. He *d. unm.* 8 June, 1808.
  5 John, *b.* 20 Nov. 1784, lieut. Hon. E. I. Co.'s service, Bengal establishment, *d. unm.* at Mallow in Ireland, 24 Oct. 1800.
  6 James-Patrick, *b.* 17 March, 1788, major in the Bengal army. He *m.* Stephannie le Mere, and had four sons and three daughters.
  1 Mary-Eliza, *m.* to her first cousin, Christopher Fagan, Esq., and *d. s. p.* in Calcutta, in 1805.
  2 Christian.
  3 Eliza-Mary, *m.* to Major-General I. L. Richardson, of the E. I. Co.'s service, and has issue.
  4 Ellen, *m.* to Lieutenant-Colonel W. H. L. Frith, of the Bengal artillery, and has issue,
  5 Catherine, *m.* to James Langdale, Esq. of London, has issue,
  6 Frances, *d.* in Tralee, October, 1801.
VII. James, who entered the French service and rose to eminence in it. In 1778, he was second in command of the Island of Dominica. At the French Revolution he emigrated, and was soon after received into the British service, in which he was employed on the staff by the late General C. Cuyler, at the reduction of several of the West India islands, and was at the period of his death in a duel at Grenada, 1 Oct. 1801, assistant-quarter-master-general.
VIII. William, *d. unm.*
I. Mary, *m.* to — Sheehy, Esq.
II. Elizabeth, *m.* to Christopher Sullivan, Esq.
III. Frances, *m.* to Matthew Moriarty, M.D. of Tralee.
IV. Ellen, *d.* in Paris, *unm.*

The 2nd son,

STEPHEN FAGAN, Esq., merchant of Cork, *m.* 16 May, 1768, Helena, dau. of James Trant, Esq. of Castle Island, co. Kerry, and had

I. Patrick, who *m.* Miss Hussey, of Dingle, and had three sons and a dau. He was killed by a fall from his horse.
II. JAMES, of whom presently.
I. Eliza, *m.* to Alexander M'Carthy, Esq. of Cork.

Stephen Fagan, *d.* 10 Oct. 1811. His 2nd son,

JAMES FAGAN, Esq., *m.* 12 June, 1799, Ellen-Teresa, dau. of Ignatius Trant, Esq. of Cork, a lineal descendant of Sir Patrick Trant, outlawed in 1691. for his adhesion to JAMES II. By this lady (who *d.* 6 Jan. 1836), Mr. Fagan left at his decease, 21 June, 1822,

  WILLIAM-TRANT, M.P. of Feltrim, Cork.
  Charles-James-Fox.
  Susan, *m.* to Henry O'Brien, Esq., M.D.

Arms—Gu., three covered cups, or.
Crest—A griffin, segreant, supporting a branch of laurel, ppr.
Motto—Deo Patriæque fidelis.
Seat—Feltrim, Cork.

FAIRFAX OF GILLING CASTLE.

FAIRFAX, CHARLES-GREGORY, Esq. of Gilling Castle, co. York, *m.* a dau. of Michael Tasburgh, Esq., of Burgh Wallis, co. York.

Lineage.—This ancient family was originally named from the "fair locks" of its members, *feax* signifying hair in the language of our Saxon ancestors and it was established before the Norman conquest at Torcester co Northumberland, whence removing into Yorkshire, there, in the vicinity of York. in the year 1205,

WILLIAM FAIRFAX son of William Fairfax, of Askam and grandson of Richard Fairfax of Askam, was bailiff of York in 1249, and purchasing from Peter de Bruce the manor of Walton, made that the place of his residence. His descendant

RICHARD FAIRFAX, of Walton, who flourished in the reigns of the fourth. fifth and sixth HENRIES, and was Chief Justice of England under the last monarch, *m.* Anastasia, dau. and co-heir of John Carthorpe. by Elizabeth his wife, dau. and co-heir of Sir William Ergham, Knt., and had, with other issue, WILLIAM, his heir, and Guy (Sir). Judge of the King's Bench, ancestor of the Fairfaxes of Newton and Steeton, and of the Lords Fairfax of Cameron. The eldest son and heir,

WILLIAM FAIRFAX, Esq. of Walton, was ancestor of the FAIRFAX's *of Walton, Viscounts Fairfax*, of Elmley, in the peerage of Ireland (*see* BURKE's *Extinct Peerage*).

WILLIAM FAIRFAX, 9th viscount, *m.* Elizabeth, dau. of Capt. Gerard, and had issue, CHARLES-GREGORY, his heir; Richard who predeceased his brother, *s. p.*; and Alathea, *m.* to Ralph Pigott Esq. of Whitton, in Middlesex. He *d.* in Nov. 1738 and was *s.* by his son,

CHARLES-GREGORY FAIRFAX 10th viscount, who left at his decease an only surviving dau. and heiress,

THE HON. ANNE FAIRFAX, who *d. unm.* in 1793, when the estates passed to her cousin,

CHARLES-GREGORY PIGOTT, 2nd son of the late Nathaniel Pigott, Esq. by Anna-Mathurina his wife, dau. of Monsieur de Beriol and grandson of Ralph Pigott, Esq. of Whitton, by ALATHEA FAIRFAX his wife. He assumed, by act of parliament in 1793, the surname of FAIRFAX only. He *m.* 1794, Mary, sister of Sir Henry Goodricke Bart. of Ribston, co. York and *d.* leaving a son, the present CHARLES-GREGORY FAIRFAX of Gilling Castle, and a dau., Harriet *m.* 22 Feb. 1839, to Francis Cholmeley, Esq. of Brandsby Hall, co. York.

Arms—Arg., three bars gemelles, gu., surmounted by a lion, rampant, sa.
Crest—On a cap of maintenance, a lion, passant, guardant, sa.
Motto—Je le feray durant ma vie.
Seat—Gilling Castle, eighteen miles north of York.

FAIRFAX OF STEETON AND NEWTON KYME.

FAIRFAX, THOMAS, Esq. of Steeton and Newton Kyme, co. York, J.P. and D.L., *b.* 1804; *m.* 29 July, 1836, Louisa-Constantia, dau. of George Ravenscroft, Esq., and has issue,

I. THOMAS-FERDINAND, *b.* 6 Oct. 1839.
II. Reginald-Guy.
III. Charles-Henry.
I. Constance-Frances.
II. Emma-Louisa.
III. Katherine-Henrietta.
IV. Isabel-Augusta.

Lineage.—SIR GUY FAIRFAX, 3rd son of Richard Fairfax, of Walton, co. York, Chief Justice of England, *temp.* HENRY VI., was constituted one of the Justices of the Court of King's Bench in 1478. He obtained from his father the manor of Steeton, and erecting a castle seated himself there. He *m.* Margaret, dau. of Sir William Ryther, of Ryther, and dying 1495, left (with two daus. Eleanor, *m.* to Sir Miles Wilstrop, of Wilstrop; and Maud *m.* to Sir John Waterton, of Medley, master of the horse to HENRY VI.) four sons, WILLIAM (Sir), his heir; Thomas serjeant-at-law; Guy; and Nicholas. The eldest son,

SIR WILLIAM FAIRFAX, of Steeton, one of the Judges of the Common Pleas *temp.* HENRY VIII., *m.* Elizabeth, eldest dau. of Sir Robert Manners, and dying in 1514 left (with four daus. Elizabeth *m.* to Sir Robert Oughtred; Ellen, *m.* to Sir William Pickering the elder, Knight Mareschal of England; Anne, *m.* to Sir Robert Normanville; and Dorothy, *m.* to — Constable, of Kexby), an only son,

SIR WILLIAM FAIRFAX Knt. of Steeton, high-sheriff of Yorkshire 26 and 31 HENRY VIII., who *m.* Isabel, only dau. of Thomas Thwayte Esq. of Denton, and dying in 1557 left, with five daus. as many sons viz., I. THOMAS (Sir) Knt. of Denton, ancestor of the LORDS FAIRFAX *of Cameron* (*see* BURKE's *Peerage and Baronetage*); II. Francis; III. Edward; IV. Henry whose eldest son was Gabriel Fairfax, Esq. of Strettonhouse; V. GABRIEL. The youngest son,

GABRIEL FAIRFAX Esq. of Steeton who distinguished his coat armour by bearing the lion, crowned or. He *m.* Elizabeth dau. of Thomas Aske, Esq. of Aughton, by Anne his wife dau. of Thomas Sutton, Esq., and had (with two daus. Anne, wife of Sir Edmund Sheffield, of Epworth; and Mary, *m.* to Sir Thomas Gower, of Stittenham) four sons, of whom the eldest,

SIR WILLIAM FAIRFAX, of Steeton was knighted by Queen ELIZABETH in 1561. He *m.* Mabel, dau. of Sir Henry Curwen, of Workington, and had by her five sons and four daus., viz., I. PHILIP (Sir) who *m.* Frances, 2nd dau. of Edmund Sheffield 1st Earl of Mulgrave, and had, with other issue, WILLIAM (Sir); II. William; III. Frederick; IV. Francis; V. Arthur; I. Mary *b.* in 1583, *m.* to Everingham Cressy Esq.; II. Priscilla *m.* to Anthony Saltmarsh, Esq.; III. Bridget, IV. Prudence. Sir William's grandson,

SIR WILLIAM FAIRFAX, Knt. of Steeton, *m.* Frances, dau. of Sir Thomas Challoner, governor and chamberlain to Prince Henry and being slain before Montgomery Castle in 1644, left (with two daus. Catharine, *m.* 1st, to Sir Martin Lister, Knt., and 2ndly to Sir Charles Lyttleton, of Hagley, Bart.; and Isabella, *m.* to Nathaniel Bladen, Esq. of Hemsworth) two sons, WILLIAM, his heir; and Thomas, major-gen. in the army, and governor of Limerick, *d.* in 1712. The elder son,

WILLIAM FAIRFAX, Esq. of Steeton, *m.* Catharine, 3rd dau. of Robert Stapleton, Esq. of Wigill, co. York, and dying in 1673, was *s.* by his eldest son,

WILLIAM FAIRFAX, Esq. of Steeton, who *d. unm.* 3 July, 1694 and was *s.* by his brother,

ROBERT FAIRFAX, Esq. of Newton Kyme, vice-admiral of the Blue, M.P. for York, and its lord mayor in 1715, the memorable year of the rising for Prince Charles. He *m.* Hester, dau. of Robert Bushell, Esq. of Ruswarpe, co. York, and *d.* 6 Oct. 1725, leaving (with a dau. Catharine, *m.* to Henry Pawson, Esq. of York) one son,

THOMAS FAIRFAX, Esq. of Newton Kyme, who *m.* Elizabeth dau. of John Simpson, Esq. of Babworth Hall, Notts, and had by her one dau. Elizabeth, and five sons I. Robert, *d. s. p.*; II. JOHN; III. Thomas, who *d.* young; IV. Guy, in holy orders, who *m.* a dau. of the Rev. John Kearney D.D., by Henrietta his wife, dau. of the Hon. and Rev. Henry Brydges, brother of James, Duke of Chandos, and had a dau. Henrietta-Catherine, *m.* to Joseph-Chamberlayne Chamberlayne, Esq. of Maugersbury; and V. William. The 2nd son and heir,

JOHN FAIRFAX Esq. of Steeton and Newton Kyme *m.* Jane, dau. and co-heir of George Loddington, Esq. of Bracebridge Hall, co. Lincoln, and was *s.* by his son,

THOMAS LODDINGTON FAIRFAX, Esq. of Steeton and Newton Kyme, *b.* in 1770, who *m.* Theophania, dau. of James Chaloner, Esq., 2nd son of Chaloner of Guisborough, and *d.* 1st July, 1840, leaving (with three daus., Jane-Frances; Elizabeth, *m.* in Feb. 1832, to the Rev. Thomas-Hart Dyke, of East Hall, Kent; and Theophania *m.* to Henry-Collingwood Blackett, Esq.) a son and successor, the present THOMAS FAIRFAX, Esq. of Steeton and Newton Kyme.

Arms—Arg., three bars gemelles, gu., surmounted by a lion, rampant, sa., crowned, or.
Crest—A lion, passant, guardant, sa.
Motto—Fare fac.
Seat—Newton Kyme, Tadcaster.

FAIRHOLME OF GREENKNOWE.

FAIRHOLME, WILLIAM, of Greenknowe, co. Berwick, *b.* 8 Aug. 1819; *m.* 15 June, 1853, Grace-Penelope, eldest dau. of Wray Palliser, Esq. of Comragh, co. Waterford, by Anne Gledstanes his wife, and has issue a dau.,

Anne-Gledstanes.

Lineage.—The late GEORGE FAIRHOLME of Greenknowe son of WILLIAM FAIRHOLME, Esq. of Chapel, co. Berwick (who *d.* 1806) by Elizabeth Compton his wife, dau. of Pringle, of Torwoodlee, co. Selkirk, *m.* 16 Nov. 1818, Caroline-Elizabeth, eldest dau. of James Ochoncar, 17th Lord Forbes, and had issue,

WILLIAM, now of Greenknowe.
James-Walter, lieut. R.N., who sailed with Sir John Franklin's expedition to the North Pole.
George-Knight-Erskine.
Charles, lieut. R.N.
Elizabeth-Margery, *m.* 6 Nov. 1851, to Lord James Murray, brother to the Duke of Athol.

Mr. Fairholme *d.* 19 Nov. 1846.

Arms—Or., an anchor, ppr.
Crest—A dove with an olive branch in its bill, ppr.
Motto—Spero meliora.
Seat—Greenknowe, co. Berwick.

FALCONER OF LEIGHTON.

FALCONER, RANDLE-WILBRAHAM, Esq., M.D., physician of the United and General Hospitals at Bath, *m.* 1st, Anne-Maria, dau. of John Wood, Esq. of Cwm and Brynhafod, Carmarthenshire, and by her (who *d.* 24 Dec. 1847) had issue,

I. JOHN-RANDLE-FALCONER.
II. Walter-Wilbraham.

He *m.* 2ndly, Sophia-Harriett Fanny, dau. of Major-General Richard-W. Howard-Vyse, of Stoke, co. Buckingham, and of Boughton, co. Northampton, heir of Field-Marshal Howard, of Effingham, and co-heir of the earldom of Strafford, and formerly

M.P. for Beverley and for Honiton, and has issue by this marriage,

I. GEORGE-THOMAS-WENTWORTH.
I. Lucy-Wentworth-Frances.
II. Sophia-Harriet-Rachael.

Lineage.—The elder line of this family is that of the Falconers of Halkerton, in Scotland, of whom was Sir Alexander Falconer, appointed a lord of session of the supreme court in 1639, and reappointed in 1661, after the restoration of CHARLES II. He was created Baron Halkerton, "to him and his heirs male whatsoever," and *d.* 1 Oct. 1671. His nephew, Sir David Falconer, also an eminent judge, was appointed a lord of session in 1676, taking the judicial title of Lord Newton, and became lord president in 1682. By his 2nd wife, Mary Nowell, he was ancestor of the Earls of Kintore, and Barons Halkerton:—he was, also, grandfather of David Hume the historian. A junior branch was Falconer of Phesdo. The lands of Phesdo were erected into a barony in 1672, in favour of Sir James Falconer, eldest son of Sir John Falconer [*m.* Agnes Spence] of Phesdo, warden of the Mint in Scotland, by whom these lands were surrendered in that year to his said son. This Sir James Falconer was appointed a lord of session in 1689, and took the judicial title of Lord Phesdo. He *d.* in 1705. He *m.* Elisabeth Trent, and had issue, John Falconer, Esq., who *d.* without issue in 1764, leaving the lands of Phesdo to his relative the Hon. Captain George Falconer, brother to the 6th and 7th Lord Halkerton. Of the Phesdo family was

JOHN FALCONER, Esq.,* who *m.* Mary Dalmahoy (who *d.* at Chester), dau. of John Dalmahoy, Esq.,† the 2nd son of Sir John Dalmahoy, of Dalmahoy, co. Edinburgh, by Rachael his wife, dau. of Thomas Wilbraham, Esq. of Nantwich. He had issue, three sons,

I. THOMAS, eighteen years in the service of the H.E.I.C. and their Resident at Cozimbuzar, and who died *unm.* in Jan. 1780, shortly after his return from India.
II. JAMES, lieut. R.N., *m.* 24 Sept. 1734, to Elizabeth Inge, dau. of William Inge, Esq. of Thorpe Constantine, co. Stafford, and had issue,
1 Elizabeth Falconer, who *m.* Thomas Pennant, Esq., the celebrated antiquary and naturalist, of Downing, Flintshire, from whom descended the late Lady Fielding, the heiress of the Pennant estates.
1 James Falconer, D.D., of Oriel College, Oxford, archdeacon of Derby, rector of Thorp, vicar of Lullington, and prebendary of Lichfield. He was *b.* in 1737, and *d.* April, 1809; he *m.* Mary, dau. of Thomas Hall, Esq. of Hermitage in Cranage, Cheshire, and sister of Mrs. Inge, of Thorpe Constantine. He had issue, four daus.,
Elizabeth, *m.* 17 Sept. 1787, the Rev. John-Batteridge Pearson, prebendary of Lichfield and vicar of Croxall, Derbyshire.
Mary, *m.* 5 Jan. 1791, the Rev. John Norbury, prebendary of Lichfield, and rector of St. Albans with St. Olave's, London.
Frances, *m.* 16 Jan. 1793, Lieut.-Col. William-Charles Madan, son of the Right Rev. Dr. Madan, bishop of Peterborough, and nephew of the 1st Marquess Cornwallis.
Catherine, *m.* 9 Oct. 1802, Col. Sir Edward Miles, C.B.
III. WILLIAM, of the Inner Temple, barrister-at-law, recorder of Chester, *b.* 1699, *m.* 7 Jan. 1731, his 2nd cousin, Elizabeth Wilbraham, dau. of Randle Wilbraham, Esq. of Nantwich, ancestor of the 1st Lord Skelmersdale, and *d.* 2 June, 1764, leaving issue,
1 THOMAS, of whom presently.
2 WILLIAM, M.D., of whom presently.
1 Mary, *m.* Charles Mainwaring, Esq. of Bromborough, co. Chester, and *d.* Sept. 1789, leaving issue.

THOMAS FALCONER, Esq. of Chester and of Lincoln's Inn, barrister-at-law (son of William Faleoner, Esq., recorder of Chester, and Elizabeth Wilbraham his wife), was the annotator of the Oxford edition of *Strabo*, and the author of several publications. He was *b.* 1736, and *d.* at Chester, *unm.* 4 Sept. 1792. His brother,

WILLIAM FALCONER, M.D., F.R.S., *b.* at Chester, Feb. 1745, *d.* at Bath, 31 Aug. 1824. He was the author of many medical and other publications. He *m.* Henrietta, dau. of Thomas Edmunds, Esq. of Worsborough Hall, co. York, and had one child,

THE REV. THOMAS FALCONER, M.A., M.D., *b.* 24 Dec. 1772, who *d.* at Bath, 19 Feb. 1839. He was formerly fellow of Corpus Christi College, Oxford, and Bampton lecturer in that University. He *m.* Frances, dau. and heir of Lieut.-Col. Robert Raitt, of the 2nd regt., and had issue,

WILLIAM, M.A., late fellow of Exeter College, Oxford, rector of Bushey, co. Hertfordshire, public examiner at Oxford in the years 1833 and 1837, *m.* Isabella, dau. of J. Robinson, Esq. and widow of W. Douglas, Esq.
Thomas, of Lincoln's Inn, barrister-at-law, appointed in October, 1850, joint arbitrator with the Right Hon. Dr. Lushington and Dr. Twiss, to determine the boundary between the provinces of Canada and New Brunswick, gazetted 26 July, 1851, Colonial Secretary of Western Australia, and appointed, 22 Dec. 1851, judge of the County Courts of the counties Glamorgan and Brecknock, and of the district of Rhayader, in Radnorshire.
Alexander Pytts, of Becton, Hampshire.
John-David. RANDLE-WILBRAHAM.
Henrietta, *m.* John-Arthur Roebuck, Esq., M.P. for Sheffield, a queen's counsel, and a bencher of the Inner Temple, and has issue an only child, Henrietta-Zipporah-Roebuck.
Frances.

Arms—Or, a falcon's head issuing from a heart, gu., between three mullets, az., and on a bordure of the last, eight plates.
Crest—A falcon perched, hooded and belled, proper.*
Motto—Vive ut vivas.

These arms were matriculated in the Lyon Office, about the year 1673, in favour of Sir John Falconer, of Phesdo, warden of the Mint.

The ancient arms of this family of Falconer are—az., an eagle displayed, ar., crowned and charged with a heart, gu., between three mullets, of the second. *Crest*—An angel kneeling within an orle of laurel.

FALKINER OF MOUNT FALCON.

FALKINER, RICHARD-HENRY-FITZRICHARD, Esq. of Mount Falcon, co. Tipperary, and Kilmakuddrick, co. Dublin, J.P., *b.* 2 Sept. 1827.

Lineage.—This, which was formerly an old Yorkshire family, and branches of which belonged to the counties of Hants, Salop, and Lincoln, settled in Ireland in the earlier part of the 17th century. About the time of the taking of the city of York by the Parliamentary army, *anno* 1644, MICHAEL FALKINER, Esq., a gentleman residing near Leeds, a cavalier, and one deeply attached to the royal cause, went over to Ireland in the army of the Marquess of Ormonde, and after the triumph of the revolutionary party, established himself in Dublin. There is still in the possession of a member of this family a signet ring presented by CHARLES I. during his residence in the north, 1642, to Michael Falkiner. He was *b.* in 1598, and *m.* 1637, Miss Anne Jackson, of Leeds, by whom he had issue, with four daus., four sons,

I. RICHARD, of whom we treat.
II. Daniel, *b.* Dec. 1642, of the city of Dublin; *m.* and had issue three sons and a dau.,
1 John, of Nangor and Terenure, co. Dublin, *m.* 1695, Mary, dau. of Charles Budden, Esq. of Terenure, and had issue three daus., co-heiresses,
Elizabeth, *m.* Freeman Rogers, Esq. of Ballynavin Castle, co. Tipperary.
Rebecca, *m.* William Gibton, Esq. of Dublin, and had issue a dau., *m.* Travers Hartley, Esq., member for Dublin in the Irish parliament, and predecessor of Henry Grattan, Esq. in the representation of that city. The eldest dau. of Travers Hartley and Miss Gibton *m.* Richard Litton, Esq., and their dau., Tempe Litton, is the mother of Mr. Falkiner of Mount Falcon.
Sarah, *m.* John Taylor, Esq., and had issue.
2 Daniel, of Dublin, sheriff of that city in 1719, and lord mayor in 1739; *m.* Eliza, dau. of George Spence, Esq., and had issue, Frederick, of Cottage and Abbotstown, co. Dublin, who *d.* 1785, having *m.* Elizabeth, dau. of James Hamilton, of Bailieborough, co. Cavan, Esq., and had issue, Daniel, of Abbotstown aforesaid, and a dau. Anne, *m.* Benjamin Geale, Esq. of Mount Geale,

---

* He was the author of a work entitled *Cryptomenysis Patefacta*, published in 1685.

† A brother of this John Dalmahoy was Thomas Dalmahoy, Esq., M.P. for Guildford, who *m.* Elizabeth, dau. and co-heir of James, Earl of Dirleton, widow of that Duke of Hamilton who was mortally wounded at the battle of Worcester. The family of Dalmahoy held the office of hereditary under-master of the royal household of Scotland.

* A similar grant of arms was made in 1720, to John Falconer, Esq., namely; Or, a falcon's head issuing from a heart, gu., between three mullets, az., and on a bordure, vert, four bezants. This John Falconer was son of David Falconer, Esq., and was grandson and heir of Sir John Falconer (who *m.* Barbara Jaffray), of Balmakellie, who was master of the Mint in Scotland. The eldest brother of this Sir John Falconer was Alexander, 1st Lord Halkerton, and his 2nd and elder brother was Sir David Falconer (who *m.* Margaret Hepburn), of Glenfarquhar, the father of Sir David Falconer, who was lord president of the court of session.

co. Kilkenny. Daniel, *m.* Dorothy, dau. of Henry Faure, of Egham, co. Surrey, Esq., and had issue, 1 Frederick-John, col. 10th regt. of foot, member for co. Dublin in the last Irish parliament, created a BARONET 15 Dec. 1812; he *m.* Anne-Frances, dau. of Sackville Gardner, Esq., but *d.* without issue. 2 Elizabeth, *m.* William Crosbie, Esq. 3 Dorothy, *m.* Major Nuttall. 4 Maria-Josepha, *m.* 1791, the Hon. Robert Moore, youngest son of Edward, 5th Earl of Drogheda. 5 Daniel, *d. unm.*

3 Caleb, of the city of Cork, *m.* Mary, dau. of — Riggs, Esq., by whom (who *d.* 1766) he had issue, 1 RIGGS, created a BARONET 24 Aug. 1777, father of Sarah-Anne, Lady Ventry, and grandfather of Sir Charles-L. Falkiner, of Annemount, co. Cork, 4th baronet (see *Peerage and Baronetage*). 2 Anne, *d. unm.* 3 Caroline, *m.* John Minchin, Esq., of the family now represented by George Minchin, Esq. of Busherstown, co. Tipperary, and had issue. 4 Elizabeth, *m.* Edward Herrick, Esq., and has issue.

4 Hannah, *m.* 1686, Trial Travers, Esq.

III. John, *b.* 23 Dec. 1644; *d. unm.*

IV. Michael, *b.* 1655; *m.* and had issue.

RICHARD FALKINER, Esq. (eldest son of Michael Falkiner and Anne his wife), was *b.* near Leeds, 2 March, 1640; he *m.* Mary, dau. of Edward Mason, Esq., and had, with a dau., Ruth, wife of — Corker, a son,

RICHARD FALKINER, *b.* 1665, who *m.* Mary, dau. of John Budden, Esq., and had a son,

RICHARD FALKINER, of Mount Falcon, *b.* 1691, who *m.* Maria, dau. of Colonel John Rogers, of Ballynavin Castle, co. Tipperary, eldest son of Colonel Freeman Rogers and Elizabeth, dau. of John Falkiner, of Nangor, and had issue,

RICHARD, his heir.

Daniel, of Ballyricard, co. Tipperary, *m.* Catherine, dau. of — Frend, Esq., and had issue.

Elizabeth, *m.* — Bayly, Esq., great-uncle of John Bayly, Esq. of Debsboro', co. Tipperary.

Maria, *m.* Samuel Barry, Esq., and had issue.

The eldest son,

RICHARD FALKINER, Esq. of Mount Falcon, *b.* 1721, barrister-at-law; *s.* his father 1783; he *m.* Mary, dau. of John Smart, Esq. of London, and had issue,

RICHARD, his heir.

Frederick, of Congor House, co. Tipperary, *b.* 1760; *m.* Louisa Fraser, and had an only dau., Judith, *m.* 1825, to the Rev. John-Rotheram Tarlton, rector of Tyholland, co. Monaghan, and has issue.

Ruth, *m.* Thomas Stoney, Esq. of Arran Hill, co. Tipperary, by whom she had issue.

Mary, *d. unm.* 1833. Charlotte, *d. unm.* 1828.

The eldest son,

THE REV. RICHARD FALKINER, of Mount Falcon, *b.* 13 June, 1751; *s.* his father, 1780. He *m.* Maria, dau. of Nathaniel Robbins, Esq. of Hymenstown, co. Tipperary, and had issue,

RICHARD, his heir.

Samuel, of Congor House, co. Tipperary, *d. unm.*

Thomas, *d. unm.*

Daniel, of Beechwood, co. Tipperary, *m.* Rebecca, dau. of Thomas Sadleir, Esq. of Castletown, co. Tipperary, and had issue; he *d.* 1852.

George, *d. unm.*

John, of Willsboro', co. Tipperary, *m.* Dora, dau. of William Hemsworth, Esq., and has issue.

Frederick, *d. unm.*

Joseph, of Rodeen, co. Tipperary, *m.* Anne, only dau. of Robert Fraser, Esq., and has issue.

Arthur, *d. unm.* Charles, *d. unm.*

Nathaniel, *m.* 1st, Marian, dau. of John Baldwin, Esq. of Castecuffa, by whom he had issue. He *d.* 1844, having *m.* 2ndly, Rebecca, dau. of Richard Litton, Esq.

The eldest son,

RICHARD FALKINER, Esq. of Mount Falcon, *b.* 1777; who served in the Peninsular campaign in the 4th royal Irish regiment of dragoon guards, *s.* his father, 1826; he *m.* June, 1825, Tempe, youngest dau. of Richard Litton, Esq. of Terrenure, co. Dublin, by his wife, the eldest dau. of Travers Hartley, Esq., M.P.; and *d.* 1833, leaving issue,

RICHARD-HENRY-FITZRICHARD, the present representative.

Travers-Hartley, *b.* July, 1829.

Frederick-John-Richard, barrister-at-law, *b.* Jan. 1831.

Robert-George, *b.* Sept. 1832.

Rebecca, *b.* 1826; *d.* 1837.

Arms—Or, three falcons close ppr., in the centre chief point a mullet gules.

Crest—A falcon's lure ppr. between two wings az.

Motto—Fortunâ favente.

Seat—Mount Falcon, co. Tipperary.

FALLON OF BALLINA HOUSE.

FALLON, ANTHONY, Esq. of Ballina House, co. Roscommon, *b.* 23 March, 1814.

Lineage.—The Fallons or O'Fallons are an old Irish family. HUGH BALLAGH O'FALLON, of Ballina, in the barony of Athlone, co. Roscommon (whose brother Malachy O'Fallon became a Franciscan friar, and founded the celebrated Irish college in Prague, A.D. 1631), *m.* Kate Keogh, of Toughmaconnel, and had three sons, HUGH, his heir; Coagh, in holy orders of the Church of Rome, parish priest of Kilcooly; and Peter, ancestor of the O'Fallons, now settled abroad. The eldest son, HUGH, of Ballina, was father, by Mary his wife, dau. of E. Coyle, of REDMOND FALLON, of Ballina, who *m.* twice, his 1st wife, Jane Brabazon, *d. s. p.*, but by his 2nd, Margaret, dau. of Col. O'Connor, he had two sons, the younger, Edward, was vicar-general of Athlone: the elder, WILLIAM FALLON, Esq. of Ballina, *m.* Anne Egan, and was father of

MALACHY FALLON, Esq. of Ballina House, *b.* 1734, who *m.* 1765, Anne Dowell, of Gort, and by her, who *d.* 1818, he left at his decease in 1820, a son and heir,

SIMON FALLON, Esq. of Ballina House, who *m.* 1806, Celia, dau. of Anthony Lynch, Esq. of Galway, and *d.* 1849, leaving issue,

ANTHONY, now of Ballina House. Patrick.

Anne, *m.* Nov. 1832, to Richard Calcut, Esq., an officer R.N.

Motto—Fortiter et fideliter.

Seat—Ballina House, co. Roscommon.

FANE OF WORMSLEY.

FANE, JOHN-WILLIAM, Esq. of Wormsley, co. Oxford, D.C.L., lieut.-colonel Oxfordshire militia, *b.* 1 Sept. 1804; *m.* 1st, 30 Nov. 1826, Catherine, dau. of the late Sir Benjamin Hobhouse, Bart., and by her (who *d.* 6 Nov. 1828) has an only dau.,

I. Sophia, *m.* 29 July, 1851, to Arthur-H.-C. Brown, Esq., jun., of Kingston, Oxfordshire.

He *m.* 2ndly, 3 Nov. 1829, Lady Ellen-Catherine Parker, dau. of Thomas, 5th Earl of Macclesfield, and by her (who *d.* 23 Sept. 1844) has issue,

I. JOHN AUGUSTUS, *b.* 10 Sept. 1830, capt. 46th foot.

I. Ellen, *m.* 24 Nov. 1858, to George Stratton, Esq.

Mr. Fane *m.* 3rdly, 18 Nov. 1845, Charlotte, dau. of the late Theodore-Henry Broadhead, Esq., and by her (who *d.* 19 May, 1855) has issue,

I. Henry-George, *b.* 10 Sept. 1846.

I. Charlotte-Elizabeth.

Lineage.—HENRY FANE, Esq. M.P., of Wormsley co. Oxford, (younger brother of Thomas, 8th Earl of Westmoreland, and son of Henry Fane, Esq., by Anne his wife, sister and co-heir of John Scrope, Esq. of Wormsley), *m.* 1st, Charlotte, only dau. of Nicholas Rowe, Esq., the poet, by whom he had an only dau., Charlotte, *m.* to Sir William St. Quintin. He *m.* 2ndly, Anne, dau. of Dr. John Wynn, bishop of Bath and Wells, and had by her a dau., Mary, *m.* to Sir Thomas Stapleton, Bart. of Greys. He *m.* 3rdly, in 1748, Charlotte, dau. and co-heir of RICHARD LUTHER Esq. of Myles's, in Essex, and had issue, JOHN, his heir; and Francis, of Spetisbury, Dorset, M.P., who *d. s. p.* The eldest son,

JOHN FANE, Esq. of Wormsley, LL.D., M.P. co. Oxford, *m.* 30 Nov. 1773 Lady Elizabeth Parker, dau. of Thomas, 3rd Earl of Macclesfield, and by her, who *d.* 10 June, 1829, had

JOHN, his heir.

Francis-William, rear-adm. R.N., of Bath, *b.* 14 Oct. 1778, *m.* 20 July, 1824, Anne, dau. of William Flint, Esq., and *d.* 23 March, 1844.

Elizabeth-Sarah, *m.* 21 Dec. 1813, to Lieut.-Col. Thomas Drake.

Mary.

Charlotte, *m.* 28 Dec. 1813, to Col. John-P. Hamilton.

Georgiana, *m.* 9 Dec. 1816, to the Right Hon. Joseph-Warner Henley, M.P.

Augusta, *m.* 25 April, 1815, to Benjamin Keene, Esq.

Mr. Fane *d.* 8 Feb. 1824, and was *s.* by his son,

JOHN FANE, Esq. of Wormsley, *b.* 9 July, 1775, high-sheriff of Oxfordshire 1836, who *m.* 6 June, 1802, Elizabeth, dau. of William Lowndes-Stone, Esq. of Brightwell Park, Oxfordshire, and *d.* 4 Oct. 1850, having had issue,

I. JOHN-WILLIAM, now of Wormsley.
II. Frederick-Adrian-Scrope, *b.* 8 Dec. 1810, *m.* 10 June, 1834, Joanna, dau. of the late Sir Benjamin Hobhouse, Bart., and has issue,
  1 Edward, *b.* 1836.
  2 Frederick-John, *b.* 30 Jan. 1840.
  1 Isabella. 2 Georgiana. 3 Charlotte.
III. George-Augustus-Scrope, *b.* 29 March, 1817, *m.* 3 June, 1843, Sophia-Frances-Pole, dau. of the late John Phillips, Esq. of Culham, Oxfordshire.
I. Elizabeth, *m.* 1842, to the Rev. John Ballard.
II. Anne, *m.* 1824, John-Billingsley Parry, Esq., Q.C., and *d.* 21 Nov. 1829.
III. Charlotte, *m.* 16 Nov. 1852, the Rev. Frederick Fyler.

Arms—Az., three dexter gauntlets, backs affronté, or.
Crest—Out of a ducal coronet, or, a bull's head, arg., pied, sa., armed of the first, charged on the neck with a rose, gu., barbed and seeded, ppr.
Motto—Ne vile Fano.
Seat—Wormsley, Oxfordshire.

FANSHAWE OF FANSHAWE GATE.

FANSHAWE, HENRY, Esq. of Dengy Hall, co. Essex, capt. R.N., *b.* 9 Dec. 1778; *m.* 1st, 1 May, 1810, Anna-Maria, dau. of Lieut.-Gen. Jenkinson; and 2ndly, 20 Jan. 1823, Caroline, dau. of F.-F. Luttrell, Esq., 2nd son of J.-F. Luttrell, Esq. of Dunster Castle, co. Somerset.

Lineage.—ROBERT FANSHAWE, Esq. of Fanshawe Gate, in the parish of Dronfield, co. Derby had two sons, I. JOHN, of whom presently; and II. Henry, remembrancer of the Exchequer, *temp.* Queen ELIZABETH, *d.* 1568, leaving, by Dorothy his wife, dau. of Sir George Stonerd, two daus., his co-heirs Anne, wife of William Fuller; and Susanna, *m.* to Timothy Lucy, Esq. The elder son, JOHN FANSHAWE Esq. of Fanshawe Gate, who *d.* in 1578, left, by Margaret his wife, dau. of Eyre, of Hassop, four sons and two daus.; of the former, the eldest,

THOMAS FANSHAWE, Esq. of Ware Park, *s.* his uncle, the remembrancer of the Exchequer. He *m.* 1st, Mary, dau. of Anthony Boucher, and had by her a son, HENRY (Sir), K.B., remembrancer of the Exchequer, who *m.* Elizabeth, 6th dau. of Thomas Smyth, Esq. of Ostenhanger, and by her was father, *inter alios*, of two sons, THOMAS, K.B. created VISCOUNT FANSHAWE, of Donamore, in the kingdom of Ireland, in 1661; and RICHARD (Sir), created a baronet in 1650. Mr. Fanshawe *m.* 2ndly, Joan Smyth, sister of Thomas, Viscount Strangford, and had by her two sons and five daus.,

Thomas (Sir), of Jenkins, co. Essex, K.B., supervisor-general, and clerk of the Crown, who *d.* in 1631, leaving, by Anne his wife, dau. of Urian Bebington, of London, a son, Thomas Fanshawe, Esq. of Jenkins, whose son, Sir Thomas Fanshawe, of Jenkins, knighted in 1660, left an only dau. and heiress, Susan, *m.* to Baptist Noel, 4th son of Baptist, Viscount Camden.
WILLIAM, of whom presently.
Alice, *m.* to Sir Christopher Hatton, K.B
Catharine, *m.* to John Bullock, Esq. of Darley and Norton, co. Derby.
Margaret, *m.* to Sir Benjamin Ayloff, Bart., of Braxstead.

Thomas Fanshawe, of Ware, *d.* 19 Feb. 1600; his youngest son,

WILLIAM FANSHAWE, Esq. of Passelews, Essex, one of the auditors of the duchy of Lancaster, *m.* Catharine, dau. of Sir John Wolstenholm, of London, and dying 4 March, 1634, was *s.* by his son,

JOHN FANSHAWE, Esq. of Passelews, *b.* in 1619, who *m.* 1st, a dau. of Kingsmill, Esq. of Sidmanton, Hants, by whom he had a son, WILLIAM, his heir. He *m.* 2ndly, Alice, dau. of Thomas Fanshawe, Esq. of Jenkins, by whom he had a son,

John, of Passelews, who *m.* a dau. of John Coke, Esq. of Melbourne, co. Derby, and dying about the year 1700, left issue,
  1 Thomas, of Passelews, who had (with two daus., Susan, *m.* to the Rev. Dr. Blackburne; and Frances, *m.* to Massingberd, Esq.) a son, Thomas, of Passelews, who *m.* Anne, dau. of Sir Crisp Gascoyne, lord mayor of London, and had, with two daus., a son, John-Gascoyne Fanshawe, Esq., who *m.* Miss Partington, and had issue, John, *b.* in 1773; Henry, *b.* in 1775; Charles-Gascoyne, *b.* in 1778; Thomas-Lewis, *b.* in 1792; and Mary.
  2 John.
  3 Charles, who *m.* Elizabeth, dau. of Sir John Rogers, Bart., and had three sons, 1 John Fanshawe, Esq., who by Penelope his wife, dau. of Dredge, Esq. of Reading, had (with three daus., Penelope; Catherine-Maria; and Elizabeth-Christiana) two sons, John, *b.* 1763; and Robert-Charles, *b.* 1780; 2 Robert Fanshawe, who *m.* Christiana, dau. of Ginnis, Esq., and by her had (with nine daus., Christiana, *m.* to the Rev. Francis Haggit; Elizabeth, *m.* to Francis Glanville, Esq. of Catchfrench; Susan, *m.* to Vice-Admiral Bedford; Catherine, *m.* to Admiral Sir T.-Byam Martin; Cordelia, *m.* to Admiral Sir T.-Chambers White; Anne; Penelope, *m.* to Col. Duckworth; Mary, *m.* to Admiral Sir Robert Stopford, G.C.B.; and Henrietta) three sons, Robert, capt. R.N., *d.* in 1804; Edward, C.B., major-gen. R.E., *m.* in 1811, Frances-Mary, sister of Sir Adolphus-John Dalrymple, Bart.; Arthur, rear-adm. R.N., *m.* a dau. of Admiral Colpoys; and 3 Charles Fanshawe, Esq., recorder of Exeter, who *m.* Elizabeth, dau. of John Seale, Esq. of Mount Boone, co. Devon, and had a son, Charles-John, *b.* 1780.
  1 Susanna.

The eldest son,

WILLIAM FANSHAWE, Esq. of St. Martin-in-the-Fields, co. Middlesex, sometime master of the Requests to King CHARLES II., *m.* Mary, dau. of Mrs. Lucy Walters, and sister of James, Duke of Monmouth, relict of William Sarsfield, of Lucan, Ireland, elder brother of Patrick, Earl of Lucan, and *d.* in the year 1707, leaving (with three daus., Ann-Dorothy, *m.* to Mathews, Esq., barrister-at-law; Lucy-Catherine, *d. unm.*; and Ann-Mary, *m.* to Mark Newdigate, of Ireland) an only son,

THOMAS-EDWARD FANSHAWE, Esq. of Great Singleton, co. Lancaster, who was next heir male of Simon, last Viscount Fanshawe, of Dengy Hall, Essex. He *m.* Elizabeth dau. of William Snelling, Esq. of Bromley, co. Middlesex, and by her had (with three daus., Elizabeth, *m.* in 1719, to Corbyn Morris, Esq.; Anne; and Mary) an only son,

SIMON FANSHAWE, Esq. of Fanshawe Gate, *b.* 4 March, 1715–16, who *m.* Althea, 2nd dau. of William Snelling, Esq., and had, with daus., of whom Frances *m.* John Jenkinson, Esq., an only son and heir,

HENRY FANSHAWE, Esq., *b.* 5 May, 1756, colonel in the British guards, and subsequently a general officer in the Russian service, under the Empress CATHERINE II. He was governor of Kioo, and subsequently of the Crimea, and served with distinction under the Duke of Wurtemberg. He *d.* a Russian senator, at Warsaw, in 1828. By his wife, Susanna-Frances (whom he *m.* 26 Feb. 1778), dau. of Charles le Grys, Esq. of Norwich, he had issue,

I. HENRY, his heir, Capt. Fanshawe, R.N., of Dengy Hall.
II. Charles-Robert, of Fanshawe Gate, co. Derby, in holy orders, vicar of Coaley, co. Gloucester, *b.* 4 April, 1780, *m.* 1st, Patty, dau. of the Rev. Mr. Faithful; and 2ndly, Jane, dau. of the Rev. Mr. Williams, by the former of whom only, who *d.* in 1823, he has issue,
  1 Charles-Simon, *b.* 9 Oct. 1806, *m.* in May, 1833, Rosa, 3rd dau. of Charles Ricketts, Esq.
  2 John, *m.* in Aug. 1842, Elizabeth, dau. of Upton, Esq.
  3 Robert, *b.* 11 April, 1814, *m.* 1st, Pamela, dau. of Gen. Boye, E. I. Co's service; and 2ndly, the dau. of Col. Wrottesley.
  1 Althea, *m.* in 1835, to John-C. Badeley, M.D., of Chelmsford.
  2 Ellen, *d.* in 1818.
  3 Susanna-Frances-Faithful.
  4 Emily, *m.* in 1841, to Henry-Georges Moysey, Esq., lieut. 11th hussars, son and heir of the Ven. Charles-Abel Moysey, D.D., archdeacon of Bath.
  5 Maria.
III. Thomas-Edward, *d. unm.*
IV. William-Simon, *b.* 25 Jan. 1784, general in the Russian service, *m.* the dau. of a Polish gentleman named Maisner, and *d.* in Russia, in 1829, leaving issue.
V. Frederick, chamberlain to the Emperors ALEXANDER and NICHOLAS. He was murdered by the Poles in 1830. He married and left issue.
VI. George, lieut.-gen. in the Russian service, and aide-de-camp to the Emperor NICHOLAS, *m.* Mademoiselle Bonet, and has issue.
I. Sophia, *d. unm.*

Arms—Or, a chev. between three fleur-de-lis, sa.
Crest—A dragon's head, erased, or, flames of fire issuing from the mouth, ppr.
Seat—Dengy Hall, co. Essex.

FARDELL OF HOLBECK LODGE.

FARDELL, THE REV. JOHN-GEORGE, M.A., rector of Sprotborough, co. York, and chaplain to the Earl of Courtown, *b.* 22 Sept. 1810; *m.* 25 May, 1837, Emma, dau. of the late John Wilson, Esq. of Sea-croft Hall, near Leeds, and of Cliffe Hall, near Darlington, and has issue,

I. JOHN-WILSON, *b.* 26 Nov. 1838.
II. Frederick-Charles, *b.* 18 July, 1843.
III. Gerald-Tunnard, *b.* 15 April, 1852.
I. Mary-Emma. II. Martha-Georgina.
III. Sarah-Louisa, *d.* young.
IV. Alice-Lydia. V. Eleanor-Maude.

Lineage.—The family of Fardell came originally from Northamptonshire, and has been settled in Lincolnshire for more than a century.

WILLIAM FARDELL, Esq., *b.* in 1707, *m.* Catherine Hubbert, and by her, who *d.* 26 Nov. 1778, left, at his decease, 23 Oct. 1745, a son,

JOHN FARDELL, Esq of Lincoln, *b.* 27 Dec. 1744, who *m.* 7 July, 1783, Eleanor-Penelope, dau. of John Hayward, Esq. of the same city, by Mary his wife, eldest dau. of Thos. Rogers, merchant, of London, and had issue,

JOHN, his heir.
Thomas, *b.* 1 Nov. 1791, of Queens' College, Cambridge, in holy orders, LL.B. rector of Boothby Pagnell, co. Lincoln, *m.* 21 Jan. 1819, Emma-Clara-Anne, only dau. of William Meyrick, Esq. of Bodorgan, co. Anglesea, and has issue.
Henry, *b.* 6 March, 1795, late of St. John's College, Cambridge, in holy orders, M.A., J.P., prebendary of Ely, and vicar of Waterbeach and Wisbech, in the Isle of Ely, *m.* 6 Jan. 1820, Eliza Sparke, eldest dau. of Bowyer Edward, Lord Bishop of Ely, and has issue.
Catherine, *m.* 1 Oct. 1811, to the Rev. Henry Bassett, B.A., rector of North Thoresby, and vicar of Glentworth and Saxby, in Lincolnshire, and has issue.
Mary, *m.* 19 Aug. 1823, to the Rev. George Moore, B.A.

Mr. Fardell, *d.* 16 Feb. 1805, and was *s.* by his eldest son,

JOHN FARDELL, Esq. of Holbeck Lodge, co. Lincoln, barrister-at-law, F.S.A. and F.A.S., *b.* 4 May, 1784, *m.* 26 Sept. 1809, Mary, youngest dau. of John Tunnard, Esq. of Frampton House, in the same shire, and had issue,

JOHN-GEORGE, present representative of the family.
Charles, resident at Holbeck Lodge, co. Lincoln, *b.* 30 March, 1813, B.A., of St. John's College, Cambridge, and of the Middle Temple.

Mr. Fardell, a magistrate, and and deputy-lieutenant for the county of Lincoln, represented the city of Lincoln in Parliament in the session of 1830. He *d.* 4 Feb. 1854.

Arms—Az., on a bend, erm., between a unicorn's head, erased, and a lion, rampant, erminois, an open book, ppr., between two roses, gu., barbed and seeded, vert.
Crest—On a mount, vert, a demi-lion, erminois, charged on the shoulder with a rose, and holding between the paws an open book, as in the arms.
Motto—Non nobis solum.
Seat—Holbeck Lodge, co. Lincoln.

FARMAR OF CLOHASS.

FARMAR, THE REV. HUGH-HOVELL-BASKERVILLE, of Clohass, co. Wexford, *b.* 24 Sept. 1822.

Lineage.—This family claims to be a branch of the noble house of Pomfret, and to have been first settled in Ireland *temp.* Queen Elizabeth.

JASPER FERMOR, Esq., was, according to the family tradition, deprived of his estates in the rebellion of 1641, and forced to seek an asylum in England. He resided for some time at Exeter, but subsequently migrated, with all his family, to America. He *m.* the eldest dau. of Anthony Gamble, Esq. of the co. of Cork, and had several children, of whom were six sons, viz.,

I. RICHARD, his heir.
II. Jasper, of Garron Kenny Fange, co. Cork, father of
THOMAS FARMER, high-sheriff of Philadelphia, and mayor of Brunswick, *m.* in 1702, Anne, dau. and co-heir of Christopher Billopp, Esq., captain R.N., and had, with daus., eight sons, viz.,
1 Jasper, R.N., *b.* 11 Feb. 1707, who had two sons, Jasper, who left several children, and Peter, father of Jasper, who *d.* in Jamaica.
2 Thomas, *b.* in 1711, who took the name of Billopp, before his own. He *m.* 1st, Miss Steele, by whom he had two daus., and 2ndly, Sarah, dau. of Samuel Leonard, Esq. of New Jersey, by whom he left at his decease, in 1750, eight children, viz., 1 Christopher Billopp-Farmer, of St. John's, New Brunswick; 2 Mary; 3 Elizabeth; 4 Rachael; 5 Thomas, who adhered to the American cause, and *d. s. p.*; 6 Sarah; 7 Catherine; and 8 Jasper, colonel 21st regt. of Royal North British Fusileers, who *m.* Susan, eldest dau. of Cortlandt Skinner, Esq. of Port Amboyna, attorney-general of New Jersey, and dying in 1798, left one son and one dau., viz., Jasper, lieutenant in the British army, who *d. s. p.*, and a dau. *m.* to W.-J. Murphy, Esq. of Jamaica.
3 Brooke, *d. s. p.* 4 Edward, *d.* young.
5 Robert, *b.* in 1718, major in the British army, *d.* in 1776, leaving issue.
6 Samuel, *b.* in 1719, *m.* Christina, dau. of — Pick, Esq., and had issue four daus.
7 William, *d.* young.
8 John, in the army, *d. unm.*
III. John, who *m.* in 1686, Mary Hayles, and was father of JOHN FARMER, of Youghall, who *d.* in 1740, leaving by Alphra Garde his wife, a son GEORGE FARMER, R.N., commander of H.M. ship Quebec, blown up, with most of the crew, whilst gallantly defending his vessel against the French frigate "La Surveillante," in 1779. His son, SIR GEORGE-WILLIAM-FARMER, was created a baronet in the October of the same year.
IV. Robert. V. Charles.
VI. Samuel, major in the army, who purchased several valuable estates in Virginia, which were lost by his children, in consequence of their adherence to the royal cause in the American war. Major Farmer *m.* Mary, dau. of Cuthbert Wilkinson, Esq., and had issue,
1 Samuel, *b.* in 1707, *m.* and had a son, Robert, of Virginia.
2 Richard, *b.* in 1709, practitioner of medicine at Philadelphia, *m.* twice, and left issue, two sons, Richard and William, who both *d. s. p.*, and one dau., Sarah, *m.* in 1778, to Capt. Bowyer.
3 Robert, an officer in the royal navy, *b.* in 1711, killed in action off Dunkirk, on board the Augusta, 74.

The elder son,

RICHARD FERMOR, or FARMER, Esq. of Arderrack, co. Cork, was obliged to leave Ireland in 1689, and retired with his family to Taunton Deane, in Somersetshire. He returned to Ireland in 1691. He *m.* in 1675, Elizabeth, eldest dau. of Lieut.-Col. Phayre, Governor of Cork under Cromwell, in 1650, and had three sons viz.,

I. JASPER, *b.* in 1676, of Kerconway, co. Cork, *m.* in 1701, Elizabeth dau. of George Rogers, Esq. of Ashgrove, co. Cork, and had a son, Richard, who *d. unm.* in 1730.
II. ROBERT.
III. John, M.D., *b.* in 1678, *m.* Lucy, 2nd dau. of Cuthbert Wilkinson, Esq., and had (with one dau., Lucy) an only son,
Jasper, who *m.* 1st, Mrs. Lasier, and 2ndly, in 1774 Grace, 2nd dau. of Hovell Farmar, M.D., and Katharina-Dorothea Russell his wife, and had three children,
1 Richard, an officer in the 8th regt., drowned at sea with his detachment, in 1814.
2 Jasper, captain Royal Marines, of Sunnybank, co. Hereford. J.P. and D.L., *m.* in 1819, Meliora, widow of P. R. Mynors, Esq. of Treago, which lady *d.* in 1829.
1 Dorah, *d. unm.* in 1831.

The 2nd son,

ROBERT FARMAR, Esq. of Fergus, co. Cork, *b.* in 1677, major in the army, *m.* in 1700, Grace, 2nd dau. and co-heir of William Hovell, Esq. of Mount Hovell, co. Cork, by Grace his wife, dau. and heir of Beare, of Beare Forest, by whom (who *d.* in 1763) he left at his decease, in 1743, the following issue,

I. HOVELL, of whom presently.
II. Edward, captain royal marines, *b.* in 1710, *m.* 1st, in 1746, Katherine, dau. of Poole St. Barbe, Esq. of Bittern Hants, and widow of Lieut. Oates, R.N., by whom he had three children, viz.,
Edward, M.D., *d. s. p.* in 1802.
Robert-Hill, of Barnhill, co. Cork, general of marines, *b.* in 1755, married three wives; by his 2nd wife, Mildred, eldest dau. of the Rev. Richard Farmar, he had four children, viz.,
1 Robert-Herring, *b.* in 1794, an officer in the 77th regt., *m.* in 1817, Mary, only dau. of Armigher Sealey, Esq. of Cork, and *d.* 22 Aug. 1843, leaving, issue, Charles-Lewis-Atterbury, in the royal marines, *b.* 23 Jan. 1831, Frances-Georgiana, and Juliana-Priscilla, *m.* 24 March, 1849, to Thomas-Osborne Stock, Esq.
2 Edward-Sterling, major in the army, *b.* in 1796, *m.* in 1836, Jane, only dau. of James Cunningham, Esq., captain R.N., and has issue, Edward-James-Cunningham, *b.* 1845; Jane-Cunningham-Mildred; Georgiana-Marianne; Florence-Lucinda-Caroline; and Helen-Theresa-Unity-Gordon.
1 Elizabeth. 2 Marianne, *d.* in 1824.
General Farmar's 3rd wife, whom he married in 1800, was Elizabeth, eldest dau. of Dr. Mallet, a physician, and relict of Thomas Symonds, Esq., captain R.N. General Farmar *d.* 32 Jan. 1839.
Katharine, *d.* in 1824.
He *m.* 2ndly, in 1779, Frances, eldest dau. of Edward Roberts, Esq. of Clover Hill, co. Cavan and had another son and dau.,

Richard-Hugh-Hovell-Sterling, of Castle Treasure, co. Cork, b. in 1782, captain royal marines, a gallant and distinguished officer, m. in 1818, Anne, 3rd dau. of Thomas Grasebrooke, Esq. of Dudbridge, co. Gloucester, and dying in 1840, left issue, 1 Richard, capt. royal marines, b. in 1819, m. 15 Feb. 1854, Eleanor, youngest dau. of John Simpson, Esq; 2 William-Edward, royal marines, b. in 1824, m. 17 Sept. 1850, Mary-Dorset, youngest dau. of William Lawrance, Esq. of Fletton Tower, co. Huntingdon; 1 Caroline; and 2 Anne-Grasebrooke.

Helen, d. unm. in 1821.

He d. in 1784.

III. Richard, in holy orders, of Barnhill, co. Cork, rector of Dunmanway and Timoleague, m. in 1759, Elizabeth, dau. of Robert Freeman, Esq. of Ballinguile, and had two daus., of whom Mildred, the elder, m. her cousin General Robert-Hill Farmar; and Mary-Anne, m. to — Herring, Esq., E. I. Co.'s service.

I. Grace, b. in 1702, m. in 1726, her cousin the Hon. Richard Hill, of Beare Forest, co. Cork, one of H.M. Council for South Carolina.

II. Elizabeth, m. John Beare, Esq., of Cork and d. in 1786, leaving issue.

III. Jane, m. to William Wakeham, Esq. of Spring Hill, co. Cork, and left issue.

IV. Hannah, m. William Keyes, Esq. d. in 1799, aged 84.

The eldest son,

Hovell Farmar, M.D. of Mount Hovell, co. Cork, b. in 1701, m. in 1739, Katharine Dorothea, eldest dau. of Christopher Russell, Esq., colonel of the 17th regt., and Governor of Minorca, where he d. in 1758, aged 57. By this lady Dr. Farmar had issue,

I. Hugh-Hovell, his heir.

II. Robert, captain in the 50th regt., m. Jane, dau. of William Wakeham, and d. s. p.

I. Elizabeth, m. Joseph Oates, Esq. of Kalnabone, co. Cork, and d. in 1810.

II. Grace, m. to Jasper Farmar, Esq.

He d. in 1770, and was s. by his elder son.

Hugh-Hovell Farmar, Esq. of Dunsinane, co. Wexford, called to the bar in 1768. He m. in 1781, Jane, dau. of Michael Roberts, Esq. of Kilmony, co. Cork, (cousin of Sir Thomas Roberts, Bart. of Britfieldstown, in the same county, and cousin of Jane Roberts, dau. and co-heir of Sir Walter Roberts Bart., and duchess of George, 3rd Duke of St. Albans,) by whom he left at his decease, in 1812,

I. Hugh-Hovell, his heir.

II. Michael-Roberts, an officer in the army, killed in action at Cuba, anno 1807.

III. William-Russell, of Bloomfield, co. Wexford, in the commission of the peace, b. in 1802, m. 1st, in 1829, Eliza, 4th dau. of Richard Donovan, Esq. of Ballymore, in the same county, and has surviving issue, 1 William-Henry, b. in 1831; 1 Anne-Jane; 2 Katherine-Elizabeth; and Elizabeth-Mary. He m. 2ndly, 29 Nov. 1853, Henrietta, 2nd dau. of Harry Alcock, Esq. of Wilton, co. Wexford.

I. Mary, m. to her cousin, Charles Hill, M.D., of St. John's, co. Wexford.

II. Katherine-Dorothea, m. to her cousin, Richard Hill, Esq. of Urrin's Fort, co. Wexford.

The eldest son and heir,

Hugh-Hovell Farmar, Esq. of Dunsinane, co. Wexford, J.P., m. in 1815, Meliora, only dau. of the late Peter-Rickards Mynors, Esq. of Treago, co. Hereford, and had issue,

Hugh-Hovell-Baskerville, present representative of the family.

William-Roberts, b. 14 March, 1825, capt. H.M. 82nd regt., severely wounded at the battle of Aliwal, m. 20 May, 1851, Alicia-Mary, only child of Edward-Stone Cotgrave, Esq., capt. R.N., and has issue, Richard-De Malpas-Cotgrave, b. 2 Dec. 1853.

Meliora-Mynors.

Anna-Catharina-Rickards, m. 12 June, 1855, to the Rev. William-Hirzel Le Marchant, vicar of Harlsfield, co. Gloucester.

Jane-Philippa-Baskerville, m. 9 Dec. 1852, to John Whitehead, Esq., barrister-at-law.

Mr. Farmar d. in 1828.

Seat—Clohass, co. Wexford.

FARMER OF NONSUCH PARK.

Farmer, William-Francis-Gamul, Esq. of Nonsuch Park, co. Surrey, high-sheriff in 1849, and a magistrate and deputy lieut.; m. in 1837, Matilda, dau. of Robert Wilkinson, Esq., and has issue,

I. William-Robert-Gamul b. 12 July 1838.

II. Thomas-Allix, b. 14 Nov. 1839.

III. George-Lancelot-McLean.

IV. Charles-Edward.

V. James-Edmund-Gamul.

VI. Henry-Lowth.

I. Matilda-Frances.

II. Margaret-Anna.

III. Emilie-Mary.

IV. Catherine-Augusta.

Lineage.—Samuel Farmer Esq., for many years M.P. for Huntingdon, claiming descent from the Fermors *of Northamptonshire*, purchased about the close of the 18th century, the beautiful seat and estate of Nonsuch, co. Surrey so long a royal residence (*see* Burke's *Visitation of Great Britain*, vol. i. p. 214). He m. Elizabeth, dau. of the late Joseph-Easton Meeke, Esq. of Rotherhithe, and sister of the late William Meeke, Esq. of Boddington, co. Surrey, and had a son,

William-Meeke, M.P. for Huntingdon, who m. Frances, dau. of Michael Barstow, Esq. of Fulford, co. York, and d. *vitâ patris*, in Oct. 1836, leaving issue,

1 William-Francis-Gamul, now of Nonsuch Park.

2 Arthur-Augustus, settled in Canada, m. Louise, dau. of the Hon. Peter De Blaquiere, and has issue,

3 George-Almond, an officer H.E.I.C.S., d. in India, 1837.

4 Thomas-McLean, late captain in the army, m. Ellen, dau. of the Rev. Henry-Curtis Cherrie, rector of Burghfield, near Reading, Berkshire.

5 Archibald-Hamilton, settled in Canada, m. Augusta, dau. of the Hon. Peter De Blaquiere, and has issue,

6 Reginald-Onslow, R.A. m. Geraldine, dau. of Captain Farrell, late R.A.

1 Elizabeth-Marie, m. to Charles Wilshere, Esq. of Hitchen, Herts.

2 Emilie-Georgiana, m. to Hippolyte Von Klenze, capt. Bavarian guards.

3 Everilda-Frances m. to Gustave Von Ascheberg, late captain Russian hussars.

4 Mary-Eugenie, m. to Maximilian, Baron Von Gumpenberg-Bayerback, of the Bavarian guards.

Arms—Arg., a fesse, sa., between three lions' heads, erased, gu.

Crest—Out of a ducal coronet, or, a cock's head, gu., crested and watt'ed, gold.

Motto—Hora e sempre.

Seat—Nonsuch Park, near Cheam.

FARNALL.

Farnall, Harry-Burrard, Esq., B.A., of Burley Villa, Lyme, co. Dorset, J.P. and D.L., b. 28 June, 1802; m. 1st, in Feb. 1829, Dorothea, 4th dau. of Alan Bellingham, Esq. of The Castle, Castle Bellingham, co. Louth; and 2ndly, Rhoda-Eleanor, dau. of the late Robert Bellamie, Esq. of Sandford House, near Taunton, by whom he has issue,

I. Harry-de la Rosa-Burrard, b. 1852.

II. Edmund-Waterton, b. 1855.

I. Eleanor-Jacintha-Mary.

Lineage.—Harry Farnall, Esq., capt. R.N. (only son of Nathaniel Farnall, Esq. an officer of the 60th regt., by Eliza-Jacintha his wife dau. of Colonel Burrard, M.P., of Lymington, and Eliza his wife dau. of De La Rosa, ambassador from the court of Spain), m. in 1800, Martha, dau. and co-heir of Philip Elliott, Esq. of Clifton, co. Gloucester, and had issue,

Harry-Burrard, his heir, 18th in direct descent from Edward I.

Philip-Elliott, of Boldnor, Isle of Wight, a magistrate, who m. 1st, Marianne-Fletcher, only surviving child, of Samuel-Pearce-Tregeare Parson, LL.D.; and 2ndly, Hannah-Frances Christie, by whom he has issue,

George-Rooke, of Burley Park, near Ringwood, Hants, J.P., who m. Mary, only child of Redstone Warner, Esq., and has issue,

Arms—Or, on a bend, gu., three annulets, of the first, within a bordure, of the second, bezantée.

Motto—Persevere.

Residence—Burley, Villa, Lyme, co. Dorset.

FARNHAM OF QUORNDON HOUSE.

Farnham, Edward-Basil, Esq. of Quorndon House, co. Leicester, J.P. and D.L., M.P. for North Leicestershire, b. 19 April, 1809; m. 5 July, 1851, Emily-Gertrude, 2nd dau. of Sir William Cradock Hartopp, Bart. of Four Oaks Park, co. Warwick, and has one son, b. 8 July, 1855.

Lineage.—By deeds without dates, there appear to have been two Lords of Querndon prior to the reign of Edward I viz.,

Robert Farnham and Sir Robert Farnham Knt. The son and heir of the latter,

SIR JOHN FARNHAM, of Querndon, co. Leicester, lived *temp.* EDWARD I., and was ancestor of

THOMAS FARNHAM, Esq. of Nether Hall, who *m.* Frances, dau. of Sir Thomas Waldron, Knt. of Charley, in Leicestershire, and dying in Aug. 1666, left, with two sons, HENRY, his heir; and Thomas, who *d. unm.*, four daus., viz., Frances, *b.* in 1630, *m.* to Clifton Rhodes, Esq. of Stocton, Notts; Margaret, bapt. 6 July, 1635, *m.* to Richard Wilson, Esq. of Knight Thorpe, in Leicestershire; Dorothy, *m.* to Henry Waldron, Esq. of Farnham Castle, co. Cavan; and Elizabeth, *m.* to the Rev. Nicholas Hall, rector of Loughborough. The elder son and heir,

HENRY FARNHAM, Esq. of Nether Hall, a captain in the army, *m.* in 1660 Martha, dau. of Thomas Mousley, Gent. of the co. Stafford, and had issue. The 4th son,

BENJAMIN FARNHAM, Esq., *m.* in 1703, Sarah one of the daus. and co-heirs of Edward Farnham, Esq. of Quorndon, and dying in 1747, aged 77, was *s.* by his son,

EDWARD FARNHAM, Esq. of Quorndon, *b.* 16 March, 1704, who *m.* 3 March, 1725, Easter Lake, of Canterbury, and by her (who was buried 1 May, 1767) had,

- WILLIAM, his heir.
- THOMAS, successor to his brother William.
- EDWARD, successor to his brother Thomas.
- Esther, *m.* to John Willows, Esq., and *d.* in 1794.
- Anne, *m.* to Noah Bolaine, Esq. of Canterbury.
- Sarah, *m.* 1st, to Sir Charles Halford, Bart., and 2ndly, to Basil, Earl of Denbigh.

Mr. Farnham *d.* 3 June, 1775, and was *s.* by his son,

THE REV. WILLIAM FARNHAM, *b.* in 1738, who *d.* issueless, and was *s.* by his brother.

THOMAS FARNHAM, captain R.N. of Quorndon House, *b.* 30 Oct. 1743, at whose decease, *unm.*, 2 Dec. 1798, the estates and representation of the family devolved on his brother.

EDWARD FARNHAM, Esq. of Quorndon House, *b.* in 1753, high-sheriff of Leicestershire in 1817, *m.* in 1795, Harriet, youngest dau. and co-heir of the Rev. Dr. Rhudde, chaplain in ordinary to his late Majesty, and by her (who *d.* 1854) had issue,

- EDWARD-BASIL, now of Quorndon.
- Sarah-Anne.
- Mary-Eliza, *m.* 28 Sept. 1842, to the late Hon. and Rev. William-Chafy Henniker, brother of John, Lord Henniker.

Mr. Farnham *d.* 7 Jan. 1835.

Arms—Quarterly, or, and az., in the two first quarters a crescent counterchanged.
Crest—An eagle, or, wings close, preying on a rabbit, arg.
Seat—Quorndon House, near Loughborough.

FARQUHAR OF GILMILNSCROFT.

GRAY-FARQUHAR, MARGARET and JANE, of Gilmilnscroft, co. Ayr.

Lineage.—The family of Farquhar has enjoyed its present possessions, in Kyle Stewart, for many generations.

ALEXANDER FARQUHAR of Gilmilnscroft (lineally descended from Robert Farquhar, laird of Gilmilnscroft at the close of the 14th century), *m.* and had, with a dau., Catherine, *m.* about the year 1546, to John Hamilton, of Camskeith, a son ANDREW, ancestor of the FARQUHARS *of Gilmilnscroft*, whose eventual heiress

JANE FARQUHAR of Gilmilnscroft (only child of Alexander Farquhar of Gilminscroft), *m.* in 1777, JOHN GRAY, Esq. of Kilmerdenny, son of James Gray, minister of Strathblane, grandson of John Gray, minister of the High Church of Glasgow, and great-grandson of Andrew Gray, whose father, John Gray, was youngest son of Sir William Gray, of Pittendrum, ancestor of Lord Gray, and had issue,

- JAMES, his heir.
- Alexander, formerly in the army, deceased.
- John, lieutenant 40th regiment, who *d.* in consequence of wounds received at Salamanca.
- William, a merchant in Glasgow, deceased.
- Andrew, comptroller of the customs at Irvine, who *m.* in 1820, Margaret, dau. of the late Benjamin Barton, Esq., late commissary-clerk of Glasgow, and has a son, John, and other issue.
- Robert, who d. in 1807.
- Eliza, *m.* to John Ashburnham, M.D. of London.

The heiress of Gilmilnscroft *d.* in 1809, and was *s.* by her eldest son,

JAMES GRAY-FARQUHAR, Esq. of Gilmilnscroft, who *m.* in 1801, Margaret-Cochrane, eldest dau. of Major James Baillie, of the 7th or royal fusiliers, and fort-major of Fort St. George by Margaret Ross his wife, eldest dau. of Lord Anchorville, late one of the senators of the College of Justice, and left issue, John, *d. s. p.*, and MARGARET and JANE, now of Gilmilnscroft. Col. Gray-Farquhar, was lieut.-col. of the royal Ayrshire militia.

Arms—Arg., a lion rampant, sa., armed and langued, or, between three sinister hands, two and one, couped paleways, gu.
Crest—A dexter hand, couped as in the arms.
Supporters—Two greyhounds, ppr.
Motto—Sto, cado, fide et armis.
Seat—Gilmilnscroft, in Kyle Stewart.

FARQUHARSON OF INVERCAULD.

FARQUHARSON, JAMES, Esq. of Invercauld, co. Aberdeen, J.P. and D.L., *m.* 30 April, 1833, Janet Hamilton, eldest dau. of the late General Francis Dundas, of Sanson, Berwickshire, 2nd son of Robert Dundas, of Arniston, Lord President of the Court of Session, and has issue,

- I. JAMES-ROSS, *b.* 9 Jan. 1834.
- II. Francis-Dundas, *b.* 16 Aug. 1835.
- III. George-Murray, *b.* 16 Aug. 1835.
- IV. John-Atholl, *b.* 7 Nov. 1837.
- V. Robert-Dundas, *b.* 29 March, 1840.
- VI. Henry, *b.* 19 Nov. 1842.
- I. Catherine. II. Henrietta-Dundas.
- III. Janet-Hamilton.

Lineage.—"The representative of this ancient family" saith Douglas, in the *Baronage*, "is the head or chief of the powerful and numerous clan FARQUHARSON, which had large possessions in the Braes of Mar (the head of Aberdeenshire), and the adjacent counties. The house of Invercauld derives its descent from

SHAW McDUFF (sprung from a younger son of the potent Thanes of Fife), who had a son called FARQUHAR, who settled in Mar, in the reign of ROBERT II. (1371), and was made baillie and chamberlain thereof; his sons, as was customary in that early period, obtaining the surname of FARQUHARSONS, sons of Farquhar, founded many opulent and powerful houses in Scotland. His great-great-grandson,

FINDLA, commonly called FINDLA MORE, from his gigantic size and great strength, a man of daring courage and of a bold and determined character, *m.* 1st, Beatrix, dau. of George Garden, of that ilk, and had (with a younger son, who founded the houses of Farquharson of Whitehouse (*see that name*), of FINZEAN, now represented by ARCHIBALD FARQUHARSON, Esq. &c.) a son and heir, ROBERT. He *m.* 2ndly a dau. of the Baron Roy, of Kincardine Stewart, and had other children seated in Perthshire. This gallant warrior was killed at Pinkie in 1547, bearing the royal banner, and was buried in the churchyard of Invercauld. He was *s.* by his son,

ROBERT FARQUHARSON, of Invercauld, who *m.* Marjory, dau. of John Reid, of Straloch, and dying *temp.* JAMES VI., was *s.* by his son,

JOHN FARQUHARSON, of Invercauld, who left by his 1st wife, a dau. of Barclay, of Garthly, an only son,

ROBERT FARQUHARSON, of Invercauld, who *m.* Margaret Erskine, of Pitodrie, and was *s.* at his decease, in the reign of CHARLES II., by his elder son,

ALEXANDER FARQUHARSON, of Invercauld, who *m.* Isabella, dau. of William Mackintosh, of that ilk, by Margaret his wife, dau. of Graham of Fintry, and had three sons and a dau., viz., WILLIAM, his heir; John, successor to his brother; Alexander, of Monaltrie; and Margaret, *m.* to John Robertson, Esq. of Lude. The eldest son,

WILLIAM FARQUHARSON, Esq. of Invercauld, *d. unm.*, and was *s.* by his brother,

JOHN FARQUHARSON, Esq. of Invercauld, who *m.* 1st, Isabella, dau. and co-heir of Sir Alexander Burnet, Bart. of Craigmyllie, and had several children, who all *d.* young. He *m.* 2ndly, Christian, dau. of Sir Robert Menzies, Bart. of Weem, and had one dau., who *d. unm.* He *m.* 3rdly, Margaret, dau. (by Ann his wife, co-heir of Sir Robert Crichton Murray, Knt. of Cockpool) of Lord James Murray, son of John, 1st Marquess of Athol, by Amelia his wife, dau. of James, 7th Earl of Derby, K.G., and had,

- JAMES, his heir.
- John, who *d.* young.
- Anne, (the celebrated Lady Macintosh, who assisted Prince CHARLES, in 1745, by heading her husband's clan,) *m.* to Eneas Macintosh, of Macintosh.
- Margaret, *d. unm.*

The Laird of Invercauld *m.* 4thly, Jean Forbes, of Waterton, and had one son, Robert, who *d. unm.*, and two daus.,

Mary, m. to Captain Oliver, and Fanny, m. to — Donaldson, Esq. He was s. at his decease, in 1750, by his son,

JAMES FARQUHARSON, Esq. of Invercauld, who m. Amelia, relict of John, 8th Lord Sinclair, and dau. of Lord George Murray, lieut.-gen. of the Chevalier's army in 1745, 5th son of John, 1st Duke of Atholl and had a large family, who all d. unm. except the youngest. Mr. Farquharson d. in 1806, and was s. by his only surviving child,

CATHERINE FARQUHARSON, of Invercauld, who m. 16 June, 1798, Captain James Ross, R.N., 2nd son of Sir John Lockhart-Ross, Bart. of Balnagowan, by Elizabeth his wife, eldest dau. of President Dundas, and by him (who took the name of Farquharson, and d. in 1810) had issue,

JAMES, now of Invercauld.
Amelia, m. Francis Grant, Esq., and d. 1837.
Elizabeth.

Arms—Quarterly: 1st and 4th, or, a lion rampant, gu., armed and langued, az. the paternal coat of the name of FARQUHARSON; 2nd and 3rd, arg., a fir tree growing out of a mount in base, seeded, ppr. on a chief, gu., the banner of Scotland in bend displayed; a canton of the first charged with a dexter hand couped at the wrist, in fesse holding a dagger, point downwards, ppr.
Crest—A lion issuant, gu., holding a sword in his dexter paw, ppr., pommelled, or.
Supporters—Two wild cats, ppr.
Motto—Fide et fortitudine.
Seats—Invercauld, Aberdeenshire; and Marlie, Perthshire.

FARQUHARSON OF HAUGHTON.

FARQUHARSON, ROBERT-FRANCIS OGILVIE, Esq. of Haughton, co. Aberdeen, b. 26 Oct. 1823.

Lineage.—This family descends from the ancient and once powerful house of CUMMING *of Altyre*, having branched, according to numerous records extant, from the parent stock about the year 1460. It also derives from the Ogilvies Earls of Findlater, whose ancestor was brother of the oldest earl in Great Britain, and brother-in-law of WILLIAM THE LION, having married that monarch's sister. The patent of the Earl of Angus bears date 1037, and he is still lineally represented by DAVID OGILVIE, *Earl of Airlie*. (*See* BURKE's *Peerage*.)

ALEXANDER CUMMING, of Altyre, m. Janet, dau. of Sir William Fraser, of Philorth (progenitor of the Lords Saltoun) and had two sons, SIR THOMAS CUMMING, his heir; and

FERQUHARD, ancestor of the Cummings of Kellas, &c. co. Moray, who, disobliged at the refusal of their chief to allow them to bury their dead in the family burial-place, and from other feuds common at that time, laid aside the surname of CUMMING, and adopted that of FARQUHARSON, as descendants of Ferquhard, from whom have sprung the FARQUHARSONS of Haughton and Balfling, in Aberdeenshire. This family of Farquharson possessed Kellas, &c. for many generations, and became allied, by marriage, to many of the best northern houses, the Grants, Inneses &c. The 4th, in direct male descent, from Ferquhard, WILLIAM FARQUHARSON, *alias* CUMMING, of Kellas, m. about the year 1580, Jean, 3rd dau. of John, grandson of FINLAY MORE (progenitor of the clan FARQUHARSON), by his 2nd wife, a dau. of Baron Roy, of Kincardine Stewart and had issue, who carried on the line. He was one of the barons of the north who signed a roll for the protection of JAMES VI. after the Gowry conspiracy.

During the civil wars, the FARQUHARSONS of Kellas followed King CHARLES I. to York, shared in his fortunes, lost their estate, were all but one killed in battle, and lie in the cathedral at Durham. The survivor,

JOHN FARQUHARSON, returned to Scotland, took up his abode in Monymusk, Aberdeenshire, and purchased the estate of HAUGHTON. He m. in 1656, a dau. of Donald Farquharson, Esq. 5th son of Invercauld, and left a son and successor,

JOHN-CUMMING FARQUHARSON, Esq. of Kellas, co. Moray, and Haughton, co. Aberdeen, who m. Janet, dau. of — Dawney, Esq. of Aberdeen, and had two sons and a dau. viz.,

I. JOHN, who m. Anne Stewart, Countess of Blessington, but predeceased his father without issue.
II. FRANCIS, his heir.
I. Mary, who m. the Rev. Alexander Ogilvie, of Cairnstown, co. Moray, son, by Janet Innes, of Culvie, his wife, of John Ogilvie, Esq. of Cairnstown (a lineal male descendant of Ogilvie of Findlater and Deskford, prior to its elevation to the peerage as Baron Deskford and Earl of Findlater), and had issue,

ALEXANDER OGILVIE, successor to his uncle.

The only surviving son,

FRANCIS FARQUHARSON, Esq., m. Grace, dau. of Francis Strachan Esq. of Edinburgh, and had a dau. Annie, who d. young. This gentleman, who purchased the two baronies of Alford, was s. at his decease by his nephew,

ALEXANDER OGILVIE, Esq., who assumed, upon inheriting the Haughton estate, the name and arms of FARQUHARSON. He m. in 1768, Mary, dau. of John Hay, Esq. of Edinburgh, and had issue, FRANCIS, his heir; JOHN, successor to his brother; Mary; and Frances-Anne, m. to Michael-Stovin Fenwick, Esq. Mr. Ogilvie Farquharson d. in 1788, and was s. by his elder son,

FRANCIS FARQUHARSON, Esq. of Haughton, at whose decease, unm. in 1806, the estates devolved upon his only brother,

JOHN FARQUHARSON, Esq. of Haughton, J.P. and D.L., b. 15 April, 1779, who m. 17 Sept. 1812, Mary-Anne, eldest dau. of Sir Archibald Grant, Bart. of Monymusk, and d. 14 May, 1854, leaving a son, the present ROBERT-FRANCIS-OGILVIE FARQUHARSON, Esq. of Haughton; and two daus., Mary-Ogilvie; and Sophia-Janet-Ogilvie, m. 22 Jan. 1845, to John Michell, Esq. of Forcett Park, co. York, and Glassel, co. Kincardine.

Arms—Quarterly: 1st, or, a lion, rampant, gu., armed and langued, az., for FARQUHARSON; 2nd and 3rd, az., a bezant betwixt three garbs, for CUMMING *of Altyre*; 4th, arg., a Scotch fir-tree growing out of a mount, ppr., also for FARQUHARSON.
Crest—A sun shining in full splendour over a cloud, ppr.
Motto—Above the sun, "Illumino." Under the arms "Memor esto majorum."
Seat—Haughton, co. Aberdeen.

FARQUHARSON OF WHITEHOUSE.

FARQUHARSON, ANDREW, Esq., J.P., of Whitehouse, co. Aberdeen, s. his father 20 Feb. 1855.

Lineage.—The families of this surname were, from the earliest accounts, located in Strathdee, in the parishes of Crathie and Kindrochit, or Braemar, co. Aberdeen, and were at one time very numerous. The first person of eminence of the name was FINDLA MHOR, so called from his great stature. He was head of the clan commonly known in the Highlands by the name of Clan Ionlay, or Farquharson of Braemar. Findla Mhor was killed at the battle of Pinkie, in 1547, in the reign of Queen MARY, carrying the Royal standard of Scotland, and was buried in the churchyard of Inveresk at a short distance from the field of battle. No monument was erected to his memory, but the place was long known in that parish by the name of the "Long Highlandman's Grave." From Findla Mhor directly descended the FARQUHARSONS *of Monaltrie*.

JAMES FARQUHARSON (the immediate younger brother of Col. Donald Farquharson, of Monaltrie, who commanded the Braemar and Strathdee men, under the illustrious Marquess of Montrose, and was highly distinguished in the wars of CHARLES I.) was a writer to the signet at Edinburgh, and purchased the lands of Whitehouse, in Cromar, co. Aberdeen. He m. 1st, a dau. of Mr. Hay, a lawyer at Edinburgh, and had two sons, James and David, whose descendants are all now extinct. He m. 2ndly, Ann, dau. of Col. Gardyne, of the Russian service, and by her acquired the lands of Ballaterauch, and had a son, HARRY, who s. him. Mr. James Farquharson d. in 1666, and was buried in the family burial-place in the church of Tullich, in Mar. His son and successor,

HARRY FARQUHARSON, of Whitehouse, m. 1st, in 1681, Barbara, youngest dau. of Francis Ross, of Auchlossen, and had issue three sons, I. FRANCIS, his heir; II. Charles, who m. a dau. of Grant of Garthenmore, and had two daus.; III. John, a surgeon in London, m. and had a dau.; and three daus., whereof the eldest m. John Forbes, of Deskrie; the 2nd, Euphemia, William Stewart, of Auchoilzie; and the 3rd, Barbara, Douglas of Blackmill. Mr. Farquharson m. 2ndly, Mrs. Elizabeth Harper, and had by her two sons, HARRY, and James, the latter of whom d. unm., and three daus. The eldest son,

FRANCIS FARQUHARSON, of Whitehouse, m. Euphemia, dau. of Robert Ross, of Auchlossen, his cousin-german, and had two sons, HARRY, and Francis, who d. unm., and several daus. He purchased the land of Shiels, in the parish of Cluny, co. Aberdeen. His eldest son,

HARRY FARQUHARSON, of Shiels, m. 1st, Jane, dau. of Rose of Tillymaught, and had three sons, Harry, Charles, and Alexander; the two first d. in Jamaica, unm.; the youngest, Alexander, m. a dau. of Irvine of Cults, but d without issue. There were also several daus.; the eldest m. John Henderson Esq. of Caskieben, co. Aberdeen; the other three m. gentlemen of the names of Edgar, Ord, and Gordon in Jamaica, the two first had issue the last none. On the death of Alexander, great-grandson of Harry Farquharson, of Whitehouse, the heirs male of his 1st family became extinct, when

HARRY FARQUHARSON, his eldest son by Mrs. Harper, his 2nd wife, became his heir. He was a captain in the regiment of infantry commanded by Col. Francis Farquharson, of Monaltrie, forming a part of the army of Prince Charles-Edward and fell at the battle of Culloden, in April, 1746. He m. in 1720, Barbara, dau of John Gordon, of Hallhead, co Aberdeen, by Mary his wife, dau. of Francis Ross, of Auchlossen and Barbara his wife, dau. of Robert Farquharson, of Invercauld. By her Capt. Farquharson had issue,

HARRY, *d. s. p.* WILLIAM, of whom we treat.
James, *d. s. p.*
Robert, a physician in Jamaica, who *d.* there, leaving a dau.
Margaret, who *d. unm.*
Grace, *m.* to the Rev. George Campbell, D.D., F.R.S., Edin., principal and professor of divinity in the University of Marischal College, and one of the ministers of Aberdeen, a man eminent for piety and literary acquirements.

The 2nd son,

WILLIAM FARQUHARSON, M.D., was a physician in Dundee, and family physician to John Lyon Bowes, Earl of Strathmore. He *m.* 1756, Margaret, eldest dau. of Patrick Souper, of Auchlunies co. Kincardine. By Margaret his wife, Dr. Farquharson had issue (with a dau., Ann, who *d. unm.*) two sons, HARRY, who *d. unm.*; and

PATRICK FARQUHARSON, Esq. of Whitehouse, J.P., who *m.* 1795, Marjory, only dau. of William Stewart, Esq. of Lesmurdie, co. Banff, and by her (who *d.* 1 April, 1849) had issue,

George-Campbell, *d. unm.* 8 Sept. 1888.
ANDREW, now of Whitehouse.
Jane-Stewart.
Margaret, *m.* to Lieut.-Col. J. Farquharson, H.E.I.C.S., of Corrachree, Aberdeenshire.

Mr. Farquharson *d.* 20 Feb. 1855.

Arms, Crest, and *Motto*—same as FARQUHARSON *of Invercauld*, but without supporters.
Seat—Whitehouse, co. Aberdeen.

FARRELL OF DALYSTON.

FARRELL, CHARLES, Esq. of Dalyston, co. Galway, J.P., *b.* in 1825; *s.* to the estates of his late maternal uncle, Charles Farrell, Esq. of Dalyston, and assumed, in consequence, by royal license, bearing date at St. James's, 1855, the surname and arms of FARRELL, instead of his patronymic, CARROLL.

Lineage.—The Farrells, now of Dalyston, spring from the O'Ferrals of Mornyng and Bawn, co. Longford, who were of the clan Boy. The old castle of Mornyng still stands and here the family was resident in 1688. Shortly after, on the defeat of King JAMES II., they were dispossessed and their property confiscated. On a tombstone in the churchyard of Moidon, co. Longford, the burial-place of the O'Ferrals of Mornyng and Bawn, are inscribed the names of Robert O'Farrell, Esq. of Bawn and of his wife Alice, and also that of James O'Farrell, Esq. of Minard (son of Robert and Alice O'Farrell of Bawn), who *d.* 26 Nov. 1771, aged 36. This James is the 1st of the name of O'Farrell who resided at Minard. He never married, and, on fixing his residence at Minard, took his sister to live with him. This lady married a namesake of her own, and had several children, viz., RICHARD O'FARRELL, who *d.* at an advanced age, in France; Robert, who *d.* at Minard; Alice, who *m.* Charles Evers, and was mother, *inter alios*, of MARY, the wife of JAMES FARRELL of Minard; Elizabeth, who *m.* Peter Farrell, of Coldragh; and another dau. who *m.* a Mr. Dalton. At the decease of James O'Farrell, of Minard, 26 Nov. 1771, the whole of his property devolved on his sister from whom it passed to her son, Robert, at whose death it was divided between the husbands (Charles Evers and Peter Farrell) of his sisters Alice and Elizabeth.

JAMES FARRELL, who *m.* sometime about 1772, Mary, dau. of Charles and Alice Evers, was son of Patrick O'Farrell, who accompanied James O'Farrell, the 1st of Minard, to that place, and resided with his wife and family at Minard, to the time of his death in 1780. Mr. James Farrell occupied a portion of the farms of Minard and Loragh, and *d.* 17 Jan. 1789, aged 38, being buried at Moidon. His son,

CHARLES FARRELL, Esq., *b.* at Minard, co. Longford, 24 Aug. 1774, took the degree of M.D. at the University of Edinburgh in 1798, who was much distinguished in the medical profession. He passed many years in high official position in the East. Dr. Farrell *d.* in 1855, having bequeathed his extensive property to his nephew, CHARLES CARROLL (son of John Carroll late of Edgeworthstown, co. Longford, by Margaret his wife, dau. of James Farrell, of Minard), who assumed in consequence the surname and arms of Farrell, and is the present CHARLES FARRELL, Esq. of Dalyston.

Arms—Per fess, or and vert, a lion rampant, counterchanged: on a canton, gu., an Irish harp, of the first.
Crest—On an Eastern crown, or, a greyhound courant, per pale, arg. and sa., gorged with a collar, gu., therefrom a broken chain, of the last.
Seat—Dalyston, near Loughrea.

FARRER OF INGLEBOROUGH.

FARRER, JAMES-WILLIAM, Esq. of Ingleborough, co. York, *b.* 11 May, 1785; *m.* 6 July, 1811, Hon. Henrietta-Elizabeth Scott, relict of the Hon. John Scott, eldest son of the 1st Earl of Eldon (Lord Chancellor of Great Britain), only dau. of Sir Matthew-White Ridley, of Blagdon, co. Northumberland, (2nd) Bart., mother of the 2nd Earl, and grandmother of the 3rd Earl of Eldon. By her, who *d.* 10 Oct. 1853, he has issue,

I. JAMES, *b.* 8 May, 1812, M.P. for South Durham, J.P. and D.L.
II. Matthew-Thomas, in holy orders, *b.* 8 Feb. 1816, vicar of Addington and perpetual curate of the chapelry of Shirley, co. Surrey, *m.* 1st, 8 Aug. 1843, Frances-Emma, eldest dau. of Edward Golding Esq of Maiden Erlegh, Berks, which lady *d. s. p.* 3 Sept. 1844; and 2ndly 8 July 1848, Mary-Louisa Anson, eldest dau. of the late Sir William Anson, Bart., K.C.B., by whom he has issue, 1. James-Anson, *b.* 1849; 2. William, *b.* 1850; 3. Matthew-George, *b.* 1852; and 1. Mary-Charlotte.
III. Oliver-William, *b.* 18 March, 1819, barrister-at-law, *m.* 8 Aug. 1848, Emily-C.-H. Cooke, only dau. of the Rev. Robert-Bryan Cooke, rector of Wheldrake, co. York, 2nd son of Philip Cooke, Esq. of Owston, near Doncaster, and has issue, Oliver-Cooke, *b.* 1829; and Philip, *b.* 1853.
IV. Henry-Richard, of Green Hamerton, barrister-at-law, late fellow of Merton College, Oxford, *m.* 29 June, 1854, Eliza-Maria, 2nd dau. of the Right Hon. Sir Thomas Fremantle, Bart of Swanbourne, co. Bucks and has a son, Richard-Ridley, *b.* 1856.
I. Frances-Sarah, *m.* 14 June, 1837 to E.-Vansittart Neale, Esq., only son of the Rev. Edward Neale, of Allesley Park, co. Warwick, late rector of Taplow, and has issue.
II. Henrietta-Louisa.

Mr. Farrer was appointed a master in Chancery, by Lord Chancellor Eldon, in 1824, and had become senior master in 1852, in which year, by the act of parliament reforming the Court of Chancery, the offices of masters in Chancery were abolished, and under the act he retired upon full pay. Mr. Farrer is J.P. for the West Riding of Yorkshire, and for the cos. of Westmorland and Lancaster, and deputy-lieut. for the first.

Lineage.—Thoresby, in his *Ducatus Leodensis*, in the description of Wortley, writes, "James Farrer, Esq., is lord of this manor, which family, like many others, has been too remiss in a timely preserving the memoirs of their predecessors and for that reason it is that this pedigree is not honoured with the name of that pious martyr Bishop Farrer, who was born within the vicarage of Halifax, within four miles of which he gave lands to his near relations."

HENRY FARRER, of Eawood Hall, Halifax, lord of the manor of Wortley, *m.* (1st and 2nd PHILIP and MARY) Anne, dau. of William Barcroft, of Barcroft, and had two sons, Henry, *d.* without issue; and John, who had two sons, Henry and John. Henry sold Eawood to his brother John, purchased lands in Lincolnshire and, in 1623, purchased and settled at Lower Greystonleigh in Chipping-in-Bolland, in Lancashire. His grandson, Richard, m. Elizabeth, dau. and customary heir of Oliver Guy, of Lanshaw in the parish of Clapham, in the county of York, whose grandson,

JAMES FARRER, m. Mary, dau. and heir of Thomas Harrison and d. at Clapham in 1766, leaving three sons and one dau.,

Oliver, m. Anne-Selina, dau. of the Right Hon. Sir William Fawcett, K.B., d 14 Aug. 1808, without issue.
Thomas, premier barrister on the erection of the Supreme Court of Judicature of Bengal, after his return from India he represented the borough of Wareham in two parliaments, d. unm. in 1797.
JAMES.
Alice, m. to Matthew Consett, Esq.

The 3rd son,

JAMES FARRER Esq., b. 15 Sept. 1751, m. Frances, only dau. of William Loxham, Esq., by Mary his wife, dau. of the Rev. Samuel Sidebottom, rector of Middleton, and granddau. of Alexander Radclyffe, Esq. of Foxdenton, Lancashire, and had issue,

I. JAMES-WILLIAM, now of Ingleborough.
II. Oliver, b. 3 Sept. 1786, also of Ingleborough, being co-proprietor with his eldest brother, J.P. for the West Riding of the county of York, and for the counties of Westmorland and Lancaster, and D.L. for the first.
III. Thomas, b. 16 Dec. 1787, m. 18 Sept. 1816, Cecilia, 3rd dau. of Richard Willis, Esq. of Halsnead, co. Lancaster, d. Sept. 1833, leaving issue,
 1 Thomas-Henry, m. Jan. 1854, Frances, 6th dau. of William Erskine, Esq., deceased, formerly master in equity, secretary to the Supreme Court, and chief magistrate of police at Bombay.
 2 William-James, b. 24 May, 1822.
 3 Frederick-Willis, b. 7 Sept. 1829.
 1 Cecilia-Frances, m. to Sir Stafford-H. Northcote, Bart., M.P. for Dudley.
 2 Mary, m. Arthur, 4th son of the late Right Hon. Henry Hobhouse, of Hapsden, co. Somerset.
 3 Ellen-Maria.
IV. William-Loxham, of Lincoln's Inn Fields, London, b. 13 Dec. 1788.
I. Mary, m. 21 April, 1808, to the Rev. Henry-Colborne Ridley, rector of Hambleden, co. Bucks, d. 3 Feb. 1832, leaving issue, and she d. in 1837.
II. Frances-Loxham, d. unm. in 1846.

Arms—Quarterly: 1st and 4th, arg., on a bend, engr., sa., three horseshoes, of the field, for FARRER; 2nd and 3rd, or, guttée de sang, a bend gu., for LOXHAM.

Crest—A horseshoe between two wings erect, ppr.

Motto—Ferrè va Ferme.

Seats—Ingleborough, Clapham, West Riding, Yorkshire.

*** The descendants of John Farrer, who purchased Eawood, have become extinct in the male line; descendants in the female line married into the families of Fawkes of Farnsley, Cooke of Wheatley, and Legard.

FARSYDE OF FYLINGDALES.

WATSON-FARSYDE, GEORGE-JAMES, Esq. of Fylingdales, co. York, barrister-at-law, assumed the additional surname of FARSYDE in 1825.

Lineage.—This is an ancient Scotch and Yorkshire family, deriving its name from the castle, lands, and villages of Easter and Wester Fawsyde, near Tranent, in East Lothian. The Fawsydes were seated at Fawsyde as early as 1253, when we find ALLAN DE FAWSYDE gives an obligation to pay yearly out of his lands to the monks of Dunfermline *quinque solidos argenti;* in 1292, ROBERTUS DE FAWSYDE swears fealty to EDWARD I. of England, for his lands of Fawsyde; in 1335, WILLIAM DE FAWSYDE, together with William de Lorreyne, has a pardon from EDWARD III. of England, for sundry raids and forays, murders, felonies, &c., committed in border warfare; in 1356, THOMAS DE FAWSYDE, *miles*, has two safe-conducts by EDWARD III. from Scotland into England, to treat concerning the liberation of David Bruce, then prisoner. From this period frequent and honourable mention is made of this family in Scottish record. They were summoned to Parliament; a Fawsyde fell on Flodden field with JAMES V. They were connected with the families of Malcolm Fleming, Earl of Wigton, and the Swintons of that ilk, and continued to hold the lands and castle of Fawsyde until the year 1644, when we find that those possessions passed by marriage out of the family into that of Douglas, Marquess of Queensbury. This is thus described in Douglas's Peerage of Scotland: "The Hon. William Douglas, of Kilhead, second son of the 1st Earl of Queensbury, m. 1st, Agnes Fawsyde, dau. and heiress of Fawsyde, of Fawsyde, a gentleman of an ancient family that had been seated four centuries at Fawsyde Castle, in the parish of Tranent, co. Haddington, by whom he had issue, &c., &c."

Prior to the marriage with Douglas, John Farsyde, or Fawsyde, a scion of this family, had come into England, either with King JAMES I. or a short time previously, and was made bow-bearer and warden of Pickering Forest, and had a lease of crown lands in Scalby and Hutton Bushell, and other places in Pickering Lythe, N. R. co. York, by King JAMES. From this person the Farsydes of Fylingdales, and the Farsyde-Watsons of Bilton Park, are lineally descended, as shewn in the pedigree preserved in the College of Arms. The father of the present male representative,

JOHN FARSYDE, Esq. of Bilton Park, co. York, J.P., son of JOHN FARSYDE, Esq. of Fylingdales, by Mary his wife, dau. of John Watson, Esq., assumed the surname of WATSON, in lieu of his patronymic. He m. Hannah, dau. of the Rev. James Hartley, of Stavely, W. R. co. York, and d. in 1810, leaving issue,

John Farsyde-Watson, Esq. of Bilton Park, near Knaresborough, who m. in 1830, Georgina, dau. of — White, Esq., and d. 1 April, 1831, leaving an only child and heiress,
 GEORGINA FARSYDE-WATSON, now of Bilton Park.
GEORGE-JAMES, of Fylingdales.
Mary, m. 7 July, 1830, to the late Rev. Edward-Sacheverell Browne-Cave, brother of Sir John-Robert Cave Browne-Cave, Bart. of Stanford, co. Northampton.

Arms—Quarterly: 1st and 4th, FARSYDE; 2nd and 3rd, WATSON.

Seat—Fylingdales, Whitby Strand, co. York.

FAULKNER OF CASTLETOWN.

FAULKNER, HUGH, Esq. of Castletown, co. Carlow, J.P. and D.L., high-sheriff in 1847; b. 7 Sept. 1802; m. 20 July, 1837, Jane-Mary-Frances, youngest dau. of Bolton Waller, Esq. of Shannon Grove, co. Limerick, and niece of John Waller, Esq. of Castletown, and had issue,

I. HENRY, b. 2 Sept. 1838.
II. Bolton-Waller, b. 21 Dec. 1841.
III. Arthur-Brooke, b. 19 Jan. 1847.
I. Anne-McLeod. II. Elizabeth-Charlotte.

Lineage.—This family claims to be a branch of the eminent Scottish family of Falconer, of Halkerton. The late HUGH FAULKNER, Esq.* of Wellbrooke and Seville Park, co. Tyrone (whose brother, Samuel, of Castletown, co. Carlow, was drowned at sea), served as high-sheriff of the co. of Wicklow, where he had a seat called Fort Faulkner. He m. 1771, Florence, dau. of the Rev. M. Cole, brother of 1st Earl of Enniskillen, and by her, who d. in 1792, left at his decease, Sept. 1801, four sons and one dau., viz.,

I. HENRY, his heir.
II. William-Cole, sometime an officer, 17th light dragoons, m. Aug. 1799, Maria, only dau. of Francis McNamara, Esq. of Ardclom, and Castletown, co. Clare, and by her, who d. 5 Dec. 1847, left at his decease, 9 July, 1812, four sons, and one dau., viz.,
 1 HUGH, successor to his uncle.
 2 Francis, m. Frances, 2nd dau. of L.-M. Simon, Esq. of Blackheath, Kent, and by her (who d. at St. Leonards, 29 Dec. 1853) has issue, Louis, Henry, Matilda, Catherine, Frances-Dyson, Louisa-Mary, Kathleen, and Jane.
 3 William, m. 1829, Miss Creagh.
 4 Henry-Cole, capt. in the army, on the staff, m. 1839, Rosalinda, dau. of Samuel Morewood, Esq., and has issue, Samuel, b. 1845; Francis-McNamara, b. 1846; William-Willoughby-Cole, b. 1851; Charlotte; and Rosalinda.
 1 Catherine, m. to Christopher Plunket, Esq., R.M., co. Louth.
III. Hugh, of Fort Faulkner, co. Wicklow, m. Henrietta, dau. of Sir Thomas Butler, Bart. of Ballintemple, co. Carlow, and d in 1848.
IV. Arthur-Brooke (Sir), Knt. of Evington, Cheltenham, physician to the forces, and physician to the Duke of Sussex; m. Anne, dau. of Donald McLeod, Esq. of Lewes, and d. 1845.
I. Catherine, m. to Captain William Martin, of the 9th dragoons.

The eldest son,

HENRY FAULKNER, Esq. of Castletown, D.L., served as high-sheriff of co. Carlow. He m. 1st, Grace-Anna, eldest

* Hugh Faulkner had three sisters, Anne, wife of Mr. Montgomery, of Naas; Letitia, wife of Mr. Morewood; and Margaret, wife of Mr. Cornwall.

dau. of Sir Charles Burton, Bart. of Pollerton, which lady *d.* 1827; and 2ndly, in 1831, Charlotte, youngest dau. of John-Snow Davis, Esq. of Summer Hill, co. Kilkenny, but *d. s. p.* 1845, and was *s.* by his nephew, HUGH FAULKNER, Esq. of Castletown.

Arms—(as registered in Ulster's Office) Az., a falcon, rising, arg., crowned with a ducal crown, or, and charged in the breast with a man's heart, gu., between two etoiles, in chief, and a trefoil, in base, of the third.
Crest—On a mount, vert, an angel in a praying posture, or, within an orle of laurel, ppr.
Motto—Vive ut vivas.
Seat—Castletown, co. Carlow.

FAUNCE OF SHARSTED.

FAUNCE, EDMUND-BARRELL, Esq. of Sharsted, co. Kent, and Newington, co. Surrey, D.L., late capt. Hon. E.I.C.S.; *m.* in Dec. 1840, Mary-Dorothy, dau. of Baldwin-D. Duppa, Esq. of Hollingbourne House, co. Kent, and has issue,

I. CHAPMAN-DELAUNE, *b.* 7 May, 1843.
II. Edmund Gladwyn, *b.* 13 April, 1846.
I. Ann-Isabella-Mary.

Lineage.—The family of FAUNCE settled in Kent in the reign of EDWARD VI., and were possessed of estates in the parishes of Rochester, Cliffe, High Alston, Aylesford, &c., in which churches monuments still exist, to different members of the family.

HARRIS, HASTED, and other historians of Kent, mention BONHAM FAUNCE, of Cliffe, co. Kent, who *d.* 1552; and his son, THOMAS FAUNCE, also of Cliffe, who *d.* and was buried there in 1609, aged 84, leaving, by his wife Alice, a son, THOMAS, who entered young into the naval service, and was present at the attack on the Spanish Armada in 1588; he *m.* Martha, dau. of J. Baynard, of Shorne, and residing at St. Margaret's, Rochester, was mayor of the city of Rochester in the year 1609. He had two sons, ROBERT and THOMAS; Thomas joined the Pilgrim Fathers, in America, in 1640, and died at New Plymouth, aged 99; his monument there has lately been restored, and is shown as that of the last Elder having authority. ROBERT FAUNCE, his elder brother, suffered considerably during the civil wars; he *m.* and had two sons, SIR ROBERT FAUNCE, his heir, knighted at the Restoration for his loyalty, who *m.* Elizabeth, dau. of Sir Richard Head, Bart. of the Hermitage, near Rochester, and

THOMAS FAUNCE, of St. Margaret's, Rochester, J.P. for the co. of Kent, who *m.* Martha Young, and had, with other issue, a son

THOMAS FAUNCE Esq. of High Halston, and St. Margaret's, Rochester, who *m.* Ann, dau. and heiress of Captain John Daniell, R.N., of St. Mary's Hall, co. Kent, and had, with a dau., a son and heir,

THOMAS FAUNCE, Esq. J.P. of St. Margaret's and St. Mary's Hall, &c., who *m.* Jane, dau. of the Rev. Edmund Barrell, prebendary of Rochester, and had issue,

EDMUND, his heir.
Thomas, major in the army, *m.* Bridget, dau. of E. Nugent, Esq. of Dublin, and had (with a dau., Jane, *m.* to J. Lonsdale, Esq.) two sons, Thomas, lieut. R.N., *d. unm.* and Alured-Dodsworth, major-general in the army, C.B., who *m.* Maria, dau of G. Goddart, Esq., and had issue, two sons and three daus.
Mary, *m.* to Alured Pincke, Esq. of Sharsted, co. Kent.
Anne, *m.* to J. Tasker, Esq., of Franks, co. Kent.
Jane, *m.* to J. Hay, Esq., Chief Justice of Quebec.

The elder son,

THE REV. EDMUND FAUNCE, of St. Mary's Hall, vicar of Sutton at Hone and Horton Kirby, co. Kent, *m.* Ann-Eleanor, dau. of James Chapman, Esq. of Paul's Cray Hill, co. Kent, and had, with a dau., a son and heir,

EDMUND FAUNCE, Esq. of St. Mary's Hall, lieut.-col. in the army, who *m.* in 1796, Brydges, dau. of Nicholas Cox, Esq., major in the army, and lieut.-governor of Gaspe, Lower Canada, and had issue,

EDMUND-BARRELL, now of Sharsted.
Thomas, *d.* young.
Robert-Nicholas, lieut.-col. E. I. Co.'s service, *m.* Caroline, dau. of Henry Dewar, Esq., and has issue two sons and three daus.
Bonham, lieutenant and adjutant 21st Fusileers *d. unm.*
Walter-Beresford, capt. 73rd regiment, killed in the Kafir war 1852.
Frances, *m.* to Edmund Longmore, Esq.
Mary, *m.* to Capt. Edmund Cox, and has issue one son and four daus.
Jane, *d. unm.*

Arms—Arg., three lions, rampant, sa., armed, and langued, gu., ducally gorged, or.
Crest—A demi-lion, rampant, sa., langued and gorged, as in the arms, between two wings, arg.
Motto—Ne tentes aut perfice.
Seat—Sharsted Court, co. Kent.

FAUSSETT OF HEPPINGTON.

FAUSSETT, GODFREY-TREVELYAN, Esq. of Heppington, co. Kent, *b.* 1840; *s.* his father in 1855.

Lineage.—The Faussetts represent several old Kentish houses, and among others that of Godfrey of Old Romney, Lydde and Heppington, part of whose estates are still retained by them. The ancient family of Godfrey was originally of Old Romney, co. Kent, where it was settled from a very early period. Their name was at first Fermor, and though several of the branches (of which there were many in the immediate neighbourhood) appear to have used the two names somewhat indiscriminately, the principal branch at length adopted that of Godfrey only. A member of one of these branches received from HENRY II. the manor of Aldington, which manor continued with them till the death of his lineal descendant, Thomas Godfrey, in the year 1490, whose two daus. and co-heirs divided the estate, Agnes marrying William de Blechynden and Rabege, John le Clerc. Another branch were lords of the adjoining manor of Hurst. The main branch remained at Old Romney till the reign of HENRY V., when they removed to Lydde, or Lid, co. Kent, where they had previously possessed lands from the earliest mention of them, and had been from time to time buried in the church, which contained many monuments to their memory.

THOMAS GODFREY, *b.* in 1553, 5th in descent from Thomas Godfrey, Esq. of Lydde, who *d.* in 1430, *m.* 1st, Mary, only dau. and heir of John Partriche, Esq. of Iden, co. Sussex, and by her (who *d.* 1580) had a son, PETER, his heir, and Mary, *m.* to Sir John Honywood, Bart. He *m.* 2ndly, Elizabeth, dau. and heir of Michael Pix, of Folkestone (by Emma his wife, dau. and heiress of Richard Strughill), and by her (who *d.* in 1589) had one son,

THOMAS, of Hodiford, father, *inter alios*, of three sons, PETER, ancestor, in the female line, of the GODFREYS *of Brook Street House*, Kent; Edmund Berry* (Sir), who being in the commission of the peace, fell a victim to the evil days of Titus Oates, and was found murdered in a ditch near Primrose Hill, in 1678; and Benjamin, of Norton Court, Kent.

Thomas Godfrey, of Lydde, *m.* 3rdly, Elizabeth, dau. of Richard Allard, Esq. of Biddenden, co. Kent, by whom he left,

Richard, M.P. for New Romney, in the reign of CHARLES I., *b.* in 1591, *d.* in 1641, who was ancestor of the Godfreys of Wye, now extinct.

The eldest son,

PETER GODFREY, Esq. of Lydde, *b.* in 1580, *m.* Dorothy, dau. of Sir Thomas Wilde, of St. Martin's, near Canterbury, and by her (who *m.* 2ndly, Sir Thomas Hamon, Knt.,) left,

THOMAS, his successor.
Peter (Sir), who *m.* Sarah, dau. of Sir Peter Heyman, Knt. of Somerfield, and by her had one son, THOMAS, afterwards heir to his uncle.
John. William.
Anne, *m.* to Sir Richard Hardres, Knt. of Hardres Court, co. Kent.
Elizabeth.

He *d.* in 1624, and was *s.* by his eldest son,

SIR THOMAS GODFREY, Knt. of Lydde, *b.* in 1607, who purchased Heppington, in 1640. He was one of the leaders of the Kentish insurrection, in favour of CHARLES I., for which he raised a troop of horse, and which was defeated by General Fairfax in 1648. By his wife, Hester, dau. of Sir John Wilde, Knt. of St. Martin's co. Kent, he left one dau., Hester who *d.* an infant, and consequently, on his death, in 1684, he was *s.* by his nephew,

THOMAS GODFREY Esq. (son of Sir Peter) of Heppington and Lydde, who *m.* Mary, relict of Sir Robert Moyle, Knt. of Buckwell, co. Kent, and dau. and co-heiress of Nicholas Toke, Esq. of Godinton. By her he left,

HENRY, his successor.
Thomas, who *d. s. p.* in 1688.
Mary, *m.* to — Wheler, Esq. of Otterden.

He was *s.* by his only surviving son,

* Erroneously called, in most histories of England, Sir Edmundbury Godfrey. He was named after the family of Berry, into which his great-aunt, Catharine Godfrey, dau. of Peter Godfrey, of Lydde, had married.

HENRY GODFREY, Esq. of Heppington and Lydde, *b.* in 1674, *m.* Catherine, dau. and heiress of the Rev. Thomas Pittis, rector of St. Botolph's, Bishopsgate, by whom he had Mary, only surviving dau, and sole heiress, who was *m.* to Bryan Fanssett, Esq. Henry Godfrey, Esq. *d.* in 1718.

Family of Faussett.

HENRY FAUSSETT, of St. Saviour's, Southwark, and of Plumstead, co. Kent, *temp.* JAMES I., by will proved in 1658, devised his estate at Plumstead to his grandson, Henry. He left by his wife, Jane, two children, JOHN, mentioned in his father's will; and a dau. *m.*, to Henry Hawkes, Gent. His son,

JOHN FAUSSETT, left three children, HENRY; Elizabeth; and Jane, *m.* to Thomas Fielder, Esq. of Dartford. The only son,

CAPTAIN HENRY FAUSSETT, heir to his grandfather, was of St. Saviour's and Plumstead. By his wife, Catharine, he left three sons and three daus. Captain Faussett, *d.* in 1679, and was *s.* by his eldest son,

WILLIAM FAUSSETT, Esq. of Plumstead and Dartford, *b.* in 1670. This gentlemen, who was the first "Receiver-General" for the co. Kent, *m.* Mary, sole dau. and heiress of John Bryan, Esq. of Rochester, and by her (who was *m.* 2ndly, to Lieut.-Gen. Robert Echlin) he had issue. He *d.* in 1711, and was *s.* by his eldest son,

BRYAN FAUSSETT, Esq. of Rochester, and afterwards of Heppington, which he rebuilt. He *m.* Mary, dau. and sole heiress of Henry Godfrey, Esq. of Heppington and Lydde, and by her had five sons and eight daus. The eldest son,

THE REV. BRYAN FAUSSETT, of Heppington and Lydde, *s.* his father, on his death in 1750. He was successively fellow of All Soul's College, Oxford, vicar of Alberbury, co. Salop, and perpetual curate of Nackington, and rector of Monk's Horton, co. Kent. This gentlemen was an antiquary of some note, and his valuable museum of Roman and Saxon remains (*see* DOUGLAS' *Nenia Britannica*) remained at Heppington till the year 1853, when it was sold by Dr. Faussett's executors; and the Saxon Collection, known to antiquaries as the "Faussett Collection," is now the property of Joseph Mayer, Esq. of Liverpool. By his wife, Elizabeth, only dau. of the Rev. Rowland Curtois, rector of Hainton, Lincolnshire, he had,

I. HENRY-GODFREY, his successor.
II. Charles, *d.* young, in 1755.
III. Bryan, who *m.* Dorothy, dau. of the Rev. John Smith, rector of Borden, Kent, and of Seirbeck, Lincolnshire, by whom he had,
   1 Bryan, *d.* young, in 1798.
   1 Elizabeth, *d.* in 1800.
   2 Anna-Maria, *m.* to Lieut. James Hesleden, R.N.
   3 Catharine-Helena, *m.* to Francis Pridham, Esq. of Bideford, co. Devon, and has issue.

I. Elizabeth, *m.* to William Bland, Esq. of Hartlip-place, co. Kent, who left a son, WILLIAM BLAND, Esq. of Hartlip-place.

He *d.* in 1775, and was *s.* by his eldest son,

HENRY-GODFREY FAUSSETT, Esq. of Heppington, *b.* in 1749, *m.* 1st, Susan, only dau. of Richard Sandys, Esq. of Northbourne Court, Kent, and had,

GODFREY, his heir,
Robert, lieut. R.N., *b.* in 1786, *d. s. p.* in 1818.
Henry, *b.* in 1788, *d. s. p.* in 1807.
Eliza, *d.* in 1820.
Mary, *d.* in 1830.
Emma, *d.* in 1850.
Anne. Susan.

Mrs. Faussett dying in 1789, he *m.* 2ndly, Sarah, only dau. and heiress of Fettiplace Nott, Esq. of Marston Hall, co. Warwick, but by her left no issue. He *d.* in 1825, and was *s.* by his eldest son,

GODFREY FAUSSETT, D.D. of Heppington, *b.* in 1780, elected Margaret Professor of Divinity in the University of Oxford, 1827: he was successively prebendary of Worcester, and canon of Christchurch, Oxford, and was also vicar of Cropthorne, co. Worcester. By his 1st wife, Marianne-Elizabeth, eldest dau. of Thomas Bridges, Esq. of St. Nicholas Court, Kent, he had,

I. BRYAN, his heir.
II. Godfrey, in holy orders, *b.* 1813, sometime fellow of Magdalene College, Oxford; *m.* Jemima-Anne-Amy, only surviving child and heiress of Thomas Edward Bridges, D.D., president of Corpus Christi College, Oxford, and eldest son of the abovementioned Thomas Bridges, Esq., and has issue,
   1 Marian-Amy-Godfrey. 2 Edith-Ellen.

I. Susan. II. Anne.

Mrs. Faussett, *d.* in 1819, and Dr. Faussett, *m.* 2ndly, Sarah, eldest dau. of Thomas Wethered, Esq. of Great Marlow, co. Bucks, by whom he had,

Henry-Godfrey, in holy orders, *b.* in 1824, perpetual curate of Littleton, co. Worcester, *m.* Helen-Melville, dau. of Rev. Edwin Sandys-Lumsdaine, of Lumsdaine (*see* family of Sandys-Lumsdaine), and had, Henry-Farmor-Godfrey, *b.* and *d.* 1855.
William, *b.* 1825, major 44th regiment.
Robert, *b.* in 1827, student of Christ Church, Oxford.
Thomas-Godfrey, *b.* in 1829, scholar of Corpus Christi College, Oxford.
Edward, *b.* in 1833, *d.* in 1841.
John-Toke, *b.* in 1835, student of Christ Church, Oxford.
Sarah.

Dr. Faussett *d.* in 1853, and was *s.* by his eldest son,

THE REV. BRYAN FAUSSETT, of Heppington, *b.* in 1811; had been (previously to his inheritance) curate of Cropthorne, Worcestershire. He *m.* Helena-Caroline, dau. of Sir John Trevelyan, Bart. of Nettlecombe Court, Somersetshire, and had,

GODFREY-TREVELYAN, present representative.
Maria-Helena.

Mr. Faussett, *d.* in 1855, and was *s.* by his only son, the present GODFREY-TREVELYAN FAUSSETT, Esq. of Heppington.

Arms—Or, a lion rampant, sa., debruised by a bend, gobony, arg. and gu. Quartering the shields of BRYAN, GODFREY, PARTRICHE, TOKE, GOLDWELL, HOLAND, MALMAYNS, HAUTE, PETO, SHELVING, BOURNE, HOUGHAM, DENNE, DE GATTON, SURRENDEN, PLUCKLEY, TONIFORD, WALWORTH, BENNETT, PITTIS, &c.

Crest—A demi-lion, rampant, sa., holding in the paws a Tuscan column, inclined bendwise, gobony, arg. and gu., the base and capital, or.

Seat—Heppington, Kent.

FAWCETT OF DURHAM.

FAWCETT, JOHN, Esq. of Durham, and of Branton, co. Northumberland, J.P. and D.L., M.A., *b.* 6 May, 1799, high-sheriff for co. Durham in 1847.

Lineage.—The family of Fawcett is of some antiquity in the co. of Durham, and held property in the parish of Boldon. This property was partly alienated, and partly descended, in the female line, to a dau. of the elder brother of the great-grandfather of the present representative of the family, who now possesses estates at Lanchester, and in the township of Framwelgate, co. Durham, as well as a property at Sunderland, chiefly occupied by the sites of Fawcett, John, Frederick, and Foyle Streets, in that town; he possesses likewise the Branton estate, in Northumberland.

CHRISTOPHER FAWCETT, Esq. of Lambton, co. Durham, who held lands in Chester and Boldon, A.D. 1669, *d.* 14 Jan. 1699-1700, leaving, by Dorothy his wife, three sons and three daus., viz.,

WILLIAM, of West Boldon, *b.* in 1675, who *m.* in 1709, Sarah, Thompson, and *d.* in 1720, leaving a son, Christopher, barrister-at-law, who *d. s. p.*, and a dau. Joan, who *m.* John Colville, Esq. of White House, in the parish of Jarrow, but *d. s. p.* in 1785.
JOHN, of whose line we treat.
Thomas, of Durham, whose will bears date, 8 March, 1741. He *d. s. p.*
Anne, *m.* to Thomas Forster, of Lumley Castle, and afterwards of Newbottle.
Margaret, *m.* to John Stephenson, Gent.
Elizabeth, *m.* to the Rev. Matthew Forster.

The 2nd son,

JOHN FAWCETT, Esq., barrister-at-law, and recorder of Durham, *b.* in 1679, *m.* Elizabeth, dau. of Richard Stonhewer, Esq. of Durham, and had issue,

I. CHRISTOPHER, his heir.
II. Richard, in holy orders, D.D., vicar of Newcastle, rector of Gateshead, and prebendary of Durham Cathedral, bapt 8 Oct. 1714, *m.* Elizabeth Brown, and *d.* 22 April, 1782, having had issue,
   1 John, who assumed the surname of PULTENEY. He *m.* Elizabeth, dau. of Sir Richard Sutton, Bart., and was the late JOHN PULTENEY, Esq. of Northerwood, Hants.
   2 Thomas, in holy orders, rector of Green's Norton, co. Northampton, *m.* Elizabeth, dau. of J. Portis, Esq.

I. Elizabeth, *m.* to Peter Bowlby, LL.D.

The eldest son,

CHRISTOPHER FAWCETT, Esq., barrister-at-law, and recorder of Newcastle-upon-Tyne, bapt. 2 July, 1713, *m.* 29 May, 1757, Winifred, dau. of Cuthbert Lambert, Esq., M.D., of Newcastle, and *d.* 10 May, 1795, having had issue,

JOHN, of whom presently.
Elizabeth, m. to Richard-William Pierse, Esq. of Thimbleby, co. York.
Julia, m. to Joseph Airey, Esq., and d. s. p.
Anne-Mary, m. to Robert Pearson, Esq.

The only son,

THE REV. JOHN FAWCETT, A.M., resident at Newton Hall, co. Durham, b. 22 Nov. 1768, m. 29 Jan. 1795, Mary-Anne, youngest dau. of Ralph Bates, Esq. of Milbourne and Holywell, co. Northumberland, by Anne his wife, dau. of Henry Ellison, Esq. of Hebburn, co. Durham, and by her (who d. 6 Dec. 1849) had issue,

I. JOHN, his heir.
II. Christopher, in holy orders, A.M., b. 4 April, 1802, of Somerford Keynes, Wilts, m. Sarah-Frances, 2nd dau. and co-heir of George-S. Foyle, Esq. of Somerford-Keynes, co. Wilts, and has issue,
1 Christopher-John-Foyle.
2 George-Foyle.
3 William.
1 Frances-Foyle.
2 Constance-Anne.
III. William, d. 27 Jan. 1829, aged 18.
IV. Henry, accidently drowned at Oxford, 18 May, 1833, aged 20.
V. Ralph-Thomas, m. 1846, Charlotte-Amelia, youngest dau. of the Hon. Charles Laurence and Lady Caroline Dundas, and has a dau. Florence.
I. Winifred-Anne, d. 7 Nov. 1850.
II. Mary-Anne, m. to John Trotter, Esq., M.D., and has issue.
III. Elizabeth, d. 12 June, 1851.
IV. Julia, d. 17 July, 1831.

Mr. Fawcett d. 18 July, 1880, aged 61, and was s. by his eldest son, the present JOHN FAWCETT, Esq. of Durham.

Arms—Or, a lion, rampant, sa., debruised by a bend, compony, gu. and arg.
Crest—A demi-lion, sa., holding between the paws an arrow, erect, or, feathered, arg.
Residence—North Bailey, Durham.

FAWKES OF FARNLEY.

FAWKES, FRANCIS-HAWKESWORTH, Esq. of Farnley, co. York, m. 6 April, 1825, Elizabeth-Anne, only dau. of the Hon. and Rev. Pierce Butler, younger son of Henry-Thomas, 2nd Earl of Carrick.

Lineage.—WALTER RAMSDEN, Esq., son of Thomas Ramsden, Esq. of Crawthorne, co. York, by Frances his wife, dau. and heir of Sir Walter Hawkesworth, Bart. of Hawkesworth, by Judith his wife, dau. (and co-heir with her sister Margaret, wife of FRANCIS FAWKES, Esq. of Farnley) of John Ayscough, Esq. of Osgodby (*see* BURKE's *Extinct Baronetage*) assumed, in compliance with the will of his grandfather, Sir Walter, who d. in 1735, the surname and arms of HAWKESWORTH. He m. Frances-Elizabeth, dau. of Joseph Hall, Esq. of Skelton Castle, and dying 17 Oct. 1760, left, with a dau., Frances, m. to Legendre Starkie, Esq. of Huntroyd, a son and successor,

WALTER-RAMSDEN-BEAUMONT HAWKESWORTH, Esq. of Hawkesworth, co. York, who took the name and arms of FAWKES, pursuant to the testamentary injunction of his cousin, Francis Fawkes, Esq. of Farnley. He m. Amelia, eldest dau. of James Farrer, Esq. and had (with two daus., Amelia, wife of Godfrey-W. Wentworth, Esq. of Woolley Park; and Frances-Elizabeth, wife of Charles-J. Brandling, Esq. of Gosforth) four sons, WALTER, Francis, Ayscough, and Richard. The eldest,

WALTER-RAMSDEN FAWKES Esq. of Farnley, b. in 1769, was elected M.P. for Yorkshire in 1806. He m. 1st, Maria, dau. of Richard Grimston, Esq. of Neswick, by whom he had, with other issue, a son and heir, the present FRANCIS-HAWKESWORTH FAWKES Esq. of Farnley. He m. 2ndly, Maria-Sophia, widow of the Hon. and Rev. Pierce Butler, and dau. of John Vernon, Esq. of Clontarf Castle, co. Dublin.

Arms, &c.—(*See* BURKE's *General Armory.*)
Seat—Farnley.

FEARNLY OF HETTON.

FEARNLY, FAIRFAX, Esq. of Hetton, co. Northumberland, and Sutton, Notts, barrister-at-law, J.P., m. Mary-Ann, dau. of the late Joseph Barton, Esq. of London, merchant, and has issue (with two daus.) three sons,

I. FAIRFAX.
II. Charles-Joseph.
III. John-Milner.

Lineage.—This family came out of Cheshire, and were settled, during the 17th, 18th, and early part of the 19th centuries, at Gomersall and Oakwell Hall, in the parish of Birstall, Yorkshire.

THOMAS FEARNLY, Esq. of Oakwell Hall, m. Susanna one of the co-heiresses of Colonel John Beckwith, of the co. York (who had m. Miss Fairfax, of the same county) and had issue two sons and one dau. The eldest son FAIRFAX, a barrister on the northern circuit, d. unm.. and was buried in Harewood Church, Yorkshire. The 2nd son,

BENJAMIN FEARNLY, Esq., m. Elizabeth eldest dau. and co-heir of John Heron, Esq. of Sutton Hall, co. Nottingham, and of Stubton and Beesthorpe, co. Lincoln, eldest brother of the late Sir Richard Heron, Bart., and uncle of the present baronet and d. in 1810, being buried in Oakwell choir, in Burstall Church. He had three sons,

THOMAS, a barrister, d. unm. 1825.
Benjamin, d. unm. 1851.
Robert, m. Eleanor, eldest dau. of the Rev. James Milner, M.A., of Leeds, and had issue a son, FAIRFAX, present representative.

Arms—Or, on a bend, vert, three bucks' heads, caboshed, arg., attired, of the first, quartering BECKWITH and HERON.
Crest—A talbot, passant, arg., through ferns, vert, collared, and lined, or.

FEILDEN OF WITTON.

FEILDEN, JOSEPH, Esq. of Witton House, co. Lancaster, J.P. and D.L., high-sheriff in 1818, b. 28 Feb. 1792; m. June, 1817, Frances-Mary, dau. of the Rev. Streynsham Master, rector of Croston, co. Lancaster, by Elizabeth his wife, dau. of Sir John-Parker Mosley, Bart., and has had issue,

I. HENRY-MASTER, J.P. and D.L., capt. 1st royal Lancashire militia, b. in 1818, m. 27 June, 1843, Caroline, dau. of Sir Oswald Mosley, Bart., and has had issue,
1 Frances-Sophia.
2 Caroline-Lætitia, d. young.
3 Cecily-Anne.
4 Randle-Mosley, d. 1856.
II. Randle-Joseph, b. in 1824, capt. 60th rifles.
III. William-Leyland, in holy orders, chaplain to the Marquess Cholmondeley, and incumbent of Knowsley, co. Lancaster, b. 1825, m. 1853, Jane, dau. of Lord Sinclair.
IV. John-Robert, in holy orders, chaplain to the Marquess Cholmondeley, student of Christchurch College, Oxford, b. in 1827.
V. Oswald-Barton, Capt. 72nd Highlanders, b. in 1832.
VI. Gilbert-Streynsham, b. in 1837.
VII. Albert-Augustus d. in 1852.
I. Frances-Mary.
II. Cecilia, m. 1854, to the Rev. R.-Atherton Rawstorne, of Hutton Hall, Penwortham, co. Lancaster.
III. Margaretta-Priscilla.
IV. Emily-Augusta, m. 1854, to Ralph Assheton, Esq., eldest son of William Assheton, Esq. of Downham Hall, co. Lancaster.
V. Louisa-Willis.
VI. Charlotte-Emma-Willoughby.

Lineage.—This family, seated in Lancashire for nearly four centuries, is a branch of the same stock as that of the ennobled house of Denbigh.

We find that HENRIE FEILDEN or FELDEN, living 1480, was, along with others, appointed a trustee for the management and appropriation of certain lands bequeathed for the purpose of establishing a chantrie and chantrie priest in the parish church of Blackburn. Next in succession was

RANDLE FELDEN, or FEILDEN b. 1510, who was appointed in the Queen's charter, dated 1567, one of the original governors of the Blackburn Grammar School. He d. at Great Harwood, in the parish of Blackburn, *anno* 1594, leaving (with a younger son, Francis, of Pythorne).

HENRIE FEILDEN, b. in 1548, who m. 1577, Alice Hyndyll, and had two sons HENRIE, his heir and Randle b. in 1583. He d. in 1610, was buried at Great Harwood, and s. by his elder son,

HENRIE FEILDEN, b. in 1578, father of another

HENRY FEILDEN, b. in 1620, who m. and had three sons, RANDLE his heir; Henry, b. in 1649; and Richard, elected a fellow of Brasennose College, Oxford, 3 Nov. 1676, who d. unm. in 1708. The eldest son,

RANDLE FEILDEN b. in 1645, m. 1st, in 1669, Ellen Pollard, by whom he had no issue; and 2ndly, Mary Bolton, by whom he had two sons and a dau., viz.,

I. HENRY, his heir.
II. Robert, b. in 1701, who m. 1st, Miss Elizabeth Howarth;

2ndly, Miss Lees, of Manchester; and 3rdly, Elizabeth, dau. of the Rev. G. Wall, vicar of Rostherne. By the last wife he left a son,

Henry, father, by Mary Broome his wife, of

Robert, who *m.* Anne, eldest dau. of Sir John-Parker Mosley, Bart. of Ancoates, and by her, who *d.* in 1810, had a son,

Robert-Mosley, in holy orders, rector of Bebington, co. Chester, who *m.* Frances-Mary, dau. of General Ramsey, and had issue.

I. Catharine, *m.* to Jonathan Patten, Esq. of Manchester.

The elder son,

HENRY FEILDEN, Esq., *b.* in 1693, *m.* Elizabeth, dau. of Mr. Sudell, and had three sons and three daus., viz.,

JOSEPH, his heir.
John, who *m.* Miss Starkey, of Redivals, but *d. s. p.*
Henry, *d. unm.*
Anne, *m.* to Mr. Craven, of Melling.
Catherine, *m.* to W. Whalley, Esq. of Orrell.
Mary, *d. unm.*

Mr. Feilden *d.* in 1741, and was *s.* by his eldest son,

JOSEPH FEILDEN, Esq. of Witton, who *m.* Margaret, dau. and co-heiress of William Leyland, Esq. of Blackburne, and had three sons and a dau., viz.,

I. HENRY, his heir.
II. JOHN, of Mollington Hall, co. Chester, *b.* 26 July, 1769, high-sheriff 1808; *m.* 20 May, 1795, Elizabeth, dau. and co-heir of the late Rev. William Loxham, of Longton, co. Lancaster, rector of Bethnal-Green, Middlesex, and had issue, John-Joseph, *d.* an infant; Priscilla, *m.* 10 May, 1842, to John Townshend, Esq. of Trevallyn, co. Denbigh; Elizabeth-Ellen; and Margaretta-Dorothea.
III. WILLIAM, of Feniscowles, created a BARONET. (*See* BURKE'S *Peerage and Baronetage.*)
Cicely, *m.* to Richard Willis, Esq. of Halsnead, co. Lancaster.

Mr. Feilden *d.* in 1792, and was *s.* by his eldest son,

HENRY FEILDEN, Esq. of Witton, *b.* in 1764, who *m.* Fanny, dau. of — Hill, Esq. of Blythe Hall, near Ormskirk, co. Lancaster, and had issue,

JOSEPH, his heir, now of Witton.
William, *b.* in 1794, deceased.
Randle-Henry, *b.* in 1802, in holy orders, rector of Ashley, in Wilts, *m.* Phœbe, dau. of Lieut.-Gen. Sir R. Arbuthnot, K.C.B.
John, *b.* in 1804, now resident in London.
Margaret, widow of Lieut.-Col. Poole, of the Scotch Greys.
Cecilia, *m.* to the Rev. Dr. Cardwell, principal of St. Alban's Hall, Oxford, &c.

Mr. Feilden *d.* in 1815.

Arms—Arg., on a fesse, cottised, az., between two martlets, in chief, and a red rose, in base, three lozenges, or. (*See* BURKE'S *Heraldic Illustrations.*)
Crest—A nuthatch, perched upon a hazel-branch, fructed, holding in its mouth a red rose, ppr.
Motto—Virtutis præmium honor.
Seat—Witton House, near Blackburn.

FELLOWES OF RAMSEY ABBEY.

FELLOWES, EDWARD, Esq. of Ramsey Abbey, co. Huntingdon, and Haverland Hall, co. Norfolk, J.P. and D.L., *b.* 14 April, 1809, lately an officer in the 15th hussars; *m.* 22 July, 1845, Mary-Julia, eldest dau. of Lord Sondes, and has issue,

I. WILLIAM-HENRY, *b.* 16 May, 1848.
II. Allwyn-Edward, *b.* 10 Nov. 1855.
I. Inna.

m **Lineage.**—WILLIAM FELLOWES, of the city of London, erchant, some time deputy-alderman of Vintry Ward (2nd son, by Anne his wife, dau. of Thomas Warfield, Esq. of Leigh, co. Worcester, of WILLIAM FELLOWES, Esq. of London), *m.* 27 Sept. 1653, Susanna, eldest dau. of William Coulson, Esq. of Greenwich, 2nd son of Christopher Coulson, Esq. of Ayton Magna, co. York, and South Mimms, co. Middlesex, and by this lady, who became eventually co-heir of her brother, Thomas Coulson, Esq., M.P. for Totness, and one of the East India Directors, and *d.* 14 Dec. 1676, Mr. Fellowes had (with a dau. Anne, *m.* 1st, to Francis Monteith, Esq. of Greenwich, and 2ndly, to John Mordaunt, of Thunderley, co. Essex), five sons, I. WILLIAM, his heir; II. Thomas, who *d. unm.*; III. George, *d. unm.* in 1712; IV. JOHN (Sir), of Carshalton, sub-governor of the South Sea Company, created a Baronet 20 Jan. 1719: he *d. unm.* 26 July, 1724; V. Edward, *d. unm.* in 1730. The eldest son and heir,

WILLIAM FELLOWES, Esq. of Lincoln's Inn, one of the masters in Chancery, and justice of the peace for co. Kent, *b.* 4 Oct. 1660, *m.* 8 Oct. 1695, Mary, dau. of Joseph Martin, Esq. of London, and *d.* 19 June, 1723–4, having had by her, who *d.* 28 Dec. 1759 (with two daus. Dorothea and Mary; and three sons, Martin, *b.* 20 July, 1702; William, *b.* in 1706; and John, *b.* in 1712), an elder son and heir,

COULSON FELLOWES, Esq. of Hampstead, co. Middlesex, Park Place, near St. Ives, Ramsey Abbey, co. Hunts. and Eggesford, co. Devon, *b.* 12 Oct. 1696, *m.* 20 April, 1725, Urania, dau. of Francis Herbert, Esq. of Oakley Park, co. Salop, and sister to Henry-Arthur, Earl of Powis, and by her, who *d.* 6 Feb. 1779, had (with three daus., viz., Mary; Dorothea; and Urania, *m.* 27 Aug. 1763, to John Wallop, 2nd Earl of Portsmouth, and *d.* 29 Jan. 1812) two sons, WILLIAM, his heir; and Henry-Arthur, of Eggesford, high-sheriff of Devonshire in 1775, who *d.* 29 Jan. 1792, having devised Eggesford to (the 2nd son of his sister, the Countess of Portsmouth) his nephew HON. NEWTON FELLOWES. (*See* BURKE'S *Peerage.*) Mr. Coulson Fellowes was *s.* by his elder son,

WILLIAM FELLOWES, Esq. of Ramsey Abbey, and of Nacton, co. Suffolk, sometime M.P. for Sudbury and Andover, who *m.* Lavinia, dau. and co-heir of James Smyth, Esq. of St. Andries, co. Somerset, and had (with two daus., Urania-Margaretta, and Frances-Lavinia, *m.* 12 Sept. 1812, to John Mayo, Esq., M.D., and *d.* in 1837) three sons, I. WILLIAM-HENRY, his heir; II. Edward, of Little Gidding, co. Huntingdon, vice-admiral R.N., *b.* 26 Feb. 1772, *m.* Hannah-Elizabeth, eldest dau. of Richard Benyon, Esq.; and III. James-Herbert, lieut. in the 3rd dragoons, *b.* 25 Feb. 1774, killed in action on the heights of Catteau, in 1794. Mr. Fellowes *d.* 4 Feb. 1804, and was *s.* by his eldest son,

WILLIAM-HENRY FELLOWES, Esq. of Ramsey Abbey, M.P. for Huntingdonshire, *b.* 15 July, 1769, who *m.* 23 July, 1805, Emma, 4th dau. of Richard Benyon, Esq. of Englefield House, co. Berks, and had issue,

William-Henry, *b.* 11 July, 1806, *d. unm.* 1836.
EDWARD, present representative.
Richard, *b.* 17 Nov. 1811, assumed by royal license, in 1854, the surname of BENYON, on succeeding to the estates of his maternal uncle, Richard Benyon de Beauvoir, Esq. of Englefield House, Berks.
James, *b.* 31 July, 1813, *m.* Gertrude, dau. of Nathaniel Micklethwait, Esq. of Taverham, Norfolk.
Emma, *m.* in 1842, to Lord Bayning.

Mr. Fellowes *d.* 23 Aug. 1837.

Arms—Az., a fesse dancettée, erm., between three lions' heads, erased, or, murally crowned, arg.
Crest—A lion's head, erased and crowned, as in the arms, charged with a fesse dancettée, erm.
Motto—Patientia et perseverantia cum magnanimitate.
Seats—Ramsey Abbey, co. Huntingdon, and Haverland Hall, co. Norfolk.

FENTON OF UNDERBANK.

FENTON, WILLIAM, Esq. of Underbank Hall, co. York, *b.* in July, 1820; *s.* his father, the late Samuel Fenton, Esq., in Sept. 1823.

Lineage.—The family of Fenton is of very ancient descent.

WILLIAM FENTON, Esq. of Underbank, son of William Fenton, Esq. of Hunslet, near Leeds, *m.* Frances, sole dau. and heiress of CAPTAIN RICHARD WEST, of Underbank, who *d.* 1 Jan. 1715, and who was son, by Frances his wife, eldest dau. of the Rev. Richard Marsh, D.D., vicar of Halifax and dean of York, of the Rev. Lewis West, M.A., archdeacon of Carlisle and vicar of Aldenham, in Cumberland, 3rd son, by Elizabeth his wife, dau. of Thomas West, Esq. of Upton, of Francis West, Esq. of Hunsholf, living 1612 and 1639, son of John West, Esq. of Little Bretton. By the heiress of Underbank Mr. Fenton had issue,

Weston, of the Inner Temple, barrister-at-law, and F.R.S. bapt. 25 Aug. 1699, *d. unm.* 5 May, 1731.
WILLIAM, of whom presently.
Lewis, fellow of Lincoln College, Oxford, and vicar of Winterborn, in Dorset, *d. unm.* in 1778.
Timothy, of the Middle Temple.
Richard, of Banktop, clerk of the peace for the West Riding, *d.* 23 Dec. 1778, aged 80, leaving by Anne his wife, dau. of the Rev. Thomas Brook, of Fieldhead, rector of Richmond, an only surviving dau., Mary, *m.* to Sir William Wake, Bart.
Samuel of Greenhead, co. York, *m.* Anne, dau. of Robert Haigh, of Storth, in the parish of Huddersfield, and *d.* 10 Nov. 1763, aged 52, having had (with four daus., Elizabeth; Frances; Anne; and Mary, *m.* to Joseph Bradley, Esq., M.D.) one son, WILLIAM, of whom hereafter, as heir to his cousin Frances.

The eldest surviving son,

William Fenton, Esq. of Underbank, m. Mary, dau. and heiress of Hatfield, Esq. of Enterclough, co. Chester, and by her, who d. 20 Sept. 1763, had issue,

William, his heir. John, d. in 1710, aged 10.
Richard, d. unm. in 1779.
Frances, of whom presently, as heir to her brother.

Mr. Fenton d. 14 April, 1783, and was s. by his eldest son,

William Fenton, Esq. of Underbank, barrister-at-law, who d. unm. 11 April, 1792, when his estates devolved on his sister,

Frances Fenton, of Underbank, who also d. unm. 6 Jan. 1794, in the 64th year of her age, when she was s. by her cousin,

William Fenton, Esq. of Spring Grove, who thus became also of Underbank. He m. Sarah, dau. of Joseph Armitage, Esq. of Honley, and had issue,

Samuel, who s. to Underbank. William, d. unm.
Richard, d. an infant.
Lewis, who s. to Spring Grove, J.P. and D.L. for co. York, a capt. in the 55th regiment, and M.P. for Huddersfield, for which borough he was the first representative. He m. Ann, dau. of Edward Hind, Esq. of Wavertree, co. Lancaster, and by her, who d. 2 Jan. 1837, left at his decease, 27 Nov. 1833, two daus., Mary-Emma and Eliza.
Harriet.
Emily, m. to Joseph Haigh, Esq., J.P., of Whitwell Hall, co. York.
Sophia, m. to Mason-Stanhope Kenny, Esq., M.D., of Halifax, co. York.
Louisa, m. to Courtney Kenny, Esq., J.P., of Ballinrobe.

The elder son,

Samuel Fenton, Esq. of Underbank, capt. in the West York militia, m. Jessy, dau. of Edward Cayley, Esq. of Whitby, and d. in Sept. 1823, leaving (with four daus., Ann, Mary, Jessy, and Charlotte) an only son and heir, the present William Fenton, Esq. of Underbank.

Arms—Quarterly: 1st and 4th, arg., a cross between four fleurs-de-lis, sa., for Fenton; 2nd and 3rd, arg., a fesse, dancettée, in chief three leopards' heads, sa., for West.
Crest—A fleur-de-lis issuing from a ducal coronet, ppr.
Seat—Underbank, co. York.

FENTON OF CASTELRIGG.

Fenton, Samuel-Greame, Esq. of Castelrigg, co. Cumberland, b. 30 May, 1795; m. 1st, 3 Jan. 1820, Eliza-Catherine, dau. of the Rev. William Metcalfe, rector of Brimpsfield, Gloucestershire; 2ndly, Susan-Agnes, dau. of Thomas Chorley, Esq. of Leeds; and 3rdly, Anne-Maria, dau. of William Bartleet, Esq. of Reddich, Worcestershire. By his 1st wife, he has issue,

I. Samuel-Greame, b. 24 Dec. 1821.
II. George-Metcalfe, b. 24 Sept. 1826.
I. Georgiana-Anne.

Lineage.—This family appears to have been very anciently settled in the neighbourhood of Leeds. Mr. Thoresby, the historian of that town, notes, that the first marriage of the ancient family of Legh of Middleton (a village adjacent to Hunslet, where they long resided and of which they were lords of the manor), after its transplanting into Yorkshire, was with Clarter, dau. of Mr. Thomas Fenton, 6 Edward III., A.D. 1332. Of the same family it appears (see p. 61, 178, also in the appendix p. 144) was Sir Geoffrey Fenton, Knt., secretary of state, who m. Alice, dau. of Richard Weston, lord-chancellor of Ireland, by whom he had one son, William, and a dau., Katharine, m. to Richard Boyle, 1st Earl of Cork, &c.; from which marriage several noble families derive their descent. He d. in 1608. In the two years immediately preceding the Restoration, William Fenton served the office of mayor of Leeds.

Thomas Fenton, who d. in 1689, aged 79, left by Anne Tatham his wife, five daus., and one son,

Thomas Fenton, Esq., who m. twice, by his 1st wife, Elizabeth, he had a son, Abraham, of whom no male issue remains; and by his 2nd, Mary, sister of James Ibbetson, Esq., father of the 1st bart. of that name, he had issue, Thomas, his heir; Naomi, d. 1756, aged 63; Tabitha, m. to John Hare, M.D.; Hannah; Mary, m. to Josiah Oates, Esq.; Anne, m. to the Rev. William Pendlebury; Mary, m. to Josiah Ryder; Lydia, d. 1756; and Rachael, m. to D. Leach, Esq. of Riddlesden Hall. Thomas Fenton d. 1705, aged 58, and was s. by his son,

Thomas Fenton, Esq., who m. Elizabeth, dau. of Sir Charles Hoghton, Bart., of Hoghton Tower, co. Lancaster, by Mary, dau. of Viscount John Massereene, and d. 1734, aged 46, leaving, with other issue, two sons, Samuel, of whom presently; and James, who m. Dorothy Greame, and d. 1804, leaving issue, James, of Hampstead. The elder of these two brothers,

Samuel Fenton, Esq., m. Ellen Leach, and d. 1794, leaving issue, three dau. and five sons, I. Thomas, barrister-at-law, d. 1794, aged 37; II. Samuel, of whom presently; III. James, of Leeds; IV. William, m. Miss Pearson, and had issue; V. Ibbotson, d. 1811, aged 44. The 2nd son,

Samuel Fenton, Esq., m. Harriet Greame, and by her (who m. 2ndly, Benjamin Sadler, Esq. of Leeds, merchant) had issue,

Samuel-Greame, now of Castelrigg.
George, lieut. in the army, d. unm. at Aracan, in India.
Anne, m. to Michael-Thomas Sadler, Esq. M.P. for Newark.
Harriet.

Arms—Arg., a cross between four fleurs-de-lis, sa.
Crest—A fleur-de-lis enfiled with a ducal coronet, or.
Seat—Castelrigg, near Keswick.

FENWICKE OF LONGFRAMLINGTON.

Fenwicke, James-Thomas, Esq. of Longframlington, co. Northumberland, B.A., of St. John's College, Cambridge, and M.D. of the University of Edinburgh, b. 15 June, 1799; m. 11 Aug. 1842, Jane, youngest dau. of Charles Hay, Esq., younger son of John Hay, Esq., formerly of Duncan Law and Gifford, co. Haddington, and has issue,

I. John-Charles-James, b. 11 July, 1845.
I. Alison-Mary-Jane.

Dr. Fenwicke s. his elder brother in 1832.

Lineage.—The Fenwickes, one of the oldest families in Northumberland, were Lords of the Castle and Tower of Fenwyke, *temp.* Henry I. (*see* Burke's *Extinct Baronetage*). The estate of East and West Matfen, which was held by Sir Robert de Fenwyke, Knt., lord of Fenwyke, in the reign of King John, passed at different times from the Fenwyke family; one portion was sold, about the year 1680, to Mr. Dagleish, or Douglas, of Newcastle, and is now the residence of Sir Edward Blackett, Bart.; and the remaining portion of the Matfen estate was sold by Mr. Fenwicke, who d. 29 Dec. 1744, aged 84, leaving issue by his wife (who d. 2 Oct. 1708) two sons and two daus.,

James, of whom presently.
A son, who d. 21 Oct., 1728, aged 34.
A dau. m. Mr. Saint, of Morpeth, and d. aged 72.
Ann, d. unm. aged 96.

The eldest son,

James Fenwicke, Esq. of Morpeth, m. about 1720, Catherine, 2nd dau. and co-heir of John Wilkinson, Esq. of Morpeth, by Barbara his wife, dau. and co-heir of William Wilson, Esq. of Longframlington and by her (who d. 20 Jan. 1773) had issue two sons

John, h
William, of The Grange House, near Morpeth, b. 22 Sept. 1735, m. Ann-Margarette, dau. of Robert Leake, Esq., and d. s. p.

Mr. Fenwicke d. 21 April, 1759, and was s. by his eldest son,

John Fenwicke, Esq., M.D., of Morpeth, b. 5 March, 1722; m. Mary, youngest dau. of John Thornton, Esq. of Netherwitton, son and heir of Nicholas Thornton, Esq. of Netherwitton Castle, co. Northumberland, by Anne his wife, 2nd dau. of Sir John Swinburne, Bart. of Casheaton Castle, and Isabel his wife, only dau. and heir of Henry Lawson, Esq. of Brough Hall, co. York, by Catherine his wife, dau. and co-heir of Sir William Fenwicke, Knt. of Meldon. By Mary his wife, who d. 9 Nov. 1778, Dr. Fenwicke had issue two sons and three daus.,

James, his heir.
John-Ralph, M.D., of the city of Durham, b. 14 Nov. 1761, a magistrate and dep.-lieut. for co. Durham, and at one time commanded the Durham Volunteers as lieut.-col. For many years a bold and eloquent advocate of constitutional freedom, and a staunch supporter of reform. He m. Dorothy, eldest dau. and co-heir of Robert Spearman, Esq. of Old Acres, by whom he had no issue. Dr. Fenwicke d. 11 Jan. 1855, aged 93, and, leaving no issue, his property went to his nephew, the present James-Thomas Fenwicke, Esq. M.D. of Longframlington.

Catherine, *d. unm.* in 1841, aged 85.
Margaret, *m.* William Charlton, Esq. of Heeleyside, co. Northumberland, and *d.* 12 March, 1833, aged 75, leaving issue one son, William-John Charlton, Esq. of Hesleyside.
Mary, *m.* Gen. De Martenne, of the French army, and left issue.

Dr. Fenwicke *d.* 23 Dec. 1783, aged 61, and was *s.* by his eldest son,

JAMES FENWICKE, Esq. of Longwitton Hall, in the parish of Hartburn, co. Northumberland, *b.* 15 Oct. 1758, *m.* Jane, only child and heir of John Manners, Esq. of Longframlington, the last of that branch of the noble house of Etal, co. Northumberland, now represented by the Duke of Rutland. By the heiress of Longframlington, Mr. Fenwicke had issue,

JOHN-MANNERS, his heir.
William, major 23rd royal Welch fusiliers, *b.* 14 Aug. 1797, and *d. unm.* 11 Sept. 1837, aged 40.
JAMES-THOMAS, M.D., now of Longframlington.
Edward, of Heckley, near Alnwick, co. Northumberland, *b.* 7 Oct. 1800, *m.* 27 March, 1845, Augusta, youngest dau. of James Crawforth, Esq. of Lynn, co. Norfolk, and *d.* 3 July, 1851, aged 50, having issue one dau., Henrietta-Jane.
Walter-Raleigh, *d.* 1 Dec. 1882.
Thornton, *b.* 2 April, 1806. Thomas, *d.* 7 May, 1825.
Manners, *b.* 24 July, 1806, *m.* 7 Oct. 1837, Eliza-Walker-Thompson, 3rd dau. of the Rev. John Collinson, of Kirkhall, co. Northumberland, and has issue, a son and a dau.
Jane, *b.* 22 Sept. 1805, *m.* 17 Feb. 1835, to Henry-Montonnier Hawkins, Esq. of The Gaer and Tredunnock, co. Monmouth, and *d.* 5 Dec. 1835, leaving an only dau., Jane-Henrietta Hawkins.

Mr. Fenwicke *d.* 3 Feb. 1837, aged 78, and was *s.* by his eldest son,

JOHN-MANNERS FENWICKE, Esq. of Longframlington, *b.* 16 May, 1796, *m.* 16 Dec. 1845, Susan-Catherine, dau. of the late John Murray, Esq. of Murraythwaites, co. Dumfries (*see family of* MURRAY), and *d.* without issue, 8 Feb. 1852, aged 55, and was *s.* by his eldest surviving brother, the present JAMES-THOMAS FENWICKE, Esq., M.D., of Longframlington.

Arms—Per fesse, gu. and arg., six martlets, counter-charged. Quartering: arg., a fesse between three martlets, sa., for BARRATT; vert., a lion, rampant, within a bordure, engrailed, or, for HEATON; as well as the arms of MANNERS.
Crest—A phœnix in flames, ppr. gorged with a mural crown.
Motto—Toujours loyal.
Seats—Longframlington, co. Northumberland, and Page Bank, co. Durham.

FERGUSON OF KINMUNDY.

FERGUSON, JAMES, Esq. of Kinmundy, co. Aberdeen, J.P. and D.L., *b.* 21 Nov. 1789; *m.* 6 Aug. 1817, Emilia, dau. of the Rev. Robert Chalmers, of Haddington, and has issue,

I. WILLIAM, *b.* 21 Dec. 1823.
II. Thomas, *b.* 20 Dec. 1826.

Lineage. — JAMES FERGUSON (3rd son of William Ferguson, of Bandyfurrow, near Inverury), entered the army in the reign of CHARLES II., rose to be a general of brigade, and *d.* in Holland in 1705, leaving a son, JAMES, and a dau., who *d. unm.* JAMES sold the estate of Balmakewan, in Kincardineshire (his father's property), and bought Kinmundy in 1724. He *m.* Elizabeth Deans, of the family of Longniddry, East Lothian, and left a son, JAMES, and a dau., Margery, who *m.* James Cumins, of Kininmouth. The son, JAMES FERGUSON, Esq. of Kinmundy, *m.* Elizabeth Urquhart, and left three sons and three daus.,

JAMES, his heir.
Thomas, *m.* his cousin, Catherine Cumins, and left a dau., Marjory, and a son, James, both *unm.*
William, *d. unm.*
Elizabeth, *m.* the Rev. David Meek, and left two sons and a dau., Andrew; James; and Elizabeth, *m.* but has no family.
Isabella, *m.* the Rev. James Aitken, and left a dau., Margaret, *unm.*, and a son, John.
Margaret, *d. unm.*

The eldest son and heir,

JAMES FERGUSON, Esq. of Kinmundy, *m.* Sept. 1787, Isabella, dau. of the Rev. William Brown, of Craydam, and by her (who *d.* 4 June, 1807) had surviving issue,

I. JAMES, now of Kinmundy.
II. William. III. John.

IV. Alexander, *m.* and has issue,
1 William. 1 Margaret.
I. Isabella.

Mr. Ferguson *d.* 20 Nov. 1816.

Arms—Arg., a buckle, az., between three boars' heads, couped, or, within a bordure, embattled of the third.
Crest—A dexter hand issuing from a cloud, grasping a broken spear, in bend, ppr.
Motto—Arte et animo.
Seat—Kinmundy, Ellon, Aberdeenshire.

FERGUSON OF HARKER LODGE.

FERGUSON, RICHARD, Esq. of Harker Lodge, co. Cumberland, J.P. and D.L., *b.* 20 May, 1784; high-sheriff in 1835; *m.* 25 May, 1809, Margaret, 3rd dau. of Capt. William Giles.

Lineage.—RICHARD FERGUSON, Esq., grandfather of the present possessor of Harker Lodge, left, by Mary his wife, a dau., Mary, and five sons, viz., John; Richard; ROBERT; Joseph; and George. Of these, the 3rd,

ROBERT FERGUSON, Esq. of Harker Lodge, *m.* 27 Dec. 1782, Anne, dau. of John Wood, Esq. of Maryport, and had issue,

RICHARD, now of Harker Lodge.
John, *d.* 3 Dec. 1829.
Joseph, *m.* Maria-Isabella, dau. of John Clark, Esq. of Bebside, co. Northumberland, and has issue, John; Robert; Joseph-Selby; Richard-William; Elizabeth; and Maria-Isabella.
Mary.
Sarah, *m.* to George-Henry Hewit, Esq. of Burgh, co. Cumberland.
Elizabeth.

Mr. Ferguson *d.* 14 Nov. 1816.

Crest—A demi-lion, holding in its paw a thistle, ppr.
Motto—Marte et arte.
Seat—Harker Lodge, co. Cumberland.

FERGUSSON OF CRAIGDARROCH AND ORROLAND.

FERGUSSON, ROBERT-CUTLAR, Esq. of Craigdarroch, co. Dumfries, and of Orroland, in the stewartry of Kirkcudbright, J.P., *b.* 3 Dec. 1836; *s.* his father, the late Right Hon. Robert-Cutlar Fergusson, 16 Nov. 1838; *m.* 26 Sept. 1854, Ella-Frances-Catherine, only dau. of Sir Archibald Alison, Bart., and has a son,

I. ROBERT-CUTLAR, *b.* 26 July, 1855.
II. Archibald-William, *b.* 3 Aug. 1856.

Lineage.—The Fergussons of Craigdarroch,

"A line that has struggled for freedom with Bruce,"

are of very ancient standing in the sheriffdom of Dumfries, and the name is familiar to all who are acquainted with the minute history of Scotland. A Fergusson of Craigdarroch was one of the first that signed the solemn league and covenant; another headed a small handful of men who defeated a portion of Cromwell's army at Glencairn, 1500 strong, in 1651; and a third fell at the battle of Killicrankie.

The old castle at Craigdarrock was burnt in a border foray, and with it most of the oldest records of the family. The oldest paper now in the family possession is a charter of confirmation, granted by John Crauford, of Balmakune, in Glencairn, of the lands of Jarbruch and Myine, to JONKINE FERGUSSON, Lord of Craigdarroch, confirming a former charter granted by John Hutcheson, of Crawford, his cousin, and another charter granted by his son, John Crawford, of Dulgarnock, cousin to the said Jonkine Fergusson. The first named charter is dated 1298, but the others have no date.

From the said Jonkine Fergusson to the present time the descent can be traced uninterruptedly from father to son.

From JOHN FERGUSSON, of Craigdarroch, son and heir of Matthew Fergusson, of Craigdarroch, living in 1484, lineally derived

ALEXANDER FERGUSSON, Esq. of Craigdarroch, chosen M.P. in 1717, who *m.* Anne, dau. of Sir Robert Laurie, of Maxweltoun, and was direct ancestor of

RIGHT HON. ROBERT-CUTLAR FERGUSSON, Esq. of Craigdarroch, son of Alexander Fergusson, Esq. of Craigdarroch, a distinguished Scottish advocate, the hero of Burns' song of *The Whistle*. Mr. Cutlar Fergusson, who was *b.* in 1769, the representative of two very ancient houses, the FERGUSSONS of Craigdarroch and the CUTLARS of Orroland, was called to the English bar in 1797, and for about twenty years practised with brilliant success at Calcutta. Returning to his native country, with a liberal fortune and a distinguished name, he offered himself to the constituency of Kirkcudbright, and, after a very severe contest with Gen. Dunlop was elected M.P. in 1826. He was distinguished by his exertions in the cause of Poland, for which a medal was struck in his honour. In 1834, he was appointed judge-advocate-general, and at the same time sworn of the Privy Council. He m. 17 May, 1832, Marie-Josephine Auger and had issue,

ROBERT-CUTLAR, now of Craigdarroch.
Adelaide, m. Monsieur De Forcade, half-brother of the late Marshal St. Arnaud, commander-in-chief of the French army in the Crimea.

Mr. Cutlar Ferguson d. at Paris, 16 Nov. 1838, and his body was carried for interment to the family vault at Craigdarroch, attended by his nephew, Lieut.-Gen. Sir James Fergusson, Governor of Gibraltar.

Arms—Arg., a lion, rampant, az., on a chief, gu., a star between a cross-crosslet fitchée and a rose, of the field.
Crest—A dexter hand, grasping a broken spear bendways, ppr.
Motto—Vi et arte.
Seat—Craigdarroch, co. Dumfries.

FERRAND OF ST. IVES AND HARDEN GRANGE.

FERRAND, WILLIAM, Esq. of Harden Grange, and St. Ives, co. York, J.P. and D.L., late M.P. for Knaresborough; m. 1st, Sarah, dau. of John Priestley, Esq., a captain in the army, and by her, who d. 3 Dec. 1832, has issue,

I. WILLIAM.
I. Sarah-Harriette.

He m. 2ndly, Fanny-Mary, a dau. of the late Lord Blantyre, and has by her a son,

Hugo, b. 1 Oct. 1848.

Mr. Busfeild, in 1839, assumed for himself and his children, by sign-manual, the surname and arms of FERRAND. He contested Bradford unsuccessfully in 1837, and was elected M.P. for Knaresborough in 1841.

Lineage.—The name of Ferrand, or Ferrant, was imported at a very early period into the Deanery of Craven, in Yorkshire, from Normandy, where it is still to be met with, and the family that it in this country designated lived as retainers to the great house of De Fortibus, Earls of Albemarle, and afterwards attached itself to that of Clifford, Earls of Cumberland.

From William de Fortibus, Earl of Albemarle, Hugh Ferrand, in the 13th century, had a deed of grant to himself and his heirs of the office of wardour of Skipton Castle.

Four different families of Ferrand, which proceeded from this common stock, are mentioned in the Yorkshire Visitations—the families of Carlton Hall, of Fleshby, of Westhall, and of Harden Grange. The three former, who in the early part of the 17th century had allied themselves by marriage to many houses of consideration, as the Tempests, the Blenkinsops, the Hebers, the Townleys, and the Percys, have now long parted with their original possessions. The last alone remains in its ancient seat.

In Dugdale's Visitation of the county of York, Christopher Ferrand, of Bingley, in Craven, is the first name of the existing line recorded.

ROBERT FERRAND, Esq. of Harden Grange, in the parish of Bingley, 3rd son of Richard Ferrand, Esq. of Bingley, and grandson of Christopher Ferrand, just mentioned, bapt. at Bingley, 6 Nov. 1597, entered his arms and pedigree 11 Aug. 1665, at Dugdale's Visitation, m. Anne, dau. of Thomas Newton, of Daventry, and had issue,

BENJAMIN, his heir.
Dorothy, m. to Ambrose Metcalfe, of Hull.
Anne, m. 1st, to Robert Milner, Esq. of Pudsey; and 2ndly, to Samuel Jenkinson, of Horbury.

The only son,

BENJAMIN FERRAND, Esq. (then of Harden Beck, a house on the Harden Grange property), was aged 41 in 1665, when his father entered the pedigree. He m. Martha, dau. of Edward Brooksbank, of Wilsden, and by her (who d. in 1699) had, with four daus., as many sons,

I. ROBERT, his heir, of St. Ives and Harden Grange, J.P. and D.L., bapt. 9 Dec. 1647, m. 1st, Barbara, dau. of Richard Bradgate, Esq. of Ullesthorp, and 2ndly, Anne, dau. of Hugh Currer, Esq. of Kildwick, and widow of William Busfeild, Esq. of Leeds. By the latter, who d. in 1712, he had one son, Robert of Harden Grange, who d. unm. in 1742. By the former, who d. in 1685, he left two sons and two daus., namely,
1 BENJAMIN, his heir, of St. Ives, Bingley, captain of the West Riding militia, bapt. 17 Sept. 1676. m. 1st, in 1707, Ann, dau. of Henry Currer, Esq. of Kildwick, son of the before-mentioned Hugh Currer, which lady, d. s. p. and was buried at Bingley, 29 July, 1727; and 2ndly, Sarah, dau. and co-heir of Thomas Dobson, Esq. of the Vicarage, near Bingley, by Ann, dau. of William Beaumont, Esq. of Darton, by whom he left, at his decease in 1731, an only child,
BENJAMIN, of St. Ives and Harden Grange, J.P., and D.L., a major in Sir George Seville's battalion of militia for the West Riding. He d. unm. 20 Oct. 1803, aged 75, having left the bulk of his property to his relative, Edward Ferrand, Esq., for life.
2 Bradgate, vicar of Bradford, d. unm.
1 Mary, m. to Thomas Roebuck, Esq. of Heath, near Wakefield.
2 Anne, m. to John Cockroft, Esq. of Bradford.
II. EDWARD, of whom presently.
III. David, a major in the army, d. s. p. in 1699.
IV. Samuel, rector of Todwich, and vicar of Rotherham, bapt. at Bingley, 24 Feb. 1664, m. 1st, Anne Marsh; 2ndly, — Dobson, by the first only of whom he had issue.

Benjamin Ferrand was buried at Bingley, 14 Feb. 1699. His 2nd son,

EDWARD FERRAND, Esq. of Harden Beck, bapt. at Bingley, 29 May, 1656, m. Jane, dau. of William Richardson, Esq. of Bierley, who was buried at Bingley, 3 April, 1716, and by her had issue,

I. RICHARDSON, of Harden, J.P., bapt. at Bingley, 21 April, 1692, m. there 24 May, 1728, Mary, dau. of William Busfeild, Esq. of Ryshworth, and d. in 1745, leaving issue,
1 Jane, m. to Robert Stansfield, Esq. of Esholt, and d. s. p. in 1772.
2 Mary, m. 1st, in 1756, to Henry Currer, Esq. of Kildwick, and 2ndly, Peter, son of Ralph Bell, Esq. of Thirsk, but d. s. p. in 1771.
JOHN, of whom presently.

JOHN FERRAND, Esq., the 2nd son, settled at Stockton, co. Durham. He was bapt. at Bingley, 29 April, 1697, and was buried there, 23 Aug. 1729. He m. at Rotterdam, 16 Sept. 1722, Maria Hewdick, or Hudig, the dau. of an eminent merchant of Rotterdam, and by her, who d. at Stockton, 1 July, 1744, aged 46, he left an only child,

RICHARDSON FERRAND, Esq. of Stockton, bapt. there 22 Nov. 1723; m. there 14 Feb. 1745, Anne, eldest dau. and co-heir of George Walker, M.A., vicar of Stockton. He was mayor of Stockton in 1751 and 1762; and d. 2 May, 1769, leaving issue,

JOHN, his heir.
Hudig Whaley, d. 23 July, 1749, in the 2nd year of his age, buried at Stockton.
George. Richardson.
Esther, m. to Benjamin Sumley, Esq., a banker, of Stockton, and a magistrate and deputy-lieutenant for the county of Durham.
Anne-Maria, m. to — Wray, Esq. of Stockton.

The son and heir,

JOHN FERRAND, Esq. of Stockton and Barnard Castle, bapt. at Stockton, 16 Jan. 1740; d. 7 Feb. 1790; having m. 5 Feb. 1772, Sarah, only dau. and heir of Edward Dale, Esq. of Stockton, and by her (who d. at Bath, 3 May, 1825) had issue,

EDWARD, heir to his father.
Walker, of Harden Grange, J.P. and D.L., a captain in the army, a brigade-major, and lieut.-col. of the Bradford local militia, and also M.P. for Tralee in two parliaments, that of 1830 and 1831. He m. 1st, his second cousin, Katherine-Maria, only child and heir of General William Twiss, colonel-commandant of the royal engineers, and 2ndly, Margaret, dau. of John Moss, Esq. of Otterspool. He was b. at Barnard Castle, 5 June, 1780, and d. s. p. 20 Sept. 1835. He was buried at Bingley.
Jane, b. in Sept. 1775, m. to the Rev. Charles Benjamin Charlewood, of Oakhill, co. Stafford, and d. in 1798, leaving a son, Charles-Benjamin, who d. unm. in 1817, aged 21, and a dau., Sarah, who m. Charles Martin, Esq. of Belvedere, Hampshire, grandson to the 3rd Duke of Athol.
Sarah, (widow of Currer-Fothergill Busfeild, Esq.)
Anne-Catharine, m. 1st, 5 Dec. 1809, to Edward Surtees, Esq. of Seatonburn, and 2ndly, George-T.-B. Monkland, Esq., a captain in the army. Of the latter marriage there is no surviving issue, but by her former husband she has an only child, WILLIAM-EDWARD SURTEES, Esq., D.C.L., barrister-at-law.

Mr. Ferrand d. 7 Feb. 1790. His eldest surviving son,

Edward Ferrand, Esq. of St. Ives, J.P. and D.L., again planted his branch of the family in Yorkshire, on becoming the principal devisee as well as male heir of the last-mentioned Benjamin Ferrand, of St. Ives. He was b. 14 Dec. 1777, and m. 31 Jan. 1809, Frances, dau. and co-heir of William Holden, Esq., by whom he had an only child,

Frances, m. to Richard Paul Amphlett, Esq. of New Hall, M.A., barrister-at-law.

Mr. Ferrand d. 21 March, 1837, and was buried at Bingley. His family estates devolved upon his sister,

Sarah (widow of Currer-Fothergill Busfeild, Esq.), who assumed in consequence, by royal license, her paternal surname and arms of Ferrand. By her husband, Currer-Fothergill Busfeild, Esq. of Cottingley Bridge, who d. 3 Dec. 1832, and who was youngest son of Johnson-Atkinson Busfeild, Esq. of Myrtle-grove, she had issue,

William, now of St. Ives and Harden Grange.
Walker, m. Emma, dau. of Edmund Broderip, Esq. of Cossington, Somersetshire, and d. 16 Sept. 1865, leaving issue.
Currer, m. Sarah, dau. of Peter Tuer, Esq., and has issue.
Johnson-Atkinson, m. Mary-Elizabeth, dau. of John Priestley, Esq., and d. 13 Sept. 1848, leaving issue.
Benjamin-Ferrand, of Magdalen College, Cambridge, accidentally drowned at Blackwall, 4 April, 1843, aged 20.
Jane-Ferrand, d. unm. in 1824.
Sarah-Dale, d. unm. in 1825.
Katharine-Maria, m. 1st, to Charles Priestley, Esq., deceased; 2ndly, to Edward-Pellew Davis, Esq.
Elizabeth-Octavia, m. in 1840, to Thomas-William Rawson, Esq., eldest son of Jeremiah Rawson, Esq. of Greenroyde, near Halifax.
Caroline, m. William Crispin, capt. R.N., of H.M. Yacht, and d. 18 Feb. 1846, leaving twin daus., for whom the Queen and Prince Albert stood sponsors.
Emily-Lucinda, m. 21 May, 1840, to Christopher-Cresswell Fenwick, Esq., son of the Rev. John-Peregrine-Lascelles Fenwick, of Bywell, Northumberland. Mr. Fenwick was drowned at Orilla, in Upper Canada, 5 Nov. 1842.

Arms—Quarterly: 1st and 4th, arg., on a chief, gu., two crosses flory, vaire, for Ferrand *of Skipton*, a cinquefoil, az., for difference, for Ferrand *of Harden Grange*, (Dugdale's Visitation;) 2nd, Walker; 3rd, Dale *of Dalton le Dale*.
Motto—Justus, propositi tenax.
Seats—St. Ives and Harden Grange.

FERRERS OF BADDESLEY CLINTON.

Ferrers, Marmion-Edward, Esq. of Baddesley Clinton, co. Warwick, J.P. and D.L., b. 13 Oct. 1813, Senior Co-Heir of the Barony of Ferrers of Chartley, and representative of the only remaining male branch of the once potent House of Ferrers.

Lineage.—This ancient family, than which few can claim a higher or more illustrious descent, derives from Walchelin, a Norman, whose son, Henry Ferrers, assumed the name from Ferriers, a small town of Gastinois, in France, otherwise called Ferrieres, from the iron mines with which that country abounded; and, in allusion to the circumstance, he bore for his arms six horses' shoes, either from the similitude of his cognomen to the French ferrier, or because the seigneurie produced iron, so essential to the soldier and cavalier in those rude times, when war was esteemed the chief business of life, and the adroit management of the steed, even amongst the nobility, the first of accomplishments. Henry de Ferrers came into England with the Conqueror, and obtained a grant of Tutbury Castle, co. Stafford. His descendant,

The Hon. Thomas Ferrers, sheriff of Staffordshire 26 Henry VI., 2nd son of William Ferrers, 5th Lord Ferrers, of Groby, m. Elizabeth, eldest sister and co-heir of Sir Baldwin Frevile, and inherited, in her right, Tamworth Castle. Sir Thomas d. 37 Henry VI., leaving issue,

Thomas (Sir), 2nd Lord of Tamworth Castle, ancestor of the family of Ferrers of Tamworth Castle, the eventual heiress of which Anne Ferrers, m. the Hon. Robert Shirley, eldest son of Robert, 1st Earl Ferrers, and 13th Lord Ferrers of Chartley, and had an only dau. and heiress, Elizabeth Shirley, Baroness Ferrers, who m. James Compton, Earl of Northampton. Their only dau. and heiress, Lady Charlotte Compton, Baroness Ferrers and Compton, m. George, 1st Marquess Townshend, and had a son and successor, George, Earl of Leicester, who became 16th Baron Ferrers of Chartley. His lordship was created Earl of Leicester in 1784, and inherited the Marquisate of Townshend at the decease of his father, as second marquess. He m. Charlotte, dau. of Eaton-Mainwaring Ellerker, Esq. of Risby Park, and had George, 2nd Marquess Townshend, and 17th Baron Ferrers of Chartley, with several other children, one of whom, the Lady Harriet-Anne Townshend (eldest dau. and co-heir), m. Edward Ferrers, Esq. of Baddesley Clinton.
Henry (Sir), of whom we are more immediately about to treat.

The 2nd son,

Sir Henry Ferrers, Knt. of Hambleton, co. Rutland, m. Margaret, dau. and co-heir of William Heckstall, Esq, of Heckstall and East Peckham, in Kent, and had (with a dau. Elizabeth) a son and successor,

Sir Edward Ferrers, b. in 1470; who m. in 1497, Constance, dau. of Nicholas Brome, Esq. of Baddesley Clinton, co. Warwick, by whom (who d. 30 Sept. 1551) he acquired that estate, and had issue four sons and six daus. Sir Edward Ferrers served the office of high-sheriff for Warwickshire in the 5th and 10th of Henry VIII.: he was s. by his grandson,

Edward Ferrers, Esq. of Baddesley Clinton, b. in 1526, only child of Henry Ferrers, by Catherine his wife, dau. and co-heir of Sir John Hampden, Knt. of Hampden. This gentleman, in the 1st of Queen Mary, represented the borough of Warwick in parliament. He m. in 1548, Bridget, dau. of William, 2nd Lord Windsor; and dying 10 Aug. 1564 (his widow survived until 1582), was s. by his eldest son,

Henry Ferrers, Esq. of Baddesley Clinton, b. 26 Jan. 1549, whom Dugdale styles an eminent antiquarian, and describes as "a man of distinguished worth, reflecting lustre on the ancient and noble family to which he belonged." Camden likewise bears testimony to his exalted character, and to the extent of his knowledge, particularly in antiquities. He m. in Oct. 1582, Jane, dau. and co-heir of Henry White, Esq. of South Warnburn, in Hampshire, son of Sir Thomas White, Knt., and by her (who d. 7 Sept. 1586, aged 23) left at his decease, 10 Oct. 1633, a dau. Mary; and a son and successor,

Edward Ferrers, Esq. of Baddesley Clinton, b. 1 Nov. 1585; sheriff of Warwickshire in the 17th Charles I. This gentleman m. 24 Feb. 1611, Anne, eldest dau. of William Peyto, Esq. of Chesterton, and by that lady (who d. 12 Sept. 1618, aged 33) had one son and two daus., namely, Henry, his heir; Eleanor; and Catherine. Mr. Ferrers d. 22 March, 1650-1, and was s. by his son,

Henry Ferrers, Esq. of Baddesley Clinton, b. 6 Dec. 1616; sheriff of Warwickshire 16 Charles II.; who, upon the death of John Ferrers, of Tamworth Castle, in 1680, became heir male of the family. He m. in April, 1638, Bridget, dau. of Edward Willoughby, Esq. of Cossell, Notts, and had a numerous family. He d. in 1682, and was s. by his eldest son,

George Ferrers, Esq. of Baddesley Clinton, b. in 1647; who d. 11 Aug. 1712, leaving, by Elizabeth his wife, only dau. of William Kempson, Esq. of Ardens Grafton, in Warwickshire, a dau., Mary-Magdalen, and a son,

Edward Ferrers, Esq. of Baddesley Clinton, b. in 1678. This gentleman m. 26 Feb. 1712, Teresa, dau. of Sir Isaac Gibson, of Worcester, and by her (who d. in 1734) had one son and one dau., viz., Thomas, his heir; and Mary, m. to — Berkeley, Esq. Mr. Ferrers was s. at his decease, in 1729, by his son,

Thomas Ferrers, Esq. of Baddesley Clinton, b. 4 April, 1713; who m. 10 June, 1737, Margaret, dau. of John Kempson, Esq. of Henley in Arden, and had two sons and five daus., viz., Edward, his heir; Henry; Mary; Teresa; Frances; Anne; and Elizabeth. The elder son,

Edward Ferrers, Esq. of Baddesley Clinton, inherited the estates upon the demise of his father, in 1760. He m. in 1763, Hester, dau. of Christopher Bird, Esq. of London, and by her (who d. in 1822) had two sons and seven daus., viz.,

Edward, his heir.
Thomas, a major in the army, who served during the whole of the Peninsular war, and was killed by a fall from the ramparts of a fortress in France, in 1817.
Hester, d. unm.
Lucy, was the 3rd wife of Robert Willoughby, Esq. of Cliff, by whom she left a dau., Madeline, m. 26 May, 1820, to Richard-Thomas Bateman, Esq. of Hartington Hall, co. Derby.
Frances, d. unm.
Maria, m. to Court Granville, Esq. of Calwich Abbey, co. Stafford.
Catherine, m. to — Edwards, Esq.
Elizabeth, m. in 1803, to John Gerard, Esq. of Windle Hall, in Lancashire, and was mother of the present Sir John Gerard, Bart. of Bryn.
Anne-Teresa, m. 1st, to Henry Clifford, Esq., barrister-

at-law, brother to Sir Thomas-Hugh-Clifford-Constable, Bart., and grandson of Hugh, 4th Lord Clifford; and 2ndly, to Edward Hebden, Esq., who *d.* 30 Jan. 1842.

Mr. Ferrers *d.* 25 Feb. 1794, and was *s.* by his son,

EDWARD FERRERS, Esq. of Baddesley Clinton, *b.* 17 April, 1765; who *m.* 18 Aug. 1788, Helena, dau. and heiress of George Alexander, Esq. of Stirtloe, co. Huntingdon, and by her (who *d.* 29 Jan. 1840) had issue,

- EDWARD, his heir.
- George-Thomas, *b.* 21 Dec. 1791, who *m.* 8 Sept. 1817, Mary, eldest dau. of George Gillow, Esq. of Hammersmith, Middlesex, and had five sons and two daus., viz., George-Joseph, *b.* in 1819; Thomas-John, *b.* in 1821; Richard-Vincent, *b.* in 1823; Edmund, *b.* in 1824; Bernard, *b.* in 1829; Mary; and Sarah.
- Mary, *m.* to John-Bruno Bowdon, Esq. of Southgate House, co. Derby.
- Magdalen, *m.* to George Pickering, Esq.
- Caroline.

Mr. Ferrers *d.* 25 Sept. 1795, and was *s.* by his son,

EDWARD FERRERS, Esq. of Baddesley Clinton, J.P. and D.L., *b.* 31 Jan. 1790; who *m.* 11 March, 1813, the Lady Harriet-Anne Ferrers Townshend, dau. and, in her issue, co-heiress of George, 2nd Marquess Townshend, and 16th Baron Ferrers of Chartley, and had issue,

- MARMION-EDWARD, now of Baddesley Clinton
- Charles, *b.* 2 Sept. 1814.
- Groby-Thomas, *b.* 19 July, 1816, *d.* 23 Sept. 1831.
- Compton-Gerard, *b.* 12 May, 1818
- Tamworth-George, *b.* 22 Sept. 1827.
- Henrietta-Elizabeth, *d.* 14 Aug. 1838.
- Margaret-Anne, *m.* April, 1846, to Lieut.-Col. Arthur-Edward Onslow, Scots fusilier-guards, 3rd son of the Hon. Col. Thomas-Cranley Onslow, of Upton House, Hants.
- Constance-Charlotte, *m.* 1845, to Boydell Croxon, Esq.

Mr. Ferrers *d.* 10 Aug. 1830.

Arms—Quarterly: 1st and 4th, vairé, or and gu. (ensigns of the feudal Earls of Derby, after the match of the 3rd Earl with Peverill); 2nd, sa., six horseshoes, arg., three, two, and one, FERRERS *ancient*; 3rd, gu., seven mascles, or a canton, erm., FERRERS OF GROBY.

Crest—A unicorn, passant, erm.

Motto—Splendio tritus.

Seat—Baddesley Clinton Hall, eight miles from Warwick.

FETHERSTONHAUGH OF HOPTON COURT.

FETHERSTONHAUGH, ALEXANDER-STEPHENSON, Esq. of Hopton Court, co. Worcester, D.L., *b.* 23 Jan. 1798; *m.* 1st, May, 1823, Emma, dau. of William Kimber, Esq. of North Cerney, co. Gloucester.

Lineage.—The first who settled on the Tyne, in Northumberland, was a chief of those Saxons who landed about the beginning of the eighth century. The house of Fetherston was formerly upon a hill, and was moated about for a defence against the Scots; but, upon the ruin of this, the son built in the holm or valley under the hill, which holm they there call "haugh," where the castle now stands; and the name of Fetherstonhaugh is thus derived. The eldest branch continued there in unbroken succession in the male line to 1659, when co-heiresses succeeded. One, ABIGAIL *m.* 1st, Peter, son and heir of Miles Dodson, Esq. of Kirkby Overblow, Yorkshire; and 2ndly, Thomas Dykes, Esq. of Gilicruce, Cumberland. The other *m.* John Blenkensopp, Esq. of Blenkensopp Castle, Haltwhistle. Younger branches, seated at Up Park, Sussex, and Stanhope Hall, Durham, became extinct on the death of the late Baronet and of Colonel Fetherstonhaugh, killed at Blenheim. Alexander Fetherstonhaugh served as high-sheriff of Northumberland: his great-uncle, Richard, D.D., chaplain and manager for Queen CATHERINE of Arragon in her divorce, refusing to subscribe to the king's supremacy, suffered death 30 July, 1540; and Sir Timothy, his nephew, raised a troop of horse at his own expense, and fought for the King at the battle of Worcester. ALEXANDER *m.* Anne, dau. of Sir Richard Lowther, ancestor of the Earl of Lonsdale; and *d.*, leaving three sons, Albany, George, and Christopher. The 2nd son, GEORGE FETHERSTONHAUGH, *m.* Margaret Musgrave, and had three sons, Albany, George, and William. ALBANY, the eldest, settled in the adjoining parish of Kirkhaugh, at Barhaugh, Northumberland, in 1638, where his descendants continued till 1813, when the co-heiresses of Albany succeeded. RICHARD FETHERSTONHAUGH, his youngest brother, *b.* at Windy Hall, Kirkhaugh; *m.* Mary, dau. of Joseph Stephenson, Esq. of Nentsbury, and sister of Thomas Stephenson, Esq. of Worcester, and left issue,

- ALEXANDER-STEPHENSON, now of Hopton Court.
- Thomas. Joseph. John, *d.* young.
- Maria. Hannah, *d.* young.

Arms—Gu., two chevrons, engrailed, between three ostrich feathers, within a bordure, also engrailed, arg.

Crest—An heraldic antelope's head, erased, gu., surmounted by two ostrich feathers, in saltire, arg.

Motto—Ne vile velis.

Seat—Hopton Court, near Worcester.

FETHERSTONHAUGH OF KIRKOSWALD.

FETHERSTONHAUGH, TIMOTHY, Esq. of The College, Kirkoswald, co. Cumberland, *b.* 5 Dec. 1840; *s.* his father 5 April, 1856.

Lineage.—The first of the Fetherstonhaughs who came to Kirkoswald was

HENRY FETHERSTONHAUGH, 2nd son of Albany Fetherstonhaugh, Esq. of Fetherstonhaugh, co. Northumberland, by Lucy his wife, dau. of Edmund Dudley, Esq. of Yanworth, co. Westmoreland. This Henry *m.* Dorothy, dau. of Thomas Wybergh, Esq. of Clifton; and *d.* in 1626, having had a dau., Dorothy, *m.* to John Stanley, Esq. of Dalegarth, and a son,

SIR TIMOTHY FETHERSTONHAUGH, Knt. of Kirkoswald, a devoted adherent to the Royalist cause, who was beheaded by CROMWELL's party in 1651. His 2nd son and heir,

THOMAS FETHERSTONHAUGH, Esq. of Kirkoswald, was thirty-seven years of age at Dugdale's Visitation in 1665. His greatgrandson,

TIMOTHY FETHERSTONHAUGH, Esq. of Kirkoswald, *d. s. p.*, and was *s.* by (the son of his sister Joyce, the wife of the Rev. Charles Smallwood, B.A.) his nephew,

CHARLES SMALLWOOD, who, in compliance with the will of his maternal uncle, assumed, by Royal license, 1 Sept. 1797, the additional surname and arms of FETHERSTONHAUGH. He *m.* 6 March, 1810, Elizabeth, dau. of Thomas Hartley, Esq. of Gillfoot, co. Cumberland, and left at his decease, 7 March, 1837,

- TIMOTHY, his heir, of Kirkoswald.
- Charles, (*see* FETHERSTONHAUGH *of Staffield Hall.*)
- Eliza, *m.* 25 April, 1837, to Thomas Tod, Esq. of Drygrange, co. Roxburgh.

The son and heir,

TIMOTHY FETHERSTONHAUGH, Esq. of The College, Kirkoswald, J.P., high-sheriff 1846, *b.* 4 March, 1811; *m.* 16 Oct. 1838, Eliza-Were, dau. of John-Were Clarke, Esq. of Bridwell, co. Devon, by Frances his wife, dau. of Sir Thomas Carew, Bart. of Haccombe, and had issue,

- TIMOTHY, present representative.
- Charles, *b.* 4 Feb. 1844.
- Albany, *b.* 10 Dec. 1845.
- Eliza. Frances. Maude.

Mr. Fetherstonhaugh *d.* 5 April, 1856.

Arms—Gu., a chev., between three ostrich feathers, arg.

Crest—An antelope's head, erased, gu., armed, or.

Motto—Valens et volens.

Seat—The College, Kirkoswald.

FETHERSTONHAUGH OF STAFFIELD HALL.

FETHERSTONHAUGH, CHARLES, Esq. of Staffield Hall, Penrith, Cumberland, J.P., *b.* 31 May, 1812; *m.* 6 April, 1847, Jane, dau. and co-heir of Francis Aglionby, Esq. of Nunnery, M.P. for eastern division of the co. of Cumberland, by Mary, his wife, dau. of John Matthews, Esq. of Wigton Hall, Cumberland, and has issue a dau.,

- Elizabeth-Aglionby.

Lineage.—REV. CHARLES SMALLWOOD, who *m.* Joyce, dau. of Heneage Fetherstonhaugh, 1760; *d.* 4 March, 1771, leaving a son,

CHARLES SMALLWOOD, who assumed the name of FETHERSTONHAUGH. He *m.* 1810, Elizabeth, dau. and co-heir of Thomas Hartley, Esq. of Gillfoot, Cumberland; which lady *d.* 8 June, 1823. Mr. Fetherstonhaugh *d.* 17 March, 1839, having had issue,

- TIMOTHY, of the College (*see* preceding family.)
- CHARLES, of Staffield Hall.
- Eliza, *m.* 25 April, 1837, Thomas Tod, Esq. of Drygrange, Roxburgshire.

Arms—Gu., a chev., between three ostrich feathers, arg.

Crest—An antelope's head, erased, gu., armed, or.

Seat—Staffield Hall, Penrith.

FETHERSTONHAUGH OF BRACKLYN CASTLE.

FETHERSTONHAUGH, HOWARD, Esq. of Bracklyn Castle, co. Westmeath, late captain 11th regiment, *b.* 23 May, 1819; *m.* 16 Aug. 1854, Lucy-Emily, dau. of William Wingfield, Esq. of Orsett Hall, Essex, and has a dau.,

CONSTANCE-LUCY.

Lineage.—This branch of the ancient family of Fetherstonhaugh, of Up Park, in Sussex, and of Newcastle, co. Northumberland, migrated to Ireland in the reign of CHARLES I., and acquired large grants of land in several counties.

THOMAS FETHERSTONHAUGH, Esq. the lineal descendant and representative of the Irish branch of the family, *m. temp.* GEORGE II., Miss Nugent, of Derrymore, co. Westmeath, and had, with a dau., wife of Francis MacEvoy, Esq. of Tobertinan, co. Meath, a son and successor,

JAMES FETHERSTONHAUGH, Esq. of Bracklyn, who *m.* Margaret, only dau. of the late Sir Richard Steele, Bart. of Hampstead, co. Dublin, and had issue,

THOMAS-JAMES, his heir.
Richard-Steele, who *m.* in 1820, the dau. of the late Mr. Baron George, of the Court of Exchequer in Ireland.
John, who *m.* in 1828, the Hon. Susan Massy, sister to the present Lord Massy.
Charlotte, *m.* to the late Major Robert Tighe, of South Hill, co. Westmeath.
Margaret-Anne, who *m.* Sir Thomas Chapman, Bart. of Killua Castle.
Harriet.

The eldest son,

THOMAS-JAMES FETHERSTONHAUGH, Esq. of Bracklyn Castle, J.P. and D.L., high-sheriff of Westmeath, *b.* 1790; *m.* 18 Dec. 1816, the Lady Eleanor Howard, 2nd dau. of William, 3rd Earl of Wicklow, and had issue,

JAMES-HOWARD, present proprietor.
Eleanor-Margaret.
Catherine-Mary. Frances-Alicia.

Mr. Fetherstonhaugh *d.* 13 Dec. 1854.

Arms—Gu., on a chevron, between three ostrich feathers, arg., a pallet.
Crest—An antelope, statant, armed, or.
Motto—Valens et volens.
Seat—Bracklyn Castle, near Kinegad.

FETHERSTON OF PACKWOOD HOUSE.

FETHERSTON, JOHN, Esq. of Packwood House, co. Warwick, represents a branch of the ancient North of England family of Fetherston-Haugh. The first notice of Fetherston of Packwood occurs in 8 EDWARD IV., from which period the pedigree is deduced in direct descent to the present proprietor.

Arms—Gu., on a chev., between three ostrich feathers, arg., three annulets, sa.
Crest—An antelope's head, erased, gu., horned and langued, vert.
Motto—Christi pennatus sidera morte peto.
Seat—Packwood House, Warwickshire.

FFARINGTON OF WORDEN.

FFARINGTON, SUSAN-MARIA and MARY-HANNAH, of Worden, co. Lancaster; *s.* their brother, James-Nowell Ffarington, Esq., 6 June, 1848.

Lineage.—The FFARINGTONS, of ffarington or Farington, in the parish of Penwortham, and Shaw Hall, in the parish of Leyland, in the county palatine of Lancaster, are a family of great antiquity. Farington Hall was their principal seat till the death of Sir Henry Ffarington in 1549. For the next two centuries they resided at Worden, and removed thence to Shaw Hall (now rebuilt and named Worden) about the year 1740.

SIR HENRY FFARINGTON, steward of the royal manor of Penwortham, and a commissioner for the suppression of monasteries (lineally descended from the marriage of John de ffarington, living *temp.* HENRY III., with Avicia Bussel, of Penwortham), *m.* 1st, Anne, dau. of Sir Alexander Ratcliffe, of Ordsall, by whom he had a son and heir, WILLIAM, whose dau. and heir, Jane, *m.* Henry Becconsal, Esq. of Becconsal. Sir Henry *m.* 2ndly, Dorothy, dau. of Sir Humphrey Okeover, of Okeover, in Staffordshire, by whom he left, at his decease (his will is dated 1549), a son,

WILLIAM FFARINGTON, living in the reign of ELIZABETH. To this gentleman, who then resided at Worden, Laurence Dalton gave the additional crest, and confirmed the arms. He *m.* Jane, only dau. of Sir Thomas Talbot, of Bashall, co. York, Knt., and had three sons, namely, I. THOMAS, his heir; II. William, *d. s. p.*; and III. Henry, who *m.* Margaret, dau. and heiress of Edward Browster, of Maxfield, and had a son, Thomas, who *m.* Anne Worrall, and was grandfather of Major-Gen. William ffarington, of Chiselhurst, who *m.* the dau. of Sir Edward Battinson, of Sudbury, and had a son, Thomas, who *d. s. p.*, and two daus., Mary, *m.* to Col. J. Selwyn; and Albinia, *m.* to Robert, 1st Duke of Ancaster. The eldest son,

THOMAS FFARINGTON (disinherited by his father), constable of Lancaster Castle, and steward of the Queen's lands at Lonsdale, *m.* Mabel, dau. and co-heir of George Benson, Esq. of Hyndhill, in Westmoreland, and had three sons and six daus., of whom the eldest son was

WILLIAM FFARINGTON, Esq. of Shawe Hall, high-sheriff for Lancashire in 1636. This gentleman, a stanch cavalier, valiantly assisted the Countess of Derby in her gallant defence of Lathom against the parliamentarians, and, in consequence, had his estate sequestered. He *m.* Margaret, dau. of Henry Worrell, Esq., and left at his decease, his will is dated 1657 (with two younger sons, George, of Knights, Middlesex, *d. s. p.*; and Henry; and four daus., Margaret, the wife of Edward Fleetwood, of Penwortham; Anne, of Clayton, of Clayton; Elizabeth, of Charnocke, of Charnocke; and Alice, of Banister, of Bank), a son and successor,

WILLIAM FFARINGTON, Esq. of Shawe Hall, named as a knight of the Royal Oak, who *m.* Catherine, dau. of Edmund Fleetwood, Esq. of Penwortham, and had issue. Mr. ffarington, whose will is dated 20 Feb. 1672, was *s.* by his son,

HENRY FFARINGTON, Esq. of Shawe Hall, who *m.* Susan, dau. of Digory Wheare, D.D., master of Gloucester Hall, professor of history at Oxford, and had, with three daus., two sons, who *d. s. p.* Mr. ffarington, whose will is dated 20 May, 1687, had a brother,

GEORGE FFARINGTON, Esq. of Shawe Hall, who *m.* Elizabeth, dau. of — Whitmore, of Thurstaston, in Cheshire, and had, with two daus., two sons, the younger, Valentine, left two daus., Elizabeth, *m.* to Col. Gardner; and Sarah, wife of Nicholas Starkie, Esq. of Riddleston. The elder son,

WILLIAM FFARINGTON, Esq. of Shawe Hall, *b.* in 1675 was sheriff of Lancashire in 1718. He *m.* Elizabeth, dau. and heir of Dr. James Rufine, of Boulogne (who fled from France, owing to the persecution of the Huguenots), and had,

GEORGE, his heir.
William, rector of Warrington, and vicar of Leigh, ancestor of FFARINGTON *of Woodvale* (*which see*).
Henry.
Elizabeth, *b.* in 1702, *m.* to Richard Atherton, Esq. of Atherton.
Margaret, *m.* to William Byssel, Esq. of Seabornes, in Herefordshire.
Isabella, *b.* in 1711, *m.* to the Rev. John Woodcock, of Staffordshire.

Mr. ffarington was *s.* by his eldest son,

GEORGE FFARINGTON, Esq. of Shawe Hall, *b.* in 1696, who *m.* Margaret, dau. and sole heir of John Bradshaw, Esq. of Pennington, and had, with several other sons, who *d.* issueless (one, Bradshaw, was killed at the battle of Fontenoy),

WILLIAM (Sir), his heir.
James, *b.* in 1773, who *m.* 1st, Jane Ashton, but by her had no child; and 2ndly, Mary, dau. of Roger Nowell, Esq. of Altham, by whom he had, WILLIAM, successor to his uncle; Mary-Isabella, *m.* to George-Watkin Kenrick, Esq. of Woore Hall, co. Stafford, and *d.* in 1829 and Charlotte, *m.* to Alexander Nowell, Esq., M.P., of Underley, in Westmoreland.
Margaret, *m.* to James-Prior Clayton, Esq.
Barbara, *m.* to the Rev. Thomas Mallory, of Mobberley.
Isabella, *m.* to Gill. Slater, Esq. of Chesterfield and Liverpool.
Mary, *m.* to Isaac Hamon, Esq. of Portarlington, in Ireland.

The eldest son,

SIR WILLIAM FFARINGTON, Knt. of Shawe Hall, *b.* in 1730, high-sheriff of Lancashire 1761, *d.* without issue, 1781, and was *s.* by his nephew,

WILLIAM FFARINGTON, Esq. of Shawe (now called Worden)

Hall, J.P. and D.L., lieut.-col. 1st regt. Lancashire militia, and high-sheriff in 1813. He m. 1st, in 1791, Sybilla-Georgiana, dau. of Edward Wilbraham-Bootle, Esq. of Lathom, and sister of Lord Skelmersdale, by whom (who d. in 1799) he had, with three sons, who all d. young, three daus., viz., Mary-Isabella, d. young; Sybilla-Georgiana, m. Thomas Scarisbrick, Esq. of Scarisbrick, and d. s. p. 1839; and Frances-Anne, d. s. p. 1831. Col. ffarington m. 2ndly, 1803, Hannah, dau. of John Matthews, Esq. of Tynemouth, and by her, who d. in 1833, had, George, who d. in 1819; William-Matthews, d. in 1827; and James-Nowell, his heir; Susan-Maria; and Mary-Hannah. Col. ffarington d. 13 June, 1837, and was s. by his only surviving son,

James-Nowell Ffarington, Esq. of Worden, b. 1813, who m. Oct. 1847, Sarah-Esther, dau. and co-heir of John Touchet, Esq. of Broom House, co. Lancaster, and dying s. p. 6 June, 1848, was s. by his sisters, Susan-Maria and Mary-Hannah.

Arms—Arg., a chevron, gu., between three leopards' heads sa.
Crest—A dragon, arg., sans wings, tail nowed, langued, and ducally gorged, gu., and wreathed with a chain, or.
Motto—Domat omnia virtus.
Seat—Worden Hall, near Preston.

FFARINGTON OF WOODVALE.

Ffarington, William, Esq. of Woodvale, Isle of Wight, a rear-admiral in Her Majesty's navy, b. 1777, m. in 1814, Frances-Ann, 2nd dau. of Edmund-Francis Green, of Medham, Isle of Wight, Esq., and has issue,

I. William, m. Cecil-Frances Harriett, eldest dau. of the Rev. James-Bradshaw Tyrwhitt, rector of Wilksby, co. Lincoln.
II. Edmund-Francis, barrister-at-law, m. Margaret, only child and heiress of James Newsham, of Preston, Esq., by whom he has issue,
1 William-James. 2 Edmund-Richard.
III. Richard-Atherton, major 51st regiment, d. 1 April, 1855, aged 32.
I. Frances-Ann, d. s. p. 1841.

Lineage.—For ancient lineage see ffarington of Worden.

William ffarington, of Worden, b. in 1675, m. Elizabeth, dau. of Dr. James Rufine, of Boulogne, one of the refugee Huguenots, by whom he had issue,

I. George, whose male line is now extinct, and who is represented by Susan-Maria, and Mary-Hannah ffarington, co-heiresses of Worden (*see* ffarington *of Worden*).
II. William, rector of Warrington and vicar of Leigh, m. Hester, dau. and co-heiress of — Gilbody, of Manchester, Esq., and had issue,
1 William, son and heir, m. Ann, dau. and co-heiress of William Nash, Esq., and d. in 1803, leaving issue,
William, son and heir, now of Woodvale.
Henry, d. s. p. at Gibralter, on board H.M.S. Triumph, 74 guns.
George, d. s. p. in the West Indies, on board H.M.S. Topaze, 32 guns.
Edward-Frazer, a lieut. in the army, d. at the capture of Java, s. p.
Esther-Frances, m. Leonard-Streete Coxe, Esq., d. 1854, leaving issue.
2 Joseph, R.A., m. Susan, dau. of the Rev. Dr. Hammond, prebendary of Norwich, and d. s. p. 1821.
3 George, d. in the East Indies, s. p. 1786.
4 Henry, m. Marianne, dau. of James Borron, of Manchester, Esq., by whom he had issue,
William, incumbent of St. James', Rochdale, m. Marianne, dau. of Dr. Haxby, of Pontefract.
Henry, m. Elizabeth, dau. of — Woodcock, of Wigan, Esq., by whom he has issue,
Henry-Borron. Richard-Atherton.
Elizabeth, m. N. Eckersley, Esq.
Marianne.
Marianne.
Elizabeth, m. John Fenton, of Dromore West, co. Sligo, a capt. in the army.
Sarah, d. s. p.
Harriett, m. Rev. Frederick Norris, rector of Gransden, co. Cambridge.
Frances, m. Lieut.-Col. Parkinson.
5 Richard-Atherton, of Parr's Wood, co. Lancaster, Esq., m. Elizabeth, dau. of James Borron, of Manchester, d. s. p.
6 Edward, d. at sea, 1796. 7 James, d. young.
8 Robert, D.D., rector of St. George's East, London, d. s. p 1841.

Arms—Same as ffarington, of Wordon.
Crest—A dragon, arg., sans wings, tai nowed, langued and ducally gorged, gu., and wreathed with a chain, or.
Motto—Domat omnia virtus.
Seat—Woodvale, Isle of Wight.

FFOLLIOTT OF HOLLYBROOK HOUSE.

Ffolliott, John, of Hollybrook House, co. Sligo, and Lickhill, co. Worcester, b. 28 Dec. 1798; m. 17 Dec. 1822, Maria-Lucie, dau. of Herbert-Rawson Stepney, Esq. of Durrow, King's County, by Alicia-Vincentia his wife, dau. of H.-P. L'Estrange, Esq. of Moystown, in the same county, and has issue,

John, b. 21 Nov. 1824.
Zaida-Maria, m. 15 June, 1847, to Sir Thomas Erskine, Bart. of Cambo.

Lineage.—In a genealogical manuscript of Sir William Dugdale's, preserved in the Ashmolean Museum in Oxford, page 70, occurs the name of William Ffolliot, husband of Agnes de Arches, foundress of Nunsectling Nunnery, in Holderness. He was her 3rd husband: her two former were Hurbertus de Sco-Quintino, and De Fauconberg. William ffolliott had, by his wife Agnes, six sons, William, Archbishop of York in the 18th of King Stephen; Pagannus; Henry; Richard; Hugh; and Jordan.

Henry Ffolliot, brother of Sir John ffolliott, who was knighted by Queen Elizabeth, and lineal descendant of William ffolliott and Agnes de Arches, commanded, in the year 1599, a company of foot, under the Earl of Ormond, at Kilkenny, and in 1601 commanded a regiment, and had great share in the victory of Kinsale, under the Lord-Deputy Mountjoy, for which he was created first Knight-Banneret and afterwards a Peer of Ireland, by the title of Baron of Ballyshannon, with a grant of large royalties and estates there. He was president of the North of Ireland; and by Anne, dau. of Sir William Stroud, of Stoke, in Somersetshire, had issue two daus., Elizabeth, m. to Sir John Ponsonby, grandfather to the Earl of Bessborough; and Frances, m. to Sir Henry King, father of the Earl of Kingston; and several sons, of whom the eldest,

Thomas, 2nd Lord ffolliott, had a company of foot in the service of King Charles I., A.D. 1641, and in 1645 commanded a regiment, and was governor of Londonderry. He had issue, by Rebecca, his wife, relict of — Waters, of Dublin, merchant, five daus., Anne, wife of John Soley, Esq.; Rebecca, wife of Job Walker, Esq.; Frances, wife to — Mason, Esq.; Elizabeth, wife to Samuel Powell, Esq.; and Mary, wife to Roland Baugh, Esq.; and one son, Henry, 3rd Lord ffolliott, m. Elizabeth, dau. and co-heiress of George Pudsey, of Langley Hall, in the co. of Warwick, Esq.; and d. without issue. The late

John Ffolliott, Esq. of Holybrook House, co. Sligo, son of Francis ffolliott, Esq., and Barbara Allen his wife, was descended from a common ancestor with the Lords ffolliott. He m. 2 Feb. 1793, Frances, sister of Sir William-Jackson Homan, Bart. of Surrock, co. Westmeath, and had issue,

John, now of Holybrook House.
Francis, in holy orders, m. Fanny-Maria, dau. of William Raymond, of Cockerham, Devon.
Philip-Homan, R.N., d. unm.
Marianne, m. to George Young, Esq., of Culdoff House, co. Donegal.
Frances, m. to George-Marmaduke Forster, Esq.
Barbara, m. to Admiral Charles-Frederick Payne, R.N.
Elizabeth, m. to Thomas Bradshaw, Esq.
Henrietta, m. to the Rev. George-Nesbitt Knox.
Lydia, m. to William Eliot, Esq.
Georgiana, m. to the Rev. James-Robert Pears, of Woodcote House, Surrey.
Susan, d. unm.

Arms—Gu., a bend, arg.
Crest—A lion rampant, per pale, gu. and arg., double queued, and murally crowned, or.
Motto—Quo virtus et fata vocant.
Seats—Hollybrook House, co. Sligo, and Lick Hill, co. Worcester.

FFOULKES OF ERIVIATT.

Ffoulkes, John-Jocelyn, Esq. of Eriviatt, co. Denbigh, J.P., b. 16 Sept. 1813; m. 18 Oct. 1843, Mary-Anne, eldest dau. of Rear-Admiral Sir William-Beauchamp Proctor, Bart. of Langley Park, co. Norfolk.

Lineage.—The lineage of this family is deduced through GRONO LLWYD AP PENWYN, living *temp.* EDWARD I. of England, chief of a younger branch of the 8th Noble Tribe of North Wales and Powys, whose founder was MARCHUDD AP CYNAN, Lord of Brynffenigl, who flourished in the ninth century. GRONO LYWYD AP PENWYN, whose chief residence was at Melai, in Denbighshire, was a prominent military leader against the patriotic cause in the wars which transferred the sovereignty of Wales to EDWARD I., and was one of the jury for taking the extent of the comote of Nant Conway, 9 July, 1352. He was father, by his 1st wife, Angharad, dau. of Heilin ap Sir Tudor, Knt., Lord of Nant and Llangynhafal, of five sons,

David Llwyd ap Grono, ancestor of the WYNNS *of Melai* and the WYNNES *of Garthewin*.
Iorwerth. Madoc. Howel. EDNYFED.

The 5th son,

EDNYFED, was great-grandfather of

GRONWY, who *m.* Margaret, dau. of Gryffydd Hanmer, and was *s.* by his son,

THOMAS AP GRONWY, whose wife was Margaret, dau. of Owen ap Griffith ap Madoc Vychan, of Plas Ucha, in Abergellen, co. Denbigh. Their son and heir,

FFOULK AP THOMAS, *m.* Alice, dau. and heir of Griffith ap Rhys ap Sir David Anwyl, of Cil Owain, and was *s.* by his son,

JOHN-WYNN FFOULKES, of ERIVIATT, co. Denbigh, who *m.* Mary, 3rd dau. of Gawen Goodman, of Ruthin, co. Denbigh, eldest son (by Sisli, dau. of Edward Thelwall, of Plas-y-Ward, co. Denbigh, Esq.) of Edward Goodman, brother of Gabriel Goodman, dean of Westminster in 1561, and cousin of Bishop Goodman, of Gloucester. By this lady he had issue (with a dau., Elizabeth, wife of John Parry, of Llanbedr) a son and heir,

PIERS FFOULKES, of Eriviatt, Esq., who *d.* 8 May, 1636. He *m.* Margaret, dau. of Edward Bellot, of Great Moreton, co. Chester, by Amy his wife, dau. and heir of Anthony Grosvenor, of Duddleston, and by her (who *d.* 4 Dec. 1631) had, with a dau., Margaret, a son and heir,

JOHN FFOULKES, Esq. of Eriviatt, who *m.* about 1618-19, Jane, dau. of Thomas ap Rhys Wynne, of Giler, co. Merioneth, Esq., high-sheriff of Denbighshire in 1624; and *d.* before his father, leaving an only son and heir,

PETER FFOULKES, Esq. of Eriviatt, who *m.* 14 Feb. 1635, Elizabeth, sister of Humphrey Lloyd, D.D., Bishop of Bangor, and dau. of Richard Lloyd, D.D., appointed canon of St. Asaph in 1611. By this lady (who *d.* in 1655-6) Mr. ffoulkes had, with other issue, a son,

PETER FFOULKES, Esq. of Eriviatt, who *s.* his father in 1701. He *m.* Margaret, dau. of R. Betton, of Shrewsbury, and niece of Lord Chancellor Jefferies, and by her (who was buried 5 Jan. 1716) left at his decease, in 1713, with other issue, a dau., Elizabeth, wife of the Rev. William Eyton, and a son and successor,

JOHN FFOULKES, Esq. of Eriviatt, *b.* Sept. 1699; who *m.* 25 Sept. 1729, Catherine, dau. and heir of Henry Roberts, of Rhyddonnen, co. Denbigh, Esq., high-sheriff of Denbighshire in 1722, and by her (who *d.* 8 Aug. 1764), had issue, of which were JOHN, his heir; and Margaret, *b.* in 1741; *m.* to Robert Peake, Esq. of the House of Perthewig; who *d.* in 1814. Mr. ffoulkes *d.* 1 May, 1758, and was *s.* by his eldest son,

JOHN FFOULKES, Esq. of Eriviatt, *b.* in Aug. 1736; high-sheriff of Denbighshire in 1778. He *m.* 12 Jan. 1767, Margaret, dau. of Hugh Clough, of Plas-Clough and Glanywern, co. Denbigh, Esq., and by her (who *d.* in March, 1826) had issue,

JOHN-POWELL, his heir.
Henry, D.D., Principal of Jesus College, Oxford, *m.* in 1825, Mary, dau. of John Horton, of Wavertree, co. Lancaster, Esq.
Hugh, an officer in the royal Cheshire militia, *d. s. p.*
Catherine, deceased. Margaret. Frances.
Diana, deceased. Mary-Anne.
Jemima, *m.* to the Rev. Mascie-Domville Taylor, of Lynn Hall, co. Chester, rector of Moreton Corbet, co. Salop.
Louisa-Matilda, deceased.

Mr. ffoulkes *d.* in Jan. 1814, and was *s.* by his eldest son,

JOHN-POWELL FFOULKES, Esq. of Eriviatt, lieut.-col. of the Royal Denbigh militia; *m.* 8 Jan. 1810, Caroline-Mary, 2nd dau. and co-heir of Robert Jocelyn, Esq., capt. R.N., of Stanstead Bury House, Herts, by Elizabeth his wife, dau. and heir of John Salusbury, of Bryn-y-Barkit, co. Denbigh, Esq. (derived from the SALUSBURYS *of Llewenі*, co. Denbigh), by Margaret his wife, dau. and heir of Eubule Wynne, of Maes-y-Coed, co. Flint. Of this marriage there was issue,

JOHN-JOCELYN.
Henry-Powell, in holy orders, *b.* 2 Jan. 1815.
Edmund-Salusbury, fellow of Jesus College, Oxford, 12 Jan. 1819.
William-Wynne, *b.* 17 July, 1821.
Elizabeth-Sophia, *b.* in 1817, *d.* 1 Jan. 1820.

Col. ffoulkes *d.* 2 Dec. 1826, aged 56, and was *s.* by his eldest son, JOHN-JOCELYN FFOULKES, Esq., now of Eriviatt.

Arms—Quarterly; 1st and 8th, gu., three boars' heads, erased, in pale, arg., for GRONO-LLWYD-AP-PENWYN; 2nd, gu., a Saracen's head, erased at the neck, ppr., wreathed about the temples, arg. and sa., for MARCHUDD AP CYNAN.
Crest—A Boar's head, erased, arg.
Motto—Jure non dono.
Seat—Eriviatt, co. Denbigh.

FINCH OF TULLAMORE PARK.

FINCH, WILLIAM, Esq. of Tullamore Park, co. Tipperary, *m.* Frances, dau. of Philip Coales, Esq. of Bath, and has had issue,

Frances-Elizabeth, *d.* young.

Lineage.—This is a branch of the ancient and eventually ennobled family of Finch, of Netherfield, in Sussex, derived from

JOHN FINCH, next brother of William Finch, of Netherfield, progenitor of the Earls of Winchelsea. John *m.* Elizabeth, dau. and heir of Richard Sewer, of Linstead, in Kent; and dying 19 May, 1442, left a son,

WILLIAM FINCH, of Linstead, ancestor of the FINCHES *of Kent and Herts.* Of the latter was

RALPH FINCH, of Watford (youngest son of John Finch, Esq. of Watford, and grandson of William Finch, Esq.), *m.* 27 Jan. 1606, Emma, dau. of Baldwyn, Esq. of Watford; and dying 1622 (his will is dated 15 March, 1621, and proved 11 May, 1622), was *s.* by his eldest son,

WILLIAM FINCH, Esq. of Watford, bapt. 23 July, 1612; *m.* twice, but had issue only by his 1st wife, Jane, viz.,

Ralph, of Chester, bapt. 2 Oct. 1632, who became by the will of (his father's younger brother) his uncle, Colonel Simon Finch, sole heir to all that gentleman's lands in Northamptonshire and in Ireland. He *m.* Elizabeth, dau. of Col William Danyel, of Chester, and *d.* in 1685, having had issue an only child, MARY, who *m.* John Earle, Esq. of Liverpool, and had (with a dau., Sarah, wife of the Hon and Rev. John Stanley, rector of Winwick, brother of the 11th Earl of Derby) four sons, of whom the eldest surviving, RALPH EARLE, Esq., assumed the surname and arms of WILLIS, (*see* WILLIS *of Halsnead.*)
EDWARD, of whom we treat.
William. Walter.
Simon, mentioned in the will of his uncle, Colonel Simon Finch.

The 2nd son,

EDWARD FINCH, Esq. of Kilcolman, co. Tipperary, *m.* Margaret, dau. of George Purdon, Esq. of Tinnerana, co. Clare, and had issue,

I. SIMON, his heir.
II. William, of Cork, *m.* Anne, dau. of William Massey, Esq. of Glenville, co. Limerick, and had issue,
  1 EDWARD, heir to his uncle, and of whom hereafter.
  2 William, of Maryville, co. Clare, *m.* Mary, dau. of Godfrey Massey, Esq. of Duntrileague, co. Limerick, but *d. s. p.*
  3 Frederick. 4 Hugh.
  5 George, *m.* Amelia, dau. of Anthony Parker, Esq. of Castlelough, co. Tipperary.
  6 John, of The Abbey, co. Limerick, *m.* Phœbe, dau. of John Browne, Esq. of Mount Browne, co. Limerick, and had issue,
    William, *m.* Marcella, dau. of Edward Singleton, Esq. of co. Clare, and relict of Henry Vereker D'Esterre, Esq., and has two sons, William and George.
    John-Browne, *m.* Maria, dau. of Edward Singleton, Esq. of co. Clare.
    Hugh, *m.* a dau. of — Brady, Esq., and is deceased.
    George, *m.* a dau. of — Langford, Esq.
  1 Anne. 2 Catherine.
I. Helena, *m.* to John Hickman, Esq. of Ballyket, co. Clare.
II. Alice.

The eldest son and heir,

SIMON FINCH, Esq. of Kilcolman, *d. s. p.* (his will is dated 10 April, 1744, and proved 15 Dec. 1758), and was *s.* by his nephew,

EDWARD FINCH, Esq. of Kilcolman, who *m.* Anne, dau. of Daniel O'Dwyer, Esq. of Tullagheady, co. Tipperary, and had issue,

WILLIAM, his heir. Daniel.

Edward, formerly capt. in the life-guards, *m.* Miss Wylde Browne, niece of Sir Lancelot Shadwell.
John.
Eliza. Anne.

Mr. Finch *d.* in Aug. 1834, and was *s.* by his eldest son, WILLIAM FINCH, Esq. of Tullamore Park.

Arms—Arg., a chevron, az., between three griffins, passant, gules.
Crest—A griffin, passant, az.
Motto—Bono vince malum.
Seat—Tullamore Park, co. Tipperary.

FINDLAY OF EASTERHILL.

FINDLAY, ROBERT, Esq. of Easterhill, co. Lanark, D.L., *b.* 19 June, 1784; *m.* 23 April, 1810, Mary, eldest dau. of John Buchanan, Esq. of Ardoch, co. Dumbarton, for some time M.P. for that shire, by Elizabeth his wife, dau. of John Parkes, Esq. of Netherton, co. Worcester, and has issue,

I. ROBERT. II. John.
III. James. IV. Charles-Bannatyne.
V. Thomas-Dunlop.
I. Elizabeth, *m.* to the Rev. Joseph Webster, rector of Hindlip, co. Worcester.
II. Dorothea. III. Mary.
IV. Amie, deceased. V. Margaret-Buchanan.
VI. Lillias-Dunlop.

Lineage.—WILLIAM FINDLAY, the only son who had issue of John Findlay, who *d.* in 1697, inherited from his father the lands of Waxford and others, co. Ayr. He *m.* in 1715, Barbara, dau. of Robert Hodzart,* chirurgeon in Kilmarnock, by his wife, a dau. of Brown, of Knockmarnock, by his wife, a dau. of Hay, of Craignethan, and by this lady (who *m.* 2ndly, Alexander Cuninghame, of Brighouse, co. Ayr, and had issue, now represented by Cuninghame of Lainshaw) he had an only son and heir,

THE REV. DR. ROBERT FINDLAY, Professor of Theology in the University of Glasgow, and author of several learned works on divinity; who *m.* in 1745, his cousin, Annabella, dau. of Robert Paterson, Esq. of Braehead, co. Ayr, and by her was father of

ROBERT FINDLAY, Esq. of Easterhill, an eminent merchant in Glasgow, who *m.* in 1781, Dorothea, youngest dau. of Robert Dunlop, Esq. of Househill, co. Renfrew (2nd son of Dunlop of Gamkirk, a branch of Dunlop, of that ilk), and Lilias his wife, only child of Robert Campbell, of Northwoodside, and Catherine his wife, sister of Margaret, Countess of Glencairn, and dau. of John Napier, of Kilmahew, whose wife, Lilias Colquhoun, was grandniece of the great Marquess of Montrose. The issue of Robert Findlay, and Dorothea his wife, consisted of three daus., Janet, *m.* to John Bannatyne, Esq.; Annabella, *m.* to J.-T. Alston, Esq.; and Dorothea, *m.* to John Donaldson, Esq.; and an only son and heir, the present ROBERT FINDLAY, Esq. of Easterhill.

Arms—Arg., on a chev. between three roses, in chief, and an eagle displayed, in base, gu., two daggers, chevron-ways, points downwards, of the first, hilted, or. The "red eagle of Dunlop" has been recently substituted for a third rose previously borne, under the authority of the Lyon Office.
Crest—A boar, passant, arg.
Motto—Fortis in arduis.
Seat—Easterhill, co. Lanark.

FINLAY OF CASTLE TOWARD.

FINLAY, ALEXANDER-STRUTHERS, Esq. of Castle Toward, *b.* 21 July, 1806; *m.* 8 Jan. 1840, Maria, dau. of Colin Campbell, Esq. of Colgraine, Dumbartonshire, and has had issue,

I. Kirkman-Alexander, *b.* 8 March, 1841; *d.* 4 Dec. 1843.
II. COLIN-CAMPBELL, *b.* 12 July, 1843.
III. Alexander-Kirkman, *b.* 4 Sept. 1844.

Lineage.—The family of the Finlays left Inverness-shire about the year 1600, and settled in Dumbartonshire, where they have for a long time possessed the estate of The Moss, near Killearn. Mr. KIRKMAN FINLAY, father of the present proprietor, being of the younger branch, settled in Glasgow, where he made a handsome fortune. He was returned M.P. for that city in 1812, and in 1819 was elected rector of the university. After a long and useful career, during which he was universally esteemed and respected, he *d.* at Castle Toward, in 1842.

Arms—Arg., on a chev. between three roses, gu., two swords, chevron-ways, points downwards, of the first, hilted, or.
Crest—A hand, holding a dagger, all ppr.
Motto—I'll be wary.
Seat—Castle Toward, Greenock.

FIRTH OF HARTFORD LODGE.

FIRTH, THOMAS, Esq. of Hartford Lodge, co. Chester, *b.* 20 April, 1786; *m.* 1st, 2 March, 1813, Eliza, dau. of John Highfield, Esq., and by her had one son,

I. Robert-Thomas, *b.* 16 Dec. 1818, *d.* 4 June, the year following.

He *m.* 2ndly, 9 June, 1821, Anne, dau. of Thomas Hand, Esq. of Middlewich, co. Chester, and by her has issue,

I. FREDERIC-HAND, *b.* 8 Aug. 1824, *m.* 15 April, 1846, Mary, dau. of Joseph Mallaby, Esq. of Birkenhead.
II. Alfred, *b.* 8 Feb. 1826, *m.* 26 June, 1850, Maria, dau. of Thomas Fletcher, Esq. of Wavertree, Liverpool.
III. Clifford, *b.* 25 Dec. 1827, *m.* 18 June, 1850, Mary-Emma, dau. of Richard Heatley, Esq. of Dodcock Grange, near Newport, Salop.
I. Emily-Anne, *m.* to George-Hatt Cook, Esq. of Castleton, Northwich.

Mr. Firth purchased Hartford Lodge and the adjoined estate of Hartford Hall, with others, in the county of Chester.

Lineage.—GEORGE FIRTH, Esq. of Northowram, co. York, *m.* 10 June, 1711, Mary Whiteley, and had two sons, Arthur and JOSEPH. The latter,

JOSEPH FIRTH, Esq., *b.* in 1715, *m.* 1st, 19 June, 1745, Anne Wilkinson, and 2ndly, Elizabeth, relict of Abraham Craven, Esq., and *d.* 30 April, 1793. By the former only (who *d.* 26 July, 1777) he had issue, three sons and three daus., Joseph; John; THOMAS; Sarah; Mary; and Anne. The youngest son,

THOMAS FIRTH, Esq., *m.* 1st, 11 April, 1784, Elizabeth, dau. of John Hemmingway, Esq. of Halifax, co. York, and 2ndly, Elizabeth, relict of John Hoyle, Esq. of Ripponden, in the same shire. He had issue by the former only, viz., three sons,

THOMAS, of Hartford Lodge.
John, *d.* 18 Dec. 1790.
Joseph, *m.* Monimia, dau. of Scipio Dyson, Esq. of Brian Royd, near Halifax, co. York, and has seven sons and six daus., viz., 1 Thomas-Dyson; 2 Scipio-Dyson; 3 John-Hoyle; 4 Edward; 5 Joseph; 6 Hemmingway; 7 Horatio-Nelson; 1 Elizabeth; 2 Sarah-Elizabeth; 3 Monimia; 4 Mary-Thomazia; 5 Elizabeth-Ann; and 6 Caroline.

Arms—Az., a chev., engrailed, erm., between two battle-axes, in chief, and a garb, in base, or.
Crest—On a mount, vert, a griffin, passant, sa., in front of hurst of six trees, ppr.
Motto—Deus incrementum dedit.
Seat—Hartford Lodge, near Northwich, co. Chester.

FISHER OF COSSINGTON AND FIELDS PLACE.

FISHER, ROBERT, Esq. of Cossington, co. Leicester, and Fields Place, co. Hereford, *b.* 9 Feb. 1795; *m.* 4 Aug. 1819, Frances, youngest dau. of Thomas Walker, Esq., one of the Registrars in the Court of Chancery, and has issue,

I. JOHN, in holy orders, *b.* 23 Aug. 1820, *m.* 7 June, 1842, Mary, dau. of John Green, Esq. deceased, late of Northampton, and has issue,
 1 Robert, *b.* 22 June, 1848.
 2 Mountjoy, *b.* 3 Nov. 1852.
 1 Frances-Mary, who *d.* in infancy, in 1845.
II. Thomas-Mountjoy, *b.* 14 Nov. 1824.
III. Robert-William, *b.* 1 March, 1833.
I. Jane-Anne, *m.* 15 July, 1851, Thomas-William Oakley, Esq. of Lydart, near Monmouth.

Lineage.—The antiquity of this Saxon family is unquestionable, and can be established by Domesday Book, which mentions the family of Piscator (the original surname)

* Robert Hodzart's mother was Annabella Boyd, dau. of Boyd of Pitcon, by his wife, a dau. of Blair of Blair.

as located and holding lands, *in capite*, in the time of EDWARD the Confessor and WILLIAM the Conqueror.

Nichols, in his history of Leicestershire, mentions, *inter alios*, Roger Piscator de Cusinton, *temp.* WILLIAM the Conqueror; William and Walter Fisher, of Mountsorrel, gave lands there in 1332 and 1340, to the abbot and convent of Garendon; and William Fisher, Clericus, was the 1st master of Wigston's Hospital, Leicester, where he *d.* in 1539.

The early pedigree of this ancient family having been imperfectly kept, we shall commence our narrative from the middle of the 16th century, when parish registers became general. The earliest register at Prestwold, co. Leicester, records the burial of ROBERT FISHER, Esq. of Burton-on-the-Woulds, 8 Feb. 1560. He was father of

JOHN FISHER, Esq. of Burton-on-the-Woulds, who was buried at Prestwold, 4 June, 1591; his widow, Aloicia Fisher was buried there 5 March, 1591. They left, among others,

ROBERT FISHER, Esq., eldest son and heir, of Burton-on-the-Woulds, who *m.* Ales, dau. of John Smalley, Esq. of Burton-on-the-Woulds, and left amongst others,

JOHN FISHER, Esq. of Burton-on-the-Woulds, their eldest son and heir. He *m.* 17 July, 1623, Anne, 3rd dau. and co-heir of Matthew Hulcock, Esq. of Cossington, where he located about 1635, and dying in 1666, left, amongst others,

MOUNTJOY FISHER, Esq., who became sole heir on the death of his elder brother John, who *d. s. p.* He *m.* 1st, in Aug. 1669, Anne, dau. and co-heir of Dabridgecourt Ward, Esq. of Little Glen, co. Leicester, and by her had three sons and two daus., viz., JOHN, his heir, of whom presently; Mountjoy; George; Anne; and Alice. He *m.* 2ndly, 20 Jan. 1684, Grace Bosse, of Segrave, co. Leicester, and by her left one dau., Grace. He was buried at Cossington 16 Sept. 1727, aged 82, and was *s.* by his eldest son and heir,

JOHN FISHER, Esq., who *m.* 18 Aug. 1719, Dorothy, eldest dau. and co-heir of Robert Smalley, Esq. of Mountsorrel, co. Leicester, and dying 25 March, 1744, aged 70, left an only son and heir,

ROBERT FISHER, Esq of Cossington, Donnington-on-the Heath, and Barrow-upon-Soar, who *m.* 19 April, 1748, Mary, eldest dau. and co-heir of Christopher Tebbutt, Esq. of Toton, co. Notts, and dying 16 Aug. 1786, aged 89, left two daus., Dorothy and Mary, who both *d. unm.*, and an only son,

THE REV. JOHN FISHER, A.M. of Cossington, Donnington, and Barrow, who *m.* 29 Dec. 1791, Charlotte, 3rd dau. (and co-heir on the death of her only brother *s. p.*) of Robert Andrew, Esq. of Harleston Park, co. Northampton, and *d.* 29 July, 1837, aged 82, leaving a son and dau., viz., ROBERT, his heir, the present proprietor of Cossington, Donnington, Barrow, and Field's Place; and Frances-Mary, *m.* 1 Feb. 1838, Joseph Tacey, Esq. of Quorndon, co. Leicester.

Arms—A shield for six quarterings: viz., FISHER, HULCOCK, WARD, SMALLEY, TEBBUTT, and ANDREW.
Crest—A kingfisher, ppr., with a fleur-de-lis, sa., on its breast.
Motto—Respice finem.
Seats—Cossington and Field's Place.

FISHER OF CHETWYND.

FISHER, ROBERT, Esq. of Chetwynd, co. Salop, J.P., *b.* 17 April, 1775; *m.* 22 Nov. 1802, Ann-Frances-Cooper, dau. and heir of Richard James, Esq. of Ludlow, by Ann his wife, dau. of Edward Fleming, Esq. of Sibdon Castle, same county, and co-heiress of her brother, Gilbert Fleming, Esq. of Sibdon Castle, and has had issue,

I. ROBERT, *b.* 10 Oct. 1808.
II. Richard-James, *b.* 21 Feb. 1814.
III. Henry, *b.* 24 May, 1815.
IV. Frederick, in holy orders, *b.* 3 July, 1816.
V. Francis, *b.* 15 Feb. 1819.
VI. Augustus, *b.* 11 March, 1826.
VII. John-Wynn, *b.* 12 Jan. 1832.
I. Ann-Fleming, *m.* 19 Oct. 1829, the Rev. John Nanney, of Maes-y-Neuadd, co. Merioneth, and of Belmont, co. Denbigh, and *d.* 11 March, 1836 (*see* NANNEY *of Maes-y-Neuadd*).
II. Georgiana-Fleming, *m.* 23 June, 1836, to Henry Urquhart, Esq. of Great Baddow, co. Essex.
III. Harriett-Fleming, *m.* 3 Aug. 1841, to John M'Cutcheon, Esq. of Canterbury Villas, Maida Vale.
IV. Rosa-Fleming. V. Catharine-Fleming.

Lineage.—In the early adaptation of the cognomen or surname, that of this family ranges among the most ancient.

OSBERNUS PISCATOR, as the surname was first assumed, held lands *in capite*, at the period of the Doomsday survey, in Sernebroc and Carlentone, Bedfordshire, where his ancestor had held lands in the time of EDWARD the Confessor. In the course of the two succeeding centuries, among the branches of this parent stock, which had dispersed into other counties, one was established in Staffordshire, were Alanus Piscator was located at Alderways, before the reign of King JOHN, and his descendant in the 6th generation, *temp.* EDWARD I., was Nicholas Piscator, *alias* Fisher, of Alderways, from whom were lineally descended Sir John Fisher, a judge of the Court of Common Pleas, who *d.* 2 HENRY VIII., seised, among other manors and estates, of the manor and advowson of Clifton, in Bedfordshire; and Thomas Fisher, who claimed Alderways, 17 HENRY VIII., two of whose descendants were created Baronets: Sir Robert Fisher, of Packington, in Warwickshire, in 1622, and Sir Thomas Fisher, of St. Giles's, in Middlesex, in 1627; but their issue male having ultimately failed, both titles became extinct. By the time of EDWARD III., the family had branched into the more northern counties, where William Fisher, in 1334, is described of Beverley, in Yorkshire (from his branch, it is supposed, was descended the pious prelate, John Fisher, bishop of Rochester and cardinal of Rome, who was the son of Robert Fisher, of Beverley, and who, for maintaining his religious principles, was beheaded on 22 June, 1535), and John Fisher, in 1361, was presented to the vicarage of Urswick, in Furness, in Lancashire, then in the patronage of the abbey and convent of Furness. During the next century, the family was established in the neighbourhood of Cockermouth, in Cumberland, where John Fisher, about the time of EDWARD IV., was seised in fee of Borrowdale Grange, within the lordship of Borrowdale (which formed part of the possessions of Furness Abbey), which estate descended, 10 ELIZABETH, to John Fisher, grandson of Edward, son of John Fisher.

JOSEPH FISHER, son of Joseph Fisher, of Cockermouth, *m.* 13 May, 1733, Elizabeth, dau. of Josiah Shaw, of Kendal, co. Westmoreland (of consanguinity to the celebrated traveller, Thomas Shaw, D.D., Regius professor of Greek, principal of Edmund Hall, Oxford, and vicar of Bramley, in Hampshire, where he *d.* in 1751), and had, besides other issue, a younger son,

ROBERT FISHER, Esq. of the Inner Temple, and of Mitcham, co. Surrey, J.P. and D.L., who *s.* his elder brother, Josiah Fisher, Esq. in 1806. He *m.* 1st, 4 March, 1769, Jane, dau. of Jabez Daniel, an eminent goldsmith of London, by whom (who *d.* 9 March, 1785) he had (besides other children who *d.* young, and a dau., Frances, *m.* to Thomas Higgins, Esq.) three sons,

I. JABEZ, barrister-at-law, *b.* 14 Feb. 1771, *d.* 25 May, 1830, *unm.*
II. ROBERT, now of Chetwynd.
III. Joseph, of Blackheath Park, co. Kent, *b.* 6 July, 1782, and *d.* 16 Jan. 1835. He *m.* 1st, 3 Feb. 1812, Mary-Ann, dau. and heiress of Edward Lamley, Esq. of Grimsbury, co. Oxford, by whom (who *d.* 14 Dec. 1814) he had a son, Edward-Lamley Fisher, Esq. of Grimsbury, *b.* 16 Nov. 1812, who *s.* to the estates of his maternal grandfather, in Oxfordshire, and *d.* 23 Oct. 1842; he *m.* 2 July, 1839, Mary-Ann, dau. of Thomas Gulliver, Esq., and left one child, Edward-Lamley, *b.* 30 Aug. 1841. Mr. Joseph Fisher *m.* 2ndly, 26 July, 1817, Julia-Ann, dau. of Charles Herley, Esq. of Cork, by whom he left issue three sons and three daus., 1 Charles, *b.* 4 May, 1818; 2 Alfred, *b.* 24 May, 1820; 3 Alponso, *b.* 16 Feb. 1823; 1 Anna-Maria; 2 Josephine; and 3 Julia-Ann.

Mr. Fisher *m.* 2ndly, 22 Aug. 1789, Mary, dau. of Charles Staples, Esq. of London, by his wife, Mary, dau. and heiress of Baron Butz, a German noble, by whom (who *d.* 6 July, 1823) he had three sons and one dau.,

I. ROGER STAPLES, of Bentworth Hall, co. Hants, *b.* 5 Sept. 1792, *m.* 20 Feb. 1819, Elizabeth, dau. and heiress of John Horman, Esq. of Finchley, and has had issue five sons and two daus., viz.,
1 Roger, barrister-at-law, *b.* 14 Dec. 1819.
2 Samuel-Sharpe-Horman, barrister-at-law, *b.* 2 Dec. 1823.
3 Robert-Blake, *b.* 31 May, 1826.
4 John, *b.* 19 July, 1831.
5 George-William, *b.* 30 June, 1839.
1 Elizabeth-Mary, *d.* 9 Sept. 1829.
2 Elizabeth.

Mr. Roger-Staples Fisher, in 1832, assumed by royal licence, under the King's sign-manual, the surname of

HORMAN before that of FISHER, and the arms of HORMAN quarterly with those of his patronymic.*

II. Josiah, b. 29 Nov. 1793.

III. Samuel, of Stockwell, co. Surrey, clerk of the Merchant Tailors' Company, b. 2 Dec. 1795, m. 16 Sept. 1829, Elizabeth, dau. of Charles Timbrell, Esq. of Berryfield House, co. Wilts, and has had issue two sons and three daus., 1 Samuel-Timbrell, b. 12 Sept. 1843; 2 Charles-Timbrell, b. 20 July, 1845; 1 Mary-Ann-Timbrell, d. 28 Oct. 1844; 2 Ellen-Timbrell; 3 Rosa-Timbrell.

I. Elizabeth-Staples, m. 10 March, 1836, to George-William Oakes, Esq. of Nottingham-place, capt. in the Bombay army, 2nd son of the late Lieut.-Gen. Sir Henry Oakes, Bart.

Arms—Arg., on a chevron, engrailed with plain cottises, between three demi-lions, guardant, gu., each supporting between the paws a dexter gauntlet, ppr., three bezants.

Crest—Issuant from a crown pallisado, or, a demi-lion, guardant, supporting a gauntlet, as in the arms.

Motto—Virtutem extendere factis.

Seat—Chetwynd, Salop.

FITZGERALD,

The Knight of Glin.

FITZGERALD, JOHN-FRAUNCEIS EYRE, **Knight of Glin**, of Glin Castle, co. Limerick, b. 1813; m. 1835, Clara, only dau. of Gerald Blennerhassett, Esq. of Riddlestown, co. Limerick, and has issue.

Lineage.—JOHN-FITZ-THOMAS FITZGERALD (ancestor, by his 1st wife, the heiress of Decres and Desmond, of the Fitzgeralds, Earls of Desmond), m. 2ndly, Honora, dau. of Hugh O'Connor, of Kerry, and had by her,

I. GILBERT FITZ-JOHN, ancestor of the **White Knight**.

II. SIR JOHN FITZ-JOHN, ancestor of the **Knight of Glin**.

III. MAURICE FITZ-JOHN, ancestor of the **Knight of Kerry**. (*See that name.*)

IV. THOMAS FITZ-JOHN, ancestor of the FITZGERALDS *of the Island of Kerry*.

John Fitz-Thomas Fitzgerald, Lord of Decies and Desmond, by virtue of his royal seigniory as a Count Palatine, created three of his sons, by the 2nd marriage, knights, and their descendants have been so styled in acts of parliament, patents under the great seal, and all legal proceedings up to the present time. He founded the monastery of Tralee, and was buried there in 1260. His 2nd son, by Honora O'Connor his 2nd wife,

SIR JOHN FITZ-JOHN, Knt., to whom his father gave the castles of Glyncorbury and Beagh, co. Limerick, was the 1st Knight of Glyn, and left issue,

JOHN FITZ-JOHN, his successor.

GERALD FITZ-JOHN, ancestor of the family of Clenlish and Castle Ishen, co. Cork, Barts.

Sir John Fitz-John was s. by his eldest son,

SIR JOHN FITZ-JOHN, del Glyn, Knt., who was s. by his son,

SIR THOMAS FITZ-JOHN, del Glyn, Knt., "custos pacis in partibus O'Connyll," 20 EDWARD III. 1346, who gave hostages for his fealty in 1345. He was s. by his son,

SIR JOHN FITZ-THOMAS, del Glyn, Knt., living in 1331, hostage for his father's fealty in 1345, who left issue,

I. THOMAS FITZ-JOHN, his successor.

II. Philip Fitz-John, who left a son,

THOMAS, successor to his uncle.

Sir John Fitz-Thomas was s. by his eldest son,

SIR THOMAS FITZ-JOHN, del Glyn, Knt., 1351, d. s. p. and was s. by his nephew,

SIR THOMAS FITZ-PHILIP FITZ-JOHN, who was s. by his son,

EDMUND FITZ-THOMAS FITZ-GERALD, Knight of Glin, who m. Mary, dau. of Thomas, Lord Kerry, and dying in 1503, was s. by his son,

THOMAS FITZ-GERALD, Knight of Glin, styled sometimes Knight of the Valley, seised of the manors of Glin and Castleton Beagh, attainted 18 HENRY VIII., and again 11 ELIZABETH, was s. by his son,

THOMAS FITZ-GERALD, who was attainted with his father, and executed 11 Queen ELIZABETH, leaving a dau., Ellen, wife of Sir Edmond Fitz-Harris, Knt., and a son, his successor,

EDMOND FITZ-GERALD, Knight of Glin, pardoned and restored to his estates, 18 June, 30 ELIZ. He m. Honora, dau. of Owen M'Carthy Reagh, and was s. by his son,

THOMAS FITZ-GERALD, Knight of Glyn, who had livery of his lands, 18 Dec. 1628. He surrendered those estates, and had them re-granted, 22 June, 1635. He m. Joan, dau. of James, Lord Dunboyne, widow of Edmond Fitz-Gibbon, son of Edmond Fitz-Gibbon, the White Knight, and was s. by his son,

GERALD FITZ-GERALD, Knight of Glyn, who made a deed of settlement of his estates, 5 Dec. 1672. He m. Joan, dau. of — O'Brien, and dying before 1700, left issue,

THOMAS, his successor. John.

Honora, wife of Henry Fitz-Gerald, Esq. of Bremore, co. Kerry.

Gerald Fitz-Gerald was s. by his eldest son,

THOMAS FITZ-GERALD, Knight of Glyn, seised of an estate in tail under the deed of settlement of 1672, m. Mary, dau. of Edmond Fitz-Gerald, and had issue,

EDMOND, his successor.

RICHARD, who s. his brother.

THOMAS, who s. his brother Richard.

Catharine, wife of Robert Fitz-Gerald, of Dublin.

Thomas Fitz-Gerald was s. by his eldest son,

EDMOND FITZ-GERALD, Knight of Glin, who d. s. p., administration 1735, and was s. by his brother,

RICHARD FITZ-GERALD, Knight of Glin, who was s. by his brother,

THOMAS FITZ-GERALD, Knight of Glin, who m. Mary, dau. of John Bateman, Esq. of Oak Park, co. Kerry, and had issue,

JOHN, his heir.

Elizabeth, m. to Thomas Plummer, Esq. of Mount Plummer, co. Cork.

Frances, m. to the Rev. Thomas Lloyd, of Castle Lloyd, co. Tipperary.

Ellen, m. to Gustavus-Matthias Hippisley, Esq.

Catharine, m. to Maurice O'Connor, Esq. co. Kerry.

Jane, m. to Joseph Sargeant, Esq. co. Limerick.

Thomas Fitz-Gerald, whose will is dated 17 Sept. 1781, and was proved 18 Feb. 1801, was s. by his eldest son,

JOHN FITZ-GERALD, Knight of Glin, who m. Margaretta-Maria, dau. of John Frauncels Gwynn, Esq. of Ford Abbey, co. Devon, and was s. by his only son,

JOHN-FRAUNCEIS FITZ-GERALD, Knight of Glin, M.A., J.P. and D.L., high-sheriff, co. Limerick, 1830, b. 28 June, 1791, who m. 28 July, 1812, Bridget, 5th dau. of the Rev. Joseph Eyre, of Westerham, in Kent, and had issue,

JOHN-FRAUNCEIS-EYRE, present Knight of Glyn.

Edmond-Urmston-McLeod.

Geraldine-Anne. Margaretta-Sophia.

Arms—Erm., a saltier, gu.

Crest—A boar, passant, gu., bristled and armed, or.

Motto—Shanit a Boo.

Seat—Glin Castle, co. Limerick.

FITZGERALD,

The Knight of Kerry.

FITZGERALD, PETER, **Knight of Kerry**, of Valentia, co. Kerry, b. in 1808; m. 1838, Julia, dau. of P.-B. Hussey, Esq. of Farrinikilla House, co. Kerry, and has issue,

I. MAURICE, b. 5 Feb. 1844.

II. Robert-John, b. 12 Jan. 1852.

III. Peter-David, b. 29 Dec. 1855.

I. Mary-Emily-Frances. II. Emily.

III. Frances-Caroline. IV. Catherine.

V. Elizabeth-Ann. VI. Julia-Emma-Isabella.

Lineage.—MAURICE FITZ-JOHN, 3rd son of JOHN-FITZ-THOMAS FITZGERALD, Lord of Decies and Desmond, by Honora his 2nd wife, dau. of Hugh O'Connor, of Kerry (*see* FITZGERALD, *Knight of Glin*), m. a dau. of O'Kenedy, and had two sons, John (Sir), of Rathanan and Inismore, whose grandson, Sir Gilbert, d. s. p. 1345; and MAURICE, father of Sir John Fitzmaurice, Knt. (heir to Sir Gilbert), whose son and heir,

SIR RICHARD FITZGERALD, generally called the 1st *Knight of Kerry*, m. and had two sons, MAURICE, his heir; and James, from whom the FITZGERALDS *of Cloyne*. The elder son,

SIR MAURICE FITZGERALD, Knight of Kerry, Lord of Rathanan and Inismore, was father of

JOHN FITZGERALD, Knight of Kerry, called the Blind Bishop of Ardfert, living 1405, whose son,

SIR MAURICE FITZGERALD, Knight of Kerry, m. and had three sons; the eldest of whom, SIR MAURICE FITZGERALD, Knight of Kerry, is styled in a record, "Domino Mauritio

* Quarterly: 1st and 4th, FISHER, as above; 2nd and 3rd, Bendy of eight, or and az., per bend, sinister, counter-changed, on a chief, gu., a lion passant, or.

Crests—FISHER, as above. HORMAN: in front of a cross-crosslet, gu., two Roman fasces, with the battle-axe in saltier, ppr.

Militi de Kerry," 12 HENRY VII; the 2nd, JOHN, was father of WILLIAM, heir to his uncle; and Robert, of Allon, whose eventual representative Joan Fitzgerald, *m.* Sir Gerald Aylmer, Bart.

SIR WILLIAM FITZGERALD, son of John, *s.* his uncle, Sir Maurice. He was father of

JOHN FITZGERALD, of Rathanan and Inismore, Knight of Kerry, who settled his estates on his heirs male, by deed, dated 8 Jan. 1578. By Shela his wife, dau. of O'Sullivan More, he left a son and successor,

WILLIAM FITZGERALD, of Rathanan, Knight of Kerry, who *m.* Mary, dau. of Charles O'Conor, of Derrymullen, and *d.* 6 Nov. 1640, leaving a son and heir,

JOHN FITZGERALD, of Rathanan, Knight of Kerry, who *m.* Catherine, dau. of Thomas Fitzmaurice, 18th Lord Kerry and Lixnau, and was father of THOMAS, who *d. v. p.*, 1667, leaving by Jane his wife, a son,

JOHN FITZGERALD, of Inismore and Rathanan, Knight of Kerry, restored to his estate by patent, dated 14 May, 1677. He *m.* Honora, dau. of Daniel O'Brien, Viscount Clare, by Catherine his wife, sister and co-heir of James Fitzgerald, last Earl of Desmond, and had a son and successor,

MAURICE FITZGERALD, Knight of Kerry, who *m.* 30 June, 1703, Elizabeth, 2nd dau. of David Crosbie, Esq. of Ardfert, by Jane his wife, younger dau. and co-heir of William Hamilton, Esq., and sister of Maurice Crosby, 1st Lord Brandon, and by her left at his decease, 15 Nov. 1762, two sons, JOHN, his heir; and ROBERT, heir to his nephew; and eight daus., viz., Jane, *m.* to George Herbert, Esq. of Currens; Honoria, *m.* to Richard Meredyth, Esq. of Tierna Bridget, *m.* 1st, to Thomas Sandes, and 2ndly, to Creagh; Margaret, *m.* to John Hewson, of Ennismore; Elizabeth, *d. unm.*; Anne, *m.* to John Stack, of Ballyconry; Mary, *m.* 1st to Robert Collis, Esq., and 2ndly to Thomas Rice, Esq. of Mount Trenchard; Lucy, *m.* to John Day, of Lohercannon; Marian, *m.* to William Meredyth, of Anna; and Barbara, married to Bastable Herbert, Esq. The elder son and heir,

JOHN FITZGERALD, Knight of Kerry, *m.* 12 April, 1732, Margaret dau. of the Rt. Hon. Joseph Deane, Lord Chief Baron of the Exchequer, and left a dau., Elizabeth (heiress to her brother), *m.* to Richard Townsend, Esq. of Castle Townsend, co. Cork; and a son,

MAURICE FITZGERALD, Knight of Kerry, who *m.* 10 June, 1764, Lady Anne Fitzmaurice, only dau. of William, 2nd Earl of Kerry, but *d. s. p.*, 1780, and was *s.* by his uncle,

ROBERT FITZGERALD, Esq., Judge of the Admiralty Court, and M.P. for Dingle, who *m.* thrice: by his first wife, Miss Leslie, an heiress, and by his 2nd, Mrs. Crosbie, dau. of the Knight of Glin, he had no issue, but by the 3rd, Catherine, dau. of Launcelot Sandes, Esq. of Kilcaven, he left at his decease in 1781 a son* and heir,

THE RT. HON. MAURICE FITZGERALD, Knight of Kerry, J.P. and D.L. a privy councillor, and M.P. for thirty-five years for co. Kerry, *b.* 29 Dec. 1774, *m.* 1st, 5 Nov. 1801, Maria, dau. of the Right Hon. David La Touche, by whom he had issue,

Robert, *d.* in infancy. Maurice, *d. unm.* 1836.
David, *b.* 1804, *d. unm.* 1848.
Robert, *b.* 1805, *m.* Ellen, eldest dau. of P.-B. Hussey, Esq. of Farrinikilla House, co. Kerry, and *d.* in 1835, leaving a dau. Maria.
Brinsley, *d.* in 1832, *unm.*
PETER, present Knight of Kerry.
Stephen, *b.* 1816.
Elizabeth, *m.* to Crofton-Thomas Vandeleur, Esq.
Maria. Gertrude, *d.* in 1828.
Catharine, *m.* to Edward-Symes Bayly, Esq. of Ballyarthur co. Wicklow.

The Knight of Kerry *m.* 2ndly, Cecilia-M. relict of Knight, Esq.

Arms—Erm., a saltier, gu.
Crest—An armed knight on horseback, all ppr.
Supporters—Dexter, a boar; sinister, a dragon.
Motto—Mullabar a Boo.
Seat—Glanleam, Valeucia.

FITZGERALD OF HOLBROOK.

FITZGERALD, WILLIAM-ROBERT-SEYMOUR-VESEY, Esq. of Holbrook, Sussex, and of Ballylinch, co. Kilkenny. M.P. for Horsham, barrister-at-law, M.A. Oriel College, Oxford, and J.P. and D.L., *b.* 1817; *m.* 1840, Maria-Tryphena, dau. of E. Seymour, Esq., M.D.

Seats—Holbrook, Horsham, and Ballylinch, Kilkenny.

* The younger son, Robert, was killed at the siege of Seringapatam, leading the grenadiers of the 33rd regt.

FIT

FITZGERALD OF TURLOUGH.

FITZGERALD, CHARLES-LIONEL, Esq. of Turlough Park, co. Mayo.

Lineage.—JOHN FITZGERALD, Esq. of Gurteens, co. Waterford, where his ancestors and he enjoyed great possessions, as well as in the co. Kilkenny, from the landing of Strongbow, in 1111, to the transplantation of the family to Mohena or Turlough, co. Mayo, forfeited his hereditary estates for his devotion to the royal cause. He *m.* the widow of General Harrison (Cromwell's General), by whom he acquired the estate of Turlough, co. Mayo, and had a son and successor,

THOMAS FITZGERALD, Esq. of Turlough, who *m.* 1st, Elizabeth Ferron (mother of Ralph Jenison, Esq., master of the buckhounds to GEORGE II.), and 2ndly, Henrietta, dau. of J. Browne, Esq. of the Neal, ancestor of the noble house of Kilmaine, by the latter of whom he had issue, six sons and four daus.; of the latter, Mary *m.* the Marquis d'Arezzo, Governor of Naples, and Bridget *m.* Thomas Leslie, of Grange, Esq. Thomas Fitzgerald, *d.* 15 July, 1747, in the 86th year of his age, and was *s.* by his eldest son,

JOHN FITZGERALD, Esq. of Turlough, who *d. unm.*, and was *s.* by his brother,

GEORGE FITZGERALD, Esq. of Turlough, a captain in the Austrian service, who *m.* Lady Mary Hervey, sister of Frederick, 4th Earl of Bristol, bishop of Derry, and by her, who was *b.* in 1726, and *d.* in 1758, had two sons,

GEORGE-ROBERT, who *m.* Miss Conolly, sister of the late Right Hon. Thomas Conolly, of Castletoun, and *d.* leaving one dau., since deceased.
CHARLES-LIONEL.

The 2nd son,

CHARLES-LIONEL-FITZGERALD, Esq. of Turlough Park, lieut.-col. of the North Mayo militia, *m.* in 1777, Dorothea, eldest dau. of Sir Thomas Butler, Bart. of Balintemple, co. Carlow, and by her, who *d.* 11 April, 1829, had issue,

I. THOMAS-GEORGE, now of Turlough.
II. Edward-Thomas, *b.* 22 Dec. 1784, lieut.-col. in the army, served as assistant quarter-master-general with the Guards at Waterloo; *m.* 20 Nov. 1811, Emma, youngest dau. of Edmond Green, Esq. of Medham, in the Isle of Wight, and, dying 1845, left surviving issue,
1 Lionel-Charles-Henry-William, *b.* 9 Sept. 1812, an officer in the army.
2 Edward-Thomas, *b.* 19 Sept. 1817.
3 Henry-Augustus-Robert, *b.* 8 Dec. 1824.
4 Desmond-Gerald, *b.* 28 Dec. 1834.
1 Louisa. 2 Emma-Mary.
3 Catherine-Dorothea. 4 Dorothea-Frances.
5 Frances-Anne.
III. Charles-Lionel, lieut.-col. in the army, *m.* Marianne, dau. of Lieut.-Col. Breedon, R.M., and left surviving issue,
1 Charles-Lionel, lieut.-col. Royal Artillery.
2 William-Hervey. 3 Henry.
4 Alfred-John. 5 Ormond.
6 Augustus-Harry.
I. Dorothea-Mary, *m.* to Patrick Kirwan, Esq. of Dalgin Park, co. Mayo, and has issue.

Col. Fitzgerald, *d.* 29 April, 1805, and was *s.* by his son,

THOMAS-GEORGE FITZGERALD, Esq. of Turlough Park, co. Mayo, and of Maperton House, Somersetshire, lieut.-col. in the army and D.L., *b.* 5 June, 1778; *m.* 1st, 6 Sept. 1806, Delia, youngest dau. of Joshua Field, Esq. of Heaton, in Yorkshire, and had by her a son,

CHARLES-LIONEL-WILLIAM, who *m.* Dorothea, 2nd dau. of Patrick Kirwan, Esq. of Dalgin Park, co. Mayo, and *d.* 9 Nov. 1834, leaving an only son, the present CHARLES-LIONEL FITZGERALD, Esq.

Colonel Fitzgerald *m.* 2ndly, 29 April, 1819, Elizabeth, only dau. of James Crowther, M.D., of Boldshay Hall, Yorkshire, and by her had,

HENRY-THOMAS-GEORGE, D.L. for co. Somerset, *m.* 23 May, 1839, Elizabeth-Harriott, eldest dau. of the Rev. Samuel-W. Yates, vicar of St. Mary's, Reading, and has issue.
Elizabeth-Geraldine. Mary-Dorothea.

Arms—Erm., a saltier, gu.
Crest—A boar, passant.
Motto—Honor probataque virtus.
Seat—Turlough Park, in Mayo.

FITZGERALD OF ADELPHI.

FITZGERALD, WILLIAM, Esq. of Adelphi, co. Clare, J.P. and high-sheriff in 1842; *m.* 8 May, 1817, Juliana-Cecilia, dau. of Maurice Fitzgerald, Esq., then of Lilford, co. Limerick, and by her (who *d.* 23 June, 1823), had two daus.,

I. Mary, *m.* 21 Feb. 1837, to Sir Lucius O'Brien, Bart. of Dromoland, (now LORD INCHIQUIN) and *d.* 26 May, 1852.

II. Anne, *m.* 5 Dec. 1839, to Richard-Basset Wilson, Esq. of Cliffe Hall, co. York.

Lineage.—GERALD FITZGERALD, Esq. of Kilcarragh, co. Clare, son and heir of Theobald Fitzgerald, Esq., an officer in the Irish brigade, *m.* 1st, Anne Perreau, of Cork, connected with the families of Daunt and Busted, and by her, who *d.* in 1734, had,

Theobald, who *m.* Miss Comyn, and *d.* leaving an only dau., who *m.* L. O'Brien, Esq.
FRANCIS, heir to his father.
Maurice, *d. s. p.*
Garrett, *m.* Juliana, dau. of Patrick Kerin, Esq., and *d.* leaving issue, 1 Gerald. 2 Maurice, of Lifford, many years Physician to the British Government and to the Nabob at Madras, *m.* 1st, Margaretta, widow of Lieut. Benjamin Frend, E. I. Co.'s service, and by her had a son, Maurice-Gerald, lieut. E. I. Co.'s Madras army, *b.* 15 Jan. 1801, *d.* at Camptee, in 1827, and a dau., Juliana-Cecilia, *m.* to William Fitzgerald, Esq. of Adelphi. Dr. Fitzgerald *m.* 2ndly, Mary, youngest dau. of the late Edward-William Burton, Esq. of Clifden, co. Clare, and by her who *d.* 30 May, 1821, had four sons, Edward-William, *b.* 16 Nov. 1804; Francis-Alexander, *b.* 5 June, 1807; Garrett, *b.* 16 June, 1809, *d.* in Oct. 1836; William, *b.* 3 Dec. 1814; and two daus., Jane, *d.* in 1829, and Anne, *d.* in 1830. 3 Terence. 4 William. 1 Eleanor. 2 Mary. 3 Margarett.

Mr. Fitzgerald *m.* 2ndly, Anne Grady, but had no further issue. He *d.* in 1762, and was *s.* by his 2nd son,

FRANCES FITZGERALD, Esq. of Kilcarragh, who *m.* Elizabeth, dau. of David Comyn, Esq. of Kilcorney, co. Clare, and had (with a dau. Elizabeth, *m.* to William Eames, Esq.) three sons, I. WILLIAM, his heir; II. George, *m.* Miss Foster, of co. Galway, and *d.* leaving a son, George-Foster, and two daus., Eliza and Barbara; and III. John, *d. unm.* The eldest son,

WILLIAM FITZGERALD, of Kilcarragh, J.P., *m.* in 1783, Anne, dau. of John Powell, Esq. of Clevcrville, co. Limerick, and dying in 1789, left issue,

FRANCIS-JOHN, of Adelphi, *b.* 27 Dec. 1788, *d. s. p.* 22 Jan. 1854.
WILLIAM, now of Adelphi.

Arms—Erm., a saltier, gu.
Crest—On a cap of maintenance, a boar, passant.
Motto—Shanet a Boo.
Seat—Adelphi, Currofin, co. Clare.

FITZGERALD OF CORKBEGG.

PENROSE-FITZGERALD, ROBERT-UNIACKE, Esq., J.P., of Corkbegg, Lisquinlan, co. Cork, and Water Castle, Queen's County, *b.* 1 July, 1800; *m.* 1830, Frances-Mary, dau. of the Rev. Dr. Austen, by the Hon. Matilda-S. Cockayne his wife, and has issue,

I. ROBERT-UNIACKE. II. Charles-Cooper.
III. James-Henry-B.
I. Matilda-S.-G. II. Geraldine-Louisa.

Lineage.—The Penroses descend from the old family of Penrose, of Cornwall. One of the Cornish house purchased a large property in Waterford, which the Irish family still hold. The Fitzgeralds of Corkbegg and Lisquinlan, are well known in the history of the county of Cork. Mr. Fitzgerald's grandfather, COOPER PENROSE, Esq., *m.* Elizabeth Dennis, and had issue,

JAMES PENROSE, *b.* 8 Oct. 1766, who *m.* 12 July, 1794, Louisa-Pettitot, dau. of Robert U. Fitzgerald, Esq. of Corkbegg and Lisquinlan, by Louisa Bullen his wife, and by her, who *d.* 28 Oct. 1854, left issue,

COOPER PENROSE.
ROBERT, who inherited the Corkbegg estates through his uncle Rice Fitzgerald, who *d.* childless, and assumed the name of Fitzgerald.
John, *m.* Harriet, dau. of Rev. J. Hardy.
William, *m.* Helena Townsend.
Louisa.
Frances, *m.* Rev. G. Gumbleton.
Geraldine, *m.* Rev. J. Gordon.
Anne, *m.* Thomas B. L. Stewart, Esq.
Gertrude, *m.* to J. T. Ingham, Esq.
Harriet.
Elizabeth, *m.* R. Atkin, Esq.

Mr. Penrose *d.* 19 April, 1845.

Arms—Erm., a saltier, gu.
Crest—A knight, on horseback.
Motto—Fortis et fidelis.
Seats—Corkbegg, Lisquinlan, co. Cork, and Water Castle, Queen's co.

FITZ-HERBERT OF NORBURY AND SWINNERTON.

FITZ-HERBERT, THOMAS, Esq. of Norbury, co. Derby, and of Swinnerton, in Staffordshire, high-sheriff in 1831, *b.* 21 Jan. 1789; *s.* his father 22 Nov. 1799; *m.* 15 July, 1809, Mary-Anne-Sophia, dau. of John-Palmer Chichester, Esq. of Arlington, co. Devon, and has issue,

CHARLES, *b.* 21 June, 1810.

Mr. Fitz-Herbert is the 26th Lord of the Manor of Norbury, and the 10th Lord of Swinnerton.

Lineage.—The family of FITZ-HERBERT, whose name appears in the Roll of Battle Abbey, descends from a Norman knight, called HERBERT, which, in conformity to a prevalent custom amongst the Normans of describing themselves as the son of some eminent ancestor, became the patronymic of the family. In Latin, *Filius Herberti*; in Norman, *Fils.* or *Fitz-Herbert*. In the year 1125, (25 HENRY I.) William, Prior of Tutbury, by his charter, attested by Robert de Ferrers, Earl of Derby, the superior lord of Tutbury, and his two sons, Robert and William de Ferrers, Hawise his wife, the Bishop of Lichfield, Abbot of Burton, and divers others distinguished persons, granted to

WILLIAM FITZ-HERBERT the manor of Norbury, co. Derby. (The original charter, with the manor, are in the possession of the present Mr. Fitz-Herbert.) He was *s.* by his son,

WILLIAM FITZ-HERBERT, lord of Norbury, living in 1166, direct ancestor of

SIR ANTHONY FITZ-HERBERT, Knt., judge of the Common Pleas, an eminent lawyer, author of the celebrated work, "De Natura Brevium," to which Blackstone refers with great commendation. He *m.* Matilda, dau. and co-heir of Sir Richard Cotton, of Hamstall Ridware, in the county of Stafford, and had with three daus., Elizabeth, *m.* to William Bassett, Esq. of Langley; Dorothy, *m.* 1st, to Sir Ralph Longford, Knt., and 2ndly, to Sir John Port, Knt. of Etwall; and Catherine, *m.* to John Sacheverel, of Morley, three sons, I. THOMAS (SIR), his heir. II. JOHN, who *m.* Catherine, dau. of Edward Restwold, of the Vache, and *d.* in 1590, leaving, with four daus., Jane, wife of Thomas Eyre, Esq. of Dunston; Matilda, wife of Thomas Barlow, of Barlow; Elizabeth; and Mary, wife of Thomas Draycot, of Sydnall, five sons, THOMAS, ANTHONY, Nicholas, secretary to cardinal Allen, Francis, and George. III. WILLIAM, *m.* Elizabeth, younger of the two daus. and co-heirs of Humphrey Swinnerton, Esq. of Swinnerton, co. Stafford, and thus acquired that manor; by this lady (who *m.* 2ndly, John Gatacre, Esq. of Gatacre, co. Salop, and *d.* in 1616) he had issue, THOMAS FITZ-HERBERT, 2nd lord of Swinnerton, who *m.* Dorothy, only dau. and heir of Edward East, Esq. of Bledlowe, in Buckinghamshire, and *d.* in 1640, having had a dau., Elizabeth, wife of Joseph Mayne, of Crestlow, Bucks, and a son, EDWARD, who *m.* Bridget, dau. of Sir John Caryll, Knt. of Agmering, in the co. of Sussex, and dying before his father (25 Nov. 1612), left a son, WILLIAM, of Swinnerton, who succeeded as 19th lord of Norbury. Sir Anthony Fitz-Herbert *d.* 27 May, 1538, and was *s.* by his eldest son,

SIR THOMAS FITZ-HERBERT, of Norbury, who *m.* in 1535, Anne, dau. and heir of Sir Arthur Eyre, of Padley, in the co. Derby, but had no issue. He was sheriff of Staffordshire, in 1547 and 1554. He *d. s. p.*, whereupon the estates of Norbury passed to his nephew,

THOMAS FITZ-HERBERT, of Norbury, who *m.* Elizabeth, dau. of John Westby, Esq. of Mowbreck, in the co. of Lancaster, but dying without issue, was *s.* by his brother,

ANTHONY FITZ-HERBERT, of Norbury, who *m.* Martha, dau. of Thomas Austen, Esq. of Oxley, in the co. of Stafford, and dying in 1613, left, with five daus., Helen; Mary, *m.* to William Lewyn, of Norfolk; Catherine, *m.* to John, 5th son of Sir Thomas Milward, Knt.; Anne, *m.* to Richard Congreve, Esq. of Stretton; and Elizabeth, *m.* to Sir John Fitz-Herbert, Knt. of Tissington, one son,

SIR JOHN FITZ-HERBERT, Knt. of Norbury, who *m.* in 1631, Dorothy, dau. of John Harpur, Esq. of Bredsall, but had no issue. Sir John was appointed colonel of dragoons, in the king's service, 16 Dec. 1642. He *d.* at Lichfield, 13 Jan. 1649, and was *s.* in the estates of Norbury, by his cousin (refer to William, 3rd son of Sir Anthony Fitz-Herbert, the judge),

WILLIAM FITZ-HERBERT, Esq., 3rd lord of Swinnerton. This gentlemen *m.* Anne, dau. of Sir Basil Brook, Knt. of Madeley, in Staffordshire, and had (with four daus., Mary,

m. to John Gower, Esq. of Colmers; Frances, m. to John Giffard, Esq. of Chillington; Bridgett, m. to Bazill Bartlett, Esq. of Castle Morton, in Worcestershire; and Anne) several sons, of whom the 2nd, Thomas, was of Shercock, in Ireland. Mr. Fitz-Herbert, who was named, in 1660, amongst the intended Knights of the Royal Oak, was *s.* by his eldest son,

Bazil Fitz-Herbert, Esq. of Norbury and Swinnerton, who m. Jane, dau. and heir of John Cotton, Esq. of Gedding Abbots, in the co. of Huntingdon, and of Boscobel and White Ladies, in Shropshire, by whom he had (with a dau., Winifred-Dorothy, *m.* in 1691, to Charles Eyston, Esq. of East Hendred, in Berkshire) a son,

William Fitz-Herbert, Esq. of Norbury and Swinnerton, who m. in 1679, Elizabeth, only dau. and heir of Robert Owen, Esq. of Weppra, in the co. of Flint, and granddau. of Dr. John Owen, Bishop of St. Asaph, and was *s.* by his eldest son,

Thomas Fitz-Herbert, Esq. of Norbury and Swinnerton, who m. in 1713, Constantia, younger dau. and co-heir of Sir George Southcote, Bart. of Blythborough, in the co. of Lincoln, and dying in 1765, was *s.* by his son,

Thomas Fitz-Herbert, Esq. of Norbury and Swinnerton, who m. 1st, in 1737, Elizabeth, dau. and co-heir of Anthony Meaborne, Esq. of Pontop, in the co. of Durham, but had no issue. He *m.* 2ndly, in 1743, Mary-Theresa, dau. of Sir Robert Throcmorton, Bart., and had (with eight daus., Mary, a nun; Constantia, *m.* 1st, to Joseph Brockholes, Esq. of Claughton, and 2ndly, to Philip Saltmarsh, Esq.; Barbara, *m.* 1st, to George Tasburgh, Esq. of Bodney, and 2ndly, to Geo. Crathorne, Esq. of Crathorne; Catherine, who *d. unm.*; Charlotte, *m.* to Sir Thomas Gage, Bart.; Anne, *d. unm.*; Teresa, *m.* to Thomas Hornyold, Esq. of Blackmore Park; and Lucy, *m.* to James Dormer, Esq.) five sons, Thomas, his successor; Basil, who *s.* his brother; William, *b.* 26 Oct. 1758, assumed, by sign-manual, 3 June, 1788, the surname and arms of Brockholes (*see* Brockholes *of Claughton Hall*); Edward, and Robert. Mr. Fitz-Herbert *d.* 3 Oct 1778, and was *s.* by his eldest son,

Thomas Fitz-Herbert, Esq. of Norbury, and of Swinnerton, *b.* 30 Aug. 1746, *m.* in 1778, Mary-Anne,* youngest dau. of Walter Smythe, Esq. of Bambridge, in the co. of Hants, niece of Sir Edward Smythe, of Acton-Burnell, Bart., and widow of Edward Weld, Esq. of Lulworth Castle, but *d.* without issue, at Nice, 7 May, 1781. He was *s.* by his brother,

Basil Fitz-Herbert, Esq. of Norbury and Swinnerton, who *m.* Elizabeth, youngest dau. and co-heir of James Windsor-Heneage, Esq. of Cadeby, in the co. of Lincoln, and of Gatcombe, in the Isle of Wight, by whom he had (with one dau., Elizabeth, who *d. unm.* in 1812) five sons, viz.,

Thomas, present proprietor.
Bazil, *b.* 2 July, 1790, *d. unm.*
John, *b.* 2 Sept. 1792.
George, *b.* 30 July, 1793.
Francis, *b.* 21 Nov. 1796; *m.* 28 July, 1828, Maria-Teresa, dau. of John-Vincent Gandolfi, Esq. of East Sheen, in Surrey, by Teresa, dau. of Thomas Hornyold, Esq. of Blackmore Park, and his wife Teresa Fitz-Herbert.

Mr. Fitz-Herbert *d.* 20 May, 1797, and was *s.* by his eldest son, the present Thomas Fitz-Herbert, Esq. of Norbury.

Arms—Arg., a chief, vaire, or and gu., over all a bend, sa.
Crest—A dexter arm, armed, and gauntlet, ppr.
Motto—Ung je serviray.
Seat—Swinnerton, co. Stafford.

FITZHUGH OF PLAS POWER.

Fitzhugh, Thomas, Esq. of Plas Power, co. Denbigh, J.P. and D.L., *b.* 14 Jan. 1770; *m.* 11 Nov. 1814, Philadelphia-Elizabeth, dau. of the late Peter Godfrey, Esq. of Old Hall, co. Suffolk, by Arabella his wife, dau. of the late Admiral Sir Joshua Rowley, Bart. of Tendring Hall, and has issue,

I. Thomas-Lloyd, *b.* 23 Aug. 1819, late of the Grenadier-guards.
II. Godfrey-William, *b.* 5 Nov. 1820.
I. Arabella-Elizabeth. II. Mary-Philadelphia.
III. Emily.

Mr. Fitzhugh has filled the office of high-sheriff for that county, as well as for Merionethshire. He is only son of the late Thomas Fitzhugh, Esq., and Mary his wife, dau. of William Lloyd, Esq. of Plas Power, co. Denbigh. He has four sisters, viz., Mary, *m.* to the late John Beauclerk, Esq.; Harriet, *m.* to James Bradshaw, Esq.; Charlotte, *m.* to Richard-Henry Cox, Esq.; and Emily, *m.* to J. Robert Udny, Esq., late lieut.-col. Grenadier-guards. The family of Fitzhugh is of very great antiquity. The senior representative is the present Rev. William-Anthony Fitzhugh, of Street, near Lewes, Sussex.

Arms—Erm., on a chief, gu., three martlets, or.
Crest—A martlet, ppr.
Motto—In moderation placing all my glory.
Seat—Plas Power, near Wrexham, co. Denbigh, N. W.

FITZMAURICE OF DUAGH.

Fitzmaurice, Oliver, of Duagh House, co. Kerry, J.P., *b.* 8 Feb. 1818; *m.* 24 April, 1855, Alice Gabbet.

Lineage.—This ancient family traces its origin to a common ancestor in a direct line with the houses of Fitzgerald, Windsor, Carew, M'Kenzie, &c., namely, Walter Fitz-Otho, Castellan of Windsor in the eleventh century.

Thomas, son of Maurice Fitz-Reymond, and a lineal descendant of Walter Fitz-Otho, the Castellan, assumed the surname of Fitzmaurice, and became Lord of Kerry of Lixnaw. His descendant.

John Fitzmaurice, 5th Lord of Kerry, *d.* at Lixnaw, in 1348. He *m.* 1st, Honora, dau. of O'Brien, of Thomond, and had by her a dau., Margaret, *m.* to Dermot M'Carthy, Lord of Carbery, and a son,

Maurice, 6th lord of Kerry, ancestor of the noble house of Kerry, now represented by the Marquess of Lansdowne.

The 5th Lord of Kerry, *m.* 2ndly, Elinor, dau. of Garret FitzPierce, Esq. of Ballymac-Equim, and had by her,

Garret, of whose descendants we have to treat.
Robert, ancestor of the Fitzmaurices of Clonealla.
Elinor, *m.* to the White Knight.

The elder son of the 2nd marriage.

Garret Fitzmaurice, founded the family of Fitzmaurice of Cosfeale, or Duaghnafealla, co. Kerry, which has preserved a male succession to the present time, being now represented by Oliver Fitzmaurice, Esq., the lineal descendant of Garret, and the proprietor of Duagh House, and a considerable portion of the once broad domains of his ancestors. His Grandfather.

Ulick Fitzmaurice, Esq. of Duaghnafealla, co. Kerry, (son and heir of John Fitzmaurice, Esq. of the same place, by Margaret, his wife, a dau. of Stack, of Ballycourcy, and grandson of Ulick Fitzmaurice, of Duaghnafealla), *m.* in 1778, Agnes, dau. of Maurice Studdert, Esq. of Elm Hill, co. Limerick, and left a son and successor,

Maurice Fitzmaurice, Esq. of Duaghnafealla, who *m.* in 1812, Margaret, dau. of Oliver Stokes, Esq. of co. Kerry, and *d.* in 1548, having had,

I. Oliver, now of Duag.
II. Maurice, *m.* Miss Mary Fisher.
III. George, in holy orders. IV. Henry.
V. Robert. VI. John. VII. Edward.
VIII. Ulick. IX. Julian.
I. Elizabeth, *m.* 1st, to James Eidington, Esq. of Gargunock, co. Stirling, and 2ndly, to the Rev. Rowland Bateman.
II. Agnes, *m.* to William Hutton, Esq. of Stirling.
III. Honoria.

Arms—Arg., a saltier, gu., and a chief, erm.
Crest—A centaur, drawing a bow and arrow, ppr., the part from the wrist, arg.
Motto—Virtute non verbis.
Seat—Duag House, Listowel.

FLANAGAN OF DRUMDOE.

Flanagan, John-Woulfe, Esq. of Drumdoe, co. Roscommon, J.P. and D.L., high-sheriff in 1851, *b.* 22 Aug. 1815; *m.* 14 Sept. 1848, Susan, 2nd dau. of the late Rt. Hon. Sir Michael O'Loghlen, Bart., Master of the Rolls in Ireland.

Lineage.—The O'Flanagans of whom J. W Flanagan, Esq. of Drumdoe, is a descendant, are a very ancient Irish

* This was the celebrated Mrs. Fitzherbert. She *d.* 27 March, 1837.

family, belonging to the co. of Roscommon. (*See Annals of Boyle by John D'Alton Esq.*) The late

TERRENCE FLANAGAN, Esq. of Drumdoe, son of JOHN FLANAGAN, Esq., and Winifred Coyne his wife, *m.* in May, 1813, Johanna Woulfe, sister of the late Lord Chief Baron Woulfe, and by her (who *d.* Jan. 1837,) left at his decease, Jan. 1846, three sons.

JOHN-WOULFE, now representative of this old and eminent family.
Stephen-Woulfe, barrister-at-law, and master in the Encumbered Estates Court in Ireland, who *m.* in Feb. 1851, Mary, dau. of J.-R. Corballis, Esq., LL.D., Q.C., and has issue.
Terence, C.E., who *m.* in 1848, Jane Hembden.

Arms—Arg., on a chev., gu., two lions, rampant, or.
Crest—A hand holding a dagger.
Motto—Audaces fortuna juvat.
Seat—Drumdoe, Boyle, co. Roscommon.

FLEMING OF CUMBERNAULD.

ELPHINSTONE-FLEMING, JOHN, Esq. of Cumbernauld House, co. Dumbarton, D.L., an officer 6th Inniskilling Dragoons, *b.* 11 Dec. 1819.

Lineage.—ADMIRAL THE HON. CHARLES ELPHINSTONE, Governor of Greenwich Hospital, and M.P. for Sterling, second son of John, eleventh Lord Elphinstone, and grandson of Charles, tenth Lord, by Clementina his wife, only dau. and heir of John Fleming, sixth Lord Wigtoun, assumed, upon inheriting the estates of the Wigtoun family, the additional surname of FLEMING. He *m.* in 1816, Donna-Catalina-Paulina Alessandro, a Spanish lady, and *d.* 30 Oct. 1840, having had (with three daus., viz. Clementina, *m.* 1845, to the Hon. Cornwallis Maude, Mary Keith, *m.* 20 April, 1843, to Alexander MacAllister, Esq. of Torridale, co. Argyll; and Anne-Elizabeth, *m.* 1851, to William Cunningham Bontine, Esq. of Ardock,) an only son, the present JOHN ELPHINSTONE-FLEMING, Esq. of Cumbernauld House.

Arms—Quarterly: 1st and 4th, arg., a chev., within a double tressure, flory and counterflory, gu., for FLEMING; 2nd and 3rd, arg., a chev., sa., between three boars' heads, erased, gu., for ELPHINSTONE.
Crest—A goat's head, erased, arg., armed, or.
Motto—Let the deed show.
Seat—Cumbernauld House, co. Dumbarton.

FLEMING OF STONEHAM.

WILLIS-FLEMING, JOHN-BROWN, Esq. of Stoneham Park, co. Hants, J.P. and D.L., *b.* 4 Oct. 1815; *m.* 27 Feb. 1840, Lady Katherine-Elizabeth Cochrane, dau. of Thomas, Earl of Dundonald.

Lineage.—This family of Fleming was established by the LORD CHIEF JUSTICE,

SIR THOMAS FLEMING, Knt.,* who was *b.* at Newport, in the Isle of Wight, in April, 1544, and *d.* in 1613. He left a son and successor,

SIR THOMAS FLEMING, of Stoneham, who *m.* Dorothy, dau. of Sir Henry Cromwell, of Hinchinbrooke, and aunt to the Protector Cromwell. By her he left at his decease, in 1623, (with a dau. Mary, *m.* to Thomas Leigh, Esq., son and heir of Sir John Leigh, of Couldrey, Hants,) a son and successor,

THOMAS FLEMING, Esq. of Stoneham, who *m.* Margaret, dau. of Edward, Lord Gorges, and had a son and dau., viz., I. EDWARD, his heir; and I. KATHERINE, who *m.* Daniel Eliot, Esq. of Port Eliot, and had by him, who *d.* in 1702, an only child, KATHERINE ELIOT, who *m.* BROWNE WILLIS, Esq. of Whaddon Hall, the celebrated antiquary, and had, with other issue, two sons, 1. THOMAS WILLIS, who *m.* twice, and had a son by each marriage, who each inherited the Stoneham property; and 2. HENRY WILLIS, who *m.* Katherine, dau. of Dr. Gregory, and had a son, THOMAS WILLIS, Esq., who *m.* Catherine, dau. of Col. Hyde, and *d.* in 1789, leaving issue, 1. JOHN BARTON, who *s.* to Stoneham; 2. Jane, *m.* to Thomas Meyrick, Esq. of Bush; 3. Charlotte; 4. Matilda; 5. Harriet, *m.* to Henry Metcalfe Wardle, Esq.; and 6. Julia, *m.* to the Rev. Edward-Orlebar Smith. Mr. Fleming was *s.* at his decease, in 1639, by his son,

EDWARD FLEMING, Esq. of Stoneham, who *m.* Katherine, dau. of Edward Hooper, Esq., and dying in 1664, was *s.* by his son,

EDWARD FLEMING, Esq. of Stoneham, who *m.* Margaret, dau. of Thomas Bland, Esq., and by her, who *d.* in 1713, left, with other issue, a son,

WILLIAM FLEMING, Esq. of Stoneham, last male representative of the family, at whose decease, *unm.*, the property of Stoneham, in Hampshire, and in the Isle of Wight, reverted to (the grandson of Browne Willis and Katherine Eliot)

THOMAS WILLIS, Esq., *b.* in 1737, who assumed, in consequence, the surname and arms of Fleming. He *d.*, however, childless, and was *s.* by his half-brother,

JOHN WILLIS, Esq., who likewise took, upon inheriting Stoneham, the surname of FLEMING. This gentleman represented Southampton in parliament. He *m.* Elizabeth, dau. of Valentine Knightley, Esq of Fawsley, in Northamptonshire, but *d. s. p.* 28 Feb. 1802, when the inheritance passed to his cousin,

JOHN BARTON WILLIS, Esq., who having assumed the additional surname of FLEMING, became

JOHN WILLIS FLEMING, Esq. of Stoneham, M.P. and high sheriff of Hants, in 1817. He *m.* Christopheria, dau. of James Buchanan, Esq. of that Ilk, and by her (who *m.* 2ndly., 4th Aug. 1846, Ulysses, Lord Downes) had issue;

JOHN-BROWNE, now of Stoneham.
Thomas-James Willis, *b.* 14 June, 1819, *m.* Miss Caroline Hunter.
Henry-William Willis, *b.* 6 Feb. 1828, *d. unm.*
Arthur-Buchanan.
Honoria, *m.* 14 Jan. 1836, to James F. Armstrong, Esq. of Castle Iver, King's county.
Catherine.
Harriet, *m.* to Lieut.-Col. Vansittart.
Charlotte-Jane, *m.* to Albert Hambrough, Esq.

Arms—Quarterly: 1st and 4th, gu., on a chev. between three owls, arg., an ermine spot, for FLEMING; 2nd and 3rd, arg., a fesse, between three lions, rampant, gu., a bordure, of the last, charged with eight bezants, for WILLIS.
Crests—1st, an eagle, displayed, sa., beaked, membered, and ducally gorged, or; 2nd, out of a mural crown, or, a demi-lion, rampant, gu., within a collar gemello, of the first, three bezants.
Seat—Stoneham Park.

FLETCHER OF SALTON.

FLETCHER, ANDREW, Esq. of Salton Hall, co. Haddington, J.P. and D.L., *b.* 20 Aug. 1796; *m.* 7 Sept. 1825, Lady Charlotte Charteris, 2nd dau. of the Earl of Wemys and March, and has issue,

I. JOHN, *b.* 7 Feb. 1827.
I. Frances-Charteris, *b.* 2 Jan. 1828. II. Margaret.

Lineage.—SIR ANDREW FLETCHER, of Innerpeffer, an eminent lawyer, and one of the senators of the College of Justice, purchased, about the middle of the 17th century, the lands of Salton, in East Lothian, from Alexander, Lord Abernethy. He *m.* a dau. of Peter Hay, of Kirkland, and had, with other issue (from William, a younger son of Sir Andrew Fletcher, descend the FLETCHERS *of Garr*, King's county)

SIR ROBERT FLETCHER, of Salton, whose eldest son was the celebrated patriot,

ANDREW FLETCHER, of Salton. This distinguished man, *b.* in 1653, first appeared in public as Commissioner for East Lothian, in the Scottish parliament, and there evinced so much spirit in opposition to the arbitrary measures of the court, that he had to retire to Holland, and was outlawed. In 1685, he participated in the enterprise of the Duke of Monmouth, and subsequently, having gone to Hungary, gained great reputation in the war against the Turks. At the Revolution, he returned to Scotland, resumed possession of his estate, and became a member of the convention for settling the new government. The political writings of Andrew Fletcher, of Salton, are much esteemed. He *d.* in 1717, and was *s.* by his brother,

HENRY FLETCHER, Esq. of Salton, who *m.* in 1688, Margaret, dau. of Sir David Carnegie, of Pitarrow, grandson of David, Earl of Southesk, and was father of

ANDREW FLETCHER, Esq. of Salton, *b.* in 1691, who being admitted an advocate at the Scottish bar, 26 Feb. 1717, was made cashier of the excise in 1718; a lord of Session in 1724; and a lord of Justiciary in 1726. He was appointed Lord Justice Clerk of Scotland in 1735, and keeper of the Signet in 1748. This gentleman *m.* Elizabeth, dau. of Sir Francis Kinloch, of Gilmerton, and had a son,

* Son of John Fleming, of Newport, by his wife Dorothy Harris, to whom he was married in 1543, and grandson of John Fleming, of the same place, who *d.* in 1531, and his wife Isabella.

GENERAL JOHN FLETCHER-CAMPBELL, of Salton, co. Haddington and Boquhan, co. Stirling, who m. in 1795, Ann Thriepland, and had two sons,

ANDREW, now of Salton.
Henry Fletcher-Campbell, of Boquhan, co. Stirling, who m. Ann, dau. of Hugh Hawthorn, Esq. of Castlewig, and has four sons.

Arms—Sa., a cross flory, between four escallops, arg.
Crest—A demi-bloodhound, az., langued, gu.
Supporters—Two griffins, ppr.
Mottoes—Dieu pour nous, and Festina lente.
Seat—Salton Hall, East Lothian.

FLETCHER OF GARR.

FLETCHER, WILLIAM-FREDERICK-HAMILTON, Esq. of Garr, in the King's County, lord of the manor of Clane, co. Kildare, b. 21 Nov. 1836.

Lineage.—This is a branch of the distinguished Scotch family of FLETCHER *of Salton*. The first who settled in Ireland was

WILLIAM FLETCHER, Esq., a younger son of Henry Fletcher, 2nd son of Sir Andrew Fletcher, of Salton, Lord Innerpeffer, an eminent Scotch judge. He went to Ireland, as officer in King WILLIAM the Third's horse-guards, and m. Miss Wilcox, dau. of a very violent presbyterian of a border family, whose brother, however, changed and became Bishop of Lichfield. By her William Fletcher was father of an only son,

WILLIAM FLETCHER, Esq., an officer in the army, who m. a dau. of Edward Gardiner, Esq., and had two sons, Edmund Fletcher, whose children all d. s. p., and

GEORGE FLETCHER, Esq., who m. Mary, eldest dau. of Stephen Myler, Esq. and left an eldest son,

WILLIAM FLETCHER, Esq., b. June, 1750, a distinguished lawyer, who became judge of the Court of Common Pleas in Ireland. He m. 28 Oct. 1780, Sarah Whitley, and d. 4 June, 1823, leaving a son,

WILLIAM FLETCHER, Esq. of Garr, lord of the manor of Clane, who m. 12 May, 1826, Franciska, youngest dau. of the late Archibald Hamilton-Rowan, Esq. of Killyleagh Castle, co. Down, lineally descended from Archibald Hamilton, brother of Sir James Hamilton, of Killyleagh, created Viscount Clanboye, 1622. By her he left at his decease, 9 Feb. 1845,

I. George, b. 1 July, 1831, d. 21 July, 1831.
II. WILLIAM-FREDERICK-HAMILTON, now of Garr.
I. Anna. II. Jeannie.

Arms—Sa., a cross flory, between four escallops, arg.
Crest—A demi-bloodhound, az., langued, gu.
Motto—Dieu pour nous.

FLETCHER OF DUNANS.

FLETCHER, ANGUS, of Dunans House, co. Argyll, b. 15 Jan. 1805, J.P. and D.L.; m. 17 April, 1845, Harriet-Eugenia, only child of Eugene Callanan, Esq., a Lisbon merchant, by Harriet Donovan his wife, and by her (who d. in 1851) has issue, Harriet and Margaret-Clementina.

Lineage.—ANGUS FLETCHER, of Dunans, b. 1719, m. 1743, Helen, dau. of Campbell, of Glenlyon, and had a son and heir,

JOHN FLETCHER, Esq., of Dunans, b. 1746, who m. in 1802, Margaret, dau. of McNab, of Inchewan, and by her (who d. 1832) had issue,

ANGUS, now of Dunans. Alexander.
Archibald-John. Andrew.
Helen, m. 1826, to Sir Charles Gordon, Bart.
Clementina-Anne.

Arms—Sa., on a cross florée, between, in the 1st and 4th quarters, an escallop, and in the 2nd and 3rd, a quiver of arrows, all arg., three crescents, in pale.
Crest—Two arms drawing a bow, all ppr.
Motto—Recta pete.
Seat—Dunans House, co. Argyle.

FLETCHER OF KEVAN ILA.

FLETCHER, JOHN, Esq. of Kevan Ila, co. Monmouth, and St. Michael's Mount, co. Lancaster, J.P., b. 24 April, 1785; m. 27 June, 1811, Eliza, only dau. of John North, Esq. of Halifax, and has issue,

I. JOHN DUNNINGTON,
II. Arthur-Pigott. III. James.
I. Eliza-Jane. II. Anne. III. Ellen.

Mr. Fletcher is son of the late William Fletcher, by Elizabeth Taylor his wife.

Arms—Arg., on a cross, engr., between four pheons, sa., an arrow in pale, the point downwards, of the field, between four bezants.
Crest—A dexter arm, embowed, encircled above the elbow by a wreath of yew, ppr., in the hand a bow, or, stringed, sa.
Motto—Sperans pergo.
Seats—Kevan Ila, co. Monmouth, and St. Michael's Mount, near Liverpool.

FLETCHER OF CORSOCK.

FLETCHER, EDWARD-CHARLES, Esq. of Corsock, Kirkcudbright, J.P., lieut.-colonel in the army, b. 27 June, 1799; m. 1st, 8 Sept. 1830, the Hon. Ellen-Mary Shore, youngest dau. of the late Lord Teignmouth, and by her, who d. in 1835, had issue,

I. HENRY-CHARLES, b. 28 April, 1833.
II. Phillip-Shore, b. 30 Dec. 1834.

He m. 2ndly, 2 Aug. 1838, the Lady Frances Marsham, 2nd dau. of Charles, Earl of Romney, and by her has a dau.,

Margaret-Isabella.

Lineage.—MAJOR PHILIP FLETCHER, great-grandson of Philip Fletcher, younger brother of Richard Fletcher, Esq., whose son, SIR HENRY FLETCHER, was created a baronet in 1640, d. in 1744, at a very advanced age, leaving (with a dau., Elizabeth, m. to Humphrey Pearson, Esq.) two sons, JOHN FLETCHER, Esq., of Clea Hall, (whose son, Sir Henry, was created a Bart. in 1782,) and

PHILIP FLETCHER, Esq., Surveyor-General of the province of Ulster, who m. Mary, dau. of the Rev. Mr. Twigg, and d. in 1758, having had issue, I. Philip, d. unm.; II. Thomas killed at the battle of Dettingen; III. Richard, who m. Anne-Helena, dau. of Archibald Edmonstone, Esq.; and d. in 1782, leaving a son, Philip, M.D.; and IV. Edward. The youngest son,

THE REV. EDWARD FLETCHER, of Lisburn, who d. in 1777, having had, by Jane Murray his wife, (with two daus., Anne-Helena, who d. unm.; and Margaret, m. to — Higginson, Esq.) three sons, who survived him, viz., Phillip, of Lisburn, in holy orders, b. in 1754, who d. unm.; EDWARD, of whom presently; and James, b. in 1768, who m. Hannah, dau. of the late Robert Bent, Esq., M.P., (she subsequently m. the Hon. and Rev. Charles Knox, Archdeacon of Armagh.) The 2nd son.

EDWARD FLETCHER, Esq. of Alresford, co. Hants, b. 7 April, 1763, in the E. I. C. civil service, m. 6 Jan. 1797, Dorothea, youngest dau. of the late Sir Charles-William Blunt, Bart., by Elizabeth Peers, his wife, and had issue,

EDWARD-CHARLES, of Corsock.
Charles-Philip, b. 2 Aug. 1805, m. 20 Feb. 1828, Francesca-Alloysa Mollica, and has issue, a son, Edward-Philip, b. 28 July, 1829, and a dau., Francesca-Louisa.
James, b. 25 April, 1820.
Charlotte-Jane, m. to the Rev. George Matthias.
Helena. Sophia, m. to Col. R. Oakes.
Emily, m. to James Arnott, Esq. Louisa.

Arms—Arg., a cross, engr., sa., between four pellets, each charged with a pheon, erect, of the first.
Crest—A horse's head, arg.
Motto—Martis non Cupidinis.
Seat—Corsock.

FLETCHER OF LAWNESWOOD.

FLETCHER, THOMAS-WILLIAM, Esq. of Lawneswood House, co. Stafford, M.A., F.R.S., F.S.A., and F.G.S., a D.L. for the co. of Worcester, and captain 1st regt. of King's Own Staffordshire militia; m. 13 Sept. 1831, Jane-Maria, dau. of James Russell, Esq. of Bescot Hall, and Endwood Court, co. Stafford, by Sarah his wife, dau. and co-heir of the Rev. John Best, M.A., fellow of Worcester College, Oxford, and prebendary of Wolverhampton, and has issue,

I. THOMAS-HOWARD KEELING. II. Walter-Bracebridge.
1. Eliza-Jane.

Lineage.—The family of Fletcher is of great antiquity in the shires of Stafford and Warwick, as in that of Cumberland, where the resident obtained a baronetcy *temp.* CHARLES I. There are proofs extant that the branch before us was seated in the county of Stafford so early as the reign of EDWARD II., but from the destruction of the early records, the pedigree can be *authentically* deduced only from the time of Queen ELIZABETH, when

THOMAS FLETCHER, of co. Stafford, *m.* Barbara, eldest dau. of Sir James Foljambe, Knt. of Walton, by Constance, his wife, dau. of Sir Edward Littleton, Knt. Their son, THOMAS FLETCHER, Esq. of Water Eyton and Shareshill, co. Stafford, acquired estates there by marriage with Margaret, dau. and eventually heiress of Ralf Alport, Esq. of Cannock, a portion of which are now held by his descendants, having always passed in the male line: of this marriage there were issue, THOMAS, his heir; and Margaret, *m.* 1st to William Chetwynd, Esq., and 2ndly to Francis Giffard, Esq. Mr. Fletcher, was buried at Shareshill, 24 Oct. 1610; his widow, 16 April, 1616. His son,

THOMAS FLETCHER, of Featherstone, co. Stafford, *b.* 2 Oct. 1590, was an officer in the army of King CHARLES I. He enlarged the estate by the purchase of lands in Wirley Magna, Wirley Parva, Saredon, Cannock and Cheslyn Hay, in the 4th CHARLES I. He *m.* 24 July, 1620, Elizabeth, dau. of William Poole, and was killed at the battle of Marston Moor, 1643, leaving a son and heir,

THOMAS FLETCHER, Esq. de Magnâ Wirley, baptized 8 Aug., 4 CAR. I. (1620), *m.* 13 Jan., 10 CAR. II., Mary Bourne, and dying 10 Sept. 1691, was *s.* by his elder son,

THOMAS FLETCHER, of Wirley Magnâ, B.A. of New College, Oxford, *b.* 21 March, baptized 14 April, 16 CHARLES II., 1664, *m.* Catherine Richards, and *d.* 21 Feb. 1718, leaving (with three daus., Catherine, wife of H. Hodgetts, Esq.; Elizabeth, *m.* in 1733, to George Keen, Esq. of Stafford; and Ann, *m.* in 1733, to Thomas Cope, Esq. of Leacroft,) an only son and heir,

THOMAS FLETCHER, Esq. of Cannock, baptized 19 March, 1707, *m.* in 1733, Mary, only dau. and heiress of William Keelinge, Esq. of Sedgeley Park, co. Stafford, by Eleanor, his wife, dau. of William Gibbons, Esq. of Ettingsall Hall (by Elizabeth, his wife, dau. of John Hawkesford, Esq., by Elizabeth, his wife, dau. and eventual heiress of Rowland Bracebridge, Esq. of Kingsbury and Winifred, his wife, dau. of Thomas Scott, Esq. of Great Bar) and had two sons,

THOMAS, his heir.
William, *b.* 2 Oct. 1740, *m.* 1770, at Oldswinford, co. Worcester, Alice, dau. of Thomas Blakemore, Esq., and aunt of Richard Blakemore, Esq., M.P. for Wells, and *d.* 21 Oct. 1804, leaving issue, THOMAS, heir to his uncle; Mary, *m.* to the Rev. John Waltham, M.A., of Jesus College, Cambridge, rector of Rock, co. Cornwall, and of Darlaston, co. Stafford, a magistrate for the latter county, and 2ndly, to the Rev. John Howells, M.A., vicar of the Holy Trinity, Coventry; Sarah, Catherine, and Frances.

He *d.* in Dec. 1790, and was *s.* by his elder son,

THOMAS FLETCHER, Esq. of Cannock, *b.* 13 May, 1730, who *d. unm.* 31 Aug. 1802, and was *s.* by his nephew,

THOMAS FLETCHER, Esq. of Handsworth, co. Stafford, *b.* 19 Feb. 1772, who *m.* 10 May, 1804, Ann, dau. of Thomas Russell, Esq., and had issue,

THOMAS-WILLIAM, now of Lawneswood House.
William, D.D., late fellow of Brasennose College, Oxford (in holy orders), *m.* 31 Dec. 1835, Hannah-Maria-Jane, dau. of Joseph Bainbrigge, Esq. of Derby, and has three sons, William-Bainbrigge, Walter John, and Edward-Blakemore; and three daus., Catherine-Anne, Lorina-Alice, and Honora.
John-Waltham, M.A. (in holy orders) *m.* Elizabeth-Sarah, dau. of the Rev. John Giles Dimock, M.A.
Henry, M.A., in holy orders. *m.* Mary-Anne-Letitia, dau. and heir of William-David Field, Esq. of Ulceby Grange, co. Lincoln, J.P. and D.L.
Anne, *m.* to the Rev. William-Henry Flowers, vicar of Ulceby, co. Lincoln.

He *d.* at Hansworth, 1 April, 1827.

Arms—Arg., a cross, engr., sa., between four pellets, each charged with a pheon, or, on a canton, az., a ducal crown, gold.

Crests—1st, A horse's head, erased, arg., gorged with a ducal crown, az; 2nd, on a chapeau, gu., a scaling-ladder, or.

Motto—Sub cruce salus.

Residence—Lawneswood House, near Stourbridge.

FLOOD OF PAULSTOWN CASTLE.

FLOOD, WILLIAM, Esq. of Paulstown Castle, co. Kilkenny, J.P., *b.* 7 April, 1817.

Lineage.—The founder of the Irish branch of the family of Flood (which claims descent from the Kentish Fludds,) was,

MAJOR FRANCIS FLOOD, of Burnchurch, who commanded a body of horse in the army of the Protector Cromwell, and went to Ireland at the same period as the Ponsonbys, Cuffes, and Wardens, all of whom settled in the co. Kilkenny, 1647. Major Flood *m.* Anne, only dau. and heir of Col. Henry Warden, M.P., granddau. of Sir Richard Warden, of Suffolk, and niece of Agmondesham Cuffe, Esq. of Desart, father of the 1st Baron Desart: by this lady, one of the greatest beauties of her day, and heiress of the estate of Burnchurch, Mr. Flood had seven sons and a dau., viz.,

I. WARDEN, his successor.
II. John, of Farmley, co. Kilkenny, M.P., who *m.* Jane, only dau. and heir of Crompton, Esq., and had two sons and a dau. viz.,
  1 JOHN, of Flood Hall, of whom presently.
  2 FREDERICK, of Newton Ormond, co. Kilkenny, LL.D., king's counsel, custos rotulorum, and M.P. for the co. of Wexford, created a baronet on the 3rd June, 1780. Sir Frederick Flood *m.* 1st, Lady Juliana Annesley, dau. of the last Earl of Anglesey, by whom (who *d.* in 1774) he had no issue. He *m.* 2ndly, Frances, dau. of the Right Hon. Sir Henry Cavendish, Bart., and had, with three sons, who *d.* young, or *unm.*, an only dau., FRANCES, who *m.* 1st, in 1799, Richard Solly, Esq. of Walthamstow, by whom (who *d.* in 1803) she had FREDERICK SOLLY, who assumed, by sign-manual, in 1818, the additional surname and arms of FLOOD, and two daus. (*See* FLOOD *of Slaney Lodge.*) Mrs. Solly, *m.* 2ndly, in 1807, John-Harward Jessop, Esq. of Doory Hall, co. Longford, and left by him two other sons and two daus. (*See* JESSOP *of Doory Hall.*) At the decease of Sir Frederick Flood, 1 Feb. 1824, the baronetcy became extinct.
  1 Elizabeth, *m.* to William Walsh, Esq.
III. Charles, of Ballymack, co. Kilkenny, *d. unm.* in 1770, and devised his estates to the Right Hon. Henry Flood, vice-treasurer of Ireland.
IV. Henry, in holy orders, *d. s. p.*
V. George, of Kilkenny, in holy orders, D.D., rector of Rathdowny, Queen's Co., *d.* in 1770, leaving issue.
VI. Francis, of Paulstown Castle, co. Kilkenny, J.P. and high-sheriff of that county, who *m.* Anne-Jane, dau. of Colonel Henry Hatton, of Great Clonard, co. Wexford, M.P., and by her (who *m.* 2ndly, John James, 1st Marquess of Abercorn) had, with a dau., Frances, *m.* to Monsr. Barthlomé de la Mothe, four sons, viz.,
  1 WARDEN, LL.D., M.P., judge of the High Court of Admiralty in Ireland, from 1790 to 1794, *m.* Anne, dau. of the Rev. Morgan Donovan, and had issue,
    WARDEN, who predeceased his father, *unm.*
    Francis, a capt. in the army, *d. unm.*
    HENRY, of Paulstown Castle, *b.* in 1769, *m.* 2 Sept. 1815, Anna-Maria Lennon, and left a son and heir, WILLIAM FLOOD, Esq., now of Paulstown Castle.
    O'Donovan, an officer in the army, served in Flanders under the Duke of York, at the sieges of Gibraltar and Minorca, *m.* Mademoiselle, Vignau, niece of the Comtesse de la Motte, maid of honour to Marie Antoinette, and left issue,
      WARDEN, late an officer in the army, *m.* 21 April, 1835, Mary-Grove, eldest dau. of the Hon. Lieut.-Gen. Arthur Grove-Annesley, and niece of Earl Annesley, and has issue.
      Marianne, *m.* to Henry-Oswald Smithe, Esq. E.I.C.S., who *d. s. p.*
    Marianne, *m.* to the Rev. Stuart Hamilton, of Tyrone, brother to Gen. Sir John Hamilton, Bart., but *d. s. p.*
  2 Hatton, colonel 1st dragoon guards, *d. unm.*
  3 Henry, a major in the army, who *m.* Miss Perkins, of Ballenshain, co Carlow. and had, with two daus., Frances and Mary, now widows, a son and heir,
    JOHN, of Viewmont, co. Kilkenny, clerk of the peace for that shire, *m.* March, 1799, Miss Brushe, great-granddau. of Dr. Maude, Bishop of Meath, and has issue surviving, viz., John, barrister-at-law; Henry; Elizabeth, *m.* to Major Stoyte, of the 24th; and Anne-Augusta, wife of John-Galway Holmes, Esq., barrister-at-law.
  4 Francis, who *m.* Miss Armstrong, and had a son, Henry, who *m.* Miss Barton, and left issue.
VII. Richard, *d. unm.*
VIII. Anne, *m.* to Dr. Henry Candler, archdeacon of Ossory, and rector of Callan.

The eldest son,

THE RIGHT HON. WARDEN FLOOD, of Flood Hall, a very distinguished Lawyer, was chief justice of the court of King's Bench in Ireland. He *m.* Miss Whiteskle, by whom he had two sons and a dau., HENRY, his heir; Warden-Jocyline, M.P., *d. unm.* in 1767; and Isabella; and dying in 1764, was *s.* by his son,

THE RIGHT HON. HENRY FLOOD, of Farmley, co. Kilkenny. This eminent person, so celebrated in the eventful history of his native country, was *b.* in 1732, and *d.* in Dec.

1795, leaving behind him the character of one of the first statesmen of the age in which he lived. He *m.* 13 April, 1762, the Lady Frances-Maria Beresford, dau. of Marcus, first Earl of Tyrone, but *d.* without issue. He devised his extensive estates to the College of Dublin, for the encouragement of the Irish language; but those estates after procrastinated litigation, reverted to his cousin and heir at law,

JOHN FLOOD, Esq. of Flood Hall, co. Kilkenny. This gentleman *m.* Elizabeth, dau. of Boyle Aldworth, Esq., of Newmarket, co. Cork, by Jane, his 1st wife, dau. of Robert Oliver, Esq. of Cloughnodfoy, and had issue, JOHN, his heir; Robert, of Farmley, *d. unm.*; and Elizabeth. Mr. Flood was *s.* at his decease by his elder son.

JOHN FLOOD, Esq., of Flood Hall, a Magistrate and deputy-lieut. for the co. of Kilkenny, who *m.* Miss Saurin, eldest dau. of the Right Hon. William Saurin, attorney-general for Ireland but *d.* without leaving issue by his marriage. His cousin is the present WILLIAM FLOOD, Esq. of Paulstown Castle.

Arms—Vert, a chevron between three wolves' heads, erased, arg.
Crest—A wolf's head, as in the arms.
Motto—Vis unita fortior.
Seat—Paulstown Castle, near Gowran, co. Kilkenny.

FLOOD OF SLANEY LODGE.

SOLLY-FLOOD, FREDERICK, Esq. of Slaney Lodge, co. Wexford, J.P., *b.* 7 Aug. 1801; *m.* 21 Aug. 1824, Mary, dau. of the Rev. Thomas Williamson, rector of Stoke Dameral, Devonport, and grand-daughter of Sir Hedworth Williamson, Bart. of Whitburn Hall, co. Durham, and has issue,

I. EDWARD-THOMAS, *b.* 3 April, 1827, *m.* 28 May, 1853, Marianne, youngest dau. of Capt. James Harvey.
II. Frederick-Richard.
III. Ferdinand-Henry.
IV. James-Douglas-Musgrave.
I. Frances-Henrietta, *m.* John-George-Cockburn Curtis, son of Captain Curtis, R.N.
II. Mary-Frederica, *m.* to Alfred Hoonloe, son of Francis, William Patterson, Esq. of Leamington Priors.
III. Julia-Anne-Adelaide.

Lineage.—SIR FREDERICK FLOOD, Bart., (*see preceding Lineage.*) *m.* 1774, for his 2nd wife, Frances, dau. of the Rt. Hon. Sir Henry Cavendish, and dying in 1824, left an only child,

FRANCES FLOOD, who *m.* 1799, RICHARD SOLLY, Esq., of York Place, London, and had issue, FREDERICK SOLLY-FLOOD, Esq. of Slaney Lodge; Frances Elizabeth, *m.* 22 Oct., 1821, Sir George Ralph Fetherston, Bart., Caroline-Jane, *m.* Capt. Samuel B. Hore, R.N.

Arms—FLOOD and SOLLY quartering.
Crests—FLOOD and SOLLY.
Motto—Vis unita fortior.
Seat—Slaney Lodge, co. Wexford.

FLOYER OF WEST STAFFORD.

FLOYER, JOHN, Esq. of West Stafford, co. Dorset, J.P. and D.L., high-sheriff 1844, and M.P. for Dorsetshire since Feb. 1846, *b.* 26 April, 1811; *s.* his brother 11 July, 1822; *m.* 20 Feb. 1844, Georgina-Charlotte-Frances, eldest dau. of the late Right Hon. George Bankes, M.P., Cursitor Baron, by Georgina-Charlotte his wife, dau. and heir of Admiral Sir Charles-Edmund Nugent, Knt., G.C.H., admiral of the fleet, and has a son and heir,

I. GEORGE-WILLIAM, *b.* 23 July, 1851.

Lineage.—The pedigree of this family is authentically deduced from

FLOIERUS, who settled soon after the Norman Conquest on the lands beyond the River Exe, co. Devon, whence the name of "Floierslands," or Floiers Hayes, his son,

RICHARD, held those lands of Richard, son of Baldwin de Courtenay, and transmitted them to his son and heir,

NICHOLAS, who was *s.* by his son,

RICHARD, who obtained a confirmation of the lands beyond the Exe, held by his grandfather, from ROBERT, natural son of King HENRY I., upon the stipulation of presenting the said Robert and his heirs with a flagon of wine, whenever they should come to dine on the Isle of Exe. This grant was afterwards confirmed, in more ample form, by Reginald de Courtenay. From this Richard derived the family of FLOYER *of Floiers Hayes*, co. Dorset,

WILLIAM FLOYER, of Floiers Hayes, a distinguished soldier, 8th in descent from Richard, attended George, Duke of Clarence, to Normandy, with three archers and thirty spears, 14 EDWARD IV. From him, the 5th in descent was,

WILLIAM FLOYER, Esq. of Floiers Hayes and Berne, who *m.* 1st, in 1641, Margaret, second dau. of Sir Edward Lawrence, Knt. of Creech Grange, Isle of Purbeck, co. Dorset, and had

ANTHONY, of Floiers Hayes, bapt. 31 May, 1642, *d.* in 1701, leaving by Sarah, his 2nd wife, dau. of John Gould, Esq. of Upway, three sons, ANTHONY, *d. s. p.*, WILLIAM, and Hubert-Charles. The 2nd, the REV. WILLIAM FLOYER, *b.* in 1676, rector of Trusham, co. Devon, *m.* Sarah, dau. of Amy Burwell, of London, and dying in 1742, left with other issue, 1 ANTHONY, of Dorchester; 2 John Gould, in holy orders, rector of Esher, in Surrey, *d. unm.* in 1777; and 3 WILLIAM FLOYER, Esq. of Reesby, in Lincolnshire, and of Athelhampton, co. Dorset, *m.* in 1752, Frances, dau. and co-heir of Edward Aiscough, Esq. of Louth, co. Lincoln, and dying in 1759, was *s.* by his son, ANTHONY, who *m.* in 1784, Elizabeth, dau. of George Brabines, Esq. of Blannington Hall, in Lincolnshire, and dying 8 March, 1814, left an only son and heir, JOHN-GOULD FLOYER, Esq. of Ketsby, co. Lincoln, *b.* in July, 1785, *m.* in 1815, Sarah, dau. of the Rev. Richard Wright, of Wrangle, and has issue, JOHN-WADHAM, *b.* in 1818; Richard-Aiscough-Martin; and Ayscough.

Mr. Floyer *m.* 2ndly, Elizabeth, dau. of Randle Mainwaring, Esq. of London, by whom (who *d.* 22 June, 1667,) he had with other issue,

WILLIAM FLOYER, Esq. of Berne, co. Dorset, who *m.* 1st, in 1677, Mary, dau. and co-heir of Sir William Pole, Knt. of Shute, co. Devon, eldest son of Sir John Pole, Bart., and 2ndly, in 1700, Grace Cossins of Broadwindson, in Dorsetshire, by the former of whom he left, at his decease in 1711, a dau. Catherine, *m.* to Humphrey Sydenham, Esq. of Dulverton, and a son,

JOHN FLOYER, Esq. of Upway, co. Dorset, and of Lincoln's Inn, barrister-at-law, *m.* 1st, 22 July, 1714, Mary, dau. of John Ellis, of St. James's, Westminster, but had no issue. He *m.* 2ndly, 11 April, 1741, Anne, dau. of James Richards, Esq. of West Knighton, co. Dorset and co-heir of her brother. By this lady he had two sons, and a dau., Anne, wife of the Rev. Charles Russell of Bath. The elder son,

JOHN FLOYER, Esq. of Upway, *b.* 28 May, 1744, *m.* Jane, only dau. of the Rev. Samuel Davison rector of Dalbury, in Derbyshire, (by Elizabeth his wife, sister of Sir Edward Wilmot, Bart. of Chaddesden, and relict of James Acton, of West Stafford.) He *d. s. p.* in 1789, when the estates devolved upon his brother,

THE REV. WILLIAM FLOYER, *b.* 5 Jan, 1746, rector of West Stafford and vicar of Stinsford, co. Dorset, who *m.* 3 Feb. 1801, Elizabeth, youngest dau. and co-heir of Stephen Barton, Esq. of Blandford, and had issue,

WILLIAM, his successor.
JOHN, heir to his brother.
Elizabeth-Margaret, *b.* 11 Aug. 1806, *d.* in 1807.
Elizabeth, *m.* in July, 1831, to Charles Wriothesley-Digby, Esq., eldest son of the Rev. Charles Digby, canon of Windsor, and *d.* 18 July, 1834, leaving a dau., Mary-Elizabeth.

Mr. Floyer *d.* 29 Dec. 1819, and was *s.* by his elder son,

WILLIAM FLOYER, Esq., *b.* 29 Dec. 1808, of West Stafford, a midshipman in the royal navy, drowned off Portland, 11 July, 1822, and was *s.* by his brother, the present JOHN FLOYER, Esq., M.P. of West Stafford.

Arms—Sa., a chevron between three arrows, arg.
Crest—A buck's head, erased, or, holding in the mouth an arrow.
Motto—Floret virtus vulnerata.
Seat—West Stafford, near Dorchester.

FLOYER OF HINTS.

FLOYER, JOHN-HUMBERSTONE, of Hints Hall, co. Stafford, *s.* his father in 1854.

Lineage.—This family is supposed to have derived from a younger branch of the Floyers of Floiers Hayes, co. Devon.

RALPH FLOYER, Esq. of the Middle Temple, son of Richard Flyer, Esq. of Blackenhall, and grandson of Thomas Flyer, Uttoxeter, purchased, HINTS, co. Stafford, in 1601. He was father, by Margery, his first wife, dau. of James Weston, Esq. of Lichfield, of

RICHARD FLOYER, Esq. of Hints, who s. his father in 1643. He d. 1679, leaving by Elizabeth, his 2nd wife, dau. of William Babington, of Coborough, a son and successor,

MATHEW FLOYER, Esq. of Hints, b. in 1646, who m. Anne, dau. and heir, of John Scott Esq. of Great Barr, and dying in 1716 left (with six daus., Elizabeth-Prudence, m. to Edward Shelden, Esq. of Wolverhampton; Susanna, m. to William Mead, Esq. of Narborough; Margaret, d. unm.; Eleanor, m. to Francis Wolferstan of Statford; and Mary, wife of George Antrobus, M.D., of Birmingham,) six sons, of whom the eldest,

RALPH FLOYER, Esq. of Hints, b. in 1676, m. in 1698, Catherine, dau. of Charles Chadwick, Esq. of Healey and Ridware, and was s. at his decease, in 1729, by his son,

SACHEVERELL FLOYER, Esq. of Hints, who m. Susanna, dau. of John Floyer, Esq. of Longdon, but by her, who m. 2ndly, George Ley, Esq. of Mathfield he had no issue. He d. in 1735, and was s. by his brother,

CHARLES FLOYER, Esq. of Hints, baptized 8 Aug, 1712, who m. Susanna, dau. and co-heir of Waldyve Willington, Esq. of Hurley, co. Warwick, and by her, who d. in 1750, had issue

I. RALPH, his heir.
II. Charles, of Sutton Coldfield, d. in 1774.
III. Sacheverell, d. unm. in 1788.
I. Susanna, d. young.
II. CATHERINE, bapt. 21 June, 1739, who m. in 1762, Thomas Levett, Esq. of Whittington and Packington, co. Stafford, and had issue,
  1 THEOPHILUS LEVETT, Esq. of Whichnor.
  2 Thomas Levett, in holy orders.
  1 Anne Levett.
  2 Catherine Levett, m. in 1794, to her cousin, William-Humberstone Cawley-Floyer, Esq. of Hints.
III. MARY, b. 16 Sept. 1742, who m. in 1763, John-Humberstone, Cawley, Esq. of Gwersylt Park, co. Denbigh, high-sheriff in 1776, and had issue, WILLIAM-HUMBERSTONE, of whom presently, as successor to his uncle at Hints; Frances, b. in 1764; John, b. in 1768, M.D., of Birmingham and Tamworth; Philip, b. in 1771; and Charles, b. in 1783.

Mr Floyer d. in 1760, and was s by his son,

RALPH FLOYER, Esq. of Hints, baptized 2 June, 1740, who served as high sheriff of Staffordshire in 1780. He d. unm., 16 Nov. 1793, having devised his estates to his nephew, WILLIAM-HUMBERLTONE CAWLEY Esq., b 17 July, 1766, who assumed the surname and arms of FLOYER. He m. Catherine, youngest dau. of Thomas Levett, Esq. of Packington, co. Stafford, and left issue, JOHN, now of Hints; Charles, in holy orders; Richard, Capt. in the army, deceased; and Catherine, d. unm.

Arms—Arg., a chev., sa., between three arrows, or.
Seat—Hints Hall, co. Stafford.

FOLEY OF PRESTWOOD.

FOLEY-HODGETTS, JOHN-HODGETTS, Esq. of Prestwood, co. Worcester, b. 17 July, 1797; m. 20 Oct. 1825, Charlotte-Margaret, dau. of the late John Gage, Esq., by Mary his wife, dau. of John Milbanke, Esq., and has issue one son,

HENRY JOHN WENTWORTH, b. 9 Dec. 1828, m. 12 Dec., 1854, Jane-Frances-Anne, 2nd dau. of the late Lord Vivian.

Mr. Foley is a magistrate and deputy-lieut. for cos. Stafford and Worcester, and represents East Worcestershire in parliament.

Lineage.—THE HON. EDWARD FOLEY, 2nd son of Thomas, 3rd Lord Foley, m. 1st, 20 Oct., 1778, Lady Anne-Margaret Coventry, dau. of the sixth Earl of Coventry, and 2ndly, in March, 1790, Eliza-Maria, dau. and heiress of John Hodgetts, Esq., by his wife, the heiress of Prestwood, and had issue,

Edward-Thomas, of Stoke Edith Park, co. Hereford, who m. 16 Aug. 1832, Lady Emily Graham, 4th dau. of James, 3rd Duke of Montrose.
JOHN-HODGETTS, of Prestwood.
Elizabeth-Maria, m. to Viscount Gage.
Anna-Maria, m. to Sir Henry-John Lambert, Bart. of Aston House, Oxon.

Arms—Quarterly: 1st and 4th, a lion, sejant, for FOLEY; 2nd and 3rd, a horse's head, erm., pierced with a spear, broken, ppr., for HODGETTS.
Crest—A lion, rampant, arg., holding between the fore-paws an escutcheon, charged with the arms.
Mottoes—Ut prosim; Vince malum bono.
Seat—Prestwood, near Stourbridge, co. Worcester.

FOLEY OF TETWORTH.

FOLEY, HENRY, Esq. of Tetworth and Wistow, co. Huntingdon, b. 12 May, 1804, late capt. in the 6th regt.; m. 2 June, 1831, Elizabeth, eldest dau. of Edward Curteis, Esq. of Glenburne, and has issue,

I. HARRY-RICHARD-STANHOPE.
I. Lizzie-Augusta-Constance.
II. Lucy-Selina-Geraldine.
III. Henrietta-Jane.
IV. Frances-Leila.
V. Marion-Alice.
VI. Florence-Maud.

Lineage.—This is a branch of the noble family of Foley, (see BURKE'S *Peerage*.)

THE REV. PHILIP FOLEY, rector of Shelsley, co. Worcester (2nd son of Robert Foley, Esq., by Mary, his wife, dau of the Rev. Ralph Markland, and grandson of Philip Foley, Esq. of Prestwood, co. Stafford, M.P., who was brother of Paul Foley, speaker of the House of Commons, ancestor of the present Lord Foley(, m. Anne, only dau of John Titmarsh, Esq. of Barrington, co. Cambridge, and had issue, Thomas-Philip, RICHARD-HARRY, Robert-Ralph, and Mary-Anne. The 2nd son,

RICHARD-HARRY FOLEY, Esq., a major-general in the army. m. in 1801, Dorothy, dau. of John Lodwick, Esq. of North Shawbury House, Essex, and had issue,

HENRY, his heir, now of Tetworth.
Horatio, d. in 1808.
Edmund, lieut. R N.
Richard, d. in 1810.
Rosa, m to her cousin, Philip Foley, Esq.
Marianne.
Helen.

Major-General Foley d. at Worcester in Feb. 1825.

Arms—Arg., a fesse, engr., between three cinquefoils, sa., all within a bordure, of the last.
Crest—A lion, rampant, arg., holding between the fore-paws an escutcheon, charged with the arms.
Motto—Ut prosim.
Seat—Tetworth Hall, co. Huntingdon.

FOLJAMBE OF OSBERTON AND ALDWARKE.

FOLJAMBE, GEORGE-SAVILE, Esq. of Osberton, Notts, and of Aldwarke, co. York, b. 4 June, 1800; m. 1st, 9 Dec. 1828, Harriet-Emily-Mary, dau. of Sir William-Mordaunt-Sturt Milner, Bart. of Nun Appleton, and by her, who d. 28 Dec. 1830, has an only child,

FRANCIS-JOHN-SAVILE, b. 9th April, 1830, m. 20 Feb. 1856, Lady Gertrude-Emily Acheson, eldest dau. of the Earl of Gosford.

He m. 2ndly, 28 Aug. 1845, Selina-Charlotte, Dowager Viscountess Milton, 2nd dau. of the Earl of Liverpool, and by her has issue,

I. Cecil-George, b. 7 Nov. 1846.
II. Henry-Savile, b. 14 Oct. 1849.
I. Elizabeth-Anne.
II. Frances-Mary.
III. Caroline-Frederica.

Lineage.—The first of this eminent family on record, SIR THOMAS FOLJAMBE, living in the reigns of HENRY III. and EDWARD I., appears either as witness or principal in many charters, and his position amongst the witnesses, either standing first, or where there are other knights named with him, near the first, shews that he was a man of principal note in his times. In 1272 he was Bailiff of the High Peak, in Derbyshire, and at his death, on the Saturday next after the feast of St Hilary, 11 EDWARD I., he held of the king an oxgang of land by the sergeantry of keeping the king's forests de Campana, which was the style of the forest of the High Peak. His eldest son and heir,

SIR THOMAS FOLJAMBE, Knt., living 16 EDWARD I., held lands in Tideswell and Wormhill, and by Catherine his wife, left a son and successor,

SIR THOMAS FOLJAMBE, Knt. of Tideswell, living 15 EDWARD II,* from whom we pass to his descendant,

THOMAS FOLJAMBE, (2nd son of Sir Godfrey Foljambe), who m. Margaret, sister and co-heir of Sir John Loudham, by whom he acquired about the time of RICHARD II., Walton with a considerable estate, and had a son and successor,

* For more ample particulars of the early progenitors of the Foljambes, as well as for the intervening descents, see *Collectanea Topographica et Genealogica*, vols. i. and ii.

THOMAS FOLJAMBE, of Walton, in Derbyshire, forty years old, 29 HENRY VI., father of

HENRY FOLJAMBE, of Walton, who *m.* Benedicta, dau. of Sir William Vernon, of Nether Hadden, and had *inter alios*, two sons,

I. GODFREY (Sir), his heir.
II. Roger, of Linacre Hall, who *m.* Ellen, dau. of John Coke, and had two sons, 1 Godfrey, of Plumley and Moor Hall, whose issue became extinct; and 2 Roger, of Linacre Hall, father of George, of Higham, whose son (by Gertrude his wife, dau. of Sir George Skipwith), PETER FOLJAMBE, of Steeton, became HEIR MALE of the family at the decease of Sir Francis Foljambe, Bart.

The eldest son,

SIR GODFREY FOLJAMBE, Knt. of Walton, *b.* there 27 March, 1472, served as sheriff of Derbyshire, 16 and 28 HENRY VIII. He *m.* 5 HENRY VII. Catherine, dau. of Sir John Leake, of Sutton in le Dale, in that co., and was *s.* by his eldest son and successor,

Sir JAMES FOLJAMBE, Knt. of Walton and Aldwarke, *b.* at Walton, 2 HENRY VIII., sheriff of Derbyshire 2nd and 3rd PHILIP and MARY. He *m.* 1st, Alice, dau. and co-heir, of Thomas Fitzwilliam, Esq. of Aldwarke (who was slain at Flodden,) by Agnes, his wife, dau. of Sir Hugh Pagenham, Knt., and had, with three daus., three sons, viz., GODFREY, his heir; George of Brimmington, co. Derby; and James, twin with George. Sir James *m.* 2ndly, Constance, dau. of Sir Edward Littleton, Knt. of Pillaton, in Staffordshire, and by her, who died in 1600, had, with five daus., a son,

FRANCIS, successor to his nephew.

Sir James Foljambe *d.* 26 Sept. 1558, and lies buried at Chesterfield, where a monument was erected to his memory. His son and successor,

SIR GODFREY FOLJAMBE, Knt. of Walton, *b.* 19 HENRY VIII. sheriff of Derbyshire, 20 ELIZABETH, *m.* Troth, dau. of Sir William, Tyrwhit, of Kettleby, and by her, who *m.* 2ndly, Sir William Mallory, Knt., left at his decease, 22 Dec. 1584, a son and successor,

GODFREY FOLJAMBE, Esq. of Walton, *b.* 21 Nov. 1558, sheriff of Derbyshire 31 ELIZABETH, who *m.* Isabel, dau. of Sir Christopher Wray, Knt., lord chief justice of England, but *d. s. p.* and was buried at Chesterfield, 14 June, 1595. His widow *m.* 2ndly, Sir William Bowes, Knt. of Barnard Castle, in Durham, and 3rdly, John, Lord Darcy of Aston. Godfrey Foljambe was *s.* by his uncle,

FRANCIS FOLJAMBE, Esq. of Aldwarke, who *m.* Frances, dau. of Thomas Burdett, Esq. of Birthwaite, and relict of Francis Wortley, Esq. of Wortley, by whom he had two sons: the elder, Sir Thomas, *d. s. p.*; the younger.

SIR FRANCIS FOLJAMBE, of Walton and Aldwarke, was created a BARONET 24 July, 1622, and served as sheriff of Derbyshire in 1633. Sir Francis *m.* 1st, to Elizabeth, dau. of Sir William Wray, of Glentworth, by whom he had an only dau. and heiress, FRANCES, *m.* 1st, to Sir Christopher Wray, and 2ndly, to John Troutbeck, M D. She *d. s. p.* He *m.* 2ndly, Elizabeth, dau. of Sir George Reresby, by whom he had no issue. (She wedded 2ndly, Edward Horner, Esq. of Mells; 3rdly, William Monson, Viscount Castlemaine; and 4thly, Sir Adam Felton Bart., of Playford.) Sir Francis Foljambe *d.* at Bath, 17 Dec. 1640, when the baronetcy expired, but the estate of Aldwarke, and the representation of the family, devolved on the male heir.

PETER FOLJAMBE, Esq. of Steeton, *b.* in 1599, who *m.* at Hope, 19 Sept 1642, Jane, dau. and co-heir of Ellis Woodruffe, Esq. of Hope, in Derbyshire, reader and bencher of the Inner Temple, and by her (who *d.* 4 Sept. 1658,) left at his decease, 26 Feb. 1668-9 a son and successor,

FRANCIS FOLJAMBE, Esq. of Aldwarke, *b.* in 1643, who *m.* Elizabeth, eldest dau. and co-heir of George Mountaine, Esq. of Wistow, by Mary, his wife, dau. of Sir Thomas Gower, Bart., of Stittenham, and by her, (who was *b.* at Wistow, 25 July, 1647, and *d.* 12 Sept, 1703,) he left at his decease, in 1707, a dau. Jane, wife of Thomas Edmunds, Esq. of Worsborough, and a son and successor,

FRANCIS FOLJAMBE, Esq. of Aldwarke, who *m.* Mary, dau of Thomas Worsley, Esq. of Hovingham, and had (with other children, who *d. s. p.*) THOMAS, his heir; and ANNE, who *m.* in 1747-8, John Moore, Esq. of Kingston-upon-Hull, and *d.* in 1751, leaving an only child, FRANCIS-FERRAND MOORE, successor to his uncle. Mr. Foljambe *d.* 6 Dec. 1752, and was *s.* by his son,

THOMAS FOLJAMBE, Esq. of Aldwarke, *b.* 23 July, 1711, sheriff of Yorkshire, in 1755, who *m.* Sarah dau. of William Spencer, Esq. of Bramley Grange, but had no issue. His widow *m.* 2ndly, Edmund Hutchinson, of Bath Mr Foljambe *d.* 28 March 1758, and was *s.* by his nephew,

FRANCIS-FERRAND MOORE, Esq., M.P. for Yorkshire, and its high sheriff, 1787, who assumed the surname and arms of FOLJAMBE. He *m.* 1st, Mary-Arabella, one of the two daus. and co-heirs of John Thornhaugh, Esq of Osberton, Notts, (who assumed the name of Hewett,) by Arabella his wife, sister of Sir George Savile, Bart., M.P., and by her, who *d.* 28 Dec. 1790, had issue,

I. JOHN-SAVILE, of Aldwarke, *b.* 13 May, 1776, *m.* 30 Oct. 1798, Elizabeth, dau. of the Rev. James Willoughby, LL.B., rector of Guiseley, brother to Henry, 4th Lord Middleton, and dying *v. p.*, 14 Jan. 1805, left issue,
  1 GEORGE-SAVILE, successor to his grandfather.
  2 Francis-Thornhaugh, *b.* 11 Sept. 1804.
  1 Mary-Arabella, *m.* 30 Dec. 1824, to the Hon. and Rev. Leland Noel, son of the Baroness Barham.
  2 Emma, *m.* 11 Sept. 1832, to Charles Anderson, Esq., only son of Sir Charles Anderson, Bart.
II. Francis-Ferrand, *b.* 20 May, 1781, barrister-at-law, *d. unm.*
III. George, 18 Oct. 1783, major in the army, *d. unm.* March, 1820.
IV. Henry-Savile, *b.* 27 Jan. 1785.
I. Mary-Beresford, *m.* 30 June, 1818, to Francis-Offley Edmunds, Esq. of Worsborough.
II. Arabella, *m.* 15 May, 1823, to the Rev. John Robinson.

Mr. Foljambe *m.* 2ndly, 12 June 1792, Lady Mary-Arabella Lumley, dau of Richard, 4th Earl of Scarborough but her ladyship *d. s. p.* in 1817. Mr. Foljambe *d.* at Osberton in 1814, and was *s.* by his grandson, the present GEORGE-SAVILE FOLJAMBE, Esq. of Osberton and Aldwarke.

Arms—Sa., a bend between six escallops, or.
Crest—A jamb unarmed (excepting the spur), quarterly, or and sa.
Motto—Soyez ferme.
Seats—Osberton, Notts, and Aldwarke Hall, West Riding of Yorkshire.

FOLLIOTT OF STAPELEY HOUSE.

FOLLIOTT, THE REV. JAMES, M.A., of Stapeley House, co. Chester, J.P., *b.* 16 July, 1799; *m.* 1835, Mary-Anne-Elizabeth, dau. of the Rev. Enoch Clementson, and has a son,

JAMES, *b.* at Rome, 1836.

Lineage.—The family of Folliott came from Normandy with WILLIAM the Conqueror, and was, at a very early period of baronial rank. The branch now before us is stated to have migrated from Yorkshire to Londonderry in 1640. It has been settled in Cheshire about a century. WILLIAM FOLLIOTT, who left Yorkshire in 1640, *m.* Jane Thompson, and had, with two other sons and one dau., a 2nd son, ROBERT FOLLIOT, of Esq. Londonderry, who *m.* Eleanor Bradshaw, of Bradshaw Hall, co. Lancaster, and was father of WILLIAM FOLLIOTT, Esq., who *m.* 1st, Rosamond Greenstreet, and 2ndly Joan Every, by the latter of whom he had with a dau. Margaret, wife of Gen. Duval, four sons who all *d. s. p.* except the 2nd, JAMES FOLLIOTT, Esq , *b.* at Londonderry, who *m.* Mary Harwood, and had a son and successor,

WILLIAM-HARWOOD FOLLIOT, Esq. of the city of Chester and of Stapeley House, near Nantwich, *b.* 7, March, 1761, who *m.* 23 Jan. 1798, Catherine, only surviving child and heiress of John Burscoe, Esq. of Stapeley House, and had two sons and two daus., viz., 1. JAMES, present representative of the family; 2. George, *b.* 12 Jan. 1801, of Vicar's Cross near Chester, who *m.* Dorothea-Elizabeth, eldest dau. of W.-J. Moore, Esq. of Dublin, and by her (who *m.* 2ndly, 12 Sept. 1854, John-Fetherstonhaugh Lowry, Esq.) he left at his decease three daus; 1. Elizabeth, *d. unm.*; and 2. Catharine, *m.* to Joseph B. Miller, Esq.

Seat—Stapeley House, Nantwich.

FONNEREAU OF CHRIST CHURCH.

FONNEREAU, THOMAS-NEALE, Esq. of Christ Church Park, co. Suffolk, *b.* 21 March, 1841.

Lineage.—This family of FONNEREAU, originally of noble descent, and presumed to have been a branch of the Earls of Ivry, of Poictiers, in Normandy, was founded in England by

ZACHARIE FONNEREAU, *b.* 10 Feb. 1636, who fled from the city of La Rochelle at the revocation of the edict of Nantes, and settled in London. His sister, Madamoiselle Gabrielle Fonnereau, of the city of La Rochelle, m. Pierre André Perache u. of Saumur, and their dau. m. Aaron Crossley, Esq. His eldest son,

CLAUDE FONNEREAU, Esq. purchased, in 1732, the manors of Christ Church, and Wicksufford, in Suffolk, of Viscount Hereford, together with a large estate at Edmonton, and the borough of Sudbury, and the borough of Aldborough, for which three of his sons sat in several successive parliaments Claude was s. by his eldest son,

THOMAS FONNEREAU, Esq of Christ Church, at whose decease, without issue, the estates devolved upon his next brother,

THE REV. DR CLAUDIUS FONNEREAU, of Christ Church, b. in 1700, who m in 1725, Ann, daughter and co-heiress of the Rev. William Bunbury, rector of Catworth, in the co. of Huntingdon (grandson of Henry Bunbury, Esq. of Bunbury and Stanny, who suffered such great hardships for his unshaken loyalty to CHARLES I.) by Anne, his wife, dau. of Sir Villiers Chernocke, Bart of Hulcote. By this lady Dr. Fonnereau acquired some of the old Bunbury property in Cheshire and had twelve children, all of whom d. in youth, or without issue, excepting Ann, m. to Sir Booth Williams, Bart of Clapton, in Northamptonshire, and

REV WILLIAM FONNEREAU, of Christ Church, the eldest son and heir, who m. in 1758, Anne, only dau. and eventually, (her brothers dying s. p.) heiress of Sir Hutchins Williams, Bart. of Clapton, in Northamptonshire, of the Friars, Chichester, of North Hall, Herts, &c. and had issue,

- CLAUDE-WILLIAMS, in holy orders, rector of Clapton, in Northamptonshire, b. in 1761, who s. his mother at the Friars, at Chichester. He m., but had no issue.
- CHARLES-WILLIAM, who inherited Christ Church.
- Harriette-Louisa-Ann, m. to Frederick Cornwallis, lieut.-col. of the 33rd regiment, cousin to the first Marquess Cornwallis.
- Mary-Anne, d. unm.

Mr. Fonnereau, who inherited in 1804, d. in 1817, and was s. by his 2nd son,

REV. CHARLES-WILLIAM FONNEREAU, of Christ Church Park, b. in 1764, who m. in 1793, Harriette-Deborah, eldest dau. of Thomas Neale, Esq. of Freston Tower, and had, with a dau., Harriette, m. in 1827, to Charles Lillingston, Esq. of the Chantry, near Ipswich, a son, WILLIAM-CHARLES, his heir. Mr. Fonnereau, served some time in His Majesty's navy, during the first American war, and was lieutenant of the Conqueror under Admiral Rodney, in the action on the 12th April, 1782. He retired afterwards, and entered holy orders. He d. in 1840, and was s. by his son,

WILLIAM-CHARLES FONNEREAU, Esq. of Christ Church, Park, J.P, and D.L., b. in 1804, m. 1832, Katherine-Georgiana, dau. of John Cobbold, Esq. of Holywells, Ipswich, and d. July, 1855, having two daus, Emily-Cordelia, and Anne-Catherine, and one son, the present THOMAS-NEALE FONNEREAU, Esq., of Christ Church Park.

Arms—Quarterly: 1st and 4th, gu., three chevronels, arg., on a chief, az., a sun in splendour, or; 2nd and 3rd, quarterly, 1st and 4th, gu., a wolf issuing out of a rock, from the sinister side of the escutcheon, all arg., 2nd and 3rd, az., three boars' heads, couped, arg.
Crest—A sun in splendour, or.
Seat—Christ Church Park, near Ipswich.

FOOT OF CARRIGACUNNA CASTLE.

FOOT, HENRY-BALDWIN, Esq. of Carrigacunna Castle, co. Cork, J.P., m. Jane, eldest dau. of the late Rev. Edward-Mitchell Carleton, of Woodside, co. Cork, by Elizabeth his wife, only child and heiress of William Withers, Esq., and has issue,

- I. HENRY.
- II. Carleton.
- III. George-Carleton.
- I. Eliza, m. to Richard Spratt, Esq. son of the late Thomas E. Spratt, Esq. of Pencil Hill.
- II. Mary-Georgiana.
- III. Penelope-Jane, d. 1st Oct., 1852.
- IV. Henrietta-Victoria.
- V. Emily.
- VI. Lucinda-Harriette.

Lineage.—This is an ancient and respectable family,

GEORGE FOOT, Esq. of Millford, co. Cork, living temp. WILLIAM III., m. Deborah, dau. of Wade, of Athy, co. Kildare, and had issue,

GEORGE, of Millford, his heir.
Thomas, of Springfort, m. Miss Podder, and had issue; George, of Springfort, d. s. p.; Thomasine, d. unm.; Deborah, d. unm.; Anne, wife of James Foot, Esq., and Martha, wife of H. Spratt, Esq., of Ballybeg.
Wade, m. Olivia, dau. of Capt. Callcott Chambre, and had issue; 1. George, m. Miss Dunscombe, and had Wade and Richard. 2 Wade, m. Margaret, dau. of Edmund Nash, Esq., of Ballyteigue, co. Limerick, and had a son, Wade (who m. Anne, dau. of Michael Scanlan, Esq., and had issue.) 3 James, m. Miss Foot, and was father of Thomas Wade, of Baltidaniel (who m. Mary, dau. of Walter Atkin, Esq., of Atkinville, and had issue.)

The eldest son,

RICHARD FOOT, Esq. of Millford, m. Juliet, dau. of Cornelius O'Callaghan, Esq., and had issue, a son,

RICHARD FOOT, Esq. of Millford, co. Cork, Colonel of North Cork Militia, m. Oct., 1771, Mary, dau. of Henry Baldwin, Esq. of Curryvody, co. Cork, by Alice, his wife, sister of Sir Robert Warren, and by her, (who d. 1841) left issue,

- George, d. s. p. 1844
- HENRY-BALDWIN, now of Carrigacunna Castle.
- Edward, m. Ellen, dau. of Cornelius O'Callaghan, Esq. of Cork, and has issue.
- Barbara, m. to Thomas E. Spratt, Esq., of Pencil Hill.
- Mary, m. to Rev. Browning Drew, and d. 1822.

Mr. Foot d. 1820.

Arms—Or, a chev., and in the dexter chief quarter, a trefoil, sa.
Crest—A pelican in her nest feeding her young, ppr.
Motto—Virescit vulnere virtus.
Seat—Carrigacunna Castle, co. Cork.

FORBES OF BERELEIGH.

FORBES, GEORGE, Esq. of Bereleigh, co. Hants, b. 13 Sept. 1805; m. 16 March, 1843, Johanna-Agnes, dau. of John-Hopton Forbes, Esq., representative of FORBES *of Waterton*, co. Aberdeen. Mr. Forbes, a magistrate and deputy-lieut. for Middlesex and Westminster, is son of Sir Charles Forbes, Bart. of Newe and Edinglassie, by Elizabeth his wife, dau. of John Cotgrave, Esq., major E.I.C.S. (*See* BURKE'S *Peerage and Baronetage.*)

Arms—Quarterly; 1st and 4th, az., three bears' heads, couped arg., muzzled, gu.; 2nd and 3rd, az., three cinquefoils, arg.
Crest—A falcon, rising, ppr.
Motto—Altius ibunt qui ad summa nituntur.
Seat—Bereleigh, near Petersfield, Hants.

FORBES OF CULLODEN.

FORBES, ARTHUR, Esq. of Culloden House, co. Inverness, D.L., b. 25 Jan. 1819; s. his father, 28 Nov. 1840; m. 28 Aug. 1849, Louisa-Sarah-Georgiana. 2nd dau. of Alexander Warrand, Esq. of Warrandfield, and granddau. of the late Hugh-Robert Duff, Esq. of Muirtown, and has issue,

- I. DUNCAN, b. 21 March, 1851.
- I. Emily-Mary-Jane.

Lineage.—The founder of the Culloden family was DUNCAN FORBES, M.P., descended paternally from the family of Lord Forbes, through that of Tolquhon, and maternally from that of Keith, Earl Marischall, (as a narrative in the hand-writing, of the President's Father informs us.) He purchased the barony of Culloden from the Laird of Mackintosh in 1626. Duncan had two brothers, JOHN, whose son Malcolm became Marquis of Montilly, in France; and PATRICK, (commonly called Black Patrick, bailie of Inverurie,) from whom descended the family of Forbes, of Foveran. Duncan Forbes d. 14 Oct. 1654, aged eighty-two. By his marriage with Janet, eldest dau. of James Forbes, of Corsinday, (a family also descended from that of Lord Forbes,) Duncan had with two daus., Elizabeth, m. to William Baillie, of Dunean; and Anna m. 1st, to Evan Macpherson, of Cluny, and 2ndly, to Alexander Mackintosh, of Connedge, three sons; JOHN, his heir; James (Capt.), of Caithness; and Duncan (Capt.), of Assynt. The eldest son.

JOHN FORBES, of Culloden, M.P., m. 1643, Anna, eldest dau. of Alexander Dunbar, of Grange, by his first wife, Jean Campbell, dau. of Sir John Campbell, of Cawdor, (a family since raised to the Earldom of Cawdor,) and by the said Anna had six sons and two daus., viz, 1. DUNCAN, his heir; 2. David (Sir), of Newhall, one of the Judges of the Court of Session, an eminent lawyer and man of letters, an influential patron of Allan Ramsay 3. Thomas; 4. Alexander who went to New England; 5. Jonathan M.D., of Elgin; 6. John (Lieut.-Col.), of Pitnacrieffe; 1. Jean m. to Sir Robert Munro; and 2. Naomi m. to Robert Dunbar, of Burgie. John Forbes was provost of Inverness, (we believe M.P. for the county) and the friend and coadjutor of the Marquis of Argyll. He d. about the year, of the Revolution, 1688, and was s. by his eldest son,

Duncan Forbes of Culloden who m. 1668, Mary dau. of Sir Robert Innes of that ilk. By this lady he had two sons John, his heir b. about the year 1672 and Duncan, afterwards lord president and seven daus. The eldest Jean was m. to Sir Harry Innes of that ilk; the 2nd Anna, to Peter Forbes of Phyline, in Assynt; the 3rd Mary (contract dated 1698,) to Robert Urquhart of Burdsyards; the fourth, Margaret, (contract dated 1699,) to George Munro, of Newmore; the fifth, Isobell to Fraser of Achnagairn; the sixth, Naomi to Dr. Alexander Paterson of Inverness; and the seventh Grizell, (contract dated 21 April 1709) to David Ross, of Kindeace. Duncan Forbes latterly served in Parliament, for the co. of Nairn, and d. in 1704. He was s. by his eldest son.

John Forbes of Culloden M.P. for Inverness-shire. He m. 1699, Jean dau. of Sir Robert Gordon, of Gordonstone, by Margaret, his wife, eldest dau of William, Lord Forbes and dying without issue in the year 1734 was s. by the Lord Advocate of Scotland, his only brother,

The Right Honourable Duncan Forbes, fifth laird of Culloden, the celebrated Lord President of the Court of Session a man whose lofty character, and eminent, but unrequited services, at a crisis of great national difficulty and gloom, are recorded by a grateful country, in some of the fairest pages of her chequered history. Of this ever memorable man the poet Thomson thus speaks;

> "Thee, Forbes, too, whom every worth attends,
> As truth sincere, as weeping friendship kind;
> Thee truly generous, and in silence great,
> Thy country feels through her reviving arts,
> Plann'd by thy wisdom, by thy soul inform'd;
> And seldom has she known a friend like thee."

Duncan Forbes, who was b. at Bunchrew, one of the family seats near Inverness, 10 Nov. 1685, m. Mary, dau. of Hugh Rose, of the ancient family of Kilravock, in Nairnshire, and dying 10 Dec. 1747, was s. by his only child,

John Forbes, Esq. of Culloden, the intimate friend of Thomson, Armstrong, and other wits and literati of his day. He served with great distinction at the battles of Fontenoy and Culloden. At the former, his horse was shot under him. By economy and judicious management he succeeded in retrieving the fortunes of his family, which had received a severe and wellnigh fatal shock from the serious extent of his father the President's losses and advances in the cause of government during the rebellion of 1745-6, losses and advances never suitably acknowledged in the proper quarter, an ingratitude still the wonder and reproach of the age. He m. 1st, Jane, dau. of Sir Arthur Forbes, Bart. of Craigievar, by whom he had two sons, Duncan, who d. in youth, and Arthur his heir; and 2ndly, in 1772, Jane, dau. of Captain Forbes, of New, by whom, (who m. afterwards, Grant, of Drumminner, Aberdeenshire) he had no issue. John Forbes d. 26 Sept. 1772, and was s. by his only surviving son,

Arthur Forbes, Esq. of Culloden, b. 15 Feb. 1760, who m, 1st, in 1779, Sarah, dau and sole heir of Edward Stratton, Esq. of Kent, and of Ripley in Surrey. By this lady who d. at Culloden House, 19 Nov. 1798, aged 36, he had one son and one dau., viz.

Duncan-George, his heir.
Sarah-Louisa, m. in 1798, to Hugh-Robert Duff, Esq. of Muirtown, Inverness-shire, and d. in 1829, leaving issue.

Mr. Forbes m. 2ndly, in 1800, Mary-Wardlaw Cumming, daughter of Admiral Sir William Cumming, but by that lady (who m. afterwards, Joseph Egerton, Esq. of Gray's Inn) had no issue. He d. 26 May, 1803, and was s. by his only son,

Duncan-George Forbes, Esq. of Culloden House, b. 17 June, 1781, who m. 29 March, 1816, Sarah, only dau. of the late Rev. Joseph Walker, of Lanchester, Ash, and Satley, co. Durham, by Eliza, his wife, dau. of Edward Boys, Esq. of St Albans and by her, who d. 18 Jan. 1838, he had three sons, Arthur, now of Culloden; Duncan, an officer N. York Rifles, b. 7 May, 1821; and Joseph-William, b. 3 Nov. 1827, who m 21 Dec. 1849, Sarah, eldest dau. of D. Dallas, Esq., and has issue, Duncan-George, b. 5 Feb. 1851, Joseph-Harding, b. 23 Nov. 1854, and Sarah-Walker. Mr. Forbes d. 28 Nov. 1840.

Arms—Az., on a chev., between three bears' heads, couped, arg., muzzled, gu., as many unicorns' heads, erased, sa.
Crest—An eagle, displayed.
Motto—Salus per Christum, or Spernet humum.
Seats—Culloden House, Inverness-shire, and Ryefield Lodge, Ross-shire.

FORBES OF ECHT HOUSE.

Forbes, James, Esq. of Echt House, co. Aberdeen, J.P. and D.L., b. 22 April, 1775; m. 20 Sept. 1800, Jane, 3rd dau. of John Niven, Esq. of Othornton, and had issue,

I. William. II. John.
I. Rachael-Anne, m. to Patrick Watson Carnegy, Esq. of Lower, co. Forfar.
II, Elizabeth.
III. Jane, m. to Clements Lumsden, Esq., Advocate, of Aberdeen.

Lineage.—This is a cadet of the Watertoun branch of the family of Tolquhon.

The Rev. William Forbes, minister of Tarvis, co. Aberdeen, son of Sir John Forbes, of Watertoun, in the same shire, m. Janet, 3rd dau. of James Gregory, Esq., Professor of Mathematics, Edinburgh, and was father of

James Forbes, Esq., physician in Aberdeen, who m. Euphemia Row, and with a dau., Euphemia, and two younger sons, John and James, had an elder son,

William Forbes, Esq. of Echt House, who m. 7 July, 1774, Elizabeth, 3rd dau. of Dr. Thomas Arbuthnott physician of Montrose, 2nd brother of the 6th Viscount Arbuthnott, and had issue,

James, of Echt House.
William, of Hazlehead, co. Aberdeen, who assumed the additional surname of Robertson, m. Helen, 2nd dau. of James Hadden, Esq. of Persley, co. Aberdeen, and has issue, seven sons.
George, of Springhill, co. Aberdeen, m. Williamina, 2nd dau. of Capt. Walker, E. I. Co.'s Service, and has issue a son and four daus.
Margaret, m. to William Gibbon, Esq. of Viewfield, Aberdeen.
Euphemia, m. to George Garden, Esq. of Montreal.
Johanna.
Elizabeth, m. to Hugh Garden, Esq. of Manan, co. of Aberdeen.
Anne.

Arms—Quarterly: 1st and 4th, az., three bears' heads, couped, arg., muzzled, gu.; 2nd and 3rd, arg., three unicorns' heads, erased, sa.; over all, an escutcheon, arg., charged with a sword and key, saltier-ways, gu.,
Crest—An eagle, displayed, sa.
Motto—Virtuti inimica quies.
Seat—Echt House, co. Aberdeen.

FORBES OF KINGERLOCH.

Forbes, Charles-Henry, Esq. of Kingerloch, co. Argyle, J.P. and D.L., b. 23 July, 1809; m. 21 Oct. 1834, Charlotte-Murray McGregor, 4th dau. of James Buchanan, Esq. of Craigend Castle, by the Lady Janet Sinclair his wife, eldest dau. of James, 12th Earl of Caithness, and has issue,

I. James Alexander b. 8 Sept. 1836.
II. Charles-Henry-Buchanan, b. 22 Sept. 1847.
I. Janet-Sinclair. II. Ida-Constance.
III. Frances-Caithness-Mellish-Abney.
IV. Helen-Meta. V. Gertrude-Emily.
VI. Aurelie-Selina-James-Sinclair.

Lineage.—Alister-Cam Forbes youngest son of Sir John Forbes, Knt., 5th laird of Driminnir and brother of the 1st Lord Forbes, m. the dau. and heir of Sir Henry Cameron of Brux, and had three sons I. Arthur, d. s. p.; II. John, of Brux; and III. Duncan. This

Duncan Forbes, of Drummellachie and Brux, m. Elizabeth, dau. of Crichton of Couland, and by her had three sons, I. William, his heir; II. John, of Brux; and III. John. The eldest son and heir,

William Forbes, Esq. of Little Kildrummie also called of Towie m. Catherine, dau. of Alexander Seton, of Meldrum, nephew of Alexander 1st Earl of Huntly and by her had with four daus. three sons viz. I. Alexander, of Towie, continuator of that line; II. John, of whom we treat; III. William, of Ardmurdo, who had a charter from George, 2nd Earl of Huntly, in 1490. The 2nd son,

THE REV. JOHN FORBES, of Barns, m. Elizabeth, dau. and heir of George Leith, Esq. of Barns, and had four sons, I. James, who fell at Pinkie in 1547; II. WILLIAM; III. Duncan; IV. John. The 2nd son,

WILLIAM FORBES, Esq., had a charter of Barns, dated 5 Dec. 1550. He m. a dau. of Andrew Lundie, of Benholm, and had two sons, ALEXANDER, his heir, who continued the family of Barns, and

GEORGE FORBES, Esq. of Skellater, which estate he got from his father. This George d. 8 July, 1632, having had, by Euphemia Skene, his wife, two sons and two daus., WILLIAM, John, Janet, and Elspeth. The elder son,

WILLIAM FORBES, Esq. of Skellater, baptized 15 Oct. 1615, distinguished himself in Montrose's army having joined the Marquis of Huntly with the warriors of Strathdon. He m. four times. He d. in 1700, aged 84. The eldest son of his 2nd marriage (with the widow of Mc Gillivray, of Dunmaglass),

JOHN FORBES, of Inverarnan and Clencowy, was a commissioner of supply for Aberdeenshire in 1704. He was taken prisoner in 1715, and d. of his wounds in Carlisle prison, having had, by his first wife, three sons,

William, who m. 1st, 19 Aug. 1708, Catherine, dau. of Alexander Forbes, Esq. of Beldornie; and 2ndly, 29 Dec. 1709, Margaret, dau. of the Rev. Thomas Alexander, and had issue only by the latter.
ALEXANDER, of Inverarnan, who continued that line.
CHARLES, of whose line we treat.

The youngest son,

CHARLES FORBES, Esq., was killed at the storming of Ticonderago, in Canada, in 1758, under General Abercromby. He m. Isabel, dau. of Donaldson, of Kinardie, and was s. by his only son and heir,

JAMES FORBES, Esq., of Kingerloch, in Argyleshire, and of Hutton Hall, co. Essex, b. in 1756, who d. in 1829, aged 78, having been m. twice; by his first wife, he left two daus., Maria-Isabella m. to Gen. David Forbes, and Charlotte, m. to Gen. Sir Charles Bruce, K.C.B. He m. 2ndly, 24 Sept. 1799, Miss Sarah Richardson, and had by her, I. JAMES, his heir; II. CHARLES-HENRY, successor to his brother, and present proprietor; III. Alexander, Civil and Session Judge, E.I. Co.'s Civil Service, Bengal; IV. William, late Major 77th regt.; V. John, deceased; I. Eliza, deceased; II. Isabel, m. to Albert Watson, Esq. of the Ceylon Rifle Brigade, and is deceased; III. Emma, m. to the Rev. Arthur-Thomas Gregory of Buckromb, co. Banff; IV. Annie; V. Sarah, who m. Admiral Williams, and is deceased; and VI. Emily, m. to Arthur Ruxton, Esq. The eldest son and heir,

JAMES FORBES, Esq. of Kingerloch survived his father only twenty months and was s. by his next brother, the present CHARLES-HENRY FORBES, Esq. of Kingerloch.

Arms—Az., three bears' heads, couped, arg., muzzled, gu.
Crest—A stag's head, attired, ppr.
Motto—Solus inter plurimos, (allusive to these, the Gordon-Forbeses, being the only Forbeses who were not Covenanters.)
Seat—Kingerloch, co. Argyle.

FORBES OF TOLQUHON.

FORBES-LEITH, JAMES, Esq. of Whitehaugh, co. Aberdeen, b. in 1828; m. 18 Nov. 1851, Mary Keith, dau. of Anthony Adrian, 8th Earl of Kintore.

Lineage.—"The Forbeses of Tolquhon have always," says Mr. Forbes, of Culloden, "had the greatest respect, next to the chief and Pitsligo, because he was lord; not but that he was the elder brother; but the estate and dependants made tocher to be large and much looked upon." The numerous alliances with families of wealth and title correspond with this statement.

SIR JOHN FORBES (3rd son of Sir John Forbes of that ilk, justiciary and coroner of Aberdeenshire temp. ROBERT III., ancestor of the Lords Forbes) m. Marjorie, dau. of Henry Preston, Thane of Formartin, and thereby became Thane of Formartin and Laird of Tolquhon: by her he had three sons, I. JOHN (Sir), his heir; II. Duncan, of Ardgeighton; and III. David, called David Foddan. The eldest,

SIR JOHN FORBES, of Tolquhon, m. Anne Straton, dau. to the laird of Lawreston, and was direct ancestor of

SIR ALEXANDER FORBES, of Tolquhon (eldest son of Walter Forbes, of Tolquhon, by Jean his wife, dau. of Alexander Forbes, 1st Lord Pitsligo.) He was one of the three colonels for Aberdeenshire in the Scotch army of CHARLES II., and is said to have rendered particular service to that monarch at the battle of Worcester, and to have been an extraordinary agent in his subsequent escape from England, for which services he received the honour of knighthood in 1653-4. He was made a burgess of Glasgow in 1685 and of St. Andrew's the same year. The Laird of Tolquhon m. in 1649, Bathia Murray, dau. of the Laird of Blackbarony, and relict of Sir William Forbes, of Craigievar, but d. s. p. in 1701–2 when Tolquhon passed to his nephew, (son of his next brother, Thomas.)

WILLIAM FORBES, of Tolquhon, b. 1685-6, who was served heir to his father and to his uncle in 1704. He m. in 1706, Anne, dau. and heiress of JOHN LEITH, of Whitehaugh, by his wife, Elizabeth, dau. of William, 11th Lord Forbes, and had a dau., Henrietta, and two sons, WILLIAM, heir to his father; and JOHN who assumed the additional surname of Leith, of whom hereafter. William Forbes d. 5 April, 1728, and was buried in Westminster Abbey. His eldest son,

THE REV. WILLIAM FORBES, Vicar of Thornbury, in Gloucestershire, in 1748; d. there in Sept. 1761, when the representation of the family devolved upon his brother,

JOHN FORBES, who assumed, as heir to his mother, the additional surname of LEITH. He m. in 1743-4, Jean, eldest dau. of Theodore Morrison, of Bogny, by Katherine Maitland, his wife, and by her, who d. in 1767, had three sons, WILLIAM, his heir; THEODORE, successor to his brother; and John who d. young, of fever, 13 Feb. 1763. He d. at Edinburgh 26 Sept. 1781, and was s. by his eldest son,

WILLIAM FORBES-LEITH, Esq. of Whitehaugh b. 1748-9 who was educated at King's College, Aberdeen, and afterwards studied civil law. He d. unm. in 1806, and was s. by his brother,

DR. THEODORE FORBES-LEITH, of Whitehaugh, an eminent physician, who m. in 1776, Marie D'Arboine, a French lady, of ancient family, and (besides three daus., viz., Mary, Harriet, and Emily) had three sons, I. Theodore, b. in Sept. 1777, d. young; II. JAMES-JOHN, heir to his father; William, post-captain R.N., m. a French lady, and had three sons. Dr. Forbes-Leith who was settled at Greenwich, previous to succeeding to Whitehaugh, d. in Aug. 1819 of lock-jaw, consequent upon a fracture of the collar-bone. He was s. by his 2nd, but eldest surviving son,

JAMES-JOHN FORBES-LEITH Esq. of Whitehaugh, b. 1780; a lieut.-col. in the E. I. Co.'s. Service, who m. 28 Nov. 1827, Williamina-Helen, only child by Williamina Kerr, his wife, of the late Lieut.-Colonel James Stewart, of the 42nd Highlanders younger son of the late Charles Stewart, Esq. of Shambelly, co. Dumfries, and thus a descendant of one of the branches of the royal family of Scotland. Col. Forbes-Leith left issue,

JAMES, present representative.
William, b. 9 April, 1833.
Thomas-Augustus, b. 25 Aug., 1834.
Henry-Stewart, b. 2 March, 1836.
Charles-Edward, b. 18 Oct. 1839.
Williamina-Stewart.
Helen-Maria.
Adelaide-Isabella.

Arms—Quarterly: 1st, az., three bears' heads, couped, arg., muzzled, gu., for FORBES; 2nd and 3rd, arg., five lozenges, conjoined, in fesse, sa., for LEITH quartering besides STEWART and PRESTON.
Crests—1st, a stag's head, attired with tynes, ppr., for FORBES; a dove, with an olive branch in its mouth, ppr.
Supporters—Two greyhounds, ppr., collared, gu.
Mottoes—Under the arms, Salus per Christum; above the Leith crest, Fidus ad extremum.
Seat—Whitehaugh, Aberdeenshire.

FORBES OF WINKFIELD PLACE.

FORBES, JOHN, Esq. of Winkfield Place, co. Berks, J.P. and D.L., post captain R.N., b. in 1780; m. 22 July, 1814, Lætitia-Mary, dau. of the late George White, Esq. of Newington House, co. Oxford, and the Isle of Thanet, Kent, and has had issue,

I. JAMES-WILLIAM, b. 7 Nov. 1815, Lieut. 13th Regt. d. on his return from India, 29 Jan. 1839, unm.
II. JOHN-GEORGE, b. 31 Jan. 1817, of Trinity College, Oxon, and of Lincoln's Inn, barrister-at-law.
III. Frederick-Edwyn, b. 3 April, 1819, commander R.N., d. unm. 23 March, 1852.
IV. George-Harrison-Anne, captain roy. art., b. 7 June, 1823.
I. Marianne, m. 1854, to the Rev Charles Willett, son of John Saltren Willett, Esq. of Petticombe, Devon.
II. Maria, m. 1851, to George Latham Browne, Esq., barrister-at-law.
III. Lætitia-Margaret, m. 1855, to John Willett, Esq., capt. roy. art.

Captain Forbes served with distinction in several actions, St. Lucia, the Nile, Genoa, Naples, &c., and was first lieutenant of the Royal George at the passage of the Dardanelles, under Sir John Duckworth.

Lineage.—George Forbes, Esq. of Colquhany, only son of Forbes of Colquhany, Strathdon, co. Aberdeen, m. Miss Gordon, and had, with a dau. m. to Alexander Innes, Esq., two sons, I. William, his heir; and II. Robert, M.D., of Banff, who m. Anne Sutherland, dau. of a cadet of the house of Sutherland, and had a son, Robert, a merchant of London, who m. his cousin, Janet Forbes, and had, with six daus., one son, Robert. The elder son and heir,

William Forbes, of Aberdeen, who m. Janet, dau. of the Rev. William Dyce, minister of Behelvie, co. Aberdeen, by Katherine his wife, dau. of Professor Anderson, of King's College, Aberdeen, and had, (with four daus., of whom the eldest m. John Abercrombie, Provost of Aberdeen; the second d. unm.; the third m. James Allardyce, brother of Alexander Allardyce, Esq. of Dunottar, M.P., and the fourth d. unm.) two sons, viz.,

George, of whom presently.
William, of Callander, co. Stirling, m. Agnes Chalmers, and had (with three daus., one of whom m. Edward-Lloyd Gatacre, Esq. of Gatacre, co. Salop) two sons, William, M.P. for Stirlingshire, b. 1806, who m. Lady Louisa Charteris, dau. of the Earl of Wemyss, and d. 10 Feb. 1855, leaving issue; and John, capt. Coldstream guards.
David, merchant in London, d. s. p.
Robert, of Castleton, co. Aberdeen, m. Elizabeth Chalmers, and left issue five sons and two daus.

The eldest son,

George Forbes, merchant in Aberdeen, m. about 1776, Jane, dau. of Lumsden of Alford and Cromar, co. Aberdeen, and had issue,

William, M.D. of the island of Jamaica, who d. leaving, by Miss Reid, of Jamaica, his wife, a dau., Ellen.
David, capt. E. I. Co.'s Service, made Governor of Ternate, for his gallant services at the capture of that island, d. unm.
John, of Winkfield Place, present representative.
George, d. unm. at Dominica.
James, capt. E. I. Co's service, d. unm.
Janet, m. to her cousin, Robert Forbes, Esq., merchant of London, and has issue.
Margaret, m. to the Rev. William Urquhart, minister of Touch, co. Aberdeen, d. leaving a dau.

Arms—Az., three bears' heads, couped, arg., muzzled, gu.
Seat—Winkfield Place, near Windsor.

FORBES OF CALLENDER.

See Forbes of Winkfield Place.

FORBES OF BALGOWNIE.

Forbes, Henry-David, Esq. of Balgownie, co. Aberdeen, J.P. and D.L., b. 12 Nov. 1790; m. 27 May, 1816, Margaret Fraser (deceased), eldest dau. and heiress of Alexander Fraser, Esq. of Fraserfield, and by her has had issue,

I. Duncan, m. Janet Dyce, only dau. of the late Robert Forbes, Esq. of Castletown.
II. Alexander, d. in infancy.
III. Henry-Erskine, Lieut. in the 1st Regt. Bombay Light Cavalry, (Lancers).
I. Mary-Isabella, d. unm.
II. Catherine-Anne, d. unm.
III. Margaret-Moir, m. to Alexander-Kinloch Forbes, youngest son of the late John Forbes Mitchell, member of the Hon. E. I. Co.'s Service, in the Presidency of Bombay.
IV. Rachel-Louisa, m. to Major Francis-George Urquhart, 1st (or Royal,) Regt. of Infantry, younger son of the late John Urquhart, of Craigston, and has issue.
V. Emmeline, m. to Rev. John-Gabriel Ryde, M.A., St. John's College, Oxon, Incumbent of St. Andrew's Episcopal Church, Aberdeen.
VI. Georgiana-Mary-Agnew

Lineage.—This is a branch of the family of Forbes-Mitchell, *of Thainston*, descending through the Forbeses, Baronets of Craigievar, and the Forbeses, lairds of Corse, from the noble family of Forbes, Lord Forbes. The present H. D. Forbes, Esq. of Balgonie, is the 6th son of Duncan Forbes-Mitchell, Esq. of Thainston, by his wife Katherine-Anne Fraser,

The estate of Balgownie, styled in the title-deeds, "antiqua baronia de Balgownie," which is near the Old Bridge of Don (or of Balgownie), built, as is usually supposed, by Henry le Chen, bishop of Aberdeen, during the reign of King Robert the Bruce, belonged to a younger branch of the family of Fraser Lord Saltoun, and was then known as "Fraserfield" On its passing into the possession of the present proprietor, however, at his marriage with the heiress of the Frasers, the estate recovered its ancient name of "Balgownie."

Arms—Az., a cross patée-fitchée, or, between three bears' heads, couped, arg., muzzled, gu.
Crest—A cock, ppr.
Motto—Watch.
Seat—Balgonie, co. Aberdeen.

Family of Fraser of Fraserfield.

For lineage, *vide* Burke's *Peerage and Baronetage*, art. Lord Saltoun.

Arms—Those of Fraser, *Lord Saltoun*, all within a bordure az., charged with eight garbs, or.

FORD OF ELLELL HALL.

Ford, William, Esq. of Ellell Hall, co. Lancaster, J.P. and D.L., b. 17 Dec. 1816; m. 8 June, 1852, Louisa, eldest dau. of William Ross, Esq. of Pendleton.

Lineage.—The family of Ford is one of very ancient settlement in Staffordshire and Cheshire. So far back as the 12th century they were established at Ford Green, in Norton-le-Moors. In the time of Henry VII., Hugh Ford, sen. (son of John, grandson of William, and great-grandson of Richard del Forde, *temp.* Richard II.), settled his estate on his grandson, Hugh Ford, son of Richard, who had died v. p. Hugh, the younger, was father of William Ford, living in 1521, whose son,

Hugh Ford, of Forde Green, co. Stafford, living in 1538 and 1564, was s. by his son, William Forde, of Forde Green, living in 1604, who m. in 1569, Alice, dau. of Richard Harblutt, of the Loyde, co. Stafford, and had a son and successor, Hugh Forde, of Forde Green who m. Margery, dau. of Michael Dickinson, of Fooker, co. Stafford, and was father of William Forde, of Forde Green, living in 1679, who m. Ellen, dau. of James Rowley, and had three sons and one dau., viz., 1 Hugh, of Forde Green, ancestor of Forde *of Ford Green*; 2 William, of Eccleshall, in holy orders, who m. and had five sons, William, Hugh, Andrew, Thomas, and James; 3 Andrew, ancestor of the Fords *of Abbeyfield*; 1 Sarah, who m. Michael Johnson, of Lichfield, and was mother of Samuel Johnson, LL.D., b. 18 Sept. 1709. The eldest son,

Hugh Forde, Esq., m. 1683, Ellen, dau. of John Mellor, Esq. of Alsop-in-the-Dale, and had a son and successor,

Josiah Forde, Esq. of the Heath House and Forde Green, b. 1694, who left, by Anne his wife, a son,

Isaac Ford, Esq., b. 1728; who m. Elizabeth, dau. of T.-H. Rawlinson, Esq. of Lancaster, and had (with two daus., Anne, m. to Robert Barclay, Esq. of Lombard-street, banker; and Mary, d. in infancy) a son,

John Ford, Esq. of Lancaster and of Morecombe Lodge, who m. 1st, Mary, eldest dau. of John Chorley, Esq. of Red Hasles, and by her had a son, John, his heir. He m. 2ndly, 1800, Mary, eldest dau. of John Lawson, of Highfield, and had issue (*see* Ford *of Enfield Old Park*). Mr. Ford d. May, 1833, and was s. by his son,

John Ford, Esq. of Ellell Hall, co. Lancaster, who m. in 1812, Elizabeth, dau. of the late John Lawson, Esq. of Lancaster, and d. March, 1819, having had (with two daus., Mary-Elizabeth, m. to her cousin, Francis Walker, Esq. of Southgate, youngest son of the late John Walker, Esq. of Arno's Grove; and Sarah Walker, m. to Charles Walker, Esq. of New Lanark) three sons, viz., Abraham-Rawlinson, of Ellell Hall, who d. s. p. 5 March, 1849, aged 36; Robert, d. s. p. 28 July, 1848; and William, now of Ellell Hall.

Arms—Az., three lions, rampant, or.
Crest—A lion, rampant, bearing a coronet.
Motto—Excitat.
Seat—Ellell Hall, co. Lancaster.

FORD OF ENFIELD OLD PARK.

Ford, Edward, Esq. of Enfield Old Park, co. Middlesex, b. 1 Dec. 1813; m. Elizabeth-Hill-Winchester, only child of the Rev. T.-W. Lewis, and has issue,

I. John-Walker, b. 12 Sept. 1838.
II. Charles-Winchester, b. 4 Nov. 1840.
III. Alfred-Lawson, b. 18 Nov. 1843.
I. Mary-Elizabeth.

Lineage.—This is a branch of the ancient family of Ford of Ford Green.

JOHN FORD, Esq. of Lancaster and of Morecombe Lodge, who *d.* May, 1833, left by Mary his 2nd wife, dau. of John Lawson, Esq., a dau., Elizabeth-Sarah, and four sons, viz., Hutton-Rawlinson, *b.* 28 Dec. 1804; Charles-Dilworth, *b.* 8 Aug. 1806; Robert-Lawson, *b.* 8 Feb. 1809, *m.* Hannah, dau. of T.-B. Pease, Esq.; and EDWARD, now of Enfield Old Park.

Arms, Crest, and *Motto*—See preceding family.
Seat—Enfield Old Park, Middlesex.

FORD OF ABBEYFIELD.

FORD, CHARLES-INGRAM, Esq. of Abbeyfield, co. Chester, J.P. and D.L., *b.* 18 July, 1797; *m.* 6 Oct. 1841, Fanny, dau. of John Holland, Esq., and has issue,

I. CHARLES, *b.* 23 Aug. 1842.
II. John-Hugh, *b.* 16 Nov. 1843.
III. Arthur-Randle, *b.* 28 Aug. 1845.

Lineage.—ANDREW FORDE, of Crewe, co. Chester, (3rd son of William Forde, of Forde Green, co. Stafford, by Ellen Rowley his wife), *m.* Hannah, dau. of John Parratt, of the same place; and dying in 1719, left two sons, JOHN and Hugh. The elder,

JOHN FORD, Esq. of Eaton, co. Chester, *m.* Anne, dau. and eventual co-heir of Charles Everard, Esq. of Somerford, Booths; and dying in 1757, aged 78, left two sons, John Ford, Esq. of the Middle Temple, barrister-at-law, who *d. s. p.* 1760, and

CHARLES FORD, Esq. of Eaton, co. Chester, and Claremont, co. Lancaster, who *m.* 1767, Anne, only child of Thomas Johnson, Esq. of Tyldesley, by Anne his 1st wife, dau. of William Sudall, Esq.; and dying 5 Jan. 1789, left (with three daus., Anne, Harriett, and Susan) a son,

JOHN FORD, Esq. of Abbeyfield, co. Chester, *b.* 23 Feb. 1768; who *m.* 8 Oct. 1796, Elizabeth, eldest dau. of Francis Ingram, Esq. of Wakefield, and by her (who *d.* 22 July, 1848), had issue,

CHARLES-INGRAM, now of Abbeyfield.
Francis-Johnson, *b.* 21 Aug. 1798; *m.* Caroline, 3rd dau. of W. Minshull, Esq. of Kentish Town, and has issue.
Frederick, in holy orders; *b.* 20 June, 1801; *m.* Anne Twemlow, of Lawton, and has issue.
Johnson, major 43rd regiment; *b.* 7 Aug. 1810; *d.* 1851.
Henry, *b.* 8 Dec. 1814; *m.* Miss Julia Marriott, of Ford Bank, and has issue.
Emily, *d. unm.*
Eleanor, *m.* to the Rev. William Hayes.

Mr Ford *d.* 14 April, 1839.

Arms—Per fesse, or and erm., a lion, rampant, az.
Crest—A lion's head, erased, az.
Seat—Abbeyfield, Sandbach, co. Chester.

FORDE OF SEAFORDE.

FORDE, WILLIAM-BROWNLOW, Esq. of Seaforde, co. Down, *b.* 5 Nov. 1823, lieut.-col. royal South Downshire militia, J.P. and D.L., high-sheriff 1858; *m.* 25 Oct. 1855, Adelaide, dau. of the late General the Hon. Robert Meade, 2nd son of the 1st Earl of Clanwilliam.

Lineage.—NICHOLAS FORDE, of Coolgreany, co. Wexford, originally of Welsh derivation, *d.* in 1605, leaving by his wife, Catherine White, five sons, of whom the 2nd,

MATHEW FORDE, of Dublin, M.P., *s.* to the estates. He *d.* before the year 1657, leaving his only son,

NICHOLAS FORDE, of Killyleagh, co. Down, *m.* Elizabeth, dau of Sir Adam Loftus, of Rathfarnham, Knt., and left an only son,

MATHEW FORDE, of Coolgreany, M P for the co. of Wexford, *m.* Margaret, dau. of Sir George Hamilton, Bart. (the 4th son of James, 1st Earl of Abercorn), by Mary Bulter his wife, dau. of Thomas, Lord Thurles, and sister of James, 1st Duke of Ormond. Mr. Forde left at his decease in 1709 (with two daus., the eldest of whom, Lucy, *m.* in 1695, Sir Laurence Esmonde, Bart. of Ballynester; and the younger, Jane, *m.* John Walsh, of Shanganah), an only son,

MATHEW FORDE, Esq. of Seaforde, M.P for Downpatrick, *m.* in 1698, Anne, dau. of William Brownlow, of Lurgan, and had, MATHEW, his heir; Francis, of Johnstown, co. Meath, col. in the army, distinguished in Lord Clive's wars in India, *m.* in 1728, Mrs. Martha George, and left issue; Arthur, rector of Lurgan, *d.* in 1767, leaving issue; Jane, *m.* to John Baillie, of Inishargie; Letitia, *m.* to Mr. Nash; and Margaret, *d. unm.* in 1773. Mr. Forde *d.* in 1729, and was *s.* by his eldest son,

MATHEW FORDE, Esq. of Seaforde and Coolgreany, M P. for Bangor. He *m.* in 1724, Christian, dau. of John Graham, Esq. of Platten, co. Meath, and had issue,

MATHEW, his successor.
John, a major in the army, *m.* in 1761, Isabella, relict of George Mathew, of Thomastown, co. Tipperary, dau. of William Brownlow, of Lurgan, by Lady Elizabeth his wife, dau. of James Hamilton, 6th Earl of Abercorn; and *d.* without issue.
William. Edward.
Arthur, a military officer. George, *d.* abroad.
Pierce, barrister-at-law.
Charity, *m.* to Francis Price, of Saintfield, co. Down.
Anne, *m.* to John Gilmore, of Dublin.
Elizabeth, *m.* to James, son of Arthur Forde, rector of Lurgan.

Mr. Forde *m.* 2ndly, Jane, relict of Sir Timothy Allen; and *d.* in 1780, when he was *s.* by his eldest son,

MATHEW FORD, Esq. of Seaforde and Coolgreany, M P. for Downpatrick, *m.* in 1750, Elizabeth, dau. of Thomas Knox, of Dungannon, and sister of Thomas, 1st Viscount Northland, and had issue,

MATHEW, his heir.
Anne, who *d. unm.*
Elizabeth, *m.* in 1785, to Thomas Douglas, Esq. of Grace Hall, co. Down; and *d.* in 1840.
Jane, *m.* in 1796, to John-Christopher Beauman, of Hyde Park, co. Wexford.
Charity, *m.* in 1795, to William Brownlow, of Lurgan, M.P. for the co. of Armagh; and *d.* in 1843.

Mr. Forde *d* in 1796, and was *s* by his only son,

MATHEW FORDE, Esq. of Seaforde and Coolgreany, high-sheriff for the co. of Down in 1808, *m.* in 1782, Catherine, eldest dau. of the Rt. Hon. William Brownlow, of Lurgan, M.P. for the co. of Armagh, and by her (who *d.* in 1808) had issue,

MATTHEW, his heir.
William-Brownlow, successor to his brother.
Thomas-Arthur, assistant-barrister of the co. of Down and co. of Roscommon, *m.* in 1814, Louisa, 10th dau. of Michael Head, of Derry, co. Tipperary; and *d.* in April, 1840, having had issue, Thomas-Head, *d. s. p.*; Matthew-Bligh; Henry-Charles; John-Vesey; Arthur-Knox, *d. s. p.*; Francis-Clayton-Octavus; Frederick-Augustus Prittie, *d. s. p.*; Catherine-Margaret; Frances-Mary-Anne, *m.* 1853, to Thos. Blacker, Esq.
Arthur, who *m.* Selina, dau of William Blundell; and *d.* in India, in 1828, leaving Mathew-William, and Arthur.
Francis-Charles, late capt. in the Royal Scots Greys, *m.* Letitia-Jane, youngest dau. of O. Jones, Esq. of Woodhall, co. Norfolk.
Anne, *m.* 1st, in 1816, Francis Hoey, of Dunganstown, co. Wicklow; who *d.* in 1818; and 2ndly, in 1825, to Captain George King, R.N.
Isabella-Jane-Octavia, *m.* in 1821, Clayton Bayley, Esq. of Norelands, co. Kilkenny.

Mr. Forde *m.* 2ndly, in 1811, Sophia, dau. of the Very Rev. Stewart Blacker, of Carrick, dean of Leighlin. but by her (who *m.* 2ndly, in 1818, William-Stewart Hamilton, of Brown Hall, and *d.* in 1829) he had no issue. He *d.* in 1812, and was *s.* by his eldest son,

MATHEW FORDE, Esq. of Seaforde and Coolgreany, *b.* in 1785; J.P. and D.L for co. Down, colonel of the Royal North Downshire militia, who served as high-sheriff for that co. in 1820, and represented it in parliament from 1821 to 1826. Colonel Forde *m.* 1st, in 1814, Mary-Anne, only child of Francis Savage, Esq. of Hollymount and Ardkeen, co. Down; and 2ndly, in 1829, Lady Harriet Savage, 3rd dau of Henry-Thomas Butler, 2nd Earl of Carrick, and widow of Francis Savage, Esq , but had no issue. He *d.* 5 Aug 1837, and was *s.* by his brother,

THE REV. WILLIAM-BROWNLOW FORDE, of Seaforde, *b.* 1786; *m.* 1812, Theodosia, dau. of Thomas Douglas, Esq. of Grace Hall, and had issue,

I. MATTHEW-THOMAS, *b.* 17 May, 1816; an officer in the army, high-sheriff of Downshire 1839; *d.* 1847.
II. WILLIAM-BROWNLOW, present representative.
III. Francis-Savage, *d.* 6 July, 1850.
IV. Charles-Arthur, *b.* 24 June, 1828; capt. Royal South Down militia.
V. Thomas-Douglass, capt. 46th regt., *b.* 19 Dec. 1830.
I. Selina-Charity. II. Elizabeth-Theodosia-Catherine.
III. Harriette-Anna.

Mr. Forde *d.* 11 March, 1856.

Arms—Az., two flaunches, or, charged with three roses in fesse, the centre rose gold, the two exterior on the (flaunches) gu., between two martlets, of the second.
Crest—A martlet, or.
Motto—Incorrupta fides nudaque veritas.
Seat—Seaforde, Devonshire.

DINGWALL-FORDYCE OF CULSH AND BRUCKLAY CASTLE.

DINGWALL-FORDYCE, ALEXANDER, Esq. of Brucklay Castle, co. Aberdeen, comm. R.N., *b.* 4 March, 1800; *m.* 14 July, 1835, Barbara, 5th dau. of James Thom, Esq. of Halifax, Nova Scotia, and has issue,

I. WILLIAM. } Twins, *b.* 31 March, 1836.
I. JAMES. }
II. Alexander, *b.* 5 Oct. 1838.
III. Arthur, *b.* 14 Jan. 1845.
I. Rachel. II. Barbara-Anne.
III. Jessy. IV. Sophia.

Mr. Dingwall-Fordyce, a deputy-lieut. for co. Aberdeen, *s.* his brother 30 Dec. 1843. He represented the city of Aberdeen in parliament from 1847 to 1852.

Lineage.—This family derives its descent on the side of the Dingwalls, from the Highland Clan of that name in Ross-shire, of whom the lairds of Kildun and Strabroke, were chief. Some of these came to Buchan, in Aberdeenshire, about the beginning of the 16th century, and settled there, apparently with the view of escaping from the interminable feuds of their own part of the country. The first of these, of whom there are authentic accounts, as ancestors of the families of Culsh and Brucklay, is WILLIAM DINGWALL, of Sealscrook, Parish of Monquhitter, co. of Aberdeen, who was *b.* about 1590. He *m.* Barbara Barclay and by her had three sons; Arthur; George; and John. The eldest of these, and the only one who left issue, was,

ARTHUR DINGWALL, who was *b.* about 1620, and in 1642, *m.* Lucres, dau. of John Irvine, of Brucklay, one of the old and well known family of Irvine, of Drum, Aberdeenshire. This ARTHUR DINGWALL (1st of Brucklay,) died in 1707, and his wife Lucres Irvine, in 1717. They had four sons and three daus., viz.

I. WILLIAM. II. George.
III. Arthur, of Brownhill, afterwards alluded to.
IV. Adam.
I. Barbara. II. Isobell. III. Helen.

The eldest son,

WILLIAM DINGWALL, Esq. of Brucklay, *b.* in 1643, *d.* in 1733, having *m.* in 1711, Anna, dau. of John Gordon, of Nethermuir. They had six sons and three daus., viz.,

I. George. II. WILLIAM. III. Alexander.
IV. JOHN. V. Arthur. VI. Patrick.
I. Anne.
II. Lucretia, married her cousin-german, William Dingwall, as afterwards alluded to.

Of these,

WILLIAM DINGWALL, Surgeon in the army, *s.* to Brucklay, on his father's death, in 1733. He was *b.* in 1721, and *d.* in 1801, having never been married. He was *s.* by his brother,

JOHN DINGWALL, Jeweller, in St. James's Street, London, who was *b.* in 1724, and *d.* in 1812, having *m.* Patience, dau. of Mr. Huddart, of London and sister to the Lady of Sir Richard Hotham, of Merton, Surrey, by whom he had no issue. A few years before his death, viz., in 1807, he entailed his lands of Brucklay, Artamford, &c., on his grand-nephew, JOHN DINGWALL, and a series of heirs, his personal property, amounting to a very large sum being vested in trustees, for the purchase of other lands in England or Scotland, to be entailed on the same series.

These consisted in the first place, of the descendants of his sister Lucretia, and her husband William Dingwall, writer in Edinburgh, who was also her cousin-german, being the 3rd son of Arthur Dingwall of Brownhill; and in the second place, of the descendants of the same William Dingwall by his second marriage in 1744, with Jean Fordyce, of Culsh, heiress of entail of her brother William Fordyce, of Culsh, and dau. of John Fordyce, of Gask and Culsh, by Lillias, dau. of William Lindsay, of Culsh, one of the Dowhill branch of the noble House of Balcarras. *See Lives of the Lindsays*, by Lord Lindsay, Vol. 1, Page 310.

By the death without issue, in 1840, of John Duff Dingwall, (who *s.* to Brucklay in 1833, on the death of his father John, the first institute of entail,) the first series of heirs, descendants of Lucretia Dingwall, became extinct, upon which,

ARTHUR DINGWALL FORDYCE, Esq. of Culsh, the representative of the second series of heirs, descendants of William Dingwall by his second marriage with Jean Fordyce of Culsh, was called to the succession. He was *b.* in 1797, *m.* in 1822, his cousin Jessy, dau. of Captain Arthur Dingwall Fordyce, of the Bengal Engineers, *s.* to Culsh, on the death of his grandfather (Commissary of Aberdeen) in 1834, and to Brucklay, as already noticed, in 1840. He *d. s. p.* 30 Dec. 1843, and was *s.* by his brother the present proprietor. This gentleman's grandfather,

ARTHUR DINGWALL FORDYCE, Esq. of Culsh, L.L.D., advocate in Aberdeen, and last judge of the Commissary or Consistorial Court there, was son of William Dingwall and Jean Fordyce of Culsh. He was *b.* 8 Dec. 1745, *m.* 14 June, 1770, Janet, sixth dau. of James Morrison, of Elsick, provost of Aberdeen, and by her, (who *d.* 15 July, 1831,) had issue,

I. William Dingwall Fordyce the younger, of Culsh, *m.* 1 Sept. 1796, Margaret, dau. and heiress of William Ritchie, Esq. of Techmuiry, co. Aberdeen, and *d. v. p.* 1 March, 1831, leaving by this lady (who survived him till 1844), four sons and two daus.
1 ARTHUR, who *s.* his grandfather.
2 William, *d. unm.* 18 April, 1839.
3 ALEXANDER, successor to his brother Arthur, and present representative.
4 George, Advocate-Depute, Edinburgh, *m.* in 1836, Sophia, 4th dau. of James Thom, Esq., sometime of Halifax, Nova Scotia.
1. Jessy.
2 Margaret, *m.* in 1835, to the Rev. Alexander Foote, one of the Ministers of Brechin, and *d.* in 1842.

Mr. Commissary Dingwall Fordyce, *d.* 21 April, 1834, and was *s.* by his eldest grandson, Arthur, as already mentioned,

Arms—Quarterly: 1st and 4th, az., three bears' heads couped, arg., muzzled, gu., for FORDYCE. 2nd, az., a buck's head, cabossed between three mullets voided, arg., for DINGWALL. 3rd, gu., a fesse chequy, arg. and az., in chief a mullet of the second, and the base wavy of the third, all within a bordure engrailed, or, for LINDSAY.
Crests—1st, an eagle, displayed. 2nd, a stag, couchant.
Mottoes—Altius ibunt qui ad summa nituntur: and, In arduis fortis.
Seat—Brucklay Castle, co. Aberdeen.

FORSTER OF LYSWAYS HALL.

FORSTER, CHARLES, Esq. of Lysways Hall, co. Stafford, M.P. for Walsall, *s.* his father, Charles-Smith Forster, Esq., 17 Nov. 1850; *m.* Aug. 1840, Frances, dau. of John Surtees, Esq. of Durham, and of Château La Colinois, in Brittany, cousin of the Earl of Eldon, and has three sons,

I. CHARLES, *b.* 1841.
II. John-Henry, *b.* 1843.
III. Villiers-Francis, *b.* 1850.

Lineage.—Until a century back, the Forsters were settled in Worcestershire.

WILLIAM FORSTER, of Birtsmorton, in that county, *m.* Margaret Smith, a descendant and co-representative of Captain John Smith, who in 1603 was in the service of Sigismond, Duke of Transylvania, from whom he received the grant of a coat of arms, "vert, a chevron gules, between three Turks heads couped," in reward for his gallantry in overcoming and cutting off the heads of three Turks on the field of battle; and which coat is confirmed to him by a record in the College of Arms. William left one son,

CHARLES FOSTER, Esq. who *d.* at Walsall, in Staffordshire, 28 June, 1815, leaving issue,

CHARLES-SMITH, his heir.
John, of Hanch Hall, co. Stafford.

The elder son,

CHARLES SMITH FOSTER, Esq. of Lysways Hall, co. Stafford, J.P., and D.L., M.P. for Walsall, served as high sheriff, 1845. He left at his decease, one son, CHARLES, now of Lysways Hall; and one dau., Ellen Catherine, *m.* to Richard Dyott, Esq. of Freeford.

Arms—Sa., on a chev., arg., between three pheons, or, as many escallops of the field.
Crest—A stag's head, erased, arg., attired, or, gorged with a collar and line of the last.
Motto—Sit fors ter felix.
Seat—Lysways Hall, Lichfield.

FORTEATH OF NEWTON.

FORTEATH, GEORGE-ALEXANDER, Esq. of Newton House, co. Elgin, a magistrate for that shire, *b.* 10 Oct. 1819; *s.* his father in 1850.

Lineage.—The late ALEXANDER FORTEATH, Esq. of Newton, a Deputy-Lieutenant for Elginshire, *m.* in 1814,

Clementina, dau. of William Robertson, Esq. of the co. Elgin, and *d.* in 1850, having had issue,

I. George-Alexander, his heir.
II. Alexander, in the army. III. James Duff.
IV. Charles-Cruickshank.
V. Frederick-Prescote, in the army.
I. Jane-Robertson.

Arms—Gu., on a chevron, or, between three bucks trippant, ppr., as many boars' heads, sa., a chief, of the second, charged with a griffin of the third.
Crest—A buck's head, erased, ppr.
Motto—Tam animo quam mente sublimis.
Seats—Newton House, co. Elgin, N.B.

FORTESCUE OF BUCKLAND FILLEIGH.

Inglett-Fortescue, John-Dicker, Esq. of Buckland Filleigh, co. Devon, J.P. and D.L., *b.* 3 Aug. 1789, M.A.

Lineage.—William Fortescue, Esq. of Buckland Filleigh, younger brother of John Fortescue, Esq., ancestor of the Earls Fortescue, *m.* Maud, dau. and heir of John Atkins, Esq. of Milton Abbot, in Devonshire, and had three sons, John, Edward, and James, and two daus., Margaret and Jaquetta, the latter *m.* to William Dennis, Esq. of Southcorne, Devon. The eldest son,

John Fortescue, Esq. of Buckland Filleigh, *m.* Christian, dau. of John Arscott, of Holdsworthy, and was grandfather of

John Fortescue, Esq. of Buckland Filleigh, *m.* 1st, Anne, dau. of Walter Porter, Esq. Thetford, in Norfolk, and widow of D. Thorn, Esq., by whom he had one son and three daus., viz.,

Roger, his successor.
Etheldred, *m.* to William Prideaux, Esq. of Langford, in Devon.
Grace, *m.* to James Bagge, Esq. of Plymouth.
Anna, *m.* to Francis Trelawny, Esq.

He *m.* 2ndly, Susannah, dau of Sir John Chichester, of Raleigh, and sister of Sir Arthur Chichester, lord deputy of Ireland, and had two other sons, namely,

John, who *d. unm.*
Faithful (Sir), who went to Ireland, and was ancestor of the Fortescues of that kingdom.

Mr. Fortescue was *s.* at his decease by his eldest son,

Roger Fortescue, Esq. of Buckland Filleigh, living in 1620, from who descended the Fortescues, of Buckland Filleigh, whose eventual heiress,

Rebecca Fortescue, of Buckland Filleigh, (dau. of George Fortescue, Esq., and Rebecca, his wife, dau. and heir of Edward Fortescue, Esq. of Spridlerton,) *m.* to Caleb Inglett, Esq., son of Caleb Inglett, Esq., by his wife the heiress of the Crewys, of Ashburton, and was *s.* by her son,

Richard Inglett, Esq., who assumed, in 1777, the additional surname, and arms of "Fortescue." He *m.* Elizabeth, dau. of Lucy Weston, Esq., of Dawlish, and granddau. of the right Rev. Stephen Weston, D.D., bishop of Exeter, by whom he left at his decease, in 1790, (with three daus., the eldest *m.* to Peter Churchill, Esq. of Dawlish; the 2nd, *m.* to John Davy Foulkes, Esq. of Medland; and the 3rd, Anne, *m.* in 1787, to John Brickdale, Esq.—*see that name* an only son,

John Inglett-Fortescue, Esq. of Buckland Filleigh, J.P., *b.* 23 Oct. 1758, lieut.-col. of the North Devon Yeomanry cavalry, and of the Tonbridge Militia, who *m.* 1st, in Sept. 1788, Anne, dau. of Thomas, Saunders, Esq., merchant of Exeter, and 2ndly, in 1818, Sarah-Bridgett. dau. and coheir of James Marwood, Esq. of Sutton, co. Devon and relict of Henry Stephens, Esq. of Cross, in the same shire; and by the former only, had issue, an only son and heir, the present John-Dicker-Inglett-Fortescue, Esq. of Buckland Filleigh Mr. Inglett-Fortescue, who was receiver-general of taxes for Devonshire, *d.* 25 Nov. 1840, and was *s.* by his only son,

Arms—Az., a bend, engrailed, arg., cottised, or.
Crest—A tiger, ppr., maned and crested, his paw resting on a shield, arg.
Motto—Forte scutum salus ducum.
Seats—Buckland Filleigh, Devon; Avishays, in Somersetshire; and Widmouth Villa, Cornwall.

FORTESCUE OF FALLAPIT.

Fortescue, William-Blundell, Esq. of Fallapit, co. Devon, J.P., *b.* 31 May, 1816; *s.* his father in July, 1821; *m.* 21 Nov. 1837, Harriet-Maria, 2nd dau. of Major-General Thomas-William Taylor, of Ogwell, co. Devon, and has issue,

I. Edmund, *b.* 3 Feb. 1839.
II. Reynell-John, *b.* 21 June, 1845.
III. Arthur-Troase, *b.* 7 April, 1848.
I. Honor-Georgina. II. Mary-Emlyn.
III. Geraldine-Eliza. IV. Frances-Amelia.

Lineage.—Sir Richard Le Forte, one of the leaders in the Conqueror's army who had the fortune to protect his chief at the battle of Hastings, by bearing before him a massive shield, hence acquired the addition of the French word "*escu*," a shield, to his surname. Sir Richard's son,

Sir Adam Fortescue, who had also a command at Hastings, obtained from his royal master grants of Wymondeston or Winston, and other lands, in the county of Devon. From him lineally descended,

William Fortescue, of Winston, whose name appears as a subscribing witness to numerous charters, and deeds in the time of Edward III. He *m.* Isabella, sister and co-heir of Thomas Beauchamp, of Ryme in the co. of Dorset, and widow of Richard Branscomb, by whom he had two sons, namely,

I. William, who inherited Winston.
II. John (Sir), one of the heroes of Agincourt, appointed in 1424, governor and captain of Meaux and Brie. He *m.* Eleanor, dau. and heir of William Norreis, Esq. of Norreis, in Devon, and had issue,
  1 Henry (Sir), Chief Justice of the Common Pleas, in Ireland, anno 1426, who *m.* 1st, Joan Wood, of Wood, and had by her a son, John, ancestor of the Fortescues *of Wood.* He *m.* 2ndly, the heiress of Fallapit, of Fallapit, and had by her a son, Richard, of Fallapit, whose granddau. and heir, Elizabeth Fortescue, *m.* Lewis Fortescue, Baron of the Exchequer.
  2 John (Sir), Chief Justice of England in 1442, ancestor of the Earls Fortescue, the extinct Earls of Clermont, of Fortescue of Ravensdale, now Baron Clermont, and of the Fortescues of Buckland Filleigh.
  3 Richard, progenitor of the Fortescues of Punsburn, in Herts, of Saldon, in Bucks, and of Faulkborne, in Essex.

The elder son,

William Fortescue, of Winston, *m.* Mabella, dau. of John Falwell, and was great grandfather of,

Lewis Fortescue, Esq., one of the Barons of the Exchequer, who *m.* Elizabeth, dau and. heir of John Fortescue, Esq. of Fallapit, by whom he acquired that estate, and had a son and successor,

John Fortescue, Esq. of Fallapit, great grandfather of

Sir Edmund Fortescue, Knt. of Fallapit, *b.* in 1610, a gallant and devoted Royalist, who *d.* in Holland, and was interred at Delph, where there was a monument erected to his memory. He *m.* Jane Southcote, of Mohoon-Ottery, and by that lady, (who *d.* in 1642) had (with three daus., Jane, who *d.* in 1641; Catherine, *m.* to Thomas Glanville, Esq.; and Mary, *m.* to George Southcote, Esq. of Buckland,) a son and successor,

Sir Edmund Fortescue, Knt. of Fallapit, created a Baronet, 31 March, 1664. This gentleman *m.* Margery, dau. of Henry, fifth Lord Sandys, of the Vine, and left (with two daus., Jane, *m.* to William Coleman, Esq., and Sarah, who *d. unm.*, in 1685, aged 21) a son and successor,

Sir Sandys Fortescue, Bart. of Fallapit, *b.* in 1660, who *m.* Elizabeth, dau. of Sir John Lenthall, Knt. of Besselsleigh, and had one only dau., Elizabeth, whereupon the title became extinct at his decease in 1682, and the estates passed to (the son of his grand uncle, Peter) his cousin,

Edmund Fortescue, Esq., *b.* in 1660, who then became of Fallapit. He *m.* Mary, dau of Sampson Wyse, Esq. of Dittisham, and by her (who *d.* in 1722, aged 62) had, with two sons who *d. unm.*, five daus., viz.,

I. Mary, heiress to Fallapit.
II. Elizabeth, who *d.* in 1768, aged 73.
III. Sarah, who *d.* in 1703, aged 5.
IV. Dorothy, who *m.* Thomas Bury, Esq., son of Sir Thomas Bury, of Exeter, Knt., and dying in 1733, aged 34, left (with a younger dau., Dorothy Bury, who *d. unm.* in 1792, aged 62) an elder,
  Catharine Bury, who was *m.* 15 Dec. 1745, to the Rev. Nathaniel Wells, rector of East Allington, co. Devon, son of Samuel Welles, of the city of Oxford. Mr. Wells *d.* 28 Sept. 1762; she in 1770, aged 43. They left issue,
    1 Edmund Wells, *b.* in 1752, of whom presently, as inheritor of Fallapit.
    2 William Wells, rector of East Allington, *b.* 19 May, 1756, *m.* 29 June, 1781, Elizabeth, dau. of John Pearse, Esq., of Euston, co. Devon, and had issue,

William-Bury, *b.* 15 April, 1782, *m.* Jane, dau. of James Pearse, Esq. of Southmolton, and. *d.* 23 Nov. 1834, leaving issue, William, who *m.* 11 Oct. 1842, Selina, 6th dau. of George Harriss, Esq. of Oaklands, co. Gloucester; and Fortescue, in holy orders. Elizabeth-Fortescue, *m.* to Capt. Arthur, R.N., C.B. Caroline-Josepha.

3 Nathaniel Wells, in holy orders, *b.* 23 Aug. 1757, *d.* in 1806; *m.* 29 Sept. 1794, Juliana, second dau. of Benjamin Hays, Esq. of Halwell, co. Devon, and had,

Nathaniel-Lawrence-Hays, of Lincoln College, Oxford, *b.* in 1796, *d.* in 1818, *unm.*; George-Leeds, *b.* in 1798, lieut. R.N., *d.* in 1827, *unm.*; Benjamin-Hays, *b.* in 1800, *d. unm.* in 1821; and Treby, *b.* in 1802, *d.* in 1833, leaving a son, Treby-Hays, who *d.* in 1834, aged six.

4 Samuel Wells, rector of Portlemouth. co. Devon, J.P., *b.* 2 Feb. 1759, *m.* 3 Jan. 1785, Elizabeth, 3rd dau. and co-heir of Robert Lake, Esq. of Scoble, by Grace, his second wife, dau. of Thomas Cornish, Esq. of West Prawl, and *d.* 26, Feb. 1839, having had,

Samuel, late an inspector in H. M. Office for Auditing the Public Accounts.
Robert-Lake, *d.* an infant.
Fortescue, captain, Royal Artillery, *m.* 13 July, 1824, Anne, 4th dau. of Richard Hepworth, Esq. of Pontefract, and has issue, Fanny-Anne, and Elizabeth-Fortescue-Mary.
Thomas-Bury, in holy orders, M.A., rector of Portlemouth, co. Devon, *m.* 23 March, 1841, Catharine-Frances, eldest dau. of the Rev. William Stockdale, vicar of Mears Ashby, and rector of Wilby, co. Northampton, and has a son, Lionel-Bury.

5 Thomas Wells, an officer of his Majesty's 46th regiment, *b.* 13 Oct. 1761, *d. unm.* in 1781, at Cork, on return from the West Indies.
1 Alice Wells, *d. unm.* in 1763, aged 16.
2 Catharine Wells, *m.* 14 July, 1772, to Christopher Searle, Esq. of Allerton, co. Devon, and *d.* in 1802.
3 Elizabeth Wells, *d.* young, in 1752.
4 Dorothy Wells, *m.* 14 Oct. 1772, to Arscott-Bickford Peppin, Esq. of Dulverton, co. Somerset, and *d.* in 1779
5 Mary Wells, *m.* to John Billingsley, Esq. of Ashwick, co. Somerset, and *d.* in 1828.
6 Elizabeth-Fortescue Wells, *m.* 13 March, 1781, to William-Henry Hatherly, Esq. of Shebbertown, co. Devon, and *d.* 18 Oct. 1838.

v. Grace, who *d. unm.* in 1743-4, aged 43.

Edmund Fortescue, of Fallapit, *d.* in 1733, and as he left no male issue, the estate devolved upon his eldest dau.,

MARY FORTESCUE, who *m.* the Right Hon. William Fortescue, of Buckland Filleigh, Master of the Rolls, and dying in 1710, aged 21, left an only dau. and heiress,

MARY FORTESCUE, *b.* in 1710, who was *m.* to John Spooner, Esq., but *d.* without surviving issue (her only child, Mary, had predeceased her in youth) when the estates reverted to her aunt,

ELIZABETH FORTESCUE, at whose decease, *unm.*, in 1768, aged 73, Fallapit passed to her grand nephew,

EDMUND WELLS, Esq., who, in compliance with the terms of her will, assumed, upon inheriting, the surname and arms of FORTESCUE only. This gentleman *m.* Mary-Anne, dau. of Peter Blundell, Esq. of Collipriest, co. Devon, by whom (who *d.* in 1807) he had,

EDMUND-NATHANIEL-WILLIAM, his heir.
Elizabeth-Wells, *m.* to Thomas-William Sturgeon, Esq., nephew to Thomas Watson Wentworth, first Marquess of Rockingham.

Mr. (Wells) Fortescue, *d.* in 1779, aged 27, and was *s.* by his son,

EDMUND-NATHANIEL-WILLIAM FORTESCUE, Esq. of Fallapit, *b.* in 1777, major of the South Devon regiment of militia. *m.* in May, 1803, Elizabeth, dau. of the late William-Long Trosse, Esq. of Trevollard, co. Cornwall, and had issue,

WILLIAM-BLUNDELL, now of Fallapit.
Henry-Reymundo, in holy orders, *b.* in 1820, *m.* 9 June, 1842, Ellen, dau. of Percival Walsh, Esq. of Stanton Harcourt, co. Oxford.
Elizabeth, *m.* to the Rev. Thomas Twysden.
Marianne-Catharine, *m.* to John Allen, Esq. of Coleridge House, co. Devon, and *d.* 2d Dec. 1842, leaving issue.
Charlotte, *m.* to Lieut.-Col. Dalgety, of H. M. 68th regt.
Mary, *m.* to J. Lloyd, Esq. of Lloydsboro'.

Mr. Fortescue *d.* in July, 1821.

Arms—Az., a bend, engrailed, arg., cottised, or.
Crest—A tiger, passant, arg., armed and maned, or.
Motto—Forte scutum salus ducum.
Seat—Fallapit, co. Devon.

FOSBERY OF CLORANE.

FOSBERY, GEORGE, Esq. of Clorane, co. Limerick, J.P., *b.* 23 March, 1806 *m.* 1st, 1829, Catherine, dau. of Thos. Leland, Esq. of Fitzwilliam Sq., Dublin; and 2ndly, 1851, Eliza, dau. of John Scott, Esq. of Firgrove, co. Clare. By the former he has an only son,

GEORGE, *b.* 30 Dec. 1830, *m.* 18 June, 1855, Sophia, 5th dau. of the Rev. Edward Herbert, of Kilpeacon Glebe.

Lineage.—The immediate ancestor of this branch of the family (anciently of Hampshire) settled in Ireland in the reign of WILLIAM III., in whose army he had held a commission in a regiment of dragoons. From him descended

GEORGE FOSBERY, Esq. of Clorane, who served the office of high sheriff of co. Limerick in 1748. His son,

WILLIAM FOSBERY, Esq., *m.* Jane, dau. of Frank Evans, Esq., and had issue (besides three daus., Anne, Jane, and Elizabeth) three sons, viz.,

I. George, *m.* 20 Oct. 1782, Christina-Mary, only dau. of Thos. Rice, Esq. of Mount Trenchard, co. Limerick, (grandfather of Thomas, Lord Monteagle,) by his wife, Mary, dau. of Gerald Fitzgerald, Knt. of Kerry, and dying 1791, left issue.

1 GEORGE, of Clorane, of whom presently.
2 Thos. Rice, in holy orders, *b.* 23 Feb. 1788, *m.* Althea-Maria, dau. of J. Smythe, Esq. of Barbavilla, co. Westmeath, and *d. s. p.* Feb. 1828.
3 William, *d.* young.
4 John-Francis, barrister-at-law.
1 Mary, *m.* to William Henn, Esq., master in Chancery.
2 Jane, *m.* to Colonel Anthony Lyster.
3 Christiana, *m.* to Colonel C. P. Leslie, M.P. of Glaslough House, co. Monaghan.

II. Francis, *m.* 1773, Phillippa, dau. of John Godfrey, Esq. of Bushfield, and had GEORGE, of Curragh Bridge, and other issue.

III. William, *m.* 1st, Margaret, dau. of R. Hoops, Esq., and by her had issue, William, who *m.* Maria, dau. of W. Ingilby, Esq., and has two sons, William and George, and four daus.; George *d. unm.*; Francis, who *m.* Meliora, dau. of R. Rose, Esq. of Adare, and had two sons, Francis and William, and two daus.; Henry; Anne, *m.* to S. Raymond, Esq. He *m.* 2ndly, in Nov. 1806, Anne, dau. of Exham Vincent, Esq., and by her had issue,

1 Thomas Vincent, in holy orders, *m.* in May, 1831, Emily-Sarah, dau. of George Gooch, Esq., by his wife, Amelia, dau. of John Kerrich, Esq., and has issue, George Vincent; William-Thomas-Exham; Henry-Thomas; Vincent-Robert, *d.* in infancy; Clement-Charles; Leonard-Arthur; Emily; Gertrude.
1 Hannah, *d.* young.
2 Georgiana, *m.* in June, 1835, to the Hon. and Rev. Musgrave A. Harris, who *d. s. p.* Aug. 1836.
3 Jane, *d.* young.

GEORGE FOSBERY, Esq. of Clorane, J.P. (son of George Fosbery and Christina-Mary, his wife) *b.* 1783, *m.* 1805, Elizabeth, dau. of Francis Fosbery, Esq. of Curragh Bridge, and *d.* 1847, leaving issue, three sons and one dau., viz.,

GEORGE, now of Clorane.
Francis, of Kilgolawn, *b.* 1808.
Thomas, of Castle Grey, *b.* 1820, *m.* 1852, Georgina, dau. of St. George Smith, Esq. of Greenhills, and has issue.
Elizabeth-Philippa, *m.* to Sir Nugent Humble, Bart.

Seat—Clorane, co. Limerick.

FOSBERY OF CURRAGHBRIDGE.

FOSBERY, GEORGE, Esq. of Curraghbridge, co. Limerick, *b.* 24 Dec. 1774; *m.* 12 May, 1812, Caroline, dau. of Richard Yielding, Esq., by Ann his wife, dau. of John Massy, Esq. of Glenville, co. Limerick, and had issue,

I. FRANCIS, *b.* 1813; *m.* 1841, Sarah-Eleanor, only dau. of Wm.-Humphreys Smith, Esq. of St. Cronans, co. Tipperary.
II. Richard, *b.* 22 Nov. 1818.
I. Catherine.
II. Anna-Philippa, *m.* to Oliver-William Mason, Esq. of Aghamore.
III. Caroline-Elizabeth.
IV. Jane-Agnes, *m.* to Joseph Smith, Esq. of St. Cronans and Clashagad.
V. Elizabeth-Barbara, *m.* to Capt. Charles-Philip Taylor, H.E.I.C.S., son of Lieut.-Gen. Henry Taylor, C.B.

Lineage.—FRANCIS FOSBERY, Esq. of Curraghbridge (2nd son of William Fosbery and Jane Evans his wife, *see preceding memoir*), *m.* 16 March, 1773, Philipa, dau. of John Godfrey, Esq., and sister of Sir William Godfrey, Bart., and dying 4 March, 1810, left issue,

GEORGE, of Curraghbridge.
William, *b.* 22 July, 1781; *m.* 1807, Elizabeth Goff, of Carrigafoy, co. Kerry, and *d.* 1851
Francis, *b.* 9 Nov. 1784; *m.* 1808, Elizabeth Creagh, widow,

dau. of Charles Widenham, Esq. of Castle Widenham, and *d.* 1826.
Henry, *b.* 11 Jan. 1789; *m.* 1820, Jane Westropp.
Barbara, *m.* Richard Parsons, Esq. of Cragbeg, and *d.* 1850.
Jane, *m.* to George Langford, Esq. of Marino, Kenmare.
Letitia, *m.* to David Jamison, Esq., an officer in the army, and *d.* 1854.
Elizabeth, *m.* 1805, to George Fosbery, Esq. of Clorane.
Phillipa.

Seat—Curraghbridge, Adare.

FOSBROOKE OF SHARDLOW AND RAVENSTONE.

FOSBROOKE, LEONARD, Esq. of Ravenstone Hall, co. Derby, barrister-at-law, *s.* his father in 1830.

Lineage.—The FOSBROOKES, who are supposed to have derived their surname and origin from Fosbrooke, in Staffordshire were settled at Cranford, in Northamptonshire, early in the reign of RICHARD II., where they acquired and for several centuries possessed, considerable estates. These lands were alienated some time in the reign of CHARLES II., and about the same period the more immediate ancestors of this branch of the family settled at Shardlow, co. Derby.

RICHARD FOSBROKE, the ultimate inheritor of the estates, *m.* Juliana dau. of William Kinsman, of Loddington, co. Northampton, and *d.* in the 33 HENRY VIII., A.D 1541, leaving a son, John then only sixteen years of age. Through this son the Fosbrookes were continued at Cranford for four generations further, in the last of which, there being no son to inherit, but a family of seven daus., (Harl. M.S., No. 1553, fo. 33,) the estates were sold.

From HENRY FOSBROKE the younger brother of the above-mentioned Richard, the Fosbrookes of Shardlow are descended. He settled in the town of Nottingham and of that place was sheriff, in the 35 Henry VIII., A.D. 1543-4, and afterwards mayor first in the 2 ELIZABETH, A.D. 1559-60, and again in the 8 ELIZABETH A.D. 1565-6.

In the year 1641 we find Leonard Fosbrooke and Robert Fosbrooke of Nottingham, gentlemen, lessees, under the Earl of Huntingdon of Wilne Ferry, on the River Trent, adjoining to the parish of Shardlow.

LEONARD FOSBROOKE, of Wilne Ferry, aforesaid, about the year 1670 purchased an estate at Shardlow. His grandson,

LEONARD FOSBROOKE, Esq. of Shardlow Hall and Ravenstone, he *m.* in 1724, Penelope only dau. of Thomas Burgh, Esq. of Coventry, barrister-at-law, and had issue. This gentleman, who served the office of high-sheriff for Derbyshire in 1725, *d.* 26 Aug. 1762, and was *s.* by his 3rd son,

LEONARD FOSBROOKE, Esq of Shardlow Hall *b.* in 1735, high-sheriff for co. Derby in 1764 who *m.* in 1766, Ann, dau. of James Winstanley, Esq. of Braunston, high-sheriff for Leicestershire, by Mary, his wife, dau. and co-heir of Sir Edmund Prideaux, Bart. and was *s.* at his decease, 1801, by his eldest son,

LEONARD FOSBROOKE Esq. of Shardlow Hall, but latterly of Ravenstone, born in 1773. He *m.* Mary, eldest dau. of the Rev. Philip Story, of Lockington Hall, and had issue,

I. LEONARD, his heir.
II. Philip.
III. Charles.
IV. Thomas.
V. Edmund, *m.* and has issue.
VI. Henry-Nathaniel, *m.* and has issue.
I. Mary-Anne, *d. s. p.*
II. Diana, *d. s. p.*
III. Frances-Sarah, *m.* and has issue.
IV. Georgina-Sibella, *d. s. p.*

He *d.* 26 March, 1830 was buried at Ravenstone, and *s.* by his eldest son, the present LEONARD FOSBROOKE, Esq. of Ravenstone Hall.

Arms—Az., a saltier, between four cinquefoils, arg.
Crest—Two bears' gambs, sa., supporting a spear, erect, ppr.
Seat—Ravenstone Hall, co. Derby.

FOSTER OF JAMAICA, EGHAM, AND KEMPSTONE.

FOSTER, JOHN-FREDERIC, Esq. of the Bogue Estate, Jamaica, and of Kempstone, co. Bedford, now resident at Alderley Edge, co. Chester, barrister-at-law, J.P. for Lancashire and Cheshire, and D.L., Chairman of the Quarter Sessions for the hundred of Salford, co. Lancaster; *b.* 18 June, 1795; *m.* 1817, Caroline, eldest dau. of the late Sir William-C. Bagshawe, of The Oaks and Wormhill Hall, co. Derby, and of Coates Hall, co. York, and has had issue,

I. John-William-Bagshawe, *b.* 1818, *d.* 1828.
II. FREDERICK-ADOLPHUS-LA-TROBE, *b.* 12 Oct. 1820, rector of Saxby, co. Lincoln, *m.* Annie-Hulbert, dau. of the Rev. William Reid, of Stone Easton, co. Somerset, and domestic chaplain to his late R.H. the Duke of Kent, and has issue,
  1 Frederic-La-Trobe, *b.* 31 July, 1853.
  1 Annie-Louisa.
  2 Caroline-Nora.
  3 Helen-Mary.
III. Thomas-Barham, civil engineer, *b.* 1827.
IV. William-Henry, commissioner of Crown Lands, warden of the Gold Fields, and protector of the Chinese, and J.P. in the colony of Victoria, *b.* 1832.
V. John-Bagshawe, *d.* an infant.
I. Caroline-Louisa, *m.* to Edward Loyd, Esq., banker, of Prestwich Lodge, co. Lancaster, and Lillesden, Kent, J.P. and D.L.
II. Mary-Eleanor, *m.* to James-Collier Harter, Esq. of Oak End, co. Lancaster.
III. Margaret-Helen.

Lineage.—This family is descended from the ancient and distinguished house of Forster or Foster, of Bamborough Castle, Northumberland, the ancestor of which, according to tradition, was WILLIAM DE FORESTIER, a Norman cavalier, who came over with WILLIAM the Conqueror in 1066.

THOMAS FORSTER, *m.* the sister of the Blind Baron of Hilton. His son,

SIR THOMAS FORSTER, in 1564 and 1572, was high-sheriff of Northumberland, and *m.* Dorothy, dau. of Lord Ogle, of Bothall.

In 1575, SIR JOHN FORSTER was a distinguished military leader in the feuds between the English and Scottish Borderers, and was governor of Bamborough, and warden of the Marches. He *m.* Jane, widow of Robert, 5th Lord Ogle, and eldest dau. of Sir Cuthbert Radclyffe and Margaret his wife, dau. of Henry, Lord Clifford, Westmoreland and Vesey.

NICHOLAS FORSTER, son of Sir John Forster, was governor of Bamborough, Lord of Blanchland. He *d.* 22 July, 1613.

SIR CLAUDIUS FORSTER, his son, *d.* in 1623. There is an inscription upon a tombstone, of that date, in Bamborough church, describing him as "Eques auratus" and "Baronettus antiquus."

SIR WILLIAM FORSTER, his son, had issue, and his nephew,

JOHN FORSTER, by whom, and from whose time, the spelling of Foster has been used, was M.P. for Northumberland. He was engaged in the rebellion of 1715, commanding the English part of the rebel forces. His estates were forfeited for the part he took in this rebellion, and were granted to Lord Crewe, bishop of Durham, who had *m.* Dorothy Forster, the aunt of the said John Forster. In 1715, he surrendered together with Lord Derwentwater and others, and was sent to London, and committed to Newgate on the charge of high treason, whence he afterwards escaped and fled to the Continent. He died, leaving no male representative of this branch of the family, but the descent is traced in the Harl. MSS. from Roger Forster, the brother of Thomas Forster, above mentioned as having married the sister of the Blind Baron of Hilton, to

SIR THOMAS FOSTER, of Egham, who was chief justice of the Court of Common Pleas, and *d.* 1612, being buried at Egham. His second son,

SIR ROBERT FOSTER, was chief justice of the Court of King's Bench, and *d.* 1663. There is a monument to him in the church at Egham, in Surrey, where there is also an estate which has remained in the family to the present time.

THOMAS FOSTER, the eldest son of Sir Thomas, had a son,

JOHN FOSTER, of Egham, who held a military command in the expedition to Jamaica under Penn and Venables, in 1655. He received a grant of extensive estates in the parish of St. Elizabeth, in that island, the greater part of which are still in the possession of the family. His son,

THOMAS FORSTER, perished in the earthquake at Port Royal, in 1692.

COL. JOHN FORSTER, his son, of Egham House, Surrey, and of Elim, The Bogue, Two Mile Wood, Lancaster, Waterford, the Island, and other estates in Jamaica, resided at Elim, in that island. He was *b.* July, 1651, and *d.* 30 July, 1731. His pedigree and descent, as above given, are shown by an inscription on an ancient tomb erected on the estate at Elim. This Col. John Foster resided on his estate at Elim, in the parish of St. Elizabeth's,

Jamaica; he was *b.* in July, 1681, *d.* 30 Aug. 1731. He *m.* Elizabeth Smith, of Barbadoes, and by her (who *m.* 2ndly, Dr. Henry Barham, of Jamaica) had issue,

I. Thomas, *b.* 1720, who *d.* without issue. He resided upon the family estate at Egham, co. Surrey, and was M.P. for Dorchester. His will gave rise to a lengthened litigation, the result of which appears in the 11th vol. of *Bast's Reports.*
II. WILLIAM, of whom presently.
III. John, *b.* 1723, *d. unm* 1744.
IV. Samuel, *b.* 1725, *m.* and had issue,
  1 John, of Egham House, Surrey, and of Elim, Lancaster, and Two Mile Wood, Jamaica, *m.* and had issue,
    George, who *m.* and had issue, a son, George-John.
    Henry, capt. 23rd regt., *m.* and had issue,
      Henry, rector of Coln Rogers, Gloucestershire, canon of Gloucester, *m* Ellen, youngest dau. of the late Rear-Adm. Sir Michael Seymour, Bart., K.C.B., and has issue.
      John, Her Majesty's Chaplain of the Savoy, *m.* Laura, dau. of Col. Lapsley, R.A., and has issue.
  2 Samuel-Warren, had issue. 3 Richard, *d. unm.*
  1 Elizabeth, *m.* to John Venner, Esq.
  2 Flora, *m.* to her cousin, John Foster, Esq. of Brickhill House, Beds.
V. Joseph, *b.* 1729, afterwards took the name of BARHAM, in addition to that of FOSTER, and had issue.
I. Mary, *m.* Florentius Vassal, Esq., whose granddau. Elizabeth Vassal, *m.* 1st, Sir Godfrey Webster, Bart., and afterwards Henry-Richard, 3rd Baron Holland.
II. Margaret, *m.* to Colin Campbell, Esq.
III. Elizabeth, *b.* 1726, *d.* 1729.
VI. Sarah, *b.* 1727, *m.* to William-Matthew Burt, governor of Santa Cruz, captain-general and governor-in-chief of the Leeward Islands, had issue.

The 2nd son,

WILLIAM FOSTER, Esq. (*b.* 1722, who *d.* 1763) *m.* Elizabeth Vassal, but by her had no issue. He *m.* 2ndly, 8 Feb. 1748, Dorothy Gale, of Acomb, near York, and of Lucena, in the island of Jamaica, of an old and distinguished family, and by her had issue,

I. THOMAS, of Grove House, Chalfont St. Giles, Buckinghamshire, and of St. Pol, in the Pyrenees, *b.* 19 Aug. 1752, had issue by his 1st wife, Deborah Senior,
  1 Thomas, *d. unm.* 2 William, *d. unm.*
  1 Elizabeth-Deborah, *m.* to Rear-Admiral Sir Thomas Ussher, K.C.B. and K.G.H.
  2 Maria-Catharine, *m.* William Pennefather, Esq.
  3 Dorothy-Valeria, *m.* 1st, Capt. Fergus, R.N.; 2ndly, Robert Strong, Esq.; and 3rdly, Baron d'Eisendecker.
  4 Emma-Louisa-Keith, *m.* to James-Esdaile Hammet, Esq.
  By his 2nd wife, Elizabeth Overend, the above-named Thomas Foster, of The Grove, had issue,
  1 John, *d.* an infant. 2 Eugene, *d.* young.
  1 Isabella, *d. unm.*
  2 Marianne, *m.* her cousin, Hermann von Zeszschwitz, capt. in the Saxon cavalry.
  3 Harriette, *m.* to her cousin, Edward von Zeszschwitz, major in the Saxon army, chamberlain to the King of Saxony.
  The male line in this the eldest branch thus became extinct.
II. Frederic-William, of the Bogue Estate, Jamaica, a bishop of the Moravian Church, *b.* 1760, *m.* 1791, Anna-Louisa-Eleanora La Trobe, of a noble refugee family from Languedoc, and *d.* at Ockbrook, co. Derby, in 1835, having had issue,
  1 JOHN-FREDERIC, now of the Bogue Estate, Jamaica, and of Kempstone, co. Bedford, representative of the eldest surviving branch of the family.
  2 William, of Ockbrook, co. Derby, *b.* 1797, *m.* Marianne, 2nd dau. of Sir William Bagshawe, of the Oaks and Wormhill Hall, Derbyshire, and *d.* 1829, having had issue one son, Frederick-William, *b.* June, 1818, *d.* April, 1838. His widow *m.* Rev. Thomas Fry, rector of Emberton, Bucks.
  3 Isaac-Henry, *b.* 1800, *d. unm.* 1827.
  1 Anna-Dorothy, *m.* John Amery, Esq., banker, at Stourbridge.
  2 Mary-Louisa, *m.* her cousin, the Rev. P. La Trobe, Ely Place, London, secretary to the Moravian Missions.
  3 Margaret-Eleanora, *d. unm.* 1833.
III. JOHN, of the Bogue Estate, Jamaica, and of Brickhill House, and lord of the manor of Marston, co. Bedford. (*See* FOSTER *of Brickhill.*)
I. Elizabeth-Dorothy, *b.* 26 Sept. 1749, *m.* to W.-H. Weber, Esq.
II. Sarah, *b.* April, 1751, *m.* Baron Christlieb Frederic von Zeszchwitz, of Taubenheim and Deutsch Baslitz, in Upper Lusatia, an ancient and distinguished Saxon family, and had issue.
III. Anna-Benigna, *b.* 1756, *d. unm.*
IV. Mary-Helden, *b.* 1762, *m.* to John Rœderer, Esq. of Neuwied, on the Rhine.

Arms—Arg., a chevron, vert, between three bugles, sa., stringed, gu.
Crest—An arm in armour, embowed, holding the head of a broken tilting spear.
Motto—Si fractus fortis.

FOSTER OF BRICKHILL HOUSE.

FOSTER, MORGAN-HUGH, Esq. of the Bogue Estate, Jamaica, and of Brickhill House, co. Bedford, *b.* 1815; *m.* 1838, Mary, dau. of George Flint, Esq., and has surviving issue

I. ALGERNON-CRAUFURD, *b.* 1 Dec. 1839.
II. Arthur, *b.* 21 July, 1843.
III. William-Erskine, *b.* 21 Oct. 1847.
I. Edith-Margaret. II. Florence-Amelia.

Lineage.—JOHN FOSTER, of the Bogue Estate, Jamaica, and of Brickhill House, Bedfordshire, lord of the manor of Marston, in the same county (*see preceding family*), a magistrate in England and in Jamaica, for many years chairman of the Central Agricultural Society in London, *b.* 21 June, 1765, *d.* 30 June, 1831. In consequence of the eminent services he had rendered to agriculture, as well by his speeches as by his writings, he was presented with two magnificent pieces of plate, one by the agriculturists of the county of Bedford, and the other by the agriculturists of the whole of England. He *m.* 1st, Margaret, dau. of Thomas Place, Esq., recorder of York, and had issue,

William, who *d. unm.*
Thomas, *d.* young. Edward, *d.* young.
Margaret, *m.* to the Rev. Maurice Farrel.

John Foster *m.* 2ndly, his cousin, Flora Foster, but by her had no issue; and 3rdly, Amelia, dau. of John Morgan, Esq., barrister-at-law, recorder of Maidstone, and sister of the Countess of Carhampton. Of this last marriage there was issue,

Algernon, *b.* 1811, *d.* 1821.
ARTHUR-FITZJOHN, heir to his father.
MORGAN-HUGH, now of Brickhill House.
Mary-Amelia, *m.* to the Rev. Henry Fuller, rector of Willington, Bedfordshire.
Flora, *m.* to the Rev. Alfred Dawson, rector of Flitwick, Bedfordshire.

The eldest surviving son,

ARTHUR-FITZJOHN FOSTER, Esq. of the Bogue Estate and of Brickhill House, barrister-at-law and member of the House of Assembly, Jamaica, *b.* 1813, *d. unm.* 1842, and was *s.* by his brother, the present MORGAN-HUGH FOSTER, Esq. of Brickhill House.

Arms, Crest, and *Motto*—Same as preceding family.
Seat—Brickhill House, Bedfordshire.

Foster-Barham Branch.

JOSEPH FOSTER, Esq (youngest son of Col. John Foster), *b.* 1729, *d.* 1789. He took the name of BARHAM: he *m.* 1stly, Dorothea, dau and eventual heir of Erasmus Vaughan, Esq. of Trecwn, co. Pembroke; and 2ndly Lady Hill, of Hawkestone. The eldest son of the 1st marriage,

JOSEPH FOSTER-BARHAM, Esq. of Trecwn, and of Stockbridge, Hants, *b.* 1760, M.P. for that borough, *m.* 1792, Lady Caroline Tufton, dau. of Sackville, 8th Earl of Thanet, and had issue, several sons and daus., the eldest son John Foster-Barham, who was M.P. for Stockbridge, and afterwards for Kendal, *m.* Lady Katharine Grimston, dau. of the Earl of Verulam, who survived her husband and is the present Countess of Clarendon. The 2nd son, William Foster-Barham, *d. unm.* The 3rd son, THE REV. CHARLES-HENRY BARHAM, now of Trecwn, nephew and sole representative of Henry, last Earl of Thanet, *m.* Miss Ince, but has no issue. There are also two daus., Mary, who *m.* Count Gacciocci; and Caroline, who *m.* the Rev. Sanderson Robins, rector of Shaftesbury.

FOSTER OF CASTLERING.

FOSTER, FREDERICK-JOHN, Esq. of Castlering, co. Louth, J.P. and D.L., *m.* 22 Oct. 1827, Isabella, 4th dau. of Peter Vere, Esq. (*see* VERE *of Carlton-upon-Trent*).

Lineage.—The Fosters, a branch of an old Berkshire family, went to Ireland during the wars of 1641.

JOHN FOSTER, Esq. of Dunleer, in the co. of Louth, *m.* 10 Dec. 1704, Mary, dau. of William Fortescue, Esq. of Newrath (sister of Thomas Fortescue, Esq. of Ravensdale

Park, whose son, William-Henry, was created EARL OF CLERMONT in 1778), and d. in 1747, having had issue,

I. Anthony (The Right Hon.), lord-chief-baron in 1766; m. in 1736, Elizabeth, dau. of William Burgh, Esq. of Birt, in the co. of Kildare, and had issue,

1 John (The Right Hon.), Speaker of the Irish House of Commons, afterwards created LORD ORIEL (see *Peerage*—title MASSEREENE).

2 William, D.D., bishop of Cork, who m. Catherine-Letitia, only dau. of the Rev. Henry Leslie, LL.D. of Ballybay (*see* LESLIE *of Leslie House*), and had, John-Leslie, a Baron of the Court of Exchequer; William, in holy orders: Henrietta, m. Jerome, Count de Salis; Letitia, m. John-Henry North, Esq., M.P.

1 Margaret, m. 1759, the Most Rev. Henry Maxwell, D.D., bishop of Meath (see *Peerage*—title FARNHAM).

II. Thomas, D.D., m. 1740, Dorn, dau. of Thomas Burgh, Esq of Oldtown, co. of Kildare, M.P. for Naas, and had issue,

1 William, M.P. for Ennis, who m. Lady Elizabeth Harvey, dau. of the Earl of Bristol, by whom (who m., after his decease, 17 Oct. 1809, William, 5th Duke of Devonshire; and d. 20 March, 1824) he had issue, Frederick-Thomas, M.P. for Bury St. Edmunds in 1817; The Right Hon. Sir Augustus-John Foster, Bart., G.C.H. (see *Baronetage*).

III. William, M.P. for Dunleer, m. 1743, Patience, dau. of John Fowke, Esq., and had issue,

1 John-William, M.P. for Dunleer, who m. in 1788, Patience, dau. of Hamilton M'Clure, Esq., and had issue,

FREDERICK-JOHN, now of Castle Ring.
Louisa-Jane, m. 26 Oct. 1819, Lord Plunket, D.D., bishop of Tuam (see *Peerage*).
Elizabeth. Emily.

2 Henry.

1 Patience, m. 1766, John M'Clintock, Esq., M.P. (*see* M'CLINTOCK *of Drumcar.*)

2 Elizabeth, m. John Longfield, Esq., M.P. (*see* LONGFIELD *of Longueville*).

IV. Samuel, d. young.

I. Margaret, m. to Stephen Sibthorpe, Esq. of Brownstown House, co. of Louth.

II. Susanna, d. unm.

III. Charlotte, m. 1738, to Nicholas Forster, Esq. of Tullaghan, co. of Monaghan, whose 3rd son was created Sir Thomas Forster, Bart. (see *Baronetge*).

Arms—Arg., a chevron, vert, between three bugles, sa., stringed, gu

Crest—A stag, ppr.

Residence—Fitzwilliam Street, Dublin.

FOSTER OF WADSWORTH BANKS.

FOSTER, HENRY, Esq. of Wadsworth Banks, and Falling Royd, co. York, J.P., b. 29 May, 1795.

Lineage.—The ancestors of this family came from Wensleydale, in the North Riding of Yorkshire, about 400 years ago, to the Slack, near Heptonstall, which they obtained by purchase. The Slack estate is still retained by a branch of the same family, and the present occupier and owner is JOHN FOSTER, Esq., who m. the only dau. and heir of Henry Lord, Esq. of Bacup, Lancashire.

JOHN FOSTER, Esq. of Slack, a son of Thomas Foster, Esq. of the same place, m. Elizabeth, dau. of Thomas Greenwood, who erected the chapel at Slack at his own expense, and preached in it gratuitously. By this lady Mr. Foster had, with a dau., three sons, John, from whom the present JOHN FOSTER, Esq. of Slack; HENRY, of whom presently; and William, who was educated for the church: he d. s. p. The 2nd son,

HENRY FOSTER, Esq., removed from Slack to his own estate at Wadsworth Banks about the year 1770. He m. Ann Townsend, of Heptonstall, and had, with a dau., Mary, who d. s. p., aged 73, and a son,

JOHN FOSTER, Esq. of Wadsworth Banks, who m. 23 Dec. 1790, Sarah, dau. of William Howorth, Gent. of White Lee, and had, with a dau., Elizabeth, who d. young, an only son, the present HENRY FOSTER, Esq. of Wadsworth Banks. Mr. Foster d. 12 Sept. 1812, aged 51.

Arms—A bend, or, between a unicorn's head, erased, in chief, and four crosses-crosslet flory, in base.

Crest—A cubit arm, erect, vested, holding in the hand a battle-axe, fesseways.

Seats—Wadsworth Banks; and Falling Royd, co. York.

FOUNTAINE OF NARFORD.

FOUNTAINE, ANDREW, Esq. of Narford Hall, co. Norfolk; s. his father, the late Andrew Fountaine, Esq., 7 June, 1835.

Lineage.—The family of Fountaine was originally of Salle, in Norfolk, and assumed the surname of DE FONTE, or FONTIBUS, from the springs or fountains near which they resided.

The first upon record who assumed the designation,

JOHN DE FONTE, called also *De Fontibus de Salle*, who flourished in the latter end of the reign of HENRY III., was much in favour with Roger Bigod, Earl of Norfolk. He d. in the beginning of EDWARD I.'s time, and was s. by his eldest son,

ROBERT DE FONTIBUS, of Salle, whose great-grandson,

JOHN FFUNTEYN, of Salle, was returned, in 1430, as one of the chief gentlemen of the county. He was a principal benefactor, if not sole founder, of the north aisle and north transept of the present church of Salle, wherein he lies buried with his three wives. He d. in 1453. From him derived, 6th in descent,

SIR ANDREW FOUNTAINE, Knt., eldest son of Andrew Fountaine, Esq. of Salle, M.P., by Sarah his wife, dau. of Sir Thomas Chicheley. This distinguished antiquary s. in 1727, upon the lamented death of Sir Isaac Newton, to the office of Warden of the Mint. He was likewise vice-chamberlain to Queen CAROLINE, and tutor to Prince WILLIAM. He d. in 1753, leaving no issue. His sister,

ELIZABETH FOUNTAINE, m. Col. Edward Clent, of the co. of Worcester, by whom she had an only dau.,

ELIZABETH CLENT, who m. Captain William Price, and left one son,

BRIGG PRICE, Esq. of Narford, who assumed, by act of parliament, the surname and arms of FOUNTAINE. He m. in July, 1769, Mary, sole dau. of George Hogge, Esq. of Lynn Regis, by whom he left at his decease, 20 April, 1825, an only surviving child,

ANDREW FOUNTAINE, Esq. of Narford Hall, high-sheriff of Norfolk in 1828, b. 13 July, 1770; who m. 7 Nov. 1806, Hannah, eldest dau. of Thomas Penrice, Esq. of Great Yarmouth, by whom (who d. in Jan. 1830) he had issue,

ANDREW, present representative.
Thomas, m. 9 Feb. 1836, Mary-Barbara, eldest dau. of Henry-Barre-De la Poer Beresford, Esq., son of the Right Hon. John Beresford.
John. Charles. Edward.
Mary, m. 10 April, 1834, to W.-George-Tyssen-Daniel Tyssen, Esq. of Foulden Hall, co. Norfolk.
Elizabeth. Caroline.

Mr. Fountaine d. 7 June, 1835.

Arms—Or, a fesse, gu., between three elephants' heads, erased, sa.

Crest—An elephant, ppr.

Motto—Vix ea nostra voco.

Seat—Narford Hall, Norfolk.

FOUNTAYNE-WILSON OF MELTON.

See MONTAGU.

FOWLER OF PENDEFORD.

FOWLER, THOMAS, Esq. of Pendeford Hall, co. Stafford, s. his father in 1815.

Lineage.—ROGER FOWLER, of Broomhill, in Norfolk, of an ancient Buckinghamshire family, derived from Richard Fowler, of Foxley, who accompanied RICHARD CŒUR DE LION to the Holy Land, m. the sister and co-heir of the Right Rev. Rowland Lee, bishop of Lichfield and Coventry, and had five sons, namely, Rowland, of Broomhill; Bryan, seated at St. Thomas's, Staffordshire; William, who seated himself at Harnage Grange, in Shropshire, ancestor of the FOWLERS *of Harnage Grange*, whose representative, Sir William Fowler, was created a Baronet in 1704; JAMES, of whose line we have to treat; Thomas, d. s. p. Roger Fowler was in the Scotch wars, and d. in the reign of HENRY VIII. His 4th son,

JAMES FOWLER, Esq., inherited from his uncle, the bishop of Lichfield, the manor of Pendeford, in Staffordshire, which, together with other lands, had been conferred upon the prelate at the dissolution of monasteries. From him descended, 4th in descent,

CHARLES FOWLER, Esq. of Pendeford, living in 1694, m. Sarah, dau. and heir of Robert Leveson, Esq. of Wolverhampton (only son of Col. Thomas Leveson, governor of Dudley Castle, by Frances, dau. of Sir William Pawlett, Knt.), and had three sons and one dau. Mr. Fowler was s. by his eldest son,

RICHARD FOWLER, Esq. of Pendeford, who m. Dorothy, dau. and heir of Humphrey Whadcock, Esq. of Corley, and had, with two sons, who predeceased him, unm., two daus., Sarah, m. to John Lane, Esq.; and Elizabeth (who d. 14 June, 1784), m. to the Rev. William Inge, A.M., canon-residentiary of Lichfield. Mr. Fowler was s. by his nephew,

THOMAS FOWLER, Esq. of Pendeford (son of Thomas Fowler, and Barbara Newton his wife), who m. Miss Leversage, and had by her one son and three daus., namely,

- THOMAS, his heir.
- Barbara, m. to Thomas Lane, Esq. of the Grange, in Essex.
- Mary, m. to her cousin, Richard Inge, Esq. of Shrewsbury, son of the Rev. William Inge, canon of Lichfield.
- Diana, m. to the Rev. Mr. Walter.

Mr. Fowler d. in 1796, and was s. by his son,

THOMAS-LEVERSAGE FOWLER, Esq. of Pendeford, who m. his cousin, Harriet Fowler, and had three sons and three daus., namely,

- I. THOMAS, his heir.
- II. Richard, who assumed the surname of BUTLER only on inheriting the estate of Barton, in Staffordshire. He m. Elizabeth, dau. of William Wynne, Esq., and niece of Owen Wynne, Esq. of Hazlewood, co. Sligo, and has issue,
  - 1 Richard-Fowler.
  - 1 Eleanor-Harriet. 2 Sarah-Catherine. 3 Mary.
- III. William, of Birmingham, m. and has issue.
- I. Elizabeth, m. to Samuel Gerrard, Esq. of Tallyho, co. Westmeath.
- II. Sarah. Mary, m.

Mr. Fowler d. in 1815, and was s. by his eldest son, the present THOMAS FOWLER, Esq. of Pendeford.

Arms—Az., on a chevron, arg., between three lions, passant-guardant, or, as many crosses formée, sa.
Crest—An owl, arg., crowned with a ducal coronet, or.
Seat—Pendeford Hall, Staffordshire.

FOWLER OF RAHINSTON.

FOWLER, ROBERT, Esq. of Rahinston House, co. Meath, b. 15 June, 1797; m. 1st, 20 Aug. 1820, Jane, eldest dau. of the Hon. John Crichton, and sister of John, 1st Earl of Erne, and by her (who d. 19 May, 1828) had issue,

- I. ROBERT, b. 15 March, 1824, m. 1856, Letitia-Mabella, dau. of Henry-Barry Coddington, Esq. of Oldbridge.
- II. John-Richard, b. 8 Oct 1826.
- I. Jane-Margaret, m. 20 March, 1844, Gartside Gartside Tipping Esq. eldest son of Thomas Tipping Esq., of Davenport Hall, co. Cheshire, by Anna Hibbert his wife, and has issue,
  - 1 Henry-Thomas, b. in Aug. 1848.
  - 2 Robert-Francis.
  - 1 Louisa-Jane-Letitia. 2 Anne-Selina.
  - 3 Mildred-Harriet.
- II. Louisa-Catharine, m. 26 Nov. 1846, James-Henry Slater, Esq., jun., only son of James-Henry Slater, Esq. of Newick Park, Sussex and has issue,
  - 1 James-Robert-Charles. 2 Francis-Saunderson.
  - 3 Cecil. 1 Catharine.

Mr. Fowler m. 2ndly, 16 May, 1831, Lady Harriet-Eleanor Wandesforde-Butler, eldest dau. of James, 2nd Marquess of Ormonde, and by her has had issue,

- I. James-Haddington, b. 28 April, 1835, and d. 19 Jan. following.
- I. Grace-Louisa. II. Harriet-Selina.
- III. Anne-Mildred IV. Mary. V. Emily.

Mr. Fowler is a magistrate and deputy-lieut. for co. Meath.

Lineage.—This family claims descent from the FOWLERS *of Harnage Grange and Abbey Cwmhir*. THE RIGHT REV. ROBERT FOWLER, D.D., Archbishop of Dublin, to which he had been translated from the see of Killaloe, having been previously prebendary of Westminster, and Chaplain to GEORGE II., m. Mildred, eldest dau. (and co-heir of her brother) of William Dealtry, Esq., of Gainsborough, co. Lincoln, and had a son, Robert, and two daus., viz., Mildred, m. in 1793 to Edmund Butler, Earl of Kilkenny, and d. in 1830, and Frances, m. 1795, to the Rev. Richard Bourke, afterwards Bishop of Waterford, whose eldest son is the present Earl of Mayo. His Grace d. 1803, and his widow in 1827. The only son,

THE RT. REV. ROBERT FOWLER, Bishop of Ossory and Ferns, m. 30 Jan. 1796, the Hon. Louisa Gardiner, eldest dau. of Luke Viscount Mountjoy, and sister of Charles John, earl of Blessington, and d. 31 Dec. 1841, aged 74 having had, by this lady, who d. in 1848, the following issue,

- I. ROBERT, now of Rahinston House.
- II. Luke, of Wellbrook, in holy orders, b. 18 Oct. 1799, Rector of Freshford, co. Kilkenny, m. Elizabeth, dau. of Owen Wynne, Esq. of Hazlewood, Sligo, and has issue,
  - 1 Charles-John. 2 Arthur-Robert.
  - 3 Edward-Willoughby.
  - 1 Laura-Frances-Florence.

Seat—Rahinston House, co. Meath

LANE-FOX OF BRAMHAM PARK.

LANE-FOX, GEORGE, Esq. of Bramham Park, co. York, m. 17 Nov. 1837, Katherine, dau. of John Stem, Esq., formerly M.P. for Bletchingley, and has issue,

- I. George-Sackville. II. James-Thomas-Richard
- I. Marcia.

Mr. Lane-Fox s. his father 1848.

Lineage.—WILLIAM FOX, living in the 14 EDWARD IV., acquired by marriage with Sibil, dau. of John de Grete, the lands of Grete, co. Worcester, and founded the family of Fox and Grete.

JOSEPH FOX, Esq., b. 27 Feb. 1617, (the 3rd son of Edmund Fox, of Birmingham, who was youngest son of Thomas Fox, of Grete, co. Worcester) held a commission in the army serving in Ireland. He m. the Hon. Thomasine Blayney, widow of Sir Henry Pierce, Bart., and dau. of Henry, 2nd Lord Blayney by Jane, his wife, dau. of Gerald Moore, Viscount Drogheda. By this lady he had (with four daus., Penelope, wife of Hugh Morgan, Esq. of Cotletstown; Mary, Jane, and Catherine) a son and successor,

HENRY FOX, Esq., who m. 1st, Jane, dau. of Robert Oliver, Esq., of Clonodfoy and had several sons who all d. young. He m. 2ndly, in 1691, the Hon. Frances Lane, dau of Sir George Lane, of Tulske, co. Roscommon, principal secretary of state in Ireland, created Viscount Lanesborough, and sister and heiress of James, Viscount Lanesborough, who d. in 1724. By her Mr. Fox had (with four daus., Denny-Henrietta, who d. young; Jane, Frances, and Anne) four sons viz.,

- Henry, who d. young.
- GEORGE, heir to his father.
- James, who d. 22 Oct. 1758, without issue.
- Sackville, who m. Ann Holloway, of Birmingham, and dying 1 Dec. 1760, left a son,
  - JAMES, heir to his uncle.

Mr. Fox was s. by his eldest surviving son.

GEORGE FOX, Esq., M.P., for the city of York, who inherited by will the extensive property of Lord Lanesborough, and assumed, by act of parliament, 22 March, 1750-1, in accordance with the testator's injunction, the additional surname and arms of Lane. He m. in 1731, Harriet, dau. and sole heiress of the Right Hon. Robert Benson, Lord Bingley, and was created on the extinction of his father-in-law's peerage, in May 1762, BARON BINGLEY, of Bingley, in the co. York. (*See* BURKE'S *Extinct Peerage*.) His Lordship had an only son,

- Robert, b. 5 Aug. 1732, who m. 1st, Mildred, dau. and heir of John Bourchier, Esq. of Beningborough; and 2ndly, the Lady Bridget Henley, eldest dau. of Robert, Earl of Northington, Lord Chancellor of England, but predeceased his father, issueless, in May, 1768. His widow m. 2ndly, the Hon. John Talmash.

Lord Bingley d. in 1772 and having survived his only child, devised his great estates in England and Ireland to his nephew,

JAMES FOX-LANE, Esq. of Bramham Park, co. York, M.P. for Horsham who m. 23 July, 1789, the Hon. Marcia-Lucy-Pitt, youngest dau. of George Lord Rivers, and had issue,

- GEORGE, his heir.
- William-Augustus, m. 31 Dec. 1817, Lady Caroline, sister of George-Sholto Douglas, Earl of Morton, and d. in 1832, leaving two sons.
- Sackville-Walter, M.P., m. 22 June, 1826, the Lady Charlotte-Mary-Anne-Georgiana Osborne, only dau. of George, 6th Duke of Leeds, and by her ladyship (who d. 17 Jan. 1836) had two sons and three daus

Thomas-Henry, in holy orders.
Marcia-Bridget, m. 5 Aug. 1815, to the Hon. Edward-Marmaduke Stourton, who assumed the surname and arms of Vavasour, and was created a Baronet. Lady Vavasour d. in 1829.

Mr. Fox-Lane d. in 1821, and was s. by his eldest son,

George Lane-Fox Esq. of Bramham Park, M.P., major of the Yorkshire Yeomanry Cavalry, and deputy-lieutenant co. York, who m. 20 Sept. 1814, Georgiana-Henrietta, only dau. of Edward Pery Buckley, Esq. of Minestead Lodge, Hants, and d. in 1848 leaving a son, the present George Lane-Fox Esq. of Bramham Park, and two daus., Georgiana-Marcia, and Frederica-Elizabeth.

Arms—Quarterly: 1st and 4th, a chevron, between three foxes' heads, erased, gu., for Fox; 2nd and 3rd, arg., a lion, rampant, gu., within a border, sa., on a canton of the first, a harp and crown, or, for Lane.
Crests—1st, Fox; 2nd, Lane.
Seat—Bramham House, near Bingley.

FOXALL OF KILLCAVY CASTLE.

Foxall, John, Esq. of Killcavy Castle, co. Armagh, J.P., b. in March, 1785; m. in May, 1803, Anna Maria, dau. of Col. Grant, of the 42nd Highlanders.

Lineage.—The estate of Killcavy, with other property in the co. of Armagh, was granted by King James I. to the ancestor of this family, Sir Marmaduke Whitechurch, by letters patent, bearing date 28 Feb., 7th of that reign. The grandfather of the present representative,

Joseph Foxall, Esq. of Cumberland, son of Joseph Foxall, LL.D., by the Hon. Frances Seymour his wife, m. Elinor Meredith, of the city of Dublin, and had, with three daus., one son,

Joseph Foxall, Esq. of Killcavy, co. Armagh, a magistrate for that co., who m. Sarah Adams, of Feversham, co. Tyrone, and had, besides the present John Foxall, Esq. of Killcavy Castle, two other sons and two daus., viz.,

Meredith, late banker of Newry, d., leaving three sons.
Powell, late of Killcavy Castle, co. Armagh, J.P., m., and had three sons and one dau.
Anne. Nicholina, m. to Richard Benison, Esq.

Seat—Killcavy Castle, Flurry Bridge, co. Armagh.

FRAMPTON OF MORETON.

Frampton, Henry, Esq. of Moreton, co. Dorset, J.P. and D.L., major Queen's Own regiment of yeomanry cavalry, b. 7 May, 1804; m. 13 May, 1833, Charlotte-Louisa, dau. of Robert-Willis Blencowe, Esq. of Hayes, co. Middlesex, and has issue,

Louisa-Mary, m. 22 Nov. 1855, to Robert-Rupert-Pennefather Fetherstonhaugh, Esq. of Balrath, co. Westmeath.

Lineage.—John Frampton, of Moreton (son of Walter de Frampton, who acquired the manor of Moreton by his marriage with Margaret, the heiress of that property, who is supposed to have been of the family of Husee), was twenty-four years of age at his father's death in 1389; and was returned six times to parliament as knight of the shire for co. Dorset, from 1387 to 1405. He was present at the battle of Agincourt; and, in the 4th Henry V., was appointed a commissioner to array the co. of Dorset against a French invasion. He was three times married. By his 1st wife, Isabel, dau. of Robert Prouse, he had one dau., Margaret, m. to Robert Bingham, of Binghams Melcombe, co. Dorset. By Edith, dau. of Sir Matthew Stawell, Knt. of Catherston, co. Somerset, his 2nd wife, he had three sons, Robert, his heir; John (father of John, of Potterne and Echilhampton, Wilts, whose son, by Joanna his wife, dau. and heir of Edward Mareschall, of Woodcote, Hants, was Roger Frampton, who eventually s. to Moreton); and William, M.P. for Dorchester. John Frampton d. 26 May, 1426, leaving Margaret, his 3rd wife, surviving him, and was s. at Moreton by his eldest son,

Robert Frampton, of Moreton, whose son (by Alianor his wife, dau. and heir of William Browning, of Melbury Sampford, co. Dorset),

James Frampton, of Moreton, b. in 1452; m. Anastasia, dau. of Sir John Newborough, Knt. of Lullworth, co. Dorset; and d. 5 June, 1523. Leaving no legitimate issue, he settled his estates on James Frampton, his bastard son, who m. Avice, dau. of Sir Thomas de la Lynde, Knt. of Winterborn, Clenston, co. Dorset; and d. s. p. before 22 Aug. 1525. On his decease, the manor of Moreton, with other appendant estates, descended to

Roger Frampton (the grandson of John, the 2nd son of John Frampton, of Moreton, who d. in 1426). He was b. in 1495, and m. Alice Trenchard; but d. s. p. 3 May, 1530, his nephew (the son of his brother Edward),

John Frampton, of Moreton, b. in 1516; d. 14 Nov. 1557, leaving by his wife, Elizabeth, dau. of Nicholas Willoughby, of Tonerspiddle, co. Dorset (with six daus.), five sons,

I. Robert, his heir.
II. John, of Upway, co. Dorset, who, by Anne his wife, dau. of Henry Willoughby, of Upway aforesaid, had,
 1 Robert, his eldest son.
 2 George, of Buckland.
III. Francis, rector of Studland, co. Dorset, d. s. p. 1646.
IV. William, who s. to the Moreton estates.
V. James, of Buckland Ripers, m. Katherine, dau. and co-heir of John Trenchard, of Warmwell, 3rd son of Sir George Trenchard, Knt. of Wolveton, in Dorsetshire; and dying in 1631, was s. by his son, James Frampton, Esq. of Buckland Ripers, father, by Katherine his 1st wife, dau. of Berkeley, of Pill, James, of Buckland, who d. unm. in 1676; and Katherine, who became the wife of George Daubeney, of Gorwell, in Dorsetshire, and by Elizabeth his 2nd wife, dau. of Henry Samways, of East Thilvington, in Dorset, he had one son, Giles Frampton, of Buckland, b. in 1643, who s. his half-brother, James, in the estate of Buckland. By Elizabeth his wife (who d. in 1706), dau. of Amias Fulford, son of Sir Francis Fulford, of Great Fulford, he had three sons, on whom, in succession, the estate of Moreton was entailed by their cousin, William Frampton, viz., Giles, of Buckland, b. in 1680, d. unm. after 1689; William, of whom hereafter; and Robert, b. in 1683, who, by Katherine his wife, dau. of Giles White, of Athelhampton, had issue, one son and four daus.

The eldest son and heir,

Robert Frampton, of Moreton, was high-sheriff of Dorset in 1588, m. Margery, dau. of Lord Thomas Paulett, of Melplash and had two sons, Thomas and Charles, who both appear to have d. s. p.; and one dau., Elizabeth, m. in 1593, to William Daccomb. Robert's uncle,

William Frampton, of Moreton, m. Elizabeth, 2nd dau. and co-heir of George Broughton, of Sampford Botfield, co. Somerset, and by her (who m. 2ndly, Thomas Hannam, of Wimbourne Minster) had a son,

William Frampton, of Moreton, b. 7 April, 1607; who m. Katharine, dau. of John Tregonwell, of Milton Abbas, co. Dorset; and dying 16 Aug. 1643, was s. in his estates by his eldest son,

William Frampton, of Moreton, b. in 1629; who d. unm. 8 Feb. 1689, and was s. by his brother,

Tregonwell Frampton, Esq. of Moreton, b. in 1641. He was keeper of the receiving horses to King William III., Queen Anne, George I., and George II.; and d. unm at Newmarket, in 1728, when the estates devolved upon his kinsman (the descendant of James Frampton, of Buckland Ripers),

William Frampton, Esq of Moreton, b. in 1681; who m. Judith, dau of Henry Arnold, Esq. of Ilsington, co. Dorset, by whom (who d. 1732) he left at his decease, in 1717, an only surviving son,

James Frampton, Esq. of Moreton, b. in 1711; high-sheriff of Dorset 17 George II.; m. 1st, 20 Aug. 1746, Mary, only dau. and heir of Joseph Houlton, Esq. of Farley Castle, co. Somerset, by whom (who d. in 1762) he had no issue. He m. 2ndly, Phillis, only dau. (and heir after her brother's death, in 1761) of Samuel Byam, Esq. of the Island of Antigua, widow of Charlton Wollaston, M.D., by whom (who d. in Feb. 1829) he had issue, James, his heir; and Mary. He d. 1784, and was s. by his son,

James Frampton, Esq. of Moreton, high-sheriff 1793, and lieut.-col., comm. of the Dorset regt. of yeomanry cavalry, b. 4 Sept. 1769; m. Sept. 9, 1799, Lady Harriot Strangways, dau. of the 2nd Earl of Ilchester, and by her (who d. 1844) he left at his decease, 8 Feb. 1855,

James, b. 28 March, 1802; d. 9 May, 1818.
Henry, now of Frampton.
William-Charlton, b. 4 June, 1811.
Harriot-Georgiana, m. 28 Oct. 1830, to William Mundy, Esq. of Markeaton, co. Derby.
Louisa-Charlotte.

Arms—Arg., a bend, gu., cottised, sa.
Crest—A greyhound, sejant, arg., collared, gu., ringed, or.
Motto—Perseverando.
Seat—Moreton, in Dorsetshire.

FRANCE OF BOSTOCK HALL.

FRANCE, JAMES-FRANCE, Esq. of Bostock Hall, co. Chester, J.P. and D.L., high-sheriff in 1821, b. 2 Feb. 1793.

Lineage.—THOMAS HAYHURST, Esq. of Liverpool, inheriting the fortune of his uncle, James France, Esq. of Everton, assumed, in 1796, in compliance with the testamentary injunction of that gentleman, the surname and arms of FRANCE. He m. Miss Cropper, sister of John Cropper, Esq. of Liverpool, and had issue,

JAMES-FRANCE, his heir.
Thomas, in holy orders, rector of Davenham, m. in 1831, Helen, eldest dau. of John Hosken-Harper, Esq. of Davenham Hall, co. Chester, and has issue, three children.
Henry-Hayhurst, capt. in the 6th dragoon-guards.
Sarah, m. to William-Wallace Currie, Esq., son of the late Dr. Currie.
Ellen.
Elizabeth m. to Stanley Perceval, Esq. of Liverpool.
Marianne, m. to Myles, eldest son of Myles Sandys, Esq. of Graythwaite Hall, co. Lancashire.
Frances.
Harriet, m. to George Littledale, Esq., late of Sandown.
Caroline, m. to John, son of John Hamilton, Esq. of Ham House, co. Dublin.

Mr. (Hayhurst) France d. 24 Jan. 1816, and was s. by his eldest son,

JAMES-FRANCE FRANCE, Esq. of Bostock Hall.

Arms—Arg., on a mount in base, a hurst, ppr, a chief, wavy, az., charged with three fleurs-de-lis, or.

Crest—A mount, thereon a hurst, as in the arms, from the centre tree a shield, pendant, gu., charged with a fleur-de-lis, or, strap, az.

Motto—Virtus semper viridis.

Seat—Bostock Hall, near Middlewich.

FRANCKLIN OF GONALSTON.

FRANCKLIN, JOHN, Esq. of Gonalston, co. Nottingham, J.P., high-sheriff 1851, b. 5 June, 1808; m. 28 Feb. 1839, Frances-Barbara, 2nd dau. of the late Harry Edgell, Esq. of Cadogan Place, barrister-at-law, and one of the benchers of Gray's Inn, and has issue,

I. JOHN-LIELL, b. 16 Oct. 1842.
II. Harry, b. Sept. 1846.
I. Caroline II. Elizabeth.

Lineage.—ROBERT FRANCKLIN, Esq. of Skipton-upon-Craven, co. York, was father of WILLIAM FRANCKLIN, of Thurleigh, co. Bedford, who m. Margaret, dau. of Risly, of Ravensdon, in the same co., and had, with three younger sons, Thomas, Richard, and William, Dean of York, Durham, and Windsor, an elder son, JOHN FRANCKLIN, who was father, by Elizabeth his wife, dau. of Barry, of Thurleigh, of a son,

JOHN FRANCKLIN, Esq. who m. 1st, Elizabeth, dau. of Halle, of Mildham, co. Durham, by whom he had two sons, John and William, and a dau. He m. 2ndly, Anne, dau. of Edward Copley, of Southill, co. Bedford, and by her had, with other issue, three sons,

GEORGE, of whom presently.
Edward, b. in 1548, in holy orders, rector of Kelshull, co. Hertford, ancestor of the present JOHN FRANCKLIN, Esq. of Gonalston.
Thomas, an alderman of the city of London.

Mr. Francklin d. in 1581. The eldest son of his second marriage,

GEORGE FRANCKLIN, m. Anne, dau of Styles, of Langley, co. Kent, and had, with three daus., Anne, m. to Richard, Gery, of Bushmead, co. Beds; Elizabeth, m. to Thomas Basse, of Berton, co. Bucks; and Margaret, m. to Thomas Bacan, of Burton, co. Northampton, four sons, viz., Edmond who, m. Elizabeth, dau. of Sir Robert Charnock, of Holcot, co. Bedford, and had one dau., Elizabeth; GEORGE, of whom presently; Nicholas, barrister-at-law, m. Bridget Street, and d. s. p.; and John, who m. Frances Blofeild. The second son,

GEORGE FRANCKLIN, Esq. of Maverne, co. Bedford, b. in 1590, m. Dorothy, only dau. of William Halsey, of Gaddesdon, co. Hants, and by her had, with a dau., Anne, m. to Richard Daston, of Wormington, co. Gloucester, three sons, viz, George, d. s. p.; William, m. the Countess of Donegall, and d. s. p.: and

SIR JOHN FRANCKLIN, a master in chancery, who m. 1st, Frances, dau of Sir Francis Clerk, of Ulcombe, co. Kent, and 2ndly, Dorothy, dau. of George Clerk, of Watford, co. Northampton, but having no issue by either, he left his estate, at his decease in Aug. 1707, to his kinsman,

THE REV. JOHN FRANCKLIN, of Mileham Rector of Gressenhall, b. 27 Oct, 1666, (son of the Rev. John Francklin, Rector of Tittleshall, co. Norfolk, by Frances his wife, dau. of Dr. Luke Skippon, and grandson, by Elizabeth, his wife, dau. of the Rev. John Montfort, of the Rev Edward Francklin, Rector of Cressingham, whose father the Rev. Edward Franklin, Rector of Kelshull, Herts, was brother of George Francklin, grandfather of Sir John Francklin, the Master in Chancery.) He m. 29 Aug. 1695 Sarah, dau. of John Neale, merchant of Wisbech, and d. 26. Nov. 1710, having had (with three younger sons, Edward, b. in 1698, d. unm. 3 Jan. 1766; Philip, b. in 1700, m. Eliza, dau. of Richard-Middleton Massey, Esq. M.D., and d. s. p.; and Luke, b. in 1707, d. 25 May, 1774, and other children, who d. young) an elder son and heir,

JOHN FRANCKLIN. Esq. of Great Barford, co. Bedford, b. 2 June, 1697, who m. 1st, 26 July, 1731, Anne, dau. of Sandra Foster, Esq. of Great Barford, and 2ndly, Elizabeth Taylor, relict of Richard Little, Esq., merchant of Wisbech, and by the former only had issue. He d. 24 July, 1740, leaving, with a dau., Anne, who d. in 1794, an only surviving son and heir,

JOHN FRANCKLIN, Esq. of Great Barford, b. in June, 1736, who m. 3 Feb. 1759, Elizabeth, dau. of Thomas Liell, Esq. of London, and by her (who d 11 June, 1787,) had twelve children, all of whom d. unm., except one dau., Mary, m. 4 Oct. 1790, to Henry Boulton, Esq. of co. Lincoln, and d., without leaving issue, 4 Sept. 1795, and his third son,

RICHARD FRANCKLIN, Esq. of Great Barford, b. 26 April, 1776, who m. 26 Feb 1807, Judith-Reddall, third dau. and co-heir of Sir Philip Monoux, of Sandy Place, co. Bedford, Bart., and by her, (who d. 9 May, 1813) had issue, JOHN, now of Gonalston; George, d. 27 Feb. 1813, young; and Elizabeth (deceased) m. in Feb. 1829, to Capt. William-Halstead Poole, R. H. Art., of Terrick Hall, co. Salop. Mr. Francklin d. 19 May, 1843.

Arms—Arg., on a bend, engr., between two lions' heads, erased, gu., a dolphin, hauriant, between two parrots, or.

Crest—A dolphin's head, or, erased, gu., between two olive branches, vert.

Motto—Sinceritate.

Seats—Gonalston, near Southwell, Notts, and Great Barford, co. Bedford.

FRANK OF CAMPSALL.

FRANK, FREDERICK-BACON, Esq. of Campsall, co. York, and Earlham Hall, Norfolk, b. 20 April, 1827; m. 14 Nov. 1854, Mary Anne, dau. of Sir Baldwin Wake Walker, Bart. K.C.B.

Lineage.—The purchases of the FRANKS, in the county of York, began in the 3 of JAMES I., when the manor of Trumflete was bought from Sir William Willoughby, by JOHN FRANK, an alderman of Pontefract, who d. about the year 1624. His eldest son,

RICHARD FRANK, Esq. of Pontefract and Campsall, b. in 1598, m. Anne, dau. of Bernard Ellis, Esq., recorder of York, and leaving no male issue, was s., in accordance with a settlement he had made, by (the son of his elder dau.) his grandson,

EDWARD ASHTON, Esq., son of Edward Ashton, Esq. of Clubcliffe, in Methley, by Ann, his wife, elder dau. and coheir of RICHARD FRANK, Esq. of Pontefract and Campsall, and grandson of the Rev. Edward Ashton, rector of Middleton, co. Lancaster, who assumed, upon inheriting Campsall, &c. at the decease of his grandfather, the surname and arms of FRANK. He m. his cousin, Ann, dau. of John Pelham, Esq. of Hull, by Jane, his wife, 2nd dau. and co-heir of Richard Frank, Esq. of Campsall and had an only dau., Anne, m. to Sir George Tempest, Bart of Tong, and d. in 1746. Edward Frank was s. by his brother,

MATTHEW ASHTON, Esq., b. 1655, who also assumed the surname and arms of FRANK. He m. Ann. dau. of Thomas Ashwin, of Hamburgh, and by her, who d. 7 Oct. 1745, had two sons and five daus. Mr. Frank d. at Campsall, 22 March, 1717, and was s. by his elder son,

RICHARD FRANK, Esq. of Campsall, recorder of Pontefract and Doncaster, one of the earliest members of the Society of Antiquaries, and the intimate associate of most of the distinguished antiquaries of his day. He m. Margaret, 3rd dau. and co-heir (with her sisters, Elizabeth, m. 1st, to Samuel Savile, Esq. of Thribergh, and 2ndly, to John Hoare, Esq.; and Catherine, m. 1st, to John Smythe, Esq. of Heath, and 2ndly, to Thomas Standish, Esq. of Duxbury) of Robert Frank, Esq. of Pontefract, M.P., son of Robert Frank, Esq., M.P., whose father, Robert, was younger brother of Richard Frank, Esq., whose dau. m.

Elward Ashton, but *d.* without issue, 22 May, 1763, aged 64, when the estates passed to his nephew,

BACON FRANK, Esq. of Campsall, J.P., for many years chairman of the quarter sessions, and high-sheriff for the co. of York in 1777. He *m.* Catherine, dau. and heir of John Hoare, Esq. of Pontefract, by Elizabeth, his wife, dau. and co-heir of Robert Frank, Esq., M.P., of the same place, and had issue,

Bacon, an officer in the army, killed by a fall from his horse at Tunbridge, 15 June, 1789, aged 18.
EDWARD, his father's heir.
Catherine. Elizabeth.
Margaret, *m.* to Rev. John Francis.
Mary, *m.* to Charles Mainwaring, Esq., capt. R.N., and has an only son, Edward-Frank-Charles Mainwaring.
Charlotte, *m.* to Thomas Bellamy, Esq.

Mr. Frank *d.* 4 April, 1812, and was *s.* by his son

REV. EDWARD FRANK, of Campsall, rector of Alderton, Suffolk, *m.* 1800, Mary Frances, dau. of Col. James Sowerby, R.A., and had issue; 1 RICHARD BACON, his heir; 2 Edward; 3 and 4 Aspinall and Adolphus, twins; 1 Jemima. The eldest son,

RICHARD-BACON FRANK, Esq. of Campsall, *m.* Caroline, dau. of S. Curteis, LL.D. and had a son, the present FREDERICK-BACON FRANK, Esq. of Campsall, and Earlham Hall.

Arms—Vert, a saltier, engrailed, or. *Crest*—A falcon.
Seats—Campsall, near Doncaster, and Earlham Hall, Norfolk.

FRANKS OF CARRIG.

FRANKS, WILLIAM, Esq. of Carrig, co. Cork, J.P., *m.* Elizabeth, dau. of Adam Newman, Esq. of Dromore, co. Cork, and has, with three daus., four sons, viz.,

I. THOMAS. II. William.
III. David. IV. John.

Lineage.—The first of the English family of Franks who settled in Ireland was an officer in Cromwell's army.

DAVID FRANKS, Esq. of Garryarthur, co. Limerick, living there, 28 Feb. 1718, was father of two sons,

I. THOMAS, his heir.
II. Matthew, of Moorestown, co. Limerick, *b.* about 1702; *m.* a dau. of — Upton, Esq. of co. Limerick, and had issue,
1 Henry, of Moorestown, co. Limerick, and of Maidstown, co. Cork, *b.* about 1728; *m.* 1776, Elizabeth, 3rd dau. of Robert Atkins, Esq. of Fountainville, co. Cork, and had issue,
ROBERT, of Maidstown, *b.* 1767; *m.* Rebecca, dau. of Robert Molloy, Esq. of Streamstown, King's County, and *d.* 26 Oct. 1843, leaving issue, 1 HENRY, of Maidstown, and now of Gortnaviders, co. Tipperary, *m.* Elizabeth, dau. of Ringrose Atkins, Esq. of Prospect Hill, co. Cork; 2 William, *d. s. p.*; 3 Robert, *d. unm.*; 4 Matthew, settled in Van Dieman's Land, and *d.* leaving issue. 1 Abigail; 2 Rebecca.
Thomas, *m.* Margaret, dau. of John Maunsell, Esq., of Ballybrood, co. Limerick, and had one son, Thomas, who *d. unm.*
Henry, *m.* and had issue.
Charles, *m.* and had issue, the Rev. James S. Franks and others,
Mathew, *d. unm.*
Elizabeth. Mary.
2 Thomas, of Ballymagooly, co. Cork, *b.* 1729, *m.* Catherine, dau. of the Rev. John Day, and dying 1787, left issue,
Mathew, of Jerpoint, co. Kilkenny, and of Merrion-square, Dublin, *b.* 1768, *m.* Mary, dau. of Robert Ferguson, Esq., and had issue; 1 Thomas, of Fitzwilliam-street, Dublin, barrister-at-law, *b.* 1808; *m.* 1834, Mary, dau. of Thomas Cuthbert Kearney, Esq., of Garratstown, co. Cork, and has issue, Matthew; Thomas; and Mary. 2 Robert Ferguson, of Jerpoint, and Upper Mount St., *m.* 1833, Henrietta, dau. of the Right Hon. Charles-Kendal Bushe, Lord Chief Justice of the King's Bench in Ireland, and has Norman; Cecil; John; Kendal; and other issue. 3 Mathew; 4 John; 1 Catherine, *m* to the Rev. Dennis Mahony, of Dromore Castle, co. Kerry; 2 Mary, *m.* to John Waller, Esq., barrister-at-law; and 3 Ellen, *m.* to Joseph Smyly, Esq., M.D.
John (Sir) Knt., barrister-at-law, *b.* 1769, judge at Calcutta 1825; *d.* 1852: *m.* 1st Catherine, dau. of Thos. Franks, Esq. of Carrig; 2ndly, Jane, dau. of John Marshall, Esq.; and, 3rdly, 1 March, 1849, Sarah-Wollaston, 2nd dau. and co-heir of Wm. O'Regan, Esq., barrister-at-law, and had issue by the first wife only, viz.; 1 John, of Ballyskiddane Castle, co. Limerick, J.P. and D.L., *m.* 1830, Eleanor, dau. of Thos. Whitmore, Esq. of Dudmaston, co. Salop, and has issue, Thomas; Henry-Whitmore; Mary, *m.* 1855, to Joseph Gubbins, Esq. of Kilfrush and Ellen; 2 Mathew, formerly an officer 11th Hussars, *m.* Louisa, dau. of Capt. Roche, H. E. I. C. S. and has issue, John, and Robert, an officer Bengal artillery; 1 Margaret, *m.* 1826, to the Ven. John Hawtayne, archdeacon of Bombay; 2 Catherine, *m.* 1818, to Thomas Montgomery, Esq.; and 3 Lucy, *m.* 1831, to Henry Holroyd, Esq.
William, an officer, R.N., *d. s. p.*
Robert, of Leeson Street, Dublin, *d. unm.* 1850.
Lucy, *m.* 1791, to Thos. Cuthbert, Esq., who took the name of Kearney.
Catherine, *m.* to Thomas Leland, Esq., of Fitzwilliam Square, Dublin.
Anne, *m.* to Hickman Kearney, Esq.
Mary, *m.* to — Palmer, Esq.
3 Welstead, of Kilfinnan, co. Limerick, *m.* 1776, Frances, dau. of William Chapman, and had a son, Thomas, of Mallow, *d. s. p.* 1805.
1 Margaret, *m.* to Noble Seyward, Esq. of Kilcannaway, co. Cork.
2 Mary, *m.* to Thomas Heffernan Esq. of co. Limerick.
3 Gertrude, *m.* to Sir John Purcell, Knt. of High Fort, co. Cork.
4 Ellen.

The elder son,

THOMAS FRANKS, Esq. of Garryarthur, co. Limerick, *b.* about 1700, *m.* Miss Hart, of the county of Clare, and was father of (with William, who *d. s. p.*, and a dau. *m.* to — Walsh, Esq. co. Limerick),

THOMAS FRANKS, Esq. of Carrig, co. Cork, J.P., who *m.* Margery, eld. dau. and co-heir of Richard Harte, Esq. of Grange, co. Limerick, *d.* 1780, leaving issue,

DAVID, his heir.
WILLIAM, successor to his brother. Thomas.
Catherine, *m.* to her cousin, Sir John Franks, and *d.* 1812.
Margaret, *m.* 1st, to Ralph Lawrenson, Esq., and 2ndly, to — Bourchier, Esq.

The eldest son,

DAVID FRANKS, Esq. of Carrig, co. Cork, J.P., *m.* a dau. of James Nash, Esq. of Bellevue, co. Cork, and by her (who *m.* 2ndly, Major-General Sir Thomas Browne, col. 8th Hussars, and *d.* in 1847) he left no issue, and was *s.* by his brother,

WILLIAM FRANKS, Esq. of Carrig, J.P., who *m.* Catherine, eldest dau. of William Hume, Esq. of Humewood, co. Wicklow, M.P., and had issue,

WILLIAM, now of Carrig.
Thomas-Harte, col. in the army, Lieut.-Col. 10th regt., and C.B., *m.* Matilda, dau. of Richard Kay, Esq. and widow of the Rev. W. Fletcher.
David-Brudenell, *m.* 1837, Catherine, dau. of — Thompson, Esq., and has issue.
Catherine-Cecilia-Jane, *m.* to Sir Denham O. Jephson Norreys, Bart, M.P.
Margaret.

Seat—Carrig, co. Cork.

FRASER OF SKIPNESS CASTLE.

FRASER, WILLIAM-THOMAS, Esq. of Skipness Castle, co. Argyll, *b.* 1 Jan. 1838; *s.* his father in 1856.

Lineage.—The late WILLIAM FRASER, Esq., of Skipness Castle, co. Argyle, son of the late Alexander Fraser and Isabella his wife, *b.* 15 Sept. 1785, *m.* 8 March, 1837, Helen-Colquhoun, eldest dau. of James Campbell, Esq. of Dunmore, and had issue,

WILLIAM-THOMAS, now of Skipness.
James-Campbell, *b.* 14 March, 1840.
Alexander-George, *b.* 28 May, 1841.
Reginald, *b.* 11 Nov. 1842.
Evan-James, *b.* 28 March, 1847.
Elizabeth-Gertrude

Seat—Skipness Castle, Argyle.

FRASER OF HOSPITALFIELD.

ALLAN-FRASER, PATRICK, Esq. of Hospitalfield, co. Forfar, Blackcraig, co. Perth, and Hawkesbury Hall, co. Warwick; *m.* Sept. 1843, Elizabeth, only dau. of Major John Fraser, of Hospitalfield, by Elizabeth his wife, dau. of Francis Parrot, M.D. of Birmingham, and assumed in 1851 the additional surname and arms of FRASER. Mr. Allan-Fraser is son of Robert Allan, Esq. of Arbroath, by Isabel his wife, dau. of Alexander Macdonald, Esq., also of Arbroath.

Arms—Quarterly: 1st and 4th, az., three frazes, arg.; 2nd and 3rd gu., a lion rampant, arg., all within a bordure, indented or; for distinction, a canton ermine.
Crest—A bush of strawberries, ppr.; for distinction, a mount, vert.
Motto—Nosce teipsum.
Seats—Hospitalfield, co. Forfar, and Hawkesbury Hall, co. Warwick.

FRASER OF CASTLE FRASER.

Fraser, Charles, Esq. of Castle Fraser, co. Ross, *b.* 9 June, 1792; *m.* 25 April, 1817, Jane, 4th dau. of Sir John Hay, Bart. of Hayston, and Mary-Elizabeth his wife, 2nd dau. of James, 16th Lord Forbes, and has issue,

I. John-Wingfield, *b.* 18 June, 1822.
II. Charles-Murray, in the 82nd regt., *b.* 8 Dec. 1825.
III. Francis-Mackenzie, R.N., *b.* 19 June, 1827.
IV. Frederick, *b.* 4 April, 1831.
I. Catherine. II. Mary-Elizabeth.
III. Eleanor-Jane. IV. Grace-Harriet.
V. Augusta-Charlotte.

Colonel Fraser, now colonel of the Ross-shire militia, served in the Peninsula in 1808-9, in the 52nd regt., and in 1812 in the Coldstream-guards. He sat in parliament for Ross-shire from 1815 to 1819.

Lineage.—The Hon. Simon Fraser, of Inverallochy, son of Simon, 8th Lord Fraser, *m.* Lady Margery Erskine, 2nd dau. of James, 7th Earl of Buchan, and by this lady he was father of

Simon Fraser, of Inverallochy, who had a son and heir,

Charles Fraser, Esq. of Inverallochy, whose eldest dau., Martha, *m.* Colin Mackenzie, Esq. of Kilcoy, and by him was mother of with other issue, Charles, (whose only son is the present Sir Colin Mackenzie, of Kilcoy, Bart.) and

Alexander Mackenzie, M.P. for co. Ross, a lieut.-general in the army, and colonel of the 78th Highlanders, who derived from his mother the estate of Inverallochy, and that of Castle Fraser from her younger sister, Elizabeth, and assumed, in consequence, the additional surname of Fraser, by Royal license. He *m.* in 1786, Helen, sister of Francis, Lord Seaforth, and *d.* in 1809, having had, with two daus., Marianne and Helen, deceased, two sons, Charles, his heir, the present Col. Charles Fraser, of Castle Fraser; and Frederick Alexander Mackenzie, Lieut.-Col. in the army, and Assist. Quarter-Master General to the forces in Canada, who *m.* 1st, Emma-Sophia, 2nd dau. of Hume Macleod, Esq. of Harris, and by her has two sons, Frederick-Charles and Colin, and one dau., Isabel: he *m.* 2ndly, Georgina, dau. of the late Sir Charles Bagot, Governor of Canada.

Arms—Quarterly: 1st and 4th, az., three cinquefoils, arg., for Fraser; 2nd and 3rd, quarterly, az. and arg., in the 1st and 4th quarters, three cinquefoils, arg., and in the 2nd and 3rd, as many antique crowns, gu., all within a bordure, erm.
Crests—1st, a mount of strawberries, fructed, ppr.; 2nd, a stag's head, couped, ppr.
Mottoes—All my hope is in God, and, Je suis prest.
Seat—Castle Fraser, co. Ross.

FRASER OF FINDRACK AND PITMURCHIE.

Fraser, Francis-Garden, Esq. of Findrack, co. Aberdeen, *s.* his father in 1824, and is heir and representative of Baird of Auchmeddan, chief of that name.

Lineage.—Francis Fraser, only son of John Fraser, who acquired the lands of Ferryhill, near Aberdeen, who was 4th son of Thomas Fraser, of Durris, co. Kincardine, and Helen, dau. of James Gordon, of Abergeldie, acquired the lands of Findrack and Pitmurchie, in Lumphanan, and at different periods the lands, of Tolmads, Drumlassie, and Birselassie, &c., in the parish of Kincardine O'Neil, co. Aberdeen.

The immediate ancestor of the family of Durris, (who were anciently designed Thanes of Cowie and Durris,) in common with the noble families of Lovat and Saltoun, (Douglas's *Peerage*, voce Saltoun and Macfarlane's' Genealogical Memoir,) was Sir Alexander Fraser, Knt., Lord High Chamberlain of Scotland in the reign of King Robert the Bruce. He *m.* Lady Mary, sister of that great prince, from whom he got many grants of land. He had a charter of the lands of Strachan in 1316, and the king afterwards gave "dilecto et fideli suo Alexandro Fraser militi," the lands of the Thanedon of Cowie to him, "et hæredibus suis inter ipsum et Mariam Bruce, sponsam suam sororem nostram." The lands of Durris were erected into a free barony, by King David Bruce in 1369.

Francis Fraser, of Findrack and Pitmurchie, *m.* Agnes Adam, by whom he had an only son,

Francis Fraser, of Findrack, *b.* in 1669, *m.* in 1704, Janet, dau. of John Fraser, Esq. of Cooperhill, by whom he had issue,

Francis, his heir.
James, *b.* 12 June, 1709.
George, *b.* 2 Feb. 1714.
William, Advocate, *b.* 22 Feb. 1719, *m.* Helen Burnett, sister of Sir Thomas Burnett, 6th Bart. of Leys.
John, *b.* 7 March, 1724.
Thomas, *b.* 18 March, 1727, *m.* Magdalena, dau. of — Dingwall, Esq., merchant in Aberdeen.
Agnes, *b.* 19 Nov. 1715, *m.* Alexander Chalmers, Esq. of Balnacraig, co. Aberdeen.

The eldest son,

Francis Fraser, of Findrack, *b.* 18 Sept. 1707, *m.* Catharine, 4th dau. of Sir Robert Gordon, Bart. of Gordonston, and sister of Sir Robert, the 4th baronet, who, on the demise of William, the 21st earl, claimed to be Earl of Sutherland, but the title was adjudged to the earl's dau. He *d.* 24 Oct. 1791, leaving issue,

Francis, his heir.
William, ensign in the army, killed in America, when carrying the regimental colours of the 42nd regiment.
John, Gordon, and Peter, } who all died without issue.
Janet, *b.* 5 Feb. 1746, *m.* 8 Nov. 1768, Charles Forbes, of Auchernack, by whom she had issue, Nathaniel Forbes, *b.* 2 Feb. 1766, now of Auchernach and Dunnottar, a lieut.-gen. H. E. I. Co. service, and Colonel of the 24th Madras, N.I., and two other sons.

The eldest son,

Francis Fraser, of Findrack, *b.* in 1737, *m.* in 1761, Henrietta, dau. of William Baird, Esq. of Auchmedden,* chief of that name, by his wife, Anne, dau. of William Duff, of Dipple, and sister of William, 1st Earl of Fife. Francis Fraser *d.* 24 Dec. 1809, having had (with seven younger sons, who all *d. unm.*, or without issue) an eldest son,

Francis Fraser, of Findrack, *b.* 22 Aug. 1762, commander, R.N., and Post Captain in the naval service of Portugal, who was an officer on board the "Formidable" at Lord Rodney's victory over Comte de Grasse, 12 April, 1782; at the relief of Gibraltar under Lord Howe; and at several other naval engagements during the late war. He *m.* Garden, dau. of Mr. Charles Winchester, of Aberdeen, and sister of Lieut.-Col. Robert Winchester, K.H., 92nd Highlanders. He *d.* 24 April, 1824, leaving (with three daus. who *d.* young) three sons,

Francis-Garden, now of Findrack.
William-Nathaniel, *m.* 1846, Philadelphia, dau. of Hugh Veitch, Esq., of Stuartfield, town-clerk of Leith, and brother of Lieut.-Col. Henry Veitch, of Eliock, co. Dumfries, and has a son, Francis, *b.* 12 Dec. 1855.
Robert-Winchester, M.D., staff surgeon, second class, army medical department, *m.* 1842, Mary-Anne, dau. of the late Arthur Anderson, Esq., of Charlton, co. Forfar, and of Deebank, co. Aberdeen.

Arms—Az., three cinquefoils, arg.
Crest—A stag's head, erased, or.
Motto—"I am ready."

*** Mr. Fraser is the only male representative of the ancient family of Durris.

FREEMAN OF PYLEWELL.

Williams-Freeman, William-Peere, Esq. of Pylewell, Hants, J.P. and D.L., high-sheriff 1838, *b.* 7 Dec. 1811; *m.* 23 July, 1833, Frances-Augusta, 3rd dau. of Wyrley Birch, Esq. of Wretham Hall, co. Norfolk, and has had issue,

I. William-Peere, *b.* 16 Oct. 1834.
II. Frederick-Peere, *b.* 29 Sept. 1836.
III. Henry-Peere, *b.* 29 April, 1838.
IV. Francis-Peere, *b.* 20 Oct. 1841.
V. Robert-Peere, *b.* 16 March, 1843.
VI. Ernest-Peere, *b.* 28 July, 1845.
VII. Herbert-Peere, *b.* 20 June, 1847.
VIII. George-Peere, *b.* 6 Aug. 1848.
I. Frances-Augusta, *d.* 18 April, 1841.
II. Mary-Katharine.
III. Julia-Margaret. IV. Flora-Jemima.

* For some account of the family of Baird, *see* Burke's *Peerage and Baronetage*, *voce* Newbyth and Sauchtonhall.

Lineage.—ANTHONY WILLIAMS, Esq. (of a family long settled at Denton, co. Lincoln) had, by his wife, a dau. of William Peere, Esq., a son,

PEERE WILLIAMS, Esq., Clerk of the Estreats, *temp.* CHARLES II., who *m.* Joanna Oyley, a lady of good family in Holland, and was father of

WILLIAM-PEERE WILLIAMS, Esq., barrister-at-law, author of three volumes of Reports. He *m.* Anne, 2nd dau. and co-heir of Sir George Hutchins, one of the Lords Commissioners of the Great Seal, *temp.* WILLIAM and MARY, and had issue,

- HUTCHINS (Sir), of Clapton, co. Northampton, created a Baronet in 1747 (*see* BURKE'S *Extinct Baronetage*).
- FREDERICK, of whom presently.
- William-Peere, of Cadleigh, Devon, who *m.* a French lady, and had two daus , Elizabeth, *m.* in 1771, to Thomas, Lord Graves; and Anne, *m.* to Sir Richard Sutton, Bart. of Norwood Park.
- George, who *m.* Diana, dau. of the Earl of Coventry.
- Anne, *m.* 1st, to George Speke, Esq. of White Lackington, by whom she had an only dau. the wife of Frederick Lord North; and 2ndly, to Sir Francis Drake, Bart. of Ash, Devon.
- Louisa, *m.* to Sir Robert Hamilton, Bart.

The 2nd son,

THE REV. FREDERICK WILLIAMS, D.D., prebendary of Peterborough, *m.* Mary, eldest dau. of the Rev. Dr. Robert Clavering, bishop of Peterborough, and had, with other issue, who *d.* in infancy, WILLIAM-PEERE, of whom presently; Robert, *b.* 26 May, 1745, *m.* 28 Aug. 1773, Miss Anne Leigh; Elizabeth, *m.* 26 Dec. 1768, to Thomas Mitchell, Esq. of Nafferton, co. Northumberland; Mary, *m.* 12 Nov. 1768, to Christopher Nesham, Esq. of Houghton le Spring. The elder son.

WILLIAM-PEERE WILLIAMS, Esq., senior admiral of the fleet, *b.* 15 Dec. 1741, *m.* 20 June, 1771, Miss Henrietta Wills, and had issue, William-Peere, *d.* 16 May, 1776; Frederick-Charles, *b.* 17 March, 1781, *d.* 1 June, 1799; WILLIAM-PEERE, of whom presently; and a dau., Anne-Eliza, *d.* young. Admiral Williams, assumed, 19 Jan. 1822, the additional surname and arms of FREEMAN, and *d.* 10 Feb. 1832, aged 90. His youngest son,

WILLIAM-PEERE WILLIAMS-FREEMAN, Esq. of Fawley Court, co. Oxford, *b.* 6 Sept. 1782, *m.* 2 March, 1811, Frances-Dorothea, eldest dau. of the late Robert-Willis Blencowe, Esq. of Hayes Park, co. Middlesex, and by her (who *m.* 2ndly, in Feb. 1839, Gen. Sir George Napier, K.C.B.) had two son and a dau.,

- WILLIAM-PEERE, late of Fawley Court, and now of Pylewell.
- Frederick-Peere, *b.* 2 Jan. 1814; *m.* 6 Oct. 1853, Sarah-Augusta, dau. of Capt. Henry Napier.
- Mary-Frances *m.* 8 Jan. 1841 to George Rooper, Esq., who *d.* 15 April, 1856.

Mr. Williams-Freeman predeceased his father, 18 July, 1830.

Arms—Quarterly: 1st and 4th, az., three lozenges, or, for FREEMAN; 2nd and 3rd, gu., a cave, ppr., therefrom issuing a wolf at full speed, regardant, arg., for WILLIAMS.
Crest—1st, a demi-lion, gu., charged with a lozenge, or, for FREEMAN; 2nd, a lion, rampant, gorged with a chaplet of oak-leaves, ppr., navally crowned, or, for WILLIAMS.
Motto—Libertas et natale solum.
Seat—Pylewell, Lymington, Hants.

FREEMAN OF CASTLE CORR.

DEANE-FREEMAN, EDWARD, Esq., late of Castle Cor, co. Cork, J.P. and D.L., high-sheriff 1846, *b.* 11 May, 1816; *m.* 26 Oct. 1841, Charlotte-Flora-Jemima, dau. of John-Lee Allen, Esq. of Errol Park, co. Perth, and has issue,

- I. JOSEPH-EDWARD, *b.* 29 Aug. 1842.
- II. Francis-Lee, *b.* 20 April, 1856.
- I. Barbara-Elizabeth-Anne. II. Edith-Maude.

Lineage.—The family of DEANE is an ancient one in Ireland, and long possessed large estates in various parts of that kingdom. Previously it was of consideration in England, and held lands in the counties of Gloucester and Northampton.

JOSEPH DEANE, Esq. of Cromlin, a partisan of CROMWELL, was appointed major of cavalry, in the parliamentary army, and received a confirmation of his original estate, besides large grants in the counties of Dublin, Wexford, Kilkenny, Cork, and Waterford. Major Deane was the only son of Edward Deane, of Cromlin, and was *b.* 2 Feb. 1623; he *m.* 8 Feb. 1652, Elizabeth, dau. of Maurice Cuffe, Esq. of Quin, co. Clare, and had, JOSEPH, his heir; Elizabeth, *m.* 1st, to Henry Grey, Esq. of Dublin, and 2ndly, in July, 1677, to Sir Donatus O'Brien, Bart. of Dromoland. Major Deane was *s.* at his decease by his only son,

JOSEPH DEANE, Esq. of Cromlin, who *m.* Elizabeth, dau. of the Right Rev. John Parker, archbishop of Dublin, and had two sons, viz.,

- I. EDWARD, his heir.
- II. Joseph, lord-chief-baron of the Irish Exchequer, *m.* Margaret, dau. of the Hon. Henry Boyle, of Castle Martyr, and *d.* 4 May, 1715, leaving five daus., his co-heirs, viz.,
  - 1 ELIZABETH, *m.* in 1722, to Hayes St. Leger, 4th Viscount Doneraile.
  - 2 BARBARA, *m.* to Arthur Hill, uncle to the Earl of Hillsborough.
  - 3 MARY, *m.* to John Bourke, Esq. of Palmerstown, created, in 1785, Earl of Mayo.
  - 4 CATHERINE, *m.* 7 Dec. 1735, to John Lysaght, 1st Lord Lisle.
  - 5 MARGARET, *m.* to John Fitzgerald, Knight of Kerry, M.P. for Dingle.
- III. Stephen, *d. s. p.*
- IV. Daniel, *d. s. p.* intestate.

The elder son,

EDWARD DEANE, Esq., M.P. for Ennisteoge, was father of

COL. EDWARD DEANE, M.P., who inherited the estates of Terrenure, co. Dublin, and of Dangan, co. Kilkenny. He *m.* Elizabeth, dau. of Amias Bushe, Esq. of Kilfane, co. Kilkenny, and had, with three daus., two sons, viz.,

- EDWARD, M.P., *d. unm.*
- Amyas, who *m.* Miss Margaret Cuffe, and had three daus., Catherine, *m.* to William Brownrigg, Esq.; Eliza, *m.* to James Burrowes, Esq.; and Anne, *m.* to Joseph Barratt Esq.
- JOSEPH, heir to his father.

Col. Deane's 3rd son,

JOSEPH DEANE, Esq. of Terrenure and Cromlin, co. Dublin, M.P. for Ennisteoge, in 1762, for the co. of Dublin in 1769, and for the co. of Kilkenny in 1778, was subsequently appointed colonel of the county of Dublin Volunteers, and occupied that distinguished position in 1782. He *m.* 1st, a sister of Sir Marcus Hill, Bart., but that lady dying soon after without issue, he *m.* 2ndly, Jane, only dau. (by Jane his wife, 3rd dau. of Sir Matthew Deane, Bart.) of WILLIAM FREEMAN, Esq. of Castle Cor, co. Cork, whose father William Freeman, Esq. of Kilbarry (son of Richard Freeman, Esq. of Kilbarry and Ballinguile) purchased Castle Cor from the Chinnery family. By Jane Freeman his wife, who became heiress to her brother, he had an only son, EDWARD, his heir. Col. Deane *m.* 3rdly, Miss Green, dau. of Col. Green, of Greenville, and had by her four sons and five daus., viz.,

- John-Berkeley, of Berkeley Forest, *m.* in 1800, Miss Knudson, an heiress, dau. of Gen. Knudson, B.I.C.S., and *d.* in 1837, leaving JOHN-ST. GEORGE DEANE, Esq. of Berkeley Forest, and other issue.
- Joseph Stokestown, who *m.* in 1810, Miss Drake, of that place, and had JOSEPH DEANE-DRAKE, Esq. of Stokestown, and other issue.
- William, who *d. unm.*
- Amias-Ferdinand, late capt. in the 96th regt.
- Frances, *m.* 1st, to Major Cliffe, of New Ross, and 2ndly, to Frances Corbet, Esq., who assumed the name of Singleton.
- Catherine.
- Eliza, *m.* to the Rev. Mr. Cliffe, of Hereford.
- Wilhelmina, *m.* to John Edwards, Esq. of Camolin Park.
- Lydia.

Col. Deane *d.* in 1801, and was *s.* by his eldest son,

EDWARD DEANE-FREEMAN, Esq. of Castle Cor, *b.* 9 Jan. 1760, who had previously, upon the demise of his maternal uncle, Matthew Freeman, Esq., inherited the large estates of the Freeman family, in the counties of Cork, Kerry, Limerick, and Tipperary, and had assumed, by sign manual, the additional surname and arms of FREEMAN. He *m.* in 1781, Mary, dau. of Richard Plummer, Esq. of Mount Plummer, co. Limerick, and Ellen, only dau. of Thomas-Bruce Brudenell, Esq., and by her had issue,

- Matthew, who *d.* under age, 6 April, 1802.
- JOSEPH, his heir.
- Richard, in holy orders, rector of Ardnageehy, co. Cork, *m.* Ellen, only dau. of the Rev. Rowland Davies, and has five sons and five daus.
- Edward.
- William, barrister-at-law, and chairman of co. Galway.
- John, *m.* 9 Aug. 1838, Anne, dau. of the late Rev. J.-C. Green, of North Grimston, co. York.
- Jane, *m.* to the Rev. Sackville-Robert Hamilton, rector of Mallow, 2nd son of the Right Hon. Sackville Hamilton (grandson of Lord Boyne), by Arabella his wife, dau. of the celebrated Bishop Berkeley.

Ellen, who *d. unm.*
Mary, *m.* to Major Thomas Poole, of the 39th regt.

Mr. Deane-Freeman was high-sheriff of the co. of Cork in 1797. He *d.* 25 March, 1826, and was *s.* by his eldest son,

JOSEPH DEANE-FREEMAN, Esq. of Castle Cor, J.P. and D.L., and high-sheriff of co. Cork in 1811, *b.* 28 Oct. 1788, who *m.* 24 Aug. 1811, Elizabeth, only dau. of Robert M'Carty, Esq. of Carrignavar, and by her (who *d.* 18 July, 1839) had issue,

I. EDWARD, present representative.
II. Robert, *m.* 2 Sept. 1842, Henrietta, dau. of — Rowley, Esq. of the co. Meath.
III. Joseph. IV. Matthew.
V. Justin, *m.* May, 1853, Maria-Marten, dau. of the Rev. Freeman-Wills Crofts, of Churchtown, co. Cork.
VI. Richard. VII. William.
I. Jane, *m.* in May, 1836, to Hewitt Poole, Esq. eldest son of Thomas Poole, Esq. of Mayfield, co. Cork, and *d.* leaving three children.
II. Mary.
III. Isabella, *m.* 23 March, 1842, to Major Henry Hamilton, 78th regt.
IV. Elizabeth.
V. Ellen, *m.* 24 Dec. 1851, Freeman Crofts, Esq. of Cloheen House, co. Cork.

Mr. Deane-Freeman, who was, at the installation of the Knights of St. Patrick in 1809, an Esquire to the Earl of Shannon, *d.* 24 Jan. 1840.

Arms—Quarterly: 1st and 4th, gu., three lozenges, arg.; 2nd and 3rd, arg., on a chev., gu., between three martlets, as many crosses of the field.
Crests—1st, a demi-lion, rampant, holding a lozenge in his paws, for FREEMAN; 2nd, a tortoise, displayed, for DEANE.
Mottoes—For FREEMAN, Liber et audax; for DEANE, Ferendo non Feriendo.

FREEMAN OF GAINES.

FREEMAN, JOHN, Esq. of Gaines, co. Hereford, J.P. and D.L., *b.* 29 Aug. 1802, high sheriff 1832; *m.* 16 May, 1826, Constantia, 2nd dau. of the Ven. Richard-Francis Onslow, Archdeacon of Worcester, by Harriet his wife, dau. of the Hon. Andrew Foley, and has issue,

I. JOHN-ARTHUR, capt. 2nd dragoons (Royal Scots Greys), *d.* in the Crimea, 29 Sept. 1854.
I. Mary-Harriet *m.* to the Rev. Arthur Childe, rector of Edwin Ralph, co. Hereford, son of William-Lacon Childe, Esq. of Kinlet, co. Salop.
II. Constance, *m.* to Francis Sutherland, Esq., son of the late John-Campbell Sutherland, Esq. of Forse, co. Caithness.
III. Cecilia-Abigail. IV. Elizabeth.

Lineage.—BELLINGHAM FREEMAN, Esq., son of Francis Freeman, of Suckley, acquired about the year 1683 the Gaines estate, situated in the parish of Whitbourne, Herefordshire, in marriage with Elizabeth, dau. of Richard Gower, Esq. of Suckley. He left at his decease a son and successor,

JOHN FREEMAN, Esq. of Gaines, who *m.* in 1727, Abigail Jones, of the Orchards, co. Hereford, and dying in 1764, left, with three daus., Betty, *m.* to John Barneby, Esq. of Brockhampton; Anne, *m.* to John Lilly, Esq. of the city of Worcester; and Abigail, *m.* to John Freeman, Esq. of Letton, two sons, JOHN and Thomas, of whom the elder,

JOHN FREEMAN, Esq. of Gaines, *m.* 30 April, 1761, Miss Anne Harris, and dying in 1801, left (with a dau., Theodosia) two sons, JOHN and Thomas-Harris, *b.* in 1771, who *m.* Mary, dau. of Richard Chambers, Esq. of Whitbourne Court, co. Hereford. The elder son,

JOHN FREEMAN, Esq. of Gaines, *m.* in 1798, Mary, eldest dau. of James Dansie, Esq. of London, and dying 22 Oct. 1831, left a son, the present JOHN FREEMAN, Esq. of Gaines, and four daus., Abigail-Mary, *m.* to Charles Sidebottom, Esq. barrister-at-law; Anne, *m.* to the Rev. Henry-Francis Sidebottom; Elizabeth, *m.* to James Plunkett, Esq.; Mary, *m.* to Fleming St. John, Esq., youngest son of the Rev. St. Andrew St. John, prebendary of Worcester.

Arms—Gu., three lozenges, arg.
Crest—A demi-lion, rampant, holding a lozenge in his paws.
Seat—Gaines, co. Hereford.

FREER OF STRATFORD-UPON-AVON.

FREER, JOHN-BRANSTON, Esq. of Stratford-upon-Avon, co. Warwick, *b.* 18 June, 1797; *m.* 1 Feb. 1820, Elizabeth-Mary, elder dau. of William-Richard Topp, Esq., capt. 14th regt. of foot, by Mary-Elizabeth his wife, dau. and co-heir of Bowyer-Leftwich Wynn, Esq., and has issue,

I. JOHN-BOWYER-WYNN.
II. William-Richard. III. Henry-Leftwich.
I. Isabella-Elizabeth-Mary. II. Maria-Eliza.
III. Caroline-Leigh. IV. Mary.
V. Jessie.

Mr. Freer, who is a magistrate and deputy-lieut. for Warwickshire, *s.* his father 8 July, 1816.

Lineage.—JOHN FREER, Esq. of Oakham, co. Rutland, who *d.* in 1806, and was buried in the family vault at Oakham, left, by Ann, his wife, a son and successor,

JOHN FREER, Esq. of Weston House, co. Rutland, high-sheriff in 1779, who *m.* 1st, in 1775, Mary, only child of John Ridlington, Esq. of Edith Weston; 2ndly, in 1795, Anne, only child of John Briggs, Esq. of Highbury Place, Islington, and 3rdly, in 1814, Jane, dau. of Boyle Vandeleur, Esq. of Ennis, in the co. Clare, which lady *m.* 2ndly, Captain Peach. Mr. Freer *d.* at Clifton, 3 July, 1816, leaving, by his 2nd wife, an only son, the present JOHN-BRANSTONE FREER, Esq. of Stratford-upon-Avon.

Arms—Sa., a chev., arg., between three dolphins, naiant, ppr.
Crest—A dolphin, naiant, ppr.
Seat—Stratford-upon-Avon.

FREKE OF HANNINGTON.

FREKE, HENRY, Esq. of Hannington, co. Wilts, J.P. and D.L.

Lineage.—ROBERT FREKE, Esq., son of Francis Freke, a person of "good repute in Somersetshire," was, for many years, auditor of the Treasury, in the reigns of HENRY VIII. and Queen ELIZABETH. He died immensely rich, leaving, besides seven daus., three sons, THOMAS (Sir), his heir; John, of Hilton; and William, great-grandfather of SIR RALPH FREKE, of West Bilney, co. Norfolk, whose only dau., GRACE, eventually sole heiress of the family, *m.* in 1741, the Hon. John Evans, second son of George, Lord Carbery. The eldest son,

SIR THOMAS FREKE, Knt., of Ewern Courtney, in Dorsetshire, "a person of considerable note, great trust, and authority, in the co. Dorset, *temp.* ELIZABETH and JAMES I." He *m.* Elizabeth, only dau. and heir of John Taylor, alderman of London, and had, with other issue, JOHN FREKE, of Ewern Courtney, and

RALPH FREKE, Esq. of Hannington, in Wiltshire, ancestor of the FREKES *of Hannington*, now represented by HENRY FREKE, Esq. of Hannington.

Arms—Sa., two bars, or, in chief, three mullets, of the same.
Crest—A bull's head, couped, sa., attired, collared and lined, or.
Seat—Hannington, Wilts.

FRENCH OF CLOONYQUIN.

FRENCH, CHRISTOPHER, Esq. of Cloonyquin, co. Roscommon, J.P., has served as high-sheriff, *b.* 15 June, 1821; *m.* 12 Feb. 1851, Susan-Emma, dau. of the Rev. W.-A. Percy, rector of Carrick-on-Shannon, and has issue,

I. ARTHUR-JOHN-ST. GEORGE, *b.* 24 Feb. 1853.
II. William, *b.* 1 May, 1854.
I. Elizabeth-Jane.

Lineage.—The family of Cloonyquin claims to be the elder branch of the FRENCHES *of Roscommon*, and is connected with the DILLONS, the FRENCHES *of Frenchpark*, the HANDCOCKS (Lord Castlemaine), and the ST. GEORGES. One branch of the family is represented by Patrick French, Esq., formerly of Knocklodge, co. Galway. The immediate ancestor of the Cloonyquin family, SIMON FRENCH, Esq. of Cloonyquin, had twelve sons; one, a Roman Catholic Bishop, resided at Foxborough, and built Foxborough House. Another descendant of this Simon French *m.* Miss St. George, and thus a branch of the family inherited the St. George estates in Galway. The great-grandfather of Mr. French, now of Cloonyquin,

COL. CHRISTOPHER FRENCH, who commanded the 52nd regt., served during the American War, and was taken prisoner, but escaped from the jail at Hartford. He went subsequently on a mission to the American Indians, and was very successful in inducing them to form an alliance with our troops. By the Indians he was much beloved, and exercised considerable influence over them during the war. He *m.* a Spanish lady, Margareta Alberti, and *d.* 1791, leaving a son and heir,

COL. JOHN FRENCH, who acted as quarter-master general under Sir G. Murray. He *m.* Anna, dau. of Archdeacon Story, of Kilmore, co. Cavan, and *d.* 1823, leaving a son and successor,

WILLIAM-ST. GEORGE FRENCH, Esq. of Cloonyquin, lieut. in the carabineers, and A.D.C. to Sir John Hope. He *m.* 1 Jan. 1819, Dorothea-Hallen Harris, and by her, who *d.* 1840, had issue,

CHRISTOPHER, now of Cloonyquin.
William. St. George.
Mary-Anne, *m.* to John Richardson, Esq., of Summerhill.
Dorothea-Jane, *m.* to Capt. Montgomorie Caulfeild.
Emily.

Arms—Erm., a chevron, sa.
Crest—A dolphin, naiant, ppr.
Seat—Cloonyquin, co. Roscommon.

FRENCH OF MONIVAE CASTLE.

FRENCH, ROBERT, Esq. of Monivae Castle, co. Galway, J.P., and D.L., high-sheriff in 1824, *b.* 6 Dec. 1799; *m.* 5 July, 1830, Katherine-Eleanor, only dau. of Nicholas Browne, Esq. of Mount Hazel, co. Galway, by Ellen, his wife (youngest dau. of Sir Thomas Burke, Bart. of Marble Hill), and by her, who *d.* 1843, has issue,

I. ROBERT-PERCY, *b.* 9 Oct. 1832, attaché to the British Embassy at Paris.
II. Acheson-Sydney-O'Brien, *b.* 8 May, 1843.

Mr. French was formerly in the army, and served in the 63rd regt.

Lineage.—This is a distinguished family of one of the fourteen ancient "tribes" of Galway. In that town still remains "French's Castle," the arms sculptured in stone in the workmanship of the seventeenth century, and the buildings disposed around a courtyard, in the style usual in Spain, with which country Galway formerly held such close mercantile correspondence (being, indeed, during the Protectorate of Richard Cromwell second in trade to London alone). There were several families of the "tribe," notably those of Castle-Ffrench, co. Galway, now Lords Ffrench; and French Park, co. Roscommon, now Lords de Freyne, the Frenchs of Rahasane Park, Curgarry, Tyrone, Brooklodge, and others, in addition to that now under notice, which suffered much during the Irish disturbances, having its estate and Castle of Monivae seized, and granted to the Lords Trimleston (the Frenchs getting them "by transplantation," and later, viz., 16 March, 30 CHARLES II., the lands of Cornidue, Derryglassane, Kilbegg, &c., still in their possession), who, returning to their ancient seat in Leinster, transferred them by sale back to the former proprietors.

The name French, Frynshe, De Ffreygne, or De Frignes (pronounced in the Norman tongue *de Freen*), appears (as last spelled) in the third list of WILLIAM THE CONQUEROR'S companions, given in Stowe's Chronicle (p. 107). The settlement of the family in Ireland dates from the English invasion, and, like it, took place in the co. Wexford, where the line of Frynshe of Ballintory, has left several descents in the Irish records. The founder in Ireland was,

SIR HUMPHREY DE FRETONE, said in different accounts to have had two and five sons. One of them,

PATRICK FREYONE or FRAYNSHE settled at Ballymacnuck, co. Wexford, and was father, with others, of

WALTER FRENCH, who about 1425 settled in the co. Galway, and *m.* a dau. and heiress of Athy, another of the fourteen "tribes," and from their issue descend the various families of the name in Galway, Sligo, Mayo, Roscommon, &c. Passing on to

PATRICK FRENCH OF MONIVAE, we find that he died testate about the year 1618, that being the date of his will, and by inquisition held at Loughreagh 30 April, 1631, it was found by the jury that

PATRICK BEGG (the small-statured) FRENCH of Monyvea, *d.* 6 Feb. 1630, possessed of the Castle of Monyvea, Carraleagh, &c., still held by the family. Patrick Begg was *s.* by his son,

ROBERT FRENCH, of Monyvea, who lived in the "evil days" of civil strife, and was deprived of his estate. He married first a dau. of the Browne "tribe," by whom he had no surviving sons; and 2ndly, Evelina Kirwan, also of a "tribe;" whose tombstone remains in the interesting ruins of Abbey Knockmoy, near the celebrated frescoes copied and displayed in the Dublin Exhibition of 1853. The inscription under the arms (impaled Baron et femme, the latter side duly bearing per fesse, in chief the arms of Browne, an eagle displayed, in base those of Kirwan, a chevron between three choughs, as second wife, with the motto "Laus Deo") is as follows:—

> "Pray for the Lady Evelyn French her soule who ordained herselfe to be interred in this Abbey, for her this monument was erected by her children Patrick French and Valentin French, and for a burial-place for themselves August the 8th, 1684."

The eldest son,

PATRICK FRENCH, Gent. above-mentioned, of Corendoe, which he had received "by transplantation*," obtained with the Lady Evelyn his mother, above mentioned, who had re-married Sir Oliver French, the lands of Derryglassam, Kilbeg, &c., as before said, 16 March, 30 CHARLES II. (deed enrolled 18 March, 1678). He was *s.* by his son,

†ROBERT FRENCH, Esq. of Corendoe and Monyvea (repurchased from the Lords Tremleston) who *m.* Elizabeth, dau. of Walter Taylor of Ballymacragh, articles dated 5 Feb. 1673. His son was,

PATRICK FRENCH, Esq. of Monivae, co. Galway, M.P. for that county, who *m.* Jane, 4th dau. of Simon Digby, bishop of Elphin, and had issue two sons, ROBERT, of whom presently, Digby, and three daus., Jane, *m.* to the Rev. Jeremy Marsh, rector of Athenry; another to — Bindon; and the 3rd to — Persse. The elder son,

ROBERT FRENCH, Esq. of Monivae, M.P. for co. Galway, *m.* in 1746, Nichola, 2nd dau. of Sir Arthur Acheson, Bart., and sister of the 1st Viscount Gosford, and had issue,

ACHESON, his heir.
Jeremiah, *m.* Lucinda, relict of Thomas St. George, Esq., and 4th dau. of Archibald, 1st Viscount Gosford.
Anne, *m.* to Sir Lucius O'Brien, Bart.

The elder son,

ACHESON FRENCH, Esq. of Monivae, *m.* 1775, Miss Miller, of the Isle of Wight, and *d.* 1779, leaving an only son,

ROBERT FRENCH, Esq. of Monivae Castle, J.P., high-sheriff, co. Galway, *b.* 1 Jan. 1776, who *m.* 1 Jan. 1799, Nichola-Maria, eldest dau of Sir Lucius O'Brien, Bart., by Anne French, his wife, and by her (who *d.* 1848) had issue,

I. ROBERT, now of Monivae.
II. Richard (twin with Robert), lieut. royal art., *d.* in 1832.
III. Lucius, capt. 9th Lancers, *d.* in India in 1842.
IV. Edward Hyde, of Hyde Park, co. Galway, *b.* in 1801; *d.* 16 Sept 1851.
V. Patrick-Digby, *b.* in 1810.
VI. Acheson, of Monivae, Hamilton, in the colony of Victoria, *b.* 24 May, 1812; *m.* 8 Feb. 1842, Anna, 2nd dau. of Dr. John Walton, of London, and has issue, 1 Acheson-Evelyn, *b.* 9 Feb. 1849; 2 Edward-Victor, *b.* 15 Dec. 1850; 3 Lucius, *b.* 9 July, 1852; 1 Amy; 2 Nichola-Frances; 3 Harriet-Maria; 4 Marianne.
I. Adelaide, *m.* to Henry Blake, Esq., only brother of Martin Blake, Esq., M.P. for Galway.
II. Mary.
III. Nichola, *m.* to Henry Blake, Esq. of Windfield.
IV. Louisa, *m.* in 1836, to William Traill, Esq. of Ballylough, co. Antrim.
V. Evelina, *m.* in 1825, to Stephen Donelan, Esq. of Killagh, co. Galway.

Mr. French *d.* 1850.

Arms—Erm., a chevron, sa.
Crest—A dolphin, naiant, embowed, ppr.
Motto—Malo mori quam fœdari.
Seat—Monivae Castle, co. Galway.

FRENCH OF CUSKINNY.

FRENCH, SAMPSON-TOWGOOD-WYNNE, Esq. of Cuskinny, co. Cork, J.P., *b.* 19 July, 1807; *m.* 12 Sept. 1837, Phebe-Maria, dau. of Samuel Perry, Esq. of Woodrooff, co. Tipperary, by the Hon. Deborah Prittie his wife, sister of the late Lord Dunalley, and has surviving issue,

I. SAVAGE, *b.* 25 June, 1840.
I. Deborah. II. Elizabeth-Anne.
III. Caroline-Mary. IV. Phebe-Maria-Catherine.

Lineage.—This family descends from RICHARD FRENCH, who *d.* in 1651, leaving a bequest to the poor of St. Finn Barr's parish, in the city of Cork, which is still paid from property belonging to the family. His son, DR. JAMES FRENCH, was mayor of Cork in 1696. The greater portion

* Bill in Exchequer Record Office.
† Report of Commissioners on Records, 1810–1815, p. 259.

of the present estates are derived from GEORGE TOWGOOD, a captain in the Cromwellian army, whose descendant,

MARY TOWGOOD (dau. of Sampson Towgood, Esq. of Goodwood, co. Cork), m. 1729, SAVAGE FRENCH, Esq., and was mother of

SAVAGE FRENCH, Esq. of Cuskinny, who m. Mary Millard, and had issue,

I. SAVAGE, his heir.
II. THOMAS-GEORGE, now of Marino, b. 8 Aug. 1780; who m. 11 May, 1811, Charlotte-Granville, dau. of Pascoe Grenfell, Esq., M.P., of Taplow House, co. Bucks, and by her (who d. in March, 1845) has issue,
  1 Pascoe-Savage, b. 1 Dec. 1815.
  1 Georgiana-Hill. 2 Emily-Grenfell.
  3 Louisa-Augusta, m. to the Hon. Robert Hare, and d. in 1853.
  4 Henrietta-Caroline. 5 Eleanor-Dorcas.
III. Sampson-Towgood, who d. unm. 1831.

The eldest son,

SAVAGE FRENCH, Esq. of Cuskinny, m. 2 Sept. 1806, Clotilda-Elizabeth Dring, and by her, who d. 9 Aug. 1832, left at his decease 28 Nov. 1834, surviving issue,

SAMPSON-TOWGOOD-WYNNE, now of Cuskinny.
Thomas-Fitz-Gerald, in holy orders.
Elinor-Elizabeth. Helen-Louisa. Charlotte-Georgina.
Georgina-Wilhelmina-Temple. Melian-Dorothea.

Arms—Vert, three foxes.
Crest—A Dolphin.
Motto—Veritas vincit.
Seat—Cuskinny, Queenstown.

FRENCH OF FRENCHGROVE.

FRENCH, JAMES, Esq. of Frenchgrove, co. Mayo, b. 16 Dec. 1791; m. 24 Jan. 1813, Margaret, only child of Thomas Kirwan, Esq. of Galway, by his wife, Margaret MacDonnell, of Ballahalla (now Moor Hall), co. Mayo, grandniece to the great Earl of Tyrconnel, and by her has issue,

I. JAMES-JOSEPH, b. 17 April, 1815; m. 26 Jan. 1836, Jane-Mary, eldest dau. of Martin-French Lynch, Esq. of Dublin, barrister-at-law.
II. Thomas-Joseph-Kirwan, b. 3 May, 1818.
I. Margaret-Josephine.
II. Mary-Josephine-Teresa, m. 6 May, 1848, to Francis-Lynch Eagur, Esq. only son of Captain Francis Eagur, of Minard, co. Kerry.

Lineage.—This is one of the oldest families of the name in Ireland, being the immediate descendants of Robert Fitz-Stephen de France (from whose cognomen they derive their name), who landed with Strongbow in the reign of HENRY II. This ROBERT FITZ-STEPHEN was lineally descended from Sir Theophilus de France, who accompanied William the Conqueror to England, and was present with him at the battle of Hastings. Robert Fitz-Steven m. Mary Brown, and had four sons, who all settled in Ireland, James, Nicholas, John, and Robert. James, the eldest, had but one son, who d. unm. John, the 3rd son, had also but one son, who d. without issue. So that from Nicholas, the 2nd, and Robert, the 4th son, doth proceed all the branches of this family now extant in Ireland. The grandfather of the present possessor of Frenchgrove,

JAMES FRENCH, Esq. m. 19 June, 1745, Sibel, only dau. of Andrew French, of Rahoon, co. Galway, and d. 25 April, 1762, having had by her (who d. 27 July, 1792), besides a son Andrew, and a dau. Anne, both of whom d. unm., another son,

JAMES FRENCH, Esq. of Frenchgrove, who m. 2 Aug. 1750, Mary-Barbara, only dau. of Francis French, Esq. of Dublin, and Mary Aylward his wife, and by her (who d. 3 Aug. 1843) had one son, JAMES, now of Frenchgrove, and two daus., Maria-Teresa, m. 24 May, 1812, to Martin-French Lynch, Esq. of Dublin, barrister-at-law; and Anna. Mr. French d. 7 July, 1793.

Arms—Erm., a chev., sa.
Crest—A dolphin, naiant, embowed, ppr.
Motto—Malo mori quam fœdari.
Seat—Frenchgrove, Kilcommon, co. Mayo.

FRERE OF ROYDON.

FRERE, GEORGE-EDWARD, Esq., F.R.S., of Roydon Hall, Norfolk, J.P., b. 29 Jan. 1807; m. 3 Dec. 1840, Isabella Tudor, and has issue,

I. JOHN-TUDOR, b. 12 Jan. 1843.
II. Richard-Tudor, b. 21 Jan. 1844.
III. Edward-Tudor, b. 4 March, 1845.
IV. William-Tudor.
I. Julia-Tudor. II. Elizabeth-Tudor.
III. Isabella-Tudor.

Lineage.—In lineal descent from ALEXANDER FRERE, of Occold, son of Alexander Frere, of Sweffling, co. Suffolk, living in 1394, was

SHEPPARD FRERE, Esq. of Roydon, Norfolk (son of Edward Frere, Esq. of Thwaite Hall, co. Suffolk, by Ellinor* his wife, dau. and co-heir, with her sister, Maria, wife of Lord Chief Baron Reynolds, of Thomas Smyth, Esq. of Thrandeston). He was b. 1712, and m. 1739, Susanna, dau. of John Hatley,† Esq. of London and Kirby Hall, Essex, by Isabella his wife, dau. of Robert Reynolds, of Bumstead Hellions (2nd son of Sir James Reynolds), and Kesie his wife, dau. of Thomas Tyrrell, of Gipping, Suffolk, by Kesia his wife, dau. of William Harvey, of Ickworth. By this lady (who d. in 1779) Mr. Frere had issue,

I. JOHN, his heir.
II. Edward, b. in 1742; m. in 1781, Mary, dau. of John Barker, of Shropham; and d. in 1819, having had by her (who d. in 1821) a son and a dau., viz.,
  Edward-Barker, b. in 1782; m. Elizabeth, dau. and heir of Hanbury Williams, Esq. of Great Yarmouth, and has issue, Edward-Hanbury, b. in 1826; Frederick, b. in 1828; Horace. b. in 1830; Edgar-Barker, b. in 1832; Augustus, b. in 1834; and Herbert, b. in 1837.
  Elizabeth-Barker, m. to Henry Barker, son of the Rev. Edward Barker, of Bacton, but had no issue.
I. Ellenor, m. to Sir John Fenn; and d. in 1813.
II. Judith, d. in 1754.

Mr. Sheppard Frere d. in 1780, and was s. by his elder son,

JOHN FRERE, Esq., F.R.S., of Roydon and Beddington, co. Surrey, b. in 1740; high-sheriff of co. Suffolk in 1776, and M.P. for Norwich in 1800; who m. in 1768, Jane, dau. and heir of John Hookham, Esq. of London, by his 1st wife, Jane, dau. of Stephen Pomfret, and Jane his wife, dau. of Thomas Flowerdew, and Margery Dee his wife, great-granddau. of Dr. John Dee, *temp.* ELIZABETH. By this lady (who d. in 1813) Mr. John Frere had issue,

I. John-Hookham (The Right Hon.), b. in 1769; fellow of Caius College, Cambridge, M.P. for West Looe in 1798, under-secretary for Foreign Affairs in 1799, envoy to Lisbon in 1800, minister to Madrid in 1802 and 1808. He m. Jemima-Elizabeth, Countess Dowager of Erroll, dau. of Joseph Blake, Esq. of Ardfry, afterwards Lord Wallscourt, and by her (who d. in 1831) had no issue; and d. at Malta, in 1846.
II. Edward, b. 16 Sept. 1770; m. 28 July, 1800, Mary-Anne, dau. of James Greene,‡ Esq. of Turton Tower and Clayton Hall, co. Lancaster, M.P. for Arundel in 1759, by Ann his wife, dau. of William Brigstock, of Blaen Pant, co. Cardigan, and by her (who d. in Jan. 1846) had issue,
  1 Edward, in holy orders, rector of Finningham, b. 30 Aug. 1805; d. 23 July, 1841.
  2 GEORGE-EDWARD, present head of the family.
  3 William-Edward, E.I.Co.'s service, b. 6 June, 1811; m. 24 March, 1838, Eliza-Jane Osborne.
  4 John-James-Bartholomew-Edward, comm. R.N., b. 28 Sept. 1812; m. in Feb. 1846, Anne, dau. of George Frere, Esq. of Twyford House.
  5 Henry-Bartle-Edward, E.I.Co.'s service, b. 29 March, 1815; m. 10 Oct. 1844, Catherine, dau. of Sir George Arthur, Bart.
  6 Richard-Edward, b. 28 Feb. 1817; d. 18 Nov. 1842.
  7 Arthur-Edward, b. 22 June, 1825; m. 11 Jan. 1847, Elizabeth-Palmer Price.
  1 Mary-Anne. 2 Jane-Ellinor-Arabella.
  3 Isabella-Susanna, m. in 1846, to Henry Mason, R.N.
  5 Frances-Anne, m. 29 Jan. 1840, to William Hart, E. I. Co.'s service.
  6 Emma.
III. GEORGE, of Twyford House (*see that family*).
IV. William, b. in 1775; m. in 1810, Mary, only dau. of Brampton-Gurdon Dillingham, by Mary his 2nd wife, dau. and co-heir of Samuel Howard; and d. in 1836, having had issue,
  1 Philip-Howard, b. in 1813.

* This lady and her sister were co-representatives of the families of Sir John Brecknock, of Berks, *temp.* HENRY V.; Paine, of Roundham, Norfolk; Long, of Livermere; and Everard, of Hawkedon, Suffolk; and were connected with the Cavendishes, afterwards Dukes of Portland.

† Mr. Hatley was of a very old family, long settled at Paxton and St. Neots, co. Hunts, and connected with the family of Hampden, the patriot.

‡ Mr. Greene was representative of the families of Sir Francis Bland, Bart. of Kippax, and Humphrey Chetham, founder of the Chetham Hospital, Manchester.

1 Ellen-Mary, *m.* in 1839, to the Hon. Stephen-Edward Spring-Rice, eldest son of Lord Monteagle.
2 Isabella.
3 Mary-Wilhelmina-Frederica, *m.* Rev. Edward Gurdon.
4 Augusta-Frederica.

v. Bartholomew, *b.* in 1776.
vi. James-Hatley, *b.* in 1779; *m.* in 1809, Merian, 2nd dau. of Matthew Martin, and has issue,

1 Hatley, *b.* in 1811; *m.* in 1840, Theodora-Amelia-Mary, dau. of the Right Rev. George-Trevor Spencer, late bishop of Madras.
2 Charles, *b.* in 1813; *m.* in 1841, Charlotte-Vansittart Neale.
3 John-Alexander, *b.* in 1814; fellow of Trinity College, Cambridge.
4 Edward-Daniel, *b.* in 1816.
5 Constantine *b.* in 1817; fellow of Corpus Christi College, Cambridge; *m.* in 1847, Antonina Gaudiano.

v. Temple, in holy orders, rector successively of Finningham, Roydon, and Burston, and prebendary of Westminster *b.* in 1781; *m.* in 1816, Jane, eldest dau. of Sir Richard Richards, lord-chief-baron of the Exchequer, by Catherine his wife, only dau and heiress of Robert Vaughan, of Cusbelmwyth, and has had issue,

1 Temple, *b.* in 1818; *d.* in 1840.
2 Robert-Temple, *b* in 1820.
3 Henry Temple, *b.* in 1821.
4 Griffith-Temple, *b.* in 1827; *d.* in 1839.
1 Catherine-Margaret-Temple.
2 Louisa-Jane-Temple.
3 Emily-Georgiana-Temple.

i. Jane, *m.* to Admiral Sir John Orde, Bart.
ii. Susanna, *d.* in 1839.

Mr. Frere *d.* 11 July, 1807.

Arms—Gu., two leopards' faces, in pale, or, between as many flaunches, of the last.

Crest—Out of a ducal coronet, an antelope's head, arg., armed, or.

Mottoes—"Traditum ab antiquis servare;" and, "Frere ayme Frere."

Seat—Roydon Hall, Diss.

FRERE OF TWYFORD HOUSE.

FRERE, GEORGE, Esq. of Twyford House, co. Herts, *b.* 1 April, 1774; *m.* 21 Aug. 1806, Elizabeth-Raper, only dau. of William Grant, Esq. of Rothiemurchus, co. Inverness, M.D., by Elizabeth his wife, only dau. and heir of John Raper, Esq. of Twyford House, and Elizabeth his wife, dau. of William Hale, Esq. of Twyford House, M.D.; by this lady Mr. Frere has issue,

i. JOHN, in holy orders, rector of Cottenham, *b.* 21 July, 1807, *m.* in 1839, Jone-Brown Dulton.
ii. George, *b.* 22 Feb. 1810, *m.* in 1842, Margaret-Anne Corrie.
iii. Bartle-John-Laurie, *b.* 1 Nov. 1814.
i. Elizabeth.
ii. Susanna-Hatley, *m.* 6 Dec. 1838, to Christopher Wordsworth, of Harrow, D.D.
iii. Anne, *m.* in 1846, John-James-Bartholomew-Edward Frere, R.N.
iv. Judith-Mary-Sophia, *b.* in 1817.

Mr. Frere *s.* to the Twyford estate, on his marriage, in 1806. He is a younger brother of the late Right Hon. John-Hookham Frere (*see preceding family*).

Seat—Twyford House, Herts.

FREWEN OF ILMER AND NORTHIAM.

FREWEN, MORETON-JOHN-EDWARD, Esq. of Ilmer, in Buckinghamshire, and Northiam, in Sussex, *b.* 14 July, 1794; *m.* 17 Dec. 1812, Sarah, dau. of the Rev. David Jenkyns, of Dryffrynbern, in Cardiganshire.

Lineage.—The name of FREWEN (variously spelt in ancient records, Frewyn, Freuen, Frewin, and Frewen) is an ancient Saxon one, and William of Malmesbury incidentally notices it, when relating an absurd story, in which one FREWEN, a chaplain of St. Wolstan, the last Saxon Bishop of Worcester, is described as playing no very creditable part.

RICHARD FREWEN, eldest son of Richard Frewen de Forthey, who was buried at Hanley Castle in 1546, and grandson of Richard Frewen, baliff of Worcester in 1478, had, by his wife, Margaret, who *d.* in 1598, with other children, a 2nd son,

THE REV. JOHN FREWEN, rector of Northiam, co. Sussex, baptized 1 July, 1560, a learned Puritan divine, who, by Eleanor his first wife, had, with other issue,

ACCEPTED, *b.* at Northiam, and there baptized, May 26, 1538; an eminent prelate, *d.* ARCHBISHOP OF YORK, *unm.* 28 March, 1664.
THANKFUL, *b.* in 1591, purse-bearer and secretary to the Lord Keeper Coventry; he purchased of Francis, Viscount Montagu, the presentation and advowson of Northiam. He *d. unm.* in 1656.
JOHN, of whom presently.
STEPHEN, ancestor of the FREWENS *of Brickwall*. (*See that family.*)

The 3rd son,

JOHN FREWEN, baptized 8 Feb. 1595, *m.* 15 April, 1623, Dorothea, dau. and co-heir of Thomas Scott, of Goatoley, in Northiam; and dying at Northiam, was buried there, 27 Jan. 1654. His 2nd surviving son,

THE REV. THOMAS FREWEN, rector of Northiam, baptized 20 June, 1630, who *m.* Mary Evernden, of Sedlescombe, Sussex, by whom (who survived him, and *m.* 2ndly, Rev. Richard Seamer, rector of East Guilford, in Sussex, and *d.* 9 Jan. 1721) he had issue,

i. THOMAS, his heir, of the Church House, Northiam, *b.* in 1666, *m.* Sarah, 5th dau. of Richard Stevens, Esq. of Culham, Berks, and dying in 1731, left two sons,

1 THOMAS of the Church House, baptized in 1691, *m.* Sarah, only dau. of Peter Bishop, Esq. of Newenden, and *d.* in 1767, leaving issue, CHARLES, of Northiam, *d. s. p.* in 1787; MARY, *m.* to the Rev. William Lord, by whom she was grandmother of the Rev. William-Edward Lord, rector of Northiam; ELIZABETH, *m.* to John Jenkins, Esq.; and ANNE, *m.* 1st, to her cousin, Charles Frewen, and 2ndly, to Admiral Charles Buckner.
2 Charles, *b.* in 1701, deputy-clerk of the Crown, and Brunswick Herald, *m.* Alice, dau. of Samuel Severn, of Shrewsbury, and *d.* in 1762, leaving one son, Charles, who *d. s. p* in 1791; and Elizabeth, who *d. unm.*

ii. THANKFUL, in whose line the representation of the family now rests.
iii. Walter *d.* in 1704.
iv. John, bapt. 11 April, 1672, of Linc.'s Inn; he *d. unm.* in 1733.
v. Stephen, bapt. 26 Feb. 1677, vicar of Fairlight, in Sussex, whose only dau., Maria, *b.* in 1705, *m.* 5 Oct. 1729, John Calvert, merchant of London, son of the Rev. John Calvert, of Stanwell, in Middlesex.
i. Mary, *m.* to George Bishopp, of Northiam.
ii. Winifred, *m.* 22 May, 1698, to Simon Ash, vicar of Salehurst, Sussex.

Rev. Thomas Frewen was buried at Northiam, 31 Jan. 1677. His 2nd son,

THE REV. THANKFUL FREWEN, bapt. 2 Feb. 1669, rector of Northiam. He *m.* Sarah dau. of Captain Luke Spenser, of Cranbrook, in Kent, and dying 2 Sept. 1749, was *s.* by his son,

THOMAS FREWEN, M.D., *b.* 20, June 1704, author of a treatise on "the Practice and Theory of Inoculation, London, 1747." He *m.* Philadelphia dau. of Joseph Tucker, of Rye, and dying in June, 1790, left issue surviving, a dau., Philadelphia, and a son,

THE REV. EDWARD FREWEN, D.D., *b.* 27 Oct. 1744, rector of Frating cum Thorington, in Essex, who *m.* 25 June, 1789, Sally, dau. of the Rev. Richard Moreton, of Little More on Hall, in Cheshire, by whom (who survived him, and *d.* 3 May, 1835) he had issue.

MORETON-JOHN-EDWARD, present proprietor.

Dr. Frewen *d.* 18 Dec. 1831.

Arms—Quarterly: 1st and 4th, erm., four bars, az., a demi-lion, rampant, ppr., issuant in chief, for FREWEN; 2nd and 3rd, quarterly; 1st and 4th arg., a cross-crosslet, fitchée, sa.; 2nd and 3rd, az., three congors' heads, erased, or, for SCOTT of Congerhurst.

Crest—A demi-lion, rampant, arg., langued and collared, gu., bearing in its paws a galltrap, az.

Motto—Mutare non est meum.

FREWEN OF BRICKWALL.

FREWEN, THOMAS, Esq. of Brickwall House, Northiam, Sussex, J.P., M.P. for South Leicestershire, *b.* 26 Aug. 1811; *m.* 4 Oct. 1832, Anne, youngest child of W.-Wilson-Carus Wilson, Esq. of Casterton Hall, Westmoreland, and has issue,

i. JOHN, *b.* 20 March, 1837.
i. Mary. ii. Selina.

Lineage.—STEPHEN FREWEN, bapt. 19 Oct. 1600, youngest son of the first marriage of the Rev. John Frewen, rector of Northiam, and brother of Accepted

Frewen, Archbishop of York, was a citizen of London, of the Skinner's Company. He realized a large fortune in trade, which was much increased by his inheriting the Archbishop's property. He *d.* at Brickwall, and was buried at Northiam, 11 Sept. 1679. Mr. Frewen *m.* 1st. 9 April, 1629, Katherine, dau. and co-heir of Thomas Scott, of Goatley, in Northiam, and had one son, THOMAS, of whom presently. He *m.* 2ndly, in 1686, Elizabeth Greene, and had by her another son, John, bapt. 28 May, 1637, buried 2 Oct. 1638. He was *s.* by his elder son,

THOMAS FREWEN, Esq., bapt. 27 Sept. 1630, M.P. for Rye, who *m.* 1st, Judith, sole dau. and heir of John Wolverstone, of Fulham, co. Middlesex, and by whom (who *d.* 29 Sept. 1666) he had five children. Mr. Frewen *m.* 2ndly, in 1671, Bridget, dau. of Sir Thomas Laton, of Laton, co. York, and co-heiress of her brother, Charles Laton, inherited in her right the large estates in the co. of York of that ancient family, and by her had issue. Mr. Frewen *m.* 3rdly, Jane, Lady Wymondsold, relict of Sir Dawes Wymondsold, of Putney, co. Surrey, and sole dau. and heir of Sir Robert Cooke, of Highnam, co. Gloucester, by his 2nd wife, Jane, relict of Mr. George Herbert; by Lady Wymondsold, (who *d.* 20 June 1718, aged 70, and lies buried at Putney) he had no issue. Mr. Frewen *d.* 8 Sept. 1702, and was buried at Putney, in the vault of the Wymondsold family. By his first wife Judith, Mr. Frewen had issue,

EDWARD, (Sir,) *b.* in 1661, and with Robert Wymondsold, received the honour of knighthood from King JAMES II. in the royal bedchamber, 4 March, 1684. Sir Edward was major of the first regiment of the Cinque Ports, and M.P. for Rye His issue is EXTINCT.
Katherine.

By his 2nd wife, Bridget he had,

Laton, (whose only son, Laton, *d. s. p.*)
Stephen, *d. unm.* John.
Mary, wife of Henry Turner, Esq. of Cold Overton, serjeant-at-law.

The 3rd son by the 2nd marriage,

THE REV. JOHN FREWEN, *b.* in 1676, rector, first of Sidbury, in Devonshire, and afterwards of Tysoe, co. Warwick, and Walton-upon-Trent, Derbyshire, *m.* Rachel dau. of Richard Stevens, of Culham, co Berks, and by her (who *d.* 21 March, 1752, aged 77, and was buried at Sapcote), had issue,

I. THOMAS, of whom presently.
II. John, *b.* in 1715, Fellow of Oriel College, Oxford, and rector of Tortworth, co. Gloucester, *m.* Elizabeth, eldest dau. and co-heir of John Townsend, of Oxford, by whom (who survived him, and *m.* 2ndly, Nathan Wright, of Englefield, co. Berks, and *d.* 2 April, 1814, aged 73) he had issue one dau.,
  1 Selina-Frewen, *b.* at Tortworth, 5 Jan. 1767, *m.* 2 Sept. 1794, to the Rev. James-Knight Moor, rector of Sapcote, Leicestershire, and dying 7 Feb. 1818, was interred at Rugby with her husband, by whom she left issue an only son, viz., Rev. John-Frewen Moor, of Bradfield House, co. Berks.
  Mr. Frewen *d.* 3 Oct. 1767, and was buried at Tortworth.
I. Bridget, *d. unm.*
II. Rachel, *b.* in 1710, *m.* to Simon Knight, of Rugby.
III. Mary, *b.* in 1715, *m.* to the Rev. Stanley Burrough, head master of Rugby school, and rector of Sapcote.

The Rev. John Frewen *d.* at Sapcote, and was there buried, 19 Feb. 1735. His elder son,

THE REV. THOMAS FREWEN, *b.* in 1708, rector of Sapcote, Leicestershire. On the death of his cousin, Laton Frewen Turner, of Brafferton Hall, Yorkshire, in 1777, he succeeded to the joint estates of the Frewen and Turner families, and assumed the name of TURNER, pursuant to the will of John Turner, of Cold Overton. He *m.* Esther Simkin, by whom, (who *d.* 6 Oct. 1808,) he left at his decease, in 1791, a son,

JOHN FREWEN, Esq., *b.*, at Sapcote, 1 Aug. 1755. High sheriff for Leicestershire, 1791; at the general election in 1807, he was returned to Parliament for Athlone, which he represented till 1812. In 1808, he *m.* Eleanor, dau. and co- heir of Charles Clarke, Esq. of London, by his 2nd wife, Elizabeth, only dau. and heir of David Hay, Esq. of Hopes, co. Haddington, and had issue,

THOMAS, his heir.
Charles-Hay-Frewen, who inherited his father's estates in the co. of York, and is a magistrate for the cos. of Leicester and Rutland.
John-Frewen.
Selina-Frewen, *m.* in 1839, to the Rev. Robert Martin, M.A., eldest surviving son of William Martin, Esq. of Anstey Pastures, co. Leicester. *(See that name.)*

Mr. Frewen Turner *d.* 1 Feb. 1829, was buried at Cold Overton, and *s.* by his elder son, the present THOMAS FREWEN, Esq. of Brickwall House.

Arms—Ermine, four bars, az., a demi-lion, rampant, ppr., issuant in chief.
Crest—A demi-lion, rampant, arg., langued and collared, gules, bearing in its paws a galltrap, az.
Motto—Mutare non est meum.
Seats—Cold Overton Hall, Leicestershire; Brickwall House, Northiam, Sussex; Innishannon, in the co. of Cork.

FRYER OF THE WERGS.

FLEEMING-FRYER, WILLIAM-FLEEMING, Esq. of the Wergs, in the co. of Stafford.

Lineage.—RICHARD FRYER, Esq., *b.* 22 July, 1693, son of RICHARD FRYER, a descendant of the Fryers, of Thornes, near Shenstone, where the old hall, surrounded by a moat, now stands, left a son and successor,

RICHARD FRYER, Esq. of Wednesfield, *b.* 26 March, 1719, who *m.* Dorothea, dau. of John Wood, Esq. of Wednesbury Hall, and granddau. of — Hope, Esq. of Neechells Hall, co. Stafford, who was a firm adherent of Royalty, and raised, for the cause of CHARLES II., a troop of horse, which he equipped and clothed at his own expense. By this lady Mr. Fryer left at his decease (with another son, John, of Wednesfield, and two daus., Elizabeth and Mary, widow of John Howard, Esq. of Chester),

RICHARD FRYER, Esq. of the Wergs, J.P., and D.L., M.P. for Wolverhampton, 1832, *b.* 11 Nov. 1771; *m.* 6 Aug. 1794, Mary, only child of William Fleeming,* Esq., and niece and sole heiress of John Fleeming, Esq. of the Wergs. By this lady he has issue,

WILLIAM-FLEEMING, who inherits the estates of the Wergs, through his mother, and under the will of his great uncle, John Fleeming, Esq.
Richard.
Elizabeth, *m.* to the Rev. Thomas Walker, A.M., Prebendary of the Collegiate Church of Wolverhampton.
Mary, *m.* to Henry Morson, Esq., co. Kent.
Dorothea, *m.* to Stubbs Wightwick, Esq. of Great Bloxwich, in Staffordshire.
Susanna, *m.* to Robert Thacker, Esq. 2nd son of William Thacker, Esq. of Minchall Hall, Staffordshire.

Arms—Or, semée of oak leaves, vert, between two flanches az., each charged with a castle, arg.
Crest—A castle, arg., encircled by a branch of oak, fructed ppr., thereon a cock, sa., combed and wattled, gu.
Motto—Mea fides in sapientiâ.
Seats—The Wergs, and New Cross House, both in Staffordshire.

FRYER OF CHATTERIS.

FRYER, JOHN, Esq. of Chatteris, Isle of Ely, *b.* 28 Aug. 1787; *m.* 2 Aug. 1814, Sarah, only child and heiress of John Richardson, Esq., and by her (who *d.* 21 Aug. 1843) has issue,

I. JOHN-RICHARDSON, of Crowe Hall, co. Norfolk, J.P., and Conservator of the Hon. Corporation of the Bedford Level, *b.* 27 Oct. 1816; *m.* 10 Jan. 1843, Mary-Agnes, youngest dau. of Steed Girdlestone, Esq., J.P. of Stebbington Hall.
II. Frederick-Daniel, of Needham Hall, co. Cambridge, *b.* 6 June, 1819; J.P. and D.L.; *m.* 23 July, 1844, Harriet-Mellicent Read, of Holbroke House, Suffolk.
I. Caroline-Sarah, *m.* 29 March, 1842, to William-Robert Chapman, Esq., youngest son of Aaron Chapman, Esq., M.P.
II. Julia-Elizabeth.

Mr. Fryer is chairman of the Hon. Corporation of the Bedford Level, J.P. and D.L., and served as

* The Fleemings have been located at the Wergs upwards of 400 years, holding their lands by prescription down to the present time, and through the ebbs and flows of succeeding generations have neither increased nor diminished their estate It is worthy of remark, as recorded in "Pit's History of Staffordshire," that the timber on the Wergs is equal to (if not the finest) any in the county of Staffordshire. "Amongst a number of well grown trees of various species," says that writer, "I could pick out a few oaks worth thirty guineas each."

Arms—Of FLEEMING, arg., a chev., engr., between three crosses-patée fitchée, sa.
Crest—A Cornish chough.

high-sheriff for the cos. of Cambridge and Huntingdon in 1835.

Arms—Arg., a chevron, sa., between three dolphins, naiant, ppr.
Crest—Out of a ducal coronet, or, an antelope's head, arg., armed, gold.
Motto—Jamais arrière.
Seat—Chatteris, Isle of Ely, co. Cambridge.

FULFORD OF GREAT FULFORD.

FULFORD, BALDWIN, Esq. of Great Fulford, Devonshire, lieut.-colonel of the Devon militia; *m.* Anna-Maria, eldest dau. of the late William Adams, Esq. of Bowdon Totness (and M.P. for that borough), and had issue,

I. BALDWIN, one of the chairmen of the Quarter Sessions.
II. Francis, rector of Trowbridge, Wilts, *m.* Mary, dau. of Andrew-Berkeley Drummond, Esq. of Cadlands, Hants, and had issue,
  1 Francis-Drummond.
  1 Alice-Mary.
III. John, an officer R.N.
IV. William, in the army. V. George.
I. Anna-Maria, *m.* to her cousin, the Rev. Dacres Adams, vicar of Pinhoe, Devon.
II. Elizabeth-Florence.
III. Eleanor, *m.* 1843, to the Rev. Herbert-George Adams.
IV. Harriet. V. Louisa. VI. Philippa.

Lineage.—The Fulfords are of Saxon origin, and held Folefort, as it is written in Domesday Book, from which place the name is derived. Here, as it appears by records, as well as registries in the College of Arms, they were seated in the time of RICHARD I., and have continued in possession of the same name, in the male line, by uninterrupted descent during a period of more than 600 years. The mansion of Fulford was garrisoned for CHARLES I., and was taken by a part of Fairfax's army under the command of Col. Okey, in Dec. 1645. Many knights of the family distinguished themselves in the Holy Land, Sir Baldwin de Fulford more particularly. Sir Thomas Fulford was one of the knights who went up with the Earl of Devon and relieved Exeter when besieged by Perkin Warbeck, in 1497.

The first of the family, according to the records in the Heralds' Office, is

WILLIAM DE FULFORD, who held Fulford *temp.* RICHARD I., and left a son,

NICHOLAS FULFORD, of Fulford, father of

WILLIAM FULFORD, of Fulford, who *m.* Mariot, dau. and co-heir of Sir Baldwin de Belston, of Parham, Devon, and had,

HENRY FULFORD, of Fulford, whose son,

WILLIAM FULFORD, of Fulford, was father of

JOHN FULFORD, of Fulford, who had a son,

SIR HENRY FULFORD, of Fulford, living *temp.* EDWARD III., said by Bishop Godwin to have sat in judgment with Chief-justice Gascoyne, and condemned Archbishop Scrope to be beheaded. He was *s.* by his son,

HENRY FULFORD, of Fulford, who *m.* the dau. and heir of Fitzurse, of Williton, Somerset, by whom he had,

SIR BALDWIN FULFORD, of Fulford, sheriff of Devon, 38 HENRY VI., knight of the Sepulchre, and under-admiral to Holland, Duke of Exeter, high-admiral of England. Prince styles Sir Baldwin "a great soldier and a traveller of so undaunted resolution, that, for the honour and liberty of a royal lady, in a castle besieged by the infidels, he fought a combat with a Saracen, for bulk and bigness an unequal match (as the representation of him cut in the wainscoat in Fulford Hall doth plainly slow), whom yet he vanquished, and rescued the lady." He *m.* Elizabeth, dau. and co-heiress of Sir John Bozom, of Bozomzeal, and by her (who *m.* 2ndly, Sir William Huddersfield, attorney-general to EDWARD IV.) had issue,

THOMAS, his heir.
John, canon of Exeter Cathedral.
Thomasin, *m.* to John Wise, Esq. of Sydenham, and had issue, Oliver Wise, ancestor of the WISES *of Sydenham*; and Alicia Wise, *m.* to John Russell, Esq., by whom she was mother of John, 1st Earl of Bedford, K.G.
Alice, *m.* to Sir William Cary, of Cockington, in Devonshire, was slain at Tewkesbury, in 1471. They left a son, Thomas Cary, father of William Cary, who *m.* Mary, dau. of Sir Thomas Boleyn, Earl of Ormond, and younger sister of Queen ANNE BOLEYN, and had a son, Henry, Lord Hunsdon, K.G., lord-chamberlain to Queen ELIZABETH.

Sir Baldwin was *s.* by his eldest son,

SIR THOMAS FULFORD, of Great Fulford, who, fighting gallantly under the banner of Lancaster at the Battle of Towton, in 1461, was taken prisoner and beheaded. He *m.* Philippa, dau. of Sir Philip Courtenay, of Powderham, by Elizabeth his wife, dau. of Walter, Lord Hungerford, high-treasurer of England *temp.* HENRY VI., and was *s.* at his decease by his eldest son,

SIR HUMPHREY FULFORD, of Great Fulford, K.B., who *m.* Florence, dau. and co-heir of Bonvile, of Shute; but dying without issue, was *s.* by his brother,

WILLIAM FULFORD, Esq. of Great Fulford, who *m.* Joan, dau. and co-heir of John Bonvile, of Combraleigh, and left a son and successor,

SIR JOHN FULFORD, knight of Great Fulford, who served the office of high-sheriff of Devon in the 26 and 32 HENRY VIII. He *m.* Lady Dorothy Bourchier, younger dau. of John, 1st Earl of Bath, by Cecilia his wife, sister and heiress of Henry D'Aubeney, Earl of Bridgewater, and had, with other issue, a dau., Faith, *m.* to Capt. Davies, the great circumnavigator, and a son and heir,

SIR JOHN FULFORD, Knt. of Great Fulford, high-sheriff of co. Down, who *m.* Ann, dau. of Sir Thomas Dennys, of Holcombe Burnell, and was father of

SIR THOMAS FULFORD, Knt. of Great Fulford, who *m.* Ursula, dau. of Richard Bampfield, Esq. of Poltimore, and had *inter alios* a dau., Bridget, *m.* to Arthur Champernoune, Esq. of Dartingdon, and a son and successor,

SIR FRANCIS FULFORD, Knt. of Great Fulford, who *m.* Elizabeth, dau. and co-heir (with her sister, Anne, *m.* to Sir Francis Ashley) of Bernard Samways, Esq. of Toller Tratrum, and Winterbouine St. Martin, and by her (who was *b.* in 1585) had, with six daus., five sons, from a younger one of whom, George, the present family descends. Sir Francis *d.* in 1664, and was *s.* by (the only son and heir of his eldest son, THOMAS FULFORD, Esq., who was slain in the civil wars, at the siege of Exeter, in 1642) his grandson,

FRANCIS FULFORD, Esq. of Great Fulford, who *m.* Susanna, dau. of John Kelland, Esq. of Painsford, in Devon, and was father of

COL. FRANCIS FULFORD, of Great Fulford, who *m.* 1st, Margaret, dau. of John, Lord Poulett, of Hinton St. George; and 2ndly, Mary, dau. and co-heir of John Tuckfield, Esq. of Little Fulford; but dying without issue, in 1700 (his widow *m.* 2ndly, Henry Trenchard, Esq.), was *s.* by his cousin (sprung from George, younger son of Sir Francis Fulford),

FRANCIS FULFORD, Esq. of Toller, who then became of Great Fulford. This gentleman *m.* Catherine, dau. of William Swete, Esq.; and dying in 1730, left a son and successor,

FRANCIS FULFORD, Esq. of Great Fulford, *b.* in 1704; who *m.* Ann, dau. of Sir Arthur Chichester, Bart. of Youlston, Devon, and had issue,

I. JOHN, his heir.
II. Francis, vicar of Dunsford.
III. Benjamin-Swete, who *m.* Joanna-Gerard, dau. of Thomas Galpine, Esq., and had issue,
  1 BALDWIN, successor to his uncle.
  1 Harriet.
  2 Elizabeth-Mary. 3 Florence-Anne.
I. Anne, *m.* to Sir John Colleton, Bart.

Mr. Fulford *d.* in 1748, and was *s.* by his eldest son,

JOHN FULFORD, Esq. of Great Fulford, who *m.* Elizabeth, dau. of John Laroche, Esq.; but dying without issue, in 1780, was *s.* by his nephew, BALDWIN FULFORD, Esq. of Great Fulford.

Arms—Gu., a chevron, arg., quartering FITZURSE, MORETON, BELSTON, BOZOM, ST. GEORGE, CANTELUPE, ST. ALBYN, and CHALBONS.
Crest—A bear's head, erased, sa., muffled, or.
Supporters—Two Saracens, ppr.
Motto—Bear up.
Seat—Great Fulford.

FULLER OF ROSE HILL.

FULLER, AUGUSTUS-ELIOTT, Esq. of Rose Hill, Brightling, and Ashdown House, co. Sussex, M.P. for East Sussex, *b.* 7 May, 1777; *m.* 5 Sept. 1801, Clara, eldest dau. and co-heir of Owen-Putland Meyrick, Esq. of Bodorgan, Anglesey, and by her (who *d.* 17 June, 1856) has issue,

I. OWEN-JOHN-AUGUSTUS, of Bodorgan, *b.* 13 July, 1804, who assumed the additional surname of MEYRICK on being left the large estates of his maternal grandfather in Anglesey. (*See* MEYRICK.)

I. Clara, *m.* 26 Sept. 1826, to Sir George-William Gervis, Bart. of Hinton House, and *d.* leaving issue.
II. Lucy-Anne, *m.* to Townsend Ince, Esq. of Christleton, near Chester.
III. Catharine-Sarah. IV. Augusta-Maria.

Lineage.—JOHN FULLER, Esq. of Waldron, and Tanners, co. Sussex, (eldest son of John Fuller, Esq. of Tanner in Waldron, and grandson of John Fuller Esq. of Heathfield, Sussex), *d.* in 1615, leaving, by Elizabeth, his wife, a son,

CAPTAIN SAMUEL FULLER, of Tanners, otherwise Tanhouse, in Waldron, bapt. 18 May, 1589, who *m.* Jane, or Joane, dau. of Stephen French, Esq. of Streame, in Chiddingley and *d.* 3 Aug. 1653, having had, with other issue, a son and heir,

CAPTAIN JOHN FULLER, *b.* 1 Aug. 1617, who *m.* Ann, dau. of John Nutt, of Mays, in Selmston, co. Sussex, and dying in 1679, was *s.* by his son,

JOHN FULLER, Esq. of Waldron, major of the Trained Bands, *b.* 20 May, 1652, *m.* Elizabeth, dau. of Samuel Fowle, Esq. of London, and was *s.* by his son,

JOHN FULLER, Esq. of Brightling, co. Sussex, J.P., and M.P., for that co., *b.* 28 July, 1680, *m.* Elizabeth, dau. and co-heir of Fulke Rose, Esq. of Jamaica, by Elizabeth, his wife, dau. and co-heir of John Langley, alderman of London, (which lady *m.* 2ndly, Sir Hans Sloane, Bart., and had issue,

I. JOHN, of Brightling, M.P., who *m.* Miss Darell, but *d. s. p.* in 1755. His widow *m.* Nashe Mason, Esq.
II. ROSE, M.P. for Romney, Maidstone, and Rye, *m.* Miss May, but *d. s. p.* in 1777.
III. HENRY, in holy orders, rector of Stoneham, *m.* Frances, dau. of Thomas Fuller, of Cattesfield, and had, with two daus., (Elizabeth, *m.* to Sir John-Palmer Acland, Bart. of Fairfield, and Frances, wife of Lancelot Brown, Esq.,) a son,
  JOHN FULLER, Esq. of Rose Hill, who inherited his uncle Rose's property, and sat in parliament for Sussex. He *d. unm.* 11 April, 1834, aged 77.
IV. THOMAS, of whom presently.
V. Stephen, a merchant in London, and many years agent for Jamaica, *m.* Miss Noakes, of Brightling, and by her had, with two daus., who *d. unm.*, three other daus., 1. Philippa, *m.* to William Dickenson, Esq. of Kings Weston, M.P. for Somersetshire, and had issue: 2. Elizabeth, *m.* to her cousin, J.-T. Fuller, Esq.; and 3. Sarah, *m.* to her first cousin, Hans Sloane, Esq., son of William Sloane, Esq. of Stoneham.
VI. Hans, *d. unm.* at Lisbon, aged 27.
I. Elizabeth, *m.* to William Sloane, Esq. of Stoneham, Hants, and had issue.

The 3rd son,

THOMAS FULLER, Esq., merchant of London, *m.* Miss Ledgitter, and by this lady (who was nearly related to the Parkers of Ratton and the Traytons of Lewes, and, through her brother, heiress to those families) had two sons, Rose, the younger, and

JOHN TRAYTON FULLER, Esq. of Ashdown House, co. Sussex, who *m.* 1st, his cousin, Elizabeth, dau. of Stephen Fuller, Esq., as before, and had a son and two daus., all of whom *d.* young. He *m.* 2ndly, in 1776, the Hon. Anne Eliott, only dau. of Gen. Eliott, 1st Lord Heathfield, the gallant defender of Gibraltar, and by her had six sons and five daus., viz.,

I. AUGUSTUS-ELIOTT, present representative.
II. Francis-John, an officer of dragoons, lost in the Bay of Gibraltar.
III. Thomas-Trayton, created a Baronet in 1821, and is the present SIR THOMAS-TRAYTON FULLER-ELIOTT-DRAKE, of Nutwell Court, co. Devon, Bart. (*See* BURKE'S *Peerage and Baronetage.*)
IV. William-Stephen, capt. R.N., *d. s. p.*, 10 Sept. 1815.
V. Rose-Henry, R.N., *m.* Margaretta, dau. of the late Sir Robert Sheffield, and has issue, one son and two daus.
VI. Robert Fitzherbert, in holy orders, rector of Chalvington, co. Sussex, *m.* Ursula, dau. of Sir Robert Sheffield, and has issue.
I. Anne, *m.* to John Hamilton, Esq. of the Island of Tobago.
II. Sarah-Maria. III. Cordelia-Sarah.
IV. Louisa. V. Charlotte.

Mr. Fuller *d.* in 1812.

Arms—Barry of six, arg. and gu., a canton, of the last.

Crest—A horse, passant, arg.

Motto—Currit qui curat.

Seat—Rose Hill, Brightling, and Ashdown House, co. Sussex.

FULLER OF NESTON PARK.

FULLER, JOHN-BIRD, Esq. of Neston Park, co. Wilts, *b.* 6 March, 1801; *m.* 22 June, 1829, Sophia-Harriet, 2nd dau. of the late William Hanning, Esq. of Dillington House, co. Somerset, and has issue,

I. JOHN-AUGUSTUS, *b.* 17 Sept. 1831.
II. George-Pargiter, *b.* 8 Jan. 1833.
I. Caroline-Sophia. II. Harriet-Georgina.

Mr. Fuller, J.P. and D.-L., for the county, and high-sheriff 1852, is eldest son of John Fuller, Esq. (*b.* in 1762), by Dinah Jeans his wife, and grandson of Gerard-Dutton-Fleetwood Fuller, Esq., who *d.* in 1795. He has one brother and two sisters, viz., Neston-Joseph, *b.* Nov. 1802, who *m.* 1826, Anne-Margaret, eldest dau. of the Hon. Colonel Browne; Georgiana, *m.* 1816, to the Rev. Thomas Heathcote; and Louisa-Mary, *m.* 1822, to the Rev. John-Andrew Methuen, brother of the late Lord Methuen.

Seat—Neston Park, co. Wilts.

FULLERTON OF THRYBERGH PARK.

FULLERTON, JOHN, Esq. of Thrybergh Park, co. York, *b.* in 1803; *m.* in 1827, Louisa, 4th dau. of Sir Gray Skipwith, Bart. of Newbold Hall, co. Warwick, and has issue,

I. THOMAS-GRAY, *b.* 30 June, 1828.
II. Charles-Garth, *b.* 26 April, 1838.
III. Arthur-George, *b.* 23 Sept. 1844.
I. Louisa. II. Sophia. III. Julia-Frances.
IV. Charlotte. V. Another dau.

Lineage.—Few families can claim so ancient and unbroken a line of ancestry as the Fullertons of Ayrshire. Their pedigree is authentically traced through six centuries, and, during the whole of that long period, no link is wanting in the chain of descent; and, what is more remarkable, no failure has occurred in the male succession.

Traditionally, it is said, the family is derived from an Anglo-Saxon or Norman origin. This seems, at least, not improbable. On the return to Scotland, or first introduction as some will have it, of Walter, son of Alan, ancestor of the High Stewards, from England, about the beginning of the twelfth century, he was accompanied by many of his friends and adherents. Soon after his arrival, Walter obtained a royal grant of the countries of Kyle and Strathgrife (now Renfrewshire), and here, as Chalmers and others affirm, many of his fo lowers obtained from him grants of land, and became resident in the country; and from them have been derived most of the principal families now inhabiting those parts. In accordance then, with tradition, it seems far from improbable that at the period here alluded to, the ancestor of the Fullertons may have so accompanied the progenitor of the High Stewards, and obtained a possession in Kyle.

ALLAN FULLARTON, living in 1240, *d.* about 1280. He was father of

ADAM FULLARTON, who received a charter of the lands of Fullarton from James, high steward of Scotland, which charter was renewed by ROBERT II. in 1371. His son,

REGINALD FULLARTON, of that ilk, living in 1310, was father of

SIR ADAM FULLARTON, of Fullarton, much in the interest of ROBERT II., and the family of Stewart. In 1346, he accompanied the army under DAVID II. into England, and was one of those created knights by that monarch before the army crossed the border; he was taken prisoner with King DAVID, at the battle of Durham, 17 Oct., and on the king's release, Sir Adam's eldest son and heir was one of the twenty hostages left in England, until the payment of the king's ransom. By Marjorie his wife, a lady of the Stewart family, Sir Adam had two sons,

JOHN, who was one of the hostages left in England for the King's ransom. He *d. v. p.*, leaving a son,
  REGINALD, successor to his grandfather.
David, who obtained a charter from Hugh Eglintoun, of that ilk, of the lands of Laithis.

Sir Adam *d.* about 1399, and was *s.* by his grandson,

REGINALD FULLARTON, of that ilk, who, by Elizabeth his wife, was father of

RANKIN FULLARTON, of that ilk, living in 1412, from whom derived in direct descent,

JAMES FULLARTON, of that ilk, who m. Agnes, dau. of John Fullarton, of Dreghorn, by Jean his wife, dau. of John Mure, of Rowallan, and had (with a dau. Helen, m. to James Blair, of Lady Kirk, co. Ayr) three sons,

JAMES FULLARTON, of that ilk, ancestor of the FULLARTONS *of Fullarton*, co. Ayr.
John, who served for some years with the army in Germany, and in 1639, went to France as lieut.-col. to the Hon. Alexander Erskine, brother to the Earl of Mar. In 1640, LOUIS XIII., King of France, advanced him to the rank of colonel in the French service. Col. Fullerton acquired the estate of Dudwick, co. Aberdeen. He m. and left issue; his descendant, Gen. John Fullerton, of Dudwick, a brave and gallant officer, greatly distinguished himself in the Prussian and Russian service, in the latter of which he attained the rank of general. He *d. s. p.*, and the estate of Dudwick passed into the family of Udny of Udny, supposed to have been related to or connected with him.
WILLIAM, of whose line we treat.

The 3rd son,

WILLIAM FULLARTON, minister of St. Quivox, m. Frances, dau. of Stewart of Reece, co. Renfrew, a cadet of the Stewarts of Lennox, and had, besides an eldest son, ROBERT, several other sons and daus.; one of the latter m. Cleland of that ilk. His eldest son,

ROBERT FULLERTON, of Craighall, living in 1660, m. Barbara, eldest dau. of Robert Hunter, of Cortoun, mayor of Ayr, and had (besides three daus. and a younger son, John, who went to India) an elder son and heir,

ROBERT FULLERTON, of Craighall, who m. Margaret, only dau. of John Wallace, merchant, of Edinburgh, and had issue, JOHN, his heir; Robert; William; Adam; George; Barbara; and Isabel. The eldest son and heir,

JOHN FULLERTON, of Craighall, *b.* 11 April, 1716, m. 1st, Miss Gowling, who *d. s. p.*; and 2ndly, Miss Weston, of West Horsley Place, co. Surrey, and by her had issue,

JOHN, his heir. Weston, *d. unm.*
JUDITH, m. Savile Finch, Esq. of Thrybergh, co. York, M.P. for Malton, son of the Hon. John Finch, by Elizabeth Savile his wife, granddau. and heiress of John Savile, Esq. of Methley, who purchased the estate of Thrybergh of Sir William Reresby, Bart. Mr. Savile Finch *d. s. p.*, having devised his estates to his wife, Judith Fullerton, who resided for twenty years after her husband's death at Thrybergh, and *d.* in 1803, having bequeathed her possessions to her nephew, the late John Fullerton, Esq.

Mr. Fullerton, who went to India, and afterwards escaped the general massacre of the English, at Gedda, on the Red Sea, was *s.* at his decease by his elder son,

THE REV. JOHN FULLERTON, many years rector of Stratford-on-Avon, who m. Rebecca Garth,* and *d.* in 1800, having had a son, JOHN, and a dau. Judith, who *d.* in 1787. The son,

JOHN FULLERTON, Esq. of Thrybergh, Dennaby, and Brinsworth, co. York, *b.* in 1778, m. 10 Dec. 1801, Louisa, dau. of Gore Townsend, Esq. of Honington Hall, co. Warwick, by Lady Elizabeth his wife, 2nd dau. of Other Lewis, 4th Earl of Plymouth, and by her (who *d.* in 1818) had issue,

I. JOHN, his heir.
II. Weston, m. Charlotte, dau. of the Rev. Thomas Trebeck, rector of Chirley, Sussex, and had issue,
  1 John-Reginald-Thomas, *b.* 10 Aug. 1840.
  1 Cecilia-Louisa-Anne. 2 Selina.
III. Thomas, *d.* in 1825.
IV. Arthur, in holy orders, rector of Thrybergh, near Rotherham.
I. Louisa, *d.* an infant.
II. Anna, m. to George Ramsden, Esq. of The Priory, Conisbrough, and *d.* in 1837.
III. Elizabeth, m. to D.-H.-W. Pickard, Esq. royal artillery.
IV. Horatia-Sophia.
V. Frances, m. to the Rev. Charles Smith, rector of East Garston, Berks, son of the late dean of Christ's Church, Oxon.

Col. Fullerton *d.* 19 Jan. 1847, and was *s.* by his eldest son, the present JOHN FULLERTON, Esq. of Thrybergh Park.

Arms—Arg., a chevron, between three otters' heads, erased, gules.
Crest—A camel's head, erased, ppr.
Motto—Lux in tenebris.
Seat—Thrybergh Park, Rotherham.

* This lady had three brothers and one sister:—
Charles Garth, father of the late Hon. Miss Garth, maid of honour to Queen CHARLOTTE; of C. Garth-Colleton, Esq.; and of Capt. Garth, R.N. of Haines Hill, Berks.
General George Garth, who *d.* at Beverley.
General Thomas Garth, who *d.* at Ilsington House, Dorset.
Elizabeth, who *d. unm.*

FULLERTON OF WESTWOOD AND BALLINTOY CASTLE.

FULLERTON, ALEXANDER-GEORGE, Esq. of Ballintoy Castle, co. Antrim, and Tockington Manor, co. Gloucester, late captain in the army, *b.* 8 Aug. 1808; m. at Paris, in July, 1833, Lady Georgiana Leveson-Gower, 2nd dau. of the late Earl of Granville, and has a son and heir,

WILLIAM-GRANVILLE, *b.* at the British Embassy, Paris, 15 July, 1834; *d.* 1855.

Lineage.—In the parish of Axminster, co. Devon, is North Wyke, once the residence and inheritance of the ancient and knightly family of Duno, de Doune, le Downe, or Downynge, the original stock, from which sprang the branch we are about to detail. In Domesday Book occurs RALPH DE DOUNE, a king's thane, and he is described as holding two manors in Devon. From him derived,

HENRY DOWNING, Esq., *b.* in 1630, the younger brother of Sir George Downing, Bart., held a commission in the guards of CHARLES II., and was living in Downing-street, London, in 1666. He m. Jane, dau., it is supposed, of the ancient family of Clotwarthy, and by her, who is buried at Bellaghy, had two sons, ADAM and George. Henry Downing *d.* about the year 1698; and was *s.* by his eldest son,

COLONEL ADAM DOWNING, *b.* in 1666, who went over to Ireland with WILLIAM III., and held the rank of colonel in his army. He was present at the siege of Derry, and there gave early and signal proofs of his courage, participating in the battle of the Boyne, and contributing eminently, by his gallantry and skill, to the success of the party with which he was engaged. He received the appointments of deputy-governor of the county of Derry, colonel of the militia, and one of the commissioners of array, and was also granted by his royal master a large tract of land in the county of Derry, still possessed by his descendant. He m. Margaret, dau. of Thomas Jackson, Esq. of Coleraine ancestor of Sir George Jackson, Bart., by Margaret Beresford, of the noble family of Waterford, and had issue,

Henry, named after his grandfather, *d.* in his minority.
JOHN, of whom presently.

Colonel Adam Downing *d.* in 1719, and was buried at Bellaghy. The inscription on his monument mentions his descent from the Devonshire family. His son and successor,

JOHN DOWNING, Esq. of Bellaghy and Rowesgift, *b.* in 1700, raised, during the rebellion of 1745, at considerable expense, a body of men to serve his king and country in a moment of great difficulty and danger. He m. Anne, dau. and heir of the Rev. J. Rowe, D.D., descended from an ancient Devonshire family, and had three sons, namely,

CLOTWORTHY, father of John and Giffard; the latter a military officer, was severely wounded at Corunna.
DAWSON, of whom presently.
John, an officer in the army, who served in the Seven Years' War, and *d. s. p.* in 1792.

The 2nd son,

DAWSON DOWNING, Esq. of Bellaghy and Rowesgift, co. Londonderry, *b.* in 1739, inherited the ancient mansion, and resided in it till his death. He m. 1st, Catherine, only child of George Fullerton, Esq., and niece and heiress of Alexander Fullerton, Esq. of Ballintoy Castle, co. Antrim, descended from a branch of the ancient Scottish family of that name, and by her had one son, GEORGE, of whom presently. Mr. Dawson Downing m. 2ndly, Sarah-Catherine, dau. of Hugh Boyd, Esq. of Ballycastle, and by her had (with six daus., of whom, Anne, m. to Robert Magee, Esq.; Margaret, m. 1st, Arthur Handcock, Esq., and 2ndly, Rear-Admiral the Hon. William La Poer Trench; and Catherine, m. Turnley, Esq.) two sons, JOHN, of Rowesgift, judge of the Supreme Court of the Kandian provinces, and David. Mr. Downing's son by his 1st wife,

GEORGE-ALEXANDER DOWNING, Esq., having inherited a considerable property from his great-uncle, assumed, in compliance with that gentleman's testamentary injunction, the surname and arms of FULLERTON, and became of Tockington Manor and Ballintoy. He was *b.* at Ballycastle, in the old family mansion of the Boyds, 30 Nov. 1775, and *d.* in 1847, leaving, by his wife, three sons and five daus., viz.,

I. ALEXANDER-GEORGE, his heir.
II. George, a military officer. III. David.
I. Catherine. II. Amy. III. Susan.
IV. Frances, m. to Sir Andrew Armstrong, Bart.
V. Mary-Anne.

Arms—Arg., three otters' head, erased, gu., for FULLERTON; barry of eight, arg. and vert; over all a gryphon, rampant, or, for DOWNING.

Crest—A camel's head and neck, erased, ppr.

Motto—Lux in tenebris.

Seats—Westwood, Hants; and Ballintoy Castle, co. Antrim.

FURNELL OF CAHIRELLY.

FURNELL, MICHAEL, Esq. of Cahirelly Castle, co. Limerick, *b.* 17 April, 1794; *m.* 1 Sept. 1820, Laura-Frances Noel, relict of John Ball, Esq., brother to Judge Ball. Mr. Furnell is a deputy-lieut. for the co. and city of Limerick, and served as high-sheriff in 1842.

Lineage.—JOHN FURNELL, Esq., son of BOUKE FURNELL, Esq., and grandson of THOMAS FURNELL, Esq., was father of PATRICK MICHAEL FURNELL, Esq., who *m.* Mary Scanlan, of Ballynaka, and had a son, JOHN FREDERICK FURNELL, Esq., who was *s.* by his son,

MICHAEL FURNELL Esq. of Cahirelly Castle, high sheriff of co. Limerick in 1787. He *m.* in 1754, Elizabeth, dau. of the Hon. and Rev. Godfrey Massy, brother of Hugh Lord Massy, and by her was father of

MICHAEL FURNELL, Esq. of Cahirelly Castle, who *m.* 20 Aug. 1791, Mary, eldest dau. of George Stackpoole, of Craigbrien Castle, co. Clare, (a direct descendant of Robert Stackpoole who in 1168 migrated to Ireland from England,) and by her had issue,

MICHAEL, present representative.
George, (treasurer of co. Limerick), *m.* Meliora Cantillon, and has issue.
John-Thomas, *m.* Arabella Wallace, and has issue.
Frederick, of Cahirelly House, *m.* Elizabeth, sister of James Brodie, Esq., of Lethen, co. Nairn.
Mary, *m.* Th. O'Brien, Esq.
Eliza, *m.* to William Gabbett, Esq.
Jane, *m.* Lawrence Marshall, Esq. of Tomoline, and is deceased.

Mr. Furnell, who served as high sheriff in 1795, *d.* 14 Jan. 1816.

Seat—Cahirelly Castle, Limerick.

FURSDON OF FURSDON.

FURSDON, GEORGE, Esq. of Fursdon, co. Devon, J.P., *b.* 14 Dec. 1802; *m.* in June, 1825, Georgiana, dau. of H. Alleyne, Esq. of Barbadoes, and has had issue,

I. CHARLES.	II. Walter.
III. George-Edward.	IV. Alfred-Henry-Marcus.
I. Margaret-Grace.	II. Ellen.
III. Lucy, *d.* in 1839.	IV. Alice.

Lineage.—ROBERT FURSDON, of Fursdon, co. Devon, living 7th EDWARD II., son of WALTER FURSDON, of Fursdon, by Johanna his wife, dau. of Robert Molins, *m.* Theophila, dau. of Philip de Dunsmore, and was father of ROBERT FURSDON, of Fursdon, under age, 7 Edward III. By Englesia, his wife, he left a son, THOMAS FURSDON, of Fursdon, 7 RICHARD II., whose son by Matilda, his wife, was ROBERT FURSDON, of Fursdon, living *temp.* HENRY IV., who *m.* Dionysia, dau. of John Sackevile, and was father of JOHN FURSDON, of Fursdon, 19 HEN. VI., whose son, WILLIAM FURSDON, of Fursdon, living 10 HENRY VII., *m.* Editha, dau. and heiress of Thomas Hayes, Esq., and had a son and successor, WILLIAM FURSDON, of Fursdon, 15 HENRY. VIII., father of JOHN FURSDON, of Fursdon, whose son, NICHOLAS FURSDON, of Fursdon, *d.* in 1618, leaving, by Maria, his wife, dau. of Roger Weeks, Esq. of Northweek, co. Devon, a son and heir, GEORGE FURSDON, Esq. of Fursdon, who, by Grace, his wife, dau. of Lovell, of Cheriton Fitzpaine, left (with two daus., Elizabeth, wife of Peter West, Esq. of Tiverton; and Grace, wife of — Hartnol of Tiverton, (a son and heir, NICHOLAS FURSDON, Esq. of Fursdon, who *m.* Elizabeth, dau. and heir of William Cullen, Esq. of Woodland, co. Devon, and was father of GEORGE FURSDON, Esq. of Fursdon, who *m.* Elizabeth, dau. and heir of Richard Elsworth, Esq. of Bickham, co. Somerset and had an only son.

GEORGE FURSDON, Esq. of Fursdon high-sheriff for Devon in 1753, who *m.* 1st, Elizabeth, eldest dau. and co-heir of Edward Cheyne, Esq. of Launceston, co. Cornwall, by whom he had a dau., Elizabeth-Penelope, *m.* to John Lyon, Esq. and *d.* in 1787. He *m.* 2ndly, in 1770, Grace, dau. of Humphrey Sydenham, Esq., of Combe, near Dulverton, co. Somerset, and left by her a son and heir,

GEORGE-SYDENHAM FURSDON, Esq. of Fursdon, who *m.* in 1797, Harriet, 2nd dau. of Francis Rodd, Esq., of Trebartha Hall, co. Cornwall, and had issue,

I. GEORGE, present representative.
II. Edward, in holy orders, *m.* Harriet-Grace, dau. of the Rev. Edward Rodd, D.D. of Trebartha Hall, and has issue, Edith and Elsworth.

I. Grace.	II. Elizabeth.
III. Frances-Jane.	IV. Penelope.

Arms—Arg., a chev., az., between three fire-balls, ppr.

Crest—A plume of five ostrich feathers issuing from a ducal coronet, all ppr.

Seat—Fursdon, co. Devon.

FURSE OF HALSDON.

FURSE, THE REV. CHARLES-WELLINGTON, of Halsdon, co. Devon, *b.* 16 April, 1821; assumed the surname and arms of his maternal uncle, the late John Henry Furse, Esq.

Lineage.—This family, whose name occurs as FERSE, in Domesday Book, is one of very long standing in the county of Devon, and was "of Furse, in the parish of Spreytown," in the reign of RICHARD I. In 1680 the Furses removed to Halsdon, in consequence of the marriage of

PHILIP FURSE, Esq. (son of Philip Furse, Esq., by his wife, a dau. of the family of Malet of Ash) with Elizabeth, heiress of that property, dau. of Philip Bellew, Esq. of Stockleigh English. By this lady who was *b.* in 1612, Mr. Furse had a son,

JOHN FURSE, Esq. of Halsdon, father, by Johanna Warren, his wife, of

PHILIP FURSE, Esq. of Halsdon, who *m.* Grace, sister of Louis Wellington, Esq. of Way, Devon, and had by her a son and successor,

THE REV. PETER-WELLINGTON FURSE, of Halsdon, a magistrate for Devon, *m.* in 1791, Miss Mary Johnson, niece of Sir Joshua Reynolds, and had a son and two daus.,

I. JOHN HENRY, J.P., *b.* 1795; *m.* 1831, Anna-Sophia, only dau. of the Rev. Richard Buller, and *d. s. p.*
I. Theresa, *m.* Charles-William Johnson, Esq., and *d.* 28 Aug. 1851, leaving issue,
1 CHARLES-WELLINGTON JOHNSON, in holy orders, who took the name and arms of Furse, and is the present possessor of Halsdon.
2 William-Johnson.
1 Mary-Theresa, *m.* to the Rev. Francis Vidal.
2 Sarah-Elizabeth.
3 Ellen-Furse, *m.* to Charles-Johnson-Anthony Deane, Esq.
II. Elizabeth, *m.* to the Rev. W. J. Yonge.

Arms—Gu., a chev., embattled, counter-embattled, between six halberds in pairs, saltierwise, or.

Crest—A castle, ppr.

Motto—Nec desit virtus.

Seat—Halsdon House, Torrington, Devon.

FYFFE OF SMITHFIELD.

FYFFE, DAVID, Esq. of Smithfield, co. Forfar, late major 44th regt., *b.* 18 April, 1781; *m.* 18 Sept. 1816, Helen, 5th dau. of William Douglas, Esq. of Brigton, in the same county, and has issue,

I. DAVID, *b.* 4 Aug. 1817, late major 46th regt.
II. William-Douglas, *b.* 7 Aug 1818.
III. James, *b.* 10 Sept. 1819.
IV. Charles; V. Robert; and VI. Graham; all three *d.* young.
I. Elizabeth-Graham.

Major Fyffe is a J.P. and D.L. for Forfarshire. He is only surviving son of the late David Fyffe, Esq., of Drumgeith, co. Forfar, by Anne his wife, only dau. of David Hunter, Esq. of Burnside, Forfarshire, his only brother, Charles, *b.* in 1785, having died in 1804. Major Fyffe has had two sisters, viz., Barbara, *d.* in 1811; and Elizabeth Bell, *m.* in 1806, to Robert Kerr, Esq. of Chatto, co. Roxburgh.

Arms—Or, a lion, rampant, gu., armed and langued, az., on a chief, of the second, a crescent, between two stars, of the first.

Crest—A demi-lion as in the arms.

Motto—Decens et honestum.

Seat—The Lodge, Broughty Ferry.

FYLER OF WOODLANDS AND HEFFLETON.

Fyler, James-Chamness, Esq. of Woodlands, co. Surrey, and Heffleton, co. Dorset, M.A., J.P. and D.L., high-sheriff of Dorsetshire in 1837; *b* 13 Aug. 1790; *m.* 1st, 19 June, 1815, Mary, 3rd dau. of Sir John Frederick, Bart. of Burwood Park, Surrey, and by her, who *d.* in 1823, had issue,

I. James, *b.* 13 Aug. 1818, B.A., in holy orders, rector of Siddington, *m.* 7 Sept. 1847, Rosalind-Charity, eldest dau. of William-Frederick Chambers, Esq., M.D., K.C.H., F.R.S., of Hordle House, Hants.
II. Frederick, *b.* 22 Feb. 1823, in holy orders, *m.* 16 Nov. 1852 Charlotte, dau. of John Fane, Esq. of Wormsley, late M.P. for Oxfordshire, and has issue, Frederick-John Fane, *b.* 14 Nov. 1853, and John-Arthur, *b.* Dec. 1855.
I. Mary.
II. Susan-Elizabeth, *m.* 16 Feb. 1847, to the Rev. Francis Pooley Roupell, rector of Walton on the Hill, Epsom, Surrey.

He *m.* 2ndly, in 1828, Mary-Elizabeth, eldest dau. and co-heir of Andrew Bain, Esq., M.D., J.P. and D.L., of Heffleton, co. Dorset, and by her has further issue,

I. Henry-I'Anson, *b.* 24 June, 1830. *d.* 28 April, 1845.
II. John-William-Townsend, Lieut. 31st Regt. *b.* 11 March, 1833.
III. William-Samuel, *b.* 19 Feb. 1835.

Lineage.—The Rev. Samuel Fyler, M.A., *b.* in 1629, Rector of Stockton, Wilts, for nearly forty years, and Precentor of Salisbury Cathedral, was author of a curious work, now in the British Museum, entitled "Longitudinis inventæ explicatio non longa." He *m.* Maria, dau. of the Rev. Thomas Hyde, D.D., 6th son of Sir Lawrence Hyde, of West Hatch, Wilts, Attorney-General to the Queen of James I., uncle to Edward, Earl of Clarendon, and by her had two sons, Samuel, *b.* in 1664, in holy orders, rector of Orcheston, Wilts, and John, of whom presently; and six daus., of whom Frances *m.* to C. Nason, Esq., and *d.* in 1719; and Repentance, the youngest, *m.* in 1713, to the Rev. Robert Morgan, rector of Linkinholt, Hants. The younger son,

The Rev. John Fyler, *b.* in 1673, *s.* his father in the Rectory of Stockton, and *d.* in 1729, leaving, with a dau., Anne, six sons,

I. John, of London, *b.* in 1701, *m.* Mary, dau. and co-heiress of John Hobbs, Esq. of Stoke Courcy, co. Somerset, by Margaret, his wife, dau. and co-heir of George Gray, Esq. of Kingston House, Dorset, and by this lady had three daus., viz., 1 Jane, *d. unm.* in 1796; 2 Frances, *m.* to John Norton, Esq., and *d.* in 1771, leaving a son and dau.; and 3 Mary, *m.* 16 March, 1762, to John I'Anson, Esq. of Epsom, and had an only child, Mary, *m.* to her cousin, Samuel Fyler, Esq.
II. Samuel, *b.* in 1702, in holy orders, curate of Dunstable.
III. Stephen. IV. Arthur. V. Arundel.
VI. George, of whom presently.

The youngest son,

George Fyler, Esq., *b.* in 1708, *m.* Mary, dau. of Thomas Bilcliffe, Esq., and had an only child,

Samuel Fyler, Esq. of Twickenham, Middlesex, and Dover Street, London, barrister-at-law, *b.* 3 July, 1759, *m.* 1st, his cousin Mary, only child of John I'Anson, Esq., and niece of Sir Thomas-Bankes I'Anson, Bart. of Corfe Castle, co. Dorset, and by her (who *d.* in May, 1794) had issue,

Thomas-Bilcliffe, his heir.
James-Chamness, now of Woodlands and Heffleton.
John I'Anson, *b.* 1 Jan. 1792, in the army, *d.* in 1815.
Mary, *d.* young.
Elizabeth, *m.* to the Rev. G. Townsend, prebendary of Durham, and vicar of Northallerton, *d.* 7 Dec. 1835, leaving issue two sons, George-Fyler Townsend, in holy orders; and James-Frederick Townsend, also in holy orders; and one dau. Mary-Susan, *m.* to G. Cator, Esq.

Mr. Fyler *m.* 2ndly, Margaret. dau. of Hugo Arnot, Esq. of Balcormo, co. Fife, descendant and representative of Robert Arnot, of Woodmyine, co. Fife, comptroller of Scotland, and captain of Stirling Castle, who was slain at Flodden, and by her also had issue,

Samuel-Arnot, in holy orders, M.A., vicar of Cornhill, Durham.
Laurence, lieut.-col. 12th Lancers, *m.* 1836, Amelia, dau. of the late Hon. John Byng, Judge in India, and niece of the late Viscount Torrington, and has issue a dau., Caroline-Amelia.
George, barrister-at-law, *m.* 12 Oct. 1841, Susan, dau. of Ralph Foster, Esq. of St. Leonard's, Sussex, and *d.* March, 1856.
Susan-Anne. Frances.
Olivia, *d.* young.
Margaret-Louisa, *d.* 21 June, 1848.
Caroline-Christiana-Bennet.
Amelia-Lillias-Jane, *m.* Dec. 1853, to Richard Donoughmore, Lovett, Esq.

Mr. Fyler *d.* 1 March, 1825, and was *s.* by his eldest son and heir,

Thomas-Bilcliffe Fyler, Esq. of Teddington, co. Middlesex, M.A., M.P. for Coventry, *b.* 12 Sept. 1788, who *m.* 26 Nov. 1828; Dorothea-Lucretia, eldest dau. of Alexander-W. Light, Esq., late col. of the 25th regt., and by her (who *m.* 2ndly, Herbert-F. Hore, Esq. of Pole Hore, co. Wexford) he left, at his decease, 4 March, 1838,

I'Anson-Annesley-Gore, *b.* 5 May, 1832.
Arthur-Evelyn, *b.* 16 June, 1833.
Dora-Elizabeth-Holwel. Eva-Rosalie.

Arms—Sa., three cinquefoils between nine cross-crosslets, or, quartering, az. and gu., a cross-patonce, and a chief, or.
Crest—A porcupine, ppr.
Motto—Volonté de Dieu.
Seats—Woodlands, Surrey, and Heffleton, co. Dorset.

GABBETT OF CAHIRLINE.

Gabbett, William-Henry, Esq. of Cahirline, co. Limerick, *m.* 1st, 1822, Rebecca, only dau. of Humphrey Jones, Esq. of Mullinabro', co. Waterford, and by her (who *d.* in 1828) had issue,

I. William, *d.* in 1841. II. Humphrey, *d.* 1852.
III. Richard-Joseph, *b.* Jan. 1828.
I. Anne-Charlotte, *m.* to the Rev. John Bowles.

Mr. Gabbett *m.* 2ndly, Sept. 1829, Frances-Margaret, dau. of Thomas Going, Esq., and has, by her,

I. Henry-Francis, *b.* 1830. II. Thomas-Richard, *b.* 1831.
I. Caroline. II. Elizabeth. III. Wilhelmina. IV. Jane.

Lineage.—John Gabbett, or Gabbett, great-grandson of John Gabbett, exon of the Yeoman-guard in 1487, went to Ireland. He *m.*, and had, besides a dau., *m.* to Manninge, two sons, Robert, who *d.* at Cashel in 1652; and

William Gabbett, Esq., who purchased Cahirline and Rathjordan, co. Limerick, from William Matthews. By Alicia his wife, dau. of Richard England, of Lifford, he left at his decease, 9 June, 1693, three daus. (Elizabeth, *m.* to William Chadwick, of Ballinard; Alicia, *m.* to Richard Sadlier, of Sopwell; and Mary, *m.* to John Hammersly) and two sons, John, of Rathjordan (whose son and heir, John, high-sheriff of the co. of Limerick 1713, *d. s. p.*), and William, of whom we treat. The 2nd son,

William Gabbett, *b.* in 1658; clerk of the peace and crown for Limerick and Clare in 1711; *m.* Mary, dau. and heir of Giles Spencer; and *d.* 27 Aug. 1713, aged 55, leaving issue four sons by her (who *d.* 18 Aug. 1718). The eldest son,

William Gabbett, Esq. of Cahirline, *s.* his cousin John, of Rathjordan. He *m.* 1st, Mary, dau. of Thomas Spiers, of Rathanny, and by her (who d. 22 Nov. 1717) had,

I. William, his heir.
II. Thomas-Spiers, of Tivoli, Glassmore, co. Cork, *m.* the eldest dau. of Boyle Davies, Esq. of Donnybrook, co. Cork.
III. John, of Anaglin, co. Cork, *m.* Marcella, dau. of William Cox, of Ballinoe, co. Limerick, and was father of Thomas Gabbett, of Castle Lake, co. Clare, mayor of Limerick, who *m.* Miss Westropp, of Fort Anna, co. Clare, and had issue,
 1 Robert, in holy orders, LL.D., rector of Castletown, and vicar-general of Killaloe, *m.* Mary, dau. of Thomas Studdert, Esq. of Bunratty, co. Clare, and had three sons and five daus., viz.,
  John, of Castle Lake, J.P. for co. Clare, *m.* Millicent, dau. of Thomas Studdert, Esq. of Bunratty, and had a son, Robert.
  Robert, went to Australia.
  Poole, of Trinity College, Dublin.
  Anna, *m.* to William Smithwick, Esq. of Youghal.
  Elizabeth, *m.* to Thomas Spaight, of Corbally, co. Clare.
  Mary, *m.* to Peter Smithwick, Esq.
  Constance, *m.* to Henry Spaight.
  Margaret, *m.* to the Rev. Standish Parker, of Castle Lough, co. Tipperary.
 2 Thomas, barrister-at-law.
 3 John, capt. in the army, of Shepperton, co. Clare, J.P., *m.* Frances, dau. of George Hallam, Esq., and had four sons and six daus., viz., John; George; Thomas, deceased; and Robert; Frances; Elizabeth; Anna; Louisa; Jane; and Margaret.
 4 Poole, of Corbally House, J.P. for co. Clare, and treasurer of co. Limerick, *m.* Mary-Anne, dau. of Edmund

Fitzgerald, Esq., and had issue four sons and three daus., viz., Thomas; Edmund, *m.* Frances, dau. of Capt. Rich, R.N.; Poole, lieut. in the army; Robert, of the Royal artillery; Abigail, *m.* to John Westropp, Esq.; Mary-Anne, *m.* to Capt. Franklin, royal artillery; Marcella, *m.* to the Rev. Richard Moore.

Mr. Gabbett *m.* 2ndly, Anne, dau. of Benjamin Frend, Esq. of Ballynetry, King's County; and 3rdly, Mary, dau. of William Freeman, Esq. of Castle Cor, and by the latter (who *m.* 2ndly, Colonel Ludovic Peterson) had a son,

Joseph, gen. in the army, col. of the 16th regt., who *m.* Adeliza, dau. and heiress of Richmoud, Esq. of Sparsholt, co. Berks; and *d. s. p.*, leaving his estate of Sparsholt, &c., to his brother William's son, JOSEPH, of High Park.

Mr. Gabbett *d.* in 1727, and was *s.* by his eldest son,

WILLIAM GABBETT, Esq. of Cahirline, *b.* in 1706; J.P. for co. Limerick; *m.* in Mary, 1730, Dorothea, dau. of the Rev. Rickard Burgh, of Dromkeen, co. Limerick, and Grove, co Tipperary, son of Ulick Burgh, bishop of Ardagh, and had, besides a dau., Elizabeth, *m.* to Bryan Mansergh, Esq., three sons,

I. WILLIAM, his heir.
II. Richard, *d.* young.
III. Joseph, *b.* 1738, of High Park, co. Tipperary, and Sparsholt, co. Berks, which latter he had from his uncle, Gen. Joseph Gabbett. He was a capt. in the 15th regt., and mayor of Limerick in 1789. He *m.* Mary, eldest dau., by Mary his wife, dau. of William Armstrong, Esq. of Mealiffe, co. Tipperary, of the Rev. Rickard Lloyd, of Castle Lloyd, son and heir of the Rev. Thomas Lloyd, of Tower-hill, chanter of Emly, who was grandson and heir of Thomas Lloyd, of Tower-hill, and Eleanor his wife, dau. of Burgh, of Dromkeen. Capt. Gabbett *d.* 16 July, 1818, having had issue by his wife (who *d.* 18 Jan. 1830),

1 Joseph, mayor of Limerick in 1818-19, who *m.* in 1806, Lucy, eldest dau., by Lucy his 2nd wife, dau. and co-heir of Philip Oliver, Esq. of Altimira, co. Cork, of the Venble. William-Wray Maunsell, of Thorpe Malsor, archdeacon of Kildare, son and heir of Col. Thomas Maunsell, who was grandson and heir of John, capt. of the life-guards of Henry Cromwell. By this lady, who was sister of Thomas Maunsell, Esq, of Thorpe Malsor, M.P. for co. Northampton, Mr. Gabbett had issue,

Joseph, in holy orders, who *m.* in 1835, Harriet, eldest dau. of Charles-Dudley Madden, Esq. of Spring Grove, 2nd son of Col. Samuel Madden, of Hilton, who was grandson and heir of Dr. Samuel Madden, D.D., called *Premium Madden*, and has issue,

Joseph. Charles-Edward-Dudley.
Lucy. Emily.

William, capt. Madras artillery.
Robert, B.A., Trinity College, Dublin.
Alicia.
Lucy, *m.* W.-S. O'Brien, Esq. of Cahermoyle, 2nd son of Sir Edward O'Brien, of Dromoland, and has issue.

2 William. 3 Thomas.
1 Mary, *m.* to the Rev. George Studdert, 2nd son of Maurice Studdert, of Elmhill.
2 Alicia.
3 Dorothea, *m.* to Robert, only son of Patrick, 2nd son Arthur Webb, Esq. of Webbsborough, co. Kilkenny.

Mr. Gabbett *d.* in 1766, and was *s.* by his eldest son and heir,

WILLIAM GABBETT, Esq. of Cahirline, *b.* in 1731; high-sheriff of co. Limerick, and mayor of Limerick in 1775; who *m.* Jane, dau. (by Helena his wife, dau. of Daniel Toler, Esq. of Beechwood) of Richard Maunsell, Esq. of Ballywilliam, who was descended from Thomas Maunsell, a Royalist officer, son of Captain Thomas Maunsell, R.N., and by this lady had, besides a dau., *m.* to W.-Faulkiner Minchin, of Annagh, co. Tipperary, three sons,

WILLIAM, his heir.
Daniel, *m.* Alicia, dau. of John Fitzgerald, Esq., and was father of John, who *m.* Anne, dau. and heir of John-Magrath Fitzgerald, Esq. of Ballinard, a lineal descendant of Archbishop Magrath, and has a son, Daniel.
Joseph, *m.* Miss Sutton, sister of Edward Sutton, Esq., Master in Chancery.

Mr. Gabbett *d.* in 1789, and was *s.* by his eldest son,

WILLIAM GABBETT, Esq. of Cahirline, high-sheriff of co. Limerick in 1813, who *m.* 1791, Jane, dau. of Richard Waller, Esq. of Castle Waller, co. Tipperary, and had a son, WILLIAM-HENRY, his heir; and two daus., Anne and Jane, who *d.* 1850. Mr. Gabbett *d.* in 1828, and was *s.* by his son, the present WILLIAM-HENRY GABBETT, Esq. of Cahirline.

Seat—Cahirline, co. Limerick.

GAEL OF CHARLTON KINGS.

GAEL, SAMUEL-HIGGS, Esq. of Charlton Kings, co. Gloucester, J.P., *b.* in Aug. 1808; *m.* Nov. 1837, Annie, youngest dau. of George Hassard, Esq. of Skea, co. Fermanagh, and has issue,

I. CHARLES-EDWARD.
I. Elizabeth-Ann. II. Jane.

Lineage.—The name of this family has been variously written, (Galle, Gale, Gael, and originally De Gales,) and the crest, "a cock" gu., is probably an illusive device.

JOHN GALE, Esq. of Charlton Kings, son of Edward Gale, Esq. of Charlton Kings, by Sarah Tuckevill his wife, and grandson of John Gale, Esq. (son of Edmond Gael, Esq. of Alstonefield, near Cheltenham), who first settled at Charlton Kings, who had, by Anna his wife, three sons, JOHN, his heir; Edward, capt. in the Maryland Artillery, *d. unm.* in New Jersey, about the year 1785; and Henry, who *d. s. p.* The eldest son,

JOHN GALE, Esq. of Charlton Kings, *m.* in 1805, Susanna, youngest dau. and last surviving child of Charles Higgs, Esq. of Charlton Kings and Deerhurst, Walton, co. Gloucester, by Susanna Cooke, his wife, heiress of the families of Cooke, Sloper, Cooper, Wager, and Deighton, of Charlton Kings, and had two sons, JOHN, who *d. unm.* at Milan, in 1829; and SAMUEL-HIGGS, now of Charlton Kings.

Crest—A cock, gu.
Motto—Vigilate.
Seat—Charlton Kings, near Cheltenham.

GAGE OF RATHLIN ISLAND.

GAGE, THE REV. ROBERT, of Rathlin Island, co. Antrim, *b.* 20 Oct. 1790; *m.* 12 Aug. 1812, Catharine, eldest dau. of Ezekiel Davis Boyd, Esq. of Ballycastle, co. Antrim, and by her (who *d.* 22 Oct. 1852) has issue,

I. ROBERT, *b.* 30 July, 1813.
II. Ezekiel, *b.* 28 July, 1819, *m.* 16 May, 1848, Maria, dau. of John Dobbs, Esq. of Waterford.
III. John, *b.* 1829; *d.* 25 Feb. 1850.
I. Catharine. II. Barbara.
III. Rosella, *m.* to Gardiner Harvey, Esq.
IV. Amelia, deceased. V. Susan, deceased.
VI. Elizabeth, *m.* to Robert-H.-Wallace Dunlop, Esq., and deceased.
VII. Adelaide. VIII. Dorothea.

Mr. Gage is a magistrate for co. Antrim.

Lineage.—This is a branch of the English family of GAGE *of Firle.* The first who went to Ireland was

The REV. ROBERT GAGE, chaplain to Queen Anne and to Lionel, Duke of Dorset, lord-lieutenant of Ireland. He was for many years prebendary of Aghadoey, in the diocese of Derry, and in which he was *s.* by his son,

The REV. JOHN GAGE, prebendary of Aghadoey, who *m.* 26 Feb. 1733, Susan, dau. of the Rev. John Johnston, rector of Clondevadogue, in the diocese of Raphoe, and *d.* 28 Jan. 1763. His son,

ROBERT GAGE, Esq., *b.* 16 Oct. 1739, *m.* 25 Dec. 1776, Barbara, dau. of John Richardson, Esq. of Somerset, near Coleraine, co. Londonderry, and had issue,

John, *d. unm.* Frederick, R.N., *d. unm.*
ROBERT, of Rathlin Island.
Barbara, *m.* to Robert Harvey, Esq. of Malinhall, co. Donegal.
Susan.
Mary-Anne, *m.* to Marcus Richardson, Esq.

Seat—Rathlin Island.

GALBRAITH OF MACHRIHANISH AND OF DRUMORE HOUSE.

GALBRAITH, DAVID-STUART, Esq. of Machrihanish and of Drumore House, co. Argyll, *b.* 9 Oct. 1782; *m.* 1812, Elizabeth, only child of James Fraser, Esq. of Skye (of the FRASERS *of Lovat*), one of the three sons of Donald Fraser and Mary Macdonald, dau. of Donald Gorn, 2nd son of Macdonald of Slate, now represented by Lord Macdonald. Mrs. Galbraith *d.* 1853, aged 56, and was buried in Glensaddell Abbey, Cantire, the adjoining Castle of that name having been a seat of Mr. Galbraith's, sold by him a few years since. Mr. Galbraith has had issue by his said wife several children, viz.,

I. James-Fraser, a magistrate, &c., of Argyllshire; m. 1844, Cecilia-Sarah, 2nd dau. of Robert de Lisle, of Acton Hall, co. Northumberland, Esq.
II. Alexander-Macdonald, also a magistrate of Argyllshire, d. at Pau, in France, 1850; m. 1848, Maria, dau. of the Rev. Alexander Scott, of Bath.
III. David-Stuart. IV. Alfred-Stuart.
V. John-Campbell, d. 1845.
VI. Albert-Stuart. VII. Henry-Louis.
I. Margaret-Fraser, m. 1838, Capt. Thomas-Hay Campbell, Madras Artillery, d. 1843.
II. Elizabeth-Fraser, m. 1843, Thomas-McMiken Craufuird, Esq. of Grange House, co. Ayr., chief of Baidland and Ardmilian, descended from the Craufurds of Loudoun.
III. Mary-Davinia-Stuart, m. 1854, Frederic-John Keeling, of Colchester, co. Essex, Esq.
IV. Flora-Stuart, m. 1840, Captain Charles-Campbell Hook, 7th Madras Cavalry.
V. Julia-Stuart, d. 1848, unm.
VI. Emma-Stuart, m. 1847, Thomas-Burton-Watkin Forster, Esq. of Holt Manor House, co. Wilts.
VII. Octavia-Stuart, m. 1848, James Vaudrey, Esq.
VIII. Adelaide-Stuart.

Mr. Galbraith is a magistrate and deputy-lieut. of Argyllshire.

Lineage.—The family of Galbraith is of the remotest antiquity; its name is derived from the celtic, and it originally belongs to the Lennox, of Scotland. It was in the parish of Baldernoch, co. Stirling, that the Galbraiths of Baldernock, chiefs of the name had their residence. The family before us is sprung from the Galbraiths of the Isle of Gigha, who descended from the Galbraiths of Baldernock, having fled there with Lord James Stuart, youngest son of Murdoch, Duke of Albany, from the Lenox, after burning Dumbarton, in the reign of James I. of Scotland. They continued to hold that island, until after 1590, from the Macdonalds of the Isles; and in Fraser's Statistical account of its inhabitants, the following occurs:—"The majority of them are of the names of Galbraith and Macneill, the former reckoned the more ancient. The Galbraiths, in the Gaelic language, are called Breatanuich or Clann a Breatanuich, i. e., Britons, or the children of the Briton, and were once reckoned a great name in Scotland, according to the following lines:—

"'Bhreatanuich, o'n Talla dhearg,
Hailse sir Alba do shloinneadh.'"

That is—

"'Galbraiths' from the Red Tower,
Noblest of Scottish sirnames.'"

Maurice Galbraith, the Galbraith, baron of Baldernoch, aforesaid, was chief of the Highland clan Bhreatanuich, or family of Galbraith, A.D. 1220. His direct descendant,

Archibald Roy Galbraith, of the Isle of Gigha, off the coast of Argyllshire, temp. Charles I., was chief of that branch of the clan which had become settled in Gigha, as aforesaid. His son and heir,

Malcolm Galbraith, of Gigha, had a son and heir,

Archibald Galbraith, of Gigha, Esq., who, as well as his father and grandfather, were leading royalists in their locality. His son and heir,

Daniel Galbraith, of Gigha, Esq., and laird of Machrihanish, in Cantire, in the county of Argyll, d. 1814, aged 84; he m. 1765, Margaret, dau. of Archibald Stuart, Esq. (son, by Flora Macalister his wife, of Archibald Stuart, Esq. of Askomilbeg, and grandson of James Stuart, of the family of Stuart of Blackhall, an officer in Montrose's army, and a devoted loyalist, who escaped to Cantire, after the defeat at Philiphaugh, in 1647.) By this marriage alone survives the present David Stuart Galbraith, his other surviving and younger brother, Daniel, who m. Marion, dau. of Macdonald, of Scothouse, first cousin of the late Glengarry, having d. 1846, aged 62.

Arms—Gu., a fesse, chequy, arg. and az., between three bears' heads, arg., erased, of the second, muzzled, of the third.
Crest—A Lion's head and neck, ppr., erased.
Motto—Vigilo et spero.
Seat—Drumore House, Argyllshire.

GALTON OF CLAVERDON.

Galton, Darwin, Esq. of Claverdon, co. Warwick, J.P. and D.L., high-sheriff 1850; b. 18 March, 1814; m. 24 Sept. 1840, Mary-Elizabeth, eldest dau. and co-heir of John Phillips, Esq. of Edstone, co. Warwick, by Mary Weir, his 2nd wife, and has had one son,

John-Samuel, b. 23 Nov. 1841, d. 20 Aug. 1842.

Lineage.—The name of Galton is of ancient occurrence in the co. of Dorset. Hutchins, in his history of that shire, makes mention of the heirs of Simon de Galton, as holding of Walter de Hogle, and he of the king in chief, by knight's service, the hamlet of Galton, surveyed in Domesday Book, in two parcels, by the designation of Galtone or Gaveltone. The Rev. John Galton, M.A., of New College, Oxford, and vicar of Lulworth, during fifty years, was b. in 1578, and the Rev. Edward Galton held the rectory of Wareham in 1661. The immediate ancestor of the Warwickshire family,

Hubert Galton, of Kingston Winterbourn, in Dorsetshire, d. in 1662, leaving, with three daus., Dorothy, b. in 1648; Mary, b. in 1655; and Edith, b. in 1658, (who all d. unm.) an only son,

John Galton, Esq. of Yatton, co. Somerset, b. in 1650, who m. Bridget relict of John Tucker, Esq., and d. in 1695, leaving a son and successor,

John Galton, Esq. of Yatton, b. in 1671, who m. in 1703, Sarah Button, and had three sons and four daus., namely,

John, of Duddeston, co. Warwick, b. in 1705; m. in 1734, Hannah Alloway, but d. without issue, in 1775.
Robert, of Bristol, merchant, b. in 1708; m. in 1734, Hannah Farmer, and d. in 1746, leaving two sons and two daus., all of whom d. young,
Samuel, of whom presently.
Edith, d. without issue, in 1784.
Sarah, m. in 1774, to William Menson, Esq. of Ilminster.
Elizabeth, Mary, } both d. s. p.

Mr. Galton d. in 1743. His 3rd son,

Samuel Galton, Esq. of Duddeston House, co. Warwickshire, b. in 1720, m. Mary, dau. of Joseph Farmer, Esq., and left at his decease, with four daus, Sarah, Mary, Elizabeth, and Hannah who all d. issueless, a son,

Samuel Galton, Esq., F.R.S., of Duddeston House, b. 18 June, 1753 who m. in 1777, Lucy, eldest dau. of Robert Barclay, Esq. of Ury, in Kincardineshire, M.P. for that co., by Lucy, his first wife, dau. of David Barclay, Esq. of London, and had issue,

Samuel Tertius, his heir.
Theodore, b. 1 April, 1784, d. 5 June, 1810.
Hubert-John-Barclay, of Warley Hall, Salop.
Ewan-Cameron, b. in 1791, d. in 1800.
John-Howard, of Hadsor House, Worcestershire.
Mary-Anne, m. 1806, to Lambert Schimmelpenninck, Esq.
Sophia, m. 19 March, 1833, to Charles Brewin, Esq.
Adele, m. in 1827, to John-Kaye Booth, M.D. of Brush House, in Yorkshire.

Mr. Galton d. 19 June, 1832, and was s. by his eldest son,

Samuel-Tertius Galton, Esq. of Duddeston House, co. Warwick, J.P. and D.L., b. 23 March, 1783; m. 30 March, 1807, Frances-Anne-Violetta, eldest dau. of Erasmus Darwin, M.D., F.R.S., author of the "Botanic Garden," &c., and had,

I. Darwin, now of Claverdon.
Erasmus, of Loxton, J.P. for Somersetshire, b. 31 March, 1815.
Francis, b. 16 Feb. 1822, m. 1 Aug. 1853, Louisa-Jane, eldest dau. of the late Dr. Butler, dean of Peterborough.
Elizabeth-Anne, m. 31 Dec 1845, to Edward Wheler, Esq., grandson of Sir Charles Wheler, Bart.
Lucy-Harriot, m. 29 March, 1832, to James Moilliet, Esq. of The Elms, Abberley, co. Worcester, d., leaving issue, 5 Nov. 1848
Millicent-Adele, m. 13 May, 1845, to the Rev. Robert Shirley Bunbury, vicar of Swansea, who d. 28 May, 1846.
Emma-Sophia.

Mr. Galton d. 23 Oct. 1844.

Arms—Erm., on a fesse, engr., gu., between six fleurs-de-lis, of the second, an eagle's head, erased, arg., between two bezants.
Crest—On a mount, vert, an eagle, erm., looking up at the sun, or, its claw resting on a fleur-de-lis, gu.
Motto—Gaudet luce.
Residence—Leamington.

GALTON OF WARLEY HALL.

Galton, Hubert-John-Barclay, Esq. of Warley Hall, co. Salop, J.P., b. 26 April, 1789; m. 15 July, 1815, Mary, dau. of Robert Barclay, Esq. of London, Banker, and has one surviving child,

Mary-Barclay.

Lineage.—*For descent and arms refer to the preceding article.*

Seat—Warley Hall, in Salop.

GALTON OF HADZOR HOUSE.

GALTON, JOHN-HOWARD, Esq. of Hadzor House, co. Worcester, J.P. and D.L., has served as high-sheriff, *b.* 8 Nov. 1794; *m.* 15 Dec. 1819, Isabella, only surviving child of Joseph Strutt, Esq. of Derby, and has issue,

I. THEODORE-HOWARD, *b.* 2 Oct. 1820, *m.* 23 April, 1853, Frances-Amelia, dau. of — Arthur, Esq.
II. Douglas-Strutt, *b.* 2 July, 1822, *m.* 26 Aug. 1851, Marianne Nicholson.
III. Herman-Ernest, *b.* 25 March, 1826, *m.* 2 June, 1851, *m.* Mary-Cameron Abercromby of Glassaugh.
IV. Robert-Cameron, *b.* 17 Nov. 1830, *m.* 21 Nov. 1854, Frances-Anne-Adele, dau. of James Moilliet, Esq. of The Elms, Abberley, co. Worcester, and has a dau., Lucy-Ethel.

Lineage.—*For descent and arms refer to preceding family.*

Seat—Hadzor House, near Droitwich.

GALWEY OF LOTA.

GALWEY, EDWARD, Esq. of Lota, co. Cork, *s.* his elder brother, the late John Galwey, Esq., who *d. s. p.* 14 Jan. 1840. He is Rear-Admiral of the Red.

Lineage.—JOHN DE BURGO, younger brother of Ulick de Burgo, ancestor of the Marquis of Clanricarde, having accredited the bills of the citizens of Galway, was commonly known by the name of John, of Galway, and for his signal services in defending Ball's Bridge, Limerick, against the great force of O'Brien, of Desmond, in 1361, received the honour of knighthood from Lionel Duke of Clarence, the lord-lieutenant of Ireland, by the name of SIR JOHN DE GALWEY, with permission to him and his heirs to carry in his arms the representation of Ball's Bridge, and the date 1361, under the same for ever. He *d.* in 1400, leaving four sons, viz.,

WILLIAM, ancestor of SIR GEOFFREY GALWEY, created a baronet of Ireland by JAMES I. (*See* BURKE'S *Extinct Baronetage.*)
Henry, killed in the Irish wars, *unm.*
Edward, also killed in the same wars, *unm.*
GEOFFREY, of whose descendants we have to treat.

The fourth son,

GEOFFREY DE GALWEY, who served the office of mayor of Cork in 1430, *m.* Elizabeth, dau. of De Courcy, Lord Kingsale, and was *s.* by his son,

EDWARD GALWEY, Esq. of Dungannon, co. Cork, ancestor of the GALWEYS *of Lota*, whose representative,

JOHN GALWEY, Esq. of Lota, one of the members for the city of Cork in the parliament of JAMES II., *m.* Elizabeth, dau. of William Meade, Esq. of Ballintobber, and sister of Sir John Meade, Bart., and grandfather of the first Earl of Clanwilliam. By this lady he had a son and dau.,

WILLIAM, his heir.
Mary, *m.* to Michael Grace, Esq. of Gracefield.

The son and successor,

WILLIAM GALWEY, Esq. of Lota, *m.* Mary, dau. and heir of John Butler, Esq. of Westcourt, co. Kilkenny, nephew of James, first Duke of Ormonde, and had issue,

JOHN, his heir. Richard.
Elizabeth, *m.* to her cousin, William Coppinger, Esq. of Ballyvolane and Barryscourt, co. Cork.
Helen, Lady Esmonde.
Mary, Mrs. Byrne, of the county of Carlow.

William Galwey *d.* in 1783, and was *s.* by his son,

JOHN GALWEY Esq. of Lota and Westcourt, who *m.* Jane, dau. of William O'Brien, Esq. of Ahacross, co. Cork, and *d.* 1793, having had issue,

I. EDWARD, his heir.
II. Richard, who *d.* in 1826, having had
 1 John, of Fort Richard, who *m.* his cousin, Jane, dau. of James Galwey, Esq., and has issue.
 2 William, lieut. 77th regiment.
 3 Edward.
 1 Mary, *m.* to James Lombard, Esq. of Kerry.
 2 Eliza. 3 Jane.
 4 Catherine. 5 Margaret.
III. John, of Doon, co. Clare, who *m.* 1st, Miss Butler, of co. Clare, by whom he had two sons, William, *d.* on board ship, and James; and 2ndly, Emily Goold, by whom he has, Edward, Jane, Catherine, Frances, Mary, Gertrude, and Elizabeth, all married.
IV. William, in holy orders, Archdeacon of Killaloe, who *m.* Lydia, dau. of Patrick Webb, Esq. of Hermitage, co. Cork, of the family of Webbsborough, co. Kilkenny, and *d.* in 1833, having had,
 1 John, who *m.* Miss Abigail Cook, of Kilternan, co. Tipperary, *s. p.*
 2 Charles, who *m.* Miss Honoria Knox, of Londonderry, and has issue.
 3 William, *d.* in 1830. 4 Robert.
 5 Edward, who *m.* Miss Anne Sankey, of co. Tipperary.
 6 Richard, who *m.* Jane, dau. of William Galwey, Esq. of Baggot Street, Dublin, *d.* 19 Oct. 1831, leaving a posthumous dau., Lydia-Anne.
I. Mary, deceased. II. Gertrude, deceased.
III. Jane, *m.* in 1788, to Sir Richard Kellet, Bart., and has issue.

The eldest son,

EDWARD GALWEY, Esq. of Lota, *m.* 1st, Jane, dau. of Mountiford Westropp, Esq. of Limerick and 2ndly, Martha, 4th dau. of Randall Roberts, Esq. of Brightfieldstown, co. Cork, and sister of Sir Thomas Roberts, first baronet. By the former he had issue,

I. JOHN, his heir.
II. EDWARD, admiral, R.N., successor to his brother.
III. William, of Lower Baggot Street, Dublin, who *m.* Anne, dau. of Hugh Norcott, Esq. of Springfield, co. Cork, uncle of the late Major-Gen. Sir Amos Norcott, and has by her, who *d.* 8 Aug. 1832, two sons and one dau., viz.,
 1 EDWARD, barrister-at-law, *m.* Cornelia-Matilda, eldest dau. of Heyward St. Leger, Esq. of Heyward's Hill, co. Cork, and has had issue,
  JOHN-EDWARD, *b.* in 1838, *d.* in 1840.
  Matilda-Anne. Isabella-Miranda.
 2 John.
 1 Jane, *m.* to her cousin, Richard Galwey, son of the Venerable Archdeacon Galwey.
IV. Richard, who *d.* leaving four daus., Mary, Charlotte, Helena, and Isabella, all married
V. Mountiford, lieut. R.N., *d.* in the West Indies about 1806.
VI. James, who *m.* Miss Marcella M'Evoy, and had issue,
 1 Edward, deceased.
 2 Christopher, ensign 93rd regiment, *d.* in 1830.
 3 James. 4 Peter, (twin with Jane.)
 5 Richard, deceased. 6 William.
 7 Michael, lieut. E. I. Co.'s service.
 1 Mary, *m.* to the Rev. Henry Williams.
 2 Jane, *m.* to John Galwey, Esq. of Fort Richard.
 3 Marcella. 4 Anna.
 5 Louisa, *m.* to Edward Galwey, second son of John Galwey, Esq. of Doon, in Clare.
 6 Antoinette.
VII. Pierce, capt. 26th regiment, who was drowned off Cork Harbour, in 1830, in a pleasure boat, with his two eldest sons. By his wife, Sarah Johnson of the island of Trinidad, he left Edward, Richard, Mary-Anne, and Susan.
VIII. Thomas, *d. unm.*

Edward Galwey *d.* in 1812, and was *s.* by his eldest son,

JOHN GALWEY, Esq. of Lota who *m.* in 1813, Susan dau. of John Grainger Esq. of co. Meath, and widow of P. E. Arthur, Esq. of Limerick, but by her, who *d.* in 1836, had no issue. He *d.* 14 Jan. 1840, and was *s.* by his next brother, the present ADMIRAL EDWARD GALWEY, of Lota.

Arms—1st and 4th, or, on a cross, gu., five mullets, of the field; 2nd and 3rd, arg., the representation of Ball's Bridge, underneath the date 1361.

Crest—A cat, sejant, ppr., collared and chained.

Mottoes—Above the crest, Vinctus sed non victus; and below the shield, Vincit Veritas.

Residence—Lower Baggot Street, Dublin.

GANNON OF LARA.

GANNON, NICHOLAS-JOHN, Esq. of Lara, co. Kildare, *b.* 18 April, 1829; *m.* 22 April, 1852, Elizabeth-Patricia, eldest dau. of Eneas MacDonnell, Esq., by Elizabeth, his 3rd wife, dau. of the Rev. Jonathan Holmes, of Thirsk, co. York, and has issue,

I. JOHN-PATRICK, *b.* May 11, 1856.
I. Pauline-Elizabeth. II. Georgina-Mary.

Mr. Gannon is a magistrate for the cos. of Meath and Kildare.

Lineage.—Lara, originally written Laragh, was purchased about half a century ago, by NICHOLAS GANNON Esq. of Balliboy, co. Meath, who *m.* Anne Caddon, and *d.* 29 Sept. 1824, leaving issue, a dau., Mary-Anne, who *m.* 1816, Christopher Drake, Esq. of Roriston, co. Meath, and three sons, of whom, the elder, JAMES-LAWRENCE GANNON, Esq. of Laragh, made many additions to the family mansion, formed extensive pleasure grounds, and effected many other improvements in the demesne. He *d.* without issue, twelve years after he inherited, in 1836. His brother

JOHN GANNON, Esq. of Laragh, *m.* 25 Sept. 1826, Elizabeth-Henrietta, youngest dau. of Myles MacDonnell, Esq. of Clonmore House, Doo Castle and Rosbeg, co. Mayo, and by her (who *d.* in 1833), left at his decease, 22 Aug. 1837, two daus., Mary-Anne, *d.* 1842, and Elizabeth-Mary, *m.* 1852, to Frederick John Long, Esq. of Wimbledon, and one son, the present NICHOLAS JOHN GANNON, Esq. of Lara.

Seat—Lara, Kilcock.

GARDE OF BALLINACURRA.

GARDE, THOMAS, Esq. of Ballinacurra House, co. Cork, and of Garryduffe, co. Waterford, *b.* 7 Nov. 1807.

Lineage.—The family of GARDE is supposed to have come originally from France, and settled in Kent. Of the Kentish line, was THOMAS GARDE, *temp.* JAC. I., who had three sons, all of whom served in the civil wars of Ireland of the 17th century. Of these three brothers, THOMAS GARDE was the eldest, and acquired a good estate by purchase and otherwise, as well as beneficial leases of land from Sir St. John Brodrick, on whose estate, in the co of Cork, he settled at the time of the Restoration. By Alice Croker, his wife, he left at his decease, in 1688, WILLIAM, his heir; John, and Christopher. The eldest son WILLIAM GARDE, of Ballybane, *m.* Jane dau. of ——, and left, at his decease, in 1713, besides daus., two sons,

I. THOMAS, his heir.
II. William, of Rathcannon, co. Cork, whose will was dated 1726; he *d.* the following year, leaving by Mary Goold his wife, three daus. and five sons, viz.,
   1 John, *m.* Elizabeth Beere.   2 Francis.
   3 Henry, of Mountbell, *m.* Ann, dau. of Valentine Harding, Esq. of Cork, and widow of William Walter, Esq. of Ballymartin.
   4 Thomas, of Garrymore, *m.* Jane, dau. of Thomas Garde, Esq. of Polemore, and had issue, Thomas, of Garrymore and Kilbarry, who *d. unm.*; John, of Kilbarry, *d. unm.*; and Richard, of Garrymore, *m.* Miss Parker.
   5 William, of Ballinvullen, *m.* Elizabeth, dau. of John Boles, Esq., and had a dau.

The elder son,

THOMAS GARDE, Esq., of Polemore, *m.* 1699, Martha, dau. of John Downing, Esq. of Broomfield, co. Cork, and had,

I. WILLIAM, his heir.
II. John, of Glin, co. Waterford, *m.* 1735, Ann, dau. of Edward Jackson, Esq. of Scart, co. Waterford, and by her, who *m.* 2ndly, William Beere, Esq. of Ballyboy, co. Tipperary, left at his decease, 4 June, 1747,
   1 THOMAS, heir to his uncle.
   2 William, *d. unm.* 1760.
   1 Sarah, *m.* to James White, Esq. of Youghal.
   2 Rebecca, *m.* 1st, to the Rev. Mr. Lymberry; and 2ndly, to the Rev. Hans Fell, both of whom she outlived to a very advanced age.
III. Thomas, of Dunsfort, *m.* 1st, 1742, Elizabeth, dau. and co-heir of Samuel Boles, Esq. of Dunsfort, and by her (who *d.* 1749) had an only son,
   Thomas, of Broomfield, and afterwards of Ballindinis, *b.* 1743; *m.* Elizabeth, dau. of Henry Garde, Esq. of Mountbell, co. Cork, and by her (who *d.* 1836, aged 97) left at his decease, in 1822, aged 79, one son and three daus., viz.,
      1 Charles, of Ballindinis, *m.* Harriet, dau. of Henry Croker, Esq. of Quartertown, co. Cork, and left at his decease,
         THOMAS, of Ballindinis, *m.* and has issue.
         Henry, of Youghal, M.D., *m.* and has issue.
         Charles, of Castlemartyr, *m.* and has issue.
         John.
         Harriott, *m.* to Thomas Cole, Esq. of Cork.
      1 Anne, *m.* 1792, to Warham Durdin, Esq. of Sunville.
      2 Elizabeth, *m.* to Robert-Atkins Durdin, Esq. of Cranemore, co. Carlow.
      3 Jane, *m.* 1814, to Francis Drew, Esq. of Frogmore, co. Cork, and Meanuss, co. Kerry.
   Thomas Garde, of Dunsfort, *m.* 2ndly, 1753, Jane, dau. of William Walter, Esq. of Ballymartin, co. Cork, and by her (who *d.* 1810) left at his decease, 1766, three sons, and a dau., viz.,
      1 William, of Rathcallen, co. Cork, *m.* Jane, dau. of T. Harding Esq. of Ballingohig, co. Cork, and *d.* 1823, aged 69, leaving an only child, JANE, *m.* to John Browne, Esq. of Cooleowre.
      2 John, of Dunsfort, *d. s. p.* 1804, aged 50.
      3 Henry, of Knockane, co. Cork, M.D., an eminent physician; *m.* 1794, Anne, dau. of the Rev. Mr. Smith, rector of Cannavee, co. Cork, and *d.* 1841, aged 83, leaving issue, Thomas of Knockane, M.D., *m.* a dau. of the Rev. Thos. Wakeham, and has issue; John, vicar of Ballinafach, *m.* Elizabeth, dau. of Robert Boles, Esq. and *d.* 1838, leaving issue; and Ellen, *m.* the Rev. Godfrey Smith, rector of Kinneigh, and *d.* 1851, leaving issue.
      1 Anne, *m.* 1784, to John Boles, Esq. of Springfield, co. Cork, and *d.* 1848, aged 91.

Thomas Garde, of Polemore, *d.* 1732, and was *s.* by his son,

WILLIAM GARDE, Esq. of Broomfield, and, afterwards, of Ballinacurra, co. Cork, a man of vigorous intellect and great knowledge of the world; *m.* 1st, Dorcas, dau. of — Peard, Esq. of Coole, co. Cork, but by her, who *d.* 1752, had no issue. He *m.* 2ndly, Aphra, dau. of Thomas Clutterbuck, Esq. of Banningstown, co. Tipperary, and by her had issue,

   Thomas, who *d.* at Trinity College, Dublin, 1775.
   William, of Broomfield, who *d.* suddenly of fever a few days before he was to have been married, 1777.
   Aphra, *d. unm.* 1794.

Mr. Garde *d.* in 1791, and was buried at Cloyne, having bequeathed the bulk of his estate to his nephew,

THOMAS GARDE, Esq. of Ballinacurra, co. Cork, and Garryduff, co. Waterford, who *m.* 8 Jan. 1761, Mary-Anne, 2nd dau. of Jeffrey Prendergast, Esq. of Mullogh Abbey, co. Tipperary, and sister and heir of Capt. Henry Prendergast, of that place, and had issue,

   JOHN, his heir.
   HENRY-PRENDERGAST, successor to his brother.
   Lucy.   Anne.   Eleanor.

Mr. Garde *d.* 24 Dec. 1806, and was *s.* by his eldest son,

JOHN GARDE, Esq. of Ballinacurra, who *m.* Anne, dau. of Sir Christopher Musgrave, Bart.; and *d. s. p.* 1832, aged 68, and was *s.* by his brother,

HENRY-PRENDERGAST GARDE, Esq. of Garryduff, co. Waterford, who then became of Ballinacurra. He *m.* 29 Oct. 1806, Catherine, 2nd dau. of Sir Edward Hoare, Bart. of Annabella, co. Cork, and had issue,

   THOMAS, present representative of the family.
   Edward-Hoare, of Carewswood, co. Cork, *m.* Eleanor, dau. of William-Massy Baker, Esq. of Fortwilliam, co. Cork, and has issue.
   Clotilda-Henrietta, *m.* Francis Rowland, Esq. of Kilkoy House, co. Cork; and *d.* 1843.

Mr. Garde *d.* 27 July, 1841.

Arms—Az., on a chevron, arg., three birds, vert, a chief, or, charged with three griffins, segreant, sa.
Crest—A demi-griffin, sa. *Motto*—Toujours fidèle.
Seats—Ballinacurra House, Midleton, co. Cork; and Garryduff, Youghal, co. Waterford.

GARDEN-CAMPBELL OF TROUP HOUSE AND GLENLYON.

GARDEN-CAMPBELL, FRANCIS-WILLIAM, Esq. of Troup House, co. Banff, and Glenlyon House, co. Perth, *b.* 23 Oct. 1840; *s.* his father 3 Oct. 1848.

Lineage.—ARCHIBALD CAMPBELL (2nd son of Sir Duncan Campbell, of Glenurchy, ancestor of the noble house of Breadalbane), was of Glenlyon, in 1502, and from him the subsequent CAMPBELLS *of Glenlyon* descended. Their eventual heiress *m.* BALNEAVES, of Edradour, co. Perth, and was mother of an only dau. and heiress,

KATHERINE BALNEAVES, who *m.* PETER GARDEN, Esq. of Delgaty, co. Aberdeen, who thus acquiring the estate of Glenlyon, assumed the name and arms of Campbell, of Glenlyon. Mr. Garden-Campbell, by the heiress of Glenlyon, had issue, Alexander, *d. unm.*; Peter, *d. unm.*; FRANCIS, his heir; Peter-Henry; David; Helen, *m.* John Burnett, Esq. of Elrick; Jean; Katherine; Margaret, *m.* to W. Farquharson, Esq. of Monaltree; Christian; and Mary, *m.* to Thomas Burnett, Esq. The eldest surviving son and heir,

FRANCIS GARDEN-CAMPBELL, succeeded to the estates of Delgaty, Troup, &c. He *m.* 1788, Penelope, dau. of Richard Smyth, Esq. of Ballynatray, co. Waterford, and by her (who *m.* 2ndly, Major-Gen. Bruce) had an only son and heir,

FRANCIS GARDEN-CAMPBELL, Esq. of Troup and Glenlyon; who *m.* 1st, 23 Dec. 1815, Christian-Forbes, dau. of Archibald Cumine, Esq. of Auchry; and 2ndly, 25 Sept. 1822, Maria, only dau. of Major-Gen. Duff, of Carnousie; and by the former had issue, FRANCIS; Archibald; Agnes, *m.* to John Kinloch, Esq. of that ilk, and Kilrie, co. Forfar; and *d.* June, 1836, and was *s.* by his elder son,

FRANCIS GARDEN-CAMPBELL, Esq. of Troup House, co. Banff, and Glenlyon, co. Perth, J. P. and D.L., *b.* 18 Nov. 1818; *m.* 18 July, 1839, Georgina-Anne, dau. of the late

W.-P. Brigstocke, Esq., M.P. for Somerset, by whom he had issue,

FRANCIS-WILLIAM, b. 23 Oct. 1840.

Family of Garden.

The family of Gardyne, or Garden, has for many centuries possessed lands in the shires of Banff and Perth, and is mentioned, at a very early period, as Gardyne, of that ilk, and of Banchory. In 1589, Gardyne, of Banchory, was one of the gentlemen sent by JAMES I. to Denmark, on the occasion of the treaty of marriage betwixt him and the Princess Anne, afterwards his queen. In the succeeding generation the lands of Banchory were sold, and Major Alexander Garden, son of the last laird of Banchory, went with the troops sent by CHARLES I. to Gustavus of Sweden, and was present at the battle of Lutzen, where that great prince lost his life, in 1632. Major Garden remained several years at the Swedish court, high in favour with Queen Christina, and, on her abdication, in 1654, returned to Scotland, and purchased the lands of Troup. He m. Betty, dau. of Alexander Strachan, Esq. of Glenbrindy, and had issue, ALEXANDER GARDEN, Esq. of Troup, who m. Bathia, dau. of Sir Alexander Forbes, of Craigievar Bart., and was s. by his eldest son,

ALEXANDER GARDEN, Esq. of Troup, who m. Jean, dau. of Sir Francis Grant, of Cullen, Bart., and had, besides three daus, Jane, m. to Alexander Forth, of Freefield and Glenbrindy; the 2nd, m. to Arthur Forbes, of Schwas; and the 3rd, m. to Joseph Cuming, of Auchry; and three sons, ALEXANDER, FRANCIS, and PETER. The eldest son and heir,

ALEXANDER GARDEN, Esq. of Troup, s. his father in 1740, and acquired great landed possessions. He represented the county in parliament for many years, and was considered the wealthiest commoner in the north of Scotland. He d. unm. in 1785, and was s. by his brother,

FRANCIS GARDEN, of Troup, Lord Gardenstown, one of the judges of the Court of Session. This gentleman was remarkable for his talents and eloquence, for the successful manner in which he conducted several important lawsuits, and particularly the celebrated "Douglas cause." In 1744, he was made sheriff of Kincardineshire; and in 1761, accepted the office of joint solicitor-general of Scotland, together with Mr. James Montgomery, under Mr. Pitt's administration. He also made great improvements in his extensive estates; built the town of Laurencekirk, co. Kincardine, and purchased a royal charter, erecting it into a burgh of barony, with a regular magistracy. Lord Gardenstown d. unm. in 1793, and was s. by his brother,

PETER GARDEN, Esq. who had purchased the estate of Delgaty. He m., as stated before, the heiress of Glenlyon, and assumed the additional surname and arms of CAMPBELL.

Arms—Quarterly: 1st and 4th, or, a boar's head, erased, sa., for CAMPBELL; 2nd, arg. a galley, oars in action and sail furled, sa., for LORN; 3rd, or, a fesse, chequy, az. and arg., for STEWART, charged on the centre with a heart, gu., royally crowned.
Crests—1st, a boar, passant, arg.; 2nd, a demi-lion, rampant, holding in the dexter paw a heart, royally crowned.
Mottoes—Above the arms, "quæ recta sequor;" below the shield, "vires animat virtus."
Supporters—Dexter, a boar, arg.; sinister, a lion, ppr.
Seats—Troup House, co. Banff; Glenlyon, co. Perth.

GARDINER OF COOMBE LODGE.

GARDINER, SAMUEL-WEARE, Esq. of Coombe Lodge, co. Oxford, D.L., b. 2 Feb. 1821; high-sheriff 1849; m. 10 Aug. 1848, Isabella-Malet, 2nd dau. of Sir Lawrence Vaughan Palk, Bart. of Haldon, Devon, and has issue,

I. CHARLES-LAWRENCE-WEARE, b. 14 Nov. 1849.
I. Isabella-Laura-Elizabeth.

Lineage.—This family claims descent from that of Gardiner, of which was Stephen Gardiner, secretary to Cardinal Wolsey, bishop of Winchester, *temp.* HENRY VIII., and chancellor of England in the reign of Queen MARY.

HENRY GARDINER, of Castle Coombe, co. Wilts, son and heir, by Joan his wife, of HENRY GARDINER, of Castle Coombe, co. Wilts, who was b. in 1596, and d. 21 Oct. 1669, m. 5 Oct. 1671, Elizabeth Woodman, and by her (who d. 26 July, 1705) had, besides other issue, Henry, b. in 1672; JOHN, of whom we treat; Francis; Mary; and Elizabeth. Mr. Gardiner d. in Jan. 1726. His younger son,

JOHN GARDINER, Esq. of Tythe Horton, co. Wilts, b. 9 Sept. 1684; d. in 1754, having had, by Catherine his wife (who d. 10 May, 1744), besides other issue, SAMUEL, of whom presently; John, b. in 1731; Anne; Mary, m. to Thomas Swanson, of Basinghall Street, and d. in 1794. The eldest son,

SAMUEL GARDINER, Esq. of Woodford, co. Essex, b. in 1724; m. 1 March, 1750, Jane-Anne Parkinson, of London; and d. 4 Jan. 1794, having had by her (who d. in 1781), with other issue who d. young, SAMUEL, of whom hereafter; John-Philip, b. 17 March, 1762, d. 4 March, 1803; Sophia, m. in 1791, to Jasper Atkinson, Esq. of The Cottage, Maidenhead, Berks, and d. in 1834; Anne, m. 30 June, 1770, to John-Fisher Weare, Esq. of Clifton, Somerset, and d. 19 Nov. 1831. The elder son,

SAMUEL GARDINER, Esq. of Coombe Lodge, co. Oxford, b. 13 Sept. 1755; m. 14 Nov. 1782, Mary, dau. and heir of Charles Boddam, Esq. of Capel House, Bull's Cross, Enfield, and niece of Governor Boddam, of Bombay, and by her (who d. 12 Jan. 1818) had, to survive youth,

CHARLES-WRIGHT, his heir.
Rawson-Boddam, b. 8 Oct. 1787; m. 17 March, 1828, Margaret, dau. of William-Baring Gould, Esq. of Lew Trenchard, Devon.
Allen-Francis, capt. R.N., b. 28 June, 1794; m. 1st, 1 July, 1823, Julia-Susanna, dau. of John Reade, Esq. of Ipeden House, Oxon; and 2ndly, Elizabeth, dau. of the Rev. William Marsh, of Maidstone, Kent, and has issue by the former.
Jane, m. 29 Aug. 1805, to the Rev. Edward Vansittart (1st cousin of Nicholas, Baron Bexley), who afterwards changed his name to Neale. She d. 13 Aug. 1806.
Emma, m. 28 July, 1818, the Rev. George Hunt, of Buckhurst House, Berks, and Barmingham, Suffolk.

Mr. Gardiner d. 10 June, 1827, and was s. by his son,

CHARLES-WRIGHT GARDINER, Esq. of Coombe Lodge, b. 13 Nov. 1783; who m. 1 May, 1810, Mary-Anne, dau. of Thomas Chase, Esq., E. I. Co.'s civil service, Madras, and has issue,

SAMUEL-WEARE, now of Coombe Lodge.
Mary-Anne-Amelia.
Laura-Emma, m. 14 April, 1841, to Sir William-Berkeley Call, Bart.

Mr. Gardiner, who for many years was military secretary to the E. I. Co.'s government at Calcutta, under Lord Hastings, d. 2 Feb. 1842.

Arms—Quarterly: 1st and 4th, or, on a chevron, gu., between three griffins' heads, erased, az., two lions, counterpassant, of the field, for GARDINER; 2nd and 3rd, gu., on a cross, or, five mullets, sa., for BODDAM.
Crest—A griffin's head, erased.
Motto—Deo non fortunæ.
Seat—Coombe Lodge, Whitchurch, Oxon.

GARDINER OF FARMHILL.

GARDINER, JOHN, Esq. of Farmhill, co. Mayo, J.P. and D.L., high-sheriff in 1833, b. 31 Oct. 1797; m. 1st, 14 May, 1819, Elizabeth, dau. of James Cuff, Lord Tyrawly, by whom he had issue a dau., HARRIET. He m. 2ndly, 14 Sept. 1832, Eleanor, dau. of James Knox Gore, Esq., and Lady Louisa Gore his wife, and by her has issue,

I. JOHN-CHARLES, b. 23 April, 1844.
II. Henry-William, b. 4 Feb. 1852.
I. Louisa-Anne.
II. Charlotte-Emily, m. Dec. 1855.
III. Eleanor-Catherine-Adelaide.
IV. Hannah-Maria-Augusta.

Lineage.—CHARLES GARDINER, Esq. of Touree, m. Maria, dau. of — Bourke, Esq. of Heathfield, co. Mayo, and had issue a son,

JOHN GARDINER, Esq. of Farmhill, co. Mayo, m. 1792, Anne, dau. of James Gildea, of Cloona Castle, and by her (who d. 1825) had issue,

JOHN, present representative.
Maria, m. to Andrew-Clarke O'Malley, Esq. of Nua Castle, co. Mayo.
Hannah-Anne, m. to Francis Evans, Esq. of Mountjoy Square, Dublin.

Motto—Virtuti et fortunæ.

GARDYNE OF MIDDLETON.

BRUCE-GARDYNE, THOMAS-MACPHERSON, Esq. of Middleton, co. Forfar, b. 23 Feb. 1831.

Lineage.—There are no records known to be in existence of the early history of this family. The first authentic document is a justiciary process in the 15th century, relating to a feud between the laird of Gardyne and the laird of Guthrie, the latter of whom was killed by the former. An account of Forfarshire, written by John Ochterlony, of Guynd, printed in the Spottiswood Miscellany, and supposed to be compiled somewhere about 1660 or 1670, calls them "Gairdyne of that ilk, a very ancient family, and chief of the name;" previous to that time the castle of Gardyne, and a great part of the barony, had passed out of their hands. The tradition of the family says it had been "wadset," to raise money for the government, in defence of the country. The GARDYNES, or GARDENS, of that ilk, the GARDYNES *of Lawton*, and the GARDYNES *of Middleton*, are all one and the same family.

DAVID GARDYNE, of Lawton, *m.* in 1603, Janet Lindsay, of Edzell, and had issue. He was *s.* by his son,

JOHN GARDYNE, who *m.* in 1643, Elizabeth, dau. of Sir John Arbuthnott, of that ilk, and had issue, four sons and twenty daus. The eldest and heir,

ROBERT GARDYNE, Esq. of Lawton, *m.* in 1676, Grizzel, dau. of Alexander Watson, Esq., and was *s.* by his elder son,

DAVID GARDYNE, Esq. of Lawton, *m.* in 1706, Anne, eldest dau. of Graham of Fintry, and had issue. The eldest son, David, after the battle of Culloden, *d.* at Newport, in Flanders. The 2nd son,

JAMES GARDYNE, Esq. of Middleton, had, by his wife, Mary, dau. of Provost Wallace, of Arbroath, whom he *m.* in 1741, five sons and eight daus. All the sons *d. s. p.* The last survivor, THOMAS GARDYNE, Esq. of Middleton, D.L., *d. unm.* 1841, and was *s.* by (the son of his sister, Ann, wife of James Bruce, Esq.) his nephew,

WILLIAM BRUCE, who assumed the name of GARDYNE in addition to that of Bruce, in accordance with his uncle's settlements. He *m.* in 1825, Catherine, dau. of Lieut.-Col. Macpherson, of Canada, and had issue,

THOMAS-MACPHERSON, now of Middleton.
James-William, *b.* 17 April, 1832.
Evan, *b.* 15 April, 1833.
David-Greenhill, *b.* 4 Aug. 1833.
Anne, *d.* in 1831. Agnes-Mary, *d.* in 1847.

Major Gardyne, major 87th regt., and a deputy-lieut. for Forfarshire, *d.* 15 June, 1846.

Arms—GARDYNE and BRUCE, quarterly.
Crests—1 GARDYNE, 2 BRUCE.
Seat—Middleton House, co. Forfar.

GARLAND OF MICHAELSTOWE HALL AND WOODCOTE GROVE.

GARLAND, EDGAR-WALTER, Esq. of Michaelstowe Hall, Essex, and of Woodcote Grove, Surrey, J.P., *b.* 26 Dec. 1814; *m.* 19 Feb. 1844, Amelia, 2nd dau. of Robert Robertson, Esq. of Auchlecks, co. Perth, and Membland, co. Devon.

Lineage.—GARLAND, of Michaelstowe Hall, Essex, and Woodcote Grove, Surrey, has, for a long succession of years, held possessions in Essex, Sussex, Surrey, and Lincolnshire: branches are also established in the cos. of Dorset and York.

NATHANIEL GARLAND, Esq. of Michaelstowe Hall and Woodcote Grove, was father of three sons, viz.,

I. James, *b.* in 1768; who *m.* Dorothy, dau. and co-heir of Thomas Allan, Esq. of Allan's Flatts, and left an only dau. and heir,
  Anna-Susanna, *m.* to Arthur Blake, brother of Sir Patrick Blake, Bart. of Langham. She had as a dowry a property at Penhurst, Sussex, which was granted to the family by King JOHN, and of which the original grant is the only title-deed.
II. Nathaniel, *d. unm.*
III. LEWES-PEAKE, of whom we treat.

The 3rd son,

LEWES-PEAKE GARLAND, Esq. of Michaelstowe, *m.* 1772; Indiana, dau. of Major-General Sherrington Talbot, niece of Lord Chancellor Talbot, and sister of Sir Charles Talbot, Bart., by whom he left two sons, NATHANIEL, of whom presently; and Lewes-Peake, who *m.* Miss Phillips, and *d.* leaving issue, Arthur, and others. The elder son,

NATHANIEL GARLAND, Esq., also of Michaelstowe, *m.* 8 March, 1814, Anna, sister and heiress of Arthur-Walter Cope, Esq. of Drummilly, co. Armagh, and had issue,

EDGAR-WALTER, now of Michaelstowe Hall and Woodcote Grove.
Nathaniel-Arthur, in holy orders, rector of Upper Deal, *m.* Mary, dau. of the Rev. Dr. Faithful, and has issue, Arthur-Nathaniel, and others.
Trevor-Lawrance.
Arabella, *m.* to the Rev. George Burmester, rector of Little Oakley, Essex, and has issue.
Indiana-Elinor.
Georgina-Catherine, *m.* to John Penniger, Esq., and has issue.
Anna-Eliza, *m.* to Captain J. De Butts, and has issue.

Nathaniel Garland *d.* in 1845.

Arms—Paly of six, or and gu., a chief, per pale, of the second, and sa.; in the dexter chief, a chaplet, ppr.; in the sinister, a demi-lion, rampant, of the field.
Crest—On a mural crown, or, a lion, sejant-reguardant, arg., his dexter paw resting on an escutcheon, of the second, charged with a garland, ppr.
Seat—Michaelstowe Hall, Essex; and Woodcote Grove, Surrey.

GARNETT OF SUMMERSEAT.

GARNETT, SAMUEL, Esq. of Summerseat, co. Meath, *b.* 10 Nov. 1775; *m.* 1st, 26 Feb. 1805, Alice, dau. of Andrew Ellard, Esq. of Newton, co. Limerick; and 2ndly, 7 Dec. 1818, Mary-Anne, dau. of Thomas Rothwell, Esq. of Rockfield, co. Meath, and had issue,

I. SAMUEL, *b.* 3 Nov. 1806, *m.* May, 1831, Martha, dau. of the Rev. George O'Connor, of Ardlunnan, co. Meath, rector of Castleknock.
II. Richard, *b.* 13 Oct. 1821.
III. William, *b.* 29 June, 1826.
I. Anne, *m.* Sept. 1833, the Rev. Richard Radcliffe, rector of Skyrne, co. Meath.
II. Helena. III. Marianne.
IV. Isabella, *m.* to Thomas-Henry Johnson, Esq. of Carnaghlis, co. Antrim.

Lineage.—The late SAMUEL GARNETT, Esq. of Summerseat, (son of John Garnett, Esq., by Anne Hatch, his wife) *m.* 1772, Mary Rothwell, and by her (who *d.* in 1817) left at his decease, in 1803,

SAMUEL, now of Summerseat.
John-Paine, *m.* in 1797.

Seat—Summerseat, Clonee, co. Meath.

GARNETT OF WYRESIDE.

GARNETT, ROBERT, Esq. of Wyreside, co. Lancaster, *b.* 1780; *m.* Louisa, dau. of Dr. Lyon, of Tamworth, and has issue,

I. CHARLES, *m.* Mary-Anne, dau. of R. P. Willock, Esq., and has Charles-Arthur, and other issue.
II. Robert, *m.* Ellen-Frances, dau. of R. P. Willock, Esq., and has Albert-Peel and other issue.
III. Henry, *m.* Harriet, dau. of the late Henry Potts, Esq., of Chester, and has Henry and other issue.
IV. Frederick-William.
I. Mary-Jane, *m.* to Frank Somerville Head, Esq., eldest son of Sir Francis-B. Head, Bart., and has issue.
II. Louisa, *m.* to Henry-Osmond Nethercoat, Esq., and *d.* 1850, leaving issue.

Lineage.—JOHN GARNETT, who resided at Casterton, near Kirby Lonsdale, left by Elizabeth, his wife, who was buried at Burton, in Kendal, a son JOHN GARNETT, merchant, formerly of Jamaica, afterwards of Ulverstone, and finally of Manchester, who *m.* Elizabeth, dau. of Arthur Studart, Esq., of Ulverstone, and *d.* in 1800, leaving issue;

I. JOHN, of Liverpool, *m.* Sarah, dau. of James Stewart, Esq. of Jamaica, and *d.* in 1850, leaving issue,
  1 John-Stewart. 2 James.
  3 Elizabeth. 4 Mary.
II. James, *d.* in Jamaica.
III. ROBERT, of Wyreside.
IV. WILLIAM, of Quernmore Park.
I. Elizabeth, *m.* to Thos. Entwistle, Esq. of Springfield, co. Lancaster.

Arms—Gu., a lion, rampant, arg., ducally crowned, and a bordure, dovetail, or; on a canton of the last, a cross-pattée-fitchée, of the field.
Crest—A demi-lion, arg., gorged with a collar, dovetail, gu., between the paws an escutcheon, or, charged with a cross-pattée-fitchée, also gu.
Seat—Wyreside, co. Lancaster.

GARNETT OF QUERNMORE PARK.

GARNETT, WILLIAM, Esq. of Quernmore Park, co. Lancaster, J.P., high-sheriff in 1843, and Master Forester of Her Majesty's Forest of Bleasdale, *b.* 17 March, 1782; *m.* 1 March, 1818, Margaret, dau. of Alexander Carson, Esq. of Liverpool, and has issue surviving,

I. WILLIAM-JAMES, *b.* 10 July, 1818, *m.* 26 June, 1846, Frances-Ann, 2nd dau. of the late Rev. Henry Hale, of King's Walden, Herts.

I. Eliza, *m.* 21 Oct. 1835, to Edward Bellasis, Esq., Serjeant-at-law.

Mr. Garnett of Quernmore Park is youngest son of the late John Garnett, merchant, formerly of the Island of Jamaica, by Elizabeth his wife, dau. of Arthur Studart, Esq.

Arms—Gu., a lion, rampant, arg., ducally crowned, a bordure, nebuly, or, on a canton, of the last, an eagle, displayed, with two heads, sa.

Crest—A demi-lion, arg., gorged with a wreath of oak, ppr., holding between the paws an escutcheon, gu., charged with a bugle horn, or.

Motto—Diligentia et honore.

Seat—Quernmore Park, near Lancaster.

GARNIER OF ROOKESBURY.

GARNIER, WILLIAM, Esq. of Rookesbury, Hants, *m.* Selina, eldest dau. of Thomas Thistlethwayte, Esq. of Southwick Park. Mr. Garnier *s.* his father in 1835.

Lineage.—GEORGE GARNIER, Esq. of Rookesbury, Hants, who *m.* 20 May, 1766, Margaret, 4th dau. of Sir John Miller, Bart., had, with other issue,

I. WILLIAM, of whom presently.
II. Thomas, Dean of Winchester, and rector of Bishop's Stoke, Hants, *m.* 8 May, 1805, Mary, dau. of Caleb Hillyer Parry, M.D. of Bath, and sister of Dr. Parry, of Summer Hill, Bath, and of Capt. Sir William-Edward Parry, R.N. By her he had issue,

1 George, *b.* 19 March, 1807; lost on board H. M. S. "Delight," off the Mauritius.
2 Thomas, rector of Trinity Church, Marylebone, *b.* 15 April, 1809, *m.* 23 May, 1835, Lady Caroline-Elizabeth Keppel, youngest dau. of the 4th Earl of Albemarle, and has issue, John, *b.* 24 Aug. 1838; Thomas-Parry, *b.* 22 Feb. 1841; Mary; Anne-Emily; Emily-Caroline; and Margaret-Gertrude.
3 Henry, *b.* 25 April, 1811, of the 4th Madras Cavalry, *m.* 10 Oct. 1835, Catherine, dau. of Col. Macleau, political resident of Travancore, East Indies, and had issue.
4 John, in holy orders, *b.* 26 April, 1813, Fellow of Merton College, and curate of St. Ebbe's, Oxford, *d.* there in 1838.
1 Maria, *m.* to the Rev. Charles Pilkington, rector of Stockton, co. Warwick, and has a son, Charles, *b.* in 1837, and a dau., Caroline-Maria.
2 Emily, *d. unm.* in 1836.

The eldest son,

THE REV. WILLIAM GARNIER, of Rookesbury, Prebendary of Winchester, and Rector of Droxford, *m.* 9 June, 1797, Henrietta, eldest dau. of Brownlow North, Bishop of Winchester, and sister of the 6th Earl of Guilford, by whom he left at his decease, 18 March, 1835, (with four daus., of whom the eldest, Harriett, *m.* in 1827, the Rev. Jonathan Phillips Carpenter; the 2nd, Frances, *m.* in 1826, Colonel Horton; and the 4th, Lucy, *m.* in 1828, John Carpenter, Esq. of Mount Tavy, co. Devon,) three sons; the eldest is the present WILLIAM GARNIER, Esq. of Rookesbury; and the 2nd, Brownlow-North, R.N., *m.* 3 Dec. 1835, Henrietta-Maria, 2nd dau. of Thomas, 4th Lord Walsingham, and *d.* 28 June, 1847.

Arms—Az., a sword, in bend, point downwards, blade ppr., hilt and pommel, or, between a fleur-de-lis, in chief, and an oak-branch, in base of the last.

Crest—A lion's head, erased, arg.

Seat—Rookesbury, Wickham, Hants.

GARRARD OF LAMER.

DRAKE-GARRARD, CHARLES-BENET, Esq. of Lamer, co. Herts, J.P., high-sheriff 1839, *b.* 14 Feb. 1806; *m.* 1 Dec. 1835, Honora-Henrietta, eldest dau. of Philip-Duncombe Pauncefort Duncombe, Esq. of Brickhill Manor, Bucks.

Lineage.—CHARLES DRAKE, Esq. 5th son of William Drake, Esq. LL.D. of Shardeloes, by Elizabeth his wife, dau. of John Raworth, Esq., (*see* DRAKE, *of Shardeloes*), and great-grandson of Montague Drake, Esq. of Shardeloes, by Jane his wife, dau. and heir of SIR JOHN GARRARD, 3rd baronet of Lamer, assumed, (on inheriting the manor and estate of Lamer, at the decease of Sir Benet Garrard, 6th baronet, in 1767,) the additional surname and arms of GARRARD. He *m.* Anne, 4th dau. of Miles Barne, Esq. of Sotterley, co. Suffolk, and had issue, 1 CHARLES-BENET, now of Lamer; 1 Anne; 2 Charlotte *m.* to G.-H., Cherry, Esq. of Denford House, Berks; 3 Caroline, *m.* to William Dawson Esq. of St. Leonards Berks; 4 Louisa, *d. unm.*, and 5 Emily, *m.* to the Rev. John Tyrwhitt-Drake, rector of Amersham. Mr. Drake Garrard, M.P., for Agmondesham, *d.* July, 1817.

Arms—Quarterly: 1st and 4th, arg., on a fesse, sa., a lion, passant, of the field; 2nd and 3rd arg., a wivern, with wings displayed, and tail, nowed, gu.

Crests—1st, a leopard, sejant, ppr.; 2nd, a naked dexter hand and arm, erect, holding a battle-axe, sa., headed, arg.

Seat—Lamer Park, Wheathampsted, Herts.

GARRETT OF JANEVILLE.

GARRETT, WILLIAM, Esq. of Janeville, co. Carlow, *b.* 10 Oct. 1783; high-sheriff 1806; *m.* 16 Nov. 1809, Margaret, dau. of Samuel Raymond, Esq. of Riversdale, co. Kerry, by Catherine his wife, dau. of Alexander Odell, Esq. of Odellville, co. Limerick, and has had issue,

I. JAMES-PERKINS, in holy orders, rector of Kellistown, co. Carlow, *b.* 10 Oct. 1810, *m.* Caroline-Anne-Elizabeth, dau. of Hugh Moore Esq. of Eglantine, co. Down (sister of the Countess of Annesley,) by Priscilla his wife, dau. of William Armitage, Esq. of Kensington, and Moraston, co. Hereford, and widow of Robert Shaw, Esq. of Terenure, co. Dublin, and has issue,

1 William-Raymond. 2 James-Hugh-Moore.
3 Annesley-John.
1 Priscilla-Cecilia. 2 Margaret-Clarissa.
3 Elizabeth-Sydney-Jane.

II. Samuel Raymond.
III. William-Thomas, in holy orders, Incumbent of East Witton, co. York, *m.* Anne, only dau. of —, Horsfall, Esq. of Bolton Rhoyd, co. York.
I. Catherine-Georgiana-Augusta, *d. unm.*
II. Jane, *d. unm.* 4 June, 1845.
III. Anna-Maria, *m.* to William-Blakeman Robertson, Esq. of Monkstown, co. Dublin.

Lineage.—CAPTAIN JOHN GARRETT descended from the same family as Sir William Garrett, lord-mayor of London in 1555, had a grant of land in the Queen's County, in pursuance of the Act of Settlement, 22 Nov. 1666. He was father of,

JAMES GARRETT, Esq. of Kilgaran and Clonferta, co. Carlow, *b.* in 1676, who *m.* Mary, dau. of Col. Blake, of Mayo, and *d. circa*, 1760, having had by her (who *d.* 7 July, 1724) two sons, THOMAS, his heir; and William, of Clonferta, who *d. unm.*; will proved, 1760. The former,

THOMAS GARRETT, Esq. of Kilgaran, otherwise Janeville, *b.* in 1711, *m.* Anne, dau. of John Cole Esq. residing at that time in the co. Wexford, and had issue,

JAMES, his heir.
Sarah, *m.* to William Meredith, Esq.
Elizabeth, *m.* to S. Brewster, Esq.
Lydia, *m.* to J. Waters, Esq.

Mr. Garrett, whose will is dated 13 Aug. 1759, and proved 16 Nov following, was *s.* by his son,

JAMES GARRETT, Esq. of Kilgarron, otherwise Janeville, *b.* 10 Oct. 1740, high-sheriff, co. Carlow 1776, who *m.* 1773, Jane, dau. and co-heir of John Perkins, Esq. of Ballintrane Castle, co. Carlow, and by her (who *d.* 7 June, 1788) had issue,

JOHN, of Janeville, *d. unm.*
WILLIAM, now of Janeville.
Anne, *m.* to Gilbert-Pickering Rudkin, Esq. of Wells, co. Carlow, captain in the army, high-sheriff, co. Carlow, 1808, and had issue, Jane, *m.* to Thomas Tench Vigors, Esq. of Erindale, and Maria, *m.* to Henry-Shaw Jones, Esq. of Randalstown.
Mary, *m.* to John Watson, Esq. of Ballydarton, co. Carlow, high-sheriff in 1834, and had John, William, Jane, and Diana.
Priscilla, *d. unm.*

Mr. Garrett *d.* 17 July, 1818.

Arms—Erm., on a fesse, az., a lion, passant, or, langued, gu.
Crest—A lion, passant, langued, gu., resting his sinister paw on a trefoil.
Motto—Semper fidelis.
Seat—Janeville, co. Carlow.

GARTSHORE OF GARTSHORE.

MURRAY-GARTSHORE, JOHN-MURRAY, Esq. of Gartshore, co. Perth, *b.* 11 Oct. 1804; *m.* 1st, 5 Aug. 1836, Mary, 2nd dau. of General Sir Howard Douglas, Bart. of Carr, and by her (who *d.* Feb. 1851), has issue,

I. JOHN. I. Mary.

He *m.* 2ndly, 29 June, 1852, Augusta-Louisa, widow of the Rev. William-Casaubon Purdon, of Tinnerana, co. Clare, and only child of the late Rev. George-Frederick Tavell, by the Lady Augusta Fitzroy his wife, dau. of Augustus, 3rd Duke of Grafton. Mr. Murray-Gartshore, 2nd son of the late Sir Patrick Murray, Bart. of Ochtertyre, by Mary-Anne his wife, youngest dau. of John, Earl of Hopetoun, assumed the additional surname he bears on succeeding to the estate of Gartshore.

Arms—Quarterly, GARTSHORE and MURRAY.
Seat—Gartshore, co. Perth.

GARSTIN OF BRAGGANSTOWN.

GARSTIN, THE REV. ANTHONY, of Bragganstown, co. Louth, J.P., *b.* in 1796.

Lineage.—THE REV. JAMES GARSTIN the great grandfather of the present representative of this respectable family, *m.* Mrs. Brabazon, and had issue Norman, ANTHONY, James, Anne and Dorcas. The second son,

ANTHONY GARSTIN, Esq. of Bragganstown, had by Anne-Jenny, his wife, CHRISTOPHILUS, William Norman, James, Anthony, Elizabeth, Anne, and Maria. The eldest son and heir,

CHRISTOPHILUS GARSTIN, Esq. of Bragganstown, *m.* in 1790, Elizabeth, dau. of Andrew Thompson, Esq., and had issue,

I. ANTHONY, his heir.
II. Christophilus, *m.* Sarah Vesey, and has issue,
1 Christophilus 2 George. 3 Anthony.
1 Eleanor. 2 Grace. 3 Emma.
III. Norman.
I. Eliza, *m.* to Digby Marsh, Esq.
II. Charlotte. III. Frances. IV. Mary. V. Anne.

Mr. Garstin *d.* in 1821, and was *s.* by his eldest son, the present REV. ANTHONY GARSTIN, of Bragganstown.

Arms—Arg., on a pale, sa., a pike's head, couped, or.
Crest—A dexter hand holding a dagger.
Motto—Gladio et virtute.
Seat—Bragganstown Castle, Bellingham.

GARVEY OF MURRISK ABBEY.

GARVEY, JOHN-CHRISTOPHER, Esq. of Murrisk Abbey, co. Mayo, high-sheriff 1853, *b.* 11 Oct. 1798; *m.* 1st, Maria, dau. of Hubert Moore, Esq. of Shannon View, co. Galway, but by her had no issue; and 2ndly, 29 Sept. 1847, Jane, eldest dau. of the Ven. William Leahy, archdeacon of Killala, by whom he left issue,

I. FRANCIS-CHRISTOPHER, *b.* 15 June, 1851.
I. Elizabeth-Rose. II. Honoria-Edith.
III. Sarah-Jane.

Lineage.—The pedigree of this ancient family which is on record in Ulster's Office, thus commences:

GARBHE or GARVEY, (that is, warlike) Prince of Morisk in the co. of Mayo, was son of Muledy son of Ferach son of Finan, the lineal descendant of Colla da Crioch or Colla of the Cross, son of Eochy or Achaius, son of Carbrey Liffechar, Monarch of all Ireland, *circiter* 300. He was father of,

FINTAN O'GARVEY, Lord of Morisk, chief of his name, and representative of the ancient sept, of tribe of O'Garbheigh, Lords of Morisk, and many other lands in the co. of Mayo. He *m.* Elizabeth, dau. of Miles Cogan, Lord of Galynge, co. Mayo, and had a son and heir,

THOMAS O'GARVEY, of Morisk, Esq., A.D. 1490, who *m.* Sabina, dau. of Simon Le Waleys or Walsh, of the co. of Mayo. He was father of,

DENIS O'GARVEY, of Morisk, chief of his name, who *m.* Gormolina, dau. of Patk. Dowdall, of Ardmas, in the barony of Fireragh Moy, and was *s.* by his son,

JOHN O'GARVEY of Morisk, Esq. who *m.* Finola, dau. of Le Botiler, or Butler, of the Ormonde family, and has issue,

JOHN, his heir.
Patrick, of Aughnagown, co. Down, secretary to Sir Nicholas Bagenal, marshal of the army of Queen ELIZABETH.

The eldest son,

JOHN GARVEY, D.D., Lord Archbishop of Armagh and Primate of all Ireland, Member of the Privy Council to Queen ELIZABETH, appointed archdeacon of Meath and Dean of Christ's Church Dublin, in 1565, consecrated Lord Bishop of Kilmore 7 April, 1585, and translated to the archdiocese of Armagh, 10 May 1589, was born in the city of Kilkenny in 1527; *d.* 2 March, 1594, and buried in Christ's Church, Dublin. He *m.* 1st, Margaret, dau. of Christopher Plunket, of Dunsoghly co. Meath, Esq., son and heir of the Hon. Thomas Plunket Justice of the Court of Common Pleas in Ireland, A.D. 1488. She was sister to the Right Hon. Sir John Plunket, Knt., Lord Chief Justice of the Queen's Bench in the time of Queen ELIZABETH, A.D. 1578, who died very old, 1 Aug. 1587. He *m.* 2ndly, Rose, youngest dau. of Thomas Usher, of Crumlin, co. Dublin, Esq., by Margaret, dau. and heir of Sir Henry Gaydon, Knt., alderman and mayor of Dublin. She was first married to John, son of Launcelot Money, of Waterford, Esq.; 2ndly, to — Davies, Esq. She was sister to Henry Usher, D.D., and aunt to James Usher, D.D., both Lords Archbishops of Armagh. She *d.* in 1612, and was buried in Christ's Church, Dublin. The archbishop's son,

SIR CHRISTOPHER GARVEY, of Lehinch, Morisk, Costello, Tully, and many other lands in Mayo, *m.* Anne, dau. of John Walsh, Esq. of Kilgobbin, co. Dublin, and was *s.* by his son,

FRANCIS GARVEY, Esq., lord of the manors of Lehinch, Morisk, Tully, &c., who *m.* and had issue;

FRANCIS, of Lehinch, *m.* Mary, dau. of Garrett O'Moore, Esq. of Bryes, and was father of JOHN GARVEY, of Lehinch, Esq., colonel in the army of King JAMES II., and M.P. He was slain in quelling an insurrection in Galway. His will, dated 17th March, 1703, was proved 9 Dec. 1708. He *m.* the Hon. Bridget Bermingham, only dau. of the Right Hon. Edward, Lord Baron of Athenry, Premier Baron of Ireland, and was father of JAMES GARVEY, of Lehinch, Kiggall, Annefield, and other lands in the co. of Mayo, *m.* Mary, dau. of Patrick Jordan, of Old Head and Elm Hall, co. Mayo, Esq., and was father of FRANCIS GARVEY, of Rossmindle, co. Mayo, Esq., who *m.* Anastasia, dau. of Henry Jordan, of Rosslevin, co. Mayo, Esq., and was father of Edmond-Francis Garvey, of Rossmindle, co. Mayo, Esq., *m.* Julia, dau. of Ignatius Kelly, of Castlegar, co. Mayo, Esq., and had FRANCIS and Biddia, wife of John Macdonnell, Esq.
JAMES, of Morisk.

The second son,

JAMES GARVEY, of Morisk, co. Mayo, Esq., had Morisk settled on him by his father. He *m.* Judith, dau. of James Lynch, of Carra, co. Mayo, Esq., and was father of,

FRANCIS GARVEY, of Morisk, Esq., who *m.* Margaret dau. of Robert Lewis, of the barony of Carra co. Mayo, Esq., and had a son and successor,

JOHN GARVEY, Esq. of Morisk &c. who *m.* Honoria, dau. of Randall McDonnell, of Rosbeg, co. Mayo, Esq., and was father of,

BONADVENTURE GARVEY, Esq. of Murrisk, who *m.* Margaret, dau. of James Merrick of Tuam, Esq., and was father of an only child and heir, the late

JOHN CHRISTOPHER GARVEY, Esq. of Murrisk

Arms—Erm., two chevs., between three crosses-pattée, gu.
Crest—A lion, passant, reguardant, gu.
Motto—Sis justus nec timeas.
Seat—Murrisk Abbey, co. Mayo.

GARVEY OF THORNVALE.

GARVEY, GEORGE, Esq. of Thornvale, King's Co., *b.* 6 July, 1794; *m.* 8 Jan. 1818, Jane, dau. of Michael Roberts, Esq. of Kilmoney Abbey, co. Cork, by Lydia, dau. and heiress of Theobald Pepper, Esq. of Mota, co. Tipperary, and has issue,

I. George-Bloomfield, lieut. R.A., *b.* 18 Feb. 1831, and *d.* at Port Royal, Jamaica, 19 Nov. 1853.
II. Toler-Roberts, *b.* 11 Feb. 1834.
III. Henry-Pepper, *b.* 6 June, 1837, a midshipman in the R.N.
I. Lydia-Anne. II. Elizabeth-Charlotte.

III. Harriett-Georgina-Charlotte, m. 8 Jan. 1849, to William Causabon, eldest son of George Frend, Esq. of Rutha, co. Limerick.
IV. Margaret-Martha, d. young. V. Jane-Mary.

Seat—Thornvale, King's County.

GASCOIGNE OF PARLINGTON.

OLIVER-GASCOIGNE, MARY-ISABELLA and ELIZABETH, of Parlington, co. York, and of Castle Oliver, co. Limerick, s. to the estates upon the demise of their father, 14 April, 1843; the elder, MARY-ISABELLA-OLIVER GASCOIGNE, m. 16 Jan. 1850, FREDERIC-CHARLES TRENCH, Esq., who assumed, on his marriage, the additional surname and arms of GASCOIGNE, and has a son and heir, b. 4 July, 1851. The younger, ELIZABETH, m. 10 Feb. 1852, Frederic-Mason, LORD ASHTOWN.

Lineage.—The family of Gascoigne is one of great antiquity, and acquired the estate of Gawthorp, at a very early period, in marriage with the dau. and co-heir of John de Gawthorp. The senior line, derived from SIR WILLIAM GASCOIGNE, the celebrated chief-justice of the reign of HENRY IV., terminated in an heiress, Margaret, wife of Thomas Wentworth, Esq. of Wentworth Wood House, grandfather of Thomas, 1st Earl of Strafford. The next branch, the GASCOIGNES OF THORPE ON THE HILL, were sprung from a 2nd son of the Gawthorp family. The co-heiresses were MARGERY, wife of Henry Procter, Esq. of New Hall, near Otley; and ELEANOR, wife of Arthur Ingram, Esq., groom of the privy chamber to CHARLES II.

The GASCOIGNES OF PARLINGTON derived their descent from NICHOLAS GASCOIGNE, of Lasingcroft, younger brother of the Chief-Justice, and were raised to the baronetcy of Scotland by King CHARLES I., in the person of SIR JOHN GASCOIGNE, of Parlington (*see* BURKE'S *Extinct Baronetage*). The last baronet, SIR THOMAS GASCOIGNE m. Mary, dau. of James Shuttleworth, Esq. of Forcet, and widow of Sir Charles Turner, Bart. of Kirkleatham, co. York, by whom he had an only child, Thomas, who d. 20 Oct. 1809. Sir Thomas d. 11 Feb. 1810, and leaving no issue, devised his estates in trust for Mr. and Mrs. Oliver (his step-dau.), for their lives, with remainder to their sons (of whom two were b. before Sir Thomas's death), and then to their daus. in tail. Under this settlement, Mr. Oliver, who was eldest son of the RIGHT HON. SILVER OLIVER, of Castle Oliver, co. Limerick, assumed the surname and arms of GASCOIGNE, and became

RICHARD OLIVER-GASCOIGNE, Esq. of Parlington. He m. Miss Turner, dau. of Sir Charles Turner, Bart. of Kirkleatham, by Mary, his wife, dau. of James Shuttleworth, Esq. and subsequently wife of SIR THOMAS GASCOIGNE, Bart., and by her, who d. about the year 1815, had issue,

THOMAS-OLIVER, d. unm. 24 April, 1842.
Richard-Silver, d. unm. 25 Dec. 1842.
MARY-ISABELLA-OLIVER, } now of Parlington.
ELIZABETH-OLIVER, }

Mr. Oliver Gascoigne, who served as high-sheriff of Yorkshire about the year 1831, d. 14 April, 1843, and was s. by his two daus. as co-heirs.

Arms—Quarterly: 1st and 4th, arg., on a pale sa., a demi-lucy, erect, couped, or, a canton, gu., for GASCOIGNE; 2nd and 3rd, arg., a chev., sa., between two pellets, in chief, and a fish, in base, gu. for OLIVER.
Seat—Parlington, co. York; and Castle Oliver, co. Limerick.

GASKELL OF KIDDINGTON HALL.

GASKELL, HENRY-LOMAX, Esq. of Kiddington Hall, co. Oxford, and of Beaumont Hall, co. Lancaster, J.P. and D.L. for the co. of Lancaster, b. 18 Sept. 1813; m. 10 Sept. 1845, Alice, dau. of Samuel Brooks, Esq. of Whalley Range, Withington, co. Lancaster, and has issue,

I. HENRY-BROOKS, b. 26 Aug. 1846.
II. Charles-Edward, b. 10 Dec. 1847.
III. James, b. 28 Aug. 1849.
IV. Walter-Edgar, b. 13 Oct. 1850.
I. Alice-Jane. II. Margaret-Caroline.

Lineage.—HENRY GASKELL, of Southworth House, near Wigan, co. Lancaster, an eminent solicitor, eldest son of John Gaskell, Esq. of Skelmersdale Hall, in the same co., by Hannah, his wife, b. 29 Oct. 1778, m. 1 June, 1807, Jane Lomax, and by her, who d. 19 Feb. 1841, had issue,

John, b. 29 Dec. 1811, d. s. p., 30 July, 1837.
HENRY-LOMAX, b. 18 Sept. 1813.
Henrietta-Hannah, m. James Close, Esq. of Naples, and d. 1837, leaving one child, Henry.
Jane, d. in infancy.
Caroline-Margaret, m. John Fowden Hodges, Esq. of Bolney Court, in the co. of Oxford, and has issue.

Mr. Gaskell d. 3 June, 1849.

Arms—Erm., three bars vert. for GASKELL; quartering, gu., on a chief, arg., a lion, passant, guardant, gu., for BROOKS.
Crest—Out of waves of the sea a dexter arm issuant, holding an anchor, cabled: over the crest, "Spes."
Motto—Spes mea in Deo.
Seats—Kiddington Hall, co. Oxford; and Beaumont Hall, co. Lancaster.

GASKELL OF THORNES HOUSE.

GASKELL, JAMES-MILNES, Esq. of Thornes House, co. York, J.P. and D.L., M.P. for Wenlock, and a Lord of the Treasury in the administration of Sir Robert Peel, b. 19 Oct. 1810; m. 16 May, 1832, Mary, 2nd dau. of the late Right Hon. Charles-W. Williams-Wynn, M.P., and has issue,

I. CHARLES-GEORGE-MILNES, b. 23 Jan. 1842.
II. Gerald-Milnes, b. 25 Oct. 1844.
I. Cecil-Grenville.
II. Isabel-Milnes, m. 8 May, 1855, to the Rev. Fitzgerald Wintour, rector of Hawerby, co. Lincoln, eldest son of the Rev. Fitzgerald Wintour, prebendary of Southwell.

Lineage.—JOHN MILNES, Esq. of Wakefield, had three sons and two daus. by his wife Miss Lapidge, of Pontefract, viz., John and Richard, d. unm.; James, m. Esther Widdowes; Mary, m. Benjamin Gaskell, Esq. of Clifton Hall, near Manchester; and Elizabeth, d. unm. JAMES and ESTHER MILNES, left an only child,

JAMES MILNES, Esq. of Thornes House, sometime M.P. for Bletchingley. He m. Mary-Ann Busk, dau. and co-heir of Hans Busk, and co-heir also of two ancient West-Riding families, that of RHODES *of Great Houghton*, and that of RICH *of Bullhouse*. He had no issue; and on his death, April 21, 1805, all the issue was exhausted of his grandfather, John Milnes, except the descendants of his aunt, Mrs. Gaskell. That lady (MARY, dau. of JOHN MILNES, Esq.) m., as already stated, BENJAMIN GASKELL, Esq. of Clifton Hall, near Manchester, son and heir of DANIEL GASKELL, Esq. of the same place, and had an only son,

DANIEL GASKELL, Esq. of Clifton Hall, who m. in 1777, Hannah, dau. of the late James Noble, Esq. of Lancaster, and by her, who d. in 1798, left at his decease, in 1787, two sons,

BENJAMIN, of Thornes House.
DANIEL, of Lupset Hall.

The elder son,

BENJAMIN GASKELL, Esq. of Thornes House, J.P., M.P. for Maldon, for many years; was b. 28 Feb. 1781, and m. 17 June, 1807, Mary, eldest dau. of the late Dr. Brandreth, of Liverpool, by whom (who d. 23 Nov. 1845) he left at his decease, 21 Jan. 1856, an only child, the present JAMES-MILNES GASKELL, Esq. of Thornes House.

Arms—Quarterly: 1st and 4th, arg., on a pale, sa., a conger-eel's head, couped and erect, or, for GASKELL; 2nd, and 3rd, az., on a chev., between three windmill sails, crossways, or, a martlet, for difference, for MILNES.
Crests—1st, a stork, ppr., collared, or, pendent therefrom an escutcheon, sa, charged with an annulet, or, and the dexter foot resting on an escallop, gu.; 2nd, a garb, or, banded by a fesse dancettée, az., charged with three mullets, pierced, or, for MILNES.
Motto—Scio cui credidi.
Seat—Thornes House, near Wakefield.

GASKELL OF LUPSET HALL.

GASKELL, DANIEL, Esq. of Lupset Hall, co. York, D.L., b. 11 Sept. 1782; m. 11 March, 1806, Mary, dau. of Benjamin Heywood, Esq. of Stanley Hall, near Wakefield. Mr. Gaskell of Lupset Hall is younger and only brother of the late Benjamin Gaskell, Esq. of Thornes House, co. York.

Seat—Lupset Hall, near Wakefield.

GASON OF RICHMOND.

GASON, RICHARD-WILLS, Esq. of Richmond, co. Tipperary, J.P. and D.L., high-sheriff in 1842; m. 15 Nov. 1811, Anne, dau. of Charles-Henry Leslie, Esq. of Wilton, co. Cork, and Lucia Izod his wife, and by her has had issue,

I. RICHARD. II. Wills-Crofts.
III. Charles-Henry, drowned, with part of his regiment, the 62nd, in crossing the Ganges, 6 Sept. 1842.
I. Lucia. II. Alicia-Ellen-Christina.
III. Catherine-Mary-Elizabeth.

Lineage.—This family, claiming to have been originally from Ickham, in Kent, settled in Ireland in the year 1640. The present representative, RICHARD-WILLS GASON, Esq., and his sister, Anna-Maria, relict of J. Houghton, Esq. of Kilmanock House, co. Wexford, are the only children of the late Richard Gason, Esq. of Richmond, co. Tipperary, by Alicia his wife (m. in 1770), dau. of Wills Crofts, Esq. of Churchtown, co. Cork, and Eleanor his wife, dau. of Robert Freeman, Esq. of Ballinguile.

Arms (granted to the Ickham family in 1589)—Az., a fesse, erm., cottised, arg., between three goats' heads, erased of the third, attired, or.
Crest—On a chapeau, az., turned up, erm., a goat's head, erased, arg., bearded and attired, or.
Motto—Fama semper vivit.
Seat—Richmond, near Nenagh, co. Tipperary.

GATACRE OF GATACRE.

GATACRE, EDWARD-LLOYD, Esq. of Gatacre, co. Salop, m. Miss Forbes, dau. of William Forbes, Esq. of Callendar.

Lineage.—It appears that in the reign of HENRY III., STEPHEN DE GATACRE possessed the manors of Gatacre and Sutton, with lands in Claverley, which he held of the king by military service, and which had been obtained by his ancestor, by grant, from EDWARD the Confessor. He d. after the year 1229, and was s. by (the son of his son Thomas) his grandson,

ROBERT DE GATACRE, lord of Gatacre, who d. unm., and was s. by his brother,

WILLIAM DE GATACRE, lord of Gatacre in 1298 and 1313, father of

GALFRY DE GATACRE, lord of Gatacre in 1314 and 1319, whose son,

THOMAS DE GATACRE, of Gatacre, living temp. EDWARD II., m. Joan, dau. of Richard de Leigh, of Leigh and Park Hall co. Stafford, and dying in 1367, was s. by his son,

THOMAS DE GATACRE, of Gatacre, temp. RICHARD II., father of

WILLIAM DE GATACRE, of Gatacre, in 1398, who dying unm., was s. by his brother,

JOHN DE GATACRE, of Gatacre, who flourished in the reigns of HENRY IV., V., and VI. He m. Joice, dau. of John Burley, Esq. of Bomcroft Castle, sheriff of Shropshire in 1409, and was s. by his eldest son,

JOHN GATACRE, Esq. of Gatacre, M.P. for Bridgenorth 12 EDWARD IV. He m. Jane, dau. of Nicholas Yonge, Esq. of Caynton, in Salop, and was father of

JOHN GATACRE, Esq. of Gatacre, who m. 1st, Eleanor, dau. of John Acton, Esq. of Aldenham, but by her had no issue; and 2ndly, Elizabeth, dau. of Sir Adam Bostock, Knt. of Bostock, in Cheshire, by whom (her will was proved in 1501) he had two sons, ROBERT, and Arthur, and one dau., Christabel, m. to John Lyster, Esq. of Rowton Castle. He d. in 1499, and was s. by his elder son,

ROBERT GATACRE, Esq. of Gatacre, in 1500, who m. Joan, 2nd dau. of John Hoord, of Bridgenorth, and had issue, WILLIAM, his heir; Richard; Francis; Mary, m. to John Wolryche, Esq. of Dudmaston; Margery, to William Middlemore, Esq. of Worcestershire; and Jane, to John Whitton, Esq. of Whitton Court. Mr. Gatacre d. in 1509, and was s. by his eldest son,

WILLIAM GATACRE, Esq. of Gatacre, who m. Helen, dau. of William Mytton, Esq. of Shrewsbury, and had, with other issue, FRANCIS, his heir; and THOMAS, ancestor of the GATAKERS *of Mildenhall*. Mr. Gatacre d. 20 Dec. 1577, and was s. by his eldest son,

FRANCIS GATACRE, Esq. of Gatacre, who m. Elizabeth, 2nd dau. and co-heir of Humphrey Swinnerton, Esq. of Swinnerton, in Staffordshire, and dying 19 June, 1590, was s. by his elder son,

WILLIAM GATACRE, Esq. of Gatacre, who m. Anne, dau. and heir of Jerome Corbet, Esq., one of the council in the marches of Wales, and dying in 1615, was s. by his son,

JOHN GATACRE, Esq. of Gatacre, who m. Mary, dau. of William Polwhele, Esq. of Polwhele, co. Cornwall, and by her, who d. in 1667, left, at his decease in 1667, a son and successor,

THOMAS GATACRE, Esq. of Gatacre, b. in 1641, who m. Sarah, dau. of Sir Walter Acton, Bart. of Aldenham, and dying in 1707, left (with six daus., Sarah; Mary; Catherine, m. to William Eaves; Frances, who d. in 1731; Elizabeth, m. in 1739, to Elias Deane, of Farmcote; and Jane, m. in 1718, to William Hall, of Stourbridge) four sons, of whom the eldest,

THOMAS GATACRE, Esq. of Gatacre, b. in 1676, was killed by a fall from his horse in 1734. He d. unm., and was s. by his brother,

EDWARD GATACRE, Esq. of Gatacre, b. in 1680, who m. 3 Oct. 1734, Margaret, eldest dau. of Benjamin Yate, Gent. of Ludstone, and dying in 1747, left, with a dau., Sarah, who d. unm. 24 July, 1787, a son and successor,

EDWARD GATACRE, Esq. of Gatacre, b. 11 Sept. 1735, who m. in 1767, Mary Pitchford, of the family of PITCHFORD *of Pitchford*, and dying 21 Aug. 1821, was s. by his only child

EDWARD GATACRE, Esq. of Gatacre, b. 16 April, 1768; m. 1st, in 1805, Annabella, eldest dau. and co-heir of the late Robert Lloyd, Esq. of Swan Hill, and by her, who d. 17 Feb. 1817, has issue,

EDWARD-LLOYD, now of Gatacre.
Annabella-Jane, m. 2 July, 1840, to the Hon. Major Charles Napier, brother of the late Lord Napier.

He m. 2ndly, in 1826, Harriet-Constantia, eldest dau. of the late Richard Jenkins, Esq. of Bicton. Colonel Gatacre, was colonel of the Shropshire militia, and a magistrate and deputy-lieutenant for that county.

Arms—Quarterly: gu. and erm., on the 2nd and 3rd, three piles, of the first, on a fesse, az., five bezants.
Crest—A raven, ppr.
Seat—Gatacre, Shropshire.

GATAKER OF MILDENHALL.

GATAKER, GEORGE, Esq. of Mildenhall, co. Suffolk, J.P. and D.L., b. 30 March, 1792; m. 1st, in 1825, Elizabeth-Harrison, 3rd dau. of Thomas Wilkinson, Esq., and by her, who d. in 1827, has a dau.,

I. Elizabeth-Mary.

He m. 2ndly, Aug. 1829, Sophia-Sarah, 2nd dau. of H.-S. Partridge, Esq. of Hockham Hall, Norfolk, and has by her surviving issue,

I. MELMOTH-WILLIAM, b. 23 Jan. 1841.
II. Charles-Frederick, b. 22 April, 1843.
III. Frank-Anthony, b. 24 Dec. 1844.
IV. Henry-Walter, b. 12 Sept. 1847.
I. Ellen-Katherine. II. Louisa-Sophia.
III. Georgina-Mary.

Lineage.—THE REV. THOMAS GATACRE, rector of St. Edmund's Lombard-street, London, 3rd son of William Gatacre, Esq. of Gatacre, was a learned and eminent divine, and is commemorated among "Fuller's Worthies." He m. Margaret, dau. of — Pigot, Esq. of co. Hertford, and dying in 1593, left, with other issue, a son and heir,

THOMAS GATAKER, B.D., rector of Rotherhithe, b. 4 Sept. 1574. He m. four times, viz., 1st, Mrs. Cupper, a widow, but had no surviving issue; 2ndly, a dau. of the Rev. Charles Vinner, and had a son,

CHARLES, in holy orders, his successor.

3rdly, Dorothy, dau. of George Farwell, Esq. of Hillbishop, in Somersetshire, and sister of Sir George and Sir John Farwell, by whom, who d. 1627, he had two daus.,

Elizabeth, m. to William Draper, Esq.
Esther.

4thly, Elizabeth, but had no other issue. He d. 29 July, 1654 (having been forty years rector of Rotherhithe), and was s. by his son,

THE REV. CHARLES GATAKER, M.A., rector of Hoggerston, co. Bucks, who d. in 1680, leaving, by his first wife, a son,

THE REV. THOMAS GATAKER, rector of Hoggerston, who m. Barbara, dau. of Sir Thomas, Hebblethwaite, of Norton, co. York, and had issue, EDWARD; Charles; Thomas; George (who m. a dau. of — Nash, Esq., and had issue); William, b. in 1691, m. Anne, eldest dau. of James Willet; Barbara, m. 1st, to John Pitcairn, of London, merchant, and 2ndly, to Withers, Esq. of Kent; and Frances, m. to the Rev. Benjamin Reynolds, rector of Hoggerston. Mr. Gataker d. in 1701, and was s. by his son,

EDWARD GATAKER, Esq., b. in 1634, who was s. by his son,

THOMAS GATAKER, Esq., who m. Anne, dau. of Thomas Hill, Esq. of Court of Hill, co. Salop, and had issue,

THOMAS, his successor.
Anne.

He was s. at his decease by his son,

THOMAS GATAKER, Esq. of Middenhall, who m. Mary, dau. of John Swale, Esq. of Middenhall, and by her (who d. 4 March, 1839, aged 92) left, at his decease, 16 March, 1844, aged 95, one surviving child, the present GEORGE GATAKER, Esq. of Mildenhall.

Arms, &c.—See preceding memoir.
Residence—Mildenhall, Suffolk.

GAUNT OF HIGHFIELD.

GAUNT, MATTHEW, Esq. of Highfield House, co. Stafford, barrister at-law, and a magistrate for the county, b. 18 Jan. 1795.

Lineage.—THE REV. JOHN GAUNT, who was rector of Dudley in 1530, by the gift of Dudley, Duke of Northumberland, was b. about 1475-80, and, by tradition, was a descendant of the dispersed and deprived family of Gaunt, Earls of Lincoln, whose possessions were forfeited *temp.* HENRY III. His grandson, ROGER GAUNT, of Rowley Regis, co. Stafford (eldest son of William Gande, or Gaunt, Gent. of the same place), was b. *circa* 1601-2 (his younger brother, Humphrey, having been christened at Rowley on the 6th May, 1604). By his 1st wife, whom he m. in May, 1628, he had no issue; but by his 2nd wife, Anne, dau. of William Colborne, or Colbrond, Gent. of Rowley, grandson of John Colbrond, of Colbrond, in Tipton, co. Stafford, by his wife, Alice, dau. and heir of Rowland Mainwaringe, of Cheshire, Esq., and great-grandson of William Colbrond, of Colbrond, Esq., who d. 30 Sept. 1506, by his wife, Maude, dau. of Richard Sheldon, of Rowley, Esq., whose sister and co-heir, Clare, m. Cornelius Wyrley, Esq. of Handsworth, co. Stafford, he had issue several children. His eldest son,

JOHN GAUNT, bapt. 19 Dec. 1641, at Rowley Regis, buried there 11 Jan. 1711, left issue, *inter alios*, his eldest son,

JOHN GAUNT, Gent., bapt. at Rowley, 4 June, 1670. He m. Sarah, dau. of John Darby, Esq., the date of the marriage settlement being 18 March, 1719. Of the grandchildren of this marriage were,

I. John Gaunt, Esq. of Leek, merchant, b. in 1760; who d. in June, 1800, leaving issue,
  1 John Gaunt, of Leek, Esq., banker.
  2 MATTHEW GAUNT, Esq. of Highfield House, Esq.
  3 Josiah Gaunt, Esq., merchant, of the Shaw, co. Stafford, who m. Mary, dau. of John Davenport, Esq. of Westood Hall, late M.P. for the Potteries; and d. s. p.
  4 Mary, m. to Henry-Charles Deakin, *vel* Dakeyne, Esq. of Hamilton-terrace, St. John's Wood, co. Middlesex.
II. Richard Gaunt, of Leek, Esq., living in 1843. He has issue.

Arms—Barry of six, or and az., a bend, gu.
Crest—A wolf's head, or, gorged with a collar, vairé.
Seat—Highfield House, co. Stafford.

GAUSSEN OF BROOKMANS PARK.

GAUSSEN, ROBERT-WILLIAM, Esq. of Brookmans Park, Herts, J.P., high-sheriff 1841, b. 7 July, 1814; m. 11 Aug. 1841, Elizabeth, dau. of James Casamaijor, Esq., and has issue,

I. ROBERT-GEORGE, b. 14 June, 1843.
II. Casamaijor-William, b. 3 Jan. 1845.

Lineage.—This family migrated to England on the revocation of the Edict of Nantes. The last survivor of the French line, the Chevalier de Gaussen, for many years French ambassador at the court of FREDERICK THE GREAT of Prussia, d. at Paris about the year 1851. Another branch still exists at Geneva.

JOHN GAUSSEN, merchant (son of Peter Gaussen, who m. in 1635, Isabeau Peissoniere, and grandson of Jean Gaussen, who m. 1589, Madlle. Barthelmy, and whose father, Louis Gaussen, m. 1564, Joanne Nogaret), m. Madlle. Margaret Bosanquet, and had issue,

Francis, d. in London 1744, *unm.*
PAUL, of whose descendants we treat.
David, of Geneva, m. Madlle. Barthelmy.
Peter, of London, m. Miss Motet. John.
Isabeau.

The 2nd son,

PAUL GAUSSEN, of Geneva, m. Catherine Valat, and had issue, PETER, David-Francis, and Paul. The eldest son,

PETER GAUSSEN, Esq., m. 1755, Anna-Maria, dau. of Samuel Bosanquet, Esq. of the Forest House, lord of the manor of Low Hall, Essex, and had issue,

SAMUEL-ROBERT, his heir.
Paul. Peter.
Mary, m. the Rev. Richard Whittingham, vicar of Potton, co. Bedford, who d. 14 June, 1845, leaving two sons, Samuel, D.D., rector of Childrey, Berks; and John, of Leytonstone, Essex; and two daus.
Anne.
Jane, m. William Franks, Esq. of Beech Hill, Berks, and had issue.

The eldest son,

SAMUEL-ROBERT GAUSSEN, Esq. of Brookman's Park, Herts, m. Eliza, dau. of Jacob Bosanquet, Esq. of Broxbournbury, by Elizabeth his wife, dau. of John Hanbury, Esq. of Kelmarsh; and d. 1812, leaving issue, SAMUEL-ROBERT, his heir; William; and Armitage, who m. Miss Sotbeby. The eldest son,

SAMUEL-ROBERT GAUSSEN, Esq. of Brookman's Park, m. 1813, his cousin, Cecilia, dau. of William Franks, Esq. of Beech Hill, Herts, and by her (who m. 2ndly, George-Jacob Bosanquet, Esq. of Broxbournbury) had issue,

ROBERT-WILLIAM, now of Brookmans.
Frederick-Charles, barrister-at-law, b. May, 1816; m. Oct. 1852, Letitia, eldest dau. of Alfred Chapman, Esq., and has a son, Alfred, b. 1855.
William-Augustus-Casamaijor, b. Oct. 1818; capt 14th light-dragoons.

Arms—Az., on ground, in base, vert, a lamb, passant, arg., on a chief of the last, three bees, ppr.
Crest—A hive with bees, volant, all ppr.
Seat—Brookman's Park, near Hatfield.

GAUSSEN OF LAKEVIEW HOUSE.

GAUSSEN, DAVID-CAMPBELL, Esq. of Lakeview House, co. Londonderry, J.P., barrister-at-law, s. his father in 1853.

Lineage. — This family, derives from a French refugee Protestant, who escaped from his native country and settled at Newry, in the north of Ireland. His name was DAVID GAUSSEN; and his wish, it is handed down, was to settle in England; but the vessel in which he sailed was obliged, by a storm, to run into Carlingford Bay for shelter. By Dorothy Fortescue his wife, he left at his decease, 6 Oct. 1751, aged 87, three daus. and one son: one of the former m. George Atkinson, Esq. of Dundalk, and another the Rev. William Lucas, vicar of Newry. The son, DAVID GAUSSEN, also of Newry. By Margaret his wife, he left at his decease, 4 July, 1802, with other issue, a dau., Elizabeth, living in 1851, then nearly ninety years of age; and a son,

DAVID GAUSSEN, Esq., who resided for sometime at Newry, and afterwards settled and d. at Ballyronan House, on the borders of Lough Neagh, co. Londonderry. He m. 1778, Elizabeth, dau. of James Campbell, Esq. of Drumbar, co. Derry, and by her (who d. in 1816) left at his decease, in 1832, with other issue, a son,

DAVID GAUSSEN, Esq. of Lakeview House, co. Derry, J.P., who m. in 1812, Anne, dau. of John Ash, Esq. of Magherafelt, and by her (who d. in 1848) had issue,

DAVID-CAMPBELL, now of Lakeview House.
Thomas-Lovett, comm. R.N., highly distinguished in the recent war with Russia, as lieut. of H.M.S. "Agamemnon."
Edmond-James, in holy orders. William-Ash.
Helena, m. to William Magill, Esq., M.D.
Jane, m. to Charles Gaussen, Esq.
Isabella. Annie. Emily-Mary.

Mr. Gaussen d. in 1853.

Arms, &c.—See GAUSSEN of Brookman's Park
Motto—Innocentiâ et industriâ.
Seat—Lakeview House, Magherafelt.

GAY OF ALBOROUGH.

GAY, JAMES, Esq. of Alborough New Hall, co. Norfolk, s. his father 5 Jan. 1852, m. Oct. 1853, Elizabeth, only surviving child of the late Thomas Parker, Esq. of Bildeston, Suffolk.

Lineage.—This family came originally from Normandy, and were settled, *temp.* ELIZABETH, at Matlask and Thurgarton, in which parishes, and the adjoining ones of

[illegible]

Lineage.—[illegible]

Arms &c.—See [illegible] of Allborough.

Seats—Thurning Hall, co. Norfolk; [illegible]

GENNYS OF WHITLEIGH.

HENN-GENNYS, EDMUND-BASTARD, Esq. of Whitleigh Hall, co. Devon, J.P., high-sheriff 1553-4, *b.* 14 Nov. 1804; *m.* 7 Jan. 1836, Ann, only child and heir of the late John Croad, Esq., by Ann his wife, 2nd dau. of the late William Chapell, Esq., and has issue,

I. EDMUND-JOHN, *b.* 18 Nov. 1836.
II. John-Croad, *b.* 15 April, 1838.
III. William-Richard-Hall, *b.* 18 May, 1841.

Lineage.—EDMUND HENN, Esq., 3rd son of William Henn, Esq. of Paradise, co. Clare (*see* HENN *of Paradise*) *m.* in 1801, Mary, only child and heir of John Gennys, Esq., and assumed, in consequence, by royal license, 26 April, 1802, the additional surname and arms of GENNYS. By Mary his wife, who *d.* 24 April, 1824, he had issue,

I. EDMUND-BASTARD, his heir, now of Whitleigh.
II. John, *m.* 1st, 1850, Catherine-Elizabeth-Caroline, only dau. of the late Vice-Admiral Richard Arthur; and 2ndly, Aug. 1855, Emily, eldest dau. of Thomas Icely, Esq. of Sydney.
III. William-Edward, *m.* 1850, Josephine, only child of Colonel Brown.
IV. Richard, *d. unm.*, 9 Feb. 1851, aged 32.
I. Mary. II. Elizabeth.
III. Bridget Charlotte.
IV. Anne, *d.* 31 Dec. 1843, aged 35.
V. Eleanor. VI. Isabella-Jane.
VII. Louisa. VIII. Cordelia.

Mr. Henn Gennys, *d.* 3 March, 1846.

Arms—Quarterly: 1st and 4th, or and arg., a lion, passant-guardant, per pale, az. and gu., for GENNYS; 2nd and 3rd, arg., a saltier, sa., bezanty, bailed, or, in the beak a sprig of myrtle, for HENN.

Crest of GENNYS—An eagle, per pale, az. and gu., the wings elevated, each charged with a crescent, from the beak an escroll, arg. thereon the words "Deo gloria."

Crest of HENN—A hen pheasant.

Seat—Whitleigh, near Plymouth.

GENT OF MOYNS.

GENT, GEORGE, Esq. of Moyns Park, co. Essex, *b.* [illegible] *m.* 1822, Jane, dau. of Thomas Willows, Esq. [illegible] and has one surviving dau.,

Susanna-Mary.

Lineage.—[illegible]

dau. of Richard Hale, Esq. of Teeving, in Hertfordshire, but had no surviving issue. He m. 2ndly, Anne, dau of Sir Thomas Playters, of Sotterley, in Suffolk, by whom he had, with two younger sons, a successor,

GEORGE GENT, Esq. of Moyns, who m. Anne, dau. of Radcliffe Todd, Esq. of Sturmere Hall, and relict of Thomas Mortlack, Esq. and dying was s. by (the son of his son George) his grandson,

GEORGE GENT, Esq. of Moyns, a justice of the peace for the co. of Essex, who m. Elizabeth, dau. and heiress of James Chaplyn, Esq., and d. in 1746, leaving (with an elder son, GEORGE, of Moyns, who m. the dau. and heir of Thomas Walford, Esq.) another son,

WILLIAM GENT, Esq. of Lincoln's-Inn, barrister at law, who m. Mrs. Baker, of Petherton, co. Somerset, and was father of

MAJOR-GENERAL WILLIAM GENT, Roy. Eng., who m. 1st, in 1785, Miss Ann-Maria Fleetwood, of Clapham, co. Surrey, and 2ndly, Miss French, of Bath, by the former of whom he left at his decease two sons and one dau., viz., GEORGE-WILLIAM, now of Moyns; John Gould, of Paris, m. in 1810, Mary, widow of Thomas Panton, Esq. of Newmarket, and has one dau.; and Anna-Maria, m. to Joseph-Sidney Tharp, Esq. of Chippenham Park, co. Cambridge. The son and heir,

GEORGE-WILLIAM GENT, Esq. of Moyns Park, b. 1786, high-sheriff of Essex 1834-5, m. 1809, Miss Vatian, of Musgrove, co. Devon, and, dying s. p., was s. by his kinsman, the present GEORGE GENT, Esq. of Moyns Park.

Arms—Erm., a chief, indented, sa., quartering the arms of MOYNE; viz., or, a cross, engrailed, sa., a label of three points, gu., in each point three bezants.
Crest—Out of a ducal coronet, an eagle, displayed.
Motto—In est clementia forte.
Seat—Moyns Park, Ridgwell, Essex.

GERARD OF ROCKSOLES.

GERARD, ARCHIBALD, Esq. of Rocksoles, co. Lanark, J.P., b. 8 July, 1812; m. 7 Aug. 1839, Euphemia-Erskine, eldest dau. (and co-heir with her sister, Mrs. Nugent) of the late Sir John Robison, K.H., and has issue,

I. JOHN, b. 30 May, 1840.
II. Montagu-Gilbert, b. 29 June, 1842.
III. Alexander, b. 5 Jan. 1845.
I. Jane-Emily. II. Anne-Mary-Margaret.
III. Dorothea-Mary-Stanislaus.

Lineage.—The first member of this family, whom we find settled in Scotland, seems to have been a GILBERT GERARD, who appeared suddenly in the north of Scotland, about the latter part of the reign of CHARLES II., and was supposed to belong to the Lancashire family of Gerard.

THE REV. GILBERT GERARD, b. in 1700, who m. Miss Majorie Mitchell, and d. in 1738, leaving two sons, ALEXANDER, of whom we treat, and Gilbert, b. 1730, who left by Agnes Hay, his wife a son John-Gray, who d. 1840, leaving twelve children, and Jean, m. to J. Mair, Esq. The elder son,

THE REV. ALEXANDER GERARD, D.D., of King's College Aberdeen, m. Jane, eldest dau. and co-heir of Dr. White, of Colnae, and had issue, 1 Gilbert, in holy orders, D.D., of Aberdeen, b. in 1760, m. Miss H. Duncan, and d. in 1815, having had issue, five sons and five daus.; 2 Alexander, d. unm.; 3 John, of Rocksoles: of him presently; 1 Marjory, who m. Patrick Cruikshank, Esq. of Stracathro; 2 Jane, d. unm. in 1833; 3 Margaret-Helen, m. to James Cruikshank, Esq. of Langley Park, co. Forfar. The 3rd son,

JOHN GERARD, Esq. of Rocksoles, co. Lanark, b. in 1765 lieut.-col. in the E. I. Co's service, and adjutant-general to the army during the campaigns under Lord Lake, m. in 1810, Dorothea-Montagu, dau. of the Rev. Archibald Alison, and had issue by her (who d. in 1819), 1 ALEXANDER, his heir; 2 ARCHIBALD, successor to his brother; 3 John, b. in 1814; 4 Alured, b. in 1815, d. in 1817; 1 Dorothea-Jane. The eldest son,

ALEXANDER GERARD, Esq. of Rocksoles, b. in 1811, lieut. 70th regt., was accidentally drowned in the Nile, 12 Sept. 1837, aged 26. He never married, and was s by his brother ARCHIBALD GERARD, Esq. the present representative of the family.

Arms—Az., a lion, rampant, or, on a chief, embattled, erm., a faulchion, in bend sinister, surmounted by the Punja, (being one of the insignia borne before the Emperor Shah Allum), saltierways, also ppr.
Crest—Out of a mural crown, a lion's gamb, holding the Punja.
Motto—Haud inferiora secutus.
Seat—Rocksoles, Lanarkshire.

GERNON OF ATHCARNE CASTLE.

GERNON, JAMES, Esq. of Athcarne Castle, co. Meath, and Hammondstown, co. Louth, b. 14 Feb. 1780, J.P., high-sheriff of Drogheda 1846; m. 26 Oct. 1807, Marianne, 2nd dau. of James O'Reilly, Esq. of Higginstown House, co. Longford, J.P., by Susan Dease his wife, and has issue,

I. JAMES, J.P., b. Jan. 1811, m. 1st, 1 Oct. 1839, Marianne dau. of George Gradwell, Esq. of Preston, co. Lancaster, and by her (who is dec.) has issue, 1 James; 2 Henry Chester: 1 Georgina; and 2 Anna-Maria. He m. 2ndly, Aug. 1849, Margaret dau. of Edmond O'Reilly, Esq. of Sylvan Lodge, Rathgar, co. Dublin.
II. Patrick, b. March, 1813. III. Thomas, b. May, 1814.
IV. William, barrister-at-law, b. Sept. 1820; Joint Secretary to the Board of Charitable Bequests in Ireland; m. Oct. 1846, Marianne, eldest dau. of the late Patrick Curtis, Esq., J.P., of Fitzwilliam Square, Dublin, and has issue; 1 William; 2 James; 3 Arthur; 4 Vincent; and 1 Louisa.
I. Judith. II. Helen.
III. Susan, m. Sept. 1852, to Stephen Stafford, Esq. of Ballymore, co. Wexford.
IV. Louisa, a nun.

Lineage.—Few families in the empire can establish so long a line of distinguished ancestry as that of Gernon, their pedigree being deducible, link by link, from ROBERT DE GERNON, who accompanied WILLIAM the Conqueror from Normandy, down to the present possessor of Athcarn Castle.

RALPH DE GERNON, living *temp.* HENRY II., son of Matthew de Gernon, and grandson of Robert de Gernon, the Norman, m. and had two sons, I. RALPH, of Prutwell, co. Derby, who had a grant thereof from King JOHN, and who was ancestor of the GERNONS of England, from whom the noble house of Cavendish claims descent; and, II. Roger, of whose line we treat. This Roger de Gernon went with Strongbow to Ireland, and was witness to a deed of Walter de Lacy, to Geoffrey Constantine. His grandson, ROGER DE GERNON, was sheriff of Louth in 1279. By Mabella, his wife, he left a son, RICHARD DE GERNON, sheriff of Louth, 1307, who held Killincowle of the Crown in capite, and Gernonstown of the Baron of Slane. By Amicia his wife, he was father of JOHN GERNON, of Killincowle, who had livery of his lands 26 Nov. 1312. In 1329 he appeared for the people of Louth, who were charged with the murder of John de Bermingham, Earl of Louth. He left, at his decease, a dau., Anne, wife of Henry Cruys, Esq. juro uxoris of Gernonstown; and a son, JOHN GERNON, of Killincowle, father of two sons, ROBERT GERNON, of Killincowle, to whom King EDWARD III. granted the manor of Douaghmaine, and who d. s. p.; and ROBERT GERNON, who succeeded to Killincowle at the decease of his brother, and became lord of Gernonstown in right of his wife and cousin Anne, dau. of Henry Cruys, Esq. By that lady he had issue, I. THOMAS, who d. v. p., leaving, by Alice, his wife, dau. and heir of Peter Peppard, a son, JOHN, of whom presently; and ROGER, ancestor of the Gernons of Gernonstown. The grandson and eventual heir of Robert Gernon,

JOHN GERNON, Esq. of Killincowle, A.D. 1421, was father of SIR JAMES GERNON, Knt. of Killincowle, who d. before 1472, leaving by Elenor Taaffe, his wife, a son and heir, SIR JOHN GERNON, Knt. of Killincowle (a minor in 1472), who m. Catherine, dau. and co-heir of Henry Drake, and was father of SIR PATRICK GERNON, Knt. of Killincowle whose son by Genet his wife, dau. of Patrick Plunket, THOMAS GERNON, Esq. of Killincowle, d. 10 Sept. 1516, leaving, by Alson, his wife, dau. of George D'Arcy, Esq. of Platten, two sons, I. JAMES (Sir) Knt. of Killincowle, whose will dated 18 Aug. 1558, was proved 1 July, 1562. He left, by Genet Plunket, his wife, four daus., of whom the eldest, Genet, m. Richard Segrave, Esq.; and JOHN. This JOHN GERNON, Esq., who inherited Killincowle from his brother, Sir James, m. Elizabeth, dau. of John Clinton, Esq. of Clintonstown, co. Louth, and was s. by his son, PATRICK GERNON, Esq. of Killincowle, who m. Anna, dau. of Edmund Harold Esq., and d. 8 Dec. 1582, leaving three sons, viz.,

THOMAS, of Killincoole, who settled his estate in remainder to Christopher Gernon, of Drogheda, and then to the heirs of Sir Patrick Gernon, of Gernonstown. He was b. 1544, and d. 9 Nov. 1613. He m. Catherine, dau. of Sir John

Bellew, of Castleton, Knt., and by her had three daus., Margaret, wife of Oliver Plunket, of Castlelompnagh, co. Louth; Catherine, and Elenor, and a son, JOHN GERNON, of Killincool, Esq., who *m.* Mary, dau. of George Plunket, of Beaulieu, Esq.; *d.* 1 Jan. 1634, and was buried at Killincool, leaving issue two sons and two daus., 1 PATRICK, of Killincool, who had a grant of confirmation, 26 June, 1638, of the manor, &c., of Killincool. He *m.* Anne, dau. of Edward Gernon, of Gernonstown, Esq., and had issue, HUGH GERNON, of Killincool, who had a confirmation of Killincool 28 Jan. 1684. He *m.* Elinor, dau. of George Peppard, Esq., alderman of Drogheda, and *d. s. p.*; Mary, wife of Thomas Stanley, of Finnon, co. Meath, Esq.; Margaret, wife of Patrick Fleming, of Ballymore, co. Dublin, Esq. 2 Christopher Gernon, Esq., *m.* Jane, dau. of James Clinton, of Clintonston, Esq.; 1 Catherine, wife of James Clinton, of Clintonston, Esq.; 2 Margaret, wife, first, of Ross Mahon, Esq. of Carfinlagh, in the co. Monaghan; 2ndly, of Patrick Bellew, Esq.

RICHARD, of whose line we treat.

Robert.

The second son,

RICHARD GERNON, Esq. of Gernonstown, *m.* Anne, dau. of Richard Plunket, Esq. of Loughcrew, and was father of

RICHARD GERNON, Esq., and of WILLIAM GERNON, Esq. of Drogheda, who *m.* Anne, dau. of John Warren, of Warrenstown, and by her was father of

CHRISTOPHER GERNON, Esq. of Drogheda, who *m.* Alicia, dau. of — Keating, and had a son,

WILLIAM GERNON, Esq. of Drogheda, who *m.* Mary, dau. of Peter Durham, of co. Meath, and was father of

CHRISTOPHER GERNON, Esq. of Drogheda, who *m.* Frances, dau. of Charles Wade, Esq. of Balscaddon, and had,

RICHARD, of Dublin, Esq., living 1738, the first of the family who settled at Bourdeaux, in France: invested there, by command of King Louis XV., with the honorary title of king's secretary. He *d.* at Bourdeaux, about the year 1770. He *m.* Mary, dau. of Martin Quody, by Lucy Petit, his wife, dau. of Christopher Petit, of Cullen, co. Meath, Esq. by Mary, his wife, dau. of Thomas Pilsworth, son of Christopher Petyt, Esq., by Mary, his wife, dau. of John Hope, of Millingar. He had issue, 1 CHRISTOPHER GERNON, of Bourdeaux, Esq., ancestor of the GERNONS *of Paris*; 2 John, chevalier of the Order of St. Louis and senior captain of the regiment of Lally, *d. unm.* 1818; and 3 Mary, wife of John O'Byrne, Esq. of Bourdeaux.

William, *d. unm.*

THOMAS, of whom we treat.

The third son,

THOMAS GERNON, Esq. of Darver, co. Louth, *m.* Miss Rose Kelly, and was father of,

PATRICK GERNON, Esq. born at Darver, co. Louth, in 1752, who *m.* Mary, dau. of James Doran, Esq. of Drogheda, and had sixteen children, all of whom died in youth or unmarried, except Marianne, who *m.* John Byrne, Esq. of Saggard, and is deceased; Elizabeth, who *m.* Thomas Coleman, Esq. of Drogheda, and is also deceased; Judith, a nun; and a son, the present JAMES GERNON, Esq. of Athcarne Castle.

Arms—Arg., an eagle, displayed, with two heads, sa., gorged with a ducal coronet, or.

Crest—A horse, passant, arg.

Motto—Parva contemnimus.

Seat—Athcarne Castle, co. Meath.

GERVAIS OF CECIL.

GERVAIS, FRANCIS-JOHN, Esq. of Cecil, co. Tyrone, J.P., *b.* 21 Aug. 1819; *m.* 16 Dec. 1852, Annie-Catherine, eldest dau. of the Rev. John Richardson Young, of Kilmarron Rectory, co. Monaghan, by Marianne his wife, dau. of John Cromie, Esq. of Cromore, co. Antrim, and has issue, KATHERINE MARY. Mr. Gervais was high-sheriff for Tyrone 1846.

Lineage.—JEAN GERVAIS, of Tournon, in Guienne, France, *m.* Anne Fabre and had two sons, PIERRE, *b.* in 1677, and Daniel, *b.* 1679, both of whom after their parents' death, and while still children, fled with an uncle at the revocation of the edict of Nantes, and settled in England. In 1710, DANIEL, the younger, was naturalized, and subsequently became a captain in the British army and gentleman usher to her Majesty Queen ANNE. He *m.* Pauline Belaguier, dau. of the Minister of the French Protestant Church in Dublin, but *d. s. p.* His brother, elder son of Jean Gervais,

PIERRE GERVAIS, *m.* in 1717, Marie-François Girard, and *d.* in 1730 having had three sons, viz., PETER, *b.* 1722; Francis-Noah, *b.* 1726; and Daniel, *b.* 1729, all of whom *d.* without leaving issue, except the eldest,

PETER GERVAIS, Esq., who *m.* 20 May, 1722, Elizabeth, 4th dau. of the Rev. Samuel Close, of Elm Park, co. Armagh. They both died in 1800, leaving a son, FRANCIS, and two daus, Mary-Anne, *m.* to the Rev. D. Kelly, and Elizabeth, *m.* to John Winder, capt. Royal Artillery. The son,

THE REV. FRANCIS GERVAIS, of Cecil, *m.* 16 March, 1807, Katherine-Jane, dau. of Michael Tisdall, Esq. of Charlesfort, co. Meath, and *d.* 6 Oct. 1849 leaving a son and two daus.,

FRANCIS JOHN, now of Cecil.

Elizabeth, *m.* 7 July, 1829, to the Hon. and Rev. John-Pratt Hewitt.

Catherine, *m.* 9 May, 1842, to Nicholas Evans, Esq. of Newton, co. Cork.

Arms—Az., a chev., or, between two lions, rampant, respectant, arg., in chief, and a white rose, leaved and slipped, ppr., in base, in the centre, chief, point, a crescent, of the third.

Crest—A lion's head, erased, a[illegible] charged with a fleur-de-lis, az.

Motto—Sic sustenta crescit.

Seat—Cecil, Augher, co. Tyrone.

GERY OF BUSHMEAD.

WADE-GERY, WILLIAM-HUGH, Esq. of Bushmead Priory, co. Bedford, J.P., *b.* 24 Aug. 1794; *m.* 2 July, 1829, Anne-Beckingham, dau. of John Milnes, Esq. of Beckingham, and has issue, WILLIAM-HUGH, *b.* 5 Aug. 1832, and Hugh, *b.* 23 Jan. 1836.

Lineage.—The family of Gery can be authentically deduced from Thomas Gery, Esq. of Royston, Herts, sheriff of Cambridgeshire, 1509. His great grandson, Richard Gery, Esq. of Bushmead Priory, was gentleman of the Privy Chamber to King CHARLES I.; and his youngest son having received the honour of knighthood, was SIR THOMAS GERY, of Bloomsbury.

THE REV. HUGH WADE, son of the Rev. Hugh Wade, vicar of Newark, in the co. of Nottingham, by Miss Martha Twentyman, and grandson of John Wade, Esq. of Cosby, in Lincolnshire, *m.* 1792, HESTER, 3rd dau. and co-heir (with her sisters, Mary-Selina, wife of John Milnes, Esq. of Beckingham, co. Lincoln, and Eleanor, wife of the Rev. Thomas Milnes) of WILLIAM GERY, Esq. of Bushmead Priory, co. Bedford, by Mary, his wife, dau. and heir of Richard Bell, Esq., and assumed, upon his marriage, by letters patent, the additional surname and arms of GERY. He was for upwards of thirty years an efficient magistrate for the counties of Bedford and Huntingdon. Mr. Wade-Gery, by the co-heiress of Bushmead, had issue,

WILLIAM-HUGH, now of Bushmead.

Charles, *b.* 9 Oct. 1795.

Hugh, in holy orders, M.A., *b.* 8 Jan. 1797, rector of Bolnhurst, co. Bedford, *m.* 17 July, 1821, Sophia-Josepha, youngest dau. of Joseph Sikes, Esq.

Thomas, *b.* 26 Sept. 1801, and *d.* 15 Dec. 1828.

Robert, *b.* 15 Dec. 1802, in holy orders, rector of Colmworth, Bedfordshire, *m.* 14 July, 1836, and has issue.

Hester, *m.* 1 May, 1827, to the Rev. J.-F. Dawson.

Mary-Hannah.

He *d.* 9 Dec. 1832.

Arms—Gu., two bars, arg., charged with three mascles, of the field, a canton, erm., quartering WADE, &c.

Crest—An antelope's head, erased, quarterly, arg. and sa., charged with four mascles, counterchanged, attired, or.

Seat—Bushmead Priory, near Eaton Socon, Bedfordshire.

GIBBS OF BELMONT.

GIBBS, GEORGE, Esq. of Belmont, co. Somerset, J.P., *b.* 27 Dec. 1779; *m.* 1st, 27 May, 1802, Salvina, dau. and heir of Henry Hendy, Esq. of Barbadoes (she *d.* 1809); and 2ndly, Aug. 1814, his cousin Harriett, dau. of Antony Gibbs, Esq.

Lineage.—In the time of RICHARD II., two brothers of this family (whose name was spelt variously Gibbe, Gibbes, or Gibbs) were settled, one at Honington, in the county of Warwick, whose descendants continued there through many generations; and the other, John Gibbe, on an estate called Venton, or Fenton, in the parish of Dartington, co. Devon, which passed, in the time of ELIZABETH, to the families of Drewe, of Hayne, and Wootton, of Inglebourne, in the same county, by the marriages of Elizabeth and Silvestra, only children and co-heirs of William Gibbs, of Fenton, a descendant of the above-named John Gibbe.

In the latter part of the 15th century, a junior branch of the Venton family had planted itself in Exeter, and, early in the reign of HENRY VIII., members of it are found in the neighbouring parishes of Woodbury and Clyst St.

George, in which latter village, John Gibbs, on the 1st of May, 1560, purchased from Thomas Lord Wentworth a small estate called Pytt (now Carsefield), which remained in the family till 1790.

William Gybbes was rector of the adjoining parish of Clyst St. Mary, in 1543, and d. in 1571, rector of Clyst St. George. Cotemporary with him were Henry Gybbes, of Woodbury, d. 1549, George Gybbe, of Clyst St. George, d. 1562, and John Gibbe, of Clyst St. George, who d. 1578.

Another George Gybbes, of Clyst St. George. m. 1st, July, 1569, Welthiana (Gwenllian) . . . , and by her had John Gibbe the elder, with two other sons and two daus. He m. 2ndly, Marie, sister of Andrew Loveringe, of Exmouth, and d. 1606, leaving by her John Gibbe, the younger, b. 1587, with three other sons and a dau.

John Gibbe, the elder, b. 1570, m. Anstitia, and d. July, 1652, leaving, besides five other sons and two daus., his eldest son, George Gibbs, of Clyst St. George; Robert Gibbs, of Woodbury; Philip Gibbs, of Fulford, in Shobrooke and Ebford, in Clyst St. George and Woodbury; and Abraham Gibbs, of Exeter, merchant, steward of the city in 1660.

This Abraham Gibbs m. Elizabeth, dau. of Isaac Manduit, of Exeter, and had (besides three other sons, who d. s. p., and three daus., of whom Elizabeth alone, wife of Simon Gandy, m. and left issue)

Isaac Gibbs, m. to Anne, dau. of John Mercer, Esq. of Heavitree, by whom he had one dau. and one son,

John, who left considerable estates in that county to his only surviving dau. (by his wife Mary, dau. of Nicholas Hall, Esq., by Elizabeth, his wife),

Anne, wife of Dr. Ballyman, which estates passed to the family of Pierce, on her re-marriage with Adam Pierce, Esq., with whose descendants they continued for several generations.

Dr. John Gibbs, of Exeter College, Oxford, fellow of All Souls, rector of Welwyn, Herts, d. unm. Jan. 15, 1698.

George Gibbs, of Clyst St. George, was b. October, 1604, and m. Alice ———, leaving three daus., Anstice, b. 1658, and d. 1675; Sarah, wife of — Goldsworthy; and Elizabeth, wife of Benjamin Brinley, of Exeter; and five sons,

John, b. 1637, and d. 1643.

George, b. 1641, had lands in Clyst St. Mary, as well as the estate of Pytt, mentioned above as purchased in 1560 by John Gibbe. He was m. in 1711, to Hannah, dau. of Robert Smith, Esq. of Heavitree, and had one only son, George, b. 1719, and d. 1720. George Gibbs was buried at Clyst St. George, Aug. 9, 1723, and was s. in the estate of Pytt by his great-nephew, George Abraham Gibbs.

John, b. 1644, and d. unm. 1677.

Abraham Gibbs, of whom presently.

Samuel, of Woodbury, b. 1654, m. 1683, to his cousin Elizabeth, dau. of Robert Gibbs, and d. s. p. 1686.

The 4th son,

Abraham Gibbs, of Topsham, Devon, b. 18 Aug. 1649, m. Tryphæna, dau. of William Rowe, Esq. of Shobbrooke, co. Devon, by Tryphæna Whitcham, his wife, and had issue,

George, baptized 1685; buried 1688.
Abraham, b. Feb. 1686.
Anna, buried 1694.
Tryphœna, baptized 1692; d. unm. 1712.
Elizabeth, wife of — Pett.
Mary, m. 1719, to Nicholas Peters.

Abraham Gibbs, the elder, d. in 1718, and was buried at Topsham. His son, the younger,

Abraham Gibbs, also of Topsham, b. Feb. 1686, d. Sept. 1726, having been twice married, 1st, to Mary, 2nd dau. of Nehemiah Monke, of Topsham; and 2ndly, to Sarah, 2nd dau. and co-heir of Robert Lyle, Esq. of Topsham (by Mary his wife, dau. of Nicholas Downe) widow of — Ewings. By this last match he had an only son,

John, also of Topsham, bapt. 1723; m. Elizabeth, dau. and heir of William Meachin, and d. July 20, 1774, leaving six sons and one dau.

I. John, bapt. July, 1755; d. unm. after 1779.

II. William, also of Topsham, bapt. June 19, 1757; m. in 1790, Susanna, dau. of the Rev. Thomas Ley, rector of Doddescombe Leigh, co. Devon, and d. in 1880, leaving five sons and two daus.

1 William-Henry, of Naples and Palermo, and afterwards of Genoa, b. 3 June, 1791, living unm. at Clyst St. George, 1856.
2 Abraham, d. young.
3 John-Ley, b. 5 June, 1793; m. Ellin-Maria, sister of Douglas Gamble, and d. at Manchester, 1837, leaving two children,
   John-Douglas-Lyle.
   Ellin-Elizabeth.
4 Lyle, b. 1800; d. 4 March, 1814.
5 Charles, of Genoa, b. 23 May, 1807; m. Stuarta, eldest dau. of Yates Brown, Esq., by Stuarta his wife, 4th dau. of David, 2nd Lord Erskine.
   1 Frances, b. 1798; d. at Tiverton, 10 Jan. 1847.
   2 Mary-Matilda, living at Tiverton, 1856.

III. Abraham, of Naples and Palermo, bapt. at Topsham, 10 Sept. 1758, m. Mary-Elizabeth, dau. of Sir James Douglas, and d. Dec. 1816, leaving Mary-Elizabeth-Catherine, his only child; m. 10 May, 1815, to lieut.-col. (now major-general) Charles Ashe à Court, of Amington Hall, co. Warwick, and has two children,

1 Charles-Henry-Wyndham, M.P. for Wilton, b. 14 Oct. 1819, m. 5 Aug. 1854, to Emily, eldest dau. of Henry Currie, Esq.
2 Elizabeth, wife of the Right Hon. Sidney Herbert.

IV. George, bapt. July 1761; d. in the West Indies, unm.

V. Lyle, of Genoa, bapt. July, 1761; d. unm. 1839.

VI. Thomas, lieut. R.N., bapt. Oct. 1767, d. unm. 1798.

I. Elizabeth, b. 1752, wife of James Richards, Esq. of Abbott's Leigh, near Bristol, d. s. p.

Abraham Gibbs, the younger, of Topsham, had by his first wife, Mary Monke, a dau., Anna, m. to Mr. Remmett, of Crediton, and two sons, viz., George, buried at Topsham, 1718, and

George-Abraham Gibbs, Esq. of Exeter, who, in 1723, s. (as heir-at-law to his great-uncle, George Gibbe) to the estate of Pytt, in the parish of Clyst St. George. He m. in 1747, Anne, dau. and co-heir of Anthony Vicary, of Exeter, by Elizabeth, his wife, dau. of Mr. Nicholas Munkley, of the same city, and had five sons and five daus.

I. George, b. 23 Sept. 1748; d. 24 Sept. 1750.

II. Sir Vicary Gibbs, of Hayes, co. Kent, M.P. for the University of Cambridge, lord-chief-justice of the Common Pleas, b. 27 Oct. 1751; d. 8 Feb 1820; buried at Hayes. He m. Frances-Cerjat-Kenneth, dau. of Major William Mackenzie, and sister of Francis-Humberstone, Lord Seaforth, and left one dau. and heiress,

Maria-Elizabeth, wife of Lieutenant-Gen. Sir Andrew Pilkington, of Catsfield Place, co Sussex (who d. 23 Feb. 1853), col. of the 20th regiment, and has two daus. and heiresses,

1 Maria-Georgina, m. 18 July, 1848, to the Rev. Burrall Hayley, rector of Catsfield, and has issue.

Andrew Burrell.	John-Newton.
Georgina-Maria-Fanny.	Blanche.

2 Louisa-Elizabeth, m. 1 Sept. 1853, to Richard-Thomas Lee, Esq. of The Grove, co. York, and has two daus.,

Sophia-Alice.	Georgina-Mary.

III. George-Gibbs, Esq. of Redland, co. Gloucester, and of the city of Bristol, merchant; m. 2ndly, Anne, dau. of William Aleyn, Esq., and Phœbe his wife, by whom he had no issue.

IV. Abraham, of Exeter, merchant, b. 19 Aug. 1754; buried at Clyst St. George, 30 May, 1782, unm.

V. Antony, of the city of London, merchant, b. 3 March, 1756. (See Gibbs, of Aldenham.)

I. Elizabeth, m. her cousin, Robert Butler Remmett, of Plymouth, M.D., b. 18 April, 1750, and had one surviving son,

Robert, barrister-at-law, m. to Elizabeth Tozor, of Totnes, and d. in 1825, leaving (with a dau., Elizabeth) three sons,

1 Robert, barrister-at-law, d. in 1852, leaving issue; and the 2nd,
2 Henry-Gibbs, captain in the Ceylon rifles; d. in 1849, leaving one dau.
3 George d., aged 20.

II. Mary, b. 2 Jan. 1759; and d. 1819; wife of the Rev. Charles Crawley, rector of Stowe Nine Churches, co. Northampton, and vicar of Broadway, co. Worcester, leaving two sons and seven daus.,

1 Charles Crawley, Esq., of Littlemore, near Oxford, b. 25 Sept. 1788, m. Eliza-Katharine, dau. of Abraham Grimes, Esq. of Coton House, co. Warwick, and has one surviving son,

Charles-Edward Crawley, b. 17 Feb. 1827.

2 George-Abraham Crawley, Esq. of Fitzroy Farm, Highgate, b. 26 Sept. 1795, m. Caroline, dau. of David Powell, Esq. of Loughton, co. Essex, and has three sons and eight daus.,

Robert-Townsend, b. 13 Feb. 1832.
George-Baden, b. 4 Sept. 1833.
Charles-David, b. 13 July, 1835.

Mary.	Caroline.
Anne, d. 1850.	Edith.
Fanny.	Agnes.
Willielmina.	Bertha.

1 Anne, wife of the Rev. John Lloyd Crawley, her cousin, rector of Heyford, co. Northampton (who d. 1850), and has had eight sons and one dau.
2 Mary, living 1854.
3 Susanna, living 1854.
4 Elizabeth, wife of the Rev. George William Daubeney.
5 Isabella, d. young.

6 Caroline, wife of her cousin, George-Henry Gibbs, of Aldenham, d. 18 Feb. 1850.
7 Charlotte, wife of her cousin, the Rev. William Crawley, has had one son and four daus.

III. Sibella, d. aged 80, at Long Ashton, co. Somerset.
IV. Anne, wife of Samuel Banfill, of Exwick House, co. Devon, d. s. p. 1828.
V. Sarah, d. unm. 1785, aged 22; buried at Clyst St. George.
VI. Catharine, wife of Mr. Burroughs, of Taunton, d. s. p. 1820, aged 53.

The 3rd son

GEORGE GIBBS, Esq. of Redland, co. Gloucester, and of the city of Bristol, b. 9 May, 1753, m. 1st, about 1776, Esther-Joanna, dau. of Richard Farr, Esq. of Bristol, and, in her children, heiress to her brothers; and, 2ndly, Anne, dau. of W. Aleyn, Esq., but had issue only by the former, viz., three sons, and two daus., all of whom are deceased, unm., except the present GEORGE GIBBS, Esq. of Belmont.

Arms—Arg., three battle-axes sa., quartering, sa., on a chief, or, 2 cinquefoils, gu., for VICARY and gu., a saltire, cotised, between 4 fleurs-de-lis, or, for Farr.
Crest—An arm embowed in armour, holding in the gauntlet a battle-axe arg.
Seat—Belmont, co. Somerset.

GIBBS OF ALDENHAM.

GIBBS, HENRY-HUCKS, Esq. of Aldenham Park, co. Herts, and Clifton Hampden, co. Oxford, b. 31 Aug. 1819; m. 6 May, 1845, Louisa-Anne, 3rd dau. of William Adams, Esq., LL.D., of Thorpe, co. Surrey, by the Hon. Mary-Anne Cockayne his wife, niece and co-heiress of Borlase, 7th and last Lord, Viscount Cullen, and by her has issue,

I. ALBAN-GEORGE-HENRY, b. 23 April, 1846.
II. Walter-Antony, b. 19 Jan. 1850.
III. Vicary, b. 12 May, 1853.
IV. Herbert-Cockayne, b. 14 May, 1854.
V. Kenneth-Francis, b. 2 April, 1856.
I. Edith-Caroline.

Lineage.—ANTONY GIBBS, 4th son of George-Abraham Gibbs, Esq. of Exeter (see GIBBS OF BELMONT), m. Dorothea-Barnetta, 2nd dau. of William Hucks, Esq. of Knaresborough (2nd son of Joseph Hucks, Esq. of Bloomsbury, and Fiducia his wife, dau. of Joshua Lomax, Esq. of Childwickbury, co. Herts), and Eleanor his wife, dau. of Thomas Barnett, Esq. of Knaresborough, which Dorothea was, in her issue, heiress to her cousins, Sarah and Anne Noyes, nieces and co-heirs of Robert Hucks, Esq. of Aldenham, co. Herts, Clifton Hampden, co. Oxon, and other estates in those counties and in Berks. Antony Gibbs d. in 1815, having had five sons and two daus.,

I. GEORGE-HENRY, his heir.
II. George-Abraham, b. 20 Jan. 1788; d. 3 March, 1789.
III. WILLIAM, now of Tyntesfield.
IV. Francis, b. 7 July, 1794; d. 16 April, 1795.
V. Joseph, in holy orders, perpetual curate of Clifton Hampden, b. 23 July, 1801; m. 14 Sept. 1831, Emily, dau. of the Rev. Charles Vaughan, of Crickhowel (representative of the family of VAUGHAN OF TRETOWER), by Emilia his wife, sister of John-Berkeley Monck, Esq. of Coley Park, near Reading, and has issue, six sons and three daus.,
1 Joseph-Henry, b. 3 June, 1832; d. 1833.
2 George-Louis-Monck, b. 28 April, 1838.
3 Joseph-Hucks, b. 14 Oct. 1840.
4 George-Henry, b. 15 Sept. 1842.
5 William-Cobham, b. 28 July, 1845.
6 Stanley-Vaughan, b. 30 Nov. 1846.
1 Emily-Harriet, wife of the Rev. Alfred Pott, principal of the Theological College, Cuddesdon, co. Oxon.
2 Dorothea-Barnetta.
3 Harriett-Theresa.
I. Harriett, wife of her cousin, George Gibbs, of Belmont.
II. Anne, d. unm. 6 Oct. 1852.

The eldest son,

GEORGE-HENRY GIBBS, Esq. of Aldenham Park, Herts and of Clifton Hampden, co. Oxford, merchant of London, b. 24 Aug. 1785; m. 7 July, 1817, Caroline, 6th dau. of the Rev. Charles Crawley, rector of Stowe Nine Churches, co. Northampton, by Mary his wife, 3rd dau. of George-Abraham Gibbs, Esq. of Exeter, and by her (who d. 18 Feb. 1850, and was buried at Clifton Hampden) had issue,

I. HENRY-HUCKS, now of Aldenham.
II. Antony b. 20 Nov. 1822, of Merry Hill, in the parish of Bushy, co. Herts; m. 7 Dec. 1854, Isabella-Margaret, 3rd dau. and co-heir of the late Charles-David Gordon, Esq., (see GORDON OF ABERGELDIE).
III. George, b. 11 Feb. 1827; drowned at Oxford, 3 June 1846, buried at Clifton Hampden.
IV. Charles, lieut. 2nd Queen's Royals, 1851, b. 28 June, 1829.
V. William-Lloyd, b. 6 Dec. 1830.
VI. John-Lomax, b. 28 March, 1832.
VII. Francis, b. 9 Aug. 1834.
VIII. Robert-Crawley, b. 4 Jan. 1839, d. 31 July, 1856.
I. Caroline. II. Mary-Dorothea.

He d. 21 Aug. 1842.

Arms—Quarterly: 1st and 4th, arg., three battle-axes, sa., for GIBBS; 2nd, sa., on a chief, arg., two cinquefoils, gu., for VICARY; 3rd, arg., a chevron between three owls, az., for HUCKS.
Crest—As GIBBS *of Belmont*.
Motto—Tenax propositi.

GIBBS OF TYNTESFIELD.

GIBBS, WILLIAM, Esq. of Tyntesfield, co. Somerset, b. 22 May, 1790; m. 1 Aug. 1839, Matilda-Blanche, dau. of Sir Thomas-Crawley Boevey, Bart. of Flanley Abbey, co. Gloucester, by Mary-Albinia his wife, dau. of Sir Thomas-Hyde Page, and has issue,

I. ANTONY, b. 10 Dec. 1841.
II. William, b. 14 Jan. 1846.
III. George-Abraham, b. 25 March, 1848.
IV. Henry-Martin, b. 30 May, 1850.
I. Dorothea-Harriett. II. Alice-Blanche.
III. Albinia-Anne.

Mr. Gibbs of Tyntesfield is 2nd son of the late Antony Gibbs, Esq. of London, by Dorothea-Barnetta his wife, dau. of William Hucks, Esq. (see GIBBS *of Aldenham*).

Arms and *Crest*—Same as the preceding.
Motto—Dios mi Amparo y Esperanza.
Seat—Tyntesfield, co. Somerset.

GIBBS OF DERRY.

GIBBS, JOHN, Esq. of The Yews, Sheffield, co. York, b. 25 May, 1811; m. 20 Jan. 1849, Anne, eldest dau. and co-heiress of Mark Skelton, Esq. of The Yews, by Anne his wife, dau. of Samuel Thorp, Esq. of Banks Hall, co. York, and has issue,

I. Louisa-Christina-Waldegrave.
II. Anna-Maria-Selina.

Lineage.—In his essay on English surnames, Lower deduces Gibbs from Gilbert, thus assigning the name a Norman origin—Gilbert (as well as Gilbard: see ROLL OF BATTLE ABBEY) being a Norman name; and it appeared, from an ancient roll in the possession of Jenking Gibbes (*temp.* HENRY VII.), of the family of Elmerstone, in Kent, a branch of Gibbes, of Fenton, in Devonshire, that the family had existed in Normandy long prior to the Conquest of England. The name De Guibes is said to be still found in France, and is deduced, by a learned Swiss clergyman, from an Arabic root; and Dumas, in his travels in the south of France, quotes one of the name as author of an archæological article in the *Journal de Trévoux*, 1729.

DANIEL GIBBES, Esq. of Cork, and of Derry, co. Cork, descended, it is presumed, from the family of Gibbs, of Devon, mentions in his will, dated 12 Jan. 1719, and proved 5 Dec. 1724, his relatives, Henry Wallis, Esq. of Drishane, Christopher Knight, sen., his brother-in-law, and his cousin Godfrey. In the records of the corporation of the city of Cork, allusion is made to this Daniel Gibbes as "an ancient freeman." He is likewise mentioned in the following curious passage, extracted from the same records:—"21st June, 1691. Whereas, the corporation is indebted unto Daniel Gibbs, in severall sumes of money by him lent towards subsisting the army, and an order of councell made for raising of the money when Mr. Gibbs shal be drawne on for the same; and whereas Mr. Gibbs is now drawne on, and wants the money, and noe publicke money in bancke to answeare the same, it is this day ordered that the mayor take money up and pay interest for the same, and give the citty seale for security, and pay the money unto Mr. Gibbs towards his discharge, or any other security that shal be demanded, and the citty seale to be given them for their security." He had issue, with five daus. (Catherine, wife of John Narcott, Esq. of Ballygarrett; Elizabeth; Judith, d. at an advanced age in 1783; Mary; and Sarah, wife of Joseph ffranklyn, Esq. of Brittas, near Cork), two sons, viz., John Gibbes, Esq. of Derry, who obtained the freedom of the city of Cork, *a gratis* 19 Sept. 1687, and *d. s. p.*; and

DANIEL GIBBES, Esq. of Derry, co. Cork, admitted a freeman at large of the city of Cork 8 March, 1725, and mentioned in Smith's *History of Cork* for his "very good improvements" at Derry. His will, dated 19 Oct. 1763, was proved 4 Jan. following. He *m.* Frances, dau. and co-heiress of George Bennett, Esq., alderman of Cork, by his 1st wife, Lucy, dau. of Edmond ffrench, Esq., alderman of Cork, and half-sister of John Bennett, Esq., justice of the King's Bench in Ireland. By her he had (with two daus., Elizabeth and Frances) two sons,

I. DANIEL, of Derry, co. Cork, J.P., deputy-governor of the co. of Cork, and colonel of a volunteer corps, *m.* 20 Feb. 1778, Mary, dau. of Sir Robert Warren, Bart. of Warrenscourt, and by her (who *d.* 27 Aug. 1807) had issue,

1 Daniel-Robert, *b.* 10 Sept. 1782; *d. unm.* 25 Jan. 1799.
2 John-Bennett, J.P., lieut. Royal Cork City regiment of militia, *b.* 14 June, 1787; *m.* (settlement dated 29 Sept. 1813), Sarah, dau. of the Rev. John Gibbs, of Inchigeelagh; but *d. s. p.*
3 Robert-Warren, of Derry, co. Cork, and of Van Diemen's Land, in holy orders, A.M., J.P., *b.* 13 April, 1790; *m.* Maria, dau. of Abraham Cross, Esq. of Shandy Hall, co. Cork, by Mary his wife, dau. of Sir Emanuel Moore, Bart.; and *d.* 30 Oct. 1853, leaving issue,

Robert-Warren. Abraham-John-Starke.
Elizabeth-Johnson.

1 Anne, *m.* to Richard Nettles, Esq., J.P. of Nettleville, co. Cork.
2 Frances, *m.* to William Crooke, Esq. of Derreen, co. Cork, J.P.
3 Mary, *m.* to Henry Cross, Esq.

II. JOHN, of whose line we treat.

The 2nd son,

THE REV. JOHN GIBBS, of Inchigeelagh and Ballynora, co. Cork, *m.* 1st, 1779, Frances, dau. of Richard Browne, Esq. of Coolcowes, co. Cork; and 2ndly, Isabella, dau. of — Connell, Esq., but had issue by the former only, viz.,

I. JOHN, his heir.
II. Richard-Browne, *m.* 2 Aug. 1821, Martha, youngest dau. of William Pierie (a member of the ancient Scotch family of PIERIE, or PIRIE, OF EDINBURGH), by Mary-Anne his wife, dau. of — Kyme, of London; and *d.* at sea, 8 Oct. 1839, leaving issue,

1 Richard-Butler, *b.* 2 Sept. 1822.
2 William-Daniel, *b.* 9 Nov. 1824; *d.* at sea, 12 May, 1844.
3 George-Sleight.
1 Martha.

III. Daniel-Henry, shipwrecked in Torres Straits in 1832, and never since heard of.
IV. George-Bennett, *d. unm.*
V. Albert, *m.* 12 Oct. 1837, Elizabeth, dau. and co-heir of Henry Douthutt, Esq. of the city of Cork; and *d. s. p.* 15 Jan. 1850.
I. Sarah, *m.* 1st, to John-Bennett Gibbs, Esq. of Derry, co. Cork, J.P., who *d. s. p.*: and 2ndly, to John-George Pyne, Esq. of Ballynacarriga, co. Cork.

The Rev. John Gibbs *d.* 3 April, 1806. His eldest son,

JOHN GIBBS, Esq. of Ballynora, co. Cork, a captain Royal Cork city militia, *m.* 5 Sept. 1810, Louisa-Anne, dau. of the Rev. Edward Cary, of Munfin, co. Wexford, by Mary his wife, dau. of Sir Edward Loftus, Bart. of Mount Loftus, and had issue,

JOHN, his heir.
Edward, *d.* an infant, 16 June, 1814.
Maria, 2nd wife of Charles-R.-W. Lane, Esq., colonel H.E.I.C.S., C.B.
Louisa, *d.* 18 May, 1836.

Mr. Gibbs *d.* 1818. His eldest son is the present JOHN GIBBS, Esq.

Arms—Arg., three battle-axes in profile, sa., quartering BENNETT.
Crest—A griffin's head, erased, arg., pierced through the back of the neck with an arrow, or, barbed and feathered, of the first.
Motto—Frapper au but.

GIBBARD OF SHARNBROOK.

GIBBARD, JOHN, Esq. of Sharnbrook, co. Bedford, J.P.

Lineage.—The late JOHN GIBBARD, Esq. of Sharnbrook, for many years a magistrate, deputy-lieutenant, and receiver-gen. for the county, major of the Bedford-militia, and colonel-commandant of the local militia, son and heir of William Gibbard, Esq. of the same place, a magistrate and high-sheriff of the county in 1785, *m.* the dau. of Leonard Hampson, Esq. (a descendant of the baronet of that name, created in 1642), by his wife, a dau. of the Rev. William Smith, vicar of St. Paul's, Bedford, rector of Barton, co. Bedford, and prebendary of Lincoln, by Mary Hawes his wife, a granddau. of the founder of charities in Bedford, descended from Sir Samuel Tuke, of Cople, and by this lady was father of the present JOHN GIBBARD, Esq. of Sharnbrook.

Seat—Sharnbrook.

GIBSONE OF PENTLAND.

GIBSONE, JOHN-CHARLES-HOPE, Esq. of Pentland, co. Edinburgh, colonel in the army, and late lieut.-col. of the 7th or Princess Royal's dragoon-guards, commanding cavalry depôt, Newbridge, co. Kildare, *b.* 21 May, 1810; *m.* 3 Nov. 1835, Jane-Louisa, only dau. of Hugh-Saye Bringloe, Esq. of Edinburgh, and has issue,

I. JOHN, an officer 17th lancers, *b.* in 1838.
II. Hugh-Francis-Hacket, *b.* in 1839.
I. Helen, *m.* 5 June, 1855, to G.-Ashby Maddock, Esq. of Naseby, co. Northampton, an officer in the 11th hussars.
II. Jane-Louisa. III. Henrietta-Anderson.

Lieut.-Col. Gibsone is only son of David-Anderson Gibsone, Esq., major-gen. in the army, by his wife, the late Mrs. Helen Gibsone, of Pentland, only child and heiress of Sir John Gibsone, Bart. of Pentland, by Henrietta his wife, dau. of James Watson, Esq. of Saughton, co. Edinburgh. At the decease of this Sir John Gibsone, the title devolved on his brother, and passed eventually to the late SIR THOMAS-GIBSON CARMICHAEL, Bart. of Skirling, co. Peebles (*see* BURKE'S *Peerage and Baronetage*).

Arms—Gu., three keys, fesseways, in pale, or.
Crest—A pelican, in her nest, and feeding her young.
Supporters—Two angels, ppr.
Motto—Pandite cœlestes portæ.
Seat—Pentland, co. Edinburgh.

GIBSON OF WHELPRIGG.

GIBSON, JOSEPH, Esq. of Whelprigg, co. Westmoreland, J.P., *b.* 28 July, 1805; *m.* 24 April, 1841, Anne, 3rd dau. of Reginald Remington, Esq. of Crowtrees Melling, co. Lancaster, and has one dau.,

I. CATHERINE.

Lineage.—JAMES GIBSON, Esq., son of JOSEPH GIBSON, Esq., by Miss Glover, his wife, *m.* Mary Wilson, and had four sons and two daus. Of the former,

WILLIAM GIBSON, *m.* in 1785, Margaret Robinson, of Rigmaden, and had with other issue, who *d.* young, a son, the present JOSEPH GIBSON, Esq. of Whelprig, and three daus., Mary, *d.* in 1809; Margaret; and Hannah, *m.* to B.-P. Gregson, Esq. of Lancaster.

Arms—Az., three storks rising, ppr.
Crest—A stork rising, ppr.
Seat—Whelprigg, Kirkby Lonsdale, co. Westmoreland.

GIBSON OF SHALFORD AND SULLINGTON.

GIBSON, GEORGE-JOHN, Esq. of Sandgate Lodge, Sullington, co. Sussex, J.P. and D.L., *m.* in 1812, Eliza, eldest dau. of Carew Elers, Esq. of Gower Street, London (Founder's kin at Wadham College), and has issue one son,

I. GEORGE-CAREW GIBSON, of Bradston Brook, Surrey, J.P. and D.L., high-sheriff for Sussex, 1855, *m.* 1st, in 1841, Eliza, youngest dau. of the late Robert Pardoe, Esq. of Park House, Bewdley, co. Worcester, D.L., major of the militia for that county, and has a son, George-Carew, *b.* 31 July, 1848, and a dau., Sidney-Elizabeth. He *m.* 2ndly, 1849, Anna-Maria-Arabella, 2nd dau. of the late John Locker, Esq., chief magistrate and registrar of the Vice Admiralty Court, Malta, and has, by her, two sons,

1 Edwin-Stillingfleet, *b.* 1850.
2 Alfred-Bradburne, *b.* 1853.

Mr. George Gibson assumed the addi[illegible] CAREW.

Lineage.—The family of Gibson was seated, *temp.* JAMES IV., in the co. of Fife, and for many generations possessed the lands of Durie in that shire, together with estates, in the neighbourhood of Glasgow.

JOHN GIBSON, an honorary freeman of Glasgow, *m.* Hester, dau. and eventual heir of Joseph Pardoe, of Halles Orchard, co. Worcester, and had an only child,

THOMAS GIBSON, Esq., of Bradston Brook, Shalford, Surrey, who *m.* in 1775, Mary, only surviving dau. of John Bradburne, Esq. of Hyde Abbey House, Winchester, and had (with two daus., Mary-Anne, who *d. unm.* in Nov. 1839, and Emma) an only son, the present GEORGE-JOHN GIBSON, Esq. of Sandgate Lodge.

Arms—Gu., three keys, fesseways, in pale, or, in chief, a portcullis, of the last.

Crest—A pelican, vuining herself, and feeding her young, ppr., gorged, with a mural crown, or.

Motto—Cœlestes pandite portæ.

Seat—Sandgate Lodge, Stonington, co. Sussex.

GIFFARD OF CHILLINGTON.

GIFFARD, THOMAS-WILLIAM, Esq. of Chillington, co. Stafford, major Staffordshire militia, *b.* 28 March, 1789; *s.* his father 1 Aug. 1823.

Lineage.—OSBORNE DE BOLEBEC, a noble Norman, living in the time of RICHARD I., surnamed Sans Peur, Duke of Normandy, *m.* Avelina, sister of Gunnora, the 2nd wife of Duke Richard, and by her had,

> WALTER, who obtained the name of "Giffard," or the Liberal, was created Count of Longueville by Duke Richard II., probably about 1025, and was constituted Earl of the county of Buckingham. (For the line of this nobleman, *see* BURKE's *Extinct and Dormant Peerage.*)
>
> OSBORNE.

The 2nd son,

OSBORNE GYFFARDE, 2nd son of Osborne de Bolebec, a noble Norman, by Avelina his wife, sister of Gunnora, the 2nd wife of Duke Richard of Normandy, and contributing together, with his distinguished brother, Walter Giffard, Count of Longueville, to placing England under the yoke of the Norman, had of course his portion of the spoil, and the fertile county of Gloucester was allotted as the locality of his reward. This Osborne *d.* about the year 1036, and was *s.* by his son,

ELIAS GIFFARDE, who, with Ala, his wife, gave lands and woods in Bockholt to the Abbey of St. Peter, in Gloucester, about the year 1100. He left two sons,

> I. ELIAS GIFFARDE, third Lord of Brimsfield, who had three sons,
>
> 1 Elias, who *d. s. p.* in 1191.
> 2 Walter, a benefactor to Gloucester Abbey.
> 3 Richard, one of the "Justices of the Court," *temp.* HENRY II. He was father of THOMAS GIFFARD, who *s.* his uncle, Elias, and carried on the line. His descendant, John Giffard, had summons to Parliament from 24 June, 1295, to 10 April, 1299, as BARON GIFFARD of Brimsfield.
>
> II. Gilbert.

The younger son,

GILBERT GIFFARDE, *m.* and left, with a dau. of Peter Corbizon, of Studley, co. Warwick, and of Chillington, co. Stafford, a son,

WILLIAM GIFFARDE, who appears to have been the first of the family who bore for arms, "Az., three stirrups, or." He was father of

PETER GIFFARDE, highly distinguished, in Ireland, under his kinsman Richard de Clare, commonly called Strongbow, Earl of Pembroke. He *m.* his cousin, Avicia Corbizon, and thus acquired the manors of Chillington and Walton, co. Stafford. He was *s.* by his son,

PETER GIFFARDE, of Chillington, who *m.* Margaret de Chuddeley, and was *s.* by his son,

SIR JOHN GIFFARD, who *m.* Ada, dau. of Hugh Courtenay, Baron of Okehampton. He *d.* in 1316, and was *s.* by his son,

SIR JOHN GIFFARD, of Chillington, who *m.* about the beginning of the 14th century, Catherine Stafford de Marston. In 1322, he was returned by the sheriff of Staffordshire as a member of the Great Council, summoned to be held at York; and in 1324, he was again elected to the parliament holden in London. He *d.* in 1366, and was *s.* by his son,

EDMUND GIFFARD, of Chillington, who *m.* a dau. of Venables, Baron of Kinderton, and dying in 1379, was *s.* by his eldest son,

JOHN GIFFARD, who was Lord of Chillington in 1394, and was *s.* by his son,

THOMAS GIFFARD, of Chillington, who *m.* Joyce, dau. and heir of Sir Robert Frauncoeys, of Whiston, co. Stafford, and had as her dowry that estate. This Thomas was sheriff of Staffordshire, in 1411. At his decease in 1416, he left an only child,

ROBERT GIFFARD, of Chillington, who *m.* 1st, Isabella Blount, but by that lady had no issue. He *m.* 2ndly, Cassandra, dau. of Thomas Humphreston, and was *s.* by his son,

SIR JOHN GIFFARD, of Chillington, who *m.* 1st, Jocosa Hoorde, and had by her two daus., Dorothea, *m.* 1st, to John Congreve, Esq. of Congreve, and 2ndly, to Francis, Earl Ferrers; and Cassandra, *m.* to Humphrey Swinnerton, Esq. of Swinnerton. He *m.* 2ndly, Elizabeth Greysoley, and had, with a dau., Frances, who *m.* to Sir John Talbot, of Grafton, two sons, viz., THOMAS, his heir; and William, Archbishop of Rheims, a duke and peer of France. This Sir John Giffard was five times sheriff of his native county; and to him HENRY VIII. granted the dissolved monastery of the Black Ladies, at Brewood, in 1539. He *d.* in 1556, and was *s.* by his son,

SIR THOMAS GIFFARD, who *m.* 1st, Dorothy, dau. and heiress of Sir John Montgomery, and had a dau., Elizabeth, *m.* to Sir John Port, of Etwall, one of the Justices of the King's Bench. Sir Thomas *m.* 2ndly, Ursula, dau. of Sir Robert Throgmorton, of Caughton, by whom he had four sons and five daus. He was sheriff of the co. of Stafford in the lifetime of his father, in 1530 and 1553. He *d.* in 1560, and was *s.* by his eldest son,

JOHN GIFFARD, Esq. of Chillington, high-sheriff of Staffordshire in 1573, who was honoured, in Aug. 1575, by a visit from Queen ELIZABETH, at Chillington. John Giffard *m.* Joyce, dau. of James Leveson, of Lilleshall and Trentham, Esq., and had eight sons and two daus. He *d.* in 1612, and was *s.* by his eldest son,

WALTER GIFFARD, Esq. of Chillington, who *m.* in 1579, Phillippa, dau. and co-heir of Henry White, Esq. of Southwarnborough, co. Southampton, and had, with other issue,

> PETER, his heir.
>
> Andrew, *m.* Catherine Leveson, and left at his decease (he was killed in a skirmish during the civil wars,) three sons, Thomas; Augustine, professor of divinity at Douay; and Bonaventure, a distinguished churchman of the reign of JAMES II. He was *b.* in 1642, and *d.* in 1733.

Walter Giffard was *s.* 29 April, 1632, by his eldest son,

PETER GIFFARD, Esq. of Chillington. This gentleman *m.* Frances, 2nd dau. of Walter Fowler, Esq. of St. Thomas, in the co. of Stafford, and had, with five younger sons and seven daus.,

> WALTER, his heir.
>
> John, of Black Ladies, who *m.* Catherine, dau. of Richard Hawkins, of Nash, co. Kent, and had, with a dau., Frances, one son, JOHN GIFFARD, of Black Ladies, who *m.* Catherine, dau. of John Taylor, Esq. of Fockbury, co. Worcester, and dying in 1709, left, with four daus., of whom the eldest, Catherine, *m.* to Thomas More, Esq. of Bamborough, three sons, PETER, who *s.* to Chillington; John, of Madeley, co. Salop; and Walter.

Peter Giffard in his extended and chequered life, saw the entire downfall and the perfect restoration of his family. From the commencement of the great rebellion, he appears to have taken an active and decided part in it, for at an early period we find his estates confiscated, and himself a prisoner. Chillington, so recently receiving a royal guest, became a royal garrison. The estates were sold by the Drury House Commissioners; and the members of the family, after fighting in the king's army as long as an army existed, were in prison, in banishment, or in concealment. When the 2nd CHARLES made his ill-advised descent on England, in 1651, several of the Giffards joined him, and fought on the fatal field of Worcester. After his defeat the King owed his safety in a great measure to the guidance of Charles Giffard, a nephew of Peter Giffard, of Chillington, and the fidelity of the Pendrills, the devoted retainers of the Giffards. He *d.* "full of days," 25 June, 1663, and was *s.* by his son,

WALTER GIFFARD, Esq. of Chillington, *b.* in 1611, *m.* 1st, Anne, dau. of Sir Thomas Holt, Bart. of Aston, by whom he had JOHN, his successor, with two other sons, and four daus. He *m.* 2ndly, Anne, dau. of Thomas Huggeford, Esq. of Solihull, but had no other issue. He *d.* in 1688, and was *s.* by his eldest son,

JOHN GIFFARD, Esq. of Chillington, *b.* in 1637, *m.* Frances, dau. of William Fitzherbert, Esq. of Swinnerton, and dying in 1694, was *s.* by his only surviving son,

THOMAS GIFFARD, Esq. of Chillington, who *m.* in 1688, Mary, dau. of John Thimelby, Esq. of Irnham, co. Lincoln, but dying without issue, in 1718, was *s.* by his kinsman,

Peter Giffard, Esq. of Black Ladies, (refer to John, 2nd son of Peter, who suffered during the civil wars and *d.* in 1663,) who thus became of **Chillington**, and representative of the family. He *m.* 1st, Winifred, dau. of Robert Howard, Esq. of Horecross, but by her had no issue. He *m.* 2ndly, Barbara, dau. of Sir Robert Throckmorton, Bart. of Caughton, and had,

Peter, his successor.
Maria, *m.* to Sir Edward Smythe, Bart. of Acton Burnell.
Anna, *m.* to —, Weld, Esq. of Lulworth.

Mr. Giffard *m.* 3rdly, Helen, dau. of Robert Roberts, Esq. of Plas-Ucha, co. Flint, by whom he had issue,

Thomas, successor to his brother Peter.
John, who inherited his mother's estate of Plas-Ucha. He *m.* Elizabeth, dau. and heir of Robert Hyde, Esq. of Nerquis, and had two daus., both of whom *d. unm.*, the last survivor at an advanced age, in 1842, when the Plas Ucha estate reverted to the present Mr. Giffard, of Chillington.
Catherine, *m.* to Francis Canning, Esq. of Foxcote.

He *d.* in 1746, and was *s.* by his eldest son,

Peter Giffard, Esq. of Chillington, who *d.* in 1748, before he had attained his majority, when the estates devolved upon his half-brother,

Thomas Giffard, Esq. of Chillington, who *m.* 1st, Barbara, dau. of Robert James Lord Petre, by whom he had one dau., Maria, *m.* to Sir John Throckmorton, Bart. Mr. Giffard *m.* 2ndly, Barbara, dau. of Sir Robert Throckmorton, Bart., and had a son, **Thomas**, his heir. He *m.* 3rdly, Frances, dau. of Thomas Stonor, Esq. of Stonor, in the co. of Oxford, by whom he left,

John, who *m.* Eleanor, dau. and heir of — Sutton, Esq. of Sutton Sturmey, in Ireland, but *d. s. p.* in 1833.
Frances, *m.* to William Throckmorton, Esq.

He *d.* in 1775, and was *s.* by his eldest son,

Thomas Giffard, Esq. of Chillington, who *m.* 23 June, 1788, Lady Charlotte Courtenay, sister of the late Earl of Devon, and had issue,

Thomas-William, his heir.
Francis-John, who *d. unm.* in 1836.
Walter-Peter, of Bilbrooke, *m.* in 1836, Henrietta-Dorothy, dau. of the late Sir John-F. Boughey, Bart. of Aqualate, and has issue a son, Walter-Thomas-Courtenay, and two daus., Henrietta-Charlotte and Selina.
Charles-Robert.
Robert-Edward, capt. 10th Hussars, *d. unm.* 1 Feb. 1836.
Charlotte, *m.* to Samuel-Campbell Simpson, Esq. of Brockton.
Lucy-Harriot.
Sophia-Elizabeth, *m.* to John, second Lord Wrottesley.
Anne-Barbara, *m.* to the Rev. Charles Whitmore, and *d.* 23 Nov. 1834.
Barbara-Denise, *m.* 26 Sept. 1839, to William-Lacon Childe Esq. of Kinlet, Salop, and *d.* in 1841.
Caroline-Mallet, *m.* to John Mytton, Esq. of Halston, and *d.* in 1841.
Louisa-Paulina-Charlotte, *m.* 27 Dec. 1832, to Sir Thomas-Fenton-Fletcher Boughey, Bart.

Mr. Giffard *d.* 1 Aug. 1823, and was *s.* by his eldest son, the present **Thomas-William Giffard**, Esq. of Chillington, the 21st Giffard of Chillington.

Arms—Quarterly: 1st and 4th, az., three stirrups with leathers, or, two and one; 2nd and 3rd gu., three lions, passant, arg.

Crests—A tiger's head, couped, full-faced, spotted various, flames issuing from his mouth, ppr., granted in 1513. A demi-archer, bearded, and couped at the knees, in armour, ppr., from his middle a short coat, paly, arg. and gu. At his middle a quiver of arrows, or, in his hands a bow and arrow drawn to the head, or, granted in 1523.

Motto—Prenez haleine, tirez fort.—Take breath and pull strong.

Seat—Chillington, co. Stafford.

GIFFARD OF BRIGHTLEY.

Giffard, Edward, Esq. of Kilcorrall, co. Wexford, *b.* 19 Dec. 1812, secretary of the Transport Board, *m.* 14 Nov. 1844, Rosamond-Catharine, dau. of William Pennell, Esq., and has,

I. John-Harding, *b.* 25 May, 1847.

I. Minnie-Rose. II. Jane-Mary.
III. Alice-Katherine. IV. Margaret-Magdalen.
V. Florence-Eliza. VI. Evelyne.

Lineage.—The family of Giffard is of great antiquity in Devonshire, where it flourished as early as the reign of **Henry II.**

Sir Roger Giffard, son of Thomas Giffard, of Halesbury, by Anne Coryton, his 2nd wife, *m.* Margaret, dau. and coheiress of John Cobleigh, of Brightley, near Caittlehampton, and was father of

John Giffard, Esq., *m.* Mary, dau. of Sir Richard Granville, of Stow, in Cornwall, by Maud, dau. and co-heir of John Beville, Esq. of Gwarnock, in that co., and by her had, besides many other children, his eldest son,

John Giffard, Esq. of Brightley, who *m.* Honor, dau. of Walter Erle, Esq. of Charborough, co. Dorset, and was father of

Arthur Giffard, Esq., who *m.* Anne, dau. of Thomas Leigh, Esq. of Borough, in Devonshire, and had a son and successor,

John Giffard, Esq., *b.* in 1602, of Brightley, one of the staunchest adherents of King **Charles I.** He was "decimated, sequestrated, and imprisoned," and paid £1136 as a composition for his estates. After the Restoration he was selected to be a Knight of the proposed Order of the Royal Oak, and *d.* in 1666. Colonel Giffard *m.* Joan, youngest dau. of Sir John Wyndham, of Orchard Wyndham, in Somersetshire, by Joan, dau. of Sir Henry Portman, and by her had three sons and several daus. The eldest son,

John Giffard, *m.* 1st, Susan, sister of Sir Coplestone Bamfylde; and 2ndly, Frances, dau. of the Honourable Doctor William Fane, 4th son of Francis, 1st Earl of Westmoreland, and *d.* in 1712. He had by her,

Henry.
Cæsar, who *s.* to the estates of Brightley under his father's will, *m.* and had issue.
Frances, *m.* to — Kenney, and left issue.

Henry Giffard, Esq., the eldest son, being disinherited by his father, settled at Wotton, in Devonshire, *m.* Martha, dau. of Edward Hill, Esq., judge of the Admiralty and treasurer of Virginia, and *d. v. p.* in 1709. His eldest son,

John Giffard, Esq. of Great Torrington, in Devonshire, settled in Ireland; *m.* Dorcas, dau. of Arthur Murphy, Esq., co. Wexford, and *d.* in 1748, leaving an only son,

John Giffard, Esq., accountant-general of His Majesty's customs at Dublin, and high-sheriff of that city in 1794, *b.* in 1746; *m.* Sarah, dau. of William Morton, Esq. of Ballynaclash, co. Wexford, *d.* in May, 1819, aged 74, and left issue,

Ambrose-Harding, his heir.
Stanley-Lees, LL.D., barrister-at-law, *m.* twice, and has issue.
William, lieut. 82nd regt., murdered by the rebels in Ireland in May, 1798.
John, *d.* young.
Harriet, *m.* 1st, to Major George King, 7th Fusiliers, who was killed at New Orleans, Jan. 1815, and 2ndly, to the Rev. James Phelan.
Mary, *m.* to the Rev. Richard Ryan.

The eldest son,

Sir Ambrose-Harding Giffard, Knt., chief-justice of Ceylon, *b.* in 1771; *m.* 1808, Harriett, dau. of Lovell Pennell, Esq. of Lyme Regis, and dying in April, 1827, left issue,

John-William, *b.* in 1811, *d. unm.* in 1833.
Edward, now of Kilcorrall.
George, capt R.N., C.B., *b.* in 1815; *married.*
William, in holy orders, *b.* 1815, *m.* and has issue.
Arthur, capt. E.I.C.S., *b.* in 1826.
Jane-Mary, *m.* to Sir William-Webb Follett, Her Majesty's solicitor-general, *d.* 1847.
Sarah. Harriet, *m.* to Wentworth Bayly, Esq.
Rose, *m.* to the Rev. G. Urquhart Fagan.
Emma, *m.* to the Rev. Francis Tate.

Arms—Sa., three lozenges conjoined, in fesse, erm.
Crest—A cock's head, erased, or.
Seat—Kilcorrall, co. Wexford.

GIFFORD OF BALLYSOP.

Gifford, Rev. William, of Ballysop, co. Wexford, *b.* 1795; *m.* 10 May, 1824, Arabella, eldest dau. of the Rev. Walton Stephens, of Hibla, co. Kildare (by Arabella his wife, dau. of William Glascott, 4th son of George Glascott, Esq. of Alderton, co. Wexford), and co-heiress of her brother, Walter Stephens, of Hibla, co. Kildare, by whom he has issue,

I. Walter-Stephens, J.P. for the co. Wexford.
II. Nicholas. III. William-James-Brownlow.

I. Anna. II. Arabella. III. Margaret.
IV. Lucy-Stephens. V. Georgina.
VI. Elizabeth. VII. Wilelmina.

Mr. Gifford, who is rector of Mageesha, co. Cork, *s.* his father 13 Sept. 1830.

Lineage.—JASPER GIFFORD, who went over to Ireland in 1641, in the same troop with William Glascote, of Aldertown, and Roger Drake, of Stokestown, got grants of property, in the co. Wexford, by patent dated 18th King CHARLES II., and fixed his residence at Polemaloe, co. Wexford. His eldest son,

WILLIAM GIFFORD, of Polemaloe, *m.* Margaret, dau. of Nicholas Bolton, of Brazeel, co. Dublin, by Anne his wife, dau. of Nicholas Loftus, of Loftus Hall, co. Wexford, and by her (who *d.* 4 May, 1718) had issue. His eldest dau., Anne, *m.* George Glascott, Esq. of Alderton, and his eldest son was

NICHOLAS GIFFORD, Esq. of Ballysop, who *m.* Katherine, dau. of Captain Sweeney, of Wexford, and He was *s.* by his son,

WILLIAM GIFFORD, Esq. of Ballysop, who *m.* 5 March, 1764, Margaret, dau. of George Glascott, Esq. of Alderton, by whom, who *d.* in March, 1791, aged 56 he left an only son,

NICHOLAS GIFFORD, of Ballysop, *b.* in 1766; *m.* Margaret, dau. of Mitchelbourne Symes, of Coolboye, co. Wicklow, by Anne his wife, dau. of George Glascott, of Alderton, by whom, who *d.* in March, 1830, he had issue,

WILLIAM, now of Ballysop.
Nicholas, *m.* Sophia, dau. of Francis Morton, Esq. of Fort Town, co. Wicklow, and has issue, Nicholas; Francis-Henry; Mary-Elizabeth; Margaret; and Frances-Anne.
Charles-Symes, *m.* Ann, dau. of Glascott Symes, Esq., and has issue, Nicholas, *m.* July, 1853, Tamzine Katherine, dau. of Alexander Grant, of Clonakitty, co. Cork, Esq.; Charles-Symes; Glascott; John; George; William-Edward; James-Richard; Alicia; Margaret-Anne; and Emma.
John-Symes, capt. H.E.I.C., *b.* Jan. 1803; *m.* 12 April, 1845, Beata, dau. of Capt. John Glascott, of Killowen, co. Wexford.
George, *d. unm.* Sept. 1841.
James, major H.E.I.C., *d. unm.* 17 May, 1853.
Thomas, *d. unm.*
Mary-Anne, *m.* to Henry-Benjamin Archer, Esq. of St. Stephen's Green, Dublin, barrister-at-law.
Margaret, *d. unm.* Elizabeth.

Nicholas Gifford, *d.* 18 Sept. 1830.

Arms—Gu., three lions, passant, in pale, arg.
Crest—A cubit dexter arm in armour, grasping a gilly flower, all proper.
Motto—Potius mori quam foedari.
Seat—Ballysop, co. Wexford.

GILBERT OF THE PRIORY.

GILBERT, WALTER-RALEIGH, Esq., J.P., lieut.-col. royal artillery, *b.* 9 April, 1813; *m.* 16 Dec. 1848, Marianne-Charlotte-Isabella, eldest dau. of William Peters, Esq. of Ashfold, Sussex, and has issue,

I. WALTER-RALEIGH, *b.* 12 Aug. 1849.
I. Mary-Marianne. II. Cecilia-Isabella.

Lineage.—Westcott observes that Gilbert, the ancestor of the present family, "possessed lands in Manadon in EDWARD the Confessor's days," and Prince adds that the Gilberts "have matched as they descended down into honourable houses, as of Champernon, Croker, Hill, Chudleigh, Agar, Molineux, Pomeroy, &c., and have yielded matches to others, in particular to the noble family of the Grenvils. They have married also divers daus. and heirs, as Compton, Champernon, Valetort, (whereby they touch the blood royal,) Reynward, Trenoch, Littleton, alias Westcott, Kelly, and others, from whose loins have proceeded many eminent persons which were of old, men of renown. Such as Otho, called also Otis Gilbert, high-sheriff of Devonshire, 15 EDWARD IV."

This OTHO or OTES GILBERT inherited Greenway, a seat beautifully situated on a bold elevation, overhanging the river Dart, about 4 miles from Dartmouth. Otho had three sons; 1 JOHN, (Sir,) knighted by Queen ELIZABETH in 1576, *m.* a dau. of Sir Richard Chudleigh, Knt. of Ashton, but *d. s. p.*; 2 HUMPHREY, (Sir,) of whose line we treat; and, 3 Adrian. The 2nd son,

SIR HUMPHREY GILBERT, knighted 1577, was eminently distinguished by his discoveries in the northern seas, where Gilbert's Straits are called after him to this day, and by the establishment of the colony of Newfoundland. This enterprising seaman, who was half-brother of Sir Walter Raleigh, *m.* Anne, dau. of Sir Anthony Agar, Knt. of Kent, and had with one dau., nine sons, the eldest, Sir John Gilbert, Knt., an officer of reputation, *m.* a dau. of Sir Richard Molyneux, of Sefton, but *d.* in 1608, without issue, as did all his brothers except

RALEIGH GILBERT, Esq. of Compton, who *m.* Miss Kelly, and left a son and successor,

AGAR GILBERT, Esq. of Compton, who *m.* Christian, dau. of Edmund Walrond, Esq. of Bovey, co. Devon, and by her, (who *d.* 8 July, 1660,) had, with a dau., Elizabeth, *m.* to Thomas Hicks, Esq. of Trevithick, two sons: the younger, John, *d.* 16 Oct. 1674; the elder,

HUMPHREY GILBERT, Esq. *s.* his father at Compton Castle, 12 April, 1661; He *m.* Joan, eldest dau. and co-heir of Roger Pomeroy, Esq. of Sandbridge, and had three sons, John, Humphrey, and Raleigh. The eldest,

JOHN GILBERT, Esq. of Compton Castle, sold the ancient seat at Greenway. He *m.* Anne, dau. of Richard Courtnay, Esq., son of Sir William Courtnay, of Powderham, and by her, who *d.* in 1775, had, (with eight daus., Anne, Catherine, Henrietta, Maria, Elizabeth-Margaret, Urania, Johan, and Lucy) four sons, John, who *d. unm.*, POMROY, Courtenay, and Humphrey. The 2nd son,

POMROY GILBERT, Esq. of Compton Castle, *m.* Mary, dau. of Admiral Edmund Williams, of Plymouth, and had by her, who *d.* in 1786, (with three daus., Mary, Elizabeth, and Lucretia,) five sons, of whom the 3rd,

The REV. EDMUND GILBERT, vicar of Constantine, and Official of the archdeaconry of Cornwall, *m.* Anne dau. of Henry Garnett, Esq. of Bristol, and had by her, who *d.* in 1822, six sons and seven daus., viz.,

JOHN-POMROY, his heir.
Henry-Garnett, lieut. R.N., lost at sea, in H.M.S. Hawk.
Walter-Raleigh, *b.* in 1786, lieut.-gen. in the E. I. Co.'s Service, G.C.B., created a BARONET in 1850, *d.* 1853 (*see* BURKE'S *Peerage and Baronetage.*)
Edmund-William, commander R.N., *b.* in 1788, *m.* in 1822, Mary, dau. of J. Simpson, Esq., and has issue, Edmund, Francis, Henry, and one dau.
Roger-Pomroy, major in the army, *b.* in 1790.
Francis-Yarde, capt. R.E., *b.* in 1794, *m.* Elizabeth, widow of William Burroughs, Esq.
Catherine-Hodgson, *m.* to Sir Walter Roberts, Bart., and has issue.
Elizabeth-Garnett, *m.* in 1813, to Joseph Hamley, Esq., *d.* in 1820, leaving issue.
Mary, *m.* in 1806, to Lord Robert Kerr, and has issue.
Anne-Garnett, *d.* young.
Lucy.
Frances-Isabella, *m.* in 1815, to William Hickey, Esq., and has issue.

Mr. Gilbert *d.* in 1816, and was *s.* by his son, the REV. JOHN-POMEROY GILBERT, M.A. of the Priory, Bodmin, Prebendary of Exeter, J.P., *b.* in 1779; *m.* in 1808, Mary, dau. of Matthew Storm, Esq., of Ilfracombe, and has had issue, EDMUND, deceased, WALTER-RALEIGH, now of The Priory, John-Pomeroy, and Otho, lieut. Royal Art.

Arms—Arg., on a chev., sa., three roses of the first, leaved ppr.
Crest—A squirrel, sejant, on a hill, vert, feeding on a crop of nuts, ppr.
Motto—Mallem mori quam mutare.
Seat—The Priory, Bodmin, Cornwall.

GILBERT OF TREDREA AND EAST-BOURN.

GILBERT, JOHN-DAVIES, Esq. of Tredrea, co. Cornwall, and of East-Bourn, co. Sussex, one of the coheirs of the Barony of Sandys, *s.* his father 16 April, 1854.

Lineage.—DAVIES GIDDY, Esq., D.C.L., M.A., F.R.S., and F.S.A., only son of the Rev. Edward Giddy, M.A. (by Catherine, his wife, dau. and eventually heir of John Davies, Esq., son of William Davies, Esq. of St. Erth, by Catherine, his wife, only child and heir of Colonel Humphrey Noye, by Hester his wife, sister and co-heir of Edwin, 8th Lord Sandys) was *b.* in 1767, and assumed the name and arms of GILBERT on his marriage, 18 April, 1808, with Mary-Anne, only dau. and heir of THOMAS GILBERT, Esq. of East-Bourn, co. Sussex. Mr. Davies-Gilbert attained a very high reputation in science and antiquities, and eventually succeeded Sir Humphry Davy in the president's chair of the Royal Academy. In 1804 he was returned to parliament by the borough of Helston, and in 1806, by that of Bodmin. By the heiress of Gilbert he left at his decease, 24 Dec. 1840, (with four daus., Catherine, *m.* 17 April, 1834, to John-S. Enys, Esq. of Enys; Mary-Susannah; Anne; and Hester-Elizabeth,) an only son,

JOHN-DAVIES GILBERT, Esq. of Tredrea and East-Bourn, *b.* 1811, who *m.* 7 Oct. 1851, the Hon. Anna-Dorothea, elder dau. of Robert, late Lord Carew, K.P., and *d.* 16 April, 1854, leaving a son and heir, the present possessor of Tredrea.

Arms—Arg., on a chev., gu., three roses, of the field.
Crest—A squirrel, sejant, gu., cracking a nut, or.
Motto—Teg Yw Hedwch.
Seats—Tredrea, Cornwall, and East-Bourn, Sussex.

GILBERT OF CANTLEY.

GILBERT, WILLIAM-ALEXANDER, Esq. of Manor House, Cantley, co. Norfolk, J.P., *b.* 24 April, 1806; *m.* 1st, 29 Sept. 1829, Maria, dau. of John-Bellamy Plowman, Esq., and by her (who *d.* 11 July, 1834) has issue,

I. WILLIAM-ALEXANDER, *b.* 3 Nov. 1831.
II. John-Bellamy, *b.* 13 April, 1834.

Mr. Gilbert *m.* 2ndly, 26 April, 1836, Mary-Anne, dau. of the Rev. John Gilbert, of Chedgrave, and by her has issue,

I. Thomas-Denny, *b.* 26 May, 1837.
II. Herbert-Henry, *b.* 17 June, 1840.
III. Walter-Edward, *b.* 4 April, 1846.
IV. Francis-Parnell, *b.* 6 Sept. 1847.
V. George-Percy, *b.* 20 April, 1849.
I. Mary-Anne. II. Alice-Jane.
III. Harriet-Helen. IV. Agnes-Anne.
V. Gertrude-Maria.

Lineage.—THOMAS GILBERT, Gent. of Chedgrave, in Norfolk, *b.* in 1694, a descendant of Thomas Gilbert, Esq. of Burlingham, in Norfolk, who had a grant of arms, *temp.* Queen ELIZABETH, *m.* Elizabeth, dau. of James Utting, Gent. of Rockland Hall, Norfolk, and by her who *d.* in 1776, aged 70, had five sons and five daus. Mr. Gilbert *d.* in 1759. His youngest son,

HENRY GILBERT, Esq. of Postwick Hall, co. Norfolk, *b.* in 1740, *m.* 1771, Anne, dau. of James Jenner, Esq. of Ashby, co. Suffolk, and by her, who *d.* 9 Feb. 1781, had issue,

I. Thomas, of Hardly, *d. unm.* 21 Aug. 1798, aged 25.
II. WILLIAM-HENRY, of Cantley.
III. Robert, of Postwick Hall, *b.* 2 June, 1776, *m.* 22 May, 1800, Lucy, dau. of John Gillett, Esq. of Halvergate, and has issue,
1 Thomas-William, *b.* 5 March, 1801.
2 Robert, *b.* 9 Feb. 1804.
3 Henry, *b.* 18 Dec. 1807.
4 Arthur, *b.* 31 Dec. 1814.
5 William-Henry, *b.* 15 July, 1816.
6 Clement, *b.* 19 March, 1822.
1 Lydia-Ann, *m.* 23 Sept. 1825, to Thomas-Gilbert Tuck, Esq.
2 Lucy. 3 Amelia. 4 Maria.
5 Helen. 6 Caroline.
IV. John, of Chedgrave, co. Norfolk, in holy orders, *b.* in 1778; *m.* Mary-Anne, dau of Richard Denny, Esq. of Bergh-Apton, Norfolk, and has issue.

Mr. Gilbert *d.* in 1812. His eldest surviving son,

WILLIAM-HENRY GILBERT, Esq. of Cantley, *b.* 1 Nov. 1774, to whom his uncle, William, devised the Cantley estate, *m.* 20 May, 1801, Elizabeth, dau. of Alexander Woods, of Westleton, Suffolk, and by her (who *d.* 6 July, 1828) had issue,

WILLIAM-ALEXANDER, now of Cantley.
Henry-Robert, *b.* 23 July, 1811, *d. unm.* 2 March, 1845.
Elizabeth-Ann, *m.* 19 March, 1833, to Alexander Woods, Esq.
Sarah, *d. unm.* 1822.

Mr. Gilbert *d.* 7 Feb. 1832.

Arms—Gu., two bars, engr., erm., in chief three fleurs-de-lis, or. The original grant to Thomas Gilbert, of North Burlingham, A.D. 1576, was:—gu., two bars, erm., in chief three fleurs de-lis, or.
Crest—A stag's head, or, on the neck a fess, engr., with plain cottises, gu.
Motto—Tenax propositi.
Seat—Cantley, Norfolk.

GILCHRIST OF OPISDALE.

GILCHRIST, DANIEL, Esq. of Opisdale, co. Sutherland, J.P. and D.L., convener of the county of Sutherland, *b.* 8 Aug. 1806; *m.* 20 Oct. 1841, Jeane, dau. of John Reork, Esq. of Gilmarton, co. Fife, and has issue one dau., MARGARET. Mr. Gilchrist is only son of Dugald Gilchrist, by Catherine-Rose his wife: he has four sisters, one of whom is *m.* to William Lyon, Esq. of London, and another to George Rose, Esq. of Pitcalvie, chief of the clan Ross.

Crest—A lion, rampant, holding in the dexter paw a scimitar, all ppr.
Motto—Mea Gloria fides.
Seat—Opisdale, co. Sutherland.

GILDEA OF PORT ROYAL.

GILDEA, JAMES-KNOX, Esq. of Port Royal and Cloncormack House, co. Mayo, high-sheriff in 1835; *b.* 24 Sept. 1804.

Lineage.—The family of Gildea, is of ancient Milesian descent, and a pedigree in the possession of the present representative, deduces it from the ancient monarchs of Ireland. At the time (1718) when that document was drawn up, the head of the house was

JAMES GILDEA, Esq. of Golough and Port Royal, chief magistrate for co. Mayo, and high-sheriff about the year 1723. He *m.* Mary Steward, of Summer Hill, and by her had (with three daus., Elenor, Anne, and Mary, and a younger son, Robert) an elder son and heir,

JAMES GILDEA, Esq. of Port Royal, who *m.* 19 Jan. 1755, Mary Ruttledge, of Cornfield, and by her, who *d.* 27 Feb. 1788, had issue, James, *b.* 19 Feb. 1756; Andrew, lieut. in the royal Irish regiment of artillery, and A.D.C. to the Duke of Rutland, *d.* in London, 16 Feb. 1787, *v. p.*; ANTHONY, of whom presently; William-Mills, *b.* 3 June, 1761, an ensign in 62nd regt., *d.* 5 Dec. 1787; George, *b.* 30 Sept. 1762; Robert, *b.* 18 Jan. 1765; Thomas, *b.* 3 Oct. 1770; Robert, *b.* 15 April, 1776; John, *b.* 24 June, 1779, lieut. in the 17th light dragoons, *d.* in Jamaica; Mary; Barbara; Margaret; Elenor; Anne; and Margaret. Mr. James Gildea *d.* at Cloonigashill, 8 Aug. 1790. His third, but eventually eldest surviving son,

ANTHONY GILDEA, Esq. of Port Royal, J.P., and twice high-sheriff, *m.* 14 Nov. 1803, Anne, 5th dau. of Francis Knox, Esq. of Rappa Castle, co. Mayo, and had issue,

I. JAMES-KNOX, present representative.
II. Anthony-Knox, barrister-at-law.
III. Robert. IV. John-Arthur, capt. 81st regt.
V. Francis, late 2nd Queen's Royals.
I. Maria.
II. Anne. III. Harriette. IV. Elizabeth.
V. Louisa. VI. Caroline. VII. Charlotte.

Arms—Arg., on a mount, vert, a stag, statant, under a bay tree, ppr.
Crest—A wolf's head, erased, ppr., langued, gu.
Mottoes—Re e merito, and Vincit qui patitur.
Seat—Cloncormack House, co. Mayo

GILL OF BICKHAM PARK.

GILL, JOHN-HORNBROOK, Esq. of Bickham Park, co. Devon, J.P. for the cos. of Devon and Cornwall, and high-sheriff of Cornwall in 1841; *b.* 10 March, 1787; *m.* in 1830, Jane, only child of Thomas Cornish, Esq. of Cholwell House, Devon, and has issue,

I. HAROLD-WRAYFORD-CORNISH, *b.* 17 July, 1831; *m.* 27 Sept. 1856, Augusta-Lucy, dau. of the late Rev. J.-P. Carpenter.
II. Reginald-Butler-Edgcumbe, *b.* 29 July, 1833.
I. Honoria-Barbara-Jane.

Lineage.—The family of Gill have been resident and possessed of landed property in the parish of Tavistock since the reign of STEPHEN, and are of Saxon origin, as denoted by the name.

JOHN GILL, Esq. (the grandfather of the present proprietor), *m.* Prothesia, dau. of Nicholas Edgcumbe, Esq., and left a son,

JOHN GILL, Esq. of Bickham Park, who *m.* in 1786, Barbara, younger dau. of Jacob Hornbrook Esq. of Tavistock, and by her (who *d.* in 1834) left at his decease, in 1841,

JOHN-HORNBROOK, now of Bickham Park.
Thomas, late M.P. for Plymouth, *m.* 1st, Rachel, dau. of Andrew Paton, Esq., and 2ndly, Jane, dau. of Robert Charles, Esq. of London, and has issue by both marriages.
William, *d. unm.* 1822.
Elizabeth, *m.* 1st, to John Smith, Esq. of Upland, Devon; and 2ndly, to Joseph Read, Esq., J.P.
Mary-Anne-Grace, *m.* to C. V. Bridgeman, Esq.
Barbara, *m.* to John Rundle, Esq., late M.P. for Tavistock.

Arms—GILL, with an escutcheon of pretence for CORNISH.
Crest—A boar, passant, resting its fore-paw on a crescent.
Motto—In te, Domine, spes nostra.
Seat—Bickham Park, Devon.

GILLBANKS OF WHITEFIELD HOUSE.

GILLBANKS, JACKSON, Esq. of Whitefield House, co. Cumberland, J.P., *b.* 5 Nov. 1819; B.A. and LL.B. of St. John's College, Cambridge, a barrister-at-law, patron of the living of Uldale.

Lineage.—This family sprung from the mountain district near Keswick. The name, spelt in old family records "Ghyllbanke," evidently shows their connection with that locality: "'Gill' or 'Ghyll,'" as an author observes, "means a mountain stream confined between steep banks and running rapidly." Several generations ago, the Gillbanks held considerable property about the Vale of St. John and Threlkeld. There is still the small ancient hamlet of Gilbank in that part where they are said to have resided, but the bulk of the property having devolved upon an heiress who married, it passed into other hands, and the family were much dispersed. One branch then settled in the east of Cumberland, where there have been a succession of clergymen of the name (under the patronage of the Howards) for many generations. The late Rev. G. Gillbanks held the living of Lanercost Priory for nearly sixty years. A distant branch is also represented by Thomas Gillbanks, Esq. of Culgaith; another branch, of which we now treat, settled at Scothwaite Close, near Ireby, which has now been in their possession about two hundred years.

JOSEPH GILLBANKS, Esq., the younger son of Joseph Gillbanks, of the above place, who *m.* Miss Elizabeth Sheffield, was *b.* 28 Jan. 1780. He went to Jamaica in 1800, and having amassed a large fortune as a merchant there, returned, in 1814, to England, when he purchased the Whitefield House, Orthwaite Hall, Haltcliff Hall, and other estates in the co. of Cumberland, which the present owner has since much improved and beautified. He *m.* 7 Jan. 1819, Mary, eldest dau. of Ralph Jackson, Esq. of Normanby-in-Cleveland, Yorkshire, and niece of Colonel Jackson, of St. Dorothy, Jamaica, and of the Hon. R. Jackson, lord chief justice of that island, which family has held large possessions there for many generations. This lady, by the sudden death of her cousin, W. Thomas Jackson (son of Colonel Jackson, of Jamaica), has succeeded to the great bulk of that gentleman's property, and by this lady, who survives him, Mr. Gillbanks had issue one son and two daus., viz.,

JACKSON, now of Whitefield House.
Mary-Elizabeth, *m.* June, 1846, to R. M. Lawrance, M.D., and has issue.
Maria-Josephine, *m.* 24 Jan. 1856, to Rev. Henry Gough, M.A., fellow of Queen's, Oxford, and rector of Charlton, Oxfordshire.

Mr. Gillbanks was for 40 years a most active magistrate and deputy-lieutenant for the county. He *d.* suddenly on the 3rd day of Feb. 1858, and was *s.* by his only son, the present JACKSON GILLBANKS, Esq. of Whitefield House.

Arms—Az., five hearts, in saltire, or, on a chief, arg., a rose, gu., between two trefoils, slipped, vert.
Crest—A stag's head, or.
Motto—Honore et virtute.
Seat—Whitefield House, near Wigton.

GILLON OF WALLHOUSE.

GILLON, ANDREW, Esq. of Wallhouse, co. Linlithgow, J.P. and D.L., *b.* 22 April, 1823; *m.* 1st, 4 April, 1848, Jane-Lillias, eldest dau. of John-Ferrier Hamilton, Esq. of Cairnhill and Westport, by the Hon. Georgina Vereker his wife, dau. of the late Viscount Gort, and has by her a son,

WILLIAM, *b.* 21 Dec. 1849.

He *m.* 2ndly, 12 Jan. 1854, Anna-Maria, only dau. of Capt. Henry-Paget Gill, late of the 50th regt., by Catherine-Cameron his wife, now Lady Maxwell, of Calderwood, dau. of Walter Logan, Esq., and by her has a son,

Henry, *b.* 10 Nov. 1854.

Lineage.—This family, one of old standing, is supposed to be of Norman origin.

JOHN GILLON, Esq. of Wallhouse, co. Linlithgow, who obtained a charter of that estate in 1572, was great-great-grandfather of

ALEXANDER GILLON, Esq. of Wallhouse, who *m.* Eleonora Montgomery, and was father of

JOHN GILLON, Esq. of Wallhouse, who *m.* Catherina, dau. of Sir Andrew Agnew, of Lochnaw, Bart., and by her was father of

ANDREW GILLON, Esq. of Wallhouse, lieutenant-colonel of Scots Fusilier Guards, who *m.* Nov. 1800, Mary-Anne, dau. of William Downe, Esq. of Downe Hall, co. Dorset, and by her (who *d.* Sept. 1801) left at his decease, 5 May, 1823, an only son and heir,

WILLIAM-DOWNE GILLON, Esq. of Wallhouse, co. Linlithgow, and Hurstmonceux, Sussex, J.P. and D.L., M.P. for the Lanark burghs in 1831-2, and for the Falkirk burghs from 1832 to 1841; *b.* 31, Aug. 1801; he *m.* 24 Oct. 1820, Helen-Eliza, dau. of John Corse Scott, Esq. of Lynton, co. Selkirk, and *d.* 7 Oct. 1846, leaving issue,

I. ANDREW, now of Wallhouse.
II. William, lieut. 72nd Bengal N.I., killed at the siege of Moultan, aged 23.
I. Helen, *m.* 29 April, 1852, to William Macfarlane Wardrop, Esq. of Bridgehouse.
II. Mary-Anne.
III. Catherine, *d. unm.*, Nov. 1852.

Arms—Gu., on a saltier, arg., five martlets, volant, of the first.
Crest—A raven, on the face of a rock, ppr.
Motto—Tutum refugium.
Supporters—Two ravens, ppr.
Seat—Wallhouse, co. Linlithgow.

GILLMAN OF OAKMOUNT.

GILLMAN, JAMES, Esq. of Oakmount, co. Cork, J.P., *b.* 14 April, 1804; *m.* 3 March, 1842, Elizabeth-Sarah, only dau. of the late Herbert Gillman, Esq., of Bennett's Grove, co. Cork, and has issue,

JAMES-HERBERT, *b.* 23 Sept. 1845.
Amelia-Davies.

Lineage.—The Gillmans of Ireland are stated, in an old family tradition, to be descended from a Christian knight of that name, who during the crusades, was engaged in single combat with a Saracen, whose right leg he cut off with a sabre cut. This exploit is commemorated in the coat of arms; and the crest, a griffin's head, with a bear's paw in its mouth, being emblematic of strength, together with the motto, "Not by word, but by deed," tend to confirm the legend. The first who settled in Ireland, were two officers in King WILLIAM'S army, 1690, one of whom survived, and received a grant of land. It is supposed that they had previously come to England from Normandy in France.

JAMES GILLMAN, Esq. of Baltembrack, co. Cork (grandfather of the present Mr. Gillman, of Oakmount), *m.* 15 March, 1754, Eliza Clarke, and by her (who *d.* 10 Feb. 1810) he left, at his death, 12 March, 1801, with other issue, a son and heir,

JAMES GILLMAN, Esq. of Oakmount, who *m.* 15 Sept. 1796, Eliza, dau. of Lander, Esq., and by her, who *d.* 14 March, 1848, had issue,

JAMES, now of Oakmount.
William, *m.*, and has issue.
Eliza, *m.*, and has issue.

Mr. Gillman, *d.* 9 June, 1814.

Arms—Az., a dexter leg cut off above the knee, ppr.
Crest—A griffin's head erased, with a bear's paw in its mouth.
Motto—Non cantu sed actu.
Seat—Oakmount, co. Cork.

GILLUM OF MIDDLETON HALL.

GILLUM, STEPHEN-FRYER, Esq. of Middleton Hall, co. Northumberland, J.P., *b.* 30 Oct. 1812; *m.* 5 May, 1837, Mary-Ann, dau. of Thomas Forster, Esq. of Adderstone House, in the same county, and has issue one dau.,

Rosamond-Ann.

Lineage.—STEPHEN FRYER, Esq., *m.* 1st, 17 Dec. 1796, Susannah Mesler, and had by her one dau., Anne, *m.* to Frederick Stale, Esq. He *m.* 2ndly, 3 Nov. 1809, Elizabeth, 2nd dau. of George Selby, Esq. of Twizell House, co. Northumberland, and by her, who *d.* 3 July, 1827, had issue,

STEPHEN, now of Middleton Hall.
Henry-George, *b.* 6 April, 1816; *d.* 23 June, 1828.
Prideaux-William, *b.* 6 July, 1824.
Elizabeth.

Margaret, *m.* to the Rev. Edmund Wills.
Marianne.
Isabella-Selby. Charlotte-Sarah.
Georgiana, Catherine, } both deceased.

Arms—Sa., on a chev., or, between three dolphins, haurient ppr. as many castles.
Crest—A dolphin, as in the arms.
Seat—Middleton Hall, Belford, co. Northumberland.

GILPIN OF HOCKLIFFE GRANGE.

Gilpin, Richard-Thomas, Esq. of Hockliffe Grange, co. Bedford, J.P. and D.L., M.P. for Bedfordshire, lieut.-col. of the county militia, *b.* 12 Jan. 1801; *m.* 13 Dec. 1831, Louisa, dau. of General Gore Browne, of Weymouth, colonel of the 44th regt.

Lineage.—This family claims to be a branch of the family of Gilpin, seated at Kentmere Hall, co. Westmoreland, *temp.* King John, in whose reign the estate was given by a Baron of Kendal to Richard Gilpin, as a reward for valuable services, and eventually came into possession (on the death of an elder brother, killed at Bosworth) of Edwin Gilpin, father of the Rev. Bernard Gilpin, rector of Houghton-le-Spring, one of the most learned divines and church reformers of that day. The immediate ancestor of the Gilpins, of Hockliffe Grange,

Robert Gilpin, Esq., son of the Rev. Robert Gilpin, rector of Hockliffe, *m.* Esther, dau. of Matthew Neale, Esq. of Exe Hall, co. Warwick, and was father, besides other children, of

Thomas Gilpin, Esq., high-sheriff of Bedfordshire in 1752, who *m.* Margaret, dau. of Pinner, Esq. of Monk-Wearmouth, co. Durham, and had an only son,

Richard Gilpin, Esq. of Hockliffe, D.L., and for upwards of forty years lieut.-col. of the Bedfordshire regt. of militia. He *m.* 1st, Mary, relict of Capt. Spencer, of Jamaica; and 2ndly, in April, 1797, Sarah, 4th dau. of William Wilkinson, Esq. of the co. of Westmoreland, and by the latter had issue,

Richard-Thomas, his heir
Sarah-Margaret, *m.* to Henry-Nelson Smith, Esq. of Great Russell-street, London, and *d.* in June, 1837.
Emma, *m.* to Thomas-T. Smith, Esq. of Bolton-street, London.

Mr. Gilpin *d.* 3 Jan. 1841.

Arms—Or, a boar, passant, sa.
Crest—Three spears, one in pale, and two in saltier, or, headed arg., tied with a scroll, bearing for
Motto—Une Foy mesme.
Seat—Hockliffe Grange, co. Bedford.

GISBORNE OF YOXALL LODGE.

Gisborne, Thomas-Guy, Esq. of Yoxall Lodge, co. Stafford, *m.* 7 Aug. 1849, Emily-Wingfield, eldest dau. of Frederic, present Lord Saye and Sele.

Lineage.—The Gisbornes, originally from Hartington, Derbyshire, migrated to the county town of Derby, and a member of the family, for more than 200 years after, almost without exception, filled the office of mayor.

John Gisborne, Esq. of Derby, *b.* in 1644, *m.* Catherine, dau. and co-heiress of John Fowler, Esq., and by her had issue,

I. John, J.P., twice mayor of Derby, *b.* in 1675, *m.*, and had issue,

Dorothy, *b.* in 1704, *m.* to Thomas-Godfrey Lushington, Esq. of Sittingbourn, in the co. of Kent, uncle of Sir Stephen Lushington, Bart., M.P.
Catherine, *b.* in 1706, *m.* to Cookin Sole, Esq. of Sittingbourn.

II. Thomas, ancestor of this branch.
III. James, in holy orders, rector of Staveley, co. Derby, prebendary of Durham, *b.* in 1687, *m.* Anne, dau. of W. Jackson, M.D., and *d.* 7 Sept. 1759, leaving issue,

1 Francis, rector of Staveley, *d. unm.* 29 July, 1821.
2 Thomas, physician to the King, and for some time president of the College of Physicians, *d. unm.* in 1806.
3 James, a general in the army, M.P., and commander-in-chief of the forces in Ireland, who *m.* Mary-Anne, dau. and co-heiress of John Boyd, Esq., and *d.* 20 Feb. 1778, leaving

Frederick, his heir.
Catherine, *m.* to the Hon. Vesey Knox, brother of Thomas, Earl of Ranfurly.
Mary-Alicia, *m.* to Major Burke.
Dorothea, *m.* to Alexander Gordon, Esq., brother of David Gordon, Esq. of Florida, co. Down.

4 Dorothy, *m.* to Samuel Foxlow, Esq. of Staveley.
5 Catherine, *m.* to the Rev. Fletcher Dixon, LL.D., vicar of Duffield, and *d.* 25 April, 1796.
6 Anne, *m.* to Isaac Hawkins, Esq.

I. Elizabeth, *b.* in 1685, *m.* to Nathaniel Edwards, M.D., of Derby.
II. Sarah, *m.* 27 April, 1707, to William Orton, Esq of Leicester.

The 2nd son,

Thomas Gisborne, Esq. of Derby, J.P., five times mayor of that town, *b.* in 1680; *m.* in Dec. 1715, Temperance, dau. of Robert Packer, Esq. of Shillingford, Berks, and *d.* 9 Dec. 1760, leaving an only son,

John Gisborne, Esq. of Yoxall, Stafford, who *m.* Anne, dau. of William Bateman, Esq. of Derby, and *d.* 15 Feb. 1779, having had issue,

Thomas, his heir.
John, of Darley Dale, who *m.* 13 Oct. 1792, Millicent, dau. of Edward-Scheverell Chandos-Pole, Esq. of Radborne, in the co. of Derby, and has issue,

John, his heir.
Harriet-Millicent, who *m.* 22 July, 1828, to the Rev. Richard-Burton Pidcock.
Caroline-Anne, *m.* to the Rev. T.-A. Rickards.
Charlotte, *m.* 20 Nov. 1872, to the Rev. Edward-George Simcox.

Temperance, *m.* to Sir Hugh Bateman, Bart.

The eldest son,

Rev. Thomas Gisborne, of Yoxall Lodge, a prebendary of Durham, was the author of many works, which obtained great favour with the public. He *m.* 1 March 1783, Mary, only dau. of Thomas Babington, Esq. of Rothley Temple, co. Leicester, and had issue,

Thomas, his heir.
Thomas-John, who *m.* Sally Krechmer, of St. Petersburgh.
William, in the Ceylon civil service, who *m.* in 1818, Mary-Elizabeth, only dau. by his 2nd marriage, of the Hon. and Rev. Thomas-James Twiselton, D.D., son of Thomas Lord Saye and Sele.
James, in holy orders, curate of Barton.
Mathew, *m.* to Anne, dau. of the Rev. David Browne, M.A.
Walter, of Horridgehouse, in the co. of Derby, Esq.
Mary, who *m.* in 1820, William Evans, Esq., M.P., of Allestree Hall.
Lydia, who *m.* 20 Dec. 1824, to the Rev. Edmund Robinson, of Thorpe Green, in the co. of York.

He *d.* in 1846, and was *s.* by his son,

Thomas Gisborne, Esq. of Yoxall Lodge, J.P. and D.L., M.P. successively for the borough of Stafford, the county of Derby, and the town of Carlow; who *m.* 1st, Elizabeth-Fysche, dau. of John Palmer, Esq. of Ickwell co. Bedford, and sister of Charles Fysche Palmer, Esq., M.P.; and 2ndly, 1826, Susan, widow of Francis Duckenfield Astley, Esq. of Duckenfield. By the former (who *d.* 20 June, 1823); he left issue,

Thomas-Guy, now of Yoxall Lodge.
Henry-Fysche, John Bowdler, } both deceased.
Elizabeth-Maria, *m.* 1835, the Hon. John-Duncan Bligh, 2nd son of John, 4th Earl of Darnley, and *d.* 1837.

Arms—Erminois, a lion, rampant, sable, collared, arg., on a canton, vert, a garb, or.
Crest—A demi-lion, ermine, collared, dovetail, or, and issuing out of a mural coronet, arg.
Seat—Yoxall Lodge, co. Stafford.

GLASCOTT OF ALDERTON.

Glascott, William-Madden, Esq. of Alderton, co. Wexford, *b.* 1806, J.P., high-sheriff 1833; *m.* 1836, Elizabeth-Harriet-Lucy, dau. of Major James Boyd, of Rosslare, co. Wexford, by Georgina his wife, dau. of Hon. George Jocelyn, and has issue,

I. William, *b.* July, 1837.
II. James-Jocelyn, *b.* April, 1845.
I. Georgina-Elizabeth. II. Bessie-Dorothea.
III. Lucy-Sophia. IV. Mary-Isabel.
V. Amy-Sarah.

Mr. Glascott *s.* his father 29 Sept. 1829.

Lineage.—This family is a branch of the ancient family of Glascock of High Estre, in Essex, and settled in Wexford during the civil wars in 1641, from which time the name has been always called Glascott.

John Glascock, of High Estre, in Essex, was living in the year 1365, the 38th of Edward III. He *m.* Alice Trenchfield, and was *s.* by his son,

Edward Glascock, of High Estre, who *m.* Isabella Wallop, and was *s.* by his son,

Thomas Glascock, of High Estre, who *m.* Agnes Fitz-Ralph, and was *s.* by his son,

William Glascock, of High Estre, who *m.* Joan, dau. of Thomas Tendering, and was *s.* by his son,

Richard Glascock, of High Estre, who *m.* Anne Channey and was *s.* by his son,

John Glascock, of High Estre, who *m.* Elizabeth, dau. of John Blount, and was *s.* by his son,

Richard Glascock, of High Estre, who *m.* Margaret, dau. of John Poyntz, and was *s.* by his son,

William Glascock, of High Estre, who *m.* Jane Wilde, and was *s.* by his son,

John Glascock, of High Estre, a lieut.-col. in the army, *m.* Joan Howe, an heiress, and had issue,

John, of High Estre, *m.* Anne Grantnam, and carried on the line in Essex.
Thomas. Edward.
William, of whom we treat, as the founder of the Glascott family in Ireland.

The 4th son,

William Glascott, went over to Ireland in the year 1649, taking with him a troop of horse. He and his soldiers were rewarded for their services with grants of land in the co. of Wexford. William Glascott purchased the debentures from the rest of the troop, and fixed his residence at Aldertown (then called by the Irish name Ballyfearnoge). He *m.* Alice, dau. of James Rowles, Esq., and had issue,

I. John, his successor.
II. James, attainted by James II. in 1689. He *d. unm.*, and administration was taken out to him by his brother, John Glascott, 23 April, 1692.
III. William.
IV. Benjamin, also attainted by James II. He was buried at Whitechurch, co. Wexford, 23 Oct. 1723.
V. Thomas, settled in Devonshire, and *m.* in 1706, Mrs. Harris, a widow, dau. of — Noel, Esq., and had a son,
Thomas Glascott, *b.* in 1709; *m.* in 1730, Elizabeth, dau. of — Deere, Esq., and left a son,
Rev. Cradock Glascott, *b.* 1742; vicar of Hatherleigh, Devon; *m.* 1784, Mary, dau. of William Edmonds, Esq., and widow of Boyle Arthur, Esq.; and *d.* in Aug. 1832, having had issue,
Rev. Cradock-John Glascott, rector of Seaton, in Devonshire, *m.* in 1814, Georgina-Goodwin, dau. of Edmond-Fearon Bourke, Esq. (of the same family as the old Viscounts Bourke *of Mayo*, now dormant), and has had issue,
Edmond-Bourke Glascott, *d. unm.*
Anne-Jane, *m.* in 1842, Frederick Elton, Esq. of Clifton.
Georgina. Edith.
Mary-Anne, *m.* 1854, to Capt. Alfred-John de Haveland Harris.
William, H.E.I.C.S., *b.* 1789; *d. unm.* 1830.
Thomas, rector of Rodborough, in Gloucestershire, *m.* Caroline, dau. of — Morris, Esq., and has, with seven daus., a son, Rev. Cholmondely-Cradock Glascott.
Mary-Anne, wife of Samuel Walkey, Esq. of Exeter.
Selina, *d. unm.*
VI. Elizabeth, wife of — Webb, Esq.
VII. Alice, wife of — Rowles, Esq.
VIII. Mary, wife of — Dodd, Esq.

William Glascott *d.* in 1679, and was *s.* by his eldest son,

John Glascott, Esq. of Aldertown, who was also attainted. He *m.* Anne, dau. of Robert Perrott, of Cooldfin, Queen's County, Esq., and co-heiress of her brother, Richard Perrott, of Darmouth, Devonshire, Esq. By her (who *d.* 24 March, 1732, and was buried at Whitechurch,) he had issue,

George, his successor. John, *d. unm.*
Juliana, wife of Quarter-master Martyn.
Hester, *d. unm.*

John Glascott *d.* in 1737, and was *s.* by his eldest son,

George Glascott, Esq. of Aldertown, who *m.* (settlement dated 24 Oct. 1729) Anne, dau. of William Gifford, Esq. of Poulmaloe (now called Pilltown), co. Wexford, and by her (who *d.* in 1773) had issue,

I. Francis, who inherited his mother's property of Pilltown. He *m.* Sarah, eldest dau. and sole heiress of William Stephens, Esq., M.D. of Chilcolm, co. Kilkenny, and *d.* 29 Dec. 1798, aged 75 years, leaving issue.

GLA

1 George-Stephens, in holy orders, lost in his yacht in the Bristol channel, *unm.* 1787.
2 William, in holy orders, successor to his uncle.
3 John, of Creaken, *m.* Susanna Tree, an American. He was buried at Whitechurch 13 April, 1817; and she was buried at the same place 13 June, 1818, leaving issue,
Francis, R.N., *d. unm.*
John, went to America.
William, went to America
Sarah. Anne.
4 Francis, *d. unm.* 5 Thomas, *d. unm.*
1 Elizabeth, wife of John Rogers, and left one dau., who *d.* young.

II. John, *s.* at Aldertown.
III. George, of Ballynamona, bapt. 17 Feb. 1732, inherited the Perrott estates under his father's will; *m.* 11 Nov. 1761, Deborah, eldest dau. of Adam Rogers, Esq. of Bolderan, co. Wexford, by whom (who *d.* in 1798. Her will was proved 10 Jan. 1799) he had issue,
1 George, of Fruit Hill, co. Wexford, *m.* 4 July, 1798, Mary-Anne, dau. of Thomas De Rinzy, Esq. of Clobemon Hall, co. Wexford; and *d.* in July, 1838, having had by her (who *d.* 11 Dec. 1820) the following issue,
Henrietta, *m.* to Pelham Babington, Esq. of Glandine, co. Wexford.
Isabella, *d. unm.* 13 Aug. 1846.
Mary-Anne, *d.* young. Julia-Anna.
2 Adam, capt. in the Wexford militia, was buried in Whitechurch, 22 April, 1816; *m.* 10 March, 1799, Sarah, dau. of Thomas Gifford, Esq. of New Ross, by whom (who *d.* in 1838) he had, George, *d. unm.* in 1834; Gifford, lieut. H.E.I.C., *d. unm.* 11 Aug. 1842; Adam-Gifford, lieut. R.N.; John, a surgeon in Constantinople; Jane, *m.* Rev. Thomas-John Jacob; and Annabella.
3 John, of whom below.
1 Isabella, *d. unm.* 17 Feb. 1831.
2 Anne, *d. unm.* 21 Feb. 1830.
3 Deborah, *d. unm.* in May, 1840.
4 Julia, *d.* young in 1802.

George Glascott made his will 10 Sept. 1780; and *d.* 30 Jan. 1788. By his will he devised Killowen to his 3rd son, viz.,

John Glascott, of Killowen, co. Wexford, captain in the Wexford militia, *b.* 1 March, 1778; *m.* 1798, Beata, eldest dau. of Henry Archer, Esq. of Ballyseskin, co. Wexford, by whom (who *d.* 22 Dec. 1850) he had issue,

John, now of Killowen.
George, *b.* 6 Jan. 1806; *m.* 31 Oct. 1835, Wilhelmina, eldest dau. of John-Lloyd Edwardes, Esq. of Camolin Park, co. Wexford, and has one dau., Wilhelmina-Eliza-Deane.
Archer, *d.* young.
Adam, *b.* 9 Dec. 1809; *m.* Aug. 1849, Susan-Emily, dau. of John Usher, Esq. of Landscape, co. Wexford; and *d.* without issue 10 Dec. 1852.
Elizabeth.
Julia, *d. unm.* 1832.
Beata, *m.* 12 April, 1845, John-Symes Gifford, captain H.E.I.C.S.

Captain John Glascott, of Killowen, *d.* 6 Sept. 1841. His eldest son is the present

John Glascott, Esq. of Killowen, barrister-at-law, *b.* 24 Nov. 1802; *m.* 9 Dec. 1829, Mary, dau. of Richard Donovan, Esq. of Ballymore, co. Wexford, and has,

John-Henry, *b.* 13 Sept. 1830.
Richard-Donovan, *b.* 12 Sept. 1833.
George-Anneslay, *b.* 1 Feb. 1835.
William-Edward, *b.* 13 June, 1838.
Robert-Richards, *b.* 24 Nov. 1840.
Anne-Beata. Mary-Donovan.

IV. William, *d.* 1776; *m.* Arabella, dau. of William Stephens, Esq. of Chilcolm, co. Kilkenny, by whom (who *d.* 16 June, 1807) he had issue,
1 William, lieut. 16th lancers, bapt. 17 Feb. 1770; *d.* in 1828; *m.* 1st, Anne, dau. of — Maguire, Esq., and had,
William, capt. 66th regt.; *m.* Sarah, dau. of Marmaduke Cramer, Esq. of Rathmore, co. Cork, by whom he left four daus., who went to Australia.
George.
He *m.* 2ndly, Sophia-Letitia, dau. of Sir George Strickland, Bart. of Boynton Hall, Yorkshire, by whom he had,
Strickland, *b.* in 1808.
Arabella, *m.* Adam Roxborough, Esq. of Gourock Castle, Renfrewshire.
1 Wilelmina, wife of John Lynn, Esq. of Fethard, co. Wexford. She *d.* in Sept. 1849.
2 Anne, *d.* in June, 1838; *m.* Francis Cherry, Esq. of Waterford, and left one dau., Frances, wife of Rev. James Hewetson.
3 Arabella, *d.* July, 1838, *m.* to Rev. Walter Stephens, of Hibla, co. Kildare.
V. Thomas, *b.* 1750; *d. unm.* 8 Feb. 177?.

I. Anne, m. to Mitchelbourne Symes, Esq. of Coolboye, co Wicklow.
II. Margaret, d. in March, 1791; m. 5 March, 1764, William Gifford, Esq. of Ballysop, co. Wexford.
III. Julia, buried at Whitechurch, 5 Feb. 1814, Major Robin Boyd.
IV. Elizabeth, d. 28 Sept. 1795; m. 6 July, 1770, Sir Edward Pickering, Bart of Titchmarsh, Northumberland.

George Glascott, of Aldertown, by his will, dated 17 May, 1750, devised his wife's property, Piltown, &c., to his eldest son, Francis Glascott, the Aldertown property to his 2nd son, John Glascott, and the Perrott property, derived from his mother, to his 3rd son, George Glascott (the ancestor of the Killowen family). He d. 10 April, 1755, and was s. at Aldertown by his 2nd son,

JOHN GLASCOTT, Esq. of Aldertown, or Alderton, bapt. 24 Jan. 1731, m. 1st, Elizabeth, sister of Richard Boyse, Esq. of Grange, near Bannow, co Wexford. She d. in 1761, aged 34, leaving no issue. He m. 2ndly, 18 July, 1769, Lucy, dau. of Rickard Donovan, Esq. of Clonmore, co. Wexford, by whom (who was buried at Whitechurch, 15 March, 1827) he had no issue. He d. himself 10 Dec. 1810, and devised all his property to the eldest surviving son of his brother, Francis Glascott, of Piltown, viz.,

THE REV. WILLIAM GLASCOTT, of Alderton and Pilltown, chaplain to his Majesty's fort of Duncannon, and rector of Ballyhack, co Wexford, b. 1755; m. Elizabeth, dau. of the Rev. Samuel Madden, by whom (who d. 22 May, 1851) he had issue,

John, b. 1798; d. young.
WILLIAM-MADDEN, his successor.
Elizabeth, m. 29 March, 1815, Rev. James-Morgan Stubbs, rector of Rossdroit, co. Wexford; and d. 1847.
Sarah, d. unm. 22 July, 1829.
Lucy, m. to John Usher, Esq. of Landscape, co. Wexford.
Cassandra, m. to Richard-Wybrants Atkinson, Esq. of Coldblow House, co. Dublin.
Wilelmina.
Margaret, d. unm. 7 Aug. 1817.
Arabella, d. unm. 30 Nov. 1823.

The Rev. William Glascott d. 29 Sept. 1829, and was s. by his only surviving son, the present WILLIAM-MADDEN GLASCOTT, of Alderton and Pilltown.

There is also at present another branch of the same family settled in Ireland, who retain the original name of Glascock. They spring from (see Morant's *History of Essex*, Library, Trinity College, Dublin) William Glascock, of Downe Hall, in Essex, which he obtained by a grant from King HENRY VIII., dated 8 June, 1540. He also purchased property from one Walter Farre, by deed, 28 June, 1579. He was a junior branch of the same family settled at High Estre. He d. 3 Dec. 1579, and was s. by his son,

RICHARD GLASCOCK, of Downe Hall, b. 1547; m. Elizabeth, dau. of William Browne, of Bobingworth, and had

I. Richard, of Downe Hall, m. Elizabeth, dau. of Thomas Rowles, of Wellington, Herts; and d. 5 Feb. 1624, leaving an only dau., his sole heiress,
Elizabeth, who d. 13 Sept. 1649, and was buried at Matching Church, Essex. She m. John Ballet, who d. 28 Dec. 1683.
II. ROBERT, of whom below. III Philip.

Richard Glascock was s. in Downe Hall by his son, who left it to his dau., and thus it went out of the family. The family treated of sprung from the 2nd son,

ROBERT GLASCOCK, who settled in Ireland, and from him descended

FRANCIS GLASCOCK, of Music Hall, co. Dublin, who m. Mary, dau. of James Whyte, Esq., and had issue,

I. James, m. 1765, Katherine, dau. of Roger Jones, Esq. of Dollardstown, co. Meath, and left one dau. and heiress,
Ellen-Katherine, who m. in July, 1787, Morley Saunders, Esq. of Saunders Grove, co. Wicklow.
II. WALTER, of whom below.
III. Charles, d. without issue.
IV. Henry, d. without issue.

As the eldest son d. without male issue, the line was carried on by the 2nd son,

WALTER GLASCOCK, who m. Jane, dau. of William Aldrick, lord-mayor of Dublin in 1741 and 1743, and had issue (with a dau., Mary, who m. the Rev. Chamberlaine Walker, rector of Rosscconnell) a son,

WILLIAM GLASCOCK, who m. Letitia, dau. of Edward Scriven, and had issue,

I. WALTER, assistant-registrar in the Registry Officer, Dublin, m. in 1806, Margaret, dau. of Thomas Webb, Esq. of Roebuck, co. Dublin; and d. 14 Aug. 1852, having had issue,
1 William, d. unm. in 1829.
1 Elizabeth. 2 Anne.

II. Edward, had a son, Edward-Molesworth Glascock, who d. 28 Jan. 1853.
III. William-Nugent Glascock, capt. R.N.
I. Elizabeth, wife of Robert Ross, of Bladensburg. She d. 12 May, 1814.

Arms—Quarterly: 1st and 4th, az., two eagles' claws, erased, barways, arg., armed, or, for GLASCOTT; 2nd and 3rd, gu., three pears, or, on a chief, arg., a demi-lion, rampant, sa., for PERROTT.
Crest—An eagle, displayed, with two heads, per pale, arg. and az.
Motto—Virtute decoratus.
Seat—Alderton, near New Ross.

ROBERTSON-GLASGOW OF MONTGREENAN,

REPRESENTING

ROBERTSON OF PRENDERGUEST AND BROWNSBANK.

ROBERTSON-GLASGOW, ROBERT, Esq. of Montgreenan, co. Ayr, a magistrate of the cos. of Ayr and Renfrew, b. 22 May, 1811; m. 11 July, 1839, Mary-Wilhelmina, dau. of John Campbell, Esq. of Stonefield, Argyllshire, by his wife, Wilhelmina, dau. of Sir James Colquhoun, of Colquhoun and Luss, Bart., co. Dumbarton, and has issue,

I. ROBERT-BRUCE, b. 8 April, 1842.
II. John-Campbell, b. 24 Aug. 1844.
I. Wilhelmina-Colquhoun.

Lineage.—This branch of the family of Robertson, which traditionally claims descent from the ancient family of Strowan, in Perthshire, has possessed lands in the county of Berwick, for considerably upwards of two centuries. In the female line, it represents the family of Seton, of Monkmyline, co. Haddington, lineally descended from Sir Christopher Seton, and Christian Bruce, sister of King ROBERT I. (ROBERT BRUCE) and also descends from Alexander, 1st Lord Home, and traces through the families of Ninewells and Bassendean, a near relationship to the two most distinguished members of that family, in the literature of Scotland, one direct ancestor of the present representative, having been cousin-german to David Hume the historian, and another standing in the same relationship, to John Home, the author of *Douglas*.

In 1624, WILLIAM ROBERTSON acquired by purchase from Alexander Meirns, certain lands and heritages in the parish of Eyemouth, in Berwickshire, sasine, dated 8 Nov. 1624. He was s. by his eldest son,

JOHN ROBERTSON, who takes sasine of the same land in 1638, and dying prior to 1668, was s. by his eldest son,

WILLIAM ROBERTSON, who m. Margaret Sinclair, in whose favour he executed a disposition of a portion of his property, in life rent, and to his eldest son WILLIAM, in fee, dated 10 Feb. 1678, he d. previous to 10 Sept. 1686, leaving with other children,

WILLIAM, afterwards of Monkmyline, and,
Elizabeth, m. Andrew Home, Esq. of Fernyside, by whom she left an only child and heiress,
Elizabeth of Fernyside, of whom afterwards,

The eldest son,

WILLIAM ROBERTSON, m. Margaret Seton, heiress of Robert Seton, of Monkmyine, co. Haddington, and acquired that property. He d. in 1720, leaving issue,

WILLIAM, his successor.
Robert, of Prenderguest, and Brownsbank, and afterwards of Fernyside, b. 4 Nov. 1713.
Isabella, m. to William Graeme, Esq. of Jordanstown, by whom she had three sons and a dau. Mr. Graeme died 11 Nov. 1775, aged 87.

The eldest son,

WILLIAM ROBERTSON, of Monkmyine, m. Anne Renton, dau. of Renton, of Lamberton, in Berwickshire, and d. s. p. 7 Aug. 1738. His widow, known as Mrs. Robertson, of Blackadder, from the place of her residence, survived him for many years. He was s. by his brother,

ROBERT ROBERTSON, of Prenderguest and Brownsbank, b. 4 Nov. 1713, m. 1st, 22 Nov. 1743, Margaret, dau. of the Rev. George Home, of Chirnside, (2nd son of Alexander Home, of Kennetsidehead, executed unjustly for high treason, 29 Dec. 1682, *(vide Woodrow's History)* by his wife, Catherine, dau. of Home, of Ninewells.) This lady was cousin-german, of David Hume the Historian. The issue of this marriage were,

I. ALEXANDER, b. Nov. 1748.
II. William-Robert, of Eyemouth b. 2 March, 1761; d.

7 July, 1833; m. 1801, Margaret, dau. of John Jameson, Esq., sheriff clerk of Clackmannanshire, by whom he had issue,

1 Robert, advocate, b. 1802; m. 1827, Alicia-Catherine, eldest dau. of the late Rev. Charles Eustace, of Robertstown, co. Kildare, heir-male and representative of the ancient Viscounts of Baltinglass, (see Burke's Peerage,) and has issue,

Robert-Jameson Eustace, capt. 60th Royal Rifles, b. 8 Jan. 1828.
Charles-Eustace, b. 7 May, 1840.
Alicia-Trimlestoun, m. 1849, James Jameson, Esq., Airfield, co. Dublin.
Helen-Margaret, b. 27 April, 1834; d. 28 Aug. 1838.

2 John-Jameson, of Gledeswood, co. Dublin, b. 1804; m. 1837, Mary-Anne, dau. of William Cairnes, Esq. of Stameen, co. Meath, and has issue,

William. Robert.
James. Albert.
Helen. Mary-Anne.
Alice-Susan.

3 William, Rev. of New Grey Friars, one of the ministers of Edinburgh, b. 1805; m. 1834, Georgiana-Touchet, dau. of John Cossins, Esq., of Weymouth, by his wife, the Hon. Elizabeth-Susanna, dau. of George, 18th Lord Audley, and has issue,

William-Buxton, b. 2 June, 1835, 79th regt.
John-Hay, b. 20 Dec. 1843.
Henry-Robert, b. 12 Jan. 1845; d. 1855.
George-Touchet, b. 14 July, 1847.
Gertrude-Susan-Audley, b. 17 July, 1849.

I. Margaret, m. her cousin, the Rev. George Home, of Monkrigg, co. Haddington and of Gunsgreen House, co. Berwick, and died Dec. 1828, leaving issue,

1 Abram, of Gunsgreen House, co. Berwick, m. Susan Anderson, of Montrave, and had issue; he d. 1856.
1 Jean, m. William-Forman Home, of Wedderburn and Billie, and had issue.
2 Elizabeth, m. Rev. George Tough, and had issue.
3 Hay, d. unm.

II. Catherine, d. unm., 15 Feb. 1815.
III. Jean, m. Thomas Potts, Esq., grandson (maternally) of Haig, of Bomerside, d. Feb. 1786, leaving issue a son,

Thomas, of the Daison, Torquay, Devonshire.

IV. Isobell, m. John Aitken, Esq. of London, merchant, d. Dec. 1806, leaving issue,

1 John, of London, merchant.
2 Alexander, lieut., R.N.

V. Robina, m. her cousin, William Murray, grandson of Home, of Kennetsidehead, d. Nov. 1832, s. p.
VI. Elizabeth, d. unm., 4 April, 1778.

Robert Robertson, of Prenderguest, m. 2nd, 15. Dec. 1761, Anne Martin, of Headrigg, co. Berwick, and 3rd, 23 Dec. 1778, his cousin-german, Elizabeth Home, of Ferneyside, widow of William McFarlane Brown, of Dalgowrie, and Kirkton, Esq., but had no issue by either of these marriages. His 3rd wife d. 9 July, 1785,* and her husband, 30 July, 1788, when he was s. by his eldest son,

Alexander Robertson, of Prenderguest, Brownsbank, and Gunsgreen, m. 24 Aug. 1773, Philadelphia Lambe, dau. and heiress of Rev. Robert Lambe, rector of Norham, and had issue,

I. Robert, his successor.
II. William, M.D., m. Isabella-Mary, dau. of — Abbs, Esq. of Newcastle, and sister of Major Abbs, s. p.
III. Alexander-Lambe, Writer to the Signet, m. Catherine, dau. of John Alison, Esq. of Wellbank, co. Forfar, and has issue.
IV. George-Home, (Rev.) of Ladykirk, m. Elizabeth, dau. of — Kenney, Esq. of St. Catherine's, co. Edinburgh; died, leaving issue.
V. John-Argyll, M.D., F.R.S., b. 12 Aug. 1800; m. 1st, 5 May, 1823, Annie, dau. and co-heiress of Charles Lockhart, Esq. of Newhall, co. Cromarty, (grandson of Sir Jas. Lockhart, Bart., of Carstairs,) and has issue,

1 Charles-Alexander Lockart, M.D., b. 4 April, 1824.
2 Frederick-Lockart (Rev.), b. 28 Dec. 1828.

He m. 2ndly, Elizabeth, dau. of Charles Wightman, Esq. of the Island of Tobago, and has issue, Charles-Edward, and other children.

VI. James-Home, (Rev.) of Coldingham, m. Jane, dau. of John Dickson, Esq. of Peelwalls, Berwickshire, d. leaving issue.
I. Philadelphia, unm.

* The estate of Ferneyside had been settled by Elizabeth Home on the 2nd son of her husband and nearest relative, William Robert, of Eyemouth, but owing to a family quarrel, this destination was revoked, and her estate was disposed by her to a more distant relative, Sir Abram Hume, of Wormlieburgh, Baronet, and is now possessed by his descendant the present Earl Brownlow, who assumes the names of Hume and Egerton. (Vide Burke's Peerage. Vide also Playfair's Baronetage, Hume, of Wormlieburgh.)

II. Margaret, m. Peter Wishart, Esq. of Foxhall, (of the ancient family of Pitarrow) and had issue.
III. Mary, m. Hugh Vietch, Esq. of Stewartfield, grandson of Vietch of Elliock, co. Dumfries, and has issue.
IV. Anne.
V. Doria, m. Joseph Hume, Esq. of Horndean, co. Berwick, and of Lochcoat, co Linlithgow, and has issue.
VI. Jane, d. unm.

Mr. Robertson d. Oct. 1804, and was s. by his eldest son,

Robert Robertson, Esq. of Prenderguest, Brownsbank, and Gunsgreen, co. Berwick, m. 2 Aug. 1804, Anne, dau. of Robert Glasgow, Esq. of Montgreenan, co. Ayr, and in consequence of that marriage, acquired the estate of Montgreenan, in Ayrshire, and also the property of Glenarbach, in the county of Dumbarton, he had issue to survive youth

Robert, now of Montgreenan.
Philadelphia-Jane.
Anne, m. George-Sherbrooke Airey, Esq., lieut. R.N., son of the late General Sir George Airey.
Charlotte-Marie-Cecilia, m. the Rev. George Drake, of Stourton rectory, Wilts, who died in 1849, leaving one dau. Alice.

Mr. Robertson, on succeeding to Montgreenan, assumed the name of Glasgow only, and dying 27 Jan. 1845, was s. by his only surviving son the present Robert-Robertson-Glasgow, of Montgreenan.

Arms—Quarterly: 1st and 4th, arg., a cocoa-nut tree growing out of a mount in base, vert; on a chief, az., a shakefork, between a martlet on the dexter and a fish naiant on the sinister, arg. 2nd, gu., three wolves' heads, erased, arg. 3rd, or, three crescents, within a tressure, flory, counterflory, gu.
Crest—A cubit arm, erect, holding an Imperial crown, all ppr.
Motto—Quo fas et gloria.
Seat—Montgreenan, co. Ayr.
Residence—Blackstone House, co. Renfrew.

Family of Seton of Monkmyline.

Dougal de Seton, temp. Alexander I. was s. by his son,

Secker de Seton, s. by his son, d. circa, 1150, leaving a son,

Philip de Seton, m. a dau. of Waldene, Earl of Dunbar, and left with other issue, a son,

Sir Alexander de Seton, d. 1248, leaving a son,

Serlo de Seton, father of,

Sir Alexander Seton, father of

Sir Christopher Seton, who m. Christian Bruce, sister of King Robert I., and relict of Gretney, 11th Earl of Mar, and left by her an only son,

Sir Alexander Seton, of Seton, d. in 1337, who was s. by his grandson,

John Lord Seton, created prior to 1449, who was father of

John, Master of Seton, (predeceased his father) who had three sons, of whom the 3rd, Alexander, was Baillie of Tranent.

The said Alexander Seton, baillie of Tranent, was father of

John Seton, of Monkmyline, who was father of

John Seton, of Monkmyline, who was father of George Seton, and of John Seton, of Monkmyline.

The said John Seton, of Monkmyline, temp. 1586, was father of

John Seton, of Monkmyline, father of

Robert Seton, of Monkmyline, (temp. 1628,) father of

Robert, of Monkmyline, temp. 1641, father of

Robert, of Monkmyline, father of

Margaret Seton, of Monkmyline, who m. William Robertson.

GLASGOW OF OLD COURT.

Glasgow, Alexander, Esq. of Old Court, co. Cork, J.P., b. 1 Nov. 1792; m. 4 April, 1826, Ellen, dau. of William Smith, Esq. of Muirbank, co. Lanark, N.B., and has had issue,

I. John, b. 1 Jan. 1827, lieut. in the 4th Dragoon Guards, d. 15 Aug. 1851.
II. William, b. 28 May, 1831, m. 31 July, 1855, Dora, eldest dau. of Bernard-Robert Shaw, Esq. of Monkstown, co. Cork.
I. Jessy, m. 7 June, 1853, to Edmund Eyre Newenham, Esq. of Maryborough Park, co. Cork.

Mr. Glasgow, formerly of Auchinraith, co. Lanark, merchant in Glasgow, and now a magistrate for the county, is eldest son of the late John Glasgow, Esq. of Glasgow (who *d.* in 1821), and Helen Smith his wife, and grandson of Alexander Glasgow, also of Glasgow, merchant, by Mary Monro his wife; he has one brother, James.

Arms—Arg., an oak tree growing out of a mount in base, vert; on a chief gu., a garb, between two crescents, or.
Crest—An eagle, rising from a rock, ppr.
Motto—Dominus providebit.
Seat—Old Court, co. Cork.

UPTON-GLEDSTANES OF FARDROSS.

UPTON-GLEDSTANES, AMBROSE, Esq. of Fardross, co. Tyrone, *b.* 22 Feb. 1802; *m.* 2 Oct. 1828, Cecilia, dau. of Richard Hornidge, Esq., D.L., of Tulfarris, co. Wicklow, and Elizabeth his wife, dau. of Hugh Henry, Esq. of Lodge Park, co. Kildare. Mr. Upton-Gledstanes has served as high-sheriff for co. Fermanagh.

Lineage.—The family of Gledstanes was settled in Tyrone before the reformation.

In 1688, CAPTAIN JAMES GLEDSTANES equipped at his own expense, a body of yeomen, and led them to the relief of Derry, for which he received a certificate, and the thanks of Governor Walker. The great-grandfather of Mr. Upton, Gledstanes,

JAMES GLEDSTANES, Esq. of Fardross, *m.* Miss Graham, of Hockley, near Armagh, and his grand-uncle, Thomas Gledstanes, *d. unm.*, leaving three sisters, his co-heirs; one *m.* Jacob, the other *m.* King, and the eldest MARGARET GLEDSTANES, *m.* in 1767, AMBROSE UPTON, Esq. Major in 18th Dragoons. They both *d.* in 1804, leaving a son,

WHITNEY UPTON, Esq. who took the surname of GLEDSTANES. He *m.* 1st, about 1795, Isabella, dau. of Moutray, Esq. of Favour Royal, co. Tyrone, which lady *d. s. p.* He *m.* 2ndly, in 1799, Emily, dau. of Michael Aylmer, Esq. of Courtown, co. Kildare, and by her, (who *d.* in 1811,) had, besides a son, who *d.* in infancy, and a dau., Frances, who *d.* in 1818, an only surviving son, the present AMBROSE UPTON GLEDSTANES, Esq. of Fardross. Mr. Upton Gledstanes, *d.* in 1805 or 1806.

Arms—Arg., a savage's head, couped, distilling drops of blood, and thereupon a bonnet composed of bay and holly leaves, all ppr., within an orle of eight martlets, sa.
Crest—A griffin issuing out of a wreath, holding a sword in its right talon, ppr.
Motto—Fide et virtute.
Seat—Fardross, co. Tyrone.

GLEGG OF OLD WITHINGTON AND GAYTON HALL.

BASKERVYLE-GLEGG, JOHN, Esq. of Old Withington, and Gayton Hall, co. Chester, J.P. and D.L., high-sheriff 1814, *b.* 27 April, 1784; *m.* 4 May, 1811, Anne, dau. of Thomas-Townley Parker, Esq. of Cuerden Hall, and Extwistle, co. Lancaster, by Susan his wife, dau. and heir of Peter Brooke, Esq. of Astley, co. Lancaster, and has issue,

I. JOHN. II. William.
I. Susan-Mary. II. Anne-Jane.
III. Susan-Fanny, *m.* Edward Hopwood, Esq., eldest son of R.-G. Hopwood, Esq. of Hopwood Hall, Lancashire.
IV. Emily. V. Lucy-Charlotte.

Lineage.—The Baskervyles were possessed of estates at Withington as early as the reign of EDWARD III. SIR JOHN BASKERVYLE, grantee of a moiety of Old Withington in 1266, was great-grandfather of

THOMAS BASKERVYLE, Esq. of Old Withington 10 RICH. II., who *m.* Idonea, dau. of John de Blurton, of Newcastle, co. Stafford, and was father of WILLIAM BASKERVYLE, Esq. of Old Withington, whose son and heir, by Catherine his wife, RANDLE BASKERVYLE, Esq. of Old Withington, *m.* Agnes, dau. and co-heir of George Bostock, of Modburleigh, 2nd son of Sir Adam Bostock, Lord of Bostock, and was grandfather of WILLIAM BASKERVYLE, Esq. of Old Withington, who *m.* 19 HENRY VII., Agnes, dau. of John Mainwaring, Esq. of Peover, and by her was father of GEORGE BASKERVYLE, Esq. of Old Withington, whose eldest son, by Elizabeth his wife, WILLIAM BASKERVYLE, Esq. of Old Withington, was father, by Emma his 1st wife, dau. of John Wynington, of Hermitage, of THOMAS BASKERVYLE, Esq. of Old Withington, who *m.* Margery, dau. and co-heiress of Thomas Kynsey, of Blackden, and by her left a son and heir, THOMAS BASKERVYLE, Esq. of Old Withington and Blackden, living in 1603, who *m.* 1st, Dorothea, dau. of Ralph Adderley, Esq. of Coton Hall, co. Stafford; and 2ndly, Dorothea, dau. of Hugh Davenport, Esq. of Calveley, and by the former left (with a dau. Margaret, *m.* to Thomas Cotton, Esq.) a son and heir, JOHN BASKERVYLE, Esq. of Old Withington, *b.* in 1599, who *m.* Magdalen, dau. of George Hope, Esq. of Queen's Hope, co. Flint, and of Dodleston, co. Chester, and by her had (with two daus., Katherine, *m.* to Thomas Hand, Esq. of Boughton; and Elizabeth, *m.* to Thomas Cowper, Esq. of Chester) a son and heir, THOMAS BASKERVYLE, Esq. of Old Withington, who *d.* in 1671, leaving, by Margaret his wife, dau. of William Hassall, Esq. an only son, JOHN BASKERVYLE, Esq. of Old Withington and of Blackden, high-sheriff of Cheshire, in 1703, who *m.* Maria, dau. of Edmund Jodrell, Esq. of Yeardsley and Twemlowe, and was father of JOHN BASKERVYLE, Esq. of Old Withington, who *m.* 1 March, 1731, Mary, dau. and finally heiress of ROBERT GLEGG, Esq. of Gayton, by Juliana his wife, dau. of Sir Roger Newdigate, Bart., and granddau. (by Elizabeth his wife, dau. of Sir Robert Cotton, Bart. of Combermere) of SIR WILLIAM GLEGG, of Gayton, knighted by King WILLIAM III. at Gayton Hall, who was the heir male and representative of the ancient Cheshire family of GLEGG, whereupon he assumed the surname of GLEGG, in lieu of his patronymic, and had a son and successor,

JOHN BASKERVYLE-GLEGG, Esq. of Old Withington and Gayton, *b.* in 1741, who *m.* 1st, Bridget, dau. and heir of John Kelsall, Esq. of Dodleston; and 2ndly, Jane, dau. of the Rev. John Parker, of Astle, by the former of whom he left at his decease, 24 Jan. 1821, an only son, the present JOHN BASKERVYLE-GLEGG, Esq. of Old Withington and Gayton.

Arms—Quarterly: 1st and 4th, sa., two lions, counter-passant, in pale, arg., for GLEGG; 2nd and 3rd, arg., a chev., gu., between three hurts, for BASKERVYLE.
Crests—1st, for GLEGG, a hawk, ppr., with wings expanded, preying on a partridge, ppr.; 2nd, for BASKERVYLE, a forester, vested, vert, edged, or, holding over the right shoulder a cross-bow, or, and with the other hand, in a leash, a hound, passant, arg.
Motto—Qui potest capere capiat.
Seats—Old Withington Hall, and Gayton Hall, co. Chester.

GLEGG OF IRBIE AND BACKFORD.

GLEGG, BASKERVYLE, Esq. of Irbie and Backford, co. Chester, late capt. 12th lancers, *s.* his father 9 Dec. 1842.

Lineage.—JOHN GLEGG, Esq. 2nd son of John Glegg, Esq. of Gayton, by his wife a dau. of Poole, of Poole, was grantee of Grange, in the co. Chester, by letters patent, dated 6th of EDWARD VI. His great-grandson, WILLIAM GLEGG, Esq. of Caldey Grange, aged *circa* 24 years of age at the Visitation of 1613. His son,

EDWARD GLEGG, Esq. of Caldey Grange, *b.* in 1622, purchased, in 1655 and 1656, the manor of Irbie, in the co. Chester. By Margaret, his 1st wife, dau. of William Glegg, Esq. of Gayton, a son, WILLIAM, of Caldey Grange, whose great-grandson, William Glegg, sold the manor of Great Caldey, to John Leigh, Esq. By Anne, his 2nd wife, only dau. of Roger Lowndes, Esq. of Overton, in Cheshire, he was father of

EDWARD GLEGG, Esq. of Irbie. This gentleman *m.* Jane, dau. of John Scorer, Gent. of Westminster, and by her left at his decease, in Dec. 1708 (with a dau., Anne, wife of the Rev. John Urmson, of Neston) two sons, JOHN, and Roger, *d. unm.* in 1777. The eldest son,

JOHN GLEGG, Esq. of Irbie, *m.* Frances, eldest dau. of Henry Birkenhead, Esq., and co-heiress of her uncle, Thomas Birkenhead, Esq. of Backford (derived from John de Birkenhead, who flourished *temp.* EDWARD III.), by whom (who *d.* 14 April, 1791) he left at his decease, in 1768, a dau., Mary, *m.* to Robert Dod, Esq. of Rowton, and an only surviving son,

JOHN GLEGG, Esq. of Irbie, who *m.* in 1762, Betty, eldest dau. of John Baskervyle-Glegg, Esq. of Withington and Gayton, by whom (who *d.* 9 July, 1810) he left two sons and a dau., viz.,

BIRKENHEAD, his heir.
John-Baskervyle, *b.* in 1773, a colonel in the army.
Juliana.

Lucy, *m.* to the Rev. J. Egerton.
Jane, *m.* to the Rev. James Bullock.

Mr. Glegg *d.* in 1804, in the 73rd year of his age, was buried at St. Mary's, and *s.* by his elder son,

LIEUT.-GEN. BIRKENHEAD GLEGG, of Backford and Irbie, *b.* 1 Nov. 1765, who *m.* 1st, 4 July, 1804, Emma, 2nd dau. and co-heir of Edward Holt, Esq. of Ince Hall, co. Lancaster, and had by her,

BASKERVYLE, his heir.
Edward-Holt, capt. Rifle Brigade.
Emma-Johanna, *m.* to Lee-Porcher Townshend, Esq.
Mary.

Gen. Glegg *m.* 2ndly, in 1814, Sarah, youngest dau. of the Rev. Henry Barnard, D.D., rector of Maghera, in Derry, and has by her three daus.,

Sarah. Isabella. Eleanor.

The General *d.* 9 Dec. 1842, and was *s.* by his son, the present BASKERVYLE GLEGG, Esq. of Irbie and Backford.

Arms—Quarterly: 1st and 4th, sa., two lions, counter-passant, in pale, arg., a crescent within a crescent, for difference, for GLEGG; 2nd and 3rd, sa., three garbs, or, within a border, arg., for BIRKENHEAD.
Crests—1st, a hawk, with wings expanded, preying on a partridge, all ppr., for GLEGG; 2nd, a goat, salient, arg., attired, or, resting its fore-feet on a garb, for BIRKENHEAD.
Seat—Backford, Cheshire.

GLENDONWYN OF PARTON.

GLENDONWYN, XAVERIA, of Parton, co. Kirkcudbright.

Lineage.—The lineage of this race is deduced by Douglas in his "Baronetage," from Sir Adam Glendonwyn, of Glendonwyn, in the time of King ALEXANDER III. The existing family are directly sprung from King ROBERT III.; their ancestor, Sir Simon Glendoning of that ilk, having *m.* Lady Mary Douglas, dau. of Archibald, 4th Earl of Douglas, by his wife, the Lady Margaret Stewart, dau. of ROBERT III., king of Scotland. The son of this marriage, SIR SIMON GLENDONING, of that ilk, *m.* the lady Elizabeth Lindsay, dau. of Alexander, Earl of Crawford. In 1449, this Sir Simon was one of the guarantees of a treaty of peace with England, together with the Earls of Douglas, Angus, Ross, Murray, Crawford, &c. He was of Parton in 1458, and perhaps yet earlier; but a charter dated in that year, and confirming the barony to him, is still extant. From him descended, in the eleventh generation, the late

WILLIAM GLENDONWYN, Esq. of Parton, who *d.* in 1809, leaving issue by his wife (Agnes Gordon, of Crogo) three daus., viz.,

Mary-Lucy-Elizabeth-Agnes, *m.* Sir James Gordon, Bart. of Letterfourie, in Banffshire, and *d.* in 1845, leaving issue, Sir William Gordon, Bart. of Letterfourie; Robert; Helen; Mary, wife of Mr. Serjeant Shee, M.P., and Alexandrina-Jane.
XAVERIA, by family arrangements the present proprietrix of Parton.
Ismene-Magdalene, wife of William Scott, of Whimpson, in Hampshire (brother of Jane-Elizabeth, countess of Oxford) by whom she has issue William-Glendonwyn, lt.-col. in the army, *m.* Jane Murray, dau. of James Ford, Esq.; Frederick-James, M.D., *m.* Miss Cameron, and has a son, William; and Charles-Glendonwyn.

Arms—Quarterly: arg. and sa., a cross, parted per cross, indented and counterchanged.
Seat—Parton, co, Kircudbright.

GLOVER OF MOUNT GLOVER.

GLOVER, JAMES, Esq. of Mount Glover, co. Cork, *m.* 1813, Ellen, only dau. of John Power, Esq. of Rosskeen, only son of Pierce Power, by Abigail Bullen his wife, and has had issue,

I. EDWARD-AUCHMUTY, J.P., barrister-at-law.
II. James, M.D., *d. unm.* III. John-Power.
IV. Marlborough-Parsons-Stirling-Freeman, *d. unm.*
V. Pierce-Power, *d.* young.
I. Ellen-Alicia-Crofts.
II. Mildred-Lavinia-Freeman, *m.* to Townsend McDermott, Esq., barrister-at-law.
III. Anna-Maria-Stirling.
IV. Mary-Georgina-Somerset, *m.* J. O'Halloran, Esq.

Lineage.—JOHN GLOVER, Esq., the first of the family who settled in Ireland, early in the 17th century, was a near relative of Robert Glover, Esq., the famous genealogist, of the 16th century, and Somerset, herald-at-arms. This JOHN GLOVER was captain in command of a large and efficient regiment of troops under one of the Percivals, and signalized himself in many battles with the native Irish, but more particularly distinguished himself by his obstinate and valiant defence of the "Rath of Anna," which he succeeded in holding against the attacks of an immense body of the Irish, who continued to charge his small but gallant band for three days, when they were compelled to retire with much slaughter. For his remarkable bravery and success on this occasion, as well as for his many other services in the local wars of the times, he obtained possession of many extensive estates in the counties of Cork and Limerick. He *m.* a Miss Mills, sister of Thomas Mills, Esq., and had issue, one son and three daus. The son,

EDWARD GLOVER, *b.* in 1663, *d.* 24 April, 1758; *m.* in 1695, Eleanor, dau. of James Barry, Esq. of Ballinvonere, and had issue, four sons,

I. Edward, *b.* in 1696, and *d.* 28 April, 1742, aged 46, *m.* Miss Quin, and left only one dau., who *m.* her first cousin, Phillip Barry, of Ballinvonere.
II. James, of Four-Mile Waters, *b.* in 1705, *d.* in April, 1753, aged 48, *m.* Miss Maunsell; he leaving no issue, his estates devolved on his 3rd brother, Thomas.
III. THOMAS, of whom presently.
IV. Philip, *m.* Frances, dau. of William Thornhill, Esq., of the family of the THORNHILLS *of Castle Kevin*, and by her he had a large family.
1 James-Philip, who *d. unm.*
2 Edmund-Thornhill, who *d.* leaving a large family.
3 William-Philip, of Burton Park, who *m.* the eldest dau. of James Magrath, Esq. of Ballyaddam, by whom he left a large family.
4 John, of John's Grove, *m.* to Miss Pole, of Kinsale, but *d.* without issue.

The 3rd son,

THOMAS GLOVER, of Mount Glover, *b.* in 1712, *d.* 22 April, 1772, aged 60 years. He *m.* 1st, in April, 1751, Mary, only dau. and heiress of William Martin, Esq. of Curroclonbro, by his wife, Ann Purdon, of Ballyclough Castle; and 2ndly, Mary, only dau. of Edward Brailing, Esq. of Dublin, and widow of Charles M'Carthy, Esq. of Rathduff: by the former only he had issue, two sons and three daus. The 2nd and eventually only surviving son,

JAMES GLOVER, Esq., *m.* Mildred,* eldest dau. of Robert Freeman, Esq. of Ballinguile Castle,† by his wife, Mildred, dau. of William Seeley, Esq., and his wife, Mildred, dau. of Col. Frederick Mullins, direct ancestor of Lord Ventry. By this lady Mr. James Glover had fourteen children, ten alive at his death, viz., six sons and four daus.,

Thomas, who *d.* in 1811, *unm.*
Edward, M.D., *d. unm.*
JAMES, of Mount Glover.
William, a lieut. in the army, *d. unm.*
Stirling-Freeman, lieut.-col. in the army, who *m.* in 1833, Georgina, 2nd dau. of Lord Charles-Henry Somerset, 2nd son of Henry 5th Duke of Beaufort.
George-Freeman, who *m.* Miss White, of Cork, and *d.* leaving two sons, Robert and George.
Mildred, who *m.* Maurice Newman, Esq.
Ellen, who *m.* William Hudson, Esq., M.D.
Mary, *d. unm.*
Bridget, *m.* to Edward Powell, Esq. of Kildare.

Arms—Sa., a chev., erm., between three crescents, arg.
Crest—An eagle, displayed, arg., charged on the breast with three spots of erminites.
Motto—Nec timeo, nec sperno.
Seat—Mount Glover, co. Cork.

GLYNN OF FAIRY HILL.

GLYNN, WILLIAM-ANTHONY, Esq. of Fairy Hill, Isle of Wight, and of Bennacot Barton, Boyton, Cornwall, J.P. for Cornwall, *b.* 22 May, 1807; *m.* 29 May, 1828, Anne Goodall, and has surviving issue,

I. WILLIAM-ANTHONY, *b.* 5 Nov. 1842.
II. Henry-Oglander-John, *b.* 5 March, 1847.
I. Anne-Matilda, *m.* to Mr. Price, of Wales.
II. Elizabeth-Susan.
III. Margaret-Gertrude-Frances.

* Her only sister, Ellen, *m.* Marlborough-Parson Stirling, col. of the 36th regt., and governor-general of Pondicherry. He left his estates to his wife, having no issue, and after death, to his nephew-in-law, Stirling-Freeman Glover, now lieut.-col. in the 12th foot.

† This Robert Freeman was eldest son of John Freeman, of Ballinguile Castle, by his wife, Alice, dau. of Henry Wrixon, grandfather of the late Sir William-Wrixon Beecher, of Ballygiblin.

Lineage.—The GLYNNS *of Cornwall*, a very ancient family, derived their name from the manor of Glynn, Cornwall, of which they became possessed at a very early period, and so continued till the time of EDWARD III. The senior male line then expired, and the dau. and heiress of Sir J. Glynn, Knt. of Glynn, *m.* Sir J. Carminow, and brought Glynn to her husband. From the Carminows it passed eventually to Sir Hugh Courtenay, who sold back the estate of Glynn to

WILLIAM GLYNN, Esq. (eldest son* of Nicholas Glynn, and the lineal descendant of Gregory Glyn, seneschall to the Duke of Cornwall, *temp.* EDWARD III., younger brother of Sir J. Glynn, of Glynn). William Glynn *m.* the dau. and co-heir of Anthony Crewe, and left a son and successor,

NICHOLAS GLYNN, Esq. of Glynn, co. Cornwall, high-sheriff, 18 JAMES I.; *m.* Jane, dau. and heir of Walter Kendall, Esq. of Pelyn, and was father of

WILLIAM GLYNN, Esq. of Glynn, aged 21 at the Herald's Visitation of 1620. By Alice his wife, dau. of Walter Harris, Esq. of Hayne, he left at his decease, Aug. 1664, a son,

NICHOLAS GLYNN, Esq. of Glynn, M.P. for Bodmin, *temp.* CHARLES II., who *m.* Gertrude Dennis, of Orlegh, Devon, niece of Sir Bevill Granville, of Stow, the royalist, and by her (who *d.* 1706) left at his decease, 26 March, 1697, aged about 70, a son and successor,

DENNIS GLYNN, Esq. of Glynn, who *m.* 1st a dau. of Foote, of Tiverton; and 2ndly, a dau. of Hohlyn, of Bodmin, and was *s.* by his son,

WILLIAM GLYNN, Esq. of Glynn, who *m.* a dau. of Prideaux, of Place, and sister of the learned Dr. Prideaux, dean of Norwich, and had with other issue, NICHOLAS GLYNN of Glynn, whose issue is EXTINCT; and

JOHN GLYNN, who was a distinguished lawyer, serjeant-at-law, recorder of London and Exeter, and M.P. for Middlesex. He was *b.* 1722, and *s.* his nephew at Glynn in 1762. He *m.* 1763, Susannah-Margaret, dau. of Sir John Oglander, Bart. of Nunwell, and by her who *d.* 1816, had three sons, viz.,

I. EDMUND-JOHN, his heir.
II. Anthony-William, B.C.L., in holy orders, of Fairy Hill, Isle of Wight, rector of Lasnewth, Cornwall, and Kingstone, Isle of Wight, *b.* 1766; *m.* Jan. 1800, Sukey-Margaret, elder dau. of the late Sir William Oglander, Bart. of Nunwell, and by her (who *d.* April, 1840) left at his decease, Feb. 1819, an only child, the present WILLIAM-ANTHONY GLYNN, Esq. of Fairy Hill.
III. Henry-Richard, admiral, R.N., *b.* 2 Sept. 1768, *m.* 1st, Maria, dau. of J. Batt, Esq. of Moditonham, Cornwall; 2ndly, Miss Speake; and 3rdly, Miss Incledon; by the last two he had no issue: by the first he left at his decease, 20 July, 1856, 1 Henry-Richard, lieut. R.N., *b.* 1806, *d. s. p.* 1848; 2 John-Edmund, a major H.E.I.C.S., owner of Nettlestone Farm, Isle of Wight, *m.* 1st, Miss Jane Reed, by whom he had two daus., Jane and Maria-Elizabeth; and 2ndly, Miss Hatherleigh, dau. of Col. Hatherleigh, by whom he has, John, Henry-Oglander-Seymour, and Sophia-Louisa; 3 Edmund, comm. R.N., *m.* Miss Templar; and two daus., 1 Susan, and 2 Elizabeth, *m.* to the Rev. Francis Begbie.

The eldest son,

EDMUND-JOHN GLYNN, Esq. of Glynn, high-sheriff of Cornwall, 1808, and major of the Cornish miners, *m.* 1790, Elizabeth, dau. and co-heir of Edward-Meux Worsley, Esq. of Gatcombe, Isle of Wight, M.P., and left issue,

ELIZABETH-ANNE, *m.* 17 July, 1818, Henry-William Petre, Esq. of Dunkenhalgh, and *d.* 18 Sept. 1828.
FANNY-MARY, *m.* to Charles-Prideaux Bruno, Esq. of Place, Cornwall.

Mr. Glynn was *s.* in the representation of the family by his nephew, the present WILLIAM-ANTHONY GLYNN, Esq.

Arms—Arg., three salmon spears, points downwards, sa.
Crest—A demi-talbot, erm., eared, or.
Seat—Fairy Hill, Isle of Wight.

GODDARD OF CLIFFE PYPARD.

GODDARD, HORATIO-NELSON, Esq. of Cliffe House, Wilts, J.P. and D.L., M.A., major Wilts militia; *b.* 8 Dec. 1806; *m.* 1st, 8 April, 1840, Anne-Elizabeth, dau. of the late Rev. Thomas Le Mesurier, B.D., rector of Haughton-le-Skerne, co. Durham, and domestic chaplain to Viscount Sidmouth, and by her (who *d.* 21 Feb. 1849) had two daus.,

I. Susan-Werden, *d.* an infant.
II. Katherine-Anne, *d.* 19 Nov. 1851, aged 10.

He *m.* 2ndly, 10 Feb. 1852, Eliza-Agnes, dau. and co-heir of W. Walford, Esq. of Sidford, Oxfordshire, and has a dau.,

I. Frances-Agnes.

Major Goddard is patron of the living of Cliffe Pypard, the gift of the rectory and vicarage having belonged to his family ever since it was first alienated from the monastery of Lacock, in the time of King HENRY VIII.

Lineage.—The family of Goddard, of Wilts, or Godard, as it was anciently spelt, is of very great antiquity. It derives its origin from a Saxon source, possessed property in England previous to the CONQUEST, and is recorded in Domesday. Subsequently to this, some of the family resided in Hants, and three Godards are recorded in the Winton Domesday, as residing and possessing land there, *temp.* HENRY I. After this period, becoming more numerous, the family appears to have separated, one branch having settled in the cos. of Leicester and Norfolk, time of King JOHN (recorded in Chancellor's Rolls, 3rd year of King JOHN, 1202).

In 1233, Thomas Godard, son of Godard, held lands in Middleton, co. Norfolk. In 31st of EDWARD III., a fine was levied on the lands of Nicholas Godard, of the same place. Lands were conveyed to Nicholas and Walter Godard, 3rd of RICHARD II. About this time Walter Godard was lord of Denvers, having *m.* the heiress of that family; his heir, Robert Godard, held a lordship in Walpole, and was buried in Terrington Church, 1448. Of this family was Sir John Godard, Governor of Louviers, in Normandy, 6th HENRY V. (*See* Bloomfield's Norf.)

In the reign of King JOHN we gain the first authentic information of the settlement, of the Godard family in Wilts.

WALTER GODARD-VILLE, or GODARD-VIL, who, for some purpose, appears to have added to his originally Saxon name the Norman termination of ville, (which his descendants as readily discarded,) held tenements and lands in Chippenham and Albourn, co. Wilts. He was father of

JOHN GODARD, de Poulton, *temp.* RICHARD II., whose son,

JOHN GODARD, de Poulton, father of

WALTER GODARD, de Cherill, living 1460, whose son,

JOHN GODARD, de Upham, in Albourn, (in which his ancestor, Walter Godard-ville, had possessed lands several centuries before,) and de Cliffe Pypard. In the visitation of Wilts, by Robert Treswell, Bleumantle, 1569, he is stated to have *m.* Elizabeth, dau. of Wm. Berenger, of Manningford Bruce. He *d.* 10 March, 1545, leaving issue,

JOHN, his heir.
Thomas, of Ogbourn, *m.* 1st, Ann, sister to Sir George Gifford, of the county of Bucks, from the eldest son of which match descends GODDARD of Swindon. He *m.* 2ndly, Jane, dau. of John Ernle, of Cannings, co. Wilts, and Ernle, Sussex, from which marriage derived the GODDARDS of Hartham, whose eventual heiress, ANNE GODDARD, *m.* to Sir William James, Bart. of Eltham.
Thomas, *m.* Mary, dau. of William Alleyne, of Calne, and was great-grandfather of John Goddard, of Berwick Bassett, whose dau. and heir, Susanna, *m.* in 1696, Caleb Bailey, Esq.
John, buried at Cliffe, in 1584.
Anne, *m.* to Thomas Hinton, Esq. of Eagle's Hall, co. Berks, of whom descended Thomas Hinton, Esq. of Chilton.
Jane, *m.* to Richard Hinton, Esq. of Bourton, Berks.

The eldest son,

JOHN GODARD, or Goddard, of Upham, inherited his father's estates at Standen-Hussey, Clyffe Pypard, and other places. He *m.* 1st, Elizabeth, dau. of Sir Robert Phetyplace, de Besylsley, co. Berks, of a very ancient family of that name, and by her, who *d.* in 1585, he had issue, two sons and three daus. He *m.* 2ndly, Alice, dau. of Thomas Goddard, Esq. of Ogbourn, St. George, by Jane, dau. of John Ernley, of Cannings, and by her had issue three sons. The eldest son,

THOMAS GODDARD, of Clyffe Pypard, whose will is dated 1609, *m.* 1st, Dorothy Stephens, who was related to the Phetyplace family, and by her had one son, FRANCIS, his heir, of whom presently. He *m.* 2ndly, Margaret, dau. of George Burley, Esq. of Pottern, Wilts, and by her had issue, four sons and three daus. The eldest son,

FRANCIS GODDARD, Esq., *s.* his father in the estates of

* From John, 2nd son of Nicholas Glynn, derived the GLYNNS *of Boyton*, Cornwall, from whom descended Dr. Glynn, a physician, fellow of King's College, Cambridge, a classical scholar and poet.

Standen-Hussey, Clyffe Pypard, and Albourn, and served as high-sheriff for Wilts, 10th year King CHARLES I., 1635. He *m.* Sarah, dau. of Sir Anthony Hungerford, of Black-Bourton, co. Oxon, and had issue, with three daus., two sons, I. EDWARD, his heir, *b.* 22 April, 1634; and II. Francis, who afterwards possessed estates at Purton, and Cowich, from whom GODDARD, of Purton. The heiress of this branch, Margaret Goddard, *m.* in 1792, to Robert Wilsonn, Esq. He *d.* 15 Jan. 1652 and was *s.* by his son,

EDWARD GODDARD, Esq. of Standen-Hussey, and Cliffe Pypard. He *m.* in 1656, Bridget, dau. of Sir Cecil Bishopp, Bart., (who, surviving her husband, *m.* 2ndly, to John Kasper Keiling, Esq., and 3rdly, in 1714, to Thomas Young, Esq.) He *d.* in 1684, and was *s.* by his son,

FRANCIS GODDARD, Esq., J.P. and D.L., who sold the ancient family estate of Standen-Hussey, in 1719. He *m.* Mary, dau. of T. Byres, Esq., who survived him, and *m.* John Harris, Esq. Mr. F. Goddard was buried in the family vault at Cliffe Pypard in 1724, and left issue, one son and one dau., EDWARD, his heir, *b.* in 1722, and Sarah, *m.* to John Mackrell, Esq., *d. s. p.* The only son,

EDWARD GODDARD, Esq. of Clyffe Pypard, high-sheriff of Wilts, 1767, *m.* 27 Aug. 1754, Johanna, dau. of Henry Read, Esq. of Crowood, near Ramsbury, Wilts. Entering into holy orders, he became vicar of Cliffe Pypard, of which living he was patron. He *d.* 6 Jan. 1791; Johanna, his wife, *d.* 22 Feb. 1802, having had issue by him,

- EDWARD, his heir.
- Francis, *b.* 15 Feb. 1763; *d. unm.* 22 Feb. 1841.
- Richard, *b.* 28 Nov. 1766; *d. unm.* 3 July, 1832, one of the senior post captains R.N.
- Sarah, *m.* 1 Jan. 1784, to Richard Hallilay, Esq., formerly of the county of York, of Wedhampton, co. Wilts, who *d.* in 1832.
- Anne, *d. unm.* 12 May, 1772.
- Elizabeth, *d. unm.* 31 Aug. 1758, very young.
- Bridget, *m.* 28 March, 1803, to T.-Weston Wadley, Esq., and *d. s. p.*, 31 Dec. 1827.
- Priscilla, *d. unm.* 18 July, 1850, aged 85.

The eldest son and heir,

THE REV. EDWARD GODDARD, of Clyffe Pypard, *b.* 10 May, 1761, M.A., vicar of Clyffe Pypard, J.P., *m.* 10 June, 1802, Annica-Susan, only dau. of Edward Bayntun, Esq., his majesty's consul-general at Algiers, and Susanna, his wife, dau. of Sir John Werden, Bart. of Cheshire, and co-heiress with her sister, Lucy, Duchess of St Albans, and had issue by her,

- Edward-John-Ambrose, of Queen's College, Oxford, capt. in the Wilts regt. of militia, *b.* 3 April, 1804; *d.* 10 Nov. 1828.
- Henry-William, *b.* 18 Dec. 1805; *d.* 3 Aug. 1818.
- HORATIO-NELSON, his heir.
- George-Ashe, (the Rev.) M.A. of Brasennose College, Oxford, Vicar of Clyffe Pypard, and a magistrate for Wilts, *b.* 15 Aug. 1809, *m.* in 1837, Catherine-Matilda, dau. and co-heiress of the late J. Sherwood, Esq. of Castle Hill, Reading.
- Thomas, Major, 44th regt. of Bengal Native Infantry, *b.* 4 Aug. 1811.
- Francis, M.A., in holy orders, Incumbent of Alderton, Wilts, *b.* 21 Jan. 1814; *m.* 18 April, 1850, Elizabeth, dau. of John Wolcott, Esq. of Knowles, Salcombe Regis, Devon, and has a son, Edward-Hungerford, *b.* 1 Jan. 1854.
- Septimus, *b.* 29 April, 1816.
- Annica-Werden, *m.* 16 Sept. 1824, to James Bradford, Esq. of Swindon, Wilts.
- Lucy-Charlotte, *d.* 6 Nov. 1833.
- Fanny, *d.* 22 July, 1834.
- Arabella, *m.* 29 April, 1851, to the Rev. R. D. Dartnell, vicar of Rodborn Cheney, Wilts.

The Rev. Mr. Goddard *d.* 22 Jan. 1839, and was *s.* by his eldest surviving son, the present HORATIO-NELSON GODDARD, Esq. of Cliffe Pypard.

Arms—Gu., a chev. vair, between three crescents, arg.
Crest—A stag's head, effronté, coupé at the neck, gu., attired, or.
Motto—Cervus non servus.
Seat—Cliffe House, Wilts.

GODDARD OF SWINDON.

GODDARD, AMBROSE-LETHBRIDGE, Esq., of The Lawn, Swindon, co. Wilts, J.P. and D.L., M.P. for Cricklade, *b.* 9 Dec. 1819; *m.* 14 Aug. 1847, Charlotte, eldest dau. of Edward-Ayshford Sanford, Esq. of Nynehead Court, co. Somerset, and has issue,

- I. AMBROSE-AYSHFORD, *b.* 7 May, 1848.
- II. Fitz-Roy-Pleydell, *b.* 29 Aug. 1852.

- III Edward-Hesketh, *b.* 19 Oct. 1855.
- I. Jessie-Henrietta.

Lineage.—THOMAS GODDARD, of Upham, co. Wilts, 2nd son of John Goddard, of Upham, (*see* GODDARD, OF CLIFFE PYPARD,) by his wife Elizabeth Berenger, living *temp.* HENRY VIII., *m.* 1st, Anna, sister of Sir George Gifford, co. Bucks, and was *s.* by his son,

RICHARD GODDARD, who resided in a handsome mansion at Upham, which had belonged to John of Gaunt, Duke of Lancaster, and was said to have been granted by him to the family of Goddard. He *m.* Elizabeth, dau. of Thomas Walrond, Esq. of Albourn, and had (with a dau., Elizabeth, *m.* to Lewis Pollard, Esq. of Newenham) three sons. I. THOMAS, his heir; II. Edward, of Englesham, who *m.* Priscilla, dau. of John D'Oyley, Esq. of Chiselhampton, and had, with other issue THOMAS, of Box, *b.* in 1620, who *d.* in 1691, leaving by Anne his wife, a son, THOMAS, of Rudloe, who *m.* in 1683, Mary, dau. of Ambrose Awdry, Esq. of Melksham, and dying in 1703, was father of AMBROSE GODDARD, who eventually *s.* to Swindon; III. Richard, of Upham, whose dau. and heir *m.* to John Yate, Esq. of Charney, Berks. The eldest son and heir,

THOMAS GODDARD, of Swindon, *m.* Jane, dau. of Sir Edmond Phetyplace, of Childrey, Berks, and dying in 1641, left a son,

RICHARD GODDARD, Esq. of Swindon, who *m.* in 1648, Anne Bowerman, and had by her a son,

THOMAS GODDARD, Esq. of Swindon, who *m.* Mary, dau. of Oliver Pleydell, of Shrivenham, and was *s.* by his eldest son,

RICHARD GODDARD, Esq. of Swindon, elected M.P. for Wotton Bassett in 1710, and for Wiltshire in 1722. He *m.*, but having no issue, was *s.* at his decease, in 1732, aged 56, by his brother,

PLEYDELL GODDARD, Esq. of Swindon, *b.* in 1686, who *d. s. p.* in 1742, and was buried at Swindon, leaving his estates to his kinsman,

AMBROSE GODDARD, Esq. who then became of Swindon, *b.* 6 Nov. 1695. He *m.* 16 Aug. 1716, Elizabeth, dau. of Ambrose Awdry, Esq. of Seend, and had three sons and five daus., of the latter, the eldest, Mary, *m.* Thomas Vilett, Esq. of Swindon; and Priscilla, *m.* John Awdry, Esq. of Melksham. Of the former, the youngest,

- Thomas, bapt. 6 March, 1722, M.P. for Wilts, *d. unm.* 12 Aug. 1770.
- Edward, bapt. 16 Oct. 1725, *d. unm.*
- AMBROSE, of whom presently.
- Mary, *m.* to Thomas Vilett, Esq., of Swindon, ancestor of Thomas Vilett, Esq., lieut.-col. in the army, now residing on his estates at Swindon, the present representative of an ancient family.
- Elizabeth, *d. unm.*
- Priscilla, *m.* to John Awdry, Esq. of Melksham, and *d.* at Lisbon.
- Lucy. Anne, *d. unm.* in 1834.

AMBROSE GODDARD, Esq., *s.*, on the death of his elder brothers, to the Swindon estates, and represented the co. Wilts in parliament from the year 1772 until 1806. He *m.* 16 Aug. 1786, Sarah, only dau. and heir of Thomas Williams, Esq. of Pilrowth, in Carmarthenshire, and had issue,

- THOMAS, his heir, *b.* in 1778; elected M.P. for Cricklade in 1806; *d. unm.* in 1814, before his father.
- AMBROSE, *s.* his father.
- Richard, in holy orders, *b.* 9 Oct. 1787, formerly Fellow of St. John's, Oxford, subsequently rector of Draycot Foliatt, and vicar of Kemble, Wiltshire. Resident at Broadstone, near Heythorp, Oxfordshire
- Henry, *b.* 4 May, 1789, *d.* young.
- Elizabeth, *d. unm.* in 1797
- Sarah.
- Lucy, *d. unm.* in 1800.
- Emma, twin with Richard, *d. unm.* in 1802.
- Ann, *m.* to Sir Thomas-Buckler Lethbridge, Bart. of Sandhill Park, Somersetshire.
- Priscilla, *d. unm.* in 1805.
- Margaret, *d. unm.* in 1799.

Mr. Goddard *d.* 19 June, 1815, and was *s.* by his eldest son,

AMBROSE GODDARD, Esq. of Swindon, captain 10th hussars, *b.* 12 Oct. 1779, J.P. and D.L., high-sheriff of Wilts, 1819-20, and M.P. for Cricklade, *m.* 1 Aug. 1818, Jessy-Dorothea, eldest dau. of Sir Thomas-Buckler Lethbridge, Bart., and by her (who *d.* 6 March, 1843), had issue,

- AMBROSE-LETHBRIDGE, now of Swindon.
- John-Hesketh, *b.* 14 Sept. 1821, 14th light dragoons.
- Charles-Richard, *b.* 12 April, 1831.
- Frederick-Fitzclarence, *b.* 4 April, 1836.
- Jessy-Dalrymple, *m.* March, 1847, to Henry Hussey Vivian, Esq. of Singleton, and *d.* Feb. 1848.

Emma-Caroline. Lucy-Clarissa.
Julia. Sarah-Adelaide.

Arms—As GODDARD OF CLIFFE.
Seat—The Lawn, Swindon.

GODFREY OF BROOK-STREET HOUSE.

GODFREY, JOHN, Esq. of Brook-Street House, co. Kent, *m.* 29 July, 1823, Augusta-Isabella, dau. of John Ingram, Esq. of Staindrop, co. Durham, and had issue,

INGRAM-FULLER, *b.* 24 Dec. 1827.
Arthur-William, *b.* 9 March, 1829.
Albert-Henry, *b.* 30 May, 1830.
Augusta-Frances-Elizabeth. Christine-Eliza.

This gentleman, whose patronymic was JULL, assumed, by sign-manual, in 1810, the surname and arms of GODFREY only.

Lineage.—The ancient family of GODFREY is supposed to derive from Godfrey le Fauconer, lord of the manor of Hurst, in Kent, as early as the reign of HENRY II.

THOMAS GODFREY, Esq. of Hodiford, son of Thomas Godfrey, of Lydd, by Elizabeth his 2nd wife, dau. and heir of Michael Pix, Esq. of Folkston (*see family of* FAUSSETT), had, by his 2nd wife, Sarah, dau. of Thomas Isles, Esq. of Hammersmith, *inter alios*, PETER, his heir, Edmund Berry (Sir), who fell a victim to the evil days of Titus Oates, and Benjamin, of Norton, whose dau. and heiress, Catherine, *m.* Stephen Lushington, Esq. The elder son,

PETER GODFREY, Esq. of Hodiford *m.* Amye, dau. of Thomas Brett Esq. of Snave, and had issue,

THOMAS, of Hodiford, who *m.* Mary, dau. of John Dallman, Esq. of Denistborpe, in Staffordshire, but dying without issue, in 1699, Hodiford passed to his cousin, Thomas Godfrey, of Woodford.
AMYE.

The only dau.,

AYME GODFREY, *m.* William Courthorpe, Esq. of Stodmarshe Court, and left at her decease, in 1742, two daus., viz., ANNE COURTHORPE, who *m.* to John Hugesson, Esq., and conveyed to him Stodmarshe Court, and SARAH COURTHOPE, who *m.* John Jull, Esq. of Ash, in Kent, and afterwards of Wodnesborough, by whom she left issue,

John-Godfrey Jull, who *d. unm.* during his passage from St. Helena to England.
THOMAS JULL.
Sarah Jull, *m.* to John-Garland Hatch, Esq. of Deal, and *d.* in 1765.

The 2nd, but only surviving son, (at Mrs. Jull's decease in 1763,)

THOMAS JULL, Esq. of Ash, *b.* in 1729, *m.* Susan, sister of W. Tully, of Sandwich, Esq., and had issue,

THOMAS, his heir.
John, of Wingham, who *m.* in 1787, Anne-Sayer, dau. of William Reynolds, Esq., and dying in 1812, left surviving issue,
JOHN, heir to his uncle.
William, *b.* 13 June, 1795.
Edward, *b.* 21 Feb. 1799.
George, *b.* 26 Sept. 1804.
Elizabeth-Anne, *m.* 7 Oct. 1812, to William Monins, Esq.
Elizabeth, who *d.* in 1817.

Mr. Jull was *s.* at his decease by his elder son,

THOMAS JULL, Esq. of Ash, *b.* in 1751, who assumed, by act of parliament, in 1799, the surname of GODFREY only. He was high-sheriff of Kent in 1802, and represented the borough of Hythe in parliament. Mr. Godfrey *m.* in Aug. 1778, Elizabeth, only surviving child of John Fuller, Esq., but dying *s. p.* in 1810, he was *s.* by his nephew, JOHN JULL, Esq., who has likewise assumed the surname and arms of Godfrey, and is the present proprietor.

Arms—Sa., a chev., between three pelicans' heads, erased, or, vulning themselves, ppr.
Crest—A demi-negro, ppr., holding in the dexter hand a cross-crosslet fitchée, arg.
Seat—Brook Street House, Kent.

GODLEY OF KILLIGAR.

GODLEY, JOHN, Esq. of Killigar, co Leitrim, J.P. and D.L., high-sheriff 1818; *b.* in 1775; *m.* in 1813, Catherine, dau. of the Right Hon. Denis Daly, of Dunsandle, co. Galway, by the Lady Harriet, his wife, and has issue,

I. JOHN-ROBERT. II. James.
III. Denis. IV. Archibald.
V. William.
I. Harriet, *m.* to the Rev. Henry O'Brien, youngest son of the late Sir Edward O'Brien, Bart. of Dromoland.
II. Charlotte.

Lineage.—The GODLEYS, of Killigar, derive from a family of the same name, seated in the co. York, where there is a township called Godley, near Halifax. The Godleys appear to have gone to Yorkshire from Cheshire in which county, as will be seen in Lyson's Magna Britannia, they were resident, in the reign of EDWARD I., at a place called Godley, (now a large manufacturing village,) which subsequently passed into the possession of the Masys.

JOHN GODLEY, Esq., who *d.* in 1710, *m.* Anne, sister and co-heir of Dr. William Eldwood, vice-provost of Trinity College, and M.P. for the University, and left a son,

WILLIAM GODLEY, Esq. who *m.* Mary, dau. of Richard Morgan, Esq. of the city of Dublin, and of Coldent, co. Dublin, second Remembrancer in the Court of Exchequer, and *d.* in 1780, having had a son,

JOHN GODLEY, Esq. of Killigar, co. Leitrim who *m.* in 1762, Rose, dau. of Alexander Macaulay, Esq. of Glenville, co. Antrim, king's counsel and judge of the Prerogative Court in Dublin, and at one time M.P. for the University of Dublin, and by this lady had issue,

William, lieut.-col. of the 83rd regt., left a son and a dau.; the former, John, settled at Oatlands, co. Dublin.
Alexander, major of the 28th regt., killed in action in Egypt, 13 March, 1801.
JOHN, of Killigar.
Anne.
Rose, *m.* the late Thomas Whitney, Esq. of New Pass, co. Westmeath, and is deceased.
Margaret.

Arms—Arg., three unicorns' heads, erased, sa., horned, gu., three trefoils, slipped, vert.
Crest—An unicorn's head, erased, arg., horned gu., charged with three trefoils, slipped, vert.
Motto—San Dieu rien.
Seat—Killigar, co. Leitrim.

GODMAN OF PARK HATCH.

GODMAN, JOSEPH, Esq. of Park Hatch, Surrey, and Merston Manor, co. Sussex, *m.* in March, 1830, Caroline, dau. of Edmund Smithe, Esq. of Horsham, and has issue,

I. JOSEPH. II. Richard-Temple.
III. Frederick-Du-Cane. IV. Percy-Sanden.
I. Caroline. II. Ellen. III. Mary.

Mr. Godman, a justice of the peace for Surrey, is only son of Joseph Godman, Esq., by Mary Hasler, his wife, (*m.* in 1788,) and grandson of Richard Godman, Esq., by Elizabeth Freeland, his wife. He has four sisters; Mary, *m.* to Godfrey Molling, Esq. of Connaught Place, London; Susan, *m.* to Edward Dorrington, Esq., Clerk of the Fees to the House of Commons; Margaret, *m.* to Patrick-Persse Fitzpatrick, Esq. of Bognor, Sussex; and Jane, *m.* to Richard-G. Kirkpatrick, Esq. of the Isle of Wight.

Arms (granted in 1579, to Thomas Godman)—Per pale, erm. and ermines, on a chief, or, a lion, passant, vert.
Crest—On a mount, vert, a black cock, wings displayed, ppr.
Motto—Cœlum quid quærimus ultra.
Seats—Park Hatch, Surrey, and Merston Manor Farm, co. Sussex.

GODSAL OF ISCOYD PARK.

GODSAL, PHILIP-LAKE, Esq. of Iscoyd Park, co. Flint, high-sheriff 1849-50; *m.* the Hon. Grace-Anne-Best, eldest dau. of William Draper, Lord Wynford.

Arms—Per pale, gu. and az., on a fesse, wavy, arg. between three crosses, pattée, or, as many crescents, sa.
Crest—A griffin's head, erased, paly of six, indented, arg. and sa., beaked, or.
Seat—Iscoyd Park, Flintshire.

GOFF OF HALE PARK.

GOFF, JOSEPH, Esq. of Hale Park, co. Hants, J.P. and D.L. for co. Dublin, high-sheriff of the co.

Tyrone in 1842, *m.* Jane, dau. of Captain T. Stannus, of Portarlington, by Caroline, his wife, dau. of J. Hamilton, Esq. of Abbotstown, near Dublin, and has had issue,

I. JOSEPH, *b.* 28 Oct. 1817, M.A., J.P., Capt. Tyrone militia; *m.* 26 Sept. 1850, Lady Adelaide-Henrietta-Louisa-Hortense Knox, youngest dau. of the Earl of Ranfurly.
II. Thomas, in holy orders, *b.* in 1818. *d.* in 1848.
III. James, *d.* in infancy.
IV. Robert. *b.* in Oct. 1823.
V. Trevor, lieut. 45th regt., *b.* in March, 1825.
VI. George, *b.* in April, 1826, M.A.
I. Sarah-Jane, *d. unm.* in 1841.
II. Caroline, *d. unm.* in 1842.
III. Sophia. IV. Eliza.
V. Harriet. *d.* young.

Lineage.—WILLIAM GOFFE, or GOUGHE, Esq., *b.* in 1619, 3rd son of Stephen Goffe, or Goughe, a Puritan Divine, Rector of Hanmer, Sussex, joined CROMWELL'S army as quarter-master, rose by his merit to the rank of colonel, and became eventually major-general of infantry. He was M.P. for Great Yarmouth, in 1654, and for the co. of Southampton in 1656, and was subsequently called up to the House of Lords by CROMWELL, with whom he was in high favour for various services rendered to him. At the Restoration, in 1660, Lord Goffe was obliged to leave England, and fled to America, where he *d.* about 1680, having undergone many vicissitudes. He had *m.* a dau. of Gen Whalley, and cousin of OLIVER CROMWELL, and by her, who remained in Ireland, had RICHARD, of whom presently; Francis, *m.* and had issue; and Judith. The son,

RICHARD GOFFE, in 1681, *m.* Hannah, dau. of J. Chamberlain, of Pontmarle, co. Wexford, and had issue, William, *b.* in 1688, *d. unm.*; Richard, *b.* in 1690, *d.* in 1767, *unm.*; Jonas, *b.* in 1693, *d. unm.*; JACOB, of whom we treat; Joseph, *b.* in 1697; Mary and Hannah, both *d.* infants; and Elizabeth, *d. unm.* in 1767. The 4th son,

JACOB GOFFE, *b.* in 1695, *m.* Mary Fade, of Wexford, and had issue,

JOSEPH, of whose line we treat.
Fade, *m.* Elizabeth Pemberton, and was father of the late Richard Goff, of Tottenham Green, co. Wexford.
JACOB, ancestor of the GOFFS *of Hordtown House*, (*see that branch.*)
Hannah, *m.* 1st, to Joseph Clibborne, of Moate Castle, co. Westmeath; and 2ndly, to W. Pigot, of Slevoy Castle, co. Wexford, and *d.* in 1789.
Sarah. Mary.
Elizabeth, *m.* to Cæsar Sutton, of Longraigne, co. Wexford.

The eldest son,

JOSEPH GOFF, Esq. of Dublin, by his wife, Miss Unthank, (who *m.* 2ndly, Fletcher, Esq. of Dublin,) had issue, JOSEPH, of whom presently; and Robert, *d. s. p.* in 1833. The elder son,

JOSEPH FADE GOFF, Esq. of Mountjoy-square, Dublin, and Newtown Park, near Dublin, *m.* Sarah dau. of George, Clibborne, Esq. of Moate Castle, co. Westmeath, and had issue,

JOSEPH, of Hale Park.
Richard, a graduate of Christ Church, Oxford, and barrister of Lincoln's Inn, *d. unm.*
John, captain in the 3rd dragoons, *d. unm.*
William, *m.* Mary, dau. of John Clibborne, Esq of Moate Castle, co. Westmeath, and has issue, three daus.
George. *m.* in 1832, Elizabeth, dau. of Peter Holmes, Esq. of Peterville, co. Tipperary, and has issue.
Edward, *d.* young. Robert.
Eliza, *d.* young.

Arms—Az., a chevron between two fleurs-de-lys, in chief, and a lion, rampant, in base, or.
Crest—A squirrel, sejant, ppr.
Motto—Fier sans tache.
Seat—Hale Park, Hants.

GOFF OF HORETOWN HOUSE.

DAVIS-GOFF, STRANGMAN, Esq. of Horetown House, co. Wexford, J.P., *b.* 27 May, 1810; *m.* 25 Feb. 1835, Susan-Maxwell, youngest dau. of Arthur Ussher, Esq. of Camphire, co. Waterford, and has issue,

I. WILLIAM-GOFF, *b.* 12 Sept. 1838.
II. Ussher, *b.* 2 Feb. 1841.
III. Charles-Edward, *b.* 30 March, 1844.
IV. Francis, *b.* 24 July, 1850.
I. Margaretta-Ussher. II. Julia-Anna.
III. Rebecca. IV. Lucy-Ussher.

Lineage.—JACOB GOFF, Esq. *b.* 1736, 3rd son of Jacob Goff, Esq., and Mary Fade, his wife, (*see* GOFF, *of Hale Park*) *m.* Elizabeth, dau. of Benjamin Wilson, Esq. of Mount Wilson, King's county, and had with several daus., two sons, WILLIAM, his heir, and Joseph Fade, of Raheenduff, whose only dau. and heiress, Jane-Colclough, *m.* Capt. Maxwell Du Pré Stronge, youngest son of Sir James M. Stronge, Bart. The elder son,

WILLIAM GOFF, Esq. of Horetown House, *b.* in 1762, *m.* in 1784, Rebecca, dau. of Edward Deaves, Esq. of North Abbey, co. Cork, and *d.* in 1840, having had issue,

I. JACOB-WILLIAM, of whom presently.
I. Rebecca, *m.* in 1809, Francis Davis, Esq. of Waterford, and by her (who *d.* 1848) has issue,
1 STRANGMAN, the present STRANGMAN-DAVIS GOFF, Esq. of Horetown House.
2 Henry, *b.* 12 July, 1825.
II. Eliza, *m.* to Jonathan Pim, Esq. of Dublin.
III. Mary, *m.* to Thomas Harvey, Esq. of Youghal.
IV. Sally, *d. unm.* V. Lucy-Anne.
VI. Arabella, *m.* to Jonathan Pim, Esq. of Mountmellic.

Mr. Goff was *s.* by his son,

JACOB-WILLIAM GOFF, Esq. of Horetown House, J.P., and D.L., *b.* in 1790, who *m.* 1st, in 1828, Eliza, dau. of Col. W.-P. Pigot, of Slevoy Castle, co. Wexford; and 2ndly, in 1833, Letitia, dau. of the Rev. A. Alcock, of Fethard Castle, co. Wexford, but dying *s. p.* in Feb. 1845, was *s.* by his nephew, STRANGMAN DAVIS, who assumed the additional surname and arms of GOFF, by royal license, 28 Feb. 1845, in compliance with the will of his maternal uncle.

Arms—Quarterly: 1st and 4th, az., a chev. between two fleurs-de-lis, in chief, and a lion, rampant, in base, or, a crescent for difference, for GOFF; 2nd and 3rd, per pale, gu. and arg., a chev., between three boars' heads, couped, counterchanged, for DAVIS.
Crest—A squirrel, sejant.
Motto—Houestas optima politia.
Seat—Horetown House, Taghmon, co. Wexford.

GOING OF BALLYPHILIP.

GOING, AMBROSE, Esq. of Ballyphilip, co. Tipperary, *b.* Oct. 1785; *m.* Feb. 1811, Margaret, 4th dau. of the late Colonel Richard Pennefather, of New Park, co. Tipperary, and has issue,

I. WILLIAM, *b.* in May, 1815, *m.* in Oct. 1841, Jane, 2nd dau. of Benjamin Frend, of Rocklow, co. Tipperary,
II. Richard-Pennefather, *b.* in 1821.
III. John, *b.* in Aug. 1822.
I. Anna, *m.* in 1835, to the Rev. Anthony Armstrong, Rector of Killoskully
II. Margaret-Isabella, *m.* in 1841, to Christopher-F. Tuthill, Esq., M.D. of Dublin.
III. Elizabeth-Frances, *m.* in 1846, to John-Harvey Adams, Esq. of Northlands, co. Cavan.
IV. Dorothea, *m.* in May, 1848, to Samuel-Murray Going, Esq. of Liskeveen House, co. Tipperary.

Mr. Going is only son of the late William Going, Esq. (who *d.* in 1844,) and Mary White, his wife, and grandson of Ambrose Going, Esq., and Bridget Hunt, his wife.

Motto—Dum spiro spero.
Seat—Ballyphilip, co. Tipperary.

GOING OF TRAVERSTON, BIRDHILL, AND MONAQUIL.

GOING, ROBERT. Esq. of Traverston, co. Tipperary, *s.* his father, the late Thomas Going, Esq. in 1841.

Lineage.—ROBERT GOING, Esq. of Tulley Moylan, co. Tipperary, *m.* Jane, 2nd dau. and co-heir of — Johnstone, Esq. of co. Cork, and had issue,

I. John, *d. unm.*
II. ROBERT, heir to his father, of whom presently.
III. James, of Belleisle, co. Clare, who *m.* Miss Marcella Walsh, of Newtown, co. Limerick, and had with other issue, 1 Robert, of Cragg, co. Tipperary, *b.* 1766, *m.* 1804, Anne, dau. of John Dwyer, Esq., and *d.* 1838, leaving issue, JOHN, now of Bird Hill, J.P., *b.* 1812, Robert-James, rector of Templeharry, King's Co., and five daus.; 2 James, of Violet Hill, co. Tipperary, *m.* Jane, dau. of

Marcus Patterson, Esq., by Mary his wife, 2nd dau. of Wyndham Quin, Esq. of Adare, M.P. for Kilmallock, and sister of Valentine-Richard, 1st Earl of Dunraven, and had issue five sons and two daus., viz., James, Marcus, Wyndham, Robert, Richard, Mary, and Marcella.

IV. Thomas, of Coolbea, co. Cork, *d. s. p.*

V. Richard, of Bird Hill, co. Tipperary, J.P., *m.* Anne, dau. of Henry White, Esq. of New Ross, same co., and had issue four sons and four daus.,

1 John, in holy orders, rector of Mealiffe, co. Tipperary, who *m.* Frances-Anne, eldest dau. of the Rev. Walter Shirley, brother of the 4th, 5th, and 6th Earl Ferrars, lineally descended from EDWARD III. The Rev. J. Going was murdered in 1829, aged 60, leaving by his wife, who survived him till 1838, with other issue, Richard, who *m.* a sister of the Rev. Peter Roe; Henry; Thomas; Charles, *m.* his cousin, Letitia, dau. of Stoney, Esq. of Oakley Park; Frances, *m.* to the Rev. J. Stoney, of Castlebar.

2 Richard, of Birdhill, *m.* and has issue.

3 Henry, *m.* his cousin, Sarah, dau. of White, Esq. of Greenhill, co. Tipperary.

4 Thomas, *m.* a dau. of Adams, Esq. of Cork.

1 Letitia, *m.* 1st, to Stoney, Esq. of Oakley Park; and 2ndly, to — White, Esq.

2 Jane, *m.* to Edward Budler, Esq. of Carlow, and deceased.

3 Rebecca, *m.* 1st, to her cousin, Thomas Going, Esq. of Santa Cruz, and 2ndly, to Captain Goodwin.

4 Eliza, *m.* to Thomas Stoney, Esq. of the co. Tipperary.

VI. Philip, of Monaquil, co. Tipperary, J.P. and M.P., and high-sheriff in 1785, *m.* Grace, dau. of Thomas Bernard, Esq., and sister of Bernard, Esq. of Castle Bernard, King's Co., and *d.* 24 April, 1820, having had by his wife, who survived him until 1836, one son and three daus.,

1 Thomas, of Santa Cruz, co. Tipperary, who *m.* Rebecca, 3rd dau. of his uncle, Richard Going, Esq. of Bird Hill, and predeceased his father, *s. p.*

1 Mary, co-heir, *m.* 10 Feb. 1794, to her cousin, John Bennett, Esq. of Ballyloughane, co. Carlow, afterwards of Viewmount, in the same co.; he *d. s. p.* 4 May, 1827.

2 Charlotte, co-heir, *m.* 31 Dec. 1798, to Robert Atkins, Esq., eldest son of Major Robert Atkins, of Firville, co. Cork, and had, with other issue, (*see* ATKINS *of Firville*,) the Rev. Philip-Going Atkins-Going, of Firville, co. Cork, and of Monaquil, co. Tipperary, to which property he *s.* by the will of his maternal grandfather, and assumed the surname of Going in addition to Atkins.

3 Jemima-Matilda, co-heir, *m.* 12 April, 1804, to Sir Amyrald Dancer, Bart. of Modereny and Cloghjordan, co. Tipperary.

Mr. Robert Going, of Taverston, was *s.* at his decease by his eldest son,

ROBERT GOING, Esq. of Taverston, who *m.* Margaret, 2nd dau. of Thomas Maunsell, Esq. of Plassy, M.P. for co. Limerick, by Dorothy, his wife, dau. of Richard Waller, Esq. of Castle Waller, co. Limerick, and was father of

THOMAS GOING, Esq. of Traverston, high-sheriff of co. Tipperary, who *m.* a sister of Caleb Powell, Esq., M.P., and *d.* 12 Feb. 1841, aged seventy-four, leaving issue,

I. ROBERT, his heir.

II. Caleb, J.P. for co. Tipperary.

I. Margaret, *m.* in 1837, to — Walsh, Esq. of co. Limerick.

II. Frances. III. Jane. IV. Sarah.

Seat—Traverston, co. Tipperary.

GOLDING OF MAIDEN ERLEGH.

GOLDING, EDWARD, Esq. of Maiden Erlegh, co. Berks, J.P. and D.L., *b.* 27 Nov. 1780; *m.* 1st, 12 Dec. 1801, Elizabeth, dau. of Col. Bailie, by whom he has a son, BAILIE, *m.* Mrs. Sealy, widow of Capt. Sealy. Mr. Golding *m.* 2ndly, 7 Nov. 1807, Frances, eighth dau. of Oldfield Bowles, Esq. of North Aston, co. Oxon, and by her has issue, Edward; Frances-Emma, *m.* in Aug. 1843, to the Rev. Matthew-Thomas Farrer, vicar of Addington, Surrey; Mary-Anne; and Laura.

Lineage.—The late EDWARD GOLDING, Esq., M.P., of Maiden Erlegh, co. Berks, purchased that estate from William Matthew Burt, Governor of the Leewards Islands. He *m.* Miss Anne English, and had two sons and two daus., viz.,

EDWARD, his heir.

Charles, in holy orders, *m.* Charlotte, dau. of Richard Palmer, Esq. of Holme Park, Berks, and has one son, Henry, in holy orders.

Charlotte, *m.* to the Rev. Henry Winch.

Caroline, *m.* to Quilt-John Greenly, R.N.

Arms—Gu., a chev., or, between three bezants.

Crest—A hind's head, with an oak-branch in the mouth, all ppr.

Motto—Pro Deo et Rege.

Seat—Malden Erlegh, co. Berks.

GOLLOP OF STRODE.

GOLLOP, GEORGE-TILLY, Esq. of Strode House, co. Dorset, J.P., *b.* 11 Oct. 1791; *m.* 19 Sept. 1815, Christina, dau. of Hubertus Vander Vliegen, of Hassel, in the district of Liege, and has issue,

I. GEORGE, *b.* 13 Aug. 1825, *m.* 5 January, 1852, Jessie Caroline, dau. of the Rev. Hugh Helyar, rector of Sutton Bingham, co. Somerset.

II. John, *b.* 27 May, 1829.

I. Christina-Georgina-Jane, *m.* 21 Aug. 1851, to Henry Reeve, Esq., registrar of the Judicial Committee of Privy Council.

Lineage.—JOHN GOLLOP, the founder of this house, was, according to some memoirs preserved in the family, a soldier of fortune from either Denmark or Sweden, who flourished in the reigns of RICHARD II. and HENRY IV., but other and more probable accounts, coinciding with the Visitation of 1623, state that he lived in 1465, and came from the north. He *m.* Alice, dau. and heir of William, or Peter Temple, of Templecombe, in Broad Windsor, and acquired thereby that estate, with the lands of North Bowood. The next upon record,

JOHN GOLLOP, of North Bowood and Temple, living *temp.* HENRY VIII., *m.* Joan, dau. of Collins, of Nailscroft, co. Dorset, and was *s.* at his decease by his son,

THOMAS GOLLOP, who, in minority, was placed under the guardianship of Sir Giles Strangeways, being then possessed of Strode, North Bowood, and Temple. He *m.* Agnes, dau. of Humphrey Watkins, of Holwel, in Somersetshire, and had issue, 1 Giles, fellow of New College, Oxford, *d.* at Rome; 2 Humphrey, who *d. s. p.*; 3 THOMAS, of whom presently; 4 John, father of John, of Mostern; 5 George, of Southampton; and 6 Richard. He *d.* in 1610, having made nearly an equal division of his estates (Strode, Bowood, &c.) amongst his sons, the third of whom,

THOMAS GOLLOP, Esq. of Strode, &c., *m.* Frances, dau. of George Poulet, Esq. of Holberne, in the co. of Dorset, and granddau. of Lord Thomas Poulet (son of William, the 1st Marquess of Winchester), and dying in 1623, was *s.* by his eldest son,

THOMAS GOLLOP, Esq. of North Bowood and Strode, barrister-at-law. This gentleman *m.* Martha, dau. of Ralph Ironside, of Longbriddy, by Jane Gilbert, only sister of Gilbert, bishop of Bristol, and dying in 1663, was *s.* by his son,

THOMAS GOLLOP, Esq. of North Bowood and Strode, *b.* in 1617, high sheriff, 27 CHARLES II., who *m.* Elizabeth, dau. and heiress of Thomas Thorne, of Candlemarsh, Gent., and had a very large family, of which the 3rd son, William, was of Candlemarsh; the 4th, JOHN, was ancestor of the GOLLOPS OF STRODE; and the 9th, George, was of Berwick The 4th son,

JOHN GOLLOP, Esq., alderman of Dorchester, *m.* 1st, Mary, dau. of Philip Stansby, of Dorchester, and 2ndly, Frances, widow of Henry Backway, Gent., by the former of whom he had issue,

JOHN, his heir.

Thomas, of London, merchant, who *m.* Mary, dau. of Walter Foy, Esq. of Bewly Wood.

Rebecca, *m.* to Edward Tucker, Esq. of Weymouth.

Mr. Gollop *d.* 25 August, 1731, and was *s.* by his son,

JOHN GOLLOP, Esq. of Strode, who *m.* 1st, Edith, dau. of, Walter Foy, Esq. of Bewley Wood; 2ndly, Penelope, dau. of John Michell, Esq. of Kingston Russell; and 3rdly, Joan, dau. of Giles Hitt, Gent. of Lorscomb. By the first lady he had issue,

THOMAS, of Lillington, who *m.* 1st Oct. 1742, Susanna, dau. of Nathaniel Tilly, of Thornford, and eventual heiress of the Tillies, by whom he had issue,

THOMAS, heir to his grandfather.

Jane, *m.* to Henry Petty, Gent. of Evershot.

He *m.* 2ndly, Miss Holloway, and had another son, John, M.D., who *m.* Miss Anne Dampier, and *d. s. p.* Mr. Gollop *d. v. p.* 10 July, 1749.

John, and Walter, both *d. s. p.*

Mr. Gollop *d.* in 1758, aged 82, and was *s.* by his grandson,

THOMAS GOLLOP, Esq. of Sherborne and Strode. This gentleman *m.* Jane, dau. of the Rev. James Sawkins, LL.B., vicar of Frampton, and rector of Bettiscombe, in Dorsetshire, and left at his decease in 1793, an only son, the present George-Tilly Gollop, Esq. of Strode.

Arms—Gu., on a bend, or, a lion, passant, guardant, sa.

Crest—A demi-lion, bendy, or, and sa., holding in his dexter paw a broken arrow, gu.

Motto—Be bolde, be wyse.

Seat—Strode House, near Bridport.

GOODALL OF DINTON HALL.

Goodall, The Rev. James-Joseph, of Hinton Hall, co. Bucks, J.P., *b.* 4 Jan. 1800; *m.* 6 Feb. 1834, Elizabeth, dau. of William Boon, Esq. of Gretton, co. Northampton, and has issue,

I. William-Alexander-George, *b.* 23 March, 1839.
II. Liebert-Edward, *b.* 22 Aug., 1842.
I. Caroline-Mary.

Lineage.—Dinton Hall, originally built A.D. 1500, by William of Warham, archbishop of Canterbury, was possessed for many centuries by the Maynes, of whom was Simon Mayne the Regicide. In 1727, another Simon Mayne disposed of Dinton Hall to John Vanhattem, a descendant of Liebert Vanhattem, who had served in the fleet, and *m.* the dau. of Admiral de Ruiter. Eventually the heiress of the Vanhattems, Rebecca, dau. of Sir John Vanhattem, of Dinton Hall, *m.* the Rev. William Goodall (brother of Dr. Joseph Goodall, provost of Eton, who *d.* 1840), and conveyed to him Dinton Hall. Of this marriage, there was issue sixteen sons and daus., of whom one son and eight daus., still survive, viz.,

James-Joseph, now of Dinton Hall.
Harriet, *m.* to Dr. Irving, prebendary of Rochester.
Anne, *m.* to the Rev. C. R. Ashfield.
Emelia, *m.* to the Rev. John Barnwell.
Frances, *m.* to the Rev. John Hooper.
Matilda, *m.* to Sackville Phelps, Esq.
Arabella. Caroline. Eliza.

Seat—Dinton Hall, Aylesbury.

GOODDEN OF OVER COMPTON.

Goodden, John, Esq. of Over Compton, co Dorset, J.P. and D.L., high-sheriff 1848; *m.* 5 Oct. 1843, Ann, dau. of the Rev. Robert Phelips, (brother of the late John Phelips, Esq. of Montacute House, co. Somerset,) by Maria, his wife, dau. of William Harbin, Esq., of Newton Surmaville, and has issue,

I. John-Robert-Phelips, *b.* 28 July, 1845.
II. Edward-Wyndham, *b.* 17 Feb. 1847.
I. Emily-Maria. II. Ann-Caroline.

Lineage.—The manor of Over Compton was held by the family of Abington from the time of Henry VIII. to the year 1736, when it passed into the possession of the Gooddens, by whom it is still enjoyed.

Robert Goodden, Esq. of Bower Hinton and Martock, co. Somerset, and Over Compton, co. Dorset, *b.* in 1708, (son and heir of John Goodden, Esq. of Bower Hinton, by Mary his wife, dau. of George Moore, Esq. of Kingsdon, and 8th in descent from John Goodwyn, who *d.* at Martock, 4 Edward VI), he served as high-sheriff of Dorsetshire in 1747. He *m.* Abigail, dau. of Wyndham Harbin, Esq. of Newton, co. Somerset, and dying in 1764, was *s.* by his eldest son,

John-Harbin Goodden, Esq of Over Compton, who *d.* unm. in 1766, and was *s.* by his next brother,

Robert Goodden, Esq. of Over Compton, high-sheriff of Dorsetshire in 1779, *d.* unm. in 1829, and was *s.* by his only surviving brother,

Wyndham Goodden, Esq. of Over Compton, who *m.* 30 Dec. 1794, Mary, 2nd dau. (and co-heir with her sister Elizabeth) of John Jeane, Esq. of Binfords, co. Somerset, and by her (who *d.* 15 April, 1844) had issue,

I. John, his heir, now of Over Compton.
II. Wyndham-Jeane, in holy orders, rector of Over and Nether Compton.
III. George, in holy orders, rector of North Barrow, co. Somerset.
IV. Henry-Charles, of Upway, co. Dorset.
V. Charles-Culliford, in holy orders, vicar of Montacute, co. Somerset, *m.* 11 March, 1851, Bessy-Curgenven, dau. of John Smith, Esq. of Plymouth, and has issue, Wyndham-Charles, *b.* 15 Feb. 1854; 1 Anne-Elizabeth; 2 Georgiana.
I. Mary.
II. Elizabeth-Harbin, *m.* 26 Sep. 1852, to the Rev. [illegible] Rogers.
III. Louisa, *m.* 2 Oct. 1856, to the Rev. [illegible] herbert.

Mr. Goodden *d.* 17 July, 1839.

Arms—Az., on a bend, between two demi-lions, [illegible] erased, or, three lozenges, vaire, gu. and arg.

Crest—A griffin's head, erased, or, with wings [illegible] vaire, arg. and gu., holding in its beak an olive-branch [illegible]

Motto—Jovis omnia plena.

Seat—Over Compton, Dorset.

GOODFORD OF CHILTON CANTELO

Goodford, Henry, Esq. of Chilton Cantelo, [illegible] Somerset, *b.* 2 April, 1811; *s.* his father, [illegible] cember, 1835.

Lineage.—Samuel Goodford, of Yeovil, *m.* [illegible] May, 1716, Ann, dau. of Philip Taylor, of Weymouth [illegible] had by her, Samuel, his heir; Ann; and Elizabeth, *m.* [illegible] Feb. 1747, to John Daniel, of Yeovil. Mr. Goodford [illegible] 2ndly, in July, 1731, Elizabeth, relict of John Old, [illegible] Yeovil, and dau. of Jeremiah Hayne, but had no [illegible] issue. His only son,

Samuel Goodford, Esq. of the Inner Temple, and [illegible] Trent, in the co. of Somerset, *m.* in Oct. 1739, Mary [illegible] surviving child of John and Elizabeth Old, and had [illegible] her (who *d.* in 1767) one dau., Mary, *m.* in July, 17[illegible] Thomas Blakemore, Esq. of Briggins Park, Herts, and [illegible] son and successor,

John-Old Goodford, Esq. of Yeovil, sheriff of Somersetshire in 1774, who *m.* in Oct. 1776, Maria, 2nd dau. [illegible] Edward Phelips, Esq. of Montacute House, and dying [illegible] 1787, left, with a dau., Elizabeth, *m.* to Lieut.-Col. Ja[illegible] Paul Bridger, of Buckenham, Sussex, a son and successor,

John Goodford, Esq. of Chilton Cantelo, *b.* 27 Dec. 17[illegible] a magistrate and deputy-lieutenant for the co. of Somerset, and high-sheriff in 1816, *m.* 4 Jan. 1810, Charlotte, 4th dau. of Montague Cholmeley, Esq. of Easton, co Lincoln, and sister of the late Sir Montague Cholmeley, Bart., by whom he had issue,

Henry, his heir.
Charles-Old, *b.* 15 July, 1812.
Montague-John, *b.* 20 Nov. 1822, *d.* 3 July, 1869.
Mary-Ann, *d.* 5 Feb. 1833.
Maria. Penelope.

Mr. Goodford *d.* 9 Dec. 1835.

Arms—Az., on a chev., between three boars' heads, arg. langued and couped, gu., as many pellets.

Crest—A boar's head, arg., langued, gu., charged on the neck with a pellet.

Seat—Chilton Cantelo, near Yeovil.

GOODLAKE OF WADLEY HOUSE.

Goodlake, Thomas-Mills, Esq. of Wadley Hous[e] Shellingford, and Letcombe, co. Berks, J.P. a[nd] D.L., high-sheriff, 1832, *b.* 2 June, 1807; *m.* 22 Jul[y] 1828, Emilia-Maria, 2nd dau. of Sir Edward [illegible] Baker, Bart., by the Lady Elizabeth-Mary, his wi[fe] dau. of Robert, Duke of Leinster, and has issue,

I. Thomas-Leinster, *b.* 13 May, 1829; *m.* 22 Nov. 18[illegible] Mary-Frederica, only dau. of the late Robert Gly[n] Esq., and niece of the present Sir Richard-Plumpt[re] Glyn, Bart.
II. Edward-Wallace, *b.* 19 Sept. 1830, barrister-at-law.
III. Gerald-Littlehales, *b.* 14 May, 1832, an officer Col[d]stream Guards, served throughout the whole war wi[th] Russia.
I. Emilia-Jane. II. Olivia-Elizabeth.

Lineage.—Goodlake is undoubtedly a Saxon patro[ny]mic. Thomas Godelac, Godlak, or Guthlac, was lo[rd] of the manor of Henworth, Middlesex, in 1378, and obtain[ed] from King Richard II., about 1394, the lordship of t[he] manor of Woxenden (now Uxonden) also in Middlese[x]. His descendant,

William Goodlake, was of Letcombe Regis in 1546. At ...tcombe Regis the family have resided from father to son ...m a period antecedent to the first institution of Registers, ... the year 1536.

Thomas Goodlake, Esq. of Letcombe Regis, J.P. (great-...eat-gandfather of the present representative), *m.* one of ...e daus. (and co-heir with her only sister, wife of John ...agrave, Esq. of Calcot Park, Berkshire) of Thomas ...urrard, Esq. of Upper Lambourne, co. Berks, and had ...numerous family. The eldest son and heir,

Thomas Goodlake, Esq. of Letcombe Regis, many years ...P. for Berks, *m.* Anne Butler, of the neighbourhood of ...ungerford, and, with a dau., Catherine, *m.* to Thomas ...ustice, Esq. of Sutton Courtnay, had a son and heir,

Thomas Goodlake, Esq. of Letcombe Regis, who *m.* in ...75, Catherine, sister of Sir Charles Price, 1st Baronet, ...d by her had, with a dau., Catherine, who *d. unm.* aged ...neteen, and two younger sons (John-Hughes, who *d.* ...aving six children; and William-Hartley), another son, ...a heir,

Thomas Goodlake, Esq. of Letcombe Regis, who *m.* ...) July, 1806, Jane, only child and heiress of William-...arnton Mills, Esq. of Wadley House, Berkshire, and by ...er (who *d.* in 1808) has an only son, the present Thomas-...ills Goodlake, Esq. of Wadley House, and Letcombe.

Arms—Per fesse, az. and or, a lion, rampant, counter-...hanged, quartering Mills.
Crest—On a mount, vert, a woodwift, or wild man, ppr., ...olding up his club, gold.
Motto—Omnia bona desuper.
Seats—Wadley House, and Shellingford, near Farringdon, ...nd Letcombe, near Wantage.

GOODWIN OF HINCHLEYWOOD.

Goodwin, The Rev. Henry-John, of Hinchley-...wood, co. Derby, *b.* 21 Nov. 1803; *m.* 1832, Frances-...Eleanora, dau. and heiress of the Rev. Richard ...Burrow-Turbutt, son of William Turbutt, Esq. of ...Ogston Hall, co. Derby, and has issue,

I. Richard-Henry, *b.* 1833.
I. Isabella-Frances. II. Helen-Emilia.

Lineage.—The first of the Gladwin family on record ...s Thomas Gladwin, who lived at Boythorpe, co. Derby, ...and was *b.* about 1605. His son, Thomas Gladwin, Esq. ...of Tupton Hall, bapt. in 1630, was sheriff for the co. of Derby in 1667, and many years a county magistrate. This gentleman had a grant of arms about 1660. By Helen his wife, he had numerous issue. The eldest son was Lemuel, from whom descended Miss Lord, of Tupton Hall; and another son was Henry Gladwin, of whose line we have to treat: he *m.* Mary, dau. of Digby Dakeyne, Esq. of Stubbing Edge, co. Derby, and had issue,

Henry, of whom afterwards.
John, *b.* in 1731, *m.* and had issue, Dorothy, who *m.* the Right Hon. the Earl of Newburgh; Mary, *m.* to Robert Cloves, Esq. of London; Jane, *m.* to Gen. William Wynyard; and Helen, *m.* to Sampson Colectough, Esq. of Beacon Hill, Notts.
Mary, *m.* to Benjamin Brocklehurst, Esq.
Dorothy, *b.* in 1736, *m.* to the Rev. Basil Beridge, and *d.* in 1792, *s. p.*

The elder son,

Henry Gladwin, Esq. of Stubbing Court, *b.* in 1730, served with great distinction in America, and became a major-general in the army. He *m.* 30 March, 1772, Frances, dau. of the Rev. John Beridge, and had,

1. Charles-Dakeyne, of Belmont and Stubbing, *b.* 29 March, 1775, lieut.-col. of the Derbyshire militia, *m.* Miss Stringer, and had issue, one dau., Frances, who *m.* Mr. Melland.
II. Henry, *d.* an infant.
I. Frances, *m.* 9 June, 1801, Francis Goodwin, Esq. of Mapleton, (son of John Goodwin, Esq., by Mary his wife, dau. and co-heir of Francis Ridgeway, Esq. of Nottingham,) and *d.* 1841, leaving issue,
 1 Henry-John, now of Hinchleywood.
 1 Frances. 2 Mary-Ridgeway.
 3 Martha-Elizabeth, *m.* 1841, to John-Goodwin Johnson, Esq.
II. Dorothy, *m.* 4 Jan. 1792, to Joshua Jebb, Esq. of Walton Lodge.
III. Mary, *m.* 29 Nov. 1800, to Baldwin-Duppa Duppa, Esq. of Hollingbourne House.
IV. Ann, *m.* 22 June, 1814, to William Turbutt, Esq. of Ogston Hall.
V. Charlotte, *m.* 28 April, 1805, to the Rev. George Hutton, D.D., of Sutterton.
VI. Martha, *d. unm.* 22 Oct. 1812.
VII. Harriet, } *d. unm.*
VIII. Ellen, }
IX. Susannah, }

Mr. Gladwin bequeathed all his estates to the Rev. Henry-John Goodwin, now of Hinchleywood.

Arms—Or, a bar, gu., between six lions' heads, erased, gu.
Crest—A griffin, sejant.
Motto—Fide et virtute.
Seat—Hinchleywood, Ashbourne.

GOOLD OF CO. LIMERICK.

Goold, The Very Rev. Frederic-Falkener, Archdeacon of Raphoe, and rector of Raymochy, co. Donegal, *b.* in May, 1808; *m.* 16 June, 1830, Caroline-Newcomen, sister of Theresa, late Countess of Eglintoun and Winton, and has issue,

I. Thomas-Francis, *b.* 2 May, 1837.
I. Augusta-Jane. II. Caroline-Mary.
III. Emily-Marianne. IV. Elizabeth-Jessie.
V. Frances-Frederica.

Archdeacon Goold is 2nd but only surviving son of the late Thomas Goold, Esq., Master in Chancery, of Merrion Square, Dublin, by Elizabeth, his wife, dau. of the Rev. Brinsley Nixon, rector of Ramstown, co. Meath, and grandson of John Goold, Esq., and his wife, Mary Quin, of Rossburn. The late Master Goold who *d.* 16 July, 1846, had an elder son, Francis, high sheriff of co. Limerick, who was accidentally drowned in Sligo Bay, 31 Aug. 1848, and a third son, Wyndham, M.P. for co. Limerick, who *d. unm.* 27 Nov. 1854, and three daus., viz., Emily-Mary, *m.* in 1830, to the Rev. John Wynne, nephew of Owen Wynne, Esq. of Hazlewood, co. Sligo; Caroline-Susan, *m.* in 1829, to Sir Robert Gore-Booth, Bart., M.P. for co. Sligo; and Augusta-Charlotte, *m.* in 1836, to Edwin, Earl of Dunraven.

Lineage.—The family is a branch of the baronetical family of Goold, and is closely connected by intermarriages with the families of Quins *of Rossbrien and Adare*, co. Limerick, the O'Briens *of Dromoland*, the Finnucanes *of Ennistymon*, and McNamaras *of Doolin*, co. Clare.

GORDON OF ABERGELDIE.

Gordon, Michael-Francis, Esq. of Abergeldie Castle, co. Aberdeen, *b.* 21 April, 1792; *m.* 31 Aug. 1820, Caroline, 5th dau. of the Rev. John Swete, of Oxton House, co. Devon, and has had issue,

I. Francis-David, *b.* 24 July, 1821.
II. John-Henry, *b.* 7 Jan. 1824; *d.* 20 April, 1848.
III. Michael-Lawrance, *b.* 3 Sept. 1833; *d.* 27 Oct. 1850.
IV. William-Herbert, *b.* 29 May, 1840; *d.* 6 Dec. 1850.
I. Caroline-Anne, *m.* 5 Jan. 1854, to Edmund Prideaux St. Aubyn, Esq., captain Madras army.
II. Margaret. III. Bertha.

Lineage.—To his 2nd son, Sir Alexander Gordon, Knt., his father, Alexander, 1st Earl of Huntly, granted by deed at Huntly, 12 Feb. 1458, all his lands, formerly parcel of the barony of Mygmar (Midmar) and Tulch, besides other estates therein mentioned. Sir Alexander acquired subsequently, by royal grant from King James III., in the 23rd year of his reign, the lands of Abergeldie, when this branch of the Gordons was ever after designated, and is styled in the deed of gift (dated at Edinburgh, 26 Dec. 1482) "dilecto familiari armigero nostro, Alexandro de Mygmair." Sir Alexander *m.* Janet, 2nd dau. and co-heir of George Leith, of Barnis, who *d.* in 1505, and relict of Alexander Seton, of Meldrum, by whom he had a son and successor,

Alexander Gordon, Esq. of Abergeldie, who *m.* Janet, dau. of Alexander Irvine, Esq. of Drum, and was *s.* by his son,

William Gordon, Esq. of Abergeldie, who *m.* Frances, dau. of Andrew, Lord Gray, who *d.* in 1514, and was *s.* by his son,

Alexander Gordon, Esq. of Abergeldie. This laird m. Katharine, dau. of Sir William Nicholson, Bart., of Carnock, king's advocate for Scotland, and had a son and heir,

Alexander Gordon, Esq. of Abergeldie, who by Euphemia, his wife, dau. of Robert Graham, Esq. of Morphy, left a son, John, his heir, and a dau., Rachel, successor to her brother. The son,

John Gordon, Esq. of Abergeldie, m. a dau. of Ross, of Kilravock, but d. without issue, when the estates and representation of the family devolved upon his sister,

Rachel Gordon, of Abergeldie, who m. Captain Charles Gordon, son of Peter Gordon, Esq. of Minmore, a cadet of the Ducal family, by Janet, dau. of Sir Alexander Gordon, of Cluny, and had a son and successor,

Peter Gordon, Esq. of Abergeldie, who m. 1st, Margaret, dau. of Peter Strachan, of Edinburgh; and 2ndly, Elizabeth, dau. of Lord Gray, by the latter of whom he had a dau., Barbara, m. to David Hunter, of Burnside. Abergeldie m. 3rdly, Margaret, sister to Sir Archibald (Foulis) Primrose, hung at Carlisle in 1745, and dau. of Sir George Foulis, Bart. of Dunipace, by Janet, dau. of Sir John Cunningham, of Caprington, king's advocate for Scotland, and had issue,

Charles, his heir,
Janet, } who both d. unm.
Rachel, }
Euphemia, m. to James, 5th Viscount Strathallan.
Jean, d. unm.

The Laird of Abergeldie was s. by his son,

Charles Gordon, Esq. of Abergeldie, who m. Alison, dau. of David Hunter, Esq. of Burnside, and widow of — Paterson, Esq., and left, at his decease, 19 March, 1796,

I. Peter, of Abergeldie, who m. 1st, Mary, dau. of John Forbes, Esq. of Blackford, and had an only child, Katharine, who d. unm. in 1802, aged 17. He m. 2ndly, Elizabeth, dau. of Alexander Leith, Esq. of Freefield, and d. without issue, in 1819. His widow d. 1855.
II. David, of whom presently.
III. Charles, Knight of the Prussian Order of Merit, d. s. p. 25 March, 1835, aged 79.
IV. Adam, of London, who m. Penelope, eldest dau. of Michael Biddulph, Esq. of Ledbury, and dying 28 May, 1800, left an only son, William Gordon, Esq. of Haffield, co. Hereford, high-sheriff in 1829, b. 8 Dec. 1794, who m. 21 Dec. 1820, Mary, eldest dau. of William Wingfield, Esq., by Lady Charlotte Digby his wife, and d. 5 Oct. 1836, leaving issue one son, Edward-William, b. 18 May, 1828, and two daus., Charlotte-Florence, and Caroline-Anne.
V. Alexander-Sinclair, d. s. p. 30 June, 1837, aged 77.
VI. William, major 60th foot, d. s. p. in 1798.
VII. John, d. young.
I. Margaret, m. to George Skene, M.D., of Aberdeen.

The 2nd son,

David Gordon, Esq. of London and Abergeldie, m. 18 June, 1789, Anne, 3rd dau. of Michael Biddulph, Esq. of Ledbury, and by her (who d. 26 Feb. 1841) had issue,

I. Charles-David, b. 30 Oct. 1790, m. 22 April, 1819, Marian, eldest dau. of Robert Phillipps, Esq. of Longworth, co. Hereford, and dying 24 Nov. 1826, left issue, 1. Anna-Maria; 2. Katharine-Frances, m. in 1842, to Duncan Davidson, Esq. of Tillychetly, co. Aberdeen; 3. Isabella-Margaret, m. 7 Dec. 1854, to Antony Gibbs, Esq. of Merry Hill, Herts; and 4. Emilia-Lucy.
II. Michael-Francis, now of Abergeldie.
III. Robert, capt. R.N., b. 7 Sept. 1796.
IV. Adam, b. 30 May, 1801, m. 8 Nov. 1825, Susan, 6th dau. of the Rev. John Swete, of Oxton House, Devon, and d. 14 Jan. 1839, leaving issue, seven sons, 1. Hugh-Mackay, b. 24 Sept. 1826; 2. Lewis, b. 28 Jan. 1828; 3. Charles-Vincent, b. in 1829, m. 1854, Emma, dau. of Charles Godwin, Esq., and has issue; 4. Adam Stephenson, in holy orders, b. in 1831; 5. Dundas-William, b. in 1833; 6. Cosmo, b. in 1837; and 7. James-Henry, b. 25 Jan. 1839; and one dau., Anne-Cecilia.
I. Anna-Penelope.
II. Harriet-Margaret.
III. Mary-Anne, m. 6 May, 1824, Rev. William Swete, 2nd son of the Rev. John Swete, of Oxton House, Devon.

Mr. Gordon d. 22 Oct. 1831, aged 78.

Arms—Quarterly: 1st, az., three boars' heads, couped, or; 2nd, or, three lions' heads, erased, gu.; 3rd, or, three crescents, gu., within a double tressure, flory, counterflory, of the second; 4th, az., three cinquefoils, arg., the whole within a bordure quarterly, arg. and gu.
Crest—A deer-hound, arg., collared, gu.
Motto—God with us; or, anciently, God with ws.
Seat—Abergeldie, co. Aberdeen.

GORDON OF CULVENNAN.

Gordon, William, Esq. of Culvennan, co. Wigton, J.P., b. 17 Aug. 1800; m. 17 Aug. 1825, his cousin-german, Agnes-Marion, dau. of John Hyslop, Esq. of Lochend, and has had issue,

I. David-Alexander, b. 29 Feb. 1828; rifle brigade, served in the Crimea; m. 1 Jan. 1855, Jane Lawrie, only dau. of Allen Bell, Esq. of Hilloton, Kirkcudbright, and has a son and heir,
William-Ainslie, b. 26 Nov. 1855.
II. John-Hyslop, b. 6 Nov. 1829.
III. James, b. 31 March, 1832.
I. Margaret, d. in 1835. II. Agnes-Marion.

Mr. Gordon is 16th in direct male descent from Sir Adam de Gordon, of Lochinvar, the companion in arms of Wallace.

Lineage.—This is a branch of the noble house of Kenmure and Lochinvar, which traces its descent from Richard de Gordoun, in 1120, and from the valiant Sir Adam de Gordounn, of Bruce's time.

Sir John Gordon, of Lochinvar, who d. in 1517, 5th in descent from the above-mentioned Sir Adam; left two sons, Sir Robert, his successor, and William. His estate of Craichlaw, co. Wigton, he settled on his 2nd son,

William Gordon, of Craichlaw, who d. in 1545, and was s. by his son,

William Gordon, of Craichlaw. He d. in 1570, and was s. by his son

John Gordon of Craichlaw, whose name we find attached to the bond by the Scottish nobility, for the establishment of James VI. on the Scottish throne. He d. in 1580, and was s. by his son,

William Gordon, of Craichlaw, who purchased the estate of Culvennan, and dying in 1636, was s. therein by his son,

Alexander Gordon, of Culvennan, who d. in 1679, and was s. by his son

William Gordon, of Culvennan, an enthusiastic presbyterian who, dying in 1703, was s. by his son,

William Gordon, of Culvennan, to whom s.,

Sir Alexander Gordon, of Culvennan lieutenant-colonel of the Kirkcudbrightshire local militia, and successively sheriff of the cos. of Wigton and Kirkcudbright. Sir Alexander, who was knighted in 1800, m. 17 July, 1769, Grace, only sister of Sir John Dalrymple Hay, of Glenluce, Bart., and had,

I. James, his heir.
II. David, b. 26 March, 1774, m. 2 Sept. 1797, Agnes, eldest dau. of William Hyslop, of Lochend, by Jean his wife, dau. of John Maxwell, Esq. of Munshes, representative of the noble house of Herries, and d. 1 Nov. 1829, leaving by her, who survived him nine years, issue,
1 William-Gordon, successor to his uncle, and present representative of the family.
2 Alexander, member of the Institution of Civil Engineers, b. 5 May, 1802, m. 14 July, 1828, Sarah, dau. of Alexander Cock, Esq. of the city of London.
3 James, b. 31 Jan. 1818; m. 1845, Amelia, 2nd dau. of James Loudon, Esq. of St. Helena, and has surviving issue, Helen-Charlotte.
1 Jean, m. 4 Feb. 1845, to the Rev. William Pitt MacFarquhar, M.A., incumbent of Bengeworth, co. Warwick.
2 Grace, m in 1828, to Charles Potter, Esq. of Earnsdale, co. Lancaster, and has issue.
3 Isabella, m. 19 Aug. 1833, to James-Richard Clark, Esq., but. d. without issue, 26 May, 1834.
I. Isabella.

Sir Alexander d. 21 Oct. 1830, at the advanced age of 83, and was s. by his eldest son,

James Gordon, Esq. of Culvennan lieut.-col. commandant of the Kirkcudbright yeomanry cavalry, and a deputy-lieut. of the co., b. 2 Dec. 1771, who m. 17 Sept. 1816, Janet, eldest dau. and co-heir of Johnstone Hannay of Balcary, Esq., and d. s. p. 27 May, 1843, when he was s. by his nephew, William.

Arms—Az., a bezant, between three boars' heads, erased, or, langued, gu.
Crest—A dexter naked arm, issuing out of a cloud, and grasping a flaming sword, ppr.
Motto—(above the crest)—Dread God.
Seat—Greenlaw House, Kirkcudbrightshire.

GORDON OF CAIRNFIELD.

Gordon, John, Esq. of Cairnfield, co. Banff, J.P. and D.L., b. 23 Sept. 1805; m. 9 Dec. 1851, Margaret, dau. of George Wright, Esq., and has a son and heir,

ADAM-STEUART, b. 10 July, 1854.

Lineage.—ROBERT GORDON, Esq. of Lunan, m. a dau. of Gordon, of Dykeside, co. Moray, and was father of ALEXANDER GORDON, Esq., who m. 1st Elizabeth, dau. of Gordon, of Cairnfield, and by her had three daus, the eldest of whom m. Gordon, of Buckie; the second m. Anderson, of Lingwood; and the third d. *unm.* Alexander Gordon, m. 2ndly, Jane, eldest dau. of Gordon, of Shillagreen, eldest son of Gordon, of Drumwhydle and Faskine, by his wife, the eldest dau. of Sir John Gordon, of Park, Bart., and by her had two sons, JOHN, and James, late of Roseburn. The 2nd son of the 2nd marriage,

JOHN GORDON, Esq., m. in 1761, Jane, dau. of George Steuart, Esq. of Tannochy, by Anne, his wife, dau. of Sir James Abercromby, Bart. of Birkenbog, and had issue,

ADAM, of Arradoul and Cairnfield.
Jane, m. to James Duff, Esq. of the island of Madeira, and had issue.
Elizabeth.

The son and heir,

ADAM GORDON, Esq. of Arradoul and Cairnfield, D.L., b. 13 Feb. 1773, m. 4 March, 1799, Elizabeth, eldest dau. of Patrick Cruickshank, Esq. of Stracathro, co. Forfar, and had issue,

JOHN, now of Cairnfield.
Patrick, lieut.-colonel N.I. Bengal; b. 27 March, 1810, m. 4 May, 1848, Charlotte-Mary, dau. of the late Capt. George Mathers, 24th foot.
George, b. 20 Sept. 1814, m. Mrs. Mary Stanley, widow, of North Carolina, U.S.
James-Gordon-Duff, E.I.C., 50 N.I. Bengal.
William, capt. E.I.C.S., 49 N.I. Bengal, b. 10 Feb. 1824, m. 19 July, 1849, Louisa-Elizabeth, eldest dau. of the Rev. Warren Mercer, vicar of Northallerton.
Jane.
Elizabeth-Marjory, m. in 1836, to the Rev. Edward Lillingston, 5th son of the late J.-W. Lillingston, of Elmdon, co. Warwick, d. in 1841, leaving two sons.
Margaret-Helen. Emma.
Harriet, m. 21 Oct. 1854, to William Terry, Esq.

Mr. Gordon d. 17 March, 1847.

Arms—Az., a pheon between three boars' heads, erased, or.
Crest—A boar's head, erased, or.
Motto—Above the crest, Byd; under the arms, Dum vigilo tutus.
Seat—Cairnfield, co. Banff.

GORDON OF PITLURG.

GORDON-CUMING-SKENE, JOHN, Esq. of Pitlurg and Dyce, co. Aberdeen, J.P., b. 9 Feb. 1827; m. 27 March, 1856, Maria, dau. of William-Henry Nares, Esq., commander R.N.

Lineage.—JOHN GORDON, of Scurdargue, or Essie, (2nd son of John de Gordon, of Strathbolgie, and brother of Adam Gordon, killed at Homildon, whose dau. and heir, Elizabeth, m. Alexander Seton, and was by his ancestor of the Gordons, Dukes of Gordon,) m Margaret, dau. of Sir Patrick Maitland, of Gight, and dying about the year 1420, was s. by his eldest son,

JOHN GORDON, who acquired the lands of Auchlenchries, in Aberdeenshire. He m. 1st, Elizabeth, dau. of Abernethy, Lord Salton, and 2ndly, Henault, dau. of Macleod, of Harris. His eldest son, by his 1st marriage,

JOHN GORDON, of Auchlenchries, m. Margaret, dau. of Sir Alexander Forbes, ancestor of Lord Pitsligo, and was slain in 1513, at the battle of Flodden, fighting under the standard of Alexander, 3rd Earl of Huntly, who commanded the victorious right wing of the Scottish army. He was s. by his only son,

JOHN GORDON, who sold the estate of Lungar, purchased the lands of Pitlurg, and exchanged Hilton for Cravethin, or Coravechin, in Aberdeenshire. He m. 1st, Lady Jane Stuart, dau. of John, Earl of Athol, brother uterine of King JAMES II. of Scotland, and son, by her 2nd marriage, of Jane, widow of JAMES I., Queen Dowager of Scotland, and granddau. of King EDWARD III. of England, being the dau. of his son, John, Duke of Lancaster. He m. 2ndly, Margaret Drummond, of the family of Perth, and d. in 1544. His eldest son,

JOHN GORDON, of Pitlurg, m Janet, dau. of James Ogilvie, of Cullen, (ancestor of the Earls of Findlater and Seafield,) by whom he acquired the estate of Broadlands, in Aberdeenshire. He fell at Pinkie, in 1547, leaving one son,

SIR JOHN GORDON, Knt. of Pitlurg, who frequently represented the county of Aberdeen in the Scottish Parliament, and bore an eminent part in the affairs of that period. Sir John m. Isabel, dau. of William, 7th Lord Forbes, and d. 16 Sept. 1600, leaving two sons and a dau. The elder son,

JOHN GORDON, of Pitlurg, inherited the esteem of JAMES IV. He m. Nicolas, dau. of Kinnaird, of Kinnaird, but dying s. p. in 1619, was s. by his brother,

ROBERT GORDON, of Pitlurg, commonly designated of Straloch. This gentleman, a poet, a mathematician, an antiquary, and a geographer, was b. 14 Sept. 1580, and d. 18 Aug. 1661, having had, with six daus., eleven sons, 1 ROBERT, his heir; 2 John, of Fechil; 3 William, who d. s. p. in 1648; 4 Alexander, who d. young, in 1615; 5 James, minister of the parish of Rothiemay, who m. the heiress of Fraser, of Techmiury, and founded a respectable family; 6 George, who d. in 1686; 7 Alexander a judge of the Court of Session, as Lord Auchintoul; 8 Hugh, who d. s. p.; 9 Arthur, an eminent barrister, who d. in 1680, leaving a son, Robert, who founded and endowed a magnificent hospital in Aberdeen; 10 Patrick, who d. in 1649; and 11 Lewis, a Physician, who d. s. p. in 1704. The eldest son,

ROBERT GORDON, of Pitlurg, b. in 1609, s. his father in 1661. He m. in 1638, Catherine, dau. of Sir Thomas Burnett, Bart. of Leys, and had,

ROBERT, his heir.
John, of Collieston, near Arbroath, a physician, who m. 1st, Katharine, dau. of John Fullerton, of Kinnebar; 2ndly, Helen, dau. of Allardyce, of Allardyce; and 3rdly, Grizel, dau. of Falconer, of Glen Farquhar. His eldest son, John, of Hilton, an eminent physician, m. Margaret, dau. of John Dowell, merchant, and had, with other issue, a son, JAMES, of whom as successor to his kinsman, Gordon, of Pitlurg.
Catherine, b. in 1644, m. to Robert, second Viscount Arbuthnot.

Pitlurg, d. in 1681, and was s. by his son,

ROBERT GORDON, of Pitlurg, b. in 1641, who m. Jean, dau. of Sir Richard Maitland, Lord Pitrichie, by whom he had a dau., m. to Baird, of Auchmedden, and a son,

ALEXANDER GORDON, of Pitlurg, who inherited the estates in 1683. He m. Jean, dau. of James Gordon, of Ellen, by whom he had a dau., who d. *unm.*, and a son, Alexander, an ensign in the British army, who dying in 1748, without issue, the property devolved on the nearest collateral male heir, his uncle's grandson,

JAMES GORDON, of Hilton, M.D., who then became of Pitlurg. He m. in 1731, Barbara, dau. of Robert Cuming, of Birnes, and dying in 1755, was s. by his son,

JOHN-GORDON CUMING, of Pitlurg, who succeeded, in right of his mother, to the entailed estates of Birnes and Leask, and added Cuming to his paternal surname. He m. Mary, dau. of John Fullerton, of Gallery, in Forfarshire, and had issue,

I. JOHN, his heir.
II. Thomas, who inherited the estate of Harperfield, in Lanarkshire, of which co. he was a deputy-lieutenant, and lieut.-col. of the militia. He m. Jane Nisbet, niece of Andrew, last Earl of Hyndford, and by her left issue, at his decease, in 1832,

1 JOHN-WILLIAM, of Harperfield, an officer in the royal engineers. 2 Hamilton.
1 Amelia.

Mr. Gordon Cuming d. in 1768, and was s. by his son,

JOHN-GORDON CUMING, of Pitlurg and Birnes, b. in 1761, who inheriting in 1815 the estates of his relative, Skene, of Dyce (eldest collateral branch of Skene, of Skene), assumed the name of Skene, in conformity with a deed of entail. He entered the army in 1779, and eventually attained the rank of Lieut.-General. He m. Lucy, 3rd dau. of Sir Hugh Crawford, Bart. of Jordan-hill, and had issue,

WILLIAM, his heir.
Thomas, who m. Harriet, third dau. of Lieut.-Gen. Sir William Hutchinson.
James, who m. Jane-Adelaide, second dau. of Sir Thos. Mackenny, Bart. of Dublin.
Crawford, m. to William Forlong, Esq. of Errins.
Isabella, m. to Francis Gordon, Esq. of Kincardine, brother of James Gordon, of Craig.
Reubina. Lucy.

Pitlurg d. in 1828, and was s. by his eldest son,

WILLIAM GORDON-CUMING-SKENE, Esq. of Pitlurg, and Dyce, J.P. and D.L., a lieut.-colonel of the Aberdeenshire militia, b. in 1786, who m. in 1825, Anne, youngest dau. of Alexander Brebner, Esq. of Learney, and had issue, JOHN, his heir; Alexander, Capt. Roy. Art., b. 30. Nov. 1823, killed at Sebastopol, June, 1855; Christian; and Lucan. Col. William Gordon entered the army at an early age, served several years with the 92nd, or Gordon Highlanders, and afterwards with the 6th regt. in France, the Peninsula, and on the staff in the West Indies. He d. 14 Jan. 1837, and was s. by his son, the present JOHN GORDON-CUMING-SKENE, Esq. of Pitlurg.

Arms—Az., three boars' heads, within a bordure, or.
Crest—A dove, arg., beaked, membered, gu., in its beak an olive branch, ppr.
Supporters—Dexter, a knight in complete armour, his visor up, with shield and lance, all ppr.; sinister, a boar, ppr.
Motto—I hope.
Seat—Parkhill, Aberdeenshire.

GORDON OF FLORIDA.

GORDON, ROBERT, Esq. of Florida, co. Down, b. 8 Sept. 1791; high-sheriff of Downshire in 1833; m. 25 Aug. 1825, Mary, 5th dau. of the late William Crawford, Esq. of Lakelands, co. Cork. Mr. Gordon s. his father 2 March, 1837.

Lineage.—This family, claiming to be a branch of the ancient and ennobled line of the same name in Scotland, is stated to have gone from Berwickshire to Ireland during the period of the civil wars in North Britain. The representative of the Irish branch, at the close of the 17th century,

ROBERT GORDON, Esq. of Ballinteggart, co. Down, m. in 1689, a sister of Robert Ross, Esq. of Rosstrevor, and had issue, 1 JOHN, his heir; 2 Robert, in holy orders. Mr. Gordon d. in 1720, and was s. by his son,

JOHN GORDON, Esq. of Ballinteggart, b. in 1690, who m. 1st, in 1720, Jane, dau. of Alexander Hamilton, Esq. of Hampton Hall, co. Dublin, and by her, who d. in 1726, had issue,

ROBERT, his heir.
Jane, m. to David Johnston, Esq.

John Gordon m. 2ndly, Grace, dau. of Thomas Knox, Esq. of Dungannon, co. Tyrone, father of the 1st Viscount Northland, and had by her,

Thomas-Knox, b. in 1728, appointed in 1771, Chief Justice of South Carolina, who d. in 1796, and was s. in Ballinteggart by his son, MAJOR JOHN GORDON.
John, b. in 1730, lieut.-col. 50th regt. (in which regiment his three nephews, Major John-Gordon Haven, Capt. John-Craford Gordon, and Capt. Robert Wallace, held commissions.) Col. Gordon, m. Elizabeth, sister of Sir Charles Bampfylde, Bart. of South Molton, in Devonshire, but d. s. p. in 1782.
Margery, m. to William Haven, Esq.
Elizabeth, m. to Joseph Wallace, Esq.

Mr. Gordon d. in February, 1771, leaving his estate of Ballinteggart to Thomas-Knox Gordon, his eldest son by his 2nd marriage. His eldest son by his 1st wife,

ROBERT GORDON, Esq., b. in 1722, m. in 1755, Alicia, only dau. of James Arbuckle, Esq., by Anne, his wife, dau. and heir of John Craford, brother and heir-at-law of David Craford, Esq. of Florida, co. Down. By this lady he had issue,

I. JOHN-CRAFORD, his heir.
II. DAVID, successor to his brother.
III. Robert, of Summerfield, co. Down, b. 1761: m. 1802, Catharine-Anne, dau. of John Clarke, Esq. of Belfast, and by her (who d. 1844.) has issue,
 1 Robert-Alexander, J.P., b. 1811.
 1 Catharine-Anne.
IV. Alexander, m. Dorothea, third dau. of Gen. James Gisborne, of Derbyshire, formerly Commander-in-Chief of the forces in Ireland, and d. 15 July, 1829, leaving issue,
 1 Robert-Francis.
 2 James-Gisborne. who entered the army, and d. in 1826.
 3 John-Frederick, in holy orders.
 4 Alexander-Thomas.
 1 Marianne. 2 Alicia-Dorothea.
I. Anne, m. in Jan. 1779, to Eldred Pottinger, Esq. of Mount Pottinger, in Downshire.

Mr. Gordon d. in 1798, and was s. by his son,

JOHN-CRAFORD GORDON, Esq. of Florida, Capt. 50th regt., b. in 1757, who d. unm. in Nov. 1797, and was s. by his next brother,

DAVID GORDON, Esq. of Florida, b. 1 June 1759, a magistrate and deputy-lieutenant for Downshire, and high sheriff in 1812, who m. 11 Sept. 1789, Mary, youngest dau. of James Crawford, Esq. of Crawfordsburn, and sister of Anne, Countess of Caledon, by whom he had surviving issue,

ROBERT, his heir.
James, in holy orders, b. 28 April, 1796.
Jane-Maria.

Mr. Gordon d. 2 March, 1837, and was s. by his son, the present ROBERT GORDON, Esq. of Florida.

Seats—Florida and Delamont, co. Down.

GORDON OF BALMAGHILL.

GORDON, JAMES-MURRAY, Esq. of Balmaghill House, co. Kirkcudbright, Capt. R.N., b. 6 March, 1782; m. 10 Dec. 1810, Sarah-Almeria, dau. of Archdeacon Caulfeild, and relict of Capt. Charlton, E. I. Co.'s Service, and by her (who d. 21 Dec. 1821) has issue,

I. THOMAS-DEMPSTER, b. 1 Nov. 1811.
II. James-Caulfeild, lieut. 92nd Highlanders, b. 5 April, 1817, d. in 1841.
I. Almeria-Caulfeild.
II. Geraldine-Caulfeild, m. to Thomas Hanyngton, Esq. Jun.

Capt. Gordon, of Balmaghill, and his brother, James-Dempster-Webster Gordon, Esq. (who m. a dau. of General Pollok, E. I. Co.'s Service, and has two sons and a dau.,) are the sole surviving issue of Thomas Gordon, Esq., by his wife, a dau. of the family of Dempster. There were two other brothers, Thomas-William Gordon, Lieut.-Col. Fusilier Guards, and George, who both d. unm.

Arms—Az., three boars' heads, erased, or.
Crest—A demi-savage, wreathed about the head and loins with laurel, ppr.
Motto—Dread God.
Seat—Balmaghill House, Kirkcudbrightshire.

GORDON OF CAIRNBULG.

GORDON, JOHN, Esq. of Cairnbulg, co. Aberdeen, b. 20 March, 1787; m. 8 June, 1812, Catharine-Anne Forbes, dau. of the late Sir William Forbes, fifth baronet of Craigievar, by his wife, the Hon. Sarah Sempill, dau. of John, twelfth Lord Sempill, and has issue,

I. GEORGE-WILLIAM-ALEXANDER, b. 1 Oct. 1814, d. 10 Dec. 1841.
II. John, b. 28 Dec. 1817, capt. 6th regt. of Bengal Native Infantry, m. 11 April, 1849, Madeline, 2nd dau. of the Rev. Dr. Roberts of Ravenden, co. Carlow, and has a son, John, b. 5 Nov. 1850.
III. Alexander-Crombie, b. 3 Dec. 1818, commander R.N.
IV. Hugh-Charles, b. 21 April, 1820, d. 12 Feb. 1821.
V. William, b. 26 June, 1821, lieut-col. in the army, and major 17th regt. of Foot.
VI. Charles, b. 20 Oct. 1823, capt. 92nd Highlanders, m. 26 April. 1849, Christina, only dau. of William Innes, Esq. of Raemoir.
I. Sarah-Janet.
II. Albinia-Isabella, m. 6 Feb. 1840, to William Gordon, Esq., eldest son of the late William Gordon, Esq. of Aberdour, co. Aberdeen, d. 3 July, 1840.
III. Catharine-Erskine.

Mr. Gordon is in the commission of the peace for the counties of Aberdeen and Banff; was appointed a deputy-lieutenant of the former county in 1808, and major of the 2nd regiment of Aberdeenshire local militia in 1809; is a member of the Scottish bar, a Fellow of the Royal Society of Edinburgh, and of the Society of Antiquaries of Scotland; is one of the deputies of the Vice-admiral of Scotland, and a director of the Highland and Agricultural Society of Scotland.

Arms—Az., three boars' heads, couped, or, within a double treasure, flowered and counterflowered with fleurs-de-lis, of the second.
Crest—Two naked arms, holding a bow at full stretch, ready to let an arrow fly, all ppr.
Motto—Fortuna sequatur.
Seat—Cairnbulg, Aberdeenshire.

GORDON OF FYVIE.

GORDON, WILLIAM-COSMO, Esq. of Fyvie Castle, co. Aberdeen, *b.* 17 May, 1810; *m.* 9 June, 1848, Mary-Grace, 3rd dau. of the late Sir Robert Abercromby, Bart. of Birkenbog. Mr. Gordon is eldest son of the late Charles Gordon, Esq. of Fyvie Castle (who *d.* 18 Feb. 1851), by Elizabeth his wife, widow of William Clutton, Esq., and grandson of the Hon. Alexander Gordon, Lord Rockville, who was 3rd son of William, 2nd Earl of Aberdeen (*see* BURKE'S *Peerage*).

Arms, Crest, and *Motto*—Those of the Earl of Aberdeen.
Seat—Fyvie Castle, co. Aberdeen.

GORDON OF PARK HOUSE.

GORDON, LACHLAN-DUFF, Esq. of Park House, co. Banff, J.P. and D.L., late capt 20th regt., *b.* 1 June, 1817; *m.* 6 March, 1847, Jane-Ellen, dau. of Thomas Butterfield, Esq. of Bermuda, and has issue,

I. THOMAS-DUFF, *b.* 11 Aug. 1848.
I. Mary-Louisa.

Lineage.—The Duffs of Drummuir derive from William Duff, third son of Adam Duff, of Clunybeg, who *d.* in 1674, ancestor of the Earl of Fife, and the Gordons of Park, from a scion of the noble house of HUNTLY.

ALEXANDER DUFF, Esq. of Drummuir, co. Banff, Provost of Inverness, and member of the Scottish parliament, had, by Katherine, his wife, three sons, ALEXANDER, of Drummuir; William, of Muirtown, co. Inverness; and JOHN, of whom we treat. The youngest,

JOHN DUFF, Esq. of Culbin, co. Moray, *m.* Helen, dau. and in her issue, heiress of SIR JAMES GORDON, of Park, Esq., by Helen, his wife, dau. of the Lord Saltoun, and by this lady had several sons and daus., all of whom *d. s. p.* except Katherine, who *m.* Alexander Morison, Esq. of Bognie, co. Aberdeen, and a son,

LACHLAN DUFF, Esq., who *m.* Rachel, dau. of Roger Hog, Esq. of West Lothian, and had (with three sons, James, *d.* in the West Indies; Roger, *d.* in Russia; and Alexander, killed at Trafalgar, in H.M.S. Mars, in 1805) another and only surviving son, THOMAS, who assumed the name of Gordon, the late THOMAS GORDON, Esq. of Park House, and a dau. Rachel, *m.* to Patrick Stewart, Esq. of Auchlincart, co. Banff. The son,

THOMAS GORDON, Esq. of Park House, *b.* 14 March, 1790, was lieut-col. of the Inverness and Banff militia, a magistrate and deputy-lieutenant, and convener of Banffshire. He *s.* to the barony of Park in 1808, through his grandmother, Helen Gordon, of Park, and assumed thereupon the surname of GORDON, in lieu of his patronymic, DUFF. He *m.* 14 Nov. 1814, Joanna-Maria, eldest dau. of David Macdowall Grant, Esq. of Arndilly, co. Banff, and had issue,

I. LACHLAN-DUFF, now of Park House.
II. David-Macdowall, R.N., deceased.
III. Alexander-Duff.
I. Mary. II. Rachel, *m.* to Dr. Mackie.
III. Eliza, *m.* to A. Steuart, Esq. of Auchlinkart.
IV. Eleanora, *m.* to the Rev. H. Walker.
V. Wilhelmina, deceased.
VI. Isabella. VII. Jemima.
VIII. Joanna, deceased. IX. Emilie.

Col. Gordon *d.* 6 Dec. 1855.

Arms—Az., a dexter arm, embowed in armour, grasping a sword, erect, in pale, ppr., hilt and pommel, or, between three boars' heads, couped, of the third, langued, gu.
Crest—A sinister gauntlet, ppr.
Mottoes—Over the crest, Sic tutus; under the arms, Salus per Christum.
Seat—Park House, co. Banff.

GORDON OF KNOKESPOCH AND TERPERSIE.

GORDON, JAMES-ADAM, Esq. of Knockespoch and Terpersie, co. Aberdeen, J.P. and D.L., high-sheriff co. Somerset, 1831, *b.* 16 April, 1791; *m.* 23 Sept. 1832, Emma-Catherine, 2nd dau. of Vice-Admiral Thomas Wolley, by Frances-Edith Francklyn, his wife. Mr. Gordon is recorder of Tregony, which borough he represented in parliament in 1830.

Lineage.—King JAMES VI. of Scotland renewed the grant of the barony of Clatt, in Aberdeenshire, in 1604, "to his beloved JAMES GORDOUN, of Knockespoke. It was first granted by JAMES IV. in 1508. The great grandfather of the present representative,

JAMES-BREBNER GORDON, Esq. of Knockespoch, son of George Gordon, Esq. of Knockespoch, and grandson of Harry Gordon, of the same place, left by Margaret his wife, a son and successor,

JAMES-BREBNER GORDON, Esq. of Knockespoch, who *m.* Jane Lavington, and had (with a dau. Mary-Anne, *m.* in 1777, to Sir William Abdy, Bart. of Felix Hall, Essex) a son and heir,

JAMES GORDON, Esq. of Knockespoch, who was M.P. successively for Stockbridge, Truro, and Clitheroe. He *m.* in 1789, Harriot, eldest dau. of Samuel Whitbread, Esq. of Arlington, M.P. for co. Bedford, by his first wife, Harriot, dau. of William Hayton, Esq. of Ivinghoe, co. Bucks, and by her left at his decease, in 1832, an only son and heir, the present JAMES-ADAM GORDON, Esq. of Knockespoch, &c.

Arms—Quarterly: 1st and 4th, az. on a fess, chequy, arg. and gu., between three boars' heads, a lion, passant, guardant, for GORDON; 2nd and 3rd, arg., a saltier, az., on a chief of the last, three boars' heads of the first, for LAVINGTON.
Crest—A stag's head, erased, ppr., attired, or; 2nd, a stag at gaze, ppr.
Mottoes—Non fraude sed laude; and, Dum vigilo tutus.
Seats—Knockespoch and Terpersie, co. Aberdeen; Naish, near Bristol, co. Somerset; Stocks House, near Tring, and Moor Place, near Ware, co. Hertford.

GORE OF PORKINGTON.

ORMSBY-GORE, WILLIAM, Esq. of Porkington, co. Salop, M.P., D.L. and J.P., *b.* 14 March, 1779; *m.* 11 Jan. 1815, Mary-Jane, only dau. and heiress of Owen Ormsby, Esq. of Willowbrook, co. Sligo, and Porkington, in Shropshire, and assumed by sign-manual, the additional surname and arms of ORMSBY. By this lady he has had issue,

I. JOHN-RALPH, *b.* 3 June, 1816, late M P. for co. Caernarvon, groom in waiting to Her Majesty, *m.* 4 June, 1844, Sarah, youngest dau. of Sir J. T. Tyrrell, Bart., M.P.
II. William-Richard, 13 Light Dragoons, M.P. for co. Sligo, *m.* 10 Sep. 1850, Emily-Charlotte, dau. of Vice-Admiral Sir George Seymour, K.C B.
III. Owen-Arthur, lieut. 43 Light Infantry, killed in the Kaffir war, *unm.*
I. Mio-Fanny, } both deceased.
II Harriet-Selina, }

Lineage.—This family derives from a common ancestor with the noble house of GORE, *Earls of Arran* in Ireland, and the Earls of Ross and Barons Annaly (now extinct).

WILLIAM GORE, Esq of Woodford, co. Leitrim, M.P. for that shire, 3rd son of Sir Arthur Gore, 1st Bart. of Newtown Gore, by Eleanor, his wife, dau. of Sir George St. George, Bart. (*See Burke's Peerage and Baronetage*), *m.* Catherine, dau of Sir Thomas Newcomen, Bart. co. Longford, and had issue,

I. WILLIAM, his successor.
II. Robert, who *m.* Letitia, dau. of Henry Brooke, Esq. of Colebrooke, co. Fermanagh, and left at his decease, in 1767, a son,
WILLIAM, who *s.* his uncle.
I. Sarah, *m.* to Sir Arthur Newcomen, Bart. of Mosstown.

Mr. Gore *d.* in 1739, and was *s.* by his elder son,

WILLIAM GORE, Esq. of Woodford, M.P co. Leitrim, who *m.* in 1733, Sarah, youngest sister of John, Earl of Darnley, and had an only son, William, who *d.* young. Mr. Gore *d.* in 1769, and was *s.* by his nephew,

WILLIAM GORE, Esq., M.P. co. Leitrim, *b.* in 1744. This gentleman *m.* 1778, Frances-Jane-Gorges Gore, only dau. and heir of Ralph Gore, Esq. of Barrow-mount, M.P. for Kilkenny, and widow of Sir Haydocke Evans Morres, Bart., and dying in 1815, left issue,

I. WILLIAM, the present proprietor.
I. Eliza-Frances, *m.* Thomas George Jaques, Esq., and *d.* leaving issue.
II. Letitia-Anne, *d. unm.* 1847.
III. Frances-Maria, *m.* Major John D. Bringhurst, and *d.* leaving issue.
IV. Selina-Isabella, *m.* 1827, a foreign marquis, and is deceased.
V. Letitia-Anne.
VI. Catherine-Sarah, now relict of the Rev. G. Sivewright.

Families of Owen and Ormsby.

MEYRICK, son of Llewellyn, lineally descended from Hwfa ap Cyndellw, founder of I. noble tribe of North Wales and Powys, *m.* Margaret, dau. of Evan Vychan, son of Evan ap Adam, of Moyston, and left a son,

JOHN AP MEYRICK, who *m.* Angharad, dau. of Griffith ap Howell ap David ap Meredith, and left a son,

ROBERT AP JOHN, who *m.* Gwenhwyvar, dau. of William ap Meredith ap Rys, and was *s.* by his son,

OWEN AP ROBERT, of Bodsilin, who *m.* Angharad, dau. and heir of David ap William ap Griffith ap Robyn, Esq., and left a son,

JOHN OWEN, Esq., secretary to Lord Walsingham, who *m.* Ellen, dau. and heir of William-Wynne Maurice, Esq., of Clenneneu, by whom (who *m.* 2ndly, Hon Sir Francis Eure, younger son of William Lord Eure, and *d.* in 1626) he had a son and successor,

SIR JOHN OWEN, Knt. of Clenneneu, a colonel in the army, a vice admiral of North Wales. This gentleman *m.* Jennet, dau. of Griffith Vaughan, Esq of Corsygedol, co. Merioneth (*See* WYNNE OF PENIARTH), and was, in 1666, *s.* by his son.

WILLIAM OWEN, Esq of Porkington, co. Salop, M P., who *m.* Katherine, only child of Lewis Anwyll, Esq. of Parke, co. Merioneth, of the royal line of North Wales, and dying in 1677-8, left a son,

SIR ROBERT OWEN, Knt. of Porkington and Clenneneu, M.P. This gentleman *m.* Margaret, dau. and heir of Owen Wynne, of Glynn. co. Merioneth, Esq., derived from Osborne Fitzgerald, lord of Ynys-y-maengwyn, in Merioneth, a scion of the great Irish house of Desmond (*See* WYNNE OF PENIARTH, and FITZGERALD, KNIGHT OF GLIN), and was *s.* at his decease, in 1698, by his son,

WILLIAM OWEN, Esq. of Porkington, who *m.* Mary, only dau. of the Very Rev. Henry Godolphin, dean of St. Paul's, and provost of Eton, sister of Francis, last Lord Godolphin of Helston, and dying in 1768, left two sons and two daus., all of whom *d. unm.*, with the exception of the eldest dau.,

MARGARET OWEN, who at length became heir, and in 1777, *m.* OWEN ORMSBY, Esq. of Willowbrook, co. Sligo, and conveyed to him the estates of Porkington (Mr. Ormsby was son and heir of William Ormsby, Esq., M.P. co. Sligo, by Hannah, dau. of Owen Wynne, Esq. of Haslewood, co. Sligo). Mr. Ormsby *d.* in 1804, and his widow in 1806, leaving an only child and heiress,

MARY-JANE ORMSBY, who represents the noble ancient family of Godolphin, and inherited such portions of the Godolphin property, as being purchased after the last Lord Godolphin made his will, did not pass under it either to the Duke of Leeds, or to Lord Francis Osborne, now Lord Godolphin. This lady *m.* WILLIAM GORE, Esq., who assumed, as already stated, the additional surname of ORMSBY, and is the present WILLIAM ORMSBY-GORE.

Arms—Quarterly: 1st and 4th, gu., a fesse between three crosses-crosslet fitchée, or; 2nd and 3rd, gu., a bend between six crosses-crosslet fitchée, or. [A canton, arg., charged with a rose of the field, for distinction.]
Crests—1st, an heraldic tiger, rampant, arg., ducally gorged, or, for GORE; 2nd, a dexter arm, embowed, in armour, ppr., charged with a rose, gu., holding in the hand a man's leg, also in armour, couped at the thigh, for ORMSBY.
Motto—In hoc signo vinces.
Seats—Porkington, Shropshire; Glynn, Merionethshire; and Willowbrooke, co. Sligo.

GORE OF TYREDAGH CASTLE.

GORE, FRANCIS, Esq. of Tyredagh Castle, co. Clare, J.P., high-sheriff 1856; *m.* 30 April, 1855, Ellen Studdert, and has a dau.,

Helen-Lettice-Elizabeth.

Lineage.—JOHN GORE, Esq. of Clonroad, co. Clare, who *m.* Jane, dau. of John Tayler, Esq. of Ballynorth, co. Limerick, had issue, FRANCIS, his heir; Charles; Ellen, *d. unm.*; Gertrude, *m.* to Thomas Hickman, Esq. of Barnstick; and Susanna, *m.* 1st, to John, son of Sir William King, Knt., and 2ndly, to Richard, 4th son of Sir Percy Smyth, of Ballynatra, co. Waterford, Knt. The elder son and heir,

FRANCIS GORE, Esq. of Clonroad, co. Clare, was made a brigadier-general in 1710. He *m.* Catherine, dau. of Sir Arthur Gore, Bart. of Newton Gore, co. Mayo, and had issue, 1 ARTHUR, his heir; 2 Francis, in holy orders, A.M., who *m.* Frances, dau. of Sir Robert Gore, of Newtown, and relict of Charles Ingoldsby, Esq., and had issue; 3 John; 1 Gertrude, who *d. unm.*; 2 Ellen; and 3 Isabella. The eldest son,

ARTHUR GORE, Esq. of Clonroad, *m.* Mabella, dau. and eventually sole heir of John Cusack, Esq. of Kilkessen, and dying in 1730, left, with a dau., Jane, *m.* to William Ryves, Esq., a son and successor,

COLONEL FRANCIS GORE, of Derrymore, co. Clare, aged 13 at the time of his father's decease, who *m.* Anne Lewis, and was father of

FRANCIS GORE, Esq. of Derrymore, who *m.* in 1797, Christianna-Emma, dau. of the late Sir Joseph Peacocke, Bart. of Barntick, co. Clare, and was father of a son,

FRANCIS GORE, Esq. of Tyredagh Castle, *b.* in Oct. 1800; *m.* 20 Dec. 1824, Mary, dau. and co-heir of the late Edmond Browne, Esq. of Newgrove, and has issue,

I. FRANCIS, now of Tyredagh. II. Edmond.
III. Thomas-Browne. IV. Poole-Hickman.
I. Anne. II. Letitia-Jane. III. Mary.
IV. Christina-Emma. V. Eliza.

Arms—Gu., a fesse, between three crosses-crosslet, fitchée, or.
Crest—An heraldic tiger, saliant, arg., collared.
Motto—In hoc signo vinces.
Seat—Tyredagh Castle, Tulla.

GORING OF WISTON.

GORING, THE REV. JOHN, of Wiston, co. Sussex, *b.* 1824; *s.* his brother 17 Nov. 1849.

Lineage.—CHARLES GORING, Esq. of Wiston, *b.* 1744, son of Sir Charles-Matthew Goring, Bart., by Elizabeth his 2nd wife, sister and co-heir of Sir Robert Fagg, Bart. of Wiston, *m.* 1st, 20 April, 1779, Sarah, dau. of Ralph Beard, Esq. of Hurstpierpoint, co. Sussex, which lady *d. s. p.* 6 Dec. 1797; and 2ndly, 7 June, 1798, Elizabeth, dau. of Edward Luxford, Esq., and by her (who *d.* 8 Aug. 1811) had a dau., Elizabeth, wife of the Rev. Walter-John Trower, bishop of Glasgow. He *m.* 3rdly, 7 May, 1812, Mary, dau. of the Rev. John Ballard, and had by her a dau., Mary, who *d. unm.* 1849, and two sons; he *d.* 1829, and was *s.* by the elder,

CHARLES GORING, Esq. of Wiston, M.P. for New Shoreham, *b.* 1817, who *m.* 19 Sept. 1849, Juliana-Mary-Caroline, dau. of Sir Willoughby-W. Dixie, Bart., and dying *s. p.* 17 Nov. 1849, was *s.* by his brother, the present REV. JOHN GORING, of Wiston.

Arms—Arg., a chevron between three annulets, gu., quartering FAGG.
Crest—A lion, rampant-guardant, sa.
Seat—Wiston, Shoreham.

GOSSELIN OF BENGEO HALL.

GOSSELIN, THOMAS LE MARCHANT, Esq. of Bengeo Hall, co Hertford, J.P., Admiral of the White, *b.* 7 May, 1765; *m.* 18 March, 1809, Sarah, dau. of Jeremiah-Rayment Hadsley, Esq. of Ware Priory, in the same county, and has issue,

I. MARTIN-HADSLEY, of Ware Priory, Herts, J.P., *b.* 5 July 1813; *m.* 1st, Feb. 1843, Frances-Arris, eldest dau. of Admiral Sir John Marshall, C.B., K.C.H., and has surviving issue,
 1 LE-MARCHANT-HADSLEY, *b.* 2 Nov. 1847.
 2 Hellier-Robert-Hadsley, *b.* 23 March, 1849.
 3 Gerard-Joshua-Hadsley, *b.* 3 Feb. 1855.
 1 Fanny-Charlotte-Hadsley.

I. Emma, *m.* 17 Aug. 1842, to Edward-Spencer Trower, 2nd son of John Trower, Esq. of Weston Grove, Hants.
II. Mary. III. Charlotte.

Lineage.—The family of GOSSELIN, of Norman origin, has long been domiciled in the island of Guernsey, but the date of its first settlement there cannot now be accurately ascertained.

ROBERT GOSSELIN, a distinguished soldier, did eminent service to King EDWARD III. at the rescue of Mont Orgueil from the French, and was in consequence appointed governor of that castle, having had at the same time a grant of the armorial ensigns, since borne by the family. From this Robert, we pass to his descendant,

JOSHUA GOSSELIN, Esq., *b.* in 1696, sworn greffier in 1737, and subsequently appointed major of the militia of Guernsey. He *m.* 1731, Anne, dau. of John Guille, of St. George, a jurat of the royal court, by whom he left at his decease, in 1775, an only surviving son,

JOSHUA GOSSELIN, Esq., *b.* in 1739. This gentleman was sworn greffier in 1768, which office he resigned in 1792. He was colonel of the north regiment of militia. He *m.*

27 July, 1761, Martha, dau. of Thomas le Marchant, Esq. of Guernsey, (son of William le Marchant, a jurat of the royal court,) by whom (who d. in 1818) he had issue,

I. JOSHUA, b. 14 Oct. 1763, m. 10 May, 1787, Mary, dau. of Thomas Priaulx, Esq. of Guernsey, and had two sons,
  1 THOMAS-WILLIAM, b. 5 Feb. 1788, m. in 1811, Elizabeth-Sophia, dau. of James le Marchant, Esq. of Rotterdam.
  2 Joshua-Carteret, of the R.N., b. 19 July, 1789.
He d. in 1789.
II. THOMAS-LE-MARCHANT, possessor of Bengeo Hall.
III. Gerard, of Mount Ospringe, co. Kent, a general in the army, b. in 1769, m. 1st, in 1791, Christian, 2nd dau. of Bonick Lipyeatt, Esq. of Faversham, and by her, who d. in 1824, had issue, GERARD-LIPYEATT, b. in 1795; George, an officer in the army, b. in 1797; Christian, m. in 1836, to J.-C. Fairman, Esq. of Lynstead: and Caroline, who d. in 1826. General Gosselin m. 2ndly, in 1835, Priscilla, dau. of J. Dimsdale, Esq.
IV. William, d. young.
V. Corbet, lieutenant R.N., d. at Trinidad, in 1808.
VI. Charles, lieutenant in the army, and aide-de-camp to General Sir Thomas Trigge, commander-in-chief in the West Indies. He d. at Trinidad, in 1803.
I. Catherine, m. to George Lamb, Esq., son of George Lamb, Esq. of Rye, in Sussex.
II. Martha, m. to George Lefebvre, Esq. of Guernsey, and d. in 1809.
III. Elizabeth-Charlotte, d. in 1789.
IV. Sarah-Anne, m. to the Rev. Nicholas Carey, rector of St. Martin's, Guernsey, and d. in 1801.
V. Emilie-Irving, m. to William-Carleton Smythies, Esq. of the army.
VI. Charlotte-Elsie, d. unm. VII. Mary, d. unm.

Arms—Gu., a chevron between three crescents, ermine. (Granted by EDWARD III. in 1359.)
Crest—A negro's head, ppr.
Seat—Bengeo Hall, near Ware.

GOULD OF LEW TRENCHARD.

GOULD, WILLIAM-BARING, Esq. of Lew Trenchard, co. Devon, J.P., b. 6 May, 1769; m. 8 March, 1801, Diana-Amelia, dau. of Joseph Sabine, Esq., by Sarah, his wife, dau. of Rowland Hunt, Esq. of Boreatton, co. Salop, and had issue,

I. EDWARD-BARING, m. Sophia, dau. of Admiral Bond, of Exeter.
II. William-Baring, R.I.C.S., m. Maria, dau. of Captain Leeson, E.I.C.S., and d. in 1839.
III. Charles-Baring, in holy orders, m. Mary-Ann, dau. of Richard Tanner, Esq.
IV. Alexander-Baring, in holy orders, m. Margaret, dau. of the Rev. J. Ireland.
I. Harriet-Baring.
II. Margaret-Baring, m. to Rawson-Boddham Gardiner, Esq.
III. Emily-Sabine.

Lineage.—"The Goulds," says Lysons, "are traceable among the municipal records of Exeter to the time of EDWARD III." In the reign of ELIZABETH, they were seated at Combe, in Staverton, and were afterwards of Hayes and Downes.

EDWARD GOULD, Esq. of Combe, in Staverton, had, by Elizabeth his wife, dau. of William Man, of Hempton, six sons, viz.

WILLIAM, of Hayes, in St. Thomas's m. Alice, dau. of Robert Taylor, Esq., and was ancestor of WILLIAM GOULD, Esq. of Dunscombe and Hayes, who m. Elizabeth, dau. of Andrew Quicke, Esq. of Newton St. Cyres, co. Devon, and left two daus., his co-heirs, viz., ELIZABETH, who m. James Buller, Esq. of Morval, and d. in 1742; and FRANCES, m. to John Tuckfield, Esq. of Little Fulford.
Edward, of Pridhamsleigh.
HENRY, of whom presently.
John, d. young.
Nicholas, merchant, of London.
James, who left, by Catherine his wife, two sons and one dau., viz., James, of Leghorn; Edward, of Highgate; and Elizabeth, m. to Thomas Reynell, Esq. of Ogwell.

The 3rd son,

HENRY GOULD, Esq. of Flowers Hays, m. Ann, dau. of Zachary Dills, and was father of EDWARD GOULD, Esq. of Lew Trenchard, who m. Elizabeth Serle, and left a son, and successor, HENRY GOULD, Esq., father, by Elizabeth his wife, of WILLIAM GOULD, Esq. of Lew Trenchard, who m. Elizabeth, dau. of Philip Drake, Esq. of Littleham, and was s. by his son, WILLIAM-DRAKE GOULD, Esq. of Lew Trenchard, who m. Margaret, dau. of Finny Belfield, Esq., serjeant-at-law, and left an only dau. and heir, MARGARET, baptised at Buckfastleigh, 23 May, 1743, who m. in 1764, CHARLES BARING, Esq., 4th son of John Baring, Esq. of Larkbeer, co. Devon, and brother of the late SIR FRANCIS BARING, Bart., and by him (who d. in 1829) left issue,

WILLIAM, of Lew Trenchard.
Charles, b. in 1775, m. Susan, widow of J. Hayward, Esq.
Jaquetta, m. to Sir Stafford Northcote, Bart.
Frances, m. to William Jackson, Esq.
Eleanor, m. to Thomas Redhead, Esq.
Lucy, m. to Lewis Mallet, Esq.
Mary, m. 1st, to Hugh Mair, Esq., and 2ndly, to J. Pellatt, Esq.
Emily, m. to Sir Samuel Young, Bart.
Caroline, m. to the Rev. William Coney.

Arms—Per saltier, or and az., a lion, rampant, counter-changed, for GOULD; quartering BARING.
Crest—A demi-lion, rampant, az., bezantée.
Motto—Probitate et labore.
Seat—Lew Trenchard, Devon.

GOWER OF BILL HILL.

LEVESON-GOWER, JOHN, Esq. of Bill Hill, co. Berks, J.P. and D.L., b. 5 April, 1802; m. 18 April, 1825, Charlotte-Gertrude-Elizabeth, dau. of Colonel and the Lady Harriet Mitchell, and has issue,

I. JOHN-EDWARD, b. 20 March, 1826, m. March, 1850, Harriett-Jane, dau. of Capt. Hunter, late of the Dragoons.
II. Hugh-Broke-Boscawen, b. 1836,
III. Sackville, b. 28 Aug. 1839.
I. Gertrude-Harriet-Mary.
II. Cecil-Henrietta-Maria.

Lineage.—THE HON. JOHN LEVESON-GOWER, admiral R.N., son of John, 1st Earl Gower, by his 3rd wife, Frances Boscawen, m. in 1773, Frances, dau. of Admiral Edward Boscawen, and had issue,

I. JOHN, his heir.
II. Edward, Rear-Admiral of the Blue, b. in 1776; m. Miss Mount, and has issue.
III. William, b. in 1779; m. in 1804, Catherine-Maria, dau. and heiress of the late Sir Thomas Gresham, Bart., and has issue,
  1 WILLIAM, now of Titsey Place, Surrey.
  1 Catherine. 2 Frances-Elizabeth.
IV. Granville, in holy orders.
I. Augusta. II. Frances, m. to John Ward, Esq.
III. Elizabeth, m. to J. T. Coryton, Esq. of Pentillie Castle, in Cornwall, and has issue.

Admiral Gower was s. at his decease by his eldest son,

JOHN LEVESON-GOWER, Esq., a general officer in the army, who m. in 1796, Isabella-Mary, 2nd dau. of the late Philip Bowes Broke, Esq., and had,

JOHN, his heir.
Edward, capt. in the Rifle brigade, b. in 1807; m. 28 March, 1839, Francis-Cecilia, dau. of the late Dr. Powell.
Mary.
Isabella, m. to John-Thomas-Ibbetson Selwyn, Esq.
Anastasia, d. 24 Dec. 1846.

General Leveson-Gower d. in 1816, and was s. by his elder son, the present JOHN LEVESON-GOWER, Esq.

Arms—Quarterly: 1st and 4th, barry of eight, arg. and gu., over all a cross-patonce, sa., for GOWER; 2nd and 3rd, az., three laurel-leaves, for LEVESON.
Crest—A wolf, passant, arg., collared and lined, or.
Motto—Frangas non flectes.
Seat—Bill Hill Berks.

GOWER OF TITSEY PARK.

LEVESON-GOWER, WILLIAM, Esq. of Titsey Park, co. Surrey, b. 23 Nov. 1806; m. 17 June, 1834, Emily-Josephine, 2nd dau. of Sir Francis-Hastings Doyle, Bart, and has issue,

I. GRANVILLE-WILLIAM-GRESHAM, b. 25 Feb. 1838.
II Arthur-Francis-Gresham, b. 25 April, 1851.
I. Emily-Katherine-Mary. II. Mary-Elizabeth.
III. Selina-Frances-Diana.
IV. Caroline-Susan-Gresham.
V. Frances-Albinia-Gresham.

For *Lineage*, *Arms*, &c., see preceding family.
Seat—Titsey Park, Surrey.

GRACE OF MANTUA.

GRACE, OLIVER-DOWELL-JOHN, Esq. of Mantua House, co. Roscommon, and Gracefield, Queen's Co., chief of his house, and male representative of the ancient feudal Lords of Courtstown, M.P. for co. Roscommon, J.P. and D.L., high-sheriff 1831, *b.* 19 Oct. 1791; *m.* 3 Sept. 1819, Frances-Mary, only dau. of the late Sir Richard Nagle, Bart of Jamestown, co. Westmeath, by his first wife, Catherine Fitzgerald, of Punchars Grange, co. Kildare, and by her, who *d.* 1 June, 1826, he has had issue,

I. JOHN-DOWELL-FITZGERALD, *b.* 20 Aug. 1821, *m.* 1 Feb. 1855, Grace, dau. of Thomas Thistlethwayte, Esq. of Southwick Park, Hants, and has issue.
II. Richard-Joseph, *b.* 8 March, 1824, *m.* Nov. 1848, Mary-Jane, dau. of William Sweetman, Esq. of Rahenny, co. Dublin.
III. Raymond-Joseph, *d.* 13 Oct. 1831.
I. Mary-Clare, *m.* 6 March, 1848, to Robert Archibald, Esq. of Davidstown, co. Kildare, who is deceased.

Lineage.—The old and eminent family of GRACE ranks amongst the earliest of the Anglo-Norman settlers in Ireland. Under the banner of Richard de Clare, the well-known Strongbow, RAYMOND, surnamed *Le Gros*, landed in that kingdom, became subsequently (*anno* 1176) its viceroy, and, marrying Basilia de Clare, Strongbow's sister, acquired the extensive district in the co. of Kilkenny, still denominated the "Cantred of Grace's country."

WILLIAM LE GROS, or Fitz-Raymond, the eldest son, of Raymond Le Gros, 2nd son of William Fitzgerald, of the Castle of Kerrin, 2nd son of Gerald Fitzwalter de Windesor, Castellan of Windsor, became Baron of Courtstown, or Tullaroan, and Lord of Grace's country. He *m.* Margaret, dau. of Robert Fitz-Warren, of Wales; but we pass from him to his descendant (the 12th in succession),

SIR JOHN LE GROS, (surnamed *Crios iarainn*, the Iron-belted) Baron of Courtstown, and Lord of Grace's country, living in 1520 and 1534. He *m.* Catherine, dau. of Pierce, Lord Le Poer, of Curraghmore, co. Waterford, and had two sons, viz.,

JOHN, who, at his father's decease, became Baron of Courtstown and Lord of Grace's country, ancestor of the senior line of the family, the GRACES, BARONS OF COURTSTOWN. The last male heir, ROBERT GRACE, *d.* at Isleworth, co. Middlesex *s. p.* in 1764, leaving his aunt, MARY, wife of JOHN LANGRISHE, Esq. of Knocktopher, his heir.
OLIVER, (Sir.)

The 2nd son,

SIR OLIVER GRACE, Knt. of Ballylinch and Legan Castles, co. Kilkenny, was Lord of Carney, in Tipperary, and M.P. for that co. in 1559. He *m.* Mary, dau. of Sir Gerald Fitzgerald, 3rd Lord Decies, by his wife, Ellice, dau. of Pierce Butler, 8th Earl of Ormonde, and, dying about 1580, was *s.* by his son,

GERALD GRACE, of Ballylinch Castle, who *m.* Margaret, dau. of Sir Robert Hartpole, of Shrule Castle, in the Queen's Co., and was *s.* at his decease, 4 March, 1618, by his son,

OLIVER GRACE, of Ballylinch Castle, who *d.* 27 Aug. 1626, leaving (by his wife Margaret, dau. of Edmond Butler, 2nd Viscount Mountgarret) a son and successor,

GERALD GRACE, of Ballylinch Castle. This gentleman fell at the battle of Kilrush, 15 April, 1642, and a confiscation, by the Commonwealth, of estates to the extent of 17,000 acres, followed. He had *m.* Ellen, eldest dau. and eventually co-heir of Edmund Butler, 3rd Lord Dunboyne, and his wife, Margaret, sole heir of Thomas, 4th Lord Caher, and was *s.* by his son,

WILLIAM GRACE, who was styled of Ballylinch Castle, but resided at Barrowmount, co. Kilkenny. He *m.* Ellinor, sister of Edward, 2nd Viscount Galmoye (by Margaret, his wife, dau. of Nicholas, 1st Lord Netterville, widow of James, eldest son of Pierce Butler, Viscount Ikerrin, ancestor of the Earls of Carrick), and had issue,

OLIVER, his successor.
John of the Grange, in the Queen's County, *m.* Anne, dau. and heiress of John Grace, Esq. of Thomastown, and had an only dau., Elizabeth, who *m.* to Richard Gamon, Esq. of Datchworthbury, co. Herts, and left two children, namely, 1 RICHARD-GRACE GAMON, of Mincheuden, co. Middlesex, M.P. for the city of Winchester, who was created a baronet in 1795, with remainder to his cousin, RICHARD GRACE, Esq. of Boley, M.P.; 2 ANNA-ELIZA GAMON, *m.* to James Brydges, 3rd DUKE OF CHANDOS, and her only dau., (the sole heiress of the Duke,) LADY ANNA-ELIZA-BRYDGES, *m.* to Robert Grenville, 1st Duke of Buckingham and Chandos.

The eldest son,

OLIVER GRACE, Esq., who was in Parliament, and held the office of chief remembrancer of the Exchequer in Ireland, settled at Shanganagh, now called Gracefield, in the Queen's Co. He *m.* Elizabeth, only surviving child of John Bryan, Esq. of Bawnmore, co. Kilkenny.* He *d.* 8 June, 1708, and was buried at Arles, where he had founded Grace's Chapel. By his wife, who *m.* 2ndly, Edmond Butler, 6th Viscount Mount Garret, great-grandfather of the 1st Earl of Kilkenny, so created 1793; he left issue,

MICHAEL, his heir.
Robert, *m.* Catherine, only child of Sheffield Grace, Esq., (2nd son of John Grace, Baron of Courtstown, who *d.* (in 1684,) by his wife, the Dowager Viscountess Dillon, dau. of Sir John Bourke, of Derrymaclaghnan, and the Lady Mary de Burgh. Robert Grace left an only child, Sir Edmund, Knt. of Malta, *d. unm.*
Sheffield, *d.* in 1699.
Lettice, *m.* to John Grace, Baron of Courtstown, who forfeited all his estates in consequence of a bill of discovery filed by his aunt, the said Dowager Viscountess Dillon, against him in 1701. Their only son, Robert, *d. s. p.*, and with him terminated the male line of Courtstown.
Anne, *m.* 1st, to Richard, eldest son of Sir Richard Nagle, secretary of state for Ireland, *temp.* JAMES II., but had no issue. She *m.* 2ndly, to Edmond Butler, 8th Lord Dunboyne, and was mother of the 9th, 10th, and 12th lords.
Ellis, or Alicia, *m.* to Samuel Gale, Esq. of Ashfield, Queen's Co.

The eldest son,

MICHAEL GRACE, Esq. of Gracefield, inherited, as co-heir-at-law, with his nephew, (the son of his sister, Lettice,) Robert Grace, of Courtstown, the undevised estates of the Sheffield family, in the cos. of Sussex, Middlesex, and York. This gentleman *m.* Mary, dau. of John Galwey, Esq. of Lota House, co. Cork, by Elizabeth, his wife, dau. of William Meade, Esq. of Ballintobber, and sister of Sir John Meade, Bart., grandfather of the 1st Earl of Clanwilliam. By her he had issue,

I. OLIVER, his successor.
II. John, of Sheffield Lodge, *d. unm.*
III. William, who resided chiefly at St. Germains, in France, *m.* Mary, dau. and heiress of Richard Harford, Esq. of Marshfield, co. Dublin, and dying 23 Nov. 1777, left two sons and a dau., viz.,
  1 RICHARD, of Boley, M.P., upon whom the baronetage conferred, in 1795, on Sir Richard-Grace Gamon was entailed. He *d.* in Jan. 1801, and his son and heir, inherited that title,
    SIR WILLIAM GRACE, Bart. (*Refer to* BURKE'S *Peerage and Baronetage.*)
  2 John, capt. of horse in the Imperial service, *d.* at the siege of Belgrade, 31 Oct. 1789.
  1 Clare-Louisa, *m.* to William Middleton, Esq. of Stockeld, co. York.
IV. Sheffield, *m.* Frances, dau. of John Bagot, Esq. of Castle Bagot, and *d.* 3 May, 1742, leaving an only child,
    Raymond, who *d.* in France, *anno* 1764, *unm.*
I. Elizabeth, *m.* to Richard Shee, Esq. of Cloran, co. Tipperary, and had issue.
II. Helena, *m.* to Simon Kavanagh, Esq. of Inch, co. Carlow, and had a son, SIR JAMES KAVANAGH, who was slain in the French war, 1795, leaving a son, HENRY KAVANAGH, a general officer in the Imperial service, who was created, in 1826, a Baron of Hungary, and appointed chamberlain to the Emperor of Austria, and chief of the military department of the council of war.

Mr. Grace *d.* 19 Nov. 1760, and was *s.* by his eldest son,

OLIVER GRACE, Esq. of Gracefield, who *m.* Mary, dau. and heiress of John Dowell, Esq. of Montagh, now Mantua, co. Roscommon, and had issue,

MICHAEL, who inherited the estate of Gracefield, *m.* Mary, dau. and co-heir (with her sisters, Catherine, Mrs. Malone, of Baronstown, and Margaret, Mrs. Dunne, of Brittas) of Nicholas Plunket, Esq. of Dunsoghly, co. Dublin, and dying 25 Aug. 1785, aged 63, left an only child, the late ALICIA GRACE KAVANAGH, of Gracefield.
JOHN, of whom presently.

Mr. Grace *d.* 24 Aug. 1781, aged 77. The 2nd son,

JOHN GRACE, Esq. of Mantua, *b.* in 1734, served several years in the Austrian army. While in the service, he had the honour of being chosen one of the guard to attend MARIE ANTOINETTE into France, on her marriage with LOUIS XVI., and the still higher honour of being the sentinel nightly at her majesty's door during the journey. He *m.* 3 Sept. 1788, Mary-Clare 2nd dau.

* By his 2nd wife, Ursula, 2nd dau. and eventually co-heiress of Walter Walsh, Esq. of Castlehoel, by his wife, the Hon. Magdalen Sheffield, sister of Edmund Sheffield 2nd Earl of Mulgrave, and ultimately sole heiress of Edmund Sheffield, last Duke of Buckingham and Normanby.

and co-heiress* of Patrick Hussey, Esq. of Ardimore, co. Kerry, by whom, who d. 1819, he had one son and two daus., viz.,

OLIVER-DOWELL-JOHN, now of Mantua.
Catherine-Eliza, m. in Aug. 1821, to Rice Hussey Esq. of Miltown, co. Kerry.
Maria, a nun.

Mr. Grace d. 25 April, 1811, at the age of 75.

Arms—Gu., a lion, rampant, per fesse, arg. and or; quartering WINDSOR, BUTLER, SHEFFIELD, DOWELL, &c. &c.
Crest—On a wreath, a demi-lion, rampant, arg.
Supporters—Dexter, a lion, ppr.; sinister, a boar, or.
Mottoes—En Grace affie, and, Concordant nomine facta.
Seats—Mantua House, near Elphin, and Gracefield, Queen's County.

GRADWELL OF DOWTH HALL.

GRADWELL, RICHARD, Esq. of Dowth Hall, in the co. of Meath, J.P., b. 29 April, 1824; m. 13 April, 1852, Maria Theresa, elder dau. of the late James MacEvoy, Esq. of Tobertinan, co. Meath, by Theresa his wife, youngest dau. and co-heir of the late Sir Joshua-Colles Meredyth, Bart., and has issue,

I. Theresa. II. Annette.

Lineage.—The GRADWELLS are an old Lancashire family, long settled in the neighbourhood of Preston, and connected, by intermarriage, with the GILLIBRANDS (now FARAKERLYS) *of Gillibrand Hall*, the Blundells, the Gregsons, the Ashhursts, and the ANDERTONS *of Buxton*. Several generations back, Mr. GRADWELL, of Hall Yards (the site of the present Clifton Hall), held a considerable portion of Clifton, co. Lancaster. He m. and had three sons and eight daus. Of the sons, the eldest d. unm.; but from one of the two younger springs the family now seated at Dowth Hall, the old mansion of the noble house of Netterville.

ROBERT GRADWELL, of Clifton, who m. Alice Holden, had a dau., Ann, the wife of Graystock, and a son,

RICHARD GRADWELL, Esq. of Clifton, b. in 1701, who m. Ann Holden, an only dau., and had issue,

Robert, who d. at the age of 21.
JOHN, of whose descendants we treat.
Helen, who m. William Brown, and had issue, George Brown, D.D., 1st Catholic bishop of Liverpool; Richard Brown; and Helen.
Dorothy. Alice.

Richard Gradwell d. 1751. His 2nd son,

JOHN GRADWELL, Esq. of Clifton, b. in 1749, m. 12 Oct. 1774, Margaret, dau. and heiress of John Gregson, Esq. of Balderstone, co. Lancaster, and niece of Mary Gregson, the wife of Christopher Crook, Esq. of Chorley, whose dau. Elizabeth m. Hawarden Gillibrand, Esq. of Gillibrand Hall, and whose son, Christopher Crook, Esq. of London, was father of Frances, m. to William-Ince Anderton, Esq. of Euxton Hall, near Chorley. By Margaret Gregson his wife, who d. 25 July, 1827, Mr. Gradwell had issue,

Richard, of Clifton, b. 4 Aug. 1775, m. 1798, Jane Marsh, of Hindley, and d. 28 Oct. 1843, leaving an only child and heiress, Margaret, who inherited the Clifton and Balderstone property, and m. Richard Carr, Esq. of Preston. She d. 18 Sept. 1851.
John, who d. unm.
Robert, a bishop in the Catholic Church.
GEORGE, of whom presently
Henry, vicar-general, Catholic Church.
Ann.

Mr. Gradwell d. 21 April, 1829. His 4th son,

GEORGE GRADWELL, Esq. of Preston, co. Lancaster, director of a bank there, colonel of volunteers, and a magistrate, b. at Clifton, 6 Feb. 1779, m. 29 June, 1819, Mary, dau. of Richard Ashhurst, Esq. of Puddington, co. Cheshire, by Helen his wife, dau. of Richard Blundell, Esq., whose father, Richard Blundell, of Carside, was a scion of the BLUNDELLS *of Ince*. By Mary Ashhurst his wife, who d. 9 April, 1848, Mr. Gradwell had issue,

JOHN, of Platten Hall, co. Meath, J.P., b. 22 April, 1822, who m. 17 June, 1851, Ellen, dau. of Peter Fitzgerald, Esq. of Soho, co. Westmeath, and has issue, GEORGE, Ellen, and Cecilia.
RICHARD, now of Dowth Hall.
Robert, in holy orders.
George, in holy orders, d. 1855.
Mary-Ann, m. to James Gernon, Esq. of Athcarne Castle, co. Meath, and d. 1848 (see p. 433).

Mr. Gradwell d. 1 Dec. 1849.

* With her sister, Mrs. Fitzgerald, of Liscarney.

Arms—Or, two foxes, courant, in pale, ppr., in the centre chief point, a rose, gu.
Crest—A stag, trippant, ppr., collared and chained, or, charged with a rose, gu.
Motto—Nil desperandum
Seat—Dowth Hall, near Drogheda.

GRÆME OF GARVOCK.

GRÆME, JAMES, Esq. of Garvock, co. Perth, J.P., b. 23 July, 1803; m. 27 June, 1837, Helena, only surviving child of Charles de Jersey, Esq. of Grange Lodge, H.M.'s attorney-general for the island of Guernsey, and has,

I. ROBERT DE GRÆME, b. 13 Feb. 1841.
II. Charles de Jersey, b. 22 Dec. 1842.
I. Mary-Elizabeth-de Jersey-Katharine.
II. Jane-Anne-Jessie.
III. Georgiana-Helena-Caroline de Jersey.
IV. Henrietta-Matilda. V. Agnes-Rollo.
VI. Charlotte-Frederica-Elizabeth-Hay.

Lineage.—WILLIAM GRÆME, 3rd son of Sir William Graham, of Kincardine, was the 1st Græme of Garvock, and direct ancestor of the present family. He was a soldier, and for his faithful services to King JAMES I., his uncle, obtained, in early life, a grant of the lands and barony of Garvock, which was afterwards confirmed in 1473. He lived to an advanced age, and left a son,

MATTHEW LE GRÆME, of Garvock, who succeeded to William in 1502, but died soon afterwards, being advanced in years before his father's death. He was s. by his son,

ARCHIBALD GRÆME, who fell at Flodden, on 9 Sep. 1513, leaving a son and successor,

JOHN GRÆME, of Garvock, who m. 1st, Mirabell, dau. of John Whyte, of Lumbany, and 2ndly, Katharine, dau. of Walter Arnot, of that ilk, in 1545. He left two sons, 1 JAMES, who s. him; 2 John, of Balgowan, ancestor of the Grahams of Balgoune, and of the gallant Lord Lynedoch, the hero of Barrosa.

JAMES GRÆME, of Garvock (the elder son), succeeded his father, John, and m. Janet Bonar, dau. of Bonar, of Kelty, in 1571, by whom he had issue. He was s. by his eldest son,

NINIAN GRÆME, who m. Elizabeth Oliphant, dau. of Laurence Oliphant, of Fergandenny, in 1606, and by her he was father of

JOHN GRÆME, of Garvock, who m. Agnes Drummond, dau. of George Drummond, of Balloch, in 1638, and was father of

JAMES GRÆME, of Garvock, who m. Anne Stewart, dau. of John Stewart, of Arntullie and Cardneys, in 1678, and was s. by his eldest son,

JAMES GRÆME, who m. 1st, Amelia, dau. of Sir Robert Moray, of Abercairney, by whom he had three sons, James, John, and ROBERT, and two daus., Anna and Elizabeth. He m. 2ndly, in 1720, Bettie Bell, sister of Charles Bell, of Craigfoodie, but by her he had no issue. He was s. by his youngest and only surviving son,

ROBERT GRÆME, who m. in 1736, Katherine, dau. of James Oliphant, Esq. of Gask, by whom he had four sons, James, Lawrence, Charles-James-Stewart, and Robert, with two daus., Amelia-Anna-Sophia and Margaret. This laird was involved in the rising of 1745, after which he escaped to France, and entered into the French service, where he remained for several years, leaving his estate to his eldest son. He returned, however, afterwards, and died in his native country. He was s. by his son,

JAMES GRÆME, of Garvock, b. 9 March, 1737, who m. 1st, in 1764, Mary, dau. of the Rev. Henry Nisbet, of the family of Dean, and by her had issue He m. 2ndly, Mary, dau. of Captain Robertson, which lady d. s. p. 1832. Garvock d. in 1812, and was s. by his only surviving son,

ROBERT GRÆME, Esq. of Garvock, J.P. and D.L., b. 4 Sep. 1766, m. 1 Sep. 1802, Jane-Anne, only dau. of William Aytoun, Esq., 2nd son of Roger Aytoun, 7th Laird of Inchdarnie, and left at his decease, 18 March, 1846,

JAMES, now of Garvock.
William, b. 30 Dec. 1806, d. 14 March, 1820.
Robert, b. 12 June, 1811, m. 28 April, 1848, Anne, 3rd dau. of Patrick, Baron Seton, of Preston, co. Linlithgow, count of Linlithgow, and Ekolsund, in Sweden, and has Agnes and Robert.
Isabella-Edmondstoun, d. 18 Jan. 1837.
Mary, m. in 1830 to Angus Turner, Esq.
Jane-Anne. Janet-Rollo. Katharine-Oliphant.

Arms—Or, three piles, gu., issuing from a chief, sa. charged with as many escallops, of the first, within a double tressure, flory, counterflory, to mark the royal descent.
Crest—A lion, rampant, gu. *Motto*—Noli me tangere.
Seat—Garvock.

GRÆME OF INCHBRAKIE.

GRÆME, GEORGE-DRUMMOND, Esq., K.H., of Inchbrakie, co. Perth, *m.* in 1842, Marianne-Jane, only surviving dau. of James, Viscount Strathallan, and had issue,

I. PATRICK-JAMES-FREDERICK, *b.* 16 March, 1849.
I. Amelia-Anne-Margaret.
II. Beatrice-Marianne-Jane.

Major Græme served in the British army during the Peninsular war, and was present at Waterloo, where he was severely wounded. He subsequently served in the Hanoverian guards, in which he attained the rank of Major. In 1816 he was created a Knight of the Guelphic Order, and has had the gold cross of WILLIAM IV. and the Hanoverian Peninsular medal conferred on him, as well as the British war medal, three clasps. Major Græme *s.* his father in 1840.

Lineage.—This ancient family derives in a direct male descent from William, the 1st earl of Montrose, who was killed at Flodden in 1513. The earl, by his third wife, Christian, dau. of Thomas Wavan, of Stevenson, and relict of Patrick, 6th Lord Hallyburton, had two sons, PATRICK, of whom we treat, and Andrew, who entered the church and became first Protestant bishop of Dunblane. The former,

PATRICK GRÆME, of Inchbrakie, *m.* Margaret Stewart, dau. of Lord Fleming, and grand-dau. of the duke of Albany, brother of King JAMES IV., and by her (who *m.* 2ndly, Sir Duncan Campbell, of Glenorchy) had issue. Patrick *d.* in 1538, and was *s.* by his eldest son,

GEORGE GRÆME, of Inchbrakie, served heir to his father in 1555. He *m.* Margaret, dau. of Andrew Rollo, baron of Duncrub, ancestor of Lord Rollo, and by her (who *m.* 2ndly, John Græme, 1st of Balgowan) had issue, PATRICK, his successor; John, the first of the family of Græmes of Bucklivie; and George, bishop of Orkney in 1615. George *d.* in 1575, and was *s.* by his eldest son,

PATRICK GRÆME, of Inchbrakie, *m.* 1st, Nicholas, dau. of Browne, of Fordell, and 2ndly, Margaret Scott, heiress of Monzie, co. Perth (a branch of the Scotts of Balweerie). Patrick Græme *d.* in 1635, and was *s.* by his eldest son (by his first wife),

GEORGE GRÆME, of Inchbrakie, who suffered severely during the civil wars, having been fined and imprisoned in 1641. He *m.* Margaret, dau. of Sir Alexander Keith, of Ludquhairn, a younger branch of the Earl Marishal's family, and *d.* in 1654; his son,

PATRICK GRÆME, of Inchbrakie, the well known loyalist of his time, in conjunction with the great Marquis of Montrose, is mentioned in all the histories of the period. The only return his loyalty met with on the Restoration, was an offer of a baronetcy, and a grant of arms, with new crest and motto. He *m.* Jean, dau. of Lord Madderty, and had issue, 1 GEORGE, his successor; 2 Patrick, captain of the Edinburgh town-guard, and afterwards colonel of dragoons in King JAMES II's army; John, postmaster-general of Scotland; James, of Newton, solicitor-general for Scotland in 1688; 1 Anne, *m.* 1st, to P. Smith, of Rapness, and 2ndly, to Sir Robert Moray, of Abercairney; 2 Margaret, *m.* to Robert, 1st Lord Nairne. Col. Græme *d.* in 1687, and was *s.* by his eldest son,

GEORGE GRÆME, of Inchbrakie, who *m.* Mary Nicol, heiress of Royston and Granton, near Edinburgh, and *d.* in 1704. His eldest son and heir,

PATRICK GRÆME, of Inchbrakie, was out of the country in 1715, but his house was burned by the duke of Argyll's army, after the battle of Sheriffmuir. He *m.* Janet, dau. of Pearson of Kippenross, and dying in 1740, was *s.* by his grandson,

PATRICK GRÆME, of Inchbrakie, captain in the Dutch service (son of George Græme and Catherine his wife, dau. of Lindsay of Cavill). In 1770, he was served "heir to Patrick, 1st of Inchbrakie, second son of William, 1st Earl of Montrose." He *m.* Amelia, eldest dau. of Lawrence Oliphant, of Gask, by his wife, the Hon. Amelia Nairne, and by her had issue,

GEORGE, his heir.
Patrick, lieut-col. 42nd Highlanders: died in India.
Lawrence, capt. R.N., drowned on returning home from the West Indies, in the Ville de Paris, after the action with Count de Grasse.
Amelia, *m.* 1st, to James Campbell, of Monzie, and 2ndly, to William Graham, of Orchill.
Margaret, *d. s. p.*
Louisa, *m.* to Robert Stewart, of Fincastle.

Capt. Græme *d.* in 1796, and was *s.* by his eldest son,

GEORGE GRÆME, of Inchbrakie, captain in 72nd Highlanders, and colonel of the Perthshire cavalry. He served at the siege of Gibraltar, where he was wounded. He *m.* Margaret, eldest dau. of Oliphant of Condie, and had issue,

Patrick, an officer in the army, killed in action in North America, in 1814.
GEORGE-DRUMMOND, his heir.
Lawrence, major in the army, and lieutenant-governor of Tobago, *m.* Miss Ridgway, and has issue, Patrick, Lawrence, Fanny, Drummond, and Margaret. He *d.* 1851.
Alexander, commander R.N., *m.* Ellenora, dau. of John Johnson, Esq. of Kirby, Lancashire.
Anthony-James, *d.* in India, in 1822.
Grace-Anne-Sophia.
Margaret, *d.* in 1802.

Col. Græme *d.* in 1840, and was *s.* by his eldest surviving son, MAJOR GEORGE-DRUMMOND GRÆME, of Inchbrakie.

Arms—Or, a dyke, fesseways, broken down in some places, and in base, a rose, gu.; on a chief, sa., three escallops of the first.
Crest—A hand holding a garland, ppr.
Motto—A Deo victoria.
Seat—Inchbrakie, Perthshire.

GRAHAM OF FINTRY.

GRAHAM, ROBERT, Esq. of Fintry, *b.* 16 Jan. 1816, *s.* to the representation of this branch of the ancient family of Graham, upon the demise of his father, 17 March, 1822.

Lineage.—SIR WILLIAM GRAHAM, Lord of Kincardine, chief of the name, and ancestor of the Dukes of Montrose, *m.* in 1406, for his 2nd wife, the Lady Mary Stuart,* dau. of ROBERT III., King of Scotland, and widow of George, Earl of Angus, and of Sir James Kennedy, of Dunure, progenitor of the Marquis of Ailsa. Of this marriage the sons were, ROBERT (Sir), who became of "Fintry;" Patrick, first archbishop of St. Andrews; William, ancestor of the Grahams, of Garvock; Harry and Walter, from whom descended the Grahams, of Knockdolian, in Carrick, and of Wallacetown, in Dumbarton. The eldest son,

SIR ROBERT GRAHAM, of Fintry, *m.* Janet, dau. and heiress of Sir Richard Lovell, of Ballumbie, by Elizabeth his wife, dau. of Sir Henry Douglas, of Lochleven, and had issue,

ROBERT, his heir.
John, ancestor of Graham, of Claverhouse and Duntroon. (*See* GRAHAM OF DUNTROON.)
Margaret, *m.* to John Erskine, of Dun.
Elizabeth, *m.* to Andrew Halliburton, of Pitcur.

Sir Robert Graham was *s.* by his eldest son,

ROBERT GRAHAM, of Fintry, who *m.* the Lady Elizabeth Douglas, dau. of John, Earl of Angus, and was *s.* by his son,

SIR DAVID GRAHAM, 3rd laird of Fintry, who *m.* a dau. of William, 1st Earl of Montrose, by Annabella his wife, dau. of John, 1st Lord Drummond, and left a son and successor,

WILLIAM GRAHAM, 4th of Fintry, who *m.* Catharine, dau. of John Beaton, of Balfour, and sister of Cardinal Beaton, archbishop of St. Andrew's, and chancellor of Scotland, and was *s.* by his son,

SIR DAVID GRAHAM, 5th of Fintry, knighted by JAS. VI. He *m.* Margaret, dau. of James, Lord Ogilvy, ancestor of the Earls of Airlie, and had three sons and one dau., Ayleon, *m.* to John Creighton, of Innermylie. His eldest son and successor,

DAVID GRAHAM, 6th of Fintry, *m.* Barbara, dau. of Sir James Scott, of Balwearie (lineal descendant of the celebrated Sir Michael Scott), and had two sons, viz., DAVID, his heir; and James, who possessed the lands of Monorgan and Craigo. Fintry was beheaded at Edinburgh, in 1592, for his participation with the Earls of Huntley and Errol in the Popish plot, and was *s.* by his son,

DAVID GRAHAM, 7th of Fintry, a devoted Royalist, who *m.* Mary, dau. of Sir James Halliburton, of Pitcour, by Margaret his wife, dau. of Sir James Scrymgeour, of Dudhope, 1st Viscount Dudhope, and left two sons and one dau., *m.* to Mackintosh, of Mackintosh. David Graham was *s.* by his son,

JOHN GRAHAM, 8th of Fintry, who *m.* the Lady Margaret

* The Lady Mary *m.* 4thly, Sir William Edmonstone

Scrymgeour, only child of James, Earl of Dundee, by the Lady Margaret Ramsey his wife, dau. of the Earl of Dalhousie, and had one son, who *d.* young. He was *s.* at his decease by his brother,

JAMES GRAHAM, 9th of Fintry. In 1679, he was lieut.-colonel of the Angus regiment, and had the offer of a baronetcy from CHARLES II., but declined the proffered honour. He *m.* Ann, dau. of Colonel Hay, of Killour, by the dau. and heiress of Whitelaw, of Whitson and Whitelaw, and was *s.* by his elder son,

DAVID GRAHAM, 10th laird of Fintry, who *m.* Anna, eldest dau of Robert Moray, of Abercairny, by Anna, his wife, dau. of Patrick Græme, of Inchbrakie, and had to survive youth one son and ten daus. The son,

ROBERT GRAHAM, 11th of Fintry, *m.* in 1735, Margaret, dau. of Sir William Murray, of Ochtertyre, by Catherine his wife, dau. of Hugh, 10th Lord Lovat, and was *s.* by his eldest son,

ROBERT GRAHAM, 12th of Fintry, *b.* 17th Jan. 1749, who *m.* Margaret-Elizabeth, dau. of Thomas Mylne, Esq. of Mylnefield, (by Isabella his wife, only dau. of Dr. George Gray, of Huntington, younger son of Gray, of Hackerton, a son of the ennobled house of Gray, and had issue,

I. Robert, who was assassinated at Benares, by the treachery of a native chief, in 1799, aged 24.
II. JOHN, heir to his father.
III. Thomas, capt. R.N., *m.* Maria, dau. of Admiral George Dundas, and *d.* at Valparaiso, while in command of the Doris frigate, 9 April, 1822.
IV. David, *b.* 28 Jan. 1785, *d. unm.* 11 Sept. 1824.
V. James-Scott, *b.* in Oct. 1796, *d.* in 1804.
I. Isabella-Gray, *d.* in infancy. II. Isabella.
III. Margaret, *d. unm.*, aged 18.
IV. Anne, *m.* to General the Hon. John Brodrick, youngest son of George, 4th Viscount Middleton, and has issue.
V. Elizabeth-Kinlock, *d.* an infant.
VI. Elizabeth, *m.* to James Keay, Esq. of Snaigon, Perthshire.
VII. Helen-Christian, *m.* to Henry Cloete, Esq., eldest son of Laurence Cloete, Esq. of Zamdvleete, C.B.S., and has issue.
VIII. Mary-Cathcart.
IX. Jemima-Agnes, *m.* to Major William-Bolden Dundas, eldest son of Admiral George Dundas (of the family of Dundas of Manor).
X. Emily-Georgina.
XI. Catharine-Margaret. XII. Roberta.
XIII. Caroline-A.-Mackay, *m.* 12 July, 1830, to A. Morton Carr, Esq., solicitor of Excise, in Scotland (of the family of Carr, of Esholt and Elton Hall, in Northumberland).

The 12th laird of Fintry *d.* 10 Jan. 1815, and was *s.* by his son,

JOHN GRAHAM, Esq., 13th of Fintry, *b.* 24 April, 1778, a military officer of distinction. He *m.* 24 July, 1812, Johanna-Catharine, dau. of Rodolph Cloete, Esq. of Westerford, Cape of Good Hope, and by her (who *m.* 2ndly, in Nov. 1836, Capt. Edward Danford, 49th regiment) had one son and three daus., viz,,

ROBERT, his heir.
Johanna-Catharina. Elizabeth-Margaret.
Isabella-Anne.

Col. Graham *d.* 17 March, 1822, and was *s.* at his decease by his son, ROBERT GRAHAM, Esq. now of Fintry.

Arms—Or, on a chief, sa., three escallops, of the first, surrounded by a double tressure, to mark the Royal descent. Three piles, sa., as representing the family of LOVEL OF BALUMBIE.
Crest—A phœnix in flames.
Motto—Bon fin.

GRAHAM OF BALGOWAN.

GRAHAM, ROBERT, Esq. of Balgowan, co. Perth, *s.* his kinsman Thomas, Lord Lynedoch, in the estate of Balgowan in 1843.

Lineage.—JOHN GRAHAM, 2nd son of John Graham, or Græme, of Garvock, purchased, in 1584, the estate of Balgowan, co. Perth, from James Lord Innermeith. He *m.* Marjory, eldest dau. of Andrew Rollo, of Duncrub, and widow of George Græme, of Inchbrakie, and was father of JOHN GRAHAM, of Balgowan, A.D. 1605, who *m.* 1st, 1605, Isabel, dau. of Ninian Bonar, of Keltie, by whom he had an only son, JOHN. He *m.* 2ndly, Helen, dau. of Thomas Blair, of Balthayock, by whom he had four sons and five daus., and was *s.* by his eldest son,

JOHN GRAHAM, Esq. of Balgowan, dying *unm.*, was *s.* by his half-brother,

THOMAS GRAHAM, Esq. of Balgowan, who *m.* 1st, 1671, Anne, dau. of Sir James Drummond, of Machany, by Anne his wife, dau. of Sir George Hay; and 2ndly, 1716, Christian, third dau. of David, 2nd Lord Newark; by the former of whom he had five sons and four daus., of whom,

JOHN, his heir.
David, *d. s. p.*
Robert, *m.* Elizabeth, dau. of Sir D. Threipland, of Fingask, and had an only son, JOHN, of Eskbank, who *m.* Mary Scott, of Usan, and was father of ROBERT, who *s.* Lord Lynedoch in the Balgowan estate, and is its present possessor.

He *d.* 1735, and was *s.* by his son,

JOHN GRÆME, or GRAHAM, Esq. of Balgowan, who *m.* 1702, Elizabeth, dau. of James Carnegie, of Balnamoon, and *d.* 1749, having had, with four daus, five sons, all of whom *d. s. p.*, except the eldest,

THOMAS GRAHAM, Esq. of Balgowan, *m.* 8 April, 1748, Lady Christian Hope, dau. of Charles, Earl of Hopetoun, and *d.* 6 Dec. 1766, leaving a son,

THOMAS GRAHAM, Esq., of Balgowan, M.P., the celebrated commander in the Peninsular war, who achieved the memorable victory of Barrosa, 5 March, 1811, and was created, 3 May, 1814, BARON LYNEDOCH. He *m.* 26 Dec. 1774, the Hon. Mary Catchcart, dau. of Charles, 9th Lord Cathcart, but by her (who *d.* 26 June, 1792), had no issue. Lord Lynedoch *d. s. p.*, 1843, and was *s.* by his kinsman, ROBERT GRAHAM, Esq. of Balgowan.

Arms, &c.—See GRÆME, of Garvock.
Seat—Balgowan, co. Perth.

GRAHAM OF DUNTROON.

STIRLING-GRAHAM, WILLIAM, Esq. of Duntroon, co. Forfar, *b.* 12 June, 1794.

Lineage.—JOHN GRAHAM, 2nd son of Sir Robert Graham, the 1st of Fintry, obtained from Archibald, Earl of Angus, a charter of the lands of Balargus, in Forfarshire. He *m.* Matilda, dau. of Sir James Scrimgeour, constable of Dundee, and was *s.* by his son,

JOHN GRAHAM, of Balargus, who acquired, in 1530, the lands of Kirkton, and subsequently those of Claverhouse. He *m.* Margaret, dau. of John Bethune, of Balfour, and had a son and successor,

JOHN GRAHAM, of Claverhouse, living in 1541, who *m.* Anne, dau. of Robert Lundin, of Balgony, in Fife, and was *s.* at his decease, about 1580, by his elder son,

SIR WILLIAM GRAHAM, of Claverhouse, who *d.* in 1642, leaving, by Marian his wife, dau. of Thomas Fotheringhame, of Powie, two sons,

GEORGE, his heir, of Claverhouse, who *d.* in 1645, leaving two sons. The elder, SIR WILLIAM GRAHAM, of Claverhouse, father of JOHN GRAHAM, the gallant Graham of Claverhouse, Viscount Dundee, killed at Killiecrankie, in 1689.
WALTER, ancestor of the Grahams of Duntroon.

Sir William *d.* in Oct. 1642. His 2nd son,

WALTER GRAHAM, Esq. of Duntroon, *m.* in 1630, Elizabeth, sister of Alexander Guthrie, Esq., and was father of DAVID GRAHAM, of Duntroon, who *d.* in 1706, leaving a son,

WILLIAM GRAHAM, of Duntroon, who assumed, at the decease of DAVID, 3rd Viscount Dundee, the title of Viscount, as heir male of the gallant Claverhouse. He was out in '15, and attainted by act of parliament His eldest son,

JAMES GRAHAM, of Duntroon, likewise assumed the title, joined in the rising of '45, and was also attainted of treason. Previously, however, in 1735, he had sold Duntroon to his uncle,

ALEXANDER GRAHAM, who settled the estate upon his brother,

DAVID GRAHAM, who then became of Duntroon. He was *b.* in 1687, and *d.* in 1766, leaving by Grisell Gardyne his wife, an only surviving son,

ALEXANDER GRAHAM, Esq. of Duntroon, who *d.* in 1782, leaving, by Clementina his wife, dau. of David Gardyne, Esq. of Middleton, co. Forfar, with several daus., one son, ALEXANDER, of Duntroon, who *d. s. p.* in 1802, whereupon his sisters became his co-heirs. Of those ladies, the only two who married were, AMELIA, who became the wife of Patrick Stirling, Esq., and CLEMENTINA, who *m.* in 1794, Gavin Drummond, Esq. and had a dau., Clementina, *m.* to the Earl of Airlie. The elder,

AMELIA GRAHAM, *m.* 18 April, 1781, Patrick Stirling, Esq. of Pittendriech, co. Forfar, son of William Stirling, Esq. of Pittendriech, had issue,

WILLIAM, her heir.
Alexander, *b.* in July, 1796, *d.* in 1801.
Clementina.

Jane, m. to John-Mortlock Lacon, Esq. of Great Yarmouth, 2nd son of the late Sir Edmund Lacon, Bart., and had issue, John-Edmund; Henry, R.N., d. in the West Indies; William-Stirling; Graham, M.D.; Mortlock; Francis, R.N., d. in the West Indies; Amelia, m. to Charles John Palmer, Esq.; Jane, Clementina; and Harriott.

Mrs. Stirling assumed, with her husband, in inheriting Duntroon, the surname and arms of GRAHAM. Her only surviving son is the present WILLIAM STIRLING GRAHAM, Esq. of Duntroon.

Arms—As GRAHAM *of Fintry*.
Seat—Duntroon, co. Forfar.

GRAHAM OF AIRTH CASTLE.

GRAHAM, WILLIAM, Esq. of Airth Castle, co. Stirling, J.P., *b.* 9 Nov. 1808; *m.* 17 Jan. 1839, Elizabeth, youngest dau. of Sir Alexander Anstruther, Knt. of Thirdpart, co. Fife, Chief Justice at Madras, and uncle to Sir Ralph-Abercromby Anstruther, Bart., and has issue,

I. THOMAS-PHILIP, *b.* at Paris, 8 Oct. 1841.
II. Janet-Caroline.

Lineage.—JAMES GRAHAM, dean of the faculty of Advocates in Scotland, and judge of the high court of Admiralty, *b.* 8 Dec. 1676, *m.* Lady Mary Livingstone, dau. of James, 3rd Earl of Callander, by Lady Anne Graham, his wife, dau. of the 2nd Marquess of Montrose, and had two sons and two daus., viz., James; WILLIAM, who *s.* his father; Elizabeth, *m.* to William Macdowall, Esq. of Castlesemple, co. Renfrew; and Anne, *m.* to Thomas Dundas, Esq. of Fingask. Mr. Graham *d.* 1746, and was *s.* by his son,

WILLIAM GRAHAM, Esq. of Airth Castle, *b.* in 1730, who *m.* Anne, dau. of Sir Henry Stirling, Bart. of Ardoch, co. Perth, and had issue. Mr. Graham *d.* 1790. His eldest son,

JAMES GRAHAM, Esq. of Airth Castle, *b.* 24 March, 1761, a Bengal civilian, *d.* 18 March, 1805, and was *s.* by his brother,

THOMAS GRAHAM, Esq. of Airth Castle, *b.* 1 March, 1768, who *s.* also, his maternal uncle, Sir Thomas Stirling, Bart., in the estate of Strowan, and in compliance with that gentleman's will, assumed the additional surname and arms of STIRLING. He *m.* 9 Feb. 1807, Caroline-Mary, only dau. of Major James Home, son of Lieut-Col. James Home, of the Royals, who was youngest son of Sir John Home, Bart. of Blackadder, co. Berwick, and by this lady (who *d.* 10 June, 1812) had issue,

WILLIAM, now of Airth Castle.
THOMAS-JAMES GRAHAM-STIRLING, Esq. of Strowan, co. Perth, *b.* 11 June, 1811, who *s.* his grand-uncle, General Sir Thomas Stirling, Bart. of Strowan. He *m.* 4 July, 1844, Mary, eldest dau. of William Stirling, Esq., 2nd son of the late John Stirling, Esq. of Kippendavie, co. Perth.
Carolus-James-Home, *b.* 24 May, 1812, a Bengal civilian.
Mary-Margaret, *d.* 14 March, 1827.

Mr. Graham Stirling *d.* 1 July, 1836.

Arms—Quarterly: 1st and 4th, or, on a chief, sa., three escallops, arg.; 2nd and 3rd, arg., a fesse, embattled, between three roses, gu.
Crest—A naked hand, holding a dagger erect, ppr.
Motto—Non immemor.
Seat—Airth Castle, co. Stirling.

CUNNINGHAME-GRAHAM OF GARTMORE.

CUNNINGHAME-GRAHAM, ROBERT-CUNNINGHAME, Esq. of Gartmore, co. Perth, and Finlaystone, co. Renfrew, *b.* 14 Sept. 1799; *m.* 24 July, 1824, Frances-Laura, dau. of Archibald Speirs, Esq. of Elderslie, by his wife, Margaret, dau. of Thomas, Lord Dundas, and has issue three sons and four daus.; the eldest son is,

WILLIAM CUNNINGHAME-BONTINE,* of Ardoch, co. Dumbarton, *b.* 11 April, 1825, late an officer in the 2nd Dragoons, *m.* in June, 1851, Anne-Elizabeth, youngest dau. of Admiral the Hon. Charles Elphinstone Fleming, of Cumbernauld House, co. Dumbarton, and has issue two sons. He is a deputy-lieut. for co. Dumbarton.

Mr. Cunninghame-Graham is vice-lieutenant of co. Dumbarton, and a deputy-lieutenant for co. Renfrew.

* The eldest son of this family, by an old entail, possesses the estate of Ardoch, and bears the name and arms of BONTINE, during the lifetime of his father.

Lineage.—SIR JOHN GRAHAM, of Kilbride, "Sir John with the bright sword," was second son of Malise, earl of Menteith, so created 6 Sep. 1427, who was son of Patrick, Earl of Strathern (in right of his wife, Euphemia, dau. and heir of Prince David, son of King ROBERT II.), and nephew of Sir Robert Graham, executed in 1437 for the murder of King JAMES I. From "Sir John with the bright sword" descended

WILLIAM GRAHAM, of Gartmore, co. Perth, who was father, besides a dau., wife of the Hon. John Alexander, 4th son of William, 1st earl of Stirling, of a son and heir, JOHN, who was father of two sons,

I. WILLIAM (SIR), of whom presently.
II. Walter, of Gallingad, who had two sons,
1 ROBERT, M.D. of Gallingad, who *s.* his cousin, Sir John Graham, of Gartmore.
2 William, of Dumbarton, who *m.* Mary, dau. and heir of James Hodge, by Mary his wife, sister and heir of Sir John Graham, of Gartmore, and had issue,
James, *d. s. p.*
William, *b.* 1720, voted as earl of Menteith, from 12 Oct. 1744, to 5 May, 1761, when the Committee of Privileges ordered him to discontinue the titles; *d. unm.* 30 June, 1783.
Grizel.
Mary, *m.* to John Bogle, of the Excise.
Margaret, *d. s. p.*

The elder son and heir,

SIR WILLIAM GRAHAM, of Gartmore, Bart., so created 28 June, 1665, *m.* 1663, the Hon. Elizabeth, 2nd dau. of John, Lord Kinpont, son and heir of William Graham, 7th earl of Menteith, and 1st earl of Airth, and sister and co-heir of William, last earl, and by this lady had a son, John (Sir), his heir, and a dau. Mary, *m.* to James Hodge, Esq., of Gladsmuir, advocate, and was mother of a dau. and heir, Mary, who *m.* William Graham of Dumbarton. Sir William was *s.* by his son,

SIR JOHN GRAHAM, 2nd bart. of Gartmore, who *d. unm.* 12 July, 1708, when Gartmore devolved on his cousin,

ROBERT GRAHAM, Esq., M.D., of Gallingad, who then became of Gartmore. He had two sons, NICOL, his heir and Thomas, M.D. of Bucchlwa, physician to George II., who *d. unm.* The elder son and heir,

NICOL GRAHAM, Esq. of Gartmore and Gallingad, *m.* 2 April, 1732, Lady Margaret Cunninghame, dau. of William Cunninghame, 12th Earl of Glencairn, and had issue,

William, *d. v. p.* 1774.
ROBERT, of whom presently.
John, col. in the army of Kipper, *d. unm. s. p.*
Elizabeth, *m.* to Sir Robert Dalyell, Bart. of Binns, co. Linlithgow.

Mr. Nicol Graham *d.* 16 Nov. 1775, and was *s.* by his only surviving son,

ROBERT GRAHAM, Esq of Gartmore, receiver-general for Jamaica. His cousin, Nicol Bontine, of Ardoch, entailed that estate upon him and his heirs, with the name and arms; but, in the event of his succeeding to Gartmore, the estate of Artoch was to go to the nearest heir of Gartmore, and at all future periods every heir of entail of Ardoch in possession was to demise in favour of any nearer heir of entail to the Gartmore estate. In 1796, on the death of John, last Earl of Glencairne, Mr. Graham succeeded to the estate of Finlaystone, &c., and assumed the name and arms of CUNNINGHAME, in addition of those of Graham, which he had resumed on his father's death. This gentleman *m.* 1st, Anne, dau. of Patrick Taylor, Esq. of Jamaica, sister of Sir John Taylor, Bart., and 2nd, Elizabeth, dau. of Thomas Buchanan, Esq., of Spittal and Leny: by the former he had issue,

WILLIAM, his heir.
Nicol Graham, of Jarbruck, Monihive, co. Dumbarton, and sometime Bontine of Ardoch, col. and marshal-de-camp in the Austrian service, Knight of Maria Theresa, and member of the Aulic Council. He *m.* twice, 1st, a French lady, by whom he had a son in the Austrian service, who *m.* a Polish lady, whose name he has assumed. By his 2nd wife Col. Graham had a son, Iwan, and a dau., *m.* to — Robertson, Esq.
Martha, *m.* to Peter Speirs, Esq. of Culcruich, co. Stirling.

The eldest son and heir,

WILLIAM CUNNINGHAME CUNNINGHAME-GRAHAM, Esq of Gartmore, Finlaystone, &c, and sometime of Ardoch, with the name of Bontine, *m.* 1st, Anna, dau. of the Venerable John Dickson, archdeacon of Down, and had issue,

ROBERT, present representative.
William-John, Bombay civil service, *d.* 1827.
Douglas, major E.I.C.S., *m.* 1st, Anne, dau. of Major Tyler, R.A., and 2ndly, Emily, dau. of Col. McNeil, E.I.C.S.

Anna, m. 1st, to Thomas Calderwood Durham, Esq. of Largo, 2ndly, to David, Lord Erskine.
Charlotte.

Mr. Cunninghame-Graham m. 2ndly, Mrs. Bogle, and by her had issue,

Thomas.
Susan, m. to Robert Bartholomew, Esq.
Matilda, m. to the Rev. W. McKellar.

He d. in Nov. 1845, and was s. by his eldest son, the present ROBERT-CUNNINGHAME CUNNINGHAME-GRAHAM, Esq. of Gartmore.

Arms, Crests, and *Mottoes*—GRAHAM and CUNNINGHAME.
Seats—Gartmore, co. Perth, and Finlaystone, co. Renfrew.

GRAHAM OF TAMRAWER.

GRAHAM, WILLIAM, Esq. of Burntshiels, co. Renfrew, J.P., late representative of the family of Tamrawer, m. 1st, Catherine, dau. of John Swanston, Esq., by whom he left five sons and two daus.,

I. WILLIAM, m. to Jane Catherine, 2nd dau. of the late John Lowndes, Esq. of Arthurlie.
II. John. III. James.
IV. Robert. V. Alexander.
I. Margaret. II. Catherine.

He m. 2ndly, Anna-Matilda, eldest dau. of the late John Lowndes, Esq. of Arthurlie, by whom he had one son and four daus.,

I. Henry-Lowndes.
I. Anna. II. Frances.
III. Elizabeth. IV. Christina.

Lineage.—The lands of Tamrawer, with several other farms forming the estate of Tamrawer, in Kilsyth parish, and county of Stirling, belonged, in the year 1427, to ROBERT GRAHAM, designed of Tamrawer, who was descended from Graham of Dundaff (of whom the Montrose family), which barony is adjacent. Robert d. in the year 1469, and was s. by his son,

WILLIAM GRAHAM, of Tamrawer, who d. in 1512, and was s. by his son,

JAMES GRAHAM, of Tamrawer, who d. in 1543, and was s. by his son,

WILLIAM GRAHAM, of Tamrawer, who d. in 1561. William was s by his son,

ROBERT GRAHAM, of Tamrawer, who, in the year 1585, built a large castellated house upon his lands. His descendant, in the fifth degree,

ROBERT GRAHAM, of Tamrawer, was an eminent agriculturist. He m. the only dau. of John Luke, Esq. of Claythorn, in Lanarkshire, by whom he had three sons, John, George, and William; also four daus. John, the eldest son, went to America, where he acquired a great extent of land, and resided there many years, but d. unm. His brothers, George and William, also d. unm. The first dau., Christian, m. Hugh M'Mutrie, Esq., and had issue; the second, Jane, m. Robert Wilson, Esq., but had no issue; the third, Helen, m. the Rev Patrick Hutchinson, A.M., and had seven sons, 1 James, m. to Annabella, eldest dau. of George Gibson, Esq. of Hampstead, and had one son, Patrick, who d young; 2 Robert; 3 John who d. unm.; 4 Peter; 5 William settled in America; 6 George, d unm; and 7 Graham, m. in 1847, to Annette-Mary, dau. of the late Archibald Crawfurd, Esq. of Ardmillan, co. Ayr; the fourth, Elizabeth, m. the Rev. James Dunn, and had issue, of whom all the sons went to America, where they settled. Robert Graham, a short time before his death, sold his estate of Tamrawer to his brother,

WILLIAM GRAHAM, an eminent merchant in London, who, as well as his brother Alexander, having d. unm., left the estate of Tamrawer to his only surviving brother,

JAMES GRAHAM, of Tamrawer. He m. Agnes Campbell, by whom he had two sons, 1 WILLIAM, of whom afterwards; and, 2 James, who married Janet Maxwell, representative of the Maxwells of Williamwood and Marksworth, co. Renfrew, and had issue (*see* MAXWELL GRAHAM *of Williamwood*); also one dau., Agnes, who m. Dr Wardrop, R.N., and had issue. He d. in 1795, and was s. by his son,

WILLIAM GRAHAM, as representative of Tamrawer, who m. Margaret, dau. of John Pattison, Esq., by whom he had five sons and four daus., 1 James, who m. Christina, dau. of John Patison, Esq of Leith, but d. before his father, leaving four daus, but no male issue: 2 WILLIAM, of whom presently; 3 Alexander m. Jane, dau. of Thomas Lancaster, Esq., and has issue; 4 John, m. Elizabeth, dau. of John-Hatt Noble, Esq. of Leckhamstead, in Berkshire, a deputy-lieut. of that county, and has issue (his eldest dau. m. in 1856, John-Frederick, only son of Sir John Croft, Bart.); 5 Robert, m. Susan, dau. of — Schuyler Esq., and has issue; 1 Agnes, m. Stewart Smith, Esq. of Glasgow, grandson of James Smith, Esq. of Craigend, Stirlingshire, and has issue; 2 Margaret, d. unm.; 3 Elizabeth; and, 4 Jessie m. Walter Crum, Esq. of Thornliebank, co. Renfrew, and has issue. William Graham d. in 1836, and was s. by his son, WILLIAM GRAHAM, Esq. of Burntshiels, late representative of the family of Tamrawer.

Arms—Or, on a chief, sa., three escallops, or.
Crest—An eagle, devouring a stork, all ppr.
Motto—Nes oubliez.

MAXWELL-GRAHAM OF WILLIAMWOOD.

MAXWELL-GRAHAM, JAMES, Esq. present representative of the families of Williamwood and Marksworth, a Magistrate and Commissioner of Supply for the co. of Renfrew.

Lineage.—JOHN MAXWELL, Esq. of Williamwood, sheriff-depute of Renfrewshire, is mentioned by Crawford, in his history of that county, as descended from the Maxwells of Aldhouse, who were sprung from a son of the ancient family of Pollock, and gives for his armorial bearings the coat of that family, viz., "Argent, on a saltier, sable, an annulet, or, stoned, azure, within a border, sable, for difference. *Crest*—A stag's head, caboseed. *Motto*—Propero sed curo.—*Lyon Register*, 1698. He m. in 1691 (*see* ROBERTSON'S *Continuation of* CRAWFURD, *p.* 270), 1st, Elizabeth, dau. of Henry Woodrop, Esq. of Dalmarnock and Dalbeth, by whom he had issue, I. JOHN, of whom presently; II. Henry, sheriff-depute, of Renfrewshire, who d. without issue; and III. John, who d. without issue; and a dau., Anna, m. to William Thomson, Esq. of Corsehill, d. also without issue. He m. 2ndly, Anne Semple, dau. of Sir William Semple, of Cathcart, but had no issue by that marriage.

JOHN MAXWELL, Esq. of Williamwood, his eldest son, m. in 1727, Annabella, dau. of Gavin Ralston, of Ralston, by Anne his wife, dau. of William Porterfield of that ilk (*see Royal Descents*), and had issue, JOHN, his heir, and four daus., the eldest, Ann, m. to Charles Maxwell, Esq. of Marksworth, in Renfrewshire, and had issue, two sons, James and Henry, and five daus., John, Janet, Ann, Annabella, and Elizabeth, of whom JOHN, the eldest, and JANET, the 2nd, will be presently taken notice of. The 2nd dau., Elizabeth, d. unm.; the 3rd, Annabella, m. Archibald Crawfurd, Esq., merchant in Greenock, and had issue; the 4th, Jacobina, m. John Baird, Esq., merchant in Glasgow, but had no surviving issue.

JOHN MAXWELL, Esq., the only son, s. his father as Laird of Williamwood. He m. in 1761, Martha, dau. of John Baird, Esq. of Craigton, in Dumbartonshire, and had issue three sons, the two younger of whom d, the one young, the other unm. He was s. by his eldest son,

JAMES MAXWELL, Esq. of Williamwood, major in the 26th regt. of dragoons. In 1788 he sold the castle and lands of Cathcart, which had been a considerable time in the family. In the same year he m. Mary, dau. of John Campbell, Esq. of Wellwood, in Ayrshire, but d. without issue in 1806. The succession now came to his cousin,

MISS JOHN MAXWELL, as above mentioned, eldest dau. of Charles Maxwell, Esq. of Marksworth, and representative of that family, her two brothers having d., the one young, the other unm. This lady, in the year 1812, sold the estate of Williamwood to Major George Morison, who, in 1817, sold it to James Stewart, Esq. Miss Maxwell d. in 1815, unm. She was s. in the representation of both the families of Williamwood and Marksworth by her next sister,

JANET, also above mentioned, who m. JAMES GRAHAM, Esq., merchant in Glasgow, 2nd son of the late James Graham, Esq. of Tamrawer, in Stirlingshire, the heir male and lineal representative of Robert Graham, proprietor of Tamrawer in the year 1427, descended of Dundaff (of whom the Montrose family), and had issue, JAMES, of whom presently; Charles, d. in 1855; and six daus., I. Ann-Maxwell, d. young; II. Agnes, m. in 1816, to James Smith, Esq. of Craigend, in Stirlingshire, and has issue (her dau., Agnes-Graham, m. David-Stuart, Lord Cardross); III. Janet, d. unm.; IV. Annabella-Maxwell; V. Ann-Maxwell; and VI. Henrietta-Maxwell, m. 1851, to James Hutchison, Esq. of Rockend, co. Dumbarton. Mrs. Graham d. in 1825, and the families of Williamwood and Marksworth are now represented by her eldest son, as above mentioned, JAMES MAXWELL-GRAHAM, Esq.

Arms—Quarterly: 1st and 4th, or, on a chief, erm., three escallops of the first, for GRAHAM; 2nd, arg., on a saltire, sa., an annulet, or, stoned, az., within a bordure, of the second, for MAXWELL *of Williamwood*; 3rd, arg., on a saltire, sa., a martlet, or, within a bordure, invected, gu., for MAXWELL *of Marksworth*.
Crests—1st, an eagle, reguardant, rising from a rock, all ppr., with the motto, "Souvenez;" 2nd, a stag's head, caboshed, with the motto, "Propero sed curo."

GRAHAM OF LEITCHTOWN.

GRAHAM, JAMES, Esq. of Leitchtown, co. Perth, J.P., *m.* in 1835, Ellenor-Smith, only surviving dau. of the late John Thwaites, Esq. of Topsham, in Devon, and has issue,

I. EDWARD-NORMAN-JAMES, *b.* 21 Dec. 1837.
II. William-Frederick, *b.* 25 Aug. 1840.
I. Emily-Louisa.

Lineage.—DAVID GRAHAM (2nd son of Walter Graham, of Gartur, which Walter was 2nd son of Alexander, 2nd Earl of Menteith, dwelt at Grahamstown, and built the house thereof. He *m.* a dau. of Kinross, Laird of Kippenross (and sister to the Lady Gartur), by whom he had, with a dau. *m.* to Campbell, of Auchterharley, in Argyllshire, a son,

PATRICK GRAHAM, who *m.* the only child of Baron Macquibbon, with whom he got the estate of Blairquhoile, of Blairchoille, in the parish of Port, of Monteith, and county of Perth, now known by the name of Leichtown. By her he had issue,

GILBERT GRAHAM, who *s.* to his father in the lands of Leichtown. He *m.* Jane, dau. of James Smith, by whom he had several sons. Gilbert *d.* in 1704, when his eldest son *s.* him, viz.,

PATRICK GRAHAM, of Leichtown, who *m.* in 1695, Margaret, only dau. of William Napier, of Culragrean, who was killed by the Camerons, at Inverary, and was *s.* by his son,

JAMES GRAHAM, who was bred a surgeon, and went early abroad. On his return he *m.* Ann, dau. of the Rev. Thomas Leckie, minister of Kilmaronock, and sister of William Leckie, of Broich, in Stirlingshire, and had two sons and three daus. The 2nd, but eldest surviving son,

JOHN GRAHAM, Esq., went to Jamaica when very young. He *s.* to the lands of Leitchtown at his father's death, in the year 1774. He *m.* Agnes, dau. of James Macewen, and *d.* in 1810, and was *s.* by his son, the present JAMES GRAHAM, Esq. of Leitchtown

Arms—Quarterly: 1st and 4th, or, on a chief, azure, three escallops of the first; 2nd and 3rd, or, a fesse, chequy, azure, and arg., in chief, a chev., az., all within a bordure, sa.
Crest—A demi-eagle, wings expanded, ppr.
Motto—Right and reason.
Seat—Leitchtown, Perthshire.

GRAHAM OF MEIKLEWOOD.

GRAHAM, GEORGE-WILLIAM, Esq. of Meiklewood, co. Stirling, *b.* July, 1835.

Lineage.—The Grahams of Meiklewood are a scion of the family of Montrose. The great-great-grandfather of the present representative,

JOHN GRAHAM, Esq. of Meiklewood, *m.* 1st, Isabella Duncan, of Lundy, and 2ndly, Bethia Colquhoun, of Camscudden. By the former he was father of

DAVID GRAHAM, Esq. of Meiklewood, who *m.* Isabella, dau. of Patrick Murray, Esq. of Ayton, and had (with four daus., Anne, Bethia, Mary, and Alison,) a son and heir,

JOHN GRAHAM, Esq. of Meiklewood, who *m.* 1st, 1782, Agnes, dau. of William Don, Esq. of Stirling, and 2ndly, Clementina, dau. of Charles Stewart, Esq. of Ardchiel, and by the former only (who *d.* 1788) had issue,

DAVID, of Meiklewood. William.
Margaret. Isabella.

The elder son,

DAVID GRAHAM, Esq. of Meiklewood, J.P. and D.L., Lieut.-Colonel, *b.* 22 March, 1785, *m.* 7 July, 1824, Honoria, dau. of Oliver Stokes, Esq. of the co. of Kerry, and had issue,

GEORGE-WILLIAM, now of Meiklewood.
David.
Agnes, *m.* to Charles Conyers, Esq. of the co. Kerry.
Henrietta-Bridget-Bowles.

Col. Graham *d.* 1847.

Arms—Or, on a chief, embattled, sa., three escallops, of the field.
Crest—A star, ppr.
Motto—Auxiliante resurgo.
Seat—Meiklewood, co. Stirling, N.B.

GRAHAM OF MOSSKNOW.

GRAHAM, WILLIAM, Esq. of Mossknow, co. Dumfries, J.P. and D.L., col. in the army, *b.* 1797; *m.* in Feb. 1830, Anne, only child of Hugh Mair, Esq. of Redhall and Wyseby, and has issue,

I. WILLIAM-MAIR, *b.* 21 May, 1832,
II. John-Gordon, *b.* 11 July, 1833.
III. Charles Steuart.
I. Rosina-Anne. II. Grace-Harriett
III. Clementina-Mary.

Lineage.—This family, "foremost in many a raid, and out in '15," has been in direct descent for more than two centuries in possession of the property and seat of Mossknow, situated on the Border. The late representative,

WILLIAM GRAHAM, Esq. of Mossknow, son and heir of John Graham, Esq. of Mossknow, by his wife, Dorothea, Hay, of the family of Hay, of Park, *m.* 18 April, 1794, Grace-Margaret, dau. of the Hon. John Gordon, 2nd son of John, 3rd Earl of Aboyne, and dying in 1832, left, (with two daus., Clementina, and Johanna-Grace, *m.* in April, 1829, to Erskine Douglas Sandford, Esq.) a son and successor, the present WILLIAM GRAHAM, Esq. of Mossknow.

Seat—Mossknow, near Annan.

GRAHAM OF EDMOND CASTLE.

GRAHAM, THOMAS-HENRY, Esq. of Edmond Castle, co. Cumberland. J.P. and D.L., high-sheriff in 1824; *b.* 25 June, 1793; *m.* 6 March, 1829, Mary, 8th dau. of the late Sir David Carnegie, Bart. of Southesk.

Lineage.—THOMAS GRAHAM, Esq. of Edmond Castle, Cumberland, descended from a branch of the Grahams, of Esk, *m.* Jan. 1749, Margaret, dau. of Thomas Coulthard, Esq. of Scotby, and by her (who *d.* aged 91, in 1816) left, at his decease, Oct. 1807,

THOMAS, his heir,
JAMES, of Kirkstall, created a BART., 1808. (*See* BURKE'S *Peerage and Baronetage*.)
William.
Mary, *m.* to Richard Graham, Esq. of Stonehouse.
Elizabeth. Margaret.

The eldest son,

THOMAS GRAHAM, Esq. of Edmond Castle, *b.* 1751, *m.* 17 Aug. 1791, Elizabeth-Susannah, dau. of John Davenport, Esq. of Clapham, Surrey, and left at his decease, 23 June, 1813,

THOMAS-HENRY, now of Edmond Castle.
John, who *m.* 1821, Caroline-Elinor, dau. of the late E. J. Curteis, Esq., M.P., of Windmill Hill, and has issue, Reginald-John; Henry-Davenport; Charles; Edward-Curteis; and Caroline-Curteis.
Elizabeth-Maria.
Emily, *m.* to the Rev. Thomas Collins.
Anne-Margaret, *m.* to Edward Pothill, Esq.

Arms—Per pale, indented, erm. and sa., on a chief, per pale of the last, and or, three escallops, counterchanged.
Crest—Two armed arms issuing out of the battlements o a tower, ppr., holding an escallop, sa.
Motto—N'oublie.
Seat—Edmond Castle, Cumberland.

GRAHAM OF DRUMGOON.

GRAHAM, ROBERT, Esq. Drumgoon, co. Fermanagh, and Ballinakill, co. Galway; *b.* May, 1786; *m.* 1st, Elizabeth, dau. of John Davis, Esq. of Summerhill, co. Kilkenny, who *d.* Feb. 1815; and, 2ndly, Jane, dau. and heiress of John Speer, Esq. of Desert Creight, co. Tyrone. By his 1st marriage he had issue,

I. FRANCIS-JOHN, *b.* Feb. 1815, J.P. and high-sheriff of Tyrone, in 1856.

Lineage.—This family, the same as that of the Historian of Derry, claims descent from the Border race of Graham; three brothers of the name settled in Ireland, in

Fermanagh, and in Monaghan. Mr. Graham's grandfather, ROBERT GRAHAM, Esq., m. Elizabeth, dau. of Robert Armstrong, of Giltagh, co. Fermanagh, and had issue, a son,

FRANCIS GRAHAM, Esq. of Drumgoon, who m. Esther, dau. of John Boyd, Esq., co. Tyrone, and dying 1836, left issue,

ROBERT, now of Drumgoon.
William, colonel in the army, m. Maria, dau. of — French, Esq.
Eliza, m. Robert Brownrigg, Esq. of Norrismount, co. Wexford.

Arms—Or, a rose, gu., barbed and seeded, ppr.; on a chief, az., three escallops of the 1st.
Crest—An arm embowed, verted, az., cuffed, arg., the hand ppr., grasping a staff, raguly, gu.
Motto—Ratio mihi sufficit.
Seats—Drumgoon, near Maguiresbridge, and Ballinakill, co. Galway.

GRANT OF GLENMORISTON.

GRANT, JAMES-MURRAY, Esq. of Glenmoriston, co. Inverness, and Moy, co. Moray, J.P. and D.L.; m. Harriet, 2nd dau. of Patrick Cameron, of Glenevis, co. Inverness, and has issue,

I. JOHN, late of the 42nd royal highlanders.
II. Evan, E.I.C.S.
III. Patrick, E.I.C. civil service.
IV. Hugh, E.I.C.S. V. James.
I. Jane, m. to William Unwin, Esq.
II. Elizabeth. III. Ellen.
IV. Harriet. V. Isabella.

Lineage.—The original grant of the lands and barony of Glenmoriston in favour of the progenitor of the present family, is the charter by King JAMES IV. to JOHN-MORE GRANT, of Culcabock, son of John Grant, of Freuchy, laird of that ilk, dated at Stirling, 8 Dec. 1509. In 1689, Patrick Grant, of Glenmoriston, was in arms at Killiecrankie, and in the risings of '15 and '45, the Glenmoriston Grants took a decided part against the government. Of the derivative branches we may mention Grant of Carron, Grant of Lynachoarn, Grant of Avimore, Croskie, &c. The great-grandfather of the existing chief of this well-known house,

PATRICK GRANT, of Glenmoriston, m. the dau. of John Grant, of Croskie, and was father of

PATRICK GRANT, Esq. of Glenmoriston, who m. Henrietta, 2nd dau. of Patrick Grant, Esq. of Rothiemurchus, and had issue four sons and four daus. The eldest son and heir,

JOHN GRANT, Esq. of Glenmoriston, lieut.-colonel in the army, and colonel of the Inverness-shire militia, m. Elizabeth-Townsend, dau. of Major John Grant, son of Mungo Grant, and grandson of Grant, of Grant, and by this lady had issue,

Patrick, who d. in 1806.
JAMES-MURRAY, of Glenmoriston and Moy.
Harriet, m. to Thomas Fraser, Esq. of Balnain.
Ann, m. to Roderick-K. Mackenzie, Esq. of Flowerburn, co. Ross.

Arms—Gu., three antique or eastern crowns, or.
Crest—A mountain in flames, ppr.
Motto—Stand firm.
Seats—Glenmoriston, co. Inverness, and Moy House, co. Moray.

GRANT OF KILGRASTON.

GRANT, JOHN, Esq. of Kilgraston, co. Perth, J.P. and D.L., b. 13 June, 1798; m. 1st, 20 June, 1820, Margaret, dau. of Francis, Lord Gray, and had by her (who d. 23 April, 1821) an only child,

Margaret, m. 10 Nov. 1840, to the Hon. David Murray, 3rd son of the Earl of Mansfield.

Mr. Grant m. 2ndly, 14 March, 1828, the Lady Lucy Bruce, third dau. of Thomas, Earl of Elgin and Kincardine, and by her has had issue,

I. FRANCIS-AUGUSTUS, b. 24 Feb. 1829; d. 1 Oct. 1854, in the Crimea, after Alma.
II. Charles-Thomas-Constantine, b. 2 July, 1831.
III. Arthur, b. 27 July, 1832; d. 15 Sept. 1853.
IV. John-Ludovick, b. 31 May, 1839; d. 10 May, 1854.
V. Robert-Henry, b. 16 Dec. 1840.
VI. Alan-Rudolph, b. 28 Feb. 1843.
VII. Alaric-Frederick, b. 17 Aug. 1844.
I. Mary. II. Annie.
III. Matilda-Catherine, d. 2 March, 1842.
IV. Lucy. V. Eliza-Louisa, d. young.
VI. Charlotte-Augusta.

Mr. Grant s. his father in 1819.

Lineage.—PETER GRANT, Esq. of Glenlochy, in Strath Spey, Inverness-shire, (an estate which he alienated after being held by his predecessors from the period when they branched off from the Grants, of Grant, chiefs of the ancient clan,) lineally descended from John Grant, of Freuchy, 4th son of John Grant, of Grant, the ninth chief of the Grants, of Grant, m. Beatrix, dau. of Donald Grant, Esq. of Inverlochy, and by her, who d. 24 Jan. 1780, aged 69, left at his decease, 15 April, 1783, aged 74, two sons, JOHN and FRANCIS. The elder,

JOHN GRANT, Esq., proceeding to Jamaica, s. Thomas French as chief justice of the island in 1783, and held the office until 1790. He purchased, towards the close of the last century, from the Murray and Craigie families, the contiguous estates of Kilgraston and Pitcaithly, situated in the east end of the beautiful and rich valley of Strath Earn, and extending over part of the Ochill Hills. Chief Justice Grant m. Margaret, dau. of Roderic Macleod, of Edinburgh, but dying issueless, 31 March, 1793, was s. by his brother,

FRANCIS GRANT, Esq. of Kilgraston and Pitcaithly, who m. Anne, eldest dau. of Robert Oliphant, Esq. of Rossie; postmaster-general of Scotland, and had issue,

JOHN, his heir.
Robert, b. in 1799, d. a midshipman R.N., in 1820.
Henry-Dundas, b. in 1801, d. unm.
Francis, b. 18 Jan. 1803, m. 1st, Emily, eldest dau. of J.-R. Farquharson, Esq. of Invercauld, and by her had one son, John-Emilius. He m. 2ndly, 21 Aug. 1798, Isabella, 5th dau. of Richard Norman, Esq., by Lady Elizabeth his wife, sister of the Duke of Rutland, and by her also has issue, Francis, Ferdinand-Hope, Isabella, Emily, and Rachel.
James-Hope, b. 22 July, 1808, major in the 9th Lancers, and C.B.
Mary-Anne, m. to Col. Lindsay, of Balcarres, and d. in 1820.
Catherine-Anne, m. in 1832, to Graham Spiers, Esq., sheriff of Edinburgh, and has issue.

Mr. Grant d. in 1819, and was s. by his eldest son, the present JOHN GRANT, Esq. of Kilgraston.

Arms—Gu., a chevron, engrailed, ermine, between three antique crowns, or.
Crest—A mountain in flames, ppr., with an escroll above, bearing the motto, "Ferte citi flammas;" but the Roman fasces, erect, ppr., was adopted by the late Chief Justice Grant.
Motto—Leges juraque serva.
Seat—Kilgraston House, Bridge of Earn, Perthshire.

GRANT OF KILMURRY.

GRANT, THOMAS ST. JOHN, Esq. of Kilmurry, co. Cork, J.P., high-sheriff co. Waterford in 1852; b. 20 Sept. 1822, m. 15 Aug. 1849, Eliza-Anna-Louis, dau. of Rev. Thomas Hoare, of Glenanore, and granddau. of Sir Edward Hoare, Bart., and has issue,

THOMAS-ST. JOHN, b. 25 Sept. 1852.

Lineage.—The first individual of this family of whom any documentary accounts are handed down, was CAPTAIN JASPER GRANT, R.N., two of whose commissions are preserved, one dated 17 April, 1669, appointing him to the command of the "Mermaid," the other, 2 April, 1672, to the command of the "Reserve." Both commissions are signed with the autograph of James, Duke of York, then lord high admiral of England (afterwards JAMES II). This officer obtained, in the year 1667, an assignment of a mortgage of the lands of Grantstown, or Ballygraunt (therein then so called), and in the following year 1668, he obtained a conveyance in fee of the same from William Dobbyn. In this document he is described as Captain Jasper Grant, of the city of Waterford. Now it appears from *Smith's and Ryland's Histories of Waterford*, that a family of Grants were from an early period residents of the city and neighbourhood of Waterford. In the year 1447 the Grants are included with the Powers (i. e. Poers), Walshes, and Duttons, in an enactment of HENRY VI., by which the citizens of Waterford are authorised to make war upon them as rebels and traitors. These two histories furnish a list of the civic officers of the city from an early date, which brings down the Waterford Grants to the year 1640, and in the year 1667 Captain Jasper Grant comes on the stage as purchaser of an estate called Ballygraunt or

Grantstown, and described as of the city of Waterford. It appears probable that in those early times of disorder and spoliation this family forfeited their paternal estate, which then passed into other hands, still retaining its name; that afterwards they regained their character for loyalty so as to entitle them to distinguished positions in the borough of Waterford, and that finally one of them was enabled to purchase back his family inheritance, and become as it were a re-founder of his race. Captain Jasper Grant, R.N., of Grantstown, *m.* sometime about the year 1667, Gillian Hely, of Kinsale, sister of Francis Hely, afterwards of the city of Cork, Gent., and had a son,

JASPER GRANT, who *m.* Annabella Fitzgerald, and was father of

JASPER GRANT, of Kilmurry, co. Cork, who *m.* Jane Vaughan, of the family of Golden Grove, but left no issue, and was *s.* by his brother,

THOMAS GRANT, Esq. of Kilmurry, who *m.* 29 July, 1719, Anne, dau. of James Uselin, of Taylorstown, co. Waterford, Esq. Their son,

THOMAS GRANT, Esq. of Kilmurry, *m.* 11 Oct. 1748, Elizabeth, dau. of Thomas Campion, of Leitrim, Esq., and was father of

THOMAS GRANT, Esq. of Kilmurry, who *m.* 28 Nov. 1792, Sarah, sister of Sir Richard Musgrave, of Tourin, in the co. Waterford, Bart., and was *s.* by his son,

THOMAS-ST. JOHN GRANT, Esq. of Kilmurry, who *m.* Sept. 1820, his cousin, Anna-Esther, dau. of the Rev. Alexander Grant, vicar of Clondallane, and *d.* 17 Jan. 1832, leaving a son and heir, the present THOMAS-ST. JOHN GRANT, Esq. of Kilmurry.

Seat—Kilmurry, co. Cork.

GRANT OF THE GNOLL.

GRANT, HENRY-JOHN, Esq. of The Gnoll, co. Glamorgan, and Wormley Bury, Herts, J.P. and D.L., high-sheriff of Glamorganshire 1834; *b.* 28 Feb. 1780; *m.* 25 May, 1822, Mary, dau. of Gen. George Warde, of Woodland Castle, younger brother of the late John Warde, Esq. of Squerries, co. Kent.

Lineage.—HENRY-GRANT, Esq. of the Gnoll, son of the Rev. John Grant, rector of Nolton, and vicar of Roch, co. Pembroke, by Elizabeth, his wife, dau. of Gilbert Davies, Esq., *m.* in 1779, Miss Alicia Camac, and by her (who *d.* 1837) left at his decease, 1831,

- HENRY-JOHN, of the Gnoll.
- Turner, colonel in the Grenadier Guards, *d.* 1845.
- Harriette, *m.* 1832, the Hon. Col. John Wingfield Stratford, who *d.* 1850.
- Maria, *d. unm.*

Seats—The Gnoll, near Neath, and Wormley Bury, Herts.

GRANTHAM OF KETTON GRANGE.

GRANTHAM, CHARLES, Esq. of Ketton Grange, co. Rutland, Capt. R.N., high-sheriff 1844, *b.* 4 Dec. 1790; *m.* 25 July, 1811, Emily-Grace, youngest dau. of the late Right Hon. James Fortescue, M.P., of Ravensdale Park, co. Louth, and sister to the late Viscount Clermont. Capt. Grantham, and his two brothers, Thomas, major-gen. Royal Artillery, and Arthur, of the R.N., and their sister, Margaret, are the children of Thomas-Bennett Grantham, Esq., capt. 15th regt., by Margaret, his wife, dau. of Captain Arthur Webber, R.N., by Margaret Robertson, his wife, and grandson of Thomas Grantham, Esq., who descended from the Granthams of Goltho', co. Lincoln. Major-Gen. Thomas Grantham, Royal Artillery, *m.* Miss Stanley, and has a son, in the Ceylon Rifles, and two daus., Charlotte, *m.* to Major Fulford, of Fulford, and Emily, *m.* to F. W. Hill, Esq., late of the 10th regt.

Arms—Erm., a griffin, segreant, gu.
Crest—A demi-griffin, gu.
Motto—Honore et amore.
Seat—Ketton Grange, near Stamford.

GRANVILLE OF WELLESBOURNE.

GRANVILLE, BERNARD, Esq. of Wellesbourne, co. Warwick, J.P. and D.L., *b.* 4 Feb. 1804; *m.* 1st, 1 June, 1828, Mathewana-Sarah, 2nd dau. of Capt. Onslow, of the Coldstream Guards, eldest son of Admiral Sir Richard Onslow, Bart, K.C.B., and has by her, who *d.* in Aug. 1829, one dau.,

Joan-Frederica-Mathewana, *m.* 1850, to Lord Charles Paulet.

Mr. Granville, *m.* 2ndly, in 1830, Anne-Catherine, dau. of Admiral Sir Hyde Parker, and has one son and a dau., viz.,

- I. BEVIL, capt. R. W. fusiliers, *b.* 20 Jan. 1834.
- II. Richard-Delabere, R.N., *d.* on board H.M.S. Bellerophon, 1855.
- III. George-Hyde, H.E.I.C.S., *b.* March, 1837.
- IV. Frederic-John, *b.* 15 Oct. 1839. V. Roger, *b.* 1848.
- I. Fanny. II. Caroline. III. Louisa.
- IV. Amy. V. Harriet.

Lineage.—The Granvilles claim descent from ROLLO, the celebrated northern chieftain, who, being driven from Norway by the king of Denmark, made a descent upon England, but was repulsed by ALFRED. He was subsequently, however, more fortunate in a similar attempt upon Normandy. Invading that country in 870, he achieved its complete conquest in 912, and was invested with the ducal dignity. He *m.* Gilbette, dau. of CHARLES the *Simple*, King of France, and had two sons. From the elder, WILLIAM, descended the CONQUEROR, and from ROBERT, the younger, created earl of Corbeil, sprang two brothers, Robert Fitzhamon, who reduced Glamorganshire (he left an only dau., Mabel, the wife of Robert de Courcil, natural son to HENRY I.), and

RICHARD, surnamed DE GRANVILLE, from one of his lordships, who came into England with Duke William, and fought at Hastings. This Richard, who, as heir male, inherited the Norman honours and estates, was earl of Corbeil, and baron of Thorigny and Granville. He likewise possessed the castle of Neath, in Glamorganshire. He *m.* Constance, only dau. of Walter Giffard, earl of Buckinghamshire and Longueville, and at his decease, in journeying to the Holy Land, left a son and successor,

RICHARD GRANVILLE, who held, *temp.* HENRY II., the lordship of Bideford, by half a knight's fee of the honour of Gloucester. He was direct and lineal ancestor of

SIR RICHARD GRANVILLE, Knt. of Stow, sheriff of Devon 24 HENRY VIII., and subsequently marshal of Calais. To this Sir Richard, who was of an active and daring spirit, and who served in the wars under the earl of Hertford, the king granted, in the 33rd year of his reign, the manor of Buckland, and rectory of Moorwinstow, formerly belonging to the monastery of Bridgewater. He *m.* Matilda, 2nd dau. and co-heir of John Bevil, Esq. of Gwarnock, and dying in 1552, was *s.* by his grandson,

SIR RICHARD GRANVILLE, Knt. of Stow, a gallant naval commander and admiral of the time of ELIZABETH, killed in action in 1591. He *m.* Mary, dau. and co-heir of Sir John St. Ledger, of Annery, in Devon, by Catherine, his wife, dau. of George, Lord Abergavenny, and had three sons and three daus. The eldest son,

SIR BERNARD GRANVILLE, Knt. of Bideford, in Devon, and of Stow, in Cornwall, was sheriff of the latter co. in the 38th ELIZABETH, and M.P. for Bodmin. He *m.* in 1608, Elizabeth, dau. and heiress of Philip Bevil, Esq., and niece and heiress of Sir William Bevil, by whom he had issue,

- BEVIL (Sir), his heir.
- Richard (Sir), a cavalier commander of great celebrity, "the king's general in the west."
- John, of Lincoln's Inn.
- Roger, drowned in the king's service.
- Gertrude, *m.* to Christopher Harris, Esq., son and heir of Sir Christopher Harris.

Sir Bernard Granville was *s.* by his eldest son, the celebrated

SIR BEVIL GRANVILLE, Knt. of Stow and Bideford, one of the boldest and most successful of the cavalier leaders. In 1642, on the first outbreaking of the civil wars, he joined the royal standard, and marching into Cornwall, rescued that whole county from the Parliament, attacked the partisans of the Commons, who had risen in great numbers in the west, and routed them at Bodmin, Launceston, and Stratton. His last and most brilliant action was at Lansdowne Hill, near Bath, where he fell, in the arms of victory, 5 July, 1643. He *m.* Grace, dau. of Sir George Smith, Knt. of Exeter, sole heiress to her mother, the dau. and co-heiress of William Vyol, Esq. of Treverder, in Cornwall, and had issue,

John, who was created, in 1661, Viscount Granville of Lansdowne, and earl of Bath (*See* Burke's *Extinct Peerage*).
Dennis, living in 1686, dean of Durham, rector of Easington and Elwycke, and chaplain in ordinary to Charles II. He *m.* Anne, 4th dau. of John Cosyn, lord bishop of Durham.
Bernard, of whom presently.
Elizabeth, *m.* to Sir Peter Prideaux, Bart. of Netherton.
Bridget, *m.* to Sir Thomas Higgins, Knt.
Johanna, *m.* to Colonel Richard Thornhill.
Grace, *m.* to Robert Fortescue, Esq. of Filley, whose dau. and co heiress *m.* Sir Haslewell Tynte, Bart

Sir Bevil's 4th son,

Bernard Granville, Esq., was master of the horse and gentleman of the bedchamber to Charles II. He *m.* Anne, only dau. and heir of Cuthbert Morley, Esq. of Haunby, co. York, and had issue,

Bevil (Sir), governor of Barbadoes, *d. unm.* in 1716.
George, of Stow, co. Cornwall, who was elevated to the peerage in 1711, as Baron Lansdowne of Biddeford. His lordship was a poet of considerable reputation (*See* Burke's *Extinct Peerage*).
Bernard, of whom presently.
Anne, *m.* to Sir John Stanley, Bart. of Grange Gorman, in Ireland, but *d. s. p.*
Elizabeth, *d. unm.*

Bernard Granville *d.* in 1701, and was buried at Lambeth. His 3rd son,

Col. Bernard Granville, of Buckland, co. Gloucester, *m.* Mary, dau. of Sir Martin Westcomb, Bart., consul at Cadiz, and by her (who *d.* in 1747, and was buried in Gloucester cathedral) had two sons and two daus., viz.,

I. Bernard, his heir.
II. Bevil, of Weedon, in Bucks, who *m.* Mary-Anne, dau. of Richard Rose, Esq., but *d.* without issue.
I Mary, *m.* 1st, to Alexander Pendarves, Esq. of Roscrow, in Cornwall, and 2ndly, to the Very Rev. Patrick Delany, dean of Down, but *d.* without issue in 1788. This lady, so justly celebrated for her great literary acquirements, was much esteemed by King George III. and Queen Charlotte, and resided constantly with their majesties both at Kew and Windsor.
II. Anne, *b.* in 1707, *m.* at Gloucester, in 1740, to John D'Ewes,* Esq., of Wellesbourne, co. Warwick (second son of Court D'Ewes, Esq. of Maplesbury, high-sheriff of Warwickshire 1714, and grandson of Richard D'Ewes, Esq. of Coughton, by Mary, his wife, dau. and co-heir of Edmund Court, Esq. of Maplebury, co. Warwick), and *d.* in 1761, leaving issue,
 1 Court D'Ewes, *d. unm.*
 2 Bernard D'Ewes, of Hagley, in Worcestershire, *b.* in 1743, *m.* in 1777, Anne, eldest dau. of John Delabere, Esq. of Cheltenham, and by her, who *d.* in 1780, left at his decease, 1822, one son and one dau., viz.,
  Court, successor to his uncle, the Rev. John Granville.
  Anne, *m.* in Jan. 1805, to George-Frederick Stratton, Esq. of Tew Park, in Oxfordshire, deceased.
 3 John D'Ewes, successor to his uncle, Bernard Granville, Esq. of Calwich Abbey.
 1 Mary D'Ewes, *m.* to John Port, Esq. of Ilam, in Staffordshire.

Col. Granville, of Buckland, *d.* in 1733, and was *s.* by his son,

Bernard Granville, Esq., who purchased from the ancient family of Fleetwood the estate of Calwich Abbey, co. Stafford, originally a cell of friars of the order of St. Benedict. Mr. Granville *d. unm.* in 1775, and bequeathed his estates to his sister Anne's 3rd son,

The Rev. John D'Ewe's, M.A., vicar of Ilam, co. Stafford, and of Norbury, in Derbyshire, *b.* in 1744, who assumed, in 1786, upon inheriting Calwich Abbey, the surname and arms of Granville. He *m.* in 1779, Harriott-Joan, 2nd dau. of John Delabere, Esq. of Cheltenham, and had one son, John, and a dau., Harriet, who both *d. unm.* Mr. Granville, *d.* in 1826, and was *s.* by his nephew,

Court D'Ewes, Esq., of Calwich Abbey, co. Stafford, and Wellesbourne Hall, co. Warwick, *b.* 1779, J.P. and D.L., who assumed the surname and arms of Granville, 1825. He *m.* 1803, Maria, dau. of Edward Ferrers, Esq., of Baddesley Clinton, co. Warwick, and by her (who *d.* 1852) had issue,

I. Bernard, now of Wellesbourne Hall.
II. Granville-John, *b.* 1807, vicar of Stratford-on-Avon; *m.* 1839, Marianne, dau. of Sir Gray Skipwith, Bart., and has, Gray; Grace; and Gertrude.
III. Court, *b.* 1808, vicar of Thexted, Essex; *m.* 1847, Lady Charlotte-Augusta Murray, sister of the Duke of Atholl.
IV. Frederic, *b.* 1810, late major R. W. fusiliers; *m.* 1854, Isabel, dau. of the late Edward Sheldon, Esq. of Brailes, M.P.
I. Harriet-Joan. II. Mary.
III. Lucy.

Arms—Quarterly: 1st and 4th gu., three horsemen's rests, or, for Granville; 2nd and 3rd, or, three quatrefoils, pierced, gu., a chief, vaire, for D'Ewes.
Crest—On a cap of maintenance, a griffin, or.
Motto—Deo Patriæ Amicis.
Seat—Wellesbourne Hall, near Warwick.

GRATTAN OF TINNEHINCH.

Grattan, Henry, Esq. of Tinnehinch, co. Wicklow, *b.* in 1789; M.P. for the city of Dublin from 1826 to 1831, and for the county of Meath from 1832 to 1851; he *m.* in 1826, Mary-O'Kelly Harvey (of the Harveys of the co. Wexford), and has had issue,

I. Henry, *d.* under age. II. James, *d.* under age.
III. Harvey, deceased.
I. Henrietta, *m.* 4 Aug. 1852, to Charles Langdale, Esq., nephew of Lord Stourton.
II. Pauline. III. Elizabeth, *d. unm.*
IV. Mary. V. Louisa.
VI. Frances. VII. Marianne.

Lineage.—Patrick Grattan, senior Fellow of the University of Dublin, *m.* in 1669, Miss Brereton, (whose family enjoyed, in the co. of Cavan, a portion of the forfeited lands held by patent from Charles II.,) and had issue,

Henry, of whom presently.
James, M.D. John, in holy orders.
Charles, in holy orders, master of the school at Enniskillen.
Richard, (Sir,) Lord Mayor of Dublin in 1735.

The eldest son,

Henry Grattan, Esq. of Garryross, *s.* to his father's property in the co. of Cavan. He *m.* into the family of the Flemyngs, and was father of

James Grattan, Esq., Recorder of, and M.P. for, the city of Dublin, who *m.* Mary, dau. of Thomas Marlay, Chief Justice of Ireland, son of Anthony Marlay, captain in the Duke of Ormonde's regiment, and grandson of Sir John Marlay, the gallant Royalist mayor of Newcastle, who held out that town to the last against the Parliamentary forces in 1644: by this lady Mr. Grattan left, at his decease in 1766, a son, the celebrated

Henry Grattan. This illustrious statesman, *b.* in Dublin, 3 July, 1746, was called to the bar in 1772, and in 1775 entered the Irish House of Commons; here he soon distinguished himself by his brilliant talents, and by his ardent patriotism. He *d.* 14 June, 1820, and his remains were deposited in Westminster Abbey. He *m.* in 1782, Henrietta-Fitzgerald (of the family of Desmond), and had issue,

James, his heir.
Henry, present representative.
Harriott, *m.* in 1826, to the Rev. Richard-William Wake, 2nd son of the late Sir William Wake, Bart. of Courteen Hall, Northamptonshire.
Mary-Anne, *m.* to John Blatchford, Esq. of Altadore, co. Wicklow, brother of Mrs. Henry Tighe, authoress of Psyche.

The Right Hon. Henry Grattan *d.* 14 May, 1820, and was *s.* by his son,

The Right Hon. James Gratton, of Tinnehinch, *b.* 1783, M.P. for the co. Wicklow for 20 years, formerly an officer in the army, who served in the Peninsula War, in the Walcheren expedition, and at Waterloo. He *m.* 7 Aug. 1847, Lady Laura-Maria Tollemache, sister of the Earl of Dysart, but *d. s. p.* 24 Oct. 1854, and was *s.* by his brother, the present Henry Gratton, Esq. of Tinnehinch.

Seat—Tinnehinch, co. Wicklow.

GRAVES OF MICKLETON.

Graves, Elizabeth-Anne, and Mary-John, daus. and co heiresses of the late John Graves, Esq., younger brother of the Rev. Morgan Graves, of Mickleton, co. Gloucester. The elder, Elizabeth-Anne, *m.* 31 July, 1838, Sir John Maxwell Steele, Bart., the younger, Mary-John, *m.* 4 May, 1854, Maxwell Hamilton, Esq. of Merrion Square Dublin.

* The D'Ewes of Wellesbourne, who became settled in the cos. of Warrick, Gloucester, and Worcester, about the commencement of the 17th century, are said to be a branch of the family of D'Ewes, originally seated in Suffolk, and of which Sir Simonds D'Ewes was so distinguished a member.

Lineage.—John Graves, of Clack Heaton, near Birdsall, West Riding, Yorkshire, *temp.* Edward IV., was father of Robert Graves, of Clackheaton, *temp.* Hen. VII., who *m.* and had three sons, viz.,

- William, of Clackheaton, *d.* 1564, leaving issue, John, of London, and James.
- John, of whose line we treat.
- Hugh, lord mayor of York, 1578, and M.P., *d.* 1588.

The 2nd son,

John Graves, of Beamesley, *d.* in 1616, aged 103, leaving by his wife, the dau. and heir of Mensier, of Croke, two sons,

- Richard, of London, of whom we treat.
- John, who *m.* and had two sons, John, Savilian Astronomer at Oxford, *d.* 1652; and Edward (Sir), Physician to Charles I., *d.* 1680.

The elder son,

Richard Graves, Esq. of London, *m.* Frances, dau. of William Gourney, of Moorehull, Yadley, Herts, and *d.* 1626, aged 54, being *s.* by his son,

Richard Graves, Esq. of Mickleton, co. Gloucester, Reader of Lincoln's Inn, and Receiver-General of Middlesex, who *m.* twice. By Eleanor, his 1st wife, dau. and co-heir of Thomas Bates, Esq. of London, and Richmond, he left at his decease, 1669, aged 59, an elder son and heir,

Samuel Graves, Esq. of Mickleton, who *m.* Susanna, dau. and co-heir of Richard Swan, Admiral in the Indian seas, and was *s.* at his decease, 1708, aged 59, by his eldest son,

Richard Graves, Esq. of Mickleton, the celebrated antiquary, who *m.* Elizabeth, dau. and co-heir of Thomas Morgan, Esq., by Elizabeth, his wife, dau. and co-heir of James Bragne, and *d.* 1729, aged 53, leaving issue,

- I. Morgan, his heir.
- II. Richard, in holy orders, of Claverton, co Somerset, author of *The Spiritual Quixote*, *b.* 4 May, 1715; *d.* 1805, leaving by Lucy Bartholomew his wife, several children, of whom the eldest,
  - The Rev. Richard Graves rector of Redgrave, Suffolk, was father, by Harriet his wife, of,
    - Richard-Charles-Head Graves, Esq. *m.* 1806, Mary-Cassandra, dau. of Thos., Lord Saye and Sele, and left with daus., a son, Capt. Twisleton Graves, of the 87th regt.
- III. Charles-Caspar, in holy orders.
- IV. Danvers, died in India, *s. p.*
- I. Mary, wife of the Rev. Dr. Taylor.
- II. Elizabeth.

The eldest son,

Morgan Graves, Esq. of Mickleton, *m.* Anne, dau. of James Walwyn, Esq. of Longworth, co. Hereford, M.P., and had issue, 1 Walwyn, *b.* 1745, *d. s. p.* 1813; 2 Richard, of whom presently; 3 Danvers, *d. unm.* 1689; 1 Catherine *m.* to the Rev. John Amphlett, D.D. of Hadsor; 2 Mary, *m.* to the Rev. William Hopton, of Canon Frome, co. Hereford; 3 Frances, *m.* Thomas Fletcher, Esq. of Goodrich, co. Hereford; and 4 Martha, who *d. unm.* 1835. The 2nd son,

The Rev. Richard Morgan Graves, D.D. of Mickleton, *m.* Elizabeth, dau. and co-heir of John Thermor, Esq. of Hannington, Wilts, and had issue,

- I. Morgan, in holy orders, of Mickleton, *d.* 1819, aged 47, *s. p.*
- II. John, *m.* Ann, dau. and co-heir of John-Thomas, Esq. of Penryn, Cornwall, and *d.* 1818, aged 36, leaving two daus., his co-heiresses, viz.,
  - 1 Elizabeth-Anne, wife of Sir John-Maxwell Steele, Bart.
  - 2 Mary-John, wife of Maxwell Hamilton, Esq.
- III. Elizabeth, *m.* to Charles-Gray Graves, Esq.

The Rev. Richard Morgan Graves, *d.* in 1815, aged 63.

Arms—Gu., an eagle displayed, or, crowned, arg., within an orle of cross-crosslets of the 2nd.
Seat—Mickleton, co. Gloucestershire.

GRAY OF CARNTYNE, FORMERLY OF DALMARNOCK.

Gray, The Rev. John Hamilton, of Carntyne, co. Lanark, D.L., *b.* 29 Dec. 1800; called to the Scottish bar in 1824; M.A. of Magdalen College. Oxford in 1824; entered into holy orders 1829; vicar of Rohover and Scarclif, co. Derby, and rural dean; *m.* 23 June, 1829, Elizabeth-Caroline, eldest dau. of James-Raymond Johnstone, Esq. of Alva, co. Clackmannan, by Mary-Elizabeth, his wife, sister of Sir Montague Cholmeley, Bart. of Easton, co. Lincoln, by whom he has issue,

- I. Caroline-Maria-Agnes-Robina, *b.* 26 June, 1833; *m.* 26 Aug. 1852, to John-Anstruther Thomson, of Charleton, co. Fife, by whom she has two sons, John-St.-Clair, and Charles-Frederick-St.-Clair.
- II. Sophia-Matilda, *b.* 1835, *d.* in the same year.

Mrs. Hamilton Gray is the authoress of *History of Etruria, History of the Roman Emperors, History of Rome, Tour to the Sepulchres of Etruria.*

Lineage.—Gray, of Carntyne, is an early cadet of the noble house of Gray, and has been established in Lanarkshire for between three and four centuries.

John Gray, of Tollcross, co. Lanark, lived before 1550. He had issue, John and James. He was *s.* by his eldest son,

John Gray, of Tollcross, who sold Tollcross, and purchased the estate of Carntyne, co. Lanark. He *d.* before 1595, and was *s.* by his son,

William Gray, of Carntyne. He *m.* 1st, Margaret Craig, by whom he had Archibald, his heir; and 2ndly, Marian, dau. of Ninian Hill, of Lambhill, by the dau. of John Hutchinson, of Gairbraid, and sister and heiress of the munificent founders of Hutchinson's hospital, in Glasgow. William Gray was *s.* by his eldest son,

Archibald Gray, of Carntyne, who *m.* Elizabeth, dau. of Colquhoun, of Kenmure, a cadet of Colquhoun of Luss. Having no issue, he was *s.* in 1628, by his brother,

John Gray, of Carntyne, who, in 1678, acquired the lands of Dalmarnock, which, for some generations, became the principal designation of his family. About the year 1680, he began to work coal in Carntyne. He *m.* Anabella, dau. of Walter Gibson, of Hillhead and Overnewton, by whom he had a son and successor,

John Gray, of Dalmarnock and Carntyne, who *s.* his father in 1687. He *m.* Janet, dau. of John Anderson, of Dowhill, who was several times lord provost of Glasgow, by Susannah his wife, dau. of James Hamilton, of Aitkenhead, lord provost of Glasgow, son of Hamilton, of Torrance. John Gray *d.* before 1715, and was *s.* by his son,

John Gray, of Dalmarnock and Carntyne, who distinguished himself as an active partisan of the exiled Royal family. He *m.* Elizabeth, dau. of James Hamilton, of Newton, an immediate cadet of Hamilton, Bart. of Silverton Hill, by Elizabeth, dau. of Gabriel Hamilton, of Westburn. Through this alliance the family of Gray now represents the Hamiltons of Newton. He had issue,

- James, his heir.
- John, heir to his brother.
- Gabriel, of Eastfield, who had one son, John, of Eastfield.
- Andrew, left issue, of whom, Elizabeth alone survives, unm. The others *d.* unm.
- Elizabeth, wife of John Spens, of Stonelaw, and mother of General John Spens, of Stonelaw.
- Anabella, wife of Henry Woddrop, of Westthorn.
- Rebecca, wife of William Ross, heir male of the family of Lord Ross.
- Jane, wife of Thomas Buchanan, of Ardoch.

John Gray *d.* 27 Jan. 1742, and was *s.* by his eldest son,

James Gray, of Dalmarnock and Carntyne, who had no issue. His 1st wife was his cousin, Elizabeth, a dau. of the family of Hamilton, of Newton. His 2nd wife was Jane, dau. of John Corbett, of Tollcross, by a dau. of Porterfield, of Duchal, and niece to the Earl of Kilmarnock. He *d.* in 1778, and was *s.* by his brother,

John Gray, of Dalmarnock and Carntyne, *b.* 1715. He *m.* Isabella, dau. and heir of John Chapman, commissary of Glasgow, by Elizabeth, dau. of David Pollock, of Balgray, an immediate cadet of Pollock, Bart. of Pollock, and maternally descended from the noble families of Boyd and Kennedy. By her he had issue three sons and three daus., who all *d.* young or unm., except Robert, his heir; and Helen, wife of William Woddropp, of Dalmarnock. In 1784, John Gray sold his estates of Dalmarnock, Newlands, and Kennyhill. He *d.* 1796, and was *s.* by his son,

Robert Gray, of Carntyne, *b.* 1756. In [illegible], he became representative of the family of Hamilton, of Newton. In 1789, he *m.* Mary-Anne, dau. of Gabriel Hamilton, of Westburn, representative of Hamilton, of Torrance, by Agnes Dundas, heiress of Duddingston, dau. of George Dundas, of Duddingston, and Magdalen-Lindsay Crawford, sister of John, Viscount Garnock, and granddau. of John, 17th Earl of Crawford, by Lady Margaret Hamilton, sister to James and William, Dukes of Hamilton. By her, who *d.* 6 Jan. 1869, he had, an only son, John. He was an active magistrate, and for nearly forty years deputy-lieutenant of the county of Lanark. He *d.* on the 11 Nov. 1833, and was *s.* by his son, JOHN-HAMILTON GRAY, now of Carntyne, and since 1824, deputy-lieutenant of Lanarkshire.

Hamilton of Newton.

SIR JAMES HAMILTON, 5th lord of Cadzow, *m.* Janet, dau. of Sir Alexander Livingston, of Calendar, governor of Scotland, ancestor of the Earl of Linlithgow, and by her had several sons. His eldest son, SIR JAMES, was, in 1445, made a peer of parliament, *m.* Princess MARY, of Scotland, dau. to King JAMES II., and was ancestor to the Duke of Hamilton. His 2nd son, Alexander, was ancestor to this family. He was proprietor of Silvertonhill, in 1449. He was *s.* by his son, James Hamilton, of Silvertonhill, who by marriage with a dau. of the house of Douglas, acquired the estate of Newton. The Hamiltons, of Silvertonhill, and their younger branch, of Newton, are the nearest legitimate cadets to the ducal house, after the branch of Abercorn. Andrew Hamilton, the 5th in descent from Alexander, the founder of this branch, was a faithful adherent of Queen MARY, was knighted by her, and *d.* 1592. His son, Sir Robert, by Elizabeth, only child of Sir William Baillie, of Prevan, lord president of the Court of Session, had issue.
I. Edward, of Silverton Hill, father to the 1st Baronet;
II. James, ancestor to this branch. James Hamilton, left issue, a son, James Hamilton, of Newton, in 1672, He *m.* 1st, Elizabeth, dau. of Gabriel Hamilton, of Westburn, by Margaret, dau. of Sir Robert Cunningham, of Gilbertfield, by whom he had a dau., Elizabeth, *b.* 1638, wife of John Gray, of Dalmarnock and Carntyne. He *m.* 2ndly, Margaret, dau. of Robert Montgomery, of Macbie Hill, cadet of Eglinton, by a dau. of Lockhart, of Lee. By her he had a son, Thomas Hamilton, of Newton, who, by a dau. of Cleland, of Cleland, had a son, James Hamilton of Newton, who *m.* Anabella, dau. of Sir Robert Pollock, Bart. of Pollock. He *d.* in 1769, and his son, James, dying *unm.*, the estate of Newton devolved, in 1775, on his cousin, Janet, wife of Colonel Richard Montgomery, cousin of Sir George Montgomery, Bart. of Macbiehill. Mrs. Montgomery *d.* in 1825, and left the estate of Newton to her husband's relation, Sir James Montgomery, Bart. of Stanhope, while the representation of this branch of the house of Hamilton was carried on by Robert Gray, of Carntyne, in right of his grandmother, Elizabeth Hamilton, of Newton.

Arms—Quarterly: 1st and 4th gu. within a border engrailed arg., a lion rampant, between three cinqfoils arg., for GRAY: 2nd and 3rd gu., within a border ermine, three cinqfoils ermine, with a crescent surmounted by a mullet for difference, for HAMILTON.
Crests—An anchor cabled, stuck in the sea, ppr., for GRAY: an oak tree, ppr., issuing from a ducal coronet, or, and transversed by a saw, for HAMILTON.
Mottoes—Fast, for GRAY; Through, for HAMILTON.
Seat—Carntyne, co. Lanark. Mr. Hamilton Gray's usual place of residence is Bolsover Castle, co. Derby.

GRAZEBROOK OF AUDNAM, AND FORMERLY OF GREYSBROOKE HALL.

GRAZEBROOK, MICHAEL, Esq. of Audnam, co. Stafford, J.P. and D.L., *b.* 6 June, 1788; *m.* May, 1821, Eliza-Wallis, only dau. and sole heiress of John Phillips, Esq. of Birmingham, and by her (who *d.* in 1833,) has issue,

I. MICHAEL-PHILLIPS, *b.* 24 Sept. 1822; *m.* 18 Sept. 1849, Mary-Ann, 3rd dau. of Richard Hickman, Esq., J.P., of Oldswinford, Worcestershire, and has issue,
  1 Michael-Hickman, *b.* Oct. 1852.
  2 William.
  1 Rosa-Mary.
II. John-Phillips, *b.* 7 April, 1826, of Hagley; *m.* 3 May, 1855, Harriette-Draffen, 2nd dau. of Thomas Francis, Esq. of Birmingham.
I. Eliza-Phillips, *m.* 1847, to John, 2nd son of William Morgan, Esq. of the Hill, near Abergavenny.

Lineage.—This family derives its name from Gereburg, Greseburg, or Gersebroc (as it is variously spelt in Domesday Book), in Yorkshire, which manor they held, with others, in fee, from the Norman conquest, successively under the great Roger de Busli, the Viponts, Lovetots, and Furnivals, and subsequently the knight-service was transferred to the Mowbrays until the reign of HENRY III. In the reign of HENRY II., Roger de Gresebrok held his lands of Alice, countess of Augie or Ewe, (dau. of William de Albini, Earl of Arundel, by Queen Alice, relict of HENRY I.) A very ancient bearing, "three conies," may probably be referred to this time. They also appear to have held the manor of Lechetone, in Gloucestershire, in capite for a short time, as we read in Domesday that Osbernus de Gerseburg had held that manor, which was then held (1084) by Humphrey Coqus, but whether it was forfeited or exchanged for other lands is not shown, and owing to the loss of some family papers cannot now be stated. The name also occurs in the Roll of Battel Abbey among those who fought at Hastings. Several legends are told relating to members of this family distinguished in different ages, among whom we may mention the son of Osbern, who, shortly after the Conquest, *m.* Ethleswytha de Hosdene, an heiress, and descended from the Saxon kings; also Roger de Gresebrok (*temp.* HENRY II.) and his son, the Angry Bear, celebrated at the 3rd Crusade, and who *d.* about 1200. (*See* BURKE's *Family Romance.*)

About 1250 (the deed is *s. d.*) Roger de Greudon granted to Bartholomew de Gresebroc the ancient mansion of the De Brays, with messuages, &c., in Senestan (now Shenstone, near Lichfield), which he had obtained as the dower of his wife, Domina Alicia de Bray, and this was afterwards called Gresbroke Hall. This Bartholomew had two sons,

Adam, who inherited Gresebroc and the Yorkshire estates, which descended from him (probably through his dau.) to the Tinsleys (who held them in 1300), and from them to the Wentworths, the present possessors.
Robert, who had Gresbroke Hall* and the estates in Senestan, Statfold, &c., co. Stafford.

From this time they are found as joint-witnesses with the Grendons, Bagods, De Astons, and other great Staffordshire families, and sometimes preceding them in the order of rotation. The more modern descent is as follows:—

MICHAEL, son of MICHAELL GRASBROOKE (who was grandson of John Greysbrooke, of Greysbrooke Hall, who *d.* 1541), left issue at his death in March, 1658, a son,

MICHAELL GRASBROOKE, who, by Dorothy his wife, had issue four sons† and three daus. Michaell *d.* April, 1689, his wife *d.* Jan. 1661. His eldest son,

---

* A portion of this ancient residence of the Grazebrook family, which remained in their possession nearly 500 years, was built before 1200, probably much earlier than that date. From the wording of the grant in 1250, it was a large mansion with outhouses, &c. It appears to have suffered much at different times; and during the Commonwealth this neighbourhood was especially over-run, although there is no express mention of its having been injured at that time. Sanders, writing in 1769, says that it was "formerly much more considerable;" indeed, since 1720, when it passed out of the family, portions have been taken down at different times, and a few years ago it was nothing more than a cottage, the kitchen, with its enormous fire-place, being all that remained, and tradition in the village says that this part was built after the old Hall had fallen to decay. It was probably an outhouse built about 1500 with older materials. In the summer of 1852 this was finally demolished, and cottages built on the site.

† From the 3rd son, Joseph, descend the Gloucestershire Grazebrooks, thus—Joseph, 3rd son of Michaell, as above *d.* 1718, leaving five sons and three daus., viz.,
Samuel, *d.* 1743.
Benjamin, *b.* Jan. 1680.
Edward, *b.* April, 1682.
Michaell, *b.* Feb. 1687.
Paul, *b.* Feb. 1691, who had a son, Joseph, buried 1728, and a dau., Elizabeth, *b.* 1720, by his wife, Elizabeth Edwards; he *d.* 1734.
The daus. were Anne, Dorothy, and Sarah.

His 2nd son,
Benjamin, *d.* young, leaving issue, Joseph who *d. s. p.*, Benjamin, and two daus., Margaret, *m.* — Watts, Esq., and Mary, *m.* to Thomas Needs, Esq. His son,
Benjamin, *m.* and had issue (with a dau., Mary, *m.* Henry Clarke, an attorney at Stroud) three sons,
Joseph, the banker of Stroud, and of Farhill, Oxfordshire, who *m.* Miss Tomb, of Coleford, near Cirencester, and left a dau., Hesther, *m.* 15 Feb. 1814, to Edward, son of Lord Chief Justice Mansfield.
Thomas, *b.* 28 June, 1756, of whom hereafter.
Benjamin, *m.* 1st, ... and 2ndly, a dau. of Sir Egerton Leigh, Bart., but *d. s. p.* in 1837.
Benjamin was buried at Bisley, in Gloucestershire. His 2nd son, Thomas, of Dudbridge, Gloucestershire, *m.* Dec. 1778, Louisa-Anna-Maria, only dau. of Durley Wintle, Esq., and left issue at his death, in 1834, three sons (his wife *d.* 1850),
Durley, *b.* 19 Dec. 1779, of Chertsey, Surrey; *m.* 24 May, 1809, Sarah, dau. of Michael Grazebrook, of Audnam, and by her who *d.* 1814, has issue a son, Henry-Goodwin Grazebrook, *b.* 24 Feb. 1810; *m.* 1848, to Lucia-Harriet, youngest dau. of Charles-W. Hallett, Esq. of Surbiton Lodge, Kingston.
Joseph, *b.* 15 June, 1793; *m.* Anne, dau. of — Froste, Esq., and by her has, besides daus., one son, William.
Henry, *b.* 10 Dec. 1804, *m.* and has issue.

John Grazebrooke, b. Feb. 1645, had issue by his first wife (with a dau., Elizabeth) two sons, viz.,

Michael, of whom hereafter.
John, b. Dec. 1676, and d. 1708, leaving two daus., Anne and Sarah.

John Grazebrooke was m. again to Elizabeth Holland, in 1704, and, at his death, was s. by his eldest son,

Michael Grazebrook, of Audnam, b. May, 1671; m. 12 May, 1718, Elizabeth, dau. of William and Anne Hunt, (sister of Thomas Hunt, lord of the manor of Hinckthull,) and by her (who d. 1751) had issue two sons and four daus. Michael Grazebrooke, d. 1756, and was s. by his only surviving son,

Michael Grazebrook, Esq. of Audnam, b. June, 1723, who m. Sarah, only dau. of Richard Worrall, Esq. of Stourton, sole heiress of the Worralls, and by her, who d. 7 June, 1799, had issue,

I. Thomas-Worrall, of whom hereafter.
II. Michael, of Audnam, and of Horsley, co. Worcester, b. 7 March, 1758; m. 21 Dec. 1785, Mary-Anne, dau. and eventual heiress of Thomas Needs, Esq., and by her, who d. 1846, had issue,
1 Michael, of whom presently.
2 William, b. 31 March, 1791, of Summerhill.
3 Henry, a merchant in Liverpool, b. 31 August, 1792; m. 15 April, 1816, Isabella, eldest dau. of Joshua Senior, Esq. of Sandyford, near Glasgow, and has issue,
Henry, b. 28 Sept. 1818; m. 5 Aug. 1847, Harriette-Moss, dau of R. W. Preston, Esq. of Beech Hill, near Liverpool.
Michael, d. s. p. 1836.
William-Joshua, b. 27 Sept. 1827.
George, b. 4 July, 1831.
Charlotte-Mary, m. 1838, to William, eldest son of Samuel Johnson, Esq. of Eltham, Kent.
Isabella, m. 1843, William-Orme, eldest son of William Foster, Esq. of Wordesley House, Staffordshire.
4 Thomas-Needs, b. 25 April, d. 27 May, 1793.
5 Frederick, b. 31 May, d. 20 Oct. 1795.
6 George, b. 21 July, 1796, of Pedmore, m. and has issue.
7 Charles, b. 23 Nov. 1802.
8 John-Worrall, b. 9 May, 1804; m. Anne, dau. of Joshua Senior, Esq., and has issue two daus., Mary-Anne, and Anna.
1 Sarah, m. to Durley Grazebrook, Esq. of Chertsey, and d. 1814.
2 Charlotte. 3 Mary-Anne.
4 Elizabeth, m. 5 Oct. 1830, to Ferdinando Smith, of Halesowen Grange, Salop, senior co-heir to the Barony of Dudley.
5 Matilda, m. to Richard, son of Richard Brettell, Esq. of Finstal House, Worcestershire.
I Mary, m. 25 March, 1786, to Richard Brettell, Esq. of Finstal House, Worcestershire.
II. Elizabeth, m. 1788, to John-Addenbrooke Homfray, Esq. of Wollaston, who took the surname of Addenbrooke, by sign-manual, in 1792, and served as high-sheriff of Worcestershire in 1798.

Michael Grazebrooke, d. 14 May, 1766, and was s. by his eldest son,

Thomas-Worrall Grazebrook, Esq. of Stourton Castle, co. Stafford, b. 11 Aug. 1756; m. Elizabeth, only dau. and heir of Robert and Mary Wilkes, of Dallicott House, Salop, and by her, who d. June, 1837, had issue,

Thomas-Worrall-Smith, of whom hereafter.
Elizabeth, m. to George-Mackenzie Kettle, Esq. of Bladen Castle, near Burton-on-Trent, and has a dau., Clara.

Thomas-Worrall Grazebrook, d. 9 Aug. 1816, and was s. by his son,

Thomas-Worrall-Smith Grazebrook, Esq. of Dallicott, co. Salop, Stourton, co. Stafford, &c., b. 5 Nov. 1809, d. s. p. in July, 1846, when the representation of the family devolved on his first cousin, Michael Grazebrook, Esq. of Audnam.

Arms—Arg., an eagle displayed, gu., armed, or, on a chief, sa., three bezants, each charged with a fleur-de-lys, az.; also a very ancient bearing—Arg., three conies, gu.
Crest—"The Angry Bear," a bear's head, enraged, or, muzzled, sa., and charged on the neck with three fleur-de-lys, fessways, az.
Residence—Audnam, co. Stafford.

GREATHED OF UDDINGS.

Greathed, Edward-Harris, Esq. of Uddings, co. Dorset, lieut.-col. in the army, b. 8 June, 1812; s. his father in Dec. 1840.

Lineage.—The late Edward Greathed, Esq. of Uddings, assumed the surname and arms of Greathed, by Royal license, in 1806, on succeeding to the estates of his maternal uncle. He m. in Aug. 1811, Mary-Elizabeth, dau. of Sir Richard-Carr Glyn, Bart. of Gaunts, co. Dorset, and d. in Dec. 1840, having had issue,

Edward-Harris, the present proprietor of Uddings.
Hervey-Harris, civil service, Bengal, m. in Dec. 1844, Eliza, dau. of Thomas Turner, Esq., civil service, Bengal.
George-Herbert-Harris, lieut. R.N.
Robert-Harris, Bengal civil service.
William-Wilberforce-Harris, Bengal engineers.
Mary-Elizabeth-Harris.
Julia-Henrietta, m. in 1842, to William-Parry Okeden, Esq.
Emily-Sarah.

Seat—Uddings, co. Dorset.

GREAVES OF AVONSIDE.

Greaves, Edward, Esq. of Avonside, co. Warwick, J.P. and D.L., b. 21 Sept. 1803; m. 15 May, 1828, Anne, dau. of John Hobbins, Esq., widow of Thomas Ward, Esq. of Moreton Morrell.

Lineage.—This family claims descent from the Worcestershire family of Greves, of Moseley. The late,

John Greaves, Esq., (son of Joseph and Rebecca Greaves), left by Mary, his wife, the present Edward Greaves, Esq. of Avonside, three other sons, and five daus., viz.,

Richard, J.P. co. Warwick.
Edward.
John-Whitehead, J.P. of the co. Carnarvon and D.L. of Merionethshire.
Joseph.
Selina, m. to Edward Flower, Esq.
Rebecca, m. to Henry Lukin, Esq.
Amelia.
Lucy, m. to Mark Jocelyn Lacy, Esq.
Sophia, m. to Stephen Smith, Esq.

Arms—Arg. on a fess, az. between three ogresses, charged with as many lions' heads erased of the field, a griffin passant between two escallops, or.
Crest—An eagle with two heads displayed sa. beaked and membered, or.
Seat—Avonbank, Barford, co. Warwick.

EMMOTT-GREEN OF EMMOTT.

Green, George-Emmott, Esq. of Emmott Hall, co. Lancaster, J.P., b. 1 March, 1813; m. 10 March, 1840, Louisa-Mary-Sheridan, dau. of the late John Macpherson, Esq., by Marianne Collete,* his wife, 2nd dau. of John Addison, Esq., and has issue

I. Charles-Richard-Emmott.
I. Marian-Caroline-Emmott.
II. Georgina-Emmott.
III. Louisa-Emmeline-Emmott.

Lineage.—Of this family, established in England since the Conquest, the first of whom any record exists is Robert de Emot, who held lands at Emmot, 4 Edward II., as appears by inquisition. His descendant, the representative of the Emmotts, in the middle of the 17th century, was

William Emmott, Esq. of Emmott, who d. in Aug. 1683, By Mary, his wife (who d. in 1677), he left four sons and one dau., viz., William, of Emmott, d. 13 May, 1720, aged 51, s. p.; John, of Emmott, who d. 21 Oct. 1746, aged 82; Thomas, d. in 1669, aged 29; Christopher, of London, merchant, d. unm. 24 Feb. 1745, aged 71; and Mary, m. to Mr. Wainhouse. This lady,

Mary Emmott, wife of Mr. Wainhouse, d. 16 Jan. 1722, aged 50, leaving a son,

Richard Wainhouse, who assumed, as heir to his uncles, the name and arms of Emmott. His death occurred 14 March, 1761, in the 60th year of his age. He left (with a dau., who m. Alexander Ross, Esq.) a son,

Richard Emmott, Esq. of Emmott, co. Lancaster, and Goldings, Herts, who entailed the former estate on his nieces. Of those ladies, the eldest is Caroline, wife of Edward Parkins, Esq. of Chesfield Lodge, Herts; and the 2nd was

Harriet-Susanna Ross, who m. in April, 1811, George Green, Esq., and had issue,

* This lady subsequently married General Sir Robert Barton.

Georgr-Emmott, now of Emmott Hall.
Charles-Alexander, lieut. horse-artillery, killed in the late war in India.
Edward-Alfred, of the Bengal native infantry
Augustus-William, in holy orders.
Walter-Emmott.
Harriet-Susanna, *m.* to the second son of John Deffell, Esq. of Upper Harley Street.
Caroline-Fanny. Gertrude-Ellen-Emmott.
Frederica-Emily.

Mrs. Green, the co-heiress of Emmott, *d.* 10 Aug. 1839.

Motto—Tenez le vrai.
Seat—Emmott Hall, Colne.

GREEN OF PAVENHAM.

Green, Thomas-Abbott, Esq. of Pavenham Bury, co. Bedford, J.P., high-sheriff 1848, *b.* 30 April, 1806; *m.* 27 May, 1834, Mary, dau. of John Green, Esq. of London, and has issue,

I. Francis-William.
II. Henry-Hylton. III. Robert-Gambier.
I. Fanny-Constantia. II. Annie-Margaret.

Lineage.—This family claims descent from the Greens of Greens Norton, co. Northampton.

John Green, Esq. of Bedford, son of Jordan Green, Esq. of Bedford, *m.* Ann, dau. of John Abbott, Esq. of Olney, co. Bucks, and was father of

Thomas-Abbott Green, Esq. of Marchmont House, co. Herts, who *m.* Elizabeth, dau. of — Lampert, Esq. of Woburn, Beds, and was father of

Henry Green, Esq. of Eyewood, co. Hereford, who *m.* in 1805, Anne dau. of William Hylton, Esq., descended from the Hyltons of Hylton Castle, co. Durham, and had,

Thomas-Abbott, now of Pavenham.
Henry, in holy orders, M.A., vicar of Hambleton, co. Rutland, *m.* Margaret, dau. of Robert Lindsell, Esq. of Fairfield, Bedfordshire.
Francis-Edward, E. I. Co.'s service, Madras.
Anne-Eliza, *m.* to William Stuart, Esq. of Prince Edward's Island.
Rosalind, *m.* to the Rev. John Foster, M.A., rector of Foxearth, Essex.

Arms—Az., a fesse, between three bucks, trippant, or.
Crest—A buck, trippant, or.
Motto—Semper viridis.
Seat—Pavenham Bury, co. Bedford.

GREENAWAY OF BARRINGTON GROVE.

Greenaway, Charles, Esq. of Barrington Grove, co. Gloucester, and Burford Priory, co. Oxford, J.P. and D.L., formerly M.P. for Leominster, *m.* 3 May, 1813, Charlotte-Sophia, youngest dau. of Robert Hurst, Esq. of Horsham Park, Sussex, M.P. Mr. Greenaway is only son and heir, by Jane his wife, eldest dau. of Charles Higgs, Esq. of Charlton Kings, co. Gloucester, of the late Giles Greenaway, Esq. high-sheriff of the last named county in 1784, who *d.* 1 Jan. 1815, leaving, with his successor, Mr. Greenaway, an only dau., *m.* to Edward Youde, Esq. of Plas-Madoc, co. Denbigh.

Arms—Gu., a chev., between three covered cups, or, on a chief, arg., three griffins' heads, erased, az., beaked, or.
Crest—A griffin's head, erased, az., pendent from the beak an amulet, or.
Seats—Barrington Grove, co. Gloucester; and Burford Priory, co. Oxford.

GREENE OF SLYNE AND WHITTINGTON.

Greene, Thomas, Esq. of Slyne, co. Lancaster, and Whittington Hall, co. Westmoreland, J.P., M.P. for Lancaster since 1824, and high-sheriff of Lancashire 1823; *b.* 19 Jan. 1794; *m.* 31 Aug. 1820, Henrietta, 3rd dau. of the Right Hon. Sir Henry Russell, Bart, and has issue,

I. Dawson-Cornelius, brevet-major 43rd lt. infantry, *b.* 23 July, 1822.
II. Thomas-Huntley, *b.* 28 Oct. 1823, in holy orders.
III. Henry-Aylmer, *b.* 16 Feb. 1827.
I. Henrietta, *m.* 1850, to the Rev. Anthony Wilson Thorold, grandson of Sir John Thorold, Bart., M.P.
II. Rose-Alice-Clotilde, *m.* 1845, to John Clerk, Esq., son of the Rt. Hon. Sir George Clerk, Bart.

Lineage.—The first notice we have of the property of Slyne being in the possession of this family, is in the 8th of James I., when two widows, Grace and Alice Greene, were jointured on it. They surrendered it, at that time, to Thomas Greene, from whom Cornelius Greene inherited the estate, in 1618. This Cornelius *d.* 14 Oct. 1669, leaving, by Dorothy, his wife, who *d.* in the following year, two sons,

Thomas, *b.* 1636, of Bolton-Holmes, who *d.* in 1714, leaving by Elizabeth his wife, a son, Cornelius Greene, *b.* in 1668, who *m.* Jane Gibson, and *d.* in 1728, leaving a son, Richard Greene, *b.* in 1727, father of the Rev. Cornelius Greene, of Terwick, near Petersfield.
Cornelius, of whose line we treat.

The 2nd son,

Cornelius Greene, Esq. of Slyne, 26 Charles II., *m.* Mary, dau. of Thomas Simpson, of Torrisholme, Gent., and by her, who *d.* in 1736, had issue, Thomas, his heir; Richard, *b.* in 1689, of St. John's College, Cambridge, *d. s. p.* in Africa; Edward, *d. s. p.* in America; William, *d. s. p.* in Asia; and Simeon, *d. s. p.* in 1771. Mr. Greene *d.* in 1712, and was *s.* by his eldest son,

Thomas Greene, Esq. of Slyne, *b.* in 1681, who *m.* Elizabeth, dau. of George Barker, Esq of Rampside, co. Lancaster, and had issue, Thomas, his heir; George, *d. s. p.* in 1758; Richard, *d. s. p.* at Calcutta; William, *d. s. p.* in 1762; and Margaret, *m.* to Robert Bradley, Esq. of Slyne. Mr. Greene *d.* in 1762, and was *s.* by his eldest son,

Thomas Greene, Esq. of Slyne, *b.* 10 Dec. 1737, who *m.* in 1792, Martha, dau. and co-heir of Edmund Dawson, Esq. of Warton, co. Lancaster, and dying 6 Dec. 1810, was *s.* by his son, Thomas Greene, Esq., now of Slyne and Whittington.

Arms—Vert, on a fesse, invecked, or, between, in chief, two pheons, and in base, a bugle-horn, arg., stringed, gu., three fleurs-de-lis, of the last.
Crest—A stag, ppr., gorged with a collar, invecked, vert, a shield suspended therefrom, or, charged with a rose, gu.
Seats—Slyne, near Lancaster; and Whittington Hall, Kirkby Lonsdale.

GREENE OF KILMANAHAN CASTLE.

Greene, Nuttall, Esq. late of Kilmanahan Castle, co. Waterford, J.P. and D.L., *m.* in 1806, Charlotte-Anne, dau. of the late William Parsons, Esq. of Dublin, and *d.* having issue,

I. William, barrister-at-law.
II. Thomas, 21st N.B. Fusiliers, *d.* in India 1840.
III. James-Parsons, *d* May, 1850.
IV. Rodolphus. V. Samuel-Parsons.
I. Sarah-Eliza, *m.* to Capt. Sneyd, H.E.I.C.S.
II. Anne, *m.* to C.-W.-H. Steward, Esq. of Suffolk, late 3rd Light Dragoons, and is deceased.
III. Susan, *m.* 1st, to T. Ringrose Atkyns, Esq., of Cork, late of the Austrian Imperial Hussars; and 2ndly, to W. Merryman, Esq.
IV. Charlotte-Frances. V. Letitia.
VI. Georgiana-Rebecca, *m.* to Capt. A. W. Hawkins, Bengal Artillery.
VII. Emma. VIII. Caroline-Cherry.

Lieut.-Col. Greene served as high-sheriff of the co. of Waterford in 1810-1811.

Lineage.—This is a junior branch of the family of Greene, so long established in high repute in the co. Waterford. The heads of the house are John Greene, Esq., M.P., for co. of Kilkenny, and Anthony-Sheppey Greene, Esq. of Malling Deanery, near Lewes, Sussex. The great-grandfather of the late Lieut.-Col. Greene, of Kilmanahan.

Colonel Rodolphus Greene, of Kilmanahan, *m.* Elizabeth Carew, of Castleborough, co. Wexford, and had issue, Rodolphus, his heir; Michael, who *m.* three times; and Elizabeth, *m.* to John Keane, Esq. of Cappoquin.

The elder son,

Rodolphus Greene, Esq. of Kilmanahan Castle, *m.* Elizabeth, dau. of Colonel Disney, of Whitechurch, co. Waterford, and had issue, William, his heir; John, Rodolphus, Frederick; Elizabeth, *m.* to the Rev. John Doyle; and Mary. The eldest son,

William Greene, Esq. of Kilmanahan Castle, m. Letitia, only child and heir of Thomas Greene, Esq. of Low Grange, co. Kilkenny, and by her, who m. 2ndly, John Greene, Esq. of Greenville, co. Kilkenny,* he had issue, besides Lieut.-Col. Nuttall Greene, of Kilmanahan Castle, another son, George, of Dublin, late of the 41st regt., who m. 1st, Eliza, dau. of the late Capt. Reynolds, 55th regt.; and 2ndly, Rose, dau. of — Nelson, Esq. of Dublin, by the former, of whom he has had issue, William, collector of Customs at Wicklow, deceased; George, late of the 55th regt.; and Letitia-Clementina.

Arms—Three stags, trippant, or.
Crest—Out of a ducal coronet, a stag's head.
Motto—Nec timeo nec sperno.

GREENE OF ROLLESTON.

Greene, Henry, Esq. of Rolleston Hall, co. Leicester, b. 4 April, 1794; s. to his maternal uncle, Henry Greene, Esq. in 1801. This gentleman whose patronymic was Thomas, assumed by sign-manual, in 1815, the surname and arms of Greene, as representative of that ancient family.

Lineage.—The family of Greene, of Rolleston, is of high antiquity in the county of Leicester.

Richard Greene, Esq. of Wykin, in the county of the city of Coventry, was father of

Richard Greene, Esq. of Wykin, who m. Joan, dau. of Edward Pell, Esq. of Rolleston, and sister and co-heir of Edward Pell, Esq. of the Middle Temple, and had issue,

Richard, of Wykin, who m. Elizabeth, dau. of Henry Smith, Esq. of Withcote, and left an only dau. and heiress,
Elizabeth, who m. her cousin, Henry Greene, Esq.
Henry, of whom presently.

The youngest son,

Henry Greene, Esq. of Rolleston. m. Mary, dau. of Abel Barker, Esq. of Hambledon, co. Rutland, and sister to Sir Abel Barker, by whom he had, with other issue, a son,

Henry Greene, Esq. of Rolleston, b. about the year 1663, who m. Elizabeth, dau. and heir of his uncle, Richard Greene, Esq. of Wykin, by whom he had an only son,

Richard Greene, Esq. of Rolleston, sheriff of Leicester in 1731, who m. Catharine, dau. of William Fortrey, Esq., and niece of James Fortrey,† Esq. of Royal Fenn, and had issue,

Henry, his successor.
Anna Maria, m. in 1759, to Edward Hickman, Esq. of Old Swinford, co. Worcester, and d. in 1779, leaving four sons and four daus.
Catherine, m. to Rev. Christopher-Hatton Walker, M.A., rector of Harrington, Northamptonshire, and of Kibworth, co. Leicester, by whom she had issue,
Richard, in holy orders, rector of Galby.
Catherine, m. in Dec. 1791, to the Rev. George Boulton, rector of Oxendon, and vicar of Weston, by whom she has issue.

Richard Greene d. in Jan. 1781, and was s. by his son,

The Rev. Henry Greene, M.A., rector of Little Burstead and Laingdon, in Essex, and prebendary of Oxted, in St. Paul's Cathedral, who m. Mary, only dau. of William Stainforth, Esq. of Stillington, near York, by Judith, one of the co-heiresses of Sir Walter Hawksworth, of Hawksworth, and had issue,

Henry, b. in Dec. 1761, who s. his father at Rolleston, 18 Sept. 1797, and m. in Aug. 1794, Elizabeth, dau. of John Glover, Esq. of Barton, in Cambridgeshire, but dying without issue, in March, 1801, the family estates devolved upon his nephew.
Catharine, who m. the Rev. Edward Thomas, M.A., vicar of Billesdon, and had issue,
Henry Thomas, (now Greene,) present proprietor.
Edward-Thomas, b. 20 Sept. 1795.
Catherine-Thomas.

Arms—Vert, three bucks, trippant, or, within a bordure of the second, quartering the ensigns of many distinguished houses, including Pell, Fortrey, Jocelyn, Bardolf, &c.
Crest—Out of park pales, in a circular form, a stag's head, ppr., attired, or.
Seat—Rolleston Hall, Leicestershire.

GREENWELL OF GREENWELL FORD.

Greenwell, The Rev. William, of Greenwell Ford, co. Durham, M.A., b. 23 March, 1820.

Lineage.—The wide spreading and ancient family of Greenwell is descended from Gulielmus Presbyter, who, in the year 1183, as appears in Boldon Buke, held the lands of Greenwall, in the parish of Wolsingham, co. Durham, and whose son, James, assumed the name of the place of his inheritance signing himself, in various charters, Jacobus de Grenisuellis and Jacobus de Grenewellis.

William Greenwell, Esq. of Stobilee, in the parish of Satley, co. Durham, (son of William, grandson of Richard, who d. in 1553, great-grandson of Thomas Greenwell, Esq. of Stobilee, living in 1503, and 6th in descent from Robert de Grenewelle, who held the vill of Satley in chief A.D. 1323,) left at his decease, in 1624, by his wife Alice, dau. of Robert Claxton, Esq., with several other children, William, of Stobilee, fined and sequestered as a recusant and royalist, (he d. in 1667, leaving issue;) 2 Richard, living in 1624; 3 Nicholas. The 3rd son,

Nicholas Greenwell, Esq. of Fenhall, purchased in 1633, Fayrhare's lands, in Ford. In 1638, he acquired another portion from Hodgson, of Manor House, and divers other parcels of various dates. He was s. at his decease by his only son,

William Greenwell, Esq. of Greenwell Ford, and sometime of Kibblesworth, who m. Barbara, dau. and heiress of Robert Cole, Esq. of Kibblesworth, and had, with several other children,

Nicholas, his heir.
John, of Newcastle, merchant, who m. Jane, dau. of Alderman William Aubone, of Newcastle-on-Tyne, and had issue, Aubone, merchant of Newcastle, who d. s. p. 1729-30; William; Nicholas, d. in 1714; and Barbara, m. to Paul Gibson, of Durham.
Robert, on whom his father and mother settled lands in Kibblesworth, in 1683. He m. in 1707, Phillis, dau. and co-heir of William Aubone, Esq. of Newcastle, and left, with junior issue, a son, William Greenwell, of Kibblesworth, who m. Mary, dau. of Joshua Twizell, Esq. of Newcastle-on-Tyne, and was s. by his son, Joshua Greenwell, Esq. of Kibblesworth, and of Newcastle-on-Tyne, who m. Mary, dau. and heiress of the Rev. Thomas Robinson, A.M., rector of Wycliffe, co. York, by Olivia, dau. of the Rev. Henry Stapylton, of Thornton Watlass, and dying in 1797, left issue,
1 William, of Kibblesworth, b. in 1775, d. unm.
2 Robinson-Robert, b. in 1778, a merchant in Newcastle, who m. in 1819, Elizabeth, dau. of John Mellar, Esq. of Whitby, and has a son, Rev. W. Greenwell.
3 Leonard (Sir), K.C.B. and K.C.H., major-general in the army, b. in 1781, d. unm.
1 Olivia, d. unm.

William Greenwell d. in 1701, and was s. by his eldest son,

Nicholas Greenwell, Esq. of Greenwell Ford, who m. Elizabeth, dau. of John Addison, Esq. of Egglestone, and was s. at his decease in 1736, by his only son,

William Greenwell, Esq. of Greenwell Ford, who m. 5 Aug. 1734, Miss Mary Saunderson, and had (with three daus., Elizabeth, m. to Edward Charlton, Esq.; Grace, m. to John Cumming, Esq.; and Anne, m. in 1761, to Robert Surtees, Esq. of Cronywell) an only son,

Alan Greenwell, Esq., who s. his father at Ford, 14 April, 1743. He m. Anne, dau. of Henry Ornsby, Esq. of Lanchester, by whom (who d. 28 April, 1783) he had issue,

William-Thomas, his heir, of Greenwell Ford.
George, who m. Mary, dau. of William Askwith, Esq. of Rippon, and has issue.
Nicholas.
Alan, who d. in 1789.
Mary, m. to Alderman John Hutchinson, of Durham.
Anne, m. to Edward Serle, Esq. of Colchester.
Jane, d. young.

---

* By her 2nd husband, John Greene, Esq. of Greenville, Mrs. Greene had a son,

Joseph Greene, Esq. of Lakeview, co. Kilkenny, J.P., m. Jane, dau. of the late William Newport, Esq., brother of the Right Hon. Sir John Newport, Bart., and has issue,
1 John-Simon, m. Eliza, dau. of Capt. Samuel Maguire, R.N. of Clonea Castle, co. Waterford.
2 William, in holy orders, m. Fanny, dau. of Latimer Whittle, Esq. of Muckamore Abbey, co. Antrim.
3 Joseph, late lieut. Bengal artillery.
4 George-Nuttall, E.I.C. service.
5 Reginald.
1 Sarah-Jane, m. to John Waring, Esq. of Springfield, co. Kilkenny.
2 Priscilla, m. to Charles Newport, Esq. of Waterford.

† By this James Fortrey, who was page of the Back Stairs to King James, many of the family pictures now at Rolleston Hall were painted; and several curiosities, still in the family, collected. He m. the celebrated Lady Bellasyse, widow of the son of John, Lord Bellasyse.

Elizabeth, m. in 1819, to John Greenwell, Esq. of Broomshields, co. Durham.

Mr. Greenwell d. 25 Feb. 1805, and was s. by his son,

WILLIAM-THOMAS GREENWELL, Esq. of Greenwell Ford, J.P. and D.L., b. 13 Feb. 1777, who m. 25 June, 1818, Dorothy, dau. of Francis Smales, Esq., by Anne, his wife, dau. and heir of Richard Radcliffe, Esq. of Cockermouth; and d. 1854, leaving issue,

WILLIAM, now of Greenwell Ford.
Francis, b. 24 May, 1823; m. Elizabeth, dau. of John Trotter, Esq., M.D., and has issue.
Alan, M.A., in holy orders, b. 19 Sept. 1824.
Henry-Nicholas, late of the 70th regt., b. 6 Dec. 1826.
Dorothy.

Arms—Or, two bars, az., between three ducal coronets, gu.
Crest—A stork, ppr., beaked and legged, gu., wreathed round the neck with a chaplet of laurel, vert.
Seat—Greenwell Ford, co. Durham.

GREENWELL OF BROOMSHIELDS.

GREENWELL, JOHN, Esq. of Broomshields, co. Durham, J.P., b. 8 Sept. 1784; m. 9 Sept. 1819, Elizabeth, dau. of Alan Greenwell, Esq. of Greenwell Ford, in the same county, and has,

THOMAS, b. 8 Feb 1821. m. 29 June, 1850.

Mr. Greenwell is in the commission of the peace for co. Durham.

Lineage.—Broomshields has been, at least for nearly four centuries, in the possession of this branch of the Greenwells. So far back as the reign of Henry VII. (22 Oct., 1488), the name of PETER GREENWELL occurs, and the family can from that period be traced in old deeds and documents. The grandfather of the present representative,

THOMAS GREENWELL, Esq. of Broomshields, only surviving son of Peter Greenwell, Esq. of Broomshields, by Rebecca Sampson, his wife, m. Mary Rippon, of Low Mills, Lanchester, co. Durham, and left at his decease, 13 Feb. 1770, a son and successor,

THOMAS GREENWELL, of Broomshields, who m. 22 March, 1774, Eleanor, dau. of John Maddison, Esq. of Hole House, co. Durham, and sister and heiress of John Maddison, Esq., secretary to Sir Joseph Yorke, and of George Maddison, Esq., under secretary of state for foreign affairs in 1782, and secretary of legation in Paris under the duke of Manchester in 1783. The estate of Hole House was purchased from the Hoppers in 1595, by Alexander Maddison, Esq. By Eleanor, his wife, Mr. Greenwell had (with three daus., Eleanor, Mary, and Elizabeth) two sons, Thomas, b. 7 Feb. 1775, who d. unm. 4 Oct. 1796, and JOHN, now of Broomshields. Mr. Greenwell d. 18 Dec. 1817; his widow, Eleanor, 11 Oct. 1820.

Arms—Or, two bars, az., between three ducal coronets, gu.
Crest—A crane's head, couped, arg., beaked, gu., with an olive-branch round the neck, vert.
Seat—Broomshields, Lanchester, co. Durham.

GREENWOOD OF KEIGHLEY AND SWARCLIFFE HALL.

GREENWOOD, FREDERICK, Esq. of Keighley and Swarcliffe Hall, both in Yorkshire, J.P. b. 15 Jan. 1797; m. 31 May, 1828, Sarah, only dau. of the late Samuel Staniforth, Esq. of Liverpool and Darnall, and has issue,

I. JOHN, J.P., and D.L., capt. Yorkshire Hussar regt. yeomanry cavalry, b. 20 Feb. 1829, m. 19 Feb. 1852, Louisa-Elizabeth, eldest dau. of Nathaniel Clarke Barnardiston, Esq. of the Ryes, Suffolk, and has issue,

1 FREDERICK-BARNARDISTON, b. 3 Jan. 1854.
1 Clara-Louisa.

I. Mary-Littledale, m. 4 Aug. 1858, to Major Rohde Hawkins, Esq. of the Privy Council Office, London, youngest son of Edward Hawkins, Esq. of the British Museum.

Lineage.—Greenwood is a very old Yorkshire name, and the family has been settled in Yorkshire from remote times; the pedigree is given at some length in *Thoresby's Leeds*. Early in the last century, JAMES GREENWOOD settled at Braithwayt, near Keighley. The late

JOHN GREENWOOD, Esq., of Keighley and Swarcliffe Hall, co. York, b. 8 Sept. 1763, only son of John Greenwood, of Keighley, by Anne, his wife, dau. of J. Barwick, Esq., m. in 1794, Sarah, eldest dau. of William Sugden, Esq. of Eastwood House, Keighley, and had issue,

FREDERICK, J.P., now of Keighley.
Edwin, J. P., of Swarcliffe, d. 28 Sep. 1852.
Ann, m. the Rev. Theodore Dury, rector of Westmill, co. Herts, and d. 1849, leaving issue.
Matilda, m. to Rawdon Briggs, Esq. of Birstwith Hall, near Harrogate, and since deceased.
Sarah-Hannah, m. to John-Benson Sedgwick, Esq. of Stone Gap, co. York, and has issue.

Arms—per chev., m., and arg., a chev., erm., between three saltiers couped, counterchanged.
Crest—A tiger, sejant, or.
Seats—Knowle, Keighley, and Swarcliffe Hall, near Harrogate: the present Frederick Greenwood, Esq., resides at Norton Conyers, near Ripon.

GREENFIELD OF BRYNDERWEN.

GREENFIELD, JAMES, Esq. of Brynderwen, co. Monmouth, b. 28 Jan. 1810; m. 22 June, 1839, Margaret, 2nd dau. of Sir Joseph Bailey, Bart., of Glanusk Park, co. Brecon, M.P. for co. Brecon, by his 1st wife, Maria, 4th dau. and co-heir of Joseph Latham, Esq., and has issue,

I. JAMES-HENRY-LATHAM, b. 5 June, 1841.
II. Charles-Bailey, b. 18 Jan. 1844.
III. Walter-Ormerod, b. 11 June, 1845.
IV. Joseph-Bailey, b. 26th July, 1847.
V. William-Crawshay, b. 8 Jan. 1851.
I. Mary-Anne-Frances-Margaret.
II. Helen-Wyatt. III. Maria-Charlotte.
IV. Annette-Crawshay.

Mr. Greenfield is a magistrate and deputy-lieut. for Monmouthshire, and served as high sheriff for the county of Anglesey, in 1839.

Lineage.—JOHN GREENFIELD, Esq. of Pulborough, co. Sussex, who d. 21 April, 1742, was father, by Mary Smart, his wife, of

JOHN GREENFIELD, Esq. of Byworth, co. Sussex, b. 1741, who m. 28 April, 1769, Hannah, eldest dau. of his cousin, Edmund Greenfield, Esq. of Haslemere, co. Surrey, and d. 14 Oct. 1802, having had issue, five sons and two daus. Of the former,

JAMES GREENFIELD, Esq. of Brynderwen, co. Caernarvon, J.P. for that shire, and deputy-lieut. for Anglesey, b. 11 March, 1775,, m. 17 April, 1804, Charlotte, second dau. of Benjamin Wyatt, Esq. of Lime Grove, co. Caernarvon, and by her, who d. in 1815, had issue,

JAMES, of Brynderwen, co. Monmouth.
Benjamin-Wyatt, M.A. of Corpus Christi Coll., Camb., barrister-at-law, b. 28 June, 1811, m. 7 Jan. 1836, Octavia-Vere-Booth, youngest dau. of George-Booth Tyndale, Esq. of Hayling, and has issue, 1 John-Tyndale, b. 18 Jan. 1840; 1 Margaret-Caroline-Tyndale; 2 Oriane-Tyndale; 3 Vere-Tyndale; 4 Dorothy-Tyndale.
Charlotte-Anne, d. unm. 29 Dec, 1824.
Mary-Wyatt, m. 31 Aug. 1828, to Charles Cooch, Esq., second son of the late Robert Cooch, Esq. of Huntingdon, and has issue.

Mr. Greenfield d. 19 Jan. 1825.

Arms—Per saltier, gu. and vert, three clarions, or.
Crest—A griphon, passant, with wings elevated, or, resting its dexter claw on a clarion, gu.
Motto—Injussi virescunt.
Seat—Brynderwen, Usk, Monmouth.

GREER OF THE GRANGE MACGREGOR.

GREER, JOSEPH, Esq. of The Grange, Moy, co. Tyrone, Major, commanding royal Tyrone marine artillery, J.P. and D.L., b. 17 April, 1795; m. 5 June, 1816, Mary, dau. of Thomas Harpur, Esq. of Moy, by Sarah his wife, dau. of Edward Clements, Esq. of Brackaville, by his wife, Mary, dau. of James Richardson, Esq. of Bloomhill, all in co. Tyrone, and has issue,

I. HENRY-HARPUR, b. 24 Feb. 1821, major 68th light infantry, m. 14 Feb. 1850, Agnes Isabella, dau. of the Ven.

Edmund D. Knox, archdeacon of Killaloe, son of the Hon. and Right Rev. Edmund Knox, bishop of Limerick, and grandson of Thomas, Viscount Northland.

II. Thomas, R.N., *b.* 5 April, 1828.

I. Emily, *m.* 15 June, 1835, James Lowry, Esq. of Rockdale, and *d.* 22 April, 1851.

II. Jane, *m.* 6 Oct. 1842, Armar Lowry, Esq. of the 80th regt.

III. Maria. IV. Anna.

Lineage.—The family Greer claims descent from the Grierson branch of the clan MacGregor.

JAMES GREER, from whom the Irish branch springs, removed, it is very probable, from the parent stock, at Lag, co. Dumfries, about the commencement of the 17th century, and settled in the neighbouring English county of Cumberland, where we find him in 1633; but the exact date when this took place is not stated, but the family records mention that James Greer, and Mary his wife, of the Rock, Cumberland, had, inter alios, a son, HENRY, and a dau., Anne, who *m.* Thomas Turner, of Turnerstead, co. Cumberland, and with her husband removing to Ireland, was ancestor of the Turners of Turner's Hill, near Newry, co. Armagh. The son,

HENRY GREER, Esq., *m.* in 1652, Mary, sister of the above-named Thomas Turner, and removed with her, in 1653, to Ireland, where they finally settled at Lurgan, co. Armagh, and dying there, left two sons, Robert, the younger, and his heir,

JAMES GREER, Esq., *b.* in 1653, *m.* 21 Aug. 1678, Eleanor, dau. and co-heir of John Rea, Esq. of Liscourran, near Lurgan, on which property he settled, and left issue, HENRY, his heir; John, *b.* in 1688, ancestor of the GREERS of Rhone Hill, and Tullylagan (*which see*); Thomas, *b.* in 1690; James, *b.* in 1693, all three *m.* and left issue; and Mary, wife of William Douglass, Esq. The eldest son and heir,

HENRY GREER, Esq., *b.* in 1681, *m.* in 1704, Sarah, dau. of Henderson, Esq. of Dunclady, co. Londonderry, and *d.* in July, 1756, leaving (with a dau., Mary) a son and heir,

HENRY GREER, Esq., *b.* in 1716, *m.* 3 June, 1741, Elizabeth, dau. of John Turner, Esq. (grandson of Thomas Turner and Ann Greer, his wife), and *d.* in Dec. 1776, leaving (with three daus., Ann, Henrietta, and Elizabeth, all of whom *m.* and left issue) a son and heir,

JOHN GREER, Esq., *b.* in 1742, who *m.* 17 Dec. 1762, Catherine, dau. of John Cuppage, Esq. of Garden Hill, co. Antrim, and had issue,

I. HENRY, *b.* 20 Nov. 1763, *m.* in 1782, Jane, dau. and only child of John Lynam, Esq. of the city of Dublin, and pre-deceased his father, 2 Aug. 1814, having had, with five other children, who *d.* young, two sons and four daus., viz.,
   1 JOSEPH, successor to his grandfather, and present representative.
   2 Richard, *b.* 10 June, 1796, in holy orders, *d. unm.* 7 June, 1825.
   1 Jane. 2 Ann.
   3 Sophia. 4 Sarah.

II. John, *d.* young.

III. John-Turner, *b.* 18 May, 1766, *d.* in 1786.

IV. Thomas, *b.* 15 Nov. 1767, J.P. and deputy-governor, *m.* but *d. s. p.* 7 April, 1837.

V. James, *b.* 31 Jan. 1775, J.P. and deputy governor *d. s. p.* 7 Aug. 1842.

VI. John-Miers, *b.* 4 April, 1778, com. R.N.

VII. George, *b.* 17 May, 1779, J.P. for Armagh.

VIII. Alexander, *b.* 20 June, 1780, half-pay of the army.

I. Elizabeth, *m.* to John Malcomson, Esq. of Clonmel, and *d. s. p.*

II. Mary, *d.* 19 Feb. 1841. III. Jane.

IV. Catherine, *m.* to John Lindsay, Esq., of Dublin.

V. Sarah-Mildred, *m.* 1st, to Major Overand, E.I.Co.'s Ser-service, and 2ndly, to the Rev. John O. Oldfield, now Archdeacon of Elphin. She *d. s. p.* 18 Jan. 1823.

Mr. John Greer, who was a justice of the peace, and deputy governor of the counties of Armagh and Tyrone for upwards of fifty years, *d.* 6 Oct. 1818, and was *s.* by his elder grandson, the present JOSEPH GREER, Esq.

Seat—Grange M'Gregor, Moy, Co. Tyrone.

GREER OF TULLYLAGAN.

GREER, THOMAS, Esq. of Tullylagan, co. Tyrone, J.P., *b.* 21 April, 1791; *m.* 27 April, 1826, Williammina, dau. of Arthur Ussher, Esq. of Camphire, co. Waterford, a direct descendant of Archbishop Ussher, and has issue,

I. FREDERICK, *b.* 17 Feb. 1829.

II. Ussher, *b.* 27 Feb. 1831, *d.* when just of age.

I. Martha-Ussher. II. Elizabeth-Jackson.

III. Priscilla-Sophia.

Lineage.—The GREERS of Tyrone claim descent (as already stated under GREER of Grange) through the Griers, or Griersons, of Lag, co. Dumfries, from the clan MacGregor in Scotland, and this claim is sustained by the strongest traditional and corroborative evidence. HENRY GREER, the first settler in Ireland, was son of James Greer, a scion of the Lag family, who left Scotland and fixed his abode in the border county of Cumberland. Henry *m.* Mary Turner, and was father inter alios of a son and heir,

JAMES GREER, Esq., *b.* in England April, 1653, who *m.* 21 Aug 1678, Eleanor, dau. and co-heir of John Rea, Esq., and had, inter alios, HENRY GREER, eldest son, ancestor of the GREERS of Grange MacGregor; and JOHN GREER, the 2nd son, who resided at Warrenstown and Tullyakan, near Lurgan; by Mary Hunks, his wife, he had several children, of whom the 2nd son,

THOMAS GREER, of Rhone Hill, became on the extinction of the male line of his elder brother, John, the head of 2nd house of the Irish Greers. He was *b.* 14 Nov. 1724, and *m.* Sarah, dau. of Thomas Greer, of Redford, his 2nd cousin, and *d.* at Rhone Hill, 5 April, 1803, leaving issue,

THOMAS, his heir.
Robert, *b.* 16 Nov. 1766, *d.* in America in 1866, *unm.*
Eleanor, *m.* to Thos. Boardman, son of Joseph Boardman, of Joneston, near Edendery.
Mary, *m.* to Richard Jacob, son of Joseph Jacob, of Waterford.
Jane, *m.* to James Clibborn, son of Burday Clibborn of Moate.
Sarah, *m.* to John Hancock, son of John Hancock, of Lisburn.
Ann, *m.* 1807, to James Nicholson.

The eldest son,

THOMAS GREER, also of Rhone Hill, *b.* 5 Sept 1761, *m.* 14 Aug. 1787, Elizabeth, dau. of William Jackson, Esq., and *d.* 26 Feb. 1840, leaving issue,

THOMAS, now of Tullylagan, co. Tyrone, J. P.
William-Jackson, *b.* 8th June, 1797, *m.* Margaret, another dau. of Arthur Ussher, Esq. and *d.* 1841, leaving issue.
John-Robert, *b.* 11th Sep., 1800, *m.* Sarah D. Strangman, and has issue.
Alfred, of Dripsey House, co. Cork, *b.* 2nd Sep., 1805, *m.* 1st, Helena Carroll, and 2ndly, Peggy, dau. of Major Colthurst of Dripsey Castle, co. Cork, and has issue by both.
Sarah, *m.* to Hugh White, of Dublin.
Mary-Jackson, *m.* to T. W. Manly.
Elizabeth, *m.* to George Thomas, of Bristol.
Caroline, *m.* to William Ridgway.
Louisa-Jane, *m.* to Joseph Rake, of Bristol.

Arms (Enrolled in Ulster's Office)—Az. a lion rampant, or, armed and langued gu., between three antique crowns of the second; on a canton arg. an oak tree eradicated, surmounted by a sword, in bend sinister, ensigned on the point with a royal crown, all ppr.

Crest—An eagle displayed ppr., charged on the breast with a quadrangular lock arg.

Motto—Memor esto.

Seat—Tullylagan, co. Tyrone.

GREG OF BALLYMENOCH.

GREG, THOMAS, Esq. of Ballymenoch, co. Down, J.P. and high-sheriff 1840, *b.* 29 Dec. 1805; *m.* 16 May, 1838, Mary, 2nd dau. of Narcissus Batt, Esq. of Purdysburn, co. Down, and Ozier Hill, co. Wexford, and has had issue,

I. HENRY-CUNNINGHAM, *b.* April, 1840, *d.* Sept. 1844.

I. Alice-Margaret.

Mr. Greg, of Ballymenoch, and his two sisters (Eliza, *m.* to the Rev. James-Stewart Blacker, M.A., rector of Keady, co. Armagh, and Alicia, *m.* to Robert Thomson, Esq), are the children of the late CUNNINGHAM GREG, Esq. of Ballymenoch, (who *d.* April, 1830), by Ellen his wife, dau. of Richard Gason, Esq.

Seat—Ballymenoch, Holywood, co. Down.

GREG OF NORCLIFFE HALL.

GREG, ROBERT-HYDE, Esq. of Norcliffe Hall, co. Chester, and Coles Park, co. Hertford, J.P., M.P. for Manchester, from 1839 to 1841, *b.* 24 Sept. 1795;

m. 14 June, 1824, Mary, eldest dau. of Robert Philips, of the Park, co. Lancaster, and Snitterfield, co. Warwick, and has issue,

I. ROBERT-PHILIPS, b. 23 March, 1826.
II. Edward-Hyde, b. 9 Nov. 1827, m. 12 March, 1856, Margaret, only dau. of the late Wm. Broadbent, Esq. of Latchford, near Warrington.
III. Henry-Russell, b. 4 July, 1832.
IV. Arthur, b. 7 July, 1835.
I. Caroline.
II. Hannah-Sophia, m. 31 March, 1852, to Benson, son of Richard Rathbone, Esq. of Liverpool.

Lineage.—The present family has its origin and derives its name from the clan MacGregor of Scotland, which claims descent from King Kenneth Mc.Alpine II., 1st King of Scotland, whose son received the name of Gregor from, his Godfather, Pope Gregory, IV. In 1603, an edict was issued by JAMES VI., against the clan Gregor, and in 1633, another by CHARLES I., denouncing the whole clan and forbidding any one from carrying or being baptized by that name. In consequence of this a complete dispersion took place, and different members of the clan adopted the names of Campbell, Gregory, Greig, &c. One of these, Andrew Greig, of Coupar, appears from a bond still in possession of the family, dated 1646, and bearing the signatures of several noted men of the time, to have lent the sum of 300 marks in aid and on account of the Parliamentary armies. His son, James Greig, of Ochiltree, had a son, John Greig, b. 1698, who, compromised in the rebellion of 1715, went over to Ireland, established himself under the name of JOHN GREG as a merchant at Belfast, and there married a Miss Cunningham. His son Thomas, b. 1718, had granted to him a right of all the minerals in the counties of Down Antrim and Derry, and refused the honour of a baronetcy. He m. 1742, Elizabeth, dau. of Samuel Hyde, of Manchester, and had issue, 12 children, most of whom married and settled in Ireland. The 6th and 9th, Thomas and Samuel, came over to England. The former, of Coles Park, Hertfordshire, married Margaret, dau. of Robert Hibbert, of Birtles Hall, Cheshire, and died without children. Samuel settled in Manchester, and m. 1790, Hannah, dau. and co-heiress of Adam Lightbody, of Liverpool, and great-great-granddau. of Philip Henry, the nonconformist, whose father John Henry, an officer in the household of CHARLES I., attended that monarch on the scaffold. They had issue,

I. Thomas, d. s. p. in 1839.
II. ROBERT-HYDE, now of Norcliffe Hall.
III. John, m. Elizabeth Kennedy.
IV. Samuel, m. Mary Needham.
V. William-Rathbone, m. Lucy Henry.
I. Elizabeth, m. to William Rathbone, Esq. of Liverpool.
II. Marianne. III. Agnes. IV. Sarah.
V. Hannah, m. to Thomas Reynolds, of Bristol.
VI. Ellen, m. to Andrew Melly, Esq. of Liverpool.

Arms—Arg., a Scotch fir, out of a mount, vert, in base, surmounted by a sword, in bend, ppr., on a dexter canton, az., a royal antique crown, ppr.; quartering TILSTON and LIGHTBODY.
Crest—An arm, embowed in armour, grasping a scimitar, az., pommel and hilt, or.
Motto—Ein doe and spair not; and also S'Rioghal mo Dhream.
Seats—Norcliffe Hall, co. Chester, and Coles Park, co. Herts.

GREGOR, OF TREWARTHENICK.

GREGOR, GORDON-WILLIAM-FRANCIS, Esq. of Trewarthenick, co. Cornwall, J.P. and D.L., high-sheriff 1829, b. 2 Oct. 1789; m. 20 June, 1814, Loveday-Sarah, only dau. of Francis Glanville, Esq. of Catchfrench, in the same shire, by Loveday-Sarah his wife, dau. and co-heiress of William Masterman, Esq. of Restormel, and has issue,

I. FRANCIS-GLANVILLE, b. 3 Sept. 1816.
I. Jane-Frances, m. 25 Sept. 1849, to the Rev. Paul William Molesworth.
II. Georgiana-Mary.
III. Elizabeth-Glanville.

This gentleman, whose patronymic is BOOKER, assumed by letters patent, in 1826, the surname and arms of GREGOR.

Lineage.—About the middle of the 17th century, we find the Gregors resident at Truro, of which town William Gregor was mayor in 1677, and at that period the family seems first to have settled at Trewarthenick, where FRANCIS GREGOR, Esq., resided in 1720.

CHARLOTTE-ANNE GREGOR, of Trewarthenick (only dau. and heir of the Rev. William Gregor, of Trewarthenick, vicar of Creed, and niece of Francis Gregor, Esq. of Trewarthenick, M.P. for Cornwall), the last of the Gregor family, d. unm. in 1825, and bequeathed her estates to LOVEDAY-SARAH, dau. of Francis Glanville, Esq. of Catchfrench, and niece of Catherine Masterman, who m. the testator's uncle, Francis Gregor, Esq., M.P. This lady (Loveday-Sarah Glanville) m. as already stated, GORDON-WILLIAM-FRANCIS BOOKER, Esq. (son, by the Lady Catherine Gordon, his wife, youngest dau. of Cosmo, 3rd Duke of Gordon, of Thomas Booker, Esq., Capt. 53rd regt., descended from a younger branch of the ancient family of Booker, of Notts, which settled in Ireland, *temp.* CHARLES II.)

Arms—Erm., a chev., gu., between three partridges, ppr., a chief of the second, thereon two escutcheons, or, each charged with an eagle, displayed, vert.
Crest—A Saracen's head, affrontée, surmounting a javelin, in bend, all ppr.
Seat—Trewarthenick, near Tregony.

GRENE OF CAPPAMURRA.

GRENE, JOHN, Esq. of Cappamurra, co. Tipperary, J.P. b. 21 Feb. 1809, m. 6 Feb. 1850, Anna-Maria, dau. of the late James Delany, Esq. of Mullingar, by Catherine, Mahon, his wife, and has issue,

I. JOHN, b. 29 Nov. 1851, and d. 18 Dec. following.
I. Catherine, b. 16 Dec. 1850.
II. Hannah, b. 27 Oct. 1852.
III. Louisa, b. 30 March, 1854.

Lineage.—GEORGE GRENE, the 2nd son of Robert Grene, of Bobbing, in the county of Kent, is mentioned in a pedigree of the "Norton" and "Grene" families, signed by "William Camden, Clarenceux," as having gone to Ireland in the reign of JAMES I, about 1609. He settled in Corstown, co. Kilkenny; it is not known whom he married, but he had one son,

PATRICK GRENE, b. in the co. Kilkenny, who m. in England, in 1641, Susan Sall, the only dau. and heiress of Sall, of Sallwood, or Sallud Hall, by whom he had two daus., Mary and Frances, and one son,

GEORGE GRENE, who m. Austace, 2nd dau. of John Purcell, of Lismarnoe, Ballyragget, co. Kilkenny, by whom he had five sons, namely, JOHN, PATRICK, George, Norton, and Thomas; and four daus., Susan, Mary, Catherine, and Jane. The 2nd son,

PATRICK GRENE, m. 1st, Ellis, dau. of Sylvester Russell, of Ballylankon, by whom he had two sons,

SYLVESTER, m. Honora Sheehy, and had, with a dau., Mary, one son, GEORGE, of Powerstown, co. Tipperary, who m. Eliza Browne, and had issue, 1 William; 2 John, m. his cousin, Hannah Grene, and has two daus., Elizabeth and Hannah; 3 George, m. Caroline Robertson, and has, William, Reginald, Sylvester, Henry, Edwin, Dorothea, and Charlotte; 1 Margaret; 2 Eliza; 3 Catherine; 4 Mary.
Michael.

Patrick Grene m. 2ndly, Susan Colpoys, and by her had,

John, m. Rose Coppinger, of Mallow, co. Cork, and had two sons, Patrick, m. Maria Arthur, of Limerick, and had issue, John, Francis, Ellen, and Rose.
JAMES, of whose descendants we treat.

JAMES GRENE, Esq., J.P., (youngest son of Patrick Grene, Esq.) m. in 1767, Ellen Ross, and by her (who d. in 1797) left at his decease, 10 April, 1807, a son,

JOHN GRENE, Esq., who m. Sept. 1797, Hannah Biddalph, and by her (who d. 30 Aug. 1839) had issue,

JOHN, now of Cappamurra.
James, b. Sept. 1798, d. 1800.
Nicholas-Biddalph, of Grene Park, co. Tipperary, J.P., b. 20 Oct. 1800; m. 30 May, 1838, Catherine, dau. of Clement Sadleir, of Shronehill, co. Tipperary, and has issue, Clement, James, John, Nicholas, Hannah, Lucinda, and Emma.
Hannah, m. 12 June, 1821, John, 2nd son of George Grene, Esq. of Powerstown, co. Tipperary (her cousin).
Ellen, d. 4 April, 1818. Eliza. Susan.
Maria, m. 30 Nov. 1837, to James Barry, co. Limerick.
Margaret, b. May, 1815; m. 9 Feb. 1847, to Jeremiah Coghlan, of the co. Cork.

Mr. Grene d. 18 Jan. 1837.

Arms—Gu., a cross, potent and border, erm.
Crest—A wolf's head, erased.
Seat—Cappamurra, co. Tipperary.

GREGORSON OF ARDTORNISH.

GREGORSON, JOHN, Esq. of Ardtornish, co. Argyll, D.L., *b.* 5 April, 1775; *m.* 22 Sept. 1820, Mary, dau. of Murdock Maclaine, Esq. of Lochbuy, by Jane, his wife, dau. of John Campbell, Esq. of Airds, and had issue,

I. ANGUS, *b.* 29 Dec. 1835.
I. Elizabeth-Campbell.
II. Margaret-Maxwell. III. Jane.

Lineage.—JOHN MACGREGOR, Esq. of Correctlet, *m.* a dau. of Graham, of Drunhim, and (with a dau., Catherine, *m.* to Eneas Macdonald) had a son and heir,

JAMES MACGREGOR, Esq. of Correctlet, who *m.* Margery, dau. of Alexander Campbell, Esq. of Airds, by his wife, the dau. of Lord Glenurchy, and had issue, Alexander, capt. in 78th regt.; ANGUS of whom presently; Dugald; and others, who *d.* young. The 2nd son,

ANGUS GREGORSON, Esq. of Ardtornish, *m.* in 1773, Elizabeth, dau. of Colin Campbell, Esq. of Achnaba, and had issue,

JOHN, his heir.
Donald, lieut.-col. 91st regt., *m.* Phœbe, dau. of Murdoch Maclaine, Esq. of Lochbuy, and has issue, Angus; Murdoch-John, 62nd regt.; John-Donald; and Elizabeth-Marjory.
Dugald, lieut. 42nd regt., killed at Burgos.
Alexander, M.D. medical staff, *d.* in Portugal.
Peter, *d.* at Barnacary, in 1834.
Eneas, *d.* a commissary in Portugal, in his 21st year.
Marjory, *m.* to Allan Maclaine, Esq. of Scallasdale.
Mary-Jane, *m.* to Donald Campbell, Esq. of Killandine.
Elizabeth, *m.* to Colin Macnab, Esq. of Dagnish.

Arms and *Crest*—Those of MACGREGOR.
Motto—Ein dæe an spair nae.

GREGORY OF STYVICHALL.

GREGORY, ARTHUR-FRANCIS, Esq. of Styvichall, co. Warwick, J. P. & D.L.; *m.* 25 Feb. 1834, the Hon. Caroline Hood, sister of Samuel, present Viscount Hood, and has issue,

I. ARTHUR, *b.* 11 Dec. 1834.
II. Francis-Hood, *b.* 29 Oct. 1836.

Mr. Gregory is the representative of the ancient Leicestershire family of Gregory of Ashfordsby, which has been settled for a considerable time at Styvichall, in Warwickshire.

Arms—Or, two bars: in chief, a lion, passant, of the last.
Crest—A demi-boar, rampant, sa., collared, or.
Seat—Styvichall, Coventry.

GREGORY OF COOLE PARK.

GREGORY, WILLIAM-HENRY, Esq. of Coole Park, co. Galway, J.P. and D.L., high-sheriff 1849, M.P. for the city of Dublin from 1842 to 1847; *b.* in 1817.

Lineage.—The ancestor of this family was a cadet of the Gregory family, of Stivic Hall, near Coventry, and went over to Ireland with Oliver Cromwell. The late

RIGHT. HON. WILLIAM GREGORY, *m.* Lady Anne Trench, sister of the late, Earl of Clancarty, and left one son,

ROBERT GREGORY, Esq. of Coole Park, who *m.* 1815, Elizabeth O'Hara, and by her left at his decease, in 1846, an only son, the present WILLIAM-HENRY GREGORY, Esq. of Coole Park.

Seat—Coole Park, near Gort.

GREGSON OF MURTON AND BURDON.

GREGSON, JOHN, Esq of Murton and Burdon, co. Durham, M.A., barrister-at-law, *b.* 12 Dec. 1805; *m.* 1st, 18 June, 1833, Isabella, dau. of the Rev. Francis Reed, rector of Hazelbury Briant, co. Dorset, brother of John Reed, Esq. of Chipchase Castle, Northumberland, and by her (who *d.* 7 July, 1842,) has issue,

I. JOHN, *b.* 20 April, 1835.
II. Lancelot-Allgood, *b.* 26 July, 1840.
I. Isabella.

Mr. Gregson *m.* 2ndly, 13 Feb. 1844, Caroline, youngest dau. of the Rev. James Dalton, rector of Croft, and by her (who *d.* 8 Feb. 1851) has issue,

I. James-Dalton, *b.* 3 Sept. 1845.
II. Charles, *b.* 5 Aug. 1848.
I. Caroline-Elizabeth-Esther.

Mr. Gregson, *m.* 3rdly, 20 Oct. 1853, Mary-Jane-Forbes, only surviving dau. of Robert Grant, Esq. of Monymusk, Aberdeen, and granddau. of Sir Archibald Grant, Bart., and has a son,

I. Francis-Robert, *b.* 7 Sept, 1854.

Lineage.—JOHN GREGSON, living in 1537, purchased the estate of Murton, co. Durham, of John-Lord Lumley, in 1566. He *d.* 20 Oct. 1607, leaving three sons.

Richard, in holy orders, aged 50 at his father's death, *m.* and had a son, JOHN, of whom hereafter, as successor to his uncle.
THOMAS, of whom presently.
Anthony, father of John Gregson, and great-grandfather of John Gregson, who purchased the estate of Lowlinn, in North Durham, and *d.* in 1779; he was grandfather of ANTHONY GREGSON, Esq. of Lowlinn, high-sheriff of Northumberland in 1825, who dying *unm.* 23 Nov. 1838, devised his estates to his cousin, Henry Knight, Esq., eldest son of the Rev. Henry Knight, rector of Ford, in Northumberland.

The 2nd son,

THOMAS GREGSON, was of Murton, having been granted that estate by his father, in 1598. By his will, dated 23 July, 1629, he devised all his estates to his nephew (son of his elder brother, Richard),

JOHN GREGSON, Esq. of Murton, who *d.* in 1674, and was *s.* by his son,

THOMAS GREGSON, Esq. of Murton, who *m.* 5 Feb. 1653, Elizabeth Smith, and by her, who *d.* in 1688, left at his decease, in 1713, (with a dau., Anne, *m.* to Mr. Todd, of Dalton; and two younger sons, George, bapt. 25 Oct. 1657; and William, bapt. 6 Feb. 1659,) an elder son and heir,

JOHN GREGSON, Esq. of Murton, bapt. 5 Feb. 1654, who *m.* 13 May, 1680, Elizabeth Johnson, of Dalden, *d.* in 1714, having previously joined with his father, in 1712, in conveying the estate of Murton to his only son and heir,

JOHN GREGSON, Esq. of Murton, and of Burdon, which latter estate he acquired under the will of his maternal uncle, George Johnson, Esq. of Burdon. He *m.* 22 May, 1712, Mary, dau. of John Johnson, Esq. of East Murton, and by her, who *d.* in Feb. 1742, had an only son and heir,

JOHN GREGSON, Esq. of Murton and Burdon, baptized 10 April, 1713, who *m.* 1st, Elizabeth, dau. and co-heir of Anthony Smith, Esq. of Ryehope, and by her had an only dau., Betty, who *d.* young. He *m.* 2ndly, 27 April, 1738, Eleanor, dau. of Giles Rain, Esq., mayor of Durham in 1720 and 1727, and by her, who *d.* in June, 1743, had two sons, John, *b.* 8 July, 1740, *d.* *unm.* in Sept. 1768; and RAIN, of whom hereafter, as heir to his father; and a dau., Mary, *m.* to Thomas Huntley, of Burdon. Mr. Gregson *m.* 3rdly, Mary, dau. of Thomas Huntley, of Burdon, and by her, who *d.* in 1768, had three sons, Thomas, *b.* 14 Dec. 1747; George, *b.* 25 May, 1749; and Selby. He *m.* 4thly, Jane, dau. of Anthony Story, Esq. of Bishopwearmouth, and dying without further issue in 1786, aged 74, was *s.* by his eldest surviving son,

RAIN GREGSON, Esq. of Murton and Burdon, *b.* 8 Aug. 1742; *m.* 14 March, 1773, Anne, dau. and heiress of George Thompson, Esq. of Seaton, and *d.* in Nov. 1807, aged 65, leaving (with a younger son, George-Rain, *b.* 4 March, 1785, and *d.* in 1794) an elder son and successor,

JOHN GREGSON, Esq. of Murton, Burdon, and Durham, *b.* 4 Jan. 1774. He *m.* 15 Sept. 1800, Elizabeth, only dau. and heiress of Lancelot Allgood, Esq. (*see* ALLGOOD *of Nunwick*), and had issue,

JOHN, present representative.
Allgood, *b.* in 1811, *d.* young.
George, *b.* 15 Dec. 1814.
Anne.
Frances, *m.* 15 Sept. 1830, to W.-E. Wooler, Esq. of Durham, and *d.* in April. 1837.
Elizabeth, *m.* 14 July, 1841, to Robert-Henry Allan, Esq. of Durham, F.S.A., 2nd son of Robert Allan, Esq. of Newbottle, and great-grandson of James Allan, Esq. of Blackwell Grange.
Eleanor, *d.* young. Mary-Matilda.

Jane-Eleanor, *d.* an infant.
Charlotte-Isabella, *m.* 21 Nov. 1844, Rev. Richard Moorsom, M.A., vicar of Seaham, co. Durham (who *d.* 5 April, 1846).

Mr. Gregson *d.* 2 May, 1840, aged 66.

Arms—Arg., a saltier, gu., a canton, chequy, or and az.
Crest—An arm, couped at the elbow, vested, bendy, wavy, of six, and environed round the wrist with ribbon, arg. and gu., holding in the hand, ppr., a battle axe, or, handle, sa.
Seat—Burdon, near Bishop Wearmouth.

GREVILLE OF NORTH MYMS PLACE.

GREVILLE, FULKE-SOUTHWELL, Esq. of North Myms Place, co. Hertford, Clonyn, and Clonteem, co. Westmeath, M.P. for co. Longford, colonel of the Westmeath light infantry regt. of militia, and high-sheriff of Hertfordshire, in 1850, *b.* 17 Feb. 1821; *m.* 28 April, 1840, Lady Rose-Emili-Mary-Anne Nugent, only dau. of the Marquess of Westmeath, and has issue,

I. ALGERNON-WILLIAM FULKE.
II. George-Frederick-Nugent.
III. Robert-Southwell.
IV. Reginald-James-Macartney.
V. Patrick-Emilius-John.
I. Mildred-Charlotte.

Lineage.—This is a branch of the noble family of Greville, represented by the Earl of Brooke and Warwick.

CAPTAIN WILLIAM FULKE GREVILLE, R.N., son and heir of Fulke Greville, Esq. of Wilbury, Wilts, by Frances, his wife dau. of James Macartney, Esq., and grandson (by Mary, his wife, dau. of Lord Arthur Somerset) of the Hon. Algernon Greville, 2nd son of Fulke, 5th Lord Brooke, *m.* Meliora, dau. of the Rev. Mr. Southwell, and *d.* 1837, leaving, with two daus., Harriet, *m.* to James Morier, Esq., and Caroline, Viscountess Combermere, two sons, Richard Greville, who *d. s. p.*, and

ALGERNON GREVILLE, Esq., *b.* 1791, who *m.* 1818, Caroline, 2nd dau. of the late Sir Bellingham Graham, Bart., and by her (who is deceased) had, with other issue (for which, *see* BURKE'S *Peerage*) a 2nd son, the present FULKE SOUTHWELL GREVILLE, Esq. of North Myms Place.

Arms—Sa., on a cross engr., or, five pellets, all within a bordure engr. of the second.
Crest—Out of a ducal coronet gu. a swan, wings expanded, arg. beaked of the 1st.
Motto—Vix ea nostra voco.
Seats—North Myms Place, Herts; Clonyn, Castle Town Delvin, and Clonteem, Drumana, Ireland.

GREY OF NORTON.

GREY, THOMAS-ROBINSON, Esq. of Norton, co. Durham, J.P. Major 1st or South Durham regt. of militia, *b.* 25 May, 1801.

Lineage.—This family of Grey is traditionally descended from a younger branch of the noble house of Grey of Northumberland, (said to have settled in the city of Durham,) and bears the arms of that race.

JOHN GREY, Gent. of the city of Durham, had, by Mary, his wife, a son, ROBERT GREY of Claypath, in the same city, an alderman thereof, who *d.* about 1698, and was *s.* by his only son, JOHN GREY, an alderman of Durham, and mayor of that city in the years 1707, 1715, 1722, and 1735. He *m.* 1st, 23 Jan. 1699, Rebecca, dau. and co-heiress of William Chipchase, Gent. of Norton, the last male representative of the family of that name, one of the most ancient stocks in the place. By this lady (who was buried 14 Jan. 1716) he had issue. Mr. Grey *m.* 2ndly, 5 Aug. 1718, Mary, dau. of George Bowes, Esq. of Bradley, and by her had further issue. Mr. Grey was buried at St. Nicholas' Church, Durham, 17 Sept. 1750, aged 80, and was *s.* by his 4th, but eldest surviving son,

JOHN GREY, Gent. of Norton, bapt. 21 July, 1709, who *m.* 28 Dec. 1727, Anne, dau. of Hugh Finch, Gent. of Billingham, co. Durham, by Anne, his wife, and by her (who was buried 17 Sept. 1767) had issue,

I. WILLIAM, of London, *b.* 9 Jan. 1729, *m.* Elizabeth Wright, of Bishopton, and by her had issue an only child, ELIZABETH, *b.* in 1757. This lady inherited the extensive estates of her great-uncle, Gascoigne Finch, Esq. She *m.* 8 June, 1783, the Rev. Christopher Anstey, of Trumpington, co. Cambridge, by whom (who *d.* 19 Dec. 1827) she had an only child, CHRISTOPHER, who lived only a few days.
II. CHIPCHASE, of whom presently.
III. John, of Norton, *b.* 14 June, 1744, *m.* 10 March, 1768, Elizabeth, dau. of John Darnell, of Billingham, and by her (who *d.* 21 Dec. 1818, aged 73) had issue,
  1. John, of Stockton, merchant, *b.* 4 Sept. 1776, *m.* 25 Nov. 1802, Margaret, dau. of Edward Alskell, of Sunderland, by whom (now living) he had issue,
    John, now of Stockton, merchant.
    Edward, now of Liverpool, merchant.
    Eleanor, *m.* 26 April, 1827, Thomas-Henry-Faber, Esq., town-clerk of Stockton, and has issue.
    Elizabeth, *m.* 6 June, 1831, Frederic-William Trevor, Esq., collector of the Customs at Montrose, and has issue.
  2. WILLIAM, the present William Grey, Esq. of Norton, (*see that name.*)
  1. Ann, of Norton.
  2. Elizabeth, *m.* in 1825, to the Rev. Christopher Anstey, before-mentioned, then vicar of Norton, for his second wife.
I. Elizabeth, *b.* 28 Jan. 1730, *d.* an infant.
II. Ann, *b.* 28 Jan. 1734, *m.* 17 May, 1764, John Ward, Gent. of Billingham.

Mr. Grey *d.* about 1760, and his 2nd son, who ultimately became the representative of the family, was, as above-mentioned,

CHIPCHASE GREY, Esq., sometime of Sunderland, and afterwards of Norton, *b.* 29 Aug. 1732, *m.* 8 Sept. 1757, Anne, eldest dau. of Thomas Robinson, Esq. of Sunderland, by Margaret, his wife, eldest dau. and co-heiress of William Ettrick, Esq. of Silksworth (*see* ROBINSON *of Silksworth*), and by her (who *d.* at Norton, 10 March, 1787,) left at his decease, 2 Aug. 1821, his then eldest surviving son,

THOMAS-ROBINSON GREY, Esq. of Norton, a lieut.-col. in the army, J.P., *b.* 1 July, 1767, *m.* 10 March, 1796, Elizabeth, dau. of Thomas Hogg, Esq. of Durham, (*see* HOGG *of Norton*, and by her (who *d.* 19 Oct. 1848,) had issue,

I. THOMAS-ROBINSON, now of Norton.
II. William, *b.* 22 April, 1803, *d.* an infant.
III. WILLIAM-ROBINSON, who has assumed the surname of ROBINSON, (*see* ROBINSON *of Silksworth*).
IV. John, of Liverpool, merchant, *m.* 6 Nov. 1835, Marianne, 3rd dau. of Elias Arnaud, Esq. of Liverpool.
I. Elizabeth-Anne. II. Margaret.
III. Harriet, *d.* in Feb. 1847.
IV. Maria, *m.* 18 July, 1839, to her second cousin, the Rev John-William Smith, M.A.

Col. Grey *d.* 17 June, 1833.

Arms—Gu., a lion rampant, within a bordure, engrailed, arg.
Crest—A scaling-ladder, arg.
Motto—De bon vouloir servir le roy.
Residence—Norton, near Stockton-on-Tees.

GREY OF NORTON.

GREY, WILLIAM, Esq. of Norton, co. Durham, J.P., *b.* in 1778; *m.* 2 July, 1807, Joanna, only child and heiress of William Scurfield, Esq. of Coatham, Mundeville, and Crindon House, co. Durham, and had,

I. WILLIAM-SCURFIELD GREY, Esq., A.M., barrister-at-law, J.P.
II. George-John Grey, Esq., M.A., assumed the name of SCURFIELD, (*see* SCURFIELD *of Ford and Hurworth-upon-Tees.*)
III. John-William Grey, Clerk, A.M., assumed the name of SMITH, (*see* SMITH *of Ryhope and Carrowbrough.*)
IV. Charles, an ensign in the 1st West India regt. He *d.* in the West Indies, in June, 1842, *unm.*
V. Henry-Anthony, of Liverpool, merchant.
VI. John-Reynolds, of Calcutta.
VII. Robert-Septimus, *d.* in infancy.
I. Sarah-Dorothy, *m.* her 2nd cousin, William Robinson Robinson, Esq. of Silksworth.
II. Joanna, } both *d.* young.
III. Anne-Elizabeth, }

Lineage.—*See* that of THOMAS-ROBINSON GREY, Esq. of Norton.

Arms, Crest, and *Motto*—*see preceding family.*
Residence—Norton, near Stockton-on-Tees.

GRIFFITH OF CASTLE NEYNOE.

GRIFFITH, HENRY, Esq. of Port Royal and Castle Neynoe, co. Sligo, J.P., high-sheriff 1847, *b.* 19 April,

1815; *m.* 29 Aug. 1843, Jemima, dau. of James Pedder, Esq. of Ashton Hall, co. Lancaster, J.P. and D.L., and has issue,

I. WILLIAM-JAMES, *b.* 8 July, 1846.
II. Henry-Thomas, *b.* 29 Jan. 1850.
I. Jane-Elizabeth. II. Brilliana-Margaretta.
III. Jemima-Pedder.

Lineage.—WILLIAM GRIFFITH, Esq. of Ballytirnan House, co. Sligo, *m.* in 1730, Alicia, dau. of John Jameson, Esq. of Sligo, and had five sons and three daus. Of the former,

HUMPHREY GRIFFITH, Esq. of Ballytirnan House, *m.* 17 March, 1775, Elizabeth, dau. of Lancelot Holmes, Esq. of Millmount, co. Roscommon, and was *s.* at his decease, 9 July, 1834, by his son,

WILLIAM GRIFFITH, Esq. of Ballytirnan House, J.P., and high-sheriff for the co. of Sligo in 1803, who *m.* 2 Sept. 1802, Brilliana, youngest dau. of Courtney Kenny, Esq. of Ballinrobe, J.P. for co. Mayo, and by her had,

HENRY, his heir, of Port Royal.
Maria-Charlotte, *m.* 1829, to Thomas Smith, Esq., M.D.
Alicia, *m.* 1829, to Samuel Stanley, Esq.
Susan, *m.* 1834, to John Craig, Esq.

Mr. Griffith *d.* 7 June, 1819.

Seats—Castle Neynoe, and Port Royal, co. Sligo.

GRIFFITH OF PENPOMPREN.

GRIFFITH, THOMAS, Esq. of Trevalyn Hall, Trevalyn, co. Denbigh, J.P. and D.L., high-sheriff 1849, *b.* 17 July, 1786; *m.* 1st, 25 Feb. 1813, Catherine, only surviving dau. of William Bond, Esq. of Edgeworthstown, co. Longford, youngest brother of Sir James Bond, Bart. She *d. s. p.* 14 Jan. 1814. He *m.* 2ndly, 17 June, 1830, Elizabeth-Mary, youngest surviving dau. of William Boscawen, Esq., and Charlotte his wife, dau. of the Rev. Dr. Ibbetson, of Bushy, Archdeacon of St. Albans, and by this lady (one of the co-heiresses of the Trevalyn estate, by virtue of the marriage of her grandfather, the Hon. Gen. George Boscawen, 3rd son of Hugh, 1st Viscount Falmouth, with Anne Trevor, dau. of John-Morley Trevor, of Trevalyn, Plas-Teg, and Glynde, by his wife, Lucy Montague, of Horton, co. Northampton, sister of George, 2nd Earl of Halifax) left at his decease one son,

BOSCAWEN-TREVOR, *b.* 14 August, 1835, an officer 23rd Royal Welsh fusiliers who served in the Crimea in 1855, and was present at the assault on the Great Redan and the fall of Sebastopol: for which he has a medal and clasp.

Lineage.—The family of Griffith of Penpompren, of which Mr. Griffith is the representative, is of great antiquity in Cardiganshire, and were seated there until 1787. THOMAS GRIFFITH, who was living at Penpompren in 1650, left an only son,

THOMAS GRIFFITH, Esq. who *m.* Anne, dau. and heiress of John West, Esq. of London and of Tredole, co. Cardigan, and dying in 1694, was *s.* by his only son,

HUGH GRIFFITH, Esq., who *m.* Susannah, dau. of Meredith Lloyd, Esq. of Cwmbwa, co. Cardigan, and *d.* in 1731, leaving by her three sons, JOHN, his heir, Cornelius, and Charles. The eldest,

JOHN GRIFFITH, Esq., *s.* his father, and resided at Penpompren, where he rendered himself highly useful as a magistrate for a long period. He served as high-sheriff of the county, in 1757, and *d.* in 1782, leaving two sons, THOMAS, his heir, and Charles, Captain Royal Marines, who *d.* in 1818, leaving issue. The former,

THOMAS GRIFFITH, Esq., *s.* his father. He *m.* 10 Dec. 1778, Jane, only child of Richard Philips, Esq. of Coedgaen, co. Carmarthen, and Wandsworth, co. Surrey, and by her was father of the late THOMAS GRIFFITH, Esq. of Trevallyn Hall.

Arms—Arg., a lion, passant, sa., between three fleurs-de-lis, gu.
Crest—A lion, passant, sa.
Seat—Trevallyn Hall, near Wrexham.

GRIGSON OF SAHAM TONEY.

GRIGSON, THE REV. WILLIAM, A.M. of Corpus Christi College, Cambridge, Lord of Howards, Harveys and Pages, in Saham Toney, and rector and patron of Whinburgh with Westfield, co. Norfolk, *b.* 25 Nov. 1809, *s.* his father 10 June, 1842; *m.* 9 July, 1844, Margaret, 3rd dau. of James Hales, Esq. of the city of Norwich, by Barbara, his wife, youngest dau. of John Greene Baseley, late mayor of Norwich, which James Hales was the youngest son of Robert Hales, Esq. of Lynn Regis, by Ann his wife, dau and co-heir of Sir John Turner, Bart. of Warham, many years M.P. for Lynn. By Margaret his wife, Mr. Grigson, has issue,

I. WILLIAM SHACKFORTH, *b.* 15 April, 1845.
II. Edward, *b.* 2 Sept. 1846.
III. Francis, *b.* 4 Aug. 1852.
IV. Baseley-Hales, *b.* 26 March, 1856.
I. Barbara-Lucy. II. Mary-Hales.
III. Ellen-Margaret.

Lineage.—The first of the family who settled in Norfolk, was,

THE REV. WILLIAM GRIGSON, M.A., instituted to the rectory of Hardingham in that co., 5 Sept. 1584. He *m.* Katherine, only sister and heir of Thomas Gesse, Gent. of Reymerstone, and *d.* in Oct. 1630, having had by this lady, who *d.* in 1651, with two daus., four sons. The 3rd son,

ROBERT GRIGSON, of Hardingham, Gent., *b.* 12 June, 1616, *m.* 1st, 18 May, 1641, Anne, dau. of Henry Payne, Gent. of Worlington, co. Cambridge, and 2ndly, Dionysia Gesse, relict of Robert Palgrave, of Garvestone, co. Norfolk, Gent., and by the former only (who *d.* 11 Sept. 1664) had, with one dau., two surviving sons, 1 Robert, of Hardingham, *m.* Elizabeth, dau. of John Jermyn, Esq. of West Tofts, co. Norfolk, cousin to Henry Jermyn, Earl of St. Alban's, K.G., and *d.* in June, 1726. From this marriage descended the Grigsons of Reymerstone and Hardingham, both of which branches are now extinct; 2 WILLIAM, whose line we treat of. The younger son,

THE REV. WILLIAM GRIGSON, A.M., rector of Morley, co. Norfolk, and lord of Shadwells, *alias* Cockerells, in that parish, bapt. 3 Jan. 1649, *m.* 29 Jan. 1677, Susan, dau. and sole heiress of Miles King, of Hardingham, and *d.* 17 Jan. 1725, having had by this lady (who *d.* 30 Aug 1713), seven daus and two sons who survived him. The elder son,

ROBERT GRIGSON, Esq., M.D., bapt. 30 Sept. 1679, *m.* 18 Dec. 1707, Frances Tawell, of Norwich, niece and one of the heirs of Robert Bene, Esq., M.P. for Norwich in the last two parliaments of Queen ANNE, and by her (who *d.* 16 March, 1746-7, aged 64) left at his decease, 10 Nov. 1747, with two daus., an only surviving son,

WILLIAM GRIGSON, Esq. of Morley, and West Wretham, co. Norfolk, D.L., bapt. 9 June, 1718, who *m.* 27 Jan. 1763, Ellen, dau. of Mr. Edward Harvey, of Watton, in the same shire, attorney-at-law, and by her (who *d.* 6 May, 1820) had,

WILLIAM, of whom presently.
EDWARD-HARVEY, late of Saham Toney, of whom hereafter.
Robert, *d.* young, *v. p.*
Ellen, *m.* 4 April, 1789, to the Rev. Leonard Shelford, B.D., rector and patron of North Tuddenham, co. Norfolk, late Fellow of Corpus Christi Coll., Camb. She *d.* 21 March, 1839, leaving issue.

Mr. Grigson sold his estate at Morley a few years before his death, which took place 17 Sept. 1787, after which the estate of Wretham was also sold, when his elder son,

THE REV. WILLIAM GRIGSON, A.B. of Corpus Christi College, Cambridge, J.P. and D.L., removed to Caston, co. Norfolk, where he resided for several years, but subsequently purchased and settled at Saham Toney. He was lord of Howards Harveys and Pages. This gentleman, who was *b.* 1 Aug. 1764, *m.* 29 Oct. 1799, Martha, eldest dau., and eventually co-heir, of the Rev. John Twells, A.M., rector of Caston, co. Norfolk, and *d. s. p.* 3 Oct. 1829. Upon the death of his widow, 17 Aug. 1839, his younger brother,

EDWARD HARVEY GRIGSON, of Broomlay Hill, in Saham Toney, *b.* 19 May, 1767, late central commissary for Norfolk, became lord of Howards Harveys and Pages. This gentleman *m.* 14 Nov. 1808, Mary, eldest dau. of Thomas Shuckforth Dixon, Gent. of Saham Toney, 3rd son of Francis Dixon, Esq. of Upwell, in the Isle of Ely, high-sheriff of cos. Cambridge and Huntingdon in 1757. By Mary Dixon, Mr. Grigson had issue,

I. WILLIAM, his successor, and present proprietor.
II. Edward-Robert, *b.* 19 April, 1814, late of Trin. Hall, Camb., now of Watton, co. Norfolk, *m.* 10 May, 1842, Mary-Jane, 4th dau. of the Rev. Richard Snape, A.B., rector of Brent Eleigh, co. Suffolk, and has issue, 1 Richard, *b.* 1843; 2 Thomas Shuckforth; 3 Robert-

Edward, b. 1846; 4 Charles-William, b. 1847; 5 Edward Snape, b. 1850; 6 Henry-Francis, b. 1851; 7 John-Septimus, b. 1853; 8 James, b. 1855.

Arms—Gu., two bars, in chief, three annulets, arg.

Crest—Out of a ducal coronet, or a griffin's head, chequy, arg. and sa.

Seat—Broomley Hill, in the parish of Saham Toney, co. Norfolk.

GRIMSHAW OF HIGH BANK.

GRIMSHAW, JOHN, Esq. of High Bank, Gorton, co. Lancaster, J.P. and D.L., b. 28 Jan. 1783; m. 14 June, 1832, Mary-Anne, dau. of Henry Ogden, Esq. of Langley Hall, near Middleton, and has issue,

I. JOHN, b. 21 April, 1833.
II. Joseph-Stanfield, b. 2 June, 1836.
III. George-Henry, b. 26 Jan. 1839.
I. Mary-Jane.

Lineage.—JAMES GRIMSHAW, Esq. of Droylsden, near Manchester, son of JAMES GRIMSHAW, Esq. of Droylsden, who d. in 1718, aged fifty-eight, by Mary, his wife, m. 1 Feb. 1721, Jane, dau. and heiress of Robert Stanfield, Esq., of Audenshaw, and with her acquired that estate. He had three sons, Robert, George, and

JOHN GRIMSHAW, Esq. of Audenshaw Lodge, who m. 28 Oct. 1779, Mary, dau. of Joseph Holt, Esq. of Wilmslow, co. Chester, and had issue,

I. JOHN, now of High Bank.
II. Joseph-Stanfield, of Stanfield Lodge, Gorton, b. 28 Jan. 1783.
III. William, of Kempsey, near Worcester, b. 8 Sept. 1784, m. 1835, Harriette, dau. of the late Robert Pattison, Esq. of Hull, and has issue, 1 William Frederick-Stanfield, b. 1838; 1 Emily-Harriette; 2 and Helena-Caroline.

Arms—Arg., a griffin, segreant, sa., beaked and membered, or.

Crest—A demi-griffin, sa.

Motto—Tenax propositi vinco.

Seat—High Bank, Gorton, Manchester.

GRIMSTON OF GRIMSTON GARTH.

GRIMSTON, CHARLES, Esq. of Grimston Garth and Kilnwich, both co. York, col. East York militia, J.P. and D.L., b. 2 July, 1791; m. 10 Nov. 1823, Jane, 3rd surviving dau. of the Very Rev. Thomas Trench, dean of Kildare, and has issue,

I. MARMADUKE-JERARD, b. 27 Nov. 1826; m. 3 July, 1856, Florence-Victoria, youngest dau. of Col. and Lady Maria Saunder on.
II. Walter-John, b. 9 Feb. 1828.
III. William-Henry, b. 1 Nov. 1830.
IV. Daniel-Thomas, b. 8 July, 1832.
I. Maria-Emma.
II. Frances-Dorothy, m. to the Rev. John Frewen Moor.
III. Jane.
IV. Catherine.
V. Elizabeth.
VI. Maude.
VII. Cicell.
VIII. Octavia.

Lineage.—SYLVESTER DE GRYMESTONE came over from Normandy as standard-bearer in the army of WILLIAM the Conqueror, to whom he did homage for Grymestone and Holmpton, and his lands elsewhere, to hold of the Lord Rosse as of his seigniore and manor of Rose in Holdernesse, which Lord Rosse was lord chamberlain of the king's household in 1066. Sylvester married, it is supposed, in Normandy, and had a son and successor,

DANIEL DE GRYMESTONE, who m. the dau. of Sir. Adam Somerville, of Brent Hall, and was father of

SIR THOMAS DE GRYMESTONE, Knt. of Grymestone, living *temp.* STEPHEN, who m. the dau. of Sir John Boeville, of Awdesley, and had a son,

SIR JOHN DE GRYMESTONE, of Grymestone, knighted by HENRY II. m. the dau. and heiress of Sir John Goodmanham, Knt. of Goodmanham, and left by her, at his decease, 12 Oct. 1165, a son,

SIR MARTIN DE GRYMESTONE, of Grymestone, Knt., living *temp.* HENRY III., who m. the dau. and co-heir of Sir John Collam, Knt. of Collam, and was s. by his son,

SIR ROGER DE GRYMESTONE, Knt. of Grymestone, who m. the dau. of Sir Fowke Constable, lord of Frishmarshe, and was s. by his elder son,

SIR GERARD DE GRYMESTONE, Knt. of Grymestone, who m. the dau of Sir John Baskerville, Knt., but having no issue, was s. by his brother,

WALTER DE GRYMESTONE, of Grymestone, who m. the dau. and co-heir of Harbarde Flinton, of Flinton, and was s. by his eldest son,

WILLIAM DE GRYMESTONE, of Grymestone, who m. Armatrude, dau. of Sir John Rysam, Knt. of Rysam, in Holderness, and had three sons, viz., 1 THOMAS, his heir; 2 Robert, ancestor of the EARL OF VERULAM; and 3 John, made second dean of Windsor in 1416. The eldest son,

THOMAS GRIMSTON, of Grimston, living in the reign of HENRY V., m. Dionesa, dau. of De Sutton, lord of Sutton, Southcotes, and Stone Ferry, and was s. at his decease by his eldest son,

SIR ROGER GRIMSTON, Knt. of Grimston, who left no issue by his wife, the dau. of Sir John Antwisle, of Lancashire, and was s. by his brother,

THOMAS GRIMSTON, of Grimston, living in 1436, who m. the dau of Sir William Fitzwilliam, Knt. of Aldwark, near Rotherham, and had (with two daus., Margaret, m. to Robert Stowthingham; and Ann, m to William Vavasour, Esq.) a son and successor,

WALTER GRIMSTON, Esq. of Grimston, m. the dau. and co-heiress of Sir John Portington, the judge of the Common Pleas in 1444, and was father of

THOMAS GRIMSTON, Esq. of Grimston, living *temp.* HENRY VII., who m. an heiress named Newark, and had, with two daus. (the elder m. to George Brigham, of Brigham, and the younger d. unm.), six sons. The eldest surviving son and heir,

WALTER GRIMSTON, Esq. of Grimston, m. the dau. of John Dakins, of Brandesburton, and had, with a dau. (Elizabeth, the wife of Marmaduke Constable), an only son,

THOMAS GRIMSTON, Esq. of Grimston, who m. the dau. of Nicholas Girlington, of Harkfurth, and had (with two daus., Ann, m. to Robert Wright, Esq. of Plowland, co. York; and Maud m. to John Thwenge, Esq. of Upper Helmesley) many sons, of whom John was ancestor of the GRIMSTONS *of Neswick*. The eldest son,

THOMAS GRIMSTON, Esq. of Grimston, living in 1540, m. the dau. and heiress of Marmaduke Thwaites, Esq. of Little Smeaton, and was s. by his son,

SIR MARMADUKE GRIMSTON, Knt. of Grimston, *temp.* Queen ELIZABETH, who m. Frances, dau. of George Gyll, Esq. of Wyddial Hall, Herts, and had by her one son, Thomas, who d. s. p. Sir Marmaduke's nephew (the only son of his brother John), another

SIR MARMADUKE GRIMSTON, of Grimston, knighted by King JAMES I., in 1603, high-sheriff for Yorkshire in 1598, m. the dau. of Sir William Dalton, of Hawkeswell, in Yorkshire, and had (with a dau., Theophania, m. to Leonard Beckwith, Esq. of Handale Abbey, in Cleveland) an only son,

WILLIAM GRIMSTON, Esq. of Grimston, who suffered severely for his royalty. He m. 1st, a dau. of Christopher Byerley, Esq. of Midridge Grange, in the county of Durham, and had by her a son, WILLIAM, his heir. He m. 2ndly, a dau. of Sir Robert Strickland, of Thornton Briggs, in Yorkshire, and had to survive youth two sons and four daus. Mr. Grimston m. 3rdly, the widow of Mr. Lalton, and dau. of Lord Evers, but by this lady had no issue. He was s. by his eldest son,

WILLIAM GRIMSTON, Esq. of Grimston, b. 16 Aug. 1640, who m. Dorothy, dau. of Sir Thomas Norcliffe, Knt. of Langton, by Dorothy, his wife, dau. of Thomas, Viscount Fairfax of Emely, and had three sons and three daus. Mr. Grimston d. 5 Aug. 1711, and was s. by his son,

THOMAS GRIMSTON, Esq. of Grimston Garth, b. 8 Oct. 1664, who m. Dorothy, dau. of Sir John Legard, Bart. of Ganton, and left at his decease, 13 April, 1729, an only surviving son,

THOMAS GRIMSTON, Esq. of Grimston Garth, b. 26 Sept. 1702, who m. 16 Oct. 1722, Jane, dau. and co-heir of John Close, Esq. of Richmond, in Yorkshire, by Jane, his wife, sister and heir of Charles Estouteville, Esq. of Hunmanby, and had, to survive youth, an only son, JOHN, his heir. Mr. Grimston d. 22 Oct. 1751, and was s. by his son,

JOHN GRIMSTON, Esq. of Grimston Garth and Kilnwick, b. 17 Feb. 1724, who m. 12th March, 1753, Jane, youngest

1815; *m.* 29 Aug. 1843, Jemima, dau. of James Pedder, Esq. of Ashton Hall, co. Lancaster, J.P. and D.L., and has issue,

1. WILLIAM-JAMES, *b.* 8 July, 1846.
II. Henry-Thomas, *b.* 29 Jan. 1850.
I. Jane-Elizabeth. II. R[illegible]
III. Jemima-Pedder.

Lineage.—WILLIAM GR[illegible] House, co. Sligo, *m.* in 1730 [illegible] Esq. of Sligo, and had fiv[illegible] former,

HUMPHREY GRIFFITH[illegible] 17 March, 1775, Eliza[illegible] of Millmount, co. R[illegible] 9 July, 1834, by hi[illegible]

WILLIAM GRIFF[illegible] high-sheriff for t[illegible] Brilliana, you[illegible] Ballinrobe, J[illegible]

HENRY, [illegible]
Maria-C[illegible]
Alicia, [illegible]
Susan [illegible]

Mr. Gr[illegible] [illegible] three mullets of six points, [illegible]

Arms—Arg. on a fess [illegible] or, pierced [illegible]
Crest—A stag's head, with a ring round the neck, arg.
Motto—Fuits provenant.
Seat—Grimston Garth, and Kilnwick, near Beverley.

GRONOW OF ASH HALL.

GRONOW, REV. THOMAS, M.A., of Ash Hall, co. Glamorgan, and Gillygudray, co. Carmarthen, J.P. (son of late Wm. Gronow, Esq. of Court Herbert, Glamorganshire, for which county he was a deputy lieutenant and magistrate, and brother of Captain Gronow, formerly of the Grenadier Guards, and late M.P. for Stafford,) *m.* 1st, Mary-Ann, eldest dau. of late John-Mins Lettsom, Esq., M.D., of London, and by her (who is deceased) has had issue four sons and three daus.; of the latter, the 2nd, Mary-Ann, is deceased; of the former, the eldest son,

WILLIAM-LETTSOM, *m.* Catherine, only dau. of the late William Norman, Esq. of Carlisle, co. Cumberland, and has issue a son and two daus.

He *m.* 2ndly, Elizabeth-Ann, eldest dau. of Wm. Grimsdale, Esq. of Wycombe, co. Bucks, and has by her, three sons and five daus.

Lineage.—The Gronows are a very ancient family, and were originally seated in North Wales where they had large landed possessions. In the reign of EDWARD III.,

SIR TUDOR AP GRONOW, an ancestor of the royal house of Tudor, claimed the honour of knighthood, for by the laws and constitution of King ARTHUR, he deemed himself entitled to that distinction upon the ground of possessing the following threefold qualifications,—birth, estate, and valour. King EDWARD III. being pleased with the bold and lordly mien of Sir Tudor ap Gronow, was induced to confer the honour upon him. Owen Tudor, the grandson of Sir Tudor ap Gronow, *m.* the widow of HENRY V., and their son, Jasper Tudor, Earl of Richmond, was the father of HENRY VII. In the choir of St. David's Cathedral there remain two recumbent effigies, in armour, representing two members of this family; in the breast and back of each figure is sculptured a lion, rampant, that in one of them being differenced by a label of five parts.

Arms—Quarterly: 1st and 4th, gu., three lions, rampant, arg.; 2nd and 3rd, or, a chev., arg., between three heads, ppr.
Crest—A lion, rampant.
Motto—Gronwi hil Gwerninion.

GROVE OF FERNE.

GROVE, JOHN, Esq. of Ferne, co. Wilts, *b.* 4 Dec. 1784; *s.* his father in 1846; *m.* 17 Jan. 1818, Jean-Helen, dau. of Sir William Frazer, Bart., and has issue,

I. THOMAS-FRASER, *b.* 27 Nov. 1821, late capt. 6th dragoons, *m.* 16 Jan. 1847, Katherine-Grace, dau. of Hon. Waller O'Grady, of Castle Garde, co. Limerick, Ireland.
II. John, *b.* 12 March 1823, *m.* 13 May, 1851, Clara-Cicely-Sarah, dau. of the late Joseph Ashton Burrow, Esq. of Carleton Hall, Cumberland.

Harvey[illegible] an[illegible] [illegible] James Hussey, Esq. [illegible] July, 1851, Frederick L. A. Selwyn, son of late Rev. Townshend Selwyn, [illegible] of Kilmington, Somerset and canon of Glou[illegible] [illegible] Sophia. V. Emma-Philippa.

Lineage.—JOHN GROVE, Esq., who settled in Wiltshire, was 5th in descent from John de Grove, of Chalfont, St. Giles, Bucks, who *d.* 26 EDWARD III., and nephew of Thomas Grove, Esq., high-sheriff of Bucks in 1434, whose only dau. and heir, Agnes, *m.* William Brudenell, Esq. of Aynho, Northamptonshire. John Grove *m.* Joan, dau. and heir of John Burhill, Esq., and was father of

THOMAS GROVE, Esq., living in 1522, who *m.* Isabel, dau. of John Luyshe, and had (with a dau., Lucie, who was thrice married) two sons, Thomas Grove, and

ROBERT GROVE, Esq., M.P., Feodary for co. Wilts, who *m.* Joane, dau. of John Comlee, Esq. of Canne, co. Dorset, and had (with a dau., Mary, *m.* to Hugh Kete, of Cheslborn, Dorset, and two junior sons, viz., Matthew, of Staple Inn, and Walter, of Honiton, co. Devon, 20th JAMES I.) an eldest son.

WILLIAM GROVE, Esq. of Gray's Inn, M.P. for Shaftesbury, *temp.* PHILIP and MARY, who purchased Ferne in 1563. He *m.* about 1563, Thomasyn, dau. and heir of Edward Mayhewe, of Fonthill, and *d.* in 1582, having had (with four daus., viz., Anne, *m.* to Sir James Bulkeley, of Burgate, Hants; Mary, *m.* to Richard Swaine, Esq. of the Middle Temple; Alice, *m.* to Thomas Butler, Esq. of Almer, Dorset; and Margaret, *m.* to Thomas Bennett, Esq. of Pithouse, Wilts) four sons, viz.,

John, *b.* in 1564, *d. s. p.* in 1629.
William, *m.* Jane, dau. and heir of John Boden, Esq., M.P., and *d.* in 1622, having had a son, John, who *m.* Mary, dau. of John Lowe, Esq. of New Sarum, and *d. s. p.*, and three daus., Mary, *m.* to John Lowe, of New Sarum; Margaret, *m.* to Francis Anketill, of Shaston; and Jane, *m.* to Hugh Grove, Esq.
ROBERT, of whom presently.
Hugh, ancestor, by Dorothy his wife, of the family of Zeals House, co. Wilts.

The 3rd son,

ROBERT GROVE, Esq., *m.* 1st, Gertrude, dau. of Cuthbert Hargill, Esq. of Cucklington, co Somerset; and 2ndly, in 1608, Honor, dau. of South, Esq. of Swallowcliff, Wilts, and, by the latter only, had issue, viz., two daus., the elder, *m.* to John Bulkeley, Esq. of Burgate, Hants, and the other, Honor, *m.* to Lewis Williams, Esq. of Henington, co. Dorset; and three sons, THOMAS, his heir; Robert, fellow of New College, Oxon, *d.* in 1663, aged 56; and William, of Morden, co. Dorset, living in 1653, who was father of ROBERT, Bishop of Chichester, *b.* in 1634, who was *m.* Elizabeth Cole, of Dover, and *d.* in 1696. The eldest son,

THOMAS GROVE, Esq., M.P. for Shaston; *m.* 1st, in 1630, Mary, dau. of John Lowe, Esq. of New Sarum, and relict of John Grove, Esq.; and 2ndly, the dau. and co-heir of Edward Lambert, Esq. of Corton, Wilts, and, by the latter only, had issue, viz., three sons: the two elder *d.* young; the 3rd and only surviving son,

ROBERT GROVE, Esq. of Ferne, *m.* 1st, in 1661, Mary, dau. of John Hanham, Esq. of Wimborne Minster, co. Dorset, and by her ,who *d.* about 1688, had (with two daus., Mary, *d.* young, and another Mary, who *d.* in 1714) two sons, THOMAS, his heir, and Robert, *b.* in 1668. Mr. Grove *m.* a second time, and *d.* in 1695. His eldest son,

THOMAS GROVE, Esq. of Ferne, *b.* in 1664, living at Martin, co. Wilts, 1713; *m.* in 1686, Elizabeth Hooke, sister and co-heir of Sir Hele Hooke, Bart. of Tangier Park, Hants, and by her, who *d.* in 1726, left at his decease, in 1738, (with a dau., Elizabeth, *m.* in 1740, to Joseph Hinxman, Esq. of North Hinton, co. Hants,) two sons, Thomas, *b.* in 1668, and *d. s. p.* in 1750; and

JOHN GROVE, Esq. of Ferne, *b.* in 1696; who *m.* 1st, about 1754, Eleanor, dau. of Sir William Hanham, of Dean's Court, Dorset, and by her, who *d.* in childbirth, had a son, William, who *d.* an infant. He *m.* 2ndly, about 1755, Philippa, eldest dau. of Walter Long, Esq. of Preshaw, Hants, and of Close Gate, Sarum, and by her had (with two daus., Philippa, living at Nether Hampton, Wilts, in 1818; and Elizabeth, *m.* in 1776, to William-Chafin Grove, Esq. of Zeals, Wilts) a son, THOMAS. Mr. Grove *d.* in 1769, aged 73. His son,

THOMAS GROVE, Esq. of Ferne, *b.* 1759; *m.* 1782, Charlotte, dau. of Charles Pilfold, Esq. of Sussex, and had, with other issue, who *d.* young,

THOMAS, b. 1789; m. 1st, Henrietta, dau. of James Farquharson, Esq. of Langton, co. Dorset: and 2ndly, 19 April, 1824, Elizabeth Hill; and dying s. p., left by his 2nd wife an only dau., Mary.
JOHN, now of Ferne.
William b. in 1790, m. Frances Grove.
George, b. in 1793, m. Charlotte, dau. of Purvis Eyre, Esq.
Charles-Henry, b. in 1794; m. 14 Feb. 1820, Eliza, dau. of Hopkins, Esq. of Alresford, Hants.
Charlotte, m. to the Rev. Richard Downes.
Emma-Philippa, m. in 1805, to John-Horsey Waddington, Esq. of Clay Hall, Herts, and d. in 1819.
Harriet, m. in 1811, to William Helyar, Esq. of Coker.

Arms—Erm., on a chev., engr., gu., three escallops, the centre one, or, the other two, arg.
Crest—A dog, passant, sa., collared, arg.
Motto—Ny dessux ny dessoux.
Seat—Ferne House, Wilts.

GRUBBE OF EASTWELL.

HUNT-GRUBBE, THOMAS, Esq. of Eastwell, Potterne, co. Wilts, J.P., major in the army; b. in April, 1793; m. 1st, 21 June, 1820, Elizabeth, dau. of the Rev. Jacob Costobadie, rector of Wensley, co. York, and by her had one son,

I. WILLIAM-HUNT, lieut. H.M. 53rd regt., served in the campaigns of the Punjaub and Sutlej; and d. in India in 1853.

He m. 2ndly, 13 May, 1834, Catherine, only dau. of Samuel Hughes, Esq. of Bath, and by this lady has further issue two sons,

I. Walter, lieut. R.N.
II. Henry-George, lieut. H.M. 9th regt.

Major Hunt-Grubbe served in the Peninsular War.

Lineage.—The family of Grubbe, spelt in the old registers Grübe or Groube, migrated from Germany about the year 1430, after the Hussite persecutions; and subsequently settled at Eastwell, in the parish of Potterne, Wilts, where they have ever since remained.

HENRY GRUBBE, Esq., M.P. for Devizes, co. Wilts, 14 ELIZABETH, 1571, d. in 1581, leaving, by his wife, a dau. of Stephens, of Burderop, co. Wilts, a son,

THOMAS GRUBBE, Esq. of Potterne, whose second son,

JOHN, of Potterne and Chernell, high-sheriff of Wilts, 14 CAR. I., m. Jenwora, dau. of Thomas Bas Kerville, Esq. of Richardston, and d. 1649, leaving a son and heir, THOMAS, who m. Thomasin, dau. of Walter Bourchier, Esq., and was father of THOMAS GRUBBE, Esq. of Potterne, who m. Mary Long, of Banton, and had an only child,

MARY GRUBBE, who m. Thomas Hunt, Esq. of Bishop's Lavington, and had a son,

WILLIAM HUNT, Esq. of Bishop's Lavington and Potterne, magistrate for Wilts, b. 14 Nov. 1696, who m. 1st, Margaret, dau. of John Smith, Esq. of Shaw House, Wilts, by whom he had a son, THOMAS-GRUBBE; and 2ndly, Anne, dau. of William Dorchester, Esq. of Etchilhampton, Wilts, which, lady, after the death of her husband, assumed the surname of GRUBBE. Mr. Hunt's son and heir,

THOMAS-GRUBBE HUNT GRUBBE, Esq. of Eastwell, co. Wilts, J.P., m. Frances, dau. of Morgan Keene, Esq. of the Close, of New Sarum, and by her, who d. in Oct. 1767, had (with a dau. Anna, m. to the Rev. Edmund Benson, M.A., and a son, Walter, in holy orders, who d. in 1807) an elder son and heir,

WILLIAM HUNT-GRUBBE, Esq., b. 16 Sept. 1760, J.P. and D.L., who m. Mary-Dorothea, dau. of the Rev. J.-A. Milnes, D.D., of Newark, Notts, and had issue,

William, lieut. Royal Horse Guards, d. with the army in Spain, in 1817. He m. Caroline, dau. of H. Griffies, and niece of Sir G.-Griffies Williams, Bart. of Llynwormwood, co. Carmarthen.
THOMAS, now of Eastwell.
James-Andrew, M.A., in holy orders, m. 1st, his cousin, only child and heir of the Rev. Thomas Milnes, rector of Burton Agnes, co. York, and by her has one dau., Elleonora; m. 1848, to Charles Wyndham, Esq. He m. 2ndly, Martha, dau. of the Rev. C. Richards, M.A., rector of Little Cheverill, co. Wilts.
John-Heneage, major-general in the army.
Anne, m. to the Rev. Samuel-Thomas Gully, M.A., rector of Berrynarber, co. Devon.
Mary-Frances, m. to Thomas Baynes, Esq., nephew of Lieut.-General Sir John Lambert.

Arms—Vert, on a chev., arg., between three demi-lions, or, as many crosses-crosslet, sa., for GRUBBE; quartering, az., on a bend, between two waterbougets, or, three leopards' faces, gu., for HUNT.
Crests—A lion's head, az., murally crowned, or, for GRUBBE; on a mount, vert, against a halberd, erect, in pale, gu., headed, arg., a talbot, sejant, or, collared, and tied to the halberd of the second, for HUNT.
Motto—Justus et tenax.
Seat—Eastwell, Potterne, near Devizes.

GRYLLS OF HELSTON.

GRYLLS, REV. RICHARD-GERVEYS, of Helston, co. Cornwall, vicar of Breage and Luxulion, b. 30 March, 1785; m. in 1816, Sophia, youngest dau. of Charles Rashleigh, Esq. of Duporth.

Lineage.—WILLIAMS GRYLLS, Esq. of Tavistock, to whom arms were confirmed in 1577, m. Elizabeth Knight, widow, and had, with a younger son, William, of Tavistock, who m. Katharine, dau. of Nicholas Westlake, Esq., an elder son,

CHARLES GRYLLS, Esq., barrister-at-law, who settled at Court, in Lanreath, Cornwall, in the reign of ELIZABETH. He m. Agnes, dau. of Charles Tubbe, Esq., and by her (who d. in 1607) was father of

SIR JOHN GRYLLS, of Court, in Lanreath, a person of great note, who was made knight banneret by King CHARLES I. He m. Grace, dau. and co-heir of William Beere, Esq., by whom he acquired the advowson, with other property at St. Neot, and had issue. Sir John d. in 1649, and was s. by his eldest son,

CHARLES GRYLLS, Esq. of Court, in Lanreath, who m. Cordelia Mohun, and had five sons and two daus. The eldest surviving son,

CHARLES GRYLLS, Esq. of Court, in Lanreath, m. 3 Aug. 1671, Elizabeth, dau. and heir of Richard Gervys, Esq. of Bonathlacke, Cornwall, and had a son and heir,

CHARLES GRYLLS, Esq., who alienated the residence of Court. Mr. Grylls m. Mary, dau. and sole heir of Edmund Spoure, Esq. of Trebartha Hall, and relict of Renatus Bellott, Esq., but d. s. p., 24 Feb. 1727, and was s. by his brother,

THE REV. RICHARD-GERVEYS GRYLLS, rector of Lanreath, who m. Anne Mohun, or Moon, and dying in 1735, left a son,

RICHARD-GERVEYS GRYLLS, Esq. of Helston, b. at Lanreath, in 1736, who m. 13 Jan. 1758, Cordelia, only dau. of Thomas Glynn, Esq., and sole heiress to her brother, by whom (who d. in 1802) he had issue,

I. RICHARD-GERVEYS, his heir.
II. Thomas, b. in 1760, m. 8 May, 1786, Mary, dau. of Humphrey Millett, Esq. of Enys, in Cornwall, and d. at Helston, 10 Nov. 1813, leaving, with three daus., as many sons, viz.,
1 Humphrey-Millett. 2 Thomas. 3 Glynn.
II. Matthew, b. 3 Aug. 1765, d. unm. in France, 3 Jan. 1795.
I. Cordelia, m. 19 Feb. 1784, to Rev. Thomas Trevenen, rector of Cardynham, and d. 24 April, 1810.
II. Sarah, d. unm. at Clifton, 20 Aug. 1823.

Mr. Grylls d. 3 April, 1771, and was s. by his eldest son,

THE REV. RICHARD-GERVEYS GRYLLS, of Helston, b. 20 Nov. 1758, who m. 24 July, 1783, Charity, eldest dau. of William Hill, Esq. of Carwythenack, and had issue,

I. RICHARD-GERVEYS, heir to his father.
II. William, b. 6 Aug. 1786, in holy orders, vicar of Crowan.
III. Henry, b. 1 Feb. 1794, in holy orders, vicar of St. Neot, m. 30 Dec. 1820, Ellen, youngest dau. of Joseph Boulderson, Esq. of John Street, Bedford Row, and by her (who d. 22 Feb. 1841) has had issue,
1 Richard-Gerveys, ensign 30th regt., d. in 1842.
2 William-Henry, midshipman R.N., H.M.S. Ganges, d. in 1839.
3 Charles-Gerveys, lieut. R.N., b. in 1826.
4 Horatio-Glynn, 64th regt., b. in 1828.
5 Shadwell-Morley, royal artillery, b. in 1831.
6 Henry-Chamond, b. in 1833.
1 Lucretia-Frances-Gerveys, d. in 1834.
2 Ellen. 3. Emma.
4 Adelaide-Frances, d. in 1841.
I. Frances, m. 6 Oct. 1814, to the Rev. William Veale, of Trevayler, in Cornwall.

The Rev. Mr. Grylls d. in Jan. 1842, aged 83, and was s. by his elder son, the present Rev. RICHARD-GERVEYS GRYLLS, of Helston.

Arms—Or, three bendlets, enhanced, gu.
Crest—A porcupine, passant, arg.
Motto—Vires agminis unus habet.
Seat—Helston, in Cornwall.

GUBBINS OF KENMARE CASTLE.

GUBBINS, JAMES, Esq. of Kenmare Castle, co. Limerick, b. 1 June, 1810; m. 13 Dec. 1815, Jane-

Hare, youngest dau. of the late Rev. Marshall Clarke, and has issue,

I. JOSEPH-MARSHALL, *b.* 10 Sept. 1846.
I. Elizabeth-Anne.

Lineage.—The first of this family, that settled in Ireland, was a native of Hertfordshire, who went over with OLIVER CROMWELL. The grandfather of the present Mr. Gubbins, of Kenmare Castle,

JAMES GUBBINS, Esq., *m.* June, 1772, Bridget Wrixon, and *d.* 18 Oct. 1805, leaving a son,

JOSEPH GUBBINS, Esq. of Kenmare Castle, *b.* 13 Oct. 1775, high-sheriff in 1806, who *m.* 14 April, 1805, Anne, youngest dau. of William Henn, Esq. of Paradise, co. Clare, and by her (who *d.* 19 March, 1848) had issue,

JAMES, now of Kenmare Castle. William.
Poole, *d.* a lieut. R.N. on board the "Scylla," at Port Royal, Jamaica, 25 April, 1843, *unm.*
Bridget, *m.* 22 April, 1-43, to Augustus Pentland, Esq., who *d.* 18 July, 1854, *s. p.*

Mr. Gubbins *d.* 3 May, 1836.

Seat—Kenmare Castle, co. Limerick.

GRATTAN-GUINNESS OF BEAUMONT AND PARK ANNESLEY.

LEE-GRATTAN-GUINNESS, THE REV. WILLIAM-SMYTH, M.A., of Beaumont, co. Dublin, and of Park Annesley, co. Wexford, principal surrogate of the diocese of Glendalough, late rector (and patron) for thirty years, of the parish of Rathdrum, co. Wicklow, *b.* 13 June, 1795; *m.* 9 March, 1826, Susan-Jane, only child of Benjamin Guinness, Esq. of Dublin, by Rebecca his wife, 2nd dau. and co-heir of Benjamin Lee, Esq. of Merrion, co. Dublin, and has issue,

I. ARTHUR-WILLIAM, of Parknashogue, co. Wexford, J.P., of Lincoln's Inn, barrister-at-law, *b.* 10 Oct. 1827.
II. Benjamin-Grattan, M.D., surgeon of the co. of Dublin militia, *b.* 27 Jan. 1829.
III. Frederick-Darley, *b.* 25 June, 1840.
I. Adelaide-Rebecca. II. Anna-Louisa.

Mr. Lee-Grattan-Guinness assumed, by royal license, in 1856, the additional surnames and arms of LEE and GRATTAN.

Lineage.—The Guinnesses of Beaumount, who have long ranked foremost amongst the merchants of the city of Dublin, paternally descend from the ancient and eminent house of Magennis, in which formerly vested the Viscounty of Iveagh (*see* BURKE'S *Extinct Peerage*). Several members of the Iveagh family lie interred, in the churchyard of St. Catherine's, Dublin, and in the parish register, the transition of the name from Magennis to McGuinness or Guinness, is clearly traceable. Maternally, the Guinnesses of Beaumount have an ancient and distinguished line of English ancestors, being sprung from the LEES *of Quarendon*, raised to the British peerage in 1674, as Earls of Lichfield. The first who bore the name, as at present spelt, was

RICHARD GUINNESS, Esq. of Celbridge, in the co. of Kildare, *b.* about the year 1680. He *m.* Elizabeth, dau. of William Read, Esq. of Hutton Read, co. Kildare, and by her (who was *b.* in 1698, and *d.* 28 Aug. 1742) had issue,

I. ARTHUR, of whom we treat.
II. Samuel, of Dublin, merchant, *m.* (license dated 1753), Sarah, dau. of Henry Jago, Gent. of Dublin, and had,
   1 Richard, barrister-at-law, *m.* Mary, dau. of George Darley, Esq. of The Scalp, co. Dublin, and left at his decease two surviving sons, viz.,
      ROBERT-RUNDELL, *b.* 14 July, 1790; *m.* 1st, 1822, Mary-Anne, dau. of the late Rev. John-Crossley Seymour, of Castletown, Queen's Co., and by her (who *d.* 1837) had three children, viz., Richard-Seymour, *b.* 1826; Henry, *b.* 1829; and Mary-Catherine, *m.* to Samuel Ferguson, Esq., barrister-at-law. He *m.* 2ndly, 1840, Mary-Anne, dau. of the Rev. Ottiwell Moore, of Liskenfere, co. Wexford, and has issue by her, Robert; Susan; Margaret; Elizabeth; Henrietta; Emily; and Edith.
      RICHARD-SAMUEL, formerly M.P. for Kinsale, and now for Barnstaple, *b.* 17 June, 1797; *m.* 25 Nov. 1835, Katherine-Frances, 2nd dau. of Sir Charles Jenkinson, Bt. of Hawkesbury, and has issue, 1 Wolfran, an officer in the army, *b.* 10 Oct. 1839; 2 Cecil, *b.* 1841; 3 Reginald, *b.* 1842; 4 Claude, *b.* 1852; 1 Mildred; 2 Edith, *m.* in 1856; 3 Geraldine; and 4 Adelaide.
   2 Samuel, barrister-at-law, *d. s. p.*

   1 Mary, *m.* Alexander Stillas, merchant, of Dublin, and *d. s. p.*
III. Richard, of Leixlip, *m.* Anne, dau. of John Foster, Esq., co. Cavan, and had issue,
   1 Jane, wife of Stanley, Esq.
   2 Matilda, wife of Major Owen.
   3 Anne, *m.* to Capt. Hewan.
   4 Olivia, *m.* to the Rev. Mr. Powell.
IV. Benjamin, merchant, *d. unm.* 1778.
I. Elizabeth, *m.* to Benjamin Clare, Esq.
II. Frances, *m.* to John Darley, of Dublin, merchant.

The eldest son,

ARTHUR GUINNESS, Esq. of Beaumont, co. Dublin, *m.* Olivia, dau. and co-heir of Edward Whitmore, Esq. of Dublin, by his wife, a dau. of John Grattan, Esq., and aunt of Mary Grattan, who *m.* William Smyth, Esq. of Bath, who built and endowed the Bethesda church and orphan school, in the city of Dublin, of which Mr. Lee-Grattan-Guinness is a trustee, as the representative of his granduncle, Mr. William Smyth, who was nephew to Arthur Smyth, archbishop of Dublin, and to the late Lord Kiltarton (*see* BURKE'S *Peerage*, GORT). By Olivia his wife (who was cousin of the Right Hon. Henry Grattan) Mr. Guinness had issue,

I. HOSEA, in holy orders, LL.D., rector of St. Werburgh's, and Chancellor of St. Patrick's Cathedral, Dublin, *m.* Jane, dau. of Lieut.-Col. Simon Hart, H.E.I.C.S., and left, with daus., three sons, Arthur, Edward, and Benjamin; the eldest of whom, ARTHUR, *m.* Catherine, dau. of the Rev. Mr. Paul, and left issue, ARTHUR-HART, now of Dublin; Thomas; and three daus.
II. ARTHUR, of whom we treat.
III. Edward, of Dublin, who *m.* Margaret, dau. of James Blair, Esq. of Lucan, co. Dublin, and by her (who *d.* 18 Aug. 1839) left at his decease, 20 Aug. 1833,
   1 Arthur-Blair, capt. 41st regt., *d. unm.* 18 March, 1835.
   2 Richard.
   1 Jane, *d. unm.* 30 Jan. 1855.
   2 Olivia.
   3 Elizabeth, *m.* 24 Feb. 1837, to her cousin, Benjamin-Lee Guinness, Esq. of St. Anne's and Ashford.
   4 Anne-Rebecca.
IV. Benjamin, of Brookville, co. Dublin, *b.* Nov. 1784; *m.* Rebecca, dau. and co-heir of Benjamin Lee, Esq. of Merrion, co. Dublin, and *d.* at Bath, May, 1826, leaving an only child and heiress,
   Susan-Jane, *m.* 9 March, 1826, to her cousin, the Rev. William-Smyth Lee-Grattan-Guinness, of Beaumont.
V. William-Lunell, of Mountjoy Square, Dublin, *m.* Susan, dau. of — Newton, Esq. of Darraghville, co. Wicklow, and had issue,
   1 William-Newton, in holy orders, rector of Ballysodare, co. Sligo, *m.* 1st, 31 March, 1835, Harriette, dau. of Rear-Admiral the Hon. William Trench, 3rd son of the 1st Earl of Clancarty; 2ndly, Miss Perceval, dau. of Alexander Perceval, Esq. of Temple House, co. Sligo; and 3rdly, Miss Day, dau. of the Rev. Mr. Day. The 2nd wife *d. s. p.*, but by the other two Mr. W.-N. Guinness has issue.
   2 Anne, *m.* to William Beattie, Esq., M.D.
VI. John-Grattan, an officer in the Hon. E.I.C.S., *m.* 1st, Susan, dau. of the late Mr. Alderman Hutton, of Dublin; and 2ndly, Mrs. D'Esterre: by the former he had issue,
   1 Arthur-Grattan, M.D., late of Dublin, and now of Exeter, F.R.C.S., *m.* Amelia, dau. of — D'Esterre, Esq., and has, Henry, and other issue.
   2 John, *m.* Miss Lamprey, dau. of the late Alderman Lamprey, and has issue,
   3 Susan. 4 Rebecca.
   5 Anne, *m.* to Dr. Siree.
I. Elizabeth, *m.* to Alderman Frederick Darley, of Dublin, high-sheriff 1808, and for many years previous to his death chief magistrate of the city of Dublin.
II. Louisa, *m.* to the Rev. William-Deane Hoare, of Limerick, and left an only dau., Olivia, *m.* to the Rev. Samuel Day, of Bristol.
III. Mary-Anne, *m.* to the Rev. John Burke, younger son of the late Michael Burke, Esq., M.P., of Ballydugan, co. Galway, and has issue.

Mr. Guinness's 2nd son,

ARTHUR GUINNESS, Esq. of Beaumount, co. Dublin, J.P. and D.L., *b.* 12 March, 1768, held for many years, honoured and respected by all classes of his fellow citizens, the foremost place amongst the merchants of his native city of Dublin. His connection with the mercantile community extended over more than sixty years, and his public services during that long period may be estimated by the universal regret of the whole country at his decease. There was not a public institution, a public or private charity, to which he was not ever ready to devote his time, and to extend the hand of benevolence; and there was not a duty of life which he did not endeavour conscientiously and unostentatiously to perform. Mr. Guinness was for very many years President of the Dublin Chamber of Commerce, filled the office of Governor of the Bank of Ireland in 1820, and was Chairman of the Metropolitan Committee for the Reformation of the Corporation of Dublin, in 1850. He d. full of years and honours, on the 9th June, 1855, and was buried at Mount Jerome Cemetery, co. Dublin. His funeral—although his family declined a public one, in accordance with Mr. Guinness's own previously-expressed wish—was attended by a procession the most numerous and respectable ever witnessed in Dublin. The lord-mayor, several of the judges and the leading members of the bar, many dignitaries and professional men of eminence, were present, as well as all the principal merchants and heads of trading firms. Mr. Arthur Guinness m. Anne, eldest dau. and co-heiress of the late Benjamin Lee, Esq. of Merrion, co. Dublin, and left issue,

William-Smyth, now of Beaumont and Park Annesley.
Arthur-Lee, of Stillorgan House.
Benjamin-Lee, of St. Anne's and Ashford (*see that family*).
Susan, m. in 1832, to the Rev. John Darley, fellow of Trinity College, who d. Dec. 1836.
Mary-Jane, m. 1845, to the Rev. David Pitcairn.
Louisa, d. unm. 18 Jan. 1856.
Elizabeth, m. 1849, to the Rev. William Jameson, of Holly-bank, co. Dublin.
Rebecca, m. 1844, to Sir Edmund Waller, Bt. of Newport, co. Tipperary; who d. 9 March, 1851.

Arms—Quarterly, 1st and 4th grand quarters, quarterly, 1st and 4th, Guinness, per saltire, gu. and az., a lion, rampant, or, on a chief, erm., a dexter hand, couped at the wrist, of the first; 2nd and 3rd, Grattan, quarterly, or and gu., in the first quarter a trefoil, vert, all within a bordure, az.; 2nd and 3rd grand quarters, Lee, arg., on a fesse, between three crescents, sa., a trefoil, or; a canton, gu., for Smyth, charged with a lion, rampant, of the first, and a chief of the same, thereon a mullet, az., between two torteaux.
Crests—1st, Guinness, a boar, passant, quarterly, or and gu.; 2nd, Grattan, on a mound, vert, a falcon, wings elevated, holding in the dexter claw a sceptre, all ppr.; 3rd, Lee, on a pillar, arg., encircled by a ducal coronet, or, an eagle preying on a bird's leg, erased, ppr.
Mottoes—Under the arms, Guinness—Spes mea in Deo. Over the crest, for Grattan—Esse quam videri.
Seat—Beaumont, near Drumcondra, co Dublin.

GUINNESS OF ST. ANNE'S AND ASHFORD.

Guinness, Benjamin-Lee, Esq. of St. Anne's, co. Dublin, and Ashford, co. Galway, b. 1 Nov. 1798, chosen first Lord Mayor of the reformed Corporation of Dublin, 1 Dec. 1850; m. 24 Feb. 1837, Elizabeth, 3rd dau. of the late Edward Guinness, Esq. of Dublin, and has issue,

I. Arthur-Edward, b. 1 Nov. 1840.
II. Benjamin-Lee, b. 4 Aug. 1842.
III. Edward-Cecil, b. 10 Nov. 1847.
I. Anne-Lee.

Mr. Benjamin-Lee Guinness, now the head of the eminent firm of Guinness of Dublin, is youngest son of the late much respected Arthur Guinness, Esq. of Beaumont, by Anne his wife, eldest dau. and co-heir of the late Benjamin Lee, Esq. of Merrion, co. Dublin, a descendant of the Lees *of Quarendon*, ennobled under the title of Lichfield. The estate of Ashford, late the property of Lord Oranmore, Mr. B.-L. Guinness purchased in 1852.

For Lineage—See preceding family.

Arms—Quarterly: 1st and 4th, Guinness, per saltire, gu. and az., a lion, rampant, or, on a chief, erm., a dexter hand, couped at the wrist, of the first; 2nd and 3rd, Lee, arg., on a fesse, between three crescents, sa., a trefoil, or.
Crests—1st, Guinness, a boar, passant quarterly, or and gu.; 2nd, Lee, on a pillar, arg., encircled by a ducal coronet, or, an eagle preying on a bird's leg, erased, ppr.
Motto—Spes mea in Deo.
Seats—St. Anne's, near Clontarf, co. Dublin; and Ashford, near Cong, co. Galway.

GULLY OF TREVENNEN.

Gully, Major William-Slade, of Trevennen, co. Cornwall, b. in 1786-7; m. Josephine Furteaux, niece of Governor Smalley, of Senegal, and has issue two daus.,

I. Cornelia-Powne.
II. Charlotte-Anne, m. 12 Oct. 1848, to John-G. St. Leger, Esq.

Lineage.—The Slades of Trevennen, from whom the Gullys derive that property, were a family of considerable antiquity and were certainly settled at Trevennen in the reign of Queen Elizabeth, if not at a much earlier period. The eventual heiress,

Mary Slade, of Trevennen, only dau. of Edward Slade, of that place, Esq., m. Samuel-Coryn Gully, Esq., b. in 1731, son of John Gully, Esq., by Susannah, his wife, dau. and co-heir of John Coryn, Esq. of Trevorder, representative of that ancient Cornish family, and by him (who d. in 1764,) left a son and successor,

William-Slade Gully, Esq. of Trevennen, who m. Jenefer-Powne, a co-heiress of the family of Thomas, of Treganunna, and had issue,

William-Slade, his heir.
Samuel-Thomas, in holy orders, rector of Berrynarber, near Ilfracombe, b. in 1789, m. Anne, dau. of William Hunt-Grubbe, Esq. of Eastwell Court, Wilts, and has, with two daus., two sons, Algernon-William, and Francis.
Peter-Thomas, d. s. p.
Anne Powne, m. to Samuel-James Fletcher, Esq.

Mr. Slade Gully d. in 1816, and was s. by his eldest son, the present William-Slade Gully, Esq. of Trevennen.

Arms—Arg., a chev., gu., between three cross-crosslets sa.
Crest—Two keys, in saltier.
Motto—Nil sine cruce.
Seat—Trevennen, Cornwall.

GUMBLETON OF GLYNNATORE.

Gumbleton, Richard-John-Maxwell, Esq. of Glynnatore, otherwise Castleview, co. Cork, b. 1834.

Lineage.—The Gumbletons of Ireland are a branch of the Kentish family, Gomeldon of Somerfield, the direct line of which failed in an heiress, Mellora Gomeldon, who m. 1st, Thomas Poole, Esq. of Cheshire, and 2ndly, Thomas Stanley, Esq. of Lancashire, attainted in 1715. The name was written variously, Gumelton or Gombeldon, by both the English and Irish houses. An ancestor of the latter, William Gomeldon, Esq., is mentioned in a bill filed in the Irish Court of Chancery, against Randal, Marquess of Antrim, bearing date 7 April, 1675. The immediate progenitor of the existing family,

Richard Gumbleton, Esq., son and heir of Richard Gumbleton, Esq. of Ballygarron, co. Waterford, served as high-sheriff of the county of Waterford in 1732. By his wife, a dau. of Drew, of Bishopstown, he left a dau., Anne, m. to Robert Daunt, Esq., and a son and successor,

Richard Gumbleton, Esq. of Ballygarron, otherwise Castle Richard, who m. Elizabeth, dau. of Daniel Conner, Esq. of Bandon, and sister of William Conner, Esq. of Connerville, co. Cork, and had issue,

I. Richard, of Castle Richard, who m. the dau. of Hamilton O'Hara, Esq., and left issue,
  1 Richard-Edward, of Castle Richard, (called by him "Glencairn Abbey,") who d. s. p. in 1819, having devised his seat, beautifully situated on the Blackwater, to his brother-in-law, Mr. Bushe.
  1 Lavinia, m. to Henry-Amyas Bushe, Esq.
  2 Rebecca, m. to Admiral Sir Tristram Ricketts, K.C.B.
II. William, of Fort William, d. unm.
III. Robert Warren, of whom presently.
IV. George, of Marston, d. s. p.
V. Henry, of Curriglass House, capt. 13th dragoons, m. in 1792, Sarah, dau. of the 2nd Lord Massy, and had issue (with several daus., of whom, Sarah, m. the Rev. G. Gumbleton; and Catherine, m. Dr. Nelligan, of Dublin) two sons, viz.,
  1 Richard, of Marston, near Tallow, m. Miss Moore, and has one dau.
  2 William, of Curriglass, near Tallow, m. Miss Purcell, and had issue.
I. Jane, m. in 1775, to William Daunt, Esq. of Kilcascan.
II. Mary, m. to Richard Peard, Esq. of Coole.
III. Anne, m. to John Rashleigh, Esq. of Ballinadee.
IV. Eliza, m. to R. Walton, Esq. of Waltoncourt.
V. Sarah, m. to M. Cramer, Esq. of Rathmore.
VI. Catherine, d. unm.

The 3rd son,

Robert-Warren Gumbleton, Esq. of Castleview, m. Margaret, dau. of John Bowen, Esq. of Oakgrave, and had issue,

I. Richard, now of Castleview.
II. John-Bowen, of Fort William, near Lismore, high-

sheriff in 1845, of the co. of Waterford, barrister-at-law, *b.* in June, 1795, *m.* 6 Jan. 1830, Ann, eldest dau. and co-heir of Henry Everard, Esq. of Spalding, co. Lincoln, and has issue,

1 Robert, *b.* 2 April, 1833, *d. unm.* 1855.
2 John-Henry, *b.* 9 March, 1841.
3 Henry-Everard, *d.* young. 4 Richard, *d.* in infancy.
1 Margaret. 2 Ann. 3 Meliora.
4 Frances. 5 Mary, *d.* in infancy.

III. George, in holy orders, of Belgrove, near Cove, *m.* 1st, his cousin Sarah, dau. of Capt. Henry Gumbleton; and 2ndly, Miss Penrose, of Woodhill: by the latter of whom he has two sons, William-Edward and George.
I. Margaret, *m.* to Capt. Richard-Gumbleton Daunt.
II. Eliza, *m.* to Benjamin Hutchins, Esq.
III. Jane, second wife of Joseph Daunt, Esq. of Kilcascan.
IV. Mary-Anne, wife of William Percy, Esq.
V. Lavinia, *m.* to Charles Colthurst, Esq. of Clonmoyle.
VI. Diana, *m.* to Richard Garde, Esq.

The eldest son,

RICHARD GUMBLETON, Esq. of Castleview, *m.* 1823, Annie, dau of — Fowke, Esq of Tewkesbury, co. Gloucester, and left surviving issue, an only son, the present RICHARD-JOHN-MAXWELL GUMBLETON, Esq. of Glynnatore.

Arms—Or, on a fesse, wavy, gu., three mullets, of the field, on a canton, az., a fleur-de-lis, gold.

Crest—A demi-griffin, with wings endorsed, arg., beaked and legged, gu., holding a mullet, or.

Motto—Memento mori.

Seat—Glynnatore or Castle View, near Tallow.

GUN OF RATTOO.

GUN, WILSON, Esq. of Rattoo, co. Kerry. J.P., *b.* 26 May, 1809; *m.* May, 1839, Gertrude-Marianne, 2nd dau. of the late Henry-E. Allen, Esq. of Bathampton, near Bath, and has two sons,

I. TOWNSEND-GEORGE, *b.* 23 May, 1840.
II. Henry-Allen, *b.* 22 April, 1842.
I. Emma-Frances.

Lineage.—The Guns were established in Ireland by a Colonel in Queen ELIZABETH's army, who went to that country from Caithness, N.B., during the early part of that monarch's reign, and got large grants of lands, the greater part of which remain still in the possession of the family.

WILLIAM GUN, Esq. of Lislahane Castle, A.D 1641, as stated in Dr. Charles Smyth's History of Kerry, had two sons,

WILLIAM, of whose line we here treat.
GEORGE, of Carrigafoile Castle, co. Kerry, ancestor of the BALLYBUNION branch, *which see.*

The elder,

WILLIAM GUN, Esq., *m.* in 1694, Catharine, dau. of Richard Townsend, one of the prisoners at Galway in 1689, and had (with three daus., Rebecca, Sarah, and Catherine, and a younger son, Francis), an elder son,

TOWNSEND GUN, Esq., who *m.* Elizabeth, dau. of Conway Blennerhassett, Esq. of Castle Conway, co. Kerry, and by her left, with one dau., Elizabeth, *m.* to Thomas, 1st Lord Ventry, an only son,

WILLIAM-TOWNSEND GUN, Esq. of Rattoo, who *m.* 1st, in 1765, Sarah, eldest dau. of Anthony Stoughton, Esq. of Ballyhorgan, co. Kerry, and had issue,

TOWNSEND, his heir.
Thomas, *d. unm.*
William, *m.* Margaret, second dau. of Sir Thomas M'Kenny, Bart., and left a dau., Sarah.
Elizabeth, *m.* 1st, in 1783, to James-Fuller Hartnet, Esq., and *m.* 2ndly, to Major William Ponsonby, of Crottoo.
Sarah, *m.* to Samuel Morris, Esq. of Ballybeggan, co. Kerry.
Frances, *m.* to Thomas Colles.
Penelope, *m.* to the Rev. James Mahon, and *d.* leaving Anthony and William.
Catherine, *m.* to the Rev. Stephen Dunlevie.

Mr. Townsend *m.* 2ndly, Eliza Kane, and by her had issue, John, George, Cherry, and Charlotte. He *d.* in 1812, and was *s.* by his son,

TOWNSEND GUN, Esq. of Rattoo, *m.* in 1803, Amelia, eldest dau. of William Wilson, Esq., and by her (who *d.* 1849) had issue,

William-Townsend, *b.* in 1808, *d. unm.* in 1837.
WILSON, of Rattoo, present representative.
Catherine, *m.* to Capt. Whitworth Lloyd, R.N.
Sarah, *m.* to Augustus Warren, Esq.

Jane, *m.* to the Rev. Edward-M. Denny, rector of Listowel.
Elizabeth, *m.* to Capt. William-Thomas Harison.

Mr. Gun *d.* 1817.

Arms—Arg., three cannon-barrels, fessways, ppr.

Crest—An open dexter hand and wrist, erect.

Motto—Vincit amor patriæ.

Seat—Rattoo, co. Kerry.

GUN OF BALLYBUNION.

GUN, GEORGE, Esq. of Ballybunion, and Plover Hill, co. Kerry, J.P., *b.* 21 Oct. 1809; *m.* 4 Sept. 1833, Belinda, dau. and co-heiress of John-Boles Reeves, Esq. of Belfort, co. Cork.

Lineage.—GEORGE GUN, Esq. of Carrigafoile Castle, co. Kerry, younger son of William Gun, Esq. of Lislahane Castle, *m.* Sarah, dau. of the Rev. Thomas Connor, Archdeacon of Ardfert, and had issue,

I. William, barrister-at-law, *m.* Eliza, dau. of William Dobson, Esq., (Six Clerk,) and co-heiress, with Dorothy, wife of Shapland Carew, Esq., and Ellen, wife of the Rev. Edward Moore. By this lady he had issue,

1 William, who *m.* Mrs. Colles, and by her (who *m.* 3rdly, Cam.-Richard Frankland) had a son, George Gun, Esq. of Newton, Mount Kennedy, co. Wicklow, who *m.* Jane Gordon, niece to General Cunningham, whose property he inherited, and assumed the additional surname of Cunningham. He was *s.* by his only son, GEORGE GUN CUNNINGHAM, Esq.
1 Sarah, *m.* in 1771, to Joshua Paul, Esq., created a baronet in 1794.

II. Richard. III. John.
IV. GEORGE, of whom we treat. V. Henry.
I. Elizabeth, *m.* to Richard Morris, Esq.
II. Honora, *m.* in 1746, to James Raymond, Esq.
III. Sarah, *m.* in 1734, to Arthur Blennerhasset, Esq.

The 4th son,

GEORGE GUN, Esq., *m.* 1st in 1747, Elizabeth, dau. of James Raymond, Esq. of Ballyegan, Listowel, and had a son and heir, GEORGE, of whom presently. He *m.* 2ndly, Joice, dau. of Robert Leslie, Esq. of Tarbert House, and by her had a son, John-Leslie, who *d. unm.* The son and heir,

GEORGE GUN, Esq. of Ballybunion, *m.* in 1774, Arabella, dau. of the Rev. Barry Denny, of Ballyvelly, Tralee, and sister of Sir Barry Denny, Bart., and by her had, with two daus., viz., Jane-Joice, *m.* 1st, in 1812, to Capt. Robert Cashell, and 2ndly, to William Hikemann, Esq.; and Arabella, *m.* to John Watts, Esq., an only son,

BARRY-WILLIAM GUN, Esq. of Plover Hill, who *m.* 5 Sept. 1807, Jane, 2nd dau of William Wilson, Esq., sister-in-law to Townsend Gun, Esq. of Rattoo, and left at his decease, 25 Aug. 1828, an only child, the present GEORGE GUN, Esq. of Ballybunion and Plover Hill.

Arms, Crest, and *Motto*—As GUN *of Rattoo.*

Seats—Ballybunion, Listowel, and Plover Hill, Tralee.

GURDON OF ASSINGTON HALL.

GURDON, JOHN, Esq. of Assington Hall, co. Suffolk, J.P., *b.* 17 Aug. 1791; *m.* 1st, 1 July, 1823, Bridget-Anna, dau. of Multon Lambarde, Esq. of Sevenoaks, and by her (who *d.* 1 June, 1826,) had a son,

JOHN-BARRETT, *b.* 15 April, 1825.

He *m.* 2ndly, 3 Jan. 1823, Anne, dau. of Colonel C.-P. Leslie, of Glasslough, co. Monaghan, M.P., and by her has, Bertrand, *b.* 3 Dec. 1829, and Philip, *b.* 11 July, 1835.

Lineage.—This family came into England with the CONQUEROR, from Gourdon, near Cahors, on the borders of Perigord, and the name is on the roll of Battell Abbey.

SIR ADAM DE GURDON, Knt., living in the time of HENRY III., was in that Monarch's reign bailiff of Alton, but was outlawed for treason and rebellion, as one of the Montford faction. He was restored, however, upon the accession of EDWARD, and constituted, in 1272, keeper of the forest of Wolmer. He *m.* 1st, Constantia, dau. and heiress of Thomas Makarel, of Selborne, co. Southampton. He resided in that shire, in a mansion-house called The Temple, which overlooked the forest. Sir Adam *m.* a 2nd wife, named Almeria, from whom he was divorced, after having had two sons, the elder of whom was seated in Wiltshire, and the younger settled himself in London. These 1 3 2 1 appear, however, to have been disinherited, for their father had a 3rd wife, Agnes, and by her a dau., JOHANNA, to whom he left his property in Selborne. This lady *m.* Richard Achard, and that estate, bearing still the name of Gurdon Manor, belongs now to Magdalen College, Oxford. The armorial ensigns of Sir Adam Gurdon are those still borne by the family of which we are treating. Sir Adam's 2nd son, (of the elder there is no further account,)

ROBERT GURDON, took up his abode in London. He *d.* in 1343, and was *s.* by his son,

JOHN GURDON, a merchant in London, who *d.* in 1385, leaving a son,

THOMAS GURDON, of Clyne, in Kent, who *d.* in 1436, and was father of

JOHN GURDON, of Clyne, who was *s.* in 1465, by his son,

JOHN GURDON, of Dedham, in Essex, who *d.* in 1487, leaving a son,

JOHN GURDON, of Dedham, father of

JOHN GURDON, of Dedham, who *m.* 1st, Mary, dau. of John Butter, Esq. of Dedham, but had no issue. He *m.* 2ndly, Anne, dau. of John Coleman, Esq. of Lynes Hall, in Suffolk, and left a son,

ROBERT GURDON, Esq., who *m.* Rose, dau. and heiress of Robert Sexton, Esq. of Lavenham, in Suffolk. This gentleman purchased Assington Hall from Sir Miles Corbet. He served the office of sheriff for the co. Suffolk, and dying in 1577, was *s.* by his son,

JOHN GURDON, Esq., who *m.* Amy, dau. and heiress of William Brampton, Esq. of Letton, in Norfolk. This gentleman was sheriff of Suffolk in 1585. He *d.* in 1623, and was *s.* by his son,

BRAMPTON GURDON, Esq. of Assington Hall and of Letton, high-sheriff for Suffolk in 1625, and M.P. for Sudbury. He *m.* 1st, Elizabeth, dau. of Edward Barrett, Esq. of Bellhouse, in Essex; and 2ndly, Muriel, dau. of Sir Martyn Sedley, of Morley, in Norfolk, by a dau. of John Knyvett, of Ashwellthorp, and had issue by both. Brampton Gurdon *d.* in 1649, and was *s.* at Assington by his eldest son,

JOHN GURDON, Esq. of Assington Hall, who represented the co. Suffolk in the Long Parliament, and was one of the committee appointed to sit in judgment upon King CHARLES I., but did not attend the trial. He *m.* Anne, dau. of Sir Calthorpe Parker, of Erwarton, and dying 9 Sept. 1679, aged 84, left, with other issue, a son,

THE REV. NATHANIEL GURDON, D.D., rector of Chelmsford, Essex, who inherited Assington at the decease of his elder brother, Philip Gurdon, Esq., M.P. for Sudbury. He *m.* Elizabeth, dau. of the Rev. Emanuel Arundell, of Stoke, co. Northampton, and *d.* 2 Feb. 1695-6, aged 64, leaving (with four daus., Anne, *m.* to Sir John Comyns, Chief Baron of the Exchequer; Elizabeth, *m.* to the Rev. William Woodroffe, B.D.; Amy; and Judith, *m.* to Richard Comyns, Esq.) a son and successor,

JOHN GURDON, Esq. of Assington, M.P. for Sudbury, who *m.* Letitia, dau. and co-heir of Sir William Cooke, Bart. of Brome, and by her, who *d.* 7 Feb. 1710, aged 37, had issue. John Gurden *d.* in 1758, aged 86. His 2nd son,

THE REV. PHILIP GURDON, vicar of Bures, *m.* Elizabeth, dau. of Herbert Pelham, Esq. of Bures, and left (with two daus., Elizabeth, *d. unm.* in 1814, aged 73; and Jemima, *m.* to the Rev. Charles Ray, vicar of Hoxne) a son,

THE REV. PHILIP GURDON, of Assington, who *m.* 1778, Sarah Richardson, and by her, who *d.* 3 Sept. 1822, aged 69, had issue,

- Brampton-Philip, 6th dragoon guards, *b.* 1779, *d.* at Coote Hill, co. Cavan, 22 Feb. 1804, aged 23.
- JOHN, now of Assington.
- Anna-Maria, *d.* in 1792, aged 13.
- Letitia, *d. unm.* in 1801.
- Jemima.
- Elizabeth, *m.* 1811, to the Rev. Joseph-Adam Stephenson, rector of Limpsham, co. Somerset.

Mr. Gurdon *d.* 7 May, 1817, aged 71.

Arms—Sa., three leopards' faces, jessant de lis, or.
Crest—A goat climbing a rock, with a sprig issuing from the top, ppr.
Motto—Virtus viget in arduis.
Seat—Assington Hall, co. Suffolk.

GURDON OF LETTON.

GURDON, BRAMPTON, Esq. of Letton, in Norfolk, and of Grundisburgh, co. Suffolk, J.P. and D.L., high-sheriff of Norfolk, 1855, *b.* 25 Sept. 1797; *m.* 12 Aug. 1828, the Hon. Henrietta-Susannah Ridley-Colborne, eldest dau. of Nicholas, Lord Colborne, and has issue,

- I. ROBERT-THORNHAGH, *b.* 18 June, 1829.
- II. William-Brampton, *b.* Sept. 1840.
- I. Charlotte. II. Amy-Louisa.

Lineage.—BRAMPTON GURDON, Esq., barrister-at-law, and representative in parliament for the borough of Ipswich from 1640 to 1654, son of Brampton Gurdon, Esq. of Assington Hall and Letton, high-sheriff for Suffolk in 1625, by Muriel Sedley, his 2nd wife, was colonel of a regiment of horse during the civil war; and at the siege of Colchester he was one of the court-martial on Sir Charles Lucas and Sir George Lisle. He *m.* Mary, dau. of Henry Polstead, of London, and dying in 1669, was *s.* by his son,

BRAMPTON GURDON, Esq. of Letton, who *m.* Elizabeth, dau. of Colonel Thornhagh, of Fenton, Nottinghamshire, son of Sir Francis Thornhagh, and was *s.* at his decease, in 1691, by his son,

THORNHAGH GURDON, Esq. of Letton, receiver-general of the co. Norfolk, in the reign of Queen ANNE, and author of an esteemed work upon the Origin and Rights of Parliament. He *m.* Elizabeth, dau. and co-heiress of Sir William Cooke, Bart. of Brome Hall, Norfolk, M.P. for that county, and left at his decease, in 1713, one son and three daus. Two of the latter *d. unm.*; the other, Letitia, *m.* the Rev. Nathaniel Saltier, of Ashdon, in Essex. The son,

THORNHAGH GURDON, Esq. of Letton, *m.* Sarah, dau. and heir of Theophilus Dillingham, Esq. of Shelton, Beds, and and was *s.*, in 1783, by his son,

BRAMPTON GURDON, Esq. of Letton, Norfolk, and of Grundisburgh, co. Suffolk, who took the surname of DILLINGHAM. He *m.* 1st, Mary, dau. of Philip Bedingfeld, Esq. of Ditchingham, and had

- THEOPHILUS-THORNHAGH, his heir.
- Thornhagh-Philip, *d.* in Nov. 1833.
- Philip-Brampton, capt. 58th foot, fell in action 1795.

He *m.* 2ndly, Mary, dau. and co-heiress of Samuel Howard, Esq. and had an only dau.,

- Mary, *m.* to William Frere, serjeant-at-law, and master of Downing College, Cambridge, who *d.* in May, 1836.

Mr. Gurdon Dillingham served the office of sheriff of Norfolk in 1789, and dying in 1820, was *s.* by his son,

THEOPHILUS-THORNHAGH GURDON, Esq. of Letton, co. Norfolk and Grundisburgh, co. Suffolk, lieut.-colonel West Norfolk Militia, J.P. and D.L., high-sheriff, 1824; *b.* 24 Aug. 1764; *m.* 25 July 1796, Anne, dau. of William Mellish, Esq., M.P., of Blyth, in Nottinghamshire, and had issue,

- BRAMPTON, now of Letton.
- John, *b.* 1799, *m.* 1st, 1835, Mary-Martin Slater, (who *d.* 17th Sept. 1842,) widow of Sir Thomas Ormsby, Bart., and dau. and heir of General Francis Rebow, and assumed, in consequence, the name and arms of REBOW; and 2ndly, Lady Georgiana Toler, dau. of the Earl of Norbury.
- Philip, in holy orders, rector of Cranworth-cum-Letton, in Norfolk, *b.* 1800; *m.* July, 1832, Henrietta-Laura, dau. of John Pulteney, Esq. of Northerwood, in Hampshire, and has two sons and seven daus.
- William, of Brantham, Suffolk, *b.* 1804, recorder of Bury, and judge of the county court in Essex.
- Edward, in holy orders, rector of Barnham Broom and Kimberly, *m.* 1st, Oct. 1846, Frederica, dau. of W. Frere, Esq., master of Downing College, Cambridge; and 2ndly, Catherine, eldest dau. of the Rev. Temple Frere, rector of Roydon, and has two sons.
- Anne, *m.* in 1825, the Hon. Henry Wodehouse, and was mother of the present Lord Wodehouse.

Colonel Gurdon *d.* March, 1849; his widow, 23 Dec. 1850.

Arms—Sa., three leopards' faces, jessant fleurs-de-lis, or, for GURDON; quartering, SEXTON, BRAMPTON, COOKE, STUART, and DILLINGHAM.
Crest—A goat climbing up a rock, all ppr.
Motto—In arduis viget virtus.
Seats—Letton, Norfolk; and Grundisburgh, Suffolk.

GURNEY OF KESWICK.

GURNEY, HUDSON, Esq. of Keswick, co. Norfolk, F.R. and A.S., *b.* 19 Jan. 1775; *m.* in 1809, Margaret, dau. of the late Robert Barclay, Esq. of Ury, Kincardineshire, M.P. for that county, by Sarah his wife, dau. of James Allardice, of Allardice, and heiress of line to the Earls of Airth and Menteith. Mr. Gurney was elected M.P. for Shaftesbury in 1812, and for Newtown, Hants, in 1816, and six successive parliaments, and was high-sheriff of Norfolk in 1835. Mrs. Gurney *d.* 16 Dec. 1855.

Lineage.—The name of Gurney, or Gournay, is derived from the town of Gournay, in Normandy.

When Normandy was ceded to Rollo by CHARLES the Simple, in 912, it is stated by the local historians that the town of Gournay, and adjacent territory of Le Brai, was given to EUDES one of his followers, from whom descended the ancient lords of Gournay. The first of these, authenticated by deed, was REGINALD, LORD OF GOURNAY, whose son, WALTER, founded the monastery of La Ferté, about the year 996, with the consent of HUGH, his elder brother. Another Hugh, called HUGH II., was one of the Norman generals at the battle of Mortemer, in 1054; he and HUGH III. were at the battle of Hastings. This latter *m.* Basilia Flaitel, and from him the descents of this family are clear; she was dau. of Gerard Flaitel, and sister (with Agnes, wife of William Giffard, Earl of Buckingham) of William, bishop of Evreux. HUGH DE GOURNAY III., held manors in Essex at the time of the survey, and *d.* at the Abbey of Bec, in Normandy, where he was shorn a monk before the year 1093.

GERARD DE GOURNAY, was his son; he *m.* Editha, dau. of William 1st Earl Warren, by Gundreda, who, according to the Warren charters, was a dau. of William the Conqueror. With her he received in frank marriage various manors. He held in Norfolk, Caistor-by-the-sea, Cantley, Hardingham, Lessingham, Kimberley, &c., from the forfeiture of Ralph Guader. Caistor was the caput baronise of the Gournays in England. Gerard de Gournay had several children, Hugh de Gournay IV. was eldest son; Walter de Gournay a younger son; and his daus. were Gundrida, who *m.* Nigel de Albini, in 1118, and a 2nd dau. *m.* Richard de Talbot, ancestor of the Earl of Shrewsbury. Gerard de Gournay *d.* about the year 1104, in the Holy Land, and Editha his widow remarried Dreux de Monceaux.

HUGH DE GOURNAY IV. was eldest son of Gerard; he *m.* twice, 1st, Beatrice, dau. of Hugh, Count of Vermandois, and 2ndly, Millicent de Maria, dau. of Thomas, Lord of Coucy; he *d.* in 1180, at a great age, leaving by his 2nd wife, Hugh de Gournay V., and a dau. Gunnora, who *m.* Nicholas de Stuteville, and had with her Kimberley and Bedingham, in Norfolk.

HUGH DE GOURNAY V., vacillated between King JOHN and Philip Augustus, and eventually lost all his Norman possessions in 1204, and took refuge in England, where he *d.* in 1214, and was buried at Langley Abbey, Norfolk. He *m.* Julia de Dampmartin, sister of Reginald, Count of Boulogne, and had a son, Hugh VI., and a dau. Milicent, *m.* 1st, to Almeric, Count of Evreux, and 2ndly, to William de Cantelupe.

HUGH DE GOURNAY VI., *d.* in 1235, having *m.* Matilda —, and left an only dau., Julia, who carried the English inheritance of this elder line of the Gournays to the Bardolfs, she having *m.* William, Lord Bardolf, of Wormegay, in Norfolk, and *d.* in 1295. These Lords of Gournay are said to have borne for arms a shield, pure sable; they are now represented, in the female line, by Lord Beaumont, through the families of Bardolf, Phelip, Beaumont, Lovel, and Stapleton.

Two younger branches of this family continued to exist from this period; the one which was the most distinguished was seated at Barew-Gurney and Inglishcombe, in Somersetshire, as early as the Survey, and retaining the name of Gournay, through two female descents, added to their territory the estates of the Harpetrees and other considerable families, and became powerful barons in the west of England. The most generally known of this family of the Gournays was Sir Thomas de Gournay, one of the murderers of EDWARD II., and his youngest son, Sir Matthew de Gournay, frequently mentioned by Froissart, who *d.* in 1406, at the advanced age of 96, after having assisted at all the great battles of EDWARD III. and the Black Prince. This gallant veteran appears to have been the last of the Somersetshire Gurneys; they bore for arms paly of six, or, and azure.

The other younger branch of the Lords of Gournay held certain manors in Norfolk as mesne lords under the Barons of Gournay, the capital tenants. These were—Runhall, Swathings-in-Hardingham, Hingham-Gurneys, and others. They also held the fief of Montigny-sur-Andelis, in Normandy, parcel of the great territory of Le Brai, which belonged to the elder line. This fief of Montigny they held by the tenure called parage, in capite of the Duke of Normandy, it having been severed in their favour on the death of Gerard de Gournay.

WALTER DE GOURNAY, younger son of Gerard and Editha de Warren, was the ancestor of this line; he lived during the civil wars in the reign of Stephen. (See *Liber Niger Scaccarii*, by Hearne. Vol. I., p. 298.)

WILLIAM DE GOURNAY I., was his son, living 1167, and was father to

MATTHEW DE GOURNAY, to whom Hameline Plantagenet, Earl Warren, gave in marriage his kinswoman, Rose de Burnham, and with her the manor of Harpley, in Norfolk, about the year 1180.

WILLIAM DE GOURNAY II., was his son and heir, living in 1235. By Katherine his wife, he was father of,

SIR JOHN DE GOURNAY, Knt., I., who fought on the side of the barons against HENRY III. at the battles of Lewes and Evesham, and forfeited the manor of South Wootton, in Norfolk, in consequence. He accompanied Prince Edward, afterwards EDWARD I., to the Holy Land, in 1270. He bore for arms argent, a cross, engrailed, gu., since borne by his descendants.

SIR WILLIAM DE GOURNAY, Knt., III., was his son, who *m.* Katherine, dau. of Edmund Baconsthorpe, and sold for an annuity, in 1294, all his estates to his brother, John de Gournay, rector and patron of Harpley, who settled them on

JOHN DE GOURNAY III., son of William III. and his wife Jane, dau. of Edmund de Lexham, who succeeded in 1332,

JOHN DE GURNEY IV., was his son, and father of

EDMUND DE GURNAY, who lived in the reign of EDWARD III. and RICHARD II. He was a lawyer of eminence, and held the situation of standing council, or recorder as it would now be called, of the city of Norwich and borough of Lynn. He *m.* Katherine de Wauncy, the heiress of the family of that name, of West Barsham, in Norfolk, and where the Gurneys were subsequently settled. He *d.* in 1385.

SIR JOHN DE GURNEY, Knt., V., was his son. He was sheriff of Norfolk and Suffolk in 1400, and knight of the shire for the former county at the parliament which met at Coventry, in 1404. He *d.* in 1408, leaving a son, Edmund, who *d.* under age.

THOMAS GURNAY I., nephew of John de Gurnay, V., and son of Robert, succeeded to the family estates. He *m.* Catharine, dau. of Robert Kerville, of Watlington, in Norfolk, and was father of

THOMAS GURNAY, Esq., II., who *m.* Margaret, dau. of Sir Thomas Jerningham, Knt. of Somerleyton, in Suffolk. His will was dated 1466, and proved 1471. He had a house in St. Gregory's parish, Norwich.

WILLIAM GURNEY, Esq., IV., was his son and heir. He was escheator for Norfolk, and lived at West Barsham and Pockthorpe, a suburb of Norwich. He *m.* Anne, dau. of Sir William Calthorpe, Knt., and *d.* in 1508, having survived his eldest son,

WILLIAM GURNEY V., who *m.* Anne, dau. of Sir Henry Heydon, of Baconsthorpe, Norfolk, Knt., who was cousin of Queen Ann Boleyn; with her he had the manor of Irstead, in Norfolk. She survived him, and remarried Sir Lionel Dymocke, Knt.

ANTHONY GURNEY, Esq., his son, was grandson and heir of William Gurney IV. He lived in the reign of HENRY VIII., and *m.* Margaret, one of the daus. and co-heirs of Sir Robert Lovel, Knt., and through her mother, of the families of Conyers of Finingham, Fitz-Ralf, and of the Barons Mortimer of Attleboro'. He resided chiefly at Great Ellingham, which he had acquired by his marriage, and at Gurney's Place, in St. Julian's parish, Norwich. His 2nd wife was Elizabeth Tyrell. He *d.* in 1556.

FRANCIS GURNEY, Esq., was his only son, born 1521, and *d.* in the lifetime of his father. He *m.* Hellen, dau. of Richard Holditch, Esq. of Ranworth, Norfolk, whose 2nd husband was John Jernegan, Gent.

HENRY GURNAY, Esq., I., was his son, and heir to his grandfather, Anthony Gurney, *b.* 1548, and *d.* in 1614, having *m.* Ellen, dau. of John Blennerhassett, Esq. of Barsham, in Suffolk. He resided chiefly at Great Ellingham, and had seven sons and five daus. Of these, Edmund Gurney, his 3rd son, was rector of Harpley, and author of several theological works. He was puritanically inclined, and took the Covenant. Francis Gurney, was Henry Gurnay's 6th son, and was a merchant, and ancestor of the present family of the GURNEYS *of Keswick*, of whom hereafter.

THOMAS GURNEY, Esq., III. of West Barsham, was eldest son of Henry. He *m.* Martha, dau. of Sir Edward Lewknor, Knt. of Denham, in Suffolk, and *d.* in 1616, leaving a large family, of whom

EDWARD GOURNAY, Esq. of West Barsham, was his eldest son. He *m.* Frances, dau. of Richard Hovell, of Hillington, in Norfolk, Esq., and *d.* in 1641, leaving,

HENRY GURNAY, Esq., II., of West Barsham, his only

son, who m. Ellen, dau. of William Adams, Esq., barrister-at-law, and d. without issue in 1661, when the direct male line of the GURNEYS *of West Barsham* became extinct, and the estates devolved to co-heiresses.

We now come to FRANCIS GURNEY, 6th son of Henry Gurney, of Great Ellingham and West Barsham, and Ellen Blennerhassett his wife. This Francis, was b. 18 Sept. 1581. He was a merchant, and was admitted a member of the Merchant Taylor's Company, in London, in 1606. He resided in the parish of St. Benet Fink, in the city, and occasionally at Norwich and Lynn, in Norfolk. He m. Ann dau. of William Browning, of Norwich, and of Maldon, in Essex, by whom he had several children, of whom, Thomas Gurney, his 3rd son, was a quaker, and the companion of George Fox. He was ancestor of the line of the late Sir John Gurney, baron of the exchequer.

FRANCIS GURNEY, of Maldon, in Essex, was 2nd son of Francis Gurney and Ann Browning, b. in 1628. He was a merchant at that place, and one of the bailiffs of the borough, in 1664. He m. Ann, dau. of Jeremy Browning, of Maldon, and had issue, with other children,

JOHN GOURNEY, or GURNEY, his eldest son, b. in 1655, who joined the Society of Quakers; he established himself as a merchant in Norwich, owing his success mainly to the new branches of commerce introduced into that city by the Protestant Refugees, who settled there after the revocation of the Edict of Nants. He m. 1687, Elisabeth Swanton, and d. in 1721, leaving four sons, John; Joseph; Benjamin; and Edmund.

JOHN GURNEY, of Norwich, was his eldest son. His descendants in the male line became extinct on the death of Bartlett Gurney, Esq. of Coltishall, in Norfolk, in 1802.

JOSEPH GURNEY, 2nd son of John and Elisabeth Swanton, was of Keswick, in Norfolk. He was b. in 1692, and m. in 1713, Hannah Middleton, of the family of Middleton, of Silksworth, in Durham, and Belsay, in Northumberland, and had three sons John. Samuel, and Joseph. He d. in 1760, and was s. by his eldest son,

JOHN GURNEY, Esq. of Keswick, who m. Elizabeth Kett, dau. of Richard Kett, Esq. of the family of the Norfolk Rebel, and d. in 1770, leaving issue,

I. RICHARD, his eldest son, of whom hereafter.
II. John, of Earlham, near Norwich, who d. in 1809, having m. Catharine, dau. of Daniel Bell, merchant in London, and left issue,
  1 John, who m. his cousin, Elizabeth Gurney, and d. s. p. in 1814.
  2 Samuel, of Upton, Essex. He m. Elizabeth, dau. of James Sheppard, Esq., and has issue,
    John Gurney, m. Laura, dau. of Rev. George Pearse, rector of Martham, Norfolk, and has issue.
    Samuel Gurney, of Carshalton, Surrey, m. Ellen, dau. of William Reynolds, Esq.
    Henry-Edmund Gurney, m. Jane, dau. of Henry Birkbeck, Esq., and has issue.
    Sarah.
    Catharine, m. Sir Edward-N. Buxton, Bart.
    Elizabeth, m. Ernest Bunsen, Esq., son of the Chevalier Bunsen.
    Priscilla, m. William Leatham, Esq. of Hemsworth, Yorkshire.
    Rachel, m. T.-Fowell Buxton, Esq.
    Richenda, m. Henry Barclay, Esq.
  3 Joseph-John, of Earlham Hall, near Norwich, having m. 1st, Jane, dau. of John Birkbeck, Esq., by whom he had two children; 2ndly, Mary, dau. of Robert Fowler, Esq.; and 3rdly, Miss Kirkbride, of Philadelphia. He d. in 1847, leaving issue,
    John-Henry Gurney, of Catton, in Norfolk, M.P. for Lynn Regis, m. Mary, only child of his cousin, Richard-Hanbury Gurney, Esq., and has issue two sons.
    Anna, m. John C. Backhouse, Esq., and d. in 1849.
  4 Daniel, of North Runcton, Norfolk, sheriff of Norfolk, 1853, m. 1822, Lady Harriet-Jemima Hay, dau. of William, 15th Earl of Erroll, who d. in 1837, by her he has issue,
    Francis-Hay Gurney, b. 1826, m. 1847, Margaret-Charlotte, dau. of Sir William-Browne Ffolkes, Bart. of Hillington, Norfolk, by Charlotte, sister of Lord Oranmore, and has issue.
    William-Hay Gurney, in holy orders, m. 1852, Anna-Maria, dau. of Sir John-P. Boileau, Bart., by Lady Catherine Eliot, dau. of the 1st Earl of Minto, and has issue.
    Charles-Henry, b. 1833.
    Somerville-Arthur, b. 1835.
    Harriet-Alicia, m. Hon. William Francis Cowper, 2nd son of 5th Earl Cowper, and d. in 1845.
    Catharine-Rachel, m. Rev. Herbert-W. Jones, youngest son of General Sir John-Thomas Jones, Bart. of Cranmer, Norfolk, K.C.B.
    Louisa-Jane, m. 1 Nov. 1855, Colonel Sir Thomas-St. Vincent Troubridge, Bart., C.B, one of Her Majesty's aides-de-camp.
    Margaret-Barclay, m. 5 June, 1856, to James-Henry Orde, Esq., son of Gen. James and Lady Elizabeth Orde.
  1 Catherine Gurney, d. single, in 1858.
  2 Rachel, d. single
  3 Elizabeth, m. Joseph Fry, Esq. This lady is well known for her exertions in the reform of prisons, &c.
  4 Richenda, m. Rev. Francis Cunningham, vicar of Lowestoff, Suffolk.
  5 Hannah, m. Sir Thomas-Fowell Buxton, Bart.
  6 Louisa, m. Samuel Hoare, Esq.
  7 Priscilla, d. single.
III. Joseph, of Lakenham Grove, near Norwich, m. Jane, dau. of Abel Chapman, Esq., and d. in 1830, leaving daus. only.

Mr. Gurney d. in 1779, and was s. by his eldest son,

RICHARD GURNEY, Esq. of Keswick, m. 1st, Agatha, dau. and heiress of David Barclay, Esq. of Youngsbury, Herts, and had by her,

  HUDSON, his heir.
  Agatha, m. to Sampson Hanbury, Esq. of Poles, Herts.

He m. 2ndly, Rachel, dau. of Osgood Hanbury, Esq. of Holfield Grange, Essex, and had other issue,

  Richard-Hanbury Gurney, of Thickthorn, Norfolk, M.P. for Norwich, m. Mary, dau. of William Jary, Esq., and d. in 1853, leaving issue a dau., Mary, m. her cousin, John-Henry Gurney, Esq., M.P. for King's Lynn, and has issue.
  Elizabeth, m. her cousin, John Gurney, Esq., jun., of Earlham, and d. in 1808.
  Anna.

Mr. Gurney d. in 1811, and was s. by his eldest son, the present HUDSON GURNEY, Esq. of Keswick.

Arms—Arg., a cross, engrailed, gu., quartering GOURNAY, WARREN, and BARCLAY.

Crests—1st, on a chapeau, gu., turned up, erm., a fish, in pale, with its head downwards; 2nd, a wrestling collar, or.

Seat—Keswick, near Norwich.

GUTHRIE OF GUTHRIE.

GUTHRIE, JOHN, Esq. of Guthrie, co. Forfar, D.L., b. 23 July, 1805; m. 23 July, 1844, Harriet, dau. of Barnabas Maude, Esq. (*see* MAUDE *of Kendal*), and has issue,

I. JOHN-DOUGLAS-MAUDE, b. 5 March, 1856.
I. Harriet-Maude. II. Edith-Douglas.
III. Mary-Berthia.

Lineage.—The surname of Guthrie, is of great antiquity in Scotland. Crawfurd, in his Lives of the Officers of State, says that the Guthries held the barony of Guthrie by charter from King DAVID II. But that they were men of rank and property long before the reign of JAMES II. is manifest, by the fact that Master Alexander, of Guthrie, is a witness, in a charter granted by Alexander Seaton, Lord of Gordon, to William, Lord Keith, afterwards Earl Marshal, dated 1 Aug. 1442; and that he obtained the lands of Kilkaudrum, in the barony of Lower Leslie, and sheriffdom Forfar, to himself and Marjory Guthrie, his spouse, by charter, from George, Lord Leslie, of Leven, the Superior, dated 10 April, 1457. By the above-mentioned Marjory he had three sons, of whom the eldest,

SIR DAVID GUTHRIE, Baron of Guthrie, was sheriff of Forfar in the year 1457. He held the high situation of armour-bearer to King JAMES III., and was constituted Lord Treasurer of Scotland in 1461, in which post he continued until 1467, when he was appointed Comptroller of the Exchequer. In 1469, he was made Lord Register of Scotland; and in 1472, we find him one of the ambassadors, on the part of Scotland, who met those of England, on the 25th April, in that year, at Newcastle, and concluded a truce till the month of July, 1473. In 1473, he was constituted Lord Chief Justice of Scotland. Sir David Guthrie, m. 1st, a dau. of Sir Thomas Maule, Lord of Panmure, but had no issue. He m. 2ndly, Janet, dau. of Sir Archibald Dundas, of Dundas, by whom he had (with a dau., Elizabeth, m. to Alexander Maule, ancestor of the Earls of Panmure) a son,

SIR ALEXANDER GUTHRIE, of Guthrie, designed, in the lifetime of his father, "of Kincaldrum." He m. the Hon. Margaret Lyon, dau. of John, 3rd Lord Glamis, by Elizabeth, dau. of Sir John Scrimgeour, of Dudhope, Constable of Dundee, and had four sons and a dau. Sir Alexander fell at Flodden (9 Sept. 1513,) with his eldest son, DAVID, his three brothers-in-law, David, William, and George Lyon, and his nephew, Sir Thomas Maule, of Panmure. He was *s.* by his grandson,

ANDREW GUTHRIE, of Guthrie, who *m.* Christian, dau. of Gairden, of Gairden, and had a son,

ALEXANDER GUTHRIE, of Guthrie, one of the subscribing barons to the articles agreed upon in the general assembly of the Kirk, in July, 1567, and also one of those to the bond or association for supporting the king and his government, after Queen MARY's resignation. He was assassinated at his house of Inverpeffer, where he was residing, by his cousin, Patrick Gairden, of Gairden, in consequence of a feud that had arisen between the two families. He had *m.* Isabel, dau. of William Wood, of Bonnytown, and left three sons, viz.,

ALEXANDER, his heir.
WILLIAM, of Gagie, who *m.* his cousin, Isabella, dau. of John Leslie, younger, of Balquhan, and dying in 1632, was father of FRANCIS GUTHRIE, of whom presently, as successor of GUTHRIE.
Gabriel, provost of the collegiate church of Guthrie.

The eldest son,

ALEXANDER GUTHRIE, of Guthrie, *s.* his father. He *m.* in 1568, Agnes, dau. of Sir Alexander Falconer, of Halkerton (great-grandfather of Alexander, 1st Lord Halkerton), by Elizabeth, his wife, dau. of Sir Archibald Douglas, of Glenbervie, and was *s.* by his eldest son,

ALEXANDER GUTHRIE, of Guthrie, who *m.* Jean, dau. of Leighton, of Ulishaven, but having no issue male, he was *s.* at his decease by his brother,

WILLIAM GUTHRIE, of Memys. This laird, having no male issue, was *s.* by his cousin,

DAVID GUTHRIE, of Guthrie, who, with his son, Alexander, disponed the barony of Guthrie to his brother,

PATRICK GUTHRIE, who became "of GUTHRIE," and was *s.* therein at his decease, by his son,

PETER GUTHRIE, whose retour bears date 24 May, 1636. This proprietor disponed the lands and barony to the Right Rev. John Guthrie, Bishop of Moray, descended from John Guthrie, of Hilltown, 4th son of Sir Alexander, Guthrie and Margaret Lyon, who, having obtained a charter of confirmation under the great seal, dated 28 Nov. 1636, and being infeft therein on the 29th Dec. following, became,

JOHN GUTHRIE, of Guthrie. This learned prelate, Bishop of Moray, *m.* a lady named Nicholas Wood, and had a dau., BERTHIA GUTHRIE, who *m.*

FRANCIS GUTHRIE (of Gagie—refer to William, 2nd son of Alexander Guthrie, of Guthrie, and Isabel Wood), under his contract of marriage he got possession of the lands, and barony of Guthrie. He had a son and heir,

JOHN GUTHRIE, of Guthrie. This laird *m.* in 1680, Cecilia, dau. of Sir John Carnegie, of Balnamoon, by the Lady Ellen Ogilvy his wife, only dau. of James 1st Earl of Airlie, and was *s.* by his son,

JAMES GUTHRIE, of Guthrie, who *m.* in 1704, Margaret, dau. of John Turnbull, of Strickathro, by whom he had (with a dau., *m.* to Rennie, of Cairny, a son and successor,

JOHN GUTHRIE, of Guthrie. This laird *m.* in 1732, Jean, dau. of the Rev. James Hodge, of Bathkimmer, minister of Lonforgan, and had issue,

JOHN, his heir.
Margaret, *m.* to William Alison, merchant in Dundee, and had issue.
Jean, *m.* to John Scrymgeour, Esq., younger son of Tealing, no issue.

The son and successor,

JOHN GUTHRIE, of Guthrie, *m.* 1768, Margaret, dau. of the Rev. Mr. Whyte, of Murrose, and was *s.* by his eldest son,

JOHN GUTHRIE, of Guthrie, Convener, and D.L., co. Forfar, who *m.* 24 June, 1798, Anne, 2nd dau. of William Douglas, Esq. of Brigton, and by her (who *d.* 2 Dec. 1845) had issue,

JOHN, now of Guthrie.
William, late Capt. 42nd Highlanders.
Elizabeth-Jane (deceased), *m.* to Thos. Mylne, Esq. of Mylneford.
Margaret. Anne, deceased. Jane.
Helen-Douglas, *m.* to John De Havilland Utermarck, Esq., H. M. Attorney-General for Guernsey.

Mr. Guthrie *d.* 12 Nov. 1845.

Arms—Quarterly: 1st and 4th, or, a lion, rampant, gu., armed and langued, az.; 2nd and 3rd, az., a garb, or.
Crest—A dexter arm issuing, holding a drawn sword, ppr.
Supporters—Two knights, armed at all points, with batons in their dexter hands, and the vizors of their helmets up, all ppr.
Motto—Above the crest, Sto pro veritate.
Seat—Guthrie Castle, Forfarshire, N.B.

GWINNETT OF WISTASTON.

GWINNETT, WILLIAM-CHUTE, Esq. of Wistaston, co. Hereford, and Penlline Castle, co. Glamorgan; *m.* Charlotte, eldest dau. of the late Henry Unett, Esq. of Marden. This gentleman, (only son of the late Thos.-Chute Hayton, Esq. of Wistaston, by Lucinda, his wife, dau. of Thomas Bayley, Esq. of Hereford, and grandson of Thomas Hayton, Esq., by Mary his wife, dau. and heir of John Price, Esq. of Wistaston, M.P. for Herefordshire, *temp.* Queen ANNE,) assumed, by sign-manual, 13 Nov. 1840, the surname and arms of GWINNETT, in compliance with the will of Miss Emilia Gwinnett of Penlline Castle, co. Glamorgan.

Arms—Az., a chev. between three spear heads, arg., embrued, ppr., within a bordure, or.
Crest—A horse's head, sa., gorged, with a wreath of oak, or, in the mouth a broken spear, in bend sinister, point downwards, embrued, ppr.
Motto—Virtus nobilitat.
Seats—Moreton Court, and Wistaston, co. Hereford; and Penlline Castle, co. Glamorgan.

GWYN OF BARON'S HALL.

GWYN, ANTHONY, Esq. of Baron's Hall, Fakenham, co. Norfolk, *b.* 29 July, 1780; *m.* 1st, 4 April, 1807, Sarah, dau. of John Stedman, Esq. of Pakenham, co. Suffolk, and by her (who *d.* 3 May, 1828) had issue,

I. ANTHONY-WILLIAM, *b.* 12 June, 1816.
II. Hamond-Stedman, *b.* 5 Nov. 1820; *m.* Harriette, dau. of James Crump, Esq., U.S.
I. Frances, *m.* to Henry-Etheridge Blyth, Esq.
II. Sarah, *m.* to Edward Dewing, Esq. of Leiston Hall, co. Suffolk.
III. Anne-Mary, *m.* to Charles Lynch, Esq. of Forest Hill.
IV. Emily, *m.* to George Watson, Esq. of Fakenham.
V. Hester, *m.* to Charles-Bye Colchester, Esq. of Milton Place, London.

He *m.* 2ndly, Mary Mercer, dau. of John Acton, Esq. of Ipswich, Suffolk, and by her has issue,

I. Thomas-Robson, *b.* 11 March, 1837, *d.* Sept. 1854.
II. Tatham, *b.* 12 March, 1839.
III. Anthony, *b.* 20 June, 1848.
I. Minna-Mary. II. Mary-Eliza. III. Anna-Acton.

Lineage.—The family of Gwyn or Gwynne, is of Welsh origin, and in the 15th century possessed considerable property in the Isle of Anglesea, and in the following century, the family intermarried with the ancient house of Bodychen. One of the collateral ancestors of the present Mr. Gwyn, was

DR. THOMAS GWYNNE, chancellor of Landaff, who, in the year 1648, by a deed of feoffment, in trust, gave to Jesus College, Oxford, the appropriate rectory of Holyhead, Isle of Anglesey, that the money arising therefrom should be given as a stipend to two fellows and as many scholars, *especially related to himself*, or at least born in the Isle of Anglesey. That gift was confirmed to the college by Dr. Justinian Lewin, who was promoted to the rank of knighthood by CHARLES II., and had *m.* the niece and heiress of the benefactor. The late

HAMOND GWYNN, Esq. (son of Anthony Gwyn, whose father, Hamond, was 2nd son by Maria his wife, dau. of Anthony Hamond, Esq. of Westacre Hall, of Rice Gwyn, who was grandnephew of Thomas Gwyn, D.D., the collegiate benefactor), *b.* in 1742, *m.* Frances, dau. of John Pigge, Esq., and had issue,

ANTHONY, present representative.
Richard, who *m.* 1st, Elizabeth, dau. of Postle, Esq., and by her has surviving five sons and two daus. He *m.* 2ndly, Elizabeth, dau. of Preston, Esq., and by her has living three sons and one dau.
Charles, *d. unm.* 14 July, 1807.
William, lieut. R.N., who *m.* Mary, dau. of Edward Rudge, Esq., and has issue living five sons and seven daus.
Elizabeth-Anne, who *d.* 9 Feb. 1793 young.

Mr. Gwyn *d.* 9 Aug. 1805, and was *s.* by his eldest son, the present ANTHONY GWYN, Esq. of Baron's Hall.

Arms—Gu., a chev. between three lions, rampant, or.
Crest—A lion, rampant, or.
Seat—Baron's Hall, Fakenham, co. Norfolk.

GWYN OF DYFFRYN.

GWYN, HOWEL, Esq. of Dyffryn, co. Glamorgan, *b.* 24 June, 1806; J.P. for the counties of Brecon, Carmarthen, and Glamorgan, and a deputy-lieut. of the last. He filled the office of high-sheriff for Glamorganshire in 1837-8, and for Carmarthenshire in 1838; *m.* 27 April, 1851, Ellen, only dau. of John Moore, Esq. of Plymouth.

Lineage.—THOMAS GWYN, Esq. of Trecastle, co. Brecon, (elder son, by Gwenllian his wife, dau. and heir of Howell ap Griffith, of Trecastle, of Rydderch ap Rhys ap Philip ap David, of Llwyn Howell, 9th in direct descent from Trahaern ap Einon, Lord of Cwmwd, co. Brecon,) *m.* Elen, dau. of Roger Vaughan, Esq. of Talgarth, in the same county, and was father of HOWEL GWYN, Esq., whose son, by Jennet his wife, dau. of Gwilym Llewelyn, Esq. of Garregfawr, THOMAS GWYN, Esq., who *d.* in 1584, leaving by Margaret his wife, dau. of Edward Games, Esq. of Newton, a son, HOWEL GWYN, Esq., who *m.* Mary, dau. of James Boyle, Esq. of Hay Castle, and was father of EDWARD GWYN, Esq. of Glyntawe, whose 2nd son (by Mary his wife, dau. of the Rev. John Llewelyn),

JOHN GWYN, Esq. of Abercrave, in Glyntawe, *m.* Anne, dau. of Thomas Price, Esq. of Abertreweren, and was father of

JAMES GWYN, Esq. of New Radnor, who *m.* Elizabeth, dau. of John Brewster, Esq. of Burton Court, co. Hereford, and had a son,

WILLIAM GWYN, Esq. of Neath, who *m.* Eliza, only dau. and heiress of Hugh Edwards, Esq. of Llanddoisant, and *d.* in 1749, leaving a son,

JOHN GWYN, Esq. of Neath, who *m.* Priscilla, dau. of Matthew Roach, Esq., and left, in 1780, a son,

WILLIAM GWYN, Esq. of Abercrave, who *m.* 1st, in 1799, Mary-Anne, eldest dau. of Edward Roberts, Esq. of Barnstaple, co. Devon, and by her, who *d.* 11 Jan. 1819, he had, with a dau. (Elizabeth, *m.* in June, 1834, to the Rev. Charles Griffith, of Breconshire, and *d.* 3 Feb. 1837), and a son, Matthew, who *d.* in Nov. 1826, another son, the present HOWEL GWYN, Esq. Mr. Gwyn, *m.* 2ndly, in 1822, and *d.* 5 Aug. 1830.

Arms—Sa., a fesse, or, between two swords, the point of that in chief upwards, the other downwards, both in pale, arg., hilted, of the second.

Crest—A hand, ppr., holding a dagger, erect, arg., hilted, or, thrust through a boar's head, couped, of the second.

Motto—Vim vi repellere licet.

Seats—Abercrave, co. Brecon; and Baglan House, co. Glamorgan.

GWYNNE OF MONACHTY.

GWYNNE, ALBAN-THOMAS-JONES, Esq. of Monachty, co. Cardigan, J.P. and D.L., *b.* in 1784; *m.* in 1808, Mary-Anne, only dau. of the late John Vevers, Esq. of Yorkhill Court, co. Hereford, and had issue,

I. ALBAN-LEWIS, of Dolayron, co. Cardigan, J.P., *b.* 5 April, 1809, late a capt. in the 62nd regt.
II. John, R.N.
III. Edward-Henly-Acton, in holy orders.
IV. William-Cust, M.D.
V. Henry.
VI. Richard.
VII. *Francis-Anthony.*
I. Jane, *m.* to Thomas-Watkin Maddy, Esq. of Hereford.
II. Maria.

Mr. Gwynne (only son of the Rev. Alban-Thomas-Jones Gwynne, of Tyglin, by his 1st wife, Martha Thomas,) had three sisters, Martha Davies, Jane Arden, and Catherine Attwood.

Motto—Conabimur.
Seat—Monachty, co. Cardigan.

GWYNNE OF GLANLERY.

EDWARDES-GWYNNE, HENRY-LEWIS, Esq. of Glanlery, co. Cardigan, J.P. and D.L., capt. half pay 62nd regt., served as high-sheriff of Cardiganshire. Mr. Edwardes-Gwynne is 2nd son of the late David-John Edwardes, Esq. of Rhyd-y-Gors. (*See that family.*)

Seat—Glanlery, co. Cardigan.

GYLL OF WYRARDISBURY.

GYLL, BROOKE-HAMILTON, Esq. of Wyrardisbury House, Bucks, and Yeovany Hall, co. Middlesex, *b.* 16 July, 1795; *m.* 3 May, 1821, Maria-Jane, dau. and co-heir of William Richardson, Esq., Accountant-General to the East India Company, by Elizabeth his wife, widow of Edward, 1st Earl of Winterton. Mrs. Gyll *d.* 21 July following her marriage, aged 27, and was buried at Wyrardisbury.

Lineage.—The name of Gill, says Camden, in his *Britannia*, means valley, and has been variously spelt according to the fluctuations of orthography in different ages. Ellis, in his *Domesday-Book*, shews that a family of this name held lands in Yorkshire antecedent to the Norman invasion. The barony and property of Gille's land, in Cumberland, prior to the Conquest, belonged to Bueth Gille, and was confiscated by WILLIAM the Conqueror, who granted them to Hubert, one of his followers. Hubert assumed the name of the original proprietor, and styled himself De Vaux, which is the French for valley, and is synonymous with Gill. Robert De Vaux, son of Hubert, barbarously murdered Bueth Gille, and his posterity resided on the territory till it passed by marriage to the family of Thomas de Multon. In the reign of HENRY III. it was conveyed to Ranulphus de Dacre, and the possessions remained in his family till the last heir male, Lord Dacre, of Gille's land, alienated it to the Duke of Norfolk. It is probable that the John Gille, whose inquis. post mortem was taken 44 EDW. III., at Greigstock, in Cumberland, was the descendant of Bueth Gille, who held the Barony of Gille's land. He left issue, John Gille, son and heir,

The immediate ancestors of the family of Gyll, or Gille, of Herts, resided in Cambridgeshire, where we find Richard, son of John Gille, holding lands under Robert de Freville, of Shelford Parva, Cambridgeshire, *temp.* EDW. I., and Walter and Bateman Gille, of Foxton, near Royston, Cambridge, at the same time. (v. Rol. Hundredorum, *temp.* EDW. I.)

RICHARD GYLLE, of Cambridgeshire, is cited in a deed of fine, Hilary, 1 RICHARD III., 1483, Westminster.

JOHN GYLL, the son of Richard, having married a lady of Buckland, migrated thither, and bought lands, messuages, &c., as appears by deeds, and his will, 1499. Members of the same family are found in Maurice Gyll, who died vicar of Shudy Camps, Cambridge, 1448; and Isabella Gyll, of Shepreth, in the same county, whose will is proved at Ely, 1485, by which she leaves to her dau. and heir, Rose, *m.* to John Marshall, Esq., all her property.

JOHN GYLL, of Buckland, *m.* Johanna, probably dau. of William Horne, Esq. of the same locality, as he says he obtained the lands he held there from him, and dying 23 Jan. 1499 (his will was proved 8 Feb. following).

RICHARD, of Buckland, his heir.
William, who left issue a son, John, cited in the will of his grandfather, John.
Andrew, had issue, two daus.
Margaret, *m.* to Thomas Veruesley, Esq. of Buckland, and had five children.
Agnes, four daus.

The eldest son,

RICHARD GYLL, of Buckland, buys lands there by deed, Hilary, 5 HENRY VII. He *d.*, and was buried at Buckland, his wife, Elizabeth, administering to his effects, 5 July, 1535. He left issue,

JOHN, of Wyddial, his heir.
Richard, of Buckland, who *d.* in 1546, and left issue, 1 John, son and heir, (who had, *inter alios*, a dau., Elizabeth, *m.* to Robert Randes, Esq. of Truswell, co. Northampton,) and two daus., 1, Margaret; and 2, Anne, cited in the will of their uncle, Leonard Gyll.
Leonard Priest, of Jesus College, Cambridge. Will proved there 14 July, 1547. Buried at St. Edward's, Cambridge.
A dau., *m.* to William Cartwright, Esq. of Buckland; and two other children.

The eldest son,

JOHN GYLL, of Wyddial, Herts, held a patent place in the Petty-bag office. He *m.* Margaret dau. and heir of George Canon, Esq. of Wyddial Hall, which he had purchased by deed, 15 HENRY VIII., Com. Plea office, and *s.* to all the estates of his father-in-law, by will proved 20 Oct. 1534. In addition to the property of George Canon, he made very large purchases in the counties of Herts, Essex, and Cambridgeshire; obtained the advowson of Wyddial, by deed 36 HENRY VIII., where he was interred,

His will was proved, 25 Jan. 1547, and the inquisitio post mortem taken 15 March, 2 EDWARD VI. He left by his wife, Margaret (who remarried, in 1547, with John Wrengham, Esq. of Hodenhoe, co. Herts), with seven daus., five sons, GEORGE; Anthony; Richard, of Bottisham, co. Cambridge, d. in 1573, leaving a dau. and heir, m. to Michael Pigot of Stratton, Beds; Francis of Haydon, Essex, m. in 1560, Marcia, dau. and co-heir of Robert Aspland, of the same place, and d. in 1595, leaving issue; and Michael, of whom presently. The eldest son,

GEORGE GYLL, of Wyddial, also held the patent place in the Petty-bag office; and made large purchases of lands, &c. in the county of Herts. He m. 1st, Gertrude, dau. and co-heir of Sir John Peryent, Knt. of Digswell, Herts, auditor of the Court of Wards and Liveries, by Elizabeth, his wife, dau. and heir of Sir John Tendering, Knt. of Badow, Essex, and had by her,

I. JOHN, of Wyddial, high-sheriff of Herts in 1575, d. 22 Oct. 1600, leaving, by Joan his wife, two sons and three daus., viz.,

1 GEORGE, (Sir,) of Wyddial, knighted at Whitehall, 23 July, 1603. He was an officer in the army, and accompanied Robert, Earl of Essex, in his expedition to Cadiz. Sir George d. 17 Nov. 1619, leaving, by Alice, his wife, who d. in 1627, dau. of Thomas, son of Sir Thomas Essex, Knt. of Lambourne, Berks, one dau., Frances, m. to Nathaniel Styles, Esq. of Walton, and two sons, JOHN, who sold Buckland and Wyddial, and George, of Littlecourt, Buntingford, who m. in 1652, Helena Baldwin, and had a son, George, b. in 1653, and a dau., Frances, b. in 1654.

2 JOHN, (Sir,) knighted 24 Nov. 1618, M.P. for Minehead in 1625, m. Joane, dau. of Hugh Trevilian, of Yarnescombe, Devon, but d. s. p. in 1650.

1 Ursula, m. in 1586, to Henry Sadleir, Esq. of Everley, co. Wilts, 3rd son of Sir Ralph Sadleir, Knt. of Standon, Herts.

2 Cordelia, m. 1st, in 1594, to Sir Thomas Harris, Knt. of Maldon, Essex, serjeant-at-law; and 2ndly, in 1622, to Capt. Robert Bacon, of Hesset, co. Suffolk.

3 Mary-Magdalene, m. 1st, in 1597, to John Dorrington, Esq. of Spaldwick; and 2ndly, to Sir — Hyde, Knt.

II. Thomas, of Chancery Lane, London. Will proved, 4 March, 1611, d. s. p.

III. Edward, of Littlecourt, Laystone, Herts, m. 1st, in 1574, Margaret Brograve, of Beckenham, and by her had a son, Edward. He m. 2ndly, 23 Sept. 1607, Lady Barbara Fludd, widow of Sir Thomas Fludd, Knt. of Milgate, and dau. of Matthew Bradbury, Esq. of Wicken, Essex. He d. in 1616, and was s. by his son,

EDWARD GYLL, Esq. of Anstey, who m. in 1604, Mary, dau of Edward Michell, Esq. of Standon, and widow of Richard Smartfoote, Esq. of Puckeridge, and d. in 1642, leaving (with two daus., Barbara, m. to Thomas Cutler, Esq. of Anstey, and Susanna, m. to John Allen, Esq. of Witham) three sons, Edward; George, of Anstey, who left issue; and John, of Braughing, Herts, who d. in 1693, leaving a son, John Gill, of Bishop Stortford, who d. in 1711, leaving a son, William, and other issue.

I. Frances, m. to Sir Marmaduke Grymstone, Knt. of Grymstone Garth, co. York.

II. Catherine, m. in 1570, to William Hyde, Esq. of South Denchworth, Berks.

George Gyll, of Wyddial, by Anne, his 2nd wife, had issue.

I. George, of Buntingford, m., and left, with other issue, Bridget, m. to William Sterne, Esq. of Barkway; and Christiana, m. to Abdias Tuer, rector of Sawbridgeworth, Herts, and d. in 1626. From this marriage maternally derived WILLIAM COLE, the antiquary.

II. Robert, of Eltham, whose dau., Sylvester, m. in 1610, Thomas Raymond, of Dunmow, Essex.

III. Henry, m Elizabeth, second dau. of Sir Philip Boteler, Knt. of Woodhall, Herts, and d. s. p.

IV. Charles, living in 1568.

I. Ann, m. in 1572, to Samuel, son of Clement Newce, Esq. of Hadham.

George Gyll of Wyddial's will was proved 2 Dec. 1568, and his inq. post mortem taken 19 Jan., 11 ELIZABETH. His brother,

MICHAEL GYLL, supposed to have settled in Kent about 1570, left a son,

JOHN GYLL, of Sutton-at-Hone, buried there 6 April, 1624. He was father of

JOHN GYLL of Sutton-at-Hone, who m. there, 14 June, 1611, Ursula, dau. of — Langridge, Esq. of Sutton, and dying in 1616, was s. by his son,

THOMAS GYLL, Esq. of Dartford, who appears in the parochial books as performing several offices in the town. By Alice, his wife, who d. in 1672, he left at his decease, 18 Sept. 1667, a son,

GEORGE GYLL, of Dartford and Boxley, Kent, who m. 25 Feb. 1676, Susanna, dau. of Thomas Cox, Esq. of Dartford, and dying in 1726, left, with other issue, a son and heir,

WILLIAM GYLL, Esq. of Boxley, baptized there 30th Sept. 1686, m. 8. Sept. 1713, Elizabeth, dau. and co-heir of John Lawrence, Esq. of Kent, niece of James Brooke, Esq. of Lewisham, Kent, high-sheriff of the county in 1731, and by her (who d. 23 April, 1750, aged 60) left at his decease 10 August, 1754, aged 68, two daus., Elizabeth, m. 1st, in 1751, to Thomas Baytop, Esq. of Rochester; and 2ndly, to James Kincaid, Esq.; and Anne, m in 1746, to Thomas Wright, son of Edward Wright, Esq. of Aldington, co. Kent, Lord Mayor of London, 1785, two sons, Brooke, who d. s. p. in 1744, and his successor,

WILLIAM GYLL, Esq. of Wyrardisbury House, co. Bucks, and Yeovany Hall, Middlesex, who m. 1st, 4 Oct. 1751, Elizabeth, eldest dau. and co-heir of Robert-Prowse Hassel, Esq. of Wyrardisbury, House, and Croydon, co. Surrey, and by her (who d. 29 June, 1769, aged 39) had issue,

I. Robert-Hutton, b. in 1758, d. s. p. in 1792.

I. Elizabeth, d. unm. 9 June, 1776.

II. Margaret, m. 7 April, 1772, to John Deschamps, Esq. of Ealing, Middlesex, and d. 9 Nov. 1799, aged 46.

III. Susanna, b. in 1756, m. 11 Feb. 1779, to Thomas-Cheadle Sanders, Esq. of Hon. E.I.C., and Charlwood, co. Surrey, who d. in 1816; and 2ndly, to William Bailey, Esq. of Tonbridge Castle, Kent, 10 June, 1819, d. 1832. She d. in 1833, aged 77, leaving issue one child, Harriet, m. to the Rev. George-Dinely Goodere, rector of Otterden, Kent.

IV. Harriet, b. in 1762, m. 11 Feb. 1784, Archibald Paxton, Esq. of Watford Place, Herts, high-sheriff of the county in 1799, brother of Sir William Paxton, Knt. of Middleton Hall, Carmarthenshire, d. in 1817, aged 80. She d. 18 Nov. 1794, aged 33, leaving issue.

William-Gill Paxton, Esq. of Henbury, co. Dorset, high-sheriff of the county in 1828, formerly M.P. for Plympton.

VI. Grace.

Mr. William Gyll m. 2ndly, 23 Dec. 1773, Mary, dau. and co-heir of John Broome, Esq. of Ludlow, co. Salop, and by her (who d. 11 March, 1820, aged 90) left at his decease, 17 March, 1798, an only child,

WILLIAM GYLL, Esq. of Wyrardisbury, b. 18 Sept 1774, capt. 2nd regt. Life-guards, and equerry to H.R.H. the Duke of Sussex. He raised a corps of volunteers in 1804, on the premeditated invasion of Napoleon. Capt. Gyll m. 13 Oct 1794, at Wyrardisbury, Lady Harriet Flemyng, only child of the Rt. Hon. Hamilton Flemyng, last Earl of Wigtoun,* and by her (who d. 6 Nov. 1813, aged 35) had issue,

I. BROOKE-HAMILTON, now of Wyrardisbury House, Bucks, and Yeovany Hall, Middlesex.

II. Bellenden-Charles, b. in 1799, d. 24 Sept. 1822, aged 24.

III. Gordon-Willoughby-James, b. in 1803, m. 20 Aug. 1839, Elizabeth-Ann, 2nd dau. of Sir Edward Bowyer Smijth, Bart., of Hill Hall, Essex, and has issue,

1 Flemyng-George, b. 3 Sept. 1841.
2 Edward-Gordon.
3 Brooke-Flemyng.
1 Letitia-Elizabeth.
2 Cordelia-Adela.
3 Lilias-Flemyng.

IV. Hamilton, b. 5 May, 1804, of Shenley Lodge, and Salisbury Hall, co. Herts, m. 30 Sept. 1835, Frances, dau. and co-heir of Sir John Murray, Bart., of Stanhope, co. Peebles, N.B., and dying 21 Feb. 1849 left issue,

1 Hamilton-Flemyng-Campbell, b. 11 Aug. 1836.
2 Bellenden-Charles-John, b. 13 March, 1838.

V. Robert, (Sir,) Knt., b. 11 July, 1805, late 15th hussars, and of the German Legion, and formerly lieut. of the Yeomen of the guard; m. 21 April, 1847, Jane-Price, dau. and co-heir of Sir John Pinhorn, Knt.

I. Louisa-Jane-Grace, m. 12 May, 1819, to Sir Jasper Atkinson, Knt., of H.M. Royal Mint, and has issue, a dau., Jane-Laura, m. to William Gowing, Esq.

Arms—Quarterly: 1st and 4th, sa., two chevrons, arg., each charged with three mullets, of the first, on a canton, or, a lion, passant, guardant, gu., for GYLL; 2nd, arg., a fesse, sa., with three martlets, of the first, between three crosses-patée, gu., for CANON; 3rd, lozengy, or and vert, a lion, rampant, gu., for GYLL.

Crest—A hawk's head, sa., between two wings, frettee, vert.

Motto—Virtutis gloria merces.

Seat—Wyrardisbury House, Bucks.

, Of the other families of Gyll, the Northamptonshire branch derived from John Gyll, only son of Richard Gyll,

* Hamilton, last Earl of Wigtoun, was son of Charles Ross, 8th earl, and grandson of James Flemyng of Castlane, Ireland, who was son of James Flemyng, of Ray, and grandson of Alexander Flemyng, 4th son of John, 1st Earl of Wigtoun.

who *d.* in 1546, of whom mention is made in the will of Leonard Gyll, Fellow of Jesus College, Cambridge, in 1547; and another branch resided at Mucking, in Essex, and held the patent office of keeper of the lions in the Tower of London for one hundred and thirteen years. (*See Collectanea Topog. et Gen.*, vol. viii.)

HACKER OF EAST BRIDGFORD.

HEATHCOTE-HACKER, JOHN, Esq. of East Bridgford Old Hall, co. Nottingham, and of Leek, co. Stafford, *b.* in 1794; assumed June, 1840, the additional surname and arms of HACKER.

Lineage.—FRANCIS HACKER, Esq., son, by Margaret, his wife, of JOHN HACKER, Esq. (who *d.* in 1620, and to whom there is a monument in the north aisle of Bridgford church), had four sons, Francis, Richard, John, and Rowland. Francis, the eldest, was Col. Hacker, who served under the Parliament, and attended King CHARLES I. to his execution. Rowland, the youngest son, served under the king during these troubles, and, after the death of his brother, who suffered as a traitor *temp* CHARLES II., left the king's army in disgust, and died in retirement, at East Bridgeford.

THE REV. RALPH HEATHCOTE, rector of Moreton, co. Derby, and vicar of Sileby, co. Leicester, *m.* Mary, dau. of the Rev. Simon Ockley, rector of Swavey, co. Cambridge, professor of Arabic, and was father of

THE REV. EDWARD HEATHCOTE, who *m.* Catherine, only surviving dau. and co-heir of Robert Hacker, Esq. of East Bridgeford, the last male descendant of the Hacker family, and had by her a numerous family, of whom

I. EDWARD, in holy orders, *m.* in 1792, Jane, only child of John Cock, Esq. late of Chesterfield, and by her, who *d.* Dec. 1810, left at his decease, April, 1844,
   1 Godfrey, *m.* Elizabeth, 3rd dau. of — Gillett, Esq.
   2 JOHN, who has assumed the additional surname and arms of HACKER, and is present proprietor of East Bridgford.
   3 Rowland, *m.* Agnes, only dau. of Samuel Harding, Esq., and has three sons, Edward, Rowland, and Godfrey.
   4 William.
   1 Jane, *m.* to Astley Holt, M.D.
   2 Frances, *m.* to the Rev. Thos. Harding.
   3 Catherine-Anne, *m.* to Benjamin Blaydes Thompson, Esq.

II. Rowland, lieut.-col. in the army, assumed, in 1819, the additional surname and arms of HACKER, under the will of his mother, and *d.* in 1840.

Arms—Erm.. three pomees, each charged with a cross, or for HEATHCOTE. Sa., a cross, vairé, between four mullets, or, pierced, of the field, for HACKER.

Crests—On a mural crown, az., a pomee, charged with a cross, or, between two wings, displayed, erm., for HEATHCOTE. A woodpecker, standing on the stock of a tree, eradicated ppr., for HACKER.

Seats—East Bridgford, Old Hall, Notts: Leek, co. Stafford.

HACKETT OF MOOR PARK.

HACKETT, THOMAS, Esq. of Moor Park, King's County and Riverstown, co. Tipperary, J.P., high sheriff of the King's County, 1844, *b.* 15 Jan. 1798; *m.* 1 July, 1830, Jane-Bernard, youngest dau. of the late Bernard Shaw, Esq. of Monkstown Castle, co. Cork, and niece of the late Sir Robert Shaw, Bart., of Bushy Park, co. Dublin, and has issue,

I. SIMPSON, capt. 28th regt. *b.* 15 June, 1831.
II. Thomas-Bernard, 23rd R. W. fusiliers, *b* 15 June, 1836.
III. Robert-Henry, 19th regt., *b.* 26 Aug. 1839.
IV. Charles, *b.* 4 Jan. 1846.

I. Jane-Louisa. II. Sara. III. Emily.
IV. Louisa. V. Alice. VI. Florence.
VII. Helena-Agnes.

Lineage.—ROBERT HACKETT, of Eglish, in the King's County, left by Anne, his wife, (with several daus. one of whom *m.* Richard Burris, Esq. of Ballintemple, King's County, and another, Deborah, *m.* Robert Robinson, Esq. of Tinnikelly,) four sons, viz.,

I. SIMPSON, of whom presently.
II. William, of Prospect, Parsonstown, deceased.
III. Michael, of Elm Grove, Parsonstown, *m.* Miss Mitchell, dau. of Adam Mitchell, Esq. and *d.* in 1856, leaving issue,
   1 Robert, a cavalry officer, *m.* Miss Steele, and *d. s. p.*
   2 THOMAS, of Whiteford, *m.* and has issue.
   3 Wellington, an officer in the army, *d. unm.*
   4 Adam, lieut. in the army.
   5 George, an officer in the army.
   6 Samuel, major in the army, and capt. 38th regt.
   7 Richard, of Elm Grove, *m.* 1st, Miss Fitzgerald, dau. of the Rev. Mr. Fitzgerald, and 2ndly, Miss Sadleir.
   1 A dau, *m.* to Capt. Davidson.
   2 Jane, *m.* to William Lewis, Esq. of Dublin.

IV. Isaac, an officer in the army, killed at Waterloo.

The eldest son,

SIMPSON HACKETT, Esq. of Riverstown, co. Tipperary (son of Robert and Anne Hackett), *b.* 28 Dec. 1763, *m.* 1 May, 1790, Sarah Mitchell, and by her (who *d.* 5 Aug. 1839) had,

Robert, 18th hussars, *b.* 1 Jan. 1796, *d.* 22 April 1816.
THOMAS, now of Moor Park.
Sarah, *m.* to Alexander A. Graydon, Esq. of Newcastle House, co. Dublin.
Anne-Maria, *m.* to John Brereton, Esq. of Old Court, co. Tipperary.
Margaret, *m.* to Thomas Hobbs, Esq. capt. 92nd Highlanders, of Barneboy, King's County.
Jane, *m.* to Robert Seymour Drought, Esq. of Ridgemont, King's County

Mr. Hackett *d.* 21 Jan. 1848.

Arms—Sa., three piles, pointing to the base, arg., the centre one charged with a trefoil, slipped, vert, on a chief, gu., a lion, passant, guardant, or.

Crest—A demi-panther, arg., spotted, az., collared, gu., charged on the shoulder with a trefoil, slipped, vert, and holding in the dexter paw a branch, of the last.

Motto—Virtute et fidelitate.

Seats—Moor Park, and Riverstown, near Parsonstown.

HAFFENDEN OF HOMEWOOD.

HAFFENDEN, ALFRED, Esq. of Homewood, co. Kent, *b.* 3 Jan, 1825.

Lineage.—The HAFFENDENS have been long resident in the county of Kent, at Tenterden and Smarden, Halden-Buggleesden, in the north part of Boresile Borough, being anciently and up to a very recent period, their property and abode; that estate, descending from Robert Haffenden, of Buggleesden, to his brother, John Haffenden, Esq. of Charing, was conveyed, by the only child of the latter, Amy Haffenden, in marriage, to William Hawker, Esq.

From Laurence Haffenden, of Buggleesden, bailiff of Tenterden, 1 RICHARD III., lineally derived,

JAMES HAFFENDEN, Esq. of Homewood and Clearwell Court, captain in the Notts militia, *b.* 1 Jan. 1788, who *m.* 28 Jan. 1813, Catharine, dau. of Joseph Walker, Esq. of Eastwood House, co. York, and dying in 1838, left issue,

ALFRED, his heir, of Homewood.
Sophia-Elizabeth, *m.* to Thomas Dickinson-Hall, Esq. of Whatton Manor, Notts.
Catherine.
Angelina, *m.* 5 May, 1841, to the Rev. Alleyne, 3rd son of Sir Henry Fitzherbert, Bart. of Tissington Hall, co. Derby.
Harriet-Cecilia.

Arms—Chequy, sa. and arg., on a bend, az., three mullets, or.

Crest—An eagle's head, couped.

Seat—Homewood, Kent.

HAGGARD OF WEST BRADENHAM.

HAGGARD, WILLIAM-MEYBOHM-RYDER, Esq. of West Bradenham Hall, Norfolk, L.L.B., barrister-at-law, J.P. and D.L., *m.* Ella, elder dau. and co-heir of Bazett Doveton, Esq., late of E.I.C. civil service, only son of the late John Doveton, Esq. of St. Helena, and has

WILLIAM, and other issue.

Lineage.—The name of this family is supposed to have been, originally Ogard, and to be descended from the Ogards of The Rye, Herts.

JOHN HAGGARD, of Royston, had by Hannah Aungier his wife, a son, JOHN HAGGARD, of Old Ford House, Bow, co. Middlesex, who *m.* 1st, Elizabeth Stretton, and 2ndly, Bridget Fellows, and had issue,

I. JOHN, his heir.
II. Mark, of Stratford-le-Bow, merchant, *m.* Mary, dau. of Peter Debonnaire, of Bromley, Middlesex, and had issue,
   1 Mark Haggard, of Stoke Newington, co. Middlesex, who *m.* Susannah Jones, and had issue (with Mark and Samuel, who both *d. unm.*, and a dau. Susannah Rachel, *m.* to C. Sanderson, stockbroker), another son,
   William Debonnaire Haggard, Esq. of the Bank of England and Lee Grove, who *m.* 1st, Mary-Frances-

Clifton, and had by her (who *d.* 1818) one son, William Debonnaire, *m.* to Sarah Nichson, and two daus., he *m.* 2ndly, Jane Copner, who *d.* 1824, leaving issue two sons, and 3rdly, Elizabeth Nodes le Cren, by whom he had a son and dau.

1 Mary, *m.* Harry Hale, merchant. 2 Hannah.

The eldest son,

JOHN HAGGARD, Esq., *m.* 1st, Mary Warner, who *d.* 1782, and was buried at Bromley Mids, and had issue by her,

John, in holy orders, rector of Bennington, Herts, who. *d.* 21 March, 1813, at 90, *s. p.*, Mary Lee, his wife, sister of Elizabeth, his father's second wife, having predeceased him, 26 Nov. 1778, æt. 58.
WILLIAM HENRY, of whom presently.

Mr. Haggard *d.* 5 Feb. 1776, æt. 75, and was buried at Bennington; his 2nd wife, Elizabeth Lee survived him and *d.* 31 Jan. 1794, at 83. The only surviving son,

WILLIAM HENRY HAGGARD, Esq., was of the city of Norwich, and *m.* Susan-Rebecca, dau. of James Barnham, Esq.; by her (who *d.* 14 Jan. 1804) he had an only son and heir,

WILLIAM HENRY HAGGARD, Esq., B.A. of Emmanuel College, Cambridge, barrister-at-law, who purchased the estate, and was of Bradenham Hall. He *m.* 16 July, 1781, Frances, only dau. of the Rev. Thos. Amyand,* rector of Hambledon, Bucks, and of Fawley, Oxon (by Frances, his wife, dau. and ultimately sole heir of Thos. Rider, of Twickenham, Esq.), which lady *d.* 21 July, 1820, æt. 60. Mr. Haggard *d.* in 1837, aged 79, leaving issue eleven children, viz. (with others who *d.* infants),

WILLIAM HARRY, of whom presently.
Thomas, *b.* 1790, *m.* Maria, dau. of William Tickell, of Bath.
John, LL.D. of Doctors' Commons, *m.* 1820, Caroline, dau. of Mark Hodgson, of Bromley, and has issue seven sons and four daus.
George, *d. unm.* 1817.
Frances, *m.* John Adolphus Young, Esq. of Great Ormond-street.
Luanda, *m.* Robt. Mapletoft, Esq., Spring Hall, Suffolk.
Caroline, *unm.*

The eldest son and heir,

WILLIAM HENRY HAGGARD, Esq., *b.* 26 Sept. 1783, *s.* his father, and *d.* 29 March, 1843, at Brighton, having *m.* 1815, Elizabeth, eldest dau. and co-heir of James Meybohm, Esq. of St. Petersburgh, and had issue. He was *s.* at Bradenham by WILLIAM MEYBOHM RIDER HAGGARD, Esq., his heir, now of Bradenham Hall, and at Amyand House, Twickenham, by his younger son, James Haggard, Esq.

Arms—Az., a mullet of six points, arg.
Crest—A mullet of six points arg.
Seat—West Bradenham, Norfolk.

HAIRE OF ARMAGH MANOR.

HAIRE, JAMES, Esq. of Armagh Manor, co. Fermanagh, high sheriff 1853, *b.* Oct. 1801.

Lineage.—The Hares are traditionally of Scottish origin, and are stated to have settled in Ireland at the period of religious persecution in Scotland. They were first established in the barony of Glenawley, co. Fermanagh, and were subsequently moved to the barony of Clonkelly, in another part of the same county, on the acquisition of the property of Armagh Manor by the late

JAMES HAIRE, Esq., who first adopted the additional *i* in the name. He *m.* Anne, dau. of William Henry, Esq., a Dublin merchant, and had issue,

ROBERT, his heir.
Hamilton, of Glassdrummon, co. Fermanagh, *m.* 1st, Frances, dau. of — Newburgh, Esq. of Ballyhaise, by whom he had, James-Hamilton, in holy orders; Frances, *m.* to William Armstrong, M.D., of Collooney, co. Sligo. He *m.* 2ndly, Anne, dau. of — Chittick, Esq. of Enniskillen, and had by her Henry, and other issue. He *d.* in Dec. 1844.
Henry, capt. 66th regt., *d.* 1809, after a long course of military service.
Mary-Anne, *m.* to Joseph Rolleston, Esq., K.C., deceased.

The eldest son,

ROBERT HAIRE, Esq. of Armagh Manor, one of H.M. Counsel; *m.* 1799, Elizabeth, dau. of William Babington, Esq. of Cavan, and by her (who *d.* 8 April, 1811) he left at his decease, 3 March, 1851, a son and a dau., viz.,

JAMES, now of Armagh Manor.
Anne, *m.* to the Rev. Hamond Dawson.

Arms—Gu., two bars, or, on a chief, indented, arg., a thistle, ppr.
Crest—A lion, rampant, arg., supporting the Roman fasces, ppr.
Motto—In te Domine speravi.
Seat—Armagh Manor, co. Fermanagh.

HALE OF ALDERLEY.

BLAGDEN-HALE, ROBERT-H., Esq. of Alderley, co. Gloucester; *m.* in 1807, Lady Theodosia-Eleanor Bourke, dau. of Joseph Deane, 3rd Earl of Mayo, Archbishop of Tuam, and by her (who *d.* 23 Aug. 1845,) had issue; his son and heir,

ROBERT-BLAGDEN, M.P. for West Gloucestershire, *b.* 1807; *m.* 1832, Anne-Jane, eldest dau. of the late G.-P. Holford, Esq. of Weston Birt, and has issue,
1 Robert, *b.* 1834. 2 Matthew-Holford, *b.* 1835.
1 Anne. 2 Theodosia. 3 Georgina.

The Hales of Alderley descend from the family of the celebrated SIR MATTHEW HALE, Chief Justice of the King's Bench, who was born at Alderley, in 1609.

Arms—Ar., a fesse, sa., in chief, three cinquefoils, of the last.
Crest—A heron's head, erased, arg.
Seat—Alderley, Wotton-under-Edge.

HALE OF KING'S WALDEN.

HALE, WILLIAM, Esq. of King's Walden, co. Hertford, *b.* Aug. 1816.

Lineage.—RICHARD HALE, eldest son of Thomas Hale, of Codicote, Herts, by Anne his wife, dau. of Edmund Michell, Esq., purchased the estate of King's Walden, Herts, in the time of ELIZABETH. His grandson,

ROWLAND HALE, Esq. of King's Walden, (eldest son of William Hale, Esq. of King's Walden, high-sheriff 1621, and brother of Archdeacon Bernard Hale, principal of Peter House, Cambridge, and also of Sir John Hale, of Stagenhoe,) *b.* 8 June, 1600, served the office of sheriff of Herts in 1647. He *m.* Elizabeth, dau. of Sir Henry Garwey, Knt., and left 7 April, 1669, a son and successor,

WILLIAM HALE, Esq. of King's Walden, M.P. for Herts, 13 and 31 of CHARLES II. He *m.* Mary, dau. of Jeremiah Elwes, Esq. of Roxby, co. Lincoln, by whom, who *d.* 28 July, 1712, at the age of 72, he had ten sons and four daus., of whom

RICHARD, *b.* 4 Nov. 1659; *m.* 3 April, 1684, Elizabeth, dau. and heir of Isaac Meynell, Esq. of Langley Meynell, co. Derby, and by her (who *m.* 2ndly, the Hon. Robert Cecil, 2nd son of James, 3rd Earl of Salisbury) left at his decease, in 1689, (with a dau., Mary, maid of honour to Queen ANNE, who *m.* Thomas Coke, Esq., and was mother of Mary Coke, the wife of Sir Mathew Lambe, whose son was elevated to the peerage as Viscount Melbourne,) a son and successor, WILLIAM HALE, Esq., M.P., whose sons, William, and Paggen, M.P. for Herts; both *d. s. p.*
BERNARD (Sir), of whom presently.

The 8th son, but in whose descendant the representation of the family is now vested,

SIR BERNARD HALE, bapt. 18 March, 1677, was constituted, in 1722, chief baron of the Exchequer in Ireland, and subsequently received the honour of knighthood. He *m.* Anne Thursby, of Northamptonshire, and by her, who *d.* 11 April, 1768, had,

I. WILLIAM, his heir.
II. Richard, who *d.* 14 Sept. 1812, in his 92nd year.
III. Bernard, a general officer, col. 20th regt., lieutenant-governor of Chelsea Hospital, 10 May, 1773, and afterwards lieutenant-governor of the Ordnance; *m.* Sept. 1750, Martha 2nd dau. of Richard Rigby, Esq. of Mistley Hall, Essex, and *d.* 18 March, 1798, leaving a son,

LIEUT.-COL. FRANCIS HALE, M.P., who, upon inheriting the estates of his maternal uncle. the Right Hon. Richard Rigby, who *d.* 8 April, 1788, assumed, by sign-manual, the surname and arms of RIGBY. He *m.* Frances, dau. of Sir Thomas Rumbold, Bart., governor of Madras, and had a dau.,

Frances, *m.* in 1808, to William Horace, 3rd Lord Rivers.

IV. John, of Plantation, near Gisborough, in Yorkshire, a general officer in the army, and colonel of the 17th light dragoons, governor of Londonderry and Coolmoreforts, in 1781; *m.* Mary, 2nd dau. of William Chaloner, Esq. of Gisborough, and *d.* 20 March, 1806, leaving a numerous issue.

* The Rev. Thos. Amyand was elder son of Claudius Amyand, Esq. surgeon to GEORGE II., whose 2nd son, George Amyand, was created a baronet.

I. Catherine, m. to Thomas Nugent, Esq., common serjeant of London.
II. Jane, m. to the Rev. Martin Madan, eldest son of Col. Madan, by Judith his wife, dau. of Mr. Justice Spencer Cowper.
III. Anne, d. unm.

Sir Bernard d. 7 Nov. 1729, and was s. by his son,

WILLIAM HALE, Esq. of King's Walden, who m. 1745, Elizabeth, youngest dau. of Sir Charles Farnaby, Bart., and by her, who d. 1780, had issue,

WILLIAM, his heir.
Paggen, a banker in London, who m. 8 Feb. 1791, Miss Mary Keet, and d. s. p. 18 Jan. 1807.
Elizabeth, m. to the Rev. Mr. Stillingfleet.
Charlotte, m. 1st, to Thomas Duncombe, Esq. of Duncombe Park, co. York: and 2ndly, to Thomas Onslow, Earl Onslow.
Sarah, m. to the Rev. James Bowles, rector of Burford, in Salop, and d. in 1783.
Anne, m. 18 April, 1782, to Sir Edward Dering, Bart.

Mr. Hale d. 14 Sept. 1793, aged 77. His son,

WILLIAM HALE, Esq. of King's Walden, m. 3 April, 1777, Mary, dau. of James, 2nd Viscount Grimston, and had issue,

WILLIAM, his heir.
Paggen, baptized 17 July, 1784, d. at Pimlico, 7 Nov. 1814.
Cecil-Farnaby-Richard, R.N., baptized 1 July, 1786, d. 17 Jan. 1801.
Henry-Jeremy, bapt. 15 Jan. 1791, curate of King's Walden, m. Frances, dau. of John Sowerby, Esq. of Putteridgebury, Herts, and d. leaving two sons and three daus.
Charlotte-Bucknall, m. her cousin, Cholmely Dering, 2nd son of Sir Edward Dering, Bart. of Surrenden Dering.
Elizabeth-Mary, m. to George Proctor, Esq. of Mardocks.

Mr. Hale d. 22 April, 1829, and was s. by his eldest son,

WILLIAM HALE, Esq. of King's Walden, b. 5 June, 1782; who m. 1st, Feb. 1815, Elizabeth, only dau. of the Hon. William Leeson, of The Node, son of Joseph, Earl of Milltown, and by her (who d. in April, 1822) had,

WILLIAM, of King's Walden.
Emily-Mary-Brand, m. 20 Jan. 1842, to the Hon. and Rev. Philip-Yorke Savile, 3rd son of the Earl of Mexborough.

He m. 2ndly, 28 Dec. 1824, Charlotte, eldest dau. of Sir Richard-Joseph Sullivan, Bart. of Thames Ditton, and had by her,

Charles-Cholmeley, b. 9 July, 1830.
Charlotte-Eliza.

Arms—Az., a chev., embattled, counter-embattled, or.
Crest—A snake, ppr., entwined round five arrows, or, headed, sa., feathered, arg., one in pale, four saltier ways.
Seat—King's Walden.

HALIDAY OF SQUIRES HILL.

HALIDAY, ALEXANDER-HENRY, Esq. of Carnmoney, co. Antrim, J.P., high sheriff 1842; b. 21 Nov. 1806.

Lineage.—This is a branch of the house of Tulliebole, Kinross-shire; the first of whom settled in Ireland was the REV. SAMUEL HALIDAY, minister of Omagh, co. Tyrone, in the general synod of Ulster, before the Revolution; of Tulliebole, Kinross-shire (and Fossaway, united parishes), from 1688 to 1691, as supposed; and of Ardstran, co. Tyrone, from 1692. He m. Lettice, dau. of John Craufurd, of Ballysavage, co. Antrim, (and of Berbel and Almuir manors, Ayrshire). His only son, SAMUEL, b. before the Revolution, ordained by the presbytery of Geneva, 1708, was chaplain to the Cameronian regiment, thenceforth to the close of the war in Flanders; and minister of the first presbyterian church of Belfast, 1719. He m. 1721, Anne, 2nd dau. of Alexander Dalway, of Ballyhill, co. Antrim, M.P., and relict, 1st of Thomas Travers, lieut.-colonel of Lord Rochford's dragoons; and 2ndly, of Arthur Maxwell, of Drum-beg, co. Antrim. He d. in 1739, leaving issue, three sons and one dau. His eldest son,

ROBERT-DALWAY HALIDAY, Esq. of Castlehill, co. Down, b. in 1724; m. in 1754, Elizabeth, eldest dau. of John Smith, of Newland, Yorkshire, (father of Sir John Sylvester Smith, the 1st Baronet), and d. in 1796, having issue by her, two sons, John Smith, and William, and one dau., Anne, surviving; besides three sons, who d. unm. in their father's lifetime, viz., Christopher, post-captain R.N.; Alexander, also in the navy, naval A.D.C. to Lord Robert Manners; and Robert, in the army, killed at Tanjore.

ALEXANDER-HENRY HALIDAY, of Belfast, M.D., the 3rd son of Samuel, b. in 1728, bore a distinguished part in the politics of Ulster during the latter half of the past century; was the original secretary of the Northern Whig Club seconder of the first public petition that was presented to the Irish parliament for the relief of Roman Catholic disabilities; and in 1771, when the "Hearts of Steel" entered the town of Belfast, and attacked the garrison in their barracks, arrested by his interposition, at the risk of his life, the conflict commenced, and saved the town from imminent destruction. He m. 1st, Martha, dau. of Randal McCollum, and (after her death, in 1778) 2ndly, in 1775, Anne, 3rd dau. of Campbell Edmonstone, lieutenant-Governor of Dumbarton Castle (brother of Sir Archibald Edmonstone, of Duntreath, the 1st Bart.), and dying in 1802, without issue, left his paternal estates, which had devolved on him, to his younger nephew,

WILLIAM HALIDAY, b. in 1763; who m. in 1805, Marian, eldest dau. and co-heir of Gilbert Webster, of Greenville, co. Down, (2nd son of Sir Godfrey Webster, of Battel Abbey Sussex, the 3rd Bart.), by his wife Marian, elder dau. and co-heir of John Boyd, of Donaghadee, co. Down, and relict of General James Gisborne, M.P., commander-in-chief of the forces in Ireland, and d. 3 June, 1836, leaving issue,

ALEXANDER-HENRY, now of Carnmoney.
William-Robert, b. 6 April, 1808, lieut.-colonel in the army.
Marion-Emily.
Elizabeth-Georgina, d. unm. 25 Jan. 1845.

Arms—Arg. a sword paleways, the pommel within a crescent in base, gu., on a canton, dexter, az., a St. Andrew's cross, of the first, quartering WEBSTER and BOYD.
Crest—A boar's head, couped, arg., langued and tusked, or.
Motto—Virtute parta.
Seat—Carnmoney, co. Antrim.

HALKETT OF HALL HILL.

HALKETT-CRAIGIE-INGLIS, CHARLES, Esq. of Cramond, co. Edinburgh, J.P., late in the 93rd regt., b. 10 Dec. 1802; m. 26 March, 1824, Susan, youngest dau. of Sir John Majoribanks, Bart. of Lees, co. Berwick, and has surviving issue,

I. JOHN-CORNELIUS, b. 19 June, 1830; m. June, 1854, Matilda-Justine, dau. of Duncan Davidson, Esq. of Tulloch.
II. David, Bengal civil service, b. 10 July, 1835.
III. Charles-Harland, b. 23 Oct. 1838.
I. Matilda, m. Oct. 1853, to Lieut.-Col. Elliot, 79th regt., eldest son of the Hon. John Elliot.
II. Anne-Catherine, m. 1851, to Major Brewster, youngest son of Sir David Brewster.
III. Mary-Stuart.

Lineage.—The Halketts were free barons in Fifeshire, and had large landed possessions in the western parts of that county six hundred years ago. The first of the family upon record, who distinguished himself by feats of arms, was

DAVID DE HALKETT, a powerful warrior, living temp. King DAVID BRUCE. He was father of

PHILIPPUS DE HALKETT, who flourished in the reigns of Kings ROBERT II. and ROBERT III. From this Philip de Halkett we pass over seven generations, observing the remarkable fact, that the chiefs of this family have always been in the military service of their own country, or that of some allied power.

GEORGE HALKETT, the 9th in direct lineal descent, and a distinguished officer, m. Isabella, dau. of Sir Patrick Hepburn, of Waughton, and had three sons and one dau., of whom

SIR JOHN HALKETT, Knt., 3rd son of George Halkett, and 10th in direct lineal descent, received the honour of knighthood from King JAMES VI.; rose to the rank of general in the Dutch service, and had the command of a Scots regiment. He was likewise president of the grand Court Marishall in Holland. Sir John m. Mary Van Loon, a lady of high rank in Amsterdam, and was killed at the siege of Bois-le-Duc in 1628, leaving a son and successor,

MAURICE HALKETT, a capt. in the army, who m. Mademoiselle Agnes Decquere, of Artois, by whom he had one son, EDWARD. Captain Maurice Halkett was killed at Maestricht, in 1675, and was s. in his estates by his only son,

EDWARD HALKETT, a major in the Dutch service, who m. Judith de Pagniet, a lady of the province of Guelderland, and had issue. Major Edward Halkett was killed at the battle of Ramilies, in 1706, and was s. by his only son,

CHARLES HALKETT, Esq., who rose to the rank of lieut.-general, and had the command of a Scots regiment in Holland. He m. 1st, Margaret eldest dau. of Brigadier-

General Corbet, by whom he had two sons, Charles and John, d. 1766, and one dau.; and m. 2ndly, Mademoiselle Anne le Faucher, a French lady, by whom he had a son,

Frederick, d. a major-gen. in the British service. He left, by his wife, a Miss Seton, with three daus., two sons,
Colin (Sir), G.C.B., a general officer.
Hugh, a general in the Hanoverian service.

The General d. in 1758, and was s. by his eldest son,

Charles Halkett, Esq., who was a colonel in the Dutch service, and governor of Namur. He m. Anne, heiress of John Craigie, Esq. of Dumbarnie, one of the lords of justiciary in Scotland, (by Susan, eldest dau. of Sir John Inglis, Bart. of Cramond, and Lady Susan Hamilton, his wife, dau. of the 4th Earl of Haddington), and by the deeds of settlement her husband and their successors were obliged to assume the name and arms of Craigie, in addition to those of Halkett. By this lady he had issue,

Charles, a major in the army, d. in India.
John-Cornelius, successor to his father.
Susanna-Judith, m. Cumin, of Relugas, (lineally descended from the ancient family of the Comines, in France.)
Margaret-Maria, m. to Colonel Lindesay, (claimant to the ancient title of Lord Lindesay, of Byres.)
Christian-Smith, m. to Major Sands.
Anna-Cockburn, m. to John Wauchope, Esq. of Niddry.
Catherine-Hermione.
Isabella-Cornelia, twin with John-Cornelius, m. the Right Hon. Robert Blair, lord-president of the Court of Session in Scotland.

The eldest surviving son and heir,

John-Cornelius Craigie-Halkett, Esq., colonel of the 55th regt., gallantly distinguished himself in the east and West Indies, as well as in Holland, and was appointed aide-de-camp to Sir Ralph Abercromby. He m. in 1800, Margaret, eldest dau. of John Davidson, Esq. of Ravelrig, and had,

Charles, now Charles Halkett-Craigie-Inglis, Esq. of Cramond.
John, Bengal N.I., b. in 1807; m. a dau. of Col. Walter, and has issue.
Robert-Blair, in the E.I.Co.'s service, b. in 1808.
Henry, b. in 1811.
Hannah-Isabella-Cornelia, m. in 1824, to William-Thomas Thornton, Esq., 2nd son of the late Edmund Thornton, Esq. of Whittington Hall, co. Lancaster, and has issue.
Anne.

Arms—Sa., three piles conjoined, in base, arg., and on a chief, gu., a lion, passant, guardant, or.
Crest—A falcon's head, erased, ppr.
Supporters—Two falcons, ppr.
Motto—"Fides sufficit," above, and "Honestè Vivo," beneath.
Seat—Cramond, co. Edinburgh.

HALL OF WESTBANK HOUSE.

Hall, Edward, Esq. of Westbank House, co. Chester, comm. R.N., m. Sarah-Miles, dau. of John-Gordon Smith, Esq. of Pomona, in Orkney, by Sarah Johnson his wife, eldest dau. of Joseph Miles, Esq. of Liverpool, and has issue,

I. Clarence-Huxley, b. 5 Sept. 1827; m. 7 March, 1855, Charlotte-B. Lyon, dau. of Edward Lyon, Esq.
II. Charles-Huxley. III. Edward-Smythe.
IV. Arthur-Francis.
I. Louisa-Margaret. II. Emily.
III. Mary-Adelaide. IV. Harriette.

Capt. Hall entered the navy in 1806. He served as aide-de-camp to his late Majesty William IV., and also to H.R.H. the Grand Duke of Wurtemberg during the Russian campaigns, and was envoy to the Court of Saxe Coburg after the peace.

Lineage.—The family of Hall is one of the oldest as well as most extensive in Cheshire. The name was originally Kingsley; the present family of Kingsley of Kingsley, being descended from a cadet of this family. Almost all the younger branches of the Halls, as well as those of the Huxleys (of whom the Halls are now the representatives), have terminated in females.

Sir Ranulphus Kingsley, Knt. of Norlegh (2nd son of Sir Ranulphus de Kingsley, of Norlegh and Kingsley, and grandson of Sir Ranulphus de Kingsley, who had a grant from Randle le Meschines before 1128), m. Mabilla de Moston, and by her (who was living a widow in 1233) had two sons, John, of whom presently; and Sir Ranulphus de Kingsley, whose great-grandson, Sir Adam de Kingsley, was escheator of the palatine of Chester and county of Flint, A.D. 1361—1399: from him descend the present family of Kingsley. The elder son,

John de Aula de Kingsley, of Norlegh, A.D. 1216, *temp.* Henry III., forester to the King in Cheshire, was great-great-grandfather of

Thomas del Hall, of Norley, who rebuilt the Hall there. He m. Margery, dau. of Sir William de Brereton, Knt. of Brereton Castle, co. Chester, and had issue. The eldest son and heir,

John del Hall, of Norley, sheriff of the city of Chester in 1387 and in 1408, m. Mary, dau. of Sir Peter le Roter de Thornton, of Thornton, and besides a younger son, Robert, prior of the Abbey of Vale Royal, co. Chester, in 1462, had an elder son and heir,

John del Hall, of Norley, who m. Agnes, dau of Sir Roger Maynwarynge, Knt. escheator of Cheshire, 2nd son of Sir Randle Maynwarynge, of Carincham, co. Chester, and by her had, besides a dau. m. to Peter Shakerley, of Shakerley, co. Chester, and a younger son, Roger, abbot of Norton, co. Chester, who rebuilt at his own expense the great window in the parish church of Great Budworth, an elder son and successor,

Thomas Hall, of Norley, who pulled down the old Hall and rebuilt it in 1500. He had two sons, of whom the elder,

Thomas Hall, of Norley, sheriff of Cheshire in 1527, and colonel of a regiment raised amongst his own tenantry, in the army sent against the Northumbrian rebels, 1569, was father of

Thomas Hall, of Norley, who m. Margaret, dau. of Sir John Egerton, of Egerton Hall and Oulton Park, co. Chester, and had two sons, John, his heir; William, of London, who left an only dau. and heiress, Mary, who m. 11 May, 1649, William Weld, of Weld House and Hassall Hall, co. Chester. Mr. Hall left large estates for the poor of Norley and its neighbourhood, and was s. at his decease, in 1639, by his eldest son and heir,

John Hall, of Norley, who m. Mary, dau. of John de Bird, of Broxton, and was father of

Peter Hall, of Norley, who, being "a Royalist Malignant," was obliged to compound for his estates by paying a heavy fine to the Commonwealth. He had issue four sons and a dau. The eldest son,

John Hall, of Norley, lord of the manors of Owlaston, Frodsham, Kingsley, Plumley, &c., in 1666, had three sons.

Peter, of Norley, left issue, which is now extinct in the male line.
Jonas, of whom we treat.
Thomas, of Prestbury, co. Chester, m. and had issue.

The 2nd son,

Jonas Hall, of Macclesfield, co. Chester, b. in 1687, m. and had issue. The eldest son,

Jonas Hall, Esq. of Macclesfield, b. in 1722, m. 1st, his cousin Martha, dau. of Thomas Hall, of Prestbury; and 2ndly, Esther, dau of Marmaduke Wyatt, and widow of S. Clowes, of Langleigh Hall, co. Chester, and by the latter only had issue. Mr. Jonas Hall d. in 1781. His eldest son,

David Hall, Esq., of Butley Hall, co. Chester, b. in 1755, captain in the Cheshire yeomanry, m. 1st, Mary, dau. of S. Huxley, Esq. of Huxley and Brindley, co. Chester; and 2ndly, Mary, dau. of the Rev. Joseph Horderne, vicar of Rosthern, co. Chester, and by the former only had issue, viz.

Charles, b. 1783, lieut-colonel 16th Madras Light Infantry, governor of the province of Wynaad, d. s. p. 1824.
William, of Butley Hall, b. 1785, d. s. p. 1842.
Samuel, b. 1786, late vice-principal of Brasennose College, Oxford, chaplain to his late Majesty William IV., rural dean of Brackley, and rector of Middleton Cheney. He m. Anne, dau. of Joseph Holdsworth, of Wakefield, and d. 24 May, 1853, having had issue, Seymour-Gilbert, Egerton-Francis, James-Edward, and Anne-Catherine, d. 1842.
Thomas, of Macclesfield.
Edward, of Westbank House, at the head of this article.
Sarah, d. unm. 1846.

Mr. David Hall d. in 1830.

Arms—Quarterly: 1st and 4th, barré, ermine and vert, on a chief, az., a talbot's head, erased, ppr., between two laurel wreaths, or, for Hall; 2nd, vert, a cross engr. erm. on an escutcheon of pretence arg. a bugle horn or, strung sa. for Kingsley; 3rd, ermine, on a bend, cotised, gu., three crescents, or, for Huxley.
Crest—A stag's head, couped at the shoulders, ppr., collared, or.
Motto—Fortitudine.
Seat—Westbank House, co. Chester.

HALL OF WHATTON MANOR.

HALL, THOMAS-DICKINSON, Esq. of Whatton Manor and of Broughton, co. Nottingham, J.P. and D.L., *b.* 18 Aug. 1808; *m.* Sophia-Elizabeth, dau. of the late James Haffenden, Esq. of Homewood, co. Kent; *s.* his grandfather 1 Oct. 1835, and is a magistrate for the counties of Notts and Leicester, and a captain in the Notts militia. He served as high-sheriff of Nottinghamshire in 1843.

Lineage.—This family came originally from Lincolnshire. The great-grandfather of the present representative, FRANCIS HALL, *m.* Miss Mary Watson, only child and heir of an opulent London merchant, and had a son and successor,

THOMAS HALL, Esq. of Nottingham and of Whatton, Notts, who *m.* Elizabeth Phillips, and by her had two sons,

I. THOMAS, an officer 7th Royal Fusiliers, *m.* Margaret Raines, a lady from the co. of Cork, but *d. s. p.*
II. WILLIAM-HENRY, an officer in the 4th or King's Own Regt., *m.* in Nov. 1807, Harriet, eldest dau. of William Dickinson, Esq. of Muskham Grange, (many years chairman of Quarter Sessions for Notts,) by Harriett, his wife, eldest dau. of John Kenrick, Esq, formerly M.P. for Bletchingley, and had issue,
  1 THOMAS-DICKINSON, successor to his grandfather.
  1 Elizabeth-Harriett.

Mr. Hall *d.* 1 Oct. 1835, and was *s.* by his grandson, the present THOMAS-DICKINSON HALL, Esq. of Whatton Manor.

Arms—Az., a bend, between three talbots' heads, erased, two in chief and one in base, arg., on a chief, or, three roses, gu., barbed and seeded, ppr.
Crest—A crescent, arg., surmounted by a griffin's head, erased, sa., in the beak three ears of wheat, or.
Motto—Persevere.
Seat—Whatton Manor, Notts, built in the Elizabethan style by the present proprietor.

HALL OF NARROW WATER.

HALL, ROGER, Esq. of Narrow Water co. Down, J.P. and D.L., high sheriff co. Armagh, 1815, and for Down 1816; *b.* 6 Nov. 1791; *m.* 10 Nov. 1812, Barbara, 4th dau. of Patrick Savage, Esq. of Portaferry, co. Down.

Lineage.—This family is of English extraction.

FRANCIS HALL, Esq. of Mount Hall, co. Down, living in the 17th century, left, by Mary his wife, four sons, ROGER, his heir; EDWARD, ancestor of the present Major-General HENRY HALL, C.B., of Knockbrack, co. Galway; Alexander; Trevor; and a dau., Frideswood, *m.* 1681, to Chichester Fortescue, Esq. of Dromiskin. The eldest son,

ROGER HALL, Esq. of Mount Hall, *m.* 1686, Christian, dau. of Sir Toby Poyntz, of Acton, co. Armagh, and had issue, TOBY, his heir; Roger; and Rose, *m.* 1708, to Richard Close, Esq., elder brother of the Rev. Samuel Close, great-grandfather of the present Colonel Maxwell Close, of Drumbanagher. The son and heir,

TOBY HALL, Esq. of Mount Hall, *m.* 1712, Margaret, dau. of the Hon. Robert Fitzgerald, and sister of the 19th Earl of Kildare, and by her (who *d.* 8 Dec. 1758), he left at his decease, 4 May, 1734, two daus., Christian and Elizabeth, and one son,

ROGER HALL, Esq. of Mount Hall, who *m.* 10 Sept. 1740, Catherine, only dau. of Rowland Savage, Esq. of Portaferry, and had issue, SAVAGE, his heir; Dorcas, *m.* to Francis Carleton, Esq.; Anne, *m.* Patrick Savage, Esq. of Portaferry; Catherine, *m.* 1765, to the Right Hon. William Brownlow, M.P.; Elizabeth, *m.* to James Moore, Esq; Sophia, *m.* to Richard Ainsworth, Esq. The son and heir,

SAVAGE HALL, Esq. of Narrow Water, *b.* 1763; *m.* 1786, Elizabeth, 4th dau. of John Madden, Esq. of Hilton, co. Monaghan, and by her (who *d.* in 1801) had issue,

I. ROGER, his heir, now of Narrow Water.
II. Savage, in holy orders, rector of Loughall, *b.* 1798; *m.* 1831, Anne, eldest dau. of the late William James O'Brien, Esq. of co. Clare, and *d.* 1851, leaving issue,
  1 SAVAGE, 89th regiment, *b.* 1834
  2 William-James, royal horse artillery, *b.* 1836.
  3 Roger; *b.* 1840.
  1 Margaret-Barbara. 2 Elizabeth-Grace.
  3 Annette. 4 Alice. 5 Emly.
III. Samuel-Madden, late major 75th regt., *b.* 1800; *m.* 1845, Anne-Margaret, youngest dau. of the late Andrew Nugent, Esq. of Portaferry.
I. Anne, *m.* to Trevor Corry, Esq. of Newry, and *d.* 1852.
II. Catharine, *m.* to Captain Nowlan.
III. Elizabeth, *m.* to the Rev. W.-B. Savage.
IV. Jane, *m.* to the Rev. Sir Hunt-Johnson Walsh, Bart.

Arms—Arg., a chev., engr., between three talbots' heads, erased, sa.
Crest—A bear's head, muzzled, ppr.
Seat—Narrow Water, Warrenpoint, Ireland.

HALL OF KNOCKBRACK.

HALL, HENRY, Esq. of Knockbrack, co. Galway, and Merville, co. Dublin, J.P., a major-general and Companion of the Bath, *b.* 11 Sept. 1789; *m.* 3 Oct. 1827, Sarah, eldest dau. of the late General Fagan, adjutant-general of the Indian army, and has had issue,

I. HENRY-EDWARD, 13th regiment, *b.* 19 Sept. 1831; served in the Crimea.
II. Christopher-James-Traill, *b.* 1839; *d.* 1854.
I. Eliza-Margaret, *m.* 30 Jan. 1855, to the Rev. Macnevin Bradshaw, only son of the late Robert Scott Bradshaw, Esq. barrister-at-law.
II. Annie-Jane.

Major-Gen. Hall is a very distinguished officer.

Lineage.—This is a collateral branch of the family of Hall, now represented by ROGER HALL, Esq. of Narrow Water.

EDWARD HALL, Esq. of Strangford, 2nd son of Francis Hall Esq. of Mount Hall, (*see preceding article*), *m.* Anne Rowley, and *d.* 1718, leaving issue,

FRANCIS, of Strangford, who *d.* 1761, leaving issue, ANNE, *m.* to James Baillie, Esq.; Elizabeth *m.* to Richard Jones, Esq.; Catherine, *m.* to Tipping, Esq.; and Rebecca, *m.* to Charles Mathew, Esq.
ROWLEY, of whom we treat.
Catherine, *m.* 1719, to William Montgomery, Esq. of Grey Abbey, co. Down, and *d.* 1723.

The 2nd son,

ROWLEY HALL, Esq. of Killeludagh, *m.* Miss Tipping, and was father of

THE VENERABLE FRANCIS HALL, D.D., archdeacon of Aughrim, co. Galway, and rector of Arboe, co. Tyrone, *m. circa*, 1780, Christian Traill, and dying *circa* 1834, left issue,

JAMES-TRAILL, barrister-at-law, chairman of the co. Galway, *m.* Anne Cockerall, only child of John Moubray, Esq., grandson of John Moubray, Esq. of Cockairny, co. Fife, and *d.* 1836, leaving issue.
Edward, William, Rowley, } all deceased.
HENRY, the present MAJOR-GENERAL HALL, C.B., of Knockbrack.
Francis Tipping, *m.* Anne-Maria Waddington, and is deceased.
Anne, deceased. Margaret, deceased.
Jane M.C.

Arms, &c., same as HALL *of Narrow Water.*
Seats—Knockbrack, co. Galway; Merville, co. Dublin.

HALL OF GRAPPENHALL.

HALL, WILLIAM, Esq. of Grappenhall Hall, co. Chester, J.P. and D.L., *b.* 29 May, 1783; *m.* 1st, 24 Oct. 1805, Hannah, youngest dau. of Joseph Goodwin, Gent. of Warrington, by whom (who *d.* in 1815,) he has issue,

I. Catharine, *m.* 29 April, 1830, to Thomas-Twanbrook Glazebrook, Esq. of Egremont, co. Chester, and of Liverpool, merchant, and has two sons and four daus.
II. Jane-Eliza, *m.* 6 March, 1832, to Lionel-Courtier Dutton, Esq. of Warrington, and has issue, two sons and two daus.

Mr. Hall *m.* 2ndly, 2 May, 1816, Martha, younger dau. of Thomas Twanbrook, of Appleton, co. Chester, Gent., by whom he has issue,

I. JOHN, *b.* 30 Sept. 1818, in holy orders, M.A. of Brasenose College, Oxford, and rector of Corley, Salop, *m.* 6 Sept. 1843, Justina, youngest dau. of the Rev. John Mills, LL.B., rector of Willoughby, co. Leicester.
II. William-Twanbrook, *b.* 6 April, 1822, of Brasennose College, Oxford.

Lineage.—This branch of the family of Hall has been settled at Warrington, in Lancashire, for nearly a century past, and claims descent from an ancient family, seated at Beverley, in the co. of York. The first of them we find at Warrington was WILLIAM HALL, who embarked in the commerce of that town, and d. at an advanced age, 4 June, 1802, leaving issue,

JOHN HALL, Gent., of Warrington, who m. 1st, Elizabeth, widow of James Reddish, (of the Reddish's of Statham Hall, co. Chester,) and by her (who d. 23 July, 1806) had an only surviving child, WILLIAM HALL, Esq. of Grappenhall Hall. Mr. Hall m. 2ndly, Mary, dau. of William Cawley, Esq., and sister of the Rev. James Cawley, M A., fellow of Brasennose College, Oxford, but by that lady had no issue. He d. 17 April 1824.

Arms—Arg., three battle-axes.
Crest—An embowed arm, holding a battle-axe.
Motto—Finem respice.
Seat—Grappenhall Hall, near Warrington.

HALLIDAY OF CHAPEL CLEEVE.

HALLIDAY, JOHN, Esq. of Chapel Cleeve, co. Somerset, J.P. and D.L., b. Oct. 1816; m. 18 June, 1845, Georgina-Eliza, dau. of Edward Coles, Esq. of Paul's House, near Taunton.

Lineage.—WALTER HALLIDAY, called "*The Minstrel*," became master of the revels to EDWARD IV., and acquired lands in the parish of Rodborough, co. Gloucester. He was father of

HENRY HALLIDAY, styled of Minchin Hampton, who m. a dau. of Payne, of Payne's Court, and left four sons, viz.,

HENRY, his successor.
EDWARD, of Rodborough, in Gloucestershire, father of William Halliday, of Rodborough, who m. Sarah Brydges, aunt of John, Lord Chandos, and had a son, SIR LEONARD HALLIDAY, lord-mayor of London in 1605.
William, of Stroud, in Gloucestershire.
John, ancestor of the late WILLIAM HALLIDAY, Esq. of Rodborough, co. Gloucester.

The eldest son,

HENRY HALLIDAY, m. and had (with another child, Edward, who d. unm.) a son,

THOMAS HALLIDAY, Esq. of Kings Stanley, father of

LAWRENCE HALLIDAY, some time mayor of the city of Gloucester, who m. Jane, dau. of Thomas Pury, and had issue,

I. William, a merchant of London, the first chairman of the United East India Company. His two daus. and co-heirs were,
 1 ANNE, m. to Sir Henry Mildmay, of Wanstead, Essex.
 2 MARGARET, m. to Sir Edward Hungerford, of Corsham, in Wilts.
II. SAMUEL, of whom presently.
III. John.
I. Margaret, m. to Mr. Jasper Clutterbooke.

The 2nd son,

SAMUEL HALLIDAY, Esq. was father of

WILLIAM HALLIDAY, Esq., who m. and had issue,

EDWARD.
Giles, of Wedington, near Devizes, ancestor of the HALLIDAYS of Urchfont and Sutton Veney, extinct in 1827.
Richard, progenitor of a branch seated at Bradford, Wilts.
Dorothy, m. to Matthew Cooke, of Frome.

The eldest son,

EDWARD HALLIDAY, Esq. of Warminster, b. in 1625, m. 1st, Mary, dau. of John Pilton, of Warminster, and had a son,

EDWARD, b. 1659, who settled at Frome, in Somersetshire, and marrying Mary, dau. of John Hippie, became ancestor of the HALLIDAYS of Frome, extinct in 1823.

Edward Halliday, m. 2ndly, Mrs. Elizabeth Gardiner, but by that lady (who d. in 1662) had no issue. He m. 3rdly, Mary, dau. of John Barton, of Warminster, and had issue, JOHN, and other issue. Mr. Halliday, d. in 1701-2. His elder son, by his third marriage,

JOHN HALLIDAY, Esq. of Yard House, co. Somerset, and of Tilshed, Wilts, b. 1671, m. Mary, dau. of Edmund Trowbridge, Esq. of Lyppeyeate, by whom (who d. 9 May, 1732) he had issue,

I. JOHN, s. to his father.
II. Edmund, b. in 1716, who m. Mary, only dau. of William Jones, of Sherborne, and dying in 1744, left issue,
 1 Edmund, b. in 1744, who m. Joanna, dau. of John Ricketts, Esq. of Gosport, and d. at Dinan, in Brittany, 24 March, 1832, leaving a son and successor,
  JOHN-EDMUND, of Warminster, who m. Mary-Jane, eldest dau. of Dr. John Seagram, of Warminster.
I. Mary, d. unm. in 1807.

Mr. Halliday d. 17 June, 1737, and was s. by his son,

JOHN HALLIDAY, Esq. of Yard House, M.P. for Taunton, high-sheriff of Somersetshire in 1745. He m. 1737, Mary, dau. of Isaac Welman, Esq. of Poundisford Park, co. Somerset, and had (with four daus.) three sons,

I. JOHN, his heir.
II. Simon, of Iford Park, Wilts, and Westcombe Park, in Kent, an eminent banker of the city of London, b. in 1738, m. Jane, dau. of John Bytheses, Esq. of Wickhouse, Wilts, and dying 18 May, 1791, left issue,
 1 SIMON-WELMAN.
 1 Mary.
 2 Harriet, m. to the Rev. Joseph Griffith, of Brompton Hall, Middlesex, rector of Turvey, in Bedfordshire.
 3 Elizabeth, m. to Michael-Dicker Saunders, Esq. of Exeter.
 4 Jane, m. to Sir John Dyer, K.C.B., colonel of the royal artillery.
 5 Louisa, m. 1st, to General Sproule, R.A.; and 2ndly, to Frederick Caulfeild, Esq. of Faulkner House, Gloucestershire.
III. Edmund Trowbridge, of Chapel Cleeve, b. 26 Oct. 1743, m. Jane, dau. of the Rev. Tilleman Hodgkinson, and left issue,
 1 John, of Chapel Cleeve, m. 1814, Anne-Innes, dau. of General Dyer, and dying in 1826, left
  JOHN, present representative of the family.
  George-Edmund, captain 82nd Foot.
  William-Leonard, captain 56th Bengal N.I.
  Jane. Anne-Innes. Susan.
 2 Trowbridge, in holy orders, now of Yard House.
 3 Mary-Elizabeth, m. to Peter Rickards-Mynors, Esq. of Treago, co. Hereford, and Enjobb, co. Radnor.

Mr. Halliday d. 9 June, 1754, and was s. by his son,

JOHN HALLIDAY, Esq. of Yard House, M.P. for Taunton, who d. unm. in April 1805, aged 68, when the representation of the family devolved upon his nephew,

SIMON-WELMAN HALLIDAY, Esq. who d. s. p. in 1842, when the representation of the family devolved on his cousin, the present JOHN HALLIDAY, Esq. of Chapel Cleeve.

Arms—Sa., three helmets, arg., garnished, or, within a border, engrailed, of the second, granted *temp.* EDWARD IV., confirmed in 1605, quartering the ensigns of TROWBRIDGE, viz., or, on a bridge of three arches, in fesse, gu., masoned, sa., the streams transfluent, ppr., a fane, arg.
Crest—A demi-lion, rampant, or, holding an anchor, as.
Motto—Quarta saluti.
Seat—Chapel Cleeve, near Dunster.

HALLIFAX OF CHADACRE HALL.

HALLIFAX, THOMAS, Esq. of Chadacre Hall, co. Suffolk, J.P. and D.L., high-sheriff, 1837, m. Annah-Maria, dau. of John Staunton, Esq. of Kenilworth, co. Warwick, and left issue,

I. THOMAS, of Berkeley Square, London, deceased.
II. John-Savile, of Edwardston House, co. Suffolk, in holy orders, m. Katharine, eldest dau. of the Rev. Thomas Godfrey, of Bury St. Edmund's.
I. Maria. II. Ellen.
III. Diana, m. to John-George Weller-Poley, Esq.

Mr. Hallifax was only surviving son of the late Sir Thomas Hallifax, Knt., lord mayor of the city of London in 1777, by Margaret his wife, dau. and co-heir of John Savile, Esq. of Clay Hill, co. Middlesex. Chadacre Hall is now the property and residence of Mr. Hallifax's two eldest daus.

Arms—Or, on a pile, engr., sa., between two fountains, ppr., three cross-crosslets, of the first, quartering, SAVILE, viz., arg., on a bend, sa., three owls, of the field.
Crest—A moor cock, with wings expanded, combed and wattled, ppr., ducally gorged, and charged on the breast with a cross-crosslet, or.
Seat—Chadacre Hall, Bury St. Edmund's Suffolk.

HALSEY OF GADDESDEN.

HALSEY, SARAH, of Gaddesden Park, co. Hertford, s. her father 9 Oct. 1788; m. 1st, 3 Aug. 1804, Joseph-Thompson Whately, Esq., 3rd son of the Rev. Joseph Whateley, D.D. of Nonsuch Park, Surrey, brother of the Archbishop of Dublin, and nephew of William Plumer, Esq. of Ware Park, M.P. for Herts. By Mr. Whateley (who assumed the surname of HALSEY in 1804, and d. 1818), she had issue,

I. THOMAS-PLUMER, M.P. for Herts, b. 26 Jan. 1815, m. Jan. 1839, Frederica, dau. of Lieut.-Col. Frederick Johnstone, of Hilton, and had a son and heir,

THOMAS-FREDERICK, b. 9 Dec. 1839.

Mr. Halsey and his wife, with an infant son, Ethelbert Arthur Sackville, were lost in the "Ercolano" steamer, 24 April, 1854.

I. Mary-Elizabeth, m. 11 Sept. 1826, to Thos. Herbert Noyes, Esq.

II. Jane, m. 1827, to the Rev. George Tyrwhitt Drake.

III. Emma, m. 1832, to Lieut Col. William Tyrwhitt Drake.

IV. Fanny.

Mrs. Halsey m. 2ndly, in Feb. 1821, the Rev. John FitzMoore, eldest son of Richard Moore, Esq. of Hampton Court Palace. Mr. Moore assumed on his marriage, the name of HALSEY, in addition to his patronymic. Mrs. Halsey has by her 2nd husband, one dau.,

I. Georgina-Theodosia Halsey.

Lineage.—"Upon the dissolution of the monastery of Dartford, in Kent, the rectory of Great Gaddesden, with the right of patronage to the vicarage, came to the crown, in which it remained vested until 36 HENRY VIII., when it was granted to William Hawse, *alias* Chamber, and it has continued ever since with that family, now called Halsey."

SIR JOHN HALSEY, Knt. of Great Gaddesden (great-grandson of William Halsey, of the Parsonage, who was buried at Great Gaddesden, 16 May, 1596), became one of the masters in Chancery. He m. Judith, eldest dau. and co-heir of James Necton, Esq., and by her, who d. aged 31, in 1658, had surviving issue, NECTON, his heir; THOMAS, successor to his brother; Dorothy, m. to Christopher Abdy, Esq., and d. in 1686, aged 41; Judith; and Lettice. Sir John Halsey, d. 29 June, 1670, was buried at Great Gaddesden, and s. by his son,

NECTON HALSEY, Esq., who d. in minority and unm., 12 Dec. 1670, and was s. by his brother,

THOMAS HALSEY, Esq. of Great Gaddesden, M.P., high-sheriff for Hertfordshire, 31 CHARLES II. He m. Anne, dau. and heiress of Thomas Henshaw, Esq. of Kensington, and left, 25 May, 1715, a son and successor,

HENSHAW HALSEY, Esq. of Great Gaddesden, who d. s. p. 13 Jan. 1738, and was s. by his brother,

CHARLES HALSEY, Esq. of Great Gaddesden, bap. 12 Dec. 1690, high-sheriff of Herts in 1746, m. Agatha, dau. of Frederick Dorrien, Esq. of London, and by her (who d. aged 75, 26 Feb. 1782) had

FREDERICK, } heirs in succession.
THOMAS, }

Anne, m. 1st, to the Rev. George Dutens; and 2ndly, to the Rev. James Willis, rector of Sopley, Hants.

Theodosia, m. 1st, to the Rev. John Perry, rector of Wyton, in Huntingdonshire; and 2ndly, to Robert Sparrow, Esq. of Worlingham, Hall, in Suffolk.

Elizabeth, m. to Thomas-Herbert Noyes, Esq.

Sophia, m. 2 April, 1766, to Richard Bingham, Esq. of Melcombe Bingham, co. Dorset.

He d. 6 April, 1748, and was s. by his son,

FREDERICK HALSEY, Esq. of Great Gaddesden, who was appointed, in 1768, commissary-general of the allied army in Germany, and was afterwards aide-de-camp to the hereditary Prince of Wolfenbuttle. He d. unm. in Hesse Darmstadt, 24 Aug. 1762, and was s. by his brother,

THOMAS HALSEY, Esq. of Great Gaddesden, b. at Hamburgh, 4 Feb. 1731, M.P. for Herts in 1768, 1774, and 1781, m. 18 March, 1784, Sarah, youngest dau. of John Crawley, Esq. of Stockwood, co. Bedford, and dying 9 Oct. 1788, left an only dau. and heiress,

SARAH HALSEY, now of Gaddesden.

Arms—Arg., on a pile, sa., three griffins' heads, erased, of the first.

Crest—A dexter hand, ppr., sleeve, gu., cuff, arg., holding a griffin's claw, erased, or.

Motto—Nescit vox missa reverti.

Seat—Gaddesden Park, Hertfordshire.

HAMBROUGH OF STEEPHILL CASTLE.

HAMBROUGH, JOHN, ESQ., of Steepbill Castle, Isle of Wight, and Pipewell Hall, co. Northampton, J.P., b. 1793; m. 11 Feb. 1820, Sophia, youngest dau. of the late Gore Townsend, Esq. of Honington Hall, co. Warwick, by the Lady Elizabeth Windsor his wife, dau. of Other Lewis, 4th Earl of Plymouth, and has issue,

I. ALBERT-JOHN, J.P. and D.L., F.G.S., &c., b. 1820; m. 1845, Charlotte-Jane, youngest dau. of John Fleming, Esq., M.P., of Stoneham Park, Hants.

II. Oscar-William, J.P., b. 1825.

III. Windsor-Edmund, B.A., b. 1830.

Lineage.—The family of Hambrough is of Hanoverian origin. The earliest recorded ancestor, HENRY HAMBROUGH, was born in 1574, and was educated at Oxford, where he distinguished himself. The epitaph on his tomb, in Huntingdonshire, records that he was of honourable ancestry. JAMES HAMBROUGH, b. 1670, was father of JOHN HAMBROUGH, b. 1694, whose son, JAMES HAMBROUGH, m. Elizabeth Nash, and was father of

JOHN HAMBROUGH, Esq., of Pipewell Hall, Northampton, and Hanwell, co. Middlesex, who m. Catherine, dau. of Robert Holden, Esq., representative of a branch of the ancient family of Holden, of Lancashire, and, maternally, a descendant of Sir Lancelot Oldisworth, of Halifax, co. York, living A.D. 1287, 15 EDWARD I.; by her he had a dau. Mary-Catherine, m. to the Rev. Edward James Townsend, rector of Ilmington, and an only surviving son, the present JOHN HAMBROUGH, Esq., of Steephill Castle.

Arms—1st and 4th: arg., semée of cross-crosslets, az., and guttes de sang, a tower sa. for HAMBROUGH; 2nd and 3rd: sa., on a fess, between two chevrons ermines, two covered cups, az. for HOLDEN.

Crest—On a mount vert, a horse current arg. powdered, with cross-crosslets and guttes de sang.

Mottoes—Over the crest: Foresight; under the arms: Honestum utili prefer.

Seats—Steephill Castle, Isle of Wight, and Pipewell Hall, Northamptonshire.

HAMERTON OF HELLIFIELD-PEEL.

HAMERTON, JAMES, Esq. of Hellifield-Peel, co. York, M.A., barrister-at-law, b. 16 May, 1779; m. 22 April, 1806, Maria, dau. of S. Chamberlayne, Esq. of Ryes, in Essex, and by her (who is deceased) has issue,

I. CHISNALL, b. 22 Feb. 1807, B.A.

II. John, b. in April, 1810, B.A.

III. Henry, b. 14 March, 1813.

I. Mary-Anne. II. Frances.

Mr. Hamerton s. his father in 1824.

Lineage.—"The town of Hamerton," says Doctor Whitaker, "gives its name to one of the most ancient families in the north of England." The first member of which, upon record,

RICHARD DE HAMERTON, living 12 HENRY II., was lineal ancestor of

SIR RICHARD HAMERTON, of Hamerton, who founded a chantry in the church of Long Preston, dedicated to our Ladye, and St. Anne. This gentleman m. Elizabeth, relict of Sir Ralph Harrington, and dau. of Sir John Assheton, K.B., of Assheton-under-Line. He d. in 1480, leaving, with a dau. (Jane, wife of Brian Rocliffe, of Cowthorpe, one of the barons of the Exchequer), a son and successor,

SIR STEPHEN HAMERTON, of Hamerton, who was made a Knight Baneret in Scotland, by Richard, duke of Gloucester, 20 Edward IV. His grandson,

SIR STEPHEN HAMERTON, of Hamerton, was in the train of Henry de Clifford, first Earl of Cumberland, and in favour at court, *temp.* HENRY VIII., but afterwards being involved in the great northern insurrection (anno 1537), he received his majesty's pardon. Rebelling a second time with the Lord Darcy, and his brother-in-law, Sir Francis de Bigod, he was taken prisoner, conveyed to London, and executed and attainted.

JOHN HAMERTON, Esq. (nephew and heir male of Sir Stephen Hamerton, of Hamerton), thus became "of Hellifield-Peel." This gentleman m. Ursula, dau. of Robert Banister, Esq. of Kilbrook, and from him derived sixth in descent,

JOHN HAMERTON, Esq. of Hellifield-Peel, b. in 1695 (eldest son of Stephen Hamerton, Esq. of Hellifield-Peel, by Anne, his wife, dau. and heir of Sir Edward Chisenhall, of Chisenhall, co. Lancaster), who m. 1st, Mary, dau. of Thomas Purchase, Esq. of Langton, by whom (who d. in 1740) he had an only surviving child,

MARY, m. to the Rev. James Brooke, of Killoughbeck.

Mr. Hamerton m. 2ndly, Mary, dau. of Gilbert Holden, Esq. of Hollins, and dying in 1763, left by this lady,

JAMES, his successor.
JOHN, A.B., d. in 1773, unm.
Gilbert, b. in 1754.
Thomas. William.
Susanna. Anne.

The eldest son,

JAMES HAMERTON, Esq. of Hellifield-Peel, b. 16 April, 1749, m. Miss Hancock, and dying in 1824, was s. by his eldest son, JAMES HAMERTON, Esq. of Hellifield-Peel.

Arms—Arg., three hammers, sa.
Crest—A greyhound, couchant.
Motto—Fixus adversa sperno.
Seat—Hellifield-Peel, co. York.

HAMILTON OF EVANDALE AND GILKERSCLEUGH.

HAMILTON, WALTER, Esq. of Gilkerscleugh, co. Lanark, colonel in the army, and lieut.-col. 78th regiment.

Lineage.—SIR JAMES HAMILTON, of Fynnart and Evandale, son of James, 1st Earl of Arran, was the first of this family. He was a person of great influence and consideration at the court of JAMES V. who appointed him cup-bearer, principal steward of the royal household, and superintendant of his palaces and castles. He was also captain of the Palace of Linlithgow, and of the Castle of Dumbarton, and was often employed by that monarch in missions, and affairs of importance. He was an extraordinary lord of the College of Justice, and high-sheriff of the shires of Renfrew, Linlithgow, and Ayr. He had extensive grants of lands from his father, the Earl of Arran; by his marriage with the heiress of the Livingstons, of Drumray, he acquired the large estates of that family, and of the Wemyss's, of Wemyss; De Valences, of Torry; and Lochores, of Lochore; and by purchase and the favour of the King, he further increased his possessions to an extent hardly equalled by the highest nobles of the land. After enjoying the confidence of the King for many years, he at last fell a victim to the intrigues of his enemies, and being falsely accused of treason, was condemned and beheaded at Edinburgh, on the 16th August, 1540, and his large estates forfeited to the Crown. He m. Margaret, sole child and heiress of Sir Robert Livingston, of Drumray, and Easter Wemyss, and had, with other children, a son and heir, JAMES. His dau. Grisel was m. to Andrew, 4th Earl of Rothes, and his dau., Agnes, to James, 6th Lord Somerville.

SIR JAMES HAMILTON, of Evandale, and Crawfordjohn, had his father's forfeiture rescinded in parliament, in 1543, and was restored to the possession of a large portion of his estates. He was sheriff of Clydesdale, and sat in parliament as Commissioner of the Barons for the shire of Lanark. He was a faithful adherent of Queen MARY, who was his guest at the castle of Craignethan, before the battle of Langside, where he was taken prisoner. He m. Helen, dau. of John Cunningham, of Caprington, and had, besides other children,

JAMES, his heir.
John, of Gilkerscleugh, of whom presently.

He d. before 1589, and was s. by his eldest son,

SIR JAMES HAMILTON, of Libberton, and Evandale, who sat in parliament as Commissioner of the barons for the shire of Lanark, and was taken prisoner with his father at Langside. He m. Christian, 3rd dau. of Robert, 4th Lord Boyd, and had issue, besides daus., two sons; 1, JAMES, his heir; and 2, Thomas, of Columby, who d. unm. He d in 1606, and was s. by his son,

SIR JAMES HAMILTON, of Evandale, and Crawfordjohn, who greatly dissipated his estate. He m. Lady Margaret Cuningham, 3rd dau of James, 7th Earl of Glencairn, and dying before 1616, left surviving issue, one dau., Jane, who m. Sir James Maxwell, of Calderwood. On the death of Sir James, the representation of the family devolved on his uncle,

JOHN HAMILTON, of Gilkerscleugh, who obtained that estate and other lands in Crawfordjohn. He was forfeited for his adherence to Queen MARY, but was subsequently restored. He m. Margaret, dau. of James Hamilton of Nielsland, and dying about 1629, was s. by his son.

JOHN HAMILTON, of Gilkerscleugh, who m. Jean, dau. of William Hamilton, of Udston, and d. about 1668, leaving a son and successor,

WILLIAM HAMILTON, of Gilkerscleugh, who m. Margaret, eldest dau. of Sir Alexander Hamilton, of Haggs, Baronet, and heir of her brother, the last Baronet. He d. before 1679, and was s. by his eldest son,

JOHN HAMILTON, of Gilkerscleugh, who, as representing the house of Evandale, carried the banner of that family, as one of the chief mourners, at the funeral of John, Duke of Rothes, Lord High Chancellor of Scotland on the 23rd of August, 1681. He m. Catharine, 6th dau. of James Hamilton, of Westport, and dying in 1700, was s. by his eldest son,

JAMES HAMILTON, of Gilkerscleugh, who acquired the barony of Monkland. He d. in 1770, leaving by his first wife, Barbara, dau. of John Mitchell, of Ledath, a son and heir,

ALEXANDER HAMILTON, of Gilkerscleugh, who m. Helen, youngest dau. of John Macqueen, of Braxfield, and had issue,

I. John, d. young.
II. James, d. young.
III. DANIEL, heir to his father.
IV. Robert, sheriff of Lanarkshire, d. s. p.
V. Charles, m. Isabella, dau. of John Campbell, Esq. of the family of Inverary, and had issue,
  1 Alexander, W.S., of Edinburgh, m. and has issue.
  2 John-Campbell, deceased.
  3 Charles, m. Janet, dau. of David Lillie, Esq. of Fifeshire, and has a son, Charles.
  4 Robert, in holy orders, chaplain to the forces, K.S.F. and K.T.S., and chaplain to the Duke of Hamilton.
  1 Margaret-Scott, deceased.
  2 Helen, deceased. 3 Isabella-Campbell.
  4 Eliza-Helen. 5 Catherine-Georgina.
VI. Alexander, R.N., deceased.
VII. Thomas, m. Elizabeth, dau. of John Parish, Esq. of Bath, and had a son, George-Lowther, in the army, deceased.
VIII. James, of Kames Castle, co. Bute, m. Harriet, dau. of Richard Wynne, Esq., and had issue, James-Alexander; Richard-Wynne; and Emma-Eugenia.
IX. Stirling, in the army, deceased.
I. Helen, d. young.
II. Barbara, m. 1st, to John Robertson, Esq. of Hallcraig; and 2ndly, to Gen. George Irving.

Alexander Hamilton d. in 1790, and was s. by his eldest surviving son,

DANIEL HAMILTON, of Gilkerscleugh, who m. Harriet, 2nd dau. of Walter Campbell, of Shawfield, and had issue,

I. Alexander-Henry, R.N., d. unm.
II. WALTER, his heir.
III. John-James, major in the 56th regt. Bengal N. I.
IV. George-William, major of the 34th regt. Bengal N. I., and commissioner of the Mooltan division, who m. Charlotte, second dau. of Colonel William Logie, and has surviving issue,
  1 George-John, 81st regt. of foot.
  2 William.
  3 Walter-Robert.
  1 Harriet, m. to Captain James-Charles Curtis.
  2 Charlotte-Helen.
V. Robert-Ker, chaplain H. E. I. C. S., m. Susan-Anne-Sophia Churchill, second daughter of the Rt. Rev. George-John-Trevor Spencer, late Bishop of Madras, and great-grandson of Charles, Duke of Marlborough, and has issue,
  1 Robert. 2 Walter.
I. Eleanora, m. to Archibald-James Hamilton, younger, of Dalzell.
II. Harriet-Carter, d. unm.

Daniel d. 1822, and was s. by his eldest surviving son,

WALTER HAMILTON, now of Gilkerscleugh, colonel in the army, and lieut.-col. of the 78th regt. of foot.

Arms—Gules, three cinquefoils pierced, ermine, within a double tressure, flowered and counter-flowered with fleurs-de-lis, argent.

Crest—In a ducal coronet, or, an oak tree fructed and penetrated transversely in the main stem by a frame saw, proper, the frame of the first.

Supporters—Two antelopes argent, attired, ducally gorged, chained and unguled, or.

Mottoes—Above: Through; below: In arduis fortitudo. The double tressure, part of the royal arms, was granted, by King JAMES V., to Sir James Hamilton, of Fynnart and Evandale, by charter dated 3rd March, 1530.

Seats—The chief seats of the family were at the castles of Craignethan or Draffan, Avathaven, Libberton, and Crawfordjohn, and at Monkland and Gilkerscleugh.

HAMILTON OF ORBISTON AND DALZELL.

HAMILTON, JOHN-GLENCAIRN-CARTER, Esq. of Dalzell, co. Lanark, D.L., capt. 2nd life-guards, *b.* 16 Nov. 1829.

Lineage.—GAVIN HAMILTON, the 4th son of Sir James Hamilton, *Dominus de Cadzow*, from whom derives the ducal house of HAMILTON, was ancestor of this family He lived during the reigns of JAMES II. and III. He *m.* Jean Muirhead, called "the fair maid of Lechbrunnock," descended of the house of Lauchope. By this lady he had issue,

- ROBERT, chancellor of Glasgow, who appears to have died before his brother John, without issue.
- II. THOMAS, who was called to the succession among the other heirs of Lord Hamilton, in the first settlement of the Hamilton estates, by charter under the great seal, of date 23rd October, 1455; but he appears to have also died before his brother John, without issue.
- III. JOHN, who succeeded to Orbistoun.
- IV. Archibald.
- V. Gavin, the ancestor of the family of Haggs.

JOHN HAMILTON, the first we have found designed by the title of Orbistoun, *m.* Jean, dau. of Hamilton, of Woodhall, by whom he had issue,

- GAVIN, his heir.
- ARCHIBALD.
- John, the first of Ferguslee.
- Patrick.
- David, the first of Bothwellhaugh.
- Daughter, *m.* to the Laird of Hawkhill.
- Daughter, *m.* to Alexander Stewart, of Race.

The eldest son,

GAVIN HAMILTON, of Orbistoun, was named one of the heirs of entail, in a deed of settlement executed by the first Earl of Arran, 16th January, 1512-13. He was again named one of the heirs of entail, in a settlement of the Hamilton estates by the Duke of Chatelherault, of date 15 Sept. 1540. He *m.* Helen, dau. of Wallace, of Cairnhill, and had issue,

- JOHN, his heir.
- Robert, provost of the College of St. Andrews.
- David.
- Arthur, the first of Parkhead.
- James, of Ruchbank, progenitor of the Hamiltons of Kilbrackmonth.

The elder son,

JOHN HAMILTON, of Orbistoun, accompanying the queen along with his kinsmen, the Hamiltons, to the battle of Langsyde, fell in that action. He *m.* Margaret, dau. of Hamilton, of Haggs, and had issue,

- JOHN, his heir.
- GAVIN, bishop of Galloway.
- Isobel, *m.* to Robert Hamilton, of Dalserf.
- A dau., *m.* to Robert Hamilton, of Barnchyith.
- A dau., *m.* to Cleland, of Knownoblehill.
- A dau., *m.* to Baillie, of Jerviston.
- Marjory, *m.* to David Dundas, of Duddingstoun.
- Margaret, *m.* to John Robertoun, brother of James Robertoun, of Ernock.

The eldest son,

JOHN HAMILTON, of Orbistown, *m.* Christian, dau. of Robert Dalziel, ancestor of the Earls of Carnwath, and had issue,

- JOHN, his heir, afterwards Sir John, Lord Justice Clerk, whose male line expired with his grandson, William Hamilton, of Orbistoun.
- JAMES, the first of Dalzell.
- Gavin.
- Marion, *m.* to James Hamilton, of Bangour.
- Margaret, *m.* to John Walkinshaw.

John of Orbistoun *d.* about 1621; his 2nd son,

JAMES HAMILTON, of Dalzell, acquired a considerable estate. He *m.* Jean, dau. of Sir John Henderson, of Fordell, and had,

- ALEXANDER, his heir.
- Robert, the first of Monkland.
- James, the first of Boggs. His tenth and youngest son, Sir David Hamilton, was chief physician to Queen Anne.
- Anne, *m.* to David Boswell, of Auchinleck.

James, of Dalzell, *d.* Feb. 1668, and was *s.* by his son,

ALEXANDER HAMILTON, of Dalzell, who had a charter of the lands and barony of Dalzell, dated 24 May, 1671. He *m.* Berthia, dau. of Sir William Henderson, of Fordell, and had issue,

- JAMES, his heir.
- William, of Greenhead.
- Jean, *m.* to Charles Stewart, of Dunearn, Esq.
- Elizabeth, *m.* to Alexander MacDougall, of Corrochtree

Alexander, of Dalziel, *d.* in 1692, and was *s.* by his son,

JAMES HAMILTON, of Dalzell, who *m.* 1693, Margaret, eldest dau. of Sir Archibald Hamilton, of Rosehall, Bart., and had issue,

- ARCHIBALD, his heir.
- James, of Muirhouse and Browncastle, appointed, in 1722, collector of taxes for the co. Lanark
- Elizabeth, *m.* to Major John Robertoun, of Ernock.
- Margaret, *b.* 22 Feb. 1700, *d.* at Muirhouse, 7th April, 1797, ætat 98.
- Jean, *m.* 20 July, 1727, to James Robertoun, of Bedley, and *d.* in April, 1784, ætat 83.
- Anne, *b.* 16th January, 1703; *d. unm.* at Muirhouse, 15th April, 1796, ætat 94.
- Violet, *d. unm.* at Orbestoun.

The eldest son,

ARCHIBALD HAMILTON, of Dalzell, *m.* 19 March, 1782, Marion, eldest dau. of Hugh Dalrymple, of Dromore, one of the Senator of the College of Justice, and descended of the family of Stair; and had issue,

- JAMES, his heir.
- JOHN, who succeeded to the estate.
- Robert, *b.* in 1746, *d.* at Dalzell, on 6th June, 1790, *unm.*
- Anne, *b.* in 1734, *d.* at Dalzell, 20th July, 1793, *unm.*
- Margaret, *m.* to William Lawson, Esq. of Cairnmuir, in Tweeddale.
- Henrietta, *d.* at Dalzell, 16 March, 1775, *unm.*

Archibald, of Dalzell, and Orbistoun, *d.* at Dalzell, 28 Dec. 1774. His widow survived, and *d.* at Dalzell, 23 Dec. 1779. Their eldest son,

JAMES HAMILTON, of Dalzell, *b.* 1733, was served heir to his father in the lands of Dalzell, &c., in 1774. He *d.* at Dalzell, 6 Dec. 1814, in his 81st year, and, being *unm.*, he was *s.* by his brother,

JOHN HAMILTON of Dalzell, *b.* 1742, a general in the army, who *m.* Miss Anne Mathews, only dau. of Dr. Mathews, and had issue,

- ARCHIBALD-JAMES, his heir, *b.* 28 Oct. 1793, an officer in the army, who served in the Peninsular war, and in the Scots Greys at Waterloo; *m.* 1st, Margaret-Sibella Ramsay, by whom (who *d.* 24 Aug. 1824) he had no surviving issue; and 2ndly, Ellinor, dau. of Daniel Hamilton, Esq. of Gilkerscleugh, by whom (whom *d.* 16 Sept. 1856) he left at his decease, 11 Jan. 1834, a son, the present JOHN-GLENCAIRN-CARTER HAMILTON, Esq. of Dalzell.
- Robert, *b.* 7th August, 1796.
- Marion, *m.* to Lieutenant-Colonel David Rattray. She *d.* 1st May, 1818.

Gen. Hamilton *d.* 9 Feb. 1832, aged 92.

Arms—First and fourth: gules, an annulet or, between three cinquefoils ermine, for ORBISTOUN; second and third: gules, a mollet argent, between three cinquefoils ermine a rose proper in chief argent, for ROSEHALL.

Supporters—On the dexter side an antelope proper, gorged with ducal crown and chains thereto affixed or; on the sinister side a savage proper wreathed, holding in sinister a club.

Crest—An antelope proper gorged, with ducal crown and chains appended.

Motto—"Quis occurrabit."

Seat—Dalzell, near Motherwell.

HAMILTON OF CRAIGHLAW.

HAMILTON, WILLIAM-CHARLES-STEWART, Esq. of Craighlaw, co. Wigton, J.P. and D.L., *b.* 1831.

Lineage.—JOHN HAMILTON, of Ladyland, who *s.* his father in 1690, sold the property to Alexander, 9th earl of Eglinton, and went to the north of Ireland, to an estate he had purchased there. He *m.* Margaret, dau. of Sir John Shaw, Bart. of Greenock, by Jane, his wife, dau. of Sir William Mure, of Rowallan, and had a numerous family. His eldest son,

WILLIAM HAMILTON, Esq., sold his Irish property, and returning to Scotland, purchased the estate of Craighlaw, co. Wigton. He *m.* Isabella, dau. of McDowal, of Logan, but had no issue. His brother,

CHARLES HAMILTON, Esq. of Craighlaw, *m.* Sarah, another dau. of McDowal, of Logan, and had several children; one of the daus., Anne, *m.* to Major John Peebles, of Irvine, and had an only child, Sarah, wife of Col. John Cunningham, of Caddel and Thornton. Mr. Hamilton *d.* in 1783, and was *s.* by his son,

WILLIAM HAMILTON, of Craighlaw, M.D., who *m.* Agnes, only child of Edward Cairns, Esq., of Girstonwood, and had (with daus., one of whom, Catherine, *m.* in 1815, William Cochrane, of Ladyland, Esq.) an only son,

WILLIAM-CHARLES HAMILTON, Esq. of Craighlaw, J.P. and D.L., formerly a capt. in the army, who served at Waterloo, *b.* 1794; *m.* 1825, Anne, dau. of the Rev. Dr. Stewart, and left issue, WILLIAM-CHARLES-STEWART, now of Craighlaw; Christina-Grace-Agnes; and Anne-Lillias.

Arms—Gu., a mullet, between three cinquefoils, all within a bordure, wavy, arg.
Crest—On waves of the sea, a dolphin in chase of a flying fish, all ppr.
Motto—Honestum pro patriâ.
Seat—Craighlaw, co. Wigton.

HAMILTON OF BANGOUR AND NINEWAR.

HAMILTON, JAMES, Esq. of Bangour, co. Ayr, and of Ninewar, East Lothian, J.P. and D.L., *b.* in Nov. 1799; *m.* in Oct. 1824, Mary, dau. of William, Lord Panmure, and *d.* 2 March, 1851.

Lineage.—The family of Hamilton of Bangour is a scion of Hamilton of Bruntwood. The great-grandfather of the present representative was the well known poet,

WILLIAM HAMILTON, of Bangour. He was *b.* at Bangour, co. Ayr, in 1704, and, in 1745, joined in the last attempt to restore the house of Stuart to the throne, was present at the battle of Culloden, and after the issue of that memorable conflict, fled to France, where he *d.* in 1754. He *m.* in 1743, Katherine, dau. of Sir James Hall, 2nd Bart. of Dunglass, and by her had one son,

JAMES HAMILTON, Esq. of Bangour, who *m.* Margaret, dau. of Bruce, of Kinnaird, and (with three daus.) was father of

WILLIAM HAMILTON, Esq. of Bangour, who *m.* in 1798, Anne, dau. of Edward Lee, of Tramore Lodge, co. Waterford, and had a son and successor, JAMES HAMILTON, Esq. of Bangour and Ninewar.

Arms—Gu., a mullet, between three cinquefoils, arg., a chief, of the second.
Crest—A ship in distress, ppr.
Motto—Immersabilis.
Seat—Ninewar, Dunbar, East Lothian.

BUCHANAN-HAMILTON OF SPITTAL, LENY, AND BARDOWIE.

BUCHANAN-HAMILTON, JOHN, Esq. of Spittal, co. Dumbarton, Leny, co. Perth, and Bardowie, co. Stirling, chief of the clan Buchanan, *b.* 14 Feb. 1822; *m.* 9 July, 1845, Margaret, youngest dau. of the late George Seton, Esq., of the family of Cariston, and has issue.

Buchanan of that Ilk.

Lineage.—The reputed progenitor of the family of Buchanan was BUEY ANSELLAN (or Absalon), son of O'Kyan, king of Ulster, in Ireland, who, having been concerned in a massacre of the Danes, in Limerick, at the beginning of the 11th century, was compelled to abandon his native country, and take refuge in Scotland (*circ.* 1016), where he lent assistance in repelling his enemies the Danes, and received from King MALCOLM II. a grant of land for his services.

SIR MAURICE BUCHANAN, 9th laird of Buchanan (son of Gilbert, 8th laird of Buchanan, seneschal to the earls of Lennox, the first of the family who assumed the surname of Buchanan), left three sons,

MAURICE (Sir), 10th laird of Buchanan.
Allan, who *m.* the heiress of the family of Leny, or Lany, of that ilk. The last lineal male descendant of the Buchanans of Leny was Henry, (*circ* 1723,) whose dau. and heiress, Catharine, *m.* Thomas Buchanan, of Spittal, as afterwards mentioned.
John, ancestor of the BUCHANANS *of Aucheiven.*

The 9th laird was *s.* by his eldest son,

SIR MAURICE BUCHANAN, 10th laird of Buchanan, in whose castle of Buchanan King ROBERT the Bruce is said to have taken refuge after his defeat, at Dalree, by Macdougall of Lorn. He left a son,

SIR WALTER BUCHANAN, 11th laird of Buchanan, whose son,

JOHN BUCHANAN, 12th laird of Buchanan, who *m.* Janet, dau. and heiress of John Buchanan, of Leny, fourth in descent from Allan, already noticed, and had three sons,

Alexander (Sir), who slew the Duke of Clarence, brother of King HENRY V., at the battle of Beaugé, in 1421. He afterwards fell at the battle of Verneuil, (*anno* 1424,) *unm.*
WALTER (Sir), who *s.* his father.
John, who inherited the lands of LENY, and carried on that family.

The 2nd son,

SIR WALTER BUCHANAN, 13th laird of Buchanan, *m.* Isabel, dau. of Murdoch Stuart, Duke of Albany, and governor of Scotland, by whom (with a dau. *m.* to Gray, of Foulis, ancestor of Lord Gray) he had three sons,

PATRICK, his successor.
Maurice, treasurer to Lady Margaret, dau. of King JAMES I., and Dauphiness of France, with whom he left Scotland.
Thomas, ancestor of the BUCHANANS *of Carbeth.*

The eldest son,

PATRICK BUCHANAN, 14th laird of Buchanan, *m.* the dau. and heiress of Galbraith of Killearn, Bamoir, &c., and (besides one dau., Annabella, who *m.* James Stuart, of Baldorrans, grandson of Murdoch, duke of Albany) left two sons,

WALTER, 15th laird.
Thomas, first of the BUCHANANS *of Drumikill,* to which family belonged the celebrated Scottish poet and historian, George Buchanan.

The eldest son,

WALTER BUCHANAN, 15th laird of Buchanan, *m.* the dau. of Lord Graham, by whom (with two daus., of whom the 1st *m.* Lamond of Lamond, and the 2nd, the laird of Ardkinglass) he had two sons,

PATRICK.
John, ancestor of the BUCHANANS *of Arnpryor.*

His eldest son,

PATRICK BUCHANAN, fell at the battle of Flodden, in 1513, during his father's lifetime; but in the history of the family he is called the 16th laird of Buchanan. This Patrick *m.* a dau. of the earl of Argyle, and (with two daus., *m.* to the lairds of Auchinbreck and Calder) had two sons,

GEORGE, 17th Laird of Buchanan, whose lineal male descendants failed, in 1682, in the person of John, 22nd and last Laird of Buchanan.
Walter, the first of the family of Spittal.

This

WALTER BUCHANAN, of Easter Catter, *m.* Isabel, dau. (or, perhaps, sister) of the 1st earl of Glencairn, by whom he had a son,

EDWARD BUCHANAN,* of Spittal, *m.* Christian, dau. of Galbraith of Culcruich, by whom he had two sons, George, and his successor,

ROBERT BUCHANAN, who left two sons, Andrew, and

WALTER BUCHANAN, who *s.* his father, and *m.* 1st, Jean, dau. of Stirling of Craigbarnet, and 2ndly, Margaret Lawson (according to Auchmar, he *m.* the dau of Galbraith of Balgair), He left two sons, Walter, and his successor,

EDWARD BUCHANAN, who *m.* 1st, Helen, dau. of Edmonstone of Balleun, by whom he had two sons, JAMES; and John, captain in the regiment of George, laird of Buchanan, killed at the battle of Inverkeithing. He *m.* 2ndly, Margaret, dau. of John Buchanan, of Ross, by whom, (with one dau., *m.* to Cuningham of Trinbeg) he had two sons, Robert and Edward. His eldest son,

JAMES BUCHANAN, *d.* before his father, having *m.* the dau. of John Buchanan, of Cashlie, by whom he had five sons, EDWARD, John (Capt.), Archibald (Capt.), Andrew, and Walter; of whom the eldest,

EDWARD BUCHANAN, *s.* his grandfather, and *m.* Christian, dau. of the Rev. Thomas Mitchell, minister of Kilmaronock, by whom (with two daus.) he had two sons,

JOHN, his heir.
Thomas, who *m.* a dau. of Napier of Ballachairn, and had by her a dau., Christina, *m.* to Mr. Thomas Napier, of Glasgow; and a son, John, M.D., who *m.* the dau. of Sir Archibald Primrose, Bart., and had a dau., Susan.

The elder son and successor,

JOHN BUCHANAN, *m.* Margaret, dau. of Patrick Muirhead, of Rashie Mill, and relict of Robert Buchanan, of Arnpryor, and had issue a dau., Christian, *m.* to Robert Buchanan, of Leny; and three sons, I. ROBERT, col.-commandant of Dundas's regt. of Scots-Dutch, who *s.* his father, but *d. s. p.*; II. PETER, who *m.* Agnes, 2nd dau. of James Hamilton, of Hutchinson, but *d. s. p.*; and, III. THOMAS, of whose line we have to treat. This

THOMAS BUCHANAN, an officer in the Dutch service, *m.* 1st, Catharine, dau. of Henry Buchanan, of Leny (the last

* Another generation is here inserted in Auchmar's account of the family. The son of Walter, first of Spittal, is there stated to have been John, who *m.* Elizabeth, dau. of Cuningham of Drumquhassle, and was father of Edward.

lineal male representative of that family), whereby the estate of Leny came into this family; and 2ndly, Elizabeth, youngest dau. of John Hamilton, of Bardowie, whence the estate of Bardowie was acquired.

Hamilton of Bardowie.

Twelfth in descent from John de Hamilton, of Bothernok, or Bardowie, was

JOHN HAMILTON, of Bardowie, who m. about 1704, Marion, dau. of Robert Buchanan, of Arnpryor, by whom he had four sons and three daus. The four brothers having d. without issue, in 1757, the daus. were served heir-portioners, and of the line, to their brother Robert; of these, Katharine and Mary having also d. s. p., the succession devolved upon

ELIZABETH, who m. THOMAS BUCHANAN, of Spittal and Leny, and left (with two daus., Elizabeth, m. 1st, to Robert Grahame, of Gartmore, and 2ndly, to Robert Fairfoul, of Strowie; and Marion, m. to J.-H.-S. Crawford, of Cowdonhill) five sons,

- Henry Buchanan, d. unm.
- JOHN BUCHANAN, who s. to the estate of Bardowie, and took the name of Hamilton. He m. Margaret, eldest dau. of Sir Hew Crawford, of Jordanhill, and Robina Pollock, representative of the Pollocks of that ilk, and d. without issue.
- ROBERT HAMILTON-BUCHANAN, a lieut. in the Royal North British Fusiliers, m. Cornelia, dau. of Commodore Tinker, and d. leaving a son, Robert Hamilton-Buchanan, capt. in the 24th regt. native infantry, who d. before his uncle, John.
- FRANCIS BUCHANAN s. his brother, John, and assumed the name of Hamilton.
- Peter Buchanan, capt. in the 23rd regt. of Fusiliers, d. unm.

The 4th son,

FRANCIS BUCHANAN-HAMILTON, M.D., of Bardowie, Spittal, and Leny, author of "An Account of Nepaul," and other works on India, m. Miss Brock, by whom he left at his decease, 1829, a dau., Catherine, who d. unm. 1839, and an only son, the present JOHN BUCHANAN-HAMILTON, Esq. of Spittal and Leny.

Arms—Quarterly: 1st and 4th, BUCHANAN. 1st, Or, a lion, rampant, sable, armed and langued, gu., within a double tressure, flowered and counterflowered, of the second, for BUCHANAN *of that ilk and Spittal*; 4th, quarterly: 1st and 4th, as BUCHANAN *of that ilk*; 2nd and 3rd, sable, on a chevron, between three bears' heads, erased, argent, muzzled, gu., a cinquefoil, of the first, for BUCHANAN *of Leny*. 2nd and 3rd, HAMILTON *of Bardowie*. Gu., on a chevron betwixt three cinquefoils, arg., a boar's head, couped, of the first, in the middle chief point an annulet, or.

Supporters—Two falcons, ppr., garnished, or.

Crests—1st, A dexter hand, holding up a duke's coronet, within two laurel branches, disposed orleways, vert, for BUCHANAN *of that ilk*; 2nd, a bent bow, held in a hand sinister, for BUCHANAN *of Spittal*. (Some of this family have carried as a crest, a dexter hand, couped at the wrist, holding a sword, with the motto, "Pro rege, et pro patria;") 3rd, a lion's paw, erased, ppr., for BUCHANAN *of Leny*; 4th, out of a ducal coronet, or, an oak-tree fructed, penetrated transversely in the main stem by a frame-saw, ppr., the frame of the first, for HAMILTON.

Mottoes—Over the crest of BUCHANAN *of that ilk*, "Clarior hinc honos;" over the SPITTAL crest, "Fortuna parcit labori;" over the LENY crest, "Nobilis est ira leonis;" over the HAMILTON crest, "Through;" under the Escutcheon, "Audaces juvo."

Seats—Leny House, co. Perth; and Bardowie, co. Stirling.

HAMILTON OF SUNDRUM.

HAMILTON, JOHN, Esq. of Sundrum, co. Ayr, J.P. and D.L., b. Sept. 1806; m. 7 May, 1845, Catherine-Barbara, eldest dau. of the late William Hobart, Esq. of Picktree, and has issue,

- I. JOHN-CLAUD-CAMPBELL, b. 1854.
- I. Mary-Dundas.

Lineage.—We know from authentic records—the town books of Ayr—that

ROBERT HAMILTON, bailie-clerk of Carrick, and Janet Blackwood, his spouse, were, on the resignation of Hew Kennedy, in 1670, admitted to the lands of Clongall, Clongall Muir, Clongall Montgomerie, Nether Clongall, Dupillburn, &c.

HUGH HAMILTON, of Clongall (now called Glengall), merchant in Ayr, m. Jean Ferguson, dau of John Ferguson, of Castlehill, and had (with seven daus.) three sons, viz.

- I. Robert, of Bourtreehill, b. 5 Jan. 1698; m. Jean Mitchell, an heiress, widow of Major Garth, and d. 4 June, 1773, leaving four daus., his co-heirs, viz.,
  1. JEAN, m. to George, Earl of Crawford.
  2. MARGARET, m. to Sir John Cathcart, Bt.
  3. FRANCES, m. to Capt. John Ferguson, of Greenvale.
  4. ELEANOR, m. to Hugh, 12th Earl of Eglinton.
- II. JOHN, from whom the Sundrum family is descended.
- III. Hugh, ancestor of the Hamiltons of Pinmore, b. 6 Jan. 1707.

JOHN HAMILTON, Esq. R.N., the 2nd son, b. 24 March, 1702, settled in Jamaica, where he and his elder brother Robert, possessed the estate of Pemberton Valley. He m. 1730, Margaret, eldest dau. of Hugh Montgomerie, of Coilsfield (by his second marriage, with Catharine Arbuckle, widow of Claud Hamilton, of Lethame), and sister of Alexander Montgomerie, of Coilsfield, father of Hugh, 12th earl of Eglinton. He was drowned in returning from the West Indies, leaving an only son,

JOHN HAMILTON, of Sundrum, who m. April, 1762, his cousin Lilias, 2nd dau. of Alexander Montgomerie, of Coilsfield, and sister of Hugh, 12th earl of Eglinton, by whom (who d. 1827) he left (with several daus., of whom the youngest, Hamilla, m. Lt.-Gen. Hughes) seven sons, viz., 1 JOHN, his successor; 2 Alexander-West, m. twice, and left issue; 3 Robert, deceased; 4 Hugh, a lieut.-colonel; 5 Archibald, of Carcluie and Rozelle, capt. E. I. Co.'s naval service; 6 Thomas-Bargany; and 7 Montgomerie, capt. in the E. I. Co.'s naval service. John Hamilton, of Sundrum, for several years vice-lieut. of the co. of Ayr, and thirty-six years covener, d. in Jan. 1821, and was s. by his son,

JOHN HAMILTON, of Sundrum, m. 4 June, 1804, Christian, eldest dau. of George Dundas, of Dundas, and d. 31 Jan. 1837, having had issue,

- I. JOHN, now of Sundrum.
- II. George-Dundas, d. 1833.
- III. Alexander, R.N.
- IV. Archibald, d. 5 June, 1846, E. I. Co.'s civil service, Madras establishment.
- V. James, E. I. C. S.
- VI. Hugh, m. Margaret Innes, and has a son, Hugh-Montgomerie.
- I. Christian, m. to Charles Sterling, Esq.
- II. Lilias, d. 1811.
- III. Margaret, d. 1811.
- IV. Lilias.
- V. Anna-Maria, m. to Capt. Charles Acton Broke, who d. 1855.
- VI. Margaret, m. 9 Aug. 1843, to the Hon. Thomas Preston, youngest son of Viscount Gormanston.
- VII. Mary, m. to John Reginald Howison Craufurd, Esq.
- VIII. Jane-Hamilla, m. to Henry Spencer, Esq.

Arms—Gu., three cinquefoils, erm., two in chief and one in base, within three fleurs-de-lis between.

Crest—Out of a ducal coronet, or, an oak-tree fructed, penetrated transversely in the main stem by a frame-saw, ppr.

Motto—Through.

Seat—Sundrum, Ayrshire.

HAMILTON OF CAIRN HILL AND WEST PORT.

FERRIER-HAMILTON, COLONEL JOHN, of Cairn Hill, co. Ayr, and Westport, co. Linlithgow, b. 6 Sept. 1786; m. in 1817, Georgina, 2nd dau. of Charles, 2nd Viscount Gort, and has issue,

- I. WALTER FERRIER, b. 1819, capt. in the army.
- II. Charles-Vereker, b. 1820, assumed the surname of CAMPBELL on succeeding to the estate of Netherplace an ancient cadetship from the Loudon family. He was in the army, and served throughout the Sutledge campaign in India.
- III. Thomas-Wallace, m. Bessie, 2nd dau. of the Hon. Sydney Stephens.
- IV. John-Prendergast.
- V. William-Archibald.
- I. Jane-Lillias, m. to Andrew Gillon, Esq. of Wallhouse, co. Linlithgow, and is deceased.
- II. Julia-Mary.
- III. Georgina-Vereker.

Colonel Hamilton is a magistrate for cos. Ayr and Linlithgow, and has served throughout the Peninsular campaign, for which he received a war medal and three clasps. He represents, through his mother and grandmother, two of the oldest families in Ayrshire, viz., the WALLACES *of Cairn Hill*, and CUNNINGHAMES *of Cunninghamehead*; and through his grandmother, the HAMILTONS *of Westport*.

Lineage.—In 1674 ANNA HAMILTON, of Westport, eldest dau. of JAMES HAMILTON, of Westport, by Anna, his wife, dau. of Sir Patrick Hamilton, of Little Preston, *m.* Walter Sandilands, eldest son of William Sandilands (2nd son of the 4th Lord Torpichen), by Elizabeth, his wife, eldest dau. and heiress of Sir William Cunninghame, Bart. of Cunninghame Head, co. Ayr, and her eldest son eventually succeeded to the baronetcy, and in 1699 is mentioned as

SIR JAMES SANDILANDS HAMILTON. He *d. s. p.* 1733, and was *s.* by his brother,

SIR WALTER SANDILANDS HAMILTON, a captain in the army, who served thirteen campaigns under Marlborough. He *m.* his cousin Helen, dau. of Thomas Hamilton, of Olivestob, and had two sons, James and Thomas, both military officers, who *d. s. p.*, and daus., of whom the eldest,

GRIZEL HAMILTON, the heiress of Westport, *m.* JOHN FERRIER, Esq. of Kirkton, co. Renfrew, and had issue,

I. WILLIAM, his heir.
II. Walter, of Glenfiner, *m.* 1784, Lillias, dau. and heir of William Wallace, Esq. of Cairnhill, co. Ayr, by Jane, his wife, dau. of Archibald Campbell, of Succoth, and had issue,
 1 JOHN, now of Cairnhill and Westport.
 2 Archibald, major 92nd regt., *d. unm.*
 3 William.
 1 Jean, *m.* to Thos. Riddell, Esq. of Camiestoun, co. Roxburgh.
 2 Margaret.
III. James, one of the principal clerks of Session, *m.* Miss Coutts, and has issue,
 1 John, *m.* Miss Wilson, and had issue.
 2 Archibald, *m.* Miss Garden, and left issue.
 3 Lorn, lieut. in the army, *d. unm.*
 4 James, lieut.-col., *d. unm.*
 5 William, capt. in the army, *d. unm.*
 6 Walter, *m.* Miss Gordon, and had issue.
 1 Jane, *m.* to lieut.-gen. Graham.
 2 Jessie, *m.* to James Connell, Esq. of Conheath.
 3 Helen, *m.* to James Kinloch, Esq.
 4 Susan.
IV. Ilay, major-gen. in the army and governor of Dumbarton Castle, *m.* 1st, Jane, only child of John Macqueen, second brother of Lord Braxfield, and had by her,
 1 Louis-Henry, advocate, *m.* Charlotte, dau. of the late Dr. Alexander Monro, and had issue.
 2 John-Macqueen, *d.* young.
 3 William-Hamilton, *d.* young.
 1 Esther-Wallace, *m.* 1805, to William Hamilton Finnie, Esq., E.I.C.S.
 2 Helen-Margaret, *m.* to Thos. Liston, Esq.
 3 Catherine-Jane, *m.* to W. J. Kemmingson, Esq. of Woodbury Lodge, Devon.
 4 Eliza-Anne, *m.* to J. MacIntyre, Esq. of Liverpool.
 5 Mary.
General Ilay Ferrier *m.* 2ndly, Agnes, only child of Roger Cutlar, Esq. of Orroland, and widow of William Lawrie, Esq. of Redcastle.
I. Helen, *d. unm.* II. Martha, *m.* to Lieut. Adamson.
III. Agnes, *m.* to Mr. Finnie.
IV. Grizel, *m.* to Mr. Burns.
V. Anne, *m.* to Dr. Glen.

The eldest son,

WILLIAM FERRIER-HAMILTON, Esq. of Westport, lieut. R.N., commanded the party of sailors who dragged the cannon up the heights of Abraham, previous to the capture of Quebec. He *m.* Miss Johnstone, of Straiton, co. Linlithgow, and dying *s. p.* 1814, was *s.* by his nephew, the present COL. HAMILTON, of Cairnhill and Westport.

Family of Wallace.

The WALLACES *of Cairnhill*, (formerly spelt Cairngell,) are one of the oldest of our Scotch families. The first was the 3rd son of Sir Richard Wallace, of Rickarton, whose 2nd son was WALLACE OF ELLERSLIE, and whose eldest son *m.* the heiress of Lindsay, of Craigie, and has ever since quartered the Wallace and Lindsay arms. The Wallaces of Cairnhill are connected by marriage with nearly every family of distinction in Ayrshire, and even with royalty itself. At Flodden one of the slain knights was Wallace of Cairnhill, and it is generally understood his eldest son, perished by his side. On the old tower at Cairnhill is a curious stone, with inscription and a coat of arms, Wallace and Muir of Rowallan, a niece of Elizabeth Muir, wife of King ROBERT II., having *m.* Sir Hugh Wallace, of Cairnhill.

Arms—Quarterly, 1st and 4th: Gu., three cinquefoils erm. within a bordure arg. charged with eight martlets of the first for HAMILTON; 2nd and 3rd: gu., a lion rampant arg. within a border arg. and az. for WALLACE.
Crest—Two branches of oak crossing each other in saltire.
Motto—Addunt robur stirpi.
Seats—Cairnhill, Ayrshire, and Westport, co. Linlithgow.

HAMILTON OF RATHOE HOUSE.

HAMILTON, DOUGLAS, Esq. of Rathoe House, co. Carlow, J.P. for that county, and also for Lanarkshire, N.B.; *b.* 5 Jan. 1814; *m.* 11 Feb. 1843, Frances-Anne, only surviving child of Hugh-Rivers Graves, Esq. of Dublin, barrister-at-law, and has issue,

I. Archibald-Douglas, *b.* 1843, *d.* young.
II. Douglas-Charles, *b.* 1846, *d.* young.
III. ALEXANDER-HAMILTON, *b.* 13 Jan. 1849.
IV. William-Douglas, *b.* 1 Oct. 1850.
V. Robert-Frederick, *b.* 17 Dec. 1852.
VI Augustus-Adolphus, *b.* 1854, *d.* an infant.
I. Idonea-Charlotte. II. Maria.

Mr. Hamilton is 4th son of the late Augustus-Barrington-Price Hamilton, Esq., lieut. R.N., 2nd son of Admiral Charles-Powell Hamilton, whose father, Lord Anne Hamilton, was 3rd son of James, Duke of Hamilton, by Elizabeth his wife, dau. and heir of Digby, Lord Gerard (*see* BURKE's *Peerage*).

Arms—Gu., three cinquefoils, pierced, erm.
Crest—Rising from a ducal coronet or, an oak tree fructed and penetrated transversely in the main stem by a frame-saw ppr: the frame or.
Motto—Through.
Seat—Rathoe House, co. Carlow.

HAMILTON OF BELTRIM.

COLE-HAMILTON, ARTHUR-WILLOUGHBY, Esq. of Beltrim, co. Tyrone, J.P. and D.L., high-sheriff 1830, *b.* 23 Nov. 1806; *m.* 16 Dec. 1831, Emily-Catherine, dau. of the Rev. Charles-Cobbe Beresford, and has issue,

I. WILLIAM-CLAUDE, 8th Foot, *b.* 8 Aug. 1833.
II. Claude, *b.* 20 Nov. 1838.
III. Charles-Richard, *b.* 6 Dec. 1842.
IV. Arthur-Henry, *b.* 17 April, 1846.
V. John-Isaac, *b.* 12 July, 1851.
I. Amelia-Harriet. II. Frances-Sophia.
III. Selina. IV. Letitia-Grace.

Lineage.—The Hon. ARTHUR COLE, 2nd son of John, 1st Lord Mountflorence, by Elizabeth, his wife, dau. of Hugh Willoughby Montgomery, Esq. of Carrow, *m.* in 1780, Letitia, dau. and heir of Claude Hamilton, Esq. of Beltrim, co. Tyrone, and assumed in consequence the additional surname of Hamilton. By her he had issue,

CLAUDE-WILLIAM, his heir.
Letitia, *m.* in Aug. 1815, to Major Stafford.
Elizabeth-Anne, *m.* in 1820, to Henry Slade, Esq.
Isabella, *m.* to James Hamilton, Esq., and *d.* in 1827.

The son and heir,

CLAUDE-WILLIAM COLE-HAMILTON, Esq. of Beltrim, *b.* 7 July, 1781, *m.* 10 Oct. 1805, Nichola-Sophia, eldest dau. of Richard Chaloner, Esq. of Kingsfort, co. Meath, and by her (who *m.* 2ndly, in 1838, Joseph Pratt, Esq. of Cabra Castle, co. Cavan) had issue,

ARTHUR-WILLOUGHBY, now of Beltrim.
Richard-Chaloner, the present RICHARD CHALONER, Esq. of Kingsfort (see page 191).

Mr. Cole-Hamilton, *d.* 25 April, 1822.

Arms—Gu., three cinquefoils, pierced, erm. quarterly with COLE.
Crests—1st, HAMILTON, rising from a ducal coronet or, an oak tree fructed and penetrated transversely in the main stem by a frame-saw ppr. the frame or; 2nd, COLE.
Seat—Beltrim, co. Tyrone.

HAMILTON OF ST. ERNANS.

HAMILTON, JOHN, Esq. of St. Ernans, co. Donegal, *b.* 25 Aug. 1800; *m.* in May, 1823, Mary, dau. of Hugh Rose, Esq. of Glastulick, co. Ross, and has had issue,

I. JAMES, of Brown Hall, co. Donegal, J.P., *b.* 8 June, 1824.
I. Isabella, *d.* in 1840. II. Mary.
III. Arabella-Rose. IV. Helen.

Mr. Hamilton is a magistrate and deputy-lieut. for co. Donegal, and served as high-sheriff in 1826.

Lineage.—JOHN HAMILTON, Esq. of Brown Hall, who *m.* Isabella, sister of James Stewart, Esq. of Killymoon,

M.P. for co. Tyrone, d. in 1811, having had by her (who d. in 1832) a son,

JAMES HAMILTON, Esq., who predeceased his father in 1805, leaving, by his wife, the Hon. Helen Pakenham, sister of the late earl of Longford, and of the 1st duchess of Wellington, the present JOHN HAMILTON, of St. Ernan's (another son, the Rev. Edward-Michael Hamilton, who m. Miss Fortesque, dau. of Chichester Fortesque, Esq. of Glyde Farm, and sister of Thomas Fortescue, created Baron Clermont, and a dau. Catherine, m. to the Rev. W. H. Foster, rector of Lough Gilly, nephew of Lord Oriel.

Arms—Gu., a sword erect in pale point upwards ppr. pomel and hilt gold between three cinquefoils arg.
Crest—A nag's head couped arg. bridled gu.
Motto—Ride through.
Seat—St. Ernans, co. Donegal.

HAMILTON OF KILLYLEAGH.

HAMILTON, ARCHIBALD-ROWAN, Esq. of Killyleagh Castle, co. Down, J.P., high-sheriff, formerly capt. 5th dragoon guards, b. 9 Aug. 1818; m. 24 Feb. 1842, Catherine-Ann, dau. of the Rev. George Caldwell, by Harriot his wife, dau. of Sir William Abdy, Bart., and has issue,

I. GAWEN-WILLIAM-ROWAN, b. 7 March, 1844.
II. George-Rowan, b. 10 April, 1845.
III. Sidney-Augustus-Rowan, b. 1 July, 1846.
IV. Frederick-Temple-Rowan, b. 17 July, 1850.
I. Harriot-Georgina.

Lineage.—This branch of the illustrious house of Hamilton springs from the same stock as the Earls of Clanbrassil and Viscounts Limerick, who derive from Thomas Hamilton, of Raplock, son of the Lord of Cadsow.

THE REV. HANS HAMILTON,* vicar of Dunlop, Ayrshire, b. 1536, m. Margaret Denham, dau. of the Laird of Weshiels; and dying 30 May, 1608, left

JAMES (Sir), of Killyleagh and Bangor, serjeant-at-law, and privy councillor to King JAMES I., who was created by patent, dated 4 May, 1622, VISCOUNT CLANEBOYE; his son and heir, James, 2nd Viscount Claneboye, was created EARL OF CLANBRASSIL, 4 March, 1647. He was father of HENRY, 2nd Earl of Clanbrassil, who d. s. p. 1675.
ARCHIBALD.
Gawen, of Ballygally.
JOHN, of Coronary, co. Cavan, and Monella, co. Armagh, ancestor of the HAMILTONS, of Abbotstown, co. Dublin. (*See that name.*)
WILLIAM, ancestor of the present GEORGE-ALEXANDER HAMILTON, Esq. of Hampton Hall, co. Dublin. (*See that name.*)
Patrick.
Jean, m. to William Mure, Esq. of Glanderstoun, Ayrshire.

The 2nd son,

ARCHIBALD HAMILTON, Esq. of Halcraig, or Harrage, co. Lanark, m. 1st, Rachel Carmichael, and had issue,

I. JOHN.
II. JAMES, of Neilsbrook, co. Antrim, who inherited one-fifth of the Earl of Clanbrassil's estates. He m. Agnes Kennedy, and had three daus.,
 1 ROSE, who m. William Fairlie, but d. without issue.
 2 RACHEL, d. unm.
 3 ANNE, m. to Hans Stevenson, Esq. of Ballyrott, and left an only son, JAMES STEVENSON, whose eldest dau. and co-heir, DORCAS STEVENSON, m. Sir John Blackwood, and was created BARONESS DUFFERIN and CLANEBOYE, in 1810.
III. GAWEN, of whom presently.

* In the churchyard of Dunlop there is a tomb erected to his memory, and on a flag-stone in the floor is the following inscription:—"Here lies Hans Hamilton, vicar of Dunlop, who deceased the 30th of May, 1608, at the age of 72 years; and Janet Denham, his spouse." Under a marble arch, within two pillars of the composite order; in front are two statues kneeling on a marble monument, in the attitude of devotion, and habited according to the fashion of the times. There is also a long inscription on a marble slab in the wall, stating that he was the son of Archibald Hamilton, of Raploch, and that his wife was Janet, 2nd dau. of Denholme, of Westshells; that they lived together 45 years, during which time he had served the cure of the church. [v. Robertson's Cunninghame.] This Archibald Hamilton was the son of James Hamilton, by Isabella, dau. of W. Blackwood, Esq., the son of William Hamilton, by Margaret, dau. of Sir William Baillie, of Leamington, the son of James Hamilton, the son of Thomas Hamilton, of Raploch, by Helen, dau. of Sir Henry Douglas, Lord of Dalkeith, ancestor to the Earls of Morton, the son of John Hamilton, of Cadzow.

IV. William, of Killyleagh, d. in 1716, without issue.
V. Hugh, of Dublin, merchant.

Archibald Hamilton m. a second time, and left a dau., Jane, who m. Archibald Edmonstone, Esq. of Braiden Island, co. Antrim. His 3rd son,

GAWEN HAMILTON, Esq. of Killyleagh, co. Down, m. Jane, dau. of Archibald Hamilton, Esq., and dying in 1703, was s. by his son,

ARCHIBALD HAMILTON, Esq. of Killyleagh, who m. Mary, dau. of David Johnstone, Esq. of Tully, co. Monaghan, and was s. at his decease, 25 April, 1747, by his eldest son,

GAWEN HAMILTON, Esq. of Killyleagh, b. 1729, who m. 28 May, 1750, Jane, only child of WILLIAM ROWAN, Esq., barrister-at-law, and widow of Tichborne Aston, Esq. of Beaulieu, co. Louth, by whom he had,

ARCHIBALD, his heir.
Sidney, m. to the Rev. Benjamin Beresford.

Mr. Hamilton d. 9 April, 1805, and was s. by his only son,

ARCHIBALD HAMILTON-ROWAN, Esq. of Killyleagh Castle, b. 12 May, 1752, who m. at Paris, 6 Oct. 1781, Sarah-Anne, dau. of Walter Dawson, Esq. of Carrickmacross, co. Monaghan, and had issue,

I. GAWEN-WILLIAM, b. at Paris, in 1783, an officer in the royal navy, and a Companion of the Bath, m. in 1817, Catherine, dau. of Gen. Sir George Cockburn; and dying 17 Aug. 1834, left issue,
 1 ARCHIBALD, the present possessor of Killyleagh Castle.
 2 George-Rowan, late capt. 5th dragoon-guards, b. 1822.
 1 Melita-Anne, m. to Jacob Sankey, Esq. of Coolmore.
II. Sydney, b. in 1789, m. a dau. of the late Henry Jackson, Esq. of Carrickmacross, and has issue.
III. Archibald, an officer in the army, d. at Gibraltar.
IV. Frederick, of the royal navy, b. in 1793; killed on the coast of Spain in 1811.
V. Dawson, b. in 1801; married, and has issue.
I. Jane.
II. Elizabeth, m. to — Beresford, Esq.
III. Mildred, m. to Sir Edward Ryan, Knight of the Order of Maria-Theresa.
IV. Harriet, m. to Crofton Fitzgerald, Esq. of the county of Clare.
V. Francesca, m. to William Fletcher, Esq., son of the late Judge Fletcher.

Mr. Hamilton-Rowan d. 1 Nov. 1834.

Arms—Gules, three cinquefoils, erm., on a chief, or, a heart.
Seat—Killyleagh Castle, Downshire.

HAMILTON OF ABBOTSTOWN.

HAMILTON, JAMES-HANS, Esq. of Abbotstown (otherwise Sheephill) and Holmpatrick, co. Dublin, M.P. D.L., and J.P. for the co. Dublin, b. Feb. 1810; m. 1853, Caroline, dau. of John-F. Trant, Esq. of Doves, co. Tipperary, by Caroline, his wife, dau. of Sir Arthur Brooke, Bart., of Cole-Brooke, co. Fermanagh, and by her (who d. Mar. 1845) had issue,

I. HANS-JAMES, b. 21 Sept. 1835.
II. Ion-Trant, b. 20 July, 1839.

Lineage.—JOHN HAMILTON Esq. of Coronary, co. Cavan, and of Monella, co. Armagh (4th son of the Rev. Hans Hamilton, Vicar of Dunlop, and brother of James, 1st Viscount Claneboye), d. at Killeleagh, co. Down, 4 Dec. 1639, and was buried at Mullaghbrack, co. Armagh, 10 Dec. 1639. He m. Sarah, dau. of Anthony Brabason, of Ballynasloe, co. Roscommon, brother to Edward, Lord Ardee, father of William, 1st Earl of Meath; and had four sons,

I. Hans, Rt. Hon. Sir, M.P., created a Baronet 6 April, 1662; d. 14 Feb. 1681, m. Magdalene, sister to Marcus, Viscount Dungannon, and left a dau.,
 Sarah, m. Robert Hamilton, Esq., created a baronet 1682.
II. Anthony, d. young.
III. JAMES, of whom below.
IV. Francis, of Tullybreck, co. Armagh, (will dated 8 Feb. 1693, proved 7 Nov. 1695), m. Eliz., sister to Henry Echlin, Esq., and had issue,
 1 Hans, of Cavan Duggan, m. and had issue.
 2 James, Rev. of Tullybreck and Castlehill, co. Down, will dated 4 Sept. 1729, proved 23 April, 1730; m. twice and had issue.

The 3rd son,

JAMES HAMILTON, Esq. of Ballyboro, co. Cavan, m. in 1639, Jane, dau. and heir of William Baillie, D.D., Bishop of Clonfert, and had issue,

I. HENRY, of whom below.
II. Hans, a brigadier-general, d. s. p.

III. William.
I. Margaret, *m.* Mr. Cuppadge.
II. Sarah, *d. s. p.* 1673.

The eldest son,

HENRY HAMILTON, Esq. of Ballyboro, killed at *Limerick*, *m.* Miss Blackwell, and had issue,

I. JAMES, his heir.
II. John, of Holmpatrick. He was M.P. for Wendover, in England, and Dundalk, in Ireland, *m.* Miss Ligoe, and had issue,
Henry, of Hacketstown, co. Dublin, *m.* Margaret, dau. of Jas. Hamilton, Esq. of Carlow, but *d. s. p.*
I. Mary, *m.* Mr. Ligoe.

The son and heir,

JAMES HAMILTON, Esq., M.P. for Carlow (will dated 27 June, 1769, was proved Nov. 1772), *m.* Anne Hall, and had issue,

I. Hans, of Carlow, called in his will dated 2 April, 1779, of Summer Hill, co. Dublin, and proved 13 June, 1738, *m.* Elinor, dau. of Benedict Arthur and sister to Daniel Arthur, of Seafield, co. Dublin, and had issue,
1 James, *d. s. p.* 2 Benedict, of Carlow.
3 Thos. Arthur, *d. s. p.*
1 Margaret, will dated 1 Sept. 1790, proved 3 Nov. 1791.
2 Anne, *m.* Chas. Siree, Esq.
II. JAMES, of whom presently.
III. John, of Straw Hill, co. Carlow, *d. s. p.*
I. Elizabeth, *m.* Fred. Faulkner, Esq. of Abbotstown, co. Dublin.
II. Rebecca, *m.* Christp. Dominick, Esq., and had issue,
Elizabeth, *m.* to St. George Usher St. George, *Lord St. George*, and had issue,
Olivia, *m.* 4 Nov. 1775, to William Robert, 2nd Duke of Leinster.
III. Margaret, *m.* Henry Hamilton, Esq. of Holmpatrick.
IV. Anne. V. Jane. VI. Sophia.

The 2nd son,

JAMES HAMILTON, Esq. of Sheephill and Holmpatrick, co. Dublin, deputy-prothonotary of the Court of King's Bench, *m.* 1st, Hannah, dau. of — Phillips, Esq., and had,

I. HANS, his heir.
II. Henry, of Ballymacool, co. Meath, *b.* 16 July, 1760; *m.* Mary, dau. of John. Wetherall, Esq. of Dublin, and had (with five daus., of whom the fourth, Harriet, *m.* Sir Erasmus D. Borrowes, Bart.) five sons, viz.,
1 James-John, *m.* 1st, Margaret, dau. of Thomas Carter, Esq. of Castle Martin, co. Kildare, and has, by her, two sons, Henry, capt. 13th lt. dragoons; and James, in holy orders; and 2ndly, 1821, Anne-Geraldine, dau. of John, 26th Lord Kinsale, by whom he has,
John De Courcy.
Thomas De Courcy, capt. 68th regt.
Gerald de Courcy.
Henry, in holy orders, of Devonshire Place, London, *m.* Frances, dau. of Ralph Peters, Esq. of Platbridge, co. Lancaster, and has issue,
Henry-Blackburne, *b.* 1841.
Frederick-William-Addison, *b.* 1845.
Arthur-John, *b.* 1846.
Harriet-Mary. F. Selina-Charlotte.
Helen-Isabel-Bruce.
3 John, *m.* Miss Smythe.
4 Hans, Q.C. of FitzWilliam Place, Dublin, *m.* 1833, Augusta, dau. of Gen. Sir Frederick Augustus Wetherall, G.C.H. of Castle Hill, Ealing, and has issue,
Augustus-Henry-Carr, lt R.A.
Roger-Adolphus, lt. H.E.I.C.S.
Edward-Pakenham-Robert. Lionel-Hans.
Douglas.
Victoria. Frederica-Mary. Florence.
Robert, *d. unm.*
III. James, of Dunboyne Castle, *b.* 1761, *d.* 24 May, 1800, having had issue, three sons and a dau.
IV. John, of Hackelstown, co. Dublin, *m.* Eliza, dau. of Sir Wm. Alexander, Bt. of Dublin, *d. s. p.*
V. Robert, *m.* Catherine, dau. of Sir William Alexander, Kt., and has issue five sons and three daus.
VI. Francis, of Dublin, *m.* Rebecca, dau. of Col. William Reynell, of Castle Reynell, co. Westmeath, and had issue three sons and three daus.
I. Charlotte, *m.* Robert White, Esq. of Aghaboe, Queen's co.
II. Caroline, *m.* Thomas Stannas, of Portarlington.
III. Elizabeth, *m.* William, son of William Irvine, Esq. of Castle Irvine, co. Fermanagh.
V. Mary, *m.* Thomas, son of Charles Henry Hendrick, of Tully, co. Kildare.
V. Sophia, *m.* Richard Jones, Esq. of Dollardstown, co. Meath.
VI. Margaret, *m.* Henry Johnson, Esq.

He *m.* 2ndly, Alice, dau. of John Hamilton, Esq. of Derry, and had issue,

I. Charles.
II. Richard, Rev., *m.* — Tipping, of co. Louth.
III. Christopher, lieut.-col. 97th foot, *m.* Hon. Sarah Handcock, sister to Richard, Lord Castlemaine.
I. Emily. II. Harriet.

He *m.* 3rdly, Miss Jane Candlir, and by his three wives had thirty-six children, several of whom *d.* young. The eldest son,

HANS HAMILTON, Esq., M.P. for the co. Dublin, for thirty years, *m.* 1st, Sarah, dau. of Joshua Lynam, Esq. of Dublin, and by her (who was *b.* 24 June, 1759) had issue,

Sarah, *m.* Geo. Woods, of Winter Lodge and Milverton, co. Dublin, Esq.
Jane, *m.* Richard Law, of Cottage, co. Dublin, *d. s. p.* 1821.

He *m.* 2ndly, Anne, dau. of Hugh Henry Mitchell, Esq. of Dublin, and had issue,

JAMES-HANS, now of Abbotstown.
Elizabeth, *m.* Robt. Law, of Dublin.
Anne, *d. unm.*
Frances, *m.* Rich. Howard Brooke, Esq., J.P. of Castle Howard, brother to Sir Arthur Brooke, Bt.
Harriet, *m.* Robt. Clayton Browne, Esq. of Browne's Hall, co. Carlow.

Mr. Hamilton *d.* Dec. 1822.

Arms—Gu., three roses, on a chief, arg., a lion, passant, guardant.
Crest—A demi-antelope, holding between the paws a human heart, gu.
Motto—Qualis ab incepto.
Seats—Abbotstown and Holmpatrick, co. Dublin.

HAMILTON OF HAMPTON HALL.

HAMILTON, GEORGE-ALEXANDER, Esq. of Hampton Hall, co. Dublin, J.P. and D.L., M.P. for the University of Dublin, *b.* 1802; *m.* 1835, Amelia Fancourt, dau. of the late Joshua Uhthoff, Esq. of Bath, a gentleman of distinguished character and service in India. In 1852, Mr. Hamilton was appointed Financial Secretary of the Treasury in the Earl of Derby's Administration, and in June, 1853, on the occasion of the installation of the Earl of Derby as Chancellor of the University of Oxford, the honorary degree of D.C.L. was conferred upon Mr. Hamilton by that University.

Lineage.—WILLIAM HAMILTON, Esq. of Bangor, co. Down (5th son of the Rev. Hans Hamilton, and brother of James, 1st Viscount Claneboye), *m.* Jane, dau. of Sir Jno. Melville, and dying 1627, left issue,

I. JAMES, of Newcastle, M.P. for Bangor, æt. 10 years 1627, killed at Blackwater fight 5 Ju. 1646, *m.* Margaret, dau. of — Kynaston, Esq. of Laule, co. Down, and had issue.
1 James, of Bangor, (will dated 20 July, 1701, proved 26 Feb. 1706), *m.* Hon. Sophia Mordaunt, dau. of John, 1st Viscount Avalon and sister to Charles, Earl of Peterborough and Monmouth, and had issue,
James, M.P. for Bangor 1692, *d. s. p.*
Anne-Catherine, *m.* in 1709, Michael Ward, Esq., M.P. for the co. Down 1715, judge of the Queen's Bench in 1727, father of Bernard Ward, VISCOUNT BANGOR.
Margaret, *m.* Thomas, Viscount Ikerrin.
2 Catherine, *m.* Vere Essex Cromwell, 4th Earl of Ardglass, Viscount Lecale, and 7th Baron Cromwell. He *d.* 1687, when the earldom and viscountcy expired, and the barony of Cromwell, originating in the writ of the 28 April 1539, devolved upon his dau.,
Elizabeth, Baroness Cromwell, *m.* 1st, Ed. Southwell, Secretary of State for Ireland; and 2ndly, Nicholas Price, Esq. of Hollymount, co. Down, by whom she had Lieut.-Gen. Michael Price.
II. John (capt.) of the co. Cavan, *m.* Jane Echlin, *d. s. p.*
III. HANS, of whom presently.
IV. William, of Erinagh, co. Down, *d.* 26 Jan. 1680, *m.* 1st, Ellen, dau. of Magennis, Esq., and had issue,
1 James, of Tullamore, co. Down, will dated 28 Dec. 1693, proved 1700, *m.* Hon. Anne Mordaunt, granddau. of John, 1st Earl of Peterborough and sister to Mrs. Hamilton, of Bangor, and had issue,
JAMES, 1st Earl of Clanbrassil and Viscount Limerick, created in 1756, *m.* Lady Harriet Bentinck, dau. of William, Earl of Portland, and had,
JAMES, 2nd Earl of Clanbrassil, Knt. of St. Patrick, *d. s. p.* in 1798, when the honours became extinct, and his lordship's sister, the Countess of Roden, inherited the estates.
Anne, *m.* Robert, Earl of Roden, grandfather of the present ROBERT, 3RD EARL OF RODEN.
Caroline.

William, *d.* young. John, *d.* young.
Sophia, *m.* Frederick Hamilton, eldest son of Visct. Boyne.
Elizabeth, *m.* Thos. Fortescue, Esq., father of William-Henry, Earl of Clermont. Cary.
2 Elinor, *m.* Matthews, Esq.

He *m.* 2ndly Christian, dau. of Joselin Ussher, son of Mark, son of the Right Rev. Henry Ussher, Archbishop of Armagh, and had issue,

1 Joselin, *d. s. p.*, will dated 17 Nov. 1689, proved 1690.
1 Christian, will dated 4 Feb. 1691, proved 19 Jan. 1692, *m.* Jas. Hamilton, of Carneyshten.

I. Ursula, married.

The 3rd son,

CAPTAIN HANS HAMILTON, M.P. of Carnisure, co. Down (will dated 2 Dec. 1655, proved 20 July, 1656), *d.* 28 Dec. 1655, and was buried at Hollywood. He *m.* Margaret, sister of David Kennedy, Esq., and had issue,

I. JAMES, *b.* 1654 (will dated 2 June, 1690, proved 10 Aug. 1691), *m.* Christian, dau. of Wm. Hamilton, of Erinagh, and had issue,

1 Margaret, *m.* John Cuffe, Lord Desart, great-grandfather o the present JOHN OTWAY O'CONNOR, 3RD EARL OF DESART.
2 Christian, *d. s. p.* 3 Anne, *d. s. p.*

II. WILLIAM, of whom presently.
III. Francis, a captain in the army.
I. Anne.
II. Jane, *m.* Hugh Montgomery, Esq. of Ballymagown.
III. Ursula, *m.* George Ross. IV. Matilda.

The 2nd son,

WILLIAM HAMILTON, Esq. of Ballybranagh, *m.* and had a son and successor,

HUGH HAMILTON, Esq. of Ballybranagh, Bright, Erinagh, and Tyrella, co. Down, *m.* Mary, dau. of Ross, of Rosstrevor, and dying 16 Nov. 1728, was buried at Killeleagh, leaving issue,

I. GEORGE, (*d.* 1770, and is buried at Rathmullan,) of Tyrella, co. Down, *m.* Eliz., dau. of Jno. Echlin, Esq. of Echlinville, co. Down, and sister to Sir Rob. Echlin, Bart., and had issue,

1 George, of Tyrella, *d. unm.* 6 July, 1796, and is buried at Rathmullan: on his death he was succeeded, at Tyrella, by his nephew, Geo. Hamilton.
2 Elizabeth, *m.* her cousin, the Hon. Baron Hamilton.

II. ALEXANDER, of whom presently.

The 2nd son,

ALEXANDER HAMILTON, Esq., M.P. of Knock, co. Dublin, and Newtown Hamilton, co. Armagh, *m.* Isabella Maxwell, and had (with three daus., Isabella, *m.* to Matthew Cassan, Esq.; Anne, *m.* to Henry Caldwell, Esq.; and Elizabeth, *m.* to Robert Law, D.D.) four sons, viz.,

I. HUGH, D.D., Lord Bishop of Clonfert 21 Jan. 1796, and Bishop of Ossory from 1798 until his death, *b.* 26 Mar. 1729. He *m.* in 1772, Isabella, eldest dau. of Hans Widman Wood, Esq. of Rosmead, co. Westmeath, by Frances, his wife, twin sister to Edward, Earl of Kingston, and had,

1 ALEXANDER, Q.C., barrister-at-law, of Newtown Hamilton, co. Dublin, *m.* 29 Jan. 1799, Julia, dau. of Michael Tisdall, Esq. of Charleville, co. Meath, and *d.* Oct. 1852, having had issue,

Isabella, *m.* Jno. Synge, Esq., D.L. of Glanmore, co. Wicklow.
Julia, *m.* Hon. and Rev. John Pratt Hewitt, 2nd son of James, Viscount Lifford.
Jane, *d. unm.* in 1824.
Catherine, *m.* Rev. Joseph Wright.
Harriet, *d. unm.* in 1834. Frances, *d. unm.* in 1837.
Alicia, *m.* Archibald Tisdall, Esq.

2 Rev. Hans, D.D., prebendary of Kilmanagh and rector of the union of Knocktopher and Kilmoganny, in the diocese of Ossory, *m.* Susan, dau. of Rt. Hon. Silver Oliver, and *d. s. p.* in 1839.
3 Henry, *m.* Sarah, dau. of Rev. Michael Sandys, rector of Powerscourt, co. Wicklow, and has issue,

Hugh, in holy orders, *m.* Mary-Charlotte, dau. of Rev. Henry Ormsby, and has issue, EDWIN, *b.* April, 1849; Henrietta, Lucy, Mary.
Francis. Henry-Alexander, J.P.
George-Hans, in holy orders, rector of Berwick-on-Tweed; *m.* Arabella, dau. of — Best, Esq., and has issue, Hans-Alfred, Henry.
Alfred, in holy orders, *m.* Henrietta, dau. of H. Cole, Esq., and has issue, Henry.
Alexander, *m.* Henrietta, dau. of Chief Baron Pollock, and has issue,
Sarah, *m.* Wm. Scriven, Esq. Frances.

4 Rev. George, rector of Killermogh, Queen's County, author of several controversial pamphlets, *m.* 1st, Sophia, dau. of George Kernan, Esq., and had issue,

Sophia, *m.* Rev. Richd. Johnson, and has issue, Sophia.
Isabella, *d. unm.* 1841.

He *m.* 2ndly Frances, dau. of Admiral Chichester Fortescue, which lady, after his decease, in 1830, *m.* Rev. Geo. Reade.

5 Rev. Hugh, *m.* Elizabeth, dau. of Jno. Staples, Esq. of Lissan, co. Tyrone, and has issue,

Hugh Staples, Rev., of Manston, Leeds, *m.* dau. of — Davis, Esq. of Killeleagh.
Richard, Rev., rector of Killeleagh, co. Down.
Albert, *d.* 1824. Hewit. Thomas, Rev.

6 Frances, *m.* Rev. Dodgson Madden, and has issue.
7 Isabella, *d. unm.* in 1845.

II. Robert, *m.* a dau. of Jonathan Chetwood, of Woodbrooke, and had issue,

1 Alexander, rector of Thomastown, co. Kilkenny, *m.* in 1801, Elinor, dau. of the Rev. Sewell Stubber, Esq. of Moyne, Queen's Co. They had issue, 1 Robert, who took the surname of STUBBER; 2 Sewell; 3 William; 4 Alexander-Chetwoode; 5 Richard-Hugh; 1 Hester-Maria, *m.* Able-J.-C. Warren, Esq. of Lowhill, co. Kilkenny; 2 Harriet; and 3 Anne.
2 Robert *m.* Sidney, dau. of Mervyn Archdall, Esq. of Castle Archdall, M.P. for Fermanagh, and had issue, MAXWELL, who *m.* 1854, dau. and co-heir of the late John Graves, Esq. of Mickleton Manor, co. Gloucester, and has issue; Robert, in holy orders, widower, with issue; Chetwode, Mervyn, Dawson, and several daus.

III. GEORGE, of whom presently.
IV. Charles, of Hamwood, co. Dublin, *m.* Elizabeth, dau. of Jonathan Chetwood, Esq. of Woodbrooke, and had issue,

Charles, of Dominick St., Dublin, *m.* Caroline, dau. of Tighe, Esq., and had Charles-William and other issue.

Mr. Hamilton represented Killileagh in Parliament from 1730 to 1759, and was one of the 124 members who successfully opposed the pretensions of the English crown in 1753, in commemoration of which, a large gold medal was struck and presented to each of the patriotic members. Mr. Hamilton's is still preserved as an heirloom in the family. The 3rd son,

HON. GEORGE HAMILTON, M.P., Baron of the Exchequer, of Hampton Hall, co. Dublin, M.P. for Belfast for many years, was raised to the Bench in 1776. He *m.* his cousin, Elizabeth, dau. of Geo. Hamilton, Esq. of Tyrella, and had,

ALEXANDER, of whom presently.
GEORGE, who succeeded his brother.
Isabella, *d. unm.*

Baron Hamilton was eminently distinguished for his public spirit: he erected the Pier at Balbriggan, principally at his private expense, and introduced the cotton and hosiery manufacture into Ireland: he *d.* 1793, and was buried in the family vault at Balrothery, and was *s.* by his son,

ALEXANDER HAMILTON, Esq., who represented Belfast, when the Union was proposed, but, the Earl of Belfast, the patron of the borough being favourable to that enactment, Mr. Hamilton resigned his seat and the lucrative office of Cursitor of the Exchequer, rather than support a measure to which he was in principle opposed. He *m.* Catherine, dau. of Thomas Burgh, Esq., and dying in 1808, *s. p.*, was *s.* by his brother,

REV. GEORGE HAMILTON, of Hampton Hall, co. Dublin, and Tyrella, co. Down, who *m.* Anna, dau. of Thomas Pepper, Esq. of Ballygarth Castle, co. Meath, by Henrietta his wife, sister of Stephen Moore, Esq. of Barn, and had issue,

GEORGE-ALEXANDER, now of Hampton Hall.
Thomas-Claude-George, J.P., *m.* 1840, Gertrude-Anne, 2nd dau. of Joshua Uhthoff, Esq. of Bath, and has a daughter, Gertrude-Uhthoff.
Harriet, *m.* J. W. Swan, Esq., M.D. of Kingstown

He *s.* his uncle at Tyrella, in 1795, and his brother at Hampton Hall, in 1808. He *d.* in 1833, and was buried in Balbriggan church, which had been built and endowed by himself.

Seat—Hampton Hall, Balbriggan.

HAMLYN OF LEAWOOD AND PASCHOE.

HAMLYN, CALMADY-POLLEXFEN, Esq. of Leawood and Paschoe, co. Devon, J.P. and D.L., *b.* 18 Jan. 1775; *m.* 27 June, 1805, Fanny Bedford, only dau. of Richard Cross, Esq. of Duryards, near Exeter, and has issue,

I. SHILSTON-CALMADY, *m.* 25 March, 1841, Sarah Carter, of Neston, co. Chester.
I. Frances-Elizabeth. II. Ellen-Mary.

Lineage.—This family, which had resided in Exeter so early as the middle of the 15th century, settled at Paschoe in 1611. The heiress of an elder branch *m.* Harris. The late

. CHRISTOPHER HAMLYN, Esq. of Paschoe, son of Robert-Paschoe Hamlyn, Esq., by Gertrude Mills his wife, m. 1st, Elizabeth-Mary, dau. (by Elizabeth his wife, dau. and eventual heir of John Pollexfen, Esq.) of Vincent Calmady, Esq., and sister and co-heir (with her sister, Pollexfen, who m. Admiral Charles-Holmes Everitt, who took the name of Calmady, of her brother, Francis Calmady, Esq. of Langdon Hall, co. Devon, and by her had an only son and heir, the present CALMADY-POLLEXFEN HAMLYN, Esq. of Paschoe and Leawood. Mr. Hamlyn m. 2ndly, Frances Marshall, but had no further issue.

Arms—Sa., two swords, in saltier, the points upwards, hilted and pomelled, or, quartering CALMADY and POLLEXFEN.
Crest—A griffin, guardant.
Motto—Caute sed strenue.
Seat—Paschoe, Colebrook and Leawood, Bridestowe, co. Devon.

HAMOND OF HALING HOUSE AND PAMPISFORD HALL.

HAMOND, WILLIAM-PARKER, Esq. of Haling House, co. Surrey, and Pampisford Hall, co. Cambridge, J.P. and D.L., high-sheriff of Cambridgeshire, 1852-3, b. 24 Nov. 1793; m. Margaret, dau. of John Maling, Esq. of Grange, Durham, and relict of Robert Nicholson, Esq. of Bradley, and has issue an only son,

WILLIAM, b. 3 Aug. 1827, barrister-at-law.

Lineage.—SIR WILLIAM HAMOND, Knt. of Carshalton, a South Sea director, d. in 1747, aged 77, leaving, by Mary his wife, three sons, WILLIAM; Peter, d. in 1753, and John, d. in 1759. The eldest son,

WILLIAM HAMOND, Esq., Turkey merchant, m. Anne, dau. of John Parker, citizen of London, and afterwards of Croydon, by Elizabeth his wife, dau. of Nicholas Ashton, citizen of London, and by her (who d. 1736) had issue,

WILLIAM.
Cordwill, drowned in his uncle's canal at Tooting, 1760.
Peter, m. Anne Jarman, and d. in Bloomsbury Square, London, in 1794, leaving a dau., Anne, m. to Somerset Davies, Esq. of Croft Castle, co. Hereford.

The eldest son,

WILLIAM HAMOND, Esq. of Carshalton, m. his cousin, Elizabeth, dau. of William Parker, Esq., by Elizabeth his wife, relict of Edward Stringer, Esq. of Haling, and dau. of John Parker, Esq. of London, and Elizabeth Ashton his wife, and d. in 1777, having had issue,

WILLIAM PARKER, of whom presently.
Edmond.
Peter-Ashton, in holy orders, rector of Widford, Herts, and South Mimms, Middlesex, d. 1806.
Francis-Thomas, in holy orders, rector of Widford, and Quidenham, Norfolk, m. Maria, dau. of Col. Lovelace, of Quidenham, and d. in 1824, leaving a son and dau. viz., William, in holy orders, m. a dau. of Gen. Budgen, and d. in 1851, and Elizabeth.

The eldest son,

WILLIAM-PARKER HAMOND, Esq. of Haling, m. Mary, dau. of Sir Robert Carr, Bart., and niece of Sir William Carr, Bart. of Etal, and had issue,

WILLIAM-PARKER, present representative.
Robert-Carr, an officer in the 14th dragoons, d. 1837.
Edmund-Glyn, in holy orders, fellow of Jesus College, Cambridge, and rector of Widford, d. 1826.
Peter, col. Madras Artillery, m. Christina-Mary, dau. of lieut.-colonel Bird, and has issue, William Parr; Robert-Thomas; Peter-Francis; Mary-Christina; Louisa-Anne; Sophia-Mary; and Christina.
Francis, b. 1799; midshipman royal navy, drowned off Winchilsea.
George, b. 1804; an officer in India; m. Mary, dau. of Lewis-William Brouncker, Esq. of Boveridge, co. Dorset.
Henry, in holy orders, rector of Widford, m. Sophia, dau. of the Rev. Dr. Edridge, and has issue, Henry Carr, and Isabella.
Isabella-Jane, m. to Capt. James Rolleston, R.N.
Eliza-Anne, d. an infant.
Louisa-Grace, m. to George Dering, Esq. of Barham Court, Kent.

Mr. Hamond d. in Sept. 1812, and was s. by his eldest son, the present WILLIAM-PARKER HAMOND, Esq. of Haling, &c.

Arms—Per pale, gu. and az., three demi-lions, pass. gard., or.
Crest—A wolf's head, erased, quarterly, or and az.
Motto—Vis fortibus arma.
Seats—Haling House, Surrey; and Pampisford Hall, co. Cambridge.

Family of Parker.

JOHN PARKER, of Frenches, Reygate, citizen of London, son of William Parker, of Sprawton, near Ipswich, co. Suffolk, m. 1st, Anne Lacy, of co. Somerset, and by her had issue,

John, of London, m. Anne, eldest dau. of N. Barnard, and d. in 1672, having had a dau., Anne, who d. young.
Joseph. d. unm.
Anne, m. to Robert Sparrow, of Ipswich.
Katherine, m. to the Rev. Charles Hampton, D.D., rector of Blechingley.
Elizabeth.

He m. 2ndly, Anne, dau. of John Ashe, Esq. of Freshford, co. Somerset, M.P. for Westbury, and widow of Nathaniel Barnard, of Shepton, Somerset, and by her (who d. in 1694) had issue,

I. Bernard, d. unm.
II. James, of Frenches, m. Elizabeth, dau. of James Ashe, of Fyfield, Wilts, and d. 1689, having had a son, John, of Frenches, and two daus., Anne and Elizabeth.
III. Augustine, who had issue, five sons,
1 William, who m. in 1712, Elizabeth, dau. of John Parker, of London, and widow of Edward Stringer, Esq. of Haling, and d. in 1727, having had issue,
William, of Haling, d. 1776.
John, d. 1734.
Grace, d. 1781.
Anne, d. 1740.
ELIZABETH, who m. William Hamond, Esq. of Carshalton, as in the text.
2 Thomas. 3 John.
4 Edward. 5 Charles.
IV. Ambrose, of Croydon, aged 29; in 1687, m. Mary-Anne, dau. of Hubbard, of the Savoy.
V. John, of London, afterwards of Croydon, m. Elizabeth, dau. of Nicholas Ashton, of London, citizen, and d. in 1706, having had issue,
1 John, of Croydon, m. Bersheba Bowyer, and has a son and dau. to survive infancy, viz., John Ashton, d. 1780, and Elizabeth, d. 1793.
1 Elizabeth, m. 1st, 1710, to Edward Stringer, Esq. of Haling, who d. the same year; and 2ndly, in 1712, to William Parker, Esq., and was mother, by the latter, of Elizabeth, who m. William Hamond, Esq.
2 Ashton, a dau., d. 1769.
3 Mary, m. to Sir Robert Kendall Cator, Bart. of Kempton, Beds.
4 ANNE, m. in 1723, to William Hamond, Esq., Turkey merchant, as in the text, and was mother of William Hamond, Esq. of Carshalton.

HAMMOND OF ST. ALBANS COURT.

HAMMOND, WILLIAM-OSMUND, Esq. of St. Albans Court, co. Kent, J.P. and D.L., high-sheriff 1846, b. 26 April, 1790; m. 15 July, 1815, Mary-Graham, eldest dau. of Sir Henry Oxenden, Bart. of Broome Park, and has,

I. WILLIAM-OXENDEN, b. 22 Dec. 1817, late of the 17th lancers.
II. Egerton-Douglas, in holy orders, vicar of Northbourne, b. 24 June, 1822; m. 6 July, 1847, Katherine-Elizabeth, eldest dau. of Robert Whitmore, Esq.
III. Maximilian-Montagu, b. 6 May, 1824, captain rifle brigade; m. 24 Aug. 1850, Ann-Rose, dau. of George Pennington, Esq., and was killed within the Redan, before Sebastopol, 8 Sept. 1855.
IV. Henry-Anthony, b. 12 June, 1829, in holy orders.
I. Mary-Elizabeth.
II. Charlotte-Anna-Maria.
III. Fanny-Anne-Charlotte, d. young.

Lineage.—EDWARD HAMMOND, Esq. of St. Albans Court, eldest son of Thomas Hammond, who purchased the manor of St. Albans, Kent, in 1551, and grandson of John Hammond, tenant to the abbot of St. Albans, *temp.* HENRY VIII., m. Katherine, dau. of John Shelly, Esq. of Patesham, in Sussex, and had issue, with two daus., six sons. The eldest son,

SIR WILLIAM HAMMOND, of St. Albans Court, knighted in 1608, m. Elizabeth, dau. of Anthony Aucher, Esq. of Bishopsbourne, by Margaret his wife, dau. of Edward Sandys, archbishop of York, and had, (with five daus., of whom Mary, m. to Sir Thomas Stanley, Knt. of Comberlow, and Elizabeth, m. to Sir John Marsham, Bart.) three sons, I. ANTHONY, his successor; II. Edward; III. William. Sir William Hammond d. in 1615, and was s. by his eldest son,

Anthony Hammond, Esq. of St. Albans Court, who m. Anne, dau. of Sir Dudley Digges, Knt. of Chilham Castle, master of the Rolls to King Charles I., and had, with several daus., four sons, viz., i. William, his successor; ii. Dudley; iii. Anthony, of Somersham Place, co. Huntingdon, whose son, Anthony, of Somersham Place, M.P. and commissioner of the navy in the reign of Queen Anne, known as *Silver-tongued Hammond*, m. Jane, dau. of Sir Walter Clarges, Bart., and had issue, 1. Thomas, of Somersham, who m. Miss Elizabeth, Adams, and d. in 1758. 2. James, the elegiac poet, M.P. for Truro; and iv. Edward, d. at sea. Anthony Hammond d. in 1661, and was s. by his eldest son,

William Hammond, Esq. of St. Albans Court, who m. twice, but had issue only by his 1st wife, Elizabeth, dau. of Sir John Marsham, Bart., viz. William, his successor; Anthony d. young; John, barrister-at-law, who left an only dau., Elizabeth, who d. unm. in 1778; Elizabeth, m. to Oliver St. John, Esq. son of the Chief Justice St. John; and Anne, m. to Dr. William Wotton, the well-known critic. He was s. at his decease by his eldest son,

William Hammond, Esq. of St. Albans Court, who m. 1st, in 1692, Elizabeth, dau. of John Kingsford, Esq., by whom, who d. in 1702, he had a son, Anthony, his successor. He m. 2ndly, Mary, dau. of Thomas Turner, Esq. of Heden, and dying in 1717, was s. by his eldest son,

Anthony Hammond, Esq. of St. Albans Court, who m. his cousin, Catherine Kingsford, and d. in 1722, when he was s. by his only child,

William Hammond, Esq. of St. Albans Court, b. in 1721, who m. Charlotte, dau. and co-heiress of William Egerton, LL.D., (grandson of John, 2nd Earl of Bridgewater,) by Ann, dau. of Sir Francis Head, Bart., and had issue. He d. 1772, and was s. by his elder son,

William Hammond, Esq. of St. Albans Court, m. in 1785, Elizabeth, eldest dau. and co-heiress of Osmund Beauvoir, D.D., by Anne, dau. and co-heiress (by Elizabeth his wife, dau. of Thomas Dalison, Esq. of Hamptons, co. Kent) of John Boys, Esq. of Hoad Court, descended from the Boys's of Fredville, and had issue,

William Osmund, now of St. Albans Court.
Maximilian-Dudley-Digges Dalyson, of Hamptons. (*See that family.*)
Elizabeth-Mary, m. to Capt. William Haig, royal marines.
Mary, m. to Charles Allix, Esq. of Willoughby Hall, co. Lincoln, and has issue.
Charlotte-Jemima, m. to John Nethercote, Esq. of Moulton Grange, Northamptonshire, and is deceased.
Julia-Jemima, d. unm.
Jemima-Julia, m. to the Rev. Thomas Clayton Glyn.

Mr. Hammond d. 1829.

*Arms**—Arg., on a chev., sa., between three ogresses, each charged with a martlet, of the field, three escallop shells, or, all within a bordure, engrailed, vert.

Crest—A hawk's head, collared, gu., rays issuing, or.

Motto—Pro rege et patriâ.

Seat—St. Albans Court, Nonington, Kent.

HAMMOND OF WISTASTON.

Hammond, James-Walthall, Esq. of Wistaston Hall, co. Chester, b. 4 May, 1805; s. his father 22 Sept. 1822.

Lineage.—Thomas Walthall, Esq., descended from the Walthalls of Walthall, co. Westmoreland, living *temp.* Henry VII, m. Margaret, dau. of Sir William Stanley, Bart. of Hooton, co. Chester, and had issue, Thomas, and Roger. The elder son,

Thomas Walthall, Esq., m. Alice, dau. and co-heiress of John Marchomley, Esq. of Marchomley, co. Salop, and was ancestor of the Walthalls of Cheshire, who frequently acted as high-sheriff, and one of whom, Richard Walthall, Esq., capt. in the king's guards, fought at Edgehill. The last male heir,

Peter Walthall, Esq. of Wistaston, m. Anne, dau. of the Rev. Dr. Brooke, Dean of Chester, by whom, who d. 26 Nov. 1802, he left no issue, at his decease, 25 April, 1818, whereupon the estates devolved upon his nephew,

James-Walthall Hammond, Esq., (son of James Hammond, Esq., and Amabelia Walthall, his wife), who m. Penelope, dau. of Thomas Hector, and had issue,

James-Walthall, present proprietor.
Penelope.

He d. 22 Sept. 1822.

Arms—Per chev., engr., gu. and arg., three oxen heads, ppr.

Crest—A boar, passant, ppr.

Seat—Wistaston Hall, near Nantwich.

HAMOND OF WESTACRE.

Hamond, Anthony, Esq. of Westacre High House, co. Norfolk, J.P. and D.L., high-sheriff, 1836, b. 4 May, 1805; m. in Feb. 1828, Mary-Anne, eldest dau. of John-Chaworth Musters, Esq. of Colwich, Notts, by Mary-Anne his wife, only dau. and heiress of George Chaworth, Esq. of Annesley Park, in the latter county, and has issue surviving,

i. Anthony. ii. Philip.
iii. Richard-Horace. iv. Thomas-Horace-Astley.
i. Mary-Anne, m. to Henry Birkbeck, Esq. of Stoke, Holy Cross, co. Norfolk.
ii. Frances. iii. Susan-Maria.
iv. Caroline-Penelope. v. Catherine-Sarah.
vi. Emily.

Lineage.—The family of Hamond is of considerable antiquity in Norfolk.

Anthony Hamond, Esq. of Wootton, great-grandson of Edmund Hamond, who d. about 1605, m. Susan, youngest dau. of Robert Walpole, Esq., M.P. for Castle Rising, and sister of Sir Robert Walpole, 1st earl of Orford, and by her had three sons. Mr. Anthony Hamond was s. at his decease, 7 Feb. 1743, by his eldest son,

Richard Hamond, Esq., who d. unm. in 1776, when the estates devolved upon his nephew,

Anthony Hamond, Esq. (son of Robert Hamond and Elizabeth Swan, his wife), who m. 1st, Polly-Amelia Payne, and by her left one son, Richard, b. in July, 1773, resident in Holland. He m. 2ndly, Sarah, one of the three daus. and co-heirs of Philip Case, Esq. of King's Lynn, and by her had (with two daus., Sarah; and Susan, m. to Henry Elwes, Esq. of Colesbourne, co. Gloucester) three sons, Anthony, d. s. p. in 1783; Philip, his successor; and Robert, d. s. p. Mr. Hamond entailed all his estates on the issue of his 2nd marriage, and was s. at his decease by the eldest surviving son of his 2nd wife,

Philip Hamond, Esq. of Westacre, who m. Anne, dau. of Charles-James Packe, Esq. of Prestwold, co. Leicester, and by her had issue,

i. Anthony, present representative.
ii. Robert-Nicholas, of Fakenham, m. Emily, second dau. of John C. Musters, Esq., and sister to his brother Anthony's wife.
iii. Richard, d. young.
iv. Philip, late a captain in the army.
i. Frances-Anne, d. young. ii. Susan-Maria.
iii. Caroline, m. to Samuel-Vere Dashwood, Esq. of Stanford Hall, co. Leicester.
iv. Catherine-Sarah, d. young.
v. Ahmeria, m. to the Rev. Robert-Scott Surtees.
vi. Emily, m. to John-George-C. Musters, Esq., eldest son of the above-mentioned J.-C. Musters, Esq.

Mr. Philip Hamond d. in July, 1824.

Arms—Az., between two chevronels, three doves, or.

Crest—On a rocky mount, ppr., a dove, arg., holding in its beak a slip of olive, vert.

Seat—Westacre High House, near Swaffham, co. Norfolk.

HANBURY OF HOLFIELD GRANGE.

Hanbury, Osgood, Esq. of Holfield Grange, Essex, b. 4 July, 1794; m. 21 July, 1817, Eleanor-Willet Hall, dau. of W. Hall, Esq., and has had issue,

i. Osgood, b. 30 May, 1826; m. Miss Newton, dau. of Wm. Newton, Esq.
ii. Sampson, b. 27 Dec. 1827; m. Anne, dau. of Mrs. Rachel Barclay.
iii. William, b 7 July, 1829, lost at sea 11 June, 1855, in H.M.S "Nirbudda."
iv. John-Osgood, b. 31 Jan. 1832; d. 26 July, 1843.
i. Eleanor-Willet, m. 1 May, 1840, to the Rev. Wm. Ayling.
ii. Susanna. iii. Anna-Emily. iv Priscilla-Rachel.

Lineage.—This family claims to be a branch of the old Worcestershire family of Hanbury *of Hanbury.*

Osgood Hanbury, Esq. of Holfield Grange, near Coggeshall, Essex, m. 18 Jan. 1757, Mary, eldest dau. of Sampson

* Granted by Barker, Garter king-at-arms, to Thomas Hamon, of Nonington, in 1548, 2 Edward VI.

Lloyd, Esq. of Birmingham, banker, and *d.* 11 Jan. 1784, having had issue,

I. John-Osgood Hanbury, *b.* 23 Nov. 1757, *d.* 23 July, 1773.

II. Osgood Hanbury, of Holfield Grange, Essex, a banker in London, *b.* 15 June, 1765, *m.* 19 Aug. 1789, Susannah-Willett, dau. of John Barclay, Esq., a banker in London, and *d.* 11 Feb. 1851, having had issue,

1 Osgood, now of Holfield Grange.
2 Robert, now of Poles.
3 Henry, *b.* 30 June, 1798.
4 Sampson, *d. unm.* 7 Nov. 1826.
5 Arthur, *b.* in 1801, rector of Bures, *m.* and has issue three sons and two daus.
6 Philip, a banker in London, *b.* 30 June, 1802, *m.* and has issue seven sons.
1 Susan, *m.* to George Field, Esq., and has issue.
2 Anna, *m.* to the Rev. John Bramston.
3 Rachael, *m.* to Robert Barclay, Esq. of Clapham, son of Charles Barclay, Esq., M.P., and has issue.
4 Mary, *m.* 1836, to Sir Francis Mackenzie, Bart.

III. Charles Hanbury, of Halstead, in Essex, a banker at Bury and Ipswich, *b.* 26 Sept. 1766, *m.* the dau. of John Bland, Esq., and *d.* in 1825, leaving issue, of whom Priscilla *m.* W.-P. Honywood, Esq., M.P. for Kent.

IV. Richard Hanbury, *b.* 23 Nov. 1767, *d.* 23 May, 1768.

V. Sampson Hanbury, of Poles Hall, Herts, a brewer in London, (Truman, Hanbury, Buxton, and Co.,) *b.* 12 March, 1769, *d.* in Aug. 1835, *m.* Agatha, dau. of Richard Gurney, Esq. of Norwich, and sister of Hudson Gurney, Esq. of Keswick Hall, in Norfolk.

I. Anna Hanbury, *m.* 12 Feb. 1782, to Thomas-Fowell Buxton, Esq.

II. Rachael Hanbury, *m.* to Richard Gurney, Esq., M.P. for Norwich, and *d.* 1 June, 1825, leaving issue.

III. Mary Hanbury, *b.* 24 Aug. 1780, *d.* in 1829, *m.* to her cousin, David Lloyd, Esq. of Kenilworth.

Seat—Holfield Grange, Coggeshall, Essex.

HANBURY OF POLES.

HANBURY, ROBERT, Esq. of Poles, co. Hertford, J.P. and D.L., high-sheriff in 1854, *b.* 2 July, 1796; *m.* 14 Aug. 1819, his cousin, Emily, dau. of the late William Hall, Esq., and by her, who *d.* 25 Dec. 1847, has issue,

I. ROBERT, *b.* 19 March, 1823; *m.* 19 July, 1849, Caroline, eldest dau. of Abel Smith, Esq. of Woodhall Park, Herts.

II. Charles-Addington, *b.* 24 June, 1828, *m.* 28 Nov. 1853, Christina-Isabella, dau. of Dr. Mackenzie, brother of the late Sir Francis-Alexander Mackenzie, Bart. of Gairloch.

III. George, *b.* 2 Oct. 1829. IV. Edgar, *b.* 5 Feb. 1834.

V. Gurney, 8th hussars, *b.* 18 March, 1835.

I. Madeline-Emily, *m.* to Alfred-Daniel, eldest son of Capt. Chapman.

Mr. Hanbury, of Poles, is next younger brother of the present Osgood Hanbury, Esq. of Holfield Grange.

Seat—Poles, Herts.

HANCOCKS OF WOLVERLEY COURT.

HANCOCKS, ALFRED-JOHN, Esq. of Wolverley Manor, co. Worcester, *m.* 1851, his cousin, Caroline-Louisa, 2nd dau. and coheiress of the late Samuel Hancocks, Esq. of Woodfield House, and has issue.

Lineage.—WILLIAM HANCOCKS, Esq., of Wolverley, an extensive ironmaster, *b.* 6 Feb. 1761, was son of William Hancocks, Esq., *b.* Aug. 1726, grandson of Samuel Hancocks, Esq., *b.* 23 Jan. 1708, and great-grandson of another Samuel Hancocks, Esq., *b.* 15 May, 1684. He *m.* Elizabeth, dau., and eventually heiress of Samuel Talbott, Esq. of Wolverley, representative of a family seated there for centuries, of whom Nash, in his *History of Worcestershire* says, they held their estates without interruption from the time of the invasion of the Conqueror, 1066. He had issue three children only,

I. JOHN HANCOCK, Esq. of Wolverley Court, of whom hereafter.

II. SAMUEL HANCOCKS, Esq., 2nd son, deceased, of Woodfield House, *m.* Teresa, dau. of John Pope, Esq. of London, and had issue six children,

1 Teresa, *d. s. p.* 2 Emily.
3 Caroline-Louisa, *m.* her cousin, Alfred-John Hancocks, Esq.
4 Ellen. 5 Victoria. 6 Harriett.

III. WILLIAM HANCOCKS, Esq., 3rd son (*see* HANCOCKS, *of Blakeshall Hall, Worcestershire*).

The eldest son,

JOHN HANCOCKS, Esq. of Wolverley Court and Manor, *m.* Elizabeth, dau. of John White, Esq., deceased, of Astley, co. Worcester, and had issue,

I. ALFRED JOHN, his heir. II. William-Frederick.
III. Arthur Annesley. IV. Augustus-Talbott.
I. Laura-Elizabeth, *m.* William Hutcheson Collins, Esq. of Cubberley House.
II. Isabella. III. Jane-Augusta.
V. Louis-Albert, deceased.

John Hancocks, Esq., who was a magistrate for the cos. of Worcester, Stafford, and Salop, *d.* and was buried at Wolverley, Sept. 1849.

Arms—As registered in Herald's College: Per chevron ar. and gules in chief a garb between two cocks respecting each other, in base a lion rampant, or.
Crest—On a mount vert, a cock gules holding with its dexter claw an ear of wheat, or.
Motto—Redeem time.
Seats—Wolverley Court and Wolverley Manor, Worcestershire.

HANCOCKS OF BLAKESHALL HALL.

HANCOCKS, WILLIAM, Esq. of Blakeshall Hall, co. Worcester, *b.* at Wolverley 1802; *m.* 1832, Hannah, dau. of John White, Esq., deceased, of Astley, co. Worcester; is a magistrate for the cos. of Worcester, Salop, and Stafford.

Lineage.—WILLIAM HANCOCKS, Esq. of Wolverley, an extensive ironmaster, *b.* 6 Feb. 1761 (son of William Hancocks, Esq. grandson of Samuel Hancocks, Esq., and great-grandson of another Samuel Hancocks, Esq.), *m.* Elizabeth Talbott, dau., and eventually heiress, of Samuel Talbott, Esq. of Wolverley, representative of a family seated there for centuries, and of whom Nash, in his *History of Worcestershire* says, they held their estates without interruption from the time of the invasion of the Conqueror, 1066. She had three children,

JOHN, of Wolverley Court.
SAMUEL, of Woodfield House.
WILLIAM, of Blakeshall Hall, as above.

Arms, Crest, and Motto—As HANCOCKS, *of Wolverley Court*, with a mullet for difference.
Seat—Blakeshall Hall, co. Worcester.

HANDLEY OF NEWARK.

HANDLEY, WILLIAM-FARNWORTH, Esq. of Newark, co. Nottingham, J.P. and D.L., high-sheriff 1822, and formerly M.P. for Newark, *b.* 9 Oct. 1780.

Lineage.—WILLIAM HANDLEY, Esq. of Newark (elder son of WILLIAM HANDLEY, Esq. of Newark, co. Notts, by his wife, Jane Moldiclough, of Kelham, in the same county), *m.* 5 Jan. 1743, Sarah Farnworth, of Newark, and was father, with other issue,* of an elder son and heir,

WILLIAM HANDLEY, Esq. who *m.* 13 Oct. 1772, Anne Marshall, of Pickering, co. York, and had issue,

I. WILLIAM-FARNWORTH.

II. JOHN, of Muskham Grange, co. Notts, *b.* 30 March, 1782, J.P., high-sheriff 1836, *m.* 17 March, 1807, Martha, dau. of Philip Story, Esq. of Lockington Hall, co. Leicester, and has,

1 JOHN, barrister-at-law, *b.* in Dec. 1807.
2 Philip, *b.* in Jan. 1809.
3 William, *b.* in Dec. 1811, in holy orders, rector of Winthorpe, Notts.
1 Martha 2 Diana-Elizabeth.

III. Benjamin, of Pointon House, co. Lincoln, J.P. and D.L., formerly M.P. for Boston, *b.* 9 Jan. 1784, capt. in the 9th lancers, with which regiment he served in South America, and in the Peninsula; subsequently he became major of the 58rd reg., from which he retired on half-pay.

IV. Charles-Richard, *b.* 6 Sept. 1786, in holy orders, vicar of Herne Hill and Sturry, co. Kent, *m.* Cassandra, dau. of Julius Hutchinson, Esq. of Hatfield Old Hall, co. Herts, and Outhorpe, co. Notts.

Arms—Arg., a fesse, gu., between three goats, current, sa., bearded, unguled, and armed, or.
Crest—A goat, as in the Arms.
Residence—Newark.

* The late HENRY HANDLEY, Esq. of Culverthorpe Hall, co. Lincoln, M.P. for that shire from 1832 to 1841, *b.* in 1797; *m.* in 1825, the Hon. Caroline Edwardes, dau. of Lord Kensington, was grandson of William Handley, Esq. of Newark, and Sarah Farnworth, his wife. He *d.* 29 June, 1846.

HANFORD OF WOOLLASHALL.

HANFORD, COMPTON-JOHN, Esq. of Woollashall, co. Worcester, J.P., *b.* 8 June, 1819; *m.* 1809, Elizabeth, 2nd dau. of the late James Martin, Esq. of Overbury, and has issue,

I. JAMES, *b.* in Feb. 1812.
II. Compton-John, *b.* in June, 1819.
I. Elizabeth-Henrietta. II. Frances.

Lineage.—This very ancient family was seated, at an early period, in the county of Chester, and at Woollashall, in Worcestershire, since 1536.

LAURENCE HANFORD, 2nd son of Robert Hanford, Esq., and 7th in descent from Sir John Hanford, of Cheshire, Knt., was father of THOMAS HANFORD, Esq., who *m.* Margaret Hungerford, and had (with two daus., Margaret, wife of Thomas Copeley, of Norton, and Catherine, wife of Whittington of Norgrove) a son, JOHN HANFORD, Esq., father of FRANCIS HANFORD, Esq. of Wooller's Hill, who *m.* Elizabeth, dau. of Walter Giffard, Esq. of Chillington, and was *s.* by his son,

WALTER HANFORD, Esq. of Woollashall, who *m.* Frances, dau. of Sir Henry Compton, Knt. of Hartpury Court, co. Gloucester, and had issue,

COMPTON, of Wooller's Hill, who *m.* 1st, Miss Chaumont, and 2ndly, Miss Slingsby, by the latter of whom he left a son, Edward, father of CHARLES HANFORD, Esq. of Woollashall, who *d.* in 1816.
EDWARD, of whose line we treat.

The 2nd son,

EDWARD HANFORD, Esq. of Redmarley, *m.* Frances, dau. of John Hornyold, Esq. of Blackmore Park, co. Worcester, by whom he had (with a dau. Elizabeth, *m.* to Samuel Niblet, Esq. of Haresfield, co. Gloucester, *see that family*) a son and heir,

CHARLES HANFORD, Esq. of Redmarley D'Abitot, co. Worcester, who *m.* Esther, dau. of John Lockley, Esq. of Derbyshire, and dying 1794, left a son,

CHARLES-EDWARD HANFORD, Esq. of Woollashall, J.P. and D.L., *b.* 1781, who *m.* 1809, Eliza, dau. of James Martin, Esq of Overbury, co. Worcester, and *d.* 17 Feb. 1854, having had issue,

Charles-Edward, *d.* under age, 1827.
James, *d. unm.* 1840.
COMPTON-JOHN, now of Woollashall.
Elizabeth-Henrietta, *d. unm.* 1835.
Frances, *m.* 1847, to William Lloyd Flood, Esq. of Farmley, co. Kilkenny.

Arms—Sa., a star of eight rays, arg.
Crest—On a chapeau, gu., turned up, erm., a wivern, gu.
Motto—Memorare novissima.
Seat—Woollashall, near Pershore, co. Worcester.

HANKEY OF FETCHAM.

HANKEY, JOHN-BARNARD, Esq. of Fetcham Park, co. Surrey, *b.* 31 March, 1784; *m.* 9 June, 1807, Elizabeth, dau. of John 1st, Lord de Blaquiere, and has issue,

I. GEORGE-JAMES-BARNARD. II. William-Barnard.
III. Frederick-Thomas-Barnard, R.N.
IV. John-Bellingham-Barnard.
V. Henry-Barnard. VI. Augustus-Barnard.
I. Mary-Barnard, *m.* to William-Holme Sumner, Esq. eldest son of George-Holme Sumner, Esq. of Hatchlands, late M.P. for Surrey.
II. Louisa-Ellinor-Barnard, *m.* 10 July, 1838, to William Davidson, Esq., 4th son of the late Henry Davidson, Esq. of Tulloch Castle, N.B.
III. Frances-Elizabeth-Barnard.
IV. Harriet-Barnard.

Lineage.—The family of HANKEY was originally seated in the county palatine of Chester. In the 14th of ELIZABETH, the right of bearing arms was conceded and granted to Henry Hankey, Esq., mayor of the city o fChester.

SIR HENRY HANKEY, an eminent citizen and alderman o fLondon, *m.* 26 Dec. 1694, Anne, dau. of Joseph Chaplin, Esq. of East Bergholt, high-sheriff of Suffolk, by Anne, his wife, dau. of Rice Price, of London, and had two sons, viz., 1 JOSEPH (Sir), Knt. and alderman (father of Joseph Chaplin Hankey, of East Bergholt, whose dau., Jane-Isabella, *m.* Sir Edward-Hyde East, Bart.); and 2, Thomas (Sir). Sir Henry Hankey *d.* in Feb. 1736-7. His 2n son,

SIR THOMAS HANKEY, Knt., alderman of London, *m.* June, 1738, Sarah, eldest dau. of the celebrated Sir John Barnard, member in 6 successive parliaments for the city of London, and had issue,

I. THOMAS, his heir.
II. Robert, *m.* Miss Penton, and left one son, Augustus-Robert, who *d. unm.*, and two daus., Matilda, *m.* to — Hartsinck, Esq., and Henrietta, to — Hirst, Esq.
III. John, who *m.* the dau. of Andrew Thomson, Esq. of Roehampton, and had three sons, namely,

1 JOHN-PETER, who *m.* Isabella, sister of Sir William Alexander, late chief baron of the Exchequer, and left three sons and one dau., viz.,

John-Alexander, *m.* Ellen, dau. of William Blake, Esq of Danesbury.
Henry, late major 8th hussars, lieut.-colonel 1st Dragoon guards, *m.* 1st, 29 June, 1839, Caroline-Maria, eldest dau. of Abraham-W. Robarts, Esq. of Roehampton, Surrey, which lady *d.* 15 April, 1844, and 2ndly, 30 Sept. 1852, Lady Emily Pennefather, widow of Richard Pennefather, Esq. of Knockevan and sister of the present Earl of Glengall.
William, captain 9th lancers.
Julia, *m.* 6 Oct. 1829, to the Hon. Thomas-Seymour Bathurst, third son of the late Earl Bathurst, and survives his widow with one son and one dau.

2 Thomson, of Portland Place, London, *m.* Martha, dau. of Benjamin Harrison, Esq., and had issue,

Thomson, M.P. for Peterborough, *b.* 1805, *m.* 1830, Appollene-Agatha Alexander, half-sister of Sir William Alexander, the chief baron.
George. Beaumont.
Louisa, *m.* to her cousin, Thomas Hankey, Esq., banker, of Fenchurch Street.
Elizabeth, *m.* to the Rev. Richard Harvey, rector of Hornsey.
Mary.
Albinia, *m.* to Dr. James Somerville.
Isabella.
Emma, *m.* to the Rev. W. Waguflr.
Martha. Caroline.

3 Frederick, (Sir,) Knt. Grand Cross of St. Michael and St. George, secretary to Government at Malta, who had a grant of supporters to his arms, in approval of his long services, *m.* 1st, his first cousin, Charlotte, dau. of Thomas Hankey, Esq. of Fetcham Park, Surrey, and by her, who *d.* in 1816, had two daus., Emma and Frederica. Sir Frederick *m.* 2ndly, a native of Corfu, and by that lady, who *d.* in 1835, had one son and one dau., viz., Frederick and Thomasine-Ionia, *m.* 27 July, 1839, to Capt. Charles-F. Maxwell, 82nd foot, nephew and military secretary to Sir Henry Bouverie, Governor of Malta.

I. Jane, *m.* to Thomas Sutton, Esq. of Moulsey, in Surrey.
II. Susannah, *m.* in 1767, to Beaumont, second Lord Hotham.

Sir Thomas *d.* in 1770, and was *s.* by his eldest son,

THOMAS HANKEY, Esq. of Fetcham Park, who *m.* Miss Wyver, of an old Cheshire family, and had issue,

JOHN-BARNARD, his heir, of Fetcham Park.
Thomas, who *m.* Louisa, dau. of Thomas Hankey, Esq.
Charlotte, *m.* to Sir Frederick Hankey, and *d.* in 1816.
Sarah, *m.* to Sir Hugh-Dillon Massey, Bart. of Doonass, co. Clare.
Louisa, *m.* to Major-General Darby Griffith, of Padworth House, Bucks.
Eliza.

Mr. Hankey *d.* 13 Sept. 1793.

Arms—Per pale, gu. and az., a wolf, salient, erminois vulned on the shoulder, of the first.
Crest—A demi-wolf, erminois.
Seat—Fetcham Park, Surrey.

HANNAY OF KINGSMUIR.

HANNAY, GEORGE-FRANCIS, Esq. of Kingsmuir, co. Fife, present male representative of the ancient Scottish family of Hannay, *m.* Miss Cunningham, (whose grandfather Capt. Cunningham, R.N., claimed the Earldom of Glencairn), and has issue.

Lineage.—HANNAY, of Sorbie, in Wigtonshire, a family of great antiquity, is traceable from the earliest period in the public records. Among the powerful chiefs of Galloway, who swore fealty to EDWARD I., occur the McCullochs, the McDowals, the HANNAYS, and the Adairs; and in the Ragman's Roll appears this entry, "1296, Gilbert de Anneth, Gilbert de Hannethe del comite de Wiggeton." Nisbet sta'es that the principal family of the name was Ahannay or Hannay, of Sorbie, and that according to Pont's MS. it bore for arms, "Arg., three Roe-bucks' heads, couped, az., collared or., with a bell pendent gu." "The lands of Sorbie," continues that learned herald, "are now possessed by others, but the family is at present represented by Mr. Robert Hannay, of Kingsmuir, in Fife; there is another family still in Galloway, descended of Sorbie, viz., HANNAY, *of Kirkdale.*" Chalmers refers, also, in his "Caledonia," to the antiquity and eminence of this family, instancing the submission of Gilbert Hannay, to King EDWARD, in 1296, and the continuous possession of Sorbie, and other lands in Wigtonshire, for many centuries. Patrick Hannay, the poet, was a grandson of Donald Hannay, of Sorbie; he served under Sir Andrew Gray, in the service of the Elector of Bohemia. In 1619, he published, "Two Elegies on the death of Queen ANNE, wife of JAMES I."; in 1622, "Poems," on the title-page of which, he styles himself M.A. A member of this family obtained a baronetcy in 1630, and assumed the title of Sir Robert Hannay, of Mochrum, Bart.; and another, Patrick, sat for the Borough of Wigton, in the famous parliament of 1639–40, which finally settled the civil and religious liberties of Scotland.

ROBERT HANNAY (who possessed Kingsmuir, in 1700), was advocate of Edinburgh, and a person of consideration in his day. He *m.* Mary Livingston, widow of Colonel Borthwick, but left no issue, whereupon the estate passed to his sister,

ANN HANNAY. This lady, (who was *m.* to Captain Erskine, of Dun, but *d.* without issue,) bequeathed Kingsmuir to her cousin,

JAMES HANNAY, son of Patrick Hannay, Esq., and from this gentleman it passed to his brother,

JOHN HANNAY, Esq. He *m.* Miss Brown, and was father of

GEORGE HANNAY, Esq. of Kingsmuir, who was an officer in the service of the Crown, in the United States. Adhering faithfully to the loyal side when the "Independence" controversy began, he was obliged to fly the country. By his wife, Miss Hambly, of Exeter, he left two sons, 1, PETER HANNAY, R.N. who served as a Lieutenant in the "Defiance," at Trafalgar, and *d. s. p.*; and GEORGE FRANCIS HANNAY, Esq., the present possessor of Kingsmuir.

Hannay of Grennan.

The HANNAYS, *of Grennan*, co. Wigtoun, a branch of HANNAY, *of Mochrum*, date the possession of their lands from the reign of JAMES V., of Scotland. They are mentioned by Wodrow, in the list of those fined for nonconformity in 1662. The last direct representative of this branch, was Alexander Hannay, of Grennan, who left two daus., co-heiresses, the eldest of whom *m.* her cousin, and had by him two sons; 1st, the late Dr. Alexander Hannay, M.D., Glasgow, who *m.* Marion, dau. of James Hannay, of Blairinnie, and by her had left two sons; 2nd, Robert Hannay, East India merchant.

In the reign of CHARLES II., Hannay, of Grennan, *m.* Margaret McCulloch, dau. of Mc.Culloch, of Myreton, for his 2nd wife, and had by her a son, John Hannay. From this John Hannay, (besides others unknown), descended,

1. The late John Hannay, of Malabay and Crochmore, in Kirkcudbrightshire, who left Alexander Hannay Esq., Banker, in Dumfries, and other sons,

2. The late James Hannay, of Blairinnie, in the same county, son of Robert Hannay, of Glasgow, by Jean Maxwell, dau. of Maxwell, of Newlaw (now represented by Maxwell, of Breoch), descended from John Maxwell, the famous Lord Herries. This James Hannay, *m.* Marion Shaw, a descendant, maternally of the Browns, of Carsluith, and McDowalls, of Glen; and of this marriage the following sons survive;

Robert Hannay, Esq., advocate.
David Hannay, *m.* and has issue, JAMES HANNAY, the distinguished writer, author of "Singleton Fontenoy" and other literary works; and Robert-Ferguson.
James Hannay, late captain of the 8th regiment, of Ballylough, co. Antrim, *m.* and has sons, Edmund, James, Robert, and Alfred.
John Hannay, Esq. of Lincluden, co. Kircudbright, *m.* and has issue, James Lennox Hannay, barrister, of the Inner Temple.
Walter Hannay.

The family of Hannay, of Rusco, co. Kircudbright, now represented by Robert Hannay of that place, also derive from the Grennan branch.

Arms—Arg. three roebucks' heads, couped, az. collared or. with a bell pendent gu.
Crest—A cross-crosslet fitchée, issuing out of a crescent sa.
Motto—Cresco et spero.
Seat—Kingsmuir, co. Fife.

HANNAY OF KIRKDALE.

RAINSFORD-HANNAY, WILLIAM-HENRY, Esq. of Kirkdale, co. Kircudbright, *s.* to the estate 1850, and thereupon added to his patronymic Rainsford, the surname of HANNAY; *m.* Maria, widow of Robert Steuart, Esq., M.P., of Alderston, co. Haddington, and dau. of Lieut.-Col. Samuel Dalrymple, C.B., descended from the noble family of Stair.

Lineage.—The family of HANNAY, originally written A'Hannay, is of very ancient descent, and the estate of Sorbie, in Galloway, was the seat of the elder branch.

ALEXANDER A'HANNAY, uncle of Patrick of Sorbie, acquired the estate of Kirkdale in 1532. He left a son,

JOHN A'HANNAY, who took an active part with his relative in the family feuds with the Murrays of Broughton, their neighbours. He was *s.* by his son,

PATRICK A'HANNAY, of Kirkdale, who *m.* Ann, dau. of of Patrick M'Kie, of Larg. Patrick was killed, 16 Dec. 1610, in a conflict when assisting the earl of Galloway against Kennedy of Blairquhan, at the Cruives of Cree. He *m.* Miss M'Kie, of Larg, and left a son and heir,

PATRICK A'Hannay, of Kirkdale, who *m.* Agnes, dau. of Gavin Dunbar, of Baldoon, a family now represented by the Earl of Selkirk, and was *s.* in 1640 by his son,

WILLIAM HANNAY, who *m.* Elizabeth, heiress of Alexander Gordon, of Castramont, a cadet of the ancient family of Lochinvar, afterwards viscounts of Kenmuir, and by her had three sons, by the eldest of whom he was *s.* viz.,

SAMUEL HANNAY, of Kirkdale, commissioner of supply, 1704, who *m.* Jean, dau. and co-heiress of Patrick M'Kie, of Larg, by his wife, Agnes, dau. of Sir Patrick Mackie, of Larg, and by her had

WILLIAM HANNAY, of Kirkdale, who was served heir to his father 13 Nov. 1716. He *m.* Margaret, dau. of the Rev. Patrick Johnston, of Girthon (represented by Col. Johnston, of Carnsalloch), and had (with daus.) two sons, viz.,

SAMUEL, his heir.
Alexander, a military officer, who took part in the German campaigns (including the battle of Minden) under the Marquess of Granby, and who became afterwards adjutant-general of the army of India.

The eldest son,

SAMUEL HANNAY, of Kirkdale, a celebrated merchant in London, in 1783, was served heir male and of line of Sir Robert Hannay, of Mochrum, Bart. (4th of the Sorbie branch), under the patent, 31st March, 1630. Sir Samuel Hannay *m.* Mary, dau. of Dr. Meade, and for some years sat in parliament. He was *s.* by his only son,

SIR SAMUEL HANNAY, of Mochrum, and Kirkdale, Bart. who *d.* a bachelor, 1 Dec. 1841, and was *s.* in the family estate by

MARY HASTINGS HANNAY, of Kirkdale, his sister, who *d.* *unm.* 20 March, 1850, and was *s.* by her nephew

WILLIAM HENRY RAINSFORD, Esq. (son of Capt. Rainsford, of the guards, by his wife, a sister of the late baronet), who assumed in consequence the surname of HANNAY. He *d.* in 1855, and his brother, MAJOR RAINSFORD HANNAY, is the present possessor of Kirkdale.

Arms and *Crest*—Same as HANNAY, *of Kingsmuir.*
Motto—Per ardua ad alta.
Seat—Kirkdale, Kirkcudbright.

HANNING OF KILCRONE.

HANNING, JAMES, Esq., of Kilcrone, co. Cork, J.P., *m.* Sept. 1851, Frances-Catherine, 2nd dau. of the late Henry Skrine, Esq. of Warleigh, co. Somerset, and Stubbings, Berks, by his wife Caroline-Anne, dau. of the Rev. Benjamin Spry, vicar of St. Mary, Redcliffe, Bristol, and prebendary of Sarum (*see that family,*) and has issue.

Lineage.—JAMES HANNING, Esq. of Kilcrone (son of JOHN HANNING, Esq., by his 2nd wife, Miss Rowland), *m.* Patience, dau. of John Wallis, Esq. of Drishane Castle, co. Cork, by his wife, Patience, eldest dau. of John Longfield, Esq. of Longueville, and had issue,

I. John, deceased.
II. JAMES, present representative.
III. Henry.
IV. Clement.
I. Patience.
II. Frances.
III. Mary-Catherine.

Seat—Kilcrone, co. Cork.

HANSON OF OSMONDTHORPE.

HANSON, JOHN-OLIVER, Esq., D.L., a director of the Bank of England, *b.* 19 May, 1791; *m.* 12 Aug. 1819, Rebecca, youngest dau. of William Scott, Esq., and has issue,

I. JOHN-OLIVER, *b.* 8 June, 1820.
II. William-Stonehewer, *b.* 13 Dec. 1821.
III. George-Scott, *b.* 2 June, 1823.
IV. Henry-Allix, *b.* 19 July, 1830.
I. Mary-Annabella. II. Louisa-Rebecca.

Lineage.—This family is descended from the Rastrickes of Rastricke, in the parish of Halifax, co. York, whose pedigree is given, from the year 1250, in WATSON's *History of Halifax*.

WILLIAM HANSON, *b.* in Sept. 1670, who purchased Osmondthorpe, was eldest son of Christopher Hanson, of Arthington, and a descendant of John de Rastricke, who assumed in 1330 the surname of HANSON. His great-grandson,

JOHN HANSON, Esq., J.P. and D.L., who was *b.* 23 April, 1759, *s.* his father, William Hanson, Esq. (who *d.* 11 Dec. 1791) at Osmondthorpe. Mr. Hanson sold the estates of Osmondthorpe and Killingbeck, and purchased the manor of Great Bromley, near Colchester. He *m.* Mary-Isabella, dau. of Thomas Oliver, Esq. of Low Layton, co. Essex, and by her (who *d.* 12 Sept. 1826) had issue,

I. WILLIAM, *b.* 7 Sept. 1788, a captain in the 20th light-dragoons, who fell at the head of his squadron, in leading a charge against a very superior force of French cavalry, at Villa Franca, in Spain, 13 Sept. 1812, aged 25.
II. JOHN-OLIVER, the present representative.
III. Henry, *b.* 1 Nov. 1792, drowned in China, 3 Oct. 1809.
IV. George, *b.* 19 April, 1794, *m.* 1st, Caroline-Eleanor, eldest dau. of William Walford, Esq. of High Beach, co. Essex. by whom (who *d.* 17 May, 1834, he has issue,
 1 George-William, *b.* 28 June, 1830.
 2 James-Oliver, *b.* 27 Sept. 1831.
 3 Alfred-Atkinson, *b.* 7 Feb. 1833.
 He *m.* 2ndly, 19 Sept. 1839, Charlotte-Douglas, dau. of the late Charles Round, Esq., and sister of Charles-Gray Round, Esq. of Birch Hall, M.P. for the co. of Essex.
V. James-Edward, *d.* an infant.
VI Edward, *b.* 14 May, 1797, and *d.* 11 March, 1835, having *m.* Lydia-Maria, dau. of John Blunt, Esq. of Woodford, co. Essex, and had issue, one son and six daus., Edward-Pardoe-Cotton, *b.* 9 March, 1834; Lydia-Mary; Isabella; Charlotte-Anne; Maria-Elizabeth; Rozanna-Innes, *d.* an infant; and Jane-Innes.
VII. James-Frederick, of Smyrna, *b.* 6 July, 1799, *m.* at Boughia, near Smyrna, 26 Jan. 1841, Eliza-Zoë, dau. of Nathaniel-W. Werry, Esq., her Majesty's consul at Damascus, and has issue, Zoë-Charlotte, and Jemima-Caroline.
VIII. Oliver, (twin with Harriet,) *b.* 13 April, 1802, *d.* 7 Sept. 1823.
IX. Charles-Simpson, of Constantinople, *b.* 19 Sept. 1803, *m.* in Sept. 1830, Charlotte, only child of the Hon. Robert Smith, speaker of the House of Assembly, Tobago, and has issue, Charles-Constantine, *b.* 16 Oct. 1832; Henry-James, *b.* 27 July, 1838; Arthur-Walker, *b.* 24 Jan. 1843; William-Wellesley, *b.* 21 Nov. 1845; Louisa-Grace; Helen-Jane; Constance-Fanny; and Adeline Eliza.
I. Mary, *m.* 16 July, 1807, Capt. Richard Bogue, R.A., who fell at the battle of Leipsic, 18 Oct. 1813, while in command of the rocket-brigade, aged 31.
II. Elizabeth, *m.* 22 Dec. 1808, Sir James-Brabazon Urmston.
III. Ann, *m.* 9 June, 1829, Henry-Bonham Bax, Esq. of Walmer, co. Kent.
IV. Harriet, (twin with Oliver,) *m.* 4 Sept. 1823, John-William Bridges, Esq., son of George Bridges, Esq. of Lawford Hall, co. Essex.
V. Maria-Louisa, *m.* 24 March, 1825, Thomas Chapman, Esq., F.R.S., F.S.A.

Mr. Hanson, who served as high-sheriff for Essex in 1795, *d.* 18 Nov. 1839.

Arms—Or, a chevron, countercomponed, arg. and az., between three martlets, sa.
Crest—On a helm, a chapeau, az., lined, arg., a martlet, volant, sa., mantled, gu., double, arg.
Motto—Sola virtus invecta.
N.B.—Certified by William Ryley, Norroy King at Arms, 17 July, 1652.

HARBIN OF NEWTON HOUSE.

HARBIN, GEORGE, Esq. of Newton House, co. Somerset, J.P., *b.* 27 Feb. 1800.

Lineage.—This family was resident in Dorsetshire more than three centuries ago.

ROBERT HARBIN, Esq. of Weeke, in the parish of Gillingham, co. Dorset, and afterwards of Newton, co. Somerset, *b.* in 1526, *m.* a dau of Sir John Mervin, of Fonthill House, Wilts, and was father of

JOHN HARBIN, Esq. of Newton, who, by Bridget, his wife, dau. of William Drury, Esq., left a son and heir,

ROBERT HARBIN, Esq. of Newton, who *m.* Gertrude, dau. of Anthony Stocker, Esq. of Chilcompton, co. Somerset, and left a son and heir,

JOHN HARBIN, Esq. of Newton, *b.* in 1610, who *m.* 1st, Isabella, dau. of William Pert, Esq. of Arnold's, co. Essex, and 2ndly, Elizabeth, dau. of Sir Richard Strode, Knt. of Newnham, co. Devon, and *d.* in 1672, when he was *s.* by his son and heir by his 1st wife,

WILLIAM HARBIN, Esq. of Newton, *b.* in 1654, who *m.* Elizabeth, dau. of Sir Francis Wyndham, Bart. of Trent, co. Somerset (who afforded CHARLES II. protection after the battle of Worcester), and dying in 1705, was *s.* by his son and heir,

WILLIAM HARBIN, Esq. of Newton, who *m.* in 1714, Abigail, dau. and sole heiress of Richard Swayne, Esq. of Gunville, co. Dorset, and had (with a dau. Abigail, *m.* to Robert Goodden, Esq. of Over Compton, Dorset) a son and successor,

SWAYNE HARBIN, Esq. of Newton, *b.* in 1718, who *m.* in 1760, Barbara, dau. and sole heiress of George Abington, Esq. of Over Compton, son and heir of Isabella Compton, dau. and sole heiress of Henry Compton, Esq. of Sutton Bingham, co. Somerset, and of Over Compton, co. Dorset. By this lady Mr. Harbin had one dau., Henrietta, and five sons, I. WYNDHAM, his heir; II. William, *b.* 18 Sept 1762, *m.* 3 Feb. 1790, Rhoda, 3rd dau. of Edward Phelips, Esq. of Montacute, M.P. for co. Somerset, and *d.* 22 Oct. 1823, having had issue, viz., 1 GEORGE, successor to his uncle, and present representative of the family; 2 Edward, M.A., in holy orders, rector of Kingweston and East Lydford, co. Somerset, *m.* Jane, eldest dau. of John Hooper, Esq. of Yeovil, and *d.* leaving issue, William, Edward, Henry, Phillip, Matilda, and Rhoda; 1 Maria, *m.* to the Rev. Robert Phelips, vicar of Yeovil, son of the Rev. William Phelips, of Montacute; 2 Elizabeth, *m.* to Thomas Potter Milles, Esq., major of the 19th light dragoons, since deceased; III. Robert; IV. John; and V. Charles. Mr. Harbin *d.* in 1781, and was *s.* by his eldest son,

WYNDHAM HARBIN, Esq. of Newton, *b.* in 1761, who *d.* *unm.* in 1837, when the estates devolved upon his nephew and heir, the present GEORGE HARBIN, Esq. of Newton.

Arms (granted to Robert Harbin, Esq., in 1618)—Az., a saltier, voided, between four spears' heads, erect, or.
Crest—A hand, ppr., holding a spear, or.
Seat—Newton House, Yeovil, co. Somerset.

HARCOURT OF ANKERWYCKE.

HARCOURT, GEORGE-SIMON, Esq. of Ankerwycke House, co. Berks, J.P. and D.L., high-sheriff 1834, and formerly M.P. for Bucks, *b.* 25 Feb. 1807; *m.* 24 June, 1833, Jessy, 2nd dau. of John Rolls, Esq. of Bryanstone-square, and has issue.

Lineage.—PHILIP HARCOURT, Esq. of Wignell, in Sussex, and of Ankerwycke, in Bucks, brother of Simon, 1st Viscount Harcourt, and eldest son of Sir Philip Harcourt, Knt. of Stanton Harcourt, co. Oxford M.P., by Elizabeth, his 2nd wife, dau. and heir of John Lee, Esq. of Ankerwycke, co. Bucks, *m*, Elizabeth, dau. and heir of Timothy, Woodroffe, Esq., and had two daus. (Elizabeth, *d.* *unm.*, and Mary, *m.* to Thomas Ringer, Esq.) and three sons. Mr. Harcourt *d.* about 1705–6, and was *s.* by his eldest son,

PHILIP HARCOURT, Esq. of Ankerwycke, who *m.* Sarah, dau. of Henry Hall, Esq. of Hutton Hall, in Essex, by whom he had an only child, Elizabeth, who *d.* *unm.* in her father's lifetime. This gentlemen *d.* in 1758, and was *s.* by his only surviving brother,

JOHN HARCOURT, Esq. of Ankerwycke, who *m.* 1st, Anne, dau. of — Parker, Esq., but had no issue. He *m.* 2ndly, Margaret Irene, dau. of John Sarney, Esq. of Somerset House, London, by whom, (who *m.* 2ndly, Lord Shuldham, and 3rdly, Lord Clanwilliam), he had,

JOHN-SIMON, his successor.
Philip, *d.* young.
George-William-Richard, colonel of the 12th foot, a brigadier-general in the army and Governor of St. Croix.

He *d.* in 1784, and was *s.* by his eldest son,

JOHN-SIMON HARCOURT, Esq. of Ankerwycke, some time

M.P. for Westbury. This gentleman *m.* 7 Dec. 1800, Elizabeth-Dale, dau. of Major Henniker, Esq., son of Sir John Henniker, Bart., who was created Lord Henniker, in 1800, and by her, who *d.* in 1810, had one dau. Elizabeth, who *d.* young, and an only son, the present GEORGE SIMON HARCOURT, Esq. of Ankerwycke.

Arms—Gu., two bars, or.
Crest—Out of a ducal coronet, or, a peacock, close, ppr.
Motto—Le bon temps viendra.
Seat—Ankerwycke House, near Staines.

HARDCASTLE OF BLIDWORTH DALE.

HARDCASTLE, JONATHAN, Esq. of Blidworth Dale, Notts, J.P., *b.* 9 April, 1816; *m.* 2 March, 1848, Mary-Francis, dau. of James Layton, Esq. of the Grove, Surrey, and has issue,

I. JOHN-NORMAN, *b.* 9 Sept. 1855.
I. Alice. II. Susan-Mary.

Mr. Hardcastle, his brother James, (who is married and has issue), and his four sisters, all married, are the surviving children of the late THOMAS HARDCASTLE, Esq. (who *d.* 15 Aug. 1839), by Ann Lever his wife, who *d.* 17th May, 1834.

Seat—Blidworth Dale, near Mansfield.

HARDEN OF HARRYBROOK.

HARDEN, JAMES, Esq. of Harrybrook, co. Armagh, J.P. and D.L., high sheriff co. Armagh, 1850, *b.* in Oct. 1805; *m.* 4 Dec. 1844, Annabella-Lloyd, eldest dau. of Col. Edwards of Nanhoron, co. Carnarvon, and has issue,

I. ROBERT-ACHESON, *b.* 2 Jan. 1846.
II. Richard-James, *b.* 28 Dec. 1846.
III. Frederick-John, *b.* 26 Oct. 1848.
IV. George, *b.* 2 Feb. 1851.

Lineage.—Mr. Harden's grandfather, JAMES HARDEN, Esq. of Harrybrook, J.P. and high-sheriff of co. Armagh, in 1792, son of Henry Harden, Esq., who was also high-sheriff in 1782, *m.* Mary Walker, and *d.* in 1806, leaving a son,

ROBERT HARDEN, Esq. of Harrybrook, *b.* in 1780, J.P. and D.L., and high-sheriff in 1809, who *m.* Anne Harley, and dying in 1840, was *s.* by his only son and heir, the present JAMES HARDEN, Esq. of Harrybrook.

Seat—Harrybrook, co. Armagh.

HARDING OF BARASET.

HARDING, WILLIAM-JUDD, Esq. of Baraset, co. Warwick, J.P. and D.L., formerly in the E.I.Co.'s civil service, Bengal, *b.* 22 Sept. 1788; *m.* 20 April, 1830, Elizabeth, 3rd dau. of the late Robert Denison, Esq. of Kilnwick Percy, co. York, by Frances, his wife, dau. of the late Sir Richard Brooke, Bart. of Norton Priory, Cheshire.

Lineage.—JUDD HARDING, of Hampton, in Arden, *b.* in 1662, son, by Susanna, his wife, of William Arden, Esq. of Hampton, *b.* in 1663, who is presumed to have been a younger son of Henry Arden, Esq. of Longcroft, co. Stafford, was father of

JUDD HARDING, of Hampton, *b.* in 1692, whose son,

JUDD HARDING, Esq. of Solihull, co. Warwick, J.P. Captain in the Warwickshire Militia, *b.* 1730, *m.* Elizabeth Hunt, of Stratford-on-Avon, and by her left (with a dau. Charlotte,) five sons,

I. JOSEPH, his successor at Solihull, a learned lawyer; father of GEORGE HARDING, Esq. of Solihull.
II. WILLIAM, of whose line we treat.
III. John, of the Royal Artillery, second in command under the Duke of Wellington at Copenhagen, and Sir John Moore at Corunna: he was honoured with the thanks of Parliament for his services there. He was father of Major-Gen. George-Judd Harding.
IV. Judd. V. Thomas

The 2nd son,

WILLIAM HARDING, Esq. went to India in the Civil Service of the E. I. C. on the Bengal establishment, and on his return to England established the estate of, and built the mansion of Baraset in 1800. He was appointed a magistrate of the county, and was gentleman of the privy chamber, to his Majesty GEORGE III. He *m.* in 1784, Harriet Sweetland, and had issue,

WILLIAM-JUDD, of Baraset.
Charles, E. I. Co.'s Civil Service, Bengal, *m.* Eliza-Anne, only dau. of Sir Frederick Hamilton, Bart. of Silverton Hill, co. Lanark.
Henry, in holy orders, *m.* the Lady Emily Fielding, dau. of the late Viscount Fielding, and has, with other issue, a son, William Fielding.
John, in holy orders, *m.* Anna, eldest dau. of the Rev. Reedstone Road, of Freckling, co. York.
Francis, captain R.N., *m.* Davidona, dau. of General Dallas, late governor of St. Helena.
Edward, Bengal Civil Service, *d.* in the East Indies.
Catherine, *m.* W.-H.-C. Plowden, Esq., an East India Director, and *d.* in China.
Charlotte-Sophia, *m.* to the Rev. William Wheler, third son of Sir Charles Wheler, Bart.
Elizabeth-Octavia, *m.* to George Baker, Esq., comm. R.N., son of Sir R. Baker, magistrate of the city of London.
Jane, *m.* to the Rev. Thomas Hunt, rector of Felton, co. Salop.
Harriet, *m.* James Molony, Esq. of Kiltanon, and *d.* 1826.
Sophia, *m.* to S. Steward, Esq. of Lincoln's Inn, son of Col. Samuel Steward, of Leamington.

Mr. Harding *d.* 22 Jan. 1822.

Arms—Erm., a fesse, chequy, or and az.
Crest—On a chapeaux, az., turned up, erm., a boar, passant, or.
Seat—Baraset, Stratford on Avon, co. Warwick.

HARDING OF TAMWORTH.

HARDING, WILLIAM, Esq. of Copeley Lodge, co. Warwick, *b.* 12 Jan. 1778; *m.* 3 Nov. 1800, Rebecca, dau. of the late Samuel Pemberton, Esq. of The Laurels, by Mary, his wife, a descendant of the noble family of Grosvenor, and has issue,

I. WILLIAM-SEXTUS, *b.* 27 June, 1806, *m.* 1 Sept. 1835, Anne, eldest dau. of Charles Harding, Esq. of Bole Hall, co Warwick.
I. Caroline, *m.* to Henry Talbot, jun., Esq. of French House, co. Warwick.

Lineage.—About 1630, an offshoot of the old Warwickshire family of Harding, removed from great Packington to Tamworth, and purchased property there. WILLIAM HARDING, in 1663, became a magistrate, and was chosen to carry the charter of the Borough to London, and deliver it up to King JAMES II. In the following year he *m.* Mary, Pickard, and was father of

WILLIAM HARDING, Esq., who *m.* in 1694, a 1st-cousin of Thomas Guy, Esq., (founder of Guy's Hospital, London, and the Almshouse and Town-Hall, Tamworth), and was father of

WILLIAM HARDING, Esq., who *m.* Mary, dau. of John Bradburn, Esq. of Winchester, and had an only son,

WILLIAM HARDING, Esq. *b.* in 1756, who *m.* Martha, dau. of Samuel Tuffley, Esq. of Leicester, and had issue,

WILLIAM, present representative of this branch of the family.
Thomas, *d.* in Hamburgh.
Charles, of Bole Hall, *b.* 24 Nov. 1782; *m.* 24 Feb. 1807, Ellen, dau. of the Rev. Borlase Willock, by Ann, his wife, only sister of Sir Robert Peel, Bt., and great-granddau. of Borlase Wingfield, Esq., by Ellen, his wife, sister of Sir Rowland Hill, Bt., and has issue, Anne, *m.* to her cousin, W. S. Harding, Esq.; Ellen; Mary; Emily, *m.* to William-Henry Lee, Esq.; and Frances-Augusta, *m.* to Edward Cripps, Esq. of Cirencester.
Samuel-Tuffley, of Manchester.
John, banker, of Bridlington, co. York.
Two daus.

Seat—Copeley Lodge, co. Warwick.

HARDING OF UPCOTT.

HARDING, THOMAS-WREY, Esq. of Upcott, co. Devon, J.P. and D.L., *b.* 29 May, 1782.

Lineage.—This family, seated at a very early period at Comb Martin, co. Devon, is supposed to have derived its origin from a branch of the house of FITZ-HARDING. The learned THOMAS HARDING, D.D., Fellow of New College, Oxford, the celebrated antagonist of Bishop Jewell, was born at Comb Martin, a son of the family. (*See* PRINCE'S *Worthies of Devon*, COLLINSON'S *History of Somersetshire, &c.*) The late

THOMAS HARDING, Esq. of Upcott, son of Robert Harding, by his wife, a dau. of the family of Limebear, m. Mary Bryan, and had issue,

Robert, his heir.
Thomas, father of the Rev. John-Limebear Harding, of Monkleigh, co. Devon, who m. Charlotte, dau. of John Goldie, Esq., and has two sons, Thomas Goldie, in the army, and Joseph Limebear, in holy orders.
John, in holy orders.
A dau., m. to Thomas Terry, Esq.

The eldest son,

Robert Harding, Esq. of Upcott, m. in 1780, Dionisia, 2nd dau. of Sir Bourchier Wrey, Bart. of Tawstock Court, Devon, and had issue,

I. Thomas-Wrey, his heir.
II. Robert, J.P., capt. Royal Artillery.
III. William, major in the army.
IV. John, in holy orders, rector of Goodleigh, near Barnstaple.
I. Dyonisia. II. Anna-Maria, deceased.

Mr. Harding d. in 1804, and was s. by his eldest son, the present Thomas-Wrey Harding, Esq. of Upcott.

Arms—Arg., on a bend, az., three martlets, or.
Crest—A falcon, displayed, ppr.
Seat—Upcott, near Barnstaple.

HARDY OF LETHERINGSETT.

Cozens-Hardy, William-Hardy, Esq. of Letheringset Hall, co. Norfolk, J.P., b. 1 Dec. 1806, m. 21 July, 1830, Sarah, dau. of Thomas Theobald, Esq. of Norwich, and has issue,

I. Clement-William-Hardy, b. 27 Feb. 1833, m. 8 May, 1856, Helen-Ferneley, dau. of T. C. Wrigley, Esq. of Huddersfield.
II. Herbert-Hardy, b. 22 Nov. 1838.
III. Theobald, b. 25 Aug. 1842.
IV. Sydney, b. 9 May, 1850.
I. Caroline. II. Cecilia-Emma.
III. Agnes. IV. Kathleen.

Mr. Cozens-Hardy, who is only son of Jeremiah Cozens, Esq. of Sprowstown Villa, by his 2nd wife, Mary-Ann, dau. of William Hardy, Esq. of Letheringsett, assumed, by sign-manual, on succeeding to the Letheringsett estates, in pursuance of the will of his maternal uncle, William Hardy, Esq., the arms and surname of Hardy, in addition to his patronymic.

Arms—Quarterly: 1st and 4th, per chev., arg. and or, in chief, two bomb-shells, fired, and in base, an eagle's head, erased, ppr., for Hardy: 2nd and 3rd, per pale, az. and gu., on a pile, or, a lion, rampant, for Cozens.
Crests—A dexter arm, embowed, ppr., charged with a pellet, between two chevronels, or, and grasping an eagle's head, fesseways, also ppr., for Hardy; a lion, rampant, or, gutté de sang, and fretty, gu., for Cozens.
Motto—Fear one.
Seat—Letheringsett Hall, co. Norfolk.

HARE OF DOCKING HALL.

Hare, Humphrey-John, Esq. of Docking Hall, co. Norfolk, b. 17 Oct. 1811, m. 11 Sept. 1833, Hannah-Elizabeth, dau. and co-heir of John Newbould, Esq. of Bramhope Hall, co. York.

Lineage.—The Hares of Docking were a younger branch of the ancient family of Hare of Stow Bardolph, in Norfolk. (*See* Burke's *Extinct Baronetage*.) The eventual heiress, Mrs. Henley, only surviving child of Hugh-Charles Hare, Esq. of Docking, devised her estates to her kinsman,

The Rev. Edward Christian, rector of Workington, co. Cumberland, son of the Rev. Humphrey Christian, by Elizabeth, his wife, dau. of Thomas Brett, Esq., and Mary, his wife, dau. of the Rev. John Basset, by Mary, his wife, which Mary was dau of John Earle, Esq. of Heydon, co. Norfolk, and Sarah, his wife, 5th dau. of Sir John Hare, Knt. of Stow Bardolph. Mr. Christian assumed, on succeeding to Docking, the name and arms of Hare, in 1798. He m. about 1772, his cousin Frances, dau. of John Christian, Esq. of Milntown and Ewanrigg Hall, co. Cumberland and had, with two daus., four sons, viz.,

Humphrey-John, his heir.
Frederick, J.P. and D.L., of Stanhoe Hall, Norfolk. He has been twice m., and has issue; his eldest son, Edward, is in the E. I. Co.'s Medical Service, and his second, Frederick-John, is Fellow of Clare Hall, Cambridge.
Edward-Henry.
Hugh-Charles, in holy orders.

Mr. (Christian) Hare d. in 1807, and was s. by his eldest son,

The Rev. Humphrey-John Hare, of Docking Hall, b. 1776, who m. 1st, 16 July, 1801, Mary, 3rd dau. of Thomas Pattenson, Esq. of Melmerby Hall, Cumberland, by whom (who d. 18 March, 1817) he had a son, Humphrey-John, now of Docking Hall; and a dau., Frances-Mary, m. to the Rev. R. Woolmer Cory. He m. 2ndly, 21 Sept. 1818, Barbara, youngest dau. of the Rev. James Mayo, of Wimbourne Minster, co. Dorset, and had by her,

I. Hugh-James, m. Anna, dau. of John Graver Browne, Esq.
II. Edward-Montague.
I. Elizabeth. II. Barbara. III. Anne.
IV. Robina, m. to Thomas Copeman, Esq.
V. Janet, m. to W. D. Chapman, Esq., Lt. Madras N.I.
VI. Lucy. VII. Catherine-Christian.

Mr. Hare d. 30 April, 1856.

Arms—Gu., two bars, and a chief, danoettée, or.
Crest—A demi-lion, rampant, ducally gorged.
Seat—Docking Hall, Norfolk.

HARE OF GRESFORD.

Hare, Francis-George, Esq. of Gresford, co. Denbigh, an officer 1st life-Guards, son and heir of the late F.-G. Hare, Esq., descended from the Hares of Hurstmonceux, co. Sussex, and nephew of Archdeacon Hare, of Lewes, who at present possesses the living of Hurstmonceux.

Seat—Gresford, Denbigh.

HARFORD OF BLAISE CASTLE.

Harford, John-Scandrett, Esq. of Blaise Castle, co. Gloucester, J.P. and D.L., high-sheriff of Cardiganshire 1824, D.C.L., F.R.S., b. 8 Oct. 1786; m. Louisa, eldest dau. of Richard-Hart Davis, Esq., many years M.P. for Bristol.

Lineage.—The Harfords are of great antiquity. The "cunabula gentis" was Bosbury, in Herefordshire, in the church of which there are several ancient and handsome monuments of the family, exhibiting their armorial bearings. The branch we are about to treat of migrated from Marshfield, in Gloucestershire, and settled at Bristol in the course of the seventeenth century.

John Harford, Esq. of Bosbury, who m. Anne, dau. of Sir John Scrope, of Castlecombe, twice high-sheriff of Wiltshire, d. 30 Aug. 1559, aged fifty-five, and was buried in the chancel of Bosbury, leaving five sons and four daus. The 5th son,

Henry Harford, Esq. of Boreham, Warminster, Wilts, whose will, dated 23 Feb. 1614, was proved 10 Nov. 1615, married twice: by his 1st wife he left a son, Henry, of whom presently; and by the 2nd, Alice Bradstone, he left another son, Bridstock, M.D., living in 1686, who m. Elizabeth, Eldest dau. of Richard Hereford, Esq. of Sufton, co. Hereford, and was great-grandfather of the present Right Hon. Sir Harford Jones-Brydges, Bart. Henry Harford, of Boreham, d. in 1615, and was buried at Warminster on the 6th April. His son by his 1st wife,

Henry Harford, had, with other issue, of whom Anne was under age in 1615, a son,

Robert Harford, who was father of two children, William and John, both of Marshfield. The former had a dau., Margaret, m. to Mr. Barnet; the latter,

John Harford, of Marshfield, had a son,

Thomas Harford, of Marshfield, living in Sept. 1657, who had issue, Thomas, of Marshfield, b. in 1646, d. in May, 1710; and

Charles Harford, of Bristol, living in 1705, who d. before 1723, leaving two sons and two daus. Of the former, the 2nd,

Edward Harford, of the city of Bristol, whose will, dated 26 July, 1705, was proved 13 Sept. following, m. Elizabeth, dau. of Charles Jones, Esq., grandson of Hugh Jones, the 1st Protestant bishop of Llandaff, and had issue,

I. Edward, his heir.
II. Mark, of Frenchay, in Gloucestershire, living in 1746, who m. Love, dau. of John Andrew, Esq. of Hill House, in the same co., and had a son, Mark, of Stoke, in Gloucestershire, who m. Sarah, dau. of Samuel Lloyd, Esq., and had issue,
  1 Mark, of Bristol; 2 Samuel Lloyd, of Sion Hill, Clifton; 3 Edward-Lloyd; 1 Sarah; 2 Susannah, m. to George Bush, Esq. of Bristol.
III. Charles, of Bristol, whose will was dated 15 Feb. 1746, and proved 9 April, 1747, m. 1st, Mary, dau. of Joseph

Beck, Esq. of Frenchay, co. Gloucester, and 2ndly, Rachael, dau. of John Reeve; by the latter he had a dau., Rachael, and by the former, a dau., Elizabeth, and a son,

Joseph, of Stapleton, in Gloucestershire, J.P., sheriff of Bristol in 1779 and 1785, who *m.* Hannah, dau. of Joseph Kill, Esq. of the same place, and had an only son,

Charles-Joseph, of Stapleton Grove, M.A., F.A.S., J.P. for Gloucestershire, who *m.* 16 June, 1795, Mary, relict of J. Marchant, Esq., and dau. of Dr. Nathaniel Coffin, of Boston, U.S., a descendant of the Coffins of Devonshire, and cousin to Admiral Sir Isaac Coffin, Bart., G.C.H., and had issue,

Charles-Joseph, captain in the army, late of the 34th regt., *d. s. p.* 16 Aug. 1838.
Henry-Charles, B.A. and F.A.S., of the Royal York Crescent, Clifton, *b.* 13 May, 1798, capt. in the Gloucester militia, who *m.* 26 July, 1825, Susan-Harriet, only surviving child of Samuel Brice, Esq. of Frenchay, in Gloucestershire, and granddau. of Edward Brice, Esq., J.P., mayor of Bristol in 1782, had issue,

Charles-Joseph, *b.* 5 May, 1826.
Frederick-Kill, *b.* 25 Jan. 1832.
Samuel-Henry, *b.* 20 April, 1833.
Susan-Harriet.
Emily-Mary. Isabella-Adelaide.

The eldest son,

Edward Harford, Esq. of Bristol, *m.* a dau. of Edward Lloyd, Esq., and dying in 1788, aged eighty-eight, was *s.* by his only son,

Edward Harford, Esq. of Frenchay, near Bristol, who *m.* Sarah, dau. and heir of John Scandrett, Esq. of that city, and left an only son and successor,

John-Scandrett Harford, Esq. of Blaise Castle, in Gloucestershire, who *m.* Mary, dau. of Abraham Gray, Esq. of Tottenham, Middlesex, and had issue,

I. John-Scandrett, his heir.
II. Abraham-Gray, who assumed the surname of Battersby, in addition to Harford, on inheriting the estate of his kinsman, William Battersby, Esq. He *m.* Elizabeth, youngest dau. of Gen. and the Right Hon. Lady Eleanor Dundas, and dying May, 1851, left issue,

1 John, M.A., of Stoke Park, co. Gloucester, J.P., *m.* Mary-C.-E., 3rd dau. of His Excellency Chevalier Bunsen, Minister Plenipo. of H. M. the King of Prussia to the Court of St. James's
2 Thomas-Dundas.
1 Eleanor.
2 Mary-Louisa, *m.* to the Rev. H. G. Bunsen, eldest son of the Chevalier Bunsen.

III. Charles-Gray. IV. Alfred, in holy orders, A.M.
V. William-Henry, who *m.* Emily, dau. of John King, Esq. of Grosvenor Place, London, many years Under Secretary of State in the Foreign Office.

Mr. Harford *d.* in Jan. 1815, and was *s.* by his son, the present John-Scandrett Harford, Esq. of Blaise Castle.

Arms—Sa., two bends, arg., on a canton, az., a bend, or.
Crest—Out of a coronet, issuing from flames, ppr., a griffin's head, or, between two wings, az., fire issuing from the mouth.
Seat—Blaise Castle, near Bristol.

HARGREAVES OF BROAD OAK.

Hargreaves, John, Esq. of Broad Oak, co. Lancaster, and Hall Barn Park, Bucks, J.P. and D.L., *b.* 1 July, 1797: *m.* 16 Nov. 1831, Grace, only dau. of William Brown, Esq. of Richmond Hill, near Liverpool, M.P., and has issue,

I. Thomas, *b.* 21 Dec. 1832, *m.* 17 Jan. 1855.
II. William, *b.* 23 March, 1837.
III. John, *b.* 30 Aug. 1839.
I. Sarah.

Lineage.—John Hargreaves, of Height, near Higham, *b.* 4 May, 1706, *m.* Mary Walsh, of Morton, in Craven, and left seven sons, viz.,

I. John, his heir. II. Jonathan.
III. James, of Liverpool, *m.* twice. By his second wife, Mary Winter, he left issue a son, Winter-Ainsworth Hargreaves, Esq., who *d. unm.* in 1827, and a dau., Mary-Catherine, who *m.* in April, 1815, the Rev. Thomas Raffles, D.D., LL.D., of Liverpool, heir male and representative of Sir Thomas-Stamford Raffles, and by her, who *d.* 17 May, 1843, has issue (*see family of* Raffles.)
IV. Robert, *b.* in 1748, *m.* Sarah, dau. of James Roberts, Esq. of Northwood, near Higham, and *d.* in 1814, leaving two sons,

1 William, *b.* in 1773, *m.* in 1806, Martha, dau. of John Holgate, Esq., and *d. s. p.* in 1832.
2 Reginald, of Spring Cottage, near Burnley, J.P. for Lancashire, *b.* in 1787, *m.* in 1817, Anne, dau. of Thomas Andrew, Esq. of Harpurhey Hall, and by her, who *d.* in 1819, has two daus., Sarah and Mary-Anne.

V. Joshua. VI. Joseph. VII. William.

The eldest son,

John Hargreaves, of Wheatley, near Burnley, co. Lancaster, *b.* 30 July, 1740, *m.* 1st, Lettice, dau. of Driver, of Subden Hall, and had by her two sons, James and George. He *m.* 2ndly, Alice, dau. of Lawrence Whittam, of Hupton, co. Lancaster, and by her (who *d.* 13 Jan. 1818) had issue,

Laurence, of Darwen, co. Lancaster, *b.* at Wheatley, 4 Feb. 1769, *m.* Jane, dau. of William Robert, of Hunterholme, near Padiham.
Thomas, of whom presently.
Mary, *m.* 25 Dec. 1800, to Adam Dugdale, Esq. of Dovecot House, near Liverpool, who is deceased.
Sarah, *m.* to James Holgate, of Burnley, merchant, who is deceased.

Mr. Hargreaves *d.* 13 April, 1810. His 2nd son,

Thomas Hargreaves, of Oak Hill, near Blackburn, *b.* 21 Dec. 1771, *m.* 1st, in 1793, Margaret, dau. of Benjamin Wilson, Esq. of Baxenden, and 2ndly, 6 June, 1803, Nancy, dau. of John Hoyle, of Haslingden. By the former he had issue,

John, his heir.
Benjamin, of Arden, Accrington, co. Lancaster.
William. James.
Alice, *m.* to Richard Kay, Esq. of Limefield, near Bury.
Helen, *m.* to James Neville, Esq. of Blackburn.

Mr. Hargreaves *d.* 12 June, 1822, and was *s.* by his son, the present John Hargreaves, Esq. of Broad Oak.

Arms—Quarterly, or and vert, on a fesse, erm., between three stags, courant, counterchanged, a fret, gu.
Crest—A buck's head, erased, vert, attired, or, with a collar, arg., charged with a fret, gu., in the mouth a sprig of oak, ppr.
Motto—Fortitudine et prudentiâ.
Seat—Broad Oak, Accrington, co. Lancaster.

HARLAND OF SUTTON HALL.

Harland, William-Charles, Esq. of Sutton Hall, co. York, J.P. and D.L., formerly M.P. for Durham, *b.* 25 Jan. 1804; *s.* his aunt, Lady Hoar Harland, in 1826, *m.* 17 May, 1827, Catherine, only dau. of Robert-Eden Duncombe Shafto, Esq. of Whitworth Park, co. Durham, by Catherine, 3rd dau. of Sir John Eden, Bart. of Windlestone Hall.

Lineage.—William Hoar, *b.* about 1680, inherited a small estate in Middlesex. He *m.* Miss Martha Baker, and dying in 1739, was buried at Stepney, leaving one son and two daus., viz., George, his heir; Martha, *m.* to Thomas Davison, Esq. of Blakiston, in Durham; Susanna, *m.* to the Rev. Joseph Butler, rector of Shadwell, and prebendary of St. Paul's. The only son,

George Hoar, Esq. of Middleton St. George, co. Durham, was keeper of the Regalia of England in the Tower of London. He *m.* 1 Jan. 1750, Frances, dau. of William Sleigh, Esq., Stockton-upon-Tees, by Mary his wife, dau. of Charles Bathurst, Esq. of Clints and Arkendale, M.P. for Richmond, and had issue,

William, his heir.
George, of Twyford Lodge, Hants, who *m.* Miss Elizabeth Cooke, but was divorced.
Charles, who assumed the surname and arms of Harland, 26 May, 1802, having *m.* Anne, only dau. and heiress of Philip Harland, Esq. of Sutton Hall, and widow of the Rev. Henry Goodrick. He was subsequently created a Baronet, but *d.* without issue, when the title expired. His widow, the heiress of Sutton Hall, survived until 24 June, 1826, when she was *s.* by the nephew of her husband, the present William-Charles Harland, Esq. of Sutton Hall.
Thomas, an admiral in the royal navy, *m.* at Marylebone, 29 May, 1788, Katherine-Dorothy, dau. of Peregrine Bertie, Esq. of Low Layton, Essex, and assumed the surname and arms of Bertie.
Ralph of Bath, *m.* 21 June, 1788, Elizabeth, dau. of Peregrine Bertie, Esq., and sister of his brother's wife.
Mary, *m.* at St. James's, Westminster, 8 Jan. 1785, to Richard-Mark Dickens, Esq., colonel of the 34th regt., and had issue.
Frances.

George Hoar's eldest son,

William Hoar, Esq., barrister-at-law, *m.* 30 Nov. 1786, Anne, dau. of John Wilkinson, Esq. of Stockton-upon-Tees, and had issue,

William-Charles, his heir.
Anne.

Mr. Hoar d. in Dec. 1834, and was s. by his son, the present WILLIAM-CHARLES-HARLAND, Esq. of Sutton Hall, who changed his name Hoar to that of Harland, in 1824.

Arms—Quarterly: 1st and 4th, arg., on a bend, between two cottises, three stags' heads, caboshed, az., for HARLAND; 2nd and 3rd, quarterly, sa. and gu., over all an eagle, displayed, with two heads, arg., within a bordure, invecked, counter-changed, for HOAR.

Crests—1st, a sea-horse, ppr., holding between his hoofs a stag's head, caboshed, az., charged with an escallop, for HARLAND; 2nd, an eagle's head, erased, arg., charged with a label of three points, pendent from the beak an annulet, for HOAR.

Motto—Constanter in Ardua.

Seat—Sutton Hall, Yorkshire.

HARPUR OF CHILVERS COTON AND BURTON HALL.

HARPUR, HENRY-RICHARD, Esq. of Chilvers Coton, co. Warwick, and Burton Hall, co. Northampton, J.P. and D.L., b. 23 Nov. 1798.

Lineage.—This is a branch of the family of Harpur, now represented by Sir John Harpur Crewe, Bart. of Calke Abbey.

ABRAHAM HARPUR, Esq., who m. Dorothy, dau. of Richard Shepherd, Gent. of Caldicote, had issue, Abraham d. unm.; Richard; John, in holy orders, rector of Shawell and Catthorpe, co. Leicester, J.P. for that shire, d. unm.; and

JOSEPH HARPUR, Esq., who m. 1st, a dau. of Purefoy, Esq. of Hinchley, a descendant of the Purefoys of Caldicote Hall, which lady d. without leaving issue. He m. 2ndly, 28 Sept. 1759, Mary, dau. of Thomas Powell, Esq. of Rugby, and by her had issue,

John, d. unm.
JOSEPH, of whom presently.
Samuel Purefoy, in holy orders, rector of Catthorpe.
Richard.
Anne, m. to Edward Oliver, Esq. of Wolscote House, co. Worcester.

Mr. Harpur d. in 1777. His eldest surviving son,

JOSEPH HARPUR, Esq., s. on the death of his cousin John, to landed property at Burton Latimer, Isham, and Watford, co. Northampton. He m. 15 Feb. 1795, Maria, only dau. of the Rev. Edward Cooper, vicar of Evesham, and by her (who d. in 1814) had issue,

I. HENRY-RICHARD, now of Chilvers Coton.
II. Latimer, in holy orders, rector of Catthorp, co. Leicester, m. in April, 1828, Anne, only dau. of the Rev. B.-G. Ebdell, vicar of Chilvers Coton, and has issue,
1 Henry. 2 Latimer.
1 Augusta.
III. John.

Mr. Harpur d. Dec. 1827.

Arms—A lion, rampant, within a bordure, engrailed, sa.

Crest—On the battlement of a tower, masoned, ppr., a boar's heads, erased, fesseways.

Seats—Chilvers Coton, co. Warwick; and Burton Hall, co. Northampton.

HARRIES OF PRISKILLY.

HARRIES, JOHN-HILL, Esq. of Priskilly, co. Pembroke, J.P. and D.L., high-sheriff 1806, b. 8 Feb. 1783; m. 19 Dec. 1807, Frances, 4th dau. and co-heir of the late Barret-Bowen Jordan, Esq. of Neeston, co. Pembroke (by Martha his wife, youngest dau. of John Adams, Esq. of Whitland, co. Carmarthen, by his wife, Elizabeth, eldest sister of the late Sir Herbert Lloyd, Bart. of Peterwell, co. Cardigan, M.P., and has issue,

I. GEORGE-JORDAN, b. 27 Sept. 1815, m. 27 Feb. 1840, Susanne-Caroline, eldest dau. of Henry Skrine, Esq. of Stubbings, Berks.
II. Owen-Hill, b. 8 Feb. 1822.
I. Frances. II. Martha-Maria.
III. Harriot-Jane.

Lineage.—The HARRIESES of Priskilly are an ancient family, and have resided from a very remote era in Pembrokeshire, where as well as in Carmarthenshire, they have long possessed considerable estates. They are a junior branch of the HARRIESES OF TREGWINT, who have been settled at their mansion there for several centuries, as appears from deeds now in possession of the family.

The immediate ancestor of the Priskilly branch was,

JAMES HARRIES, Esq. (2nd son of JOHN HARRIES, Esq. of Tregwint, whose descendants have intermarried with the most respectable families in the counties of Pembroke, Carmarthen, and Cardigan). This gentleman m. in 1640, Ellen, dau. and heiress of Eynon Griffith, Esq. of Tresissilt, by whom he acquired the Tresissilt, and other contiguous estates, which are still in the family, and were their principal residence until 1726, when they removed to Priskilly. Mr. Harries was s. at his decease by his son,

JOHN HARRIES, Esq., who m. 12 Dec. 1670, Letitia, dau. of John Owen, Esq. of Priskilly, and had a son and successor,

GEORGE HARRIES, Esq., who, by the will, dated 6 Oct. 1726, of his maternal uncle, Thomas Owen, Esq., became possessed of the Priskilly Forest estate, held *in capite* under the Bishop of St. David's, and also valuable landed property in the parishes of St. David's, Fishguard, and Letterson. He m. Margaret, eldest dau. of John Symmons, of Llanstinan, Esq., M.P. for the borough of Cardigan, and had issue,

JOHN, his successor.
George, an officer in the army, d. in 1758.
Martha, m. 1st, in 1739, to John Williams, Esq. of Corngavan, co. Carmarthen; m. 2ndly, in 1749, Alexander Scurlock, Esq.
Anne, m. to Rowland Edwardes, Esq., of Little Trefgarn.
Margaret, m. to William Gardner, Esq., barrister-at-law.

George Harries, Esq. d. 18 Sept. 1732, and was s. by his elder son,

JOHN HARRIES, Esq. of Priskilly, who m. 29 June, 1749, Harriot-Mountjoy, only child and heir of the Rev. Joseph Hill, D.D., of Colebrook, co. Carmarthen, precentor of St. David's, by whom he had issue,

John-Hill, capt. of grenadiers, 33rd regiment of foot, who fell, mortally wounded, in the battle on the Brandy Wine, in America, 11 Sept. 1777.
GEORGE, successor to his father.
Joseph, m. in 1799, Jane, sole heiress of her grandfather, Gilbert James, Esq. of Llanunwas, and dying in 1824, left a son,
Gilbert-James Harries, Esq., of Llanunwas, m. Cecilia, eldest dau. of Charles-Allen Philipps, of St. Bride's Hill, Esq., and has two daus., Jane and Mary.
Margaret-Theodosia, m. 30 Sept. 1791, to Thomas Williams, Esq. of Trelethin, and d. s. p. 7 June, 1811.
Harriot, m. in 1784, to the Rev. William James, vicar of Mathry, and had issue, four sons and four daus.

John Harries d. 1 Nov. 1801, and was s. by his son,

GEORGE HARRIES, Esq. of Priskilly, who m. 9 June, 1781, Mary, second dau. of William Bowen, Esq. of Leweston, and had issue,

JOHN-HILL, of Priskilly.
George, in holy orders, A.M., rector of Letterston and Nolton, vicar of Roch, prebendary and canon-residentiary in the Cathedral of St. David's.
William-Thomas, first lieut. royal marines, deceased.
Joseph-Delebere, lieut. 3rd foot guards, deceased.
Charles-Richard.
Harriot-Elizabeth. Mary-Ann.
Margaret-Jane-Martha, m. in Sept. 1816, to George Lloyd, Esq. of Brunant, co. Carmarthen, and has issue.

Mr. Harries d. 21 June, 1808.

Arms—Az., three mullets, pierced, or, quartering the arms of OWEN: gu., a boar, arg., chained to a holly-bush, vert, armed and langued, or, the chain and collar gold.

Crest—A mullet, pierced, or.

Motto—Integritas semper Tutamen.

Seat—Priskilly, Pembrokeshire.

HARRIES OF CRUCKTON.

HARRIES, FRANCIS, Esq. of Cruckton Hall, and Broseley Hall, co. Salop; J.P. and D.L.; m. Harriet, dau. and co-heir of Thomas Boycott, Esq. of Rudge.

Lineage.—Descended from JOHN HARRIES, of Cruckton, who was living in 1468, was

THOMAS HARRIES, Esq. of Weston Lizard (son of Thomas Harries, Esq. of Prescot, and grandson of Arthur Harris, Esq. of Prescot, near Baschurch, who was 3rd son of John Harries, Esq. of Cruckton, co. Salop, and brother of Sir Thomas Harries, Bart. of Tong Castle, co. Salop), s. to Cruckton, and served as high-sheriff of Shropshire in 1730. He m. Elizabeth, dau. of William Hawkins, Esq., and had three sons, JOHN, Arthur, and William. The eldest, JOHN HARRIES, Esq. of Cruckton, was father (by Sarah his wife, dau. and co-heir of Robert Hill, Esq. of Tern) of THOMAS HARRIES, Esq. of Cruckton, who m. 1738, Mary, dau. and heir of Robert Phillips, Esq., and had issue, EDWARD,

Richard (father of an only dau. and heir, Margaret, wife of Cornwell-Baron Wilson, Esq.), and William. The eldest, son,

The Rev. Edward Harries, of Cruckton, A.M., b. 27 Nov. 1743; m. 1771, Lucia, dau. and heir of Francis Turner Blithe, Esq. of Broseley Hall, co. Salop, and dying 31 Jan. 1812, left two sons, viz.,

I. Thomas, of Cruckton, J.P. and D.L., high-sheriff in 1802, b. 1774; m. 1798, Barbara-Mary-Anne, dau. and co-heir of John Smitheman, Esq., and d. s. p. 1848.
II. Francis-Blithe, of Benthall Hall, co. Salop, b. 1776; m. 1802, Emma-Gertrude, dau. of Edward Jenkins, Esq. of Charlton Hill, co. Salop, and dying in 1848, left issue, 1 Francis, now of Cruckton; 2 Thomas, lieut.-col. in the army, Knt. of the Legion of Honour; 3 John-Henry-Acton, in holy orders; and one surviving dau., Lucia, widow of the Marchese Stefano Di Negro.

Arms—Barry of eight, erm. and az., over all three annulets, or.
Crest—A hawk, arg., beaked and belled, or, preying on a curlew, of the first.
Seat—Cruckton Hall, co. Salop.

HARRIS OF HAYNE.

Harris, Christopher-Arthur, Esq. of Hayne, co. Devon, b. 14 Jan. 1801, m. 15 Feb. 1825, Louisa-Eleonora, 3rd dau. of the late Rev. Thomas Watkins, of Pennoyre, in Brecknockshire, and granddau. of Richard Vaughan, Esq. of Golden Grove, Carmarthenshire, by whom he has issue,

I. Arthur-Vaughan-Donnithorne, b. 17 Dec. 1825.
I. Elizabeth-Caroline. II. Louisa-Penelope.

Lineage.—John Harris, a younger son of the Harrises of Radford, was father (by his wife, the heiress of Stone, of Stone) of

William Harris, who m. Thomasine, dau. and heiress of Walter Hayne, of Hayne, and was s. by his son,

John Harris, Esq. of Stone, a king's serjeant and recorder of the city of Exeter, who m. the dau. of Michael Kelly, Esq. of Ratcliffe, in Devonshire, and had issue. The eldest son,

William Harris, Esq. of Hayne, m. Mary, dau. of Sir Fulk Grevill, Knt. of Beauchamp's Court, in Warwickshire, and had, with four daus., a son and successor,

Arthur Harris, Esq. of Hayne, and of Kenegie, m. Margaret, dau. and heiress of John Davils, Esq. of Totely, in Devon, and had issue, John, his successor; and Arthur, father of Christopher, heir to his cousin, Sir Arthur Harris, Bart. Mr. Harris d. 1628, and was s. by his son,

John Harris, Esq. of Hayne and Kenegie, who m. 1st Florence, dau. of Sir John Windham, but by her had no issue. He m. 2ndly, Cordelia, eldest dau. of Sir John Mohun, of Boconnoc, created in 1628, Lord Mohun of Oakhampton, by whom he had an only son and successor,

Arthur Harris, Esq. of Hayne and Kenegie, created a baronet in 1673, who d. s. p., when the estates passed to his cousin,

Christopher Harris, Esq. of Hayne and Kenegie, who m. Elizabeth, dau. of William Martin, Esq. of Linderidge, and was s. by his son,

William Harris, Esq. of Hayne, M.P., sheriff for Devon in 1703; dying in 1709, he left issue,

Christopher, his successor.
John, successor to his brother.
William, father of
Christopher, who inherited the estates from his uncle.
Jane, m. to William Arundel, Esq. of Trengwainton and Menedarva, both in the county of Cornwall.

The eldest son and heir,

Christopher Harris, Esq. of Hayne, M.P. for Oakhampton, m. Mary, dau. of John Buller, Esq. of Keveral, but dying without surviving issue in 1718, he was s. by his brother,

John Harris, Esq., master of the household to their Majesties George II. and George III., who thus became of "Hayne." He m. 1st, Margaret, dau. of Roger Tuckfield, Esq. of Raddon, and relict of Samuel Rolle, Esq. of Heanton, and 2ndly, Anne, dau. of Francis Seymour, Lord Conway. but had no issue. He d. in 1767, and was s. by his nephew,

Christopher Harris, Esq. of Hayne. This gentleman m. Penelope, dau. of the Rev. Isaac Donnithorne, of St. Agnes, in Cornwall, and had two daus., namely,

I. Penelope.
II. Elizabeth, who m. her cousin, Isaac Donnithorne, Esq., who assumed the surname of Harris, and had issue,

1 Christopher-Arthur, now of Hayne.
2 John-James, m. Frances, dau. of the late Edward Acton, Esq. of Gataure Park, co. Salop.
1 Cordelia-Elizabeth, d. in 1809.

On the decease of this Christopher Harris with only these daus., the entailed estates of the family passed to his cousin, William Arundel, Esq of Trengwainton, and Menedarva, while Hayne descended to those ladies, Miss Harris and Mrs. (Donnithorne) Harris, as co-heirs.

Arms—Sa., three crescents, within a bordure, arg.
Crest—An eagle, rising, erm., beaked and spurred, or.
Motto—Kur, deu, res, pub, tra, (old Cornish;) English, For God and the commonwealth.
Seat—Hayne, Devon.

HARRISON OF RAMSAY AND DINTON.

Harrison, The Rev. John, M.A., vicar of Dinton, Bucks, J.P., m. 1816, Henrietta-Elizabeth Wollaston (of whom hereafter), devisee of her relations, Mrs. Euphemia Gifford and Mrs. Elizabeth Gulston, and has issue, two daus.,

I. Henrietta-Euphemia, m. 1846, Acton Tindal, Esq. of the Manor House, Aylesbury, and has issue,
1 Nicholas. 2 Acton-Gifford. 3 Charles-Harrison.
II. Margaret Mary.

Lineage.—Richard Harrison, Esq., inherited from his father Richard Harrison (whose only child he was by Anne Morland, his wife), lands in the county of Westmoreland, which were in possession of his forefathers, *temp.* Elizabethæ. He m. Hannah Bird, co-heiress of Thomas Bird, citizen of London. and had an only son, the Rev. John Harrison, LL.B. of Trinity College, Cambridge, rector of Wrabness, co. Essex, who m. Margaret Mary, sole dau. and heiress of Maurice Gough, LL.D. of Magdalen College, Cambridge, rector of Wrabness, vicar of Little Clacton, and prebendary of Armagh, and had issue by her,

John, his heir.
Margaret, d. unm.
Hannah, d. unm.
Mary, m. Rev. Rev. Robert Marratt Miller, D.D., vicar of Dedham, co. Essex, and had a son, John Harrison, barrister-at-law, and a dau., Mary Marratt, m. to S. C. Alston Swinton, Esq. of Swinton, co. Berwick.
Elizabeth.

Mrs. Harrison was eventually heiress and representative of her uncle, Robert Carrington, Esq. of Southhouse, in Ramsey, co. Essex.

Arms—Quarterly: Harrison, Gough, and Carrington.
Motto—Secundis dubiisque rectus.

Family of Wollaston.

(For preceding pedigree, see Wollaston *of* Shenton*).*

Henry Wollaston, great-grandson of Thomas Wollaston, of Perton, co. Stafford, "a person of rank and influence in the reign of Henry VII.," was alderman of London; "Knowing that the road to honour was by humility, he traded in a way that was plain, honest, and punctual, he raised a fair estate." He purchased the manor of Wollaston, in Staffordshire, which had been sold by his ancestors in the reign of Richard II., and he laid out his money in buying those estates which are now in the possession of the Wollastons of Shenton. Henry Wollaston attained the great age of ninety-two. "We know not," writes his descendant, William Wollaston, author of *The Religion of Nature*, "We know not what presages good men may have before death, but he ordered that his eldest son, William, should come to him, and proposed that they two, according to the fashion of devotion in those days, should sing a psalm together, and on this psalm he chose to lay out his last breath; for, in the middle of it he expired in his chair, 1617." Henry Wollaston m. twice. From his 1st marriage, with Sarah, dau. of William Burgess, of Kippington, Kent, descend the Wollastons of Shenton; by his 2nd marriage, with Alice Smith, widow, he had issue,

Henry, called "Justice Wollaston" in the family memoirs, of Waltham Abbey, in the commission of the peace for the county of Essex: he m. Ursula, dau. of Samuel Fox, of Warlies, and had issue by her,

Henry Wollaston, of Waltham Holy Cross, Esq. captain in the trained bands, 1664; he m. Anne, dau. of Oliver Boteler, Esq. of Harrold, Beds, and by her he had issue,

Henry, in holy orders, bapt. 1669; deceased 23 May, 1702.
Oliver, bapt. and buried 1665.
Richard Wollaston, bapt. 1663, and buried 1737. He

m. Elizabeth Wollaston, and had issue by her, 1 Richard, receiver-general of taxes for the county of Salop, m. Anne, dau. of Robert Clive, of Styche, Esq., aunt of the 1st Lord Clive, and d. s. p. 2 JOHN, of whom presently. 1 Elizabeth, m. 1709, the Rev. John Gifford (of Yester, N.B.) chaplain to his relative, John, 2nd Marquis of Tweeddale, rector of Mainstone, Salop. She, who d. in 1763, had issue, Richard Gifford, B.A. of Balliol College, Oxford; vicar of Duffield, co. Derby; rector of North Ockendon, co. Essex; and chaplain to John, 4th Marquis Tweeddale. Mr. Gifford m. Elizabeth Woodhouse, cousin and devisee of the Rev. Thomas Alleyne, rector of Loughborough, co. Leicester, and had issue, an only child, Euphemia, who d. unm., aged 89, 6 Dec. 1853.

JOHN WOLLASTON, M.D., bapt. 9 Sept. 1691, 2nd son of Richard and Elizabeth Wollaston, had issue by Sarah Weaver, his wife,

John, m. Eliza Baskerville, of Weobly, co. Hereford, and was ancestor of the Venerable John Ramsden Wollaston, Archdeacon of Albany, N.S.W. Richard Wollaston, m. Mary, only child of John Acton M.D., (by Mary, dau. of Humphrey Sandford, Esq. of the Isle, near Shrewsbury. This gentleman was 4th in descent from Margaret Plowden, sister of Edward Plowden, of Plowden, the eminent lawyer.) Richard Wollaston had issue, by Mary his wife, (inter alios) Thomas Wollaston, an officer in the army, m Henrietta, dau. of Richard Gulston, Esq. of Wyddial Hall, Herts, by Wilhelmina Mary, his first wife, and great-great-granddau. of Francis Turner, Bishop of Ely, and Lord High Almoner, who was one of the seven bishops sent to the Tower, 8 June, 1688, by JAMES II., and one of the non-jurors, deprived in 1689, by WILLIAM and MARY. Thomas Wollaston had issue, by his wife, inter alios, a dau., Henrietta-Elizabeth Wollaston, who m. the Rev. John Harrison, as stated above.

HARRISON OF GREEN BANK.

HARRISON, BENSON, Esq. of Green Bank, co. Westmorland, and Water Park, co. Lancaster, J.P. and D.L., b. 12 Feb. 1786; m. 1st, 16 July, 1816, Louisa-Lennox, dau. of the late Alexander Johnston, Esq. of Dublin, and by her (who d. 4 Jan. 1820) had one dau.,

I. Mary-Anne, m. 1840, the Rev. William Dobson, M.A., late fellow of Trinity College, Cambridge, and principal of the Proprietary College, Cheltenham, and has issue.

He m. 2ndly, 27 Sept. 1823, Dorothy, dau. of the late Richard Wordsworth, Esq. of Whitehaven (cousin to the poet), by Mary his wife, only child and heir of the late J. Scott, Esq. of Branthwaite Hall, Cumberland, and by her has issue,

I. MATTHEW-BENSON, of Belle Vue, Ambleside, b. 30 July, 1824, J.P., m. Dec. 1845, Catherine-Jones, dau. of the late Rev. George Day, rector of Earsham, Norfolk, and has issue,
  1 Benson-Day, b. 1848. 2 George, b. 1849.
  3 Frederick-Faber, b. 1850.
II. Wordsworth, of the Lund, co. Lancaster, b. 13 Aug. 1826, m. May, 1852, Charlotte-Emily, dau. of the Rev. Thomas Bartlett, vicar of Luton, Bedfordshire, and has issue,
  1 Gilbert-Henry-Wordsworth, b. 1853.
  2 Dorothy-Wordsworth.
III. Benson, capt. R. Westmoreland militia, b. 11 March, 1828.
IV. Richard, b. 25 Sept. 1832.
V. John-Wordsworth-Faber, b. 1835, d. 1849.
I. Dorothy, m. 3 July, 1849, to the Rev. John Bolland, M.A., 3rd son of the late Sir William Bolland, Baron of the Exchequer.

Mr. Harrison is only son of the late Matthew Harrison, Esq. of the Lund, Ulverston, by Mary Benson his wife, and descends through his maternal grandmother from the Braithwaites, of Brathay, Ambleside Hall, and Baysbrown, which last estate and manor are now in his possession. Mr. Harrison is head of the oldest iron works establishment in England and Scotland.

Arms—Az., three demi-lions, rampant, or.
Crest—A demi-lion, rampant, arg.
Motto—Vincit qui patitur.
Seat—Greenbank, Ambleside, co. Westmorland.

HARRISON OF WINSCALES AND STAINBURN.

HARRISON, JOHN, Esq. of Winscales and Stainburn, co. Cumberland, m. in 1834, Anne, eldest dau. of Allison Crosthwaite, Esq. of Workington, and has issue, two sons and one dau. This gentleman is the eldest son of William Falcon, Esq., by Jane his wife, 2nd dau. of Thomas Harrison, Esq. of Winscales, and great grandson of Michael Falcon, Esq., a ship-builder of great eminence at Workington, who was the descendant of a very ancient family in Cumberland. The surname he now bears, Mr. Harrison assumed, by royal licence, dated 19 Aug. 1844, on succeeding to the estates of his maternal ancestors, at the decease of his uncle, John Harrison, Esq.

Arms—Quarterly: 1st and 4th, arg., two bars gemelles, sa., between three hares, courant, ppr., for HARRISON; 2nd and 3rd, erm., two chevronels, paly, az. and sa., between three falcons, ppr., belled, or, and holding in the beak a lure, of the last, for FALCON.
Crests—Upon a mount, vert, a stag, courant, regardant, sa., semée of quatrefoils, attired and unguled, or, holding in the mouth an arrow, in bend, sinister, ppr. for HARRISON; on a fret, sa., a falcon, rising, ppr., belled, or, and holding in the beak a lure, of the last, for FALCON.
Motto—Vite, courageux, fier.
Seat—Stainburn, Workington.

HARRISON OF SNELSTON HALL.

HARRISON, JOHN, Esq. of Snelston Hall, co. Derby, J.P. and D.L., b. 15 June, 1782; m. 16 Sept. 1813, Elizabeth, only surviving dau. and heiress of Edmund Evans, Esq., late of Yeldersley House, co. Derby, (by Dorothy his wife, only child of Francis Coles, Esq. of Birmingham, and Ellen his wife, dau. of William Bowyer, Esq.) and by this lady has had issue a son and four daus., viz.,

I. JOHN, b. 20 March, 1819.
I. Elizabeth, d. 1 May, 1834.
II. Ellen-Bowyer.
III. Juliana-Bowyer, m. to Henry Stanton, Esq. of Thelwall, co. Chester.
IV. Dorothy-Sarah.

Mr. Harrison is only son of the late John Harrison, Esq. of Derby, by his 1st wife, Juliana Saxelby, which lady d. 20 June, 1782, having had, besides the present Mr. Harrison, two daus., Anne, m. 14 Dec. 1801, to James Stanton, Esq.; and Juliana, m. 3 June, 1813, to John Stanton, Esq. The late Mr. Harrison m. 2ndly, 4 Jan. 1796, Mary, dau. of the Rev. Geo. Almond, and d. 3 Jan. 1808, having had by this lady (who d. 9 April, 1850) a dau., Mary, m. 4 Aug. 1821, to Major George Young, son of Sir William Young, Bart.

Arms—Azure, three demi-lions. or, a canton, arg., with an escutcheon of pretence, quartering the arms of EVANS, COLES, BOWYER, STEBBING, &c.
Crest—A demi-lion, or, supporting a chaplet of roses, vert.
Seat—Snelston Hall, near Ashbourne, co. Derby.

HARRISON OF MERTON HALL.

HARRISON, JOHN, Esq. of Merton Hall, and Ardkeen, co. Down, J.P. and D.L., b. July, 1790; m. 1st, 22 Dec. 1822, Catharine, eldest dau. of Wm. Thompson, Esq. late of Belfast, and by her (who d. 27 April, 1836) has had issue,

I. HENRY, b. 8 Nov. 1827, m. 15 Jan. 1851, Mary, dau. of Richard Davison, Esq., M.P. for Belfast, and d 1 Jan. 1855, leaving issue, 1 John, b. 2 Jan. 1852; 2 Richard-Davison, b. 22 Dec. 1854; and, 1 Margaret.
II. John, b. 20 May, 1833.
I. Eliza. II. Mary-Catherine.

Mr. Harrison m. 2ndly, 17 March, 1840, Ann-Elizabeth, dau. of Henry Purdon, Esq., M.D., of Sans Souci, co. Down.

Lineage.—The late JOHN HARRISON, Esq. of Merton Hall, co. Down, only son of Robert Harrison, of Yorkshire, by Sarah his wife, dau. of B. L. Lee, Esq. of Coton Hall, co. Salop, m. Elizabeth, only dau. of John Harrison, Esq., by Margaret Stewart, his wife, and had issue,

I. JOHN, now of Merton Hall.
II. James, lieut.-colonel Madras horse artillery, m. 1832, Marianne, dau. of Abraham Collis, Esq., M.D., of Dublin, and by her, who d. Nov. 1850, has issue,
1 Abraham-St.-John.
2 Emily-Sophia, m. 1852, to Henry Dwyer, Esq.
III. Henry, R.N., d. 1818.
IV. Robert, M.D., professor of anatomy, T.C., Dublin, m. 1821, a dau. of Henry Cope, and by her had issue, Henry Cope, deceased; William-James, m 1851 Sophia-Emily, dau. of — Auchmuty, Esq. of the co. Leitrim; Abraham; Sophia-Mary; Marianne and Anne.
I. Anne, d. 1853.

Seats—Merton Hall, and Ardkeen, co. Down.

FISKE-HARRISON OF COPFORD HALL.

FISKE-HARRISON, FISKE-GOODEVE, Esq. of Copford Hall, co. Essex, *b.* 2 Sept. 1793; *m.* 27 March, 1826, Jane, dau. of James-Goodeve Sparrow, Esq. of Gosfield-place, co. Essex. This gentleman, whose patronymic is HARRISON, *s.* his father 2 Dec. 1839, in the family estates, as well as his maternal property, and assumed thereupon his mother's surname of FISKE, in addition to and before that of HARRISON. He is a magistrate for the county, and has served as high-sheriff.

Lineage.—THE REV. JOHN HARRISON, of Copford Hall, incumbent of Faulkbourn and East Hanningfield, co. Essex, son of the REV. JOHN HARRISON, m. Anne, dau. of the Rev. Thomas Bernard, and by her, who d. in 1783, had issue, JOHN-HAYNES, his heir; Thomas Bernard, in holy orders, rector of Little Bardfield; Hezekiah-Goodeve, in holy orders, rector of Little Stambridge, d. in March, 1840; and Elizabeth, twin with her eldest brother, John-Haynes, d. unm. in Dec. 1839. Mr. Harrison d. in 1797, and was s. by his eldest son,

JOHN HAYNES HARRISON, Esq. of Copford Hall, who m. 11 Dec. 1783, Sarah-Thomas, only child and heiress of the Rev. John Fiske, of Thorpe Morieux, co. Suffolk, and grand-dau. and heiress of Samuel Thomas, Esq. of Lavenham, and by her, who d. 12 Dec. 1825, had issue,

FISKE-GOODEVE, now of Copford Hall.
Thomas-Thomas, in holy orders, rector of Thorpe Morieux, co. Suffolk, m. 2 Oct. 1827, Anne, dau. of Rear-Admiral Nicholas Tomlinson, and has issue.
Mary-Ann.
Anne-Bernard.
Catherine, m. in 1824, to John Ruggles-Brise, Esq. of Spains Hall, Essex.
Jane-Dulcibella-Eldred.

Mr. Harrison d. 2 Dec. 1839.

Arms—Quarterly: 1st and 4th, az., two bars, erm., between six estoiles, three, two, and one, arg.; 2nd and 3rd, arg., three crescents, barry undée, az. and gu.
Crest—A stork, wings expanded, arg., beaked and membered, or.
Motto—Ferendo et feriendo.
Seat—Copford Hall, near Colchester.

HARRISSON OF TYDD ST. MARY'S.

HARRISSON, EVERSON, Esq. of Tydd St. Mary's, co. Rutland, J.P. and D.L., *b.* 10 March, 1796; *m.* 21 Oct. 1824, Matilda, only child of Francis Millns, Esq. of Horncastle, and has issue,

I. CHARLES-MILLNS, b. 20 April, 1826.
II. Francis-Joseph, b. 2 June, 1830.
III. George-Augustus, d. young.
IV. Arthur-Everson, b. 21 July, 1833.
V. George-Alexander, b. 18 June, 1836.
VI. Henry-Albert, b. 10 April, 1841.
I. Mary-Katherine. II. Elizabeth-Matilda.

Mr. Harrisson is only son of Joseph Harrisson, Esq., by Charlotte his wife, dau. of Thomas Everson, Esq., and coheir of John Everson, Esq. of Holbeach, and grandson of Robert Harrisson, Esq. of Tydd St. Mary's, by Katherine his wife, dau. of the Rev. Roger Stevens.

Arms—Az., a fleur-de-lis.
Crest—An ostrich, with a small serpent in its mouth.
Motto—Deo non fortunâ.

HART OF KILDERRY HOUSE.

HART, GEORGE-VAUGHAN, Esq. of Kilderry House, co. Donegal, J.P. and D.L., *b.* 7 June, 1805; *m.* 23 Sept. 1835, Jane-Maria, dau. of the Rev. G.-V. Hart, rector of Castlebar, and has issue,

I. WILLIAM-EDWARD, b. 24 Dec. 1844.
II. John-Hume. III. George-Percival.
I. Maria-Henrietta. II. Charlotte.
III. Elizabeth-Jane, d. young, 1849.
IV. Marianna-Vaughan. V. Josephine-Francis.
VI. Catherine-Grace.
VII. Adelaide-Elizabeth-Jane.
VIII. Georgiana-Susanna.

Lineage.—This family was founded in Ireland by Captain HENRY HART, who went from England with the Earl of Essex, in the reign of ELIZABETH, and since then it has been connected by intermarriages with the Boswells, Beresfords, and Vaughans. This Capt. Hart's son, Colonel GEORGE HART, was father of Colonel Henry Hart, whose son, GEORGE HART, likewise attained the rank of Colonel, and was father of the Rev. EDWARD HART, who m. Elizabeth Ramsay, and was father of

GEORGE-VAUGHAN-HART, Esq., a General in the army, and military governor of Londonderry, and Culmore Fort, who m. 1792, Charlotte Ellerker, and by her (who d. in 1827) had issue,

GEORGE VAUGHAN, now of Kilderry House.
John-Richard, d. unm. 1833.
Henry, d. unm. 1850. Edward, d. unm. 1836.
William, E. I. C. S., m. Frances Frere.
Elizabeth Grant, accidentally burned to death in 1824.
Charlotte, m. to George Gough, Esq., and d. in 1827.
Frances-Alicia-Anne, m. to the Rev. R. Chichester.
Georgina-Susan, m. to the Rev. Edward Hamilton.

General Hart represented the county of Donegal in Parliament for nearly 18 years, and d. in 1832.

Arms—Arg., three fleurs-de-lis, gu.
Crest—A tower with a flaming heart, ppr.
Motto—Cœur fidele.
Seat—Kilderry House, co. Donegal.

HARTCUP OF UPLAND GROVE AND DITCHINGHAM LODGE.

HARTCUP, WILLIAM, Esq. of Upland Grove, co. Suffolk, and Ditchingham Lodge, co. Norfolk, *b.* 23 March, 1814; *m.* 13 June, 1843, Louisa-Jane, eldest dau. of James-Taylor Margetson, Esq., and has issue,

I. HERBERT-JAMES, b. 13 Oct. 1844.
II. William-Thomas, b. 30 March, 1848.
I. Lucy-Jane.

Lineage.—The family of Hartcup is of German extraction.

GENERAL THOMAS HARTCUP, senior officer of the Royal Engineers, m. Ann-Monins Monroe, and d. 28 March, 1829, leaving two daus., Ann, m. to Col. William Gravatt, R.A., and Catharine, m. to Thomas Green, Esq. of Ipswich, two sons, THOMAS, his heir; and William, Capt. R.E., d. unm. 20 Sept. 1805. The eldest son,

THE REV. THOMAS HARTCUP, m. 8 May, 1810, Jane, only dau. of John Parker, Esq., and d. 21 Jan. 1829, having had by this lady (who d. 20 March, 1820)

Thomas-Wilson, b. 1 Sept. 1811, d. unm. 30 Jan. 1842.
WILLIAM, of Upland Grove House and Ditchingham.
Elizabeth, m. to Narcisse Bretel, Esq.
Jane.

Arms—Arg., a chevron, gu., between three Saracens' heads, each collared with a bow.
Crest—A warrior's head, in profile, helmeted, between two wings.
Residences—Upland Grove House, Bungay, co. Suffolk, and Ditchingham Lodge, co. Norfolk.

HARTLEY OF BUCKLEBURY.

HARTLEY, WINCHCOMBE HENRY-HOWARD, Esq. of Bucklebury House, co. Berks, and Little Sodbury, co. Gloucester, D.L., *b.* 5 Oct. 1810; *s.* his father 9 Sept. 1832.

Lineage—At the dissolution of the Abbey of Reading, in 1539, Bucklebury (anciently spelt Buryhalbury) was granted by HENRY VIII. to

JOHN WINCHCOMBE, Esq., son of the opulent clothier of

that name, well known as the famous "Jack of Newbury." He was father of

HENRY WINCHCOMBE, Esq. of Bucklebury, Berks, who was created a baronet in 1661. He m. Frances, dau. and co-heir of Thomas Howard, Earl of Berkshire, and d. in 1667, leaving a son and successor,

SIR HENRY WINCHCOMBE, of Bucklebury, m. Miss Rolls, but d. without male issue, in Nov. 1703, when the baronetcy became extinct. The estates devolved on Sir Henry's eldest dau., FRANCES, wife of the celebrated Viscount Bolingbroke, who occasionally resided at Bucklebury. As her ladyship left no child, the property passed by her younger sister, to the family of the Packers, knights of the shire in succession for the county of Berks. HENRY PACKER, Esq., the last male heir, devised it to his sister's son,

WINCHCOMBE-HENRY HARTLEY, Esq., (son of David Hartley, M.A. of Bath, by Elizabeth, his wife, dau. of Robert Packer, Esq. of Shillingford, Berks, by Mary, his wife, dau. and co-heir of Sir Henry Winchcombe, Bart., of Bucklebury), who for many years represented Berkshire in parliament. He m. in 1787, Ann, eldest dau. of Samuel Blackwell, Esq. of Williamstrip Park, co. Gloucester, and d. 12 Aug. 1794, leaving a son,

THE REV. WINCHCOMBE-HENRY-HOWARD HARTLEY, of Bucklebury, who m. 21 Aug. 1809, Elizabeth, eldest dau. of Thomas Watts, Esq. of Bath, and d. 9 Sept. 1832, leaving a dau., Elizabeth-Ann, and a son, the present WINCHCOMBE-HENRY-HOWARD HARTLEY, Esq. of Bucklebury, and Little Sodbury.

Arms—Arg., on a cross, gu., pierced, of the field, four cinque-foils, or, in the 1st and 4th quarters, a martlet, sa. Quartering PACKER, STEVENS, WINCHCOMBE, HOWARD, BROTHERTON (PLANTAGENET), WARREN, MOWBRAY.
Crest—A martlet, sa., holding in the beak a cross-crosslet, fitchée, or.
Motto—Vive ut vivas.
Seats—Bucklebury House, Berks; and Little Sodbury, Gloucestershire.

HARTLEY OF GILLFOOT.

HARTLEY, THOMAS, Esq. of Gillfoot, co. Cumberland, J.P., high-sheriff 1839, b. 29 Sept. 1802; m. 10 April, 1839, Georgianna, youngest dau. of George Rimington, Esq. of Tyne Field House, in the same county. Mr. Hartley is son of the late Thomas Hartley, Esq., by Anne, his wife, eldest dau. of Thomas Hartley, Esq. of Gilfoot, and grandson of John Hartley, Esq. of Whitehaven, and Elizabeth Milham, his wife. Mr. Hartley has had two brothers, Wilfrid, M.A., in holy orders, and Grayson, d. in New South Wales, Oct. 1838; and three sisters, viz., Elizabeth, m. in Nov. 1836, to the Rev. J. Carter; Catherine, m. in July, 1831, to the Rev. R. Parkinson, B.D.; and Ann-Eliza, m. in May, 1834, to D'Arcy Boulton, Esq.

Arms—Arg., on a cross, gu., pierced, of the field, four cinquefoils, or, in the 1st and 4th quarters, a martlet, sa.
Crest—A martlet, sa., holding in the beak a cross-crosslet, fitchée, or.
Seat—Gillfoot, near Whitehaven.

HARTOPP OF DALBY.

HARTOPP, EDWARD-BOURCHIER, Esq. of Dalby House, co. Leicester, J.P. and D.L., high-sheriff, 1832, b. 14 Dec. 1809; m. at Naples, 18 Feb. 1834, Honoria, second dau. of the late Major-General William Gent, and has a son and heir,

GEORGE, b. 15 Feb. 1835.

Lineage.—The Hall at Little Dalby has been the residence of this branch of the ancient family of Hartropp since the reign of ELIZABETH.

WILLIAM HARTOPP, Esq., baptized in 1625 (eldest son of George Hartopp, Esq. of Little Dalby, younger brother of Sir Edward Hartopp, Bart. of Freathly), m. Dorothy, dau. of Sir Thomas Hartopp, Knt. of Burton Lazars, and by her (who d. in 1707, aged 70) had, *inter alios*, a son,

THE REV. SAMUEL HARTOPP, b. in 1665, vicar of Little Dalby, who d. in 1717, leaving by Elizabeth, his wife, (who d. in 1721, aged 47), two sons and one dau. The elder son,

SAMUEL HARTOPP, Esq. b. in 1709, m. in 1730, Letitia, dau. of Edward Wigley, Esq. of Scraptoft, and dying in 1752, left a son and successor,

EDWARD-WILLIAM HARTOPP, Esq. b. in 1731, high-sheriff for Leicestershire in 1763. He m. Elizabeth, dau. of Thomas Boothby, Esq. of Potters Marston, and by her (who d. in 1769) left issue, three sons and five daus. Mr. Hartopp d. in 1773, and was s. by his son,

EDWARD HARTOPP, Esq. of Little Dalby, who assumed the additional surname and arms of WIGLEY. He m. the Hon. Juliana Evans,* dau. of George, Lord Carbery, and by her (who d. 20 May, 1807) had issue,

EDWARD, his heir.
William-Evans, in holy orders, rector of Harby, Leicestershire, who m. Eliza-Georgiana, dau. of — Gubbins, Esq., and had an only child,
Edward-Samuel Evans.
Juliana d. unm.

Mr. Hartopp Wigley, d. 30 June, 1808, was buried at Little Dalby, and s. by his son,

EDWARD HARTOPP, Esq. of Little Dalby, who m. in 1808, Anna-Eleanora, eldest dau. of Sir Bouchier Wrey, Bart., and by her (who m. 2ndly, 9 Dec. 1815, Sir Lawrence-Vaughan Palk, Bart.) had two sons,

EDWARD-BOURCHIER, his heir.
Robert-Palk, b. in Oct. 1812, bapt. at Tawstock, Devon.

Mr. Hartopp d. in 1813, and was s. by his son, the present EDWARD-BOUCHIER HARTOPP, Esq. of Dalby.

Arms—Sa., a chev., erm., between three otters, arg.
Crest—Out of a ducal coronet, or, a pelican, vulning herself, arg.
Seat—Dalby House, co. Leicester.

HARVEY OF BARGY CASTLE.

HARVEY, JOHN, Esq. of Bargy Castle, and Mount Pleasant, co. Wexford, captain R.A., and major of the Donegal artillery, J.P., b. 27 Oct. 1816; m. 1st, 11 Nov. 1837, Jane, dau. of Lieut. William Miller, R.A., and has issue,

I. Elizabeth-Jane. II. Henrietta.
III. Mary-Elizabeth.

He m. 2ndly, 8 June, 1852, Anne, dau. of the late Pierce-William Hughes, Esq. of Wexford, and by her has issue,

I. JOHN-MACLACHLAN, b. 27 Sept. 1853.
II. Edward-George-Colebrooke, b. 1 Feb. 1855.

Lineage.—The Harveys, of whom we are about to treat, came originally, it is supposed, from Bosworth, in Leicestershire. AMBROSE HARVEY, styled "the elder of Bridge of Bargy," the name of the townland on which the castle is built, was father of

AMBROSE HARVEY, styled "the younger of Gregheels," who was buried at Pomhaggard, where, in a distinct and separate portion of the burying-ground, his grave, and that of his wife beside it, are still to be seen. He was father of

THE REV. WILLIAM HARVEY, rector of Mulrankan, and prebendary of Edermine, who m. 1st, Susannah, 5th. dau. of John Harvey, Esq. of Killiane Castle, M.P. for Wexford, in 1695, and had issue,

I. The Rev. Ambrose Harvey, disinherited by his father's will. His great-grandson, Jaffray, settled in Canada.
II John, of Tagunnan, co. Wexford, who was also disinherited by his father's will. He m. Jane Russel, and was buried at Maglass, 18 Aug. 1794, having had issue,
1 JOHN, of Mount Pleasant, *alias* Tagunnan, who eventually succeeded to the Bargy estates, under the will of his first cousin, James of Bargy.
2 Richard, an officer in the army, d. unm.
3 William, of Killiane Lodge, co. Wexford, treasurer of the county, m. 9 Dec. 1797, Dorothea, third dau. of John Harvey, Esq. of Killiane Castle, and d. 5 Sept. 1828, leaving issue seven sons and two daus., viz.,
John, b. 16 Feb. 1803, now treasurer of the co. of Wexford, m. Harriett, dau. of John Farran, Esq. of Sherrington, co. Dublin, and has issue.
William, b. 31 Oct. 1807, settled at Buenos Ayres South America.
Joseph, b. 30 Aug. 1809.
Richard, b. 7 June, 1815.
Vigors, b. 15 Oct. 1817.
Robert, b. 17 Nov. 1819.
James, b. 7 Dec. 1821.
Sarah, m. 4 July, 1829, to Robert Percival, Esq. of Great Hayestown, co. Wexford, and has issue, three daus. Anne.

* Through this marriage the present Mr. Hartopp was one of the co-heirs to the Barony of VAUX.

III. FRANCIS, who *s.* to the estates of his father, of whom presently.
I. Elizabeth, *m.* to John Boxwell, of Lingstown Castle, co. Wexford.
II. Susannah, *m.* 1st, to — Thornton; 2ndly, to — Bennett.
III. Catharine, *m.* 17 Sept. 1737, to Thomas Hore, Esq. of Pole Hore, co. Wexford; she *d.* in 1777.
IV. Mary, *m.* 1st, to — Allen; 2ndly, to James Moore, Esq. of Milne Hall, co. Cavan.

The Rev. William Harvey *m.* 2ndly, Dorothea, dau. and heiress of Christopher Champney, Esq. of Kyle, co. Wexford, and had issue, CHRISTOPHER, of Kyle, and other issue (*See* HARVEY OF KYLE). The Rev. William Harvey was mayor of Wexford about 1753. His will was proved in Dublin, in 1765, and he was *s.* in his estates by his 3rd son,

FRANCIS HARVEY, Esq. of Bargy Castle, who *m.* Martha, eldest dau. of the Rev. James Harvey, of Killiane Castle, and had issue. Francis Harvey was one of the six clerks in Chancery. His will was proved in Dublin, in 1792, and he was *s.* by his eldest son,

BEAUCHAMP-BAGENAL HARVEY, Esq. of Bargy Castle, barrister-at-law. This misguided gentleman suffered the extreme penalty of the law for the prominent part he took in the rebellion of 1798, and an act of attainder passed against his property, and received the royal assent 6 Oct. 1798 (38 GEO. III.) He *d. unm.*, and his brother,

JAMES HARVEY, Esq., received a re-grant of the old family estates twelve years after the attainder; dying *unm.*, he bequeathed by his will, which was proved in Dublin, the chief part of the old family estates to his first cousin,

JOHN HARVEY, Esq. of Mount Pleasant, J.P., barrister-at-law, who *m.* Mary (who *d.* 20 March, 1837), dau. of William Harrison, Esq. of Castle Harrison, co. Cork, and had issue,

I. John, in the Royal navy, *d. unm.*
II. William-Harrison, lieut. R.A., who lost an arm at Waterloo, *m.* Elizabeth-Mary,* dau. of Colonel Paulet Colebrooke, R.A., and *d.* 18 Aug 1826, leaving issue,
  1 JOHN, now of Bargy Castle.
  2 William-Henry, *m.* Maria, dau. of the late Rev. Mr. Black, of Cornwall, and has four sons.
  3 James-Colebrooke, lt. 39th regt., A.D.C. to Sir J. Littler, G.C.B., killed at the battle of Ferozeshahur 21 Dec. 1845.
  1 Agnes-Mary.
III. George, in the Royal Navy, drowned at Cork by the upsetting of a boat, *unm.*
I. Sarah. II. Eliza.
III. Anne, *m.* 2 June, 1835, to Conolly M'Causland Lecky, Esq. of the city of Londonderry.

Mr. Harvey *d.* 4 June, 1834, and was *s.* in his estates by his grandson, the present JOHN HARVEY, Esq. of Bargy Castle.

Arms—Or, on a chief, indented, *sa.*, three crescents, arg.
Crest—A dexter arm, embowed in armour, grasping a sword, ppr., pommel and hilt, or.
Motto—Semper idem.
Seats—Bargy Castle and Mount Pleasant, co. Wexford.

HARVEY OF KYLE.

HARVEY, PERCY-LORENZO, Esq. of Kyle, co. Wexford, *b.* 8 Oct. 1806; captain H.E.I.C. service, J.P. for co. Wexford, *m.* 1st, Anne, dau. of James Cuppage, Esq., and 2ndly, July, 1854, Mary-Arabella, dau. of Francis Leigh, Esq., son of the late Francis Leigh, Esq. of Rosegarland, by the latter of whom he has a son,

I. PERCY-LEIGH, *b.* 2 Oct. 1855.

Lineage.—THE REV. CHRISTOPHER HARVEY, D.D. of Kyle, eldest son of the Rev. William Harvey, of Bargy Castle (by his 2nd marriage with Dorothea, dau and heiress of Christopher Champney, Esq. of Kyle), was incumbent of Rathdowney, diocese of Ossory, and of Ross, near Ross Carberry, co. Cork, and prebendary of Edermine, diocese of Ferns. He *m.* Rachel, dau. of Lorenzo Nickson, Esq. of Munny, co. Wicklow, eldest sister of Christiana, 1st Baroness of Donoughmore, and niece and heiress of Richard Hutchinson, Esq. of Knocklofty, co. Tipperary, and had issue,

WILLIAM, his heir.
Dorothea, *m.* in 1797, Percy Evans-Freke, Esq., and was mother of the present Lord Carbery.
Rachel, *m.* to Capt. Charles Randall.

* She *m.* 2ndly, in 1832, Lieut.-Col. Maclachlan, of the Royal Artillery, Knight of the Order of St. Maurice, and St. Lazar of Sicily.

The Rev. Dr. Christopher Harvey inherited only the estates brought into the family by his mother. He was buried 20 April, 1796, his will being proved in Dublin the same year, and was *s.* by his only son,

WILLIAM HARVEY, Esq. of Kyle, barrister-at-law, *b.* about 1767; *m.* 22 Aug. 1795, Dora, 3rd dau. of the Hon. Maurice Crosbie, dean of Limerick, 3rd son of Sir Maurice Crosbie, who was created Lord Brandon, and had issue,

I. CHRISTOPHER-GEORGE, *b.* 18 Sept. 1797, Mayor of Wexford in 1832.
II. James-William, *b.* 20 Aug. 1798, of Park House, near Wexford, latterly a captain of Dragoons, *m.* 10 March, 1824, Frances, dau. and subsequently only child of Joshua-John Pounden, Esq. of Fairfield, co. Wexford, who was sheriff of Dublin in 1,98. She *d.* 8 May, 1835, leaving issue,
  1 Crosbie-William, *b.* 3 Nov. 1831.
  1 Sophia-Pyne. 2 Julia-Maria.
  3 Dora-Adalaide. 4 Mary-Anne.
III. Maurice-Crosbie, R.N., J.P., *b.* 25 Aug. 1799, *d. unm.* 23 Nov. 1830.
IV. PERCY-LORENZO, now of Kyle.
V. Henry-Robert, *b.* 22 June, 1802, J.P., *m.* Eugenie-Fannie-Felicité, dau. of Monsr. Simon-Jaques Rochard, of London, and has issue,
  1 William-Crosbie, *b.* 12 March, 1835.
  2 James-Henry, *b.* 24 Feb. 1836.
  3 Cavendish-Gore, *b.* 21 Aug. 1838.
  1 Dorothea-Eugenia.

Arms—Or, on a chief, indented, sa., three crescents, arg.
Crest—A dexter hand, couped at the wrist, and erect, ppr., above which a crescent, reversed, arg.
Motto—Semper idem.
Seat—Kyle, on the river Slaney.

HARVEY OF ICKWELL BURY.

HARVEY, JOHN, Esq. of Ickwell Bury, co. Bedford, and of Finningley Park, co. York, J.P. and D.L., high-sheriff of Beds. 1839, *b.* 14 Nov. 1815; *s.* his father, 20 June, 1819; *m.* in 1842, Annie-Jane, dau. of Henry Tennant, Esq. of Cadoxton Lodge, near Neath, co. Glamorgan, and has issue,

JOHN-EDMOND-AUDLEY, *b.* 1850.
Beatrice-Susan-Audley.

Lineage.—ROBERT HARVEY, Esq., descended from a common ancestor with the noble family of Bristol, *m.* about the year 1637, Sarah, sister of Hugh Audley, Esq. of the Inner Temple, and of Cole Park, in the parish of Malmesbury, co. Wilts, and had a son and heir, ROBERT HARVEY, Esq., D.C.L., who *d.* in 1712, leaving three sons, I. JOHN; II. Hugh, of Cole Park, Wilts, whose male representative is ALFRED-AUGUSTUS HARVEY, Esq., M.D., of the Lodge, Bathampton, near Bath, grandson and heir of Audley Harvey, Esq. of Cole Park; and III. Robert, whose son, Robert Harvey, Esq. of Stockton, Wilts, *m.* MARY THURSBY. The eldest son,

JOHN HARVEY, Esq., became possessed of the estates of Ickwell Bury, co. Bedford, and Finningley Park, co. York. He *m.* Mary Vassalf, widow, and had issue,

JOHN, *b.* in 1667. Robert. William.
Edmond. Samuel.

The eldest son,

JOHN HARVEY, Esq., M.P., of Ickwell Bury, *b.* in 1677, *m.* Sarah Gore, widow, dau. and co-heir of Sir John Robinson, Bart. of Farming Woods, co. Northampton, and had issue. The only son to leave issue,

JAMES HARVEY, Esq., *m.* Elizabeth Fairie, and had two sons,

I. JOHN, his heir.
II. Edmond, in holy orders, rector of Finningley, who *m.* Mary, dau. and co-heir of the Rev. George Brooke, of Willian, Herts, and had issue.
  1 John, who *s.* his father as rector of Finningley. He is deceased.
  2 William, *d. unm.*
  3 Edmond, rector, first, of Willian, Herts, and afterwards of Stapleford, in the same co. He *m.* Christiana, dau. of Thomas, brother of John Greame, Esq. of Sewerby in Yorkshire, and left issue one son, Edmond-George, and three daus.
  4 James, in holy orders, who *m.* Catherine, dau. of the Rev. Henry Venn, rector of Yelling, in Huntingdonshire, and had one son, Edmond, and four daus.
  1 Elizabeth, *m.* to Gervas Woodhouse, Esq. of Owston House, in Lincolnshire, and had a son, the Rev. Gervas-Henry Woodhouse.

The elder son,

JOHN HARVEY, Esq. of Ickwell Bury, high-sheriff of

Bedfordshire in 1781, m. Sarah Silcock, and had (with a dau., Sarah, m. to William Astell, Esq. of Everton House, co. Beds) an only son and heir,

JOHN HARVEY, Esq., of Ickwell Bury and Finningley, who m. Susannah, youngest dau. of John Gibbard, Esq. of Sharnbrook, in Bedfordshire, and had issue, JOHN, his heir; Susan, deceased; Sarah; Mary; Elizabeth, m. to Thomas Kington Bayly, Esq. of Abbots Leigh, co. Somerset. Mr. Harvey was a deputy-lieut. for Bedfordshire, and served as its high-sheriff in 1795. At the period of the French Revolution he raised and supported, chiefly at his own expense, a troop of volunteers, called the Dismounted Bedfordshire Horse Artillery. He d. 20 June, 1819, and was s. by his son, the present JOHN HARVEY, Esq. of Ickwell Bury and Finningley.

Arms—Or, on a chev., gu., between three leopards' heads, of the first, three trefoils, ppr.

Crest—A leopard, passant, bezantée, gorged with a ducal coronet, and chained, or, holding in his dexter paw a trefoil, slipped, ppr.

Motto—Recte faciendo neminem timeas.

Seats—Ickwell Bury, Bedfordshire, and Finningley Park, Yorkshire.

HARVEY OF CASTLESEMPLE.

HARVEY, JAMES, Esq. of Castlesemple, co. Renfrew, Mousewald, co. Dumfries, and the Upper and Lower Conference Estates in the Island of Grenada, lieut.-col. (h. p.) of the 92nd regt., K.H., J.P. and D.L.; m. 1816, Margaret, dau. and heiress of the Hon. John Harvey, of the island of Grenada, and Castlesemple, in Scotland, and on the death of Mr. Harvey, in 1820, assumed the name of HARVEY, in lieu of his patronymic, LEE. They had issue,

I. JOHN-RAE LEE.
II. James-Octavius Lee.
III. Henry Lee.
I. Catherine Lee.
II. Margaret Lee.

Lineage.—WILLIAM LEE, Esq. of the city of Dublin, a descendant of the distinguished family of Lee of Ditchley, co. Oxford, which was raised to the rank of baronet in 1611, and ennobled, in 1674, by the title of earl of Lichfield, m. Elizabeth Widdrington, and had

THOMAS LEE, Esq., his son and heir, who m. 1st, Susannah, dau. of Michael Lewis, of Tullagorey, co. Kildare, Esq., and 2ndly, Catharine, dau. of Andrew Hamilton, of Ballymodonell, co Donegal, Esq., of which last-mentioned marriage the eldest son, JAMES LEE, afterwards HARVEY, was of Castle Temple.

Arms of the family of LEE—Sa., a fesse, erminois, two crescents in chief, arg., and a crescent, in base, of the last.

Crest—A crescent, erminois.

Motto—Fides non timet.

Arms of HARVEY—Gu., on a bend, erminois, three trefoils, slipped, vert, on a chief, arg., a buck's head, caboshed, az., between two mullets, of the first, and in the sinister chief point of the field, a cross-patée, of the fourth.

Crest—Out of a crescent, or, charged with a buck's head, as in the arms, a cubit arm ppr., the hand grasping a trefoil, slipped, erect, vert, the arm charged with an ermine spot, gold.

Motto—Omnia bene.

Seat—Castlesemple, Renfrewshire.

HARVEY OF CARNOUSIE.

HARVEY, WILLIAM-JAMES, Esq. of Carnousie, J.P. and D.L., co. Banff, b. 13 Nov. 1799; m. 7 April, 1835, Isabel, dau. of Charles Barclay, Esq., by Elizabeth Williamson his wife, and has issue,

I. JOHN, b. 5 Jan. 1841.
II. William-James, b. 5 Dec. 1845.
III. James-Charles, b. 12 Aug. 1848.
IV. Isaac-Alexander, b. 8 June, 1850.
V. George-Samuel-Abercromby, b. 21 Oct. 1854.
I. Elizabeth-Alexandrina.
II. Antonia-Mary.
III. Mary-Edith-Jane.
IV. Isabella-Constance.

Mr. Harvey, of Canousie, and his sister, Anne-Mary m. 30 Sept. 1828, to the Rev. John-P. Hetherington, are the children of the late John Harvey, Esq. and Janet MacAndrew his wife.

Seat—Carnousie House, Banffshire.

HARVEY OF MALIN HALL.

HARVEY JOHN, Esq. of Malin Hall, co. Donegal, J.P. and D.L., high-sheriff 1836, b. 24 Jan. 1802; m. 19 April, 1831, Emily, dau. of the Rev. George Miller, D.D., of Armagh, and by her (who d. 22 June, 1839) has issue,

I. ROBERT, b. 30 June, 1833.
II. George-Miller, b. 14 Aug. 1838.

Lineage.—This family is descended from the Harveys of Essex, and its present representative, John Harvey, Esq. of Malin Hall, has still in his possession the confirmation of arms given by William Dethicke, garter, and William Camden, clarenceux, to his ancestor, George Harvey, of Malden, in Essex, youngest of the four sons of Roger Harvey, "whose father, for approved services to her late most excellent princess, Elizabeth, Queen of Englande, of famous memorie, was advanced and rewarded with landes and tenementes in those parts of Essex where they have continued by manie descentes." And the confirmation of arms further narrates that "the saide George Harvey had been, by the king's highnesse, made a captaine in the troope now raising for the good service of his highnesse in the kingdome of Irelande."

REV. JOHN HARVEY, of Malin Hall, the lineal descendant of Capt. George Harvey, b. 27 Dec. 1742, m. 16 Oct. 1766, Elizabeth, dau. of Robert Young, Esq. of Culdaff House, co. Donegal, and by her (who d. 29 June, 1811) left at his decease, 12 May, 1794, a son,

ROBERT HARVEY, Esq. of Malin Hall, b. 21 Aug. 1770, m. 14 April, 1801, Barbara-Frances, dau. of Robert Gage, Esq. of Rathlin Island, co. Antrim, and by her had issue,

JOHN, now of Malin Hall.
Robert, m. Anne Smith.
George, m. Jane Richardson.
Gardiner, m. Rosetta Gage.
Marc.
Marianne, m. Rev. Charles Miller.
Barbara.
Susan.
Catharine, m. James Alexander, Esq., B.C.S.

The Rev. John Harvey, d. 1 Dec. 1820.

Arms—Gu. a bend dexter arg. charged with three trefoils, vert.

Crest—A lion ppr. holding in his dexter paw a trefoil, vert.

Seat—Malin Hall, co. Donegal.

HARVEY OF THORPE.

HARVEY, SIR ROBERT-JOHN, Knt., C.B., K.T.S., K.C.B.A. of Mousehold House, co. Norfolk, J.P. and D.L., lieut.-general in the army, b. 21 Feb. 1785; m. June, 1815, Charlotte, dau. of Robert Harvey, Esq. of Watton, and has issue,

I. ROBERT-JOHN, b. 16 April, 1817, m. Aug. 1845, Lady Henrietta-Augusta Lambart, granddau. of Richard, 7th Earl of Cavan, and has three sons and two daus.
II. John, b. 2 April, 1822.
III. Edward-Kerrison, b. 21 Dec. 1826, m. 1856, Emma-Susanna, dau. of the late Rev. Clement Chevallier, rector of Badingham and Cransford, Suffolk.
I. Julia, m. 14 Nov. 1837, to Major Samuel Ives Sutton, eldest son of the late Rear-Admiral Sutton.
II. Charlotte-Emma, m. 18 Sept. 1838, to the Rev. Henry Churchman Long, rector of Newton and Swainsthorpe, 2nd son of the Rev. Robert Churchman Long, of Dunston Hall, co. Norfolk.
III. Maria-Frances, d. 1845.

Sir Robert Harvey, a distinguished soldier, was present at the battles of Oporto, Busaço, Salamanca, Vittoria, Nive, Nivelle, Orthes and Toulouse, and at the sieges of Cuidad Rodrigo, Badajos, Burgos, and St. Sebastian.

Lineage.—JOHN HARVEY, Esq. of Beacham Well, in Norfolk, inherited a considerable estate in that parish, and was buried there in 1569. This estate passed in direct descent from father to son, to his great-grandson,

ROBERT HARVEY, Esq. of Beacham Well, who d. in 1678, leaving (with a younger child, William, ancestor of THOMAS HARVEY, Esq. of Northwold) a son and heir,

ROBERT HARVEY, Esq. of Beacham Well, who left at his decease, in 1695, two sons, viz.,

ROBERT, great-grandfather of ROBERT HARVEY, Esq. of Watton, whose dau., CHARLOTTE-MARY, m. her cousin, SIR ROBERT-JOHN HARVEY, C.B.
JOHN.

The 2nd son,

JOHN HARVEY, Esq., an eminent merchant of Norwich, was twice mayor of that city. He *m.* 1st, Ann, dau. of William Straham, Esq., and had a son, ROBERT, his heir. He *m.* a 2nd time,* and had further issue. Mr. Harvey, *d.* in 1742, and was *s.* by his eldest son,

ROBERT HARVEY, Esq., mayor of Norwich, who *m.* Lydia, dau. of John Black, Esq. and dying in 1773, was *s.* by his son,

ROBERT HARVEY, Esq., twice mayor of Norwich, who *m.* Judith, dau. of Capt. Onley, R.N., and sister of the Rev. Charles Onley, of Stisted Hall, in Essex, and had issue,

- ROBERT, his heir. JOHN, successor to his brother.
- Charles, who took the surname and arms of SAVILL-ONLEY. (*See family of* SAVILL-ONLEY.)
- Sarah.

Mr. Harvey *d.* in 1816, and was *s.* by his eldest son,

ROBERT HARVEY, Esq. of Catton, mayor of Norwich, lieut.-col. of the East Norfolk militia, and subsequently Colonel-Commandant of the Norwich regiment of volunteers, *m.* Ann, dau. of Jeremiah Ives, Esq., mayor of Norwich, but dying *s. p.* in 1820, he was *s.* by his brother,

JOHN HARVEY, Esq. of Thorpe Lodge, *b.* 17 May, 1755, Lieut.-Colonel Commandant of the 3rd Norfolk cavalry volunteers, and high-sheriff for the co. in 1825, who *m.* in Dec. 1783, Frances, dau. of Sir Roger Kerrison, and had issue,

- ROBERT-JOHN (Sir), now of Mousehold House.
- George, of Thorpe Grove, Norfolk, *b.* in 1793, *m.* Marianne, only child of Dr. Beevor, D.D., and niece of the late Sir Thomas Beevor, Bart., and had issue. Mr. Harvey was drowned while bathing, 4 Oct 1831.
- Roger-Kerrison, who *m.* Eliza, dau. of Sir Edmund Lacon, Bart., and had issue.
- Fanny, *m.* to the Rev. Edward Bellman.
- Emma, *m.* to Richard Day Squire, Esq.
- Marianne, *m.* to the Rev. Charles Day.
- Caroline, *m.* 16 April, 1818, to her cousin, Onley Savill-Onley, Esq.
- Harriott, *m.* to Capt. Blakiston.
- Rosa, *m.* to John Ranking, Esq.
- Augusta, *m.* to Harry Goring, Esq., eldest son of Sir Charles Goring, Bart.
- Charlotte, *m.* 9 Aug. 1838, to R. Blake, Esq. of Swafield.

Col. Harvey *d.* 9 Feb. 1842.

Arms—Erminois, on a chief, indented, gu., three crescents, arg. The augmentation to SIR ROBERT HARVEY is, in lieu of the crescent in the centre in chief, the representation of the gold medal presented to him by command of H.R.H. the Prince Regent, for his services at the battle of Orthes, pendent from a riband, gu., fimbriated, azure, beneath it the word "Orthes," and a canton, erm., charged with a representation of the insignia of a knight of the Royal Portuguese order of the Tower and Sword, pendant from a riband. To the crest of HARVEY, the augmentation of a mural crown, or, out of which the arm is issuant.

Crest—Over a dexter cubit arm, erect, ppr., a crescent, arg., between two branches of laurel, also ppr.

Motto—Alteri si tibi.

Seat—Mousehold House, Norwich.

HASELL OF DALEMAIN.

HASELL, EDWARD-WILLIAMS, Esq. of Dalemain, co. Cumberland, J.P. and D.L., chairman of quarter sessions for Cumberland and Westmorland, lieut.-col. commandant of the Westmorland and Cumberland yeomanry cavalry, and high-sheriff for the latter county in 1830, *b.* 10 July, 1796; *m.* 12 July, 1826, Dorothea, youngest dau. of Edward King, Esq. of Hungrill, co. York, and has issue surviving,

- I. WILLIAMS, *b.* 4 March, 1836.
- II. John-Edward, *b.* 19 Sept. 1839.
- III. George-Edmund, *b.* 26 Sept. 1847.
- I. Dorothea. II. Elizabeth-Julia. III. Alice-Jane.
- IV. Mary, *m.* to William Parker, Esq.
- V. Henrietta-Maria. VI. Frances-Anne.

Lineage.—The Hasells were first settled in Cambridgeshire, where several burials of members of the family occur, in the register of Bottisham church, in that county; as, John Hasell, 1572; Agnes, his widow, 23 Oct. 1575, &c.

SIR EDWARD HASELL, knighted by King WILLIAM III., was the first of the family who settled in Cumberland, Dalemain being purchased by him from the co-heiresses of the ancient family of De Layton, in 1665. Sir Edward, who was *b.* 27 Nov. 1642 (the son of the Rev. Edward Hasell, rector of Middleton Cheney, co. Northampton, by Martha, his wife, dau. of Dr. Henry Smith, Master of Saint Mary Magdalen, Cambridge), was elected, in 1701, M.P. for the county of Cumberland. He *m.* 1st Jane, eldest dau. of Sir Timothy Fetherstonhaugh, Knt. (who *d.* on the scaffold, for his loyalty to King CHARLES I.), and widow of Bernard Kirkbride. This lady dying *s. p.* in 1695, he *m.* 2ndly 24 Nov. 1696, Dorothy, dau. of William Williams, Esq. of Johnby Hall, and by her left at his decease, 12 Sept. 1707, a son and successor,

EDWARD HASELL, Esq. of Dalemain, *b.* in 1706, who *m.* Julia, 2nd dau. of Sir Christopher Musgrave, Bart. of Edenhall, Cumberland, and had issue. The 3rd son,

CHRISTOPHER HASELL, Esq., *m.* Miss Goade, and had (with two daus., Julia, who *d. unm.*; and Eliza, *m.* to her cousin, Richard Houghton, Esq.) a son,

EDWARD HASELL, Esq. of Dalemain, *b.* in 1765, who *m.* 1st, in 1792, Elizabeth, dau. of William Carus, Esq. of Kirkby Lonsdale, and by her (who *d.* in 1810) had issue,

- EDWARD-WILLIAMS, now of Dalemain.
- Christopher, *b.* in 1814, capt. in the Bengal army.
- William-Lowther, capt. in the Bengal army, *d.* at Cairo, June, 1849.
- Marianne, *m.* to the Rev. Sir J.-C. Musgrave, Bart. of Edenhall, who *d.* in 1835.
- Julia. Jane.
- Maria, *m.* to George Graham, Esq., son of the late Sir James Graham, Bart., and *d.* March, 1855.

Mr. Hasell *m.* 2ndly, in 1812, Jane, dau. of the Rev. R. Whitehead, of Ormside Lodge, which lady *d.* in Nov. 1816. Mr. Hasell himself *d.* at Dalemain, 24 Dec. 1825.

Arms—Or, on a fesse, az., between three hazel-nuts, ppr., as many crescents, arg.

Crest—A squirrel, arg., feeding on a hazel-nut, ppr., encircled with hazel-branches.

Seat—Dalemain, co. Cumberland.

HASLER OF ALDINGBOURNE.

HASLER, RICHARD, Esq. of Aldingbourne and Barkfold, co. Sussex, J.P. and D.L., *b.* 2 Dec. 1795; *m.* 27 April, 1830, Julia, dau. of the late Hon. William Wyndham, and has had issue,

- I. WILLIAM-WYNDHAM, *b.* 18 May, 1833.
- II. John-Vaughan, who *d.* in Dec. 1837.
- III. Richard-Charles, lieut. R.N., *d.* 5 June, 1856.
- IV. Henry-Gratwicke, *b.* 14 Feb. 1841.
- I. Fanny-Georgina-Jane, *m.* 12 April, 1856, to Alexander Mitchell, Esq. of Stowe N.B., late capt. gren.-gds.

Mr. Hasler, the representative of a family which has been settled in Sussex, for many generations, is only surviving son of the late Richard Hasler, Esq., high-sheriff of Sussex in 1821 (who *d.* Sept. 1836), by Martha his wife, only child of Thomas Newland, Esq. of Slindon, and grandson of Richard Hasler, Esq., by Jane Batcock his wife. Mr. Hasler has one surviving sister, Emma.

Arms—Per chev., gu. and sa., three lions, rampant, arg., each charged on the shoulder with a cross-patée, az.

Crest—A squirrel, sejant, cracking a nut, ppr., collared, gemel, az., between two branches of palm.

Motto—Qui nucleum vult, nucem frangat.

Seats—Aldingbourne, Chichester; and Barkfold, Petworth.

HASSARD OF GARDENHILL.

HASSARD, ALEXANDER-JASON, Esq. of Gardenhill, co. Fermanagh, *b.* 1 Sept. 1837, *s.* his uncle, William Hassard, Esq., 15 Nov. 1847.

Lineage.—The family of Hassard is of Norman extraction, and of considerable antiquity. The orthography was originally "Hassart." The long extinct title of Duke de Charanté was in this family. Two members thereof visited the Holy Land as Crusaders. Soon after the Conquest a branch became seated in Gloucestershire, and afterwards removed to Dorsetshire. The first English ancestor from whom an unbroken succession can be traced was,

JOHN HASSART OR HASSARD, A.D. 1469, lord of the manor of Seaton, 7 miles from Lyme. He left issue,

- JOHN Hassard, of whom hereafter.
- Gilbert, rector of Trusham, co. Devon, 31 July, 1541.

* From the second marriage lineally descended,

HENRY HARVEY, Esq. of the co. Suffolk, and

GEORGE HARVEY, Esq. (his younger brother) of Catton, near Norwich, late a capt. in the 18th hussars, who *m.* Lady Honora-Elizabeth-Hester Lambart, dau. of the Earl of Cavan.

The elder son,

JOHN HASSARD, *b.* 1498, mayor of Lyme in 1550 and 1557, left issue,

- JOHN, of whom hereafter.
- Robert, several times mayor of Lyme and M.P. for the borough in 1589 and 1598.
- Anne, *m.* to Robert, 3rd son of John Yonge.

The elder son,

JOHN HASSARD, *b.* 1531, mayor of Lyme in 1567, 1572, 1578, 1582, 1588, 1594, 1601, and 1606, altogether seven times, was returned M.P. for the Borough in 1585, 1586, and 1606. The gallery at the West end of the nave of the church of Lyme Regis, bears the following inscription on its front, in capital letters:—

> "John Hassard built this to the glorie of Almightie God, in the eightieth year of his age, Anno Domini 1611."

And on the South side appears:—

> "John Hassard, seven times maior, deceased the seventh day of November, Anno Domini 1612."

He left issue,

- ROBERT, of whom hereafter.
- John, vicar of Awliscombe, co. Devon.
- Mary, *m.* Roger Hill, of Tounsford, co. Somerset, Esq.
- Alice, *m.* Alexander Hill, Esq., second brother of Roger.

The elder son,

ROBERT HASSARD, M.P., *b.* 1582, *m.* Elizabeth, dau. of Peter Clarke, Esq. of Suffolk, and left issue,

- JOHN, ancestor of the HASSARD-SHORTS, of Edlington Grove, co. Lincoln. They assumed the name and arms of Short in 1794.
- JASON, of whom we treat.
- GEORGE, ancestor of the HASSARDS, *of Skea*, co. Fermanagh.

Jason and George Hassard, accompanied by some of the Caldwells, went over to Ireland in the reign of CHARLES II., after having previously raised troops in the South of England. They assumed the 2nd motto of "Fortuna viam ducit," on landing. They had eventually large tracts of land granted them in Fermanagh, and other adjoining counties. The Hassards were distinguished at the sieges of Enniskillen and Londonderry.

JASON HASSARD, of Gardenhill and Toam, *b.* 1617, was mayor and M.P. for Lyme, before he departed for Ireland. His will bears date 21 Oct. 1690. He left issue,

- RICHARD, his heir.
- John, the supposed ancestor of the family of the late MAJOR-GENERAL HASSARD, of the Royal Engineers.

The eldest son,

RICHARD HASSARD, Esq. of Gardenhill and Toam, *b.* 1671, *m.* 1706, Mary, dau. of John Enery, Esq. of Ballyconnel, co. Cavan, and left a son and successor,

RICHARD HASSARD, Esq. of Gardenhill and Toam, *b.* 1709. He *m.* 1733, Jane, dau. of James Little, Esq. of the co. Fermanagh, and left issue,

- JASON, his heir.
- John, of Toam, ancestor of the HASSARDS, *of Waterford.*
- William.
- Catharine, *m.* in 1771, Alexander Young, Esq. (*see* YOUNG *of Coolkeiragh*, co. Derry).
- Anne, *m.* Thomas Stewart, Esq., M.D. of Enniskillen, and was mother of the late LIEUT.-GENERAL THOMAS STEWART, of the Madras army.
- Frances, *m.* Beresford Burston, Esq., K.C. of the Irish Bar.

The eldest son,

JASON HASSARD, Esq. of Gardenhill, *b.* 1734; *m.* 1777, Anne, dau. of Alexander Montgomery, Esq. of Clontarf, co. Dublin, and *d.* about 1812, leaving issue,

- I. RICHARD, of Gardenhill, *b.* 1778, capt. 74th Highlanders, *d. unm.*
- II. JASON, of Gardenhill, *b.* 1780, *d. unm.*
- III. WILLIAM, of Gardenhill, *b* 1781, for many years treasurer for the county Fermanagh, assassinated in the avenue of Gardenhill, 13th November, 1847, *unm.*
- IV. ALEXANDER, captain 6th Inniskilling dragoons, *m.* in 1836, Elizabeth Bolton, daughter of the late Jason Hassard, capt. 74th Highlanders, and *d.* Sept. 1845, leaving issue,
  - 1 ALEXANDER JASON, the present representative.
  - 2 Francis-William, *b.* 1841.
  - 1 Anne-Frances-Deey, deceased.
  - 2 Elizabeth-Sophie Marshall. 3 Arabella-Jane.
- V. John, of Bawnboy House, co. Cavan, high-sheriff for co. Cavan, in 1824, *m.* 1818, Charlotte, youngest dau. of the late Robert Deey, Esq of Ravensdale, near Maynooth, and Merrion Square, Dublin, and was killed from his horse in 1830, leaving issue,
  - 1 JASON, deceased. 2 RICHARD, *b.* 1820.

  - 3 Robert-Deey, *b.* 1822, 2nd Bombay European Light Infantry.
  - 4 Francis, deceased. 5 William, *b.* 1825.
  - 6 John, *b.* 1830.
  - 1 Marianne. 2 Eliza.
- VI. Francis, of Rockwood, co. Cavan.
- I. Mary, *m.* 1819, the Rev. Henry Cottingham, of Holywell, co. Cavan.
- II. Anne-Frances, *m.* 1818, William Deey, Esq. of St. Marks, co. Dublin.

Arms—Gu., two bars, arg., on a chief, or, three escallops of the first.
Crest—An escallop, or.
Mottoes—"Vive en espoir," above the crest, and "Fortuna viam ducit," beneath the shield.
Seat—Gardenhill, county Fermanagh.

HASSARD OF WATERFORD.

HASSARD, MICHAEL-DOBBYN, Esq. of Waterford, *b.* 1817; *m.* in 1846, Anne, dau. of the late Sir Francis-John Hassard, and has issue,

I. Anna-Maria. II. Jane.

Lineage.—This family is a branch of the Hassards of Gardenhill, co. Fermanagh.

JOHN HASSARD, *b.* 1736, 2nd son of Richard Hassard, Esq. of Gardenhill and Toam, *m.* 1st, 1767, Elizabeth, dau. of Cornelius Bolton, Esq. of Ballycanvan, co. Waterford, and by her, who *d.* in 1770, had issue,

- I. RICHARD, *b.* 1768, lieut. in the Royal Irish artillery and afterwards capt. in the Waterford militia, *m.* 1812, Frances-Margurette, dau. of Michael Dobbyn, Esq. of the city of Waterford, and left issue,
  - 1 Richard-Henry, *d. unm.*
  - 2 MICHAEL DOBBYN, the present representative.
- I. Jane. II. Elizabeth, *d. unm.*

He *m.* 2ndly, 1778, Samuella, dau. and co-heir of Samuel Barker, Esq. of the city of Waterford, and by her he had issue,

- I. FRANCIS-JOHN (Sir), *b.* 1780, recorder of the city of Waterford, knighted in 1810. He *m.* 1816, Anne, dau. of Charles Hudson, Esq. of Stackenny, co. Kildare, and widow of the late James Johnston, Esq. of Carrickbreda, co. Armagh, and *d.* in 1822, leaving issue,
  - 1 FRANCIS-CHARLES, *b.* 1817, *m.* 1846, Margarette-Frances, dau. of Richard Hudson, Esq. of Springfarm, co. Wicklow, and *d.* in 1850, leaving issue,
    - Francis-John, *b.* 1847.
    - Charles-Alexander-Joseph, *b.* 1851.
  - 2 Richard-John, of Belfield, co. Wicklow, *b.* 1820, *m.* in 1840, Charlotte-Augusta, dau. of Charles Quintin Dick, capt. 80th regiment, and had issue,
    - Francis-John, *b.* 1841. William-Charles, *b.* 1843.
    - Charles-Quintin, *b.* 1846.
    - Elizabeth-Rose. Anna-Margaret.
    - Charlotte-Augusta. Maria-Louisa.
  - 1 Anne, *m.* in 1846, Michael-Dobbyn Hassard, Esq.
- II. John, capt. 74th Highlanders, *b.* 1782, *d. unm.* 1825.
- III. Jason, also capt. 74th Highlanders, *b.* 1785, *m.* Eliza, daughter of Hugh Marshall, Esq. of Waterford, *d.* in 1842, leaving issue,
  - 1 John-William, *b.* 1822.
  - 2 Jason, *b.* 1826, major 57th regt.
  - 3 Henry-Bolton, *b.* 1828, asst.-surgeon Cape Mounted Rifles.
  - 4 William, 90th regt., *b.* 1830.
  - 5 Francis, 6th regt., *b.* 1834.
  - 1 Samuella, *m.* John Robinson, Esq., M.D.
  - 2 Elizabeth-Bolton, *m.* Alexander Hassard, capt. 6th Inniskilling dragoons.
- IV. William-Henry, *b.* 1790, recorder of the city of Waterford in 1828, *m.* same year, Catherine-Jane, dau. of the late John Hewson, capt. 89th regt., and widow of the late Capt. Roger Sheely, and had issue, Anne-Julia.
- I. Samia, *m.* James Burkett, Esq., M.P.

Arms—Gu. two bars, ar., on a chief, or, three escallops of the first.
Crest—An escallop, or.
Mottoes—"Vive en espoir," over the crest, and "Fortuna viam ducit," beneath the shield.
Residence—Glenville, Waterford.

HASSARD OF SKEA.

HASSARD, THE REV. EDWARD, Rector of Rathkeale, and Chancellor of the diocese of Limerick, *s.* to the representation of the family of Hassard of Skea, at the death of his father, 10 Aug. 1847; *m.* 15 Sept. 1855, Miss Mary-Anne Gibb, of Norfolk Square, Brighton.

Lineage.—The family of HASSARD OF SKEA is a branch of the old English stock of HASSARD OF LYME. (*See Hassard of Gardenhill*).

JASON HASSARD, Esq. of Skea, co. Fermanagh, a descendant of Capt. Jason Hassard, who took an active part in the sieges of Enniskillen and Londonderry, *m.* Anne, dau. of Col. Johnston, and left a son,

ROBERT HASSARD, Esq. of Skea, who *m.* 1762, Jane, dau. of George Nixon, Esq. of Nixon Hall, co. Fermanagh and *d.* 1800, leaving two sons, viz.,

JASON, *m.* a dau. of Dr. Murray, late of Dungannon, and niece of the Provost of Trinity College, Dublin, and is deceased.
GEORGE, of whom presently.
Catherine, *m.* to Capt. Gerrard Irvine.
Anne. Letitia. Rose, *m.* to — Adkins, Esq.

The 2nd son,

GEORGE HASSARD, Esq. of Skea, *b.* May, 1775, J.P., served as high-sheriff of co. Fermanagh in 1818 and 1828. He *m.* 1799, Miss Jane Maguire, and by her (who d. March, 1846) had issue,

EDWARD, present head of the Skea family.
Henry, barrister-at-law, *d. unm.*
William, of Mountjoy Square, Dublin.
George, of Mountjoy Square, Dublin, barrister, *b.* 10 Sept. 1811.
Richard, *d. unm.* John, who went to Australia.
Charles.
Francis, in holy orders, rector of Fuerty, co. Roscommon.
Mary, *m.* 1822, to George Campbell Williams, Esq.
Anne, *m.* to Samuel Gale, Esq., barrister of Battledown, near Cheltenham.
Elizabeth. Jane, *d.* young. Charlotte, *d.* young.

Arms—See HASSARD *of Gardenhill.*
Seat—Skea, co. Fermanagh.

HATCH OF ARDEE CASTLE.

HATCH, WILLIAM, Esq. of Ardee Castle, co. Louth, *b.* 1 July, 1795; a magistrate for the county.

Lineage.—JEREMIAH HATCH, of Ardee, son of JEREMIAH HATCH, of the same place, by Jane Pepper, his wife, *m.* 20 Aug. 1793, Anne, dau. of Thomas Hatch, of Ardee, by his wife, Rose Williams, of Coolderry, and *d.* 30 May, 1814, aged fifty-six, having had, by this lady, who survived him, and *d.* 10 Aug. 1840, aged eighty-five, the following issue,

Thomas, A.B. Trin. Coll., Camb., *b.* 23 July, 1794, *d.* 18 Aug. 1817.
WILLIAM, of Ardee Castle.
John, M.D., *b.* 20 July, 1796; *m.* Harriet Freeman.
Jeremiah, A.B., *b.* in 1797, went to Australia in 1824.
Rose-Anne, *m.* to James Cuthbertson, Esq., M.D., of Dublin.

Arms—Gu., two demi-lions, passant-guardant, couped in pale, or, on a chief, arg., a cannon, mounted, ppr.
Crest—A demi-lion, rampant, or, armed and langued, gu., charged on the breast with a pile of shot, ppr., holding a staff, also ppr., thereto affixed a flag, arg., charged with a cross of the second.
Motto—Fortis valore et armis.
Seat—Ardee Castle, Ardee, co. Louth.

HATFEILD OF THORP ARCH AND LAUGHTON.

HATFEILD, RANDALL-WILMER, Esq. of Thorp Arch Hall, co. York, *b.* 8 July, 1828; lieut. 10th hussars; *m.* Aug. 1856, Miss FitzGibbon.

Lineage.—NICHOLAS HATFEILD, of Shiregreen, in the parish of Ecclesfield, co. York (son of ROBERT HATFEILD, grandson of WILLIAM HATFEILD, and great-grandson of ROBERT HATFEILD, whose father, WILLIAM HATFEILD, was son of RICHARD HATFEILD, grandson of RALPH HATFEILD, and great-grandson of ADAM DE HATFIELD, of Glossopdale), possessed an estate in the parish of Glossop. He *m.* Ann Sanderson, and left (his will was dated 2 Aug. 1558, and proved 26 Sept. following) a son,

ALEXANDER HATFEILD, of Hatfeild House, Shiregreen, who *m.* at Ecclesfield, 11 Aug. 1558, Isabel Shiercliffe, and was father of

RALPH HATFEILD, of Shiregreen, and afterwards of Laughton-en-le-Morthen, who administered to his mother in 1610. From him descended his great-grandson,

AURENGZEBE HATFIELD, of Laughton, bapt. 4 June, 1710, who *m.* in Dec. 1746, Susanna, dau. of John Hatfeild, and by her (who *m.* 2ndly, William Marshall, of Newton Kyme) he left at his decease, Aug. 1752, an only surviving son,

JOHN HATFEILD, of Laughton, *b.* 29 April, 1748, who *d. unm.* 11 Jan. 1791, and was *s.* by his half-brother,

WILLIAM MARSHALL, of Newton Kyme and Laughton, lieut.-col. of the 3rd West Yorkshire militia, *b.* 17 July, 1764 (son of William Marshall, Esq. of Newton Kyme, capt. of dragoons, by SUSANNA HATFEILD, his wife, and grandson of Henry Marshall, Esq. of Newton Kyme, by Elizabeth Hatfeild, aunt of Aurengzebe Hatfeild, of Laughton). Col. Marshall *m.* in 1798, Christiana, dau. of Godfrey Higgins, of Skellow Grange, and by her (who *d.* 2 Oct. 1832) left at his decease, 17 Jan. 1815, a son and dau.,

WILLIAM, his heir.
CHRISTIANA, heir to her brother.

The son,

WILLIAM HATFEILD (which surname he assumed, by royal licence, 26 Dec. 1833), of Newton Kyme and Laughton, *b.* 17 June, 1799, *d. unm.* 7 Sept. 1844, and was *s.* by his sister,

CHRISTIANA, who *m.* Randall Gossip, who assumed the surname and arms of HATFEILD, and was the late RANDALL HATFEILD, Esq. of Thorp Arch and Laughton.

Family of Gossip.

WILLIAM GOSSIP, of Hatfeild and Thorpe Arch, *b.* 6 March, 1704, *m.* 13 Nov. 1731, Anne, dau. and co-heir of George Wilmer, eldest son of Randall Wilmer, of Overhelmsly, and by her (who *d.* 9 July, 1780) had, with other issue, George, *b.* 29 June, 1735, an officer in the Buffs (ancestor of WILLIAM HATFEILD GOSSIP, Esq., who took the name of DE RODES); THOMAS, of whom presently, and Wilmer, of Thorp Arch Mr. Gossip *d* 25 March, 1772. His 3rd son,

THOMAS GOSSIP, *b.* 21 June, 1744, *m.* in 1770, Johanna, dau. and heir of Richard Cartwright, of Oadly, co. Leicester, and by her (who *d.* 11 Oct. 1825) had issue,

William, of Thorp Arch, *b.* in 1770, *m.* twice, but *d. s. p.* 21 Aug. 1833.
RANDALL, of whom we treat.

Mr. Gossip *d.* in 1776. His younger son,

RANDALL GOSSIP, lieut.-col., *b.* 5 Feb. 1774, *m.* 30 Nov. 1798, Leah, dau. of the Rev. John Currey, rector of Dartford, co. Kent, and *d.* 29 Sept. 1832, having had issue,

RANDALL, who *m.* CHRISTIANA, dau. of Lieut.-Col. William Marshall, of Newton Kyme and Laughton, and assumed the surname and arms of HATFEILD, and is the present RANDALL HATFEILD, of Thorp Arch, &c., as above.
William, *b.* 22 Oct. 1801, lieut. 41st regt., killed in action, in the Burmese war, 1 Dec. 1825.
Wilmer, *b.* 2 Sept. 1804, assumed, by Royal licence, the surname and arms of WILMER, in 1832, *m.* 12 Dec. 1832, Anne, dau. and co-heir of the Rev. Thomas Wingfield, and has issue,
Augustus-Henry.
Anna-Maria.
Thomas-George, in holy orders, *b.* 10 Oct. 1808, assumed, by Royal licence, the surname and arms of Wilmer, in 1833, *m.* in 1840, Emma, dau. of Raven, and *d. s. p.* 25 Dec. 1845.
Leah-Fortrie, *m.* 3 April, 1830, to Charles-William Minet, of Baldwins, co. Kent.
Georgina. Frances-Anne, *d.* young.

The eldest son,

RANDALL GOSSIP, Esq., of Thorp Arch, *b.* 28 May, 1800, *m.* 9 Sept. 1825, Christiana, only dau. of the late William Marshall, Esq. of Newton Kyme and Laughton, lieut.-col. 3rd West York militia, and sister and sole heir of William Hatfeild, Esq. of Laughton-en-le-Morthen and Newton Kyme, and had issue,

RANDALL-WILMER, now of Laughton.
William, 88th regt., *b.* 3 Dec. 1834.
Thomas-Godfrey, *b.* 29 Nov. 1837.
John, *b.* 15 June, 1846.
Christina-Leah. Elizabeth.
Jane. Lucy. Frances.

This gentleman, formerly an officer in the fusilier-guards, assumed the surname of HATFEILD, by royal licence, 16 Oct. 1844, on succeeding, *jure uxoris*, to the estates of his wife's brother, William Hatfeild, Esq. of Newton Kyme and Laughton. He *d.* 1853.

Arms—Quarterly: 1st and 4th, erm., on a chev., engrailed, sa., three cinquefoils, or, for HATFEILD; 2nd and 3rd, per fesse, indented, arg. and sa., a pale, counterchanged, three goats' heads, erased, two and one, az., and as many crosses-patée, fitchée, one and two, of the first, for GOSSIP.
Crests—1st, a dexter cubit arm, vested, sa., cuffed, arg., the hand, ppr., holding a cinquefoil, slipped, or, for HATFEILD; 2nd, Two goats' heads, erased, addorsed, the dexter, sa., the sinister, arg., for GOSSIP.
Motto—Pax.
Seat—Thorp Arch.

HATTON OF CLONARD.

Hatton, Villiers-Francis, Esq. of the co. Wexford, vice-admiral, late M.P. for that county, *b.* 20 Aug. 1787; *m.* 24 May, 1817, Harriet, dau. of the late Right Hon. David La Touche, M.P. for co. Carlow, by the Lady Cecilia Leeson his wife, dau. of the 1st Earl of Miltown, and has issue,

I. Villiers La Touche, *b.* 24 April, 1824, late of the 1st Royals, *m.* Nov. 1850, Rosea, only dau. of Sir William de Bathe, Bart., and has two son and two daus.

I. Cecilia.

II. Elizabeth-Frances, *m.* 29 Nov. 1854, to Arthur-Lowry Cole, Lieut.-Col., 17th Regt. eldest son of the late General the Hon. Sir Galbraith-Lowry Cole, brother of the Earl of Enniskillen.

Lineage.—The family of Hatton was anciently of great repute in Cheshire, Cambridgeshire, and Northamptonshire. Its most distinguished members were the celebrated lawyer, Sir Christopher Hatton, K.G., Lord Chancellor, *temp.* Queen Elizabeth, and Christopher, Lord Hatton of Kirkby, a gallant Royalist in the time of Charles I. The Wexford Branch, which has, since its settlement in the sister island, maintained a leading influence in that county, was there established in the reign of Elizabeth. The grandfather of the present representative.

John Hatton, Esq. of Clonard, co. Wexford, son of Henry Hatton, Esq. of Clonard, had, by Elizabeth, his wife, four sons, viz.,

Henry, his heir.
William, *m.* Elizabeth Ross and had issue, 1 William, deceased; 1 Louisa, *m.* to Mr. Sandwith, of the Royal Marines; and 2 Isabella-Elizabeth-Mary, m. to the Rev. John-B. Hildebrand, rector of Saxby and Stapleford, co. Leicester.
George, M.P. for Lisburne, who *m* the Lady Isabella-Rachael-Seymour Conway, youngest dau. of Francis first, Marquess of Hertford, and had, with a dau., Isabella-Elizabeth, *m.* to Baron Grumker, and *d. s. p.* in 1831, and a son, Henry-John, Com. R.N., deceased, another son, the present Villiers-Francis Hatton, Esq., vice-adm.
John, major-gen. in the army, *m.* a dau. of Col. Hodges, and is deceased. His eldest son resides at Ballisalla House, Isle of Man.

The eldest son and heir,

Henry Hatton, Esq. of Clonard, co. Wexford, *m.* in 1783, the Hon. Anne-Jane, eldest dau. of the 2nd Earl of Arran, by his 1st wife, Catherine, only dau. of William, Viscount Glerawley, but by her (who *m.* 2ndly, John, 1st Marquess of Abercorn) had no issue. He was *s.* by his nephew, the present Vice-Admiral Villiers-Francis Hatton.

Arms—Az., a chev. between three garbs, or.
Crest—A hind, passant, ppr.

HAVERS OF THELTON HALL.

Havers, Thomas, Esq. of Thelton Hall, co. Norfolk, *b.* in July, 1787; *m.* in Sept. 1809, Dorothy, dau. of Forster Charlton, Esq. of Alndyke, in Northumberland, and has issue,

I. Thomas.	II. William	III. Robert.
IV. John.	V. Charles.	VI. Richard.
VII. George.	VIII. Arthur.	

Lineage.—John Havers was gentleman of the horse to John, Duke of Norfolk, and attended him in the battle of Bosworth Field, wherein that nobleman was slain. His successor, another

John Havers, of Winfarthing, was steward of the Howard family. His eldest son,

Thomas Havers, of Winfarthing, purchased, in 1592, the mayor of Thelton, and erected the present mansion. Mr. Havers, who was steward to the Duke of Norfolk, *d.* in 1605, and was *s.* by his eldest surviving son,

John Havers, Esq. of Thelton Hall, who was bailiff to the Earl of Arundel in 1610. He *m.* Elizabeth, dau. of John Tindall, of Banham, and had issue,

William, his heir.
Clere, of Brakendale, who *m.* and had issue,
Richmond, *d. s. p.*
John, of Norwich, who *m.* Miss Mary Collins, and had issue.

The elder son,

William Havers, Esq. of Thelton Hall, lord of the manor in 1664, *m.* Susan, dau. of Brooke, Esq. of Whitechurch, and had issue; Thomas, of whom presently; John; Susan, *m.* to T. Risden, Esq.; and, Elizabeth, *m.* to H. Huddleston, Esq. of Sawston in Cambridgeshire. The elder son,

Thomas Havers, Esq. of Thelton Hall, *m.* 1st, Mary Englefield, of Berkshire, and 2ndly, Alice, dau. and coheiress of Sir E. Moore, Bart. of Kittington, co. Notts. He was *s.* by his eldest son,

William Havers, Esq. of Thelton Hall, who *m.* Miss Mary Dormer, and had (with a dau., Mary, *m.* to H. Bedingfield, Esq. of Stoke Ash, in Suffolk), three sons, of whom the eldest,

Thomas Havers, Esq. of Thelton Hall, lord of the manor in 1737, *m.* Henrietta-Maria, dau. of Sir Symonds D'Ewes, of co. Suffolk, and had issue, Thomas, his heir; William; Edward; and Henrietta-Maria. Mr. Havers was *s.* by his eldest son,

Thomas Havers, Esq. of Thelton Hall, who *m.* Catherine, dau. of John Dutry, Esq., and had issue Thomas, his successor; John; William; Edward; Catherine, *m.* to Francis Bedingfield, Esq. of Ditchingham, in Norfolk; Mary, *m.* to Jeremiah Norris, Esq. of Colney Hall, Norfolk; Lucretia, *m.* to Thomas Wright, Esq. of Henrietta Street, London, banker; Henrietta-Maria; Rosa-Lelia, *m.* to John Needham, Esq. of Bickham, Somersetshire; Anna; and Maria-Henrietta. The eldest son,

Thomas Havers, Esq. of Thelton Hall, *m.* Elizabeth, dau. of Robert Cliffe, Esq. of Glandford Briggs, co. Lincoln, and had issue,

Thomas, his heir.	Robert.
Edward.	Richard.
Henry.	William.
Eliza.	Lucretia.
Harriott.	Charlotte.

Mr. Havers was *s.* at his decease by his eldest son, the present Thomas Havers, Esq. of Thelton Hall.

Arms—Or, on a fesse, sa., three chess rooks, of the field.
Crest—A griffin, sejant, erm., crowned and collared.
Seat—Thelton Hall, Norfolk.

DE HAVILLAND OF HAVILLAND HALL.

De Havilland, Thomas-Fiott, Esq. of Havilland Hall, Guernsey, lieut.-col. H.E.I.C.S., jurat of the royal court of Guernsey, 1842, *b.* 10 April, 1775; *m.* 1st, 8 Sept. 1808, Elizabeth, dau. of Thomas de Saumarez, Esq., first cousin of the late Lord de Saumarez, and by her had issue,

I. Thomas, Captain 55th Regt., *d.* of fever at Hong-Kong, 6 Sept. 1843.

II. Charles-Ross, in holy orders, *m.* Grace-Anna, dau. of David Verner, Esq., and niece of Colonel Verner.

I. Emilia-Andros.

II. Elizabeth-Martha, *m.* to St. John Gore, son of the Rev. Thomas Gore, and nephew of the late Sir Ralph Gore, Bart.

He *m.* 2ndly, Harriet, dau. of Anthony Gore, Esq., and niece of the late Sir Ralph Gore, Bart.

Lineage.—The ancient Guernsey family of De Havilland, is of Norman origin, and came from Cotantin, in Normandy, *temp.* William the Conqueror. It has been known in the Isle of Guernsey since 1176, and members of the family have been solicitors and attorneys-general, jurats and bailiffs of the Royal Court, from the earliest records. In a charter under the great seal of England, still extant, granted by Edward IV., in the 1st year of his reign, the king confirms the ancient constitution of the island, and adds many new privileges, in consideration of the gallantry displayed, and the heavy losses sustained, by "Le Sieur Thomas de Havilland," and others, gentlemen of Guernsey, and their followers, in recovering Mont Orgueil Castle, in Jersey, from the French, by whom it had been held during the last 6 years of Henry VI's reign, in commemoration of which was added "a laurel branch," above the shield, as an honourable augmentation to the island arms. The Havillands in England are descended from Christopher de Havilland, who left Guernsey, and established himself at Pool, *temp.* Henry VIII. He was grandson of James de Havilland, who was sworn a jurat of the Royal Court, A.D. 1527. The eldest son of this James, the jurat of 1527, was

James de Havilland, attorney-general of the island, in

1583. He *m.* Thomasse, dau. of Richard Maindonal, and was father of

JAMES DE HAVILLAND, of Guernsey, who *m.* Martha, dau. of John de Vic, and had a son and heir,

JAMES DE HAVILLAND, jurat of the Royal Court of Guernsey, *b.* in 1612, who *m.* in 1640, Mary, dau. of Josias de Marchant, and was father of

JOHN DE HAVILLAND, of Guernsey, who *m.* Anne, dau. of John de Saumarez, jurat of the Royal Court of Guernsey, and left a son and successor,

JAMES DE HAVILLAND, Esq. of Guernsey, who *m.* Catherine, dau. of the Rev. John Martin, by Catherine Gibault, his wife, and *d.* in 1719, having had (besides three daus.) one son,

JOHN DE HAVILLAND, Esq. of Guernsey, who *m.* Mary, dau. of Peter Dobree, Esq., and Martha Carey, his wife, and had four sons and several daus. The youngest, but survivor of all the other children,

SIR PETER DE HAVILLAND, Knt. barrister, magistrate, and bailiff of Guernsey for many years. *m.* 1st, in 1771, Carteretta, dau. of the Rev. Thomas Fiott, and by her (who *d.* in 1789) had issue,

I. THOMAS-FIOTT, of Havilland Hall.
II. Charles, *m.* Martha, dau. of Richard Saumarez, Esq., brother of the late Lord de Saumarez, and *d.* in 1845, leaving issue,
  1 Charles-Richard, in holy orders, of Downside, co. Somerset.
  2 Saumarez, a cadet in the E. I. Co.'s service, drowned in the Ganges.
  3 James, Royal Artillery. 4 John.
  1 Harriet.
III. Peter, } both *d.* young.
IV. James, }
I. Carterette, *m.* to Col. Sir George Smith, who *d.* at Cadiz, in 1809: she *d.* in 1844.
II. Catherine, *m.* to the late Thomas de Saumarez, attorney-general of Guernsey.
III. Ann, *m.* to Daniel de Lisle.
IV. Mary, *m.* to Thomas Andros, Esq., a descendant of Sir Edmund Andros.

Sir Peter *m.* 2ndly, in 1796, Emilia, dau. of Elisha Tupper, but by her he had no issue. He *d.* in 1821.

Arms—Arg., three triple-turreted towers, sa.
Motto—Dominus fortissima turris.
Seat—Havilland Hall, Guernsey.

HAVILAND OF CAMBRIDGE.

HAVILAND, JOHN, Esq., M.D., of Ditton Hall, co. Cambridge, regius professor of physic, professor of anatomy, and fellow of St. John's College, Cambridge, *b.* in 1785; *s.* to the estate at the decease of his father; *m.* 31 March, 1819, Louisa, youngest dau. and co-heir of the late Rev. George Pollen, of Little Bookham manor house, co. Surrey, and had issue,

I. JOHN, in holy orders, vicar of Pampesford, co. Cambridge, *m.* in 1846, Harriett, 3rd dau. of the Marchese di Spineto, the only surviving member of the Neapolitan branch of the Doria family.
II. George-Edward. III. Henry-James.
IV. Francis-Gregory. V. Arthur-Coles.

Lineage.—JAMES DE HAVILLAND, Esq. sworn a jurat of the Royal Court in 1516, lineally descended from Le Sieur Thomas de Havilland, so distinguished at the recovery of Mont Orgueil, in Jersey, *temp.* EDWARD IV., was grandfather of

CHRISTOPHER DE HAVILLAND, who settled at Poole, in Dorsetshire, early in the reign of ELIZABETH. He *m.* Amy, only dau. and heiress of John Mann, Esq. of that place, and by her had issue; MATTHEW, alderman and many times mayor of Bristol; and John. The 2nd son,

JOHN HAVILLAND, Esq. of Charlinch Hall, co. Somerset, *m.* Elizabeth, dau. of Richard Everard, Esq., and by her had issue. The elder son,

ROBERT HAVILLAND, was father of

MATTHEW HAVILAND, Esq. of Goathurst Place, a Cavalier officer. He *m.* Lucretia, a co-heiress, and had issue,

JOHN, of whom hereafter.
Matthew, of Wellisford House.
William, a captain in the army, who served with honour during the revolutionary war of 1688, in Ireland, where he *m.* and left an only son,
  WILLIAM HAVILAND, Esq. of Penn, co. Bucks, lieut.-general and colonel of the 45th. He *d.* 16 Sept. 1784, and left issue, by Mary, dau. of Thomas Dodge, Esq. of co. Meath, Ireland, a dau., Mary, *m.* in 1785, to Samuel-Ruxton Fitzherbert, Esq. of Swinnerton, co. Meath, and a son,
    WILLIAM, of Penn, co. Bucks, lieut.-col. of the 45th, *m.* a niece of the great statesman, Edmund Burke; *d.* at Martinico, leaving an only son
      THOMAS HAVILAND BURKE, Esq. of Penn, co. Bucks, and of Lincoln's Inn, whose son and heir is the present EDMUND HAVILAND BURKE, Esq.

The elder son,

JOHN HAVILAND, Esq. of Gundenham, *b.* in 1658, *m.* Joan, dau. of Alexander Webber, Esq. of co. Somerset, *d.* 22 July, 1746, and left issue,

EDWARD HAVILAND, Esq., 5th son, *b.* in 1692, *m.* 12 Dec. 1718, Mary, dau. of C. Clotworthy, Esq. of Clotworthy, co. Somerset, and by her he left, at his death, 1 Oct, 1783, a son and successor,

JOHN HAVILAND, Esq. of Gundenham, *b.* 3 Jan. 1720, who *s.* his cousin, Mary Haviland. He *m.* Mary, dau. of Walter Prior, Esq., and *d.* 14 March, 1786 (will proved 2 April of the same year) leaving issue,

JOHN HAVILAND, Esq. of Gundenham, *b.* in 1754, who *m.* Mary, dau. and co-heir of Samuel Glover, Esq. of Dunham, Notts, by whom he left at his decease, in 1817, an only son, DR. HAVILAND, of Cambridge.

Arms—Arg., three towers, triple towered, sa.
Crest—A cubit arm, in armour, or, grasping a battle-axe, ppr.
Motto—Dominus fortissima turris.
Estates—In the counties of Somerset and Cambridge.
Residence—Cambridge.

HAWKESWORTH OF FOREST.

HAWKESWORTH, JOHN, Esq. of Forest, Queen's County, *b.* 28 Aug. 1801; *m.* 1st, 29 Sept. 1827, Henrietta Magan, who *d.* without issue, 7 April, 1829, dau. of Arthur Magan, Esq. of Clonearl, King's County, and Georgina his wife, co-heiress (with her sister, Eliza-Anne, wife of Charles Henry, Lord Castle Coote) of the Very Rev. Dean Tilson, of Eagle Hill, co. Kildare, and Cork Abbey, co. Wicklow He *m.* 2ndly, 1 Sept. 1834, Florentina, dau. of John Walmesley, Esq. of the Hall of Ince, Lancashire, by his second marriage with Ellen, dau. of Richard-Godolphin Long, Esq. of Rood Ashton, Wiltshire; by this marriage he has had issue,

I. JOHN-WALTER, *b.* 13 Feb. 1839.
I. Florence, *d.* 29 July 1841.

Lineage.—This family is a younger branch of one long settled at Hawkesworth Hall, in Yorkshire, and now represented in the elder line by WALTER FAWKES, Esq. of Farnley Hall, Yorkshire, who is descended from Frances, only dau. and heir of Sir Walter Hawkesworth, of Hawkesworth, Bart. upon whose death, in 1735, the baronetcy created in 1678, became extinct.

THOMAS HAWKESWORTH, Esq., in the law (a younger son of William Hawkesworth, of Hawkesworth, Esq., by Rosamond, his wife, dau. of Thomas Lister, of Westby, Esq.), *b.* in 1585, *m.* Mary, dau. of William Hickman, Esq., by whom he had several sons, Walter, the eldest, *d.* before himself, and PETER, the 2nd, *b.* in 1635, *m.* 23 April, 1667, Ann Bayly. He held a commission in the army of King WILLIAM III., who made him a grant of lands in the county of Clare, which grant was not afterwards confirmed. He had three sons and two daus. The eldest son, WALTER, *d.* without issue, in 1720, at Limerick, and the 2nd, THOMAS, *b.* in 1691, *d.* in 1739. He *m.* Ellen, dau. of Capt. Eyre, one of the English officers of the garrison of Limerick, after the revolution of 1688: his eldest son, Thomas, *d. unm.*, the 2nd,

JOHN HAWKESWORTH, Esq., J.P., *b.* Aug. 1730, *m.* 10 May, 1773, Jane, dau. of John Cunningham, Esq., and by her, who *d.* 14 Sept. 1773, had issue, JOHN, his heir; and Thomas, rector of Kilmane, in the diocese of Killaloe, and vicar-general of Tuam, *m.* Miss Fitzgerald, but *d. s. p.* Feb. 1841. The eldest son and heir,

JOHN HAWKESWORTH, Esq. of Forest, J.P. and deputy-governor, *b.* 3 June, 1775; *m.* 23 May, 1799, Ellen, dau. of Richard Steele, Esq., and by her (who *d.* 2 May, 1838) had issue,

JOHN, now of Forest.
Richard, J.P. of the Queen's County, *b.* 28th May, 1808; *m.* Caroline, daughter of the Rev. John Tidd Moore, of Lamberton Park, Queen's County, eldest son of the Right

Hon. Arthur Moore, and has issue two sons, John, *b.* 1 April, 1852; and Richard, *b.* March, 1854.

Thomas, of East Stoke, Somersetshire, *b.* 29 June, 1806; *m.* 28 June, 1831, Sarah Frances, co-heiress with her sister, Mrs. Fyler, of their father, Andrew Bain, Esq. of Heffleton, Dorsetshire, and of his wife, Elizabeth, co-heiress with her sister, Sarah, wife of Sir Eyre Coote, of West Park, Hampshire, of John Rodbard, Esq. of East Stoke, Somersetshire, and has issue one son and two daughters,

John-William-Bain, *b.* 19 Sept. 1834.
Frances. Caroline.

Jane, *m.* 18 February, 1834, Rev. William Truell, second son of Rev. Dr. Truell, of Clonmannon, co. of Wicklow.

Mary, *m.* 31 Oct. 1835, Rev. Nathaniel Bond, of the Grange, Dorsetshire.

Mr. Hawkesworth *d.* 25 April, 1824.

Arms—Sa., three falcons, close, ppr.
Seat—Forest, Queen's Co.

HAWKINS OF THE GAER.

HAWKINS, HENRY-MONTONNIER, Esq. of The Gaer, co. Monmouth, J.P., *b.* 17 Sept. 1805; *m.* 1st, 17 Feb. 1835, Jane, only dau. of James Fenwicke, Esq. of Longwitton Hall, co. Northumberland, and had by her, who *d.* at Ross, co. Hereford, 5 Dec. 1835, a dau.,

Jane Henrietta.

He *m.* 2ndly, 14 Jan. 1851, Lucy, youngest dau. of David Lambe, Esq., youngest son of Lacon Lambe, Esq. of Henwood, co. Hereford, and has a son,

HENRY MONTONNIER, *b.* 21 Nov. 1851.

Lineage.—The HAWKINSES are a family of great antiquity in the co. of Kent; the name being local from the parish of Hawking, in the hundred of Folkestone, written in the time of the Saxons, "Hawkyngge. The first of the name on record is Osbert de Hawking, *temp.* HENRY II.; and, in EDWARD III.'s reign the Hawkinses took up their residence at Nash Court, in the parish of Boughton-under-Bleane, co. Kent, and in the parish church are still to be seen some of the monuments. The family resided at Nash Court till the year 1800, when Thomas Hawkins, of Nash Court, Esq., died, and the estate became the property of his four daus. as co-heirs. Being of the Roman Catholic persuasion, they suffered greatly at different times. The house of Nash was scandalously plundered by some of the neighbourhood, in 1715, during the ferment the nation was thrown into on account of the rebellion in Scotland, when the furniture, pictures, and writings of the estate were burnt, and an excellent library of books, and plate carried off and never heard of afterwards. They experienced great losses at different periods, when younger members of the family were obliged to quit Kent and become located in other counties; one branch settled about 1554 in Cornwall, another in Somersetshire, from which Sir John Cæsar Hawkins, Bart., and a third was established in Wales; from the latter was descended

HENRY HAWKINS, Esq. of Mount Street, Grosvenor Square, London, *b.* in 1712, *m.* 19 Nov. 1742, Margaret, dau. of Anthony Montonnier, Esq. of Llanedarn, co. Glamorgan, and sister and heir of Anthony Montonnier, Esq. of Newport, co. Monmouth. By this lady, who was buried at Newport, 18 Sep. 1785, aged 69, he had issue,

James, *b.* 6 Jan. 1746, *d.* in New York in 1780.
HENRY-MONTONNIER, of whom presently.
Mary-Catherine, *b.* 15 October, 1744; *d. unm.* 14 Oct. 1816.
Margaret, *b.* 15 May, 1749; *d.* Feb. 1787, aged 37.

Mr. Hawkins *d.* 20 May, 1749, aged 37, from a fall from his horse whilst riding in Hyde Park. The 2nd son,

HENRY MONTONNIER HAWKINS, Esq. of Newport, co. Monmouth, *b.* 10 Dec. 1747, *m.* 4 April, 1767, Florence, 3rd dau. and co-heir of William Seys, Esq. of The Gaer, in the parish of St. Woollos, co. Monmouth, who was high-sheriff for the county in 1738, and lineally descended from Roger Seys, Esq. of Boverton, co. Glamorgan, attorney-general of all Wales, *temp.* Queen ELIZABETH. By this lady, who was bapt. 12 Jan. 1740, and *d.* 2 April, 1802, he had issue one only child, viz.,

ANTHONY MONTONNIER, of whom presently.

Mr. Hawkins *d.* at Newport, 12 May, 1814, aged sixty-six, and was *s.* by his only son,

ANTHONY MONTONNIER HAWKINS, Esq., M.D., of The Gaer, co. Monmouth, *b.* 19 Feb. 1771, *m.* 26 Oct. 1800, Jane, only surviving child and heir of William Nicholl, Esq. of Tredunnock, co. Monmouth, who was high-sheriff for the county in 1775 (*see Nicholl of Tredunnock*), by whom he had issue thirteen children,

William, *b.* 4 October, 1801, *d.* at Sidmouth, co. Devon, 28 April, 1815.
Henry-Montonnier, *b.* 22 Sept. 1804, *d.* 28 March, 1805.
HENRY-MONTONNIER, his heir.
Anthony-Nicholl, *b.* 18 Nov. 1807, *d.* 6 March, 1808.
Anthony-Nicholl, of the Middle Temple, barrister-at-law, *b.* 14 April, 1809.
Charles, F.R.C.S., *b.* 29 May, 1812.
Robert-Ralph-Augustus, M.A. of Trinity College, Cambridge, and of Lincoln's Inn, barrister-at-law, *b.* 18 April, 1814.
Jane-Anna, *b.* 15 August, 1802, *d.* 15 March, 1808.
Jane-Frances.
Maria, *b.* 29 August, 1810, *d.* Sept., 1811.
Florence-Rose, *b.* 19 Feb. 1816, *d. unm.* 25 April, 1841.
Harriet-Elizabeth, *b.* 1818, *d.* the same year.
Katherine-Eugenia.

Dr. Hawkins *d.* at his house in Upper Brook Street, Grosvenor Square, London, 22 July, 1838, aged sixty-two, and was *s.* by his eldest surviving son, the present HENRY MONTONNIER HAWKINS, Esq.

Arms—Argent, on a saltier, sable, five fleur-de-lis, or, quartering, sable, a chevron between three spear-heads, argent, imbrued gules, for Seys, of the Gaer, with numerous other quarterings.
Crest—On a mount, vert, a hind lodged, or.
Motto—Toujours prêt.
Seat—The Gaer House, near Newport, Monmouthshire. The present house was modernised by the late Anthony Montonnier Hawkins, Esq., M.D., the old mansion having been built by Alexander Seys, Esq., in Queen Elizabeth's reign. It is situated near a Roman fort: the Welsh for a fort being Gaer, gave the name to the estate.

HAWKINS OF MIDDLESEX.

HAWKINS, CHARLES-SIDNEY, Esq. of Cantlowes, co. Middlesex, D.L., M.A., *b.* 16 Oct. 1817; *m.* 30 Oct. 1844, Thomasine, eldest dau. of the Rev. J.-G. Maddison.

Lineage.—The first person of this family of whom anything is known is ANDREW HAWKINS, Esq., who was resident at Nash Court, *temp.* EDWARD III. He *m.* Joan de Nash, by whom he had issue, two sons, Richard and John. From him descended

JOHN HAWKINS, Esq. of Tavistock, Devon, who *m.* Joan, dau. of William Amydas, Esq. of Launceston, Cornwall, by whom he was father of

WILLIAM HAWKINS, Esq. of Plymouth, who *m.* Joan, dau. of William Trelawny, Esq. of Cornwall, and granddau. of Sir John Trelawny, descendant of Edwin, who held the lordship of Trelawny, *temp.* EDWARD the Confessor; by her he had issue, a son,

SIR JOHN HAWKINS, *b.* in 1520, admiral and treasurer of the navy, *temp.* Queen ELIZABETH. He *d.* at Porto Rico, 21 Nov. 1595, having been three times elected member of parliament. Sir John *m.* the dau. of — Gunson, Esq., and by her was father of

ADMIRAL SIR RICHARD HAWKINS, who also distinguished himself. He was the sixth person that passed the Straits of Magellan. He *d.* suddenly, in 1622, being seized with apoplexy, while at the privy council. His widow, the Lady Judith, survived him seven years; by her he had two sons and three daus., 1 JOHN; 2 Richard; 1 Margaret; 2 Joan; and 3 Mary. The eldest son,

JOHN HAWKINS, Esq., by Hester, his wife, had four sons, 1 Robert, *d.* in 1644; 2 John, *b.* in 1639, *d.* in 1642; 3 JOHN, *b.* in 1643; and, 4 William, *b.* in 1644. The 3rd son,

JOHN HAWKINS, Esq., *m.* Elizabeth, dau. of — Phillips, Esq. of Herefordshire, and was *s.* by his son,

JOHN HAWKINS, Esq., who *m.* Elizabeth, dau. of Thomas Gwatkin, Esq. of Townhope Herefordshire, and dying in 1771, was *s.* by his youngest and only surviving son,

SIR JOHN HAWKINS, *b.* in 1719, author of the *Science and Practice of Music*, published in 1776, in 5 vols. 4to. Sir John Hawkins was for many years a magistrate and chairman of the quarter sessions of Middlesex, and was knighted for his conduct in his magisterial capacity. He *m.* Sidney, second dau. of Peter Storer, Esq. of Cantlowes, and Ashford, in Middlesex, who, on the death of her brother, Peter Storer, jun., Esq., became one of his co-heiresses. By her he had issue. Sir John *d.* 21 May, 1789, and was *s.* by his son,

JOHN-SIDNEY HAWKINS, Esq., F.S.A., *b.* 14 Jan. 1758, the author of *The History of the Origin and Establishment of*

Gothic Architecture, published in 1813, and of other works; also the editor of the Latin play of *Ignoramus*. He *m.* Emily, dau. of M. Mackenzie, Esq., by whom he had issue,

CHARLES-SIDNEY, his heir.
Emily-Louisa, *b.* 5 Nov. 1825.

Mr. Hawkins *d.* 12 Aug. 1842, and was *s.* by his son, the present CHARLES-SIDNEY HAWKINS, Esq. of Cantlowes.

Arms—Quarterly: 1st, and 4th, sable, on a point, wavy, a lion, passant, or, in chief, three besants, on a canton, or, a scallop, between two palmers' staves, sa., for HAWKINS; 2nd and 3rd, arg., three storks, passant, for STORER.
Crest—A demi-Moor in his proper costume, bound and captive, with annulets on his arms and ears, or.
Motto—Nil æquo plus.
Seat—Cantlowes, Middlesex.

HAWKINS OF ALRESFORD HALL.

HAWKINS, WILLIAM-WARWICK, Esq. of Alresford Hall, Essex, J.P. and D.L., M.P. for the borough of Colchester, *b.* 11 March, 1816; *m.* 11th May, 1842, Jane-Harriet, youngest dau. of Francis Smythies, Esq. of "The Turrets," Colchester.

Lineage.—In 1611, we find the manor of Alresford held by William Tabor, doctor of civil law, whose only dau. and heiress conveyed it by marriage to John Browne, Esq. By him it was sold to JOHN HAWKINS, Esq. of Braintree, who left the estate by will, bearing date 1633, to his son, John Hawkins, Esq., whose only dau. and heiress, Christian, *m.* Sir John Dawe, Bart. of Lyons Boking, Essex. By Sir John, the property was divided and sold, partly to Benjamin Field, Esq. of London. Eventually the principal portions of the estate and manor were repurchased and leased by the late

WILLIAM HAWKINS, Esq. of Colchester. This gentleman *m.* 11 April, 1815, Mary-Anne, dau. of John Warwick, Esq., and by her (who *d.* 19 Nov. 1834) had issue,

WILLIAM-WARWICK, M.P., now of Alresford.
John-Alfred, deceased.
Charles-Henry, *m.* Sarah-Jane, dau. of John Bawtree, Esq. of Abberton, Essex.
George-Mason, *m.* Emma, dau. of Rev. I. Reeve, rector of Raydon, Suffolk.
Thomas-Cooper. Frederick-Parker.
Septimus-Moore, capt. 97th regt., *m.* Harriet Lavinia, dau. of the late Col. Dennie, A.D.C. to H.M., C.B., which marriage was dissolved by Act of Parliament, 1852.
Octavius, deceased.

Arms—Sa. a lion passant, or, on waves of the sea, ppr., in chief, three bezants.
Crest—A demi-Moor, in his proper colour bound and captive, with annulets on his arms and ears, or
Seat—Alresford Hall, near Colchester.

HAWLEY OF WEST GREEN HOUSE.

HAWLEY, WILLIAM-HENRY-TOOVEY, Esq. of West Green House, co. Hants, *b.* 4 Dec. 1793; *m.* 12 April, 1821, Elizabeth-Mary, eldest dau. and co-heir of John Broughton, Esq. of Blackwater House, admiral of the red. Mr. Hawley is a magistrate and deputy-lieut. of Hampshire, and one of the Assistant Poor Law Commissioners.

Lineage.—HENRY HAWLEY, Esq., lieut.-general in the army, stated to have been grandson of Lord Hawley, a peer in the reign of CHARLES I., *m.* Anne Toovey, and was father of

CAPTAIN WILLIAM HENRY-TOOVEY HAWLEY, who *m.* Jane Baker, and was father of

HENRY-WILLIAM-TOOVEY HAWLEY, Esq., lieut.-col. of the 1st king's dragoon-guards, who *m.* in 1793, Catherine, dau. of George Jepson, Esq. of Lincoln, and had issue,

WILLIAM-HENRY-TOOVEY, present representative.
Robert-Toovey, late 1st dragoon-guards, *m.* Louisa, only dau. of John-Hanbury Beaufoy, Esq. of Upton Gray, co. Hants, and has issue four sons and four daus., viz., Henry-John, *m.* and has issue; Robert-Beaufoy major 89th regt.; Trevor; and William-Hanbury, capt. 14th regt.; Louisa, *m.* to the Rev. George Hustler, rector of Appleton; Julia-Georgiana, Ellen-Margaret, and Maria-Annabella.
John-Toovey, in holy orders, rector of Eversley, Hants.
Catherine-Toovey, *m.* to John Breedon, Esq. of Delabere, co. Berks.
Jane-Toovey, deceased.

Arms—Vert, a saltier, engr., arg.
Crest—A winged thunderbolt, ppr.
Motto—Et suivez moy.
Seat—West Green House, co. Hants.

HAY OF DUNSE CASTLE.

HAY, WILLIAM, Esq. of Dunse Casele, co. Berwick, J.P. and D.L., col. of the militia, and convener of Berwickshire, *b.* 29 Feb. 1788; *m.* 13 May, 1816, Mary, dau. of John Bradstreet Garstin, Esq. of Harold House, co. Bedford, and has issue,

I. WILLIAM-JAMES, *b.* 1827.
II. Alexander-Charles, *b.* 1829.
III. Robert-Mordaunt, *b.* 1833.
I. Mary, *m.* 1840, to G. Home Drummond, Esq., jun. of Blair Drummond, and *d.* 4 April, 1855.
II. Christian-Henrietta.
III. Anne-Elizabeth, *m.* 1855, to Robert-Graham Moir, Esq. of Leckie, co. Stirling.
IV. Cordelia, *m.* 28 June, 1848, to J. B. Yonge, Esq. of Puslinch, co. Devon.
V. Janet-Matilda *m.* 1856, to Charles-Thomas-Constantine, eldest son of John Grant, Esq. of Kilgraston, co. Perth.
VI. Harriet-Scott.

Lineage.—ROBERT HAY, Esq. of Drumelzier, Whittinghame and Linplum, *b.* 18 April, 1731, for thirty-eight years in the East India Company's civil service, was son of Alexander Hay, Esq., of Drumelzier and Whittinghame, by Anne, his wife, dau. of Alexander, 5th Lord Blantyre, and grandson of the Hon. William Hay (son of John, 1st earl of Tweeddale), by Elizabeth, his wife, dau. of Alexander Seton, 1st viscount of Kingston. He *m.* 7 Feb. 1787, Janet, eldest dau. of James Erskine, Esq. of Cardross, and by her, who *d.* 29 Aug. 1808, had issue,

WILLIAM, now of Dunse Castle.
James, of Linplum, *b.* 2 May, 1790, *d.* at Ketton Hall, Lincolnshire, 2 Dec. 1819.
Alexander, of Nunraw, *b.* 6 Sept. 1796, killed at Waterloo, 18 June, 1815.
Robert, of Linplum, *b.* 6 Jan. 1799, *m.* in 1836, Kalitza Psarakée, a Greek lady, and has issue,
Robert-James-Alexander, *b.* 14 May, 1840.
James-William, *b.* 5 Aug. 1841.
Kalitza-Janet. Henrietta-Maria.
Charles-Erskine, of Nunraw, *b.* 20 Oct. 1801, *d.* at Paris, 5 May, 1827.
Christian.
Henrietta, *m.* to Charles-Alexander Moir, Esq. of Leckie, and *d.* 1854.
Anne. Elizabeth-Seton.

Mr. Hay *d.* 21 Aug. 1807.

Arms—1st and 4th, az., three cinquefoils, arg.; 2nd and 3rd, gu., three bars, erm. Over all on an escutcheon, arg., three escutcheons, gu.
Crest—A goat's head erased arg.
Motto—Spare nought.
Seat—Dunse Castle, Berwickshire.

HAY OF HOPES.

HAY, WILLIAM, Esq. of Hopes, co. Haddington, J.P. and D.L., *b.* 9 Nov. 1774; *m.* 23 Sept. 1820, Frances-Anne, dau. of Robert Ogle, Esq. of Eglingham, co. Northumberland, and has issue,

I. JOHN-CHARLES, 60th Bengal infantry, *b.* 5 Sept. 1821.
II. William-Augustus, Bengal civil service, *b.* 8 June, 1823, *d.* 1843.
I. Frances-Amelia, *m.* 1850, Cavaliere Luigi dei Frescobaldi, son of Marchese Frescobaldi, of Florence.
II. Caroline.

Lineage.—JOHN HAY, Esq. of Hopes (son of the Hon. Edmund Hay, of Hopes, youngest son of John, 1st earl of Tweeddale), *m.* 9 March, 1698, Margaret, dau. of Sir James Holburn, of Menstrie, co. Fife, and sister of Lady Clerk and Lady Inglis, and had issue,

John, *b.* 1702, *d. s. p.*
CHARLES, of whom presently.
William, *b.* 1707.
James, condemned to be executed 1745, for being out with Charles-Edward, but pardoned.
David. Holbourne.

The 3rd son,

CHARLES HAY, Esq. of Hopes, *b.* 1704, who *m.* 10 March, 1730, Christian Ross; and their son,

JOHN HAY, Esq. of Hopes, *b.* 1732, *m.* 2 Nov. 1761, Margaret, dau. of — Reid, Esq. of Georgie, and had issue,

I. James, *b.* 1764, *m.* 1788, and *d.* 1821, leaving a son,
William Falconer Hay, 3rd Bombay lt. inf., who is *m.* and has two sons, twins,
John. Edward.

II. Charles, b. 1766, father of Charles Crossland Hay.
III. John, b. 1770, m. Miss Anne Walker and had issue,
1 John.
2 Edward, Bengal infantry, killed at Cabul.
IV. WILLIAM, now of Hopes.
V. Robert, (Capt.,) m. Miss Leonora Nutting and had issue,
1 John-Monckton, Bengal Civil Service.
2 William, Bengal artillery.
VI. Edward, colonel commanding H.E.I.C.S. Depot at Chatham, b. 1784.
I. Christian, m. to Lieut.-Gen. Hardyman.
II. Frances, m. to Capt. Nelson.
III. Isabella, m. to Major Brougham.
IV. Catherine, m. to Capt. Hardyman.

Mr. Hay sold Hopes to his son William.

Arms and *Crest*—*See* HAY *of Dunse Castle.*
Motto—Spare nought.
Seat—Hopes, co. East Lothian, or Haddingtonshire.

HAY OF LEYS.

HAY-BALFOUR, DAVID, Esq. of Leys, co. Perth, and of Randerston, in Fifeshire, s. his father in 1790.

Lineage.—WILLIAM DE HAYA, a younger son of David de Haya, and brother of Gilbert Hay, ancestor of the noble house of Erroll, obtained from his brother Gilbert, in 1255, a grant of Leys. He was grandfather of

EDMUND DE HAYA, of Leys, an eminent patriot, who distinguished himself in favour of King ROBERT I. His great-great-grandson,

EDMUND HAY, of Leys, to whom William, earl of Errol, granted a charter of confirmation in 1451, had two sons, EDMUND, his heir; and Peter, from whom descend the families of KINNOUL, Melginch, Pitfour, Seggieden, &c. The elder son,

EDMUND HAY, of Leys, who had seisine of his estate in 1496, was ancestor of

GEORGE HAY-BALFOUR, Esq., b. in 1682, who m. his cousin Mary, dau. of JAMES BALFOUR, Esq. of Randerston, in Fifeshire, and thus acquired that estate. By this lady he had issue,

PETER, his heir.
Catherine, b. in 1723, m. to George Clephan, Esq. of Carslogie.
Mary, b. in 1727, m. to Sir Robert Gordon, of Gordonstown.
Elizabeth, b. in 1729, m. to — Sinclair, Esq.

The son and successor,

PETER HAY, Esq. of Leys, b. in 1717, was served heir to his father in 1752. He m. in 1739, Elisabeth, dau. of David Scott, Esq. of Scottstarvit, by Lucy, dau. of Sir Robert Gordon, of Gordonstown, and had issue,

DAVID, } JOHN, } successive proprietors.
Lindsay, b. in 1743, m. to John Dalziel, Esq. of Lingo, and had issue.
Catherine, m. to Henry Butter, Esq. of Pitlochrie, and had issue.
Elizabeth, m. to Peter Stewart, Esq. of Collarnie, and had issue.
Lucy, m. to Patrick Moncrieff, Esq. of Reidie, eldest son of Col. George Moncrieff, of Reidie, and had issue.

The eldest son,

DAVID HAY-BALFOUR, Esq. of Leys and Randerston, in 1757, was served heir to his father in the lands of Leys, and to his great-grandfather, James Balfour, of Randerston. He d. without issue, in 1760, and was s. by his brother,

JOHN HAY-BALFOUR, Esq. of Leys and Randerston, who m. in 1777, Catherine, dau. of Col. George Moncrieff, of Reidie, in Fifeshire, and had issue,

DAVID, his heir of Leys.
Peter, late a captain of the 18th dragoons.
Jane, m. to James Paterson, Esq. of Carpow, and has issue.

Mr. Hay-Balfour d. in 1790.

Arms—Quarterly: 1st and 4th, erm., three escutcheons, gu., for HAY of Leys; 2nd and 3rd, or, on a chev., sa., between two trefoils, in chief, and a garb, in base, vert, banded, of the first, an otter's head, erased, arg., for BALFOUR of Randerston.
Crest—A Lowland Scots countryman demi-figure, vested, grey, waistcoat, gu., bonnet, az., and feather, ppr., bearing on his right shoulder an ox-yoke, ppr., broken at one extremity.
Supporters—(Granted, as the patent states, in respect of the great antiquity of the family.) Two Danish soldiers of the tenth century, habited in chain mail, on their head a helmet or skull-cap, and holding in their exterior hands javelins, all ppr., at the top of each javelin a peunencle, gu., and on their arms a round shield, az., bordered and spiked, or, their tunic or under-vest of orange colour reaching to the knee, their mantles, vert, fastened on each shoulder by a round buckle, gold, and half-boots or buskins turned down, of a buff colour.
Motto—Primus è stirpe, in allusion to this family being the immediate younger branch of the noble House of HAY *of Errol*.
Seats—Leys and Randerston.

HAY OF SEGGIEDEN.

HAY, JAMES, Esq. of Seggieden, co. Perth, D.L., b. 5 May, 1771; m. 1st, in 1801, Margaret, dau. of John Richardson, Esq. of Pitfour, by whom (who d. 14 March, 1819) he had,

I. JAMES-RICHARDSON, b. 29 Dec. 1802, a captain in the army, half-pay, unattached, a deputy-lieut., who inherited the estate of Aberargie, in Perthshire, on the decease of his mother. He m. 7 Feb. 1833, Margaret-Lothian-Douglas, youngest dau. of the late Lieut. Col. Thomas Inglis, and had a dau., CHARLOTTE-ELIZABETH, who inherits Seggieden.
II. John, lieut. R.N. III. Thomas, M.D. of London.
IV. Patrick, 42nd native infantry, Bengal.
V. William, of Edinburgh.
I. Barbara. II. Jane.

He m. 2ndly, in 1821, Christina-Craigie, dau. of James Stewart, Esq. of Urrard.

Lineage.—JAMES HAY, Esq. of Pitfour (8th of that house, in a direct male line from PETER HAY, 2nd son of Edmund Hay, of Leys, living *temp.* JAMES III.), m. 1st, Jean, dau. of Sir Andrew Hay, of Keillor, and had, with a dau., a son,

JOHN, who s. at Pitfour, whose grandson, JOHN HAY, sold Pitfour to John Richardson, Esq. The present representative of the Great House of Hay, of Pitfour, is WILLIAM EDMUND HAY, Esq., H.E.I.C.S.

James Hay m. 2ndly, Anne, dau. of Sir George Preston, Bart. of Valleyfield, and widow of Oliphant, of Gask, by whom he had another son,

PATRICK HAY, Esq., who m. Barbara, 3rd dau. of John Nairn, Esq. of Seggieden, by Elizabeth Fowler, his wife. She (Barbara) eventually succeeded her sister as heiress of Seggieden, and entailed the property on the only son of her marriage, viz.,

JOHN HAY, Esq. of Seggieden. This gentleman m. Lillias, youngest dau. of John Hay, Esq. of Pitfour, by Mary, the heiress of Ross, and had, with several other children, a son and successor,

JAMES HAY, Esq. of Seggieden, b. 17 May, 1739, who m. 15 Aug. 1770, Jean, dau. of the Rev. James Donaldson, minister of Glammis, and left, at his decease, 23 March, 1781, an only son and successor, the present JAMES HAY, Esq. of Seggieden.

Arms—Quarterly: 1st and 4th, arg., three inescutcheons, gu., within a bordure, chequy, of the second and first, for HAY; and for difference, in the centre of the quarters, a bull's head, couped, gu., second and third, party per pale, sa. and arg., on a chaplet, four quatrefoils, all counter, changed, in the centre, chief, a martlet, arg., for difference, for NAIRN *of Seggieden*.
Crest—A demi-countryman, ppr., holding over his shoulders an oxen-yoke, or, the boughs, gu.
Motto—Diligentia fit ubertas.
Supporters—Dexter, a countryman, ppr., holding over his shoulders an oxen-yoke, or, boughs, gu.; sinister, a talbot, ppr.
Seats—Seggieden, Perth, and Killicranky Cottage, in the Pass of Killicranky.

HAY OF RANNES.—(*See* LEITH-HAY.)

HAYMAN OF MYRTLE GROVE AND SOUTH ABBEY.

HAYMAN, THE REV SAMUEL, of South Abbey, Youghal, co. Cork, B.A. (and formerly fellow commoner) of Trinity College, Dublin, b. 27 July, 1818; m. at St. Anne's Church, Belfast, 26 Sept. 1854, Emily, dau. (by Henrietta his wife, dau. and coheiress of Samuel Jackson, Esq. of Stormount, co. Down) of the late Rev. Mark Cassidi, M.A., Chancellor of Kilfenora and incumbent of Newtown-ards.

Lineage.—The family of HEYMAN, or HAYMAN (for it has been spelled both ways), is of Norman descent; and their genealogical roll embraces a period of more than nine centuries.

ROLLO, the Sea King, by his marriage with Gisla, dau. of CHARLES the Simple, king of France, left issue at his death, in 917, two sons, WILLIAM LONGSWORD, Duke of Normandy (through whom derived WILLIAM the Conqueror of England, and the English kings), and

ROBERT, created Earl of Corbeil; in direct succession from whom was

HAIMON DENTATUS, 6th earl of Corbeil and baron of Tourney and Granville. He was slain at the battle of Val des Dunes, near Caen, in 1037, leaving (along with two daus., Crespina, wife of Grimaldus, prince of Monaco, and Gerletta, wife of William, duke of Aquitaine), four sons, who all accompanied the duke of Normandy in his English invasion of 1066,

ROBERT FITZ-HAMON, or (as Thierry writes it) FITZ-AYMON, the conqueror of South Wales.
Haimon, surnamed in the Domesday Survey, *Dapifer*.
Richard, ancestor of the GRANVILLE family.
CREUQUERE, or CREVE-CŒUR, Lord of Chatham, whose line we follow.

Créve-cœur-en-Ange, in the arrondissement of Lisieux, gave its title to the earl of Corbeil's youngest son, whose Christian name seems, from the family records, to have been HUGO, or HUGH. In the Battel Abbey roll he is called "Creuquere;" and he appears in an old French chronicle, relative to the battle of Hastings, as "Le Sire de Crévecœur." From him two lines proceeded; one, that of the barons of Redburn, benefactors of the priory of Bolington, was seated in Lincolnshire; the other line, established in Kent, had for its chief,

ROBERT DE CREPITO CORDE, or DE CREVE-CŒUR, who, in 1119, founded the priory of Black Canons, at Leeds, in Kent, the manor of which (along with the hundred of Chatham) he inherited from his uncle, Sir Robert Fitz-Hamon. Here, also, during the feud between the king and Odo, bishop of Baieux, he erected a strong castle, to preserve the district confided to him by John Fynes, constable of Dover and warden of the Cinque Ports. He received, at the same time, many of Haimon Dapifer's possessions, and had his lands erected into a barony, called by distinction, "Baronia de Créveguer," consisting of five knights' fees. The head of this barony was Chatham, for which reason his descendants generally wrote themselves *Domini de Cëtham*. His great-grandson,

HAIMON DE CREVE-CŒUR, was lord of Ightham, in the reign of King JOHN (now the property of the JAMES family. See that name). This, and his other landed possessions, he bequeathed to his son,

HAIMON DE CREVE-CŒUR, called likewise Sir Hamo del Blen, from his manor of Bleane. He was also seised of Farleigh, Teston, and Leeds, and the hereditary lordship of Chatham. Of his valorous deeds in Palestine, in the crusade under CŒUR DE LION, an interesting account is given in *Anecdotes of the Aristocracy*, vol. ii. pp. 25, 26. The field of Ascalon cost him his three sons, who successively perished while defending the English banner. He returned to his native land on the truce then made with the Soldan; and *d.* peaceably in 1203, being *s.* by his grandson,

ROBERT HAIMON, who, according to prevailing fashion, converted his patronymic into a surname, and thus led the way to the disuse, and finally to the extinction, of the Norman affix, "de Créve-cœur." He sided with the discontented barons in the reign of HENRY III. and, in 1258, was one of the league, under Simon Montfort, Earl of Leicester, formed against that pusillanimous monarch. His lands were in consequence escheated in 1265, but were (excepting Chatham) restored some years after. Undeterred by this precedent, his son,

ROBERT HAIMON, surnamed "de Créve-cœur," was one of the leaders in the revolt against Gaveston, EDWARD II.'s minion; and, during the temporary triumph of that unhappy monarch, was compelled to surrender his fief of Leeds, which, about 1318, was conveyed by the king, in exchange, to BARTHOLOMEW, LORD DE BADLESMERE. The opposition of the nobles was ultimately successful; and the unfortunate EDWARD was cruelly murdered in Berkeley Castle, 22 Sept. 1327. Omitting five intervening generations, during which the orthography of the name was unsettled, and, by successive owners, was used as "Haimon," "Haymon," and "Hayman," indifferently, we come to

RALPH HEYMAN, or HAYMAN, who, in the reign of HENRY VII. (1485-1509), possessed considerable estates in Kent, and was ancestor of a line that received a baronetcy from CHARLES I., under patent, dated 12 Aug. 1641. (*See* HEYMAN OF SOMERFIELD, *Extinct Baronetcies*). In the list of the Justices of the Peace and their Dwelling Parishes," which Lambard, in his curious *Peregrination of Kent*, originally written in 1570, furnishes, we find the name of "RALPH HAYMAN," in Sellynge, Baylywicke of Shypwey; and among "Such of the Nobilitie and Gentrie as the Heralds recorded in their Visitation, 1574," he mentions "RALPH HAYMAN." He was grandson of the first-mentioned Ralph Hayman. The Somerfield branch subsequently adopted the spelling "Heyman," probably for distinction's sake, but at what period it is difficult to say. Ralph Hayman's very near kinsman, if not son, was

ROBERT, or ROGER HAYMAN, Esq., *b. circ.* 1524, *temp.* HENRY VIII, who, to avoid religious persecution in Queen MARY's reign, fled from Kent, and found refuge in Devonshire. He settled at or near Exeter; and here, *circ.* 1566, he *m.* Joan, 2nd dau. of Walter Yonge, Esq. of Sudburie. By this marriage he had four sons,

I. John, *b. circ.* 1568, an opulent merchant of Minehead, in Somersetshire. He was living anno 16 JACOBI I. (1619), as, in a deed still extant, we find him then purchasing an estate from the Luttrell family. He seems to have *d.* soon after, probably *s. p.*
II. ROBERT, of whom presently.
III. William, of Bristol, who had issue,
 1 Thomas, *d. s. p. ante* 1670.
 2 John, settled in Virginia.
 3 WILLIAM (Sir), mayor of Bristol in 1684, in which year he was knighted at Whitehall, by King JAMES II., *m.* 1 Nov. 1670, Mary, dau. of William Colston, sheriff of Bristol, only surviving sister and heir of EDWARD COLSTON, the philanthropist, by whom, at his death, 1 Aug. 1702, he had issue,
  Sarah, *m.* in 1689, to Thomas Langton, Esq., son of Sir Thomas Langton. She *d. in vitâ patris.*
  Mary, *m.* in 1698, Thomas Edwards, Esq. of Filkins, near Lechlade, co. Gloucester, and had issue,
   Sarah, *m.* to John Pullen, Esq., *s. p.*
   Mary, *m.* in 1723, to FRANCIS, second BARON MIDDLETON (*see Peerage*).
   Sophia, *m.* to Alexander-Ready Colston, Esq. (*see* COLSTON *of Roundway Park.*)
 1 Phillis. 2 Elizabeth.
IV. George, *vivens* 1649, who is believed to have founded a branch in Devonshire.

The 2nd son,

ROBERT HAYMAN, Esq., was *b. circ.* 1570, at Minehead, where he *m. circ.* 1599, Elizabeth [Gibbons?], and by her (who *d.* in 1647) had issue. Mr. Hayman held the commission of captain in the army during the civil wars; and two suits of armour, reputed to have been his, were, until lately, preserved at the old family seat, Bye Farm. He seems to have been occasionally employed in Ireland, and, on the conclusion of hostilities, to have settled there. He was resident at Youghal, co. Cork, 5 Nov. 1651; but appears to have returned to England a year or two afterwards. He *d.* at Minehead, in 1654, being *s.* by his eldest son,

GEORGE HAYMAN, Esq. of Minehead, was *b. circ.* 1600; *m. circ.* 1626, Miss Mary Atkins, of Minehead, and by her (who was buried at Minehead, 4 June, 1685) had issue, George, of Minehead; Simon, of Minehead; Robert, of Minehead; and SAMUEL; and one dau., Joan, *m.* 30 Dec. 1662, to John Ball, Esq. He *d.* at Minehead, 12 Nov. 1670. His younger son,

SAMUEL HAYMAN, Esq. of South Abbey, Youghal, *b.* 17 April, 1636; *m. circ.* 1659, his cousin, Elizabeth, dau. of John Atkin, Esq. of Minehead, and afterwards of Polemore, near Youghal, and by her (who *d.* 22 Feb. 1676-7) he had issue,

JOHN, his heir.
George, of Bye Farm, co. Somerset, ancestor of the HAYMANS *of Bye Farm, and Bilbrook, co. Somerset.*
SAMUEL, of the College, Youghal, of whom hereafter.
Jane, *m.* 1st, 20 July, 1682, to John Vaughan, Esq. of Youghal; and 2ndly, 11 May, 1685, Jasper Lucas, Esq. of the same town.
Frances, bapt. 18 Nov. 1672, *m.* 9 April, 1700, Alderman John Luther,* of Youghal, who *d.* in the year of his mayoralty, 26 Feb. 1709.

He *d.* at Youghal, 23 Dec. 1672, and was *s.* by his eldest son,

JOHN HAYMAN, Esq. of Cloynepriest, M.P. for Youghal for ten years, 1703-1713. He was *b.* in 1664, and lived for some time at his grandfather's seat, Polemore, which was bequeathed to him, and subsequently at Cloynepriest, in its vicinity, a manor which he purchased. Among his English estates were Somerliere, near the village of Bilbrook,

* The LUTHER family, who were kin to the great Reformer, settled in England in the reign of HENRY VIII.

co. Somerset, which he purchased, in 1717, of Sir Hugh Stukeley, Bart.; Parracombe, near Combmartin, co. Devon; and South Hill manor, in the same county. He *m.* in 1687, Hannah, dau. of James Crockford, Esq. of Ellscombe, cousin-german to his brother George's wife, and by her (who *d.* at Minehead, 25 Sept. 1688) had issue an only child,

Atkin, *d.* 11 March, 1688, and was buried with his mother, in the aisle of Minehead Church, where is their gravestone.

Mr. Hayman was among the Protestants attainted by King James's parliament held in Dublin, 7 May, 1689, and was constrained to flee to his relatives in Somersetshire. He *d.* 21 Aug. 1731, and was buried at Cloynepriest, when the representation of the family in Ireland devolved on the issue of his youngest brother,

Samuel Hayman, Esq. of The College, Youghal, bapt. at Youghal, 1 Sept. 1668; *m.* 5 Nov. 1700, Elizabeth, eldest dau. of Richard Paradice, Esq. of Youghal, and by her (who was *b.* 9 Dec. 1681, and *d.* 14 April, 1756) had issue, sixteen children. Of the daus., the eldest, Jane, *m.* 31 Aug. 1732, Valentine Browning, Esq. of Affane; the 2nd, Elizabeth, *m.* her cousin, Samuel Luther, Esq. of Youghal; the 5th, Mary, *m.* John Hayman, Esq.; and the 7th, Hannah, *m.* 1741, Thomas Gimlett, Esq. He *d.* at his seat, The College, Youghal, 2 Dec. 1722, when he was *s.* by his eldest son,

John Hayman, Esq. of The College, Youghal, now called Myrtle Grove, *b.* 10 May, 1702; mayor of Youghal in 1750 and 1751. He *d. unm.* 14 April, 1770, at his seat, Myrtle Grove, and was *s.* by his next surviving brother,

The Rev. Atkin Hayman, A.M., *b.* 11 June, 1714; for eleven years officiating minister of St. Mary's Collegiate Church, Youghal, in 1754, chaplain to the Earl of Hillsborough, and finally vicar of Ballyclogh and Castlemagner, near Mallow, which he retained until his death. In 1742, he had *m.* his cousin, Elizabeth, youngest dau. of the Rev. Walter Atkin, of Leadington, incumbent of Middleton, and vicar-general of the diocese of Cloyne (by Elizabeth Coningsby his wife, of Hampton Court, co. Hereford, cousin to Earl Coningsby), and by her (who *d.* 30 Jan. 1756) had issue. He *m.* 2ndly, 12 Aug. 1757, Elizabeth, dau. of Frank Wilson, Esq. of Youghal, but by that lady (who *d.* 3 Oct. 1776) had no issue. The Rev. Atkin Hayman *d.* 18 April, 1793, and was buried in the chancel of St. Mary's Church, Youghal. His elder surviving son succeeded,

Walter-Atkin Hayman, Esq. of Myrtle Grove, bapt. at Middleton, 30 June, 1750; *m.* 28 July, 1789, Eliza, dau. of Henry White, Esq. of New Ross, co. Tipperary (by his wife, Elizabeth, 3rd dau. of Thomas Maunsell, Esq., M.P. for Kilmallock), who *d. s. p.* 22 Aug. 1800, at Carmarthen, South Wales, on her journey home from the Bristol hot wells. He *d.* at his seat, Myrtle Grove, 5 June, 1816. His only brother,

Samuel Hayman, Esq., M.D., was bapt. at Middleton, 26 Sept. 1753. He *m.* 17 Nov. 1782, Melian, younger dau. and co-heiress of Matthew Jones, Esq., collector of Youghal (by Audriah his wife, 2nd dau. of James Roch, Esq. of Woodbine Hill, co. Waterford, descended from the Lords Roche *of Fermoy*), and by her (who *d.* 25 Feb. 1835) he had issue,

I. Atkin, lieut. R.N., *b.* at Prospect Row, Cork, 17 Sept. 1783. He *m.* 6 Feb. 1813, at Douglas Church, near Cork, Eliza, younger dau. of the late Walter Atkin, Esq. of Leadington, high-sheriff of co. Cork in 1766, (by Mary, his wife, second dau. of George Dunscombe, Esq. of Mount Desert) and by her (who *m.* 2ndly, 17 May, 1821, William-Andrews Lamb, Esq., J.P., of Kilcolman Park, Bandon) left issue, at his death, 25 March, 1817, at Sunday's Well, Cork,

1 Samuel, a posthumous son, *d.* in infancy.
1 Mary-Harriette, *m.* 27 Feb. 1838, her cousin, Sobieski Kildahl, Esq. of Youghal, and *d.* 23 Aug. 1850.
2 Elizabeth, *d. unm.* at Chelsea, 11 Nov. 1852.

II. Matthew, his heir.
I. Elizabeth, *b.* at Prospect Row, Cork, 17 Nov. 1786, *d. unm.* 3 Feb. 1831.

Dr. Hayman *d.* at his seat, Prospect Hill, near Youghal, 20 March, 1834, and was *s.* by his 2nd son,

Matthew Hayman, Esq. of South Abbey, *b.* 28 Dec. 1789; *m.* 22 Jan. 1816, Helen, 2nd dau. of Arundel Hill, Esq. of Doneraile, and by her (who *d.* 27 July, 1850) has had issue,

Samuel, his heir.
Matthew-Jones, major 18th Royal Irish, gallantly distinguished and severely wounded at the siege of Sebastopol.
Arundel-Hill, *b.* 16 Jan. 1832, *d.* 8 Aug. 1836.
Helen-Maria.
Melian-Jones, *m.* 6 Sept. 1851, Alexander Durdin, Esq. of Huntington Castle, co. Carlow.
Elizabeth.
Maria-Lucy-Anne, *m.* 2 June, 1853, Capt. Frank P. Cassidi, late of 16th regt., of Glenbrook, Magherafelt, co. Derry.
Susan.

Mr. Hayman, who is in the commission of the peace for the co. of Cork, represents, through his mother, the ancient family of Jones, of Lloynririd, co. Montgomery.

Arms—Arg., on a chevron, engrailed, az., between three martlets, sa., as many cinquefoils, pierced, or.
Crests—1st, a demi-Moor, full-faced, wreathed round the temples, holding in the dexter hand a rose, slipped and leaved, all ppr.; 2nd, a martlet, as in the arms.
Motto—Cœlum, non Solum.
Residence—South Abbey, Youghal, co. Cork.

HAYNES OF THIMBLEBY LODGE.

Haynes, Robert, Esq. of Thimbleby Lodge, co. York, formerly a magistrate and representative for the department of St. John Barbadoes, *m.* 1st, 25 May, 1815, Sarah Anne, dau. of the Rev. Mr. Payne, of Barbadoes, and by her has issue surviving, Robert, Sarah-Anne, and Jane-Alleyne. He *m.* 2ndly, 26 Sept. 1825, Elizabeth, dau. of Robert Reece, Esq., and by her has issue surviving, viz.; William, Henry-Higginson, Edmund-Lee, Jonathan-Wynyard, Elizabeth, and Caroline-Anne.

Lineage.—This family is one of high respectability, their ancestors having been forced to emigrate to Barbadoes in the time of Cromwell, being loyalists, where they have held landed property, which has descended from father to son ever since, and is now in the possession of Richard Haynes, Esq. The grandfather of the present Mr. Haynes, of Thimbleby Lodge,

Richard Haynes, Esq. of Barbadoes, son of Robert Haynes, Esq., *m.* Anne Elcock, and had issue, Robert, of whom presently; Richard-Downes, deceased; Henry, post-capt. R.N., deceased; Edmund; and Anne-Elcock. The eldest son,

Robert Haynes, Esq., represented the parish of St. John, Barbadoes, for 35 years, during which he acted as a magistrate, and was lieut.-general of militia. He was for several years speaker of the House of Assembly of Barbadoes. He *m.* Thomasine-Anne, dau. of — Clarke, and widow of Nathaniel Barrow, and by her had,

Richard, *m.* Jane-Alleyne Payne, and has issue.
Robert, of Thimbleby Lodge, co. York.
George-Barrow, *m.* Ann Walker Oughterson, and left issue.
William-Clarke, *m.* Margaret Crichton, and *d.* leaving three sons and one dau.
Thomasine, *m.* 1st, to John-Hathersall Pindar, and 2ndly, to Frederick-Christian Lordy, major of infantry, unattached.

Arms—Quarterly: 1st and 4th, arg. three crescents, paly wavy gu. and az.; 2nd and 3rd, gu. two billets arg.
Crest—A stork, wings displayed, ppr., in the beak a serpent of the last.
Seat—Thimbleby Lodge, co. York.

HAYWARD OF QUEDGELEY HOUSE.

Curtis-Hayward, John, Esq. of Quedgeley House, co. Gloucester, J.P. and D.L., *b.* 28 Sept. 1804; *m.* 20 Aug. 1840, Elizabeth, youngest dau. of Benjamin Harrison, Esq. of Clapham Common, Surrey, and has issue,

I. John-Frederick, *b.* 19 Sept. 1842.
II. Arthur-Cecil, *b.* 8 March, 1846.
I. Albinia-Mary.
II. Margaret-Frances.
III. Emily-Lucy.
IV. Isabella-Elizabeth.
V. Catharine-Anne.

Lineage.—William Hayward, Esq., son of Thomas Hayward, Esq., and Susan his wife, dau. of George Shoyle, Esq. of Dymock, co. Gloucester, and grandson of Thomas Hayward, alias Cox, of Forthampton, living in 1690, *m.* Eleanor, dau. of Richard Rogers, Esq. of Dowdeswell, in the same shire, and had issue, three sons and three daus. Mr. Hayward, whose will bears date 1 May, 1694, and was proved in 1697, was *s.* by his son,

William Hayward, Esq. of Quedgeley, *b.* 23 Feb. 1670, who *m.* Margaret, dau. of Major-General Selwyn, of Matson, co. Gloucester, and *d.* in 1709, having had (with a dau., Albinia, *m.* to Thomas Winstone, Esq.) two sons, Thomas, his heir; and John, in holy orders, rector of Withington, who m. in 1740, Bridget, eldest dau. of Richard Southby, Esq. of Carswell, co. Berks, and had a son, Sir Thomas Hayward, of Carswell, (*see family of* Hayward-Southby.) The elder son of William,

Thomas Hayward, Esq. of Quedgeley, m. Mercy, dau. of Charles Parsons, Esq. of Bredon, co. Worcester, and d. in 1782, leaving two sons; Charles, the elder, who d. in 1803; and

William Hayward, Esq. of Quedgeley, who assumed the additional surname of Winstone, on inheriting the property of his uncle. He m. in 1770, Elizabeth, dau. of Gabriel Wayne, Esq. of Frenchay, co. Gloucester, and had, with a son, Thomas, b. in 1771, and d. in 1793, three daus. and co-heirs, Albinia-Frances, of whom presently; Louisa, m. to Capt. Thomas Sykes, R.N.; and Lucy, m. to the Rev. William Forster, vicar of Southpoole, Devon, both deceased. The eldest dau. and eventual heiress,

Albinia-Frances Hayward, m. in 1799, to the Rev. John Adey Curtis, vicar of Bitton, co. Gloucester (son of Thomas Curtis, Esq., F.R.S., by Anne his wife, dau. of John Jobbins, Esq.), and by him, who assumed the surname of Hayward, and d. 1812, had issue,

John, of Quedgeley House.
William-Winstone, in holy orders, b. 1811; m. 1845, Elizabeth-Esther, dau. of the Rev. James Phelps, rector of Alderley, and has three daus., Albinia-Frances; Alice-Elizabeth; and Eleanor-Winstone.
Albinia.
Anne, m. to Harry Nisbet, Esq., Bengal Civil Service.
Lucy, m. 1847, to the Rev. Samuel Lysons, of Hempsted Court.
Frances, m. in 1840, to the Rev. Thomas Peters, rector of Eastington, co. Gloucester.
Elizabeth-Anna-Maria, m. 1843, to Philip Smith, Esq.

Arms—Arg., on a bend, sa., three fleurs-de-lis, or, on a chief, of the second, a lion, passant, of the third.
Crest—Or, a demi-lion, rampant, sa., holding a fleur-de-lis.
Motto—Virtute non sanguine.
Seat—Quedgeley House, co. Gloucester.

HEAD OF MODREENY HOUSE.

Head, William-Henry, Esq. of Modreeny House, co. Tipperary, J. P., b. 8 Sept. 1809. (His late Majesty William IV. stood sponsor.)

Lineage.—John Head, Esq. of Ashley Park, co. Tipperary, who d. 23 June, 1817; m. Phœbe Toler, sister of the 1st Earl of Norbury, and left a son,

Lieutenant-General Michael Head, Modreeny House, who m. Oct. 1808, Elizabeth, dau. of Edward Ravenscroft, Esq., Portland Place, London, and died, leaving an only child, William-Henry Head, Esq. of Modreeny House.

Seat—Modreeny House, co. Tipperary.

HEALE OF HIGHFIELD HOUSE.

Heale, Henry-Newton, Esq. of Highfield House, Hemel Hempstead, Herts, J.P., b. 5 Nov. 1814; m. 8 Feb. 1849, Anne-Judith, eldest dau. of the late Charles-Aston Key, Esq., and has four daus. Mr. Heale is son of Mr. William Heale, merchant of London.

Seat—Highfield House, Hemel Hempstead.

HEARD OF KINSALE.

Heard, John-Isaac, Esq. of Kinsale and Ballydaly, co. Cork, M.P., J.P., and D.L., high-sheriff, 1839, b. 1788; m. 1808, Mary, dau. of Hope Wilkes, Esq. of Lofts Hall, Essex, and has issue,

I. Robert, m. Charlotte, dau. of John B. Warren, Esq. of Warren's Grove, co. Cork, and niece of Sir Augustus Warren, Bart., and has two sons and two daus.
I. Catherine-Jane.
II. Mary, m. to Achilles Daunt, Esq., J.P., co. Cork.

Lineage.—This family is a branch of the stock from which also derived the late Sir Isaac Heard, Garter King-of-Arms. The full pedigree and arms appear on record in the Heralds' Office, London. The present Mr. Heard, M.P., is son of the late John Heard, Esq., by Rachel Servatt, his wife, and grandson of John Heard, and Rose Wyatt, his wife.

Residence—Kinsale.

HEATHCOTE OF CONNINGTON CASTLE.

Heathcote, John-Moyer, Esq. of Connington Castle, co. Huntingdon, J.P. and D.L., b. 9 Nov. 1800; m. April, 1833, the Hon. Emily-Frances Ridley-Colborne, dau. of Lord Colborne, and has issue,

I. John-Moyer, b. 12 July, 1834.
II. William-George, b. 6 Feb, 1836.
III. Charles-Gilbert, b. 2 March, 1841.
IV. Henry-Francis, b. 11 Aug. 1849.
I. Mary-Emily

Mr. Heathcote has served as high-sheriff of Huntingdonshire.

Lineage.—John Heathcote, Esq., second son of Sir John Heathcote, Bart., by Bridget his wife, dau. of John White, Esq. of Wallingwells, M.P., and grandson of Sir Gilbert Heathcote, Bart., M.P. for the city of London, m. 24 Oct. 1764, Lydia, dau. and heir of John Moyer, Esq., and had (besides a dau., Lydia, m. to the Hon. John Dawnay) a son,

John Heathcote, Esq. of Connington Castle, b. in 1767, who m. 5 Nov. 1799, Miss Mary-Anne Thornhill, and by her (who d. 27 July, 1854) had issue,

John-Moyer, his heir.
Robert-Boothby, m. 1st, Miss Charlotte Sotheby, and by her (who is deceased) has issue, a son and two daus. He m. 2ndly, Miss Elizabeth-Bridget Wells
George, m. Miss Catherine-Sophia Sotheby, and d. s. p.
Mary-Anne, Lydia, m. to George-Hussey Packe, Esq.
Frances-Catherine, m. to the Rev. William Rooper.

Mr. Heathcote d. 3 May, 1838.

Arms—Erm., three pomeis, each charged with a cross, or.
Crest—On a mural crown, az., a pomeis, as in the arms, between two wings, displayed, erm.
Seat—Connington Castle, near Stilton, co. Huntingdon.

HEATON OF PLAS HEATON.

Heaton, John-Richard, Esq. of Plas Heaton, co. Denbigh, major in the army, b. 29 May, 1816.

Lineage.—The Heatons, now of Plas Heaton, and formerly of Lleweny Green, co. Denbigh, are a branch of the Heatons of Heaton, co. Lancaster, and first settled in Wales as officers under Henry de Lacy, the great Earl of Lincoln, who was Constable of Chester, and Lord of Rhos and Rhyfoniog, co. Denbigh. From

Sir Alexander Heaton, Lord of Heaton, co. Lancaster, lineally descended,

Richard Heaton, Esq. of Lleweny Green, living *temp.* Elizabeth, who m. Elizabeth, dau. (by Winifred, dau. of Kenelm Throckmorton, Esq.,) of Cadwallader Wynn, of Voelas, co. Denbigh, Esq., and by her (who m. 2ndly, Hugh Peake, Esq.), was great-grandfather of

Richard Heaton, Esq. of Lleweny Green, who m. in 1693, Margaret, dau. and co-heir of Edward Davies, Esq of Denbigh, a cadet of the ancient Denbighshire House of Wygfair, derived from Ednowain Bendew, Lord of Tegaingl, Founder of the XIII. Noble Tribe of North Wales and Powys. By this lady Mr. Heaton was father of,

John Heaton, Esq. of Lleweny Green, who m. 16 July, 1734, Martha, only dau. of Christopher Adamson, of Wereham, co. Norfolk, Esq. His son,

Richard Heaton, Esq. of Plas Heaton, co. Denbigh, m. 11 Aug. 1783, Sarah Venables, of Oswestry, co. Salop, whose family now resides at Wood Hill, near Oswestry. Of this marriage there was issue,

I. John.
II. Sarah-Elizabeth.
III. Margaret, m. Joseph-Venables Lovett, of Belmont, co Salop, Esq.
IV. Mary, m. Richard-Lloyd Williams, of Henllan Place, co. Denbigh, and Hafod Duryd, co. Caernarvon, Esq.

Mr. Heaton was s. by his only son,

John Heaton, Esq. of Plas Heaton, b. 16 May, 1787; who m. 1st Aug. 1814, Elizabeth, sister of Wilson Jones, of Cefn-Coch, co. Denbigh, Esq., late M.P. for Denbigh, and dau. of the late John Jones, Esq. of Cefn-Coch, (*see that name,*) and by her had issue,

John Richard, now of Plas Heaton.
Charles-Wilson, in holy orders, b. 1 Feb 1820.
Hugh-Edward, in holy orders, b. 13 May, 1821.
Sarah-Elizabeth.

Mr. Heaton m. 2ndly, 21 April, 1824, Anne-Eliza, dau. of John, Lord Henniker, and by her has had issue,

I. William-Henniker, lieut. R.N., b. 13 July, 1835.
II. Frederick-Luxmore, b. 30 April, 1837.
III. Arthur, b. 11 Jan. 1839.
IV. Llewelyn-Francis, b. 15 Sept. 1840.
I. Mary. II. Anne-Eliza, deceased.
III. Emily-Margaret. IV. Frances.
V. Anna-Maria, deceased. VI. Jessy.

Mr. Heaton, J.P., and chairman of Quarter Sessions of Denbighshire, served the office of high-sheriff for that county in 1837, and d. 14 May, 1855.

Arms—Arg., on a bend, engrailed, sa., three bucks' heads of the field.
Crest—A buck's head, as in the arms.
Motto—Er cordiad y caera. (From the foundation of the fortress.)
Seat—Plas Heaton, co. Denbigh.

HEBER OF HODNET.

HEBER-PERCY, ALGERNON-CHARLES, Esq. of Hodnet Hall, co. Salop, J.P. late high-sheriff, b. 29 June, 1812; m. 29 July, 1839, Emily, dau. and co-heir of Reginald Heber, Bishop of Calcutta, and has issue,

I. ALGERNON, b. 23 Feb. 1845.
II. Reginald-Josceline, b. 3 May, 1849.
III. Hugh-Louis, b. 6 Jan. 1853.
I. Blanche-Emily. II. Ethel-Cecilia.

Lineage.—The Hebers take their name from a place in Craven called Haybergh, where the earliest of the family are supposed to have risen. The oldest tradition refers to ERNULPHUS DE HAYBURGH, of Saxon descent, living towards the end of the 12th century at Milnethorpe, in the parish of Sandale. His descendants seem to have continued there as gentlemen of very small fortune for six generations, intermarrying with respectable families in the north of England. In 1461,

THOMAS HEBBIRE, Gent., is mentioned by Dodsworth. He lived at Adwalton, in Craven, in 1463. His brother, Oswald, had a commission in the Duke of York's army, and was slain at the battle of Wakefield. Thomas d. at Keytheley, in 1499, and was s. by his son,

THOMAS HEIBER, b. in 1478, who was possessed of land at Keytheley and at Elslach, and was the purchaser of the estate of West Marton, in Craven, where he d. in 1548. His eldest son,

REGINALD HEBER, succeeded him at Marton. He m. in 1558, Anne, dau of John de Malholme, of Elslach; and d. 14 Nov. 1600. His son, Thomas Heber, dying in his lifetime, all his estates descended to his grandson,

THOMAS HEBER, b. 8 June, 1566, J.P. He m. Elinore, dau. of Thomas Ferrand, Esq. of Carlton; and dying at Marton, in 1633, was s. by his eldest son,

THOMAS HEBER, J.P. temp. CHARLES I., who m. Anne, dau. of Sir William Lowther, of Ingleton, and was buried at East Marton, 26 Jan. 1659. He was s. by his son,

THOMAS HEBER, Esq., who m. Bridget, dau. of Sir John Pennington, of Muncaster; and d. in 1668, leaving a son,

THOMAS HEBER, Esq. of Marton, b. in 1643; who m. Rebecca, dau. of Sir Robert Markham, Bart. of Sedgebrooke, Lincolnshire; and was buried at Marton, 2 Dec. 1679. His son,

REGINALD HEBER, b. at York in 1675, m. in 1696, Hester, dau. of Sir William Cayley, Bart. of Brompton; and was buried at Marton, in 1715, leaving a son and heir,

THOMAS HEBER, of Marton, b. in 1697; J.P. and D.L.; m. in 1722, Elizabeth, eldest dau. of John Atherton, of Atherton and Beausey, in Lancashire, and heiress (through her mother, Elizabeth Cholmondeley, and her grandmother, Elizabeth Vernon) to the manors and estates of her ancestor, SIR HENRY VERNON, Bart. of Hodnet. (*See* BURKE'S *Extinct Baronetage*). Thomas Heber d. 21 Oct. 1752, and was s. by his eldest son,

RICHARD HEBER, Esq., who d. without male issue in 1766, when the estates devolved upon his brother,

THE REV. REGINALD HEBER, rector of Chelsea, and afterwards of Malpas, Cheshire, and Hodnet, Salop, b. in 1729; who m. 1st, in 1773, Mary, dau. and co-heir of Martin Bayley, M.A., rector of Kelsale, Lord of the Manor of Wicklewood Ampnors, in Norfolk, and by her (who d. in 1774) had an only son,

RICHARD, his heir.

He m. 2ndly, in 1782, Mary, dau. of Cuthbert Allanson, D.D., of Middleton Hall, Yorkshire, and Adlington, in Lancashire, by whom he had three children,

I. REGINALD, b. in 1785; consecrated bishop of Calcutta in 1823, and eminent alike for his virtues and talents. He d. in Southern India, April, 1826, leaving, by Amelia his wife, dau. of William-Davies Shipley, Dean of St. Asaph, two daus.,
1 EMILY, m. 29 July, 1839, Algernon-Charles Percy, Esq.
2 HARRIOT-SARAH, m. 22 Nov. 1842, to John, eldest son of John Thornton, Esq. of Clapham, Surrey.
II. Thomas, in holy orders, rector of Marton; d. unm. in 1816.
I. Mary, m. to the Rev. Charles-Cowper Cholmondeley. This lady inherited the estates in Yorkshire and Shropshire, under the will of her eldest brother.

The Rev. Reginald Heber d. in 1804, and was s. by his eldest son,

RICHARD HEBER, Esq. of Hodnet and of Marton, lieut.-col. of yeomanry, and high-sheriff of Shropshire in 1821, who was, in the latter end of that year, elected M.P. for the university of Oxford. Mr. Heber, an accomplished scholar, d. unm. 4 Oct. 1833, leaving by his will all his hereditary property and personality to "his only sister, Mary, widow of Charles Cowper Cholmondeley, rector of Hodnet, with remainder to his nieces, the daus. of his late brother Reginald." His sister,

MARY HEBER, m. 1st, 22 June, 1822, the Rev. Charles-Cowper Cholmondeley, rector of Hodnet, nephew of Thomas, Lord Delamere, and by him (who d. 1831) had four sons. She m. 2ndly, 1841, The Rev. S.-H. Macaulay, rector of Hodnet, and was s. at her decease by her niece, EMILY, now of Hodnet, wife of ALGERNON-CHARLES HEBER-PERCY, Esq.

Arms—Quarterly: 1st and 4th, grand quarterings, 1 and 4, quarterly, 1st and 4th, or, a lion, rampant, az., for BRABANT; 2nd and 3rd, gu., three lucies, laurient, ppr., for LUCY; 2 and 3, az., five fusils, in fesse, or. for Percy; 2nd and 3rd, grand quarterings, per fesse, az. and gu., a lion, rampant, or, in the dexter chief-point a cinquefoil, az., a cross-crosslet for difference, for HEBER: an escutcheon of pretence—HEBER without the difference.
Crest—1st, for PERCY, on a chapeau, gu., turned up, erm., a lion, statant, az., the tail, extended; 2nd, for HEBER, out of a ducal coronet, or, a lady's head and shoulders, ppr., in profile, crined, or.
Motto—Esperance en Dieu.
Seat—Hodnet Hall, near Shrewsbury.

HEDDLE OF MELSETTER.

HEDDLE, JOHN-GEORGE, Esq. of Melsetter and Hoy, co. Orkney, J.P. and D.L., m. in 1843, Mary, 2nd dau. of William Traill, Esq. of Woodwick, by Harriet Sarle, his 1st wife, and has issue,

I. JOHN-GEORGE, b. 11 Dec. 1844.
II. Robert-William, b. 1848.
III. Charles-Traill, b. 1850. IV. Alexander-Dunbar.
I. Harriot-Traill. II. Mary.

Lineage.—The surname Heddle is a local one of Scandinavian origin. In the ancient rentals we find it variously spelt—Haidale, Hedal, and Heddell; from the same document, it appears that this family held lands in Harray and Stennis prior to 1503. Charters, or written titles, were not in use in Orkney until sometime after the annexation of those islands to the Scottish crown; and the Haidales and other udallors held their lands "on payment of scot and tiend conform to the rentals."

JOHN HEDDLE, of Cletts, m. 1772, Elizabeth Hett, only child of Alexander Hett, of Gruthay, by Barbara Hett, of Kirkhouse, and had issue, sixteen children. He was s. in the estate of Cletts and Gruthay by his eldest son,

JOHN HEDDLE, M.D., who entered the army, served with distinction, and was wounded at the taking of Senegal; and, after rising to the rank of inspector-general of hospitals, d. unm., and was s. by his brother,

ROBERT HEDDLE, Esq. of Cletts and Melsetter, m. 1st Henrietta, dau. of Major James Moodie, of Melsetter (an ancient family in the north, descended from Bishop William Moodie), and had issue,

I. JOHN-GEORGE, of Melsetter and Hoy.
II. James-Alexander, d. young s. p.
III. Robert. IV. Matthew-Foster, M.D.
I. Elizabeth-Dunbar, m. John Traill, and left issue.
II. Henrietta-Moodie, m. Wm. Traill, of Woodwick, and has issue.
III. Mary-Bury, d. in infancy.
IV. Mary-Bury, d. young.

He m. 2ndly, Elizabeth, dau. of Captain Sutherland; and d. in 1842, without issue by this marriage, and was s. in his estates by his son, JOHN-GEORGE.

Arms—HEDDLE and MOODIE quarterly.
Crest—A leopard's or cat's head, erased.
Motto—Virtute et labore.
Seats—Melsetter, by Kirkwall; and Cletts, Orkney.

HEIGHAM OF HUNSTON.

HEIGHAM, JOHN-HENRY, Esq. of Hunston, Suffolk, J.P. and D.L., *b.* 24 July, 1798; *m.* 14 Aug. 1827, Maria-Catherine, eldest dau. of William Gould, Esq. of St. Edmundsbury, lieut.-colonel in the army, and by her (who *d.* in 1837) had issue,

I. CLEMENT-HENRY-JOHN, *b.* 11 July, 1829.
II. Henry.
I. Maria-Elizabeth.
II. Mary-Anne-Charlotte.
III. Catherine-Gould.
IV. Fanny.
V. Henrietta.

Lineage.—The family of Heigham takes its name from Heigham, a hamlet of Gaseley, in Suffolk, where they for a long time had considerable possessions. We have, however, no uninterrupted pedigree of the family, except from the time of Richard Heigham, who *d.* in 1340. His son, by Joane his wife,

THOMAS HEIGHAM, had, by Maude his wife, three sons, THOMAS; Robert, *d.* 5 Nov. 1388; and John, in holy orders, of Tuddenham, *d.* 18 Oct. 1393. The eldest son,

THOMAS HEIGHAM, of Heigham, *m.* Alice, dau. and heir of John Hune, of Tunstall, in Suffolk; and *d.* 7 Feb. 1409, leaving by her (who *d.* 1 March, 1448) a son,

THOMAS HEIGHAM, of Heigham, who *m.* Alice, dau. and heir of Boys, and had issue, THOMAS, his heir; John, parson of Burwell and Elvedon, *d.* in 1467; Joane, *m.* to Robert Harewell; and Margaret, *m.* to William Mounteney. The elder son,

THOMAS HEIGHAM, of Heigham, *m.* Isabel, dau. and co-heir of Sir Hugh Francis, Knt. of Gyffordes Hall, in Wickhambrook, co. Suffolk, and by her (who *d.* 26 March, 1452) had issue, THOMAS, his heir; Clement, of Gyffordes Hall, co. Suffolk;* William, in holy orders, of Elveton and Gaseley, elect bishop of Ely, *d.* in 1490; Richard, of Lincoln's Inn, serjeant-at-law, reader of Lincoln's Inn, *d.* 21 Oct. 1500. Mr. Heigham *d.* 21 March, 1480, and was *s.* by his eldest son,

THOMAS HEIGHAM, of Heigham, who *m.* Catherine, dau. of William Cotton, of Lindwade, co. Cambridge; and *d.* 23 April, 1492, leaving issue. From John, the 2nd son, derived the HEIGHAMS *of Heigham*, whose eventual heiress, Susan Heigham, *m.* Sir Edward Lewkenor, Knt. The 4th son,

CLEMENT HEIGHAM, of Lavenham, *m.* Matilda, dau. of Lawrence Cooke; and dying in 1500, left an eldest son and heir,

SIR CLEMENT HEIGHAM, of Barrow, co. Suffolk, *m.* 1st, Anne, dau. of John de Moonines, of Seamer Hall, in Suffolk, and by her had five daus. Sir Clement *m.* 2ndly, Anne, dau. of Sir George Waldegrave, Knt. of Smalbridge, co. Suffolk, and widow of Henry Buers, of Acton, in Suffolk, and by her had, JOHN (Sir), his heir; Thomas, buried in Dec. 1797, *s. p.*; William, of East Ham, Essex; Judith, *m.* to John Spelman, of Narburgh, in Norfolk; and Dorothy, *m.* to Sir Charles Framlingham, Knt. of Crowes Hall, in Suffolk. Sir Clement *d.* in 1570, and was *s.* by his eldest son,

SIR JOHN HEIGHAM, Knt. of Barrow, who *m.* 1st, 9 Dec. 1562, Anne, dau. and co-heir of Edmund Wright, of Sutton Hall, in Brutfield, co. Suffolk; and 2ndly, Anne, dau. of William Poley, of Boxted, in Suffolk, and by the former (who *d.* in 1000) had issue. Sir John *d.* in 1626, aged 98, and was *s.* by his eldest son,

SIR CLEMENT HEIGHAM, Knt. of Barrow, M.P. of Suffolk in 1598 and 1614. He *m.* 1st, Anne dau. and sole heir of William Cardinal, of Great Bromley, Essex, and by her had, with other issue, JOHN, ancestor of the HEIGHAMS *of Barrow*. Sir Clement *m.* 2ndly, Anne, dau. of John Appleyard, of Dunston, and relict of Robert Bedingfield, of Ditchingham, in Norfolk, and by her had a son,

THE REV. ARTHUR HEIGHAM, rector of Redgrave, in Suffolk, *m.* 6 Feb. 1658, Anne, dau. of Thomas Cecil, of Depden, in Suffolk, and *d.* 28 Jan. 1698, having had (besides a dau., Susan, *m.* to the Rev. Maurice Moseley, rector of Weston Market, in Suffolk, and a son, Clement, *d.* an infant) an elder son and heir,

THE REV. ARTHUR HEIGHAM, rector of Hepton, in Suffolk, bapt. 11 May, 1643; who *m.* in 1678, Hannah, dau. of John Symonds, of Gislingham, in Suffolk, and *d.* in 1690, leaving a son,

JOHN HEIGHAM, Esq. of Rougham and Hunston, bapt. 20 July, 1679; who *m.* 1st, 10 April, 1701, Mary, dau. and sole heir of John Larkin, of Hunston, and by her (who *d.* 19 Aug 1718) had two sons and two daus. Mr. Heigham *m.* 2ndly, Anne, dau. and co-heir of John Pell, of Darsingham, in Norfolk, and relict of William Ellis, of Cotton, co. Suffolk, and by her (who *d.* 28 July, 1738) had (besides a dau., Anne, who *d.* in infancy, in 1724) a son,

PELL HEIGHAM, Esq. of Rougham, bapt. 9 May, 1725; who *m.* 2 Oct. 1757, Penelope, dau. of George Dashwood, Esq. of Peyton Hall, co. Suffolk; and *d.* 27 Aug. 1781, having had by her (who *d.* 17 Sept. 1806) three sons and two daus. The 2nd son,

THE REV. HENRY HEIGHAM, of Hunston, who *s.* his brother John, was *b.* 21 Jan. 1768; *m.* 13 July, 1790, Elizabeth, dau. of Thomas Symonds, Esq. of St. Edmundsbury, capt. R.N., and by her (who *d.* 9 Dec. 1832) had issue,

I. JOHN-HENRY, now of Hunston.
II. George-Thomas, of Houghton Hall, in Cavendish, Suffolk, J.P., late capt. 4th dragoon-guards; *b.* 25 Aug. 1800; *m.* in 1830, Mary-Anne-Elizabeth, only dau. of the Rev. Henry Hasted, rector of Honingsheath, co. Suffolk, and had issue,
   1 George-Henry-John, *b.* 16 May, 1831.
   2 Charles-Pell, *b.* 17 Nov 1837.
   3 Arthur-Linzee-Chatterton, *b.* 23 March, 1839.
   1 Mary-Anne-Eliza.
   2 Emily-Penelope-St. George.
III. Charles-William, of Lincoln's Inn, barrister-at-law; *b.* 18 Aug. 1802.
I. Mary-Anna-Penelope, *m.* in 1829, to the Rev. Edward Gould, rector of Sproughton, in Suffolk.
II. Elizabeth-Sophia, *m.* in 1835, to Alexander-Henry-Augustus-John, Comte de St. George, of Changins, in the Canton de Vaud, Switzerland.

Mr. Heigham *d.* 29 Dec. 1834.

Arms—Sa., a fesse, chequy, or and az., between three horses' heads, erased, arg.
Crest—A horse's head and neck, erased, arg.
Seat—Hunston, Suffolk.

HELYAR OF COKER COURT.

HELYAR, WILLIAM-HAWKER, Esq. of Coker Court, co. Somerset, and of Sedgehill House, co. Wiltshire, *b.* 24 Aug. 1812; *m.* 29 April, 1843, Theodora-Adelaide, dau. of Colonel Theodore de Risnel. Mr. Helyar *s.* at the decease of his father, 10 Dec. 1841.

Lineage.—This family came originally from the co. of Devon, where it appears to have been of importance, for we find one William Helyar representing Molcombe Regis in parliament, in the reigns of RICHARD II. and HENRY IV. In 1616,

WILLIAM HELYAR, Esq. of East Coker, *b.* 5 March, 1621, son of Henry Helyar, Esq., by Christian his wife, dau. of William Cary, Esq. of Clovelly, and grandson of the Ven. William Helyar, archdeacon of Barnstaple, was a zealous Cavalier; he *m.* Rachel, dau. of Sir Hugh Wyndham, Bart. of Pilsdon, co. Dorset, by whom (who *d.* 20 May, 1673) he had, with other children, who all *d.* young or unm., WILLIAM, his heir; and John, of Yatley, co. Surrey, *b.* in 1654, whose only dau. and heiress *m.* William Wyndham, Esq. Mr. Helyar, high-sheriff for Somersetshire in 1661, was *s.* at his decease by his eldest surviving son,

WILLIAM HELYAR, Esq. of East Coker, in Somersetshire, and of Canonteign, in Devon, *b.* 10 July, 1662; high-sheriff for the co. of Somerset in 1701, and M.P. for the same shire in 1714. He *m.* Joanna, dau. and co-heiress of — Hele, Esq. of South Tawton, in Devonshire, and had issue, WILLIAM, his successor; Robert, barrister-at-law, *d. s. p.* in [illegible]; Rachel, *m.* to Sir John Coryton, Bart. of Newton Park, in Cornwall, and *d. s. p.*; Mary, *d.* unm.; and Joanna. The elder son and heir,

WILLIAM HELYAR, Esq. of East Coker, *m.* Mary, dau. and heiress of John Goddard, Esq. of Gillingham, in Dorsetshire, and had, with three daus., an only son, his successor, in 1753.

WILLIAM HELYAR, Esq. of Coker Court, co. Somerset, and of Bucknall, in Devon, *b.* in 1722; who *m.* Betty, dau. and co-heir of William Weston, Esq. of Weston, in Dorsetshire, and had, with four daus., six sons. Mr. Helyar was sheriff of Somersetshire in 1764. He *d.* in 1780, and was *s.* by his eldest son,

WILLIAM HELYAR, Esq. of Coker Court, in Somersetshire, and of Sedgehill, co. Wilts, J.P., *b.* 8 Sept. 1746, *m.* in 1777,

* Thomas Heigham, of Wickhambrook, great-grandson of Clement, of Gyffordes Hall, was a distinguished soldier. He served in Holland and France, and in Ireland against the rebels. A large brass, with a recumbent figure in coat-armour, erected in [illegible] by his nephew, Sir Robert [illegible], Knt. of [illegible], in [illegible]shire, records his deeds.

Elizabeth, 2nd dau. and co-heir of William Hawker, Esq. of Luppitt, co. Devon, by Elizabeth his wife, dau. and heiress of Thomas Welman, Esq. of Poundisford Lodge, co. Somerset, youngest son of Isaac Welman, Esq. of Poundisford Park, and by her (who *d.* 24 May, 1834) had surviving issue,

- WILLIAM, his heir.
- Henry, *b.* 29 Nov. 1784; in holy orders, rector of Hardington; *m.* Maria, eldest dau. of J. Perring, Esq. of Combe Florey, co. Somerset, and has issue.
- George, *b.* 6 Aug. 1786; barrister-at-law; *d. s. p.*
- Hugh-Welman, *b.* 23 March, 1793; rector of Sutton and Bingham, in Somersetshire, and of Beer Hacket, co. Dorset, and J.P. for Somersetshire; *m.* Honoria, youngest dau. of John Perring, Esq. of Combe Flory, and has issue.
- CHARLES-JOHN, now of Poundisford Lodge.
- Elizabeth, *m.* Gen. Farrer.
- Harriet.
- Caroline.
- Emily-Lucy.

Mr. Helyar *d.* 30 Aug. 1820, and was *s.* by his eldest son,

WILLIAM HELYAR, Esq. of Coker Court, and of Sedgehill, co. Wilts, J.P for Somerset, Wilts, and Devon; *b.* 14 May, 1778; who served as high-sheriff of the first-named co. in 1829. He *m.* in Nov. 1811, Harriet, dau. of Thomas Grove, Esq. of Ferne House, co. Wilts, and had issue,

- I. WILLIAM-HAWKER, his heir.
- II. Albert.
- III. Charles.
- IV. Edwin-Grove.
- I. Agnes-Grove, *m.* 18 July, 1844, to William-Charles Lambert, Esq. of Knowle House, co. Dorset.
- II. Ellen-Harriet, *m.* to William Phelips, Esq. of Montacute House, Somerset.
- III. Lucy-Elizabeth, *d.* 12 April, 1836.
- IV. Anne.

Mr. Helyar *d.* 10 Dec. 1841, aged 63, and was *s.* by his eldest son, the present WILLIAM-HAWKER HELYAR, Esq.

Arms—Az., a cross-fleury, arg., between four mullets, pierced, or.
Crest—A cock, sa., beaked, combed, and wattled, gu., under a cross-fleury, fitchée.
Motto—In labore quies.
Seat—Coker Court, near Yeovil.

HELYAR OF POUNDISFORD LODGE.

HELYAR, CHARLES-JOHN, Esq. of Poundisford Lodge, co. Somerset, J.P., *b.* 15 May, 1796; *m.* 5 June, 1839, Charlotte-Anne, 2nd dau. of General Michel, of Dewlish House and Kingston Russell, co. Dorset, by Anne his wife, dau. of the Hon. Henry Fane, of Fulbeck, co. Lincoln, and has issue,

- I. CHARLES-WELMAN, *b.* 13 Aug. 1843.
- II. Frederic-William, *b.* 6 April, 1846.
- I. Cecily-Caroline.

Mr. Helyar is youngest son of the late William Helyar, Esq. of Coker Court, co. Somerset.

Arms, Crest, and *Motto*—See preceding article.
Seat—Poundiford Lodge, co. Somerset.

HEMSWORTH OF ABBEVILLE.

HEMSWORTH, THOMAS-GERARD, Esq. of Abbeville, co. Tipperary, *s.* his father, 1 Sept. 1856.

Lineage.—This family was originally of Hemsworth, co. York.

THE REV. HENRY HEMSWORTH left Yorkshire about 1650, and became rector of St. Anne's, Dublin. He *d.* in April, 1696, leaving two sons. The elder,

THE REV. THOMAS HEMSWORTH, of Abbeville, co. Tipperary, rector of the parishes of Birr, Kinnetty, St. Clerens, and Lockeen, *m.* Lucy, dau. of Godfrey Boate, Esq., one of the justices of the King's Bench in Ireland, and by her (who *d.* 10 April, 1758) had, THOMAS, his heir; John, M.D., *m.* Mary Minchin; Godfrey, who, by Mabel Gubbins his wife, was father of Godfrey, of Dorrass, co. Clare, who *m.* 14 Sept. 1802, Eliza Fitzgibbon; Denton-Boate; and Jane, wife of George Minchin, Esq. The eldest son,

THE REV. THOMAS HEMSWORTH, of Abbeville, *m.* 1st, Miss Plunkett, of Dillonstown, co. Louth, by whom he had an only dau., Lucy, who *d. unm.*, and 2ndly, Elizabeth, dau. of Lucius Wilson, of Deer Park, co. Clare, Esq., and by her had (with two daus., Ellen, wife of William Newstead, of Derrignaston, co. Tipperary, and Mary) three sons, THOMAS, his heir; Richard, who *d. s. p.*; William, of Loughrea and Ash Park, who *m.* in 1780, Anne Newman, and had, with other issue, a son and heir, THOMAS, capt. in the army, who *m.* Miss Bicknell, and had, Thomas, and other children. The Rev. Mr. Hemsworth's will was proved 15 April, 1769. He was *s.* by his eldest son,

THOMAS HEMSWORTH, Esq. of Abbeville, who *m.* 8 Jan. 1782, Mary, eldest dau. of Henry D'Esterre, Esq. of Rosmanagher, co. Clare, and by her (who *d.* 1837) had issue,

- THOMAS, late of Abbeville.
- HENRY-D'ESTERRE, of Shropham Hall (*see that family*).
- Mary, *m.* to Lieut.-Col. John Campbell, of Blackhall, co. Kincardine.
- Eliza, *m.* to Lieut.-Col. Sir Thomas-Noel Harris, groom of the privy-chamber.
- Darkay, *m.* to Major William Izod, of Chapel Izod, co. Kilkenny.

Mr. Hemsworth *d.* 8 Nov. 1811, and was *s.* by his eldest son,

THOMAS HEMSWORTH, Esq. of Abbeville, J.P., *b.* 24 Oct. 1783; *m.* 4 March, 1808, Jane, eldest dau. of Gerard Irvine, Esq. of Rockfield, co. Fermanagh, and had issue,

- THOMAS-GERARD, now of Abbeville.
- John.
- Henry.
- William, *m.* 1850, Frances-Delap, 2nd dau. of Nathaniel Robbins, Esq. of Hymenstown, co. Tipperary.

Arms—Per saltier, arg. and or, a leopard's face, sa.
Crest—A dexter arm, embowed, in armour, the gauntlet grasping a sword, ppr., hilt and pommel, or, transfixing a leopard's face, sa.
Motto—Manus hæc inimica tyrannis.
Seat—Abbeville, co. Tipperary.

HEMSWORTH OF SHROPHAM HALL.

HEMSWORTH, HENRY-WILLIAM, Esq. of Shropham Hall, co. Norfolk, *b.* 6 May, 1815; *m.* 24 May, 1851, Ellen, dau. of the late Francis Kemble, Esq. of Chesterfield Street, Mayfair.

Lineage.—HENRY-D'ESTERRE HEMSWORTH, Esq. of Shropham Hall, Norfolk, J.P. and D.L., 2nd son of Thomas Hemsworth, Esq. of Abbeville, co. Tipperary, who *d.* in 1811, by Mary his wife, dau. of Henry D'Esterre, Esq. of Rosmanagher, co. Clare; *m.* Aug. 1813, Jane-Maria, 2nd dau. and co-heiress of Gen. James Barker, of an old Norfolk family, who took the name of Hethersett (he was aide-de-camp to the Marquess Townshend at the battle of Quebec, and received a large grant of land in Prince Edward's Island for his services); by her had issue,

- I. HENRY-WILLIAM, now of Shropham Hall.
- II. Augustus-Barker, in holy orders, M.A.; *m.* 17 March, 1847, Duncana, eldest dau. of the late Alexander Campbell Esq. of Kilmartin, co. Argyll, and has issue,
  - 1 Augustus-Noel-Campbell, *b.* 21 Jan. 1853.
  - 1 Laura-Anne-Maria.
  - 2 Louisa-Augusta.
- I. Amelia, *m.* to Francis-Henry, youngest son of the late John-Barker Huntington, Esq. of Somerton Hall, co. Norfolk.
- II. Eliza-Anna-Maria, *m.* to the Rev. Addison Hemsworth, of Rockland Rectory, Norfolk.
- III. Jane-Maria, *m.* to the Rev. Samuel-Frederick Bignold, of Tivetshall Rectory, Norfolk, 2nd son of Sir Samuel Bignold, M.P.

Arms and *Crest*—As HEMSWORTH OF ABBEVILLE, quartering, az., a lion, rampant, or, in the paw a battle-axe, arg., for HETHERSETT.
Motto—Manus hæc inimica tyrannis.
Seat—Shropham Hall, co. Norfolk.

HENEAGE OF HAINTON.

HENEAGE, GEORGE-FIESCHI, Esq. of Hainton, co. Lincoln, D.L., M.P. for Lincoln, *b.* 22 Nov. 1800; *m.* 16 Jan. 1833, Frances, dau. of Michael Tasburgh, Esq. of Burghwallis, in Yorkshire, and by her (who *d.* in 1842) has two sons and one dau.

Lineage.—The period of the first settlement of the family of Heneage in Lincolnshire may be nearly defined by the circumstance of Sir Robert de Heneage being witness, together with Sir Richard de Angemine, of the same co., and several others, to a grant of land, *temp.* WILLIAM RUFUS, from Nicholas Bassett to the monks of Brucria.

JOHN DE HENEAGE (son of Sir William de Heneage, Knt., grandson of Walter de Heneage, and great-grandson of John de Heneage, living *temp.* HENRY III.) appears, by deed, to have been possessed of the manor of Haynton, in Lincolnshire, 10 EDWARD III. From him derived, 6th in descent,

JOHN HENEAGE, Esq., who inherited Hainton from his brother, Sir Thomas Heneage, Knt. He was 2nd son of John Heneage, Esq. of Hainton, and great-grandson of William

Heneage, Esq. of Hainton, (whose 2nd son, ROBERT, auditor of the Duchy of Lancaster, was father of Sir Thomas Heneage, of Copt Hall, Essex, whose dau. and heir, Elizabeth, m. Sir Moyle Finch, Bart.) He m. Anne, dau. and sole heir of Edward Coke, Esq. of Helmeden, in Northamptonshire, and had issue. The 3rd son,

WILLIAM HENEAGE, Esq. of Benworth, m. Anne, dau. and co-heir of Ralph Fishbourne, of Fishbourne, in Durham, and had (with two daus., Anne, m. to Nicholas Wilson, of Sheepwash; and Catherine, m. to William Ascough), two sons, THOMAS (Sir), his heir; and George (Sir), who m. Mary, dau. of John Bussy. The elder son,

SIR THOMAS HENEAGE, Knt. of Hainton, m. Barbara, dau. of Sir Thomas Guilford, Knt. of Leamstead, in Kent, and had four sons and two daus., Mary, m. to Andrew Boyd; and Jane, m. to Patrick, Lord Dunsany. The eldest son,

SIR GEORGE HENEAGE, Knt. of Hainton, m. Elizabeth, dau. of Francis Tresham, of Rushton, in Northamptonshire, and was s. by his son,

GEORGE HENEAGE, Esq. of Hainton, who m. Faith, dau. of Sir Philip Tyrwhitt, of Stainfield, and was s. by his son,

GEORGE HENEAGE, Esq. of Hainton, who m. Mary, only dau. and heiress of Thomas Kemp, Esq. of Slindon, co. Sussex, and was father of

GEORGE HENEAGE, Esq. of Hainton, who m. Elizabeth, dau. of Sir Henry Hunloke, Bart. of Wingerworth, by Catherine his wife, dau. and heir of Francis Tyrwhitt, Esq. of Kettleby, and had six sons and two daus. He was s. at his decease by his eldest son,

THOMAS-HENRY HENEAGE, Esq. of Hainton, who m. 1st, 14 July, 1728, Anna-Maria, only dau. of Roboaldo Fieschi, Count de Lavagna, in Genoa, by whom he had issue,

GEORGE-FIESCHI, his heir.
Elizabeth-Maria.

He m. 2ndly, Katherine, eldest dau. of John-Francis Newport, Esq. of St. John's, Pelham, in Herts, by whom he had issue, Thomas, and Katherine. The eldest son and successor,

GEORGE-FIESCHI HENEAGE, Esq. of Hainton, m. 18 Sept. 1755, the Hon. Katherine Petre, eldest dau. of Robert-James, Lord Petre, and had issue,

I. GEORGE-ROBERT, his heir.
II. Thomas-Fieschi, b. in London, 28 Sept. 1771; m. in July, 1802, the Hon. Arabella Pelham, dau. of Charles, Lord Yarborough, and has issue,
   1 Charles-Fieschi, m. in Aug. 1837, Louisa, dau. of Lord Graves, and has issue,
      Algernon. Cecil.
      Mary. Louisa.
   2 Dudley Robert. 3 Henry-Pelham, in holy orders.
   4 Windsor.
   1 Arabella-Sophia, m. in Dec. 1834, to George-Carey, 3rd son of Charles Elwes, Esq. of Billing, Northamptonshire.
   2 Georgiana.
III. Edward, b. in London, 21 July, 1775.
I. Mary-Anne-Winifred, m. March, 1797, to F. Aicken, Esq.
II. Teresa, m. in March, 1797, to John Carpenter, Esq.
III. Barbara, deceased.

The eldest son,

GEORGE-ROBERT HENEAGE, Esq. of Hainton, b. 21 Dec. 1768, m. 18 Aug. 1798, Frances-Anne, 2nd dau. of Lieut.-Gen. George Ainslie, colonel of the 13th regiment of foot, and had issue,

I. GEORGE-FIESCHI, now of Hainton.
II Edward, late M.P. for Grimsby, m. 1st, Charlotte-Frances-Ann, dau. of Col. Rolleston, of Watnall, Notts; and 2ndly, Miss Hoare.
I. Frances-Anne, m. 11 Nov. 1826. to Edward Howard, Esq. of the 2nd life-guards, nephew to the Duke of Norfolk.
II. Catherine, m. 19 Dec. 1833, to William Beresford, Esq. of the co. of Wicklow.

Mr. Heneage d. 16 June, 1833.

Arms—Or, a greyhound, courant, sa., between three leopards' heads, az., a border, engrailed, gu.
Crest—A greyhound, courant, sa.
Motto—Toujours firme.
Seat—Hainton, Lincolnshire.

MERCER-HENDERSON OF FORDELL.

MERCER-HENDERSON, GEORGE-WILLIAM, Esq. of Fordell, in the parish of Dalgetty in the shire of Fife, D.L., late a captain in the Scots fusilier guards.

Lineage.—The family of Henderson has been settled at Fordell for about four centuries. (*See* DOUGLAS'S *Baronage*.)

JAMES HENDERSON, of Fordell, lord-justice-clerk, was killed in 1513, at Flodden Field, as well as his eldest son, whilst in attendance on JAMES IV.

GEORGE HENDERSON, of Fordell, was killed, in 1547, at the battle of Pinkie.

In the reign of CHARLES II., the eldest son of Sir John Henderson, who held a command in the army of CHARLES I., was created a Baronet in 1694. which honour continued in the family until the year 1833, when, on the death of Sir Robert-Bruce Henderson, without issue, the title became EXTINCT.

The estate of Fordell was left by Sir John Henderson (the elder brother of the said Sir Robert Bruce-Henderson), successively M.P. for the co. of Fife and for Stirling, to his only child and heir, ISABELLA-ANNE, who m. in 1818, the late Admiral of the Fleet, Sir Philip-Charles Henderson-Calderwood Durham, G.C.B. She d. 18 Dec. 1844; and he 1 April, 1845, both having d. without issue. The estate of Fordell descended to her first-cousin, GEORGE MERCER, who thereupon assumed the surname of HENDERSON in addition to, and after, that of MERCER.

GEORGE MERCER, lieut.-colonel of the 1st life-guards (son of George Mercer, J.P. for the cos. of Surrey and Middlesex, descended from a younger branch of the house of Mercer of Aldie, co. Perth), m. Jean, the eldest dau. of Sir Robert Henderson, and sister of the above-mentioned Sir John Henderson and Sir Robert-Bruce Henderson, Barts. She d. in 1814; and he in Paris, in 1822, having had issue,

I. GEORGE MERCER, afterwards George Mercer-Henderson, who succeeded to Fordell on the death of Sir Philip-Charles Henderson, Durham; and d. unm. 13 Oct. 1852.
II. Robert Mercer, lieut.-col. of the 3rd foot-guards, killed whilst in command of the light-infantry battalion of the guards at the siege of Bergen-op-Zoom, in 1814. He received a medal for his services in Egypt.
III. Douglas Mercer, afterwards Douglas Mercer-Henderson, C.B., lieut.-gen. in the army, and colonel of the 68th foot, succeeded to Fordell on the death of his brother, and by Royal license, bearing date 14 Jan. 1853, he and his issue were authorized to take the surname of HENDERSON in addition to that, and after that, of Mercer, and to bear the arms of Henderson quarterly with those of Mercer. He m. 2 Nov. 1820, Susan-Arabella, 2nd dau. of Sir William Rowley, of Tendring Hall, Bart. (Lieut.-Gen. Mercer-Henderson accompanied the 3rd guards on the expedition to Hanover in 1805, and on that to Walcheren in 1809: served in the Peninsula from March, 1810, to May, 1811, and again from July, 1811, to March, 1814, including the affair of Sobral, wounded whilst acting as aide-de-camp to Sir Brent Spencer, battle of Barrosa; wounded whilst aide-de-camp to Brig.-Gen. Dilkes, siege of Ciudad Rodrigo, battle of Salamanca, capture of Madrid, siege of Burgos, passage of the Bidassoa, and battles of the Nive and Nivelle; served also in the campaign of 1815, including the battles of Quatre Bras and Waterloo, and capture of Paris; at Waterloo he commanded the 3rd guards in the latter part of the action; in addition to the decoration of C.B., he received the Waterloo medal, as also the war-medal with five clasps). He d. at Naples 21 March, 1854, having had issue,
   1 GEORGE-WILLIAM MERCER-HENDERSON, the present possessor of Fordell.
   2 Douglas Mercer, d. young.
   3 Robert-Philip Mercer-Henderson, a lieut. in the royal navy, d. unm. 10 March, 1855.
   1 Jane, m. 26 June, 1851, James Clerk, Esq., eldest son of the Right Hon. Sir George Clerk, of Penicuick, Bart., and has issue.
   2 Edith.
IV. James Mercer, d. young.
I. Elizabeth-Isabella. II. Isabella-Anne.

Arms—Quarterly: 1st and 4th, HENDERSON, viz., gu., three piles issuing from the sinister, arg., on a chief of the last, a crescent, az., between two ermine spots; 2nd and 3rd, MERCER, viz., or, on a fesse, between three crosses-patée, in chief, gu., and a mullet of six points, in base, az., as many bezants, all within a bordure, of the third.

Crests—For HENDERSON, viz., a cubit-arm, ppr., the hand holding an estoile, radiated. or, and surmounted by a crescent, az.; and for MERCER, viz., the head and neck of a heron, erased, holding in its beak an eel, seizing the neck of the former. ppr.

Mottoes—Over the Crest of HENDERSON, "Sola virtus nobilitat;" over that of MERCER, "The Grit Poul."

Seat—Fordell, co. Fife.

HENDERSON OF STEMSTER.

HENDERSON, DAVID, Esq. of Stemster, co. Caithness, b. 10 April, 1788; m. 25 May, 1816, Margery, dau. of lieut.-col. Williamson, of Banniskirk, by Janet Sinclair his wife, co-heiress of Miss Catherine Sinclair, of Southdun, and has issue,

I. ALEXANDER, b. 29 April, 1820.
II. Benjamin, b. 29 Aug. 1823.
III. David, b. 22 April, 1833.
I. Janet-Sinclair, deceased.
II. Margaret, m. to James Williamson, Esq. of Port Philip, Australia.
III. Donaldina-Jamesina-Williamson, m. to Staff-Surgeon Patrick-Sinclair Laing.
IV. Williamina-Mary.

Mr. Henderson is a magistrate and deputy-lieutenant for co. Caithness, and s. his father in 1842.

Lineage.—DAVID HENDERSON, Esq. of Stemster, b. in 1714; m. in 1754, Cecilia, dau. of William Honeyman, Esq. of Græmsay, Orkney;* and d. in 1778, when he was s. by his son,

ALEXANDER HENDERSON, Esq. of Stemster, b. 1763; who m. in 1787, Margaret, dau. of William Duthie, Esq. of Arduthie, co. Kincardine, and by her (who d. in 1824) had issue,

DAVID, his successor.
Alexander, E.I.C.S., d. in India.
William-Honyman, capt. R.N., and C.B., m. 1844, Elizabeth Wallis, widow of Lord James Townshend.
James, of Biltster, co. Caithness, m. Elizabeth, dau. of the late Kenneth Mackay, Esq. of Newmore, co. Ross.
Patrick, major E.I.C.S.
Margaret. Johanna. Cecilia-Honyman.
Mary, m. to Charles Chalmers, Esq. of Monkshile, co. Aberdeen, advocate.

Mr. Henderson d. in 1842.

Arms, Crest, Motto—As HENDERSON OF FORDELL.
Seat—Stemster, by Thurso, co. Caithness.

HENDERSON OF WESTERTON.

HENDERSON, JOHN ALEXANDER, Esq. of Westerton, co. of Stirling, Scotland, late major rifle brigade, s. his uncle, John Henderson, Esq.

Lineage.—WILLIAM MAYNE, of Powis, co. Clackmannan, had several sons and daus., one of whom, EDWARD, succeeded to Powis; another, WILLIAM, being a distinguished lawyer, was created a Baronet, and subsequently Lord Newhaven, in Ireland; and another, JAMES, of St. Ninians, left an only dau.,

EUPHEMIA MAYNE, who m. 1st, James Henderson, Esq. of Westerton, and had two sons, John and William (both of whom served in the army in India); and 2ndly, James Alexander, Esq., provost of Stirling (descended from the ALEXANDERS *of Menstrie*, afterwards Earls of Stirling), and had a son, Edward, who acquired the estate of Powis (the late proprietor of which, Major James Mayne, left an only dau., Helen-Elphinston Mayne). This

EDWARD ALEXANDER, Esq. of Powis, m. 1st, H. Colquhoun; and 2ndly, Catherine Glas: by the latter there were two sons and three daus. (*see* p. 9). The 2nd son, MAJOR JOHN ALEXANDER, succeeded to Westerton on the demise of his uncle John.

Crest—A tilter at the ring.
Motto—Practise no fraud.
Seat—Westerton, Bridge of Allan.

HENLEY OF WATERPERY.

HENLEY, THE RIGHT HON. JOSEPH-WARNER of Waterpery, co. Oxford, J.P. and D.L., M.P. for that county since 1841, and President of the Board of Trade from March to Dec. 1852, b. in 1793; m. in 1817, Georgiana, dau. of John Fane, Esq. of Wormsley, and has issue surviving,

I. JOSEPH-JOHN.
II. Francis-George. III. Arthur.
I. Georgiana, m. to the Rev. G. Denison.
II. Ann-Maria-Augusta.
III. Grace-Elizabeth. IV. Ellen-Mary.
V. Nancy. VI. Adelaide-Charlotte.

Mr. Henley is only son of Joseph Henley, Esq., by Anne his wife, dau. of C. Rooke, Esq. of Wandsworth.

Arms—Az., a lion, rampant, arg., supporting a rudder, or, on a chief of the second, an anchor, sa., between two trefoils, ppr.

* Andrew Honeyman, bishop of Orkney, m. Mary Stuart, heiress of Græmsay, and a descendant of the Earls of Orkney.

Crest—An eagle, wings displayed, or, holding in the claw an anchor and cable, sa., and in the beak a trefoil, ppr.
Motto—Perseverando.
Seat—Waterpery, co. Oxford.

HENN OF PARADISE.

HENN, THOMAS-RICE, Esq. of Paradise, co. Clare, barrister-at-law, m. Oct. 1845, Jane, Isabella, 2nd dau. of the Right Hon. Francis Blackburne, late Lord Chancellor of Ireland, and now Lord Justice of the Court of Appeal in Chancery in that country, and has,

I. WILLIAM. II. Francis-Blackburne.
And other issue.

Lineage.—The family of Henn, one of English origin, has been settled in the county of Clare for nearly two centuries. The name was originally Hene, subsequently Henne, and lastly, about the year 1685, the final *e* was dropped, leaving the name as it is spelt at the present day. The founder of the Irish branch was Henry Hene, a distinguished Englishman, Lord Chief Baron of Ireland in the reigns of CHARLES II. and JAMES II., and a Commissioner of Forfeited Estates for the counties of Clare and Galway. Henry Hene was himself descended from an English line as ancient as any of which there are authentic records. The name is to be found in Doomsday Book, vol. i, p. 28. Title subsexe XIII. Terra Willi de Braiose in BRESBOK HYND' Radulf ten *de Willo Hene*, and to this family belonged a baronetcy, now extinct, created by JAMES I., anno 1642. Henry Hene, Lord Chief Baron of the Irish Court of Exchequer, is stated to have been nephew to Sir Henry Hene, the 1st baronet, being the son of his elder brother William, who was himself the eldest son of Henry Hene, Esq. of Barking, in Surrey. The history of this baronetcy may be read in BURKE's *Extinct Peerage*, p. 256. It is sufficient to state here that the 2nd baronet, Sir Henry, spelt his name HENNE, and that in the time of the 3rd and last bart., Sir Richard, the name became what it is at present. Richard Henn, the eldest son of the Lord Chief Baron settled at Paradise, anno. 1685, having in that year obtained a grant of "Paradise Hill," from the then Earl of Thomond. Richard dying without issue in the year 1717, devised his estates to his brother Thomas, who, in 1714, m. Miss Barbara Darby, and had issue by her, Richard, William, Thomas, Mary, Eliza, Anne, and Catherine. Thomas (the father) d. in 1735, and was s. by his son Richard, who m. in 1731, Bridget Hickman, by whom he had issue, Thomas, who d. young; William, who succeeded to his property; Mary, who m. Dough O'Brien, and Anne, who d. unm. WILLIAM HENN m. Bridget Browne, and had issue by her, 1. RICHARD HENN, who m. Miss Mary Arthur of Glenomera. 2. William, who m. but d. without issue; 3. Edmund, who m. Miss Gennys, (an English heiress of Devonshire, whose name he took, becoming Edmund Henn-Gennys); 4. Thomas, who m. Miss Blakeney, but had no issue; 5 Poole, who m. Miss Pentland, by whom he left issue, William-Poole, and other children; 1. Jane, who m. John Hunt; 2. Eliza, who m. Bolton Waller, Esq. of Shannon Grove, in co. Limerick; and 3. Anne, m. to — Bambrick, Esq., her first husband, and to — Gubbins, Esq., her 2nd husband. RICHARD HENN, Esq., who m. Miss Arthur, and who on the death of his father, William, s. to the estates, had issue, William, Thomas, and Lucy, who all d. without issue; and he himself dying subsequently, devised the lands of Paradise to his wife Mary, who, in her turn, devised them to her own brother, the late THOMAS ARTHUR, Esq. of Glenomera, in the co. of Clare.

This beautiful property, however, after remaining in the possession of Mr. Arthur for about thirty years, has been recently restored to the name of the ancient proprietors, having been repurchased from Mr. Arthur's younger children by THOMAS RICE HENN, Esq., whose descent from the original grantee of the estate is derived as follows.

WILLIAM HENN, 2nd son of Thomas Henn, the brother and devisee of Richard the grantee, was called to the Irish bar, and created a judge of the King's Bench in 1768. He was father of

WILLIAM HENN, who became a Master of the Irish Court of Chancery 10 July, 1793, and m. Susanna, sister of the late Sir Jonathan Lovett, Bart., of Lipscombe Park, in Buckinghamshire, by whom he left issue, 1 William, his eldest son, now the senior Master in Chancery in Ireland; 2 Jonathan, the celebrated Queen's Counsel; and several other children.

WILLIAM HENN, the present Master in Chancery, m. Mary-

Rice Fosberry, eldest dau. of George Fosbery of Clorane, in the co. of Limerick, Esq., by Christiana his wife, dau. of Thomas Rice, Esq. of Mount Trenchard, in the same co., by whom he has issue; 1. William, who *d. unm.* in 1853; 2. Thomas-Rice, the present proprietor of the Paradise estate; 3. Jonathan-Lovett, and five daus.; 1. Christiana; 2. Susanna; 3. Mary, *m.* to John Stanford, Esq.; 4. Ellen; 5. Jane, *m.* to Robert Holmes, Esq.

The Paradise estate is situate on the River Fergus, at its present junction with the Shannon, and is described by Lloyd, in his survey of the co. Clare, published in the year 1760, as being "one of the most beautiful seats in this kingdom."

It is an interesting fact connected with this distinguished legal family, that Henry Hene, the Lord Chief Baron, a man of known attachment to the Protestant faith, was removed from his high office by King James the 2nd, in order to make way for Mr. Henn's maternal ancestor, Sir Stephen Rice, created Lord Chief Baron, A.D. 1686, upon whom the same sovereign afterwards bestowed the Barony of Mounteagle. The title of Mounteagle, denied by Parliament to Sir Stephen Rice, has been recently restored, as is well known, in the person of his patriotic and gifted descendant, the present Lord Monteagle of Brandon.

Arms (duly registered)—Gu., a lion, rampant, arg., a canton, of the last, thereon a wolf, passant, sa.
Crest—On a mount, vert, a hen-pheasant, ppr.
Motto—Gloria deo.
Seat—Paradise, Killiadysart, co. Clare.

HEPWORTH OF PONTEFRACT.

Hepworth, William, Esq. of Ackworth Lodge, Pontefract, co. York, J.P. and D.L., late captain 3rd W. Y. lt. inf., and mayor of Pontefract in 1833 and 1838, *b.* 6 Dec. 1801; *m.* 18 Aug. 1827, Mary, eldest dau. of John Crossley, Esq. of Scaitcliffe.

Lineage.—John Hepworth, Esq., mayor of Pontefract in 1795, son of Richard Hepworth, Esq. of Armley Heights, co. York, *m.* Anne Townend, sister and, in her issue, heir of William Townend, Esq. (who *d. unm.* 1 April, 1817, when his estates devolved upon his grand-nephew, the present Mr. Hepworth), and by her, with a dau., Anne, *m.* to John Hill, Esq. of Ripley, co. York, was father of

Richard Hepworth, Esq., who *m.* 5 June, 1799, Frances, eldest dau. of Richard Chamberlain, Gent. of Skipton, co. York, and by her (who *d.* 6 June, 1813) left at his decease, 5 Feb. 1817,

William, now of Pontefract.
Frances, *m.* 27 April, 1824, to Thomas Hall, Esq. of Purston Lodge, J.P., and has issue.
Elizabeth-Foss.
Anne, *m.* 13 July, 1824, to Fortescue Wells, Esq. of Slade, co. Devon, capt. royal horse-artillery, and has issue. (*See* Fortescue of Fallapit).

Arms—Arg., a bend, sa., between two lions, rampant, gu.
Crest—Out of a ducal coronet, ppr., a wyvern, vert.
Motto—Loyal à mort.
Residence—Ackworth Lodge, Pontefract.

HERBERT OF LLANARTH.

Herbert, John-Arthur-Edward, Esq. of Llanarth Court, co. Monmouth, J.P. and D.L., *m.* 1846, Augusta-Charlotte-Elizabeth, only child of the Right Hon. Sir Benjamin Hall, Bart, M.P., and has issue,

I. Ivor-John-Caradoc, *b.* in 1851.
I. Henrietta-Mary-Arvanwen.
II. Florence-Catherine-Mary.

Lineage.—This very ancient family, from which the chivalrous house of Herbert and other eminent houses sprang, derived originally in England from Herbert styled Count of Vermandois, who came over at the Conquest with the first William, and filled the office of chamberlain to the second (William Rufus). He is mentioned in the Battle Abbey Roll, and was rewarded by a grant of lands in Hampshire. His wife was Emma, dau. of Stephen, Earl of Blois, by Adela, dau. of William the Conqueror, and by that lady he left a son and heir, Herbert Fitz-Herbert, called Herbert of Winchester, chamberlain and treasurer to King Henry I., and the first of his family born in England. He *m.* Adela, or Lucy, dau. and co-heir of Sir Robert Corbet, Knt., Lord of Alcester, co. Warwick, and was father of Herbert Fitz-Herbert, who obtained from Henry II. a confirmation of the landed possessions of his father, and likewise the office of chamberlain. His great-grandson,

Peter Fitz-Reginald, *b.* in 1275 (brother of John Fitz-Reginald, summoned to parliament as a Baron in 1294, and 3rd son, by Joan his wife, dau. and co-heir of William de Vivonia, Lord of Chewton, co. Somerset, of Reginald Fitz-Peter, Lord of Blenlevenny, son of Peter Fitz-Herbert, Baron of Berstaple, co. Devon, by Alice his 1st wife, dau. of Robert Fitz-Roger, Lord of Warkworth and Clavering), had a grant from his mother, Joan de Vivonia, of the manor of Cheuyton, or Chewton. He *m.* Alice, dau. and heir of Blethin Broadspere, Lord of Llanlowell, near Uske, in Monmouthshire, and had issue,

Roger Fitz-Peter, who *d.* before his father, leaving an only son and heir, Sir Henry Fitz-Roger, Knt., whose granddau. and heir, Elizabeth, *m.* John Boneville.
Herbert Fitz-Peter.

He *d.* in 1323. His younger son,

Herbert Fitz-Peter, *m.* Margaret, dau. of Sir John Walsh, Knt., and left a son and heir,

Adam Fitz-Herbert, Lord of Llan-Howell, or Llanllowell, near Uske, and of Betesley, or Beachley. His grandson,

William ap Jenkin, *alias* Herbert, Lord of Gwarindee, living at Perthir, near Monmouth, from 20 to 50 (1337) of Edward III., *m.* Gwenllian, dau. of Howell Ichon, Esq., and had four sons viz.,

I. John, or Jenkyn ap Gwillim, of Gwarindee, or Werndu, ancestor of the family of Progers.
II. David ap Gwillim ap Jenkin, of the Chapell, *m.* Anne, dau. of Watkin Rees, of that place, and was ancestor of the Morgans of Arxton.
III. Howell ap Gwillim, of whom presently.
IV. Thomas ap Gwillim, Knt., *m.* Maud, dau. and co-heir of Sir John Morley, Knt., Lord of Ragland Castle, and acquired thereby, Llansaintfraed, where he afterwards resided, and was buried at his decease, 8 July, 1438. His youngest* son,

Sir William ap Thomas, Knt., *alias* Herbert, of Ragland Castle, co. Monmouth, knighted by Henry V., at Azincourt. He *m.* the dau. of Sir David Gam, Knt., and had issue, from which derived the Herberts, Earls of Powis, the Herberts *of Coldbrook House*, the Herberts, Lords Herberts, *of Chirbury*, the Herberts *of Muckruss*, co. Kerry (*which see*), the Herberts *of St. Julians*, &c.

The 3rd son,

Howell ap Gwillim, *m.* Maud, dau. of Howell ap Rhys, and was *s.* by his son,

Jenkin ap Howell, who *m.* Constance, dau. of Roger Vychan ap Walter Says, Esq., and left a son and heir,

David ap Jenkin, who fell at the battle of Banbury, fighting under the standard of his cousin, the Earl of Pembroke. He *m.* Margaret, dau. and co-heir of Thomas Huntley, Esq. of Treowen, Llanarth, &c., son of Thomas Huntley, Esq. of Treowen, by Alice his wife, dau. and heir of William Wallis, Esq. of Llanarth, and was *s.* by his son,

Thomas ap David ap Jenkin, of Treowen, who *m.* Margaret, dau. of Morgan Kemeys, and left a son and heir,

John ap Thomas, of Treowen, who *m.* in 1481, Anne, dau. of David ap Gwillim Morgan, Esq. of Arxton, co. Hereford, and had issue, William, his heir; David, of Chepstow, co. Monmouth, ancestor of the Viscounts Ranelagh; and other issue. The eldest son and heir,

William ap John, *alias* Jones, lord of Hendre Obeth, Castle Arnold, Llanarth, and Cefn Dugloid, *m.* 1st, Constance, dau. of Thomas Morgan, Esq., and sister of Rowland Morgan, Esq. of Machin, and by that lady had issue, John, his heir; William; Charles; and Walter. Mr. Jones *m.* 2ndly, Anne, dau. of Sir Walter Hawley, Knt. of Sussex, and by her had, Philip, of London and Llanarth; John; and Elizabeth. He *m.* 3rdly, Elizabeth, dau. of Richard Herbert, Esq. of Penkelly, and had another son, namely, William; and a dau., Blanch, who *m.* Rowland Morgan, Esq. of Machen, and conveyed the estate of Castle Arnold to the Morgans. He was *s.* by his eldest son,

John Jones, Esq. of Treowen, living in 1563, and dead before 1609; who *m.* Anne, dau. of Giles Doddington, Esq. of the co. of Somerset, and had (with three daus., Florence, *m.* to Edward Points, Esq.; Jane; and Elizabeth, *m.* to Sir Charles Jones, of Dingestow, in Monmouthshire) a son and heir,

* The elder sons were, Philip, of Llansaintfraed; Evan, ancestor of the Gwyns and Raglands *of Glamorganshire*; David, progenitor of the family of Hughes *of Kilcurt*; and Howell, of Perthyr, near Monmouth, ancestor of the Powells *of Perthyr*.

WILLIAM JONES, Esq. of Treowen, Hendre, Obeth, and Llanarth, who m. Jane, only dau. and heir of Moor Gwillim, Esq. of Monmouth, M.P. for that borough in 1586, and was s. by his eldest son,

SIR PHILIP JONES, Knt. of Treowen, lieut.-col. of the troops raised in the co. of Monmouth for CHARLES I., and M.P. for the same county in 1653. He m. Elizabeth, dau. of Sir Edward Morgan, Bart. of Llantarnan Abbey, in the co. of Monmouth, and had three sons and nine daus. Dying in 1660, he was s. by his eldest son,

WILLIAM JONES, Esq. of Llanarth Court, Treowen, who m. Mary, dau. of Christopher Anderton, Esq. of Lostock, co. Lancaster; and dying in 1667, was s. by his elder son,

PHILIP JONES, Esq. of Llanarth Court, who m. Anne, dau. and heir of Anthony Bassett, Esq. of Kamain, co. Glamorgan, and had, with five daus., of whom the eldest, Elizabeth, m. in 1705, John Vaughan, Esq. of Courtfield, co. Monmouth, four sons, of whom the eldest,

JOHN JONES, Esq. of Llanarth Court, Treowen, and Penllwyn, co. Monmouth, m. Florence, sister and heir of Henry Morgan, Esq. of Penllwyn (a branch of the MORGANS *of Tredegar*), by whom (who d. in Dec. 1756) he had, with five daus., of whom the eldest, Mary, m. in 1768, Richard Lee, Esq. of Great Delce, Kent, of Clytha, and Llanfoist, co. Monmouth, six sons, of whom three d. under age: the others were, PHILIP, the heir; John, major in the Hanoverian service, b. in 1728, d unm. in 1808; and William, of Clytha House, co. Monmouth, which he purchased from his brother-in-law, b. in 1733–4, m. in 1767, Elizabeth, dau. of Sir William Morgan, K.B., but d. s. p. in 1805. Mr. Jones d. in March, 1775, aged 88, and was s. by his son,

PHILIP JONES, Esq. of Llanarth Court, b in 1723, who, m. Catherine, youngest sister and co-heir of John Wyborne, Esq. of Hawkwell Place, in Kent. He d. 16 May, 1782 leaving a son, his heir,

JOHN JONES, Esq. of Llanarth Court, co. Monmouth, and of Upton Court, Berks, who m. 18 Sept. 1789, his cousin, Mary, eldest dau. and co-heir (with her sisters, Elizabeth, who d. unm.; and Apollonia, m. in 1792, to Robert Berkeley, Esq. of Spetchley, co. Worcester) of Richard Lee, Esq. of Llanfoist House, near Abergavenny by Mary Jones his wife, and by her (who d. 1854) had issue,

- JOHN, his heir.
- Philip of the Hill House, Abergavenny, and of Perthyre House, near Monmouth, b. 7 Dec. 1791; high-sheriff of Monmouthshire in 1837.
- William, of Clytha House, which estate he inherited under the will of his grand-uncle of the same name, b. in Dec. 1798; m. Frances, eldest dau. of Edward Huddleston, Esq. of Purse Caundle, co. Dorset, and niece of the late Richard Huddleston, Esq. of Sawston Hall, in Cambridgeshire, and has, William-Reginald-Joseph-Fitzherbert, and other issue.
- Edward-Basil, b. 14 June, 1800. Henry-Wyborne.
- Richard, b. in 1806, capt. Hanoverian hussars.
- Thomas, b. in 1808; d. and buried at Llanarth, in 1823.
- Mary, m. 21 June, 1821, to Simon-Thomas Scrope, Esq., eldest son of Simon-Thomas Scrope, Esq. of Danby-upon-Yore, co. York; and d. 25 April, 1830, leaving issue.
- Elizabeth. Florence, d. unm. in 1807.
- Anne, d. unm. in 1808. Jane-Mary.
- Apollonia, m. at Llanarth, 5 Feb. 1834, to Mons. Rio, of Brittany.

Mr. Jones dying in June, 1828, was s. by his eldest son,

JOHN JONES, Esq. of Llanarth Court, b. 5 June, 1790; who m. 11 Sept. 1817, Lady Harriet Plunkett, only dau. of Arthur-James, 8th Earl of Fingall, K.P.; and dying 22 April, 1848, left issue,

- JOHN-ARTHUR, now of Llanarth.
- Arthur-James, lieut.-col. in the army, b. 21 Jan. 1820.
- Edmund-Philip, b. 24 Jan. 1823; major R. M. militia.
- Gerald-Herbert, b. 9 Feb. 1826; deceased.
- Frances-Mary, d. 1843. Mary-Louisa.

Arms—Per pale, az. and gu., three lions, rampant, arg. The Quarterings are very numerous.

Crest—A Moorish woman's head, affrontée, with long hair, sa., a wreath about the head, or and gu., tied at the end by a button.

Motto—Asgre lân Diogell ei Pherchen.

Seat—Llanarth Court, Monmouthshire.

HERBERT OF MUCKRUSS.

HERBERT, HENRY-ARTHUR, Esq. of Muckruss, co. Kerry, M.P. for that county, m. Mary, dau. of the late James Balfour, Esq. of Whittinghame, East Lothian, by Lady Eleanor, his wife, dau. of James Maitland, 8th Earl of Lauderdale, and has issue,

- I. HENRY-ARTHUR. II. Charles.
- I. Louisa.

Lineage.—The name of Herbert (her-Bert, *illustrious Lord*) stands so prominent upon the records of British history, and has been ennobled, at various times, in so many of its branches, and by so many ancient and renewed creations, that it has become a matter of as much interest as difficulty, in the present day, to ascertain the legitimate and chief stem of this long descended family.

Since the merging of the elder branch in the family of CLIVE, by the marriage of the heiress of the last Herbert, Earl of Powis, with the son of the celebrated General Lord Clive, the chieftainship of the name seems indubitably to rest with HERBERT *of Muckruss*, in the county of Kerry, descended from Thomas Herbert, of Kilcuagh, who went to Ireland under the care and patronage of his relative Lord Herbert, of Cherbury and Castle Island, A.D. 1656; which Thomas was the son of Mathew, the son of Sir John, the son of Sir William, the son of Sir Mathew, of Colebroke, the lineal descendant from the eldest son of Sir Richard Herbert, of Colebroke, only brother of the Earl of Pembroke, of the first creation. These brothers, (as may be read in the pages of Speed and Hollinshed), suffered as Yorkists in the wars of the Roses. The heir general of the Earl of Pembroke married into the family of Somerset, Earl and Marquess of Worcester, and Duke of Beaufort. From Sir Richard descended, in the younger branches, the Lords Herbert, of Cherbury, after Earls of Powis, and Herbert, Earl of Torrington, both extinct in the male line, while from a senior, but never ennobled branch, the family of Muckruss and Kilcuagh, now remains the existing and legitimate male representative of this long-descended house.

THOMAS HERBERT, of Kilcuagh aforesaid, served as high-sheriff of the co. Kerry, 1659. He m. Mary, dau. of Edward Kenny, of Cullen, co. Cork, and had issue,

- EDWARD, his heir. John, d. s. p.
- Arthur, m. Mary Bastable, of whom came the wide-spread branches of HERBERT *of Currens, of Cahirnane, and Brewsterfield*, and their collaterals.

The eldest son,

EDWARD HERBERT, Esq. of Muckruss, high-sheriff of Kerry, m. 1684, Agnes Crosbie, dau. of Patrick Crosbie, of Tubrid, and had issue,

- EDWARD, his heir.
- John, d. s p. Arthur, d. s. p.
- Elizabeth, m. to William Hull, of Lemcon, eldest son of Sir William Hull.
- Arabella, m. to Sir Francis Brewster, Knt.
- Margaret, m. 1st, to John Leader, of Mount Leader, co. Cork; and 2ndly, to the Rev. Stanley Craven.

The eldest son,

EDWARD HERBERT, Esq. of Muckruss, M.P. for Ludlow, in Salop, A.D. 1756, m. the Hon. Frances Browne, dau. of Nicholas, 2nd Viscount Kenmare, and had issue,

- THOMAS, his heir.
- Nicholas, in holy orders; m. Hon. Martha Cuffe, dau. of John, 1st Lord Dysart, and from him descend the HERBERTS *of the co. Tipperary*.
- Edward, M.P. 1760, for Inistioge, co. Kilkenny.
- Agnes, m. 1st, to Florence McCarthy-More;* and 2ndly, to Edward Herbert, of Currens, s. p.
- Helena, m. to Hedges, Esq. of Macroom Castle, co. Cork.
- Frances, m. to John Blennerhassett, Esq. of Ballyseedy.
- Arabella, d. unm.
- Thomasine, m. Thomas Cuffe, Esq., and was mother of Grace Cuffe, wife of Barry-Maxwell, Earl of Farnham.
- Catherine, m. to Robert Herbert, of the Currens family.

The eldest son,

THOMAS HERBERT, Esq. of Muckruss, M.P. for Ludlow, m. 1st, Anne Marten, of Overbury, co. Worcester, and by her had issue,

- HENRY-ARTHUR, his heir.
- Edward, in holy orders, m. to Mary Herbert, of Brewsterfield, dau. of Bastable Herbert and Barbara-Fitzgerald, dau. of the Knight of Kerry, and hence descends the REV. EDWARD HERBERT, now vicar of Killarney.
- Frances, m. to the Rev. Edward Kenny.
- Catherine, m. to the Rev. Mr. Dawson.
- Mary, m. Rev. Arthur Herbert, brother of R.-T. Herbert, of whom descend Rev. Thomas Herbert, rector of Killentierna, and his brothers.
- Anne, m. to Col. James Kearney.
- Emily, m. Richard-Townsend Herbert, of Cahirnane, as his 1st wife.

---

* The only son of this marriage, Charles McCartie-More, d. unm. 1770, and bequeathed the remnant of his once-territorial estates, including Pallace, once the famed residence of the McCarties, to his kinsman, Thomas Herbert, of Muckruss.

Thomas Herbert m. 2ndly, Agnes, dau. of Rev. Francis Bland, vicar of Killarney, and by her had issue,

Thomas, d. s. p. 1798, buried in Worcester cathedral
Francis, killed in a duel at Gibraltar, 1797.
Cherry, d. unm. Elizabeth.

The eldest son,

HENRY-ARTHUR HERBERT, Esq. of Muckruss, m. Elizabeth, dau. of Lord George Sackville, and sister to the last Duke of Dorset, and had issue a dau., Elizabeth, wife of Major Henry Verelst, and a son and successor,

CHARLES HERBERT, Esq. of Muckruss, who m. 1814, Louisa Middleton, and had issue,

HENRY-ARTHUR, now of Muckruss.
Charles, d. s. p.
Louisa, m. Hon. and Rev. H. Stuart, brother to the Earl of Galloway, and has issue.
Emily, m. to Colonel Long.
Maria, m. to Hon. White Hedges, of Macroom Castle, and has issue.

Arms—Per pale, az. and gu., three lions, rampant, arg., armed and langued, or.
Crest—A bundle of arrows, or, headed and feathered, arg., six in saltire, one in pale, girt round the middle with a belt, gu., buckle and point extended, of the first.
Seat—Muckruss, co. Kerry.

HERBERT OF CAHIRNANE.

ARTHUR HERBERT, 3rd son of Thomas Herbert, of Kilcuagh, and Mary Kenny (*see* HERBERT *of Muckruss*), m. Mary, dau. of George Bastable, of Castle Island, and had issue,

GEORGE, his heir.
John, of Knockanagore, m. Anne Blennerhasset; and d. s. p.
Thomas, m. Mary Biggs: male issue extinct.
Edward, m. Agnes Herbert, widow of McCarthy-More, s. p.
Arthur, m. Lucy Brewster, dau. of Francis Brewster, of Brewsterfield.
Bastable, m. Barbara-Fitzgerald, dau. of Maurice, Knt. of Kerry, and from him descend the HERBERTS *of Brewsterfield*.
Francis, d. s. p. Charles, d. s. p.
Lucy, m. to Francis Markham.
Agnes, m. Orpen, of Kilowen.
Mary, m. 1st, Supple; 2ndly, Lucy.
Margaret, m. Saunders.
Charity, m. Richard Chute, of Chute Hall.

GEORGE HERBERT, Esq., eldest son of Arthur Herbert and Mary Bastable, m. Jane Fitzgerald, dau. of Maurice Fitzgerald, Knt. of Kerry, and had issue,

ARTHUR, his heir.
Maurice, s. p., served in the American War.
John, d. s. p.
George, d. s. p., served in the American War.
Edward, s. p. Thomas, s. p. John, s. p.
Elizabeth, m. Francis Brewster, of Brewsterfield.
Jane, m. Talbot.
Lucy, m. Gorham, of Obrennan.
Agnes, m. Eusebius Chute, of Obrennan.

The eldest son,

ARTHUR HERBERT, Esq. of Cahirnane and Currans, m. Frances, dau. of Colonel Richard Townsend, of Castle Townsend, co. Cork, and had issue,

RICHARD-TOWNSEND, his heir.
Arthur, in holy orders, m. Mary Herbert, of Muckruss, and had issue. Helen.

Arthur Herbert, m. 2ndly, Agnes Colles, widow of Frederick Mullins, of Burnham, eldest brother of the 1st Baron Ventry, and had issue by her,

Frances, m. 1794, to Richard Digby, Esq.

The eldest son,

RICHARD TOWNSEND-HERBERT, Esq. of Cahirnane, m. 1st, Emily Herbert, of Muckruss, and by her had issue, Emily and Anne. He m. 2ndly, Jane, dau. of Anthony Stoughton Esq. of Ballyhorgan, and Elizabeth Bateman his wife, and had issue,

ARTHUR, his heir.
THOMAS (Sir), K.C.B., rear-admiral R.N., b. 1793; who served with distinction in the Chinese War of 1840-1, was a lord of the Admiralty from Feb. to Dec. 1852, and has been M.P. for Dartmouth since 1852. Sir Thomas was high-sheriff, co. Kerry, 1829, and is a deputy-lieut.
Richard, in holy orders, d. unm.
Charles, major in the army.
Elizabeth, m. to Rear-Adm. Wm. Butcher, and has issue.
Helen, m. to Rev. Barry Denny, and has issue.
Jane.
Penelope, m. to Francis Chute, Esq. of Chute Hall.
Frances.
Anne, m. to Rev. Browning Drew; and d. 1853.
Letitia, m. to — Jackson, Esq., co. Tipperary.
Mary, m. to John Bouchier, Esq.

The eldest son,

REV. ARTHUR HERBERT, rector of Castle Island, co. Kerry, m. Jane, dau. of Rev. Maynard Denny, of Churchhill, by Penelope Stoughton his wife, and has issue,

RICHARD, in holy orders.
Edward, captain Kerry regiment of militia.
Penelope, m. to Arthur-Maynard Denny, Esq., grandson of Admiral Lord Collingwood, and has issue.

HERBERT OF PILL HOUSE.

HERBERT, WALTER-OTWAY, Esq. of Pill House, co. Tipperary, J.P., b. 8 Oct. 1798; m. 19 Sept. 1822, Mary, only dau. of John Miles, Esq. of Damereu House, co. Dorset, and has issue,

I. JOHN-OTWAY, in holy orders.
II. Nicholas.
I. Margaret-Jane, m. to Nicholas Valentine Maher, Esq. of Turtulla, late M.P. co. Tipperary.
II. Honoria.

Lineage.—THE REV. NICHOLAS HERBERT, younger son of Edward Herbert, Esq. of Muckruss, M.P. for Ludlow, 1756, by Frances his wife, dau. of Nicholas, Viscount Kenmare, m. Hon. Martha Cuffe, dau. of John, 1st Lord Desart, and by her, who d. in 1808, left at his decease, in 1802, JOHN-OTWAY, his heir; Thomas, m. Lucinda, dau. of the Hon. and Rev. Hamilton Cuffe; Nicholas, J.P., in holy orders; Lucinda, m. to William Bradshaw, Esq.; Sophia, m. to John Mandeville, Esq. of Anner Castle; and three other daus., who d. unm.

THE REV. JOHN-OTWAY HERBERT, who m. 1796, Honoria-Ann, only dau. of Captain James Russell, H.E.I.C.S., and had an only child, WALTER-OTWAY HERBERT, Esq.

Arms and *Crest*—See HERBERT OF MUCKRUSS.
Seat—Pill House, near Carrick-on-Suir.

HERCY OF CRUCHFIELD.

HERCY, JOHN, Esq. of Cruchfield House, Berks, J.P. and D.L., b. 10 July, 1790; m. 21 Nov. 1815, Frances, only child of Thomas-Joseph Moore, Esq. of Stafford House, Chiswick, Middlesex, and has surviving issue,

I. THOMAS-JOSEPH, b. 31 Dec. 1824.
II. Francis-John, b. 22 Nov. 1835.
III. Eustace-Lovelace, b. 27 July, 1838.
I. Frances-Bridget, m. 21 Sept. 1840, to Joseph-Francis Tempest, Esq., fourth surviving son of the late Stephen Tempest, Esq. of Broughton, co. York.
II. Elizabeth, twin with her sister Frances.
III. Mary-Anne. IV. Theresa.
V. Emma-Lucy. VI. Catharine-Joanna.

Lineage.—In the reign of HENRY III.,

MALVEYSIN DE HERCY was constable of Tykhill. He m. Theophania, dau. and co.-heir (with her sister Isabel,* wife of Sir William Rufus, Knt.) of Gilbert de Arches, Baron of Grove, Notts, and had two sons, Robert, who d. s. p., and

SIR HUGH HERCY, Knt. of Grove, co. Nottingham, from whom descended the HERCYS *of Grove, Notts*, and the HERCYS *of Cruchfield*; the latter preserved a male succession up to the death in 1794, of LOVELACE HERCY, Esq. of Cruchfield, Berks, and of Newman Street, London, banker, His nephew and heir,

THOMAS-HERCY SMALLWOOD, Esq. of Great Portland Street, London, b. 1 Feb. 1756, (elder son of Henry Smallwood, of the Strand, Westminster, by Rebecca-Sophia his wife, dau. of William Hercy, Esq. of Cruchfield), assumed the surname and arms of HERCY only, by sign-manual, 10 Dec. 1821. He m. 23 Jan. 1785, Bridget, dau. of Thomas Barker, Esq. of Great Thornham, Suffolk, and had issue,

JOHN, now of Cruchfield.
Henry-Edward, b. 23 Nov. 1792; m. Miss Pugh, and had issue.
Elizabeth, m. to John Brydon, Esq. of Welbeck Street, Cavendish Square.
Bridget, m. to John Devey, Esq. of Wolverhampton.

Mr. Hercy d. in 1823.

Arms—Gu., a chief, arg., quartering ARCHES, LEKE, TOWERS, STAVELEY, TALBOT, and DE FREIGN.
Crest—Out of a ducal coronet, or, a man's head, ppr., wreathed about the temples.
Seat—Hawthorn Hill, Berks.

* Her great grandson, Eustace de Mortaine, sold his lands to Robert de Hercy.

HEREFORD OF SUFTON COURT.

Hereford, Richard, Esq. of Sufton Court, co. Hereford, J.P., *b.* 6 July, 1808; *m.* 5 June, 1828, Harriot-Arabella, dau. of the late Capt. Sir Robert Mends, Knt., R.N., and has issue,

I. Richard-James, *b.* 1 April, 1833.
I. Harriot-Mary.

Lineage.—The family of Hereford, one of very great antiquity, derived its surname, according to an old manuscript, from "the name of a city on the borders of the Principality of Wales, formerly very well fortified, and the ordinary residence of the ancient Earls of Hereford."

Contemporaneous with the potent feudal Earls of Hereford, there resided in the city of Hereford, in the time of Henry II., A.D. 1170,

Roger Hereford, "a famous philosopher, (says the same manuscript,) who published during the period that Henry of Hereford, and Mabel, his brother, enjoyed the co. of Hereford, the books quoted by John Pits.

This eminent man flourished about the year 1170, in the reign of the second Henry, and sixteen years after the death of Roger, Earl of Hereford, one of the brothers of the heiresses who divided the great estates of these earls; so that he seems to have been born at the close of Henry the First's time. He left at his decease a son,

Henry de Hereford, of whom there is an entry in the Pipe Roll, in the 8th of John, *anno* 1201, "that Master Henry of Hereford owes a palfrey, for a fief of the king, to William of Braieuse, for the land of Witton." This appears to have been the first estate in the family. From this Henry descended the eminent Herefordshire family of Hereford *of Sufton* and *Mordiford*.

Sir Henry de Hereford, of Sufton and Mordiford, distinguished himself in the Scottish wars, and received the honour of knighthood from King Edward III., with a general pardon for all offences committed by him against the State. In 1352, he was present in the parliament held at Westminster, as one of the representatives of the county of Hereford; and the same year he was a second time summoned to the great parliament which was to be held at the same place.

Sir James Hereford, Knt. of Sufton, *b.* 1718, the last male heir of this long-descended line, *m.* twice, 1st, Martha, dau. of — Skinner, and 2ndly, Frances, dau. of — Hopton, Esq. of Cannon Frome, but dying issueless, in 1780, devised his estates, by will, to (the son of his eldest sister) his nephew,

James Caldicott, Esq. of Holmer House, *b.* in 1756, (son of John Caldicott, Esq. of Holmer House, co. Hereford, by Frances, his wife, dau. of Roger Hereford, Esq. of Sufton,) who assumed, in consequence, the surname and arms of Hereford. He *m.* Mary, dau. of John Scudamore, Esq. of Kentchurch Court, in the co. of Hereford, and had issue,

Richard, his heir.
Mary.
Sarah, *m.* to David Lambe, Esq. of Hereford.
Frances. Catharine, *d. unm.* in 1826.
Anne, *m.* to John-Kelly Tudor, Esq., R.N., of Penally, Pembrokeshire.
Lucy.

Mr. Hereford *d.* in Feb. 1823, and was *s.* by his son, the present Richard Hereford, Esq. of Sufton.

Arms—Gu., three eagles, displayed, arg.
Crest—An eagle, displayed.
Seat—Sufton Court, near Hereford.

BURCHELL-HERNE OF BUSHEY GRANGE.

Burchell-Herne, Humphrey-Harper, Esq. of Bushey Grange, co. Hertford, M.A. Trinity College, Cambridge, and of the Middle Temple, barrister-at-law, *b.* 2 Sept. 1797, *m.* 1 June, 1837, Harriet, younger dau. of Richard Miles, Esq. of Kensington, and has issue,

I. Humphrey-Frederick-Herne, *b.* 1 Oct. 1843.
I. Harriet-Sarah II. Dorothea-Louisa.

Mr. Burchell-Herne is in the commission of the peace for the counties of Hertford and Middlesex, a deputy-lieutenant of the former, and in 1847 served the office of high-sheriff of Herts. In 1854, as grand-nephew and heir of Sir William Herne, he assumed by sign-manual the additional surname of Herne.

Lineage.—Richard Herne, an alderman, and in 1618 sheriff of London, *m.* Susanna, dau. of John Woodward, of Hampstead, in the co. of Middlesex, Esq., and left a son and successor,

Nicholas Herne, of Hampstead, who had two sons,

Basil, his heir.
Nathaniel (Sir) Knt., Alderman, and 1674 sheriff of London, *m.* Judith, dau. of Sir John Frederick, lord-mayor of that city, and had, with other issue, a son,
Frederick-Herne, whose dau., Judith Herne, *m.* at Hampstead Church, 22 March, 1704, William, second Earl of Jersey.

The elder son,

Basil Herne, Esq. of Hampstead, *m.* Dorothy, dau. of Hugh Wilbraham, Esq. of Woodhey, co. Chester, brother of Sir Richard Wilbraham, Baronet, and dying 1692, left, with four daus., a son and successor,

Basil Herne, Esq., one of the six clerks of the Court of Chancery, who *d.* in 1728, leaving, by his wife, Susanna, two daus., Elizabeth and Dorothy, and a son and successor,

Basil Herne, Esq. of Hampstead, who *m.* in 1737, Sophia, dau. of Lewis Barbar, Esq. of Dover Street, Piccadilly, and dying in 1774, left issue three sons and a dau., viz.,

Basil, of Hampstead, who *d.* in 1806, *unm.*
Lewis, who *m.* Honor, dau. of Thomas Ashton, Esq., and *d.* without issue.
William (Sir) Knt., of Hampstead and Oldfield Lodge, Berks, alderman, and in 1797 sheriff of London, who *m.* twice, but *d.* without issue, in 1854.
Susanna, *m.* in 1762, John Blount Burchell, only son of Matthew Burchell, of Hunton, in the co. of Kent, and left issue,
Basil Burchell, of Bushey Grange, Esq., *b.* in 1764, *m.* in 1793, Sarah, dau. of Lieut.-Colonel Humphrey Harper, of the Madras army, and dying 1838, left issue,
Humphrey-Harper Burchell, now Herne.
Basil Herne Burchell, lieut.-col. in the army.

Arms—Quarterly: 1st and 4th, for Herne, arg., a chevron erminée, between three herons. 2nd and 3rd, for Burchell, argent, a chevron, sable, charged with three fleurs-de-lys, between three cross-crosslets fitchée.
Crests—Out of a ducal coronet, or, a heron's head proper, and a lion rampant, az., supported by a tree, vert.
Motto—Usque ad aras.
Seat—Bushey Grange, Herts.

HERON OF MOOR HALL.

Heron, The Rev. George, of Moor Hall, co. Chester, *s.* his father 15 Nov. 1848.

Lineage.—This is a branch of the Herons of Chipchase Castle, Northumberland. The first member of the family possessed of landed estates in Cheshire was

George Heron, Esq., who purchased the manor of Daresbury, with other estates, in 1755. He *m.* Felicia, eldest dau. of Peter Brooke, Esq. of Mere, in that county, and by her had issue,

George, in holy orders, a fellow of Brasennose College, Oxford, and rector of Warburton, Cheshire, *d. s. p.*
Peter-Kyffen, of whom presently.
William, in holy orders, vicar of Middlewich.

The second son,

Peter-Kyffen Heron, Esq. of Daresbury Hall, sheriff of Cheshire in 1777, *m.* 20 Oct. 1768, Rebecca, only dau. and heiress of Richard Rutter, Esq. of Moor Hall, co. Chester, by whom the family acquired the estates they now possess in that township. By her, Mr. Heron had issue,

Peter, his heir.
Elizabeth, who *d. unm.* in 1837.

The son and heir,

Gen. Peter Heron, of Moor Hall, D.L., M.P. for Newton, *b.* 19 May, 1770; *m.* 29 May, 1799, Catherine, dau. of Edward Gregge-Hopwood, Esq. of Hopwood Hall, Lancashire, and had issue,

George, in holy orders, now of Moor Hall.
Harry, captain in the army, *m.* Elizabeth, dau. of Dr. Freeman, M.D. of Chester.
Catherine.
Mary-Felicia, *m.* to John Smith Barry, Esq. of Marbury Hall, co. Chester, and Foaty, co. Cork.

General Heron *d.* 1848.

Arms—Gu., a chev. between three herons, close, arg.
Crest—A heron, close, arg.
Motto—Ardua petit ardea.
Seat—Moor Hall, co. Chester.

HERRICK OF BEAUMANOR.

PERRY-HERRICK, WILLIAM, Esq. of Beaumanor, co. Leicester, J.P. and D.L., *b.* in 1794; barrister-at-law, M.A. of University College, Oxford, high-sheriff, of Leicestershire, in 1835.

Lineage.—"There is a tradition," says Dean Swift,* "that the most ancient family of the ERICKS derive their lineage from ERICK, the forester, a great commander, who raised an army to oppose the invasion of WILLIAM the Conqueror, by whom he was vanquished; but afterwards employed to command that Prince's forces, and in his old age retired to his house in Leicestershire, where his family hath continued ever since." Though the earliest ancestor of the family is only recorded by tradition, we learn from ancient writings of unquestionable authority, that the EYRICKS were seated, at a very remote period, at Great Stretton, in Leicestershire, in that respectable line of life, so justly the pride of an Englishman, free tenants of their own lands, two virgates of which they held under the Abbey of Leicester, on the payment of an annual quit rent to the king of a pound of pepper. These virgates had been given to the abbey by Ralph Friday, Lord of Wibtoft, and were successively held by Roger Torr, Sir Ralph Neville, Alan and Henry Eyryk, and Robert Eyryk, the son of Alan.

HENRY EYRYK (the above named) was grandfather of

ROBERT EYRYK, of Stretton, who, by Joanna, his wife, had three sons, viz.,

WILLIAM, (Sir,) his heir.
Robert, known by the name of Robert de Stretton, who entering into holy orders, obtained the degree of LL.D., was appointed chaplain to EDWARD the Black Prince, and was eventually consecrated Bishop of Lichfield. His lordship *d.* in 1385.
John, of Stretton.

From the eldest son,

SIR WILLIAM EYRIK, Knt. of Stretton, descended,

ROBERT EYRICK, of Houghton-on-the-Hill, living about 1450, who left, by Agnes, his wife, two sons, Robert, who *d. s. p.*, and

THOMAS EYRICK, of Houghton, who settled at Leicester, and is the first of the name that appears in the corporation books, where he is mentioned as a member of that body, in 1511. He died about six years after, leaving two sons and a dau. The second son,

JOHN EYRICK, or HEYRICK, of Leicester, *b.* in 1518, was twice mayor of that corporation, in 1559 and 1572. He *m.* Mary, dau. of John Bond, Esq. of Wardend, in Warwickshire, and by her (who *d.* 8 Dec. 1611, aged ninety-seven) had, with seven daus., five sons, viz.,

ROBERT, thrice mayor of Leicester, and representative of the borough in parliament. He *d.* in 1618, leaving a numerous family. He is now represented by the REV. SAMUEL HEYRICK, rector of Brampton, in Northamptonshire.
Nicholas, of London, who *m.* in 1582, Julian, dau. of William Stone, Esq. of Segenhoe, in Bedfordshire, and dying in 1592, left issue, 1 William, *b.* in 1585, *d. s. p.*; 2 Thomas, *b.* in 1588, who *m.* and had issue. He is presumed to have been grandfather of Thomas Heyrick, curate of Harborough, who published some sermons and poems; 3 Nicholas, of London, merchant, living in 1664, aged 75, *m.* Susanna, dau. of William Salter, and had issue; 4 ROBERT, *b.* in 1591, in holy orders, a poet of considerable merit; and 5 William, *b.* in 1593.
Thomas, *d.* in 1623, *s. p.*
John, alderman of Leicester, *d.* in 1613, leaving issue.
WILLIAM, (Sir,) of whom we treat.

The fifth son,

SIR WILLIAM HEYRICKE, M.P. for Leicester, *b.* about the year 1557, removing to London, in 1574, to reside with his brother Nicholas, then an eminent banker in Cheapside, attached himself to the court, and for a considerable time "resided constantly there." He was a man of great abilities and address; remarkably handsome, as appears by a small picture still preserved of him, in his younger days; was high in the confidence of Queen ELIZABETH, as well as of King JAMES, and by honourable service to both, acquired large property. In the reign of the former sovereign he was despatched on an embassy to the Ottoman Porte, and on his return rewarded with a lucrative appointment in the Exchequer. He *d.* 2 March, 1652-3, having had by his wife, Joan, dau. of Richard May, Esq. of London, and sister of Sir Humphrey May, Chancellor of the Duchy of Lancaster five daus. and seven sons, 1 WILLIAM, his heir; 2 Robert, *d. s. p.*; 3 Richard, who *d.* warden of Manchester, in 1667; 4 Thomas; 5 Henry; 6 Roger, Fellow of All Souls'; and 7 John, *b.* in 1612. Sir William (who was aged ninety-six at his decease) was *s.* by his son,

* The dean's father married Mrs. Abigail Erick, of Leicestershire, descended from this family.

WILLIAM HERRICK, Esq. of Beaumanor, *b.* in 1597, who was appointed, in 1633, by King CHARLES I., to repair the Castle of Leicester, and place it in a proper state of defence. He *m.* in 1623, Elizabeth, dau. of Humphrey Fox, Esq. of London, and dying in 1671, left an only son and successor,

WILLIAM HERRICK, Esq. of Beaumanor, *b.* in 1624, who *m.* 1st, in July, 1649, Anne, eldest dau. of William Bainbrigge, Esq. of Lockington, in the county of Leicester, by Elizabeth, his wife, dau. of Gervas Pigott, Esq. of Thrumpton, Notts, and had by her (who *d.* in 1655) three sons and one dau. He *m.* 2ndly, in 1657, Frances, dau. of William Milward, Esq. of Chilcote, in Derbyshire, (son and heir of Sir Thomas Milward, the Judge,) and had by her one son and three daus. Mr. Herrick *d.* in 1693, and was *s.* by his eldest son,

WILLIAM HERRICK, Esq. of Beaumanor, *b.* in 1650, who *m.* Dorothy, dau. of James Wootton, Esq. of Weston, in Derbyshire, and by her (who *d.* in 1749, aged one hundred) had two daus. and three sons, 1 WILLIAM, his heir; 2 John, *d.* in 1760, leaving two sons and two daus., all deceased; 3 Thomas, of Leicester, father, by his second wife Katherine Bakewell, of William, of Knighton, and Katherine, *m.* to Richard Dyott, Esq. of Freeford Hall, Staffordshire. Mr. Herrick *d.* in 1705, and was *s.* by his eldest son,

WILLIAM HERRICK, Esq. of Beaumanor, *b.* in 1689, who *m.* in 1740, Lucy, dau. of John Gage, Esq. of Bentley Park, Sussex, derived from James, second son of Sir John Gage, K.G. of Firle, and by her (who *d.* 25 March, 1778) had to survive infancy, three sons and one dau., viz.,

I. WILLIAM, his heir.
II. John, *b.* 9 Nov. 1749, sometime of the Middle Temple, London, *d. unm.* 14 May, 1819.
III. Thomas-Bainbrigge, of Gray's Inn, *b.* 23 Nov. 1754, *m.* 15 Aug. 1793, Mary, only dau. of James Perry, Esq. of Erdesley Park, co. Hereford, and by her (who *d.* 29 Aug. 1836) he left, at his decease, 24 Sept. 1824,
1 WILLIAM, successor to his uncle.
1 Mary-Anne. 2 Lucy, *d. unm.*, 11 Oct. 1832.
I. Lucy, *m.* in March, 1768, to Richard Gildart, Esq. of Norton Hall, co. Stafford, and had issue, one son, Richard, who *d. unm.* 24 Nov. 1802.

Mr Herrick, who was high-sheriff of Leicestershire in 1753, *d.* 27 Sept. 1773, and was *s.* by his eldest son,

WILLIAM HERRICK Esq. of Beaumanor Park, *b.* 14 Dec. 1745, served as sheriff for Leicestershire in 1786. He *m.* in 1789, Miss Sarah Stokes, of Woodhouse, and dying without issue, 18 Feb 1832, (his wife predeceased him, 29 Aug 1823,) was *s.* by his nephew, the present WILLIAM PERRY-HERRICK, Esq. of Beaumanor Park.

Arms—Arg., a fesse, vairé, or and gu., quarterly with PERRY.
Crests—1st, a bull's head, arg., issuing from a laurel garland, the muzzle, horns, and ears, tipped, sa.; 2nd, a hind's head, erased, or, holding in the mouth a sprig of peartree, vert.
Motto—Virtus omnia nobilitat.
Seat—Beaumanor Park.

HERRICK OF SHIPPOOL.

HERRICK, WILLIAM-HENRY, Esq. of Shippool, co. Cork, J.P., Capt. R.N., *b.* 13 Feb. 1784; *m.* 8 Sept. 1814, Mary, only dau. of Robert De la Cour, Esq. of Bear Forest, co. Cork, and by her (who *d.* 1 July, 1854) has issue,

I. THOMAS-BOUSFIELD, *b.* 25 Feb. 1819; *m.* 23 April, 1844, Eliza-Annie, 2nd dau. of John-Tonson Rye, Esq. of Rye Court, co. Cork, and has issue, Mary-Eliza; Eliza-Sophia; Georgiana-Adelaide; Anne.
II. William-Henry, *b.* 9 Feb. 1824, lieut. 8th regt. of foot; *m.* 21 June, 1848, Anna-Sophia, 2nd dau. of the late Chambre Corker, Esq. of Cor Castle, co. Cork.
III. Benjamin-Bousfield, *b.* 18 Feb. 1826, captain royal marines; *m.* 21 Feb. 1856, Caroline, youngest dau. of Captain Biggs, late of the 60th rifles.
IV. James-Hugh, *b.* 13 Dec. 1830; capt. W. Cork artillery.
I. Mary-De-la-Cour, *m.* 6 Jan. 1836, to Richard Corbett, Esq., M.D., of Cork; and *d.* 31 March, 1847.
II. Anne-Harriet, *m.* 21 Aug. 1841, to John-Campbell Meade, Esq. of Innishannon, co. Cork.
III. Louisa-Josephine Pettitot
IV. Georgiana-Henrietta. V. Catherine-De-la-Cour.

Lineage.—From the exact coincidence of name, arms, and dates, there can exist but little doubt that this is a junior branch of the HERRICKS *of Beaumanor*, in Leicestershire.

JOHN HERRICK, Esq. *b.* in 1612, accompanied the Duke of Ormonde to Ireland in 1641. He *m.* twice, and *d.* 8 Aug. 1689, leaving, by the 1st wife, a son, GERSHOM, and by the 2nd, two sons and a dau. viz., John, Francis, and Mary. To his 2nd son, John, he bequeathed an estate in the barony of Ibane. To his eldest son,

GERSHOM HERRICK, *b.* in 1665, he devised his estate of Shippool. He *m.* in 1693, Susanna, only child and heir of Swithen Smart, Esq., by Frances his wife, eldest dau. of Edward Riggs, Esq. of Riggsdale, co. Cork, and left, at his decease in 1730, a son and successor,

EDWARD HERRICK, Esq. of Shippool, *b.* in 1694, who *m.* in 1728, Elizabeth, dau. of Caleb Falkiner, Esq. of the city of Cork, and had six sons and two daus. The 2nd son, Edward, lieut. R.N., was killed on board, "the Dorsetshire," in Sir Edward Hawke's action, 20 Sept. 1759. The eldest son,

FALKINER HERRICK, Esq. of Shippool, *b.* in 1729; *m.* June, 1753, Sarah, eldest dau. of Thomas Bousfield, Esq of Cork, and had issue,

THOMAS-BOUSFIELD, his heir.
Francis, capt. 27th regt., killed at the taking of Guadaloupe, 1795.
Jane, *m.* to the Rev. Ambrose Hickey.
Elizabeth, *d. unm.*, aged 36.

Mr. Herrick *d.* 1780, and was *s.* by his son,

THOMAS-BOUSFIELD HERRICK, Esq. of Shippool, *b.* 1754; who *m.* 1783, Anne, only dau. of Henry Moore, Esq. of Frankfort House, co. Cork, and by her, (who *m.* 2ndly, in 1798, Daniel Cudmore, Esq., and *d.* 1820) had issue,

WILLIAM-HENRY, now of Shippool.
Henry-Moore, capt. 45th regt. killed at the storming of Badajoz, *unm.*
Edward, captain R N.; *m.* in 1836, Charlotte, only dau. of the late Capt. Thomas Alexander, R.N., C.B., and has issue, Arthur, 54th regt., *b.* 20 Dec. 1836; Edward, *b.* 17 June, 1845; Charlotte; Henrietta.
Ann, *m.* in Jan. 1818, to Richard-Plummer Davies, Esq., captain R.N.

Mr. Herrick *d.* in 1796.

Arms, Crest, and *Motto*—See HERRICK *of Beaumanor.*
Seat—Shippool, near Innishannon.

HERVEY OF KILLIANE.

HERVEY, CHARLES-JOHN-VIGORS, Esq. of Killiane Castle, co. Wexford, *b.* 29 Nov. 1817; *m.* 24 July, 1839, Martha, dau. of the late Thomas-Read Kemp, Esq., M.P. of Kemp Town, Brighton, by Frances his wife, dau. of Sir Francis Baring, Bart., and has issue,

I. CHARLES-WILLIAM-ARTHUR, *b.* 26 Jan. 1855.
I. Lydia. II. Blanche-Maud.
III. Marie-Augusta.

Lineage.—This family claims to be a branch of the noble house of Bristol.

FRANCIS HARVEY (3rd son of Richard Harvey, of Lyme Regis, co. Dorset, merchant, and grandson of John Harvey, of Meldreth) having been taken in arms by Prince Rupert, was committed with other prisoners to the jail at Exeter, at the beginning of the rebellion; and on being liberated, he went to Lyme Regis and also became a merchant in that town, of which he was chosen mayor in 1644, and admitted a freeman. After the year 1649, he obtained a grant of lands in the county of Wexford from CROMWELL, which were confirmed to him by CHARLES II.; and in 1666 he passed patent for 1898 English (863 Irish) acres in the barony of Forth. He was representative in parliament for the borough of Clonmines in 1661, and Mayor of Wexford in 1671, of which county he was high-sheriff, 26 and 27 CHARLES II. (1673 and 4). He *m.* Katharine Plunket, and had issue. Mr. Harvey was buried in the chancel of St. Iberius' Church, in Wexford, 23 Nov. 1692, and was *s.* by his eldest son,

JOHN HARVEY, Esq. of Killiane Castle, M.P. for Wexford in 1695, and high-sheriff of the county, 5 WILLIAM and MARY (1692). He *m.* 19 Oct. 1675, Elizabeth, dau. of James Stopford, Esq. of New Hall, co. Meath, ancestor of the Earl of Courtown, and had issue. Mr. Harvey was buried in the chancel of St. Iberius' Church, Wexford, 21 Sept. 1707, and was *s.* by his eldest son,

THE REV. JAMES HARVEY, of Killiane Castle, co. Wexford, rector of Rathaspeck, in that county *b.* 1676; *m.* Martha, dau. of John Beauchamp, Esq. of Ballyloughane, co. Carlow, by a dau. of Bartholomew Vigors, bishop of Leighlin and Ferns, and had issue,

I. JOHN, his heir.
II. Vigors, lieut. 16th regiment of foot, *d. s. p.*
III. James, of Wigan, Lancashire, capt. in the 7th regt. of foot; *m.* Cecily, dau. and heiress of Robert Leigh, eldest son of Alexander Leigh, of Hindly Hall, Esq., and had issue,
 1 Robert-John, of Farnham, Yorkshire. Esq., colonel in the army, who took by royal permission, in 1818, the name of Hervey. He *m.* Elizabeth, dau. and heiress of Thomas Bickerdyke, Esq. of Farnham, Yorkshire, and had (with a dau. who was married) two sons,
  James-Vigors, formerly capt. Coldstream-gds., married.
  Beauchamp, formerly of the 20th light drags., married.
 2 James-Leigh, late capt. 33rd regiment.
 1 Martha-Cecilia, *d. unm.*
IV. Francis, *d. s. p.* V. Bartholomew, *d. s. p.*
I. Martha, *m.* to Francis Harvey, of Bargy Castle, co. Wexford, Esq.
II. Katharine, *m.* to Philip Palliser, Esq. of Castletown, co. Wexford.

The Rev. James Harvey *d.* 16 June, 1760, aged 84, and was *s.* by his eldest son,

JOHN HARVEY, Esq. of Killiane Castle, capt. 16th regt. of foot; who *m.* Martha Roe, and dying in 1763, left an only child,

JOHN HARVEY, Esq. of Killiane Castle, *b.* in 1751, high-sheriff of county Wexford 1772; *m.* Dorothy, *b.* 2 Jan. 1756, eldest dau. of Major Loftus Cliffe, and by her (who *d.* in 1813) had issue,

VIGORS, his heir.
Anne, *m.* 1st, to James Gilldea, Esq. of Coslough, co. Mayo; and 2ndly, to Ralph Nash, Esq. of Cahirconlist, co. Limerick.
Martha, *d. unm.*; her will was proved in Dublin in 1800.
Dorothy, *m.* 7 Dec. 1798, to William Harvey, Esq. (brother of John Harvey, Esq. of Bargy Castle.)
Barbara, *m.* 1st. in 1798, to Richard Lambart, Esq. of Bristol; and 2ndly, Arthur Meadows, of Hermitage, co. Wexford.
Mary, *m.* to Henry Archer, Esq. of Ballyseskin, co. Wexford.
Frances, *m.* 1809, to the Very Rev. Samuel Adams, of Northlands, co. Cavan, Dean of Cashel.

Mr. Harvey *d.* 29 May, 1796, and was *s.* by his son,

VIGORS HARVEY, Esq. of Killiane Castle, co. Wexford, and of Hammerton Hall, Yorkshire, *b.* 12 Dec. 1794; who, in 1818, assumed by royal permission the name of HERVEY. He *m.* 1816, Frances-Margaretta, sister of Sir Charles Shakerley, Bart., and by her (who *m.* 2ndly, 1832, T.-R. Kemp, Esq., M.P., of Kemp Town Brighton) he left at his decease in 1827, an only child, CHARLES-JOHN-VIGORS HERVEY, Esq., now of Killiane.

Arms—Gu., on a bend, arg, three trefoils, slipped, vert.
Crest—A cat-a-mountain ppr., holding in the dexter paw a trefoil, slipped, vert.
Motto—Je n'oublieray jamais.
Seat—Killiane Castle, near Wexford.

BAMFORD-HESKETH OF GWYRCH CASTLE.

BAMFORD-HESKETH, LLOYD-HESKETH, Esq. of Gwyrch Castle, co. Denbigh, high-sheriff 1828, *b.* 9 Aug. 1788; *m.* 28 Oct 1825, Lady Emily-Esther-Anne Lygon, youngest dau. of William, 1st Earl Beauchamp, and has issue,

I. ROBERT, *b.* in June, 1826. II. William-Reginald.
I. Anna-Maria.

Lineage.—A younger son of the Rossall family,

ROBERT HESKETH, Esq., who resided at his seat, Upton, in Cheshire, *m.* an heiress named Nicholson, and thus acquired the Bamford estates. By an act of parliament, in 1806, he was compelled to change his name for BAMFORD, but by a second act, he obtained permission to resume that of HESKETH. His son and successor,

ROBERT BAMFORD-HESKETH, Esq. of Bamford Hall, and Upton, *m.* in 1785, Frances Lloyd, heiress of Gwyrch Castle, in Denbighshire, derived from the marriage, in 1611, of Griffith Lloyd, with Catherine, dau. of Edward Morgan, Esq. of Golden Grove, and had issue,

LLOYD, now of Gwyrch Castle.
Robert, an officer in the guards, major, by brevet, in the army, *d.* of a wound received at Waterloo. He never married.
John, *m.* the dau. of the Rev. Gilbert Ford, rector of North Meols, Lancashire.
Frances, *m.* to Thomas Hudson, Esq., M.P. for Evesham.

Ellen, m. to Sir James Robertson-Bruce, Bart. of Down Hall, co. Derry.

Mr. Bamford-Hesketh d. 16 Jan. 1816.

Arms—Or, on a bend, sa., between two torteaux, three garbs of the field; quartering BAMFORD and LLOYD.
Crests—1st, a garb, or, charged with a cross-patée; 2nd, a rose, arg.; 3rd, a dexter arm, couped at the shoulder, and embowed in armour, holding a scythe.
Motto—In Deo mea spes.
Seat—Gwyrch Castle, Denbighshire.

HEWETT OF TYR MAB ELLIS.

HEWETT, JOHN, Esq., sometime of Chalderton, Hants, and now of Tyr Mab Ellis, co. Glamorgan, J.P. and D.L., major in the army, b. 28 July 1787; m. 1st, 2 Nov. 1816, Frances, dau. of John Pritchard, Esq. of Oldcastle, co. Glamorgan, but by her had no issue. He m. 2ndly, 29 Nov. 1829, Frances, dau. of Thomas Thornewill, Esq. of Dove Cliff, co. Stafford, and by her has issue,

I. JOHN-FREDERICK-NAPIER, b. 20 June, 1833, J.P., lieut. 72nd highlanders; m 17 Aug. 1859, Elizabeth-La Motte, dau. of the Rev. S.-J. Jackson, of Ayton, St. David's, Jamaica, representative of the family of the loyal Bishop Juxon, *temp.* CHARLES I.
II. Edward-Osborne, b. 25 Sept. 1835, lieut. R.E.
III. Thomas-Meyrick, b. 3 July, 1838, lieut. R.M.
I. Frances-Mary, m. 17 May, 1855, to Henry Pickering-Clarke, Esq. of Treweme House, Hounslow, eldest son of Thomas Pickering-Clarke, Esq. of Perrymeade, co. Somerset, late capt. R.N.

Major Hewett claims to be male representative of the Hewetts of Headley Hall, co. York, and as such to be entitled to their Baronetcy.

Lineage.—WILLIAM HEWETT, Esq. of St. Neots, 7th son of Sir John Hewett, 2nd Bart., by Frances Tyrrell his wife, m. Miss Savile, and is stated to have had, besides WILLIAM and TYRRELL, who became 4th and 6th Baronets, a third son,

THOMAS HEWETT, Esq. R.N., who m. Margaret, dau. of Richard Moses, Esq. of Yorkshire (grandaunt of the Miss Moses, who m. Aubrey Beauclerk, Earl of Burford), and had issue, 1 Thomas, d. unm.; 2 JOHN, heir; 3 Richard, R.N.; 4 William, of the Foreign Office; 1 Sarah; and 2 Margaret, m. to — Reubens, Esq. The eldest son to survive,

JOHN HEWETT, Esq., R.N., of Yallons, co. Devon, m. 18 June, 1746, Sarah, dau. of Henry Meyrick, Esq. of Ilfordcombe, and niece of Sir Edward Meyrick, of Cottrell, co. Glamorgan, and had (with two daus., Amelia, and Honoria, m. to — Leeworthy, Esq.) four sons, 1 John, who is supposed to have married; 2 WILLIAM, of whom presently; 3 Henry-Meyrick, m. and left one dau.; 4 Richard, capt. R.N., d. unm. Mr. Hewett d. 26 Feb. 1768. His 2nd son,

WILLIAM HEWETT, Esq., R.N., m. Mary-David, dau. of David Thomas, Esq of Glynn Nedd, co. Glamorgan, and had, with other children, who d. young,

William, comm. R.N., m. Rosa, dau. of Vavasour Montgomorie, Esq. of Dominica, and dying in command of the "Thetis" brig, at Dominica, left an only child, William, d. at sea, æt. 12, in charge of his step father, Captain Bailey.
Richard, R.N., drowned at sea, unm., 1806.
John, now of Tyr Mab Ellis.
Thomas, lieut. R.N., m. Anne-Newin, dau. of Newin Barlowe, Esq. of Parke, Hants, and d. 14 June, 1839, leaving one son, Vincent-Bowen, lieut. royal marines, and two daus.
Marianne, m. 1st, to Charles-Harcourt White, Esq., lieut. R.N.; and 2ndly, Samuel Barber, Esq., late capt. in the Northumberland militia.

Mr. Hewett d. 1806.

Arms—Gu., a chev., engr., between three horned owls, arg.
Crest—The stump of a tree, sprouting, ppr., thereon a falcon, close, arg., legged and belled, or.
Mottoes—Ne te quæsiveris extra; and Une pure foy.
Seat—Tyr Mab Ellis, Pont y Pridd, co. Glamorgan.

HEWGILL OF HORNBY GRANGE.

HEWGILL, HENRY, Esq. of Hornby Grange, co. York, J.P. and D.L., b. 6 June, 1788; m. in 1812, Harriet, youngest dau. of the late Col. Lovelace, and has issue,

I. EDWIN-HENRY, b. 24 Aug. 1814.
II. Percy-William, b. 13 Feb. 1816; m. Jane, dau. of Lieut.-Col. Petley, R.A.
III. Henry-Frederick, b. 20 Oct. 1818, in holy orders; m. Fanny, dau. of the late Charles de Coetlogon, Esq.
IV. Frederick-Charles, b. 12 Sept. 1825, Midshipman R N.
V. Arthur-Scott, b. 1 Jan. 1831.
I. Elizabeth-Mary. II. Harriet.

Lineage.—THE REV. HENRY HEWGILL, M.A., rector of Great Smeaton, co. York, only son of Henry Hewgill, Esq., by Cordelia Place his wife; m. 1st, in 1758, Catherine, dau. of Thornicroft, Esq. of Cheshire, and by her had one son, EDWIN, of whom presently. He m. 2ndly, in 1765, Antonina, youngest dau. of the Hon. Thomas and Elizabeth Willoughby, of Birdsall, co. York, and by her had (with a dau. Antonina, m. to William-B. Bayley, Esq., M.D.) two sons, James, M.A., in holy orders, rector of Great Smeaton; and Francis, M.A., in holy orders, rector of Wollaton, Notts. The only son of the first marriage,

EDWIN HEWGILL, Esq of Hornby Grange, a general in the army; m. in 1785, Elizabeth-Mary, dau. of William Fraser, Esq., some time under-secretary of state, *temp.* GEORGE III., and by her had one son, the present HENRY HEWGILL, Esq. of Hornby Grange, and one dau., Catherine-Antonina, m. to Henry Hinde, Esq., late a major in the army.

Arms—Sa., two battle-axes (hoes), in saltier, arg., quartering THORNICROFT, vert, a mascle, between four cross-crosslets, arg.
Crest—A nag's head, erased, sa.
Motto—Marte et labore.
Seat—Hornby Grange, co. York.

HEXT OF TRENARREN.

HEXT, THOMAS, Esq. of Trenarren, Cornwall, m. 21 Aug. 1845, Rhoda-Charleton, dau. of Rev. Harry-Farr Yeatman, of Stock House, co. Dorset, by Sarah his wife, only dau. and heiress of James Huish Wolcott, Esq. of Widworthy, co. Devon, and has issue,

I. ARTHUR STANIFORTH, b. 9 Sept 1847.
II. Henry-Yeatman b. 22 May, 1849.

Lineage.—The family of Hext was resident for several centuries at Kingston, in Devonshire. Late in the sixteenth century two younger sons settled in Cornwall, and the elder branches failing at Kingston, in Devon, and at Constantine, in Cornwall, the line was continued through the youngest son, from whom the present Thomas Hext, of Trenarren, is descended.

JOHN HEXT, of Kingston, m. Jane, dau. of John Fortescue, and had, with two sons, John and Thomas, five daus., viz., Agnes, m. to Sir Lewis Pollard, Knt., one of the judges of the Common Pleas, of whom it is remarkable that they had eleven sons and eleven daus., and that of these eleven sons four were made knights, viz., Sir Hugh, Sir John, Sir Richard, and Sir George, (the last created for his gallant conduct in the defence of Boulogne;) and of the eleven daus. four married knights, viz., Sir Hugh Stukeley, of Affton, Sir Hugh Courtenay, of Powderham, Sir Hugh Pawlett, of Stampford-Peveril, and Sir John Crocker, of Lineham. Sir Lewis Pollard and his wife, Agnes, lie buried in King's Nympton church, in Devonshire. Elizabeth, second dau. of John Hext, of Kingston, m. John Ackland; Jane, m. Nicholas Holway; Catherine, and Eleanor. The eldest son,

JOHN HEXT, of Kingston, m. Jane, dau. and co-heir of Stephen Tilley, of Broadclist, in Devonshire, and had issue, four sons and three daus., of whom the two eldest sons were, I JOHN, his heir, of whom presently; and II. Thomas, grandfather of Sir Edward Hext, of Netherham, Somersetshire, sheriff of Somersetshire, 1 James I., and knight of the shire in several parliaments. Elizabeth, his sole dau. and heiress, m. 1st, Sir Joseph Killigrew, and 2ndly, Sir John Stawell, father of Ralph, Lord Stawell. The son and heir,

JOHN HEXT, of Kingston, m. Elizabeth, dau. and heir of Peter Colswell, of Exeter, and left a son and heir,

JOHN HEXT, of Kingston, who m. Philippa, dau. of William Denham, of Wortham, Devon, and had issue three sons, I. John, of Kingston; II. William, of Constantine, in Cornwall (living in 1620); III. Arthur, who m. the dau. of — Merret, of Trelowtha in Probus, Cornwall, and had issue, a son,

SAMUEL HEXT, the first possessor of Trenarren, who was bapt. at St. Burians, 2 Nov. 1606, and was buried at St.

Austel, 28 Dec. 1680. By Jane, his wife, he had, with junior issue, SAMUEL, his heir, and FRANCIS, who m. Miss Smith, and dying 1673, left a son Francis, who m. Elizabeth, dau. and heir of Thomas Waddesden, of Bourton, and left two sons, THOMAS, successor to Trenarren, and FRANCIS, ancestor of the HEXTS *of Tredithy*. The eldest son,

SAMUEL HEXT, *b.* in 1639, *d.* in 1714. He *m.* Jane, dau. of David Mole, of Trevissick, in 1665, and had two children, Nathaniel and Jane, who *d.* both young. Mr. Hext having survived his children, entailed Trenarren, in 1709, on his grand-nephew.

THOMAS HEXT, Esq., *b.* in 1699, who *m.* 1725, Gertrude, dau. and co-heiress of Henry Hawkins, Esq., and had issue. Mr. Hext *d.* in 1767, and his two eldest sons deceasing *unm.*, the estates devolved on the youngest,

SAMUEL HEXT, Esq.. *b.* in 1733, who *m.* in 1757, Margery, dau. and heiress of John Tayldor, of Helland, Cornwall, and by her (who *d.* in 1795) left at his decease, in 1800, a son and successor,

THOMAS HEXT, Esq. of Trenarren and Lostwithiel, *b.* in 1762, at whose decease in 1822, *unm.*, the estates passed to his brother,

JOHN HEXT, Esq. of Trenarren, *b* 1766, who *m.* 1799, Elizabeth, dau. of Thomas Staniforth, Esq. of Darnall, co. York, (an estate possessed by that family *temp.* RICH. II.) He died 1838, and left issue,

THOMAS, the present possessor of Trenarren.
Samuel-Henry.
John-Hawkins, vicar of Morval, who *m.* in 1841, Susannah Catherine, dau. of the late Rev. John-Lane Kitson, rector of Staverton, in Devonshire, and who by her has issue, besides four daus., two sons, John and Edward.
Charles-Staniforth, captain in the 8th regt. of foot.
Elizabeth, *m.* in 1821, John Daintry, Esq. of North Rode, Cheshire, since rector of Patney, Wilts, and subsequently incumbent of North Rode.
Alethea, *m.* in 1835, James-George Crab, Esq. of Shidfield House, Hampshire, who has since adopted, by sign-manual, the name and arms of Boucher, and has issue.
Mary, *m.* in 1845, Samuel Hawkins, Esq. of Shidfield.
Gertrude, *m.* in 1845, Rev. Daniel Parsons, M.A., of Beg-brook, Gloucestershire.
Frances-Margery.

Arms—Or, a tower, triple-towered, porte ouverte, between three battle-axes, sa.

Crest—A demi-lion, or, rising from a tower, sa., holding in the dexter-paw a battle-axe, of the last.

Seat—Trenarren, Cornwall.

HEXT OF TREDITHY.

HEXT, WILLIAM, Esq. of Tredithy and Lancarfe, co. Cornwall, Capt. R.N., *b.* 8 July, 1780; *m.* 15 Sept. 1812, Barbara, youngest dau. and last surviving child and heir of the late James Read, M.D., of Tremeare, and has issue,

I. FRANCIS-JOHN, *b.* 28 Aug. 1817.
II. George, *b.* 15 Jan. 1819, M.A., Fellow of Corpus Christi College, Oxford.
I. Susanna-Read.

Lineage.—FRANCIS-JOHN HEXT, Esq., brother of Thomas Hext, Esq. of Trenarren, *b.* 8 Jan. 1703, *m.* Catherine, sister of Hender Mounsteven, Esq. of Lancarfe, high sheriff in 1764, and had issue (with two daus., Eliza and Anne, and a younger son, Samuel, who *d. unm.*) an elder son,

FRANCIS-JOHN HEXT, Esq. of Tredithy, who *m.* in Jan. 1769, Margaret, dau. of Elias Lang, Esq. of Plymouth, and heir of her brother, Elias Lang, of Tredithy, and left issue, with three daus., Anne, *m.* to the Rev. Charles Kendall; Jane, and Margaret, four sons, of whom two succeeded him,

FRANCIS-JOHN, of Tredithy, rector of Holland, and deputy-lieutenant, who *d.* in Bath, 1842, aged 63, unmarried.
WILLIAM, the present representative.
Samuel, major in the army. He received a gold medal for Badajos, where he stormed the citadel, and two clasps for Orthes and Toulouse, with the cross and order as companion of the Bath. He died in consequence of an accident, 24 July, 1822, aged 40.
George, lieut. R.N., who fell by a rifle-shot, leading a boat attack in America, in 1813, aged 28.

Arms—Or, a tower, triple-towered, porte ouverte, between three battle-axes, sa.

Crest—A demi-lion, or, rising from a tower, sa., holding in the dexter-paw a battle-axe, of the last.

Seats—Tredithy and Lancarfe.

HEYCOCK OF EAST NORTON.

HEYCOCK, JOHN-HIPPISLEY, Esq. of East Norton, co. Leicester, *b.* 3 Feb. 1793; *m.* 18 May, 1819, Martha, only child of Thomas Lewin, Esq. of Thrussington Grange, same county, and by her (who *d.* 1840) has had issue,

I. JOHN, *b.* 5 March, 1822; *d.* 1837.
II. HENRY, *b.* 6 April, 1825.
III. Charles, captain 89th foot, *b.* 11 Oct. 1827.
IV. Thomas, in holy orders, *b.* 1 June, 1831.
I. Mary-Anne, *d.* 1846. II. Susanna.
III. Emma, *d.* 1850.

Lineage.—THE REV. JOSEPH HEYCOCK, of Mortimer, Berks, *m.* and had two sons, Joseph, of Reading, who *d. unm.*, leaving his estate to his brother, and

NICHOLAS HEYCOCK, Esq. of Tilton, in Leicestershire, *b.* at Mortimer, about the year 1672. He *m.* 1710, Mary, only dau. of — Palmer, Esq. of Saddington, co. Leicester, and had issue,

JOHN, his heir.
Mary, *b.* in 1711, *m.* to Edward Muxloe, Esq. of Pickwell, high-sheriff of Leicestershire.
Catherine, *b.* in 1715, *m.* to John Dawson, Esq.
Elizabeth, *m.* to Henry Hensman, Esq. of Pytchley.

Nicholas Heycock *d.* 1763, was buried at Tilton, and *s.* by his son,

JOHN HEYCOCK, Esq. of East Norton, co. Leicester, *b.* in 1713, *m.* 1st, 1744, Mary, second dau. and co-heir of Benjamin Clarke, Esq. of Hardingstone, in Northamptonshire, brother of Bartholomew Clarke, Esq., whose only dau. *m.* Sir Jacob Bouverie, 1st Earl of Radnor. By Mary Clarke, his wife (who *d.* 1752), had issue,

JOSEPH, *b.* in 1748, *m.* Mary Black, of Leveden, co. Northampton, and had two sons, Nicholas and John, who both *d. unm.*
Mary, *b.* in 1745, *m.* to Richard Raworth, Esq. of Owston.
Elizabeth, *b.* in 1746, *m.* to John Smith, Esq. of Uppingham, in Rutlandshire, and *d. s. p.*

He *m.* 2ndly, in 1755, Elizabeth, dau. of — Brown, Esq. of Skeffington, in Leicestershire, and had by her (who *d.* in 1758) a dau., Dorothy, *b.* in 1756, the wife of Henry Hensman, Esq. of Pitchley, Northamptonshire, and a son,

JOHN HEYCOCK, Esq. of Owston, *b.* in 1758, who *m.* in 1790, Susanna, second dau. of Tobias Hippisley, Esq. of Hambleton, high-sheriff of Rutlandshire in 1800, 3rd son of Thomas Hippisley, eldest brother of Sir John Hippisley: by her (who *d.* in 1816) had issue,

JOHN-HIPPISLEY, his heir.
Charles, in holy orders, who *s.* his cousin, Mr. Hensman, at Pytchley, Northamptonshire; *b.* in 1795; *m.* Catherine, only dau. of F. Bissill, Esq., and niece of the Rev. William Bissill, of Wissendine, in Rutlandshire, and has issue.
Thomas, of Braunstone, co. Rutland, *b.* in Sept. 1796.
William, of New York, United States of America, *d. s. p.* 1847.
Henry, of Pendleton, near Manchester, *m.* Jane, eldest dau. of — Cockshot, Esq.
Edwin, *m.* Mary, dau. of — Cockshot, and has issue.
Frederick, of Bourne, co. Cambridge, *m.* Mary, only dau. of — Heywood, Esq.
Alfred, *d.* aged about 16, and was buried at Owston.
Susanna, *d. unm.* in 1810.
Elizabeth, *m.* to Rowland-Maurice Fawcett, M.D.
Emma, *m.* to Ayscough Smith, Esq. of Leesthorpe Hall, co. Leicester, and has issue.

Mr. Heycock *d.* in 1823, was buried at Owston, and *s.* by his eldest son, the present JOHN-HIPPISLEY HEYCOCK, Esq. of Norton.

Arms—Or, a cross, sa., in the first quarter a fleur-de-lis, quartering HIPPISLEY.

Seat—Manor House, East Norton, co. Leicester.

HEYLAND OF GLENDARAGH AND TAMLAGHT.

HEYLAND, LANGFORD-ROWLEY, Esq. of Glendaragh, co. Antrim and Tamlaght, co. Derry, J.P., *b.* 7 March, 1807.

Lineage.—This is a branch of the Suffolk family of HEYLAND, and has long been settled in the north of Ireland in high repute and position.

ROWLAND HEYLAND, Esq. of Castle Roe, co. Derry, *m.* 1st, Miss Galt, and by her had,

LANGFORD, his heir.
Mary-Anne, wife of the Rev. Richard-Henry Symes, of Ballybeg, co. Wicklow.

He m. 2ndly, Miss MacDonnell, and by her had,

I. Arthur, major 40th regt., killed at Waterloo, leaving, by Miss Mary Kyffin, his wife, five sons and two daus., viz.,
1 John-Rowley, of Ballintemple, co. Derry, J.P., lt.-col. in the army, severely wounded while in command of the 7th fusiliers, in the attack on the Redan, m., and has issue.
2 Arthur, E.I.C.S., deceased.
3 Macdonnell, deceased.
4 Kyffin, capt. 25th regt., deceased.
5 Alfred, lieut.-col. 95th regt., lost an arm at the battle of Alma.
1 Mary-Anne, m. to James Browne, Esq.
2 Anne, m. to the Rev. Mr. Smyth.

II. Hercules-John, capt. 14th regt., d. s. p.

The eldest son and heir,

LANGFORD-ROWLEY HEYLAND, Esq. of Glendaragh and Tamlaght, lieut.-col. commanding Londonderry militia, and a magistrate for the counties of Derry and Antrim, m. in 1792, Charlotte Alexander, of Caledon, and by her (who d. 31 July, 1833) had issue,

I. LANGFORD ROWLEY, present representative.
II. Alexander-Charles, b. 7 March, 1807, of the Bengal Civil Service, late judge of Ghazepore, m. 1st, 30 March, 1835, Anne-Alexander, dau. of the Rev. Samuel Montgomery, of Moville, co. Donegal, and by her (who d. 11 Oct. 1839) had issue,
1 Langford-Rowley, b 11 July, 1837, lieut. 33rd regt., a young officer of great promise, d., pierced with seven wounds, before Sebastopol, 18 June, 1855.
2 Alexander-Samuel, b. 11 Oct. 1839.
1 Maria-Susan, m. to the Rev. R. McClintock, son of John McClintock, Esq. of Drumcar, by the Lady Elizabeth his wife.

He m. 2ndly, 23 Feb. 1841, Emily, dau. of John Montgomery Hill, Esq., commissioner of Port Elizabeth, Cape of Good Hope, and has, by her, a son,
1 Edward-Obré, b. 4 Oct. 1842.

III. Arthur-James, late of the Belgian Cavalry.
I. Sophia-Florence, m. to A. O. B. Bellingham, Esq. of Dunany, co. Louth.
II. Charlotte, m. to E. Curry, Esq., H. B. M.'s consul at Ostend, and is deceased.
III. Mabella.
IV. Marianne, m. to E. M. Dunne, Esq of Brittas, Queen's Co.
V. Catherine, m. to Edouard Vander Noot, Baron de Moorselles, Belgium, and is deceased.

Col. Heyland d. 1 Nov. 1829.

Arms—Az., a lion rampant, arg., surmounted by a bend, gu., charged with a tower, ppr.
Crest—Out of battlements, ppr., charged with a cross-crosslet, gu., a nag's head, ppr.
Motto—Favent fortuna.
Seats—Glendaragh, co. Antrim, and Tamlaght, co. Derry.

HEYWOOD OF HOPE END.

HEYWOOD, THOMAS, Esq. of Hope End, co. Hereford, J.P. and D.L., high-sheriff 1840, b. 3 Sept. 1797; m. 2 Oct. 1823, Mary-Elizabeth, dau. of John Barton, Esq. of Swinton, co. Lancaster, and Saxby, co. Lincoln, and has issue,

I. THOMAS, late capt. 16th lancers, J.P. and D.L., b. 28 Sept. 1826, m. 16 Aug 1853, Mary-Emily, dau. of M. G. Beresford, D.D., bishop of Kilmore, and has issue.
I. Margaret, m. to Thomas Percival Heywood, Esq., eldest son of Sir Benjamin Heywood, Bart.
II. Mary-Elizabeth, m. to the Rev. George-Henry Sumner, M.A., rector of Old Alresford, son of the bishop of Winchester.

Mr. Heywood is younger brother of the present Sir Benjamin Heywood, Bart. of Claremont, co. Lancaster, and 3rd son of the late Nathaniel Heywood, Esq. of Manchester, by Anne his wife, dau. of the celebrated Thomas Percival of that town, M.D., F.R.S.

Arms—Arg., three torteaux, in bend, between two bendlets, gu., on a canton, of the last, a cross-patée, or.
Crest—On a mount, vert, the trunk of a tree, with two branches sprouting therefrom, and entwined by ivy, thereon a falcon, with wings displayed, ppr.
Motto—Alte volo.
Seat—Hope End, near Ledbury, co. Hereford.

HEYWOOD OF STANLEY HALL.

HEYWOOD, ARTHUR, Esq. of Stanley Hall, co. York, m. Miss Duroure, dau. of Colonel Duroure. Mr. Heywood s. his father in 1822.

Lineage.—BENJAMIN HEYWOOD, b. at Ormskirk, (the son of Nathaniel Heywood, Gent. of that place, by Isabel Lynford, his 1st wife, grandson of the Rev. Nathaniel Heywood, M.A., Vicar of Ormskirk, from which he was ejected in 1662, and great-grandson of Richard Heywood, Gent. of Little Lever, son of Oliver Heywood, Gent. of the same place, who d. aged 72, in 1628,) settled as a merchant at Drogheda, and d. in 1725, aged 36. He m. Anne, sister of General Arthur Graham, of Armagh, and had, with four daus., three sons, viz.,

ARTHUR, his heir.
Benjamin, of Liverpool, merchant, and afterwards of Manchester, banker, grandfather of the present SIR BENJAMIN HEYWOOD, Bart. of Claremont, co. Lancaster.
Nathaniel, lieut.-colonel Coldstream guards, and gentleman of the bed-chamber to the Duke of Gloucester, m. 1st, Maria, dau. of General Bowles; and 2ndly, a sister of Admiral Sir Richard Hughes, and left issue.

The eldest son,

ARTHUR HEYWOOD, of Liverpool, banker, m. 1st, Sarah, dau. of Samuel Ogden, Esq. of Mossley Hill, co. Lancaster; and 2ndly, Hannah, dau. of Richard Milnes, Esq. of Wakefield. He d. in Feb. 1795, aged 78, having had, by his 1st wife, one dau., Sarah, m. to James Mason, Esq. of Shrewsbury; and by his second wife, four sons and two daus., viz.,

Richard, of Larkhill and Liverpool, banker, m. Mary, sister of Thomas Earle, Esq. of Spekelands, but d. s. p.
BENJAMIN, of whom presently.
Arthur, of Larkhill and Liverpool, banker, d. unm. in 1836.
John-Pemberton, of Wakefield, barrister-at-law, m. Margaret, dau. of Peter Drinkwater, Esq. of Irwell House, and left issue.
Anna-Maria, } both d. unm.
Bridget, }

The 2nd son,

BENJAMIN HEYWOOD, Esq. of Stanley Hall, Wakefield, Yorkshire, m. Elizabeth, dau. of Mr. Thomas Hobson, of York, and relict of William Serjeantson, Esq. of Hanleth, in Craven, and d. in 1822, leaving issue. His son and successor is the present ARTHUR HEYWOOD, Esq. of Stanley Hall, and his eldest dau., Elizabeth, is widow of the late Hugh Jones, Esq. of Lark Hill, West Derby.

Arms—Arg., three torteaux, in bend, between two bendlets, gu., on a canton, of the last, a cross-patée, or.
Crest—On a mount, vert, the trunk of a tree, with two branches sprouting therefrom, and entwined by ivy, thereon a falcon, with wings displayed, ppr.
Motto—Alte volo.
Seat—Stanley Hall, Wakefield.

HIBBERT OF BIRTLES HALL.

HIBBERT, THOMAS, Esq. of Birtles Hall, co. Chester, J.P. and D.L., m. Caroline-Henrietta, eldest dau. of Charles Cholmondeley, Esq. of Knutsford, and niece of Lord Delamere, and has issue,

I. HUGH-ROBERT, major 7th royal fusiliers, b. Dec. 1828.
II. Reginald, B.A., in holy orders, b. Dec. 1829.
III. Francis.
I. Caroline-Essex.
II. Dorothea-Letitia.
III. Georgina-Charlotte.
IV. Octavia-Letitia.

Mr. Hibbert has been high-sheriff of Cheshire.

Lineage.—The ancient family of Hibbert, of Marple (vide Harl. MSS., and Ormerod's History of Cheshire), claim descent from Paganus, or Payne Hubert, who accompanied King RICHARD CŒUR DE LION to the Crusades, A.D. 1190.

ROBERT HIBBERT, Esq. of Booth and Stockfield Hall, (7th in descent from Nicholas Hibbert, of Marple, Cheshire, who d. July 1506), b. 1684; m. at the Collegiate Church of Manchester, 3 March, 1708, Margaret Tetlow, and d. 15 April, 1762, having had issue,

THOMAS, b. 1710; resided 46 years in Jamaica, where he d. unm., 29 May, 1780.
ROBERT, of whom presently.
Samuel, b 1719; d. unm. 15 March, 1752.
JOHN, b 1732; d 1769, having m. Janet, dau. of Samuel Gordon, Esq., he was ancestor of JOHN-HUBERT-WASHINGTON HIBBERT, Esq. of Bilton Grange, co. Warwick, and of John Hibbert, Esq. of Braywicke Lodge, Berks.
And three daus.

The 2nd son,

ROBERT HIBBERT, Esq. of Stockfield Hall, co. Lancaster, b. 1717; m. 1743, Abigail, dau. and co-heir of William Scholey, Esq. of Yorkshire, and d. 28 Jan. 1784, having had issue, besides Robert, of Birtles, five other sons, and three daus., viz.,

Thomas, of Chalfont House, *d. s. p.* 1817.
George, of Munden House, Herts, father of the late William Hibbert, Esq. of Hare Hill, Cheshire.
Samuel, *d.* at Nantes, 1786, leaving issue.
John, *d. unm.* 1770.
Anne, *m.* to Lieut.-General John Prince.
Margaret, *m.* to Thomas Gregg, Esq.
Elizabeth, *m.* to Robert Markland, Esq.

Robert Hibbert, Esq. of Birtles Hall, co. Chester and Chalfont House, Bucks, *b.* 12 Oct. 1750, (son of Robert Hibbert and Abigail Scholey his wife), *m.* 3 Sept. 1785, Letitia-Hamilton, dau. of Ballard Nembhard, Esq. of the Island of Jamaica, and by her (who *d.* 1 April, 1854), had issue,

I. Thomas, his heir, now of Birtles Hall.
II. Robert, of Chalfont Lodge, Bucks, *m.* 1st, Letitia, only dau. of Harry-Augustus Leicester, Esq. of Chester, brother of John, 1st Lord de Tabley; and 2ndly, Charlotte, eldest dau. of John Drummond, Esq. of Denham, Bucks. He *d.* 17 Dec. 1829, leaving by his second wife,
1 Frederick-Drummond, J.P., late of the Scots Greys, *b.* 9 Dec. 1824.
2 Leicester, late of the Queen's Bays, *b.* 6 March, 1826; *m.* 29 April, 1851, Arethusa-Jane, dau. of Charles Calvert, Esq. M.P. of Kneller Hall, and has issue.
III. John-Nembhard, of Chalfont House. (*See that name*).
I. Anna, *m.* to Thomas Tipping, Esq. of Davenport Hall, Cheshire.
II. Letitia-Hamilton.

Arms—Erm., on a bend, sa., three crescents, arg.
Crest—An arm, erect, couped below the elbow, vested, az. cuff, erm., hand ppr., grasping a crescent, arg.
Motto—Fidem rectumque colendo.
Seat—Birtles Hall, Cheshire.

HIBBERT OF CHALFONT PARK.

Hibbert, John-Nembhard, Esq. of Chalfont Park, co. Bucks, major in the army, late capt. King's dragoon-guards, J.P. and D.L., high-sheriff 1837; *m.* 6 Aug. 1833, Jane-Anne, eldest dau. of Sir Robert Alexander, Bart. Mr. Hibbert is 3rd son of the late Robert Hibbert, Esq., and younger brother of the present Thomas Hibbert, Esq. of Birtles Hall.

Arms, Crest, and Motto—As Hibbert of Birtles Hall.
Seat—Chalfont Park, co. Bucks.

HIBBERT-WARE. (*See* Ware.)

HIBBERT OF BILTON GRANGE.

Hibbert, John-Hubert-Washington, Esq. of Bilton Grange, co. Warwick, captain in the army, *m.* 10 Jan. 1839, Julia, 3rd dau. of the late Sir Henry-Joseph Tichborne, Bart., widow of Lieut.-Col. Charles-Thomas Talbot, and mother of Bertram-Arthur, last Earl of Shrewsbury, and has issue. Captain Hibbert derives descent from John Hibbert, Esq., *b.* 1732, 4th son of Robert Hibbert, Esq. of Booth and Stockfield Hall. (*See* Hibbert *of Birtles.*)

Arms, Crest, and Motto—*See* Hibbert *of Birtles.*
Seat—Bilton Grange, Rugby.

HIBBERT OF BRAYWICK LODGE.

Hibbert, John, Esq. of Braywick Lodge, Berks, *b.* 29 Jan. 1811; *m.* 15 Sept. 1836, Charlotte-Elizabeth, dau. of Lieut.-Gen. Charles Turner, col. of the 19th regt. Mr. Hibbert, of Braywick Lodge, is son of the late John Hibbert, Esq. (who *d.* 11 Sept. 1855), by Charlotte his wife (who *d.* 28 June, 1825), dau. of Thomas Sumpter, Esq. of Histon Hall, co. Cambridge, and grandson (by Janet Gordon his wife) of John Hibbert, Esq., youngest son of Robert Hibbert, Esq. of Booth and Stockfield Hall. (*See* Hibbert *of Birtles Hall.*)

Arms, &c.—Same as Hibbert *of Birtles Hall*
Seat—Braywick Lodge, Maidenhead.

HICKMAN OF THONOCK HALL.

Bacon-Hickman, Henry, Esq. of Thonock Hall, co. Lincoln, *b.* 29 Oct. 1788. Mr. Bacon-Hickman, who is youngest son of the late, and second brother of the present Sir Edmund Bacon, Bart. of Redgrave, and Mildenhall, *s.* in 1826, to the Hickman estates, under the will of Frances Hickman, only surviving dau. of the last Sir Nevil Hickman, Bart., and assumed thereupon, by Royal license, the additional surname and arms of Hickman. He served the office of high-sheriff of Lincolnshire in 1831.

Arms—Quarterly: 1st and 4th, per pale, indented, arg. and az., a canton, of the last, for Hickman; 2nd and 3rd, gu., on a chief, arg., two mullets, pierced, sa., for Bacon.
Crests—A talbot, couchant, arg., collared and lined, az., at the end of the line a knot, for Hickman; a boar, passant, erm., for Bacon.
Motto—Toujours fidèle.
Seat—Thonock Hall, near Gainsborough, co. Lincoln.

HICKS OF WILBRAHAM TEMPLE.

Hicks, Edward, of Wilbraham Temple, co. Cambridge, J.P., *b.* 10 Aug. 1814; *m.* 10 Oct. 1838, Grace, eldest dau. of Stanley-Pipe Wolferstan, Esq. of Statfold and Pipe Halls, co. Stafford, by his wife Elizabeth Jervis, of Seal, co. Leicester, and has issue,

I. Stanley-Edward, *b.* in Jan. 1843.
II. Henry-John, *b.* in April, 1844.
I. Emily-Grace. II. Eda

This gentleman (only son of the late Edward Simpson, Esq. of Lichfield,* by Elizabeth his wife, dau. of William Anderton, Esq. of Moseley, co. Worcester, and Rebecca his wife, dau. of Gregory Hicks, Esq.), assumed, by royal licence in 1835, the surname and arms of Hicks, on succeeding to the estate of his kinsman, James Hicks, Esq. of Wilbraham Temple. The family of Hicks, of Wilbraham Temple, was a branch of the ancient stock of Hicks, of Campden.

Arms—Quarterly: 1st and 4th, gu., a fesse, between three fleurs-de-lis, or, for Hicks; 2nd and 3rd, per bend, sinister, or and sa., a lion, rampant, counterchanged, holding between the paws a gauntlet, az., for Simpson.
Crests—1st, a buck's head, couped, or, gorged with a chaplet of roses, leaved, vert, for Hicks; 2nd, an ounce's head, ppr., erased, and ducally crowned, gu., charged on the neck with a gauntlet, or, for Simpson.
Motto—Tout bien ou rien.
Seat—Wilbraham Temple, Cambridge.

HICKSON OF LETTEROUGH.

Hickson, Robert-Conway, Esq. of Fermoyle, co. Kerry, *b.* 25 Nov. 1812; high-sheriff of Kerry, 1855-6; *m.* 1st, in Aug. 1831, Agnes, only dau. of the late John Mahony, Esq. of Dromore Castle, by his wife Margarette, dau. of Sir William Godfrey, Bart., but by her had no surviving issue. Mr. Hickson *m.* 2ndly, 20 April, 1841, Jane, only dau. of Patterson O'Hara, Esq. late of H.M. 59th foot, of the ancient family of the O'Haras, of Antrim, by his wife Araminta Erskine, of the Mar family, and sister of the late Col. Jas. Erskine of H.M. 48th foot, and by her has issue,

I. James-Robert-Conway, *b.* 2 Jan. 1844.
II. Patterson-O'Hara, *b.* 5 Oct. 1845.
III. Robert-Conway, *b.* 17 Sept. 1847; *d.* 28 Feb. 1850.
IV. George-Archibald Erskine, *b.* 1854.
I. Araminta-Theresa. II. Jane-Sarah-Victoria.
III. Theresa-Georgina-Adelaide.

Lineage.—This family, which came originally from Cambridgeshire, and spelled the name Hixon, have long

* Edward Simpson was youngest son of Charles Simpson, Esq of Lichfield, by Mary his wife, dau. of Edward Cheney, Esq. of Yoxall, and grandson of Stephen Simpson, Esq., the son of Stephen Simpson, Esq. of Sheriff Hales Manor.

been of high standing in the co. of Kerry. The first on record there, we have been able to trace, is

THE REV. JOHN HICKSON, who was appointed rector, by patent, of the parishes of Killiney and Kilgobbin, in the diocese of Ardfert. His son,

THOMAS HICKSON, m. Frances Hussey, dau. of Walter Hussey,* of Castle Gregory, by his wife, Catherine, dau. of FitzGerald, of Kilmurry, and had issue (besides a dau., Catherine, m. to Walter Langdon, son of the Rev. Nathaniel Langdon, dean of Ardfert, previous to 1641) three sons, viz., RICHARD, whose issue is extinct; JOHN, of whom presently; and Robert, ancestor of the family of The Grove.

JOHN HICKSON, 2nd son of Thomas Hickson and Frances Hussey, m. Mary Rice, and left issue,

I. CHRISTOPHER, of whom hereafter.
II. James, high-sheriff for co. Kerry in 1765, who m. Miss Kean, and left issue,
  1 MARY, m. to her cousin, Robert Hickson.
  2 Catherine, m. Arthur Blennerhassett (Robert) of Fortfield, co. Kerry.
III. John, of Tierbrim, m. in 1743, Ellen, dau. of Dominick Trant (grandfather of the late Sir Nicholas Trant, who commanded the native force in Portugal, during the late war), by Mary, dau. of Pierce Ferriter, of Ballyferriter, and Ferriter's Island, now called The Blasketts, head of the ancient family of that name, and had issue,
  1 Robert, a capt. in the 5th foot, m. Mary Blake, of the co. Galway, and had issue,
    George-Blake, a barrister of eminence, and one of Her Majesty's counsel-at-law; m. Anne Watts, relict of William O'Neil, Esq., and has issue, a son, William. Mr. Hickson m. 2ndly, Julia, dau. of Christopher Delmege, of Castlepark, co. Limerick, but has no issue.
    Robert, m. Margaret Lynch, dau. of Mark Lynch, Esq. of Drumcorry, co. Galway, relict of — Watts, Esq., and has issue, Robert, John, Cecilia, Mary, and Anne.
  2 James, m. Mary, dau. of John O'Connell, of Newtown, co. Cork, by his wife Avis Hilliard, and left issue,
    John-James, m. Sarah, dau. of the Rev. James Day, rector of Tralee, and vicar-general of Ardfert, by his wife, Margaret, dau. of McGillycuddy, of The Reeks; and dying in 1839, left issue surviving,
      James-John, of Hillville, J.P. for co. Kerry, m. in 1839, his cousin, Deborah Godfrey, dau. of the Rev. Edward Day, rector of Kilgobbin, and has issue.
      John.
      Mary-Agnes.
    Ellen, m. to Morgan-O'Connell Busteed, Esq., M.D., of Tralee; but d. s. p.
    Maria, m. William Busteed, Esq. of Castlebar.
  3 Christopher, m. Miss Moriarty, and had issue (with a son, Robert, who d. unm.),
    John-Christopher, of the city of Dublin, m. Miss Wright, and has issue, two daus.,
      Eliza, m. David Robertson, Esq., H.E.I.C.S.
      Catherine-Charlotte.
    Catherine. Mary.
  4 John, m. Miss Poor, and had issue,
    Thomas, d. unm.
    Eliza, m. to Mr. Coppinger, of the city of Cork.
  5 George, of Hillville, J.P. for co. Kerry, d. unm.
  1 Katharine, m. — Mahoney, Esq., but left no issue.
  2 Mary, m. Thomas Day, Esq., and had issue.
IV. George, m. in 1747, Mary, only dau. of George Gould, Esq., and niece of Dominick Trant, Esq. of the city of Cork, and left a dau.,
    Elizabeth, m. to John Fagan, of Kiltallagh, co. Kerry.

The eldest son,

CHRISTOPHER HICKSON, Esq. of Fermoyle, m. in 1740, Elizabeth, dau. of Thomas Conway, Esq. of Castle Conway, co. Kerry, and was s. by his eldest son,

ROBERT HICKSON, Esq of Fermoyle, high-sheriff for Kerry in 1778. He m. (settlement dated 30 Oct. 1770) his cousin, Mary, dau. of his uncle, James Hickson, Esq.; and d. in the year 1812, leaving issue,

JAMES-ROBERT, of whom presently.
Robert-Conway, high-sheriff of Kerry in 1811, d. unm.
George, J.P., d. unm.
Mary, m. Jeremiah Leyne, Esq. of Tralee, M.D.
Catherine, m. to her cousin, Robert Blennerhassett, son of Arthur Blennerhassett (Robert), and Catherine Hickson.
Anne, m. John Hilliard, Esq. of Scrahan Lodge, co. Kerry (settlement dated 19 Jan. 1824).

The eldest son,

JAMES-ROBERT HICKSON, Esq. of Fermoyle, m. 10 Feb. 1808, Teresa-Maria, eldest dau. of John Pearl, Esq. of the city of Cork, and had issue,

ROBERT-CONWAY, present representative.
George-James, d. unm., aged 24, 30 May, 1837.
Jane-Elizabeth.
Sarah-Maria, m. 8 Aug. 1835, to Richard Norris, Esq. of Cork.

Mr. Hickson d. in Feb. 1817.

Arms (originally confirmed by Camden, in 1617, to Thomas Hixon, of Greenwood, keeper of the king's wardrobe, who descended out of Cambridgeshire, and now duly registered in the Office of Arms, Dublin Castle)—Or, two eagles' legs, erased, à-la-quise, in saltier; the dexter surmounted of the sinister, sa.; in the centre chief point a trefoil, vert.

Crest—Out of a ducal coronet, a griffin's head, ppr., charged with a trefoil, vert.

Motto—Fide et fortitudine.

Seat—Fermoyle House, near Tralee.

HICKSON OF GROVE, DINGLE.

HICKSON, ROBERT-ALBERT, Esq. of Grove, Dingle, co. Kerry.

Lineage.—ROBERT HICKSON, Esq. of Dingle, 3rd son of Thomas Hickson, by Frances Hussey, his wife, m. Barbara Trant, and was father of

JOHN HICKSON, Esq., who m. Ellen Rice, and had a son,

ROBERT HICKSON, Esq. of Dingle, J.P., and deputy-governor of co. Kerry, and high-sheriff in 1794, who m. in 1776, Judith, dau. of William Murray, Esq., and had issue,

JOHN, his heir.
Samuel-Murray, of Dingle, J.P. for Kerry, d. s. p.
Robert, in holy orders, m. Miss Hewson, and has a son, William.
James, J.P., of Lansdowne Lodge, d. leaving Robert-James and other issue.
George, in holy orders, m. and has a son, Robert, and daus.
Mary, m. to the late Peter-Bodkin Hussey, Esq., barrister-at-law.
Anne, m. to Sir William Cox, of Coolcliffe, co. Wexford.

The eldest son,

JOHN HICKSON, Esq. of Grove, Dingle, J.P. and D.L., b. 20 May, 1782; served as high-sheriff 1826. He m. 4 May, 1813, Barbara, eldest dau. of John Mahony, Esq. of Dromore Castle, Kenmare, and d. , having had issue,

ROBERT, J.P., m. Julia-Sophia Bruyere, and d. leaving a son,
  ROBERT-ALBERT, now of Grove, Dingle.
John, who has assumed the surname of MAHONY.
Richard-Mahony, m. Lucy, dau. of John Curry, Esq., and has issue.
Margaret, m. to William Norcock, Esq.
Barbara, m. to Capt. James Bower, R.N. Julia.
Mary-Anne, m. to Charles Blennerhassett, Esq. of Ballyseedy, co. Kerry.
Sarah.

Motto—Fide et fortitudine.

Seat—Grove, Dingle, co. Kerry.

HIGGINS OF SKELLOW GRANGE.

HIGGINS, GODFREY, Esq. of Skellow Grange, co. York, J.P. and D.L., b. 9 July, 1801; s. his father 9 Aug. 1833.

Lineage.—GODFREY HIGGINS, Esq., (son of Richard Higgins, Esq. of York, by Anne, his wife, dau. and co-heir of Lionel Copley, Esq. of Wadsworth, derived from Christopher, 3rd son of Sir William Copley, Knt., by Dorothy, his wife, dau. and co-heir of Sir William Fitzwilliam, of Sprotborough,) purchased from the family of Anne, of Burgh Wallis, the manor of Skellow, and certain demesne lands which lay close to the Grange. He m. Miss Christeana Matterson, and had issue,

GODFREY, his heir.
Christiana, m. to William Marshall, Esq. of Newton Kyme.

Mr. Higgins, d. 23 May, 1794, when sole representative of his grandfather, Lionel Copley, and was s. by his son,

GODFREY HIGGINS, Esq., F.S.A., of Skellow Grange, co. York, J.P. This gentleman m. in 1800, Jane, only dau. and heiress of Richard Thorpe, Esq. of Milnthorpe, near Wakefield, and had one son and two daus., viz.,

GODFREY, now of Skellow Grange.
Jane, m. to Lieut.-Gen. Sharpe, of Hoddam Castle, Dumfries-shire, M.P. for the Dumfries boroughs.
Charlotte, d. young.

* This Walter Hussey (proprietor of Castle Gregory, Ballyheggan and The Magheries) was 2nd son of Meyler Hussey, who founded the castle of Castle Gregory, by his wife, Frances Spring: the elder son, Nicholas, was killed in the wars.

Mr. Higgins, who enjoyed considerable literary reputation, d. 9 Aug. 1833.

Arms—Erm., on a fesse, sa., three towers, arg.
Crest—Out of a tower, sa., a lion's head, arg.
Seat—Skellow Grange, near Doncaster.

HIGGINS OF TURVEY HOUSE.

HIGGINS, THOMAS-CHARLES, Esq. of Turvey House, Beds, J.P. for Beds, Bucks, and Northamptonshire, D.L. of the counties of Bedford and Buckingham, and Chairman of Quarter Sessions in Beds, m. in 1838, Charlotte, 2nd dau. of Sir Rose Price, Bart. of Trengwainton, in Cornwall, and has issue,

I. WILLIAM-FRANCIS.
II. Dennis-Lambert.
I. Harriet-Anna.
II. Emily-Kathleen.
III. Louisa-Blanche.

Lineage.—JOHN HIGGINS, Esq., the father of the present Thomas Charles Higgins, Esq. of Turvey House, was grandson of Ann Clarke, co-heiress and dau. of Marchant Clarke, of Hardingston, co. Northampton, Esq., whose elder dau. was married to Lord Folkestone, afterwards Earl of Radnor. The said John Higgins m. Martha, dau. of William Farrer, of Brafield House, Bucks, Esq., by whom he had issue,

THOMAS-CHARLES, now of Turvey House.
William-Bartholomew, lt.-col. of Beds militia, residing at Picts Hill, in Beds.
Harriet, who m. General Scott.
Ann-Maria, deceased.

Arms—Vert, three cranes' heads, erased, arg.
Crest—A griffin's head, erased, or, gorged with a collar, gu.
Motto—Nihil quod obstat virtuti.
Seat—Turvey House, Beds.

HIGGINS OF TURVEY ABBEY.

HIGGINS, CHARLES-LONGUET, Esq. of Turvey Abbey, co. Bedford, J.P. and D.L., b. 30 Nov. 1806; m. 26 July, 1853, Helen-Eliza, dau. of Thomas Burgon, Esq. of the British Museum, by Catharine-Margaret, his wife, only dau. of the Chevalier Ambrose Hermann de Cramer, Austrian Consul at Smyrna.

Lineage.—JOHN HIGGINS, son of Hugh and Susanna Higgins, had, by Ann, his wife, five sons, JOHN; CHARLES, sheriff of London in 1787, who purchased the manor of Turvey, co. Bedford; Bartholomew; William; and THOMAS. The youngest son,

THOMAS HIGGINS, Esq. of Turvey Abbey, m. in 1762, Mary Parrott, and dying 24 May, 1794, left (with a dau., Sarah, who d. in 1802) a son,

JOHN HIGGINS, Esq. of Turvey Abbey, b. 1768, J.P. and D.L., high-sheriff 1801, who m. 1 Nov. 1804, Theresa, dau. of Benjamin Longuet, Esq. of Bath, and by her (who d. 5 Sept. 1845) left at his decease, 14 Nov. 1846, two sons and one dau., viz.,

CHARLES-LONGUET, now of Turvey Abbey.
Henry-Hugh, in holy orders, m. 3 Aug. 1852, Anne Gouthwaite.
Mary, m. 13 Oct. 1846, to the Rev. Edwin-Horatio Steventon.

Arms—Vert, three cranes' heads, erased, arg.
Crest—A griffin's head, erased, or, gorged with a collar, gu.
Seat—Turvey Abbey, co. Bedford.

HIGGINS OF BOSBURY HOUSE.

HIGGINS, THE REV. EDWARD, of Bosbury House, co. Hereford, J.P. and D.L., b. 1803; m. 7 Feb. 1833, Georgiana-Esther, dau. and co-heir of George Meredith, Esq. of Berrington Court, co. Worcester, J.P. high-sheriff for Worcestershire 1828, and has an only child,

ELLEN-GRAY, m. Robert-Baskerville R. Mynors, Esq. of Evancoyd, co. Radnor, eldest son of Peter Rickards-Mynors, Esq. of Treago, co. Hereford, and has a son and heir, WILLOUGHBY-BASKERVILLE MYNORS.

Lineage.—The Clyntons of Castleditch, now represented by the family of HIGGINS, owned, in early times, the greater part of the parish of Eastnor, and had large possessions in other parts of the co. of Hereford, but, about the year 1603, they sold the Mansion House of Castleditch, and the lands in Eastnor, to Mr. Richard Cocks, alderman of London, ancestor of the present Lord Somers.

EDWARD HIGGINS,* Esq., m. in 1563, Mary, dau. and co-heir of Thomas Clynton, Esq. of Castleditch, high-sheriff of Herefordshire 1568, by Margery, his wife, dau. of Richard Tracy, Esq. of Toddington, and had a son,

THOMAS HIGGINS, of the Birchen and Hillende, Eastnor, co. Hereford, mentioned in the will of his grandfather, Thomas Clinton. He m. in 1601, Anne, dau. of James Parry, Gent. of Ledbury, and had, with other issue, a son and successor,

ROBERT HIGGINS, who m. Joan Machan, of English Bicknor, and had (with four daus., Anne, m. to the Rev. W. Hanbury; Eleanor, m. to T. Morley, Esq.; Mary, m. to — Grinsell, Esq.; and Elizabeth) three sons, THOMAS, Simon, and Robert. The eldest son,

THOMAS HIGGINS, Esq. of Eastnor, m. Dorothy, living in 1680, dau. and heir of Thomas Yonge, Esq. of Hanley Castle, co. Worcester, by Editha, his wife, dau. of Anthony Stoughton, Esq. of St. John's, near Warwick, and grand-dau. (by Mary, his wife, dau. and heir of William Pinnock, Esq.) of John Yonge, Esq. of Hanley Castle, whose great-grandfather, John Yonge, Esq. of Crombe Dabitot, co. Worcester, (grandson of Sir Philip Yonge, Knt. of Taynton, co. Salop,) m. Jane, dau. and co-heir of Richard Jennets, Esq., by Jane, his wife, dau. of Hugh Wrottesley, of the co. of Stafford. By Dorothy, his wife, Mr. Higgins had a son and heir,

THOMAS HIGGINS, Esq. of Eastnor, who m. Winifred, dau. of T. Barnes, Gent. of Longdon, and had issue, THOMAS, Michael, John, Robert, Winifred, Mary, Donna-Catherine, Anne, and Elizabeth. The eldest son,

THOMAS HIGGINS, of Eastnor, b. in 1701, m. Elizabeth, dau. of Joseph Allen, Gent., and had (with three daus., Elizabeth, Anne, and Mary) a son,

THOMAS HIGGINS, Gent. of Hillend, Eastnor, b. in 1730, who m. Sarah, dau. of Mr. Wood, of Preston Court, co. Gloucester, and dying in 1809, left, with other issue, a son and heir,

THE REV. JOSEPH HIGGINS, of Eastnor, J.P. and D.L., rector of Eastnor, co. Hereford, who m. 27 June, 1796, Mary, dau. of Thomas Hussey, Esq., and d. 2 Sept. 1847, having had issue,

THOMAS, in holy orders, of Pangbourne, J.P. co. Hereford, m. 1st, Mary-Stanley, dau. of John Mills, Esq. of Stratford Hall, co. Worcester; and 2ndly, Maria, dau. of Browne, Esq. of London.
Joseph-Allen, of West Bank, near Ledbury, J.P. and D.L., m. Eliza, dau. of Thomas Perkins Hill, Esq. of Cheltenham.
Samuel, of Berrow Court, co. Worcester, m. Elizabeth, dau. of Mathews, Esq. of Linton, co. Hereford, and has a son, Samuel-Meyrick, rector of Icomb, co. Gloucester, and two daus.
EDWARD, now of Bosbury House, near Ledbury.
James, d. unm.
Robert, m. Maria-Agnes, dau. of Col. Crosse, and d. leaving a dau., Mary.
William.
Francis, m. in 1842, Miss Elizabeth Williams, dau. of the late Earl of Coventry.
Anne, m. to the Rev. Joseph Lawson Whatley, J.P., rector of Aston Ingham.
Mary.
Penelope, d. unm.

Arms—Quarterly, 1st and 4th: Paly of six, or and az., on a chev., cottised, erm., three crosses-patée, gu. 2nd and 3rd: Vert, three cranes' heads, erased, arg., quartering CLINTON, PARLIES, and YONGE.
Crest—A garb, ppr., charged with two crosses-patée, gu.
Motto—Patriam hinc sustinet.
Residence—Eastnor, co. Hereford.

HIGGINS OF WESTPORT.

HIGGINS, FITZGERALD, Esq. of Westport, co. Mayo, J.P., captain in the army, b. 6 Jan. 1789; m. 22 Feb. 1811, Mary, only child of William Ouseley, Esq. of Rushbrook, (of the family of the Right Hon. Sir Gore Ouseley, Bart.), by Marianne his wife, sister to the late M.-G. Prendergast, Esq. of Ballyfair, M.P. for Galway, and by her (who d. 15 April, 1834) has issue,

I. CHARLES-FITZGERALD, J.P., b. 31 July, 1815, m. 1 July, 1842, Amelia-Vertue, only dau. of Sir Richard Paul

* He is called Edward Higens, or Higgins, in Cooke's Visitation of 1569, and is supposed to have been descended from the family of Higgins, or Higons, of Church Stretton, co. Salop.

Jodrell, Bart. of Sall Park, Norfolk, and has RICHARD GEORGE-JODRELL, b. 11 Nov. 1843, and other issue.
George-Gore-Ouseley, late civil service, Jamaica, now of Glen Corribb, co. Mayo, J.P. and M.P. for that county, lieut.-col. of the North Mayo militia, b. 15 Oct. 1818.
I. Margaret. II. Mary. III. Ellen-King.

Lineage.—The family of Higgins, or O'Higgins, formerly possessed extensive territories in Connaught, and so far back as the end of the 14th century, we find mention made of the O'Higgins of Murh O'Higgin, co. Sligo. During the wars of the Commonwealth, PHELIM O'HIGGINS, a stanch Royalist, had his estates confiscated.

HUGH-ROE HIGGINS, Esq. of Moyna, co. Mayo, (son of Charles Higgins, of Moyna, whose father, Col. Hugo O'Higgins, was killed at the siege of Athlone, fighting for King JAMES II.) m. Kate, sister of John Browne, Esq. of Aughagower, and d. in 1746, leaving two sons, CHARLES, of whom presently; and Philip, who d. unm. in 1764. The elder son,

CHARLES HIGGINS, Esq. of Moyna, co. Mayo, m. in 1749, Mary, dau. of Patrick Fitzgerald, Esq. of Turlough, and had issue,

I. HUGH, who m. in 1774, Frances, only dau. of John Garvey, Esq. of Murrisk Abbey, and d. in 1776, leaving a son, Charles-Garvey, in the army, who d. in 1837, and a dau., Mary.
II. CHARLES, of whom presently.
III. Patrick, d. in 1824.
IV. Luke, b. in 1760, who m. 1st, Caroline, sister of Sir William Boyd, of Mount Gordon, co. Mayo, by whom he had an only child,
1 Alexander-Boyd, captain in the army, m. in 1812, Eliza, sister of Dr. Hodgkinson, Provost of Trinity College, Dublin.
He m. 2ndly, Catherine, sister of Sir Anthony Brabazon, Bart., M.P., of Brabazon Park, by whom, who d. in 1821, he had issue,
1 Hugh Brabazon, Esq., now of Brabazon Park (*see* p. 124).
1 Sarah, m. in 1826, to the Rev. Denis Bingham, of Killala, nephew of John, Lord Clanmorris.

The 2nd son,

CHARLES HIGGINS, Esq., J.P., and a deputy-governor of Mayo, b. in Feb. 1752, m. 10 Nov. 1777, Margaret, dau. of Henry Macdonnell, Esq. of Mount Pleasant, by Jane, his wife, dau. of Owen O'Malley, Esq. of Burrishoole, and had issue,

Charles, J.P., d. unm. at Madeira, in 1808.
FITZGERALD, now of Westport.
Henry, m. in 1819, Emily, widow of Governor Isaac, and dying in 1827, left a son, Henry-William, an officer in the army.
Luke, R.N., d. of wounds received at Trafalgar.
John-Browne, major in the army, d. unm. in 1812.
George-Martin, J.P., an officer in the army, d. unm. in June, 1837.
Catherine, d. unm. in 1809.
Eliza, d. unm. in 1806.

Mr. Higgins d. 3 March, 1837.

Arms—Arg., guttée, sa., on a fesse, of the second, three towers, double-turretted, or. The present Capt. Higgins, of Westport, bears, in right of his wife, Mary, only child of William Ouseley, Esq. of Rushbrook, the arms of Ouseley, on an escutcheon of pretence.
Crest—Out of a tower, double-turretted, sa., a demi-griffin, arg., holding in the dexter paw a dagger, of the last, hilt and pommel, or.
Motto—Pro patriâ.
Seat—Westport, co. Mayo.

HIGGINSON OF LISBURN.

HIGGINSON, HENRY-THEOPHILUS, Esq. of Lisburn, co. Antrim, and Carnalea House, co. Down, J.P., m. Charlotte, only surviving child and heiress of John McConnell, Esq. of Belfast, by Charlotte his wife, only dau. of James Potter, Esq. of Ardview, co. Down, by Dorothea his wife, sister and co-heiress of Henry-William Shaw, Esq. of Ballytweedey House, co. Antrim, who served the office of high-sheriff of the counties of Down and Antrim. Mr. McConnell claimed the earldom of Menteath in right of his ancestor, the Hon. Mr. Graham who fled from Scotland after the rising of 1745.

Lineage.—The ancestor of this highly respectable family, an English gentleman, accompanied the army of King WILLIAM III. to Ireland in the commissariat department. The grandfather of the present Henry-Theophilus Higginson, Esq., the late REV. THOMAS HIGGINSON, was rector of Lisburn, and possessed the lands of Ballinderry.

Arms (as duly registered)—Sa., three towers, in fesse, arg., between six trefoils, slipped, three in chief and three in base, or.
Crest—Out of a tower, ppr., a demi-griffin, segreant, vert, armed and beaked, or.
Motto—Malo mori quam fœdari.
Seat—Carnalea House, near Bangor, co. Down.

HILDYARD OF WINESTEAD.

HILDYARD, THE REV. WILLIAM, rector of Market Deeping, co. York, m. 1 May, 1838, Sophia, 4th dau. of the late Rev. John Hildyard, vicar of Bonby, co. Lincoln.

Lineage.—This family, styled by Camden a knightly one, traces its origin from an early period. The first on record, ROBERT HILDYARD, or HILDHEARD (as the name was originally spelt), of Normanby, was living 10 HENRY I., 1109.

SIR CHRISTOPHER HILDYARD, son of Richard Hildyard, Esq., by Jane, dau. and heir of Marmaduke Thwenge, Esq., and grandson of Martin Hildyard, Esq. of Winestead, by Emma his wife, dau. of Sir John Rudston, Knt., became, at the decease of his uncle, heir male of the family. He m. Elizabeth, dau. and sole heir of Henry Welby, Esq. of Goxhill, and had, with several daus., three sons, viz.,

HENRY, his heir. Christopher.
ROBERT (Sir), of Patrington, co. York, a gallant and distinguished Royalist commander, made a banneret by the Duke of Newcastle, and created a Baronet at the Restoration. (*See* BURKE'S *Extinct Baronetage*.)

The eldest son,

HENRY HILDYARD, Esq. of Winestead, co. York, and East Horsley, co. Surrey, was one of the severest sufferers in the Royal cause. He m. Lady Anne Leke, dau. of Francis, 1st Earl of Scarborough, and had, with daus., four sons,

HENRY, of Kelsterne, in Lincolnshire, raised and commanded a troop of horse for JAMES II. He m. 1st, Dorothy, dau. of Vincent Grantham, Esq. of Goltho, co. Lincoln, by whom he had a son, Christopher, who m. Jane, dau. of George Pitt, Esq. of Strathfieldsaye Hants, and left only four daus. Henry Hildyard m. 2ndly, Elizabeth, dau. of John Hilder, Esq., and had by her, Francis, Thomas, and Michael.
Charles.
Edward, of the Inner Temple, barrister-at-law, d. s. p.
PHILIP, of whose descendants we have to treat.

The 4th son,

PHILIP HILDYARD, Esq. of East Horsley, co. Surrey, one of the chamberlains of the Exchequer, m. Elizabeth, dau. of Sir Francis Vincent, Bart. of Stoke Dabernon; and dying in 1692, was buried in the Temple Church. His elder son,

HENRY HILDYARD, Esq of Goxhill, co. Lincoln, m. Frances, 2nd dau. and co-heir of William Long, Esq., and was father of two sons, Henry Hildyard, and

WILLIAM HILDYARD, Esq. of Great Grimsby, who m. in 1761, Frances, only dau. of the Rev. John Whichcote, rector of Scotton and Scotter, co. Lincoln, and his son,

THE REV. WILLIAM HILDYARD, rector of Winestead, b. 6 July, 1762; m. 12 Dec. 1793, Catherine, 3rd dau. of Isle Grant, Esq. of Ruckland, co. Lincoln, and by her (who d. 1855) had issue,

WILLIAM, in holy orders, now rector of Market Deeping.
John, barrister-at-law, recorder of Stamford, Grantham, and Leicester, m. 6 Nov. 1824, Jane, 2nd dau. of Lord John Townshend, of Balls Park, co. Hertford, and d. 13 Feb. 1855.
Robert-Charles, Q.C., A.M., M.P. for Whitehaven, b. 1800.
Henry, a merchant at Rio de Janeiro, b. 1801.
Frederick, rector of Swanington, co. Norfolk, m. 9 July, 1840, Lætitia, only dau. of John Shore, Esq. of Guilford Street, London, and has one son and two daus.
Horatio-Samuel, in holy orders, rector of Loftus, co. York.
Francis, barrister-at-law, d. May, 1846.
James, B.D., of Ingoldsby Rectory, near Grantham, J.P., b. 11 April, 1809; m. 19 Aug. 1847, Eliza-Matilda, only dau. of George Kinderley, Esq. of Lincoln's Inn, and has two surviving daus., Nora-Catharine and Evelyn-Matilda.
Richard, rector of Winestead, b. 5 March, 1811.
Alexander-Grant, in holy orders, curate of Holt and Blaston, co. Leicester, m. 12 June, 1851, and has two sons, GEORGE and Robert.
Catherine-Frances. Charlotte.

Arms—Az., three mullets, or.
Crest—Originally, a reindeer, ppr.; subsequently, a cock, sa., beaked, legged, and wattled, gu.

HILDYARD OF FLINTHAM HALL.

THOROTON-HILDYARD, THOMAS-BLACKBORNE, Esq. of Flintham Hall, co. Nottingham, J.P., and formerly M.P. for South Notts, *b.* 8 April, 1821; *m.* 3 May, 1842, Anne-Margaret, second dau. of Colonel Rochfort, of Clogrenane, co. Carlow, and has issue,

I. THOMAS-BLACKBORNE THOROTON, *b.* 10 March, 1843.
II. Robert-Charles Thoroton, *b.* 3 Nov. 1844.
III. Henry-John Thoroton, *b.* 5 July, 1846.

Lineage.—SIR ROBERT-D'ARCY HILDYARD, 4th bart. of Pattrington, lineally descended from Sir Robert Hildyard, the 3rd son of Sir Christopher Hildyard, of Winestead (*see preceding memoir*), served as high-sheriff of Yorkshire in 1783. He *m.* Mary, dau. of Sir Edward Dering, Bart. of Surrenden-Dering, but *d. s. p.* 6 Nov. 1814, when the baronetcy became extinct. The estates and representation of the family devolved on Sir Robert's niece and heiress,

ANNE-CATHERINE WHYTE (dau. of James Whyte, Esq., and Anne-Catherine his wife, dau. of Sir Robert Hildyard, 3rd bart., M.P., by Maria-Catherine, his wife, only child of Henry D'Arcy, Esq. of Sedbury), who *m.* THOMAS-BLACKBORNE THOROTON, Esq., who assumed, in consequence, the surname and arms of HILDYARD, and had by her,

THOMAS-BLACKBORNE, now of Flintham.
Robert-D'Arcy. Henry-Charles.
John-George-Bowes.
Anne-Catharine, deceased. Mary-Anne.
Elizabeth, *m.* 17 March, 1841, to Sir John-Charles Thorold, Bart.
Esther-Sophia.

Colonel Hildyard was *s.* by his eldest son, the present THOMAS-BLACKBORNE THOROTON-HILDYARD, Esq., M.P., of Flintham Hall.

Arms—HILDYARD and THOROTON, quarterly.
Crests—1st, HILDYARD; 2nd THOROTON.
Seat—Flintham Hall, near Newark.

HILL OF DONERAILE.

HILL, ARUNDEL, Esq. of Graig, near Doneraile, co. Cork, *b.* in 1801; *m.* Thomasine, 4th dau. of the late Sir James-Laurence Cotter, of Rockforest, Bart., (*see Baronetage*) and has issue,

I. JAMES, his heir.
II. Arundel, in holy orders, of Fermoy, co. Cork.
III. William, an officer in the army.

Mr. Hill *s.* to the representation of the family, on the decease of his father, the late James Hill, Esq. of Graig, 25 Sept. 1850.

Lineage.—The family of Hill, of Doneraile, is derived lineally from the Featherstone* branch of the Hills, or Hylls, of Littlepipe, co. Stafford, and was established in Ireland at the period of the Commonwealth. At first they fixed themselves at Kilmallock, co. Limerick (in the old abbey of which many monuments of the house may be found), and thence, a century afterwards, removed to Doneraile, in the co. of Cork, where they have since flourished.

WILLIAM HILL, of Featherstone, co. Stafford, Esq., *b. circa* 1580; *m. circa* 1610, Miss Judith Taylor, of Winchester, called for her unrivalled loveliness "The Phœnix of Winchester," by whom he was father of

WILLIAM HILL, captain of cavalry in Cromwell's army before Chester. He went to Ireland along with the parliamentary forces, and bore an active part in the campaigns of the Protector. He *m. circa* 1652, Catherine, dau. and sole heiress of the Rev. Henry Coyne, of a Staffordshire family, vicar of the collegiate church of Kilmallock, co. Limerick; and by this lady obtained several fee-simple estates in, or near to, Kilmallock, which, at his death in 1693, he left to his only son,

WILLIAM HILL, Esq. of Kilmallock, who *m. circa* 1686, Anne, dau. of Arundel Coke, or Cooke, Esq. of the co. Suffolk. By this lady, who *d.* in 1729, he had six sons and three daus.,

I. WILLIAM, who *m.* in 1718, and *d.* in 1739, leaving an only dau., Margaret, who *m.* — Lee, Esq., co. Clare, but had no issue. On her father's decease, in 1739, Mrs. Lee assumed the family estates; but when the next brother Thomas' son (William), came of age, he commenced a suit against her, and recovered them.
II. Thomas, *m.* 14 March, 1719, Margaret, dau. of John Davenport, Esq. of Ennis; and *d.* in 1740, leaving a son, in minority,

WILLIAM HILL, *m.* 1st, Aphra, sister of the late John Crone, Esq. of Doneraile, and by her had an only child, Aphra, who *m.* — Gregg, Esq. of Ennis, barrister-at-law, and had one child, Aphra Gregg, who *d. unm.* He *m.* 2ndly, Isabella, dau. of John Gibbings, Esq. of Gibbings Grove, co. Limerick (by Anne, his wife, dau. of Robert Conran, Esq.); and by this marriage had two sons, Thomas, *b.* in 1739; *d. unm.* at Cove, now Queenstown, co. Cork, 5 Sept 1813; Downes, *d. unm.* in 1781; and a dau., Anne, who *d.* young. Mr. Hill *d.* intestate, in 1758.

III. Richard, *m.* Miss Sarah Davenport; and, dying in 1747, left a son, William, who *d.* in 1793, leaving a son, William, who was accidentally shot, in Oct. 1815, at Pallaskenry, co. Limerick, by a serjeant of the 74th regt.
IV. ARUNDEL, of whom presently.
V. James, *m.* Miss Baldwin, of the Queen's co., and had a dau. Anne, who was *m.* to Thomas Morton, Esq. of Castletown, in said co. She *d. s. p.*, in widowhood, at Clonmel, in July, 1816.
VI. Samuel, of Pallaskenry, co. Limerick, *m.* Miss Lucas, of Ballingaddy, co. Clare, sister of the well-known Dr. Lucas, M.P. for Dublin, and had an only son,

GEORGE HILL, of Pallaskenry, who *m.* Agnes, dau. of the Rev. Philip Gayer, of Ballingrane; and by this lady, who *d.* in 1817, he, dying in 1791, had issue,

1 Samuel Hill, who went to Harrisburgh, America, in 1787 or 1788, and *d.* there.
2 Thomas, of Mount Pleasant, co. Limerick, who *m.* 1st, Catherine, dau. of — Pratt, Esq. of Pallas, by whom he had a dau., Catherine. He *m.* 2ndly, Elizabeth, dau. of Thomas Tydd, Esq. of Cloghyddan, and had further issue, Arundel, of Bolane cottage, *m.* Miss Franklin, dau. of the Rev. Mr. Franklin, of Kildimo; Thomas, now of Mount Pleasant, *m.* Miss Hawkshaw; George, of Limerick; and four daus.
3 William.
4 Arundel, *m.* Miss Bold, by whom he had a son, in holy orders, resident in America.
5 Richard, *m.* Miss Watson, of the city of Limerick.
6 Rowland, *d. unm.* 7 Charles, *d. unm.*
1 Margaret, *m.* to Mr. Bull, of Silvermines.
2 Mary, *m.*
3 Catherine, *m.*
4 Anne, *m.* — Ryan, Esq. 5 Agnes, *d. unm.*

I. Elizabeth, II. Catherine, III. Anne, } Alive in 1718, and then mentioned in their father's will.

Mr. Hill's last will bears date 19 Dec. 1717, and his decease followed soon after. His fourth son, whose line we follow, was

ARUNDEL HILL, Esq. of Doneraile, co. Cork, *b.* in 1694; *m.* Mary, dau. and sole heir of James Collins, Esq. of Buskot, co. Limerick, by whom he had two sons,

ARUNDEL, his heir.
James, an officer in the 3rd dragoon guards; *d. s. p.* in 1800 or 1801.

He *d.* at Doneraile 6 Feb. 1780, and was *s.* by his elder son,

ARUNDEL HILL, Esq. of Doneraile, *b.* in Sept. 1739; *m.* 1st, Mary, dau. of John Crone, Esq. (by his wife, Mary Armstead, who had been previously *m.* to Dr. Richard Creagh, of Newmarket, co. Cork, and had by that union a son, William Creagh, and a dau., Sarah, *m.* to JOHN-PHILPOT CURRAN, Esq., the distinguished advocate): by her he had,

JAMES, his heir. Arundel, *d.* in childhood.
Anne, *d.* young.

His wife dying, Nov. 1774, Mr. Hill *m.* 2ndly, in 1776, Helen, dau. of Garret Nagle, Esq of Ballyduffe, or Shanballyduffe, co. Cork; and by her, who *d.* 22 May, 1830, he had further issue,

I. Arundel, of Cloheen House, co. Cork, lieut.-col. of the South Cork militia, and for many years a magistrate of the county, *b.* 12 Dec. 1777; *m.* in 1796, Susan, dau. of Captain Kiggell, 53rd regt.; and, dying 28 March, 1840, had issue three daus.,

1 Helen.
2 Susan-Maria, *d. unm.* in Dec. 1827.
3 Margaret-Anne.

II. William, of Donnybrook, *b.* 12 Dec. 1780; *m.* Eliza, dau. of William Parker, Esq of Lansdowne, co. Tipperary; and, dying 27 April, 1847, had issue,

1 Arundel, now of Donnybrook, *m.* 2 Sept. 1844, Elizabeth-Georgina, dau. of Jonas Stawell, Esq. of Old Court, co. Cork (by his wife, Anna, dau. of the Hon.

* Another of their seats was Shenstone Castle, in the same shire. The heiress of Shenstone, Elizabeth Hill, *d.* in 1743. She had *m.* John Egerton, Esq. of Tatton Park, from whom the present William-Tatton Egerton, Esq. of Tatton.

and Right Rev. William Foster, D.D., bishop of Clogher, brother of John, Lord Oriel and Ferrard), and has issue, William; Anne-Letitia.
2 William, who was murdered by the Moors near Cape Spartel, on the African shore, 20 March, 1830. (See "*United Service Journal*," vol. ii., 1830, pp. 35-37.)
3 James, now of Dublin.
4 Matthew-Franks, *d.* in childhood.
1 Alicia, *d. unm.* 2 Helen, *d. unm.*
3 Emma, *d. unm.* in London, in 1830.
4 Eliza, *d. unm.*
5 Anne, *m.* June, 1854, to Robert Wilson, Esq. of Richmond, near Monkstown, Dublin, and has issue two daus.
6 Maria, *m.* to the Rev. Mark Clarke, rector of Shronell, co. Tipperary. He *d.* at Kilkie, co. Clare, 6 Sept. 1848.

III. Thomas, M.A., in holy orders, *b.* 28 Dec. 1779; *d. unm.* at Tipperary, 21 May, 1813.
IV. St. Leger, captain of the 12th lancers, and previously of the 3rd dragoon-guards, *b.* 8 Sept. 1782; *m.* Catherine, dau. of the late John Nugent, Esq. (whose sister, Jane-Mary Nugent, became the wife of the statesman, EDMUND BURKE), by whom he had issue,
1 Arundel-Edmund, capt of the 89th regt., slain before Sebastopol, 26 March, 1855.
1 Lucy-Nugent, *d. unm.* of consumption, at Richmond, Surrey, 15 Sept. 1853.
V. Richard of Doneraile, a magistrate for the co. Cork, *b.* 20 Sept. 1791; *d. unm.* at his residence in Doneraile, 18 Jan. 1845.
VI. Samuel, *b.* 16 June, 1794; *d.* 1 April, 1806.
I. Maria-Nagle Hill, *b.* 20 April, 1781; *d. unm.* at Doneraile, 6 Jan. 1845.
II. Helen, *b.* 4 Aug. 1786; *m.* 22 Jan. 1816, to Matthew Hayman, Esq. of South Abbey, Youghal (*see that family*).
III. Lucy-Anne, *b.* 3 Dec. 1787; *m.* to Launcelot-James Kiggell, Esq. of Birchwood, near Tarbert, co. Limerick; and *d.* 17 March, 1844, having had issue (with a dau. *d.* in infancy),
1 Launcelot-John-Kiggell, *b.* 14 June, 1829; an officer of the South Cork militia.
IV. Anne, *b.* 8 March, 1789; *m.* 9 June, 1810, to Captain Henderson Boyle, of the Londonderry militia; and by him, who *d.* 9 Jan. 1845, in his 57th year, she, dying 8 March, 1836, has issue,
1 James-Boyle, C.E.
1 Helen, *m.* to A.-C. Montgomery, Esq., and has issue.
2 Anne, *m.* to the Rev. Samuel Twigg, of Magherafelt, and has issue.
3 Lucy-Maria-Elizabeth, *m.* 21 Dec. 1847, to John-Stuart Vesey, Esq., M.D., son of the late Rev. Thomas-Agmondisham Vesey, rector of Magherafelt, and has issue.

Mr. Hill *d.* at Doneraile, 17 Oct. 1820 (his last will bears date 21 Oct. 1813), and was *s.* by his eldest son,

JAMES HILL, Esq. of Graig, co. Cork, *b.* 9 Nov. 1771; *m.* in 1800, Mary, dau. of Hugh Norcott, Esq. of Cork, and by her, who *d.* 7 Nov. 1844, had issue,
I. ARUNDEL, the present representative.
II. Hugh, of the Inner Temple, Q.C.; *m.* Audriah, dau. of Col. Webb, of London, and has issue,
1 Donald. 2 Eardley.
III. James, *m.* 1st, *s. p.* Margaret, dau. of the late John Nugent, Esq. of London; and 2ndly, Elizabeth, eldest dau. of Charles-Deane Oliver, Esq. of Rockmills, co. Cork, by whom he has issue,
1 Sarah. 2 Georgina.
IV. William, in holy orders, minister of Trinity Church, Leicester; *m.* 1st, Dorothea-Scott, dau. of Dr. Lorraine (M.D.), of Rothesay, Isle of Bute, and by her, who *d.* in 1841, had a son, William. He *m.* 2ndly, Mary, dau. of — Watts, Esq. of Bramblehill, co. Devon.
V. Thomas, *d. unm.*
VI. George, *m.* Anne Watts, sister of his brother William's wife.
I. Anne, *m.* to Francis Browne, Esq. of Mount Southwell, co. Limerick (grandson of the Rev. John Browne, of Danespit and Mount Browne, who in 1752, *m.* Meliora, dau. of the Hon. Col. Southwell, brother of VISCOUNT SOUTHWELL (*See* BROWNE *of Clonboy*), by whom,
1 Henry-Southwell. 2 James.
1 Frances. 2 Mary.
II. Mary, *m.* John-Hastings Otway, Esq. of Leeson Street, Dublin, barrister-at-law, and Q.C.; and has issue,
1 Cæsar. 2 John-Hastings.
1 Mary. 2 Elizabeth. 3 Frances.
III. Sarah, *m.* 8 Feb. 1842, to George Chatterton, Esq. of Ballinamought, co. Cork, and has issue,
1 James.
1 Anne. 2 Mary-Amelia, *d.* an infant. 3 Catherine.

Mr. Hill *d.* at Devonshire Place, Youghal, 25 Sept. 1850; and was *s.* by his eldest son and heir, Arundel Hill, Esq., now of Graig.

Arms—(Confirmed, in 1560, by Sir Gilbert Dethick, Garter.) Az., a chevron, between three fleurs-de-lis, or, a canton of the last.
Crest—A lion, rampant, arg., pierced through the breast by a broken spear, in bend, ppr., the head guttée de sang.
Motto—Ne tentes, aut perfice.
Seats—Graig and Donnybrook, near Doneraile, co. Cork.

HILL OF GRESSENHALL HALL.

HILL, JOHN-DAVID-HAY, of Gressenhall Hall, co. Norfolk, J.P., *b.* 26 June, 1805; *m.* 21 Nov. 1827, Margaret, 2nd dau. of E.-J. Collett, Esq. of Lockers House, Hemel Hempsted, Herts, and niece of Richard Alsager, Esq., late M.P. for co. Surrey, and has issue,

I. JOHN-DAVID-HAY. II. Alsager-Hay.
III. Reginald-Hay.
I. Margaret II. Julia-Hay.
III. Henrietta-Hay. IV. Florence-Hay.
V Mary-Henrietta-Hay. VI. Elizabeth-Hay.

Mr. Hill is only son of John Hill, Esq., by Julia-Anna, dau. of Lieut.-Col. David Hay, royal artillery, and grandson of John Hill, Esq., who was son of another John Hill, Esq.

Arms—Gu., two bars, erm., in chief, a lion, passant, arg.
Crest—A boar's head, sa., in the mouth a trefoil, slipped, ppr.
Motto—Spe labor levis.
Seat—Gressenhall Hall, near East Dereham, Norfolk.

HILL OF STALLINGTON HALL.

HILL, RICHARD-CLARKE, Esq. of Stallington Hall, co. Stafford, J.P., *m.* in 1811, Sarah, dau. of — Bird, Esq. of Eyam, in Derbyshire, by whom (who *d.* in 1818) he had two daus., viz., Mary-Anne and Sarah.

Lineage.—This family derives, according to Nash, from the De Montes of Castle Morton, in the parish of Longdon, and co. Worcester. "John De Monte, 20th EDWARD III., *anno* 1346, held lands in Castle Morton which Odo de Monte lately held, and the heir of John de Monte, 7th HENRY VI., (1429,) held the same lands. His heirs, the Hylls, lived in this Morton. The Hylls before this were in Hill-Cromb, 27th EDWARD I. (1299.)"

ANTHONY HILL, Esq. of Pepperhill, *b.* 23 Oct. 1690, (son of William Hill, of Pepperhill, muster master for Staffordshire, by Elizabeth, his wife, dau. of John Arden, Esq., and grandson of John Hill, Esq. of Castle Morton, an officer in the army of King CHARLES I.) *m.* 8 July, 1710, Catharine, dau. of Mark Coyney, Esq., and had, with other issue, Edward, whose elder son, WALTER-WILLIAM HILL, assumed the surname of COYNEY, (*see family of* COYNEY,) and RICHARD, of whom presently. The youngest son,

RICHARD HILL, Esq., *b.* 30 March, 1729, *m.* Mary, only dau. and heir of William Clarke, Gent. of Caverswall, co. Stafford, by whom, who *d.* in 1802, he had an only son. RICHARD-CLARKE. Mr. Hill purchased the estate and mansion of Stallington Hall, and dying 2 April, 1794, was *s.* by his son, RICHARD-CLARKE HILL, Esq. of Stallington Hall.

Arms—Sa., a chevron, or, between three wild cats, passant, guardant.
Crest—A hawk, ppr., with bells on the legs.
Seat—Stallington Hall, co. Stafford.

HILLS OF COLNE PARK.

HILLS, ROBERT, Esq. of Colne Park, co. Essex, J.P. and D.L., high-sheriff 1856, *b.* 15 Aug. 1796; *m.* 8 July, 1819, Mary, dau. of James Cole, Esq. of Great Holland, Essex, and has had issue,

ROBERT-ASTLE, *b.* 2 Oct. 1821, *m.* 22 Oct. 1846, and *d.* 25 Aug. 1855, leaving issue, one son and two daus.
Mary-Frances, *m.* 14 May, 1844, to the Rev. James-Farr Reeve, rector of Great and Little Thornham, Suffolk.

Lineage.—This family claims descent from a younger branch of the ancient house of Astley of Patshall.

THOMAS ASTLE, Esq., Keeper of the Records in the Tower of London, son of David Astley, Esq., and grandson of Thomas Astley, Esq. of Faude, near Tutbury, *m.* Anna-

Maria, dau. and heir of the Rev. Philip Morant, of Colchester, and had issue,

I. Thomas, of Gosfield Hall, co. Essex, b. 20 Jan. 1767, whose dau., Louisa, m. Charles-Robert Sperling, Esq. of Etchingham Lodge, Sussex.
II. PHILIP, of whom presently.
III. Edward, b. 4 Nov. 1770, m. in 1800, Harriet, dau. of Nathaniel Bateman, of the city of Gloucester, and d. s. p. 2 June, 1816.
IV. George, b. 27 Nov. 1773, rear-admiral of the Blue, d. in 1830.
V. William, b. 15 Jan. 1776, lieut. E.I.C.S., d. at Bombay, 15 July, 1797.
I. Maria, m. to the Rev. Matthew Bloxham, of Ide Hill Kent.
II. Charlotte, d. unm. in 1826.

The 2nd son,

PHILIP ASTLE, Esq. of Colne Park, co. Essex, b. 26 Jan. 1768, assumed the surname and arms of HILLS, by Royal licence, 9 Jan. 1790, in compliance with the will of Michael-Robert Hills, Esq. of Colne Park. He m. 15 May, 1794, Frances, dau. of the Rev. Thomas Banks, of Wimbledon, Surrey, and had,

I. ROBERT, his heir, and present proprietor.
I. Frances, d. 22 Sept. 1846.
II. Anna-Maria, m. to Henry Downes, Esq. of Colchester, capt. R.N. She d. s. p. in 1823.
III. Harriet, m. to Charles Haselfoot, Esq. of Boreham Manor, Essex.
IV. Eleanor. V. Charlotte. VI. Emma.
VII. Caroline, m. 22 July, 1852, to Charles Meredith, Esq. of Lincoln's Inn.

Mr. Hills d. 8 April, 1830.

Arms—Quarterly: 1st and 4th, erm., on a fesse, sa., castle, with turrets, ppr., for HILLS; 2ndly, az., a cinquefoil, pierced, erm., a label of three points throughout, or, for ASTLE; 3rdly, gu., on a chev., arg., three talbots, passant, sa., for MORANT.
Crests—Of HILLS, a castle, as in the arms; of ASTLE, on a chapeau, gu., turned up, erm., a ducal coronet, with cap, ppr., therefrom issuant a plume of five ostrich feathers, arg.
Motto—Fide sed cui vide.
Seat—Colne Park, near Halstead, co. Essex.

HILTON OF PRESTON HOUSE.

HILTON, GILES, Esq. of Preston House, co. Kent, J.P., b. in 1779; m. 1st, in 1803, Mary, dau. of the late John Shepherd, Esq. of Faversham; and, 2ndly, Sarah, dau. of the late Captain Waller, R.N. Mr. Hilton s. the late Thomas-Gibbs Hilton, Esq. of Marshes Selling. The family claims descent from the old baronial house of Hilton, of Hilton Castle, co. Durham.

Arms—Arg., two bars, az.
Crest—(As over Hilton Castle) Moses's head in profile, glorified, adorned with a rich diapered mantle, all ppr.
Motto—Tanq. je puis.
Seat—Preston House, Faversham.

HINCKS OF BRECKENBROUGH.

HINCKS, THOMAS-COWPER, Esq. of Breckenbrough, North Riding of York, J.P., M.A., barrister-at-law, b. 17 Jan. 1788; m. 17 Sept. 1835, Marianne, 6th dau. of Henry-Percy Pulleine, Esq. of Crake Hall, co. York, and has had issue,

I. THOMAS-COWPER, b. 20 Aug. 1840.
I. Mary-Joanna. II. Elisabeth-Esther.
III. Maria. IV. Henrietta-Pulleine.

Lineage.—WILLIAM HINCKS, Esq., an alderman of the city of Chester in 1643, was father (by his first wife, a dau. of Jansan, whom he married in 1596) of

EDWARD HINCKS, b. 15 June, 1617, who m. in 1644, Elizabeth, dau. of — Jones, Esq., and d. in 1666, leaving, with other issue, an eldest son,

JOSEPH HINCKS, Esq., who m. in 1672, Eunice, dau. of the Rev. Samuel Slater, and d. in 1680, leaving (with two daus., Sarah and Elizabeth,) two sons, Joseph, the elder, who m. Anne, dau. of Ryder, Esq., by whom he had issue; and the younger,

EDWARD HINCKS, Esq., baptized 5 April, 1676, m. 1st, in 1699, Mary, dau. of Robert Sparke, Esq. of Chester, by whom he had issue,

THOMAS, his heir, grandfather of the late Rev. THOMAS DIX HINCKS, of Belfast.

Mr. Edward Hincks m. 2ndly, Hannah, dau. of Robert Murrey, Esq., alderman of Chester, and by her had, with other issue, a son. The second son,

JOHN HINCKS, Esq. of Chorlton, co. Chester, banker in the city of Chester, and a deputy-lieut. for the county, b. 4 Dec. 1716, m. 10 Oct. 1755, Arbella, second dau. and eventually sole heir of Thomas Cowper, Esq., by Esther, his wife, second dau. and eventual sole heir of John Alleyne, Esq. of Gresley, co. Derby, and granddau. of Thomas Cowper, Esq., M.P. for Chester in 1697, who was second son (by Elizabeth, his wife, dau. of John Baskervyle, Esq. of Old Withington,) of Thomas Cowper, Esq. of Overleigh, seventh in lineal descent from Thomas Cowper, page of honour to Prince Arthur, eldest son of King HENRY VII. By this lady, Mr. Hincks left at his decease, 1 June, 1772, (with two daus., Esther, who d. unm., and Arbella, who d. young,) a son,

THOMAS-COWPER HINCKS, Esq., D.L., of Marefield, co. Leicester, and of Mancetter and Baddesley, co. Warwick, capt. in the King's dragoon-guards, b. 5 Jan. 1758, who m. 15 Jan. 1787, Joanna, eldest dau. of Colonel Roger Morris, of York, one of H. M. council for New York, and by her (who d. 30 Dec. 1822) had issue,

THOMAS-COWPER, of Breckenbrough.
John, of Huntington, co. Chester, b. 4 Jan. 1789, capt. royal art., resident at Cowling Hall, near Bedale, m. 31 May, 1826, Henrietta, second dau. of Henry-Percy Pulleine, Esq. of Crake Hall, in Yorkshire, and d. 14 Oct. 1842.

Mr. Hincks d. 4 March, 1819.

Arms—Gu., a lion, rampant, erm., within an orle of bezants and plates alternately, quartering COWPER, ALLEYNE, CALLYS, &c.
Crest—A demi-lion, gu., guttée de larmes, gorged with a collar, dancettée, arg., the sinister paw resting on an annulet, or.
Motto—In cruce et lachrymis spes est.
Seat—Breckenbrough, co. York.

HINDE OF ACTON HOUSE.

HODGSON-HINDE, JOHN, Esq. of Stella Hall and Acton House, in Northumberland, J.P. and D.L., high-sheriff 1849, M.P. for Newcastle-on-Tyne, in seven parliaments, b. 30 July, 1806; m. 31 Jan. 1833, Isabella, eldest dau. and co-heir of the late Anthony Compton, Esq. of Carham Hall, in Northumberland, assumed by sign-manual, in 1836, in compliance with the testamentary injunction of of Miss Elizabeth-Archer Hinde, the additional surname of HINDE.

Lineage.—The earliest notice which we have of the family of Hodgson, is in the records of the town of Newcastle, in the reign of EDWARD I. John Hodgson was one of the bailiffs of that town in 1276, and served the office of mayor in 1278, 1280, and 1281; in the last year he was knighted. Richard Hodgson, his son, was twice bailiff, in 1281 and 1288.

THOMAS HODGSON, with whom a connected pedigree must commence, was b. in 1424, and s. to the estates of Collierley and Hermon on the death of his mother, Johanna, dau. and heiress of John de Gilford. He had a son,

HUGH HODGSON, who s. his father in 1505, and d. in 1508, leaving two sons, GEORGE (for whose descendants see Surtees' Durham, vol. ii.) and

WILLIAM HODGSON, who had two sons, William and GEORGE. He d. before 1566. His second son,

GEORGE HODGSON, living in 1590, had a son,

WILLIAM HODGSON, who was one of the lessees, with Sir William Riddell and others, of the manors of Gateshead and Whickham, held under the crown in trust for the corporation of Newcastle, A.D. 1590; m. Agnes, widow of John Harrison, Esq., and had four sons, RICHARD, GEORGE, Samuel, and Henry. The second,

GEORGE HODGSON, s. to the property of his brother Richard, on the death of the latter in 1649. He d. in 1669, leaving by Jane his wife, a son,

LUKE HODGSON, Esq., who d. in 1691, leaving by his wife Susan, three sons, Luke, a physician in Newcastle; Samuel, a merchant in the same place; and JOHN. The youngest,

JOHN HODGSON, Esq., was father of

THOMAS HODGSON, Esq., who, by his wife Mary, had a son JOHN, and two daus., Jane, d. 23 March, 1797, and Mary d. 5 Sept. 1769, both unm. The only son,

JOHN HODGSON, Esq., m. Anne, only child of James

Appleby, Esq. of Askerton, co. Cumberland, (eldest son of Joseph Appleby, Esq. of Kirklinton, in the same shire, by Dorothy his wife, dau. and ultimately sole heiress of Henry Dacre, Esq. of Lanercost Abbey,) and by this lady, who *d.* 28 May, 1773, had issue. Mr. Hodgson *d.* 4 Nov. 1749, and was *s.* by his son,

JOHN HODGSON, Esq., who *m.* 24 July, 1773, Alice, dau of Thomas Wilkinson, Esq. of Walbottle, and by her, who *d.* 27 July, 1832, left at his decease, 13 Aug. 1781, an only son,

JOHN HODGSON, Esq. of Elswick, who *m.* 3 May, 1803, Sarah, dau. of Richard Huntley, Esq. of Friarside, co. Durham, and had issue,

- JOHN, now of Acton House.
- Richard, *b.* 1 April, 1812, for some time M.P. for the borough of Berwick, *m.* Catherine-Monypenny, second dau. and co-heir of the late Anthony Compton, Esq. of Carham Hall, and has one dau.
- Thomas, J.P., *b.* 3 Oct. 1814, *m.* Marianne, second dau. of the Rev. J.-T. Huntley, vicar of Kimbolton, and rector of Swineshead, Huntingdonshire, and has issue.
- Sarah, *m.* to the Rev. W.-C. King, vicar of Norham.
- Alice. Anne-Jane, *d.* 7 March, 1826. Mary.

Mr. Hodgson *d.* 12 July, 1820.

Arms—Per chev., embattled, or and az., three martlets, counterchanged.

Crest—On a rock a dove, az., winged, or, in the beak an olive-branch, ppr.

Motto—Miseris succurrere disco.

Seats—Acton House, and Stella Hall, Northumberland.

HINGSTON OF HOLBETON.

HINGSTON, JOSEPH, Esq. of Holbeton and Dodbrooke House, co. Devon, *b.* 5 May, 1788; *m.* 8 Sept. 1825, Elizabeth-Talwin, dau. of James Kenway, Esq. of Bridport, and has surviving issue,

- Josephine, *m.* 1851, Robert Dymond, Esq. of Exeter, and has issue.

Lineage.—ANDREW HINGSTON, Esq. of Scotscombe, in the parish of Holbeton, son of WALTER HINGSTON, who *d.* in 1627, and grandson of ANDREW HINGSTON, *m.* in 1623, Grace Hingston, of Ringmore, and *d.* in 1643, having had by her, who *d.* in 1675, with a dau. Jane, five sons, I. Walter, *b.* in 1624, *m.* in 1652, Sarah Rowe, and *d.* in 1684; II. JAMES, of whom presently; III. Josias, *b.* in 1631; IV. Abel, *b.* in 1637, *d.* in 1676; and V. William. The second son,

JAMES HINGSTON, *b.* in 1626; *d.* in 1659, leaving, by Alice his wife, (with a younger son, Andrew, *b.* in 1659,) an elder son,

JAMES HINGSTON, Esq., *b.* in 1654, who *d.* in 1733, leaving a son and heir,

JAMES HINGSTON, Esq. of Hobleton, who *m.* 1st, Anne Rowe; and 2ndly, Elizabeth Brooking, and by the latter, who *d.* in 1746, had (with a dau. Sarah, *m.* to William Hele) an only son,

JOHN HINGSTON, Esq. of Kingsbridge, co. Devon, *b.* in 1737, who *m.* 1st, in 1760, Rachel, dau. of George Fox, Esq. of Par, co. Cornwall; she *d.* the following year *s. p.* He *m.* 2ndly, in 1763, Rachel, dau. of Joseph Collier, Esq. of Plymouth, and Dorothy his wife, and by this lady had (with a dau. Dorothy, *m.* to Robert Were Fox, Esq.), a son,

JOSEPH HINGSTON, Esq. of Dodbrooke, co. Devon, *b.* in 1764, who *m.* 22 Nov. 1785, Sarah, dau. of Joseph Ball, Esq. of Bridgewater, and by her, who *d.* in 1790, had issue,

- JOSEPH, of Dodbrooke House.
- Sarah-Ball, *m.* in 1805, to Walter Prideaux, Esq. son of George Prideaux, Esq. of Kingsbridge, and by him (who *d.* 24 June, 1832) had numerous issue.

Mr. Hingston *m.* 2ndly, in 1796, Catherine-Phillips, dau. of Joseph Tregelles, of Falmouth, and by her also had issue,

- Frederick-Collier, *b.* in 1803, *d.* in 1810.
- Charles, *b.* in 1805, M.D., of Plymouth, *m.* 1st, in 1830, Mary, dau. of George Braithwaite, Esq. of Kendal, co. Westmoreland, and by her (who *d.* in 1833) had issue two daus., Marianne, and Georgina Braithwaite, who *d.* 1854. He *m.* 2ndly, in 1837, Louisa-Jane, dau. of Sir William-George Parker, Bart, capt. R.N., and by her has issue, 1 Charles Albert; 2 Ernest-Allison; 1 Louisa; 2 Charlotte-Parker, 3 Fanny-Catherine; 4 Clara-Gertrude; 5 Sophia-Elizabeth.
- Alfred, of Plymouth and Marsh House, co. Devon, *b.* in 1807; *m* in 1831, Mary, dau. of James Barton Nottage, Esq. of Lancaster, and has issue, 1 Alfred Nottage; 2 Joseph-Tregelles; 3 Frederick-Collier; 4 George; 5 Augustus; 1 Jane-Catherine; 2 Mary-Elizabeth, *d.* 1851; 3 Esther Margaret; 4 Emma-Rachel; 5 Rosetta.
- Catherine-Tregelles, *m.* in 1829, to William Browne, son of John Browne, Esq. of Longbarne, co. Devon.
- Rachel-Collier, *m.* in 1819, to George, son of Edward Fox, of Wadebridge, co. Cornwall, and has numerous issue.
- Susanna-Anna.
- Sophia-Price, *m.* in 1836, to Alfred Gilkes, son of Benjamin Gilkes, Esq. of London.
- Louisa-Ellen, *m.* in 1835, to Gilbert Gilkes, another son of Benjamin Gilkes, Esq. of London.

Mr. Hingston *d.* 30 April, 1835.

Arms—Gu., an arm in armour, ppr., holding a Danish battle-axe, arg.

Crest—A hind's head, couped, or holding in the mouth a holly slip, ppr.

Seat—Dodbrooke House, Devonshire.

HIPPISLEY OF STONEASTON.

HIPPISLEY, JOHN, Esq., F.R.S., F.R.A.S., of Stoneaston, co. Somerset, J.P. and D.L., high-sheriff 1856, *b.* 29 Oct. 1804; *m.* 1st, 19 May, 1830, Anne-Elizabeth, dau. of the Rev. Thomas Clare, rector of St. Andrews, and by her had issue,

- I. JOHN, *b.* 13 March, 1832.
- II. Henry-Edward, *b.* 3 Sept. 1838.
- III. Clare-Robert, *b.* 2 July, 1842.
- I. Anne-Catherine. II. Charlotte-Mary.

He *m.* 2ndly, 1 Aug. 1843, Georgiana, dau. of the late Rev. John Dolphin, rector of Wakes Colne and Pedmarsh, Essex, and by her has issue,

- I. Frederic-Thomas, *b.* 28 April, 1847.
- II. Richard-Lionel, *b.* 2 July, 1853.
- I. Martha-Sybil. II. Georgiana.

Lineage.—The family tradition holds that the chief part of the Somersetshire estates were given to Richard Hippisley by JOHN OF GAUNT; and an ancient parchment pedigree is headed with the following rhyme, purporting to be the form of grant of several manors therein named:—

"I, John a Gaunt, do give and grant unto Richard Hippisley,
All the manners herein named, as I think in number seven,
To be as firm to be thine, as ever they were mine, from Heaven above to Hell below,
And to confirm the truth, I seal it with my great tooth, the wax in doe.
Stone Easton, Camley, Wakam, Toddlhouse, Brasket Charde, Hinton, Bluet."

According to Collinson's *Somersetshire*, the manor of Ston Easton was granted at the dissolution of the monasteries, 36 HENRY VIII., to JOHN HIPPISLEY, the lineal descendant of the Richard Hippisley of the rhyming grant. This

JOHN HIPPISLEY, Esq. of Ston Easton, in Somersetshire, *m.* Mary, dau. of J. Flowre, and had issue,

- I. JOHN, his heir.
- II. William, who *d.* in 1630, leaving three sons, viz.,
  - 1 Thomas, who *d.* in 1640, leaving issue.
  - 2 Richard, captain of Standgate Castle.
  - 3 John (Sir), ranger of Bushey Park, who, on the breaking out of the civil wars, sided with the parliament, and was a commissioner sent to treat with the king. Sir John Hippisley sold Marston House to the Earl of Cork.

Mr. Hippisley was *s.* by his eldest son,

JOHN HIPPISLEY, Esq. of Ston Easton, who *m.* Dorothy, dau. of Sir John Horner, of Cloford and Wells, and was *s.* by his eldest son,

JOHN HIPPISLEY, Esq. of Ston Easton, who *m.* Eliza, dau. and heiress of John Organ, Esq. of Lamborne, Berks. and had issue,

- I. JOHN, of Ston Easton, who *m.* Margaret, dau. and heiress of John Preston, Esq. of Cricket St. Thomas, co. Somerset, and had, with other issue,
  - 1 John, eldest son, *d. s. p.*
  - 2 RICHARD, of Ston Easton and Camley, 2nd son, who *m.* Miss Elizabeth Yorke, and was *s.* by his son,
    - PRESTON HIPPISLEY, Esq. of Ston Easton, who *m.* Susan, dau. and heiress of Charles Yorke, Esq. of Bassets Down, in Wilts, and was *s.* by his only dau.,
    - MARGARET HIPPISLEY, who *m.* John Coxe, Esq. of Lee, and conveyed to him the estates of the principal branch of Hippisleys. The son and heir of this marriage,
    - JOHN HIPPISLEY-COXE, *m.* Mary, dau. of Stephen Northleigh, Esq. of Peamore, in Devon, and had issue,
    - RICHARD HIPPISLEY-COXE, of Ston Easton, M.P. for Somersetshire in 1768, who *d. s. p.*

John, *d. s. p.*
Henry, of Ston Easton, M.P. for Somersetshire, who *m.* Elizabeth-Anne, dau. of Thomas Horner, Esq. of Mells Park; but *d. s. p.* in 17.5, having devised his estates to his kinsman, the present John Hippisley, of Ston Easton. Mr. Henry Hippisley's widow *m* 2ndly, Sir John Coxe-Hippisley, Bart.; and *d* 25 March, 1843.
Margaret, *m.* to the Rev. John Hippisley, of Stow, in Gloucestershire.
Mary, *m.* to John Buller, Esq. of Downes.
Anne, *m.* to William James, Esq. of Ash.
Susannah, *m.* to Francis, Lord de Dunstanville.

3 George (7th son of John Hippisley, of Ston Easton, by Margaret Preston) was father of
John Hippisley, who *m.* Miss Mary Atkyns, of the co. of Hereford, and was *s.* by his son,
Richard Hippisley, who *m.* Jane, dau. of the Rev. Henry Edwards, vicar of Chard, in Somersetshire, and had a son,
John, in holy orders, of whom presently, as heir to the Lamborne branch.

II. Richard.

The 2nd son,

Richard Hippisley, Esq., inherited the estate of Lamborne, in Berkshire. He *m.* Anne Orlebar, and had two sons,

Richard, who *d. s. p.*; and

John Hippisley, Esq. of Lamborne, who *m.* Miss Catherine Southby, and was *s.* by his son,

John Hippisley, Esq. of Lamborne, who *m* Cotton, dau. of — Bowles, Esq., and had a son and heir,

Organ Hippisley, Esq. of Lamborne, who *d.* in 1735, without surviving issue, and was *s.* by his brother,

John Hippisley, Esq. of Lamborne. This gentleman *m.* Miss Maria Odam; but dying *s. p.* in 1769, devised his estates to his kinsman,

The Rev. John Hippisley, of Stow, co. Gloucester, who thus became of Lamborne. He *m.* Margaret, dau. of John Hippisley-Coxe, Esq. of Ston Easton, co. Somerset, and had issue,

Richard, who assumed the additional surname and arms of Tuckfield (*see* Hippisley of Shobrook).
Henry.
Frances-Anne.

Mr. Hippisley, who *d.* in 1822, bequeathed his estates at Lamborne to his 2nd son,

The Rev. Henry Hippisley, M.A., of Lamborne Place and Sparsholt House, *b.* 7 April, 1776; who *m.* 21 Dec. 1803, Anne, 3rd dau. and co-heiress of Lock Rollinson, Esq. of Chadlington, co. Oxford, and by her (who *d.* 7 Nov. 1855) had issue,

John, now of Ston Easton.
Henry, now of Lamborne Place.
Robert-William, rector of Stow, co. Gloucester, *b.* 17 July, 1818; *m.* 10 June, 1841, Grace-Louisa, eldest dau. of Thomas Raikes, Esq. of Welton, co. York, and has issue.
Margaret. Anne, *d.* 1855.
Mary, *m.* to the Rev Henry Mills.
Frances, *d.* 5 Jan. 1836.
Charlotte-Martha, *m.* to the Rev. Frederic Shelley.
Jane. Emma-Elizabeth.
Isabella-Maria, *m.* to Dr. Luther.

The Rev. Henry Hippisley *d.* 1 June, 1838.

Arms—Sa., three mullets, pierced, in bend, between two bendlets, or.

Crest—A hind's head, erased, ppr., gorged, with a collar, sa., charged with three mullets, pierced, or.

Seat—Ston Easton, co. Somerset.

HIPPISLEY OF LAMBORNE.

Hippisley, Henry, Esq. of Lamborne Place and Sparsholt House, co. Berks, and Cote House, co. Oxford, J.P. and D.L., high-sheriff of Berks, 1840, *b.* 6 March, 1808; *m.* 1st, 9 Feb. 1839, Elizabeth-Agnes, dau. and heiress of the Rev. John Nelson, D.D., prebendary of Heytesbury, Wilts, and, by her, has issue,

I. Henry-Nelson, *b.* 15 Oct. 1839.
I. Catherine. II. Agnes.
III. Eleanor-Anne. IV. Beatrix.

He *m.* 2ndly, 8 May, 1851, Elizabeth-Mary, eldest dau. of the Right Hon. Laurence Sulivan, by Elizabeth, his wife, dau. of Henry, 2nd Viscount Palmerston, and has by her,

I. Lawrence-Temple, *b.* 28 March, 1854.
II. William-Henry, *b.* 1 Dec. 1855.
I. Emily-Sulivan.

Lineage.—See Hippisley of Ston Easton, the present Henry Hippisley, Esq. of Lamborne, being the next brother of John Hippisley, Esq., now of Ston Easton.

Arms and *Crest*—See Hippisley of Ston Easton.

HIPPISLEY OF SHOBROOK PARK.

Hippisley, John-Henry, Esq. of Shobrook Park, co. Devon.

Lineage.—Richard Hippisley, Esq. of Fulford, Devon (eldest son of the Rev. John Hippisley, of Stow, co. Gloucester, by Margaret his wife, dau. of John Hippisley-Coxe, Esq. of Ston Easton—*see* preceding memoir), assumed the surname of Tuckfield. He *m.* 15 April, 1800, Charlotte, dau. of Sir John Mordaunt, Bart., M.P., and by her (who *d.* May, 1848) had issue, John-Henry, now of Shobrook Park; and Richard-Hippisley Tuckfield.

Arms—Same as Hippisley of Ston Easton.

Seat—Shobrook Park, Devon.

HIPPISLEY OF CAMELY AND STANTON.

(*See* Hippisley Trenchard.)

HOBHOUSE OF HADSPEN HOUSE.

Hobhouse, Henry, Esq. of Hadspen House, co. Somerset, J.P. and D.L., barrister-at-law, M.A. Oxon, *b.* 13 July, 1811; *m.* 7 April, 1853, Charlotte-Etruria, youngest dau. of James, 3rd Lord Talbot of Malahide, and by her (who *d.* 17 April, 1855) has issue,

I. Henry, *b.* 1 March, 1854.
I. Margaret-Eliza.

Lineage.—Henry Hobhouse, Esq. (younger brother of John Hobhouse, Esq. of Wesbury College, grandfather of Sir John Cam Hobhouse, Bart., Lord Broughton), *b.* in 1714, *m.* 1st, in 1738, Jane, dau. of James Banister, Esq., and by her, who *d.* in 1756, had issue,

Henry, his heir.
Jane, who *m.* in 1774, John Freeman, Esq. of Letton, co. Hereford.

He *m.* 2ndly, in 1761, Mary, dau. of Michael White, Esq., and had by her a son, Thomas, who *d. unm.* in 1820. Mr. Hobhouse *d.* in 1773, his widow in 1810, and was *s.* by his son,

Henry Hobhouse, Esq. of Hadspen House, co. Somerset, *b.* in 1742, who *m.* in 1775, Sarah, dau. of the Rev. Richard Jenkins, M.A., canon-residentiary of Wells, and by her, who *d.* in July, 1777, left, at his decease, 2 April 1792, a dau., Sarah, who *d. unm.* in 1810, and a son,

Right Hon. Henry Hobhouse, *b.* 12 April, 1776, *m.* 7 April, 1806, Harriet, 6th dau. of John Turton, Esq. of Sugnall Hall, Staffordshire, and left issue,

Henry, M.A., now of Hadspen House.
Edmund, *b.* 17 April, 1817.
Reginald, *b.* 16 March, 1818.
Arthur, *b.* 10 Nov. 1819.
Harriet, *m.* 31 March, 1834, to Henry Jenkyns, M.A., professor in the University of Durham.
Catherine. Eliza. Eleanor.

Mr. Hobhouse was Under Secretary of State for the Home Department from 1817 to 1827. He was sworn of the Privy Council in 1828.

Arms—Party per pale, az. and gu., three estoiles, or, issuing out of as many crescents, arg.

Crest—Out of a mural coronet, party, per pale, as the arms, an estoile, issuing, or.

Motto—Mutare sperno.

Seat—Hadspen House, Somerset.

HOBLYN OF COLQUITE.

(*See* Peter-Hoblyn.)

HODDER OF HODDERSFIELD.

MOORE-HODDER, WILLIAM-HENRY, Esq. of Hoddersfield, co. Cork, m. 1st, Charlotte, of Ardrum, co. Cork, sister to the late Sir Nicholas-Conway Colthurst, Bart., and 2ndly, (his first wife having d. 7 March, 1832,) 14 Feb. 1839, Lucy, dau. of Colonel Need, of Mansfield Woodhouse, co. Notts. Colonel Hodden is col. of the North Cork militia, and a magistrate and deputy lieutenant for the county.

Lineage.—It appears, from *Hutchins' History of Dorsetshire*, that the Hodders were originally of that county, where they held the manor of Longbridy, and other estates. Colonel John Hodder, of Bridgetown, and his brother, William Hodder, of Coolmore, were settlers in the co. of Cork before 1641. The former was some time agent to Sir Philip Perceval. William, as appears from his will, was b. at Millcome, (Melcome Regis, in Dorsetshire?) They had a brother, Edward Hodder, whose dau. was living at Weymouth in 1671, and a sister, m. to William Smart. Both of them made large purchases of soldiers' allotments of land, and passed patent for them under the Act of Settlement. John obtained two grants to the extent of 4,133 acres, and William a grant of 7,364 acres, in the co. of Cork, including the seats of the family, viz., Coolmore, Ringabrow or Hoddersfield, Ballea, Ringabella, and Fountainstown. John was mayor of the city of Cork in 1656, and high-sheriff of the co. of Cork in 1657, and William was mayor in 1657, and high-sheriff of the county in 1661. The latter was called before the House of Commons in 1662 for breach of privilege towards a member of the house, being then styled "of Fountainstown," though this might have been his son, of the same name. John m. Jane ——, but d. without issue in 1673, leaving his estates to Francis, second son of his brother, William having, however, by deed in his lifetime given Dunkettle and other large estates to his nephew, William Smart.

WILLIAM HODDER d. in 1665. He m. 1st, ——; and 2ndly, Margery Carthy, and had two sons and two daus.,

WILLIAM. Francis, of whom hereafter.
Sarah, m. Swithin Walton, Esq.
Jane, m. John Newenham, alderman of Cork, ancestor of the Coolmore family.

WILLIAM HODDER, the eldest, was of Ballea Castle, co. of Cork He d. in England in 1689, leaving issue, by his wife, Hannah,

I. THOMAS, bred to the bar, high-sheriff of the county of Cork, in 1697. He sold Coolmore, &c., to the Newenhams, in 1691, and d. about 1738. He m. 1st, ——, and 2ndly, Barbara, widow of — Cockerell, and had three daus.,

1 Sarah, m. Francis Power, of Cork, merchant, and had issue. Her eldest son, Hodder Power, of Ballea, d. in 1775, leaving his portion of Ballea to George Hodder, Esq. of Mountainstown.
2 Elizabeth, m. 1st, — Cotterell, 2ndly, — Eustace.
3 Elinor, m. Wm. Fuller, of Cork, merchant.

II. John, of Cork, merchant, m. Elizabeth, dau. of Bate French, and d. 1726, leaving issue, Bate, who d. s. p., and two daus., Sarah and Frances.

III. Samuel, of Fountainstown, m. in 1694, Elizabeth, dau. of John Boles, of Inch, Esq., and d. 1737, leaving issue, besides daus., viz., Elizabeth, d. 1743; Anne, m. Alderman William Busteed; and Mary, m. Benjamin Barter, of Anagh, five sons, viz.,

1 John Hodder, of Ringabella, m. 1722, Mary, dau. of Edward Bullen, of the Old Head, Esq., and d. 1742, leaving four daus., Elizabeth, Mary, Anne, and Hannah, and four sons, viz.,

John, m. 1747, Martha, dau. of Francis Woodley, Esq., and had a dau., Sarah, who m. — Saunders, Esq., and d. s. p., and a son,

Samuel Hodder, of Ringabella, m. 1793, Jane, dau. of George Hodder, of Fountainstown, Esq., and had,

Francis Hodder, of Ringabella, m. Alicia, dau. of William Martin, Esq., and had issue,

Francis Hodder, Esq., now of Ringabella.

William. Edward. Thomas, who left issue.

2 Francis, of Fountainstown, d. 1744, s. p.
3 William, a lieut. in Major-General St. Clair's regt. of foot, d. 1748.
4 George, of Fountainstown, mayor of Cork, in 1754, m. ——, dau. of — Baker, Esq., and had a dau., Elisabeth, m. Francis Woodley, Esq., and a son.

George Hodder, of Fountainstown, Esq., J.P. for the co. of Cork, m. a dau. of William Norris, Esq. of Old Court, and left issue, George Hodder, Esq., now of Fountainstown, J.P., and other issue.

5 Jonathan.

IV. Benjamin Hodder, captain in Lord Mark Kerr's regiment, in 1729, d. s. p.

William Hodder had also by his wife, Hannah, six daus., viz.,

I. Margery, m. 1669, Walter Lane.
II. Sarah, m. Edward Boyle, Esq.
III. Elizabeth, m. in 1681, Robert Gookin, of Courtmac Sherry, Esq.
IV. Mary, m. John Honner, Esq. of Cloghane.
V. Hester, m. Robert Francis, Esq., grandson of Sir Robert Travers, who fell at the battle of Knocknanoss.
VI. Rebecca.

We now return to

FRANCIS HODDER, 2nd son of the 1st William. He s. to large estates by his father's and uncle's wills, and was of Bridgetown and Ringabrow or Heddersfield. He had issue by his wife, Jane, besides three daus., Martha, m. 1st, in 1682, Lovegrove Willard, Esq., 2ndly, in 1692, Randal Roberts, Esq.; Jane, m. Roger Power, of Currabinny, Esq.; and Mary, m. 1693, Thomas Tuckey, Esq.; three sons, viz., John of Hoddersfield and Killeagh,* m. 1703, Anne Farmer, by whom he had a dau., Sarah, wife of — Marshal; William, b. 1659, m. in 1679, Jane, dau. of John Grove, Esq. of Ballyhimock, by whom he had a dau., Jane, m. to Thomas Roberts, Esq. of Britfieldstown, ancestor of the baronets of that name; and FRANCIS HODDER, Esq. of Cork, who d. 1726, leaving issue, besides four daus., Jane, m. Joseph Bullen, Esq., Alicia-Hannah, m. John Bayly, of Ballymoney, Esq., and Elizabeth, three sons, viz., Captain William Hodder, of whom presently, George, who probably d. without issue, and Francis, who m. 1723, Anne, widow of — Webb, Esq., and dau. (probably) of — Newenham, of Coolmore, and had a dau., Anne.

CAPTAIN WILLIAM HODDER s. eventually at Hoddersfield. He m. Anne, sister of Captain Daniel Webb, and had issue,

WILLIAM, who m. 1st, ——, 2ndly, Anne, dau. of — Grey, Esq., and 3rdly, the Hon. Margaret Lysaght, dau. of Lord Lisle, and d. s. p. 1787, leaving his estates to his nephew, William-Henry Moore, Esq., on condition that he should bear the name and arms of Hodder.
Hannah.
ANNE, m. HENRY MOORE, Esq., capt. in the 48th foot, and had (with a dau., Anne, m. to Thomas B. Herrick, Esq. of Shippool, co. Cork) a son,

WILLIAM-HENRY MOORE, Esq., who assumed the additional surname of HODDER upon the death of his maternal uncle, and became of Hoddersfield. He m. in 1789, Harriet, dau. of the Right Hon. Henry-Theophilus Clements, (brother to the 1st Earl of Leitrim,) by Mary, his wife, dau. and heir of General Webb, and had issue,

I. WILLIAM-HENRY, now of Hoddersfield.
II. Theophilus-Henry. III. Thomas-Eyre.
IV. John-Francis, m. and has issue.
I. Catherine, widow of the Rev. John Johnson.
II. Harriet. III. Anna-Maria. IV. Selina.

Arms—Quarterly: 1st and 4th, arg., three pole-axes, erect, in fess, ppr., for HODDER; 2nd and 3rd, az., on a chief, indented, or, three mullets, pierced, gu., for MOORE.
Crest—A fire-ship with her courses set, fire issuing from below the rigging, all ppr., for HODDER; out of a ducal coronet, or, a Moor's head, in profile, all ppr., for MOORE.
Motto—Per ignem ferris vicimus.
Seat—Hoddersfield, co. Cork.

HODGES OF HEMSTED.

HODGES, THOMAS-LAW, Esq. of Hemsted, co. Kent, J.P. and D.L., major West Kent militia, M.P. for that county in several parliaments, b. 3 June 1776; m. 16 Feb. 1802, Rebecca, only child of Sir Roger Twisden, Bart. of Bradbourn Park, by Rebecca his wife, dau. of Isaac Wildash, Esq. of Rochester, and had issue,

I. THOMAS-TWISDEN, m. Mary, dau. of Thomas Chandless, Esq. of London.
I. Ann-Rebecca, m. 12 June, 1821, to Cooke Tylden Pattenson, Esq. of Ibornden, Kent, and d. 11 Feb. 1836.
II. Frances-Dorothea, m. 26 March, 1833, to the Hon. Robert Forbes, younger son of General Lord Forbes, of Castle Forbes, co. Aberdeen.
III. Caroline-Cordelia.

---

* This John was probably the youngest son, though the birth of a John, son of Francis, appears in 1657.

IV. Julia-Elizabeth, m. 29 Dec. 1825, to the Rev. William-Marriott Smith-Marriott, second son of Sir John-Wyldbore Smith, Bart. of the Down House, co. Dorset, and d. 11 March, 1842.
V. Katherine, m. 1 June, 1830, to William Peareth, Esq. of Usworth House, co. Durham.
VI. Charlotte-Lydia, m. 9 March, 1837, to Edward-Barrett Curties, Esq., M.P. for Rye, second son of Edward-Jeremiah Curties, Esq. of Windmill Hill, co. Sussex, M.P., and d. 8 June, 1838.

Lineage.—This family was, for many generations, resident in Dorsetshire and Gloucestershire.

THOMAS HODGES, Esq., son of THOMAS HODGES, Esq. of Bredy, co. Dorset, m. Miss Hallett, and d. while Governor of Bombay, 22 Feb. 1771, leaving an only son,

THOMAS-HALLETT HODGES, Esq., high-sheriff of Kent in 1786, who m. Dorothy, youngest dau. of John Cartwright, Esq. of Marnham, co. Notts, and d. 23 June, 1801, aged 47, having had by this lady (who d. 21 Jan. 1800) five sons and two daus., viz.,

THOMAS-LAW, of Hemsted.
John, b. 30 May, 1777; d. 9 Oct. 1793.
Henry, b. 25 July, 1779; m. Cordelia, eldest dau. of Lieut.-Gen. the Hon. James Murray, and d. 1 July, 1837, leaving one son and one dau.
Francis-Willoughby, b. 21 Oct. 1783, lieut. R.N.; d. 15 July, 1800.
Edmund, b. 5 Nov. 1792, lieut. R.A.; d. in Ireland.
Ann-Elizabeth, m. to the Rev. Frederic Hotham, second son of Sir Beaumont Hotham, Knt., one of the Barons of the Exchequer.
Julia-Frances, m. to Sir William Darley, Knt.

Arms—Or, three crescents, sa., on a canton of the second, a ducal crown of the first.
Crest—Out of a ducal coronet, or, an heraldic antelope's head, arg., horned and tufted, gold.
Motto—Praevisa mala pereunt.
Seat—Hemsted, Kent.

HODGETTS OF HAGLEY.

HODGETTS, THOMAS-WEBB, Esq. of Hagley, co. Worcester, b. 12 Dec. 1788, m. 27 Sept. 1814, Isabella, 4th dau. of Robert Hankin, Esq. of Newcastle-on-Tyne, and has an only dau.,

Eliza-Anne, m. 13 Oct. 1842, to Captain William-Wylly Chambers, R.N.

Mr. Hodgetts is a magistrate for the counties of Worcester and Stafford. His father, the late Booth Hodgetts, Esq., son of Thomas Hodgetts, by Ann his wife, m. in 1787, Elizabeth, 2nd dau. of Thomas Webb, of Warwickshire, and had (with two daus., Mary and Elizabeth) two sons, THOMAS-WEBB HODGETTS, Esq. of Hagley; and Booth, who m. Miss Hope, of Kent, and had issue, Thomas, Booth, William, Joseph, and Mary.

Arms—Per fesse, az. and gu., on a chev., engr., between three doves, in chief, and a fleur-de-lis in base, or, three annulets.
Crest—An eagle, wings expanded, in the beak an annulet.
Motto—Confido conquiesco.
Seat—Hagley, near Stourbridge.

HODGSON OF HOUGHTON HOUSE.

HODGSON, WILLIAM, Esq. of Houghton House, co. Cumberland, J.P. and D.L., five times mayor of Carlisle, b. 9 Feb. 1773; m. 17 June, 1806, Anne, eldest dau. of Thomas Young, Esq., and by her (who d. 22 Dec. 1854) he left at his decease, 14 Jan. 1854,

I. THOMAS-HOUGHTON, now of Houghton House, b. 2 Jan. 1813; m. 19 April, 1842, Elizabeth, eldest dau. of the Rev. Robert Gutch, of Seagrave, co. Leicester.
II. William-Henry, b. 10 June, 1815.
III. Joseph-Lowther, b. 27 Sept. 1818; m. Jane-Eleanor, widow of James-R. Grant, Esq., and dau. of John Dixon, Esq., and has issue, Annie and Mabel.
IV. George-Courtenay, b. 25 Dec. 1821; m. Elizabeth, dau. of John Bircham, Esq., and has, William-George-Courtenay; Henry-Bernard; and Annette-Isabel.
V. Charles-Bernard, b. 21 May, 1824.
I. Annette, m. 1st, Lieut.-Col. Cowper, C.B.; and 2ndly, the Rev. William-Deacons Isaac, of Harts Hill.
II. Elizabeth, m. the Rev. William-M. Thompson, of Woolwich.
III. Jane.
IV. Isabel-Sarah, m. to William Carruthers, Esq.
V. Mary.

Lineage.—WILLIAM HODGSON, Esq. son of George Hodgson, by Jane his wife, and granddau. of Joseph Hodgson, by Elizabeth, his wife, m. in 1767, Elizabeth, dau. of Joseph Stordy, and had, besides the late WILLIAM HODGSON, Esq. of Houghton House, another son and two daus, viz.,

I. Joseph, m. Sarah Nicholson, of Bat House, parish of Crosby, and had issue,
1 William-Nicholson, m. Mary, dau. of Thomas Irwin, Esq., J.P.
Joseph-Stordy, in holy orders, m. 6 Aug. 1840, Sophia-Elizabeth, dau. of Sir Thomas-Dalrymple Hesketh, Bart. of Rufford Hall, and has issue.
Sarah-Grace, m. to John Fawcett, Esq. of Petterill Bank, barrister-at-law.
I. Isabella, m. to Thomas Atkinson, Esq. of Carlisle, J.P.
II. Elizabeth, m. to David Donald, Esq.

Arms—Sa., a chev., between three martlets, or.
Crest—A dove, close, az., holding in his beak a sprig of laurel, ppr.
Motto—Dread God.
Seat—Houghton House, Stanwix, co. Cumberland.

HOG OF NEWLISTON.

HOG, JAMES-MAITLAND, Esq. of Newliston, co. Linlithgow, J.P. and D.L., b. 7 Aug. 1799; m. 7 Aug. 1827, Helen, 4th dau. of Sir Alexander-Charles-Maitland Gibson, Bart. of Clifton Hall, and has issue,

THOMAS-ALEXANDER, b. 14 Jan. 1835.
Helen-Maitland.

Lineage.—The surname of Hog, one of local origin, is of great antiquity in Scotland: coeval with the retirement of Cospatrick, Earl of Northumberland, into North Britain, about the Norman Conquest, it became hereditary in the reign of MALCOLM CANMORE, and was first assumed by the proprietors of the lands of Hogstown, in the shire of Angus. ALEXANDER HOG, of Hogstown, gave a charter of alienation to Sir Alexander Hume, in the reign of JAMES III. (1484.) He was founder of the house of Harcarse, in Berwickshire, from which sprung Sir Roger Hog, senator of the College of Justice, and also,

JOHN HOG, Esq. of Cammo, (now New Saughton), co. Mid-Lothian, and Ladykirk, co. Berwick, son and heir of WILLIAM HOG, Esq., (immediate younger brother of Sir Roger Hog, Knt of Harcarse, one of the senators of the College of Justice,) by Janet his wife, dau. of Sir Robert Douglas, Knt. of Glenbervie, grandson of Archibald, 5th Earl of Angus. He m. 27th June, 1707, Mary, dau. of Alexander Cochrane, Esq. of Barbauchlaw, co. Linlithgow, and had two sons. The younger,

ROGER HOG, Esq. of Newliston, b. 22 Nov. 1715, described in the certificate, in 1783, from the Lyon Office of Scotland, of the matriculation of his arms, as "ROGER HOG, Esq., heir male and representative of the ancient families of Hog of Harcarse and Bogend, and chief of the surname;" m. 14 March, 1738, Rachel, dau. of Thomas Missing, Esq. of Stubbington Park, co. Hants, and had issue. He d. March, 1789, and was s. by his eldest surviving son,

THOMAS HOG, Esq. of Newliston, b. 4 Sept. 1742, who m. 1st, 9 March, 1770, Lady Maria-Julian, third dau. of James, 7th Earl of Lauderdale, and by her (who d. in 1795) had, with other issue, who d. unm., ROGER, his heir; and Mary-Turner, m. 29 May, 1800, the late Sir John-Buchanan Hepburn, Bart. of Smeaton Hepburn, and d. 1854. Mr. Hog m. 2ndly, 17 March, 1798, Mary, dau. of James Stewart, of the Stewarts of Athol, and by her had,

I. JAMES-MAITLAND, present representative.
II. Thomas, b. 1 March, 1806; m. in Sept. 1830, Katherine-Maynard, dau. of Archibald Swinton, Esq. of Warsash House, co. Hants, and by her had,
1 Thomas-Ignatius, b. 26 Sept. 1832.
2 James-Maitland, b. 6 March, 1834.
3 Archibald-Francis, b. 20 April, 1835.
4 Roger, b. 22 June, 1838.
1 Katharine. Louisa.
III. Eleanor-Julian, m. 7 Aug. 1827, to David Maitland-Makgill-Crichton, of Rankeillour, and d. in Jan. 1833.
IV. Rachel-Elizabeth, m. in March, 1826, to Patrick-Frazer Tytler, son of Alexander-Frazer Tytler, of Woodhouselee, one of the senators of the College of Justice, d. in April, 1835.

v. Margaret-Charlotte, m. 7 Nov. 1837, to Robert-Gilmore Colquhoun, of Camstradden, H.B.M. consul-general at Bucharest, and d. s. p. in 1838.

Mr. Hog d. in March 1827, and was s. by his eldest son,

ROGER HOG, Esq. of Newliston, b. 25 Oct. 1771, who d. unm. 31 Dec. 1833, and was s. by his half-brother, the present JAMES MAITLAND HOG, Esq. of Newliston, co. Linlithgow.

Arms—Arg., three boars' heads, erased, az., armed, or.
Crest—An oak-tree, ppr.
Supporters—Two boars, ppr.
Motto—Dat gloria vires.
Seat—Newliston, co. Linlithgow.

HOGG OF NORTON HOUSE.

HOGG, JOHN, Esq., M.A., of Norton House, co. Durham, barrister-at-law, F.R.S., b. 21 March, 1800, m. 30 April, 1850, Anne-Louisa-Sarah, 2nd dau. of the late Major Goldfinch, of the Priory, Chewton Mendip, and Belmont, Bath, and has one surviving dau.,

Louisa-Julia-Jefferson.

Lineage.—THOMAS HOGG, Esq. of Norton and of the College, in the city of Durham, son of John Hogg, of Norton, Gent., by Isabel his wife, m. Ann, only child and heiress of John Jefferson, Esq. of Norton and Elton, co. Durham, whose ancestor was Sir John Jefferson, Knt., a judge of the Common Pleas in Ireland in 1691, and one of the lord keepers of the Great Seal of Ireland in 1697. By Ann his wife, Mr. Hogg had issue, JOHN, his heir; and Elizabeth, m. to the late Lieutenant-Colonel Grey, of Norton, D.L. and J.P. The son and heir,

JOHN HOGG, Esq. of Norton House, barrister-at-law, D.L., m. in 1791, Prudentia, eldest dau. of the Rev. Watkin Jones, M.A., rector of Derwen, co. Denbigh, by Sarah his wife, dau. of Robert Ewer, capt. 69th comp. Marines; and by her, who was also niece of Dr. John Ewer, bishop of Llandaff, and subsequently of Bangor, in 1768, had issue,

Thomas-Jefferson, barrister-at law, of the Middle Temple, late one of the Municipal Corporation Commissioners.
JOHN, now of Norton House.
William, late scholar of Clare Hall, Cambridge, d. unm. in 1821.
Robert-Ewer, d. unm. in 1817.
Sarah-Isabella, d. an infant.
Prudentia-Ann, d. unm., July, 1851.
Elizabeth-Sarah.

Mr. Hogg d. in 1823.

Arms—Quarterly: 1st, arg., three boars' heads couped, sa., for HOGG; 2nd, az., a fret, arg., on a chief of the last, three leopards' faces, gu., for JEFFERSON; 3rd, or, on a mount, vert, a lion, rampant, az., for JONES; 4th, arg., a wolf, statant, sa., on a chief, az., three crosses formée, of the first, for EWER.
Crest—A boar, statant, ppr., pierced in the side with an arrow, or, against an oak tree, ppr., fructed, or.
Motto—Dat gloria vires.
Seat—Norton House, Norton, Stockton-on-Tees.

HOLBECH OF FARNBOROUGH.

HOLBECH, WILLIAM, Esq. of Farnborough, co. Warwick, b. 22 Jan. 1774; m. 16 April, 1805, Lucy, 6th dau. of Oldfield Bowles, Esq. of North Aston, co. Oxford, and had issue,

I. HUGH, b. 15 Aug. 1814; m. 4 Jan. 1838, the Hon. Jane-Sarah Hood, 3rd dau. of Samuel, Lord Bridport; and d. 8 June, 1849. His widow m. 10 Dec. 1853, Sir Charles Hotham, K.C.B.
II. Charles-William, b. 30 July, 1816.
III. Henry, b. 23 March, 1818.
I. Mary.
II. Louisa-Anne, m. 12 Feb. 1828, to William Markham, Esq. of Becca Hall, co. York.
III. Laura. IV. Frances.
V. Jane, } twins.
VI. Emma, }

Lineage.—AMBROSE HOLBECH, Esq. of Mollington and Farnborough, both in Warwickshire (elder son of Ambrose Holbech, Esq. of Mollington, by Joan his wife, dau. of Thomas Holloway, Esq. of Cropedy, co. Oxford, and lineal descendant of Oliver Holbech, of Holbech, living *circa* 1223), purchased, in 1678, the manor of Radston. He m. Sarah, dau. of William Harvey, Gent. of London, by whom (who d. 4 May, 1682) he had issue, WILLIAM, his heir; Ambrose, of Mollington, d. s. p. in 1737; Hugh, m. Elizabeth Woodhall, a widow; Sarah, wife of Sir Thomas Powys, Knt. of Lilford, one of the judges of the Court of King's Bench; Mary, of Richard Jennens, Esq. of Long Wittenham, Berks; Anne, of Tobiah Harvey, Gent.; and Finetta, d. unm. in 1758. He d. 2 March, 1701, and was s. by his eldest son,

WILLIAM HOLBECH, Esq. of Farnborough, co. Warwick, and of Radston, Notts, who m. Elizabeth, dau. and heir of William Allington, Esq. of London, and by her (who d. in 1708-9) he had, with other issue, WILLIAM, his heir; Hugh, of Mollington, who m. Catherine, dau. of Col. Cornwall, and d. in 1675, leaving a son, WILLIAM, heir to his uncle; Jane, wife of John Blencowe, Esq. of Marston, St. Lawrence, Notts; Elizabeth, wife of George Tost, Esq.; Anne, wife of Toby Chauncy, Esq. Mr. Holbech d. 7 July, 1717, and was s. by his eldest son,

WILLIAM HOLBECH, Esq. of Farnborough and Radston, who d. unm. in 1771, and was s. by his nephew,

WILLIAM HOLBECH, Esq. of Mollington, who m. in 1772, Anne, dau. of William Woodhouse, of Lichfield, M.D., and had issue,

WILLIAM, of Farnborough.
Henry-Hugh, barrister-at-law, b. in 1779.
Charles, b. in 1782; in holy orders, vicar of Farnborough, and perpetual curate of Radston; d. 28 Nov. 1837.
Edward, b. in 1785; an officer in the army.
George, lieutenant R.N.
Mary-Anne, m. in 1807, to Sir Charles Mordaunt, Bart. of Walton D'Evile, co. Warwick.
Caroline.

Mr. Holbech, M.P. for Banbury from 1792 to 1796, d. 6 July, 1812.

Arms—Vert, six escallops, three, two, and one, arg.
Crest—A maunch, vert, charged with escallops, arg.
Seat—Farnborough, near Banbury.

HOLDEN OF ASTON.

HOLDEN, EDWARD-ANTHONY, Esq. of Aston Hall, co. Derby, J.P. and D.L. high-sheriff 1838, b. 2 Aug. 1805; m. 22 Nov. 1832, Susan-Drummond, dau. of George Moore, Esq. of Appleby Hall, co. Leicester, and has issue,

I. EDWARD-SHUTTLEWORTH, b. 5 Dec. 1836; killed at Sebastopol, 8 Sept. 1855.
II. Charles-Shuttleworth, b. 16 July, 1838.
III. James-Shuttleworth, b. 13 Nov. 1843.
IV. John-Shuttleworth, b. 27 June, 1847.
V. Francis-Shuttleworth, b. 6 April, 1852.
I. Susan-Elizabeth. II. Anne-Shuttleworth.
III. Mary-Shuttleworth.
IV. Rosamond-Shuttleworth.
V. Emma-Shuttleworth. VI. Caroline-Shuttleworth.

Lineage.—The first of the family of Holden, of whom we find mention in Derbyshire, was of Wilne; his son, ROBERT HOLDEN, Esq., settled at Aston, and d. in 1659.

THE REV. CHARLES SHUTTLEWORTH, of Aston, youngest son of James Shuttleworth, Esq. of Gawthorp, by Mary his wife, only dau. and heir of ROBERT HOLDEN, Esq. of Aston, took the name and arms of HOLDEN in 1791. He m. 1st, the Hon. Mary Cockburn, dau. of Lord Forester, and by her (who d. in 1777) had one son, who d. an infant. He m. 2ndly, Elizabeth, dau. of Sir Thomas Whitmore, which lady d. s. p. in 1795; and 3rdly, Rosamond-Amelia Dean, by whom (who d. 11 Aug. 1820) he had issue,

EDWARD-ANTHONY, now of Aston Hall.
Charles-Shuttleworth, d. 2 March, 1817.
James-Richard, in holy orders, m. Mary, only dau. of Thomas Moore, Esq. of Ruddington, Notts.
Sophia-Elizabeth-Rosamond.
Antonia-Henrietta, m. to Col. Clowes, of Broughton Hall, Manchester.
Teresa-Amelia. Rosamond-Adeline, d. in 1829.
Emma, m. to J. Doneian, Esq.
Isabel-Clare, m. to G. Moore, Esq. of Appleby Hall.

Arms—Sa., a fesse, engrailed, erminois, or, between two chevrons, erm.
Crest—A moor-cock, rising, sa., winged, or.
Seat—Aston Hall, near Derby.

HOLDEN OF PALACE HOUSE.

HOLDEN, HENRY, Esq. of Reedly House, and Palace House, co. Lancaster, J.P. and D.L., b. 8 Aug.

1824; capt. in the 13th light dragoons; *s.* his father, the late John Greenwood, Esq., who *d.* 2 Oct. 1834, and by royal licence, dated 28 July, 1840, has resumed the family name of HOLDEN; *m.* 10 June, 1854, Ellen, eldest dau. of Col. White, of Woodlands, near Dublin, lord-lieutenant of the co. of Longford, and has a dau., EVELEEN.

Lineage.—ROBERT HOLDEN, Esq. of Holden, co. Lancaster, aged 63, *anno* 1665. Representative of the ancient Lancashire family of Holden, of Holden, recorded in the Visitations, *m.* Mary, dau. of Alexander Chorley, Esq. of Lincoln's Inn, and had a son and heir,

RALPH HOLDEN, Esq. of Holden, *b.* in 1629; who *m.* Mary, dau. and co-heir of the Rev. Edmund Ryshton, and was father of

ROBERT HOLDEN, Esq. of Holden, *b.* in 1655, living in 1677, who, by Catherine his wife, who survived him, had (with two daus., Catherine and Susanna, and a younger son, Robert, bapt. 24 July, 1684) an elder son and heir,

RALPH HOLDEN, Esq. of Holden, bapt. 26 May, 1681, who *d.* in 1706, leaving, by Frances his wife, a son and heir,

ROBERT HOLDEN, Esq. of Holden, bapt. 18 Jan. 1700, who *d.* 21 March, 1729-30, leaving, by Martha his wife, two daus., Frances and Martha, and a son,

RALPH HOLDEN, Esq. of Holden Hall, of Stockport, co. Chester, and of Palace House, *b.* 6 June, 1722; who *m.* 24 Dec. 1744, Mary, dau. and co-heir of John Holden, Esq. of Palace House, co. Lancaster; and *d.* in 1777, having had issue,

- ROBERT, his heir.
- Betty, *m.* 20 June, 1780, to Henry Greenwood, Esq. of Burnley, co. Lancaster; and *d.* in 1781, leaving a son, JOHN, of whom hereafter, as successor to his uncle.
- Frances, *m.* 13 May, 1784, to Hugh Taylor, Esq. of Liverpool; and *d. s. p.* 6 May, 1817.

The son and heir,

ROBERT HOLDEN, Esq. of Palace House, *d. unm.* 8 April, 1792, and was *s.* by his sister's only son,

JOHN GREENWOOD, Esq. of Palace House, J.P., *b.* 1781; who *m.* 13 Oct. 1821, Elizabeth, dau. of Henry Aspinall, Esq. of Reedly House, and by her (who obtained the Royal license, dated 28 July, 1840, for herself and children to take the name and arms of HOLDEN only) had issue,

- HENRY, present representative.
- Ralph, *b.* 11 Sept. 1827.
- William, *b.* 7 Sept. 1831; *m.* Miss Paulet, dau. of J. Paulet, Esq. of Seaforth House, co. Lancaster, and has a dau., Blanche.
- Bessie, *m.* to Ernest, youngest son of Sir Thomas Lavie, Governor of Greenwich Hospital.
- Rhoda.

Mr. Greenwood *d.* 2 Oct. 1834, and was *s.* by his eldest son, Henry, who, with his mother and brother and sisters, has resumed the surname of HOLDEN.

Arms—Sa., a fesse, between two chevrons, erm., between the fesse and upper chevron, a covered cup, or.
Crest—A moor-cock, ppr., charged on the breast with a cinquefoil, or.
Motto—Nec temere nec timide.
Seat—Reedly House, and Palace House, near Burnley, co. Lancaster.

HOLDEN OF DARLEY ABBEY.

(*See* LOWE OF LOCKO.)

HOLFORD OF WESTONBIRT.

HOLFORD, ROBERT-STAYNER, Esq. of Westonbirt, co. Gloucester, J.P. and D.L., high sheriff 1843, and present M.P. for East Gloucestershire, *b.* 16 March, 1808; *m.* 5 Aug. 1854, Mary-Anne, dau. of General James Lindsay, of Balcarres, co. Fife, by Anne his wife, dau. of Sir Coutts Trotter, Bart., and has a dau., Margaret.

Lineage.—This family claims descent from the ancient Cheshire family of HOLFORD, of Holford.

SIR RICHARD HOLFORD, Knt., Master in Chancery, came into possession of the estate of Westonbirt, by his 1st marriage, with the heiress of the family of Crewe, in that co., towards the close of the 17th century. He *m.* 2ndly, Elizabeth, dau. of Vice-Admiral Sir Richard Stayner; and 3rdly, Susanna, dau. of Samuel Trotman, Esq.; and by his 2nd wife was father of

ROBERT HOLFORD, Esq., a Master in Chancery, who *m.* Sarah, dau. of Sir Peter Vandeput, and was father of

PETER HOLFORD, Esq., also a Master in Chancery, who *m.* Anne, dau. of William Nutt, Esq. of Buxsted, co. Sussex, and *d.* 1803, having had issue,

- Robert, of Westonbirt, *d. unm.* in 1838.
- GEORGE-PETER, of whom presently.
- Sarah, *m.* to Sir Charles-Grave Hudson, Bart. of Wanlip, co. Leicester.
- Charlotte, *m.* to Charles Bosanquet, Esq. of Rock, co. Northumberland.

The younger son,

GEORGE-PETER HOLFORD, Esq. of Westonbirt, *m.* Anne, dau. of the Rev. Averell Daniell, of Lifford, co. Donegal, and by her (who *d.* 18 March, 1849) left at decease, 29 April, 1839.

- ROBERT-STAYNER, now of Westonbirt.
- Anne-Jane, *m.* 1832, to Robert-Blagden Hale, Esq. of Alderley, co. Gloucester.
- Georgina, *m.* 1856, to Peter-Robert Burrell, Esq. of Stoke Park, co. Suffolk.
- Emily-Elizabeth, *m.* to Sir George-Joseph Palmer, Bart. of Wanlip Hall, co. Leicester.

Arms—Arg., a greyhound, passant, sa.
Crest—A greyhound's head, couped, sa.
Seat—Westonbirt, Tetbury, co. Gloucester.

HOLFORD OF BUCKLAND.

GWYNNE-HOLFORD, JAMES-PRICE-WILLIAM, Esq. of Kilgwyn, co. Carmarthen, and Buckland and Tre Holford, co. Brecknock, an officer 16th lancers, *b.* 25 Nov. 1833.

Lineage.—JOSIAH HOLFORD, Esq. of Hampstead, who *m.* Magdalen, dau. of William Price, Esq., son of James Price, Esq. of Kilgwyn, had by her, who *d.* 19 Jan. 1812, five daus., who all *d. unm.*, except the 4th, Charlotte, wife of Jeremiah Olive, Esq., and two sons,

- JOHN-JOSIAH, his heir.
- Charles, of Hampstead, co. Middlesex, *b.* 16 May, 1774, *m.* 1st, in 1796, Mary, dau. of Thomas Roberts, Esq. of Charterhouse-square, and by her, who *d.* in 1820, had an only child, Mary, *m.* to Charles-Henry Pilgrim, Esq., son of Charles Pilgrim, Esq. of Southampton. Mr. Charles Holford *m.* 2ndly, in May, 1824, Mary-Anne, dau. of Edward Toller, Esq. of Doctors' Commons and Hampstead, and by her has, with a dau., who *d.* in infancy, three sons and three daus., viz., Charles-Edward, *b.* 22 Feb. 1830; John Henry, *b.* 1 June, 1831; George, *b.* 7 Feb. 1832; Ellen; Matilda; and Mary-Anne.

The eldest son,

JOHN-JOSIAH HOLFORD, Esq. of Kilgwyn, co. Carmarthen, *b.* 5 Feb. 1765, *m.* 24 Jan. 1789, Jane-Margaret, dau. of Charles Jackson, Esq. of the General Post-office, London, and had issue,

- JAMES-PRICE, his heir.
- John Josiah, lieut. R.N., *d. unm.* 28 Feb. 1781.
- Henry, *b.* 16 April, 1799, *d.* 12 April, 1803.
- George Charles, late of the Inniskillen dragoons, *b.* 2 Aug. 1803, *m.* in Aug. 1834, Harriet-Sophia, dau. of John Stevenson, Esq. of Binfield Place, co. Berks, and has a son, Henry, and a dau.
- Louisa, *m.* 28 July, 1824, to George Stevenson, Esq.
- Sophia, *m.* to Francis-Anthony Morris, Esq.

The eldest son,

JAMES-PRICE HOLFORD, Esq. of Kilgwyn, lieut.-col. in the army, J.P., *b.* 25 Sept. 1791, high-sheriff of Breconshire in 1840, *m.* 4 Sept. 1830, Anna-Maria-Eleanor, dau. of Roderick Gwynne, Esq., son of Thynne-Howe Gwynne, Esq., and grandson of Roderick Gwynne,* Esq., by Anne his wife, dau. and co-heir of Lord Chedworth, and had,

- JAMES-PRICE-WILLIAM, now of Buckland.
- Jane-Eliza-Anna-Maria.
- Louisa-Mary-Ermine-Eleanora.

* In the year 1405, RHYDDERCH AP RHYS, of Llwyn Howel, descended from Trahaern ap Einon, Lord of Cwmwd, co. Brecon, *m.* Gwenllian, dau. and heir of Howell ap Griffith, of Trecastle, younger brother of the renowned Sir David Gam, one of the companions in arms of HENRY V. at Agincourt, and had two sons, I. THOMAS, styled Gwynne, from his fair complexion, who remained in the possession of his maternal estate, and resided in the mansion house of Trecastle. He was ancestor of the present HOWEL GWYN, Esq. of Abercrave, co. Brecon; and II. DAVID, who, from his fair complexion and red hair, is called in the family pedigree, DAVID COCH GWYNNE. He inherited the paternal property, and was ancestor of the GWYNNE of *Glanbran*, and the GWYNNES of *Buckland*.

Elizabeth-Sophia, *d.* in infancy.
Thynne-Howe. Harriett.

Arms—Quarterly: 1st and 4th, arg., on a mount, vert, a greyhound, passant, sa., collared, or, for HOLFORD; 2nd and 3rd, sa., a fesse, cottised, or, between two swords, arg., hilts and pomels of the second, for GWYNNE; and an escutcheon of pretence, of twenty-one quarterings, in right of his wife.

Crests—1st, from the sun in splendour, or, rising from behind a hill, vert, a greyhound's head, issuant, sa.; 2nd, a dexter arm in armour, ppr., issuant from a crescent, arg., holding a sword, erect, also ppr., hilt and pomel gold, enfiled by a boar's head, or, erased and vulned, ppr.

Motto—Over the 2nd crest, Vim vi repellere licet; and under the arms, Toujours fidèle.

Seats—Kilgwyn, co. Carmarthen; Buckland, and Tre Holford, co. Brecknock.

HOLLEY OF BURGH HALL.

HUNT-HOLLEY, JAMES, Esq. of Burgh Hall, Norfolk, J.P., *b.* 1804; *m.* 1832, Horatia, 3rd dau. of the late Vice-Admiral Windham, of Felbrigg, and has issue,

I. WILLIAM, *b.* 23 Jan. 1835.
II. James. III. George.
IV. Edmund. V Charles.
I. Horatia-Anne. II. Sophia-Caroline.
III. Marianne. IV. Maria-Katharine.
V. Emily-Georgina. VI. Gertrude-Charlotte.

The family of Holley is of ancient repute in the county of Norfolk. The name of Hunt was added to their surname upon the marriage of Miss Hunt with the great-grandfather of the present owner of the estate. He resided at Blickling in the same neighbourhood, as did also his son, but the place was afterwards sold. Burgh Hall was built in 1849 by the present James Hunt-Holley, Esq., who is son and heir of the late James-Hunt Holley, Esq. of Blickling, J.P., who *d.* 1828.

Seat—Burgh Hall, Aylsham.

HOLLINSHEAD OF HOLLINSHEAD HALL.

BROCK-HOLLINSHEAD, HENRY, Esq. of Hollinshead Hall, co. Lancaster, J.P., *b.* 22 March, 1819; *m.* 11 Sept. 1845, Margaret, eldest dau. of James Neville, Esq. of Beardwood, near Blackburn, and has,

I. HUGH-NEVILLE, *b.* 30 Sept. 1846.
II. Henry-Clifford, *b.* 31 May, 1852.
I. Beatrice-Emma. II. Margaret-Edith.
III. Margaret-Neville. IV. Florence-Helen.

Lineage.—The very ancient family of Holynshed of Holynshed in Sutton, co. Chester, can be traced as seated there up to the reign of HENRY III.; of the senior line was RALPH HOLYNSHED of Cophurst, the Chronicler. From his uncle, WILLIAM HOLLYNSHED, of Bugiawton, descended the family of Hollinshed, of which the last male heir, JOHN HOLLINSHEAD, Esq. of Hollinshead Hall, *d.* 10 July, 1802, *unm.*, and bequeathed his property and name to his cousin, WILLIAM BROCK, Esq., 4th son of Edward Brock, of Stockport, and grandson of Edward Brock, Esq. of Bakewell, by EMMA, his wife, only dau. of EDWARD HOLLINSHEAD, Esq. Mr. Brock took the surname of HOLLINSHEAD, and *d. s. p.* 1803, having devised his estates to (the son of his brother Laurence) his nephew,

LAURENCE BROCK, of Hollinshead Hall, *b.* 8 March, 1778, who *d.* 25 July, 1838. He took the surname of HOLLINSHEAD, in addition to his own, in 1803. He *m.* 1st, in 1806, Margaretta, the dau. of Edward Edwards, Esq. of Plas Fran, near Wrexham, by whom he had one son, Edward, who *d.* an infant in 1820. He *m.* 2ndly, in 1818, Mary, the dau. of Roger Potts, Esq. of Serjeants-inn, London, by whom he had,

HENRY BROCK-HOLLINSHEAD, now of Hollinshead.
Laurence, who *d.* an infant.
Clifford, *b.* 6 Dec. 1824, *d. s. p.* 24 March, 1858.
Frederick, *b.* 8 Aug. 1826, late 12th Royal lancers, *m.* 16 Aug. 1851, and has issue, Frederick and Lizzie-Emma.
Emma, *m.* 22 April, 1847, James Whigham, Esq., barrister-at-law, and has Laurence-Robert, James-Gilbert, William-Henry-Coote, and Emma.

He *m.* 3rdly, Eliza the dau. of the Rev. William Hampson, of Bolton-le-Moors, by whom he had one dau., Eliza.

Arms—Quarterly: 1st and 4th, per bend, arg. and ermine, on a cross, sable, a cross-crosslet, fitchée, or, (in the dexter chief point an escallop, az., for distinction,) for HOLLINSHEAD; 2nd and 3rd, az., a brock, or, between three bezants, two and one, for BROCK.

Crests—Of HOLLINSHEAD: A heron, arg., in the beak a cross-crosslet, fitchée, sable, behind the heron an arrow and bow in saltier, ppr., (the heron charged on the breast with an escallop, az., for distinction.) Of BROCK: A boar's head, couped, or, between two bucks' horns, sable.

Motto—Nemo me impune lacessit.

Seat—Hollinshead Hall, near Blackburne.

HOLLIS OF SHIRE NEWTON.

HOLLIS, WILLIAM, Esq. of Shirenewton House, co. Monmouth, J.P., high-sheriff 1831, *b.* 21 March, 1797; *m.* 31 May, 1836, Annette, eldest dau. of the Rev. James-Ashe Gabb, rector of Shirenewton, and has issue,

I. Marianne-Charlotte. II. Annette-Susanne.
III. Sophia-Mary.

Mr. Hollis is only son of William Hollis, Esq., and Sarah, his wife, 2nd dau. of William Collins, Esq. of Thornbury, co. Gloucester, and grandson, by Susan his wife, dau. of Thomas Davis, merchant, of Bristol, of William Hollis, Esq., elder son of William Hollis, Esq., and Mary his wife. Mr. Hollis has one sister, Susannah, *m.* in May, 1821, to Thomas Luce, Esq.

Arms—Sa., a bend, between two talbots, passant, arg.

Crest—A dexter arm, embowed, in armour, garnished, holding a branch of holly, berried, all ppr.

Seat—Shirenewton House, near Chepstow, co. Monmouth.

HOLLIST OF LODSWORTH.

HOLLIST, HASLER, Esq. of Lodsworth House, co. Sussex, J.P. and D.L., *b.* 5 Oct. 1797; *m.* 13 Dec. 1825, Frances-Georgiana, eldest dau. of the late Sir Francis-Molyneux Ommanney, and has issue,

I. EDWARD-OMMANNEY, } twins, *b.* 9 July, 1838.
II. George. }
I. Frances-Georgiana. II. Margaret-Anne.
III. Elizabeth-Mary. IV. Agnes-Ash.
V. Marian-Beatrice.

Lineage.—This family, it is believed, were settled in the immediate neighbourhood of Lodsworth early in the 12th century, if not before—probably in the time of HENRY I. The direct ancestor, "Ricciardus le Capron," took the inquisiciones post mortem Johannis, in 1216, in respect of lands at Ambersham, about a mile thence; when he held the manor and lived in the manor house. "Rogerus le Kaperon" lived there *temp.* EDWARD III., and the family migrated from the old house to one or another part of the property, called Moore, in the reign of ELIZABETH. Here they continued to reside till the late Anthony Capron, afterwards Hollist, went to Midhurst to live, in 1806, and where he *d.* in 1836.

ANTHONY CAPRON, Esq., *b.* in 1707, sixth in direct descent from THOMAS CAPRON, of Ambersham Manor House, who *d.* in 1543; *m.* in 1733, Elizabeth Lee, and *d.* in Nov. 1735. His only issue,

ANTHONY CAPRON, Esq., a posthumous son, *b.* 31 Jan. 1736; *m.* in 1760, Anne Vincent; and *d.* in 1811, leaving an only son,

ANTHONY CAPRON, Esq., *b.* 30 Jan. 1762; who *m.* in 1796, Margaret, youngest dau. of Richard Hasler, Esq., and had issue, HASLER, now of Lodsworth; Anne; and Mary, *m.* to William-Henry Watson, Esq., Q.C., M.P. for Hull. Mr. Capron assumed, in Sept. 1833, the surname of HOLLIST, in lieu of his patronymic, in compliance with the will of a distant relative, and *d.* 30 Sept. 1836.

Arms—Sa., on a bend, between a greyhound, courant, bendways, in chief, and a dolphin, hauriant, in base, arg., three torteaux, on a chief, of the second, three sprigs of strawberry, fructed, ppr.

Crest—Between two sprigs of strawberry, as in the Arms, a dexter arm, embowed, in armour, the hand within a gauntlet, holding a sprig of holly, all ppr.

Mottoes—Currendo; over the crest, Gardez le Capron.

Seat—Lodsworth, near Petworth, co. Sussex.

HOLLOND OF BENHALL LODGE.

HOLLOND, THE REV. EDMUND, of Benhall Lodge, co. Suffolk, *m.* 1st, 6 Feb. 1839, Isabella-Esther, youngest dau. of the late Rev. Sir John Robinson, Bart. of Rokeby, co. Louth, Ireland, and by her (who d. 23 Jan. 1848) has issue,

I. EDMUND-WILLIAM, b. 18 April, 1841.
II. John-Robert, b. 2 Nov. 1843.
I. Mary-Isabella. II. Esther-Harriet.
III. Fanny-Louisa.

Mr. Hollond m. 2ndly, 10 Feb. 1852, Fanny, dau. of John Reade, Esq. of Holbrook House, Suffolk, and has by her a dau., Caroline-Elizabeth.

Lineage.—MAJOR HOLLOND, son of Richard and Susannah Holland, was in command of the East India Company's troops in Bengal, where he d. about the year 1756, leaving by his wife, a sister of Edward Fowke, Esq. of Horley, Kent, four sons, viz.,

I. RICHARD, in the army, killed in India in a skirmish with the natives.
II. John, of the E. I. Co.'s civil service at Madras, of which he was acting governor. He m. Eliza, dau. of Joseph Hinchman, Esq., and d. 31 Jan. 1806, leaving issue,
 1 Edward, who purchased the estate of Benhall Lodge from the trustees of Sir Hyde Parker, Bart., and d. unm. 7 Dec. 1829.
 2 Thomas-Stanhope, d. without issue, 22 May, 1836.
III. Edward-John, in the E. I. Co.'s civil service at Madras; d. unm. 19 Aug. 1821.
IV. WILLIAM, in the E. I. Co.'s civil service at Bengal; m. Harriet, dau. of Thomas Pope, Esq., and d. 14 Feb. 1836, leaving, besides the present REV. EDMUND HOLLAND, of Benhall Lodge, three other sons and two daus. viz.,
 1 Richard.
 2 Frederick, d. unm. 4 Feb. 1838.
 3 Robert, late M.P. for Hastings; m. 18 March, 1840, Ellen-Julia, dau. of the late Thomas Teed, Esq. of Stanmore Hall, Middlesex.
 1 Mary, m. 14 May, 1834, to Henry Blackden, Esq. (who d. 24 Dec. 1853), son of the late Benjamin Blackden, Esq., by Elizabeth his wife, dau. of Sir Richard Cayley, Bart.
 2 Sophia, m. 8 Sept. 1825, the Rev. Thomas-Ward Franklyn, son of the late George Franklyn, Esq. of Bristol, and has issue, Thomas-Edmund, m. 1854, Selina, eldest dau. of Capt. George Hope, R.N., and has issue; Frederick; Hollond; Sophia; and Fanny.

Arms—Az., a lion rampant, within an orle of trefoils, arg.
Crest—Out of a ducal coronet, or, a demi-lion, rampant, arg.
Motto—Vincit qui se vincit.
Seat—Benhall Lodge, Saxmundham.

HOLLYNGWORTHE OF HOLLYNGWORTHE.

DE HOLLYNGWORTHE, ROBERT, Esq. of Hollyngworthe Hall, co. Chester, J.P. and D.L., b. in 1791; late capt. in the 6th dragoon-guards.

Lineage.—This family has been seated at Hollyngworthe Hall, from the Saxon times—from the year 1022, as set forth in a very ancient pedigree.

JOHN HOLLINGWORTH, Esq. of Hollingworth, son of Jacob Hollingworth, Esq., by his wife, Mary Leigh, of Cranbrook, disposed of the estate of Hollingworth, &c., to the ancestor of the Rev. Daniel Whittle, who sold back the property, in 1831, to the present Capt. de Hollyngworthe. By Mary his wife, dau. of — Rayner, Esq. of Bearsted, co. Kent, he had a son,

THOMAS-ROBERT HOLLINGWORTH, Esq., who m. in 1788, Mary, dau. and co-heiress of John Green, Esq. of Maidstone, and had a son, the present ROBERT DE HOLLYNGWORTHE, Esq., who purchased back, in 1831, the estate of Hollingworth, and has resumed the spelling of the name of the time of Queen ELIZABETH.

Arms—Az., on a bend, arg., three holly-leaves, vert.
Crest—A stag, lodged, ppr.
Motto—Disce ferenda pati.
Seat—Hollyngworthe Hall, Cheshire.

HOLME OF PAUL-HOLME.

HOLME, BRYAN-HOLME, Esq. of Paul Holme, co. York, late capt. 88th regt., b. 4 May, 1821; m. 6 Sept. 1849, Catherine-Margaret, 2nd dau. of Gen. the Hon. Sir Patrick Stuart (son of the 10th Lord Blantyre) by Catherine-Henrietta, granddau. of the 1st Lord Rodney, and has issue,

I. CHARLES-HENRY, b. 27 Sept. 1853.
II. Bryan-Francis, b. 13 June, 1856.
I. Catherine-Mary. II. Louisa-Stuart.

Lineage.—This ancient and distinguished family has been established in the county of York since the period of the Norman Conquest.

OLENOR HOLME, grandson of JOHN, living *temp.* CONQUEST, was comptroller to the Empress Maud, and received the honour of knighthood from that princess. From him derived, 6th in descent,

SIR BRYAN HOLME, of Paull-Holme, who was knighted by EDWARD III., and appointed master of the King's buckhounds in 1328. He m. Dame Helen, of Blois, and had a son, ROBERT, his heir. At the taking of the King of Scots prisoner, in 1346, Sir Bryan had given him for his crest, A hound's head, erased, or, out of a coronet embattled, gu. He d. soon after. His descendants the Holmes, of Paul-Holme, intermarrying with the Ellikers, Constables, Hildyards, Aslabys, Tyrwhitts, Stricklands, Grimstons, Langtons, Rodes, &c., continued to preserve a male succession until the deaths of Henry and John Holme, who had no issue, and devised their property to their grand-nephew,

THE REV. NICHOLAS TORRE, rector of Rise, in Holderness, b. 14 Dec. 1756 (3rd son of the Rev. James Torre, of Snydall, co. York, by Betty his wife, only dau. of STEPHEN HOLME, Esq. of Paul-Holme), who assumed in consequence the surname and arms of HOLME. He d. 1 Sept. 1833, and was s. by (the son of his next brother Henry) his nephew, Henry-James Torre, who assumed, on inheriting, the surname and arms of HOLME, and became,

THE REV. HENRY-JAMES HOLME, of Paul-Holme. This gentleman, b. 11 Sept. 1793, m. 20 Nov. 1817, Margaret, only dau. and heiress of Capt. George Mangles, 60th regt., and by her (who m. 2ndly, 1853, Rev. Robert Machell, of Marton Vicarage, and of Little Weighton and Beverley) had issue,

BRYAN-HOLME, now of Paul-Holme.
Edward-Ferdinand-Holme, lieut. R.N., b. 26 Sept. 1827.
Emily-Rosellen, m. 18 July, 1851, Capt. Lawrence-Trent Cave, 54th regt.; and d. 19 April, 1852.

Mr. Holme d. 28 Dec. 1850.

Arms—Barry of six, or and az., on a canton, arg., a chaplet, gu.
Crests—1st, a holly-tree, fructed, ppr.; 2nd, out of a mural coronet, gu., a hound's head, erased, or.
Motto—Holme semper viret.
Seat—Paul-Holme, co. York.

HOLMES OF ST. DAVID'S.

HOLMES, BASSETT-W., Esq. of St. David's, co. Tipperary, J.P., b. 20 Dec. 1821.

Lineage.—The first of this family who settled in the sister kingdom is stated to have been a private secretary to the lord-lieutenant, Wentworth, Earl of Strafford, and to have accompanied that nobleman to Ireland in 1630. The present representative is a minor, who possesses the old family place, Peterfield. The late

GILBERT HOLMES, Esq. of Bell Mount, King's co., m. 1764, Mary, dau. of Francis Saunderson, Esq. of Castle Saunderson, and by her (who d. in 1788) left at his decease, in 1810, a son,

THE VERY REV. GILBERT HOLMES, dean of Ardfert, co. Kerry, who m. Lydia-Waller, eldest dau. of the late Colonel Saunderson, of Castle Saunderson, who, for many years, represented Cavan; and d. 28 Dec. 1846, having had, besides the present BASSETT-W. HOLMES, Esq. of St. David's, four other sons and one dau.,

FRANCIS-S., major 8th regiment, d. at Kurrochee, in Scinde, India, Aug. 1849.
Peter, capt. Madras native infantry, d. at Mangalor, 1834.
Alexander, R.N., d. 1839.
Hardress-R., 66th regiment, d. at St. Ann's, Barbadoes, in Sept. 1848.
Lydia-Catherine, m. 1842, Capt. Bayly, late 68th regiment, son of John Bayly, Esq., Debsbro, co. Tipperary.

Seat—St. David's, co. Tipperary.

HOLMES OF SCOLE HOUSE.

HOLMES, THE REV. WILLIAM, M.A., of Scole House, co. Norfolk, rector of Scole, m. 11 Aug. 1845, Jemima, youngest dau of the late Sir Charles Flower, Bart., and has a son and heir,

WILLIAM-JAMES OWEN, b. 2 Sept. 1850.

Lineage.—The ancestors of this gentleman, who is the only son of the late William Holmes, Esq., an officer in the army, of Mundham, in Norfolk, have monuments in the churches and churchyards of Ashby, Mundham, and Beccles.

Arms—Barry of eight, or and az., on a canton, arg., three garlands, ppr.

Crest—A lion's head, erased, or.

Motto—Ora et labora.

Seat—Scole House, Norfolk.

HOLT OF ENFIELD.

HOLT, WILLIAM-HENRY, Esq., M.D., of Enfield and Red Bank, near Kendal, Westmoreland, *m.* 1st, a dau. of Alderman Charles Hamerton; and 2ndly, Harriet, widow of the late Thomas Browning, Esq. of Enfield and London, and by the former only (who *d.* in 1826) had issue,

- I. ASTLEY, M.D., *b.* in 1803; *m.* Jane, eldest dau. of the Rev. Edward Heathcote, of Rose Hill, Chesterfield.
- II. William, *b.* in 1806; *m.* Miss Adams.
- III. Charles, *b.* in 1808; *m.* Georgiana, dau. of Thomas Britt, Esq., and has issue, a son.
- IV. Edward, *b.* in 1810; *d. s. p.* abroad.
- V. Frederick, *b.* in 1817; *d. s. p.*
- I. Emily, *m.* to O.-B.-B. Woolsey, Esq.
- II. Mary, *m.* to J. Jameson, Esq.
- III. Louisa, *m.* to W.-T. Martin, Esq.
- IV. Fanny, *m.* to E. Tyte, Esq., and has issue.

Lineage.—The HOLTS *of Tottenham and Enfield* are a branch of the HOLTS *of Grislehurst*, Lancashire, where they have resided and possessed large landed property for centuries.

JOHN HOLT, Esq., *b.* at Grantham, co. Lincoln, about 1759, settled in early life at Tottenham. He *m.* twice, and had issue by both wives. By his 2nd wife, Hannah Elizabeth, dau. of William Glover, Esq. of Reigate, who was grandson, maternally, of Lord Santry, had three sons and three daus. Mr. Holt *d.* in 1795, and was buried at Tottenham. The eldest son of the 2nd marriage,

WILLIAM HOLT, Esq., *m.* 1st, Sarah, dau. of J. Rose, Esq. of London; and 2ndly, Jane, only child of William Cook, Esq. of Kendal, and by the former only (who *d.* in 1811) had issue,

- WILLIAM-HENRY, his heir.
- George-Palmer, M.D., of Jesus College, Cambridge, *m.* a dau. of Wharton, Esq.; and *d.* in 1837, leaving issue two sons and a dau.
- Joseph, *m.* a dau. of Humphries, Esq., and has issue three daus.
- Henry, *d. s. p.* in 1826, aged 30.
- Sarah, *m.* to C. Harris, Esq.

Mr. Holt *d.* in 1835, aged 74.

Arms—Arg., on a bend, engrailed, sa., three fleurs-de-lis, of the first.

Crest—A spear-head, ppr.

Motto—Ut sanem vulnera [illegible].

Seats—Enfield, Red Bank, near Kendal, Westmoreland; and the Green, near Manchester.

HOLT OF STUBBYLEE.

HOLT, JOHN, Esq. of Stubbylee, co. Lancaster, J.P., *b.* 22 Aug. 18[illegible]4; *m.* 25 June, 182[illegible], Judith, 3rd dau. of James Maden, Esq. of Greens, also in Lancashire, and by her (who *d.* 24 March, 184[illegible]) has issue,

- I. JAMES-MADEN, M.A., Christchurch, Oxon, *b.* 18 Oct. [illegible]
- I. [illegible]-Anne-Elizabeth, *d.* 26 Oct. 184[illegible].
- II. [illegible]

Lineage.—This family claims to be an offshoot of [illegible]

[illegible] H[illegible] [illegible] M[illegible] Esq. [illegible] [illegible] by his son.

JAMES HOLT, Esq. of Stubbylee, [illegible] March, 17[illegible], who *m.* [illegible], Jenny, dau. of Thomas H[illegible], Gent.

of Lee; and 2ndly, 9 Sept. 1803, Anne, dau. of James Heyworth, Esq. of Greensnook, and by the latter only (who *d.* 4 Feb. 1819) an only child, JOHN, now of Stubbylee.

Arms—Arg., on a bend, engrailed, sa., three fleurs-de-lis, of the first.

Crest—A dexter arm, embowed, in armour, ppr., garnished, or, holding in the gauntlet a pheon, sa.

Seat—Stubbylee, Bacup, near Manchester.

BINNING-HOME OF ARGATY AND SOFTLAW.

BINNING-HOME, GEORGE-HOME-MONRO, Esq. of Argaty, co. Perth, and Softlaw, co. Roxburgh, J.P., *b.* 28 May, 1804; *m.* 20 Feb. 1839, Catharine Burnett, of Gadgirth, co. Ayr, and has issue,

- I. DAVID-GEORGE, *b.* 18 Feb. 1843.
- II. George-Joseph, *b.* 22 May, 1845.
- I. Sophia-Margaret.
- II. Catherine-Jane-Agnes.

Family of Binning.

Lineage.—The chief family of this name in Scotland was Binning, of Binning, whose ancestors acquired those lands lying in the county of Linlithgow, and, when surnames became hereditary, assumed the territorial name as a patronymic. The immediate ancestor of whom we have certain information was

WILLIAM BYNNIE, who, in the year 1308, took the castle of Linlithgow from the English, by concealing himself and seven sons in a waggon of hay, which was stopped in the threshold, when the porter and those with him were instantly slain, and a large party of friends, lying in ambush, was admitted, and the garrison put to the sword. The castle was delivered by its captor to King ROBERT BRUCE, who rewarded him with a gift of lands, and assigned to the family, to perpetuate the memory of this hardy adventure, an augmentation of a loaded waggon to their armorial bearings. From William Bynnie lineally descended

CHARLES BINNING, Esq., solicitor-general for Scotland in 1722, 4th son of Sir William Binning, of Walliefoord, a great merchant, and provost of Edinburgh); who *m.* Margaret, dau. of Montgomery, of Broomlands, co. Ayr, by whom he had a son,

WILLIAM BINNING, Esq., who *m.* Elizabeth, dau. of Archibald Stewart, Esq. of Torrance, and by her had a son, Charles, who *d. unm.* in 1754, and three daus., Elizabeth, CATHARINE, and Isabella. The 2nd dau.,

CATHARINE BINNING, *m.* David Inglis, Esq., and had by him two daus., Margaret, *d. unm.*; and

CATHARINE INGLIS, who *m.* ALEXANDER MONRO, Esq. of Craiglockart and Cockburn, 3rd son of Alexander Monro, Esq. of Auchenbowie, by Isabella his wife, eldest dau. of Sir Donald M'Donald, of The Isles, and by him had two sons, Alexander; and

DAVID MONRO, Esq. of Softlaw, who, by deed of entail, assumed the surname and arms of BINNING. He *m.* 1st, in 1803, his cousin, Sophia, only child, and heiress of George Home, Esq. of Argaty (lineally descended from George Home of Argaty, son of Sir Patrick Home, of Polwarth), by Jane his wife, eldest dau. and co-heir of John Monro, Esq. of Auchenbowie, eldest son of Alexander Monro, Esq. of Auchenbowie, and his wife, Isabella M'Donald, of The Isles. By this lady (who *d.* in 180[illegible]) he had,

- GEORGE-HOME-MONRO, his heir.
- Alexander-R[illegible] Monro, of Auchenbowie, *m.* Harriet, dau. of Dr. Alexander Monro, and has issue four sons and a dau.

Mr. Binning *m.* 2ndly, in 18[illegible], Isabella Blair, and by her had a son,

- Robert-Blair-Monro, *b.* in 18[illegible], E.I. Co.'s civil service.

Mr. Binning *d.* in 18[illegible], and was *s.* by his eldest son, the present GEORGE HOME-MONRO BINNING-HOME, Esq. of Argaty and Softlaw, who is eldest representative and heir [illegible] of Sir Donald M'Donald, of The Isles, and consequently of the earldom of Ross.

Family of Home of Argaty.

[illegible] HOME, of Argaty and [illegible] Feb. [illegible] Shaw his wife of Sir Patrick Home, of Polwarth, who [illegible] Argaty and [illegible] granted him by charter dated in 1604: *m.* Margaret, [illegible] dau. of Robert, 3rd Lord Erskine, of Mar, who [illegible] at Fa[illegible], and had three sons.

ALEXANDER, his heir.
Patrick (Capt.), of Correquhormbie, *d.* in Sept. 1572.
David, attainted, and sentenced to be executed, 8 Dec. 1584.

The eldest son and heir,

ALEXANDER HOME, of Argaty, *s.* his father sometime after July, 1562, and *d.* about 1574, leaving by Manot his wife, dau. of Sir John Campbell, of Glenurchy, a son and heir,

PATRICK HOME, of Argaty, who *d.* in Jan. 1629, leaving, with other issue, an eldest son and heir,

HENRY HOME, of Argaty, served heir to his father in Argaty, and to his great-uncle, Patrick, in Correquhormbie, 13 March, 1629. He *m.* Mary Mushett; and *d.* sometime before Oct. 1659, having had,

GEORGE, his heir, of Argaty, which estate he granted to his brother JOHN, in Oct. 1659.
JOHN, major in the army, obtained a grant of Argaty from his elder brother, GEORGE, *m.* in 1660, Jean-Drummond; and *d.* in 1670.
Patrick, bapt. 24 May, 1631.
HENRY, of whom we treat.
David, living 12 Oct. 1659.
Alexander, bapt. 23 Nov. 1635.
William, bapt. 25 Nov. 1842.

Mr. Home lost the half of his estates from his adherence to the cause of CHARLES I. His 4th son,

HENRY HOME, bapt. 27 July, 1633, *s.* to Argaty on the death of his brother, John, and was served heir to his father in those lands, 26 Oct. 1682. He *m.* before 1680, Janet Moir; and *d.* in July, 1689, having had issue (besides two daus.),

1 GEORGE, of Argaty, bapt. 12 March, 1686-7, served heir to his father, 5 Aug. 1700; resigned Argaty, and obtained a new charter, 1 April, 1709. He *d. s. p.* before Sept. 1751.
1 MARY, of Argaty, *m.* George Stewart, of Ballachallen, and by him (who *d.* before Sept. 1751) had, with other issue,
   1 David Home-Stewart, *d. s. p.*
   2 George Home-Stewart, who *m.* Anne Digges, of Chilham Castle, Kent, and was father of
      GEORGE HOME, of Argaty, who *s.* his uncle David. He *m.* Jane, dau. of John Monro, of Auchenbowie (by his wife, Sophia Inglis, of Auchendenny), son of Alexander Monro, of Auchenbowie, by Isabella his wife, sister of Sir Donald M'Donald, Bart. of the Isles, who *d. unm.* in 1729. By this lady Mr. George Home, of Argaty, had a dau.,
         SOPHIA HOME, of Argaty, who *m.* her cousin, DAVID MONRO BINNING, Esq. of Softlaw.

Arms—Quarterly: I. Quarterly, HOME, Polwarth: St. Clair, and Steuart. II. BINNING and HOME, quarterly. III. Monro. IV. Inglis. V. MacDonald. VI. Douglas.

Crests—I. HOME. II. BINNING.

Mottoes—True to the end; and Christo duce feliciter.

Seat—Argaty, co. Perth.

HOME OF WEDDERBURN.

(*See* MILNE-GRADEN.)

HOME OF BROOM HOUSE.

HOME, GEORGE-LOGAN, Esq. of Broom House, and Edrom, co. Berwick, J.P., Knight of the Legion of Honour, and Knight of the Redeemer of Grace, *b.* 17 Oct. 1805, *s.* his uncle, Lieut.-General James Home, of Broom House, 5 Dec. 1849; *m.* 17 Dec. 1844, Annie, eldest dau. of Major Doran, 18th Royal Irish regiment, and has issue,

I. WILLIAM-JAMES HOME, *b.* 26 Sept. 1847.
II. Cospatrie-Robert, *d.* young.
III. George-John-Ninian, *b.* 30 Jan. 1855.

Lineage.—SIR DAVID HOME, of Wedderburn, slain at the battle of Flodden, 1531, had seven sons called the "Spears of Wedderburn," one of whom, Patrick, received assignation and charter of the lands of Broom House from Adam, prior of Coldingham, (with consent of the convent, and Robert, abbot of Holyrood,) dated 1530, which was confirmed afterwards by the pope's commissioners, 1536. Patrick was *s.* by his son Ferdinand in 1556, who was *s.* by his son Patrick in 1563, *s.* by his son Patrick in 1617, *s.* by his son John 1654, *s.* by his son John in 1691.

PATRICK HOME, writer to the Signet, got a charter from Queen ANNE of the lands of Bartlerig, and *s.* his uncle John in the estate of Broom House, 1705. He appears to have had three sons, William, Alexander, and Patrick, of Bughtrig, and by his will disposed his estate of Broom House to his second son, Alexander, who sold it to his elder brother, William, 1718. William dying without issue, was *s.* by his nephew, William, son of Patrick, of Bartlerig and Bughtrig, 1774. This

WILLIAM HOME, Esq., joined the army of Charles Edward in the rebellion of 1745, and served on the personal staff of the Prince at Culloden, where he was taken prisoner and condemned for high treason at Stirling, but was reprieved on account of his being a minor. He afterwards served in the Prussian army, but returned to Broom House on the death of his uncle in 1774. He *m.* Jane, dau. of James Hunter, Esq., by whom he had issue,

I. William, lieut. in the army, *d.* in the West Indies.
II. JAMES, who succeeded him.
III. Helen, *m.* 1801, Major George Logan, eldest son of George Logan, Esq. of Edrom, by him (who *d.* 1826) she left at her decease, 1815,
   1 William, lieut. 45th regt. Madras infantry, *d.* in the East Indies, in 1829.
   2 GEORGE, only surviving son.
   3 James, *d. unm.* in Jamaica, 1844.
   4 Ninian-Home *d.* in Canada, 1839.

The 2nd son and heir,

JAMES HOME, of Broom House, lieut. general in the army, *s.* his father, William, in 1794, and dying *unm.* 5 Dec. 1849, was *s.* by his nephew, GEORGE LOGAN, of Edrom, the present proprietor.

Arms—Per fesse, vert and az., a lion rampt., within a bordure, arg.

Crest—A lion's head, erased, arg., gorged with a collar, gemel vert, and in front thereof a thistle, slipped, ppr.

Motto—True to the end.

Seat—Broom House, co. Berwick.

HOMFRAY OF PENLLINE CASTLE.

HOMFRAY, JOHN, Esq. of Penlline Castle, co. Glamorgan, J.P. and D.L., high-sheriff in 1843, *b.* 10 Sept. 1793; *m.* 1 Nov. 1819, Ann-Maria, only child and heiress of John Richards, Esq. of the Corner House, Cardiff, Glamorgan, by Mary his wife, dau. and co-heir of Peter Birt, Esq. of Wenvoe Castle, and has issue,

I. JOHN-RICHARDS, *b.* 9 Oct. 1824.
II. Mary-Jane-Richards.
III. Ann-Maria, *m.* 24 Oct. 1843, to Richard Bassett, Esq. of Bonvilstone, co. Glamorgan.

Lineage.—The name of Homfray is derived from the French words, *homme vrai*. The Homfrays were distinguished amongst the soldiers of the Cross, and they were eminent in the early wars of the Plantagenet kings. The portrait of John Homfray, living in 1390, and a gallant warrior of that day, is still preserved in the British Museum.

WILLIAM HOMFRAY, who resided at Wales, near Rotherham, in Yorkshire, in 1590, was lineal ancestor of

FRANCIS HOMFRAY, of Wales, near Rotherham, who had (by Elizabeth, his wife, who was buried at Wales, 3 Jan. 1724,) three sons, viz.,

FRANCIS, his heir.
THOMAS (*see* HOMFRAY *of The Place.*). John.

The eldest son,

FRANCIS HOMFRAY, of Wales, near Rotherham, *m.* 1st, Sarah Baker, by whom he had issue, the male line of which is now extinct. He *m.* 2ndly, Mary, dau. of Thomas Jeston, Esq. of The Heath, co. Worcester, by whom, who *d.* in 1758, he left at his decease, in 1736, with five daus., four sons, viz.,

JESTON, who *m.* Mary, dau. of Thomas Cotton, Esq. of the Combermere family, and left a son,
   FRANCIS, in holy orders, rector of Lanvayer, and vicar of Llanarth, co Monmouth, who *m.* Harriet, dau. of Jeston Homfray, Esq., and *d.* in 1813, leaving a son, KENYON HOMFRAY, in holy orders, *b.* 6 Jan. 1812, and a dau., Maria, *m.* in 1831, to the Rev. Robert-James Smith.
Thomas, who *d.* 11 May, 1797, leaving, by Elizabeth, his first wife, only child of Edmond Jones, Esq., a dau., Elizabeth, *m.* in 1774, to Peter Fry, of Axbridge.
FRANCIS, of whom presently.

John, who *m.* Mary, dau. and co-heir of the Rev. Jeremiah Addenbrooke, M.A., and *d.* in 1760, leaving a son, JOHN-ADDENBROOKE, who took the name of ADDENBROOKE by sign-manual, in 1792, and was sheriff of Worcestershire in 1798. He *m.* in 1788, Elizabeth Grazebrooke, and had issue.

The 3rd son,

FRANCIS HOMFRAY, Esq. of Wollaston Hall, co. Worcester, *m.* 1st, Hannah, dau. of Popkin, Esq. of Coitrehen, co. Glamorgan, and left one son and a dau., viz.,

JESTON, of Broadwaters, in Worcestershire, *b.* 11 June, 1752, *m.* in 1776, Sarah, dau. of Pidcock, Esq. of the Platts, and *d.* 2 March, 1816, leaving issue, 1 GEORGE, *b.* in 1778; 2 Charles, *b.* in 1781, *m.*, and has issue; 3 David, *b.* in 1792, *m.*, and has issue; 4 William, *d.* in 1821; 5 Popkin, *b.* in 1796; 6 Henry, *b.* in 1799, *m.*, and has issue; 1 Harriet, *m.* in 1805, to the Rev. F. Homfray; 2 Caroline; 3 Henrietta; and 4 Sarah, *m.* to Dr. Ogle, M.D.

Mary, *m.* to Thomas Barker, Esq.

He *m.* 2ndly, 1756, Catherine, dau. and co-heiress of Jeremiah Caswell, Esq. of The Hyde, co. Stafford, and had further issue,

I. Francis, of the Hyde, who *m.* Mary, dau. of John Pidcock, Esq. of the Platts, co. Stafford, and *d.* in 1809, leaving issue, 1 Jeremiah-Caswell, in holy orders, *d. s. p.*; 2 Francis, *b.* in 1784; 3 Harry, *b.* in 1789, *m.* Miss Catherine Jones, and has issue; 1 Mary, *m.* in 1808, to Richard Crawshay, Esq.; 2 Catherine, *m.* to Thomas Stringer, Esq.; 3 Jane; 4 Elizabeth, *m.* to William Crawshay, Esq.; 5 Eleanor, *m.* to Jos. Attwood, Esq.; 6 Louisa; 7 Clara, *m.* in 1826, to William-B.-E.-Gibbs Crawford, Esq.; and 8 Mira.

II. JEREMIAH, (Sir,) of Llandaff House.

III. Thomas, of the Hill, in Worcestershire, *m.* in 1785, Miss Elizabeth Stephens, and *d.* in 1825, leaving, with other issue, a son, John, who assumed the name of Stephens.

IV. Samuel, M.P. for Stafford, sheriff of Monmouthshire in 1813, who *m.* Jane, eldest dau. of Sir Charles-Gould Morgan, Bart. of Tredegar, and *d.* 20 May, 1822, leaving issue,

SAMUEL, high-sheriff of Monmouthshire in 1841, *b.* 7 Dec. 1795, *m.* 14 Dec. 1822, Miss Charlotte Stable, and has issue, SAMUEL-GEORGE, *b.* 7 Dec. 1830; Lorenzo-Augustus, *b.* 21 May, 1832; Charles-Gould-Morgan, *b.* 12 Dec. 1836; William-Henry-Wickey, *b.* 12 May, 1838; and Charlotte-Jane.

2 Watkin, *b.* 30 Dec. 1796, *m.* in Sept. 1822, Miss Eliza-Lee Thomson, and has, Watkin, Frederick-Samuel, William-Henry, Charles-Augustus, and Eliza-Jane.

3 Jane, *m.* in 1818, to J. K. Pickard, Esq.

4 Amelia, *m.* in 1817, William Thomson, Esq., M.P. of Perrydaron, co. Glamorgan, and had one child, Amelia, *m.* 20 July, 1842, to Thomas, Earl of Bective.

5 Maria, *m.* to George Darby, Esq., M.P., and has issue.

I. Catherine, *m.* to Thomas Wilson, Esq., and *d.* 24 March, 1801, leaving a son, Melville Wilson, who *m.* Miss Stevenson, dau. of Sir B. Stevenson, and has issue.

Mr. Francis Homfray *d.* Dec. 1798. His 3rd son,

SIR JEREMIAH HOMFRAY, Knt. of Llandaff House, co. Glamorgan, *b.* 16 Feb. 1759, high-sheriff in 1809, *m.* 2 May, 1787, Mary, dau. of John Richards, Esq. of Cardiff, and by her, who *d.* 17 March, 1830, had issue,

JEREMIAH, *b.* 1 Sept. 1790, *d.* 6 Oct. 1850.

JOHN, now of Penlline Castle.

Francis, *d. unm.* in 1813.

George, *d. unm.* in 1815.

Jeston, *b.* 22 July, 1797, *m.* 17 Aug. 1843, Esther-Amelia-Isabella, eldest dau. of Sir Francis Desanges, Knt., and *d.* 16 May, 1851.

Anthonio, M.D., *b.* 4 Oct. 1799, *m.* 5 June, 1831, Eustatia, dau. of Rear-Admiral Sir Ross Donnelly, and had by her, who *d.* in 1838, a son, Ross-Richards, *b.* 30 April, 1833, and a dau., Eustatia-Donnelly. Dr. Homfray *d.* 23 March, 1848.

Robert-Shedden, *b.* 22 Jan. 1804, *m.* in 1832, Miss Catherine Denham, and *d.* Feb. 1845, leaving issue.

Marianne, *m.* in 1806, to Thos.-M. Newte, Esq., and *d. s. p.* in 1819.

Charlotte, *m.* in 1824, to James Lewis, Esq., and *d.* 1855.

Catherine-Diana, *m.* to Jacob-Æmilius Irving, Esq., and has issue.

Harriet-Newte.

Arms—Quarterly: 1st, gu., a cross-bottony, ermine; 2nd, quarterly, arg. and sa.; 3rd, sa., four pales, ermine; 4th, arg., three bars gemelles, sa.

Crest—An otter, ppr., wounded in the shoulder with a spear.

Motto—Vulneratur, non vincitur.

Seat—Penlline Castle, in Glamorganshire.

HOMFRAY OF THE PLACE.

HOMFRAY, HENRY-REVEL, Esq. of the Place, near Newmarket, Suffolk, *b.* 25 Mar. 1809; *m.* 27 Sept. 1838, Frances-Alice, dau. and co-heiress of William Rayner, Esq. of Shadishall, by Frances his wife, dau. of Thomas-Fuller English, Esq. of Bocking, Essex, and has a dau.,

Martha-English-Rayner.

Lineage.—THOMAS HOMFRAY, Esq., bap. 1764, the 2nd son of Francis Homfray, of Wales, near Rotherham, Yorkshire, (*see preceding memoir*,) *d.* 1733, leaving by Anne Revel, his wife, a son,

JOHN HOMFRAY, *b.* 1723, who *m.* Sarah, dau. of John Parr, and by her, who *d.* 20 Feb. 1798, he left at his decease, 2 Feb. 1804, a son,

THE REV. JOHN HOMFRAY, rector of Sutton, co. Norfolk, *m.* 13 June, 1797, Hetty, dau. of James Symonds, Esq. of Ormsby, co. Norfolk, and by her (who *d.* Jan. 1843) left at his decease, Dec. 1842, a son and successor, HENRY-REVEL HOMFRAY, Esq. of The Place.

Arms—Gu., a cross bottony, erm.

Crest—An otter, ppr., wounded in the shoulder with a spear.

Seat—The Place, near Newmarket.

HONYWOOD OF MARK'S HALL.

HONYWOOD, WILLIAM-PHILIP, Esq. of Mark's Hall, Essex, married.

Lineage.—Mr. Honywood of Marks Hall is a descendant of the ancient and distinguished family of HONYWOOD *of Kent*. The Marks Hall estate was purchased, in 1605, from the Devaughs by Robert Honywood, Esq. of Charing, an ancestor of the present owner.

Arms—Arg., a chev., between three hawks' heads, erased az.

Crest—A wolf's head, couped, erm.

Motto—Omne bonum desuper.

Seat—Mark's Hall, Essex.

HOOD OF BARDON PARK.

JACOMB-HOOD, ROBERT, Esq. of Bardon Park, co. Leicester, *b.* 8 July, 1794; *m.* 29 March, 1821, Susan, dau. of John Kemp, Esq. of Broom Hills, Essex, and has issue,

I. ROBERT, *b.* 25 Jan. 1822.

II. John-Kemp, *b.* 3 Feb. 1823.

III. George-Frederick, *b.* 19 May, 1831.

IV. Francis-Randolph, *b.* 27 March, 1838.

I. Eliza-Hood. II. Mary-Randolph.

III. Emma. IV. Susan. V. Louisa.

This gentleman whose patronymic is JACOMB, inherited Bardon Park in 1833, at the decease of William Hood, Esq., and assumed, by that gentleman's desire, the additional surname and arms of HOOD.

Lineage.—In 1569 Bardon Park was granted by Queen ELIZABETH to Sir Henry Hastings, Knt., and Henry Cutler, Gent., from whom it was alienated to the family of HOOD, originally settled at Wilford, near Nottingham, by whom it was possessed for several generations; the last male heir,

WILLIAM HOOD, Esq. of Bardon Park, *b.* in 1744, barrister-at-law, and, at the period of his decease, senior bencher of the Inner Temple; *m.* in 1782, Mary, dau. of Charles Buxton, Esq. of Braxted, in Essex, but dying without issue, 16 May, 1833, devised his estates to (his mother's grand-nephew) his cousin, ROBERT JACOMB, Esq., who has assumed the surname and arms of HOOD, and is the present ROBERT-JACOMB HOOD, Esq. of Bardon Park.

Families of Snell and Jacomb.

WILLIAM SNELL, Esq. of Laurence Pountney Hill, and of Walthamstow, *m.* Cecilia, 2nd dau. and co-heir of Sir Edmund Harrison, Knt., of London, by Mary his wife, dau. of the Hon. Nathaniel Fiennes, younger brother of James, 2nd Viscount Saye and Sele, and dying 4 July, 1759, aged 67, left issue,

WILLIAM SNELL, of Clapham, many years a director of the East India Company, and afterwards of the Bank of England, m. Elizabeth, dau. of Benjamin Bond, Esq. of London, and relict of Joseph Brooksbank, Esq. of Healaugh Manor, Yorkshire, but d. s. p. 16 Jan. 1789, aged 69.
CECILIA SNELL, co-heir to her brother, m. to John Hood, Esq. of Bardon Park, and d. in 1790, leaving, with other issue, a son, WILLIAM HOOD, Esq. of Bardon Park.
MARY SNELL, co-heir to her brother, m. to William Jacomb, Esq. of Laurence Pountney Hill, and dying 10 Dec. 1784, left issue,

THE REV. ROBERT JACOMB, of Wellingborough, in Northamptonshire, who m. 1st, Sarah, dau. of Daniel Danvers, Esq., but by that lady had no issue; and 2ndly, in 1793, Elizabeth, dau. of William Hilhouse, Esq. of Clifton, by whom, who d. at Bath, 13 Oct. 1806, he had

ROBERT JACOMB, who assumed the surname of HOOD.
Thomas Jacomb, who m. Janet, 4th dau. of Nathaniel Pierce, Esq. of Wellingborough, in Northamptonshire, and has, Thomas; William; Henry; Janet; Lucy; and Cecilia.

Cecilia-Lucy Jacomb, m. to William-Wilkin Wilkin, Esq. of Costessy, in Norfolk, and had issue.

Arms—Quarterly: 1st and 4th, az., a fret, or, on a chief, of the last, three crescents, of the field; 2nd and 3rd, per chevron, az. and erm.; in chief, two lions' heads, erased, arg., langued, gu.
Crests—1st, a demi-talbot, gu., collared and lined, arg.; 2nd a lion's head, erased, barry of six, arg. and az.
Motto—Manners makyth man.
Seat—Bardon Park, Leicestershire.

HOOD OF NETTLEHAM HALL.

HOOD, JOHN, Esq. of Nettleham Hall, co. Lincoln, lord of the manor of West Firsby, co. Lincoln, b. 25 Jan. 1788, m. 14 May, 1818, Anne, dau. of Ralph Robb, Esq. of Menstrey, N.B., and has had issue,

I. John, d. young, 1837.
II. WILLIAM FRANKLAND, M.A., in holy orders, m. 1847, Elizabeth, dau. of the late Rev. J.-W. Sinclair, M.A., vicar of Hutton Bushell, co. York, and has issue.
III. Francis-Fothergill, lieut. 64th regt., d. at Malaga, 2 March, 1853.
IV. Charles-Ralph, of Toghe House, co. Mayo, b. 1830, m. 1853, Sophia, dau. of Robert Odell, Esq.
I. Grace-Sophia.
II. Mary-Elizabeth, m. to the Rev. R. G. Simpson, M.A.
III. Elizabeth. IV. Anne-Maria.
V. Margaret. VI. Helen.

Lineage.—This family is descended from John Hood, who in Jan. 1660, accompanied Gen. Monk from Scotland, when on his way to restore CHARLES II. They separated at York, Hood being left with one regiment, under Col. Fairfax. He eventually settled in that county.

JOHN HOOD, of Craike, co. York, m. a dau. of Francis Radclyffe, 1st Earl of Derwentwater, and aunt of the last unfortunate Earl, and was father of

JOHN HOODE, of Craike, who m. Mary, dau. of — Theakstone, of Craike, and had a son,

JOHN HOOD, of Kirkbridge, co. York, who m. Elizabeth, dau of William Wright, of Baldersby, co. York, and had issue, John and WILLIAM. The younger son,

WILLIAM HOOD, of Kirkbridge, co. York, lord of the manor of West Firsby, co. Lincoln, m. Grace, dau. of Francis-Firby Fothergill, of Aiskew, co. York, and granddau. of William Frankland, of Trinity College, Cambridge, and lord of the manor of Yafforth, co. York, and had issue,

JOHN, his heir, of Nettleham.
Elizabeth, m. to Capt. J.-A. Moore, R N.
Grace, m. to William Danby, Esq., co. Lincoln.

Arms—Az., a fret, arg., on a chief, sa., three crescents, or.
Crest—A hooded crow, in its beak, a Scotch thistle; in its dexter claw, a sword.
Motto—Esse quam videri.
Seat—Nettleham Hall, co. Lincoln.

HOOD OF STONERIDGE.

HOOD, JOHN, Esq. of Stoneridge, co. Berwick, J.P. and D.L., b. 8 July, 1795; m. 1st, 10 Nov. 1818, Janet-Anne, 2nd dau. of Alexander Lowe, Esq. of Leadenurquhart, co. Fife, by his wife, Anne, 2nd dau. of George Thomson, Esq. of Nuthill and Falkland, and by her (who d. in 1836) he has issue,

I. THOMAS HOOD, b. 31 Dec. 1819; m. 21 Feb. 1843, Charlotte, 2nd dau. of Col. John Shapland, C.B., by his wife, Elizabeth-Flora Nicholetts, and has issue,

1 John-Shapland-Elliott, b. 15 Jan. 1844.
2 Thomas-Cockburn.

II. Alexander-Charles.
III. John, Hon. E. I. Co.'s service. IV. James-Lowe.
I. Anne.
II. Agnes, m. in 1846, to George-Ferguson Fullerton, Esq., E. I. Co.'s civil service at Madras, 2nd son of the Hon. Lord Fullerton.
III. Isabella. IV. Rachel.
V. Cecilia-Charlotte. VI. Janet-Keith.

He m. 2ndly, in 1844, Mrs. Elizabeth Cosens, of Kames.

Lineage.—The surname of Hood, in Scotland, is almost entirely confined to the eastern district of Berwickshire, where it has existed for a long period.

There has ever been a tradition and belief in this family, that their progenitor came from England, and was descended from Nobilis ille Exlex famosissimus Robertus Fitsooth, vel Hoode, Comes de Huntingtun, *temp.* HENRY II. et RICHARD I.

JAMES HOOD, and his predecessors, possessed property in the parish of Eymouth in the Merse, in the reigns of JAMES VI. and CHARLES I., called by their name, "Hoodsland," part of which, although sold in 1697, is still in the county records under that designation. He survived his younger brother,

THOMAS HWDE, b. in 1648, whose name is so spelled on his tombstone in Ayton, where several generations of the family are interred. He left two sons, JOHN and THOMAS. John, the eldest, was b. in 1677, and d. in 1732, leaving also two sons; THOMAS, the younger of the two, b. in 1727, acquired the estate of Stoneridge, and was s. by his elder brother, JOHN, of Stoneridge, b. in 1719, and who d. in 1810, and bequeathed his property to his 3rd cousin, the present JOHN HOOD, Esq. of Stoneridge.

THOMAS HOOD, 2nd son of Thomas Hwde, was b. in 1683, and d. in 1725, leaving, by his wife, Catherine Rutherford, one son,

THOMAS HOOD, b. in 1714, who m. Mary Cockburn, dau. of David Cockburn, Esq., Langton, and d. in 1777, leaving two sons and three daus.

THOMAS HOOD, of Hardacres, co. Berwick, the eldest son, was b. in 1749, and d. in 1834. He was a person of singular ability and worth. His opinion and sound judgment as a magistrate and referee, were much respected, and few have ever been more esteemed in the county they lived in. He m. in 1788, his cousin-german, Agnes Cockburn, 3rd dau. of Thomas Cockburn,* of Rowchester, by Agnes his wife, dau. of John Scott, of Belford, co. Roxburgh, and had two sons and two daus. The eldest son, Thomas Hood, capt. in 75th regt., d. in Santa Maura, in 1818, and by his wife, Rebecca Walker, of Wooden, left one dau. The 2nd son, JOHN HOOD, of Stoneridge, succeeded to that property in 1810, and survived his father. He is the present possessor.

Arms—Per cross, sa. and arg., quarterly, over all, a bend, or.
Crest—A demi-archer, accoutred, ppr.
Motto—Olim sic erat.
Seat—Stoneridge, co. Berwick.

HOPE OF DEEPDENE.

HOPE, HENRY-THOMAS, Esq. of Deepdene, co. Surrey, and of Trenant Park, Cornwall, J.P., late M.P. for Gloucester, b. in 1808; s. his father in 1831.

Lineage.—HENRY HOPE,† Esq., 2nd son of Sir Thomas Hope, of Kerse, and younger brother of Sir Alexander Hope, of Kerse, created a baronet in 1672, founded the great and opulent branch of the Hopes, long settled as merchants at Amsterdam. He m. Anna Hope, and was father of

* THOMAS COCKBURN, of Rowchester, b. in 1723, from whom the present John Hood, of Stoneridge, is thus paternally and maternally descended, was deputy-keeper of the Great Seal of Scotland. His great-grandfather, James Cockburn, of Selburnrig, descended in direct line from Cockburn of that ilk, and Langton, chief of that very ancient Border family, lost, in the time of the troubles, his property of Selburnrig, in Lammermoor, originally a part of the estate of Langton, which a predecessor, a younger son, acquired from his father.

† Sir Robert Douglas deduces the Hopes of Amsterdam differently, and calls Henry Hope their immediate ancestor, not son of Sir Thomas Hope, of Kerse, but younger brother of Sir Thomas Hope, the eminent lawyer, the first Baronet of Craighall.

ARCHIBALD HOPE, Esq., who m. Anne Claus, and had nine sons and two daus. The 3rd son,

THOMAS HOPE, Esq. of Amsterdam, m. Margaret Marselis, and had four children, who all d. young, excepting

JOHN HOPE, Esq. of Amsterdam, who m. P. B. Van Der Hoeven, and had three sons,

THOMAS, his heir. Adrian, d. unm. Henry-Philip.

The eldest son,

THOMAS HOPE, Esq. of Deepdene, in Sussex, and of Duchess-street, London, the author of *Anastasius*, was a distinguished patron of literature and the fine arts. He m. 16 April, 1806, the Hon. Louisa Beresford, youngest child of the Right Rev. Lord Decies, Archbishop of Tuam, and by that lady, who m. 2ndly, Viscount Beresford, and d. 21 July, 1851, had issue,

HENRY, now of Deepdene.
Adrian-John, late capt. 4th dragoon-gds, who m. Matilda, Countess Rapp, dau. of General Rapp, one of Napoleon's commanders.
Alexander-James-Beresford Beresford-Hope, m. 7 July, 1842, Lady Mildred-Arabella-Charlotte-Henrietta-Cecil, eldest dau. of the Marquess of Salisbury.

Mr. Hope d. 3 Feb. 1831.

Arms—Az., a chevron, or, between three bezants.
Crest—A broken globe, surmounted of a rainbow, with clouds at each end, ppr.
Motto—At spes non fracta.
Seats—Trenant Park, near East Looe, and the Deepdene, near Dorking.

HOPES OF BRAMPTON CROFTS.

HOPES, WILLIAM, Esq. of Brampton Crofts, co. Westmorland, J.P., b. 2 Dec. 1800; m. 12 March, 1838, Jane, dau. of Thomas Swanwick, Esq. of Macclesfield, co. Chester, and has issue a dau., JANE. Mr. Hopes is only son of Wililam Hopes, Esq. of Stainmore, co. Westmoreland, and Jane his wife, dau. of William Dickinson, of the same place.

Seat—Brampton Crofts, near Appleby.

HOPE OF CARRIDEN.

HOPE, JAMES, Esq., capt. R.N., of Carriden, co. Linlithgow, J.P. and D.L., b. 8 March, 1808; m. 16 Aug. 1838, the Hon. Frederica Kinnaird, dau. of Charles, 8th Lord Kinnaird.

Lineage.—REAR-ADMIRAL SIR GEORGE HOPE, K.C.B., b. 4 July, 1767, son of the Hon. Charles Hope-Vere, 2nd son of Charles, 1st Earl of Hopetoun (*see* BURKE'S *Peerage*), m. 1st, 28 Jan. 1803, Lady Jemima Hope-Johnstone, 5th dau. of James, 3rd Earl of Hopetoun, and by her, who d. in 1808, had a son, the present CAPT. JAMES HOPE, of Carriden, and a dau., Helen. He m. 2ndly, 30 Nov. 1814, the Hon. Georgiana-Mary-Anne Kinnaird, 2nd dau. of George, 7th Lord Kinnaird, and by her, who survives, left, at his decease, in 1818, a dau., Eliza, m. 3 June, 1835, to Sir Harry Verney, Bart.

Arms—Az., on a chev., or, between three bezants, a laurel leaf, slipped, vert.
Crest—A broken globe, surmounted of a rainbow, with clouds at each end, all ppr.
Motto—At spes non fracta.
Seat—Carriden, co. Linlithgow.

HOPER OF THORNHILL.

HOPER, GEORGE, Esq. of Thornhill, Sussex, J.P., b. 2 Sept. 1784; m. 1 Jan. 1834, Henrietta-Louisa, dau. of Sir George Shiffner, Bart., of Coombe, Sussex.

Lineage.—The family of Hoper was established in St. Andrew's, Holborn, and possessed the manor of Lucton, co. Hereford, in 1635. RICHARD HOPER, of Lucton, served as high-sheriff of Herefordshire in 1707. The Hopers resided also at Sunning, co. Berkshire, in the early part of the last century.

THE REV. JOHN HOPER, vicar of Steyning and rector of Piecombe, Sussex, m. July 7, 1757, Mary, dau. of Moses Griffith, M.D., and by her, (who d. July, 1784), he left at his decease, 1790, a son,

JOHN HOPER, Esq. of Lewes, Sussex, m. 9 Oct. 1783, Sarah Cossam, of Hastings, and dying 1845, left issue,

I. GEORGE, now of Thornhill.
II. Henry, rector of Hangleton and vicar of Portslade, m. 1 June, 1820, Sarah, dau. of Rev. Richard Constable, vicar of Cowfold, Sussex, and has two sons,
  1 Richard, b. 9 Oct. 1830.
  2 Henry, b. 23 March, 1834.
III. John, of Lewes and Shermanbury, m. 20 July, 1831, Harriet Merry, of Uckfield.
I. Mary-Ann. II. Winifred.

Arms—Sa., a chev., or, between three tulips, ppr.
Crest—A cubit arm, vested and cuffed in the hand, ppr., a tulip, also ppr.
Seat—Thornhill, East Grinsted.

HOPKINS OF OVING HOUSE.

NORTHEY-HOPKINS, WILLIAM-RICHARD, Esq. of Oving House, co. Bucks, J.P., formerly a captain in the army, and aide-de-camp to the late Duke of Richmond, when Lord-Lieutenant of Ireland, m. Anne-Elizabeth, dau. of Gerald Fortescue, Esq. of the co. Louth, and has had,

I. Richard-Arthur-Fortescue, an officer in the army, who d. on service in the 17th year of his age.
I. Fanny-Elizabeth, m. 25 Jan. 1830, to George-Ives Lord Boston, and has issue.
II. Geraldine, m. in 1838, to Joseph-Pratt Tynte, Esq., second son of Col. Pratt, of Cabra Castle, co. Cavan, by Jemima-Roberta, his wife, dau. of Sir James Tynte, Bart.
III. Adelaide-Grace. IV. Antoinette. V. Eulalie-Emily.

Lineage.—This family, through both lines, NORTHEY and HOPKYNS,* establishes antiquity and eminence;—through both it has enjoyed, for a long series of years, parliamentary rank—through both it has served a succession of monarchs—and through both, acquired civic and military distinction.

SIR RICHARD HOPKINS, Knt., eldest son of Sampson Hopkyns, mayor of Coventry in 1609, and 4th in descent from William Hopkyns, mayor of Coventry 22 EDWARD IV., became eminent at the bar, and attained the rank of serjeant-at-law. He represented Coventry in parliament at the Restoration. He m. Sarah, dau. and co-heir of John Button, Esq. of Buckland, in Hampshire, by Mary, his wife, dau. of William Jesson, Esq., mayor of Coventry in 1631, and had issue,

RICHARD, his heir.
Thomas, secretary to Lord Sunderland, steward of Coventry, and commissioner of salt duties.
Sarah, who m. Sir John Goodricke, Bart. of Ribston, co. York.

Sir Richard, who was a faithful servant of King CHARLES I., and enjoyed the confidence of that unhappy prince in an eminent degree, as a series of letters addressed to him by the king, in his majesty's extremity, still extant, and in the possession of the family, fully attests, d. at Lymington, in Hampshire, and was buried there, in 1682. He was s. by his elder son,

RICHARD HOPKINS, Esq., M.P. for Coventry in 1660, 1669, 1678, 1689, 1696, and 1698. He m. Mary, dau. of Mr. Alderman Johnson, and sister of Lady Hale, by whom he had a son, EDWARD, his heir; and a dau., Mary. Mr. Hopkins was a person of considerable importance in the time of JAMES II., and was an active opponent of the court, and promoter of the revolution. He d. 1 Feb. 1707, in the 68th year of his age, and his widow, 13 Oct. 1711. Both are interred in St. Michael's Church, Coventry. Their son and heir,

THE RIGHT HON. EDWARD HOPKINS, was M.P. for Coventry, *temp.* WILLIAM III. and Queen ANNE, and Secretary of State for Ireland. This distinguished statesman m. Anna-Maria, dau. and co-heir (with her sister, Charlotte, the wife

* The name was originally written Hopkyns—it was so spelt by John Hopkyns, who filled a civic office in the city of Coventry, in 1567. From the strong resemblance between the armorial bearings of the Wykehams, of Swalcliffe, co. Oxon, and the Hopkyns' of Oving, it has been conjectured that, in early times, some bond of connexion may have existed between the two families. In confirmation, too, of this surmise, there is in Sibford Gower, in Swalcliffe parish, a small estate, which is charged with a quit-rent of a hundred pence, that tradition has assigned to the late owner, as the 19th John Hopkins, who has successively and lineally inherited it, without the intervention of any other Christian name than John; it now belongs to Mr. D.-D Hopkins, who has a deed in his possession of the 9th year of ELIZABETH'S reign, when the name is written Hopkyns. As this estate joins immediately to Warwickshire, it may be fairly assumed that the family of Hopkyns, at Coventry, and that in Swalcliffe, derive from a common ancestor.

of Richard Luther, Esq. of Myles's, in Essex,) of Hugh Chamberlen, M.D. of Alderton Manor and Hinton Hall, both in the co. Suffolk, by Mary, his 2nd wife, only child and heiress of Nathaniel Bacon, Esq. of Friston Hall, in the same county, and had issue,

RICHARD, his heir.
Edward, *d. s. p.* in 1748, under age.
Benjamin, *d. s. p.* in 1779, aged 45.
Mary, *d.* in 1712, aged 17.
ANNE, who *m.* WILLIAM NORTHEY, Esq., M.P., of Ivey House, in Wiltshire, and *d.* in 1822, leaving, with other issue, a third son,

RICHARD NORTHEY, of whom presently, as inheritor of the Hopkins' estates.

This eminent person, who, as stated above, filled the important office of Secretary of State for Ireland, left behind him an interesting manuscript, entitled "Travels of the Right Hon. Edward Hopkins, written by himself, for the amusement of his descendants." Mr. Hopkins had afterwards the high honour of accompanying the ambassador on a visit to the Prince of Condé, at Chantilly, and describes several days' sojourn there. He *d.* 17 Jan. 1735-6, in the 62nd year of his age; his widow survived him 35 years, and *d.* 9 Feb. 1768. They were interred in St. Michael's, Coventry. He was *s.* by his eldest son,

RICHARD HOPKINS, Esq., M.P. for Coventry, and Lord Commissioner of the Admiralty and Lord of the Treasury. He *d.* without issue, 18 March, 1799, aged 71, and was *s.* by (the 3rd son of his sister, Anne) his nephew, Richard Northey, who has assumed the additional surname and arms of HOPKINS, and was the late

GENERAL RICHARD NORTHEY-HOPKINS, of Oving House, *b.* 1756, who *m.* 1st, 1777, Frances, dau. of John Wray, Esq. of Monaghan, and by her had issue,

WILLIAM-RICHARD, now of Oving House.
Anne. Frances.

He *m.* 2ndly, Miss Thompson, and by her had issue,

Richard, late capt. 8th hussars.
Lucy, *m.* to J. Rowley, Esq., and *d. s. p.*
Harriett, *m.* to Charles Shrader, Esq.
Julia, *m.* to Capt. H. Hamilton Shum, of the 31st regt.
Emma, *m.* to Henry Le Patourel, Esq. of Sidbury Castle, Devon.

Gen. Northey Hopkins *d.* 26 April, 1845.

Arms—Quarterly: 1st and 4th, sa., a chev., arg., charged with three roses, gu., between three matchlocks, or, for HOPKINS: 2nd and 3rd, or, on a fesse, az., between three panthers, statant, semées of estoiles, arg., two lilies, of the last, with a rose in centre gold, stem vert, for NORTHEY; quartering CHAMBERLEN, BACON, QUAPLADDE, DE KIRTON, LUDHAM, and THORPE.

Crests—1st, a tower, per bend, indented, ar. and gu., from the battlements flames issuant, ppr., for HOPKINS; 2nd, a cockatrice, flames issuant from the mouth, ppr., for NORTHEY.

Seats—Oving House, Bucks; and Barston Park, Warwickshire.

HOPKINS OF TIDMARSH HOUSE.

HOPKINS, JOHN, Esq. of Tidmarsh House, co. Berks, J.P. high-sheriff 1848, *b.* 6 July, 1803; *m.* 1 May, 1828, Jane, 2nd surviving dau. of the Rev. John-Symonds Breedon, D.D., of Bere Court, Berks, and has issue,

I. ROBERT-JOHN, *b.* 18 Feb. 1829, *m.* 10 Aug. 1853.
I. Jane. II. Sarah-Maria. III. Julia. IV. Emily.

Lineage.—The family of Hopkins traces founders' kin to St. John's College, Oxford. Its ancestors lived on the same estate at Steventon for six hundred years. The estate of Tidmarsh was purchased, in 1798, from Charles Butler, Esq., by the late

ROBERT HOPKINS, Esq., son of John Hopkins and Anna, his wife. He *m.* in 1799, Miss Sarah Law, and had, with a son, Robert, who *d. s. p.* in 1838, and a dau., Sarah, *m.* to the Rev. B.-D. Hawkins, of Rivenhall, Essex, another son, the present JOHN HOPKINS, Esq. of Tidmarsh House. Mr. Hopkins served as high-sheriff of Berkshire in 1814.

Arms—Sa., on a chev., between three pistols, or, as many roses, gu.

Crest—A castle in flames, ppr.

Motto—Inter primos.

Seat—Tidmarsh House, near Reading.

HOPPER OF WALWORTH.

HOPPER, (now SHIPPERDSON) THE REV. EDMUND-HECTOR, of Walworth and Pittington Hall, Garth, co. Durham, J.P., M.A., formerly fellow of Christ's College, Cambridge, *b.* 25 Sept. 1806; *m.* 1 Nov. 1838, Adeline, dau. of John Kerrich, Esq. of Harleston, co. Norfolk, and has issue,

I. THOMAS-HENRY, *b.* 26 Aug. 1839.
I. Mary-Adeline. II. Isabella-Henrietta.

Lineage.—This family was for many generations seated at Wolsingham, co. Durham, in which parish they held lands at a very early period.

JENKIN HOPPER, *temp.* HENRY VIII., possessed the estate of Todcpotts, and other lands in Wolsingham, which remained with his descendants for two centuries. From him descended,

JOHN HOPPER, of Todcpotts and Wigside (will dated 25 April, 1603), who left by his wife, Alice, with three other sons, a son and successor,

ANTHONY HOPPER, who was father of

THOMAS HOPPER, who had issue six sons, of whom Robert purchased the estate of The Eshes. The eldest son and heir,

JOHN HOPPER, *b.* 1627, left at his decease, 10 Nov. 1700, two sons,

JOHN, *b.* 1655; *d.* 12 Oct. 1712, leaving by his wife, Isabel, a son, Richard, *b* 1687; who *m.* Isabella, dau. of William Coulson, of Cleadon, Esq., and left at his decease, June, 1735 (with a dau., Isabella, *m.* Robert Bates, Esq. of Fawnlees), a son, Richard, who *m.* his second-cousin, Thomasine Hopper, and *d. s. p.* 1791.
ANTHONY, of whom presently.

The 2nd son,

ANTHONY HOPPER, bapt. 2 April, 1665, sold the family estates in Wolsingham. He *m.* 9 May, 1691, Frances, dau. of Thomas Coulson, Esq., and by her left issue a son,

THOMAS HOPPER, who settled at Durham, and *m.* 1st, 15 Dec. 1723, Mary, dau. of — Burletson, Esq., by whom he had no issue. He *m.* 2ndly, 6 Jan. 1729, Elizabeth Paxton, widow of — Fulthorpe, Esq., and left issue by her, with one dau., Thomasine, *m.* to her cousin, Richard Hopper, Esq., six sons,

I. John, bapt. 22 Aug. 1731, mayor of Durham, 1764; *m.* Margaret, dau. of David Johnson, and *d. s. p.*
II. Thomas, bapt. 12 Oct. 1732, vicar of Bowdon, rector of Barley, and prebendary of Ely; *m.* 31 Jan. 1771, Alice Massey, widow of — Robinson, Esq.; and *d.* 23 Oct. 1779, leaving issue a son,

1 Thomas, of Silksworth House, co. Durham, bapt. 20 Aug. 1772; *m.* 1st, Wilhelmina-Dorothy, dau. of the Rev. Richard Hammett, of Bideford, co. Devon, by whom he had, with a younger dau., Harriet, who predeceased him *unm.*, a dau. and heiress, Priscilla-Maria, now of Silksworth House, *m.* to Col. William Beckwith, K.H., of Trindon, co. Durham. He *m.* 2ndly, Everalid, dau. of Thomas Hustler, of Acklam, co. York, Esq.; and 3rdly, his cousin, Elizabeth Hopper; by neither of whom he had issue. He *d.* 14 June, 1830.

III. Christopher, bapt. 17 July, 1734; *m.* Miss Mary Norris, and left at his decease, Sept. 1823, with a dau., Elizabeth, *m.* to her cousin, Thomas Hopper, Esq., a son,

1 Thomas, of Sharow Lodge, co. York, and of Walworth, co. Durham, *m.* Catharine, dau. of Henry Richmond, M.D., and *d.* March, 1849, without issue.

IV. GEORGE, of whom presently.
V. Hendry, bapt. 6 June, 1737, of Silksworth House. He purchased and entailed the estate of Walworth. He *m.* 20 Nov. 1770, Elizabeth, dau. and co-heir of William Steele, Esq. of Lamb Abbey, co. Kent, M.P., and *d.* 21 June, 1812, without issue.
VI. Anthony, bapt. 30 Dec. 1738, *d.* 28 Feb. 1823, *unm.*

The 4th son,

GEORGE HOPPER, Esq., bapt. 11 Nov. 1735; *m.* 1st, Anne, only dau. and heiress of the Rev. Walter Carles,* vicar of Sandon (by Anne, his wife, sister of Edmund Hector, Esq. of Birmingham, the friend of Samuel Johnson), by whom he acquired the estate of Fiveways House, near Birmingham,

* He was the only son of Richard Carless, Esq. of Birmingham, by Anne, dau. of Walter Moseley, Esq. of Enfield, co. Stafford, by Jane, only dau. and heir of William Acton, Esq., 3rd son of Sir Edward Acton, of Aldenham, Bart.; who was the son of Richard Carless, Esq., the near kinsman and legatee of Colonel William Carles, the preserver of King CHARLES II. in the Royal Oak at Boscobel. This was a branch of the ancient family of Carles, of Albrighton, co. Shropshire. On 18 Jan. 11 EDWARD I., Roger Carlis had a grant of free warren in Albrighton. In 1370, Sir William Carles, of Albrighton, was sheriff of Shropshire.

with lands at Harborne, Marston Culey, and Longdon, and by her had issue an only child and heir,

WALTER-CARLES.

He m. 2ndly, Anne, dau. of Henry Perkins, Esq., but by her had no issue; and dying 14 April, 1787, was s. by his son,

WALTER-CARLES HOPPER, Esq. of Belmont, co. Durham, heir also to his great-uncle, Edmund Hector, Esq., b. 25 July, 1772; who m. 9 Aug. 1808, Margaret, dau. of Ralph Shipperdson, Esq. of Pittington Hall Garth, and by her had issue,

I. EDMUND-HECTOR, his heir, who has succeeded to the estates of Pittington Hall Garth, and assumed the name and arms of SHIPPERDSON.
II. Walter-Anthony, b. 16 Dec. 1810, of Lincoln's Inn, barrister-at-law d. unm. 15 Oct. 1845.
III. Ralph-Shipperdson, b. 18 Feb. 1815, M.D.
IV. Augustus-Macdonald, b. 11 Aug. 1816, M.A., late fellow of St John's College, Cambridge, rector of Starston, co. Norfolk, and a magistrate for that county; m. 15 April, 1847, Charlotte, younger dau. of Rev. John Holmes, of Gawdy Hall, co. Norfolk, and by her has issue,
  1 Richard-Carles, b. 4 Feb. 1848.
  1 Annie-Margaret, b. 12 June, 1849.
  2 Sarah, b. 12 Nov. 1851.
  3 Constance, b. 11 May, 1853.
I. Mary-Anne-Frances.
II. Caroline-Elizabeth, m. Rev. James Boucher, nephew of Viscount Molesworth.
III. Isabella-Margaret, m. her cousin, F.-Russell Apletre, Esq. of Goldings, co. Hants.
IV. Frances.

Mr. Hopper inherited the estate of Walworth at the decease of his cousin, Thomas Hopper, Esq. of Sharow Lodge, and dying 15 Jan. 1853, was s. by his eldest son, the present REV. EDMUND-HECTOR HOPPER (now SHIPPERDSON), of Walworth, representative of the family.

Arms—Quarterly: 1st and 4th, gyronny of eight, sa. and erm., over all a tower, triple towered, arg., masoned, of the first, for HOPPER; 2nd and 3rd, or, on a mount, in base, an oak-tree, vert, over all, on a fesse, gu., three regal crowns, of the first, for CARLES or CARLOS. These bearings of Carlos were granted, 21 May, 1658, by CHARLES II. to his preserver, in the Royal Oak after the battle of Worcester, Col. William Carlos, "in perpetuam rei memoriam" as it is expressed in the patent.

Crests—1st, a tower, as in the arms, for HOPPER; 2nd, a sword, arg., hilt and pomel, or, and a sceptre, of the second, crossed, in saltire, enfiled with an oaken civic crown, vert, fructed, of the second, for CARLES.

Motto—Subditus fidelis regis et salus regni.

HOPPER-WILLIAMSON OF SHINCLIFFE.

HOPPER-WILLIAMSON, THE REV. ROBERT, rector of Hurworth, co. Durham, J.P., b. 9 Aug. 1784; m. 18 June, 1811, Elizabeth, dau. of William Barras, Esq., and has issue,

I. ROBERT, in holy orders; b. 8 July, 1813.
II. William, major 85th regiment, b. 25 May, 1823.
I. Elizabeth.
II. Ann-Alice, m. 11 April, 1839, to John-George Scurfield, Esq., and has issue.
III. Frances-Barras. IV. Mary.

Lineage.—Surtees, in his "*History of Durham*," several times makes mention of the respectable family of Hopper, of Shincliffe, and the records of the Dean and Chapter of Durham, under whom nearly the whole of the property at Shincliffe is held, state that the lease of the premises where the Hopper lived, was granted "11 May, 1594, to John Hopper, of Shincliffe, Janet his wife, and Sampson Hopper their son." On this property the Hoppers resided for several generations, till JOHN HOPPER, of Shincliffe, left two sons, JOHN and HENDRY; the latter,

HENDRY HOPPER, of Durham, purchased (A.D. 1720) Crook Hall, the manor of Sidgate; the lordship of Thrislington; and the estates of Heugh Hall and Quarrington Grange, in the parish of Kelloe. He d. 1750, s. p. His brother,

JOHN HOPPER, Esq. of Shincliffe, m. Anne Colling, of Long Newton; and d. 1743, leaving issue,

JOHN, his heir.
Ralph, who m. Philadelphia Cuthbert, and was father of an only son, the late JOHN-THOMAS-HENDRY HOPPER, Esq. of Wilton Castle, co. Durham, who m. and had issue. Of his daus., Mary-Anne m. Sir Joseph Bailey, Bart. of Glanusk Park, co. Brecon, M.P.; and of the sons, the eldest, the REV. JOHN HOPPER, sold Wilton Castle to Sir William Chaytor, Bart.
Hendry.
Mary.

The eldest son,

JOHN HOPPER, Esq. of Shincliffe, heir to his uncle, Hendry Hopper, Esq., m. 25 June, 1752, Elizabeth, only child of Robert Hilton, Esq., and had issue, JOHN, who d. unm.; ROBERT, of whom presently; and Ralph, in holy orders, who m. Elizabeth Artby; and d. 3 May, 1834, leaving one son. The second son,

ROBERT HOPPER, Esq., a barrister of great provincial eminence, chancellor of the county palatine of Durham, and recorder of Newcastle-upon-Tyne, m. 28 October, 1782, Anne, only dau. of Dr. William Williamson, rector of Whickham, third son of Sir William Williamson, Bart., and assumed in consequence the additional surname of WILLIAMSON. He d. 12 Jan. 1835. Of this marriage the issue were two sons, viz., the present REV. ROBERT HOPPER-WILLIAMSON, rector of Hurworth, and JOHN-WILLIAM WILLIAMSON, Esq. of Whickham, b. 17 Sept. 1789, J.P. and D.L., who served as high-sheriff co. Durham, and d. unm. 15 April, 1850.

Arms—Quarterly: 1st and 4th, gyronny of eight, sa. and erm., over all a tower, triple-towered, arg., masoned; 2nd and 3rd, or, a chev., gu. between three trefoils, slipped, sa.

Crest—A tower, triple-towered, arg. masoned.

Residence—Hurworth Rectory, near Darlington.

HOPTON OF CANON FROME.

HOPTON, THE REV. JOHN, of Canon Frome Court, co. Hereford, J.P. vicar of Canon Frome and prebendary of Hereford, b. 5 Oct. 1782; m. 3 May, 1807, Grace-Anne, eldest dau. of John Williams, Esq. of Wilcroft, co. Hereford, and by her (who d. 1 Oct. 1839) had issue,

I. JOHN, A.M., J.P., and D.L., late captain 3rd dragoon-guards; b. 1809; m. 1843, Maria, dau. of Edward Dixon, Esq.
II. Richard, in holy orders, d. unm. 1835.
III. Conan, lieut. 22nd regt., d. unm. 1838.
IV. Charles-Edward, b. 1823; capt. 23rd Welsh fusiliers; wounded at the Alma; m. 1845, Mary-Jane, dau. of David Vaughan, Esq.
I. Grace-Anne, m. 1841, to James, eldest son of Edward Poole, Esq. II. Mary.
III. Frances, twin with Richard, d. an infant, 20 Jan. 1812.
IV. Lydia, m. 1840, to the Rev. John Graves, vicar of Stretton Grandison, co. Hereford.
V. Susannah, d. unm.
VI. Ellen-Elizabeth, m. 1849, to the Rev. John Buckle.
VII. Caroline-Anne, m. 1845, to Charles Guy Trafford, Esq.
VIII. Anna-Maria.

Lineage—The family of Hopton came originally from Normandy with the CONQUEROR, and settled at Hopton, in Shropshire. A descendant of that eminent house,

SIR RICHARD Hopton, of Cherbury, high-sheriff of Herefordshire in 1610, m. his kinswoman, Elizabeth, dau. of John Hopton, and niece and devisee of Michael Hopton, of Canon Frome, son of William Hopton, of Hopton and Dounton, co. Salop. By this lady he had issue, five sons and two daus. The 2nd son,

SIR EDWARD HOPTON, of Canon Frome, M.P. for the city of Hereford, and yeoman of the stirrup to CHARLES I. in 1634, was created a knight banneret by his Majesty, on the field of battle. He acted likewise as a deputy-lieutenant for Herefordshire, was colonel of the county militia, and gentleman-pensioner in ordinary to the king. He m. 20 July, 1654, Deborah, widow of Isaac Jones, and dau. of Robert Hatton, of Thames Ditton, Surrey, serjeant-at-law, by whom (who d. 13 July, 1702, aged 77,) he had EDWARD, his heir, father of RICHARD HOPTON, Esq. of Canon Frome, M.P. for Hereford, who m. Elizabeth, widow of William Gregory, Esq. of How Caple, in Herefordshire, and dau. of Thomas Geers, serjeant-at-law, of the Marsh, by Elizabeth his second wife, dau. and heir of William Cope, of Icomb, in Gloucestershire, by the Lady Elizabeth Fane, dau. to the 1st Earl of Westmoreland. By this lady, who d. 3 Sept. 1747, aged 65, he had, with other issue, a dau., DEBORAH, b. 1708, who m 1730, JOHN PARSONS, Esq. of Kemerton Court, co. Gloucester, a descendant of Conan Parsons, of Kemerton, A.D. 1584, and left a son,

THE REV. WILLIAM PARSONS, of Kemerton Court, co. Gloucester, to whom his mother's nephew, Richard Cope Hopton,* Esq., devised by will the Canon Frome estates,

* This Richard Cope Hopton (son of Edward Cope Hopton) had one sister, Anne, who m. Michael Clements, Esq., capt. R.N., and d. 1786, leaving one son and one dau., Michael Hopton Clements, and Mary-Anne Clements.

and who assumed in consequence, by sign-manual, the surname and arms of HOPTON, 21 March, 1817. He m. 1st, 1781, Mary, dau. of Morgan Graves, Esq. of Mickleton, co. Gloucester, and by her, who d. in 1800, had issue,

JOHN, now of Canon Frome.
Charles, capt. 27th regiment of foot, d. of a wound received in Spain, buried at Stretton Grandsome, 13 Sept. 1813, unm.
Mary-Anne.

Mr. (Parsons) Hopton m. 2ndly, 25 Aug. 1801, Anne, dau. of James Poole, Esq. of Homend, in Herefordshire, barrister-at-law, and had by her,

William, in holy orders, vicar of Bishop's Frome, in Herefordshire, J.P., m. 8 Sept. 1830, Diana-Christian, second dau. of the Rev. Charles Shuckburgh, of The Moat, in Wiltshire, and has three surviving children, Edward, Michael, and Diana.
James-Michael.
Charlotte. Elizabeth. Catherine. Deborah.

Mr. Hopton d. 1841.

Arms—Gu., between nine-crosses-patée, fitchée, or, a lion, rampant, of the second.
Crest—On a ducal coronet a gryphon's head, holding in his mouth a bleeding hand.
Seat—Canon Frome Court.

HOPWOOD OF HOPWOOD.

GREGGE-HOPWOOD, EDWARD-JOHN, Esq. of Hopwood Hall, co. Lancaster, D.L., capt. in the army, b. 27 April, 1807, m. 20 April, 1839, Susan-Fanny, dau. of John-Baskervyle Glegg, Esq. of Old Withington and Gayton, co. Chester, and has a son, EDWARD-ROBERT, b. 6 Feb. 1846, and four daus., Cecilia, Lucy, Mary-Rose, and Evelyn.

Lineage.—The family of Hopwood has been seated at Hopwood since the reign of KING JOHN. In 1359 Adam de Hopwood was one of an inquisition at Preston; and in 1442, Galfridus Hopwood was styled gentleman among the witnesses to the licence for the foundation of the church at Manchester. At the death of Dr. Hopwood, early in the 18th century, by which the original family became extinct, the Hopwood estates passed by will to Edward Gregge, of whom hereafter. JOSEPH GREGGE, Esq. of Chamber Hall, co. Lancaster, second son of Robert Gregge, Esq., barrister-at-law, m. circa 1680, Martha, dau. and heir of Henry Wrigley, Esq. of Chamber Hall, co. Lancaster, (a residence which will have much future historical interest as the birth-place of the 2nd Sir Robert Peel), and was father of

BENJAMIN GREGGE, Esq. of Chamber Hall, who m. Elizabeth Gill, of Carr House, co. York, and had (with a dau. Martha, who m. Thomas Perceval, Esq., F.S.A., of Royton Hall, co. Lancaster, and d. 1760, leaving an only child, Katherine, m. 1763, to Joseph Pickford, Esq. of Royton Hall), a son,

EDWARD GREGGE, Esq., who assumed the additional surname of HOPWOOD. He m. Judith, dau. of — Sunderland, Esq. of Whittington Hall, and by her had issue,

ROBERT, his heir.
Mary, m. to James Starky, Esq. of Heywood Hall, co. Lancaster.
Catherine, m. to General Heron, of Moor Hall, co. Chester.

His only son,

ROBERT GREGGE-HOPWOOD, Esq. of Hopwood Hall, co. Lancaster, b. 30 Nov. 1773; m. 31 Dec. 1805, the Hon. Cecilia Byng, dau. of John, 5th Viscount Torrington, and has issue,

EDWARD-JOHN, now of Hopwood Hall.
Frank, in holy orders, m. 11 June, 1835, Lady Eleanor-Mary Stanley, dau. of Edward, Earl of Derby.
Hervey, capt. in the grenadier-guards.
Mary-Augusta, m. 18 June, 1834, to Charles-William, Earl of Sefton.

Mr. Gregge-Hopwood, a magistrate and deputy-lieut. for Lancashire, and high-sheriff in 1802, d. 1854.

Arms—Quarterly: 1st and 4th, paly of six, arg. and vert; 2nd and 3rd, or, three trefoils, slipped, between two chevronels, sa.
Crest—Out of a ducal coronet, an eagle's head, holding in the beak a trefoil, slipped, all ppr.
Seat—Hopwood Hall, co. Lancaster.

HORDERN OF OXLEY HOUSE.

HORDERN, ALEXANDER, Esq. of Oxley House, co. Stafford, barrister-at-law, J.P. and D.L., b. in 1786; m. in Feb. 1827, Jane-Hickman, dau. of Benjamin Hill, Esq. of Wolverhampton, and had issue a son,

JAMES, b. in Aug. 1828.

Mr. Hordern, who s. in 1825, his father, the late James Hordern, Esq. of Wolverhampton, banker, high-sheriff of Staffordshire in 1823; he had one brother, Henry Hordern, Esq. of Dunstall Hall, co. Stafford, J.P. and D.L., who m. a dau. of Francis Holyoake, Esq.

Arms—Gu., on a cross, raguly, arg., an arrow, in pale, the pheon upwards, sa.; in the 1st and 4th quarters, a wolf's head, erased, erminois.
Crest—An ox's head, caboshed, gu., armed, or, surmounting two arrows, in saltier, of the last, barbed and flighted, arg.
Motto—Fortiter ac sapienter.
Seat—Oxley House, co. Stafford.

HORE OF POLE-HORE.

HORE, HERBERT-FRANCIS, Esq. of Pole-Hore, co. Wexford, b. 14 March, 1817; m. Jan. 1840, Dorothea-Lucretia, dau. of Alexander-Whalley Light, Esq., late colonel of the 25th regt., and widow of Thomas-Bilcliffe Fyler, Esq. of Teddington, Middlesex, M.P. for Coventry, and has issue,

I. PHILIP-HERBERT, b. 14 Nov. 1841.
II. Herbert-William. III. Walter. IV. Gerald.
I. Edith-Catherine. II. Ismay.

Lineage.—SIR WILLIAM LE HORE, one of the Norman knights who invaded Ireland in 1170, obtained grants of land in the county of Wexford, and established the family before us. His descendant,

THOMAS LE HORE (with whom the pedigree, in the Visitation of the county, begins), of The Pole, held that manor by the service of "keeping a passage over the Pill-water, as often as the sessions should be held at Wexford." He had three sons, 1 RICHARD; 2 DAVID (Sir), of The Pole, high-sheriff 1334; and 3 WALTER, of whom hereafter.

WALTER LE HORE, the 3rd son, was father of

WILLIAM LE HORE, chief-serjeant of Wexford before 1382, who had several sons; from the 3rd derived the HORES OF SHANDON, co. Waterford. The eldest son,

SIR NICHOLAS LE HORE, Knt., seneschal of the Earl of Pembroke's lands, and sheriff of the co. Wexford, in 1390 and 1396, m. Matilda, dau. of Sir William, Lord Loundres of Naas, co. Kildare, and had issue, Thomas, abbot of Dunbrody in 1447; and CHRISTOPHER. This

CHRISTOPHER HORE, of The Pole, m. Maude, dau. of John Neville, Baron of Rosgarland, and from him derived, 6th in descent,

CHRISTOPHER HORE, Esq. of Pole Hore, a small portion of whose patrimony, sequestrated by CROMWELL, was recovered at the Restoration: dying in 1682, he left, by his wife, Margaret, Sutton, of Fethard and Clonard (who m. 2ndly, William Esmonde, Esq. of Johnstown), a son,

PHILIP HORE, Esq. of Pole Hore, b. in 1678, who m. in 1705, Jane, dau. of Thomas Richards, Esq. of Rathaspeck, and The Park, and (having become a Protestant) d. in 1749, leaving issue. The eldest son,

THOMAS HORE, Esq. of Pole Hore, m. in 1737, Catherine, dau. of Rev. William Harvey, of Bargy Castle, rector of Mulrankan, and d. in 1774, leaving three co-heirs, all married. His brother,

CÆSAR HORE, Esq. of Pole Hore, m. in 1745, Anastasia, dau. of Thomas Clare, Esq., and dying in Dublin in April, 1791, left issue. The eldest son,

PHILIP HORE, Esq. of Pole Hore, b. in 1750; m. in 1779, Elizabeth, dau. of William Woollett, Esq. of Chiselhurst, Kent, and dying in 1802, left an only child,

HERBERT-WILLIAM HORE, Esq. of Pole Hore, capt. of His Majesty's ship "Freija," in 1814, m. that year, Eliza, dau. and co-heir (with Sarah, wife of Colonel Brandreth, R.A.) of George Curling, Esq. of West Hatch, Essex. Capt. Hore dying in 1823, left issue,

HERBERT-FRANCIS.
Edward-George, b. 17 Sept. 1823, comm. R.N.
Eliza-Sarah.

Mrs. Hore m. 2ndly, in 1826, Henry Bedford, Esq.

Arms—Arg., an eagle, az.
Crest—A demi-eagle, az.
Motto—Constanter.

HORE OF HARPERSTON.

HORE-RUTHVEN, WALTER, Esq. of Harperston, co. Wexford, and Freeland House, co. Perth, J.P. high-sheriff co. Wexford, 1828, *b.* 6 June, 1784; *m.* Mary-Elizabeth-Thornton, BARONESS RUTHVEN, dau. of James, Lord Ruthven, and has issue,

I. WILLIAM, *m.* Della-Honoria, dau. of Major Lowen, and *d.* 12 May, 1847, leaving,

WALTER-JAMES, of the rifle brigade.
And other issue.

II. Ruthven, *d.* 1839.
III. Walter, major H.E.I.C.S., deceased.
IV. Leslie-Melville.
V. Cavendish-Bradstreet, lieut. R.N., *d.* 22 Oct. 1854, of wounds received before Sebastopol.

I. Mary. II. Eleanor-Catherine.
III. Anna. IV. Wilhelmina.
V. Jane. VI. Georgina.

Lineage.—NICHOLAS HORE, Esq. of Harperston (son of William Hore, Esq. of Harperston, by his wife, a dau. of Nicholas Browne, Grand Seneschal of Wexford, and lineal descendant of THOMAS LE HORE, living in 1272), flourished *temp.* HENRY VIII., and was a great actor in the border warfare of that period in the co. of Wexford. His brother,

DAVID HORE, became Lord of Harperston, *m.* a dau. of William Sutton, Lord of Ballykeroge, and had issue,

ROBERT, his heir, *d. s. p.* in 1547.
WILLIAM, who *s.* his brother.
Richard, of Taghmon, living in 1569, from whom descended David Hore, Esq. of Aghfada, M.P. for Taghmon in 1634, whose dau., Ellen, *m.* Christopher Bryan, Esq. of Skarr.

The 2nd son,

WILLIAM HORE, Esq. of Harperston, *m.* Joan, dau. of Sir Nicholas Chevers, Knt. of Balyhaly, co. Wexford, and was great-grandfather of

WILLIAM HORE, Esq. of Harperston, *b.* in 1587; who *m.* 10 Dec. 1607, Margaret, dau. of Oliver Keating, Esq. of Kilcoan, by Joan, dau. of Hon. Pierce Butler, BARON OF KAYER, 2nd son of Sir Richard, 1st Viscount Mountgarrett. He signed the great roll of the Catholic Confederation, and took an active part in the civil wars; was a member of the General Assembly of the Supreme Council of Kilkenny, in 1643; and in 1644, was appointed commissioner of the revenue of Ireland, and the previous year, receiver of the public money, and treasurer of the county. His great-grandson,

COL. WILLIAM HORE, of Harperston, was M.P. co. Wexford in 1711, and M.P. for his borough of Taghmon, from 1731 till his death. He *m.* Anne, dau. of the Rev. Thomas Bunbury, of Baleaker, and had issue,

WILLIAM, his heir.
Walter, of Drinagh, *d.* in 1762.
Thomas, *m.* a dau. of John Tench, Esq. of Bryonstown, and dying before 1762, left William; Walter; and Anne.
Martha.
Jane, *m.* to Richard Waddy, Esq. of Clougheast Castle, co. Wexford.

Col. Hore *m.* 2ndly, Catherine, co-heir of John Shapland, Esq., sister of Elizabeth, wife of Robert Carew, Esq. of Castleboro', ancestor of LORD CAREW, and had one dau., Ellen. He *d.* 13 April, 1741, and was *s.* by his son,

WILLIAM HORE, Esq., D.C.L., appointed in 1729, advocate-general and judge-martial; in 1730, a commissioner of appeals; in 1732, a master in Chancery, and subsequently, king's attorney-general and one of the chief-justices of Ireland. He was M.P. for Taghmon from 1727 to 1731, and from 1741 till his death. He *m.* 1st, Dorothy, 5th dau. of William Ponsonby, Viscount Duncannon, sister to Brabazon, 1st Earl of Besborough, by whom he had issue an only son and two daus., viz.,

Walter, his heir.
Mary, *m.* 17 April, 1746, to John Cox, Esq. of Coolcliffe.
Anne, *b.* in 1732, *m.* to Gen. Anthony Cliffe, of Ross.

He *m.* 2ndly, 29 Aug. 1743, Mary, dau. of John Grogan, Esq. of Johnstown Castle, widow of Major Andrew Knox, of Rathmacknee Castle. She survived him, and *m.* 3rdly (as 2nd wife to), Charles Tottenham, Esq. of Tottenham Green, Wexfordshire, grandfather of Sir Charles-Tottenham Loftus, Bart., 1st Marquis of Ely, and *d.* in 1777. Mr. Hore *d.* in 1746. His son,

COL. WALTER HORE, of Harperston, judge-martial and advocate-general of Ireland, col. of the yeomanry cavalry of the county, and high-sheriff in 1793; *m.* 28 May, 1758, Lady Anne Stopford, 4th dau. of James, 1st Earl of Courtown, and had several children, viz.,

I. WILLIAM. II. James, *d. unm.*
III. Walter, of Seafield, near Courtown, Wexfordshire, capt. in the army, J.P., *m.* Catherine, dau. of John Conroy, Esq., and aunt of the late Sir John Conroy, Bart., and has issue,

1 Walter, in holy orders, *m.* in 1812, Harriet, co-heir of the Hon. George Jocelyn, 2nd son of Robert, 1st EARL OF RODEN, and dying 28 Sept. 1843, left issue, Walter; George; Georgina; Harriet; Catherine; Tamasina.
2 James.
1 Elizabeth. 2 Frances. 3 Louisa.

IV. Thomas, rector of Kiltennel, co. Wexford, of Ham, in Surrey, *m.* Lady Mary Howard, aunt of the present Earl of Wicklow.
V. Ponsonby, late of the 9th light dragoons, *m.* Rachel, dau. of Mr. Coxe, of Castletown, co. Kilkenny, and is buried at Taghmon.
I. Elizabeth, *m.* to James Boyd, Esq. of Rosslare House.

Col. Hore who was for many years M.P. for Taghmon, *d.* 26 Feb. 1795, and was *s.* by his son,

WILLIAM HORE, Esq., of Harperston, J.P., high-sheriff in 1788, who *m.* 5 Jan. 1782, Eleanor-Catherine, dau. and heiress of Sir Simon Bradstreet, Bart. and left issue,

WALTER, the present WALTER HORE-RUTHVEN, of Harperston.
William, major 67th foot, *d.* in 1830.
Samuel-Bradstreet, of Lamberton, co. Wicklow, comm. R.N., *b.* in April, 1791; *m.* 8 Sept. 1821, Jane-Carolina, dau. of Richard Solly, Esq., granddau. of Sir Frederick Flood, Bart., and is deceased.
James-Stopford, comm. R.N., *b.* in April, 1795, and is deceased.
Henry-Cavendish, lieut. R.N., *m.* and has two sons and one dau.
Thomas, lieut.-col. royal engineers, *m.* Miss Leigh, dau. of Francis Leigh, Esq. of Rosegarland, co. Wexford.
Anna, *m.* to the Rev. John Hunt.

Mr. Hore was murdered by the rebels on the bridge of Wexford, 20 June, 1798. His eldest son is the present WALTER HORE RUTHVEN, Esq. of Harperston.

Arms—Arg., an eagle, az., a crescent, gu.
Crest—A demi-eagle, az.
Motto—Constanter.
Seats—Harperston, co. Wexford (the residence of Cromwell for some days, when at the head of his army, in 1649) and Freeland House, co. Perth.

HORNBY OF DALTON HALL.

HORNBY, EDMUND, Esq. of Dalton Hall, co. Westmorland, J.P. and D.L., high-sheriff 1828, *b.* 17 June, 1773; *m.* 22 Aug. 1796, Lady Charlotte Stanley, dau. of Edward, 12th Earl of Derby, and has one son,

EDMUND-GEORGE, late M.P. for Warrington, *b.* 16 Nov. 1799, *m.* 30 Jan. 1827, Sarah, dau. of Thomas Yates, Esq. of Irwell House, in Lancashire, 1st cousin to Sir Robert Peel, and has,

1 Elizabeth-Sarah. 2 Lucy-Francesca.

Lineage.—The family of Hornby were settled in the Fylde country, in the north of Lancashire, from a very remote antiquity.

JOHANNES DE HORNEBY was receiver-general of the duchy rents under John of Gaunt; and the records in the duchy-office give the seals of the arms such as they have been ever since borne by their descendants. In the reign of JAMES I., HUGH DE HORNBY, Esq. of Bankfield, in Fylde, was rated to find service and men of arms. He was ruined by the civil wars, and sold Bankfield to the family of Harrison. His son,

GEOFFREY HORNBY, followed the profession of the law, and settled at Poulton, in the Fylde, where he acquired considerable property. He was father of

EDMUND HORNBY, Esq., who *m.* Dorothy, dau. of Geoffrey Rishton, of Antley, in co. Lancaster, M.P. for Preston, and sister of Edward Rishton, Esq. of Antley, of good Lancashire descent. She *d.* 1722. This Edmund Hornby left issue, by Dorothy his wife, GEOFFREY; George, in holy orders, rector of Whittington, *d. s. p.*; Anne, wife of Edmund Cole, of Beaumont, near Lancaster, by whom she had a dau., Dorothy, wife of Butler, of Kirkland. Edmund Hornby had other issue, who *d.* young. The eldest son,

GEOFFREY HORNBY, Esq. of Poulton and Scale Hall, near Lancaster, *m.* Susanna, dau. and heir of Edward Sherdley, of Kirkham, Gent., by Ellen his wife, dau. and co-heir of John Veale, Esq. of Whinney Heyes, in Fylde, and Susanna

Rishton his wife, and left issue two sons, Geoffrey, *d. s. p.* 1801; and

EDMUND HORNBY, Esq. of Poulton and Scale Hall, *b.* Oct. 1728; *m.* Margaret, 2nd dau. of John Winckley, Esq. of Preston, by his wife, Elizabeth Starkie, of Huntroyde, co. Lancaster. By her (with three daus., Margaret, *d.* 1815; Susan, *d.* 1799; and Dorothy, *d.* young) he had issue,

GEOFFREY HORNBY, only son and heir, sometime colonel of one of the regiments of Lancashire militia; he afterwards took orders, and was rector of Winwick, Lancaster, 1782. He *m.* 25 April, 1772, Lucy, dau. of James, Lord Strange, and sister of Edward, 12th Earl of Derby, and had issue seven sons and six daus.,

EDMUND, his heir, of Dalton Hall.
James-John, in holy orders, rector of Winwick, *m.* 1st, Esther, youngest dau. and co-heir of Robert-Vernon Atherton, Esq. of Atherton, by Harriet his wife, dau. and co-heir of Peter Legh, Esq. of Lyme; and 2ndly, Catherine, dau. of — Boyle, Esq.; and *d.*, leaving issue.
Geoffrey, in holy orders, rector of Bury, Lancashire, *m.* the Hon. Georgiana Byng, sister of the late Lord Torrington, and has issue.
Edward-Thomas-Stanley, in holy orders, *d. unm.*
PHIPPS (Sir), K.C.B., of Littlegreen.
George, in holy orders.
Charles, lieut.-col. Scots fusilier-guards, now in holy orders.
Lucy, *m.* to the Rev. H.-W. Champneys, rector of Badsworth.
Charlotte, *m.* 30 June, 1798, to Edward, Lord Stanley, late Earl of Derby; and *d.* in 1817.
Georgiana. Frances-Susannah.
Louisa. Henrietta-Elizabeth.

Mr. Hornby *d.* 31 July, 1812.

Arms—Or, a chevron, between three bugle-horns, sa.
Crest—A bugle-horn.
Seat—Dalton Hall, near Burton.

HORNBY OF LITTLEGREEN.

HORNBY, SIR PHIPPS, K.C.B., of Littlegreen, co. Sussex, rear-admiral, R.N., *m.* 22 Dec. 1814, Maria-Sophia, eldest dau. of the late Right Hon. Lieut.-General Burgoyne; succeeded by the will of his godfather Thomas-Peckham Phipps, Esq. of Littlegreen, to his estates in Sussex. He has issue,

I. PHIPPS-JOHN, capt. royal engineers, *b.* 20 April, 1820; *m.* 7 March, 1844, Frederica, dau. of Capt. Briton; and *d.* 8 April, 1848, leaving two daus.
II. Geoffrey-Thomas-Phipps, capt. R.N., *b.* 20 Feb. 1825; *m.* 27 April, 1853, Emily-Frances, only dau. of Rev. John Coles, of Ditcham, Hants.
III. James-John, a fellow of University College, Oxford, *b.* 18 Dec. 1826.
I. Caroline-Lucy, *m.* 29 Nov. 1838, to Sir Wm. Denison, R.E., Governor of Van Diemen's Land.
II. Susan-Charlotte-Margaret, *m.* 18 April, 1844, the Rev. William Hornby, of St. Michaels, Lancashire.
III. Maria-Elizabeth.
IV. Lucy-Hester. V. Elizabeth.

Arms—See HORNBY OF DALTON HALL.
Seat—Littlegreen, Sussex.

HORNBY OF RIBBY HALL.

HORNBY, HUGH, Esq. of Ribby Hall, co. Lancaster, *b.* 13 July, 1799; *m.* 7 July, 1836, Anne, dau. of Samuel-Chetham Hilton, Esq., by Martha his wife, dau. of Samuel Clowes, Esq. of Broughton, and has issue,

I. HUGH-HILTON, *b.* 10 Sept. 1838.
I. Margaret-Anne, *b.* 12 June, 1837.

Lineage.—RICHARD HORNBY, of Newton, in the parish of Kirkham, *b.* about 1613; *m.* in 1653, Elizabeth, dau. of Christopher Walmesley, of Elston, and was father of

WILLIAM HORNBY, of Newton, *b.* in 1656; who *m.* 3 Sept. 1681, Isabel Horscarr; and *d.* in 1710, leaving an eldest son,

ROBERT HORNBY, Esq., *b.* in 1690; who *d.* in 1768, leaving, by Elizabeth his wife, three sons, William and Richard, whose lines are extinct; and

HUGH HORNBY, Esq., *b.* in 1719, who settled at Kirkham. He *m.* Margaret, dau. and eventually sole heiress of Joseph Hankinson, of Kirkham, by Alice his wife, dau. of John Sudell, Esq. of Blackburn, and by this lady (who *d.* in Aug. 1804) had issue,

JOSEPH, of whom presently.
Robert, *b.* 18 July, 1750; *d.* in 1776, *unm.*
THOMAS, of Kirkham (*see* HORNBY OF LIVERPOOL).
William, of Kirkham, *b.* in 1761; *d. unm.* in 1824.
JOHN, of Blackburn (*see* HORNBY OF RAIKE'S HALL).
HUGH, in holy orders, M.A. (*see* HORNBY OF ST. MICHAEL'S).
Alice, *m.* to Richard Birley, of Blackburn.
Elizabeth, *d.* in infancy.

Mr. Hornby *d.* in Feb. 1781. His eldest son,

JOSEPH HORNBY, Esq. of Ribby Hall, D.L. for Lancashire, *b.* 22 Sept. 1748; *m.* 16 Aug. 1796, Margaret, dau. of Robert Wilson, of Preston, and by her (who *d.* 26 March, 1838) had issue,

HUGH, his heir, now of Ribby.
Margaret, *m.* to William Langton, Esq. of Manchester.
Alice, *d. unm.*

Mr. Hornby *d.* 19 March, 1832.

Arms—Arg., a chevron, vert, in base, a bugle-horn, stringed, sa., on a chief, of the second, two bugle-horns, of the field.
Crest—A bugle-horn, stringed, sa., and passing through the knot, in fesse, an arrow, point towards the sinister, or.
Motto—Crede cornu.
Seat—Ribby Hall, co. Lancaster.

HORNBY OF LIVERPOOL.

HORNBY, HUGH, Esq. of Sandown, near Liverpool, merchant, J.P., *b.* 26 Dec. 1792; *m.* in 1828, Louise, dau. of Luc François Cortazzi, sometime Venetian Consul at Smyrna, by Elizabeth, his wife, dau. of Anthony Hayes, British Consul at the same place, and has issue,

I. HUGH-FREDERICK, *b.* 4 Jan. 1826.
II. Edward-William, *b.* 21 Oct. 1829.
III. Richard-Cortazzi, *b.* 3 May, 1839.
I. Louise-Elizabeth, *m.* 30 March, 1848, to Benjamin-Heywood, 2nd son of Hugh Jones, Esq. of Larkhill, co. Lancaster.
II. Helen-Cicely, *d.* in 1838.
III. Marianne, *d.* in 1833. IV. Matilda-Theresa.
V. Helen-Cicely. VI. Mary-Jane.

Lineage.—THOMAS HORNBY, of Kirkham, the 3rd surviving son of Hugh Hornby, of Kirkham (*see preceding article*), *b.* 16 July, 1759; *m.* 15 May, 1786, Cicely, dau. of Thomas Langton, of Kirkham. He *d.* 31 March, 1824; and his widow in 1838. Besides several children, who *d.* in infancy, they left issue,

I. HUGH, the present representative of this branch of the family.
II. Joseph, of Liverpool, *b.* 19 April, 1794; *m.* 18 Jan. 1821, Elizabeth-Baldwin, dau. of Thomas-Fournis Dyson, of Liverpool, and of Willow Hall, near Halifax, by his wife, Anne Baldwin, dau. of Richard Sealy, of Lisbon; and *d.* 28 May, 1853, having had issue,
1 Thomas-Dyson, *b.* 1 Feb. 1822.
2 William, *b.* 6 July, 1823; *d.* 6 Jan. 1824.
3 William-Joseph, *b.* 6 June, 1827; *d.* 18 Jan. 1842.
4 Henry-Hugh, *b.* 30 Nov. 1821; *m.* 31 July, 1856, Sophia, 5th dau. of Thomas Haigh, Esq. of Elm Hall, Liverpool.
5 Charles-Edward, *b.* 20 Oct. 1833.
6 Richard-Dyson, *b.* 29 Nov. 1836; *d.* 10 Jan. 1837.
1 Anne-Mary. 2 Harriet-Elizabeth.
III. Thomas, in holy orders, M.A., *b.* 10 Nov. 1801; *m.* 8 May, 1832, Margaret, dau. of William Rigby, of Liverpool, by Alice, dau. of James Rigg, of the same place. Their issue are,
1 Edmund, *b.* 11 May, 1837; *d.* in the same year.
1 Emily. 2 Mary-Louisa.
3 Edith-Agnes. 4 Frances-Margaret.
IV. Hankinson, *b.* 21 May, 1803.
I. Jane, *m.* Joseph Birley, Esq. of Fordbank, near Manchester, who *d.* 24 Jan. 1847. She *d.* 16 Feb. 1856.
II. Margaret.
III. Elizabeth, *d. unm.* in 1832.
IV. Cicely, *m.* to Hugh-Hornby Birley, of Manchester; and *d.* 15 Jan. 1843.
V. Marianne, *m.* to John, 3rd son of L.-F. Cortazzi.

Arms, Crest, and Motto—See HORNBY OF RIBBY HALL.

HORNBY OF RAIKES HALL.

HORNBY, DANIEL, Esq. of Raikes Hall, co. Lancaster, *b.* 28 June, 1800; *m.* Frances, dau. of John Birley, by his wife Margaret, dau. of Daniel Backhouse, of Liverpool, and has issue,

FANNY-BACKHOUSE.

Lineage.—JOHN HORNBY, of Blackburn and of Raikes Hall, 5th surviving son of Hugh Hornby, of Kirkham, (*see* HORNBY *of Ribby Hall*,) *b.* 2 July, 1763, *m.* Alice Kendall, widow, dau. of Daniel Backhouse, of Liverpool, and by her (who d. 8 Dec. 1827) had issue, beside children who d. in infancy,

I. DANIEL, the present representative of this branch of the family.
II. Robert, in holy orders, J.P., incumbent of Walton-le Dale, b. 20 June, 1804, m. 22 June, 1830, Maria-Leyland, dau. of Sir William Feilden, Bart., M.P., by his wife, Mary-Haughton, dau. of Edmund Jackson, of the Island of Jamaica. They have issue,

1 Robert-Montague, b. 23 April, 1835.
2 William-St. John-Sumner, b. 31 Aug. 1836.
3 Leyland, b. 18 Jan. 1845.
4 Frederick-Feilden, b. 25 April, 1846.
1 Maria-Catherine. 2 Georgiana. 3 Alice.
4 Mary-Letitia. 5 Frances-Harriet.
6 Mary-Eliza. 7 Emily-Caroline.
8 Elizabeth-Haughton.

III. William-Henry, of Blackburn, J.P., b. 2 July, 1805, m. 19 May, 1831, Margaret-Susannah, dau. and sole heir of Edward Birley, of Kirkham, and has had issue,

1 John, b. 2 Dec. 1832.
2 Edward-Kenworthy, b. 16 June, 1839.
3 Henry-Sudell, b. 4 July, 1840, d. in the same year.
4 William-Henry, b. 29 Aug. 1841.
5 Cecil-Lumsden, b. 25 July, 1843.
6 Albert-Neilson, b. 10 Feb. 1847.
1 Elizabeth-Henriana. 2 Frances-Mary.
3 Augusta-Margaret. 4 Caroline-Louisa.

IV. John, M.P. for Blackburn, b. 19 Aug. 1810, m. Margaret, dau. of the Rev. Christopher Bird, vicar of Chollerton, in co. Northumberland, and has issue,

1 John-Frederick, b. 1 June, 1846.

Mr. Hornby d. 29 Jan. 1841.

Arms, Crest, and *Motto*—*See* HORNBY *of Ribby Hall.*

HORNBY OF ST. MICHAEL'S.

HORNBY, REV. WILLIAM, M.A., vicar of St. Michael's, co. Lancaster, b. 26 Feb. 1810: m. 17 Jan. 1837, Ellen, dau. of William Cross, of Redscar, by Ellen his wife, dau. of Edward Chaffers, of Liverpool, and by her (who d. 15 March, 1840) had issue,

I. William-Hugh, b. 1 June, 1838, d. 22 Nov. 1842.
II. STARKY, b. 12 July, 1839.

He m. 2ndly, 18 April, 1844, Susan-Charlotte, dau. of Admiral Sir Phipps Hornby, K.C.B., by Maria-Sophia, his wife, dau. of General Burgoyne, and has issue,

I. William, b. 15 Oct. 1845.

Lineage.—THE REV. HUGH HORNBY, M.A., vicar of St. Michael's, youngest son of Hugh Hornby, of Kirkham, (*see* HORNBY *of Ribby Hall*,) b. 22 Aug. 1765, m. 9 Aug. 1792, Ann, dau and co-heir of Joseph Starky, M.D. of Redvales, by Elizabeth, his wife, and d. 3 Jan. 1817, leaving a son, WILLIAM, the present representative of this branch of the family, and Elizabeth, d. *unm.*

Arms, Crest, and *Motto*—*See* HORNBY *of Ribby Hall.*

HORNER OF MELLS PARK.

HORNER, THE REV. JOHN-STUART-HIPPISLEY, M.A. of Mells Park, co. Somerset, prebendary of Wells, and rector of Mells, b. 9 Oct. 1810; m. 22 Sept. 1840, Sophia-Gertrude, eldest dau. of the late William Dickinson, Esq., M.P., and has issue,

I. JOHN-FRANCIS-FORTESCUE, b. 23 Dec. 1842.
II. George-William, } b. 10 June, 1849.
III. Maurice, }
IV. John-Stuart, b. 30 Sept. 1855.
I. Elizabeth-Gertrude. II. Margaret-Maria.
III. Caroline-Sophia. IV. Muriel.

Lineage.—JOHN HORNER, steward to the Abbot of Glastonbury at the Dissolution of the Monasteries, m. and left a dau., Anne, wife of Thomas Bamfylde, and two sons, JOHN, of whose line we treat, and Thomas, living at Cloford, 1540. The elder son,

JOHN HORNER, left by Elizabeth, his wife, two sons, JOHN, his heir; and George, of Leigh, who d. 1570, leaving issue. The elder son,

SIR JOHN HORNER, Knt., who settled at Mells, co. Somerset, and served as high-sheriff in 1564 and 1573. An old local distich records that—

"Horner, Popham, Wyndham, and Thynne,
When the abbot came out, then they came in."

Sir John m. Mary A'Holt, widow, heiress of John Matte, tailor to King HENRY VIII., and d. 1587, leaving THOMAS, his heir; Dorothy, m. to John Hippisley, Esq. of Cameley; Joane, b. 1561, m. about 1593, to Bishop Still, and other issue. The son and heir,

THOMAS HORNER, Esq. of Mells Park, b. 1547, M P. for Somersetshire 1585, and high-sheriff 1607, m. 1st, Elizabeth Pollard; 2ndly, Jane, dau. of Sir John Popham, Knt. of Littlecott, Wilts; and 3rdly, Elizabeth . . . . . . By his 2nd wife, Jane Popham, who d. 1591, he left at his decease, in 1612, an eldest son and heir,

SIR JOHN HORNER, Knt. of Mells, M.P. for Dorsetshire, b. about 1580, a devoted Royalist, who was honoured with a visit by King CHARLES I., in July, 1644. He m. Anne, dau. of Sir George Speke, of White Lackington, and by her, who d. 1666, left at his decease, in 1659, with other issue, a dau., Anne, m. 1662 to John Harrington, Esq., and a son and heir,

SIR GEORGE HORNER, Knt. of Mells, b. 1604, M.P. from 1642 to 1660, who m. Anne, dau. of Sir Henry Pool, and had GEORGE, his heir; Anne, m. to Baldwin Malet, Esq.; Francis, m. to Thomas Bere, Esq., Jun. of Huntsham, Devon, and other issue. The son and heir,

GEORGE HORNER, Esq. of Mells, b. 1646, M.P. from 1685 to 1688, m. Elizabeth, dau. and co-heir of Col. Robert Fortescue, of Filleigh, and by her (who d. in 1693) had, with junior issue,

I. THOMAS, of Mells Park, b. 1688, m. Susannah, dau. and co-heir of Thomas Strangways, Esq. of Melbury, co. Dorset, and d. 1741, leaving issue,

Thomas Strangways, of Melbury, co. Dorset, who d. s. p.
Elizabeth, eventually sole heiress, m. to Sir Stephen Fox, 1st EARL OF ILCHESTER.

II. JOHN, of whose line we treat.

The second son,

JOHN HORNER, Esq, b. 1689, m. Ann, dau. of Edward Philipps, Esq. of Preston Plucknett, and dying 1746, left, with other issue, a son and heir,

THOMAS HORNER, Esq. of Mells Park, b. 1737, m. 1759, Elizabeth, dau. of the Rev. Thomas Paget, (*see* PAGET *of Cranmore Hall*,) and by her (who d. 1802) left at his decease, in 1804, a dau., Elizabeth-Anne, m. 1st, to Henry-Hippisley Coxe, Esq.; and 2ndly, to Sir J.-Coxe Hippisley, Bart.; and a son,

THOMAS-STRANGWAYS HORNER, Esq. of Mells Park, who m. 6 July, 1805, Margaret-Frances, dau. of Sir John-Coxe Hippisley, Bart., and had issue,

THOMAS-STRANGWAYS, d. in 1843.
JOHN-STUART-HIPPISLEY, now of Mells Park.
George-Charles-Boyle, d. 1820.
William-Windham, d. 1855. Charles-Edward-Boyle.
Elizabeth-Margaret-Maria. Margaret-Frances-Lilias.
Louisa-Mary, d. 1828. Isabella-Harriet, d. 1820.

Mr. Horner d. 1844.

Arms (Granted 1584)—Sa., three talbots, passant, arg.
Crest—A talbot, sejant, arg., collared and lined, or.
Seat—Mells Park, co. Somerset.

HORNOR OF THE HOWE.

HORNOR, EDWARD, Esq. of the Howe, Essex, J.P., b. 3 June, 1811; m. 24 Aug. 1842, Anne, dau. of Robert Moline, merchant, of Stone House, Kent, and has issue,

I. FRANCIS-BIRKBECK, b. July 2, 1843.
II. Lewis, b. March 5, 1845.
III. Allan-Moline, b. Jan. 10, 1848.
IV. Charles-Ernest, b. Dec. 23, 1849.
I. Alice. II. Edith-Anne. III. Florence.

Mr. Edward Hornor, and his brother Charles-Birkbeck Hornor are the sons of Benjamin Hornor by Alice Birkbeck his wife, sister of the celebrated Dr. Birkbeck, and grandsons of Edward Hornor, by Jane Emson his wife.

Arms—Or, three talbots, passant, sa.
Crest—A talbot, sejant, collared and lined, or.
Seat—The Howe, near Halstead.

HORNYOLD OF BLACKMORE.

HORNYOLD, THOMAS-CHARLES, Esq. of Blackmore Park and Hanley Castle, co. Worcester, J.P. and

D.L., *b.* 29 Jan. 1791; *m.* 1st, in Oct. 1812, Bridget-Mary, dau. of John-Webb Weston, Esq. of Sutton Place, co. Surrey; she *d.* in 1827. He *m.* 2ndly, in May, 1828, Lucy, eldest dau. of William Saunders, Esq. of Worcester, and grandniece of Arthur, 1st Earl of Mountnorris.

Lineage.—The Hornyolds, or, as their name was originally written, Horniold, possessed lands in Hanley Castle, *temp.* HENRY III.

THOMAS HORNYOLD, Esq. of Hanley Castle, son of JOHN HORNYOLD (killed at Worcester), and grandson of Ralph Hornyold, Esq., was a great sufferer for his attachment to the royal cause, *temp.* CHARLES I. He *m.* 1st, Margaret, dau. of Robert Gower, Esq. of Colemers, and 2ndly, Frances, dau. of J. Skynner. By the former he had a son,

ROBERT HORNYOLD, Esq. of Hanley Castle, who *d.* in 1712, and was buried at Hanley, leaving, by Bridget, his wife, dau. of Anthony Windsor, Esq., a son,

JOHN HORNYOLD, Esq. of Hanley Castle, who *m.* Mary, eldest dau. of Sir Piers Mostyn, Bart. of Talacre, co. Flint, by Frances, his wife, dau. and co-heir of Sir George Selby, and *d.* in 1771, when he was *s.* by his son,

THOMAS HORNYOLD, Esq. of Blackmore Park, who *m.* Mary-Catherine, *b.* in 1721, only dau. of Richard Towneley, Esq. of Towneley, by Mary, his wife, dau. of William, Lord Widdrington, and by her, who *d.* in 1762, had issue, a dau. Bridget, and two sons, THOMAS and CHARLES. The elder son and heir,

THOMAS HORNYOLD, Esq. of Blackmore Park, *m.* Teresa, dau. of Thomas Fitzherbert, Esq. of Swinnerton Hall, co. Stafford, and by her, who *d.* in 1815, had issue,

- THOMAS-CHARLES, of Blackmore Park.
- Teresa, *m.* to John-Vincent Gandolfi, Esq. of East Sheen, co. Middlesex.
- Maria, a nun.

Mr. Hornyold *d.* in 1813.

Arms—Az., on a bend, embattled, arg., a greyhound, courant, between two escallops, sa.

Crest—A demi-unicorn, gu., crined and armed, or.

Seats—Blackmore Park and Hanley Castle, co. Worcester.

HORTON OF HOWROYDE.

HORTON, JOSHUA-THOMAS, Esq. of Howroyde, co. York, *b.* 10 May, 1836.

Lineage.—The antiquity of the family of HORTON is established by the fact, that one ROBERT DE HORTON manumitted a bondman to his manor of Horton long before the time of Henry Lacy, Earl of Lincoln, who *d.* in 1310; it is also ascertained that the Hortons had a manor house in Great Horton, with a mill and certain demesne lands thereunto belonging, at a very remote period.

JOSHUA HORTON, Esq. of Sowerby, J.P., *b.* in 1619 (the 3rd son of William Horton, Esq. of Frith House, in Barkisland, and brother of William Horton, Esq. of Barkisland Hall, who purchased HOWROYDE), bought the manor of Horton, in Bradforddale, Stansfield Hall, &c. He *m.* Martha, dau. and co-heir of Thomas Binns, Esq. of Rushworth, and by her (who *d.* in 1694) had issue. Mr. Horton *d.* in 1679, and was *s.* by his eldest son,

JOSHUA HORTON, Esq. of Sowerby, *b.* 22 Jan. 1657, who purchased, and resided at, Chadderton. He *m.* in 1678, Mary, dau. of Robert Gregg, Esq. of Bradley, and had thirteen children. Mr. Horton *d.* 15 Dec. 1708. The eldest son and heir,

THOMAS HORTON, Esq. of Chadderton, *b.* 4 May, 1685, J.P., governor of the Isle of Man for the Earl of Derby; *m.* Anne, dau. and co-heir of Richard Mostyn, Esq. of London (a younger branch of the Mostyns of Mostyn), and by her (who *d.* in 1725) had issue,

- I. WILLIAM (Sir), his successor, at Chadderton, created a Baronet, 14 Jan. 1764. His male issue is *extinct*.
- II. Thomas, *d.* young.
- III. THOMAS-JOSHUA, of whom presently.
- I. Mary. II. Anne. III. Jane.
- IV. Susannah, *m.* to George Lloyd, Esq. of Hulme Hall, near Manchester, and *d.* 16 March, 1797.
- V. Sarah.

The 3rd son,

THOMAS-JOSHUA HORTON, Esq. of Howroyde, *b.* in 1720; *m.* 1st, Anne, dau. of George Clarke, Esq., lieut.-governor of New York, but had no issue. He *m.* 2ndly, in 1765, Mary-Bethia, dau. of the Rev. John Woollin, rector of Emley, co. York, and vicar of Blackburn, co. York, and by her, who *d.* 8 Feb. 1806, had,

- THOMAS, his successor.
- Joshua-Sidney, *b.* 7 March, 1768, admiral R.N.; who *m.* Grace, dau. of — Treacher, Esq., and relict of Henry Whorwood, Esq., and *d.* 24 Nov. 1835, leaving two sons and a dau., viz., Sidney-Lloyd, William, and Mary-Emily.
- William, in holy orders, vicar of St. Mary's, Rochdale, *b.* 5 May, 1769; who *m.* 7 Nov. 1793, Elizabeth, dau. of John Lyon, Esq., M.D., of Liverpool, and left at his decease a son, Richard-George, of Leeds, who *m.* 3 April, 1828, Emily Boulton, and had three daus., viz., Mary-Anne; Charlotte, *m.* in 1830, to Stephen Davy, Esq. of Redruth, Cornwall; and Elizabeth-Maria.
- Richard-Henry, a lieut.-col. in the army, *d. unm.*
- Anna-Maria, Jane, } both *d. unm.*
- Charlotte, *m.* to the Rev. William Richardson, of Ferrybridge, in Yorkshire, and has issue.
- Frances, *m.* twice, 1st, to Major Richard-Henry Horton, of the 84th regt., who *d.* in 1813.
- Harriett.

Mr. Horton was *s.* at his decease, in 1793, by his eldest son,

THOMAS HORTON, Esq. of Howroyde, J.P. and D.L., *b.* 26 Aug. 1766; who *m.* March, 1789, the Lady Mary Gordon, youngest dau. of George, 3rd Earl of Aberdeen, and had issue,

- JOSHUA-THOMAS, in holy orders, his heir.
- George-William, lieut.-col. in the army, who *m.* in 1826, Frances-Esther, 2nd dau. of the Rev. William Garnier, of Rookesbury, co. Hants, by whom he had issue, George-William, William-Thomas, Henry, Harriet-Mary, Frances-Elizabeth, and Lucy.
- Mary, *m.* in 1816, to Francis-Beynon Hacket, Esq. of Moor Hall, co. Warwick, and has issue.

Mr. Horton *d.* in 1828, and was *s.* by his elder son,

THE REV. JOSHUA-THOMAS HORTON, of Howroyde, vicar of Ormskirk, co. Lancaster, J.P. and D.L., *b.* in 1791; *m.* 6 Nov. 1832, Harriet, eldest dau. of Sir Thomas-Dalrymple Hesketh, Bart. of Rufford Hall, and by her who *d.* 10 May, 1836, had issue one son,

JOSHUA-THOMAS, now of Howroyde.

Mr. Horton *d.* Nov. 1845.

Arms—Gu., a lion, rampant, arg., charged on the shoulder with a boar's head, couped, az., within a bordure, engrailed, of the second.

Crest—A red rose, seeded, barbed, and surrounded by two laurel branches, ppr.

Motto—Pro rege et lege.

Seat—Howroyde, near Halifax.

HOSKEN OF ELLENGLAZE.

HOSKEN, JAMES-THEODORE, Esq. of Ellenglaze, co. Cornwall, *b.* 15 Dec. 1838.

Lineage.—The HOSKENS have been respectable landowners in the county of Cornwall for a series of years. They were formerely seated at the Barton of Hoskens, in the parish of St. Enedor, whence they removed, in the 16th century, to Hendra Green, in the parish of St. Stephen's, near Launceston.

JOHN HOSKEN, Esq., the lineal descendant and representative of the family, was buried in the parish church of St. Stephen's, 9 Jan. 1742. By his wife, Jane (dau. of — Hosken, Esq. of Eglaskerry), he left several children. The eldest son,

RICHARD HOSKEN, Esq., *b.* in 1708; *m.* in 1732, Edith, eldest dau. of John Edgecombe, Esq. of Cargantle, in Cornwall (of the noble family of Edgecumbe of Mount Edgecumbe), and was *s.* by his only son,

JOHN HOSKEN, Esq., *b.* in 1744; who *m.* in 1770, Johanna, dau. of John Hutchings, of Woodcotte, co. Devon, by his wife, Joan Gay (of an ancient family in the parish of Black Torrington, related to the poet Gay). In 1780, upon the demise of his cousin, Joseph Hosken, Esq. of Carines, in the parish of Cubert, he removed to that place. Mr. Hosken *d.* 12 April, 1810, leaving three sons and two daus., viz.,

- JOSEPH, his heir.
- JOHN, of Davenham Hall, Cheshire, *b.* 17 Nov. 1782; *m.* 18 Dec. 1809, Anne, dau. of William Harper, Esq. of Everton, near Liverpool, and assumed, in compliance with that gentleman's will, the surname of HARPER, in 1815. He had issue a son, William, *b.* 23 July, 1814, and three daus., Helen, Maria, and Emily-Anne.
- Richard, *b.* in 1784, who *m.* Anne, widow of John Furniss, Esq. of Lamellen, Cornwall; their dau., Maria, *m.* 15 Jan.

1835, the Rev. S.-M. Walker, M.A., vicar of St. Enodor, son of Lieut.-Gen. Walker.
Jane, m. to John James, Esq. of Truro.
Maria, m. to H.-P. Andrew, Esq.

The son and heir,

JOSEPH HOSKEN, Esq. of Carines, and Ellenglaze, b. 20 Nov. 1778, J.P. and D.L.; m. 28 June, 1796, Jean, only dau. of James Harvey, Esq., alderman, and twice mayor of Bristol, and d. 1833, having had issue,

JAMES-HARVEY, his heir. John, b. 17 May, 1808.
Richard Finlay, b. 17 Sept. 1811, m. Frances, dau. of — Booth, Esq.
Charles-Henry, b. 18 Dec. 1814, in holy orders; m. Lætitia, widow of Edward James, Esq., lieut. H.E.I.C.S.

The eldest son,

JAMES-HARVEY HOSKEN, Esq. of Ellenglaze, b. 21 Nov. 1808; m. 5 Aug. 1834, Caroline, youngest dau. of Lieut.-Col. Sandys, of Lanarth, Cornwall, and by her, who m. 2ndly, 7 Dec. 1843, the Rev. J.-George Venables, M.A., left at his decease, 9 May, 1839, an only child, the present JAMES-THEODORE HOSKEN, Esq. of Ellenglaze.

Arms—Per pale, gu. and az., a chev., or, charged with three cinquefoils, between as many lions, passant, arg.
Motto—Vis unita fortior.
Seat—Ellenglaze, Cornwall.

HOSKINS OF HIGHAM.

HOSKINS, THOMAS-ALISON, Esq. of Higham, co. Cumberland, J.P. and D.L., high-sheriff, 1854, b. 29 March, 1800; m. 16 Oct. 1827, Sarah, dau. of Thomas Irwin, Esq. of Justicetown, and sister of Thomas Irwin, Esq. of Calder Abbey, Cumberland, and has issue,

I. GEORGE-RICHARD, b. 26 Sept. 1828.
II. Thomas-Alison, b. 19 Dec. 1829.
III. William-Senhouse, b. 18 Dec. 1833, d. 1850.
IV. Louis-Irwin, b. Nov. 1835.
V. Reginald, b. 20 Oct. 1837.
I. Mary. II. Ellen. III. Sarah, deceased.

Lineage.—ALEXANDER HOSKINS, Esq. b. at Moor Park, Hertfordshire, Aug. 1722, descended from the family of HOSKINS *of Barrow Green, Oxted, Surrey*, was great-grandson of Sir William Hoskins, knight-banneret of Youghal, who escaped from the Irish massacre in 1641. Alexander Hoskins, Esq., settled at Great Broughton, Cumberland, in 1748, and was for many years chairman of the quarter-sessions. He d. in 1800. His youngest son, GEORGE HOSKINS, Esq., m. Mary Alison, of Liverpool, and left issue the present THOMAS-ALISON HOSKINS, Esq. of Higham; George-Alexander, of Gloucester Square, London, who m. in 1843, Mary Thornton; and Mary-Anne Hoskins.

Arms—per pale, gu. and az., a chev., engr., or, between three lions, rampant, arg.
Crest—A cock's head, erased, or, pellettée, combed and wattled, gu., between two wings, expanded, of the first.
Motto—Virtute non verbis.
Seat—Higham, near Cockermouth.

HOSKYNS OF WROXHALL ABBEY.

WREN HOSKYNS, CHANDOS, Esq. of Wroxhall Abbey, co. Warwick, J.P. and D.L., high-sheriff 1855, b. 15 Feb. 1812; m. 1st, 20 April, 1837, Theodosia-Anne-Martha, dau. and heir of the late Christopher-Roberts Wren, Esq. of Wroxhall Abbey, and has issue one dau.,

CATHERINE.

He m. 2ndly, 6 July, 1846, Anna-Fane, youngest dau. of Charles Milner Ricketts, Esq. late First member of the Supreme Council of Bengal, and has by her,

1. HUNGERFORD-CHANDOS, b. 12 Sept. 1852.
1. Clara-Amelia.

Mr. Wren Hoskyns, who is second son of the present Sir Hungerford Hoskyns, Bart. of Harewood, co. Hereford, assumed, by sign-manual, the additional surname and arms of WREN on his marriage with the heiress of Wroxhall, which estate he then acquired.

Lineage.—For HOSKYNS, see BURKE'S *Peerage and Baronetage*.

Family of Wren.

CHRISTOPHER WREN, Esq., son (by his 1st wife, Faith, dau. of Sir Thomas Coghill) of SIR CHRISTOPHER WREN, Knt, the celebrated architect, (who was born 10 Oct. 1632, the son of the rector of East Knoyle, Wilts, and who d. 25 Feb. 1723,) m. 1st, Mary, dau. of Philip Musard, Esq. of London, and had a son, CHRISTOPHER, of whom presently. He m. 2ndly, Constance, dau. of Sir Thomas Middleton, Bart., and relict of Sir Roger Burgoyne, Bart., and by her had one son, Stephen. The elder son,

CHRISTOPHER WREN, Esq. of Wroxhall, m. Mary, dau. of Bartlett, Esq., and had, with two daus., (Harriet, m. to Clement Newsam, Esq., and Sarah, m. to James West, Esq. of Alscot Park, co. Gloucester,) a son and heir,

CHRISTOPHER WREN, Esq. of Wroxhall, who m. Martha, dau. of David Roberts, Esq. of Kinmell, co. Denbigh, and had, with a dau., (Martha, m. to Thomas Day, Esq. E.I. Co.'s service), a son and heir,

CHRISTOPHER-ROBERTS WREN, Esq. of Wroxhall Abbey, b. 13 Sept. 1775, who m. 4 April, 1815, Anne, dau. of Thomas Biggs, Esq. of Pedmore, co. Worcester, and d. 4 March, 1828, leaving an only dau. and heiress, THEODOSIA-ANNE-MARTHA, who m. CHANDOS HOSKYNS, Esq., as stated above.

Arms—Quarterly: 1st and 4th, per pale, az. and gu., a chev. between three lions, rampant, or, for HOSKYNS; 2nd and 3rd, arg., a chev. between three lions' heads, erased, az., on a chief, gu., three crosses-crosslet, or, cantoned, of the first, for WREN.
Crests—1st, Out of a ducal coronet, a lion's head, erased, or, flames of fire issuing from the mouth, ppr., crowned, of the first, for HOSKYNS; 2ndly, a lion's head, erased, arg., collared, gu., pierced through the neck by a broken spear, or, the head towards the sinister, of the first, vulned of the second, for WREN.
Mottoes—For HOSKYNS, Vincula da linguæ, vel tibi lingua dabit. For WREN, (ancient,) Numero pondere et mensura; (modern,) Virtuti fortuna comes.
Seat—Wroxhall Abbey, co. Warwick.

HOSTE OF BARWICK HOUSE.

HOSTE, DERICK, Esq. of Barwick House, co. Norfolk, J.P. and D.L., b. 2 Jan. 1799; m. 30 Oct. 1828, his cousin, Anne, dau. of the Rev. Dixon Hoste, and youngest sister of the late Sir William Hoste, Bart., and dying 24 Nov. 1847, left two daus.,

I. SOPHIA-MARGARET, present possessor of Barwick House.
II. Elizabeth-Marianne.

Lineage.—WILLIAM HOSTE, Esq., younger son of Theodore Hoste, Esq., by Mary Helmore, his wife, grandson of James Hoste, Esq., by Elizabeth, his wife, dau. of Sir Edward Walpole, K.B., and uncle of Sir William Hoste, Bart., m. 31 Dec. 1787, Anne, only child and heir of Robert Glover, Esq. of Barwick, and d. in 1834, and was s. by his only son, the late DERICK HOSTE, Esq. of Barwick House.

Arms—Az., a bull's head, cabossed, couped at the neck, arg., between two wings, or, quartering GLOVER, sa., a fess, embattled, erm., betw. three crescents, arg.
Crest—Two wings, addorsed, or.
Seat—Barwick House, near Docking.

HOUBLON OF HALLINGBURY.

HOUBLON, JOHN-ARCHER, Esq. of Hallingbury Place, co. Essex, and Culverthorpe, co. Lincoln, J.P. and D.L., col. of the Essex militia, m. in 1828, Anne, dau. of Vice-Admiral Sir James Whitley-Deans Dundas, G.C.B., of Barton Court, Berks, and grand-dau. of the late Lord Amesbury.

Lineage.—JAMES HOUBLON, Esq. of London, merchant, who m. Mary Ducane, had, with other issue,

CHARLES, his heir.
James, Sir, M.P. for the city of London, m. [illegible], Sarah, dau. of Charles Wynne, Esq., and had a dau. ELIZABETH, m. to John Harvey, Esq. of Norwich.
John, Sir, first governor of the Bank of England, and mayor of London in 1695, and one of the [illegible] of the Admiralty, m. Mary Jurion, of London, and had, with a dau., ARABELLA, m. to Richard [illegible], Esq. of Hanson, co. Salop, a son, THE REV. [illegible], rector of Moreton, in Essex, who m. Elizabeth, only dau. and heir of the Rev. Thomas W[illegible], and had issue, Anne, m. to the Rev. Lilly Butler, D.D., [illegible]

St. Anne's, London; and Elizabeth, m. to the Rev. Thomas Wragge, M.A.
Jacob, in holy orders, rector of Bobbingworth, d. unm.

The eldest son,

CHARLES HOUBLON, Esq., m. Mary, dau. of Daniel Bates, Esq. of Abingdon, and had issue, JACOB; John, barrister-at-law; and Lætitia. The elder son,

JACOB HOUBLON, Esq. m. Mary, only dau. of Sir John-Hynde Cotton, Bart., by Lettice his first wife, dau. of Sir Ambrose Crawley, Knt. of Greenwich, and had issue, a dau. and two sons. The elder son and heir,

JACOB HOUBLON, Esq., m. Susannah, dau. and heir of John Archer, Esq. of Coopersale, co. Essex, by Mary his wife, dau. of John, 2nd Earl Fitzwilliam, and by her had, with two daus., Maria and Letitia, an only son,

JOHN-ARCHER HOUBLON, Esq. of Hallinbury, co. Essex, and Welford, Berks, M.P. for the former county, who m. Mary-Ann, dau. of Thomas Bramston, of Skreens, co. Essex, and had issue,

I. JOHN-ARCHER, his heir.
II. Charles, who assumed the surname of EYRE, in lieu of his patronymic, on succeeding his father in the estates of Welford, Berks. (*See* EYRE, *of Welford*).
III. Thomas-Archer, m. in July, 1839, Eleanor, dau. of the Rev. John Deedes, of Willingale, Essex.
IV. Richard-Archer. V. Frederick-Archer.
I. Susannah-Letitia. II. Mary-Ann.
III. Harriet.

Mr. Houldon d. in 1831, and was s. at Hallinbury, by his eldest son, the present JOHN ARCHER HOUBLON, Esq. of that place.

Arms—Quarterly: 1st and 4th, HOUBLON, arg., the base, vert, issuing therefrom three hop-poles, sustaining their fruit, all ppr; 2nd and 3rd, quarterly; 1st and 4th, erm., a cross, sa., for ARCHER; 2nd and 3rd, arg., on a chev., sa., three quatrefoils, or, for EYRE.
Crests—A lion's head, erased, or, for HOUBLON; a wyvern, arg., for ARCHER; a leg, in armour, couped at the thigh, ppr., garnished and spurred, or, for EYRE.
Seats—Hallingbury Place, co. Essex, and Culverthorpe, co. Lincoln.

HOUGHTON OF KILMANOCK HOUSE.

HOUGHTON, GEORGE-POWELL, of Kilmanock House, co. Wexford, J.P. and D.L., sheriff in 1839, b. 15 June, 1813; m. 25 April, 1833, Anne-Coote, dau. of John Greene, Esq. of Greenville, co. Kilkenny, by Anne-Coote his wife, dau. of John Knox-Grogan, Esq. of Johnstown Castle, Wexford, and has had issue,

I. GEORGE-POWELL, lieut. 11th hussars, who d. at Scutari from the effects of a wound received at Balaclava, 22 Nov. 1854.
I. Anne-Coote. II. Anna-Maria-Alicia.
III. Charlotte.

Lineage.—THOMAS HOUGHTON, who is stated to have been son of Sir Richard Hoghton of Haughton Tower, co. Lancaster, by Katherine Gerard his wife, settled in Ireland, in 1641. He m. Mary, dau. of Valentine Smyth, of Dama, co. Kilkenny, and by her had issue,

THOMAS, his heir.
Mary, m. to Valentine Savage, of Dublin.

The son and heir,

THOMAS HOUGHTON, of Bally Anne, m. Katherine, dau. of — Lambert, and had,

VALENTINE, of Kilmanock. Henry. John.

HENRY HOUGHTON, Esq., the 2nd son, of New Ross, got a lease of Kilkenny from George Glascott, 1761. He m. Mary, dau. of — Grubb, and was father of,

THOMAS HOUGHTON, Esq. of Kilmanock, who m. Margaret, dau. of Thomas Wyse, of the manor of St. John Waterford, and was father of,

HENRY-THOMAS HOUGHTON, Esq. of Kilmanock, (will dated 10 July, 1798), m. Mary, dau. of Richard Powell, Esq. of New Garden, co. Limerick, and by her had issue,

I. THOMAS-RICHARD, his heir.
II. Henry-George, m. Sarah, dau. of — Jackson, by whom he had issue,
  1 George-Henry, who m. Grace, dau. of Charles Maunsell, Esq., and had two sons and three daus., viz.,
    Henry-George. Charles-Frederick.
    Marion. Anna-Maria. Georgina.
  1 Sarah, wife of the Rev. Matthew Enright.
  2 Phœbe, wife of Samuel Maunsell, Esq.
  3 Maria, wife of Charles Maunsell, Esq.

I. Ellen, m. 20 Dec. 1794, to Col. William Pemberton Pigot, of Slevoy Castle, Wexford.
II. Anne, m. to Col. Goddard Richards, of Bath.
III. Maria, wife of Lewis Thomas, Esq. IV. Charlotte.

The elder son and heir,

THOMAS-RICHARD HOUGHTON, Esq. of Kilmanock, m. July, 1808, Anna-Maria, dau. of Richard Gason, Esq., and d. 22 April, 1824, leaving issue,

I. Henry-Thomas, of Kilmanock, d. April, 1826.
II. GEORGE-POWELL, now of Kilmanock.
III. Alicia-Richarda, m. July, 1833, to Lyon Campbell, Esq.

Mr. Houghton d. 22 April, 1824.

Arms—Sa., three bars, or.
Crest—A bull's head, collared.
Motto—Nobilitat.
Seat—Kilmanock House, co. Wexford.

HOULTON OF FARLEY CASTLE.

HOULTON, JOHN-TORRIANO, Esq. of Farley Castle, co. Somerset, D.L., b. 10 Nov. 1799; m. 3 Jan. 1854, the Baronne Ferdinandine de Fürstenberg, eldest dau. of the Baron de Fürstenberg and the Baronne Marie de Lilien his wife, and has issue,

FRANCIS-FERDINAND, b. 24 Jan. 1856.
Caroline-Mary-Ann.

Lineage.—The ancestors of this family were of Bradford, co. Wilts, in 1598.

JOSEPH HOULTON, Esq. of Trowbridge, Wilts, living 1623; m. Anne, dau. of — Yorke, Esq., recorder, and sometime M.P. for Devizes, and left a son,

JOSEPH HOULTON, Esq. of Trowbridge, high sheriff of Wilts in 1696, who purchased, about the year, 1700, the estate of Farley Hungerford, in Somerset and Wilts, lately belonging to the Hungerford family. He m. 1st, a dau. of Cooper, of Beckington, and had by her a son, JOSEPH, his heir; and 2ndly, Mary Ewer, by whom he had a son, Robert, of Trowbridge, who d. s. p. Mr. Houlton d. in 1720, and was s. by his son,

JOSEPH HOULTON, Esq. of Farley Castle, who m. 1st, Mary, dau. of Nicholas Green, Esq. of Brook, in Wilts, M.P., colonel in the army of the Parliament, and had issue,

I. JOSEPH, his heir.
II. John, of Bristol and of Monckton Combe, who m. Susannah, dau. of William Watts, Esq. of Bristol, and d. in 1767, having had issue,
  1 Joseph, of Trowbridge, who m. Mary, dau. of Philip Gibbs, Esq.; their issue is extinct.
  2 ROBERT, heir to Farley Castle, of whom presently.
  3 Nathaniel, of Bristol, d. s. p. in 1767.
  4 John, of Seagry and Grittleton, rear-adm. R.N., d. unm. in 1791. There is a memoir of him in the *History of Grittleton*, by Rev. J. E. Jackson, published by the Wiltshire Topographical Society, 1843.
III. Nathaniel, of Seagry House, Wilts, which he built, m. Mary, dau. of Francis Newton, Esq. of Taunton, but d. s. p. in 1754.
IV. Robert, of Grittleton, d. s. p. 1771.

Mr. Houlton, m. 2ndly, Priscilla, dau. of Walker White, Esq. of Grittleton, (to which estate she s. as co-heiress on the death of her brother Walter, 1705.) He d. in 1731, and was s. by his son,

JOSEPH HOULTON, Esq. of Farley Castle, and Grittleton, a magistrate for Wilts, and high-sheriff in 1724; who m. Anna, dau. of Abraham Hooke, Esq. of Bristol, and d. in 1750, leaving an only dau. and heir,

Mary, of Farley Castle, who m. 20 Aug. 1746, James Frampton, Esq. of Moreton, in Dorsetshire, high-sheriff of that co. in 1744, but d. s. p. in 1762. The Houlton estate, at Farley, passed, at the decease of Mr. Frampton, in 1784, to

ROBERT HOULTON, Esq. of Farley Castle and Grittleton, son of John and Susannah Houlton. He m. Susannah, dau. of Thomas Tysdale, of The Fort, Bristol, Esq., and dying in 1785, was s. by his son,

JOSEPH HOULTON, Esq. of Farley Castle, a capt. in the army, who m. at Gibralter, Dorothea-Sarah, dau. of Charles Torriano, Esq., capt. R.A., and had issue,

JOHN, his heir.
Robert, of Bath, capt. R.N.
Joseph, lieut. 40th reg. infantry, d. unm. in 1795.
Charles Torriano.
Samuel, capt. 11th reg. of native infantry, d. at Dinapore, E.I. in 1827.

George (Sir) Knt., capt. 43rd regt., ensign of the yeomen of the guard, m. Anna, dau. of John Cruickshank, Esq. of Bath.

Mr. Houlton d. in 1806, and was s. by his son,

JOHN HOULTON, Esq. of Farley Castle and Grittleton, (which latter estate he sold in 1827, to Joseph Neild, Esq.); b. 29 May, 1773; colonel 1st regiment Somerset militia a deputy-lieutenant for that co., high-sheriff of Wilts, 1808; m. 2 Jan. 1799, Mary-Ann, sole dau. and heiress of Thomas Ellis, Esq. of Rollestone, Devon, and had issue,

I. JOHN-TORRIANO, now of Farley Castle.
II. Charles-Gore, in the Bombay Civil Service, d. 1826.
III. George-Frederick, in the civil service of Bengal, m. 6 June, 1837, at Dinapore, Eliza-Anne, dau. of Henry Hart, Esq., M.D. of 31st reg. inf., by whom he had,
1 Ellis Hart Torriano Houlton, b. 12 Aug. 1841.
2 Vivian-M.-T. Houlton, d. at Weston-super-Mare, 23 Sept. 1848, æt. 5.
3 Ella, d. young. 4 Flora, b. 1840.
Mr. G.-F. Houlton d. at Patna, 20 May, 1844.
IV. Arthur, b. 1817.
V. Edward, d. young, at Brussells, 1822, æt. 3.
VI. Edward-Victor-Lewis, b. 1823, some time founder's kin fellow of St. John's Coll., Oxon; Government secretary at Malta.
I. Dorothea-Frances, m. to Henry Shirley, Esq. of Peppingford House, Sussex, d. in 1828.
II. Amelia-Elizabeth Bridgman, m. 1824, to Col. Sir John Morillyon Wilson, C.B. and K.H. of Chelsea College.
III. Isabella-Jane, m. in Jan. 1834, to Quintus Vivian, Esq., then of 8th hussars, some time of Knuston Hall, near Wellingborough.
IV. Eliza, m. to Rev. James Jackson, M.A. of B. N. C., Oxon, eldest son of James Jackson, Esq. of Doncaster, and (1856) vicar of St. Sepulchre's, London.
V. Mary-Ann Maxwell. VI. Ella-Catharine.
VII. Catharine-Ann Murray, m. 1836, to Arthur-W. Ward, eldest son of John Ward, Esq. of Holwood, and Calverley Park, Tunbridge Wells.
VIII. Florentine-Louisa, m. 1839, to Neville Ward, Esq., youngest son of the aforesaid John Ward, Esq.

Lieutenant-Colonel Houlton d. 17 Feb. 1839, and was s. by his eldest son, the present JOHN TORRIANO HOULTON, Esq.

Arms—Arg., on a fess, wavy, between three talbots' heads, erased, az., as many bezants.
Crest—A talbot's head, erased, azure, gorged with a collar, wavy, or, charged with three torteaux.
Motto—Semper fidelis.
Seat—Farley Castle, co. Somerset.

HOUSTOUN OF JOHNSTONE.

HOUSTOUN, LUDOVIC, Esq. of Johnstone Castle, co. Renfrew, J.P. and D.L., b. 10 May, 1780; m. 6 Nov. 1809, Ann, eldest dau. of John Stirling, Esq. of Kippendavie, co. Perth, and by her (who d. 12 July, 1851) had issue,

George, b. 31 July, 1810; D.L., and M.P. for co. Renfrew in two parliaments; d. unm. 14 Sept. 1843.

Lineage.—The family of Houstoun, a very old one in the co. of Renfrew, derive their descent from Hugo de Padvinan, who acquired a grant of land in that shire in the reign of MALCOLM IV. of Scotland. They settled on the lands of Houstoun, in Renfrewshire, and continued there a long line of knights, as Barons of Houstoun. Sir Ludovic Houstoun, of Houstoun, who d. in 1662, had a numerous issue, and one of his younger sons was George, the first of the HOUSTOUNS *of Johnstone*. This

GEORGE HOUSTOUN, Esq., 2nd son of Sir Ludovic Houstoun, of Houstoun, m. Elizabeth, dau. of Alexander Cunninghame, Esq of Craigends, and had one son,

LUDOVIC HOUSTOUN, Esq., who m. Agnes, dau. of Walkinshaw, of Walkinshaw, and had two sons, William; and

LUDOVIC HOUSTOUN, Esq. of Johnstone, who m. Jean Rankine, of Drumdow, co. Ayr, and was father of

GEORGE HOUSTOUN, Esq. of Johnstone, convener of Renfrewshire, who m. 1st, in 1778, Mary, eldest dau. of Colonel William Macdowall, of Garthland, M.P., and by her (who d. 1782), and had issue two sons,

I. LUDOVIC, his heir.
II. William, b. 18 Sept. 1781; m. 8 July, 1845, Marion-Douglas, only surviving dau. of the late Col. Russell, of Woodside; and d. 6 Feb. 1856, leaving issue,
1 GEORGE-LUDOVIC, b. 31 Aug. 1846.
2 William-James, b. 25 Oct. 1848.
1 Mary-Erskine. 2 Anne-Margaret.

He m. 2ndly, in 1805, Anne, dau. of Walkinshaw, of Walkinshaw, but by her (who d. in 1810) he had no issue. Mr. Houstoun d. 1 Jan. 1816, and was s. by his elder son, the present LUDOVIC HOUSTOUN, Esq. of Johnstone Castle.

Arms—Or, a chevron, chequy, az. and arg., between three martlets, sa.
Crest—A sand-glass, ppr.
Motto—In time.
Supporters—Two hinds.
Seat—Johnstone Castle.

HOUSTON OF CONNEYWARREN.

HOUSTOUN, THOMAS, Esq. of Conneywarren, co. Tyrone, high-sheriff of the co. Tyrone in 1839, b. in 1795; m. 1st, Sophia, dau. of Lord Boyne; and 2ndly, in 1832, Charlotte, dau. of Major-General Thomas-Gerard Elrington, by his wife, a dau. of the Very Rev. Robert Burrows, dean of Cork, and has a son,

CLAUDIUS-CRIGAN, b. in 1834.

Lineage.—This family derives from the branch of the ancient Scottish house of Houstoun, which is established in the cos. of Ross and Sutherland. One of its descendants,

THOMAS HOUSTOUN, Esq., adopting the military profession—a profession in which so many of his ancestors had gained distinction—served as major in the 17th regiment, and was killed at the storming of St. Domingo, in 1795-6. He m. 30 July, 1791, Margaret, dau. of Charles Crigan, Esq. of Omagh, co. Tyrone, elder brother of the Right Rev. Claudius Crigan, bishop of Sodor and Man, and by her (who d. in 1826) left a son, the present THOMAS HOUSTOUN, Esq.

Arms, *Crest*—As the preceding.
Seat—Mount Pleasant House, Omagh.

*** Another highly respectable branch of the Houstoun family is established at Belfast.

BLAKISTON-HOUSTON OF ORANGEFIELD AND RODDENS HOUSE.

BLAKISTON-HOUSTON, RICHARD-BAYLY, Esq. of Orangefield and Roddens House, both in co. Down, b. 13 May, 1793; m. 11 July, 1827, Mary-Isabella, dau. of John-Holmes Houston, Esq. of Orangefield, co. Down, and has issue,

I. JOHN-HOUSTON, b. 11 Sept. 1829.
II. Thomas, b. 12 Nov. 1833.
III. Charles-William, b. 11 May, 1836.
I. Anne, m. in 1848, to Matthew Blakiston, Esq. eldest son of John Blakiston, Esq. of Mobberley, co. Chester.

This gentleman who is 5th son of the late Sir Matthew Blakiston, Bart., by Anne his wife, dau. of John Rochfort, Esq. of Clogrenane, co. Carlow, assumed by royal license on the death of his father-in-law, in March, 1843, the surname of HOUSTON, in addition to his patronymic BLAKISTON.

Arms—Quarterly: 1st and 4th, or, a chevron, chequy, sa. and arg., between three martlets, of the second, for HOUSTON; 2nd and 3rd, arg., two bars, and in chief, three cocks statant, gu. for BLAKISTON.
Crests—1st, a sand glass, ppr.; 2nd, a cock, statant, gu.
Motto—Over the first Crest, "Time;" under the Arms, "Do well and doubt not."
Seats—Orangefield, and Rodden's House, co. Down.

HOWARD OF GREYSTOKE.

HOWARD, HENRY, Esq. of Greystoke Castle, co. Cumberland, and Thornbury Castle, co. Gloucester, J.P. and D.L., high-sheriff of Cumberland, 1834, M.P. for Steyning 1824, and for Shoreham from 1826 to 1832, b. 25 July, 1802; m. 6 Dec. 1849, Charlotte-Caroline-Georgiana, eldest dau. of Henry-Lawes Long, Esq. of Hampton Lodge, Surrey, by the Lady Catharine his wife, sister of Horatio, 3rd Earl of Orford, and has issue,

I. HENRY-CHARLES, b. 17 Sept. 1850.
II. Edward-Stafford, b. 28 Nov. 1851.
III. Robert-Mowbray, b. 23 May, 1854.
I. Elizabeth-Catherine.

Mr. Henry Howard s. his father 17 June, 1824.

Lineage.—LORD HENRY-THOMAS HOWARD-MOLYNEUX-HOWARD, *b.* 7 Oct. 1766, 2nd son of HENRY HOWARD, Esq. of Glossop, co. Derby, by Juliana his wife, 2nd dau. of Sir William Molyneux, Bart., and younger brother of BERNARD-EDWARD, late DUKE OF NORFOLK, was advanced to the precedency of a duke's younger son, in 1817. He *m.* 12 Sept. 1801, Elizabeth, 3rd dau. of Edward Long, Esq., chief-justice of the Vice-Admiralty Court, Jamaica, and by her (who *d.* 24 May, 1834) had issue,

HENRY, his heir, now of Greystoke.
Henrietta-Anne, *m.* in 1830, to Henry-John-George, 3rd Earl of Carnarvon.
Isabella-Catherine-Mary, *m.* to Charles-John, 17th Earl of Suffolk and 10th Earl of Berkshire.
Charlotte-Juliana-Jane, *m.* 5 Oct. 1831, to James-Wentworth Buller, Esq. of Downes, co. Devon; and *d.* in 1855.
Juliana-Barbara, *m.* 7 July, 1831, to Sir John Ogilvy, Bart.; and *d.* 27 Dec. 1833.

Lord Molyneux-Howard, who was deputy earl-marshal, M.P. for Steyning, and high-steward of the city of Gloucester, *d.* 17 June, 1824, and was *s.* by his only son, the present HENRY HOWARD, Esq. of Greystoke Castle.

Arms—1 HOWARD, same as HOWARD OF CORBY; 2 BROTHERTON; 3 WARREN; 4 MOWBRAY; 5 DACRE; 6 GREYSTOKE.
Crest—On a chapeau, gu., turned up, erm., a lion, statant-guardant, the tail extended, or, gorged with a ducal coronet, arg.
Motto—Sola virtus invicta.
Seats—Greystoke Castle, co. Cumberland; and Thornbury Castle, co. Gloucester.

HOWARD OF CORBY.

HOWARD, PHILIP-HENRY, Esq. of Corby Castle, co. Cumberland, *b.* 22 April, 1801; *s.* his father, 1 March, 1842; *m.* 16 Nov. 1843, Miss Eliza-Minto Canning, of Foxcote, co. Warwick, eldest dau. of the late Major John Canning, E.I.Co.'s service, and niece of the late Francis Canning, Esq. of Foxcote, and has issue,

I. PHILIP-JOHN-CANNING, *b.* 14 March, 1853.
I. Mary-Frances. II. Margaret-Jane.
III. Agnes-Julia.

Mr. Howard was for sometime M.P. for Carlisle.

Lineage.—This is a distinguished branch of the illustrious house of Norfolk.

SIR FRANCIS HOWARD, Knt. of Corby Castle, co. Cumberland *b.* 29 Aug. 1588, 2nd son of Lord William Howard, "Belted Will" (2nd son of Thomas, 4th Duke of Norfolk), by Elizabeth his wife, sister and co-heir of George, Lord Dacre, of Gillesland, was next brother of Sir Philip Howard, ancestor of the EARLS OF CARLISLE. He was colonel in the service of CHARLES I., and in the Royal cause raised a regiment of horse, and sold two estates (Newsham, co. Durham, and Bereton, near York) for its support. He *m.* 1st, Margaret, dau. of John Preston, Esq. of the manor of Furness, of Lancaster, and by her (who *d.* in 1625) had issue,

Thomas, colonel of his father's regt., who fell at Atherton Moor, in 1643.
Elizabeth, *m.* to Edward Standish, Esq. of Standish, co. Lancaster.

Sir Francis *m.* 2ndly, Mary, dau. of Sir Henry Widdrington, Knt. of Widdrington Castle, co. Northumberland, by Mary his wife, dau. of Sir Richard Curwen, Knt., and by her had issue,

FRANCIS, his heir. WILLIAM.
Margaret, *m.* to Thomas Haggerston, Esq. of Haggerston.
Alethia, *d. unm.* Catherine, *d. unm.*
Anne, *d. unm.* in 1683.

Sir Francis *d.* in 1660, and was *s.* by his eldest son,

FRANCIS HOWARD, Esq. of Corby Castle, *b.* 29 June, 1635, capt. in the army, and governor of the city of Carlisle; who *m.* 1st, Ann, dau. of William Gerard, Esq. of Bryn, and had by her (who *d.* in 1679), Elizabeth, *m.* 1st, to William Errington, Esq. of Walwich Grange, and 2ndly, to Michael Ann, Esq. of Bramanbiggin; and Mary, *m.* to Francis Warwick, Esq. of Warwick, co. Cumberland. Capt. Howard, *m.* 2ndly, Mary-Ann-Dorothy, dau. of Richard Towneley, Esq. of Towneley, and by her had two daus., Ann, *m.* to Marmaduke Langdale, Esq. of Howton; and Frances, who *d. unm.* Capt. Howard *d.* in 1702, having devised his estate to his brother,

WILLIAM HOWARD, Esq. of Corby Hall, who *m.* Jane, dau. of John Dalston, Esq. of Acornbank, co. Westmorland; and dying in 1739, was *s.* by his son,

THOMAS HOWARD, Esq. of Corby Castle, who *m.* 1st, Barbara, dau. of John, Viscount Lonsdale, by whom he had (with a son, Thomas, who *d.* in youth) three daus.,

Elizabeth, *d. unm.* in 1799.
Jane, *m.* to Francis Warwick, Esq. of Warwick Hall; and *d. s. p.* in 1778.
Mary, *d.* young.

He *m.* 2ndly, in 1720, Barbara, sister of Sir Christopher Musgrave, of Edenhall, by whom he had, *inter alios*, a son and heir, PHILIP. He *m.* 3rdly, in 1734, Mary, sister of Francis-Carrington Smith, Esq.; but by her (who *d.* in 1735) had no child. He *d.* in 1740, and was *s.* by his son,

PHILIP HOWARD, Esq. of Corby Castle, *b.* in 1730; who *m.* in 1754, Ann, eldest dau. of Henry Withim, Esq. of Cliffe, co. York, and by her (who *d.* at Bath, in 1794) had issue,

HENRY, his heir.
Philip, *b.* in 1766; in the Sardinian service; *d. unm.* in Piedmont, in 1786.
Catherine, *m.* in 1776, to John Gartside, Esq. of Crumpsall, co. Lancaster.
Maria, *m.* 1st, in 1786, to the Hon. George Petre; and 2ndly, to Col. Henry Espinasse.

Mr. Howard *d.* 8 Jan. 1810, and was *s.* by his son,

HENRY HOWARD, Esq. of Corby Castle, *b.* 2 July, 1757; high-sheriff of Cumberland in 1832; *m.* 1st, 4 Nov. 1788, Maria, 3rd dau. and co-heir of Andrew, Lord Archer, of Umberslade, but by her (who *d.* 9 Nov. 1789) had no issue. He *m.* 2ndly, 18 March, 1793, Catherine-Mary, 2nd dau. of Sir Richard Neave, Bart. of Dagnam Park, Essex, and had by her two sons and three daus., viz.,

I. PHILIP-HENRY, his heir.
II. Henry-Francis, envoy-extraordinary and minister-plenipotentiary at Lisbon, *b.* 3 Nov. 1809; *m.* 1st, 23 Dec. 1830, Sevilla, 4th dau. of David, Lord Erskine, and by her (who *d.* 12 March, 1835) has two daus., Isabella and Adela. He *m.* 2ndly, 30 Aug. 1841, Marie-Ernestine, Baroness Von der Schulenburg, fourth dau. of the late Baron Wilhelm-Leopold Von der Schulenburg, of Priemern, in the kingdom of Prussia and has by her, Henry, *b.* 11 Aug. 1843; Francis, *b.* 26 March, 1848; Sevilla-Catherine, *d.* 1846; Catherine-Mary; and Mary-Louisa.
I. Catherine, *m.* in 1829, to the Hon Philip Stourton.
II. Emma-Agnes, *m.* in 1823, to William-Francis, late Lord Petre.
III. Adeliza-Maria, *m.* in 1830, to her cousin, Henry-Petre, Esq. of Dunkenhalgh, co. Lancaster, who *d.* 26 Nov. 1852.

Mr. Howard *d.* 1 March, 1842, in the enjoyment of the highest reputation for piety, patriotism and virtue, and was not less distinguished by his courtesy and kindness than by his literary attainments and his correct taste. His eldest son and successor is the present PHILIP-HENRY HOWARD, Esq. of Corby Castle.

Arms—Gu., on a bend, between six cross-crosslets, fitchée, arg., an escutcheon, or, charged with a demi-lion, rampant, pierced through the mouth with an arrow, within a double tressure, flory, counter-flory, of the first, quartering, BROTHERTON, WARREN, MOWBRAY, DACRE, and GREYSTOCK.
Crest—On a chapeau, gu., termed-up, erm., a lion, statant-guardant, the tail extended, or, ducally crowned, arg., gorged with a label of three points, of the last.
Motto—Sola virtus invicta.
Seat—Corby Castle, Cumberland.

HOWELL OF PRINKNASH.

HOWELL, THOMAS-JONES, Esq. of Prinknash Park, co. Gloucester, J.P. and D.L., *b.* 24 Dec. 1793; *m.* 4 Sept. 1817, Susanna-Maria, eldest surviving dau. of Alexander Macleod, Esq. of Harris, co. Inverness, and by her, who *d.* 15 Oct. 1842, had issue,

I. WILLIAM-CHARLES, *b.* 3 Aug. 1818.
II. Frederick-Donald, *b.* 10 Jan. 1820.
III. Edward, *b.* 13 Sept. 1828.
IV. Henry-Hyett, *b.* 13 July, 1830.
V. Willoughby-Wintle, *b.* 1 Jan. 1833.
VI. John-Davies, *b.* 18 Oct. 1837.
VII. Frances-Weston-Macleod, *b.* 15 Oct. 1842.
I. Emelyn-Jane. II. Laura. III. Constance.

In 1822, he was judge-advocate and judge of the vice-admiralty court at Gibraltar; in 1830, secretary to the commissioners of colonial inquiry; in 1832, commissioner for the West India Islands' relief; and in 1833, inspector of factories.

Lineage.—JOHN HOWELL, Esq., who purchased the estate of Prinknash in 1770, from Henry-Toye Bridgeman, Esq., *m.* in 1755, Elizabeth-Charlotte, widow of Isaac Grove, Esq., barrister-at-law, and dau. and heir of John Demetress, Esq., one of the assistant judges of Jamaica, by his wife, a dau. of Thomas Trengrouse, and Catherine his wife, dau. of Thomas Chafe, Esq., and great-granddau. of William Paulet, Esq. of Poultons, grandson of the 1st Marquess of Winchester. Through this alliance, a claim exists to the Barony of St. John of Basing. Mr. Howell *d.* 2 Nov. 1802, and was *s.* by his son,

THOMAS-BAYLY HOWELL, Esq. of Prinknash Park, F.R.S., F.A.S., *b.* 6 Sept. 1767, who *m.* 24 May, 1790, Lucy-Anne, youngest dau. and co-heir of Robert Long, Esq., and by that lady, who was declared, by a decision of the House of Lords, to be one of the co-heirs of the Barony of Zouch of Harryngworth, Mr. Howell left at his decease a son and successor, the present THOMAS-JONES HOWELL, Esq. of Prinknash Park.

Arms—Sa., a chevron, between three fleurs-de-lis, arg.
Crest—A stag lodged, sa., in the mouth a leaf, ppr.
Seat—Prinknash Park, co. Gloucester.

HOWES OF MORNINGTHORPE.

HOWES, EDWARD, Esq. of Morningthorpe, co. Norfolk, J.P. and D.L., one of the chairmen of quarter sessions for the county, *b.* 7 July, 1813; *m.* 1 March, 1842, Agnes-Maria, dau. of Richard Gwyn, Esq., who *d. s. p.* Feb. 1843; and 2ndly, Fanny, 4th dau. of Robert Fellowes of Shotesham Park, Esq.

Lineage.—This family has been settled in Norfolk for several centuries, having removed from Berkshire, where their ancestor, John de Huse, had a grant of manors in 1066. His descendant, John Howse or Howys, held land in Besthorpe, co. Norfolk, *anno* 35 HENRY VI., from which time Besthorpe was the seat of the family for seven generations until

ROBERT HOWSE, Esq., removed to Carleton Rode, he *d.* in 1618. His eldest son,

JOHN HOWSE, Esq., was of Carleton Rode, co. Norfolk, and dying in 1668, was *s.* by his only son,

THOMAS HOWSE, Esq., who *m.* Tabitha, only dau. of John Roope, Esq. of Morningthorpe, and had, with other issue,

JOHN, his successor.
Anne, *m.* to J. Dalling, Esq. of Denton.
Tabitha, *m.* to William Holmes, Esq. of Mundham.

He *d.* in 1671, and was *s.* by his son,

JOHN HOWSE, Esq., who settled in the old mansion house of the ROOPE family at Morningthorpe, in 1697, and purchased adjoining property at Shelton and Tritton, from Maurice Shelton, Esq., and Sir Peter Gleane, Bart., who was ruined in the Civil Wars. Mr. Howse served the office of sheriff for the county of Norfolk, in 1718, and then altered his name to HOWES, in conformity with an error in the writ by which he was so designated. He *m.* Elizabeth, dau. of H. Keddington, Esq. of Hockham, and had issue,

I. JOHN, his successor.
II. Thomas, *m.* Elizabeth, dau. of John Colman, Esq. of Hardingham, and was father of
  Thomas, a literary person, author of *Observations on Books, ancient and modern.*
  Elizabeth, *m.* to George Wegg, Esq. of Colchester.
III. Elizabeth, *m.* to J. Colman, Esq. of Hardingham, and had a dau.,
  Elizabeth Colman, who *m.* the Rev. Richard Potter, prebendary of Norwich, and the translator of Æschylus.

Mr. Howes *d.* in 1737, and was *s.* by his elder son,

JOHN HOWES, Esq. of Morningthorpe, who *m.* Barbara, dau. of Thomas Sydnor, Esq. of Honingham (who had a grant of arms in 1519), and had, with six daus. two sons,

JOHN, who was commandant of Negrais, and *d.* there in 1756.
THOMAS.

He *d.* in 1673, and was *s.* by his only surviving son,

THE REV. THOMAS HOWES, of Morningthorpe, who *m.* in 1758, Susan, only dau. of Francis Longe, Esq. of Spixworth, co. Norfolk, and had issue,

I. John, of Gray's Inn, *d. s. p.* in 1787.
II. THOMAS, in holy orders, his successor.
III. George, rector of Spixworth, in Norfolk, *m.* 1st, in 1811, Elizabeth, dau. of Robert Fellowes, of Shotisham, Esq., who *d.* 1816, leaving issue
  1 George, *d.* in 1827, *s. p.*
  2 EDWARD, now of Morningthorpe.
  3 Henry, rector of Barton St. Andrew, Norfolk.
  1 Henrietta.
  2ndly, Maria-Margaret, dau. of Thomas Blake, of Scottow, Esq., who *d.* 1818, leaving one son, Frederic.
IV. Francis, in holy orders, author of a translation of *Persius*, and other works, *d.* in 1844, leaving issue.
I. Anne, *d.* 1850, *unm.*
II. Margaret, *m.* Rev. Edward Hawkins, younger son of Sir Cæsar Hawkins, of Kelston, Bart.

THE REV. THOMAS HOWES, rector of Fulton, co. Norfolk, *s.* his father in 1796; *m.* in 1798, Anne, only dau. of the Rev. John-Fairfax Francklin, of Attleborough; and *d. s. p.* 12 Dec. 1848.

Arms—Quarterly: 1st and 4th, arg., a chevron, between three griffins' head, erased, sa.; 2nd, gu., a lion, rampant, within an orle of eight pheons, arg., for ROOPE; and 3rd, arg., a fesse, undè, az., between three fleurs-de-lis on three crescents, sa., in a bordure, engrailed, gu., for SYDNOR.
Crest—A demi-unicorn, issuing out of a ducal crown, ppr.
Seat—Manor House, Morningthorpe.

HOWLIN OF BALLYHYLAND.

HOWLIN, JOHN, Esq. of Ballyhyland, and Carna House, co. Wexford, J.P. and D.L., *b.* Oct. 1797; *m.* 6 Dec. 1826, Alicia-Jane, dau. of the Rev. Edward Lloyd, of Castle Lloyd, co. Limerick, and has issue,

I. JAMES, *b.* 14 Oct. 1828.
II. Abraham-John, *b.* 1 Aug. 1839.
I. Dania-Mary.

Lineage.—ABRAHAM-JAMES HOWLIN, Esq. J.P. co. Wexford, *m.* 1760, Alice (who *d.* 1799), dau. of Rev. M. Finn, rector of Castle Durrow, Queen's Co., and *d.* 1816, leaving a son,

JAMES HOWLIN, Esq. of Ballyhyland, who *m.* 1794, Anna, dau. of John James, Esq., J.P., of Ballycrystal, co. Wexford, and *d.* 1825, leaving issue,

JOHN, now of Ballyhyland.
James, *m.* 1821, Anne, dau. of Benjamin Howlin, of Hilltown, co. Wexford.
Anne, *m.* 1827, Capt. John Baker Graves.

Seat—Ballyhyland, co. Wexford.

HOZIER OF NEWLANDS.

HOZIER, JAMES, Esq. of Newlands and Mauldsley Castle, co. Lanark, and of Newlands, *m.* Catherine-Margaret, 2nd dau. of Sir William Feilden, Bart. of Finniscowles (so created 1846), and has issue.

Lineage.—The grandfather of the present proprietor of Mauldsley Castle, whose name was Maclehose, acquired a fortune in the city of Glasgow, and in 1784, purchased the estate of Newlands from Mr. Gray, of Dalmarnock and Carntyne. Mr. Maclehose was *s.* by his son, who abandoned his original surname of Maclehose, and adopted that of HOZIER. He *m.* the dau. of Mr. Coats, provost of Glasgow, the paternal grandfather of Mr. Campbell Colquhoun, and by her had a son and heir, the present JAMES HOZIER, Esq. of Newlands, who has acquired, by purchase, several properties in Lanarkshire, including the beautiful residence of Mauldsley Castle.

Seat—Mauldsley Castle, co. Lanark.

HUBAND OF IPSLEY.

HUBAND, GEORGE, Esq., M.A., late captain 8th hussars, representative of the Hubands of Warwickshire and Derbyshire, *s.* his grandfather in 1835, in his landed property in the co. of Dublin, *m.* 1 May, 1844, Marianne, youngest dau. of Admiral Croft, of Stillington, co. York, and has issue.

I. WILLIAM-GEORGE.
I. Fanny-Harriett-Augusta.
II. Georgina-Maria-Louisa.

Lineage.—"This family," says Wotton, "is of very ancient and worthy extraction, and descended from HUGO HUBOLD, who held Ipsley, of Osbernus, at the Norman invasion, &c.; and they have continued lords of this manor in a lineal succession until now," (1727.) The name, written successively Hubald, Hubold, Hubande, and Huband, is derived from HUGH, the appellation of the Saxon progenitor, and BALD, the Saxon spelling of the word bold. Hugo appears in Doomsday Book as holding the lands of Ipsley at the Norman invasion, in 1066; and Dugdale mentions him as ancestor of the Hubands of Warwickshire and Derbyshire. From this Hugo descended WILLIAM HUBOLD, sometimes written HUBANT, living 5 STEPHEN, 1140, and HUGH HUBOLD, who held the manor of Ipsley in 1189.

ANTHONY HUBAND, Esq., (fourth son of Nicholas Huband, Esq. of Ipsley, by Dorothy his wife, dau. and co-heir of Sir John Danvers, of Calthorpe; and youngest brother of Ralph Huband, of Ipsley, ancestor of the HUBANDS *of Ipsley*,

EXTINCT BARONETS), inherited estates in Worcestershire under his mother's will. He m. a dau. of the Rev. John Tibotts, rector of Inkberrow, in the same co., (to which living he had been presented by Sir John Huband,) and was father of

JOHN-TIBBOTS HUBAND, Esq. of Inkberrow, who d. in 1624, (his will bears date in the previous year,) leaving, by Mary his wife, an only son,

EDWARD HUBAND, Esq. of Egyoke House, co. Worcester, who m. Isabella, dau. of Thomas Dyson, Esq. of Morton Hall, in the same co., and left by her, (who d. 5 June, 1702,) at his decease, 29 Dec. 1670, a son and successor,

EDMOND HUBAND, Esq., who accompanied the Duke of Ormonde, lord-lieutenant of Ireland, to that country as his private secretary, and settled there. He m. Hester, dau. of Thomas Spring, Esq. of Egyoke, Worcestershire, and of Springfield, co. Dublin, and d. in June, 1729, leaving two son, viz.,

I. FRANCIS, heir to his father, who m. Anne, dau. of John Hayes, Esq. of Avondale, co. Wicklow, by Ann his wife, dau. of John Parnell, Esq., M.P. for Granard, and aunt of the late Lord Congleton, whose brother, William Parnell, s. to Avondale, under the will of Samuel Hayes, Esq., M.P. for Wicklow, brother of the above John. Mr. Huband d. in 1729, leaving an only son,

1 JOHN-HAYES HUBAND, Esq., in whom the representation of the Hayes family vested. He m. twice. His first wife d. s. p., but the second, whom he married when upwards of 80, left an only son, Francis, who d. s. p. in 1835.

II. EDWARD.

The younger son,

EDWARD HUBAND, Esq., m. Eliza, dau. of Thomas Willcocks, Esq. banker of the city of Dublin, of the firm of Sir Charles Burton, Bart., and Co., and left two sons, I. JOSHUA, of the co. of Westmeath, lieut. R.N.; d. without lawful issue; and II. JOSEPH. This

JOSEPH HUBAND, Esq., m. Katherine, dau. of George Reynolds, Esq. of Crumlin, co. Dublin, by his wife Catherine Noy, of the family of William Noy, attorney-general to CHARLES I., and by her, who d. in 1841, had (with three daus., Catherine, m. to Edward Smith, Esq. of Smith Park, co. Meath, now deceased; Eliza, m. to the Rev. Philipps Griffith, of Roscrea, co. Tipperary, also deceased; and Sarah, m. to George Bonynge Rochfort, Esq. of Woodville, co. Westmeath,) an only son,

WILCOCKS, a gentleman of extensive literary attainments, and a zealous patron of the fine arts; m. in 1806, Frances, eldest dau. (by Anna his wife, dau. of Samuel Lindesay, Esq. of Hollymount, co. Mayo), of Arthur Chichester Macartney, Esq. of Murlough, co. Down, elder brother of the late Sir John Macartney, Bart., and eldest son of William Macartney, Esq., forty years M.P. for Belfast; and dying v. p. in 1834, left issue,

GEORGE, successor to his grandfather.
Arthur, late of the Royal Navy; m. 1 Aug. 1850, Anne, dau. of Admiral Croft, of Stillington, co. York, and has a dau., Caroline-Harriet.
Anna, d. unm. in 1822.
Catherine, m. to Arthur-Burgh Crofton, Esq. of Roebuck Castle, co. Dublin, high-sheriff in 1842, and d. 30 Dec. 1849, leaving a son, George-James, and four daus., two of whom survive.
Letitia, and Georgiana-Augusta, both d. unm.

Mr. Huband d. in 1835, and was s. by his grandson, the present CAPTAIN GEORGE HUBAND, now male representative of the Ipsley family.

Arms—Sa., three leopards' faces, jessant de lis, arg., quartering DANVERS, BRULY, and PURYE.
Crest—A wolf, passant, or.
Motto—Cave lupum.

HUDDLESTON OF SAWSTON.

HUDDLESTON, FERDINAND, Esq, of Sawston, co. Cambridge.

Lineage.—This branch of the ancient family of HODELSTON, or HUDDLESTON, of Millum Castle, in Cumberland, became fixed in Cambridgeshire some time in the 15th century, through an alliance with the once potent house of NEVIL, which it now partly represents.

SIR WILLIAM HODLESTON, Knt., youngest son of Sir John Hodleston, Knt. of Millum, by Joane his wife, dau. and co-heir of Sir Miles Stapleton, m. Lady Isabel Nevill, fifth dau. of John, Marquess of Montacute, and sister and coheir of George, Duke of Bedford, and had two sons. The elder son and heir,

SIR JOHN HODLESTON, Knt. of Salston, m. the Hon. Dorothy Sutton, dau. of Edward, Lord Dudley. He was sheriff of the cos. of Cambridge and Huntingdon in 3 RICHARD III., and was s. at his decease by his son,

SIR JOHN HODLESTON, Knt., privy.councillor to Queen MARY, vice-chamberlain to King PHILIP, and captain of his Majesty's guard, m. Bridget, dau. of Sir Robert Cotton, Knt, of Lanwood, in Cambridgeshire, and left at his decease, 4 Nov. 1557, a dau., Alice, m. to Sir Thomas Lovel, Knt. of East Harling, Norfolk; and a son,

SIR EDMUND HODELSTON, Knt. of Salston, co. Cambridge, who m. Dorothy, dau. and heir of Henry Beconsall, Esq. of Beaconsall, in Lancashire, and had one son and four daus., viz.,

HENRY, his heir.
Frances, m. to George Wild, Esq. of the co. of Worcester, serjeant-at-law, and d. 29 Nov. 1630.
Jane, m. to Sir Walter Wiseman, Knt. of Brodon, in Essex.
Isabel, m. to Sir Edward Fortescue, Esq. of Faulkborn, in Essex.
Dorothy, m. to Henry Hastings, Esq., son of Sir Henry Hastings, Knt. of Leicestershire.

Whilst the house at Salston was erecting, Sir Edmund resided on his estates in Essex, and served the office of sheriff for that county in 20, 21, and 30 ELIZABETH. He d. at his sister's, Lady Lovel, in 5 JAMES I., and was s. by his son,

HENRY HODELSTON, of Salston, m. Dorothy, dau. of Robert, 1st Lord Dormer, by his wife the Hon. Elizabeth Brown, dau. of Sir Anthony Brown, Viscount Montagu, and had four sons and two daus. He d. in 1617, and was s. by his elder son,

SIR ROBERT HODELSTON, of Salston, gamekeeper to King CHARLES I., at Newmarket, who m. 1st, the Hon. Mary Roper, dau. of Christopher, Lord Tyenham, by whom he had a son, HENRY, who predeceased him, unm. Sir Robert m. 2ndly, Mary, dau. of Richard Tufton, Esq., and niece of Nicholas, Earl of Thanet, but had no issue. His brother,

HENRY HODELSTON, Esq., lieut.-colonel in the service of King CHARLES I., m. Mary, dau. of William Havers, Esq. of Thelton Hall, in Norfolk, and dying in 1659, was s. by his son,

RICHARD HUDDLESTON, Esq. of Sawston, who m. Mary, dau. of Richard Bostock, Esq. of Wexhall, co. Salop, by whom (who d. 30 Aug. 1729) he had (with seven daus, of whom, Mary, m. Sir Francis Fortescue, Bart.; Catherine, m. Charles Bodenham, Esq. of Rotherwas; and Constantia, m. the Rev. Robert Harding) four sons,

RICHARD, his successor.
William, m. Frances Beaumont, and was father of General William-Orcher Huddleston, of the artillery.
John, in holy orders.
Henry, M.D., m. Mary, dau. of Sir William Gage, Bart. of Hengrave, and had a dau., Lelia, m. to James Farril, Esq., and d. without issue.

Mr. Huddleston d. 10 May, 1713, and was s. by his eldest son,

RICHARD HUDDLESTON, Esq. of Sawston, who m. Mary, dau. and co-heir of John Ayloffe, Esq. of Ewhurst, Hants, and dying in 1717, left, with two daus., Barbara and Frances, nuns at Bruges, a son and successor,

RICHARD HUDDLESTON, Esq. of Sawston, b. 30 Aug. 1716, m. 23 Feb. 1735, Jane, dau. and sole heir of Thomas Belchier, Esq. of Monmouth, by Ursula his wife, dau. of R. Needham, Esq. of Helston, and had issue,

I. FERDINAND, his successor.
II. Thomas, of Milton, in Cambridgeshire, m. Elizabeth, dau. of Sir Henry Mackworth, Bart. of Normanton, and his wife, the Lady Anne Hamilton, dau. of James, 7th Earl of Abercorn, and had a son and three daus., viz.,

1 Francis, late captain in the army, m. 30 Dec. 1810, Hannah, eldest dau. of Robert Pike, Esq. of the city of Dublin, and left, with younger children, a son and heir, JOHN-FOLLIOTT HUDDLESTON, Esq. of Her Majesty's Customs, Dublin.
1 Elizabeth. 2 Mary. 3 Frances.

III. Richard, of Gray's Inn, m. Sarah, dau. of J. Doffkin, merchant of London, and left an only dau. and heir, Mary-Jane, wife of Basil Eyston, Esq. of East Hendred, Berks.
I. Mary, m. to Henry Bostock, Esq. of the co. of Salop.

Mr. Huddleston d. in 1760, and was s. by his eldest son,

FERDINAND HUDDLESTON, Esq. of Sawston, who m. Mary, dau. and sole heir of Timothy Lucas, Esq. of Marlborough, and had issue,

RICHARD, his heir, of Sawston, J.P. and D.L., b. 1768, high-sheriff, 1834; who d. s. p., 1847.
Henry, of Gray's Inn, barrister-at-law, m. Miss Ann Goodchild, and d. s. p.
EDWARD, of Purse Caundle, in Dorsetshire, and afterwards

of Sawston, m. Miss Sarah Barton, and had issue. His eldest son is the present FERDINAND HUDDLESTON, Esq. of Sawston.
Mary, m. to Denis Scully, Esq. of Kilfeade, and d. s. p. 12 April, 1806.
Jane, m. Francis Canning, Esq. of Foxcote, co. Warwick.

Mr. Huddleston d. 6 April, 1808.

Arms—Gu., fretty, arg., quartering, among many others, the ensigns of MILLUM, *Lord of Millum;* FENWICK *of Fenwick;* STAPLETON *of Ingham;* FITZALAN; INGHAM *of Norfolk;* NEVILL, MARQUIS OF MONTAGUE; NEVILL, admiral to WILLIAM the Conqueror; BULMER, BARON BULMER; FITZRANDOLPH; FITZROGER; INGLETHORPE; MONTAGUE *Earl of Salisbury;* HOLLAND, *Earl of Kent;* PLANTAGENET, &c. (See BURKE'S *General Armory*.

Crest—Two arms holding up a bloody scalp.

Motto—Soli Deo honor et gloria.

Seat—Sawston Hall, near Cambridge.

HUGESSEN OF PROVENDER.

KNATCHBULL-HUGESSEN, EDWARD-HUGESSEN, Esq. of Provender, co. Kent.

Lineage.—This family originally came from the town of Dunkirke, in Flanders, where HUGHE HUGESSINE, for service done in battle, received from the Duke of Vandomme, hereditary lord of that town, a grant of a coat of arms, which bearings were subsequently confirmed to his descendants in England, by Sir William Segar in 1624.

MARY HUGESSEN, 2nd dau. (and co-heir with her sister, Dorothea, who m. Joseph Banks, Esq. of Revesby Abbey, and d. s. p. 1828) of William-Western Hugessen, Esq. of Provender, by Thomasine his wife, 2nd dau. of Sir John Honywood, Bart., was 5th in descent from SIR WILLIAM HUGESSEN, of Linsted, high-sheriff of Kent, in 1671, whose father, James Hugessen, Esq. of Linsted, Kent, merchant adventurer, purchased the estate of Provender in 1633. She m. 1780, Edward Knatchbull, eldest son of Sir E. Knatchbull, 7th baronet of Mersham Hatch, co. Kent. He s. as 8th baronet in 1789, and d. in Sept. 1819, having had by her (who d. in 1785), besides a younger son, Norton-Joseph, lieut. R.N., who d. s. p. in 1801, an elder son and heir,

THE RIGHT HON. SIR EDWARD KNATCHBULL, 9th baronet, b. 20 Dec. 1781, M.P. for co. Kent; who m. 1st, 25 Aug. 1806, Annabella-Christiana, dau. of Sir John Honywood, Bart., and by her (who d. in 1814) had, with other issue,

NORTON-JOSEPH, b. in 1808, present and 10th baronet of Mersham Hatch.

The Right Hon. Sir Edward Knatchbull m. 2ndly, in 1820, Fanny-Catherine, eldest dau. of Edward Knight, Esq. of Godmersham Park, and by her had five sons and three daus.,

I. EDWARD-HUGESSEN, now of Provender.
II. Reginald-Bridges. III. Richard-Astley.
IV. Herbert-Thomas. V. William-Western.
I. Matilda-Catherine. II. Louisa-Susanna.
III. Fanny-Elizabeth-Alicia-Sophia, d. s. p. in 1845.

Sir Edward d. in 1849, and was s. in the baronetcy by his eldest son by his 1st wife. The Hugessen property derived from his mother and aunt, the two co-heirs of William-Western Hugessen, Esq. of Provender, he left to his widow for life, and entailed it upon his children by her. They have consequently assumed the additional surname and arms of HUGESSEN.

Arms as granted to Hughe Hugessine by the Duke of Vandomme, and subsequently confirmed to his descendants in England, by a grant in 1624 from Sir William Segar. Arg., on a mount, vert, in base an oak-tree, ppr., between two boars, combattant, sa., armed and tusked, or.

Crest—A tree, as in the arms, between two wings, az.

HUGHES OF ALLTLWYD.

HUGHES, JOHN, Esq. of Alltlwyd, co. Cardigan, J.P. and D.L., high-sheriff, co. Cardigan, 1837, b. 15 July, 1805; m. 1st, 6 March, 1833, Mary-Anne, eldest dau. of Albar-T.-J. Gwynne, Esq. of Monachty, co. Cardigan, and by her had an only dau., who d. an infant. He m. 2ndly, 10 Aug. 1836, Elizabeth, 2nd dau. of George-Williams Parry, Esq. of Llidiarde, co. Cardigan, and by her has issue,

I. John-George-Parry, b. 20 Oct. 1837.
II. William-Thomas, b. 5 Nov. 1838.

Lineage.—WILLIAM HUGHES, Esq. of Rhôs Tyddin (now better known by the name of the Devil's Bridge), was father of

THE REV. WILLIAM HUGHES, of Glanravon, vicar of Lanilar, who m. Dorothy, dau. of Thomas Evans, Esq. of Tymawr Talsarn, co. Cardigan, and by her had a son and heir,

JOHN HUGHES, Esq. of Glanravon, who m. in 1801, Jane Edwards, relict of Thomas Evans, Esq. of Lanilar, co. Cardigan, and by her had issue,

JOHN, his heir.
Jane, m. to the Rev. John Jones.
Elizabeth, m. to John Syme, Esq. of Edinburgh.

Arms—Arg., a chev., between three fleurs-de-lis, az., on a chief, of the last, a mullet, pierced, of the field.

Crest—On a chapeau, gu., turned up, erm., a demi-lion, rampant, holding in the dexter paw a fleur-de-lis.

Motto—Y cyfiawn sydd by megis Llew.

Seat—Alltlwyd, co. Cardigan.

HUGHES OF DONNINGTON PRIORY.

HUGHES, JOHN, Esq. of Donnington Priory, co. Berks, J.P. and D.L., M.A. of Oriel College, Oxford, b. 2 Jan. 1790; m. 14 Dec. 1820, Margaret-Elizabeth, 2nd dau. of Thomas Wilkinson, Esq. of Stokesley Hall, co. York, and by her has,

I. GEORGE-EDWARD, D.C.L., b. 18 Sept. 1821; m. 31 Aug. 1852, Anne-Salusbury, eldest dau. of Samuel Steward, Esq. of Connaught Square.
II. Thomas, b. 19 Oct. 1822; m. 17 Aug. 1847, Anne-Frances, eldest dau. of the Rev. James Ford, of Hirondels, Devon.
III. John, b. 24 March, 1824; m. 18 Aug. 1853, Elizabeth-Howard, dau. of the late Right Hon. Thomas Peregrine Courtenay.
IV. William-Hastings, b. 15 Dec. 1833.
V. Henry-Salusbury, b. 26 Aug. 1836.
VI. Arthur-Octavius.
I. Jane-Elizabeth, m. 10 Aug. 1848, to Nassau-John Senior, Esq., M.A., barrister-at-law.

Mr. Hughes is the author of an "Itinerary of Provence and the Rhone," to which Sir Walter Scott refers with much commendation in his preface to "Quentin Durward."

Lineage.—The surname of Hughes was first adopted in this line of Welsh gentry, by the sons of HUGH AP THOMAS AP MWYNDEG, of Pantgwyn, in the parish of Ysceiviog, of the XIIth Noble Tribe of North Wales and Powys, founded by Edwin of Tegiangl. Of this family was MYNDEC (or properly MWYNDEG) HUGHES, merchant of Liverpool, and son of the last possessor of the estate of Galle Ffawler, in the parish aforesaid. He m. the sister and co-heir of Thomas Wood, Esq. of Hillingdon, Middlesex, and was father of

THE REV. THOMAS HUGHES, rector of Llanfwrog and Llansilyn, co. Denbigh, J.P. He m. Elizabeth, dau. of Norfolk Salusbury, Esq. of Plas-y-Ward, co. Denbigh, and aunt to the late Sir Robert Salusbury, Bart. of Llanwern, and had issue, Robert, in the Hon. E.I.Co.'s service (whose dau. and heiress, Frances, m. her cousin, Archdeacon Newcome, warden of Ruthin, North Wales); THOMAS, of whom presently. Anne, m. to John Fryer, Esq. of Taplow Lodge, Bucks; and Elizabeth, m. to Rev. H. Newcome, rector of Gresford, co. Denbigh (nephew of the then Bishop of St. Asaph). The 2nd son,

THE REV. THOMAS HUGHES, D.D., preceptor in the royal family of GEORGE III., subsequently canon residentiary of St. Paul's, and one of the clerks of the closet to GEORGE III. and GEORGE IV., m. Mary-Anne, dau. and heiress of the late Rev. George Watts * and granddau. of the Rev. George Watts, chaplain to GEORGE II., and master of the Temple Church, London, and by her had an only son, JOHN HUGHES, Esq. of Donnington Priory.

Arms—Quarterly: 1st and 4th, sa., a fesse, cottised, between three lions' heads, erased, arg.; 2nd, az., three arrows, points downwards, or, on a chief of the second, three Moors' heads, couped, sidefaced, sa.; 3rd, arg., a chev., erm., between three unicorns' heads, caped, sa.

Seat—Donnington Priory, Berks.

* Mrs. Watts, the maternal grandmother of the present Mr. Hughes, was dau. and heiress of Richard Head, Esq., descendant and representative of the Mr. Head mentioned in the "History of Newbury" as the host of Lord Falkland before the battle, with whom he received the sacrament. The meaning of "Mwyndeg" is "courteous." It appears only to occur in this line as a baptismal name.

HUGHES OF GWERCLAS.

HUGHES, WILLIAM, Esq., REPRESENTATIVE, in the male line, of the HUGHES'S OF GWERCLAS, BARONS OF KYMMER-YN-EDEIRNION, b. 18 April, 1801; m. 11 July, 1835, Eliza-Anne, dau. of William-Henry Worthington, of Sandiway Bank, co. Chester, Esq., formerly an officer in the Royal Horse guards Blue, and has issue,

I. WILLIAM-O'FARRELL, b. 18 Feb. 1838.
I. Frances-Elizabeth-Margaretta.

Lineage.—Few families can establish a loftier lineage, or deduce descent through more numerous stocks of historic distinction, than the HUGHES's *of Gwerclas, Lords of Kymmer-yn-Edeirnion*, and *Barons of Edeirnion*, within the ancient Principality of Powys and Kingdom of Wales.

Derived, by uninterrupted lineal male succession, from OWAIN BROGYNTYN, Lord of Edeirnion, Dinmael, and Abertanat in Powys, son of Madoc, last Sovereign Prince of Powys, the existing heir of the Hughes's deduces, through the Baronial Lords of Kymmer, and the Royal Line of Powys, a genealogy of twenty-eight descents, extending over ten centuries, transmitted, in common with the lineage of the monarchs of North Wales and South Wales, (the two other Sovereign Dynasties of Cambria,) from RHODRI MAWR, renowned in the annals of the Cymri as the Egbert of his race, who, uniting, by inheritance and marriage, the several states of North Wales, South Wales, and Powys, became King of all Wales, A.D. 843.

OWAIN-BROGYNTYN AP MADOC, third son of Madoc ap Meredith, Prince of Powys, 10th in descent from Rhodri Mawr, bore the prefix of *Brogyntyn*, from the place of his birth, a locality of that name near Oswestry in Shropshire. In 1160, when the Sovereign Diadem, of the Madocian line of Powys, was buried in the tomb of Madoc ap Meredith, last Prince of Powys, and his dominions were apportioned among his children, his chivalrous son, OWAIN BROGYNTYN, became LORD OF EDEIRNION, DINMAEL AND ABERTANAT, in Powys-Fadoc, and inherited from his father the Royal Arms of Powys, "Arg., a lion, rampant, sa., armed and langued, gu.," which have been transmitted to his descendants. This chief, one of the most distinguished warriors of his age, who took a conspicuous part in the most prominent incidents of a period peculiarly eventful in the annals of Cambria, made a grant to Basingwick Abbey of Bala Lake, in Penllyn, which was witnessed by Reiner, bishop of St. Asaph from 1186 to 1224, and by Ithel Owain's chaplain. Owain Brogyntyn married Maredd, dau. of Einion ap Seisylt, Lord of Mathafern, in Montgomeryshire, progenitor of the powerful family of Pugh Mathavern, and of the Pryces of Gunley. By this lady he had three sons: I. Griffith, living in 1200, who succeeded to Half Edeirnion, ancestor of the Barons of Crogen and Branas, in Edeirnion, represented by the Barons of Kymmer and Barons of Hendwr, in Edeirnion; II. Bleddyn, Lord of Dinmael, living 25 May, 2 HENRY III., 1218, from whom derived, 1 The Barons of Rûg, in Edeirnion; 2 Maesmores of Maesmore, in Dinmael; 3 The House of Plas Issa, in Edeirnion; III. IORWERTH. The 3rd son,

IORWERTH AP OWAIN BROGYNTYN inherited half Edeirnion. He m. Efa, dau. and heir of Madoc, Lord of Mawddwy in Merionethshire, younger son of Gwenwynwyn, Prince of Powys-Wenwynwyn. By a writ tested at Westminster, 6 Jan., 29 HENRY III., 1244, "Maddok filius Wenvwen," with other barons of North Wales, who performed homage to the King, is ordered to appear before the King at Westminster (Rymer's Fœd. I. 258); and "Maddok filius Wenwywyn" is party to a treaty of confederation dated 42 HEN. III. 1258 (ib. 370). Iorwerth ap Owen, by Efa verch Madoc, had issue: I. GRIFFITH AP IORWERTH; II. Elisau ap Iorwerth, living 42 HENRY III., 1258, and 22 July, 12 EDWARD I., 1284, whose son, Madoc ap Elisar, living 9 August, 17 EDWARD III., 1343, was father of Llewelyn ap Madoc, elected Bishop of St. Asaph, 31 EDWARD III. (Le Neve's Fasti Ecclesiæ Anglicanæ, by Duffus Hardy, i., 68-9). Iorwerth ap Owain Brogyntyn was s. by his eldest son,

GRIFFITH AP IORWERTH, a Baron of Edeirnion, who strenuously co-operated with the Cambrian patriots in asserting the independence of his country against EDWARD I. of England. In 42 HENRY III., 1258, we find him and his brother Elisau, by the designation of "Elisse and Grufud fil Iorwerth," and their uncle, Griffith Madoc, Lord of Bromfield, Madoc ap Gwenwynwyn, Lord of Mawddwy, as also Llewelyn ap Griffith, Prince of Wales, and other "Magnates Walliæ," in conjunction with certain "Magnates Scotiæ," parties to a convention not to make peace with the King of England without mutual consent (Rymer, i., 370). Compelled at length to submission, after the death of Llewelyn ap Griffith, by the conquest of Wales by EDW. I.; he accepted a pardon from that monarch, dated at Carnarvon, in the 12th year of his reign, 20 July, 1284 (Rot. Wall. in Turr. Lond., 12 EDWARD I., n. 5), and two days afterwards received from EDWARD a grant to hold his lands "per Baroniam sicut antecessores sui eas tenuerunt" (*ibid*). Griffith ap Iorwerth m. Gwenllian, dau. of David Goch, Lord of Penmachno in Caernarvon, son of David ap Griffith, Lord of Denbigh, who assumed the Welsh throne on the death of his elder brother, Llewelyn ap Griffith, 10 Dec., 8 EDWARD I., 1282. From Llowarch ap David, brother of Gwenllian, derived the Pughs of Penmachno, represented by the Baroness Le Despencer, and another brother, Griffith ap David Goch, who *temp.* HENRY III., was foreman of a jury appointed to take the extent of Wales at Nant Conway, was buried at Bettws, where his figure is to be seen in armour, with the inscription, "Agnus Dei miserere mei." Griffith ap Iorwerth was father of

DAVID AP GRIFFITH, a Baron of Edeirnion, who m. Agnes, dau. of Madoc Vychan, Baron of Main-yn-Meifod, co. Montgomery, paternal progenitor of the Powys's, Lords Lilford, derived from Iorwerth Goch, Lord of Marchmont, ancestor of the Kynastons of Hardwick, Barts., and was father of,

LLEWELYN DDU AP DAVID, II. BARON OF KYMMER-YN-EDEIRNION, "Owen [I. recorded BARON OF KYMMER] ap David ap Griffith," with his brother, "Llewelyn ap David ap Griffith," "Barones de Edyernion," performed fealty to Edward the Black Prince, 9 Aug. 17 EDWARD III., on receiving from his father a grant of the Principality of Wales (*Arch. Cambr.*, No. 7, p. 244). About 24 EDWARD III. Llewelyn and his brother Owen were summoned as "Llewelin ap Dauid et Oweyn ap David freius" to the sessions held at Conway before the Justiciary of North Wales, to answer by what warrant they claim to exercise BARONIAL rights, "APUD THLANGAYR [Langar] IN TERRIS SUIS IN EDEIRNION." (Record of Caernarvon, published by the Record Commissioners, page 188.) Llewellyn Ddu m. Anne, dau. of Ieuan ap Iorwerth, of Llanwyllyn, in Merionethshire, and was father of

IEUAN AP LLEWELYN DDU, III. BARON OF KYMMER-YN-EDEIRNION, m. Maredd, "Lady of Crogen and Branas," co. Merioneth (living under age Wednesday, on the morrow of All Saints, 8 EDWARD III., and also under age *circa* 24 EDWARD III.), dau. and heir of Ievan ap Llewelyn, Baron of Crogen and Branas, and was s. by his son,

RHYS AP IEUAN, IV. BARON OF KYMMER-YN-EDEIRNION, and Baron of Crogen and Branas, m. Angharad, dau. and heir of Howel ap Meuric Vychan, V. Lord of Nannau, in Merionethshire, and had two sons: the elder,

DAVID AP RHYS, V. BARON OF KYMMER-YN-EDEIRNION, appears as one of the Jurors in an Inquisition held at Bala 24 Oct. 1427: he m. Mali, dau. of David ap Ieuan, the heroic Constable and defender of Harlech Castle in 1468. David ap Rhys was dead 25 Oct., 23 HENRY VI., 1444, as appears by his Inquis. post-mortem, and was s. by his elder son,

GRIFFITH VYCHAN AP DAVID, VI. BARON OF KYMMER-YN-EDEIRNION, who m. Margaret, dau. of William ap Meredith of Mochnant-yn-Rhaiadr, and had an only son,

WILLIAM AP GRIFFITH VYCHAN, VII. BARON OF KYMMER-YN-EDEIRNION, living June, 15 HENRY VIII., 1523, who m. Margaret, 3rd dau. of Meredith ap David of Melai, and Vronheulog, both in Denbighshire, ancestor of the Wynns of Melai and Maenan, represented by Lord Newborough. His son and successor,

HUGH AP WILLIAM, VIII. BARON OF KYMMER-YN-EDEIRNION, substituted for Kymmer, the seat of his ancestors, the mansion of Gwerclas within the barony: he m. Alis, dau. of Richard ap Thomas of Caerwalwch, in Llanynys, who was living 3 Dec. 1602. This gentleman d. 23 Feb. 1600, as appears by his Inquis. post-mortem, and was s. by his eldest son,

HUMFFREY HUGHES, Esq. of GWERCLAS, IX. BARON OF KYMMER-YN-EDEIRNION, high-sheriff of Merionethshire in 1618. This gentleman, who assumed the surname of "HUGHES," from this time hereditary in the family, and was living 7 Oct., 36 ELIZ. 1594, the date of Lewis Dwn's Visitation Pedigree, d. s. p., and was s. by his brother,

RICHARD HUGHES, Esq. of GWERCLAS, X. BARON OF KYMMER-YN-EDEIRNION, living 7 Oct. 36 ELIZ. 1594, who m. 2 Nov. 1601, Frances, widow of Richard Evers, Esq., "dau. to John Volpe" [Iovanni Volpe,] "an Italian Doctor, famous in Queen ELIZABETH's time;" and dying 21 March, 1641, was succeeded by his eldest son,

HUMFFREY HUGHES, Esq. of Gwerclas, XI. BARON OF

Kymmer-yn-Edeirnion, b. 14 Aug. 1605, high-sheriff of Merionethshire in 1670. Mr. Hughes, a stanch Royalist, m. 1st, 13 Aug. 1615, Magdalen, dau. and heir of John Rogers-Wynn, of Bryntangor, in Bryneglwys, co. Denbigh, Esq., and by her alone had issue. Mr Hughes m. 2ndly, 18 May, 1659, Ellenor, dau. of John Savage, Esq. of Barrow, co. Chester, and widow of Francis Fitton, Esq. of Carden. She d. 5 Aug. 1661, aged fifty-five. He m. 3rdly, 31 May, 1662, Sarah, dau. of Richard Franklin, of Ebsworth, co. Cambridge, Esq., which lady d. 22 Oct. 1666; and 4thly, 12 Feb. 1667, Ellenor, (who survived him,) widow of James Mytton, Esq. of Pontyscowryd, co. Montgomery, sister of Sir Thomas Jones, Knt., M.P. for Shrewsbury, and chief-justice of the Common Pleas, dau. of Thomas Jones, of Sandford, co. Salop, Esq. The third, but eventually eldest surviving son, by the heiress of Bryntangor, who was co-heir of the monarchs of North Wales, South Wales, and Powys, viz.,

Thomas Hughes, Esq. of Gwerclas, and jure uxoris of Hendreforfydd, in Edeirnion, b. 18 Sept. 1628; m. 1st, Mary, dau. and heir of John Griffith, of Hendreforfydd, Esq., and by her (who d. 24 Sept. 1656) had issue a son, John, b. and d. 26 Dec. 1652, and two daus.: Joyes, heiress of her mother, b. 16 Nov. 1654, m. to John Maurice, Esq., and had issue, living 2 June, 1708; and Dorothea, b. 18 Aug. 1656, m. to William Middleton, of Tir-y-Llanerch, Esq., and had issue, living 2 June, 1703. Mr. Hughes m. 2ndly, Margaret, dau. of Griffith ap Thomas ap Roger, of Llanfair Dyffryn Clwyd, co. Denbigh, and by her had issue,

Hugh Hughes, Esq. of Gwerclas and Bryntangor, xii. Baron of Kymmer-yn-Edeirnion, high-sheriff of Merionethshire in 1720, who s. his grandfather, Humffrey Hughes. This gentleman, b. 31 July, 1659, m. 1st, his cousin, Dorothy, dau. of Thomas Yale, of Plas-yn-Yale, co. Denbigh, Esq.; and 2ndly, his cousin Jane, dau. of John Maesmor, of Maesmor, co. Denbigh, Esq. By the latter he had no issue; by the former he left at his decease (he was buried 2 April, 1725) two daus. and co-heiresses, Dorothy and Magdalen; the latter d. unm., and was buried at Llangar, 18 Aug. 1733. The former,

Dorothy Hughes, heiress of Gwerclas, Kymmer-yn-Edeirnion, and Bryntangor, b. 20 March, 1684-5, m. Edward Lloyd, of Plymog, co. Denbigh, Esq., high-sheriff of Merionethshire in 1732, and of Denbighshire in 1736, and was mother of Hugh Hughes-Lloyd, Esq. of Gwerclas and Plymog, high-sheriff of Merionethshire in 1747, who m. Margaret, dau. and heiress of Richard Walmsley, of Coldcoates Hall, co. Lancaster, and of Bashall, co. York, representative of the knightly and historic Talbots of Bashall, and had a son and heir, Richard Hughes-Lloyd, Esq. of Gwerclas, Plymog, and Bashall, father of the present Richard-Walmsley Lloyd, Esq.

Thomas, b. 27 Feb. 1660, d. 15 Nov. 1661.
John, of whom presently, as continuer of the male line.
Humffrey, b. 22 March, and d. 19 Sept. 1663.
Humffrey, b. 12 Aug. 1667, d. unm. and was buried 14 March, 1684.

Mr. Hughes d. 2 April, 1670. His third, and eventually only surviving younger son,

John Hughes, Esq., b. 28 Aug. 1662, was seated at Kymmer-yn-Edeirnion. He m. 3 Nov. 1693, Dorothy, dau. of Andrew Lloyd, of Plymog, co. Denbigh, Esq., and d. 1 July, 1694, (having been drowned in the River Dee,) leaving issue a son and successor,

Daniel Hughes, Esq. of Pen-y-Clawdd, co. Denbigh, b. 2 July, 1694, succeeded as heir male of the Hughes's of Gwerclas, Barons of Kymmer-yn-Edeirnion, at the decease, without issue male, of his uncle, Hugh Hughes, Esq. He m. 14 Feb. 1740, Catherine, dau. and heir of the Rev. John Wynn, of Pen-y-Clawdd, co. Denbigh, of the Race of Edwin, Lord of Tegaingl, in Flint, and by her (who d. 2 April, 1769) had John, his heir; Samuel, and Sarah, of whom the two last d. in youth. Mr. Hughes d. 14 Aug. 1754, and was s. by his son,

John Hughes, Esq. of Pen-y-Clawdd, b. 25 June, 1742, who m. 22 July, 1764, Mary, dau. of John Jones, Esq. of Plas Hen, co. Montgomery, a younger branch of the Denbighshire house of Llwynon, and by her (who d. 10 Feb. 1823) had a son and successor,

William Hughes, Esq. of Pen-y-Clawdd, b. 8 Feb. 1779, who m. 27 March, 1800, Elizabeth, dau. of Thomas Davies, Esq. of Trefynant, co. Denbigh, derived from the ancient family of Davies, of Gwysaney, and by her (who d. 4 April, 1844) had issue,

William, present representative.
Thomas, M.D., b. 22 Aug. 1803.
John, of the Inner Temple, barrister-at-law, b. 6 Oct. 1805, m. 6 July, 1832, Dorothea, eldest surviving dau. of Richard Hughes Lloyd, Esq. of Plymog, Gwerclas, and Bashall, and by her (who d. 27 Jan. 1848) has an only son, Talbot de Bashall, an officer in the Cape Mounted Rifles, b. 15 Dec. 1836.
Edward, d. young.

Mr. Hughes d. 18 Jan. 1836.

Arms—Those of the sovereign princes of Powys, viz., arg., a lion, rampt., sa., armed and langued, gu. ("the black lion of Powys.")

Crest—Out of a ducal coronet, or, a demi-lion, rampt., sa., armed and langued, gu.

Supporters—Dexter, a lion, rampant, sa., armed and langued, gu. Sinister, a dragon, gu., with wings, displayed.

Motto—Kymmer-yn-Edeirnion.

HUGHES OF KINMEL AND DINORBEN.

Hugh-Robert Hughes, Esq. of Kinmel and Dinorben, co. Denbigh, J.P. and D.L., b. 11 June, 1827; m. 18 April, 1853, Florentia, 2nd dau. of Henry-Thomas, Lord Ravensworth, and has issue. Mr. Hughes s. at the death of his first-cousin, William-Lewis, 2nd Lord Dinorben, 6 Oct. 1852, to the estates of the family, under the entail created by his grandfather.

Lineage.—From Hwfa ap Cynddelw, Lord of Llys Llifon, in Anglesey (of ancient British descent) founder of the 1st Noble Tribe of North Wales living in the time of Owen Gwynedd, Prince of North Wales (who succeeded to the crown A.D. 1137, and d. 1169), lineally descended

Hugh Lewis, Esq. of Presadfedd (son of John Lewis, by Elizabeth Vaughan his wife, and grandson of Hugh Lewis Hên, by Janet, dau. of William Bulkeley), who m. Agnes, sister of Sir Rhys Griffith, Knt. of Penrhyn, co. Carnarvon, high-sheriff of Carnarvon in 1537, and dau. of Sir William Griffith, Knt. of Penrhyn, Chamberlain of North Wales, and was father of two sons, William, of whom presently; and John Lewis Bach, who m. Ellen, dau. of Hugh ap Llewelyn ap Meredith, which lady m. 2ndly, Sir William Maurice, of Clenenneu. The elder son and heir,

William Lewis, Esq., J.P., and high-sheriff of Anglesey in 1549, 1557, and 1572, and M.P. for that county in two parliaments, certified his pedigree in the Visitation, 6 Nov. 1588. He m. 1st, Margaret, dau. of Sir John Puleston, Knt. of Bersham, Constable of the Castle of Carnarvon, and by her had, Hugh Lewis, of Presadfedd and other issue. William Lewis m. 2ndly, Ellen, sister of John ap Edward, Esq. of Bodewryd, high-sheriff of Anglesey in 1613, dau. of Edward ap Hugh Gwyn, Esq. of Bodewryd, and by her (who m. 2ndly, Harry Mostyn, Esq. of Calcot, co. Flint) had (with a dau., Margaret, m. to Robert Pugh, of Creuddyn) a son,

Robert Lewis, of Cemlyn, who m. Gaenor, dau. of William Roberts, of Caerau, co. Anglesey, and was father of

William Lewis, of Cemlyn, who m. Anne, relict of the Rev. Richard Hughes, rector of Llanfair-ynghornwy, and dau. (by Anne his wife, dau. of Rhys Wynn, of Llwydiarth) of William Bulkeley, Esq. of Brynddû son (by Jane his wife, sole heir of Rhys ap William, of Coedon) of the Rev. Arthur Bulkeley, son of Sir Richard Bulkeley, Knt. of Baron Hill, co. Anglesey, derived through the families of Needham, Talbot, Butler, and Bohun, from King Edward I. (*see* Burke's *Royal Families, Vol. III.*) By this lady Mr. Lewis had two sons and a dau., viz., Robert, of Cemlyn, d. s. p.; Ambrose, of whom we treat; and Sage, m. to John Bulkeley, of Bwlchanan. The younger son,

The Rev. Ambrose Lewis, rector of Llanrhudd, to which he was inducted in 1704, m. Martha, dau. and co-heir of the Rev. Hugh Humphreys, rector of Trefdraeth, by Jane his wife, sister and co-heir of Owen Hughes, Esq. of Beaumaris, M.P., who d. s. p. in 1708, and dau. of Thomas Hughes, Esq. of Porthllongddu, derived from Gweirydd ap Rhys Goch. By this lady (who d. in 1725) Mr. Lewis had issue,

William, of Llysdulas, and also of Madryn, co. Carnarvon, who left his nieces his co-heiresses.
Hugh, } both d. s. p.
Owen, }
Robert, of whom presently.
Anne, m. to William Lewis, Esq. of Trysallwyn, co. Anglesey.
Jane, m. to William Bulkeley, Esq. of Brynddû.
Margaret, d. unm.

The youngest son,

The Rev. Robert Lewis, chancellor of Bangor, m. 18 April, 1734, Margaret, dau of Hugh Price, Esq. of Beaumaris, by Sidney his wife, only child of William Williams, of Treiarddur, co. Anglesey, descended from Hwfa ap Cynddelw,

Lord of Llys Llfon, and by this lady had three daus. and co-heirs,

SIDNEY, co-heir to her uncle, William, from whom she inherited Madryn. She m. Love Parry, Esq. of Peniarth, M.P., and was mother of two daus. and co-heirs. The elder, Margaret, b. in 1783, s. to Madryn, and m. Thomas Parry Jones, Esq. of Llwynon, co. Denbigh, who assumed the additional surname of Parry.
ANNA-MARIA, d. unm.
MARY, of whom we treat.

The youngest dau. and co-heir,

MARY LEWIS, also co-heir to her uncle, William Lewis, from whom she inherited Llysdulas, co. Anglesey, m. the REV. EDWARD HUGHES, A.M., of Kinmel Park, co. Denbigh, and of Dinorben, in the same county, son of Hugh Hughes, Esq. of Lliniog, in Anglesey, and had issue,

I. WILLIAM-LEWIS, his heir, 1st Lord Dinorben.
II. HUGH-ROBERT, seated at Bache Hall, co. Chester, who m. 1st, Barbara, dau. of John-Bodychan Sparrow, Esq. of Red Hill, co. Anglesey, by Anne his wife, only child and heiress of Ambrose Lewis, Esq. of Trwysclwn, co. Anglesey, and by her had four daus., viz.,
1 Mary-Anne, m. 7 Jan. 1834, to Richard Massie, Esq., eldest son of the Rev. Richard Massie, of Coddington, co. Chester, and d. 20 Feb. 1841.
2 Margaret-Grace, d. unm. 14 Jan. 1838.
3 Elizabeth-Henrietta, m. 29 Oct. 1840, to Philip Stapleton Humberston, Esq. of Chester.
4 Anne-Barbara, d. unm. 18 March, 1847.
Mr. Hughes m. 2ndly, 12 June, 1826, Anne, dau. of Thomas Lance, Esq. of Wavertree, co. Lancaster, and by her had,
1 HUGH-ROBERT HUGHES, Esq. now of Kinmel Park and Dinorben.
2 Edward-Owen, b. 29 June, 1829; d. 25 Sept. following year.
1 Adelaide-Elinor.
III. James, col. in the army, C.B.; b. 12 Nov. 1778; m. 16 March, 1841, Fanny, eldest dau. of the Hon. Sir Francis Charles Stanhope, K.C.H., 6th son of Charles, 3rd Earl of Harrington, and d. s. p. 29 Nov. 1845.
I. Margaret, m. in July, 1792, to Owen Williams, Esq. of Temple House, Berks, and Craigydon, co. Anglesea, M.P. for Great Marlow, and d. in 1821, leaving issue: her eldest son is Thomas-Peers Williams, Esq. of Temple House and Craigydon, M P.
II. Anne, m. 11 June, 1799, to Sir Robert Williams, Bart. of Penrhyn, co. Carnarvon, and d. in Sept. 1837, leaving by him (who d. 1 Dec. 1830) issue, of whom the eldest son is the present Sir Richard Williams Bulkeley, Bart. of Penrhyn, M.P.
III. Martha, m. 1st, in 1809, to Cynric Lloyd, Esq., 3rd brother of Edward Price Lloyd, Baron Mostyn. He d. s. p. 1822. She m. 2ndly, in 18?9, Sir Henry Wyatt, lieut.-col. in the 2nd guards, and d. 9 April, 1839.

The eldest son,

I. WILLIAM-LEWIS HUGHES, of Kinmel Park, Dinorben, and Llysdulas, Esq., M.P., b. 10 Nov. 1767, created BARON DINORBEN, 10 Sept. 1831; m. 1st, 8 March, 1804, Charlotte-Margaret, 3rd dau. of Ralph William Grey, Esq. of Backworth, co. Northumberland, and by her (who d. 21 Jan. 1835), had issue,

EDWARD, b. 5 Nov. 1806; d. 3 March, 1814.
WILLIAM-LEWIS-HUGHES, 2nd Baron Dinorben.
Charlotte-Mary, m. 27 May, 1828, to Sir Richard Williams-Bulkeley, Bart. of Penrhyn, co. Carnarvon, and d. s. p. 17 May, 1829.
Frances-Margaret, m. in 1835, to Alan Legge, 3rd Baron Gardner, and d. s. p. 8 Dec. 1847.
Martha-Mary.
Eliza-Anne, d. young, 1815.
Laura, also d. young, 1816.
Caroline-Anne, d. unm. 19 April, 1832. Emily.
Augusta, d. young, 1852.

Lord Dinorben m. 2ndly, in 1840, Gertrude, youngest dau. of Grice Smyth, Esq. of Ballynatray, co. Waterford, and sister of Penelope, consort of H.R.H. the Prince of Capua, son of the King of Naples, and by her had two daus.,

Gertrude-Cecilia, d. an infant, 1843.
Gwen-Gertrude.

Lord Dinorben d. 10 Feb. 1852, and was s. by his only surviving son.

II. WILLIAM-LEWIS, 2nd baron, b. 5 Nov. 1821, who d. unm. 6 Oct. 1852, when the title became EXTINCT. The entailed estates devolved on his first-cousin and heir male, the present HUGH-ROBERT HUGHES, Esq. of Kinmel and Dinorben.

Arms—Gu., two lions, passant, and a rose in chief, arg.
Crest—Out of a baron's coronet, a demi-lion, rampant, arg., holding between the paws a white rose, ppr.
Motto—Heb Dduw heb ddym Dduw a Digon.
Seat—Kinmel Park, St. Asaph.

HUGHES OF ELY HOUSE.

HUGHES, ROBERT, Esq. of Ely House, co. Wexford, J.P., b. 10 Sept. 1772; m. 1 Jan. 1797, Anne, 2nd dau. of Captain Frederick Sparks, of Croshue, in the same county, and had issue,

I. ROBERT-WIGRAM, in the Hon. E. I. C. Bengal civil service.
II. Frederic, capt. in the 7th Madras cavalry, and Knight of the First Class of the Royal Persian Order of the Lion and Sun.
I. Georgiana, m. 21 March, 1821, to John Doran, Esq., major in the 18th Royal Irish regt., and has issue.

Lineage.—The first of this family who settled in Ireland was COL. ABRAHAM HUGHES, who came from Wales with CROMWELL. He m. Sarah Dean, of princely Danish descent, owner of the estates of Ballytrent and St. Margaret's, and by her had two sons, Abraham-Thomas, high-sheriff of the co. Wexford *temp.* WILLIAM III.; and Dean; and seven daus., of whom, the eldest, m. to — Nixon, Esq. of Belmont, co. Wexford, collector of Kilkenny, an ancestor of the Earl of Donoughmore; the 2nd, m. to Dr. Hawleston, of Kilscorn; the 3rd, to Richard Newton, of Ballynahallo; the 4th, to Richard Donovan, of Clogmore; and the 5th, to Robert Phaire, of Killough. Abraham Hughes was father of

ABRAHAM HUGHES, Esq. of Ballytreut, co. Wexford, who m. Euphemia, dau. of Brigadier-General Haughton, of Birmount, in the same county, and had by her (who m. 2ndly, Captain Ball), Harry, whose son, Henry Hughes, Esq., cut off the entail, and sold the estate; Abraham; and Euphemia. The younger son,

ABRAHAM HUGHES, Esq., m. 8 Jan. 1767, Jane, youngest dau. of Colonel Robert Clifford (*see* CLIFFORD OF CROMWELL'S FORT, co. Wexford), by Mary Boyd his wife, dau. of Highgate Boyd, Esq. of Roslare, and Margaret his wife, sister of Nicholas Loftus, 1st Viscount Loftus, great-grandfather of the present Marquess of Ely, and had issue,

Henry, capt. in the E.I.Co.'s maritime service, d. unm.
Abraham, lieut. R.N., d. unm.
ROBERT.
William, lieut. 53rd regt., d. unm.
James, who d. leaving by his wife, Miss Lawrence, a son, Henry, lieut. 18th Madras native infantry.
Nicholas-Loftus, E.I Co.'s maritime service, d. unm.
George, half-pay lieut. 73rd regt.
Mary, m. to Robert Donovan, Esq.
Eleanor, d. unm. Euphemia.

Mr. Hughes d. in 1824, and was s. by his son, the present ROBERT HUGHES, Esq. of Ely House.

Arms—Or, on a chevron, sa., between three griffins' heads, erased, gu., as many mullets, pierced, of the field.
Crest—A griffin's head, erased, gu.
Motto—Verus amor patriæ.
Seat—Ely House, Wexford.

HUGHES OF PLAS COCH.

HUGHES, WILLIAM-BULKELEY, Esq. of Plâs Côch, co. Anglesey, and Brynddû, in the same county, b. 26 July, 1797. Mr. Hughes, who is a magistrate for the cos. of Anglesey and Carnarvon, and a deputy-lieut. of the latter county, was elected M.P. for the Carnarvon District of Boroughs, 26 July, 1837, which he has uninterruptedly continued to represent. Mr. Hughes m. 19 April, 1825, Elizabeth, widow of Harry Wormald, Esq. of Woodhouse House, co. York, dau. and heiress of Jonathan Nettleship, of Mattersey Abbey, co. Nottingham, Esq., and s. to the representation of his family 28 Nov. 1836, on the decease of his father, Sir William Hughes.

Lineage.—This ancient line, which has, from remote antiquity, enjoyed an honourable rank among the aristocracy of the northern Principality, inherits paternal lineage with its ancestral domain from LLYWARCH AP BRAN, lord of the Commot of Menai in Anglesey, who flourished in the 12th century. This noble m. Rymel, dau. of Grono, son of Owen ap Edwin, Lord of Tegaingl, and had issue,

I. Llywarch Goch, of whom no particulars appear to have been transmitted.
II. Iorwerth ap Llywarch, progenitor of 1 Family of Porthamel, represented by Bulkeleys, of Porthamel. 2 House of Rhosgolyn. 3 Prices, of Bodowyr, represented by Fitzgeralds, of Bodowyr. 4 House of Gorsedd-Wyd

ryn, represented by Johnsons, of Gorsedd Wydryn. 5 Wynns, of Marsogim, represented by Owens, of Bodion, Barts. 6 House of Berw Ucha, represented by Griffith, of Carrogllwyd, Trygan, and Berw. 7 House of Plas Gwyn and Bryn Celli, represented by Thomas, of Bryn Celli. 8 House of Carreg Wydryn. 9 Lloyds, of Rhiw Goch, co. Merioneth, represented by Wynns, of Gwydyr, Barts. 10 Owens, of Tranmynydd. 11 House of Gelli Lydon. 12 Family of Hendre Mawr, co. Merioneth.
III. CADWGAN AP LLYWARCH.

The 3rd son,

CADWGAN AP LLYWARCH was seated at Porthaml, in Menai, in the parish of Llanedwin, as indicated by the designation, Wele ap Cadwgan ap Llywarch, in that locality, derived from his name, which Wele was inherited, as coheir, by his descendant, Howel ap Gwyn, 26 EDWARD III. By Eva, his wife, dau. of Einion ap Seissyllt, Lord of the Cantred of Merioneth, Cadwgan had, with a younger son, Meredith, of Bodorgan, represented as heir general by Augustus Fuller Meyrick, Esq. of Bodorgan, an elder son,

IORWERTH AP CADWGAN, who *m.* Jane, dau. of Meredith ap Rys ap Meredith Hen, and had issue,

I. Llywelyn, of Myfyrian, living A.D. 1300, ancestor of that house, represented by Prytharch, of Myfyrian, whose heiress *m.* Pierce Lloyd, of Lligwy, Esq.
II. GWYN AP IORWERTH.
III. Philip, from whom derived Wynns, of Llanedwin; Lloyds, of Henblas, represented by Morgans, of Henblas, and William Lloyd, successively Bishop of St. Asaph, Lichfield, and Worcester.
IV. Adda, progenitor of Lloyds, of Plas Bach and Meirion Heilyn, and Williams, of Trivet.

The 2nd son of Iorwerth ap Cadwgan, viz.,

GWYN AP IORWERTH, was living Tuesday, the morrow of the Feast of St. Hilary, 2 EDWARD II., the date of a deed given at "Rhossur" (Newborough) whereby, by the description of "Gwyn ap Iorwerth ap Cadwgan liber tenens de Villa de Porthamel," he makes a grant of certain lands. His son, by Janet, dau. of Ieuan ap Cynric, derived from Marchudd, Lord of Abergelleu, viz.,

HOWEL AP GWYN, was one of the jurors for taking the extent of the Commot of Menai, at Rhosvair, Monday, in the second week of Lent, 26 EDWARD III., and as appears by the same extent, then co-heir of Wele Cadwgan ap Llywarch, in Porthaml. Howel ap Gwyn *m.* Addyn dau. of Meredith Ddu ap Gronwy (he was party to a deed dated Tuesday, on the morrow of the Feast of St. Hilary, 2 Edward II.) derived from Llywarch ap Bran, Lord of Menai. Their son,

IEVAN AP HOWEL, living *circa* 1375, *m.* Agnes, dau. of Howel ap Cynric of Llywidiarth, co. Anglesey, and was father of

MADOC AP IEVAN living *circa* 1400 He *m.* Jane, dau. and heir of David ap Hwfa, of Coed Hwfa, of the line of the Lord of Menai, and was father of

IEVAN AP MADOC, witness of a grant of lands to be held from the Feast of All Saints, 2 Edward IV. (1462) and of a grant of lands in consideration of four marks to be paid on the Feast of All Saints, 4 Edward IV. (1464). By a deed dated 12 EDWARD IV., lands were granted him, by the designation of Ievan ap Madoc ap Ievan ap Howel, free tenant of the Lord the King in the Ville of Porthaml, in the Commot of Menai, and by his will, dated 10 Nov. 1482, he directs that he shall be buried in the Church of Llanedwin. He *m.* Matilda, dau. of Madoc, 3rd son of Hwlkin, of Llyslew, and Plas Newydd, in Porthaml, derived through the house of Bodowyr, from Llywarch ap Bran. Their son,

LLYWELYN AP IEVAN, was living 20 January, 18 Edward IV. (1479), the date of letters patent dated at Carnarvon, of grant and appointment, by Edward, Prince of Wales of the office of Reingelt of the Commot of Menai, to, among others, Llywelyn ap Ievan ap Madoc. He was also grantee of lands, by a deed dated at Porthaml, 1 May 17 Henry VII. (1502). His wife was Elen dau. of Tudyr ap David, of Penwnllys, in Tyndaethwy, co. Carnarvon, derived from Iarddur ap Cynddelw, Lord of Allechwedd, in Carnarvon. Llywelyn ap Ievan was succeeded by his son,

HUGH AP LLYWELYN, Gent. of Porthaml, grantee, with others, of the office of Reingild, of the Commot of Menai, under letters patent of Arthur, Prince of Wales, dated at Carnarvon, 8 February, 15 HENRY VII. His will, dated 12 April, 1557, and proved at Bangor, the 30th of the same month, directs that he shall be buried at Llanedwin. He *m.* Masli, dau. of David ap Ievan, of Myfyrian, co. Anglesey, and by her, whose will, dated 9 February, 1561-2, was proved at Bangor, 22 May, 1562, he had an eldest son,

DAVID LLOYD AP HUGH, Gent. of Porthaml, party to a deed dated 18 Nov., 33 HENRY VIII. (1541), whose will, dated 11 March, 1574, was proved at Bangor, 26 April, in the same year. His wife was Agnes dau. of John Owen, Gent. of Llanfacthly, co. Anglesey, ancestor of the Owens of Bodsilin, and subsequently of Clenenneu, co. Carnarvon, and Porkington, co. Salop, younger brother of Owen ap Meiric of Bodeon, ancestor of the Owens of Orielton and of Bodeon Barts. By this lady, who was executrix of her husband's will, David Lloyd ap Hugh had an eldest son,

HUGH HUGHES, Esq. of Porthaml, the first who assumed the family surname. He rebuilt, 1569, the family residence, which, from the colour of the stone, acquired the name of Plâs Côch (Red Hall), which has been since substituted for that of Porthaml Issa. This gentleman, who was high-sheriff for Anglesey, 1581, 1592, and 1600, and represented that county in the parliament assembled at Westminster 9 ELIZABETH, was a bencher of Lincoln's Inn, attorney-general to Queen ELIZABETH for North Wales, and was appointed by JAMES I. lord-chief-justice for Ireland; but *d.* in London before he proceeded to that country. He *m.* Elizabeth, dau. and co-heir of Simon Montagu, Esq., brother of Edward, Lord Montagu, of Boughton, and of Henry, Earl of Manchester, and by her (who *m.* 2ndly, the Rev. Robert White, D.D., prebendary of Worcester) left a son and heir,

ROGER HUGHES, Esq. of Plâs Côch, barrister-at-law (whose will, dated 29 May, 1646, was proved 1 May, 1650). He *m.* Winifred, dau. of David Owen, of Llandegfair, and had a son and successor,

HUGH HUGHES, Esq. of Plâs Côch, living 1645, father, by Jane his wife, dau. of Owen Wynn, Esq. of Glascoed, of a son and heir,

ROGER HUGHES, Esq. of Plâs Côch, high-sheriff 1685, who *m.* 1677, Margaret, dau. and heir of Henry Jones, Esq. of Plas-yn-Llangoed, and had issue, I. HUGH; II. Henry; III. ROGER; IV. David; V. Owen; VI. Robert, B.A., who *m.* Jane, dau. of James Kelsall, Esq. of Bradshaw Hall, Cheshire, and *d.* in 1756, leaving issue, 1 Robert, who *m.* 1761, Emma, dau. of William Jones, Esq. of Penheskin, Ucha (he *d.* without issue: she *m.* 2ndly, Col. Peacock); 2 William, heir to his uncle; 1 Margaret, who *m.* Robert Bulkeley, Esq. of Gronant, Anglesey; VII. John; VIII. William; I. Margaret, *m.* John Hughes; II. Jane, who *m.* 1st, Owen Williams, and 2ndly, Hugh Lewis; III. Dulcibella, who *m.* Samuel Weigh. Mr. Hughes *d.* in 1716, and was *s.* by his son,

HUGH HUGHES, Esq., of Plâs Côch, high-sheriff 1719, who *m.* 1718, Emma, dau. of William Griffith, Esq. of Carrigllwyd, but dying *s. p.* 1765, was *s.* by his nephew,

WILLIAM HUGHES, Esq. of Plâs Côch and Plas-yn-Llangoed, who *m.* Anna, dau. and heir of Fortunatus Wright, of Liverpool, merchant, by Mary his wife, dau. and heir of William Bulkeley, Esq. of Brynddû co. Anglesey, and by her had issue,

WILLIAM-BULKELEY (Knt.) his heir.
Hugh-Robert, in holy orders, *d. unm.* 1804.
ROBERT (*see* HUGHES OF PLAS-YN-LLANGOED).
John, *d. unm.*
Mary, *d. unm.* 1826.
Anne, *m.* to Richard Jones, Esq, and *d. s. p.* 1833.
Jane, *m.* George Martin, Esq. of Stockport, and *d.* 1833, leaving a son, George-Henry, and a dau., Jane.
Margaret, *m.* Captain M'Donald, of Edinburgh, and left a dau., Margaret-Hughes, *m.* to Capt. Cuppage.

Mr. Hughes was *s.* by his eldest son,

SIR WILLIAM-BULKELEY HUGHES, Knt. of Plâs Côch *b.* 7 Dec. 1766, who *m.* 2 July, 1792, Elizabeth, 2nd dau. and co-heir of Rice Thomas, Esq. of Coed-helen, co. Caernarvon, and by her (who *d.* 1839) had issue,

WILLIAM-BULKELEY, his heir.
Rice-Robert, M.A. of Jesus College, Oxford, rector of Newborough, and vicar of Llanidan, co. Anglesey, *b.* 19 March, 1800, *m.* 5 Dec. 1838, Charlotte, 2nd dau. of the Very Rev. John Warren, dean of Bangor, and left issue three sons, Rice-William, *b.* 1 Nov. 1841, who has taken the name of THOMAS, and is the present Rice-William-Thomas, of Coedhelen; Lloyd-Warren-George, *b.* 27 Aug. 1846, and Trevor-Charles, *b.* 1 Oct. 1848.
Robert-George, lt.-col. 52nd foot, *b.* 1 Nov. 1801, *m.* 5 Aug. 1830, Hannah, 2nd dau. of John Jordan, Gent. of Shrewsbury, and has issue, a son, George-William-Bulkeley, capt. 52nd foot; Goodman, Sarah-Elizabeth, Helen, *d. unm.* 1855, and Maria.
Thomas, *d.* young. Margaret, *d. unm.*
Elizabeth, *m.* 1817, Pierce-Wynne Yorke, Esq. of Dyffryn-Aled, co. Denbigh.
Mary, *m.* 1821, Osgood Gee, jun., Esq. of Earl's Colne House, co. Essex.
Ellen-Catherine.
Sidney-Jane, *m.* Frederick-Charlton Marsden, major 29th Bengal native infantry.

Sir William-Bulkeley Hughes *d.* 28 Nov. 1836, and was *s.* by his son, the present WILLIAM-BULKELEY HUGHES, Esq., M.P., of Plâs Côch.

Arms—Arg., a chevron, erm., between three Cornish choughs, ppr., each holding in his beak an ermine spot; quartering, 1st, sa., a chevron, between three bulls' heads, caboshed, arg.; 2nd, gu., a lion, rampant-guardant, or; 3rd, arg., three boars' heads, couped, sa.; 4th, vert, a stag, trippant, arg., attired, or; 5th, gu., a chevron, between three stags' heads, arg., attired, or; 6th, gu., a chevron, erm., between three Saracens' heads, couped, ppr.; 7th, arg., on a chevron, sa., three mullets, of the first.

Crest—A Cornish chough, ppr., holding in his claw a fleur-de-lis, arg.

Motto—Duw a Ddarpar i'r Brian.

Seat—Plâs Côch, co. Anglesey.

HUGHES OF PLAS-YN-LLANGOED.

HUGHES, ROBERT-JONES, Esq., B.A., of Plâs-yn-Llangoed, co. Anglesey, J.P., *b.* 5 Oct. 1810; high-sheriff in 1845.

Lineage.—WILLIAM HUGHES, of Plâs Côch, was *s.* in the estate of Plas-yn-L'angoed, and the impropriate rectory, advowson, and patronage of Llaniestyn, with the chapelries of Llangoed and Llanfihangel-tyn-Sylw, by his 2nd son,

THE REV. HUGH-ROBERT HUGHES, B.C.L., who *d.* 4 May, 1804, and was *s.* by his brother,

ROBERT HUGHES, Esq., lieut. R.N., high-sheriff of Anglesey in 1815, who *m.* Dorothy-Philadelphia, 5th dau. of Herbert Jones, Esq. of Llynon co. Anglesey, by Dorothea his wife, dau. of the Rev. William Sutton, rector of Llanuchan, Denbighshire, and left issue,

- ROBERT-JONES, his heir.
- William-Henry, *m.* Charlotte, dau. of — Riteon, Esq. of Liverpool, and has issue,
  - William-Henry. David-John. James-Llewelyn.
- Herbert-Jones, *m.* Helen Hunt, eldest dau. of John-R. Greig, Esq. of Lethangie, Kinross, N.B., and has Herbert, and other issue.
- Hugh-Robert, of Bangor, *m.* 1847, Catherine, dau. of John Rutherford Greig, Esq., and has issue.
- Dorothea-Emma, *m.* John Cattermole, Esq. of Norfolk, and has issue three sons.
- Mary-Elizabeth, *m.* Thomas Morris, Esq. of Liverpool, and has issue.

Robert Hughes *d.* 29 Nov. 1827, and was *s.* by his son, the present ROBERT-JONES HUGHES, Esq. of Plas-yn-Langoed.

Arms, Crest, and *Motto*—*see* HUGHES *of Plâs Côch.*

Seat—Plas-yn-Llangoed, co. Anglesey.

HUGHES OF YSTRAD.

HUGHES, THOMAS, Esq. of Ystrad, co. Denbigh, *b.* 7 Dec. 1799; *m.* 20 Nov. 1827, Margaret, only dau. of Robt. Williams, late of the city of Chester, and of Pentremawr, Denbighshire, Esq., and by her (who *d.* 1 April, 1854) has issue,

- I. HUGH-ROBERT, *b.* 17 Jan. 1835.
- I. Sarah-Mary. II. Martha-Elizabeth.
- III. Selina-Margaret.

Mr. Hughes is a magistrate of the counties of Denbigh and Flint, and D.L. of the former county, for which he has served the office of sheriff: he is also by letters patent, steward of the crown for the lordship of Denbigh.

Lineage.—Mr. Hughes' ancestors in the paternal line descend from Iorwerth Sais, of Llanynys, who bore for arms, or, three lions, couchant, sa. He was son of Iorwerth ap Llewelyn ap Iorwerth ap Heilin ap Cowryd ap Cadvan, of Dyffryn Clwyd. Einion Vychan ap Ieuan, the great-grandson of Iorwerth Sais, was father of David ap Einion Vychan, whose wife was Margaret, dau. of Howel ap David Lloyd ap Griffith. Their son, Hugh ap David, *m.* Margaret, dau. of Tudyr ap Grono, of Penllyn, and was father of Robert ap Hugh, of Segroyt, in Llanrhaiadr, co. Denbigh, an ancient inheritance still belonging to Mr. Hughes, and upon which his ancestors resided for many generations.

From ROBERT AP HUGH descended

ANDREW HUGHES, Gent. of Segroyt, *temp.* JAMES I., who appears to have been the first who assumed the family surname. He *m.* Katherine Lloyd, of Brynlluarth, and was *s.* by his eldest son and heir,

HUGH HUGHES, who *m.* Grace, dau. of Evan Lloyd, of Erivistt, Gent., by whom he left issue an eldest son, EVAN HUGHES, and a dau., Margaret, who *m.* Robert Price, and left issue a dau., Jane, who *m.* — Maurice, of Lys whose son, — Maurice, of Ystrad, Esq., had a dau., Margaret, *m.* to John Conway, Esq., from whose descendants the present Mr. Hughes purchased the Ystrad estate in 1830.

EVAN HUGHES, the eldest son of Hugh, *m.* in 1685, Mary, dau. and heiress of David Roberts, Gent., of Penybryn, St. Asaph, co. Flint, by Ellin Conway, of Pentre-llech, and left issue,

HUGH, his heir, who resided at Penybryn, and in 1707, *m.* Mary, sole dau. of Meriana Jones, of Meriadog, co. Denbigh, Widow. The eldest son of this marriage was JOHN, who dying *unm.* was *s.* by the 2nd son.

THE REV. DAVID HUGHES, A.M. Jesus College, Oxon, in holy orders, rector of Llandd get, in Denbighshire, and vicar of Aghrim, in the diocese of Clonfert, in Ireland, where he *d.* in 1767, having *m.* Margaret, dau. of Edward Hughes, of Keidiog, and sister of John Hughes, Esq. of Plas-draw, by whom he left issue,

- HUGH, his heir (afterwards of Llainwen).
- Edward, in holy orders. And three daus.

HUGH HUGHES, Esq., the eldest son, *s.* his father, and in 1758, *m.* Mary, dau. and heiress of Rice Roberts, Gent. of Llainwen, co. Denbigh, by Anne, eldest dau. of Jonathan Parry, of Llangollen-fechan, Esq. Mr. Hughes of Llainwen, was *s.* by his eldest son,

JOHN HUGHES, Esq., *b.* in 1763, who *m.* 30 April, 1795, Mary, eldest dau. and co-heiress of John Matthews,* of Willington, in Hanmer, co. Flint, Gent., by Mary his wife, dau. of John Maddox, Gent. of Preesheulle, co. Salop, which Mary afterwards, upon the death, without issue of her brother, Thomas Maddox, *s.* to her father's estate in Shropshire. By Mary his wife, Mr. Hughes left at his decease, 18 April, 1830, a son and two daus.,

- THOMAS, now of Ystrad.
- Mary-Ann, *d.* 7 Jan. 1854.
- Margaret, *m.* April, 1833, to Robert Read, Esq., who *d.* in March, 1846, leaving three daus.

Mr. Hughes *d.* 12 April, 1830, and was *s.* by his only son, the present THOMAS HUGHES, Esq.

Arms—1st, or, three lions, couchant, sa.; 2nd, erm., a lion, rampant, sa.; 3rd, sa., on a bend, arg., between two cottises, erm., a rose, gu.; 4th, az., three lions, rampant, or, and on a chief, arg., three cross-crosslets, sa.; 5th, arg., on a fesse, gu., between two cottises, wavy, sa., three crescents, or; 6th, arg., a chevron, between three towers, sa., flaming with fire.

Crests—1st, a lion, couchant, sa.; 2nd, a lion's paw, holding a cross-crosslet, sa.

Seat—Ystrad, co. Denbigh.

HUGHES OF THE GROVE.

HUGHES, JAMES-FREEMAN, Esq of the Grove, near Stillorgan, co. Dublin, A.B., Trinity College, Dublin, barrister-at-law, *b.* 19 Feb. 1808, *m.* 15 Sept. 1842, Martha, 4th dau. of the late William Redfern, Esq. of Churchfield House, co. Warwick, and has issue,

- I. JOHN-DE COURCY, *b.* 15 May, 1850.
- II. James-De Courcy-Ireland, *b.* 19 May, 1856.
- I. Constant-Grace-Martha.
- II. Eleanor-Anne-Catharine, *d.* 31 Dec. 1845.
- III. Anna-Maria-De Courcy. IV. Honoria.
- V. Martha-Rosa. VI. Edith-Redfern.

* MATTHEWS, OF ERBISTOCK AND WILLINGTON.

Maurice Matthews, 4th son of John Matthews, of Harnage, co. Salop, Esq., was rector of Erbistock in 1669, and *m.* Catherine, dau. of John Powell, of Bodylling, who was brother of Sir Thomas Powell, of Horsley, Bart. His 2nd son, John, *b.* Aug. 1665, was of Willington. By his wife, Ellen Partin, he left issue an eldest son, John, who, in 1729, *m.* Christiana, eldest dau. and co-heiress of Robert Dod,* of Bersham, by his wife Elizabeth, dau. of Jonas Dod, of Harnage. The eldest son of this marriage, John Matthews, *m.* Mary Maddox as above stated. John and Ellen Matthews had a 2nd son, George, who was grandfather of Mrs. Roberts, wife of the Rev. Nathaniel Roberts, of Cefn Park, co. Denbigh, and of Lady Palmer, wife of Sir Roger Palmer, Bart. of Kenure Park, co. Dublin.

* The family of Dod of Harnage, were a branch of the ancient Cheshire family of that name, and derived more immediately from William Dod, of the Lower Hall, Broxton His great-grandson, Richard Dod, *m.* Eleanor, dau. of Robert Matthews, of Harnage, *temp.* ELIZABETH, and became seated at Harnage, where the elder line of his male descendants continued, until Jonas Dod, great-grandson of Richard, who having only daus. and co-heirs, the eldest of those daus., Elizabeth, carried the Harnage estate in marriage to Robert Dod, of Bersham, co. Denbigh, whose eldest dau. and co-heir, Christiana, *b.* in 1694, *m.* John Matthews, as in the preceding note.

Lineage.—The first of the present family, who went over from Wales and settled in Ireland, was

JOHN HUGHES, Esq., an officer in the army of CHARLES II. He subsequently held a government appointment in one of the military departments of that period. He purchased the estate of Elm Park, co. Mayo; and *m.* about the year 1682, Miss Wynne, of an ancient Welsh family, and had issue several children. He was *s.* by his eldest son,

JAMES HUGHES, Esq. of Elm Park, J.P., *b. temp.* CHARLES II., about 1684; *m.* 1714, Miss Giles, a branch of the family of GILES *of Gileston*, and had issue,

JOHN, his heir, of whom presently.
George. William, an officer in the army.

The eldest son,

JOHN HUGHES, Esq., *b.* 1716; *m.* 1737, Mary Blakeney, an heiress, of the co. of Cavan; and *d.* 28 April, 1779, aged 63, leaving issue,

JOHN, his heir. JAMES, of whom presently.
Douglas. Alexander.
Eleanor.

The 2nd son,

JAMES HUGHES, Esq. of Ballinrobe, co. Mayo, *b.* 1740; *m.* May, 1774, Letitia, dau. of the Very Rev. William Ireland, a distinguished divine, rector of Cong co. Mayo, warden of Galway, and J.P. for several cos., and great-great-granddau. of William Ireland, Esq., by the Hon. Margaret De Courcy his wife youngest surviving dau. of John De Courcy, 21st Lord Kingsale, and sole surviving sister and heiress of Almericus, 22nd Lord Kingsale. Mr. Hughes, dying 9 Nov. 1786, aged 46 left issue, by Letitia his wife,

I. JOHN, of the Grove, *b.* 1 May, 1775; *m.* 10 May, 1806, Eleanor, eldest dau. of the late James Collins, Esq., an officer of the barrack department of Ireland, granddau. of the Rev. Emanuel Collins, A.M., and great-granddau. of Major Samuel Collins, of Chew-Magna, Somersetshire, a distinguished officer of dragoons in the army of WILLIAM III. Mr. Hughes held, for many years, the government appointment of secretary to the barrack-department of Ireland, and previously that of inspector-general of barracks; and dying 9 Feb. 1852, in the 77th year of his age, left issue, by Eleanor his wife,
 1 JAMES-FREEMAN, now of The Grove.
 2 John-Emanuel, A.B., Trinity College, Dublin, *b.* 8 Nov. 1809.
 1 Henrietta.
 2 Eleanor-Jane, *d.* 21 Sept. 1825.
 3 Constant-Grace, *m.* Aug. 1840, William Graves, Esq., and has issue, John-Hughes, *b.* 29 Sept. 1844, *d.* 18 Dec. 1846; William-Alexander, *b.* July, 1846; James-Yoxall, *b.* 11 Nov. 1849; Martha-Grace.
 4 Mary. 5 Anna-Maria
 6 Eleanor-Martha-Jane, *d.* 21 Feb. 1829.

II. William, an officer in the 64th regiment, *b.* 1776; *m.* Margaret, dau. of — Carr, Esq., and widow of Colonel Duncan; *d.* 1822.

III. James, of Strabane, co. Tyrone, *b.* 1780; *m.* Jane, dau. of the Very Rev. John Brocas, dean of Killala, and granddau. of the Very Rev. Theophilus Brocas.

I. Mary, *m.* Stephen Hughes, Esq., and has, with other issue, William, in holy orders, A.M., and ex-scholar of Trinity College, Dublin, rector of Aughanloo, co. Londonderry, *b.* 5 April, 1801, *m.* Rebecca Mathewson, of Ardstraw, co. Tyrone (whose grandfather *d.* in 1828, at the age of 101, having, at the time of his death, 165 descendants living), and has issue surviving, George, William, Mary, Lavinia-Mathewson, Isabella, Rebecca, Madeline, Jemima.

II. Letitia, *m.* Major Edward-Harman Pope, of Popefield, Queen's Co., J.P., and has issue, Thomas Harman; James-Hughes; Jane-Mary; Ellen-Thomasina; Harriet-Anne *m.* Joseph-L. Beasley, Esq. of Salisbury, co. of Kildare, and has issue; Letitia-Lucinda.

III. Magdalene, *m.* — Tunbridge, Esq., and had, with other issue, John, an officer of the Ordnance Department; and Jane, *m.* the Rev. Kenneth Fraser, rector of Astley Bridge, Lancashire.

Seat—The Grove, co. Dublin.

HULTON OF HULTON.

HULTON, WILLIAM, Esq. of Hulton Park, co. Lancaster, deputy-lieut., high-sheriff 1809, *b.* 23 Oct. 1787; *m.* 25 Oct. 1808, Maria, youngest dau. and co-heir of Randall Ford, Esq. of Wexham, in Bucks, by Elizabeth his wife, eldest dau. of Peter Brooke, Esq. of Mere, in Cheshire, and has issue,

I. WILLIAM-FORD, *m.* 15 Oct. 1839, Georgiana, youngest dau. of the late Sir John-Lister Kaye Bart., by his wife, Lady Amelia Grey, dau. of George-Harry, 5th Earl of Stamford, and has issue,

 1 WILLIAM-WILBRAHAM. 2 Edward.
 1 Jessie. 2 Georgiana-Maria.

II. Arthur-Hyde.

III. Frederick-Bleythin, an ensign in the 48th regt., *d.* abroad in 1839.

IV. Charles-Norleigh. V. Hugh-Thurstain.

VI. Alfred-Lacy.

I. Amelia-Maria, *m.* 31 Jan. 1837, to the Hon. and Rev. H.-Montague Villiers, Bishop of Carlisle.

II. Sophia-Frances-Anne, *m.* 7 Dec. 1836, to E.-R.-Gale Braddyll, Esq., eldest son of Lieut.-Col. Braddyll, of Conishead Priory, co. Lancaster.

III. Gertrude-Mary, *m.* to George Wilson, Esq. eldest son of Col Wilson of Dallam Tower, co. Westmoreland.

IV. Emma-Louisa, *d.* in 1841.

Mr. Hulton is likewise Constable of Lancaster Castle.

Lineage.—This family possesses the most unerring proof of antiquity in the title-deeds of their estate of Hulton, from which the Hultons derive their surname, and of which they have been uninterrupted lords since the Conquest. The first feudal proprietor on record,

BLEYTHIN DE HULTON, living *temp.* HENRY II., was father of

JORVETH, *alias* YARWIT DE HULTON, who flourished in the reigns of RICHARD I. and JOHN, and obtained from the latter a grant by charter of the town of Penelton in Lancashire in exchange for other lands which the king, when Earl of Morton, had given him. He had, with other issue, a son,

RICHARD DE HULTON, who had a grant of lands in Barton from Edith de Barton, by consent of Gilbert de Norton, her husband, which lands Jorveth de Hulton, father of Richard, had some time held of her. To his son and successor,

DAVID DE HULTON, Lord of Hulton, his cousin, Robert de Hulton, granted all his lands in Hulton, and William de Ferrers gave all his possessions in Flixton, together with his manor of Hordeshale, by homage and service of two marks of silver four times a-year, and by the sixth part of a knight's fee, A.D. 1219. David de Hulton *m.* Agnes, dau. of Adam de Blackburne, and was father of several sons,* of whom the eldest,

RICHARD DE HULTON, of Hulton, was ancestor of the very eminent family of HULTON *of Hulton*, whose representative *temp.* HENRY VIII.,

ROGER HULTON, Esq. of Hulton Park, *m.* Katharine dau. and co-heir of Sir Jame Harrington, of Wolfedge, and by her (who was living a widow 29 Sept. 16 HENRY VII.) had three sons, and one dau. Emma *m.* to Richard Parr, of Kempsnough. The eldest son,

ADAM HULTON, Esq. of Hulton Park living 20 Jan. 21 HENRY VIII., *m.* by license, Alice, only child and heiress of John Hulton, Esq. of Farnworth, and had four sons and three daus.: of the latter the eldest Elena, was *m.* to Ralph Assheton, Esq. of Great Lever; and the 2nd, Clemence, to John Walmesley, of Blackyhurst. Adam Hulton was *s.* at his decease by his eldest son.

WILLIAM HULTON Esq. of Hulton Park, who *m.* Elizabeth, dau. of Thomas Legh, Esq of Adlington, and had (with other issue, of which John was of Stapleford, and Ellen the wife of John Hordeyne, of Woolstone) a son,

ADAM HULTON, Esq. of Hulton, *m.* 21 HENRY VIII., Clemence dau. of Sir William Norris of Speke, co. Lancaster; and dying 15 ELIZABETH was *s.* by his son,

WILLIAM HULTON, Esq. of Hulton Park, aged 32 at his father's decease. He *m.* Margaret dau. and co-heir of Henry Kighley Esq. of Inskip, and had with other issue (of whom, Katherine, *m.* Assheton Potter, Esq. of Croston; and Elizabeth, Robert Dalton, Esq. of Thornham), a son and successor,

ADAM HULTON, Esq. of Hulton Park who *m.* previously to 4 Feb. 29 ELIZABETH, Alice Baguley, of Manchester, and was *s.* by his eldest son.

WILLIAM HULTON, Esq. of Hulton Park who *m.* Katherine, 5th dau. of Robert Hyde of Hyde and Norbury, in Cheshire, by Beatrix his wife, dau. of Sir William Calverley, of Calverley in Yorkshire, and had issue,

ADAM, his heir. Edward, *d. unm.* in 1645.
Beatrix, *m.* to George Rigby, Esq. of Peel, 4th son of Alexander Rigby, of Middleton.

William Hulton *d.* 6 Sept. 1613 (his widow *m.* 2ndly, Roger Nowel, of Read; and 3rdly, Saville Radcliffe), and was *s.* by his son,

* From John de Hulton, the youngest son, descended the HULTONS *of Farnworth*.

ADAM HULTON, Esq. of Hulton Park, b. 1 July, 1607; who m. Grace, only dau. of Edmund Howarth, Esq. of Howarth, and had issue,

WILLIAM, his heir.
Anne, m. to Thomas Lacy, Esq. of Longworth.
Beatrix, m. to Edward Copley, Esq. of Batley.

Mr. Hulton, whose will bears date 16 Sept. 1651, was s. by his son,

WILLIAM HULTON, Esq. of Hulton Park and Farneworth, b. 9 Sept. 1625; who m. Anne, only child and heir of William Jessop, Esq. of Warwick House, Holborn, M.P. for Stafford and had issue. Mr. Hulton d. 27 March 1694, was buried in the chancel of Dean Church, and s. by his son,

HENRY HULTON, Esq. of Hulton Park, bapt. 3 Feb. 1665; who m. at Thornhill, 29 Sept. 1735, Eleanor, eldest dau. and co-heir of the Rev. John Copley, rector of Elmley, but dying without issue, the estates passed to his brother,

JESSOP HULTON, Esq. of Hulton Park and Farneworth, bapt. at Dean, 18 Feb. 1667-8. He m. Mary, dau. of William Haselden, co. Hereford, and had issue. Mr. Hulton d. about the year 1726, and was s. by his son,

WILLIAM HULTON, Esq. of Hulton Park and Farneworth, bapt. at Dean, 22 June, 1717; who m. Mary dau. and co-heir of William Leigh, Esq. of Westhoughton House, and by her (who m. 2ndly, Edward Clowes, Esq. of Broughton) left at his decease, in April, 1741, an only son and successor,

WILLIAM HULTON Esq. of Hulton Park and Farneworth, b. in Ireland, 6 Oct. 1739. He m. 25 April, 1759, Anne, dau. and heir of John Hall, Esq. of Droylsden, in Lancashire, and by her (who d. 23 June 1802) had issue,

I. WILLIAM, his heir.
II. Henry, b. 27 Nov. 1765; lieut.-col. commandant of the Blackburne regiment of local militia, m. Louisa-Caroline, 4th dau. of John-Hooke Campbell, Esq. of Bangeston, in Pembrokeshire, Lord Lyon, King at Arms, Scotland, and had issue,
1 Henry-William, d. s. p. in 1822.
2 William-Adam, barrister-at-law, m. Dorothy-Anne, youngest dau. of Edward Gorst, Esq. of Preston, and has issue,
William-Jessop, b. 5 Feb. 1837, d. an infant.
Henry-Edward, b. 21 June, 1839.
Frederick-Campbell, b. 24 June, 1841.
George-Eustace, b. 11 July, 1842.
Eliza-Louisa. Mary-Caroline.
3 Jessop-George-De Blackburne, M.D., E.I.Co.'s service, d. s. p. off Arabia, in Sept. 1836.
4 Campbell-Basset-Arthur-Grey, in holy orders.
5 Frederick-Blethyn-Copley.
1 Louisa-Caroline-Mary-Anne, m. to John Addison, Esq. of Preston, barrister-at-law; and d. in 1825, leaving a dau., Anne-Agnes.
2 Anne-Beatrice.
3 Eleanor-Eustatia, d. in April, 1842, s. p.
4 Henrietta-Maria. 5 Charlotte-Frances-Mona.
I. Anne, m. to Banastre Parker, Esq. of Extwistle and Cuerden; and d. s. p in 1830.

Mr. Hulton d. in France, 1 Jan. 1773 and was s. by his son,

WILLIAM HULTON, Esq. of Hulton Park, b. 23 May, 1762; who served as high-sheriff in 1789. He m. 28 Aug. 1785, Jane, 3rd dau. of Peter Brooke Esq. of Mere, co. Chester, and by her (who m. 2ndly, Major Thomas-William Boyce) had issue,

WILLIAM, his heir.
Frances-Anne, m. 4 May, 1810, to the Rev. John Rowles Browne, vicar of Prestbury, in Cheshire.

Mr. Hulton d. 24 June, 1800, and was s. by his son, the present WILLIAM HULTON, Esq. of Hulton Park.

Arms—Arg., a lion, rampant, gu.
Crest—In a mural crown, a stag's head, with a branch of hawthorn.
Motto—Mens flecti nescia.
Seat—Hulton Park, near Bolton.

HUME OF NINEWELLS.

HUME, AGNES, of Ninewells, co. Berwick, dau. and heiress of David Hume, of Ninewells, one of the barons of the court of Exchequer in Scotland; m. Matthew Norman Macdonald, Esq., brother of the late Sir John Macdonald, Adjutant-General.

Lineage.—THOMAS HUME, or HOME, 2nd son of Sir Alexander Home, of Dunglass who was slain at the battle of Verneuil, in 1424, founded the family of HOME *of Tyninghame and Ninewells*, of which the representative in the 17th century.

JOHN HUME, Esq. of Ninewells, m. and left, with a dau., Catherine, wife of the Rev. George Home (*see family of* ROBERTSON, p. 449), a son, JOSEPH HOME, Esq. of Ninewells, who m. Catherine, dau. of Sir David Falconer, lord president of the Court of Session, 1681, and sister of David, 5th Lord Falconer, and had issue,

JOHN, his heir.
DAVID, the celebrated historian, b. at Edinburgh, in 1711, and d. unm. in 1776.
Catharine.

The elder son,

JOHN HUME, Esq. of Ninewells and of Ferney Castle, Berwick b. in 1724; m. in 1751, Agnes, only dau. of Robert Carre, Esq. of Cavers, in Roxburghshire (by Helen his wife, sister of Sir Walter Riddell, Bart. of Riddell) and had issue,

JOSEPH, his heir.
DAVID, who s. on the death of his brother, to the family estates.
John, a writer to the Signet in Edinburgh.
Catherine, m. to Capt. Robert Johnston, of Hilton and Hutton Hall, co. Berwick.

Mr. Hume d. 14 Nov. 1786 and was s. by his eldest son,

JOSEPH HUME, Esq. of Ninewells, early in life capt. in the 2nd dragoon-guards, d. unm. 14 Feb. 1832, and was s. by his next brother and heir, the very eminent lawyer,

DAVID HUME, Esq., formerly one of the barons of the Court of Exchequer in Scotland, from which office he retired in 1834, having held it for a period of twelve years. He was successively sheriff-depute of Berwickshire and of West Lothian, and was a professor of the Scotch laws in the University of Edinburgh. Baron Hume m. Jane Alder, and had issue,

Joseph, advocate, d. unm. 1819.
Elizabeth, of Ninewells, which she rebuilt in 1841, d. unm.
AGNES, now of Ninewells.
CATHERINE, m. 1819, Adolphus M'Dowall Ross,* M.D., and has issue,
Andrew-Ross. David Hume.
Adolphus-M'Dowall. John-Abercromby.
Jane-Alder, m. 1851, to Henry Gordon Dickson, Esq.
Isabella, m. 1847, to John-George Chancellor, Esq.
Catherine-Agnes, m. 1850, to Richard Pynsent, Esq.
Elizabeth-Mary.
Dr. Ross d. 1842; Mrs. Ross d. 1851.

Arms—Vert, a lion, rampant, arg., within a bordure, or, charged with nine fountains, or wells, ppr.
Crest—A lion's head, erased, arg., collared, gu.
Motto—True to the end.
Seat—Ninewells, Berwickshire.

*** GEORGE HOME, Esq. of Whitfield, derived from a brother of Home of Ninewells, was possessed of a very considerable landed property in Berwickshire, and long represented that county in parliament, but owing to the

---

* FAMILY OF ROSS.—The branch of the family of Ross, from which the future representatives of Ninewells descend, has been seated in Galloway for many centuries, and in the possession of extensive estates, amongst others Balniel (carried into the family of Stair by the marriage of Margaret Ross, the heiress, 21st Sept. 1643, with James, 1st Viscount of Stair) Galston, Balkail, Balsarrock, and Balgreen, and connected, by marriage, with the noble families of Lindsay, Earls of Crawford and Balcarres, Campbell, Earls of Loudon, M'Gill, Viscounts of Oxfurd, Dalrymple, Earls of Stair, &c.

Andrew Ross (great-grandfather of Dr. Adolphus M'Dowall Ross) possessed the estates of Balkail, Balsarroch, and Balgreen, all in the co. Wigton, and left three sons,

I. Alexander, of Balkail, grandfather of General Sir Hew Dalrymple Ross, G.C.B.
II. Andrew, of Balsarroch, grandfather of Admiral Sir John Ross, and great-grandfather of Captain Sir James Ross, R.N., the distinguished Polar navigators.
III. James, of Balgreen, m. Isabella Allan, dau. of Captain Allan, Royal Navy, and had, with other issue,
1 Andrew, colonel in the army, m. Isabella Macdonell, of Aberhallader, and had issue,
Alexander-James, lt.-colonel in the army.
Adolphus M'Dowall, M.D., *ut supra.*
James Kerr, of Laurence Park, co. Stirling, colonel in the army, K.H., aide-de-camp to General Sir John Buchan, during the Peninsular War, m. in 1827, Margaret, 2nd dau. of James M'Turvy, Esq. of Lude, co. Perth.
Isabella, m. George Bell, Esq. of Hunthill, co. Roxburgh.
Mary-Anne, m. Dr. Bartlett Buchanan.
Eleanora-Jane, m. Robert Bell, Esq., advocate-procurator of the Church of Scotland, and sheriff of the counties of Berwick and Haddington.
Margaret, m. David Welsh, Esq. of Collin, co. Wigton, and of Nuthill, co. Dumfries.
Clementina Blair, m. Thomas Corrie, Esq. of Newton Aird, co. Dumfries.

prominent part he took in the rising of '45, the estate of Whitfield was confiscated. This George Home, who inherited the lands of Manderston, near Dunse, from his mother's brother, Alexander Cairncross, bishop of Raphoe, was *s.* by his brother,

ALEXANDER HOME, of Manderston, who *m.* the heiress of Drummond of Kildees, with whom he obtained a small fortune, but being of an extravagant disposition, he soon involved his property. Manderston was sold, and with the residue he purchased a property between Edinburgh and Leith, which he denominated Whitfield, in order to preserve the family title. He *d.* without issue, and was *s.* by his nephew (the son of his deceased brother), at that time a midshipman, R.N., who *d.* in 1805, in the Island of Dominica, of which he was a member of council, leaving a widow and an infant son, the present ALEXANDER-GEORGE HOME, Esq. of Whitfield, fellow of the Royal College of Physicians, and assistant-surgeon of the 2nd dragoon-guards.

HUME OF HUMEWOOD.

HUME, WILLIAM-WENTWORTH-FITZWILLIAM, Esq. of Humewood, co. Wicklow, *b.* 28 Oct. 1805; *m.* 8 June, 1829, Margaret-Bruce, eldest dau. of Robert Chaloner, Esq. of Guisboro', co. York, by the Hon. Frances-Laura Dundas, his wife, dau. of the late Lord Dundas, and has surviving issue,

I. Charlotte-Anna, *m.* to Richard-P. Long, Esq. of Dolforgan, co. Montgomery, eldest son of Walter Long, Esq. of Rood Ashton, co. Wilts, M.P. for that county.

Mr. Hume, who is a magistrate and D.L. for co. Wicklow, *s.* his father in Nov. 1815.

Lineage.—ANDREW HUME (son and successor of Gavin Hume, "Captain of Tantallon," distinguished in the French service, and grandson of Alexander Hume, 3rd Baron of Polworth), returned to Scotland and purchased the estate of the Rhodes, near to the lands of his cousin, the 1st Sir John Hume, of North Berwick. He *m.* Mosea Seaton, dau. of Seaton of Barnes, and niece to the Earl of Winton, by whom he had, with a dau., supposed to have *m.* George Hume, of Pinkerton, four sons, viz., ROBERT, his heir; Thomas; John; and William. Andrew Hume *d.* in 1594 or 1595, and was *s.* by his eldest son,

ROBERT HUME, who *m.* Anne, dau. of Dr. Michelson, Laird of Brackness, and granddau. of Sir Bruce Semple, of Cathcart, by whom he had a son,

THOMAS HUME, Esq., who purchased the estate of Humewood, co. Wicklow. He *m.* 1st, Miss Jane Lauder, co. Leitrim; and 2ndly, Elizabeth Galbraith, widow of Hugh Galbraith, of St. Johnstown, co. Fermanagh. By the 1st only he had issue, viz.,

WILLIAM, his heir. George, *d.* young.
Robert, ancestor of the Humes of Lisanure Castle, co. Cavan, and of Cariga, in Leitrim, and of the Humes of Dublin.

Mr. Hume *d.* in 1718, an was *s.* by his eldest son,

WILLIAM HUME, Esq. of Humewood, who *m.* Anna dau. of John Dennison Esq. of the city of Dublin, and had two sons and four daus., viz.. GEORGE, his heir; Dennison, who *d.* without issue; Isabella; Sarah; Catherine; Margaret. He *d.* 26 May. 1752, having previously settled, by deed, dated 6 Dec. 1744, his estate on his eldest son,

GEORGE HUME, Esq. of Humewood, who *m.* Anna, dau. of Thomas Butler, Esq. of Ballymurtagh, co. Wicklow, and had five sons and two daus , viz., WILLIAM, his heir; George *d. s. p.*; Dennison, *d. s. p.*; John-La Touch, who *m.* and left issue; Clement, who also *m.* and left issue; Isabella; and Anna, who *m.* Benjamin Wills, Esq. of the city of Dublin. He *d.* in Aug. 1765 and was *s.* by his eldest son,

WILLIAM HUME, Esq. of Humewood, M.P. co. Wicklow, shot by a party of rebels in the Wicklow mountains 8 Oct. 1798. He *m.* Catherine, dau. of Sir Joseph Hoare, Bart., M.P., of Annabella, co. Cork, and had two sons and four daus., viz.,

WILLIAM-HOARE, his heir.
Joseph-Samuel, who *m.* Miss Smith, and left issue one son, now settled in America, and three daus.
Catherine, *m.* to William Franks, Esq. of Carrig, co. Cork.
Anne, *m.* to the Rev. Dominick-E. Blake.
Jane, *m.* to the Hon. and Rev. Maurice Mahon, now Lord Hartland; she *d. s. p.* 12 Dec. 1838.
Grace.

The eldest son,

WILLIAM-HOARE HUME, Esq. of Humewood, M.P. for Wicklow, co. He *m.* Charlotte-Anna only dau. of the late Samuel Dick, Esq. of Dublin, and sister to Quintin Dick Esq. M.P. for Maldon and had issue.

WILLIAM-WENTWORTH-FITZWILLIAM, now of Humewood.
Quintin-Dick, in holy orders, married.
George Ponsonby, major 58th regt.
Charlotte-Isabella-Forster, *m.* to T. Crowe, Esq. of Dromore Castle, co. Clare.
Charlotte-Jane.

Mr. Hume *d.* in Nov. 1815.

Arms—Quarterly: 1st and 4th, vert, a lion, rampant, arg.; 2nd and 3rd, arg., three ravens, vert.
Crest—A lion's head, erased, arg.
Motto—True to the end.
Seat—Humewood, Baltinglass, co. Wicklow.

HUMFFREYS OF LLWYN.

HUMFFREYS, WILLIAM, Esq. of Llwyn, co. Montgomery, *s.* his brother, 14 Aug. 1824.

Lineage.—The Humffreys of Llwyn deduce lineage from Edwin, Lord of Tegaingl, in Flint, founder of the Twelfth Noble Tribe of North Wales and Powys. From this chief derived, eleventh in succession,

IEVAN VOELVRYCH (AP IORWERTH VAUGHAN), of Maesgwynedd, who *m.* Efa, dau. Cyhelyn, son of Rhun ap Einion Efell, Lord of Cynllaeth, and had issue,

Ievan, surnamed Caereinion, ancestor of the OWENS *of Tedsmore*, OWENS *of Bettws*, OWENS *of Woodhouse*, and OWENS *of Condover*.
Einion. LLEWELYN.
Iorwerth-Goch, ancestor of REAR-ADMIRAL SIR SALUSBURY DAVENPORT (originally HUMFFREYS), C.B. and K.C.H., of Bramall Hall.

The 3rd son,

LLEWELYN, was father of IEVAN, whose son, WILLIAM AP IEVAN, was seated at Llangar, co. Merioneth. His son,

ELISAU AP WILLIAM, *m.* Margaret, dau. of Ievan ap Richard, and was *s.* by his son,

HUMFFREY AP ELISAU of Glanalwen, in Llangar, and of Maerddu, in Gwyddelwern, both in the co. of Merioneth, whose wife was Eleanor, dau. of Edward Lloyd, Esq. of Llysvassy. Their son,

WILLIAM AP HUMFFREY, who first adopted the family surname of HUMFFREYS, served by the name of William Humffreys, Esq., as a captain for CHARLES I. and sold the Glanalwen estate to his wife's brother, Edmund Meirick. Mr. Humffrey *m.* Dorothy dau. of Peter Meyrick, Esq. of Ucheldre, and was father of

WILLIAM HUMFFREYS, of Merddu, who *m.* Jane, dau. of Edward Wynne, of Llangynhafal, and was *s.* by his son,

WILLIAM HUMFFREYS, of Maerddu, *b.* in 1666. This gentleman *m.* Grace, dau. of Robert Lloyd, of Porth, Gent., descended from Osborne Fitzgerald Lord of Ynysymaengwyn, and had issue. Mr. Humffreys *d.* 7 Jan. 1718. His son,

ROGER HUMFFREYS, Esq. of Llanfyllin, co. Montgomery, who was *b.* in 1695, left at his decease, in 1733, a son,

WILLIAM HUMFFREYS, Esq. of Llwyn, co. Montgomery, father of

JOHN HUMFFREYS, Esq. of Llwyn, who *m.* Rebecca, dau. of William-Mostyn Owen, of Woodhouse, co. Salop, Esq.; *d.* 17 Sept. 1817, having had issue,

John Humffreys, Esq. of Llwyn, who *d. s. p.* at Arcot, Madras, 14 Aug. 1824.
WILLIAM, successor of his brother.
Roger-Mostyn. Thomas-Henry.
Edward-Arthur.
Harriet-Rebecca. Frances-Anne.

John Humffreys was *s.* at his death by his brother, the present WILLIAM HUMFFREYS, Esq.

Arms—Quarterly: 1st and 4th, arg., a cross-flory, engrailed, sa., between four Cornish choughs, ppr., on a chief, az., a boar's head, couped, arg., tusked, or, langued, gu., for HUMFFREYS; 2nd and 3rd, erm., a saltier, engrailed, gu., thereon a crescent, or, for LLOYD OF FORTH.
Crest—On a chapeau, a boar, passant, arg., fretty, gu., more usually described and depicted as a boar in a net, or toils.

HUMFREY OF WROXHAM HOUSE.

BLAKE-HUMFREY, ROBERT, Esq. of Wroxham House, co. Norfolk, J.P. and D.L., *b.* 23 Nov. 1795; *m.* 9 Aug. 1838, Charlotte, youngest dau. of Col. Harvey, of Thorpe Lodge, Norwich, by Frances his wife, dau. of Sir Roger Kerrison, Knt., and has issue,

I. ROBERT-HARVEY *b.* 23 Jan. 1843.
II. Thomas, *b.* 8 March, 1844. III. John *b.* 23 Jan. 1847.

I. Margaret. II. Eleanor.
III. Caroline. IV. Isabel-Charlotte.

This gentleman (who served with the army in the Peninsula, was severely wounded at the passage of the Nive, and has a medal with two clasps) is 2nd son of Thomas Blake, of Norwich, Esq., barrister-at-law, a magistrate and D.L. co. Norfolk. (*See pedigree of* BLAKE, *of Horstead.*)

In August, 1847, he assumed by royal licence the surname and arms of HUMFREY in addition to his paternal name and coat, in compliance with the will of the REV. JOHN HUMFREY, of Wroxham, rector of Great Dunham, and Crostwick, in co. Norfolk.

The REV. JOHN HUMFREY, descended from an ancient family at Rishangles, co. Suffolk, was son of the Rev. Richard Humfrey, rector of Thorpe, near Norwich, and brother of the Rev. Richard Humfrey, sometime preceptor to the royal Dukes of Clarence and Kent, sons of GEORGE III.

Arms—Quarterly: 1st and 4th, gu., a lion, rampant, and above the head a ducal coronet, or, with a canton, of the last, for distinction, for HUMFREY; 2nd and 3rd, arg., a chevron, between three garbs, sa., within a bordure, of the last, thereon eight fleurs-de-lis of the first, for BLAKE.

Crests—1st, on a ducal coronet, an eagle, wings elevated, holding in the dexter claw a sceptre, or, and charged on the breast (for distinction) with a cross-crosslet, gu., for HUMFREY; 2nd, on a morion, a martlet, ppr., for BLAKE.

Motto—Coelestem spero coronam.

Seat—Wroxham House, Norfolk.

HUMFREY OF CAVANACOR.

HUMFREY, BENJAMIN-GEALE, Esq. of Cavanacor, co. Donegal, lieut.-colonel in the army, served in the 45th regiment., during the Peninsular war, for which he has a medal and nine clasps; J.P. and high-sheriff in 1848, *b.* 28 Sept. 1793; *m.* 3 July, 1823; Mary, only child and heiress of William Keys, Esq. of Cavanacor, and has issue,

I. WILLIAM, *b.* 16 July, 1824; *d.* April, 1826.
II. John-Keys, *b.* 16 June, 1828; an officer 53rd regiment.
III. Alexander *b.* 9 Aug. 1831; an officer 77th regiment.
IV. Benjamin-Geale, *b.* 25 Dec. 1833; in the royal artillery.
I. Jane. II. Mary.
III. Marion *m.* 11 Aug. 1853, Joseph Fishbourne, Esq. of Ashfield Hall, Queen's Co., and has a dau., Mary-Josephine.
IV. Elizabeth. V. Kate. VI. Annie-Frances.

Lineage.—The first settlement of the Humfrey family in Ireland was made by Richard Humfrey, who was *b.* in 1614. He was the son of Richard Humfrey, of Rettenden, Essex by his wife, the dau. of Sir Samuel Sandys, of Ombersley, co. Worcester, and landed in Ireland 1655 where he settled at Donard, co. Wicklow. His wife *d.* there in 1666; and he in 1665. His eldest son,

HENRY HUMFREY, *m.* 13 Jan. 1675, Catharine dau. of Frances Rolleston, Esq. of Frankfort Castle; and *d.* 4 July, 1709, leaving a son

HENRY HUMFREY, Esq., who *m.* 19 July 1712, Elizabeth Henthorn; and *d.* 12 March 1741, leaving a son,

THOMAS HUMFREY, Esq. *b.* 28 Jan. 1717, who was father, by Elizabeth Stewart his wife, of an only son, HENRY HUMFREY, Esq. *b.* 1757, who, dying *unm.* 1 May 1843 left, by will, his property in Wicklow, Louth, and the King's Co., to his kinsman, Benjamin-Geale Humfrey Esq. His ancestor,

MATTHEW HUMFREY, Esq., was brother of Henry Humfrey who *m.* Miss Rolleston. He *m.* 1685, Deborah, dau. of Benjamin Bunbury, Esq. of Killerig co. Carlow, and by her (who *m.* 2ndly Thomas Bernard, Esq. of Clonmulst) left five sons of whom the eldest, Matthew, *d. unm.* 1744. The 2nd son,

JOHN HUMFREY, Esq. *m.* 27 April, 1747, Elizabeth, dau. of John Geale, Esq. of Mount Geale, co. Kilkenny; and dying 1758 left a son,

WILLIAM HUMFREY, Esq. *b.* 1750; who *m.* 5 Feb. 1774, Mary, dau. of Alexander Kirkpatrick, Esq., and by her (who *d.* 1802) left at his decease 20 Oct. 1829,

ALEXANDER, *b.* 1775; *d.* Aug. 1845; *m.* Catherine, dau. of Major Craven, and had issue, William-Charles, *b.* 1802, *m.* Collins, dau. of Major Fortye, and has four sons and two daus.; Alexander-John, *b.* 1803, *m.* Caroline, dau. of John Bayley, Esq.; Thomas-Craven, *b.* 1811; Benjamin, *b.* 1818, *m.* Harriet, dau. of D. O'Rorke, Esq.; Ellen, *m.* Rev. J. F. Morton.
BENJAMIN-GEALE, now of Cavanacor.
Anne, *m.* R. Stotesbury, Esq.; *d.* 1820.
Margaret, *d.* 1815. Eliza, *m.* J. M. Reade, Esq.
Catherine, *d.* 9 Dec. 1815. Mary-Anne.

Arms—Gu., on a cross, botonné, arg., five pellets.

Motto—Sic olim.

Seat—Cavanacor, co. Donegal.

HUMPHRYS OF BALLYHAISE HOUSE.

HUMPHRYS, WILLIAM, Esq. of Ballyhaise House, co. Cavan, J.P. and D.L., has served as high-sheriff, *b.* Dec. 1798; *m.* Jan. 1827, Anna-Maria, dau. of John Pratt Winter, Esq. of Agher, co. Meath, and has issue,

I. WILLIAM, *b.* Nov. 1827.
II. John-Winter, *b.* Sept. 1829; *m.* Feb. 1854, Priscilla-Cecilia dau. of the Rev. J.-P. Garrett, of Janeville, co. Carlow.
III. Mervyn-Archdall, *b.* March, 1830.
I. Anne-Elizabeth.

He *m.* 2ndly, Feb. 1838, Maria-Clarissa, dau. of Hugh Moore, Esq. of Eglantine House, co. Down, by whom he had,

I. Hugh, *b.* 10 Nov. 1838.
II. Armitage-Eglantine, *b.* Aug. 1843.
I. Cecilia-Letitia. II. Clara.
III. Sylvia-Priscilla.

Mr. Humphrys is son of the late William Humphrys by Letitia his wife.

Arms—Gu., a lion, rampant, and above the head a ducal coronet, or, on a canton, of the last, a trefoil, vert.

Crest—On a ducal coronet, an eagle, wings elevated, holding in his dexter claw a sceptre, or.

Motto—Optima sperando spiro.

Seat—Ballyhaise House, co. Cavan.

HUNGERFORD OF INCHODONY.

HUNGERFORD, THOMAS, Esq. of Inchodony, (The Island) co Cork, *b.* 16 Jan. 1795; *m.* 1 Dec. 1842, Caroline, dau. of George Sandes, Esq. of Dunowen, co. Cork, and has issue,

I. Mary-Sandes.
II. Frances-Eyre.

Lineage.—This is an undoubted branch of the illustrious house of Hungerford of England.

CAPT. THOMAS HUNGERFORD, of Rathbarry, or The Little Island, about four miles westward of Inchodony, the seat of his descendants, served in Ireland in the civil wars ensuing 23 Oct. 1641 (as did also Col. Anthony Hungerford) and eventually purchased considerable estates, among others Inchipun, Clashetariffe, Ballyvolane Lissicurrane and West Cappoen. He was living in 1680. By Mary his wife, he had,

RICHARD, his heir.
John, in holy orders, *b.* in the co. Cork, 1658; of Cahirmore, co. Cork, A.D. 1658.
THOMAS, ancestor of the CAHIRMORE branch.
Elizabeth, *m.* to Achilles Daunt, Esq., ancestor of the DAUNTS *of Tracton Abbey*, co. Cork.
Margaret, *m.* to Francis Poole, of Mayfield.
Jane, *m.* Thomas Hewitt, jun.

The eldest,

COLONEL RICHARD HUNGERFORD, of Inchodony, or The Island, near Clonakilty, is called "cousin," in the will, dated 24 May, 1729, of John Hungerford, lord of the manor of Hungerford, in England. His own will was dated on or about 5 April, 1725. He *m.* Mary, dau. of Sir Emanuel Moore; and *d.* about 1729, leaving issue,

THOMAS, his heir.
Emanuel, in holy orders, *m.* twice, by his 1st wife, he had a dau., Mary, *m.* to Richard Hungerford, of The Island. By his 2nd wife, he had three sons, viz., Richard, John, Thomas.
Richard, also a legatee in the will of John Hungerford, of Hungerford. He *d.* 1755, leaving, by Rachel his wife, an only dau., Rachel, who was *m.* to Grady, of Elton, co. Limerick.
A dau., *m.* to — Daunt.
Katherine, *m.* 1715, to Thomas Knowles, of Killeghy, co. Cork.
Jane.

The son and heir,

Thomas Hungerford, *d. vita patris*, having *m.* in 1719, Susannah Becher, and having left issue,

Richard, his heir.
Elizabeth, *m.* in 1738, to Capt. Philip Townsend, of Derry, near Ross-Carbery.
Mary (a legatee in the will of John Hungerford, of Hungerford), *m.* in 1739, to the Rev. Horatio Townsend, of Coolmona.

The only son,

Richard Hungerford, Esq. of The Island, and for many years of Foxhall, *m.* 1st, Mary Becher, and by her had,

I. Thomas, his heir.
II. John, who *m.* in 1771, Anne Daunt; and *d.* in 1803, leaving issue,
1 Richard, of Cappeen, *m.* in 1808, his cousin, Jane Hungerford, and had, Becher, of Clonakilty, and other issue.
2 Thomas, *m.* Louisa Campbell, in 1809.
3 Henry, *m.* Johanna Daunt.
4 John, *d. s. p.* 5 Becher, *d. s. p.*
6 Emanuel, *m.* Catherine Loane.
1 Eliza, *m.* to Dr. George Hungerford.
2 Anne, *m.* in 1794, to Robert Sealy, Esq.
3 Mary. 4 Susan.

He *m.* 2ndly, Mary, dau. of the Rev. Emanuel Hungerford, and by her was father of

Richard, in holy orders, *m.* 1775, Mary Hungerford, and by her (who *m.* 2ndly, Michael French) had an only child, Richard, *b.* 1776, who *m.* 1794, Isabella Masters, and left issue, Richard, of Carrigeen, who *m.* Mary-Cranfield, dau. of Capt. Colin Campbell, and left issue; Thomas; John; Henry; Stephen; Michael-French; Maria; Catherine; Isabella.
Emanuel, *d. s. p.* Becher, *d. s. p.*
Letitia, *m.* 1769, to Richard Becher.
Elizabeth, *m.* to Capt. Jeremiah Donovan.
Susan, *d. s. p.*

Richard Hungerford *d. circa* 1784, and was *s.* by his son.

Thomas Hungerford, Esq. of The Island, who *m.* 1770, Mary-Cranfield Becher, and by her (who *d.* 1836) had issue,

Richard, his heir.
George (Dr.), of Clonakilty, *m.* in 1802, Eliza Hungerford, his 1st cousin, and by her (who *d.* in 1828) had issue, Thomas, who *d. s. p.*; Richard, who *m.* in 1843, Mary, dau. of William Daunt, of Spring Hill, and had issue. Dr. George *d.* 15 Sept. 1882.
Thomas, of Broomley, near Carrigoline, *m.* 1st, Johanna, widow of Henry Hungerford; and 2ndly, Eliza, dau. of the late Dr. George Daunt, of the city of Cork, and had issue, by his 1st wife, Thomas-William, *m.* Miss O'Hea; Eliza-Charlotte, *m.* to O'Donovan Becher, Esq.; and Mary-Cranfield. By the 2nd wife he had, George-Daunt; Georgina-Daunt; Catherine-Maria; Susanna-Letitia; and Charlotte.

The son and heir

Richard Hungerford, of The Island, *b.* 1771; *m.* July, 1793, Frances, dau. of Richard Becher, Esq. of Hollybrooke, and by her (who *d.* 12 Sept. 1843) had issue,

Thomas, now of Inchodony, or The Island.
Richard-Becher, *m.* 18 Sept. 1837, Frances, dau. of John Becher, Esq. of Hollybrooke, and has Richard, and other issue. John, *d. s. p.*
William, *m.* 22 March, 1831, Jane-Foye, and has three sons, Richard, William, and Winspear.
George, *m.* 7 Oct. 1845, to Mary-Elizabeth Sandes, and has issue.
Henry, *d. s. p.* 10 Oct. 1855.
Becher, *m.* 14 Feb. 1845, Jane Crossley, and has issue.
Fanny.
Susan, *m.* 4 June, 1836, to Wintrop-Baldwin Sealy, Esq.

Mr. Hungerford *d.* 16 Feb. 1833.

Arms—Sa., two bars, arg., in chief, three plates.
Crest—Out of a ducal coronet, or, a pepper garb, between two reaping-hooks, all ppr.
Motto—Et Dieu mon appuy.

HUNGERFORD OF CAHIRMORE.

Hungerford, Thomas, Esq., A.M., of Cahirmore, co. Cork, J.P., *b.* 1789; *m.* 1814, Alicia, dau. of the Rev. Henry Jones, of Drombeg, rector of Lislee and Kinsela, and by her (who is deceased) has had issue,

I. Thomas, *d.* aged 18 in 1840.
II. Henry-Jones, barrister-at-law, *b* 1825; *m.* Dec 1856, Mary-Boone, eldest dau. of Henry-Augustus Cowper, Esq., H.B.M., consul at Pernambuco.
III. Edward *d.* 1849.
I. Catherine-Charlotte.
II. Jane, *d.* 1855. III. Harriette-Alicia
IV. Martha-Terry, *d.* 1842. V. Alice.

Lineage.—As stated under the history of Hungerford, of Inchodony, there exists no doubt as to this being a branch of the great English family of Hungerford, so illustrious in our annals.

Captain Thomas Hungerford (descended from Sir Edmund Hungerford, of Down Ampney, co. Gloucester, second surviving son (by Catherine his wife, dau. and coheir of Sir Thomas Peverell, descended from the Peverells of Sandford Peverell, co. Devon, seated there early in the reign of Edward II.) of Walter, Lord Hungerford, K.G., and lord-treasurer, 6 Henry VI., who derived, from Sir Thomas Hungerford, sheriff of Wilts, and speaker of the House of Commons, and Joan his wife, dau. and co-heir of Sir Edmund Hussey, of Holbrooke) died in 1680,* leaving, by Mary his wife, a 3rd son,

Thomas Hungerford, *b.* 1663, of Trinity College, Dublin, 1679, who *m.* in 1684, Francis Synge, sister to the Archbishop of Tuam, and had issue,

I. Thomas, his heir.
II. John, who *m.* Catherine, dau. of Henry Jones, Esq. of Drombeg House, and was father of
1 Thomas Hungerford, Esq., whose son, by Ellen his wife, dau. of Captain Payne, of Tralee, was
2 John-Townsend Hungerford, Esq., solicitor to the Hon. E. I. Co. at Bombay. He *m.* Mary-Anne, dau of J. Payne, Esq., and niece of T. Price, Esq. of Ardmoyle, and Clonmore, co. Tipperary, and *d.* leaving issue,
1 John-Hayes, who *d.* in 1823.
2 Townsend-James-William, capt. Bengal artillery, *b.* in 1814.
1 Ellen, who *m.* Rawson-Hart Boddam, Esq., Bengal civil service, eldest son of R.-H. Boddam, Esq., governor of the Bank.
2 Mary-Anne, *m.* 1st, Ewan Law, Esq., Bengal civil service, son of Ewan Law, Esq. of Horsted Place, Sussex, who *d.* in 1818; and 2ndly, in 1826, to George Williamson, Esq., lieut. H.M.'s 11th dragoons, and capt. H. H., the Nizam's cavalry.
3 Catherine, *m.* Welby Jackson, Esq., of the Bengal civil service, son of Sir John Jackson, Bart.

The eldest son,

Colonel Thomas Hungerford, of Cahirmore, *m.* in 1724, Barbara, dau. of Colonel Bryan Townsend, M.P., of Castle Townsend, co. Cork, and by her had a son,

Thomas Hungerford, Esq, of Cahirmore, J.P., who *m.* in 1761, Sarah, dau. of Dr. John Boisseau, a Huguenot, and was father of (his will is dated 17 Jan. 1799),

Thomas Hungerford, Esq. of Cahirmore, who *m.* in 1787, Jane, dau. of Jonas Travers Esq., of Butlerstown, co. Cork, and by her (who *m.* 2ndly, 1791, the Rev. William Stuart, of Welfield, co. Cork), left at his decease, *v. p.*, a son and heir, the present Thomas Hungerford, Esq. of Cahirmore.

Arms, &c.—Same as Hungerford *of Inchodony.*
Seat—Cahirmore, Ross Carberry, co. Cork.

HUNGERFORD OF DINGLEY PARK.

Holditch-Hungerford, Henry-Hungerford, Esq. of Dingley Park, co. Northampton, J.P. and D.L., high-sheriff 1828, *b.* 9 Jan. 1803; *s.* by will to the estates of the late John-Peach Hungerford, Esq., M.P. for Leicestershire in three successive parliaments, from 1775 to 1790, who *d.* 4 June, 1809, aged 90; *m.* 4 Aug. 1846, Honoria, dau. of Francis Forester, Esq., (brother of the 1st Lord Forester) by the Lady Louisa-Catherine-Barbara Vane his wife, eldest dau. of the 1st Duke of Cleveland, and has issue,

I. Henry-Vane-Forester, *b.* 8 May, 1852.
II. Powlett-Henry-Edward, *b.* 5 July, 1853.
III. Edward-Lytton, *b.* 15 Aug. 1855.

* Copy of inscription on the monument erected to the memory of Capt. Hungerford, in Ross Carbery Cathedral:—

"In memory of Captain Thomas Hungerford, who died March 2nd, 1680, and was interred in this Cathedral He was descended from Sir Edmund Hungerford, of Downe Ampney, in the county of Gloucester. Sir Edmund was second son of Walter, Lord Hungerford, of Farley Castle, co. Wilts, who took the Duke of Orleans prisoner at the battle of Agincourt; was lord-high-steward in the reign of Henry V., one of the executors to his will, and lord-high-treasurer in the reign of Henry VI. Lord Hungerford was the only surviving son of Sir Thomas de Hungerforde, who, in 51 Edward III., was the first who took the chair as Speaker of the House of Commons. This tablet is erected by Thomas Hungerford, of Cahirmore, the 6th in descent from the above Captain Thomas Hungerford, this 21st day of February, 1837.

I. Julia-Mary-Anne.
II. Louia-Erica. II. Clara-Constance.

Lineage.—The Holdich's, from whom the present Henry-Hungerford, Holdich-Hungerford, Esq., paternally derives, are a branch of the family of Holdich, Holditch, or Holdiche, which at an early period possessed considerable estates in the co. of Norfolk.

Edward Holdich, living in 1700, had three sons: Edward, of Sidney College, Cambridge, A.B. *d. unm.*; Thomas, of whom presently; and Jeffery, of Clare Hall, Cambridge, rector of Stibbington, Huntingdonshire, many years, and *d.* in 1779, leaving issue.

Thomas Holdich (second son) lived at Thrapston, where he *d.* in 1752. His son,

Edward Holdich, *s.* him, and in 1756, *m.* Anne, eldest grand-niece and co-heiress of Thomas Peach, Esq. of Dingley Park, and had, with other issue, a son,

The Rev. Thomas Holdich, A.M., rector of Burton Overy, co. Leicester, which he resigned in 1811, and rector of Maidwell, co. Northampton, to which he was presented, in 1808, by the late John Peach Hungerford, Esq.; and also of Draughton, to which he was presented, in 1841, by H.-H. Hungerford, Esq. He *m.* 1st, in 1802, Anne, eldest dau. of Henry Haynes, Esq. of Whittlesea, co. Cambridge and by, her who *d.* 20 Feb. 1806, had issue,

Henry-Hungerford, the present proprietor of Dingley who, upon attaining the age of 21, (in 1824), assumed the name and arms of Hungerford, in compliance with the will of the late John Peach Hungerford, Esq.
Thomas Peach, A.M., rector of Dingley, *b.* 21 Dec. 1804; *m.* 1st, 25 Nov. 1830, Katherine, dau. of the Rev. F.-J. Corrance, vicar of Great Glenn, co. Leicester, which lady *d. s. p.* 28 Feb. 1834; and 2ndly, in 1839, Susan, dau. of — Garrard, Esq. and has issue.
Mary-Anne, *m.* to C. Boultbee, Esq. of Whittlesea.

Mr. Holdich *m.* 2ndly, in 1808, Elizabeth-Laura, dau and co-heiress of the late Henry-Lawrence Maydwell, Esq. of Whittlesea, and had by her several children.

Arms—Quarterly: 1st and 4th, sa., two bars, arg., in chief, three plates, for Hungerford; 2nd and 3rd, or, on a chev., sa., cottised, gu., three martlets, of the field, a chief, vaire, for Holdich.
Crests—1st, out of a ducal coronet, or, a pepper garb, of the first, between two sickles, erect, ppr., for Hungerford; 2nd, a martlet, sa., in front of a cross patée, fitchée, between two branches of palm, or, for Holdich.
Mottoes—Et Dieu mon appui, for Hungerford; Stet fortuna domus, for Holdich.
Seat—Dingley Park, co. Northampton.

HUNT OF PITTENCRIEFF.

Hunt, James, Esq. of Pittencrieff and Logie, co. Fife, J.P. and D.L., *b.* 20 March, 1785; *m.* 5 Oct. 1813, Margaret, dau. of John Grieve, Esq., and has issue,

I. William.
II. John, advocate, *d.* 10 June, 1841.
III. James-Alexander. IV. Andrew.
V. Robert. VI. Ralph.
I. Thomasina-Agnes, *m.* 3 Feb. 1841, to Sir Alexander-Charles Gibson Maitland, Bart. of Clifton Hall.
II. Janet, *m.* to B. R. Bell, Esq., advocate, sheriff of Elgin and Moray.

Mr. Hunt is eldest son of the late William Hunt, of Pittencrieff, by Janet his wife, dau. of James Alexander, Esq. of Balrudery, and grandson of William Hunt and Ellen Young, his wife. He has one brother, William, and a sister, Christina, *m.* to James Harrowar, Esq. of Inzievar, advocate.

Crest—A lion's head, erased.
Motto—Vi et virtute.
Seats—Pittencrieff and Logie, co. Fife.

HUNT OF BOREATTON.

Hunt, Rowland, Esq. of Boreatton, co. Salop, *b.* 8 Nov. 1828.

Lineage.—This family, as well as the Hunts of Staffordshire, derive from Richard de Venator, living *temp.* Edward I. Fifth in descent from him was

Thomas Hunt, of Stoke Dawbenny, co. Rutland, living A.D. 1430, son of Nicholas Hunt, of the same place, and grandson of Thomas le Hunt, living 40 Edward III. From him derived in direct descent,

Thomas Hunt, Esq., *b.* in 1599, member for Shrewsbury in the parliament of the Commonwealth, high-sheriff of Shropshire in 1656, who, after the restoration of Charles II., purchased the estate of Boreatton. He *m.* Elizabeth, dau. of Owen of Woodhouse, and had issue,

Rowland, his heir.
John, of Chester, who *m.* Anne, dau. of Richard Amphlett, Esq. of Hadsor, and was father of
Thomas Hunt, Esq. of Mollington, who *m.* Mary, sister of Henry Robartes, Earl of Radnor, and had issue (*see* Robartes).
Thomas, *b.* in 1645, *d. s. p.*
Elizabeth, *b.* in 1631, who *m.* Bartholomew Beale, Esq.
Martha, *m.* to Palmer, of Wanlip, co. Leicester.
Mary, *b.* in 1646, *d.* in 1660.

He *d.* in 1669 and was *s.* by his eldest son,

Rowland Hunt, Esq. of Boreatton, *b.* in 1629, who *m.* Frances, dau. of Lord Paget, and was father of

Thomas Hunt, Esq. of Boreatton, *b.* about 1669, who *m.* 1st, Jane, eldest dau., and, in her issue, heiress of Sir Edward Ward, Lord Chief Baron; and 2ndly, Miss Haswell: by the former of whom he had issue. Mr. Hunt *d.* in 1752, and was *s.* by his son,

Thomas Hunt, Esq. of Boreatton, *b.* in 1704, who *m.* Sarah, dau. of Edward Witts, Esq., and had issue. Mr. Hunt was *s.* by his son,

Rowland Hunt, Esq. of Boreatton, *b.* in 1753, who *m.* Ann, dau. of Mark Cornish, Esq. of London, and had issue,

I. Rowland, his heir.
II. George, of Wadenhoe, co. Northampton, in holy orders, who *m.* 28 July, 1818, Emma, dau. of Samuel Gardiner, Esq. of Coombe Lodge, co. Oxford, and had issue,
1 George-Ward.
1 Mary. 2 Eliza-Frances.
3 Jane-Emilia. 4 Julia-Henrietta.
5 Emily-Ellen. 6 Matilda-Selina.
7 Ellen. 8 Laura.
III. Thomas, *m.* Jane, dau. of William Harding, Esq. and had issue,
1 Thomas-Henry. 2 Charles-John.
3 William-Cornish.
1 Harriet-Susanna-Anne. 2 Caroline-Emma.
IV. Edward, deceased. V. John deceased.
I. Susanna-Frances. II. Sarah-Elizabeth, deceased.

Mr. Hunt *d.* in 1811, and was *s.* by his son,

Rowland Hunt, Esq. of Boreatton, who *m.* in 1823, Mary, dau. of Thomas Lloyd, Esq. of Shrewsbury and Glangwna, Carnarvonshire, and had issue,

Rowland, now of Boreatton.
Thomas-Edward-Lloyd, *b.* 15 June, 1830.
Annabella-Eliza. Charlotte-Frances.

Arms—Per pale, arg. and sa., a saltier, counterchanged.
Crest—A talbot, sejant, sa., collared, or, lined, az., the line tied to a halbert, in pale of the second, headed, of the last.
Seat—Boreatton, Shrewsbury.

HUNTER OF THAT ILK.

Hunter, Robert, Esq. of Hunter, or Hunterston, co. Ayr, J.P. and D.L., *b.* 29 Aug. 1799, *m.* 22 Nov. 1836, Christian Macknight, eldest dau. of William Craufurd, Esq. of Cartsburn, co. Renfrew, and has issue,

I. Jane. II. Eleanora.

Lineage.—Two ancient families of the name of Hunter existed in Scotland for many centuries—Hunter, of Polmood, in Tweeddale, now extinct, and Hunter, of Hunter, the present chief of the Hunters.

The patriarch of the race was one of the companions in arms of William the Conqueror.

Of the Hunterston line, Craufurd states that he had "very carefully perused their writs," and that ' from charters they appear to have had at least a part of the estate they still possess in Cunninghame, while the Morvilles were lords of that country, as far back as the reign of Alexander II." In the remarks on the Rag. Roll, it is stated, that in an ancient bounding charter, the lands of Arnele-Hunter, adjoining to Hunterston, are bounded with "terris Normani Venatoris."

Norman Hunter, living between the years 1215 and 1249, is the first ancestor mentioned in any deed. The Hunterston estate has been in the possession of the family for more than eight hundred years, though only entailed by the father of the present proprietor.

Robert Hunter, of Hunterston, chief of this ancient house in the 17th century, was served heir of conquest to his

The son and heir,

THOMAS HUNGERFORD, *d. vita patris*, having *m.* in 1719, Susannah Becher, and having left issue,

RICHARD, his heir.
Elizabeth, *m.* in 1738, to Capt. Philip Townsend, of Derry, near Ross-Carbery.
Mary (a legatee in the will of John Hungerford, of Hungerford), *m.* in 1739, to the Rev. Horatio Townsend, of Coolmona.

The only son,

RICHARD HUNGERFORD, Esq. of The Island, and for many years of Foxhall, *m.* 1st, Mary Becher, and by her had,

I. THOMAS, his heir.
II. John, who *m.* in 1771, Anne Daunt; and *d.* in 1803, leaving issue,
   1 Richard, of Cappeen, *m.* in 1803, his cousin, Jane Hungerford, and had, Becher, of Clonakilty, and other issue.
   2 Thomas, *m.* Louisa Campbell, in 1809.
   3 Henry, *m.* Johanna Daunt.
   4 John, *d. s. p.* 5 Becher, *d. s. p.*
   6 Emanuel, *m.* Catherine Loane.
   1 Eliza, *m.* to Dr. George Hungerford.
   2 Anne, *m.* in 1794, to Robert Sealy, Esq.
   3 Mary. 4 Susan.

He *m.* 2ndly, Mary, dau. of the Rev. Eman ... and by her was father of

Richard, in holy orders, *m.* 1775, M... by her (who *m.* 2ndly, Michael F... Richard, *b.* 1776, who *m.* 1794, ... issue, Richard, of Carrigeen, ... of Capt. Colin Campbell, ar... Henry; Stephen; Mich... Isabella.
Emanuel, *d. s. p.*
Letitia, *m.* 1769, to Ri...
Elizabeth, *m.* to Cap...
Susan, *d. s. p.*

Richard Hungerfor...
THOMAS HUNGE...
Mary-Cranfield ...

RICHARD, hi... who *m.* Margaret Stewart, George (Dr... a dau., Marion, the wife of his 1st c... Thomas ...nghame, of Carlung, and had dau. o... Dr. G... of Craufield, but *d. s. p.* Thom... by his elder son, wido... of Hunterston, who *m.* Marion, late ... Craufurd, of Cartsburn, and had five by ... Cha... Cra... Ge... Ch... predeceased his father.

The s... Miss Milliken, of Port Glasgow, and Ri... 1793, ... *m.* Rebecca Fleming, and had five sons and ...

... 1 Jan. 1782, *d. unm.* in 1846.
... *b.* 7 Dec. 1784, *m.* Jane, dau. of William ... Esq., and had (with a dau., Jane, who *d.* in infancy) a son,
CHARLES FLEMING, *b.* in 1829, present male representative of the Hunters of Hunterston.
Patrick, *b.* 23 Sept. 1787.
Milliken, *b.* 7 March, 1791, *m.* Margaret, dau. of — Walker, Esq. of Irvine.
Robert, *b.* 26 Aug. 1793.
Mary. 2 Marion. 3 Margaret.
Elizabeth, *m.* William Steuart, Esq. of Glenormiston, and had issue.
5 Agnes.

IV. Henry. V. Thomas.
I. Rebecca, *d. unm.*
II. Elizabeth, *m.* to John Hyndman, of Lunderston.
III. Marion, *m.* to Hugh Muir, Esq.
IV. Dorothea, *m.* 1st, 19 Dec. 1741, W. Kelso, Esq. of Hullerhirst, grandfather of Alexander Hamilton, of Hullerhirst, co. Ayr, and The Retreat, co. Devon, and 2ndly, Hugh Weir, Esq. of Kirkwall.
Margaret, *m.* Mr. Caldwell, merchant of Greenock.

Hunterston *d.* in 1733, and was *s.* by his son,

ROBERT HUNTER, Esq. of Hunterston, who *m.* Janet Aitchison, of Glasgow, and dying in 1796, left, with a younger dau., Marion, who *d. unm.*,

ELEANORA HUNTER, of Hunterston, who *m.* in 1796, her cousin, Robert Caldwell, Esq., who became, by assumption, HUNTER "of Hunterston," and by him, who *d.* 22 Aug. 1826, had issue,

I. ROBERT, heir, now of Hunterston.
II. Patrick, deceased. III. Norman.
I. Eleanora. II. Marion-Craufurd, *d. unm.*
III. Margaret. IV. Janet.

Lineage.—As stated under the b... courant, arg., col. of Inchodony, there exists no do... hunting-horns, of branch of the great English fam... trious in our annals. ..., collared, or.

CAPTAIN THOMAS HUNG... ...astle, and Hunterston House, EDMUND HUNGERFORD, of ...805. second surviving son ... heir of Sir Thomas P... Sandford Peverell. of EDWARD II.) ... treasurer, 6 H... gerford, ... Common... Husse... wife ...

...R OF STRAADARRAN.

...CHARD, Esq. of Straadarran, co. Lon...P. and D.L., *b.* 24 March, 1788; *m.* ...19, Dorothea-Maria, 3rd dau. of John-Frederick Waring-Maxwell, Esq. of Finne...e, co. Down, and has had issue,

I. Nathaniel-Maxwell, *b.* 28 Oct. 1819, lieut. 17th regt., *d.* at Aden, June, 1844.
II. JOHN-CHARLES-FREDERICK, *b.* 18 March, 1822; *m.* 18 June 1853, the Hon. Meliora-Emily-Anna, youngest dau. of Viscount Combermere.
I. Anna-Maria-Dorothea, *d.* in 1837, *unm.*
II. Maria-Margaret-Jane.

Lineage.—This family of Hunter sprang originally from Hunterston, in Ayrshire, N.B., but at what period they settled at Derry is not known. Three brothers however, distinguished themselves at the siege of that place, viz., Captain Henry Hunter,* John Hunter, and James Hunter. The first-named received the thanks of parliament and a pension for his services. The grandfather of the present Richard Hunter, Esq.,

RICHARD HUNTER, Esq. of Troy House, co. Londonderry, *m.* Anne Allen, and was *s.* at his decease by his son,

NATHANIEL HUNTER, Esq. of Troy House, *b.* 2 March, 1762; who *m.* 16 March, 1786, Margaret, only child of Henry Boyle,* Esq. of Drumcovit, co. Londonderry, by his wife, Jane Stephenson, of Knocken, in the same county, and by this lady (who *d.* in 1799) had issue,

RICHARD, now of Straadarran.
Henry-Boyle, *d. unm.*
Nathaniel, capt. Madras horse artillery, *d. unm.* at St. Helena.
Stevenson, in holy orders, rector of Loughguile, co. Antrim; *m.* Eliza, dau. of Henry Clarke, Esq. of Turnaroberts, co. Antrim, and has issue a son, Nathaniel.
William, *m.* Miss Magee, dau. of the Archbishop of Dublin, and has issue three sons, William, Henry, and Charles.
James-Stephenson, *m.* Margaret, dau. of James Stephenson, Esq. of Fort William, co. Londonderry, and has issue five sons, Henry; John; James; Arthur; and Robert.
John, of the Madras infantry, *d. unm.*
Robert-Alexander, 29th regt., *d. unm.*
Jane.
Margaret, *m.* to James Stevenson, Esq. of Ash Park, co. Londonderry.

Mr. Hunter *d.* 28 July, 1811.

Arms—Arg., three bugle-horns, bendways, gu., garnished and furnished, vert.
Crest—A stag's head, caboshed, ppr.
Motto—Arte et marte.
Seat—Straadarran, co. Londonderry.

HUNTER-ARUNDELL OF BARJARG.

HUNTER-ARUNDELL, WILLIAM-FRANCIS, Esq. of Barjarg Tower, co. Dumfries, J.P., *b.* 16 June, 1820; *m.* 20 Sept. 1849, Mary, eldest dau. of David Dickson, Esq. of Kilbucno and Hartree.

Lineage.—JAMES HUNTER, a younger son of Hunter of Hunterston, acquired the lands of Abbotshill, in the parish

* The said Captain Henry Hunter, after the siege of Derry, marched to the county Down and defeated Con Bucah O'Neil at Killinchey in the Woods, and having heard that Henry Maxwell, Esq. of Finnebrogue, had been seized and put into Downpatrick gaol, by order of Tyrconnell, for his adherence to King WILLIAM, Hunter immediately marched and relieved him from gaol, and placed him in safety at his own residence of Finnebrogue, for which he got the thanks of parliament and a pension, and Henry Maxwell was made a privy-counsellor. Richard Hunter, Esq., now of Straadarran, is *m.* to Dorothea-Maria Waring Maxwell, great-granddau. to the Right Hon. Henry Maxwell, of Finnebrogue, co. Down.

* The Boyles, or O'Boyles, a very ancient Irish family, came from the Barony of Boylagh, co. Donegal, and settled at Drumcovit some hundred years ago, and had great possessions in the co. of Derry.

om Alan Stewart, Abbot of Crossraquel, by a
d 19 May, 1569. He was father, by Janet Neil
n and heir,
, of Abbotshill, who got a new charter
93, and acquired, by his wife, a dau. of
w, the lands of Roddingrood. He

bbotshill and Roddingrood, who
son,
hill, provost of Ayr who m.
ns,
came extinct.
on s. to his father's lands.
Adam, of Glentaig, but

whom presently.
st of Ayr; m. in 1657, Agnes,
y whom he had five daus., all of
Barbara, who m. Robert Fullarton,
x sons, of whom
ER, b. in 1665, m. in 1688, Agnes, dau. of
ith, magistrate of Glasgow, and d. in 1708,
by her (who d. in 1702) an only surviving son,

AMES HUNTER, provost of Ayr, b. in 1698; who m. in 1726, Janet, eldest dau. of James Hunter, of Abbotshill and Park, and d. in 1784, having by her, who d. in 1746 (with three daus., Mary, Sarah, and Jean-Isabella), four sons,

1 James, banker in Ayr, b. in 1727; m. in 1750, Sarah, dau. of Patrick Ballantine, of Ayr, and by her (who d. in 1806) had, with other issue, who d. young or unm., a son and three daus., Patrick, capt. Bengal infantry, who m. the Hon. Jean Rollo, 2nd dau. of James, 7th Lord Rollo, by whom he has six sons, James; Patrick; John; William; Hugh, who m. Eliza, dau. of Henry Veitch, of Elliock; and Roger-Rollo: Ann, m. to William Wood; Grace, m. to George Charles; and Marian, m. to James Mair.

2 ROBERT, who s. to Thurston.

3 Andrew, m. Stewart, dau. of the Rev. Robert Cunninghame, of Bowerhouses, near Dunbar.

4 John, b. in 1746, settled in Virginia. He m. Jane, dau. of Col. Broadwater, and had (with a dau., Ann, m. to Mr. Cundell, in Virginia) four sons, James, of Virginia; Robert, of Virginia; George-Washington; and John, E. I. Co.'s service.

The 2nd son,

ROBERT HUNTER, s. to Thurston, by the will of his aunt, Agnes Hunter. He m. 1st, in 1764, Margaret, dau. of James Robertson, of Calcutta, and by her (who d. in 1776) had a son, Robert, who d., and three daus., Margaret; Janet, m. 1st, to Michael Riddel, Esq., and 2ndly, to Henry Irving, Esq.; and Sarah, m. to W. Robertson, Esq. of Ladykirk. Mr. Hunter m. 2ndly, Isabella, dau. of the Hon Lord Chief Baron Robert Ord of the Court of Exchequer, Scotland, and by her had (with three daus., Eleanor, m. to Peter Sandilands, of Barnyhill; Isabella, m. to Dugald Campbell, Esq. of Ballinaby, in the Isle of Islay; and Agnes, m. to Archibald-George Campbell, of Shirvan) four sons, JAMES, his successor; John and Andrew both deceased; and Richard, who m. Margaret Walker, and had several sons and daus. The eldest son,

JAMES HUNTER, now of Thurston, East Lothian, m. Elizabeth, dau. of Ross Jennings, Esq., by whom he has issue, 1 JAMES-WILLIAM; 2 Robert-Francis; 3 Richard; 4 John-Alexander; 1 Isabella; 2 Sarah-Elizabeth; 3 Margaretta-Eleanor.

V. William, who got Bromberry Yards. He m. in 1667, Anna, dau. of John Adamson, of Woodlands.

The 3rd son,

ADAM HUNTER, s. his brother John in Abbotshill. He m. 1st, Marion Blair dau. of Blair, of Balthyock in the Carse of Gowrie; and 2ndly, Janet, dau. of Wallace of Mainholm and Woodhead, and was s. by the eldest son of his 1st marriage,

JAMES HUNTER of Abbotshill b. 5 Aug. 1672; who m. in 1694, Janet, dau. of John Fergusson (of the family of Craigdarroch) by Janet Cochran his wife, and by her had (with two daus. Agnes, m. to Robert Hunter, of Thurston, in East Lothian, who, predeceasing her. left her the disposal of his estate, which at her death she bequeathed to Robert, 2nd son of her sister; and Janet, m. to James, 3rd son of Robert Hunter. provost of Ayr) five sons: the eldest three d. s. p.; the 4th, ANDREW, we treat of; and the 5th, John, of Mainholm and Millquarter (now Craigie House), b. 11 Aug. 1702; m. Anne, dau. and heiress of William Cunninghame, of Broomhill. by Anne Hamilton his wife, 2nd dau. and co-heiress of Sir Archibald Hamilton, Bart. of Rosehall, M.P. for the county of Lanark, and by this lady was ancestor of Sir David-Hunter Blair, Bart. Mr. Hunter d. 1 Nov. 1739, and was s. by his eldest surviving son,

ANDREW HUNTER, of Abbotshill, b. in 1695; who m. Grace, dau. of Col. William Maxwell, of Cardoness by whom he had with other issue, a son, ANDREW, of whom presently; JOHN, ancestor of the DOONHOLM branch, *which see*; and five daus., Janet, m. to Robert Aiken; Grizel, m. to Col. Christopher Maxwell, of the 30th regt., brother of Sir David Maxwell, of Cardoness; Henrietta, m. to Alexander Copland, M.D., younger son of Copland of Collieston; Agnes, and Nicholas. Mr. Hunter d. in 1770, and was s. by his son,

THE REV. ANDREW HUNTER, D.D. of Abbotshill, which property he sold, and purchased Barjarg. He was b. in 1744, and being bred to the church, became professor of Divinity in the University of Edinburgh. He m. 14 April, 1779, the Hon. Mainie-Schaw Napier, eldest dau. of William 6th Lord Napier, and by her, who d. 9 Oct. 1806, had (with three daus., Mainie-Anne-Charlotte, d. young; Grizel, m. 27 June, 1808, to George Ross, Esq. advocate, and a commissary of Edinburgh, 4th son of the late Admiral Sir John Lockhart Ross, Bart.; Henrietta-Hope) three sons, Andrew d. in infancy; WILLIAM-FRANCIS, his heir; and John, in holy orders, who m. Caroline, dau. of the late Hepburn Mitchelson, of Middleton. Dr Hunter d. 21 April, 1809, and was s. by his elder surviving son,

WILLIAM-FRANCIS HUNTER-ARUNDEL, Esq. of Barjarg, advocate; who m. Nov. 1813, Jane, dau. and eventually heiress of Francis St. Aubyn, of Collin Mixton, by Jane Arundell, his wife, co-heiress of the ARUNDELLS *of Tolverne and Truthall*, in Cornwall, and by her had GODOLPHIN, d. s. p.; Arundell, deceased; WILLIAM-FRANCIS, now of Barjarg Tower; Frances-St. Aubyn, m. to the Rev. W. Murray, now of Salcombe; Marianne-Schaw Napier, widow of W.-A. Woodcock, Esq.; and Jane-Arundell, deceased.

Arms—Vert, three dogs' collars, or, on a chief, arg., three hunting-horns, of the first, stringed and tipped, gu.
Crest—A stag's head, erased.
Motto—Vigilantia, robur, voluptas.
Seat—Barjarg, Tower, near Dumfries.

HUNTER OF BONNYTOUN.

HUNTER, ANDREW, Esq. of Bonnytoun and Doonholm, co. Ayr, D.L., b. 7 Aug. 1776; m. 21 April, 1814, Helen, eldest dau. of John Campbell, Esq. of Ormidale, co. Argyll, and has had issue

I. John d. unm. 1846. II. Campbell, d. unm. 1846.
III. WILLIAM-FRANCIS, capt. Bombay cavalry.
IV. Andrew capt. 2nd regt. Bengal infantry. m. 1854, Caroline-Cherry, youngest dau. of Lieut.-Col. Nuttall Greene, of Kilmanahan Castle, co. Waterford.
I. Helen.

Lineage.—JOHN HUNTER, writer to the Signet, b. 1746, 2nd surviving son of Andrew Hunter, of Abbotshill, by Grace, dau. of Col. William Maxwell, of Cardoness; m. in 1773. Jane, dau. and co-heir of William Ferguson, Esq. of Bonnytoun and Doonholm, by whom he acquired the latter property, and afterwards purchased the former from Fleming of Barochan, his brother-in-law. By this lady he had, with other issue who d. young,

I. ANDREW, his heir, now of Bonnytoun.
II. Alexander, of Edinburgh, clerk to the Signet, m. in 1819, Maria, dau. of Alexander Maclean, Esq. of Coll, co. Argyll, and has six sons and two daus.
III. Francis, lieut.-col. of cavalry, E.I.Co.'s service, now resident at Taunton, Somerset, m. Elizabeth, 3rd dau. of Thomas Tulloh, Esq. of Elliestoh, co. Roxburgh, and has three daus., viz.,
1 Jane. 2 Eleanora-Elizabeth.
3 Anna-Maria-Margaret-Helen.
I. Elizabeth, m. John Carr, Esq. of St. Anne's, co. York, who is deceased.
II. Eleanora-Garvine.

Mr. Hunter d. in 1823.

Arms—Vert, three dogs of the chase, courant, arg., on a chief of the second, three hunting horns of the first, stringed and tipped, gu.
Crest—A stag's head, cabossed.
Motto—Vigilantia, robur, voluptas.

HUNTER OF SEASIDE AND GLENCARSE.

HUNTER, CHARLES, Esq. of Seaside and Glencarse, co. Perth, J.P. and D.L., b. 31 May, 1782; m. in Dec. 1815, Agnes, dau. of Andrew Thomson, Esq. of Kinloch, co. Fife, and has issue,

I. JAMES, b. in Sept. 1816, 42nd highlanders; m. 24 Aug. 1843, Jane, dau. of the late Hugh Gordon, Esq. of Manar, co. Aberdeen.
II. Andrew, b. in May, 1818.
III. Thomas, b. in Feb. 1820. IV. Charles, b. Nov. 1827.
I Agnes d. in 1840.

Lineage.—JAMES HUNTER, Esq., b. in 1701; m. in 1720, Janet-Mathew, dau. of James-Matthew Mains, of Fintrie, and had (besides other issue who d. young or unm., with four daus., Margaret, m. 1st, to Charles Hill, Esq., and 2ndly, to Robert Webster, Esq. of Cransley; Anne, m. to Charles Kinnear, Esq. of Kinnear; Janet, m. to James Miller, Esq. of New Miln; and Elizabeth, m. to Patrick Kinnear, Esq. of Lochton), five sons, viz., James, a merchant in London; CHARLES, of whom presently; Patrick, a planter in Jamaica; Thomas who purchased the estate of Glencarse; and Alexander, a merchant in London. The 2nd son,

CHARLES HUNTER, Esq., m. 22 Aug. 1751, his cousin Agnes, eldest dau. of Robert Hunter, Esq. of Ballo, and had (with three daus., Janet; Catherine; and Margaret, m. to Robert Blair) an only surviving son,

JAMES HUNTER, Esq. of Seaside b. in 1757, who m. in Feb. 1778, Elizabeth dau. of Patrick Crow, Esq. of Hillside of Logie, and had issue,

CHARLES, his heir.
Patrick, lieut. in the E.I.C.'s service, d. at Bombay, in 1804, from a wound received at Assaye.
James.
Agnes, m. to James Webster, Esq. of Balruddery.
Margaret, m. to George Seton, Esq.
Helen, d. young.
Barbara, m. to Andrew Thomson, Esq., jun., of Kinloch.

Arms—Vert, three greyhounds, in pale, in full speed, arg., collared, gu., within a bordure, or, on a chief, wavy, of the second, a fleur-de-lis, az., between two bugles, of the field, stringed, of the third, and viroled, of the fourth.
Crest—A greyhound's head and neck, arg., collared, gu.
Motto—Dum spiro spero.
Seats—Seaside and Glencarse, co. Perth.

HUNTER OF MEDOMSLEY.

HUNTER, MATTHEW-DYSERT, Esq. of Medomsley, co. Durham, and Anton's Hill, co. Berwick, J.P., m. 1852, Isabella, eldest dau. of John Buckle, Esq. of Wharton House, co. Edinburgh, by Isabella his wife, dau. of Edward Hay Mackenzie, Esq. and has issue,

I. MARTIN, b. June, 1854. II. James, b. Oct. 1855.

Lineage.—WILLIAM HUNTER, Esq. of Medomsley, co. Durham (which estate has been in the possession of the family since 1584), d. in 1712, having had, by Barbara his wife (with two daus., Anne, m. to John Hislop, Esq.; and Catherine, m. to Smith, Esq.), five sons, Richard, of Clarewood, co. Northumberland; Luke, of Chollerton, in the same co.; Thomas, of Bellingside, co. Durham; Peter; and ROBERT. This

ROBERT HUNTER, Esq. of Medomsley, m. in 1715, Dorothy, dau. of Johnson, Esq. of Ebchester Hill, co. Durham, and left at his decease (with two daus., Jane, d. unm.; and Isabella, m. to Ralph Smith, Esq. of Cliffordsfort, co. Northumberland), a son,

CUTHBERT HUNTER, Esq. of Medomsley, who m. in 1749, Anne, dau. of the Rev. Martin Nixon, rector of Wooler, and vicar of Haltwhistle, and d. in 1800, leaving by her, who d. in 1791, three sons and five daus., viz.,

MARTIN (Sir), his heir.
Robert, of Bunker Hill, co. Durham, m. Sarah, dau. of N. Clayton, Esq., and d. in 1793, leaving two daus., Sarah and Isabella.
Peter, King's advocate at Sierra Leone, d. unm. in 1817.
Elizabeth, m. to — Richley, Esq., deceased.
Isabella, d. unm. in 1831. Dorothy, d. unm. in 1793.
Anne, m. to — Jobling, Esq. of Corbridge, d. in 1809.
Jane, m. to John Surtees, Esq., d. in 1827.
Mary, m. to Thomas Harvey, Esq., d. in 1843.

The eldest son,

GEN. SIR MARTIN HUNTER, G.C.M.G. and G.C.H., of Medomsley, governor of Stirling Castle, b 6 Sept. 1757; m. 13 Sept. 1797, Jean, only dau. and heir of James Dickson, Esq. of Anton's Hill, co. Berwick, and by her (who d. 1844) had issue,

James, a major in the army, deceased.
MATTHEW DYSART, now of Medomsley.
Robert-MacKeller, capt. E.I.C.S., Bengal, deceased.

George-Martin, lieut. R.N., commanding H. M. brig "Cameleon," deceased.
William, E.I.C. Civil service, Bengal, d. 8 May, 1838.
Thomas-Harvey, an officer E.I.C.S., Bengal.
Jean, m. in 1830, to George Dickson, Esq. of Belchester, co. Berwick.
Anne. Mary-Grey, deceased.
Margaret-Dysert, m. to Charles-Samuel Grey, Esq., only brother of the Right Hon. Sir George Grey, Bart., M.P.

Sir Martin Hunter d. 1846.

Arms—Gu., on a chevron, or, between three bucks' heads, as many bugle horns.
Crest—A deer's head.
Motto—Vigilantia, robur, voluptas.
Seats—Medomsley, co. Durham, and Anton's Hill, co. Berwick.

HUNTER OF BLACKNESS.

HUNTER, DAVID, Esq. of Blackness, co. Forfar, J.P. and D.L.

Lineage.—Mr. Hunter, of Blackness, is son and heir of ALEXANDER GIBSON HUNTER, Esq., by Anne, his wife, dau. of Gibson, of Clifton Hall, and grandson of David Hunter, Esq. of Blackness, by Elizabeth, his wife, dau. of Gibson, of Durie.

The Hunters are a family of considerable antiquity in Forfarshire, and their names appear in the rolls of the Scottish Parliament.

The present Mr. Hunter's great-grandmother, on the male side, was a dau. of Robert Graham, of Fintry, and Anne Moray, of Abercairney. Sir William de Graham, ancestor of the Fintrys, m. Mary Stewart, 2nd dau. of King ROBERT III. of Scotland, and relict of George, Earl of Angus. His great-grandmother, on the female side was Helen (niece of the 1st Earl of Hyndford) m. to John Gibson, of Durie, a family of great antiquity and now represented by Sir Thomas-Gibson Carmichael of Castle Craig, Bart.

The Grahams of Fintry were ancestors of John Graham, Viscount Dundee, killed at Killicrankie.

Seat—Blackness by Dundee.

HUNTLEY OF BOXWELL.

HUNTLEY, THE REV. RICHARD-WEBSTER, A.M. of Boxwell Court, co. Gloucester, J.P., b. 2 April, 1793; m. 8 July, 1830, Mary, eldest dau. of the late Richard Lyster, Esq. of Rowton Castle, M.P. for Shropshire, and has issue,

RICHARD-FREVILLE, B.A. of the Inner Temple, b. 15 Dec. 1833.
Henry, of Exeter College, Oxford, b. 23 Feb. 1835.

Lineage.—Thomas Wakeman, Esq. of the Graig, Monmouth, in his collections for the history of that county, by reference to the public records deduces this family from William Fitz-Baderon grantee from WILLIAM the Conqueror, of the manor of Huntley, co. Gloucester, and of the town castle and barony of Monmouth. Since the reign of HENRY VIII., the family of Huntley has been recorded to the present day in the College of Arms, London.

JOHN HUNTLEY, of Standish and Boxwell living 34 HENRY VIII., m. Alice, dau. and co-heir of Edmund Langley of Siddington son of Walter Langley, of Knowlton by Isabel, his wife, dau. and sole heir of William Pope, Esq., serjeant-at-law, by Margaret, his wife dau. and heir of Sir John de Langley, of Siddington. By Alice, his wife, Mr. Huntley, who d. in 1543, had two sons and a dau., viz., I. GEORGE, of Frocester, grandfather of SIR GEORGE HUNTLEY Knt. of Frocester, who d. 23 Sept. 1622, having had issue three sons, who d. s. p., and three daus.; II. HENRY, of whom presently; and I. Ann, m. to Henry Baskerville. The second son,

HENRY HUNTLEY, Esq. of Boxwell, whose will bears date 1556, m. Elizabeth, dau. of William Throgmorton, of Tortworth, and dying in 1556, was s. by his son,

GEORGE HUNTLEY, Esq., who acquired the manor and free-warren of Boxwell, in Gloucestershire, temp. JAMES I., by purchase from Sir Walter Raleigh, grantee from the crown, and was high-sheriff of Gloucestershire in 1599. He m. Constance, dau. and co-heir of Edward Ferrers, Esq. of Wood Bevington, co. Warwick, 2nd son of Sir Edward Ferrers, of Baddesley Clinton, and had issue. The youngest son and eventual heir,

MATTHEW HUNTLEY, Esq. of Boxwell, m. twice. By his 1st wife Jane Algini, he had a son, MATTHEW, his heir;

and by his 2nd wife, Frances, dau. of Sir George Snigge, Knt., baron of the Exchequer, George successor to his brother, several other sons who d. issueless, and four daus. Mr. Huntley d. in 1653, capt. in Prince Rupert's horse, was buried at Boxwell, 3 Oct. in that year, and s. by his son,

Matthew Huntley, Esq., bapt. at Boxwell in 1613, at whose decease, without issue, the estates devolved upon his brother,

George Huntley, Esq. of Boxwell, b. in 1619, who m. Silvestra, dau. and heir of Edward Wykes, Esq. of Wells and Shiplate, in Somersetshire, and by her (who d. 25 Feb. 1675) had an eldest son,

Matthew Huntley, Esq. of Boxwell, summoned by the Heralds at the Visitation in 1682. He m. Elizabeth dau. John Chandler, Esq. of Aldermanbury, and eventually one of the co-heirs of the Right Rev. Dr. Chandler, bishop of Durham, by whom he had left, at his decease 1712, a son and heir,

The Rev. Richard Huntley, of Boxwell, bapt. there in 1689, rector of Boxwell, co. Gloucester, and of Castlecombe, co. Wilts, who m. Anne, dau. of Col. Henry Lee, of the Donjohn, Canterbury, and of Walsingham Abbey, Norfolk, and had issue. Mr. Huntley d. 17 April, 1728, and was s. by his son,

The Rev. Richard Huntley, of Boxwell, M.A., who m. Anne, dau. and heiress of Nicholas Beaker, Esq. of Nettleton House, co. Wilts, and had, to survive infancy, two sons and five daus. Mr. Huntley d. in 1794, and was s. by his son,

The Rev. Richard Huntley, A.M., of Boxwell, b. 26 March, 1776, who m. 3 May, 1790, Anne, dau. and sole heiress of the Ven. James Webster, LL.B., Archdeacon of Gloucester, by Sarah, his wife, dau. and heiress of Richard Iwells, Esq. of Newark, and of Elizabeth, his wife, sister and heiress of William Warburton, D.D., lord bishop of Gloucester. By her, who d. 25 Feb. 1856, Mr. Huntley left at his decease, 25 Oct. 1831,

- I. Richard-Webster, now of Boxwell Court.
- II. James-Webster, M.A., vicar of Thursby, Carlisle, and of Clanfield, co. Oxford, who m. Anne, eldest dau. of the Rev. Samuel-James Goodenough, D.D., canon of Carlisle, and has two daus.
- III. Henry-Veel, (Sir,) capt. R.N., m. Anna, dau. of Lieut.-Gen. Skinner, and has,
  - 1 Spencer-Robert. 2 Henry-Ferrers.
  - 1 Constance.
- IV. William-Warburton, major 3rd dragoon-guards, m. Emily-Theresa, dau. of Sir Lewis Versturme, and d. s. p. 26 June, 1843.
- V. Edmund, m. 3 Jan. 1833, Harriet-Louisa, dau. and co-heir of the late William Goode, Esq., and d. 4 May, 1839, leaving one son surviving, viz., Osmond-Currie, of Exeter Coll., Oxon, b. 23 March, 1837.
- VI. Osmond-Charles, d. unm. in 1840.
- VII. George-Henry.
- I. Anne, d. unm. 1 June, 1856.
- II. Clara-Jane, m. to William Mills, Esq., of Great Saxham Hall, Suffolk.
- Frances, m. to William-Bird Brodie, Esq., M.P., of the Close, Salisbury.

Arms—Arg., on a chev., between three stags' heads, erased, sa., as many bugle-horns, stringed, of the field.
Crest—A talbot, ppr., collared and lined, or.
Motto—Je voul. droit. avoir.
Seat—Boxwell Court, Gloucestershire.

HURT OF ALDERWASLEY AND WIRKSWORTH.

Hurt, Francis, Esq. of Alderwasley, co. Derby, J.P. and D.L., b. 20 Oct. 1803; m. 22 Aug. 1829, Cecilia-Emily, dau. of Richard Norman, Esq. of Melton Mowbray, co. Leicester, by his wife the Lady Elizabeth Manners, sister of the Duke of Rutland, and has had issue,

- I. Francis-Richard, an officer in the army, b. 12 July 1832, killed at the attack on the Redan, Sebastopol, 18 June, 1855.
- II. Henry-Francis-Eden, an officer in the army, b. 17 March, 1834, killed at Inkerman, 5 Nov. 1854.
- III. Albert-Frederic, b. 7 March, 1835.
- IV. Charles-Manners, d. young.
- V. John-Frederic, b. 22 April, 1833.
- VI. Theodore-Octavius, b. 20 Oct. 1839.
- VII. George-Edward, b. 29 Dec 1843.
- VIII. Louis-Charles, b. 23 Feb. 1845.
- IX. Richard-Norman, b. 23 July, 1847.
- X. James-Nicholas, b. 15 June, 1849.
- XI. Norman-Anthony, b. 27 July, 1850.
- I. Cecilia-Isabella, m. to John, 2nd son of Major Hurt, of Wirksworth.
- II. Alice-Mary-Sophia. III. Grace-Selina-Frances.
- IV. Henrietta-Maria.

Lineage.—Roger Hurt, Esq. of Castern, co. Stafford, youngest son of Nicholas Hurt, Esq. of Ashbourne and Kniveton, co. Derby, and grandson of Thomas Hurt, Esq., m. Edith, dau. of John Cockayne, Esq. of Baddesley, co. Warwick, and had a son and heir, Nicholas Hurt, Esq. of Castern, b. in 1569, who m. in 1588, Ellen, dau. of John Beresford, Esq. of Newton Grange, and d. in 1642, leaving issue the second, but eldest surviving son,

Roger Hurt, Esq. of Castern, m. Frances, dau. of Edward Brudenell, Esq. of Stanton Wyvil, co. Leicester, and d. about 1667, aged 76, having had three daus and three sons. The eldest son and heir,

Nicholas Hurt, Esq. of Castern, aged 42 in 1663, m. Isabella, dau. of Sir Henry Harper, Bart. of Calke, co. Derby, and d. in 1676, leaving a son and heir,

Nicholas Hurt, Esq. of Castern, who m. 12 Jan 1670, Elizabeth, dau. and heir of John Lowe, Esq. of Alderwasley, co. Derby, and sister and heir of John Lowe, Esq. of the same place, and by her, who d. 20 April, 1713, aged 62, left at his decease, in 1711, in his 63rd year, his eldest son and heir,

Charles Hurt, Esq. of Alderwasley, bapt. 11 July, 1678, high-sheriff of Derbyshire in 1714, m. Catherine, dau. of Gervase Rosell, Esq. of Ratcliffe-on-Trent, Notts, and by her, who d. 29 May, 1756, had a dau., Grace, m. 21 May, 1749, to Richard Milnes, Esq. of Dunston, co. Derby, and two sons, Nicholas, his successor; and Francis, successor to his brother. Mr. Hurt d. in 1763, and was s. by his second, but eldest surviving son,

Nicholas Hurt, Esq. of Alderwasley, bapt. 24 Feb. 1710, high-sheriff of Derbyshire in 1756, who d. s. p. in May, 1767, when he was s. by his brother,

Francis Hurt, Esq. of Alderwasley, who had previously been of Wirksworth: he was b. about 1722, m. 17 Aug. 1751, Mary, dau. of Thomas Gell, of Gatehouse, Wirksworth, and by her, who d. 6 March, 1801, aged 81, had issue,

- I. Francis, his heir, of whom presently.
- II. Charles, of Wirksworth, b. 5 Oct. 1758, high-sheriff of Derbyshire in 1797, and m. 12 June, 1780, Susanna, dau. of Sir Richard Arkwright, of Cromford, co. Derby, Knt., and d. 30 Aug. 1834, having had by her, who d. 4 May, 1835,
  - 1 Charles, of Wirksworth, b. 29 June, 1782.
  - 2 Richard, of Wirksworth, b. 1 March, 1785, m. 19 March, 1808, Caroline, fourth dau. of Robert Shuttleworth, Esq. of Barton Lodge, co. Lancaster, and by her (who d. 20 Aug. 1827) had, to survive infancy, three sons and four daus., viz., Robert-Charles, b. 25 Oct. 1815, killed by the accidental discharge of his gun, 1 Feb. 1838; Richard-Stephen, b. 28 Feb. 1817, a midshipman on board H.M.S. Snake, from the maintop of which he fell and d. 22 July, 1834; Philip-Anthony, b. 1 April, 1821; Caroline, m. 8 Nov. 1830, to Edward-Davies Davenport, Esq. of Calveley; Sophia-Elizabeth, m. 21 May, 1838 to Capt. William-Fanshawe Martin, R.N., eldest son of Admiral Sir T.-B. Martin, G.C.B.; Margaret-Emma, m. 24 Jan. 1838, to the Rev. Nathan Hubbersty, of Wirksworth, M.A.; and Georgiana-Susan.
  - 3 Frederick-Nicholas and 4 John-Octavius, both d. young
  - 5 Edward-Nicholas, of Dorset Square, London, b. 17 Jan. 1795, m. 7 Aug. 1823, Caroline, youngest dau. of Joseph Strutt, Esq. of Derby: she d. s. p. 21 Oct. 1834.
  - 6 John-Francis-Thomas, b. 26 Sept. 1796, in holy orders, vicar of Beeston, co. Notts, m. 6 Aug. 1822, Mary, dau. and co-heir of Adam Wolley, Esq. of Matlock, co. Derby, and has issue surviving, John, b. 13 May, 1823; George, b. 28 Oct. 1824; Charles, b. 21 March, 1826; Edward, b. 10 Nov. 1831; Francis, b. 2 June, 1835; and Emma. This gentleman, on the death of his father-in-law, in 1827, assumed, by Royal sign-manual, 25 Sept. 1827, the surname and arms of Wolley.
  - 1 Susanna, m. 6 Feb. 1811, to John Ryle, Esq. of Park House, Macclesfield.
  - 2 Mary-Anne, m. 2 Sept. 1805, to Peter Arkwright, Esq. of Rock House, Cromford, co. Derby.
  - 3 Margaret, d. an infant.
  - 4 Frances, d. unm. in Aug. 1831.
  - 5 Margaret-Anne, d. 31 Dec. 1799.
- I. Catherine, m. 23 Feb. 1781, to the Rev. George Holcombe, D.D., rector of Matlock, co. Derby, and of East and West Lake, co. Notts, and prebendary of Westminster. She d. 3 April, 1841.
- II. Cassandra, m. 8 July, 1776, to her cousin, Philip Gell, Esq. of Wirksworth, and d. s. p. 14 Nov. 1776.
- III. Mary, m. 4 July, 1780, to the Rev. John Moore, of Appleby, co. Leicester, and d. s. p. 23 Feb. 1823.
- IV. Mercy, d. young.

v. Elizabeth, m. 24 May, 1785, to Thomas Webb, Esq. of Strelley, Notts, who took the name and arms of Edge, by Royal licence. She d. 7 May, 1803.

Mr. Hurt d. 7 Aug. 1783, aged 61, and was s. by his elder son and heir,

Francis Hurt, Esq. of Alderwasley and Castern, b. 2 Sept. 1753, high-sheriff of co. Derby in 1778, who m. 1 Sept. 1778, Elizabeth, dau. of James Shuttleworth, Esq. of Gawthorpe and Barton Lodge, co. Lancaster, and by her, who d. 7 May, 1831, had issue,

Francis-Edward, present representative.
James, of Wirksworth, b. 16 June, 1785, late a major in the 9th lancers, m. 11 Oct. 1825, Mary-Margaret, dau. of Thomas-Webb Edge, Esq. of Strelley, Notts, and has issue four sons and four daus., viz., James-Thomas, b. 14 Aug. 1827; John-Francis, b. 22 Jan. 1829, m. Cecilia-Isabella, dau. of Francis Hurt, Esq. of Alderwasley; Charles, b. 31 Oct. 1833; Henry-Richard, b. 6 Aug. 1836, twin with his sister, Susan-Emma; Mary-Elizabeth; Cassandra; Catherine-Anne; and Susan-Emma, twin with her brother, Henry-Richard.
Henry, b. 18 Aug. 1786, lieut in the Royal Marines, lost in H.M.S Hero, off the Texel, 24 Dec. 1811.
Mary, m. 27 June, 1820, to Sir Richard Goodwin Keats, G.C.B., vice-admiral of the Red, and governor of Greenwich Hospital.
Elizabeth, m. 20 April, 1815, to George Moore, Esq. of Appleby, co. Leicester, and d. 15 June, 1841.
Cassandra, m. 5 June, 1828, to the Rev. John-Fleming St. John, vicar of Spondon, co. Derby.
Catherine Emma, d. in 1793.
Anne-Emma, m. 28 May, 1833, to Thomas Gell, Esq. of Wirksworth, late major in the 29th regt.
Catherine, m. 2 Nov. 1815, to John Broadhurst, Esq. of Foston, co. Derby, and d. 3 Sept. 1816.

Mr. Hurt d. 5 Jan. 1801, in his 48th year, and was s. by his eldest son,

Francis-Edward Hurt, Esq. of Alderwasley and Castern, high-sheriff 1814; b. 11 Feb. 1781, who m. 27 Oct. 1802, Elizabeth, dau. of the late Richard Arkwright, Esq. of Willersley Castle, co. Derby, and by her, who d. 30 Jan. 1838, had issue,

Francis, now of Alderwasley.
Mary, m. 1828, to Robert-John, Lord Auckland, Bishop of Bath and Wells.
Emma. Elizabeth. Selina. Frances.
Anne, m. to Edmund Wilmot, Esq.

Arms—Quarterly: 1st, sa., a fesse between three cinquefoils, or, for Hurt; 2nd, gu., a wolf, preyant, arg., for Lowe *of Alderwasley*; 3rd, az., a hart, trippant, arg., for Lowe *of Denby*, and likewise for Lowe *of Alderwasley*; 4th, arg., a bugle-horn between three crescents, sa., each charged with a bezant, for Fawne *of Alderwasley*.
Crest—A hart, passant, ppr., horned, membered, and hurt in the haunch with an arrow, or, feathered, arg.
Motto—Mane prædam vesperi spolium.
Seat—Alderwasley, Belper, co. Derby.

HUSSEY OF NASH COURT.

Hussey, John, Esq. of Nash Court, co. Dorset, J.P., b. 23 Oct. 1794; m. 1st, in May, 1817, Catherine, dau. of John Knapp, Esq. of Bath, and by her had a son, Hubert, b. in 1818, who d. 7 Feb. 1831. He m. 2ndly, in Feb. 1820, Christina, eldest dau. of Thomas-Raymond Arundell, Esq. of Ashcombe, Wilts, and by her has surviving issue,

i. Giles, b. 6 May, 1827. m. Mary Nichol.
ii. Reginald, b. 2 Sept. 1832. iii. Hubert, b. 8 Aug. 1835.
i. Agnes, m. 1855. to Robert Freame, Esq.
ii. Louisa, m. Oct. 1854, to Theodore Arundell, Esq.

Lineage.—The family of Hussey, distinguished by many noble and equestrian alliances, derived its origin, as appears by the registry of the pedigree in the Visitation of Dorset, A.D. 1623, as well as by a manuscript in ancient French, said to have been found in the Abbey of Glastonbury at its dissolution, from Hubert Hussey, a Norman noble, who, having married the Countess Helen, dau. of Richard, 5th Duke of Normandy, accompanied the Conqueror to England, and had a grant of the office of high-constable, with considerable possessions.

Sir James Hussey, Knt., LL.D., principal of Magdalen College, and chancellor to the Bishop of Salisbury, was father of

James Hussey, Esq. of Blandford St. Mary, living in 1622, who m. Elizabeth, dau. of George Hovenden, D.D. of Canterbury, and had three sons, George; Thomas; and Robert, who m. Susan, dau. of Emanuel Gauntlet, of Salisbury. The eldest son,

George Hussey, Esq. of Marnhull, co. Dorset, b. in 1623, purchased the manor of Marnhull in 1651. He m. 1st, Elizabeth, dau. of Charles Walcott, Esq. of Shropshire, by whom he had a dau., Cicely; and 2ndly, Grace, dau. of Sir Lewis Dive, of Bromham, co. Bedford, by whom he had (with four daus. Susan, Mary, Martha, and Anne) one son,

John Hussey, Esq. of Marnhull, who m. Mary, dau. of Thomas Burdet, Esq., and had issue. Mr. Hussey d. in 1736. His 5th son.

Giles Hussey, Esq., b. at Marnhull, 10 Feb. 1710, who possessed great ability as a painter, eventually, at the decease of his brother, James, in 1773, s. to the family estate. He d. s. p. in June, 1788, and was s. by (his sister's son) his nephew,

John Rowe, Esq. of Marnhull, who assumed the surname and arms of Hussey. He m. Anne, dau. of George Rowe, Esq. of Cranbourne, and had issue,

John, now of Nash Court.
George, m. Miss Baily, of London, but had no issue.
Mary-Ann, m. to Herman Scruers, Esq.
Teresa, m. 1st, to Spry Bartlett, Esq., and 2ndly, to Monsr. Mastraca.
Frances, m. to Monsieur Cornett; and d. in 1839, leaving two children.
Grace-Victoria, m. to G. Shaw, Esq., and has issue.

Mr. Hussey d. in 1811.

Arms—Barry of six, erm. and gu.
Crest—A boot, sa., spurred, or, topped, erm.
Seat—Nash Court, Marnhull, Dorset.

HUSSEY OF SCOTNEY CASTLE.

Hussey, Edward, Esq. of Scotney Castle, Lamberhurst, Sussex, J.P. and D.L., high-sheriff 1844, b. 13 July, 1807; m. 24 Nov. 1853, the Hon. Henrietta-Sarah, eldest dau. of the Hon. Robert-H. Clive and his wife, the Lady Harriet Clive, now Baroness Windsor, and has a son and heir,

Edward-Windsor, b. 5 Oct. 1855.

Lineage.—This branch of the old Norman family before us derives from

Edward Hussey, Esq. of Little Shelsley, co. Worcester, who m. in 1641, and was s. by his son.

Edward Hussey, Esq. of Norgrove's End, in Bayton co. Worcester, who m. twice, and left at his decease, 27 May, 1707, an only son (by his 1st wife, Elinor, 3rd dau. of Edward Cresset, Esq. of The Cotes, in Shropshire), viz.,

Thomas Hussey, Esq. of Burwash, co. Sussex who m. Frances, dau. and co-heir of Thomas Lake, Esq. of Taywell, by whom he had (with two younger sons, John, who d. in 1754; and Edward, d. in 1742; and a dau., Frances, wife of George Weller, Esq. of Tunbridge, who subsequently took the surname of Poley) a son and heir, his successor in 1735,

Thomas Hussey, Esq. of Burwash and of Ashford, both in Kent, b. in 1722; who m. 8 Oct. 1747, Anne, only child of Maurice Berkeley Esq., by Anne, only dau. and eventually heir of the Rev. Roger Calow, of Warbleton, in Sussex, and had several children, of whom the following married, viz., Edward, his heir; John in holy orders m. Miss Jennings, an heiress, and left an only son, Thomas-John, in holy orders, rector of Hayes, Kent; William, M.A., rector of Sandhurst, m. Charlotte dau. of William Twopenny, Esq. of Rochester and has issue;* Frances, wife of S. Streatfield, Esq.; Philadelphia, wife of Thomas Rutton, Esq., d. s. p.; Harriet, m. to John Austen, Esq. Thomas Hussey d. in 1779, was s. by his eldest son,

Edward Hussey, Esq. of Scotney Castle, who m. in 1775, Elizabeth-Sarah, only dau. and heir of Robert Bridge, Esq. of Bocking co. Essex, and dying 4 July, 1816, was s. by his son,

Edward Hussey, Esq. of Scotney Castle, who m. Anne, dau. and co-heir of William Jemmett Esq. of Ashford, and left at his decease, 6 Sept. 1817, a dau., Eleanor-Louisa, who d. in 1820; and a son, the present Edward-Hussey, Esq. of Scotney Castle.

Arms—Or, a cross, vert, charged with a mullet, pierced, arg.
Crest—A hind, ducally gorged and chained, at lodge, under an oak-tree, ppr.
Seat—Scotney Castle, Lamberhurst.

* Of the Rev. William Hussey's children, William, the eldest son, of Hawkhurst, m. Mary-Anne Law, co-heir of her father, and granddau. of the Rev. Archdeacon John Law, and had issue, Arthur; the 2nd is a clergyman; Henry, the 3rd, m. 21 Aug. 1838, Eliza-Adamy, youngest dau. of J.-G. Walford, Esq. of Woodlands; Charlotte, the eldest dau., m. Alexander-H. Sutherland, Esq., F.S.A. There are several other sons and daus.

HUSSEY OF WYRLEY GROVE.

HUSSEY, PHINEAS-FOWKE, Esq. of Wyrley Grove, co. Stafford, late 98th regt. of foot, *b.* 14 Jan. 1822; *m.* 15 Oct. 1850, Elizabeth-Clementina, 2nd dau. of Archibald-Nisbet Carmichael, Esq., and has one surviving dau., Elizabeth.

Lineage.—The manor of Little Wyrley, and a considerable estate in land and coal-mines therein, has been held by this family many years, passing through four generations to the present possessor.

The Husseys became lords of Little Wyrley by marriage of JOSEPH HUSSEY, of London, with Sybil, heiress of Walter Fowke, of Brewood.

SYBIL FOWKE, dau. and co-heir of Walter Fowke, Esq. (whose father, Roger Fowke, Esq. of Brewood, the representative of an old Staffordshire family, bought Little Wyrley of John Leveson), who *m.* JOSEPH HUSSEY, citizen, of St. Bride's, London, son of Joseph Hussey, of Southampton, and a descendant probably of the HUSSEYS *of Wilts and Dorset*, and was mother of

FOWKE HUSSEY, of Little Wyrley, in 1714, who *m.* Elizabeth, dau. of William Jesson, Gent. of Lichfield and sister of William Jesson, barrister-at-law. Of this marriage, the 4th son,

RICHARD HUSSEY, of Wolverhampton, *b.* in 1722, *m.* Anne Beckett, and by her (who *d.* 17 July, 1789) left at his decease, 23 Oct. 1774, a son,

PHINEAS HUSSEY, Esq. of Wyrley Grove, in 1799, who inherited Little Wyrley by will of his uncle, Phineas Hussey. He *m.* 1st Fanny Fowler, by whom he had no issue; and 2ndly, 24 Sept. 1814, Sophia Ray, by whom he left at his decease, with a dau. (Fanny-Sophia, who *m.* in 1843, Edward Kellaart, Esq. of Ceylon, army medical staff; and *d.* in 1847) a son, the present PHINEAS-FOWKE HUSSEY, Esq. of Wyrley Grove.

Arms—Barry of six, erm. and gu.
Crest—A boot, sa., the spur, or, turned down, erm.
Motto—Ut tibi sic aliis.
Seat—Wyrley Grove, Staffordshire.

HUSSEY OF UPWOOD.

HUSSEY, RICHARD-HUSSEY, Esq. of Upwood, co. Huntingdon, J.P. and D.L., *b.* 22 Oct. 1815; *s.* his father in 1843.

Lineage.—For this gentleman's paternal family, refer to MOUBRAY OF COCKAIRNY.

VICE-ADMIRAL RICHARD-HUSSEY MOUBRAY, 2nd son of Robert Moubray, Esq. of Cockairny, co. Fife, by Arabella his wife, dau. of Thomas Hussey, Esq. of Wrexham, co. Denbigh, and co-heir (with her sister, Maria-Anne, wife of Sir Richard Bickerton, Bart.) of her brother, Lieut.-Gen. Vere Warner, of Wood Wood, assumed the surname of HUSSEY, and became SIR RICHARD-HUSSEY HUSSEY, K.C.B., G.C.M.S., of Wood Walton, at the decease of his cousin, Admiral Sir Richard Bickerton, Bart., K.C.B., of Upwood, in 1832. He *m.* 5 Jan. 1815, Emma, 6th dau. of William Hobson, Esq. of Markfield, co. Middlesex, and had issue, RICHARD-HUSSEY, his heir; Emma; Eleanor, *m.* 12 March, 1838 to Lord St. John, of Bletshoe; and Laura, *m.* to Captain S.-W. Buller, E.I.C.S. Sir Richard *d.* in 1843.

Arms—Quarterly: per a cross of pearls, or and gu., in the 1st and 4th quarters, a cross, az.; in the 2nd and 3rd, three lions, passant-guardant, or, on the centre chief point (as an honourable augmentation) on a plate, the turban of an omrah of the Mogul empire, ppr.
Crest—A hind, trippant, ppr., ducally gorged and chained, or.
Seat—Upwood, Huntingdonshire.

HUSSEY OF WESTOWN.

HUSSEY, ANTHONY STRONG, Esq. of Westown, co. Dublin, *b.* 24 Aug. 1782; *m.* 19 Aug. 1811, Mable, eldest dau. of Malachy Donelan, Esq. of Ballydonelan, co. Galway, and by her has issue,

I. GERALD.
II. Malachy, *m.* Miss Fitzgerald, and has issue.
III. Anthony, an officer in Prince Coburg's regt. of lancers, Austrian service.
IV. Edward.
V. Richard, in the Austrian service.
I. Mary, a nun.
II. Mable, a nun.
III. Margaret.
IV. Isabella.

Mr. Hussey, who *s.* his father, the late Gerald-Strong Hussey, Esq., 30 Nov. 1811, is a magistrate for the cos. of Meath and Dublin, and a deputy-lieutenant of the former.

Lineage.—SIR HUGH HUSSEY, who went to Ireland 17 HENRY II., *m.* the sister of Theobald FitzWalter, the first Butler of that kingdom, and *d.* seised of large possessions in the co. of Meath, from the grant of Hugh de Lacie. His son WALTER HUSSEY, was father, by Agnes his wife, dau. and heir of Hugh de Lacie, sen., Earl of Ulster, of HUGH HUSSEY, who *m.* a dau. of Adam de Hereford, and had a son, WILLIAM HUSSEY, who by Catherine Fitzgerald his wife, a dau. of the house of Kildare, was father of SIR JOHN HUSSEY, Knt., 1st Baron of Galtrim, summoned to parliament 25 March and 22 Nov. 1374, and 22 Jan. 1377. From him descended the great house of HUSSEY, *Barons of Galtrim.*

PETER HUSSEY, Esq., 2nd son of James Hussey, Baron of Galtrim, by Mary his wife, dau of Richard Aylmer, Esq. of Lyons, *m.* Mary, only dau. of Bartholomew Bellew, Esq. of Westown, co. Dublin, and had a son,

LUKE HUSSEY, Esq. of Westown, father of

COL. EDWARD HUSSEY, of Westown, who *m.* Mabel Barnewall, and had issue,

I. JAMES, his heir.
II. George, *d. unm.*
III. Luke, *d. unm.*
IV. Nicholas, who *d. unm.*
I. Mabel, *m.* to Matthias Barnewall, Esq. of Castletown, co. Meath.
II. CATHERINE, who *m.* SIR ANDREW AYLMER, Bart. of Balrath, co. Meath, and by him, who *d.* 5 Nov. 1740, left at her decease, in 1746, with other issue, a dau.,
   MABEL AYLMER, who *m.* JOHN STRONG, Esq. of Mullafin, co. Meath, and had five sons, ANDREW; Simon; John; GERALD, of whom presently, as inheritor of the Westown estates; and Robert.

The eldest son,

JAMES HUSSEY, Esq. of Westown, co. Dublin, and of Courtown, co. Kildare, *m.* Catherine, dau. of Richard Parsons, Viscount Rosse, and by her, who in 1766, had issue (with four daus. Frances, Elizabeth, Mabel, and Mary) three sons, who all *d. s. p.* Mr. Hussey, *d.* in 1759, and was *s.* by his son,

EDWARD HUSSEY, Esq. of Westown, who *m.* in 1743, Isabella, eldest dau. and co-heir of John, Duke of Montague, and relict of William Montague, Duke of Manchester, and assumed, at the decease of his father-in-law, the name and arms of MONTAGUE. In 1753, he was installed a Knight of the Bath; in 1762, created a peer of Great Britain, as BARON BEAULIEU, of Beaulieu; and in 1784, advanced to be EARL BEAULIEU. By the co-heiress of Montague, his lordship had an only son, JOHN, who *d. unm.*, and one dau., Isabella, who also *d. unm.* in 1772. He *d.* in 1802 (when the peerage expired), and was *s.* in the Irish estates by his brother,

RICHARD HUSSEY, Esq. of Westown, who *d. unm.*, having devised his property to his cousin (the grandson of Catherine Hussey, by her husband, Sir Andrew Aylmer, Bart.),

GERALD STRONG, Esq., who assumed, in consequence, the name and arms of HUSSEY. Owing, however, to the will of Lord Beaulieu, who had bequeathed the estates to Lord Sidney Osborne, youngest son of the Duke of Leeds, litigation ensued, and was at length terminated by a compromise and division of the property under an act of parliament, 51 GEORGE III. Mr. Strong-Hussey *m.* in 1781, Mary, dau. of Anthony Lynch, Esq. of LaVally, co. Galway, and had issue,

ANTHONY, his heir, now of Westown.
Margaret, *m.* in 1812, to Francis Magan, Esq. of Emo, co. Westmeath.
Isabella, *m.* in 1813, to Lieut.-Col. William Meall, E.I.Co.'s service, and *d.* leaving two daus.

Mr. Strong-Hussey *d.* 30 Nov. 1811.

Arms—Barry of six, erm. and gu., on a canton of the last, a cross, or.
Crest—A hind, passant, arg., on a mount, vert, and under a tree, ppr.
Motto—Cor immobile.
Seat—Westown, near Balbriggan.

HUSSEY OF DINGLE.

HUSSEY, JAMES, Esq. of Dingle, co. Kerry, J.P., *b.* 1816.

Lineage.—This family, of Norman descent, settled in Ireland, in the reign of HENRY II. A branch established itself in Kerry, and got a grant of the land from Castledrum to Dingle. In 1613, MICHAEL HUSSEY, represented the borough of Dingle in parliament. In 1641, WALTER HUSSEY was lord of the castle of Dingle, called from thence Dangean in Hushey, or the fortress of Hussey: he was also owner of The Magheries and Ballybeggan, and had the castles of Castle Gregory and Minard. He was besieged in the latter by Cols. Le Hunt and Sadleir, of CROMWELL'S army, and blown up; his estate was thus confiscated. From Walter came RICHARD, from whom was descended PETER HUSSEY, who m. Helen Rice, and had issue, MAURICE HUSSEY, who m. Mary Hussey, and had issue, JOHN; Edward; and Alice, m. 23 Nov. 1748, to James Fitzgerald, of Liscarney.

JOHN HUSSEY, the eldest son, m. Miss Bodkin, and had issue, Maurice, Connolly, Edward, and PETER-BODKIN, all d. unm., except

PETER-BODKIN HUSSEY, Esq., barrister, who m. 10 Dec. 1804, Mary, eldest dau. of Robert Hickson, Esq. of Dingle, J.P. and deputy-governor of Kerry, and left issue,

John, who d. unm. at St. Malo, France.
JAMES, J.P., of Dingle.
Edward, J.P., of Dingle, m. to Julia, dau. of the Rev. Robert Hickson, and has issue, Peter, Edward, and Julia.
Robert, d. unm. in India.
Samuel-Murray, J.P., of Cloghroe House, Cork, b. 1825, m. 1853, Julia-Agnes, 3rd dau. of John Hickson, Esq., D.L., and has issue, Robert-John and Mary.
Ellen, m. to Robert, 3rd son of the Right Hon. Maurice Fitzgerald, Knight of Kerry.
Anne.
Julia, m. to Peter Fitzgerald, Knight of Kerry.

Arms—Barry of six, erm. and gu., on a canton of the last, a cross, or.
Crest—A hind, passant, arg., on a mound, vert, and under a tree, ppr.
Motto—Cor immobile.
Seat—Farranikella, co. Cork.

HUSTLER OF ACKLAM HALL.

HUSTLER, THOMAS, Esq. of Acklam Hall, co. York, J.P., b. 1 Aug. 1801; m. 12 Aug. 1822, Charlotte-Frances-Eliza, only dau. of the late Richard Wells, Esq. of Demerara, West Indies, and has issue,

I. WILLIAM-THOMAS, b. 29 May, 1823.
II. Richard, b. 5 Oct. 1824.
III. George, b. 12 June, 1826. IV. James, d. young.
I. Evereld-Catherine-Eliza.

Lineage.—This family was founded at Acklam, by WILLIAM HUSTLER, of Bridlington, co. York, who flourished *temp.* JAMES I., and purchasing the estate of Acklam of Sir Matthew Boynton, Bart., *temp.* CHARLES I., became seated there. He m. Eleanor, dau. of William Simpson, of Ryton, co. York, and d. 5 Nov., 20 CHARLES I., and by her (who m. 2ndly, Sir Edward Buckhoole, Knt. of Kent) he had a son and heir,

WILLIAM HUSTLER, Esq. of Acklam, who m. Grace, dau. of Sir John Savile, of Lupset, near Wakefield, in Yorkshire, and was s. by his son,

SIR WILLIAM HUSTLER, Knt. of Acklam, in Cleveland, knighted at Whitehall, 14 May, 1673, m. 8 July, 1680, Dame Anne Wentworth, relict of Sir Matthew Wentworth, Bart. of Bretton, and dau. of William Osbaldiston, Esq. of Hunmanby; and d. about 1730, leaving,

JAMES, eventual heir.
ANNE, eventually co-heiress, with her sisters, to her father's lands, m. 1700, THOMAS PEIRSE, Esq. of Hutton Bonville.
Another co-heir, m. to — Hodgson.
Third co-heir.
EVERELD, of whom presently.

JAMES HUSTLER, Esq. of Acklam, the youngest son of Sir William, was the last male heir of the old stock; he dying s. p., the whole of the estates at Acklam and Middlesbro', in Cleveland, devolved upon his sisters as co-heirs: of whom

EVERELD HUSTLER, was the eventual survivor and last resident at Acklam. This lady was b. 18 Aug. 1698, and was never married. She made her will, devising Acklam to her nephew, Thomas Peirse, Esq., and d. 11 Jan. 1784. was s. by him, who soon after taking the name and arms of HUSTLER, became

THOMAS HUSTLER, Esq. of Acklam. He m. 1st, 1737, Jane, dau. and co-heiress of Staines, of Sowerby, and by her had an only son,

THOMAS, his successor at Acklam.

He m. 2ndly, Mary, dau. of Sir Tancred Robinson, Bart.; and 3rdly, Constance, dau. of Ralph Lutton, Esq. of Knapton, and granddau. of Sir Griffith Boynton, Bart. By his last wife he had issue,

I. William, who m. 1st, in 1800, Charlotte, dau. of William Meade, Esq. of Philadelphia, and had issue,

THOMAS, now of Acklam.

He m. 2ndly, Sarah, dau. of the Rev. John Bostock, rector of East Grinstead, Sussex, and by her had a dau.,

Evereld-Catherine, m. 17 Nov. 1835, to the Rev. Thomas-Watkyn Richards, rector of Puttenham, Surrey.

He m. 3rdly, Mary, widow of — Wylam, Esq., and by her had issue,

William, barrister-at-law, d. abroad, 1 June, 1845.

Mr. William Hustler d. in 1818.

I. Constance, d. unm.
II. Evereld, m. to Thomas Hopper, Esq. of Shincliffe Grange, co. Durham, and d. in 1811.

Thomas Hustler, Esq. was s. by his eldest son,

THOMAS HUSTLER, Esq. of Acklam, who d. unm., in 1819, when Acklam devolved upon his nephew and heir, the present THOMAS HUSTLER, Esq. of Acklam.

Arms—Arg., on a fesse, az., between two martlets, sa., three fleurs-de-lis, or.
Crest—A talbot, sejant, arg., gorged with a collar, az., thereon three fleurs-de-lis, or.
Motto—Aut nunquam tentes aut perfice.
Seat—Acklam Hall, in Cleveland.

HUTCHINSON OF TIMONEY.

HUTCHINSON, JOHN-DAWSON, Esq. of Timoney, co. Tipperary, m. 1st, 15 Dec. 1840, Elizabeth, youngest dau. of John Lloyd, Esq. of Lloydsborough, in the same co., but by her, who d. 3 March, 1842, has no issue. He m. 2ndly, Eliza-Hannah, dau. of George Waller, Esq. of Prior Park, co. Tipperary, and has by her a dau.,

ANNA-CHRISTINA.

Lineage.—The founder of this family in Ireland was JAMES HUTCHINSON, captain in Cromwell's army, (son of John and Isabel Hutchinson), b. in 1613, at Kirkbystephen, co. Westmorland, m. Mary, dau. of John Godfrey, Esq. of King Wilton, co. Hereford, settled at Knockballymagher, near Roscrea, co. Tipperary. Captain Hutchinson d. 20 Sept. 1689, and was s. by his elder son.

JAMES HUTCHINSON, Esq. of Knockballymagher and Timoney, who m. 1st, 10 Jan. 1661, Mary, dau. of John Bennet, Esq. of co. Kildare, and by her (who d. 12 Oct. 1690) had (with two daus., Mary d. 17 April, 1706; and Elizabeth, d. in 1705) two sons,

JAMES, who inherited Knockballymagher. His great-grandson,

WILLIAM-HENRY HUTCHINSON, Esq. of Knockballymagher, who m. 1st, in 1821, Sarah, dau. of John Birch, Esq. of the Shee Hills, co. Tipperary, and by her had an only dau., and, by the marriage settlement, sole heiress to his landed property, SARAH-ANNE. He m. 2ndly, in 1832, Eliza-Hannah, dau. of George Waller, Esq. of Prior Park, co. Tipperary, and by her had issue, a son and two daus.; Thomas William-Henry, b. in 1833; Eliza-Selina, and another dau. Mr. Hutchinson d. 21 Nov. 1842, and was s., according to the terms of his marriage settlement, by the only child of his first marriage, SARAH-ANNE HUTCHINSON, now of Knockballymagher.

JOHN, to whom his father left Timoney.

Mr. Hutchinson m. 2ndly, 8 Aug. 1694, Sarah, relict of Richard Poard, of Limerick, and d. 18 Sept. 1718, dividing his estates between his two sons.

JOHN HUTCHINSON, Esq. of Timoney, second son, by Mary Bennet his wife m. 18 June, 1715, Mary, dau. of Paul Chambers, Esq., and d. 18 May, 1758, leaving JAMES, his heir; Benjamin, b. in 1720, d. in 1791; John, b. in 1731; Mary; Elizabeth, d. in 1792. The son and heir,

JAMES HUTCHINSON, Esq. of Timoney, b. 20 July, 1716, m. 15 Oct. 1748, Christiana, dau. of John Pim, Esq. of Larra, Queen's County, and d. 11 Aug. 1791, and had by her (who d. in 1795), with other issue,

WILLIAM, his heir.
John, b. 2 Jan. 1763.
Mary, m. in 1779, to Robert Powell, Esq. of the city of Dublin.
Sarah, m. to Thomas Hutchinson, Esq. of Knockballymagher.

The son and heir,

WILLIAM HUTCHINSON, Esq. of Timoney, J.P., high-sheriff co. Tipperary, b. 9 Sept. 1757, m. 10 June, 1791, Anne, dau.

and co-heiress of John-Dawson Coates, Esq. of the city of Dublin, banker, and by her, by whom he became possessed of considerable estates in the counties of Dublin, Carlow, Meath, Wexford, King's and Queen's Counties, had issue,

I. JOHN DAWSON, now of Timoney.
II. James, d. 9 March, 1839.
III. William, d. in 1814.
IV. Dawson.
V. Frederick.
VI. Joseph.
VII. Summers.
VIII. Samuel.
IX. William, d. in 1836.
I. Eliza-Dawson.
II. Christiana, m. in 1826, to Frederick Lidwill, Esq. of Dromard, co. Tipperary, and d. in 1833, leaving issue.
III. Sarah-Summers, m. in 1819, to John-Dawson Duckett, Esq. of Duckett's Grove, co. Carlow.
IV. Maria.
V. Anne, m. 7 June, 1840, to Michael-Head Drought, Esq. of Harristown, Queen's County.
VI. Sophia, m. in 1831, to John Pim, Esq. of Larra, Queen's County.
VII. Henrietta.
VIII. Louisa, m. 20 Feb. 1840, to Frederick-Adolphus Jackson, Esq. of Inane, co. Tipperary.
IX. Amelia.
X. Charlotte, m. in 1844, to Samuel-John Goslin, Esq., captain 49th regiment.

Mr. Hutchinson d. 6 June, 1832, and was s. by his eldest son, the present JOHN-DAWSON HUTCHINSON, Esq. of Timoney.

Seat—Timoney, co. Tipperary.

HUTCHINSON OF WHITTON HOUSE.

HUTCHINSON, GEORGE-THOMAS, Esq. of Whitton House, co. Durham, b. 15 March, 1794; m. 1826, Elizabeth, only dau. of Capt. John Mercer, E.I.C.S.

Lineage.—A family of Hutchinsons was settled at Cowlam, or Cowland, in Yorkshire, about the middle of the 13th century, and from that descended Richard and John Hutchinson, who went to Ireland, and the celebrated Colonel Hutchinson, the parliamentary governor of Nottingham Castle.

THOMAS HUTCHINSON, of Cornforth, in Durham, (son of Thomas Hutchinson, and — Allanson,) m. 18 Jan. 1579, Janet Armstrong, and had issue,

I. ROBERT, ancestor of WILLIAM HUTCHINSON, the historian of Durham.
II. Thomas, b. 26 Dec. 1585, who m. in 1633, Elizabeth Richardson, and had a son,
  1 Henry, who m. 8 May, 1677, Mary Legge, and had issue.
III. Cuthbert, b. in 1590.
IV. RICHARD.

The 4th son,

RICHARD HUTCHINSON, Esq., bapt. 30 April, 1592 m. Agnes-Meriall, and left (with a dau., Meriall, m. in 1640, to Cuthbert Speke) a son and successor,

WILLIAM HUTCHINSON, Esq., bapt. 11 March, 1620, who m. in 1648, Ann, dau. of — Woodhouse, Esq. of Brandon House, and had issue. The 3rd son,

THOMAS HUTCHINSON, Esq., bapt. 20 April 1661, purchased the estate of Whitton. He m. 18 June, 1705, Sarah, dau. and co-heiress of Henry Law, Esq. of Billingham, and was s. by his son,

HENRY HUTCHINSON, Esq. of Whitton and Bishopton, b. in 1706, who m. in 1728, Mary, dau. of George Scurfield, Esq. of Crimdon House, and had issue,

I. GEORGE, his heir.
II. Thomas, of Bishopton, who m. in 1781, Miss Mary Brown, of Welbourn, in Lincolnshire, and had a son,
  Thomas, of Stockton and Brunton, who m. in 1809, Mary-Sarah, dau. and co-heiress of John Stuart, Esq., and granddau. of Thomas Dawson, Esq. of Tanfield, by whom he had four sons and five daus., viz.,
   1 Henry, b. in 1810.
   2 Thomas, b. in 1811.
   3 John-Alexander, b. in 1820.
   4 George-Stuart-Dawson, b. in 1826.
   5 Mary.
   6 Charlotte.
   7 Susannah-Maria.
   8 Agnes.
   9 Emily.
III. Henry, of Stockton and Kirklevington, who d. unm. 28 Jan. 1811, aged 77.
IV. John, of Penrith, Cumberland, who m. Miss Mary Monkhouse, of the same town, and had issue. (*See* SUTTON *of Bilton*.)

The eldest son and heir,

GEORGE HUTCHINSON, Esq. of Whitton and Stockton, banker, m. Catherine, dau. of Francis Forster, Esq. of Buston, by Frances his wife, dau. of Charles Bathurst, Esq. of Skutterskelf, M.P. for Richmond, and granddau. of Joseph Forster, Esq. of Buston, 4th in descent from Florence Forster, a younger son of the Edderstone family, and had issue,

GEORGE, his heir.
Henry, b. 13 May, 1778.
Frances-Mary, who m. 15 July, 1800, Charles Swain, Esq.

Mr. Hutchinson d. 24 Feb. 1804, aged 74, and was s. by his son,

GEORGE HUTCHINSON, Esq. of Whitton, b. 20 Sept. 1768; m. 16 May, 1793, Charlotte-Barbara, dau. and co-heiress of Thomas Dawson, Esq. of Tanfield, Durham, and had issue,

GEORGE-THOMAS, now of Whitton House.
Charles-Francis, b. 22 July, 1796.
Charlotte, d. young.
Catherine-Mary, m. to Jose-Luis Fernandes, grandson and representative of the late Marquis of Tavora.

Mr. Hutchinson was a deputy-lieutenant for the Palatinate.

Arms—Per pale, gu. and az., semée of cross-crosslets, and a lion, rampant, or.
Crest—Out of a ducal coronet, a cockatrice, az.
Motto—Nihil humani alienum.
Seat—Whitton House, Durham.

HUTCHISON OF ROCKEND.

HUTCHISON, JAMES, Esq. of Rockend, co. Dumbarton, J.P., m. 1st, Annabella, eldest dau. of the late George Gibson, Esq. of Hampstead, and by her had issue, one son, Patrick, who d. young. He m. 2ndly, in April, 1851, Henrietta-Maxwell, youngest dau. of the late James Graham, Esq. of Glasgow, (2nd son of the late James Graham, Esq. of Tamrawer,) by Janet-Maxwell of Williamwood his wife.

Lineage.—THE REV. PATRICK HUTCHISON, A.M., m. Helen, 3rd dau. of Robert Graham, Esq. of Tamrawer, co. Stirling, by whom he had seven sons, viz.,

I. JAMES, of Rockend.
II. Robert.
III. John, d. unm.
IV. Peter, d. unm.
V. William, settled in America.
VI. George, d. unm.
VII. Graham, m. in 1847, Annette-Mary, dau. of the late Archibald Crawfurd, Esq. of Ardmillan, co. Ayr, and has issue.

Arms—Arg., a fesse, az., surmounted by three arrows, points downwards, one in pale, the other two meeting in point, counterchanged, in chief, a boar's head, erased, sa., impaling with those of his wife, viz.: Quarterly, 1st and 4th, or, on a chief, ermines, three escallops of the first, for GRAHAM; 2nd, arg., on a saltire, sable, an annulet, or, stoned, az., for MAXWELL *of Williamwood*; 3rd, arg., on a saltire, sa., a martlet, or, within a border, invecked, gu., for MAXWELL *of Marksworth*.
Crest—A stag's head, erased, gu., attired, or.
Motto—Memor esto.

HUTTON OF MARSKE.

HUTTON, TIMOTHY, Esq. of Marske and Clifton Castle, co. York, b. 14 Oct. 1779; m. 12 Dec. 1804, Elizabeth, dau. of William Chaytor, Esq. of Spennithorne.

Lineage.—This family is descended from the HUTTONS *of Priest Hutton*, in Lancashire. In the grant of arms to the family, dated 1 May, 1584, the following assertion is made by Glover, the herald: "Ex antiquâ Huttonorum familiâ in Lancastriensi Palatinatu nobilibus satis parentibus oriundus."

MATTHEW HUTTON, of Priest Hutton, in the parish of Warton, m., and had three sons, viz.,

EDMUND, of Warton, father of ROBERT HUTTON, D.D., prebendary of Durham, and rector of Houghton-le-Spring, ancestor of the HUTTONS *of Houghton-le-Spring*.
MATTHEW, of whom presently.
Robert, D.D., rector of Houghton-le-Skerne, co. Durham.

The 2nd son,

MATTHEW HUTTON, elected bishop of Durham 1589; was translated to the archiepiscopal see of York 24 March, 1594. He m. thrice, but by his 1st and 2nd wives, Catherine Fulmesby, niece of Dr. Goodricke, bishop of Ely (m. in 1564), and Beatrice, dau. of Sir Thomas Fincham, Knt. (she d. in 1582) he had no issue; by the 3rd, Frances, dau. of Sir Martin Bowes, Knt., who d. 10 Aug. 1620, he was father of two sons, TIMOTHY (Sir), his heir, and Thomas (Sir), of Popleton, co. York; and three daus., Thomasine, m. to Sir William Gee, of Bishops' Burton, in Yorkshire; Elizabeth,

m. to Richard Remington, archdeacon of York; and Anne, m. to Sir John Calverley, Bart. There is a monument to the archbishop in the Cathedral of York. His elder son and heir,

Sir Timothy Hutton, of Marske, in 1598, was sheriff of the co. of York in 1605, and then received the honour of knighthood. He m. Elizabeth, dau. of Sir George Bowes, of Streatlam, co. Durham, knight marshal, by his 2nd wife, Jane, dau. of Sir John Talbot, Knt., and had issue. Sir Timothy d. in 1629, was buried in St. Mary's Church, Richmond, where there is a splendid monument to his memory, and s. by his eldest son,

Matthew Hutton, Esq. of Marske, b. 22 Oct 1597; m. 22 April, 1617, Barbara, eldest dau. of Sir Conyers D'Arcy, afterwards Lord D'Arcy, and sister of Conyers, 1st Earl of Holderness, by whom he had two sons and four daus. Mr. Hutton was s. at his decease by his elder son,

John Hutton, Esq. of Marske, who m. in 1651, Frances, 2nd dau. of Bryan Stapylton, Esq. of Myton, co. York; and dying in March, 1663-4, left, with five daus., an only son,

John Hutton, Esq. of Marske, b. 14 July, 1659; m. in 1680, Dorothy, dau. and co-heir of William Dyke, Esq. of Frant, in Sussex, and d. in Feb. 1730-1 (he was buried on the 2nd of March following), leaving, with five daus., four sons, viz., John, his heir; Matthew, D.D., archbishop of Canterbury, b. in 1692, d. 19 March, 1758. (His Grace m. Mary, dau. of John Lutman, Gent. of Petworth, co. Sussex, and had two daus., Dorothy, m. to Francis Popham, Esq. of Littlecott, and Mary; Timothy; and Thomas. The eldest son and heir,

John Hutton, Esq. of Marske, b. in 1691; m. 1st, in 1720, Barbara, dau. of Thomas Barker, Esq. of York, and by her, who d. in 1723, had no issue. Mr. Hutton m. 2ndly, in 1726, Elizabeth, dau. of James, Lord D'Arcy, of the kingdom of Ireland, and by her who d. in 1739, had issue,

- John, his successor.
- Matthew, b. in 1732, d. unm. 31 Dec. 1782.
- James, b. in 1739, d. at Aldborough, co. York, 2 March, 1798. He m. Mary, dau. of John Hoyle, Esq. of Ashgill, in Yorkshire, and left issue a son, James-Henry-D'Arcy Hutton, Esq., now of Aldburgh, who m. in 1821, Harriet Aggas, and by her, since deceased, had (with a dau., Harriet-Emma) two sons, John-Timothy, b. in 1822, and James-Henry, b. in 1823.
- Anne, b. in 1731, m. to her cousin, George-Wanley Bowes, Esq. of Thornton, co. York.
- Elizabeth, m. to Henry Pulleine, Esq. of Carleton Hall, co. York.

He d. in 1768, and was s. by his eldest son,

John Hutton, Esq. of Marske, b. 30 Sept. 1730; m. Anne, dau. of Mr. Richard Ling, of Appleby, and had four sons, viz.,

- John, his heir, of Marske, high-sheriff, 1825, d. unm. 14 Aug. 1841.
- James, a captain in the army, b. 24 Jan. 1776, d. at Marske, 24 Jan. 1809.
- Matthew, a captain in the army, b. 31 Dec. 1777, d. 12 Dec. 1813, buried at Marske.
- Timothy, now of Marske and Clifton Castle.

Mr. Hutton d. on the 24th Sept. 1782.

Arms—Gu., on a fesse, between three cushions, arg., fringed and tasselled, or, as many fleurs-de-lis, of the field.
Crest—On a cushion, gu., placed lozenge-ways, an open book, the edges gilt, with the words *Odor Vitæ* inscribed.
Motto—Spiritus gladius.
Seats—Marske, and Clifton Castle, Yorkshire.

HUTTON OF OVERTHWAITE.

Hutton, William, Esq. of Overthwaite, co. Westmorland, b. 28 May, 1781; m. 16 June, 1803, Catherine, dau. of Edward Pedder, Esq. of Bishham Lodge, and Preston, co. Lancaster, and had issue,

- i. William, in holy orders, now vicar of Beetham; m. Margaret-Denton, dau. of James-Bramall Toosey, Esq. of Lynn Regis, and has issue, William-James; Catherine-Mary; Margaret-Toosey; Lucy-Elizabeth; and Frances-Jane.
- ii. Edward.
- iii. Thomas, deceased.
- iv. George, royal artillery, deceased.
- v. Molyneux, deceased.
- vi. James.
- vii. Charles, M.D., m. Henrietta, dau. of Dr. Seymour, of Charles Street, Belgrave Square.
- viii. Richard.
- i. Margaret, m. to the Rev. William Mason, A.M., vicar of Normanton.
- ii. Eleanor, m. to William Brayshay, Esq. of Bradford.
- iii. Catherine.
- iv. Isabella-Jane, m. to the Rev. James Cookson, incumbent of Marton parsonage, near Blackpool.

Mr. Hutton d. in 1853, and his widow now has the family property.

Lineage.—About the time of Henry VII. it appears, from deeds and other records, that the Huttons *of Overthwaite*, and the Huttons *of Goldsborough*, in Yorkshire, branched from the ancient family of Hutton *of Hutton Hall*, Penrith, which derived from Adam de Hoton, living *temp.* Edward I.*

Thomas Hutton, Esq. of Overthwaite, in the parish of Beetham, Westmorland, who d. in 1588, at a very great age, left a son and successor, George Hutton, Esq. of Overthwaite, who d. in 1621, and was father of Thomas Hutton, Esq. of Overthwaite, at whose decease, in 1650, the property devolved on his son, George Hutton, Esq. of Overthwaite, who d. in 1678, and had two sons, Thomas, his heir; and John, ancestor of the Rev. John Hutton, vicar of Burton, whose only dau. and heir, Agnes, m. to Capt. Johnson, of Mains Hall, co. Hereford. The elder son, Thomas Hutton, Esq. of Overthwaite, m. Eleanor, dau. of William Tenant, Esq. of York, by Eleanor his wife, dau. of Roger Crowle, Esq.,† by Eleanor his wife, dau. of Edward Wilson, Esq. of Dalham Tower, and d. in 1732, leaving a son, George Hutton, Esq. of Overthwaite, who left at his decease, in 1786, two sons, George Hutton, Esq. of Overthwaite, who d. unm. in 1802, and

The Rev. William Hutton, vicar of Beetham, who built Cappelside House, near Beetham, and fixed his residence there. He m. Lucy, 3rd dau. and co-heir, by Mary his wife, dau. of Oliver Marton, Esq. of Lancaster, of Rigby Molyneux, Esq., M.P. for Preston, only son of Thomas Molyneux, Esq. of Preston, by Mary his wife, dau. of Gilbert Mundy, Esq. of Allestree, co. Derby, and grandson of Sir John Molyneux, Bart. of Teversall, by Lucy his wife, dau. of Alexander Rigby, Esq. of Middleton, one of the barons of the Exchequer, and d. in 1811, having had two sons, Thomas-Molyneux Hutton, who d. unm. 20 May, 1796, and the late William Hutton, Esq. of Beetham.

Arms—Arg., on a fesse, sa., three bucks' heads, caboshed, or.
Crest—Issuant from a tower, ppr., three arrows, sa.
Seat—Beetham, co. Westmoreland.

HUTTON OF GATE BURTON.

Hutton, William, Esq. of Gate Burton, co. Lincoln, J.P. and D.L., high-sheriff 1832, b. 17 July, 1805; m. 9 May, 1832, Jane, dau. of Nicholas Bacon, Esq., 2nd son of Sir Edmund Bacon, Bart., by Jane his wife, dau. of Alexander Bowker, Esq. of Lynn Regis, and has had issue,

- i. William-Frederick, b. in July, 1833, and d. in 1849.
- ii. George-Morland, 46th regt., b. 3 Dec. 1834.
- iii. Edmund-Bacon, b. in June, 1840.

Lineage.—This highly respectable family has been long seated in Lincolnshire.

Thomas Hutton, Esq., b. in 1690 (son of Thomas Hutton, of Treswell, by Mary, his wife, dau. of Joshua Cooper, and 4th in descent from Thomas Howton, of Headon, owner of land in Treswell, Notts, A.D. 1612) m. Elizabeth, dau. of John Rayner, Esq., and d. in 1740, having had issue,

- i. Thomas, of whom presently.
- ii. George, D.D., b. 1716, rector of Gate-Burton, d. unm. Dec. 1804.
- i. Frances, d. unm.
- ii. Elizabeth, m. to William Morgan Darwin, Esq., M.D.

The eldest son,

Thomas Hutton, Esq. of Gate Burton, b. 1715, m. Elizabeth, dau. of William Morland Esq. of Court Lodge, Lamberhurst, co. Kent, and d. in 1774, having had issue,

- i. William, of whom we treat.
- ii. John, b. 1754, m. Mary, dau. and heir of Francis Stones, Esq. of Gainsboro', and left at his decease, 1789, an only child,

* The last direct male heir of the Huttons of Hutton Hall, was Dr. Addison Hutton, who d. in 1745. Sir Richard Hutton, a younger son of the Hutton Hall family, was judge of the Common Pleas, *temp.* Hen. VIII.

† Roger Crowle was eldest son of George Crowle, Esq. of Hull, by Eleanor, his wife, dau. of Lowther of Swillington.

Frances-Mary, m. to the Rt. Hon. Charles Tennyson d'Eyncourt, of Bayons Manor, co. Lincoln.

III. George, D.D., d. s. p.

IV. Henry, m. twice, and, by his first wife, Mary-Judith Dell, had issue,

1 Henry-William, b. 1787, m. 1811, Marianne, dau. of John Fleming, Esq., and left issue,

Edward-Thomas, m. and left issue.
Thomas, major 4th lt. drgs., took part in the memorable charge at Balaclava, m. 1856, Georgina-Maria, only child of Edward Everard, Esq. of Middleton, Norfolk.
Alfred.
Mariann-Eleanor.
Harriet-Susan, m. to George Holland Ackers, Esq. of Moreton Hall, co. Chester.

2 Thomas, colonel 4th dragoon guards, m. Sarah, dau. of the Rev. John Gilby, and has issue,
Charles-Thomas-Dell. Herbert-William-Dell.
Augustus-Henry-Dell.
Adelaide-Sarah Dell.

3 Mary, m. to Captain Tozer, R.N.

4 Harriett, m. 1st, to George Ackers, Esq. of Moreton Hall, co. Chester; and 2ndly, Col. Powell, of Nanteos, M.P.

I. Judith, m. to Ambrose Cookson, Esq., M.D. of Lincoln.

The eldest son,

William Hutton, Esq. of Gate Burton, b. in 1750; m. 1st, Eliza, dau. of Capt. Carr Scrope, R.N.; and 2ndly, in 1802, Mary-Anne, dau. of T. Pyke, Esq. of Baythorne Park, co. Essex, by Mary his wife, dau. of Algernon Massingberd, Esq. of Gunby Park, co. Lincoln: by the latter lady he had issue,

William, his heir, now of Gate Burton.
George-Thomas, in holy orders, rector of Gate Burton, m. Caroline, dau. of Robert Holden, Esq. of Nuthall Temple, co. Notts, and has issue.
Henry-Frederick, in holy orders, rector of Spridlington, co. Lincoln, m. Louisa, dau. of the Rev. T. Wollaston, rector of Scotter, in the same county, and has issue.
Sophia, m. to George-Clayton Atkinson, Esq. of West Denton, near Newcastle-on-Tyne.
Emily, m. to the Rev. Charles Hensley, of Gainsborough.
Maria, m. to Edward Symons, Esq. of South Ferriby, captain E.I.C.S. Bengal artillery.
Caroline.

Mr. Hutton d. 1821.

Arms—Arg., on a fesse, sa., three bucks' heads, cabossed, or.
Crest—A buck's head, as in the arms.
Motto—Spero.
Seat—Gate Burton, near Gainsborough.

HUYSHE OF SAND AND CLISTHYDON.

Huyshe, the Rev. John, of Sand, in Devonshire, rector of Clisthydon, b. 15 Sept. 1800; m. Ann-Lydia, dau. of William Greaves, Esq., M.D. of Mayfield, co. Derby.

Lineage.—This is a branch of the ancient family of Huyshe, of Doniford, in Somersetshire, whose name, originally spelt Hywis, was taken from their residence, Lod Hywis, in the same county.

Richard de Hywis, of Lod Hywis, living *temp.* King John, had two sons, Richard de Hywis; and

John de Hywis, of Lynch, in the parish of Luxborough, father of

John de Hywish, who had a grant of a house and a caracute of land, in Doniford, from John Fitzurse, 33 Henry III. From him descended the family of Hewish of Doniford, whose representative, *temp.* Henry VII.,

Oliver Hewish, of Doniford (son of Oliver Hewish, of Doniford, by Johanna his wife, dau. and co-heir of John Avenall, of Blackpoole, Devon, and great-grandson of Oliver Hywish, of Doniford, by the dau. and heir of Simon de la Roche), m. a Cavendish, and had (with a dau., m. to Chichester, of Hawle, in Devonshire) three sons, viz., John, his heir; Humphrey; and Thomas, ancestor of the Huyshes *of Tetton*, in the parish of Kingston, and "of those other Huyshes about Taunton; and so of Richard Huyshe, who lyeth buried in Taunton." This Richard was of New Inn in 1589. Oliver Hewish's eldest son,

John Hewyshe, Gent. of Doniford, whose will, dated 24 July, 1551, was proved in the Prerogative Court, of Canterbury, 8 Feb. 1552, m. Grace, dau. of Richard Walrond, Esq., and had issue, William, of Doniford, ancestor of the Huyshes *of Doniford and Wells*; Roger, whose son, William, was of Aller, in Somersetshire; James, of whom presently; Dorothy, m. to Edward Hensley, of Devonshire; and Alice, m. to John Bourne. The youngest son,

James Huyshe, sometime of Cheapside, London, a member of the Grocers' Company, d. 20 Aug. 1590, and was buried in St. Pancras, Soper Lane. His monumental inscription is preserved in Stowe's *London*. By his 1st wife he had eleven children; and by the 2nd, eighteen. Of these Rowland, William, James, and Thomas, are the only sons named in his will. His 1st wife was Margaret, dau. and heir of Robert Bowser, or Bourchier, of London. His 2nd wife, Mary, dau. of Moffytt, of Barnet, in Herts. The eldest son by the 1st wife,

Rowland Huyshe, sometime of South Brent, in Somersetshire, and afterwards of Sand, in the parish of Sidbury, Devon, was bapt. 11 April, 1560, and named after his godfather, Sir Rowland Hill. He m. Anne,* dau. of John Wentworth, Esq. of Bocking, in Essex, by Elizabeth his wife, dau. of Sir Edward Capel, Knt., and had by her (who d. 1629) a son and successor,

James Huyshe, Esq. of Sand, bapt. at Sidbury, 2 May, 1604, who, during the civil wars, engaged most actively in support of the Royal cause, and thereby sacrificed a considerable portion of his private fortune. He m. Deborah, co-heir of her brother, Periam Reynell, Esq., and dau. (by Mary his wife, dau. and co-heir of Sir John Periam, Knt.) of Richard Reynell, Esq. of Creedy Widger, co. Devon, 5th son of George Reynell, Esq. of Malston. James Huyshe thus acquired the manor and advowson of Clisthydon. By her Mr. Huyshe had issue, James, his heir; John, a merchant of Dublin in 1668, d. unm. at Barbadoes; Richard, a merchant in Dublin, bapt. 29 Nov. 1638, m. Elizabeth More, of the Queen's Co., and had two sons, Richard and Francis, of whom presently; Anne, bapt. 9 May, 1625, m. 1st, to John Vernon, Esq., captain in the parliamentary army, and m. 2ndly, — Courtenay, Esq.; Mary, bapt. 1 March 1626, d. in Dublin before 1657, wife of William Allen, adjutant-general in Ireland, living in 1657; Deborah, bapt. 5 Sept. 1628, buried 21 Aug. 1661; Rebecca, bapt. 20 Jan. 1632, m. 26 June, 1663-4, to the Rev. Elijah Dene, rector of Clisthydon; Jael, m. 2 Feb. 1663, to Francis Drake, of Ide, merchant; Tryphoena, wife of John Gay, of Frithelstock, d. in 1731. The eldest son,

James Huyshe, Esq. of Sand, bapt. 15 July, 1630; m. 25 July, 1684, Urith, dau. of Edmund Walrond, Esq. of Bovey, and had issue, James, his heir; Deborah, m. to John Woolcott, of Bossel; Anne; Mary, m. to the Rev. William Symons, vicar of Otterton; Urith, m. to — Wilsman. Mr. Huyshe was buried 5 June, 1708, and was s. by his son,

James Huyshe, Esq. of Sand, bapt. 25 June, 1689; who m. Catherine Drake, of Yarborough, and had a son, James, bapt. 31 March, and buried 14 April, 1717; and a dau., Anne, bapt. 24 Aug. 1720, buried 6 May, 1721. He d. in 1724, and was s. by his cousin,

Richard Huyshe, Esq. of Sand, eldest son of Richard Huyshe, of Dublin, who m. Marianne Synot, widow; but dying s. p., was s. by his brother,

The Rev. Francis Huyshe, b. 6 May, 1672; M.A., rector of Clisthydon; m. 16 Aug. 1706, Sarah, dau. of Richard Newte, of Duval, in Devon, son of the Rev. Richard Newte, rector of Tiverton, and by her (who d. 19 March, 1747, in her 70th year) had four sons and four daus. His 3rd son,

The Rev. John Huyshe, rector of Pembridge, co. Hereford, b. 29 June, 1717, changed the spelling of his name to Huish. He m. 20 March, 1766, Elizabeth, dau. of Thomas Hornsby, Esq. of Durham, and by her (who d. in June, 1792) had issue,

I. Francis (who resumed the ancient spelling of the name), of Sand, sometime rector of Clisthydon, and prebendary of Cutton, in the castle of Exeter, b. 29 Feb. 1768; m. 18 May, 1803, Harriet, 3rd dau. of John Waterhouse, Esq. of Wellhead, Halifax, and had issue, Wentworth, b. 29 May, 1812, d. 22 Nov. 1829; Harriet, m. 20 Feb. 1838, to Arthur Abbott, Esq.

II. John, in holy orders, sometime of Heathenhill, parish of Clisthydon, now of Exeter, b. 10 Dec. 1772; m. at Eardisley, Herefordshire, Oct. 1799, Milborough-Anne, dau. of Thomas Harris, Esq., and by her (who d. 13 July, 1824) had issue,

1 John, now of Sand and Clisthydon.
2 Rowland, vicar of East Coker, co. Somerset, b. 26 Aug. 1801; m. Hannah, dau. of John Bullock, Esq. of East Coker.
3 George, b. 2 Feb. 1804; major, 26th Bengal native infantry, late assistant-commissary-gen.; m. in India, Harriette-Matilda Lightfoot, and has a son, John-

* This lady, through Spencer and Clare, was descended from King Edward I.

Troughton Huyshe, *b.* 10 Feb. 1832; and a dau., *b.* 20 Jan. 1837.

4 Alfred, *b.* 8 Aug. 1811; in the Bengal horse-artillery; *m.* in India, in 1836, Julia-Maria, 3rd dau. of the Rev. Mr. Hagar, and has issue, a son, *b.* 10 May, 1837.

1 Milborough-Anne, *m.* 25 Jan. 1832, to the Rev. Charles Walkey, of Lucton, in Herefordshire.

I. Sarah, *m.* at Pembridge, 1 Jan. 1798, to Richard Whitcombe, Esq. of Bollingham, in Herefordshire, of the WHITCOMBES *of Berwick Maveyn*, Salop.

The Rev. John Huish *d.* 17 May, 1802.

Arms—Arg., on a bend, sa., three luces, of the first.

Crest—An elephant's head, couped, arg., crowned and tusked, or.

Huish of Nottingham.

IN this family there is a tradition that its ancestor, having joined in Monmouth's rebellion fled after the battle of Sedgmoor; and to escape the persecution of Judge Jeffreys, quitted altogether his native place, Taunton, and settled at Leicester. The arms of Huish and Avenell* have been borne quarterly by this family, and they possess a Bible of the date 1676, with the name "Elizabeth Huish Taunton, Somersetshire," on the binding. These traditions, coupled with the coincidence of the rather uncommon Christian name of Mark recurring with that of Robert at that precise period, afford the strongest grounds for believing this to be the truth, although no direct evidence exists of the fact.

MARK HUISH, of St. James's, Taunton, and who was a direct descendent of Richard Huyshe, of New Inn, (for whom, *see* before page 606) whose will was proved in 1651, had issue, Robert and Mark, the latter baptised 14 Nov. 1630. Robert was father of Mark, baptised 18 June, 1654, and Robert, baptised in 1659.

ROBERT HUISH or HEWISH, *m.* 30 April, 1698, Sarah Cooke, and had issue. The eldest son,

ROBERT HUISH, Esq. of Nottingham, sheriff of that town in 1736; alderman in 1759; and mayor in 1760; *m.* Alice, dau. of Alderman Richard Weston, of Leicester, and by her, who survived him, had issue,

I. Robert, *unm.* drowned in his passage to Guernsey.

II. MARK, of whom presently.

I. Elizabeth, *m.* Nathaniel Denison, Esq. of Daybrook, Notts, (*see* DENISON, *of Ossington*), and *d.* in 1811, aged 90, leaving issue,

1 Alice, *m.* to John Davison, M.D. of Leicester, and had issue.

2 Mary, *m.* to Sir Robert Bewicke, Knt. of Close House, Northumberland, and had issue.

3 Anne, *d. unm.*

Mr. Huish, whose will was proved at York, 23 Dec. 1765, was buried at St. Nicholas, Nottingham, and *s.* by his son,

MARK HUISH, Esq of Nottingham, bapt. 16 Dec. 1725; *m.* 1774, Margaret, dau. of Charles Stuart, Esq., and by her had issue,

I. MARK, *b.* 1 March, 1776; a deputy-lieutenant for Nottinghamshire; *m.* 5 Aug. 1799, Eliza, dau. of John Gainsborough, Esq. of Worksop, and by her, who *d.* in 1824, had issue,

1 MARK, captain 74th regiment Bengal native infantry; *b.* 9 March, 1808; *m.* 1841, his cousin, Margaret.

2 Henry, *d.* in 1831.

1 Eliza.

Mark Huish *d.* 14 Jan. 1833, and was buried at St. Nicholas.

II. Robert, author of "*The History of Bees*," and various other works; *m.* 1805, Maria Petty, dau. of Robert Greening, Esq. of the Customs, and *d.* 1850, leaving issue.

1 Robert, *b.* 16 June, 1811.

2 John, *b.* 14 June, 1814.

3 Calverley, *b.* 26 Oct. 1821.

1 Margaret-Eliza.

2 Harriett-Maria.

III. John, *b.* 14 July, 1780; *m.* in 1809, Mary, dau. of Henry-Norton Gamble, Esq. of Willoughby, Leicestershire, capt. R.N., and by her, who *d.* 30 April, 1825, had issue,

1 John, *b.* 17 March, 1813; *m.* 20 Sept. 1848, Alice, dau. of Titus Bourne, Esq. of Alford, Lincolnshire, and by her, who *d.* 10 May, 1854, has issue,

Alice-Maud-Mary.

Margaret-Edith.

Eliza-Caroline-Mabel, *b* and *d.* 1854.

2 Marcus, *b.* 19 July, 1815; *m.* 1st, 29 Oct. 1840, Margaret-Jane, dau. of Titus Bourne, Esq., and by her, who *d.* 24 Dec. 1847, has issue,

Marcus-Bourne, *b.* 1843.

John-Hall, *b.* 1847.

Mary-Gertrude.

Margaret-Stuart.

And 2ndly, 15 Sept. 1849, Frances-Sarah, dau. of Sir Francis Sacheverel Darwin, Knt., and has issue,

Francis-Darwin, *b.* 1850.

Florence.

1 Mary, *d.* 3 Oct. 1821.

2 Margaret, *m.* her cousin, Mark (above.)

3 Eliza.

4 Anne-Caroline, *m.* 25 Aug. 1853, the Rev. William Singleton, rector of Worlington, Suffolk.

John Huish *d.* October, 1823, and was buried at Sneinton, Notts.

IV. Calverley, *b.* 15 July, 1786; *m.* 26 May, 1809, Harriet, dau. of John Youle, Esq. of Nottingham, and had issue,

1 Calverley, *b.* 27 April, 1817; *d.* 18 Sept. 1818.

1 Harriet, *m.* 1851, the Rev. George Park, vicar of Hawkshead Lancashire.

2 Margaret-Ann.

V. William, lieut. 6th regt. dragoons carbineers, *b.* 23 Nov. 1787; and *d.* 3 June, 1822.

I. Eliza, *m.* in 1809, to Francis Hart, Esq. of Nottingham, banker, and *d.* 1851, having had issue,

1 Frank, *b.* in 1816; *d.* 26 April, 1836.

2 Eliza, *m.* in 1846, to Sir Charles Fellows, Knt., and *d.* 3 Jan. 1847, leaving issue,

Frank Hart, *b.* 25 Dec. 1846.

II. Margaret, *m.* 9 Nov. 1806, to J. B. Smith, Esq. of Newark, who *d.* in 1807, leaving a dau.,

Josepha Smith, *b.* in 1807; *d.* 23 July, 1823.

Mrs. Smith *d.* at Bath, 30 Jan. 1850.

HYDE OF CASTLE HYDE.

HYDE, JOHN, Esq. late of Castle Hyde, and now of Craig, co. Cork.

Lineage.—ARTHUR HYDE, Esq., 2nd son of WILLIAM HYDE, Esq. (living in 1566) of Denchworth, by Alice his wife, dau. of Sir Thomas Essex, of Lambourne, settled in Ireland *temp.* ELIZABETH, and was living in 1623. He *m.* Elizabeth, dau and sole heir of John Pate, Esq. of Buckingham, and (with four daus., Susan, wife of Sir Richard Southwell, Knt. of Limerick; Helen, wife of Thomas Hyde; Catherine, *m.* 1st, to Robert Gore, Esq., and 2ndly, to Cornelius O'Garvan; and Frances, *m.* to Richard Pilkington) was father of two sons. Thomas, the younger; and the elder, SIR ARTHUR HYDE, Knt., of Carrigoneda, co. Cork, who, by Helen his wife, dau. of Anthony Power, Esq. of co. Waterford, left an elder son and heir,

WILLIAM HYDE, Esq. of Carrigoneda, who *m.* Catherine, dau. of Robert Tynte, Esq. of co. Cork, eldest son of Sir Robert Tynte, Knt., and, with other issue, had ARTHUR, of whom presently; John, *m.* Susannah Rowlston, and had two sons and two daus., viz., Arthur, William, Katharine, and Ellen; Katherine, wife of Sir Henry Spottiswood, eldest son of James Spottiswood, lord bishop of Clogher; Elizabeth, wife of James Spottiswood, 2nd son of the bishop of Clogher; Susan, wife of Anthony, son of Sir John Dowdall, of Kilfinny, co. Limerick, Knt. The elder son,

ARTHUR HYDE, Esq. of Castle Hyde, co. Cork, living in 1669; *m.* Elizabeth, dau. of Sir Richard Gethin, Bart., and *d.* in 1688, leaving, with five daus. (Sarah, wife of William Causabon, Esq. of Youghal; Deborah, wife of John Brown, of Kilbolan; Elizabeth, wife of Foulke, Esq. of Kilvokery, co. Cork; Catharine; and Gertrude, *m.* in 1699, to Robert Gore, Esq. of Sligo) and two younger sons, William and Richard, an elder son and heir,

ARTHUR HYDE, Esq. of Castle Hyde, who *m.* 1st, 3 Oct. 1695, Joan, dau. of Richard Yeats, Esq. of Youghal, and by her had, with a dau., Elizabeth, wife of Alderman John Lucas, of Youghal, a son and heir, ARTHUR, of whom presently. He *m.* 2ndly, Mary, dau. of Col. George Evans, of Carrass, co. Cork, and by her had, with two daus , Mary and Jane, two sons, viz.,

George, who *m.* and was father of the Rev. Arthur Hyde. John, of Creg Castle, co. Cork, who *m.* Joanna Condon, and had a son and three daus., William, of Templenoe, co. Cork, *m.* Catherine Lane, and *d.* in 1790; Elizabeth, wife of — Pooley, Esq.; Sarah, wife of Ambrose Lane, Esq. of Kilkenny; and Mary, wife of John Alleyne, Esq. of Coolprebane, co. Tipperary.

Mr. Hyde *d.* 6 Oct. 1720, and was *s.* by his eldest son,

ARTHUR HYDE, Esq. of Castle Hyde, who *m.* Anne, only dau. and heir of Richard Price, Esq. of Ardmayle, and of

* Oliver Hewish, of Doniford, 30 HENRY VI., *m.* Johanna, dau. and co-heir of Avenell, of Blackpoole, Devon.

Clonmore, co. Tipperary, and had issue (with three daus., Jane, m. in May, 1749, to the Hon. Richard Barry, son of James, Earl of Barrymore, and d. 19 Oct. 1751; Anne and Deborah, both d. unm.) three sons, viz., ARTHUR, of Castle Hyde, who d. unm.; William; and JOHN, eventual successor to the family estate. The last,

JOHN HYDE, Esq. of Castle Hyde and of Creg, m. Sarah, dau. of Benjamin Burton, Esq. of Burton Hall, co. Carlow, by Lady Anne Ponsonby his wife, dau. of William, Earl of Besborough, and had issue,

- JOHN, late of Castle Hyde.
- William, d. in the East Indies, in 1790.
- Anne, m. to Col. William Stewart, son of Sir Annesley Stewart, Bart. of Fort Stewart, co. Donegal.
- Catherine, m. to John Leslie, Esq.
- Mary, m. to Benjamin Woodward, Esq.
- Sarah, m. 9 June, 1798, to the Right Hon. Henry, Earl of Shannon, and d. 6 Sept. 1820.

The elder son,

JOHN HYDE, Esq. of Castle Hyde, one of the esquires of the Order of St. Patrick to the Earl of Shannon, at the Installation, 29 June, 1809; m. in 1801, Elizabeth, 2nd dau. of Cornelius O'Callaghan, Lord Lismore, and by her (who d. 18 Aug. 1824) had issue surviving,

- JOHN, present representative of the family.
- Cornelius.
- Frances.
- Sarah, m. to William-Cooke Collis, Esq. of Castle Cooke, co. Cork.
- Elizabeth, m. to Robert McCarty, Esq. of Carrignavar, co. Cork.
- Louisa.

Arms—Gu., two chevrons, arg.
Crest—A lion's head, erased, sa., bezantée.
Motto—De vivis, nil nisi verum.
Seat—Craig, co. Cork.

HYETT OF PAINSWICK.

HYETT, WILLIAM-HENRY, Esq. of Painswick House, co. Gloucester, J.P. and D.L., formerly M.P. for Stroud, b. 2 Sept. 1795; m. 25 Oct. 1821, Anne-Jane, dau. of Joseph-Seymour Biscoe, Esq., and has issue,

- I. WILLIAM-HENRY ADAMS, b. 14 Dec. 1825.
- I. Frances-Stephana. II. Josephine.
- III. Mary-Clementina. IV. Annie-Grace.
- V. Sarah-Jane. VI. Stephana-Ingl's.

Mr. Hyett, whose patronymic was ADAMS, assumed by Act of Parliament, in 1815, his present surname, upon succeeding to the estates of the late Benjamin Hyett, Esq. of Painswick, who d. 21 June, 1810.

Lineage.—This family of Adams, long settled and connected with Shrewsbury, is a younger branch of the ancient and worshipful house of ADAMS *of Longdon*, in Salop, so long seated in that county; and which bore for arms, "Ermine, three cats, passant, in pale, azure."

Their pedigree and arms ("Ermine, three cats, passant, in pale, azure") were recorded at the Visitation in 1623, by Francis Adams, Esq. of Longdon. The immediate ancestor of this branch was Robert Adams, of Great Chatwall, in the parish of Gnosall, co. Stafford. He bought an estate at Hadley, in Salop, 26 Nov., 20 CHARLES II., and was s. by his son and heir, William, who left, by will dated 2 Feb. 1696, the property at Hadley to his younger sons, JOHN and Thomas, whilst that at Great Chatwall was inherited by his eldest son, Robert. This

JOHN ADAMS, b. in 1675, alderman of Shrewsbury, and mayor thereof in 1726; m. 1705, Elizabeth, dau. of Edward Jorden, Esq. of Prior's Leigh, co. Salop, sheriff of Shropshire in 1720, d. in 1752, leaving issue by his said wife,

- WILLIAM, D.D., master of Pembroke College, Oxon, archdeacon of Llandaff, and prebendary of Gloucester Cathedral, b. 1706, and d. 13 Jan. 1789, aged 82. He m. 12 Jan. 1742, Sarah, dau. of Thomas Hunt, Esq. of Boreatton, co. Salop, and had by her only two children, Thomas, who d. an infant; and SARAH, b. 28 March, 1746, who m. 10 July, 1788, BENJAMIN HYETT, Esq. of Painswick House, but d. s. p. in June, 1804. Her husband d. 1809-10.
- JOHN, of whom hereafter.
- Henry, m. Susanna, sister of the Rev. Crispus Green, of Colchester.
- Elizabeth, d. unm.
- Catherine, m. to the Rev. Rowland Hunt, D.D.
- Mary, m. to G. Jorden, Esq. of Tinterne, co. Monmouth.
- Sarah, m. to — Woodford, Esq.

JOHN ADAMS, Esq. of Shrewsbury (2nd son of John Adams, Esq., and Elizabeth) m. Grace, dau. of John Cay, Esq., judge of the Marshalsea, brother of Robert Cay, Esq. of Charlton House, co. Northumberland, and by her was father of

THE REV. HENRY-CAY ADAMS, of Shrewsbury, A.M., m. Frances, dau. of Richard Marston, Esq. of Willenhall, co. Stafford, by Barbara his wife, dau. of Thomas Kirby, Esq. of Bambrough Grange, Yorkshire, and d. before 1810, having had issue,

- WILLIAM-HENRY ADAMS, to whom the late Benjamin Hyett, Esq., devised his estates in 1809-10, and who taking the name and arms of Hyett in 1813, is the present WILLIAM-HENRY HYETT, Esq. of Painswick House, co. Gloucester.
- John Adams, in holy orders, deceased.
- Sarah-Adams, m. J.-W. Walters, Esq., and d. 16 Sept. 1824.
- Mary-Clementina Adams, m. to Samuel-M. Barrett, Esq. of Carlton Hall, near Richmond, in Yorkshire, M.P. for Richmond, and d. s. p. 8 June, 1831.

Arms—Quarterly: 1st and 4th, arg., a lion, rampant, az., on a chief, dancettée, sa., two roses, arg., for HYETT; 2nd and 3rd, erm., three cats, passant, in pale, az., for ADAMS.
Crests—1st, a castle, ppr., charged with four pellets, issuing therefrom a lion's head, in the mouth a rose, slipped, gu., for HYETT; 2nd, a greyhound's head, erased, erm., for ADAMS.
Motto—Cor immobile, for HYETT.
Seat—Painswick House.

ILBERT OF HORSWELL HOUSE AND BOWRINGSLEIGH.

ILBERT, WILLIAM-ROOPE, Esq. of Horswell House and Bowringsleigh, both in Devonshire, J.P. and D.L., high-sheriff in 1837, b. 15 April, 1805; s. his uncle in Nov. 1825; m. 31 March, 1830, Augusta-Jane, 2nd dau. of James Somerville (Fownes) Somerville, Esq. of Dinder House, co. Somerset, and has surviving issue,

- I. WILLIAM-ROOPE, b. 2 April, 1833.
- II. Somerville-Peter, b. 1 June, 1845.
- I. Frances-Anne. II. Augusta-Charlotte.
- III. Catherine-Sophia.

Lineage.—WILLIAM ILBERT (the first of the name on record) left two sons. The elder son,

WILLIAM ILBERT, m. in 1605, Alice Hansford, and was father of

PETER ILBERT, b. 1616; m. 1646, Katherine, dau. of Henry Dotin, Esq. of Slapton, and dying in 1691, was s. by his son,

WILLIAM ILBERT, Esq., m. in 1668, Mary, dau. of Henry Luscombe, Esq. of Rattery, and d. in 1679, leaving, with other issue, of whom Katherine m. in 1695, John Tinkham, a son and successor,

WILLIAM ILBERT, Esq., (major of the Devon militia, commanded by Sir Francis Drake), who m. 1st, Jane Osborne, of Crebar, in Devonshire, an heiress, by whom he had a son, WILLIAM, his heir, and a dau., Jane. He m. 2ndly, in 1719, Catherine, dau. of Jonathan Elford, Esq. of Bickham. Major Ilbert was s. by his son,

WILLIAM ILBERT, Esq. of Bowringsleigh, in Devon, who m. in 1734, Bridget, 6th dau. of Sir William Courtenay, of Powderham Castle, by the Lady Anne Bertie his wife, dau. of James, 1st Earl of Abingdon, and had issue, WILLIAM, his heir; William-Elford, twin with his elder brother, Col. of the South Devon militia; Catherine, m. to Richard Prideaux, Esq. of Kingsbridge; Bridget-Anne, m. to William Birdwood, M.D. of Totness; and Jane, m. to J.-G. Pearse, Esq. of South Molton. Mr. Ilbert was s. in 1751 by his eldest son,

WILLIAM ILBERT, Esq. of Bowringsleigh, high-sheriff for Devon, in 1768. He m. in 1761, Frances, dau. and sole heir of William Roope, Esq. of Horswell House, Devon, (son of John Roope, Esq. of Horswell, by Frances his wife, dau. of Andrew Cholwich, Esq. of Odston, of Cholwich, and had issue, I. William Roope, R.N., b. in 1762, drowned in 1781; II. ROOPE, his heir; III. Peregrine, archdeacon of Barnstaple, and rector of Farringdon, d. in 1805; IV. PETER, heir to his brother Roope; V. Willoughby, in the E.I.Co.'s naval service, d. in 1795; VI. Courtenay, capt. R.A., b. in 1780; m. in 1804, Anne, dau. of Geoffrey Taylor, Esq. of Sevenoaks, and d. in 1816, leaving two sons, WILLIAM-ROOPE, heir to his uncle, and Peregrine-Arthur, in holy orders, rector of Thurlestone, co. Devon, m. 30 April, 1840, Rose-Anne, eldest dau. of George-Welsh Owen, Esq. of Lowman Green, Tiverton, Devon, and has issue, 1 Courtenay-Peregrine, b. 12

June, 1841; 2 Arthur, b. 23 March, 1843; 3 Owen, b. 13 Jan. 1846; 4 Willoughby, b. 22 Feb. 1848; 5 Donald, b. 8 June, 1850; 1 Marian-Lucy; 2 Helen; 3 Bridget-Mary, wife of Francis Cross, Esq. of Great Duryard, co. Devon, and d. in 1834; 4 Frances, m. to J. Somerville Fownes, afterwards Somerville of Dinder House, co. Somerset, and d. in 1824; 5 Sophia-Maria, wife of Robert-John Harrison, Esq. of Caer Howel, co. Montgomery, and d. in 1836; and, 6 Augusta, wife of John-Lort Phillips, Esq. of Haverfordwest, co. Pembroke. Mr. Ilbert was s. by his eldest son,

The Rev. Roope Ilbert, of Bowringsleigh, rector of Stockleigh Pomeroy and Cheriton Bishop, co. Devon, b. in 1763, who d. in 1823, and was s. by his next brother,

Peter Ilbert, Esq. of Bowringsleigh and Horswell House, captain in the North Devon militia, b. in 1765, who d. s. p. in 1825, and was s. by his nephew, the present William-Roope Ilbert, Esq. of Bowrinsleigh and Horswell House.

Arms—Quarterly: 1st and 4th, or, two chevronells, engr., vert, between three roses, gu., seeded and barbed, ppr., for Ilbert; 2nd, arg., a lion, rampant, per fesse, gu. and vert, between seven pheons, az., for Roope; 3rd, quarterly, erm. and az., over all a cross, or, charged with five annulets, sa., for Osborne.

Crest—A cock pheasant, arg., combed and wattled, gu.

Motto—Nulla rosa sine spinis.

Seat—Horswell House, co. Devon.

INGE OF THORPE-CONSTANTINE.

Inge, William, Esq. of Thorpe-Constantine, co. Stafford, formerly a capt. in the army, s. his father in Feb. 1838.

Lineage.—Richard Inge, of Leicester, said to be descended from the Knighton family of Inge, m. Jane, dau. and co-heir of William Ives, alderman of Leicester, (who purchased Thorpe in 1681), and was s. by his son,

William Inge, Esq. of Thorpe, who was appointed by parliament in 1654, one of the judges of Leicestershire. He m. 1st, Elizabeth, dau. of George Ashby, Esq. of Quenby, but by her had no surviving issue. He m. 2ndly, Elizabeth, dau. of Thomas, and sister of Richard Tunsted, Esq. of the co. of Derby, and had William, his heir, with other children. He m. 3rdly, Martha, dau. of Walter Ruding, Esq. of Westcotes, in Leicestershire, and widow of Sir Henry Hungate, Knt. He d. in 1662, and was s. by his eldest son,

William Inge, Esq. of Thorpe, sheriff of Staffordshire, in 1684. He m. Frances, eldest dau. of Sir Thomas Gresley, Bart. of Drakelow, co. Derby, and had, with other issue, William, his heir; Richard, in holy orders, rector of Netherseile, co. Leicester, m. Elizabeth Mugeston, and left issue; and Frances, wife of Richard Dyott, Esq. of Freeford. Mr. Inge d. in 1690, and was s. by his eldest son,

William Inge, Esq., distinguished as a scholar and an antiquary, who m. Elizabeth, dau. and co-heir of Robert Phillips, Esq. of Newton, co. Warwick and had Theodore-William, his successor; Elizabeth, m. in 1734, to James Falconer, Esq. of Chester, and had a son, James, LL.D., rector of Thorpe and Lullington, archdeacon of Derby, and prebendary of Lichfield, m. Miss Hall, dau. of Thomas Hall, Esq. of Hermitage, co. Chester. Mr. Inge d. in 1731, and was s. by his son,

Theodore-William Inge, Esq. of Thorpe, sheriff of Staffordshire, 12 George II., m. Henrietta, dau. of Sir John Wrottesley, of Wrottesley, in the same co., and had William, his heir; Frances, wife of John Cave Brown, Esq. of Stretton, and d s.p.; and Henrietta, m. to Robert Bakewell, Esq. of Swenston, co. Leicester, and left an only dau., the heiress of Bakewell. Mr. Inge d. in 1753, and was s. by his son,

William Inge, Esq. of Thorp, J.P., sheriff of Staffordshire, 7 George III. He m. Anne, dau. of Thomas Hall, Esq. of Hermitage, co. Chester, and had surviving issue,

William-Phillips, his successor.
Henrietta.
Anne, b. in 1771; d. in 1790.

Mr. Inge was s. at his decease by his only son,

William-Phillips Inge, Esq. of Thorpe, b. 26 Aug. 1773, high-sheriff of Staffordshire in 1807, who m. 5 Jan. 1798, Lady Elisabeth-Euphemia Stewart, fourth dau. of John, 8th Earl of Galloway, and had issue,

William, his successor.
George, in holy orders, rector of Thorpe-Constantine.
Charles, an officer in the 53rd regiment.
Harriet.
Susan, m. to George Moore, Esq. of Appleby Hall, and d. in 1836.

Mr. Inge d. 5 Feb. 1838, and was s. by his eldest son, William Inge, Esq. of Thorpe.

Arms—Or, on a chevron, vert, three leopards' heads, arg.

Crest—Two battle-axes, in saltier, ppr. enfiled with a ducal coronet, or.

Seat—Thorpe-Constantine, in the co. of Stafford.

INGHAM OF MARTON.

Ingham, Theophilus-Hastings, Esq. of Marton House, co. York, J.P., Judge of the County Court, barrister-at-law, b. 15 July, 1808, m. 23 Sept. 1829, Mary, only child of the late John Thomson, Esq. of Lancashire. Mr. Ingham is son and heir of the late Ignatius Ingham, Esq. of East Marton, by Elizabeth Moone, his wife, and grandson of the Rev. Benjamin Ingham, rector of Aberford, near Leeds, (the friend and coadjutor of John Wesley) by the Lady Margaret Hastings his wife, dau. of Theophilus Hastings, 7th Earl of Huntingdon.

Arms—Quarterly, or and vert, a cross-moline, quarterly, counterchanged, on a chief, arg., a maunch, sa.

Crest—Two arms, embowed, vested, vert, cuff, or, holding between the hands a maunch, sa.

Motto—In veritate victoria.

Seat—Marton House, near Skipton, co. York.

INGRAM OF SWINSHEAD ABBEY.

Ingram, Herbert, Esq. of Swinshead Abbey, co. Lincoln, and Loudwater, Herts, M.P. for Boston, and a magistrate for the co. of Hertford, b. 27 May, 1811; m. 4 July, 1843, Miss Anne Little, of Eye, Northamptonshire, and has issue,

Herbert, b. 1845.
Two younger sons.
And five daus.

Mr. Ingram is the originator and chief proprietor of *The Illustrated London News*, and was returned to Parliament by the borough of Boston in 1856. Mr. Ingram, and his sister, Harriet, wife of N. Cooke, Esq. of Notting Hill, Bayswater, are the children of Herbert Ingram and Jane his wife.

Seats—Swinshead Abbey, co. Lincoln; and Loudwater, Herts.

INGRAM OF HOAR CROSS.

(*See* Meynell-Ingram.)

INNES OF RAEMOIR.

Innes, William, Esq. of Raemoir, co. Kincardine, b. 29 March, 1781; m. 19 Oct. 1809, Jane, eldest dau. and co-heir of Alexander Brebner, Esq. of Lairney, and has issue,

I. Alexander, of Cowie, co. Kincardine, b. 29 March, 1812; m. 5 April, 1842, Ann-Katherine, eldest dau. of Gen. Sir Alexander Leith, K.C.B., of Freefield, co. Aberdeen, and has two sons and one dau.
II. Thomas, of Edinburgh, advocate, b. 31 Oct. 1814; m. 29 July, 1839, Helen-Christian, dau. of Thomas Burnett, Esq. of Aberdeen, and has, William, b. 27 May, 1841, and two other sons.
I. Christian, m. 26 April, 1849, to Capt. Charles Gordon, 92nd Royal Highlanders, son of John Gordon, Esq. of Cairnbulg.

Mr. Innes, formerly a merchant of the city of London, is a deputy-lieutenant for the cos. of Kincardine and Aberdeen, and Convener of the former shire.

Lineage.—Alexander Innes, Esq. of Cowie, co. Kincardine, and of Breda, co. Aberdeen, b. in 1728 (2nd son, by Jane, his wife, dau. of Duff, of Craigstone, of John Innes, 7th of Edengight, whose ancestor, John, the 1st of Edengight, was 4th son of Robert Innes, of Invermarkie, living 1503, and grandson of Walter Innes, 2nd son of Sir Robert Innes, of Innes, the 11th generation of the family), m. in 1767, Elizabeth, dau. of Provost Davidson, of Aberdeen, and had issue,

I. John, of Cowie, b. in 1776; m. in 1802, Une-Cameron, eldest dau. of Robert Barclay, Esq. of Ury, M.P., and d. in April, 1832, having had issue,

1 John, who d. in 1810.
1 Cameron, m. to Col. P.-A. Lautour.
2 Elizabeth, m. to Arthur Abercromby, Esq. of Glassaugh, co. Banff.
3 Margaret, m. to Alexander Gibson, Esq. of Johnston, co. Kincardine.

II. William, of Raemoir.
I. Jane, m. to George More, Esq., provost of Aberdeen.
II. Elizabeth, m. to James Hadden, Esq. of Persley.
III. Helen, m. to James Farquhar, Esq., M.P., of Johnston.
IV. Margaret, m. to Alexander More, Esq.
V. Hannah, m. to Alexander Allardyce, Esq. of Dunnottar, M.P.
VI. Ann, m. to Alexander Hadden, Esq. of Nottingham.
VII. Hope, m. to Gavin Hadden, Esq.
VIII. Violet, m. to John Hadden, Esq. of Nottingham.

Mr. Innes d. in 1778.

Arms—Arg., three stars, az., within a bordure, chequy, of the first and second.
Crest—A branch of palm, slipped, ppr.
Motto—Ornatur radix fronde.
Seat—Raemoir, Kincardineshire.

IRBY OF BOYLAND HALL.

Irby, Frederick-William, Esq. of Boyland Hall, co. Norfolk, J.P. and D.L., high-sheriff 1852, b. 28 July, 1806; m. 17 March, 1846, Isabella-Harriet, only dau. of R.-N. Bruce, Esq. of Chester Square, London.

Lineage.—The Hon. Frederick-Paul Irby, rear-admiral R.N., C.B., b. 18 April, 1779, younger son of Frederick, 2nd Lord Boston, m. 1st, in 1803, Emily-Ives, youngest dau. and co-heir of William Drake, Esq. of Amersham, Bucks, son of William Drake, Esq. of Shardeloes, Bucks, M.P., by Elizabeth Raworth his wife, only child of John Raworth, Esq., who s. to Boyland Hall, at the decease of his maternal uncle, Wentworth Garneys, Esq. of Boyland Hall, the last direct representative of the eminent family of Garneys *of Kenton and Boyland*. By Emily-Ives (who d. 7 Aug. 1806) Admiral Irby had an only son,

Frederick-William, now of Boyland Hall.

Admiral Irby m. 2ndly, in 1816, Frances, 2nd dau. of Ichabod Wright, Esq. of Mapperley Hall, Notts, and had by her,

Charles-Paul, b. in 1818, d. 14 May, 1836.
Montagu-Henry-John, b. in 1828.
Leonard-Howard-Lloyd, b. in 1836.
Frances-Harriet. Margaret-Amelia.
Adeline-Paulina.

Arms—Of Irby, arg., fretty, sa., on a canton, gu., a chaplet, or; of Garneys, arg., a chev. between three escallops, az.
Crests—A Saracen's head, ppr., for Irby; a cubit arm, erased, grasping a scimetar, imbrued, all ppr., hilt and pommel, or, for Garneys.
Motto—Honor fidelitatis præmium.
Seat—Boyland Hall, near Long Stratton, co. Norfolk.

IRELAND OF OWSDEN HALL.

Ireland, Thomas-James, Esq. of Owsden Hall, co. Suffolk, J.P. and D.L., high-sheriff 1849, b. 10 Jan. 1792; m. 14 Feb. 1829, Elizabeth, dau. of Sir William-Earle Welby, Bart. of Dunton, co. Lincoln, and has issue,

I. Thomas-James, b. 27 Nov. 1829; d. 17 April, 1843.
I. Elizabeth-Mary.
II. Agnes, m. 8 June, 1852, to the Rev. Henry Warburton, rector of Sible Hedingham, Essex.
III. Beatrice. IV. Emily. V. Caroline-Charlotte.

Lineage.—This family is presumed to derive from a younger son of the ancient house of Ireland *of Hale Hall*. The late

Thomas Ireland, Esq., son of Thomas Ireland, Esq., m. 23 June, 1787, Bridget, dau. of the Rev. Christopher Hand, B.D., rector of Aller, co. Somerset, by Bridget his wife, dau. of the Rev. Thomas Harris, of Duxford, co. Cambridge, and had an only child, the present Thomas-James Ireland, Esq. of Owsden.

Arms—Gu., six fleurs-de-lis, three, two, and one, or.
Crest—A dove and olive branch, ppr.
Seat—Owsden Hall, near Newmarket.

IREMONGER OF WHERWELL PRIORY.

Iremonger, William, Esq. of the Priory, Wherwell, co. Hants, b. 18 Nov. 1808; m. 1844, Mary-Anne-Widmore, only dau. of W.-H. Kilpin, Esq. of Longparish and King's Clere, and has issue,

I. William-Henry, b. at Florence, 20 April, 1845.
I. Mary-Delicia. II. Elfreda-Harriet.
III. Mildred-Helen.

Lineage.—The family of Iremonger was of considerable antiquity in the counties of Salop, Lancaster, and Berks. William Iremonger, Esq. of Goldingsfield, or Golden Acre, near Binfield, son of James Iremonger, of Rudge, Shropshire, was a justice of the peace for Berks in 1601, and mayor of Reading in 1617 and 1626; his will is dated 4 May, 1637. He was twice married; his son by his 1st wife, Juliana Butler, was John Iremonger, Esq. of London. Of his numerous issue by his 2nd wife, Alice, dau. of Thomas Davis, of Maidenhead, Samuel Iremonger, of London, and of Donnington, co. Berks, was 16 years old at the Visitation in 1623; another son, Edward Iremonger, was of West Woodhay, and had a son, Edward; a 3rd son, Alphonso Iremonger, m. Dorothy, dau. of John Greene, of London, and had a son and heir, John Iremonger. The Iremongers, of Wherwell Priory, derive from Joshua Iremonger, Esq. (son, by Sarah his wife, dau. of Edward Lascelles, of Joshua Iremonger, of London, and grandson of another Joshua Iremonger, of London, whose will, dated 26 Feb. 1711, was proved 12 Nov. 1713.) He m. 1st, 28 Sept. 1742, Delicia, dau. of Sir John Fryer, Bart., and had by her, who d. in 1744, a son, Joshua, his heir. He m. 2ndly, Mrs. Elizabeth Lacey; and 3rdly, Penelope, dau. of Mark-Anthony Morgan, Esq. of Cottelstown, co. Sligo, M.P., and widow of Charles Dunbar, Esq.; by the former of whom he had a son, Lascelles, in holy orders, prebendary of Wherwell, and vicar of Goodworth Chatford, who d. 6 Feb. 1830, leaving, by Catharine his 1st wife, dau. of Chidley Morgan, Esq., a dau., Catharine-Penelope, m. in 1805, to Walter Jones, Esq.; and by Harriet his 2nd wife, sister of Lord Gambier, a dau., Henrietta-Georgiana-Marcia, wife of Sir William Chatterton, Bart. of Castle Mahon. Mr. Joshua Iremonger d. 31 Dec. 1804, aged 83, and was s. by his son,

Joshua Iremonger, Esq. of The Priory, Wherwell, an officer in the guards, who m. 8 Oct. 1765, Anne, dau. and eventually heiress of Col. Joseph Dussaux, and by her (who d. 1 June, 1806) had issue,

Joshua-Lascelles, b. 24 July, 1766, lost at sea in the Swan sloop of war, in 1782.
William, heir to his father.
Richard, b. 9 July, 1779; m. 11 June, 1801, Eleanora, 3rd dau. of Sir Thomas Crawley Boevey, Bart. of Flaxley Abbey, co. Gloucester, and dying 31 May, 1819, left an only child, Richard, b. in 1802.
Frederick, b. 26 Feb. 1782, d. 11 May, 1820, unm.
Anne-Delicia, m. to Capt. James Towers, 5th light drags. (who afterwards went into holy orders.)
Elizabeth-Sophia.

Mr. Iremonger d. 6 July, 1817, and was s. by his son,

William Iremonger, Esq. of The Priory, Wherwell, lieut.-col. of the Queen's royal regt. of infantry, b. 31 Aug. 1776, who served with distinction at Toulon, Buenos Ayres, Egypt, and Walcheren, and commanded the 2nd (or Queen's Own) foot throughout the Peninsular war. He was a Knight of the Crescent in Turkey. Col. Iremonger m. 4 Jan. 1808, Pennant, youngest dau. of Rice Thomas, Esq. of Coed Helen, co. Carnarvon, and left issue,

William, now of The Priory, Wherwell.
Thomas-Lascelles, b. 24 April, 1815.
Frederick-Assheton, b. 2 June, 1816.
Pennant-Athelwold, b. 18 Feb. 1821.
Henry-Edward, b. 25 March, 1826.
Margaret-Sophia. Helen-Frances.
Elfrida-Susannah-Harriet, m. 23 April, 1844, to Sir William Eden, Bart.

Arms—Sa., on a chevron, or, between three boars, passant, arg., as many falcons' heads, erased, of the field.
Crest—A phœnix, or, issuant from flames of fire, ppr.
Seat—The Priory, Wherwell, Hants.

IRTON OF IRTON.

Irton, Samuel, Esq. of Irton Hall, co. Cumberland, J.P. and D.L., M.P., for the Western Division of the county since 1833, b. 29 Sept. 1796; m. 25 July, 1825, Eleanor, 2nd dau. of Joseph-Tiffin Senhouse, Esq. of Calder Abbey.

Lineage.—The Irtons have been seated at Irton, co. Cumberland, from a period antecedent to the Conquest, and have, since that period, been, in a direct line, successive lords thereof. The first of the family mentioned by Mr. Warburton, Somerset herald, is

BARTRAM D'YRTON, who lived in the beginning of the reign of HENRY I.; and Richard is mentioned soon after the Conquest, as appears by a deed of gift in the Exchequer of lands given to the abbey at York by Andrew de Morwick, to which Bartram was an evidence. He was *s.* by

ADAM D'YRTON, of Yrton, who was one of the knights of St. John of Jerusalem, and attending Godfrey of Boulogne and the other Christian princes to the Holy Land, was at the siege of Jerusalem. During the war, he slew a Saracen general, and is said to have severed, at one blow, the infidel's head from his body. He *m.* Joan Stutville, and was father of

HUGH D'YRTON, who *m.* Gertrude Tiliol, of an ancient and eminent family, which possessed Scaleby Castle and a large estate on the borders, and was *s.* by his son,

EDMUND D'YRTON, who joined the crusade under RICHARD I., and participated in all that monarch's wars. He lost his life in the journey to Jerusalem, and left, by his wife, the dau. of Edmund Dudley, of Yanwick, in Westmoreland, a son and successor,

STEPHEN D'YRTON, who *m.* Jane Dacre, and had two sons, namely, ROGER, his heir; and Randolph, constituted, in 1280, bishop of Carlisle. The elder son,

ROGER D'YRTON, *m.*, and had a son and successor,

WILLIAM D'YRTON, who *m.* Grace Hanmer, of Shropshire, a near relative of the HANMERS *of Hanmer*, in Flintshire, and was *s.* by his son,

ROGER D'YRTON, living in 1292, who *m.* Susan, dau. of Sir Alexander Basinthwaite. By this lady, Roger D'Yrton acquired the manors of Basinthwaite, Loweswater, Unthank, and divers other lands of considerable value, and had a son and heir,

ADAM D'YRTON, who *m.* Elizabeth, sole heiress of Sir John Copeland, and obtained with her the manors of Berker, Berkby, and Senton. He left two sons, of whom the younger, Alexander, *m.* a lady of the family of Odingsels, and settled at Wolverley, in Warwickshire. The elder,

RICHARD D'YRTON, *m.* Margaret, dau. of John Broughton, of Broughton, in Staffordshire, and was father of

CHRISTOPHER IRTON, of Irton, who *m.* Margaret, dau. of Richard Redman, of Herwood Castle, and was *s.* by his son,

NICHOLAS IRTON, of Irton, who *m.* a dau. of William Dykes, of Wardell, in Cumberland, and was *s.* by his son,

JOHN IRTON, Esq. of Irton, living *temp.* EDWARD IV., who *m.* Anne, dau. of Sir Thomas Lamplugh, Knt., by Eleanor his wife, dau. of Sir Henry Fenwick, of Fenwick, and had, with another son, Joseph (who left two daus., Elizabeth, *m.* to William Armorer, Esq.; and Mary, *m.* to John Skelton, Esq. of Armathwaite Castle), a son,

WILLIAM IRTON, Esq. of Irton, who was appointed, in 1493, general to the Duke of Gloucester, and (as appears by an old grant in the family) his deputy-lieutenant. He *m.* a dau. of the ancient house of Fleming of Rydall, and was *s.* by his son,

THOMAS IRTON, of Irton, who received the honour of knighthood from the Earl of Surrey, at Flodden Field, and was slain in a skirmish at Kelso with the Scotch. He *d. s. p.*, and was *s.* in 1503, by his brother,

RICHARD IRTON, of Irton, who served as sheriff for Cumberland 22 HENRY VIII. He *m.* Anne, dau. of Sir William Middleton, Knt. of Stokeld Park, and left a son and heir,

CHRISTOPHER IRTON, Esq. of Irton, who *m.* in 1543, Elizabeth, dau. of Sir William Millory, Knt. of Studley Park, and was *s.* by his son,

JOHN IRTON, Esq. of Irton, who *m.* in 1577, Anne, dau. of Richard Kirby, Esq. of Kirby, by Mary his wife, dau. of Sir Roger Bellingham, and was father of

JOHN IRTON, Esq. of Irton, who *m.* in 1638, Anne, sister of Sir Harry Ponsonby, ancestor to the Earls of Bessborough, and left a son and successor,

JOHN IRTON, Esq. of Irton, who *m.* in 1658, Elizabeth, dau. of Musgrave, of Meatrig, younger brother of Sir William Musgrave, Knt. of Crookdale, and was *s.* by his son,

GEORGE IRTON, Esq. of Irton, who *m.* Eliza, dau. of Thomas Lamplugh, Esq. of Lamplugh, and was *s.* by his son,

GEORGE IRTON, Esq. of Irton, high-sheriff of Cumberland in 1753, who *m.* in 1695 Elizabeth, dau. of David Poole, Esq. of Knottingley and Syke House, co. York, and had two sons and five daus. He was *s.* by the eldest,

SAMUEL IRTON, Esq. of Irton, who *m.* Frances, only dau. and heiress of Robert Tubman, Esq. of Cockermouth, and had three sons, with as many daus. The eldest surviving son,

EDMUND-LAMPLUGH IRTON, Esq. of Irton, *m.* 1st, Miss Hodgson, of Hawkshead, and by her had a dau., Anne-Frances, *m.* to Joseph Gunson, Esq. of Ingwell. He *m.* 2ndly, 2 Aug. 1787, Harriet, dau. of John Hayne, Esq. of Ashbourn Green, co. Derby. By the latter (who *d.* 8 Nov. 1849) he had issue,

SAMUEL, his heir,
Richard, lieut.-colonel in the rifle-brigade, *m.* Selina, dau. of Joseph Sabine, Esq., and is deceased.
Frances, *m.* 6 Oct. 1842, to Sir E.-S. Prideaux, Bart.; and *d. s. p.*

Mr. Irton *d.* 2 Nov. 1820, and was *s.* by his son, the present SAMUEL IRTON, Esq. of Irton, M.P. for West Cumberland.

Arms—Arg., a fesse, sa., in chief, three mullets, gu.
Crest—A Saracen's head.
Motto—Semper constans et fidelis.
Seat—Irton Hall, situated on the river Irt.

IRVINE OF DRUM.

IRVINE, ALEXANDER-FORBES, Esq. of Drum, co. Aberdeen, J.P. and D.L., *b.* 10 Jan. 1777, *s.* in 1807 to the estate of Schivas, as heir to his cousin, Miss Francis Forbes; *m.* 19 Dec. 1816, Margaret, dau. of the late James Hamilton, Esq., and has three sons and two daus., viz.,

I. ALEXANDER-FORBES.
II. James-Hamilton.
III. Charles, E.I.C.S.
I. Bertrice-Wood.
II. Jane-Christina.

Lineage.—The name of Irwin, Irwyn, or Irvine, appears to have been of long standing in the south and south-west of Scotland.

A member of the family of Irwin early acquired the lands of Bonshaw, in Dumfriesshire, which his descendants still possess; and when ROBERT BRUCE took the field against EDWARD I. for the crown of Scotland, he appointed

WILLIAM DE IRWIN of that line (but whether its chief or not has not been ascertained) his armour-bearer, gave him his own devise or arms, when Earl of Carrick, viz., "three holly-leaves," and made him a grant, by charter under the great seal, of the forest of Drom, or Drum, in Aberdeenshire. Thus originated the great house of IRVINE OF DRUM, so highly allied, and so conspicuous in the family records of Scotland. Tradition tells of a bloody feud that broke out between the Irvines and the Keiths, hereditary grand-marshals of Scotland; and of a battle fought upon a moor on the north side of the Dee, which, in consequence, is still called "the Keiths' Muir." The Irvines defeated their enemies and drove them across the river.

ALEXANDER IRVINE, of Drum, grandson of the grantee, was a commander of the lowland forces at the battle of Harlow, *anno* 1411, where he was killed. Alexander Irvine was *s.* by his brother,

ALEXANDER IRVINE, of Drum, who changed his Christian name upon inheriting, a precedent for which alteration being established by King ROBERT III., whose baptismal name had been JOHN. This laird of Drum was one of the commissioners deputed by the states of Scotland to treat concerning the ransom of JAMES I., and was knighted by that monarch in 1424. He *m.* Elizabeth, dau. of Sir Robert Keith, great-marishall of Scotland and had two sons: the elder was ALEXANDER, his heir; and the younger, to whom he gave the lands of Whiteriggs and Redmires, and who had a charter from the Earl of Huntly of the lands of Beltie, distinguished himself at the battle of Brechin, in 1452, under that nobleman, against the Earl of Crawfurd. From this gallant person descend the IRVINES *of Lentuck*, and the IRVINES in Germany. The elder son,

ALEXANDER IRVINE, of Drum, *m.* Abernethy, dau. of the Lord Saltoun, and was *s.* by his son,

ALEXANDER IRVINE, of Drum, father, by his 1st wife, Elizabeth, 3rd dau. of Alexander, Lord Forbes, of

ALEXANDER IRVINE, of Drum, who *m.* Janet, only dau. of Allardyce, of that ilk, and had a son and heir,

ALEXANDER, living in 1527. He *m.* Elizabeth Ogilvie, dau. of the laird of Findlater, and falling at the battle of Pinkie, *anno* 1547, his father then living, left six sons and three daus., viz.,

1 ALEXANDER, successor to his grandfather
2 William, of Ardlogie.
3 Robert, of Tillylair, from whom the IRVINES *of Fortrie*.
4 Gilbert, of Colairlie, predecessor of Murthill and Cults.
5 JAMES, a knight of Malta, ordained, by the Grand Master, prior of the order in Scotland.
6 John, *d.* young.

1 Janet, *m.* to Gordon, of Abergeldie.
2 Elizabeth, *m.* to Seton, of Meldrum.
3 Margaret, *m.* to Cheyne, of Arnage.

The laird was *s.* at his decease by his grandson,

ALEXANDER IRVINE, of Drum. He *m.* the Lady Elizabeth Keith, 2nd dau. of William, Earl Marishall, and had, with four daus., five sons, viz.,

I. ALEXANDER, who *s.* him.
II. Robert, of Fornett and Moncoffer; line now extinct.
III. James, of Brucklaw, predecessor of Saphock; extinct.
IV. William, of Beltie; extinct.
V. JOHN, of Artamford, who *m.* Beatrix, dau. of Irvine, of Pitmurchie and Lumphanan, by whom he had eight sons, who all *d.* without issue, except JAMES, the 2nd, who, by a transaction with his eldest brother, *s.* to the estates, and became,

JAMES IRVINE, of Artamford. He *m.* Anne, dau. of Keith, of Ravenscraig, by whom he had a son and successor,

JAMES IRVINE, of Artamford, *m.* in 1673, Margaret, dau. of James Sutherland, of Kinminily, and had,

ALEXANDER, bought Crimond, in 1703. Of him hereafter, as inheritor of Drum.
William, of Artamford. Robert.
Thomas, of Auchmunziel.
Charles, was already engaged as a merchant in the first establishment of the Swedish East India Company.
Margaret, *m.* to Hugh Rose, of Clova.

This laird of Drum was *s.* by his son,

ALEXANDER IRVINE, of Drum, living *temp.* JAMES VI. He *m.* the Lady Marion Douglas, dau. of Robert, Earl of Buchan, and had two sons and five daus. The elder son,

SIR ALEXANDER IRVINE, of Drum, sheriff-principal of Aberdeen, *m.* 1617, Magdalen, eldest dau. of Sir John Scrimgeour, of Dudhop, Knt., constable of Dundee, and had issue,

ALEXANDER, his successor.
Marion, *m.* to James, Viscount Frendraught.
Jean, *m.* to George Crichton, brother of Lord Frendraught.
Margaret, *m.* to Charles, Earl of Aboyne.

Sir Alexander had a patent from King CHARLES I., creating him Earl of Aberdeen, which the breaking out of the rebellion prevented from passing the great seal. Sir Alexander was *s.* by his son,

ALEXANDER IRVINE, of Drum, who *m.* 1st, the Lady Mary Gordon, 4th dau. of John, Marquess of Huntly, and had, ALEXANDER, his heir; Mary, *m.* to Patrick, Count Leslie, of Balquhain; Margaret, *m.* to Gilbert Menzies, of Pidfodlee; JEAN, *m.* to ALEXANDER IRVINE, of Murthill, eventually of Drum; and Henrietta, *m.* to Alexander Leslie, of Pitcapple. The laird *m.* 2ndly, Margaret Couts, and had a dau., Katharine, *m.* to John Gray. DRUM, with his father, as already stated, was actively engaged in upholding the royal cause, and suffered in consequence incarceration, expatriation, and confiscation. The laird *d.* 1687, and was *s.* by his eldest son,

ALEXANDER IRVINE, of Drum, who *m.* Margaret Forbes, dau. of Forbes, of Auchreddie; and dying in 1696, without issue, was *s.* by his kinsman

ALEXANDER IRVINE, of Murthill, who thus became Laird of Drum. He *m.* Jean, the entailer's 3rd dau., and dying in 1720, was *s.* by his son,

ALEXANDER IRVINE, of Drum, who *d.* in 1735, *unm.*, when he was *s.* by his uncle,

JOHN IRVINE, of Drum, who *m.* Katharine, dau. of Robert Fullerton, of Dudwick; but *d.* in 1737, without issue, when the male line of the Murthill branch became extinct. The succession then opened to the descendants of JOHN IRVINE, of Artamford, and devolved upon his great-grandson,

ALEXANDER IRVINE, of Crimond, who thus became of Drum. He *m.* in 1698 Isabel, dau. of Thomas Thomson, of Faichfield; and dying 1744, was *s.* by his only surviving son,

ALEXANDER IRVINE, of Drum and Crimond, who *m.* 1751, Mary, 2nd dau. of James Ogilvie, of Auchiries, and had,

ALEXANDER, his successor.
Charles, a major general in the army, who *m.* Diana, dau. of Sir Alexander Gordon, Bart. of Lesmore, and had three sons, now deceased, and five daus., of whom the 2nd, Mary, *m.* the Rev. Charles Wimberley. Gen. Irvine *d.* in 1819.
James, *m.* a Roman lady, the widow of — Manley, painter, but had no issue. He *d.* at Rome, in 1831.
Margaret.
Isabella, *m.* to the Rev. Alexander Allen, and had issue; but herself, her husband, and children, are all dead.
Rebecca, *m.* to George Ogilvie, of Auchiries, and had issue.

The laird of Drum *d.* in 1761, and was *s.* by his eldest son,

ALEXANDER IRVINE, Esq. of Drum, *b.* 4 Oct. 1754; who *m.* 31 Dec. 1775, Jean, only dau. of Hugh Forbes, Esq. of Schivas, and had issue,

ALEXANDER-FORBES, now of Drum.
Charles, of London.
Hugh, *d.* in 1829. This gentleman was a landscape-painter.
Francis, capt. in the E.I.Co.'s service, *m.* in 1815, Frances-Sophia, dau. of the late John-Herbert Harrington, Esq., and has one son and two daus.
Christian.

Mr. Irvine was a deputy-lieutenant in Aberdeen.

Arms—Arg., three bunches of holly-leaves, three in each, two and one, vert, banded, gu.
Crest—A bunch of nine holly-leaves.
Supporters—Two savages, with clubs in their hands, and wreathed about the head and loins with holly.
Motto—Sub sole, sub umbrâ virens.
Seat—Drum, co. Aberdeen.

IRVINE OF INVERAMSAY.

IRVINE, PATRICK, Esq. of Inveramsay, co. Aberdeenshire, in the civil service of the East India Company, on the Madras Establishment, *b.* 21 Aug. 1814.

Lineage.—JOHN IRVINE, of Gottenburgh, merchant, afterwards residing in Aberdeen, eldest son of Thomas Irvine, of Auchmunzel, younger brother of Alexander Irvine, of Drum, co. Aberdeen, *m.* 10 Jan. 1757, Margaret, dau. of William Chalmers, of Aldbar, Forfarshire, and by her (who *d.* 12 March, 1822) left, at his decease, 23 Feb. 1795, a son,

PATRICK IRVINE, of Inveramsay, a writer to Her Majesty's Signet, Edinburgh, and a deputy-lieutenant of Aberdeenshire, *b.* 23 Sept. 1773, *m.* 1 June, 1803, Margaret, dau. of Patrick Orr, of Budgelin, Kincardineshire, and by her (who was *b.* 1 Feb. 1784, and *d.* 10 June, 1851) had a son,

PATRICK, now of Inveramsay.

Patrick Irvine *d.* 3 Feb. 1854.

Arms—Arg., three small sheafs of hollin 2 and 1, vert, each consisting of as many leaves, slipped and tied, bands, gu., within a bordure, nebule of the second.
Crest—A dexter hand holding two hollin branches, of three leaves each, crossways, ppr.
Motto—Color fidesque perennis.
Seat—Inveramsay, co. Aberdeen.

IRVINE OF ROCKFIELD.

IRVINE, JOHN, Esq. of Rockfield, co. Fermanagh, Esq., J.P. and D.L., late major in the Royal Tyrone Fusiliers, high-sheriff of the county Fermanagh 1819, *m.* in 1817, Sarah, eldest dau. of Thos. Towers, of Bushy Park, co. Tipperary, Esq., has issue,

I. GERARD, *d.* in 1840.
II. JOHN-GERARD.
III. Christopher.
IV. Thomas, *d.* in 1840.
V. Charles-Dopping.
VI. Malcolm-Edward, *d.* in 1839.
VII. Arthur-Benjamin.
VIII. Duncan-Malcolm.
I. Mary.
II. Kathleen, *d.* in 1845.
III. Caroline-Sophia.
IV. Sarah-Elizabeth, *d.* in 1841.

Lineage.—CHRISTOPHER IRVINE, laird of Bonshaw, co. Dumfries, Scotland, commanded the light cavalry at the battle of Flodden Field in 1513, where he was killed, as was also his son, Christopher, father of Christopher, next laird of Bonshaw, who held a command, and was killed at the battle of Solway Moss, but left issue two sons, Edward and Christopher, the younger of whom (Christopher) was laird of Robbgill and Annan, in Scotland, and father of John, who *d.* leaving a son,

CHRISTOPHER IRVINE, of Castle Irvine, co. Fermanagh, Ireland, who had issue three sons, viz.,

Gerard Irvine (Sir), of Castle Irvine, Bt., lieut.-col. (now changed by the proprietor, William Darcy, Esq., to Necarn Castle). He *d.* in command in Duke Schomberg's camp, near Dundalk, in 1689, and left surviving only one dau., named Mary, who *m.* John Creighton, or Crichton, Esq., ancestor of the Earl of Erne.
Christopher Irvine, Dr., of Edinburg, historiographer of Scotland, who *d.* about the year 1692, leaving only one son, Dr. Christopher, of Castle Irvine, M.P. for the co. Fermanagh, from 1693 to 1711, *d. unm.* in the year 1714.
William Irvine, of Ballindulla, co. Fermanagh, Esq., who *d.* in the year 1693, leaving issue five sons and two daus., viz.,

Christopher Irvine, of Cooles and Castle Irvine, who succeeded his cousin, Dr. Christopher, to the Castle Irvine estates in co. Fermanagh.
JOHN, of whom afterwards.
Charles, lt.-col., *m.* in 1698, Margaret, sister of Dr. King, Archbishop of Dublin, *d.* in 1745, without issue.
Launcellot, *d. unm.*
Gerard, *d.* in 1755, without issue.
Rebecca. Elizabeth.

JOHN IRVINE, of Cooles and Rockfield, co. Fermanagh, Esq., the 2nd son of the above mentioned William, *d.* in 1716, leaving issue—I. CHRISTOPHER, his successor; II. John, *d.* a minor and *unm.*; Sophia, and four other daus. The eldest son,

MAJOR CHRISTOPHER IRVINE, of Cooles and Rockfield, *m.* Jane, dau. of Rev. Dr. Green, of cos. Fermanagh and Limerick, and *d.* in 1760, leaving issue,

JOHN, his successor. Gerard.

The elder son,

JOHN IRVINE, of Rockfield, co. Fermanagh, Esq., *m.* in 1745, Catherine, eldest dau. of Rev. Dr. Story, bishop of Kilmore. He served as high-sheriff of Fermanagh in the year 1768, and *d.* in 1787, leaving issue—I. CHRISTOPHER, *d. unm.*; II. JOSEPH, *d. unm.*; III. Gerard, his successor; IV. William, capt. in the 5th dragoons, afterwards major in the Royal Tyrone regiment of militia, *d.* in 1830; and three daus., namely, Deborah, Elizabeth, and Sophia, all dead. The 3rd son,

GERARD IRVINE, of Rockfield, co. Fermanagh, Esq., deputy-governor of co. Fermanagh, half-pay capt. from the 47th regiment, with which regiment he served in the American war, and was at the battle of Bunker's Hill; was high-sheriff of the co. in 1803. He *m.* Catherine, dau. of Robert Hassard, of Stoneville, co. Fermanagh, Esq., and *d.* 3 March, 1835, leaving issue,

I. JOHN, his successor, now of Rockfield.
II. Robert, *d.* in 1823. III. William, *d.* in 1850.
IV. Arthur-Henry, of Spring Hill co. Tyrone, in holy orders.
V. George, late captain in the 83rd regt. of Bengal Native infantry.
Jane. Catherine.

Arms—Arg., a fesse, gu., between three holly-leaves, vert.
Crest—A dexter arm in armour, fesseways, issuing out of a cloud, hand, ppr., holding a thistle, likewise ppr.
Motto—Dum memor ipse mei.
Seat—Rockfield, near Enniskillen, co. Fermanagh.

IRVINE OF GREEN HILL.

IRVINE, HAMILTON, Esq. of Green Hill, co. Fermanagh, *b.* 21 Oct. 1768; *m.* in Feb. 1798, Elizabeth, dau. of John Sandys, Esq. of the co. of Longford, and by her had issue,

I. ARTHUR-HENRY. II. Hamilton-John.
I. Letticia. II. Elizabeth.
III. Anne-Hannah. IV. Catherine-Angelina.

Mr. Irvine, a magistrate and deputy-lieutenant for co. Fermanagh, served as high-sheriff in 1799.

Lineage.—GERARD IRVINE, Esq. of Green Hill, co. Fermanagh, *m.* Jane, dau. of the Rev. William Green, of Sallysgrove, in the same county, and was father of

GERARD IRVINE, Esq. of Green Hill, who *m.* 1st, 28 Dec. 1751, Anne, dau. of Andrew Hamilton, Esq. of Balimadonnell, co. Donegal; and 2ndly, Sarah, dau. of John Moutray, Esq. of Faver Royal, co. Tyrone, and had issue,

I. HAMILTON, of Green Hill.
II. Christopher. III. Arthur-Henry, married.
IV. Andrew. V. William, *m.* and has issue.
VI. John. VII. Thomas-Gledstane.
I. Catherine. II. Elizabeth.
III. Anne. IV. Sophia-Jane.
V. Letticia, *m.* to James King, Esq.

Arms—As IRVINE *of Drum*.
Crest—A dexter arm in armour, fesseways, ppr., holding a thistle, also ppr.
Motto—Dum memor ipse mei.
Seat—Green Hill, co. Fermanagh.

IRWIN OF JUSTUSTOWN AND CALDER ABBEY.

IRWIN, THOMAS, Esq. of Justustown, and *jure uxoris*, of Calder Abbey, both in co. Cumberland, J.P., high-sheriff 1836, *b.* 19 Nov. 1789; *m.* 16 April, 1823, Mary, only dau. and heiress of the late Joseph Senhouse, Esq. of Calder Abbey, who *d.* 15 March, 1803. Mr. Irwin is captain on half-pay of the Enniskillen dragoons. He is son of the late Thomas Irwin, Esq. of Justustown, (who *m.* in 1788, Jane, 2nd dau. of John Senhouse, Esq. of Calder Abbey, and *d.* 3 Jan. 1832,) and grandson of Thomas Irwin, Esq. of Mosside and Justustown. Capt. Thomas Irwin has had two brothers and three sisters, viz., John, lieut. E. I. Co.'s service, *d.* 21 Sept. 1824; Joseph, lieut. R.N., *m.* Emily Dillon, (of an Irish family); Jane; Mary, wife of W.-N. Hodgson, Esq. of Carlisle; and Sarah, wife of T.-A. Hoskins, Esq. of High Setmurthy, near Cockermouth.

Arms—Arg., three holly leaves, ppr.
Crest—A dove holding an olive-branch in its beak.
Motto—Haud ullis labantia ventis.
Seats—Justustown, near Carlisle, and Calder Abbey.

IRWIN OF TANRAGOE.

IRWIN, JOHN-LEWIS, Esq. of Tanragoe, co. Sligo, *s.* his uncle in 1846.

Lineage.—The Irwins of Tanragoe have maintained a position of great respectability amongst the gentry of the co. of Sligo, since their settlement in Ireland, but from which branch of the Scottish Irvines or Irvings they descend, has not been ascertained. The peculiar name of *Crinus*, borne by members of the family, is traditionally derived from *Krynin* Abethnæ, the second husband of the mother of DUNCAN, King of Scotland, to whom and his descendants that monarch granted the privilege of bearing the *thistle* as a crest.

JOHN IRWIN, Esq. who *m.* a dau. of Col. Lewis Jones, of Ardnaglass, held a command in the parliamentary army in which his father-in-law also served, and accompanying CROMWELL into Ireland, settled in the co. of Sligo. He was father of

ALEXANDER IRWIN, Esq. of the co. of Sligo, who *m.* the sister of — Griffith, Esq. of Ballincar, and aunt of Colonel Griffith, father of Anne, Countess of Harrington, and of Lady Rich. By this lady Mr. Irwin had six sons, who all *d.* without issue, excepting the eldest,

JOHN IRWIN, Esq. of Tanragoe, *b.* in 1680, a col. in the army. He *m.* 1st, Lady Mary Dilkes, widow of — Dilkes, Esq. of the co. of Cork, but had no issue; and 2ndly, Susanna Cadden, of an ancient Cavan family, by whom he had one son and two daus., viz.,

LEWIS-FRANCIS, his heir.
Letitia, *m.* to Capt. Thomas Webber, of the 4th horse, and had one son and a dau.
Margaret, who *m.* Robert Browne, Esq. of Fortland, co. Sligo.

Col. Irwin *d.* in 1752, and was *s.* by his son,

LEWIS-FRANCIS IRWIN, Esq. of Tanragoe, *b.* in 1728, who *m.* in 1766, Elizabeth, only sister of the late John Harrison, Esq. of Norton Place, co. Lincoln, and by her, who *d.* in 1815, aged 82, had issue,

I. JOHN, his heir.
II. Crinus, in holy orders, archdeacon of Ossory, who *m.* in 1807, Amy, eldest dau. of the late Mr. Justice Chamberlain, judge of the King's Bench, in Ireland, and had, with four daus., two sons,
1 John-Lewis, of Tanragoe. 2 Lewis-Chamberlain.
I. Elizabeth, *m.* to Robert Jones, Esq. of Fortland, co. Sligo, and *d.* in 1822, leaving issue.
Margaret, *m.* to the late Rev. Shuckburgh Upton, of the Templetown family, and has issue.
III. Beatrice-Susanna, *m.* to Benjamin Agar, Esq. of Brockfield, co. York, and has issue.

Mr. Irwin *d.* in 1785, and was *s.* by his elder son,

JOHN IRWIN, Esq. of Tanragoe, col. of the Sligo militia, *b.* 17 April, 1770; who served as high-sheriff 1822. He *d.* 1846, and was *s.* by his nephew.

Arms—Arg., three holly-leaves, ppr.
Crest—A hand issuing out of a cloud, grasping a branch of thistle, ppr.
Motto—Nemo me impune lacessit.
Seat—Tanragoe, Collooney.

ISHERWOOD OF MARPLE.

BRADSHAW-ISHERWOOD, THOMAS, Esq. of Marple Hall, Cheshire, and of Bradshaw Hall, co. Lancaster, J.P. and D.L., *b.* 10 Feb. 1820; *m.* 22 July, 1840, Mary-Ellen, eldest surviving dau. of the Rev. Henry Bellairs, of Bedworth, co. Warwick, and has issue,

I. JOHN-HENRY, *b.* 27 Aug. 1841.
II. Arthur-Salusbury, *b.* 21 May, 1848.

Lineage.—Mr. Bradshaw-Isherwood inherits the property of and represents the ancient family of Bradshaw of

Bradshaw Hall, co. Lancaster, an estate which was held at the time of the Conquest by SIR JOHN BRADSHAW, who was repossessed of it by the CONQUEROR. It went to his descendants for twenty-five generations in uninterrupted male succession, when it reverted, A.D. 1690, to the Bradshaws of Marple, in which family it has since continued. It has been a wide-spreading family, and is now represented in its several branches by the Earls of Crawford and Balcarres, by the Bradshaws of Barton Blount, the Bradshaw-Bowles of Bradshaw Edge, and the Isherwoods of Marple. Passing over the earlier history of the family, which is recorded in *Wotton's Baronetage*, and other works we come to the period when this branch of the family settled at Marple.

HENRY BRADSHAW, Esq., 2nd son of William Bradshaw, Esq. of Bradshaw Hall, by Margaret, dau. of Christopher Clayton, Esq. of Stryades Hall, Cheshire, having *m.* Dorothy, the heiress of Christopher Bagshaw, Esq. of The Ridge, co. Derby, purchased Marple Hall, 1606, from Sir Edward Stanley, K.B., having previously resided there as tenant. He *d.* 1611, and left issue a dau., who *m.* John Milton, father of the poet, and

HENRY BRADSHAW, Esq., who *m.* Catherine, dau. and co-heiress of Ralph Winnington, Esq. of Offerton Hall, Cheshire, and dying 1654, left issue,

HENRY.
John, the celebrated judge, who presided at the trial of King CHARLES I., born 1602. He was M.P. for Cheshire, chief justice of Chester, and chancellor for the Duchy of Lancaster. He *d.* without issue, 1659, leaving the remains of his immense wealth to his nephew, Henry Bradshaw.

The elder son,

HENRY BRADSHAW, Esq. colonel in Cromwell's army, wounded at the battle of Worcester, and one of the judges who condemned the Earl of Derby, *m.* 1st, Mary, dau. and heiress of Barnard Welles, Esq. of Wyberslegh Hall, Cheshire; and 2ndly, Anne, dau. of George Bowden, Esq. of Bowden, Cheshire. He *d.* 1661, and left issue, by his 1st wife,

HENRY BRADSHAW, Esq., who, on failure of the senior branch of the family, became possessed of Bradshaw Hall, A.D. 1690. He *m.* Magdalene, eldest dau. and co-heir of Thomas Barcroft, Esq. of Barcroft Hall, co. Lancaster, and had issue,

HENRY BRADSHAW, Esq., high-sheriff for Derbyshire 1701, who *m.* Elizabeth, dau. of Richard Legh, Esq. of High Legh, Cheshire, and dying without issue, was *s.* by his brother,

THOMAS BRADSHAW, who *d. unm.* 1743, when his estates went to his only sister,

MARY BRADSHAW, who was twice *m.*, 1st, to John Pimlot, Esq. (whose only child, Mary, *m.* Lindon Evelyn, Esq., M.P. for Dundalk, whose only child *m.* Lord Dunsany); and 2ndly, to NATHANIEL ISHERWOOD, Esq. of Bury, co. Lancaster, by whom she had issue. Her eldest son,

NATHANIEL ISHERWOOD, Esq., *m.* Mary, dau. of John Brabin, Esq. of Brabin's Hall, co. Cheshire, and dying without issue, 1765, was *s.* by his only brother,

THOMAS ISHERWOOD, Esq. of Bradshaw and Marple, who *m.* 1st, Elizabeth, dau. of Thomas Attcroft, Esq. of Gillibrand House, near Blackburn, by whom he had one son, who *d.* an infant, and six daus. He *m.* 2ndly, Mary, dau. of Thomas Orrel, Esq. of Salterley, co. Chester, and had issue,

THOMAS BRADSHAW, his successor, *d. unm.* 5 Jan. 1791.
HENRY BRADSHAW, successor to his brother, *d. unm.* 1801, aged 26.
JOHN, of whom presently.
Magdalen-Barcroft, *m.* to Henry Salvin, Esq. of Thorpe Salvin.
Mariann, *m.* to George Salvin, Esq.
Hannah, who *d. unm.* in 1798.
Mary-Anne, who *d. unm.*
Margaret, *d. unm.* in 1793.

The 3rd son,

JOHN ISHERWOOD, Esq. of Marple Hall, co Chester, and Bradshaw Hall, co. Lancaster, *b.* 19 June, 1776, high-sheriff of Cheshire in 1815, *m.* 19 Oct. 1812, Elizabeth, dau. and co-heir of the Rev. Thomas Bancroft, M.A., vicar of Bolton, J.P., and chaplain to Viscount Castle-Stuart, and by her (who *d.* 1856) had issue,

THOMAS-BRADSHAW, present representative.
Anna-Maria, *m.* 1839, to the Rev. Charles Bellairs, of Bedworth, co. Warwick.
Miriam.
Anne-Magdalen, *m.* 1843, to the Rev. John Vaughan Lloyd, vicar of Mold, co. Flint.
Margaret-Sarah. Esther-Alice. Jemima.

Mr. Isherwood *d.* in 1839.

Arms—Quarterly: 1st and 4th, ISHERWOOD, arg., a fesse, dancettée azure, on a chief, azure, a lion, passant, or; 2nd and 3rd, BRADSHAW, arg., two bendlets, sable, between as many martlets, of the 2nd.

Crests—1st, ISHERWOOD, a wolf's head, erased, pr. out of a crescent, azure; 2nd, BRADSHAW, on a mount, vert, a stag at gaze, pr. under a vine branch, fructed, or.

Motto—Bona benemerenti benedictio.

Seats—Marple Hall, Cheshire; Bradshaw Hall, co. Lancaster.

ISTED OF ECTON.

ISTED, AMBROSE, Esq. of Ecton, co. Northampton, baptized there 22 Feb. 1797; *m.* 1st, at Barton-Seagrave, 26 July, 1832, Eleanor-Elizabeth, eldest dau. of the Hon. and Rev. Richard-Bruce Stopford, canon of Windsor, youngest brother of James-George, Earl of Courtown, which lady *d.* in 1851; and 2ndly, 10 Sept. 1853, Frances-Elizabeth, dau. of Thomas, Viscount Anson, and widow of the Hon. Charles-John Murray. Mr. Isted *s.* his father 12 Aug. 1827.

Lineage.—"ISTED of ECTON came from Eysted, a large maritime town in the province of Schonen, in the kingdom of Sweden, and settled at Framfield, in Sussex, probably in the time of EDWARD III., where they enjoyed a considerable estate, some part of which continued in the family till 1718, when it was sold by Thomas Isted, Esq. of Ecton."

JOHN ISTED, of Framfield, in Sussex, was father of another JOHN ISTED, of Framfield, whose son,

RICHARD ISTED, of Framfield, *m.* Anne, dau. of William Warnet, of the same place, and had a son and successor,

THOMAS ISTED, of Framfield, who *m.* Elizabeth, dau. and heiress of Thomas Twine, M.D. of Lewes, in Sussex, and had two sons, Thomas, of London (who *m.* Elizabeth Oliver, and was father of a son, Oliver, and a dau. Elizabeth, who both *d. s. p.*), and

RICHARD ISTED, Esq. of Framfield. He *m.* Anne, dau. and co-heir of Edward Goodwyn, of Dorking, in Surrey, by Anne his wife, sister of Sir Anthony Benn, Knt., recorder of London, and had issue. The 2nd son,

AMBROSE ISTED, Esq. of St. John's Square, Middlesex *m.* Sarah dau. of Thomas Feltham, Esq., descended from the Felthams of Sculthorp, in Norfolk, and by her who *d.* about 1725, left at his decease, in 1692, a dau. Anne, *b.* in 1682, who *d. unm.* at Northampton, 28 Jan. 1768, and a son and successor,

THOMAS ISTED, Esq. of St. John's Square, Middlesex, and of Ecton, co. Northampton, *b.* 9 Dec. 1677, who sold Framfield in 1718. He *m.* Anne, dau. and co-heir of Fulk Rose, Esq. of the island of Jamaica, and of Elizabeth his wife, dau. and co-heir of John Langley, alderman of London (who *m.* 2ndly, Sir Hans Sloane, Bart.) By this lady, who *d.* 26 Dec. 1722, Mr. Isted had issue. Mr. Isted *d.* in 1731, was buried at Ecton, and *s.* by his son,

AMBROSE ISTED, Esq. of Ecton, *b.* 6 March, 1717-18, who *m.* 16 Sept. 1746, Anne, dau. of Sir Charles, and sister and co-heir of Sir Charles Buck, Bart. of Hanby, in Lincolnshire, and of The Grove, Herts, by whom (who *d.* at Bath, 21 Nov. 1800) he had issue,

SAMUEL, his heir.
George, of St. James's Place, Westminster, bencher of the Inner Temple, bapt. at Ecton, 7 Sept. 1754, who *d. unm.* 3 Nov. 1821.
Anne, *m.* in 1792, to Robert Corbet, Esq. of Longner, Salop, but *d. s. p.* in 1822.
Harriet, *d. unm.* at Bath, in 1809. Rose-Sarah.
Charlotte, *m.* 26 Feb. 1805, to the Rev. Thomas Howell, of Chalton, Hants, and *d. s. p.* 2 Dec. 1826.
Mary, *m.* 17 July, 1780, to William Sotheby, Esq. of Sewardstone, Essex, and of Lower Grosvenor-street, and has issue.

Mr. Isted *d.* 6 May, 1781, and was buried at Ecton. He was *s.* by his son,

SAMUEL ISTED, Esq. of Ecton, baptized there 17 May, 1750, who *m.* 20 Oct. 1795, Barbara, eldest dau. and co-heir of Thomas Percy, Lord Bishop of Dromore, and *d.* 12 Aug. 1827, having had a dau. Anne, who *d.* an infant in 1801, and a son, the present AMBROSE ISTED, Esq. of Ecton.

Arms—Gu., a chevron, vaire, between three talbots' heads, erased, or.

Crest—A buck's head, erased, ppr., attired and ducally gorged, or.

Seat—Ecton, co. Northampton.

Blair, co. Ayr, M.P., and by her, who *d.* in 1817, left at his decease, in 1822, an only dau. and heir.

MADELINE-EGLANTINE, *m.* in 1834, to Mervyn Pratt, Esq. of Cabra Castle, co. Cavan.

II. GEORGE of whom presently.
III. James, lieut.-col. 6th dragoon-guards, served in the Peninsula, at Waterloo, in India, &c.
IV. Francis, major 85th regiment, served in the campaigns of Holland.
V. Andrew, in holy orders, *m.* Mary-Louisa, dau. of the Rev. Edwin Stock, son of Dr. Stock, Bishop of Waterford, and has issue.
VI. Oliver.
I. Barbara, *m* to Thomas Carey, Esq. of Rozel, Guernsey.
II. Jane, *m.* to Christopher Carleton, Esq. of Market Hill.
III. Mary.
IV. Elizabeth, *m.* to Thomas Orme, Esq. of Abbeytown.
V. Anne, *m.* to William Orme, Esq. of Glenmore.
VI. Sarah, *d. unm.* VI. Belinda-Cuff.

Col. Jackson *d.* in 1805. His 2nd son,

GEORGE JACKSON, Esq., Col. of the North Mayo militia, *m.* in 1804, Sidney, only child and heir of Arthur Vaughan, Esq. of Curramore, co. Mayo, a descendant of the Vaughans of Wales, and had issue,

GEORGE-VAUGHAN, his heir, of Carramore, M.A., *b.* 19 Sept. 1806, *d unm.*
William, in holy orders.
Francis, in the Indian army.
OLIVER-VAUGHAN, an officer in the army, now of Carramore.
James-Sidney.
Maria-Louisa.

Colonel Jackson *d.* in 1836.

Arms—Arg., on a chev., sa., between three hawks' heads, erased, az., as many cinquefoils, of the field, quartering CUFF, AUNGIER, RUTLEDGE, VAUGHAN, and VAUGHAN *of Wales.*
Crest—A horse, passant, arg.
Motto—Celer et audax.
Seat—Carramore, co. Mayo.

JACKSON OF GLANBEG.

JACKSON, GEORGE-BENNETT, Esq. of Glanbeg, co. Waterford, J.P.

Lineage.—THOMAS JACKSON, Esq., *m.* Mary, dau. of Henry Wallis, Esq. of Westwood, co. Cork, and was father of

JOHN JACKSON, Esq., who *m.* Ellen, dau. of Thomas Cochran, Gent., and had, with a dau., Ellen, who *d. unm.* in 1837, at an advanced age, two sons, John, of Glenmore, captain 11th foot, and

GEORGE JACKSON, Esq. of Glanbeg, who *m.* Susanna, dau. and sole heiress of Joseph Bennett, Esq. of Ballymore, co. Cork, recorder of Cork, and by her, who survived him, had issue,

JOSEPH-HENRY, who assumed the surname and arms of BENNETT (*see* BENNETT).
GEORGE-BENNETT, of Glanbeg.
Thomas.
John, in holy orders, rector of Tallow, co. Waterford; *m.* Rosa, dau. of William Poole, Esq. of Ballyanchor, and has issue three sons and a dau.
Edward-Bennett, capt. 2nd or Queen's regiment, *m.* dau. of Grier, Esq. of co. Wexford, and had a son, who *d.* in Bombay, in 1837.
Georgina.
Charlotte, *m.* to Richard Martin, Esq., M.D., of co. Somerset.
Anna, *d. unm.*
Maria, *m.* to William Smart, Esq., R.N.
Elizabeth-Warren.

Arms—Arg., a lion, passant, gu., on a chief, of the last, three pole-axes, of the first.
Crest—An arm in armour, embowed, in the hand, a battle-axe, all ppr.
Seat—Glanbeg, near Lismore, co. Waterford.

JACSON OF BARTON.

JACSON, CHARLES-ROGER, Esq. of Barton, co. Lancaster, J.P. and D.L., *b.* 29 Nov. 1817; *m.* 16 June, 1846, Catherine, only dau. of Henry-Grenehalgh Formby, Esq., 2nd son of the late Rev. Richard Formby, LL.B., of Formby Hall, in the same county. Mr. Jacson *s.* his father, George Jackson, Esq., 14 March, 1846.

Lineage.—MICHAEL JACSON, of East Briggeford, or Bridgeford, co. Notts, kinsman of the parson of the church of that place, *m.* Frances, dau. of — Poole, of Spreston, in the same county, and by her left four sons, viz., 1 WILLIAM, whose only child, WILLIAM, parson of Screveton, co. Notts (described by Dr. Thoroton, in his antiquities of the county of Notts, as a man of great worth, who left but few equals for prudence, piety, and learning, in that country), *d.* 27 Feb. 1661, and left issue by Dorothy his wife, sister of the said Dr. Thoroton's father, four sons, viz., William, in 1677, one of the coroners of the county of Notts, Michael, Roger, John, and a dau., Elizabeth, *m.* to her cousin, Richard White, of London; 2 ROGER, parson of Langford, co. Derby (of whom we treat); 3 George, a citizen of London; 4 John, of Burton Fors.

THE REV. ROGER JACSON, of Langford, co. Derby, 2nd son of Michael Jacson, of East Bridgeford, *b. circ.* 1600; *m.* Sancta, sister of John Hansou, Esq., an opulent citizen of London (who at his death devised his estates in Suffolk, Derbyshire, and Yorkshire, to his sister's sons), and had issue five sons and two daus., viz.,

WILLIAM, S.T.P., of Jesus College, Cambridge, *d. unm.* in 1680.
John, minister of Etwall; left issue.
Roger, of London, *d. unm.* 1698.
GEORGE (of whom we treat).
Marah, *m.* to Thomas Brailsford, a merchant in London.
Frances, *m.* to Francis Morley.

GEORGE JACSON, M.D. of Derby, 4th son of Rev. Roger Jacson, of Langford, *b.* 1646, inherited the estates of his uncle, Mr. Hanson, by various successions. He *m.* Anne, dau. of Thomas Adshead, Esq. of Millwich, co. Stafford, descended maternally from Thomas Beresford, Esq. of Bentley, whose 16th son, James, was the founder of a fellowship at St. John's College, Cambridge. Dr. Jacson *d.* in 1699, and left issue three sons and two daus., viz., 1 George, clerk of Leek, co. Stafford, *b.* 1682, *m.* Joyce Hollins. He inherited his father's estates, which were sold after his death in 1719. He left issue an only child, Anne, who *d. unm.* at Staveley, co. Derby, in 1749. 2 Roger, M.B., *b.* 1687, *m.* in 1721, Frances, dau. and co-heiress of Colonel John Shallcross,* of Shallcross Hall, co. Derby, and Anne Arderne, of Harden, his wife; and *d. s. p.* in 1743, leaving his estates to the son of his brother Simon; 3 SIMON (of whom we treat); 1 Dorothy, *m.* to John Gisborne, Esq. of Derby, *b.* 1675; and 2 Anne, *m.* to Rev. James Gisborne, rector of Staveley, and prebendary of Durham, who was father of Dr. Thomas Gisborne, physician to King GEORGE III., and sometime president of the College of Physicians; who *d. unm.* in 1806. The 3rd son,

SIMON JACSON, of Chester, *b.* 1691, was, in 1715, one of the representatives of the merchants of the port of Liverpool deputed by them to treat with the corporation of Chester, at the invitation of the latter, for the freedom of the city to a certain number of their body (who should remove to the city of Chester), and for the exemption from all tolls and duties payable to the city, with a view to the extension of the commerce of the River Dee. Simon *m.* in 1721, Mary, sister of Rev. Hugh Poole, rector of Bebington, co. Chester, who at his death, in 1739, devised that rectory and other estates to his sister's son, Simon Jacson, the younger (of whom we treat presently), who with a dau., *m.* to Mr James Perrin, a merchant of Flint, were the issue of the marriage. The son and heir,

THE REV. SIMON JACSON, of Bebington, Somersall, and Shallcross, *b.* 1728; *m.* 1749, Anne, elder dau. of Richard Fitzherbert, Esq. of Somersall, co. Derby, and Margaret his wife, dau. and co-heiress of Col. John Shallcross, of Shallcross Hall. Rev. Simon Jacson *s.* his uncle, Rev. Hugh Poole, in the advowson (1739) and became rector (1753) of

* The ancient family of SHALLCROSS *of Shallcross* is believed to be extinct, the above-named John Shallcross, who was sheriff of the co. in 1686, and *d.* in 1733, having been the last heir male. Six generations of this family are described in the Visitation of 1611 (see *Lysons' Derbyshire*). A MS. pedigree traces the family back to a period antecedent to the 23rd EDWARD I. (A.D. 1294.) The first ancestor therein named is Suanie de Shakelcros. To "Richard de Schalcros, sonne of Suanij," an inheritance in Ferneleigh was conveyed in 1294. Two other deeds in the margin of the pedigree relate to lands in Tacysal or Taxal. These estates appear to have remained in the family to the end of its existence. The MS. records intermarriages with the families of Beresford, of Bentley (thus forming a double connection with the Jacsons), Jodrell, of Cheshire, Bagshawe, of the Ridge, co. Derby, Davenport, Cressy, Brereton, Rowley, of Rowley, co. Salop, Arderne, of Harden, Fitzherbert, of Somersall, and others of distinction. Col. John Shallcross, the last male heir, who *d.* in 1733, left issue three daus., of whom Margaret, was *m.* to Richard Fitzherbert, Esq. of Somersall Herbert, co. Derby; Frances, was *m.* to Roger Jacson, Esq. of Ashborne, who *s.* his father-in-law in the possession of the Shallcross estates; and Anne, who *d. unm.* at Stockport, in 1774.

Bebington. He was devisee of his uncle Roger Jacson's estates in Shallcross, &c. Rev. Simon Jacson had issue three sons and four daus.,

Simon. *d. unm.*
Roger (of whom presently).
Shallcross, vicar of Rostherne, co. Chester, and of Somersall, co. Derby, *b.* 1757; *d. unm.* 1821.
Anne, *m.* in 1774, to John Atherton, Esq. of Walton Hall, co. Lancaster; *d.* 1805, leaving issue.
Frances-Margaretta, authoress of *Rhoda* and other works, *d. unm.* in 1842.
Maria-Elizabetha, authoress of *The Florist's Manual*, and some botanical works, *d. unm.* in 1829.
Letitia, *d. unm.* Isabella, *d. unm.*

Mr. Jacson sold the Shallcross estate in 1794, to Foster Bower, Esq. He *d.* in 1808, and was *s.* in his estates of Bebington by his eldest surviving son,

THE REV. ROGER JACSON, patron and rector of Bebington, chairman of the Court of Quarter Sessions of the co. of Chester for forty years, *b.* 9 July, 1758. He *s.* to Somersall, in 1806, on the death of his aunt, Mrs. Frances Fitzherbert who was devisee of that estate under the will of her brother, Richard Fitzherbert, Esq., the last heir male who d. *unm.* in 1803. This very old branch of the ancient family of Fitzherbert thus became extinct. The family traces its descent from the chamberlain of HENRY I., about 1120, a very early descendant of whom, William, the father of Sir William Fitzherbert, lord of Norbury, "to whom HENRY III. granted free warren in Norbury, A.D. 1252," and who had three sons, viz., Henry, his heir; Thomas, lord of Somersall, ancestor of the FITZHERBERTS *of Tissington*, co. Derby; and Richard, of Twycross, co. Leicester" (see *Baronetage*), was "William Fitzherbert of Summershall Herbert, in the countie of Derbie."—(*MS Pedigree.*) Mr. Jacson *m.* 19 March, 1777, Frances, a descendant of the FULFORDS *of Fulford*, co. *Devon*, dau. of Rev. John Gibson, of Romaldkirk, co. York (N.R.), and of Preston, co. Lancaster; and 2ndly, 27 May, 1801, Mary-Anton Johnson, of Wallasey, co. Chester; by the former of whom he had issue, viz.,

I. { John, twin-brother of Roger, *d. unm.* in 1799.
{ Roger, in holy orders, *m.* Elizabeth, dau. of William Leche, Esq. of Carden Park, co. Chester, *d.* 1819, and had issue, Roger, H.E.I. Co.'s service, who *d. unm.* in 1845; Frances, *m.* to Dominy Rasbotham, Esq.; Anne; Mary.
II. George, *b.* 1783, *d.* 14 March, 1846. He acquired the estate of Barton, co. Lancaster, in 1834, by purchase from the late James Shuttleworth, Esq. He *m.* in 1813, his cousin, Charlotte, eldest dau. of Charles Gibson, Esq. of Quernmore Park, in the same county, by Charlotte his wife, dau. of Edward Wilson, Esq. of Dalham Tower, co. Westmorland, and had issue eight sons and four daus., viz.,
1 George, *d. unm.* in 1831.
2 CHARLES-ROGER, present representative and proprietor of the Barton estate.
3 Simon-Fitzherbert, *m.* Georgina, dau. of Charles Winchester, Esq. of Aberdeen.
4 John, *m.* Mary-Jane, dau. of Henry Newbery, Esq. of Manchester, sprung from a Devonshire family.
5 Roger, *d. unm.* in 1853. 6 Henry, *d. unm.* in 1839.
7 Edward, in holy orders, *m.* Marianne-Eliza-Frances, dau. of Thomas-Bulkeley Owen, Esq. of Tedsmore Hall, co. Salop.
8 William-Shallcross, in holy orders.
1 Charlotte-Anne, *d. unm.* in 1889.
2 Frances, *m.* to John Richardson, Esq. of Poplar Vale, co. Monaghan, and *d.* in 1851, leaving issue.
3 Mary Isabella, *d. unm.* 1841.
4 Maria-Margaretta.
III. Shallcross, of Newton Bank, co. Chester, late captain in the 3rd light-dragoons; *m.* Frances, dau. of the Rev. Joseph Cook, of Newton Hall, co. Northumberland, and had issue, viz.,
1 Shallcross-Fitzherbert, *d.* in 1824, *unm.*
2 Widdrington, *d. unm.* in 1845.
3 Shallcross-Fitzherbert, who inherited the estates of his maternal uncle, Samuel-Edward Widdrington, Esq. of Newton and Hauley (see *Widdrington*), and, in compliance with his will, took the name and arms of WIDDRINGTON in 1856.
1 Eliza, *m.* in 1841, to James-Hugh-Smith Barry, Esq. of Marbury, co. Chester, and Foaty, co. Cork.
2 Frances-Isabel, *m.* 7 July, 1853, to Charles-William Orde, Esq. of Nunnykirk, co. Northumberland.
I. Frances, *d. unm.* in 1837.

Arms—Gu., a fesse, between three sheldrakes, arg.
Crest—A sheldrake, rising, ppr.
Seat—Barton Hall, Preston, co. Lancaster.

GREVIS-JAMES OF IGHTHAM COURT.

GREVIS-JAMES, DEMETRIUS, Esq. of Ightham Court, co. Kent, J.P. and D.L., high-sheriff, co. Kent 1833, *b.* 21 May, 1776; *m.* 21 March, 1812, Mary, dau. of the late James Shutt, Esq. of Humbleton, in Holderness, and has surviving issue,

I. DEMETRIUS-WYNDHAM, major 2nd regt. Queen's Royals *b.* 3 June, 1819.
II. Arthur, *b.* 28 Feb. 1833.
I. Frances-Maria, *m.* to T. Charlton, Esq.
II. Emily. III. Mary, *m.* to Capt. H. B. Wilson.
IV. Caroline.
V. Rosa, *m.* to the Rev. B. P. Thompson.
VI. Lavinia.
VII. Isabella, *m.* to F. W. Springett, Esq.
VII. Adelaide-Margaret.

This gentleman whose patronymic is GREVIS, assumed, by sign manual, in 1817, the additional surname and arms of JAMES.

Lineage.—The manor of Ightham was possessed, *temp.* King JOHN, by Hamon de Crevequier, from whom it passed. through the families of De Criol, De Inge, Zouch of Harringworth, Read, and Willoughby, to the house of JAMES, by which it is now enjoyed.

The JAMESES were originally, says Philpot called Hæstrecht,* from a lordship of that name which they possessed near Utrecht.

ROGER, son of JACOB VAN HÆSTRECHT, emigrated into England in the reign of King HENRY VIII.; and being known, after the Dutch manner, by the name of Roger Jacobs, the English at length called him Roger James. He *m.* Sarah, only dau. and heir of Henry Morskin, Esq of London, and had issue,

I. ROGER, of Upminster, in Essex, who *m.* Sarah, dau. of John Smith, Esq. of London, and was *s.* by his son,
SIR ROGER JAMES, of Reigate, in Surrey, who *m.* Elizabeth, dau. of Anthony Aucher, and had a dau., ELIZABETH.
II. Arnold, of London, who *m.* Mary, dau. of John Van hulst, of that city.
III. WILLIAM.
IV. Thomas, who *m.* the dau. of Fulke.
V. Richard, who *m.* Gertrude, dau. of John Smyth, and had, with other issue, a son, Sir John, of Cresshill, in Essex, and a dau., Emlin, who *m.* Mr. James Cane; and their son inheriting the estates of his uncle, Sir John was advanced to the dignity of a Baronet, 34 CHARLES II. This branch of the family is now EXTINCT.
VI. John, of Grove Manor, who *m.* Susanna, dau. and co-heir of Peter Vandewall, of Antwerp, and had issue.
VII. George, of Malendine, near Rochester, who *m.* Audrey, dau. of John Smyth, and had issue.
I. Sarah, *m.* 1st, to Thomas Draper, Esq. of Islington; and 2ndly, to Sir Nicholas Kempe, Knt.

The 3rd son,

WILLIAM JAMES, Esq., acquired, *temp.* Queen ELIZABETH, by purchase, the manor of Ightham Court, co. Kent. He *m.* Jane, dau. and heir of Henry Kule, and had issue,

WILLIAM, his heir. Thomas.
Jane, *m.* to Henry Dixon, Esq. of Hilden; and *d.* in 1602,

The elder son,

WILLIAM JAMES, Esq. of Ightham Court, *b.* in 1601, was a person of great influence during the Protectorate, and enjoyed the confidence of CROMWELL. He was a member of the committee appointed for the sequestration of delinquent estates, and was, in five years, thrice chosen knight of the shire for Kent. He *m.* Jane, dau. of Nicholas Miller, Esq. of Crouch, and was *s.* by his only son,

SIR DEMETRIUS JAMES, of Ightham Court, who received the honour of knighthood from King CHARLES II. He *m.* Anne, only dau. of the famous physician, Dr. George Bate and had (with other issue, who *d. unm.*),

WILLIAM, his successor.
Jane, *m.* to Sir John Rainey, Bart.
Anne, *m.* to Thomas Puckle, Esq. of the Middle Temple.

Sir Demetrius was *s.* by his eldest son,

WILLIAM JAMES, Esq. of Ightham Court, living in 171 This gentleman *m.* Anne, only dau. and heir of Sir Thomas Wyndham,† Bart. of Trent, in Somersetshire (son of th

* The family of Hæstrecht was allied by marriage to the ancient and eminent houses of Wassanaer and Waermont.

† Sir Thomas Wyndham, Bart., was sixth in descent from the marriage of Sir John Wyndham, Knt., with Margaret, dau. of John, Duke of Norfolk, and thus derived, in direct line from MARGARET PLANTAGENET, Duchess of Norfolk, dau. and heir of Thomas Plantagenet (5th son of King EDWARD I.), by his 2nd consort, Margaret, dau. of PHILIP III. of France.

Sir Francis Wyndham who, with his family, was so signally instrumental in the preservation of King CHARLES II. after the battle of Worcester). By this lady he had, with two daus., three sons,

I. WILLIAM, his heir.
II. Richard, of the Middle Temple, d. unm.
III. Demetrius, a colonel in the army, whose dau., Elizabeth, m. Charles Grevis, Esq. (of the ancient family of the Greves, or Grevis, of Moseley Hall, co. Worcester, whose ancestor came into England with the Conqueror), and by him (who d. in 1835) left issue,
  1 DEMETRIUS GREVIS, who eventually inherited the estates; and assuming the surname and arms of JAMES, is the present DEMETRIUS GREVIS-JAMES, Esq. of Ightham Court Lodge.
  1 Elizabeth. 2 Caroline. 3 Eleanor.

The eldest son,

WILLIAM JAMES, Esq. of Ightham Court, was high-sherif for Kent in 1732. He m. Elizabeth, dau. of Demetrius James, of Reigate, and had (with a dau., Sarah-Bella-Elizabeth, who m. Josiah-Wood Hindman, Esq. of Greenwich, and of Upton, Essex, and by him (who d. in 1784) had two daus. and co-heirs, Sophia, m. to William Turner, Esq.; and Frances-Maria, m. to Joseph Newell) two sons, viz.,

RICHARD, his heir.
Demetrius, in holy orders, rector of Ightham, d. in 1781, s. p.

Mr. James who was Usher of the Black Rod in Ireland, was s. at his decease by his elder son,

RICHARD JAMES, Esq. of Ightham Court, who d. without issue in Nov. 1817, when the family estates devolved upon his first-cousin, the present DEMETRIUS GREVIS-JAMES, Esq. of Ightham Court.

Arms—Quarterly: 1st and 4th, arg., two bars, embattled, gu., for JAMES; 2nd and 3rd, arg., on a fesse, az., between three pellets, each charged with a lion's head, erased, of the first, a griffin, passant, between two escallop-shells, or, for GREVIS.
Crest—1st, for JAMES, out of a ducal coronet, or, a demi-swan, wings expanded, arg., beak, gu.; 2nd, for GREVIS, a squirrel, holding between its paws an escallop-shell, or.
Motto—Fide et constantiâ.
Seat—Ightham Court Lodge, co. Kent.

JAMES OF BARROCK AND WEST AUCKLAND.

JAMES, WILLIAM, Esq., of Barrock, co. Cumberland, J.P. and D.L., high-sheriff in 1827, M.P. for Carlisle and East Cumberland successively from 1820 to 1847, m. Feb. 1816, Fanny, dau. of Wm.-Calton Rutson, of Allerton, co. Lancaster, Esq., and sister of Wm. Rutson, Esq. of Newby Wiske, and Nunnington Hall, high-sheriff of Yorkshire in 1851, and has issue,

I. WILLIAM-EDWARD, b. 7 Dec. 1816; late capt. in the 84th regiment; m. Sept. 1841, Elizabeth, dau. of William Hill, Esq. of Ryhope, co. Durham, and has issue,
  1 William-Edward-Ashton, b. 1842.
  2 Arthur-Cecil-Rutson.
  3 Evans-Henry-Murchison. 4 Philip-Herbert.
  1 Lucy-Caroline.
  2 Frances-Alethea. 3 Edith-Priscilla.
II. Francis-Herbert, b. April, 1822; living in Jamaica.
III. John-Henry, b. 18 Sept. 1826; fellow of Brazennose College, Oxford; m. July, 1853, Jane Ramsden, dau. of the Rev. Thomas-Ramsden Ashworth, of the family of ASHWORTH *of Ashworth*, co. Lancashire, and has issue, Janet-Marion, b. July, 1854.
IV. Alfred, b. 20 Aug. 1832.
I. Caroline. II. Frances-Adela.

Lineage.—JOHN JAMES, of West Auckland, b. 1664, d. aged 83, 1747, leaving (by Jane his wife) three daus., Anne, wife of Joseph Appleby; Jane, wife of William Wilson; and Margaret, who d. unm.; and two sons, William-James, who m. and had issue, and

JOHN JAMES, of West Auckland and Killerly, who, by his wife, Jane, dau. of Thomas Todd, of Whoriton, co. York, Esq., by Jane Hunter his wife, had issue,

I. JOHN, of West Auckland and Killerly, b. 1730; m. Sarah, dau. of Thomas Ward, Esq., and had issue.
II. William, of Finch House, near Liverpool, an eminent West India merchant, b. 1734; m. Elizabeth, dau. and heir of the Rev. Mr. Evans, who d. 1789, and had issue,
  1 WILLIAM EVANS, of whom presently, ob. v. p.
  2 John-James, of Houghton Lodge, co. Hants, m. Margaret, dau. of William Wilson, of Liverpool, Esq., and had issue,
  Elizabeth-Alethea, m. to Rev. John Penleaze, rector of Black Torrington, co. Devon.
  Mary-Frances, m. to Hon. G.-Rolle-Walpole Trefusis, capt. R.N., son of George, 15th Baron Clinton.
  3 Alethea, m. to Richard Walker, of Liverpool, Esq.
I Jane, m. James Allen, Esq., and had issue.

WILLIAM-EVANS JAMES, b. 1763 (son of William James, of Finch House aforesaid); d. 1795, in his father's lifetime. He m. Elizabeth, dau. of Nicholas Ashton, of Woolton Hall, Lancashire, Esq., by Mary his wife, dau. and heiress of John Philpot, of Chester, Esq., grandson and heir of Rev. Matthew Henry, author of a *Commentary on the Bible*, and Mary Warburton his wife, sole heiress of the WARBURTONS *of Hefferston Grange*, a younger branch of the great Cheshire house of WARBURTON *of Warburton and Arley*. This lady remarried Lieut.-Col. George-M. Williams. By her 1st husband she had issue,

WILLIAM, now of Barrock.
John, of Burnville, co. Devon, J.P. and D.L., b. 1794; d. 1854; m. 1st, Anne, dau. of Thomas Herring, Esq.; and 2ndly, Patience, dau. of G. Luxmore, Esq., and niece of the Bishop of St. Asaph, and had issue, Evans-Luxmore-James, b. 1836.
Alethea, m. Fergus, eldest son of the Rev. Fergus Graham, rector of Arthuret, co. Cumberland, brother of the first Sir James Graham, of Netherby, Bart.

Arms—Quarterly: 1st and 4th, az., a dolphin, embowed, ppr., for JAMES; 2nd and 3rd, arg., three boars' heads, couped, sa., langued and armed, gu., for EVANS.
Crest—A bull, passant, ppr.
Motto—Vincit amor patriæ.
Seat—Barrock, Cumberland.

JAMES OF OTTERBURN.

JAMES, THOMAS, Esq. of Otterburn Tower, co. Northumberland, J.P. and D.L., b. 12 May, 1807; m. 25 June, 1833, Margaret-Bernard, 3rd dau. of the Rev. John Collinson, of Boldon, co. Durham, and has issue,

I. WILLIAM, b. 28 Feb 1838.
II. Thomas, b. 6 May, 1844.
III. Harry-Redesdale, b 23 Sept. 1845.
IV. John-Collinson, b 22 Dec. 1846.
V. Richard, b. 9 April, 1848.
VI. Charles-Woodhouse, b. 13 Sept. 1851.
VII. Christian-Hugh-Septimus, b. 25 Dec. 1852.
VIII. Octavius, b. 9 April, 1855.
I. Emily. II. Margaret Sybel.

Lineage.—JOHN JAMES, Esq. of Newcastle, co. Northumberland, son of THOMAS JAMES, Esq. of Cargo and Stenton, co. Cumberland, m. twice, and had, with a dau., Elizabeth, and a son, Thomas, another son,

WILLIAM JAMES, Esq., who m. in 1803, Elizabeth, eldest dau. of Joseph Woodhouse, Esq. of Scotswood, co. Northumberland, and by her, who m. 2ndly, in 1822, Charles Bulmer, Esq., and d. 19 July, 1852, had issue,

THOMAS, of Otterburn.
William, capt. in the army, m. Susanna Knight, and has issue, Frederick; Gerald; and Susan.
Edward, m. and has issue, Walter; Theodosia; Elizabeth; Susan; and Herbert.
John, m. Eleanor, only child of — Tharpe, Esq.
Hugh-Septimus, m. Alexandrina, 2nd dau. of Dr. Hamilton.
Octavius, in holy orders, m. Helen Bowlby, and has issue, Lewis; Martha; Mabel; and Elizabeth.
James, M.D., m. Georgina Brodhurst.
Elizabeth, m. 1st, to the Rev. John Fox; and 2ndly, to Henry Hewetson, Esq.
Susan, m. to Major Brooksbank. Emma.

Arms—Sa., on a chevron, arg., between three dolphins, embowed, erminois, as many cross-crosslets, gu.
Crest—A buffalo, passant, gu., armed, ppr., the dexter forefoot resting on an escocheon, arg., charged with a pheon, sa.
Motto—Deo semper confido.
Seat—Otterburn Tower, co. Northumberland.

JAMES OF PANTSAISON.

JAMES, JOHN-TAUBMAN-WILLIAM, Esq. of Pantsaison, co. Pembroke, J.P. and D.L., b. 31 Oct. 1812; m. 28 Dec. 1836, Margaret-Elizabeth, eldest dau. of the late Captain Jones-Parry, R.N. of Llwyn Onn, co. Denbigh, and niece of the late General Sir Love Parry, of Madryn, co. Caernarvon, and has issue,

I. WILLIAM-PARRY, b. 6 Aug. 1839.
II. John-Alexander, b. 3 April, 1841.
III. Robert-Lloyd, b. 9 Nov. 1844.
I. Dora-Emily. II. Margaret-Ellen.

Lineage.—The Jameses have been seated for some centuries at Pantsaison, and a tradition in the family states that there were thirteen William Jameses, of Pantsaison, in succession.

William James, Esq. of Pantsaison, who *m.* Margaret, dau. and heiress of Vaughan Thomas, Esq. of Poste, co. Pembroke, had three sons, the eldest of whom,

William James, Esq. of Pantsaison, *m.* Rebecca Bateman, only surviving sister and heir of John Bateman, Esq. of Robeston Wathen, co. Pembroke, and had, with four daus., eight sons. Of the latter,

Col. John James, *m.* 1811, Margaret-Christian, dau. of the late Major Taubman, of The Nunnery, Isle of Man, by Dorothy his wife (*m.* in 1774), dau. of John Christian, Esq. of Ewanrigg Hall, co. Cumberland, and Miltown, Isle of Man, and by her (who *d.* 1837) two sons, John-Taubman-William, now of Pantsaison; and Mark-Wilks-William, in holy orders, *b.* 27 Oct. 1818, *m.* 1846, Charlotte Ellen, 3rd dau. of the late Capt. Jones-Parry, R.N., of Llwyn Onn, and has issue, John-Taubman, Dora-Margaret, Mary-Christian, and Emily-Georgina.

Arms—Sa., a dolphin, naiant, embowed, between three crosses-crosslet, or, quartering Taubman, Bateman, and Vaughan.
Crest—A demi-bull, rampant, sa., horned and hoofed, or, langued, gu.
Motto—Fyddylon at y gorfin. In English—Faithful to the end.
Seat—Pantsaison, co. Pembroke.

JAMESON OF WINDFIELD.

Jameson, Rev. John, of Windfield, co. Galway, M.A. of Queen's College, Oxford, *b.* 17 July, 1816; *m.* Jan. 1846, Isabella-Anne, eldest dau. of Major-General Sir Harry-David Jones, royal engineers, K.C.B., commander of the legion of honour of France, and has issue,

I. James-Francis, *b.* 5 June, 1848.
II. Harry-William, *b.* 5 Sept. 1851.
I. Charlotte-Elizabeth.
II. Edith-Sophia-Inkerman.

Lineage.—William Jameson, of Alloa, Clackmannanshire, *m.* 25 Nov. 1737, Helen Horne, of Thomanean, Kinross-shire, and had, with other issue, a son,

John Jameson, Esq., sheriff-clerk of Clackmannanshire, *b.* 1740, who *m.* 1768, Margaret, eldest sister of James Haig, Esq. of Blairhill, Perthshire, and Lochrin, Midlothian, and had issue,

I. Robert, *b.* 17 June, 1771, sheriff-clerk of Clackmannanshire, *d. unm.* 1847.
II. John, of Prussia Street, Dublin, *b.* Aug. 1773, *m.* Isabella, dau. of John Stein, Esq., and had issue,
 1 John, of Prussia Street, director of the Bank of Ireland; *m.* Anne, dau. of Wm. Haig, Esq., and has issue.
 2 James, of Delvin Lodge, *m.* Lucy, dau. of William Cairnes, Esq. of Stameen, co. Meath, and has issue.
 3 William, in holy orders, of Hollybank Bank, *m.* 1849, Elizabeth, dau. of the late Arthur Guinness, Esq. of Beaumont, co. Dublin, and has issue.
 4 Andrew, sheriff-clerk of Clackmannanshire, *m.* Miss Cochrane, and has issue.
 5 Henry, *m.* Margaret, dau. of Andrew Phelp, Esq., and has issue.
 1 Isabella.
III. William, of Merrion Square, Dublin, *b.* 29 July, 1777, *d. s. p.* Dec. 1822.
IV. James, of whom presently.
V. Andrew, *b.* 18 Aug. 1783, *m.* and has issue.
I. Margaret, *m.* 1801, William-Robert Robertson, Esq. (*see family of* Robertson *of Prendergues*t.)
II. Helen, *d. unm.*
III. Anne, *m.* Major Francis Stupart, of the 2nd North British dragoons (Scots Greys).
IV. Janet, *m.* John Woolsey, Esq. of Milestown, co. Louth.

Mr. Jameson *d.* 1824. His 4th son,

James Jameson, Esq., *s.* to the fortune of his immediate elder brother, William, of Merrion Square, and purchased the estate of Winfield, co. Galway, and the demesne of Mont Rose, co. Dublin. He *m.* 17th July, 1816, Elizabeth-Sophia, youngest dau. of the Rev. William Woolsey, of Priorland, co. Louth, by his wife, Mary-Anne, youngest sister of Sir William Bellingham, of Castle Bellingham, in the county of Louth, Bart., in lineal descent from the Plantagenet kings, and had issue,

I. John, now of Windfield.
II. William, of Mont Rose, co. Dublin, *b.* 19 Dec. 1818, *m.* March, 1855, Emily St. Leger, 2nd dau. of Colonel Arthur-Henry O'Niell, of St. Anne's, co. Dublin, and has issue, a son,
 James-Arthur-Henry, *b.* 24 Dec. 1855.
III. James, of Airfield, co. Dublin, *b.* 4 Aug. 1821, *m.* 10 Jan. 1849, Alicia Trimleston, dau. of Robert Robertson, Esq., advocate and sheriff-substitute of Stirlingshire, by Alicia-Catherine, his wife, eldest dau. of the Rev. Charles Eustace (*see* p. 351) and has issue,
 1 James-Robert, *b.* 4 Dec. 1849.
 2 William-Frederick, *b.* 27 Jan. 1851.
 3 John-Eustace, *b.* 22 March, 1852.
 1 Helen-Lucy.
IV. Robert O'Brien, lieut. 2nd life guards, now of the 11th hussars, *b.* 17 June, 1828.
I. Mary-Anne. II. Elizabeth-Sophia.

Mr. Jameson, who was a director of the Bank of Ireland, *d.* deputy-governor 24 Aug. 1847, and was *s.* in his estate of Windfield, by his eldest son, the present Rev. John Jameson.

Arms—Azure, a saltier or, cantoned with three Roman galleys, ppr. and a bugle in base or.
Crest—A Roman galley ppr. the sail gu. charged with a lion passant guardant or.
Motto—Sine metu.

JARRETT OF CAMERTON COURT.

Jarrett, John, Esq. of Camerton Court, co. Somerset, J.P. and D.L. high-sheriff 1840-1, *b.* 4 July, 1802; *m.* 15 July, 1823, Anna-Eliza, younger dau. of Sir Jonathan Waller, Bart., G.C.H., of Pope's Villa, Twickenham, and has issue,

I. Anna-Mary. [illegible] [illegible]-beth.

Lineage.—[illegible] retts derive their [illegible] the massacre of [illegible] whence they mig[illegible]

Herbert-New[illegible] island of Jamaica, [illegible]

John Jarrett, [illegible] Reid, of Jamaica, [illegible]

Herbert-Newton Jarrett, Esq., who *m.* Anne, dau. of James Stephens, Esq. of Hinton-on-the-Green, co. Gloucester, and of Camerton Court, co. Somerset, by his wife, Elizabeth-Paterson Wallen, of Jamaica, and granddau. of Philip Stephens, Esq. of Hinton and Camerton Court, son of the Rev. George Stephens, prebendary of Highworth, co. Wilts. By this lady Mr. Jarrett had issue,

John, of Camerton Court. Stephen, *d. unm.* Oct. 1855.
Anne, *m.* 9 July, 1822, to the Rev. William Gooch, son of Col. William Gooch, and grandson of Sir Thomas Gooch, Bart.
Mary, *d.* young.

Arms—Az., a lion, rampant, erm., ducally crowned, or, quartering Stephens and Ridley.
Crest—A lion's head, erased, or, ducally crowned and collared, gu.
Motto—Consilio et armis.
Seat—Camerton Court, near Bath.

JARVIS OF DODDINGTON HALL.

Jarvis, George-Knollis, Esq. of Doddington Hall, co. Lincoln, *s.* his father, 14 June, 1851; *m.* Emily, eldest dau. of the Rev. George-Thomas Pretyman, Chancellor of Lincoln, by Emily his wife, dau. of Christopher Tower, Esq. of Weald Hall, Essex.

Lineage.—George Ralph Payne Jarvis, Esq. of Doddington Hall, co. Lincoln, J.P. and D.L., lieut.-col. in the army, *b.* 18 May, 1774, *m.* 1st, 2 Dec. 1802, Philadelphia, 3rd dau. of Ebenezer Blackwell, by Mary, his wife, dau. of the Rev. Robert Eden, prebendary of Winchester; and 2ndly, 24 June, 1830, Frances dau. of the Rev. John Sturges, LL.D., chancellor of Winchester, by Judith, his wife, dau. of Richard Bourne, Esq. of Acton Hall, co. Worcester; and by the former had issue,

George-Knollis, now of Doddington Hall.
Charles-Macquarie-George, in holy orders, *m.* Augusta, second dau. of Robert Cracroft, Esq. of Hackthorn, co. Lincoln, by Augusta, his wife, dau. of Sir John Ingilby, Bart.
Henry-George, captain in the army, *d.* in the West Indies.
John-George, captain in the 52nd light infantry.
Edwin-George, *m.* Frances, eldest dau. of Robert Cracroft Esq. of Hackthorn, co. Lincoln.
Mary-Eden, *m.* to Robert Cole, Esq., major in the army.
Anne-Fector, *m.* to John Bromhead, Esq. of Lincoln.

Col. Jarvis *d.* 14 June, 1851.

Arms—Sa., on a chev., engr., between three martlets, arg., as many cinquefoils, pierced, of the first, on a chief, of the second, a fleur-de-lis, between two escallops, of the field.

Crest—An unicorn's head, arg., gorged with a collar, charged with three cinquefoils.

Seat—Doddington Hall, co. Lincoln.

JEAFFRESON OF DULLINGHAM HOUSE.

JEAFFRESON, CHRISTOPHER-WILLIAM, Esq. of Dullingham House, co. Cambridge, *b.* 23 Jan. 1836; *s.* to the estates upon the death of his mother, in 1838, and has assumed the surname and arms of JEAFFRESON.

Lineage.—CHRISTOPHER JEAFFRESON, Esq. of Dullingham *b* 12 July, 1699 J.P., M.P. for the town of Cambridge, *m.* Elizabeth 3rd dau. of Sir John Shuckburgh, Bart. of Shuckburgh, and *d.* 18 Jan. 1748, leaving a son and heir,

CHRISTOPHER JEAFFRESON, Esq. of Dullingham, who *m.* Sarah, dau. of Francis Dayrell, Esq. of Shudy Campè, co. Cambridge and by her, who *d.* in June, 1792, he left at his decease, 26 Sept. 1789, (with a dau., Sarah-Elizabeth, who *d. unm.* 11 May, 1804,) a son and heir,

CHRISTOPHER JEAFFRESON, Esq. of Dullingham, a lieut.-gen. in the army, and col. of the Cambridgeshire local militia, who *m.* in 1794, Harriet, Viscountess Gormanstown, relict of Anthony, 11th viscount, and dau. of John Robinson Esq. of Denston Hall, co. Suffolk and by her, who *d.* in 1826, had an only dau. and heiress, HARRIET. Lieut.-gen. Jeaffreson, J.P. and D.L., *d.* 22 Oct. 1824, and was *s.* by his dau.,

HARRIET JEAFFRESON, also eventual heiress to her maternal grandfather, John Robinson, Esq. of Denston Hall. She *m.* 23 June, 1827, William Pigott, Esq., J.P. and D.L., 3rd son of Sir George Pigott, Bart. of Knapton, and *d.* 12 March. 1838, leaving by him (who *m.* 2ndly, 18 Oct. 1847, Charlotte-Maria, widow of the late Gen. Lord Keane, G.C.B.) a son and two daus., viz.,

- CHRISTOPHER-WILLIAM, who has assumed the surname and arms of Jeaffreson, and is the present representative.
- Ada, *m.* 15 March, 18[illegible]3, to John Dunn Gardner, Esq. of Chatteris, co. Cambridge.
- Harriet.

Arms—Az., a fret, arg., on a chief, of the last, three leopards' heads, gu.

Crest—A talbot's head, erased, arg., eared, gu.

Seat—Dullingham House, co. Cambridge.

JEFFREYS OF WEM.

JEFFREYS, WILLIAM-EGERTON, Esq. of Wem, co. Salop, residing at Coton Hill, near Shrewsbury, *b.* 22 Dec. 1806.

Lineage.—This family claims descent from the Jeffreys of Acton, co. Denbigh.

WILLIAM JEFFREYS, of Wem, co. Salop, a member of the Society of Friends, resided in the present house at Wem, which was built in 1656. He was father of WILLIAM JEFFREYS, of Wem, whose son, WILLIAM JEFFREYS. of Wem, *m.* Margaret Allen, and left at his decease in 1774, a son, WILLIAM JEFFREYS, of Wem, *b.* in 1716, who *m.* Ann, dau. of Hugh Egerton, Esq., and by her, who was *b.* in 1718, and *d.* 6 May, 1790, had issue. Mr. Jeffreys *d.* 6 May, 1761, and was *s.* by his 3rd son and eventual heir,

WILLIAM JEFFREYS, Esq. of Wem, *b.* 23 March, 1741, *d. unm.* 20 Jan. 1822. and was *s.* by his brother and heir,

THOMAS JEFFREYS, Esq. of Wem, *b.* 2 May, 1743, *m.* 30 Sept. 1771, Mary, dau. of William Bayley, Esq., and by her, who was *b.* 5 June, 1748, and *d.* 19 Dec. 1802, had issue,

- I. WILLIAM-EGERTON.
- II. Thomas, M.D., *b.* 28 Dec. 1774, *m.* 25 May, 1815, Elizabeth Percival, of Lancashire.
- I. Anne, *b.* 2 Sept. 1772, and *d.* the same year.
- II. Mary, *b.* 6 Oct. 1776, *m.* 24 Dec. 1797, Overbury-Whitley Badger, Esq., and by this gentleman, who was *b.* 5 Oct. 1773, and *d.* 14 Aug. 1815, has issue,
  - 1 Thomas-Jeffreys, *b.* 6 Jan. 1802.
  - 2 Susannah Margaret, *m.* 30 March, 1824, to John Beck, Esq., and has had issue.
- III. Susannah, *b.* 1 April, 1778, *d.* 8 Nov. 1802, *unm.*

Mr. Jeffreys *d.* 22 Aug. 1818, and was *s.* by his son,

WILLIAM-EGERTON JEFFREYS, Esq. of Wem, J.P. and D.L., *b.* 11 Sept. 1773, *m.* 4 Sept. 1799, Sarah, dau. and co-heir of William Corfield, Esq. of Shrewsbury, and has issue,

- WILLIAM-EGERTON, of Wem.
- Harriet.
- Marianne, who *m.* 4 Sept. 1824 Richard-Bryan Smith, Esq., F.S.A., of Lydiate.
- Susanna-Emma, *m.* to Charles Whitmore, Esq.
- Sarah-Ellen.

Arms—Quarterly: 1st and 4th, erm., a lion, rampant, sa., a canton, of the last, for JEFFREYS; 2nd and 3rd, gu., a fesse, erm., between three pheons, arg., for EGERTON.

Crest—A lion's head, erased, sa., gorged with a wreath.

Motto—Supra spem spero.

Residence—Coton Hill, near Shrewsbury.

JENKINS OF BICTON HALL.

JENKINS, RICHARD, Esq. of Bicton Hall and Abbey House, both in the co. of Salop, *b.* 8 Sept. 1828, in the Bengal Civil Service, *m.* Mrs. Sophia Mayne, widow, 2nd dau. of Horace Aylward. Esq.

Lineage.—RICHARD JENKINS, *b.* in 1621, of Blandford, co. Dorset sprung from a family anciently located in Yorkshire, attaching himself to the celebrated Royalist, Lord Colepeper. was with that nobleman at St. Germains in 1649, and subsequently accompanied him when amb assador extraordinary to the Emperor of Russia and the United Provinces. In 1651 he returned to England, and settled at Charlton Hill, near Wroxeter holding several employments under Lord Newport, lord-lieutenant of the county. He *m.* in 1668, Mary. dau. and co-heir of Richard Bagot, Esq. of Hargrave, in Shropshire and with her acquired that and other estates in the parish of Alberbury. He *d.* in 1697, and was *s.* by his son,

THOMAS JENKINS. Esq. of the Abbey Foregate, Shrewsbury. who *m.* 7 Feb. 1708, Gertrude. dau. of Capt. Richard Wingfield, 2nd son of William Wingfield, Esq. of Preston Brockhurst, Salop, and had issue,

- I. RICHARD, his heir.
- II. Thomas, *m.* Rachael, dau. of Sir Edward Leighton, Bart., and had, with other issue,
  - Edward, of Charlton Hill.
- III. Robert.
- I. Emma. to John Jenkins, Esq. of Bicton.

Mr. Jenkins, who was high-sheriff for Salop in 1720, *d.* 29 Dec. 1730, and was *s.* by his son,

RICHARD JENKINS, Esq.. *b.* 28 Aug. 1709, who *m.* 1st, Letitia, dau. and heiress of John Muckleston, Esq. of Bicton, and by her, who *d.* 16 July, 1740 had two sons, Richard, who *d. unm.*; and JOHN, his heir. He *m.* 2ndly, Emma, dau. of Sir Francis Charlton, of Ludford, and relict of John Lloyd. Esq. of Aston Hall Salop, and had a dau., Mary-Gertrude, *m.* to the Venerable Edward Browne archdeacon of Ross, son of the archbishop of Tuam. Mr. Jenkins was *s.* at his decease by his son,

JOHN JENKINS Esq. of Bicton *b.* 16 July, 1740, who *m.* 16 April 1759, Emma, dau. of Thomas Jenkins. Esq. of Shrewsbury, by Rachel his wife, dau. of Sir Edward Leighton, Bart. of Loton Park, and had by her, who *d.* in 1764, four sons, viz.,

- RICHARD, his heir.
- William, *d. unm.*
- Edward, who *m.* Elizabeth, eldest dau. of George Ravenscroft, Esq. of Wrexham, and had issue. The eldest son, Col. Richard Boycott Jenkins, *m.* Miss Ord, and left two sons and two daus.
- Thomas, who *m.* Mary Hale, of Macclesfield, and left no issue.

Mr. Jenkins *d.* 28 June. 1771, and was *s.* by his son:

RICHARD JENKINS, Esq. of Bicton, *b.* there 6 March, 1760, who *m.* in Oct. 1781, Harriet-Constantia, dau. of George Ravenscroft, Esq. of Wrexham. in Denbighshire, and by her. who *d.* at Bicton. 19 April, 1822, had issue,

- RICHARD, (Sir), his heir, G.C.B , of Bicton.
- Charles-Edward-Orlando, *b.* 19 Jan. 1789. who *d. unm.*, 16 July, 1823, in India, a captain of artillery in the Company's service.
- Harriett-Constantia, *m.* to Edward Gatacre, Esq. of Gatacre Hall.
- Elizabeth, *m.* to Robert Jenkins, Esq. of Charlton Hill, Salop.
- Frances-Mary-Gertrude.
- Letitia-Emma-Sally, *m.* to the Rev. Charles Wingfield, of The Gro, co. Montgomery.

Mr. Jenkins *d.* at Bicton, 8 Nov. 1797, and was *s.* by his son.

SIR RICHARD JENKINS, G.C.B , D.C.L., J.P., and D.L., a director E.I.C., *b.* 18 Feb. 1785; *m.* 31 March, 1824 Elizabeth-Helen dau. of Hugh Spottiswoode Esq., of the Hon. E.I.Co's Civil Service, and had issue,

- RICHARD, present representative.
- Charles, *b.* 20 May, 1831.
- Arthur, *b.* 20 Jan. 1833.
- Edward-Gordon, *b.* 11 March, 1838.
- Emily, *m.* to Frederick Baring, Esq.
- Cecilia-Harriet-Theophila, *m.* to John-Archibald Pym, Esq.
- Helen. Melanie.

Arms—Or, a lion, rampant, regardant, sa. Quartering BAGOT and MUCKLESTON.
Crest—On a mural crown, sa., a lion, passant, regardant, or.
Motto—Perge sed caute.
Seats—Bicton Hall, and Abbey House, both near Shrewsbury.

Arms (granted to Sir Richard Jenkins, G.C.B.)—"Or," a lion rampant, regardant, sable, a chief, embattled, az., thereon a representation of two hills flanking a valley—that on the sinister side surmounted by a building called an "end Gah," or place of festival, proper, the whole surmounted with the word "Seetabuldee," in letters of gold.
Crest—On a mural crown, sable, a lion, passant, regardant, crowned with an eastern crown, or, the dexter paw supporting a flag, swallow-tailed, gu., inscribed with the word "Nagpore," in letters of gold.
Supporters—A soldier of the Bengal and Madras native service, whose regiments distinguished themselves in the battle of Seetabuldee.
The said chief in the arms and eastern crown and flag on the crest being intended to bear allusion to the distinguished ability manifested by the said Sir Richard Jenkins in discharge of the important functions of president at the Court of Nagpore, and especially to the memorable defence of the British presidency at Seetabuldee, near the capital of Nagpore, against a formidable attack by the forces of the Rajah Appah Sahib, in the month of November, 1817, and to his subsequent administration, during a series of years, of the Government of that state.

JENKINS OF CHARLTON HILL.

JENKINS, EDWARD-LEIGHTON, Esq. of Charlton Hill, co. Salop, *b.* 20 Jan. 1816; *s.* his father, 2 May, 1836. Mr. Jenkins is in the Bombay civil service.

Lineage.—EDWARD JENKINS, Esq. of Charlton Hill, (only surviving son of Thomas Jenkins, Esq., by Rachel his wife dau. of Sir Edward Leighton, Bart., and grandson of Thomas Jenkins, Esq. of the Abbey Foregate, Shrewsbury) *m.* Sarah, dau. of the Rev. Richard Boycott; and *d.* 20 May, 1820, having had issue,

Robert-Charlton, *b.* in 1772, deceased.
ROBERT-BOYCOTT-CRESSETT, heir.
Emma-Gertrude, *m.* to Francis-Blithe Harries, Esq. of Benthall Hall.
Louisa-Elizabeth-Sarah, *d.* in 1794.

Mr. Edward Jenkins was in the army and served in the first American war. His son ahd successor,

ROBERT-BOYCOTT-CRESSETT-LEIGHTON JENKINS, Esq. of Charlton Hill, *b.* 13 March, 1781, a major in the army, *m.* 26 Feb. 1808, Elizabeth, second dau. of Richard Jenkins, Esq. of Bicton Hall, and *d.* 2 May, 1636, having had issue,

I. EDWARD-LEIGHTON, present representative of the family.
II. Charles-Vanbrugh, *b.* 4 March, 1822, captain 1st Bengal light cavalry, in which regt. he served in the expedition to Cabul for the release of Sir Robert Sale from Jellallabad, and in the battles of Maharajpore and Aliwal; *b.* 4 March, 1822; *m.* 24 March, 1847, Annette-Louise-Robertina, eldest dau. of Horace Aylward, Esq., and has issue,
 1 Robert-Edward-Arthur, *b.* 5 Feb. 1848.
 2 Edgar-Francis, *b.* 17 Dec. 1850.
 3 Charles-Bradford-Harries, *b.* 17 March, 1856.
 1 Mary-Louise.
III. Robert, *b.* 22 Jan. 1825, Comm. R.N., promoted for his services.
I. Louisa-Harriett.
II. Mary-Elizabeth, *d.* 19 June, 1853.

Arms—Or, a lion rampant, regardant, sa.
Crest—On a mural crown, sa., a lion passant, regardant, or.
Motto—Perge sed caute.
Seat—Charlton Hill, Shropshire.

JENNER OF WENVOE CASTLE.

JENNER, ROBERT-FRANCIS, Esq. of Wenvoe Castle, co. Glamorgan, J.P. and D.L., high-sheriff 1828, *b.* 13 Jan. 1802; *m.* 10 Aug. 1824, Elizabeth-Lascelles Jenner, eldest dau. of the late Right Hon. Sir Herbert Jenner-Fust, dean of the Arches, and Judge of the Prerogative Court, and by her (who *d.* 29 Sept. 1850) has issue,

I. ROBERT-FRANCIS-LASCELLES, *b.* 16 Sept. 1826.
II. Alfred-Herbert, in holy orders, rector of Wenvoe, *b.* 16 Feb. 1828.
III. Hugh, *b.* 18 July, 1831.
IV. Edmund, *b.* 20 Oct. 1833.
V. Frederic, *b.* 19 May, 1839.
VI. Herbert-Augustus-Rous, *b.* 6 May, 1842.
VII. Algernon-Romilly, *b.* 1 May, 1845.

I. Emma-Elizabeth-Vivian, *m.* 5 March, 1856, to Captain H. Wily, late 50th foot.
II. Frances-Anne-Jane.
III. Gertrude.
IV. Harriet-Georgina.
V. Isabel.

Lineage.—ROBERT JENNER, Esq. of Chiselhurst, co. Kent, *m.* 1775, ANNE, eldest dau. and co-heiress of PETER BIRT, Esq. of Wenboe Castle, co. Glamorgan, who had purchased that estate from Sir Edmund Thomas, Bart, in 1765, and had by her two sons, viz.,

ROBERT, his heir.
Herbert, (Sir,) D.C.L., dean of the Arches, and judge of the Prerogative Court of Canterbury, *b.* in 1778, *m.* in 1808, Miss Lascelles, youngest dau. of the late General Lascelles, and has issue. Sir Herbert assumed, 14 Jan. 1842, the additional surname and arms of FUST, pursuant to the testamentary injunction of his kinsman, Sir John Fust, Bart., of Hill Court.

The eldest son,

ROBERT JENNER, Esq. of Wenvoe Castle, *m.* 18 Jan. 1801, Frances, eldest dau. of the late Gen. Lascelles, and by her (who *d.* 7 Aug. 1841) had issue,

I. ROBERT-FRANCIS, now of Wenvoe Castle.
II. Herbert-Charles.
III. George-Peter.
IV. Gill-Birt-Price, *m.* Ann, dau. of H. Martin, Esq.
V. Albert-Lascelles, *m.* Henrietta-Julia, eldest dau. of Sir John Morris, Bart., and has issue two sons,
 1 George.
 2 Cecil-Armine.
VI. Birt-Wyndham-Rous, *m.* Ann, dau. of Langley St. Albyn, Esq. of Alfoxton, co. Somerset, and has,
 1 Birt-St. Albyn.
 2 Frances-Anne-Caroline.

Arms—Az., two swords, erect, in chev., arg., hilts and pommels, or, between three covered cups, of the last.
Crest—A covered cup, or, standing between two swords, in saltier, arg., hilts and pommels, of the first.
Seat—Wenvoe Castle, near Cardiff.

JENNEY OF BREDFIELD.

JENNEY, EDMUND, Esq. of Bredfield House, co. Suffolk, J.P. and D.L., bapt. 1768; *s.* his father in Aug. 1801.

Lineage.—The name of this family was originally spelt GYNEY.

SIR WILLIAM JENNEY, Knt. of Knodishall, co. Suffolk, one of the judges of the King's Bench in 1477, son of John Jenney, Esq. of Knodishall, by Maud, his wife, dau. and heir of John Bokill, of Friston, *m.* 1st, Elizabeth, dau. of Thomas Cawse, Esq., and by her, who was living in 1466, had four sons and four daus. The Judge, *m.* 2ndly, Eleanor, widow of Robert Ingleys, Esq., and dau. of John Sampson, Esq.; but by her, who *d.* in 1496, and was buried at Norwich, he had no issue. He *d.* 23 Dec. 1483, and was *s.* by his eldest son,

SIR EDMUND JENNEY, Knt. of Knodishall, who *m.* about 1467, Catherine, dau. and heir of Robert Boys, Esq. (by Jane his wife, dau. and heir of Edward Wychingham, Esq.) and had issue,

WILLIAM, *b.* 24 May, 1470, *m.* 1st, Audrey, dau. of Sir Robert Clere, Knt. of Ormsby, in Norfolk, but by that lady, who *d.* in 1502, had no issue. He *m.* 2ndly, Elizabeth, dau. of Mr. Alderman Thomas Button, of London, and left at his decease, 28 Feb., 10 HENRY VIII., a dau., Elizabeth, and a son, FRANCIS, heir to his grandfather.
Robert, *b.* in 1484, *d. s. p.* in 1560.
CHRISTOPHER, (Sir,) of Cressingham, *b.* in 1486, one of the judges of the Common Pleas, in 1539, *m.* Elizabeth, dau. and co-heir of William Eyre, Esq. of Bury St. Edmund's.
John, *b.* in 1488, *m.* in 1512, Anne, widow of William Bocher, Esq. of co. Suffolk, and left issue.
Jane, *m.* to William Playters, Esq. of Sotterley, and *d.* in 1540.
Elizabeth, *b.* in 1471.
Anne, *m.* to Thomas Billingford, Gent. of Stoke, in Norfolk.
Rose, *b.* in 1474, *m.* in 1493, to John King, Gent of Shelley.
Thomasse, *m.* to William Duke, Esq. of Brampton, in Suffolk.
Isabella, *m.* to Richard Littlebury, Gent., and living in 1521.

Sir Edmund *d.* in 1522, and was *s.* by his grandson,

FRANCIS JENNEY, Esq. of Knodishall, *b.* in 1510. This gentleman *m.* twice, 1st, Margaret, dau. of Sir Robert Peyton, Knt. of Iselham, and 2ndly, Mary, dau. of Robert Brograve, Esq. of Kent. By the latter he had no issue, but by the former was father of a numerous family. He *d.* in 1590, and was *s.* by his eldest son,

ARTHUR JENNEY, Esq. of Knodishall, *b.* in 1533, who *m.* before 1559, Elye, dau. of George Jerningan, Esq. of Somerleyton, in Suffolk, and was *s.* at his decease, in 1604, by his grandson,

SIR ARTHUR JENNEY, Knt. of Knodishall, (son of Francis Jenney, Esq., by Anne his wife, dau. and co-heir of George Bede, Esq. of Thorington.) He was sheriff of Suffolk in 1645, and of Norfolk in 1654. This gentleman *m.* 1st, in 1616, Anne, dau. of Sir Robert Barker, and by that lady had, with other issue, I. ROBERT, (Sir,) his heir; II. George, of Morton, in Norfolk, *b.* in 1630, *m.* and had a son, George, who *d.* in 1749, leaving, by Bridget, his wife, four daus., his co-heirs, viz., 1. Mary, *m.* to the Rev. Richard Tapps, of Norwich; 2. Bridget, *d. unm.*; 3. Sarah, *d. unm.*; and 4. Anne, *m.* to Rev. Mr. Greete. Sir Arthur *m.* 2ndly, Catherine, dau. of Sir John Porter, and by her had a son, Thomas, of Campsey Ash, who *d. s. p.* in 1675. He *m.* 3rdly, Helen, widow of John Freeman, Esq., and dau. of Francis Stonard, Esq. of Knowleshill, in Essex, by whom he had two daus., Susann, who *d. s. p.*; and Isabella, who *m.* the Rev. John Talbot, of Icklingham. Sir Arthur *m.* 4thly, Mary, dau. of Thomas Hall, Esq. of Godalming, in Surrey, and by her (who survived him, and re-married William Nicholls, Gent.) had a son, Edmund. He *d.* 24 March, 1667-8, aged seventy-five, was buried at Knodishall, and was *s.* by his eldest son,

SIR ROBERT JENNEY, Knt. of Knodishall, who *m.* in 1640, Elizabeth, dau. of Sir John Offley, Knt. of Madeley, co. Stafford, and had issue,

I. OFFLEY, his heir.
II. EDMUND, of Campsey-Ash, *m.* in 1683, Dorothy, dau. and co-heir of Robert Marryott, Esq. of Bredfield, and relict of Thomas Knight, of London, and by her he left at his decease, 17 Feb. 1694-5,
 1 ARTHUR, of Woodbridge, who *m.* in 1711, Mirabella, dau. of Henry Edgar, Gent. of Eye, in Suffolk, and widow of Robert Burley, Gent. of Wisbech, and dying in 1729, left
  EDMUND, of Bredfield, of whom presently.
  Edgar, *d.* in 1746.
  Arthur, of Rendlesham, in Suffolk, *m.* a dau. of — Langley, and left at his decease in 1742, a son, Edmund, of Bungay, who *m.* Elizabeth, dau. of — Denny, of Eye, in Suffolk, and left in 1800, with two daus., (Elizabeth, *m.* to Thomas Crowther, Esq.; and Marianne, *m.* to Philip Bell, Gent.,) an only surviving son, William, *b.* 9 Dec. 1779, living in 1834, *m.* Caroline-Frances, dau. of Major Archibald Stewart, of the Blues, and granddau. maternally of Sir Henry Harpur, of Calke Abbey, and has issue, Stewart-William, *b.* 28 Dec. 1816; Arthur-Henry, *b.* 31 March, 1819; Frances-Caroline, *m.* 25 Sept. 1827, to the Rev. Henry-R. Crewe, brother of Sir Geo. Crewe, Bart.; Lucy-Elizabeth; Caroline-Maria; Georgiana-Selina.
I. Catherine, *m.* to Nicholas son of Arthur Drury, Esq.

Sir Robert *d.* in 1660, and was *s.* by his eldest son,

OFFLEY, JENNEY, Esq. of Knodishall, bapt. 4 April, 1641, *m.* in 1666, Alethea, eldest dau. of Sir Edward Duke, Bart. of Benhall, and by that lady (who *m.* 2ndly, Ralph Snelling, Esq., and 3rdly, William Foster, Esq.) left at his decease in 1670, an only child,

ROBERT JENNEY, Esq. of Leiston, bapt. 3 Dec. 1677, *m.* Deborah, dau. of John Braham, Esq. of Ash, and had a son, OFFLEY, who *d.* in 1735, *unm.* Mr. Jenney *d.* in 1741, and was *s.* by his cousin,

EDMUND JENNEY, Esq. of Bredfield, who *m.* in 1765, Anne, dau. of Philip Broke, Esq. of Nacton, by whom, who *d.* 19 Oct. 1821, aged eighty-four. Mr. Jenney left at his decease, in 1801, with other issue, now deceased, a son, the late EDMUND JENNEY, of Bredfield.

Arms—Erm., a bend, gu., cottised, or.
Crest—On a glove, in fesse, arg., a hawk or falcon, close, or, belled, of the last.
Seats—Bredfield House, and Hasketon, near Woodbridge.

JENYNS OF BOTTISHAM HALL.

JENYNS, GEORGE, Esq. of Bottisham Hall, co. Cambridge, *b.* in 1795; *m.* in 1820, Maria-Jane, dau. of Sir James Gambier, Knt., and has surviving issue,

I. SOAME-GAMBIER, C.B., major 13th lt. drgs., *b.* in 1826.
II. Charles-Fitzgerald-Gambier, *b.* in 1827, *m.* 1st, Fanny, dau. of William Murril, Esq., who *d.* 1854; and 2ndly, 1856, Rose-Emily, dau. of William Earle Lytton Bulwer, Esq. of Heydon, co. Norfolk.
I. Jemima-Maria-Hicks. II. Isabel-Charlotte.

Lineage.—In the year 1563, Sir William St. Loe, Knt., released all his right in the Manor of Churchill, in Somersetshire, to RALPH JENYNS, of Islington, in Middlesex, whose descendant, Richard Jenyns, sold it to John Churchill, Esq. of Lincoln's Inn.

SIR JOHN JENYNS, knighted in 1603, the representative of Ralph, *m.* 1st, Anne, dau. of Sir William Brounker, and had by her one son,

JOHN (Sir), who was made K.B. at the creation of Charles, Prince of Wales, served as sheriff of Herts in 1626, and was M.P. for St. Albans. He *m.* Alice, 3rd dau. of Sir Richard Spencer, and had several children, of whom
 RICHARD, of Sandridge, in Herts, *d.* in 1744, leaving, by his wife, Frances, dau. and co-heir of Sir Gifford Thornhurst, Bart., three daus., Frances ("La Belle Jenyns"), *m.* to Richard, Duke of Tyrconnel; Barbara, *m.* to Edward Griffith, Esq.; and Sarah, the celebrated Duchess of Marlborough.

Sir John Jenyns *m.* 2ndly, Dorothy, widow of John Latch, Esq., and dau. of Thomas Bulbeck, by Ursula, dau. of Robert Gray, and had (with a dau., Elizabeth, who *d. unm.*) a son,

THOMAS JENYNS, Esq. of Hayes, in Middlesex, *b.* in 1609; who *m.* Veare, dau. of Thomas Palmer, Esq., and by her (who *d.* in 1644) left at his decease, in 1650 (with other children, who *d. s. p*), a son and successor,

ROGER JENYNS, Esq. of Hayes, *b.* in 1636; who *m.* Sarah, dau. of Joseph Latch, Esq., and had issue,

I. JOHN, who *d.* in 1715, leaving, by Jane his wife, dau. of James Clitherow, Esq., *inter alios*, a son, Roger, who *m.* Miss Harvey, and was father of John-Harvey, who *m.* Elizabeth, dau. of the Rev. Edward Chappelow, and *d.* in 1789, leaving, with a dau., Charlotte-Elizabeth, *m.* to the Rev. John Vachell, a son, GEORGE-LEONARD, of whom presently.
II. ROGER (Sir), of whom we treat.
III. Thomas, *d. unm.*

Roger Jenyns *d.* in 1693. His 2nd son,

SIR ROGER JENYNS, Knt., *b.* in 1663; purchased the estate of Bottisham, in the co. of Cambridge, and became an active magistrate of that shire. He *m.* 1st, Martha, widow of John Mingay, by whom (who *d.* in 1701) he had two sons and a dau., Roger, Veare, and Sarah. He *m.* 2ndly, Elizabeth, dau. of Sir Peter Soame, of Heyden, in Essex, and by her, who *d.* in 1728, left, at his decease in 1740, a son and successor,

SOAME JENYNS, Esq. of Bottisham Hall, *b.* in 1704, M.P. for Cambridgeshire, the well known writer and wit. Mr. Jenyns *m.* 1st Mary only dau. of Col. Soame, of Dereham, in Norfolk, and 2ndly, Elizabeth, dau. of Henry Grey Esq. of Hackney, but *d. s. p.* 18 Dec. 1787. He devised his estates, after the demise of his widow, to his cousin,

THE REV. GEORGE-LEONARD JENYNS of Bottisham, *b.* 19 June, 1763, who *m.* 1788, Mary, dau. of the late William Heberden, M.D., and had issue,

Soame, *d.* in 1803.
GEORGE, now of Bottisham.
Charles, *b.* 15 Aug. 1798; *m.* 1st, Marianne, only dau. of Samuel Vachell, Esq.; and 2ndly, in 1842, Louisa, eldest dau. of Walter Young, Esq.
Leonard, *b.* 25 May, 1800, *m.* Jane, dau. of Rev. Edward Daubeny, of Ampney, co. Gloucester.
Mary.
Harriet, *m.* to the Rev. John-Stephen Henslow, professor of Botany at Cambridge.
Elizabeth.

Arms—Arg., on a fesse, gu., three bezants.
Crest—A demi-lion, rampant, or, supporting a spear, erect, of the first, headed, as.
Motto—Ignavis nunquam.
Seat—Bottisham Hall.

JERVOISE OF HERRIARD.

ELLIS-JERVOISE, FRANCIS-JERVOISE, Esq. of Herriard Park, co. Hants, and The Moat, Britford, co. Wilts, J.P. and D.L., *b.* 18 March, 1809; *m.* 1st, 6 Feb. 1838, Mary-Frances, youngest dau. of Sir William Knighton, Bart., which lady *d. s. p.* 26 June, 1839. He *m.* 2ndly, 20 July, 1841, Mary-Louisa, 2nd dau. of George Marx, Esq., and by her has issue,

I. FRANCIS-MICHAEL, *b.* 29 Sept. 1844.
II. John-Purefoy, *b.* 8 Sept. 1846.
III. Arthur-Tristram, *b.* 19 Sept. 1848.
I. Selina-Mary. II. Emma-Gertrude, *d.* young.
III. Constance-Catharine. VI. Edith-Purefoy.
V. Ethel-Madeline.

Mr. Ellis-Jervoise served as high-sheriff of Hants 1852, during which year he attended in state the funeral of the late Duke of Wellington, lord-lieutenant of the county.

Lineage.—RICHARD JERVEYS, Esq. of Northfield and Weoly Park, co. Worcester, *b.* in 1500, son of THOMAS JERVEYS, Esq. of Northfield, and Joan Gower, his wife, was possessed of estates situated in Chelmarsh, Nether Court,

Quatt Jerveys, Quatt Malvern, co. Salop, and purchased, 28 March, 1542, of George, Earl of Huntingdon, and his son, Francis, Lord Hastings, the manor and estate of Britford, otherwise Birtford, co. Wilts. He m. 26 Oct. 1525, Winefride, dau. of John Barnard citizen of London and d. 28 Dec. 1557, and was buried at Chelsea. His son and successor,

THOMAS JERVEYS, Esq. b. 28 Dec. 1532, m. Cicely, dau. of — Ridley, Esq. of Bould co. Salop, and by her (who d. 1 July, 1595) left at his decease, 27 Dec. 1588, a son,

SIR THOMAS JERVOISE, Knt., b. 11 June, 1587, who m. 21 July, 1601, Lucy, eldest dau. of Sir Richard Powlet, Knt. of Herriard, co. Hants, and d. 20 Oct. 1654, leaving a son,

THOMAS JERVOISE, Esq., b. 16 March, 1616, who m. 30 July, 1657, Mary, second dau of George Purefoy, Esq. of Wadley House, near Farringdon, co. Berks, and d. 13 May, 1693, having had by this lady (who d. 24 May, 1687) a son and heir,

THOMAS JERVOISE, Esq. of Herriard, b. 6 Sept. 1667, who m. 1st, 18 Feb. 1691, Elizabeth, dau. of Sir Gilbert Clarke, Knt. of Chilcot, co. Derby, (which lady d. 21 July, 1695.) He m. 2ndly, 9 Aug. 1700, Elizabeth, dau. and heiress of Sir John Stonehouse, Bart. of Amerden Hall, co. Essex, and d. 10 May, 1743, leaving by the latter lady (who d. 7 July, 1706) a son,

RICHARD JERVOISE, Esq. of Herriard, b. 5 Jan. 1703-4, who m. 2 Jan. 1733-4, Ann, dau. and heiress of Tristram Hudleston, Esq. of Croydon, co. Surrey, and d. 17 March, 1762, leaving by her (who d. 25 Sept. 1756) two sons. The elder,

TRISTRAM-HUDLESTON JERVOISE, Esq., b. 1 June (O.S.), 1736, d. unm. 31 Dec. 1794, and was s. by his brother,

THE REV. GEORGE-HUDLESTON-JERVOISE-PUREFOY JERVOISE, of Herriard Park, who m. 22 May, 1769, Mary, second dau. and co-heiress of the Rev. Wright Hawes, rector of Shalston, co. Bucks, and of Stretton in Fosse, co. Warwick, and had issue, (beside two daus., who d. young,)

GEORGE-PUREFOY, his heir.
Jervoise-Purefoy, d. unm.
Richard-Purefoy, d. leaving a dau., m. to Thomas Fitzgerald, Esq. of Shaltons House, co. Bucks.
MARY-PUREFOY, of whom hereafter, as successor to her brother.

Mr. Jervoise d. 3 Nov. 1805, and was s. by his eldest son,

GEORGE PUREFOY-JERVOISE, Esq. of Herriard, b. 10 April, 1770, who m. 1st, Elizabeth, dau. and heiress of Thomas Hall, of Preston Candover, co. Hants, which lady d. in 1821. He m. 2ndly, Anna-Maria-Selina, eldest dau. of Wadham Locke, Esq. of Rowdeford, co. Wilts. Mr. Jervoise d. s. p. 1 Dec. 1847, when the family estates devolved on his sister,

MARY-PUREFOY JERVOISE, who had m. the Rev. FRANCIS ELLIS, M.A. rector of Lasham, co. Hants, and vicar of Long Compton, co. Warwick. Mr. Ellis in thus acquiring through his wife, the family estates of the Jervoises, assumed by Royal licence, in March, 1848, the additional surname and arms of JERVOISE. The issue of this marriage were,

FRANCIS-JERVOISE, now of Herriard Park.
Harriet-Purefoy, m. to the Rev. Charles Causton, rector of Stretton-on-Fosse, co. Warwick.
Mary-Elizabeth, m. to William-Harriot Roe, Esq. of Manor House, Holybourne, co. Hants.
Catharine-Anne, d. unm.
Caroline-Jervoise, m. to the Rev. George-F. Smith.
Julia-Georgiana, d. unm.

Mrs. Ellis-Jervoise d. 30 April, 1849.

Arms—Quarterly: 1st and 4th, sa., a chevron, between three eaglets, close, arg., for JERVOISE; 2nd and 3rd, three eels, sa., for ELLIS.
Crests—An heraldic tiger's head, sa., for JERVOISE; a plume of five ostrich feathers, arg., for ELLIS.
Motto—Virtutis premium laus.
Seats—Herriard Park, Hants; The Moat, Britford, co. Wilts.

JESSE OF LLANBEDR HALL.

JESSE, JOHN, Esq. of Llanbedr Hall, co. Denbigh, J.P., F.R.S., high-sheriff in 1856, b. 6 Jan. 1801; m. 1st, 28 Oct. 1840, Sarah, dau. of John Garratt, Esq. of Bishop's Court, Devon, and Cleveland House, Cheltenham, formerly alderman and lord mayor of London, and by her has one son,

FRANCIS-ABLETT, b. 29 Jan. 1845.

He m. 2ndly, 1 March, 1848, Eliza, dau. of Edward Milne, Esq. of Manchester, and has issue,

I. John-Fairfax, b. 30 June, 1851.
I. Sarah-Margaret. II. Eliza-Stephenson.

Lineage.—This family is clearly traced up to Thomas Jesse, who settled in Manchester, and who was nephew of Harry Jesse, the "Godly Preacher to His Highness Oliver Cromwell." The late

JOHN JESSE, Esq., b. 17 Nov. 1759, m. July, 1796, Sarah, dau. of Ambrose Smith, Esq., by Phœbe, his wife, of Cheil, co. Stafford; and by her, who d. 16 Oct. 1838, he left at his decease, 27 Feb. 1817, two sons,

JOHN, now of Llanbedr Hall.
Joseph-Ablett, b. 16 April, 1808, d. 15 March, 1845.

Arms—Arg., three dogfish.
Crest—A demi-lion, rampt.
Seat—Llanbedr Hall, Ruthin.

JESSOP OF DOORY HALL.

JESSOP, FREDERICK-THOMAS, Esq. of Doory Hall, co. Longford, J.P. and D.L., high-sheriff 1835, b. 26 Aug. 1811; m. 12 July, 1836, Elizabeth, dau. of Peter Low, Esq., by Louisa his wife, dau. of the late Sir Richard Butler, Bart. of Garryhundon House, co. Carlow, and has issue,

I. FRANCIS-JOHN, 2nd regt., b. 30 May, 1837.
II. Frederick-Flood, b. 17 Sept. 1844.
III. George-Henry, b. 5 Feb. 1852.
I. Louisa. II. Elizabeth.
III. Frances-Flood. IV. Mary.

Lineage.—The Doory Hall Estates, situated in the cos. of Longford, Westmeath, and Roscommon, were granted to this family (descended from the Jessops of Derbyshire and Yorkshire) by King CHARLES II.

ANTHONY JESSOP, Esq., who m. Bridget, dau. and heir of William Donnelly, Esq. of Portumna Castle, and by her had, with three daus. and a son, William, who d. unm., another son,

JOHN JESSOP, Esq. of Doory Hall, who m. Mary-Anne, dau. and co-heir of Robert Fetherston, Esq. of White Rock, and had two sons, JOHN-HARWARD, his heir, and Robert-Fetherstone, in holy orders. The elder,

JOHN-HARWARD JESSOP, Esq. of Doory Hall, m. in 1806, Frances, only child and heiress of Sir Frederick Flood, Bart., M.P., and relict of Richard Solly, Esq. of co. Essex (by whom she had a son, Frederick Solly, Esq., and two daus., Frances, m. to Sir George-R. Fetherston, Bart., M.P.; and Caroline, m. to Capt. Samuel-B. Hore.) By this lady, Mr. Jessop had issue,

FREDERICK-THOMAS, now of Doory Hall.
Robert, in holy orders, m. 1st, Susan, dau. of Mr. Baron Pennefather, and by her (who d. 1837) has one son, William, b. 1833; and 2ndly, Isabella, dau. of Capt. Hort, and by her had a son, Robert.
Frances-Flood, m. to the Hon. and Rev. John Gustavus Handcock, rector of Annaduff, co. Leitrim, third son of the late Lord Castlemaine.
Maria, m. to the Rev. Nicholas Devereux, rector of Annatress, only son of Major Devereux, of Ballyrankin House, co. Wexford.
Jane, m. to Matthew-Thomas Derinzy, Esq. of Clobemon Hall, co. Wexford.

Mr. Jessop d. in Aug. 1825.

Arms—Or, two bars, gu., in chief, three leopards' heads, of the second.
Crest—A dove, holding in its beak an olive-branch, ppr.
Motto—Pax et amor.
Seat—Doory Hall, Ballymahon, Ireland.

JEX-BLAKE OF SWANTON ABBOTTS.

JEX-BLAKE, THE REV. WILLIAM-JEX, of Swanton Abbotts, co. Norfolk, J.P., b. 23 Nov. 1786, m. 11 June, 1811, Maria, dau. of William Lubbock, Esq., and sister of Sir John-William Lubbock, Bart., and has issue,

I. WILLIAM-LUBBOCK, b. 15 June, 1818; m. 30 Sept. 1847, Susan-Margaret, youngest dau. of Francis Blake, Esq. of Norwich, and has issue.
II. Charles-Thomas, b. 8 March, 1820; m. 4 June, 1850, Fanny, eldest dau. of the Rev. Richard Johnson, and has issue.
I. Maria, m. to the Rev. Townley Blackwood Price.
II. Anna-Eliza, m. to William Blackwood Price, Esq.

Lineage.—JOHN BLAKE, Gent. of Bunwell, co. Norfolk, b. in 1583, was buried there 4 Aug. 1646, leaving, by Martha, his wife, a son and heir,

JOHN BLAKE, Gent. of Bunwell, b. in 1622, m. 1st, in 1644, Anne, dau. of John Welles, Esq.; and 2ndly, (settlement dated 2 May, 1662,) Susanna, dau. of John Stubling, Esq. of Stoke, co. Suffolk, and d. in 1686, leaving a son and heir,

ROBERT BLAKE, Esq. of Scottow, b. at Bunwell, 7 Dec. 1655, m. Margaret, eldest dau. of William Durrant, of Scottow, Esq., and, with other issue, was father of

Thomas Blake, Esq. of Scottow, *b.* 7 Nov. 1689, who *m.* Elizabeth, dau. of John Jex, Esq. of Lowestoft, co. Suffolk, by Mary, his wife, (eldest dau. and co-heir of William Coulson, Esq.) and by her was father of

Thomas Blake, Esq. of Scottow, *b.* 18 June, 1726, who *m* 23 July, 1754, Judith, dau. of William Clarke, Esq. of Loddon, and *d.* 26 June, 1806, leaving two sons,

Thomas, of Norwich, Esq., barrister-at-law, justice of the peace, and deputy-lieut. for co. Norfolk, *b.* 22 June, 1755, *m.* 1st, Margaret, only child of the Rev. Thomas Weston, rector of Cookely and Halesworth; and 2ndly, Theodora, eldest dau. of David Columbine, Esq., by whom (who *d.* 26 July, 1801) he had four sons and three daus. This gentleman *d.* 27 Sept. 1813.
William, of Swanton Abbotts.

The second son,

William Blake, Esq. of Swanton Abbotts, J.P. and D.L., *b.* 31 May, 1758, who assumed, 1837, the additional surname and arms of Jex, *m.* 21 Dec. 1785, Catharine, dau. of Robert Ferrier, Esq., and *d.* Feb. 1843, having had issue,

William-Jex, now of Swanton Abbotts.
Robert-Ferrier, in holy orders, rector of Great Dunham, Norfolk, *b.* 5 March, 1789, *m.* 20 Oct. 1828, Elinor-Sarah-Elizabeth, youngest dau. of William Hoey, Esq. of Dunganstown, co. Wicklow, J.P., and has issue.
Thomas, of Cumberland Terrace, Regent's Park, Esq., J.P., proctor in Doctors' Commons, *b.* 17 Dec. 1790, *m.* 1st, in Jan. 1821, Elizabeth, only child of William Palmer, Esq.; she *d.* 6 July, the same year. He *m.* 2ndly, in 1824, Maria-Emily, youngest dau. of Thomas Cubitt, Esq. of Honing Hall, co. Norfolk, and has issue.
Judith, *d.* young.
Catherine-Charlotte, *d. unm.* 1855.
Elizabeth, *m.* to the Rev. John Gunton.

Arms—Quarterly: 1st and 4th, arg., a chev., between three garbs, sa., within a bordure, of the last, charged with eight fleurs-de-lis, of the field, for Blake; 2nd and 3rd., arg., on a fesse, engr., sa., between two plain cottises, gu., three escallops, of the field, for Jex.
Crest of Blake—A morion, ppr., thereon a martlet, arg.; of Jex, a horse's head, arg., maned, or, erased, gu., in the mouth a broken tilting-spear, gold.
Motto—Bene præparatum pectus.
Seat—Swanton Abbott's, co. Norfolk.

JODRELL OF YEARDSLEY.

Jodrell, John-William, Esq. of Yeardsley, co. Chester, *b.* in 1808; *s.* to his estates upon the demise of his father, 5 March, 1829; entered the grenadier guards in 1825, and retired from them in 1831.

Lineage.—The Jodrells of Yeardsley were settled at Yeardsley, in the county of Chester, towards the middle of the reign of Edward III.

The first of the name on record was possessed, together with his sons, of lands in several townships within the manor of High Peak, in the co. of Derby, 14 Edward I., A.D. 1286. His great-grandson,

William Jauderell, the immediate ancestor of the family, served as an archer under Edward the Black Prince, Earl of Chester, in the French wars. He had his pass for England dated from Bordeaux, 28 Edward III., A.D. 1355, and was possessed at his death (as appears by several authentic records) of lands in the townships of Yeardsley cum Whaley, Disley, and Kettleshulme, in the co. of Chester, which lands have continued ever since in the family. He *m.* in 1356, Agnes, dau. of Robert de Bradshawe, and left issue, Roger, Thomas,* John, Robert, and Alice. He was *s.* by his eldest son,

Roger Jaudrell, of Yeardsley, Esq., who was for many years one of the four esquires of the king's body, in the reign of Richard II, and for his good service had granted to him for life, 17 Richard II, the town of Wheston, in Leicestershire. The fourth in descent from him, Roger Jodrell, of Yeardsley and Twemlow, Esq., *m* during the reign of Henry VII, Ellen, dau. and co-heir of Roger Knutsford, of Twemlow, Esq., through whom that estate (which subsequently became a residence of the family) was acquired. The family afterwards intermarried with the Burdetts of Foremark, the Molyneux's of Teversal, and other ancient houses; and the tenth in direct male descent from the first possessor of Yeardsley, viz.,

Francis Jodrell, of Yeardsley and Twemlow, Esq., high sheriff of Cheshire in 1715, *m.* 1st, in 1713, Hannah, only dau. and heiress of John Ashton, Esq.; and 2ndly, Mary, one of the daus. and co-heiresses of Edward Gregge, Esq. of Hopwood, in Cheshire, but had no issue by her. His eldest and only remaining son, by his 1st wife,

Francis Jodrell, Esq., *m.* Jane, dau. and co-heiress of Thomas Butterworth, Esq., and predeceasing his father, about 1750, left issue,

Frances, of whom presently.
Elizabeth, who inherited the Twemlow estate, and *m.* in 1778, Egerton Leigh, Esq. of High Leigh, co. Chester.

Frances Jodrell, eldest dau. and heiress of the Yeardsley estate, *m.* in 1775, John Bower, of Manchester, Esq, who assumed, by sign-manual, in compliance with the testamentary injunction of his wife's grandfather, the surname and arms of Jodrell, and had issue,

Francis, his successor.
Thomas-Marsden, captain in the 35th regt. of foot, who fell at Rosetta, in Egypt, while acting as aide-de-camp to Gen. Oswald.
Edmund-Henry, late col. commanding the 2nd battalion of grenadier-guards, served thirty-four years in that regiment; was on foreign service in Sicily in 1806 and 1807; in the Peninsula, in 1810, 1811, and 1812; was present at the battle of Barrosa; at the passage of the Bidassoa, the Nive, and the Nivelle; the actions in front of Bidart; the passage of the Adour; and at Bayonne.
Harriet, *m.* to Shakspeare Phillips, Esq.
Maria, *m.* to John Stratton, Esq.

Mr. Bower-Jodrell *d.* in 1796, and was *s.* by his eldest son,

Francis Jodrell, of Yeardsley and Henbury, Esq., who was high-sheriff of Cheshire in 1813. He *m.* in 1807, Maria, dau. of Sir William Lemon, of Carclew, co. Cornwall, Bart. (by Jane, dau. of James Buller, of Morval, Esq., by his 2nd wife, Lady Jane Bathurst, dau. of Allen, 1st Earl Bathurst), and had issue,

John-William, present proprietor.
Foster-Bower, *b.* in 1810, *d.* at Oxford, in Nov. 1830.
Francis-Charles, *b.* in 1812, lately capt. in the grenadier-gds.

Mr. Jodrell *d.* 5 March, 1829, and was *s.* by his eldest son, John-William Jodrell, Esq., present representative of the family.

Arms—Sa., three round buckles, arg.
Crest—A cock's head and neck, couped, or, wings elevated and endorsed, arg., combed and jelloped, gu.
Seat—Yeardsley Hall, co. Chester.

JOHNES OF DOLAUCOTHY.

Johnes, John, Esq. of Dolaucothy, co. Carmarthen, J.P. and D.L., barrister-at-law, *b.* 6 Feb. 1800; *m.* 8 Oct. 1822, Elizabeth, only dau. of the Rev. John Edwardes, of Gileston Manor, Glamorganshire, and has two daus.,

I. Charlotte-Anna-Maria, *m.* to Charles-Cæsar Cookman, Esq., eldest son of Edward-Rogers Cookman, Esq. of Monart House, co. Wexford.
II. Elizabeth.

Lineage.—This family, a very ancient one, and one of long standing in the counties of Carmarthen and Cardigan, derives its lineage from Rees ap Gronow ap Einon. His son,

Elydyr ap Rees, *m.* Gwladys, dau. of Phillip ap Bach ap Gwaithvoed, Lord of Egairfach, in Glamorganshire, but according to others, of Cadwgan ap Iorworth ap Llywarch ap Bran, and had a son,

Sir Elydyr Ddu, or Leonard Ddu, Knight of the Sepulchre, who *m.* Cecil, dau. of Sitsyllt ap Llewellyn ap Moreiddig Warwin, Lord of Cantreselyff, and had a son,

Phillip ap Eydyr, who *m.* Gwladys, dau. of Dav d Vras ap Enion Goch ap Griffith ap Enion Vychan, and had, *inter alios*,

Nicholas ap Phillip, who *m.* Jemmett, dau. of Griffith ap Llewellyn, and was father of

Griffith ap Nicholas, of Newton, in Carmarthenshire, who *m.* 1st, Mably, dau. of Meredith Dunn, of Kidwelly; 2ndly Margaret, dau. of Sir John Perrot, of Pembrokeshire; and 3rdly, Jane, dau. and co-heir of Jenkin ap Rees. Griffith was slain at Wakefield, on the side of York, leaving a numerous issue by his three wives. The eldest son,

Thomas ap Griffith, of Newton, *m.* 1st, Elizabeth, dau. and heiress of Sir John Griffith, of Abermarles, in Carmarthenshire, and 2ndly, Elizabeth, dau. of Francis, or James, 2nd son of Philip, Duke of Burgundy. He was killed in a duel, and buried at Bardsey Island, leaving issue,

Morgan ap Thomas, fought on the side of York, *d. s. p.*
David ap Thomas, called David *Cyffyl Cwtta* (or short-tail horse), fought on the side of Lancaster; he left no legitimate issue.
Jenkin ap Thomas.

---

* From this Thomas, who *m.* the dau. of Bailey, of Moor House, co. Stafford, Sir Richard-Paul Jodrell is supposed to be descended.

David ap Thomas, the younger.
Rhys ap Thomas (Sir), Knight of the Garter, lord and proprietor of large estates in the counties of Pembroke, Carmarthen, Glamorgan, and Cardigan. He was ancestor of LORD DYNEVOR.
JOHN AP THOMAS, of whom we have to treat.

The 6th son (issue of the 2nd marriage),

JOHN AP THOMAS of Abermarles, m. Elizabeth, dau. of Thomas Vaughan, of Bredwardine, by Elinor his wife, dau. of Robert, Lord Whitney, and had a son and successor,

SIR THOMAS JOHNES, Knt. of Abermarles and Haroldston, in Pembrokeshire, sheriff of Carmarthenshire in 1541, and of Cardiganshire in 1544, was first knight for the co. of Pembroke. He m. Mary, dau. and heir of James Berkeley, 2nd son of Maurice, Lord Berkeley, and widow of Thomas Perrot, of Haroldstown, and by her, who m. 3rdly, Sir Robert Whitney, had issue,

HENRY (Sir), of Abermarles, from whom sprang the family of JOHNES of that place, now EXTINCT in the male line.
Richard, of Cwmgwilly, in Carmarthenshire; issue EXTINCT in the male line.
JAMES, of whom presently. Samuel.
Catherine, m. to John Vaughan, Esq. of Pembrey.
Eleanor, m. to Griffith Rice, Esq. of Newton.
Mary, m. to Rudderch Gwynne, Esq. of Glanbrane.

The 3rd son,

JAMES JOHNES, Esq. of Llanbadarn-fawr, Cardiganshire, was high-sheriff of that county in 1586. He m. Anne, dau. of John Thomas, Esq. of Cryngae, in Cardiganshire, and Dolaucothy, in Carmarthenshire, and widow of James-Lewis, of Llanbadarn-fawr. By this lady he left (with a dau., Mary, m. to David Lloyd, of Glanswin, in Carmarthenshire) a son,

THOMAS JOHNES, Esq. of Llanbadarn-fawr and Dolaucothy, sheriff of Cardiganshire in 1618, who m. Mary, dau. of James Lewis, Esq. of Abernantbychan, and by her, who m. 2ndly, Rowland Pugh, Esq. of Mathavarn, left a dau., Winifred, the wife of David Lloyd, Esq., and a son,

JAMES JOHNES, Esq. of Dolaucothy, sheriff of Carmarthenshire in 1667, and of Cardiganshire in 1670, who m. 1st, a dau. of Rowland Pugh, Esq. of Mathavarn, and 2ndly, Mary, dau. of Sir John Pryce of Gogerthan. He had issue; the eldest son,

THOMAS JOHNES, Esq. of Dolaucothy, was sheriff of Cardiganshire in 1673. He m. Elizabeth, dau. and heir of Thomas Lloyd, of Llanvairclydoge, and had issue. The eldest son,

THOMAS JOHNES, Esq. of Llanvairclydoge, sheriff of Cardiganshire in 1705, m. Anne, dau. of David Lloyd, of Crynoryn, and had (with two daus., Grace, the wife of Lewis Vaughan, Esq.; and Elizabeth, m. 1st, to Gwyn Williams, of Penpont, and 2ndly, to John Williams, of Edwinsford) a son and successor,

THOMAS JOHNES, Esq. of Llanvairclydoge, who represented Cardiganshire in parliament, from 1713 to 1722. He m. 1st, Jane, dau. and heiress of William Herbert, of Hafodychtryd, and 2ndly, Blanch, dau. of David Van, Esq. of Lanwern, but dying issueless, in 1733, he devised his estates (will dated 28 May, 1733) to his cousin,

THOMAS JOHNES, Esq. of Dolaucothy and Penybont (son of James, and grandson of Thomas Johnes, Esq. of Dolaucothy), who m. Mary-Anne, dau. and co-heir of Jeremiah Powell, of Cwmele, Radnorshire, and had issue,

I. THOMAS, of Llanvairclydoge, and Croft Castle, Herefordshire, M.P. for Radnorshire, m. Elizabeth, dau. and heir of Richard Knight, Esq. of Croft Castle, and had,
  1 THOMAS, of Hafodychtryd, in Cardiganshire, M.P. and lord-lieutenant for Cardiganshire. Mr. Johnes m. 1st, Maria Burgh, of Monmouthshire; and 2ndly, his cousin, Jane, dau. of John Johnes, Esq. of Dolaucothy, but d. without surviving issue, 23 April, 1816, aged 67, his only dau., Maria-Anne, having predeceased him unm.
  2 Samuel, in holy orders, fellow of All Souls', Oxford, and rector of Welwyn, Herts. This gentleman took the surname of KNIGHT. His dau. Louisa, m. to John Shelley, Esq., eldest son of Sir John Shelley, Bart.
  1 Elizabeth, m. to John-Hanbury Williams, Esq.
  2 Anne.
II. JOHN, of whom presently.
I. Elizabeth, m. to John Lewis, Esq.
II. Mary-Anne, m. to John Hughes, Esq. of Tymawr, d. s. p.
III. Grace, d. unm.
IV. Catherine, m. to George Lewis, Esq of Barnesfield, co. Carmarthen.

The 2nd son,

JOHN JOHNES, Esq. of Dolaucothy, m. Jan. 1758, Jane, dau. of Hector Rees, Esq. of Killymaenllwyd, Carmarthenshire, and had issue. Mr. Johnes d. in 1781, and was s. by his son

JOHN JOHNES, Esq. of Dolaucothy, who m. in 1797, Elizabeth, dau. and heir of John Bowen, Esq. of Maes Llanwrthol, and had issue,

JOHN, now of Dolaucothy.
Elizabeth, m. to William Bonville, Esq. of Carmarthen.
Jane, m. to Capt. James Beek.
Mary-Anne, m. to Jeremiah-Walter Lloyd, Esq. of London.
Charlotte, d. unm. in 1836.

Mr. Johnes d. 12 Sept. 1815, and was s. by his son, the present JOHN JOHNES, Esq. of Dolaucothy.

Arms—Arg., a chevron, sa., between three ravens, ppr. within a bordure, invected, gu., bezantée.
Crest—Two battle-axes, saltierwise, sa.
Motto—Deus pascit corvos.
Seat—Dolaucothy, in Carmarthenshire.

JOHNSON OF AYSCOUGH-FEE HALL.

JOHNSON, MAURICE, Esq., B.A., of Ayscough-Fee Hall, Spalding, co. Lincoln, J.P., m. 1841, Elizabeth, only dau. and heir of the Rev. Thomas Mills, M.A., canon of Peterborough, and by her (who d. in 1844) has a dau., ELIZABETH-JOHNSON.

Lineage.—This family derived from the Norman house of FitzJohn, or Johnson, as mentioned by Gwillim, and have been settled at Spalding from an early period. Willus Johnson de Spalding, as appears by the rolls in the Tower, was appointed assessor of the poll-tax, co. Lincoln, A.D. 1381. From him descended,

THOMAS JOHNSON, of Althorpe and Spalding, *temp.* RICHARD III, who m. Alice, dau. and heir of Redhead, of Grimbleby, co. Lincoln, by a dau. and heir of William Atkirke, of Grimbleby, and had issue,

JOHN, from whom descended the JOHNSONS *of Aldborough*, whose eventual heiress, ANNE, only child of SIR HENRY JOHNSON, M.P. for Aldborough, m. Sir Thomas Wentworth, Earl of Strafford.
WILLIAM-HENRY, from whom the JOHNSONS *of Spalding*.

The 2nd son,

WILLIAM-HENRY JOHNSON, m. Eliza de St. Martyn, sister and heir of Geoffrey de St. Martyn, Lord of Aunsby, co. Lincoln, and was father of

MARTYN JOHNSON, Esq., who m. in 1570, a dau. of Atkin, of Sutterton, co. Lincoln, and had issue.

MARTYN JOHNSON, Esq. of Spalding, his eldest son, m. 1st, Ellinor Burton, who d. s. p. in 1609; and m. 2ndly, in 1617, Jane, dau. of George Lynn, Esq. of Southwick Hall, co. Northampton, and had issue. The eldest son,

WALTER JOHNSON, Esq. of Spalding, captain of the train-bands commanded by Robert, Earl of Lindsey (1672), m. 1st, Agnes, dau. of William Willesby, Esq. of Borquery House, and had issue,

I. Martyn, of Spalding, m. Mary, dau. of John Lynn, Esq., and granddau. of Sir Anthony Cade, and had issue,
  Walter, LL.B., rector of Redmarshall, co. Durham, m. Miss Cox, niece of Gen. Williamson, and had issue,
    George, B.D., prebendary of Lincoln, and vicar of Norton, co. Durham, m. Isabella Wilson; and d. in 1786, leaving issue,
      George-Francis, of Southwick Hall, took the name and arms of LYNN.
      Walter, of Star Cross, Devon.
      Robert, of Eastbourne, a commander in the E.I.Co.'s maritime service.
      Elizabeth, m. to Gilbert Crompton, Esq.
      Caroline, m. to the Rev. Charles E. Isham.
      Isabella, m. to Gen. Sir Charles Wale, K.C.B.
      Grace-Martha, m. to Robert Sherard, Esq.
I. Mary, m. 1st, to John Green, Esq. of Dunsby; and 2ndly, to Francis Pilliad, Esq., capt. dragoon-guards.

Mr. Walter Johnson m. 2ndly, Katherine, dau. and heir of William Downes, Esq. of Debenham, co. Suffolk; and d. in 1692, leaving issue, a son,

MAURICE JOHNSON, Esq. of Ayscough-Fee Hall, barrister-at-law, who m. 1st, in 1683, Jane, dau. and co-heir of Francis Johnson, Esq. of Ayscough-Fee Hall son and heir, by a dau. and co-heir of Sir Richard Ogle, Knt., of John Johnson, descended of the JOHNSONS *of Wytham*. Mr. Johnson m. 2ndly, Elizabeth, eldest dau. of Sir Anthony Oldfield, Bart., and widow of Fabian Phillips, Esq.; and 3rdly, Anne, widow of William Gouville Esq. but by neither of these had he any issue. By his 1st wife he left, MAURICE, his heir; and John, barrister-at-law, of Fulney Hall, d. in 1690, unm. The elder son,

MAURICE JOHNSON, Esq., F.A.S., of Ayscough-Fee Hall, barrister-at-law, founder of the Gents. Society, Spalding, deputy-recorder of Stamford, m. Elizabeth, dau. and heir of William Ambler, Esq. of Kirton, and granddau. of Sir

Anthony Oldfield, Bart., and Elizabeth his wife, dau. of Sir Edward Gresham, Knt. of Limpsfield. Mr. Johnson d. in 1755, aged 67, and by his wife (who d. in 1754, aged 65) had issue, twenty-six children. The elder son,

MAURICE JOHNSON, Esq. of Ayscough-Fee Hall, and Stanway Hall, co Essex, colonel of 1st regiment of guards, commanded by the Duke of Cumberland, serving at Dettingen and Culloden, m. 1st, Elizabeth, dau. of Sir Edward Bellamy, lord-mayor of London, which lady d. s. p.; and 2ndly, in 1755, Mary Baker, by whom he had issue,

I. MAURICE, his heir.
II. Walter-Maurice, lieut. 3rd dragoon-guards, afterwards vicar of Weston, m. Frances, dau. of George Foley, Esq. of Boxted Hall, Suffolk, and had issue,
 1 George, lieut. 41st foot, d. at Madras s. p.
 2 William, M.A., vicar of Billesby, d. s. p.
 1 Frances, m. to the Rev. George Osborn, vicar of Stainby, co. Lincoln.
 2 Eliza. 3 Mary-Anne.
I. Mary, d. unm.
II. Elizabeth, m. to Samuel Dinham, Esq.
III. Ann, m. to Fairfax Johnson, Esq.

The eldest son,

THE REV. MAURICE JOHNSON, D.D., of Ayscough-Fee Hall, prebendary of Lincoln, rector of Spalding, and vicar of Moulton, J.P. and D.L., m. Ann-Elizabeth, dau. of Theophilus Buckworth, Esq. of Spalding, and had issue,

I. MAURICE, his heir, M.A., in holy orders, of Moulton, fellow commoner of St. John's College, Cambridge, m. in 1814, Frances, dau. of Beale Post, Esq. of Beddows Place, co. Kent; and d. in 1820, in the lifetime of his father, leaving issue,
 MAURICE JOHNSON, Esq., the present representative.
II. Theophilus-Fairfax, J.P., high-sheriff co. Lincoln in 1847, m. Millicent-Anne, dau. and sole heir of Stephen Moore, Esq., and has issue, Theophilus-Maurice-Stephen.
I. Anne-Elizabeth, m. to the Rev. William Moore, D.D.

Arms—Or, a water-bouget, sa.
Crest—A ducal coronet.
Motto—Onus sub honore.
Seat—Ayscough-Fee Hall.

JOHNSON OF DEANERY.

JOHNSON, EDWARD, Esq. of Deanery, Chester-le-street, co. Durham, J.P., b. 22 March, 1798; m. 29 Oct. 1828, Jane, 3rd dau. of George Atkinson, Esq. of Morland, co. Westmoreland.

Lineage.—FRANCIS JOHNSON, Esq., D.L. b. 9 June, 1748 (eldest surviving son of Francis Johnson, M.D., by Mary, dau. of Jean Huet, of Whickham), m. 6 June 1782, Anne, only child of Robert Cook, Esq. of Low Newton, co. Northumberland, by his 2nd wife, Dorothy, dau. of William Lawson, Esq. of Longhirst, and had issue,

FRANCIS, his heir, now of Low Newton, co. Northumberland, b. 5 Jan. 1784; m. 6 June, 1820, Eleanor, eldest dau. of Charles Bacon, Esq. of Styford.
Robert, b. 21 June, 1785; d. 16 Feb. 1822.
John-Huet, b. 28 July, 1796; d. young.
EDWARD, now of Deanery.
Dorothy. Maria. Sarah.

Arms—Gu., on a chevron, arg., between three savages' heads, ppr., as many pheons.
Crest—A savage's head, couped at the shoulders, bearded and wreathed about the temples, all ppr.
Motto—Nil admirari.
Seat—Deanery, Chester-le-Street, co. Durham.

JOHNSON OF MONKS-FIELDS.

JOHNSON, JAMES-PROUD, A.M., M.D., of Monks-fields, co. Montgomery, and Belmont House, Salop, J.P., b. 14 July, 1784; m. 18 Jan. 1816, Jane, eldest dau. and co-heir of John Simpson, Esq. of Steuhouse, co. Midlothian, and Brounckers Court, Wilts, by Jane Perrott, his wife, and by her has issue,

I. JOHN-SIMPSON, b. 29 June, 1818; m. 13 Aug. 1847, Margaret Windsor.
I. Louisa-Jane. II. Eliza-Jean.
III. Anne-Susannah-Augusta, d. 22 March, 1847.

Doctor Johnson served as high-sheriff for Montgomeryshire in 1836.

Lineage.—JAMES JOHNSON, Esq., son of Richard Johnson, Esq. of Booden Hall, co. Stafford, by Ann his wife, dau. of John Aston, Esq. of Whiston, co. Stafford, m. 1st, Jane Pooler, co-heir of J. Pooler, Esq. of Cooksland, co. Stafford; and 2ndly, in 1781, Susanna, only surviving dau. of Joseph Proud, M.D. of Bilstone, co. Stafford, and Honor Trevor his wife; and by the latter only had issue, besides two sons, who d. infants,

JAMES-PROUD, his heir.
John, lieut. R.N., m. thrice, and has an only dau., Honoria.
Richard-Francis, lieut. R.N., d. in 1811.
William-Proude, lieut. half-pay, 41st regiment, m. twice, and d. 1855, and leaving issue four daus.,
Henry, ensign, Salop militia, d. in 1822.
Ann. Honor, d. 9 Feb. 1851.
Susanna, m. to J.-D. Sheppard, Esq., Hanoverian consul at Glasgow, d. 1841.

Mr. Johnson d. in 1808, and was s. by his eldest son the present JAMES-PROUD JOHNSON, M.D.

Arms—Quarterly: 1st and 4th, arg., a chevron, sa., between three lions' heads, couped, gu., langued, az., ducally crowned, or; 2nd and 3rd, or, a chevron, gu., and three bars, sa., an escutcheon of pretence, arg., on a chief, vert, three crescents, of the first.
Crest—A lion's head, couped, gu., langued, az., ducally crowned, or, between two ostrich feathers, arg.
Motto—Securior quo paratior.
Seat—Monks-fields, co. Montgomery; Brounckers Court, and Belmont House, co. Salop.

JOHNSTON OF SHIELDHALL.

JOHNSTON, ROBERT, Esq. of Shieldhall, resident at Plean House, co. Stirling, b. 17 Oct. 1825; m. 3 Oct. 1848, Eliza, dau. of John Ker, Esq. of Glasgow, and has issue,

HENRY-WILLIAM, b. May, 1852.
Edith-Ker.

Lineage.—The late ALEXANDER JOHNSTONE, Esq., M.P. for the Kilmarnock burghs, m. 1816, Agnes Ronald; and d. 8 May, 1844, leaving issue,

ROBERT, now of Shield Hall.
Alexander, of Corneiston Lanarkshire, m. 1852, Catherine, dau. of William Brown, Esq. of Dundee.
Elizabeth, m. 1841, to Robert Ker, Esq. of Auchenfraith, Lanarkshire.
Rachel, m. 1849, to Walter Paterson, Esq. of Glasgow.

Residence—Plean House, co. Stirling.

JOHNSTON OF CARNSALLOCH.

JOHNSTON, THOMAS-HENRY, Esq. of Carnsalloch, co. Dumfries, J.P., a colonel in the army; s. his mother in 1852.

Lineage.—This is a very ancient branch of the family of Johnston of Johnston, and held, until the latter end of the 16th century, considerable possessions in that district of the county called Annandale. About the year 1560,

ROBERT JOHNSTON alienated the greater part of his Annandale property, and removed to Nithsdale, since which period this district has become their usual abode. He m. Marion Maxwell, a very considerable heiress, and was great-grandfather of

PATRICK JOHNSTON, of Carnsallock, b. 1634; who m. 1669, Jane, dau. of Francis Scott, of Thirlstane, in Selkirkshire, grandfather of Francis, 5th Lord Napier, and had issue. The 4th son,

PATRICK JOHNSTON, b. 1667; m. 1698, Jane, dau of Samuel Brown, a younger brother of Archibald Brown, of Mollanes, Kirkcudbright, and had a dau., Margaret, wife of William Hannay, of Kirkdale, and other issue. The eldest son,

ALEXANDER JOHNSTON, of Carnsalloch, M.P for Kirkcudbright, m. in 1748, Janet, dau. of James Gordon, of Campbellton, Kirkcudbright, and had, with other children, who d. unm.,

I. PETER, his heir.
II. Alexander, b. 10 Nov. 1750; m. 1774, the Hon. Hester-Maria, sole dau. of Francis, 5th Lord Napier, and had,
 1 THE RIGHT HON. SIR ALEXANDER JOHNSTON, heir to his uncle.
 2 Major-Gen. Francis Johnston, C.B., b. 5 Aug. 1776; and d. 5 Jan. 1844.
III Samuel, b. in Feb. 1752; d. in 1798, unm. He was paymaster-general of the forces in the West Indies.
I. Jane-Margaret, b. 1761; m. 1797, Johnston Hannay, Esq. of Balcarry; and d. 6 April, 1836.

He d. 15 Nov. 1775, and was s. by his eldest son,

PETER JOHNSTON, of Carnsalloch, b. 5 Aug. 1749, M P. for Kirkcudbright, one of the Commissioners of Bankruptcy in England; d. at Carnsalloch, 3 Oct. 1837, and was s. by his nephew,

RIGHT HON. SIR ALEXANDER JOHNSTON, of Carnsalloch, b. 25 April, 1775; formerly chief-justice and president of the Council of the Island of Ceylon; m. Louisa, sole surviving dau. of Lord William Campbell, son of John, 4th Duke of Argyll, and by her (who *d.* 7 May, 1852) had issue,

THOMAS-HENRY, now of Carnsalloch.
Patrick-Francis, D.L. of Dumfriesshire, one of H.M. late Commissioners of Charities in England, and subsequently British Commissioner on a Special Mission to Portugal.
Alexander-Robert, late H.M deputy-superintendent and lieut.-governor of the Island of Hong Kong, *m.* 30 Sept. 1856, Frances-Ellen, dau. of the late Richard Bury Palliser, Esq.
Frederick-Erskine, a commander in the Royal navy, *m.* 6 June, 1855, Clementina-Frances, dau. of Rear-Admiral Henry-T.-B. Collier, C.B., and has a son, Alexander-William Campbell, *b.* 8 April, 1856.
Caroline-Hester
Janet-Mary, *d.* 15 Sept. 1846.
Frederica-Maria-Paulina.

Sir Alexander *d.* 6 March, 1849.

Arms—Arg., a saltire, sa., on a chief, gu., three cushions, or, in base, a man's heart, ensigned with an imperial crown, ppr.
Crest—A spur, with wings, or, leather, gu.
Motto—Nunquam non paratus.
Seat—Carnsalloch, co. Dumfries.

M'DOWAL-JOHNSTON OF BALLYWILLWILL.

M'DOWAL-JOHNSTON, THE REV. GEORGE-HENRY, J.P.. of Ballywillwill, co. Down, rector of Donegore and Kilbride, co. Antrim; *m.* 12 March, 1811, Lady Anna-Maria Annesley, 2nd dau. of Richard, Earl of Annesley, which lady *d. s. p.* 20 March, 1835.

Lineage.—RICHARD M'DOWALL JOHNSTON, Esq., son of WILLIAM JOHNSTON, Esq. of Netherlaw Park, co. Kirkcudbright (whose sister *m.* Captain, subsequently Colonel, James M'Dowal, son of Colonel John M'Dowal, and Janet Ross his wife, sister of the Countess of Stair), assumed the surname and arms of M'DOWAL, in compliance with the will of his uncle, Colonel James M'Dowal, who bequeathed him the estates of Gyllespie and Craignargit, co. Galloway. He *m.* Jane Crooks, and had two sons, WILLIAM, his heir; and Henry, *d.* young. He *d.* in 1772, and was *s.* by his son, WILLIAM M'DOWAL-JOHNSTON, Esq. of Ballywillwill, who *m.* in Nov. 1768, Rebecca, dau. of the Rev. George Vaughan, rector of Dromore, co. Down (whose father, John Vaughan, and grandfather, George Vaughan, had been rectors of the same place; and *d.* in 1784, leaving a son and heir, the present GEORGE-HENRY M'DOWAL-JOHNSTON, of Ballywillwill.

Arms—Quarterly: JOHNSTON and M'DOWAL.
Crests—1st, JOHNSTON; 2nd, M'DOWAL.
Motto—Nunquam non paratus
Seat—Ballywillwill, Castlewellan, co. Down.

JOHNSTON OF FORT JOHNSTON.

JOHNSTON, HENRY-GEORGE, Esq. of Fort Johnston, co. Monaghan, *b.* March, 1799; *m.* 5 Oct. 1820, Maria, dau. of Walter Young, Esq. of Monaghan, and has issue,

I. WALTER, *b.* 5 Oct 1823. II. Henry, *b.* 1 Sept. 1827.
III. William-Young, *b.* 7 April, 1833.
I. Maltida, *m.* to J.-B. Travers, Esq. of the 31st regt.
II. Elizabeth, *m.* to Robert McKinstry, Esq., M.D.
III. Louisa-Martha, *m.* to Edward-W. Lucas, Esq. of Raconnell, co. Monaghan.
IV. Maria-Alicia.

Lineage.—GEORGE JOHNSTON, Esq., son of James Johnston, Esq. of Tullycallick, by Margery his wife, had two sons, John, M D. of Cork; and

THOMAS JOHNSTON, Esq. of Fort Johnston, co. Monaghan, who *m.* 1st, in 1796, Martha, eldest dau. of the Rev. Dr. Hingston, vicar-general of Cloyne, by whom he had, HENRY-GEORGE, now Fort Johnston; Thomas-Hodnet, *d. unm.*; Anne-Matilda, *m.* in 1830, to Nicholas Dunscombe, Esq. of Greaville-place, Cork, grandson of Nicholas Dunscombe, Esq. of Mount Desert, co. Cork; Maria, *m.* to the Rev. Richard-G. Meredith, of Cove, co. Cork. Mr. Johnston *m.* 2ndly, Rosalinda, only dau. of John O'Connell, Esq. of Dublin, and by her had one dau., Rosalinda.

Seat—Fort Johnston, Glasslough, co. Monaghan.

JOHNSTON OF HOLLY PARK.

JOHNSTON, HAMILTON-TRAIL, Esq. of Holly Park, co. Down, J.P., *b.* 1796.

Lineage.—ROBERT JOHNSTON, Esq, *b.* at Gilford Castle, about 1741, only brother of Sir Richard Johnston, Bart., and younger son of Sir William Johnston, of Gilford Castle, co. Down, by Nicholina his wife, dau. of Sir Nicholas Acheson, *m.* 1774, Jane, dau of the Rev. Hamilton Trail, rector of Killinchy, co. Down, by Susannah his wife, dau. of William Hamilton, Esq. of Killyleagh Castle, co. Down, and had, ROBERT, Myrtella, and HAMILTON-TRAIL, living *unm.*

Arms—Arg., a saltire, sa., on a chief, gu., three cushions, or.
Crest—A winged spur.
Motto—Nunquam non paratus.
Seat—Holly Park, Killinchy, co. Down.

JOHNSTON OF MAGHEREMENA CASTLE.

JOHNSTON, JAMES, Esq. of Magheremena Castle. co. Fermanagh, J.P. and D.L., high-sheriff, *b.* 16 Sept. 1817; *m.* 24 May, 1838, Cecilia, dau. of Thomas-Newcomen Edgeworth, Esq. of Kilshrewly, and has issue,

I. ROBERT-EDGEWORTH, *b.* 17 Dec. 1842.
I. Letitia-Marian. II. Rosetta.

Lineage.—This family, originally from Scotland, has been seated in the co. of Fermanagh more than two centuries. The grandfather of the present representative,

CAPT. JOHN JOHNSTONE, left by Anne his wife (*m.* in 1756), one son,

ROBERT JOHNSTONE, Esq., Q.C., who *m.* 14 Oct. 1806, Letitia, dau. of Sir William Richardson, Bart., and dying 15 Aug. 1833, left issue,

I. JAMES, now of Magheremena Castle.
I. Anna-Maria, *m.* to the late George Knox, Esq. of Prehen, co. Londonderry, and has issue,
1 George, *b.* 1834.
1 Letitia. 2 Harriet.
II. Harriette, *m.* to Henry Daniel, Esq. of Auburn, co. Westmeath.

Seat—Magheremena Castle, co. Fermanagh.

JOHNSTONE OF ANNANDALE.

JOHNSTONE-HOPE, JOHN-JAMES, Esq. of Annandale; of Raehills, co. Dumfries, M.P., J.P. and D.L., *b.* 29 Nov. 1796, *m.* 8 July, 1816, Alicia-Anne, eldest dau. of George Gordon, Esq. of Hallhead, co. Aberdeen, by Anne, his wife, dau. of Baird of Newbyth, and has issue,

I. WILLIAM-JAMES, *b.* 1 July, 1819; *m.* 7 Dec. 1841, Hon. Octavia-Sophia-Bosvile Macdonald, youngest dau. of the late Lord Macdonald; and *d.* 17 March, 1850, leaving issue.
II. George-Gordon, late of the 92nd Highlanders, *m.* 1845, Adelaide, dau. of Sir George Sinclair, Bart. of Ulbster, and has issue.
III. John-Charles, in the diplomatic service.
IV. Robert-Gordon, H.E.I.C.S., *m.* 1855, Agnes, dau. of Colonel Swanson, H.E.I.C.S.
V. Charles, lieut. R.N., *d.* 17 June, 1855.
VI. David-Baird, 92nd regiment.
I. Anne-Jemima. II. Lucy-Williamina.
III. Alice, *m* 1845, to Sir Graham Graham-Montgomery, Bart., M.P.

Mr. Hope-Johnstone, who is a claimant of the Annandale peerage, is hereditary keeper of Lochmaben Castle.

Lineage.—SIR WILLIAM JOHNSTON-HOPE, vice-admiral, G.C.B., *b.* 16 Aug. 1766 (youngest son of John Hope-Vere, Esq., who was younger son of the Hon. Charles Hope, 2nd son of Charles, 1st Earl Hopetoun); *m.* 1st, 8 July, 1792, Lady Anne Hope-Johnstone, eldest dau. of James, 3rd Earl of Hopetoun, and by her (who inherited the Annandale estates, and *d* 28 Aug. 1818) had issue,

JOHN-JAMES, of Raehills, M.P.
William-James, rear-admiral R.N., *b.* in 1798; *m.* in 1826, Ellen, eldest dau. of Sir Thomas Kirkpatrick, Bart., and has issue, three daus.
Charles-James, capt. R.N., *b.* 29 Jan. 1801; *m.* 23 April, 1827, Eliza, 3rd dau. of Joseph Wood, Esq.; and *d.* 14 April, 1835, leaving issue, one son and two daus.
George-James, capt. R.N., *b.* 30 July, 1802; *m.* in July, 1826, Maria, dau. of Joseph Ranking, Esq.; and *d.* 1842, leaving issue, one son and two daus.
Elizabeth.
Mary (Hon.), late maid of honour to Queen ADELAIDE, *m.* 3 Feb. 1840, the Hon. and Right Rev. Hugh Percy, Lord Bishop of Carlisle; and *d.* 22 Nov. 1851.

Admiral Johnstone-Hope *m.* 2ndly, 30 Oct. 1821, Maria, Countess Dowager of Athlone, second dau. of the late Sir John Eden, Bart.; and *d.* 2 May, 1831.

Arms—Quarterly: 1st and 4th, arg., a saltier, sa., on a chief, gu., three cushions, or, for JOHNSTONE; 2nd and 3rd, az., on a chevron, or, between three bezants a laurel-leaf, slipped, vert, for HOPE.
Crests—1st, a spur, erect, or, winged, arg., for JOHNSTONE; 2nd, a globe, fractured at the top, under a rainbow, with clouds at each end, all ppr., for HOPE.
Mottoes—At spes non fracta; and, Nunquam non paratus.
Seat—Raehills, co. Dumfries.

JOHNSTONE OF ALVA.

JOHNSTONE, JAMES, Esq. of Alva, co. Clackmannan, and of Hangingshaw, co. Selkirk, *b.* 4 July, 1801, D.L. of the cos. of Clackmannan, Stirling, and Selkirk, M.P. for the cos. of Clackmannan and Kinross; *m.* 9 Jan. 1846, the Hon. Augusta-Anne Norton, sister of Lord Grantley, by whom he has issue,

I. AUGUSTUS-JOHN-JAMES, *b.* 3 May, 1847.
I. Caroline-Mary-Elizabeth.

Lineage.—The JOHNSTONES of Westerhall, are descended from MATTHEW JOHNSTONE, son, of Sir Adam Johnstone, who *d.* 1455, by his 2nd wife, Lady Janet Dunbar, dau. of George, 11th Earl of March, and widow of Lord Seton. From Sir Adam's son, by his 1st marriage, descended the MARQUESSES OF ANNANDALE.

On the death of George, 3rd Marquess of Annandale, in 1792, the Baronet of Westerhall became head of the family of Johnstone, and claimant of the dormant marquessate. This claim is still before the House of Lords.

Matthew Johnstone *d.* in 1491, and from him descended a long line of knights of Westerhall, who intermarried with the families of Douglas, Earl of Angus, Somerville of Camnethan, Oliphant, Lord Oliphant, Scott of Harden, Bannatyne of Corehouse.

SIR WILLIAM JOHNSTONE, 2nd baronet of Westerhall, who *d.* in 1728, had by his wife, Henrietta Johnstone, of Warriston, two sons, JAMES, his heir; and John, a colonel in the army, who *d.* in 1743, and by his wife, Charlotte, Dowager Marchioness of Annandale (mother of the late marquess), a dau. and heiress of John-Vanden Bempdè, had issue, a son, who, in 1792, inherited the great Vanden-Bempdè fortune of his half-brother, the marquess, was created a Baronet, and was father of Sir John-V.-B. Johnstone, Bart. of Hackness. Sir William was *s.* by his eldest son,

SIR JAMES JOHNSTONE, 3rd baronet of Westerhall, who *m.* the Hon. Barbara Murray, dau. of Alexander, 4th Lord Elibank, by whom he had,

JAMES (Sir), 4th baronet.
WILLIAM (Sir), 5th baronet.
George, who carried on the line of the family, and was father of SIR JOHN, 6th baronet.
JOHN, of whom hereafter, as ancestor to the Alva branch.
Barbara, wife of Charles, 6th Lord Kinnaird, mother of the 7th lord.
Margaret, wife of David, Lord Ogilvie, mother of David, Earl of Airlie, and of Lady Margaret, wife of Sir John Wedderburn, Bart. of Ballendean.
Charlotte, wife of J. Balmain, and maternal grandmother to Lord Grantley, and to the Hon. Mrs. Johnstone, of Alva.

Sir James Johnstone *d.* 1772, and was *s.* by his eldest son, Sir James, who, dying *unm.*, was *s.* by his brother, Sir William, 5th bart. of Westerhall. He was for many years a distinguished member of parliament, and acquired an immense fortune by his wife, Frances Pulteney, dau and heir of Daniel Pulteney, cousin and heir of the Earl of Bath. Sir William assumed the surname of Pulteney. He had an only child, Henrietta-Laura Johnstone-Pulteney, created COUNTESS OF BATH, and *d.* in 1808, without issue by her husband, Gen. Sir James Murray, Bart. Sir William Johnstone-Pulteney having no male issue, was *s.* in the Johnstone title, estates, and claim to the Annandale marquessate, by his nephew, SIR JOHN-LOWTHER JOHNSTONE, 6th baronet, grandfather of the present Sir Frederick, 8th baronet of Westerhall, a minor.

The 4th son of Sir James Johnstone and the Hon. Barbara Murray was

JOHN JOHNSTONE, *b.* 28 April, 1734, who held important appointments in India in the service of the East India Company. He commanded the artillery at the battle of Plassy in 1757, and by his skilful management, contributed to that victory. He *m.* Elizabeth-Caroline, dau. of Colonel Keene, and niece to Dr. Keene, bishop of Ely, and Sir Benjamin Keene, British minister at the Court of Spain. He purchased the estates of Alva, Hangingshaw, and others, in Scotland and was for some years in parliament. He *d.* at Alva, in Dec. 1795, and left, with a dau., Elizabeth, wife of James Gordon, of Craig, an only son and successor,

JAMES-RAYMOND JOHNSTONE, of Alva, who *m.* 20 June, 1799, Mary-Elizabeth, sister of Sir Montague Cholmeley, Bart. of Easton, co. Lincoln, and had,

JAMES, his successor.
John, *b.* 1802; a colonel H.E.I.C.S.; *m.* Caroline, dau. of the Rev. Pannel, by whom he had a dau., Mary-Elizabeth. Colonel Johnstone perished with half of his regiment in the Indian seas, in May, 1854.
Montague-Cholmeley, *b.* 1804; a major-general; *m.* Louisa, dau. of Gen. Sir Henry Somerset, and granddau. of Lord Charles Somerset, by whom he has issue, three sons and a dau.
George-Dempster, *b.* 1805; in holy orders; *m.* Mary-Anne Hawkins, of Bignor, in Sussex, niece of Sir Christopher Hawkins, and Colonel Sibthorp, of Canwick, by whom he has issue, a son, Herbert, and another son and dau.
Charles-Kinnaird, *b.* 1806; capt. in the E.I.Co.'s navy, knight of the Persian Order of the Lion and Sun; *m.* Elizabeth, only dau. of Francis Gordon, of Craig, by whom he has issue, four daus.
Henry-Wedderburn, *b.* 1810; captain R.N.
Robert-Abercrombie, in holy orders, *b.* 1811; *m.* Anne Walker, without issue.
Francis-William, *b.* 1818; a capt. in the army; *m.* Maria Mahoney, by whom he has issue, several children.
Elizabeth-Caroline, *m.* 23 June, 1829, the Rev. John-Hamilton Gray, of Carntyne, co. of Lanark. She has an only dau., who *m.* 1852, John-Anstruther Thomson, of Charleton, in the co. of Fife. Mrs. Hamilton Gray has acquired distinguished literary reputation by her historical works.
Emily-Sarah.
Mary-Anne, *m.* 1839, James Dewar, and has issue.
Catherine-Lucy.
Sophia-Matilda, *m.* 1832, Sir John-Muir Mackenzie, Bart. of Delvine, Perthshire, who *d.* Feb. 1855, by whom she has issue SIR ALEXANDER, the present bart. of Delvine, five other sons, and three daus.
Jemima-Eleanora, *m.* Feb. 1848, Lord Frederick Beauclerk, of Grimsby Hall, in the co. of Lincoln, 2nd son of William, 8th Duke of St. Albans, by whom she has issue, two sons, Nelthorp and Frederick.
Mary-Cecilia, *m* May, 1837, the Hon. Laurence Harman-King, 2nd son of Viscount Lorton. He has assumed the surname of HARMAN on succeeding to his grandmother, the Countess of Rosse's estates of Newcastle, in the co. of Longford. By him she has issue, Edward, an officer in the army; Wentworth; Frances; and other sons and daus.
Charlotte-Octavia, *m.* 1845, James-Harrison Cholmeley, a major in the army, 2nd son of Sir Montague Cholmeley, Bart. of Easton, co. Lincoln, who *d.* in 1854.

Mr. Johnstone *d.* at Alva April, 1830, and was *s.* by his eldest son, JAMES JOHNSTONE, now of Alva and Hangingshaw.

Arms—Arg., a saltire, sa., on a chief, gu., three woolpacks, or, in base a man's heart, ppr., royally crowned, or.
Crest—A spur, with wings, or, leather, gu.
Motto—Nunquam non paratus.
Seats—Alva House, co. Clackmannan; Hangingshaw, co. Selkirk.

JOHNSTONE OF MAINSTONE COURT.

JOHNSTONE, JOHN, Esq. of Mainstone Court, co. Hereford, J.P. (3rd son of Charles Johnstone, Esq. of Ludlow, by Mary his wife, dau. of John Beddoe, Esq., and nephew of the 1st Sir Richard Vanden Bempde-Johnstone, Bart. of Hackness), *b.* 16 March, 1784; *m.* 14 Sept. 1813, Agnes, only child and heiress of the late Rev. John Hutton, of Burton, co. Westmoreland, and had surviving issue,

I. GEORGE-HENRY, *b.* 20 Dec. 1818, and in holy orders.
II. Geoffrey, *b.* 8 Aug. 1823.
III. Charles-Octavius, *b.* 11 Aug. 1827.
IV. Robert-Bruce, *b.* 8 Sept. 1829.
I. Louisa-Rebecca. II. Anna.

Arms—Arg., a saltier, sa., in base, a human heart, ensigned with a regal crown, or, on a chief, gu., three woolpacks of the third.
Crest—A winged spur, erect, or, straps, gu., buckle, arg.
Motto—Nunquam non paratus.
Seat—Mainstone Court, near Ledbury, co. Hereford.

JOHNSTONE OF GALABANK.

JOHNSTONE, EDWARD, Esq. of Edgbaston Hall, co. Warwick, barrister-at-law.

Lineage.—EDWARD JOHNSTONE (2nd son of John Johnstone, of Galabank, by Janet his wife, dau. of Thomas Kirkpatrick, of Auldgirth, and grandson, by his wife, Agnes Graham, of Dumfries, of George Johnstone, whose father, John Johnstone, of Mylnefield, purchased, in 1625, the lands of Galabank, in Annan, N.B.), m. Isabella Carlisle, and had two sons, JOHN and Edward The younger, Edward, was a merchant in London, and d. s. p The elder,

JOHN JOHNSTONE, s. as Laird of Galabank. He was b. 30 Aug 1688; and m. 1712, Anna Ralston, and had issue,

Edward, A.M., minister of Moffat, d. s. p. 1761.
JAMES, heir to his father.
Isabella, m. to John Murray, Esq.

Mr. Johnstone d. 12 Oct. 1774, and was s. by his son,

JAMES JOHNSTONE, M.D. of Galabank, b. 14 April, 1730; who m. in 1753, Hannah, dau. of Henry Crane, Esq. of Kidderminster, and had issue,

I. James, M.D., d. unm. in 1783, of jail fever at Worcester.
II. Thomas, A.M., rector of Aston Bottevil, who m. Sarah Hale, and left an only surviving dau., Catherine.
III. EDWARD, of Edgbaston Hall.
IV. Henry, lieut.-colonel in the army, d. unm.
V. John, M.D., F.R.S., of Monument House, Edgbaston, Warwickshire, and of Galabank, b. 22 Oct. 1768; m. 26 Dec. 1809, Anna-Delicia, only dau. of Capt. George Curtis, and niece of Sir William Curtis, Bart. By this lady he left at his decease, in 1837, two daus., viz.,
  1 ANNA-DELICIA, m. 4 June, 1829, to the Rev. Walter-Farquhar Hook, A M., vicar of Holy Trinity, Coventry.
  2 AGNES-MARY, m. 24 June, 1834, to the Rev. Henry Clarke, A.M., rector of Cofton Hacket.
VI. Lockhart, bencher of Lincoln's Inn, m. Miss Eliza Green, of Poole, and has two sons and two daus., viz., John, a physician at New York; William, in the E.I.Co.'s military service; Anna; and Janet.
I. Mary.

Dr. Johnstone d. 28 April, 1802. His 3rd son,

EDWARD JOHNSTONE, Esq., M.D. of Edgbaston Hall, co. Warwick, m. 1st, Catherine-Letitia, dau. of the Rev. Thomas Wearden, and heiress maternally of the family of Holden, of Erdington, in the same shire, and has by her one dau., Catharine. He m. 2ndly, Elizabeth, dau. of Thomas Pearson, M.D., of Tittenhal, and had two sons,

EDWARD, of Edgbaston.
James, M.D., m. Maria-Mary Payne, dau. of Joseph Webster, Esq. of Penns, and has one dau., Maria-Mary.

Arms—Arg., a saltier, sa., on a chief, gu., three cushions, or.
Crest—A spur, with wings, or, leather, gu.
Mottoes—Nunquam non paratus; and, I make sure.
Seat—Edgbaston Hall, near Birmingham.

JOHNSTONE OF SNOW HILL.

JOHNSTONE, JOHN-DOUGLAS, Esq. of Snow Hill, co. Fermanagh, and of the co. Tyrone, b. 5 Aug. 1839.

Lineage.—This family of Johnstone claims (as descended in the male line) the honours of the noble house of Annandale.

WILLIAM JOHNSTONE, Esq., who settled in Ireland, m. Prudence, dau. of William Goodfellow, Esq. of co. Derry, and had one son,

JAMES JOHNSTONE, Esq. of the co. Fermanagh, who m. Joanna, dau. of Gunnis, Esq. of co. Donegal, and (with a younger son, Christopher, surgeon of the 17th lancers, who was father of Christopher Johnstone, col. of the 8th hussars) had an elder son and heir,

JAMES JOHNSTONE, Esq. of Snow Hill, who m. Anne, dau. of John Johnstone, Esq. of Adragoold House, co. Leitrim, and had issue,

JOHN-DOUGLAS, his successor.
Andrew, lieut. 8th hussars, d. unm. at Calcutta, in 1810.
Margaret, m. 1st, to Capt. W. Johnston, of the 63rd regt.; and 2ndly, to Gilbert Burrington, Esq.
Mary, m. to Francis Lloyd, Esq., eldest son of George Lloyd, Esq. of Mount Catharine, co. Limerick.

Mr. Johnstone d. in 1808, and was s. by his elder son and heir,

JOHN-DOUGLAS JOHNSTONE, Esq. of Snow Hill, b. in May, 1769; m. in 1798, Sammina, youngest dau. of Samuel Yates, Esq. of Moone Abbey, co. Kildare, and had issue,

JAMES-DOUGLAS, b. in 1803, m. in 1828, Charlotte, eldest dau. of John Devereux, Esq. of Ballyrankin House, co. Wexford, major Wexford militia, and d. 3 Aug. 1840, leaving a dau., Samina-Maria, and an only son, the present JOHN-DOUGLAS JOHNSTONE, Esq. of Snow Hill.
Richard-Gosford, b. in 1807, d. in Upper Canada, in April, 1840.
John-Douglas, b. in 1809, lieut.-col. 83rd regt., C.B., served through the campaign in the Crimea, and lost an arm at the first attack on the Redan, 18 June, 1855; m. 1830, Caroline, eldest dau. of the Rev. A. O'Beirne, D.D., and has a son, John-Douglas, lt. 83rd regt., b. 1833, and two daus., Samina and Caroline.
Fairholme, d. in 183?.
Samuel-Yates, b. in 1815, barrister-at-law.
Catherine, d. unm.
Anna-Douglas, m. 1837, to her cousin, Francis-Bateman Lloyd, Esq.
Samina, m. 1829, to William Worthington, Esq., eldest son of the late Sir William Worthington, of the city of Dublin, lord-mayor 1795-6.

Mr. Johnstone d. Nov. 1842.

Arms—Arg., a saltier, sa., on a chief, gu., three cushions, or.
Crest—A winged spur, ppr.
Motto—Nunquam non paratus.
Seat—Snowhill, co. Fermanagh.

JOLIFFE OF AMMERDOWN PARK.

JOLIFFE, THE REV. THOMAS-ROBERT, of Ammerdown Park, co. Somerset, J.P. and D.L.; s. his brother in 1854.

Lineage.—The family of Joliffe, originally Joli, is of considerable antiquity in the counties of Stafford and Worcester, and the pedigree, in possession of the senior members, comprises intermarriages with many eminent and noble houses. One branch, established in the North, enjoyed, it appears, from authentic records, power and affluence, even before the institution in Europe of hereditary honours.

JOHN JOLIFFE, Esq. (3rd son of Benjamin Joliffe, Esq. of Cofton Hall, co. Worcester, and grandson of Thomas Joliffe, Esq. of Cofton, by Margaret his wife, dau. of Richard Skinner, Esq., by Margaret his wife, dau. of Edward Lyttelton, Esq.), represented the borough of Petersfield in parliament, anno 1763. He m. 1st, Katherine, dau. of Robert Mitchell, Esq. of Petersfield, but had no issue. He m. 2ndly, Mary, dau. and heiress of Samuel Holden, Esq. of London, by whom he had,

WILLIAM, M.P., who m. Eleanor, dau. and heiress of Sir Richard Hylton, Bart. (formerly Musgrave) of Hayton Castle, in Cumberland, and was s. by his eldest son,
  THE REV. WILLIAM JOLIFFE, who m. Julia, dau. of Sir Abraham Pytches, Knt. of Streatham, and was s. at his decease by his eldest son, the present SIR WILLIAM-GEORGE-HYLTON JOLIFFE, Bart.
THOMAS-SAMUEL, of whom presently.

Mr. Joliffe was s. at his decease, in 1771, by his son,

THOMAS-SAMUEL JOLIFFE, Esq., M.P. for Petersfield, who m. in 1778, Mary-Anne, dau. and heir of the Rev. Robert Twyford, of Kilmersdon, co. Somerset, and had issue,

JOHN-TWYFORD, his heir.
THOMAS-ROBERT, now of Ammerdown Park.
Charles, an officer in the army, who fell at Waterloo, honourable mention is made of his conduct as an officer.
Mary-Anne.

Mr. Joliffe d. 6 June, 1824, at the close of the 78th year of his age, and was s. by his elder son,

JOHN-TWYFORD JOLIFFE, Esq of Ammerdown Park, who d. deeply lamented, 1854, and was s. by his only surviving brother, the present REV. THOMAS-ROBERT JOLIFFE, of Ammerdown Park.

Arms—Arg., on a pile, az., three dexter gauntlets, of the field.
Crest—A cubit arm, erect, vested and cuffed, the sleeve charged with a pile, arg., the hand grasping a sword, ppr.
Seat—Ammerdown Park, near Bath.

JONES OF FONMON CASTLE.

JONES, ROBERT-OLIVER, Esq. of Fonmon Castle, co. Glamorgan, J.P., high-sheriff 1838, b. 16 Dec. 1811; m. 1st, 13 Sept. 1843, Alicia, dau. of Evan Thomas, Esq. of Llwynmadoc, co. Brecon, and Sully, co. Glamorgan, and by her (who d. 1 April, 1851) has surviving issue,

OLIVER-HENRY, b. 7 Jan. 1846.
Edith-Alicia.

He m. 2ndly, 30 Aug. 1853, Sarah-Elizabeth, 3rd dau. of John-Bruce Pryce, Esq. of Duffryn, co. Glamorgan.

Lineage.—COL. PHILIP JONES, M.P. for Glamorgan and Brecon, governor of Swansea and Cardiff, and one of OLIVER CROMWELL's privy council, purchased the estate of

Fonmon Castle from the Earl of Bolingbroke. Col. Jones, who was descended from a son of Bethin ap Maenarch, the last Lord of Brecon, was one of those called to the Upper House by CROMWELL. After the Restoration, he served as high-sheriff of the county: he left, by Jane Pryce his wife, of the family of Pryce of Gellyher and Courtcarney, in Gower, a son and heir,

OLIVER JONES, Esq. of Fenmon Castle, who *m.* Mary Button, of Duffryn, and was father of

ROBERT JONES, Esq. of Fonmon Castle, M.P. for co. Glamorgan, who *d.* 1 GEORGE I., leaving, by Mary his wife, dau. of Sir Humphrey Edwin, of Llanfihangel, co. Glamorgan, two sons and three daus., all of whom *d. s. p.*, except the eldest,

ROBERT JONES, Esq. of Fonmon Castle, who *m.* Mary Forrest, of Minehead, co. Somerset, and had (with four daus., viz., Mary, *m.* to William Thomas, Esq. of Llanbradock; Charlotte, *m.* 1st, to Thomas Ashby, Esq. of London, 2ndly, to the Hon. Col. Maude, and 3rdly, to C. Edwin, Esq. of Dunraven Castle, co. Glamorgan; Diana, *m.* to Thomas Matthews, Esq. of Landaff and Bath; and Catherine, *m.* to John Coghlan, Esq. of Bristol), an only son and heir,

ROBERT JONES, Esq. of Fonmon Castle, who *m.* 1st, Jane, heiress of the Rev. Evan Seys, of Boverton Place, co. Glamorgan, and by her had two daus., who *d.* young. He *m.* 2ndly, April, 1770, Joanna, dau. of Edmund Lloyd, Esq. of Cardiff, and by her (who *d.* 1812) had issue,

I. ROBERT, his heir.
II. Oliver-Thomas, *b.* 8 Sept. 1776, major-gen. in the army, and lieut.-col. of the 18th hussars, which regiment he commanded under Sir John Moore, in the Peninsula, *m.* 1st, Louisa, dau. and heiress of Col. Stanley, of Lincolnshire, and by her (who *d.* 28 Jan. 1810) had two daus., Louisa, *d. unm.*; and Laura-Anne, *m.* to the Rev. William Annesley, 3rd son of the Rev. Arthur Annesley, of Clifford Chambers, co Warwick. Gen. Jones *m.* 2ndly, 20 Feb. 1811, Maria-Antonia, youngest dau. of the late Henry Swinburne, Esq. of Hamsterly Hall, co. Durham, and granddau. of Sir John Swinburne, Bart. of Capheaton, co. Northumberland, and by this lady had issue,
  1 ROBERT-OLIVER, successor to his uncle, and present proprietor.
  2 Oliver-John, capt. R N., *b.* 15 March, 1813.
  1 Rosa-Antonia, *m.* 1838, Rev. John Cholmley.
  Major-Gen. Jones *d.* 15 Nov. 1815.
III. John, *b.* in Oct. 1782, capt. E. I. Co.'s service, *m.* Cordelia Ferguson, and *d.* Oct. 1820, leaving two daus., Anna, *m.* to James Wapshare, Esq., and Joanna.
I. Mary, *m.* to the Rev. J.-T. Casberd, D.C.L.
II. Diana, *m.* 6 Nov. 1810, to John Richards, Esq. of co. Glamorgan.
III. Charlotte, *d.* in 1839.
IV. Anna, *m.* to Frederick Villebois, Esq. of Adbury Lodge, and Benham Place, Berks, and *d. s. p.* in 1840.

Mr. Jones was *s.* by his eldest son,

ROBERT JONES, Esq. of Fonmon Castle, *b.* in Nov. 1773, who *d. unm.* in 1834, and was *s.* by his nephew, the present ROBERT-OLIVER JONES, Esq. of Fonmon Castle.

Arms—Quarterly: 1st, sa., a chevron, arg., between three spear heads, arg., the points embrued with blood; 2nd, arg., a wivern's head, erased, vert, holding in its mouth a dexter hand, gu.; 3rd, gu., a chevron, erm.; 4th, arg., a stag, couchant, gu., the horns and hoofs, or, holding in its mouth a branch, vert.

Crest—A cubit arm, erect, in armour, ppr., in the gauntlet a spear of the first, headed, arg., embrued, gu.

Motto—

Seat—Fonmon Castle, co. Glamorgan.

JONES OF GWYNFRYN.

JONES, WILLIAM-TILSLEY, Esq. of Gwynfryn, co. Cardigan, J.P. and D.L., *b.* 18 July, 1782; *m.* 8 March, 1821, Christiana, dau. of the late Henry Tickell, Esq. of London, and Leytonstone, co. Essex, and had issue,

I. WILLIAM-BASIL. II. Everard-Whiting.
I. Dorothea. II. Catherine-Emily.

Mr. Jones, son of William Jones, Esq. of Gwynfryn, by Mary his wife, dau. of the Rev. William Tilsley, grandson of William Jones, Esq., by Jane his wife, dau. and co-heir of Evan Watkins, Esq., and great-grandson of William Jones, by his wife, a dau. of John Griffith, Esq. of Penpompren; served as high-sheriff in 1838.

Arms—Arg., a cross-moline, sa., between four Cornish choughs, ppr.

Crest—A demi-lion, rampant.

Motto—Mors mihi lucrum.

Seat—Gwynfryn, co. Cardigan.

JONES OF GURREY.

JONES, GRIFFITH-BOWEN, Esq. of Gurrey, co. Carmarthen, J.P., *b.* Jan. 1793.

Lineage.—WILLIAM JONES, Esq. of Cilsane, *b.* in 1765, J.P. and D.L. for Carmarthenshire, *m.* Anne, dau. and co-heir of Griffith Bowen, Esq. of Gurrey, whose mother, the only dau. and heir of Marmaduke Lloyd, was great-granddau. of Sir Marmaduke Lloyd, of Maesfelin, one of the judges of the Brecon Circuit, and had issue,

I. WILLIAM-WALTER, *b.* in 1791, who *m.* in 1815, Sarah, dau. of John Place, Esq. of Caddiston, near Neath, and *d. vitâ patris*, 18 June, 1828, leaving issue,
  1 WILLIAM-PLACE, *b.* 12 March, 1823, who *m.* in Oct. 1844, Susannah-Amelia, dau. of the Hon. Admiral Gardner, 2nd son of the 1st Lord Gardner.
  1 Frances-Sarah-Place, *m.* 29 June, 1836, to Richard Ouseley, Esq., major 50th Bengal army, and governor of Burghagur, 3rd son of Sir William Ouseley, Knt.
II. GRIFFITH-BOWEN, now of Gurrey.
I. Anne, who *m.* 13 Oct. 1824, James Thomas, Esq. of Mount Pleasant, and *d.* 24 May, 1844, leaving issue,
  1 James-William-Bowen Thomas, *b.* 12 Sept. 1828.
  2 Edward-Griffith-Bowen Thomas, 1st lieut. R. W. fusiliers, *b.* 19 Dec. 1831, *d.* 15 Nov. 1854.
  1 Anne, *m.* 4 Nov. 1847, to Henry Bedwell, Esq.
  2 Maria-Theresa.

Seat—Gurrey, co. Carmarthen.

JONES OF LLWYNON.

See JONES-PARRY.

JONES OF HARTSHEATH.

JONES, WILSON, Esq. of Hartsheath, co. Flint, of Cefn Coch, co. Denbigh, and of Gelli Gynan, in the same co., J.P. and D.L., high-sheriff of Denbighshire 1831; *b.* 3 July, 1795; *m.* 14 May, 1822, Cecil, dau. of the late John Carstairs, of Warboys, co. Huntingdon, Esq., F.R.S. and D.C.L., and had issue,

I. JOHN-CARSTAIRS. II. Hugh-Maurice.
III. Wilson-Henry. IV. Alexander-Fair.
I. Cecil-Elizabeth. II. Elizabeth-Jane.
III. Margaret-Helen. IV. Johanna.

Mr. Jones was twice elected M.P. for Denbigh, and retired from parliament in 1831.

Lineage.—The lineage of this family is deduced from COWRYD AP CADVAN, a chieftain of Dyffryn Clwyd, in Denbighland.

MAURICE JONES, Esq. of Cefn Coch, co. Denbigh, and Gelli Gynan (only child of Hugh ap John, of Ddol, co. Merioneth, who first assumed the surname of JONES, and was descended in a direct line from David ap Cowryd ap Cadvan, of Dyffryn Clwyd), *m.* Catherine, dau and heiress of Peter Williams, of Bala, co. Merioneth, Esq., and had issue. The eldest son,

JOHN JONES, Esq. of Cefn Coch and Gelli Gynan, who *m.* Elizabeth, dau. and heiress of Edward Wilson, of Liverpool, Esq., and by her (who *m.* 2ndly, William-M. Thackeray, of Chester, M.D., had issue,

WILSON, of Hartsheath. John-Maurice, *d.* in 1813.
Elizabeth, *m.* John Heaton, of Plas Heaton, co. Denbigh, Esq., and *d.* in 1822, leaving issue.

Mr. Jones *d.* in 1797.

Arms—Arg., a chevron between three boars' heads, couped, gu.

Crest—A boar's head, couped, gu.

Motto—Heb nevol nerth, nid sicr saeth: "Without help from above the arrow flies in vain."

Seats—Hartsheath, co Flint, and Cefn Coch, co. Denbigh.

JONES OF LLANARTH COURT.

See HERBERT.

JONES OF LLANERCHRUGOG HALL.

JONES, THOMAS, Esq. of Llanerchrugog Hall, co. Denbigh, and Old Marton Hall, co. Salop, *b.* 27 July,

1781; m. 1 Aug. 1814, Frances-Esther, only dau. of Charles Morrall, Esq. of Kilhendre Park, and Plas Iolyn, Shropshire, by Frances his wife, sister and heiress of William Challnor, Esq. of Plas Iolyn, and by her (who d. 8 March, 1843) had issue,

I. THOMAS barrister-at-law.
II. William-Charles-Hussey, m. 25 Nov. 1854, Helen, dau. of Dr. Bernays, of King's College.
III. Henry m. 10 Aug. 1854, Elizabeth-Rebecca, dau. of William Taylor, Esq. of Humberston Lodge, co. Leicester.
IV. John-Morrall.
I. Emily.

Lineage.—This very ancient family, descended, in direct paternal line, through EDNOWAIN BENDEW, one of the Fifteen Noble Tribes of North Wales, from Gwaithvoed, Lord of Cardigan and Gwent, A.D. 921, and the Pendragons and kings of the Britons, was allied, throughout many ages, with some of the most ancient houses in Wales and Shropshire.

ROBERT AP IORWARTH AP RIRID AP IORWARTH AP MADOC AP EDNOWAIN BENDEW lived in 1339; his brother, Gwyn, in 1313 (witness to deed). Ithel Vychan ap Kenrick, grandson of Robert, m. Angharad, dau. and heiress of Robert ap Howel, of Holt (of the great house of Gwydir). The Anglicised name of Jones (originally "ap John" and "Jones de Chilton," in the Visitation of Shropshire, 1623) was first borne by his great-grandson, Richard, 6th son of John, son of Kenrick, 3rd son of Ithel Vychan. Richard, son of William, son of Richard, was of Chilton, near Shrewsbury, which remained a family seat for several centuries (till 1816). The heads of the Llanerchrugog family, in four successive generations, m. daus. of the neighbouring houses of Llwynon, Eyton of Eyton, and Watstay (since called Wynnstay, on being left to Sir John Wynn, ancestor of Sir W.-W. Wynn), Erthig of Erthig, and Trevor of Trevor. Llanerchrugog Hall has been a seat of the family from time immemorial—at least two generations before 1459. The present Mr. Jones is the fourteenth in succession from "Dio of Llanerchrugog." Old Marton Hall is also a very ancient mansion. In one of the rooms there is a dais for the seat of the head of the house. The black lion of the princes of Powys appears, as the Old Marton arms, in a very ancient Old Marton pedigree painted on vellum in the possession of the family.

RICHARD JONES, Esq., b. 1711 (son of John Jones, who was b. 1667, and d. 1733), m. Margaret, eldest dau. of Richard Higgons, Esq. of The Leasowes, co. Salop (descended from the very ancient Shropshire families of Higgons, or Hugons, Maddocks, Wycherley, &c.), and sister of William Higgons, Esq. of Llanerchrugog, who, by Mary his wife, widow of William Pennant, Esq., and dau. and heir of John Payne, Esq., had an only child, Elizabeth Higgons, who d. unm. 19 April, 1811. The son and heir of Richard Jones and Margaret Higgons his wife,

WILLIAM JONES, Esq. of Llanerchrugog Hall and Old Marton Hall, b. 5 May, 1752; m. Georgiana, dau. and heir of Thomas Wood, Esq. of Goodnestone Kent, by Rebecca his wife, dau. of the Rev. Mr. Howley, and aunt of William Howley, D.D., archbishop of Canterbury. By this lady (who was b. 4 Aug. 1757, and d. 19 Sept. 1823) he had three daus., Rebecca, d. unm. 1828; Charlotte; and Lucretia, d. unm. 1828; and one son, the present THOMAS JONES, Esq. of Llanerchrugog Hall.

Arms—Arg., a lion rampant, vert, vulned in the shoulder, gu. (otherwise; mouth imbrued, gu.)
Crests—1. A sun in splendour, or. 2. On an eastern crown a dragon, passant, guardant.
Mottoes—Virtutis præmium felicitas; and also, Esto sol testis.
Seat—Llanerchrugog Hall, co. Denbigh

JONES OF NASS.

JONES, EDWARD-OWEN, Esq. of Nass, co. Gloucester, J.P. and D.L., Knight of St. Ferdinand of Spain, b. 19 Oct. 1808; m. 14 Oct. 1840, Catherine-Sophia, dau. of John Fortescue-Brickdale, Esq. of Birchamp House, co. Gloucester, and by her has issue,

I. WILLIAM-CHARLES-NIGEL, b. 30 Jan. 1849.
II. Edward-Cholmeley, b. 30 Jan. 1852.
I. Catherine-Elizabeth.
II. Frances-Alice.
III. Isabel-Mary.

Lineage.—This is a family of considerable antiquity, and one of long standing in Gloucestershire.

ROYNON JONES, Esq. who m. Anne dau. and co-heir of Edward Cooke, of Highnam Court, co. Gloucester, was father, by her, of WILLIAM JONES, Esq., who m. Cholmeley, dau. of Sir John D'Oyly, Bart., and had a son, ROYNON JONES, Esq., who m. his cousin, Mary Jones, and was s. by his son,

EDWARD JONES, Esq. of Nass, who m. 12 Sept. 1814, Elizabeth, dau. of the Rev. Edward Owen, of Ty Gwyn, co. Merioneth; and d. 3 May, 1847, having issue,

Roynon, b. 4 Oct. 1806; d. 17 Nov. 1835. He was in the rifle-brigade.
EDWARD-OWEN, now of Nass.
William-Wynn, b. 13 Aug. 1813; an officer of the horse-artillery. He d. 14 May, 1843.
Mary-Elizabeth, m. 18 Oct. 1849, to the Rev. Henry Wood, rector of Boroughbridge, Somersetshire.
Emma-Diana.

Seat—Nass, near Lydney.

JONES OF PANTGLAS.

JONES, DAVID, Esq. of Pantglâs, co. Carmarthen, J.P. and D.L., M.P. for Carmarthenshire, and high-sheriff in 1845, b. Nov. 1810; m. 29 July, 1845, Margaret-Charlotte, eldest dau. of the late Sir George Campbell, of Edenwood, co. Fife, and niece of Lord Campbell, lord-chief-justice, and has issue,

I. ALFRED-CAMPBELL-HALLYBURTON, b 10 March, 1849.
I. Mary-Eleanor-Margaret-Geraldine.
II. Louisa-Madeline-Maria.

Lineage.—This family has been settled in the neighbourhood of Landovery, where they have been landed proprietors for upwards of three centuries. Some property in present possession has descended, by direct succession, from the time of Queen ELIZABETH. Mr. Jones's grandfather,

DAVID JONES, Esq. of Blaenos, and of Pantglâs, J.P. m. 1st, 1786, Anne, dau. and eventually sole heiress of the Rev. John Jones, of Gwalvhedyr, and by her had issue,

I. Evan, b. 1785; d. unm. 1820.
II. John, b. 6 Feb. 1788; m. 1809, Mary, youngest dau. of William Jones, Esq. of Ystradwalter, and by this lady left, at his decease in 1812 three sons, viz.,
1 DAVID, now of Pantglâs and Penlan.
2 William, J.P. and D.L., of Glanderrina, co. Cardigan.
3 John, barrister-at-law, J.P. of Blaenôs co. Carmarthen, m. his cousin, Anne, 2nd dau. of David Thomas, Esq. of Wellfield House, co. Radnor, who d. 29 Sept. 1844.

Mr. David Jones m. 2ndly, Catherine, eldest dau. of Morgan-Pryse Lloyd, Esq. of Glansevin, by Catherine his wife, granddau. of the 1st Viscount Hereford, but had no issue. He d. 29 Sept. 1840.

Arms—Gu., on a chevron, arg., between three bucks' heads, erased, or, a falcon, sa., belled.
Crest—On a mount, vert, a bull's head, erased, sa., bezantée.
Motto—Da ei fydd.
Seat—Pantglâs, near Landilo, co. Carmarthen.

JONES OF TREWYTHEN.

JONES, WYTHEN, Esq. of Rhiewport, co. Montgomery, high-sheriff in 1829, b. 13 Dec. 1789; m. 12 July, 1814, Mary, eldest dau. of the late Rev. William Thornes, vicar of Alberbury, co. Salop, and has issue one dau.,

CHARLOTTE.

Lineage—This a younger branch of the eminent house of Nannau, in Merioneth, derived from CADWGAN, Lord of Nannau, son of Bleddyn ap Cynfyn, King of Powys.

THE REV. EVAN JONES, of Trewythen (son of Bowen Jones, Esq. of Penyr Altgoch, by Mary his wife, dau. and heir of Evan Jones, Esq. of Trewythen, and great-great-grandson of Evan Jones, who was 2nd son of Wythen Jones, Esq. of Trewythen, by Margaret his wife, dau. of Thomas Johnes, Esq. of Dolaucothi) m. Charlotte dau. of Hervey Combe, Esq. of Andover, and had issue WYTHEN, of Trewythen; Hervey-Bowen, who m. Sophia, dau. of the late John-Frederick Pike, Esq. of Enfield; Charlotte, m. to John Hunter, Esq. of Mountscvern; Caroline, m. to Boyce Combe, Esq.

Arms—Quarterly; 1st and 4th, or, a lion, rampant, gu.; 2nd and 3rd, sa., three nags' heads, erased.

Crest—A lion, rampant, gu.
Motto—Frangas non flectes.
Seat—Rhiewport, co. Montgomery.

JONES OF WEPRE HALL.

JONES, HOWEL-MADDOCK-ARTHUR, Esq. of Wepré Hall, co. Flint, J.P. and D.L., major of the royal Flintshire rifles, *b.* 29 May, 1819; *m.* 1st, 9 Feb. 1843, Louisa-Creighton, dau. of Major Robert M'Crea, 5th Royal Veterans, and has issue,

TREVOR-LOUIS, *b.* 22 Feb. 1844.

Mr. Jones *m.* 2ndly, 3 Sept. 1845, Matilda, dau. of Simon Barrow, Esq. of Bath, and by her has issue,

I. Trevor-Randulph, *b.* 16 Oct. 1847.
II. Arthur-Wepré, *b.* 24 March, 1854.
III. Edward-Maddock, *b.* 23 Oct. 1855.
I. Gwynedd-Ellen. II. Evelyn-Tryphena.
III. Honora-Sidney.

Lineage.—The immediate ancestor of this respectable Welsh family,

EDWARD JONES, Esq., *m.* Lucy, dau. of Edward Tottie, Esq. of Wongla, by his wife, Lucy Lloyd, of Cornist, and granddau. of George Tottie, Esq. of Pen-y-pylle, by his wife, Jane Percivall, of Bagilt; and *d.* in 1780, leaving (with two sons, Edward and John, who *d. s. p.*) a dau.,

MARY JONES, who *m.* Humphrey Jones, Esq., and was mother of two sons, EDWARD, of Wepre; and Trevor, M.D., of Lichfield. The former,

EDWARD JONES, Esq of Wepre Hall (who *d.* 16 Oct. 1815), had by Hannah his wife, five sons and four daus. The youngest son but the only one to leave issue,

HOWEL-WEPRE OWEN-JONES, Esq., *m.* 1st, Henrietta-Maria, eldest dau of the Rev. William Williams, canon of St. Asaph; and 2ndly, Anne-Elizabeth, dau. of the Rev. T. Ward, prebendary of Chester, and by the former only had issue,

HOWELL-MADDOCK-ARTHUR, of Wepre Hall.
Mary-Charlotte, *m.* Nicholas Roskell, Esq.
Sidney-Eliza, *m.* to Thomas Flintt, Esq.
Frances-Harriett, *m.* to John Simpson, Esq.

Seat—Wepre Hall, Northop, co. Flint.

JONES OF YSTRAD.

JONES, MARY-ANNE, of Ystrad, co. Carmarthen, *b.* 1781; *s.* to the representation of the family upon the decease of her brother, the late John Jones, Esq., M.P.

Lineage.—The JONESES *of Llansadwrn*, from whom the JONESES *of Ystrad* descend, are a younger branch of the very ancient and once highly-distinguished knightly family of JONES OF ABERMARLES, co. Carmarthen. The late

JOHN JONES Esq. of Capeldewy and Ystrad (2nd son of Thomas Jones, Esq. of Ystrad, by Anna-Maria his wife, eldest dau. and co-heir of John Jones, Esq. of Crynfryn, co. Cardigan, descended from Rees Chwith, Esquire of the Body to King EDWARD I), *s.* to the estates at the death of his brother, Thomas. This gentleman, who was *b.* 15 Sept. 1777 sat in parliament for a long series of years; first for Pembroke, subsequently for the borough of Carmarthen, and finally for the county of Carmarthen, of which he was a deputy-lieut. He *d. unm.* 12 Nov. 1842, deeply regretted by his friends, constituency, and the community at large.

Arms—Arg., a chevron, gu., between three stags' heads, ppr., quartering REES OF CAPELDEWY, JONES OF TYGLYN, and LEWIS OF LLYNYCRWR.
Crest—A stag's head, erased, ppr.
Residence—Ystrad Cwm, Llanelly.

JONES OF CHASTLETON.

WHITMORE-JONES, JOHN-ARTHUR, Esq. of Chastleton House, co. Oxford, *b.* 1822.

Lineage.—The Chastleton estate was purchased by WALTER JONES Esq., from Catesby, the well-known conspirator in the Gunpowder Plot, who sold it to procure the required funds. For an account of Chastleton House, *see* Skelton's *Antiquities of Oxfordshire*, and Nash's *Ancient Mansions*.

ARTHUR JONES, Esq. of Chastleton, co. Oxford, the last male heir of the family of JONES OF CHASTLETON, son of Henry Jones, Esq. of Chastleton who *d.* in 1761, and grandson of Walter Jones, Esq. of Chastleton, by ANNE his wife sister of WILLIAM WHITMORE, Esq. of Apley, co. Salop, M.P. for Bridgnorth, *d.* 21 Nov. 1828, having bequeathed the Chastleton estate to his kinsman JOHN-HENRY WHITMORE Esq., only son, by his 2nd wife, of William Whitmore, Esq. of Dudmaston, and grandson of Charles Whitmore Esq. of Southampton, who was 4th son of William Whitmore, Esq. of Apley, whose sister, Anne, *m.* Walter Jones, Esq. of Chastleton (*see* WHITMORE OF APLEY). Mr. Whitmore, on succeeding to that property, assumed, in 1828, the surname and arms of JONES. He *m.* 1 Jan. 1821, Dorothy, dau. of Thomas Clutton, Esq. of Pensax Court, co Worcester, and had issue,

I. JOHN-ARTHUR, now of Chastleton.
II. William. III. Walter-Thomas, *b.* 1831.
IV. Wolryche-Harry.
I. Mary-Elizabeth. II. Jennetta.
III. Frances-Barbara, *m.* 1855, to the Rev. Charles-Alan Dickins.
IV. Joanna-Dorothea, *m.* 1851, to the Rev. Thomas Harris.
V. Louisa-Georgiana. VI. Elinor-Marian.

Mr. Whitmore-Jones, who was a magistrate and deputy-lieutenant, *d.* 1853.

Arms—Quarterly: 1st and 4th, gu., a lion, rampant, within a border, indented, or, a canton, ermine; 2nd and 3rd, vert, fretty, or, for WHITMORE.
Motto—Incorrupta fides.
Seat—Chastleton House, Oxfordshire.

JONES OF LARK HILL.

JONES, RICHARD-HEYWOOD, Esq. of Lark Hill, West Derby, co. Lancaster, J.P., *b.* 20 Oct. 1810; *m.* 11 Oct. 1836, Margaret, only dau. of John Harrison, Esq. of Ambleside, and has issue,

I. RICHARD-HEYWOOD, *b.* 28 July, 1853.
I. Catherine. II. Mary-Venetia.
III. Elizabeth.

Lineage.—THOMAS JONES, Esq., captain in the Merionethshire militia, *b.* in 1740, eldest son of John Jones, by Maria-Margaretta his wife, eldest dau. and co-heir of Sir Thomas Longueville, Bart. (*see* family of LONGUEVILLE OF PRESTATYN), *m.* 1st, Miss Jane Jones, by whom he had a son, Thomas-Longueville (*see* LONGUEVILLE OF PRESTATYN); and 2ndly, Anne Lloyd, by whom he left issue (with two daus., Mrs Barker and Mrs. Boydell) three sons (for whom, *see* LONGUEVILLE). The 4th,

HUGH JONES, Esq. of Lark Hill, West Derby, co. Lancaster, *b.* 20 Sept. 1777; *m.* 24 March, 1806, Elizabeth eldest dau of Benjamin Heywood, Esq of Stanley Hall and Wakefield, Yorkshire, and niece to Arthur Heywood, Esq. of Lark Hill, by which lady he had issue,

RICHARD-HEYWOOD his heir.
Benjamin-Heywood, J.P. and D.L., *m.* Louisa, dau. of Hugh Hornby, Esq. of Liverpool.
Hugh-Longueville.
Elizabeth-Anne, *m.* to Samuel Bright, Esq., 5th son of the late Richard Bright, Esq. of Ham Green, Bristol, by Sarah, dau. of Benjamin Heywood, Esq. of Liverpool.
Anna-Maria, *m.* to John Pemberton Heywood, Esq. of Norris Green, co. Lancaster.
Mary-Ellen, *m.* to Robertson Gladstone, Esq. of Liverpool.
Harriette, *m.* to Daniel Neilson, Esq. of Liverpool.
Emma, *m.* in 1840, to the Hon. Richard Denman, 3rd son of Lord Denman.

Mr. Jones *s* to Lark Hill on the death of the late Arthur Heywood, Esq., in 1837.

Arms—Or, a lion, rampant, az., quartering LONGUEVILLE.
Crest—A talbot's head, couped at the shoulders, gu., gorged with a collar, dancettée, arg.
Motto—Till then thus
Seat—Lark Hill, Liverpool.

JONES OF BEALANAMORE AND HEADFORT.

JONES, WALTER, Esq. of Bealanamore, co. Dublin, of Headfort, co. Leitrim, and of Hayle Place, co. Kent, col. of the Leitrim militia, *b.* 29 Dec. 1754; *m.* 8 Oct. 1805, Catherine-Penelope, dau. and co-heir of the Rev. Lascelles Iremonger, vicar of Chatford, Hants, by Catharine his wife, dau. of Chidley Morgan, Esq., and left five daus.,

I. Maria-Sophia, *m.* 1833, to Capt. Henry-Shovel Marsham, R.N.
II. Catherine-Penelope.
III. Elizabeth-Martia, *m.* to the Rev. George Marsham

(son of the Hon. Dr. Marsham, uncle to the Earl of Romney), rector of Allington and Halden, in Kent.
IV. Sophia. V. Anne.

Colonel Jones was formerly representative in parliament for Coleraine, and one of the Governors of the county of Leitrim.

Lineage.—BRYAN JONES, Esq. of the city of Dublin, auditor of war, descended from an ancient family in Wales, had a grant of lands from King JAMES I. in 1622. His great-grandson,

WALTER JONES, Esq. of Headfort, co. Leitrim, *m.* in 1722, Olivia, only dau. and co-heir of the Hon. Chidley Coote, of Coote Hall, co. Roscommon, and had issue,

THEOPHILUS, his heir.
Margaret, *b.* 21 March, 1724; *m.* 22 March, 1754, to Chidley Morgan, Esq.
Catherine, *m.* 3 Jan. 1758, to Sir Nicholas Barry, Bart.
Elizabeth, *m.* to Edward Crofton, Esq.
Frances, *m.* in Oct. 1760, to Lieut.-Gen. Thomas Bligh.

The only son,

THE RIGHT HON. THEOPHILUS JONES, of Headfort, M.P. for the co. of Leitrim, and subsequently for the borough of Coleraine, *m.* 1st, 29 March, 1754, the Lady Catherine Beresford, dau. of Marcus, Earl of Tyrone, and widow of Thomas Christmas, Esq., by whom (who *d.* in March, 1763) he had issue,

I. WALTER, his heir.
II. Theophilus, of Bolton Row, London, vice-admiral of the Red, *b.* in Sept. 1760; *d. unm.*
III. James, of Merrion Square, Dublin, in holy orders, rector of Urney, in the diocese of Derry, *m.* 1st, Lydia, dau. of Theobald Wolfe, and had by her (who *d.* in 1793) four sons and two daus., namely,
1 Theophilus, of Dublin, barrister-at-law, assistant-barrister of the co. Down.
2 Theobald, rear-admiral R.N., of Bovagh, co. Derry, M.P. for co. of Londonderry, *b.* 1790.
3 James, in holy orders.
4 Walter, of Dublin, *m.* and has issue.
1 Elizabeth. 2 Catherine, *d. unm.*
The Rev. James Jones *m.* 2ndly, 1 Oct. 1796, Anne, dau. of Sir Robert Blackwood, Bart. (by Dorcas his wife, Baroness Dufferin and Clanboyne), and relict of the Very Rev. John Ryder, dean of Lismore, son of John, Archbishop of Tuam. Mr. Jones *d.* in 1835, and was buried at Urney.

The Right Hon. Theophilus Jones *m.* 2ndly, in 1768, Anne, dau. of Col. John Murray, sometime M.P. for Monaghan (by Mary his wife, dau. of Sir Alexander Cairnes, Bart., and widow of Cadwallader, Lord Blayney), and had by her one son, Henry, who *d.* young, and two daus., Maria, *d. unm.*, and Anne, *d.* in infancy. Mr. Jones *d.* 8 Dec. 1811.

Arms—Gu., two lioncels, rampant-guardant, or, armed and langued, az., on a quarter, of the second, a fret, of the first.
Crest—A talbot's head, couped, arg., langued and chained, gu.
Motto—Deus fortitudo mea.
Seats—Headfort, co. Leitrim; and Hayle Place, near Maidstone.

JONES OF LISSELAN.

JONES, WILLIAM-BENCE, Esq. of Lisselan, co. Cork, J.P., M.A., barrister-at-law, *b.* 5 Oct. 1812; *m.* 6 July, 1843, Caroline, dau. of the late William Dickinson, Esq. of Kingsweston, M.P. for Somersetshire, and has issue,

I. WILLIAM-FRANCIS-BENCE, *b.* 9 March, 1856.
I. Caroline-Sophia. II. Mary-Lilias.
III. Philippa-Frances.

Lineage.—WILLIAM JONES, Esq. of Blackrock and city of Cork, *d.* 23 Feb. 1831, leaving issue, by his wife, Eleanor Winthrop, a son,

WILLIAM JONES, Esq., lieut.-colonel 5th dragoon-guards, who *m.* Matilda, dau. of the Rev. Bence Bence, of Thorington Hall, Suffolk, rector of Beccles; and dying 6 Aug. 1843, left issue,

WILLIAM-BENCE, now of Lisselan.
Henry-Bence, M.D., of Brook Street, London, *m.* Lady Millicent Acheson, dau. of the late Earl of Gosford.
Frederick-Pembroke, *m.* Emma, dau. of W. Delmar, Esq. of The Elms, Canterbury.

Seat—Lisselan, co. Cork.

JONES OF MONEYGLASS HOUSE.

HAMILTON-JONES, THOMAS-MORRIS, Esq. of Moneyglass House, co. Antrim, J.P., *b.* 2 April, 1821. Mr. Jones has served as high-sheriff in the several counties of Armagh, Antrim, Down, and Fermanagh.

Lineage.—THOMAS-MORRIS JONES, Esq., the grandfather of the present possessor of Moneyglass, *m.* LETITIA HAMILTON, and by her had issue a son,

KENRICK-MORRIS JONES-HAMILTON, Esq. of Moneyglass, who *m.* 12 July, 1818, Mabella, dau. of — Hill, Esq., and by her (who *m.* 2ndly, Lieut.-Col. Kennedy, late of the 18th hussars) had issue.

THOMAS-MORRIS-HAMILTON, now of Moneyglass.
John-Charles-Hill-Morris, *b.* 30 March, 1824, capt. 54th regiment.
Mabella, *m.* to Meredith Chambre, Esq. of Hawthorn Hill, co. Armagh.

Mr. Jones-Hamilton *d.* 31 March, 1831.

Arms—JONES and HAMILTON, quarterly.
Seat—Moneyglass, co. Antrim.

JONES OF MULLINABRO'.

JONES, JOHN-HAWTRY, Esq. of Mullinabro', co. Kilkenny, J.P. and D.L., high-sheriff in 1833, *b.* 23 Dec. 1803; *m.* Aug. 1840, Annie, dau. of William Milward, Esq. of Waterford, and has issue,

I. JOHN-HUMPHRY, *b.* 20 Oct. 1843.
II. William, *b.* 12 March, 1849.
III. Henry, *b.* 19 April, 1851.
IV. Francis, *b.* 18 April, 1854.
I. Marion-Jane. II. Annie-Eliza. III. Emily.

Lineage.—Mr. Jones's grandfather, JOHN JONES, Esq., who *m.* Rebecca, dau. of Alderman William Morris, of Waterford, *d.* Dec. 1788, and by her (who *d.* 1801) left issue a son,

HUMPHRY JONES, Esq. of Mullinabro', who *m.* 1st, 1790, Anne, dau. of Rev. Ralph Hawtry, and by her had issue,

John-Hawtry, *d.* Sept. 1803.
JOHN-HAWTRY, now of Mullinabro'.
Ralph-Hawtry, *d.* 25 Jan. 1817.
Humphry, *d. unm.* Nov. 1825.
Sarah, *m.* Sept. 1812, to Major Oliver-Cuffe Jackson.
Rebecca, *m.* Jan. 1822, to William-Henry Gabbett, Esq.
Marianne, *m.* Nov. 1826, to Dr. George Ormsby.
Ellen, *d.* Jan. 1826. Anne-Charlotte.

Mr. Humphry Jones *m.* 2ndly, 1811, Lucy, dau. of Samuel Newport, Esq., and by her had issue,

Samuel-Humphry. Marmaduke, *d.* 1852.
Lucy-Jane.

Seat—Mullinabro', co. Kilkenny.

JORDAN OF PIGEONSFORD.

JORDAN, GEORGE-BOWEN-JORDAN, Esq. of Pigeonsford, co. Cardigan, and Dumpledale, co. Pembroke, J.P. and D.L., high-sheriff of Cardiganshire in 1836, *b.* 6 Sept. 1806; *m.* 31 July, 1831, Ellen, 3rd dau. of Sir John Owen, Bart. of Orielton, co. Pembroke, and by her (who *d.* 12 Nov. 1856) has had issue,

I. GEORGE-PRICE, *b.* 3 April, 1835; *d.* 3 May, 1850.
II. Barrett-Price, *b.* 8 April, 1842.
I. Ellen-Evelyn-Elizabeth.
II. Elizabeth-Maria. III. Angelina.

This gentleman, whose patronymic was PRICE, took the name of JORDAN under the will of the Rev. John Jordan, of Dumpledale, co. Pembroke.

Lineage.—The family of Jordan is of Anglo-Norman origin. The first settler in Wales was Jordan de Cantington, one of the companions of Martin de Tours, in his conquest of Kemmes, *temp.* WILLIAM I. At the close of the 14th, or beginning of the 15th, century, LEONARD JORDAN *m.* the heiress of Dumpledale, and thus acquired that estate; the Jordans were thenceforth widely spread over the co. of Pembroke, but are now extinct in the male line.

GEORGE PRICE, Esq. of Pigeonsford, co. Cardigan, captain in the army, and colonel of the County Local Militia (son of David Price, Esq. of Penygraig, co. Cardigan, by Dorothea his wife, only dau. of James Bowen, Esq. of Llwyngwair, co. Pembroke, and grandson of John Price, Esq., by Bridget, dau. and co-heir of Lewis Parry, Esq. of Cwymeynon, co. Cardigan), m. 1805, Elizabeth, eldest dau. and co-heir of BARRETT-BOWEN JORDAN, Esq. of Neeston, whose mother was one of the co-heiresses of William Bowen, Esq. of Haverfordwest, by one of the co-heiresses of William Fowler, Esq. of Robeston Hall, and left at his decease an only surviving son, the present GEORGE-BOWEN-JORDAN JORDAN, Esq. of Pigeonsford.

Arms—Gu., a lion, rampant, between eight cross-crosslets, fitchée, or, a chief, of the second.
Seats—Pigeonsford, co. Cardigan; Dumpledale, co. Pembroke.

JOYCE OF MERVUE.

JOYCE, PIERCE, Esq. of Mervue, co. Galway, J.P., *b.* 17 Oct. 1809; *m.* 12 Jan. 1842, Jane-Mary, eldest dau. of Francis Blake, Esq. of Cregg Castle, co. Galway, and has issue,

I. PIERCE. II. Walter.
III. Francis. IV. John.
I. Georgina. II. Helena.

Lineage.—The late WALTER JOYCE, Esq. of Mervue,* J.P. (son of Pierce Joyce, Esq., by Fanny Kelly his wife, and grandson, by his wife, Mary Elward, of Ballinagar, of Walter Joyce, son of John Joyce, and Eliza Lynch his wife), was *b.* in 1769, and *m.* in 1806, Helen Appleyard, by whom he had issue,

I. WALTER, *m.* 1829, Christina Kelly, and *d. s. p.*
II. PIERCE, now of Mervue.
III. THOMAS-APPLEYARD, now of Rahasane Park.
I. Helen, *m.* 1835, to Charles Lynch, Esq.
II. Christina.
III. Eliza, *m.* 1832, Cornelius-J. O'Kelly, Esq., and is dead.
IV. Theresa, *m.* 1838, Ambrose O'Kelly, Esq., and is dead.
V. Mary-Aloysia, deceased.

Mr. Joyce *d.* 4 July, 1858.

Motto—Mors aut honorabilis vita.
Seat—Mervue, co. Galway.

JOYCE OF RAHASANE.

JOYCE, THOMAS-APPLEYARD, Esq. of Rahasane Park, co. Galway, J.P., high-sheriff 1852, *b.* 18 June, 1819; *m.* Julia-Frances, only child of Major Bisshopp, K.H., by Julia his wife, dau. of William Talbot, Esq. of Castle Talbot, co. Wexford, and has issue,

I. WILLIAM-WALTER, *b.* 26 Feb. 1845.
II. Thomas-Appleyard, *b.* 22 July, 1848.
III. Frederick-Talbot, *b.* 2 Jan. 1850.
IV. Arthur-Edward, *b.* 7 May, 1851.
I. Elizabeth. II. Julia. III. Agnes.

Mr. Thomas Joyce, of Rahasane, is 3rd son of the late WALTER JOYCE, Esq. of Mervue.

Seat—Rahasane Park, co. Galway.

JUSTICE OF HINSTOCK.

JUSTICE, HENRY, Esq. of Hinstock, co. Salop, J.P. and D.L., *b.* 23 Nov. 1790; *m.* 26 Oct. 1839, Louisa-Anne, dau. of Alexander Radford, Esq., and has issue,

PHILIP-WILLIAM.
Louisa.

Mr. Justice served as high-sheriff in 1842. He is son of Philip Justice, Esq., and Judith Rottor his wife, and grandson, by Avis his wife, of Philip Justice, Esq., only son of William Justice and Beatrice his wife. Mr. Justice has four brothers and two sisters, viz., Philip, Robert, William, and John; Elizabeth, and Caroline.

Crest—A falcon.
Motto—Justitiæ soror fides.
Seat—Hinstock, co. Salop.

* The late Walter Joyce, Esq. of Mervue, had one sister, Jane, *m.* 1787, to James Blake, Esq. of Cregg Castle.

KAVANAGH OF BORRIS.

KAVANAGH, ARTHUR-MACMORROUGH, Esq. of Borris House, co. Carlow, J.P., high-sheriff of co. Kilkenny in 1856, *b.* 25 March, 1831; *m.* 15 March, 1855, Frances-Mary, only surviving dau. of the Rev. Joseph-Forde Leathley, and has a son and heir,

WALTER-MACMURROUGH, *b.* 14 Jan. 1856.

Lineage.—In ancient times the ancestors of this eminent house were monarchs of all Ireland, and at the period of the invasion of that country by HENRY II., were Kings of Leinster. The family bore the name of MACMURROUGH; in 1171, that of CAOMHANACH, or KAVANAGA, was given to Donall, son of Dermot MacMorrough, and from him was continued to his descendants. Dermot MacMorrough's dau., Eva, *m.* Strongbow, Earl of Pembroke. In the reign of PHILIP and MARY, CAHIR MAC ART KAVANAGH, was created Baron of Ballyane for life. He *m.* Alice dau. of the Earl of Kildare, lord-lieutenant of Ireland, by Elizabeth Grey his wife, dau. of the Marquess of Dorset, and *d.* before 1555, having had three sons, Murrough, *d. s. p.*; Dermot, also *d. s. p.*; and BRYAN KAVANAGH, who *d.* before 1572, leaving, by Elinor his wife, dau. of George Byrne, of Roscrea, a son, MORGAN KAVANAGH, of Borris who *d.* in 1636, leaving a son, BRYAN KAVANAGH, of Borris, who *m.* Elinor, dau. of Sir Thomas Colclough, Knt. of Tintern Abbey, and *d.* in 1662, leaving a son, MORGAN KAVANAGH, of Borris, who *m.* Mary, dau. of John Walsh, Esq. of Pilltown, and was father of MORGAN KAVANAGH, of Borris, who *m.* Frances, dau. of Sir Laurence Esmonde, Bart., and had issue, BRYAN, his heir; Henry, *d.* in 1741; and Charles, general in the Austrian service, and governor of Prague; and Mary. The eldest son,

BRYAN KAVANAGH, Esq. of Borris, *m.* Mary, dau. of Thomas Butler, Esq. of Kilcash, and dying in 1741, left, with six daus., of whom the eldest, Margaret, *m.* Richard Galway, Esq., a son,

THOMAS KAVANAGH, Esq. of Borris, who *m.* in 1755, Lady Susanna Butler, sister of the Earl of Ormonde, and *d.* in 1790, having had issue,

Walter, who *d. s. p.* in 1813.
Brian, *d. s. p.*
Morgan, *m.* in 1792, Alicia, only child of Michael Grace, Esq. of Gracefield, in the Queen's County, and *d. s. p.* 1804.
THOMAS, of whom presently.
Helena, *m.* to James Archbold, Esq. of Davidstown.
Mary, *m.* to George Butler, Esq. of Ballyragget.
Honora.

The 4th son, and eventual inheritor,

THOMAS KAVANAGH, Esq. of Borris House, *b.* 10 March, 1767, M.P. for the city of Kilkenny in the last Irish parliament, and subsequently representative for the co. of Carlow in the last two parliaments of GEORGE IV. and 1st of WILLIAM IV., *m.* 1st, 24 March, 1799, Lady Elizabeth Butler, dau. of John, Earl of Ormonde, and by her, who *d.* in 1822, had issue, a son, Walter, who *d.* 1836, and nine daus., of whom six *d. unm.*, the other three were, Anne, who *m.* Henry Bruen, Esq. of Oak Park, co. Carlow, and *d.* 1830; Susanna, *m.* to Major Doyne; and Grace, who *m.* John-St. George Deane, Esq. of Berkeley Forest, co. Wexford, and *d. s. p.* Mr. Kavanagh *m.* 2ndly, 28 Feb. 1825, Lady Harriet-Margaret Le Poer Trench, dau. of Richard, Earl of Clancarty, and by her had issue,

THOMAS, his successor, of Borris House, *d. unm.* in Australia, March, 1852
CHARLES, of Borris, *b.* 28 Jan. 1829; *d. unm.* Feb. 1853.
ARTHUR, now of Borris.
Harriet-Margaret, *m.* to Capt. W. A. Middleton, R.A.

Mr. Kavanagh *d.* 20 Jan. 1837.

Arms—Arg., a lion, passant, gu., in base two crescents, of the last.
Crest—Issuant between the horns of a crescent, gu., a garb, or.
Seat—Borris House, co. Carlow.

KAY OF MANNINGHAM.

LISTER-KAY, JOHN, Esq. of Manningham Hall, co. York, *b.* 17 Dec. 1810; *s.* his father 24 Nov. 1853; *m.* and has issue. This gentleman assumed the surname of LISTER-KAY on succeeding to the family estates.

Lineage.—This family and that of SIR ROBERT-HENRY CUNLIFFE, Bart. of Liverpool, derive from a common ancestor.

JOHN CUNLIFFE, Esq. of Fairfield Hall, Addingham, *b.* in 1742, was eldest son of Ellis Cunliffe, Esq. of Ilkley and High House, Addingham (by Elizabeth his wife, dau. of the Rev. Thomas Lister, uncle of Samuel Lister, Esq. of Manningham), and grandson of Nicholas Cunliffe, Esq. of Whycollar, co. Lancaster, who went to reside at Ilkley in 1695. He *m.* 23 Nov. 1772, Mary, only dau. of the Rev. William Thompson, rector of Addingham, and *d.* in 1818, having had by her, who *d.* 13 June, 1834,

- ELLIS, of Manningham and Fairfield Hall.
- William, of Fairfield Hall, J.P. and D.L., *d. s. p.*
- John, *d.* young.
- Thomas-Lister-Thompson.
- Mary, *m.* to the Rev John Coates, rector of Addingham.
- Eliza, *m.* to Richard Parr, of Algarkirk.
- Harriott, *m.* to John Ellis, Esq. of High House, Addingham.
- Phœbe, *m.* to John Outhwait, of London.
- Sophia, *m.* to John Pickersgill, Esq. of Tavistock-square.

The eldest son,

ELLIS CUNLIFFE-LISTER-KAY, Esq. of Manningham and Fairfield Hall, co. York, J.P. and D.L., M.P. for Bradford, *b.* 13 May, 1774; *m.* 1st, in 1794, his cousin, Ruth Myers, niece and heiress of Samuel Lister, Esq. of Manningham, and 2ndly, in Feb. 1809, Mary, only child of William Kay, Esq. of Haram Grange and Cottingham, near Hull, and by the latter only had issue,

- William, barrister-at-law, late M.P. for Bradford, *b.* 13 Dec. 1809; *d.* 12 Aug. 1841.
- JOHN, now of Manningham Hall.
- Ellis, *b.* in 1813, *d.* in 1833.
- Samuel, *b.* in 1815.
- Thomas-Thompson, *b.* in 1821.
- Mary, *m.* to Joshua Ingham, Esq. of Blake Hall.
- Harriotte, *m.* to — Esdaile, Esq.
- Anne, *m.* 12 Oct. 1847, to the Hon. Richard-Gilbert Talbot.
- Elizabeth-Emily.

Mr. Cunliffe-Lister-Kay *m.* 3rdly, 11 Nov. 1844, Hon. Elizabeth Talbot, widow of George Mellefont, Esq., and dau. of the late Baroness Talbot de Malahide, and *d.* 24 Nov. 1853.

Arms—Quarterly: KAY, LISTER, and CUNLIFFE.
Crests—Of KAY, a griffin's head, collared; of LISTER, a stag's head, ppr.; of CUNLIFFE, a greyhound, sejant, arg., collared, sa.
Motto—Fidem parit integritas.
Seats—Manningham and Fairfield Hall, Addingham.

KEANE OF BEECH PARK.

KEANE, MARCUS, Esq. of Beech Park, co. Clare, J.P., *b.* 7 Feb. 1815; *m.* 9 Nov. 1847, Louisa-Isabella, dau. of Nicholas Westby, Esq. and the Honourable Mrs. Westby, of York Gate, Regent's Park, London, and has issue,

- I. PERCEVAL-WILLIAM, *b.* 12 Sept. 1848.
- II. Robert-Charles-George, *b.* 5 Nov. 1851.
- III. Marcus-Thomas-Francis, *b.* 30 July, 1854.
- I. Jane-Mary. II. Louisa-Caroline.

Lineage.—OWEN KEANE, Esq. the head of this branch of the Keane family, came from the co. of Londonderry, and settled at Ballyvoe, near Ennis, about the middle of the 17th century. He *m.* Judith, a dau. of Sir Robert Shaw, of Galway, and had one son, ROBERT KEANE, *b.* 1690. This Robert *m. circa* 1730, Mary, dau. of Robin Keane, of Ross, in the co. Clare, and had three sons, Robert, whose sons *d. s. p.*; CHARLES, of whom we treat; and Patrick, who *m.* Anne, dau. of Robert Crowe, Esq. of Ennis. The 2nd son,

CHARLES KEANE, Esq. of Corbally, co. Clare, *m.* 1766, Anne, dau. of Robert Harding, Esq. of Limerick, and, dying in 1802, left (with two daus., Mary, *m.* to Robert Creagh, Esq. of Dangan, and Anne, *m.* to William Power, Esq.) two sons, CHARLES KEANE, major royal art., who *d.* in the West Indies, in 1812, without issue, and

ROBERT KEANE, Esq. of Beech Park, J.P., *b.* 1774, *m.* Dec. 1799, Jane, eldest dau. and co-heiress of Thomas Delahunty, Esq. of Crusheen, and by her (who *d.* Feb. 1842) had issue,

- I. Charles, M.D., *m.* 1832, Sarah, dau. of Andrew-James Watson, Esq., and *d. vitâ patris, s. p.* 16 Aug. after. His widow *m.* 2ndly, George Ellis, Esq., M.D., of Dublin.
- II. FRANCIS-NATHANIEL, of Hermitage, near Ennis, J.P., *b.* Oct. 1803; *m.* July, 1827, Hannah-Maria, dau. of Sir Christopher Marrett, Knt. of Limerick, and has issue, 1 Christopher-Marrett; 2 Charles; 3 Francis-Burton; 4 William-Henry; 1 Hannah-Maria; 2 Jane; 3 Sarah; 4 Susanna.
- III. Thomas, of Kilballyowen, co. Clare, J.P., *m.* Anne, dau. of Thomas Crowe, Esq. of The Abbey, Ennis.
- IV. Giles, major 86th regt.
- V. Robert, of Dublin, *m.* Mary-Anne, dau. of John Code, Esq., and has three daus.
- VI. MARCUS, now of Beech Park.
- VII. William, in holy orders, rector of Whitby, Yorkshire, *m.* Elizabeth, dau. of the Hon. John Fryer Thomas, Esq., member of council at Madras, and has two sons,
  - 1 John-Thomas. 2 Robert-Charles.
- VIII. Henry.
- I. Anne, *m.* to Thomas Pilkington, Esq. of Waterpark, Ennis.
- II. Susanna, *m.* Armaud Dubourdieu, Esq.
- III. Maria, *m.* to the Rev. Charles Ward, vicar of Kilmaley.
- IV. Jane, *m.* to John Rutherford, Esq. of Kingsborough, Parsonstown.
- V. Charlotte.

Arms—Quarterly: gu. and or, in the first and fourth quarters, a salmon naiant, arg.; in the second and third quarters a tree, vert.
Crest—A wild cat, rampt., guardant, ppr., gorged with an antique Irish crown, or, and charged on the shoulder with a trefoil, vert.
Motto—Felis demulcta mitis.
Seat—Beech Park, Ennis.

KECK OF STAUGHTON GRANGE.

LEGH-KECK, GEORGE-ANTHONY, Esq. of Staughton Grange, co. Leicester, and Bank Hall, co. Lancaster, J.P. and D.L., formerly M.P. for Leicestershire, and lieut.-col. comm. of the Leicestershire regiment of yeomanry; *m.* 1802, Elizabeth, 2nd dau. of Robert-Vernon Atherton, Esq. of Atherton, co. Lancaster, but by her (who *d.* in 1837) had no issue.

Lineage. — ANTHONY KECK, Esq., nephew of Sir Anthony Keck, and cousin and devisee of Francis Keck, *d.* 23 Nov. 1736, leaving a dau., MARTHA, who *m.* David James, Esq., and by him, who *d.* 8 Jan. 1746, left at her decease, a son,

ANTHONY JAMES (devisee of his grandfather), who assumed the surname and arms of KECK in 1737. By Ann Busby his 1st wife, who became eventually an heiress in right of her mother, one of the daus. of Sir Henry Beaumont, Bart., and was buried at Staughton, 17 Feb. 1705, he left at his decease, 30 April, 1786, a son,

ANTHONY-JAMES KECK, Esq. of Staughton Grange, co. Leicester, sometime M.P. for Newton, who *m.* 18 July, 1765, Elizabeth, 2nd dau. and co-heir of PETER LEGH, Esq. of Lyme, in Cheshire, by Martha his wife, only dau. and heir of Thomas Bennett, Esq. of Salthrop, Wilts, and by her, who *m.* 2ndly, William-Bathurst Pye, Esq., had a dau., Elizabeth-Ann, *m.* to Thomas Calley, Esq. of Burderop, co. Wilts, and two sons, PEERS-ANTHONY and GEORGE-ANTHONY LEGH. The former,

PEERS-ANTHONY KECK, Esq. of Staughton Grange and Bank Hall, *d. unm.*, 12 March, 1797, and was *s.* by his brother, GEORGE-ANTHONY LEGH-KECK, Esq.

Arms—Sa., a band, erm., between two cottises, flory, counterflory, or.
Crest—Out of a mural crown, a maiden's head, erm., purfled, or, her hair disheveiled, of the same, and flotant, adorned with a chaplet, vert, and garnished with roses, ppr.
Motto—En Dieu est ma foy.
Seats—Staughton Grange and Bank Hall.

KEIR OF KINMOUTH.

SMALL-KEIR, PATRICK, Esq. of Kinmouth, co. Perth, J.P. and D.L., an advocate at the Scotch bar, *b.* 31 Dec. 1782; *m.* 7 Aug. 1807, Jane, dau. of John Stewart, Esq. of East Craigs, co. Linlithgow, 2nd son of Robert Stewart, of Binny, and had issue surviving, one son,

PATRICK, *b.* 9 May, 1810, who *m.* 26 April, 1836, Amelia-Balfour, dau. of Sir Niel Menzies, Bart., and has issue a son, William-Augustus, and two daus., Catharine-Menzies, and Jane-Amelia.

Lineage.—WILLIAM SMALL, Esq. of Kindrogan (son of William Small, of Kindrogan, by Agnes his wife, dau. of James Stewart, Esq. of Urrard, and grandson of William Small, of Kindrogan, by Isabel Farquharson his wife), *m.* in 1776, Margaret, dau. of WALTER KEIR, Esq. of Balcairn, co. Perth, and by her had a son, PATRICK SMALL-KEIR, Esq. of Kindrogan.

Arms—Per fesse, wavy, gu. and arg., a lion, passant, sa., pierced with a dagger, in bend, ppr., entering at the shoulder, hilted, or, for SMALL; arg., a cross, eng., sa., between four roses, gu., for KEIR.
Crests—A branch of palm, ppr., erect, for SMALL; a hand, holding a sword, in pale, ppr., for KEIR.
Mottoes—Ratione non irâ, for SMALL; Alterum non lædere, for KEIR.
Seat—Kindrogan, co. Perth.

KEKEWICH OF PEAMORE.

KEKEWICH, SAMUEL-TREHAWKE, Esq. of Peamore, co. Devon, J.P. and D.L., high-sheriff 1834, and M.P. for Exeter from 1826 to 1830; *b.* 31 Oct. 1796; *m.* 1st, 3 April, 1820, Agatha-Maria-Sophia, 4th dau. of John Langston, Esq. of Sarsden, co. Oxford, and sister of James-Haughton Langston, Esq., M.P. for Oxford city, and by her had issue,

I. TREHAWKE, *b.* 22 Jan. 1823, who is married.
II. Arthur, fellow of Exeter College, Oxford, *b.* 26 July, 1832.
III. Lewis, 20th regt., *b.* 3 Sept. 1836, was at Alma, Balaclava, and Inkerman; was wounded at Inkerman, and died at Corfu, 16 Feb. 1855.
I. Henrietta, *m.* to Henry Ley, Esq., jun., Clerk of the House of Commons.
II. Agatha, *m.* to Henry-Hall Dare, Esq., 23rd fusiliers.
III. Elizabeth, *m.* to Ralph-Ludlow Lopes, Esq., 2nd son of Sir Ralph Lopes, Bart., late M.P. for South Devon.
IV. Julia-Frances, *m.* to James-Thomas Edge, Esq of Stretty Hall, Notts.

He *m.* 2ndly, 9 June, 1840, Louisa, dau. of Lewis-William Buck, Esq. of Moreton, co. Devon, M.P., and by her has,

I. George-William, *b.* 1 April, 1841.
Emma. II. Louisa. III. Anna-Maude.

Lineage.—This family, originally of Lancashire, settled about the middle of the 16th century in Cornwall, in consequence of a marriage with the heiress of Talvarne.

GEORGE KEKEWICH, resident at Catchfrench, at the time of Carew, rebuilt the mansion in the castellated style; the stately embattled entrance, and some other parts of which are still standing, and bear the words, "George Kekewich, 1580," cut in stone. The manor of Catchfrench continued in the Kekewich family until the time of CHARLES II., when it was sold by John Kekewich, Esq., to Hugh Boscawen, Esq. of Tregothnan. In the same reign Peter Kekewich, Esq., possessed the manor of Trehawke; and Samuel Kekewich, Esq., was seated at Polmartin; subsequently the representatives of the family were resident at Hall, near Fowey. The great-grandfather of the present head of the house,

PENDARVES KEKEWICH, Esq., *m.* Mary Hills, and had (besides two daus.) one son,

WILLIAM KEKEWICH, Esq., who *m.* Susanna Johnstone, and had thirteen children; of whom, the eldest, SAMUEL, was his heir; of the others, Charles, in holy orders, was of Lymmouth, co. Devon; and George, for many years judge at the Cape of Good Hope. The eldest son,

SAMUEL KEKEWICH, Esq. of Peamore, *m.* Salome, dau. of George Sweet, Esq. of Tiverton, co. Devon, and by her (who *d.* 29 March, 1844) had a son, SAMUEL-TREHAWKE, now of Peamore; and one sister, Salome, *m.* to Sir Thomas-William Blomefield, Bart. Mr. Kekewich *d.* 26 Aug. 1822.

Arms—Arg., two lions, passant, in bend, sa., between two cottises, gu.
Crest—A leopard's head and neck, affronté.
Motto—Fructus virtutis.
Seat—Peamore, near Exeter.

KELHAM OF BLEASBY HALL.

KELHAM, ROBERT-KELHAM, Esq. of Bleasby Hall, co. Notts, and Great Gonerby, Billingborough, and Allington, co. Lincoln, J.P., *b.* 26 Sept. 1787; *m.* 1st, Oct. 1812, Dorothea, only child and heir of John Phillips, Esq. of The Homewood and Willands, co. Surrey, and has issue,

I. ROBERT, *b.* 12 July, 1813.
II. Marmaduke, *b.* 27 July, 1814; *m.* 17 Dec. 1845, Julia-Ann, dau. of Robert Christie, Esq., and *d.* 28 Feb. 1852, leaving issue,
  1 Marmaduke-Langdale, *b.* 12 Oct. 1847.
  2 Robert-Maunsell, *b.* 21 Oct. 1849.
  3 Henry-Phillips, *b.* 24 July, 1851.
III. Augustus, *b.* 14 Nov. 1819; *m.* 4 July, 1850, Susan-Mary, eldest dau. of Samuel Aldersey, Esq. of Aldersey Hall, Cheshire, and has issue,
  1 Hugh-Aldersey-Langdale, *b.* 24 Aug. 1852.
  1 Lucy-Avice-Maud.
IV. Phillips, *b.* 21 Oct. 1824, *m.* Anne, eldest dau. of E. Y. Griffith, of Bangor, Esq.

V. Henry, *b.* 24 Sept. 1828, a lieut. R.N., served in the China War in 1842, on board H. M. ship "Endermion;" *m.* 7 Sept. 1852, Fanny-Goldie, youngest dau. of James Hall, Esq., M.D., R.N., and *d.* of the yellow fever, at Grand Quay, Turk's Island, West Indies, 28 Oct. 1852.
  Henry-Robert (posthumous), *b.* 21 June, 1853.
I. Avice, *m.* 9 Sept. 1852, the Rev. William Morgan, M.A., of Llandegai, co. Carnarvon, and has issue.
II. Jane, *m.* T.-B. Sands, Esq. of Liverpool, and has issue.
III. Arabella.

This gentleman, whose paternal name is LANGDALE, assumed by act of parliament, in 1812, the surname of KELHAM only, and the arms of Kelham, in compliance with the will of his maternal uncle, Robert Kelham, Esq., dated 29 Aug. 1808.

Lineage.—The Kelhams descend from a younger branch of an ancient family which was very early seated at Kelham, near Newark-upon-Trent, co. Nottingham, and bore for arms, "Az., three covered cups, or," allusive to the office they filled, of cup-bearer to Allan, 1st Earl of Richmond, son-in-law of WILLIAM the Conqueror.

THOMAS KELHAM, Esq. of Great Gonerby, son and heir of Robert Kelham, Esq. of Great Gonerby, and the lineal descendant of Richard Kelum, of Allington, co. Lincoln, living 1428, *b.* 13 Sept. 1638, *m.* Mary Lee, of Woodborough, Notts, and was *s.* at his decease, April, 1699, by his only son,

THE REV. ROBERT KELHAM, of Great Gonerby, *b.* 23 Jan. 1676, vicar of Billingborough, Threckingham, and Walcot, co. Lincoln, *m.* his cousin, 5 Feb. 1709, Mary, dau. and co-heir of John Kelham, Esq. of Gonerby, and had issue. The 3rd but eldest surviving son,

ROBERT KELHAM, Esq. of Hatton-garden, London, Great Gonerby and Billingborough, co. Lincoln, and Bush Hill, Edmonton, co. Middlesex, *b.* 9 Nov. 1717; *m.* 21 Dec. 1752, Sarah, youngest dau. of Peter and Joanna Gery, descended from an ancient family long seated at Bilston, co. Leicester, who *d.* 28 Sept. 1774, aged 58; he *d.* 29 March, 1808, in his 91st year. They had issue,

I. ROBERT, of Great Gonerby, Billingborough, and Bush Hill, *b.* 8 Jan. 1755, who *d. unm.* 11 Nov. 1811. His will was dated 29 Aug. 1808, and by it he devised his estates to his nephew, ROBERT-KELHAM LANGDALE, of whom presently.
I. Sarah-Augusta, *m.* 20 Dec. 1778, Marmaduke Langdale, Esq., New Ormond-street, London; traditionally descended from a younger branch of the Langdales of Houghton, co. York, from whom also derived the famed Cavalier commander, Sir Marmaduke Langdale, created in 1658, Baron Langdale, of Holme. Mrs. Langdale *d.* 2 Aug. 1832, having had, with younger issue,
  1 MARMADUKE-ROBERT LANGDALE, Esq. of Garston House, Surrey, and Pix Hall, Kent.
  2 ROBERT-KELHAM LANGDALE, Esq. (heir to his uncle, Robert Kelham, Esq. of Bush Hill), the present ROBERT-KELHAM KELHAM, Esq. of Bleasby Hall.
III. Avice, of Enfield, *b.* 8 April, 1762, *d. unm.* 27 July, 1841.

Arms—Quarterly: 1st and 4th, per pale, gu. and az., three covered cups, two and one, or, on a chief, engrailed, arg., three estoiles, sa., KELHAM; 2nd, az., three covered cups, or, KELHAM, ancient; 3rd, sa., a chevron, between three estoiles, arg., LANGDALE.
Crest—On a wreath of colours, a demi-eagle, with two heads, displayed, az., semée of ermine spots, and charged on each wing with a covered cup, or.
Motto—Beneficiorum memor.
Seat—Bleasby Hall, Notts.

KELLY OF CASTLE KELLY.

See O'KELLY.

KELLY OF KELLY.

KELLY, ARTHUR, Esq. of Kelly, co. Devon, J.P., high-sheriff 1836, *b.* 11 Sept. 1804; *m.* 27 Oct. 1829, Sophia, dau. of the late Robert Maitland, Esq. of Thaxted, Essex, formerly a merchant of the city of London, and has issue,

I. REGINALD, *b.* 10 Jan. 1834.
II. Maitland *b.* 21 Aug. 1842.
I. Juliana, *m.* 14 July, 1853, to Harry-Reginald, 2nd son of the late Sir William Trelawny, Bart.
II. Mary-Anne. III. Edith.
IV. Blanche. V. Sophy-Maitland.

Lineage.—"This family," we quote from their authenticated pedigree, "may look back beyond the Conquest, and derive themselves from the ancient Britons."

NICHOLAS DE KELLY, living *temp.* HEN. II., was father of WILLIAM DE KELLY, who was *s.* by his son, WARREN DE KELLY, father of SIR WILLIAM KELLY, of Kelly, *temp.* HEN. III., whose son, RICHARD KELLY, of Kelly, living in 1220, was *s.* by his son, SIR JOHN KELLY, of Kelly, Knt., living *temp.* EDW. I. He was father of JOHN KELLY, of Kelly, *temp.* EDW. II., who left by Margaret his wife, a son,

SIR JOHN KELLY, Knt., of Kelly, living 44 EDW. III., who *m.* Elinor, dau. and co-heiress of John Crewes, of Bradstone, and was father of JOHN KELLY, of Kelly, whose son MATTHEW KELLY, of Kelly, was *s.* by his son, JOHN KELLY, of Kelly, father of

THOMAS KELLY, of Kelly, *m. temp.* HEN. VI., Elizabeth, dau. and heir of William Talbot, Esq. of Talbotswyke, co. Devon, and had a son,

RICHARD KELLY, of Kelly, which estate he inherited at the decease of his elder brother, Nicholas. He *m.* Jane, dau. of Thomas Bratton, of Bratton, co. Somerset, and was direct ancestor of

WILLIAM KELLY, Esq. of Kelly, living at the Herald's Visitation in 1620, then aged 32. His 2nd son,

JOHN KELLY, Esq. of Kelly, *d. unm.* in 1689, and devised his estates to his cousin-german,

FRANCIS KELLY, Esq. of Tredown, in Bradstone, who then became of Kelly. He *m.* Elizabeth, dau. of — Tucker, Esq. of Holdsworthy, in Devon, and dying in Dec. 1690, was buried at Kelly, and left (with two dau., Joan, *m.* 14 Sept. 1693, to John Tillam; and Phillippa) an only son and successor,

ARTHUR KELLY, Esq. of Kelly, who *m.* Susanna, only dau. and heir of William Handcock, Esq. of Hendra St. Germains, in Cornwall, and by that lady had issue. Mr. Kelly *d.* 18 Oct. 1712, and was *s.* by his only son,

ARTHUR KELLY, Esq. of Kelly, bapt. 23 Oct. 1712, who *m.* Mary, eldest dau. of William Tucker, Esq. of Coryton, co. Devon, and had by her (who *d.* in 1781) six sons and two daus., viz.,

I. ARTHUR, his heir.
II. Francis-John, a capt. in the 18th, or royal Irish regt., bapt. 12 May, 1749, *m.* in 1782, Elizabeth, dau. of Thomas Oakeley, Esq. of Deal, in Kent, and had issue, Henry, capt. royal African corps, *d. unm.*; Elizabeth; Catharine; Mary; and Agnes, *m.* to Samuel Laing, Esq. of Orkney, N.B.
III. William-Handcock, vice-admiral of the Blue, baptised 6 April, 1751, *m.* Sally, dau. of Magnus Morton, Esq., judge of the Isle of Nevis, and *d.* 2 May, 1811, leaving a son, Magnus-Morton, lieut. R.N., *d. s. p.*, and a dau., Mary-Anne, wife of Theophilus Clive, Esq.
IV Benedictus-Marwood, of Holsworthy, Devon, bapt. 12 Aug. 1752, O.S., *m.* 30 April, 1780, Mary, dau. of Arscott Coham, of Holsworthy, and dying in Feb. 1836, left issue,
1 William, comm. R.N., *b.* 27 Feb. 1782, *m.* in 1821, Sarah Cole.
2 Benedictus-Marwood, rear-admiral R.N., *b.* in 1790, *m.* 31 Aug. 1837, Mary-Ann, eldest dau. and co-heir of Richard Price, Esq. of Highfields Park, co. Sussex, which lady *d.* 14 July, 1838.
3 John-Tucker, lieut. horse artillery at Madras, *d. unm.* in 1818.
4 Francis-Coham.
1 Mary.
2 Juliana, *m.* in 1823, to George Braund, Esq. of Exeter.
3 Sarah. 4 Elizabeth.
V. Thomas, of Burrington, in Devonshire, bapt. 3 Sept. 1760, *m.* in 1788, Miss Vinning, of Stoke, in Cornwall, and *d. s. p.*
I. Susannah, bapt. 3 June, 1746, *d.* in 1769.
II. Mary, *m.* to Lewis Robertson, Esq., capt. R.N.

Mr. Kelly *d.* in March, 1762, and was *s.* by his eldest son,

ARTHUR KELLY, Esq. of Kelly, col. of the South Devon militia, bapt. 15 July, 1742. He *m.* Dorothea-Juliana, dau. of Edward Drewe, Esq. of Exeter, by Dorothea-Juliana, his wife, dau. and eventual co-heiress of the Rt. Hon. George Treby, of Plympton, co. Devon, and had issue,

ARTHUR, bapt. 15 June, 1778; *m.* 16 June, 1808, Mary, only child of John Godwin, Esq. of Portsmouth, Hants, banker, and dying 23 March, 1822, in the lifetime of his father, left an only child, ARTHUR, now of Kelly.
Edward, capt. 51st regt., bapt. 26 Jan. 1779; *m.* Sarah, dau. of Edward Braddon, Esq. of Skisdon, St. Kew, Cornwall, and dying 24 May, 1831, left an only child, Edward-Henry, *b.* in 1821.
Mary, *m.* to the Rev. Edward Morshead, rector of Calstock, in Cornwall, and of Kelly, co. Devon.
Elizabeth. Susanna, *d. unm.*
Juliana, *d. unm.*

Phillippa, *m.* 1st, to Thomas Sowdon, Esq. of Whitstone, and 2ndly, 28 March, 1839, to Thomas, son of the late John Yarde, Esq. of Trowbridge House, Devon.

Col. Kelly *d.* in 1823.

Arms—Quarterly: 1st and 4th, arg., a chevron between three billets, gu., for KELLY; 2nd and 3rd, arg., a chevron between three talbots, sa., for TALBOT.
Crest—Out of a ducal coronet, gu., an ostrich's head holding in the beak a horseshoe, or.
Seat—Kelly, Devon.

KELLY OF NEWTOWN.

KELLY, JAMES, Esq. of Newtown House, co. Galway, *m.* Mary-Frances, only dau. of Augustine Fallon, Esq., and left surviving issue,

I. JOHN. II. Charles, barrister-at-law.
III. Joseph, *m.* Marianne, 5th dau. of the late Sir Michael-Dillon Bellew, Bart. of Mount Bellew, co. Galway, and has issue.
I. Mary-Theresa. II. Ellen-Mary.
III. Anne-Mary. IV. Sabina-Mary.
V. Matilda-Mary.

Lineage.—The Kellys of Newtown are derived from the ancient family of Kelly of Aughrim Castle, co. Galway About the close of the 17th century, there were two brothers of the family, BRYAN and JOHN. The younger was ancestor of the KELLYS *of Newtown;* the elder, BRYAN had two sons, General O'Kelly, of the Austrian service, who *d. unm.*; and John O'Kelly, father, by Miss Donelan his wife, of an only dau., *m.* to Count Marcolini. Reverting to the younger brother,

JOHN KELLY: he *m.* and had (with a dau., mother of Capt. William Kelly, of the Irish brigade) two sons,

JOHN, father of PATRICK O'KELLY, colonel in the Austrian service, who *d. unm.*
JAMES.

The younger son,

JAMES KELLY, Esq., *m.* Miss Kelly, and had two sons and a dau., John, who *d. unm.*; JAMES; and Bridget, who *m.* J. Kelly, Esq., and had one dau., *m.* to John Callanan, M.D. of Cork. The 2nd son,

JAMES KELLY, Esq. of Cork, son of James Kelly, of the co. of Galway, *m.* Mary, dau. of Robert French, Esq. of French Grove, co. Mayo, and had issue,

JOHN, of Newtown, co. Galway, and Greencastle, Island of Jamaica, *d. unm.*
Robert, *d. unm.*
JAMES, of Newtown.
Mary, *m.* to Patrick Taafe, Esq. of Foxborough, co. Roscommon.

Arms—Gu., on a mount, ppr., two lions, rampant, supporting a tower, arg.
Crest—A griffin, passant.
Motto—Turris fortis mihi Deus.
Seat—Newtown House, co. Galway.

KELSO OF KELSOLAND.

KELSO, EDWARD-JOHN-FRANCIS, Esq. of Kelsoland of Horkesley Park, co. Essex, late a captain in the 72nd Highlanders, *m.* 10 June, 1841, Frances-Lætitia-Philippa, only child and heiress of the late Barrington Purvis, Esq. of Beccles, co. Suffolk, and Amy-Lætitia his wife, eldest dau. of the Rev. Nathaniel Colville, D.D., of Lawshall, Bury St. Edmunds and has issue,

I. EDWARD-BARRINGTON-PURVIS, *b.* 21 March, 1842.
II. Edward-Archibald-Robert, *b.* 21 May, 1844.
III. Edward-Henry-George, *b.* 1850.
I. Philippa-Charlotte-Mary.

Lineage.—The Kelsos, one of the most ancient families of Ayrshire, came originally, it is stated, from Normandy, and that traditionary origin is corroborated by the fact that Yuelsoe is a surname still preserved in that province.

HUGO DE KELSO, the first of the name mentioned in the public records of Scotland, appears in the Ragman Roll, *anno* 1296, and is called by the continuator of Nisbet "ancestor of the KELSOS *of Kelsoland.*" From him derived the eminent Scottish family of KELSO OF KELSOLAND, whose male representative, about the middle of the 18th century, was CAPT. JOHN KELSO, of the 32nd regiment, son of Capt. Robert Kelso, whose father, JOHN KELSO, of Kelsoland, sold the old family estates, in 1671, to James Brisbane, of

Bishopton, who altered the name to BRISBANE. Capt. John Kelso m. 13 June, 1758, Margaret, dau. of William Mowatt, Esq., provost of Aberdeen in 1754, and had issue,

I. WILLIAM, his heir, of Dankeith, major of the 23rd light-dragoons, subsequently colonel of the Ayrshire militia, J.P. and D.L., who m. 30 Aug. 1784, Susanna, dau. of William Fergusson, Esq. of Doonholm, and had issue,

1 John, d. unm.
2 WILLIAM, of Dankeith, lieut.-col. H.E.I.C.S., d. s. p.
3 Fleming, lieutenant 13th light-dragoons, d. unm.
1 Elizabeth, m. to John-H. Martin, Esq. of Glencree, co. Wigton, son of Samuel Martin, Esq. of Antigua, and has issue.
2 Margaret.
3 Mary-Susanna, m. to the Rev. Alfred-G. Utterson (son of John Utterson, Esq. of Mile End House, Sussex, and Marwell Hall, Hants), rector of Layer Marney, co. Essex.

Colonel Kelso d. 22 April, 1836.

II. Robert, major-gen. in the army, who m. Marianne-Susan, dau. of Nelson Burtsell, Esq. of Suffolk, and had issue,

1 EDWARD-JOHN-FRANCIS, of Horkesley Park, now KELSO OF KELSOLAND.
1 Margaret-Augusta, m. to the Rev. Courtenay-Boyle Bruce, rector of St. Cross, Homersfield, and St. James, co. Suffolk.
2 Louisa-Marianne-Susan-Frances, m. to the Rev. Wm. Colvill, rector of Bytham, St. Peter's, and Brome, co. Suffolk.

Gen. Kelso d. at his residence at Bungay, in Suffolk, 13 Oct. 1823.

III. John, an ensign in the 51st regt., deceased.
IV. Millar, R.N., drowned in the river Ganges, near Calcutta.
V. Alexander-Stuart, } who both d. in the West Indies.
VI. Berrie, }
VII. Archibald, J.P. and D.L., b. 18 Feb. 1771; who purchased the estate of Sauchrie, in Carrick, Ayrshire; m. Feb. 1805, Miss Macharg, dau. of Macharg of Kiers, an ancient Ayrshire family, and had issue, Archibald; Andrew-John; John; Cecilia-Margaret; Margaret-Georgiana, deceased; Jane, deceased; and Elizabeth, deceased.
VIII. George, captain of an Indiaman, who m. Miss Plumb, but d. s. p.
IX. Andrew, d. unm.
I. Jane. II. Frances, d. unm.
III. Mary, m. to the late Patrick Ballentyne, Esq. of Castle Hill, in Ayrshire.
IV. Margaret, d. unm. V. Charlotte-Christina.

Capt. Kelso d. in 1781.

Arms—Sa., a fesse, engrailed, between three garbs, or.
Crest—A garb, or.
Supporters—Two lions rampt., gu., each charged on the shoulders with a garb, or.
Motto—Otium cum dignitate.
Seat—Horkesley Park, Essex.

KEMMIS OF SHAEN.

KEMMIS, THOMAS, Esq. of Shaen Castle and Straboe, Queen's County, patron of Rosenallis, b. 1837.

Lineage.—This family claims descent from the ancient family of Kemeys, of Keven Mabley.

THOMAS KEMMIS, Esq. of Shaen Castle, Killeen, Straboe, and Clonin, Queen's Co., who was b. 1710, and d. 1774, left, by Susan, his wife, dau. of George Long, Esq. of Derrynaseery, five sons, viz.,

JOHN, of Straboe, Treasurer of the county, b. 6 July, 1747, m. Margaret, dau. of Charles White, Esq. of Charleville, and by her who d. 1820, left, at his decease, 1806, three daus. and two sons, Charles, of Derrynaseery, and Thomas, in holy orders, of Straboe, both of whom d. s. p.
James, major-general in the army, d. 2 April, 1820.
THOMAS, of whose descendants we treat.
Joshua, of Knightstown, b. 6 Feb. 1755, J.P., high-sheriff 1795, m. Catherine, dau. of the Ven. Archdeacon Smyth, D.D., and d. 1818, leaving issue, Joshua, of Knightstowne, J.P., d. 1842; Alicia, m. to the Rev. Gustavus Warner, and Catherine, m. to the Rev. William Betty.
William, of Killeen, Clonin, &c., Treasurer of the Queen's Co., d. s. p. 1848.

The third son,

THOMAS KEMMIS, Esq. of Shaen Castle, Killeen, &c., Crown Solicitor for Ireland and Solicitor to the Treasury, patron of Rosenallis, b. 4 May, 1753, m. Anne, dau. of Henry White, Esq. of Dublin, and d. 15 Jan. 1823, having had issue,

I. THOMAS, his heir.
II. Henry, M.A., Q.C., assistant barrister and Chairman of the Quarter Sessions of Kilmainham, M.P. for Tralee 1800, m. 1804, Maria, dau. of Arthur Dawson, Esq. of Castle Dawson, co. Londonderry, M.P., and d. 1857, having had issue,

1 Thomas-Arthur, of Croham Hurst, Croydon, Surrey, J.P., late capt. Gren. gds., M.P. for East Looe, b. 16 March, 1806, m. 14 Sept. 1833, Henrietta-Anne, dau. of Col. Charles Kemeys Kemeys-Tynte, of Halswell House, co. Somerset, and has a son, Arthur-Henry-Nicholas, lt. Somerset militia, b. 1834.
2 Henry-Richard, barrister-at-law, b. 1811, m. Miss Laura Male, and has issue.

III. WILLIAM, now of Ballinacor* (*See that family*).
IV. James, of Derry and Meelick, Queen's Co., d. s. p. 1841.
I. Anne, m. 1800, to Richard Warburton, Esq. of Garryhinch, Queen's Co., J.P. and D.L.
II. Susan, m. 21 Dec. 1802, to William Talbot, Esq. of Mount Talbot, co. Roscommon, who d. s. p. 1851.
III. Mary, m. 1st, to Sir Arthur Carden, Bt., and 2ndly, to Capt. Smith, of Mount Butler, co. Tipperary.

The eldest son,

THE REV. THOMAS KEMMIS, of Shaen Castle and Brockley Park, Queen's Co., patron of Rosenallis. b. 6 Aug. 1775, m. Mary, dau. and heir of Arthur Riky, Esq. of Airfield, co. Dublin, and d. 4 Oct. 1827, leaving issue,

THOMAS, his heir.
Arthur, of Sidney, Australia, m. Miss Redmond, of Limerick, and has issue.
Henry, of Tankerville, near Melbourne, Australia, m. twice and had issue.
Mary, m. to Charles Hogan, Esq. of Dublin.

The eldest son,

THOMAS KEMMIS, Esq. of Shaen Castle and Straboe, patron of Rosenallis, J.P., high-sheriff 1832, m. Mary, dau. of the Rev. Robert Jelly, of Portarlington, and by her (who m. 2ndly, 1856, Sir Henry Marsh, Bart., M.D.) had issue I. THOMAS, now of Shaen Castle and Straboe, patron of Rosenallis; II. Robert, R.N., b. 1839; III. William; IV. Arthur; and I. Jane, who d. unm. 1857. Mr. Kemmis d. 1844.

Seat—Shaen Castle, Queen's Co.

KEMMIS OF BALLINACOR.

KEMMIS, WILLIAM, Esq. of Ballinacor, Rathdrum, co. Wicklow, J.P. and D.L., high-sheriff of that county 1835, and of the Queen's County 1851, Crown Solicitor and Solicitor to the Treasury, b. 28 Oct. 1777; m. 11 May, 1805, Ellen, 2nd dau. of Nicholas-Southcote Mansergh, Esq. of Greenane, co. Tipperary, and has issue,

I. WILLIAM-GILBERT, b. 11 June, 1806, J.P. and D.L., high-sheriff of Wicklow 1835 and of Queen's Co. 1852.
II. Thomas, barrister-at-law, Crown Solicitor of Leinster, b. 19 April, 1807; m. 17 June, 1839, Elizabeth-Anne, dau. of the Rev. Charles-Lambe Palmer, of Rahan, co. Kildare, and has issue.
III. George, in holy orders, vicar of Rosenalis, b. 4 June, 1808; m. 23 April, 1835, Caroline, dau. of the Rev. John Olphert, of Ballyconnell, co. Donegal, and has William, Lt. R.A., and other issue.
IV. Richard, b. 20 Feb. 1812.
I. Elizabeth, m. 16 Jan. 1826, to William-Charles Quin, Esq., an ecclesiastical commissioner.

Mr. Kemmis of Ballinacor is 3rd son of Thomas Kemmis, Esq. of Shaen Castle, by Anne White, his wife.

Seat—Ballinacor, Rathdrum.

KEMP OF LEWES.

KEMP, THOMAS-READ, Esq. of Lewes, co. Sussex, formerly M.P. for Lewes, b. 23 Dec. 1782; m. 1st, Frances, dau. of the late Sir Francis Baring, Bart.; and 2ndly, 26 Nov. 1832, Frances-Margaretta, dau. of the late Charles-Watkin-John Shakerley, Esq. of Somerford Park, co. Chester, and widow of Vigors Hervey, Esq. of Killiane Castle. By the 1st wife, he had four sons and six daus.; and by his 2nd, one son,

FREDERICK-SHAKERLEY, d. 30 Dec. 1834.

Mr. T.-R. Kemp, who sat in parliament for Lewes, d. 21 Dec. 1844.

Lineage.—GEORGE KEMP, of Lewes, descendant of a branch of the ancient family of Kemp of Olanteigh, m. in the earlier portion of the 18th century, Grace, dau. of Thomas Stonestreet, Esq. of Lewes, who d. in 1749, and had issue,

THOMAS, his heir.
Nathaniel, of Rottingdean.
John. George.
Grace, m. to John Paine, of Patcham Place.
Elizabeth, b. in 1760.

The elder son,

THOMAS KEMP, Esq. of Lewes Castle and Hurstmonceaux Park, co. Sussex, M.P., m. Anne Read, of Brookland, an heiress, and left at his decease, with a dau., Anne, m. 1st, to the Rev. George Bythesea, rector of Ightham, Kent, and 2ndly, to Capt. A.-C. Sober, of the dragoon-guards, a son and successor, THOMAS-READ KEMP, Esq.

Arms—Gu., three garbs within a bordure, engrailed, or. *Crest*—A hawk.

KENDALL OF AUSTREY.

KENDALL, EDWARD, Esq. of Austrey, co. Warwick, J.P. co. Gloucester, high-sheriff of Breconshire 1818, *b.* 8 Sept. 1789; *m.* 1st, 20 Nov. 1810, Anna-Maria, eldest dau. of Christopher Darling, Esq., of the 45th regt., and by her (who *d.* April, 1831) has surviving issue,

I. Georgiana, *m.* to Count John-Sobieski Stuart.
II. Rosa-Julianna-Harriet, *m.* to William Nurse, Esq. of Barbadoes.
III. Angelina, *m.* to Jelinger-Cookson Symons, Esq., barrister-at-law.

He *m.* 2ndly, Eliza-Lee, dau. of Thomas Lane Thompson, Esq. of Blackheath, and widow of Watkin Homfray, Esq.

Lineage.—The ancient family of Kendall was seated at a very early period at Smytheebye, in Derbyshire, and is recorded in the Visitation of that county, made in the year 1611. By an original deed, dated 10 May, 1495, it appears that JOHN KENDALL, of Smythesbye, became entitled, in right of Margaret his wife, to a third share of the estate (which share was Austrey, co. Warwick) of Henry Alstrie, Gent., and Edyth his wife, one of the three daus. of Henry Alstre the younger. Among the earlier alliances of the Kendalls of Smythesbye, may be mentioned Fitzherbert, Shepey, and Sacheverell.

HENRY KENDALL, Esq. of Austrey, a lineal descendant of Kendall of Smythesbye, as shown in the Visitation of 1611, *m.* in 1573, Margaret, dau. of George Kendall, Esq., and by her (who *m.* 2ndly, — Orton, Esq.) had twelve children, viz., Nathaniel, *b.* 1574, *d.* in the following year; HENRY, of whom presently; William, *b.* 1580 George, *b.* 1584; Robert, *b.* 1586; Christopher, *b.* 1590; Mary; Margaret; Ruth; Elizabeth; Joan; and Dorothy. The 2nd but eldest surviving son,

HENRY KENDALL, Esq. of Austrey, *b.* in 1578, *m.* about 1600, Lucy, dau. of Robert Brooke, Esq. of Haslecover, co. Stafford, and sister of William Brooke, Esq. of the same place, the lineage of whose family (intermarried with the Huddlestones of Elford, and related through them to Sir William Smith and Sir John Stanley, of Elford) is set forth in Shaw's *Staffordshire*. He *d.* about 1658, leaving a son, HENRY, his heir, and four daus., viz, Hester, Rebecca, Lucy, and Blanche, *m.* to Thomas Austrey, of London, Esq. The son,

HENRY KENDALL, Esq. of Austrey, *b.* in Sept. 1608, *m.* in 1646, Elizabeth, dau. of the Rev. Robert Dowley, of Elford, and by her had,

JONATHAN, his heir.
Rebecca, *m.* to William Brian, Esq. of Shardlow, co Derby.
Elizabeth, *m.* to the Rev. Mr. Potter, of Feckenham, co. Worcester.
Lucy, *m.* to Crawshaw, Esq. of London.
Mary, *m.* to — Bromley, Esq. of London.

Mr. Kendall *m.* 2ndly, Mary, dau. of the Rev. Mr. Hucksop, of Yorkshire, and by her had a dau., Sarah, *m.* to — Whyte, Esq. of co. Stafford. Mr. Kendall *d.* in 1678, his son and heir,

JONATHAN KENDALL, Esq. of Austrey, *m.* in 1675, Jane, dau. of — Dyson, Esq. of Hollow Fields, parish of Inkberrow, co. Worcester, and *d.* about 1717, having had issue,

Jonathan, *b.* 1676, *d. unm.* aged 32.
Nathaniel and Henry, both *d.* in infancy.
EDWARD, of whom presently.
Elizabeth, *m.* to Samuel Ballard, of Austrey.
Mary, *m.* to William Wright, Esq. of Doddlespool.

The eldest surviving son,

EDWARD KENDALL, Esq. of Austrey, *b.* in 1684; *m.* in 1712, Anna, dau. of William Cotton, Esq. of Haigh, co. York, and had issue,

I. Jonathan, *b.* 1714, *m.* in 1741, Elizabeth, dau. of Joseph Smith, Esq. of Birmingham, which lady *d.* 5 March, 1764. He *d. s. p.* 7 March, 1791.
II. Edward, *b.* 19 Sept. 1714, *d. s. p.* in his 26th year.
II. William, *b.* 1717, *d.* an infant.

IV. HENRY, of whom we treat.
V. John, *b.* 14 Feb. 1723, *d.* an infant.
VI. George, *b.* 10 Feb. 1724, *m.* about 1755, Martha Hyde and had issue,
1 Edward-Jonathan, *m.* Lucy Gill, and *d. s. p.*
2 Henry, *m.* Ann Belton, and *d.* leaving issue,
Henry.
William, *m.* Miss Greenhill, and has issue.
Thomas, *d. unm.*
3 George, *m.* Sarah Hill, and *d.* leaving issue,
Edward.
George, *m.* Theresa Glass, and *d.* leaving three sons, George, Henry, Edmund, and Charles, and one dau., Sarah, deceased.
William, *m.* Eliza Clayton, and has a son, Percy.
Henry, *m.* Eliza-Anne Jackson, and has issue, Henry, John-Broughton, Edward, Arthur-George, Eliza-Margaret, Lucy, Caroline-Jane-Rose, Alice-Mary, Agnes, and Emily-Blyth.
4 William-Jones, *m.* Jane-Campbell Kettle, and *d.* leaving issue,
James.
John, *m.* the widow of Harrop, and has issue,
Martha, *m.* to John-T. Smith, Esq.
Lucy-Lumb.
1 Mary, 1st, Judgson, Esq., and 2nd, to Atchison, Esq.
2 Lucy, *m.* to Thomas Lumb, Esq. of Silcoates, co. York, and *d. s. p.*
VII. Thomas, *b.* 18 May, 1730, *d. s. p.* aged 33.
I. Anna, *d.* an infant.
II. Jane, *m.* to William Jones, Esq. of London.
III. Elizabeth, *m.* to Samuel Noton, Esq. of London, and *d.* at Nottingham, leaving issue.
IV. Mary, *d.* an infant.

The 4th son,

HENRY KENDALL, Esq., *b.* 25 Dec. 1718, *m.* Ellen Jacques and *d.* in 1787, having had issue,

EDWARD, his heir.
Jonathan, *m.* Mercy West, and *d.* in 1810, *s. p.*
Henry, *d.* in London, *unm.*
George, drowned at Lancaster, aged 18.
Anna, *m.* to Edward-Kendall Jones, Esq., son of William Jones, Esq. of London, and has issue, Ellen-Jane, *m.* to Charles Manby, Esq., and *d. s. p.*; Edward-Henry, *m.* Mary Collier; and William West.

The eldest son,

EDWARD KENDALL, Esq. of Austrey, *b.* in 1750; *m.* Elizabeth, 2nd dau. of Samuel Irton, Esq. of Irton Hall, Cumberland, by Frances his wife, dau. and heiress of Robert Tubman, Esq. of Cockermouth, and had issue, an only son, the present EDWARD KENDALL, of Austrey, Esq.

Arms—Gu., fesse, chequy, or and az., between three eagles, displayed of the second.
Crest—An eagle displayed, as in the arms.
Motto—Aquila petit solem.

KENNEDY OF BENNANE AND FINNARTS.

KENNEDY, HEW-FERGUSSONE, Esq. of Bennane and Finnarts, co. Ayr.

Lineage.—Nisbet, author of the excellent work on Heraldry, whose authority must be considered good, is of opinion that the Kennedys sprung from the family of the old Earls of Carrick, before the Macdonalls or the Bruces had that title. In confirmation of this, Sir David Lindsay, of the Mount, Lyon King-at-Arms in the reign of JAMES V., has given in his blazons, in 1549, the arms of the "Erle of Carrik of ald" thus—"Argent, a cheveron, gules." Those borne by the name of Kennedy are the very same, with the addition of three crosslets.

The first of the family mentioned in any charter, Nisbet informs us, is DUNCAN DE CARRICK, and, from the document, it appears that he lived in the reign of MALCOLM IV, which began about 1150. The grandson of Duncan, ROLAND, of Carrick, had a grant of the country of Carrick, from Neil, Earl of Carrick, and was declared chief of his name. This grant was confirmed by ALEXANDER III.

The sixth in lineal descent from this Roland was SIR JOHN KENNEDY, of Denure. He *m.* the heiress of Sir Neil Montgomerie, of Cassilis, and had two sons, SIR GILBERT, who succeeded him; and SIR HEW, of Ardstinchar, whom the King of France distinguished for his gallant conduct at the battles of Baugé and Verneuil. Sir Hew *d. unm.* Sir Gilbert, the elder son, was twice married. By his 1st wife, Marion, dau. of Sir James Sandilands, of Calder, he had two sons, Gilbert, who *d.* in the French service, without issue; and THOMAS, of Bargany, who *s.* also to the estates and honours of his uncle, Sir Hew, of Ardstinchar. We find the arms of Kennedy of Bargany emblazoned, in

1549, by Sir David Lindsay, as quartered with the Royal arms of France. From Nisbet, it appears that Sir Gilbert again had, by his 2nd marriage, one son, James, who was preferred to his father's inheritance in consequence of his matching with the Royal Family. By the Princess Mary, dau. of ROBERT III, and widow of the Earl of Angus, he had issue, and his eldest son was created LORD KENNEDY.

The ninth in descent from Thomas of Bargany, was

HEW KENNEDY, of Bennane, who m. his cousin-german, Agnes, dau. of David Fergussone, of Finnarts, and had issue,

DAVID KENNEDY, of Bennane, who m. his cousin-german, Mary, dau. of John Forsythe, of Belliston, co. Antrim, and had issue a son and successor,

HEW-FERGUSSONE KENNEDY, of Bennane and Finnarts, 23rd in descent from Duncan de Carrick.

Arms—Quarterly: 1st and 4th, KENNEDY, arg., a chev., gu., between three crosslets, fitchée, sa.; 2nd and 3rd, FRANCE, az., three fleurs-de-lis, or. The shield supported on the dexter side by a female, and on the sinister by a wyvern.

Crest—A fleur-de-lis, or, issuing out of two oak leaves, ppr.

Motto—Fvimvs.

Seat—Finnants, Ayrshire.

KENNEDY OF DUNURE.

KENNEDY, RIGHT HON. THOMAS-FRANCIS, of Dalguharran Castle, and Dunure, co. Ayr, J.P. and D.L., b. 1788; m. 1820, Sophia, only dau. of Sir Samuel Romilly, and has a son,

FRANCIS-THOMAS-ROMILLY, b. 1842.

Mr. Kennedy, M.P. for the Ayr District of Burghs from 1818 to 1834, was Clerk of the Ordnance in 1832, and a Lord of the Treasury in 1833 and 1834. In 1837, he was appointed Paymaster of Civil Services in Ireland, and was a Commissioner of the Woods and Forests from 1850 to 1854.

Mr. Kennedy is son of the late Thomas Kennedy, Esq., by Jane Adam his wife, and grand-nephew of Thomas Kennedy, of Dunure, who was Lord Advocate of Scotland in the reign of Queen ANNE.

He descends from Gilbert Kennedy, 2nd son of Alexander Kennedy, of Bargeny and Ardstinchar, by Mariot his wife, dau. of Sir John Dunbar, of Mochrum.

Arms, *Crest*, *Motto*—Same as KENNEDY *of Bennane*.

Seats—Dalquharran Castle, and Dunure, Ayrshire.

KENNEDY OF KNOCKNALLING.

KENNEDY, JOHN, Esq. of Knocknalling, co. Ayr, J.P. for Lancashire, b. 4 July, 1769; m. Mary, dau. of — Stuart, Esq. of Manchester, and left issue,

I. JOHN, of Lincoln's Inn, barrister-at-law, m. Eliza, dau. of George Murray, Esq. of co. Wigton.
I. Margaret, m. to Henry McConnell, Esq.
II. Elizabeth, m. to John Greg, Esq.
III. Mary, m. to Samuel Robinson, Esq.
IV. Marianne.
V. Rachael, m. to Edward Chadwick, Esq. of London.
VI. Anne, m. to Albert Escher, Esq. of Zurich.

Lineage.—From title-deeds in possession of the family, beginning with the precept by Kennedy of Bargeny, for infefting Thomas Kennedy in the lands of Knocknalling and Knockreoch, dated 20 July, 1476, it appears that the Kennedys have been proprietors of Knocknalling for upwards of four hundred years.

ROBERT KENNEDY, Esq. of Knocknalling (son of David Kennedy, Esq. of Knocknalling, and grandson of John Kennedy, Esq. of Dumfries), who m. 11 Oct. 1768, Margaret Alexander, and by her (who d. 17 Dec. 1801, aged 73) had issue,

DAVID, his heir.
JOHN, successor to his brother, and present representative.
Alexander, m. Isabella, dau. of Robert Hope, Esq.
Robert, m. the dau. of Robert Henderson, Esq. of Jamaica.
James, m. Jane, dau. of Matthew Brown, Esq. of Crossfat.
Elizabeth, m. to Robert Whigham, Esq. of Haliday Hill, Provost of Sanquhar.
Barbara, m. to John Crichton, Esq. of Sanquahar.

The eldest son and heir,

DAVID KENNEDY, Esq. of Knocknalling, m. Mary, dau. of James M'Millan, Esq. of Corlac and Dalshangar; but dying s. p. in Nov. 1836, was s. by his brother, JOHN KENNEDY, Esq. of Knocknalling.

Arms—Arg., a chev., gu., between three crosses-crosslet, fitchée., sa., all within a double treasure, flory counterflory, of the second, two crescents in flank and one in base, for difference.

Crest—A dolphin, naiant, or.

Motto—Avise la fin.

Seat—Knocknalling.

KENNEDY OF CULTRA.

KENNEDY, ROBERT-JOHN, Esq. of Cultra, co. Down, b. Dec. 1851.

Lineage.—This branch of the noble house of Ailsa left Ayrshire in 1668, and settled in the co. of Down, at Cultra, where they have since remained.

HUGH KENNEDY, Esq. of Cultra (son of John Kennedy and Martha Stewart his wife), m. Mabel Curteis, of the co. Meath, and was father of

JOHN KENNEDY, Esq. of Cultra, who m. Elizabeth, dau. of Henry Cole, Esq. (brother of the 1st Lord Mount Florence), by Mary his wife, dau. of Sir Arthur Brooke, Bart.; and d. in 1802, leaving a son and heir,

HUGH KENNEDY, Esq. of Cultra, b. 1775; who m. 1st, 1800, Grace-Dorothea, only child of Thomas Hughes, and granddau. of Sir Edward Newenham, M.P., and by her (who d. in 1819) had issue,

JOHN, d. 1839.
ROBERT-STEWART, of whom presently.
Henry.
Arthur-Edward, Governor and Commander-in-Chief of West Australia, m. 1839, Georgiana, dau. of J. Macartney, Esq., and has issue, Arthur, Elizabeth, and Georgina.
William-Hugh, captain R.N., deputy comptroller-general of coast guard, m. 8 April, 1841, Georgiana, dau. of Vice-Admiral the Hon. Sir Charles Paget, G.C.H., son of 1st Earl of Uxbridge, and has issue, Elizabeth-Frederica.
Dorothea, m. 1831, to Capt. Price, R.N.
Elizabeth-Selina, m. 1833, to the Rev. Herbert Kynaston, D.D., high master of St. Paul's, and prebendary of St. Paul's Cathedral.
Frances-Matilda, m. 1833, to the Rev. Frederick Panter.
Emily-Jane, m. 1847, to Donald Mackenzie Douglas, Esq., son of General Sir Kenneth Mackenzie Douglas, Bart.
Grace, m. 1844, to Arthur Woodgate, Esq., son of the Rev. Stephen Woodgate, of Pembury, Kent.

Mr. Kennedy m. 2ndly, 1824, Sophia, dau. of Wm. Low, Esq., by Sophia his wife, dau. of Richard, 4th Viscount Boyne, and had issue by her. He d. in 1852, and was s. by his only surviving son,

ROBERT-STEWART KENNEDY, Esq. of Cultra, b. 1804; who m. Sept. 1849, Anne-Catherine, only dau. of Edward Ward, Esq. of Bangor Castle, co. Down, by the Lady Matilda his wife, dau. of Robert, 1st Marquess of Londonderry; and d. July, 1854, leaving issue,

ROBERT-JOHN, present representative of the family.
Edward-Henry, b. Sept. 1854.
Grace-Emily.

Arms—Arg. a chev., between three cross-crosslets, fitchée, sa., all within a double treasure, flory, counterflory of the second.

Crest—A dolphin, naiant, ppr.

Motto—Avise la fin.

Seat—Cultra, co. Down.

KENNEDY OF KNOCKGRAY.

CLARK-KENNEDY, ALEXANDER-KENNEDY, Esq. of Knockgray, co. Kirkcudbright, a major-general in the army, aide-de-camp to the Queen, C.B., and Knight of the Hanoverian Guelphic Order, b. 1782; m. 21 Dec. 1816, Harriet-Rebekah, dau. and co-heir (with Margaret-Eleanor, who m. her cousin, Lieut.-Colonel Purvis, of Darsham) of John Randall, Esq., and has issue,

I. JOHN, b. 21 Sept. 1817; lieut.-col. 18th Royal Irish regt.
II. Alexander-Kennedy, b. 12 Jan. 1821, Hon. E.I.C.S; m. 1842, Harriet, 2nd dau. of the late Archibald Ewart, Esq. of the Hon. E. I. Co.'s service, and has issue.
I. Harriet-Sarah. II. Mary-Jane.
III. Charlotte-Anne.

Major-General Clark-Kennedy is eldest son of the late John Clark, Esq. of Nunland, D.L. for Kirkcudbrightshire, by Anne his wife, dau. and eventual co-heir of Alexander Kennedy, Esq. of Knockgray, son of John Kennedy, of Knockgray, *b.* 1689, and grandson of Alexander Kennedy, minister of Straiton, and chaplain to the Earl of Cassilis, who acquired the property of Knockgray. Major-General Clark-Kennedy had two brothers and two sisters, viz., John Clark, M.D., of Speddoch, co. Dumfries, deputy inspector-general of army hospitals; Walter Clark, H.E.I.C.S., lost in the "Hindostan," 11 Jan. 1803; Jane Clark, who *m.* Lieut.-Col. George Maxwell, of Carruchan, and *d.* 1839; and Christiana Clark.

Arms—Arg., a chevron, gu., between three cross-crosslets, fitchée, sa., in chief, a fleur-de-lis. Honourable augmentation granted to Colonel Clark-Kennedy, in commemoration of his having, when in command of the centre squadron of the royal dragoons at the battle of Waterloo, captured the eagle and colours of the 105th regt. of French infantry, with his own hand, (*vide* SIBORNE'S *History of the Battle of Waterloo*, vol. ii. p. 33.) On a canton of honourable augmentation, erm., the eagle and colours of the 105th regt., inscribed, "L'Empereur Napoleon, au 105me regiment d'infantrie de ligne," and a sword, crossed, ppr., and above them the word "Waterloo." *Crest*—A demi-dragoon, of the royal dragoons, holding, dexter, a sword, and, sinister, an eagle, all ppr.
Crest—A dolphin.
Motto—Avise la fine.
Seat—Knockgray, co. Kirkcudbright.

KENNEY OF KILCLOGHER.

KENNEY, JAMES-CHRISTOPHER-FITZGERALD, Esq. of Kilclogher, co. Galway, J.P., A.B., M.R.I.A., called to the bar in 1848, *s.* 29 Feb. 1852. Mr. Kenney is of Founder's kin to William of Wykeham, has a Royal descent from EDW. I and III, and represents the ancient houses of FitzGerald of Rathrone and Tecroghan, Hope of Hopestown, Ledwich of Carrick, and others; among which is a branch of the Taylors of Swords, as well as the Milesian line of O'Kelly of Kilclogher, seated there since about 1352.

Lineage.—The first patent of lands granted to this family in the co. Galway, is dated 29 Jan. 22 JAMES I. Their early descents compiled by Collinson, the historian of Somersetshire, begin with

JOHN DE KENNE, who, 12 HENRY II., held two knights' fees at Kenne, co. Somerset. He was father of Richard and William de Kenne or Kenei, who, 24 June, 1199, had a lawsuit with William, son of Richard de Kaines, and in the year 1200 was given by King JOHN as a hostage to the King of France. Richard was father of Sir Richard de Kenne, one of the barons minor, father of Sir John, living 26 EDWARD III., and M.P. for Lancaster in 1327; and probably of Henry Kenny, sent into Scotland under safe conduct by the King, 10 Aug. 8 EDWARD II. Sir John's son was John, father of John, father of Robert, father of John, living 12 EDWARD IV., and bearing arms, erm., three crescents, gu. He had several sons; John, the eldest was grandfather of Christopher, the last of the senior branch, whose heiress brought the estates into the family of the Marquesses of Winchester; and among the descendants of Christopher's three brothers, Thomas, John, and Edmund, mentioned in the MSS. Visitations in the British Museum, as founders of the houses of London, Clevedon, and Hutton, lies the representation of the eldest lines of the family. We revert to

NICHOLAS KENNE *vel* KENNEY, 5th son of the John Kenne living 12 EDWARD IV., 1472. He is supposed to have added the fleur-de-lis to the arms, as now borne and on legal record since the 42nd ELIZABETH. He went over to Ireland, where he *m.* Anne Nevill, of Wexford, an old Anglo-Norman family, and had issue by her,

- John Kenney, who had issue two sons, Robert, father of Robert, who seems to have returned to England; and Nicholas, father of Nicholas, who apparently had only one dau., Anne Kenney, wife of Edmund, 2nd son of Robert Barnewall, Esq. of Dunbroe. She *d.* in Dec. 1636, having issue, Mark Barnewall, Mathew and James Barnewall, and another son, said in the funeral entry in the British Museum, to have *d.* young.
- Richard Kenney, father of one only child, believed to have *m.* — Baldwyn, Esq. of Southampton, as given in Camden's Visitation.
- NICHOLAS KENNEY, who follows.

NICHOLAS KENNEY, of Kenney's Hall, Wexford, *m.* Anne Synott, of an ancient Wexford family, and had issue,

NICHOLAS KENNEY, of Kenney's Hall and Dublin, who *d.* in or about 1590, father of

NICHOLAS KENNEY, Esq. of Kenney's Hall and Edermine co. Wexford, several times a Royal Commissioner, and Escheator and Feodary General of, and last who held that office for, all Ireland, to Queen ELIZABETH (in 1596) and JAMES I. He received Edermine Manor co. Wexford, and large grants of lands by patents dated 18 Feb. 1610, and 16 Jan. 1616. His arms, exactly as now borne by his descendants, are still well preserved under his signature, on the seals of several inquisitions taken before him, and on record in the Exchequer Office, Dublin. He *d.* 1621, having had issue by his wife, a dau. of the old English family of Kettlewell or Kettleby,

- Edward Kenney, Esq. of Newcastle, near Lyons, co. Dublin, deputy-escheator 1610, *m.* Margaret, dau. of — Neale, Esq., and *d.* 13 June, 1617, having had issue, Michael, William, Cicely, and Jane, who *m.* her cousin, Capt. William Kenney, of Kenneyswood.
- HENRY, of whom presently.
- Michael.
- Jane.

The 2nd son,

HENRY KENNEY, Esq. of Kenney's Hall and Edermine, re-granted the estates, together with letters of naturalisation, in Ireland, legalizing the grants, he being of English blood, by patents from JAMES I. He was M.P. for Newcastle, near Lyons. He *d.* at his mansion house in Dublin, 10 July, 1650, survived by his wife and administratrix, Frances Barry, sister of Lord Santry, by whom (*d.* July, 1668) he had issue,

- RICHARD (Col.), of whom presently.
- EDWARD, of Cullen, of whom hereafter.
- WILLIAM (Capt.), of Kenneyswood, of whom later.
- Bridget, *d. unm.*
- Mary, *m.* Thomas Herbert, Esq. of Mucruss.
- Elizabeth, *m.* Hon. Raymond Fitzmaurice, son of Lord Kerry.

The eldest son,

COL. RICHARD KENNEY, of Kenney's Hall and Edermine, high-sheriff for Wexford and M.P., *m.* Judith, dau. of William Hawkins, Esq., aunt to Sir William Hawkins, Ulster king of arms, and sister to the Viscountess Loftus. He *d.* 1 Oct. 1682, his will dated 28 Aug. in that year, leaving issue one dau. and heiress, Frances, required by her father's will to marry her cousin, Edward Kenney, of Curerrow or Carrow, which she did, thus uniting the lines of Edermine and Cullen. We revert to this Edward's grandfather, viz.,

EDWARD KENNEY, Esq. of Ballymartle and Cullen, co. Cork, 2nd son of Henry and Frances Barry, *m.* Mary, dau. of — Merriell, Esq. His will is dated 24 Aug. 1683, leaving legacies to his cousins, Jenkin Conway, Robert Saunders, and others, with, after his own issue, his heirs, the Kenneys, descendants of his brother William. He had issue,

- EDWARD, of Cullen, of whom presently.
- William, of Cork, *m.* Catherine, dau. of Sir Peter Courthorpe, of Courtstown and Little Island, co. Cork, governor of Munster (by his 2nd wife, Elizabeth Giffard), and sister of the Viscountess Midleton. He had issue, with other children, William Kenney, J.P. of Coolkeareene, co. Cork.
- Jane, *m.* Martin Supple, Esq. of Dromada, co. Cork.
- Mary, *m.* Capt. Richard Meade, of Tasaxon, co. Cork.

EDWARD KENNEY, Esq. of Cullen, *m.* Sarah, dau. or sister of Capt. Swithin Walton, of Dromore Castle, co. Cork, and had issue (with Jane, William, Richard, and Thomas, R.N., capt. of the Falmouth, killed in action off Brest, in 1704) an eldest son,

COL. EDWARD KENNEY, of Carrow, which he disposed of to the Herberts, subsequently of Cullen, which he sold to the Meade family, and finally of Newford House or Ballinra, co. Wexford, which he built after obtaining the Kenney's Hall and Edermine property by his marriage with his cousin, Frances, heiress of Col. Richard Kenney, of Edermine, was high-sheriff of Wexford about 1696, and J.P. He survived his wife and *m.* a 2nd time, and *d.* about 1730. By Frances his wife he had issue,

- Richard, *d. s. p., v. p.*
- HENRY, of whom presently.
- Thomas, who *d.* about 1732, had issue, COL. EDWARD KENNEY, of Newford, of whom hereafter.
- Mary.
- Elizabeth, *m.* John Goodisson, Esq. of Bellisland, co. Wicklow.
- Catherine, *m.* Charles Morton, of Ballynescar, co. Wexford, Esq.

The eldest surviving son,

HENRY KENNEY, Esq. of Newford, Edermine, Kenney's Hall, &c., *b.* 1699; *d.* 12 Dec. 1751; *m.* Elizabeth, dau. and co-heiress of Henry Dodwell, Esq. of Manor Dodwell, co. Roscommon, aunt of Lord Sidney, and sister of Lady Browne, of the Neale. She re-married Thomas Morgan, Esq. recorder of Dublin, and 3rdly, the Rev. James Edkins. Mr. Kenney *d. s. p.*, and was *s.* by the son of his brother Thomas, viz.,

COL. EDWARD KENNEY, of Newford, Kenney's Hall, Edermine, &c., killed in a duel by — Colclough, Esq., *d. s. p.*, believed the last male representative of the Cullen branch. We revert to the 3rd son of Henry and Frances Barry,

CAPT. WILLIAM KENNEY, of Kenneyswood, co. Cork, *m.* his cousin-german, Jane, dau. of Edward Kenney, of Newcastle, and had issue,

JAMES (Capt.), of whom presently.
Thomas Kenney.

CAPT. JAMES KENNEY, of Grange, co. Wexford, *b.* 1658; *d.* 9 Jan. 1679; *m.* Alice, only child of Robert Taylor, Esq. of Dublin (son of Robert, son of Francis, son of Robert Taylor, by Elizabeth Golding, granddau. of Lord Howth, and through him inheriting, by two lines, the Plantagenet blood, son of James Taylor, Esq. of Swords, co. Dublin), and by her who *d.* 6 May, 1698, had issue, with sons, who *d. s. p.*, a dau., Catherine, *m.* to Patrick Daly, Esq. The eldest son,

JAMES KENNEY, Esq. of Wexford, who *d* 14 Jan. 1764; *m.* Ellen, dau. of Edward Whitmore, of Ballyteignie, co. Wexford, and was *s.* by his son,

JAMES KENNEY, Esq. of Wexford, *b.* 1710; *d.* 1771; *m.* Catherine, (*d.* 1782) dau. of Capt. Thomas O'Kelly, of King JAMES's army (by his wife, Catherine Masterson, of the Fernes family) grandnephew of Col. Richard O'Kelly, of Kilclogher, co. Galway, who forfeited that estate, purchased back by William Kenney, Esq., of whom later. Mr. Kenney had issue,

Thomas, of Wexford and Dublin, *d. unm.* 14 Jan. 1805.
WILLIAM, of whom presently.
James, *d.* 1798, father of Thomas, who *d. unm.*

The 2nd son,

WILLIAM KENNEY, Esq. of Kilclogher and Keelogues, &c., co. Galway, Ballytarusney, co. Wexford, Longwood, co. Meath, and Gardiner's Place, Dublin, *b.* 1755, *m.* 1789, Bridget Fitzgerald, dau. and heiress of John Daly, Esq. of Dalybrook, &c., co. Kildare, by Julia Fitzgerald his wife, dau. of Gerald Fitzgerald, Esq. of Rathrone co. Meath, and Clare, dau. of Sir John Bellew, Bart. Mr. Kenney *d.* 22 Jan, 1830, leaving issue, by his wife, who *d.* 28 Aug. 1842,

JAMES-FITZGERALD, of whom presently.
William, *d. unm.* 15 April, 1850.
THOMAS-HENRY. *See* KENNEY *of Ballyforan.*
Anthony, in holy orders, *b.* 13 June, 1802, *d.* 21 July, 1846.
Julia, *b.* 1794, *d. unm.* 31 Oct. 1832.
Clare, *m.* 16 July, 1823, the Hon. Gonville Ffrench, of Claremont, co. Roscommon, but has no issue.

The eldest son,

JAMES-FITZGERALD KENNEY, Esq. of Kilclogher and Keelogues, &c., co. Galway, Longwood, co. Meath, and Merrion-square, Dublin, J.P. for the co. Galway, lieut. 8th or King's regt., war medal for services in West Indies, lieut.-col. in foreign service, Gr: In: Gen:, and 33rd in Ireland, and of the Grand Orient of France, *b.* 21 April, 1790; *m.* 24 Jan. 1814, Jane-Olivia, only dau. of William-Thomas Nugent, of Pallas, called Lord Riverston (*see* BURKE's *Peerage, title* WESTMEATH), and by her, who *d.* 27 Dec. 1842, had,

William-Nugent, capt. 11th regt., *b.* 23 March, 1815; *d. unm.* 18 Dec. 1850.
JAMES-CHRISTOPHER-FITZGERALD, now of Kilclogher.
NUGENT-THOMAS. *See* KENNEY *of Correndoo.*
Francis, *d.* 31 March, 1830, æt. 3 months.
Mary-Jane, *b.* 8 July, 1816, *d.* 11 Dec. 1817.
Olivia-Emily, *b.* 12 June, 1817, *d.* 20 Nov. 1823.
Jane-Olivia, *b.* 14 July, 1825, *d.* 21 Sept. 1839.
Julia-Mary-FitzGerald.

Lieut.-Col. Kenney *d.* 29 Feb. 1852.

Arms—(Registered and confirmed in Ulster's office) Per pale, or and az., a fleur-de-lis between three crescents, all counterchanged, quartering Kenne, Taylor, O'Kelly, O'Daly, FitzGerald, and many others.

Crests—Out of an earl's coronet, or, a cubit arm erect, vested, gu., cuffed, arg., the hand, ppr., grasping a truncheon, of the first, for KENNEY; a deer-hound, courant, arg., traversing a tree, ppr., for DALY; a monkey at gaze, the tail extended, chained about the middle, or, for FITZGERALD.

Mottoes—In 1677, over the crest, "Teneat, luceat, floreat"; and beneath the shield "Vi virtute et valore;" now the former alone.

Seat—Kilclogher, Monivea, co. Galway.

Town Residence—Merrion Square, South, Dublin.

KENNEY OF CORRENDOO.

KENNEY, NUGENT-THOMAS, Esq. of Correndoo, co. Galway, and Merrion Square, Dublin, second surviving son of the late Lieut.-Col. Kenney, of Kilclogher, co. Galway, and his wife, Jane-Olivia, only dau. of William-Thomas Nugent, Lord Riverston, of Pallas, co. Galway.

Lineage, *Arms, Crest, Motto*—*As* KENNEY *of Kilclogher.*
Seat—Correndoo, Monivea, co. Galway.

KENNEY OF BALLYFORAN.

KENNEY, THOMAS-HENRY, Esq. of Ballyforan, co. Roscommon, A.B., barrister-at-law, *m.* 2 April, 1827, Sophie-Aimée-Armande-Guyon de Montlivault, youngest dau. of Jacques-Marie-Cecile, Comte de Montlivault, chevalier de St. Louis, &c., (and of Catherine de la Charmoise, dau. of the Marquis de la Charmoise, his wife) one of the representatives, by the decision of the Parliament of Paris, of the Lusignans, Kings of Jerusalem, and kin of His Imperial Majesty Napoleon III. Mr. Kenney has issue,

I. JAMES-LOUIS-LIONEL, lieut. in the Imperial navy of France, Knight of the Legion of Honour.
II. Marie-Claire. II. Adele.

Lineage, *Arms, Crest, Motto*—*As* KENNEY *of Kilclogher.*
Seat—Ballyforan House, Ballyforan, Ballinasloe.

KENNY OF BALLINROBE.

KENNY, COURTNEY, Esq. of Ballinrobe, co. Mayo, J.P., *b.* 26 Sept. 1781; *m.* 16 Dec. 1816, Louisa, dau. of William Fenton, Esq. of Spring Grove, Yorkshire, and by her (who *d.* 15 Aug. 1841) has issue,

I. Courtney, *b.* March, 1818; *d.* 1824.
II. George-Frederick, *b.* June, 1821; *d.* 1826.
III. STANHOPE-WILLIAM-FENTON, *b.* 1 July, 1827.
IV. Lewis-Fenton, C.E.; *b.* 18 June, 1831.
I. Sarah-Louisa. II. Susan-Anne.
III. Emma-Sophia. IV. Maria.
V. Caroline.

Lineage.—The ancestor of this family is stated to have come to England on the expulsion of the Huguenots from France. The first who settled in Ireland *circa* A.D. 1680, *m.* a dau. of John Gray, an Englishman, and was father of

THOMAS KENNY, Esq., who *m.* 20 Oct, 1698, Anne, dau. of David Courtney, and granddau. of the Rev. John Courtney, M.A., rector of Ballinrobe, and by her (who *d.* 25 Feb. 1766) he left at his decease, 11 Dec. 1725, a son,

COURTNEY KENNY, Esq. of Roxborough, Ballinrobe, capt. in Colonel Cuff's regiment of militia dragoons; *b.* 14 April, 1702; who *m.* 1st, Eliza Thompson, who *d. s. p.*; and 2ndly, Anne, dau. of the Rev. John Rogers, co. Down, and by her (who *d.* 5 Dec., 1782) had issue,

I. THOMAS, *b.* 11 Oct. 1734, *m.* 12 Jan. 1757, Eliza, dau. of the Very Rev. William Crowe, D.D., dean of Clonfert, by Emilia his wife, sister of George, Lord Carbery. He *d.* 28 Oct. 1812, aged 78, and his wife, 29 July, 1814, aged 78, having had issue

1 William, lieut.-col. 11th Madras Native Infantry, *m.* Martha, relict of George Cuming, Esq., chief at Cuddledore, and *d.* in 1803, of wounds received leading the storming party at Gawilghur, having had issue,

William, late major 73rd regiment, *m.* Miss Inge of Leicestershire.
Eyre, lieut.-col. 60th regt., unatt.

2 Thomas, *m.* a dau. of the Rev. Vesian Pick, rector of Johnstown, and had issue,

Edward, of Ballyoman, co. Wicklow, major 89th regt. retired full pay; *m.* Mary Anne, dau. of Captain Courtney Kenny, and has issue, Edward, lieut. 84th regt., Henry and Mary-Jessie.

3 David-Crowe, lieut.-gen. E.I.C.S., *d.* 20 Aug. 1847, æt. 65, leaving William and Maria.

4 Courtney, capt. 9th regt., *m.* a dau. of Gen. Geils. He was shot acting as engineer at the siege of Burgos, leaving issue,

Henry, who *m.* and had two daus., Euphemia and Edith.
Thomas, lieut.-colonel and assistant adjutant-general 2nd Madras European Infantry, has issue, Courtney, 88th regiment, and others.
William, major 13th Madras Native Infantry.
Mary-Anne, *m.* to Major Edward Kenny.
Jessie, *m.* to Capt. Geils, *d. s. p.*

II. COURTNEY, of whom presently.
III. John, *m.* Frances, dau. of Lemuel Shuldham, Esq.
I. Frances, *m.* Arthur Stanhope, Esq.
II. Anne, *m.* Gregory Cuff, Esq., J.P., Creagh, co. Mayo.
III. Hannah, *m.* to John Garnet, Esq.

Mr. Courtney Kenny *d.* 17 Sept. 1779. His 2nd son,

COURTNEY KENNY, Esq., J.P. of Roxborough, Ballinrobe, *b.* 21 April, 1736, *m.* 23 April, 1775, Susanna, dau. of Stanhope Mason, Esq. of Moira, co. Down, and by her (who *d.* 10 March, 1809, æt. 78) had issue,

I. COURTNEY, now of Ballinrobe.
II. Mason-Stanhope, M.D., J.P. of Halifax, Yorkshire; *b.* 29 Nov. 1786; *m.* Aug 1812, Sophia, dau. of William Fenton, Esq. of Spring Grove, Yorkshire, and has issue,
  1 William-Fenton, *b.* 18 Sept. 1815, *m.* Agnes-Ramsden, dau. of John Ralph, Esq., J.P. of Halifax, and has issue, Courtney Stanhope, *b.* 18 March, 1847.
  2 Lewis Stanhope, M.A., in holy orders, Lancaster, *b.* 3 Jan. 1827.
  1 Emily-Anne, *m.* to the Rev. Godfrey R. Ferris, M.A., Halifax.
III. John, *m.* Miss Lovelock, and *d.* 27 Oct. 1819, leaving a son, C. Bermingham.
I. Anne, *m.* to Major Maxwell, Northampton Fencibles.
II. Susan, *m.* to Thomas Gildea, Esq., clerk of the peace, Mayo.
III. Maria, *m.* to John Clarke, Esq.
IV. Brillianna, *m.* William Griffith, J.P. of co. Sligo.

Mr. Courtney Kenny *d.* 10 March, 1809, aged 78,

Residence—Ballinrobe, co. Mayo.

KENRICK OF NANTCLWYD WOORE.

KENRICK, RICHARD-KYFFYN, Esq. of Nantclwyd, co. Denbigh.

Lineage.—DAVID KENRICK *temp.* EDWARD III., was companion to the Black Prince in the battles of Crecy and Poitiers. He founded the church of Ashley, co. Stafford, and from him descended

JOHN KENRICK, of Woore, co. Salop, who *d.* 9 May, 1628, having *m.* Elizabeth, dau. and heir of Jaspar Lodge, alias Littleton, of Woore, Esq., by Ellenor, dau. of Nicholas Grosvenor, of Wethen. This John left ten sons and two daus. The four eldest sons died without issue, and the property devolved upon

ANDREW KENRICK, of Woore, the 5th son, who *m.* Mary, dau. of William Whiteway, of Dorchester Esq., and left, (along with two daus., Mary, the wife of Ralph Triplet, Esq., and Elizabeth, wife of Anthony Whitwell, Esq.) two sons, Andrew, 2nd son, who *m.* Sarah, dau. of Joseph Perry of London, Esq.; and

RICHARD KENRICK, Esq., elder son and heir, who *m.* 1604, Rebecca, dau. and heir of Maurice Gethin of Kenioge, Esq. and left six sons and six daus.

ANDREW KENRICK, the 2nd son and heir, *d.* 12 Nov. 1747, aged 80, leaving, by his first wife Dorothy Baker, of Birthdin, co. Sussex, a dau. Dorothy, wife to Randle Wilbraham, of Rode Hall, Esq., M.P., and deputy high steward of Oxford, grandfather of Edward, Lord Skelmersdale, and a son,

ANDREW KENRICK, Esq. of Woore, who *m.* Martha, dau. and heir of Eubule Thelwall of Nantclw'd, co. Denbigh, Esq., and left, with four daus., Martha, Mary, Dorothy, and Ann, a son and heir,

RICHARD KENRICK, Esq. of Woore and Nantclwd. He *m.* Elizabeth, dau. of J. Fardell, Esq. and left issue,

I. RICHARD-HARRY, of Nantclwd, of whom hereafter.
II. George-Watkin, of Woore, *m.* 1st, Mary, dau. and heir of J. ffoulkes, Esq. of Llanrydd, co Denbigh, and of Mertin, co. Flint, by whom he left a dau., MARY-ELIZABETH, *m.* 2 May, 1820, to Sir William Henry Clerke, Bart. of Hitcham, co. Bucks. His 2nd wife was Mary Isabella, dau. of James ffarington, of Worden, co. Lancaster, by whom (who *d.* 1829) he left two sons and six daus.
  1 George Kenrick, of Woore, who *m.* Louisa, dau. of J. Posthlewaite, Esq.
  2 William.
  1 Isabella Harriett, *m.* to H. F. Way, Esq.
  2 Sophia-Margaret-Ford.
  3 Charlotte-Louisa-Alexandrina, *m.* to William Gladstone, Esq.
  4 Mary-Hannah-Albina, *m.* to the Rev. H. W. Bellairs.
  5 Ermine-Elizabeth, wife of Allan Edward, Esq.
  6 Fanny-Georgina-Catharine, *m.* to James Edward, Esq.
III. Charles-Gethin, of Cefn y Gadda, who *m.* Eliza, dau. of Butler Clough, Esq., but *d. s. p.*
I. Elizabeth, *m.* to Richard Price, of Rhulias, Esq.
II. Harriett, *m.* to Thomas Ikin, Esq.
III. Sophia, *m.* to Sir George Farmer, Bart.
IV. Maria, *m.* 1st, Price Jones, Esq.; and 2ndly, J. Nicholls, Esq.
V. Louisa *d. unm.*

The eldest son,

RICHARD-HARRY KENRICK, of Nantclwy'd, *m.* Ermine, dau. and co-heir of Sir Thomas Kyffin, of Maenan and Bemont, and left issue,

I. RICHARD-KYFFIN, of Nantclwyd.
II. Thomas, who *d. unm.* 1855.
III. Henry-Kyffin, of Belmont, *d. unm.*
I. Margaret-Kenrick, *d.* 1851.
II. Elizabeth-Kenrick, now Kyffin of Belmont, co. Denbigh.
III. Harriet, *m.* to Henry Hawarden Fazakerley, of Gillibrand, co. Lancaster, Esq.

The present representative is RICHARD KYFFYN-KENRICK above.

Arms—Erm., a lion, rampant, sable.
Crest—A sparrow-hawk, with five arrows in his claws.
Seat—Nantclwyd, co. Denbigh.

KEOGH OF KILBRIDE.

KEOGH, JOHN-HENRY, Esq. of Kilbride, co. Carlow, J.P., lieut.-col. of the co. of Carlow militia, and late capt. 30th foot, *b.* 10 June, 1820, *m.* 1857, a dau. of Capt. Edwin Richards, R.N.

Lineage.—The family of Keogh, or more properly MacEochaid, derives its descent from Fergus, King of Ulster, grandson of Roderick the Great, monarch of all Ireland, and Mea, dau. of Eochaid Feidlioch, King of Connaught, A.M. 3850.

A branch of this family were chiefs of Owney Tire, now the baronies of Owney and Arra, in Tipperary, and Owney beg, in Limerick, thus mentioned by O'Heerin.

"Over Owney Tire, of rich produce,
Rules MacKeogh, as his chosen place."*

MAHONY MACKEOGH, Esq. of Cloonclieve, co. of Limerick, was father of

JOHN MACKEOGH, Esq. of Castle Troy, co. of Limerick, father of

DENIS MACKEOGH, Esq. of Castle Troy, who *m.* Mrs. Eyre, by whom he had

The REV. JOHN KEOGH, D.D., of Strokestown, co. of Roscommon, author of several scientific works; he *m.* Miss Clopton, daughter of the Rev. Rous Clopton, D.D. of Clopton Hall, Warwickshire, and had issue, 1 The Rev. Michael Keogh, of Strokestown, co. of Roscommon; and 2 The Rev. John Keogh, D.D., of Mitchellstown, co. of Cork, author of the *Antiquities of Ireland*, &c., *m.* Miss Jennings, cousin-german of Sarah the great Duchess of Marlborough. The eldest son,

The REV. MICHAEL KEOGH, *m.* Miss Dodd, of Clearly Hall, Hampshire, and had

JOHN KEOGH, Esq. of Loughlinstown, co. of Kildare, by whose exertions the right of renewal for ever was obtained for the tenantry of Ireland; he *m.* Elizabeth, dau. of Christophilus Clynch, Esq. of Peamount House, co. of Dublin, and, dying in 1803, left

GEORGE ROUS.
Henry Clopton, in holy orders, *m.* Elizabeth, dau. of Nicholas Aylward, Esq. of Shankhill Castle, co. of Kilkenny, and has issue.
Annie, *m.* to Lieut.-Colonel Hamlet Obins, and has issue.

The eldest son,

GEORGE ROUS KEOGH Esq. of Kilbride, co. of Carlow, *m.* Marianne, dau. of General Sir Thomas Molyneux, Bart. of Castledillon, co. of Armagh, and, dying in 1850, left

JOHN-HENRY, now of Kilbride, co. Carlow.
Thomas-Molyneux, captain 78th Highlanders, *m.* Henrietta, dau. of Charles Butler, Esq.
William-Somerset.
Elizabeth Margaret.
Georgiana-Mary, *m.* Shapland Swiney, Esq. of Clohamon House, Wexford.
Emuy-Blanche. Adelaide-Maria.

Arms—Argent, a lion rampant gules, between a dexter hand apaumée in the sinister, and a crescent in the dexter chief point, both of the second—for KEOGH, quarterly with CLOPTON and CLYNCH.
Crest—A boar passant.
Motto—Resistite usque ad sanguinem.
Seat—Kilbride, co. Carlow.

* *See* Dean Keogh's *Antiquities of Ireland, Annals of the Four Masters*, &c.

KER OF GATESHAW.

KER, WILLIAM, Esq. of Gateshaw, co. Roxburgh, J.P., *b.* in 1775; *m.* his cousin-german, Jane, dau. of Ellis Martin, Esq., and had issue,

I. GILBERT.
II. Ellis-Martin.
I. Elizabeth.
II. Margaret-Cecilia.
III. Jane-Mary-Scott.
IV. Essex.
V. Wilhelmina-Eliott, *d.* young.
VI. Anna-Maria.
VII. Georgiana-Augusta-Wilkinson.

Lineage.—LANCELOT KER, of Gateshaw and Crookedshaws, living in 1595, (younger son of GILBERT KER, of Primside, son of ANDREW KER, of Primside, whose father, RALPH KER, of Primside, living in 1502, was second son of ANDREW KER, of Cessford, living in 1474, from whom the noble houses of Roxburgh and Lothian derive,) was father of GILBERT KER, of Gateshaw and Crookedshaws, whose son and heir, ANDREW KER, of Crookedshaws, living in 1648, left a son, GILBERT KER, of the same place father of ANDREW KER, of Kelso, living in 1698, who left a son,

WILLIAM KER, Esq. of Gateshaw, *b.* in 1707, who *m.* Elizabeth, dau. of Gilbert Eliott, Esq. of Stonedge, and had issue, 1 GILBERT, his heir; 2 Charles (Sir); 3 William, of Edinburgh; 4 Robert, lieut.-col. E.I.C.S.; 1 Mary; 2 Elizabeth, *m.* to Ellis Martin, Esq.; 3 Essex, *m.* to Capt. Turner, E. I. Co.'s service. The eldest son and heir,

GILBERT KER, Esq. of Gateshaw, *b.* in 1749, *m.* Margaret, dau. of John Hood, Esq. of Stoneridge, by whom he had, 1 WILLIAM, of Gateshaw; 2 John, lieutenant 19th regt., *d.* in Ceylon; 3 Gilbert, R.N., deceased; 4 Thomas, merchant, *d.* in Jamaica; 1 Jane; 2 Eliza; 3 Cecilia; 4 Margaret, *m.* to Francis Brodie, Esq.; and 5 Agnes.

Arms—Vert, on a chev. between three unicorns' heads, erased, arg., armed and maned, or, as many mullets, sa.

Crest—An unicorn's head, erased, arg., armed and maned, or.

Motto—Pro Christo et patriâ.

Seat—Gateshaw, co. Roxburgh.

KER OF NEWBLISS HOUSE.

See MURRAY.

KERR OF MONTALTO.

KERR, DAVID-STEWART, Esq. of Montalto, co. Down, M.P. for that county since 1852, J.P. and D.L., *m.* 1 March, 1842, Hon. Anna-Dorothea Blackwood, youngest dau. of Hans, 3rd Lord Dufferin.

Lineage.—DAVID KER, Esq. of Portavo and Montalto, co. Down, J.P. and D.L., M.P. for Downpatrick, descended from a branch of the Scottish Kers. He *m.* 22 Feb. 1814, Lady Selina-Sarah Stewart, sister of the late Marquess of Londonderry, and *d.* 30 Dec. 1844, leaving an only son, the present DAVID-STEWART KERR, Esq., M.P. of Montalto, and daus., of whom the eldest dau., Frances-Anne, was *m.*, 6 Feb. 1840, to Matthew-John Anketell, Esq., eldest son of William Anketell, Esq. of Anketell Grove.

Seat—Montalto, Ballynahinch, co. Down.

SCOTT-KERR OF CHATTO.

SCOTT-KERR, WILLIAM, Esq. of Chatto and Sunlaws, co. Roxburgh, J.P. and D.L., *b.* 3 Oct. 1807; *m.* 1st, 19 Dec. 1837, Hannah-Charlotte, only child and heiress of Henry Scott, Esq. of Horsleyhill and Belford, and relict of Sir John-James Douglas, Bart. of Springwood Park, and has issue, ELIZABETH-MARY-CHARLOTTE. He *m.* 2ndly, Jan. 1855, Frances-Louisa, 2nd dau. of the late Robert Fennesy, Esq., and has by her a dau., Frances-Edith.

Lineage.—This family, that of SCOTT *of Thirlestaine*, in Roxburghshire (distinct from SCOTT *of Thirlestaine*, in Selkirkshire, represented by Lord Napier) is a branch of the great Scottish family of Scott of Sinton, from which spring in the female line the Ducal house of Buccleugh, and in the male the Scotts of Harden (represented by Lord Polwarth) and the Scotts of Abbotsford.

ALEXANDER SCOTT, of Thirlestaine son of WILLIAM SCOTT, of Thirlestaine, and Christian Don, his wife, and grandson of JAMES SCOTT, (brother-german of Sir William Scott, of Harden,) by Agnes Riddel, his wife, (and which James acquired the lands of Thirlestaine, Histon, and others, from Sir Andrew Ker, of Greenhead, in the year 1661,) *m.* 28 Jan. 1729, Barbara Kerr, of Frogden, and had issue five sons and six daus. The eldest son and heir,

WILLIAM SCOTT, Esq. of Thirlestaine, *m.* 24 June, 1762, Elizabeth Græme, of Balgowan, co. Perth, and had issue, ALEXANDER, *d. unm.* in 1790; ROBERT, of whom presently; Elizabeth, *m.* to Dr. Mackcurin, and *d.* in 1846; Barbara-Christian, *d. unm.* in 1845; Jessy-Murray, *m.* to Sir Patrick-Murray Thriepland, Bart. This gentleman assumed, by Royal licence, the name and arms of KERR, on succeeding to the entailed estates of Sunlaws and Chatto, on the decease of Christian Kerr, commonly called Lady Chatto, who *d. s. p.* and who was lineally descended from a brother of Sir William Kerr, of Greenhead, brother-german of the Earl of Ancrum. He *d.* 4 May, 1782, and was *s.* by his eldest son,

ALEXANDER SCOTT-KERR, of Sunlaws and Chatto, lieut. in the 62nd regt., who *d. unm.* in Philadelphia, in 1790, and was *s.* by his brother,

ROBERT SCOTT-KERR, Esq. of Sunlaws, who *m.* 17 Dec. 1806, Elizabeth Bell, younger dau. of David Fyffe, Esq. of Drumgeith, co. Forfar, and had issue,

I. WILLIAM, his heir and present representative.
I. Anne.
II. Elizabeth-Græme.
III. Margaret.
IV. Rebecca-Agnes, *m.* May, 1855, to John Lewis Bayley, Esq.
V. Madeline.

He *d.* in 1831, and was *s.* by his only surviving son, the present WILLIAM SCOTT-KERR, Esq. of Chatto, representative of the Kerrs of Greenhead, and of the Scotts of Thirlestaine, in Roxburghshire.

Arms—Quarterly: 1st and 4th, KERR; 2nd and 3rd, SCOTT.

Crests—1st, KERR; 2nd, SCOTT.

Mottoes—1st, over the KERR crest, "Regulier et vigoureux;" 2nd, over the SCOTT crest, "Pacem amo."

Seat—Sunlaws, near Kelso, co. Roxburgh.

KERRICH OF GELDESTON HALL.

KERRICH, JOHN, Esq. of Geldeston Hall, co. Norfolk, J.P. and D.L., *b.* 21 Dec. 1798; *m.* 26 Dec. 1826, Mary-Eleanor, eldest surviving dau. of John Fitzgerald, Esq. of Naseby, co. Northampton, and Little Island, co. Waterford, and has issue,

I. WALTER-FITZGERALD, *b.* 16 Dec. 1829.
II. Edmund, *b.* 25 April, 1833.
III. Charles-Augustus, *b.* 6 Aug. 1836.
IV. John, *b.* 6 Feb. 1841.
I. Eleanor-Frances.
II. Elizabeth.
III. Amelia-Jane.
IV. Mary.
V. Andalusia.
VI. Anna-Maria-Theresa.

Lineage.—This family was settled at Dunwich, in Suffolk, as early as 1299, as appears from the records of that borough, which was represented in Parliament by Johannes Kerriche, 2 EDWARD II., A.D. 1308.

JOHN KERRICH, M.D., of Bury St. Edmunds (elder son of Walter Kerrich, Esq. of Harleston, by Ann, his wife, dau. and co-heir of John Dove, Esq. of Harleston, and grandson of John Kerrich, Gent. of Mendham) *m.* Mary, fourth dau. and co-heir of Symon Patrick, of Cambridge, and had issue, 1 JOHN, of whom we treat; 2 Walter, canon of Salisbury; 3 Thomas, in holy orders, rector of Horinger, co. Suffolk; and 4 Mary-Catherine, *m.* to Richard Reynolds, of Paxton, Hants. Mr. Kerrich *d.* 9 Oct. 1762. His eldest surviving son,

JOHN KERRICH, Esq. of Harleston, *b.* 18 Aug. 1733, *m.* his cousin, Amelia, dau. of Simon Kerrich, Esq. of Geldeston, and *d.* in 1795, leaving (with a dau., Amelia, *m.* to George Gooch, Esq. of Brunswick-square, capt. in the E. I. Co.'s service, and an Elder Brother of the Trinity House, and *d.* in 1807; and a son, Edward, of Southampton-buildings, London, *d. s. p.*, 5 Jan. 1821) an elder son and heir,

JOHN KERRICH, Esq. of Harleston, J.P. and D.L., who *m.* 21 Feb. 1798, Elizabeth, dau. of John Walker, Esq. of Wall's End, co. Northumberland, and by her, who *d.* 19 Nov. 1822, had issue,

JOHN, his heir.
Thomas, *b.* 20 Dec. 1804, *m.* 10 March, 1827, Harriet-Frances, dau. of George Baring, Esq., and has issue, Leonard, and Walter-D'Oyly.
Edward, *b.* 14 Jan. 1807, *m.* 17 Sept. 1829, Mary-Evelyn-Susan, second dau. of Richard Fuller, Esq. of the Rookery, co. Surrey, and has issue, Henry Walker *b.* 25 April, 1832, and six daus.

Amelia, deceased.
Adeline, m. to the Rev. Edmund-Hector Hopper.
Jane, d. unm. Anne, d. unm.

Mr. Kerrich d. 25 April, 1812, and was s. by his eldest son, JOHN KERRICH, Esq. of Geldeston Hall.

Arms—Sa., on a pile, arg., a calthrap, of the first.
Crest—A calthrap on a hill, ppr.
Motto—Nunquam non paratus.
Seat—Geldeston Hall, co. Norfolk.

KINCHANT OF PARK HALL.

KINCHANT, RICHARD-HENRY, of Park Hall, co. Salop, J.P. and D.L., high-sheriff 1846, b. 6 Jan. 1804; late an officer in the 69th regt.; m. 2 Dec. 1831, Eliza-Maria, only dau. of the Rev. Richard-Bewley Caton, M.A., of Binbrook, co. Lincoln, and has issue,

I. CHARLTON-JOHN, b. 27 May, 1834.
II. Job-Henry, b. 20 Aug. 1835.
III. Richard-Caton, b. 4 April, 1841.
I. Eliza-Power, m. 23 April, 1851, Edward Venables, Esq., son of L. J. Venables, Esq. of Woodhill, co. Salop.
II. Myra-Catherine-Ann.

Lineage.—JOHN QUINCHANT, a native of France, became a captain in Gen. Harry Pulteney's regiment of foot, and fell at the battle of Fontenoy, 11 May, 1745. He m. Elizabeth, 3rd dau. of Benjamin Scott, Esq. of Eltham, co. Kent, and had a son,

JOHN QUINCHANT, who altered the spelling of his paternal name to KINCHANT, and was a captain in the 32nd regiment of infantry. He resided first at Stone House, near Ludlow, and afterwards at Park Hall, near Oswestry, which estate he acquired in right of his wife, Emma, dau. of Sir Francis Charlton, Bart of Ludford, relict of Richard Jenkins, Esq. of Bicton Hall, co. Salop,* and co-heiress of her brother, Job Charlton, of Park Hall, sheriff of Shropshire in 1748. Capt. John Kinchant d. 9 June, 1789, aged 68, leaving issue, by the above lady (with two daus., Emma, m. to John Gardner, Esq. of Sansau, co. Salop; and Eliza, m. to Richard Bock, Esq. of Shrewsbury and Trefnanny,) three sons, viz.,

I. JOHN-CHARLTON, his successor.
II. Francis, in holy orders, of Easton, near Middleton-on-Hill, co. Hereford, m. Mary, only child of Samuel Patshull, Esq. of Easton, by whom he had issue, Francis-Charlton, a cornet in the Scots Greys, killed at the battle of Waterloo, 18 June, 1815; and Mary-Emma, m. 1st, to Captain Henry Andrews, of the 4th, or King's Own, regiment; and 2ndly, to the Rev. John Langley, curate of St. Chad's, Salop, and afterwards rector of Wallingford, Oxfordshire.
III. Richard, of the civil service, E.I.Co., m. 1802, Myra-Catherine-Anne, dau. of John Wilkinson, Esq., Recorder of Bombay, and d. in 1809, leaving issue,
  1 RICHARD-HENRY, present representative.
  2 John-Robert-Nathaniel, b. 28 June, 1805, in holy orders, incumbent of Llanvair, Waterdine, and Bettws, co. Salop, m. May, 1835, Maria, dau. of Richard Phayre, Esq., H.E.I.C.S., and has issue, Robert, Francis, Charlton, Catherine, Maria and Rose.
  1 Myra-Catharine-Anne, m. to Charles J. Ellis, Esq. of the E.I.Co.'s civil service.

The eldest son,

JOHN-CHARLTON KINCHANT, Esq. of Park Hall, high-sheriff of Salop in 1775, m. Jane Stukeley, dau. of — Fowler, Esq., co. Berks, and dying s. p. in 1832, was s. by his nephew, the present RICHARD-HENRY KINCHANT, Esq. of Park Hall.

Arms—Az., three lions' heads, two and one, erased, arg., ducally crowned, or.
Crest—Issuant, from a ducal coronet, or a demi-lion, arg.
Motto—Virtus pyramidis.
Seat—Park Hall, Oswestry, co. Salop.

KING OF UMBERSLADE.

KING, EDWARD-BOLTON, Esq. of Umberslade, co. Warwick, J.P., high-sheriff 1830, and formerly M.P. for Warwick, b. 1801; m. 1828, Georgiana, 2nd dau. of Robert Knight, Esq. of Barrells, M.P., and has issue,

I. EDWARD-RALEIGH, b. in 1833.
I. Georgiana. II. Frances-Dorothea.
III. Jane. IV. Catherine.
V. Isabella. VI. Henrietta.

Lineage.—This is presumed to have been originally a Westmoreland family, and is stated to descend from Sir Ralph King, who fought at Azincourt. The first of its members out of that county,

THOMAS KING, whose father garrisoned the church of Malhamdale for the parliament, erected Church End in Kirby. He had two sons and a dau. His 2nd son,

THOMAS KING, settled at Skellands, in the parish of Kirby Malhamdale, and co. of York. His great-great-grandson,

EDWARD KING, Esq. of Hungerhill, co. York, vice-chancellor of the duchy of Lancaster, and bencher of Gray's Inn, (4th son of the Very Rev. James King of Skellands, co. York, dean of Raphoe, by Anne his wife, dau. and co-heir of John Walker, Esq. of Hungerhill; and brother of Captain James King, the circumnavigator, of Walter King, D.D., bishop of Rochester, and of John King, Esq., Under Secretary of State), m. 1st, Miss Lang, by whom he had three daus.,

Henrietta, m. to the Hon. George Carleton, colonel in the army, killed at Bergom-op-Zoom, and had, with three daus., a son, Guy, the present Lord Dorchester.
Ann, m. to — Sunderland, Esq.
Mary, m. to — Radcliffe, Esq.

He m. 2ndly, Miss Dorothy Myers, and had issue,

EDWARD-BOLTON, his heir.
John Myers, in holy orders, vicar of Catcombe, co. Somerset, m. his first cousin, Miss Frances King, dau. of the bishop of Rochester, and has one son and a dau., John and Frances.
Susan-Alice, m. to the Rev. James Formby, vicar of Frindsbury, Kent.
Dorothea, m. 12 July, 1826, to Edward-Williams Hasell, Esq. of Dalemain, in Cumberland, and has issue.

Mr. King d. in 1824,

Arms—Sa., a lion, rampant, between three cross-crosslets, or.
Crest—Out of a ducal coronet, a demi-lion, rampant.
Seat—Umberslade, near Henley-in-Arden.

KING OF NORTH PETHERTON.

MEADE-KING, RICHARD, Esq. of The Rectory, North Petherton, co. Somerset, J.P. and D.L., high-sheriff 1846, b. 2 March, 1776; m. 23 May, 1804, Elizabella, only dau. of John Warren, M.D., of Taunton, by Betty his wife, 3rd and youngest dau. and co-heir of James Woolcott, Esq. of Shearston, in the parish of North Petherton, co. Somerset, and by this lady (who d. 6 Jan. 1826) has issue,

I. RICHARD, of Walford, near Taunton, J.P., b. 27 April, 1806; m. 2 Feb. 1831, Catherine, 2nd dau. and co-heir of the late William Oliver, Esq. of Hope Corner, near Taunton, and has issue,
  1 Richard-Meade, b. 27 Oct. 1831.
  2 William-Oliver, b. 17 March, 1833.
  3 Frederick-Meade, b. 21 Nov. 1835.
  4 Henry-Herbert, b. 16 Feb. 1837.
  5 Walter, b. 1 April, 1842.
  1 Eliza-Catherine.
  2 Henrietta.
II. Frederick, b. 28 March, 1818; d. unm. 3 Oct. 1834.
III. Henry-Warren, b. 1 April, 1817; m. 28 Sept. 1847, Mary-Anne, 2nd dau. of Joseph Higgin, merchant of Manchester, and has issue,
  1 Richard-Robert, b. 3 Feb. 1852.
  1 Jessie-Marion.
IV. Charles-James, b. 9 Aug. 1822; m. 1 May, 1855, Catherine Hall, eldest dau. of William Newton, merchant of Birkenhead, and has issue,
  1 Agnes-Gertrude.
V. William-Thomas-Pearse, b. 24 Nov. 1824; m. 14 April, 1852, Ellen-Catherine, dau. of Isaac Lovell, Esq. of West Haddon, co. Northampton.
I. Elizabella-Warren.
II. Clara-Theresa.
III. Ellen, m. 29 Sept. 1835, to the Rev. George Bodley Warren, of Dulverton, co. Somerset.
IV. Jessie-Louisa, m. 8 Nov 1835, John-Clitsome Warren, Esq. of Taunton, and d. 8 May, 1845.

Lineage.—JOHN MEADE, of Lyng, co. Somerset, m. 3 June, 1697, Mary Morse, of North Petherton, and with a dau., Mary, had three sons, John baptized 2 April, 1700; RICHARD, of whom presently; and William, bapt. Nov. 1703. The 2nd son,

* Previously relict of John Lloyd, Esq. of Aston, co. Salop.

RICHARD MEADE, Gent. of North Petherton, bapt. 11 Nov. 1701, *m.* Joan Hydon, of the same place, and by her, who *d.* in 1754, had (with two daus, Hannah, *m.* 15 Nov. 1774, to her cousin, John Meade of Lyng, and *d. s. p.* 2 Feb. 1781; and Mary, *m.* to Francis Coombe, Gent. of North Petherton, and *d. s. p.*, and three sons who *d.* young) an only surviving son and heir,

WILLIAM MEADE, Gent. of North Petherton, bapt. 19 May, 1751, who *m.* 21 June, 1775, Elizabeth, younger dau. and co-heir of John Ling, Gent. of North Petherton, and by her, who *d.* in May, 1786, left, at his decease in March, 1789, an only son and successor, the present RICHARD MEADE-KING, Esq. of the Rectory of North Petherton, who assumed, by royal license, 5 Oct. 1830, the additional surname and arms of King, in compliance with the will of the late Richard King, Esq. of the Rectory, North Petherton.

Arms—Quarterly: 1st and 4th, a lion, rampant, between three crosses-crosslet, sa., and as many escallops, gu., for KING; 2nd and 3rd, gu., on a chev., arg., between three leopards' faces, or., two arrows, in saltier, az., barbed and flighted, ppr., between two bows, chevronwise, of the fourth, for MEADE.
Crests—A mount, vert, thereon an arm, in bend dexter, couped at the elbow, the hand supporting a tilting-spear, erect, the head broken, the arm surmounting a branch of oak, fructed, in bend sinister, all ppr., for KING; a demi-griffin, az., wings elevated, erm., in the dexter claw a fleur-de-lis, or, for MEADE.
Motto—Cadenti porrigo dextram.
Residence—Pyrland Hall, co, Somerset.

KING OF BALLYLIN.

KING, REV. HENRY, of Ballylin, King's County, *b.* 1779; *m.* 5 June, 1821, Harriett, youngest dau. of John Lloyd, Esq. of Gloster, King's County, for many years M.P. for that county, and had issue,

I. JOHN-GILBERT, *b.* 19 Dec. 1822, J.P. and D.L. at one time, high-sheriff for the King's County.
I. Harriett.
II. Jane, *m.* to Sir William R. Mahon, Bart.
III. Mary, *m.* to Hon. Henry C. Ward, son of the late Viscount Bangor.

Lineage.—This family and that of Sir Gilbert King, Bart., of Charlestown is one and the same.

GILBERT KING, Esq., who *m.* Sarah, dau. of John French, of French Park, co. Roscommon, had a son,

GILBERT KING, Esq., major 5th dragoon-guards, *m.* Rebecca, his cousin, dau. of John King, Esq. of Ballylin, and sister of John King, Esq. of the same place, M.P. for Jamestown, and left, with a dau., Harriett, *m.* to the Rev. John Eagles, a son and heir, the present REV. HENRY KING, who *s.* to Ballylin at the decease of his maternal uncle.

Arms—Sa., a lion, rampant, double queued, or.
Crest—An escallop, gu.
Motto—Spes tutissima cœlis.
Seat—Ballylin, King's County.

KING OF STAUNTON PARK.

KING, JAMES-KING, Esq. of Staunton Park, co. Hereford, M.P. for that shire, J.P., *b.* 6 Nov. 1806; *m.* 17 March, 1835, Mary-Cochrane, 4th dau. of Kenneth-Francis Mackenzie, Esq. (a younger branch of the Mackenzies of Redcastle, co. Ross, N.B.), and has issue,

I. FRANCIS-JAMES, *b.* 13 Oct. 1838.
I. Emma-Anne. II. Eleanor-Mary.
III. Adeline. IV. Katherine-Julia.

Lineage.—THE REV. JAMES SIMPKINSON, M.A., rector of St. Peter-le-Poor, Old Broad Street, London, son of Roger Simpkinson, Esq. of London, by Elizabeth his wife, dau. of William King, Esq of Staunton Park, assumed, by royal lincence, April 1837, his maternal surname and arms of KING only. He *m.* 1st July, 1802, Emma, 4th dau. of Edward Vaux, Esq. of the city of London, and had issue,

I. JAMES-KING, now of Staunton Park.
II. Thomas, in holy orders, M.A., of Balliol College, Oxon, *m.* 12 Oct. 1838, Amelia-Frances, 6th dau. of Kenneth-Francis Mackenzie, Esq., and has issue, a dau., Rose-Margaret.
I. Margaret. II. Mary. III. Elizabeth.
IV. Frances, *m.* to the Rev. James Garbett, M.A., rector of Clayton, co. Sussex, and professor of poetry in the University of Oxford.
V. Louisa-Decima.

Arms—Quarterly: arg. and az., in the 2nd and 3rd quarters, a mullet of six points, or, pierced, of the field, over all a bend barry of six, of the second, charged with a cinquefoil, of the third and gu.
Crest—A lion, rampant, bendy, or and az. supporting two branches composed of two roses, gu., and three cinquefoils, vert., slipped and leaved, of the last.
Motto—Floreo in ungue leonis.
Seat—Staunton Park, near Leominster, co. Hereford.

KINGDON OF LAUNCELLS.

KINGDON, GEORGE-BOUGHTON, Esq. of Launcells, co. Cornwall, and Compton Hall, co. Devon, J.P. and D.L., *b.* 10 March, 1775; *m.* 29 June, 1837, Christiana, dau. of the late Rev. William-Holland Coham, of Coham, Dunsland, and Upcott Avenell, all in co. Devon. Mr. Kingdon is one of the gentlemen of her Majesty's most honourable Privy Chamber.

Lineage.—The Kingdons are an old and respectable family of the counties of Cornwall and Devon. Their most ancient residence, of which there is now any authentic account, was at TREHUNSEY, in the parish of Quithiock, Cornwall, where they flourished in the 12th, 13th, 14th, and 15th centuries.

The eldest branch of the Kingdon family became extinct at Trehunsey, about the middle of the 16th century, when the two co-heiresses married Chiverton and Vivian.

ROGER KINGDON (son of Roger Kingdon, Esq., descended from one of the sons of the Trehunsey family), settled at Holsworthy, co. Devon, about the year 1730, and engaged in commerce. He *m.* 18 June, 1733, Judith, dau. of John Cory, Esq., and had issue,

I. JOHN, in holy orders, J.P., *b.* 4 Nov. 1735; *m.* in 1766, Jane, dau. of the Rev. John Hotkin, patron and vicar of Okehampton, and had issue,
1 JOHN, in holy orders, rector of the parishes of Marhamchurch and Whitstone, Cornwall, J.P., *m.* Miss Marsh, sister-in-law to Richard Preston, Esq., barrister-at-law, the late eminent conveyancer, and has several children, one of whom, the Rev. William Kingdon, rector of Whitstone, *m.* Miss Hawker, dau. of the Rev. Jacob Hawker, vicar of Stratton.
2 Roger, in holy orders, patron and rector of Holsworthy, Devon, *m.* the widow of the Rev. Leonard Herring, and has several children, of whom one, the Rev. John Kingdon, is rector of Michaelstow, Cornwall.
3 Richard, *m.* his 1st cousin, Mary, dau. of the late Richard Kingdon, Esq., and has a son, the Rev. Roger-George Kingdon.
4 Thomas-Hockin, in holy orders, J.P., rector of Pyworthy, Devon. He *m.* Miss Nicholson, dau. of Samuel Nicholson, Esq., late of Ham, and sister of George Nicholson, Esq. of Waverley Abbey, and has issue, the Rev. Samuel Kingdon, *m.* Miss Napier, dau. of the late Gen. Napier, H.E.I.C.S.; the Rev. George-Thomas Kingdon, *m.* Miss Badcock; and Paul Kingdon, Esq., barrister-at-law, late fellow of Exeter College, Oxford, *m.* Miss Foulkes, dau. of the Rev. Peter-D. Foulkes.
5 Francis, *m.* Miss Palmer, dau. of the late Very Rev. Dr. Palmer, dean of Cashell, and has several children.
6 Dennis, late major in the 80th regt., *m.* Miss Herring, only child of the late Rev. Leonard Herring.
1 Elizabeth-Dennis, *m.* to Capt. Usherwood, R.N.
II. RICHARD, of whom presently.
III. Roger, who *d.* young.
I. Mary, II. Judith, both deceased.

The 2nd son,

RICHARD KINGDON, Esq. of Holsworthy, co. Devon, was for many years an active magistrate for that shire. He *m.* in 1770, Rebecca, only dau. of the Rev. George Boughton, of the ancient family of Boughton, of Lawford Hall, in Warwickshire, and had issue,

Roger, in holy orders, *d. unm.*
GEORGE-BOUGHTON, now of Launcells.
Richard, M.D., *m.* Jane, dau. of the late Dr. Parson, M.D., and sister of Dr. Parson, LL.D., and has, Broughton, and other issue.
Cory, M.D., *m.* Elizabeth, dau. of the Rev. James Buckingham, and has, Alfred-Cory, in holy orders; Clement-Broughton; and other issue.
Judith, *m.* to John Braddon, Esq., J.P. and D.L.
Mary, *m.* to her cousin, Richard Kingdon, Esq.

Arms—Quarterly: 1st and 4th, arg., a chevron, sa., between three magpies, ppr., for KINGDON; 2nd and 3rd, sa., three crescents, or, for BOUGHTON.
Crest—An eagle displayed, with two necks and heads, sa.
Seats—Launcells House, near Stratton, Cornwall; and Compton Hall, near Plymouth, Devon.

KINGSCOTE OF KINGSCOTE.

KINGSCOTE, THOMAS-HENRY, Esq. of Kingscote, co. Gloucester, J.P., high-sheriff 1841, *b.* 19 Jan. 1799; *m.* 1st, 8 April, 1828, Isabella-Frances-Anne, 6th dau. of Henry, 6th Duke of Beaufort, and by her (who *d.* 4 Feb. 1831), has issue,

I. ROBERT-NIGEL-FITZHARDINGE, *b.* 28 Feb. 1830; *m.* 1st, Caroline-Sophia, dau. of Col. Wyndham, of Petworth, Sussex; and 2ndly, Lady Emily-Marie, dau. of Earl Howe.

I. Isabella-Charlotte-Louisa, *m.* 29 Nov. 1854, to Capt. Marcin, of Bloomfield, co. Sligo, late of the 3rd light dragoons.

He *m.* 2ndly, 5 June, 1833, Harriott-Mary-Anne, eldest dau. of Benjamin, 1st Lord Bloomfield, and by her also has issue,

I. Fitzharding, *b.* 16 March, 1837.
II. Henry-Bloomfield, *b.* 28 Feb. 1843.
III. Thomas-Arthur-Fitzhardinge, *b.* 16 Jan. 1845.
IV. William-Anthony, *b.* 26 Nov. 1848.
V. John-Bloomfield, *b.* 27 Feb. 1851.
I. Georgina-Emily. II. Louisa-Harriott.
III. Caroline-Frances.

Lineage.—NIGELL FITZ-ARTHUR, grandson of ANSGERUS, the Saxon, living in 985, *m.* Adeva, dau. of Robert Fitz-Hardinge, grandson of SUENO, the 3rd King of Denmark, by Eva, niece of WILLIAM the Conqueror. With this lady he received as dower the manor of Kingscote (called in Domesday Book, Chingescote).

ADAM DE KINGSCOTE, of Kingscote (son of Nigell Fitz-Arthur, by Adeva his wife), had a confirmation of that manor in 1188, from his uncle, Lord Maurice FitzHardinge. He was buried in Bristol Cathedral, and from him descended the KINGSCOTES *of Kingscote*, whose chief in the time of HENRY V. shared in the glory of AZINCOURT. The eventual representative,

WILLIAM KINGSCOTE, Esq. of Kingscote, son of William, who *d.* in 1706, and great-grandson of Anthony, who *d.* in 1645, and lies interred in the church of Kingscote, under a monument bearing an interesting inscription referential to the family history.* He *m.* Catherine Barnsley, and had issue,

I. NIGELL, his heir.
II. Robert-Fitzhardinge, of London, who *m.* Mary Hammond, a co-heiress, and dying in 1770, left, with two daus. (Hannah, *m.* to Robert Ladbroke, Esq., M.P.; and Catherine, *m.* to Edward Jenner, Esq., M.D., F.R.S.) and a son, Nigell, who *d. s. p.*, two elder sons, viz.,
  1 ROBERT, who inherited the estates from his uncle.
  2 Thomas, who *m.* Oct. 1794, Harriet, 4th dau. of the late Sir H. Peyton, Bart., of Doddington, and dying in 1811, left issue,
    THOMAS-HENRY, present proprietor.
    Henry-Thomas, *b.* in 1802, *m.* 11 July, 1833, Harriett, eldest dau. of Christopher-T. Tower, Esq. of Weald Hall, co. Essex, and has issue, five sons and four daus.
    Robert-Arthur-Fitzhardinge, *b.* 1811, *m.* Rosamund, dau. of — Daniell, Esq., and has one son and two daus.
    Emily-Frances, *m.* to Sir John Kennaway, Bart.
    Caroline-Marianne, *m.* in 1828, to the Rev. Alan-Gardner Cornwall, A.M., 2nd son of the late John Cornwall, Esq. of Hendon, Middlesex.
I. Elizabeth, *m.* to Thomas, Earl of Suffolk, and *d.* in 1769.

Mr. Kingscote *d.* in 1731, aged forty-one, and was *s.* by his elder son,

NIGELL KINGSCOTE, Esq. of Kingscote, *b.* in 1720, major of the Gloucester militia, who *d. unm.* in 1773, and was *s.* by his nephew,

ROBERT KINGSCOTE, Esq. of Kingscote, col. of the North Gloucester militia, who, never having married, entailed his estates upon the children of his brother Thomas. He *d.* in Feb. 1840, and was *s.* in Kingscote by his nephew, the present THOMAS-HENRY KINGSCOTE, Esq.

Arms—Sa., ten escallop shells, in pile, arg.; on a canton, gu., a mullet pierced, or.
Crest—An escallop shell.
Seat—Kingscote Park, co. Gloucester.

* In the same church a tombstone records the death of THOYLUS KINGSCOTE, "who did service as a commander for the Prince of Orange forty years, and, being eighty years old, ended this life upon the 10th of December, 1656."

KIRKE OF MARKHAM.

KIRKE, WILLIAM, Esq. of Markham Hall, co. Notts, J.P., *b.* 29 March, 1799; *m.* 1st, 1820, Miss Harriet Bowmer, and by her (who *d.* in 1826) he had John-Montague, who *d.* an infant. Mr. Kirke *m.* 2ndly, Anne, dau. of Sir Thomas-Woollaston White, Bart. of Wallingwells, Notts, and by her, who survives her husband, he left at his decease, 15 March, 1848,

I. JOHN-HENRY, lieut. 19th regt., *b.* 16 Dec. 1838, served before Sebastopol in 1854-55.
I. Anne. II. Harriott.

Lineage.—NICHOLAS KIRKE, of Anstan, in the parish of Laughton-en-le-Morthen, Yorkshire, had his estate sequestered "for his delinquency to the Commonwealth," but restored to him on payment of a fine of £169 11*s.* 5*d.*, to the parliament of England; the release and receipt for which is dated 2 Dec. 1653. He *d.* 14 April, 1659; his son,

JOHN KIRKE, Gent. of Anstan, purchased an estate and settled at Markham in 1685. He *d.* 3 Dec. 1710, and was buried at Markham. By Sarah his wife (who *d.* 1724), he left, with a younger son, William, *b.* in 1688, another son,

JOHN KIRKE, Gent. of Markham, *b.* in 1679, who, by Eleanor his wife, had issue, WILLIAM, of whom presently; Edmund, J.P. for Notts, who *d.* 4 Dec. 1786, and was buried at Markham, *s. p.*; Anne, *m.* to John Bright, Gent. of East Retford; and Eleanor, who *d. unm.* The eldest son,

WILLIAM KIRKE, Esq. of Markham, J.P. for Notts, bapt. at Markham, 1 June, 1715, *d.* 25 May, 1773, aged 58, and was buried in the church there. He had two sons, JOHN and William, the latter of whom *d.* in 1785. The elder,

JOHN KIRKE, Esq. of Markham and Retford, *d.* 8 March, 1779, aged 27, and was buried at Markham. His wife was Dorothy-Tye, dau. and heiress of Joseph Bright, Esq. of Retford and Eckington, co. Derby, by Dorothy, dau. of John Tye, Esq., and co-heir of her brother, Thomas Tye. His son and heir,

JOHN KIRKE, Esq. of Markham and Retford, *b.* in 1777, J.P., sometime capt. in the 24th light-dragoons, and afterwards colonel of the Sherwood rangers, *d.* 23 Feb. 1826. He *m.* 1st, Ann-Mervyn, dau. of Sir William Richardson, Bart. of Augher, co. Tyrone, and by that lady (who *d.* 21 Dec. 1815) had issue,

I. WILLIAM, who *s.* at Markham, and commences this article.
II. John, lieut. 11th light dragoons, *b.* in April, 1800, *d.* at Meerut, in 1825, *unm.*
III. James, lieut. R.N., *b.* in 1805, *d.* at Jersey, *unm.*
IV. Henry, col 12th Bengal native infantry, *b.* in 1806, *m.* 1829, Margaret, dau. of Col. Blair, and had issue, 1 Henry; 2 St.-George; 1 Ellen-Mervyn, *m.* to R. Faithful, Esq., Bengal cavalry; 2 Anna-Maria, *m.* to Mark Thornhill, Esq., E.I.C. Civil Service; 3 Norah-Letitia, *m.* to P. Harris, Esq., Bengal infantry, *d.* 1856; and 4 Margaret-Kathleen.
V. St.-George, in holy orders, rector of Marten, co. Lincoln, *m.* 1843, Mary, eldest dau. of the Rev. Joseph Cooke, D.D., and has issue, St.-George-Mervyn; Mary-Elina; and Dora-Elizabeth.
I. Dorothea-Letitia, *m.* 1828, the Rev. Taylor White, B.A., vicar of Cuckney, Notts, and *d.* 1840.
II. Eliza, *d. unm.*
III. Diana-Maria, *m.* 1831, Rev. Thomas-W. Wrench, M.A., rector of St. Michael's, Cornhill.
IV. Harriet, *m.* 1832, Thomas-Bigsby Chamberlin, Esq., J.P. of Brighton.
V. Ann, *m.* to the Rev. Charles-Vere Hodge, M.A., of St. Edmund Hall, Oxford, vicar of Clarborough, near Retford.
VI. Charlotte, *m.* to the Rev. Francis-Arthur Jackson, B.A., vicar of Riccall, co. York.
VII. Eliza, *d. unm.* in 1827.

The 2nd wife of Col. Kirke was Maria, sister of the Rev. Richard Almond, vicar of St. Peter's, Nottingham; by her he had,

I. Robert-Piercy, *d.* young, 1835.
II. John, barrister-at-law, *b.* 27 May, 1826.
I. Mary-Georgina-Bettina, *m.* 1 May, 1844, to Charles Thorold, Esq. of Welham, near Retford.

Arms—Arg., a chevron, between three boars' heads, couped, sa.
Crest—A boar's head, erect, couped, sa.
Seat—Marfield Hall, East Markham, Notts.

KIRSOPP OF THE SPITAL.

KIRSOPP, JAMES, Esq. of The Spital, co. Northumberland, J.P., *b.* 6 March, 1814; *m.* 24 May, 1848,

Eliza Dunn, of Bath House, Newcastle-on-Tyne, and has a son,

JAMES-JOSEPH, b. 18 May, 1852.

Lineage.—JAMES GIBSON, Esq. (son of John Gibson, Esq., and Elizabeth Leadbitter his wife), assumed the surname of KIRSOPP, in compliance with the will of William Kirsopp, Esq. of Hexham. He m. 26 July, 1809, Eliza, only dau., by his 2nd wife, of Sir Alexander Livingstone, Bart. of Westquarter, co. Stirling, and had surviving issue,

JAMES, now of The Spital.
Frank, b. 24 June, 1822.
Mary-Ann.
Elizabeth-Janet, m. 30 May, 1842, to Edward, 2nd son of William-John Charlton, Esq. of Hesleyside, co. Northumberland.

Arms—Gu., a saltier, erm., between two cranes, in pale, arg., and two garbs, in fesse, or.
Crest—A mount, vert, thereon a crane, as in the arms, the dexter claw reposing on an escutcheon, arg., charged with the letter K., sa.
Motto—Credo.
Seat—The Spital, near Hexham, co. Northumberland.

KIRKWOOD OF WOODBROOK.

KIRKWOOD, JAMES, Esq. of Woodbrook, co. Roscommon, b. 1808, J.P., high-sheriff 1848; m. 7 Oct. 1839, Sarah-Mary-Dodd, eldest dau. of the late Capt. James-Nicholson Soden, 24th regt., J.P. and D.L., only son of Thomas Soden, Esq., J.P., of Money Gold, co. Sligo, for fifty years provost of Sligo, and has issue,

I. THOMAS-YADEN-LLOYD, b. 19 Sept. 1843.
II. James Nicholson-Soden, b. 4 Jan. 1846.
III. Kingson-Dodd-Lloyd, b. 20 July, 1851.
I. Isabella-Matilda-Emily.
II. Annina-Mary.
III. Sarah-Carey-Lydia-Adelaide.
IV. Joanna.

Lineage.—This family, one of considerable antiquity, has been seated in Roscommon for centuries.

JAMES KIRKWOOD, Esq. of Woodbrook, J.P., b. 1731, (son of Thomas Kirkwood, Esq. of Woodbrook, by Eleanor his wife, dau. of the first Archdeacon Carey, and grandson of Michael Kirkwood, Esq. of Killukin, by his wife Elizabeth Jackson, of Enniscoe, co. Mayo), m. Catherine, only dau. of Samuel Kirkwood, Esq. of Moyne Abbey, co. Mayo, and d. in 1791, leaving a son and successor,

THOMAS KIRKWOOD, Esq. of Woodbrook, J.P., high-sheriff co. Roscommon, 1806, who m. 15 Feb. 1798, Anne, dau. of James Knott, Esq. of Battlefield, co. Sligo, and by her (who d. 1836, aged 68) had a son, JAMES, now of Woodbrook, and the following issue,

Thomas, m. Jude, eldest dau. of John Kirkwood, Esq. of Rathfarnan House, co. Dublin, and d. 2 May, 1854, leaving two sons and four daus.
Harloe, d. unm. July, 1850.
Joanna, m. to Charles Galagher Moore, Esq., 2nd son of the late George Moore, Esq., barrister-at-law, of Mountjoy Square, Dublin.
Mary, m. to Edward Fraser, Esq. of Annagh, co. Sligo.

Arms—Gu., on a chev., or, between three fetterlocks, arg., a pheon, between two mullets, pierced, sa.
Crest—A pheon, sa.
Motto—Spes mea in Deo.
Seat—Woodbrook, Carrick-on-Shannon, co. Roscommon.

KIRWAN OF BLINDWELL.

KIRWAN, MARTIN-STAUNTON, Esq. of Blindwell, co. Galway, J.P. and D.L.; s. his father in 1828.

Lineage.—The Kirwans of Blindwell, of Milesian origin, bore the surname of O'Quirivane until the time of Queen ELIZABETH. They have been settled at Tubber-Keagh, literally Blindwell, time immemorial, and in the confirmatory grant of CHARLES II. reference is made to their recognition by HENRY VII. and King JOHN.

MARTIN KIRWAN, Esq. of Blindwell, (son of Martin Kirwan, of Blindwell, by his wife Anne Lynch, of Drimcong, grandson of Martin Kirwan, Esq. of Blindwell, by his wife, a dau. of Sir John Browne of the Neale, great-grandson of Martin Kirwan, Esq. of Blindwell, by his wife, a dau. of George Bingham, Esq. of Castlebar, great-great-grandson of Martin Kirwan, Esq. of Blindwell, by his wife, dau. of Lynch, of Lydecon, and great-great-great-grandson of Martin Kirwan, Esq. of Blindwell, by his wife, a dau. of Burke, of Derry-Macloghny Castle, (m. Alice, dau. of Charles Blake, Esq. of Merlin Park, co. Galway, and had, with a dau., Mary, (who m. George Shee, Esq., and d. in 1706,) several sons, of whom one of the younger, John Kirwan, became eminent as a jurisconsult in Spain, and another settled in the island of Porto Rico, where his only dau. survived until lately, possessed of a large property. The eldest son,

MARTIN KIRWAN, Esq. of Blindwell, high-sheriff of the county of Galway, m. Mary, eldest dau. and co-heir of Thomas Coleman, Esq. of the Grove House, co. Galway, and had, with a dau., who m. M. Blake, Esq. of Ballinafad, co. Mayo, a son and successor,

MARTIN KIRWAN, Esq. of Blindwell, also high-sheriff of the county of Galway, who m. Mary, eldest dau. and co-heir of James Staunton, Esq. of Waterdale, co. Galway, and had issue three sons, MARTIN, his heir; James, who d. in India, where he held a high civil appointment; and Thomas, lost in the Centurion, of which vessel he was first lieutenant; and two daus., Harriet, m. to John Bodkin, Esq. of Annagh; and Mary, m. to D.-J. Wilson, Esq. of Belvoir Castle. The eldest son,

MARTIN KIRWAN, Esq. of Blindwell, m. Mary, 3rd dau. of William Burke, Esq. of Keelogues, 3rd son of Richard Burke, 4th son of Sir John Burke, 4th Bart. of Glinsk, and by her had issue,

I. MARTIN-STAUNTON, now of Blindwell.
II. James. III. Thomas. IV. William.
I. Catharine. II. Charlotte. III. Margaret.

Mr. Kirwan d. in 1828.

Arms—Arg., a chev., sa., between three coots, ppr., quartering STAUNTON.
Crest—A coot, as in the arms.
Seat—Blindwell, co. Galway.

KIRWAN OF CREGG.

KIRWAN, RICHARD-A.-HYACINTH, Esq. of Knockdoe, co. Galway, J.P., b. 30 May, 1813; m. 29 April, 1839, Agnes-Jane, 3rd dau. of J. Thompson, Esq. of Lauriston, co. Down.

Lineage.—WILLIAM KIRWAN, who went to Galway in 1488, d. there in 1499, leaving two sons, THOMAS-REAGH, of whom presently, and Patrick, warden of Galway. The elder,

THOMAS-REAGH KIRWAN, d. in 1545, and was ancestor of

MARTIN KIRWAN, Esq. of Cregg, eldest son of Patrick Kirwan, Esq. of Cregg, and grandson of Martin Kirwan, Esq. of Cregg (from whose youngest son, Thomas, descend the KIRWANS *of Hillsbrook*) m. Mary French, and had four sons viz., 1 Patrick, who d. in 1756; 2 Richard, LL.D., of Cregg, Pres. Roy. Irish Society, a distinguished writer on chemistry, geology, and the kindred sciences, and one of the first natural philosophers of his time, m. in 1757, Anne, dau. of Sir Thomas Blake, Bart. of Menlo; and d. in 1812, leaving two daus., Maria-Theresa, m. in 1793, to John-Thomas, fifteenth Lord Trimlestown and Elizabeth, m. to Mr. Hill; 3 Andrew, major in the army, d. in 1813; 4 HYACINTH. The youngest son,

HYACINTH KIRWAN, Esq., m. Elizabeth-Frances, dau. of Patrick Blake, Esq., a younger son of the family of Blake, of Tower Hill, co. Mayo, and d. in 1800, having had issue, 1 Martin, R.N., lost in H.M.S. Yorke; 2 PATRICK; 3 Richard, capt. half-pay 94th regt., m. Ellen, dau. of the late — Bond, Esq., barrister-at-law; 4 Andrew, capt. half-pay 66th regt., m. Charlotte, 2nd dau. of — Eld, Esq. of Seighford Hall, co. Stafford; 5 John, R.N., d. in 1825; and 1 Elizabeth-Frances, m. in 1818, to T. Macquoid, Esq. The 2nd son,

PATRICK KIRWAN, Esq. of Cregg, co. Galway, b. 19 Dec. 1787; m. 9 Aug. 1811, Louisa-Margaret, dau. of Geoffrey Browne, Esq. of Castle Macgarratt, co. Mayo, and sister of Lord Oranmore, and by her, who d. in 1826, had issue,

RICHARD, A.-H., present representative of the family.
Edward, in holy orders, b. Aug. 1814.
John-Henry, in holy orders, b. 25 Dec. 1816.
Hyacinth, b. 28 July, 1820
Henrietta-Theresa, m. in Feb. 1838, to the Rev. G.-D.-A. Tyler.
Louisa-Margaret, m. in April, 1838, to H.-B. Brownlow, Esq., Bengal civil service, youngest brother of Lord Lurgan, d. in 1840.
Elizabeth-Frances-Charlotte.
Mary-Anne-Georgiana.
Isabella-Catherine-Louisa.

Mr. Kirwan d. 31 Dec. 1847.

Arms—Arg., a chevron, gu., between three Cornish choughs, sa.
Crest—A Cornish chough, as in the arms.
Motto—Mon Dieu, mon roi, et ma patrie.

KIRWAN OF CASTLE HACKET.

KIRWAN, DENIS, Esq. of Castle Hacket, co. Galway, J.P. and D.L., high-sheriff 1844, *b.* 4 Sept. 1808; *m.* 11 April, 1844, Anne-Margaret, only child of Major Thomas Macan, of Greenmount, co. Louth, and has issue,

JOHN-THOMAS, *b.* 23 Feb. 1851.
Mary-Lizzy.

Lineage.—STEPHEN KIRWAN, Esq., 2nd son of Thomas Oge Kirwan, Esq. (*see* KIRWAN *of Cregg*) had, with other issue, a son, RICHARD KIRWAN, father of STEPHEN KIRWAN, Esq., whose son, SIR JOHN KIRWAN, Knt., left a son, SIMON KIRWAN, Esq., whose son, JOHN KIRWAN, Esq. of Castle Hacket, *d.* in 1781, leaving by his wife, a Miss Daly, of Dalystown, co. Galway, three sons, JOHN, Denis, and James, of whom the eldest,

JOHN KIRWAN, Esq. of Castle Hacket, *m.* Mary, dau. of Henry-Boyle Carter, Esq. of Castle Martin, co. Kildare, by Susanna, his wife (*m.* in 1750), dau. and co-heir of Sir Arthur Shaen, Bart. of Kilmore, and dying in June, 1821, left, with a dau., two sons, JOHN, his heir, and Henry, who *m.* Miss Bingham, and had issue. The elder son,

JOHN KIRWAN, Esq. of Castle Hacket, *b.* 1780; *m.* 1806, Penelope, eldest dau. of James-H. Burke, Esq. of St. Clerans, and by her (who *d.* 19 Nov. 1842) had issue,

DENIS, now of Castle Hacket.
John, *d.* aged 20, 10 June, 1827.
Elizabeth, *m.* in 1839, Hon. Edward Lawless, now Lord Cloncurry.

Mr. Kirwan *d.* 22 June, 1842.

Arms, &c.—*See* KIRWAN *of Cregg*.
Motto—J'aime mon Dieu, mon roi, et mon pays.
Seat—Castle Hacket, co. Galway.

KIRWAN OF HILLSBROOK.

KIRWAN, JOHN-JOSEPH-ANDREW, Esq. of Castlecomer, co. Kilkenny, resident magistrate of that county, J.P. and D.L. co. Galway, *b.* 31 Oct. 1811; *m.* 11 June, 1832, Mary-Isabella, only dau. of Major William Burke, of Quansborough, by the Lady Matilda his wife, dau. of William, 2nd Earl of Howth, and co-heiress of her mother, Lady Elizabeth Bermingham, dau. and co-heir of Thomas, Earl of Louth. By this lady he has,

I. MARTIN-FITZ-JOHN. II. William-Fitz-John.
III. Andrew-Fitz-John. IV. Henry.
I. Matilda-Harriet-Josephine, *m.* to her cousin, Joseph-Blake Burke, Esq. of Roscommon.

Lineage.—THOMAS KIRWAN, Esq., 2nd son of Martin Kirwan, Esq. of Cregg, by Eliza Bodkin, his wife, *m.* his cousin, a dau. of John Kirwan, Esq. of Knock, and had three sons, Martin-Fitz-Thomas, who *d.* in 1771; Ambrose; and JOHN. The youngest,

JOHN KIRWAN, Esq. of Hillsbrook, *m.* Mary Mahon, and had two sons, I. JOSEPH, who *d.* without male issue, in 1827: of his daus. and co-heiresses, Mary, *m.* Capt. John Kirwan; Julia, *m.* Edward Browne, Esq.; and Eliza, *m.* James, Viscount Netterville; and II. MARTIN, of whom presently; and three daus., Matilda, *m.* to Walter Blake, Esq. of Menlo; Theresa, *m.* in 1775, to William Burke, Esq. of Ower; and Harriet, *m.* to George-William Lyster, Esq. The 2nd son,

MARTIN-JOHN KIRWAN, Esq. of Knockdromadough and Stowe, co. Galway; *m.* in or about the year 1807, Mary, dau. of Miles Burke, Esq. of the island of St. Eustatia, by Catherine his wife, dau. of Sir Walter Blake, Bart. of Menlo, and had issue,

JOHN-JOSEPH-ANDREW, his heir.
Miles, barrister-at-law, *m.* in 1838, Miss Kirwan, only dau. of John Kirwan, Esq.
Martin. Henry.
Mary, *m.* in 1838, to James Blakeney, Esq., and has issue.
Barbara, *m.* to Henry, M'Donell, Esq. of Streamsfort, and has issue.

Arms, Crest, &c.—As KIRWAN *of Cregg*.

KIRWAN OF DALGIN.

MAITLAND-KIRWAN, CHARLES-LIONEL, Esq. of Gelston Castle, Castle Douglas, N.B., and late of Dalgin Park, co. Mayo, J.P. and D.L., at one time high-sheriff, co. Mayo; *b.* July, 1811; *m.* 25 Oct. 1842, Matilda-Elizabeth, dau. of William Maitland, Esq. of Auchlane and Gelston, and has issue,

I. CHARLES-LIONEL. II. William-Francis.
III. Lionel. IV. James-Maitland.
I. Mary-Agnes. II. Dora-Fitzgerald.
III. Matilda-Douglas.

Lineage.—The KIRWANS *of Dalgin* descend from EDMUND-ABIGID KIRWAN, Esq., 2nd son of Patrick Kirwan, Esq. of Cregg, who *d.* in 1608. He *m.* Anastasia Blake, and had a son and successor, ALEXANDER KIRWAN, Esq., father of EDMOND KIRWAN, Esq., whose son, MARTIN KIRWAN, Esq. of Dalgin, co. Mayo, *m.* and had six sons, Edmund, Valentine, PATRICK, Alexander, Andrew, and Martin. The 3rd of whom,

PATRICK KIRWAN, Esq. of Dalgin, *m.* and had three sons, MARTIN, who *d.* in 1825; PATRICK; and George. The 2nd son,

PATRICK KIRWAN, Esq. of Dalgin, *m.* Dorothea-Mary, dau. of Charles-Lionel Fitzgerald, Esq. of Turlough Park, co. Mayo, and had issue,

CHARLES-LIONEL, his heir, late of Dalgin, and now of Gelston Castle.
Martin.
Caroline.
Dorothea, *m.* to her cousin, Charles-Lionel-William Fitzgerald, Esq., who *d.* 9 Nov. 1834.
Mary. Julia-Emma.

Arms, &c.—As KIRWAN *of Cregg*.
Seat—Gelston Castle, Castle Douglas, N. B.

KITTERMASTER OF MERIDEN.

KITTERMASTER, JAMES, Esq. of Meriden, co. Warwick (eldest and only surviving son of James Kittermaster, of Meriden, and Margaret his wife), *b.* 5 March, 1789; entered the 49th regt. as ensign, in 1807, was made lieutenant 1810, and retired from the army 1812. He afterwards graduated in medicine, taking, in 1826, the degree of M.D. He inherited, in 1838 (on the death of Ann Marshall, who had a life interest in the property), the estate of the Rev. Anthony Bliss, vicar of Meriden, and incumbent of Castle Bromwich, both in the co. of Warwick, who *d.* 1815. He inherited also, at the same time, the estate of Mary Marshall, who *d.* 1828, dau. and co-heiress of the Rev. Francis Marshall, of Allesley, co. Warwick. He *m.* 6 Jan. 1813, Mary, dau. of William and Mary Zachary, of Meriden, and has issue,

I. Henry-Fitz James, *b.* 31 Dec. 1813, *d. s. p.* 1858.
II. FREDERICK-WILSON, M.A. Pemb. Coll. Oxford, *b.* 18 May, 1820, in holy orders.
III. Anthony Bliss, C. E. Moore, Canada West, *b.* 17 Jan. 1829.
IV. Albert-Reuben, Moore, Canada West, *b.* 3 March, 1830.
I. Anna-Maria, *m.* Charles Marshall, Esq. of London.
II. Edith-Harriet.

Lineage.—THOMAS KYDERMISTER was prior of Kenilworth in 1402. Dugdale has preserved a singular inscription which was upon the great bell of Kenilworth, the gift of this Thomas Kydermister.

RICHARD KYDERMISTER, a native of Romsley, near Kidderminster, was educated at Oxford (Gloucester Hall, now Worcester College) and afterwards elected Abbot of Winchcombe, 1487. He became a celebrated preacher, and, in 1500, travelled to Rome. In 1510 he received, by Royal grant, the Manor of Sudeley, co. Gloucester. In 1515 he preached a remarkable sermon at St. Paul's Cross, in defence of the privileges of the Clergy, which aroused the anger of the King and Parliament. He wrote a history of the Abbots of Winchcombe, and other works, among which was a *Tract against the Doctrine of M. Luther*. He *d.* 1531, and was buried in the Abbey at Winchcombe.

JOHN KYDERMISTER, a nephew of the above-named Richard, settled in London and became a member of the Drapers' Company. He *m.* Annys Wenthame, and had issue one son, JOHN. He *d.* 1543.

JOHN KYDERMISTER, his son, b. 1520, purchased an estate at Langley Marsh, co. Bucks, to which he retired. He m. Elizabeth Welford, of Enfield, and had issue, EDMUND, Thomas, and three daus. He built several alms'-houses at Langley, and d. 1558. His son,

EDMUND KYDERMISTER, b. 1548, was one of the six clerks in Chancery. He m. 1574, Ann, sister of Sir Oliph Leigh, of Addington, and d. 1607, leaving issue, JOHN, Robert, and several daus.

SIR JOHN KYDERMISTER, his son, b. 1576, m. Mary, dau. of Sir William Garrard, of Dorney. He was knighted at Hampton Court, 3 Oct. 1609, and received from King CHARLES I. the manor and park of Langley Marsh. He restored the church there, and built, at the west end, a room for a library, in which, afterwards, the Royalists were accustomed to meet. He had issue only one dau., Elizabeth, who m. Sir John Parsons, of Boveney, the heiress of which family m. Thomas Lambarde, ancestor of the present William Lambarde, Esq., Beechmont, co. Kent. Another nephew of Richard, Abbot of Winchcombe, remaining at Romsley, left a son.

WILLIAM KYDERMISTER, who, in a suit with Sir John Lyttleton, obtained an order from the Court of Chancery "to maintain quiet possession of his lands at Romsley." Afterwards becoming possessed of property at Coleshill, he removed thither about 1550. He left issue, by his wife, Isabella, Thomas, Richard, and three daus.

THOMAS KYDERMASTER, his son, b. 1563, had, by his wife, Elnor, one son. Thomas Kittermaster, b. 1606, who left several children, one of whom m. Catherine, dau. of Sir Edward Holt, of Aston.

RICHARD KYDERMASTER (brother of Thomas) b. 1576, had also one son, Thomas, b. 1607, who, by his wife, Elizabeth, left issue. Thomas, John, RICHARD, and William.

RICHARD KITTERMASTER, his son, b. 1649, left four sons and two daus., of whom,

RICHARD KITTERMASTER, his son, b. 1679, had issue, by Susannah, his wife, John, THOMAS, Richard, and William.

THOMAS KITTERMASTER, his son, b. 1709, had, by his wife, Sarah, three sons and two daus., of whom,

RICHARD KITTERMASTER, his son, b. 1742, left issue, by Elizabeth, his wife, JAMES, Henry, Richard, and George.

JAMES KITTERMASTER, his son, b. at Coleshill, 1763, m. Margaret, dau. of William Harper, of Meriden, and was the father of JAMES KITTERMASTER, the present representative. He d. 1814.

Arms—Az., two chev., erminois, betw. three bezants.

Crest—On a chap., azure, turned up, erm., an eagle rising, erminois.—Confirmed by Sir William Segar Garter, to Thomas Kydermaster, of Coleshill, co. Warwick, and by a subsequent Herald in a visitation of Warwickshire, to his son, Thomas Kittermaster. Also to Kydermister of Langley, in the visitation of Bucks, 1634.

KNATCHBULL OF BABINGTON.

KNATCHBULL, WILLIAM-FRANCIS, Esq. of Babington, co. Somerset, J.P. and D.L., high-sheriff 1841, M.P. for East Somerset; b. 30 July, 1804; m. April, 1829, Emma-Louisa, dau. of the late Charles-Gordon Gray, Esq. of Virgin Valley, Jamaica.

Lineage.—THE REV. WADHAM KNATCHBULL, Chancellor and Prebendary of Durham, third son (by Alice his wife, dau. of John Wyndham, Esq. of Nonington) of Sir Edward Knatchbull, 4th Bart., and M.P. for co. Kent, m. Harriet, dau. of Charles Parry, Esq., and d. in 1760, leaving (with a dau. Catherine, m. to Thomas Knight, Esq. of Godmersham, and a son, Charles, of the Royal navy, who m. his cousin, Frances, dau. and heir of Major Norton Knatchbull) an elder son,

WYNDHAM KNATCHBULL, who m. 12 June, 1790, his cousin, Catherine-Maria, dau. of Sir Edward Knatchbull, Bart., and by her (who d. 30 Jan. 1807) left at his decease, 29 June, 1833, two sons,

- WADHAM, in holy orders, prebendary of Wells, m. in 1825, Louisa-Elizabeth, third dau. of William Wyndham, Esq. of Dinton, and by her (who d. 1845) has six sons and four daus.
- Wyndham, ensign Gren. gds., d. 1813.
- Norton-Charles, lt. 1st Royals, d. 1823.
- WILLIAM-FRANCIS, now of Babington.

Arms—Az., three crosses-crosslet, fitchée, between two bendlets, or.

Crest—On a chapeau, az., turned up, erm., a leopard, statant, arg., spotted, sa.

Motto—In crucifixa gloria mea

Seat—Babington, co. Somerset.

KNIGHT OF GODMERSHAM.

KNIGHT, EDWARD, Esq. of Chawton House, co. Hants, and of Godmersham Park, co. Kent, J.P. and D.L., high-sheriff for Hants 1822, b. 1794; m. 1st, May, 1826, Mary-Dorothea, dau. of the Right Hon. Sir Edward Knatchbull, Bart., and by her (who d. 1838) has had issue,

- I. WYNDHAM-WILLIAM, b. 1828; m. 1849, Henrietta-Frances, dau. of Lieut.-Col. Armstrong.
- II. Philip-Henry, lieut. R. W. fusiliers, b. 1835.
- III. Charles-Ernest, b. 1836; d. before Sebastopol, Oct. 1855.
- IV. William-Broadnax, b. 1833.
- I. Georgina-Elizabeth.

Mr. Knight m. 2ndly, March, 1840, Adela, dau. of John Portal, Esq. of Freefolk Priors, Hants, and by her has issue,

- I. Montague-George, b. 1844.
- II. Charles-Edward, b. 1846.
- III. Henry-John, b. 1848.
- I. Elizabeth-Adela.
- II. Adela-Louisa-Cassandra.
- III. Adela-Mary-Margaretta.
- IV. Helen-Adela.
- V. Ethel-Adela.

Lineage.—The family of Knight is of high respectability in Hampshire. WILLIAM KNIGHT, of Chawton, living about the middle of the 16th century, was great-grandfather of NICHOLAS KNIGHT, Esq., who left issue by his wife, Elizabeth, three sons, of whom the youngest,

STEPHEN KNIGHT, of Chawton, Esq., d. in 1628, leaving, by Judith his wife, one son and a dau., viz., RICHARD, and Dorothy, who m. Richard Martin, Esq. of Ensham, in Oxfordshire. Stephen Knight's son,

RICHARD KNIGHT, Esq. of Chawton, m. Elizabeth, dau. of J. Fielder, Esq. of Barrow Court, in Berks, and was s. at his decease, in 1642, by his son,

SIR RICHARD KNIGHT, Knt., who m. Priscilla, only dau. of Sir Robert Reynolds, of Elvetham, in Hants, but dying s. p. in 1679, he devised his estates to his kinsman,

RICHARD MARTIN, Esq. This gentleman, upon inheriting, assumed the surname of KNIGHT. He d. unm. in 1687, and was s. by his brother.

CHRISTOPHER MARTIN, Esq., who likewise took the name of KNIGHT. He also d. unm. in 1702, and bequeathed his estates to his sister,

ELIZABETH KNIGHT. This lady m. 1st, William Woodward, Esq., son of Edward Woodward, Esq. of Fosters, in Surrey, by Elizabeth, dau. of Sir Christopher Lewkenor and his wife, Mary May. She m. 2ndly, Bulstrode Peachey, Esq., uncle of the 1st Lord Selsey, but dying s. p. in 1737, devised her estates to

THOMAS BROADNAX, Esq. of Godmersham, who had relinquished his patronymic and assumed the surname of MAY. In 1729, this gentleman kept his shrievalty for the county of Kent, and rebuilt, three years after, the mansion of Godmersham. In 1738, Mr. May again changed his name to that of KNIGHT, in conformity with the testamentary injunction of Mrs. Elizabeth Knight widow of Bulstrode Peachey Knight, Esq. He m. in 1729, Jane eldest dau. and co-heir of William Monk, Esq. of Buckingham, in Sussex (by Hannah, dau. and co-heir of Stephen Stringer, Esq. of Goudhurst, and Jane Austen* his wife), and had, with younger children, a son and heir, THOMAS. Mr. Knight d. in 1781, at the advanced age of 80, and was s. by his eldest son,

THOMAS KNIGHT, Esq. of Chawton and Godmersham, b. in 1735, who m. Catherine, dau. of Dr. Wadham Knatchbull, dean of Canterbury, but dying issueless in 1794, devised his lands to his cousin,

EDWARD AUSTEN, Esq., who changed his name to that of KNIGHT, and became of Godmersham. He m. 1791, Elizabeth, 3rd dau. of Sir Brook Bridges, Bart., by whom, who d. in 1808, he had issue,

---

* This JANE AUSTEN was eldest dau. of John Austen, Esq. of Grovehurst, in Kent; which JOHN AUSTEN, Esq., had a son,

JOHN AUSTEN, Esq., who m. Elizabeth, dau. of Thomas Weller, Esq. of Tonbridge, and d. v. p. in 1704, leaving, with other issue,

WILLIAM AUSTEN, Esq., who m. Miss Rebecca Hampson, and had a son,

THE REV. GEORGE AUSTEN, who m. Miss Cassandra Leigh, and had issue,

JAMES, who m. 1st, Anne, dau. of Gen. Mathew, by Lady

EDWARD, now of Chawton House and Godmersham.

George-Thomas, *m.* 7 Feb. 1837, the Countess Nelson, relict of William, 1st Earl Nelson.

Henry, a major in the army, *m.* 1st, Sophia, dau. and co-heir of Lewis Cage, Esq., by whom he has a son; and 2ndly, 12 Jan. 1836, Charlotte, eldest dau. of the late Rev. Edward Northey, canon of Windsor, and by her (who *d.* 28 June, 1839) has a dau.

William, in holy orders, of Steventon, Hants, *m.* 1st, Caroline, eldest dau. of John Portal, Esq. of Freefolk House, in Hants, and by her has issue four sons and three daus. He *m.* 2ndly, Mary, dau. of the Rev. Edward Northey, by whom he had three daus., *d.* in infancy; and 3rdly, Hester, relict of General Sir John Hope.

Charles-Bridges.

Brook-John, *m.* Margaret, dau. of Charles Pearson, Esq.

Fanny-Catherine, *m.* in 1820, to Sir Edward Knatchbull, Bart. M.P.

Elizabeth, *m.* to Edward Rice, Esq. of Dane Court, Kent, M.P.

Marianne.

Louisa, *m.* to Lord George-Augustus Hill.

Cassandra-Jane, *m.* 21 Oct. 1834, to Lord George-Augustus Hill.

Mr. Knight *d.* 19 Nov. 1852.

Arms—Vert, a bend, fusilly, or, in base a cinquefoil, arg., a canton, gu., quartering the AUSTEN arms, viz., Or, a chev., gu., between three lions' gambs, erect, sa.

Crests—1st, a friar, habited ppr., holding in the dexter hand a cinquefoil, slipped, arg., and in the sinister, a cross, sa., suspended from the wrist, the breast charged with a rose, gu., for KNIGHT; 2nd, on a mural crown, or, a stag, sejant, arg., attired, gold, for AUSTEN.

Seats—Godmersham Park, Kent; Chawton House, Hants.

KNIGHT OF GLEN PARVA.

KNIGHT, JOSEPH, Esq. of Manor House, Glen Parva, co. Leicester, capt. H.M. 26th Leicestershire regt. of militia, *b.* 3 Feb. 1803; *m.* 11 March, 1830, Mary, dau. of the late John Gregory, Esq. of Aylestone Hall, co. Leicester, and has issue,

I. GREGORY, *b.* 30 Aug. 1832.
II. Joseph-Gay, *b.* 8 Sept. 1837.
I. Mary-Ada } both *d. unm.*
II. Ida-Anne }

Lineage.—THOMAS KNIGHT, of the city of Bath, and of Weston, near Bath, *m.* at Tamworth, 28 Nov. 1591, Elizabeth Buttrye, and was *s.* by his eldest son,

THOMAS KNIGHT, *b.* 13 Aug. 1599, who inherited real property in the counties of Warwick and Stafford, as heir both to his father and his mother. He had a son,

RYCHARD KNIGHT, who *d.* in 1708, leaving an only son,

SAMUEL KNIGHT, *b.* 28 June, 1686. He *m.* 1 July, 1714, Judith, only child of Thomas Voughton, of Tamworth by his 1st wife, Isabel: Judith was the granddau. of John Voughton, Gent. of Wiggington, co. Stafford, who was the maternal uncle of Thomas Guy, Esq., M.P., the founder of Guy's Hospital; by this marriage, the senior relationship to the founder became vested, (at the decease of Mrs. Clarke,) in 1848, in their descendants, (*see* BURKE's *Founder's Kin.*) They had issue,

I. JOSEPH, *b.* in 1715, *m.* in 1737, Katharine Rhys, an only child, and had issue,

1. JOSEPH, *b.* in 1750; *m.* 1 Feb. 1775, Mary, only child and heir of John Rogers, Esq. of Monmouth: they had issue an only child and heir,

ANN, *b.* 1 Nov, 1775; *m.* in 1800, to her kinsman, Samuel Knight, Esq. of Edmonton, co. Middlesex.

Jane Bertie, dau. of Peregrine, Duke of Ancaster, and had an only child, Jane-Anna-Elizabeth, *m.* to the Rev. B. Lefroy. He *m.* 2ndly, Mary Lloyd, and left at his decease, a dau., Caroline, and an only son, the Rev. James-Edward Austen, of Tring Park, Herts, who *m.* Emma, dau. of Charles Smith, Esq. of Suttons, and had issue.

EDWARD, successor to his cousin, THOMAS KNIGHT, as in the text.

Henry-Thomas, in holy orders, who *m.* Eleanor, dau. of Henry Jackson, Esq. of London, by Sarah, dau. of David Papillon, Esq. of Acrise.

Francis-William (Sir), admiral of the Red, and K.C.B., *b.* in 1774, who *m.* 1st, Mary, only child of John Gibson, Esq. of Ramsgate, by whom, who *d.* in 1823, he has issue. Admiral Austen *m.* 2ndly, Martha, dau. and co-heir of the Rev. N. Lloyd, rector of Hinton.

Charles-John, a captain R.N., *m.* twice, and has issue.

Cassandra-Elizabeth.

Jane, *b.* 16 Dec. 1775, and *d. unm.* 18 July, 1817. This lady acquired high reputation as a novelist, and has left behind her some of the best modern productions in that walk of literature. We need only name *Sense and Sensibility*, *Pride and Prejudice*, and *Emma*.

2 Katharine.

II. John, *b.* in 1716; *d.* in 1756, *unm.*

III. Samuel, *b.* in 1717.

IV. Thomas, *b.* in 1719.

V. Charles, *b.* in 1721, *d. unm.*

VI. Henry, *b.* in 1723; *d.* at Islington, co. Middlesex, in 1806, leaving issue by his wife Anne,

Henry, *b.* 4 May, 1748, who *m.* in 1777, Mary Potter, of Great Bedwin, co. Wilts, and by her (who *d.* in 1780) had issue,

Edward, *b.* in 1780; *d.* in 1819, *unm.*

Ann, *b.* in 1778; *d.* in 1815, *unm.*

Henry Knight *m.* 2ndly, in 1781, Elizabeth,* only dau. of Thomas Parry, of St. Katherine's Hall, co. Somerset, who *d.* in 1828: the issue by this marriage was, Henry-Parry, *b.* in 1783; *d.* in 1810, *unm.*; John, *b.* in 1787; *m.* in 1811, Ann, dau. of Ralph and Johanna Hodgkinson, of Eckington, co. Derby, by whom he has left issue, one only child, Annie-Elizabeth, *b.* in 1817, *m.* to Henry Revell, Esq. of Darfield, co. York; and Elizabeth, *b.* in 1782, *d.* in 1785.

VII. Edward, *b.* in 1725; *d.* in 1787, *unm.*

VIII. Richard, *b.* in 1729; *d.* in 1742, *unm.*

IX. William, of Tamworth, *b.* in 1732; *m.* 22 Dec. 1754, Mary Thorpe, of Leicester, and had issue,

SAMUEL, *b.* in 1770; *m.* in 1800, Ann, dau. and heir of Joseph Knight, by his wife Mary, the heiress of John Rogers, Esq., and had issue,

1 Joseph, now of Glen Parva, only son, the last male representative of the family of Knight, heir of his mother, the only child of Anne, dau. of Joseph Knight, whose mother was Mary, the only child of John Rogers, of Charter House Square, London, a descendant of John Rogers—the proto-martyr burned in Smithfield, 1555. Captain Knight is also senior descendant of the Voughton family in the eldest surviving branch.

1 Marian.

2 Maria, *m.* 1827, Richard W. Webb, Esq. of Hampstead, Middlesex, and *d.* 1829, leaving one dau.

3 Betsy, *m.* 1833, John Walker Wood, Esq. of Rothley Grange, co. Leicester, and has issue,

I. Anne, *b.* in 1737, *d. unm.*

Arms—Paly, arg. and gu., within a bordure, engrailed, sa., on a canton of the first, a spur, or.

Crest—Between two wings, a spur, or, rowel downwards, leathered and buckled.

Residence—The Manor House, Glen Parva.

KNIGHT OF WOLVERLEY.

KNIGHT, FREDERICK-WINN, Esq. of Wolverley, co. Worcester, M.P. for West Worcestershire, *b.* 1812; *m.* 1850, Maria-Louisa Couling, dau. of the late E. Gibbs, Esq., and has a son and heir,

FREDERIC-SEBRIGHT-WINN, *b.* 11 May, 1851.

Lineage.—RICHARD KNIGHT, Esq., founder of this family, (son of Richard Knight, of Madeley, co. Salop, who was engaged in the iron trade at the time of the Commonwealth, and who is believed to have been the grandson of Thomas Knight de Salop, who represented Shrewsbury in the 1st Parliament of HENRY VIII.) acquired great wealth by the iron works of Shropshire, and settled at Downton, co. Hereford. He *m.* Elizabeth, dau. of Andrew Payne, of Shawbury, co. Salop, and by her (who was baptized 7 Nov. 1671, and *d.* 19 Oct. 1754) had issue,

I. Richard, of Croft Castle, who *m.* Elizabeth, dau. of Samuel Powell, Esq. of Stanedge, co. Radnor, and had an only dau. and heiress, ELIZABETH, who *m.* Thomas Johnes, Esq. of Llanvairclydoge, M.P. for Radnorshire, and had (with two daus., Elizabeth, *m.* to John Hanbury Williams, Esq.; and Anne) two sons,

1 Thomas, of Hafod, M.P., lord-lieutenant of Cardiganshire, who *d.* without surviving issue, in 1816.

2 Samuel, in holy orders, who assumed the surname of KNIGHT, *m.* Ann-Maria, dau. of Sir Cornelius Cuyler, Bart., and *d.* 1852, leaving a dau., Louisa-Elizabeth, wife of Sir John Shelley, Bart., M.P.

1 Elizabeth, *m.* 1770, to Hanbury Williams, Esq.

2 Ann, of Portman Square and Torquay, *d. unm.*

II. Thomas, in holy orders, rector of Bewdley and Ribbes-

---

* The estate of St. Katherine's Hall, near Bath, became the property of Elizabeth Parry, after her marriage with Henry Knight, as the heiress of her mother, who was the only child of — Blanchard, who died there, on the day following a visit paid to him on his death-bed by King CHARLES I., when the monarch presented to him a silver token, taken from his own neck, bearing the effigies of his Majesty and the Queen. The medal is in perfect preservation, retaining the likenesses in a very striking manner, and is covered with the remains of very rich gilding. It is in the possession of Mrs. Revell, to whom it has descended as an heir-loom.

ford, m. Ursula Nash; and d. 1764, aged 67, leaving two sons,

1 RICHARD-PAYNE, M.P., an eminent patron of learning and the fine arts, distinguished likewise as a classical writer and poet. He d. 28 April, 1824, aged 76.

2 Thomas-Andrew, F.R.S., of Downton Castle, co. Hereford, first president of the Horticultural Society of London, b. 10 Oct. 1758; m. Frances-Felton, and had issue an only son, Thomas-Andrew, who d. s. p.; and three daus., Frances, m. to Thomas Pendarves Stackhouse, Esq.; Elizabeth, m. in 1828, Francis Walpole, Esq.; and Charlotte, m. in 1824, Sir William-Edward-Rouse Boughton, Bart. of Lawford Hall, co. Warwick. Mr. Knight d. 11 May, 1838.

III. EDWARD, of whom presently.

IV. Ralph, of Bringwood, co. Hereford, m. Mary Duppa, and d. 27 Feb. 1754, aged 50, leaving a son,

Thomas Knight, Esq. of Henley Hall, who d. unm. 22 Aug. 1808.

I. Anne, m. to Abraham Spooner, Esq. of Birmingham.
II. Elizabeth, m. to Edward Baugh, Esq. of Ludlow.
III. A dau., m. to — Careless, of Birmingham.
IV. A dau., m. Rogers, of Shutt End, co. Stafford, and was grandmother of SAMUEL ROGERS, the poet.

The 3rd son,

EDWARD KNIGHT, Esq. of Wolverley, co. Worcester, m. Elizabeth James, of Olton End, near Solihull, co. Warwick, and had,

I. Edward, of Wolverley, who d. unm., 1812.
II. James, of Ludlow, who d. s. p., 1815.
III. JOHN, of whom presently.
I. Elizabeth, m. 1st, to — Palmer, Esq.; and 2nd, to Charles Baldwyn, Esq. of Aqualate.
II. Mary, m. to Colonel Bampfylde, of Hestercombe.
III. Sarah, m. to Sir John Sebright, Bart.

The 2nd son,

JOHN KNIGHT, Esq. of Lea Castle, co. Worcester, b. 1740, m. Henrietta Cunyngham, and had two sons,

I. JOHN, his heir.
II. Thomas, of Pap Castle, Cumberland, who m. Isabella Walker, and left issue,

1 Thomas, barrister-at-law, b. 1798; m. Miss Hobler; and d. 1850, leaving two daus.
2 John, of Henley Hall, b. 1803; m. Catherine Levyson, and has issue, John; James-Thomas; Charles; and Henrietta.
3 Robert, deceased.
4 Edward, in the army, b. 1806; m. Catherine Pemberton, and has Edward-Frederic, b 1852, and other issue.
5 James, in the army, b. 1807; killed 184–.
6 Humphrey. 7 Charles, deceased.
1 Isabella. 2 Henrietta. 3 Marianne.
4 Catherine. 5 Elizabeth. 6 Maria.

Mr. Knight was s. by his elder son,

JOHN KNIGHT, Esq. of Wolverley and Exmoor Forest, who s. to the representation of the Knight family at the decease of his cousin, Thomas-Andrew Knight, Esq. of Downton Castle in 1838. He m. 1st, Helen-Charlotte, sister of Adm. Sir George Hope, which lady d. s. p.; and 2nd, the Hon. Jane Elizabeth Winn, dau. of Lord Headley, by whom (who d. at Rome 1841) he had issue,

I. FREDERIC-WINN, now of Wolverley.
II. Charles-Allanson, b. 1814.
III. Edward-Lewis, capt. in the army, b. 1817; m. 1851, Elizabeth Harris, of Canada, and by her (who was accidentally drowned, 1854) had two sons, both drowned with their mother.
I. Margaret. II. Isabella-Jane.
III. Helen-Georgiana.

Mr. Knight d. at Rome, 1850.

Arms—Arg., three pales, gu., within a bordure, engr., az., on a canton, of the second, a spur, or.

Crest—On a spur, lying fesseways, or, an eagle, per fesse, arg. and az., wings expanded, of the first, beaked and legged, gu.

Seats—Simonsbath, co. Devon, and Wolverley, co. Worcester.

KNOLLES OF KILLEIGHY AND OATLANDS.

KNOLLES, THOMAS-WALTON, Esq. of Oatlands, co. Cork, J.P., s. his father, the late THOMAS KNOLLES, Esq., in 1840.

Lineage.—THOMAS KNOLLES, Esq. of Killeighy and Knockahowlea, co. Cork (traditionally claiming descent from the family of Lord Knollys in England), m. circiter 1657, Dorothy, eldest dau. of Giles Busteed, Esq. of Mount Long, in the same county, by whom he had (with four daus., Elizabeth, m. in 1684, Wallis Warren, Esq.; Dorothy, m. in 1692, to George Daunt, Esq. of Knockatowr, co Cork; Rachel, m. in 1697, to William Daunt, Esq. of Kilcascan; and Leah, wife of — Snow, Esq. of Kinsale)

THOMAS KNOLLES, Esq. of Killeighy, son and heir, who was b. on 6 Dec. 1660; and m. 1st (circiter 1682), Margaret, dau. of Thomas Hungerford, Esq. of Inchidony Island, co. Cork, and had issue three daus., viz., Mary, m. in 1702, to Michael Shuler, of Kinsale, merchant; Anne, m. in 1706, to Henry Daunt, Esq. of Knocknamana, co. Cork; Margaret. Mr. Knolles m. 2ndly, in 1692, Rachael, dau. (by Anne Cooke) of Francis Shuler, of Kinsale, merchant, by whom he had issue two sons and three daus. Mr. Knolles was attainted by King JAMES II.'s Irish parliament of 1689, for his adherence to King WILLIAM. Dying in 1707, he was s. by his eldest son,

THOMAS KNOLLES, Esq. of Killeighy, b. 1693; m. in 1715, Catherine, dau. of Colonel Richard Hungerford, of Inchidony, and dying 1756, was s. by his eldest son,

THOMAS KNOLLES, Esq. of Killeighy, b. 1719; m. 1740, Joanna, dau. of Robert O'Callaghan, Esq. of Clonmeen, co. Cork, by Mary Towgood, dau. of Sampson Towgood, Esq., by Melian, dau. of Sir Matthew Deane, Bart., ancestor of Lord Muskerry. By her he had issue two sons and seven daus. Dying in 1770, Mr. Knolles was s. by his eldest son,

THOMAS KNOLLES, Esq. of Killeighy, who m. in 1781, Miss Sarah Meade; and dying in 1807, was s. by his eldest son,

THOMAS KNOLLES, Esq. of Killeighy and Oatlands, b. in 1784; m. in 1807, Frances-Susanna, dau. of Thomas Walton, Esq. of Walton Court, co. Cork, and co-heir with her sister Anne, 2nd wife of Sir Thomas Roberts, of Brittfieldstown, Bart. By this lady he had issue,

THOMAS-WALTON, now of Oatlands.
Richard Walton.
Robert-William, who emigrated to Australia, in 1836.
Francis-Charles.
Elizabeth, wife of Robert Nettles, Esq. of Nettleville, co. Cork.
Anne. Sarah-Frances.

Mr. Knolles d. 1840.

Seat—Oatlands, near Kinsale.

KNOX OF RAPPA CASTLE.

KNOX, ANNESLEY, Esq. of Rappa Castle, co. Mayo, J.P. and D.L., high-sheriff 1829; m. Oct. 1833, Miss Elizabeth Knox.

Lineage.—This family is of very ancient descent, and claims to derive from UCHTRE, the Saxon prince, who founded the Anglo-Saxon kingdom of Northumberland, and who was brother of Hengist and Horsa.

In 1610 ANDREW KNOX, being then Bishop of the Isles, was translated to the see of Raphoe; and since that time others of the same family have settled in Ireland, and acquired large estates and high position.

WILLIAM KNOX, Esq. of Lifford, co. Donegal, of Scottish parentage, m. a lady named Campbell, and by her, left at his decease, in 1650 (with three daus.), two sons, JOHN (Sir) sheriff of Dublin in 1675, and lord-mayor in 1685-6, knighted 6 Feb. 1685; he d. s. p. 1687; WILLIAM, of whose descendants we have to treat. The 2nd son,

WILLIAM KNOX, Esq. of Castlerea, co. Mayo, b. in 1630, whose name appears to the loyal addresses from that county to CHARLES II., in 1682 and 1683; m. 1st, Mary, only dau. of Roger Palmer, Esq. of Castle Lacken, co. Mayo, and had by her,

FRANCIS, of Moyne Abbey, in Mayo, his heir.
ARTHUR, see KNOX, of Castlerea.
Richard, of Lissadrone, co. Mayo, m. Mary, 2nd dau. and co-heir of Roger Palmer, Esq. of Palmerstown, co. Mayo, by Charity his 2nd wife, dau. and co-heir of Maurice Annesley, Esq. of Little Rath, but d. s. p. 1754.
Mary, m. in 1705, to Thomas Bell, Esq., alderman of Dublin, and lord-mayor in 1702.

He m. 2ndly, the dau. and heir of Crofton, of Rappa Castle, and had issue,

William, of Dublin, clerk of the Crown, of the Peace, and of Assizes, for the province of Connaught.
John.

William Knox's eldest son,

FRANCIS KNOX, Esq. of Moyne Abbey, co. Mayo, sheriff 1718, m. Dorothy, 4th dau. and co-heir of Maurice Annesley, Esq. of Little Rath, in Kildare, nephew of Arthur, 1st Earl of Anglesea, and had by her,

I. Thomas, d. unm. v. p.
II. JAMES, of Moyne Abbey, b. 22 July, 1724, high-sheriff of Mayo; m. Dorothea, 2nd dau. of Peter Rutledge, Esq. of Cornfield, in that county, and d. in 1806, having had issue.

1 Francis, of Moyne Abbey, b. in 1754, assistant-barrister for the county of Sligo, and king's counsel. In 1797, he represented Philipstown in Parliament. He d. unm. 12 April, 1821, and was buried in Moyne Abbey.
2 John, of Summer Hill, Dublin, m. Sarah, dau. of Daniel Graham, Esq. of the county of Mayo, and had issue.
3 William, in the E. I. Co.'s service, d. aged 19.
4 James, capt. 51st foot, d. at Armagh.
1 Elizabeth, m. to Dowell O'Reilly, Esq. of The Heath, Queen's County.
2 Dorothea, d. unm. in Aug. 1807.
3 Mary-Anne. 4 Charity.

III. Francis, of whom presently.
I. Sarah, wife of Francis Blake, Esq.
II. Dorothy, b. 15 Nov. 1729; m. to Thomas Rutledge, Esq. of Killala.
III. Elinor, b. 22 Nov. 1730, d. unm.
IV. Mary-Anne, b. 3 May, 1728, d. unm. in 1800.

Francis Knox, whose will, dated 28 Feb. 1729, was proved 16 Feb. 1731, d. in 1730, and lies buried at Killala. His 3rd son,

Francis Knox, Esq., b. 16 July, 1726, settled at Rappa Castle, in Mayo, of which co., as well as of Sligo, he served as high-sheriff. He m. 25 March, 1761, Mary, dau. and co-heir of Annesley Gore, Esq. of Belleek, M.P. co. Mayo, (brother of Arthur, 1st Earl of Arran), and by her, who d. 31 Oct. 1818, had issue,

Annesley-Gore, of Rappa Castle, his heir.
Francis, J.P., d. unm. in 1803.
James. (See Knox-Gore.)
Henry-William, of Netley Park. (See Knox *of Netley Park*.)
Arthur, of Bushfield, in Mayo, b. in 1785; m. Barbara, only dau. of Joseph Lambert, Esq. of Brookhill, and had issue.
John, of Greenwood Park, in Mayo, b. 3 Nov. 1786; m. Jane, dau. of Samuel Handy, Esq.
Eleanor-Anne, m. 24 Dec. 1786, to John Knox, Esq., major Sligo militia, and had issue.
Dorothea-Henrietta, m. 16 Oct. 1787, to Henry Bruen, Esq., of Oak Park, co. Carlow, lieut.-col. in the army, and M.P. for that county.
Elizabeth, m. 28 Aug. 1787, to Robert Rutledge, Esq. of Bloomfield, in Mayo, M.P. for Duleck, in 1797.
Mary, m. to William Handy, Esq. of Bracca Castle.
Anne, m. 14 Nov. 1808, to Anthony Gildea, Esq. of Port Royal, in Mayo.
Charity, m. 23 May, 1815, to William Orme, Esq. of Glenmore.

Mr. Knox d. in 1818, and was s. by his eldest son,

Annesley-Gore Knox, Esq. of Rappa Castle, m. 28 July, 1793, Harriette, sister of Sir Ross Mahon, Bart., and had issue,

I. Francis, d. in March, 1810, aged 16.
II. Annesley, now of Rappa Castle.
III. St. George-Henry, in holy orders, m. in Dec. 1836, Miss Ann-C. St. George.
IV. James-Annesley, J.P., m. 28 March, 1833, Mary-Mina, dau. of Henry-William Knox, Esq. of Netley Park, and left issue.
V. John.
VI. Henry-Augustus, m. Eleanor, dau. of Henry-William Knox, Esq., and has issue.
VII. Francis-William.
I. Anne-Elizabeth. II. Maria.
III. Harriette, m. in April, 1833, to James-Knox Gore, Esq.
IV. Jane. V. Emily.

Arms—Gu., a falcon, wings expanded, within a bordure, engrailed, or, on a canton of the same, a fesse, chequy, arg. and az.
Crest—A falcon, close, on a perch, all ppr.
Seat—Rappa Castle, co. Mayo.

KNOX-GORE OF BELLEEK MANOR.

Knox-Gore, Francis-Arthur, Esq. of Belleek Manor, co. Mayo, lord-lieut. and custos-rotulorum co. Sligo, colonel of the Sligo rifles, high-sheriff of the co. of Mayo in 1840, b. 23 June, 1803; m. 4 Aug. 1829, Sarah, dau. of Charles-Nesbitt Knox, Esq. of Castle Lacken, in the same shire, and has issue,

I. Charles-James, b. 20 Sept. 1831.
II. Arthur-William, b. 28 Oct. 1833.
I. Jane-Louisa.
II. Matilda, m. to Captain William Boyd Saunders, Roy. Horse Art.
III. Sarah-Jane.
IV. Elizabeth-Louisa.

Colonel Knox-Gore s. to the estates of his great-grandfather, Annesley Gore, Esq., brother to the 1st Earl of Arran, on the demise, in Feb. 1821, of the Right Hon. Henry King, who had a life-interest in the property.

Lineage.—James Knox, Esq., M.P. for Taghmon, b. 25 March, 1774, third son of Francis Knox, Esq. of Rappa Castle, co. Mayo, was called to the bar in 1797. He settled at Broadlands Park, in Mayo, and became a magistrate in 1803, and deputy-governor of that co. In 1818, he assumed, by sign-manual, in compliance with the will of his maternal grandfather, Annesley Gore, Esq., the surname and arms of Gore, in addition to those of Knox. He m. 19 Jan. 1800, Lady Maria-Louisa Gore, eldest dau. of Arthur Saunders, second Earl of Arran, by Anna, his second wife, dau. of the Rev. Boleyn Knight, of Ottley, in Yorkshire, and by her (who d. 6 March, 1827) had issue,

Francis-Arthur, his heir.
James, who m. in April, 1833, Harriette, dau. of Annesley Gore-Knox, Esq. of Rappa Castle.
Henry-William, in the army.
Annesley, E. I. C. M. S. George-Edward, R.N.
Anna-Maria, m. to John-Frederic Knox, Esq. of Mount Falcon, co. Mayo.
Louisa-Maria, m. to Capt. Cuff, of Deal Castle, co. Mayo.
Eleanor-Adelaide, m. to Major Gardiner, of Farm Hill, co. Mayo.
Charlotte-Catharine, m. to Ernest Knox, Esq. of Castlerea.

Mr. Knox-Gore, who was ranger of the Curragh of Kildare, d. 21 Oct. 1818, and was s. by his eldest son, the present Francis-Arthur Knox-Gore, Esq. of Belleek Manor.

Arms—1st and 4th, gu., a fesse between three crosses-crosslet, or, for Gore; 2nd and 3rd, gu., a falcon, wings expanded, within a bordure, engr., or, on a canton of the same, a fesse, chequy, arg. and az., for Knox.
Crests—1st, a wolf, salient, arg., collared, gu., for Gore; 2nd, a falcon, close, on a perch, ppr., for Knox.
Motto—In hoc signo vinces.
Seat—Belleek Manor, co. Mayo.

KNOX OF NETLEY PARK.

Knox, Henry-William, Esq. of Netley Park, co. Mayo, J.P. and D.L., high-sheriff 1845, b. 9 Dec. 1809; m. 1st, 7 Dec. 1835, Isabella-Antoinette, youngest dau. of John Peel, Esq. of Burton-on-Trent, Staffordshire, which lady d. 19 Dec. 1838; and 2ndly, in 1842, Eliza, eldest dau. of the O'Grady of Kilballyowen.

Lineage.—Henry-William Knox, Esq. of Netley Park, in the co. of Mayo (fourth son of Francis Knox, Esq. of Rappa Castle) capt. 6th dragoon-guards, served as high-sheriff for Mayo in 1810. He m. Jane, eldest dau. of the Rev. William Rogers, D.D., of Kells, in Meath, and by her, who d. 13 Feb. 1835, had issue,

Henry-William, now of Netley Park.
William-Henry, d. 1847. Annesley-Gore
Mary-Mina, m. to James A. Knox, Esq. (deceased) and has issue.
Harriette, m. to Charles Kirkwood, Esq. of Bartra House, co. Mayo, capt. R.N.
Eleanor, m. H. A. Knox, Esq., and has issue.

Mr. Knox d. 6 Oct. 1816.

Arms, Crest, &c.—As Knox *of Rappa Castle*.
Seat—Netley Park, Mayo.

KNOX OF CASTLEREA.

Knox, John, Esq. of Castlerea, co. Mayo, J.P. and D.L., b. 13 May, 1783; m. 12 March, 1808, Maria-Anne, only dau. of Major John Knox, and has issue,

I. Arthur-Edward, late an officer in the 2nd life-guards, m. 12 Dec. 1835, Lady Jane Parsons, elder dau. of Laurence, Earl of Rosse, and has issue.
II. Ernest, m. Charlotte-Catharine, dau. of James Knox-Gore, Esq.
III. Robert-Augustus, in holy orders, m. in 1842, Octavia-Gertrude, youngest dau. of the late Rev. R.-J. Hallifax, only son of Samuel Hallifax, Bishop of St. Asaph.
IV. Edward-William-John. V. Alfred-Charles.

Mr. Knox, who s. his father 23 Oct. 1798, served the office of sheriff for Wicklow in 1809, and for Mayo in 1821.

Lineage.—Arthur Knox, Esq. (2nd son of William Knox, Esq. of Castle Rea, by Mary Palmer, his wife) served as high-sheriff co. Mayo, 1732-3. He m. 8 May, 1724, Hannah, 3rd dau. and co-heir of Roger Palmer, Esq. of Palmerstown, co. Mayo, by Charity, his 2nd wife, 2nd dau. and co-heir of

Maurice Annesley, Esq. of Little Rath, co. Kildare, and *d.* 16 May, 1748, leaving a dau., Sydney, *m.* to Matthew Vaughan, Esq. of Carramore, and a son,

JOHN KNOX, Esq. of Castlerea, *b.* 1728, J.P., M.P. for Donegal, from 1761 to 1769, and Castlebar, from 1769 to 1774; served as high-sheriff for Sligo in 1762, and for Mayo in 1768. He *m.* 25 May, 1750, Anne, fourth dau. of the Rt. Hon. Sir Henry King, Bart., by Isabella, his wife, sister of Richard, Viscount Powerscourt and had by her, who *d.* 27 March, 1808, two sons and three daus., namely,

- ARTHUR, his heir.
- John, of Castlerea, co. Mayo, and afterwards of Dublin. (*See* KNOX *of Mount Falcon.*)
- Isabella, *m.* to Xaverius Blake, Esq. of Oranmore, co. Galway.
- Hannah, *m.* 29 July, 1775, to James Wilson, Esq. of Parsonstown, co. Meath.
- Anne, *d. unm.* 14 Sept. 1788.

Mr. Knox *d.* 24 Feb. 1774, and was *s.* by his son,

ARTHUR KNOX, Esq., *b.* 18 Sept. 1759, who settled at Woodstock, in Wicklow (an estate he purchased from Lord St. George) and served the office of high-sheriff for that co. in 1791. He was also high-sheriff for Mayo, and a magistrate for both counties. He *m.* 23 June, 1781, Lady Mary Brabason, eldest dau. of Anthony, eighth Earl of Meath, and had issue,

- JOHN, his heir.
- Edward, *b.* 2 Nov. 1786, a field-officer in the army.
- Arthur, *b.* 22 Nov. 1793, in holy orders, *m.* in Nov. 1820, Mary, dau. of the Right Hon. Denis Daly, of Dunsandle, co. Galway.
- Mary, *d. unm.* at Bristol, in July, 1798.
- Anne, *m.* to Edward-William Scott, Esq., barrister-at-law.

Mr. Knox *d.* at Bristol, 28 Oct. 1796, and was buried at New Castle, co. Wicklow, in a vault which he had built for the use of his family. His eldest son is the present JOHN KNOX, Esq. of Castlerea.

Arms—Gu., a falcon, wings expanded, within a bordure, engr., or, on a canton, of the last, a fesse, chequy, arg. and az., or, within an orle, wavy, arg., on a canton, of the second, a fesse, chequy, arg. and az.
Crest—A falcon, close, perched, ppr.
Seat—Castlerea, co. Mayo.

KNOX OF MOUNT FALCON.

KNOX, JOHN-FREDERIC, Esq. of Mount Falcon, co. Mayo, Lieut.-Col. of the Sligo militia, J.P. and D.L. counties of Mayo and Sligo, high-sheriff of Mayo 1823, and of Sligo 1824, *b.* 28 Feb. 1789; *m.* 28 Jan. 1819, Anna-Maria, eldest dau. of James Knox-Gore, Esq. of Broadlands Park, co. Mayo, by his wife, Lady Maria-Louisa, dau. of Arthur-Saunders, 2nd Earl of Arran, and by this lady has issue,

- I. FREDERIC-EDGAR, *b.* 29 April, 1822.
- II. Utred-Augustus, *b.* 19 April, 1825.
- III. Albert-Henry, *b.* 10 Feb. 1827.
- IV. Alfred-William, *b.* 5 May, 1829.
- V. Alberic-Edward, *b.* 17 Sept. 1831.
- VI. Ernest-Adolphus, *b.* 25 April, 1834.
- VII. John-Ethelred *b.* 7 March, 1836.
- I. Eleanor-Louisa.

Lineage.—JOHN KNOX, Esq., *b.* 10 March, 1764, major in the Sligo regt. of militia, second son of John Knox, Esq. of Castlerea, M.P., by Anne, his wife, dau. of the Rt. Hon. Sir Henry King, Bart., M.P. co. Roscommon, *m.* 1st, 24 Dec. 1786, Eleanor-Anne, eldest dau. of Francis Knox, Esq. of Rappa Castle, co. Mayo, by Mary, his wife, fourth dau. and co-heir of Annesley Gore, Esq., M.P. for co. Mayo (brother to Arthur, first Earl of Arran) and by this lady who *d.* 20 March, 1790, had (with a dau., Maria-Anne, *m.* 12 March, 1808, to John Knox, Esq. of Woodstock, co. Wicklow, and Castlerea, co. Mayo) two sons, JOHN-FREDERIC, now of Mount Falcon; and Francis, *b.* in 1790, *d.* young (in 1793.) Major Knox *m.* 2ndly, 14 April, 1811, Catharine, second dau. of Richard Chaloner, Esq. of Kingsfort, co. Meath, and by her had further issue, Richard, Edward-Chaloner, and Robert-John; Frances-Maria; Elizabeth, *m.* to Sir John Blunden, Bart.; and Catherine, deceased. Major John Knox *d.* 11 July, 1821. His eldest son is the present JOHN-FREDERIC KNOX, Esq. of Mount Falcon.

Arms—Gu., a falcon, wings expanded, within a bordure, engr., or, on a canton, of the last, a fesse, chequy, arg. and az.
Crest—A falcon, close, on a perch, all ppr.
Motto—Moveo et proficio.
Seat—Mount Falcon, near Ballina, co. Mayo.

KNYFTON OF UPHILL.

KNYFTON, THOMAS-TUTTON, Esq. of Uphill, co. Somerset, J.P. and D.L., high-sheriff 1851; *m.* 1st, 15 Dec. 1836, Eliza-Maria, eldest dau. of Major-General Sir Love Jones-Parry, of Madryn, co. Carnarvon, by whom (who *d.* 29 Sept. 1838) he had a son,

Thomas-Parry, *b.* 23 Sept. 1838; *d.* 13 Oct. in the same year.

He *m.* 2ndly, 12 July, 1855, Georgiana-Sophia, only surviving child of William-Hungerford Colston, D.D., rector of West Lydford, co. Somerset.

Lineage.—THOMAS KNIVETON, of Mugginton, co. Derby, descended from a junior branch of the Knivetons of Mercaston, *m.* his kinswoman, Elizabeth, dau. of Sir William Kniveton, Bart. of Mercaston, co. Derby, M.P. for the county in the 1st of JAMES I., created a Baronet in 1611. They had, with other issue, a son,

THOMAS KNIVETON OR KNYFTON, of Mugginton, who *m.* twice. By his 1st marriage he had no issue. He *m.* 2ndly, about 1661, Ann Pegge, and had (with three daus.) two sons, I. Thomas, who *d.* at Derby about 1705, leaving two daus.; and GEORGE. The younger son,

GEORGE KNYFTON, Esq. *m.* 1698, Mary, only child of Thomas Hobbs, of Uphill, co. Somerset, and settled there. He *d.* in March, 1744, having had a numerous family, all of whom *d.* young or *unm.*, except one dau., Ann, *m.* to the Rev. Benjamin Hancock, rector of Uphill, and *d.* 11 July, 1765, and two sons, THOMAS, of whom presently; and George, bapt. 16 Nov. 1722, in holy orders, vicar of St. Decumans, co. Somerset, *d.* in Nov. 1797, having had three sons, George, Charles, and Thomas, who all *d. unm.* in his lifetime. The elder son,

THOMAS KNYFTON, Esq. of Uphill, bapt. 24 Jan. 1716, *m.* 28 Aug. 1765, Miss Tutton, and *d.* in June, 1776, having had, with a dau., Mary, a son,

THOMAS-TUTTON KNYFTON, Esq. of Uphill, bapt. 27 Jan. 1770, *m.* 25 May, 1797, Miss Chappell, and *d.* at Wells, 18 Jan. 1810, having had,

- THOMAS-TUTTON, now of Uphill.
- Mary, *m.* 14 Feb. 1837, to Robert Graves, Esq. of Charlton House, in the parish of Donhead St. Mary, in the county of Wilts, and has issue.

Arms—Gu., a chevron, vaire, az. and sa.
Crest—An eagle's head, erased, or, between two wings, displayed, sa.
Motto—In te Domine confido.
Seat—Uphill Castle, co. Somerset.

KYAN OF BALLYMURTAGH.

KYAN, THE REV. WILLIAM-EDWARD, of Ballymurtagh, co. Wicklow, *b.* in 1814; *s.* his father in 1850.

Lineage.—The O'Cahans, princes of Derry, a younger branch of the illustrious house of O'Neill, of Tyrone, descended, through Fergal, monarch of all Ireland A.D. 700-718, from Niall of the Nine Hostages. Their genealogy is to be found in MacFerbish and other Irish authorities, and their history down to the 17th century is minutely chronicled by the national annalists. Donal O'Cahan, the last chieftain of Derry, was appointed A.D. 1598, and dispossessed of his territory in 1607.

THE REV. JAMES KYAN, of Rathbeggan, co. Meath, whom unvarying tradition records to have been son of the dispossessed chieftain, and to have been placed (according to the policy at that time pursued by the English government) at Trinity College, Dublin, to be educated as a Protestant, entered holy orders of the Church of England, and was settled at Rathbeggan, in 1628. He *m.* Jane, dau. of Christopher Plunkett, Esq., and had two sons, ADAM, of whose descendants we treat; and Christopher, whose line is extinct. The elder son,

THE REV. ADAM KYAN, of Rathbeggan, *m.* Joyce, dau. of W. Flood, Esq., and by her (who *m.* 2ndly, Dr. Thomas Seele, dean of St. Patrick's, provost of Trinity College) left, with a dau., Jane, an only son,

THE REV. JAMES KYAN, of Cushinstown, co. Meath, *b.* in 1646, who entered Trinity College in 1663, and became senior fellow in 1671, and afterwards 1680, prebendary of Stragond, in the cathedral of St. Patrick. He *m.* Elizabeth, dau. of R. Nelson, Esq., and *d.* in 1682, leaving issue, ADAM, his heir; John, in holy orders, *b.* in 1680, vicar of Esker and rector of Lucan 1714, his descendants are extinct; Joyce; and Ann. The elder son,

Adam Kyan, Esq. of Cushinstown, co. Meath, Mount Howard, co. Wexford, and Ballymurtagh, co. Wicklow, acquired the two last named estates in marriage with Mary, dau. and heir of John Howard, Esq. By her he left, at his decease in 1738, two sons; the younger son, John, *d. unm.* 1736. The elder,

Howard Kyan, Esq. of Mount Howard and Ballymurtagh, *b.* 1711; *m.* in 1735, Frances, dau. of Laurence Esmonde, Esq. of Ballynastray, co. Wexford, and by her, who *d.* in 1785, had issue,

I. John Howard, his heir.
II. James, of Carlow, *b.* 1748; who *m.* 1777, Ellen, dau. of Thomas MacCarthy, Esq., and by her (who *d.* in 1824) had issue,
 1 Dennis, lieut. H.E.I.C.S., *b.* 1778; *d.* in India, *unm.* 1812
 2 John-Howard, capt. 2nd regt. Bengal cavalry, *b.* 1779, who *m.* Mary, sister of Lieut.-Col. Baldock, H.E.I.C.S., and left at his decease, 1844, an only child, Ellen.
 3 James-Esmonde, *b.* 1793, *m.* Julia, dau. of — Dunn, Esq., and *d.* 1859, leaving issue,
  Algernon. John-Howard.
  Julia. Ellen.
 4 Francis-Daniel, *b.* 1799.
 1 Fanny, *m.* 1802, to Matthew Redmond, Esq.
 2 Ellen, *m.* 1804, to John-Howard Kyan, Esq. of Ballymurtagh.
 3 Jane. 4 Margaret.
III. Esmonde, *b.* 1750, who was engaged in the rebellion of 1798, and was executed with Colclough, Grogan, and Bagenal Harvey, at Wexford, half an hour before the arrival of the express sent from Dublin Castle with his pardon, obtained by his brother, Francis. He was twice *m.*; by his 1st wife, Mary-Ann, dau. of — Byrne, Esq., he had five daus., Mary, *m.* to Purcell, Esq.; Fanny, *m.* to Richard Edgeworth, Esq.; Eliza; Theresa; and Mary-Ann; and by his 2nd, two sons, John-Howard, and Esmonde, who both *d.* young, and one dau., Margaret. This unfortunate gentleman was not less distinguished for humanity than bravery and military science; and Sir Richard Musgrave has recorded a few of the many instances in which his interference saved the lives of his opponents.
IV. Francis, major-general, H.E.I.C.S., *b.* 1752, who *m.* 1798, Jane, dau. of James Blackney, Esq., and dying in 1814, left issue,
 1 Francis, *b.* in 1799, who *m.* Catherine, dau. of Richard Galloway, Esq., and has issue, Francis, *b.* 1830; Gertrude; and Margaret, *m.* 1855, to Thomas Hayes, Esq.
 2 James. 3 Adam-Howard.
 4 Alexander, in holy orders.
 5 John-Walter, *b.* 1813, *m.* 1832, Miss Murphy.
 1 Gertrude, *m.* to Michael Keating, Esq. of Tinny Park, co. Kilkenny.
I. Mary, *m.* Richard Doyle, Esq., and *d. s. p.* 1806.
II. Elizabeth. III. Ann.
IV. Joyce, *m.* Redmond Lanigan, Esq. R.N., and *d.* 1794.

Mr. Kyan *d.* 1766, and was *s.* by his eldest son,

John-Howard Kyan, Esq. of Mount Howard and Ballymurtagh, *b.* 1743, who *m.* 1768, Phillis, dau. of Thomas Sutton, Comte de Clonard, and by her, who *d.* 1808, had issue,

John-Howard, his heir.
Thomas-Sutton, lieut. H.E.I.C.S., *b.* 1785; *d. unm.* in India, 1813.
Phillis, *m.* 1809, John Broome, Esq., and *d.* 1830.
Fanny.
Mary, *m.* 1798, Capt. Henry-Michael Ormsby, and *d.* 1849.
Ellen, *m.* 1797, Charles Baggs, Esq., barrister-at-law, and *d.* 1827.
Elizabeth.

Mr. Kyan *d.* 1801, and was *s.* by his son,

John-Howard Kyan, Esq. of Ballymurtagh, *b.* 1774, who *m.* 1804, his cousin, Ellen, dau. of James Kyan, Esq. of Carlow, and had issue,

I. William-Edward, present representative of the family.
II. Howard, *b.* 1819; *d.* 1825.
III. John-Howard, *b.* 1829; *m.* 1853, Mary, dau. of John Cantwell, Esq. of Dublin, and has issue, John-Howard, *b.* 17 Jan. 1854.
I. Sarah. II. Mary-Ann. III. Eliza.
IV. Fanny. V. Cecilia.
VI. Phillis. VII. Helen.

Mr. Kyan *d.* 1850, and was *s.* by his eldest son, the present Rev. William-Edward Kyan, of Ballymurtagh.

Arms—Gu., an antique Irish crown, ppr., between three fishes, haurrant, arg.
Crest—A wild cat, saliant, ppr., gorged with an antique Irish crown.
Motto—Inclytus virtute.

SNEYD-KYNNERSLEY OF LOXLEY PARK.

Sneyd-Kynnersley, Clement-Thomas, Esq. of Loxley Park, co. Stafford, *b.* 21 Oct. 1833.

Lineage.—According to an old pedigree, "the family of the Kynnersleys is very ancient, being seated long before the Conquest in com. Hereford, in a castle soe called at present. In Doomesday Booke it is recorded, that when the Conqueror was possessed of his newe kingdome of England, hee sent his Comiss[rs] throughout y[e] remote parts thereof, to know howe every man held his lands. In which tyme there was an ould gentleman that lived and was owner of Kynnardsley Castle, in com. Hereford: by name John de Kynnardsley, and by title a knight (if any knights were before the Conquest.) This ould gentleman was blind, he had then liveing with him twelve sonnes, whom with himself he armed, and stood in his castle gate, his halberd in his hand, attending the coming of sheriffs and other comiss[rs] from y[e] king, who being arrived, demanded of him by what tenure he held his castle and lands; y[e] old kn[t] replyed by his armes, showing to them his halberd."

Hugo de Kynnardsleye is mentioned in several charters, in the time of Henry III., and was seized of the manor of Newland and other estates in the cos. of Gloucester and Hereford. This Hugh, a soldier of the Cross, accompanied Prince Edward to the Holy Land, and received the honour of knighthood, upon which occasion he added the Jerusalem crosses to his arms, which were before "Az., a lion rampant, arg."

For centuries after the Kynnersleys of Loxley preserved a male succession, and still continue to be one of the leading families of Leicestershire. The last male representative,

Clement Kynnersley, Esq. of Loxley (son of Thomas Kynnersley, Esq. of Loxley, an officer R.N., by Penelope, his wife, only dau. of John Wheeler, Esq. of Wootton, and grandson of Thomas Kynnersley, Esq. of Loxley, by Barbara, his wife, dau. of Sir Gilbert Clarke, of Chilcote) *m.* Rosamond, dau. of Sir Wolstan Dixie, Bart. of Bosworth Park, co. Leicester, but dying issueless, in 1815, willed his property to his nephew, Thomas Sneyd (youngest son of John Sneyd, Esq. of Bishton, co. Stafford, by Penelope his wife, eldest dau. of Thomas Kynnersley, Esq. of Loxley Park, co. Stafford). Mr Thomas Sneyd, J.P. and D.L., who was born 6 May, 1774, assumed, by Royal licence, 1815, the additional surname and arms of Kynnersley. He *m.* 1st, Miss Maria Stokes Kynnersley, and by her (who *d.* 16 March, 1821) had two sons and two daus. He *m.* 2ndly, Miss Harriet Potts, and by her had issue three sons and five daus. The eldest son of the first marriage,

Clement-John, *m.* 4 Jan. 1830, Mary, dau. of William, Sneyd, Esq. of Ashcombe, and *d.* 3 March, 1840, leaving issue,
 Clement-Thomas, now of Loxley Park.
 William-Henry.
 Mary-Jane, *m.* to the Rev. W. Fraser.

Mr. Sneyd Kynnersley *d.* 5 Sept. 1844.

Arms—Quarterly: 1st and 4th, for Kynnersley, az., semée of crosses-crosslet, a lion rampant, arg.; 2nd and 3rd, for Sneyd, arg., a scythe, the blade in chief, the sned, or handle in bend sinister, sable; in the fesse, point, a fleur de-lis, of the second.
Crests—For Kynnersley, a mount, vert, thereon a greyhound, sejant, arg., collared, or, under a hawthorn-tree, ppr.; for Sneyd, a lion, statant, guardant, the tail extended, sa.
Motto—Nec opprimere nec opprimi.
Seat—Loxley Park, in the co. of Stafford.

KYRLE OF MUCH MARCLE.

Money-Kyrle, William, Esq. of Homme House, Much Marcle, co. Hereford, of Whetham, co. Wilts, and of Pitsford, co. Northampton, *b.* 1 May, 1808; high-sheriff of Herefordshire 1853, M.A., J.P.

Lineage.—In the oldest writings relative to the Kyrles the name is variously written, *Crul*, *Crull*, and *Crulle*; afterwards *Cryll*, and sometimes *Curl*; until at last it was universally spelt Kyrle. The first of the family on record,

Robert Crul, of Altone, or Old Town, near Ross, resided, in 1295, at Homme, now Hom Green, in the same neighbourhood. From him descended Walter Kyrle, who was seated at "the Hulle," or Hill, near Ross, in the year 1489. Dying at the close of the same century this gentleman bequeathed the Hill to his eldest son, Walter, who left an only dau. and heir, Alice, *m.* to Christopher Clarke, Esq., and to his second son, James, the estate of Walford, near Ross. James thus became founder of the Walford branch of the Kyrle family.

Thomas Kyrle, of Walford Court, son and heir of the above-mentioned James, lived *temp.* Henry VII., and by his marriage with Johan, dau. and heir of Hugh Abraball (by Alice his wife, dau. of John Rudhall, of Rudhall) had, with four daus., nine sons. From the eldest of these sons, viz., WALTER, of Walford (who *m.* Joan, dau. of Richard Warncombe, Esq.) descended JOHN KYRLE, the celebrated "MAN OF ROSS" (who was born at the White House, Dymock, in May, 1637, and *d. s. p.* at Ross, 7 Nov. 1724) and from the fourth of them, viz., THOMAS KYRLE, who seated himself at Much Marcle early in the reign of ELIZABETH, the line, which, through the female representative, still retains possession of that ancient seat.

SIR JOHN KYRLE, of Much Marcle, 2nd Bart., grandson of Thomas Kyrle, the first of Much Marcle, *m.* 16 Dec. 1647, Rebecca, dau. of Daniel Vincent, Esq., and by her (who *m.* 2ndly, John Booth, Esq. of Letton) had four daus. Sir John Kyrle, who was M.P. for Herefordshire, at the period of his decease, *d.* 4 Jan. 1679-80, and was *s.* by his eldest dau. and co-heir,

VINCENTIA KYRLE, *b.* 2 Oct. 1651, who *m.* 6 Dec. 1674, Sir John Ernle, Knt. of Bury Town, Wilts (son of Sir John Ernle, of Whetham, Knt., Chancellor of the Exchequer, *temp.* CHARLES II. and JAMES II.) and had issue,

JOHN KYRLE ERNLE, the heir.
Hester Ernle, *b.* 8 Feb. 1675-6, *m.* to William Washbourne, Esq., son and heir of William Washbourne, of Wychenford and Pytchley, Esq., and was mother of

ELIZABETH WASHBOURNE, who *m.* 1 Oct. 1723, FRANCIS MONEY, Esq. of Wellingborough, and *d.* 2 March, 1726, leaving an only son,

JAMES MONEY, Esq., of whom presently.

Vincentia Lady Ernle was *s.* by her son,

JOHN KYRLE ERNLE, Esq. of Whetham and Much Marcle, bapt. 10 May, 1683, who *m.* 1704, Constantia, only dau. of Sir Thomas Rolt, Knt. of Saccombe, Herts, and dying Oct. 1725, left an only dau. and heir,

CONSTANTIA ERNLE, who *m.* 1741, Thomas, Viscount Dupplin, afterwards 8th Earl of Kinnoul, and had an only child, Thomas-John-Ernle Hay, *b.* 12 Aug. 1742, who *d.* 14 Oct. 1743. The countess herself *d.* in 1753, and was interred at Calne on the 7th July. Leaving no issue, she settled her estates upon the next heir, and sole representative of her ancestors, as shown above (the son of her first cousin, Elizabeth)

JAMES MONEY, of Pitsford, Northamptonshire, Esq., lieut.-col. in the army, bapt. 25 Sept. 1724 who *m.* Eugenia, eldest dau. and co-heir of George Stoughton, Esq. of St. John's, Warwick, and dying 14 June, 1785, left an only surviving son,

WILLIAM MONEY, Esq. of Much Marcle, *b.* 23 Feb. 1748, who *m.* Mary, dau. of William Webster, Esq. of Stockton-on-Tees (by Mary, his wife, dau. of Roland Burdon, Esq.) and by her (who *d.* 20 June, 1813, aged 69) had issue,

I. JAMES, his heir.
II. WILLIAM, successor to his brother.
III. George, late master in equity, accountant-general, and keeper of the records in the Supreme Court of Judicature, Calcutta, *m.* 21 Jan. 1817, Pulcherie, dau. of Henri, Marquis de Bourbel, and has issue,
  1 William-Bayley. 2 George-Henri.
  3 Alonzo. 4 Edward Mortimer.
  5 Aurelian.
IV. Kyrle Ernle, M.A., vicar of Much Marcle, and prelector and prebendary of Hereford Cathedral, *m.* 16 Jan. 1806, Mary-Thomasina, dau. of Dominick Ffrench, Esq., and had surviving issue,
  1 Kyrle Ernle Aubrey, *m.* in 1841, Emma Kemp Mitford, relict of the Rev. John Reveley Mitford.
  2 Rowland-William-Taylor, *m.* in 1840, Katherine, dau. of Major Peyton, of the Indian army, and has issue.
  1 Mary Ernle, *m.* in 1830, to Oswald, son of Thomas Grimston, Esq. of Grimston Garth, co. York.
  2 Ellenor, *m.* in 1827, to the Rev. Richard-Coke Wilmot, son of Sir Robert Wilmot, Bart. of Chaddesden, co. Derby.
  3 Eugenia-Jane, *m.* in 1840, to the Rev. Henry Huntingford, M.A., rector of Hampton Bishop, co. Hereford, canon of Hereford, and fellow of Winchester College.
  4 Vincentia-Sybilla.
V. Rowland, rear-admiral R.N., C.B., *m.* 12 Sept. 1805, Maria, dau. of William Money, Esq. of Walthamstow, Essex, and has issue,
  1 Rowland. 2 Ernle Kyrle.
  3 William-Taylor. 4 David-Inglis, *d.* in 1848.
  1 Maria Rowlanda, *m.* in 1830, to the Rev. Samuel-James Gambier, nephew to the late Lord Gambier.
  2 Amelia-Mary, *m.* in 1841, to the Hon. H.-F. Pery, son of the late Viscount Glentworth, and grandson to the Earl of Limerick.
  3 Angelica-Mary. 4 Emma-Martha.
  5 Eva-Maria, *m.* in 1843, to H.-E.-M. Palmer, Esq. of the Indian army.
VI. John, commander in the East India Company's maritime service, *d. unm.* 6 Aug. 1825.

I. Hester. II. Mary, *d.* in childhood.
III. Eugenia, *m.* 3 June, 1797, to William-Taylor Money, Esq. of Walthamstow, Essex, Knight of the Guelphic Order, M.P., and subsequently H. B. M. Consul-General at Venice and Milan, and had issue.
IV. Susannah, *m.* 17 July, 1800, to the Rev. Robert Chatfield, D.C.L., vicar of Chatteris, Cambridgeshire.
V. Dorothea. VI. Alice, *d. unm.* 27 Oct. 1802.
VII. Vincentia, *d. unm.* 1 April, 1816.

Mr. Money *d.* 6 Nov. 1808, and was *s.* by his eldest son,

SIR JAMES MONEY, of Much Marcle, a major-general in the army, *b.* 15 Aug 1775 and *m.* 27 Dec. 1811, to Anne-Caroline, eldest dau. of Robert Taylor, of Gloucester Place, Portman Square, London, Esq. He assumed by Royal licence, dated 26 April, 1809, the additional surname and arms of KYRLE, and was created a Baronet at the coronation of Her Majesty Queen Victoria, in 1838. Major-General Sir James Kyrle Money *d.* 26 June, 1843, without issue, and was *s.* by his next brother,

REV. WILLIAM MONEY KYRLE, M.A., J.P., *b.* 13 Oct. 1776; *m.* 16 July, 1805, Emma, dau. of Richard Down, of Halliwick Manor House, co. Middlesex, Esq. (by Rose, his wife, dau. and heir of Henry Neale, of London, Esq., lineally descended from the ancient house of NEALE, of Dean, in Bedfordshire) and had issue,

WILLIAM, now of Homme House.
Edward Kyrle, lt. 2nd regt. Bengal lt. cavalry, *b.* 29 Jan. 1810, *d. unm.* at Loodianha, East Indies, 17 Nov. 1841.
John Ernle, capt. 32nd regt., *b.* 1 March, 1812, *m.* 16 July, 1842, Harriet-Louisa, eldest dau. of William Sutton, of Hertingfordbury, co. Herts, Esq., and has issue.
James Stoughton, of Emmanuel College, Cambridge, in holy orders, Fellow of the Society of Antiquaries, and rector of Yatesbury, co. Wilts, *b.* 31 Oct. 1813, *m.* 17 Jan. 1839, Rose-Elizabeth, dau. of John Drake Pridham, of Plymouth, co. Devon, Esq., and *d. s. p.* 1852. His widow *m.* 2ndly, — Phillips, Esq.
George Washbourne, M.A., Fellow of King's College, Cambridge, *b.* 22 Oct. 1815.
Richard-Walter, *b.* 16 Nov. 1825; in the 32nd regt.
Charles-Septimus, *b.* 26 Sept. 1827.
Emma, *m.* 1841, to the Rev. George Prothero.

Mr. Money-Kyrle *d.* 18 Jan. 1848.

Arms—Quarterly: 1st and 4th, vert, a chev. between three fleurs-de-lis, or, for KYRLE; 2nd and 3rd, chequy, arg. and gu., on a chief, sa., three eagles, displayed, or, for MONEY.
Crests—1st, on a mount, vert, a hedgehog, or, for KYRLE; 2nd, an eagle's head, sa., erased, arg., collared, gemelle, holding in the beak a fleur-de-lis, or, for MONEY.
Motto—Nil moror ictus.
Seats—Hom House, Herefordshire; Whetham, Wiltshire; and Pitsford, Northamptonshire.

LABOUCHERE OF OVER STOWEY.

LABOUCHERE, THE RIGHT HON. HENRY, of Over Stowey, co. Somerset, and of Stoke Park, Bucks, M.A., Secretary of State for the Colonies, M.P. for Taunton, *b.* 15 Aug. 1798; *m.* 1st, 10 April, 1840, Frances, youngest dau. of Sir Thomas Baring, Bart. of Larkbeer, co. Devon, and by her (who *d.* 25 May, 1850) has issue, MARY. He *m.* 2ndly, 13 July, 1852, Lady Mary-Matilda-Georgiana Howard, dau. of the 6th Earl of Carlisle. Mr. Labouchere was a Lord of the Admiralty from 1832 to 1834, Vice-President of the Board of Trade and Master of the Mint from 1835 to 1839, Chief Secretary for Ireland from 1846 to 1847, and again President of the Board of Trade from 1847 to 1852. He became Secretary of State for the Colonies in 1855.

Lineage.—The family of Labouchere left France at the period of the revocation of the edict of Nantes, and became established in Holland. The first who settled in England was the late

PETER-CÆSAR LABOUCHERE, Esq., a partner in the great mercantile house of Hope, who purchased the estates of Hylands, in Essex, and Over Stowey, co. Somerset. He *m.* 26 Nov. 1796, Dorothy-Elizabeth, 4th dau. of the late Sir Francis Baring, Bart.; and dying 16 Jan. 1839, left two sons, HENRY, now of Over Stowey; and John, J.P., of Broome Hall Dorking, Surrey, *b.* 1799, *m.* 1830, Mary, dau. of James Du Pré, Esq. of Wilton Park, co. Bucks, and has, Henry, *b.* 1831; Arthur, *b.* 1842; and six daus.

Seats—Over Stowey, near Bridgewater; and Stoke Park, Bucks.

LADE OF BOUGHTON HOUSE.

LADE, JOHN-PRYCE, Esq. of Boughton House, co.

Kent, J.P., and major in the East Kent regiment of militia.

Lineage.—Robert Lade, Esq. of Barham, recorder of Canterbury in 1668 (eldest son of Vincent Ladd, Esq. of Barham, by Agnes Denne his wife, and brother of Thomas of Barham, grandfather of Sir John Lade, Bart., M.P.), m. in July, 1619, Mary, dau. of William Lovelace, of The Friary, Canterbury; and d. in 1666, leaving, with younger issue, a son,

Lancelot Lade, Esq., barrister-at-law, who d. in 1687, leaving, by Elizabeth Barrett his wife, with other issue, a son and heir,

Vincent Lade, of the Archbishop's Palace, and afterwards of Burgate, who m. Ann Kite, of Hoad House, in Bleane, and by her (who d. in 1720) left at his decease, in 1730, with other issue, a younger son,

Michael Lade, Esq., b. in 1698, father, by Elizabeth Dadd his wife, of

John Lade, Esq. of Boughton, b. 18 April, 1734; who m. 12 June, 1757, Hester, dau. of Hills Hobday, of Faversham, and had (with one dau., Hester, m. to Will.Stacey Coast, of Chartham Deanery) three sons, John-Hobday, of whom presently; William, of Jesus College, Cambridge; and Charles, an officer in the army. The eldest,

John-Hobday Lade, Esq. of Boughton, an officer in the army, m. 2 Jan. 1791, Eliza, dau. of Evors, Esq., and niece of Sir John-Powell Pryce, Bart. of Newton Hall, co. Montgomery, and by her had (with a dau., Maria, m. to Wastel Brisco, Esq. of Bohemia, co. Sussex) a son, the present John-Pryce Lade, Esq. of Boughton House.

Arms—Arg., a fesse, wavy, between three escallops, sa.
Crest—A leopard's head, ppr.
Seat—Boughton Hall, near Faversham, Kent.

LALOR OF CREGG.

Lalor, Thomas, Esq. of Cregg, co. Tipperary, J.P. and D.L., formerly gentleman-at-large to H.E. the late Earl of Bessborough, when Lord-Lieutenant of Ireland.

Lineage.—The O'Lalors or Lalors, are of Milesian origin. At an early period they migrated with the O'Mores from Ulster to the extensive district of Leix, in the Queen's County, of which country the O'Mores became powerful Princes, and, under them, the O'Lalors were influential chieftains, possessing considerable landed property between Stradbally and Maryborough. Their principal seat was at Disert, near the rock of Dunamase. Thence a branch sprung, which settled in the county of Tipperary. In the "Four Masters," the O'Lalors are enumerated with the O'Mores, the O'Dempseys, &c., amongst the leading Irish Gentry basely murdered at the Hill of Mullaghmaestan, co. Kildare, in 1577; and by virtue of an Act passed at Dublin 3rd and 4th Philip and Mary, the possessions of O'Lalor, along with those of O'More and others, were confiscated. In 1599, the O'Lalors took part, along with Anthony O'More, against the forces of Queen Elizabeth, and fought with great gallantry at the Pass of Plumes. In 1600, the O'Lalors were received into the royal protection by the Lord-Deputy.

Dionysius Lalor, of Ballywoney, was a member of this family. His name was signed to the new form of oath and declaration of the Confederate Catholics of Ireland, dated 10 Jan. 1646, o.s., amongst the signatures of several other personages, who are styled by historians, "veluti comitiales in Domo Communium."

The first member of the O'Lalor family who became a resident of the county Tipperary, was Jeremiah Lalor, b. in 1626. He came from Disert, in the Queen's County, about the year 1666, after having taken a prominent part in defending the fortress of Dunamase against the Parliamentarians during the war of 1641. He held the rank of major in the Irish forces, and his father was nephew to Winafred, dau. of O'Lalor, of the Queen's County, and wife of the Rev. John Crosbie, incumbent of Disert, consecrated lord bishop of Ardfert in 1600, who d. in 1621. The lands of Farran-g-cahill, near Templemore, and also several other denominations in that neighbourhood, were Major Jeremiah Lalor's estates. Farrenagahill at the present day pays a chief-rent to his descendant Capt. Edmund Power-Lalor, of Longorchard after-mentioned. Major Jeremiah Lalor, although then far advanced in years, fought as a volunteer under the banner of King James at the battle of the Boyne. After he had become resident in the county Tipperary, he m. Judith, dau. of Kedragh O'Meagher, Esq. of Boulebane Castle, same county, and had issue,

Jeremiah of Barnagrotty, of whom hereafter.
John, ancestor of Mrs. Laffan.
Patrick, who d. without issue.
Mathew of Killough. He m. the dau. of — Kiely, Esq. of the co. Cork, and had issue, 1 John, of Oldcastle; 2 Elizabeth, wife of James Butler, Esq. of Park, co. Tipperary, and by him grandmother of Capt. James Butler, also of Park, who m. Gertrude, dau. of Sir John Craven-Carden, Bart., deceased, of The Priory, Templemore; 3 Mary, wife of Edmund Thompson, Esq. of Thurles; 4 James, of Clonamuckoge, father of James, Mathias, and John, all officers in the army; 5 Richard, of Shanakill, who m. Eleanor, sister of Thomas Lidwill, Esq. of Clonmore, co. Tipperary, by whom he had issue, viz., Capt. Richard, who served in the siege of Buenos Ayres; Thomas, a capt. in the 82nd regt.; and Mary; Richard, of Shanakill, d. 15 June, 1776, as did his wife Eleanor, the 8 Aug. 1782.
Martin, of Gortnagoona, who m. Miss Doyle, of the co. Kilkenny, aunt to Major-General Doyle, and had issue by her, Ellen, wife of William, son of Theobald Butler, Esq. of the co. Carlow.

Major Jeremiah Lalor d. 9 July, 1709, aged 83 years, and was, with his wife, interred at Templemore. His eldest son,

Jeremiah Lalor, Esq. of Barnagrotty, in the King's County, m. the dau. of Samuel Smith, Esq. of Lisduffe, co. Tipperary, descended from an ancient Irish family, and had two sons, viz.,

I. John, of Longorchard, of whom presently.
II. Jeremiah, of Barnagrotty, grandfather of Thomas Lalor Cooke, Esq. of Parsonstown, King's County.

The eldest son,

John Lalor, Esq. of Longorchard, co. Tipperary, m. Elizabeth, sister of John Doherty, Esq. of Outrath, co. Tipperary, and d. 9 May, 1782, aged 75 years, leaving issue,

I. Thomas, his heir.
II. Nicholas, of Dunmore and Ballyragget, co. Kilkenny, m. Cecilia, dau. of Ulick Burke, Esq. of Meelick, co. Galway, and d. 29 June, 1796, s. p.
III. John, of Crannagh and Longorchard, co. Tipperary, a deputy governor and justice of the quorum for that county. (*See* Power-Lalor.)
IV. Jeremiah, of Glasshouse, m. 1st, Lydia, dau. of William Smith, Esq. of Burriscastle, Queen's County, by whom he was father of John, of Gurteen, co. Tipperary, who m. Sarah, dau. of Edward Kennedy, Esq. This Jeremiah m. 2ndly, Anne, dau. of John Doherty, Esq. of Outrath, co. Tipperary, of which marriage no issue survives.
V. James, of Riverstown, m. Miss Bray, a niece to the late Most Rev. Dr. Thomas Bray, Roman Catholic archbishop, and has a dau., Alicia.
VI. Joseph, a law student, who d. young and unm.
I. Bridget, wife of Noble Luke Usher, Esq. of Gurteen, co. Tipperary. She d. without issue.
II. Alice, wife of William Keating, Esq. of Brookley, co. Tipperary. She d. without issue.
III. Susan, who d. unm.

The eldest son,

Thomas Lalor, Esq. of Cregg, co. Tipperary, J.P., and a deputy-governor of the counties of Tipperary and Kilkenny, m. Bridget, dau. of Edmund Power, Esq. of Garnavilla, and d. 27 May, 1812, leaving issue,

Thomas-Edmund, his heir.
Maria, m. to D'Arcy Mahon, Esq.
Alice, m. to John Power, Esq. of Churchtown.

The son and heir,

Thomas-Edmund Lalor, Esq. of Cregg, J.P. and D.L., served as high-sheriff of the co. Tipperary, 1840–1. He m. Anne, dau. of Richard Power, Esq. of Carrick-on-Suir, and had issue,

Thomas, now of Cregg.
John, 12th infantry, d. 11 Nov. 1850, aged 26.
Nicholas, d. 18 Oct. 1848, aged 22.
Mary-Anne.
Eliza, m. 1856, William O'Meagher, Esq. of Kilmoyler, co. Tipperary.
Louisa, wife of Clement Sadlier, Esq. of Castle Blake, co. Tipperary.

Mr. Lalor d. 22 Feb. 1847, aged 62; his widow survived until 31 Jan. 1848.

Arms—(Duly registered.) Vert, a lion rampt., or, armed and langued, gu.
Crest—An arm embowed, vested, gu., cuffed, vert, the hand ppr., grasping a short sword, also ppr.
Motto—Fortis et fidelis.
Seat—Cregg, co. Tipperary.

POWER-LALOR OF LONG ORCHARD.

Power-Lalor, Edmund-James, Esq. of Long Orchard, co. Tipperary, b. 18 Oct. 1817, J.P. and D.L., high-sheriff 1857.

Lineage.—Paternally Capt. Power-Lalor is a descendant of the very eminent and very ancient family of De La Poer, which was established in Ireland by SIR ROGER LE POER, one of the companions in arms of Strongbow (*see* POWER *of Gurteen*). Capt. Power-Lalor being 2nd son of the late EDMUND POWER, Esq. of Gurteen, by Anastasia-Phelan his wife, dau. and heir of John Lalor of Long Orchard, and grandson of JOHN POWER, Esq. of Gurteen, whose father Edmund Power, was son of James Power, of Kurraghkilly, the son of James Power, who was 3rd son of Richard Power, nephew of Richard, 1st Earl of Tyrone. Maternally, Capt. Power-Lalor descends from the old Milesian family of O'Lalor.

JOHN LALOR, Esq. of Crannagh and Long Orchard, co. Tipperary, J.P. and deputy-governor, 3rd son of John Lalor, Esq. of Long Orchard (*see* LALOR *of Cragg*), *m.* Mary, dau. of Thomas Phelan, Esq. of Nodstown, co. Tipperary, and had issue,

I. John-Thomas, *b.* 1793, *d.* 1823, *unm.*
II. Thomas-Phelan, barrister-at-law, *d. unm.* at Bath, 4 June, 1825.
III. Nicholas, *d.* young, 1809.
I. ANASTASIA-PHELAN, *m.* 1st, 1815, EDMUND POWER, Esq. of Gurteen, co. Waterford, by whom (who *d.* 29 May, 1830) had issue,
1 John Power, Esq. of Gurteen, D.L., *m.* Frances, dau. of Sir John Power, Bart. of Kilfane, co. Kilkenny, and *d.* 12 May, 1851, leaving issue, four sons and four daus.
2 EDMUND POWER-LALOR, Esq. now of Long Orchard.
3 Richard-Francis-Lalor Power, Esq., *m.* Miss Jane Hutton, of the United States.
1 Mary, *m.* to Henry Petre, Esq. of Dunkenhalgh, Lancashire.
2 Ellen, *m.* to Patrick Power, Esq. of Tramore, co. Waterford.
Anastasia, Mrs. Power, *m.* 2ndly, the Right Hon. Richard-Lalor Shiel, M.P., and *d.* 4 Aug. 1852.
II. Mary, *m.* 1828, to Richard-Montesquieu Bellew, Esq., deceased, son of the late Sir Edward Bellew, Bart., and *d. s. p.*

John Lalor, of Crannagh and Long Orchard, *d.* 7 Sept. 1828.

Arms—Quarterly: 1st and 4th, or, a lion rampt., gu.; 2nd, arg., a chief, indented, sa.; 3rd, arg., on a chief, gu., three escallops, of the 1st.
Crests—1st, an arm embowed, vested, gu., cuffed, vert, the hand ppr., grasping a short sword, also ppr.; 2nd, a stag's head, affronté, or, between the horns a crucifix, ppr.
Mottoes—Fortis et fidelis and per crucem ad coronam.
Seat—Long Orchard, co. Tipperary.

LAMB OF WEST DENTON AND TERNON.

LAMB, JOSEPH, Esq. of West Denton, Northumberland, and Ternon, Cumberland, J.P. and D.L., *b.* 11 Nov. 1781; *m.* 4 May, 1824, Amelia-Mary, dau. of Joseph Michael, Esq. of Stamford, Lincolnshire, and has had issue,

I. Joseph, *b.* 12 May, 1825; *d.* 31 July, 1842.
II. RICHARD, D.L., *b.* 11 Aug. 1826; *m.* 6 Feb. 1855, Georgiana-Elizabeth, dau. of Stephen Eaton, Esq. of Ketton Hall, Rutland, and has issue one dau., Mary-Georgiana.
III. William-Wentworth, *b.* 14 July, 1830; a capt. in the 7th dragoon-guards.
IV. John, *b.* 21 July, 1834; *d.* 12 Aug. 1851.
V. Robert-Ormston, *b.* 5 Nov. 1836.
I. Amelia-Mary, *m.* 16 April, 1856, Capt. Nugent Chichester, eldest son of Joseph Chichester-Nagle, Esq. of Calverleigh Court, Devon.
II. Josephine-Mary-Agnes.
III. Mary-Emma-Alice-Blanche.

Lineage.—This family is a younger branch of the Lambs of Seat Hill, Cumberland, in which county they have held land for centuries.

RICHARD LAMB, Esq. of Seat Hill, Cumberland, *b.* 1680; *m.* Alice Graham, of Edmond Castle, Cumberland, and had issue a numerous family, of which the youngest son,

JOSEPH LAMB, Esq. of Ryton Hall, Durham, *b.* 1732, J.P., *m.* 1st, the heiress of the Humble family, of Ryton, Durham, and had issue two daus., who *d.* in infancy; and 2ndly, Sarah, dau. of Warren Maude, Esq. of Sunnyside, co. Durham, and had issue,

I. HUMBLE, J.P., *b.* 1774, was 6th wrangler, and B.A. of Emmanuel College, Cambridge; *m.* Jane, dau. of Alexander Chatto, Esq. of Main House, Roxburghshire, and had issue,
1 Joseph-Chatto, *m.* Eleanor, dau. of William-Oliver Rutherford, Esq. of Edgerstone, Roxburghshire, and has issue.
2 Alexander.
3 Charles, *m.* Frances Ongley, dau. of Capt. Frederick Burgoyne, R.N., and has issue.
1 Elizabeth, *m.* William Maude, Esq. of Selaby Park, Durham.
2 Sarah.
3 Jane, *m.* John Stravenson, Esq. of Ryton, Durham, and has issue.
4 Isabella, *m.* Bewick Blackburn, Esq., and has issue.
II. Warren, *b.* 1778; *m.* 1811, Sarah, dau. of Robert Hunter, Esq. of Bunker Hill, Durham, and has issue,
1 Warren-Maude, *d.* 1840.
2 Frederick, *m.* Lilla-Louisa, dau. of Adam-Wallace Elmslie, Esq. of London, and has issue.
3 Thomas.
1 Sarah-Maude.
2 Louisa, *m.* Colonel St. Aubyn, of Belvedere House, Jersey, and has issue.
3 Harriet, *m.* George Falle, Esq.
4 Caroline-Laura, *m.* Colonel St. Aubyn, jun., and has issue.
III. JOSEPH, of whose line we treat.
I. Harriet, *m.* Robert Scott, Esq. of Shincliffe Hall, Durham, and had issue,
1 William, *b.* 1804; *m.* Georgina, dau. of Col. Herries, and has issue.
2 Dudley, *b.* 19 May, 1831.
1 Georgina, *d.*
II. Sarah, *m.* George Broadrick, Esq. of Hamphall Park, Yorkshire.
III. Helen, *m.* Capt. Fead, R.N., and has issue.

Arms—Sa., on a fesse, erm., between three cinquefoils, arg., two mullets, of the field.
Crest—The holy or paschal lamb.
Motto—Palma non sine pulvere.
Residence—Axwell Park, Durham.

LAMBARDE OF SEVENOAKS.

LAMBARDE, WILLIAM, Esq. of Beechmont, Sevenoaks, co. Kent, J.P. and D.L., *b.* 18 Nov. 1796; *m.* in Oct. 1818, Harriet-Elizabeth, 5th dau. of Sir James Nasmyth, Bart. of Posso, co. Peebles, and has issue,

I. MULTON, *b.* in 1821; *m.* March, 1848, Teresa-Livesay, dau. of Edmund Turton, Esq. of Brasted Place, Kent, and has issue, John-Bell-William-Edmund; Multon-Thomas-George; Mary-Louisa-Lucinda.
II. John, *b.* in 1823; *m.* 1847, Mary, dau. of Capt. Haslam; and *d.* 1848, leaving a dau., Harriet-Charlotte.
III. William, *b.* in 1824.
IV. Francis, *b.* in 1830.
V. Charles-James, *b.* in 1833.
VI. Thomas-Murray, *b.* in 1836.
VII. Henry, *b.* March, 1840.
I. Eleanora, *m.* 1854, to Robt.-W.-P. Battiscombe, eldest son of the Rev. R. Battiscombe, rector of Barkway, Herts.
II. Julia.
III. Harriet.
IV. Jane-Aurea.
V. Alice-Mary.

Mr. Lambarde *s.* his father in April, 1836.

Lineage.—JOHN LAMBARDE Esq., sheriff of London in 1551, son of WILLIAM LAMBARDE, of Ledbury, co. Hereford, and grandson of THOMAS LAMBARDE, of the same place, Gent., *m.* Juliana, dau. and heir of William Herne, of London; and *d.* in 1554, leaving (with a younger son, Giles, of London, who *m.* Margaret, dau. and co-heir of John Stevenson, Esq. of London) an elder son,

WILLIAM LAMBARDE, Esq. of Greenwich, who *m.* 1st, Jane, dau. of George Multon, Esq.; and 2ndly, Silvestria, dau. and heir of Robert Deane, of Hallinge, co. Kent, and widow of William Dalison, Esq.; and by the latter had (with a dau., Margaret, *m.* to Thomas, 2nd son of Thomas Godfrey, of Lid) an only son,

SIR MULTON LAMBARDE, Knt. of Westcombe, in Greenwich, who *m.* Ann, dau. of Sir Thomas Lowe, Knt., alderman of London; and *d.* in 1634, leaving a son,

THOMAS LAMBARDE, Esq., who sold his estate at Greenwich. He *m.* in 1638, Isabella, dau. of Sir John Garrard, Bart. of Lamer, by whom he had (with two daus., Isabella, *m.* to Alington Paynter, Esq. of Gillingham, Kent; and Mary, *m.* to Thomas Hatton, of London) two sons, Thomas Lambarde, *b.* in 1642, who *d. s. p.*; and

WILLIAM LAMBARDE, Esq. of Sevenoaks, who *d.* in 1711, leaving, by Magdalen Humfreys, of Leicestershire, his wife (with a younger son, Sir Multon Lambarde, Knt., who *m.* Jone, sole heir of Fowler, of Ash, near Ridley, Kent; and *d. s. p.* in 1758) an elder son,

Thomas Lambarde, Esq. of Sevenoaks, who m. Mary, youngest dau. and co-heir of Sir John Beale, Bart. of Farningham, in Kent; and d. in 1745, having had, with other issue, who d. young or unm., a son

Thomas Lambarde, Esq. of Sevenoaks, who m. in 1747, Grace, dau. of Sir William Parsons, Bart. of Stanton, Notts, and had (with four daus., Grace; Mary, m. to the Rev. John Hallward; Amie, m. to the Rev. Sackville Austen; and Jane, m. to John Randolph, bishop of London) two sons, Multon, of whom presently; and Thomas, in holy orders, rector of Ash, near Wrotham, who m. 3 June, 1783, Miss Otway. Mr. Lambarde d. in 1769, and was s. by his elder son,

Multon Lambarde, Esq. of Sevenoaks b. in 1757; who m. in 1778, Aurea dau. and co-heir of Francis Otway, Esq. of Spalding, co. Lincoln, and had issue, two sons and two daus., viz., William, his heir; Thomas; Bridget-Aurea, m. John Gurdon, Esq. of Assington Hall, Suffolk, and d. 1826; Juliana, m. to Admiral C.-G. Randolph, R.N.; and Mary, m. to the Rev. Richard Salway, rector of Fawkham, Kent. Mr. Lambarde, d. in April, 1836, and was s. by his elder son, the present William Lambarde, Esq. of Beechmont.

Arms—Gu., a chevron, vaire, between three lambs, arg.
Crest—A reindeer's head, erased, arg.
Motto—Deo patriæ tibi.
Seat—Beechmont, Sevenoaks, co. Kent.

LAMBART OF BEAU PARC.

Lambart, Gustavus-William, Esq. of Beau Parc, co. Meath, J.P., late major of the royal Meath militia, b. 1814; m. 5 June, 1847, Lady Frances-M.-C. Conyngham, 2nd dau. of the Marquess Conyngham, and had issue,

I. Gustavus-Francis-William, b. 25 March, 1848.
I. Amy-Gwendaline. II. Cecil-Jane.

Lineage.—Charles Lambart, Esq. of Painstown, M.P. for Kilbeggan, son (by Eleanor his 2nd wife, only child of Simon Creame Esq.) of the Hon. Oliver Lambart, of Painstown, M.P., 3rd son of Charles, 1st Earl of Cavan, m. Elizabeth, only dau. of Gustavus-Hamilton, Viscount Boyne, and had issue, Charles, M.P., d. unm. in 1740; Gustavus, heir to his father; Hamilton, major-general in the army; Elizabeth, m. in 1754, to Nicholas Ogle, Esq.; Eleanor, m. to Thomas Elrington, Esq.; Mary, m. to Christopher Nicholson Esq. of Balrath; and Sophia, m. to the Rev. Robert Gregory. Mr. Lambart d. in 1753, and was s. by his son,

Gustavus Lambert, Esq. of Beau Parc, co. Meath, M.P. for Kilbeggan, who m. Thomasine, dau. of George Rochefort, Esq. of Rochefort, co. Westmeath, and had a son and successor,

Charles Lambert, Esq. of Beau Parc, who m. Frances, dau. of James-Lenox Naper-Dutton, Esq. of Sherborne, co. Gloucester, and left at his decease (with two daus., Frances-Thomasine, m. to Charles Chetwynd, Earl Talbot; and Elizabeth, m. to Sir Rose Price, Bart. of Trengwainton) an only son,

Gustavus Lambart, Esq. of Beau Parc, J.P. and D.L., b. 16 Sept. 1772; who m. Anna-Butler, dau. of Sir John Stevenson, and had issue.

Gustavus-William, now of Beau Parc.
Charles-James, in holy orders, b. 4 Feb. 1817; m. Maria Smith and has issue, Rudolph.
Olivia-Frances.
Frances-Anne-Catherine, m. to Robert-Westley-Hall Dare, Esq. of Theydon Bois, Essex.

Mr. Lambert d. 22 Sept. 1850.

Arms—Gu., three narcissuses, arg., pierced, of the field.
Crest—A centaur, ppr., drawing his bow, gu., arrow, or.
Motto—Ut quo cunque paratus.
Seat—Beau Parc, co. Meath.

LAMBE OF BIDNEY AND HENWOOD.

Lambe, Lacon-William, Esq., M.D., of Bidney and Henwood, co. Hereford, J.P., b. in 1797; m. in 1834, Amelia, 2nd dau. of the Rev. George Foxton, of Twyning, co. Gloucester, and by her (who d. 1840) has issue,

I. Lacon.
I. Jessy. II. Mary.

Lineage.—The family of Lambe, of Bidney, came originally from Yorkshire, and was probably a branch of the ancient family of Lambe established at an early period in the co. of Kent. The founder of the family appears to have been Flemish; for Lambe Lane, near the High Street, Canterbury, took its name from an old house, formerly the property of one Lambin, a Fleming and in the 20th year of the reign of Henry III., 1236, we find Lambin de Langham held the manor of Lambin, in the parish of Rolvenden, near Tenterden, Kent; and a John Lambyn was sheriff of London, 1318. In the early part of Edward III.'s reign the estate of Lambyn was sold to the family of Holden; and in 1470, William Lambe, of the parish of Chart, in the same county, made his will. Of this family was William Lambe, a gentleman of the chapel of King Henry VIII., and a great favourite of that prince. William Lambe, out of his great love of learning, erected in 1578, a free grammar school at Sutton Valence, the place of his birth, in the co. of Kent; he also founded alms-houses and many other extensive charities. His London residence in Cripplegate and the chapel of St. James, which had been granted him by Henry VIII., he gave to the Clothworkers of London. This worthy benefactor d. in 1577, and was buried in St. Faith's Church, under St. Paul's; shortly before his death he finished his conduit for bringing water to the city of London, which was called Lambe's Conduit, and gave the name to the street so called. On the front of his alms-house are carved the founder's arms, which are the same as those borne by the Lambes of Herefordshire, as well as the Lambes of the co. of Suffolk, who were living there in 1559: the late Viscount Melbourne, who was descended from Peniston Lambe, of Lincoln's Inn, bore similar ensigns; thus making the Kent family the source from which the different branches took their origin.

William Lambe Esq., who resided at Acworth, co. York, and had a residence also in London, m. Anne, dau. of Clement Stonor, Esq., by his wife Mabel, and sister of Frances Stonor, Esq. of Knoleshill and Stapleford, co. Essex, and left issue a son, William Lambe, Esq., who had, with two daus., Ann, wife of Mr. Mott, of London, and Mabell, wife of Mr. Field, a son and heir,

William Lambe, Esq. of Lincoln's Inn, London, and of Bidney, parish of Dilwyn, co. Hereford, which he purchased in 1661. He m. Margaret, eldest dau. of Sir William Childe, Knt., LL.D., a master in chancery, by his wife, Anne Lacon,* the heiress of Kinlett, co. Salop, and had issue. Mr. Lambe was a magistrate for co. Hereford, and alive in 1683, at the time of the Visitation of Herefordshire, and was s. by his eldest son,

William Lambe, Esq. of Bidney, b. in 1659, who m. Mary, dau. of — Thowgood, Esq., and by her (who d. in 1742) had issue three sons, I. William, d. a minor; II. John, his heir; III. Lacon, A.M., b. 1700, vicar of Caerleon, co. Monmouth, where he d. 12 June, 1742, aged 41; having m. 29 June, 1723, Elizabeth, eldest dau. of the Rev. William Tyler, vicar of Dilwyn, co. Hereford, who d. at Bristol, 28 Feb. 1766, aged 63, having had issue, Lacon, who s. his uncle John; Sarah, who m. Samuel Miles, Esq. of Bristol, where she d. 30 April, 1801; and other issue. Mr. Lambe d. in 1729, aged 70, and was s. by his eldest surviving son,

John Lambe, Esq. of Bidney, co. Hereford, who m. a dau. of — Rogers, Esq. of Broomy Close, Herefordshire, and had an only dau., Sarah, who d. unm. Mr. Lambe d. from an accident in 1751, and was s. by his nephew,

Lacon Lambe, Esq. of Bidney, b. 26 April, 1729, m. 1st, Margaret, dau. of — Wilkins, Esq., who d. s. p.; and 2ndly, 14 April, 1762, Elizabeth, dau. of John Berington, Esq. of Winsley and Devereux Wootton, co. Hereford, by Winifred his wife, dau. of John Hornyold, Esq. of Blackmore Park, co. Worcester. By her, who d. 30 Sept. 1828, aged 86, he had issue,

I. Lacon, his heir.
II. William, who s. his brother Lacon.
III. John, capt. in the Hon. East India Co.'s navy, b. 4 Sept 1768, d. at Brussels, 26 Feb. 1803, aged 35, having m. Augusta, dau. of — Thomas, Esq., by whom he left issue, Perceval-John, and Augusta.
IV. David, formerly of The Moor, near Hereford, subsequently of Usk, co. Monmouth, b. 20 Jan. 1771, m. 26 March, 1818, Sarah, 2nd dau. of James Hereford, Esq. of Sufton Court, co. Hereford, by his wife Mary, dau. of John Scudamore, Esq., M.P. of Kentchurch Court, in the same co., and had issue,
   1 James, b. 11 Sept. 1819, d. unm. at The Moor, near Hereford, 18 Aug. 1848, aged 28.
   2 David, in holy orders, b. 31 Aug. 1821.

*Anne Lacon was dau. and heiress of Rowland Lacon, Esq. of Kinlet, co. Salop, son and heir of Sir Francis Lacon, Knt. of Willey and Kinlet, co. Salop, by his wife, Jane, youngest dau. of Anthony Browne, Viscount Montague (*see pedigree of* Lacon Childe, *of Kinlet*).

3 Henry, *b.* 8 June, 1827, *d. unm.* at Sydney, Australia, 1 July, 1854, aged 27.
4 John, *b.* 9 June, 1832.
1 Sarah, *d. unm.* 2 Anna-Caroline.
3 Lucy, *m.* 14 Jan. 1851, Henry-Montonnier Hawkins, Esq. (*see* HAWKINS *of The Gaer.*)

I. Elizabeth, *b.* 1 Feb. 1763, *d.* at Ghent, 1830, aged 67.
II. Winifred, *d.* young. III. Frances, *d.* young.
IV. Mary, *b.* 20 Jan. 1789, *m.* at Dilwyn Church, 4 Nov. 1789, William Blount, Esq., M.D., of Orleton, co. Hereford, and had issue (*see Pedigree of* BLOUNT *of Orleton*).
V. Frances, *d. unm.* 26 June, 1776.

Mr. Lambe *s.* to the Bidney estate, at the death of his uncle, John Lambe, Esq., in 1751, and built Henwood House, on the Bidney estate. He *d.* in Castle Street, Hereford, 7 Sept. 1807, aged 78, and was *s.* by his eldest son,

LACON LAMBE, Esq. of Bidney and Henwood, *b.* 2 March, 1764; *d. unm.* 25 June, 1828, aged 64, at Worthing, Sussex, was buried at Broadwater, and was *s.* by his next brother,

WILLIAM LAMBE, Esq., M.D., of Bidney and Henwood, *b.* 26 Feb. 1765; *m.* 1st, in 1794, Harriot-Mary, eldest dau. of John Welsh, Esq. of Warwick, and afterwards of Plymstock, co. Devon, and by her (who *d.* in 1804) had issue two sons and five daus.,

LACON-WILLIAM, his heir, now of Bidney and Henwood.
David, *b.* 1803; *d.* in Australia, leaving by his wife, Harriet Bannister, an only dau., Harriet.
Harriet, *m.* to John-Alfred-Chastel de Boinville, and has had issue.
Mary, *m.* Saxe Bannister, Esq., and has a dau., Marian.
Elizabeth, *d.* young.
Anne, *m.* M.-A. Aymond, and has issue a son and dau.
Augusta, *m.* Frederick Foerster, and has issue.

He *m.* 2ndly, in 1810, Catherine, dau. of — Saunders Esq., M.D., of Upper Berkeley-street, London, and had issue by her one dau.,

Catherine.

Dr. Lambe *d.* at Henwood, 2 June, 1847, aged 82.

Arms—Sa., on a fesse, or, between three cinquefoils, erm., a lion, passant-guardant, gu., between two mullets, pierced, of the field.
Crest—A demi-lion, rampant, gu., collared, or, holding in the dexter paw a mullet, sa.
Seat—Henwood, near Weobly, co. Hereford.

LAMBERT OF CARNAGH.

LAMBERT, HENRY, Esq. of Carnagh, co. Wexford, J.P. and D.L., late M.P. for the co. of Wexford, *b.* 1 Sept. 1786; *m.* 11 June, 1835, Catherine, youngest dau. of William Talbot, Esq. of Castle Talbot, in the same county, and sister of the late Countess of Shrewsbury, and has issue,

I. HENRY, *b.* 2 Dec. 1836.
II. George-Thomas, *b.* 9 Nov. 1837.
I. Mary-Jane. II. Anne.
III. Catherine. IV. Juliana-Margaret.

Lineage.—This family was established in Ireland by Milo de Lamberte, *temp.* HENRY II. His descendant, Philip de Lamberte, of Ballyhire, in the barony of Forth, *m.* Marian, dau. of John Synnott, Esq., and from him the fourth in descent was

JAMES LAMBERT, Esq. of Ballyhire, who *d.* in 1631, leaving, by Mary, his wife, eldest dau. of Robert Esmonde, Esq. of Johnstown, co. Wexford, a son and heir, PATRICK LAMBERT, Esq., father, by Mary, his wife, dau. and heir of Peter Barnewall, Esq. of Drimnagh, of NICHOLAS LAMBERT, Esq. of Carnagh, who *m.* Marian, dau. and eventual co-heir of Richard Stafford, Esq., and left a son, JAMES LAMBERT, Esq. of Carnagh, who *m.* Anstace, dau. and heir of Nicholas Sutton, Esq., and was father of

PATRICK LAMBERT, Esq. of Carnagh, who *m.* Catherine White, acquired with her estates in the co. Kilkenny, and had two sons and a dau. The elder son,

JAMES LAMBERT, Esq. of Carnagh, dying at Bath without issue, in 1757, was *s.* by his brother,

HENRY LAMBERT, Esq. of Carnagh, who *m.* Margaret FitzSimon, of the house of Glancullen, co. Dublin, and had three sons and two daus. The eldest son,

PATRICK LAMBERT, Esq. of Carnagh, *m.* in 1781, Mary-Anne, eldest dau. of George Lattin, Esq. of Morristown Lattin, co. Kildare, representative of the very ancient family of Lattin, and had issue,

HENRY, his heir, now of Carnagh.
Ambrose, of Newgrove, co. Kilkenny, *b.* 1789, *m.* 1823, Eliza, dau. of John Snow, Esq., and cousin-german of Thomas Wyse, Esq., M.P., and *d.* 5 July, 1856, leaving issue.
Catherine, *m.* in 1811, to Gerald Aylmer, Esq. head of the ancient house of Lyons, in Kildare, and brother to the late Countess of Kenmare.
Margaret. Letitia, a nun, *d.* 1854.
Jane, *m.* to A. Banon, Esq., M.D., of Irishtown, co. Westmeath.

Mr. Lambert *d.* in July, 1808.

Arms—Quarterly: 1st and 4th, vert, a lamb, arg.; 2nd and 3rd, erm., an eagle, displayed, gu.
Crest—A sagittary, gu. and arg., charged with a trefoil, vert, the bow and arrow, or.
Motto—Deus providebit.
Seat—Carnagh, co. Wexford.

LAMBERT OF BROOKHILL.

LAMBERT, ALEXANDER-CLENDINNING, Esq. of Brookhill and Cong Abbey, co. Mayo, D.L., treasurer of the county; *m.* 12 Sept. 1848, Emma-Mary, dau. of Guy-Lenox Prendergast, Esq., formerly member of council, Bombay, and M.P. for Lymington, and has issue,

I. A son and heir, *b.* 1857.
I. Emma-Mary-Louisa. II. Flora-Marion.

Lineage.—This family descends from that of GENERAL JOHN LAMBERT, so distinguished in the civil wars of England and Scotland during the Protectorate. His nephew,

JOHN LAMBERT, Esq., settled in the west of Ireland. He was father of two sons, of whom the younger,

JOSEPH LAMBERT, Esq. of Toher and Thomastown, established himself in the co. of Mayo, in the year 1690. He *m.* Anne, sister of Peter Rutledge, Esq. of Cornfield, and had a son,

FRANCIS LAMBERT, Esq. of Toher and Thomastown, who *m.* 1st, Rebecca, dau. of Thomas Lindsey, Esq. of Turin Castle, co. Mayo, and sister of Thomas Lindsey, Esq. of Hollymount, and had by her a son, JOSEPH, his heir, and two daus.: the elder, Letitia, *m.* to Thomas Elwood, Esq. of Ashford, co. Galway; and the younger, to Francis Goodwin, Esq. Mr. Lambert *m.* 2ndly, Miss Ormsby, of the co. Mayo, and had by her a son, Francis, an officer in the Royal navy, who *d.* leaving issue. The only son of the first marriage,

JOSEPH LAMBERT, Esq. of Brookhill, who served as high-sheriff of the co. Mayo, *m.* 1st, Barbara, dau. of the late Thomas Ruttledge, Esq. of Bloomfield, and sister and heir of Robert Ruttledge, Esq. of the same place, and by her had issue,

THOMAS, who *d. unm.*
FRANCIS, in holy orders, of Bloomfield, co. Mayo, J.P., who assumed the name and arms of RUTTLEDGE. He *m.* about 1822, Margaret, 2nd dau. of the late Col. Bruen, of Old Park, co. Carlow, and has four sons and four daus. (*see* RUTTLEDGE *of Bloomfield.*)
Barbara, *m.* to Arthur Knox, Esq. of Bushfield, co. Mayo.

Mr. Lambert *m.* 2ndly, Mary, dau. of the Rev. Alexander Clendinning, D.D., rector of Westport, and by her had issue,

JOSEPH, late of Brookhill, J.P., *d. unm.*
ALEXANDER-CLENDINNING, now of Brookhill.
Eleanor, *m.* to David-Ruttledge Courtenay, Esq., barrister-at-law.
Rebecca, *d. unm.*
Letitia, *m.* to John Veevers, Esq. of Dublin.
Elizabeth.
Georgina, *m.* to Charles Bowen, Esq. of Hollymount.

Mr. Lambert *d.* in 1818.

Arms—Gu., a cross-crosslet, or, between three cinquefoils, pierced, arg.
Crest—A centaur, ppr., charged on the shoulder with a cross-crosslet, or.
Seat—Brookhill, co. Mayo.

LAMBERT OF WATERDALE, LATE OF CREG CLARE.

LAMBERT, JAMES-STAUNTON, Esq. of Waterdale, co. Galway, J.P. and D.L., high-sheriff 1813, and M.P. for the co. of Galway from 1826 to 1833; *b.* 5 March, 1789; *m.* 25 Sept. 1832, the Hon. Camden-Elizabeth Macclellan, only dau. of Camden-Gray, Lord Kirkcudbright, and by her has issue,

I. WALTER-MACCLELLAN, capt. 41st regt., *b.* 31 Aug. 1833.
II. Charles-James, *b.* 11 Oct. 1837; *d.* 6 Feb. 1855.
III. Thomas-Camden, *b.* 5 Oct. 1841.
IV. Robert, *b.* 4 Feb. 1844.
V. James-Henry, *b.* 6 Sept. 1851.

I. Sarah-Elizabeth. II. Harriette.
III. Katherine-Isabella, *d.* 1854.

Lineage.—This family, which trace their descent from John Lambert, 2nd son of Lambert, of Calton, co. York, settled in the co. of Galway, in 1630, on a lease they held of the Deer Park, at Portumna, from the Earl of Clanricarde, with which nobleman the first of the name, JOHN LAMBERT, went over from England. This John Lambert's son, who *m.* Janet, dau. of Walter Taylor, Esq., was killed at the siege of Derry, leaving a son,

WALTER LAMBERT, Esq. of Creg Clare, who *m.* 1st, Miss Hamilton, and by her had one son, CHARLES, of whom presently. He *m.* 2ndly, Miss Martyn, of Tullyra, by whom he had (with several daus., of whom one *m.* Francis Butler, Esq. of Cregg; and another *m.* —Morgan, Esq. of Monksfield) several sons, ancestors respectively of the LAMBERTS *of Castle Lambert* (*see that family*), LAMBERTS *of Kilquain*, LAMBERTS *of Castle Ellen*, &c. The eldest son,

CHARLES LAMBERT, Esq. of Creg Clare, *m.* in 1742, Margaret, dau. of Dominick Browne, Esq. of Castle Macgarrett, co. Galway, and by her had (with six other children, who *d. unm.*) a son, WALTER, of whom presently, and three daus., viz., Elizabeth, *m.* to John Burke, Esq. of Tyaquin; Catherine, *m.* to Wilson, Esq. of Belvoir, co. Clare; and Ellice, *m.* to — Donnelan, Esq. of Killagh, co. Galway. The son

WALTER LAMBERT, Esq. of Creg Clare, *m.* 1st, in 1779 Honoria Dillon, sister to the 1st Lord Clonbrook, by whom he had no issue; and 2ndly, in 1784, Catherine, dau. and co-heiress of James Staunton, Esq. of Waterdale, descended in direct line from the STAUNTONS *of Nottinghamshire*, but by her had three daus., Harriet, *d.* 1829; Maria, *d.* 1858; and Emma, *d.* 1831; and two sons, JAMES-STAUNTON, his heir, and Thomas-Dominick, *b.* July, 1791. Mr. Lambert *d.* 25 Sept. 1832, and was *s.* by his elder son, the present JAMES-STAUNTON LAMBERT, Esq. of Waterdale.

Arms—Quarterly: 1st and 4th, gu., three cinquefoils, pierced, arg., for LAMBERT; 2nd and 3rd, arg., two chevrons, sa., for STAUNTON.
Crest—A centaur, ppr., bow, gu., arrow, or.
Motto—Ut quocunque paratus.
Seat—Waterdale House, co. Galway.

LAMBERT OF CASTLE LAMBERT.

LAMBERT, WALTER, Esq. of Castle Lambert, co. Galway, J.P., high-sheriff 1828, *b.* 10 Sept. 1795; *m.* 21 Oct. 1817, Ann, dau. of Colonel Giles Eyre, of Eyre Court Castle, and has issue,

I. THOMAS-EYRE. II. Giles-Eyre. III. Walter.
IV. Richard. V. Burton.
I. Annie, *m.* to Edward, 2nd son of Garrett O'Moore, of Cloughan Castle, King's County.
II. Anchoretta-Maria. III. Ada.

Lineage.—THOMAS LAMBERT, Esq., son, by his 2nd wife, Miss Martyn, of Walter Lambert, Esq. of Creg Clare, *m.* Miss E. Wood, dau. of Wood, of Chappel Field, co. Sligo, and had (with two daus., Margaret, *m.* to — Boat, Esq. of Ducks Pool, co. Waterford; and Anne, *m.* to Henry Lambert, Esq. of the co. Galway) a son and successor,

WALTER LAMBERT, Esq. of Castle Lambert, who *m.* in 1791, Eliza, dau. of Burton Persse, Esq. of Persse Lodge, co. Galway, and had issue,

WALTER, now of Castle Lambert.
John, *m.* a dau. of Col. Peyton, and has issue six sons and two daus.
Richard, *m.* Elizabeth-Charlotte-Louisa, dau. and heir of the late John Campbell, Esq. of Lyston Hall, Essex (*see* LAMBERT *of Lyston Hall.*)
Parsons. Charles. Robert.
Sarah, *m.* 1st, to Charles Barry, 2nd Baron Clanmorris; and 2ndly, in 1830, to Edward-S. Hickman, Esq.
Bessy, *m.* to St. George, Esq. of Kilcolgan Castle, co. Galway.
Anna, Mrs. Rathborne, of Ballymore, co. Galway.

Arms—Gu., three cinquefoils, pierced, arg.
Crest—A centaur, ppr., bow, gu., arrow, or.
Motto—Ut quocunque paratus.
Seat—Castle Lambert, near Athenry.

LAMBERT OF LYSTON HALL.

LAMBERT, RICHARD, Esq. of Lyston Hall, co. Essex, *b.* 7 April, 1807; *m.* 27 June, 1828, Elizabeth-Charlotte-Louisa, eldest dau. and heir of the late John Campbell, Esq. of Lyston Hall, accountant-general of the Court of Chancery, and by her has issue,

LAM

I. JOHN-CAMPBELL.
II. Richard-Blake. III. Walter-Miller.
I. Elizabeth-Blackwell-Campbell, *m.* 27 May, 1851, to W.-R. Williams, Esq., 4th dragoon-guards, eldest son of Robert-Vaughan-Wynne Williams, Esq. of Bedford-place.
II. Anne-Henrietta-Campbell. III. Julia-Campbell.

Mr. Lambert is 4th son of the late Walter Lambert, Esq. of Castle Lambert, co. Galway.

Arms—Gu., three cinquefoils, pierced, arg.
Crest—A centaur, ppr., bow, gu., arrow, or.
Motto—Ut quocunque paratus.
Seat—Lyston Hall, Essex.

LAMBERT OF AGGARD.

LAMBERT, JOHN-WALTER-HENRY, Esq. of Aggard, co. Galway, J.P., high-sheriff 1850, *b.* 5 Oct. 1811; *m.* Feb. 1833, Anne, dau. of William Fetherston Haugh, Esq. of Derrahing, co. Galway, by whom he has issue,

I. THOMAS-WALTER, *b.* 24 March, 1841.
II. John-Henry, *b.* 16 Dec. 1844.
III. William-Fetherston, *b.* 20 Nov. 1853.
I. Anne-Caroline. II. Charlotte.
III. Emily. IV. Elizabeth-Jane.
V. Marian. VI. Adelaide.
VII. Fanny. VIII. Alice.

Lineage.—THOMAS LAMBERT, Esq. of Aggard, son of John Lambert, Esq., by Mary Burke his wife, *m.* 5 Sept. 1805, Lydia, dau. of — Fetherston-Haugh, Esq.; and *d.* 1822, leaving issue,

JOHN-WALTER-HENRY, now of Aggard.
Cuthbert-Fetherston.
Lydia, *m.* to Capt. Cuthbert Barlow.
Cecilia, *m.* to W. Nixon, Esq.
Charlotte, *m.* to Capt. Henry Marshall.

Seat—Aggard, co. Galway.

LAMONT OF LAMONT.

LAMONT, ARCHIBALD-JAMES, Esq. of Lamont, co. Argyll, J.P. and D.L., *b.* 1818; *m.* 1st, Sept. 1839, Adelaide, dau. of Jas.-Hewitt Massy-Dawson, Esq., son of the Hon. Jas. Massy-Dawson, and has issue,

Adelaide-Augusta.

He *m.* 2ndly, March, 1844, Harriet, dau. of Colonel Alexander Campbell, of Possil, and has issue,

I. JOHN-HENRY, *b.* 10 March, 1854.
I. Harriet, *d.* 26 Feb. 1852. II. Joclyn.
III. Amelia-Georgina-Adelaide. IV. Marion-Alice.

Lineage.—The family of LAMONT *of Lamont* dates from the eleventh century. Interesting details are given of them in SKENE's *Highland Clans*. The grandfather of the present representative of this long descended line,

JOHN LAMONT, Esq. of Lamont, *m.* 1773, Helen, dau. of D. Campbell, of South Hall, and by her (who *d.* in 1840) had a son,

MAJOR-GEN. JOHN LAMONT, of Lamont, who *m.* in 1805, Rebecca Hobbs, and had issue,

ARCHIBALD-JAMES, now of Lamont.
John, *d.* in infancy.
Amelia, *m.* I.-G. Davidson, Esq.; and *d.* in 1840.
Augusta-Charlotte-Matilda, *d.* 1830.
Georgina, *d.* in 1847.

Arms—Az., a lion, rampant, arg., within a bordure, of the second.
Crest—An open hand, couped, ppr.
Supporters—Two wild men.
Motto—Ne parcas nec spernas.
Seat—Lamont.

LAMPLUGH OF LAMPLUGH.

LAMPLUGH-RAPER, JOHN-LAMPLUGH, Esq. of Lamplugh, co. Cumberland, and of Lotherton, in Yorkshire, *b.* 19 July, 1790; *m.* 25 Oct. 1818, Jane, 2nd dau. of Benjamin Brooksbank, Esq. of Healaugh Hall, W. R. of York.

Lineage.—ADAM DE LAMPLUGH, son of Sir Robert de Lamplugh, Lord of Lamplugh, in Cumberland, and of Hallkord, in Lancashire, *temp.* HENRY II. and RICHARD I., had a confirmation, with many privileges, from Richard de Lucy, Lord of Coupland. From him lineally descended

THOMAS LAMPLUGH, D.D., archbishop of York, who m. Catherine, dau. of Edward Davenant, D.D., nephew of John Davenant, bishop of Salisbury, and had a son and successor, THOMAS LAMPLUGH, D.D., archdeacon of Richmond, b. in 1661, who was father, by Margaret his wife, of

THE REV. THOMAS LAMPLUGH, rector of Bolton Percy and canon-residentiary of York Minster, to whom his cousin, Thomas Lamplugh, Esq. of Lamplugh, co. Cumberland, (grandson of Col. Lamplugh* the royalist, so gallantly distinguished at Marston Moor), bequeathed by will, dated 1734, Lamplugh Hall and demesne. This gentleman m. 17 April, 1721, Honor, dau. of William Chaloner, Esq. of Guisborough, co. York, and was s. by his only son,

THE REV. THOMAS LAMPLUGH, of Lamplugh, rector of Copgrove and Goldesborough, and prebendary of Wistow, who m. Mary, dau. of James Collins, Gent. of Knaresborough and Foleyfote, but, dying without issue, in 1783, was s. by (the son of his sister Anne, and her husband, John Raper, Esq. of Abberford), his nephew,

JOHN RAPER, Esq. of Abberford and Lotherton, who then became also "of Lamplugh." He m. at Fulford, 16 Oct. 1789, Katherine, 3rd dau. of the Rev. Godfrey Wolley, by Katherine his wife, dau. of the Rev. Thomas Lamplugh, of Lamplugh, and had two sons and one dau., viz.,

JOHN-LAMPLUGH RAPER, his heir.
Henry Raper, of Lincoln's Inn, barrister-at-law, b. 12 Feb. 1795, m. 16 Dec. 1824, Georgiana, 3rd dau. of John Moore, Esq., capt. in the 5th regt. of dragoon-guards.
Ann Raper, m. to James Brooksbank, merchant, of London, 2nd son of Benjamin Brooksbank, Esq. of Healaugh Hall, in the West Riding of York.

Mr. Raper d. 3 July, 1824.

Arms—Or, a cross-fleury, sa.
Crest—A goat's head, arg., attired and bearded, or.
Seats—Lamplugh Hall, Cumberland; Lotherton, in Yorkshire.

L'AMY OF DUNKENNY.

L'AMY, JOHN-RAMSAY, Esq. of Dunkenny, co. Forfar, J.P. and D.L., b. 9 April, 1813; m. 10 June, 1845, Mary-Riche-Macleod, only dau. of William-Mitchell Innes, Esq., of Ayton, and has issue,

I. JAMES, b. 19 Aug. 1847.
II. William, b. 11 Aug. 1850.
III. John-Alexander-Ramsay, b. 10 June, 1852.
I. Christina.
II. Mary-Milliamina.

Lineage.—The family of L'Amy, of Dunkenny, is one of considerable antiquity. The writings, or land rights, by which the present possessor holds the lands of Dunkenny, and in which occur the names of his ancestors who succeeded to the inheritance, go back as far as 1520; and in the Lord Lyon's patent of arms it is mentioned, that a "Lamy, of Dunkenny," was one of the witnesses to a Royal Charter in 1401. The surname appears at a much earlier period (1329) in the Chamberlain's Roll, in the Scotch Exchequer Records. The late

JOHN-RAMSAY L'AMY, Esq. of Dunkenny, m. in 1760, Agnes, dau. of Robert Hamilton, Esq. of Kilbrackmont, co. Fife, and by her, who d. in 1782, had issue,

JAMES, his heir.
Agnes, m. to the Rev. Dr. Lyon, D.D.
Margaret, m. to George Kerr, Esq., younger, of Dumbarrow, co. Fife.
Hamilton, m. to Gore Daly, Esq.
Helen, d. unm.

Mr. L'Amy d. in 1814, and was s. by his son,

JAMES L'AMY, Esq. of Dunkenny, D.L., an advocate at the Scotch bar, and sheriff of Forfarshire, b. 8 July, 1772; who m. 5 Nov. 1811, Mary, dau. of Joseph Carson, Esq., M.D., of Philadelphia, and by her (who d. 1836) had issue,

JOHN-RAMSAY, now of Dunkenny.
Sylvester, H.E.I.C.S.
Helen. Mary-Georgina, d. 1848.

Mr. L'Amy d. 15 Jan. 1854.

Arms—Az., three croziers, paleways, in fesse, or, and in base, a saltier, couped, arg.
Crest—A dexter hand, erect, ppr. holding a crosier, or.
Motto—Per varios casus.
Supporters—Two naked savages, wreathed about the head and middle with laurel, and holding clubs over their shoulders, all ppr.
Seat—Dunkenny, co. Forfar.

LANDOR OF IPSLEY COURT.

LANDOR, WALTER-SAVAGE, Esq. of Ipsley Court, co. Warwick, b. Jan. 1775; m. May, 1811, Julia, dau. of Jean Thuillier, Baron Neuveville, of Bath, a lady of Swiss extraction, and has,

I. ARNOLD-SAVAGE.
II. Walter-Savage. III. Charles-Savage.
I. Julia-Elizabeth-Savage.

This gentleman, the distinguished poet, is known in the world of letters as the author of *Imaginary Conversations of Literary Men and Statesmen*, and several other productions.

Lineage.—This family, designated indifferently LAUNDE and LAUNDER, claim to derive from the De la Laundes. In the time of CHARLES I., JOHN LAUNDER, of Rugeley, was a captain in the royal army; and in the following reign the name began to be spelt as it now appears; under WILLIAM and MARY, WALTER LANDOR, Esq. of Rugeley, was high-sheriff for Staffordshire.

WALTER LANDOR, Esq. (son and successor of Robert Landor, Esq. of Rugeley, by Mary his wife, dau. and co-heir of Walter Noble, Esq. of Longdon, and grandson of Robert Llandor, Esq. of Rugely, b. 6 June, 1680, by Elizabeth his wife, dau. and heir of the Rev. John Taylor), m. 1st, in May, 1760, Mary, only child of Richard Wright, Esq. of Warwick, and had by her an only dau., Maria, m. to her cousin, Humphrey Arden, Esq. He m. 2ndly, Elizabeth, dau. and co-heir of Charles Savage, Esq. of Tachbrook, co. Warwick, and had by her

WALTER-SAVAGE, of Ipsley Court.
Charles-Savage, in holy orders, rector of Cotton, in Staffordshire, m. in January, 1812, Catherine, only child of — Wilson, Esq. of Marston Montgomery, Derbyshire, and has, with three daus., one son, Charles-Wilson.
Henry-Eyres.
Robert-Eyres, in holy orders, rector of Birlingham, in Worcestershire.
Elizabeth-Savage. Mary-Anne, d. unm.
Ellen.

Arms—Arg., two bends, gu., each surmounted with a cottise, dancettée, or.
Crest—A dexter arm, gu., banded with two cottises, or, holding in the hand a fleur-de-lis, arg.
Seat—Ipsley Court, in Warwickshire.

LANE OF KING'S BROMLEY.

LANE, JOHN-NEWTON, Esq. of King's Bromley Manor, co. Stafford, b. 4 Dec. 1800; m. 8 Jan. 1828, the Hon. Agnes Bagot, 2nd dau. of William, 2nd Lord Bagot, by the Lady Louisa Legge, his wife, dau. of George, 3rd Earl of Dartmouth, K.G., and has had issue,

I. JOHN-HENRY-BAGOT, b. 24 Feb. 1829.
II. Albert-William, b. 12 April 1830; and d. 7 Jan. 1831.
III. Sidney Leveson, b. 13 April, 1831.
IV. William, b. 14 Feb.; and d. 15 April, 1832.
V. Cecil-Newton, b. 27 May, 1833.
VI. Greville-Charles, b. 4 Nov. 1834.
VII. Ernald, b. 3 March, 1836.
VIII. Arthur-Louis, b. 18 July, 1840; and d. 3 March, 1846.
IX. Edward-Alfred-Reginald, b. 12 Aug. 1841, d. 29 Sept. 1854.
X. Ronald-Bertram, b. 19 Feb. 1847.
I. Agnes-Louisa, d. 15 June, 1842.
II. Alice-Frances-Jane, d. 17 Feb. 1846.
III. Edith-Emmeline-Mary.
IV. Isabel-Emma-Beatrice.

Mr. Lane s. his father 21 Dec. 1824.

Lineage.—The ancient family of Lane came into England, according to Hollinshed, with the CONQUEROR. Its pedigree commences with

SIR REGINALD DE LONE, grandfather of

ADAM DE LONA of West Hampton, co. Stafford, whose grandson,

RICHARD DE LA LONE, 9 EDWARD II., living at Hampton, was direct ancestor of

* Colonel Lamplugh's dau., Elizabeth, wife of Henry Brougham, Esq., of Scales, co. of Cumberland, is now represented by her eldest male descendant Henry, LORD BROUGHAM and VAUX.

JOHN LANE, Esq. of Bentley, who *m.* Margaret, dau. and heiress of Thomas Partrich, of King's Bromley, and dying 19 ELIZABETH, was *s.* by his son,

THOMAS LANE, Esq. of Bentley and Hyde, who *m.* Catherine, dau. of Richard Trentham, Esq. of Rochester, and aunt of Elizabeth de Vere, Countess of Oxford, and had issue, JOHN, his successor; Thomas; Richard, of Kearns, in Monmouthshire; and Cassandra, *m.* to Thomas Littleton, 3rd son of Sir Edward Littleton, of Pillaton. He *d.* 31 ELIZABETH, and was *s.* by his eldest son,

JOHN LANE, Esq. of Bentley and Hyde, who *m.* Jane, dau. of Sir Edward Littleton, of Pillaton, and had issue, THOMAS, his successor; and Alice, *m.* to Alexander Wightwick, Esq. He *d.* 3 JAMES I., and was *s.* by his son,

THOMAS LANE, Esq. of Bentley and Hyde. This gentleman *m.* Anne, eldest dau. of Sir Walter Bagot of Blithfield, co. Stafford, and sister of Sir Hervey Bagot, Bart. He assisted in the preservation of King CHARLES II., after the battle of Worcester and suffered severely for his attachment to the royal cause. He had several children, I. JOHN, his successor; II. William, of Shetton, from whom the Irish family spring; III. Richard, a groom of the bed-chamber; I. Jane, celebrated for her heroic conduct in saving the life of King CHARLES II., after the battle of Worcester, *m.* subsequently, Sir Clement Fisher, of Packington, in Warwickshire, Bart.; II. Withy, *m.* to — Petre, Esq.; III. Anne, *m.* to Edward Birch, Esq. of Leacroft; IV. Mary, *m.* to Edward, son of Sir Oliver Nicholas, (cupbearer to JAMES I., and carver to King CHARLES I.) Mr. Lane *d.* in 1660, and was *s.* by his eldest son,

COLONEL JOHN LANE, who was so instrumental in saving King CHARLES II., after the battle of Worcester, and received him at his seat at Bentley, from which place he was conveyed in disguise by Miss Lane, to Mrs. Norton's at Abbot's Leigh, near Bristol. For these signal services the family was dignified with an especial badge of honour, viz., the arms of England in a canton, in augmentation of its paternal coat, and a crest, a strawberry roan horse, bearing between his fore legs the royal crown. There is a tradition, that Col. Lane was likewise offered a peerage, but declined it. He *m.* Athaliah Anson, and had, with other issue, SIR THOMAS, his successor; Lettice, who *d.* 23 Nov. 1709; Frances, *m.* to William Offley, of Madeley Manor, co. Stafford; Mary, *m.* to Sir Humphrey Jervis, lord-mayor of Dublin. Col. Lane *d.* in 1667, and was *s.* by his eldest son,

SIR THOMAS LANE, Knt. of Bentley, who *m.* Abigail, Lady Williams, widow of Sir Henry Williams, Bart. of Gwernevet, and dau. of Samuel Wightwick, prothonotary of the King's Bench, and dying 25 Jan. 1715, was *s.* by his only surviving son,

JOHN LANE, Esq. of Bentley, *b.* 12 Dec. 1669, who *m.* 30 April, 1702, Mary, dau. and co-heiress, with her sister, Sybill (wife of the Rev. Dr. Birch,) of Humfrey Wyrley, Esq. of Hampstead, co. Stafford, by Mary, his wife, eldest dau. and co-heir (with her sister, Jane, *m.* to William de Zulstein, Earl of Rochford) of Sir Henry Wroth, Knt. of Durance, co. Middlesex, and had issue. Mr. Lane *d.* 25 Oct. 1748, and was *s.* by his son,

THOMAS LANE Esq. of Bentley, *b.* 28 April, 1703, who *m.* 1st, Miss Anne Austen, and had issue, JOHN, his successor; Thomas, *d.* young; Mary, *m.* to John Taylor, Esq. of Walsal; Ann, *d.* young; Elizabeth-Sybilla, *m.* to Roger Holmes, Esq. Mr. Lane *m.* 2ndly, Miss Anne Sayer, and had issue, I. Thomas, in holy orders, rector of Handsworth, *m.* in 1779, Esther-Barbara, dau. of Sir Thomas Birch, judge of the Common Pleas; II. Charles, *d.* young; III. William, colonel in the army, and for some time governor of St. Helena, *m.* Miss Camac, of Greenmount Lodge, in Ireland; IV. EDWARD, *d.* in 1784; I. Jane, *m.* to John Freer, of Birmingham; II. Anna, *m.* in 1776, to George Birch, Esq. of Harborne and Hampstead, co. Stafford. Mr. Lane *d.* in 1775, and was *s.* by his eldest son,

JOHN LANE, Esq., *b.* in 1723, who *m.* 1750, Sarah, dau. and co-heiress of Richard Fowler, Esq. of Penford, co. Stafford, and had issue,

I. JOHN, his successor.

II. Thomas, of Leyton Grange, in Essex, clerk of the Goldsmiths' Company, *b.* 30 Sept. 1754, *m.* 4 Sept. 1784, Barbara, dau. of Thomas Fowler, of Pendeford, Esq., by whom he had issue,

1 Thomas-Goldsmith Fowler, *b.* 5 Nov. 1786, *m.* Rebecca, relict of Capt. Napier, and *d.* 10 April, 1819, *s. p.*

2 John, *b.* 6 June, 1788, who *s.* his father as clerk of the Goldsmiths' Company, and in the estate of Leyton Grange, Essex: *m.* 1st, 19 Aug. 1817, Jane, 2nd dau. of the Rev. John Williams, M.A., vicar of Marston Magna, co. Somerset, and prebendary of Wells, she *d.* 7 July, 1818. He *m.* 2ndly, 17 Jan. 1825, Elisabeth, only surviving dau. and heir of William Carter, Esq., *d.* 17 June, 1852. Mr. John Lane *d.* 16 Jan. 1852, leaving issue by his 1st wife,

Mary-Jane, *m.* 12 June, 1839, John Salt, Esq.

By the 2nd marriage,

Newton-John, *b.* 25 Nov. 1828.
William-Goldsmith-Lister, *b.* 7 Dec. 1835.
Charles-Leveson, *b.* 21 March, 1839.
Harry-Thomas-Fowler, *b.* 3 July, 1842.
Mary, *m.* 9 Jan. 1850, William-Fowler-Mountford Copeland, Esq., eldest son of William-Taylor Copeland, Esq., M.P., *b.* 4 Nov. 1828.
Adelaide-Lucy, *d.* 21 July, 1831.
Florence, *d.* 31 Dec. 1851.
Ada-Barbara. Amelia-Sarah-Lucy.
Alice-Julia.

3 Charles, in holy orders, *b.* 2 Feb. 1793, rector and vicar of Wrotham, and rural dean of Shoreham, co. Kent, &c., *m.* 1 July, 1816, Frances-Catherine, 2nd dau. of the Right Rev. Daniel Sandford, D.D., bishop of Edinburgh, and has issue,

Thomas-Sandford, *b.* 28 Sept. 1818, *d.* 10 July, 1830.
Charles-Edward, *b.* 23 July, 1820, *d.* 20 Aug. 1822.
Richard-Douglas-Hay, late capt. 17th lancers, *b.* 9 Dec. 1823, *m.* 30 April, 1851, Elizabeth-Middleton, only dau. and heir of the late Thomas Ward, Esq. of Heath House, co. Middlesex, and has issue,

Reginald-Charles-Douglas, *b.* 6 April, 1852.
Beaufort-Cosmo-Douglas, *b.* 5 July, 1854.

Charles-Henry, *b.* 16 Jan. 1829, *d.* 29 May, 1832.
Thomas-Bruce, Hon. E.I.C. civil service, Bengal Presidency, *b.* 29 April, 1831, *m.* 20 July, 1853, Adelaide-Fanny-Spring, 4th dau. of William-Hallows Belli, Esq. of the Hon. E.I.C. civil service.
Henry-Murray, Bluemantle Pursuivant-of-Arms, *b.* 3 March, 1833.
Francis-Charles De Lona, *b.* 21 June, 1834.
Jane, *m.* 24 Aug. 1843, Col. Edward-Charles Warde, C.B., R.H.A., eldest surviving son of the late Gen. Sir Henry Warde, G.C.B., *b.* 13 Nov. 1810.
Eleanor-Sarah, *m.* 22 June, 1854, John-Bourryau Broadley, Esq., late capt. 17th lancers.
Frances-Lennox Heneage, *m.* 23 Nov. 1853, Arthur-Vandigaid Davies-Berrington, Esq., only surviving son and heir of J. Davies-Berrington, Esq. of Woodland Castle, co. Glamorgan.
Louisa-Anne.
Alice-Howley, *d.* 1 Jan. 1850.
Blanche-Emma.

4 Richard, *b.* 2 Oct. 1794, *m.* 24 April, 1827, Sarah Pink, 3rd dau. of George-Thomas Tracy, Esq. of Liskeard, co. Cornwall, and has issue,

Richard-Stuart, *b.* 14 July, 1829, *m.* 31 Aug. 1852, Emily-Eliza, eldest dau. of Samuel Levison, Esq.
Charles-Stuart, lieut. 26th regt. native light infantry, *b.* 9 Feb. 1831, *m.* 23 Sept. 1852, Anne-Josephine, 3rd dau. of the Rev. Richard-Bethuel Boyes.
Thomas-Blomefield, Hon. E.I.C. civil service, Bengal Presidency, *b.* 9 June, 1832.
Wilmot, *b.* 19 Sept. 1833.
Henry, *b.* 26 May, 1835.
Frances-Bain, *d.* 26 Oct. 1835.
Sarah-Magdalene. Emily.

1 Sarah, *m.* 4 Feb. 1812, William Cotton, Esq. of Walwood House, co. Essex, one of the directors of the Bank of England, and governor in the years 1842-3-4, *b.* 12 Sept. 1786.

2 Jane, *b.* 21 May, 1791, *d.* 21 July, 1791.

Mr. Thomas Lane *d.* 10 Jan. 1824.

III. Richard, capt. R.N. *b.* 6 June, 1761, *d.* 28 Feb. 1799, *s. p.*

IV. Newton-Charles, in holy orders, *b.* 16 Feb. 1763, rector of Ingoldsby, co. Lincoln, *d.* 6 March, 1844, *s. p.*

I. Sarah, *b.* 2 Nov. 1751, *d.* young.

II. Maria, *b.* 29 Jan. 1757, *m.* 28 April, 1788, the Rev. John Lucy, of Charlecote Park, co. Warwick, and had issue.

III. Sarah, *b.* 30 March, 1759, *d.* young.

Mr. Lane *d.* 28 June, 1782, and was *s.* by his eldest son,

JOHN LANE, Esq., *b.* 25 Dec. 1752, fellow of Queen's College, Cambridge, barrister-at-law, deputy-lieut. of the county of Stafford, high-steward of the town of Burton-upon-Trent &c. &c., who *m.* 20 Jan. 1800, Sarah, only surviving dau. of Thomas Lloyd, Esq., and widow of John Amler, Esq. of Ford Hall, co. Salop, and by her, who *d.* 1 April, 1855, had issue,

JOHN-NEWTON, his successor.
Thomas-Leveson, in holy orders, *b.* 28 Sept. 1802, vicar of Baswick, co. Stafford, and of Wasperton, co. Warwick.

Mr. Lane *d.* 31 Dec. 1824, and was *s.* by his eldest son, the present JOHN-NEWTON LANE, Esq.

Arms—Per fesse, or and az., a chevron, gu., between three mullets, counterchanged; on a canton of the third, th royal lions of England. Quartering De la Hyde, Wyrley, Fowler, and many others.

Crest—A strawberry roan horse, saliant, couped at the flanks, bridled, sa., bitted and garnished, or, supporting between the feet an imperial crown, ppr.

Motto—Garde le Roy.

Seat—King's Bromley Manor, near Lichfield.

LANE OF BADGEMORE.

Lane, Charles, Esq. of Badgemore, co. Oxford, J.P. and D.L., barrister-at-law, *b.* 27 Oct. 1793; *m.* 3 Jan. 1824, Emily-Maria, 2nd dau. of the late John Thornhill, Esq., an East India Director, and has issue,

- i. Charles-Powlett, *b.* 8 Feb. 1826.
- ii. Thomas-Thornhill, *b.* 17 Nov. 1833.
- iii. John-Reynolds, *b.* 14 Nov. 1836.
- iv. Cudbert-William-Jones, *b.* 10 March, 1842.
- i. Francina-Maria. ii. Henrietta-Catherine.
- iii. Emily-Rose. iv Anna-Maria, *d.* in 1836.
- v. Helena-Ursula-Catharine, *m.* 28 April, 1856, to Valentine-Dudley-Henry-Cary Elwes, Esq., late of the 12th lancers, only son and heir of Cary-Charles Elwes, Esq. of Billing Hall, co. Northampton.

Lineage.—Thomas Lane, of Hitchenden, co. Buck, descended from the Lanes *of Holibar*, co. Northampton, was grandfather of

Robert Lane, who *m.* Alice, dau. of Robert Saunders, of Hambledon, co. Bucks, and had issue. The 4th son,

Francis Lane, of London, merchant, bapt. 5 Nov. 1587, *m.* twice, and had issue by both wives. His 2nd son, by the first, John Lane, also of the city of London, *b.* about 1621, fined for sheriff and alderman, *m.* 1st, Elizabeth Taylor, of Staffordshire; and 2ndly, Anne, eldest dau. of Sir John Trevor, Knt. of Trevalyn, and widow of Alderman Weldon. By the former (who *d.* 22 Nov. 1677) Mr. Lane left (with a dau., Mary, *m.* to Paul Foley, of Stoke Edith, co. Hereford, speaker of the House of Commons) a son and successor,

Sir Thomas Lane, Knt., alderman of London, sheriff of that city in 1693, and lord-mayor in 1695. He *m.* 1st, Mary, sister of Sir Henry Ashhurst, Bart.; and 2ndly, Elizabeth, relict of Sir Thomas Cudden, Knt., chamberlain of London. By the former, who *d.* 29 Nov. 1698, he had (with several daus., one of whom, Elizabeth, *m.* Sir David Hamilton, M.D.) four sons, of whom the eldest,

John Lane, Esq., *b.* in 1677, *m.* Elizabeth, dau. of Henry Hovener, merchant of London, and by her (who *d.* 21 Dec. 1732) had, with other issue, Thomas, a master in Chancery; and a 4th son,

William Lane, Esq., *b.* in 1709, *m.* Elizabeth Pynsent, of the family of Sir William Pynsent, Bart. of Burton Pynsent, co. Devon, and by her (who had been previously *m.* to Mr. Anderson, and *d.* in 1807) had issue,

- i. William, who *m.* twice: by his 1st wife he had, William; Thomas; Mary; and Eliza, *m.* to Benjamin Whitelock, Esq.; and by his 2nd (Susan, dau. of the Rev. Dr. Pollock) he had, Charlton, in holy orders; Charles Thomas, barrister-at-law, deceased; and Susan.
- ii. Thomas, of whom presently.
- iii. John, rector of Sawbridgeworth, Herts, and High Roadings, Essex, *m.* Molly Impey, niece of Sir Elijah Impey, and *d.* in 1817, leaving issue.

Mr. Lane *d.* in 1785. His 2nd son,

Thomas Lane, Esq., *b.* 2 Jan. 1759, *m.* 28 May, 1789, Sarah-Charlotte, only dau. of John Williams, Esq. of Dorsetshire, and of Wimpole Street, by Charlotte Thornhill his wife; and *d.* 15 Nov. 1822, leaving an only surviving son, the present Charles Lane, Esq. of Badgemore.

Arms—Per pale, az. and gu., three saltiers, couped, arg.

Crest—Two griffins' heads, one gu., the other az., issuing out of a crescent.

Motto—Nec degenero.

Seat—Badgemore, near Henley-on-Thames.

LANE OF COFFLEET.

Lane, The Rev. Richard, of Coffleet and Bradley, co. Devon, *b.* 18 Feb. 1772; *m.* 18 Feb. 1800, Lucy, dau. of Nicholas Dennys, Esq. of Ashley, near Tiverton, and had issue,

- i. Thomas-Veale. ii. Richard.
- iii. Dennys. iv. Lascelles. v. Reginald.
- i. Lucy, *m.* 18 May, 1826, to Samborne-Stucley Palmer, Esq. of Timsbury House, co. Somerset.
- ii. Penelope. iii. Emily.
- iv. Jacquesta. v. Frances.

Lineage.—Early in the last century, the estate of Coffleet was purchased by Thomas Veale, Esq. of Bradley, who *d.* in 1780, and was *s.* by (the son of his sister, Charity, who *m.* Richard Lane, Esq.) his nephew,

Thomas Lane, Esq. of Bradley and Coffleet, a magistrate for Devonshire for upwards of thirty-seven years, and high-sheriff in 1784. He *m.* Penelope, only dau. and heir of Thomas Tothill, Esq. of Begtor, and left at his decease surviving issue, a dau., Penelope, and a son, Rev. Richard Lane, of Coffleet and Bradley.

Arms—Quarterly: 1st and 4th, per pale, gu. and az., three saltiers, arg., for Lane; 2nd, arg., on a bend, sa., three calves, passant, of the first, for Veale; 3rd, arg., on a bend, sa., cottised, of the same, a lion, passant-guardant, of the first, for Tothill.

Crest—In a crescent, or, two griffins' heads, dexter, gu., sinister, az., conjoined and couped, beaked, or.

Seats—Coffleet and Bradley, Devon.

LANE OF RYELANDS.

Lane, Robert, Esq. of Ryelands, co. Hereford, J.P., high-sheriff 1841, *b.* March, 1785; *m.* Oct. 1813, Ann, dau. of John Livesey, Esq. of Coppul Hall, co. Lancaster, by Mary his wife, dau. of Samuel Clewes, Esq. of Broughton Hall, and has had issue,

- i. Robert, *b.* 1815; *d. unm.* 1836.
- ii. Theophilus-William, *b.* 1817; *m.* 1848, Emily, dau. of Charles Bowen, Esq. of Kilna Court, Queen's Co.
- i. Juliana, *m.* to Capt. Godfrey-Colpoys Bloomfield, son of John Bloomfield, Esq. of Castle Caldwell, co. Fermanagh.
- ii. Mary-Harriet, *m.* to the Rev. Vernon-George Guise, rector of Longhope, co. Gloucester, 4th son of Gen. Sir John Guise, Bart., K.C.B.

Lineage.—This branch of the family of Lane has been settled for many generations in the co. of Hereford, and represents the very ancient house of Rodd *of the Rodd.*

Theophilus Lane, Esq. (elder son, by Anne his wife, of Theophilus Lane, Esq.), *m.* Juliana, dau. and co-heir of Bampfylde Rodd, Esq. of the Rodd, in Herefordshire, and of Stoke Canon, co. Devon, by his wife, the only dau. of Mr. Justice Price, of the Common Pleas, of Foxley, co. Hereford, and had, with two daus. and a son, another son,

Robert Lane, Esq. of Ryelands, who *m.* 1780, Anne, sister of William Symons, Esq. of Chaddlewood, Devon, and was father of an only surviving son, the present Robert Lane, Esq. of Ryelands.

Arms—Per pale, az. and gu., three saltiers, couped, arg.

Crest—Out of a crescent, or, two griffins' heads, one gu., the other az.

Motto—Celeriter.

Seat—Ryelands, co. Hereford.

LANE-FOX OF BRAMHAM.

See Fox.

LANGDALE OF GARSTON HOUSE.

Langdale, Marmaduke-Robert, Esq. of Garston House, Godstone, Surrey, and of Pix Hall, Hawkhurst, Kent, *b.* 6 April, 1785, F.R.A.S., F.R.B.S.; *m.* 1 Oct. 1812, Louisa, dau. and co-heir of George Jourdan, Esq., and has had issue,

- i. Marmaduke, lieut. 41st foot, *b.* 11 Aug. 1813; *m.* Henrietta, eldest dau. of George Chapman, Esq. of Madras; and *d.* 1 Oct. 1842, leaving two sons and one dau.,
  - 1 Marmaduke-Robert, *b.* 2 March, 1839.
  - 2 Albert, *b.* 8 Sept. 1842.
  - 1 Louisa.
- ii. Alfred, *b.* 20 Sept. 1815; *m.* Charlotte, eldest dau. of William Keene, Esq., barrister-at-law, and has issue.
- iii. George-Augustus, M.A., in holy orders, *b.* 15 Jan. 1817; *m.* and has issue.
- iv. William-Atkinson, *b.* 6 Nov. 1818.

Lineage.—George Langdale, Esq. of March, Isle of Ely, descended from the Langdales *of Houghton*, co. York, *d.* 1674, leaving, by Margaret his wife (who *m.* 2ndly, Isaac

St. Gens, Esq., youngest brother of Sir Francis St. Gens, Knt. of Thorp House, near Peterborough, co. Northampton), his 2nd, but only surviving son,

GODFREY LANGDALE, Esq. of Longthorpe, *b.* in 1674, who was always addressed by Marmaduke, the 3rd Lord Langdale (who *d.* 12 Dec. 1718), as *cousin*. He *m.* Margaret, dau. of George Sayer, Esq. of Huntingdon, and by her (who *d.* 20 Oct. 1744) had issue. Mr. Langdale dying 1 Jan. 1737, was *s.* by his 3rd but only surviving son,

MARMADUKE LANGDALE, Esq. of Southampton Row, Bloomsbury, *b.* 12 Oct. 1719; who *d.* 26 Aug. 1782, leaving, by his wife, Mary, only child and heir of John Lighthasel, Esq., a son and successor,

MARMADUKE LANGDALE, Esq. of New Ormond Street, Queen Square, Holborn, *b.* 5 May, 1756; who *m.* 20 Dec. 1778, Sarah-Augusta, eldest dau. of Robert Kelham, Esq. of Great Gonerby and Billingborough, co. Lincoln, and of Bush Hill, Edmonton, co. Middlesex, senior member of the Hon. Society of Lincoln's Inn; and *d.* 2 Aug. 1832, leaving issue,

I. MARMADUKE-ROBERT, now of Garston House and Pix Hall.
II. Robert-Kelham, who assumed the name and arms of KELHAM only (*see* KELHAM *of Bleasby*).
III. George, *b.* 24 Aug. 1791; *m.* Eliza, dau. of — Cooper, Esq., and has issue, Eliza-Langdale, *b.* in July, 1796.
IV. William-John, in holy orders, *b.* 9 May, 1796; *m.* Marian, dau. of — Jackson, Esq. of Lewes, co. Sussex, and has issue,
1 William-Augustus, *b.* 12 Feb. 1834.
2 Marmaduke-Albert, *b.* 4 Nov. 1839.
1 Margaretta-Charlotte, *b.* 26 April, 1835.
I. Sarah, *m.* 1st, the Rev. Edward Smith, of Folkingham; 2ndly, the Rev. Charles Day.
II. Avice, *m.* William-James May, Esq. of Southwell.
III. Elizabeth, *m.* 12 Aug. 1815, William Belt, Esq. of the Crown Office, Temple.

Arms—Party, per chevron, az. and sa., a chevron, ermine, between three estoiles, arg.
Crest—An estoile, arg., between two oak-branches, ppr.
Motto—Post tenebras lucem.
Seat—Garston House, Godstone.

LANGSTON OF SARSDEN HOUSE.

LANGSTON, JAMES-HAUGHTON, Esq. of Sarsden House, co. Oxford, J.P. and D.L., M.P. for the city of Oxford; *m.* 6 July, 1834, Lady Julia Moreton, dau. of Thomas, 1st Earl of Ducie, and has issue.

Arms—Or, on a chevron, between two roses, in chief, gu., and a dolphin, in base, ppr., three cross-crosslets, or.
Seat—Sarsden House, near Chipping Norton.

GORE-LANGTON OF NEWTON PARK.

GORE-LANGTON, WILLIAM-HENRY-POWELL, Esq. of Newton Park and Hatch Beauchamp, co. Somerset, J.P. and D.L., M.P. for West Somerset, *b.* 25 July, 1824; *m.* 9 June, 1846, Lady Anne-Eliza-Mary Grenville, dau. of the present Duke of Buckingham and Chandos, and has issue,

I. WILLIAM-STEPHEN, *b.* 11 May, 1847.
II. Henry-Powell, *b.* 14 Dec. 1854.
I. Mary-Jane. II. Frances-Anne.

Lineage.—SIR JOHN GORE, Knt., lord-mayor of London in 1624, 4th son of Mr. Alderman Gerard Gore, of London, and brother of Paul Gore, ancestor of the EARLS OF ARRAN, *m.* Hester, dau. of Sir Thomas Campbell; and dying in 1636, left, *inter alios*, a son,

SIR JOHN GORE, Knt. of Gilstone, co. Herts, who *m.* Bridget, dau. of Sir Edward Harington, Bart.; and *d.* in 1659. His brother,

WILLIAM GORE, of Morden, co. Surrey, afterwards of Barrow Court, in Somersetshire, *m.* Jane, dau. of Thomas Smith, Esq. of Tedworth, Wilts, by whom he left at his decease, in 1662, a son, his successor,

SIR THOMAS GORE, Knt., who *m.* Philippa, sister and co-heir of Sir Giles Tooker of Maddington, in Wiltshire; and dying in 1675, left issue, William, *d.* in 1718, leaving issue; Thomas, *d.* before 1725, leaving issue; EDWARD, of whom presently; Jane, *m.* to Richard Baskerville, Esq. of Richardston; and Anne, *m.* to — Stear. Sir Thomas's 3rd son,

EDWARD GORE, Esq. *m.* Arabella, sister and co-heir of Sir John Smyth, Bart. of Long Ashton, co. Somerset; and *d.* in 1742. His 2nd son and eventual heir,

EDWARD GORE, Esq., *m.* Barbara, widow of Sir Edward Mostyn, Bart., and dau. and sole heiress of Sir George Browne, of Kiddington Park, Oxfordshire (by the Lady Barbara Lee, dau. of Edward, 1st Earl of Lichfield), by whom he left at his decease, in 1801,

I. WILLIAM, his successor.
II. Charles, in holy orders, *m.* in 1798, Harriet, dau. of Richard Little, Esq. of Grosvenor Place, and had surviving issue,
1 MONTAGUE, of Barrow Court, late M.P. for Barnstaple.
2 William-Charles. 3 George.

Mr. Gore *d.* in 1801, and was *s.* by his elder son,

WILLIAM GORE-LANGTON, Esq. of Newton Park, co. Somerset, colonel of the Oxford militia, *b.* in Dec. 1760; *m.* 1st, in 1783, Bridget, only child and heiress of Joseph Langton, Esq. of Newton Park (upon which occasion he assumed, by Royal permission, the additional surname and arms of LANGTON), and had issue,

WILLIAM, late M.P. for East Somerset, *b.* in 1787; *m.* in 1822, Jacintha-Dorothea, only child of H.-Powell Collins, Esq. of Hatch Beauchamp, and had one son, WILLIAM-HENRY-POWELL-GORE-LANGTON, Esq. of Newton Park.
Edward, *b.* in 1789, an officer in the army.
John, an officer in the army, *d.* at Ceylon.
Frances-Matilda.

Colonel Gore-Langton *m.* 2ndly, Mary, only dau. of John Browne, Esq. of Salperton, co. Gloucester, and had by that lady,

William-Henry, J.P. and D.L., M.P. for Bristol, *b.* 1802; *m.* 1824, Maria, dau. of John Lewis, Esq.
John-Frederick, capt. grenadier-guards, *d.* 27 Oct. 1834.
Mary-Henrietta, *m.* in 1831, to Sir J.-M. Burgoyne, Bart. of Sutton Park.
Caroline-Maria, *m.* 5 July, 1836, to Col. D'Oyly, of the grenadier-guards.

Arms—Quarterly: LANGTON and GORE, quarterly.
Motto—In hoc signo vinces.
Seat—Newton Park, near Bath.

LATHAM OF BRADWALL.

LATHAM, GEORGE-WILLIAM, Esq. of Bradwall Hall, co. Chester, M.A., of the Inner Temple, barrister-at-law, J.P., *b.* 4 May, 1827.

Lineage.—This is a junior branch of the ancient Cheshire house of LATHOM, of Lathom and Knowsley, which terminated in an heiress, ISABELLA LATHAM, who *m.* Sir John Stanley, Knt., ancestor of the Earls of Derby, in the reign of HENRY VIII., ALEXANDER DE LATHAM occurs in existing deeds, as seized of lands in Astbury, and using the same arms; and from him property descended lineally to the Lathams of Bradwall.

THE REV. JOHN LATHAM, rector of Lawton, in Cheshire, *b.* in 1636 (son of John Latham, of Congleton, whose father, John Latham, of the same place, was grandson of Alexander Latham, also of Congleton, living *temp.* HENRY VIII.) *m.* 31 March, 1692, Maria Moreton, and *d.* 5 June, 1705, leaving (with a dau. Hester, *m.* to the Rev. William Hall, rector of Gawsworth, and *d. s. p.*) an only son and heir,

THE REV. JOHN LATHAM, minister of Bunney, co. Notts, and of Woolstrop, co. Leicester, *b.* 11 Nov. 1694, *m.* Margaret, dau. of William Knott, Esq. of Great Gonerby, in Lincolnshire, and had two sons, JOHN, his successor; and Charles, of Waltham, in Leicestershire, *m.* and had issue. The elder son,

THE REV. JOHN LATHAM, B.A., minister of Siddington, in Cheshire, *b.* 28 Nov. 1725, *m.* 9 June, 1753, Sarah, dau. of Richard Podmore, Esq. of Sandbach, and had issue,

JOHN, M.D., his heir.
Richard, of Sandbach, *m.* Sarah, dau. of Charles Latham, Esq. of Waltham, co. Leicester, and had issue four sons, living.

Mr. Latham *d.* 21 June, 1783, and was *s.* by his son.

JOHN LATHAM, Esq. of Bradwall Hall, M.D., at some time President of the Royal College of Physicians, London, F.R.S., L.S., &c., *b.* 29 Dec. 1761; *m.* 12 April, 1784, Mary, eldest dau and co-heiress of the Rev. Peter Meyer, vicar of Prestbury, (descended from Mere of Mere co. Chester) by Martha, his wife, second dau. and co-heir of John Arderne, Esq. of Sutton, sprung from a scion of Arderne of Alvanley, and had issue,

JOHN, D.C.L., sometime fellow of All Souls' College, Oxford, his heir.
Peter-Mere, M.D., Fellow of the Royal College of Physicians, *b.* 1 July, 17-9; *m.* 1st, in Sept. 1824, Diana-Clarissa, dau. of Major-Gen. the Hon. Granville-Anson Chetwynd-Stapyilton; and that lady dying *s. p.* 28 Sept. 182-

he m. 2ndly, 14 Feb. 1833, Grace-Mary, third dau. of David Chambers, Esq., com. R.N., and by her has issue.
Henry, M.A., in holy orders, b. 4 Nov. 1794, m. 27 July, 1824, Maria, third dau. and co-heir of James Halliwell, Esq. of Broomfield, in Lancashire, and has issue.
Sarah, m. 2 Aug. 1808, to George Ormerod, Esq. of Sedbury Park, co. Gloucester, and Tyldesley, co. Lancaster.
Frances, d. unm. in 1829.

Doctor Latham d. 1843, and was s. by his son,

JOHN LATHAM, Esq. of Bradwall Hall, b. 18 March, 1787, who m 24 May, 1821, Elizabeth-Anne, eldest dau. of Sir Henry Dampier, Knt., late one of the judges of the Court of King's Bench, and by her (who d. 31 May, 1839) had,

John-Henry, b. 14 Feb. 1823, d. 4 July, 1843.
GEORGE-WILLIAM, now of Bradwall Hall.
Thomas-Dampier, d. young, 1837.
Francis-Law, of Brasenose College, Oxford, b. 5 Aug. 1837.
Mary-Frances, m. to the Rev. A. Jones.

Mr. Latham d. 30 Jan. 1853.

Arms—Erminois, on a chief, indented, az., three bezants, over all, a bend, gules.
Crest—On a rock, ppr., an eagle with wings elevated, erminois, preying on a child, ppr., swaddled, az., banded, arg.
Motto—Secundâ alite.
Seat—Bradwall Hall, Cheshire.

LA TOUCHE OF MARLAY.

LA TOUCHE, DAVID-CHARLES, Esq. of Marlay, co. Dublin, colonel of the county Dublin militia, J.P. and D.L., b. 18 April, 1800; high-sheriff of Wicklow in 1838, and of the county of the city of Dublin in 1843.

Lineage.—The family of La Touche was established in Ireland by

DAVID DIGUES DE LA TOUCHE, a Huguenot, who settled in that kingdom after the Revocation of the Edict of Nantes, having served first as volunteer, and afterwards as lieutenant and captain, in the Princess Anne's regiment of infantry. He was the fourth son of a noble Protestant family of the Blesois, which possessed considerable estates between Blois and Orleans, and in other parts of France. He first fled to Holland, where a branch of his family had for some time been established, and shortly afterwards embarking with the Prince of Orange, served the Irish campaign under him. At the conclusion of the war, Mr. La Touche, with many of his countrymen, settled in Dublin. He m. twice: by his second wife he had no issue; but by the first, whom he m. 5 July, 1690, Judith Biard, dau. of Noé Biard, and Judith Chevalier, his wife, he had issue, 1 David; 2 James-Digges, who m. twice, and dying in 1763, left surviving issue three sons, William, E.I.C.C.S.; James, of Jamaica; and Peter; 1 Martha, and 2 Judith. Mr. La Touche d. 17 Oct. 1745, and was s. in the Bank which he had established in Dublin, by his son,

DAVID-DIGUES LA TOUCHE, Esq., b. 31 Dec. 1703, who had been educated in Holland with his relation, Digues de la Motte, at Rotterdam. He m. 8 Feb. 1724-5, Mary-Anne, dau. of Gabriel Canasilhes, and had issue, Gabriel-David, b. in 1728, who d. v. p.; DAVID, of whom presently; James, b. 1730, d. v. p.; JOHN (see LA TOUCHE *of Harristown*;) PETER (see LA TOUCHE *of Bellevue*;) Gabriel, b. 26 Dec. 1734; Matthew, b. in 1738; Mary-Anne, b. in 1726; Martha, b. in 1736; Elizabeth, twin with Martha; and Judith, b. in 1742. Mr. La Touche d. in Feb. 1785. The eldest son,

THE RIGHT HON. DAVID LA TOUCHE, of Marlay, co. Dublin, many years M.P. for his own borough of Newcastle and other places, m. in 1762, Elizabeth, dau. of George Marlay, D.D., bishop of Dromore, son of Chief Justice Marlay, and by her (who was first-cousin to the Right Hon. Henry Grattan) he had issue, 1 DAVID, his heir; 2 George, d. unm. in 1823; 3 John-David, b. 2 Jan. 1772; 4 Peter, b. in 1777 (see LA TOUCHE *of Bellevue*;) 5 Robert, lieut.-col. of the Carlow militia, and for some years M.P. for Carlow, b. in 1783; 6 William, d. young; 1 Elizabeth, m. in 1781, to the Earl of Lanesborough; 2 Harriet, m. to Sir Nicholas Colthurst, Bart. of Ardrum, co Cork; 3 Emily, m. to Col. George Vesey, of Lucan; 4 Anne, m. to George Jeffreys, Esq. of Blarney Castle, co. Cork; 5 Maria, m. to the Knight of Kerry. The eldest son,

DAVID LA TOUCHE, Esq. of Marlay, col. of the Carlow militia, and, for many years, M.P. for that county, m. 24 Dec. 1789, Lady Cecilia Leeson, dau. of the Earl of Milltown, and left issue, 1 DAVID, d. unm. in 1830; 2 JOHN, in holy orders, vicar of Mountrath, m. and has issue; 3 George, b. in 1798, m. and has children; 4 Peter, col. E.I.C.S., m. a dau. of General Maxwell, and has issue; 5 William, d. unm.; 6 Robert, capt. in the army, m. and has issue; 7 Cecil, d. unm.; 1 Elizabeth, m. to Lord Brandon; 2 Harriet, m. to Villiers Hatton, Esq., rear-adml. R.N.; 3 Frances, d. unm.; 4 Emily; and 5 Mary. Col. La Touche sold Marlay to his brother,

JOHN-DAVID LA TOUCHE, Esq., who m. in 1799, Anne-Caroline, dau. of Charles Tottenham, Esq. of New Ross, co Wexford, and had issue,

DAVID-CHARLES, now of Marlay.
Charles-John, b. 21 March, 1811.
Frances-Caroline. Elizabeth-Louisa.
Anne-Caroline.

Arms—Arg., a pomegranate, ppr., couped, gu., on a chief, of the last, two mullets, of the field.
Crest—A mullet of five points, pierced, arg.
Motto—Quid verum atque decens curo et rogo.
Seat—Marlay, co. Dublin.

LA TOUCHE OF BELLEVUE.

LA TOUCHE, PETER, Esq. of Bellevue, co. Wicklow, s. his father in 1830.

Lineage.—PETER LA TOUCHE, Esq. of Bellevue, 3rd surviving son of David-Digues La Touche, Esq., by Mary-Ann Canasilhes his wife, sat for many years in parliament as knight of the shire for Leitrim. He m. 1st, in 1766, Rebecca, only dau. of Robert Vicars, Esq. of Grantstown, Queen's County, which lady d. s. p. in 1786; and 2ndly, Elizabeth, dau. of Richard Vicars, Esq. of Lavalley, which lady, who had no children, survived her husband a considerable time. Having no issue, Mr. La Touche adopted (the 4th son of his brother, the Right Hon. David La Touche, of Marlay) his nephew,

PETER LA TOUCHE, Esq. This gentleman, who was b. in 1777, m. in 1806, the Hon. Charlotte Maude, dau. of Cornwallis, Viscount Hawarden, and has issue,

I. PETER, his heir.
II. Cornwallis, d. in India.
III. William-Robert. IV. Ashley.
V. Charles-Henry.
VI. Francis, late high-sheriff of the county of Leitrim.
VII. James. VIII. Octavius.
IX. John-Alexander.
I. Isabella. II. Charlotte. III. Mary.
IV. Eliza. V. Elizabeth, d. young.

Mr. La Touche d. in 1830, and was s. by his son, the present PETER LA TOUCHE, Esq. of Bellevue.

Arms, &c.—As LA TOUCHE *of Marlay*.
Seat—Bellevue, co. Wicklow.

LA TOUCHE OF HARRISTOWN.

LA TOUCHE, JOHN, Esq. of Harristown, co. Kildare, J.P. and D.L., at one time high-sheriff, b. 16 Sept. 1814; m. 16 May, 1843, Maria, only child of Rose-Lambart Price, Esq. of Trengwainton, by his wife Catherine, Countess Dowager of Desart, and has issue,

I. PERCY-O'CONNOR, b. 12 July, 1846.
I. Emily-Maria. II. Rose-Lucy.

Lineage.—JOHN LA TOUCHE, Esq. of Harristown, co. Kildare, M.P., 2nd surviving son of David-Digues La Touche, Esq., by Mary-Anne Canasilhes his wife, m. in 1763, Gertrude-Fitzgerald, dau. of Robert Uniacke, Esq. of the co. Cork, who took the name and arms of Fitzgerald, and had issue,

ROBERT, his heir.
John, many years M.P. for the county of Leitrim, d. unm.
Gertrude, m. to Francis Mathew, 2nd Earl of Llandaff, and d. s. p.
Marianne, m. to Ralph-Peter Dundas, Esq.

The elder son,

ROBERT LA TOUCHE, Esq. of Harristown, M.P. for the co. Kildare, m. 17 April, 1810, Lady Emily Le Poer Trench, youngest dau. of William Power Keating, 1st Earl of Clancarty, and by her, who d. 8 April, 1816, has issue,

JOHN, now of Harristown.
Robert, twin with John, d. 8 Sept. 1846.
William, b. in 1815.
Anne, d. young.
Gertrude, m. 1841, to her cousin, Stanley McClintock, Esq., son of John McClintock, Esq. of Drumcar, by his wife the Lady Elizabeth Le Poer Trench.
Emily, d. young.

Mr. La Touche d. May, 1844.

Arms, &c.—As LA TOUCHE *of Marlay*.
Seat—Harristown, Kilcullen.

LASLETT OF ABBERTON HALL.

LASLETT, WILLIAM, Esq. of Abberton Hall, co. Worcester, M.P. for the city of Worcester, *b.* 9 Oct. 1801; *m.* 3 Feb. 1842, Maria, eldest dau. of the Right Rev. Dr. Carr, Bishop of Worcester.

Lineage.—THOMAS LASLETT, Esq., who *m* 20 July, 1760, Jane, only child of Ralph Emmerson, Esq., *d.* 3 Aug. 1788, leaving a son and heir,

THOMAS-EMMERSON LASLETT, Esq. of Worcester, who *m.* 23 Dec. 1798, Sophia Jenkins; and *d.* 19 Dec. 1816, (his widow survived until 30 July, 1836) leaving issue,

WILLIAM, now of Abberton Hall.
Thomas-Emmerson, *d. unm.*
Sophia, *d. unm.*, 4 Dec. 1851.

Seat—Abberton Hall, near Pershore.

LAUTOUR OF HEXTON HOUSE.

LAUTOUR, JOSEPH-ANDREW, Esq. of Hexton House, co. Herts, J.P. and D.L., formerly an officer 1st foot-guards, high-sheriff of Herts 1827, *b.* 1785; *m.* 1809, Caroline, only surviving dau. and heir (her sister and co-heir, Jane, wife of Sir George Shee, Bart., having *d.s.p.*), of William Young, Esq. (natural son of Patrick, 5th Lord Elibank), and by this lady, with whom he acquired the Hertfordshire and other estates, had issue,

I. WILLIAM-FRANCIS-JOSEPH, formerly capt. grenad.-gds., *m.* Eliza, dau. of William Turton, Esq. of East Sheen, and has issue.
II. Edward, H.E.I.Co.'s civil service, *m.* Catherine, dau. of Archibald Sconce, Esq. of Stirlingshire, and has issue.
III. Edgar-Frederic, H.E.I.Co.'s civil service, *m.* Louisa, dau. of William Davidson, Esq.
IV. Albert, an officer in the rifle brigade.
I. Jane, *m.* to Col. Louis de Tavares Osorio of the kingdom of Portugal, and has issue.
II. Caroline-Georgiana, *m.* to Theophilus-John, eldest son of Sir Richard St. George, Bart., and *d.*, leaving issue.
III. Barbara-Maria. IV. Maria-Douglas.
V. Gertrude-Emily.

Lineage.—The De Lautours came originally from Alsace, and were of highly-distinguished ancestry. They took their rise from the Compté de Cominges; and so early as the time of Amarius, 1st Count of Cominges, who lived about the year 900, the name of the "Sire de La Tour, Chevalier," occurs.

RAYMOND, called Gausseraud, Seigneur de la Tour, living 1130, *m.* and had two sons, I. BERNARD DE LATOUR, from whom descended the DE LAUTOURS, Seigneurs de Cayriech, of whom the ENGLISH LAUTOURS are a branch; and II. BERTRAND, ancestor of Henry de la Tour d'Auvergne, Vicomte de Turenne, marshal of France.

JOSEPH FRANCOIS LOUIS DE LAUTOUR, *b.* 1730 (grandson of Andre Louis de la Lautor, who was in the service of the Duc de Lorraine, and 1st cousin of Pierre Jacques de Lautour, lieut.-gen. des Eaux et Forêts at Rouen), came in early life to England, and thence proceeded to the East Indies, where, at Madras, he established himself as a banker and merchant. He subsequently returned to England, and wished to revisit his native country, but the war prevented him. He *m.* 1779, Anne Hordle, and had three sons, I. JOSEPH-ANDREW, of Hexton House; II Peter-Augustus, C B., K.H., colonel half-pay of the 20th light dragoons, who served with distinction at Waterloo, *m.* Cameron, dau. of John Innes, Esq. of Cowie, and had a dau; III. James-Oliver, an officer of the 1st guards, killed in action at Bayonne, 24 Dec. 1813; and four daus., viz., I. Amelia, *m.* to Lieut.-General Sir W. Cumming; II. Barbara, *m.* to C. Teesdale, Esq. of Bognor, Sussex; III. Georgiana, *m.* to Edward Majoribanks, Esq. of the firm of Coutts and Co.; IV. Maria, *m.* 1st, to Sir Robert Farquhar, Bart.; and 2ndly, to the late Thomas Hamilton, Esq., author of "Cyril Thornton," brother of Sir W. Hamilton, Bart.

Arms—Erminois, a fesse crenellée cottised, gu. in chief, a tower tripled towered, ppr., masoned, arg.
Crest—A dexter arm, embowed in armour, arg., holding in the hand, gauntletted, the ancient escutcheon of La Tour, viz., az., a tower, as in the arms.
Supporters—Two angels, ppr.
Motto—Pour Dieu et mon pays.
Seat—Hexton House, Herts.

LAWES OF ROTHAMSTED.

LAWES, JOHN-BENNET, Esq. of Rothamsted Manor House, co. Herts, J.P., *b.* 28 Dec. 1815; *m.* 28 Dec. 1842, Caroline, dau. of the late Andrew Fountaine, Esq. of Narford Hall, Norfolk, and has issue,

I. CHARLES-BENNET, *b.* Oct. 1843.
I. Caroline.

Lineage.—JOHN BENNET, Esq, J.P., (grandson of Thomas Bennet, Esq, by Elizabeth his wife, dau. of James Wittewrong, Esq. of Rothamsted, recorder of St. Albans, son of Sir John Wittewrong, Bart., by Elizabeth Middleton his wife), derived Rothamsted from his cousin, Thomas Wittewrong, Esq., the last of the Wittewrongs, who *d. unm.* in 1763, and dying *s.p.*, was *s.* in the estates by his nephew, (son of his sister Mary, by Thomas Lawes, Esq. her husband)

JOHN-BENNET LAWES, Esq. of Rothamsted Manor House, D.L., who *m.* Aug. 1812, Marianne, dau. of J. Sherman, Esq. of Drayton, co. Oxford, and relict of the Rev. David-George Knox, and had issue,

JOHN-BENNET, his heir.
Marianne, *m.* 30 Oct. 1834, to Charles-Thomas Warde, Esq. of Welcombe House, co. Warwick.
Emily-Catharine, *m.* to Lewis Mathias Esq. of Lamphey Court, co. Pembroke.

Mr. Lawes *d.* 22 Oct. 1822, and was *s.* by his only son, the present JOHN BENNET LAWES, Esq. of Rothamsted.

Arms—Or, on a chief, az., three estoiles, of the field.
Crest—On a ducal coronet, or, an ermine, passant, ppr.
Seat—Rothamsted Manor House, co. Herts.

LAWRENCE OF SEVENHAMPTON.

LAWRENCE, WALTER-LAWRENCE, Esq. of Sandywell Park, co. Gloucester, J.P. and D.L., *b.* 21 May, 1799; *m.* 24 July, 1824, Mary, only dau. of Christian Speldt, Esq. of Stratford, in Essex, and has three daus., viz.,

I. MARY-ELIZABETH.
II. Alice. III. Agatha.

This gentleman, whose patronymic is MORRIS, assumed in its stead the surname and arms of LAWRENCE, by the desire of his maternal grandfather, Walter Lawrence, Esq.

Lineage.—From SIR ROBERT LAWRENCE, Knt., great-grand-son of James Lawrence, of Ashton Hall, co. Lancaster, living 37 HENRY III., lineally descended.

WALTER LAWRENCE, Esq. of Sevenhampton, who *m.* Mary, dau. of John Cocks, Esq. of Woodmancote, co. Gloucester, a branch of the family of Cocks of Dumbleton, progenitors of the ennobled house of Somers, and was *s.* at his decease by his elder surviving son,

WALTER LAWRENCE, Esq. of Sevenhampton, who *m.* Mary, only surviving child of Thomas Hayward, Esq., by Dorothy his wife, another dau. of the said John Cocks, Esq. of Woodmancote, and left, at his decease, an only surviving child,

MARY LAWRENCE, of Sevenhampton, representative, through her two grandmothers, of the family of Cocks of Woodmancote. She *m.* in 1797, William Morris, Esq., brother of Robert Morris, Esq., M.P., for Gloucester, and has an only surviving child, WALTER-LAWRENCE-LAWRENCE, Esq. of Sandywell Park.

Arms—Arg., a cross raguly, gu.
Crest—The tail and lower part of a fish, erected and couped, ppr.
Seat—Sandywell Park, Andoversford.

LAWRENCE OF LISREAGHAN.

LAWRENCE, WALTER, Esq. of Lisreaghan, co. Galway, J.P., high-sheriff 1820-1, *b.* 15 Dec. 1793; *m.* 1 March, 1818, Georgiana, 3rd dau. of the late Charles Blake, Esq. of Moyne, co. Mayo, and of Merlin Park, co. Galway, and has had issue,

I. WALTER, late of the 41st regt., *m.* Olivia, eldest dau. of the late Sir Michael D. Bellew, Bt.
II. Charles, *d.* 1816. III. John.
IV. Peter-Charles, *d.* in 1842. V. Charles.
VI. Peter. VII. Denis-John.
VIII. George. IX. Henry-William.

I. Georgiana-Anastasia. II. Catherine-Elizabeth.
III. Maria-Jane. IV. Matilda, *d.* in 1835.
V. Margaret-Eleanora. VI. Frances-Anne.
VII. Anne-Letitia-Helena.
VIII. Adelaide-Octavia-Maria.
IX. Julia, *d.* in 1837. X. Elizabeth, *d.* in 1838.

Lineage.—This family claims to be a younger branch of the very ancient and distinguished family of the LAWRENCES *of Lancashire*, descended from Sir Richard Lawrence, of Ashton Hall, in that county, and was established in Ireland *temp.* Queen ELIZABETH.

JOHN LAWRENCE settled at Ballymore, co. Galway, and had issue, WALTER, his heir; John; Edward; Peter; Joseph.

WALTER LAWRENCE, of Ballymore, *s.* his father, for whose distinguished services he was rewarded with large grants of lands, under patent from JAMES I., dated 1617. He *m.* in 1603, Cicely, dau. of Garrett Moore, Esq. of Briese, co. Mayo; and *d.* in 1635, when he was *s.* by his only son,

JOHN LAWRENCE, of Ballymore and Lisreaghan, who *m.* 1st, in 1640, a dau. of John O'Donelan, Esq. of Ballydonelan, co. Galway, by whom he had no issue; and 2ndly, Mabella, dau. of Killagh O'Kelly, Esq. of Aughrim, co. Galway, eldest son and heir of Feartanah O'Kelly, last chief of his name, and had (with a dau., Mabella, *m.* to J. Kelly, Esq. of Ballagh, co. Galway) a son, WALTER, of whom presently. He *d.* in 1675 (his widow *m.* 2ndly, James Deane, Esq.), and was *s.* by his son,

WALTER LAWRENCE, Esq. of Lisreaghan, who *m.* in 1673, Cicily, dau. of Colonel Garrett Moore, of Cloghan Castle, King's County, by his wife, the Lady Margaret, 2nd dau. of Richard, 6th Earl of Clanricarde, and by her (who *m.* 2ndly, John Kelly, Esq.) left at his decease, in 1677 (with a dau., Honoria, *m.* to H. Pelly, Esq. of Kill, co. Galway), two sons, minors, John, *d. s. p.*, under age; and

WALTER LAWRENCE, Esq. of Lisreaghan, who *m.* in 1699, Mary, dau. of Nicholas Archdekrene, Esq. of Gortnamona, co. Galway; and dying in 1706, was *s.* by his eldest son,

JOHN LAWRENCE, Esq. of Lisreaghan, who *m.* 20 April, 1727, Mary, only dau. and heiress of John Scott, Esq. of Greenish and Cappavarnagh, co. Galway, and of Mont Serat, West Indies, by his wife, Anastasia, dau. of Robert Ffrench, Esq. of Rahasane, co. Galway; and dying in 1730, was *s.* by his only son,

WALTER LAWRENCE, Esq. of Lisreaghan, *b.* 1729; who *m.* 1st, in May, 1760, Margery, only dau. of Edmond Netterville, Esq. of Longford, co. Galway, and had issue, Peter, *b.* Aug. 1762, *d. s. p.* July, 1790; and Maria, *d. unm.* in 1823. Mr. Lawrence *m.* 2ndly, in Aug. 1791, Catherine, dau. of John D'Arcy, Esq. of Ballykine, co. Mayo, and by her had issue,

WALTER, now of Lisreaghan.
Matilda-Margaret, *m.* to Thomas Seymour, Esq. of Ballymore Castle, co. Galway, and has issue.

Mr. Lawrence *d.* in Oct. 1796.

Arms—Quarterly: 1st and 4th, arg., a cross-raguly, gu., for LAWRENCE; 2nd and 3rd, sa., a catherine wheel, between two crescents, in chief, and a trefoil in base, or, for SCOTT.
Crest—A demi-turbot, tail erect, ppr.
Motto—Pro rege, et pro patriâ, semper.
Seat—Lisreaghan (or Bellevue), Lawrencetown, co. Galway.

LAWSON OF ALDBOROUGH AND BOROUGHBRIDGE.

LAWSON, ANDREW-SHERLOCK, Esq. of Aldborough Manor and Boroughbridge Hall, both in the county of York, *b.* 1 Nov. 1824; *m.* 1 July, 1852, Isabella, youngest dau. of the late John Grant, Esq. of Nuttall Hall, co. Lancaster, and has issue,

I. ANDREW-SHERLOCK, *b.* 22 Feb 1855.
II. John-Grant, *b.* 28 July, 1856.
I. Jane-Grant.

Lineage.—In 1530,

SIR GEORGE LAWSON, Knt., treasurer of Berwick, was mayor of the city of York. He left a dau., Anne, *m.* to William Lawson, and a son, his successor,

THOMAS LAWSON, of York, mayor of that city in 1562. He *m.* Christian, dau. of Hugh Atkinson, of Castleford, in Yorkshire, and had, with two daus., three sons, of whom the eldest,

PETER LAWSON, of Poppleton, living in 1584, *m.* Elizabeth, dau. of Ambrose Beckwith, of Stillingfleet, and had two sons and two daus. The elder son,

GEORGE LAWSON, *b.* in 1575, of Poppleton, and subsequently of Moreby, *m.* Anne, dau. of George Twisleton, of Barley, near Selby, and had issue three sons and eight daus. The eldest son,

THE REV. GEORGE LAWSON, of Moreby, bapt. 13 Nov. 1606, rector of Eakring, Notts; *m.* in 1656, Eleanor More, of Normanton, co. Lincoln, by whom (who was buried in 1686) he had a son and heir,

GEORGE LAWSON, Esq. of Morby, who *m.* in 1680, Elizabeth, only dau. and heir of Marmaduke Bosville, Esq. of Seaton Rosse, in the East Riding, and by her (who *d.* in 1698) had two sons, viz.,

I. MARMADUKE, his heir.
II. RICHARD, *b.* in 1697; mayor of York in 1741 and 1754. He *m.* Barbara, dau. of the Rev. Thomas Burton, M.A., vicar of Halifax, by Elizabeth his wife, dau. of Francis Jessop, Esq. of Broom Hall, great-great-grandson of Richard Jessop, Esq., by Anne his wife, eldest dau. and co-heir of Robert Swyft, Esq. of Broom Hall, descended from Robert Swyft, "the rich mercer of Rotherham," and had issue,
 1 MARMADUKE, of whom presently.
 1 Dorothy, *m.* to her cousin, Andrew Wilkinson, Esq. of Boroughbridge, capt. R.N., eldest surviving son of Andrew Wilkinson, Esq., member for Aldbro' in many parliaments, by Barbara, sister to the last Lord D'Arcy, of Navan, being dau. and co-heir of William Jessop, Esq. of Broom Hall, M.P., and the Hon. Mary Jessop.

Mr. Lawson *d.* in 1699, and was *s.* by his elder son,

MARMADUKE LAWSON, Esq. of Moreby, bapt. in 1685, who had, by Susannah his 1st wife (who *d.* in 1711) two sons, who both *d. s. p.* Mr. Lawson's nephew,

THE REV. MARMADUKE LAWSON, M.A., rector of Sprostley and prebendary of Ripon, *b.* in 1749; *m.* Barbara-Isabella, dau. of John Wilkinson, Esq. of the Middle Temple, brother of the Rev. James Wilkinson, vicar of Sheffield, of Broom Hall, near that place, and of Boroughbridge Hall, Yorkshire, and had issue,

MARMADUKE, his heir. ANDREW, heir to his brother.
James, vicar of Buckminster, co. Leicester.
John, incumbent of Seaton Carew, co. Durham.
Barbara.
Dorothy, *m.* in 1831, to the Rev. Edward Bird, rector of Tattenhall, Cheshire.
Mary, *m.* in 1835, to the Rev. Alexander Stewart, M.A., rector of Burford, Worcestershire, eldest son of the Hon. Montgomerie Stewart, and nephew to the Earl of Galloway. He *d.* in 1836.

Mr. Lawson *d.* in 1814 (Mrs. Lawson *d.* in 1838), and was *s.* by his eldest son,

MARMADUKE LAWSON, Esq. of Boroughbridge Hall, J.P., M.P., a gentleman distinguished by his literary pre-eminence at Cambridge. He *d. unm.* 10 March, 1823, when the Wilkinson estates devolved upon his next brother,

ANDREW LAWSON, Esq. of Aldborough Lodge and Boroughbridge Hall, M.P. for Knaresborough, *b.* in 1800; *m.* in 1823, Marianne-Anna-Maria, eldest dau. of Thomas-Sherlock Gooch, Esq. of Bramfield Hall, in Suffolk, M.P., and had issue,

ANDREW-SHERLOCK, present head of the family,
Edward-John, *b.* 8 April, 1826.
Marmaduke-Charles, *b.* 16 Oct. 1827.
James-George, *b.* 14 Nov. 1828.
Thomas-William, *b.* 1 March, 1833.
Richard, *b.* 11 April, 1835. Septimus, *b.* 1 July, 1836.
Octavius-Ridley, *b.* 23 March, 1840.
Mary, *m.* 9 Dec. 1847, to John-Dunn Gardner, Esq. of Chatteris, co. Cambridge; and *d.* April, 1851.
Anne-Matilda.

Arms—Paly of four, gu. and vert, on a chevron, or, a greyhound's head, erased, sa., between two cinquefoils, az., a chief, gold, charged with an ogress, thereon a demi-lion, rampant, arg., between two crescents, sa., on each three plates.
Crest—A wolf's head, erased, ppr., charged on the neck with three bezants, a collar, vert.
Motto—Loyal secret.
Seats—Aldborough Manor, and Boroughbridge Hall, Yorkshire.

LAWSON OF LONGHIRST.

LAWSON, WILLIAM-JOHN, Esq. of Longhirst Hall, co. Northumberland, *b.* 5 March, 1822.

Lineage.—WILLIAM LAWSON, Esq. of Longhirst, living in 1652, son of Robert Lawson, of Longhirst, whose will bears date in 1632, and grandson of Robert Lawson, of Longhirst, had by Margaret his wife (who *m.* 2ndly, Anthony Mitford, Esq.), a 2nd son,

JOHN LAWSON, Esq. of Longhirst, who m. 4 Dec. 1679, Barbara, dau. of Edward Cook, Esq. of Amble New Hall, and had issue, WILLIAM, his heir; Edward, b. in 1686; John, whose son, John, sold Old Moor, in 1828; Margaret, b. in 1682, wife of Mr. Henry Atkinson, and mother of Jane Atkinson, who m. William Scott, merchant, of Newcastle, and had, with other issue, the Lords Stowell and Eldon; Jane, m. to Ralph Watson, Esq. of North Seaton; Mary, m. to Mr. George Barker; and Sarah, m. in 1741, to the Rev. John Walton. The eldest son,

WILLIAM LAWSON, Esq. of Longhirst, b. 21 May, 1684; m. 29 Dec. 1722, Ann, dau. of Robert Carnaby, Esq. of Fullwell, in Durham, and had issue. Mr. Lawson d. 1 March, 1769, and was s. by his eldest son,

JOHN LAWSON, Esq. of Longhirst, b. 31 Dec. 1731; who d. unm. 17 Sept. 1822, and was s. by his nephew,

WILLIAM LAWSON, Esq. of Longhirst, J.P. and D.L. (son of William Lawson, and his wife, Jane Smith, of Togston). He was b. 21 Jan. 1775; and m. 24 Feb. 1831, John-Hester, dau. of the late Mr. John Clark, of Haddington, by whom he left at his decease, 20 Oct. 1855, two sons and three daus., viz.,

WILLIAM-JOHN, now of Longhirst.
Edward, in holy orders, m. 20 Oct. 1853, Mary-Eliza, dau. of the late George Maule, Esq., solicitor to the Treasury, and has issue, William-Edward, b. 5 April, 1855; and Mary-Louisa.
Susannah. Jane-Hester. Louisa-Caroline.

Arms—Arg., a chevron, between three martlets, sa.
Crest—Two arms, embowed, couped at the elbow, vested, erm., cuff, arg., supporting in the hands, ppr., the sun in splendour, gold.
Seat—Longhirst, Morpeth.

LAWTON OF LAWTON.

LAWTON, CHARLES-BOURNE, Esq. of Lawton Hall, co. Chester, J.P.; m. 1st, Anne, dau. of Henry Featherstonhaugh, Esq. of Tooting, co. Surrey; and 2ndly, Marianne-Percy, dau. of William Belcombe, M.D., of York, but has no issue.

Lineage.—This family have possessed the manor of Lawton since the reign of HENRY VI., and, by a well-founded tradition, from a much earlier period. The pedigree, however, prior to that date cannot be perfectly traced; we shall, therefore, begin with the earliest member of the family from whom there is a clear deduction, viz.,

HUGH LAWTON, of Lawton, who m. Isabella, dau. of John Madoc, and widow of Bekyn Bernys.

JOHN LAWTON, Esq. of Lawton, b. in 1606 (eldest son and heir of William Lawton, Esq. of Lawton, and grandson of John Lawton, Esq. of Lawton, living in 1580); m. Clare, dau. of Ralph Sneyd, Esq. of Keel, co. Stafford, by whom he had an eldest son and successor,

WILLIAM LAWTON, Esq. of Lawton, b. in 1630; sheriff of Cheshire in 1672; who m. Hester, 2nd dau. of Sir Edward Longueville, Bart., by Margaret, dau. of Sir Thomas Temple, of Stowe, and by her had issue. Mr. Lawton d. Sept. 1693, and was s. by his eldest son,

JOHN LAWTON, Esq. of Lawton, b. 7 May, 1656; who m. 1st, Anne, dau. of George, younger son of Henry, 1st Earl of Manchester, and sister of Charles, Earl of Halifax. By this lady Mr. Lawton had issue,

William, who d. s. p. in 1714.
Edward, m. Charlotte, dau. of William Trafford, Esq. of Swithamley, and d. in 1730.
John, M.P. for Newcastle-under-Lyme, d. 18 June, 1740.
Anne, m. in 1735, to John Lawton, Esq. of Wybunbury.
Mary, m. to Ralph Trafford, Esq.; with several other children, who d. unm.

Mr. Lawton m. 2ndly, Mary, relict of Sir Edward Longueville, Bart., by whom he had an only son, his successor,

ROBERT LAWTON, Esq. of Lawton, bapt. 6 May, 1723; sheriff of Cheshire in 1754; who m. Sarah, dau. of John Offley, Esq. of Madeley, M.P. for the co. of Chester, who assumed afterwards the surname of CREWE. By this lady Mr. Lawton had an eldest son and successor,

JOHN LAWTON, Esq. of Lawton, b. in Sept. 1746. He m. Anne, dau. and co-heiress of Charles Crewe, Esq., M.P. for Cheshire; and d. 25 March, 1804, leaving issue,

WILLIAM, his heir.
CHARLES-BOURNE, of Lawton.
John, m. Elizabeth, dau. of John Carter, Esq., and has issue.
Philip, a lieut. in the 83rd light infantry, d. on his passage to the West Indies.

The eldest son,

WILLIAM LAWTON, Esq. of Lawton, succeeded, on the death of his father, in 1804, to the family estates; but, dying issueless, was therein s. by his next brother, CHARLES-BOURNE LAWTON, Esq. of Lawton Hall.

Arms—Arg., on a fesse, between three cross-crosslets, fitchée, sa., a cinquefoil, of the first.
Crest—A demi-wolf, rampant, arg., licking a wound in the right shoulder.
Seat—Lawton Hall, Cheshire.

LAWTON OF CAPE VIEW.

LAWTON, HUGH, Esq. of Cape View, co. Cork, J.P., b. 11 May, 1778; m. 30 May, 1799, Anna-Maria, only child (by his 1st wife, Margaret, dau. of Robert Gordon, Esq. of New Grove, by Anne his wife, sister of General Robert Cunningham, 1st Lord Rossmore) of William Warren, Esq. of Lisgoold, co. Cork, 2nd son of Sir Robert Warren, 1st Bart., of Crookstown, co. Cork. By her Mr. Lawton has issue,

I. CHRISTOPHER, b. 1800; m. 1822, Mary-Anne Knowles, of the co. Worcester.
II. Robert-Shaw, b. 1810; m. 1833, Dorothy FitzSymonds.
III. Charles-Palmer, b. 1811.
IV. William-Henry, b. 1813.
V. Augustus, b. 1818. VI. Edward, b. 1819.
VII. William-Warren, b. 1821.
I. Anna-Maria.
II. Mercy, m. to the Rev. Christopher-Somers Clarke, rector of Lindsell, Dunmow, co. Essex.
III. Margaret-Gordon. IV. Catherine-Rye.
V. Mary-Bushe.

Lineage.—This is a scion of the ancient Cheshire family of Lawton, of Lawton Hill, which went over to Ireland with WILLIAM III. A branch settled at Bordeaux, in France, and is still resident there. The great-grandfather of the present representative,

HUGH LAWTON, Esq., m. in Cheshire, and had (with a dau., mother of Judge Carleton, created VISCOUNT CARLETON) a son,

HUGH LAWTON, Esq. of Castle Jane, co Cork, who m. 27 July, 1734, his cousin, Jane Lawton; and d. in 1784, leaving (with a dau., Anne, m. to Peter Carey, Esq. of Careysville Castle, Fermoy, co. Cork) three sons, William, CHRISTOPHER, and Hugh. His 2nd son,

CHRISTOPHER LAWTON, Esq. of Mercyville, co. Cork, m. in 1774, Mercy, dau. of Col. Samuel Hutchinson, of Black Rock, Bantry, and of Affadown, co. Cork, and by this lady (who d. in 1813) had (with two sons and a dau., all of whom d. young) another son and dau., viz., the present HUGH LAWTON, Esq. of Cape View; and Jane, m. to Robert Shaw, Esq., first-cousin of Sir Robert Shaw, Bart. of Dublin; and d. leaving issue. Mr. Lawton d. in 1789.

Arms—Arg., on a fesse, between three crosses-crosslet, fitchée, sa., a cinquefoil, of the first.
Crest—A demi-wolf, salient, regardant, arg., and licking a wound on the shoulder, three drops of blood dropping therefrom.
Motto—Honor.
Seat—Cape View, co. Cork.

LAWLOR OF GRENAGH HOUSE.

SHINE-LAWLOR, DENIS, Esq. of Castlelough and Grenagh House, co. Kerry, J.P., b. 30 March, 1808; m. 4 June, 1840, Isabella, eldest dau. of Edward Huddleston, Esq. of Sawston Hall, co. Cambridge, and has issue,

I. DECIES-ALEXANDER, b. 8 July, 1843.
I. Isabella-Ellen. II. Mary-Jane.
III. Frances-Mary.

Mr. Lawlor served as high-sheriff in 1840.

Lineage.—DENIS SHINE, Esq. of Killarney, son of Denis Shine, Esq. of Mount Infant, co. Cork, by Eliza Barrett his wife, m. 21 Jan. 1807, Ellen, only dau. of Martin Lawlor, Esq. of Killarney, and left issue,

DENIS, now of Castlelough and Grenagh House.
Martin, M.D.
Mary-Anne, a nun.

Mr. Shine was killed by a fall from his horse, 17 June, 1812.

Seat—Grenagh House, co. Kerry.

LAYTON OF CHETTISHAM HALL.

LAYTON, WILLIAM, Esq. of Chettisham Hall, Isle of Ely, J.P. and D.L., high-sheriff 1838, *b.* 6 Oct. 1797; *m.* 18 Oct. 1826, Anne, dau. of John Tilden, Esq. of Ifield Court, Kent. Mr. Layton is son of William Layton, Esq., by Mary Tomson his wife. He has one brother, Edward, who *m.* in May, 1821, Amelia, dau. of Charles Miller, Esq., late consul of Bencoolen, and one sister, Mary, *m.* to the Rev. William Tilden, rector of Downham, near Ely, formerly of Ifield Court.

Seat—Chettisham Hall, Ely.

LEA OF ASTLEY HALL.

LEA, THOMAS-SIMCOX, Esq. of Astley Hall, co. Worcester, J.P. and D.L., high-sheriff 1845, *b.* 17 June, 1788; *m.* 1st, 12 Aug. 1818, Elizabeth-Pratt, eldest dau. of George Simcox, Esq., J.P., of Harborne, co. Stafford, and by her (who *d.* 13 Feb. 1834) had issue,

I. FREDERIC-SIMCOX, *b.* 24 Dec. 1823; incumbent of Trinity Church, Stepney; *m.* 11 Dec. 1855, Elizabeth-Catherine, 2nd dau. of the Rev. Henry Clark, vicar of Harmston, co. Lincoln.

I. Harriet-Eliza, *m.* 8 Jan. 1845, to the Rev. S.-R. Waller, incumbent of Lower Mitton, co. Worcester.

II. Margaret. III. Anne-Maria. IV. Lavinia.

Mr. Lea *m.* 2ndly, 21 April, 1835, Lavinia-Anne, dau. of W.-B. Tarbutt, Esq. of London, and by her has,

I. Reginald-Stephen, *b.* 21 Jan. 1846.

I. Caroline. II. Laura-Sophia.

III. Augusta. IV. Charlotte. V. Clara-Jane.

Lineage.—JOHN LEA, of Kidderminster (eldest son of Francis Lea, of Kidderminster, by Hannah his wife, dau. of John Broom, and grandson of John Lea, whose grandfather, Stephen Lea, of Kidderminster, clothier, purchased a freehold, in 1636, from Abraham Chamberlain) *m.* 14 March, 1786, Ann, dau. of Thomas Simcox, Esq. of West Bromwich and Birmingham; and *d.* 21 Sept. 1843, having had (besides the present THOMAS SIMCOX LEA, Esq. of Astley Hall) two other sons and three daus., viz.,

John, *m.* Ann-Maria, 2nd dau. of George Simcox, Esq.; and *d.* leaving two sons, Arthur-Augustus, and John-Walter, both of Wadham College, Oxford.

George, in holy orders, canon of Lichfield, and incumbent of Christ Church, Birmingham, *m.* Sophia, dau. of the late Hon. Mr. Baron Gurney.

Hannah-Maria, *m.* to Thomas-Green Simcox, Esq. of Harborne House, co. Stafford.

Louisa.

Ann, *m.* to William Hogan, Esq. of Dublin, barrister-at-law.

Arms—Erm., a fesse, dancetté, vert, fleury, counterfleury, or, between, in chief, two lions, passant, sa., and in base, a stag, lodged, ppr., collared, and chain reflexed over the back, of the third.

Crest—A beaver, ppr., semée-de-lis, or, holding in the mouth a branch of willow, also ppr.

Motto—Spe vitæ melioris.

Seat—Astley Hall, near Stourport.

LEADER OF DROMAGH CASTLE.

LEADER, NICHOLAS-PHILPOT, Esq. of Dromagh Castle, co. Cork, J.P.; *s.* his father in 1836.

Lineage.—About the middle of the 17th century, two brothers, HENRY and JOHN LEADER, settled in the co. Cork, in Ireland. The younger brother, JOHN, was ancestor of the LEADERS, of Keale, co. Cork: the elder,

HENRY LEADER, Esq., purchased very considerable estates in the co. Cork, amongst others, the family residence of Mount Leader. He *m.* 1689, Margaret, dau. of Thomas Radley, Esq., by Mavella Chinnery his wife, and *d. circa* 1738, having had issue,

JOHN, of Mount Leader, *b.* 1698; *m.* 1718, Margaret, 3rd dau. of Edward Herbert, of Kilcow, co. Kerry, and *d. circa* 1732, leaving, by his wife (who *m.* 2ndly, Rev Craven Stanley), with six daus., of whom the eldest, Mary, *m.* Richard-Edward Hull, Esq. of Lenmcon, three sons, EDWARD, whose only son, John Leader, Esq., sold Mount Leader to his cousin, William Leader; Thomas; Richard, capt. in the army, of Oldcastle, co. Cork.

Thomas, *b.* in 1700, *d.* in 1727, being murdered by his cousins, the O'Keefes.

HENRY, of Tullig, co. Cork, of whom presently.

Mary, *m.* 1711, to John Purcell, Esq. of Gurteenard, co. Cork.

Margaret, who *m.* Daniel O'Keefe, Esq. of Cullen, co. Cork.

Marcella, who *m.* John Leader, of Keale.

The 3rd son of Henry Leader, by Margaret Radley his wife,

HENRY LEADER, Esq. of Tullig, co. Cork, *b.* 1705, *m.* 1741, Christabella, dau. of William Philpott, of Dromagh, co. Cork, and by her (who *d.* in 1794) left issue,

I. JOHN, *b.* in 1742, *d.* in 1801. He *m.* in 1767, Deborah, eldest dau. of Emanuel Hutchinson, Esq., and had an only son, HENRY LEADER, Esq., formerly of Illy, co. Donegal, and late of Adelaide Road, Dublin, *b.* in 1768. He *m.* Mary, dau. of the Rev. Thomas Stewart, and *d.* in 1844, leaving a son, HENRY, of Dromaneen, near Kanturk, co. Cork, *m.* 1835, Sarah, dau. of Thomas Woodcock, Esq., banker, of Wigan, and had, William, and other issue; and five daus., Elizabeth, *d. unm.*; Deborah, *m.* in 1845, to John Allen, Esq.; Mary, *m.* in 1844, to William-Ribton Ward, Esq.; Charlotte, *m.* Francis Forster, Esq. of Rushine Lodge, co. Donegal; and Margaret, *m.* in Aug. 1884, John-H. Orpen, Esq., M.D.

II. William, of Mount Leader, J.P., *b.* in 1743; *d.* in 1828; *m.* April, 1768, Margaret, dau. of Warham St. Leger, Esq. of Heyward's Hill, and had issue,

1 NICHOLAS-PHILPOT, M.P. for Kilkenny, who *m.* Margaret, dau. and co-heir of Andrew Nash, Esq. of Nashville, co. Cork, and *d.* 1836, leaving issue,

NICHOLAS-PHILPOT, now of Dromagh Castle.

William, of Nashville, *m.* Miss McGillicuddy of the Reeks.

Henry, who *m.* Margaret, dau. of John-Birmingham Miller, Esq., Q.C., and has issue.

Margaret, *m.* John Newman, Esq., eldest son of Adam Newman, Esq. of Dromore, co. Cork.

Elizabeth.

2 Warham, rector of St. Anne's, Shandon, Cork, *m.* Henrietta, dau. of Robert Atkins, of Firville, and *d. s. p.*

3 William, curate of St. Peter's, Cork, *d. unm.*

4 HENRY, now of Mount Leader, co. Cork.

1 Elizabeth, *m.* in 1799, the Rev. Mathew Purcell, eldest son of Sir John Purcell. The Rev. Mr. Purcell *d.* in 1845.

2 Harriett, *m.* to Mathias Headley, Esq. of Mount Rivers, co. Cork, and *d. s. p.* in 1833.

3 Emilia, *m.* to John-Rye Coppinger, Esq. of Carhue, co. Cork, and *d. s. p.* in 1832.

4 Louisa, *m.* Richard-Harris Purcell, Esq. of Annabella, and has issue.

III. Henry, of Tullig, *m.* Mary Kearnery, and *d.* in 1809, leaving issue an only child, Henry, who *d. s. p.*

IV. Nicholas, who went to America.

I. Elizabeth, *m.* Joseph Barry, Esq., M.D. of Mallow.

II. Christabella, *d.* in 1838, *m.* in 1773, Christopher Headley, Esq. of Mount Rivers.

III. Catherine, *d. s. p.* in 1772.

IV. Mavella, *d. s. p.* in 1773.

Arms—Arg., on a fesse, sa., between three ogresses, each charged with an escallop of the field, a lion's head, erased, between two boars' heads, also erased, or, all within a bordure, engrailed, az.

Crest—An arm, habited, paly of six, vert and gu., holding in the hand, ppr., a branch of three roses, barbed and leaved, ppr.

Seat—Dromagh Castle, co. Cork.

LEADER OF MOUNT LEADER.

LEADER, HENRY, Esq. of Mount Leader, co. Cork, J.P., *b.* 4 June, 1793; *m.* Aug. 1830, Elizabeth, 2nd dau. of the late Rev. Charles Eustace, of Robertstown, co. Kildare, claimant of the Baltinglass Peerage, and by her has an only child,

HENRY-EUSTACE, capt. 16th lancers, *b.* in 1833.

Lineage.—WILLIAM LEADER, Esq., *b.* 1743 (2nd son of Henry Leader, Esq. of Tullig, co. Cork, by Christabella his wife, dau. of William Philpott, Esq. of Dromagh, co. Cork), purchased Mount Leader from the elder branch of the family. He *m.* in 1768, Margaret, dau. of Warham St. Leger, Esq. of Heyward's Hill, co. Cork, and by her (who *d.* in Feb. 1828) had, with other issue,

NICHOLAS-PHILPOT, M.P. for Kilkenny, *d.* in 1836, leavin issue.

HENRY, of Mount Leader.

Mr. Leader *d.* in April, 1828.

Seat—Mount Leader, co. Cork.

LEAHY OF SHANAKIEL.

Leahy, Francis-Robert, Esq. of Shanakiel House, co. Cork, J.P., b. 31 May, 1825; m. 17 Jan. 1850, Mary, dau. of the late Edmond Scully, Esq. of Bloomfield House, co. Tipperary.

Lineage.—Daniel Leahy, Esq. of Shanakiel House, co. Cork,* J.P. and D.L., b. 1782, eldest son of David Leahy, Esq. of Shanakiel House, by Catherine his wife, dau. of James O'Sullivan, Esq., m. 1st, Catherine, dau. of the late Robert-Warren Gumbleton, Esq. of Castle-View, co. Waterford, which lady d. s. p.; and 2ndly, Margaret-Jane, dau. of the late Francis Arthur, Esq. of Limerick, by whom he had issue,

David, b. 16 Oct. 1820, who assumed the surname and arms of Arthur, in compliance with the will of his grandfather, to whose estates he succeeded. He m. 5 Nov. 1846, Amelia, dau. of Sir Joseph Radcliffe, Bart. of Rudding Park, co. York. Mr. Arthur is a magistrate for the co. Cork, and has served the office of high-sheriff for the cities of Cork and Limerick.
Francis-Robert, now of Shanakiel House.
James-Edmund, lieut. H.M. 84th regt. killed in India, by a fall from his horse, Aug. 1849.
Daniel-Francis, of Woodlawn, J.P., b. 31 Oct. 1832, m. 23 Feb. 1856, Mary, only dau. of William-Trant Fagan, Esq., M.P.
Edmund-John, b. 1 March, 1834.
Alice-Mary, m. Sept. 1855, to John N. Murphy, Esq. of Clifton, Cork, J.P. and D.L., high-sheriff of the city of Cork.

Arms—Gu., a lion, rampt., and, in chief, two sceptres, in saltire, or.
Crest—Out of a mural crown, ppr., a demi-lion, rampt., or, charged on the shoulder with a tower, gu., and holding in the dexter paw a sceptre, gold.
Motto—Tout vient de Dieu.
Seat—Shanakiel House, Cork.

LEAKE OF THORPE HALL.

Martin-Leake, John, Esq. of Thorpe Hall, co. Essex, J.P. and D.L., b. 5 Dec. 1773; m. 29 March, 1810, Helen, dau. of James Ore, Esq., and relict of Captain Lacy, royal engineers, and has issue,

I. Mary.
II. Helen, m. to the Rev. Frederic Pyndar Lowe, son of the Rev. Robert Lowe, rector of Bingham, Notts.

Mr. Martin-Leake is a Bencher of the Middle Temple, and Chairman of the Quarter Sessions of Essex.

Lineage.—Stephen Martin, Esq., capt. R.N., who d. in 1730, aged 70, took by Royal licence the additional surname and arms of Leake, in honour of his brother-in-law, Admiral Sir John Leake. He m. Catherine Hill, and was father of

Stephen-Martin Leake, Esq. of Thorpe Hall, co. Essex, b. 1702, Garter King-of-Arms, who m. Anne, dau. of Fletcher Powell, Esq. of New Radnor, and by her, who d. in 1803, aged 88, had six sons and three daus. Mr. Martin Leake was the author of some works of Heraldry and Numismatics. He d. in 1773, aged 72, and was s. by his son,

John-Martin Leake, Esq. of Thorpe Hall, who m. in Sept. 1761, Mary, dau. of Peter Calvert, Esq. of Hadham, Herts, and by her, who d. 27 Oct. 1821, had issue,

John, now of Thorpe Hall.
William, late lieut.-col. Roy. Art., F.R.S. and honorary LL.D., Oxford, b. 1776, who m. Charlotte, dau. of Sir Charles Wilkins, and relict of W. Marsdon, Esq., F.R.S., but has no issue.
Stephen-Ralph, b. 1782, m. Georgiana, dau. of George Stevens, and has issue three sons and two daus.
Mary.
Susanna-Maria, m. to Admiral R.-G. Middleton, and d. 1834, leaving issue.

Mr. Martin Leake d. in April, 1836, aged 97.

Arms—Quarterly: 1st and 4th, or, on a chev., engr., az., eight annulets, arg., on a canton, gu., a castle, triple-towered, of the third, for Leake; 2nd and 3rd, paly of six, or and az., on a chief, gu., three merlins, of the first, for Martin.
Crest—A ship gun-carriage, on it a piece of ordnance, mounted, all ppr.
Motto—Pari animo.
Seat—Thorpe Hall, co. Essex.

* Daniel Leahy had a brother, John Leahy, Esq., who m. Catharine, dau. of William O'Shea, Esq of Limerick, and has issue.

LEARMONTH OF DEAN AND MURRISTON.

Learmonth, John, Esq. of Dean and Murriston, co. Edinburgh, D.L., formerly Lord Provost of Edinburgh, b. 26 May, 1789; m. Feb. 1824, Margaret, dau. of the late James Cleghorn, M.D., state physician in Dublin, and has issue,

I. Alexander, major 17th lancers, b. 22 Aug. 1829.
I. Agnes.

Lineage.—The late John Learmonth, Esq. of Edinburgh, son of John Learmonth and Jessy Cleland, his wife, m. Grace Young, and by her (who d. 1848) left, at his decease, in 1812, a son and three daus., viz.,

John, now of Dean and Murriston.
Elizabeth. Jessy, m. to Charles Parker, Esq., R.N.
Margaret, m. 1821, to Sir John Sinclair, Bart. of Dunbeath.

Arms—Or, on a chev., sa., three mascles, of the first.
Crest—A dove and olive branch, ppr.
Motto—Dum spiro spero.
Seat—Dean, co. Edinburgh.

LEATHAM OF HEMSWORTH HALL.

Leatham, William-Henry, Esq. of Hemsworth Hall, co. York, J.P. and D.L., b. 6 July, 1815; m. 21 Feb. 1839, Priscilla, dau. of the late Samuel Gurney, Esq. of West Ham, Essex, and has surviving issue,

I. Samuel-Gurney, b. 13 Dec. 1840.
II. William-Henry, b. 30 Dec. 1844.
III. Edmund-Ernest, b. 3 Dec. 1847.
IV. Charles-Alfred, b. 11 Sept. 1849.
V. Gerald-Arthur-Buxton, b. 30 April, 1851.
VI. Herbert-Barclay, b. 15 Nov. 1852.
VII. Octavius, b. 17 April, 1854.
VIII. Claude, b. 18 April, 1856.

Lineage.—The late William Leatham, Esq. of Heath, banker at Wakefield, Pontefract, and Doncaster, m. Margaret, dau. and heir of Joshua Walker, M.D., by his wife, Mary Arthington, of Leeds, and d. 19 Oct. 1842, leaving,

John-Arthington.
William-Henry, now of Hemsworth Hall.
Charles-Albert, m. Miss Rachel Pease, of Southend, Darlington.
Edward-Aldam, m. Miss Mary-Jane Fowler, of Elm Grove, Melksham.
Margaret-Elizabeth, m. to John Bright, Esq., M.P., of One Ash, Rochdale.
Mary-Walker, m. Joseph Gurney Barclay, Esq. of Lombard Street, London, and d. 10 Feb. 1848.

Arms—Per saltire, erm. and or, on a chief, engrailed, az., three bezants, each charged with a saltire, gu.
Crest—A nest, thereon an eagle, wings elevated, or, the nest and wings fretty, vert.
Motto—Virtute vinces.
Seat—Hemsworth Hall, W. R. Yorkshire.

LEATHES OF HERRINGFLEET.

Leathes, Henry-Mussenden, Esq. of Herringfleet Hall, co. Suffolk, b. 13 Aug. 1789; s. his brother, John-Francis, in 1848; was formerly in the royal horse artillery, and has received honorary medals for the Peninsular War and Waterloo; m. 1827, Charlotte, dau. of the late Thomas Fowler, Esq. of Gunton Hall, co. Suffolk, and has issue,

Hill-Mussenden, b. 1829, capt. in the 2nd Suffolk militia.
Carteret-Henry, b. 1832.
Henrietta-Katherine, m. 1850, to Richard Drought Graves, Esq.
Jane-Charlotte.

Lineage.—The family of De Mussenden came over with William the Conqueror, and became possessed of the lordship and lands of Mussenden, or as it is now written, Missenden, co. Bucks, about that period. About the year 1660, The Rev. Francis Mussenden of Leak and Leverton, co. Lincoln, a descendant of the Buckinghamshire family, passed over into Ireland, became prebendary of the diocese of Down and Connor, and settled at Hillsborough. He had two sons, John, of whom presently; and Francis, registrar of the same diocese, ancestor of William Mussenden, Esq. of Larchfield, co. Down. The elder son,

John Mussenden, vicar-general of Down and Connor, m. Penelope Hill, of Hillsbro', and had a son,

John Mussenden, Esq., who m. Jane, dau. of Adam Leathes, Esq., and sister of William Leathes, Esq., minister at the Hague (descended from a very ancient family, originally settled at Leatheswater, Cumberland) and *d.* in 1700, leaving issue,

CARTERET, his heir.
Hill, *b.* in 1699, M.P. for Harwich, *d. s. p.* in 1772, having bequeathed Herringfleet to his brother, CARTERET.
Jane, who *m.* William Johnstone, Esq. of the county of Antrim.

The eldest son,

CARTERET MUSSENDEN, Esq., M.P. for Harwich and Sudbury, *b.* in 1698, took the surname and arms of LEATHES. He *d.* in 1787. By his marriage with Loveday, dau. of S. Garrod, Esq. of the co. of Lincoln, who *d.* in 1758, he had, with one dau., three sons, viz.,

JOHN, his heir.
GEORGE, successor to his brother.
Edward, rector of Reedham, co. Norfolk, *m.* Elizabeth, dau. of the Rev. James Reading, of Woodstock, co. Oxford, and dying in 1786, left issue,
EDWARD, in holy orders, rector of Reedham, *d. s. p.* 1847.
George-Reading, in holy orders, *m.* in 1821, Sarah, eldest dau. of Lieut.-Gen. Hethersett, of Shropham Hall, Norfolk, but *d. s. p.* in 1836.
Elizabeth, *m.* to the Rev. James Tompson, of Norwich, and has had issue, James, in holy orders, *d.* in 1819; Edward, *d.* in India; Elizabeth, *m.* to the Rev. Frederick Leathes; Hannah, *m.* to J. Kitson, Esq., secretary to the Bishop of Norwich and registrar of that diocese; Maria; and Amelia, *m.* 1852, to Lt.-Col. Prior, H.E.I.C.S.
Mary, *m.* 1st, to Horatio, son of James Beevor, Esq., and nephew of Sir Thomas Beevor, Bart., and 2ndly, to Sir John Mortlock, one of the commissioners of excise. By her first marriage, she had one son, Horatio, capt. E.I. Co.'s Service; Mary, who *d.* in 1837; and Harriet; and by her second, six daus., viz., Elizabeth, *m.* Major Prior, and *d.* 1839; Agnes; Eleanor, *m.* to the Rev. J. Donaldson, D.D., and *d.* 1850; Louisa, *m.* to William Harcourt Ranking, Esq., M.D., and *d.* 1848; Matilda, *m.* 1846, to D. Maitland, Esq.; and Gertrude.

The eldest son,

JOHN LEATHES, Esq. of Reedham, co. Norfolk, and of Herringfleet, co. Suffolk, *m.* Miss Death, and *d. s. p.* in 1788. His widow re-married Anthony Merry, Esq., many years minister-plenipotentiary at the courts of France, Sweden, Denmark, and the United States. Mr. Leathes was *s.* by his next brother,

GEORGE LEATHES, Esq. of Bury St. Edmunds, *b.* in 1745, many years a major of dragoons, who served in the German war from 1760 to 1763. He *m.* Mary, dau. of J. Moore, Esq. of the co. of Worcester, and *d.* in 1817, having had issue,

I. George-Augustus, lieut.-col. in the 96th regt. of infantry, who *d. unm.* at the island of Antigua, in 1808.
II. JOHN-FRANCIS, late of Herringfleet Hall and Reedham, *d. s. p.* 1848.
III. HENRY-MUSSENDEN, present Lord of Herringfleet.
IV. Frederick, in holy orders, rector of Reedham and Wickhampton, *m.* in 1821, his cousin, Elizabeth, dau. of the Rev. James Tompson, by Elizabeth, his wife, dau. of the Rev. Edward Leathes, of Reedham, and by her, who *d.* in 1842, he has issue,
1 George-Cergnt. 2 Frederick de Mussenden.
3 John-Thurlow. 4 James. 5 William.
1 Elizabeth. 2 Georgina. 3 Ellen.
4 Louisa. 5 Augusta. 6 Jane.
V. Edward, of Normanstone, co. Suffolk, a magistrate of that county, *m.* Eliza, dau. of G. Galloway, Esq., by whom he has,
1 George, an officer H.E.I.C.S. 2 Edward.
3 Joseph. 4 Francis, *d.* 1848. 5 William.
1 Harriett. 2 Fanny.
3 Millicent, *m.* 1850, to Thomas, eldest son of Thomas Grisell, Esq. of Norbury Park, co. Surrey.
4 Katherine, *m.* to the Rev. Daniel Wilson, grandson of Daniel Wilson, Bishop of Calcutta.
5 Jane. 6 Mary.
I. Louisa-Mary, *d.* 1855.
II. Harriet-Elizabeth, *d.* 1852.

Arms—Az., on a bend, between three fleurs-de-lis, or, as many mullets, pierced, gu., quartering MUSSENDEN.
Crests—1st, a demi-griffin, rampant, armed and langued, gu., for LEATHES; 2nd, a dove, with an olive-branch in its beak, all ppr., for MUSSENDEN.
Mottoes—In ardua virtus, for LEATHES; Tending to peace, for MUSSENDEN.
Seat—Herringfleet Hall, Lowestoft, Suffolk.

LECHE OF CARDEN.

LECHE, JOHN-HURLESTON, Esq. of Carden, co. Chester, *b.* 25 Feb. 1827; *m.* 1st, 18 July, 1850, Caroline, youngest dau. of Edwin Corbett, Esq., younger brother of Corbett of Darnhall, co. Chester, and by her has two daus.,

I. Caroline-Maude. II. Florence-Anna.

He *m.* 2ndly, 18 June, 1855, Eleanor-Frances-Stanhope, 2nd dau. of the late Charles-Stanhope Jones, Esq. of Anglesey.

Lineage.—JOHN LECHE, living in the reign of HEN. IV., a scion of the family of Leche, of Chatsworth, co. Derby, *m.* LUCY, dau. and co-heir of WILLIAM DE CAWARDEN, of Carden, co. Chester, and was father of

JOHN DE L'LECHE, living *temp.* HEN. IV., father, by Maud, his wife, of JOHN LECHE, Esq. of Carden, whose name, with that of his wife, Isabel, dau. and heir of William Johnson, of Farndon, occurs in a deed in 1 EDWARD IV. His son and successor,

JOHN LECHE, Esq. of Carden, *m.* 14 EDWARD IV., Margaret, dau. and sole heir of George Mainwaring, Esq. of Ightfield, and had issue, 1 JOHN, his heir; 2 Henry, who *m.* Mary, dau. of Andrew Wilson, and was father of JOHN, who *s.* his uncle at Carden; 3 George, alderman of Chester, ancestor of the LECHES *of Mollington*; 4 William; 5 Robert; 1 Anne; and 2 Margaret, *m.* to Hugh Catherall. The eldest son and heir,

JOHN LECHE, Esq. of Carden, survived until 6 EDWARD VI., as appears by his will dated in that year, and dying without issue, was *s.* by his nephew,

JOHN LECHE, Esq. of Carden, who *m.* before 27 HEN. VIII., Jane, dau. of Robert Fitton, Esq., and was *s.* by his son,

JOHN LECHE, Esq. of Carden, bapt. in 1558, who *m.* Ursula, dau. of the Rev. John Mainwaring, of Drayton, and had (with two daus., Mary, the elder, *m.* to Thomas Bebington, of Chorley; and the younger, *m.* to John Hinde, of Stanney) a son and heir,

JOHN LECHE, Esq. of Carden, who *m.* in 1613, Alice, dau. of William Alderrey, alderman of Chester, and, dying in 1657, was *s.* by his son,

JOHN LECHE, Esq. of Carden, aged fifty, 29 July, 1664, who *m.* 1st, Elizabeth, dau. of John Newton, of Highley, in Salop, and by her, who *d.* in 1654, had four sons and four daus., viz., 1 JOHN, his heir; 2 Francis, deputy-registrar of the diocese of St. Asaph; 3 Thomas, a minister in Cambridge; 4 Charles, of Chester, *m.* Frances, dau. of George Buckley, Esq., and had a son, Samuel; 1 Mary; 2 Sarah, *m.* 10 Dec. 1682, to Humphrey Walley, of Chester; 3 Elizabeth; and 4 Alice. Mr. Leche *m.* 2ndly, 20 April, 1665, Elizabeth, dau. of — Best, Esq., and relict of Richard Alport, Esq. of Overton, by whom he had Richard and Bridget. He was *s.* by his eldest son,

JOHN LECHE, Esq. of Carden, *m.* 23 Sept. 1674, Grace, dau. of Hugh Currer, Esq. of Kildwick, in Yorkshire, and had issue, 1 JOHN, his heir; 2 Thomas, bapt. in 1679, rector of Tilston; 3 Henry; and 1 Elizabeth, *m.* to the Rev. Thomas Lloyd, of Plas Power, in Denbighshire, and *d.* in 1746. The eldest son,

JOHN LECHE, Esq. of Carden, high-sheriff of Cheshire in 1712, *m.* Sarah, dau. and heiress of Thomas Hargrave, Esq. of Helsby, and was *s.* by his eldest son,

JOHN LECHE, Esq. of Carden, high-sheriff 1753, who *m.* 7 May, 1728, Mary, second dau. of John Hurleston, Esq. of Newton, and co-heir of her uncle, Charles Hurleston, Esq., and by her, who *d.* 29 Dec. 1763, left at his decease (with three daus., 1 Penelope, *m.* to Thomas Puleston, Esq. of Emral, but *d. s. p.*; 2 Sarah; and 3 Mary, *m.* to Thomas Roberts, Esq. of Mollington) several sons, all of whom *d. s. p.*, except

WILLIAM LECHE, Esq. of Carden, high-sheriff for Cheshire in 1774, *m.* 26 April, 1805, Hannah, dau. of James Newell, by whom he left, at his decease, 8 May, 1817, aged 83, a son, JOHN-HURLESTON, his heir.

JOHN-HURLESTON LECHE, Esq. of Carden, *b.* 23 May, 1805, high-sheriff of Cheshire 1832, who *m.* 25 May, 1826, Elisabeth-Antonia, eldest dau. of Anthony-Innys Stokes, Esq. of St. Botolph's, in Pembrokeshire, and had issue,

JOHN-HURLESTON, now of Carden.
William-Randolph, *b.* 10 Feb. 1828, and *d.* 7 Jan. 1830.
William-Edward, *b.* 4 Aug. 1830, *m.* Mary, dau. of Samuel Harrison, Esq. of the co. Cork.
Hugh-Richard-Anthony-Evergreen, *b.* 5 April, 1832.
Charles-Henry, *b.* 30 May, 1833.
Randal, *b.* 22 Jan. 1835.
James-Thomas, *b.* 30 May, 1837.
Victoria-Penelope. Johanna-Hurleston.

Arms—Erm., on a chief, indented, gu., three ducal coronets, or.
Crest—On a ducal coronet, or, a cubit arm, ppr., the hand grasping a snake, vert.
Motto—Alla corona fidisimo.
Seat—Carden Park, Chester.

LECHMERE OF HILL HOUSE.

Lechmere, John, Esq. of Hill House, co. Oxford, J.P. and D.L., *b.* 9 Jan. 1793; *m.* 3 March, 1823, Anna-Maria, youngest dau. of the Hon. Andrew Foley, M.P., of Newport House, co. Hereford.

Lineage.—William Lechmere, Esq., admiral R.N., a descendant of the ancient Worcestershire family of Lechmere, *m.* Elizabeth Dashwood, youngest dau. of Sir John-Dashwood King, Bart. of West Wycombe, co. Bucks, and had issue,

Charles, *b.* 4 Dec. 1789, Com. R.N.; *d. unm.*, on board His Majesty's ship Leven, 9 Nov. 1822.
John, of Hill House. Richard, *b.* 1 Aug. 1799.
Lucy, *m.* to Richard Parkinson, Esq. of Kinnersley Castle, co. Hereford; and *d.* leaving issue.
Mary, *m.* 5 Oct. 1814, to James, Lord de Saumarez.
Elizabeth, *m.* to Monro, Esq.
Georgiana-Sarah, deceased. Caroline-Amelia.
Augusta, *m.* to James-Moncrieff Melville, Esq. of Hanley.

Arms—Gu., a fesse, or, in chief, two pelicans vulning themselves, of the last.
Crest—A pelican, az., vulning herself, ppr.
Motto—Ducit amor patriæ.
Seat—Hill House, Steeple Aston, co. Oxford.

LECHMERE OF FOWNHOPE COURT.

Lechmere, Thomas, Esq. of Fownhope Court, co. Hereford, J.P., *b.* 21 Dec. 1818; *m.* 7 May, 1846, Elizabeth, only dau. of the Rev. John Eckley, of Credenhill Court, co. Hereford, by Elizabeth his wife, eldest dau. of John Williams, Esq. of Velin Newydd House, co. Brecon, and has issue,

I. John-Scudamore, *b.* 8 Sept. 1850.
II. Edmund-Sandys, *b.* 18 March, 1852.
III. Capel-Thomas, *b.* 4 April, 1854.
I. Mary-Jane. II. Elizabeth.

Lineage.—Sandys Lechmere, Esq. of Fownhope, co. Hereford (2nd son of Sir Nicholas Lechmere, Knt., baron of the Exchequer, by Penelope his wife, dau. of Sir Edwin Sandys, of Northborne), *m.* Joanna, widow of John Holmes, Esq., and only dau. of Robert Clarke, Esq., by whom he left, at his decease in 1694, an only son,

Nicholas Lechmere, Esq. of Fownhope, who *m.* Martha, dau. and co-heir of John Scudamore, Esq. of Treworgan; and dying in 1711, was *s.* by his son,

Scudamore Lechmere, Esq. of Fownhope, who *m.* Jane, 2nd dau. of Edmund Pateshall, Esq. of Allensmore, co. Hereford, and had, with two daus., five sons, viz.,

John-Scudamore, his heir.
Edmund, of Allensmore, assumed the surname and arms of Pateshall. (*See that family.*)
Edwyn-Sandys, *m.* Elizabeth, dau. of the Rev. Mr. Jones, of Foy, co. Hereford: and by her, who *d.* in 1822, had issue.
Nicholas, *d.* at sea.
Thomas-Allen, *m.* Jane, youngest dau. of John Whitmore, Esq. of the Haywood, and left issue.

The eldest son,

John-Scudamore Lechmere, Esq. of Fownhope, *m.* Catherine, 2nd dau. of John Whitmore, Esq. of the Haywood; and *d.* 8 Jan. 1801. His son,

Capel Lechmere, Esq. of Fownhope Court, who *m.* 26 May, 1817, Mary Walker, of Mordiford, co. Hereford, and left at his decease three sons, Thomas, now of Fownhope; Capel-Thomas; and George-Scudamore, *m.* 1846, Sophia Drew, of Taunton, co. Somerset.

Arms—Gu., a fesse, or, and in chief, two pelicans, arg.
Crest—A pelican, az., vulning herself, ppr.
Motto—Ducit amor patriæ.
Seat—Fownhope Court, Herefordshire.

LECKY OF BALLYKEALEY.

Lecky, John-James, Esq. of Ballykealey, co. Carlow, J.P. and D.L., high-sheriff 1828, *b.* 2 Oct. 1802; *m.* 25 July, 1825, Sarah-Lucia, only dau. of John Smith, Esq. of Baulby, Yorkshire, and of Marlborough-place, Surrey, and has issue,

I. John-Frederick, *b.* 25 May, 1826; *m.* 28 July, 1853, Frances-Margaret-Fetherston-Haugh, only dau. of J.-Beauchamp Brady, Esq. of Myshall Lodge, co. Carlow.

II. Francis-Smith, *b.* 21 April, 1828, *d.* young.
I. Mary-Elizabeth-Adelaide, *m.* 21 June, 1853, to the Rev. Francis-Metcalf Watson.

Lineage.—This is an ancient and influential family deriving originally from Stirlingshire, N.B. The estate of Kilnock, co. Carlow, has been in their possession for nearly 300 years.

Robert Lecky, Esq. of Kilnock, co. Carlow, son of James Lecky, Esq. of the same place, *d.* in 1780, leaving a son,

John Lecky, Esq. of Ballykealey, who *m.* 1780, Elizabeth, dau. of Jacob Goff, Esq. of Goff's Bridge, co. Wexford, and by her (who *d.* Jan. 1841) had issue,

Robert, *d.* young.
John-James, now of Ballykealey.
Eliza, *m.* June, 1800, to John Watson, Esq. of Kilconner House, co. Carlow, and has issue.
Mary, *m.* James-Forbes Russell, Esq., and has issue.
Anne, *m.* J. Phelps, Esq., and has issue.
Jane-Sophia, *d. unm.*
Sarah-Maria, *m.* J. Christy, Esq. of Stramore House co. Down, and has issue.
Hannah-Matilda, *d. unm.*
Lydia, *m.* A. Goff, Esq. of Tottenham Green, co. Wexford.

Mr. John Lecky, of Ballykealey, *d.* Dec. 1802.

Seat—Ballykealey, co. Carlow.

LECKY OF CASTLE LECKY AND BALLYHOLLAND HOUSE.

Lecky, Holland, Esq. of Castle Lecky, co. Londonderry, and Ballyholland House, co. Down, *b.* 27 Feb. 1794; *m.* 29 Sept. 1816, Diana, dau. of John McMullin, Esq., banker, and sister of John McMullin, Esq., deputy inspector-general of the forces, and has issue,

I. Marcus-Daly. II. Averell-William.
III. Robert-Daniel. IV. Alexander-Conolly.
V. Squire-Thornton. VI. Stratford.
I. Jane-Elizabeth. II. Diana-Maria.
III. Louisa-Victoria. IV. Albertina.

Lineage.—This family, which has been settled in the north of Ireland for nearly two centuries, and members of which took part, as military officers, in the memorable siege of Derry, is of Scotch extraction. During the popular tumults of Scotland two brothers of the name, passed over into Ireland; one settled in co. Londonderry, and the other in co. Carlow. From the former derives Holland Lecky, Esq. of Castle Lecky; and from the latter John-James Lecky, Esq. of Ballykealey.

A hundred and fifty years since, the name of Lecky is associated with the high official appointments of Derry, for which city the late Alderman William Lecky (cousin of Averell Lecky, Esq. of Castle Lecky) was twice returned in 1790. Connolly-M'Causland Lecky, Esq., the inheritor of his property, *m.* in 1835, Anne, dau. of John Harvey Esq. of Bargy Castle, co. Wexford.

Holland Lecky, Esq. of Castle Lecky and Ballyholland House, capt. 2nd drag.-guards (whose mother was dau. of John Averell bishop of Limerick), *m.* Elizabeth, dau. of the Rev. Thomas Daniel, of co. Derry, an heiress, and had issue, Averell, his heir; Holland; William; and Catherine. The eldest son,

Averell Lecky, Esq. of Castle Lecky and Ballyholland House, capt. 14th light-drags., *m. circa* 1790, Jane, widow of Mr. Aylward, of Ballinagar, co. Galway, and dau. of the late Hyacinth Daly, Esq. of Killimur Castle, in the same co., and by her left at his decease, 29 Jan. 1834, an only child, Holland Lecky, Esq. of Castle Lecky and Ballyholland House.

Seat—Castle Lecky and Ballyholland House.

LECKY OF BEARDIVILLE.

Lecky, Hugh, Esq. of Beardiville, Bushmills, co. Antrim, J.P., high-sheriff 1835, *b.* 29 Aug. 1804; *m.* Aug. 1837, Matilda, dau. of George Hutchinson, Esq. of Ballymoney (by Elizabeth his wife, dau. of Thomas Lecky, Esq. of Ballymoney, co. Antrim), and has issue,

I. Hugh, *b.* 21 Oct. 1839.
II. George, *b.* 1841.

III. John-Gage, b. 1844. IV. Harry, b. 1846.
I. Elizabeth.

Lineage.—This family is of Scotch extraction, and settled in the county of Derry, towards the latter end of the 16th century.

CAPT. ALEXANDER LECKY, who served at the siege of Londonderry, was father of

HARRY LECKY, of Agivy, co. Derry, who m. 1724, Mary, dau. of John McCollum, Esq. of Limnalavy Glenarm, co. Antrim, and had a son,

HUGH LECKY, Esq. of Agivy, who m. 1765, Elizabeth, dau. of the Rev. John Gage, of Rathlin, co. Antrim, and had issue,

John-Gage, of Agivy, b. 1772, m. 1818, Elizabeth, dau. of the Rev. Oliver McCausland, and d. 1819, s. p.
HUGH, of whom presently.
Mary, m. John Caldwell, Esq., M.D., Londonderry.
Anne, m. John Ball, Esq. of Dublin, barrister-at-law.

The 2nd son,

HUGH LECKY, Esq., b. 1773, m. 1808, Elizabeth, dau. of James Orr, Esq. of Keely, and d. 1817, having had issue,

HUGH, now of Beardiville.
James-Orr, m. 1855, Harriet, dau. of John Knox, Esq. of Rushbrook.
John-Gage, lieut.-col., late of the 38th regt., m. 1846, Tamazina, dau. of William Edie, of Thornhill, co. Tyrone.
Andrew, William, d. } twins.
Conolly.

Seat—Beardiville, Bushmills, co. Antrim.

LEDSAM OF CHAD HILL.

LEDSAM, JOSEPH-FREDERICK, Esq. of Chad Hill, co. Warwick, and of Northfield, co. Worcester, J.P. and D.L., high-sheriff of Worcestershire 1848, b. 16 April, 1791; m. 4 Dec. 1817, Elizabeth-Ann-Ashton, only dau. and heir of James Goddington, Esq. of Camp Hill, near Birmingham, Banker, and by her (who d. 17 July, 1855) has had issue,

I. JOSEPH, b. 24 Dec. 1823, m. 27 Oct. 1853, Frances-Barbara Jackson, of Harborne, co. Stafford, and has a son, Joseph-Frederick, b. 10 Dec. 1854.
II. Frederick-George, M.A., in holy orders, b. 23 Nov. 1826.
III. Thomas-Moreton, b. 10 May, 1830, d. unm. April 1854.
IV. William, b. 27 Oct. 1832.
V. James-Goddington, b. 9 Aug. 1836.
I. Mary-Elizabeth, m. 14 July, 1846, to William, 2nd son of William Chance, Esq. of Spring Grove, Birmingham.
II. Emily-Agnes.

Lineage.—This family is of very considerable antiquity in the counties of Chester and Flint. Ormerod, in his history of the former shire, mentions that "Richard, son of Letitia de Ledsham, occurs in a grant of lands in Moston, in the time of Thomas, abbot of Chester, in the 13th century;" and Willet, in his memoirs of Hawarden states that "the earliest documents the parish possesses, save the Register is a copy of the Will of GEORGE LEDSHAM, late of the Inner Temple, London, bearing date 24 Feb. 1606. By this will," continues Mr. Willet, "George Ledsham, left £300 to erect and maintain a grammar-school for ever, in the west corner of the churchyard of Hawarden. Mr. Ledsham was a freeholder of this parish, and the proprietor of that estate in Ewloe known by the name of Farm-Stile, the which he gave to his sister, Ann Ledsham, who m. a Mr. Robert Jones, of Farm-Stile." Among the names of the ancient families of the city of Chester, in 1646, when it surrendered to the parliamentary forces, is mentioned Thomas Ledsham.

GEORGE LEDSHAM, of the Inner Temple, of Hawarden, co. Flint, and of the Farm-Stile estate, in Ewloe, d. about 1606, leaving a son,

DANIEL LEDSHAM b. at Weppera, co. Flint, who went to Ireland about 1655, as secretary to Col. Harrison, in CROMWELL'S army. He d. in that kingdom, leaving three sons, DANIEL; JOHN, of Hawarden; and Thomas. The eldest son,

DANIEL LEDSHAM, Esq. of Cloghjordan, co. Tipperary, served as high-sheriff of that county. He subsequently removed to Flintshire, and finally settled at Birmingham, where he d. in 1783, aged ninety-three. He m. 23 May, 1727, Ann, dau. of John Moreton, Esq. of Northop, co. Flint, and had issue. The 4th son,

THOMAS LEDSAM, Esq., b. at Hawarden, co. Flint, 12 Feb. 1740, m. Charlotte, eldest dau. of William Ward, Esq. of Allestree Hall, co. Derby, by Mary his wife, dau. of Richard Smith, Esq. of Enderby Hall, co. Leicester, and had issue,

I. John-Moreton, b. 19 Oct. 1762, of Farringdon, co. Berks, and Lechlade, co. Gloucester, m. Mary-Barbara, dau. of Coffin, of Blackladies, co. Stafford, and d. 6 Nov. 1832, leaving issue,
1 John-Joseph, b. 14 Nov. 1796, m. 9 July, 1828, Selina Jones, of Packington, co. Warwick.
1 Barbara-Maria, m. 27 Dec. 1823, to Gabriel-Jean-Marie De Lys, M.D., only son of the Marquis De Lys, of La Vilder, Brittany, and had issue.
2 Frances-Anne, m. to George-Elwell Jackson, Esq.
II. JOSEPH, of whom presently.
III. Daniel, of the Moors and Nonsuch, co. Worcester, b. 29 March, 1772, m. Sarah-Elizabeth, dau. of Thomas Soden, Esq. of Allesley, co. Warwick, and had issue, DANIEL, in holy orders, b. 26 Jan. 1813, and Sarah, m. in 1832, to Charles Hopkins, Esq., lieut. R.N.
IV. William, b. 10 March, 1778, d. at Lisbon, 13 July, 1814.

The 2nd son,

JOSEPH LEDSAM, Esq., b. 5 March, 1767, m. Mary, eldest dau. of John Bullock, Esq., by his wife, Mary Blythe, of Saltley, co. Warwick, and dying 9 Nov. 1816, left (with a dau., Mary-Anne-Moreton, who m. 23 Jan. 1818, Joseph Hodgson, Esq. of Birmingham, F.R.S., and has one dau., Marianne, m. 12 May, 1858, to Lieut.-Col. Shakespeare) an only surviving son, the present JOSEPH-FREDERICK LEDSAM, Esq. of Chad Hill.

Arms—Quarterly: sa. and arg., four leopards' faces, counterchanged.
Crest—A Cornish chough.
Motto—Fac et spera.
Seat—Chad Hill, Edgbaston.

LEE OF HARTWELL.

LEE, JOHN, Esq., LL.D., of Hartwell, co. Buckingham, b. 28 April, 1783; s. his maternal uncle, William-Lee Antonie, Esq., in 1815, and assumed, under that gentleman's will, his present surname of Lee, in lieu of his patronymic, FIOTT. To the Hartwell property he succeeded, by the bequest of his kinsman, the Rev. Sir George Lee, 6th Bart.

Lineage.—This family, supposed to have been a younger branch of the Leghs of Cheshire, settled in Bucks in the beginning of HENRY IV.'s reign.

THOMAS LEE, Esq. of Hartwell, co. Bucks, (eldest son of Thomas Lee, Esq. of Moreton and Hartwell, by Elizabeth his wife, dau. of Sir George Croke), was created a Baronet, 16 Aug. 1660. His direct male descendant (for *intermediate pedigree, see* BURKE'S *Extinct Peerage*),

THE REV. SIR GEORGE LEE, rector of Hartwell, and vicar of Stowe, b. in 1767, d. unm. in 1827, when the Baronetcy expired, and the estates devolved, by Sir George's will, on their present possessor, JOHN LEE, Esq., LL.D., the next heir in blood. He is son of the late John Fiott, Esq., by Harriet his wife, 2nd dau. of William Lee, Esq. of Totteridge, who was son of the Right Hon. Sir William Lee, Chief Justice of England, 2nd son of Sir Thomas Lee, 2nd Bart. of Hartwell.

Arms—Az., two bars, or, a bend, chequy, or and gu.
Crest—A bear, passant, sa., muzzled, collared and chained, or.
Motto—Verum atque decens.
Seat—Hartwell, Bucks.

LEE OF BALSDON LODGE.

LEE, JOHN-HUTCHINSON, Esq. of Balsdon Lodge, Torquay, Devon, b. 27 Aug. 1810; m. 2 Feb. 1847, Caroline, youngest dau. of the late Charles Hives, Esq. of Gledhow Grove, Leeds, and has issue,

I. JOHN-THEOPHILUS, b. 8 May, 1850.
II. Henry-Hives, b. 9 Feb. 1856.
I. Alice-Jane. II. Margaret-Caroline.

Mr. Lee was for some years aide-de-camp to the late Sultan Mahmoud, who conferred on him the Order of the Crescent; he is also a magistrate for Middlesex and Westminster.

Lineage.—JOHN LEE, Esq., an officer in R.N., descended from the Lees of Dumbale, co. Cheshire; d. in 1786, leaving issue,

JOHN, of whom presently.
Richard, colonel in the army.
Esther, m. Gen. Theophilus Lewis.

The elder son,

JOHN LEE, Esq., capt. R.N., m. 12 Jan. 1786, Margaret Hay, granddau. of Dr. John Hay, physician to GEORGE I., and dau. of James Maclellan, of Annan, of the Kircudbright family, and d. 23 March, 1800, having had, by this lady, who d. 24 June, 1810,

John Theophilus, b. 28 Aug. 1786.
Henrietta-Maria, d. young.

His only son,

SIR JOHN THEOPHILUS LEE, of Lauriston Hall, s. his father on the 23 March, 1800. He m. 24 Dec. 1807, Sophia, dau. of Major Lawler, of Greenwich, and had issue,

I. Horatio William Pitt, b. Sept. 1808; d. in active service R.N., on board H.M. Tartar, Capt. Sir Thomas Hardy, in 1828.
II. JOHN-HUTCHINSON, now of Baledon Lodge.
III. Melville-Lauriston, b. 27 April, 1821, of Magdalene College, Cambridge, in holy orders; rector of Bridport, Dorset, m. 14 April, 1852, Emily, dau. of J. Dicker, Esq. of Lewes, and has issue,
1 Alicia-Marion.
2 Emily-Theresa-Josephine.
IV. Alfred-Theophilus, in holy orders, scholar of Christ's College, Cambridge; m. 4 Aug. 1853, Euphemia, only dau. of Marriott Dalway, Bella Hill, Carrickfergus, and has issue,
1 Marriott Dalway, b. 17 May, 1854.
2 Robert-Maclellan-Lauriston, b. 11 Dec. 1855.
I. Henrietta-Margaretta-Hay, m. 27 April, 1848, the Rev. Guy Bryan, eldest son of the Rev. Guy Bryan, rector of Woodham Walter, Essex, by Selina-Elizabeth his wife, dau. of John Eardley Wilmot, Esq.
II. Sophia-Townshend, m. 19 April, 1842, Rev. G. W. B. Wills, of Woodham College, Oxford; rector of St. Leonard, Exeter.
III. Emma-Louisa-Berry, m. 28 June 1842, the Rev. Thomas John Main, fellow of St. John's College, and professor of Royal Naval College, Portsmouth.
IV. Augusta.
V. Euphemia, m. 2 Feb. 1847, Donald Sinclair, M.D., brother of Sir John Sinclair, Bart., of Barrock House, Caithness.

Sir John Theophilus Lee entered the Royal Navy under Lord St. Vincent, in 1795, and was present at the battles of Cape St. Vincent and the Nile, and in eighteen other actions with frigates, forts and boats. He was knighted in 1827, and was presented by the Sultan Mahmoud with the order of the Crescent, in diamonds; and had also conferred on him the orders of Christ of Portugal, St. Louis of France, St. Andrew of Russia, and Waldimir of Prussia. He was a magistrate for Middlesex, Hants, and Devon, and deputy-lieutenant for the two former counties. He d. at Lauriston Hall, Torquay, 25 Oct. 1843.

Arms—Arg., a chev., engr., between three leopards' heads, sa.
Crest—A leopard's head, sa., surmounting a ducal coronet.
Motto—Dum spiro spero.
Seat—Baledon Lodge, Torquay.

LEE OF THE ABBEY.

LEE, CHARLES-BENJAMIN, Esq. of The Abbey, Knaresborough, b. 16 Feb. 1797; m. 28 Aug. 1839, the Hon. Mary-Stuart Forbes, dau. of James Ochoncar, 18th Lord Forbes, and has issue,

I. CHARLES-WALTER, b. 13 Sept. 1840.
I. Isabella-Ann.

Lineage.—JOHN LEE, Esq. of The Abbey, Knaresborough, D.L., son of the late Thomas Lee, Esq., by Ann Foster his wife, b. 6 Sept. 1766; who m. 4 Feb. 1794, Maria Mainwaring, of Goltho' Hall, co. Lincoln, and had issue,

JOHN, b. 1795, d. unm.
CHARLES-BENJAMIN, now of The Abbey.
Frederick, b. in 1800; m. in Jan. 1832, Elizabeth Cole, and has issue.
George, b. 13 Feb. 1802, m. in Oct. 1831, Mary Stark, and had issue.
Charlotte.
Emma-Maria, d. unm.

Arms—Sa., three crowns, or.
Crest—An arm in armour, holding a battle-axe.
Motto—Dum spiro spero.
Seat—Old Pa'ace, Richmond, Surrey.

LEE OF BARNA.

LEE, HENRY-ALBERT, Esq. of Barna, co. Tipperary, b. 2 Aug. 1818; m. 31 July, 1852, Susan-Kate, eldest dau. of the late John Benn, Esq., and has issue,

I. ALBERT-HENRY, b. 26 April, 1853.
II. William-Alexander, b. 18 Aug. 1854.
III. John-Francis, b. 12 April, 1856.

Lineage.—This family was settled in Ireland by CAPT. RICHARD LEE, (stated to have been nephew to the Earl of Lichfield), who accompanied CROMWELL to Ireland; and a letter of the Lord Protector still remains in the possession of the present Mr. Lee, of Barna, appointing him captain in the 62nd regiment of Foot. CROMWELL afterwards bestowed on him large estates in the co. of Tipperary. The great-grandfather of the present Mr. Lee,

HENRY LEE, son of EDWARD LEE, Esq., by Elizabeth Ryan his wife, m. Mary Philips, and was father of (with three other sons),

GEORGE LEE, Esq. of Barna, who m. 11 Feb. 1778, Alice Norris, and had issue,

HENRY, his heir.
Edward, who m., and by his wife, who is deceased, had one dau.
Anna, m. to James Dickson, Esq., barrister-at-law.

Mr. Lee d. June, 1816, and was s. by his son,

HENRY LEE, Esq. of Barna, J.P., b. 2 March, 1789, who m. 2 Jan. 1808, Maria, dau. of Christopher Crofts, Esq. of Stream Hill, co. Cork, and had issue,

I. HENRY-ALBERT, now of Barna.
II. Charles-Edward.
III. George-Augusta.
I. Anne.
II. Alicia-Maria.
III. Catherine-Louisa.
IV. Charlotte, deceased.
V. Emily.
VI. Maria.

Mr. Lee d. 18 Jan. 1848.

Arms—Arg., a fesse between three crescents, sa.
Crest—On a column, arg., encircled with a ducal coronet, or, a falcon, close, ppr., standing on a bird's leg, sa., erased, gu.
Motto—Fide et constantiâ.
Seat—Barna, co. Tipperary.

LEE OF DILLINGTON HOUSE.

LEE, JOHN-LEE, Esq. of Dillington House, co. Somerset, and Orleigh Court, co. Devon, J.P. and D.L., high-sheriff 1845, b. 11 Dec. 1802; m. 1st, 18 Feb. 1834, Jessy, dau. of John-Edwards Vaughan, Esq. of Rheola, co. Glamorgan, late M.P., and by her (who d. 1836) has one son,

I. VAUGHAN-HANNING-LEE, 21st Fusiliers, b. 25 Feb. 1836.

He m. 2ndly, 17 Aug. 1841, the Hon. Mary-Sophia Hood, eldest dau. of Lord Bridport, and has by her,

I. Edward-Hanning, b. 26 Aug. 1845.
II. William-Hanning, b. 9 Dec. 1846.
I. Emily-Mary.
II. Alice-Georgina.

Mr. Lee, whose patronymic is HANNING, assumed the surname of LEE, by sign-manual, in 1822. He is only son of William Hanning, Esq. of Dillington House, by his wife, HARRIET LEE, of Orleigh Court, co. Devon (m. in 1800), and grandson of John Hanning, Esq. of Dillington, by Susan his wife, dau. of T. Harvard, Esq. of Whitelackington, co. Somerset. He has two sisters, Georgina-Elizabeth, m. Nov. 1824, to William Speke, Esq. of Jordans; and Sophia-Harriet, m. June, 1828, to John-B. Fuller, Esq. of Neston Park, Wilts. Mr. Lee-Lee was M.P. for Wells in the reign of WILLIAM IV.

Arms—Quarterly: 1st and 4th, LEE; 2nd and 3rd, HANNING.
Crests—1st, for LEE; 2nd, for HANNING.
Seats—Dillington House, near Ilminster, and Orleigh Court, near Bideford.

LEE OF HOLBOROUGH.

LEE, WILLIAM, Esq. of Holborough, co. Kent, J.P. and D.L., b. 23 Aug. 1801; m. 2 April, 1820, Christiana, dau. of S. Reynolds, Esq. of Thoydon Hall, Essex, and has issue,

I. Anne, m. June, 1845, W.-H. Roberts, Esq., capt. R.E., who is deceased.
II. Sarah, m. Oct. 1853, to Alfred Smith, Esq. of Rochester.

Mr. Lee, of Holborough, is 3rd son of Henry and Susannah Lee, of Camps Hill, Lewisham, Kent.

Arms—Az., two bars, erminois.
Crest—A bear, statant, ppr., muzzled, gu., collared and chained, arg.
Motto—Verum atque decens.
Seat—Holborough, Kent.

LEE OF THE MOUNT.

LEE, EDWARD-HERBERT, Esq. of The Mount, Dynas Powis, co. Glamorgan, J.P., *b.* Oct. 1786; *m.* June, 1810, Mary-Anne, 2nd dau. of Thomas Thompson, Esq. of London, and by her (who *d.* 26 April, 1811) has an only son,

HENRY-THOMAS, *b.* 21 April, 1811; *m.* in Aug. 1837, Catherine-Frances, 5th dau. of James Broadwood, Esq. of Lyne House, Surrey, and has issue,

1 HENRY-HERBERT.
2 John-Robert. 3 Francis-Ashmore.
1 Mary-Anne-Elizabeth. 2 Barbara-Stewart.

Lineage.—HENRY LEE, merchant of Hull, and at one time mayor of that town, *m.* Catherine Freeman, great-grand-aunt of Lord Brougham, and had issue, HENRY, *b.* in 1727; Thomas, capt. R.N., lost at sea in 1770, while in command of the Aurora frigate; Catherine, *m.* to Sir Arthur Clarke, Bart. of Snailwell. The elder son,

THE REV. HENRY LEE, vicar of Willoughby-with-Wolfhamcote, co. Warwick, *b.* in 1727, *m.* Margaret, dau. of Edward Hurst, Esq. of Upton, Bucks, and sister of William Hurst, Esq., high-sheriff of Glamorganshire in 1776, and had two sons, HENRY, his heir; and Thomas, in the navy, lost at sea in 1770. Mr. Lee *d.* in 1768, and was *s.* by his son,

HENRY LEE, Esq., *b.* in 1758, J.P. and D.L. who *m.* in May, 1779, Sarah, only dau. of the Rev. Samuel Roberts, of Salisbury, and dying in Dec. 1832, left (with three daus., Sarah-Margaretta, *m.* in Dec. 1796, to Thomas-Lane Thompson, Esq. of Blackheath; Arthuretta-Clarke; and Anna-Maria) an only son, EDWARD-HERBERT LEE, Esq. of The Mount, Dynas Powis.

Arms—Arg., on a chev., engr., between three leopards' heads, sa., a crescent.
Crest—A leopard's head, sa., surmounting a ducal coronet.
Motto—Fortiter, sed suaviter.
Residence—The Mount, Dynas Powis, Glamorganshire.

LEE OF COTON HALL.

LEE, REV. HARRY, of Kingsgate House, Hants, represents the very ancient family of Lee of Coton Hall, co. Salop, which has continued, in a direct line, from father to son, from the reign of EDWARD I. to the present time, and in which the same property remained until conveyed by an heiress to the Wingfields of Tickencote, co. Rutland.

LEECH OF RATHKEALE ABBEY.

LEECH, GEORGE-WILLIAMS, Esq. of Rathkeale Abbey, co. Limerick, barrister-at-law, J.P., *b.* 30 Aug. 1810; *m.* 1st, 12 Nov. 1834, Anna-Maria, dau. of General George Bellasis, and by her has a son,

ROBERT-S.-B., 94th regt., *b.* 21 May, 1836.

He *m.* 2ndly, 28 Sept. 1846, Catherine, dau. of Hunt-Walshe Chambre, Esq. of Hawthorne Hill, co. Armagh, by whom he has issue,

I. Hunt-Chambre, *b.* 20 Dec. 1847.
II. John-Bourke-Massy, *b.* 21 July, 1854.
I. Helena-E.-Susanna. II. Catherine-Rebecca.
III. Eliza-Georgina.

Lineage.—This family which claims to be a branch of that of LECHE *of Carden*, co. Chester, settled in Ireland about the middle of the 17th century. It was long established in Mayo, and intermarried with the BOURKES, PAGETS, and ORMES, of that county. The late

JOHN-BOURKE LEECH, Esq., *b.* 19 Dec. 1763, son of Robert Leech Esq., by his wife Julie Bourke, and grandson of John Leech Esq. of Frankford, co. Sligo, by Mary his wife, eldest dau. of Robert Orme, Esq. of Carne, co. Mayo, left, by Helena-E.-Susannah his wife, six sons, viz.,

WILLIAM, *b.* 1798, *m.* E.-C. Macdougall, and had one son, William, deceased.
GEORGE-WILLIAMS, now of Rathkeale Abbey.
James, of Somerset House, London.
John, of Liverpool. Robert, of Bombay.
Arthur.

Seat—Rathkeale Abbey, co. Limerick.

LEEKE OF LONGFORD.

LEEKE, RALPH-MERRICK, Esq. of Longford Hall, co. Salop, J.P. and D.L., high-sheriff 1850, *b.* 4 Sept. 1813; *m.* 26 Oct. 1847, Lady Hester-Maria, dau. of Newton-Fellowes, 4th Earl of Portsmouth, by Catharine his wife, dau. of Hugh, 1st Earl Fortescue, and has issue,

I. RALPH, *b.* 1849. II. Thomas-Newton, *b.* 1854.
III. Walter-Harvey, *b.* 1856.
I. Hester-Catharine. II. Charlotte-Urania.

Lineage.—This family has, for several centuries, been of importance in the county of Salop. The immediate ancestor of the present line,

RALPH LEEKE, of Ludlow, was living in 1534. His seal is represented in a pedigree of the family, which is attested by Sir William Segar, as bearing his shield of arms, the same as now used with the legend, "Sigill. Radi Leeke Armigeri." From him descended

RALPH LEEKE, Esq., 2nd son of Thomas Leeke, Esq. of the Vineyard, near Wellington, and 6th in descent from Ralph Leeke, whose eldest son, THOMAS, was one of the barons of the Exchequer, acquired a large fortune in the civil service of the E. I. Company. Returning to England in 1786, he purchased, the following year, from the Earl of Shrewsbury, the manors and estates of Longford and Church Aston, in Shropshire, and was high-sheriff of that county 1796. He *m.* 18 Dec. 1787, Honoria-Frances, only dau. of Walter Harvey-Thursby, Esq., and by her (who *d.* 1843) had issue, THOMAS, his heir; Ralph-Harvey, rector of Longford, *b.* 4 Oct. 1794; Augusta; Caroline *m.* 7 Sept. 1824, to the Hon. and Rev. William Nevill; Emily-Frances-Anne, *m.* 29 Oct. 1835 to the Rev. Sir Henry Thompson, Bart. He *d.* 30 Sept. 1829, and was *s.* by his elder son,

THOMAS LEEKE Esq. of Longford Hall, barrister-at-law, J.P., *b.* 21 Nov. 1788, who *m.* 1st, 13 Nov. 1812, Louisa, youngest dau. of the late Brig.-Gen. Robert Shawe, and by her, who *d.* 16 April, 1816, had issue,

RALPH-MERRICK, present representative.
Egerton, *b.* 23 March, 1816.
Charlotte, *m.* to the Rev. Wyndham Madden.

Mr. Leeke *m.* 2ndly, 21 Jan. 1822, Anna, only dau. of the late Hon. Matthew Plunkett, brother to the 10th Lord Louth.

Arms—Arg., on a chief, gu., a fleur-de-lis, or, over all, a bend, engr., as.
Crest—A leg, couped at the thigh, charged with two fleurs-de-lis.
Motto—Agendo gnaviter.
Seat—Longford Hall, near Newport, Shropshire.

LEFEVRE OF HECKFIELD PLACE.

SHAW-LEFEVRE, THE RIGHT HON. CHARLES, of Heckfield Place, co. Hants, M.P. for North Hants, and for eighteen years SPEAKER OF THE HOUSE OF COMMONS, *b.* 22 Feb. 1794; *m.* 24 June, 1817, Emma-Laura, dau. of Samuel Whitbread, Esq., M.P., by the Lady Elizabeth, his wife, sister of Charles, Earl Grey, and has had, with three sons, who all *d.* young, three daus.,

I. Emma-Laura.
II. Helena, *m.* 26 Feb. 1851, to Sir Henry B.-P.-St. John Mildmay Bart.
III. Elizabeth.

Mr. Shaw-Lefevre is a magistrate and deputy-lieut. for Hampshire, High Steward of Winchester, and lieut.-col. of the Hants Yeomanry.

Lineage.—The Lefevres came from the neighbourhood of Rouen, in Normandy, and established themselves in England at the Revocation of the Edict of Nantes. About the same period, a member of this family, Pierre Lefevre, son of Isaac Lefevre, suffered death, after thirty years' imprisonment, on account of his religious tenets.

JOHN LEFEVRE and ISAAC LEFEVRE, were the two members of the family who first came to England, of whom, JOHN, the eldest, served as a lieut.-colonel in Marlborough's army, and settled in Essex. The younger, ISAAC LEFEVRE, *m.*, and had, with daus., of whom Madeline, *m.* William Currie, Esq., banker, London, four sons, of whom the eldest,

JOHN LEFEVRE, Esq. of Heckfield Place, Hants, m. twice, had by his 2nd wife, Helena, dau. of Lister Selman, Esq. of Old Ford, co. Middlesex, an only child,

HELENA LEFEVRE, who m. Charles Shaw, Esq., M.P. for Reading, barrister-at-law, son of George Shaw, Esq., by Maria Green his wife, and grandson of George Shaw, Esq., of an old Yorkshire family, and had by him (who took the name of LEFEVRE) three sons, viz.,

CHARLES, the present RIGHT HON. CHARLES SHAW LEFEVRE.
John-George, (Sir) K.C.B., formerly M.P. for Petersfield, and Under Secretary for the Colonies, and now clerk of Parliament, m. 29 Dec. 1824, Rachel-Emily, dau. of Ichabod Wright, Esq. of Mapperley, Notts, and has six daus., and one surviving son, GEORGE-JOHN, of the Inner Temple, barrister-at-law.
Henry-Francis, m. 1st, Helen, dau. of General Sir John G. Le Marchant, by whom he has three daus., Helen, Anna-Maria, and Sophia; and 2ndly, Elizabeth-Emma, dau. of the Rev. John and the Hon. Emma Foster.

Mr. Shaw-Lefevre sat for the first time in parliament for Newton, in 1796, and subsequently represented Reading. He d. 27 April, 1823.

Arms—Quarterly: 1st and 4th, sa., a chev., arg., between two trefoils, slipped, in chief, and a bezant in base, therefrom issuant a cross-patée, or, for LEFEVRE; 2nd and 3rd, sa., a chev., erm., on a canton, or, a talbot's head, erased, gu. for SHAW.
Crest—Six arrows, interlaced saltierwise, three and three, ppr., within an annulet, or.
Motto—Sans changer.
Seat—Heckfield Place, near Winchfield.

LEFROY OF CARRICKGLASS.

LEFROY, THE RIGHT HON. THOMAS-LANGLOIS, of Carrickglass, co. Longford, Lord Chief Justice of Ireland, b. 1776; m. 1799, Mary, only dau. and heir of Jeffry Paul, Esq. of Silver Spring, co. Wexford, member of a younger branch of the family of Sir Robert Paul, Bart., and has issue,

I. ANTHONY, D.L., and for many years M.P. for the county of Longford, for which he served as high-sheriff, in 1850, m. 1824, Hon. Jane-King, eldest dau. of the late Viscount Lorton, and granddau. of Robert Earl of Kingston, and has issue,
  1 Frances, m. to Col. David-Carrick Buchanan, of Drumpellier, co. Lanark.
  2 Mary, m. to Hon. W. Talbot, capt. 9th regt.
II. Thomas-Paul, Q.C., m. Hon. Elizabeth Massy, dau. of Hugh, 3rd Lord Massy, and has issue, Thomas-Langlois, and several other children.
III. Jeffry, in holy orders, m. Helena, eldest dau. of the Rev. Frederick Trench, by Lady Helena his wife, sister of George-James, 6th Earl of Egmont, and has issue, Charles, and other children.
IV. George-Thomson, who served as high-sheriff of Longford, in the year 1846.
I. Jane.
II. Anne.
III. Mary.

Lord Chief Justice Lefroy, one of the most distinguished lawyers of his time, sat in parliament as member for the University of Dublin for many years previously to his elevation to the Bench, which took place in 1841, when he was appointed a Baron of the Exchequer. He became Chief Justice in 1852.

Lineage.—The Lefroys are of Flemish extraction, and emigrated to England in the time of the Duke of Alva's persecutions. The first who settled in this country, A.D. 1569, was ANTHONY LEFROY. His descendant,

THOMAS LEFROY, of Canterbury,* m. Phœbe, b. in 1679, dau. of Thomas Thomson, Esq. of Kenfield, by Phœbe his wife, dau. of William Hammond, Esq. of St. Alban's Court, Kent, and by her, who d. in 1761, had a son,

ANTHONY LEFROY, of Leghorn, who m. Elizabeth Langlois, sister of Benjamin Langlois Esq., M.P., many years Under-Secretary of State, and had (with one dau., Phœbe, m. to an Italian nobleman, Staffetti Del Medico, Count di Carrara)* two sons,

I. ANTHONY, lieut.-col. 9th dragoons, m. 15 Nov. 1765, Anne Gardiner, and d. 8 Sept. 1819, having had issue,
  1 RIGHT HON. THOMAS LEFROY, the present chief-justice of Ireland.
  2 Anthony, late capt. 65th regt. m. and has issue.
  3 Benjamin, capt. roy. art., m. and issue.
  4 Henry, rector of Santry, near Dublin, m. and has issue.
  1 Lucy, m. to Hugh-Ryves Baker, Esq.
  2 Phœbe, m. to Capt. Butler.
  3 Sarah, m. to Capt. Courtenay.
  4 Anne, m. to Major Power.
  5 Eliza, m. to Richard Sadleir, Esq.
II. Isaac-Peter-George, fellow of All Souls', Oxford, rector of Ash and Compton, co. Surrey, m. Anne, eldest dau. of Edward Brydges, Esq. of Wootton Court, co. Kent, by Jemima his wife, dau. and co-heir of William Egerton, LL.D., grandson of John, 2nd Earl of Bridgewater, and by her (who d. in 1804) left at his decease, Jan. 1806, three sons and one dau.,
  1 John-Henry-George, of Ewshot House, rector of Ash and Compton, b. 1782, m. Sophia, youngest dau. of the Rev. Charles-Jeffreys Cottrell, and d. 1823, leaving issue, George, d. unm.; Charles-Edward, m. Janet, dau. of James Walker, Esq.; Anthony-Cottrell, m. Anne, dau. of John Rickman, Esq., and has three daus.; John-Henry, m. Emily-Mary, dau. of Chief Justice Robinson, of Toronto, Canada, and has one son and one dau.; Henry-Maxwell; Frederick, deceased: Ann, m. to John McClintock, Esq.; Frances-Phœbe, m. to George-K. Rickards, Esq., barrister-at-law; Anna-Sophia; Isabella-Elizabeth; and Lucy, deceased.
  2 Christopher-Edward, b. 1785.
  3 Benjamin, in holy orders, rector of Ash, m. Jane-Anna-Elizabeth, eldest dau. of the late Rev. James Austen, rector of Steventon, Hants, and dying 1829, left issue, George-Benjamin-Austen, and six daus.
  1 Lucy, m. to the Rev. Henry Rice, of Norton Court, near Faversham.

Arms—Quarterly: 1st and 4th, vert, fretty, arg., on a chief, of the second, a hood or cap (allusive to the badge assumed by the party opposed to the Duke of Alva), between two wyverns, gu., for LEFROY; 2nd and 3rd, az., a chevron, or, between three crescents, arg., on a chief, gu., three mullets, of the third, for LANGLOIS.
Crest—A demi-wyvern, gu., gorged with a collar, dancettée, arg., fretty, vert.
Motto—Mutare sperno (adopted at the period of the Huguenot persecutions).
Seat—Carrickglass, co. Longford.

LEGGE OF MALONE HOUSE.

LEGGE, WILLIAM-WALLACE, Esq. of Malone House, co. Antrim, D.L., high-sheriff 1823, s. his uncle, William Legge, in 1821, and adopted the surname of LEGGE; m. 27 Sept. 1838, Eleanor-Wilkie, 3rd dau. and co-heiress of Thomas Forster, of Adderstone, Northumberland, and has issue,

I. WILLIAM-WALLACE. II. Florence-Wallace.

Lineage.—In 1676, WILLIAM LEGGE, an officer in the army, with recommendations from JAMES II., then Duke of York, served under the Duke Schomberg in Flanders, and accompanied him to Ireland in 1690. His son,

WILLIAM LEGGE, settled at Malone, co. Antrim, and d. 7 Nov. 1723, leaving, with other sons,

WILLIAM LEGG, who d. in Nov. 1750.

ALEXANDER LEGGE (his eldest son) then s., and served as high-sheriff for the co. Antrim. He d. in 1777, leaving issue,

WILLIAM, his heir, who served as high-sheriff for co. Antrim, and d. 20 Sept. 1821.
Elinor, who m. HILL-WALLACE, Esq., an officer in the army, claiming descent from the Wallaces of Ellerslie, and had issue,
  WILLIAM, present possessor.
  Hill, m. 2nd dau. of Major Topham, of Yorkshire.
  Ellen.
Marcella, who m. Anthony Semple, Esq. of Malahide, and d. without issue.

Seat—Malone House, co. Antrim.

LEGH OF NORBURY BOOTHS HALL.

LEGH, PETER, Esq. of Norbury Booths Hall, co. Chester, J.P. and D.L., formerly high-sheriff, b. 11 June, 1794.

Lineage.—AGNES DE LEGH, (only dau. and heir of Richard de Legh, great-grandson of Hamon, Lord of the

* Monument to this Thomas Lefroy, in the parish church of Potham, Kent:—

Sacred
to Thos. Lefroy, of Canterbury,
who died 3 Nov. 1723, aged 43;
of a Cambresian Family
that preferred
Religion and Liberty
To their Country and Property,
In the time of Duke Alva's Persecution.

* This family retain their rank and large possessions at Carrara.

Mediety of High Legh, *temp.* HENRY II., *m.* 1st, RICHARD DE LYMME and had by him a son, THOMAS, who took the name of LEGH, and half the mediety of High Leigh; his son, THOMAS LEGH, was progenitor of the LEIGHS of the West Hall, High Leigh. Agnes *m.* 2ndly, William de Hawardyn, and had another son, RALPH DE HAWARDYN who had the other half of the mediety of High Legh, and sold it to Sir Richard Massey, of Tatton, in 1206. Agnes *m.* 3rdly, Sir William Venables, Knt., 2nd son of Sir William Venables, Baron of Kinderton, and by him had a 3rd son, JOHN, who took the name of Legh, and purchased Knutsford Booth before 28 EDWARD I. By his 1st wife he had a son, JOHN (Sir.) He *m.* 2ndly, Ellen, dau. of Thomas de Corona, of Adlington, and by her had, ROBERT, progenitor of the Leghs of Adlington, Annesley, Lyme, Ridge, Stoneleigh, Stockwell, &c.; William (Sir), ancestor of the Leghs of Isall; Peter, founder of the Leghs of Bechton; and Gilbert, whose son, John, *m.* Cecilia de Towneley, and was ancestor of the TOWNELEYS of Towneley.

SIR JOHN DE LEGH, living *temp.* EDWARD III., eldest son of John Legh, the 1st of Knutsford Booth, was direct ancestor of the family of LEGH, of Booths, whose eventual heiress,

RUTH LEGH, of Booths, only dau. of Peter Legh, Esq. of Booths, *m.* Thomas Pennington, Esq. of Chester, and was *s.* at her decease, in 1715-16, by her only surviving son,

THOMAS PENNINGTON, Esq. of Booths, who assumed the surname and arms of Legh. He *m.* Helena, dau. of Sir Willoughby Aston, Bart. of Aston, and was *s.* by his only son,

PETER LEGH, Esq. of Booths, *b.* 4 March, 1722-3, who, in 1745, completed the erection of Norbury Booths' Hall. He *m.* 20 June, 1744, Anne, dau. and co-heir of Peter Wade, Esq., by whom, who *d.* in 1794, he had, with other issue, who *d. s. p.*, WILLOUGHBY and JOHN, and Anne-Helena, who *m.* in 1792, John Matthews, Esq., capt. R.N., and *d.* next year *s. p.* He *d.* 12 Aug. 1804, and was *s.* by his eldest surviving son,

WILLOUGHBY LEGH, Esq. of Norbury Booths Hall, *b.* 25 May, 1749, who, dying *unm.*, was *s.* by his brother,

JOHN LEGH, Esq. of Bedford Square, London, and Torkington, in Cheshire, barrister-at-law, who *m.* 29 March, 1792, Isabella, dau. and co-heir of Edmund Dawson, Esq. of Wharton, in Lancashire, and by her (who *d.* 19 Feb. 1849), had issue,

I. PETER, now of Norbury Booths Hall.
II. Edmund-Dawson, *b.* in 1801, in holy orders; *m.* Catherine Robinson, and *d.* 9 March, 1845, leaving issue,
   1 John-Pennington. 2 William-Dawson.
   3 Christopher. 4 Henry-Edmund.
   1 Catherine-Louisa, *m.* to Edward Penrose Hathaway, Esq.
   2 Isabella-Helen. 3 Frances-Ann.
I. Ann, *m.* to William Clowes, Esq., and *d.* 21 April, 1855.
II. Isabel, *m.* to the Rev. Bertie Johnson, rector of Lymme, Cheshire, and *d.* 26 May, 1855.

Mr. Lee *d.* in April, 1826.

Arms—Az., two bars, or, over all a bend, gules.
Crest—An arm embowed, couped at the shoulder, vested, gules, hand, ppr., holding a sword erect, also ppr., a snake twisting round the same, arg.
Motto—Prudens, fidelis, et audax.
Seat—Norbury Booths Hall, near Knutsford.

LEGH OF ADLINGTON.

LEGH, CHARLES-RICHARD-BANASTRE, Esq. of Adlington Hall, co. Chester, *b.* 4 March, 1821.

Lineage.—ROBERT DE LEGH, 2nd son of John Legh, of Booths, by Ellen his wife, dau. and heir of Thomas de Corona, of Adlington, living *temp.* EDWARD II., *m.* Matilda, dau. and heir of Adam de Norley, and was father of

ROBERT LEGH, of Adlington, who *m.* Matilda, dau. and co-heir of Sir John de Arderne, Knt. of Aldford and Alvanley, and had two sons, viz., ROBERT (Sir), his heir; Piers (Sir), ancestor of the LEGHS *of Lyme*. From the elder son,

SIR ROBERT LEGH, Knt. of Adlington, sheriff of Cheshire 17 and 22 RICHARD II, the 8th in descent was

SIR URIAN LEGH, Knt. of Adlington, aged thirty-five 44 ELIZABETH, who was knighted by the Earl of Essex at the siege of Cadiz, and, during that expedition, is traditionally said to have been engaged in an adventure which gave rise to the well-known ballad of "The Spanish Lady's Love." Another gallant knight, Sir John Bollo, however, disputes the fact of being the hero of that romantic affair. Sir Urian was sheriff of Cheshire in the year of Sir Richard St. George's Visitation of the county, in 1613, and survived until 3 CHARLES I., when his inquisition was taken. His direct male descendant,

CHARLES LEGH, Esq. of Adlington (only son of John Leigh, Esq. of Adlington, by Lady Isabella Roberts his wife, sister of the Earl of Radnor, and grandson of Thomas Leigh, Esq. of Adlington, high-sheriff of Cheshire 14 CHARLES II.), *m.* Hester, dau. and co-heir of Robert Lee, Esq. of Wincham, in Cheshire, and had an only child,

Thomas, of Wincham, who *m.* Mary, dau. of Francis Reynolds, Esq. of Strangeways, in Lancashire; and *d. s. p.* in 1775, aged 40, without surviving issue.

Mr. Legh *d.* at Buxton in July, 1781, and was *s.* under settlement by his niece,

ELIZABETH DAVENPORT, who *m.* in 1752, John Rowlls, Esq. of Kingston, receiver-general for Surrey, and by him (who *d.* in 1779) had issue,

I. John Rowlls, who *m.* Harriet, sister and co-heir of Sir Peter Warburton, Bart. of Arley, and, predeceasing his mother, left an only dau. and heir,
   Elizabeth-Hester Rowlls, *m.* to Thomas-Delves Broughton, Esq., 4th son of Sir Thomas Broughton, Bart.
II. William-Peter Rowlls, slain in a duel at Cranford Bridge.
III. Charles-Edward Rowlls, *d.* without issue.
I. Elizabeth Rowlls, *m.* 1st, in 1778, to Thomas-Browne Calley, Esq. of Burderop, Wilts; and 2ndly, to Thomas Haverfield, Esq.

Mrs. Rowlls, who assumed the surname of LEGH, *d.* in 1806, leaving no surviving male issue, when the Adlington estates devolved, in accordance with the settlement of her predecessor, on her kinsman,

RICHARD CROSSE, Esq. of Shaw Hill, near Preston, in Lancashire (only son of Thomas Crosse, Esq., by Sarah his wife, and grandson of Richard Crosse, Esq. of Crosse Hall, co. Lancaster, by Ann his wife, eldest dau. of Robert Leigh, of Chorley, 2nd son of Thomas Leigh, Esq. of Adlington, the high-sheriff of Cheshire, 14 CHARLES II.) Mr. Crosse assumed, in consequence, the surname and arms of LEGH. He *m.* in 1787, Anne, only surviving dau. of Robert Parker, Esq. of Cuerden Hall, by Anne his wife, dau. and heir of Thomas Townley, Esq. of Royle, and by her (who *d.* in 1807) had issue (with a younger son, Richard-Townley, who *d. unm.* in 1825, and three daus.) a son and successor,

THOMAS LEGH, Esq. of Adlington, *b.* Sept. 1792; who *m.* Louisa, dau. of George Newnham, Esq. of New Timber Place, Sussex, and by her (who *m.* 2ndly, 12 May, 1830, the Hon. Thomas-Americus Erskine, eldest son of David Montague, Lord Erskine) had issue,

CHARLES-RICHARD-BANASTRE, now of Adlington.
Mary-Anne, *m.* 6 Dec. 1830, to the Hon. and Rev. Augustus Cavendish, 4th son of the late Lord Waterpark.
Marcella-Louisa. Emily-Anne.

Mr. Legh *d.* 25 April, 1829.

Arms—Az., two bars, arg., debruised by a bend, compony, or and gu., for difference.
Crest—A unicorn's head, couped, arg., armed and maned, or, on the neck a cross patonce, gu.
Seat—Adlington Hall, Cheshire.

LEGH OF LYME.

LEGH, THOMAS, Esq., LL.D. and F.A.S. of Lyme Park, co. Chester, and of Haydock Lodge and Golborne Park, co. Lancaster, J.P., *m.* 14 Jan. 1829, Ellen, dau. of William Turner, Esq. of Shrigley Park, co. Chester, M.P. for Blackburne, and by her (who *d.* in 1831) has an only dau.,

Ellen-Jane, *m.* 1847, to Brabazon Lowther, Esq., 4th son of the late Gorges Lowther, Esq.

Mr. Legh represented the family borough of Newton in parliament from 1819 to 1831.

Lineage.—SIR PIERS LEGH, Knt., younger son of Robert Legh, of Adlington, who *d. temp.* RICHARD II., and of Matilda his wife, dau. and co-heiress of Sir John de Arderne, Knt., *m.* in Nov. 1388, Margaret, only dau. and heiress of Sir Thomas Danyers, Knt. of Bradley, and left two sons, PETER (Sir), of Lyme; and John, of Ridge. The elder son of Sir Piers,

SIR PETER LEGH, of Lyme, knight-banneret, accompanying King HENRY to France, distinguished himself in the wars of that valiant prince, and met his death wound on the field of Azincourt, of which he died soon after at Paris. His remains were brought over to England, and interred with his father, at Macclesfield. Sir Peter *m.*

Joan, dau. and heiress of Sir Gilbert Haydock, of Haydock, a Lancashire knight of ancient descent and extensive possessions by whom he left a son and successor,

SIR PETER LEGH, Knt. of Lyme and Haydock, who, enrolling himself under the banner of York, in the wars of the Roses, received the honour of knighthood, at the battle of Wakefield. His descendants were the LEGHS *of Lyme*, one of the most eminent and distinguished of the Cheshire families.

THOMAS-PETER LEGH, Esq. of Golborne (son of the Rev. Ashburnham Legh, of Golborne Park, co. Lancaster), inherited the estates, and became representative of this very ancient family. He represented the borough of Newton in parliament, and was colonel of the Lancashire fencible cavalry. He *d.* 7 Aug. 1797, and was *s.* at Lyme by the present THOMAS LEGH, Esq., who has the following brothers and sisters,

William, *m.* the dau. and heiress of John Wilkinson, Esq. of Castlehead, the celebrated iron-master; and *d.* leaving issue.
Peter, incumbent of Newton.
Maria, *m.* Thomas Claughton, Esq., and has issue.
Margaret, *m.* 8 Jan. 1828, Robert Dalzell, Esq., barrister-at-law.
Emma. Mary.

Arms—Gu., a cross, engrailed, arg., in the chief point, on an inescutcheon, sa., semée of estoiles, arg., an arm in armour, embowed, of the second, the hand ppr., holding a pennon, silver, the whole within a bordure, wavy, arg.
Crest—Issuant out of a ducal coronet, or, a ram's head, arg., armed, or, in the mouth a laurel slip, vert, over all a pallet, wavy, gu.
Seat—Lyme Park, Cheshire.

LEGH OF HIGH LEGH.

LEGH, GEORGE-CORNWALL, Esq. of High Legh, co. Chester, high-sheriff 1838, and M.P. for the northern division of that county, *s.* his father in 1832; *m.* in 1828, Louisa-Charlotte, 2nd dau. of Edward Taylor, Esq. of Bifrons, co. Kent, and niece of Lieut.-Gen. Sir Herbert Taylor, G.C.B., G.C.H.

Lineage.—THOMAS DE LEGA, of Easthall, in the parish of Rostherne, co. Chester, son of Hugh de Lega, son of Oswald de Lega de Easthall, was father of THOMAS DE LEGA, of Easthall, whose son, ADAM LEGH, of the Easthall, was father of HUGH DE LEGH, of the Easthalls, who had a son,

JOHN DE LEGH, of Easthall, in Highlegh, who *m.* Jane, dau. and co-heir of Mathew, Lord of Alpraham, co. Chester, and had three sons. The 2nd son,

JOHN DE LEGH, of Alpraham, had a son and heir, JOHN DE LEGH, who was father of THOMAS DE LEGH, of Northwood, father of THOMAS LEGH, of Northwood, 30 HENRY VI., 1451, whose son, THOMAS LEGH, *m.* Elizabeth, dau. of Godfrey Mellington, and was father of another THOMAS LEGH, living 4 HENRY VIII., who *m.* Margaret, dau. of Richard Charlton, and by her had a son, ROBERT LEGH, who, by Alice his wife, dau. of Hugh Starkey, of Olton, left a son and heir,

THOMAS LEGH, of High Legh, who *m.* Isabel, dau. and heir of Rafe Trafford, of Lancashire, and was *s.* by his son and heir,

ROBERT LEGH, of High Legh, who *m.* Eleanor, dau. of Randoll Spurstow, of Spurstow, and by her had an elder son and heir,

GEORGE LEGH, of High Legh, who *m.* 1st, a dau. of Leycester, of Tabley; and 2ndly, Anne, dau. of John Booth, of Barton, and left a son and successor,

THOMAS LEGH, of High Legh, Esq., who *m.* Barbara, dau. of Thomas Brooke, Esq. of Norton, co. Chester, and by her had (with three daus.) three sons, HENRY, his heir; Thomas, *d. unm.*; and George, a cavalier, slain in the civil war. The eldest son,

HENRY LEGH, Esq. of High Legh, fifty-two years old *anno* 1663, *m.* Dorothy, dau. and sole heir of the Rev. Gregory Turner, of Manley, rector of Sephton, co. Lancaster; and *d.* in 1684, leaving an eldest son and heir,

RICHARD LEGH, Esq. of High Legh, thirty-one years old in 1663, who *m.* in 1675, Mary, dau. of Thomas Legh, Esq. of Adlington, co. Chester; and dying in 1705, was *s.* by his son,

HENRY LEGH, Esq. of High Legh, *b.* in 1679; who *m.* Letitia, dau. of Sir Richard Brooke, of Norton, Bart.; and *d.* in 1757, having had two sons and a dau., viz., GEORGE, his heir; Henry, *d. unm.* in July, 1752, aged about 71; and Mary, wife of the Rev. Legh Richmond, rector of Stockport, co. Chester, who *d.* in 1789. The son and successor,

GEORGE LEGH, Esq. of High Legh, *b.* 10 July, 1703; *m.* Anne-Maria, dau. and heir of Francis Cornwall, Baron of Burford, and by her (who *d.* in 1741) had (with two daus., Letitia, *m.* to the Rev. Egerton Leigh, archdeacon of Salop; and Anna-Maria) two son, HENRY-CORNWALL, his heir; and George-Langton, *b.* 21 May, 1739, *d.* an infant. Mr. Legh *d.* in 1790, and was *s.* by his son and heir,

HENRY-CORNWALL LEGH, Esq. of High Legh, *b.* 24 May, 1734; high-sheriff in 1791; who *m.* in 1761, Elizabeth, dau. and co-heir of Robert Hopkinson, Esq. of Heath, co. York, and by her (who *d.* in April, 1808) had (with two daus., Elizabeth-Dorothea, *d. unm.* in 1777; and Anna-Maria, *m.* 3 Jan. 1788, to Thomas Pitt, Esq. of St. James's, Westminster) two sons, GEORGE-JOHN, his heir; Henry-Cornwall, who *d. unm.* in the West Indies in 1793. Mr. Legh *d.* in 1791, and was *s.* by his elder son,

GEORGE-JOHN LEGH, Esq. of High Legh, *b.* in 1768; high-sheriff in 1805; who *m.* 14 July, 1803, Mary, dau. of John Blackburne, Esq. of Hale, co. Lancaster, M.P., and had issue,

GEORGE-CORNWALL, his heir and present representative.
Henry-Cornwall, in holy orders, *m.* Miss Williams, of Bryngwyn, and has issue.
Anna-Elizabeth, *m.* 8 March, 1832, to Sir Philip de Malpas Grey-Egerton, Bart.
Frances, *m.* to the Rev. Beilby-Porteous Hodgson, son of the dean of Carlisle.
Harriet, *m.* to Herbert Taylor, Esq., captain 85th light-infantry, eldest son of Edward Taylor, Esq. of Bifrons.

Mr. Legh *d.* in 1832.

Arms—Arg., a lion, rampant, gu., langued, az., quartering.
Crest—A demi-lion, rampant, gu., langued, az., collared, or.
Motto—Pour Dieu, pour terre.
Seat—High Legh, co. Chester.

LE HUNTE OF ARTRAMONT.

LE HUNTE, GEORGE, Esq. of Artramont, co. Wexford, J.P., high-sheriff 1836, *b.* 15 June, 1815; *m.* 5 Aug. 1845, Mary, 5th dau. of the Right Hon. Edward Pennefather, and has issue,

I. GEORGE-RUTHVEN, *b.* 20 Aug. 1852.
II. Richard, *b.* 8 Sept. 1854.
I. Mary-Harriet. II. Ellen.

Lineage.—RICHARD LE HUNTE (youngest son of Sir George le Hunte, Knt. of Little Bradley, co. Suffolk, high-sheriff of Suffolk, 1610, by Elizabeth his wife, dau. of Sir John Peyton, Knt. and widow of Sir Anthony Irby), *b.* 10 Aug. 1620, went to Ireland a colonel in the army of CROMWELL, and eventually settling at Cashel, co. Tipperary, represented that city in parliament, *anno* 1661. He *m.* Mary, dau. of Thomas Lloyd, Esq. of Cilcyfedd, co. Pembroke, and was *s.* at his decease (will dated 29 March, 1668) by his eldest son,

GEORGE LE HUNTE, Esq., who *m.* Alice, dau. and heir of Francis Leger, Esq. of Cappagh, in Tipperary, by whom (who re-married, in Sept. 1698, Robert Stewart, Esq. of Castle Rothray, co. Wicklow) he had issue, RICHARD, M.P., *d. s. p.* in 1747; Francis; GEORGE; William, in holy orders; Thomas, barrister-at-law (who left, in 1775, three daus., viz., Anne, wife of the Rev. Dr. Symes; Alice, wife of Samuel Hayes, Esq. of Avondale, co. Wicklow; and Jane, wife of John Lloyd, Esq. of Gloster, King's Co.); Anne, *m.* to Alderman French, of Dublin; Elizabeth, *m.* to the Rev. Mr. Buchanan; and Jane, *m.* to George Warburton, of Garryhinch. Mr. Le Hunte, *d.* at Haverfordwest, 27 May, 1627. His 3rd son,

GEORGE LE HUNTE, Esq. of Ballymartin, co. Wexford, *m.* Editha Jones, an heiress, and was father of

GEORGE LE HUNTE, Esq. of Artramont, co. Wexford. He *m.* Alicia-Maria Corry, and dying in 1799, left, with three daus., of whom, Anne, *m.* S. Purdon, Esq., and Editha, *m.* Sir Henry Meredyth, Bart., five sons, RICHARD, WILLIAM-AUGUSTUS, George, Charles, and Francis. The eldest,

RICHARD LE HUNTE, Esq. of Artramont, *b.* 25 Feb. 1769, *m.* Miss Morgan, and had one son, Richard, who *d.* a minor; and three daus., Maria, *m.* to J.-M. Hobson, Esq., barrister-at-law; Sophia, *m.* to W. Doyle, Esq.; and Louisa, the wife of William-H.-B.-Jordan Wilson, Esq. of Knowle Hall, co. Warwick. Mr. Le Hunte was *s.* at his decease by his brother,

WILLIAM-AUGUSTUS LE HUNTE, Esq. of Artramont, *b.* in 1774, who *m.* 1st, Patty, only dau. of Col. Warburton, of Garryhinch, but by her had no issue; he *m.* 2ndly, Miss J.-M. Huson, eldest dau. of Lieut.-Col. Huson, by whom he had a dau., Alicia; and 3rdly, Henrietta, dau. of the Rev.

Miller, by whom he had issue, George; William-Augustus; Francis; Harriet-Josephine, deceased; Patty-Warburton, deceased; Maria; Marianne; and Edith, m. 7 May, 1839, to the Rev. Yarburgh-Gamaliel LLoyd, 2nd son of George LLoyd, Esq. of Stockton, Yorkshire. Mr. Le Hunte d. 1820.

Arms—Vert, a saltier, arg.
Crest—A lion, sejeant.
Motto—Parcere prostratis.
Seat—Artramont, co. Wexford.

BAINBRIGGE-LE HUNT OF BURGH.

Bainbrigge Le Hunt, Peter, Esq. of Burgh, co. Lincoln, J.P. and D.L., assumed the surname of Le Hunt in 1832, and s. to the estates of his kinswoman, Florence-Matilda Fallows, née Le Hunt.

Lineage.—Thomas Bainbrigge, Esq. of Derby (2nd son of William Bainbrigge, Esq. of Lockington, by his wife, Barbara Wilmot), m. Catherine Parker, of Derby (stated to have been of the noble family of Macclesfield), and had issue. The eldest son,

Thomas Bainbrigge, Esq. of Woodseat, co. Stafford, m. Anne, dau. of Isaac Borrow or Borough, Esq. of Castlefields, co. Derby, and had issue,

Thomas, d. unm.
Joseph, m. 1st, Honor Gell; and 2ndly, Hannah Harrison, but by the latter only had issue.
John, d. unm.
Philip, of whom we treat.

The youngest son,

Philip Bainbrigge, Esq. of Ashbourne, lieut.-col. in the army, m. 19 March, 1781, Rachel, 2nd dau. of Peter Dobree, Esq. of Guernsey, and by her (who d. 4 May, 1842) had,

Philip, lieut.-gen. in the army, C.B., m. Sarah-Mary Fletcher, of Liverpool, and has issue.
John-Hankey, col. in the army, fort-major of Guernsey, m. his cousin, Sophia Dobree, and has issue.
Peter, the present Peter Bainbrigge Le Hunt, Esq.
Thomas, late capt. 57th regt., m. Miss Sarah Bate, and d. at sea, in April, 1834, leaving issue.
Harriet, m. to Lieut.-Col. Robert Dale, who was killed at New Orleans in 1815; she d. s. p. in April, 1836.
Honor-Elizabeth, d. unm. in 1833.
Rachel-Dobree.
Anne, m. to Samuel Dobree, Esq., jun., of Walthamstow, d. in 1815.

Col. Bainbrigge was killed in battle in Holland, 6 Oct. 1799.

Arms—Quarterly: 1st and 4th, az., a bend, between six leopards' faces, or, on a canton of the field, a gauntlet of the second, for difference, for Le Hunte; 2nd and 3rd, arg., a chevron, embattled, between three battle-axes, sa., for Bainbrigge.
Crests—1st, a leopard's face, between two wings displayed, for Le Hunte; 2nd, a goat, sa., horned and hoofed, arg., a collar about his neck, standing on a hill, vert, for Bainbrigge.
Motto—Deus mihi providebit.
Residence—Ashbourn, co. Derby.

LEIGH OF WEST HALL, HIGH LEIGH.

Leigh, Egerton, Esq. of the West Hall, High Leigh, and of Jodrell Hall, co. Chester, J.P. and D.L., high-sheriff 1836; b. 23 Aug. 1779; m. 26 Dec. 1809, Wilhelmina-Sarah, dau. of the late George Stratton, Esq. of Tew Park, co. Oxford, and has had issue,

I. Egerton, b. 1815, late a capt. 2nd drag.-guards, and now major 1st royal Cheshire militia, m. 20 Sept. 1842, Lydia-Rachel, dau. and co-heir of John-Smith Wright, Esq. of Rempstone Hall, Notts, and has issue,
   1 Egerton, b. 18 July, 1843.
   2 John-Jodrell, b. 21 April, 1845.
   3 Edward-Egerton. 4 Neville-Egerton.
   5 Arthur-Egerton.
   1 Eleanor-Egerton-Sophia.
I. Eleanor-Agnes, d. unm. 20 Nov. 1837.
II. Anna-Elizabeth.
III. Beatrice-Julia, m. 1845, to the Rev. John-Oliver Hopkins, of Uffington, co. Salop.
IV. Caroline.
V. Augusta, m. to Charles Gresley, Esq. of The Close, Lichfield.

Lineage.—Old and honourable as is the descent of the Leghs of the West Hall, the Lymmes, from whom they originally sprang, were even still more ancient. Ormerod conjectures Lymme to have been a collateral branch of the Barons of Halton. Agnes de Legh, heiress of the West Hall, in High Leigh, m. temp. Henry III., Richard de Lymme, and was mother of

Thomas de Legh, named from the place of his residence, from whom descended the eminent and highly allied family of Leigh, of West Hall, High Leigh; the male representative of which, towards the close of the 17th century was

The Rev. Peter Leigh, M.A., vicar of Great Budworth, rector of Lymme and of Whitchurch, co. Salop. He m. Elizabeth,* dau. of the Hon. Thomas Egerton, of Tatton Park (3rd son of John, 2nd Earl of Bridgewater, by his wife, Elizabeth, dau. of William Cavendish, Duke of Newcastle), and had issue, Egerton, heir to his uncle Austine; John; Thomas, rector of Murston, co. Kent, and ancestor of the Leighs of Leatherlake House; Peter, ancestor of Sir Egerton Leigh, Bart.; Jane; Hester; and Mary, m. to the Rev. Sir John Head, Bart., archdeacon and prebendary of Canterbury. Peter Leigh d. in 1719. His eldest son,

The Rev. Egerton Leigh, LL.D., of the West Hall, rector of Lymme and Middle, co. Salop, canon-residentiary of Hereford, and master of the hospital of St. Katherine, at Ledbury, bapt. 30 March, 1702, m. 1st, Anne dau. and co-heiress of Hamlet Yates, Esq. of Crowley, and had issue, I. Peter, his heir; II. Thomas; III. Hamlet; IV. Egerton, M.A., forty years rector of Lymme, canon-residentiary of Lichfield, and archdeacon of Salop, m. 1st, Letitia, dau. of George Legh, Esq. of the East Hall, by whom he had no issue, and 2ndly Theodosia, dau. of Ralph Leycester, Esq. of Toft, and d. in Sept. 1798, aged 66, leaving two daus., Susanna, m. to Ralph Leycester, jun., Esq., M.P., and Theodosia; I. Mary; II. Anne, m. 1st, to the Rev. Mr. Felton, and 2ndly, to the Rev. Mr. Cockayne; and III. Elizabeth. Dr. Egerton Leigh m. 2ndly, Elizabeth Drinkwater, and had by her, I. John; II. William; III. Austine; IV. Samuel; V. George, d. unm. in 1816; VI. William; I. Hester; and II. Jane. He m. 3rdly, Cassandra Phelps, and had issue, Henry, Cassandra, Ariana, and Catherine. He d. at Bath, in 1760. His son and successor,

The Rev. Peter Leigh, LL.B., rector of Lymme and Middle, m. Mary, dau. and co-heiress of Henry Doughty, Esq. of Broadwell, co. Gloucester. He d. before his father, in 1758, leaving issue, I. Egerton, his heir; II. Thomas-Hodges; III. Peter-Neve; IV. Timothy, d. unm. in the East Indies, in 1814; I. Mary, m. to Robert Lancaster, vicar of Arlsey, co. Bedford; II. Anne, m. to John Frodsham, capt. R.N.; and III. Elizabeth, who d. unm. The son and heir,

Egerton Leigh, Esq. of the West Hall, High Leigh, and of Twemlow, b. 25 Oct. 1752, m. 21 Sept. 1778, Elizabeth, dau. and co-heiress of Francis Jodrell, Esq. of Yeardsley and Twemlow, co. Chester, and by her (who d. 12 March, 1807) had issue, I. Egerton, now of the West Hall, High Leigh; II. Peter, M.A., rector of Lymme, b. 20 Aug. 1782, m. 10 Nov. 1812, Mary, dau. of Thomas Blackburne, clerk, LL.D., warden of Manchester College: she d. 19 July, 1819, aged 30 and Peter Leigh m. 2ndly, 18 March, 1828, Jane, dau. of Harriot Steward, Esq. of Watford, Herts; III. Jodrell, capt. R.N. of Broadwell, co. Gloucester, b. 15 Jan. 1790; I. Mary-Anne, m. 14 June, 1802, the Right Hon. James Abercromby, Lord Dunfermline; II. Charlotte, m. Joseph Jellicoe, Esq. of Finchley, co. Middlesex, she d. at Rome, in 1823; III. Emma, m. 1 May, 1811, John Smith, Esq., M.P., of Dale Park, co. Sussex (brother of Lord Carrington); IV. Augusta, m. in 1821, to Thomas Dumbleton, Esq. of Hall Grove, co. Surrey; V. Caroline; and VI. Harriet, d. unm. in 1809. Mr. Leigh d. 22 June, 1833.

Arms—Or, a lion rampant, gu.
Crest—A cubit arm, vested, paly of five pieces, or and sa., cuffed, arg., hand, ppr., grasping the upper and lower fragments of a broken tilting-spear, the point upwards.
Motto—Force avec vertu.
Seat—West Hall, High Leigh, and Jodrell Hall, co. Chester.

LEIGH OF LEATHERLAKE HOUSE.

Leigh, The Rev. James-Allett, of Leatherlake House, Runnymeade, Surrey, M.A., b. 21 Sept. 1770; m. 26 Dec. 1796, Sarah, eldest dau. of Robert Smith, Esq. of Butts Lodge, Bishop's Waltham, by Sarah his wife, dau. of Robert Friend, Esq. of Wellow, and

* In direct descent from Henry VII., by his dau., Mary, Queen-Dowager of France, and Duchess of Suffolk, and her posterity.

first-cousin of Dr. Newcome, archbishop of Armagh. By this lady (who *d.* 29 Sept. 1824) he has had issue,

I. JAMES-ALLETT, *b.* 27 Feb. 1799, *m.* 1831, Susanna-Frances-Lurania, eldest dau. of John Birch, Esq., and Susanna, his wife, one of the last descendants of the poet Milton, and by her (who *d.* 10 March, 1854) has issue,

1 EGERTON-PIERS-ALLETT, bapt. 21 Sept. 1832.
2 Walter-Edward-Egerton, *b.* 10 April, 1843.
1 Augusta-Susanna-Egerton.
2 Ada-Egerton. 3 Alice-Egerton.
4 Laurette-Egerton.

II. Frederick-Augustus, *b.* 3 Nov. 1800, *d.* in 1806.
I. Arabella-Diana, *m.* 26 Dec. 1847, John-Henry Nelson, Esq. of Dublin, and *d.* a widow, 13 Sept. 1852.
II. Georgiana-Caroline, *d.* 3 Jan. 1811.

Lineage.—This is a branch of the LEIGHS of West Hall, in High Leigh.

THE REV. THOMAS LEIGH, M.A., *b.* 1706, rector and patron of Murston, in Kent, and rector of St. Margaret's, in Canterbury, was third son of the Rev. Peter Leigh, M.A. of the West Hall, High Leigh, by Elizabeth, his wife, dau. of the Hon. Thomas Egerton, of Tatton Park, co. Chester, 3rd son of John, 2nd Earl of Bridgewater. He *m.* Jane, dau. of J. Barnes, Esq., and widow of Thomas Allett, Esq., brother of John Allett, Esq. of Leatherlake House, Runnymeade, high-sheriff of Berks in 1750. By her he had issue,

EGERTON, in holy orders, his heir.
Elizabeth, *d. unm.*
Charlotte, *m.* 1762, to the Rev. Johnson Lawson, M.A., vicar of Throwley, in Kent, and Dean of Battle.

The Rev. Thomas Leigh *d.* 19 April, 1774, and was *s.* by his son,

THE REV. EGERTON LEIGH, LL.S., rector and patron of Murston, in Kent, and vicar of Tilmanstone, bapt. 25 Jan. 1735, *m.* 1768, Sarah, youngest dau. of John Stone, Esq. of Langley, in Bucks, and had issue,

JAMES-ALLETT, of Leatherlake House.
Egerton-Peers, of Langley Place, Bucks, and Chertsey Abbey, Surrey, *b.* 23 April, 1774, *d. unm.* 20 May, 1832.
Elizabeth-Jane, *m.* 29 Sept. 1792, Anthony-Harvest Isaacson, Esq., and *d.* 24 July, 1839, leaving issue.
Charlotte-Priscilla, *m.* to Solomon Hudson, of Chertsey, in Surrey, and *d.* 10 April, 1837, leaving an only dau.

The Rev. Egerton Leigh *d.* in 1788.

Arms, &c.—See LEIGH *of West Hall.*
Seat—Leatherlake House, Egham.

LEIGH OF PONTY-POOL.

HANBURY-LEIGH, CAPEL, Esq. of Ponty-Pool Park, co. Monmouth, lord-lieutenant of that county, *b.* 6 Oct. 1776; *m.* 1st, 13 April, 1797, Molly-Anne, only dau. of Nathaniel Myers, Esq. of Neath, co. Glamorgan, and relict of Sir R.-H. Mackworth, Bart.; and 2ndly, 20 Aug. 1847, Emma-Elizabeth, 4th dau. of the late Thomas-Bates Rous, Esq. of Courtyrala, co. Glamorgan, and by her has issue,

I. JOHN-CAPEL, *b.* 14 May, 1853.
I. Emma-Charlotte. II. Frances-Elizabeth.

This gentleman assumed the surname and arms of LEIGH in 1797.

Lineage.—This family derives, in the male line, from the Hanburys of Hanbury, an old Worcestershire house, which had been there seated from a remote period. In the female line the present Capel Hanbury Leigh, Esq., descends from an heiress of the Lords Leigh, of Stoneleigh, the representatives of a distinguished branch of the great Cheshire house of Leigh.

HENRY DE HANBURY, son of Geoffrey de Hanbury, of Hanbury, and grandson of Geoffrey de Hanbury, living at Hanbury, *temp.* JOHN, was lord chief-justice of the Common Pleas in Ireland, *temp.* EDWARD II., and *d.* about the year 1353. His son and heir,

REGINALD DE HANBURY, M.P. for Worcestershire, 37 EDW. III., was father of

ROGER DE HANBURY, M.P. for Worcestershire, living at Hanbury, *temp.* RICHARD II., whose son and successor,

JOHN DE HANBURY, of Hanbury, A.D. 1400, *m.* and had issue,

WILLIAM, of Hanbury Hall, father, by Margery his wife, of JOHN HANBURY, Esq. of Hanbury Hall, co. Worcester, ancestor of the HANBURYS of that place.
JOHN, of Beanhall, manor of Feckenham, co. Worcester, whose son, EDWARD HANBURY, Esq. of Bean Hall, was ancestor of the HANBURYS *of Kelmarsh*, now represented by LORD BATEMAN.
RICHARD, of whose descendants we treat.

The 3rd son,

RICHARD HANBURY, Esq., *m.* and was father of

RICHARD HANBURY, Esq., who *m.* 1st, Catharine Smyth, by whom he had a son, RICHARD, of Elmley Lovett; and 2ndly, Margery Tynter, by whom he had a son, Henry, ancestor of the HANBURYS *of Hampshire*. The eldest son,

RICHARD HANBURY, Esq. of Elmley Lovett, co. Worcester, *m.* a lady named Basset, and had issue three sons, John, Thomas, and William. The eldest,

JOHN HANBURY, Esq., was of Elmley Lovett. He *m.* 1st, Edith, dau. of John Broade, of Elmley Lovett, and by her had issue,

RICHARD, of Riding Court, Datchet, Bucks, *m.* Alice, dau. of Jasper Fisher, Esq., and *d.* 1608, having had two daus., his co-heirs, Alice, who *m.* William Combes, Esq., but *d. s. p.*; and Elizabeth, *m.* to Sir Edmund Wheler, Knt. of London.
Alice, *m.* to Francis Barnard, of London.

Mr. Hanbury *m.* a second time, and had further issue,

RICHARD, of whom presently. Philip, *d. s. p.*
Joyce, *m.* and had issue.
Fortune, *m.* and had issue.

The eldest son of the 2nd marriage,

RICHARD HANBURY, Esq. of Elmley Lovett, *m.* Margery, dau. of Francis Bradley, Esq., and left issue, 1 JOHN, his heir; 2 Philip, *m.* and had issue; 3 Rose, *m.* to Richard Budd, Esq., auditor to JAMES I. and CHARLES I.; and 1 a dau., *m.* to Rev. John Cole, B.A., vicar of Elmley Lovett. The son and heir,

JOHN HANBURY, Esq. of Fakenham, co. Worcester, M.P. for the city of Gloucester, in 1626, was a stanch parliamentarian, high in the confidence of OLIVER CROMWELL by whom he was appointed sheriff of Worcester, in 1649–50. In 1623 he recorded his pedigree in the Visitation of Gloucestershire, and obtained the crest of Hanbury from Camden, being described as of Purcell's Green, co. Worcester. He *m.* Anne, dau. of Christopher Capel, Esq. of Capel House, in Herefordshire, alderman and M.P. of Gloucester; and dying in 1659, left issue, 1 John, *d. v. p.*; 2 Richard, *d. s. p.* 1661; 3 Christopher, *d. v. p.*; 4 CAPEL, of whom we treat; 5 John, living 1657, and a dau., *m.* to Gregory Wiltshire. The fourth son,

CAPEL HANBURY, Esq. of Gloucester and of Whorestone, in Worcestershire, purchased Pontypool 1665. He *m.* 1st, Elizabeth Capel, 2ndly, Honor, dau. of Edward Salwey, Esq. of Stanford, M.P., and 3rdly Elizabeth, dau. of Sir — Smith, Knt. of Kent, widow of 1st of William Ackworth, Esq., and 2ndly, of Robert Foley, Esq. of Stourbridge. His second and third wives *d. s.p.* By the first wife he left a dau., Mary, *m.* to Mr. Serjeant John Hoo, and a son and successor,

JOHN HANBURY, Esq. of Ponty-Pool Park, in Monmouthshire, M.P. for that co., and a major in the army; who *m.* in 1703, Bridget eldest dau. and co-heir of Sir Edward Ayscough, of Stallinborough, co. Lincoln, and *d.* 13 June, 1734, leaving (with other children who *d. s. p.*)

I. CAPEL, of whom presently.
II. Charles (Sir) K.B. of Coldbrook Park, co. Monmouth, *b.* 8 Dec. 1709; M.P. for Monmouth; *m.* in 1732, Frances, 2nd dau. and co-heir of Thomas, Earl of Coningsby, and had two daus., his co-heirs,

1 FRANCES, *m.* in 1754, to William, 4th Earl of Essex.
2 CHARLOTTE, *m.* in 1759, to the Hon. Robert Boyle.

Sir Charles, who assumed the surname of WILLIAMS, *d.* 17 Nov. 1759.

III. George, of Coldbrook, *b.* 23 Sept. 1715, who assumed the surname of WILLIAMS at the decease of his brother, Sir Charles Hanbury Williams. He *m.* Miss Chambrè, dau. of John Chambrè, Esq. of Lanfoist, and *d.* in 1764, leaving issue.
IV. Thomas, *d.* in 1778, leaving issue.

The eldest son, to leave issue,

CAPEL HANBURY, Esq. of Ponty-Pool Park, M.P. for Monmouth, *b.* 2 Dec. 1707, *m.* 7 Oct. 1743, Jane, dau. of Thomas-Charles, fifth Viscount Tracy, and great-granddau. of John, third Viscount Tracy, by ELIZABETH, his wife, eldest dau. of Thomas Leigh, first LORD LEIGH, of Stoneleigh, and dying 7 Dec. 1765, left, with two daus., Henrietta and Frances, one son,

JOHN HANBURY, Esq. of Ponty-Pool Park, M.P. for the co. Monmouth, *b.* 5 Aug. 1744, who *m.* Jane, dau. of Morgan Lewis, Esq. of St. Pierre, in that shire, and by her (wh

2ndly, Thomas Stoughton, Esq. of Ballyhorgan, co. Kerry) left at his decease, 4 April, 1784,

John-Capel, *d. unm.*, aged 21, in 1796.
CAPEL, now of Ponty-Pool Park.
CHARLES, created BARON SUDELEY. (*See* BURKE's *Peerage.*)

Arms—Quarterly: 1st and 4th, gu., a cross, engr., arg., in the first quarter a lozenge, of the second, for LEIGH; 2nd and 3rd, or, a bend, engr., vert, plain, cottised, sa., for HANBURY.
Crests—1st, a unicorn's head, erased, arg., armed, and crined, or, for LEIGH; 2nd, out of a mural crown, sa., a demi-lion, rampant, or, holding in the paws a battle-axe, sa., helved, gold, for HANBURY.
Seat—Ponty-Pool Park, Monmouthshire.

LEIGH OF BARDON.

LEIGH, ROBERT, Esq. of Taunton, *b.* in 1774; late captain 1st Somerset militia, and a deputy-lieut. for that county.

Lineage.—This is a branch of an ancient Devonshire family, Walter de Lega having, as appears by Sir William Pole's collections towards a description of Devon, held lands therein in the reign of HENRY II. Lysons, in the sixth volume of his "Magna Britannia," in his account of families extinct since 1620, or removed out of the county, states, that "Leigh, of Ridge, in Bishop's Morchard, married the heiress of Ridge. Ten descents are described in the Visitation of 1620, when there was male issue."

ROBERT LEIGH, a scion of the Leighs of Ridge, removed out of Devonshire, and settled at Bardon, in Somersetshire, A.D. 1525. His direct descendant,

ROBERT LEIGH, Esq. of Bardon (second son of William Leigh, Esq., by his wife Rebecca Sanders, of Yeovil, whose mother was Susanna Dampier, of the Bruton family) *m.* in 1770, Maria Bourget, a native of Berlin, and had issue,

ROBERT, his heir.
William, of Bardon, having purchased the estate from his elder brother, *m.* Frances-Wilson, eldest dau. of Thomas Oliver, Esq. of London, and had two sons and five daus. Robert, the elder son, *m.* in 1828, Charlotte, third dau. of the late Samuel Cox, Esq. of Beaminster, in Dorset.
Henry-James, of Taunton, who *m.* Miss Anne-Whitmarsh Waters, of Blandford, in Dorsetshire.
Frederick, who *m.* Anna Kennaway, of Exeter, niece of Sir John Kennaway, Bart.
John, in holy orders, *d. unm.*
Mary, *m.* to the Rev. Robert Tripp.
Anne, *m.* 1st, to Montague-Bere Baker Bere, Esq. of Morebath, in Devon; 2ndly, to John-Burgess Karslake, Esq. of the same county; and 3rdly, to Richard-C. Campion, Esq. of Exeter.

Mr. Leigh *d.* in 1798, and was *s.* by his eldest son, the present ROBERT LEIGH, Esq.

Arms—Arg., two bars, az., a bend, componé, or and gu.
Crest—A demi-lion, rampant, armed and langued, gu.
Motto—Legibus antiquis.

LEIGH OF HINDLEY HALL.

(*See* PEMBERTON-LEIGH.)

LEIGH OF BELMONT.

LEIGH, JOSEPH, Esq. of Belmont, co. Chester, *b.* 7 May, 1830; *m.* 6 Oct. 1852, Fanny-Penelope, eldest dau. of the Rev. F.-Streynsham Master, rector of Chorley, and canon of Manchester.

Lineage.—This family claims to be a branch of the ancient family of Leigh of High Leigh.

JOSEPH LEIGH, Esq. of Belmont, *b.* 25 Oct. 1768, *m.* 21 Oct. 1794, Margaret Sherlock, and had issue,

I. JAMES-HEATH, of Belmont and Grappenhall Lodge, J.P. and D.L., high-sheriff in 1835, *m.* 9 Oct. 1827, Frances, 3rd dau. of Sir Oswald Mosley, Bart. of Rolleston Hall, co. Stafford, by whom he had,
1 JOSEPH, his heir, now of Belmont.
2 James-Mosley, *b.* 16 March, 1832, *m.* 28 June, 1855, Susan-Mary, 2nd dau. of Captain Wynyard, R.N., and niece of the late Edward Lloyd, Esq. of Oldfield Hall, co. Cheshire.
3 Oswald-Peter, *b.* 20 Sept. 1833, lieut. 22nd regt.
4 John, *b.* 5 July, 1835. 5 Albert, *b.* 26 Aug. 1841.
6 Henry-Alfred, *b.* 14 March, 1846.
1 Frances. 2 Amy-Sophia.
II. John, in holy orders, rector of Egginton, co. Derby, *b.* 8 Feb. 1798.

Mr. Leigh *d.* 5 Aug. 1848.

Arms—Gu., a cross, engr., arg.; in the 1st quarter, a lion, rampant, or; and in the 2nd, a lozenge, of the second.
Crest—A lozenge, gu., charged with an unicorn's head, couped, arg., crined, or.
Motto—Leges juraque servo.
Seat—Belmont, co. Chester.

LEIGH OF BROWNSOVER HALL.

WARD-BOUGHTON-LEIGH, JOHN, Esq. of Brownsover Hall, co. Warwick, J.P. and D.L.; *m.* in 1811, Theodosia de Malmsburgh, only dau. and heir of Sir Egerton Leigh, Bart., by Theodosia his wife, dau. of Sir Edward Boughton, Bart., and has had,

I. JOHN, late 1st dragoon-guards, deceased.
I. Theodosia. II. Grace. III. Jemima.
And other issue.

This gentleman, who is 4th son of the late William-Zouch Lucas-Ward, Esq. of Guilsborough Park, co. Northampton, assumed, by sign-manual, in 1831, the additional surnames and arms of BOUGHTON and LEIGH.

Lineage.—*See* WARD.

Arms—Quarterly, LEIGH, BOUGHTON, and WARD.
Crest—LEIGH, BOUGHTON, and WARD.
Seat—Brownsover Hall, co. Warwick.

LEIGHTON OF BAUSELEY.

LEIGHTON, THE REV. FRANCIS-KNYVETT, M.A., of Bausley, or Ballsley, co. Montgomery, late fellow of All Souls' College, and now rector of Harpeden, co. Oxon, *b.* 2 July, 1806; *m.* 23 Feb. 1843, Catherine, 2nd dau. of the Hon. and Rev. James St. Leger, 3rd son of the 1st Viscount Doneraile, and has had issue,

I. FRANCIS ST. LEGER-KNYVETT, *b.* 27 Aug. 1850, *d.* 28 Aug. 1855.
II. Charles-Arthur-Baldwin-Knyvett, *b.* 9 Nov. 1854.
I. Louisa-Catherine-Clare. II. Caroline-Alice-Jane.

Lineage.—The family of LEIGHTON was in England long before the Norman Conquest, and Camden, in his "Britannia," styles it *Nobilem et Equestrem Familiam.*

DANIEL LEIGHTON, Esq., a lieut.-col. in Gen. Evans's horse, 2nd son of Sir Edward Leighton, 1st Bart. of Watlesborough, *m.* Jane, dau. of Nathaniel Thorold, Esq. of the city of London, and had (with two daus., Jane, *m.* 1st, to Capt. Cathcart, and 2ndly, to Jonathan, eldest son of Sir John Cope, Bart.; and the younger, *m.* to Captain Sabine) two sons, HERBERT, his heir; and Edward, lieut. R.N., *d. unm.* Col. Leighton was *s.* at his decease by his elder son,

HERBERT LEIGHTON, Esq., a capt. in the army, gentleman-usher to Frederick, Prince of Wales (father of King GEORGE III.), and page to the Princess Dowager of Wales. He *m.* Harriet, eldest dau. of Henry Wilson, Esq. of Ashwelthorpe, co. Norfolk, by Elizabeth, eldest dau. and co-heir of John Knyvett, and had a son and successor,

THE REV. FRANCIS LEIGHTON, who *m.* Clare, sister and co-heir of John-Boynton Adams, Esq. of Camblesforth, co. York, by whom he had a son and heir,

COL. FRANCIS-KNYVETT LEIGHTON, *b.* 1772, who *m.* July, 1805, Hon. Louisa-Anne St. Leger, dau. of St. Leger Aldworth, 1st Viscount Doneraile, and by her (who *d.* 1849) had issue,

FRANCIS-KNYVETT, present representative.
Louisa-Anne, *m.* 23 April, 1833, to Thomas-H. Hope-Edwardes, Esq. of Notley, high-sheriff of the co. of Gloucester in 1837.
Clare.

Col. Leighton *d.* 19 Nov. 1834.

Arms—Quarterly, per fesse, indented, or, and gu.
Crest—A wyvern, with wings expanded, sa.
Motto—Dread shame.
Residence—Harpeden Rectory, Henley-on-Thames.

LEIR OF JAGGARD'S HOUSE.

LEIR, THOMAS-MACIE, Esq. of Jaggard's House, co. Wilts, *b.* 19 Nov. 1795; *m.* Miss Collard, of Swansea, and has issue,

I. THOMAS. II. Charles. III. Henry.
I. Anne. II. Jane. III. Maria.
IV. Isabella.

Lineage.—This family, originally of German descent, riving, it is said, its patronymic from the town of Leer, the Ems, in Westphalia, has been seated many centuries the co. of Devon. Sir Peter Lear, its chief, was created Bart. in the year 1660, and possessed very extensive operty and manors. The first that settled in Somersetire was the Rev. Richard Leir, rector of Charlton Musgrove, great-great-grandfather of

The Rev. Thomas Leir, b. 14 April, 1738 (son of the Rev. Thomas Leir, incumbent of Ditcheat and Charlton Musgrove, by Elizabeth his wife, dau. of Paul Methuen, Esq.), who s. his father in the livings of Ditcheat and Charlton, in 1781. He m. Mary, dau. of John Shore, Esq., Mary his wife, dau. of John Kington, Esq. of Jaggard's House, Wilts, and had issue six sons and three daus., several of whom d. s. p.: the others were,

Thomas, his heir.
William, b. 10 Sept. 1768, s. his father in the living of Ditcheat, in 1812, m. Harriott, dau. of Randolph Marriott, Esq. of Leases Hall, Yorkshire, by Elizabeth his wife, dau. of Christopher Wilson, lord bishop of Bristol, and had two sons and seven daus., viz., William-Marriott, M.A., m. Mary-Anne, dau. of Edward Langford, Esq. of Trungle; Charles-Marriott, B.A.; Harriett-Mary, wife of George-Augustus Woodforde, Esq.; Elizabeth; Charlotte; Marianne; Sophia, m. to Capt. Charles Dawe; Emma; Frances; and Hester, m. to William-Frederick Robinson, Esq.
Paul, b. 9 June, 1770, s. his father in the living of Charlton Musgrove, in 1812, m. Fanny, widow of William-Morton Pleydell, Esq. of Whatcombe, Dorset, and dau. of William Frake, Esq. of Hannington House, Wilts.
Richard, b. 17 Jan. 1772, barrister-at-law.

The eldest son,

Thomas Leir, Esq. of Weston, J.P., b. 17 Oct. 1765, m. Anne, dau. of the Rev. John Jekyll, D.D., Vicar of Evercreech, and precentor of St. David's Cathedral, and left issue, Thomas-Macie, his heir; John-Macie; Jane-Elizabeth; Mary, wife of the Rev. Edward Wilkins; Anne; and Helen. Mr. Leir d. 9 May, 1836.

Arms—Az., a fesse, raguly, between three unicorns' heads, erased, or.
Crest—A demi-unicorn, rampant, having between his legs a staff, raguly.
Seats—Jaggard's House, Wilts, and Weston, co. Somerset.

LEITH OF WHITEHAUGH.

(*See* Forbes-Leith).

LEITH-HAY OF RANNES AND LEITH HALL.

Leith-Hay, Sir Andrew, Knt. of Rannes and Leith Hall, co. Aberdeen, K.H., J.P. and D.L., lieut.-col. in the army, late M.P. for the Elgin district of burghs, b. 17 Feb. 1785; m. 1816, Mary-Margaret, dau. of William Clark, Esq. of Buckland House, and has issue,

I. Alexander-Sebastian, b. 12 Feb. 1818.
II. William, b. 31 July, 1819; married.
III. James, b. 26 Nov. 1820; married.
IV. Norman, b. 19 Aug. 1829.
V. Charles, b. 18 Oct. 1831.
I. Caroline-Elizabeth.

Lineage.—The surname of Leith is of great antiquity in Scotland, and those who bore it held, in a remote era, vast possessions, including the Barony of Restalrig, and others in the shire of Mid-Lothian and territory of Leith, whence, it is presumed, the name was assumed. The immediate ancestor of the family before us,

William Leith, of Barnis, living in the time of David Bruce, and said to have been the male representative of the Leiths *of Edingarrock*, was provost of Aberdeen in 1350, and proprietor of the lands of Caprington, in Aberdeenshire. He m. a dau. of Donald, 12th Earl of Marr, and had two sons, Laurence, his heir; and John, ambassador to the court of England in 1412. William Leith d. some time in the reign of Robert II., and was s. by his elder son,

Laurence Leith, of Barnis, co. Aberdeen. Provost of Aberdeen in 1401, 1403, and 1411, from whom descended

James Leith, of New Leslie, who m. Margaret, dau. of Alexander Strachan, of Glenkindy, and had issue, John, his heir; Alexander, ancestor of the Leiths *of Glenkindy and Freefield;* William, d. s. p.; Margaret, m. to Gordon, of Beldornie; and Jean, m. to John Grant, of Tomavillion. He was s. at his decease by his eldest son,

John Leith, Esq. of Leith Hall, who m. Janet Ogilvie, dau. of George, 2nd Lord Banff, by Agnes Falconer his wife, dau. of Alexander, 1st Lord Halkerton, and had issue, John, his successor; Patrick; George, of Blackhall; Laurence; Anthony; and Elizabeth, m. to Richard Gordon, Esq. of Craigmile. Mr. Leith, acquiring the whole estate of Leslie, in the Garrock, regained possession of the lands of Edingarrock, his ancient patrimonial inheritance. He d. in 1727, and was s. by his eldest son,

John Leith, Esq. of Leith Hall, who m. Mary, dau. of Charles Hay, Esq. of Rannes; and dying in 1736, left (with a dau., Janet, m. to James Gordon, of Ardmilie) a son and heir,

John Leith, Esq. of Leith Hall, who augmented his estate by the lands of Lair and Ardlair. He m. Harriot, dau. and heiress of Alexander Steuart, of Auchluncart, and had three sons, viz.,

John, } heirs in succession.
Alexander, }
James (Sir), a lieut.-gen. in the army, G.C.B., K.T.S., Grand Cordon of the Order of Merit of France, governor of Barbadoes, and commander of the forces in the Windward and Leeward Islands. Sir James Leith d. 16 Oct. 1816.

John Leith d. in 1763, and was s. by his eldest son,

John Leith, Esq. of Leith Hall, at whose decease, without issue, in 1778, the estates devolved on his brother,

Alexander Leith, who, having s. Andrew Hay, of Rannes, was the late Gen. Alexander Leith-Hay, of Rannes and Leith Hall. This gentleman, who was b. in 1758; m. in 1784, Mary, dau. of Charles Forbes, Esq. of Ballogie, and by her (who d. 1824) had issue,

Andrew, his heir.
John, rear-admiral R.N., d. Oct. 1854, leaving two sons and two daus.
Harriet-Christian, m. to Sir Harry-N. Lumsden, Bart.; and d. in 1820.
Mary, widow of Major Mitchell, of Ashgrove.
Elizabeth, m. to Alexander Forbes, Esq. of Blackford.
Margaret.

Gen. Hay d. 11 May, 1838.

Arms—Quarterly: 1st and 4th, or, a cross-crosslet, fitchée, sa., between three crescents, in chief, and as many fusils, in base, barways, gu.; 2nd and 3rd, quarterly, 1st and 4th, arg., three inescutcheons, gu.; 2nd and 3rd, gu., three cinquefoils, arg.
Crests—A cross-crosslet, fitchée, sa., and a goat, trippant, ppr.
Supporters—Two naked men, wreathed about the loins, each holding in his exterior hand a club.
Mottoes—Trustie to the end; spare nought.
Seats—Leith Hall, and Leslie House, Aberdeenshire.

LEMAN OF BRAMPTON HALL.

Orgill-Leman, Rev. George, of Brampton Hall, co. Suffolk, b. 1789.

Lineage.—The Rev. Naunton-Thomas Orgill, of Brampton Hall, b. 11 Dec. 1759, (son of William Orgill, Esq. of Beccles, and Susan Leman his wife, 3rd dau. and co-heir of William Leman, Esq., by Sarah, his wife, dau. of Thomas Leman, Esq. of Brampton Hall, grandson of Thomas Leman, Esq. of Brampton, nephew of Sir John Leman *see* Burke's *Extinct Baronetage*) assumed the surname of his maternal ancestors in addition to his patronymic. He m. 3 Dec. 1783, Henrietta-Jane, 4th dau. of Sir William Anderson, Bart. of Lea, co. Lincoln; and d. 1837, having had issue,

George, his heir, now of Brampton Hall.
Naunton, b. 1792; d. unm. 1818.
Robert, b. 1799; in holy orders; m. 25 March, 1824, Isabella-Camilla, dau. of the late Sir William-Jervis Twysden, Bart., and by her (who d. 7 March, 1850) has issue, Robert, Francis, and John.
Charles, b. 1801; d. unm. 1815.
William, b. 1802; d. unm. 1843.
Thomas, in holy orders, b. 1804; m. 1838, Emily, dau. of the Rev. J. Guerin.
Elizabeth-Mary, d. unm. 1842.
Charlotte, d. 1796.
Susan, d. unm. 1856.
Harriet, d. unm. 1834.
Frances, m. 1820, to Molyneux Shuldham, Esq.
Anne, m. 1812, to Thomas Geo, Esq.
Charlotte, m. 1821, to George Barlee, Esq.

Arms—Az., a fesse, between three dolphins, naiant, arg.
Crest—Arg., on a lemon-tree, a pelican in her piety, ppr.
Motto—Volens semperque juvare paratus.
Seat—Brampton Hall, Suffolk.

LENDRUM OF JAMESTOWN.

LENDRUM, JAMES, Esq. of Jamestown, co. Fermanagh, J.P. and D.L., high-sheriff for co. Fermanagh 1835, and for co. Tyrone 1837, *b.* 12 Jan. 1806; *m.* 2 Nov. 1843, Anne, eldest dau. of Samuel Vesey, Esq., and has issue,

I. GEORGE-COSBY, *b.* 2 April, 1846.
II. James-Vesey, twin with his brother George.
III. William-Trevor, *b.* 4 July, 1854.
I. Rosabelle-Frances. II. Mary-Jane-Waller.
III. Elizabeth-Alice.

Lineage.—GEORGE LENDRUM, Esq. of Moorfield, co. Tyrone, son and heir of JAMES LENDRUM, Esq. of the same place, *m.* Mary, dau. of Thomas Story, Esq. of the city of Clogher, co. Tyrone, and had issue. JAMES, his heir; Thomas, in holy orders; Joseph, in holy orders; John, a major E.I.C.S.; Mary, *m.* to John Prichard, Esq. of co. Wexford; Anne, *d. unm.*; and Rebecca, *m.* to the Rev. Dr. Nun. The eldest son and heir,

JAMES LENDRUM, Esq. of Jamestown, *m.* 1st, Nov. 1770 Ann Young, of Carrick, co. Donegal; and 2ndly, in July, 1812, Margaret Young, of Lougheak, co. Donegal. By the former lady, Mr. Lendrum had (with a dau., Letitia, who *d. unm.*) an only son,

GEORGE LENDRUM, Esq. of Jamestown *b.* 24 Aug. 1776; *m.* 28 April, 1805, Mary-Jane, 3rd dau. of Henry Coddington, Esq. of Oldbridge, co. Meath, and had issue,

JAMES, now of Jamestown.
Elizabeth, *m.* in Aug. 1831, to the Rev. Cosby-Stopford Mangan, incumbent of the parish of Derrynoose, co. Armagh.

Mr. Lendrum was a magistrate and deputy-lieutenant for co. Fermanagh, but resigned in 1841. He served as high-sheriff of co. Fermanagh 1806, and of Tyrone in 1819. He *d.* 22 Oct. 1855.

Arms—Gu., three garbs, or, on a chief, arg., as many wool-packs, sa.
Crest—On a mount, vert, a dove, holding an olive-branch in its beak, all ppr.
Motto—La paix.
Seat—Jamestown, Enniskillen, co. Fermanagh.

LENIGAN OF CASTLE FOGERTY.

LENIGAN, JAMES, Esq. of Castle Fogerty, co. Tipperary, J.P. and D.L., *m.* Eleanor-Frances, dau. of John Evans, Esq., and sister of William Evans, Esq., late M.P. for Leominster, by whom he has had two daus., viz.,

I. Sarah-Ellen-Henrietta, *d.* at Munich, in Bavaria.
II. PENELOPE-ELIZABETH-MARIE.

Lineage.—The ancient family of FOGARTY, now represented by the LENIGANS *of Castle Fogerty*, was of importance in Ireland antecedently to the descent of the English in the reign of HENRY II. The chief of the sept, in 1583,

CONOHER NA SURY O'FOGARTA, of Munroe, co. Tipperary, was father of

DONOUGH O'FOGARTY, who was slain in battle at Lateragh, his father then living. 26 Nov. 1583, and was the Donough who *m.* Ellen Purcell, of the ancient baronial family of Loghmoe and lies buried in the abbey of Holy Cross, to which he was a considerable benefactor. From him, 4th in descent,

TEIGE, or TIMOTHY O'FOGARTY, of Bally Fogarty, *m.* Margaret, dau. of Burke, of Barrycurry, and had issue,

CORNELIUS, his heir.
Thomas, *m.* Anne, dau. of James Magrath, Esq. of Derrymore, and had a son, Magrath Fogerty, who was father of Thomas Fogerty, and grandfather of Magrath Fogerty, Esq. of Ballinlonty, and of Philip Fogerty, Esq., barrister-at-law.
John. Dionysius, a priest.
Malachy, doctor of the Sorbonne, and prefect of the College of Lombard, in Paris, *anno* 1705.

The eldest son and heir,

CORNELIUS FOGARTY, Esq. of Castle Fogarty, *b.* 14 May, 1661, captain in the army of King JAMES II., *m.* in 1696, Mary, dau. of Michael Kearney, Esq. of Milestown, co. Tipperary, and dying in 1730, was *s.* by his son,

TEIGE, or TIMOTHY FOGARTY, Esq. of Castle Fogarty, who *d. s. p.* at the age of fifty, in 1747, and was *s.* by his brother,

THOMAS FOGARTY, Esq. of Castle Fogarty, who *m.* Christian, dau. and eventual heir of James Moyler, Esq of Sallymount, co. Kildare, and had issue,

JAMES, his heir.
Thomas, capt. of the regiment of Uttonia, in the Spanish service, *d. unm.* in 1781.
ELIZABETH, *m.* to WILLIAM LANIGAN, Esq. of Zoar, co. Kilkenny (elder son of George Lanigan, Esq. of Zoar, by Mabella, his wife, dau. of Edmund Shee, Esq. of Cloran, co. Tipperary, and grandson of William Lanigan, by Mary Gore his wife, granddau. of Sir Paul Gore, Bart.), and by him (who *d.* 23 Nov. 1768) left an only son, THOMAS LANIGAN.

Mr. Fogarty *d.* in 1756, and was *s.* by his elder son,

JAMES FOGARTY, Esq. of Castle Fogarty, high-sheriff for the co. of Tipperary in 1783, who *d. unm.* in 1788, when his sister, ELIZABETH LANIGAN, became his heir, and the estates passed through her to her only son,

THOMAS LENIGAN, Esq., who thus became "of Castle Fogarty." This gentleman *m.* 1st, in 1794, Penniel, dau. of Edmund Armstrong, Esq. of Buncraggy, co. Clare (by his wife, Hannah, sister of Robert-Henry Westropp, Esq.) and had issue,

JAMES, now of Castle Fogerty. Edmund.
Anna, *m.* to John-Dennis Ryan, Esq., lieut. 13th dragoons, 2nd surviving son of the late George Ryan, Esq. of Inch, co. Tipperary.
Elizabeth. Henrietta.

Mr. Lenigan *m.* 2ndly, Clarinda, dau. of John O'Reilly, Esq. of Mount Street, Dublin, and had by her two other daus., viz.,

Mary, a nun. Rosetta.

He *d.* 2 Aug. 1825.

Arms—Quarterly: 1st, az., on a pallet, arg., three trefoils, in pale, vert, between two lions, rampant, or, each between three fleurs-de-lis, two and one, arg., for LENIGAN; 2nd, az., in chief, two lions, rampant, supporting a garb, all or, in the dexter base a crescent, and in the sinister an Irish harp, gold, stringed, arg., for FOGERTY (*ancient*); 3rd, vert, a fesse, arg., between three garbs, two and one, or, for FOGERTY (*modern*); 4th. arg., a chief, vert, for MYLER.
Crests—1st, a lion, rampant, or, leaning on a sword, arg., hilted, gold; 2nd, an arm, embowed in armour, ppr., garnished, or, holding a dagger, arg., hilted, gold.
Seat—Castle Fogerty, co. Tipperary.

LENTHALL OF BESSELS LEIGH.

LENTHALL, KYFFIN-JOHN-WILLIAM, Esq. of Bessels Leigh Manor, co. Berks, and Maynan Hall, co. Caernarvon, high-sheriff of Caernarvonshire 1828, *b.* 12 Oct. 1789; *m.* 28 April, 1818, Mary-Anne, eldest dau. of John Ashton, Esq. of The Grange, co. Chester, and has issue,

I. EDMUND-KYFFIN, *b.* 30 Aug. 1821.
II. William-Kyffin, *b.* in 1822.
III. Francis-Kyffin, *b.* in 1824, called to the bar at Lincoln's-Inn, 1846.
I. Mary-Anne.

Lineage.—SIR ROWLAND LENTHALL, of Lenthall and Hampton Court, co. Hereford (whose family had been seated at Lenthall, from the reign of EDWARD I.), was Master of the Robes to King HENRY IV. He was a lord-marcher, and was associated with Thomas Chaucer (the poet's son), as one of the ambassadors to the Parisian court, to negotiate the marriage of Queen KATHARINE with HENRY V. Sir Rowland accompanied HENRY V. to France, and having a command at the battle of Azincourt, made so many prisoners in that celebrated conflict, that he completed, with the produce of their ransom, the new buildings at Hampton Court. In that mansion was preserved a picture (still extant), engraved by Vertue, and said by Walpole to be an undoubted original, of HENRY IV. Pendant from the neck is a chain with medallion, on which are depicted the arms of the Fitz-Alans, Earls of Arundel, and underneath the following inscription: "HENRY IV., King of England, who laid the first stone of this house, and left this picture in it when he gave it to Lenthall." Sir Rowland, who was also deputy-governor of Alençon under the Duke of Gloucester, and constable of Wigmore and Bolsover Castles, *m.* Margaret, dau., and eventually coheiress, of Richard Fitz-Alan, Earl of Arundel; upon which marriage, Lady Margaret being related to the king, Sir Rowland, "being a gallant fellow," (*vide* LELAND'S *Itin.*) had given to him "a thousand by the year," for the maintenance of them and their heirs, of which grant, says Leland, the town of Ludlow forms a part. By Lady Margaret, who *d.* 1422, Sir Rowland had issue,

Edmund, who having *m.* Margaret, dau. of William, 5th Lord Zouch, of Harringworth, *d. s. p.* 1447; and
Henry, who also *d. s. p.* in the same year; both being buried in the Grey Friars, London.

r Rowland *m.* 2ndly, Lucy, dau. and co-heir of Richard, h Lord Grey de Codnor, by whom he had issue,

Rowland, *m.* to Isabella, dau. of Sir Walter Devereux, and *d.* 1488.
John, *m.* Anne, dau. of Humphrey Bessels, of Bessels Leigh, co. Berks.
Katharine, *m.* to William, Lord Zouch, of Harringworth.
Elizabeth, *m.* to Sir Thomas Cornwall, of Burford, by which last alliance Hampton Court eventually vested in the Cornwall family.

r Rowland was high-sheriff of Hereford in 1428, and *d.* ov. 1450.

A few years later, the Lenthalls, retaining a portion only their possessions in Herefordshire, settled at Latchford id Great Haseley, in Oxfordshire, which manors and tates they acquired in the reign of EDWARD IV., by the arriage of William Lenthall (described in his will as of Lenthall"), who *d.* June, 1497, with the heiress of the ipards. Thomas Lenthall, the eldest son of William last-entioned, *m.* Elizabeth, dau. and heir of John Willie, of sau Tracie, and had issue, William, living, says Francis ain, "of reverent age," in 1584, and several daus., of hom one *m.* Sir John Tempest, of Bollinghall, co. York. 1580, these estates were possessed by John Lenthall, sq., whose son (by Elinor, dau. of Ed. Lee, of Pitston, co. ucks, Esq.),

SIR EDMUND LENTHALL, was one of those fined, under an t of parliament passed in the reign of JAMES I., for straining persons of quality from residing so much of the ar in London. Sir Edmund *m.* Elizabeth, dau. of Sir rancis Stonor, of Stonor, co. Oxford, but *d. s. p.* and the ne of the family was continued through his uncle,

WILLIAM LENTHALL, Esq., who *m.* Frances, dau. of r Richard Southwell, of St. Faith's, in Norfolk, and who, his decease, 2 Dec. 1596, aged 44, left issue,

I. JOHN (Sir), who inherited the family estates upon the demise of his cousin, Sir Edmund. This gentleman, who held the office of marshal of the King's Bench Prison, *m.* Bridget, dau. of Sir Thomas Temple, Bart. of Stow, and had (with eight daus., of whom Catherine, *m.* to Lord Paisley, and Frances, *m.* to Edward, eldest son of Sir Edward Moore, of Odiham, Hants) six sons, of whom the eldest,
   EDMUND, *m.* Elizabeth, dau. of Sir William Wade, lieutenant of the Tower of London, and had issue three sons and a dau: William Lenthall (M.P. for Wallingford, 1679, and for Cricklade, 1681), the elder son, *m.* twice, 1st Stephanie, dau. of Admiral Sir S. Harvey, K.C.B.; and 2ndly, Lucy, dau. of Ed. Dunch, first-cousin to Oliver, Lord Protector, but had no issue by either marriage, and selling the old family estates at Latchford and Great Haseley, terminated this branch of the family; Edmund, the 2nd son, *d.* 1644; John, the 3rd son, *d.* 14 May, 1641, without issue; and Bridget, the only dau., *d. unm.* 1641.
II. WILLIAM, of whom hereafter.
III. Thomas. IV. Francis.
And four daus., one of whom *m.* into the family of Warcup, and was mother of Sir Edmund Warcup, the historian of Italy.

he 2nd son,

THE RIGHT HON. WILLIAM LENTHALL, *b.* June, 1591, was, 1633, admitted a bencher of Lincoln's-Inn, made recorder f Gloucester, Woodstock, and London, and Master of the olls. In 1639, he was returned member for Woodstock; nd when the Long Parliament met, 3 Nov. 1640, he was hosen Speaker, which important office he continued to old after the king's death, and until the dissolution of iat assembly. In the first parliament called by CROMWELL, s Protector, he had no seat; but in the second, he was sturned for two places, the city of Gloucester and the co. f Oxford, and was again elected Speaker. He subsequently as appointed chamberlain of Chester, chancellor of the uchy of Lancaster, and keeper of the Great Seal. He eceived a patent of peerage from Oliver, Lord Protector, 656, and in the single parliament assembled by RICHARD ROMWELL, he sat in the upper house by the title of Villiam, Lord Lenthall, and so great was his influence and reight at the Restoration, that General Monck assured Cing CHARLES, that he could not have brought about hat desirable event without Mr. Lenthall's concurrence. his eminent lawyer and statesman *m.* Elizabeth, dau. of mbrose Evans, Esq. of Lodington, co. Northampton, by rhom (who was first cousin of Lucius Cary, Lord Falkland) e had issue,

JOHN, his successor.
William. Francis.
Elizabeth, *m.* to Sir Rowland Lacey, of Puddlecote and Shipton, in Oxfordshire.
Frances.

Mr. Speaker Lenthall *d.* at his seat, the Priory, Burford, 1 Sept. 1662, and was privately buried at Burford, the advowson of which church, with the manor and estate, he had purchased of the great Lord Falkland. His only surviving son and successor,

SIR JOHN LENTHALL, was member for Gloucester in the Long Parliament, and also for the same place in the parliament called by RICHARD CROMWELL. Sir John, who was colonel in the army, governor of Windsor Castle, and one of the six clerks in Chancery, was created a baronet by OLIVER CROMWELL. He *m.* 1st, Mary, dau. of Sir William Ayshcombe, of Alvercot, Oxon, but had by her no issue. He *m.* 2ndly, Mary Blewet, relict of Sir John Stonehouse, Bart., by whom he had one son, WILLIAM, and a dau. Elizabeth, *m.* to Sir Sandys Fortescue, of Buckland Filleigh, co. Devon. Sir John *m.* 3rdly, Catherine, dau. of Colonel Eusebius Andrews, of Edmonton, Middlesex, but had no further issue. He served the office of sheriff for the co. of Oxford in 1672, and dying 9 Nov. 1681, was buried in the chancel of Bessels Leigh Church, and was *s.* by his only son,

WILLIAM LENTHALL, Esq., to whom General Monck stood sponsor, who *m.* his first cousin, the Hon. Catherine Hamilton, only child of James, Lord Paisley, son and heir of James, 2nd Earl of Abercorn, by whom (who *m.* after his decease, the Earl of Abercorn) he left issue at his demise, 5 Sept. 1686, at the early age of 27, two sons, JOHN, his heir; and James, so named after his grandfather, Lord Paisley. The elder,

JOHN LENTHALL, Esq., who served the office of sheriff for Oxfordshire, and *m.* Jane, dau. of Sir W. Hill, had two sons and two daus.,

WILLIAM, his successor.
JOHN, successor to his brother.
Jane. Mary.

The elder son,

WILLIAM LENTHALL, Esq. of Burford, sheriff of Oxfordshire, dying *unm.* in 1781, the family representation devolved upon his brother,

JOHN LENTHALL, Esq., bapt. 29 Jan. 1722, who *m.* Anne, dau. of the Rev. Christopher Shute, and had two sons,

I. JOHN, of Burford, sheriff for Oxfordshire, in 1787, who *m.* Sarah, dau. of the Rev. John Caswall, rector of Swacliffe, by whom (who *d.* 2 March, 1837) he left at his decease, in 1820, with three daus., two sons, viz.,
   1 WILLIAM-JOHN, *m.* Frances-Mary, eldest dau. of T. Terry, Esq. of Beverley, and has one surviving son, Edmund-Henry, of Lincoln's Inn.
   2 Rowland-Henry, of Kemsey, in Worcestershire, who has been twice married.
II. WILLIAM-JOHN.

The 2nd son,

WILLIAM-JOHN LENTHALL, Esq. of Bessels Leigh, in Berkshire, *b.* in Jan. 1764, was high-sheriff for the counties of Caernarvon and Merioneth. He *m.* in Jan. 1789, Elizabeth, dau. and co-heiress (with Anne, wife of the Rev. John Nanney, of Maes-y-neuadd, co. Merioneth and Ermine, wife of Richard-Hughes Kenrick, of Nantclwyd, co. Denbigh, Esq.) of Sir Thomas Kyffin, of Maynan, co. Caernarvon, by whom (who *d.* in June, 1791) he had two children,

KYFFIN-JOHN-WILLIAM, now of Bessels Leigh.
Ann-Margaret, *d.* young.

Mr. Lenthall *d.* in March, 1855.

Arms—Arg., on a bend, cottised, sa., three mullets, or.
Crest—A greyhound, salient, sa., collared, or.
Motto—Azincourt.
Seats—Bessels Leigh, near Abingdon; Maynan Hall, Caernarvonshire; Yelford Hastings, Oxon.

LESLIE OF BALQUHAIN.

LESLIE, CHARLES, Esq. of Balquhain, Fetternear, and Inch, all in the co. Aberdeen, colonel in the army, K.H.; *m.* 1st, Nov. 1826, Mary, dau. of Major-General Sir Charles Holloway, and had by her one surviving son,

I. CHARLES-STEPHEN, *b.* 1832, who is married.

Colonel Leslie *m.* 2ndly, 21 July, 1836, Dorothy, sister and heiress of Francis, 8th Earl of Newburgh, but by her (who *d.* 22 Nov. 1853) has no issue. Colonel Leslie served in the Peninsular war, and was severely wounded at Talavera.

Lineage.—BARTHOLOMEW, the founder of the family, was a noble Hungarian, who came to Scotland with Queen MARGARITE, 1067. He was much esteemed by King MALCOLM CANMORE, who conferred upon him grants of lands in various parts of Scotland, but particularly in the district of the Garioch, co. Aberdeen, where the ruins of the old castle of Leslie still remain, in the parish of Leslie. Bartholomew's son, MALCOLM, was father of NORMAN, whose grandson SIR NORMAN DE LESLEY, Dominus de Lesley, *m.* Elizabeth Leith, heiress of Edengarrioch, and had an only son,

SIR ANDREW DE LESLEY, styled 6th *Dominus ejusdem*, or Lesley, who *m.* 1st, about 1313, Mary, dau. and co-heir of Sir Alexander, Lord Abernethy of Abernethy, and by her had issue, from which the noble house of ROTHES springs. Sir Andrew *m.* 2ndly, Elizabeth Douglas, dau. of Lord Douglas, by whom he had a son, GEORGE, founder of the Balquhain family; and a dau. Margaret, *m.* to David Abercromby. This son,

GEORGE LESLIE, Baron of Balquhain, *m.* Elizabeth Keith, dau. of the Baron of Inverugie, and *d.* about 1351, having had a son and successor,

HAMELIN LESLIE, 2nd Baron of Balquhain, who had a passport to travel abroad, in 1356. He *m.* a dau. of Maxwell, Baron of Carlaverock, and *d.* about 1378, leaving a son and successor,

SIR ANDREW LESLIE, 3rd Baron of Balquhain, who *m.* Isabel Mortimer, dau. of the Baron of Craigievar, and had a son, WILLIAM (Sir), his heir, and four daus. Sir Andrew's son and heir,

SIR WILLIAM LESLIE, 4th Baron of Balquhain, distinguished at the battle of Brechin, in 1452. He *m.* 1st, the Hon. Eliza Fraser, of Lovat, by whom he had two sons, ALEXANDER, his heir, and William of Kincraigie. He *m.* 2ndly, Agnes Irvine of Drum, by whom he had ALEXANDER, 1st of Wardes, ancestor of the LESLIES of Warthill, Glasslough, &c. The great-great-grandson of the eldest son, ALEXANDER LESLIE, 5th Baron of Balquhain, was

WILLIAM LESLIE, 9th Baron of Balquhain, who *m.* 1st, Janet, dau. of John, 6th Lord Forbes, and widow of John, Earl of Atholl; and 2ndly, Margaret Leslie; and *d.* in 1571, having had issue. Queen MARY, in her progress from Aberdeen to the north, honoured Leslie at Balquhain Castle with a visit, and passed the night there, 9 Sept. 1562. His eldest son,

JOHN LESLIE, 10th Baron of Balquhain, *m.* 1st, in 1564, Eliza Grant, of Grant, by whom he had, JOHN, his heir; WILLIAM, successor to his nephew. He *m.* 2ndly, 1597, Eliza, dau. of the Earl of Erroll; and 3rdly, 1598, Johanna Erskine, sister to the 1st Earl of Kelly: by the latter had two sons, ALEXANDER, successor to his half-brother, William; and Walter, who served with great distinction in the Austrian army, and was created a Count of the Holy Roman Empire. He *m.* the Princess Ann-Francisca de Dietrichstein. Walter *d. s. p.* in 1667. John Leslie *d.* in 1622, and was *s.* by his eldest son,

JOHN LESLIE, 11th Baron of Balquhain, who *m.* 1st, the widow of Duguid of Auchinhove, and dau. of Gordon; and 2ndly, Jean Innes; and by the latter had a son and heir,

JOHN LESLIE, 12th Baron of Balquhain, who entered the Muscovite service, became a colonel, and fell at the siege of Igolwitz, in 1655, leaving no male issue by his wife, a dau. of Crawford. He was *s.* by his uncle,

WILLIAM LESLIE, as 13th Baron of Balquhain, who was in the service of CHARLES II., whom he accompanied to Holland. He *m.* Margery Bernard, by whom he had a dau., Mary, *m.* to Sir Elias Lechton, a colonel in the army. Having had no male issue, he was *s.* about 1660, by his half-brother,

ALEXANDER LESLIE, as 14th Baron of Balquhain, who was created a Count of the Roman Empire. He *m.* Jean Elphinston, of Glack, and *d.* in 1677, having had issue,

James, field-marshal in the Austrian service, who *s.* his uncle, Count Walter, as second count: he *m.* the Princess Maria-Theresa de Leichtenstein, and *d. s. p.* in 1694.
PATRICK, of whom presently, as 15th Baron of Balquhain.
Alexander, Count Leslie, colonel in the Austrian army, killed at the siege of Vienna, in 1683, leaving by his wife, the Countess Heberstein, a son, Francis-Jacob, Count Leslie, who *d. s. p.* in 1700.
William, in holy orders, author of "Laurus Leslæana," published in 1692.

The 2nd son,

PATRICK LESLIE, 15th Baron of Balquhain, *m.* 1st, Ellen Douglas, by whom he had,

I. James-Ernest, 3rd Count Leslie, in Germany. He *m.* the Princess Berne de Leichtenstein; and *d.* in 1728, having had issue, Charles-Cajetan, 4th Count Leslie, who *m.* 26 June, 1719, the Princess Maria-Theresa D'Eggenberg, and *d.* in 1760, having had, with other issue, ANTHONY, of whom hereafter, as 19th Baron of Balquhain.
I. Margery, *m.* to Alexander Leslie, of Pitcaple.
II. Ann-Francisca, *m.* to John Grant, of Ballindalloch, and had issue, John Grant (Capt.) father of PETER LESLIE-GRANT, of whom hereafter, as 20th Baron of Balquhain, and of Eliza Grant, *m.* to Patrick Leslie Duguid.
III. Theresa, *m.* to Robert Duguid, of Auchinhove, and had issue, PATRICK LESLIE-DUGUID, who *s.* as 21st Baron of Balquhain, and of whom hereafter.
IV. Betty, abbess of the Ursuline Convent at Lisle.

The 15th Baron *m.* 2ndly, Mary Irvine, of Drum, and by her had GEORGE, who *s.* his father as 16th Baron, and four daus. Count Patrick Leslie finding the ancient castle of Balquhain incommodious, removed to Fetternear, beautifully situated on the banks of the Don. Thus Fetternear became the family residence, and the old castle of Balquhain fell to decay. He *d.* in 1710, and was *s.* by his 2nd son,

GEORGE LESLIE, 16th Baron of Balquhain, and Count Leslie, who *m.* in 1706, the Hon. Margaret Elphinston, dau. of Lord Elphinston, and dying 17 June, 1715, was *s.* by his elder son,

JAMES LESLIE, Count Leslie, 17th Baron of Balquhain, who dying *unm.*, at Paris, in 1731, was *s.* by his brother,

ERNEST LESLIE, Count Leslie, 18th Baron of Balquhain, who *d. unm.* in 1739. The estate was claimed by Sir James Leslie, of Pitcaple, in right of his mother, Margery, eldest dau. of Count Patrick Leslie the 15th Baron; and by Count Anthony Leslie, as 2nd son of Count Charles Cajetan Leslie. But the House of Peers decided in favour of the latter, and accordingly, in 1743,

ANTHONY LESLIE, Count Leslie, 2nd son of Count Charles Cajetan Leslie, *s.* as heir male, as 19th Baron of Balquain; but his father dying in 1760, he *s.* to the German estates, and the entail made by Count Patrick Leslie precluding him from holding both the German and Scottish estates, the Balqubain lands went, according to the entail, to

PETER LESLIE-GRANT, (son of Captain John Grant, and grandson of Anne Francisca, 2nd dau. of Count Patrick Leslie,) who then became 20th Baron of Balquhain. He *d. unm.* in 1775, and was *s.* by

PATRICK LESLIE-DUGUID, of Auchinhove, as 21st Baron of Balquhain, in right of his mother, Theresa, 3rd dau. of Count Patrick Leslie, 15th Baron of Balquhain, the entailer. He was *b.* in 1700, and *m.* in 1740, Amelia, dau. of J. Irvine, Esq. of Kingcausey, and had issue. He took a very active part in the cause of the Stewarts, and was engaged in the struggles of 1715 and 1745. He *d.* in April, 1777, and was *s.* by his son,

JOHN LESLIE, 22nd Baron of Balquhain, *b.* in 1751. He *m.* 17 Nov. 1774, Violet, dau. of John Dalzell, Esq., by his wife the Hon. Harriet Gordon, dau. of William, Lord Kenmure, and by her, who *d.* 23 Sept. 1836, he had issue,

I. ERNEST, his successor.
II. John, of the Austrian service; lost at sea.
III. JAMES-MICHAEL, who *s.* as 25th Baron of Balquhain.
IV. CHARLES, now of Balquhain.
V. Anthony, now an officer in the army; *m.* Jan. 1840, Ann Monaghan.
VI. Edward, an officer in the army, *d. s. p.* in 1813.
VII. Francis, also in the army; served in Spain and France; was present at Waterloo; *d. s. p.* 17 July, 1831.
VIII. Louis-Xavier, (twin with Francis), likewise in the army.
I. Amelia, *m.* in 1801, to Alexander Fraser, Esq. of Strichen, and has a son, Thomas-Alexander, Lord Lovat.
II. Violet.

Mr. Leslie *d.* in Feb. 1828, aged 77, and was *s.* by his son,

ERNEST LESLIE, 23rd Baron of Balquhain, *b.* in 1775, who entered the Austrian army, and served in the various campaigns from 1796 to 1813, and was present at most of the great battles, from Hohenlinden to the battle of Dresden, in Oct. 1813, where he was severely wounded. This gentleman *m.* 22 Jan. 1812, the Baroness Fanny Stilfried, dau. of Emanuel, Baron Stilfried chamberlain to the Emperor of Austria, and Knight of Malta, and by her had issue,

JOHN EDWARD, his successor.
Augusta, *d. unm.* at Prague, in 1837.
Mary, *m.* in 1839, to her cousin, Edward, Baron Stilfried.

Count Ernest Leslie *d.* at Frankfort, 15 March, 1836 and was *s.* by his son,

JOHN-EDWARD LESLIE, Count Leslie, 24th Baron of Balquhain, b. 22 June, 1820, an officer in the Austrian service, who d. unm., at Fetternear, 19 Aug. 1844, and was s. by his uncle,

JAMES-MICHAEL LESLIE, Esq., 25th Baron of Balquhain, J.P. and D.L., who d. unm., and was s. by his brother, the present COLONEL LESLIE, of Balquhain.

Arms—Arg., on a fesse, az., three buckles, or.
Crest—A demi-griffin, erased, ppr.
Supporters—Two griffins, ppr.
Motto—Grip fast.
Seats—Fetternear House, co. Aberdeen, and Hassop Hall, Derbyshire.

LESLIE OF WARTHILL.

LESLIE, WILLIAM, Esq., J.P. and D.L., 10th Laird of Warthill, and 22nd lineal male descendant of the original progenitor of the ancient family of Leslie, b. 29 June, 1770; m. 16 Jan. 1818, Jane, 3rd dau. of the late Rev. Patrick Davidson, D.D., of Rayne, and niece of the late Sir Walter Farquhar, Bart., and by this lady has had issue six sons and two daus., viz.,

I. WILLIAM, b. 16 March, 1814, formerly a member of the house of Dent and Co., in China, m. 1848, Matilda-Rose, second dau. of the late William Rose Robinson, Esq. of Clermiston, sheriff of Lanarkshire, and has issue a son, WILLIAM DOUGLAS, b. 12 Aug. 1849, and three daus.
II. Patrick, in New South Wales, b. 25 Sept. 1815, m. 1840, Katherine, 3rd dau. of Hannibal H. Macarthur, Esq. of Vineyard, and has issue, a son, WILLIAM NORMAN, b. 11 June, 1841.
III. Walter-Stevenson-Davidson, b. 11 Dec. 1818.
IV. George-Farquhar, b. 19 Aug. 1820, a member of the Legislative Council of New South Wales, m. 1848, Emmeline, 5th dau. of Hannibal H. Macarthur, Esq.
V. James, b. 5 Dec. 1824, d. 8 Oct. 1829.
VI. Thomas-Coats, b. 28 Sept. 1826, in China.
I. Mary-Anne, m. 1836, to Patrick Davidson, of Inchmarlo, Esq., LL.D.
II. Catherine, m. 1854, to Christopher Rolleston, Esq., son of the Rev. John Rolleston, of Burton Joyce and Shelford, Notts.

Lineage.—According to the best authorities, the original progenitor of the families of the surname of Leslie, was an Hungarian knight, named Bartholomew, who appeared in Scotland in 1067, during the reign of Malcolm Caenmore, and, among other distinguished marks of royal favour, obtained from that monarch a grant of the lands of Fitchie, now called Leslie, in Fifeshire, Innerlepad, in Angus Cushnie, in Marr, and those now called Leslie in the Garioch. He had also the good fortune to rescue from imminent danger Malcolm's Queen, Margaret, sister to Edgar Atheling, and granddau., maternally, of Solomon King of Hungary when carried away by the stream in crossing a river on horseback, dragging her to land by her belt or girdle. Hence, a belt and three buckles were assigned to him for a coat of arms, with *Grip Fast* as the motto, from the queen calling out in these words when in danger, and two griffins rampant, for supporters.

ALEXANDER LESLIE, 1st of Wardes, eldest son of William Leslie, 4th Baron of Balquhain, by Agnes Irvine, his 2nd wife, got two holly-leaves added to his armorial bearings as a distinctive mark of his family. He m. the heretrix of Balcomie, in Fife, and had a son and heir,

JOHN LESLIE, of Wardes, who m. 1st, Stuart, dau. of the Bishop of Moray, who d. s. p.; 2ndly, Margaret Crichton, dau. of the Baron of Frendraught, by whom he had only one son, who s. him, named Alexander, whose descendants continued the Wardes succession, and his great-grandson, John, sixth Baron, was included among the first creation of Nova Scotia baronets, 1625; 3rdly, Forbes, dau. of the Laird of Echt, by whom he had two sons, WILLIAM and Alexander. The elder,

WILLIAM LESLIE, who got from his father the Kemmels of Durno &c., m. 1st, a dau. of William Rowan, burgess in Aberdeen, by whom he had only one son, John, slain at the fatal battle of Pinkie, in 1547. He m. 2ndly, in the year 1518, Janet Cruickshank, heiress of Warthill, she being only surviving child of John, son of Andrew Cruickshank, of Tillymorgan. By this lady he is reported to have had twenty-one children. The youngest dau., Elizabeth, was m. to Andrew Lyall, of Middlehill, and at her wedding all the children danced together in the "Ha' of Warthill," along with both parents, who were then hale and strong. This 1st Laird of Warthill d. in 1561, and was s. by his son,

STEPHEN LESLIE, second Laird of Warthill, who m. 1st, Margaret Leith, of Lickleyhead, and 2ndly, Bessie Spens, dau. to the Laird of Boddam. By his first lady he had two sons, WILLIAM, his heir; and Alexander, who m. Isabel Rundiman, dau. to Sir John Priest, of Oyne; also two daus., Julia, m. to John Anderson, son to William, of Bonnyton, and Margaret, m. to Andrew-Edward, son of William, in old Rayne. This Stephen dying in his 90th year, was s. by his son,

WILLIAM LESLIE, third Laird of Warthill, who m. Margaret, dau. to Gilbert Gray, of Tullo, by whom he had two sons, JAMES, his heir, and William; also two daughters, Margaret, the eldest, m. to her cousin-german, John Gray, and Beatrix, m. Gordon, Laird of Tillichoudie. He d. in his 80th year. The elder son,

JAMES LESLIE, fourth Laird of Warthill, m. Beatrix Abercrombie, dau. of Walter, Archdeacon of Aberdeen, son of Birkenbog, by whom he had many children—some say twenty-one. James Leslie d. in 1679, after attaining the great age of 105. His eldest son,

WILLIAM LESLIE, fifth Laird of Warthill, who m. Ann Elphinstone, dau. of the laird of Glack, and grandniece to the celebrated Bishop Elphinstone, of Aberdeen, and had by her four sons, viz., I. ALEXANDER, his heir; II. William, professor of Theology in the University of Padua, bishop of Laybach, metropolitan of Carniola, and a prince of the empire, and privy councillor to his Imperial Majesty; III. James, merchant in Aberdeen, who d. s. p.; and IV. John, a writer in Edinburgh. The eldest son,

ALEXANDER LESLIE, sixth Laird of Warthill, m. 1st, Elizabeth Gordon, dau. of the Laird of Badenscoth, by whom he had three sons, George, who d. a youth at College; JOHN, his successor; and William, who d. unm. He m. 2ndly, Janet Gordon, dau. of the Laird of Cocklarachie, and sister of Gordon, of Auchintoul, made general in the Muscovite army by the Czar, Peter the Great; but she predeceased her husband without leaving any issue. Dying in 1721, aged 66, he was s. by his only surviving son,

JOHN LESLIE, seventh laird of Warthill, who m. 1st, Mary Gordon, dau. of George, Laird of Rothney, who d. s. p., and 2ndly, Margaret, dau. of Patrick Dun, Laird of Tarty, by whom he had an only son, ALEXANDER, his successor. He d. 15 May, 1747, aged 64.

ALEXANDER LESLIE, eighth Laird of Warthill. He m. (1730) at the age of 19, Helen, only dau. of George Seton, of Mounie, by his first wife, Ann Gibson, dau. of Sir Alexander Gibson, of Addiston, in Mid Lothian, and had by her six sons and five daus. This Alexander d. in 1764, and his two eldest sons having predeceased him, he was s. by his third son,

ALEXANDER LESLIE, ninth Laird of Warthill, who m. Isabel Milne, dau. of Milne, in Fraserburgh. He d. s. p. 16 Jan. 1799, when the succession devolved on his nephew,

WILLIAM LESLIE, tenth Laird of Warthill, eldest surviving son of George Leslie, of Folla, and in right of his mother, Mary, eldest married dau. of Alexander, eighth of Warthill, was both the heir of his uncle and grandfather, and also the lineal male representative of the family through his father, the latter being the direct male descendant of William, second son of William, third of Warthill.

Family of Leslie of Folla.

WILLIAM LESLIE of Folla, second son of William, third of Warthill, was father, by his 1st wife, Marjory, dau. of William Crichton, brother of the Viscount of Frendraught, of an only son,

JAMES LESLIE, II. of Folla, whose eldest son, by his 1st wife, Isabel, dau. of William Milne, of Monkshill,

THE REV. WILLIAM LESLIE III. of Folla, s. his father in 1698, who having been provided in the church living of Aquareigh, co. Fermanagh, in Ireland, resided there till 1714. He d. unm. Sept. 1722, aged 71, and was s. by his next brother,

GEORGE LESLIE, IV. of Folla. He m. Isabel, dau. of William Cheyne, of Kaithen, and d. 21 June, 1730, aged 75 leaving a son and successor,

THE REV. WILLIAM LESLIE, V. of Folla, who d. unm. 31 July, 1748, in his 64th year, and was s. by his only brother,

JOHN LESLIE, VI. of Folla. He m. Elizabeth Gordon, dau. of Hugh, Laird of Culto, by whom he had ten children. Of this numerous family, GEORGE, the eldest son, alone left any descendants, and he s. to the property on his father's death, 25 April, 1783, aged 86.

GEORGE LESLIE, VII. of Folla, having had the lands made over to him in his father's lifetime, m. 12 June, 1768, Mary, third dau. of Alexander Leslie, eighth of Warthill, by whom he had two sons and one dau.,

WILLIAM, (now of Warthill) who *s.* to the Warthill estate, in right of his mother, after the death of his uncle Alexander, in 1799, and in him the male line of the Warthill and Folla branches were again united.
George, who *d.* in 1798, aged 26, *unm.*
Helen, *m.* in 1818, to the Rev. James Innes, Episcopal minister of Meicklefolla, by whom she had one son, James, who *d.* in infancy.

Arms—Arg., on a bend, az., three buckles, or; and (in consequence of descent from WARDES) two holly-leaves.

Crest—A griffin's head, erased, ppr.

Motto—Grip fast.

Seat—Warthill, Aberdeenshire.

LESLIE OF BALLIBAY.

LESLIE, EMILY-ELEANORA-WILHELMINA, of Ballibay, co. Monaghan, only surviving dau. and heiress of the late Charles-Albert Leslie, Esq. of Ballibay, *m.* 1st, Arthur French, Esq., and by him (who *d.* March, 1843) has issue,

I. ROBERT-CHARLES FRENCH.
II. Charles-Albert-Leslie French.
I. Helen-Charlotte, *m.* James Blake, Esq. of Cregg Castle.
II. Albertina-Caroline, *m.* to James Ryan, Esq.

The heiress of Ballibay *m.* 2ndly, 1844, the Rev. J.-Charles-W. Leslie, 4th son of James Leslie, Esq. of Leslie Hill, co. Antrim, and has issue,

I. Ferdinand-Seymour, *b.* Oct. 1845.
I. Marion-Adelaide.

Lineage.—The Irish LESLIES descend from the noble family of Rothes, and are allied by blood to many of the nobility of Scotland. Their first settlement in Ireland took place in the reign of JAMES I.; and different members of the family now possess considerable estates in the counties of Monaghan, Antrim, Down, Donegal, and Meath.

HENRY LESLIE, *b.* in 1580, removing from Scotland, settled in Ireland in 1614, and *d.* in 1661, leaving a son,

JAMES LESLIE, *b.* 21 Nov. 1624, who *m.* Jane Echlin, of Downshire, and was *s.* by his eldest son,

THE VEN. HENRY LESLIE, archdeacon of Down, *b.* 4 Nov. 1651, who *m.* Margaret Beachan, of an English family, and had, with other issue, a son and a dau., viz.,

PETER, his heir.
Penelope, who *m.* E.-F. Stafford, Esq., and had a dau., Anne, wife of Arthur, 1st Viscount Dungannon.

Mr. Leslie was *s.* at his decease by his son,

THE REV. PETER LESLIE, *b.* in 1686, rector of Ahoghill, co. Antrim, who *m.* Jane, dau. of the Right Rev. Dr. Dopping, bishop of Meath, and had issue,

HENRY, LL.D., his heir, of Ballybay, co. Monaghan.
James, of Leslie Hill, co. Antrim, *b.* in 1728; *m.* 1st, Mrs. Hamilton; and 2ndly, Sarah Fleming; but *d. s. p.* in 1796.
Samuel, major in the 14th regt., *d. unm.*
EDMOND, archdeacon of Down (*see* LESLIE *of Leslie Hill*).
Margaret, *m.* to the Very Rev. Hill Benson, dean of Connor.
Jane, *m.* to the Rev. Mr. Stewart.

The eldest son,

THE REV. HENRY LESLIE, of Ballybay, co. Monaghan, LL.D., *b.* in Oct. 1719, rector of Tandragee, in Armagh, *m.* in 1753, Catherine, dau. of the Very Rev. Charles Meredyth, dean of Meath, and had issue,

I. Peter-Henry, *b.* in 1755; killed in action in America.
II. CHARLES-ALBERT, of Ballybay, co. Monaghan, *b.* 23 May, 1765; *m.* July, 1799, Ellen, youngest dau. of Richard Magenis, Esq. of Waringstown, co. Down, and left at his decease, in 1838, an only surviving dau., EMILY-ELINORA-WILHELMINA, now of Ballibay.
I. Catherine-Letitia, *m.* to the Right Rev. William Foster, bishop of Clogher.

Arms—Quarterly: 1st and 4th, arg., on a bend, az., three buckles, or, for LESLIE; 2nd and 3rd, or, a lion, rampant, gu., debruised by a riband, sa., for ABERNETHY.

Crest—An angel.

Motto—Grip fast.

Seat—Ballibay, co. Monaghan.

LESLIE OF LESLIE HILL.

LESLIE, JAMES-EDMUND, Esq. of Leslie Hill, co. Antrim, J.P. and D.L., high-sheriff co. Antrim 1854-55, *b.* 3 April, 1800; *m.* 14 April, 1823, Sarah, youngest dau. of the Right Rev. Daniel Sandford, D.D., bishop of Edinburgh, by Helen-Frances-Catherine his wife, eldest dau. and co-heir of Erskine Douglas, Esq., and has issue,

I. JAMES-SANDFORD, *b.* 10 Aug. 1824; *d.* 27 Jan. 1829.
II. Henry-Erskine, *b.* 15 Nov. 1825; *d.* 10 Feb. 1829.
III. EDMUND-DOUGLAS, capt. Royal Antrim rifles, *b.* 22 Sept. 1828.
IV. Daniel-Sandford, *b.* 8 March, 1830; *d.* 28 Dec. 1830.
V. Seymour-Montague, *b.* 14 Nov. 1835.
VI. Francis-Macnaghten, *b.* 7 Feb. 1837.
VII. Erskine-Douglas, *b.* and *d.* June, 1839.
I. Frances-Mary. II. Mary-Wilhelmina.
III. Sarah-Agnes. IV. Jane-Elizabeth.

Lineage.—THE VEN. EDMUND LESLIE, archdeacon of Down, *b.* in Nov. 1735, 4th son of the Rev. Peter Leslie (*see* LESLIE *of Ballibay*); *m.* 1st, Jane, dau. of John Macnaughten, Esq. of Benvarden, co. Antrim, and had by her,

Peter, *d.* in London. Bartholomew, *d.* in India.
JAMES, now of Leslie House. Edmund, *d.* in India.
Mary, *m.* Rev. Mr. Boraston.

Archdeacon Leslie *m.* 2ndly Eleanor, dau. of George Portis, Esq. of London, and had by her three sons and one dau., viz.,

I. George, who *m.* Elizabeth, dau. and heir of Francis Hutcheson, D.D. of the co. of Down, by whom he left at his decease, in 1831,
1 Edmund-Francis, J.P.
2 George, capt. royal artillery.
1 Mary-Elinor, *m.* William-Thomas Poe, Esq. of Soulsboro'; and *d.* leaving issue.
2 Elizabeth, *d.* young.
3 Ellen, *m.* to Daniel De la Cherois, Esq. of Donaghadee, co. Down.
II. Henry, dean of Connor, *d. s. p.* 1848.
III. Samuel, rear-admiral R.N., *m.* Martha, dau. of George Vaughan, Esq.; and *d. s. p.* Sept. 1851.
I. Ellen, *m.* to the Rev. Stephen Dickson, youngest son of Dr. William Dickson, lord-bishop of Down and Connor; and *d.* in giving birth to her dau., Ellen, *m.* to Dr. Christian.

Archdeacon Leslie's eldest surviving son,

JAMES LESLIE, Esq. of Leslie House, *s.* to the estates of Leslie Hill upon the demise of his uncle, James Leslie, Esq. 1796. In 1797 he was high-sheriff for the co. of Antrim. He was *b.* 17 July, 1768, and *d.* 17 April, 1847, having *m.* 28 Feb. 1795 Mary, dau. of Adam Cuppage, Esq. of co. Armagh, by whom, who *d.* 1 Feb. 1847, he had issue,

JAMES-EDMUND, now of Leslie Hill.
Henry, *m.* Harriet-Ann, eldest dau. of Capt. Thomas-Job-Syer Hanmer, R.N., of Holbrook Hall, Suffolk, and has issue, Henry-Hanmer, *b.* 1853, and Mary-Emily.
Frances-Seymour, of the Home Office; married.
John-Charles-William, in holy orders, *m.* Emily-Eleanor-Wilhelmina, widow of A. French, Esq., and dau. of Charles-Albert Leslie, Esq. of Ballibay, and has issue.

Arms, &c.—See LESLIE *of Ballibay*.

Seat—Leslie Hill, co. Antrim.

LESLIE OF GLASSLOUGH.

LESLIE, CHARLES-POWELL, Esq. of Glasslough, co. Monaghan, M.P. for that county, *b.* 13 Sept. 1821; *s.* his father 15 Nov. 1831.

Lineage.—JOHN LESLIE, the founder of the Glasslough branch of the Leslie family, in Ireland, a descendant of the house of Balquhain, in Aberdeenshire, was *b.* in the north of Scotland, and educated first at Aberdeen, and then at Oxford. Of this distinguished divine, there is an interesting account in Sir James Ware's *History of Ireland*, edited by Harris. His chief preferment in the church of Scotland was the bishopric of Orkney, whence he was removed to Raphoe, in 1633, and thence translated to the see of Clogher, 17 June, 1661. He *d.* at his seat at Castle Lesley, *alias* Glasslough, in Sept. 1671. His lordship's son and successor,

THE REV. CHARLES LESLIE, M.A., chancellor of the cathedral of Connor, *d.* March, 1722, at his seat, Glasslough. His son and successor,

ROBERT LESLIE, Esq. of Glasslough, *m.* Frances, dau. of John Rogerson, chief-justice of the Court of King's Bench, in Ireland, and had (with a dau., Annabella, *m.* to the late

Robert Leigh, Esq. of Rose Garland, co Wexford) a son and successor,

Charles-Powell Leslie, Esq. of Glasslough, M.P. for the co. of Monaghan, who *m.* 1st, 22 May, 1765, Prudence-Penelope, dau. of Arthur-Hill Trevor, 1st Viscount Dungannon, and had two sons,

- I. Charles Powell, his heir.
- II. John, D.D., consecrated Bishop of Dromore, in 1812, and translated to the see of Elphin, in 1820. His lordship *m.* 1 Aug. 1808, Isabella, 2nd dau. of the Hon. and Right Rev. Thomas St. Lawrence, Bishop of Cork and Ross, and by her (who *d.* 30 Nov. 1830) had issue,
  - 1 Charles, in holy orders, *m.* 8 April, 1834, the Hon. Frances King, 3rd dau. of Viscount Lorton, but became a widower 28 July, 1835. He *m.* 2ndly, 22 Aug. 1837, Louisa-Mary, 2nd dau. of Major-Gen. the Hon. Sir Henry King, K.C.B., brother of the Earl of Kingston.
  - 2 John, of Christ Church, Oxford.
  - 3 Thomas. 4 Arthur.
  - 1 Frances-Anne-Prudentia.
  - 2 Emma, *m.* 4 July, 1837, to the Rev. Nicholas Toke, M.A.
  - 3 Charlotte. 4 Isabella. 5 Harriet.

Mr. Leslie *m.* 2ndly, Mary-Anne, dau. of the Rev. Joshua Tench, of Bryanstown, co. Wexford, and by that lady had,

- Edward, in holy orders, *m.* Margaret, dau. of the Rev. Mr. Higginson, of Lisburne, in the co. of Antrim.
- Emily-Jane, *m.* to the Rev. John Hallward, vicar of Assington, in Suffolk.
- Harriet, *m.* to the Rev. William Hallward, rector of Minden, in Suffolk.
- Mary-Anne, *d. unm.*
- Isabella-Frances, *m.* to Anthony Cliffe, Esq. of Bellevue, co. Wexford.

Mr. Leslie *d.* in 1800, and was *s.* by his eldest son,

Col. Charles-Powell Leslie, of Glasslough, J.P., who was high-sheriff in 1788, and M.P. for the co of Monaghan. He *m.* 1st, Anne, dau. of the Rev. Dudley-Charles Ryder, of Merrion Square, Dublin, and had by her,

- Alicia-Maria. Charlotte, *d. unm.*
- Anne, *m.* to John Gurdon, Esq. of Assington, in Suffolk.

He *m.* 2ndly, 24 May, 1819, Christiana, dau. of George Fosberry, Esq. of Clorane, co. Limerick, and by that lady had,

- Charles-Powell, now of Glasslough.
- John. Thomas.
- Christiana, *m.* in 1843, to the Rev. Lord John Beresford.
- Prudentia-Penelope. Julia. Emily,

Col. Leslie *d.* 15 Nov. 1831.

Arms—Quarterly: 1st and 4th, arg., in base, three thistle leaves, conjoined, vert, on a fesse, gu., three oval buckles, or; 2nd and 3rd, quarterly, 1st and 4th, arg., on a bend, az., three oval buckles, or; 2nd and 3rd, or, a lion rampant, gu., over all a bendlet, sa.
Crest—A griffin's head, ppr.
Motto—Grip fast.
Seat—Glasslough, in the co. of Monaghan.

LE STRANGE OF HUNSTANTON,

See Styleman-Le Strange.

LEVETT OF MILFORD HALL.

Levett, Richard-Byrd, Esq. of Milford Hall, co. Stafford, J.P., formerly an officer 60th royal Rifles, and now major 3rd regt. Staffordshire militia, *b.* 24 Nov. 1810; *m.* 1 Aug. 1848, Elizabeth-Mary, dau. of John Mirehouse, Esq. of Brownslade, co. Pembroke, by Elizabeth his wife, dau. of Dr. Fisher, Bishop of Salisbury, and has issue,

- I. Richard-Walter-Byrd, *b.* 5 May, 1849.
- II. William-Swinnerton-Bird, *b.* Jan. 1856.
- I. Louisa-Mary. II. Evelyn-Honora.

Lineage.—William Levett, Esq. of Savernake, co. Wilts, page to King Charles I. at the time of that monarch's death, was father of Sir Richard Levett, Knt., lord-mayor of London in 1700, who had, with other issue, a dau., Elizabeth, *m.* in 1713, to Sir Edward Hulse, Bart., M.D., and a son, Richard Levett, Esq., alderman of London, who *m.* Anne Sweetaple, and had a son and successor, the Rev. Richard Levett, rector of Blithfield and Leigh, co. Stafford, who *m.* Catherine Walcot, of Walcot, co. Salop, and was father of

The Rev. Richard Levett, vicar of West Wycombe, Bucks, who *m.* Lucy, dau. and heir of Edward Byrd, Esq. of Field and Brocton, co. Stafford and of Smallwood, co. Chester, and by her (through whom came the Milford estate) left at his decease, in 1805, a son and successor,

The Rev. Richard Levett, of Milford Hall, *b.* 17 Nov. 1772, who *m.* 16 Jan. 1804, Louisa-Frances, 4th dau. of the Rev. Walter Bagot, of Blithfield, co. Stafford (brother of the 1st Lord Bagot), by Anne his wife, dau. of William Swinnerton, Esq. of Butterton Hall, co. Stafford, and had issue,

- Richard-Byrd, now of Milford Hall.
- Frances-Mary.

Mr. Levett *d.* in 1843.

Arms—Arg., a lion, rampant, sa., murally crowned, or, and two crosses-fitchée, in pale, between two piles, issuing from the dexter and sinister chiefs, sa., each pile charged with three crosses-crosslet fitchée, of the third.
Crest—A demi-lion, or entwined with a sprig of laurel, vert, and supporting a cross-crosslet fitchée, sa.
Seat—Milford Hall, co. Stafford.

LEVETT OF WICHNOR PARK.

Levett, Theophilus-John, Esq. of Wichnor Park, co. Stafford, J.P., capt. 1st life-guards, *b.* 11 Dec. 1829; *m.* 10 Jan. 1856, Lady Jane-Lissey-Harriet Feilding, 2nd dau. of the present Earl of Denbigh.

Lineage.—Theophilus Levett, Esq. of Winchnor Park, co. Stafford, derived from a common ancestor with the Levetts *of Milford Hall*, *m.* Mary, 2nd dau. and co-heir of John Babington, Esq. of Packington, co. Warwick, and dying in 1746, left issue, Thomas; John, who purchased Wichnor, in 1765; Richard, in holy orders; and Anne, *m.* to the Rev. Richard Levett, of West Wycomb. The eldest son,

Thomas Levett, Esq. of Wichnor Park, *m.* in 1762, Catherine, dau. and eventually co-heir of Charles Floyer, Esq. of Hints, co. Stafford, by Susanna his wife, dau. and co-heir of Waldyve Willington, Esq. of Hurley, co. Warwick, and had issue,

- Theophilus, his heir.
- Thomas, in holy orders, of Packington, *m.* Wilmot-Maria, dau. of Sir N.-B. Gresley, Bart.; but *d. s. p.* in 1843.
- Anne, *d. unm*,
- Catharine, *m.* in 1794, to her cousin, William Humberstone Cawley-Floyer, Esq. of Hints Hall, co. Stafford.

The son and heir,

Theophilus Levett, Esq. of Wichnor Park, high-sheriff of Staffordshire 50 George III., and recorder of the city of Lichfield, *m.* Frances, dau. of Thomas Prinsep, Esq. of Croxall Hall, co. Derby, and had issue, I. John, his heir; II. Theophilus, *m.* Henrietta, dau. of the Rev. John Templer, of Devonshire; III. Thomas, who took the surname of Prinsep: he *m.* 1st, Margaret, dau. of David Monro, Esq., by whom he had one surviving dau., and 2ndly, Caroline, dau. of the Rev. John Templer; IV. Arthur, married; I. Frances, *m.* to William Gist, Esq.; II. Mary, *m.* to the Rev. John Mucklestone; and III. Anne. Mr. Levett *d.* 3 Dec. 1839, and was *s.* by his son,

John Levett, Esq. of Wichnor Park and Packington Hall, who *m.* 19 Feb. 1829, Sophia-Eliza, niece of the Marquess of Ailsa, and dau. of the Hon. Robert Kennedy, by Jane his wife, sister of Gen. Alexander Macomb, commander-in-chief of the armies of the United States in America, and had issue,

- Theofilus-John, now of Wichnor Park.
- Robert-Thomas-Kennedy, *b.* 29 April, 1831.
- Edward, *b.* 18 Dec. 1832.
- Charles-Richard, *b.* 14 June, 1834.
- Henry-Gordon, *b.* 26 July, 1841.
- Sophia-Frances-Margaret.

Arms—Arg., a lion, rampant, between three crosses-crosslet fitchée, sa., a bordure, engrailed, az., charged with four crosses-crosslet fitchée, and four fleurs-de-lis, alternately, or.
Crest—A demi-lion, arg., ducally crowned, or, gorged with a collar, az., in the dexter paw a cross-crosslet fitchée, sa., the sinister paw resting on an escutcheon, of the third, charged with a fleur-de-lis, gold.
Seat—Wichnor Park, co. Stafford.

LEWIN OF CLOGANS.

Horsfall-Lewin, Christopher-Henry, Esq. of Cloghans, co. Mayo, assumed the name and arms of Lewin, at the desire of his maternal grandfather, Thomas Lewin, Esq. of Cloghans. Mr. Horsfall-Lewin is only son of the late Captain Horsfall, by Jane his wife, eldest dau. and co-heir (with her sister, Barbara, *m.* to Ralph Benson, Esq. of Lut wyche Hall, co. Salop, M.P.) of THOMAS LEWIN, Esq. of Clogans, co. Mayo.

Arms—Arg., a bend, engr., sa., between two trefoils, slipped, vert.
Crest—A demi-lion, holding between his paws a trefoil.
Motto—Spes mea in Deo.
Seat—Cloghans, co. Mayo.

LEWIN OF THE CO. CLARE.

See ROSS-LEWIN.

LEWIN OF WOMASTON.

LEWIN, SAMUEL, Esq. of Womaston House, co. Radnor, J.P., *b.* 4 Dec. 1799; *m.* 27 July, 1837, Sarah, eldest dau. of John Smart, Esq. of Manor House, Chigwell, Essex, and has issue,

I. SAMUEL, *b.* 6 May, 1838,
II. Percival-John, *b.* 1 Nov. 1840.
I. Sophia.

Lineage.—SAMUEL LEWIN, son of Samuel Lewin, *m.* Mary-Millar, dau. of Mr. Pollard, consul at Aleppo, and had two sons, SAMUEL and Charles-Devereux, and three daus., Elizabeth, Henrietta, and Sophia. The elder son,

SAMUEL LEWIN, Esq. of Womaston, *m.* in 1795, Mary Furmage, and had issue, I. SAMUEL, now of Womaston; II. Alexander-Percival; III. James-Davies; I. Elizabeth; II. Mary; III. Sophia; and IV. Hannah-Puget.

Arms—Or, a chev., engr., az., between three escallops, in chief, gu., and a buck's head, erased, in base, of the last.
Crest—A sea-lion, ppr., the tail nowed, holding in the paws a shield, gu., charged with an escallop, or.
Seat—Womaston House, co. Radnor.

LEWIS OF GREENMEADOW.

LEWIS, HENRY, Esq. of Greenmeadow, co. Glamorgan, *b.* 11 March, 1815; *m.* Anne, dau. of Walter Morgan, Esq. of Merthyr, and has issue,

I. HENRY, *b.* 1847.
II. Thomas-Wyndham, *b.* 1848.
I. Mary-Price. II. Blanche-Eliza.
III. Dorothy-Anne.

Lineage.—GWAETHVOED, son of Gwlydden, by Morfydd his wife, dau. and sole heir of Owain ap Teithwalch, Lord of Cardigan, and the 12th in descent from Ieon, of the lineage of the Princes of Britain, was contemporary with EDGAR, King of the Saxons, and on being ordered by the Saxon King Edgar to row his barge upon the Dee, refused, saying, "*Fear him who fears not death*"—(Ofner na ofno angau.) Gwaethvoed *m.* Morfydd, dau. and co-heir of Ivor, Lord of Gwent, by whom he was father of

KINDRYCH, who *m.* Nest, dau. of Tangno ap Cadwgel, Lord of Ardudwy, in North Wales, and was father of

CEDIVOR, Lord of Llancaysach, in Morganwg, (Glamorganshire), who *m.* Gwenllian, dau. and heir of Madoc ap Caradoc, heiress of Senghenydd. His son,

MEURIC AP CEDIVOR, was father of

IVOR AP MEURIC, known in Welsh history as IVOR BACH, (that is, Ivor Petit or Little Ivor), who, though a man of low stature, was of high mind and courage; he *m.* Eleanor, dau. of Rys ap Griffith ap Rys ap Tudor, Lord of South Wales, and had issue GRIFFITH AP IVOR, Lord of Senghenydd, living 1174, father by Mabel his wife, dau. of the Earl of Gloucester, of RHYS AP GRIFFITH, Lord of Senghenydd, who *m.* a dau. of Yorath, Lord of Caerleon, and had a son,

GRIFFITH AP RHYS, of Senghenydd, was taken in Castel Coch, by De Clare, who put out his eyes, probably about 1257, and seised upon the lands of Senghenydd. He was father of

HOWEL VELYN AP GRIFFITH, who *m.* Sarah, dau. of Sir Mayo le Soer, Knt., Lord of St. Fagan's, and was father of

MADOC AP HOWEL VELYN, Lord of St. Fagan's and Emrych, who *m.* Everydd, dau. and co-heir of Lewis ap Rhys ap Rosser, descended from Bleddyn ap Maenarch, and had a son,

LLEWELYN AP MADOC, of Merthyr, father, by Joan his wife, dau. of Llewelyn ap Rys ap Grono, Lord of Glyn Nedd, of

LLEWELYN VYCHAN AP LLEWELYN, who *m.* Anne, dau. of Evan ap Einion, of Prysedwyn, and was direct ancestor* of

EDWARD LEWIS, of the Van, sheriff 1548, 1555, and 1559, who first adopted the family surname. He *m.* Anne, dau. of Sir William Morgan, of Pencoed, and was *s.* by his son,

THOMAS LEWIS, of The Van, sheriff, 1569, who *m.* 1st, Margaret, dau. of Robert Gamage, Esq. of Coyty; and 2ndly, Catherine, dau. of Sir George Mathew, Knt. of Radr, high-sheriff for Glamorganshire in 1546. By his first wife he left an eldest son and successor,

SIR EDWARD LEWIS, Knt. of the Van, Penmark, St. Fagan's, Corntown, and Liantrithyd, *b.* 1560; sheriff 1601 and 1612, knighted at Theobald, 1603, who *m.* Blanch, sister of Sir William Morgan, of Tredegar, and had four sons, viz.,

I. Edward (Sir), of The Van, who *m.* Anne, dau. of Robert, Earl of Dorset, and widow of Lord Beauchamp, and was ancestor of Lewis of Borestal, Bucks, of Edington, Wilts, and of Van, co. Glamorgan, now represented by BARONESS WINDSOR.
II. William (Sir), Knt.
III. Nicholas.
IV. THOMAS (Sir), of whom presently.

The youngest son,

SIR THOMAS LEWIS, of Penmark Place, knighted at Whitehall, 1628, *m.* the dau. of Edmund Thomas, Esq. of Wenvoe, and dying 19 Dec. 1669, left issue,

Thomas, of Penmark Place, sheriff, 1674, *d. s. p.*, 1689.
Gabriel Edmund.
Katherine, *m.* to Edward Kemeys, Esq.

The 2nd son,

GABRIEL LEWIS, Esq. of Llanishen, sheriff in 1614, M.P. for Cardiff, *m.* Elizabeth, dau. of William Carne, Esq. of Nash, and left a dau., Elizabeth, *m.* to Edward Herbert, Esq. of Cogan, and a son and successor,

THOMAS LEWIS, Esq. of Llanishen, sheriff in 1639, who *m.* Eleanor, dau. of William Jones, of Abergavenny, and was *s.* by his son,

GABRIEL LEWIS, Esq. of Llanishen, sheriff in 1662, who *m.* Grace, dau. of Humphrey Wyndham, Esq. of Dunraven Castle, co. Glamorgan, and was father of

THOMAS LEWIS, Esq. of Llanishen, high-sheriff in 1683. He *m.* 1st, Elizabeth Van, by whom he had a son,

THOMAS, sheriff in 1745, who left one son, Wyndham, *b.* in 1752, and two daus., Elizabeth and Blanche, who all *d. s. p.*
Jane, *m.* William Bruce, Esq. of Llanblethian.
Grace, *m.* to Dr. Bates, of Cowbridge.

Thomas Lewis, *m.* 2ndly, Elizabeth, dau. of Henry Morgan, Esq. of Penllwyn, co. Monmouth, and had, with a dau., Grace, a son,

THOMAS LEWIS, Esq of Newhouse, high-sheriff of Glamorganshire in 1757, who *m.* Elizabeth, dau. of Morgan Thomas, Esq. of Rubina, and left at his decease, 1764, aged sixty-five, two sons, WYNDHAM, his heir; and William, of The Forge and Greenmeadow; sheriff, 1790, *d. s. p.* The elder son,

THE REV. WYNDHAM LEWIS, of Newhouse, *m.* Margaret, dau. and eventual heir of Samuel Price, Esq. of Park, co. Glamorgan, by Katharine his wife, dau. and heir of John Williams, Esq. of Llanvair, and had issue,

I. THOMAS, of Newhouse, *m.* 7 April, 1802, Dorothy-Augusta, dau. of John Goodrich, Esq. of Energlyn, co. Glamorgan, and left (with two daus., Dorothy-Price, wife of J.-H. Langley, Esq., and Mary Shadden, deceased.), one son, JOHN LEWIS, Esq. of Newhouse, who *d. s. p.*
II. Henry, of whom presently.
III. Wyndham, of Greenmeadow, co. Glamorgan, *b.* 7 Oct. 1780, M.P. for Cardiff in 1820, for Aldburgh in 1827, and for Maidstone in 1835; *m.* in 1815, Mary-Anne, only dau. of John Evans, Esq. of Brampford Speke, Devonshire, and *d. s. p.* 14 March, 1838. His widow *m.* 2ndly, the Right Hon. B. D'Israeli, M.P.

---

* The intervening descent follows:—

LLEWELYN VYCHAN=Anne, dau. of Evan ap Einion.
|
RYS AP LLEWELYN VYCHAN=Margaret, dau. of Thomas Liasset, of St. Hillary.
|
LLEWELYN ANWYL AP RYS=Janet, dau. of Griffith ap Howel Gam, of Llanvrynach.
|
RICHARD GWYN AP LLEWELYN, of Merthyr=Cecil, dau. of Evan Trahearn ap Meyrick, of Merthyr.
|
1. Dau. of Lewis ap Rosser ap Llewelyn=LEWIS AP RICHARD GWYN=2. Gwladys, dau. and heir of Ievan-John ap Ievan ap Philip, of Merthyr, and widow of Morgan Thomas.

RICHARD, ancestor of the Pritchards of Llancaysach. (by 1st wife)
EDWARD LEWIS, of the Van. (by 2nd wife)

IV. William-Price, in holy orders, vicar of Llanishen; d. 1849, leaving issue.
I. Mary-Anne, m. to Richard-Rice Williams, Esq.
II. Katherine, m. 1st, to Thomas Williams, Esq.; and 2ndly, to James Bradley, Esq. of Bristol.

The 2nd son,

HENRY LEWIS, Esq., of Park and Greenmeadow, an officer in the army; b. 26 May, 1774, d. 26 Sept. 1838. He m. Mary, dau. of George, and sister to the Rev. Charles Emerson, and by her (who d. at Greenmeadow, 10 Aug. 1841) had issue,

HENRY, now of Greenmeadow.
Wyndham, d. young.
Wyndham-William, of The Heath, co. Glamorgan, b. 10 Aug. 1827; sheriff, 1855-6; m. Annie, dau. of George Overton, of Merthyr, and has issue, Annie-Mary Price.
Charles, d. young.
Mary-Jane, m. Henry Andrew Vaughan, Esq., and has issue.
Anne-Price, m. George-Thomas Clark, Esq. of Frimhurst, co. Surrey, and has issue.
Catherine Price, m. George Collins Jackson, Esq., major in the 7th hussars, and has issue.

Arms—Quarterly: 1st, sa., a lion, rampant, arg.; 2nd, sa., a chev., between three spear heads, az., embowed, gu.; 3rd, sa., a chev., between three fleurs-de-lis, or; 4th, or, on a quarter, gu., two lions, passant-guardant.
Crest—LEWIS—A lion, sejant, arg. PRICE—A paschal lamb glorified, or, bearing a pennon of St. George.
Mottoes—"Patriæ fidus;" and "Ofner na ofne angua."
Seat—Greenmeadow, co. Glamorgan.

LEWIS OF GILFACH.

LEWIS, THE REV. DAVID-PRICE, of Gilfach, co. Carmarthen, J.P., b. 10 Jan. 1805.

Lineage.—DAVID HOWELL, of Penyrhin, Landdansaint, co. Carmarthen (descended from Owen Gethin, grandson of Cradoc ap Gwillym, of Glyntawe, to whom King JOHN gave for arms, "Az., a buck, tripping, arg., bearing a royal crown, between his horns"), was father of

LEWIS DAVID, of Panthowel, in Llanddansaint, who m. Elizabeth, dau. of Rees Price, of Brynwhyth Gwinfe, co. Carmarthen, derived, in the female line, from a branch of the Aubreys of Coedmawr, and dying 16 Feb. 1745, left, with a dau., Jane, m. to John-Reps Morris, two sons, DAVID, his heir; and Rees, accidentally killed. The elder son,

DAVID LEWIS, of Panthowel, m. 15 Jan. 1738, Anne, dau. of Rees Llewellyn, of Lliewel, Brecon, and by her, who d. in 1785, had issue, LEWIS; Rice, a clergyman, d. at Usk, s. p.; John, of Pencryg, who m. Elinor, dau. of John Jones, Esq.; Thomas, of Neath, d. unm. 9 Oct. 1791; Magdalen, m. to Owen Bowen, of Cwmydw, Mothvey, co. Carmarthen; Elizabeth, m. to David Evans, of Llansadurn, co. Carmarthen; Anne, m. to Griffith Morgan, of Clynhir, Llandilo Talybont; Gwladis, m. to Richard Prichard, of Llanwrda. The eldest son,

LEWIS LEWIS, Esq. of Panthowel, m. 30 Dec. 1772, Mary, dau. of Henry Jones, Esq. of Brunant Cayo, and by her (who d. 15 April, 1834, aged 84) had issue,

DAVID-JONES, of Gilfach.
Thomas, of Llanddansaint, and has issue, Lewis, Morgan, David, Martha, Mary, and Louisa.
Rice, of Merthyr Tydvil, m. Magdalen, dau. of Thomas Llewellyn, of Lliewel, co. Brecon, and has issue, Thomas, David, Lewis, Rice, William, Henry, Mary-Anne, Margaret, Elizabeth, Sarah, and Catherine.
Margaret, m. to William-David Jeffrey, Esq., and d. 4 Jan. 1796, aged 21, leaving issue.
Anne, m. 1st, to William Williams, Esq. of Llanddansaint, and 2ndly, to William Howell, Esq.
Mary, m. to Evan Evans, of Llansadurn.

Mr. Lewis d. 20 Sept. 1796, aged 54, and was s. by his son,

DAVID-JONES LEWIS, Esq. of Gilfach, J.P., b. 16 Oct. 1773, who m. 3 July, 1798, Mary, only child of David Price, Esq. of Blaenycwm, co. Carmarthen, and by her (who d. 9 Dec. 1823, aged 50) had issue,

DAVID-PRICE, now of Gilfach.
Lewis, of Wymondham, Norfolk.
Frederick, resident at Llwynelyn, m. Anna-Letitia, only dau. of Robert-Middleton Williams, Esq. of Carmarthen, and has issue, David-Jones, b. 17 July, 1848; Frederick-Williams, b. 8 May, 1851; Charles-Prytherch, b. 20 Aug. 1853; Arthur-Middleton, b. 20 July, 1855; Anna-Letitia-Price; Mary-Agnes.
Margaret, d. unm.

Mr. Lewis d. 28 Nov. 1848.

Arms—Quarterly: 1st and 4th, az., a buck, trippant, arg. bearing a royal crown between his horns; 2nd and 3rd, az. a chevron, between three eagles' heads, erased, or.
Crest—A buck, trippant, and an eagle's head, as in the arms.
Motto—Byddwch gyfiawn ac nag ofnwch (Be just and fear not).
Seat—Gilfach, Carmarthenshire.

LEWIS OF HENLLAN.

LEWIS, JOHN-LENNOX-GRIFFITH-POGER, Esq. of Henllan, co. Carmarthen, J.P. and D.L., barrister-at-law, b. 22 Oct. 1819.

Lineage.—The early pedigree of the family of Lewis is given in the Book of Golden Grove, penes the Earl of Cawdor.

RICHARD LEWIS, Esq. of Henllan (son of Roger Lewis, who was son of Lodwich, and grandson of Roger, the last named in the Golden Grove MS.), m. in 1744, Mary, dau. of John Griffiths, Esq. of Glan-y-rhydd, and had issue, John, DAVID, Catherine, Margaret, and Mary. The 2nd, but only surviving son,

DAVID LEWIS, Esq., m. in 1785, Elizabeth, dau. of Morgan Lewis, of Carmarthen, and had, JOHN, Owen-Evan, Mary, Margaret, Elizabeth, and Elinor. The eldest son,

JOHN LEWIS, Esq. of Henllan, m. 1st, in 1818, Eliza, dau. of Charles-P. Callen, Esq. of Grove, co. Pembroke, and by her had,

JOHN-LENNOX-GRIFFITH-POGER, now of Henllan.
Richard, in holy orders, rector of Lampeter, m. Georgiana, dau. of Capt. Lewis, H.E.I.C.S., and has one son, ARTHUR-GRIFFITH-POGER.

He m. 2ndly, in 1824, Elizabeth, dau. of William Humphreys, of Pembroke, and by her had,

Frederick, deceased. Charles, deceased.
Herbert.
Elizabeth, m. to the Rev. Mr. Garbett.

Motto—Be wise as serpents.
Seat—Henllan, co. Carmarthen.

LEWIS OF STRADEY.

LEWIS, DAVID, Esq. of Stradey, co. Carmarthen, J.P. and D.L., high-sheriff 1833, and sometime M.P. for the Carmarthen boroughs, m. 9 June, 1836, Lætitia, youngest dau. of the late Benjamin Way, Esq. of Denham Place, Bucks, and has issue,

I. CHARLES-WILLIAM-MANSEL, b. 2 Dec. 1845.
I. Fanny-Louisa.
II. Rowena-Harriet-Mansel, d. 2 Oct. 1844.

Mr. Lewis is only son and heir, by Catherine his wife, 2nd dau. of William Lloyd, Esq. of Laques, co. Carmarthen, of Thomas Lewis, Esq. of Stradey, who s. to that estate, in 1807, under the will of Mrs. Mansel, dau. and eventually sole heir of Sir Edward-Vaughan Mansel, Bart.

Seat—Stradey, co. Carmarthen.

LEWIS OF GWINFE.

LEWIS, LEWIS, Esq. of Gwinfe, co. Carmarthen, J.P. and D.L., b. 23 Dec. 1805; m. 9 March, 1830, Miss Sarah-Simmons Barnes Colborne, niece of the late William Barnes, Esq. of Redland Court, co. Gloucester, and has issue,

I. CHARLES-BASSETT, an officer in the army, b. 13 Dec. 1831.
II. Lewis-Gwyn, lieut. Indian navy, b. 21 Sept. 1834.
III. Edward-Studley, an officer in the army, b. 21 Nov. 1836.
IV. Frank-Davie, b. 31 May, 1838.
V. George-Septimus, b. 21 Sept. 1843.
I. Eleanora-Jane. II. Eustatia-Harriette.
III. Augusta-Blanche.

Lineage.—THE REV. THOMAS LEWIS, J.P. for co. Brecon, and D.L. for co. Carmarthen, rector of Pemboyr, co. Brecon, son of Lewis Lewis, Esq., a deputy-lieut. for Carmarthenshire, and his wife, Barbara Lloyd, of Llancomthou, co. Glamorgan, m. 11 Aug. 1762, Elizabeth Studley, of Shropshire, and had (besides two daus., Elizabeth and Susanna) a son,

The Rev. Lewis Lewis, of Gwinfe, co. Carmarthen, J.P. and D.L., rector of Clovelly, co. Devon, who *m.* 22 Sept. 1802, Eleonora, eldest dau. of the late John Davie, Esq. of Orleigh, co. Devon, and had issue,

I. Lewis, now of Gwinfe.
II. Thomas, *m.* 19 April, 1836, Victoire-Maria, 4th dau. of Andrew Houston, Esq. of the island of Grenada, and has issue,
  1 Andrew-Courtenay, *b.* 31 Jan. 1837.
  2 George-May, *b.* 23 Aug., and *d.* in Oct. 1840.
  3 Charles-Houston, *b.* 17 Feb. 1844.
  1 Eleonara-Harriette.
I. Eleonora-Elizabeth, *m.* in Oct. 1827, to Charles Bishop, Esq., eldest son of John-Rees Bishop, Esq. of Dalcaney. co. Carmarthen.

Mr. Lewis *d.* in 1826.

Arms—Quarterly: 1st and 4th, gu., a griffin, segreant, or, for Lewis; 2nd and 3rd, sa., three nags' heads, erased, or, for Lloyd.
Crest—A demi-griffin, segreant, couped, or.
Motto—Facta non verba.
Seat—Gwinfe, co. Carmarthen.

LEWIS OF HENLLYS AND BODIOR.

Hampton-Lewis, John-Lewis, Esq. of Henllys and Bodior, co. Anglesey, J.P. and D.L., late capt. 5th dragoon-guards, high-sheriff of Anglesey 1846, *b.* 18 Oct. 1798; *m.* 2 Sept. 1833, Frances-Elizabeth, only child and heiress of Thomas I'Anson, Esq. of Harnby, co. York, and has issue,

I. Thomas-Lewis-Hampton, *b.* 9 Aug. 1834 (the elder son will take name of Lewis at his father's death, the other children bear and will continue to bear the surname of Hampton).
II. John-Vivian-Hampton, *b.* 18 June, 1835.
I. Fanny-Mary-Hampton.
II. Mary-Freeman-Grace-Hampton.

Lineage.—William Hampton, descended from an ancient Lancashire family, formed one of the garrison of Beaumaris Castle in 1460, and held there the rank of deputy-governor, as appears from a document bearing his name, giving orders to the inhabitants of the town to extinguish their fires at an appointed hour. He received a grant of Henllys, co. Anglesey, anciently the seat of Gweirydd ap Rhys Goch, chief of one of the Fifteen Tribes of North Wales. The eventual heiress of the Hamptons of Henllys,

Mary Hampton, of Henllys (only child of Robert Hampton, Esq., high-sheriff of Anglesey 1732), *m.* 11 April, 1746, John Jones, Esq. of Trefollwyn, son of Hugh Jones, Esq. of the same place, by Ann his wife, dau. of William Lloyd, of Llansadwrn, and had (with a dau., Mary, *m.* to William Lloyd, Esq. of Rockville, co. Roscommon) a son and successor,

John Hampton-Jones, Esq. of Henllys, *b.* 24 Feb. 1746, high-sheriff of Anglesey in 1770, who *m.*, 25 June, 1770, Emma, only dau. of the Rev. John Lewis, A.M., of Plas Llanfihangel, rector of Llandegfain, by Elizabeth his wife, dau. of Thomas Roberts, Esq. of Bodior, and had issue, I. John-Hampton, his heir; II. Robert-Edward, in holy orders, *b.* in April, 1779, B.A. Wadham College, Oxford, chaplain to H.M. forces at the Mauritius, *m.* in 1811, Susanna-Dorothea, 2nd dau. of John Williams, Esq. of Peniarth Uchaf, co. Merioneth, and has issue, Henry Berkeley; and Maria-Dorothea-Wilhelmina Sidney, *m.* to Robert Webster, Esq. of the 99th regt.; I. Elizabeth-Margaret, *d. unm.*; II. Jane-Lewis. The elder son,

John-Hampton Hampton-Lewis, Esq. of Henllys, *b.* 21 Nov. 1775, *s.* his father 12 Sept. 1806. He *m* 19 Dec. 1796, Mary, dau. of Richard Chambers, Esq. of Whitbourn Court and Cradley Hall, co. Hereford, and had issue,

John-Lewis, the present John-Lewis Hampton-Lewis, Esq. of Henllys and Bodior.
Joseph, *b.* 2 Feb. 1800, lieut.-col. 50th regt. of native infantry, H. E. I. C. S., *m.* Ellen, dau. of Major Hall, E.I. Co.'s service, and has issue, John-Lewis, *b.* 27 March, 1827.
Emma, *d.* in Aug. 1819.
Mary-Margaret, *m.* 22 Nov. 1825, to Alexander Anderson, Esq. of Kingask, co. Fife, major E.I. Co.'s engineers, and has issue.
Anna-Maria Surnam, *m.* 16 June, 1835, to Charles Longman, Esq. 2nd son of Thomas-Norton Longman, Esq. of Mount Grove, Hampstead, Middlesex, and has issue.

Mr. Hampton-Lewis *d.* 23 Jan. 1843.

Arms—Quarterly: 1st and 4th, quarterly, 1st and 4th, arg., a chevron, sa., between three Cornish choughs, ppr., in the beak of each an ermine spot, for Lewis, 2nd and 3rd, gu., on a chevron, between three bucks' heads, caboshed, ar., a crescent, of the field, for difference, for Roberts *of Bodior*; 2nd and 3rd, gu., on a fesse, or, between a mullet, in chief, and an escallop, in base, arg., three martlets, sa., for Hampton.
Crests—1st, a Cornish chough, ppr., in the dexter claw a fleur-de-lis, az., for Lewis; 2nd, a wyvern amidst bulrushes, ppr., for Hampton.
Motto—A Deo et rege.
Seats—Henllys and Bodior, co. Anglesey.

LEWIS OF KILCULLEN.

Lewis, J.-Harvey, Esq. of Kilcullen, co. Kildare, and of 24, Grosvenor-street, Grosvenor-square, London, high-sheriff of the co. of Kildare, in 1857; *m.* 27 Aug. 1840, Emily-Owen, only child of George Ball, Esq. of Richmond, Surrey, which lady *d. s. p.* 11 Nov. 1850.

Lineage.—The family of Lewis or Llewys is one of great antiquity in Wales. A descendant of the ancient stem,

Francis Lewis, of Cardigan, who *m.* Elizabeth Budurds, settled in Ireland about the middle of the 17th century, and acquired property in the county of Kildare, Meath, and the Queen's County. He was father of

William Lewis, Esq. of Tullygory, co. Kildare, who *m.* Margaret, dau. of Francis Roberts, Esq., by Jean O'Kelly, his wife, and was *s.* by his son,

Michael Lewis, Esq. of Tullygory, who *m.* Susanne, dau. of Edmund Jones, Esq., M P. for Duleek, A.D. 1695, by Rebecca, his wife, dau. of William Crutchley, Esq. of Crutchley Hall, co. Stafford, and had a son and successor,

Robert Lewis, Esq. of the City of Dublin, and of the Queen's County, who *m.* Anne, dau. of Arthur Gambell, Esq. of Washford, co. Westmeath, M.P. for Ballyshannon, by Elizabeth, his wife, dau. of Major John D'Alton, of Duneel Castle, co. Westmeath. By Anne Gambell, his wife, Robert Lewis had a son and heir,

Michael Lewis, Esq. of Spring Hill, co. Dublin, who *m.* Anne, only dau. of R. Frisell, Esq., descended from the Frasers of Lovat, and had issue,

William, his heir.
Arthur-Gambell, lieut.-col. Monaghan militia (*see his name*).
Richard, *m.* 1st, Emily, dau. of — Osborne, Esq. of London; 2ndly, a dau. of Thomas Taylor, Esq. of Polygon House, Southampton; and 3rdly, Frances Tyler, niece of Admiral Sir Charles Tyler, and left issue.
Robert, R.N., *m.* Elizabeth, dau. of Sir Richard Onslow, Bart., K.B., Vice-Admiral of England and general of Marines, and *d.* in 1840, leaving issue.
Edward, *m.* his cousin, Henrietta, dau. and co-heir of H. Loftus Frizell, Esq., and has issue.
Edmond-Jones, in holy orders, *m.* Elizabeth, dau. of the Rev. William Lyster, and niece of James, Lord Bishop of Dromore, and has issue.
Anne, *m.* to Major J. Fielding Sweeny, and has issue.
Eleanor, *m.* to F. Bernard Sweeny, Esq.
Charlotte, *m.* to Captain Stuart.

Michael Lewis *d.* in 1824. His eldest son,

William Lewis, Esq. of Harlech, co. Dublin, and of Kilcullen, co. Kildare, *m.* Dora, dau. of John Cassidy, Esq. of Monasterevan, and *d.* in 1850, leaving issue,

J.-Harvey, now of Kilcullen.
William, of Dublin, *m.* Jane, dau. of Michael Hackett, Esq. of Elm Grove, King's County, and has issue.
Mary-Anne, *m.* in 1832, to Robert Morellet Alloway, Esq. of Ballyshanduffe, otherwise The Derries, Queen's County.

Arms—As duly registered in Ulster's office—Sa., a chev., erm., between three spear heads, arg.
Crest—Out of a ducal coronet, a plume of feathers, charged with a chev., or.
Motto—"Bidd Llu Hebb Llidd."
Residence—24, Grosvenor Street, Grosvenor Square, London.

LEWIS OF SEATOWN AND CLANAMULLY.

Lewis, Arthur-Gambell, Esq. of Seatown, co. Dublin, and Clanamully Scottstown, co. Monaghan, J.P. and D.L., lieut.-col. Monaghan militia; high-sheriff for co. Monaghan, 1847, and for co. Longford 1854; *m.* 1st, Hester, 2nd dau. of Richard Westenra, Esq. of Rutland-square, Dublin (uncle to Lord Rossmore), by Bridget his wife, sister and co-heiress of Maurice-Peppard Warren, Esq. of Lara, co. Carlow, and granddau. of Lady Hester Westenra, who was dau. to Ford, Earl of Cavan. Colonel Lewis m. 2ndly, Henrietta, relict of the Hon. Richard Westenra, 2nd son to Warner-William, Lord Rossmore, and sole heiress of Henry-Owen Scott, Esq. of Clanamulla Scottstown, co. Monaghan (a younger branch of Scott, Lord Polwarth), granddau. and co-heiress of John Owen, Esq. of Newgrove, co. Monaghan. By his 1st marriage, Colonel Lewis has an only child, viz., MAURICE-PEPPARD-WARREN, barrister-at-law, who, by his mother, is descended from the great Earl de Warren (whose arms he bears), as also from the ancient baronial family of Peppard, co. Louth, and from Ford, Earl of Cavan. By his 2nd marriage, Colonel Lewis has an only child, Henry-Owen, who is, through his mother, descended by a common descent from the Scotts, Lord Polworth, and in a direct line from Edward, 1st Lord Blayney, Baron of Monaghan, and Garrett, Viscount Drogheda.

Colonel Lewis is 2nd son of Michael Lewis, of Spring Hill, co. Dublin, who d. in 1824, by Anne his wife (who d. in 1825), only dau. of R. Frizell, Esq., or Frazer, descended from Frazer of Lovat, in Scotland. (*See* LEWIS *of Kilcullen*).

Arms and *Crest*—Same as LEWIS *of Kilcullen*.
Residence—Fitzwilliam Sq., West.
Seats—Seatown, co. Dublin, and Clanamully, co. Monaghan.

LEWIS OF ST. PIERRE.

LEWIS, CHARLES-JAMES, Esq. of St. Pierre, co. Monmouth, J.P. and D.L., b. 26 Jan. 1781; s. his eldest brother, Colonel Lewis, in 1847.

Lineage.—This family derives, in a direct male line, from CADIFOR, prince or chieftain of Divet, a portion of country which comprised Pembrokeshire and part of Caermarthenshire. Cadivor flourished about the period of the Norman Conquest, and was buried in the priory of Caermarthen. He m. Ellen, dau. and heiress of Llwchlawen, the great Lord of Kilsant, and had a son, BLEDRI, Lord of Blaencuch, who m. Clydwen, dau. and heir of Griffith ap Cydrick ap Gwaithvoed; and their great-great-grandson, IVOR AP LLEWELYN, m. Tanglwrst, dau. and heir of Howel Sais ap Rhys ap Griffith ap Rhys ap Tewdwr Mawr, and was great-grandfather of

LLEWELYN AP IVOR, Lord of St. Clare, co. Caermarthen, and Tredegar, co. Monmouth, who m. Angharad, dau. and heir of Sir Morgan Meredith, descended from Rhys, King of South Wales. Angharad was called the beauteous maid of Caerleon upon Uske, and was the representative of the old Welsh Lords of Caerleon. They had issue three sons, viz.,

MORGAN, Lord of St. Clare and Tredegar, living 1374, 48 EDW. III., from whom the MORGANS *of Tredegar, Pen-y-Coed, Llantarnam, &c. &c.*
IVOR HAEL, of Gwern-y-cleppa, who d. of the plague, 1361.
PHILIP ap Llewelyn ap Ivor.

The third son,

PHILIP AP LLEWELYN, m. Nest, dau. of Gwillym Sais ap Madoc, and had issue, Gwillym Philip Llewelyn, John-Philip Llewelyn, Gwenllian, m. David Gwillym-Jenkin, and an elder son,

SIR DAVID AP PHILIP, who m. Christy, dau. of David ap Ievan ap Rhys Voel, and their grandson,

THOMAS LEWIS, Esq. of Cheptow, co. of Monmouth, killed at Banbury, 1469, m. Elizabeth, dau. of Morgan-Jenkin-Philip, of Langston, co. Monmouth, and his great-grandson,

HENRY LEWIS, Esq. of St. Pierre, living 1536, high-sheriff in 1544, d. 1547, having m. Bridget, dau. and heir of Thomas Kemeys, and widow of Thomas Herbert, of Caldicot, by whom he was father of

WILLIAM LEWIS, Esq. of St. Pierre, living in 1583, who m. Margaret, dau. of Robert Gamage, of Coity, co. Glamorgan, and was s. by his son,

HENRY LEWIS, Esq. of St. Pierre, high-sheriff 1609, d. 7 Feb. 1637, 12 CHAS. I., having m. Joan, dau. and co-heir of Henry Herbert, Esq. of Wonastow, by whom he had a son and heir,

GEORGE LEWIS, Esq. of St. Pierre, who m. Mary, dau. of Sir William Morgan, of Tredegar, and d. v. p. 17 Nov. 1634, leaving issue, William, who d. a minor; Elizabeth, who m. Roger Oates, of Cefn Tilla, co. of Monmouth, and a son and heir,

THOMAS LEWIS, Esq. of St. Pierre, a stanch and devoted Royalist, 11 years old in 1639, living 1673. He m. Johanna, dau. of Joseph Langton, Esq. of Newton Park, co. Somerset, and was s. by his eldest son,

THOMAS LEWIS, Esq. of St. Pierre, who m. De la Riviere or De la Rivers, dau. of General Sir Thomas Morgan, Knt. and Bart. of Llangattock, co. of Monmouth, which lady m. 2ndly, Thomas Williams, Esq., 4th son of Sir Trevor Williams, Bart. of Llangibby Castle, co. of Monmouth, ancestor of the present William A. Williams, Esq. of Llangibby Castle. Mr. Lewis left issue a son,

THOMAS LEWIS, Esq. of St. Pierre, who m. 1st, Frances, dau. of Sir Richard Levett, Knt. of Kew, who d. in 1707; 2ndly, Katharine, only dau. and heir of Hugh Calveley Cotton, eldest son of Sir Robert Cotton, Bart. of Combermere, co. Chester; and 3rdly, Jane-Rachel, only dau. and heir of William Becher, Esq. of Howberry, co. Bedford. Mr. Lewis d. 29 May, 1732, aged 47, having had issue, by his 3rd wife, Craven, who m. and d. s. p. before 1764; Mary, d. 1734; Fanny, d. 9 May, 1767, having m. Thomas Lewis, Esq. of Crick, who d. Feb. 1803, aged 68; and an elder son,

MORGAN LEWIS, Esq. of St. Pierre, who d. 17 August, 1779, aged 57, having m. Rachel, only dau. of Charles Van, Esq. of Llanwern, co. Monmouth, and by her, who d. 28 Jan. 1797, aged 70, had seven sons and three daus.

I. THOMAS, his heir.
II. CHARLES, who s. his brother.
III. John-Craven, of Henbury, co. Gloucester, who m. and left a dau., who m. Capt. Crowdy, and left issue a dau.
IV. George, drowned in the Severn, 6 Nov. 1774, æt. 16.
V. Edward, in holy orders, rector of Portskewet and St. Pierre, d. 1 March, 1839, aged 79, having m. Mary, eldest dau. and co-heir of William Freke, Esq. of Hannington, co. Wilts, who d. 29 Dec. 1846, aged 76, and had issue one son and three daus., viz.,
  1 Edward Freke, in holy orders, rector of Portskewet and St. Pierre, m. 31 August, 1853, Caroline-Mary, 2nd dau. of Thomas Bates Rous, Esq. of Court-y-rala, co. Glamorgan.
  1 Mary, m. her cousin, Rev. Francis Lewis.
  2 Frances. 3 Anne, m. Capt. John King, R.N.
VI. Francis, in holy orders, LL.B., d. 17 Sept. 1794, aged 32, m. Fanny, younger dau. and co-heir of William Freke, Esq. of Hannington, co. Wilts, who survived her husband, and m. 2ndly, William Morton Pleydell, Esq. of Whitcomb, co. Dorset; and 3rdly, Rev. Paul Leir.
VII. James, d. 4 June, 1787, aged 22.
I. Jane, m. 1st, 12 Feb. 1774, John Hanbury, Esq. of Pont-y-Pool, co. Monmouth, who d. 4 April, 1784, having had three sons, viz.,
  1 John Capel, d. unm. 1796.
  2 Capel, now of Pont-y-Pool, lord-lieutenant of the co. of Monmouth (*see* HANBURY LEIGH).
  3 Charles, created Baron Sudeley,
  She m. 2ndly, Thomas Stoughton, Esq. of Ballyhorgan, co. Kerry, and had issue.
II. Ellen, who m. Rev. Thomas Leyson, M.A. of Jesus College, Oxford, vicar of Bassaleg, and rector of Panteague and Tredunnock, co. of Monmouth.
III. Frances, d. 30 March, 1795.

Morgan Lewis d. 17 August, 1779, aged 57, and was s. by his eldest son,

THOMAS LEWIS, Esq. of St. Pierre, who m. 1st, Margaret, dau. of John Cope, Esq of Petherton, in the parish of Westmoreland, Jamaica, which lady was accidentally burnt to death at St. Pierre, 26th January, 1788, aged 19. He m. 2ndly, Anne, dau. of Rev. Thomas Leyson, who survived her husband, and m. 2ndly, 25 April, 1798, Charles Kemeys Kemeys Tynte, Esq., and d. April, 1835. Mr. Lewis d. 17 June, 1796, s. p., aged 45, when the family estates devolved upon his next brother,

CHARLES LEWIS, Esq. of St. Pierre, who m. 16 June, 1777, Susanna, dau. of Francis Davis, Esq of Chepstow, and Anne, his wife, dau. and co-heir of James Higford, Esq. of Dixton, co. Gloucester, and had issue,

I. THOMAS, his heir.
II. CHARLES-JAMES, the present possessor of St. Pierre.
III. Francis, in holy orders, J.P. and D.L., rector of Llanvair Kilgidin, co. of Monmouth, and vicar of Hom Lacy, co. Hereford, b. 4 July, 1782, m. 1st, 25 March, 1828, his cousin, Mary, eldest dau. of the Rev. Edward Lewis, rector of Portskewit, who d. 31 May, 1846, leaving issue.
  1 Charles-Edward, J.P., b. 26 April, 1830.
  2 Thomas-Freke, b. 16 May, 1831, lieut. 23rd R. W. Fusiliers.
  3 Francis Higford, b. 24 Sept. 1832, d. 10 April, 1855
  4 Henry Leece, b. 8 Sept. 1834, d. 15 Feb. 1835.
  5 George-William, b. 23 June, 1840.
  1 Mary-Fanny-Susanna.

He *m.* 2ndly, 7 Jan. 1863, Jane, only dau. of Vice-Admiral Charles Gordon and widow of the Rev. J.-H. S. Bevor.

IV. Edward Higford, *b.* 27 July, 1788, *d.* on board H.M.S. Neptune, off Barbadoes, 27 April, 1810, aged 22.

V. Henry, *b.* 1 Nov. 1794, *d.* 30 June, 1814.

I. Frances-Susanna, *b.* 22 Jan. 1791, *m.* John Baldwyn, Esq. of The Mount, Chepstow, and *d.* 25 Sept. 1828.

Mr. Lewis *d.* 16 Dec. 1840, aged 86, and was *s.* by his son,

THOMAS LEWIS, Esq. of St. Pierre, colonel of the Monmouth militia, *b.* 12 May, 1779, *m.* 1st, Maria-Anne, dau. of Thomas Daniel, Esq. of Henbury, co. Gloucester; and 2ndly, Caroline, dau. and co-heir of Thomas Dyot Skip-Bucknall, Esq. of Hampton Court, co. Middlesex. She *d.* 29 March, 1850, aged 52, and Colonel Lewis *d. s. p.* at Clifton, 21 April, 1847, aged 67, and was *s.* by his brother, the present CHARLES-JAMES LEWIS, Esq. of St. Pierre.

Arms—Or, a lion rampant, sa., with many quarterings.
Crest—A griffin, segreant, sa.
Motto—Ha persa la fide, ha perso l'honore.
Seat—St. Pierre Park, near Chepstow.

LEWTHWAITE OF BROAD GATE.

LEWTHWAITE, JOHN, Esq. of Broad Gate, co. Cumberland, J.P. and D.L., *b.* 1792; *m.* 1820, Anne, dau. of William Kirkbank, Esq., D.L., of Beckside, and has issue,

I. WILLIAM, *m.* Mary, dau. of William Chalinor, Esq.
II. Joseph.
III. George.
I. Mary, *m.* to Walter Buchanan, Esq. of Liverpool.
II. Elizabeth.
III. Eleanor, *m.* to Robert-Francis Calrow, Esq.
IV. Ann.
V. Agnes.

Lineage.—This name seems to import Anglo-Saxon derivation; Thwaite, signifying a piece of ground cleared of wood, and the prefix, Lowe, a hill, give the ancient orthography of the name. The family appears from ancient documents, to have held lands in various parts of Cumberland from an early period.

WILLIAM LEWTHWAITE, Esq. of Broad Gate and of Whitehaven, J.P., 2nd son of William Lewthwaite, of Broad Gate, by Elizabeth his wife, dau. of John Towers, Esq. of Hockler Hall, co. Lancaster, and grandson (by Eleanor his wife, dau. of George Wingfield, Esq. of Woodland), of John Lewthwaite, Esq., whose grandfather, Thomas Lewthwaite, purchased Broad Gate, and *d.* 1667, *m.* Mary, dau. and co-heir of Joseph Nicholson, Esq. of Milholme, and had issue,

WILLIAM who succeeded his father at Broad Gate.
John, *m.* Margaret, eldest dau. of Roger Taylor, Esq. of Stott Park, in the co. Lancaster, and had issue, William; Gilfrid; Marianne; and Frances-Jane.
George, rector of Adel, co. York, J.P., *m.* Martha, dau. of Thomas Birley, Esq. of Kirkham, co. Lancaster, and had issue, William-Henry; George; and Margaret.
Joseph, a merchant in the West Indies, *d.* in 1816, *unm.*
Agnes, *m.* to the Rev. R. Armitstead, rector of Moresby.
Mary, *m.* Milham Hartley, Esq. of Rose Hill, Cumberland.
Ann, *m.* to Peter Dixon, Esq. of Newington, Surrey; and *d.* in 1803, *s. p.*
Margaret, *m.* to Peter Taylor, Esq. of Belfield, Westmoreland, major in the Royal Westmoreland militia; and *d.* in 1835, *s. p.*
Frances, *d.* young.
Betsy, of Hazel Mount.

The eldest son,

WILLIAM LEWTHWAITE, Esq. of Broad Gate, J.P., *m.* Eleanor, dau. of Thomas Cragg, Esq. of Lowscales, and by her (who *d.* 1830) had issue,

JOHN, of Broad Gate.
Mary, *m.* to William Postlethwaite, merchant of Ulverstone.
Agnes, *m.* to Robert Postlethwaite, Esq. of Broughton.
Eleanor, *d. unm.*
Elizabeth, *d. unm.*

Mr. Lewthwaite *d.* 1845.

Arms—Erm., a cross-flory, az., fretty, or.
Crest—A garb, bound by a serpent, nowed, ppr., holding in the mouth a cross-crosslet, fitchée, gu.
Motto—Tendens ad æthera virtus.
Seat—Broad Gate, Cumberland.

LEYCESTER OF TOFT.

LEYCESTER, RALPH-OSWALD, Esq. of Toft Hall, co. Chester, *b.* July, 1844.

Lineage.—RALPH LEYCESTER, younger brother of John Leycester, of Tabley, *m.* Joan, dau. and heiress of Robert Toft, of Toft, and dying *temp.* RICHARD II. was *s.* by his son,

ROBERT LEYCESTER, father of

ROBERT LEYCESTER, whose great-great-grandson,

SIR RALPH LEYCESTER, of Toft, was knighted at Leith, in Scotland, 11 May, 1544, at which time the Earl of Hertford, being then General, knighted several Cheshire gentlemen. Sir Ralph's grandson,

SIR GEORGE LEYCESTER, Knt., of Toft, *m.* Alice, eldest dau. of Peter Leycester, Esq. of Tabley, and had issue. Sir George was made sheriff of Cheshire by patent, dated 29 Dec., 45 ELIZABETH. He *d.* in 1612, and was *s.* by his only surviving son,

RALPH LEYCESTER, Esq. of Toft, father, by his wife, Mary, dau. of Anthony Woodhull, Esq. of Mollington, co. Oxford, of a son and heir,

GEORGE LEYCESTER, Esq. of Toft, who *m.* Dorothy, dau. of John Clayton, Esq., and sister and co-heir of Richard Clayton, Esq. of Crooke, in Lancashire, and had several children, the eldest of whom,

RALPH LEYCESTER, Esq. of Toft, *m.* Eleanor, dau. of Sir Peter Leycester, Bart. of Tabley, the well-known historian of Cheshire, and dying in March, 1685, was *s.* by his elder son,

GEORGE LEYCESTER, Esq. of Toft, who *m.* Jane, dau. of Oswald Mosley, Esq. of Ancoats, by whom he had three sons, RALPH his successor; George, a merchant in London, ancestor of the family of LEYCESTER, of White Place, Berks; and Oswald. The eldest son and successor,

RALPH LEYCESTER, Esq. of Toft, *b.* in 1699, *m.* Katherine, dau. and co-heiress of Edward Norris, Esq. of Speke, co. Lancaster, by Anne, dau. and heiress of Peter Gerard, Esq. of Crewood, and by her (who *d.* in 1799, at the advanced age of ninety) he had issue,

GEORGE, his successor.
RALPH, heir to his brother.
Edward, *d. unm.* in 1756.
Hugh, *b.* in 1748, King's counsel, and one of the judges of North Wales, *d.* 2 Jan. 1836.
Oswald, *b.* in 1752; in holy orders, M.A., rector of Stoke-upon-Tern; who *m.* 1st, Mary, dau. of P. Johnson, Esq. of Semperly; and 2ndly, Eliza, dau. of Charles White, Esq. of Manchester.
Anne, *m.* to the Rev. Dr. Norbury.
Theodosia, *m.* to the Rev. Egerton Leigh, archdeacon of Salop, and rector of Lymme.
Susannah, *m.* to the Hon. John Grey, 3rd son of the Earl of Stamford.

Mr. Leycester *d.* in 1777, and was *s.* by his eldest son,

GEORGE LEYCESTER, Esq. of Toft, at whose decease, *unm.* in 1809, the family estates devolved upon his brother,

RALPH LEYCESTER, Esq. of Toft, who *m.* in 1762, Charlotte, 3rd dau. of the Rev. Dr. Lushington, of Eastbourne, Sussex, and had issue,

RALPH, his heir.
Henry, a capt. in the navy, *d.* at Pisa.
George, fellow of King's College, Cambridge.
William, *m.* in the East Indies, —, dau. of — Friel, Esq., and has issue.
Charlotte, *m.* to Charles Dumbleton, Esq. of Bath.
Harriet, *m.* to the Rev. Robert Cox, vicar of Bridgenorth.
Susanna.

Mr. Leycester was *s.* at his decease by his eldest son,

RALPH LEYCESTER, Esq. of Toft, *b.* in 1764, M.P. for Shaftesbury, who *m.* Susanna, eldest dau. of the Rev. Egerton Leigh, of the family of the West Hall, High Leigh, and left at his decease (with three daus., Charlotte, Emma-Theodosia, and Laura-Susanna, which last *d.* 6 Jan. 1835) an only son and heir,

RALPH-GERARD LEYCESTER, Esq. of Toft Hall, *b.* 11 Oct. 1817, who *m.* 10 June, 1840, Emily-Elizabeth, dau. of Chas.-Tyrwhitt, Jones, Esq., and dying April 1851, left issue, I. RALPH-OSWALD, now of Toft; II. Charles-Hugh; III. Ernest-Gerard; I. Georgina-Susanna; and II. Amy-Theodosia.

Arms—Az., between two fleurs-de-lis, or, a fesse, of the second, fretty, gu.
Crest—A roebuck, per pale, or and gu., attired, of the second, holding in his mouth an acorn-branch, ppr.
Seat—Toft Hall, Knutsford, Cheshire.

LEYCESTER OF WHITE PLACE.

LEYCESTER, HENRY-HANMER, Esq. of White Place, co. Berks, *b.* 4 March, 1808; *m.* 28 April, 1852, Clara-Priscilla, dau. of Francis-John Norris, Esq., only son of John Norris, Esq. of Hemstead, in Kent, M.P., and grandson of Sir John Norris, admiral of the fleet *temp.* Queen ANNE, and has issue,

I. ARTHUR-HANMER, *b.* 18 Jan. 1853.
II. Lionel de Walden-Henry, *b.* 18 Oct. 1856.

Lineage.—GEORGE LEYCESTER, Esq., 2nd son of George Leycester, Esq. of Toft Hall, by Jane, his wife, dau. of

Oswald Mosley, Esq. of Ancoats, m. Martha, dau. of John Dodson, Esq., high-sheriff of co. Berks, and by her had an only son and heir,

THE REV. RALPH LEYCESTER, of White Place, who m. in 1761, Susannah, sister of Sir Walden Hanmer, Bart., M.P. for Sudbury, and d. in 1803, leaving with a dau. Martha Elizabeth, m. to John Adolphus, Esq. barrister-at-law, an only son and successor,

GEORGE-HANMER LEYCESTER, Esq. of White Place, b. 12 July, 1763, who m. 1796, Charlotte-Jemima, youngest dau. of the late Hans-Wintrop Mortimer, Esq. of Caldwell, co. Derby, M.P. for Shaftesbury, by Ann his wife, only dau. of Lord Anne Hamilton, 3rd son of James, Duke of Hamilton, and had issue,

GEORGE-RALPH, now of White Place.
Henry-Hanmer.
Edmund-Mortimer, comm. R.N., m. Henrietta, dau. of Capt. Neville, R.N., and has issue, Ralph-Neville, and Isabel.
Oswald-Walden. Augustus-Adolphus.
Henrietta-Maria, m. to Wm. Ward, Esq.
Louisa-Genevieve, m. to Francis Lyne, Esq.
Susannah, m. to Capt. Poulton, Madras army, and is since deceased.

Mr. Leycester d. 6 Oct. 1838.

Arms—Az., a fesse, or; fretty, gu., between two fleurs-de-lis, of the second.
Crest—A roebuck, statant, per pale, or and gu., attired, of the second, holding in his mouth an acorn-branch, ppr.
Motto—Dominus illuminatio mea.
Seat—White Place, near Maidenhead, Berks.

LILLINGSTON OF ELMDON.

See SPOONER-LILLINGSTON.

LIND OF RYDE.

LIND, JAMES-PLAYER, Esq. M.D., of Corstorphine Lodge, Ryde, Isle of Wight, J.P., b. 16 Sept. 1790; m. 17 Oct. 1822, Mary-Anne, dau. of William Reeks, Esq. of Bourne, Sussex.

Lineage.—The surname of Lynne was assumed by the proprietors of the lands and barony of Lynne, in Ayrshire, as soon as surnames became hereditary in Scotland. WALTER DE LYNNE obtained a grant of the lands of Pitmadie, in Perthshire, from King ALEXANDER II., A.D. 1244. From the Lynnes of Ayrshire descended,

JAMES LIND, M.D., b. in Edinburgh, in 1716, so well known for his medical works, especially his treatise on the scurvy, and his discovery of the mode of procuring fresh water at sea by distillation. He m. Isabel, dau. of John Dickie, Esq. of Corstorphine Hill, accountant-general of excise in Scotland, and d. in 1794, leaving two sons and one dau.,

JOHN, of whom we treat.
James (Sir), K.C.B., captain R.N.
Margaret, who m. Dr. Thomas Meek.

The elder son,

JOHN LIND, Esq., M.D., b. 1751, m. 1789, Elizabeth-Lydia, dau. of William Player, Esq. of Ryde, Isle of Wight, and sister and co-heiress of George Player, Esq. of Ryde, and had surviving issue,

JAMES-PLAYER, of Corstorphine Lodge.
Elizabeth, m. 1820, to Jean-Beat-Albert du Thon, lieut.-colonel, Lausanne, Switzerland; since deceased.
Anne.

Arms—Gu., two lances or spears, in saltier, betwixt a mullet, in chief, and a crescent, in base, arg., all within a border of the last, charged with four fleurs-de-lis, and as many annulets, alternately, az.
Crest—Two laurel-branches, in saltier, ppr.
Motto—Semper virescit virtus.
Seat—Corstorphine Lodge, Ryde, Isle of Wight.

LINDSAY-CARNEGIE OF SPYNIE.

LINDSAY-CARNEGIE, WILLIAM-FULLARTON, Esq. of Spynie, and Boysack, in North Britain, J.P. and D.L., b. 13 May, 1788; m. 27 Dec. 1820, Lady Jane-Christian Carnegie, dau. of William, 7th Earl of Northesk, G.C.B., and by her (who d. 1 Oct. 1840) has issue surviving,

I. John, b. 14 Feb. 1833.
II. Henry-Alexander, b. 5 July, 1836.
III. Donald-Christian-Strachan, b. 9 July, 1840.
I. Mary-Elizabeth, m. in Jan. 1845, to Major George Gordon, 50th regt., Bengal native infantry, son of Gordon of Halmyre, co. Peebles.
II. Jane, m. 1850, to Alexander Lindsay, Esq., formerly capt. 8th hussars.
III. Susan, m. 1856, to Robert Ramsay, Esq.
IV. Helen.

Mr. Carnegie, late a captain in the royal artillery, and hereditary fowler to the Kings of Scotland, is representative of Lady Catherine, sister of King ROBERT III., wife of David Lindsay, 11th Earl of Crauford; of the Fullartons of that ilk, and of the Carnegies of Boysack; is the oldest cadet of the noble house of Northesk, patron of the parish of Spynie, co. Moray, and heir to the Barony of Spynie.

Lineage.—GODFRIDUS FULLERTON, of Fullerton, in the counties of Perth and Forfar, got from King ROBERT the Bruce a charter of the office of King's Fowler, the grantee and his successors being "obliged to serve the king's house with wild fowl, when the king and his successors shall come to Forfar, where Fullerton shall be entertained, with a servant and two horses." From him descended

WILLIAM FULLERTON, of Fullerton, who m. about 1650, Margaret Lindsay, eldest dau. of the 2nd Lord Spynie, and sister to George, the 3rd and last Lord Spynie. Their only son,

WILLIAM FULLERTON, of Fullerton, by Susan his wife, was father of

JOHN FULLERTON, of Fullerton, who m. Margaret Carnegie, and had (besides a dau., Jean, m. to Sir John Wedderburn, Bart. of Blackness) a son,

WILLIAM FULLERTON, of Fullerton, who m. Susanna Ogilvy, and was father of a son, WILLIAM, and a dau., Margaret, m. to Walter, commonly called Earl of Airlie, and d. s. p. The son,

WILLIAM FULLERTON, of Fullerton and Glenquich, who assumed the surname of LINDSAY, claimed the title of Lord Spynie, but was unsuccessful, under the supposition that the original grant had been made only to the 1st Lord Spynie's issue male; this has at last been clearly proved to have been wrong, by Mr. Riddell, the distinguished writer on Scotch peerage law. Mr. Fullerton-Lindsay m. 1st, Stewart, only dau. and heir of James Carnegie, of Boysack, representative of the Hon. Sir John Carnegie, 2nd son of the 1st Earl of Northesk, and by her had an only son, JAMES, his heir. He m. 2ndly, Margaret, only dau. and heir of James Blair, Esq. of Ardblair, co. Perth, but by her had no issue. Mr. Fullerton-Lindsay, who was a lieut.-col. in the Spanish service, was s. by his only son,

JAMES FULLERTON-LINDSAY-CARNEGIE, Esq. of Boysack, Fullerton, Glenquich, Spynie, and Kinblethmont, who m. in 1786, Mary-Elizabeth, only dau. and heir of James Strachan, Esq., of the Thornton family, and by her had issue,

WILLIAM, his heir, and present laird.
Alexander, who m. 31 Oct. 1820, Amy, only dau. of Alexander Cruikshank, Esq. of Strackathrow, co. Forfar, and had an only son, Alexander-Cruikshank, b. 1 Nov. 1821. Mr. Lindsay, who was captain of the "Kelly Castle," Indiaman, d. 25 July, 1822.
John-Mackenzie, a writer to the signet in Edinburgh, m. Florence, dau. of the Rev. Charles Brown, and has a dau., Emily.
Donald, b. 1794.
Susan, m. at Edinburgh, 15 March, 1814, to Thomas Tod, Esq., advocate.
Margaret-Northesk, d. unm. 23 Feb. 1818.

Arms—Quarterly: 1st, CARNEGIE; 2nd, LINDSAY; 3rd, FULLERTON.
Crests—1st, CARNEGIE; 2nd, LINDSAY; 3rd, FULLERTON.
Seat—Kinblethmont, near Arbroath, co. Forfar.

LINDSAY OF BALCARRES.

LINDSAY, JAMES, Esq. of Balcarres and Leuchars, co. Fife, J.P. and D.L., lieut.-gen. in the army, b. 17 April, 1793; m. 2 April, 1823, Anne, eldest dau. of the late Sir Coutts Trotter, Bart., and has issue,

I. COUTTS LINDSAY, (Sir), Bart., b. 2 Feb. 1824, an officer in the Grenadier-guards.
II. Robert, b. 17 April, 1833.
I. Margaret, m. 23 July, 1846, to Alexr. William, Lord Lindsay.
II. Mary-Anne, m. 1854, to Robert-Stayner Holford, Esq. of Weston Birt, co. Gloucester.

General Lindsay is eldest son of the Hon. Robert Lindsay, 2nd son of James, 5th Earl of Balcarres.

Arms—Quarterly: 1st and 4th, gu., a fesse, chequy, arg. and az., for LINDSAY; 2nd and 3rd, or, a lion, rampant, gu., debruised of a riband, in bend, sa., for ABERNETHY; all within a bordure, of the third, semée of stars, or.

Crest—A tent, ppr., semée of stars, or.

Motto—Astra castra, numen lumen.

Seats—Balcarres, and Leuchars, both in the co. of Fife.

LINDESAY OF LOUGHRY.

LINDESAY, FREDERICK, Esq. of Loughry, co. Tyrone, J.P. and D.L., *m.* 1856.

Lineage.—The first of the Loughry and Tullahoge family of Lindesay was ROBERT LINDESAY, chief harbinger and comptroller of the artillery to King JAMES I., of England; he was son of Thomas Lindesay, collector depute within the bounds of Lothian, and searcher-general at Leith and Snowdon Herald in the years 1562, 1580, and 1592. He was a descendant of the Lords Lindesay of the Byres, progenitors of the late Earl of Crawfurd and Lyndesay, who *d.* in 1808. The chief harbinger, Robert Lindesay, had two sons, ROBERT, ancestor of the Loughry family; and ALEXANDER, M.D., ancestor of LYNDESAY *of Cahoo*, stated to have been killed at the siege of Derry. The eldest son,

ROBERT LINDESAY, Esq. of Loughry, co. Tyrone, an officer in the royal army at Worcester, *d.* 1674, aged 70, leaving a son,

ROBERT LINDESAY, Esq. of Loughry, a refugee in Derry, during the siege of 1689, who *d.* 1691, leaving issue, ROBERT LINDESAY, of Loughry, Judge of the Common Pleas, *d. s. p.* 1742, and

JOHN LINDESAY, Esq. of Loughry, who *d.* 1761, and was *s.* by his son,

ROBERT LINDESAY, Esq of Loughry, who *d.* 1823, leaving a son,

JOHN LINDESAY, Esq. of Loughry, who *d.* 1826. His son,

JOHN LINDESAY, Esq. of Loughry, J.P. and D.L., *d.* 1848, and was *s.* by his son, the present FREDERICK LINDESAY, Esq. of Loughry.

Arms—Gu., a fesse, chequy, arg. and az., three mullets in chief, of the second, and a crescent, ppr., in base.

Crest—A swan, ppr., standing, his wings closed.

Seat—Loughry, co. Tyrone.

LINDESAY OF CAHOO.

LINDESAY, WALTER, Esq. of Greenville, co. Dublin, and Glen View, co. Wicklow, J.P., barrister-at-law, *b.* 10 April, 1808; *m.* 28 March, 1838, Harriet Cole, 2nd dau. of William Cornish, Esq. of Marazion, Cornwall, and has issue,

I. WALTER-BROCAS, *b.* 25 Dec. 1848.

I. Nora-Cole. II. Harriet-Mary-Anne-Foster.

III. Frances-Honora.

Lineage.—ALEXANDER LINDESAY, M.D., 2nd son of Robert Lindesay, Esq., the chief harbinger (*see* LINDESAY *of Loughry*), *m.* Miss Cheevers, of Desertcrete, and had a son,

WALTER LINDESAY, Esq. of Cahoo, co. Tyrone, J.P., who *m.* Miss Stewart, and *d.* 1742, leaving two sons, ALEXANDER, of whom presently; and John, in holy orders, ancestor of the Rev. John Lindesay, vicar of Stanford in Avon. The elder son,

THE REV. ALEXANDER LINDESAY, rector of Kilmore, co. Monaghan, *m.* Miss E. Richardson, dau. of the Rev. Mr. Richardson, of Somerset, co. Derry, and had a dau., Hannah, wife of John Richardson, Esq., J.P., of Farlough House, co. Tyrone, and two sons, WALTER, his heir; and Robert, grandfather of the late Gen. Effingham Lindesay, of Constance, Switzerland. The elder,

THE REV. WALTER LINDESAY, *b.* 1733, rector of Bellaghy, co. Derry, *b.* 1733; *m.* 1757, Elizabeth, dau. of Sir Nicholas Forster, Bart., and dying in 1775, left two sons, I. ALEXANDER, in holy orders, rector of Rathdrum, co. Louth, *b.* in 1757, father of an only dau., Louisa; and II. ROBERT, *b.* in 1766, who *m.* 1804, Georgina, dau. and heir of the Very Rev. John Brocas, dean of Killala (the representative of the noble French family of Brocas), and dying in 1839, left issue, WALTER, now of Greenville, and one dau., Eleanor-Maria, who *d. unm.* 1845.

Arms—As LINDESAY *of Loughry*.

Seats—Greenville, co. Dublin, and Glenview, co. Wicklow.

LINDSEY OF HOLLYMOUNT HOUSE.

LINDSEY, THOMAS-SPENCER, Esq. of Hollymount House, co. Mayo, J.P. and D.L., high-sheriff 1822, *b.* 31 July, 1790; *m.* 11 May, 1818, Margaret-Hester, only dau. of the late Richard-Alexander-Oswald, Esq. of Auchencruive, and has issue,

I. RICHARD-ALEXANDER, late an officer in the army, *b.* 15 March, 1823.

II. Thomas-Spencer, *b.* 7 May, 1828.

I. Anne-Eleanor-Matilda-Nina, *m.* 4 Nov. 1841, to the Baron Godefroy de Blonay, of Blonay and Vevey, in the Canton de Vaud, Switzerland.

II. Lucy. III. Elizabeth-Frances.

IV. Lillias-Margaret-Jane. V. Catherine-Mary.

Lineage.—THOMAS LINDSEY, Esq., a younger son of THOMAS LINDSEY, Esq. of Turin Castle, co. Mayo, and a descendant of the great Scottish house of Lindsay, *m.* in 1757, Frances-Muschamp Vesey, granddau. of Dr. John Vesey, archbishop of Tuam, and had an only son,

THOMAS LINDSEY, Esq. of Hollymount, who *m.* in 1784, Lady Margaret-Eleanor Bingham, dau. of Charles, 1st Earl of Lucan, and by her (who *d.* in 1839) had issue,

THOMAS-SPENCER, now of Hollymount.

Charles-Richard, in the royal navy, went down in the old Blenheim, in 1807, with Sir Thomas Trowbridge.

William-Henry-Bingham, lieut. in the 10th hussars, at Waterloo, *d.* in India, in 1822.

Margaret-Louisa, *m.* to the Rev. J.-G. Porter, eldest son of the late bishop of Clogher.

Anne, *m.* to the Hon. and Rev. J.-G. Browne, brother of Lord Oranmore.

Eleanor, *m.* to James Reed, Esq., and *d.* in 1840.

Emily *m.* to the Rev. Edmund Dowdney.

Louisa.

Arms—Gu., a fesse, chequy, arg. and az., between three mullets, of the second.

Crest—An eagle, displayed, with two necks.

Seat—Hollymount House, Hollymount, co. Mayo.

LINGEN OF PENLANOLE.

LINGEN, HENRY, Esq. of Penlanole, co. Radnor, J.P., high-sheriff 1839-40, barrister-at-law, *b.* 16 Aug. 1803; *m.* 7 May, 1837, Priscilla, dau. of Joseph Jones, Esq. of Aberystwith, co. Cardigan, and has issue,

I. HENRY-JONES, *b.* 3 Oct. 1839.

II. Charles-Nelson, *b.* 21 Oct. 1843.

Lineage.—The Penlanole family is descended from SIR JOHN LINGEN, of Stoke Edith, in the county of Hereford, who was owner of great possessions in Herefordshire. In the struggle between CHARLES I. and his Parliament Sir Henry Lingen espoused the Royal cause and for some time maintained a troop of horse for the king's service. By this and consequent fines and confiscations Sir Henry's estates were much reduced. At one time he was fined £5000, the highest sum levied on a commoner. These losses were never remembered by CHARLES II.

JAMES LINGEN, Esq. of Thinghill Court, co. Hereford, *m.* Miss Birt, of London, and had (with three daus. Margaret, *m.* to Mr. Godshall; Eleanor, *m.* to F. Lane, Esq. of Hampton; and Fanny, *m.* to W.-A. Adams, Esq. of Pinhalt, co. Hereford) an only son,

WILLIAM LINGEN, Esq. of Sutton, co. Hereford, who *m.* Jane, second dau. of Richard Heming, Esq. of the Duffields, in the same shire, and by her had a son, WILLIAM, of whom presently, and three daus., viz. Jane, *m.* to Henry Unett, Esq. of Frenes Court, co. Hereford; Margaret, *m.* to John Griffiths, Esq., twice mayor of Hereford; and Nancy, *m.* to William Cook, Esq. of Munderfield, co. Hereford. The only son,

WILLIAM LINGEN, Esq. of Burghill Lodge, co. Hereford, *m.* 1796, Anne, only dau. and heir of John Barrett, Esq. of Hollins Hill, and had issue,

I. HENRY, of Penlanole.

II. Charles, M.D., fellow of the Roy. College of Surgeons, and senior surgeon to the Hereford County Infirmary, *m.* Ellen, 3rd dau. of the late Rev. Charles Taylor, D.D., chancellor of the diocese of Hereford, and has issue,

1 Charles-James. 2 John Taylor.
1 Eliza-Jane. 2 Ellen-Mary.
3 Alice-Margaret. 4 Blanche-Sophia.
5 Florence-Anna.

I. Mary-Anne, *d.* 17 May, 1837. II. Sophia.
III. Eliza. IV. Margaret.
V. Jane, *m.* to the Rev. Joseph-Henry Barker, M.A.

Arms—Barry of six, or and az., on a bend, gu., three roses, arg.
Crest—Out of a ducal coronet, or, a garb, vert.
Seat—Penlanole, co. Radnor.

LISTER OF BURWELL PARK.

LISTER, MATTHEW-HENRY, Esq. of Burwell Park, co. Lincoln, *b.* 1801; *m.* 1823, Arabella, youngest dau. of the late John Cracroft, Esq. of Hackthorn Hall, co. Lincoln, and has issue,

I. MATTHEW-HENRY.
I. Emily-Sophia, *m.* to the Rev. William D. Marsden.
II. Lucy. III. Florence-Arabella.
IV. Augusta-Penelope-Anne.

Mr. Lister is one of the co-heirs of the Barony of Kyme.

Lineage.—This is the senior line of the ancient family of Lister, of which the noble house of Ribblesdale is a junior branch.

SIR WILLIAM LISTER, Knt. of Thornton (son of Laurence Lister, Esq. of Midhope, by Evereld, his wife, dau. of Sir John Sayer, and grandson of William Lister, Esq., who purchased Thornton, in Craven, and who was elder brother of Thomas Lister, ancestor of the LISTERS *of Gisburne Park*, co. York) *m.* Mary, dau. of Sir Henry Bellasys, Bart. of Newborough, and left at his decease, in 1650, with other issue, I. WILLIAM LISTER, Esq. of Thornton; and II. SIR MARTIN LISTER, Knt., the well-known physician. His successor at Burwell,

MATTHEW LISTER, Esq. of Burwell Park, *m.* 1689, Eleanor, dau. and eventual heir of Sir Charles Dymoke, Knt. of Scrivelsby, champion to JAMES II., great-great-grandson of Sir Edward Dymoke, Knt., champion to Queen ELIZABETH, by Anne Talboys, his wife, sister and co-heir of GILBERT TALBOYS BARON TALBOYS OF KYME, and was father of

MATTHEW LISTER, Esq. of Burwell Park, who *d.* 1744, and was *s.* by his son,

MATTHEW LISTER, Esq. of Burwell Park, *m.* Grace, widow of Sir Edward Boughton, Bart., and dau. of Sir John Shuckburgh, Bart., and *d.* in Jan. 1786, having had a son,

MATTHEW-DYMOKE LISTER, Esq. of Burwell Park, who *m.* Lydia, only child and heiress of Joseph Bancroft, Esq., and by her (who *m.* 2ndly, Joseph Livesey, Esq.) left, at his decease, in 1772, a son,

MATTHEW-BANCROFT LISTER, Esq. of Burwell Park, who claimed the barony of Kyme. He *m.* 1799, Miss Sophia Brunton, and by her (who *d.* 1851) had issue,

MATTHEW-HENRY, now of Burwell.
John-Samuel, *m.* Elizabeth, dau. of William Wilcox, Esq. of Halifax, and has William, Matthew, and four daus.
Joseph-Martin. George-Arthur, barrister-at-law.
Alfred-Edward.
Lydia Boughton, *m.* to the Rev. G. Jackson.
Sophia, *m.* to the Rev. Francis Pickford.
Mary, *m.* to George Marmaduke Alington, Esq. of Swinhope, co. Lincoln.
Ellen-Frances.

Mr. Lister *d.* Oct. 14, 1842.

Arms—Erm., on a fesse, sa., three mullets, or.
Crest—A stag's head, erased, ppr.
Motto—Est modus.
Seat—Burwell Park, near Louth, Lincolnshire.

LISTER OF OUSEFLEET GRANGE.

LISTER, ROBERT-CORNELIUS, Esq. of Ousefleet Grange, co. York, J.P., *b.* 17 April, 1818; *m.* 26 April, 1842, Elizabeth-Cornwall, dau. of Jarvis Empson, Esq. of Goole Hall, and has issue,

I. JAMES-EMPSON, *b.* 7 July, 1851.
I. Elizabeth-Empson. II. Alice.

Lineage.—GEORGE STOVIN, Esq. son of GEORGE STOVIN, Esq. of Tetley House, co. Lincoln, took the surname and arms of LISTER, under the will of Thomas Lister, Esq. of Girsby House, co. Lincoln. By Elizabeth his wife, he was father of

JAMES LISTER, Esq., who *m.* in 1800, Alice, dau. of Robert Spofforth, Esq. of Howden, E.R. co. York, and by her had a son, the present ROBERT-CORNELIUS LISTER, Esq. of Ousefleet Grange.

Arms—Erm., on a fesse, sa., three mullets, or.
Crest—A stag's head, issuing from a ducal coronet.
Motto—Retinens vestigia famæ.
Seat—Ousefleet Grange, near Goole, co. York.

LITTLE OF LLANVAIR GRANGE.

LITTLE, WILLIAM-HUNTER, Esq. of Llanvair Grange, co. Monmouth, J.P., high-sheriff 1852, *b.* Oct. 1790; *m.* 1st, Aug. 1831, Mary-Katharine-Newman, dau. of the Rev. Dr. Rogers, of Rainscombe House, co. Wilts; and 2ndly, May, 1836, Georgiana, dau. of Winchcome-Henry Hartley, Esq., formerly Judge of the Vice-Admiralty Court at the Cape of Good Hope, and his wife, Lady Louisa Lumley, dau. of Richard, 4th Earl of Scarborough. By his 1st wife he had one dau., Louisa-Elizabeth-Katharine, *m.* 1854, to Frederick-Townley Parker, Esq., son of Thomas-Townley Parker, Esq., M.P., of Cuerden Hall, co. Lancaster. By his 2nd wife he has,

I. GEORGE-SAVILE-LUMLEY, *b.* Feb. 1837.
II. James-Law-Charles-Hunter, *b.* Aug. 1844.
III. William-Hunter-Buller, *b.* Nov. 1847.
I. Emma-Georgiana-Charlotte.
II. Henrietta-Hannah-Louisa.
III. Barbara-Elizabeth-Maria.

Lineage.—GEORGE LITTLE, Esq., who *m.* Henrietta-Maria, dau. of Samuel Forth, Esq., barrister-at-law, had two sons, SIMON, and Samuel, D.D., who *m.* Georgiana-Augusta, dau. of Augustus, 4th Earl of Berkeley, and relict of the Earl of Granard. The elder son,

SIMON LITTLE, Esq., *m.* Letitia, sister of Sir James Bond, Bart. of Coolamber House, co. Longford, and had issue, GEORGE, of whom presently; James; and Elizabeth. The elder son,

GEORGE LITTLE, Esq. of Llanvair Grange, *m.* in 1789, Louisa, youngest dau. of William Hornby, Esq. of The Hook, co. Hants, many years governor of Bombay, while Warren Hastings was governor of Bengal, and by her (who *d.* 1834) had issue,

WILLIAM-HUNTER, of Llanvair Grange.
John-Hornby, E. I. C. civil service, *d. unm.* in 1829.
James, barrister-at-law.
Emma, *m.* in 1842, to Charles-Reginald Buller, Esq. of the civil service, Ceylon, son of the late James Buller, Esq., clerk of the Privy Council.
Georgiana, *d. unm.*

Mr. Little *d.* 1826.

Arms—Sa., a chev., engr., arg.
Crest—A leopard's head, ppr.
Motto—Magnum in parvo.
Seat—Llanvair Grange, co. Monmouth.

LITTLEDALE OF BOLTON HALL.

LITTLEDALE, MARY, of Bolton Hall, co. York, *b.* 16 Nov. 1779. This lady is the eldest dau. of the late PUDSEY DAWSON, Esq. of Langcliff Hall and Bolton Hall (*see* page 284), and widow of ANTHONY LITTLEDALE, Esq. By him, who was *b.* 2 Oct. 1777, and *d.* 20 Jan. 1820, Mrs. Littledale has issue,

I. HENRY-ANTHONY, J.P., *b.* 19 March, 1810, barrister-at-law, *m.* 4 Sept. 1845, Mary-Elizabeth, eldest dau. of John Armytage, Esq. (eldest son of Sir George Armytage, Bart.), by Mary his wife, dau. of William Assheton, Esq. of Downham Hall, co. Lancaster, and has issue,
   1 HENRY-WILLIAM-ASSHETON, *b.* 6 Sept. 1846.
   2 Godfrey-Armytage, *b.* 15 Sept. 1854.
   1 Edith. 2 Mary-Georgiana.
II. William-Dawson, *b.* 27 June, 1811, *m.* 26 Feb. 1835, Frances-Florinda-Matilda-Murray, dau. of Major-Gen. Charles Cobbe, R.H.A., and has issue,
   1 AMBROSE-DAWSON, *b.* in 1840.
   2 Harold-Dawson, *b.* 1849.
   1 Florinda-Mary-Cobbe. 2 Georgina-Beresford.
I. Elizabeth-Anne, *m.* to the Rev. Robert-William Good enough.
II. Mary-Jane, *m.* to Gwalter-Boranskill-Congrove Lonsdale, Esq.
III. Caroline, *m.* to the Rev. Willoughby-John-Edward Rooke.

Lineage.—Oughtred de Bolton, living *temp.* Henry I., held among other possessions the manor of Bolton by Bowland. Seventh in descent from him was John de Bolton, bow-bearer of the forest of Bowland, upon whose death, without issue, *temp.* Edward III., the manor of Bolton devolved upon his cousin, John de Pudsey, son of his aunt, Catherine de Bolton (the eldest dau. and eventually co-heiress of his grandfather, John de Bolton) by, Simon de Pudsey. For fourteen generations it remained with his male descendants (of whom we may in passing name Sir Ralph Pudsey, Knt., the entertainer of King Henry VI. at Bolton, and Thomas Pudsey, the friend of the gallant Earl of Surrey), until the demise of Ambrose Pudsey, Esq., whose nephew (the son of his sister, Jane Pudsey,* and her husband, William Dawson, Esq. of Langcliff), Ambrose Dawson, Esq. of Llancliff Hall, co. York, eventually inherited the property. Mr. Dawson *d.* in 1794, leaving by Mary his wife, sister of Sir Willoughby Aston, Bart., a son and successor, Pudsey Dawson, Esq. of Langcliff and Bolton Hall, *b.* in 1752, who *m.* Miss Elizabeth-Anne Scott, and dying in 1816, left amongst other surviving issue, the present Pudsey Dawson, Esq. of Langcliff Hall and Hornby Castle (*see that name*), and Mary, the present Mrs. Littledale, of Bolton Hall.

Family of Littledale.

Of the family of Littledale, which appears to have resided at Ennerdale, in Cumberland, at the date of the Reformation, was Joseph Littledale, who removed to Whitehaven. His eldest son, Joseph Littledale, *m.* Mary, eldest dau. and co-heir of Isaac Langton, Esq. of The How, in Ennerdale, by Frances, his wife, eldest dau. and co-heir of Anthony Patrickson, Esq. of The How and Linethwaite, and had issue,

I. Isaac, who *m.* Mary, dau. of Hartley, Esq., and had issue,

1 Isaac, *d.* in 1843.
2 Thomas, of Braystones, co. Cumberland, and Highfield House, co. Lancaster, *m.* Sarah, dau. of Thomas, Molyneux, Esq., and has issue, Thomas, who *m.* a dau. of Clement Royds, Esq.; Alfred, who *d.* in 1842; John-Bolton; and Annie.
1 Elizabeth, *m.* to Wordsworth, Esq.
2 Mary, *m.* to Atkinson, Esq.

II. Henry, who *m.* Sarah, dau. of John Wilkinson, Esq. of Whitehaven, and had issue,

1 Joseph (Sir), Knt., one of the judges of the court of Queen's Bench, and a privy councillor, *b.* 26 May, 1767, *m.* Miss Hannah Timberlake, and *d.* 26 June, 1842, leaving a dau. Elizabeth, wife of Thomas Coventry, Esq.
2 John, *m.* 1st, Miss Whiteley, and had by her two sons, Harold, who *m.* Margaret, dau. of Sir John Tobin, Knt., and has issue; and Edward. He *m.* 2ndly, Hannah, dau. of — Moore, Esq.
3 Johnson-Wilkinson, *m.* and had issue.
4 Isaac, *d.* 31 May, 1828.
5 Henry, *d. unm.* 6 Thomas, *d. unm.*
7 Anthony, who *m.* Mary, eldest dau. of Pudsey Dawson, Esq., and had issue.
8 Alfred, *d. unm.* 9 Edward, *d.* in 1837.
10 George-Decimus, *m.* Harriet, dau. of T.-H. France, Esq., and *d.* in 1826, leaving issue, George, *b.* in 1824; Harriet; and Emily, *m.* to — French, Esq.

1 Elizabeth, *m.* to John Bolton, Esq. of Storr's Hall.
2 Mary, *m.* to Samuel Stainiforth, Esq.
3 Annabella, *m.* to J.-D. Case, Esq.

III. Thomas, *m.* Susannah, dau. and co-heir of Charles Allen, Esq. of Rotterdam, and *d.* in 1809, leaving issue,

1 Charles, of Portland Place, *b.* 1778, *m.* 5 May, 1803, Louisa, dau. of S. Castell, Esq., and *d.* 18 April, 1849, leaving issue,

Charles-Richard, of Scarlets, near Maidenhead, *b.* 1807, *m.* 1835, Emily, dau. of Charles Hammersley, Esq.
Edward, major 1st royal dragoons.
Arthur, *b.* 1815, *m.* 1st, 1835, Henrietta, dau. of George Law, Esq., H.E.I.C.S., and by her (who *d.* 1847) has, Arthur, *b.* 1842, and other issue; he *m.* 2ndly, 1853, Miss Emily Barnes, by whom he has issue.
Louisa-Sophia, *m.* to John-Lloyd, son of the late Sir William Clayton, Bart.

2 Joseph, of Norfolk Street, Park Lane.
3 Henry, of Kempston Grange, Beds.
1 Mary, *m.* to Godfrey Thornton, Esq. of Muggerhanger.
2 Julia *m.* to the Rev. Richard Dawkins.
3 Susan, *m.* to John Dixon, Esq.

Arms—For Littledale—Quarterly: 1st and 4th, arg., a lion, passant, gu., on a chief, az., three cross-crosslets, of the field, Littledale; 2nd, per pale, arg. and or, three chevronels, gu., Langton; 3rd, or, a fesse, between three greyhounds, courant, sa., Patrickson. For Dawson—Quarterly of eight coats: I. Dawson, az., on a bend, engrailed, arg., three daws, sa.; II. Pudsey, vert, a chev. between three spur rowels, or; III. Bolton, gu., a chev., between three mullets, arg., in chief, two bird bolts, palewise, feathered upwards, or; IV. Laton, arg., a fesse, between six cross-crosslets, fitchée, sa.; V. Strabolgi, paly of six, or and sa., on a canton, in chief, quarterly, or and gu., a bend, sa. (for Eure); VI. Pilkington, arg., a cross-patonce, voided, gu.; VII. Scrope, az., a bend, or; VIII. Sandford, per chev., sa. and erm., in chief, two boars' heads, arg.
Crest—Of Littledale—A demi-lion, gu., gorged with a collar, gemelle, arg., holding in the dexter paw a cross-crosslet, of the second.
Motto—Fac et spera.
Seat—Bolton Hall, near Skipton in Craven.

LLEWELLIN OF HOLM WOOD.

Llewellin, Richard, Esq. of Holm Wood, co. Gloucester, and Tregwynt, co. Pembroke, J.P., high-sheriff 1840, *b.* 29 March, 1802.

Lineage.—Richard Llewellin, Esq. of Holm Wood, *b.* 1 Nov. 1759, son and heir (by Mary his wife dau. of John Williams, Esq. of Trearchid, co. Pembroke) of Richard Llewellin, Esq. of Holm Wood, who migrated from Pembrokeshire to Bristol, *m.* 14 Jan. 1800, Anna-Maria Ames, sister of Lionel Lyde, Esq. of Ayott St. Lawrence, Herts, and Levi Ames, Esq. of the Hyde, Beds, and by her had issue,

Richard, of Holm Wood.
Thomas, *b.* 8 Dec. 1805, of Olveston Court, co. Gloucester.
Anna-Maria, *m.* 30 May, 1839, to the Rev. William Purcell.
Elizabeth, *m.* 1834, to Captain Thomas-Digby Roberts, H.E.I.C.S.
Phœbe, and Emma, both *d. unm.*

Mr. Llewellin *d.* 17 Dec. 1825.

Crest—A griffin.
Motto—Fuimus.
Seat—Holm Wood, Westbury, near Bristol; and Tregwynt, near Fishguard, co. Pembroke.

LLOYD OF BRONWYDD.

Lloyd, Thomas-Davies, Esq. of Bronwydd, co. Cardigan, J.P. and D.L., high-sheriff 1850, *b.* 19 May, 1820; *m.* Dec. 1846, Henrietta-Mary, dau. of the late George Reid, Esq. of Watlington Hall, Norfolk, by Louisa his wife, dau. of Sir Charles Oakeley, Bart., and has a son and heir,

Martyne-Owen-Mowbray, *b.* 8 Feb. 1851.

Mr. Lloyd is 23rd Lord of the Barony of Kemes, co. Pembroke, in hereditary descent from Martin de Tours, one of the companions in arms of William the Conqueror. The Barony of Kemes is the only "Lordship Marcher" now in existence in the kingdom; and the lords thereof still exercise a portion of their rights, and annually appoint, under their hands and seals, the mayors of Newport, co. Pembroke.

* Jane Pudsey, the wife of William Dawson, Esq., was dau. of Ambrose Pudsey, Esq. of Bolton, grandson of Ambrose Pudsey, of Bolton, Esq., by Bridget his wife, dau. of Sir Richard Sandford, of Howgill Castle, co. Westmoreland, and 5th in lineal descent from Thomas Pudsey, of Bolton, Esq., by Elizabeth his wife, dau., and, in her issue, co-heiress of John, Lord Scrope, of Bolton Castle. Thomas Pudsey was son and heir of Henry Pudsey, of Bolton, and Joan his wife, dau. of Sir Ralph Eure, and grandson of Thomas Pudsey, Esq. of Bolton, and Margaret his wife, dau. and co-heir of Roger Pilkington, Esq. of Pilkington, co. Lancaster. The last-named Thomas Pudsey, Esq., was son of Henry Pudsey, Lord of Bolton, by Margaret his wife, dau. of Sir John Conyers, Knt. of Hornby Castle, co. York, and great-grandson of Sir Ralph Pudsey, Knt., Lord of Bolton, 31 Henry VI., by Margaret Tunstall, of Thirland Castle (by Eleanor, dau. of Henry, Lord Fitz-Hugh, K.G.); this lady was sister to Sir Richard Tunstall, K.G., and aunt to Cuthbert Tunstall, bishop of Durham, and Sir Brian Tunstall, who was killed at Flodden. Sir Ralph Pudsey was son of Sir John Pudsey, Knt. of Bolton and Barforth (by Margaret his wife, only child of Sir William Eure, Knt., by Isabella, only child of Sir Adomar de Athol, brother and representative of David de Strabolgi, Earl of Athol), grandson of Henry Pudsey, living 27 Edward III., by Elizabeth his wife, dau. and heir of John Layton, of Barforth Castle, and 5th in descent from Simon Pudsey, who *m. temp.* Edward I., Catherine de Bolton

Lineage.—MARTIN DE TOURS, a Norman, who accompanied the Conqueror to England having as one of the Lords-Marchers, acquired, by conquest, a large district in Pembrokeshire, called CEMAES or KEMES, became PALATINE BARON thereof He made Newport the head of his Palatinate, and there erected his castle (the ruins of which still exist). He was *s.* by his son, ROBERT MARTIN, Lord Palatine of Kemes, who *m.* Maud Peverel, and had a son and successor,

WILLIAM MARTIN Lord Palatine of Kemes, 16 HEN. II. He *m.* the dau. of Rhys ap Griffith, and was *s.* by his son,

WILLIAM MARTIN, Lord Palatine of Kemes, who *d.* 17th King JOHN, leaving his son and heir,

NICHOLAS MARTIN, Lord Palatine of Kemes who *m.* Maud, dau. of Guy de Brien, by Eve his wife, dau. and heir of Henry de Tracey, and, in her right, became possessed of the lordship of Berstaple Devon. In 29 HENRY III., Nicholas received command to assist the Earl of Gloucester, and other the Barons-Marcher, against the Welsh. He was *s.* by his grandson

WILLIAM MARTIN, Lord Palatine of Kemes (son of Nicholas, who *d. v. p.*) He was summoned to Parliament from 23 EDWARD I. to 18 EDWARD II., and dying in the latter year, was *s.* by his son,

WILLIAM MARTIN, Lord Palatine of Kemes, at whose decease the barony of Martin fell into abeyance between his heirs, Eleanor, his sister, wife of William de Columbers, and James de Audley, his nephew, son of Joane, his sister, by Nicholas de Audley, Lord Audley.

In the family of Audley, the barony of Kemes continued vested for several successive generations, until it passed, by right of inheritance, to the OWENS *of Henllys*, descended from the Martins, ancient Lords-Marcher of Kemes.

With the OWENS *of Henllys* the lordship of Kemes remained, until conveyed by the daughter and heiress of WILLIAM LLOYD, of Penpedwast, Esq., Lord of Kemes, who was heir general of the Owens, in marriage to THOMAS LLOYD, Esq. of Bronwydd, co. Cardigan. This gentleman was son of THOMAS LLOYD, Esq. of Bronwydd (living in 1700), by Ann his wife, dau. of Lewis Morgan, Esq. of Wiston, co. Pembroke, grandson of THOMAS LLOYD, Esq. of Bronwydd, by Magdalen his wife, dau. of Col. John Robinson, of Gwersylt, co. Denbigh, and great-grandson, by his wife, a dau. of John Parry, of Blaenpant, of RHYS LLOYD, Esq. of Bronwydd, who was son of the REV. THOMAS LLOYD, rector of Llangunllo, by a dau. of Brwyn, of Pant David, which REV. THOMAS LLOYD was 2nd son (by Margaret his wife, heiress of Bronwydd, dau. of Thomas ap Owain), of David ap Rhys, of Crynfryn, a descendant of the ancient Lords of Dyfed. By his wife, the heiress of Kemes, Mr. Lloyd had issue,

THOMAS, of whom presently.
Owen, colonel in the army, who *m.* Mary, dau. and heir of Thomas Lloyd, Esq. of Abertrinant, co. Cardigan, by Elizabeth his wife, sister to the Earl of Lisburne.
Anne-Louisa. Bridget.
Joan, *m.* to William Lewes, Esq. of Llysnewidd, co. Caermarthen, and had issue.
Beatrice.

The elder son and heir,

THOMAS LLOYD, Esq. of Bronwydd, capt. in the 10th foot, and subsequently colonel, commanding the Fishguard and Newport regiment, *m.* Mary, dau. and heiress of John Jones, Esq., M.D., of Haverfordwest, and by her, who *d.* 1830, left at his decease, 13 July, 1807, a son and heir,

THOMAS LLOYD, Esq. of Bronwydd, *b.* Jan. 1788, J.P., and D.L., high-sheriff of Cardiganshire 1814, who *m.* 23 July, 1819, Ann-Davies, dau. of John Thomas, Esq. of Llwydcoed and Lletty Mawr, co. Caermarthen, and had issue,

THOMAS-DAVIES, now of Bronwydd.
James-John, late 1st regt. of foot, *m.* a dau. of David-Arthur-Saunders Davies, Esq. of Pentre, co. Pembroke, M.P., and has issue, Owen-George-James, and Alice.
Rhys-Jones, in holy orders, *m.* Anna, dau. of Lewis Lloyd, Esq. of Nantgwilt, co. Radnor, and has issue, George-Evan, and Edith-Anna.
Owen-William. George-Martin.

Arms—Az., a wolf, salient, arg.
Crest—A boar chained to a holly-bush, ppr.
Motto—I Dduw B'or Diolch—in English, To God be thanks.
Seat—Bronwydd, co. Cardigan.

LLOYD OF PLYMOG, GWERCLAS, AND BASHALL.

LLOYD, RICHARD-WALMESLEY, Esq., representative of the Houses of Plymog, Gwerclas, Coldcoates, and Bashall, *b.* 3 Aug. 1801; *m.* 14 Aug. 1828, Emma, dau. of the late William Thompson, of Linacre House, co. Lancaster, Esq., and had issue,

EDWARD-WALMESLEY, *b.* 7 July, 1829, *d. unm.* 25 Feb. 1848.
Emma-Margaretta, *d. unm.* 22 May, 1848.

Lineage.—Among the eminent families illustrating the rolls of Cambrian genealogy, few are of higher consideration than the LLOYDS *of Plymog*, who, in point of antiquity, both male and female, vie with the most ancient houses in the kingdom. Paternally they derive from MARCHUDD AP CYNAN, Lord of Brynffenigl, in Denbighland, founder of the VIII. Noble Tribe of North Wales and Powys, who flourished in the middle of the ninth century; while, through heiresses, they represent several eminent houses, including the Hughes's of Gwerclas, Barons of Kymmer-yn-Edeirnion, scions of the Sovereign Princes of Powys; the Coldcoates line of the Lancashire Walmesleys; a younger branch of the Ferrers's, Earls of Derby; and also the chivalrous and Knightly Talbots de Bashall, senior line of the great House of Shrewsbury.

MARCHUDD AP CYNAN, whose chief seat was Brynffenigl, in Denbighland, was father of KARWEDH AP MARCHUDD, Lord of Brynffenigl, whose son, JAFETH AP KARWEDH, Lord of Brynffenigl, was father of NATHAN AP JAFETH, Lord of Brynffenigl, who had two sons, I. EDRYD, II. Edwin, and a dau., Efa, wife of Madoc Crwm, Lord of Llechwedd, Issaf. The elder son, EDRYD AP NATHAN, Lord of Brynffenigl, had, with other issue,

IDNERTH AP EDRYD, Lord of Brynffenigl, whose eldest son,

GWGAN AP IDNERTH, Lord of Brynffenigl, had three sons, I. IORWERTH; II. Rhys, ancestor of HOEL MOELINYDD; III. Kendrig. The eldest son,

IORWERTH AP GWGAN, Lord of Brynffenigl, *m.* Gwenllian, dau. of Ririd ap Paagen, and had a son and a dau. viz., KENDRIG AP IORWERTH, and Gwenllian, who *m.* Iorwerth, son of Hwfa ap Cynddelw, founder of the I. Noble Tribe of North Wales and Powys. Iorwerth was *s.* by his son,

KENDRIG AP IORWERTH, Lord of Brynffenigl and Llansadwrn, who *m.* Angharad, dau. and heir (by Gwenllian, dau. of Ievan, son of Owen Gwynedd, Prince of North Wales) of Hwfa ap Kendrig ap Rhywalon, Lord of Christionydd-Cynrig and Maelor Cymraigh, of the Tribe of Tudor-Trevor, Lord of Hereford. By this lady, Kendrig ap Iorwerth had, with junior issue,

EDNYFED VYCHAN AP KENDRIG, Lord of Brynffenigl, in Denbighland, and Krigeth in Efinoydd, chief counsellor, chief justice, and general of Llewelyn ap Iorwerth, King of North Wales, who was one of the most prominent historical characters of the period. Commanding in the wars between Llewelyn, Prince of North Wales, and JOHN, King of England, he attacked the army of Ranulph, Earl of Chester, and achieving a signal victory, killed three chief captains and commanders of the enemy, whose heads he laid at the feet of his sovereign. For this exploit he had conferred on him new armorial ensigns emblematic of the occasion, which continue to be borne by the LLOYDS *of Plymog*, and other families derived from him. He *m.* twice, 1st, Tangwystyl, dau. of Llowarch ap Bran, Lord of Menon, in Anglesey, founder of the II. Noble Tribe of North Wales and Powys, cotemporary with Owen Gwynedd, Prince of North Wales, and by her had issue,

I. Tudor (Sir) ap Ednyfed Vychan, of Nant and Llangynhafal, one of the commissioners for the conclusion of peace between EDWARD I., King of England, and LLEWELYN AP IORWORTH, King of North Wales. He *m.* Adlais, dau. of Richard, son of Cadwallader, 2nd son of GRIFFITH AP CYNAN, King of North Wales, and was father of HEILIN AP SIR TUDOR, Knt.
II. Llewelyn ap Ednyfed Vychan, who had a moiety of Creuthyn, in Yale.
III. KENDRIG AP EDNYFED VYCHAN, of whose line we have to treat.
IV. Rhys ap Ednyfed Vychan, of Garth Garmon.
V. Howel ap Ednyfed Vychan, consecrated Bishop of St. Asaph 25 HENRY III.
VI. Rhys ap Ednyfed Vychan, of Garth Garmon, ancestor of the LLOYDS *of Gydros*.
VII. Iorwerth ap Ednyfed Vychan, Lord of Abermarlais, in Glandowi, co. Caermarthen.
I. Angharad, *m.* Einion Vychan ap Einion, of Plas yn-nant, in Llanganhafel, co. Anglesey.
II. Gwenllian, *m.* Llewelyn, the great Prince of North Wales.

Ednyfed Vychan *m.* 2ndly, Gwenllian, dau. of Rhys ap Griffith, Lord of South Wales, representative of the Sovereign Princes of South Wales, by whom he had issue,

I. Grono ap Ednyfed Vychan, Lord of Tref-Gastell, in Anglesey, chief-counsellor of Llewelyn ap Griffith, Prince of North Wales, who m. Morfydd, dau. of Meuric ap Ithel, Lord of Gwent, and had, with junior issue,

Tudor ap Grono, of Penmynedd, who built the priory of Bangor, and did homage for his lands to EDWARD I. at Chester. His great-great-grandson SIR OWEN TUDOR, Knt., m. Catherine of Valois, youngest dau. of CHARLES VI., King of France, widow of HENRY V., King of England, and by him mother of HENRY VI., King of England. By this illustrious alliance, Sir Owen Tudor, who was beheaded in 1461, left, with other issue, an elder son,

EDMUND TUDOR, created by HENRY VI., 23 Nov. 1452, Earl of Richmond, who m. the Lady Margaret Beaufort, dau. and heir of John, Duke of Somerset, and great-granddau. of John of Gaunt, by Catherine Swynford; and dying in 1546, left an only son,

Henry VII., King of England, founder of the Royal Line of Tudor.

II. Griffith ap Ednyfed Vychan, of Henglawdd, father of Sir Rhys Griffith, Knt., whose son, SIR GRIFFITH LLWYD, received from EDWARD I. the honour of knighthood on bringing him intelligence of the birth of his son, Edward of Caernarvon.

The 3rd son of Ednyfed Vychan, by his first marriage, viz.,

KENDRIG AP EDNYFED VYCHAN, who had a moiety of Creuthyn, in Yale, was father of three sons. The eldest,

KENDRIG VYCHAN AP KENDRIG, had issue, I. KENDRIG BRAWD; II. Howel Goch ap Kendrig Vychan, ancestor of the FAMILY OF BRYN IEVAN, in Garthgarmon; and III. Griffith Goch ap Kendrig Vychan. The eldest son,

KENDRIG BRAWD AP KENDRIG VYCHAN, m. the dau. of Grono Llwyd ap Penwyn, a conspicuous military chieftain, instrumental in obtaining for EDWARD I. of England the Sovereignty of Wales. Kendrig Brawd was s. by his son,

EDNYFED AP KENDRIG BRAWD, who m. Ellen, widow of Iolyn ap Ievan, of Yale, in Denbighshire, and dau. of Iorwerth Sais ap Iorwerth, of Llanynys, co. Denbigh, and by her had two sons. The elder,

RHYS AP EDNYFED, was father of two sons, I. GRIFFITH; II. John ap Rhys; and was s. by the elder,

GRIFFITH AP RHYS, who m. Margaret, dau. and heir of Rhys ap Griffith, derived from Sandde Hardd, Lord of Burton, in Denbighland, and had a son and heir,

TUDOR AP GRIFFITH, of Plymog, in the Lordship of Yale, parish of Llanferres, and county of Denbigh, living 22 HENRY VII., 1506-7. He m. Ellen, widow of David ap Rhys, of Pentrehobyn, co. Flint, of the Tribe of Edwin, Lord of Tegaingl, and dau. of Griffith Vaughan, of Cors-y-Gedol, co. Merioneth, Esq., and by her had issue. The elder son,

JOHN LLOYD, Esq. of Plymog (the first of the family who assumed the family patronymic), m. Gwenhwyfar, dau. of Llewelyn ap Griffith ap Howel, of Llanarmon, in Yale, co. Denbigh, and had issue. The eldest son,

ROBERT LLOYD, Esq. of Plymog, m. Gwenhwyfar, dau. of Edward ap Bell Lloyd, of Treflownydd, co. Flint, and had issue. The eldest son,

HUGH LLOYD, Esq. of Plymog, m. Catherine, dau. of Kendrig ap David, of Golstyn-Argoed, co. Flint, and by her, who was buried at Llanferres, 1 May, 1619, left at his decease (he was buried at Llandwrnog, in Yale, 8 April, 1636), a son,

NICHOLAS LLOYD, Esq. of Plymog, who m. Jane, dau. of Edward Pryce, of Ffynogion, in Llanfair-Duffryn-Clwyd, co. Denbigh, Esq., and had an elder son and heir,

ANDREW LLOYD, Esq. of Plymog, living in 1676, who left, by Elizabeth his wife, who was buried at Llanferres, 18 Sept. 1674, three sons and a dau., viz., I. NICHOLAS; II. ROBERT, successor to his brother; III. Edward, Gent., seated at Plymog during the minority of his nephew, of the same name. He d. prior to 25 Nov. 1695; I. Dorothy, m. 3 Nov. 1693, John Hughes, Esq., seated at Kymmer-yn-Edeirnion, co. Merioneth, only surviving younger child of Thomas Hughes, Esq., of Gwerclas and Kymmer. Andrew Lloyd's eldest son,

NICHOLAS LLOYD, Esq. of Plymog, bapt. 10 May, 1648, d. 23 March, 1678, leaving no surviving issue, and was s. by his brother and heir,

ROBERT LLOYD, Esq. of Plymog, who m. 25 May, 1684, Ann, dau. and co-heir of Edward Davies, Esq. of Denbigh, a cadet of the ancient Denbighshire House of Wygfair. By her, Robert Lloyd, who was buried at Llanferres, 4 Feb. 1689, had an only son and successor,

EDWARD LLOYD, Esq. of Plymog, high-sheriff of Merionethshire in 1732, and of Denbighshire in 1736, who m. (Settlement dated 9 Dec. 11 GEORGE I.) Dorothy, dau. and eventually sole heiress of Hugh Hughes, of Gwerclas, in Edeirnion, co. Merioneth, Esq., and dying 16 May, 1762, was s. by his son,

HUGH-HUGHES LLOYD, Esq. of Plymog and Gwerclas, b. 22 Oct. 1725, high-sheriff of Merionethshire in 1747. He m. 18 April, 1766, Margaret, dau. and heiress of Richard Walmesley, of Coldcoates, Hall, co. Lancaster, and of Bashall, co. York, Esq., son and heir of Richard Walmesley, Esq. of Coldcoates Hall, by Dorothy his wife, sister and co-heir of William Ferrers, Esq. of Bashall, grandson and representative of Edward Ferrers, Esq. (derived from William de Ferrers, 7th Earl of Derby), and of Jane, his wife, heiress of Bashall, dau. and heir of William White, Esq. of Duffield, co. Derby, colonel in the service of the Long Parliament, by Margery his wife, co-heiress of Bashall, dau. and co-heir of THOMAS TALBOT, Esq. of Bashall, last male representative of the knightly and historic family of Talbot de Bashall, senior line of the Great House of Shrewsbury. By the heiress of Bashall, who was buried 26 May, 1800, Mr. Lloyd left at his decease, 31 March, 1788, his eldest son and heir,

RICHARD-HUGHES LLOYD, Esq. of Plymog, Gwerclas, and Bashall, major of the royal Merioneth militia, b. 4 Nov. 1768, who m. 9 Oct. 1798, Caroline, dau. of Henry Thompson, Esq., and by her, who d. 23 Nov. 1816, had issue,

RICHARD-WALMESLEY, present representative.
John-Hughes, lieut. R.N., b. 7 July, 1803; m. 18 Feb. 1843, Mary, only child of Lucas Ward, Esq.
Edward-Salusbury, col. H.E.I.C.S., b. 23 Feb. 1806, m. 1844, Catherine-Anne, dau. of the Rev. Robert Wynell Mayow, and d. 1851, leaving two sons.
Hugh-Hughes, major H.E.I.C.S., b. 5 Nov. 1807.
William-Heston, b. 14 June, 1811; d. unm. 26 Sept. 1827.
Caroline-Margaret, d. unm. 8 May, 1827.
Sarah-Margaretta, d. young, 25 Nov. 1815.
Dorothea, m. 5 July, 1832, her relative, John Hughes, of the Inner Temple, Esq., barrister-at-law (see HUGHES of *Gwerclas*, p. 590), left a son, TALBOT DE BASHALL HUGHES, an officer, Cape Mounted Rifles, b. 15 Dec. 1836.
Frances-Yale, d. unm. 29 Sept. 1829. Jane.
Sarah-Margaretta, d. unm. 17 July, 1842.

Mr. Lloyd, d. 24 Jan. 1822.

Arms—Gu., on a chevron, erm., between three Englishmen's heads, couped at the neck, in profile, ppr., bearded and crined, sa.
Crest—An Englishman's head, as in the arms.
Motto—Heb Dduw heb ddim a Dduw a ddigon—With God everything; without God, nothing.

LLOYD OF GLANSEVIN.

LLOYD, EDWARD-PRYSE, Esq. of Glansevin, co. Caermarthen, J.P. and D.L., high-sheriff of Cardiganshire 1825, b. 12 Oct. 1786; m. 30 Nov. 1818, Anne, dau. of William Hughes, Esq. of Tregib, and Eliza his wife, dau. of Richard Gwynne, Esq. of Taliaris, co. Caermarthen, and has had issue,

I. MORGAN-PRYSE, b. 2 July, 1820, m. 28 Sept. 1843, Georgiana-Caroline, 8th dau. of the late Colonel Sackville Gwynne, of Glanbrane Park.
II. Edward-Pryse, b. 30 Oct. 1822.
I. Catherine-Elizabeth-Florentia.
II. Caroline-Frances, deceased.
III. Anna-Maria-Charlotte.

Lineage.—The LLOYDS of Glansevin are stated to derive from IDIO WYLLT, son of Suthrie, Lord of Desmond, in Ireland, by Nest his wife, dau. of Tudwr Mawr, King of South Wales. The late MORGAN-PRYSE LLOYD, Esq. of Glansevin, only son of Edward Pryse Lloyd, Esq. of Glansevin, and the lineal descendant of David Lloyd, Esq. of Glansevin, in 1596; m. 10 Nov. 1783, Catherine, dau. of Price Jones, Esq. of Glanhafren, co. Montgomery, by Bridget his wife, eldest dau. of Edward Devereux, 11th Viscount Hereford, and had issue,

EDWARD-PRYSE, of Glansevin.
Catherine-Martha.
Margaretta-Juliana.

Arms—Arg., a lion, rampant, sa., the tail introverted, the head, paws, and brush of the tail, of the first.
Crest—A lion, rampant.
Motto—Fiat justitia, ruat coelum.
Seat—Glansevin, co. Caermarthen.

LLOYD OF LEATON KNOLLS.

LLOYD, JOHN-ARTHUR, Esq. of Leaton Knolls, co. Salop, b. 2 Feb. 1787.

Lineage.—This family is a branch of the distinguished line of TUDOR TREVOR, Lord of Hereford.

RANDLE LLOYD, of Croesmere, co. Salop, living in 1604, (2nd son of Robert ap John, of Bangor, by Matilda, his wife, dau. and heir of David Lloyd, Esq. of Penley, co. Flint), was father of

RANDLE LLOYD, Esq. of Croesmere, who *m.* in 1608, his cousin Matilda, dau. of William Lloyd, of Penley, and had a son,

FRANCIS LLOYD, Esq. of Croesmere, who *m.* in 1638, Sarah, dau. of Edward Muckleston, Esq. of Penylan, co. Salop, recorder of Oswestry, and was *s.* by his son,

EDWARD LLOYD, Esq. of Leaton Knolls, near Shrewsbury, who *m.* Elizabeth, dau. of Isaac Cleaton, Esq., and by her, who *d.* in 1721, left at his decease, in 1698, a son,

EDWARD LLOYD, Esq. of Leaton Knolls, *b.* in 1689, high-sheriff of Shropshire in 1727; who *m.* Susan, dau. of Peter Scarlett, Esq. of Hogstowe, and dying 1764, was *s.* by his son,

EDWARD LLOYD, Esq. of Leaton Knolls, *b.* 1714, who *m.* Jane, eldest dau. and heir of Thomas Lloyd, Esq., of Domgay, co. Montgomery, and was father of

FRANCIS LLOYD, Esq. of Leaton Knolls, who *m.* Elizabeth, dau. of Arthur Graham, Esq. of Hockly Lodge, co. Armagh, and co-heiress of her maternal grandfather, John, Viscount Ligonier. By this lady, Mr. Lloyd had issue,

FRANCIS, his heir.
JOHN-ARTHUR, present representative.
Charles Spencer.
Henry-James, in holy orders, *m.* Elizabeth, dau. of Philip Miles, Esq. of Leigh Court, co. Somerset, and has issue, Arthur-Philip, Elizabeth, and Graham.
Maria-Penelope. Jane-Emma.
Elizabeth, *d.* 1 Aug. 1843. Charlotte-Sophia.

The eldest son,

FRANCIS LLOYD, Esq. of Leaton Knolls, *d. s. p.*, 14 July, 1814, and was *s.* by his brother, the present JOHN-ARTHUR LLOYD, Esq.

Arms—Per bend, sinister, erm. and ermines, a lion, rampant, or, and a bordure, gu.
Crest—A demi-lion, rampant, or.
Motto—Retinens vestigia famæ.
Seat—Leaton Knolls, near Shrewsbury.

LLOYD OF ACOMBE.

LLOYD, GEORGE, Esq. of Stockton Hall, near York, sometime a captain in the 2nd Lancashire militia, *b.* 21 May, 1787; *m.* 17 May, 1810, Alicia-Maria, dau. of John Greame, Esq. of Sewerby House, co. York, and has issue,

I. GEORGE-JOHN, *b.* 28 July, 1811; *m.* Miss Mary Hilton.
II. Yarburgh-Gamaliel, *b.* in 1813, in holy orders; *m.* 7 May, 1839, Editha, dau. of the late W.-A. Le Hunte, Esq. of Artramont, co. Wexford.
III. Henry, *b.* 30 Dec. 1815.
IV. Edward, *b.* 27 May, 1823.
I. Alicia-Maria.

Lineage.—This family is supposed to descend from the Lloyds of Llanynys, co. Denbigh.

GEORGE LLYOD, Esq., F.R.S., D.L., only child of Gamaliel Lloyd, of Manchester, merchant and manufacturer, by Elizabeth his wife, dau. and co-heir of John Carte, M.B. of Manchester, and grandson of George Lloyd, *b.* 1650 (eldest son of Gamaliel Lloyd, of Mattersey, Notts), who settled at Manchester; he *d.* at Barrowby, near Leeds, 4 Dec. 1783. He *m.* 1st, Eleanor, elder dau. of Henry Wright, Esq. of Offerton, in Cheshire, by Purefoy, his wife, dau. of Sir Willoughby Aston, Bart., and had an only child,

JOHN, F.R.S., of Snitterton, co. Warwick, *m.* Anne, dau. and heir of James Hibbins, M.D., and had issue,
GEORGE, of Welcombe House, co. Warwick, *b.* 7 March, 1768, high-sheriff in 1806, *d. unm.* 11 July, 1831.
JOHN-GAMALIEL, of Welcombe House, Bencher of the Middle Temple, high-sheriff of Warwickshire in 1832, *d. unm.* in 1837.
Charlotte, who *m.* the Rev. Thomas Warde, and had a son, CHARLES-THOMAS WARDE, Esq., now of Welcombe House.

Mr. Lloyd *m.* 2ndly, Susannah, dau. of Thomas Horton, Esq. of Chadderton, in Lancashire, (sometime governor of the Isle of Man, under the Earl of Derby, and father of Sir William Horton, Bart.,) by his wife Anne, dau. and co-heiress of Richard Mostyn, of London, and had issue,

I. GAMALIEL, alderman of Leeds, and mayor in 1799, *d.* in Great Ormonde Street, London, 31 Aug. 1817. He *m.* Elizabeth, dau. of James Attwood, Esq., and had issue,
1 WILLIAM-HORTON, F.L.S., possessor of estates in the counties of York, Lancaster, and Derby, *b.* 10 Feb. 1784, who *m.* 13 April, 1826, Mary, 4th and youngest dau. of George Whitelocke, Esq. of Seymour Place Bryanston Square, London, by Mary, dau. of David Roche, Esq., an alderman of the city of Limerick, and had issue,
GAMALIEL, *b.* 12 June, 1827; *d.* 6 Nov. 1839.
George-Whitelocke, *b.* 30 May, 1830.
2 Mary-Horton, *m.* to Stephen-John Winthrop, M.D.
3 Anne-Susannah, *m.* to Leonard Horner, Esq., F.R.S.
II. GEORGE, of whom presently.
III. Thomas, of Hosforth Hall, lieut.-colonel commandant of the Leeds volunteers, *d.* at Kingthorp House, near Pickering, 7 April, 1828. He *m.* Anne, dau. of Walter Wade Esq. of New Grange, co. York, and had issue,
1 GEORGE, of Coatham, Yorkshire, *b.* 25 May, 1786. He *m.* 1st, 1820, Marian-Christina, 5th dau. of Alexander Maclean, Esq. of Col, in Argyllshire, by whom (who *d.* in 1821) he has no issue. He *m.* 2ndly, 7 June, 1825, Elizabeth, 2nd dau. of William-Rookes-Leeds Serjeantson, Esq. of Camp Hill, near Ripon, and has issue, 1 THOMAS-WILLIAM; 2 George-Walter; 3 John-George; 1 Caroline-Anne; 5 Marianne-Jane.
1 Mary-Anne, *m.* 16 Nov. 1815, to Mr. John Priestly, of Thorpe, merchant, and *d.* in 1823.
I. Anne.
II. Susannah, *m.* to the Rev. Henry Wray.
III. Elizabeth, *m.* to Thomas Bateson, Esq., and had a son, SIR ROBERT BATESON, of Belvoir Park, M.P.

The 2nd son,

GEORGE LLOYD, Esq., barrister-at-law, long resident at Manchester, and afterwards at York, *m.* Elizabeth dau. of Jeremiah Naylor, of Wakefield, merchant, and had issue,

GEORGE, now of Acombe.
Edward-Jeremiah, of Oldfield Hall, co. Chester, barrister-at-law, *b.* 22 June, 1790; *m.* in 1822, Elizabeth, 2nd dau. and co-heiress of William Rigby, Esq. of Oldfield Hall, and has no surviving issue.
Elizabeth, *m.* 1st, to William Butler Laird, Esq. of Strath Martin, near Dundee, a captain in the 17th dragoons, by whom (who *d.* in 1810) she has issue. She *m.* 2ndly, Robert Alison, Esq. of Dundee, and has other children.
Susannah-Georgiana.
Mary-Anne, *m.* 4 Aug. 1831, to her cousin, the Rev. Cecil-Daniel Wray, Canon of the Collegiate Church at Manchester.

Arms—Argent, three lions, dormant, in pale, sa.
Crest—A demi-arm in scale armour, the hand naked, ppr., the cuff, arg., grasping a lizard, vert.
Seat—Stockton Hall, near York.

LLOYD OF ASTON.

LLOYD, WILLIAM, Esq., J.P. and D.L., high-sheriff 1810, of Aston, co. Salop, *b.* 1780; *m.* 1805, Louisa, eldest dau. and co-heir of the late Admiral Sir Eliab Harvey, G.C.B., of Rolls Park, in Essex, and by her (who is now of Aston Hall), left at his decease, 1843,

I. EDWARD-HARVEY,
II. Richard-Thomas, *m.* in 1852, Lady Frances Hay, 3rd dau. of the Earl of Kinnoull, and has a son and a dau.
I. Louisa-Eliza.
II. Charlotte, *m.* 30 Oct. 1838, to George Granville Pigott, of Doddershall.

Lineage.—The Lloyds of Aston have been seated at Aston from an early period, and derive from the roya house of Powys, through their immediate progenitor, EINION EFELL, Lord of Cynllaeth, son of Madoc, last Prince of Powys.

ANDREW LLOYD, Esq. of Aston, like his neighbour, Mytton, of Halston, adopted the cause of the Parliament, against King CHARLES I., and held a captain's commission in the army. Capt. Lloyd *m.* Margaret, dau. of Thomas Powell, Esq. of Whittington Park, and had, with other issue, THOMAS, his heir, and Richard, (Sir,) Chancellor of Durham, and Judge of the Admiralty Court, father of Sir Nathaniel Lloyd, Knt., a liberal benefactor to the colleges of Trinity Hall and All Souls, Oxford. The elder son,

THOMAS LLOYD, Esq. of Aston, acquired, by marriage with Sarah, dau. and co-heir of Frances Albany, Esq., the lordship and estate of Whittington, in Shropshire, and had *inter alios*, ROBERT, his heir. ELIZABETH, *m.* to Foulk Lloyd, Esq. of Foxhall, co. Denbigh, (descended, in the male line, from William Rosindale, grandson of Henry Rosindale, of Rosindale, co. Lancaster, who adopted the surname. Of the Henllan and Foxhall family, Humphrey

Lloyd, the celebrated antiquary, was a descendant.) Elizabeth and Foulk Lloyd had three sons, viz.,

John Lloyd, } successively of Aston.
Thomas Lloyd, }
Rosindale Lloyd, who m. Jane, dau. of Robert Davies, Esq. of Llannerch, and d. in 1734. He had, William, (the Rev.), who s. his uncle at Aston.

Mr. Lloyd d. in 1692, and was s. by his son,

Robert Lloyd, Esq. of Aston, M.P. co. Salop, who m. Mary, eldest dau. of Sir John Bridgeman, Bart., and left a son and heir,

Robert Lloyd, Esq. of Aston, M.P. co. Salop. He d. unm. 7 June, 1734, when the Aston and other estates devolved upon (the eldest son of his aunt) his cousin,

John Lloyd, Esq. of Foxhall, who dying without issue, in 1741, was s. by his brother,

Thomas Lloyd, Esq. of Aston, at whose decease, unm., in 1754, the estates passed to his nephew,

The Rev. William Lloyd, of Aston. This gentleman m. Elizabeth, dau. of William Sneyd, Esq. of Bishton, co. Stafford, and had an only son and heir,

The Rev. John-Robert Lloyd, of Aston, who m. Martha, 4th dau. of John Shakespeare, Esq. of London, and had issue,

William, his heir.
Charles-Arthur-Albany, rector of Whittington, co. Salop, b. 1785; m. Mrs. Hannah-Simpson Cowan; and d. 1851, leaving three children.
George-Newton-Kynaston, rector of Selattyn, co. Salop, b. 1786; m. Miss Corrie; and d. 1848, leaving three children.
Elizabeth, m. to Robert Curtis, Esq. of Ireland; and d., leaving issue.
Charlotte, m. in 1808, to the Hon. Thomas Kenyon, brother of Lord Kenyon, and has issue.

Mr. Lloyd d. in 1803, and was s. by his eldest son,

William Lloyd, Esq., late of Aston, whose widow now holds that estate.

Arms—Per fesse, sa. and arg., a lion, rampant, counterchanged, of the field.

Motto—Hwy pery clôd na golud. (In English, Longer wil fame last than wealth).

Seat—Aston Hall, in Shropshire.

LLOYD OF CROGHAN.

Lloyd, Guy, Esq. of Croghan House, co. Roscommon, J.P. and D.L., high-sheriff for co. Roscommon 1833, and for Leitrim 1847; b. 30 Dec. 1803; m. 26 May, 1827, Susanna-Martha, youngest dau. of John-Stephenson Cann, Esq. of Wramplingham, Norfolk, and has issue,

I. Guy, b. 13 April, 1833.
II. John-Merrick, b. 1846.
III. William-Richard, b. 1848.
I. Sarah-Martha.
II. Susan-Ellen.
III Mary-Anne.
IV. Elizabeth-Bertha.
V. Emma-Jane.
VI. Katharine-Edith.
VII. Frances-Dorothea.
VIII. Alice-Octavia.
IX. Emily-Muriel-Knyvett.

Lineage.—Capt. Owen Lloyd, the first possessor of the Roscommon estates, was eldest son of Thomas Lloyd, Esq., of the co. of Leitrim, who migrated from Wales to Ireland, under the auspices of his kinsman, Sir Ralph Bingley. He m. Elizabeth Fitzgerald, granddau. of Sir Luke Fitzgerald, of Tycroghan, co. Kildare, and left at his decease, 1664, three sons and three daus.; the eldest son,

Thomas Lloyd, col. in the army, chosen commander in the field by the Inniskillen forces, in the war against James II., d. in 1689. He m. Margaret, dau. of Sir John Cole, Bart., ancestor of the Viscounts Cole, Earls of Enniskillen, but left no issue. Col. Thomas Lloyd was s. by his brother,

Richard Lloyd, Esq., Speaker of the Upper House of Assembly in Jamaica, and Lord Chief Justice of that island, where he m. Mary Guy, an heiress, and had two sons and two daus. Chief Justice Lloyd was s. by his 2nd, but eldest surviving son,

Guy Lloyd, Esq., who m. Mary Copping, of Essex, and had issue,

Richard, successor to his father.
Henry, in holy orders, m. Diana, dau. of Thomas Bullock, Esq. of Hingham, in Norfolk.
Mary, m. to Thomas St. John, Esq.

Mr. Lloyd was s. by his son,

Richard Lloyd, Esq. of Bylaugh, co. Norfolk, colonel of the East Norfolk militia, m. Elizabeth, dau. and sole heiress of Thomas Jecks, Esq. of Bawdeswell Hall, and had issue,

Guy, his successor.
Richard, b. in 1772; m. Sarah-Harriet, dau. of Peter Elvin, Esq. of Thurning Hall, Norfolk, and had, with other issue, Richard-Hastings-Edward.
Henry, m. Sarah, eldest dau. of J.-Stephenson Cann, Esq.
Merrick, R.N., killed on board H.M.S. the "Sirius," under Nelson, in 1805, before Malta, s. p.
Bridget, m. to the Rev. Dr. Bulwer, rector of Cawston, co. Norfolk.
Katharine, } of Bawdeswell Hall, and demesne lands
Letitia, } thereto annexed.
Eliza, }
Margaret, m. to Robert Bircham, Esq.
Diana, m. to the Rev. James Stoughton A.M., rector of Sparham.
Jane, m. to the Rev. Thomas Dade, rector of Broadway and Bincombe, Dorsetshire.

Colonel Lloyd d. 1811, and was s. by his eldest son,

Guy Lloyd, Esq., J.P., of Croghan House, co. Roscommon, b. 19 Aug. 1766, who m. 17 Dec. 1799, Martha, dau. of William Bircham, Esq. of The Ollands, co. Norfolk, and had issue,

Guy, now of Croghan House.
Sarah-Bircham, m. 14 Dec 1835, the Rev. William Atthill, of Brandiston Hall, co. Norfolk; and d. 1837.
Elizabeth, m. 10 Dec. 1825, to the Rev. Philip Francis, A.B., of Stibbard Lodge, co. Norfolk.
Martha.

Arms—Gu., a chevron, or, and on a chief, erm., a canton, arg., thereon an eagle with two heads, displayed, sa.

Crests—A stag's head, couped, ppr., with a neck, surcharged with a laurel chaplet; and on a ducal coronet, or, a double eagle, displayed, sa.

Mottoes—Over the stag's head, "Spectemur agendo;" and over the eagle, "Eò altius quò profundius."

Seat—Croghan House, co. Roscommon.

LLOYD OF DAN-YR-ALLT.

Lloyd, John-William, Esq. of Dan-yr-allt, co. Caermarthen, J.P., b. 3 Sept. 1781; m. 29 Jan. 1807, Anna-Maria, 5th dau. of John Longley, Esq., recorder of Rochester, and has had issue,

I. John-Philipps, b. 27 April, 1808; d. 17 Sept. 1849, unm.
II. Henry-Robert, M.A., in holy orders, vicar of Owersby, co. Lincoln, b. 9 Aug. 1809, m. 17 Oct. 1848, Harriet, 4th dau. of the Hon. and Rt. Rev. Edward Grey, bishop of Hereford, and granddau. of Charles, 1st Earl Grey.
III. St. Vincent, b. 23 Dec. 1810.
IV. Joseph-Howard-Francis, b. 29 May, 1812; m. 2 June, 1837, Emmeline Rogers, dau. of Charles Searle, Esq. of Dominica.
V. William-Christopher, lieut. 53rd regt. Bengal native infantry, b. 26 Aug. 1815, d. unm. 14 June, 1841.
VI. Herbert, b. 26 Dec. 1821, capt. 21st regt. Madras native infantry.
I. Anna-Maria, m. 6 Sept. 1836, to William, only son of Robert Peel, Esq. of Taliaris, in Caermarthenshire.
II. Charlotte-Louisa-Frances, m. 14 March, 1843, to John Peel, Esq., 7th son of Robert Peel, Esq. of Accrington House and Hyndburn, co. Lancaster.
III. Sophia-Catherine-Martha.
IV. Rosamond-Elizabeth, m. 17 Aug. 1854, to Frederick Layard, Esq. of Ceylon C.S.

Lineage.—Cadivor ap Dyfnwal, Lord of Castle Howel, ninth in descent from Rhodri Mawr, or the Great, King of Wales, took by escalade, 11th Henry II., the castle of Cardigan from the Earl of Clare and the Flemings, for which service his kinsman, the great Lord Rhys, of South Wales, gave him considerable lands and a new shield of arms, viz., "Sa., three scaling-ladders, and between the two uppermost a spear's head, arg., its point imbrued, on a chief, gu., a tower triple-turretted, of the second." By his wife, Katherine, dau. of his prince and kinsman, the Lord Rhys, he had, with other issue, a son,

Rhydderch ap Cadivor, Lord of Castle Howel, who m. Jennet, dau. of Sir Aron ap Rhys ap Bledri, Lord of Kilsaint, and Knight of the Sepulchre, who went with Richard Cœr-de-Lion to Palestine against the Infidels. Rhydderch's son,

Rhys ap Rhydderch, of Bodyr Ychan and Castle Howel, m. Catherine, dau. of Sir Elydyr Ddû, Knt., and had issue. The 3rd son,

Cadwgan Fawr ap Rhys, was father of

Cadwgan Vychan, of Carrog, co. Cardigan, whose son,

Cadwgan Grach, of Carrog, m. Eva, dau. of Meredydd

Vychan ap Meredydd ap Richard Rhydderch ap Bledri, and had a son,

Llewellin ap Cadwgan Grach, who m. Gwladys, dau. of Meredydd Fawr ap Meredydd ap Richard, of Iraenau, in Caermarthenshire, and was direct ancestor of

John Lloyd, Esq. of Foes-y-Bleiddied, who m. Elizabeth, dau. and co-heir of Thomas Lloyd, Esq. of Wernvylyg and Llanllyr, and had (with two daus., Lettice, m. to Thomas Edwards, Esq. of Rhyd-y-Gors; and Catherine, m. to Jenkin Lloyd, of Llanvaughan) a son and successor,

David Lloyd, Esq. of Foes-y-Bleiddied, who was a favourite of James II., and attended that king in all his troubles. He m. Sage, dau. of John Lloyd, of Cilgwynne, co. Cardigan, and left (with a dau., Margaret, wife of Charles Lloyd) a son and successor,

John Lloyd, Esq. of Foes-y-Bleiddied, b. in 1700, who m. Mary, dau. of James Philipps, Esq. of Penty Park, in Pembrokeshire, and had issue,

James, of Foes-y-Bleiddied, who m. Anna-Maria, dau. and heir of Richard Lloyd, Esq. of Ystrad Tello, and Mabws, in Cardiganshire, and dying 6 June, 1800, left a son and successor,

John, of Mabws, who m. Elinor, dau. and heir of John Allen, Esq. of Dale Castle, Pembrokeshire, and was grandfather of the present John-Philipps-Allen-Lloyd Philipps, Esq. of Dale Castle.

John, of whom presently.

Vaughan, general of artillery, who commenced his military career at Minden, and distinguished himself at the memorable defence of Gibraltar by Gen. Elliott. He m. Mrs. Sarah Beaumes, a widow, and d. s. p. in 1817.

Thomas, d. s. p.

Briana, d. unm.

Mr. Lloyd d. in 1781. His 2nd son,

John Lloyd, Esq., clerk of the check of Plymouth Dockyard: m. Jane Atkins, and by her (who d. 2 Sept. 1784) had issue,

William, d. unm. 13 July, 1776, aged 22.

John, of whom presently.

Louisa-Maria, m. 7 July, 1792, to Admiral Sir Herbert Sawyer, K.C.B., and d. 20 December, 1828, having had issue.

Mr. Lloyd d. 12 Dec. 1806, aged 82, and was s. by his son,

John Lloyd, Esq., major in the 46th regt., and aide-de-camp to Sir Henry Clinton during the American war, in which he received three wounds, the ultimate cause of his death. He m. 30 July, 1777, Corbetta, dau. of the Rev. George Holcombe, archdeacon of Caermarthen, and rector of Pwllcrochon, in Pembrokeshire, and had issue,

I. William-John, major in the Royal artillery, b. 2 Dec. 1778, d. unm. at Brussels, 29 July, 1815, of a wound received at Waterloo.

II. John-William, now of Dan-yr-allt.

III. George, rear-adml. R.N., b. 13 Oct. 1793, m. 1st, 1 May, 1817, Elizabeth, dau. of John Morgan, Esq. of Burfield House, co. Gloucester, and by her (who d. 1828) had issue,

1 John-Sawyer, b. 6 Feb. 1818, midshipman H.M.S. Thunder, drowned in the West Indies, by the upsetting of one of her boats, Jan. 1834.

2 Charles, lt. Indian navy. 1 Ellen, d. 1848.

2 Elizabeth, d. 1855.

Adml. Lloyd m. 2ndly, 13 March, 1832, Marianne, dau. of Jacob Richards, Esq. of Tenby, and by her (who d. Dec. 1849) had issue,

1 Jacob-Richards, lt. Roy. marines.

1 Susannah-Munday. 2 Harriette-Richards.

He m. 3rdly, 2 Jan. 1851, Catherine, dau. of John Stokes Stokes, Esq. of Cuffern, co. Pembroke, and by her had issue,

1 Martha-Sophia. 2 Louisa-Corbetta.

IV. Vaughan, lieut. R.N., b. 29 June, 1795, m. 6 Feb. 1827, Augusta, only dau. of John Adams, Esq. of Pembroke, and by her (who d. 1828) had issue,

Frances.

I. Louisa-Jane, m. 22 April, 1823, to George Bowling, Esq. of Pembroke.

Mr. Lloyd d. 24 Nov. 1801.

Arms—Sa., a spear's head, imbrued, ppr., between three scaling-ladders, arg., and on a chief, gu., a castle, triple-towered, ppr., for Lloyd *of Llanllyr*.

Crests—1st, a wolf, rampant, arg., holding between its paws a spear's head, point downwards, imbrued, and three drops of blood under the sinister paw; 2nd, a lion, rampant, reguardant, sa.

Motto—"Heb dduw heb ddim a Duw a digon."

Seat—Dan-yr-Allt, Caermarthenshire.

LLOYD OF COEDMORE.

Lloyd, Thomas, Esq. of Coedmore, co. Cardigan, lord-lieut. and custos-rotulorum of that county, and its high-sheriff 1817, b. 1 Nov. 1793; m. 23 March, 1819, Charlotte, 2nd dau. of the late Captain Edward Longcroft, R.N., of Havant, co. Hants, and has issue,

I. Thomas-Edward, b. 12 April, 1820; married.

II. Edmund, b. 29 Jan. 1822.

III. Walter, b. 7 Dec. 1823.

IV. Charles-Oliver, b. 9 June, 1825.

Lineage.—Griffith ap Grono ap Elydir ap Gwrgeney ap Idnerth ap Cadwgan ap Elystan, Prince of Ferlys, m. Margaret, dau. of Cadwgan ap Idnerth, and was father of David Griffyd, who m. Joan, dau. and heir of Morgan Winter, of Caermarthen, and had a son, Thomas ap David, who m. Gwenllian, dau. and heir of Gryfyd ap Jenkin, and was father of Rhys ap Thomas, who m. the dau. and co-heir of Jenkin ap Rhys David, of Gilvachwer, and was father of a 4th son, Howel Vychan, who m. a dau. of Jenkin ap Rhydderch, and had a son, David ap Howel, whose wife was Nest, dau. and heir of David ap Jenkin Lloyd Gruffydd, and whose son was David Lloyd, who m. a dau. of Thomas ap Howel Vawr, of Gilvachwerissa, and was father of Jenkin Lloyd, who m. Elizabeth, dau. of David ap Jenkin Lloyd Ychan, of Llanvair Clydogan, and had a son, David Lloyd, who m. Elinor, dau. of Thomas Lloyd; the second son, Thomas Lloyd, high-sheriff of Cardiganshire, *temp.* Queen Elizabeth, m. Mary, dau. and co-heir of Rhys Lloyd, of Cylgwyn, and had John Lloyd, who m. Dorothy, dau. of Walter Vaughan, of Llanelly, and had a son, Capt. Thomas Lloyd, living in 1693, who m. Jane, dau. of John Lewis, Esq. of Coedmawr, and had a son, John Lloyd, who m. Elinor, dau. of John Lloyd, of Llangeuyth, and was father of

John Lloyd, Esq. of Coedmore, who m. Miss Lloyd, o Mabws, and was father of

Walter Lloyd, Esq. of Coedmore, who m. Anna-Posthuma Thomas, of the co. of Caermarthen, and by her left, at his decease, *circa* 1786, with two daus., a son and heir,

Thomas Lloyd, of Coedmore, who m. *circa* 1790, Elizabeth, 4th dau. of the late Edmund Probyn, Esq. of Newland, co. Gloucester, and by her (who d. 1851) had issue,

Thomas, present representative.

Oliver, b. 16 July, 1801, m. 1st, 1828, Anna-Maria, only child of Capt. James-Richard-Lewes Lloyd, of Dolhaidd, co. Caermarthen, by whom he had two daus., Maria, m. to Thomas Elliott, Esq.; and Emeline, m. to William Brigstocke, Esq.

Sophia.

Anna, m. to John Probyn, Esq. of Manor House, co. Gloucester.

Mr. Lloyd d. 1810.

Arms—Quarterly: 1st and 4th, sa., a spear-head, arg., erect, embrued, ppr., between three scaling-ladders, in bend, of the second; 2nd and 3rd, quarterly, 1st and 4th, arg., a lion, rampant, gu.; 2nd and 3rd, az., a lion, rampant, within an orle of quatrefoils, arg.

Crest—A lion, rampant, arg.

Motto—Fide et fortitudine.

Seat—Coedmore, near Cardigan.

LLOYD OF CLOCHFAEN AND PLAS MADOG.

Julia, elder dau. of the late Rev. Thomas Youde, by Sarah his wife, only dau. and heir of Jenkyn Lloyd, Esq. of Clochfaen, is the present possessor of Clochfaen and Plâs Madog, co. Denbigh.

Lineage.—Ynyr ap Cadfarch, Lord of Chirk, Whittington, Oswestry, and both the Maelors, by his wife Rhiengar, dau. and heiress of Lluddoccaf ap Caradog, Earl of Hereford, had, besides a younger son, Ynyr Frych, abbot of Abbey d'Or, an elder son,

Tudor Trefor, Earl of Hereford, Lord of Chirk, &c., and the Tribe of March. He d. A.D. 948, and by his wife Angharad, dau. of Howel Dha, King of Wales, had one dau. and three sons; the 3rd of whom, Dyngad, m. Cicilia, dau. of Severus ap Cadifor Wynwyn, Lord of Buallt, and had issue, Rhiwallon, who, by Laetitia his wife, dau. of Cadwaladr ap Perydyr Goch, was father of

Cynwrig ap Rhiwallon, who was slain A.D. 1074, and is buried at Wrexham. He bore "Erm., a lion rampant, sa. By Agnes his wife, dau. of Idnerth Benfras, Lord of Maesbrook, he had a 6th son, David, father of Madog, whose grandson Ieuan ap Meredydd, was father of

Madoc Danwr, of Llangurig, which parish, together with an augmentation to his arms of a border, gu., semée of annulets, arg., was given him for his services in battle by Gwenwynwn, Prince of Powys, A.D. 1197. By his wife, a dau. of the house of Elystan Glodrudd, he had a son, Meredydd, who m. Dyddgu, dau. of Llewelyn ap Einion ap Llewelyn, Esq., descended from Brochwel, King of Powys, by whom he had a son, Howel Lloyd, of Llangurig, whose grandson, Ieuan ap Gruffydd, of Llangurig, by his 1st wife, Gwenllian, dau. and heiress of Jenkyn ap Gruffyd Goch, of the line of Madog Danwr, had one son,

Jenkyn Goch, of Clochfaen, in Llangurig, Esq., who m. Catherine, dau. and heiress of Maurice Fychan ap Maurice ap Madog, of Kerry, Esq., descended from Elystan Glodrudd, Prince of Fferlis, Founder of the Fifth Royal Tribe of Wales, by whom he had a son,

Maurice ap Jenkyn, of Clochfaen, Esq., who, by Margaret his wife, dau. of Llewellyn ap Rhys Lloyd, of Creuddyn, Esq., descended from Gwaethfoed, Lord of Cardigan, had issue, Jenkyn ap Maurice, who m. Catherine, dau. of Morgan ap Rhys ap Howel, by whom he had a son, David, who, by Catherine his wife, dau. of Evan ap David ad Guto, of Rhaiadr, descended from Llowdden, Lord of Uwch-Aeron, was father of

Evan ap David, of Clochfaen, Esq., who m. Margaret, dau. of David Lloyd-Blaeney, of Grugynog, Esq., by whom he had issue,

Rhys Lloyd, of Clochfaen, Esq., who m. Margaret, dau. of Jenkyn Lloyd, of Berthlloyd, Esq., and had a son, Jenkyn Lloyd, of Clochfaen, Esq., who by Mallt his wife, dau. of Morgan David, of Llanbrynmair, was father of Rhys Lloyd, of Clochfaen, Esq. who d. 1699, and by Mary his wife, dau. of John Thomas, of Llanlloddian, Esq., descended from Brochwel, King of Powys, was father of

Jenkyn Lloyd, of Clochfaen, Esq., who, by Rachael his wife, sister and heir of Edward, and dau. of John Fowler, of Abbey Cwmhir, Esq., in co. Radnor (*see* Burke's *Royal Descents, art.* Youde Lloyd), had issue,

Rhys Lloyd, of Clochfaen, Esq., who m. Sarah, only dau. and heir of William Platt, of Rhydonen, in the parish of Llanynys, and co. of Denbigh, Esq. (by Mary his wife, eldest dau. and co-heir of Thomas Hughes, of Pen-y-nant, in the parish of Rhiwabon, Esq.), by whom he had three daus. and one son,

Jenkyn Lloyd, of Clochfaen, Esq. He m. Elizabeth, dau. and heir of Edward Lloyd, of Plas Madog, co. Denbigh, Esq., by whom he had one only dau. and heiress, Sarah, *b.* A.D. 1746, and *d.* A.D. 1837; she m. 1st, John Edwards, of Crogen Iddon and Yspytty, co. Denbigh, Esq., by whom she had no issue; and 2ndly, she m. the Rev. Thomas Youde, of Ruthin, by whom she had three sons and two daus., Julia, the present possessor of Clochfaen and Madog; and Harriet, m. to Jacob-William Hinde, Esq., D.L. for Middlesex, by whom she has two sons, Jacob-Youde-William, and Charles-Thomas-Edward, an officer in the Bengal service, and two daus., Harriet-Esther-Julia, and Mary-Charlotte.

Lloyd of Plas Madog.

This family descends likewise from Tudor Trefor, through Awr ap Ieuaf ap Cyhelyn, 3rd son of Tudor ap Rhys Sais, Lord of Chirk.

Awr, of Tref-awr, *i.e.* Trefor, had two sons, 1 Adda, ancestor of the Trevors *of Trevor*; and 2 Iorwerth ap Awr, who, by Margaret his wife, dau. of Ednyfed ap Iorwerth ap Meilyr Eyton, had one son, Iorwerth Fychan, living A.D. 1332, who m. 1st, Agnes, dau. of Hwfa ap Iorwerth, of Hafod-y-Wern, by whom he had two sons, Howel and Ieuan; and 2ndly, he m. Margaret, dau. of Madog ap Llewelyn, Lord of Eyton, by whom he had a dau., Lucy, wife of Madog Lloyd, of Iscoed, and one son, Ednyfed Lloyd, Esq., who m. the sister and heir of Ednyfed ap Iorwerth ap Madog, of Horsley, in the parish of Gresford, Esq., by whom he had a son, Llewelyn, living A.D. 1393, who, by Gwenllian his wife, dau. of Adda ap Howel ap Ieuaf, of Trevor, was father of

David ap Llewelyn, of Plas Madog, who m. Margaret, dau. and heir of Dio ap Hwfa ap Ieuaf ap Hwfa ap Madog yr Athro, of Plas Madog, descended from Cynwrig ap Rhiwallon, and had issue,

Iohn ap David, of Plas Madog, Esq., who m. Angharad, dau. of Howel ap Ieuan ap Gruffydd, of Bersham, Esq., and Philippa his 1st wife, dau. of Sir Randle Brereton, of Malpas, Knt., by whom he had one dau., Angharad, and one son, Randle, who m. Angharad, dau. of Iohn ap Ieuan ap Deicws, of Llanerch-Rugog, Esq., and was father of

John Lloyd, of Plas Madog, Esq., who by Jannette his wife, dau. of Geoffrey Bromfield, of Bryn-y-Wiwair, Esq., in the parish of Rhiwabon, had a son,

William Lloyd, of Plas Madog, Esq., who m. Catherine, dau. of Owain Brereton, of Borasham, Esq., and Elizabeth his 1st wife, dau. of Iohn Salusbury, Esq. of Lleweny, and by her had two daus. and five sons, the eldest of whom,

Edward Lloyd, of Plas Madog, Esq., m. Anne, dau. of John Eyton, of Leeswood, Esq. (and Jane his wife, dau. of Iohn Lloyd, of Bodidris, Esq.) and had an elder son, Edward Lloyd, of Plas Madog, Esq., who, by Rebecca his wife, dau. of the Rev. Mostyn Piers, of Cambridge, was father of Edward Lloyd, of Plas Madog, Esq., who m. Elizabeth, dau. of Owain Lloyd, Esq.* (and Jane his wife, dau. and heir of John Brereton, Esq., and relict of John Fachnallt, of Fachnallt, Esq.), by whom he had issue three sons, 1 Capt. John Lloyd, of Plas Madog, killed in London with Sir Evan Lloyd, of Bodidris; 2 William Lloyd, of Plas Madog, who, as well as his brother John, left no children. The 3rd son,

Samuel Lloyd, of Plas Madog, Esq., m. Sarah, dau. and co-heir of Luke Lloyd, jun., of The Bryn, in the parish of Hanmer, Esq., by whom he had a son, Edward Lloyd, of Plas Madog, Esq., who, by Anne his wife, dau. and co-heir of William Lloyd, of Plas Benion, Esq., had a dau., Elizabeth, heiress of Plas Madog, who m. Jenkyn Lloyd, of Clochfaen, Esq.

Arms—Quarterly: 1st and 4th, Erm., a lion rampant, sa., armed and langued, gu., in a border of the second, semé of annulets, arg., for Madoc Danwr; 2nd and 3rd, party, per bend sinister, erm. and erms., a lion rampant, or, for Tudor Trefor, Earl of Hereford.

Crest—On a wreath, arg. and gu., a lion rampant, of the second.

Motto—In te Domine speravi.

LLOYD OF TRALLWYN.

Lloyd, John-Ellis, Esq. of Trallwyn, co. Caernarvon, *b.* 10 May, 1819; *m.* 21 Aug. 1845, Eleanor, dau. of John Sothern, Esq. of Liverpool, and has issue,

I. John-Ellis, *b.* 12 July, 1846.
II. Charles-Henry, *b.* 6 Aug. 1847.
I. Edith-Mary. II. Annie-Elizabeth.
III. Harriet-Jane. IV. Mary-Ellen.

Lineage.—John Ellis, Esq., *b.* 1 Nov. 1786 (son of Hugh Ellis, Esq. of Caernarvon, by Anne his wife, dau. of Samuel Wright, Esq. of Knutsford, and grandson of the Venerable John Ellis, archdeacon of Merioneth, by Ann his wife, dau. and heir of Hugh Lloyd, Esq. of Trallwyn), assumed by royal licence, 1811, the surname and arms of Lloyd, in compliance with the testamentary injunction of his granduncle the Rev. William Lloyd, son of Hugh Lloyd, Esq. of Trallwyn. He was a magistrate and deputy-lieut. for Carnarvonshire, and served as high-sheriff 1817. He m. 5 Dec. 1815, Jane, dau. the Rev. Griffith Jones, and had issue,

John-Ellis, now of Trallwyn.
Hugh, *b.* 7 Dec. 1825.
Robert, *b.* 16 April, 1833.
Richard, *b.* 8 Sept. 1834.
Margaret-Ann.
Mary-Catherine, m. 1854, to Alfred Jones, Esq.
Cordelia. Elizabeth.

Arms—Az., on a chevron, or, between three spear heads arg., a torteau, between two bulls' heads, caboshed, sa.

Crest—A lion, rampant, arg., gutté de sang, surmounting two spears, in saltire, ppr.

Motto—Instanter perfectus.

Seat—Trallwyn, co. Caernarvon.

LLOYD OF LAQUES.

Lloyd, Elizabeth, of Laques, co. Carmarthen, *s.* her brother, Aug. 1854.

Lineage.—This is a younger branch of the very ancient Cambrian family of Lloyd, of Plâs Llanstephan, who traced a direct lineal descent from Tudwal Glof, and of which the eventual heiress, Elizabeth, dau. of Francis Lloyd, Esq. of Llanstephan, m. Hugh Meare, Esq.

Daniel Lloyd, Esq. of Laques (2nd son of Rees Lloyd, Esq. of Plâs Llanstephan, who *d.* 4. Jan. 1622), m. Sarah Evans, of Petterwell, and was father of

The Rev. William Lloyd, of Laques, M.A., rector of

* Second son of William Lloyd, of Plas Madog, Esq.

Llansadwrnen, and vicar of Laugharn, co. Carmarthen, who d. 24 Jan. 1706, leaving, by Susanna his wife, dau. of John Davies, Esq., a son and heir,

WILLIAM LLOYD, Esq. of Laques, barrister-at-law, who d. in May, 1747, leaving, by Jane his wife, dau. of John Davies, Esq. of Dolegwynddon, a son and successor,

DANIEL LLOYD, Esq. of Laques, barrister-at-law, J.P., high-sheriff of co. Cardigan in 1760, who m., March, 1760, Katherine, dau. of Francis Meare, Esq. of Corston, co. Pembroke, and had (with six daus., of whom Katherine m. Thomas Lewis, Esq. of Stradey; Jane m. Jeremiah Price, Esq. of Glangwilly; and Anne m. John Conway Hughes, Esq.), six sons. Mr. Lloyd d. in 1792, and was s. by his eldest son,

WILLIAM LLOYD, Esq. of Laques, J.P. and D.L., high-sheriff in 1807, who m in 1792, Maria-Elenora, only child of John Colborne, Esq. of Swindon, co. Stafford, and by her (who d. in Sept. 1829), left at his decease, 1840, a son, WILLIAM LLOYD, Esq. of Laques, who d. s. p. Aug, 1854, and a dau., ELIZABETH, now of Laques.

Arms—Quarterly: 1st, Gu, on a bend between three daggers, arg., a lion, passant, sa; 2nd, arg., on a chev., gu., three garbs, or; 3rd, arg., two lions, reguardant, sa; 4th, sa., an eagle with two heads displayed, or.

Crest—An eagle preying on a bird.

Seat—Laques, in the parish of Llanstephan, co. Carmarthen.

LLOYD OF PALE.

LLOYD, REV. DAVID-MORRIS, of Palè, co. Merioneth, J.P., b. 1777; m. 12 May, 1814, Martha, dau. of James Taylor, Esq. of Church Hill House, Doddington, co. Kent, and has issue,

I. DAVID MORRIS.
II. John. III. James-Lushington.
I. Jane-Martha, m. to William-George Duncan, Esq. of Great Houghton House, co. Northampton.

Lineage.—The present LLOYDS of Palè, derive paternally from HELD MOLWYNOG, Lord of Uwch Aled, a Chieftain of Denbighland, founder of IX Noble Tribe of North Wales and Powys. From this Noble descended

IEVAN LLOYD, son of Jeffrey Lloyd, a distinguished Bard, of Dyffryn Brethlyn, in Egiwys Fach, co. Denbigh, who m. Margaret, dau. and heir of Maurice Lloyd, of Palè, in Edeirnion, co. Merioneth, who d. in 1614, son of John Lloyd, of Palè, derived from Griffith ap Rhys, of Crogen and Branas, co. Merioneth, younger son of Rhys ap Ievan, IV. Baron of Kymmer-yn-Edeirnion, under age 15-16 RICHARD II., 1391-2, representative of Owen Brogyntyn, Lord of Edeirnion, Dinmael, and Abertanat, son of Madoc ap Meredith, last Prince of Powys. By the heiress of Palè, who was buried at Llandderfel, 18 April, 1664, Ievan Lloyd, who was buried at the same place, 8 July, 1639, had issue, with an elder son, Jeffrey, who d. s. p., another son,

MAURICE LLOYD, Esq. of Palè, b. 10 Jan. 1618, grandfather of

MAURICE LLOYD, Esq, of Palè, whose eldest son,

JOHN LLOYD, Esq. of Palè, who d. 7 Nov. 1742, aged 42, m. Margaret, dau, of William Vaughan, Esq. of Caynog, and had issue, I. John; II. MAURICE; I. JANE; II. Margaret; III. Catherine. The 2nd son and eventual heir,

MAURICE LLOYD, Esq. of Palè, m. Jane, dau. of David Morris, of Ty-ucha Ciltalgarth, co. Merioneth, and had issue,

DAVID-MORRIS, of Palè.
John, m. the dau. of Admiral Roddam.
Maurice, in holy orders, vicar of Lenham, m. Elizabeth, youngest dau. of the late James Best, Esq. of Park House, co. Kent.
William.
Jane.
Margaret, m. to William Radley, Esq. of Highfield House, co. Middlesex.
Sarah. Bridget. Susan.

Arms—Sa., a stag, trippant, arg., attired, or.

Crest—A lion, rampant, sa., armed and langued, gu.

LLOYD OF GLOSTER.

LLOYD, HARDRESS, Esq. of Gloster, in the King's County, J.P. and D.L., b. about the year 1782; for some years lieut.-col. of the South Down militia, M.P. for the King's County from 1807 to 1816.

Lineage.—TREVOR LLOYD, (youngest son of Evan Lloyd, Esq. of Bodidris-yn-Yale, co. Denbigh, by Mary his wife, dau. and co-heir of Sir Richard Trevor, Knt. of Allington, and brother of John Lloyd, Esq. of Bodidris, whose son, Sir Evan Lloyd, of Bodidris, was created a BARONET, 1646), a captain in the army of CHARLES I.; m. in 1639, Miss Medhop, an heiress, by whom he acquired estates in the King's County, and in the county of Tipperary, and had a son and successor,

MEDHOP LLOYD, Esq. of the King's County, who m. Mary, 3rd dau. (by Frances O'More his wife, descended from the Princes of Leix), of Christopher Lovett, Esq., lord mayor of Dublin, 3rd son of Sir Robert Lovett, of Liscombe, high-sheriff of Bucks in 1606, and had fourteen children, all of whom d. s. p., with the exception of

TREVOR LLOYD, Esq., who, inheriting the family estates, became of Gloster, in the King's County. He m. Miss Waller, of Castletown, co. Limerick, (a descendant of Sir Hardress Waller, governor of Limerick during the Commonwealth), and had, with other issue,

JOHN, his heir.
Hardress, who d. s. p.
Waller, m. to Lovat Ashe, Esq. of Ashgrove, co. Tipperary.
Rose, m. to Alexander Saunderson, Esq. of Castle Saunderson, co. Cavan.

Mr. Lloyd was s. by his eldest son,

JOHN LLOYD, Esq. of Gloster, M.P. for the King's County from 1768 until 1790, and subsequently for the borough of Inistiogue. Mr. Lloyd m. circa 1777, Jane, youngest dau. and co-heir (with her sisters, Anne, wife of the Rev. Abraham Symes, D.D., and Alice, wife of Samuel Hayes, Esq. of Avondale) of Thomas Le Hunte, Esq., who d. in 1775, 5th son of George Le Hunte, of Artramont, co. Wexford, Esq., and had issue,

HARDRESS, now of Gloster.
Trevor, who d. at Cambridge in 1796.
Thomas, lieut.-colonel in the army, killed at the passage of the Nivelle, 10 Nov. 1813, at the head of his regiment, the 94th.
Evan.
John, of Parsonstown, King's Co., who m. Miss Vaughan, dau. of William-Peisley Vaughan, Esq. of Golden Grove, in the King's County, and left one dau., MARY, m. 1848, Samuel-Dawson Hutchinson, Esq. of Mount Heaton, King's County, who assumed, in consequence, the surname of LLOYD-VAUGHAN.
Alice, m. 5 April, 1797, to Laurence, late Earl of Rosse.
Harriet, m. to the Rev. Mr. King, of Ballylin.

Mr. Lloyd was s. at his decease by his eldest son, the present HARDRESS LLOYD, Esq. of Gloster.

Arms—I. LLOYD OF GLOSTER: Paly of eight, arg. and gu., the ensigns of LLEWELYN AP YNYR O'IAL.—II. LLOYD OF GLOSTER, (ancient ensigns of SANDDE HARDD, Lord of Morton:) Vert, semée of broomslips, or, over all, a lion, rampant, or.

Crest—A lion, rampant, arg., holding a snake in his paw.

Motto—Respice prospice.

Seat—Gloster, near Shinrone, King's County.

LLOYD OF CASTLE LLOYD.

LLOYD, THOMAS, Esq. of Castle Lloyd, co. Limerick, b. Aug. 1814; m. June, 1838, Mary, eldest dau. of the Rev. Charles-Philip Coote, rector of Doon, co. Limerick, and niece of the late Chidley Coote, Esq. of Mount Coote, and has issue,

I. WILLIAM-THOMAS-LLEWELYN, b. 1839.
II. Charles-Thomas-Cadwalader, b. 1841.

Lineage.—THOMAS LLOYD, Esq. of Tower Hill, co. Limerick, of ancient Welsh descent, m. Eleanor, dau. of the Rev. Rickard Burgh, D.D., and was father of WILLIAM LLOYD, Esq., who m. Jane, dau. of Thomas Fitzgerald, Esq., and had a son, the REV. THOMAS LLOYD, who m. 1st, his cousin, Mary, dau. of the Rev. Rickard Burgh, of Dromkeen, and had by her, three sons, RICKARD, of whom presently; William, of Tower Hill; and Edward. He m. 2ndly, Miss Bateman, of Altavilla, and by her was father of Colonel Lloyd, who m. the dau. and heiress of Lloyd of Dromsalla, and had a son, THOMAS LLOYD, Esq. of Beechmount, co. Limerick, M.P. for that shire in 1826, and K.C., who m. in 1792, Katherine, dau. of Eyre Evans, Esq. of Miltown Castle, and had issue. The eldest son of the 1st marriage of the Rev. Thomas Lloyd, was

THE REV. RICKARD LLOYD, of Castle Lloyd, who m. Mary, dau. of William Armstrong, Esq. of Mealliffe, and had issue,

I. THOMAS, in holy orders, who m. Elizabeth, dau. of Thomas Fitzgerald, Knight of Glin, and had, with two elder sons, who d. unm., another son,

The Rev. William-Edward Lloyd, rector of Fenor, who

m. 1812, Anne, dau. of Thomas Peacocke, Esq. of Fort Etna, and d. Nov. 1858, leaving issue, 1 Thomas, now of Castle Lloyd; 2 Rickard; 3 John; 4 Edward-William-Cadwallader, 7th Fusiliers; 1 Mary, m. to the Rev. Henry Smyth; 2 Elizabeth, m. to Henry Cooper Reide, Esq.; 3 Louisa, m. to the Rev. Peter Marsh; 4 Anna, m. to John Pierce; 5 Wilhelmina, deceased; and 7 Geraldine m. to Richard Dawson, Esq.

II. Edward, rector of Fethard.
III. William, barrister-at-law, d. in 1783.
IV. John, serjeant-at-law, d. in 18:5.
I. Alice. II. Eliza.
III. Mary, m. to Joseph Gabbett, Esq. of High Park, 2nd 2nd son of William Gabbett, Esq. of Cahirline, co. Limerick.

Seat—Castle Lloyd, Ulla, co. Limerick.

LLOYD OF LLOYDSBORO'.

Lloyd, John, Esq. of Lloydsboro' and Cranagh, co. Tipperary, b. 16 March, 1790; m. 21 July, 1810, Debby-Ann, dau. of John Lloyd, Esq. of Cranagh, and has issue,

I. John-Jesse, J.P., m. Mary, youngest dau. of Edmund-N.-W. Fortescue, Esq. of Fallapit, co. Devon, and has issue, three sons and one dau.
II. Richard-Jesse, lieut. 50th regiment, d. unm. 14 Oct. 1846.
I. Elizabeth-Ann, m. to John-Dawson Hutchinson, Esq. of Timoney Park, and d. 3 March, 1843.
II. Ellen-Eliza, m. John-Stratford Collins, Esq. and d. 1852, leaving issue.

Lineage.—John Lloyd, Esq. of Lloydsboro, co. Tipperary, son of Joseph Lloyd, Esq., by Mary Otway his wife, claimed to derive his descent from the great Welsh family of Lloyd of Bodidris. He m. Elizabeth, dau. of Sir John Blunden, Bart., and was father of

John Lloyd, Esq. of Cranagh, who m. Deborah Clutterbuck, and had issue,

I. John, of Cranagh and Lloydsboro', m. Amy Brazier, and left an only dau., Debby-Anne, m. to her cousin, John Lloyd, Esq. of Lloydsboro'.
II. Thomas, m. Judith Meagher, and had issue, George-Richard, m.; Horatio, m., and d. leaving issue; Robert, deceased; and Debby, m. to George Newton, Esq., capt. 3rd light dragoons, killed at Moodkee, 18 Dec. 1845.
III. Richard, A.M., rector of Clonouty, co. Tipperary, afterwards of Northam Cottage, North Devon, b. 9 Dec. 1754; m. 16 Sept. 1788, Priscilla, dau. of the Rev. John Lord, rector of Clonkelly; and d. 8 Jan. 1830, leaving issue,
  1 George-William-Aylmer, C.B., major-gen. H.E.I.C.S., b. 4 July, 1789; m. 1 March, 1824, Caroline, 2nd dau. of the late Capt. William Bruce, H.E.I.C.S., which lady d. 1845.
  2 John, lieut. R.N., and J.P. of Panbula, near Eden, Twofold Bay, New South Wales, m. 19 Jan. 1824, Sarah Robinson, and had issue,
    Arthur, of Northam House, co. Devon, and Adelaide, South Australia, b. 30 Oct. 1824.
    William, civil engineer, East Indies, b. 24 May, 1826.
    Priscilla-Emilia, m. 1847, to Major William-Ellison Warden.
  3 Arthur-Forbes, M.A., rector of Instow, Devon, m. Harriet, dau. of Thomas-Furley Forster, Esq. of Walthamstow, and had issue,
    Arthur-Forster, of Morpeth Vale, South Australia, m. 1851, Jean, youngest dau. of James-Gordon Morgan, Esq., M.D., of Barnstaple, and has issue.
    Richard, of Morpeth Vale, South Australia, m. 19 June, 1856, Marcella-Adelaide-Cornelia, dau. of James Elton, Esq.
    Benjamin-Furney. George-Aylmer.
    Thomas-Furney. Edward.
    Harriet-Mary, m. 1855, to Charles-Constantine Bruce, Esq.
    Isabella. Emily. Adelaide.
    Susanna. Priscilla-Lord. Marion.
  1 Isabella-Anne.
IV. Henry-Jesse, of whom presently.
V. Frederick, m. Julia, dau. of Thomas Vereker, Esq. of Roxborough, and left issue, John, of Lisheen Castle, m. and has issue; Frederick, lieut. R.N., deceased; Henry-Vereker, m. Miss Jopp; Charles, in holy orders, m. and has issue; Julia, m. George Duncan, Esq.; Camilla; and Harriet, d. unm.
I. Elizabeth, m. to the Rev. Charles Tuckey.
II. Debby, m. to Gorges Hely, Esq.

The 4th son,

Henry-Jesse Lloyd, Esq. of Castle Iney, co. Tipperary, who m. Ellen, dau. of Thomas Garde, Esq. of B..lina Curra co. Cork, and, dying 1816, left issue,

I. John, of Lloydsboro'. II. Thomas, d. unm.
III. Henry-Jesse, of Farrinrory, co. Tipperary, m. 1st Harriet-Amelia, youngest dau. of Sir John-Craven Carden, Bart., and has issue,
  1 Jesse, of Ballyleck House, co. Monaghan, J.P., late capt. 47th regiment, b. 23 Feb. 1824, m. 14 Dec. 185.. Ellen, eldest dau. of George Vincent, Esq. of Erinagh, co. Clare, and has a son,
    Henry-Craven-Jesse, b. 8 Feb. 1855.
  1 Frances-Maria, m. 26 March, 1840, to Andrew Wauchope, Esq. of Niddrie.
  2 Josephine-Julia-Helen, m. 19 May, 1846, to Henry, Lord Rossmore.
  3 Coralie-Augusta-Frederica, m. 17 June, 1848, to Wm.-FitzWilliam Burton, Esq. of Burton Hall, co. Carlow.
IV. William, m. Kate, only dau. of John Harris, Esq. of Waterford, and had issue.
I. Mary-Anne, m. to the Rev. Thomas Hoare, youngest son of the late Sir Edward Hoare, Bart.
II. Eliza-Lucy, m. Mr. Morris, and is deceased.

Arms—Paly of eight, or and arg.
Crest—A lion, rampant, holding in the dexter paw a snake.
Motto—Ynir o yale.
Seat—Lloydsboro', near Templemore, co. Tipperary.

LLOYD OF ALLTYR ODIN.

(*See* Davies of Blaendyffryn.)

LOCH OF DRYLAW.

Loch, James, Esq. of Drylaw, co. Edinburgh, b. 7 May, 1780, an advocate, and M.P. for Kirkwall; m. 10 Aug. 1810, Ann, youngest dau. of P. Orr, Esq. of Kincardineshire, and left issue,

I. George, b. in 1811. II. Granville-Gower, b. in 1813.
III. William-Adam, b. in 1814.
IV. Thomas, b. in 1816.
V. James-Patrick, b. in 1819, and d. in 1834.
VI. John-Charles, b. in 1825.
VII. Henry-Brougham, b. in 1827.
I. Anne-Marjory. II. Mary-Clementina-Marion.

Lineage.—James Loch, merchant and burgess of Edinburgh, m. 11 Oct. 1610, Margaret Barclay, of the same city, and was s. by his eldest son,

James Loch, Esq. of Drylaw, Treasurer of Edinburgh, b. 27 Aug. 1612, who was s. by his son,

James Loch, Esq. of Drylaw, b. 2 May, 1650, who m. Isabel, dau. of Sir George Foulis, of Ravelston, and had issue, (with three daus., the eldest of whom Janet, m. in 1710, Edward Marjoribanks, Esq. of Hallyards, George, his heir; John, of Edinburgh, merchant, who m. Margaret, dau. of Sir William Menzies, of Gladstone, and left at his decease, in 1756, an only son, William, father of John, of Rarham, and James, Joint King's Remembrancer for Scotland. He d. 12 Nov. 1690, and was s. by his eldest son,

George Loch, Esq. of Drylaw, b. 28 March, 1678, who m. Jean, dau. of George Foulis, Esq. of Ravelston, and was s. by his elder son,

James Loch, Esq. of Drylaw, b. 16 Aug. 1693, who m. 14 Jan. 1748, Frances, dau. of the Hon. William Erskine, son of David, 4th Earl of Buchan, and dying 14 Nov. 1759, left a dau., Margaret, m. to her cousin, James Lock, Esq., and a son and successor,

George Loch, Esq. of Drylaw, who m. Mary, dau. of John Adam, Esq. of Blair, co. Kinross, and sister of the Lord Chief Commissioner Adam, by whom he had issue,

James, late of Drylaw.
John, formerly M.P. for Hythe, a director of the East India Company, of the Australian Society, &c., who m. Marion, dau. of Archibald Cullen, Esq., K.C., and has a son, George-John, and a dau., Marion.
William, in the Bengal civil service, who left issue, George-William, William, Charles, Mary, Eliza, and Charlotte.
Francis-Erskine, capt. R.N., who m. Miss Jesse Robertson, and has issue.

Mr. Loch d. in 1788.

Arms—Arg., a saltier, engrailed, sa., between two swans, naiant, in locks, ppr., in the flanks.
Crest—A swan devouring a perch, ppr.
Motto—Assiduitate non desidiâ.
Seat—Drylaw.

Lightning Source UK Ltd.
Milton Keynes UK
UKHW020148090223
416651UK00002B/637

9 781297 505959